CHILTON'S

TRUCK and VAN
SERVICE
MANUAL

Vice President & General Manager John P. Kushnerick
Editor-In-Chief Kerry A. Freeman, S.A.E.
Managing Editor Dean F. Morgantini, S.A.E. □ **Managing Editor** David H. Lee, A.S.E., S.A.E.
Senior Editor Richard J. Rivele, S.A.E. □ **Senior Editor** W. Calvin Settle, Jr., S.A.E.
Senior Editor Ron Webb
Project Manager Nick D'Andrea □ **Project Manager** Wayne A. Eiffes, A.S.E., S.A.E.
Service Editors Lawrence C. Braun, S.A.E., A.S.C., Peter M. Conti, Jr., Thomas B. Dallett,
Robert E. Doughten, Thomas G. Gaeta, Ken Grabowski, A.S.E., Michael Grady,
Martin J. Gunther, Steven Horner, Neil Leonard, A.S.E., Robert McAnally,
Steven Morgan, Michael J. Randazzo, Richard T. Smith,
James B. Steele, Larry E. Stiles, Jim Taylor, Anthony Tortorici, A.S.E., S.A.E.
Editorial Consultants Edward K. Shea, S.A.E., Stan Stephenson

Manager of Production John J. Cantwell
Supervisor Mechanical Paste-up Margaret A. Stoner
Mechanical Artist Andrea Steiger
Mechanical Artist Lorraine Martinelli
Special Projects Peter Kaprielyan

Sales Director Albert M. Kushnerick □ **Assistant** Jacquelyn T. Powers
Regional Sales Managers Joseph Andrews, Jr., David Flaherty, Larry W. Marshall

OFFICERS
President Gary R. Ingersoll
Senior Vice President, Book Publishing & Research Ronald A. Hoxter

CHILTON BOOK COMPANY
*ONE OF THE **ABC PUBLISHING COMPANIES**,*
*A PART OF **CAPITAL CITIES/ABC, INC.***

Manufactured in USA   ©1990 Chilton Book Company ● Chilton Way, Radnor, Pa. 19089
ISBN 0–8019–8048–8
1234567890   9876543210

SAFETY NOTICE

Proper service and repair procedures are vital to the safe, reliable operation of all motor vehicles, as well as the personal safety of those performing repairs. This manual outlines procedures for servicing and repairing vehicles using safe, effective methods. The procedures contain many NOTES, CAUTIONS and WARNINGS which should be followed along with standard safety procedures to eliminate the possibilty of personal injury or improper service which could damage the vehicle or compromise its safety.

It is important to note that the repair procedures and techniques, tools and parts for servicng motor vehicles, as well as the skill and experience of the individual performing the work vary widely. It is not possible to anticipate all of the conceivable ways or conditions under which vehicles may be serviced, or to provide cautions as to all of the possible hazards that may result. Standard and accepted safety precautions and equipment should be used when handling toxic or flammable fluids, and safety goggles or other protection should be used during cutting, grinding, chiseling, prying, or any other process that can cause material removal or projectiles.

Some procedures require the use of tools specially designed for a specific purpose. Before substituting another tool or procedure, you must be completely satisfied that neither your personal safety, nor the performance of the vehicle will be endangered

PART NUMBERS

Part numbers listed in this reference are not recomendations by Chilton for any product by brand name. They are references that can be used with interchange manuals and aftermarket supplier catalogs to locate each brand supplier's discrete part number.

Although information in this manual is based on industry sources and is complete as possible at the time of publication, the possibilty exists that some car manufacturers made later changes which could not be included here. While striving for total accuracy, Chilton Book Company cannot assume responsibility for any errors, changes or omissions that may occur in the compilation of this data.

SPECIFICATIONS

VEHICLE IDENTIFICATION CHART

It is important for servicing and ordering parts to be certain of the vehicle and engine identification. The VIN (vehicle identification number) is a 17 digit number visible through the windshield on the driver's side of the dash and contains the vehicle and engine identification codes. The tenth digit indicates model year and the eighth digit indicates engine code. It can be interpreted as follows:

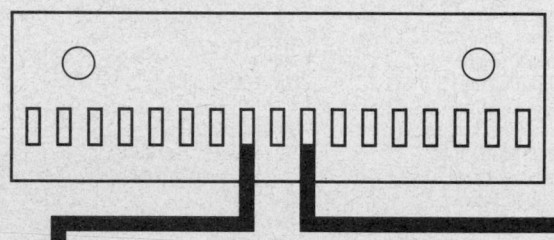

Engine Code

Code	Cu. In.	Liters	Cyl.	Fuel Sys.	Eng. Mfg.
H	225	3.7	6	1 BBL carb.	Chrysler
X	239	3.9	6	EFI	Chrysler
T	318	5.2	8	2 BBL carb.	Chrysler
Y	318	5.2	8	EFI	Chrysler
W ①	360	5.9	8	4 BBL carb.	Chrysler
I ②	360	5.9	8	4 BBL carb.	Chrysler
Z	360	5.9	8	EFI	Chrysler
5 ③	360	5.9	8	EFI	Chrysler
8	360	5.9	6	Turbo Diesel	Cummins

Model Year

Code	Year
G	1986
H	1987
J	1988
K	1989
L	1990

① Federal
② California
③ Heavy Duty Chassis

ENGINE IDENTIFICATION

Year	Model	Engine Displacement cu. in. (liter)	Engine Series Identification (VIN)	No. of Cylinders	Engine Type
1986	B150 Van	225 (3.7)	H	6	OHV
	B150 Van	318 (5.2)	T	8	OHV
	B250 Van	225 (3.7)	H	6	OHV
	B250 Van	318 (5.2)	T	8	OHV
	B250 Van	360 (5.9)	W	8	OHV
	B350 Van	318 (5.2)	T	8	OHV
	B350 Van	360 (5.9)	W	8	OHV
	B350 Van	360 (5.9)	I	8	OHV

ENGINE IDENTIFICATION

Year	Model	Engine Displacement cu. in. (liter)	Engine Series Identification (VIN)	No. of Cylinders	Engine Type
1986	D100 Pick-Up	225 (3.7)	H	6	OHV
	D100 Pick-Up	318 (5.2)	T	8	OHV
	D100 Pick-Up	360 (5.9)	W	8	OHV
	D100 Pick-Up	360 (5.9)	I	8	OHV
	W100 Pick-Up	225 (3.9)	H	6	OHV
	W100 Pick-Up	318 (5.2)	T	8	OHV
	W100 Pick-Up	360 (5.9)	W	8	OHV
	AD100 Ramcharger	318 (5.2)	T	8	OHV
	AW100 Ramcharger	318 (5.2)	T	8	OHV
	AW100 Ramcharger	360 (5.9)	W	8	OHV
	AW100 Ramcharger	360 (5.9)	I	8	OHV
	D250 Pick-Up	225 (3.7)	H	6	OHV
	D250 Pick-Up	318 (5.2)	T	8	OHV
	W250 Pick-Up	225 (3.7)	H	6	OHV
	W250 Pick-Up	318 (5.2)	T	8	OHV
	W250 Pick-Up	360 (5.9)	W	8	OHV
	W250 Pick-Up	360 (5.9)	I	8	OHV
	D350 Pick-Up	318 (5.2)	T	8	OHV
	D350 Pick-Up	360 (5.9)	W	8	OHV
	D350 Pick-Up	360 (5.9)	I	8	OHV
	W350 Pick-Up	318 (5.2)	T	8	OHV
	W350 Pick-Up	360 (5.9)	W	8	OHV
	W350 Pick-Up	360 (5.9)	I	8	OHV
1987	B150 Van	225 (3.7)	H	6	OHV
	B150 Van	318 (5.2)	T	8	OHV
	B250 Van	225 (3.7)	H	6	OHV
	B250 Van	318 (5.2)	T	8	OHV
	B250 Van	360 (5.9)	W	8	OHV
	B350 Van	318 (5.2)	T	8	OHV
	B350 Van	360 (5.9)	W	8	OHV
	B350 Van	360 (5.9)	I	8	OHV
	D150 Pick-Up	225 (3.7)	H	6	OHV
	D150 Pick-Up	318 (5.2)	T	8	OHV
	D150 Pick-Up	360 (5.9)	W	8	OHV
	D150 Pick-Up	360 (5.9)	I	8	OHV
	W150 Pick-Up	225 (3.7)	H	6	OHV
	W150 Pick-Up	318 (5.2)	T	8	OHV
	W150 Pick-Up	360 (5.9)	W	8	OHV
	AD150 Ramcharger	318 (5.2)	T	8	OHV
	AW150 Ramcharger	318 (5.2)	T	8	OHV
	AW150 Ramcharger	360 (5.9)	W	8	OHV
	AW150 Ramcharger	360 (5.9)	I	8	OHV
	D250 Pick-Up	225 (3.7)	H	6	OHV
	D250 Pick-Up	318 (5.2)	T	8	OHV

ENGINE IDENTIFICATION

Year	Model	Engine Displacement cu. in. (liter)	Engine Series Identification (VIN)	No. of Cylinders	Engine Type
1987	W250 Pick-Up	225 (3.7)	H	6	OHV
	W250 Pick-Up	318 (5.2)	T	8	OHV
	W250 Pick-Up	360 (5.9)	W	8	OHV
	W250 Pick-Up	360 (5.9)	I	8	OHV
	D350 Pick-Up	318 (5.2)	T	8	OHV
	D350 Pick-Up	360 (5.9)	W	8	OHV
	D350 Pick-Up	360 (5.9)	I	8	OHV
	W350 Pick-Up	318 (5.2)	T	8	OHV
	W350 Pick-Up	360 (5.9)	W	8	OHV
	W350 Pick-Up	360 (5.9)	I	8	OHV
1988	B100 Van	239 (3.9)	X	6	OHV
	B100 Van	318 (5.2)	Y	8	OHV
	B150 Van	239 (3.9)	X	6	OHV
	B150 Van	318 (5.2)	Y	8	OHV
	B250 Van	239 (3.9)	X	6	OHV
	B250 Van	318 (5.2)	Y	8	OHV
	B250 Van	360 (5.9)	W	8	OHV
	B350 Van	318 (5.2)	Y	8	OHV
	B350 Van	360 (5.9)	W	8	OHV
	D100 Pick-Up	239 (3.9)	X	6	OHV
	D100 Pick-Up	318 (5.2)	Y	8	OHV
	D100 Pick-Up	360 (5.9)	W	8	OHV
	W100 Pick-Up	318 (5.2)	Y	8	OHV
	W100 Pick-Up	360 (5.9)	W	8	OHV
	D150 Pick-Up	239 (3.9)	X	6	OHV
	D150 Pick-Up	318 (5.2)	Y	8	OHV
	D150 Pick-Up	360 (5.9)	W	8	OHV
	W150 Pick-Up	318 (5.2)	Y	8	OHV
	W150 Pick-Up	360 (5.9)	W	8	OHV
	AD150 Ramcharger	318 (5.2)	Y	8	OHV
	AD150 Ramcharger	360 (5.9)	W	8	OHV
	AW150 Ramcharger	318 (5.2)	Y	8	OHV
	AW150 Ramcharger	360 (5.9)	W	8	OHV
	D250 Pick-Up	239 (3.9)	X	6	OHV
	D250 Pick-Up	318 (5.2)	Y	8	OHV
	D250 Pick-Up	360 (5.9)	W	8	OHV
	W250 Pick-Up	318 (5.2)	Y	8	OHV
	W250 Pick-Up	360 (5.9)	W	8	OHV
	D350 Pick-Up	318 (5.2)	Y	8	OHV
	D350 Pick-Up	360 (5.9)	W	8	OHV
	W350 Pick-Up	318 (5.2)	Y	8	OHV
	W350 Pick-Up	360 (5.9)	W	8	OHV

ENGINE IDENTIFICATION

Year	Model	Engine Displacement cu. in. (liter)	Engine Series Identification (VIN)	No. of Cylinders	Engine Type
1989	B100 Van	239 (3.9)	X	6	OHV
	B100 Van	318 (5.2)	Y	8	OHV
	B150 Van	239 (3.9)	W	8	OHV
	B150 Van	318 (5.2)	Y	8	OHV
	B250 Van	239 (3.9)	X	6	OHV
	B250 Van	318 (5.2)	Y	8	OHV
	B250 Van	360 (5.9)	Z	8	OHV
	B350 Van	318 (5.2)	Y	8	OHV
	B350 Van	360 (5.9)	Z	8	OHV
	D100 Pick-Up	239 (3.9)	X	6	OHV
	D100 Pick-Up	318 (5.2)	Y	8	OHV
	D100 Pick-Up	360 (5.9)	Z	8	OHV
	W100 Pick-Up	318 (5.2)	Y	8	OHV
	W100 Pick-Up	360 (5.9)	Z	8	OHV
	D150 Pick-Up	239 (3.9)	X	6	OHV
	D150 Pick-Up	318 (5.2)	Y	8	OHV
	D150 Pick-Up	360 (5.9)	Z	8	OHV
	W150 Pick-Up	239 (3.9)	X	6	OHV
	W150 Pick-Up	318 (5.2)	Y	8	OHV
	W150 Pick-Up	360 (5.9)	Z	8	OHV
	AD150 Ramcharger	318 (5.2)	Y	8	OHV
	AD150 Ramcharger	360 (5.9)	Z	8	OHV
	AW150 Ramcharger	318 (5.2)	Y	8	OHV
	AW150 Ramcharger	360 (5.9)	Z	8	OHV
	D250 Pick-Up	239 (3.9)	X	6	OHV
	D250 Pick-Up	318 (5.2)	Y	8	OHV
	D250 Pick-Up	360 (5.9)	Z	8	OHV
	D250 Pick-Up	360 (5.9)	8	6	OHV Turbo diesel
	W250 Pick-Up	318 (5.2)	Y	8	OHV
	W250 Pick-Up	360 (5.9)	Z	8	OHV
	W250 Pick-Up	360 (5.9)	8	6	OHV Turbo diesel
	D350 Pick-Up	360 (5.9)	Z	8	OHV
	D350 Pick-Up	360 (5.9)	8	6	OHV Turbo diesel
	W350 Pick-Up	360 (5.9)	Z	8	OHV
	W350 Pick-Up	360 (5.9)	8	6	OHV Turbo diesel
1990	B150 Van	239 (3.9)	X	6	OHV
	B150 Van	318 (5.2)	Y	8	OHV
	B250 Van	239 (3.9)	X	6	OHV
	B250 Van	318 (5.2)	Y	8	OHV
	B250 Van	360 (5.9)	Z	8	OHV
	B250 Van	360 (5.9)	5	8	OHV
	B350 Van	318 (5.2)	Y	8	OHV
	B350 Van	360 (5.9)	Z	8	OHV
	B350 Van	360 (5.9)	5	8	OHV

ENGINE IDENTIFICATION

Year	Model	Engine Displacement cu. in. (liter)	Engine Series Identification (VIN)	No. of Cylinders	Engine Type
1990	D150 Pickup	239 (3.9)	X	6	OHV
	D150 Pickup	318 (5.2)	Y	8	OHV
	D150 Pickup	360 (5.9)	Z	8	OHV
	W150 Pickup	239 (3.9)	X	6	OHV
	W150 Pickup	318 (5.2)	Y	8	OHV
	W150 Pickup	360 (5.9)	Z	8	OHV
	AD150 Ramcharger	318 (5.2)	Y	8	OHV
	AD150 Ramcharger	360 (5.9)	Z	8	OHV
	AD150 Ramcharger	360 (5.9)	5	8	OHV
	AW150 Ramcharger	318 (5.2)	Y	8	OHV
	AW150 Ramcharger	360 (5.9)	Z	8	OHV
	AW150 Ramcharger	360 (5.9)	5	8	OHV
	D250 Pickup	239 (3.9)	X	6	OHV
	D250 Pickup	318 (5.2)	Y	8	OHV
	D250 Pickup	360 (5.9)	Z	8	OHV
	D250 Pickup	360 (5.9)	5	8	OHV
	D250 Pickup	360 (5.9)	8	6	OHV Turbodiesel
	W250 Pickup	318 (5.2)	Y	8	OHV
	W250 Pickup	360 (5.9)	Z	8	OHV
	W250 Pickup	360 (5.9)	5	8	OHV
	W250 Pickup	360 (5.9)	8	6	OHV Turbodiesel
	D350 Pickup	360 (5.9)	Z	8	OHV
	D350 Pickup	360 (5.9)	5	8	OHV
	D350 Pickup	360 (5.9)	8	6	OHV Turbodiesel
	W350 Pickup	360 (5.9)	Z	8	OHV
	W350 Pickup	360 (5.9)	5	8	OHV
	W350 Pickup	360 (5.9)	8	6	OHV Turbodiesel

GENERAL ENGINE SPECIFICATIONS

Year	VIN	No. Cylinder Displacement cu. in. (liter)	Fuel System Type	Net Horsepower @ rpm	Net Torque @ rpm (ft. lbs.)	Bore × Stroke (in.)	Compression Ratio	Oil Pressure @ rpm
1986	H	6-225 (3.7)	1bbl	90 @ 3600	160 @ 1600	3.40 × 4.12	8.4:1	25–70 @ 3000
	T	8-318 (5.2)	2bbl	120 @ 3600	245 @ 1600	3.91 × 3.31	9.0:1	30–80 @ 3000
	W	8-360 (5.9)	4bbl	120 @ 3600	245 @ 1600	4.00 × 3.58	8.5:1	30–80 @ 3000
	I	8-360 (5.9)	4bbl	185 @ 4000	275 @ 2000	4.00 × 3.58	8.0:1	30–80 @ 3000
1987	H	6-225 (3.7)	1bbl	90 @ 3600	160 @ 1600	3.40 × 4.12	8.4:1	25–70 @ 3000
	T	8-318 (5.2)	2bbl	120 @ 3600	245 @ 1600	3.91 × 3.31	9.0:1	30–80 @ 3000
	W	8-360 (5.9)	4bbl	120 @ 3600	245 @ 1600	4.00 × 3.58	8.5:1	30–80 @ 3000
	I	8-360 (5.9)	4bbl	185 @ 4000	275 @ 2000	4.00 × 3.58	8.0:1	30–80 @ 3000

GENERAL ENGINE SPECIFICATIONS

Year	VIN	No. Cylinder Displacement cu. in. (liter)	Fuel System Type	Net Horsepower @ rpm	Net Torque @ rpm (ft. lbs.)	Bore × Stroke (in.)	Compression Ratio	Oil Pressure @ rpm
1988	X	6-239 (3.9)	EFI	125 @ 4000	195 @ 2000	3.91 × 3.31	9.2:1	30–80 @ 3000
	Y	8-318 (5.2)	EFI	170 @ 4000	260 @ 2000	3.91 × 3.31	9.2:1	30–80 @ 3000
	W	8-360 (5.9)	4bbl	185 @ 4000	283 @ 1600	4.00 × 3.58	8.1:1	30–80 @ 3000
1989	X	6-239 (3.9)	EFI	125 @ 4000	195 @ 2000	3.91 × 3.31	9.0:1	30–80 @ 3000
	Y	8-318 (5.2)	EFI	170 @ 4000	260 @ 2000	3.91 × 3.31	9.2:1	30–80 @ 3000
	Z	8-360 (5.9)	EFI	193 @ 4000	285 @ 1600	4.00 × 3.58	8.1:1	30–80 @ 3000
	8	6-360 (5.9)	Turbo diesel	160 @ 2500	400 @ 1700	4.02 × 4.72	17.5:1	30–70 @ 2500
1990	X	6-239 (3.9)	EFI	125 @ 4000	195 @ 2000	3.91 × 3.31	9.2:1	30–80 @ 3000
	Y	8-318 (5.2)	EFI	170 @ 4000	260 @ 2000	3.91 × 3.31	9.2:1	30–80 @ 3000
	Z	8-360 (5.9)	EFI	193 @ 4000	292 @ 2400	4.00 × 3.58	8.1:1	30–80 @ 3000
	5	8-360 (5.9)	EFI	193 @ 4000	292 @ 2400	4.00 × 3.58	8.1:1	30–80 @ 3000
	8	6-360 (5.9)	Turbo diesel	160 @ 2500	400 @ 1700	4.02 × 4.72	17.5:1	30–70 @ 2500

GASOLINE ENGINE TUNE-UP SPECIFICATIONS

Year	VIN	No. Cylinder Displacement cu. in. (liter)	Spark Plugs Type	Spark Plugs Gap (in.)	Ignition Timing (deg.) MT	Ignition Timing (deg.) AT	Compression Pressure (psi) ①	Fuel Pump (psi)	Idle Speed (rpm) MT	Idle Speed (rpm) AT	Valve Clearance In.	Valve Clearance Ex.
1986	H	6-225 (3.7)	RBL16Y	.035	12B	16B	100	3.5–5.0	725	750	Hyd.	Hyd.
	T	8-318 (5.2)	RN12YC	.035	8B	8B	100	5.0–7.0	650	650	Hyd.	Hyd.
	W	8-360 (5.9)	RN12YC	.035	13B	10B	100	5.0–7.0	750	750	Hyd.	Hyd.
	I	8-360 (5.9)	RN12YC	.035	13B	10B	100	5.0–7.0	700	700	Hyd.	Hyd.
1987	H	6-225 (3.7)	RBL16Y	.035	12B	16B	100	3.5–5.0	725	750	Hyd.	Hyd.
	T	8-318 (5.2)	RN12YC	.035	8B	8B	100	5.0–7.0	650	650	Hyd.	Hyd.
	W	8-360 (5.9)	RN12YC	.035	13B	10B	100	5.0–7.0	750	750	Hyd.	Hyd.
	I	8-360 (5.9)	RN12YC	.035	13B	10B	100	5.0–7.0	700	700	Hyd.	Hyd.
1988	X	6-239 (3.9)	RN12YC	.035	10B	10B	100	13.0–16.0	750	750	Hyd.	Hyd.
	Y	8-318 (5.2)	RN12YC	.035	10B	10B	100	13.0–16.0	700	700	Hyd.	Hyd.
1989	W	8-360 (5.9)	RN12YC	.035	13B	10B	100	5.0–7.0	750	750	Hyd.	Hyd.
	X	6-239 (3.9)	RN12YC	.035	10B	10B	100	13.0–16.0	750	750	Hyd.	Hyd.
	Y	8-318 (5.2)	RN12YC	.035	10B	10B	100	13.0–16.0	700	700	Hyd.	Hyd.
	Z	6-360 (5.9)	RN12YC	.035	10B	10B	100	13.0–16.0	700	700	Hyd.	Hyd.
1990	X	6-239 (3.9)	RN12YC	.035	10B	10B	100	13.0–16.0	750	750	Hyd.	Hyd.
	Y	8-318 (5.2)	RN12YC	.035	10B	10B	100	13.0–16.0	700	700	Hyd.	Hyd.
	Z	8-360 (5.9)	RN12YC	.035	10B	10B	100	13.0–16.0	700	700	Hyd.	Hyd.
	5	6-360 (5.9)	RN12YC	.035	10B	10B	100	13.0–16.0	700	700	Hyd.	Hyd.

① Minimum specification

DIESEL ENGINE TUNE-UP SPECIFICATIONS

Year	VIN	No. Cylinder Displacement cu. in. (liter)	Valve Clearance		Intake Valve Opens (deg.)	Injection Pump Setting (deg.)	Injection Nozzle Pressure (psi)		Idle Speed (rpm)	Cranking Compression Pressure (psi)
			Intake (in.)	Exhaust (in.)			New	Used		
1989	8	6-360 (5.9)	0.010	0.020	NA	①	3550 ②	NA	③	NA
1990	8	6-360 (5.9)	0.010	0.020	NA	①	3550 ②	NA	③	NA

① Align the alignment marks on the pump flange and gear housing.
② Injector operating or pop pressure
③ Automatic transmission, air conditioning ON—700
   Manual transmission, air conditioning ON—750

FIRING ORDERS

NOTE: To avoid confusion, always replace spark plug wires one at a time.

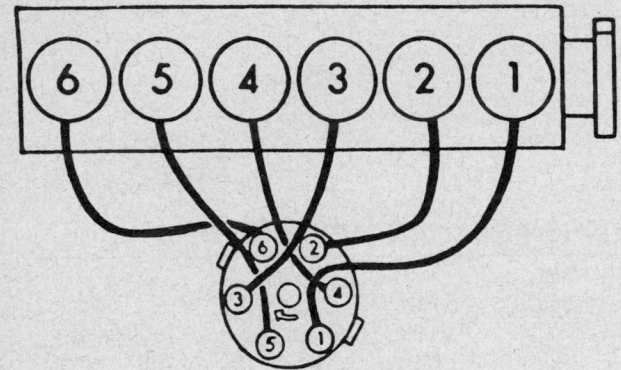

Chrysler 3.7L (225 cu. in.)
Firing order: 1–5–3–6–2–4
Distributor rotation: clockwise

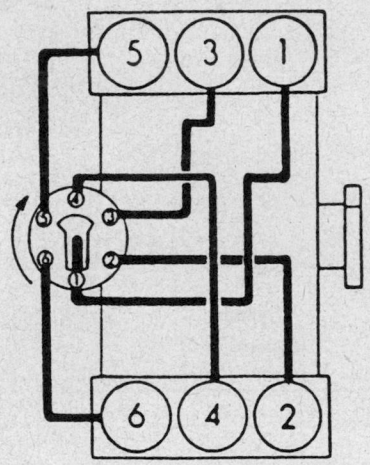

Chrysler 3.9L (239 cu. in.)
Firing order: 1–6–5–4–3–2
Distributor rotation: clockwise

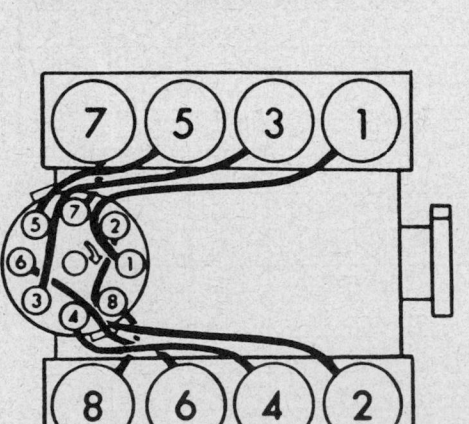

Chrysler 5.2L (318 cu. in.) and 5.9L (360 cu. in.)
Firing order: 1–8–4–3–6–5–7–2
Distributor rotation: clockwise

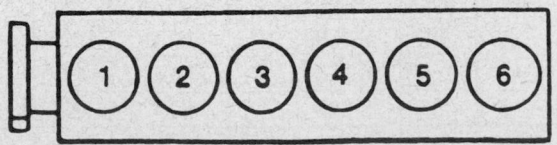

Cummins 5.9L (360 cu. in.) Turbodiesel
Firing order: 1–5–3–6–2–4

CAPACITIES

Year	Model	VIN	No. Cylinder Displacement cu. in. (liter)	Engine Crankcase with Filter	Engine Crankcase without Filter	Transmission (pts.) 4-Spd	Transmission (pts.) 5-Spd	Transmission (pts.) Auto.	Drive Axle (pts.)	Fuel Tank (gal.)	Cooling System (qts.)
1986	B150 Van	H	6-225 (3.7)	6	5	7.5	—	①	②	④	12 ⑥
	B150 Van	T	8-318 (5.2)	6	5	7.5	—	①	②	④	16 ⑥
	B250 Van	H	6-225 (3.7)	6	5	7.5	—	①	②	④	12 ⑥
	B250 Van	T	8-318 (5.2)	6	5	7.5	—	①	②	④	16 ⑥
	B250 Van	W	8-360 (5.9)	6	5	7.5	—	①	②	④	14.5 ⑥
	B350 Van	T	8-318 (5.2)	6	5	7.5	—	①	②	④	16 ⑥
	B350 Van	W	8-360 (5.9)	6	5	7.5	—	①	②	④	14.5 ⑥
	B350 Van	I	8-360 (5.9)	6	5	7.5	—	①	②	④	14.5 ⑥
	D100 Pick-Up	H	6-225 (3.7)	6	5	7	—	①	②	⑤	13
	D100 Pick-Up	T	8-318 (5.2)	6	5	7	—	①	②	⑤	17
	D100 Pick-Up	W	8-360 (5.9)	6	5	7	—	①	②	⑤	15.5
	D100 Pick-Up	I	8-360 (5.9)	6	5	7	—	①	②	⑤	15.5
	W100 Pick-Up	H	6-225 (3.7)	6	5	7	—	①	②③	⑤	13 ⑦
	W100 Pick-Up	T	8-318 (5.2)	6	5	7	—	①	②③	⑤	17 ⑦
	W100 Pick-Up	W	8-360 (5.9)	6	5	7	—	①	②③	⑤	15.5 ⑦
	AD100 Ramcharger	T	8-318 (5.2)	6	5	7	—	①	②	⑤	17
	AW100 Ramcharger	T	8-318 (5.2)	6	5	7	—	①	②③	⑤	17 ⑦
	AW100 Ramcharger	W	8-360 (5.9)	6	5	7	—	①	②③	⑤	15.5 ⑦
	AW100 Ramcharger	I	8-360 (5.9)	6	5	7	—	①	②③	⑤	15.5 ⑦
	D250 Pick-Up	H	6-225 (3.7)	6	5	7	—	①	②	⑤	13
	D250 Pick-Up	T	8-318 (5.2)	6	5	7	—	①	②	⑤	17
	W250 Pick-Up	H	6-225 (3.7)	6	5	7	—	①	②③	⑤	13 ⑦
	W250 Pick-Up	T	8-318 (5.2)	6	5	7	—	①	②③	⑤	17 ⑦
	W250 Pick-Up	W	8-360 (5.9)	6	5	7	—	①	②③	⑤	15.5 ⑦
	W250 Pick-Up	I	8-360 (5.9)	6	5	7	—	①	②③	⑤	15.5 ⑦
	D350 Pick-Up	T	8-318 (5.2)	6	5	7	—	①	②	⑤	17
	D350 Pick-Up	W	8-360 (5.9)	6	5	7	—	①	②	⑤	15.5
	D350 Pick-Up	I	8-360 (5.9)	6	5	7	—	①	②	⑤	15.5
	W350 Pick-Up	T	8-318 (5.2)	6	5	7	—	①	②③	⑤	17 ⑦
	W350 Pick-Up	W	8-360 (5.9)	6	5	7	—	①	②③	⑤	15.5 ⑦
	W350 Pick-Up	I	8-360 (5.9)	6	5	7	—	①	②③	⑤	15.5 ⑦
1987	B150 Van	H	6-225 (3.7)	6	5	7.5	—	①	②	④	13.5 ⑧
	B150 Van	T	8-318 (5.2)	6	5	7.5	—	①	②	④	16.5 ⑧
	B250 Van	H	6-225 (3.7)	6	5	7.5	—	①	②	④	13.5 ⑧
	B250 Van	T	8-318 (5.2)	6	5	7.5	—	①	②	④	16.5 ⑧
	B250 Van	W	8-360 (5.9)	6	5	7.5	—	①	②	④	15 ⑧
	B350 Van	T	8-318 (5.2)	6	5	7.5	—	①	②	④	16.5 ⑧
	B350 Van	W	8-360 (5.9)	6	5	7.5	—	①	②	④	15 ⑧
	B350 Van	I	8-360 (5.9)	6	5	7.5	—	①	②	④	15 ⑧
	D150 Pick-Up	H	6-225 (3.7)	6	5	7	—	①	②	⑤	14
	D150 Pick-Up	T	8-318 (5.2)	6	5	7	—	①	②	⑤	17 ⑨
	D150 Pick-Up	W	8-360 (5.9)	6	5	7	—	①	②	⑤	15.5
	D150 Pick-Up	I	8-360 (5.9)	6	5	7	—	①	②	⑤	15.5

CAPACITIES

Year	Model	VIN	No. Cylinder Displacement cu. in. (liter)	Engine Crankcase with Filter	Engine Crankcase without Filter	Transmission (pts.) 4-Spd	Transmission (pts.) 5-Spd	Transmission (pts.) Auto.	Drive Axle (pts.)	Fuel Tank (gal.)	Cooling System (qts.)
1987	W150 Pickup	H	6-225 (3.7)	6	5	7	—	①	②③	⑤	13.5
	W150 Pickup	T	8-318 (5.2)	6	5	7	—	①	②③	⑤	17
	W150 Pickup	W	8-360 (5.9)	6	5	7	—	①	②③	⑤	15.5 ⑨
	AD150 Ramcharger	T	8-318 (5.2)	6	5	7	—	①	②	⑤	17 ⑨
	AW150 Ramcharger	T	8-318 (5.2)	6	5	7	—	①	②③	⑤	16.5 ⑨
	AW150 Ramcharger	W	8-360 (5.9)	6	5	7	—	①	②③	⑤	15.5 ⑨
	AW150 Ramcharger	I	8-360 (5.9)	6	5	7	—	①	②③	⑤	15.5 ⑨
	D250 Pickup	H	6-225 (3.7)	6	5	7	—	①	②	⑤	14
	D250 Pickup	T	8-318 (5.2)	6	5	7	—	①	②	⑤	17 ⑨
	W250 Pickup	H	6-225 (3.7)	6	5	7	—	①	②③	⑤	13.5
	W250 Pickup	T	8-318 (5.2)	6	5	7	—	①	②③	⑤	17
	W250 Pickup	W	8-360 (5.9)	6	5	7	—	①	②③	⑤	15.5 ⑨
	W250 Pickup	I	8-360 (5.9)	6	5	7	—	①	②③	⑤	15.5 ⑨
	D350 Pickup	T	8-318 (5.2)	6	5	7	—	①	②	⑤	17 ⑨
	D350 Pickup	W	8-360 (5.9)	6	5	7	—	①	②	⑤	15.5 ⑨
	D350 Pickup	I	8-360 (5.9)	5	4	7	—	①	②	⑤	15.5 ⑨
	W350 Pickup	T	8-318 (5.2)	6	5	7	—	①	②③	⑤	17
	W350 Pickup	W	8-360 (5.9)	6	5	7	—	①	②③	⑤	15.5 ⑨
	W350 Pickup	I	8-360 (5.9)	6	5	7	—	①	②③	⑤	15.5 ⑨
1988	B100 Van	X	6-239 (3.9)	4	4	7	4	①	②	⑩	14.6
	B100 Van	Y	8-318 (5.2)	5	4	7	4	①	②	⑩	16.5
	B150 Van	X	6-239 (3.9)	4	4	7	4	①	②	⑩	14.6
	B150 Van	Y	8-318 (5.2)	5	4	7	4	①	②	⑩	16.5
	B250 Van	X	6-239 (3.9)	4	4	7	4	①	②	⑩	14.6
	B250 Van	Y	8-318 (5.2)	5	4	7	4	①	②	⑩	16.5
	B250 Van	W	8-360 (5.9)	5	4	7	4	①	②	⑩	15 ⑧
	B350 Van	Y	8-318 (5.2)	5	4	7	—	①	②	⑩	16.5
	B350 Van	W	8-360 (5.9)	5	4	7	—	①	②	⑩	15 ⑧
	D100 Pickup	X	6-239 (3.9)	4	4	7	4	①	②	⑪	15.1
	D100 Pickup	Y	8-318 (5.2)	5	4	7	4	①	②	⑪	17
	D100 Pickup	W	8-360 (5.9)	5	4	7	4	①	②	30	15.5
	W100 Pickup	Y	8-318 (5.2)	5	4	7	—	①	②③	⑪	17
	W100 Pickup	W	8-360 (5.9)	5	4	7	4	①	②	30	15.5
	D150 Pickup	X	6-239 (3.9)	4	4	7	4	①	②	⑪	15.1
	D150 Pickup	Y	8-318 (5.2)	5	4	7	4	①	②	⑪	17
	D150 Pickup	W	8-360 (5.9)	5	4	7	—	①	②③	30	15.5
	W150 Pickup	Y	8-318 (5.2)	5	4	7	—	①	②③	⑪	17
	W150 Pickup	W	8-360 (5.9)	5	4	7	—	①	②	34	15.5
	AD150 Ramcharger	Y	8-318 (5.2)	5	4	7	—	①	②	34	17
	AD150 Ramcharger	W	8-360 (5.9)	5	4	7	—	①	②③	34	15.5
	AW150 Ramcharger	Y	8-318 (5.2)	5	4	7	—	①	②③	34	17
	AW150 Ramcharger	W	8-360 (5.9)	5	4	7	—	①	②	30	15.5

CAPACITIES

Year	Model	VIN	No. Cylinder Displacement cu. in. (liter)	Engine Crankcase with Filter	without Filter	Transmission (pts.) 4-Spd	5-Spd	Auto.	Drive Axle (pts.)	Fuel Tank (gal.)	Cooling System (qts.)
1988	D250 Pickup	X	6-239 (3.9)	4	4	7	—	①	②	⑪	15.1
	D250 Pickup	Y	8-318 (5.2)	5	4	7	—	①	②	⑪	17
	D250 Pickup	W	8-360 (5.9)	5	4	7	—	①	②	30	15.5
	W250 Pickup	Y	8-318 (5.2)	5	4	7	—	①	②③	⑪	17
	W250 Pickup	W	8-360 (5.9)	5	4	7	—	①	②③	30	15.5
	D350 Pickup	Y	8-318 (5.2)	5	4	7	—	①	②	⑪	17
	D350 Pickup	W	8-360 (5.9)	6	5	7	—	①	②	30	15.5
	M350 Pickup	Y	8-318 (5.2)	5	4	7	—	①	②③	⑪	17
	M350 Pickup	W	8-360 (5.9)	5	4	7	—	①	②③	30	15.5
1989	B100 Van	X	6-239 (3.9)	4	4	—	4	①⑫	②	⑩	14.6
	B100 Van	Y	8-318 (5.2)	5	4	—	4	①⑫	②	⑩	16.5
	B150 Van	W	6-239 (3.9)	4	4	—	4	①⑫	②	⑩	14.6
	B150 Van	Y	8-318 (5.2)	5	4	—	4	①⑫	②	⑩	16.5
	B250 Van	X	6-239 (3.9)	4	4	—	4	①⑫	②	⑩	14.6
	B250 Van	Y	8-318 (5.2)	5	4	—	4	①⑫	②	⑩	16.5
	B250 Van	Z	8-360 (5.9)	5	4	—	4	①⑫	②	⑩	15 ⑧
	B350 Van	Y	8-318 (5.2)	5	4	—	—	①⑫	②	⑩	16.5
	B350 Van	Z	8-360 (5.9)	5	4	—	—	①⑫	②	⑩	15 ⑧
	D100 Pickup	X	6-239 (3.9)	4	4	7	4	①⑫	②	⑪	15.1
	D100 Pickup	Y	8-318 (5.2)	5	4	7	4	①⑫	②	⑪	17
	D100 Pickup	Z	8-360 (5.9)	5	4	7	4	①⑫	②	30	15.5
	W100 Pickup	Y	8-318 (5.2)	5	4	7	—	①⑫	②③	⑪	17
	W100 Pickup	Z	8-360 (5.9)	5	4	7	—	①⑫	②③	30	15.5
	D150 Pickup	X	6-239 (3.9)	4	4	7	4	①⑫	②	⑪	15.1
	D150 Pickup	Y	8-318 (5.2)	5	4	7	4	①⑫	②	⑪	17
	D150 Pickup	Z	8-360 (5.9)	5	4	7	4	①⑫	②	30	15.5
	W150 Pickup	X	6-239 (3.9)	4	4	7	—	①	②③	⑪	15.1
	W150 Pickup	Y	8-318 (5.2)	5	4	7	—	①	②③	⑪	17
	W150 Pickup	Z	8-360 (5.9)	5	4	7	—	①	②③	30	15.5
	AD150 Ramcharger	Y	8-318 (5.2)	5	4	7	4	①⑫	②	34	17
	AD150 Ramcharger	Z	8-360 (5.9)	5	4	7	4	①⑫	②	34	15.5
	AM150 Ramcharger	Y	8-318 (5.2)	5	4	7	—	①	②③	34	17
	AM150 Ramcharger	Z	8-360 (5.9)	5	4	7	—	①	②③	34	15.5
	D250 Pickup	X	6-239 (3.9)	4	4	7	4	①⑫	②	30	15.1
	D250 Pickup	Y	8-318 (5.2)	5	4	7	4	①⑫	②	⑪	17
	D250 Pickup	Z	8-360 (5.9)	5	4	7	4	①⑫	②	30	15.5
	D250 Pickup	8	6-360 (5.9)	12	11	—	7	22	7	30	⑭
	W250 Pickup	Y	8-318 (5.2)	5	4	7	—	①	②③	⑪	17
	W250 Pickup	Z	8-360 (5.9)	5	4	7	—	①	②③	30	15.5
	W250 Pickup	8	6-360 (5.9)	12	11	—	7	22	⑬	30	⑭
	D350 Pickup	Z	8-360 (5.9)	5	4	7	4	①	②	30	15.5
	D350 Pickup	8	6-360 (5.9)	12	11	—	7	22	7	30	⑭
	W350 Pickup	Z	8-360 (5.9)	5	4	7	—	①	②③	30	15.5
	W350 Pickup	8	6-360 (5.9)	12	11	—	7	22	⑬	30	⑭

CHRYSLER CORPORATION
D/W SERIES (PICK-UP) • RAMCHARGER • B SERIES (VAN)

CAPACITIES

Year	Model	VIN	No. Cylinder Displacement cu. in. (liter)	Engine Crankcase with Filter	Engine Crankcase without Filter	Transmission (pts.) 4-Spd	5-Spd	Auto.	Drive Axle (pts.)	Fuel Tank (gal.)	Cooling System (qts.)
1990	B150 Van	X	6-239 (3.9)	4	4	7	4	①⑫	②	⑩	14.6
	B150 Van	Y	8-318 (5.2)	5	4	7	4	①⑫	②	⑩	16.5
	B250 Van	X	6-239 (3.9)	4	4	7	—	①⑫	②	⑩	14.6
	B250 Van	Y	8-318 (5.2)	5	4	7	—	①⑫	②	⑩	16.5
	B250 Van	Z	8-360 (5.9)	5	4	7	—	①⑫	②	⑩	15⑧
	B250 Van	5	8-360 (5.9)	5	4	7	—	①⑫	②	⑩	15⑧
	B350 Van	Y	8-318 (5.2)	5	4	7	—	①⑫	②	⑩	16.5
	B350 Van	Z	8-360 (5.9)	5	4	7	—	①⑫	②	⑩	15⑧
	B350 Van	5	8-360 (5.9)	5	4	7	—	①⑫	②	⑩	15⑧
	D150 Pickup	X	6-239 (3.9)	4	4	7	4	①	②	⑪	15.1
	D150 Pickup	Y	8-318 (5.2)	5	4	7	4	①	②	⑪	17
	D150 Pickup	Z	8-360 (5.9)	5	4	7	4	①	②	30	15.5
	W150 Pickup	X	6-239 (3.9)	4	4	7	—	①	②③	⑪	15.1
	W150 Pickup	Y	8-318 (5.2)	5	4	7	—	①	②③	⑪	17
	W150 Pickup	Z	8-360 (5.9)	5	4	7	—	①	②③	30	15.5
	AD150 Ramcharger	Y	8-318 (5.2)	5	4	7	—	①	②	34	17
	AD150 Ramcharger	Z	8-360 (5.9)	5	4	7	—	①	②	34	15.5
	AD150 Ramcharger	5	8-360 (5.9)	5	4	7	—	①	②	34	15.5
	AW150 Ramcharger	Y	8-318 (5.2)	5	4	7	—	①	②③	34	16.5
	AW150 Ramcharger	Z	8-360 (5.9)	5	4	7	—	①	②③	34	15
	AW150 Ramcharger	5	8-360 (5.9)	5	4	7	—	①	②③	34	15
	D250 Pickup	X	6-239 (3.9)	4	4	7	4	①	②	⑪	15.1
	D250 Pickup	Y	8-318 (5.2)	5	4	7	4	①	②	⑪	17
	D250 Pickup	Z	8-360 (5.9)	5	4	7	4	①	②	30	15.5
	D250 Pickup	5	8-360 (5.9)	5	4	7	4	①	②	30	15.5
	D250 Pickup	8	6-360 (5.9)	12	11	—	7	22	7	30	⑭
	W250 Pickup	Y	8-318 (5.2)	5	4	7	4	①	②③	⑪	17
	W250 Pickup	Z	8-360 (5.9)	5	4	7	4	①	②③	30	15.5
	W250 Pickup	5	8-360 (5.9)	5	4	7	4	①	②③	30	15.5
	W250 Pickup	8	6-360 (5.9)	12	11	—	7	22	⑬	30	⑭
	D350 Pickup	Z	8-360 (5.9)	5	4	7	4	①	②	30	15.5
	D350 Pickup	5	8-360 (5.9)	5	4	7	4	①	②	30	15.5
	D350 Pickup	8	6-360 (5.9)	12	11	—	7	22	7	30	⑭
	W350 Pickup	Z	8-360 (5.9)	5	4	7	4	①	②③	30	15.5
	W350 Pickup	5	8-360 (5.9)	5	4	7	4	①	②③	30	15.5
	W350 Pickup	8	6-360 (5.9)	12	11	—	7	22	⑬	30	⑭

① A-904T/A-999/A-998 Transmissions—17.1 pts.
A-727 Transmission with lockup—16.7 pts.
A-727 Transmission without lockup—17.1 pts.
② Chrysler 8³⁄₈ in.—4.5 pts.
Chrysler 9¼ in.—4.5 pts.
Spicer or Dana 60—6.0 pts.
Dana 70—7.0 pts.
③ Front axle except W250 and W350—5.6 pts.
Front axle—W250 and W350—6.5 pts.

④ Standard—22 gals. (metal)
Optional—36 gals. (plastic)
⑤ Sport Utility—35 gals.
Light truck standard—20 gals.
Light truck optional—30 gals.
⑥ Add 2 qts. with air conditioning or max cooling
⑦ Add 1 qt. with air conditioning or increased cooling
⑧ Add 1 qt. when equipped with rear heater
⑨ Add ½ qt. with 20 inch tall radiator

⑩ Standard—22 gals.
Optional—35 gals.
⑪ Standard—22 gals.
Optional—30 gals.
⑫ A500 Transmission—20.4 pts.
⑬ Rear axle—7.0 pts.
Front axle—6.3 pts.
⑭ With manual transmission—15.5 qts.
With automatic transmission—16.5 qts.

CAMSHAFT SPECIFICATIONS
All measurements given in inches.

Year	VIN	No. Cylinder Displacement cu. in. (liter)	Journal Diameter 1	2	3	4	5	Lobe Lift In.	Ex.	Bearing Clearance	Camshaft End Play
1986	H	6-225 (3.7)	1.998–1.999	1.982–1.983	1.967–1.968	1.951–1.952	—	0.378	0.378	0.001–0.005	—
	T	8-318 (5.2)	1.998–1.999	1.982–1.983	1.967–1.968	1.951–1.952	1.561 1.562	0.373	0.400	0.001–0.005	0.002–0.010
	W	8-360 (5.9)	1.998–1.999	1.982–1.983	1.967–1.968	1.951–1.952	1.561 1.562	0.410	0.410	0.001–0.005	0.002–0.010
	I	8-360 (5.9)	1.998–1.999	1.982–1.983	1.967–1.968	1.951–1.952	1.561 1.562	0.410	0.410	0.001–0.005	0.002–0.010
1987	H	6-225 (3.7)	1.998–1.999	1.982–1.983	1.967–1.968	1.951–1.952	—	0.378	0.378	0.001–0.005	—
	T	8-318 (5.2)	1.998–1.999	1.982–1.983	1.967–1.968	1.951–1.952	1.561 1.562	0.373	0.400	0.001–0.005	0.002–0.010
	W	8-360 (5.9)	1.998–1.999	1.982–1.983	1.967–1.968	1.951–1.952	1.561 1.562	0.410	0.410	0.001–0.005	0.002–0.010
	I	8-360 (5.9)	1.998–1.999	1.982–1.983	1.967–1.968	1.951–1.952	1.561 1.562	0.410	0.410	0.001–0.005	0.002–0.010
1988	X	6-239 (3.9)	1.998–1.999	1.967–1.968	1.951–1.952	② ③	—	0.373	0.400	0.001–0.005	0.002–0.010
	Y	8-318 (5.2)	1.998–1.999	1.982–1.983	1.967–1.968	1.951–1.952	1.561 1.562	0.373	0.400	0.001–0.005	0.002–0.010
	W	8-360 (5.9)	1.998–1.999	1.982–1.983	1.967–1.968	1.951–1.952	1.561 1.562	0.410	0.410	0.001–0.005	0.002–0.010
1989	X	6-239 (3.9)	1.998–1.999	1.967–1.968	1.951–1.952	② ③	—	0.373	0.400	0.001–0.005	0.002–0.010
	Y	8-318 (5.2)	1.998–1.999	1.982–1.983	1.967–1.968	1.951–1.952	1.561 1.562	0.373	0.400	0.001–0.005	0.002–0.010
	Z	8-360 (5.9)	1.998–1.999	1.982–1.983	1.967–1.968	1.951–1.952	1.561 1.562	0.410	0.410	0.001–0.005	0.002–0.010
	8	6-360 (5.9)	2.125 ①	2.125	2.125	2.125	—	1.852 ②	1.841 ②	0.001–0.005	0.006–0.010
1990	X	6-239 (3.9)	1.998–1.999	1.967–1.968	1.951–1.952	② ③	—	0.373	0.400	0.001–0.005	0.002–0.010
	Y	8-318 (5.2)	1.998–1.999	1.982–1.983	1.967–1.968	1.951–1.952	1.561 1.562	0.373	0.400	0.001–0.005	0.002–0.010
	Z	8-360 (5.9)	1.998–1.999	1.982–1.983	1.967–1.968	1.951–1.952	1.561 1.562	0.410	0.410	0.001–0.005	0.002–0.010
	5	8-360 (5.9)	1.998–1.999	1.982–1.983	1.967–1.968	1.951–1.952	1.561 1.562	0.410	0.410	0.001–0.005	0.002–0.010
	8	6-360 (5.9)	2.125 ①	2.125	2.125	2.125	—	1.852 ②	1.841 ②	0.001–0.005	0.006–0.010

① Minimum wear limit
② Minimum diameter at peak of lobe

CRANKSHAFT AND CONNECTING ROD SPECIFICATIONS

All measurements are given in inches.

Year	VIN	No. Cylinder Displacement cu. in. (liter)	Crankshaft				Connecting Rod		
			Main Brg. Journal Dia.	Main Brg. Oil Clearance	Shaft End-play	Thrust on No.	Journal Diameter	Oil Clearance	Side Clearance
1986	H	6-225 (3.7)	2.4795–2.7505	0.0010–0.0025	0.004–0.010	3	2.187–2.188	0.0010–0.0025	0.007–0.013
	T	8-318 (5.2)	2.4995–2.5005	①	0.002–0.010	3	2.124–2.125	0.0005–0.0022	0.006–0.014
	W	8-360 (5.9)	2.8095–2.8105	①	0.002–0.010	3	2.124–2.125	0.0005–0.0022	0.006–0.014
	I	8-360 (5.9)	2.8095–2.8105	①	0.002–0.010	3	2.124–2.125	0.0005–0.0022	0.006–0.014
1987	H	6-225 (3.7)	2.4795–2.7505	0.0010–0.0025	0.004–0.010	3	2.187–2.188	0.0010–0.0025	0.007–0.013
	T	8-318 (5.2)	2.4995–2.5005	①	0.002–0.010	3	2.124–2.125	0.0005–0.0022	0.006–0.014
	W	8-360 (5.9)	2.8095–2.8105	①	0.002–0.010	3	2.124–2.125	0.0005–0.0022	0.006–0.014
	I	8-360 (5.9)	2.8095–2.8105	①	0.002–0.010	3	2.124–2.125	0.0005–0.0022	0.006–0.014
1988	X	6-239 (3.9)	2.4995–2.5005	①	0.002–0.010	2	2.124–2.125	0.0005–0.0022	0.006–0.014
	Y	8-318 (5.2)	2.4995–2.5005	①	0.002–0.010	3	2.124–2.125	0.0005–0.0022	0.006–0.014
	W	8-360 (5.9)	2.8095–2.8105	①	0.002–0.010	3	2.124–2.125	0.0005–0.0022	0.006–0.014
1989	X	6-239 (3.9)	2.4995–2.5005	①	0.002–0.010	2	2.124–2.125	0.0005–0.0022	0.006–0.014
	Y	8-318 (5.2)	2.4995–2.5005	①	0.002–0.010	3	2.124–2.125	0.0005–0.0022	0.006–0.014
	Z	8-360 (5.9)	2.8095–2.8105	①	0.002–0.010	3	2.124–2.125	0.0005–0.0022	0.006–0.014
	8	6-360 (5.9)	3.2662 ②	0.0047 ③	0.005–0.012	6	2.715 ②	0.0035 ③	0.004–0.012
1990	X	6-239 (3.9)	2.4995–2.5005	①	0.002–0.010	2	2.124–2.125	0.0005–0.0022	0.006–0.014
	Y	8-318 (5.2)	2.4995–2.5005	①	0.002–0.010	3	2.124–2.125	0.0005–0.0022	0.006–0.014
	Z	8-360 (5.9)	2.8095–2.8105	①	0.002–0.010	3	2.124–2.125	0.0005–0.0022	0.006–0.014
	5	8-360 (5.9)	2.8095–2.8105	①	0.002–0.010	3	2.124–2.125	0.0005–0.0022	0.006–0.014
	8	6-360 (5.9)	3.2662 ②	0.0047 ③	0.005–0.012	6	2.715 ②	0.0035 ③	0.004–0.012

① No. 1—0.0005–0.0015 in.
　 Nos. 2–5—0.0005–0.0025 in.
② Minimum wear limit
③ Maximum clearance

VALVE SPECIFICATIONS

Year	VIN	No. Cylinder Displacement cu. in. (liter)	Seat Angle (deg.)	Face Angle (deg.)	Spring Test Pressure (lbs.)	Spring Installed Height (in.)	Stem-to-Guide Clearance (in.)		Stem Diameter (in.)	
							Intake	Exhaust	Intake	Exhaust
1986	H	6-225 (3.7)	45–45.5	①	137–150	1.625–1.688	0.001–0.017	0.002–0.017	0.372–0.373	0.371–0.372
	T	8-318 (5.2)	45–45.5	44.5–45	②	③	0.001–0.017	0.002–0.017	0.372–0.373	0.371–0.372
	W	8-360 (5.9)	45–45.5	44.5–45	②	③	0.001–0.017	0.002–0.017	0.372–0.373	0.371–0.372
	I	8-360 (5.9)	45–45.5	44.5–45	②	③	0.001–0.017	0.002–0.017	0.372–0.373	0.371–0.372
1987	H	6-225 (3.7)	45–45.5	①	137–150	1.625–1.688	0.001–0.017	0.002–0.017	0.372–0.373	0.371–0.372
	T	8-318 (5.2)	45–45.5	44.5–45	②	③	0.001–0.017	0.002–0.017	0.372–0.373	0.371–0.372
	W	8-360 (5.9)	45–45.5	44.5–45	②	③	0.001–0.017	0.002–0.017	0.372–0.373	0.371–0.372
	I	8-360 (5.9)	45–45.5	44.5–45	②	③	0.001–0.017	0.002–0.017	0.372–0.373	0.371–0.372
1988	X	6-239 (3.9)	45–45.5	44.5–45	②	③	0.001–0.017	0.002–0.017	0.372–0.373	0.371–0.372
	Y	8-318 (5.2)	45–45.5	44.5–45	②	③	0.001–0.017	0.002–0.017	0.372–0.373	0.371–0.372
	W	8-360 (5.9)	45–45.5	44.5–45	②	③	0.001–0.017	0.002–0.017	0.372–0.373	0.371–0.372
1989	X	6-239 (3.9)	45–45.5	44.5–45	②	③	0.001–0.017	0.002–0.017	0.372–0.373	0.371–0.372
	Y	8-318 (5.2)	45–45.5	44.5–45	②	③	0.001–0.017	0.002–0.017	0.372–0.373	0.371–0.372
	Z	8-360 (5.9)	45–45.5	44.5–45	②	③	0.001–0.017	0.002–0.017	0.372–0.373	0.371–0.372
	8	8-360 (5.9)	④	④	65 ⑤	2.19 ⑥	0.002–0.006	0.002–0.006	0.313–0.314	0.313–0.314
1990	X	6-239 (3.9)	45–45.5	44.5–45	②	③	0.001–0.017	0.002–0.017	0.372–0.373	0.371–0.372
	Y	8-318 (5.2)	45–45.5	44.5–45	②	③	0.001–0.017	0.002–0.017	0.372–0.373	0.371–0.372
	Z	8-360 (5.9)	45–45.5	44.5–45	②	③	0.001–0.017	0.002–0.017	0.372–0.373	0.371–0.372
	5	8-360 (5.9)	45–45.5	44.5–45	②	③	0.001–0.017	0.002–0.017	0.372–0.373	0.371–0.372
	8	6-360 (5.9)	④	④	65 ⑤	2.19 ⑥	0.002–0.006	0.002–0.006	0.313–0.314	0.313–0.314

① Intake—44.5 degrees–45 degrees
   Exhaust—42.5 degrees–43 degrees
② Intake—170–184 lbs.
   Exhaust—318 CID (5.2L) and 239 CID (3.9L)—180–194 lbs.
   Exhaust—360 CID (5.9L)—181–197 lbs.
③ Intake—1.625–1.688 in.
   Exhaust—1.453–1.516 in.
④ Intake—30 degrees
   Exhaust—45 degrees
⑤ Minimum acceptable load at 1.94 in.
⑥ Free standing length

PISTON AND RING SPECIFICATIONS

All measurements are given in inches.

Year	VIN	No. Cylinder Displacement cu. in. (liter)	Piston Clearance	Ring Gap			Ring Side Clearance		
				Top Compression	Bottom Compression	Oil Control	Top Compression	Bottom Compression	Oil Control
1986	H	6-225 (3.7)	0.0005–0.0015	0.010–0.020	0.010–0.020	0.015–0.055	0.0015–0.0030	0.0015–0.0030	0.0002–0.0050
	T	8-318 (5.2)	0.0005–0.0015	0.010–0.020	0.010–0.020	0.015–0.055	0.0015–0.0030	0.0015–0.0030	0.0002–0.0050
	W	8-360 (5.9)	0.0005–0.0015	0.010–0.020	0.010–0.020	0.015–0.055	0.0015–0.0030	0.0015–0.0030	0.0002–0.0050
	I	8-360 (5.9)	0.0005–0.0015	0.010–0.020	0.010–0.020	0.015–0.055	0.0015–0.0030	0.0015–0.0030	0.0002–0.0050
1987	H	6-225 (3.7)	0.0005–0.0015	0.010–0.020	0.010–0.020	0.015–0.055	0.0015–0.0030	0.0015–0.0030	0.0002–0.0050
	T	8-318 (5.2)	0.0005–0.0015	0.010–0.020	0.010–0.020	0.015–0.055	0.0015–0.0030	0.0015–0.0030	0.0002–0.0050
	W	8-360 (5.9)	0.0005–0.0015	0.010–0.020	0.010–0.020	0.015–0.055	0.0015–0.0030	0.0015–0.0030	0.0002–0.0050
	I	8-360 (5.9)	0.0005–0.0015	0.010–0.020	0.010–0.020	0.015–0.055	0.0015–0.0030	0.0015–0.0030	0.0002–0.0050
1988	X	6-239 (3.9)	0.0005–0.0015	0.010–0.020	0.010–0.020	0.015–0.055	0.0015–0.0030	0.0015–0.0030	0.0002–0.0050
	Y	8-318 (5.2)	0.0005–0.0015	0.010–0.020	0.010–0.020	0.015–0.055	0.0015–0.0030	0.0015–0.0030	0.0002–0.0050
	W	8-360 (5.9)	0.0005–0.0015	0.010–0.020	0.010–0.020	0.015–0.055	0.0015–0.0030	0.0015–0.0030	0.0002–0.0050
1989	X	6-239 (3.9)	0.0005–0.0015	0.010–0.020	0.010–0.020	0.015–0.055	0.0015–0.0030	0.0015–0.0030	0.0002–0.0050
	Y	8-318 (5.2)	0.0005–0.0015	0.010–0.020	0.010–0.020	0.015–0.055	0.0015–0.0030	0.0015–0.0030	0.0002–0.0050
	Z	8-360 (5.9)	0.0005–0.0015	0.010–0.020	0.010–0.020	0.015–0.055	0.0015–0.0030	0.0015–0.0030	0.0002–0.0050
	8	8-360 (5.9)	NA	0.016–0.028	0.010–0.215	0.010–0.215	0.0030–0.0060	0.0030–0.0060	0.0020–0.0050
1990	X	6-239 (3.9)	0.0005–0.0015	0.010–0.020	0.010–0.020	0.015–0.055	0.0015–0.0030	0.0015–0.0030	0.0002–0.0050
	Y	8-318 (5.2)	0.0005–0.0015	0.010–0.020	0.010–0.020	0.015–0.055	0.0015–0.0030	0.0015–0.0030	0.0002–0.0050
	Z	8-360 (5.9)	0.0005–0.0015	0.010–0.020	0.010–0.020	0.015–0.055	0.0015–0.0030	0.0015–0.0030	0.0002–0.0050
	5	8-360 (5.9)	0.0005–0.0015	0.010–0.020	0.010–0.020	0.015–0.055	0.0015–0.0030	0.0015–0.0030	0.0002–0.0050
	8	8-360 (5.9)	NA	0.016–0.028	0.010–0.215	0.010–0.215	0.0030–0.0060	0.0030–0.0060	0.0020–0.0050

TORQUE SPECIFICATIONS

All readings in ft. lbs.

Year	VIN	No. Cylinder Displacement cu. in. (liter)	Cylinder Head Bolts	Main Bearing Bolts	Rod Bearing Bolts	Crankshaft Pulley Bolts	Flywheel Bolts	Mainfold Intake	Mainfold Exhaust	Spark Plugs
1986	H	6-225 (3.7)	70	85	45	NA ①	55	②	②	10
	T	8-318 (5.2)	105	85	45	100 ③	55	45	④	30
	W	8-360 (5.9)	105	85	45	100 ③	55	45	④	30
	I	8-360 (5.9)	105	85	45	100 ③	55	45	④	30
1987	H	6-225 (3.7)	70	85	45	NA ①	55	②	②	10
	T	8-318 (5.2)	105	85	45	100 ③	55	45	④	30
	W	8-360 (5.9)	105	85	45	100 ③	55	45	④	30
	I	8-360 (5.9)	105	85	45	100 ③	55	45	④	30
1988	X	6-239 (3.9)	105	85	45	135 ③	55	45	④	30
	Y	8-318 (5.2)	105	85	45	100 ③	55	45	④	30
	W	8-360 (5.9)	105	85	45	100 ③	55	45	④	30
1989	X	6-239 (3.9)	105	85	45	135 ③	55	45	④	30
	Y	8-318 (5.2)	105	85	45	100 ③	55	40	④	30
	Z	8-360 (5.9)	105	85	45	100 ③	55	40	④	30
	8	6-360 (5.9)	⑤	⑥	⑦	92 ③	101	⑧	32	NA
1990	X	6-239 (3.9)	105	85	45	135 ③	55	45	④	30
	Y	8-318 (5.2)	105	85	45	100 ③	55	40	④	30
	Z	8-360 (5.9)	105	85	45	100 ③	55	40	④	30
	5	8-360 (5.9)	105	85	45	100 ③	55	40	④	30
	8	6-360 (5.9)	⑤	⑥	⑦	92 ③	101	⑧	32	NA

① Press fit using special tool
② Intake to exhaust manifold screws—260 inch lbs.
   All manifold to head nuts—120 inch lbs.
③ Vibration dampener bolt
④ Bolts—20 ft. lbs.
   Nuts—15 ft. lbs.
⑤ Stage 1—29
   Stage 2—62
   Stage 3—93

⑥ Stage 1—45
   Stage 2—88
   Stage 3—129
⑦ Stage 1—26
   Stage 2—51
   Stage 3—73
⑧ Intake manifold cover

BRAKE SPECIFICATIONS

All measurements in inches unless noted.

Year	Model	Lug Nut Torque (ft. lbs.)	Master Cylinder Bore	Brake Disc Minimum Thickness	Brake Disc Maximum Runout	Standard Brake Drum Diameter	Minimum Lining Thickness Front	Minimum Lining Thickness Rear
1986	B150 Van	85–110	1.125	1.180	0.004	11	0.062	0.062
	B250 Van	85–110	1.125	1.180	0.004	11	0.062	0.062
	B350 Van	①	1.125	②	0.004	12	0.062	0.062
	D100 Pickup	①	1.125	1.180	0.004	11	0.062	0.062
	W100 Pickup	①	1.125	1.180	0.004	11	0.062	0.062
	AD100 Ramcharger	①	1.125	1.180	0.004	11	0.062	0.062
	AM100 Ramcharger	①	1.125	1.180	0.004	11	0.062	0.062

CHRYSLER CORPORATION
D/W SERIES (PICK-UP) • RAMCHARGER • B SERIES (VAN)

BRAKE SPECIFICATIONS
All measurements in inches unless noted.

Year	Model	Lug Nut Torque (ft. lbs.)	Master Cylinder Bore	Brake Disc Minimum Thickness	Brake Disc Maximum Runout	Standard Brake Drum Diameter	Minimum Lining Thickness Front	Rear
1986	D250 Pick-Up	①	1.125	②	0.005	12	0.062	0.062
	W250 Pick-Up	①	1.125	1.125	0.005	12	0.062	0.062
	D350 Pick-Up	①	1.125	1.125	0.005	12	0.062	0.062
	W350 Pick-Up	①	1.125	1.125	0.005	12	0.062	0.062
1987	B150 Van	85–110	1.125	1.180	0.004	11	0.062	0.062
	B250 Van	85–110	1.125	1.180	0.004	11	0.062	0.062
	B350 Van	①	1.125	②	0.004	12	0.062	0.062
	D150 Pick-Up	①	1.125	1.180	0.004	11	0.062	0.062
	W150 Pick-Up	①	1.125	1.180	0.004	11	0.062	0.062
	AD150 Ramcharger	①	1.125	1.180	0.004	11	0.062	0.062
	AW150 Ramcharger	①	1.125	1.180	0.004	11	0.062	0.062
	D250 Pick-Up	①	1.125	②	0.005	12	0.062	0.062
	W250 Pick-Up	①	1.125	1.125	0.005	12	0.062	0.062
	D350 Pick-Up	①	1.125	1.125	0.005	12	0.062	0.062
	W350 Pick-Up	①	1.125	1.125	0.005	12	0.062	0.062
1988	B100 Van	85–110	1.125	1.180	0.004	11	0.062	0.062
	B150 Van	85–110	1.125	1.180	0.004	11	0.062	0.062
	B250 Van	85–110	1.125	1.180	0.004	11	0.062	0.062
	B350 Van	①	1.125	②	0.004	12	0.062	0.062
	D100 Pick-Up	①	1.125	1.180	0.004	11	0.062	0.062
	W100 Pick-Up	①	1.125	1.180	0.004	11	0.062	0.062
	D150 Pick-Up	①	1.125	1.180	0.004	11	0.062	0.062
	W150 Pick-Up	①	1.125	1.180	0.004	11	0.062	0.062
	AD150 Ramcharger	①	1.125	1.180	0.004	11	0.062	0.062
	AW150 Ramcharger	①	1.125	1.180	0.004	11	0.062	0.062
	D250 Pick-Up	①	1.125	②	0.005	12	0.062	0.062
	W250 Pick-Up	①	1.125	1.125	0.005	12	0.062	0.062
	D350 Pick-Up	①	1.125	1.125	0.005	12	0.062	0.062
	W350 Pick-Up	①	1.125	1.125	0.005	12	0.062	0.062
1989	B100 Van	85–110	1.125	1.180	0.004	11	0.062	0.062
	B150 Van	85–110	1.125	1.180	0.004	11	0.062	0.062
	B250 Van	85–110	1.125	1.180	0.004	11	0.062	0.062
	B350 Van	①	1.125	②	0.004	12	0.062	0.062
	D100 Pick-Up	①	1.125	1.180	0.004	11	0.062	0.062
	W100 Pick-Up	①	1.125	1.180	0.004	11	0.062	0.062
	D150 Pick-Up	①	1.125	1.180	0.004	11	0.062	0.062
	W150 Pick-Up	①	1.125	1.180	0.004	11	0.062	0.062
	AD150 Ramcharger	①	1.125	1.180	0.004	11	0.062	0.062
	AW150 Ramcharger	①	1.125	1.180	0.004	11	0.062	0.062
	D250 Pick-Up	①	1.125	②	0.005	12	0.062	0.062
	W250 Pick-Up	①	1.125	1.125	0.005	12	0.062	0.062
	D350 Pick-Up	①	1.125	1.125	0.005	12	0.062	0.062
	W350 Pick-Up	①	1.125	1.125	0.005	12	0.062	0.062

BRAKE SPECIFICATIONS
All measurements in inches unless noted.

Year	Model	Lug Nut Torque (ft. lbs.)	Master Cylinder Bore	Brake Disc Minimum Thickness	Brake Disc Maximum Runout	Standard Brake Drum Diameter	Minimum Lining Thickness Front	Rear
1990	B150 Van	85–110	1.125	1.180	0.004	11	0.062	0.062
	B250 Van	85–110	1.125	1.180	0.004	11	0.062	0.062
	B350 Van	①	1.125	②	0.004	12	0.062	0.062
	D150 Pick-Up	①	1.125	1.180	0.004	11	0.062	0.062
	W150 Pick-Up	①	1.125	1.180	0.004	11	0.062	0.062
	AD150 Ramcharger	①	1.125	1.180	0.004	11	0.062	0.062
	AW150 Ramcharger	①	1.125	1.180	0.004	11	0.062	0.062
	D250 Pick-Up	①	1.125	②	0.005	12	0.062	0.062
	W250 Pick-Up	①	1.125	1.125	0.005	12	0.062	0.062
	D350 Pick-Up	①	1.125	1.125	0.005	12	0.062	0.062
	W350 Pick-Up	①	1.125	1.125	0.005	12	0.062	0.062

① ½ × 20 cone lug nut—105 ft. lbs.
⅝ × 18 cone lug nut—200 ft. lbs.
⅝ × 18 flanged lug nut—325 ft. lbs.
② With 3300 lb. or 3600 lb. front axle—1.180 in.
With 4000 lb. front axle—1.125 in.

WHEEL ALIGNMENT

Year	Model	Caster Range (deg.)	Caster Preferred Setting (deg.)	Camber Range (deg.)	Camber Preferred Setting (deg.)	Toe-in (in.)	Steering Axis Inclination (deg.)
1986	B150 Van	1.25P–3.75P	2.5	0.6N–0.6P	0	0	NA
	B250 Van	1.25P–3.75P	2.5	0.6N–0.6P	0	0	NA
	B350 Van	1.25P–3.75P	2.5	0.6N–0.6P	0	0	NA
	D100 Pick-Up	1N–2P	0.5	0P–1P	0.5	0.25	NA
	M100 Pick-Up	0.5P–3.5P	2	0.5P–1.5P	1	0.20	NA
	AD100 Ramcharger	1N–2P	0.5	0–1P	0.5	0.25	NA
	AW100 Ramcharger	0.5P–3.5P	2	0.5P–1.5P	1	0.20	8.5 ①
	D250 Pick-Up	1N–2P	0.5	0–1P	0.5	0.25	NA
	M250 Pick-Up	0.5P–3.5P	2	0.5P–1.5P	1	0.20	8.5 ①
	D350 Pick-Up	1N–2P	0.5	0–1P	0.5	0.25	NA
	W350 Pick-Up	0.5P–3.5P	2	0.5P–1.5P	1	0.20	8.5 ①
1987	B150 Van	1.25P–3.75P	2.5	0.6N–0.6P	0	0	NA
	B250 Van	1.25P–3.75P	2.5	0.6N–0.6P	0	0	NA
	B350 Van	1.25P–3.75P	2.5	0.6N–0.6P	0	0	NA
	D150 Pick-Up	1N–2P	0.5	0–1P	0.5	0.25	NA
	M150 Pick-Up	0.5P–3.5P	2	0.5P–1.5P	1	0.20	8.5 ①
	AD150 Ramcharger	1N–2P	0.5	0–1P	0.5	0.25	NA
	AW150 Ramcharger	0.5P–3.5P	2	0.5P–1.5P	1	0.20	8.5 ①

CHRYSLER CORPORATION
D/W SERIES (PICK-UP) • RAMCHARGER • B SERIES (VAN)

WHEEL ALIGNMENT

Year	Model	Caster Range (deg.)	Preferred Setting (deg.)	Camber Range (deg.)	Preferred Setting (deg.)	Toe-in (in.)	Steering Axis Inclination (deg.)
1987	D250 Pick-Up	1N–2P	0.5	0–1P	0.5	0.25	NA
	M250 Pick-Up	0.5P–3.5P	2	0.5P–1.5P	1	0.20	8.5 ①
	D350 Pick-Up	1N–2P	0.5	0–1P	0.5	0.25	NA
	M350 Pick-Up	0.5P–3.5P	2	0.5P–1.5P	1	0.20	8.5 ①
1988	B100 Van	1.25P–3.75P	2.5	0.6N–0.6P	0	0	NA
	B150 Van	1.25P–3.75P	2.5	0.6N–0.6P	0	0	NA
	B250 Van	1.25P–3.75P	2.5	0.6N–0.6P	0	0	NA
	B350 Van	1.25P–3.75P	2.5	0.6N–0.6P	0	0	NA
	D100 Pick-Up	1N–2P	0.5	0–1P	0.5	0.25	NA
	M100 Pick-Up	0.5P–3.5P	2	0.5P–1.5P	1	0.20	8.5 ①
	D150 Pick-Up	1N–2P	0.5	0–1P	0.5	0.25	NA
	M150 Pick-Up	0.5P–3.5P	2	0.5P–1.5P	1	0.20	8.5 ①
	AD150 Ramcharger	1N–2P	0.5	0–1P	0.5	0.25	NA
	AW150 Ramcharger	0.5P–3.5P	2	0.5P–1.5P	1	0.20	8.5 ①
	D250 Pick-Up	1N–2P	0.5	0–1P	0.5	0.25	NA
	M250 Pick-Up	0.5P–3.5P	2	0.5P–1.5P	1	0.20	8.5 ①
	D350 Pick-Up	1N–2P	0.5	0–1P	0.5	0.25	NA
	M350 Pick-Up	0.5P–3.5P	2	0.5P–1.5P	1	0.20	8.5 ①
1989	B100 Van	1.25P–3.75P	2.5	0.6N–0.6P	0	0	NA
	B150 Van	1.25P–3.75P	2.5	0.6N–0.6P	0	0	NA
	B250 Van	1.25P–3.75P	2.5	0.6N–0.6P	0	0	NA
	B350 Van	1.25P–3.75P	2.5	0.6N–0.6P	0	0	NA
	D100 Pick-Up	1N–2P	0.5	0–1P	0.5	0.25	NA
	W100 Pick-Up	0.5P–3.5P	2	0.5P–1.5P	1	0.20	8.5 ①
	D150 Pick-Up	1N–2P	0.5	0–1P	0.5	0.25	NA
	W150 Pick-Up	0.5P–3.5P	2	0.5P–1.5P	1	0.20	8.5 ①
	AD150 Ramcharger	1N–2P	0.5	0–1P	0.5	0.25	NA
	AM150 Ramcharger	0.5P–3.5P	2	0.5P–1.5P	1	0.20	8.5 ①
	D250 Pick-Up	1N–2P	0.5	0–1P	0.5	0.25	NA
	W250 Pick-Up	0.5P–3.5P	2	0.5P–1.5P	1	0.20	8.5 ①
	D350 Pick-Up	1N–2P	0.5	0–1P	0.5	0.25	NA
	W350 Pick-Up	0.5P–3.5P	2	0.5P–1.5P	1	0.20	8.5 ①
1990	B150 Van	1.25P–3.75P	2.5	0.6N–0.6P	0	0	NA
	B250 Van	1.25P–3.75P	2.5	0.6N–0.6P	0	0	NA
	B350 Van	1.25P–3.75P	2.5	0.6N–0.6P	0	0	NA
	D150 Pick-Up	1N–2P	0.5	0–1P	0.5	0.25	NA
	W150 Pick-Up	0.5P–3.5P	2	0.5P–1.5P	1	0.20	8.5 ①
	AD150 Ramcharger	1N–2P	0.5	0–1P	0.5	0.25	NA
	AW150 Ramcharger	0.5P–3.5P	2	0.5P–1.5P	1	0.20	8.5 ①
	D250 Pick-Up	1N–2P	0.5	0–1P	0.5	0.25	NA
	W250 Pick-Up	0.5P–3.5P	2	0.5P–1.5P	1	0.20	8.5 ①
	D350 Pick-Up	1N–2P	0.5	0–1P	0.5	0.25	NA
	W350 Pick-Up	0.5P–3.5P	2	0.5P–1.5P	1	0.20	8.5 ①

① King pin inclination

ENGINE ELECTRICAL

NOTE: Disconnecting the negative battery cable on some vehicles may interfere with the functions of the on board computer systems and may require the computer to undergo a relearning process, once the negative battery cable is reconnected.

Distributor

Removal and Installation

1. Disconnect the negative battery cable.
2. Disconnect the distributor pickup lead wires and vacuum hose, if equipped.
3. Unfasten the distributor cap retaining clips and lift off the distributor cap with all ignition wires still connected. Remove the coil wire if necessary.
4. Matchmark the rotor to the distributor housing.

NOTE: Do not crank the engine during this procedure. If the engine is cranked, the matchmark must be disregarded.

5. Remove the hold-down bolt and clamp.
6. Remove the distributor from the engine.

To install:

7. Install a new distributor housing O-ring.
8. Install the distributor in the engine so the rotor is lined up with the matchmark on the housing. Make sure the distributor is fully seated and that the distributor shaft is fully engaged.
9. If the engine has been cranked, position the engine so that the No. 1 piston is at TDC of the compression stroke and the mark on the vibration damper is lined up with **0** on the timing indicator. Then install the distributor so the rotor is aligned with the position of the No. 1 ignition wire on the distributor cap.
10. Install the hold-down clamp and snug the hold-down bolt.
11. Connect the distributor pickup lead wires.
12. Install the distributor cap and snap the retaining clips into place.
13. Connect the negative battery cable.
14. Adjust the ignition timing and tighten the hold-down bolt.

Ignition Timing

Adjustment

1. Start the engine, set the parking brake and run the engine until at normal operating temperature. Keep all lights and accessories **OFF**.
2. If a magnetic timing unit is available, insert the probe into the receptacle near the timing scale. The scale is located on the timing chain cover above and to the left of the vibration damper on Pick-Ups and below the damper on Vans.
3. If a magnetic timing unit is not available, connect a conventional power timing light to the No. 1 cylinder spark plug wire.
4. Connect the red lead of a tachometer to the negative primary terminal of the coil and connect the black lead to a good ground.
5. If the vehicle is equipped with a carburetor, ground the carburetor switch with a jumper wire. Set the idle speed according to the Vehicle Emission Control Information (VECI) label. Disconnect and plug the distributor vacuum advance hose at the distributor or computer, if equipped.
6. If the vehicle is equipped with Electronic Fuel Injection (EFI), connect the Diagnostic Readout Box II (DRBII) and access the Basic Timing Mode. If the DRBII is not available, disconnect the coolant sensor located near the thermostat housing

and confirm that the Check Engine lamp on the instrument panel is **ON**.
7. Aim the timing light at the timing scale or read the magnetic timing unit.
8. If the timing is advanced (higher than the specification on the VECI label), the distributor should be turned clockwise. If the timing is retarded, (lower than the specification on the VECI label), the distributor should be turned counterclockwise.
9. Loosen the distributor hold-down bolt just enough so the distributor can be rotated. Turn the distributor in the proper direction until the specified timing is reached. Tighten the hold-down bolt and recheck the timing and idle speed.
10. Turn the engine off. Remove the jumper wire, if used. Connect the vacuum hose or coolant sensor (make sure the Check Engine lamp does not come on when the vehicle is started). Disconnect the timing apparatus and tachometer.
11. If the coolant temperature sensor was disconnected, erase the created fault code using the Erase Fault Code mode on the DRBII. If the DRBII is not available, the code can be erased by disconnecting the battery, although it is not recommended.

NOTE: If the battery is disconnected, radio memory will be lost and other fault codes that may have been stored in the computer's memory will be erased. If the coolant sensor code is not erased at this point, it will disappear after 50–100 vehicle key on/off cycles providing there is no problem with that circuit.

Alternator

For further information, please refer to "Electrical" in the Unit Repair section.

Belt Tension Adjustment

NOTE: The belt tension is automatically adjusted by the tensioner on the 5.9L diesel engine. Periodic adjustment is not necessary.

1. Loosen the pivot bolt slightly.
2. Loosen the adjuster strap nut or bolt just enough so the alternator can be moved.
3. If the alternator bracket is not equipped with an adjuster bolt, use a suitable pry bar and apply tension to the alternator until the belt(s) deflect about ¼–½ in. under a 10 lb. load. Torque the adjuster strap bolt to 200 inch lbs. (23 Nm). Torque the pivot bolt to 30 ft. lbs. (41 Nm).
4. If the bracket is equipped with an adjuster bolt, tighten it until the belts deflect about ½ in. under a 10 lb. load. Torque the adjuster strap nut to 200 inch lbs. (23 Nm). Torque the pivot bolt to 30 ft. lbs. (41 Nm).

Removal and Installation

1. Disconnect the negative battery cable.
2. On the 5.9L diesel engine, use a ⅜ in. drive breaker bar to lift the belt tensioner and remove the belt. On all other engines, loosen the mounting bolts, move the alternator toward the engine and remove the drive belt(s).

NOTE: On some Vans, it may be easier to remove the alternator through the right front wheelwell since the fan shroud and possibly air conditioning and heater plumbing under the hood will prevent removal from in front of the vehicle. Lift the vehicle and safely support to remove the right front wheel and gain access to the alternator on these applications.

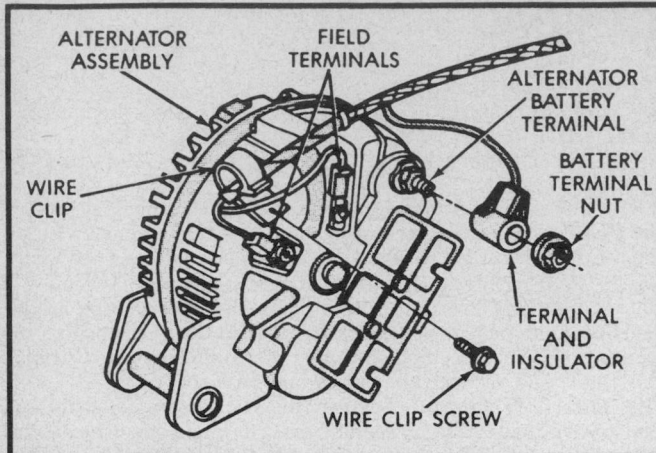

Chrysler 60 and 78 amp alternator terminals

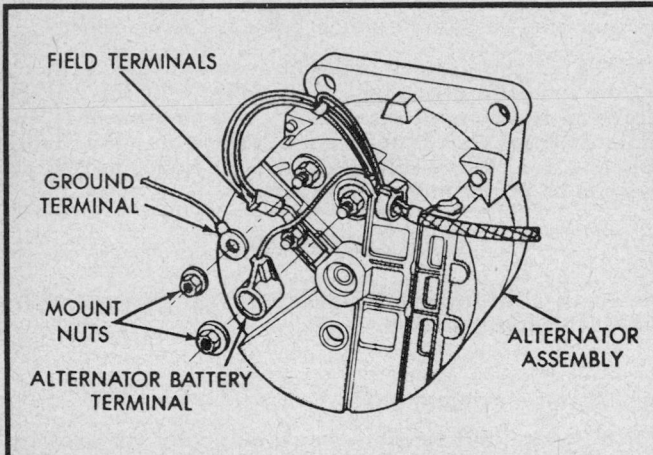

Chrysler 114 amp alternator terminals

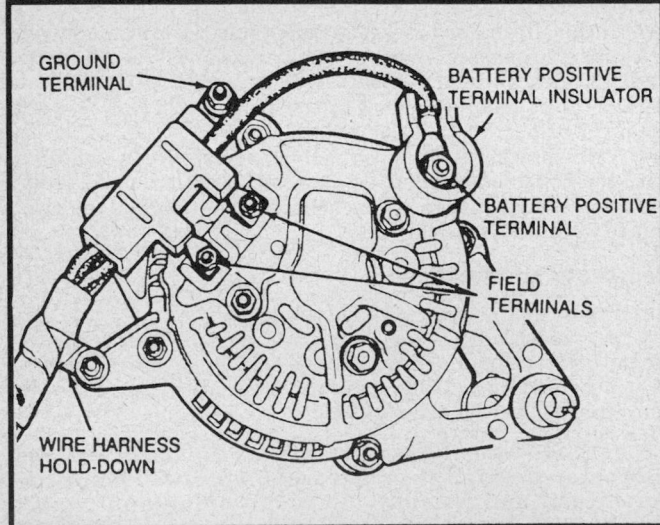

Chrysler 90HS, 120HS and Nippondenso alternators terminals

3. Remove the mounting bolts, spacers and adjuster bolt, if equipped and remove the alternator from the brackets.

4. Remove the battery positive, field and ground terminals from the rear of the alternator. Remove the wire harness hold-down screw from the alternator, if equipped.

To install:

5. Connect all wiring to the proper terminals on the rear of the alternator and install the wire harness hold-down screw, if equipped.

6. Position the alternator in the mounting brackets.

7. Install the spacers, pivot bolt, adjuster strap bolt or nut and adjuster bolt, if equipped.

8. On the 5.9L diesel engine, torque the upper bolt to 18 ft. lbs. (24 Nm), the lower bolt to 32 ft. lbs. (43 Nm) and install the belt. On all other engines, install the drive belt(s) and adjust to specification. Torque the adjuster strap nut or bolt to 200 inch lbs. (23 Nm). Torque the pivot bolt to 30 ft. lbs. (41 Nm).

9. Connect the negative battery cable.

Voltage Regulator

For further information, please refer to "Electrical" in the Unit Repair section.

Removal and Installation

NOTE: The voltage regulator is integrated into the circuitry of the Single Module Engine Controller (SMEC) or Single Board Engine Controller (SBEC) on vehicles with EFI and is not serviceable.

1. Disconnect the negative battery cable.
2. Unplug the connector from the voltage regulator.
3. Remove the retaining screws and remove the regulator from the vehicle.
4. The installation is the reversal of the removal procedure. Make sure the connector retainer is properly clipped in place.

Starter

For further information, please refer to "Electrical" in the Unit Repair section.

Removal and Installation

1. Disconnect the negative battery cable.
2. Raise the vehicle and support safely, unless equipped with a 3.7L engine.
3. Remove the heat shield from the starter, if equipped.
4. Disconnect the solenoid lead wires from the starter.
5. Unbolt the starter, remove the exhaust bracket and automatic transmission oil cooler tube bracket, if equipped and remove the starter from the vehicle.

To install:

6. Install the starter to the bellhousing and install the upper mounting bolt loosely.
7. Install the automatic transmission oil cooler tube bracket and exhaust bracket, if equipped. Install the lower mounting nut or bolts. Torque the mounting nut and bolt evenly to 50 ft. lbs. (68 Nm) on all engines except the 5.9L diesel engine. On that engine, torque the mounting bolts to 32 ft. lbs. (43 Nm).
8. Connect the solenoid lead wires.
9. Install the heat shield, if equipped.
10. Connect the negative battery cable and check the starter for proper operation.

Intake Manifold Heater

Removal and Installation

5.9L DIESEL ENGINE

1. Disconnect the negative battery cable.
2. Disconnect the throttle rod from the throttle lever.

Rotating the throttle bracket away from the engine

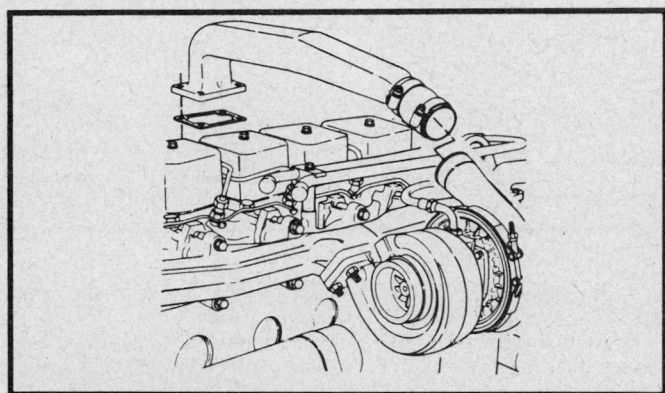

Air crossover tube and turbocharger

3. Remove the 4 bolts that attach the air crossover to the intake manifold. Loosen the lower throttle control bracket mounting bolt and move the bracket away from the engine.
4. Loosen the hose clamps on the turbocharger end of the

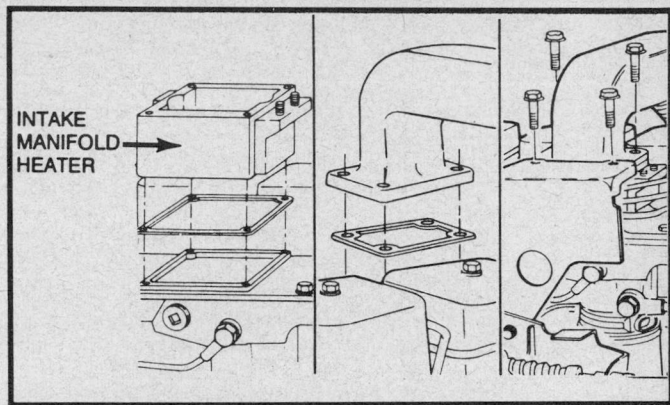

Intake manifold heater and related parts

crossover tube and remove the tube and gasket. Cover the turbocharger opening with a clean shop towel.
5. Disconnect the electrical wiring from the intake manifold heater, remove the heater and remove the gasket.
To install:
6. Clean the gasket mounting surface and install a new gasket.
7. Install the intake manifold heater and connect the wiring.
8. Remove the towel from the turbocharger opening and install the air crossover tube and gasket. Tighten the hose clamps.
9. Rotate the throttle control bracket back into place. Torque all mounting bolts to 18 ft. lbs. (24 Nm).
10. Attach the throttle rod to the throttle lever.

Testing

1. Disconnect the negative battery cable.
2. Disconnect the wires from the intake manifold heater.
3. Using an ohmmeter, check the resistance from a good ground to each heater terminal.
4. If there is any resistance, or if the circuit is open, inspect the assembly for dirty or corroded connections.
5. If the resistance is 0Ω, the heater is functioning properly.
6. If the circuit is open, the heater is defective.

CHASSIS ELECTRICAL

Heater Blower Motor

Removal and Installation
VAN WITHOUT AIR CONDITIONING

1. Disconnect the negative battery cable.
2. Remove the air intake duct and top half of the fan shroud, if necessary. Disconnect the blower connector.
3. Remove the 7 screws that fasten the back plate to the heater housing.
4. Remove the blower motor from the vehicle.
5. Remove the spring clip fastening the blower wheel to the blower shaft and pull off the wheel.
6. Remove the vent tube.
7. Remove the nuts fastening the blower motor to the back plate and remove the motor.
To install:
8. Check the seal for breaks and adhesion; repair as necessary.
9. Install the blower motor to the back plate.
10. Install the vent tube.

11. Install the blower wheel to the shaft and secure the spring clip.
12. Install the assembly to the heater housing and install the 7 screws.
13. Connect the conector.
14. Install the fan shroud and air duct, if they were removed.
15. Connect the negative battery cable and check the blower motor for proper operation.

VAN WITH AIR CONDITIONING

1. Disconnect the negative battery cable.
2. Remove the air intake duct and top half of the fan shroud.
3. Disconnect the blower connector.
4. Remove the blower motor cooling tube.
5. Remove the retaining nuts and washers from the studs holding the blower.
6. Pull the air conditioning lines inboard and upward while removing the blower assembly from the vehicle. Remove the spring clip fastening the blower wheel to the blower shaft and pull off the wheel.

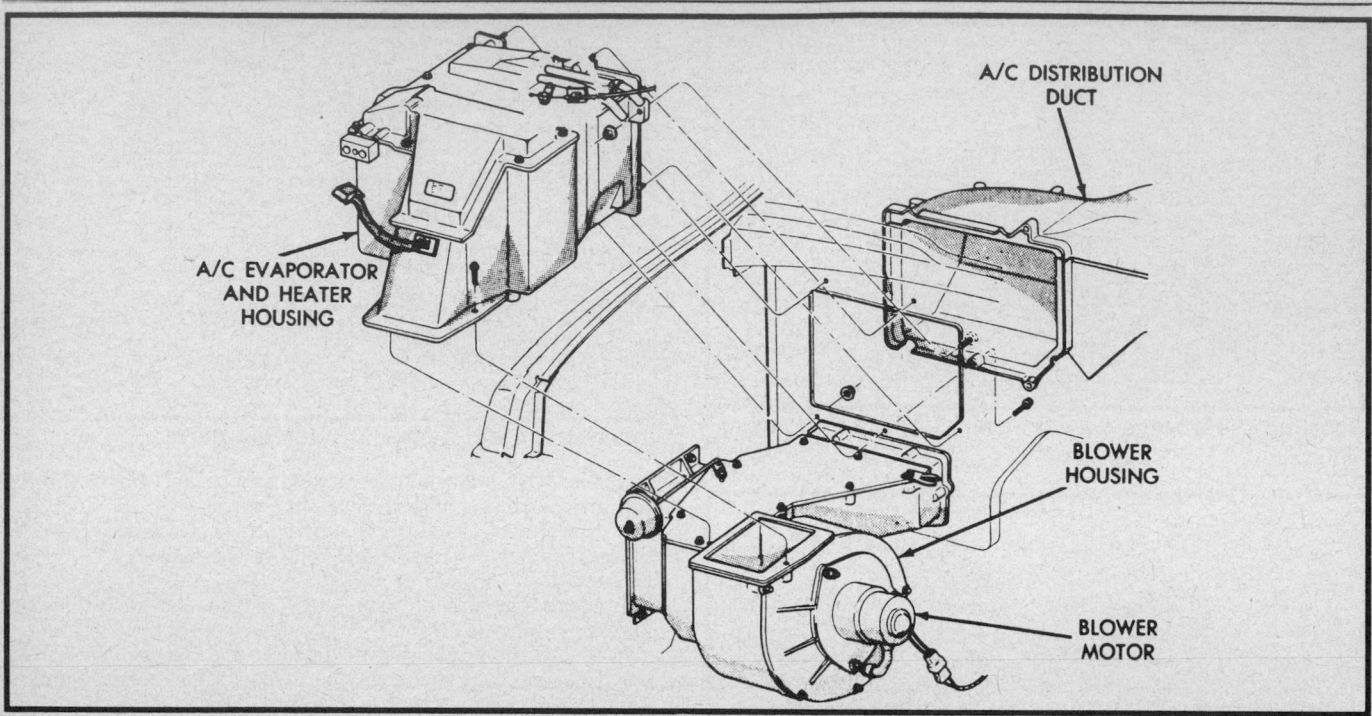

Underhood location of the blower motor—Van with air conditioning

To install:

7. Install the blower wheel to the shaft and install the spring clip. Inspect the blower mounting plate seal and repair as necessary. Apply rubber adhesive to the seal to aid in assembly.

8. Install the blower into the housing and install the washers and nuts.

9. Install the cooling tube.

10. Connect the connector.

11. Install the fan shroud and air intake duct.

12. Connect the negative battery cable and check the blower motor for proper operation.

PICK-UP AND RAMCHARGER

1. Disconnect the negative battery cable.
2. Disconnect the blower connector.
3. Remove the blower motor cooling tube.
4. Remove the screws or retaining nuts retaining the blower plate to the housing.
5. Remove the assembly from the housing.
6. Remove the spring clip fastening the blower wheel to the blower shaft and pull off the wheel. Remove the blower from the plate.

To install:

7. Inspect the blower mounting plate seal and repair as necessary.

8. Install the blower to the plate. Install the blower wheel to the shaft and install the spring clip.

9. Install the blower into the housing and install the screws or washers and nuts.

10. Install the cooling tube.

11. Connect the connector.

12. Connect the negative battery cable and check the blower motor for proper operation.

Windshield Wiper Motor

Removal and Installation

1. Disconnect the negative battery cable.
2. Disconnect the wires from the wiper motor.
3. Remove the mounting bolts.

4. Pull the motor out far enough to gain access to the crank arm to motor link retainer bushing.

5. Remove the crank arm from the drive link by prying the retainer bushing from the crank arm pin with a suitable prying tool.

6. Remove the motor from the vehicle.

7. Hold the crank arm with a wrench while removing the crank nut to prevent from overloading the gears.

8. Remove the crank arm from the motor.

To install:

9. Index the slot correctly and position the crank arm on the motor shaft. Start the crank nut making sure the crank arm does not move from its slotted position.

10. Hold the crank arm with a wrench and torque the nut to 95 inch lbs. (11 Nm).

11. Lubricate the drive link retainer bushing and install the crank arm pin to the bushing by snapping them together suitable pliers.

12. Install the motor to the vehicle and torque the mounting bolts to 65 inch lbs. (7 Nm).

13. Connect the wires to the motor.

14. Connect the negative battery cable and check the wiper motor for proper operation.

Windshield Wiper Switch

Removal and Installation

DASH MOUNTED

Van

1. Disconnect the negative battery cable.
2. Remove the lower column cover, if equipped.
3. Remove the 2 screws retaining the switch from under the instrument panel.
4. Disconnect the connector and illumination lamp.
5. Remove the assembly from under the instrument panel and remove the switch from the housing.
6. The installation is the reversal of the removal procedure.
7. Connect the negative battery cable and check the switch for proper operation.

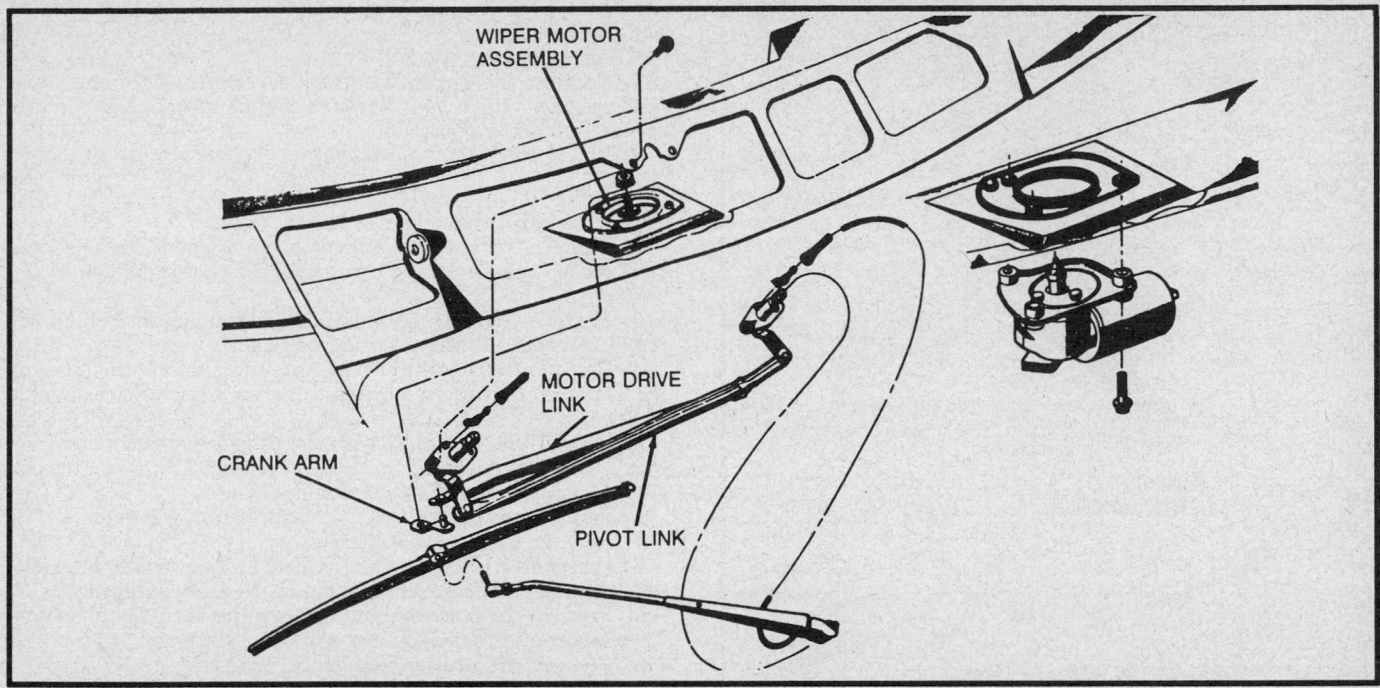

Typical Van windshield wiper motor and linkage

Pick-Up and Ramcharger

1. Disconnect the negative battery cable.
2. Remove the map light.
3. Remove 6 screws which attach the faceplate to the base panel. There is a screw below the heater-air conditioning control panel which is not visible from above.
4. If equipped with automatic transmission, place the shift lever in its lowest position.
5. Remove the faceplate by pulling the top edge rearward to clear the brow and pulling the bottom out, disengaging the attaching clips. If the vehicle is equipped with 4WD, disconnect the indicator wires.
6. Reach under the instrument panel, depress the spring button and remove the headlight switch knob.
7. Pull the wiper switch knob off the lever. Remove the power mirror switch knob, if equipped.
8. Remove the bezel.
9. Remove the screws attaching the wiper switch to the instrument panel, disconnect the wiring and remove the switch from the vehicle.

To install:

10. Connect the wiring to the switch and install the switch to the instrument panel.
11. Install the bezel.
12. Install the headlight stem and wiper switch knob. Install the power mirror switch knob, if removed.
13. Connect the 4WD indicator if equipped, install the cluster faceplate and map light.
14. Connect the negative battery cable and check the switch for proper operation.

COLUMN MOUNTED

Except Tilt Wheel

1. Disconnect the negative battery cable.
2. Remove the lower steering column cover, if equipped.
3. Remove the horn pad mounting screws from behind the steering wheel and remove the horn pad.
4. Remove the steering wheel nut, matchmark the steering wheel to the shaft and remove the steering wheel with a suitable puller.
5. Remove the plastic wiring channel from the underside of the steering column.
6. Disconnect the wiper switch connector, intermittent wipe module connector and cruise control connector, if equipped.
7. Remove the side lock housing cover.
8. Remove the slotted hex-head screw that attaches the wiper switch to the turn signal switch and remove the switch.
9. Remove the control knob from the end of the stalk. Pull the round nylon hider up the control stalk and remove the re-

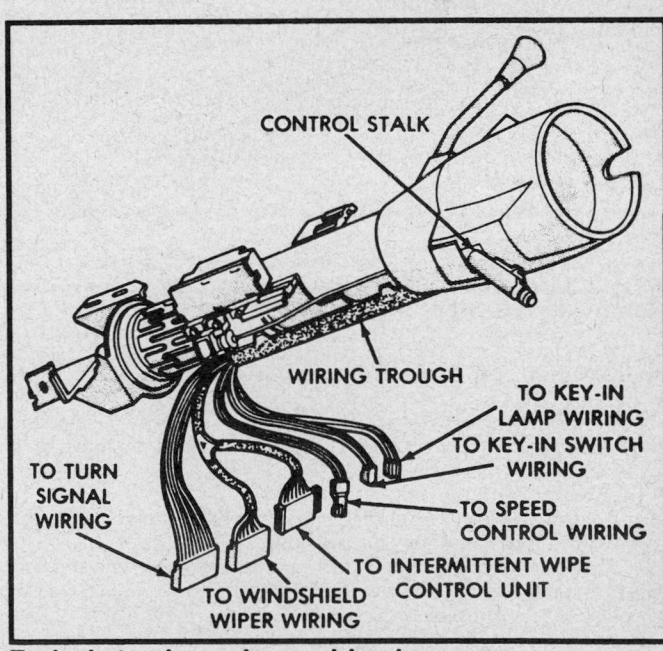

Typical steering column wiring harness

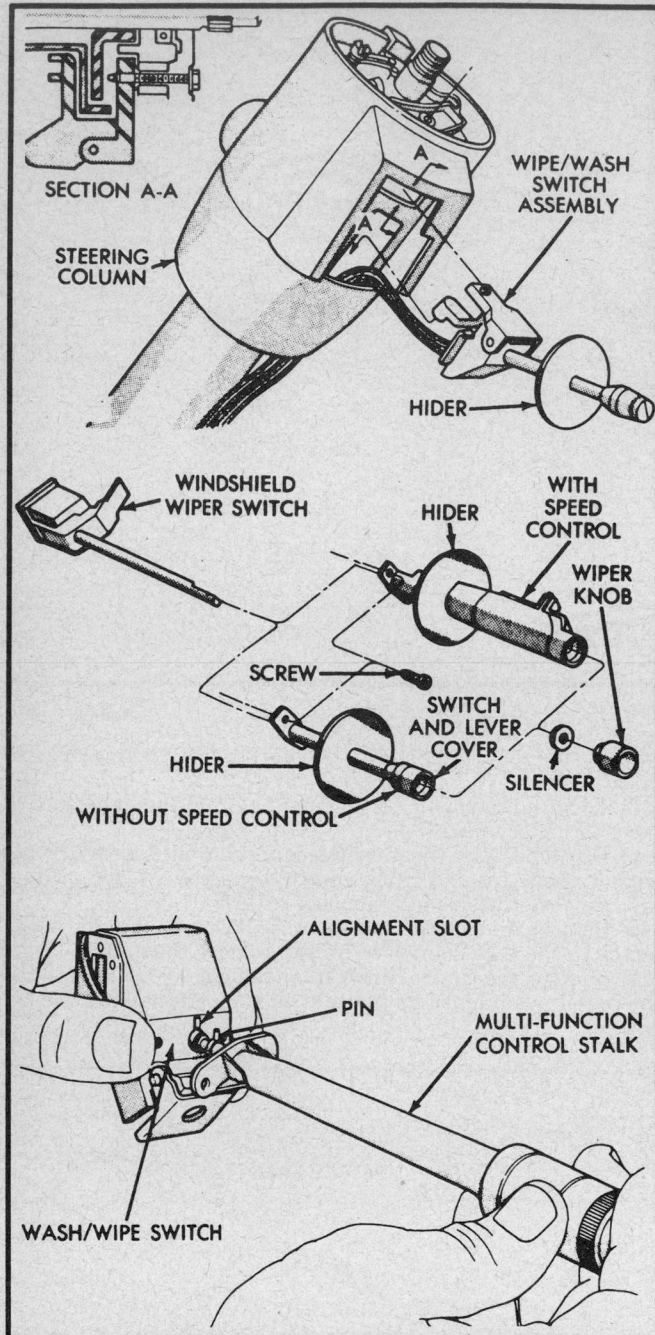

Removing the wiper switch—standard column

vealed screws that attach the control stalk sleeve to the wiper switch.

10. Rotate the control stalk shaft to the full clockwise position and remove the shaft from the wiper switch by pulling it straight out.

To install:

11. Install the control shaft to the wiper switch, install the screws, the hider and the control knob.

12. Run the wiring through the opening and down the steering column, position the switch and install the hex-head screw. Make sure the dimmer switch rod is properly engaged.

13. Install the side lock housing cover.

14. Connect the wires and install the wiring channel.

15. Install the steering wheel torque the nut to 45 ft. lbs. (61 Nm).

16. Install the horn pad.

17. Connect the negative battery cable and check the wiper and washer, cruise control, turn signal switch and dimmer switch for proper operation.

18. Install the lower column cover, if equipped.

Tilt Wheel

1. Disconnect the negative battery cable.

2. Remove the lower steering column cover, if equipped and remove the plastic wiring channel from the underside of the steering column.

3. Remove the horn pad mounting screws from behind the steering wheel and remove the horn pad.

4. Remove the steering wheel nut, matchmark the steering wheel to the shaft and remove the steering wheel with a suitable puller.

5. Depress the lock plate with the proper depressing tool, remove the retaining ring from its groove and remove the tool, ring, lock plate, cancelling cam and spring.

6. Remove the switch stalk actuator screw and arm.

7. Remove the hazard switch knob.

8. Disconnect the turn signal switch, wiper switch, intermittent module and cruise control connectors, if equipped.

9. Remove the 3 screws and remove the turn signal switch. Tape the connector to the wires to aid in removal.

10. Remove the ignition key lamp.

11. Place the key in the **LOCK** position and remove the key. Insert a thin tool into the slot next to the switch mounting screw boss, depress the spring latch at the bottom of the slot releasing the lock. Remove the lock cylinder.

12. Remove the buzzer switch and wedge spring.

13. Remove the 3 housing cover screws and remove the housing cover.

14. Remove the wiper switch pivot pin with a punch and remove the switch.

15. Remove the control knob from the end of the stalk. Pull the round nylon hider up the control stalk and remove the revealed screws that attach the control stalk sleeve to the wiper switch.

16. Rotate the control stalk shaft to the full clockwise position and remove the shaft from the wiper switch by pulling it straight out.

To install:

17. Install the control shaft to the wiper switch, install the screws, the hider and the control knob.

18. Run the wiring through the opening and down the steering column, position the switch and install the wiper switch pivot pin.

19. Install the housing cover.

20. Install the buzzer switch and wedge spring.

21. Install the lock cylinder.

22. Install the ignition key lamp.

23. Install the turn signal switch, switch stalk actuator arm and hazard switch knob.

24. Install the spring, cancelling cam, lock plate and ring on the steering shaft. Depress the plate with the depressing tool and install the ring securely in the groove. Remove the tool slowly.

25. Connect the turn signal switch, wiper switch, intermittent module and cruise control connectors, if equipped. Install the channel.

26. Install the steering wheel torque the nut to 45 ft. lbs. (61 Nm).

27. Install the horn pad.

28. Connect the negative battery cable and check the wiper and washer, cruise control, turn signal switch and dimmer switch for proper operation.

29. Install the lower column cover, if equipped.

Instrument Cluster

Removal and Installation

VAN

1. Disconnect the negative battery cable.
2. Open the glove box. Remove the screws that fasten the hood and bezel assembly. Pull the bezel off of the upper retaining clips.
3. Disconnect the gearshift pointer cable from the arm on the steering column, if equipped.
4. Remove the cluster screws. Pull the cluster out far enough to disconnect the speedometer cable by releasing the spring clip.
5. Remove all printed circuit board multiple connectors and the message center connector.
6. Remove the cluster assembly.
7. To remove the speedometer, remove the cluster lens, unplug the Emissions Maintenance Reminder (EMR) timer wires from the speedometer, if equipped and remove the retaining screws.

To install:

8. Install the speedometer if removed and connect the EMR wiring, if equipped. Position the cluster to the panel and connect the speedometer cable, multiple connectors and message center connector.
9. Push the cluster in place and install the retaining screws.
10. Connect the gearshift pointer cable to the arm on the steering column, if equipped and adjust if necessary.
11. Install the hood and bezel assembly and install the retaining screws.
12. Connect the negative battery cable.

PICK-UP AND RAMCHARGER

1. Disconnect the negative battery cable.
2. Remove the map light.
3. Remove 6 screws which attach the faceplate to the base panel. There is a screw below the heater-air conditioning control panel which is not visible from above.
4. If equipped with automatic transmission, place the shift lever in its lowest position.
5. Remove the faceplate by pulling the top edge rearward to clear the brow and pulling the bottom out, disengaging the attaching clips. If the vehicle is equipped with 4WD, disconnect the indicator wires.
6. Remove the upper and lower steering column covers. Disconnect the shift indicator actuator cable from the steering column, if equipped.
7. Loosen the heater and air conditioning control and pull it out enough to clear the cluster housing.
8. Remove the screws that retain the cluster and pull the cluster out far enough to disconnect the speedometer cable by releasing the spring clip.
9. Remove all printed circuit board multiple connectors.
10. Remove the cluster assembly.
11. To remove the speedometer, remove the cluster lens, unplug the EMR timer wires from the speedometer, if equipped and remove the retaining screws.

To install:

12. Install the speedometer if removed and connect the EMR wiring, if equipped. Position the cluster to the panel and connect the speedometer cable and multiple connectors.
13. Push the cluster in place and install the retaining screws.
14. Install the heater air conditioning control screws.
15. Connect the shift indicator actuator cable and check for alignment.
16. Install the upper and lower steering column covers.
17. Connect the 4WD indicator if equipped, install the cluster faceplate and map light.
18. Connect the negative battery cable.

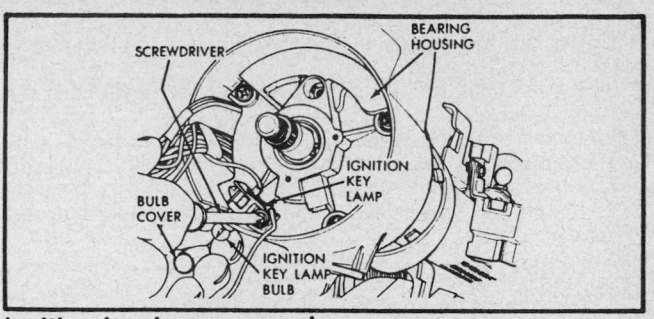

Ignition key lamp removal

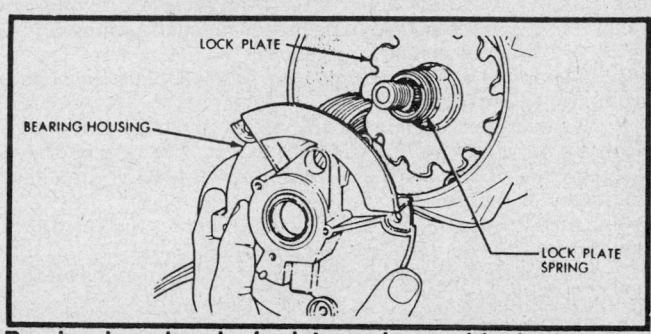

Bearing housing, lock plate spring and lock plate location

Headlight Switch

Removal and Installation

VAN

1. Disconnect the negative battery cable.
2. Remove the lower steering column cover, if equipped.
3. Unscrew the hood release handle and lower it.
4. Working under the instrument panel, depress the spring button on the headlight switch and pull the stem out.
5. Open the glove box. Remove the screws that fasten the dash bezel assembly. Pull the bezel off of the upper retaining clips.
6. Remove the switch bezel and remove the illumination bulb socket.
7. Remove the switch mounting nut from the panel, remove the switch and disconnect the wiring.

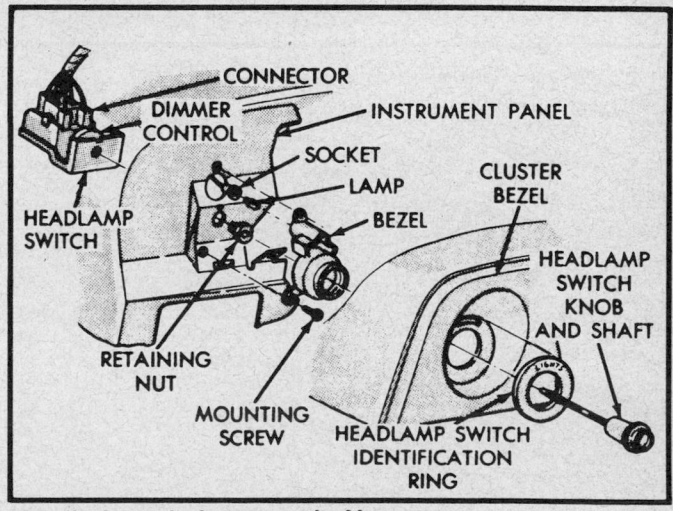

Headlight switch removal—Van

To install:

8. Connect the switch, install the switch to the panel and install the mounting nut.

9. Install the illumination bulb socket to the switch bezel and install the bezel.

10. Install the dash bezel and headlight switch stem.

11. Connect the negative battery cable and check the switch for proper operation.

12. Install the hood release handle and lower steering column cover.

PICK-UP AND RAMCHARGER

1. Disconnect the negative battery cable.

2. Remove the map light.

3. Remove 6 screws which attach the faceplate to the base panel. There is a screw below the heater-air conditioning control panel which is not visible from above.

4. If equipped with automatic transmission, place the shift lever in its lowest position.

5. Remove the faceplate by pulling the top edge rearward to clear the brow and pulling the bottom out, disengaging the attaching clips. If the vehicle is equipped with 4WD, disconnect the indicator wires.

6. Reach under the instrument panel, depress the spring button and remove the headlight switch knob.

7. Remove the wiper and power mirror switch knobs off their levers, if equipped.

8. Remove the bezel.

9. Remove the switch mounting nut from the panel, remove the switch and disconnect the wiring.

To install:

10. Connect the switch, install the switch to the panel and install the mounting nut.

11. Install the bezel.

12. Install the headlight stem and wiper and power mirror switch knobs, if removed.

13. Connect the 4WD indicator if equipped, install the cluster faceplate and map light.

14. Connect the negative battery cable and check the switch for proper operation.

Dimmer Switch

Removal and Installation
FLOOR MOUNTED

1. Disconnect the negative battery cable.

2. Raise the carpeting around the switch.

3. Unbolt the switch from the floor.

4. Unplug the switch and remove it from the vehicle.

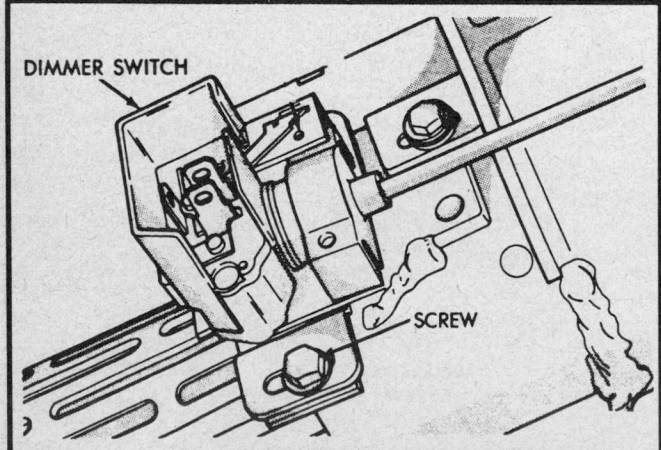

DIMMER SWITCH

SCREW

Column mounted dimmer switch location

5. The installation is the reversal of the removal procedure.

6. Connect the negative battery cable and check the switch for proper operation.

COLUMN MOUNTED

1. Disconnect the negative battery cable.

2. Remove the lower steering column cover, if equipped.

3. Unplug the switch.

4. Holding the actuating rod against its upper seat, remove the bolts that attach the switch to the column and remove the switch.

5. The installation is the reversal of the removal procedure. Adjust the switch as required.

6. Connect the negative battery cable and check the switch for proper operation.

Turn Signal Switch

Removal and Installation
STANDARD COLUMN

1. Disconnect the negative battery cable.

2. Remove the lower steering column cover, if equipped.

3. Remove the horn pad mounting screws from behind the steering wheel and remove the horn pad.

4. Remove the steering wheel nut, matchmark the steering wheel to the shaft and remove the steering wheel with a suitable puller.

5. Remove the plastic wiring channel from the underside of the steering column and disconnect the turn signal switch connector.

6. Remove the hazard switch knob. Remove the slotted hex-head screw that attaches the wiper switch to the turn signal switch.

7. Remove the 3 screws and pull the turn signal switch out of the column.

To install:

8. Run the wiring through the opening and down the steering column, position the switch and install the hex-head screw. Make sure the dimmer switch rod is properly engaged.

9. Install the 3 screws and the hazard switch knob.

10. Connect the wires and install the wiring channel.

11. Install the steering wheel torque the nut to 45 ft. lbs. (61 Nm).

12. Install the horn pad.

13. Connect the negative battery cable and check the turn signal switch and dimmer switch for proper operation.

14. Install the lower column cover, if equipped.

TILT COLUMN

1. Disconnect the negative battery cable.

2. Remove the lower steering column cover, if equipped and remove the plastic wiring channel from the underside of the steering column.

3. Remove the horn pad mounting screws from behind the steering wheel and remove the horn pad.

4. Remove the steering wheel nut, matchmark the steering wheel to the shaft and remove the steering wheel with a suitable puller.

5. Depress the lock plate with the proper depressing tool, remove the retaining ring from its groove and remove the tool, ring, lock plate, cancelling cam and spring.

6. Remove the stalk actuator screw and arm.

7. Remove the hazard switch knob.

8. Disconnect the turn signal switch connector.

9. Remove the 3 screws and remove the turn signal switch. Tape the connector to the wires to aid in removal.

To install:

10. Run the wiring through the opening and down the steering column, install the turn signal switch, switch stalk actuator arm and hazard switch knob.

11. Install the spring, cancelling cam, lock plate and ring on the steering shaft. Depress the plate with the depressing tool and install the ring securely in the groove. Remove the tool slowly.

12. Connect the turn signal switch connector and install the channel.

13. Install the steering wheel torque the nut to 45 ft. lbs. (61 Nm).

14. Install the horn pad.

15. Connect the negative battery cable and check the turn signal switch and dimmer switch for proper operation.

16. Install the lower column cover, if equipped.

Ignition Lock

Removal and Installation
STANDARD COLUMN

1. Disconnect the negative battery cable.

2. Remove the horn pad mounting screws from behind the steering wheel and remove the horn pad.

3. Remove the steering wheel nut, matchmark the steering wheel to the shaft and remove the steering wheel with a suitable puller.

4. Remove the hazard switch knob. Remove the slotted hex-head screw that attaches the wiper switch to the turn signal switch.

5. Remove the 3 screws and pull the turn signal switch out of the column as far as it will go. Unplug it below if necessary.

6. Remove the ignition switch key lamp.

7. Place the key in the **LOCK** position and remove the key.

8. Insert 2 suitable small diameter tools into both release holes and push inward to release the spring loaded lock retainers while simultaneously pulling the key lock cylinder out of its bore.

To install:

9. Install the key cylinder.

10. Install the ignition switch key lamp.

11. Install the turn signal switch and hazard switch knob. Connect the wires if they were disconnected.

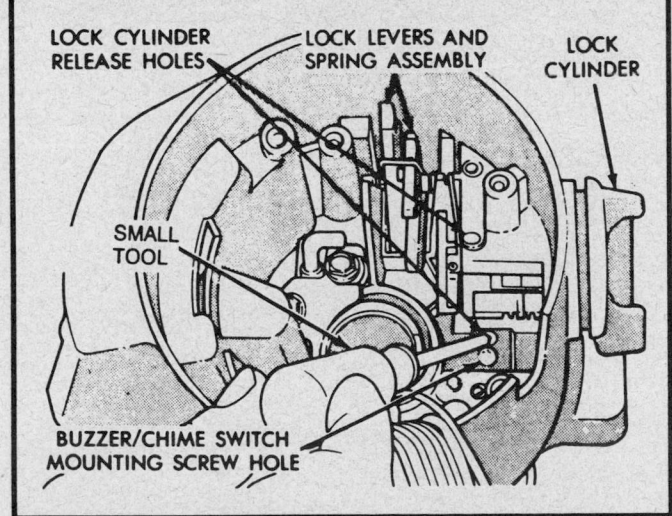

Removing the key lock cylinder—standard column

12. Install the steering wheel torque the nut to 45 ft. lbs. (61 Nm).

13. Install the horn pad.

14. Connect the negative battery cable and check the lock cylinder for proper operation.

15. Install the lower column cover, if equipped.

TILT COLUMN

1. Disconnect the negative battery cable.

2. Remove the horn pad mounting screws from behind the steering wheel and remove the horn pad.

3. Remove the steering wheel nut, matchmark the steering wheel to the shaft and remove the steering wheel with a suitable puller.

4. Depress the lock plate with the proper depressing tool, remove the retaining ring from its groove and remove the tool, ring, lock plate, cancelling cam and spring.

5. Remove the stalk actuator screw and arm.

6. Remove the hazard switch knob.

7. Remove the 3 screws and pull the turn signal switch out of the column as far as it will go. Unplug it below if necessary.

8. Remove the ignition key lamp.

9. Place the key in the **LOCK** position and remove the key. Insert a thin tool into the slot next to the switch mounting screw boss, depress the spring latch at the bottom of the slot releasing the lock and remove the lock cylinder.

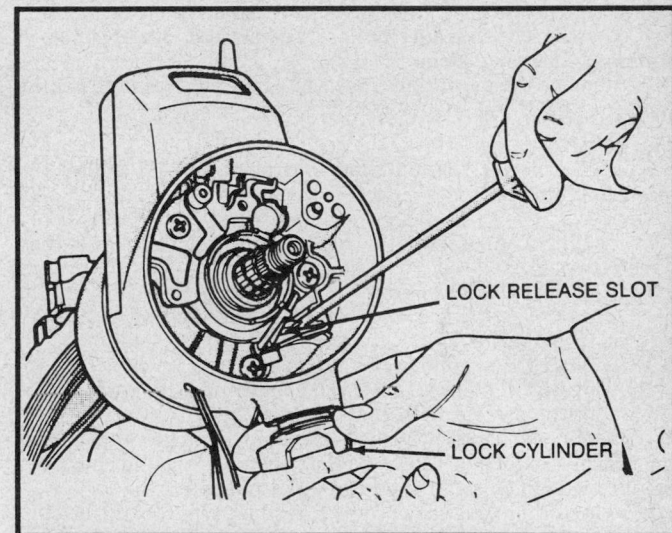

Removing the key lock cylinder—tilt column

To install:

10. Install the lock cylinder.

11. Install the ignition key lamp.

12. Install the turn signal switch, switch stalk actuator arm and hazard switch knob.

13. Install the spring, cancelling cam, lock plate and ring on the steering shaft. Depress the plate with the depressing tool and install the ring securely in the groove. Remove the tool slowly.

14. Connect the wires if they were disconnected.

15. Install the steering wheel torque the nut to 45 ft. lbs. (61 Nm).

16. Install the horn pad.

17. Connect the negative battery cable and check the turn signal switch for proper operation.

18. Install the lower column cover, if it was removed.

Stoplight Switch

Removal and Installation

1. Disconnect the negative battery cable.
2. Remove the switch mounting bracket assembly from the brake pedal bracket.
3. Remove the switch from its bracket.
4. The installation is the reversal of the removal procedure.

5. Connect the negative battery cable and check the switch for proper operation.

Fuses and Circuit Breakers

Location

The fuse box is located to the left of the glove box on Vans and directly under the steering column on Pick-Ups and Ramchargers.

ENGINE COOLING

Radiator

Removal and Installation

1. Disconnect the negative battery cable.
2. Open the radiator petcock and drain the antifreeze. Once the antifreeze has stopped draining, close the petcock.
3. Remove the upper hose and coolant reserve tank hose from the radiator.
4. Remove the shroud from the radiator and position it away from the radiator.
5. On Vans, remove the upper mounting screws, raise the vehicle and support safely.
6. Remove the lower hose from the radiator.
7. Disconnect the automatic transmission cooler lines, if equipped and plug them.
8. Remove the mounting screws and carefully lift or lower the radiator out of the engine compartment.

To install:

9. Lift or lower the radiator into position and install the mounting screws.
99,
10. Connect the automatic transmission cooler lines, if they were removed.
11. Connect the lower hose.
12. Lower the vehicle and install the remaining mounting screws, if applicable.
13. Install the shroud.
14. Connect the upper hose and coolant reserve tank hose.
15. Fill the system with coolant.
16. Connect the negative battery cable, run the vehicle until the thermostat opens, fill the radiator completely and check the automatic transmission fluid level, if equipped.
17. Once the vehicle has cooled, recheck the coolant level.

Heater Core

Removal and Installation

VAN WITHOUT AIR CONDITIONING

1. Disconnect the negative battery cable.
2. Drain the cooling system. Disconnect and plug the heater hoses.
3. Disconnect the temperature control cable from the heater core cover and the blend door crank. Disconnect the vent cable.
4. Disconnect the blower motor connector.
5. Remove the screws retaining the heater assembly to the side cowl and the nuts fastening the heater assembly to the dash panel.
6. Remove the heater unit from the vehicle.
7. Remove the back plate and remove the screws holding the heater core cover to the heater housing. Lift the cover from the housing.

8. Remove the retaining screws from the heater core and remove the core from the heater housing.

To install:

9. Clean out the inside of the housing. Place the heater core into the housing and fasten.
10. Position the blend air door and right vent door in the housing and fasten the heater core cover to the housing.
11. Check the dash panel and side cowl seals for breaks and lack of adhesion. Repair as required.
12. Install the heater assembly to the vehicle.
13. Connect the blower connector.
14. Connect the cables.
15. Connect the heater hoses.
16. Refill the radiator.
17. Connect the negative battery cable, run the vehicle until the thermostat opens, fill the radiator completely and check the operation of the heater.
18. Once the vehicle has cooled, recheck the coolant level.

VAN WITH AIR CONDITIONING

1. Disconnect the negative battery cable. Properly discharge the air conditioning system completely.
2. Disconnect the freeze control connector from the wire harness at the H-valve, if equipped.
3. Drain the cooling system. Place a layer of non-conductive waterproof material over the alternator to prevent coolant from

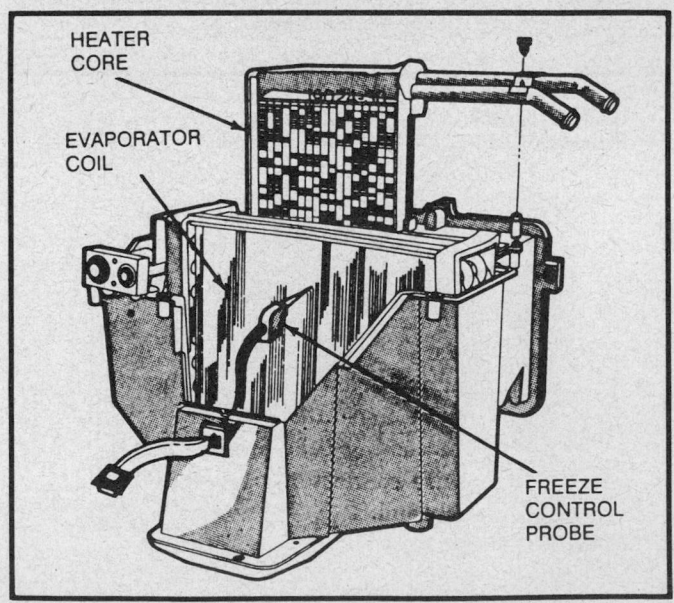

Heater core removal—van with air conditioning

spilling on it when disconnecting the heater hoses. Disconnect and cap the heater hoses.

4. Slowly disconnect the refrigerant plumbing from the H valve. Remove the 2 screws from the filter drier bracket and swing the plumbing out of the way towards the center of the vehicle.

5. Remove the temperature control cable from the cover.

6. Working from inside the vehicle, remove the glove box, spot cooler bezel and the appearance shield. Working through the glove box opening and under the instrument panel, remove the screws and nuts attaching the evaporator core housing to the dash panel.

7. Remove the 2 screws from the flange connection to the blower housing. Separate the evaporator core housing from the blower housing.

8. Carefully remove the evaporator core housing from the vehicle.

9. Remove the cover from the housing and remove the screw retaining the strap to heater core. Remove the heater core from the housing.

To install:

10. Clean the inside of the housing. Place the heater core into the housing and install the retaining strap and screw.

11. Install the housing cover.

12. Install the blower housing to the evaporator housing.

13. Inspect all air seals and mating surfaces for possible breaks and leaks and repair as required.

14. Install the assembly to the dash panel and from inside the vehicle, install the screws and nuts attaching it to the dash panel.

15. Install the appearance shield, spot cooler bezel and glove box.

16. Attach the temperature control cable to the cover.

17. Position the plumbing and install the 2 screws onto the filter drier bracket.

18. Install a new gasket and connect the refrigerant plumbing to the H-valve.

19. Connect the heater hoses and remove the waterproof material from the alternator. Connect the freeze control wire harness, if equipped.

20. Evacuate and recharge the air conditioning system. Refill the radiator.

21. Connect the negative battery cable, run the vehicle until the thermostat opens, fill the radiator completely and check the operation of the entire climate control system.

22. Once the vehicle has cooled, recheck the coolant level.

PICK-UP AND RAMCHARGER WITHOUT AIR CONDITIONING

1. Disconnect the negative battery cable.

2. Drain the cooling system. Remove and plug the heater core hoses.

3. Remove the right side cowl trim panel, if equipped. Remove the glove box assembly. Remove the structural brace through the glovebox opening.

4. Remove the right half of the instrument panel lower reinforcement and disconnect the ground strap.

5. Disconnect the control cables from the heater housing and the blower motor wires on the engine side.

6. Remove the retaining screw between the package to cowl side sheet metal.

7. Remove the 6 heater housing retaining nuts on the engine side of the heater assembly and remove the heater housing assembly.

8. Remove the heater housing cover retaining screws and the mode door crank. Separate the cover from the housing.

9. Carefully lift the heater core from the heater housing.

To install:

10. Clean the inside of the housing. Install the heater core into the housing.

11. Install the housing cover.

11. Inspect the dash panel seal for damage and repair as required.

12. Install the assembly to the dash panel and install the retaining nuts.

13. Install the cowl side retaining screws.

14. Connect the blower motor connector.

15. Connect the control cables.

16. Install the right lower instrument panel reinforcement, structural brace, glove box and cowl side trim panel, if equipped.

17. Connect the heater hoses.

18. Refill the radiator.

19. Connect the negative battery cable, run the vehicle until the thermostat opens, fill the radiator completely and check the operation of the heater.

20. Once the vehicle has cooled, recheck the coolant level.

PICK-UP AND RAMCHARGER WITH AIR CONDITIONING

1. Disconnect the negative battery cable. Properly discharge the air condition system. Drain the cooling system. Disconnect and plug the heater hoses and the refrigerant lines.

2. Remove the condensation tube from the housing.

3. Move the transfer case and gear shift levers away from the instrument panel, if equipped.

4. Remove the right side cowl trim panel, if equipped. Remove the glove box and swing it out from the bottom.

5. Remove the structural brace from the through hole in the glove box opening. Remove the ash tray.

6. Remove the right lower half of the dash reinforcement by removing the retaining screws holding it to the instrument panel and to the cowl side trim panel.

7. Disconnect the radio ground strap, if equipped. Remove the center and floor air distribution ducts.

8. Disconnect the temperature control cable from the assembly and tape it out of the way.

9. Disconnect the vacuum lines from the extension on the control unit and unclip the vacuum lines from the defroster duct.

10. Remove the wiring connector from the resistor block. Remove the blower motor electrical connector from the engine side of the assembly.

11. Disconnect the vacuum lines on the engine side and make sure the grommet is free from the dash panel.

12. Remove the retaining nuts on the engine side. Remove the screw that retains the assembly to the cowl side of the sheetmetal.

13. Remove the assembly from the vehicle.

14. Remove the vacuum actuators, door crank levers, evaporator case cover retaining nuts and screws and the heater core retaining screws. Lift the cover off of the asembly and remove the heater core from its mounting.

To install:

15. Clean the inside of the housing. Install the heater core into the housing.

16. Install the housing cover, retaining screws and nuts, levers and actuators.

17. Inspect the dash panel seals for damage and repair as required.

18. Feed the vacuum lines through the hole in the dash panel, install the assembly to the dash panel and install all retaining nuts and screws.

19. Connect the resistor block and blower motor.

20. Connect the vacuum lines to the extension on the control unit and clip the vacuum lines to the defroster duct.

21. Connect the temperature control cable to the assembly.

22. Connect the radio ground strap, if equipped. Install the center and floor air distribution ducts.

23. Install the dash reinforcement, structural brace, glove box and right side cowl trim panel, if equipped. Install the ash tray.

24. Install the condensation tube.

25. Connect the heater hoses and vacuum lines.

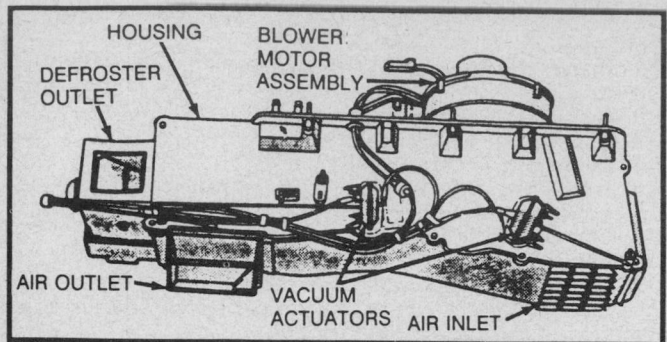

Evaporator heater assembly—Pick-Up and Ramcharger with air conditioning

26. Install a new gasket and connect the refrigerant lines.
27. Evacuate and recharge the air conditioning system. Refill the radiator.
28. Connect the negative battery cable, run the vehicle until the thermostat opens, fill the radiator completely and check the operation of the entire climate control system.
29. Once the vehicle has cooled, recheck the coolant level.

Water Pump

Removal and Installation

——— CAUTION ———

If the water pump is being replaced due to bearing or shaft damage, the mechanical cooling fan should be carefully inspected for fatigue cracks, loose blades or loose rivets resulting from excessive vibration. If the fan is damaged in any way, it could snap at any time, possibly causing serious personal injury or damage to the vehicle.

3.7L ENGINE

1. Disconnect the negative battery cable.
2. Drain the coolant and remove the lower radiator hose. Remove the shroud and radiator if necessary.
3. Remove the fan, spacer, pulley and bolts together.

NOTE: Do not place the viscous fan in an upright position because the silicone fluid in the drive could drain into the bearing and contaminate its lubricant.

4. Loosen the alternator, power steering pump or idler pulley and remove all belts. Remove the air pump and bracket, if equipped.
5. Position the bypass hose clamp in the center of the hose.
6. Disconnect the heater hose.
7. Remove the water pump retaining bolts and remove the pump from the engine.
To install:
8. Clean and dry the pump mating surfaces. Install a new bypass hose.
9. Install a new gasket and install the water pump. Install any bolts that do not attach a bracket. Tighten the bypass hose clamps. Install the heater hose.
10. Install the air pump and bracket, power steering pump and bracket and alternator. Torque all water pump bolts to 30 ft. lbs. (41 Nm).
11. Install the fan, spacer, pulley and bolts together.
12. Adjust all belt tensions.
13. Install the shroud and radiator, if they were removed. Fill the radiator with coolant.
14. Connect the negative battery cable, run the vehicle until the thermostat opens, fill the radiator completely and check for leaks.
15. Once the vehicle has cooled, recheck the coolant level.

3.9L, 5.2L AND 5.9L GASOLINE ENGINES

1. Disconnect the negative battery cable. Drain the coolant.
2. Remove the shroud from the radiator and slide it over the fan if it is 1-piece.
3. Remove the radiator and lower hose.
4. Remove the fan blade, spacer or viscous drive unit, pully, bolts and shroud (if it was not removed in Step 2) together. Remove the air pump belt and power steering pump belt.

NOTE: Do not place the viscous fan in an upright position because the silicone fluid in the drive could drain into the bearing and contaminate its lubricant.

5. Loosen the alternator mounting bolts and remove the alternator/air conditioner belts.
6. Remove the alternator bracket. On some 1988–90 vehicles, this bracket also supports the air conditioner compressor or idler pulley, which will remain supported by its rear mount.
7. Remove the air pump(s). Remove the air pump bracket and unbolt the power steering pump bracket with the pump still attached and position it out of the way.
8. Disconnect the heater and bypass hoses.
9. On 1986–88 vehicles with air conditioning, remove the air conditioner compressor pulley and field coil assembly, if necessary to remove the water pump to compressor front mount bolts and bracket.
10. Remove the remaining pump retaining bolts (if any) and remove the pump from the engine.
To install:
11. Clean and dry the pump mating surfaces. Install a new bypass hose to the engine.
12. Install a new gasket and install the water pump to the engine.
13. Install any bolts that do not retain a bracket. Tighten the bypass hose clamps. Install the heater hose.
14. Install the water pump to compressor front mount bolts and bracket, if it was removed.
15. Install all remaining brackets and components that were removed during the removal procedure. Torque all water pump retaining bolts that do not go through adjusting slots to 30 ft. lbs. (41 Nm).
16. Install the air conditioner compressor pulley and field coil assembly, if it was removed. Install and adjust the alternator/air conditioner belts. Place the remaining belts over their components.
17. Install the fan blade, spacer or viscous drive unit, pully and bolts along with the shroud (if it is a 1-piece unit) together.
18. Install the radiator, lower hose and shroud.
19. Adjust all belts and torque the remaining water pump retaining bolts to 30 ft. lbs. (41 Nm).
20. Fill the radiator with coolant.
21. Connect the negative battery cable, run the vehicle until

5.9L diesel engine water pump

the thermostat opens, fill the radiator completely and check for leaks.

22. Once the vehicle has cooled, recheck the coolant level.

5.9L DIESEL ENGINE

1. Disconnect the negative battery cable.
2. Drain the coolant.
3. Use a ⅜ in. drive breaker bar to lift the belt tensioner and remove the belt.
4. Remove the 2 water pump retaining bolts and remove the pump from the engine.
5. Remove the O-ring from the pump groove.

To install:

6. Clean the O-ring groove and install a new O-ring.
7. Clean the pump mating surfaces and install the pump to the engine.
8. Torque the mounting bolts to 18 ft. lbs. (24 Nm). Fill the radiator with coolant.
9. Install the drive belt.
10. Connect the negative battery cable, run the vehicle until the thermostat opens, fill the radiator completely and check for leaks.
11. Once the vehicle has cooled, recheck the coolant level.

Thermostat

Removal and Installation

EXCEPT 5.9L DIESEL ENGINE

1. Disconnect the negative battery cable. Drain the coolant down to thermostat level or below.
2. Remove the thermostat housing.
3. Remove the thermostat and discard the gasket.
4. Clean the housing mating surfaces and use a new gasket.
5. The installation is the reversal of the removal procedure.
6. Connect the negative battery cable, run the vehicle until the thermostat opens, fill the radiator completely and check for leaks.
7. Once the vehicle has cooled, recheck the coolant level.

5.9L DIESEL ENGINE

1. Disconnect the negative battery cable.
2. Drain the coolant.
3. Use a ⅜ in. drive breaker bar to lift the belt tensioner and remove the belt.

4. Disconnect the upper radiator hose from the thermostat housing.
5. Loosen the alternator mounting bolts and lower the alternator.
6. Unbolt the thermostat housing and remove the housing, engine lifting bracket and thermostat with seal.

To install:

7. Install the new thermostat to the housing, making sure the tang on the thermostat is aligned with the slot in the housing. This will ensure correct positioning of the jiggle pins in the housing. This is important because during filling, air vents through the jiggle pin openings through the upper hose and out the radiator fill neck.
8. Clean the pump mating surfaces.
9. Install the engine lifting bracket, new seal, thermostat and housing. Make sure the seal is installed with the beveled side facing out.
10. Torque the thermostat housing bolts to 18 ft. lbs. (24 Nm). Connect the upper hose to the housing.
11. Reinstall the alternator into position. Torque the upper bolt to 18 ft. lbs. (24 Nm) and the lower bolt to 32 ft. lbs. (43 Nm).
12. Install the drive belt.
13. Connect the negative battery cable, run the vehicle until the thermostat opens, fill the radiator completely and check for leaks.
14. Once the vehicle has cooled, recheck the coolant level.

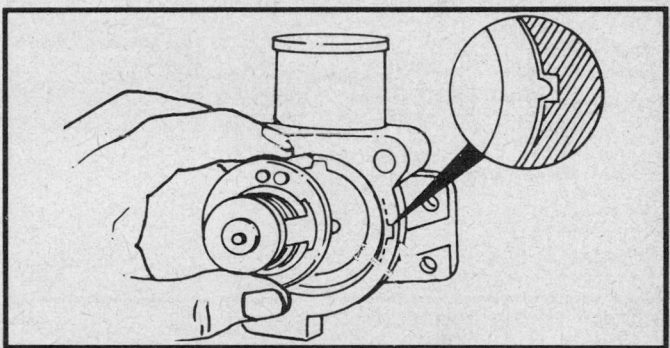

Installing the thermostat in the housing

5.9L diesel engine thermostat

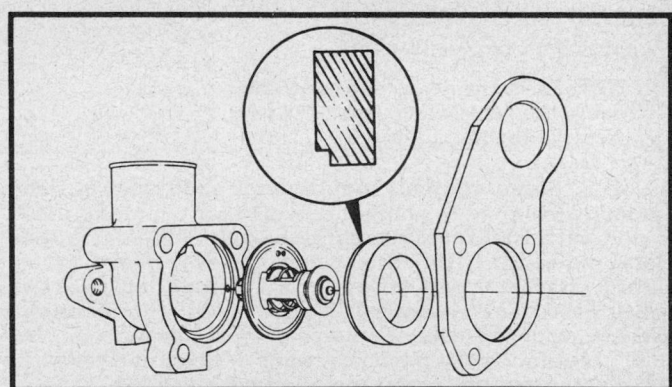

Proper positioning of the rubber seal

GASOLINE FUEL SYSTEM

Fuel System Service Precautions

Relieving Fuel System Pressure

1. Loosen the fuel filler cap to release fuel tank pressure.
2. Disconnect the injectors wiring harness from the engine harness.
3. Connect a jumper wire from either of the end pins in the connector to ground.
4. Being careful not to allow contact between the jumper leads, connect a jumper wire to the pin next to the one that is grounded and touch the other end of the jumper to the positive battery post for no longer than 5 seconds. This will relieve fuel pressure.
5. Remove the jumper wires and connect the connector.

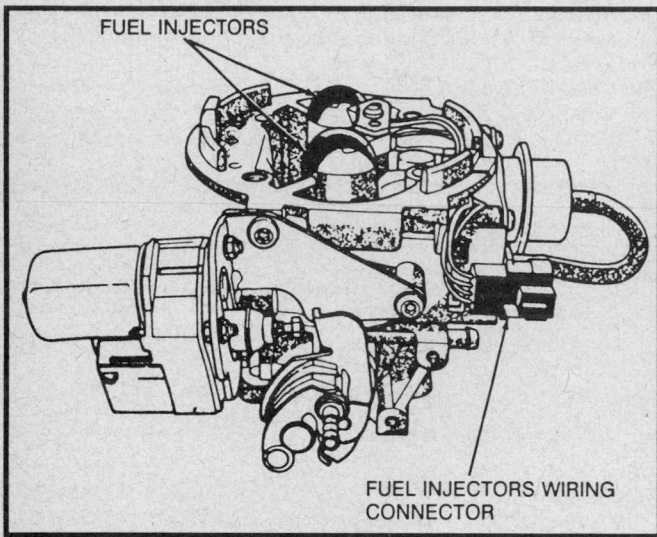

Injector wiring connector location

Fuel Filter

Removal and Installation
CARBURETED ENGINE

1. Disconnect the negative battery cable.
2. Raise the vehicle and support safely.
3. Remove the fuel filter with hoses.

NOTE: Some vehicles may be equipped with a field package designed to combat driveability problems associated with fuel foaming. Affected vehicles have a special replaceable filter/reservoir mounted inboard on the right front frame rail. When the kit is installed, the conventional filter is discarded. Do not install a conventional filter or conventional clamps or hoses in place of the special replacement parts; they are not compatible with the electronic fuel pump installed with the kit.

4. Install the new filter, hoses and clamps.
5. If the vehicle is equipped with a Rochester Quadrajet carburetor, a second filter mounted in the carburetor can also be replaced. Remove the air cleaner assembly, disconnect the fuel line, remove the fuel inlet nut, gasket, filter and spring. The installation is the reversal of the removal procedure.
6. Connect the negative battery cable, start the engine and check for leaks.

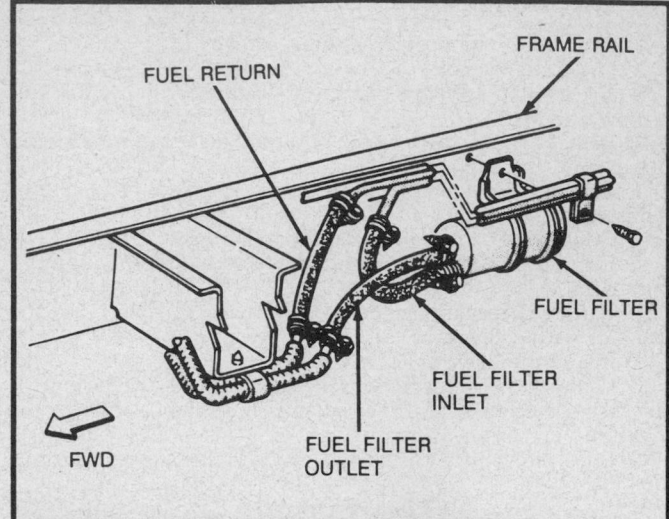

Fuel filter location

FUEL INJECTED ENGINE

--- **CAUTION** ---

Do not use conventional fuel hoses or clamps when servicing this fuel system. They are not compatible with the injection system and could fail, causing personal injury or damage to the vehicle. Use only hoses and clamps specifically designed for fuel injection.

1. Relieve the fuel pressure.
2. Disconnect the negative battery cable.
3. Remove the filter retaining screw and remove the filter assembly from the mounting plate.
4. Loosen the outlet hose clamp on the filter and inlet hose clamp on the rear fuel tube.
5. Wrap a shop towel around the hoses to absorb fuel. Remove the hoses from the filter and fuel tube and discard the clamps and the filter.

To install:

6. Install the inlet hose on the fuel tube and tighten the new clamp to 10 inch lbs. (1 Nm).
7. Install the outlet hose on the filter outlet fitting and tighten the new clamp to 10 inch lbs. (1 Nm).
8. Position the filter assembly on the mounting plate and tighten the mounting screw to 75 inch lbs. (8 Nm).
9. Connect the negative battery cable, start the engine and check for leaks.

Mechanical Fuel Pump

Pressure Testing

1. Raise the vehicle and support safely.
2. Connect a pressure gauge (0–15 psi minimum range) to the fuel pump outlet fitting.
3. Crank the engine several times while observing the gauge.
4. The 3.7L engine should develop 4.0–5.5 psi. The 5.2L and 5.9L engines should develop 5.75–7.25 psi. If the vehicle is equipped with the field package noted above, fuel pressure should be 13–15 psi.

Removal and Installation

1. Disconnect the negative battery cable.
2. Raise the vehicle and support safely.
3. Disconnect the fuel lines from the pump and plug them.

4. Remove the fuel pump retaining bolts and remove the pump from the engine.

5. Clean and dry the mounting surfaces and bolt holes.

6. The installation is the reversal of the removal procedure.

7. Connect the negative battery cable, start the engine and check for leaks.

Electric Fuel Pump

Pressure Testing

1. Relieve the fuel pressure.

2. Disconnect the larger diameter fuel supply hose from the engine fuel line assembly.

3. Connect the fuel system pressure tester C–4799A, or equivalent between the fuel supply hose and the engine fuel line assembly.

4. With the key in the **RUN** position, put the DRB I or II in the activate auto shutdown relay mode; this will activate the fuel pump and pressurize the system.

5. The pressure specification is 13.5–15.5 psi. If the pressure is within specifications, reinstall the fuel hose.

6. If fuel pressure is below specifications, install the tester in the fuel supply line between the tank and the filter and repeat the test.

7. If the pressure is 5 psi higher than in Step 5, replace the fuel filter. If no change is observed, squeeze the return hose. If pressure increases, replace the pressure regulator. If no change is observed, the problem is either a plugged in-tank sock filter or a defective pump.

8. If fuel pressure is above specifications, remove the fuel return line hose from the chassis line at the fuel tank and connect a 3 foot piece of fuel hose to the return line. Put the other end into a 2 gallon minimum capacity approved gasoline container. Repeat the test. If pressure is now correct, check the in-tank return hose for kinking. Replace the fuel pump assembly if the in-tank reservoir check valve or aspirator jet is obstructed.

9. If pressure is still above specifications, remove the fuel return hose from the throttle body. Connect a substitute hose to the throttle body return nipple and place the other end of the hose in a clean container. Repeat the test. If pressure is now correct, check for a restricted fuel return line. If no change is observed, replace the fuel pressure regulator.

Removal and Installation

The fuel pump module is installed in the top of the fuel tank. It contains the fuel pump, fuel pump reservoir, pressure relief/rollover valve, electrical connector for the sending unit, fuel filler vent, supply and return tube connections and the drain tube nipple.

1. Relieve the fuel pressure.

2. Disconnect the negative battery cable.

3. Raise the vehicle and support safely. Remove the skid plate, if equipped.

4. Using the proper equipment, drain the fuel tank.

5. Disconnect the vent hoses and filler hose from the tank and remove the hoses from the bracket attached to the top of the frame rail, if equipped.

6. Place a transmission jack or equivalent under the center of the tank and apply slight pressure.

7. Remove the retaining strap J-bolt nuts and remove the straps.

8. Lower the tank enough to reach in and disconnect the electrical connector and the remaining fuel tubes from the top of the module.

9. Lower the tank and remove the module. When the module is released from the tank it will spring up. Remove the pump from the module.

To install:

10. Clean the seal area of the tank. Install the new pump to the module so the filter is in the same position as before removal. Install a new O-ring on the module.

11. Align the module with the retaining bracket on the bottom of the tank. It is normal for the module to have a slight interference fit with the bracket.

12. Push the module down and install the retaining clamp.

13. Install the fuel tank and skid plate, if equipped.

14. Connect the negative battery cable, start the engine and check for leaks.

Carburetor

Removal and Installation

1. Disconnect the negative battery cable.

2. Remove the air cleaner assembly.

3. Remove and install the fuel tank cap to relieve any pressure in the tank.

4. Matchmark all vacuum hoses and electrical connectors and remove from the carburetor.

5. Disconnect the throttle, cruise control, choke and kickdown cables and linkages, if equipped.

6. Disconnect and plug the fuel inlet line.

7. Remove the mounting bolts and/or nuts and remove the carburetor from the intake manifold.

To install:

8. Clean the mounting surface of the manifold and install a new base gasket.

9. Install the mounting bolts and/or nuts and tighten them alternately to compress the base gasket evenly.

10. Connect the fuel line.

11. Connect the throttle, cruise control, choke and kickdown cables and linkages, if equipped.

12. Install all vacuum hoses and electrical connectors in their proper locations.

13. Install the air cleaner.

14. Connect the negative battery cable, start the engine and perform all necessary adjustments.

Idle Speed Adjustment

1. Start the engine and run until at normal operating temperature. Check and adjust the ignition timing. Turn the engine off.

2. Disconnect and plug the EGR hose. Disconnect the oxygen sensor, if equipped.

3. Disconnect and plug the 3/16 in. hose at the canister.

4. Remove the PCV hose from the valve cover and allow it to draw underhood air.

5. Ground the carburetor switch with a jumper wire, if equipped.

6. Disconnect the vacuum hose from the computer, if equipped and connect an auxiliary vacuum supply of 16 Hg.in.

7. Make sure all accessories are off. Install a tachometer and start the engine.

8. Allow the engine to run for 2 minutes to stabilize. Turn the idle speed screw until the correct idle speed according to the VECI label is reached.

9. Connect all wires and hoses that were previously disconnected. It is normal for the idle speed to vary after all hoses and wires are reconnected; do not readjust.

Idle Mixture Adjustment

1. Disconnect and plug the EGR hose. Disconnect the oxygen sensor, if equipped.

2. Disconnect and plug the 3/16 in. hose at the canister.

3. Remove the PCV hose from the valve cover and allow it to draw underhood air.

4. Ground the carburetor switch with a jumper wire, if equipped.

5. Disconnect the vacuum hose from the computer, if

equipped and connect an auxiliary vacuum supply of 16 Hg.in.

6. Remove the concealment plug. Disconnect the vacuum supply hose to the tee and install a propane supply hose in its place.

7. Make sure all accessories are off. Install a tachometer and start the engine. Allow the engine to run for 2 minutes to stabilize.

8. Open the main propane valve. Slowly open the propane metering valve until the maximum engine rpm is reached. When too much propane is added, the engine will begin to stumble; at this point back off until the engine stabilizes.

9. Adjust the idle rpm to obtain the specified propane rpm. Fine tune the metering valve to obtain the highest rpm again. If there has been a change to the maximum rpm, readjust the idle screw to the specified propane rpm.

10. Turn the main propane valve off and allow the engine to run for 1 minute to stabilize.

11. Adjust the mixture screw to obtain the smoothest idle at the specified idle rpm.

12. Open the main propane valve. Fine tune the metering valve to obtain the highest rpm. If the maximum engine speed is more that 25 rpm different than the specified propane rpm, repeat the procedure.

13. Turn the propane valves off and remove the propane canister. Reinstall the vacuum supply hose to the tee.

14. Perform the idle speed adjustment procedure.

15. Connect all wires and hoses that were previously disconnected.

Service Adjustments.

For all carburetor service adjustment procedures and Specifications, please refer to "Carburetor Service" in the Unit Repair section.

Fuel Injection

Idle Speed Adjustment

1. Start the engine and allow it to reach normal operating temperature. If it is already hot, run it for 2 minutes.

2. Turn the engine off and allow 1 minute for the Idle Speed Control (ISC) actuator shaft to fully extend.

3. Disconnect the ISC actuator connector and the coolant temperature sensor.

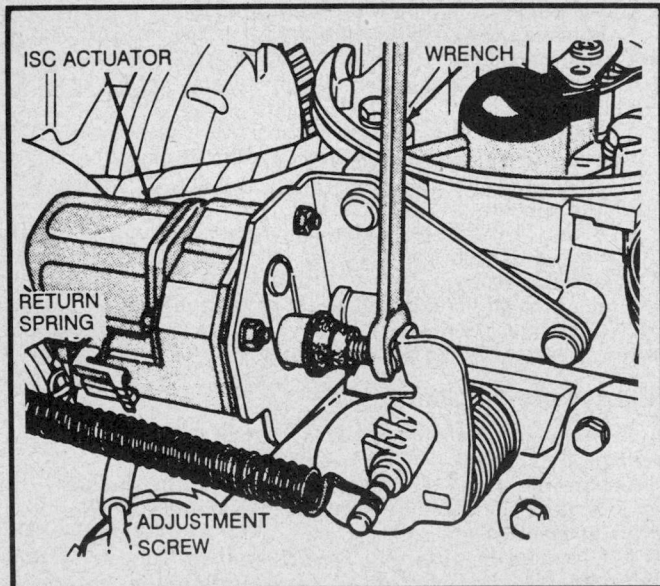

Adjusting the idle speed

4. Connect a tachometer to the engine and start the engine.

5. Adjust the extension screw on the actuator shaft until the rpm is within specifications:
   - 3.9L engine—2500–2600 rpm
   - 5.2L and 5.9L engines—2750–2850 rpm

6. Turn the engine off. Reconnect the ISC actuator connector and the coolant temperature sensor. Remove the tachometer.

Idle Mixture Adjustment

There is no idle mixture adjustment provided with this fuel injection system.

Fuel Injector

Removal and Installation

1. Remove the air cleaner assembly.
2. Relieve the fuel pressure.
3. Disconnect the negative battery cable.

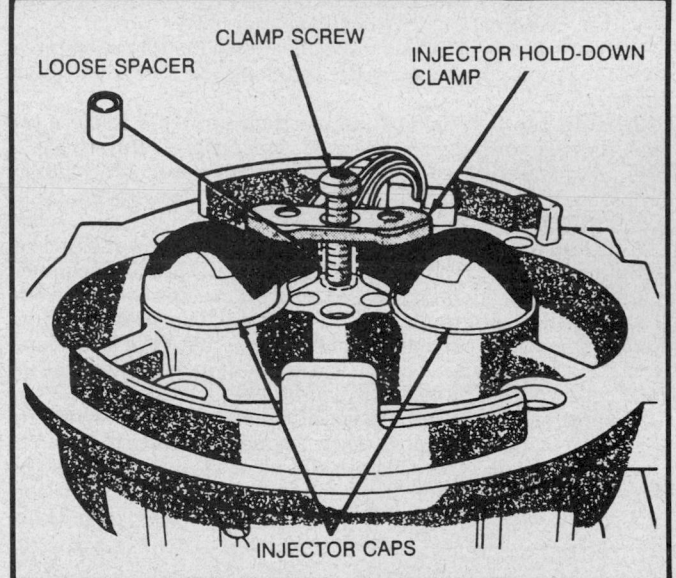

Injector hold-down and spacer

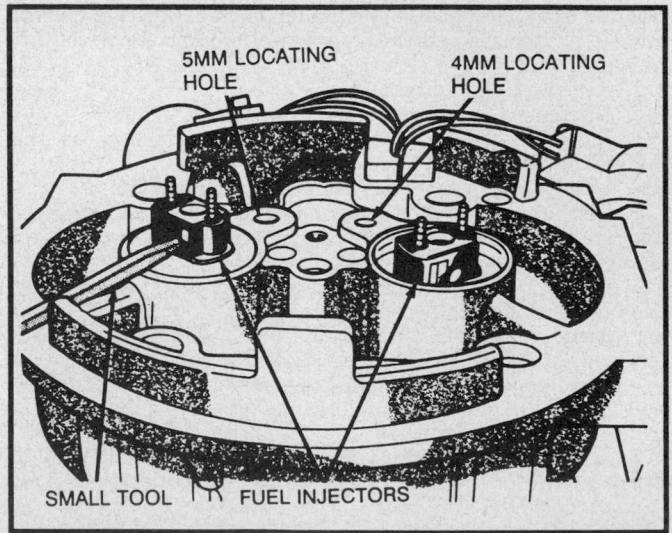

Removing the injector from its pod

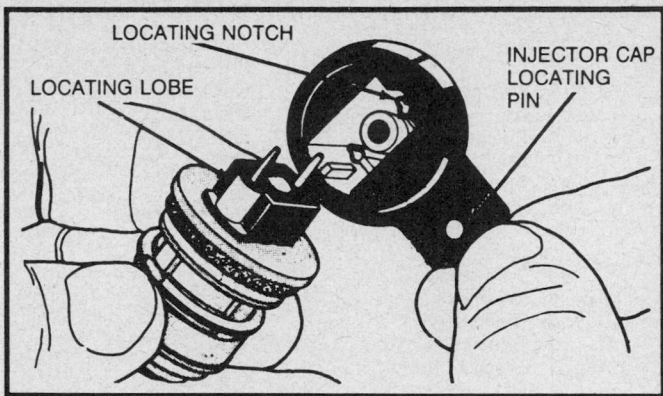

Installing the injector to the cap

NOTE: There is a small spacer below the injector hold-down clamp. Take the proper precaution to prevent this spacer from falling into the throttle body.

4. Remove the injector hold-down Torx® screw, the hold-down and the spacer.

5. Using a small flat-tipped tool, lift the caps off of the injector.

6. Using the same tool, gently pry the injector from its pod.

7. Remove the lower O-ring from the pod.

To install:

8. Install the new lower O-ring on the injector.

9. Align the injector terminal housing with the locating socket in the injector cap.

10. Press the injector cap so that the upper O-ring flange is flush with the lower surface of the cap.

11. Spray the inner surfaces of the injector pod with suitable carburetor parts cleaner to remove residual varnish and gasoline.

12. Lubricate the O-rings sparingly with unmedicated petroleum jelly.

13. Place the injector and cap into the injector pod and align the cap locating pin with the locating hole in the casting. The right side locating pin in 5mm in diameter and will not fit into the other hole. The left side pin is 4mm in diameter and will be loose in the other hole.

14. Press firmly on the injector cap until it is flush with the casting surface.

15. Install the spacer and align the holes in the hold-down with the pins on the caps and install.

16. Push down on the caps, install the screw and torque to 35 inch lbs. (4 Nm).

17. Connect the negative battery cable and check for leaks using the DRB I or II to activate the fuel pump.

18. Install the air cleaner.

DIESEL FUEL SYSTEM

Fuel/Water Separator Filter

Removal and Installation

1. Disconnect the negative battery cable.
2. Disconnect the Water In Filter (WIF) sensor connector.
3. Remove the separator filter assembly from the filter head with a standard oil filter wrench.
4. Remove the square cut O-ring from the filter mounting bushing.
5. Drain the fuel/water separator filter and remove the assembly from the fuel filter.

To install:

6. Install a new O-ring to the WIF assembly and install to the new separator filter.
7. Install a new square cut O-ring to the mounting bushing.
8. Fill the fuel/water separator filter with clean diesel fuel.
9. Apply a light coat of oil to the sealing surface of the separator filter.
10. Install the assembly and tighten it ½ turn after the seal contacts the filter head.
11. Reconnect the WIF sensor connector.
12. Connect the negative battery cable, start the engine and check for leaks.

Draining Water From the System

Filtration and separation of water from the fuel is important for trouble free operation and long life of the fuel system. Regular maintenance, including draining moisture from the fuel/water separator filter is essential to keep water out of the fuel pump. To remove the collected water, simply unscrew the drain at the bottom of the WIF assembly located at the bottom of the filter separator.

Diesel Injection Pump

Removal and Installation

NOTE: The Bosche VE lever is indexed to the shaft during pump calibration. Do not remove it from the pump during removal.

1. Disconnect the negative battery cable.
2. Remove the throttle linkage and bracket.
3. Disconnect the fuel drain manifold.
4. Remove the injection pump supply line.
5. Remove the high pressure lines.
6. Disconnect the electrical wire to the fuel shut off valve.
7. Remove the fuel air control tube.
8. Remove the pump support bracket.
9. Remove the oil fill tube bracket and adapter from the front gear cover.
10. Place a shop towel in the gear cover opening in a position that will prevent the nut and washer from falling into the gear housing. Remove the gear retaining nut and washer.
11. Install the turning tool into the flywheel housing opening on the exhaust side of the engine. Place a ½ in. drive universal joint in the turning tool and attach enough extensions to the joint to make it convenient to turn the tool.
12. Using a ratchet to turn the turning tool, turn the engine until the key way on the fuel pump shaft is pointing approximately in the six o'clock position.
13. Locate TDC for cylinder No. 1 by turning the engine slowly while pusing in on the TDC pin. Stop turning the engine as soon as the pin engages with the gear timing hole. Disengage the pin after locating TDC and remove the turning equipment.
14. Loosen the lockscrew, remove the special washer from the injection pump and wire it to the line above it so it will not get

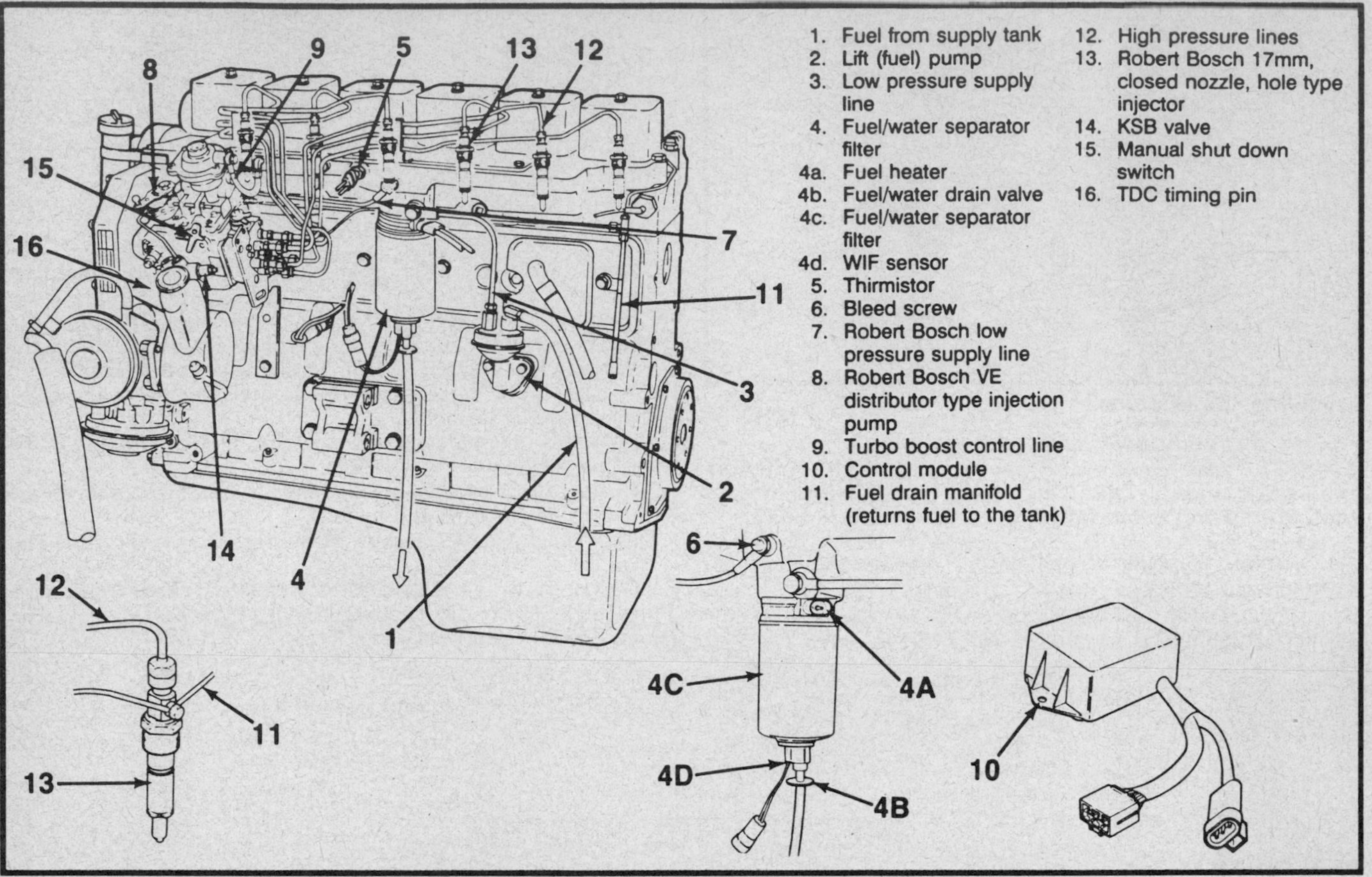

1. Fuel from supply tank
2. Lift (fuel) pump
3. Low pressure supply line
4. Fuel/water separator filter
4a. Fuel heater
4b. Fuel/water drain valve
4c. Fuel/water separator filter
4d. WIF sensor
5. Thirmistor
6. Bleed screw
7. Robert Bosch low pressure supply line
8. Robert Bosch VE distributor type injection pump
9. Turbo boost control line
10. Control module
11. Fuel drain manifold (returns fuel to the tank)
12. High pressure lines
13. Robert Bosch 17mm, closed nozzle, hole type injector
14. KSB valve
15. Manual shut down switch
16. TDC timing pin

Fuel system components—5.9L diesel engine

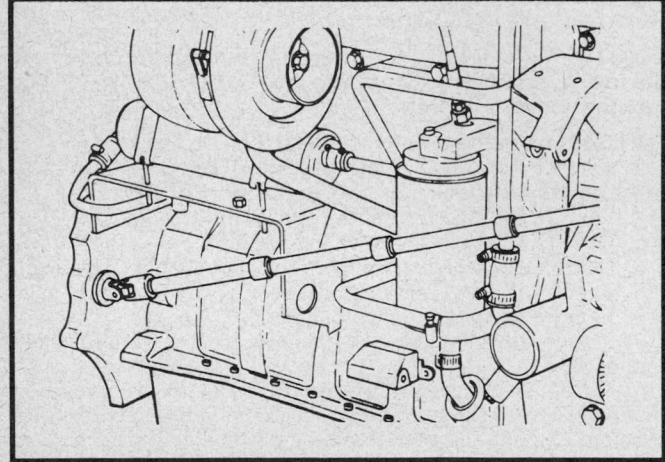

Installing the turning tool

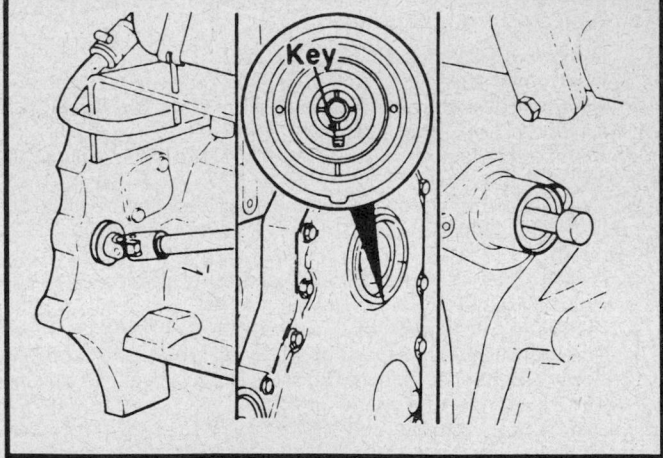

Locating TDC with the TDC pin

misplaced. Retighten the lockscrew to 22 ft. lbs. (30 Nm) to lock the driveshaft.

15. Using a suitable puller, pull the pump drive gear from the driveshaft.

NOTE: Be careful not to drop the drive gear key into the front cover when removing or installing the pump. If it does drop in, it must be removed before proceeding.

16. Remove the 3 mounting nuts and remove the injection pump from the vehicle.

17. Remove the gasket and clean the mounting surface.
To install:
18. Install a new gasket.

NOTE: The shaft of a new or reconditioned pump is locked so the key aligns with the drive gear keyway with cylinder No. 1 at TDC.

19. Install the pump and finger tighten the mounting nuts; the pump must be free to move in the slots.
20. Install the pump drive gear, washer and nut to the drive-

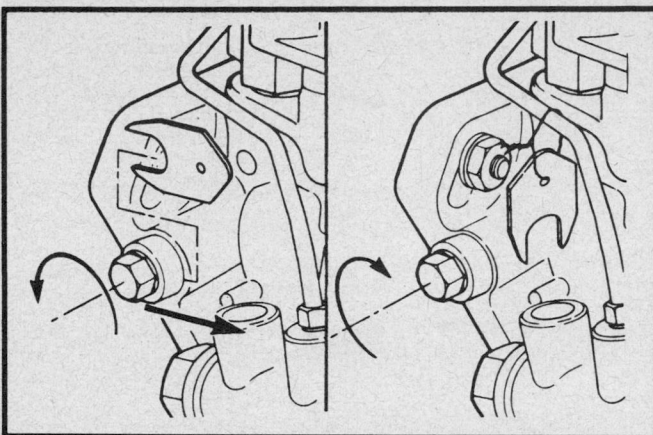

Removing the special washer from the injection pump

shaft. The pump will rotate slightly because of gear helix and clearance. This is acceptable providing the pump is free to move on the flange slots and the crankshaft does not move. Torque the nut to 11–15 ft. lbs. (15–20 Nm). This is not the final torque; do not overtighten.

21. If installing the original pump, rotate the pump to align the original timing marks and torque the mounting nuts to 18 ft. lbs. (24 Nm).

22. If installing a replacement pump, take up gear lash by rotating the pump counterclockwise toward the cylinder head, and torque the mounting nuts to 18 ft. lbs. (24 Nm). Permanently mark the new injection pump flange to match the mark on the gear housing.

23. Loosen the lockscrew and install the special washer under the lockscrew. Torque to 19 ft. lbs. (13 Nm). Disengage the TDC pin.

24. Install the injection pump support bracket. Finger tighten the bolts initially, then torque them to 18 ft. lbs. (24 Nm) in the following sequence
   a. Bracket to block bolts.
   b. Bracket to injection pump bolts.
   c. Throttle support bracket bolts

25. Now perform the final torque of the pump drive gear retaining nut to 48 ft. lbs. (65 Nm).

26. Install the oil filler tube assembly and clamp. Torque the bolts to 32 ft. lbs. (43 Nm).

27. Install all fuel lines and the electrical connector to the fuel shut off valve. Tighten the high pressure lines to 18 ft. lbs. (24 Nm).

28. Install the fuel air control tube. Torque the banjo fitting bolt to 9 ft. lbs. (12 Nm).

29. Install the throttle bracket and linkage. When connecting the cable to the control lever, adjust the legnth so the lever has stop-to-stop movement.

30. Connect the negative battery cable.

CAUTION

Do not place any part of the hand near the base of the high pressure line. A fuel leak from a high pressure fuel line has sufficient pressure to penetrate the skin and cause serious bodily harm. Do not bleed the lines if the engine is hot. Fuel spilling onto a hot exhaust manifold creates the danger of fire.

31. To bleed air from the system, run or crank the engine and carefully loosen the high pressure fitting from each injector one at a time. Retighten the fitting after the air has expelled before going on to the next injector fitting. The operation is complete when the engine runs smoothly. If the air cannot be removed, check the pump and supply line for suction leaks.

32. Adjust the idle speed if necessary.

Idle Speed Adjustment

1. Start the engine and run until at normal operating temperature.

2. An optical tachometer must be used to read engine speed; a conventional tachometer connected to the coil is useless in this instance.

3. Turn the air conditioning **ON**, if equipped.

4. Turn the idle speed screw until the desired idle speed is obtained. The specification for a vehicle equipped with automatic transmission is 700 rpm. The specification for a vehicle equipped with manual transmission is 750 rpm.

Injection Pump Timing

Adjustment

1. Install the turning tool into the flywheel housing opening on the exhaust side of the engine. Place a ½ in. drive universal joint in the turning tool and attach enough extensions to the joint to make it conveneient to turn the tool.

2. Using a ratchet to turn the turning tool, turn the engine until the key way on the fuel pump shaft is pointing approximately in the six o'clock position.

3. Locate TDC for cylinder No. 1 by turning the engine slowly while pusing in on the TDC pin. Stop turning the engine as soon as the pin engages with the gear timing hole. Disengage the pin after locating TDC.

4. Remove the plug from the end of the pump.

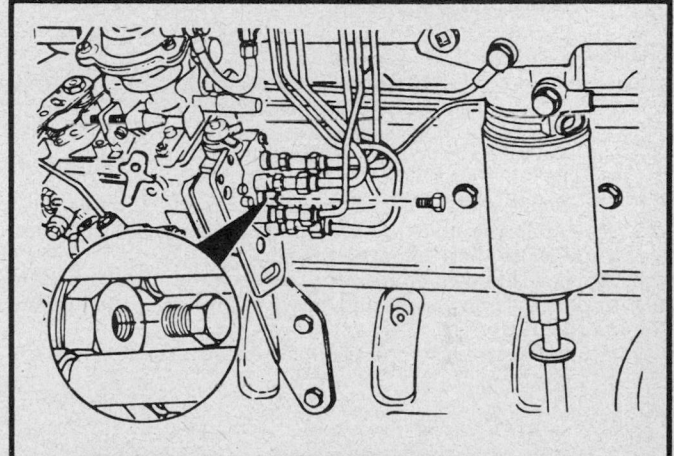

Removing the plug from the pump

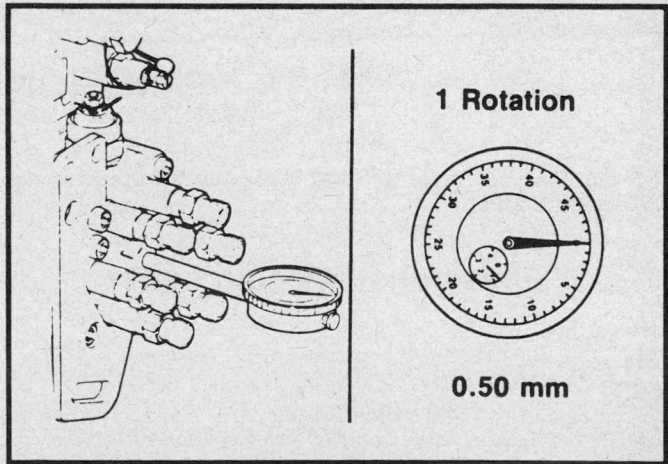

1 Rotation

0.50 mm

Installing the timing indicator

5. Install the special timing indicator, allowing for adequate indicator pin travel. It may be necessary to disconnect 1 or more fuel lines to properly install the indicator.

NOTE: The indicator is marked in increments of 0.01mm. One revolution of the indicator needle is equal to 0.050mm.

6. Turn the engine counterclockwise until the indicator needle stops moving. Adjust the indicator face to read zero.

7. Rotate the engine back to TDC and count the number of revolutions of the indicator needle. The reading shown when the engine timing pin engages is the amount of plunger lift the pump has at that point.

8. Readjust the indicator face to read zero. Loosen the pump mounting nuts and rotate the pump clockwise toward the cylinder head until the indicator reads the correct value for plunger lift (the reading in Step 7). Torque the mounting nuts to 18 ft. lbs. (24 Nm).

9. Remove the engine turning equipment and timing indicator. Install the timing plug and torque to 7.5 ft. lbs. (10 Nm). Connect any fuel lines that were disconnected.

10. Road test the vehicle.

Fuel Injector

Removal and Installation

1. Disconnect the negative battery cable. Remove the throttle linkage and bracket if necessary.

2. Disconnect the high pressure fuel supply line to the injector.

3. Disconnect the fuel drain manifold.

4. Clean the area around the injector.

5. Using a 24mm deepwell socket, remove the injector from the cylinder head.

To install:

6. Clean the injector bore with a bore brush.

7. Assemble the injector and 1 new copper sealing washer. Never use more than 1 copper washer.

8. Apply a thin coat of anti-sieze compound to the threads of the injector hold-down nut and between the top of the nut and the injector body.

9. Align the protrusion in the injector with the notch in the

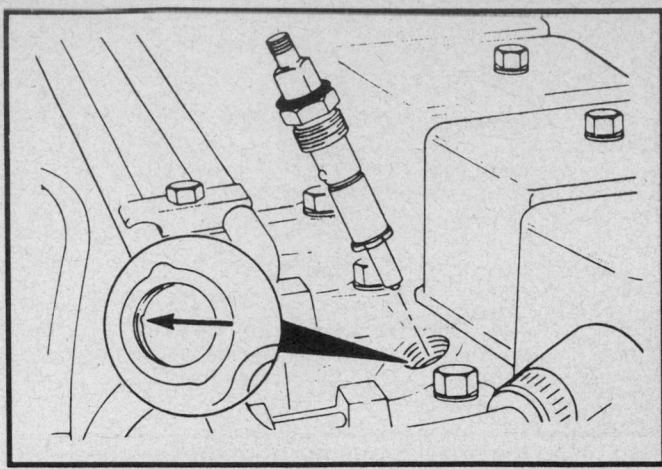

Installing the fuel injector

bore and install the injector. Torque the injector retainer nut to 44 ft. lbs. (60 Nm).

10. Push the O-ring into the groove at the top of the injector.

11. Using new sealing washers, assemble the fuel drain manifold and high pressure lines. Torque the banjo fitting bolt to 6 ft. lbs. (8 Nm). Leave the high pressure line loose temporarily.

—————————— **CAUTION** ——————————

Do not place any part of the hand near the base of the high pressure line. A fuel leak from a high pressure fuel line has sufficient pressure to penetrate the skin and cause serious bodily harm. Do not bleed the lines if the engine is hot. Fuel spilling onto a hot exhaust manifold creates the danger of fire.

————————————————————————————————

12. To bleed air from the system, run or crank the engine and tighten the fitting after the air has expelled. If more than 1 injector was replaced, tighten each fitting after the air has expelled before going on to the next injector fitting. Torque the fittings to 18 ft. lbs. (24 Nm). The operation is complete when the engine runs smoothly. If the air cannot be removed, check the pump and supply line for suction leaks.

13. Install the throttle linkage and bracket if they were removed.

EMISSION CONTROLS

Please refer to "Professional Emission Component Application Guide".

Emissions Warning Lamp

Resetting

1986–88 VEHICLES

1. Locate the EMR switch module. It is a red, green or tan plastic box located either on the lower portion of the steering column or to the left of the steering column on Vans and behind the right side of the glove box on Pick-Up and Ramcharger.

2. Remove the 9 volt battery (under the small black panel) from the module. 1988 vehicles do not have the 9 volt battery.

3. Reset the switch by inserting a small rod into a hole in the case of the module, which closes a switch and turns the lamp off.

4. Install a new 9 volt battery, if equipped.

1989–90 VEHICLES

1. Connect the DRBII to the diagnostic connector.

2. Turn the ignition switch to the **RUN** position and access the Emissions EMR Tests on the DRBII.

3. Select EMR Memory Check.

4. Select Reset EMR Light. This will reset the EMR timing in the computer and turn the light off.

5. Disconnect the DRBII.

GASOLINE ENGINE MECHANICAL

NOTE: Disconnecting the negative battery cable on some vehicles may interfere with the functions of the on board computer systems and may require the computer to undergo a relearning process, once the negative battery cable is reconnected.

Engine

Removal and Installation

1. Relieve the fuel pressure if the vehicle is equipped with fuel injection. Disconnect the negative battery cable from the battery and from the engine.
2. Remove the hood and the oil dipstick. Discharge the air conditioning on Vans. It is not necessary to discharge the air conditioning on Pick-Up or Ramcharger.
3. Raise the vehicle and support safely. Drain the engine oil and coolant. Remove the lower radiator hose.
4. Remove the starter. Remove the engine to transmission struts, if equipped.
5. Remove the air pump tube from the exhaust pipe on 3.7L engine. Remove the exhaust pipe from the exhaust manifold(s).
6. If the vehicle is equipped with a manual transmission, remove the transmission and all related parts.
7. If the vehicle is equipped with an automatic transmission, remove the inspection plate, matchmark the flex plate to the converter, remove the torque converter bolts and push the torque converter backwards as far as it will go. Remove the lower bell housing bolts.
8. Remove the engine mount lower nuts. Remove only the right side mount insulator nut on 3.7L engine.
9. Disconnect and plug the rubber fuel inlet and return hoses from the fuel lines at the right front of the vehicle. Lower the vehicle.
10. Remove the air cleaner assembly, disconnect all linkages and cables and remove the carburetor or throttle body. Stuff a clean shop towel into the intake manifold opening to prevent foreign objects from entering. Remove the left exhaust manifold and heat shield on Vans.
11. Remove the discharge and suction lines from the compressor on Vans. Cap the openings on the compressor to prevent foreign objects from entering. Unbolt the compressor from the engine on Pick-Up and Ramcharger and position it to the side.
12. On Vans, remove the front bumper, grille and support brace. Remove the radiator, shroud, condenser and support as an assembly. On Pick-Up and Ramcharger, remove the radiator and shroud. Remove the fan and all related parts.
13. Unbolt the power steering pump brackets from the engine and position it to the side.
14. Remove the alternator, air pump and all brackets. Disconnect the heater hoses.
15. Remove the distributor cap with all spark plug wires attached.
16. Disconnect all remaining electrical connectors, vacuum hoses and check for any other items preventing engine removal.
17. Attach an engine removal device to the intake manifold or cylinder head.
18. If the vehicle is equipped with an automatic transmission, support the transmission with a floor jack, or equivalent. Remove the remaining bell housing bolts. Remove the upper left engine mount nut on 3.7L engine.
19. Remove the engine from the vehicle slowly and carefully. Vans may need to be raised slightly, depending on the size of the removal device.

To install:

20. Lower the engine into position and install the upper bell housing bolts. Install the left side engine mount nut on 3.7L engine. Remove the engine removal device. Install the left side exhaust manifold, if it was removed. Install the oil dipstick.
21. Raise the vehicle and support safely.
22. Install the engine mount nuts and the remaining bell housing bolts.
23. If the vehicle is equipped with a manual transmission, install the transmission and all related parts.
24. If the vehicle is equipped with an automatic transmission, align the torque converter and flex plate and install the bolts. Install the inspection plate, starter and the engine to transmission struts, if equipped.
25. Connect the rubber fuel inlet and return hoses to the fuel lines at the right front of the vehicle.
26. Install the exhaust pipe to the exhaust manifold(s). Install the air pump tube to the exhaust pipe on 3.7L engine. Lower the vehicle.
27. Connect the heater hoses.
28. Make sure the negative battery cable is not connected to the battery. Connect the engine side of the negative cable to the engine. Install the alternator, air pump, power steering pump and all brackets.
29. Install the air conditioning compressor and connect the lines with new gaskets, if they were disconnected.
30. Install the throttle body or carburetor using a new base gasket and connect all linkages and cables. Connect all electrical connectors, vacuum hoses, etc. that were disconnected during the engine removal procedure.
31. Install the lower radiator hose. Install the fan and all related parts. Adjust all belt tensions.
32. On Vans, install the radiator, shroud, condenser and support as an assembly. Install the support brace, grille and bumper. On Pick-Up and Ramcharger, install the radiator and shroud.
33. Install the distributor cap with all spark plug wires attached.
34. Install the air cleaner assembly.
35. Install the hood.
36. Fill the engine with the specified amount of oil and fill the radiator with coolant.
37. Connect the negative battery cable and set all adjustments to specification.
38. Evacuate and recharge the air conditioning system if it was opened.

Cylinder Head

Removal and Installation

3.7L ENGINE

1. Disconnect the negative battery cable and drain the cooling system.
2. Remove the air cleaner assembly and fuel line.
3. Disconnect all wires, hoses, linkages and cables from the carburetor.
4. Disconnect the vacuum line from the distributor.
5. Disconnect the ignition wires from all 6 spark plugs.
6. Disconnect the heater hose and the upper clamp around the bypass hose.
7. Disconnect the coolant temperature sending unit wire.
8. Disconnect the exhaust pipe from the manifold.
9. Disconnect the diverter valve vacuum line from the intake manifold and remove the air tube assembly from the cylinder head, if equipped.
10. Remove the PCV hose from the valve cover and remove the valve cover.
11. Note the positioning of the oil hole and remove the rocker

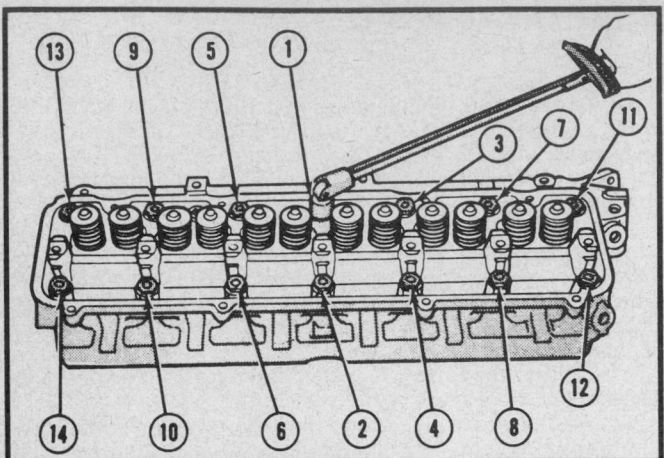

Cylinder head bolt torque sequence — 3.7L engine

arms and shaft assembly. Do not disassemble unless service is required.

12. Remove the pushrods and identify them to ensure installation in their original locations.

13. Remove the head bolts and remove the cylinder head with the manifolds as an assembly. Remove the manifolds from the head.

To install:

14. Clean and dry all gasket surfaces of the cylinder block and head. Inspect all surfaces with a straightedge. If the flatness exceeds 0.0075 times the length of the span measured (in any direction), replace or machine the head gasket surface.

15. Using no sealer whatsoever, install a new head gasket to the block. Clean, dry and lightly oil all head bolt threads. Engaging the bypass hose, position the head assembly — without the manifolds — on the block and install the head bolts.

16. Torque the head bolts in sequence to 35 ft. lbs. (47 Nm). Repeat the sequence retightening the bolts to a final torque of 70 ft. lbs. (95 Nm).

17. Install the pushrods. Assemble the rocker shaft assembly, if it was serviced. Install the assembly with the oil hole positioned to provide proper lubrication to the rocker assemblies. Install the rocker shaft retainers between the rocker arms and not on the extended bushings of the arms; the long retainer belongs in the center position only. Install the special shaft bolt at the rear of the shaft and install the rest of the bolts to the shaft. Torque the bolts evenly and gradually to 25 ft. lbs. (34 Nm).

18. Clean and dry the valve cover mating surfaces, bolts and bolt holes. Install the valve cover with a new gasket. Install the PCV valve.

19. Install the manifolds to the head and snug all nuts to about 20 inch lbs. Make sure the conical washers are installed with the cup side in.

20. Tighten the inner nut holding the manifolds together to 300 inch lbs. (34 Nm), then torque the outer 2 bolts to 260 inch lbs. (31 Nm).

21. Starting at the center and working outward, torque the manifold nuts on the head to 120 inch lbs. (14 Nm). Do not overtorque these nuts.

22. Connect the heater hose and bypass hose clamps.

23. Connect the wires, hoses, linkages and cables to the carburetor. Connect the fuel line.

24. Connect the spark plug wires, the distributor vacuum line and the sending unit wire.

25. Install the air tube with a new gasket and install the diverter valve vacuum line, if equipped.

26. Connect the exhaust pipe to the manifold.

27. Install the air cleaner assembly.

28. Fill the cooling system.

29. Connect the negative battery cable and set all adjustments to specification.

3.9L, 5.2L AND 5.9L ENGINES

1. Relieve the fuel pressure if the vehicle is equipped with fuel injection. Disconnect the negative battery cable from the battery and drain the cooling system.

2. Raise the vehicle and safely support. Disconnect the exhaust pipe from the manifolds.

3. Remove the alternator if the right head is being removed and the air pump and battery ground cable if the left head is being removed.

4. Remove the air cleaner assembly. Remove the air conditioning compressor or unbolt it and lay it to the side, if equipped. Remove the distributor cap with all wires attached.

5. Disconnect all wires, hoses, linkages and cables from the carburetor or throttle body. Disconnect the fuel line.

6. Disconnect the ignition coil, coolant temperature sending unit wire and all other connectors along the wiring harness connected to items on the intake manifold.

7. Disconnect the heater hose, upper radiator hose and the lower bypass hose clamp.

8. Remove the valve cover(s).

9. Remove the intake manifold assembly. Remove the exhaust manifold(s).

10. Remove the rocker arm and shaft assembly from the head(s). Do not disassemble unless service is required.

11. Remove the pushrods and identify them to ensure installation in their original locations.

12. Remove the head bolts and remove the cylinder head(s).

To install:

13. Clean and dry all gasket surfaces of the cylinder block and head. Inspect all surfaces with a straightedge. If the flatness exceeds 0.0075 times the length of the span measured (in any direction), replace or machine the head gasket surface.

14. Using no sealer whatsoever, install the new head gasket(s) to the block. Clean, dry and lightly oil all head bolts threads. Install the head(s) and install the head bolts.

15. Torque the head bolts in sequence to 50 ft. lbs. (68 Nm). Repeat the sequence retightening the bolts to a final torque of 105 ft. lbs. (143 Nm) and repeat the second step to ensure all bolts are accurately torqued.

16. Assemble the rocker shaft assembly, if it was serviced. Make sure all rocker arms with an **RH** stamped on them are installed to the right of those with an **LH**. Install the pushrods, rocker arms and shaft(s) with the notch on the end of the shaft pointing to the engine centerline and to the rear of the right

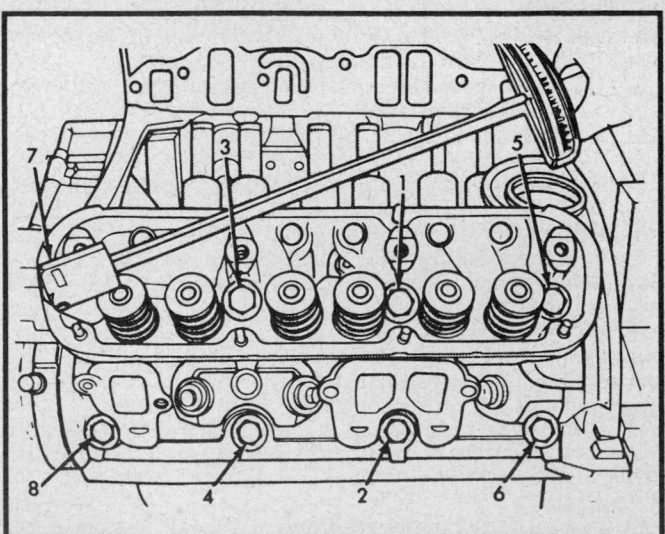

Cylinder head bolt torque sequence — 3.9L engine

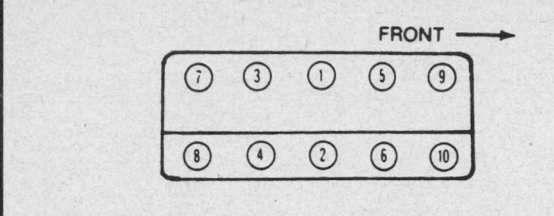

Cylinder head bolt torque sequence—5.2L and 5.9L engines

bank or to the front of the left bank. Make sure the long stamped steel retainers are at the number 2 and 4 positions. Torque the bolts evenly and gradually to 200 inch lbs. (23 Nm).

17. Clean and dry the intake manifold contact surfaces. Coat the intake manifold side gaskets very lightly with sealer and install the gaskets to the heads. Cutouts at the front of the gaskets differentiate the right and left sides.

18. Apply a thin uniform coat of quick dry cement to the front and rear intake manifold gaskets and mounting surfaces on the block and apply a thin bead of sealer to each of 4 the corners. Install the front and rear gaskets engaging the hole in the block and the tangs from the head gaskets. Apply a second thin bead of sealer above the gaskets in the 4 corners.

19. Carefully lower the intake manifold into position engaging the bypass hose; after it is satisfactorily in place, inspect the gaskets to make sure they have not become dislodged.

20. Install the intake manifold bolts and torque in sequence to 25 ft. lbs. (34 Nm). Repeat the sequence retightening the bolts to a final torque of 40 ft. lbs. (54 Nm) and repeat the second step to ensure all bolts are accurately torqued.

21. Install the exhaust manifold(s) and torque the bolts to 20 ft. lbs. (27 Nm). Torque the end nuts to 15 ft. lbs. (20 Nm).

22. Clean and dry the valve cover mating surfaces, bolts and bolt holes. Install the valve cover(s) each with a new gasket.

23. Connect the heater hose, upper radiator hose and the lower bypass hose clamp.

24. Connect the ignition coil, coolant temperature sending unit wire and all other connectors that were disconnected along the wiring harness.

25. Install the air conditioning compressor, if equipped. Install the distributor cap and all spark plug wires.

26. Install the alternator, battery ground and air pump, if they were removed.

27. Connect all wires, hoses, cables and the fuel line to the carburetor or throttle body. Install the air cleaner assembly.

28. Raise the vehicle and safely support. Connect the exhaust pipe to the manifolds.

29. Fill the cooling system.

30. Connect the negative battery cable and set all adjustments to specification.

Rocker Arms and Shaft

Removal and Installation

1. Disconnect the negative battery cable.
2. Remove the valve cover and gasket.
3. Note the positioning of the oil hole (3.7L engine) or notch (3.9L, 5.2L and 5.9L engines) and remove the rocker arms and shaft assembly from the head.
4. Disassemble the assembly as required and replace all worn parts.

NOTE: On engines with exhaust valve rotators, the exhaust rocker arm must have relief for clearance.

To install:

5. On 3.7L engine, install the assembly with the oil hole posi-

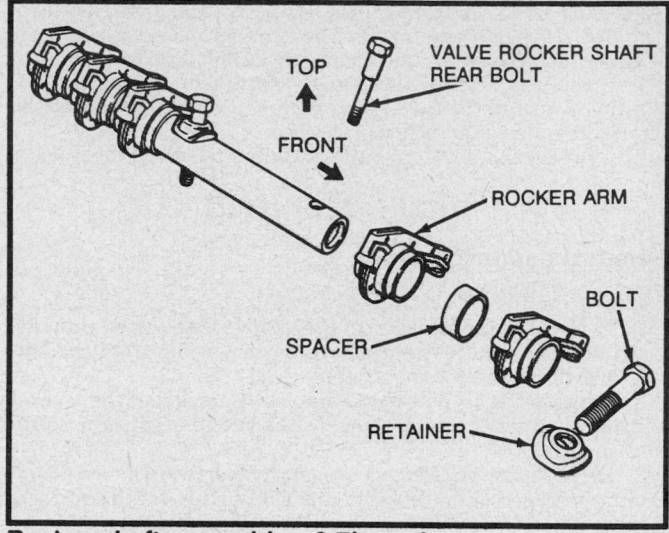

Rocker shaft assembly—3.7L engine

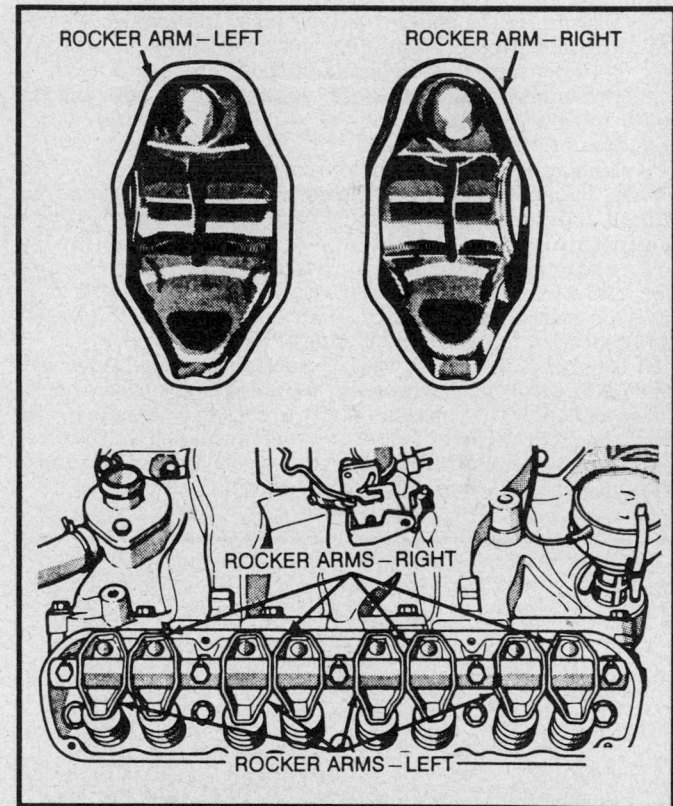

Identifying and assembling the rocker assembly—5.2L and 5.9L engines; 3.9L engine parts are similar

tioned to provide proper lubrication to the rocker assemblies. Install the rocker shaft retainers between the rocker arms and not on the extended bushings of the arms; the long retainer belongs in the center position only. Install the special shaft bolt at the rear of the shaft and install the rest of the bolts to the shaft. Torque the bolts evenly and gradually to 25 ft. lbs. (34 Nm).

6. On 3.9L, 5.2L and 5.9L engines, make sure all rocker arms with an **RH** stamped on them are installed to the right of those with an **LH**. Install the assembly with the notch on the end of the shaft pointing to the engine centerline and to the rear of the

right bank or to the front of the left bank. Make sure the long stamped steel retainers are at the number 2 and 4 positions. Torque the bolts evenly and gradually to 200 inch lbs. (23 Nm).

7. Clean and dry the valve cover mating surfaces, bolts and bolt holes. Install the valve cover with a new gasket. Torque the screws or nuts to 95 inch lbs. (11 Nm).

8. Connect the negative battery cable and check for leaks.

Intake Manifold

Removal and Installation

3.9L, 5.2L and 5.9L ENGINES

1. Relieve the fuel pressure if the vehicle is equipped with fuel injection. Disconnect the negative battery cable from the battery and drain the cooling system.

2. Remove the air pump and bracket. Removal of the bracket will allow for easier installation of the left front corner of the intake manifold.

3. Remove the air cleaner assembly. Remove the air conditioning compressor or unbolt it and lay it to the side, if equipped. Remove the distributor cap with all wires attached.

4. Disconnect all wires, hoses, linkages and cables from the carburetor or throttle body. Disconnect the fuel line.

5. Disconnect the ignition coil, coolant temperature sending unit wire and all other connectors along the wiring harness connected to items on the intake manifold.

6. Disconnect the heater hose, upper radiator hose and the lower bypass hose clamp.

7. Remove the valve covers.

8. Unbolt the intake manifold from the heads and remove the intake manifold assembly. Disassemble the manifold as required and clean out the exhaust crossover passages.

To install:

9. Clean and dry the intake manifold contact surfaces. Coat the intake manifold side gaskets very lightly with sealer and install the gaskets to the heads. Cutouts at the front of the gaskets differentiate the right and left sides.

10. Apply a thin uniform coat of quick dry cement to the front and rear intake manifold gaskets and mounting surfaces on the block and apply a thin bead of sealer to each of 4 the corners. Install the front and rear gaskets engaging the hole in the block and the tangs from the head gaskets. Apply a second thin bead of sealer above the gaskets in the 4 corners.

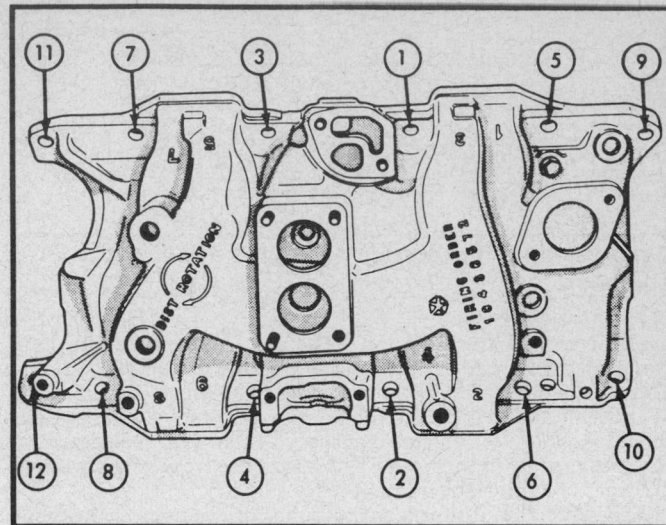

Intake manifold bolt torque sequence—5.2L and 5.9L engine

11. Carefully lower the intake manifold into position engaging the bypass hose; after it is satisfactorily in place, inspect the gaskets to make sure they have not become dislodged.

12. Install the intake manifold bolts with the aspirator tube, air pump bracket and kickdown linkage bracket in place, if equipped. Torque the bolts in sequence to 25 ft. lbs. (34 Nm). Repeat the sequence retightening the bolts to a final torque of 40 ft. lbs. (54 Nm) and repeat the second step to ensure all bolts are accurately torqued.

13. Clean and dry the valve cover mating surfaces, bolts and bolt holes. Install the valve covers with a new gasket. Torque the screws or nuts to 95 inch lbs. (11 Nm).

14. Connect the heater hose, upper radiator hose and the lower bypass hose clamp.

15. Connect the ignition coil, coolant temperature sending unit wire and all other connectors that were disconnected along the wiring harness.

16. Install the air conditioning compressor, if equipped. Install the distributor cap and all spark plug wires.

17. Install air pump.

18. Connect all wires, hoses, cables and the fuel line to the carburetor or throttle body. Install the air cleaner assembly.

19. Fill the cooling system.

20. Connect the negative battery cable and check for leaks.

Exhaust Manifold

Removal and Installation

3.9L, 5.2L and 5.9L ENGINES

1. Disconnect the negative battery cable. Remove the hot air tube and heat shield, if necessary.

2. Raise the vehicle and support safely. Remove the exhaust pipe from the exhaust manifolds. Lower the vehicle.

3. Take note of all conical washer locations and remove the bolts, nuts and washers attaching the manifold to the head.

4. Remove the manifold.

To install:

5. If either of the end studs came out with the nuts, install a new stud using sealer on the coarse threads.

6. Position the manifold on the end studs. Install conical washers and nuts on the studs.

7. Install the remaining bolts and washers in their proper locations. The inner bolts are not mounted with washers. Work-

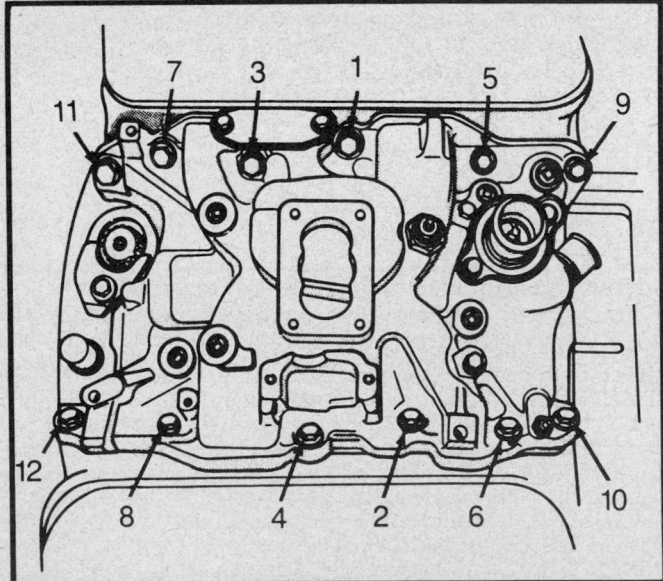

Intake manifold bolt torque sequence—3.9L engine

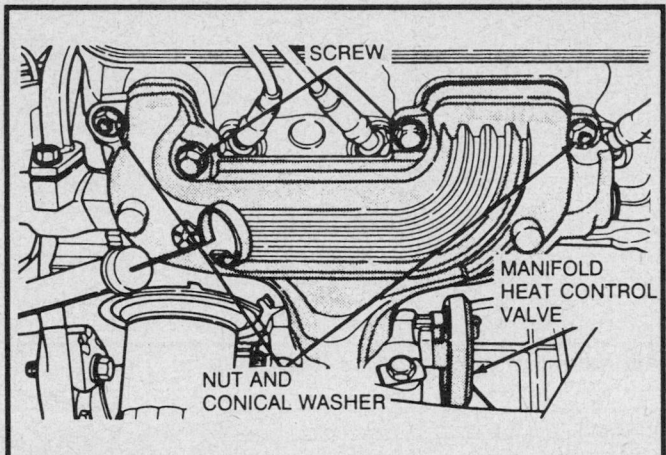

Exhaust manifold installation—3.9L engine (right side shown)

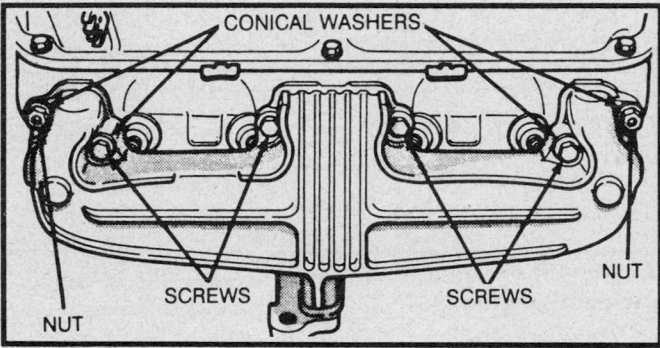

Exhaust manifold installation—5.2L and 5.9L engines

ing outward from the center, torque the bolts to 20 ft. lbs. (27 Nm) and the nuts to 15 ft. lbs. (20 Nm).

8. Install the exhaust pipe to the manifolds.
9. Connect the negative battery cable and check for exhaust leaks.

Combination Manifold

Removal and Installation

3.7L ENGINE

1. Disconnect the negative battery cable and drain the cooling system.
2. Remove the air cleaner assembly and fuel line.
3. Disconnect all wires, hoses, linkages and cables from the carburetor.
4. Disconnect the diverter valve vacuum line from the intake manifold, if equipped.
5. Disconnect the exhaust pipe from the exhaust manifold. Unbolt the manifolds from each other and remove both manifolds from the vehicle.
To install:
6. Install a new combination intake and exhaust manifold gasket to the head.
7. Install the manifolds to the head using a nw gasket between them and snug all nuts to about 20 inch lbs. Make sure the conical washers are installed with the cup side in.
8. Tighten the inner nut holding the manifolds together to 300 inch lbs. (34 Nm), then torque the outer 2 bolts to 260 inch lbs. (31 Nm).
9. Starting at the center and working outward, torque the

manifold nuts on the head to 120 inch lbs. (14 Nm). Do not overtorque these nuts.
10. Connect the heater hose and bypass hose clamps.
11. Connect the wires, hoses, linkages and cables to the carburetor. Connect the fuel line.
12. Install the air tube with a new gasket and install the diverter valve vacuum line, if equipped.
13. Connect the exhaust pipe to the manifold.
14. Install the air cleaner assembly.
15. Fill the cooling system.
16. Connect the negative battery cable and check for leaks.

Timing Chain Cover

Removal and Installation

1. Disconnect the negative battery cable.
2. Drain the cooling system.
3. Remove the radiator, fan and all related parts. Remove the water pump from all engines except the 3.7L. The cover can be removed without removing the water pump on the 3.7L engine.
4. Remove the crankshaft pulley.
5. Remove the vibration damper using the proper puller. The cover can be removed from the 3.7L engine at this point.
6. Disconnect the fuel lines from the fuel pump, if equipped.
7. Remove the 2 front bolts from the oil pan.
8. Unbolt the chain cover from the block and remove, using caution to avoid damaging the oil pan gasket. Remove the fuel pump from the cover, if equipped.
To install:
9. Clean and dry the mating surfaces of the cover and block. Apply a thin bead of sealer to the oil pan gasket.
10. Install a new cover gasket and install the cover. Torque the bolts to 200 inch lbs. (23 Nm) on 3.7L engine and to 30 ft. lbs. (41 Nm) on 3.9L, 5.2L and 5.9L engines.
11. Install the water pump with a new gasket, if it was removed.
12. On 3.7L engine, install the vibration damper using tool C–3237A. On all other engines, install the damper with tool C–3638, install the bolt and washer and torque to specification. Apply a small amount of sealer to the bolts and install the crankshaft pulley.
13. Install the fuel pump using a new gasket, if equipped and connect the fuel lines. Install the 2 oil pan bolts, if they were removed.
14. Install the radiator, fan and all related parts.
15. Fill the cooling system.
16. Connect the negative battery cable and check for leaks.

Front Cover Oil Seal

Removal and Installation

1. Disconnect the negative battery cable.
2. Remove the belts from the crankshaft pulley.
3. Remove the fan and shroud from the vehicle.
4. Remove the crankshaft pulley.
5. Remove the vibration damper using the proper puller.
6. Using a suitable tool behind the lips of the oil seal, pry outward. Take care not to damage the crankshaft seal surface of the cover.
To install:
7. Install the new seal by installing the threaded shaft part of the special tool C–4251 into the threads of the crankshaft.
8. Place the seal into the opening with the spring toward the engine. Place the installing adapter C–4251-2 (3.7L engine) or C–4251-3 (3.9L, 5.2L and 5.9L engines) with the thrust bearing and nut on the shaft. Tighten the nut until the tool is flush with the timing chain cover. Remove the tool.
9. On 3.7L engine, install the vibration damper using tool C–3237A. On all other engines, install the damper with tool C–

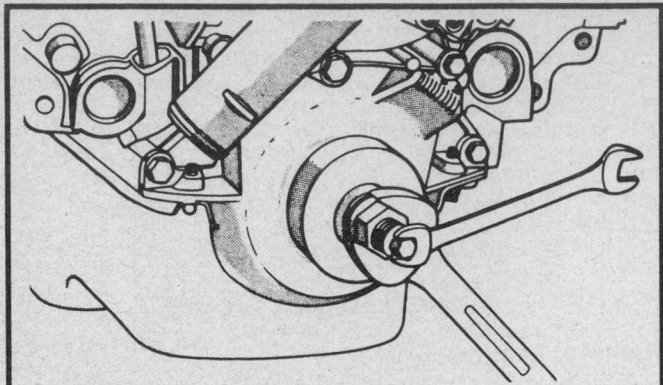

Installing the front cover oil seal—3.9L, 5.2L and 5.9L engines

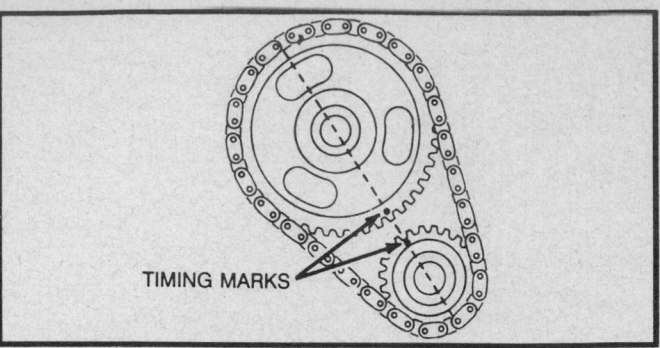

Alignment of timing marks—3.7L engine

3638, install the bolt and washer and torque to specification.

10. Apply a small amount of sealer to the bolts and install the crankshaft pulley.

11. Install the fan and shroud.

12. Connect the negative battery cable and check for leaks.

Timing Chain and Gears

Removal and Installation

1. If possible, crank the engine around so that the No. 1 cylinder is at TDC on the compression stroke. Remove the distributor cap to confirm and line the timing mark on the damper pulley with **0** on the timing scale. This will aid in aligning timing marks when installing the timing gears. Disconnect the negative battery cable.

2. Drain the cooling system.

3. Remove the radiator, fan and all related parts. Remove the water pump from all engines except the 3.7L engine. The cover can be removed without removing the water pump on the 3.7L engine.

4. Remove the crankshaft pulley.

5. Remove the vibration damper using the proper puller. The cover can be removed from the 3.7L engine at this point.

6. Disconnect the fuel lines from the fuel pump, if equipped.

7. Remove the 2 front bolts from the oil pan.

8. Unbolt the chain cover from the block and remove, using caution to avoid damaging the oil pan gasket. Remove the fuel pump from the cover, if equipped.

9. Remove the camshaft gear retaining bolt, cup washer and fuel pump eccentric, if equipped. Remove the timing chain and gears.

To install:

10. Place both camshaft and crankshaft gears on the bench with the timing marks on the exact imaginary center line through both gear bores as they are installed on the engine. Place the timing chain around both sprockets.

11. Turn the crankshaft and camshaft so the keys line up with the keyways in the gears when the timing marks are in proper position.

12. Slide both gears over their respective shafts and use a straightedge to check timing mark alignment.

13. Install the fuel pump eccentric and cup washer, if equipped. Torque the camshaft gear retaining bolt to 35 ft. lbs. (47 Nm).

14. Clean and dry the mating surfaces of the timing chain cover and block. Apply a thin bead of sealer to the oil pan gasket.

15. Install a new cover gasket and install the cover. Torque the bolts to 200 inch lbs. (23 Nm) on 3.7L engine and to 30 ft. lbs. (41 Nm) on 3.9L, 5.2L and 5.9L engines.

Alignment of timing marks—3.9L, 5.2L and 5.9L gasoline engines

16. Install the water pump with a new gasket, if it was removed.

17. On 3.7L engine, install the vibration damper using tool C-3237A. On all other engines, install the damper with tool C-3638, install the bolt and washer and torque to specification. Apply a small amount of sealer to the bolts and install the crankshaft pulley.

18. Install the fuel pump using a new gasket, if equipped and connect the fuel lines. Install the 2 oil pan bolts, if they were removed.

19. Install the radiator, fan and all related parts.

20. Fill the cooling system.

21. Connect the negative battery cable, set all adjustments to specifications and check for leaks.

Camshaft

Removal and Installation

1. If possible, crank the engine around so that the No. 1 cylinder is at TDC on the compression stroke. Remove the distributor cap to confirm and line the timing mark on the damper pulley with **0** on the timing scale. This will aid in aligning timing marks when installing the timing gears. If the vehicel is equipped with fuel injection, relieve the fuel pressure. Disconnect the negative battery cable.

2. Drain the cooling system.

3. Remove the valve cover(s).

4. Remove the rocker shaft assembly(s). Identify and remove the pushrods.

5. On 3.9L, 5.2L and 5.9L engines, remove the intake manifold. Identify and remove all lifters.

6. Remove the distributor. On 3.9L, 5.2L and 5.9L engines, lift out the oil pump and distributor driveshaft.

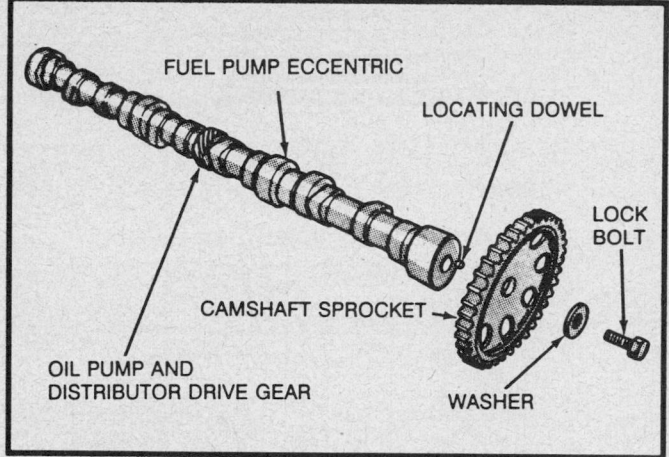

3.7L engine camshaft and gear

7. On 3.7L engine, remove the oil pump.

8. Remove the radiator, fan and all related parts.

9. Remove the fuel pump, if equipped. Remove the timing chain cover, timing chain and gears.

10. On 3.9L, 5.2L and 5.9L engines, note the location of the oil tab and remove the camshaft thrust plate.

11. Install suitable long bolt into the front of the camshaft to facilitate removal. Remove the camshaft, being careful not to damage any of the cam bearings with the cam lobes.

To install:

12. On 3.7L engine, lubricate the camshaft lobes and journals and install the camshaft into the block.

13. On 3.9L, 5.2L and 5.9L engines, install the camshaft to within 2 in. of its final installation position. Install the camshaft blocking tool C–3509 and bolt it in place with the distributor hold-down bolt. This will prevent the camshaft from being pushed in too far and knocking out the welch plug at the rear of the block. This tool should remain in place until the timing chain installation has been completed.

14. Install the camshaft thrust plate and chain oil tab, if equipped. Make sure the tang of the oil tab enters the hole in the thrust plate at the lower right. Torque the bolts to 210 inch lbs. (24 Nm). Make sure the top edge of the oil tab is flat against the thrust plate or it will not feed oil to the chain.

15. Place both camshaft and crankshaft gears on the bench with the timing marks on the exact imaginary center line through both gear bores as they are installed on the engine. Place the timing chain around both sprockets.

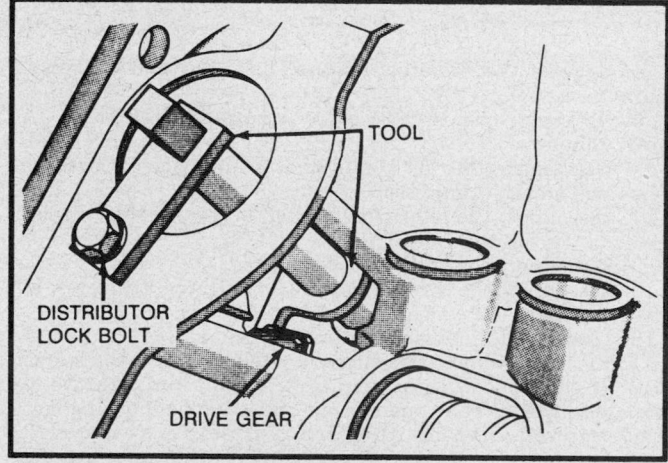

Installing the camshaft blocking tool

16. Turn the crankshaft and camshaft so the keys line up with the keyways in the gears when the timing marks are in proper position.

17. Slide both gears over their respective shafts and use a straightedge to check timing mark alignment.

18. Install the fuel pump eccentric and cup washer, if equipped. Torque the camshaft gear retaining bolt to 35 ft. lbs. (47 Nm). Remove the camshaft blocking tool, if it was installed.

19. Measure camshaft endplay, if applicable. Replace the thrust plate if not within specifications.

20. On 3.9L, 5.2L and 5.9L engines, coat the oil pump and distributor driveshaft with oil. Install 3.9L engine shaft so that when the gear spirals into place and drops into the oil pump, the slot in the top of the gear is pointing directly to the left front intake manifold bolt hole. Install 5.2L and 5.9L engine shaft in a similar manner, except position it so that the slot is parallel with the center line of the camshaft.

21. If the camshaft was not replaced, lubricate and install the lifters in their original locations. If the camshaft was replaced, new lifters must be used.

22. Install the pushrods and rocker shaft assembly(s).

23. Install the intake manifold, if it was removed. Install the valve cover(s).

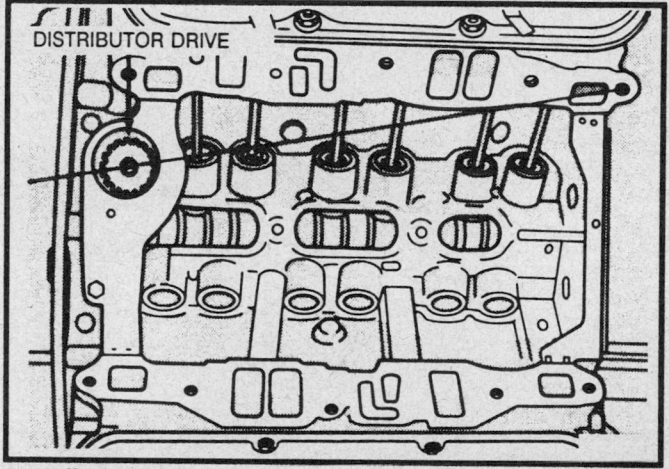

Installed distributor drive gear position—3.9L engine

Installed distributor drive gear position—5.2L and 5.9L gasoline engine

24. Install the distributor so the rotor points to the No. 1 spark plug wire position on the cap.

25. On 3.7L engine, install the oil pump.

26. Install the timing chain cover and all related parts, fuel pump if equipped, and radiator.

27. When everything is bolted in place, change the engine oil and replace the oil filter.

NOTE: If the camshaft or lifters have been replaced, add 1 pint of Mopar crankcase conditioner, or equivalent when replenishing the oil to aid in break in. This mixture should be left in the engine for a minimum of 500 miles and drained at the next normal oil change.

28. Fill the radiator with coolant.

29. Connect the negative battery cable, set all adjustments to specifications and check for leaks.

Piston and Piston Rings

Positioning

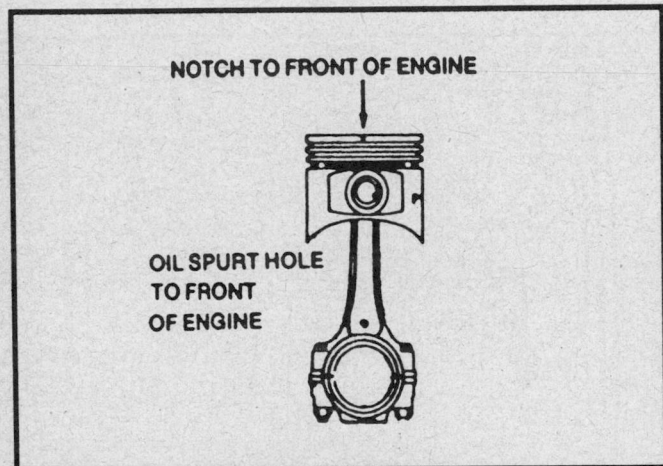

Piston positioning—3.7L engine

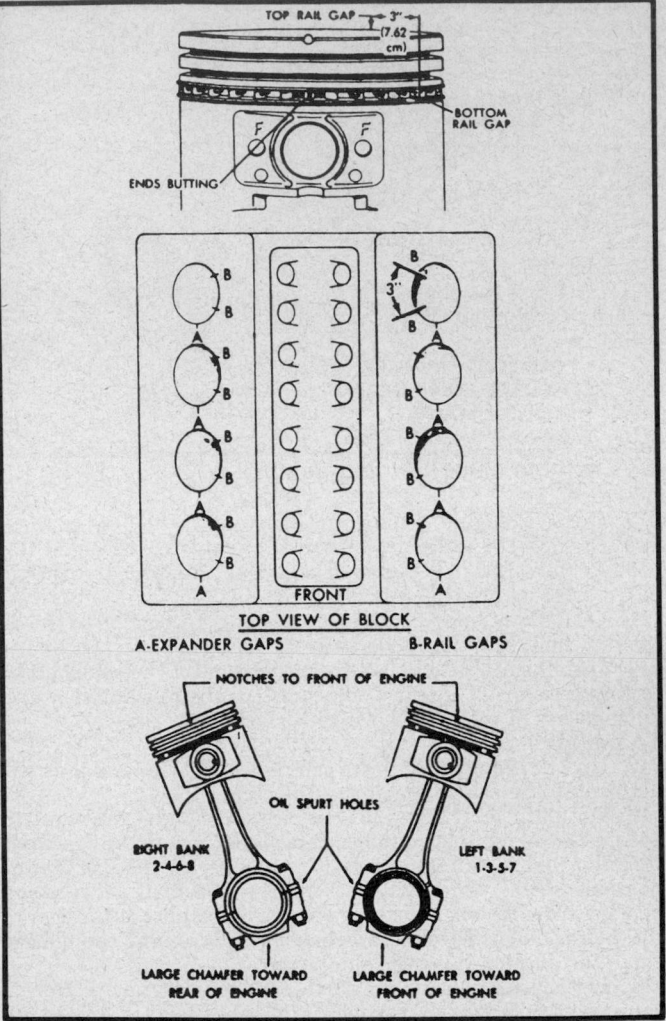

Piston ring and piston installation—5.2L and 5.9L gasoline engines; 3.9L engine is is similar

DIESEL ENGINE MECHANICAL

NOTE: Disconnecting the negative battery cable on some vehicles may interfere with the functions of the on board computer systems and may require the computer to undergo a relearning process, once the negative battery cable is reconnected.

Engine

Removal and Installation

--------- CAUTION ---------

This engine has a dry weight of 880 lbs. Make sure the engine removal equipment is rated adequately, or personal injury may result.

1. Remove the hood.

2. Disconnect the negative cable from the battery and from the engine.

3. Drain the coolant.

4. Remove the radiator, shroud, belt, fan and all related parts.

5. Remove the intake and exhaust pipes from the turbocharger.

6. Disconnect the air conditioner connections. Cover the openings on the compressor.

7. Disconnect the alternator and all other electrical connections to the engine.

8. Disconnect the acclerator linkage.

9. Disconnect the throttle linkage from the control lever, but do not remove the control lever from the injection pump.

10. Disconnect all engine driven accessories.

11. Raise the vehicle and support safely. Remove the starter.

12. If equipped with automatic transmission, remove the torque converter bolts and remove the lower bellhousing bolts. If equipped with manual transmission, remove the transmission.

13. Drain the oil from the engine.

14. Disconnect the transmission oil cooler lines from their brackets, if equipped.

15. Disconnect the exhaust pipe from the turbocharger. Lower the vehicle.

16. Disconnect and plug the fuel lines.

17. Using the proper equipment, hoist the engine slightly using the lifting eyes and support the transmission, if still installed.

18. Remove the motor mounts.

19. Remove the upper bellhousing bolts.

20. Remove the engine from the vehicle.

To install:

21. Position the engine in the engine compartment and install the motor mounts. Torque the nuts and bolts to 57 ft. lbs. (77 Nm).

22. Install the bellhousing bolts and torque converter bolts, if equipped. Install the manual transmission, if equipped.

23. Install the starter.

24. Connect the exhaust pipe.

25. Connect the transmission oil cooler lines to their brackets, if equipped.

26. Connect the fuel lines.

27. Connect the power steering lines.

28. Connect all engine driven accessories.

29. Connect the accelerator linkage.

30. Connect the throttle linkage to the control lever.

31. Connect the air conditioner connections.

32. Connect the alternator and all other electrical connections to the engine.

33. Install the intake and exhaust pipes to the turbocharger.

34. Install the fan and all related parts, shroud and radiator.

35. Fill the enine with the proper amount of diesel engine oil.

36. Fill the radiator with coolant.

37. Connect the negative battery cable, set all adjustments to specifications and check for leaks.

Cylinder Head

Removal and Installation

1. Disconnect the negative battery cable.

2. Drain the coolant.

3. Disconnect the radiator hose and heater hoses.

4. Remove the turbocharger and air crossover.

5. Remove the exhaust manifold.

6. Remove all fuel lines from the injection pump and injector nozzles. Remove the fuel filter.

7. Remove the valve covers.

8. Remove the rocker arms and pushrods.

9. Unbolt the cylinder head from the block. Remove the cylinder head.

10. Inspect the coolant passages. A large accumulation of rust or lime will require service to the block.

11. Inspect the surface of the head for flatness. The maximum variation is 0.0004 in. (0.010mm) within any 2 in. diameter area or 0.012 in. (0.30mm) overall end to end or side to side.

To install:

12. Thoroughly clean and dry the mating surfaces of the head and block. Position the new head gasket on the dowels.

13. Install the head onto the dowels on the block.

14. Lubricate the pushrod sockets and install the pushrods and rocker arms.

15. Clean, dry and lightly lubricate the head bolts. Install and torque in sequence first to 29 ft. lbs. (40 Nm), then to 62 ft. Lbs. (85 Nm) and finally to 93 ft. lbs. (126 Nm).

16. Install the rocker arm pedastal bolts. Torque to 18 ft. lbs. (24 Nm).

17. Adjust the valve clearance.

18. Install the valve covers with new gaskets. Torque the bolts to 18 ft. lbs. (24 Nm).

19. Install all fuel lines and the fuel filter.

20. Install the exhaust manifold.

21. Install the turbocharger and air crossover.

22. Connect the radiator hose and heater hoses.

23. Fill the radiator with coolant.

24. Connect the negative battery cable, set all adjustments to specifications and check for leaks.

Valve Clearance

Adjustment

1. Perform the adjustment when the engine is below 140°F (60°C).

2. Disconnect the negative battery cable.

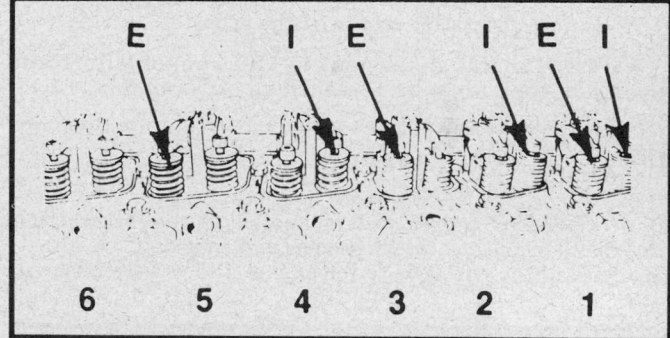

First group of valves to be adjusted—5.9L diesel engine

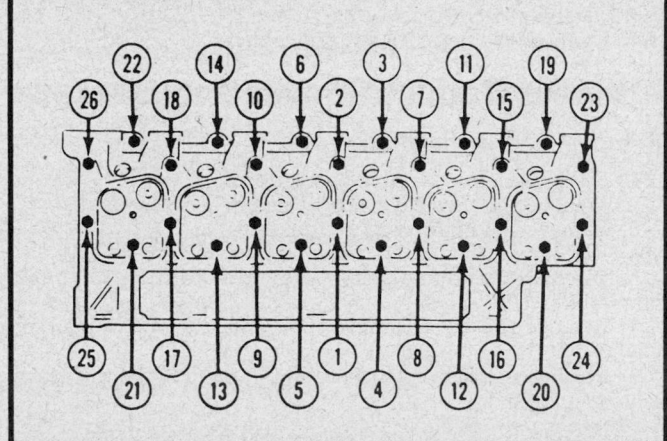

Cylinder head bolt tightening sequence—5.9L diesel engine

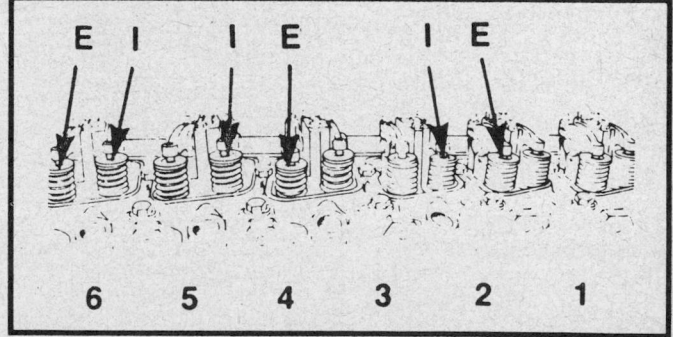

Second group of valves to be adjusted—5.9L diesel engine

3. Use the timing pin to locate TDC for cylinder No. 1. Disengage the pin.

4. Remove the valve covers.

5. With the engine is in this position, the first group of valves may be adjusted:

No. 1 intake: 0.10 in. (0.254mm)
No. 1 exhaust: 0.20 in. (0.508mm)
No. 2 intake: 0.10 in. (0.254mm)
No. 3 exhaust: 0.20 in. (0.508mm)
No. 4 intake: 0.10 in. (0.254mm)
No. 5 exhaust: 0.20 in. (0.508mm)

6. Mark the pulley and rotate the engine 360 degrees.

7. With the engine is in this position, the second group of valves may be adjusted:

No. 2 exhaust: 0.20 in. (0.508mm)
No. 3 intake: 0.10 in. (0.254mm)
No. 4 exhaust: 0.20 in. (0.508mm)
No. 5 intake: 0.10 in. (0.254mm)
No. 6 intake: 0.10 in. (0.254mm)
No. 6 exhaust: 0.20 in. (0.508mm)

8. Torque all locknuts to 18 ft. lbs. (24 Nm).

9. Install the valve covers with new gaskets. Torque the bolts to 18 ft. lbs. (24 Nm).

10. Connect the negative battery cable.

Rocker Arm and Pedastal Assembly

Removal and Installation

1. Disconnect the negative battery cable.
2. Remove the valve cover.
3. Loosen the adjusting screw locknuts. Loosen the screws until they stop.
4. Remove the 8mm bolt and 12mm head bolt from the pedastal.
5. Remove the pedastal and rocker arm assembly. Remove the pushrods if necessary.
6. Remove the retaining ring and thrust washer.
7. Remove the rocker arm from the pedastal.

NOTE: Do not disassemble the rocker shaft and pedastal; they must be replaced as an assembly.

8. Remove the locknut and adjusting screw from the rocker arm.

To install:

9. Install the adjusting screw and locknut.
10. Lubricate the shaft with oil and install the rocker arm to the shaft. Install the thrust washer and snapring.
11. Install the pushrods to the engine if they were removed.

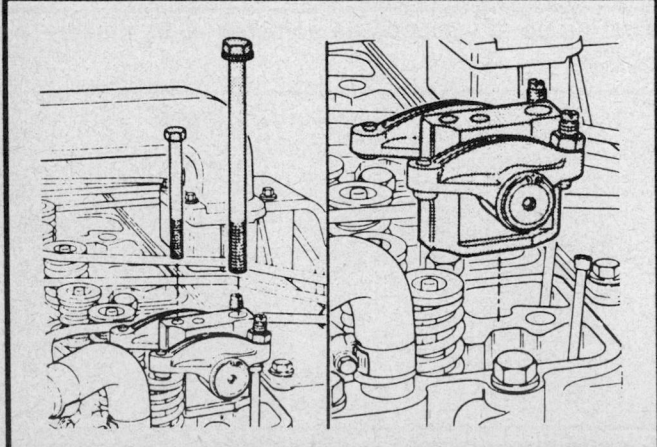

Removing the rocker arm and pedastal assembly

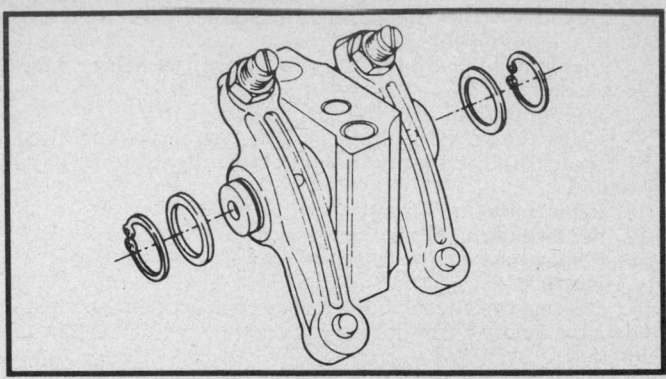

Removing or installing the rocker arm from the pedastal

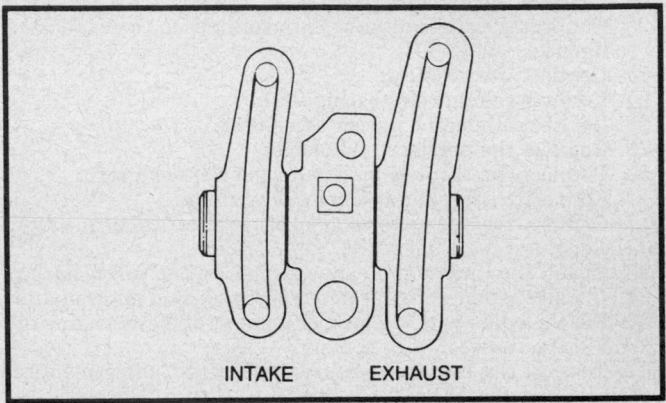

INTAKE   EXHAUST

Proper rocker arm installation—5.9L diesel engine

12. Install the pedastal and rocker arm assembly to the head aligning the dowel in the pedastal with the dowel bore in the head. If the pushrod is holding the pedastal oof of the head, turn the engine until the pedastal will set on the head without interference.

13. Lubricate the threads of the bolt with oil. Install and torque first to 29 ft. lbs. (40 Nm), then to 62 ft. Lbs. (85 Nm) and finally to 93 ft. lbs. (126 Nm). If all of the pedastals were removed, follow the entire head bolt torque sequence including those head bolts that were not removed in this procedure.

14. Tighten the 8mm bolts to 18 ft. lbs. (24 Nm).

15. Adjust the valves.

16. Install the valve cover with a new gasket. Torque the bolts to 18 ft. lbs. (24 Nm).

17. Connect the negative battery cable.

Intake Manifold Cover and Gasket

Removal and Installation

1. Disconnect the negative battery cable.
2. Remove the throttle control bracket and linkage.
3. Remove the high pressure fuel lines.
4. Disconnect the intake manifold heater.
5. Disconnect the fuel heater ground wire from the intake manifold.
6. Remove the air crossover tube and the intake manifold heater.
7. Remove the manifold cover and gasket. Clean the gasket sealing surface.

To install:

8. Install the new gasket and cover. Some of the bolt holes are drilled through. Apply liquid teflon sealant to these bolts. Torque all bolts to 18 ft. lbs. (24 Nm).

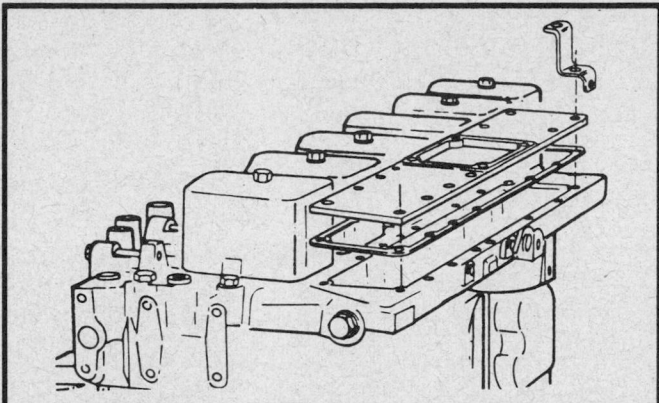

Intake manifold cover and gasket—5.9L diesel engine 3M

9. Assemble all intake piping and intake manifold heater with the throttle control bracket and linkage.
10. Connect the fuel heater ground wiring.
11. Install and bleed the high pressure fuel lines.
12. Connect the negative battery cable.

Exhaust Manifold

Removal and Installation

1. Disconnect the negative battery cable.
2. Disconnect the air intake hose and exhaust pipe from the turbo.
3. Remove the turbocharger and gasket.
4. Remove the cab heater supply and return lines.
5. Remove the exhaust manifold and gasket. Clean the gasket sealing surface.
To install:
6. Install the new gasket and manifold. Torque the exhaust manifold bolts in sequence to 32 ft. lbs. (43 Nm).
7. Install the cab heater supply and return lines.
8. Install the turbocharger and gasket.
9. Connect the air intake and exhaust piping.
10. Connect the negative battery cable and check for exhaust leaks.

Turbocharger

Removal and Installation

1. Disconnect the negative battery cable.
2. Loosen the air crossover hose.
3. Disconnect the intake hose and exhaust pipe.
4. Remove the oil drain tube bolts.
5. Remove the oil supply line from the turbocharger.

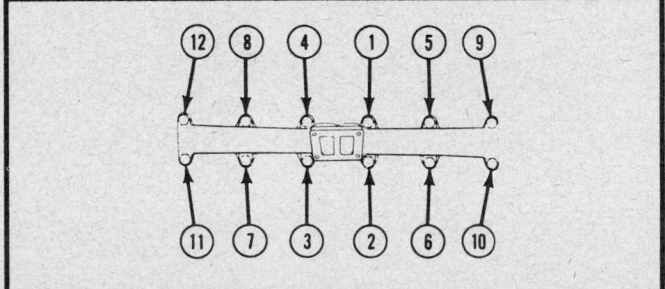

Exhaust manifold bolt torque sequence—5.9L diesel engine

6. Remove the turbocharger mounting nuts and remove the turbocharger.
To install:
7. Inspect the mounting surface for cracks and damage.
8. Install a new gasket and apply anti-sieze compound to the mounting studs.
9. Install the turbocharger and torque the mounting nuts to 24 ft. lbs. (32 Nm).
10. Install the air crossover hose.
11. Install a new gasket and install the oil drain tube. Torque the bolts to 18 ft. lbs. (24 Nm).
12. New turbochargers must be prelubricated with fresh engine oil before operation. To do so, poor about 2 or 3 oz. of oil into the supply fitting and rotate the turbine wheel to circulate the oil.
13. Install the oil supply line to the turbocharger.
14. Connect the intake and exhaust piping.
15. Connect the negative battery cable and check for exhaust leaks.

Timing Gear Cover

Removal and Installation

1. Disconnect the negative battery cable.
2. Remove the fan drive assembly and belt.
3. Remove the belt tensioner.
4. Remove the oil fill tube and adaptor.
5. Remove the crankshaft pulley.
6. Remove all bolts that attach the cover to the gear housing.
7. Gently pry the gear cover away from the housing and remove from the engine.
To install:
8. Clean the gasket sealing surfaces.
9. Lubricate the gear train with oil.
10. Thoroughly clean and dry the seal area of the crankshaft.
11. Install the front cover and a new gasket. Install the bolts finger tight.
12. Using the alignment/installation tool, align the cover to the crankshaft.
13. Torque the cover bolts to 18 ft. lbs. (24 Nm). Remove the tool.
14. Install the oil fill tube and adaptor.
15. Install the crankshaft pulley, but do not torque the bolts at this point.
16. Install the fan, belt tensioner and belt.
17. Torque the crankshaft pulley bolts to 92 ft. lbs. (125 Nm).
18. Connect the negative battery cable and check for leaks.

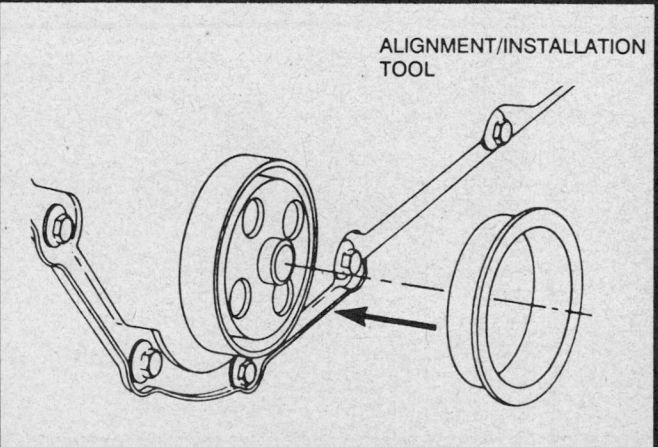

ALIGNMENT/INSTALLATION TOOL

Aligning the cover with the crankshaft

Front Cover Oil Seal

Replacement

1. Disconnect the negative battery cable.
2. Remove the drive belt.
3. Remove the crankshaft pulley.
4. Drill two ⅛ in. holes into the seal face, 180 degrees apart.
5. Using a slide hammer with a No. 10 sheet metal screw, pull the seal out alternating from side to side until the seal is out.
6. Thoroughly clean and dry the crankshaft.
7. Apply a bead of Loctite®277 to the outside diameter of the seal.
8. Install the pilot from the seal kit ont the crankshaft.
9. Install the seal onto the pilot and start it into the front cover seal bore. Remove the pilot.
10. Use the alignment/installation tool and a plastic hammer to fully install the seal.
11. Install the crankshaft pulley, but do not torque the bolts at this point.
12. Install the drive belt.
13. Torque the crankshaft pulley bolts to 92 ft. lbs. (125 Nm).
14. Connect the negative battery cable and check for leaks.

Camshaft

Removal and Installation

1. Disconnect the negative battery cable.
2. Remove the valve covers.
3. Remove the rocker pedastal and arm assemblies.
4. Remove the pushrods.
5. Remove the drive belt.
6. Drain the cooling system. Remove the fan assembly, radiator and all related parts.
7. Remove the crankshaft pulley.
8. Remove the front gear cover.
9. Remove the fuel pump.
10. Insert the special dowels into the pushrod holes and onto the top of each lifter. When properly installed, the dowels can be use to hold the tappets up securely. Wrap rubber bands around the top of the dowels to prevent them from dropping down.
11. Rotate the crankshaft to align the crankshaft to camshaft timing marks.
12. Remove the bolts from the thrust plate.
13. Remove the camshaft and thrust plate.
14. Press the gear from the camshaft and remove the key.

To install:

15. Install the key on the camshaft.
16. Heat the camshaft gear to 250°F (121°C) for 45 minutes.

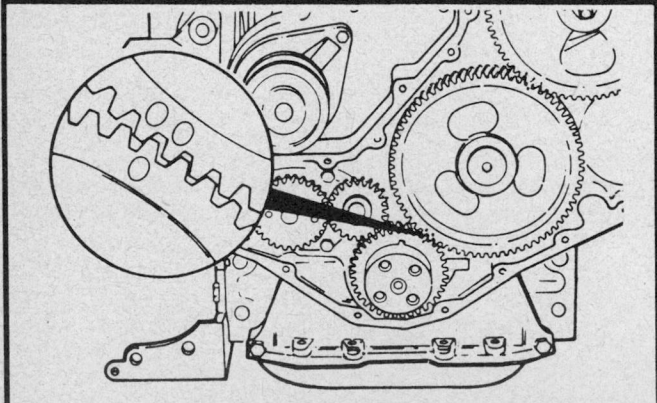

Crankshaft gear and camshaft gear timing marks— 5.9L diesel engine

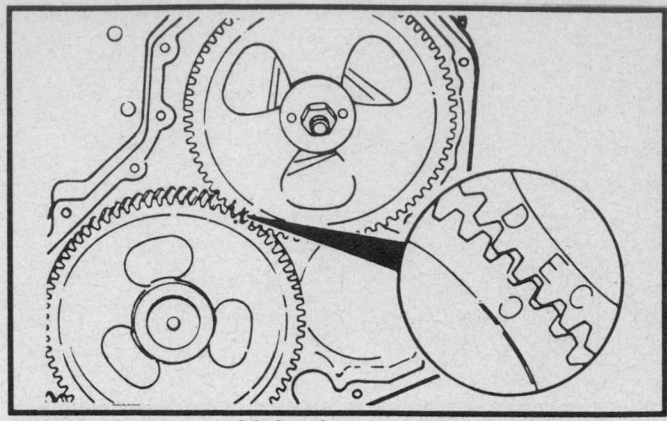

Camshaft gear and injection pump gear timing marks—5.9L diesel engine

Lubricate the gear mount surface with Lubriplate 105. Install the gear to the camshaft with the timing marks facing away from the shaft.

17. Lubricate the camshaft bores, lobes, journals and thrust washer with Lubriplate 105.

NOTE: Do not push the camshaft in too far or it may dislodge the plug in the rear of the camshaft bore, possibly creating a leak.

18. Install the camshaft and thrust washer so the **E** timing mark on the injection pump gear aligns with the **C** timing mark on the camshaft gear and the timing mark on the crankshaft gear align with those on the camshaft gear.
19. Install the thrust washer bolts and torque to 18 ft. lbs. (24 Nm).
20. Check the endplay of the camshaft. The specification is 0.006–0.010 in. (0.152–0.254mm).
21. Check the backlash of the camshaft gear. The specification is 0.003–0.013 in. (0.080–0.330mm).
22. Install the tappets and pushrods.
23. Install the rocker pedastal and arm assemblies.
24. Install the front cover and crankshaft pulley.
25. Install the drive belt and fan assembly.
26. Install the fuel pump.
27. Adjust the valves.
28. Install the valve covers.
29. Connect the negative battery cable and check for leaks.

Piston and Connecting Rod
Positioning

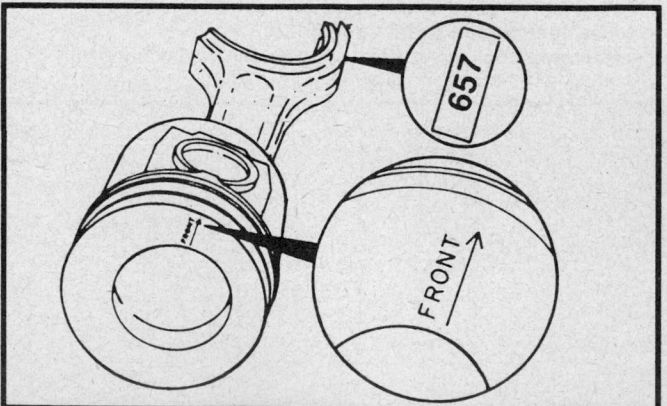

The "FRONT" marking and the number on the rod should be oriented as shown—5.9L diesel engine

ENGINE LUBRICATION

Oil pan

Removal and Installation

3.7L ENGINE

1. Disconnect the negative battery cable.
2. Remove the oil dipstick.
3. Raise the vehicle and support safely. Drain the engine oil.
4. Remove the engine to transmission strut.
5. Remove the torque converter inspection cover, if equipped.
6. Remove the oil pan bolts and remove the pan from the vehicle.

To install:

7. Using a new pan gasket set, apply a thin bead of sealer to the 4 corners where the rubber seals and cork gasket meet.
8. Thoroughly clean and dry all bolts and bolt holes. Install the pan and tighten the bolts to 75 inch lbs. (4 Nm), then re-tighten to 200 inch lbs. (23 Nm).
9. Install the torque converter inspection cover, if equipped.
10. Install the engine to transmission strut. Lower the vehicle.
11. Install the dipstick.
12. Fill the engine with the proper amount of oil.
13. Connect the negative battery cable and check for leaks.

EXCEPT 3.7L ENGINE

1. Disconnect the negative battery cable.
2. Remove the engine oil dipstick.
3. On Vans, remove the engine cover. Remove the air intake duct.
4. Raise the vehicle and support safely. Drain the engine oil.
5. Remove the transmission support braces.
6. Remove the starter and torque converter inspection cover, if equipped.
7. Remove the oxygen sensor and air injection tube, if equipped.
8. Lower the exhaust crossover pipe.
9. Remove the engine mount nuts.
10. Using the proper quipment, support the transmission. Remove the transmission mount bolts.
11. Support the engine with a jackstand. Raise the engine and transmission as required to allow for pan removal.
12. Remove the oil pan bolts and remove the pan from the vehicle.

To install:

13. Using a new pan gasket set, apply a thin bead of sealer to the 4 corners where the rubber seals and cork gasket meet.
14. Thoroughly clean and dry all bolts and bolt holes. Install the pan and tighten the bolts to 75 inch lbs. (4 Nm), then re-tighten to 200 inch lbs. (23 Nm).
15. Lower the engine and transmission and install the engine mount nuts and transmission mount bolts.
16. Install the exhaust crossover pipe. Install the oxygen sensor and air injection tube, if equipped.
17. Install the torque converter inspection cover, if equipped. Install the starter and support braces. Lower the vehicle.
18. Install the dipstick, air intake duct and engine cover, if it was removed.
19. Fill the engine with the proper amount of oil.
20. Connect the negative battery cable and check for leaks.

Oil Pump

Removal and Installation

3.7L ENGINE

1. Disconnect the negative battery cable.
2. Raise the vehicle and support safely.
3. Remove the oil filter.

4. The outer rotor will drop out when the pump cover is removed. Remove the oil pump cover and outer rotor.
5. Remove the oil pump.

To install:

6. Prime the pump by pouring fresh oil into the pump intake and turning the driveshaft until oil comes out the pressure port. Repeat a few times until no air bubbles are present. Using a new gasket, install the oil pump to the engine without the rotor and cover. Torque the bolts to 200 inch lbs. (23 Nm).
7. Install the outer rotor, seal and cover. Torque the cover bolts to 130 inch lbs. (15 Nm).
8. Install a new oil filter.
9. Connect the negative battery cable and check the oil pressure.

3.9L, 5.2L AND 5.9L GASOLINE ENGINES

1. Disconnect the negative battery cable.
2. Remove the oil pan.
3. Remove the screen.
4. Unbolt the oil pump from the rear main bearing cap and remove it from the vehicle.

To install:

5. Prime the pump by pouring fresh oil into the pump intake and turning the driveshaft until oil comes out the pressure port. Repeat a few times until no air bubbles are present. Install the oil pump with a rotating motion to ensure proper pump driveshaft engagement.
6. Hold the pump flush against the main cap and finger tighten the attaching bolts.
7. Torque the bolts to 30 ft. lbs. (41 Nm).
8. Install the screen.
9. Install the oil pan with a new gasket.
10. Connect the negative battery cable and check the oil pressure.

5.9L DIESEL ENGINE

1. Disconnect the negative battery cable.
2. Remove the drive belt.
3. Remove the radiator.
4. Remove the fan assembly.
5. Remove the oil fill tube and adaptor.
6. Remove the crankshaft pulley.
7. Remove the front cover.
8. Remove the 4 pump mounting bolts and remove the pump from the block.

To install:

9. Prime the pump by pouring fresh oil into the pump intake and turning the driveshaft until oil comes out the pressure port. Repeat a few times until no air bubbles are present. Align the idler gear pin with the locating bore in the block and install the pump.
10. Tighten the mounting bolts in the proper sequence to 44 inch lbs. (5 Nm), then repeat the sequence torquing to 18 ft. lbs. (24 Nm).

NOTE: When the pump is correctly installed, the flange on the pump should not touch the block; the back plate on the pump seats against the bottom of the bore.

11. Measure the backlash of the idler to pump drive gears. The specification is 0.003–0.013 in. (0.08–0.33mm).
12. Measure the backlash of the idler to crankshaft gears. The specification is 0.003–0.013 in. (0.08–0.33mm).
13. Install the front cover and crankshaft pulley.
14. Install the oil fill tube and adaptor.
15. Install the fan assembly, radiator and drive belt.
16. Connect the negative battery cable and check the oil pressure.

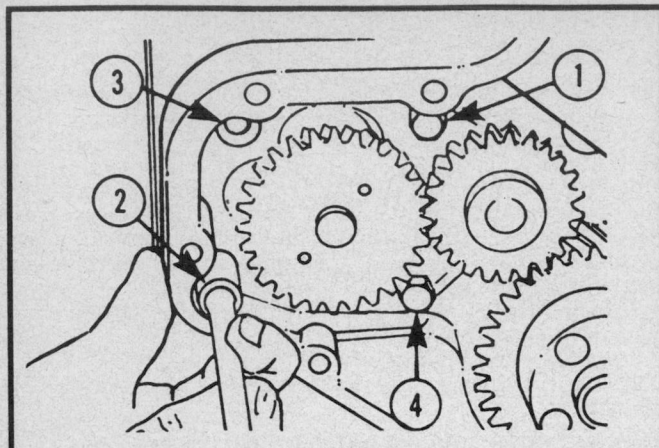

Oil pump attaching bolts tightening sequence—5.9L diesel engine

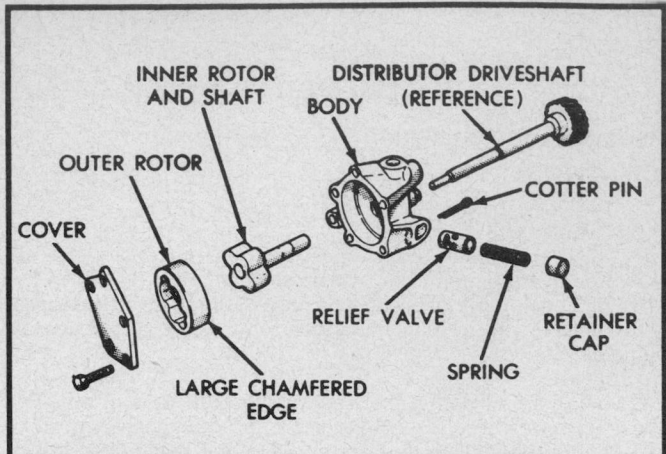

Exploded view of the oil pump—5.2L and 5.9L gasoline engines

Checking

3.7L ENGINE

1. Press off the drive gear. Disassemble the remainder of the pump.

2. Replace the pump assembly if the cover is scratched or grooved or if the cover is warped more than 0.0015 in. (0.038mm).

3. The minimum thickness of the outer rotor is 0.825 in. (20.96mm). The minimum diameter of the outer rotor is 2.469 in. (62.70mm). The minimum thickness of the inner rotor is 0.825 in. (20.96mm). If any of the above measurements are not within specifications, replace the shaft and both rotors.

4. The maximum clearance between the outer rotor and the pump body is 0.014 in. (0.356mm). Replace the pump assembly if not within specifications.

5. Install the inner rotor and place a straightedge across the bolt holes. If a feeler gauge of 0.004 in. (0.101mm) or more fits, replace the pump assembly.

6. The maximum clearance between the rotors is 0.010 in. (0.254mm). Replace the shaft and both rotors if not within specifications.

7. Inspect the relief valve plunger for scoring. Small marks may be removed with 400-grit wet of dry sandpaper.

8. The relief valve spring should have a freelength of 2¼ in. Replace the spring if it fails to meet the specification.

9. Assemble the pump using new parts where necessary.

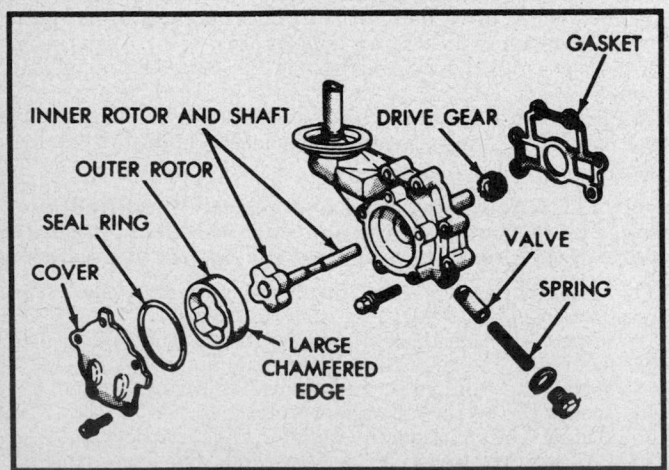

Exploded view of the oil pump—3.7L engine

3.9L, 5.2L AND 5.9L GASOLINE ENGINES

1. Disassemble the pump.

2. Replace the pump assembly if the cover is scratched or grooved or if the cover is warped more than 0.0015 in. (0.038mm).

3. The minimum thickness of the outer rotor is 0.825 in. (20.96mm) for 3.9L and 5.2L engine and 1987–90 5.9L engine. The specification is 0.943 in. (23.90mm) for 1986 5.9L engines. The minimum diameter of the outer rotor is 2.469 in. (62.70mm). The minimum thickness of the inner rotor is 0.825 in. (20.96mm) for 3.9L and 5.2L engine and 1987–90 5.9L engine. The specification is 0.943 in. (23.90mm) for 1986 5.9L engines. If any of the above measurements are not within specifications, replace the shaft and both rotors.

4. The maximum clearance between the outer rotor and the pump body is 0.014 in. (0.356mm). Replace the pump assembly if not within specifications.

5. Install the inner rotor and place a straightedge across the bolt holes. If a feeler gauge of 0.004 in. (0.101mm) or more fits, replace the pump assembly.

6. The maximum clearance between the rotors is 0.010 in. (0.254mm). Replace the shaft and both rotors if not within specifications.

7. Inspect the relief valve plunger for scoring. Small marks may be removed with 400-grit wet of dry sandpaper.

8. The relief valve spring should have a freelength of about 2 in. Replace the spring if it fails to meet specifications.

9. Assemble the pump using new parts where necessary.

5.9L DIESEL ENGINE

1. Inspect the drive and idle gears for damage of any type. The maximum backlash between the gears is 0.015 in. (0.38mm).

2. Remove the back plate.

3. The maximum tip clearance of the rotors is 0.007 in. (0.178mm).

4. Place a straightedge across the rotors. The maximum clearance is 0.005 in. (0.127mm).

5. The maximum rotor to body clearance is 0.015 in. (0.381mm).

6. Remove the rotor and inspect all parts for visible damage.

7. Assemble the pump using new parts where necessary.

Rear Main Bearing Oil Seal

The 3.9L and 5.2L engine rear main seal is a 2 piece, fitted rope type seal. The 3.7L and 5.9L engine rear main seal is a split rub-

ber type. In all cases, the upper half can be installed with the crankshaft in place. The 2 halves should always be replaced as a set.

Removal and Installation

3.7L ENGINE

1. Disconnect the negative battery cable.
2. Raise the vehicle and support safely. Drain the engine oil. Remove the oil pan.
3. Remove the rear seal retainer and the rear main bearing cap.
4. Remove the lower seal from the retainer.
5. To remove the upper seal, press on one end of the seal with a small blunt tool, rotate the crankshaft slightly and pull out the other end of the seal.

To install:

6. Wipe the crankshaft surface clean and coat it lightly with oil.
7. When installing the upper seal, hold the seal (with the paint stripe to the rear) tightly against the crankshaft and position the shim protector supplied with the seal package between the seal lip and the sharp edge of the groove in the block.
8. Rotate the crankshaft while sliding the seal into the groove. If any rubber has peeled off of the back of the new seal, do not use it; it will leak.
9. When installing the lower seal, apply a ⅛ in. bead of sealer in the bottom of the groove extending up to within ½ in. from the top of the groove.
10. Install the seal in the retainer with the paint stripe facing the rear.
11. Install the side seals on the retainer using super bonder, or equivalent.
12. Apply a very small amount of sealer to the areas around the bolt holes on the top of the retainer. Do not allow any sealer to get onto the top surface of the seal lip.

13. Install the retainer and torque the bolts to 30 ft. lbs. (41 Nm).
14. Install the main cap and torque the bolts to 85 ft. lbs. (115 Nm).
15. Install the pan and fill the engine with the proper amount of oil.
16. Connect the negative battery cable and check for leaks.

3.9L AND 5.2L ENGINE

1. Raise the vehicle and support safely. Drain the engine oil. Remove the oil pan and oil pump.
2. Remove the rear main bearing cap.
3. Remove the lower seal from the cap.
4. To remove the upper rope seal, use oil seal remover and installer kit KD–492, or equivalent, following the instructions provided with the tool.

To install:

5. Wipe the crankshaft surface clean and coat it lightly with oil.
6. Use oil seal remover and installer kit KD–492, or equivalent to install the upper rope seal. Trim the ends of the upper seal to eliminate frayed ends.
7. Install the lower rope seal in the main cap so that both ends protrude. Use tool C–3511 to seat the seal in its groove. Cut of the portions of the seal that extend above the cap on both sides and install the end seals to the cap.
8. Install the main cap to the block and torque the bolts to 85 ft. lbs. (115 Nm).
9. Install the pan and fill the engine with the proper amount of oil.
10. Connect the negative battery cable and check for leaks.

5.9L GASOLINE ENGINE

1. Raise the vehicle and support safely. Drain the engine oil. Remove the oil pan and oil pump.
2. Remove the rear main bearing cap.
3. Remove the lower seal from the cap.
4. To remove the upper seal, press on one end of the seal with a small blunt tool, rotate the crankshaft slightly and pull out the other end of the seal.

To install:

5. Wipe the crankshaft surface clean and coat it lightly with oil.
6. When installing the upper seal, hold the seal (with the paint stripe to the rear) tightly against the crankshaft and rotate the crankshaft while sliding the seal into the groove. If any rubber has peeled off of the back of the new seal, do not use it; it will leak.
7. When installing the lower rubber seal, make sure the paint stripe is positioned to the rear and place a drop of sealer next to both ends of the seal.

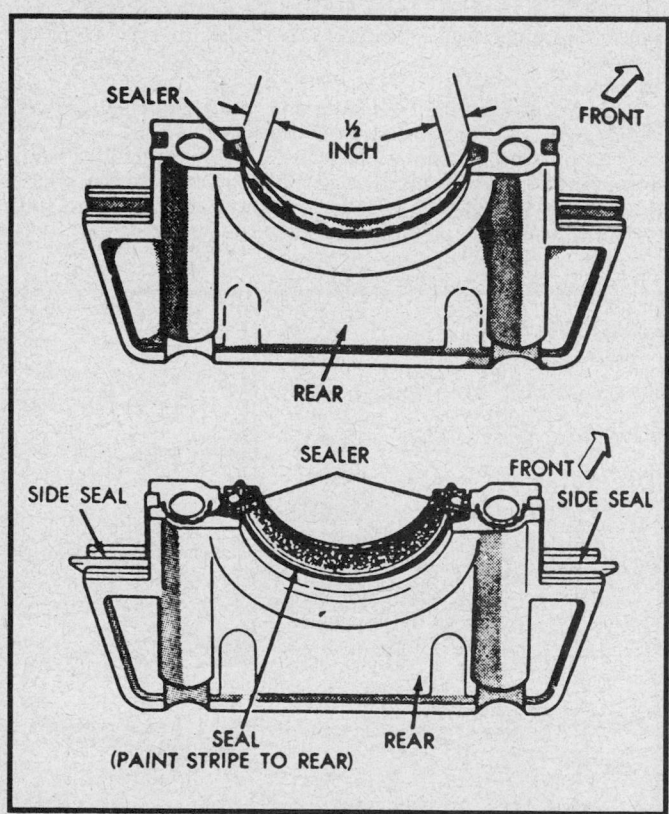

Apply sealer to these locations—3.7L engine

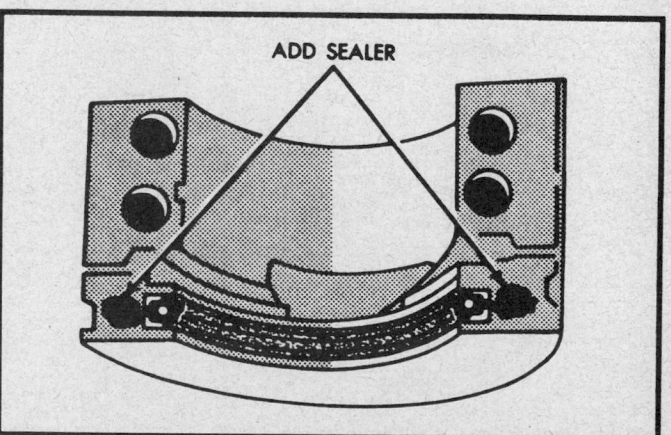

Lower rear main seal—5.9L gasoline engine

8. Install the main cap to the block and torque the bolts to 85 ft. lbs. (115 Nm).

9. Install the oil pump and pan and fill the engine with the proper amount of oil.

10. Connect the negative battery cable and check for leaks.

5.9L DIESEL ENGINE

The rear crankshaft seal is mounted in a housing that is bolted to the rear of the block. A double lipped teflon seal is used.

1. Disconnect the negative battery cable.
2. Remove the transmssion.
3. Remove the clutch cover and plate, if equipped.
4. Remove the flywheel.
5. Drill two ⅛ in. holes 180 degrees apart into the seals. Be extremely careful not to drill against the crankshaft.

6. Using a No. 10 sheet metal screw and a slide hammer, remove the rear seal.

To install:

7. Thoroughly clean and dry the crankshaft surface. Do not oil the crankshaft or seal prior to installation or the seal will leak.

8. Install the seal pilot included in the replacement seal kit, on the crankshaft. Push the seal on the pilot and crankshaft. Remove the pilot.

9. If the new seal has a rubber outer diameter, lubricate it with soapy water. If the seal does not have a rubber outer diameter, use Loctite®277, or equivalent on the outer diameter.

10. Use the alignment tool to install the seal to the proper depth in the housing. Drive the seal in gradually and evenly until the alignment tool stops against the housing.

MANUAL TRANSMISSION

For further information, please refer to "Professional Transmission Manual".

Transmission Assembly

Removal and Installation

1. Disconnect the negative battery cable.
2. Remove the shift lever. If the vehicle is equipped with the NP–435 4 speed, push the retainer (not the gearshift lever itself) down and rotate it counterclockwise slightly to release. If the vehicle is equipped with the NP–2500 5 speed, unbolt the shifter base assembly from the transmission. If the vehicle is equipped with the A–833 4 speed, label and disconnect the linkages to the shifter assembly and unbolt the shifter from its support.
3. Raise the vehicle and support safely. Remove the skid plates, if equipped. Drain the transmission and transfer case, if equipped.
4. Disconnect the distance sensor, if equipped and disconnect the speedometer cable from the transmission or transfer case.
5. Matchmark and remove the driveshaft(s). Disconnect the PTO, if equipped.

6. If equipped with 4WD, disconnect all linkage, electrical connectors and vacuum lines from the transfer case. Using a suitable jack, support the transfer case, unbolt the transfer case from the transmission and slide it backwards to remove it from the vehicle.

7. Disconnect the reverse light switch connector and remove all wiring from any clips on the transmission case.

8. Install an appropriate engine support fixture to hold the engine in place when the transmission is out of the vehicle.

9. Support the transmission with a suitable transmission jack.

10. Remove the transmission crossmember.

11. Remove the transmission to bell housing bolts.

12. Slide the transmission backwards until the input shaft clears the clutch disc. Remove the transmission from the vehicle.

To install:

13. Lubricate the pilot bushing and input shaft splines very lightly with high temperature lubricant.

14. Mount the transmission securely on a suitable transmission jack and lift it in place until the input shaft is centered in the bell housing opening. Roll the transmission forward until the input shaft splines fully engage with the clutch disc.

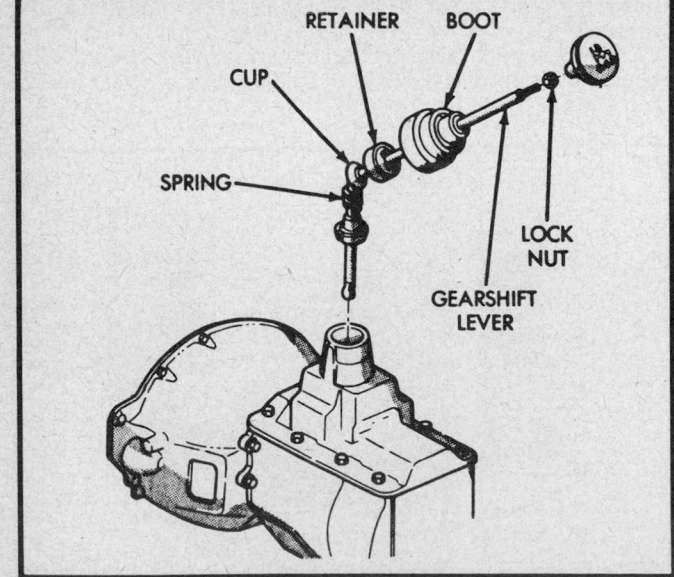

New Process 435 shifter components

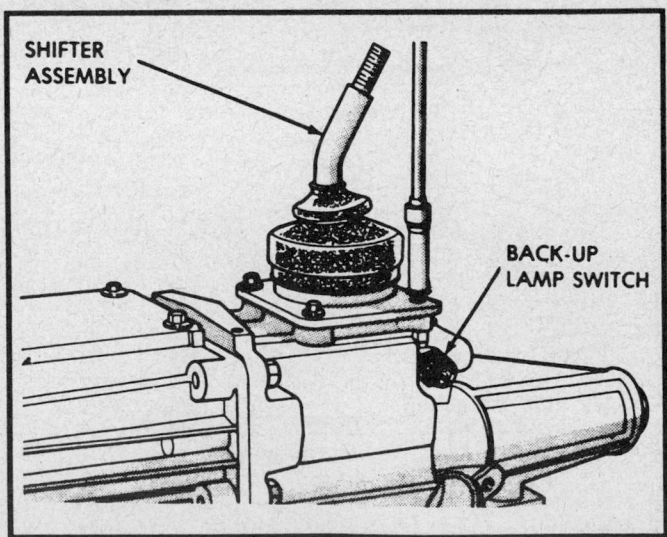

New Process 2500 transmission

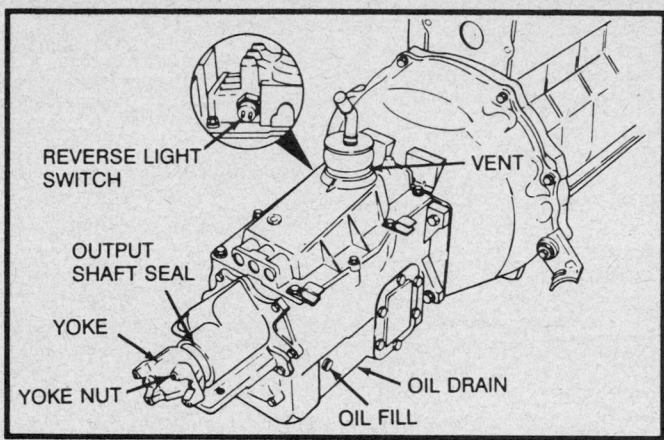
Getrag G-360 transmission coupled with the 5.9L diesel engine

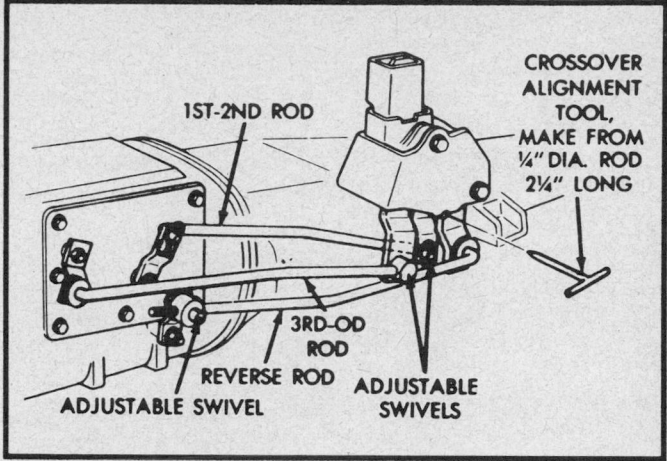
A-833 shifter and linkage

15. Install the transmission to bell housing bolts. Torque the bolts to 50 ft. lbs. (68 Nm).
16. Install the transmission crossmember. Remove the transmission and engine support fixtures.
17. Install the transfer case and connect all linkage, electrical connectors and vacuum lines to the transfer case.
18. Connect the reverse light switch connector and clip all wiring to the transmission case.
19. Connect speedometer cable and distance sensor, if equipped.
20. Install the driveshaft(s) and connect the PTO, if equipped.
21. Fill the transmission and transfer case, if equipped, with the proper lubricant.
22. Install the shifter assembly and linkages, if equipped.
23. Install the skid plates, if equipped.
24. Connect the negative battery cable and check the transmission for proper operation.

Linkage Adjustment

A-833 4 SPEED

1. Place the shifter in the neutral position.
2. Raise the vehicle and support safely.
3. Install the fabricated aligning tool to hold the levers in the neutral crossover position.
4. Disconnect the control rods from the levers in the shifter assembly. Make sure the levers are still in the neutral position.
5. Rotate the threaded ends of the shift control rods to adjust the rod length. Starting with the 1/2 rod, adjust it so the fabricated tool does not bind. Repeat with the 3/4 and the reverse rods.
6. Install the rods to their levers with the washers and clips.
7. Remove the alignment tool and check the shifting action for smoothness.

CLUTCH

Clutch Assembly

Removal and Installation

1. Disconnect the negative battery cable.
2. Raise the vehicle and support safely.
3. Remove the transmission and transfer case, if equipped.
4. Remove the inspection cover at the bottom of the bell housing.
5. Rotating the engine with a flywheel turner, remove the clutch cover bolts gradually as they appear.
6. Remove the clutch cover and disc by lowering it through the opening at the bottom of the housing.
To install:
7. Raise the clutch cover and disc into place and use a suitable clutch aligning tool or spare input shaft to center the disc. Tighten all of the bolts finger tight.
8. The cover bolts must be turned gradually, evenly and to the proper torque to avoid distorting the cover. Torque $^5/_{16}$ in. diameter bolts in the aforementioned manner to 17 ft. lbs (23 Nm). Torque $^3/_8$ in. diameter bolts similarly to 30 ft. lbs. (41 Nm).
9. Install the transmission and transfer case, if equipped.
10. Install the inspection cover.

11. Connect the negative battery cable and check the clutch for proper operation.

Pedal Free-play Adjustment

NOTE: Chrysler has used a hydraulic clutch release system on their full size trucks since 1988. There is no adjustment for free-play on vehicles with this system.

1. Inspect the clutch pedal rubber stop and replace if it is damaged.
2. Raise the vehicle and support safely.
3. Adjust the fork by turning the self-locking nut on the actuating rod to provide about $^3/_{32}$ in. of movement at the end of the fork. This will provide about 1 in. of free-play at the clutch pedal.

Clutch Master Cylinder and Slave Cylinder

The clutch master cylinder, remote reservoir, slave cylinder and connecting lines are all serviced as a complete assembly. The cylinders and connecting lines are sealed units. They are prefilled

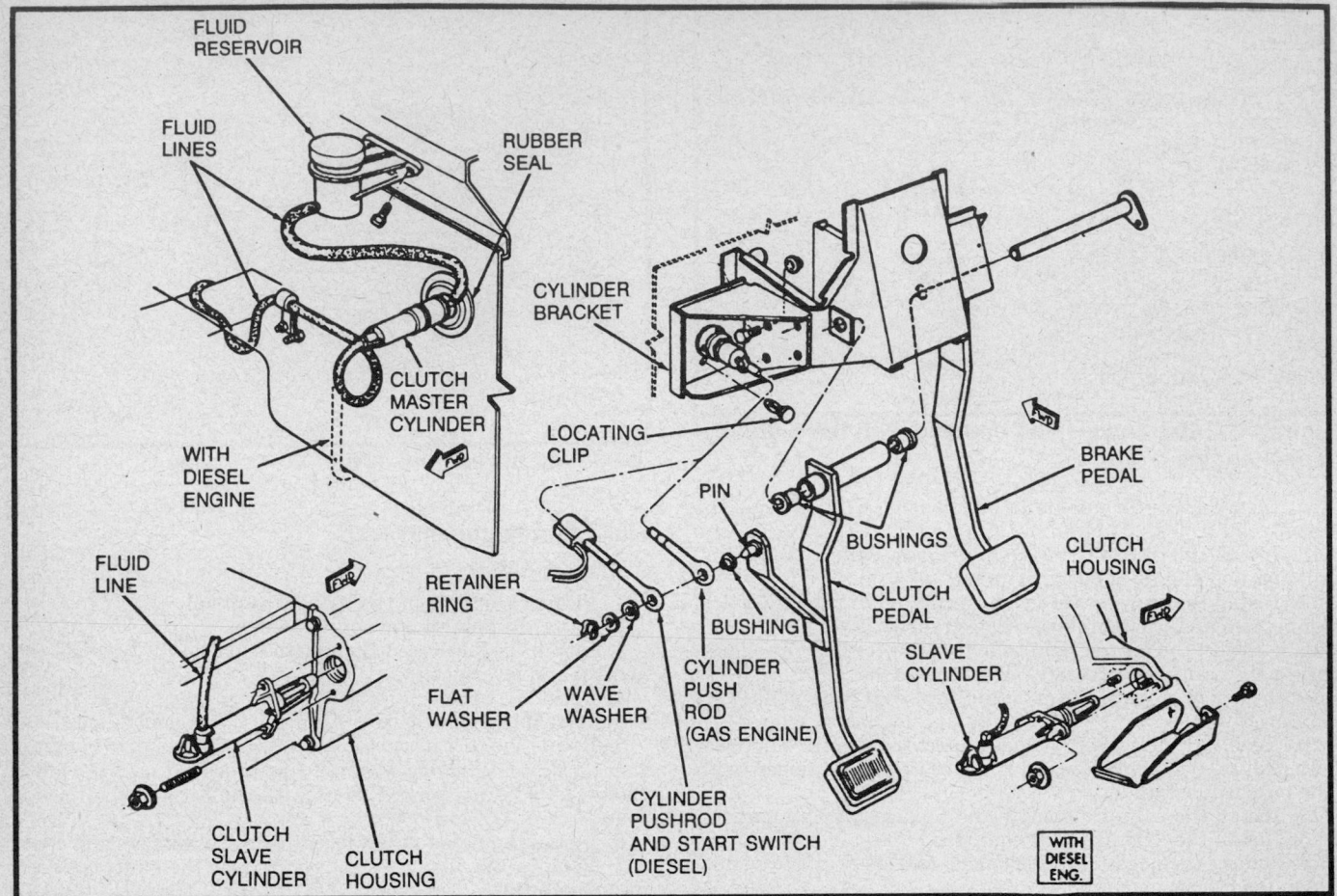

Hydraulic clutch release components—Pick-Up and Ramcharger

with fluid from the factory and cannot be disassembled or serviced separately.

Removal and Installation

1. Disconnect the negative battery cable.
2. Raise the vehicle and support safely.
3. Remove the nuts attaching the slave cylinder to the bell housing.
4. Remove the slave cylinder and clip from the housing.
5. Lower the vehicle.
6. Remove the locating clip from the clutch master cylinder mounting bracket.
7. Remove the retaining ring, flat washer and wave washer that attach the clutch master cylinder pushrod to the clutch pedal. Slide the pushrod off of the pedal pin. Inspect the bushing on the pedal pin and replace if it is excessively worn.
8. Verify that the cap on the clutch master cylinder reservoir is tight so that fluid will not spill during removal.
9. Remove the screws attaching the reservoir and bracket, if equipped, to the dash panel and remove the reservoir.
10. Pull the clutch master cylinder rubber seal from the dash panel.
11. Rotate the clutch master cylinder 45 degrees to unlock it. Remove the cylinder from the dash panel.
12. Remove the clutch master cylinder, remote reservoir, slave cylinder and connecting lines from the vehicle.

To install:

13. Verify that the cap on the fluid reservoir is tight so that fluid will not spill during installation.
14. Position the components in the replacement kit in their places on the vehicle.
15. Insert the master cylinder in the dash. Rotate it 45 degrees to lock it in place.
16. Lubricate the rubber seal with a suitable lubricant to ease installation. Seat the seal around the cylinder in the dash.
17. Install the fluid reservoir and bracket, if equipped, to the dash panel.
18. Install the master cylinder pushrod to the clutch pedal pin. Secure the rod with the wave washer, flat washer and retaining ring. Install the locating clip. Do not remove the plastic shipping stop from the pushrod until the slave cylinder has been installed.
19. Raise the vehicle and support safely.
20. Insert the slave cylinder pushrod through the opening and make sure the cap on the end of the pushrod is securely engaged in the release lever before tightening the attaching nuts. Torque the nuts to 200 inch lbs. (23 Nm).
21. Lower the vehicle. Remove the plastic shipping stop from the master cylinder pushrod.
22. Operate the clutch pedal a few times to verify proper operation of the system.
23. Connect the negative battery cable and road test the vehicle.

AUTOMATIC TRANSMISSION

For further information, please refer to "Professional Transmission Manual".

Transmission Assembly

Removal and Installation

1. Disconnect the negative battery cable.
2. Raise the vehicle and support safely. Drain the transmission and transfer case, if equipped.
3. Disconnect and lower or remove any exhaust parts as required.
4. Remove the skid plates, if equipped.
5. Matchmark and remove the driveshaft(s).
6. Disconnect the distance sensor, if equipped and the speedometer cable.
7. If equipped with 4WD, disconnect all linkage, electrical connectors and vacuum lines from the transfer case. Using a suitable jack, support the transfer case, unbolt the transfer case from the transmission and slide it backwards to remove it from the vehicle.
8. Remove the engine to transmission struts.
9. Remove the starter and the fluid cooler lines bracket.
10. Remove the torque converter inspection cover.
11. Matchmark the converter to the flex plate. Remove the torque converter bolts.
12. Disconnect the wires to the neutral safety switch, and lock-up solenoid, if equipped.
13. Disconnect the oil cooler lines from the transmission.
14. Disconnect the gearshift rod and torque shaft assembly from the transmission.
15. Disconnect the throttle rod from the lever.
16. Unbolt the oil filler tube brace and lift the oil filler tube out of its bore.
17. Install an appropriate engine support fixture to hold the engine in place when the transmission is out of the vehicle.
18. Raise the transmission slightly using a suitable transmission jack.
19. Remove the transmission crossmember.
20. Remove the oil filter, if necessary. Remove all bell housing bolts and remove the transmission from the vehicle.
To install:
21. Install the transmission securely on the transmission jack. Rotate the converter so it will align with the positioning of the flex plate.
22. Apply a coating of high temperature grease to the torque converter pilot hub.
23. Raise the transmission into place and push it forward until the dowels engage and the bell housing is flush with the block.
24. Install the oil filler tube. Install the bell housing bolts and torque to 30 ft. lbs. (41 Nm). Install the oil filter, if it was removed.
25. Install the transmission crossmember. Remove the engine support fixture and the transmission jack.
26. Install the torque converter bolts and torque to 23 ft. lbs. (31 Nm).
27. Connect the oil cooler lines.
28. Connect the throttle rod to the lever and adjust if necessary.
29. Connect the gearshift rod and torque shaft assembly to the transmission and adjust if necessary.
30. Connect the wires to the neutral safety switch, and lockup solenoid, if equipped. Make sure all wires are routed correctly and clipped in place.
31. Install the torque converter inspection cover, starter and transmission struts.
32. Install the transfer case, if equipped.

33. Connect the distance sensor, if equipped.
34. Connect the the speedometer cable.
35. Install the driveshaft(s).
36. Install exhaust parts that were removed in order to remove the transmission.
37. Fill the transfer case, if equipped. Lower the vehicle.
38. Connect the negative battery cable.
39. Fill the transmission with the proper amount of Dexron®II.
40. Road test the vehicle, check for leaks and recheck the fluid level.

Shift Linkage Adjustment

NOTE: Do not attempt to adjust the linkage if any of the parts are excessively worn. If any rods are removed from the plastic grommets, new grommets should be installed. Pry only where the grommet and rod attach, not on the rod itself. Use pliers to snap the rod into the new grommet.

1. Shift the transmission into **P**.
2. Raise the vehicle and support safely.
3. Loosen the shift rod adjusting swivel lock screw. Make sure the swivel turns freely on the rod.
4. Make sure the valve body is in the **PARK** position by moving it all the way rearward.
5. Adjust the swivel position on the shift rod to obtain a free pin fit in the toque shaft lever. Tighten the lock screw.
6. If the vehicle starts in any gear other than **P** or **N**, or does not start in both **P** and **N**, then either the adjustment is wrong or another problem exists.

Throttle Linkage Adjustment
EXCEPT 5.9L DIESEL ENGINE

1. If the vehicle is carbureted, perform the adjustment with the engine at normal operating temperature and off of the fast idle cam.
2. If the vehicle is fuel injected, retract the ISC actuator by doing one of the following:
   a. If the DRBII is available, connect its connector to the diagnostic connector. Start the engine and place the DRBII in the "Throttle Body Minimum Air Flow Test" mode. Disconnect the electrical connector on the ISC actuator. Shut off the engine and disconnect the DRBII; the actuator is now fully retracted.

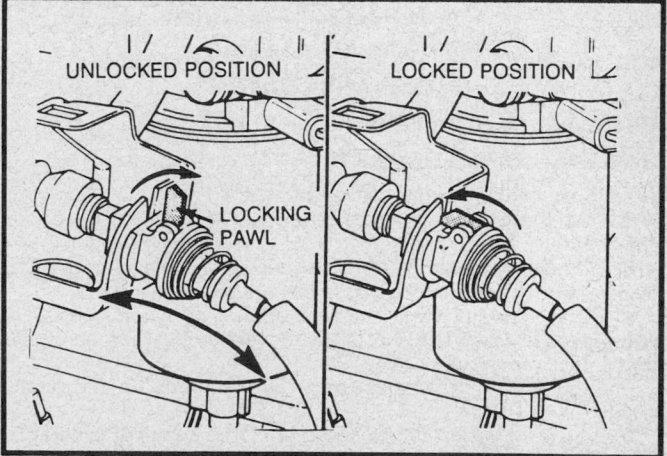

Unlocking and locking the throttle cable pawl

b. If the DRBII is not available, 2 jumper wires may be used. With the engine off, disconnect the connector to the ISC actuator. Connect a pair of jumper wires to the battery. Connect the negative jumper to the top pin of the ISC actuator and the positive jumper to the other pin. Do not leave the jumpers connected for more than 5 seconds. Disconnect the jumpers and the ISC actuator is fully retracted.

3. Raise the vehicle and support safely.

4. Loosen the adjustable swivel lock screw on the throttle rod enough so the rod travels freely in the swivel.

5. Hold the throttle lever firmly forward against its internal stop and tighten the lock screw. Lower the vehicle.

6. Reconnect the ISC actuator, if equipped.

7. If equipped with fuel injection, turn the ignition key to the RUN position for at least 5 seconds, but do not start the engine. Turn the key to the OFF position.

8. Start the engine and road test the vehicle.

Throttle Cable Adjustment
5.9L DIESEL ENGINE

1. Perform the adjustment with the engine at normal operating temperature.

2. While the throttle lever is seated against the low idle stop screw, the clearance between the actuation pin and the rear end of the slotted cable should be about $^7/_{32}$ in.

3. If it is not at specification, lift the locking pawl and slide the cable to the proper position to obtain the specified clearance.

4. Lock the pawl back into place and road test the vehicle.

TRANSFER CASE

Transfer Case Assembly
Removal and Installation

1. Disconnect the negative battery cable.

2. Raise the vehicle and support safely.

3. Remove the skid plates, if equipped. Drain the transfer case fluid.

4. Disconnect the distance sensor, if equipped and disconnect the speedometer cable from the transfer case.

5. Matchmark and remove the driveshafts.

6. Disconnect the PTO, if equipped.

7. Disconnect the linkage, electrical connectors and vacuum lines from the transfer case. Using a suitable jack, support the transfer case, unbolt the transfer case from the transmission and slide it backwards to remove it from the vehicle.

8. The installation is the reversal of the removal procedure.

Linkage Adjustment
NEW PROCESS 205

1. Shift the transfer case into neutral.

2. Move the shift rod boot upward for access.

3. Loosen the shift bracket bolts and move the bracket as far forward as possible. Tighten the bolts.

4. Check the smoothness of operation of the transfer case.

NEW PROCESS 208 AND 241

1. Move the transfer case shift lever boot aside for access to the shift lever and gate.

2. Move the shift lever into the 4H position. Make sure the lever is against the 4H gate.

3. Raise the vehicle and support safely.

4. Loosen the shift rod clamp screw until the shift rod is free to slide in the swivel.

5. Verify that the lever is in the 4H position and move it if it has moved out of position.

6. Tighten the clamp screw.

7. Check the smoothness of operation of the transfer case.

DRIVE AXLE

Rear Driveshaft
Removal and Installation
ONE-PIECE DRIVESHAFT

1. Raise the vehicle and support safely.

2. Matchmark the driveshaft and the rear axle drive pinion gear shaft yoke.

3. Remove the rear U-joint attaching bolts and both strap clamps from the rear axle drive pinion gear shaft yoke.

4. Fluid may run from the rear of the extension housing or transfer case when the shaft is removed, so position a suitable drain pan under the area.

5. Remove the driveshaft from the transmission or transfer case.

6. The installation is the reversal of the removal procedure. Torque ¼–28 clamp bolts to 14 ft. lbs. (19 Nm) and $^5/_{16}$–24 to 25 ft. lbs. (34 Nm).

TWO-PIECE DRIVESHAFT

1. Raise the vehicle and support safely.

2. Matchmark the driveshaft and the rear axle drive pinion gear shaft yoke.

3. Remove the rear U-joint attaching bolts and both strap clamps from the rear axle drive pinion gear shaft yoke.

4. Detach the protective boot clamp from the front shaft splines, if equipped and slide the rear shaft slip yoke from the front shaft at the center bearing. Remove the rear shaft from the vehicle.

5. Matchmark the yokes at the transmission or transfer case and remove the clamp retaining bolts and clamp straps.

6. Remove the center bearing retaining bolts and nuts and remove the front shaft with center bearing from the vehicle.

7. The installation is the reversal of the removal procedure. Torque ¼–28 clamp bolts to 14 ft. lbs. (19 Nm) and $^5/_{16}$–24 to 25 ft. lbs. (34 Nm).

8. Torque the center bearing bolts and nuts to 50 ft. lbs. (68 Nm).

Front Driveshaft

Removal and Installation

1. Raise the vehicle and support safely.
2. Remove the skid plate, if equipped.
3. Matchmark the driveshaft and the front axle drive pinion gear shaft yoke.
4. Remove the CV joint to transfer case flange capscrews and lockwashers.
5. Remove the front U-joint attaching bolts and both strap clamps.
6. Remove the front driveshaft from the vehicle.
7. The installation is the reversal of the removal procedure. Torque the CV joint to transfer case flange capscrews to 25 ft. lbs. (34 Nm).
8. Torque ¼–28 clamp bolts to 14 ft. lbs. (19 Nm) and ⁵⁄₁₆–24 to 25 ft. lbs. (34 Nm).

Rear Driveshaft Center Bearing

Removal and Installation

1. Remove the shafts and center bearing from the vehicle.

NOTE: Do not clamp the driveshaft tube in a vise. Clamp only the forged portion of the welded yoke in a vise. Do not overtighten the vise jaws.

2. Clamp the front shaft in a vise and remove the bearing support and rubber insulator from the center bearing.
3. Bend the slinger away from the center bearing to provide sufficient clearance for installing a puller.
4. Remove the bearing from the front shaft with a suitable puller and remove the slinger. The replacement package contains the bearing, slinger and retainer.
5. The installation is the reversal of the removal procedure.

Single Cardan Universal Joint

Removal and Installation

1. Remove the driveshaft and slip yoke, if equipped from the vehicle.

NOTE: Do not clamp the driveshaft tube in a vise. Clamp only the forged portion of the welded yoke or the slip yoke in a vise. Do not overtighten the vise jaws.

2. Clamp the yoke in a vise and remove the bearing cap retainers.
3. Place a socket which has an inside diameter larger than the outside diameter of the bearing cap, against the yoke around the perimeter of the first cap to be removed. Place a socket which is slightly smaller than the cap, on the cap opposite the cap to be removed. Then position the yoke in a vise.
4. Compress the jaws until the smaller socket has driven the other cap into the larger socket.
5. Release the jaws and remove the cap that is partially out of the yoke.
6. Repeat the procedure for the remaining cap(s).

To install:

7. Clean and remove any rust from the yoke bores and lubricate lightly with suitable lithium based grease.
8. Position the spider cylinders in the yoke bores. Insert the seals into the yoke bores and against the spider cylinders. Tap the bearing caps into the yoke bores far enough to keep the spider in place.
9. Place the socket that is slightly smaller than the cap against the first cap and position the assembly in a vise.
10. Compress the jaws to force the bearing caps into the yoke bores far enough so the retainer grooves are visible.
11. Repeat the procedure for the remaining caps, if necessary.
12. Install the retaining clips.
13. Install the driveshaft assembly to the vehicle.

Double Cardan Constant Velocity Joint

Removal and Installation

1. Remove the front driveshaft from the vehicle.
2. Matchmark the yokes before disassembling so they will be installed in their original locations to retain driveshaft balance.
3. To expedite removal, remove the bearing caps in the sequence indicated.
4. Support the driveshaft horizontally and aligned with the base plate of the press. Shear the bearing cap plastic retaining ring and position the first link yoke rear arm over a 1⅛ in. sock-

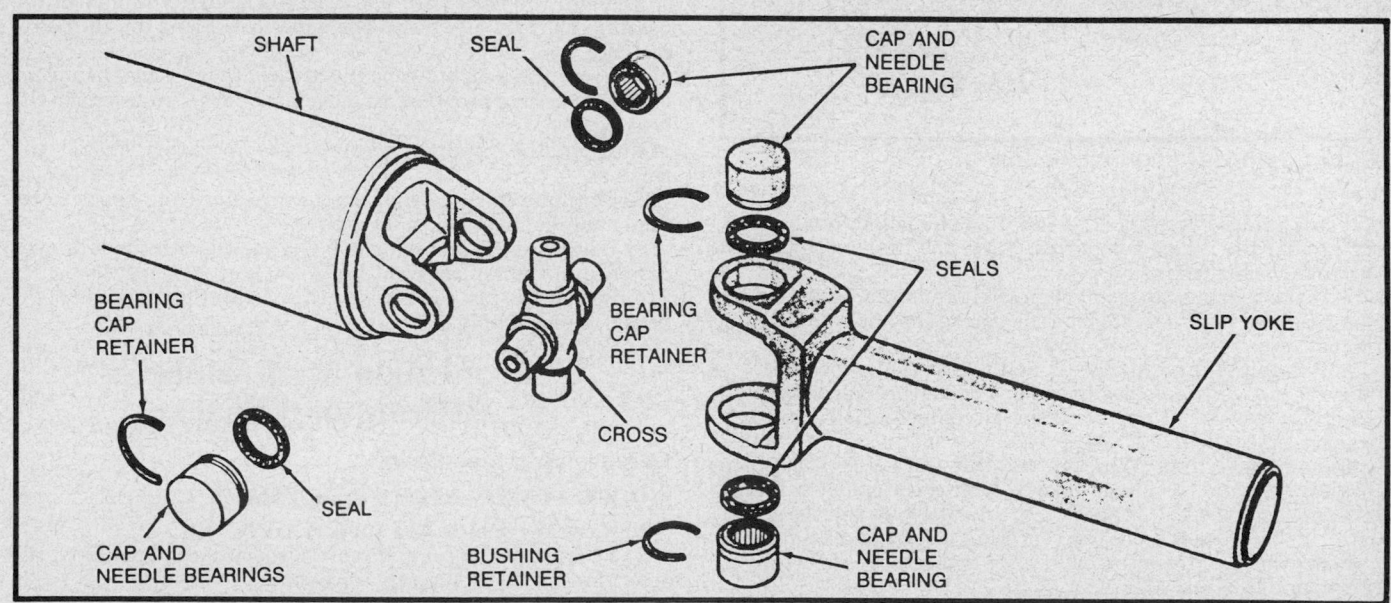

Single cardan universal joint components

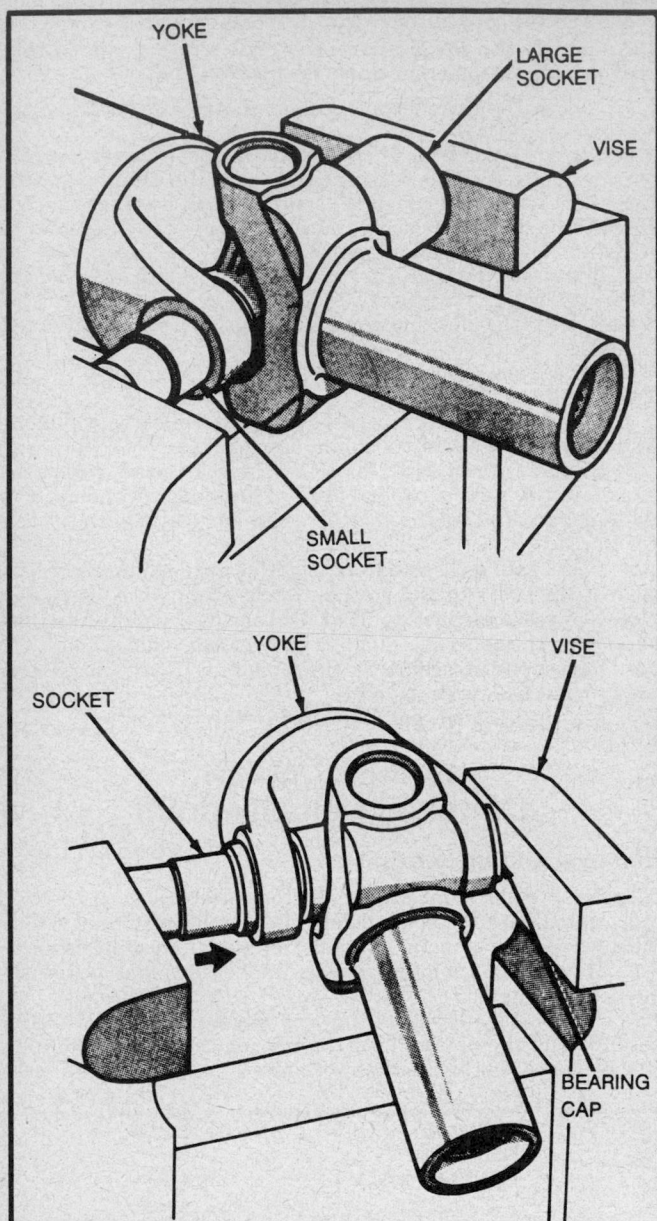

U-joint removal and installation

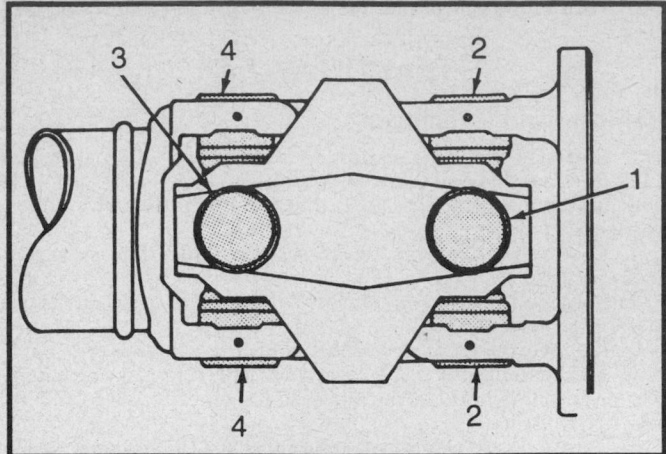

Bearing cap removal sequence

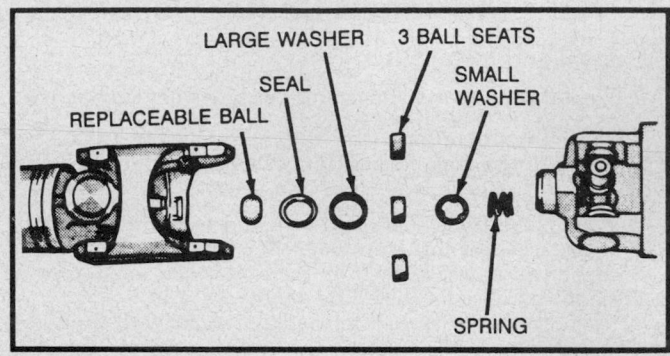

Double cardan joint components

et. Place Spider Press Tool C–4365–1, or equivalent on the bearing caps in the flange yoke arms. Force the bearing cap out of the yoke with a press.

5. If the bearing cap is not completely removed, insert a suitable spacer between the spider and bearing cap and complete the removal.

6. Rotate the driveshaft 180° and repeat the procedure.

7. Disengage the spider trunnions from the link yoke. Pull the flange yoke and the spider from the centering ball on the ball support tube yoke.

8. To remove the ball socket, separate the CV joint between the link yoke and the flange yoke by forcing the spider trunnion bushing from the link yoke. Pull the flange yoke and the spider with the ball socket from the centering ball as an assembly.

9. Pry the seal from the ball socket and remove the washers, spring and 3 ball seats.

10. Remove the centering ball from the ball socket using Tool set C–4365.

To install:

11. Install the centering ball in the socket using special tool C–4365–3. Force the ball into the socket until it is seated firmly against the shoulder at the base of the socket.

12. To install the spider, insert one bearing cap partially into one of the yoke bores and then rotate the yoke 180°. Insert the spider into the yoke bore and seat the spider trunnion in the bearing cap. Partially insert the opposite bearing cap in the remaining yoke bore.

13. Force the bearing caps inward while pivoting the spider back and forth to provide free movement of the trunnions in the bearing.

14. When the retainer grooves become visible, install the retainer.

15. Continue to force the caps inward until the opposite retainer can be installed in its groove.

16. Lubricate the centering ball and socket with the lubricant provided in the replacement kit.

17. Repeat the installation procedure with the remaining portion of the assembly.

Front Axle Shaft, Hub, Bearing and Seal

Removal and Installation

MODEL 44-8FD – RIGHT SIDE SHAFT

1. Raise the vehicle and support safely.

2. Remove the wheel and remove the brake caliper from the rotor. Do not allow the caliper to hang by the hose.

3. Remove the dust cap and driving hub snapring.

4. Remove the driving hub and retaining ring.

5. Remove the wheel bearing nut lock using tool C–4170–A, or equivalent. Remove the retaining washer and the wheel bearing adjusting nut.

6. Remove the rotor/hub with wheel bearings and retainer spring plate. Remove the grease seal and bearing from the rotor.

7. Remove the splash shield and spindle from the steering knuckle..

8. Remove the brake caliper adaptor from the knuckle.

9. Remove the axle shaft from the axle housing. Remove the seal and stone guard from the shaft.

To install:

10. Install the seal on the axle shaft stone shield with the lip facing toward the axle shaft splines.

11. Insert the axle assembly into the axle housing making sure not to damage the differential seal.

12. Install the brake caliper adaptor to the knuckle. Install the spindle and splash shield and torque the nuts to 30 ft. lbs. (41 Nm).

13. Lubricate and install the inner wheel bearing in the rotor and install a new seal.

14. Install the assembly to the spindle. Install the adjusting nut and tighten it with 50 ft. lbs. (68 Nm) of torque. Loosen the nut and tighten with 35 ft. lbs. (48 Nm) of torque. Loosen the adjusting nut about ¾ turn. Position the retaining washer on the adjusting nut by rotating the nut so that the alignment pin pressed into the nut will enter the nearest hole in the retaining washer. Install and tighten the nut lock with 50 ft. lbs. (68 Nm) of torque. The final bearing endplay should be 0.001–0.010 in.

15. Install the retaining spring, driving hub and retaining ring.

16. Apply sealant to the edge of the dust cap and install.

17. Install the brake components and wheel.

18. Road test the vehicle and check for leaks.

MODEL 44-8FD – LEFT SIDE SHAFT

1. Raise the vehicle and support safely.

2. Remove the wheel and remove the brake caliper from the rotor. Do not allow the caliper to hang by the hose.

3. Remove the dust cap and driving hub snapring.

4. Remove the driving hub and retaining ring.

5. Remove the wheel bearing nut lock using tool C–4170–A, or equivalent. Remove the retaining washer and the wheel bearing adjusting nut.

6. Remove the rotor/hub with wheel bearings and retainer spring plate. Remove the grease seal and bearing from the rotor.

7. Remove the splash shield and spindle from the steering knuckle..

8. Remove the brake caliper adaptor from the knuckle.

9. Disconnect the vacuum hoses and electrical connector from the disconnect housing assembly.

10. Remove the disconnect housing assembly cover and shield.

11. Remove the intermediate axle shaft from the axle tube.

12. Remove the shift collar from the disconnect housing.

13. Remove the inner axle shaft seal from the axle tube and remove from the housing. If the vehicle is equipped with a seal guard, discard it; the guard is not used with the replacement seal.

14. Remove the front differential cover.

15. Force the inner axle shaft toward the center of the vehicle and remove the C–lock from the recessed groove in the shaft.

16. Remove the inner axle shaft using tools D–354–4 and D–354–3, or equivalent.

To install:

17. Install the inner axle shaft using D–354–4 and D–354–2, or equivalent. Slide the axle shaft into the side gear and install the C–lock in the groove.

18. Install the replacement seal using the proper replacing tools.

19. Install the shift collar on the splined end of the inner axle shaft.

20. Install the intermediate axle shaft through the axle tube.

21. Install the disconnect housing assembly cover. Make sure the shift fork is properly guided into the shift collar groove. Install the shield.

22. Connect the vacuum hoses and electrical connector to the diaphram and switch on the disconnect housing assembly.

23. Install the brake caliper adaptor to the knuckle. Install the spindle and splash shield and torque the nts to 30 ft. lbs. (41 Nm).

24. Lubricate and install the inner wheel bearing in the rotor and install a new seal.

25. Install the assembly to the spindle. Install the adjusting nut and tighten it with 50 ft. lbs. (68 Nm) of torque. Loosen the nut and tighten with 35 ft. lbs. (48 Nm) of torque. Loosen the adjusting nut about ¾ turn. Position the retaining washer on the adjusting nut by rotating the nut so that the alignment pin pressed into the nut will enter the nearest hole in the retaining washer. Install and tighten the nut lock with 50 ft. lbs. (68 Nm) of torque. The final bearing endplay should be 0.001–0.010 in.

26. Install the retaining spring, driving hub and retaining ring.

27. Apply sealant to the edge of the dust cap and install.

28. Install the brake components and wheel.

29. Road test the vehicle and check for leaks.

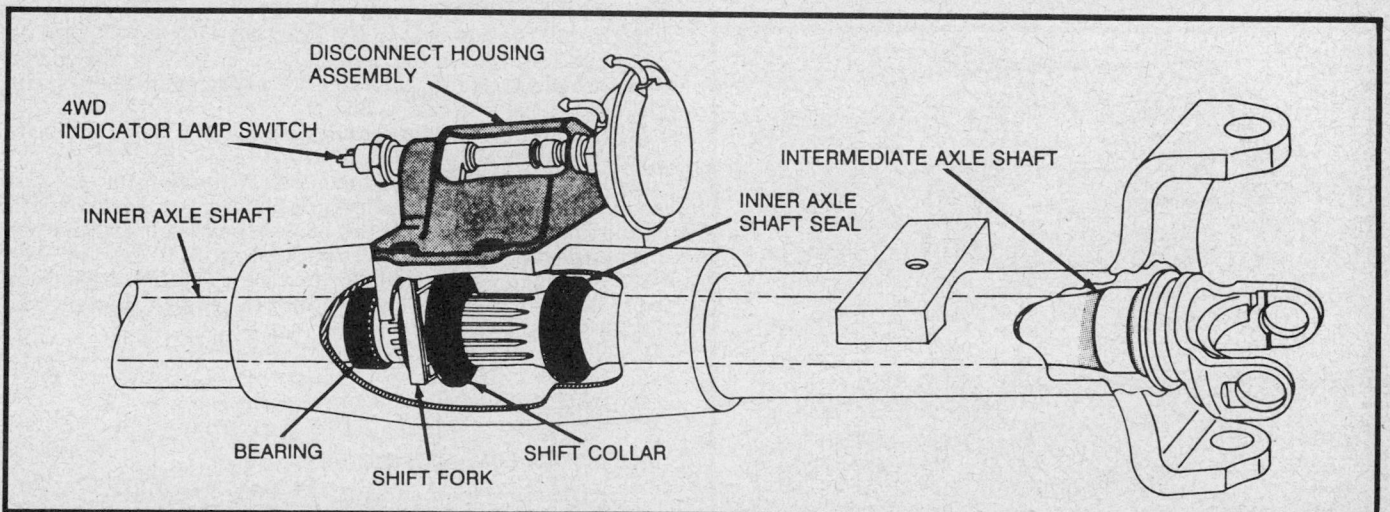

Model 44-8FD left side front axle

DANA 60

1. Raise the vehicle and support safely.
2. Remove the wheel and remove the brake caliper and pads from the rotor. Do not allow the caliper to hang by the hose.
3. Turn the shift knob to the **ENGAGE** position.
4. Apply pressure to the face of the shift knob and remove the 3 retaining screws located nearest to the flange. Pull outward and remove the shift knob from the base.
5. Remove the snapring from the axle shaft.
6. Remove the capscrews and lockwashers from the base flange.
7. Remove the locking hub from the rotor/hub. Remove and discard the gasket.
8. Straighten the lock ring tangs and use tool DD–1241–JD, or equivalent to remove the outer locknut and the lock ring. Remove the inner locknut and the outer wheel bearing.
9. Remove the rotor/hub with the inner wheel bearing. Remove the grease seal and bearing from the rotor.
10. Remove the splash shield, caliper adaptor and spindle from the steering knuckle.
11. Slide the inner and outer axle shafts with the bronze spacer, seal and slinger from the axle shaft tube and the steering knuckle.

To install:

12. Position the bronze spacer on the axle shaft with the chamfer facing the U–joint. Slide the axle shaft into the steering knuckle and the axle shaft tube.
13. Install the spindle, the brake adaptor and the splash shield. Torque the nuts to 65 ft. lbs. (86 Nm). Position the inner pad on the adaptor.
14. Lubricate and install the inner wheel bearing in the rotor and install a new seal. Install the rotor to the spindle. Install the outer wheel bearing and inner locknut.
15. Install the locknut nut and tighten it with 50 ft. lbs. (68 Nm) of torque. Loosen the nut and tighten with 35 ft. lbs. (48 Nm) of torque. Loosen the adjusting nut about ¾ turn. Install the lock ring and outer locknut. Install and tighten the nut lock with 65 ft. lbs. (88 Nm) of torque. Bend one tang over each of the locknuts. The final bearing endplay should be 0.001–0.010 in.
16. Install a new gasket on the hub. Install the drive flange and torque the nuts to 35 ft. lbs. (48 Nm). Install the snapring.
17. Position the locking hub shift knob on its base. Align the splines by pushing inward on the shift knob and rotating it clockwise to lock it in place.
18. Install and tighten the 3 screws.
19. Install the brake components and wheel.
29. Road test the vehicle and check for leaks.

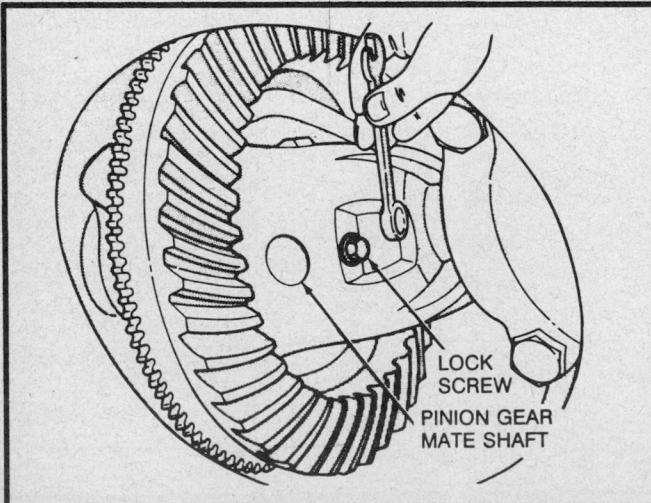

Removing the lock screw

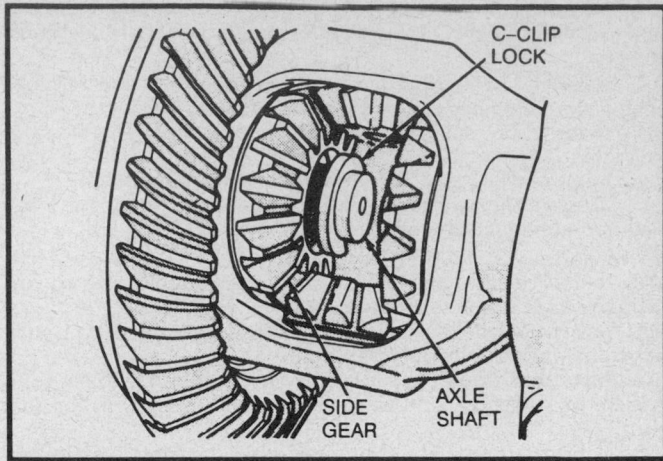

Removing the C–clip lock

Rear Axle Shaft, Bearing and Seal

Removal and Installation

CHRYSLER 8⅜ IN. AND 9¼ IN.

1. Raise the vehicle and support safely.
2. Remove the wheel and brake drum.
3. Remove the differential housing cover.
4. Rotate the differential case as required to expose the lock screw and remove it. Remove the pinion mate gear shaft from the case.
5. Force the axle shaft toward the center of the vehicle and remove the axle shaft C–clip lock from the recessed groove in the axle shaft.
6. Remove the axle shaft from the axle housing.
7. Pry the axle shaft seal from the end of the axle tube using a suitable pry bar.
8. To remove the bearing from an 8⅜ in. rear, use removal tool C–637 attached to a suitable slide hammer. To remove the bearing from an 9¼ in. rear, use removal tool C–4828 attached to a suitable slide hammer.

To install:

9. Clean the bearing bore in the axle tube.
10. Insert the new axle shaft bearing onto the pilot of tool C–4198 for 8⅜ in. rear or tool C–4826 for 9¼ in. rear. The bearing is fully installed when it is seated firmly against the shoulder in the axle tube.
11. Install the new seal to the axle tube.
12. Lubricat the bearing bore and seal lip with grease and insert the axle shaft into the axle tube engaging its splines with the differential side gear splines.
13. Install the C–clip lock in the groove at the end of the shaft. Force the shaft outward to seat the C–clip.
14. Insert the differential pinion gear mate shaft into the case and through the thrust washers and pinion gears. Align the hole in the shaft with the lock screw hole in the differential case and install the lock screw. Torque the screw to 14 ft. lbs. (19 Nm).
15. Thoroughly clean and dry the case cover, mating surface, bolts and bolt holes. Apply silicone sealer to the cover and install.
16. Install the drum and wheel.
17. Fill the differential with the proper lubricant.
18. Road test the vehicle and check for leaks.

MODEL 60, 60M AND 70

1. Raise the vehicle and support safely.
2. Remove the axle flange bolts.
3. Remove the axle shaft.

4. Remove the nut lock and remove the special adjustment nut.

5. Remove the outer bearing, brake drum and inner bearing. Remove the inner seal from the drum.

To install:

6. Lubricate and install the inner bearing to the drum and install a new seal.

7. Install the drum to the axle housing. Install the outer bearing to the drum.

8. Tighten the adjustment nut with 130 ft. lbs. (175 Nm) while rotating the wheel.

9. Loosen the adjustment nut one-third of a turn to provide about 0.005 in. of bearing endplay. Install the nut lock.

10. Install the axle with a new flange gasket.

11. Install the axle flange bolts and torque to 70 ft. lbs. (95 Nm).

Pinion Seal

Removal and Installation

1. Raise the vehicle and support safely.

2. Matchmark and remove the driveshaft.

3. Remove the rear wheel and brake drums to prevent any drag.

4. Using an inch lb. torque wrench, measure the pinion bearing preload. Read the torque while the handle of the wrench is moving through several complete revolutions.

5. Using the proper tools, hold the companion flange and remove the drive pinion nut and washer.

6. Remove the companion flange using tool C–452, or equivalent. Lower the rear of the vehicle to prevent fluid loss.

7. Using a seal remover tool, remove the seal from the carrier and clean the seal seat.

To install:

8. The outside diameter of the seal is precoated with a special sealer so no sealing compound is required for installing. The seal is properly installed when the flange contacts the housing flange face.

9. Install the companion flange and the washer with the convex side out.

10. For 8⅜ and 9¼ rears, tighten the pinion nut to 210 ft. lbs. (285 Nm) and check the pinion bearing preload. If the preload is less than the original preload measured, continue tightening the nut in very small increments until the proper preload is reached.

11. For 60, 60M and 70 rears, torque the pinion nut to 260 ft. lbs. (350 Nm).

12. Install the driveshaft, drums and rear wheels.

13. Refill the differential with the proper lubricant.

14. Road test the vehicle.

Differential Case

Removal and Installation

CHRYSLER 8⅜ IN. AND 9¼ IN.

1. Raise the vehicle and support safely.

2. Remove the wheels and the brake drums.

3. Remove the housing cover and drain the lubricant.

4. Remove the rear wheel anti-lock brake sensor, if equipped.

5. Remove both axle shafts.

6. Matchmark the bearing caps to the differential housing.

7. Remove the differential bearing threaded adjuster lock from each cap.

8. Loosen but do not remove the bearing caps.

9. Loosen the side adjusters using tool C–4164.

10. Remove the bearing caps, the threaded adjusters and the differential case.

To install:

11. Position the assembled differential case in the housing.

12. Install the bearing caps in their original positions according to the matchmarks made during the disassembly.

13. Torque the upper bolts to 10 ft. lbs. (14 Nm) and finger tighten the bottom bolts.

14. Tighten the side adjusters until the proper side play specifications are reached.

15. Torque the bearing caps bolts to 70 ft. lbs. (95 Nm) for 8⅜ in. rears or 100 ft. lbs. (136 Nm) for 9¼ in. rears.

16. Install both axle shafts.

17. Install the rear wheel anti-lock brake sensor, if equipped.

18. Install the housing cover and fill with the proper lubricant.

19. Install the drums and wheels.

20. Road test the vehicle.

MODEL 60, 60M AND 70

1. Raise the vehicle and support safely.

2. Remove both axle shafts. Remove the wheels and the brake drums.

3. Remove the housing cover and drain the lubricant.

4. Remove the rear wheel anti-lock brake sensor, if equipped.

5. Matchmark the bearing caps to the differential housing.

6. Remove the bearing caps.

7. Position a suitable housing spreader in the housing with the dowels seated securely in the locating holes.

8. Spread the case no more than 0.015 in. (0.38mm).

9. Remove the differential case from the housing using a small prying tool, if necessary.

10. Spread the housing and install the assembled case.

11. Install the bearing caps in their original positions according to the matchmarks made during the disassembly.

12. Torque the cap bolts to 85 ft. lbs. (115 Nm).

13. Check and adjust all measurements to specifications.

14. Install the rear wheel anti-lock brake sensor, if equipped.

15. Install the housing cover and fill with the proper lubricant, including suitable hypoid gear lubricant if the differential is a TraC–Lok.

16. Install the drums and wheels.

17. Install both axle shafts.

18. Road test the vehicle.

Axle Housing

Removal and Installation

1. Disconnect the negative battery cable. Raise vehicle and support safely.

2. Remove the rear wheel anti-lock brake sensor, if equipped.

3. Remove the rear wheels.

4. Disconnect the brake hose at the T-fitting.

5. Disconnect the parking brake cables.

6. Remove the driveshaft.

7. Support the weight of the assembly with the proper equipment. Disconnect the shock absorbers and remove the leaf spring nuts and U-bolts.

8. Remove the assembly from vehicle.

9. The installation is the reversal of the removal procedure.

STEERING

Steering Wheel

Removal and Installation

1. Disconnect the negative battery cable.
2. Remove the horn pad.
3. Remove the steering wheel hold-down nut. Matchmark the steering wheel to the shaft.
4. Using a suitable steering wheel puller, pull the steering wheel off of the shaft.

5. The installation is the reversal of the removal procedure.

Manual Steering Gear

Removal and Installation

1. Disconnect the negative battery cable.
2. Remove the 2 bolts from the wormshaft to steering shaft coupler.
3. Raise the vehicle and support safely.

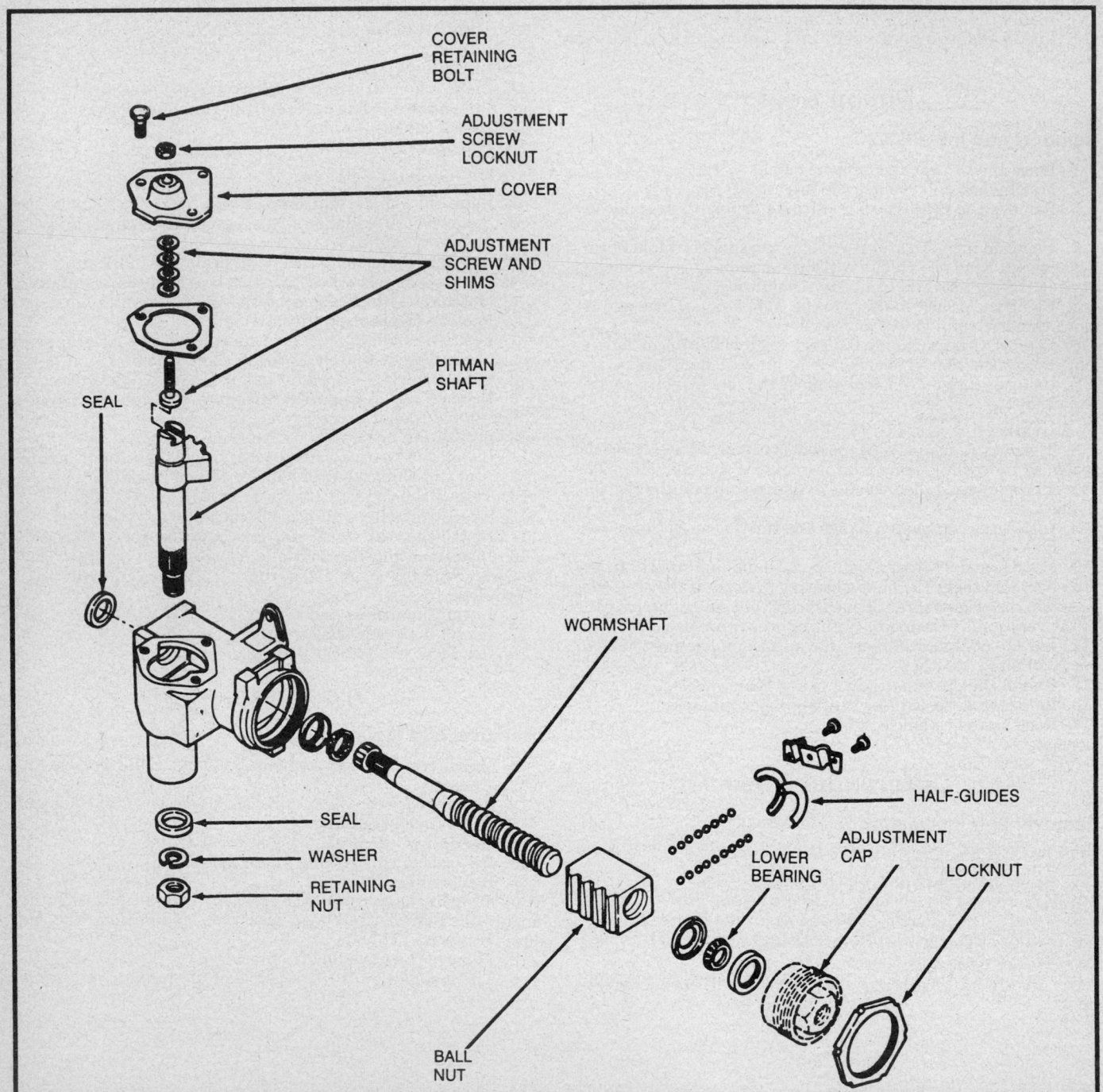

Exploded view of the manual steering gear

4. Matchmark and remove the pitman arm from the pitman shaft using tool C–4150, or equivalent.

5. Remove the steering gear mounting bolts and remove the gear from the vehicle.

6. The installation is the reversal of the removal procedure. Torque the pitman arm nut to 175 ft. lbs. (237 Nm).

Wormshaft Preload Torque Adjustment

1. Raise the vehicle and support safely.
2. Remove the pitman from the pitman shaft.
3. Remove the horn pad.
4. Loosen the sector shaft adjusting screw locknut and back off the adjusting screw about 1½ turns.
5. Turn the steering wheel to the right stop and then back ½ turn. Measure the torque required to turn the steering while back to the straight ahead position. The specification is 4–6 inch lbs.
6. If not within specifications, loosen the large adjustment cap locknut and turn the adjustment cap until the proper preload is reached. Turning the adjuster clockwise increases the preload torque.
7. Tighten the locknut and recheck the preload.
8. Tighten the sector shaft adjuster screw locknut.

Sector Shaft Adjustment

1. Perform the wormshaft preload procedure.
2. Center the steering wheel.
3. Loosen the sector shaft adjuster screw locknut and screw the adjuster screw all the way down. Tighten the locknut.
4. Rotate the steering wheel ¼ turn away from the overcenter position. Measure the torque required to rotate the wheel over the overcenter position. The specification is 14 inch lbs.
5. If not within specifications, adjust the screw accordingly and tighten the locknut.
6. Install the horn pad.
7. Install the pitman arm.

Power Steering Gear

Removal and Installation

1. Place the wheels in the straight ahead position.
2. Remove the windshield washer solvent reservoir and the coolant overflow tank, if necessary.
3. Position a drain pan under the steering gear.
4. Disconnect the fluid hoses from the gear and plug them.
5. Raise the vehicle and support safely. Matchmark and remove the pitman arm.
6. Disconnect the steering column shaft from the stub shaft.
7. Remove the retaining bolts and remove the steering gear from the vehicle.
8. The installation is the reversal of the removal procedure. Torque the pitman arm nut to 175 ft. lbs. (237 Nm).

Adjustment

1. If the vehicle wanders of the steering has too much play, the sector shaft can be adjusted.
2. Loosen the adjusting screw locknut and turn the screw all the down.
3. Back the screw off ¼–½ turn.
4. Tighten the locknut.
5. Road test the vehicle. If the steering wheel does not return easily after a turn, back the screw off until the wheel returns easily.

Power Steering Pump

Removal and Installation

1. Disconnect the negative battery cable.

2. Position a drain pan under the power steering pump.
3. Disconnect the fluid hoses from the pump and plug them.
4. Remove the front bracket attaching bolts and remove the belt from the pulley.
3. Remove the rear pump to bracket nut and remove the pump.
4. Remove the bracket from the pump.
5. Remove the pulley from the pump with the proper puller. Install the pulley on the new pump using the special installation tools.
6. The installation is the reversal of the removal procedure.

Belt Adjustment

1. Loosen the bracket mounting bolts.
2. Using a ½ in. drive breaker bar in the square hole provided in the bracket, move the pump away from the engine. Do not pry against the fluid reservoir.
3. With the pump moved enough so that the belt deflects about ¼–½ in. under a 10 lb. load, tighten the bolts.

System Bleeding

1. Fill the reservoir with power steering fluid.
2. Turn the wheels to the full left turn position and add fluid until the reservoir is full.
3. Start the engine and add fluid to bring the level to the correct level.
4. To purge the system of air, turn the steering wheel from side to side without contacting the stops.
5. Return the wheel to the straight ahead position and operate the engine for 2 minutes before road testing. This should bleed the system completely.

Tie Rod Ends

Removal and Installation

1. Raise the vehicle and support safely.
2. Remove the cotter pin and nut from the tie rod end.
3. Using a suitable puller, remove the tie rod from the steering knuckle of center link.

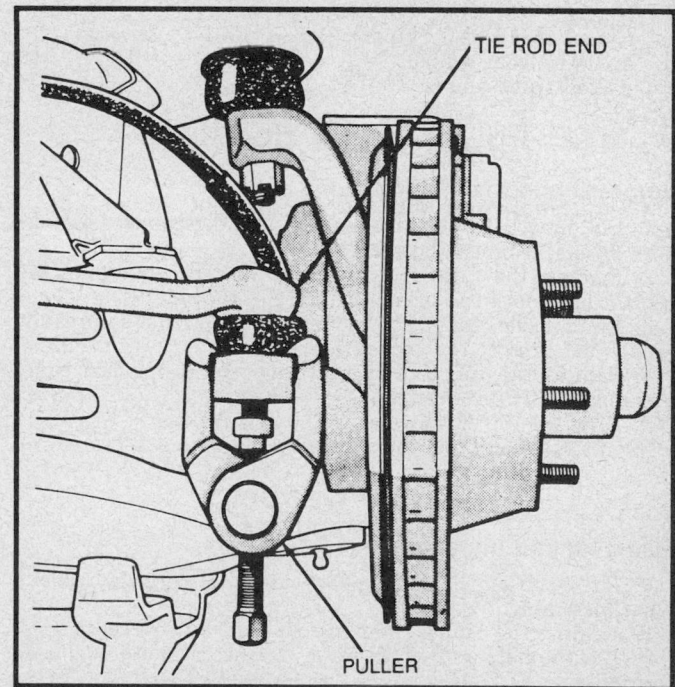

Removing the tie rod end

4. Loosen the sleeve clamp nut and bolt and unscrew the tie rod end from the sleeve.

5. The installation is the reversal of the removal procedure.

Torque the stud nuts to 45 ft. lbs. (61 Nm) and install a new cotter pin.

6. Perform a front end alignment as required.

BRAKES

For all brake system repair and service procedure not detained below, please refer to "Brakes" in the Unit Repair section.

Master Cylinder

Removal and Installation

1. Disconnect the negative battery cable.
2. Disconnect and plug the brake lines from the master cylinder.
3. Remove the nuts attaching the master cylinder to the power booster.
4. Remove the master cylinder from the mounting studs.

To install:

4. Bench bleed the master cylinder.
5. Install to the studs and install the nuts.
6. Install the brake lines to the master cylinder.

Combination Valve

Removal and Installation

1. Disconnect the negative battery cable.
2. Raise the vehicle and support safely.
3. Tag and disconnect the brake lines from the valve.
4. Disconnect the wires to the pressure switch.
5. Remove the combination valve from the frame bracket.
6. The installation is the reversal of the removal procedure.
7. Bleed the brakes in the following order:
   a. Rear Wheel Anti-Lock valve
   b. Right rear wheel cylinder
   c. Left rear wheel cylinder
   d. Right front caliper
   e. Left front caliper

Power Brake Booster

Removal and Installation

1. Disconnect the negative battery cable. Disconnect the vacuum hose(s) from the booster.
2. Remove the nuts attaching the master cylinder to the booster and move the master cylinder to the side.
3. From inside of the vehicle, remove the clip that secures the booster pushrod to the brake pedal.
4. Remove the nuts that attach the booster to the dash panel and remove it from the vehicle.
5. Transfer the check valve to the new booster.
6. The installation is the reversal of the removal procedure.

Brake Caliper

Removal and Installation

1. Raise the vehicle and support safely. Remove the tire and wheel assembly.
2. Remove the caliper retaining clips and anti-rattle springs.
3. Lift the caliper off of the rotor. Remove the outer pad from the caliper.
4. Remove the brake hose retaining bolt from the caliper.

To install:

5. Install the brake hose to the caliper using new copper washers.
6. Adjust the ears of the outer pad to provide a tight fit in the caliper recesses.
7. Position the caliper over the rotor so the caliper engages the adaptor correctly.
8. Install the anti-rattle springs and retaining clips.
9. Fill the master cylinder and bleed the brakes.

Disc Brake Pads

Removal and Installation

1. Remove some of the fluid from the master cylinder. Raise the vehicle and support safely. Remove the tire and wheel assemblies.
2. Remove the caliper and remove the outer pad from the caliper.
3. Remove the inner pad from the adaptor.

To install:

4. Use a large C–clamp to compress the piston back into the caliper bore.
5. Adjust the ears of the outer pad to provide a tight fit in the caliper recesses.
6. Install the inner pad to the adaptor.
7. Position the caliper over the rotor so the caliper engages the adaptor correctly.
8. Install the anti-rattle springs and retaining clips.
9. Refill the master cylinder.

Brake Rotor

Removal and Installation

1. Raise the vehicle and support safely.
2. Remove the wheel.
3. Remove the caliper and disc brake pads.
4. Remove the dust cap.
5. Remove the cotter pin, castelated nut lock, wheel bearing nut and washer from the spindle.
6. Remove the outer wheel bearing.
7. Remove the rotor with the inner wheel bearing from the spindle. Remove the grease seal.

To install:

8. Lubricate and install the inner wheel bearing. Install a new grease seal.
9. Install the rotor to the spindle.
10. Lubricate and install the outer wheel bearing, washer and nut. When the bearing preload is properly set, install the nut lock and a new cotter pin.
11. Install the grease cap.
12. Install the brake pads and caliper.
13. Install the wheel.

Brake Drums

Removal and Installation

EXCEPT DANA AXLE

1. Raise the vehicle and support safely.
2. Remove the wheel.

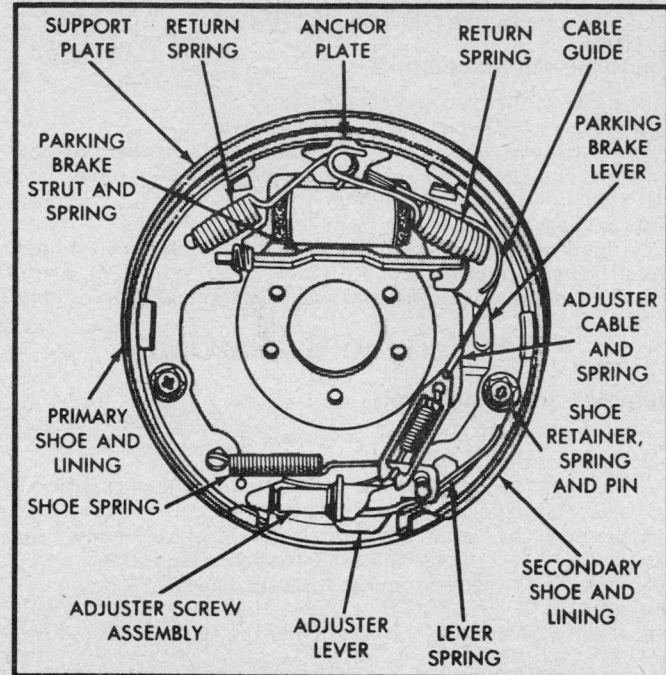

11 in. drum brakes

3. Remove the factory clips from the wheel studs, if equipped.

4. Remove the drum. If the drum is difficult to remove, remove the plug from the rear of the backing plate and push the self adjuster lever away from the star wheel. Rotate the star wheel to retract the shoes.

5. The installation is the reversal of the removal procedure.

DANA AXLE

1. Raise the vehicle and support safely.

2. Remove the axle shafts.

3. Remove the bearing adjuster nut and the outer bearing.

4. Remove the drum. If the drum is difficult to remove, remove the plug from the rear of the backing plate and push the self adjuster lever away from the star wheel. Rotate the star wheel to retract the shoes.

5. The installation is the reversal of the removal procedure.

Brake Shoes

Removal and Installation

11 INCH BRAKE DRUM

1. Raise the vehicle and support safely. Remove the wheels and drums. Remove the primary and secondary shoe return springs from the anchor pin.

2. Lift the adjuster lever and disconnect the actuator cable.

3. Remove the shoe retainers and springs.

4. Remove the shoes (held together by the lower spring) while

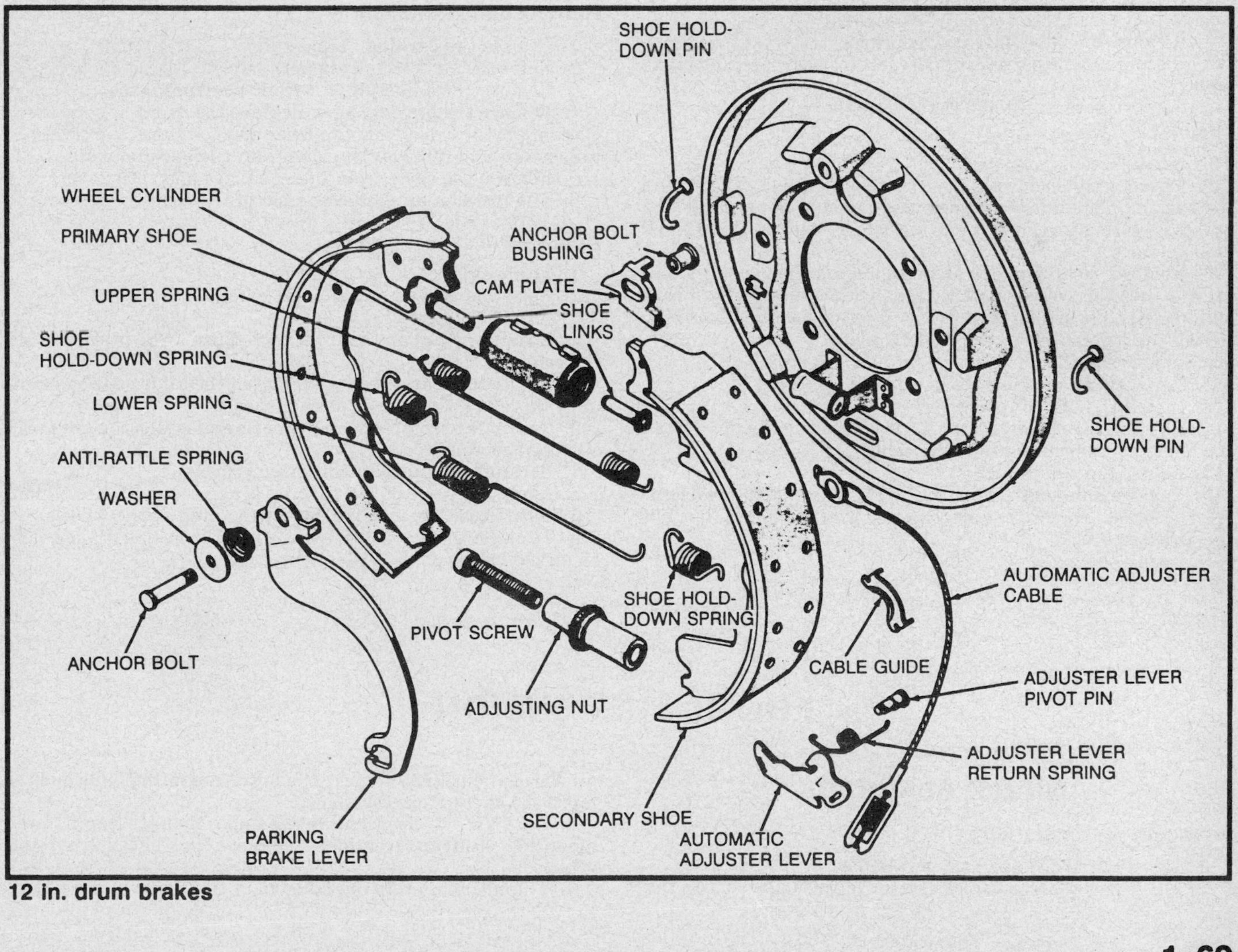

12 in. drum brakes

separating the parking brake actuating lever from the shoe with a twisting motion.

To install:

5. Thoroughly clean and dry the backing plate. To prepare the backing plate, lubricate the bosses, anchor pin and parking brake actuating lever pivot surface lightly with lithium based grease.

6. Remove, clean and dry all parts still on the old shoes. Lubricate the star wheel shaft threads with anti-sieze lubricant and transfer all parts to their proper locations on the new shoes.

7. Spread the shoes apart, engage the parking brake lever and position them on the backing plate so the wheel cylinder pins engage and the anchor pins hold the shoes.

8. Install the parking brake strut and hold-down spring assemblies.

9. Install the anchor plate. Lubricate the sliding surface of the actuator cable plate lightly and install the cable.

10. Install the shoe return spring opposite the cable, then install the remaining cable.

11. Adjust the star wheel.

12. Remove any grease from the linings and install the drum.

13. Complete the brake adjustment with the wheels installed.

12 INCH BRAKE DRUM

1. Raise the vehicle and support safely. Remove the axles and drums.

2. Unhook the adjuster lever return spring from the lever.

3. Remove the lever and return spring from the lever pin.

4. Unhook the adjuster cable from the lever.

5. Remove the upper shoe to shoe spring.

6. Remove the shoe hold-down springs.

7. Disconnect the parking brake cable from the parking brake lever.

8. Remove both brake shoes, the lower spring and star wheel assembly.

To install:

9. Thoroughly clean and dry the backing plate. To prepare the backing plate, lubricate the bosses, anchor pin and parking brake actuating lever pivot surface lightly with lithium based grease.

10. Remove, clean and dry all parts still on the old shoes. Lubricate the star wheel shaft threads with anti-sieze lubricant and transfer all parts to their proper locations on the new shoes. Install the assemblies to the backing plate.

11. Install the shoe hold-down springs and pins.

12. Connect the parking brake cable to the lever.

13. Install the upper spring.

14. Position the adjuster lever return spring on the pin. Install the adjuster lever and attach the cable.

15. Adjust the star wheel.

16. Remove any grease from the linings and install the drum.

17. Complete the brake adjustment with the wheels (but not the axles) installed.

18. Install the axles.

Wheel Cylinder

Removal and Installation

1. Raise the vehicle and support safely.

2. Remove the wheel, drum and brake shoes.

3. If equipped with a 12 in. drum, remove the anchor bolt and nut, washer, spring, parking brake lever, adjuster cable, cam plate and anchor spring bushing.

4. Remove the brake line from the wheel cylinder.

5. Remove the wheel cylinder bolts and remove the cylinder from the backing plate.

6. The installation is the reversal of the removal procedure.

Front Parking Brake Cable

Removal and Installation

1. Raise the vehicle and support safely.

2. Remove the front cable adjusting nut.

3. Remove the clip securing the cable to the anchor bracket and slide the cable out of the bracket.

4. Remove the retainer attaching the cable to the pedal assembly frame. Disengage the cable from the pedal clevis.

5. Remove the cable grommet from the floor pan and remove the cable.

6. The installation is the reversal of the removal procedure.

Rear Parking Brake Cable

Removal and Installation

1. Release the parking brakes fully.

2. Raise the vehicle and support safely.

3. Remove the adjusting nut from the front cable.

4. Remove the brake drums. Remove the shoes, if necessary. Disconnect the cable from the lever and compress the cable retainer tabs and remove the cable from the backing plate.

5. Remove the cable from the equalizer and ratio lever.

6. The installation is the reversal of the removal procedure.

Adjustment

1. Release the parking brakes fully.

2. Raise the vehicle and support safely.

3. Adjust the rear brakes.

4. Loosen the nut on the front cable until there is slack in all the cables.

5. Rotate the rear wheels and tighten the cable adjusting nut until there is a slight drag at the wheels.

6. Continue to rotate the rear wheels and loosen the nut until all drag is eliminated.

7. Back off the nut an additional 2 turns.

8. Apply and release the parking brake several times. Upon the least release, verify that there is no drag at the wheels.

9. To check the operation, make sure the parking brake holds on an incline.

FRONT SUSPENSION

Shock Absorbers

Removal and Installation

1. Raise the vehicle and support safely.

2. On 2 wheel drive vehicles, remove the upper shock nut, washer and bushing. Remove the lower mounting bolts and remove the shock from the vehicle.

3. On 4WD vehicles, remove the upper mounting nut, lower mounting stud and retainers. Remove the shock from the vehicle.

4. The installation is the reversal of the removal procedure.

Coil Springs

Removal and Installation

1. Raise the vehicle and support safely.
2. Remove the shock absorber.
3. Remove the strut bar and disconnect the sway bar from the lower control arm, if equipped.
4. Install spring compressor tool DD–1278, or equivalent to the coil spring and tighten the nut finger tight, then back off half a turn.
5. Remove the cotter pin and lower ball joint nut.
6. Release the lower ball joint taper using ball stud loosening tool C–3564–A, or equivalent.
7. Remove the tool and remove the ball stud from the control arm. Release the compressor tool from the coil spring.
8. Pull the arm down and remove the spring with the rubber isolation pad from the vehicle.

To install:

9. Install the spring with the rubber isolators. Install the compressor tool and compress it enough so the lower ball joint can be inserted through the knuckle.
10. Torque $^{11}/_{16}-16$ lower ball joint nuts to 135 ft. lbs. (183 Nm). Torque $^3/_4-16$ nuts to 175 ft. lbs. (237 Nm). Install a new cotter pin. Remove the spring compressor.
11. Install the strut bar and connect the sway bar from the lower control arm, if equipped.
12. Install the shock absorber.

Leaf Springs

Removal and Installation

1. Raise the vehicle and support safely.
2. Using the proper equipment, support the weight of the front axle.
3. Remove the nuts, washers and U-bolts attaching the springs to the axle housing. Remove the spring pad.
4. Remove the spring shackle bolts, shackle and spring front bolt.
5. Remove the spring from the vehicle.
6. The installation is the reversal of the removal procedure. Torque the U-bolt nuts to 110 ft. lbs. (149 Nm).

Upper Ball Joint

Inspection

To inspect the ball joints, unload the suspension. Upper ball joints on 2WD vehicles and any ball joint on 4WD vehicles should be replaced if any play exists at all.

Removal and Installation

2WD VEHICLES

1. Raise the vehicle and support safely.
2. Position a support at the outer end of the lower control arm and lower the vehicle so that the support compresses the coil spring.
3. Remove the tire and wheel assembly.
4. Release the upper ball joint taper using ball stud loosening tool C–3564–A, or equivalent.
5. Unthread the ball joint from the control arm with tool C–3561, or equivalent.
6. The installation is the reversal of the removal procedure. Torque the ball joint itself to 125 ft. lbs. (169 Nm).
7. Torque the upper ball stud nut to 135 ft. lbs (183 Nm).

4WD VEHICLES

1. Raise the vehicle and support safely.
2. Remove the front axle shaft.
3. Disconnect the tie rod end from the steering knuckle. On

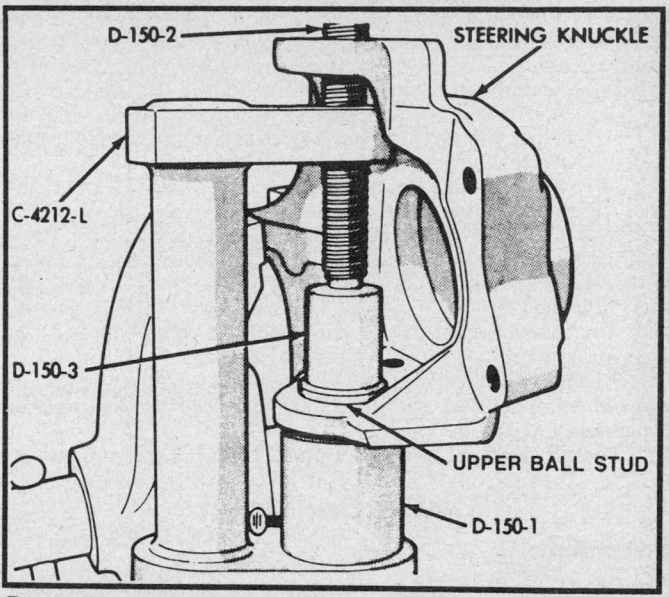
Removing the upper ball joint from the knuckle

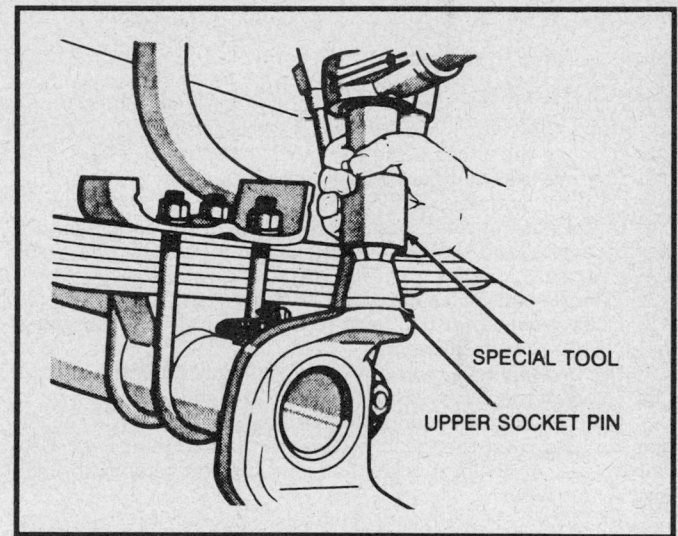
Removing or installing the upper socket pin

the left side, disconnect the drag link ball stud from the steering knuckle.
4. On the left side, remove the nuts and washers from the steering knuckle arm and remove the arm and spring, if equipped, from the knuckle.
5. If equipped with a Model 44 front axle, remove the ball joint nuts and discard the lower nut. Use a brass drift and hammer to separate the steering knuckle from the axle tube yoke. Use tool C–4169 to remove the sleeve from the upper yoke arm.
6. Remove the snapring from the ball joint. Install the knuckle in a vise and use tools D–150–1, D–150–3 and C–4212–L to remove the ball joint from the knuckle.
7. If equipped with a Dana 60 front axle, remove the bolts from the knuckle lower cap. Dislodge the cap from the steering knuckle and axle tube yoke. Remove the steering knuckle. Use tool D–192 to remove the upper socket pin from the axle tube upper arm bore. Remove the seal.

To install:

8. If equipped with a Model 44, use tools C–4212–L and C–4288 to force the upper ball joint into the steering knuckle. In-

stall the snapring and install a new rubber boot. Thread the replacement sleeve into the upper yoke bore so that 2 threads are exposed at the top of the yoke. Position the knuckle on the axle tube yoke and install a new lower ball stud nut. Torque to 80 ft. lbs. (108 Nm). Using the special socket, torque the sleeve to 40 ft. lbs. (54 Nm). Install the upper ball stud nut and torque to 100 ft. lbs. (136 Nm) and install a new cotter pin.

9. If equipped with a Dana 60 front axle, use tool D–192 to install the upper socket pin to the axle tube upper arm bore. Install a new seal. Torque to 500–600 ft. lbs. (668–813 Nm). Position the knuckle over the socket pin. Fill the lower socket cavity with grease. Install the lower cap and torque the bolts to 80 ft. lbs. (110 Nm).

10. On the left side, install the spring, if equipped and the steering knuckle arm to the steering knuckle.

11. Connect the tie rod to the end of the steering knuckle. On the left side, connect the drag link ball stud to the steering knuckle.

12. Install the front axle shaft and all related components.

Lower Ball Joint

Inspection

To inspect the ball joints, unload the suspension. Lower ball joints on 2WD vehicles should be replaced if the have more than 0.020 in. play. Any ball joint on 4WD vehicles should be replaced if any play exists.

Removal and Installation

2WD VEHICLES

1. Raise the vehicle and support safely.
2. Remove the shock absorber.
3. Remove the strut bar and disconnect the sway bar from the lower control arm, if equipped.
4. Install spring compressor tool DD–1278, or equivalent to the coil spring and tighten the nut finger tight, then back off half a turn.
5. Remove the cotter pin and lower ball joint nut.
6. Release the lower ball joint taper using ball stud loosening tool C–3564–A, or equivalent.
7. Remove the tool and remove the ball stud from the control arm. Release the compressor tool from the coil spring.
8. Pull the arm down and remove the spring with the rubber isolation pad from the vehicle. Remove the ball joint boot. Use tool C–4212, or an appropriate ball joint press to remove the ball joint from the arm.

To install:

9. Use the remover tool to press the ball joint into the arm. Install a new rubber boot. Install the spring with the rubber isolators. Install the compressor tool and compress it enough so the lower ball joint can be inserted through the knuckle.

10. Torque $^{11}/_{16}$–16 lower ball joint nuts to 135 ft. lbs. (183 Nm). Torque $^3/_4$–16 nuts to 175 ft. lbs. (237 Nm). Install a new cotter pin. Remove the spring compressor.

11. Install the strut bar and connect the sway bar from the lower control arm, if equipped.

12. Install the shock absorber.

4WD VEHICLES

1. Raise the vehicle and support safely.
2. Remove the front axle shaft.
3. Disconnect the tie rod end from the steering knuckle. On the left side, disconnect the drag link ball stud from the steering knuckle.
4. On the left side, remove the nuts and washers from the steering knuckle arm and remove the arm and spring, if equipped, from the knuckle.
5. If equipped with a Model 44 front axle, remove the ball joint nuts and discard the lower nut. Use a brass drift and hammer to separate the steering knuckle from the axle tube yoke.

6. Remove the snapring from the ball joint. Install the knuckle in a vise and use tools D–150–1, D–150–3 and C–4212–L to remove the ball joint from the knuckle.

7. If equipped with a Dana 60 front axle, use tools C–4212–L, C–4366–1 and C–4366–2 to remove the lower ball joint.

To install:

8. If equipped with a Model 44, use tools C–4212–L and C–4288 to force the lower ball joint into the steering knuckle. Install the snapring and install a new rubber boot. Position the knuckle on the axle tube yoke and install a new lower ball stud nut. Torque to 80 ft. lbs. (108 Nm). Install the upper ball stud nut and torque to 100 ft. lbs. (136 Nm) and install a new cotter pin.

9. If equipped with a Dana 60 front axle, use tools C–4212–L, C–4366–3 and C–4366–4 to install the seal and lower bearing cup into the axle tube yoke lower bore. Reposition the tools and install the lower bearing and seal into the bore. Position the knuckle over the socket pin. Fill the lower socket cavity with grease. Install the lower cap and torque the bolts to 80 ft. lbs. (110 Nm).

10. On the left side, install the spring, if equipped and the steering knuckle arm to the steering knuckle.

11. Connect the tie rod to the end of the steering knuckle. On the left side, connect the drag link ball stud to the steering knuckle.

12. Install the front axle shaft and all related components.

Upper Control Arm

Removal and Installation

1. Raise the vehicle and support safely.
2. Remove the shock absorber.
3. Remove the strut bar and disconnect the sway bar from the lower control arm, if equipped.
4. Install spring compressor tool DD–1278, or equivalent to the coil spring and tighten the nut finger tight, then back off half a turn.
5. Remove the cotter pin and upper ball joint nut. Suspend the rotor assembly with a wire so there is not excessive pull on the brake hose.
6. Release the upper ball joint taper using ball stud loosening tool C–3564–A, or equivalent.
7. Remove the tool and remove the ball stud from the control arm.
8. Remove the pivot bar retaining bolts on Vans or the cam

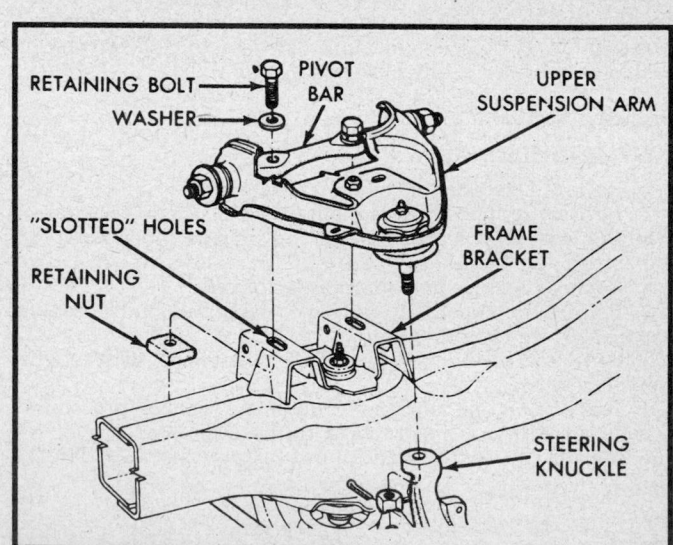

Upper control arm—Van

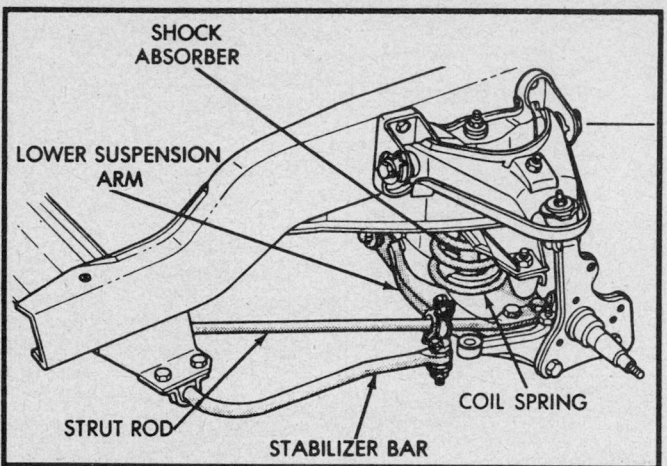

Upper control arm and related components— 2 wheel drive Pick-Up and Ramcharger

bolt assemblies on Pick-Up and Ramcharger and remove the arm from the vehicle.

To install:
9. Install the arm to the frame rail bracket and install the retaining bolts.
10. Torque the ball joint nut to 135 ft. lbs. (183 Nm). Install a new cotter pin. Remove the spring compressor.
11. Install the strut bar and connect the sway bar from the lower control arm, if equipped.
12. Install the shock absorber.
13. Align the front end. When all settings are at specifications, torque the pivot bar retaining bolts on Vans to 195 ft. lbs. (264 Nm). Torque the cam bolts to 70 ft. lbs. (95 Nm) on Pick-Up and Ramcharger.

Lower Control Arm

Removal and Installation

1. Raise the vehicle and support safely.
2. Remove the shock absorber.
3. Remove the strut bar and disconnect the sway bar from the lower control arm, if equipped.
4. Install spring compressor tool DD–1278, or equivalent to the coil spring and tighten the nut finger tight, then back off half a turn.
5. Remove the cotter pin and lower ball joint nut.
6. Release the lower ball joint taper using ball stud loosening tool C–3564–A, or equivalent.
7. Remove the tool and remove the ball stud from the control arm. Release the compressor tool from the coil spring.
8. Pull the arm down and remove the spring with the rubber isolation pad from the vehicle. Remove the lower control arm pivot bolt from the crossmember and remove the arm from the vehicle.

To install:
9. Install the arm to the crossmember finger tight. Install the

spring with the rubber isolators. Install the compressor tool and compress it enough so the lower ball joint can be inserted through the knuckle.
10. Torque $^{11}/_{16}-16$ lower ball joint nuts to 135 ft. lbs. (183 Nm). Torque $^{3}/_{4}-16$ nuts to 175 ft. lbs. (237 Nm). Install a new cotter pin. Remove the spring compressor.
11. Install the strut bar and connect the sway bar from the lower control arm, if equipped.
12. Install the shock absorber.
13. Lower the vehicle completely. When the weight of the vehicle is off of the lifting apparatus, torque the lower arm pivot bolts to 175 ft. lbs. (237 Nm) on Vans or 225 ft. lbs. (305 Nm) on Pick-Up and Ramcharger.
14. Align the front end as required.

Sway Bar

Removal and Installation

1. Raise the vehicle and support safely.
2. Remove the front sway bar brackets and retainers.
3. Remove the sway bar connecting links to the control arm or front axle. Remove the sway bar from the vehicle.
4. The installation is the reversal of the removal procedure. Tighten the nuts just enough so the bushings compress to the same outer diameter as the washer adjacent to it.

Front Wheel Bearings

Removal and Installation

1. Raise the vehicle and support safely.
2. Remove the tire and wheel assembly.
3. Remove the caliper and disc brake pads.
4. Remove the dust cap.
5. Remove the cotter pin, castelated nut lock, wheel bearing nut and washer from the spindle.
6. Remove the outer wheel bearing.
7. Remove the rotor with the inner wheel bearing from the spindle. Remove the grease seal.

To install:
8. Lubricate and install the inner wheel bearing. Install a new grease seal.
9. Install the rotor to the spindle.
10. Lubricate and install the outer wheel bearing, washer and nut. When the bearing preload is properly set, install the nut lock and a new cotter pin.
11. Install the grease cap.
12. Install the brake pads and caliper.
13. Install the wheel.

Adjustment

1. Tighten the wheel bearing nut to 240–300 inch lbs. (27–34 Nm) while turning the rotor.
2. Loosen the wheel bearing adjusting nut completely.
3. Tighten the nut finger tight.
4. Check the wheel bearing endplay. The specification is 0.0001–0.003 in.
5. Install the nut lock and cotter pin.

REAR SUSPENSION

Shock Absorber

Removal and Installation

1. Raise the vehicle and support safely.

2. Remove the bolts that attach the shock to the frame or bracket.
3. Remove the shock from the vehicle.
4. The installation is the reversal of the removal procedure.

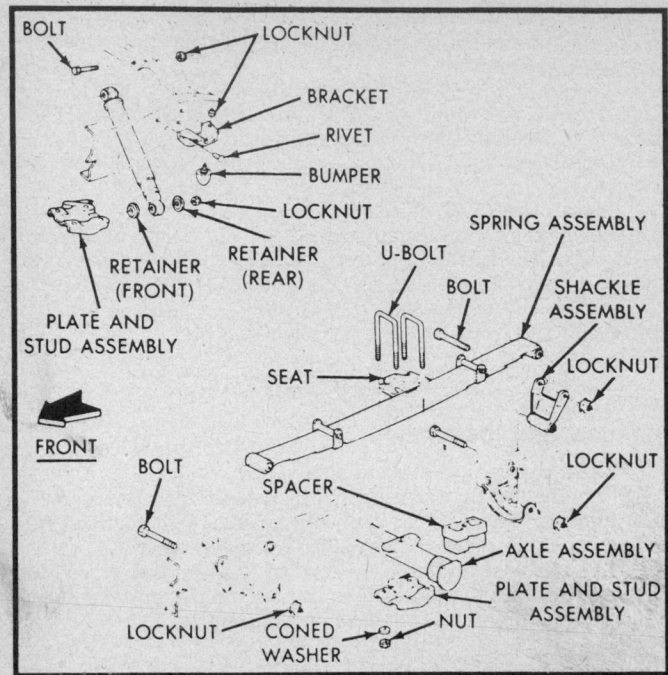

Rear suspension components—150 models

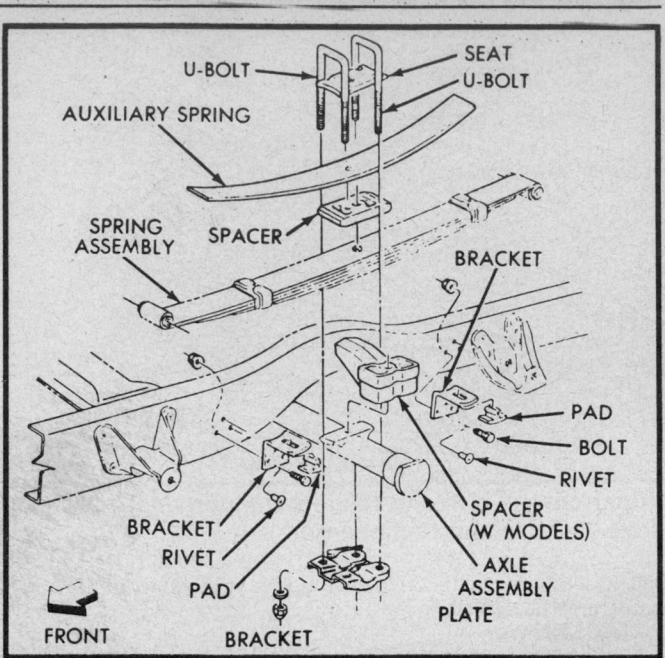

Rear suspension with auxiliary springs—D and W 250 and 350 models

Leaf Springs

Removal and Installation

1. Raise the vehicle and support safely.
2. Using the proper equipment, support the weight of the axle.

3. Remove the nuts, washers and U-bolts attaching the springs to the axle housing. Remove the spacer.
4. Remove the spring shackle bolts, shackle and spring front bolt.
5. Remove the springs and auxiliary spring, if equipped, from the vehicle.
6. The installation is the reversal of the removal procedure.

SPECIFICATIONS

VEHICLE IDENTIFICATION CHART

It is important for servicing and ordering parts to be certain of the vehicle and engine identification. The VIN (vehicle identification number) is a 17 digit number visible through the windshield on the driver's side of the dash and contains the vehicle and engine identification codes. The tenth digit indicates model year and the eighth digit indicates engine code. It can be interpreted as follows:

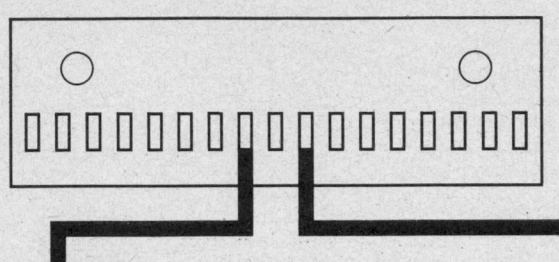

Engine Code						Model Year	
Code	Cu. In.	Liters	Cyl.	Fuel Sys.	Eng. Mfg.	Code	Year
C	135	2.2	4	Carb	Chrys	G	1986
K	153	2.5	4	EFI	Chrys	H	1987
J	153	2.5	4	Turbo	Chrys	J	1988
G	156	2.6	4	Carb	Mitsubishi	K	1989
3	181	3.0	6	EFI	Mitsubishi	L	1990
R	201	3.3	6	EFI	Chrys		
M	239	3.9	6	Carb	Chrys		
X	239	3.9	6	EFI	Chrys		

ENGINE IDENTIFICATION

Year	Model	Engine Displacement cu. in. (liter)	Engine Series Identification (VIN)	No. of Cylinders	Engine Type
1986	Caravan	135 (2.2)	C	4	OHC
	Caravan	156 (2.6)	G	4	OHC
	Voyager	135 (2.2)	C	4	OHC
	Voyager	156 (2.6)	G	4	OHC
1987	Caravan	135 (2.2)	C	4	OHC
	Caravan	153 (2.5)	K	4	OHC
	Caravan	156 (2.6)	G	4	OHC
	Caravan	181 (3.0)	3	6	OHC
	Voyager	135 (2.2)	C	4	OHC
	Voyager	153 (2.5)	K	4	OHC
	Voyager	156 (2.6)	G	4	OHC
	Voyager	181 (3.0)	3	6	OHC
	Dakota	135 (2.2)	C	4	OHC
	Dakota	239 (3.9)	M	6	OHV

ENGINE IDENTIFICATION

Year	Model	Engine Displacement cu. in. (liter)	Engine Series Identification (VIN)	No. of Cylinders	Engine Type
1988	Caravan	153 (2.5)	K	4	OHC
	Caravan	181 (3.0)	3	4	OHC
	Voyager	153 (2.5)	K	6	OHC
	Voyager	181 (3.0)	3	6	OHC
	Dakota	135 (2.2)	C	4	OHC
	Dakota	239 (3.9)	X	6	OHV
1989	Caravan	153 (2.5)	K	4	OHC
	Caravan	153 (2.5)	J	4	OHC
	Caravan	181 (3.0)	3	6	OHC
	Voyager	153 (2.5)	K	4	OHC
	Voyager	153 (2.5)	J	4	OHC
	Voyager	181 (3.0)	3	6	OHC
	Dakota	153 (2.5)	K	4	OHC
	Dakota	239 (3.9)	X	6	OHV
1990	Caravan	153 (2.5)	K	4	OHC
	Caravan	153 (2.5)	J	4	OHC
	Caravan	181 (3.0)	3	6	OHC
	Caravan	201 (3.3)	R	6	OHV
	Voyager	153 (2.5)	K	4	OHC
	Voyager	153 (2.5)	J	4	OHC
	Voyager	181 (3.0)	3	6	OHC
	Voyager	201 (3.3)	R	6	OHV
	Town & Country	201 (3.3)	R	6	OHV
	Dakota	153 (2.5)	K	4	OHC
	Dakota	239 (3.9)	X	6	OHV

GENERAL ENGINE SPECIFICATIONS

Year	VIN	No. Cylinder Displacement cu. in. (liter)	Fuel System Type	Net Horsepower @ rpm	Net Torque @ rpm (ft. lbs.)	Bore × Stroke (in.)	Compression Ratio	Oil Pressure @ rpm
1986	C	4-135 (2.2)	2 bbl	96 @ 5200	119 @ 3200	3.44 × 3.62	9.5:1	50 @ 2000
	G	4-156 (2.6)	2 bbl	101 @ 5600	140 @ 2800	3.59 × 3.86	8.7:1	85 @ 2500
1987	C	4-135 (2.2)	2 bbl	96 @ 5200	119 @ 3200	3.44 × 3.62	9.5:1	50 @ 2000
	K	4-153 (2.5)	EFI	100 @ 4800	135 @ 2800	3.44 × 4.09	8.9:1	30–80 @ 3000
	G	4-156 (2.6)	2 bbl	101 @ 5600	140 @ 2800	3.59 × 3.86	8.7:1	85 @ 2500
	3	6-181 (3.0)	EFI	142 @ 5000	173 @ 2800	3.59 × 2.99	8.9:1	30–80 @ 3000
	M	6-239 (3.9)	2 bbl	125 @ 4000	195 @ 2000	3.91 × 3.31	9.0:1	30–80 @ 3000
1988	C	4-135 (2.2)	2 bbl	96 @ 5200	140 @ 2800	3.44 × 3.62	9.5:1	50 @ 2000
	K	4-153 (2.5)	EFI	100 @ 4800	135 @ 2800	3.44 × 4.09	8.9:1	30–80 @ 3000
	3	6-181 (3.0)	EFI	142 @ 5000	173 @ 2800	3.59 × 2.99	8.9:1	30–80 @ 3000
	X	6-239 (3.9)	EFI	125 @ 4000	195 @ 2000	3.91 × 3.31	9.0:1	30–80 @ 3000

GENERAL ENGINE SPECIFICATIONS

Year	VIN	No. Cylinder Displacement cu. in. (liter)	Fuel System Type	Net Horsepower @ rpm	Net Torque @ rpm (ft. lbs.)	Bore × Stroke (in.)	Compression Ratio	Oil Pressure @ rpm
1989	K	4-153 (2.5)	EFI	100 @ 4800	135 @ 2800	3.44 × 4.09	8.9:1	30–80 @ 3000
	J	4-153 (2.5)	Turbo	150 @ 4800	180 @ 2000	3.44 × 4.09	7.8:1	30–80 @ 3000
	3	6-181 (3.0)	EFI	142 @ 5000	173 @ 2800	3.59 × 2.99	8.9:1	30–80 @ 3000
	X	6-239 (3.9)	EFI	125 @ 4000	195 @ 2000	3.91 × 3.31	9.0:1	30–80 @ 3000
1990	K	4-153 (2.5)	EFI	100 @ 4800	135 @ 2800	3.44 × 4.09	8.9:1	30–80 @ 3000
	J	4-153 (2.5)	Turbo	150 @ 4800	180 @ 2000	3.44 × 4.09	7.8:1	30–80 @ 3000
	3	6-181 (3.0)	EFI	142 @ 5000	173 @ 2800	3.59 × 2.99	8.9:1	30–80 @ 3000
	R	6-201 (3.3)	EFI	150 @ 4000	185 @ 3600	3.66 × 3.19	8.9:1	30–80 @ 3000
	X	6-239 (3.9)	EFI	125 @ 4000	195 @ 2000	3.91 × 3.31	9.0:1	30–80 @ 3000

GASOLINE ENGINE TUNE-UP SPECIFICATIONS

Year	VIN	No. Cylinder Displacement cu. in. (liter)	Spark Plugs Type	Gap (in.)	Ignition Timing (deg.) MT	AT	Compression Pressure (psi)	Fuel Pump (psi)	Idle speed (rpm) MT	AT	Valve Clearance In.	Ex.
1986	C	4-135 (2.2)	RN12YC	.035	6B	6B	100	4.5–6	850	900	Hyd.	Hyd.
	G	4-156 (2.6)	RN12YC	.040	—	7B	150	4.5–6	—	800	0.006	0.010
1987	C	4-135 (2.2)	RN12YC	.035	6B	6B	100	4.5–6	850	900	Hyd.	Hyd.
	K	4-153 (2.5)	RN12YC	.035	12B	12B	100	15	850	850	Hyd.	Hyd.
	G	4-156 (2.6)	RN12YC	.040	—	7B	150	4.5–6	—	800	0.006	0.010
	3	6-181 (3.0)	RN11YC4	.040	—	12B	178	48	—	700	Hyd.	Hyd.
	M	6-239 (3.9)	RN12YC	.035	7B	7B	100	5.75–7.25	①	①	Hyd.	Hyd.
1988	C	4-135 (2.2)	RN12YC	.035	6B	—	100	4.5–6	850	—	Hyd.	Hyd.
	K	4-153 (2.5)	RN12YC	.035	12B	12B	100	15	850	850	Hyd.	Hyd.
	3	6-181 (3.0)	RN11YC4	.040	—	12B	178	48	—	700	Hyd.	Hyd.
	X	6-239 (3.9)	RN12YC	.035	10B	10B	100	13–16	750	750	Hyd.	Hyd.
1989	K	4-153 (2.5)	RN12YC	.035	12B	12B	100	15	850	850	Hyd.	Hyd.
	J	4-153 (2.5)	RN12Y C	.035	12B	12B	100	55	950	900	Hyd.	Hyd.
	3	6-181 (3.0)	RN11YC4	.040	—	12B	178	48	—	700	Hyd.	Hyd.
	X	6-239 (3.9)	RN12YC	.035	10B	10B	100	13–16	750	750	Hyd.	Hyd.
1990	K	4-153 (2.5)	RN12YC	.035	12B	12B	100	15	850	850	Hyd.	Hyd.
	J	4-153 (2.5)	RN12Y C	.035	12B	12B	100	55	950	900	Hyd.	Hyd.
	3	6-181 (3.0)	RN11YC4	.040	—	12B	178	48	—	700	Hyd.	Hyd.
	R	6-201 (3.3)	RN16YC5	.050	—	16B	100	43–53	—	750	Hyd.	Hyd.
	X	6-239 (3.9)	RN12YC	.035	10B	10B	100	13–16	750	750	Hyd.	Hyd.

① Refer to Vehicle Emissions Label

FIRING ORDERS

NOTE: To avoid confusion, always replace spark plug wires one at a time.

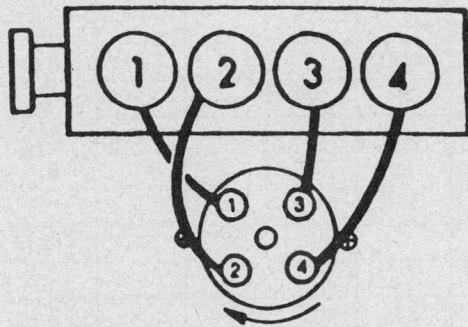

Chrysler Corp. 2.2L and 2.5L engines
Engine firing order: 1–3–4–2
Distributor rotation: clockwise

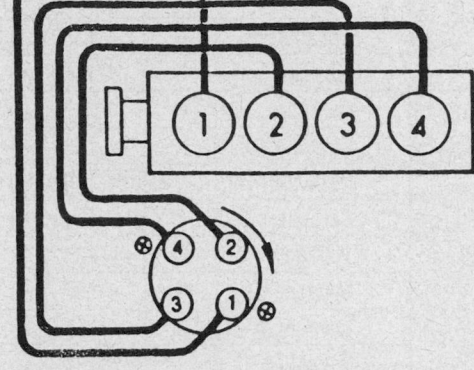

Chrysler Corp. (Mitsubishi) 2.6L engine
Firing order: 1–3–4–2
Distributor rotation: clockwise

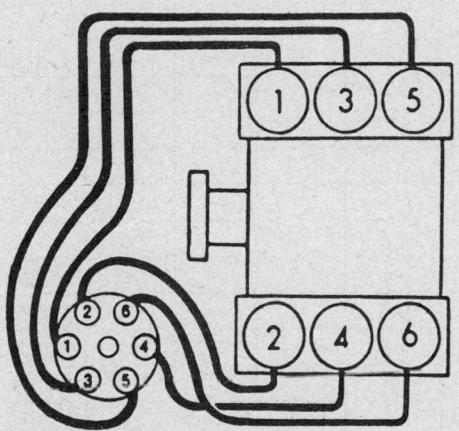

Chrysler Corp. (Mitsubishi) 3.0L engine
Firing order: 1–2–3–4–5–6
Distributor rotation: counterclockwise

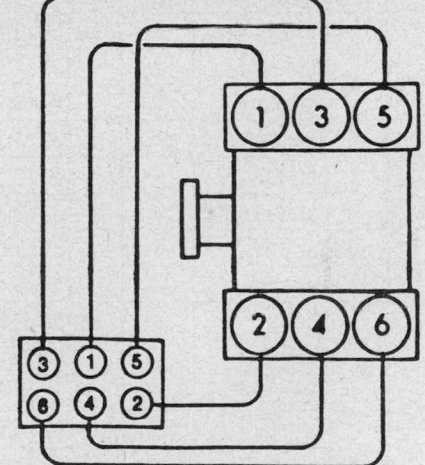

Chrysler Corp. 3.3L engine
Firing order: 1–2–3–4–5–6

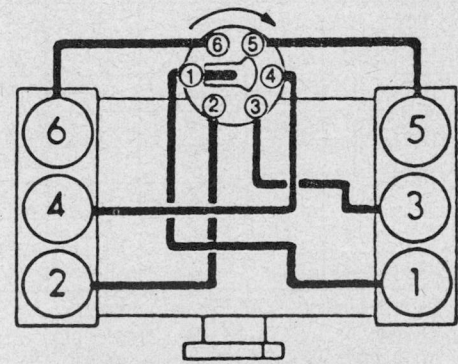

Chrysler Corp. 3.9L engine
Firing order: 1–6–5–4–3–2
Distributor rotation: clockwise

CAPACITIES

Year	Model	VIN	No. Cylinder Displacement cu. in (liter)	Engine Crankcase with Filter	Engine Crankcase without Filter	Transmission (pts.) 4-Spd	Transmission (pts.) 5-Spd	Transmission (pts.) Auto.	Drive Axle (pts.)	Fuel Tank (gal.)	Cooling System (qts.) ⑥
1986	Caravan	C	4-135 (2.2)	4	4	4.0	4.8	①	—	④	8.5
	Caravan	G	4-156 (2.6)	5	4.5	—	—	①	—	④	9.5
	Voyager	C	4-135 (2.2)	4	4	4.0	4.8	①	—	④	8.5
	Voyager	G	4-156 (2.6)	5	4.5	—	—	①	—	④	9.5
1987	Caravan	C	4-135 (2.2)	4	4	4.0	4.8	①	—	④	8.5
	Caravan	K	4-153 (2.5)	4	4	—	4.8	①	—	④	8.5
	Caravan	G	4-156 (2.6)	5	4.5	—	—	①	—	④	9.5
	Caravan	3	6-181 (3.0)	4	4	—	—	①	—	④	10.5
	Voyager	C	4-135 (2.2)	4	4	4.0	4.8	①	—	④	8.5
	Voyager	K	4-153 (2.5)	4	4	—	4.8	①	—	④	8.5
	Voyager	G	4-156 (2.6)	5	4.5	—	—	①	—	④	9.5
	Voyager	3	6-181 (3.0)	4	4	—	—	①	—	④	10.5
	Dakota	C	4-135 (2.2)	4	4	—	4.0	15.6	②	⑤	9.8
	Dakota	M	6-239 (3.9)	5	5	—	4.0	17.2	②③	⑤	⑦
1988	Caravan	K	4-153 (2.5)	4	4	—	4.8	①	—	④	8.5
	Caravan	3	6-181 (3.0)	4	4	—	—	①	—	④	10.5
	Voyager	K	4-153 (2.5)	4	4	—	4.8	①	—	④	8.5
	Voyager	3	6-181 (3.0)	4	4	—	—	①	—	④	10.5
	Dakota	C	4-135 (2.2)	4	4	—	4.0	15.6	②	⑤	9.8
	Dakota	X	6-239 (3.9)	4	4	—	4.0	17.2	②③	⑤	⑦
1989	Caravan	K	4-153 (2.5)	4	4	—	4.8	①	—	④	8.5
	Caravan	J	4-153 (2.5)	4	4	—	4.8	①	—	④	8.5
	Caravan	3	6-181 (3.0)	4	4	—	—	①	—	④	10.5
	Voyager	K	4-153 (2.5)	4	4	—	4.8	①	—	④	8.5
	Voyager	J	4-153 (2.5)	4	4	—	4.8	①	—	④	8.5
	Voyager	3	6-181 (3.0)	4	4	—	—	①	—	④	10.5
	Dakota	K	4-153 (2.5)	4	4	—	4.0	15.6	②	⑤	9.8
	Dakota	X	6-239 (3.9)	4	4	—	4.0	17.2	②③	⑤	⑦
1990	Caravan	K	4-153 (2.5)	4	4	—	4.8	①	—	④	8.5
	Caravan	J	4-153 (2.5)	4	4	—	4.8	①	—	④	8.5
	Caravan	3	6-181 (3.0)	4	4	—	—	①	—	④	10.5
	Caravan	R	6-201 (3.3)	4	4	—	—	①	—	④	10.5
	Voyager	K	4-153 (2.5)	4	4	—	4.8	①	—	④	8.5
	Voyager	J	4-153 (2.5)	4	4	—	4.8	①	—	④	8.5
	Voyager	3	6-181 (3.0)	4	4	—	—	①	—	④	10.5
	Voyager	R	6-201 (3.3)	4	4	—	—	①	—	④	10.5
	Town & Country	R	6-201 (3.3)	4	4	—	—	18.2	—	④	10.5
	Dakota	K	4-153 (2.5)	4	4	—	4.0	—	②	⑤	9.8
	Dakota	X	6-239 (3.9)	4	4	—	4.0	20.4	②③	⑤	⑦

① A413/A470 automatic transaxles (except fleet): 17.8 pts.
A413/A470 automatic transaxles (fleet): 18.4 pts.
A413/A670 automatic transaxles with lockup: 17.0 pts.
A604: 18.2 pts.
② 7¼ in.: 3.0 pts.

8¼ in.: 4.4 pts.
③ Front axle: 2.6 pts.
④ Standard: 15 gal.
Optional: 20 gal.
⑤ Standard: 15 gal.

Optional: 22 gal.
⑥ Add 1 qt. when equipped with rear heater
⑦ Standard radiator: 14 qts.
Heavy duty radiator: 14.3 qts.

CAMSHAFT SPECIFICATIONS

All measurements given in inches.

Year	VIN	No. Cylinder Displacement cu. in. (liter)	Journal Diameter 1	2	3	4	5	Lobe Lift In.	Ex.	Bearing Clearance	Camshaft End Play
1986	C	4-135 (2.2)	1.375–1.376	1.375–1.376	1.375–1.376	1.375–1.376	1.375–1.376	NA	NA	—	0.005–0.020
	G	4-156 (2.6)	NA	NA	NA	NA	NA	①	①	0.002–0.004	0.004–0.008
1987	C	4-135 (2.2)	1.375–1.376	1.375–1.376	1.375–1.376	1.375–1.376	1.375–1.376	NA	NA	—	0.005–0.020
	K	4-153 (2.5)	1.375–1.376	1.375–1.376	1.375–1.376	1.375–1.376	1.375–1.376	NA	NA	—	0.005–0.020
	G	4.156 (2.6)	NA	NA	NA	NA	NA	①	①	0.002–0.004	0.004–0.008
	3	6-181 (3.0)	NA	NA	NA	NA	NA	②	②	—	NA
	M	6-239 (3.9)	1.998–1.999	1.967–1.968	1.951–1.952	1.561–1.562	—	0.373	0.400	0.001–0.005	0.002–0.010
1988	C	4-135 (2.2)	1.375–1.376	1.375–1.376	1.375–1.376	1.375–1.376	1.375–1.376	NA	NA	—	0.005–0.020
	K	4-153 (2.5)	1.375–1.376	1.375–1.376	1.375–1.376	1.375–1.376	1.375–1.376	NA	NA	—	0.005–0.020
	3	6-181 (3.0)	NA	NA	NA	NA	NA	②	②	—	NA
	X	6-239 (3.9)	1.998–1.999	1.967–1.968	1.951–1.952	1.561–1.562	—	0.373	0.400	0.001–0.005	0.002–0.010
1989	K	4-153 (2.5)	1.375–1.376	1.375–1.376	1.375–1.376	1.375–1.376	1.375–1.376	NA	NA	—	0.005–0.020
	J	4-153 (2.5)	1.375–1.376	1.375–1.376	1.375–1.376	1.375–1.376	1.375–1.376	NA	NA	—	0.005–0.020
	3	6-181 (3.0)	NA	NA	NA	NA	NA	②	②	—	NA
	X	6-239 (3.9)	1.998–1.999	1.967–1.968	1.951–1.952	1.561–1.562	—	0.373	0.400	0.001–0.005	0.002–0.010
1990	K	4-153 (2.5)	1.375–1.376	1.375–1.376	1.375–1.376	1.375–1.376	1.375–1.376	NA	NA	—	0.005–0.020
	J	4-153 (2.5)	1.375–1.376	1.375–1.376	1.375–1.376	1.375–1.376	1.375–1.376	NA	NA	—	0.005–0.013
	3	6-181 (3.0)	NA	NA	NA	NA	NA	②	②	—	NA
	R	6-201 (3.3)	1.997–1.999	1.980–1.982	1.965–1.967	1.949–1.952	—	0.400	0.400	0.001–0.005	0.005–0.012
	X	6-239 (3.9)	1.998–1.999	1.967–1.968	1.951–1.952	1.561–1.562	—	0.373	0.400	0.001–0.005	0.002–0.010

① Height of cam lobe: 1.661 in.
② Height of cam lobe: 1.604–1.624 in.

CHRYSLER CORPORATION
DAKOTA • CARAVAN/VOYAGER/TOWN & COUNTRY • RAM VAN

CRANKSHAFT AND CONNECTING ROD SPECIFICATIONS
All measurements are given in inches.

Year	VIN	No. Cylinder Displacement cu. in. (liter)	Crankshaft				Connecting Rod		
			Main Brg. Journal Dia.	Main Brg. Oil Clearance	Shaft End-play	Thrust on No.	Journal Diameter	Oil Clearance	Side Clearance
1986	C	4-135 (2.2)	2.362–2.363	0.0003–0.0031	0.002–0.007	3	1.968–1.969	0.0008–0.0034	0.005-0.013
	G	4-156 (2.6)	2.362	0.0008–0.0028	0.002–0.007	3	2.866	0.0008–0.0028	0.004–0.010
1987	C	4-135 (2.2)	2.362–2.363	0.0003–0.0031	0.002–0.007	3	1.968–1.969	0.0008–0.0034	0.005–0.013
	K	4-153 (2.5)	2.362–2.363	0.0003–0.0031	0.002–0.007	3	1.968–1.969	0.0008–0.0034	0.005–0.013
	G	4-156 (2.6)	2.362	0.0008–0.0028	0.002–0.007	3	2.866	0.0008–0.0028	0.004–0.010
	3	6-181 (3.0)	2.361–2.363	0.0006–0.0020	0.002–0.010	3	1.968–1.969	0.0008–0.0028	0.004–0.010
	M	6-239 (3.9)	2.500–2.501	①	0.002–0.010	2	2.124–2.125	0.0005–0.0022	0.006–0.014
1988	C	4-135 (2.2)	2.362–2.363	0.0003–0.0031	0.002–0.007	3	1.968–1.969	0.0008–0.0034	0.005–0.013
	K	4-153 (2.5)	2.362–2.363	0.0003–0.0031	0.002–0.007	3	1.968–1.969	0.0008–0.0034	0.005–0.013
	3	6-181 (3.0)	2.361–2.363	0.0006–0.0020	0.002–0.010	3	1.968–1.969	0.0008–0.0028	0.004–0.010
	X	6-239 (3.9)	2.500–2.501	①	0.002–0.010	2	2.124–2.125	0.0005–0.0022	0.006–0.014
1989	K	4-153 (2.5)	2.362–2.363	0.0003–0.0031	0.002–0.007	3	1.968–1.969	0.0008–0.0034	0.005–0.013
	J	4-153 (2.5)	2.362–2.363	0.0004–0.0023	0.002–0.010	3	1.968–1.969	0.0008–0.0034	0.005–0.013
	3	6-181 (3.0)	2.361–2.363	0.0006–0.0020	0.002–0.010	3	1.968–1.969	0.0008–0.0028	0.004–0.010
	X	6-239 (3.9)	2.500–2.501	①	0.002–0.010	2	2.124–2.125	0.0005–0.0022	0.006–0.014
1990	K	4-153 (2.5)	2.362–2.363	0.0003–0.0031	0.002–0.007	3	1.968–1.969	0.0008–0.0034	0.005–0.013
	J	4-153 (2.5)	2.362–2.363	0.0004–0.0023	0.002–0.010	3	1.968–1.969	0.0008–0.0034	0.005–0.013
	3	6-181 (3.0)	2.361–2.363	0.0006–0.0020	0.002–0.010	3	1.968–1.969	0.0008–0.0028	0.004–0.010
	R	6-201 (3.3)	2.519	0.0007–0.0022	0.001–0.007	2	2.283	0.0008–0.0030	0.005–0.015
	X	6-239 (3.9)	2.500–2.501	①	0.002–0.010	2	2.124–2.125	0.0005–0.0022	0.006–0.014

① No. 1: 0.0005–0.0015 in.
 Nos. 2-5: 0.0005–0.0025 in.

VALVE SPECIFICATIONS
All measurements given in inches.

Year	VIN	No. Cylinder Displacement cu. in. (liter)	Seat Angle (deg.)	Face Angle (deg.)	Spring Test Pressure (lbs.)	Spring Installed Height (in.)	Stem-to-Guide Clearance (in.) Intake	Exhaust	Stem Diameter (in.) Intake	Exhaust
1986	C	4-135 (2.2)	45	45	95	1.65	0.001–0.003	0.0030–0.0047	0.3124	0.3103
	G	4-156 (2.6)	45	45	61	1.59	0.001–0.004	0.002–0.006	0.3150	0.3150
1987	C	4-135 (2.2)	45	45	95	1.65	0.001–0.003	0.0030–0.0047	0.3124	0.3103
	K	4-153 (2.5)	45	45	115	1.65	0.001–0.003	0.0030–0.0047	0.3124	0.3103
	G	4.156 (2.6)	45	45	61	1.59	0.001–0.004	0.002–0.006	0.3150	0.3150
	3	6-181 (3.0)	44.5	45.5	73	1.59	0.001–0.002	0.002–0.003	0.313–0.314	0.312–0.313
	M	6-239 (3.9)	45	45	①	②	0.001–0.017	0.002–0.017	0.372–0.373	0.371–0.372
1988	C	4-135 (2.2)	45	45	95	1.65	0.001–0.003	0.0030–0.0047	0.3124	0.3103
	K	4-153 (2.5)	45	45	115	1.65	0.001–0.003	0.0030–0.0047	0.3124	0.3103
	3	6-181 (3.0)	44.5	45.5	73	1.59	0.001–0.002	0.002–0.003	0.313–0.314	0.312–0.313
	X	6-239 (3.9)	45	45	①	②	0.001–0.017	0.002–0.017	0.372–0.373	0.371–0.372
1989	K	4-153 (2.5)	45	45	115	1.65	0.001–0.003	0.0030–0.0047	0.3124	0.3103
	J	4-153 (2.5)	45	45	115	1.65	0.001–0.003	0.0030–0.0047	0.3124	0.3103
	3	6-181 (3.0)	44.5	45.5	73	1.59	0.001–0.002	0.002–0.003	0.313–0.314	0.312–0.313
	X	6-239 (3.9)	45	45	①	②	0.001–0.017	0.002–0.017	0.372–0.373	0.371–0.372
1990	K	4-153 (2.5)	45	45	115	1.65	0.001–0.003	0.0030–0.0047	0.3124	0.3103
	J	4-153 (2.5)	45	45	115	1.65	0.001–0.003	0.0030–0.0047	0.3124	0.3103
	3	6-181 (3.0)	44.5	45.5	73	1.59	0.001–0.002	0.002–0.003	0.313–0.314	0.312–0.313
	R	6-201 (3.3)	45	44.5	60	1.56	0.002–0.016	0.002–0.016	0.311–0.312	0.311–0.312
	X	6-239 (3.9)	45	45	①	②	0.001–0.017	0.002–0.017	0.372–0.373	0.371–0.372

① Intake: 170–184 lbs. Exhaust: 180–194 lbs.
② Intake: 1.625–1.688 in. Exhaust: 1.453–1.516 in.

PISTON AND RING SPECIFICATIONS
All measurements are given in inches.

Year	VIN	No. Cylinder Displacement cu. in. (liter)	Piston Clearance	Ring Gap Top Compression	Ring Gap Bottom Compression	Ring Gap Oil Control	Ring Side Clearance Top Compression	Ring Side Clearance Bottom Compression	Ring Side Clearance Oil Control
1986	C	4-135 (2.2)	0.0005–0.0015	0.010–0.021	0.011–0.021	0.015–0.035	0.0015–0.0031	0.0015–0.0031	0.0002–0.0080
	G	4-156 (2.6)	0.0008–0.0016	0.011–0.018	0.011–0.018	0.008–0.035	0.0024–0.0039	0.0024–0.0039	NA
1987	C	4-135 (2.2)	0.0005–0.0015	0.010–0.021	0.011–0.021	0.015–0.035	0.0015–0.0031	0.0015–0.0031	0.0002–0.0080
	K	4-153 (2.5)	0.0005–0.0015	0.010–0.021	0.011–0.021	0.015–0.035	0.0015–0.0031	0.0015–0.0031	0.0002–0.0080
	G	4-156 (2.6)	0.0008–0.0016	0.011–0.018	0.011–0.018	0.008–0.035	0.0024–0.0039	0.0008–0.0024	NA
	3	6-181 (3.0)	0.0008–0.0015	0.012–0.018	0.010–0.016	0.012–0.035	0.0020–0.0035	0.0008–0.0020	NA
	M	6-239 (3.9)	0.0005–0.0015	0.010–0.020	0.010–0.020	0.015–0.055	0.0015–0.0030	0.0015–0.0030	0.0002–0.0050
1988	C	4-135 (2.2)	0.0005–0.0015	0.010–0.021	0.011–0.021	0.015–0.035	0.0015–0.0031	0.0015–0.0031	0.0002–0.0080
	K	4-153 (2.5)	0.0005–0.0015	0.010–0.021	0.011–0.021	0.015–0.035	0.0015–0.0031	0.0015–0.0031	0.0002–0.0080
	3	6-181 (3.0)	0.0008–0.0015	0.012–0.018	0.010–0.016	0.012–0.035	0.0020–0.0035	0.0008–0.0020	NA
	X	6-239 (3.9)	0.0005–0.0015	0.010–0.020	0.010–0.020	0.015–0.055	0.0015–0.0030	0.0015–0.0030	0.0002–0.0050
1989	K	4-153 (2.5)	0.0005–0.0015	0.010–0.021	0.011–0.021	0.015–0.035	0.0015–0.0031	0.0015–0.0031	0.0002–0.0080
	J	4-153 (2.5)	0.0006–0.0018	0.010–0.020	0.008–0.019	0.015–0.055	0.0016–0.0030	0.0016–0.0030	0.0002–0.0080
	3	6-181 (3.0)	0.0008–0.0015	0.012–0.018	0.010–0.016	0.012–0.035	0.0020–0.0035	0.0008–0.0020	NA
	X	6-239 (3.9)	0.0005–0.0015	0.010–0.020	0.010–0.020	0.015–0.055	0.0015–0.0030	0.0015–0.0030	0.0002–0.0050
1990	K	4-153 (2.5)	0.0005–0.0015	0.010–0.021	0.011–0.021	0.015–0.035	0.0015–0.0031	0.0015–0.0031	0.0002–0.0080
	J	4-153 (2.5)	0.0006–0.0018	0.010–0.020	0.008–0.019	0.015–0.055	0.0016–0.0030	0.0016–0.0030	0.0002–0.0080
	3	6-181 (3.0)	0.0008–0.0015	0.012–0.018	0.010–0.016	0.012–0.035	0.0020–0.0035	0.0008–0.0020	NA
	R	6-201 (3.3)	0.0009–0.0022	0.012–0.022	0.012–0.022	0.010–0.040	0.0012–0.0037	0.0012–0.0037	0.0005–0.0089
	X	6-239 (3.9)	0.0005–0.0015	0.010–0.020	0.010–0.020	0.015–0.055	0.0015–0.0030	0.0015–0.0030	0.0002–0.0050

TORQUE SPECIFICATIONS
All readings in ft. lbs.

Year	VIN	No. Cylinder Displacement cu. in. (liter)	Cylinder Head Bolts	Main Bearing Bolts	Rod Bearing Bolts	Crankshaft Pulley Bolts	Flywheel Bolts	Manifold Intake	Manifold Exhaust	Spark Plugs
1986	C	4-135 (2.2)	①	30 ②	40 ②	50	70	17	17	26
	G	4-156 (2.6)	70	58	34	87	70	13	13	18
1987	C	4-135 (2.2)	①	30 ②	40 ②	50	70	17	17	26
	K	4-153 (2.5)	①	30 ②	40 ②	50	70	17	17	26
	G	4.156 (2.6)	70	58	34	87	70	13	13	18
	3	6-181 (3.0)	70	60	38	110	70	17	17	20
	M	6-239 (3.9)	105	85	45	135	55	45	④	30
1988	C	4-135 (2.2)	①	30 ②	40 ②	50	70	17	17	26
	K	4-153 (2.5)	①	30 ②	40 ②	50	70	17	17	26
	3	6-181 (3.0)	70	60	38	110	70	17	17	20
	X	6-239 (3.9)	105	85	45	135	55	45	④	30
1989	K	4-153 (2.5)	①	30 ②	40 ②	50	70	17	17	26
	J	4-153 (2.5)	①	30 ②	40 ②	50	70	17	17	26
	3	6-181 (3.0)	70	60	38	110	70	17	17	20
	X	6-239 (3.9)	105	85	45	135	55	45	④	30
1990	K	4-153 (2.5)	①	30 ②	40 ②	50	70	17	17	26
	J	4-153 (2.5)	①	30 ②	40 ②	50	70	17	17	26
	3	6-181 (3.0)	70	60	38	110	70	17	17	20
	R	6-201 (3.3)	③	30 ②	40 ②	40	70	17	17	30
	X	6-239 (3.9)	105	85	45	135	55	45	④	30

① Sequence: 45, 65, 65 plus ¼ turn
② Plus ¼ turn
③ Sequence: 45, 65, 65 plus ¼ turn, torque the small bolt in the rear of the head to 25 ft. lbs. last.
④ Bolts: 20 ft. lbs.
　 Nuts: 15 ft. lbs.

BRAKE SPECIFICATIONS
All measurements in inches unless noted

Year	Model	Lug Nut Torque (ft. lbs.)	Master Cylinder Bore	Brake Disc Minimum Thickness	Brake Disc Maximum Runout	Standard Brake Drum Diameter	Minimum Lining Thickness Front	Minimum Lining Thickness Rear
1986	Caravan	95	0.94	0.80	0.005	9	0.06	0.06
	Voyager	95	0.94	0.80	0.005	9	0.06	0.06
1987	Caravan	95	0.94	0.80	0.005	9	0.06	0.06
	Voyager	95	0.94	0.80	0.005	9	0.06	0.06
	Dakota	85	NA	0.81	0.004	9	0.06	0.06
1988	Caravan	95	0.94	0.80	0.005	9	0.06	0.06
	Voyager	95	0.94	0.80	0.005	9	0.06	0.06
	Dakota	85	NA	0.81	0.004	9	0.06	0.06
1989	Caravan	95	0.94	0.80	0.005	9	0.06	0.06
	Voyager	95	0.94	0.80	0.005	9	0.06	0.06
	Dakota	85	NA	0.81	0.004	9	0.06	0.06

BRAKE SPECIFICATIONS

All measurements in inches unless noted

Year	Model	Lug Nut Torque (ft. lbs.)	Master Cylinder Bore	Brake Disc Minimum Thickness	Brake Disc Maximum Runout	Standard Brake Drum Diameter	Minimum Lining Thickness Front	Minimum Lining Thickness Rear
1990	Caravan	95	0.94	0.80	0.005	9	0.06	0.06
	Voyager	95	0.94	0.80	0.005	9	0.06	0.06
	Town & Country	95	0.94	0.80	0.005	9	0.06	0.06
	Dakota	85	NA	0.81	0.004	9	0.06	0.06

WHEEL ALIGNMENT

Year	Model		Caster Range (deg.)	Caster Preferred Setting (deg.)	Camber Range (deg.)	Camber Preferred Setting (deg.)	Toe-in (in.)	Steering Axis Inclination (deg.)
1986	Caravan	front	①	②	0.25N–0.75P	0.30P	0.06	—
		rear	—	—	1.00N–0.50P	0.25N	0.00	—
	Voyager	front	①	②	0.25N–0.75P	0.30P	0.06	—
		rear	—	—	1.00N–0.50P	0.25N	0.00	—
1987	Caravan	front	①	②	0.25N–0.75P	0.30P	0.06	—
		rear	—	—	1.00N–0.50P	0.25N	0.00	—
	Voyager	front	①	②	0.25N–0.75P	0.30P	0.06	—
		rear	—	—	1.00N–0.50P	0.25N	0.00	—
	Dakota		0.50P–2.50P	1.50P	0–1P	0.50P	0.25	—
1988	Caravan	front	①	②	0.25N–0.75P	0.30P	0.06	—
		rear	—	—	1.00N–0.50P	0.25N	0.00	—
	Voyager	front	①	②	0.25N–0.75P	0.30P	0.06	—
		rear	—	—	1.00N–0.50P	0.25N	0.00	—
	Dakota		0.50P–2.50P	1.50P	0–1P	0.50P	0.25	—
1989	Caravan	front	①	②	0.25N–0.75P	0.30P	0.06	—
		rear	—	—	1.00N–0.50P	0.25N	0.00	—
	Voyager	front	①	②	0.25N–0.75P	0.30P	0.06	—
		rear	—	—	1.00N–0.50P	0.25N	0.00	—
	Dakota		0.50P–2.50P	1.50P	0–1P	0.50P	0.25	—
1990	Caravan	front	①	②	0.25N–0.75P	0.30P	0.06	—
		rear	—	—	1.00N–0.50P	0.25N	0.00	—
	Voyager	front	①	②	0.25N–0.75P	0.30P	0.06	—
		rear	—	—	1.00N–0.50P	0.25N	0.00	—
	Town & Country	front	①	②	0.25N–0.75P	0.30P	0.06	—
		rear	—	—	1.00N–0.50P	0.25N	0.00	—
	Dakota		0.50P–2.50P	1.50P	0–1P	0.50P	0.25	—

① Not adjustable; maximum variation between sides should not exceed 1.5°
② Van: 0.40P   Wagon: 0.70P

ENGINE ELECTRICAL

NOTE: Disconnecting the negative battery cable on some vehicles may interfere with the functions of the on board computer systems and may require the computer to undergo a relearning process, once the negative battery cable is reconnected.

Distributor

Removal and Installation

EXCEPT 3.3L ENGINE

1. Disconnect the negative battery cable.
2. Disconnect the distributor pickup lead wires and vacuum hose(s), if equipped. Remove the splash shield, if equipped.
3. Unfasten the distributor cap retaining clips or screws and lift off the distributor cap with all ignition wires still connected. Remove the coil wire if necessary.
4. Matchmark the rotor to the distributor housing.

NOTE: Do not crank the engine during this procedure. If the engine is cranked, the matchmark must be disregarded.

5. Remove the hold-down bolt and clamp.
6. Remove the distributor from the engine.

To install:

7. Install a new distributor housing O-ring.
8. Install the distributor in the engine so the rotor is lined up with the matchmark on the housing. Make sure the distributor is fully seated and that the distributor shaft is fully engaged.
9. If the engine has been cranked, position the engine so that the No. 1 piston is at TDC of the compression stroke and the mark on the vibration damper is lined up with **0** on the timing indicator. Then install the distributor so the rotor is aligned with the position of the No. 1 ignition wire on the distributor cap.

NOTE: There are distributor cap runners inside the cap on 3.0L engines. Make sure the rotor is pointing to where the No. 1 runner originates inside the cap and not where the No. 1 ignition wire plugs into the cap.

10. Install the hold-down clamp and snug the hold-down bolt. Connect the vacuum hose(s), if equipped.
11. Connect the distributor pickup lead wires. Install the splash shield, if equipped.
12. Install the distributor cap and snap the retaining clips into place or tighten the screws.
13. Connect the negative battery cable.
14. Adjust the ignition timing and tighten the hold-down bolt.

3.3L ENGINE

Ignition Coil

1. Disconnect the negative battery cable.
2. Remove the spark plug wires from the coil.
3. Disconnect the electrical connector.
4. Remove the coil fasteners.
5. Remove the coil from the ignition module.
6. The installation is the reverse of the removal procedure.

Crank Position Sensor

1. Disconnect the negative battery cable.
2. Disconnect the sensor lead at the harness connector.
3. Remove the sensor retainer bolt.
4. Pull the sensor straight up and out of the transaxle housing.
5. If the removed sensor is being reinstalled, clean off the old spacer completely and attach a new spacer to the sensor. If a

new spacer is not used, the sensor will not function properly. New sensors are equipped with a new spacer.

To install:

6. Install the sensor in the transaxle housing and push the sensor down until contact is made with the drive plate.
7. Hold in this position and install the retaining bolt. Torque to 9 ft. lbs. (12 Nm).
8. Connect the sensor lead wire.

Cam Position Sensor

1. Disconnect the negative battery cable.
2. Disconnect the sensor lead at the harness connector.
3. Loosen the sensor retaining bolt enough to allow the slot to slide past the bolt.
4. Pull the sensor (not by the wire) straight up and out of the chain case cover. Resistance may be high due to the presence of the rubber O-ring.

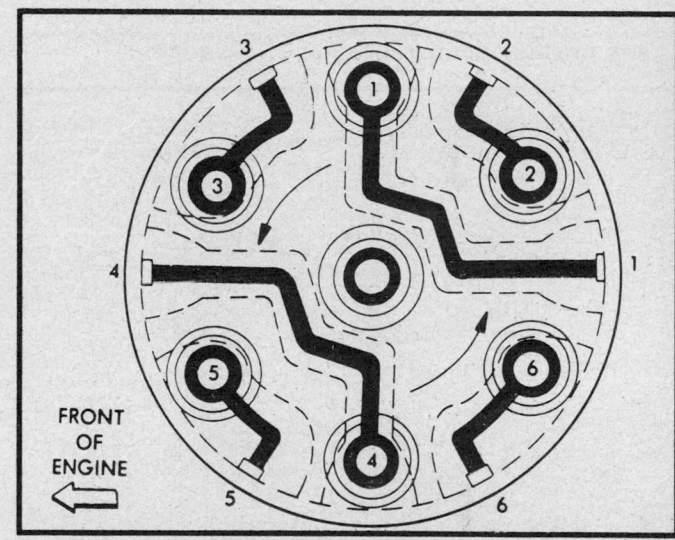

Distributor cap terminal routing—3.0L engine

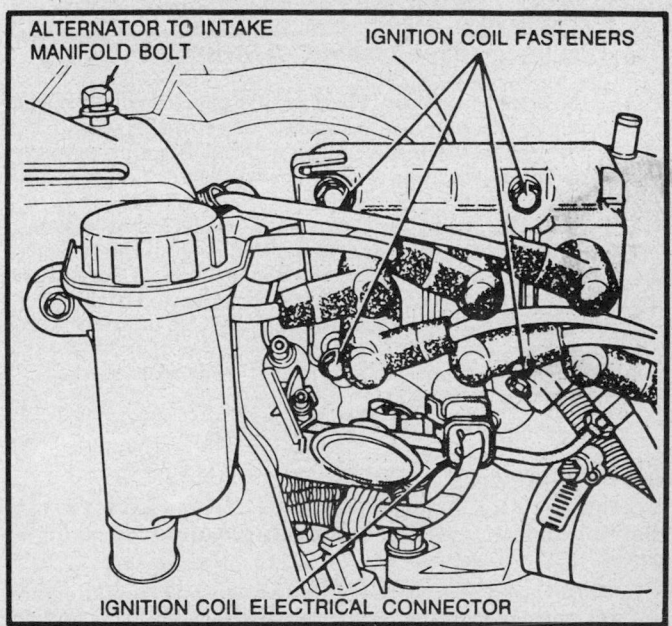

Ignition coil removal and installation—3.3L engine

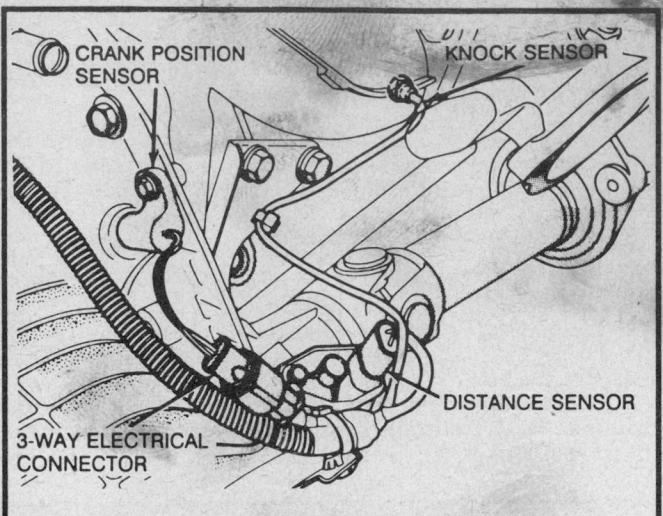

Crank position sensor location—3.3L engine

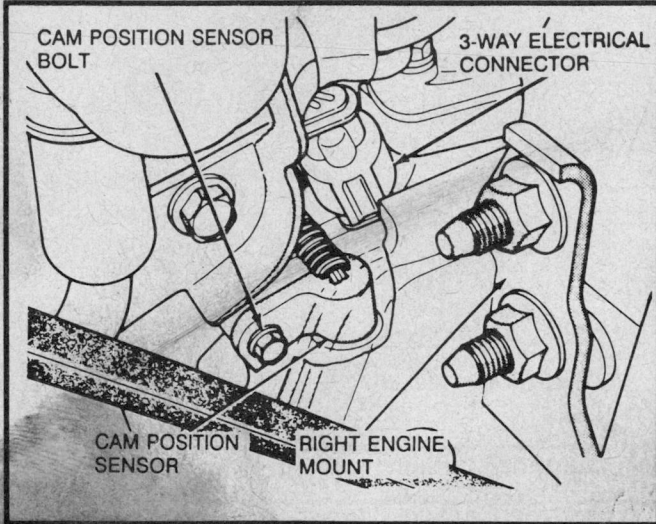

Cam position sensor location—3.3L engine

5. If the removed sensor is being reinstalled, clean off the old spacer completely and attach a new spacer to the sensor. If a new spacer is not used, the sensor will not function properly. New sensors are equipped with a new spacer.

To install:

6. Inspect the O-ring for damage and replace if necessary.

7. Lubricate the O-ring lightly with oil. Install the sensor to the chain case cover and push the sensor into its bore in the chain case cover until contact is made with the cam timing gear.

8. Hold in this position and tighten the bolt to 9 ft. lbs. (12 Nm).

9. Connect the connector and rout it away from the belt.

Ignition Timing

Adjustment

NOTE: The 3.3L engine is equipped with distributorless ignition; the timing cannot be changed or set.

1. Start the engine, set the parking brake and run the engine until at normal operating temperature. Keep all lights and accessories OFF.

2. If a magnetic timing unit is available, insert the probe into the receptacle near the timing scale. The scale is located near the crankshaft pulley on 2.6L, 3.0L and 3.9L engines and on the bell housing on 2.2L and 2.5L engines.

3. If a magnetic timing unit is not available, connect a conventional power timing light to the No. 1 cylinder spark plug wire.

4. Connect the red lead of a tachometer to the negative primary terminal of the coil and connect the black lead to a good ground.

5. Disconnect and plug the distributor vacuum advance hose at the computer or distributor. If the vehicle is equipped with a carbureted 2.2L engine, disconnect the carburetor 6-way electrical connector and remove the violet wire from the connector and reconnect the connector. This disables the electronic spark advance. Set the idle speed according to the Vehicle Emission Control Information (VECI) label.

6. If the vehicle is equipped with Electronic Fuel Injection (EFI), disconnect the coolant sensor located near the thermostat housing. The Check Engine lamp on the instrument panel must be ON. On 1989–90 vehicles, connect the Diagnostic Readout Box II (DRBII) and access the Basic Timing Mode. If the DRBII is not available, disconnect the coolant sensor located near the thermostat housing. The Check Engine lamp on the instrument panel must be ON.

7. Aim the timing light at the timing scale or read the magnetic timing unit.

8. Loosen the distributor hold-down bolt just enough so the disributor can be rotated.

9. Turn the distributor in the proper direction until the specified timing according to the VECI label is reached. Tighten the hold-down bolt and recheck the timing and idle speed.

10. Turn the engine off. Remove the jumper wire, if used. Connect the vacuum hose(s) or coolant sensor (make sure the Check Engine lamp does not come on when the vehicle is restarted). Disconnect the timing apparatus and tachometer. Reinstal the violet wire into the carburetor connector, if it was removed.

11. If the coolant temperature sensor was disconnected, erase the created fault code using the Erase Fault Code mode on the DRBII. If the DRBII is not available, the code can be erased by disconnecting the battery, although it is not recommended.

NOTE: If the battery is disconnected, radio memory will be lost and other fault codes that may have been stored in the computer's memory will be erased. If the coolant sensor code is not erased at this point, it will disappear after 50–100 vehicle key on/off cycles providing there is no problem with that circuit.

Alternator

For further information, please refer to "Electrical" in the Unit Repair section.

Belt Tension Adjustment

NOTE: The belt tension is automatically adjusted by a dynamic tensioner on the 3.0L and 3.3L engines. Periodic adjustment is not necessary.

1. Loosen the pivot bolt slightly.

2. Raise the vehicle and support safely, if necessary. Remove the splash shield, if equipped. Loosen the adjuster slot nut or bolt just enough so the alternator can be moved.

3. On 1987 Dakota, use a suitable pry bar and apply tension to the alternator until the belt(s) deflect about ¼–½ in. under a 10 lb. load. Torque the adjuster strap bolt to 17 ft. lbs. (23 Nm). Torque the pivot bolt to 30 ft. lbs. (41 Nm).

4. If the bracket is equipped with an adjuster bolt, first loosen the locknut, if equipped and tighten the bolt until the belt(s) de-

flect about ¼–½ in. under a 10 lb. load. Tighten the adjuster slot bolt and pivot bolt.

Removal and Installation

1. Disconnect the negative battery cable.
2. On some 2.2L and 2.5L engines, remove the air conditioning compressor and position it to the side. Remove the oil filter to allow the alternator to be removed from above, if possible.
3. On 3.0L and 3.3L engines, release the dynamic belt tensioner and remove the belt. On all other engines, loosen the mounting bolts, move the alternator toward the engine and remove the drive belt(s).
4. Remove the mounting bolts, spacers and adjuster bolt, if equipped and remove the alternator from the brackets.
5. Remove the battery positive, field and ground terminals from the rear of the alternator. Remove the wire harness hold-down screw from the alternator, if equipped.

To install:
6. Connect all wiring to the proper terminals on the rear of the alternator and install the wire harness hold-down screw, if equipped.
7. Position the alternator in the mounting brackets.
8. Install the spacers, pivot bolt, belt(s), adjuster slot bolt or nut and adjuster bolt, if equipped. Install the air conditioning compressor and oil filter, if they were removed.
9. Adjust the belt tension, if necessary.
10. Connect the negative battery cable.

Voltage Regulator

For further information, please refer to "Electrical" in the Unit Repair section.

Removal and Installation

NOTE: The voltage regulator is integrated into the circuitry of the Single Module Engine Controller (SMEC) or Single Board Engine Controller (SBEC) on vehicles equipped with EFI and is not serviceable. The voltage regulator is internally mounted in the alternator on vehicles equipped with the 2.6L engine.

1. Disconnect the negative battery cable.
2. Unplug the connector from the voltage regulator.
3. Remove the retaining screws and remove the regulator from the vehicle.
4. The installation is the reverse of the removal procedure. Make sure the connector retainer is properly clipped in place.

Starter

For further information, please refer to "Electrical" in the Unit Repair section.

Removal and Installation

1. Disconnect the negative battery cable.
2. On 2.2L and 2.5L engines, remove the attaching nut and bolt at the top of the bell housing. Raise the vehicle and support safely.
3. Remove the rear mount from the starter, if equipped. Remove the heat shield from the starter, if equipped.
4. Unbolt the starter, remove the exhaust bracket and automatic transmission oil cooler tube bracket, if equipped and remove the starter from the vehicle.
5. Disconnect the solenoid lead wires from the starter.

To install:
6. Connect the solenoid lead wires and install the heat shield, if equipped.

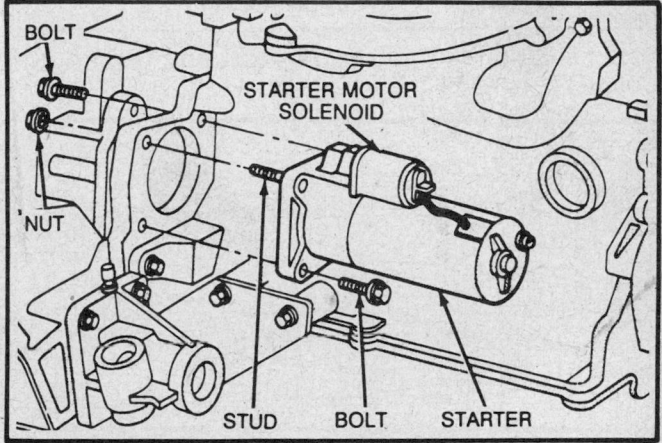

Removing or installing the starter—2.2L and 2.5L engines

7. On the 3.9L engine, install the starter to the bellhousing and install the mounting bolt loosely. Install the automatic transmission oil cooler tube bracket and exhaust bracket, if equipped. Install the lower mounting nut. Torque both to 50 ft. lbs. (68 Nm).
8. On the 2.2L and 2.5L engines, install the lower bolt loosely, then lower the vehicle and install the nut and bolt from above and torque to 40 ft. lbs. (54 Nm). Then raise the vehicle again and torque the bottom bolt to the same value. Install the rear mount to the starter.
9. On 3.0L and 3.3L engines, install all mounting bolts and torque to 40 ft. lbs. (54 Nm) evenly.
10. Connect the negative battery cable and check the starter for proper operation.

CHASSIS ELECTRICAL

Heater Blower Motor

Removal and Installation

CARAVAN, VOYAGER AND TOWN & COUNTRY

1. Disconnect the negative battery cable.
2. Disconnect the blower motor lead under the right side of the instrument panel.
3. Remove 5 attaching screws securing the blower to the heater A/C housing.
4. Lower the blower from its cavity and remove it from the vehicle.
5. Remove the fan from the blower.
6. The installation is the reverse of the removal procedure.
7. Connect the negative battery cable and check the blower motor for proper operation.

With Rear Heater

1. Disconnect the negative battery cable.
2. Remove the middle bench, if equipped. Remove the left lower quarter trim panel.

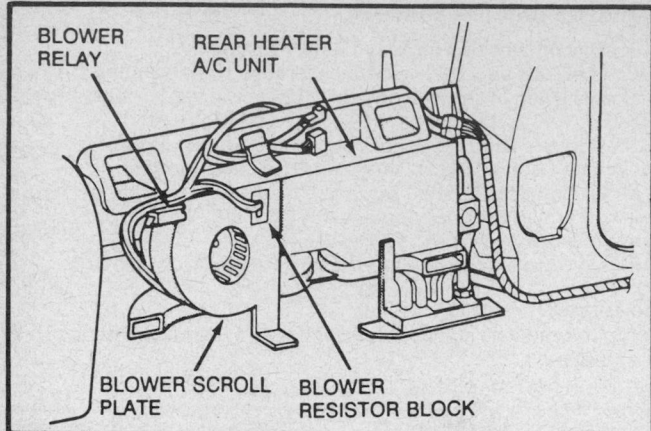

Rear heater unit—Caravan, Voyager and Town & Country

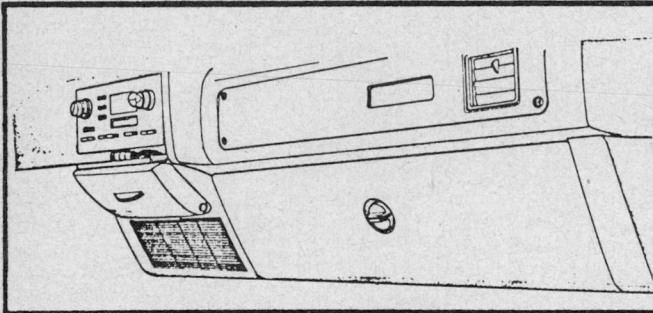

Lower instrument panel module—Dakota

3. Remove 1 blower scroll cover to floor screw and 7 schroll to unit screws.
4. Remove the blower relay.
5. Rotate the blower scroll cover from under the unit.
6. Remove the fan from the blower motor, remove the 3 motor attaching screws and remove the motor from the unit.
7. The installation is the reverse of the removal procedure.
8. Connect the negative battery cable and check the blower motor for proper operation.

DAKOTA

1. Disconnect the negative battery cable.
2. Remove the steering column cover, intermittent wiper control and the lower instrument panel module retaining screw to the right of the steering column.
3. Remove the center distribution duct retaining screws and panel support screw at the bottom of the module.
4. Remove the courtesy lamp at the lower right corner of the module and the screw near the ash receiver.
5. Open the glovebox and remove the screws along the top edge.
6. Move the module out and down far enough to unclip the wiring harness and antenna cable and disconnect the speaker wire (if equipped with monaural radio) and glovebox light wire. Remove the module from the vehicle.
7. If the vehicle is equipped with air conditioning, disconnect the 2 vacuum lines from the recirculating air door actuator and disconnect the blower lead wires.
8. Remove 2 screws at the top of the blower housing, 5 screws from around the housing and remove the blower housing from the unit.
9. Remove 3 screw attaching the blower to the unit and remove the blower from the vehicle.

10. Remove the fan from the blower motor.
To install:
11. Install the fan to the blower motor and secure the clip.
12. Install the blower to the unit and install the blower housing.
13. Connect the 2 vacuum lines from the recirculating air door actuator, if equipped and connect the blower lead wires.
14. Hold the module in position and clip the wiring harness and antenna cable in place and connect the speaker wire (if equipped with monaural radio) and glovebox light wire.
15. Install the retaining screws along the top of the inside of the glovebox.
16. Install the courtesy lamp at the lower right corner of the module and the screw near the ash receiver.
17. Install the panel support screw at the bottom of the module and the center distribution duct retaining screws and .
18. Install the lower instrument panel module retaining screw to the right of the steering column, intermittent wiper control and the steering column cover.
19. Connect the negative battery cable and check the blower motor for proper operation.

Windshield Wiper Motor

Removal and Installation

CARAVAN, VOYAGER AND TOWN & COUNTRY

1. Disconnect the negative battery cable.
2. Remove the wiper arms.
3. Open the hood and remove the cowl top plenum grille and the plastic screen.
4. Remove the wiper pivot retaining screws and push the pivots down into the plenum chamber.
5. Remove the nut from the wiper motor output shaft and remove the linkage assembly from the motor.
6. Disconnect the wiper motor harness, remove the mounting nuts and remove the motor from the vehicle.
7. The installation is the reverse of the removal procedure.
8. Connect the negative battery cable and check the wipers for proper operation.

DAKOTA

1. Disconnect the negative battery cable.
2. Disconnect the connector from the motor.
3. Remove the wiper arms, raise the hood and remove the cowl panel.
4. Hold the drive crank with a wrench while remove the crank nut. Remove the drive crank.
5. Remove the mounting nuts and remove the motor from the vehicle.
6. The installation is the reverse of the removal procedure.
7. Connect the negative battery cable and check the wipers for proper operation.

Liftgate Wiper System

Removal and Installation

CARAVAN, VOYAGER AND TOWN & COUNTRY

1. Disconnect the negative battery cable.
2. Remove the liftgate wiper using the special removal tool.

--- **CAUTION** ---

Prying the arm off of the shaft with a prying device could damage the arm permanently and possibly cause it to pop off of the shaft while in operation causing poor rear vision for the driver and a dangerous situation for the driver behind. Do not bend or push the spring clip at the base of the arm to release the arm; it is self-releasing. Use only the indicated tool.

3. Open the liftgate and remove the trim panel.

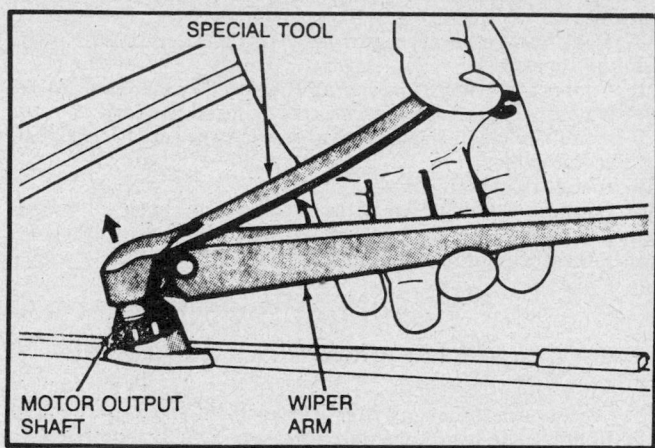

Removing the liftgate wiper arm

4. Remove the motor mounting screws, disconnect the wiring harness and remove the motor from the liftgate.
4. The installation is the reverse of the removal procedure.
5. Connect the negative battery cable and check the rear wiper for proper operation.

Windshield Wiper Switch

Removal and Installation
EXCEPT TILT WHEEL

1. Disconnect the negative battery cable.
2. Remove the lower steering column cover, if equipped.
3. Remove the horn pad mounting screws from behind the steering wheel and remove the horn pad.
4. Remove the steering wheel nut, matchmark the steering wheel to the shaft and remove the steering wheel with a suitable puller.
5. Remove the plastic wiring channel from the underside of the steering column.
6. Disconnect the wiper switch connector, intermittent wipe module connector and cruise control connector, if equipped.
7. Remove the side lock housing cover.
8. Remove the slotted hex-head screw that attaches the wiper switch to the turn signal switch and remove the switch.
9. Remove the control knob from the end of the stalk. Pull the round nylon hider up the control stalk and remove the revealed screws that attach the control stalk sleeve to the wiper switch.
10. Rotate the control stalk shaft to the full clockwise position and remove the shaft from the wiper switch by pulling it straight out.
To install:
11. Install the control shaft to the wiper switch, install the screws, the hider and the control knob.
12. Run the wiring through the opening and down the steering column, position the switch and install the hex-head screw. Make sure the dimmer switch rod is properly engaged.
13. Install the side lock housing cover.
14. Connect the wires and install the wiring channel.
15. Install the steering wheel torque the nut to 45 ft. lbs. (61 Nm).
16. Install the horn pad.
17. Connect the negative battery cable and check the wiper and washer, cruise control, turn signal switch and dimmer switch for proper operation.
18. Install the lower column cover, if equipped.
TILT WHEEL

1. Disconnect the negative battery cable.

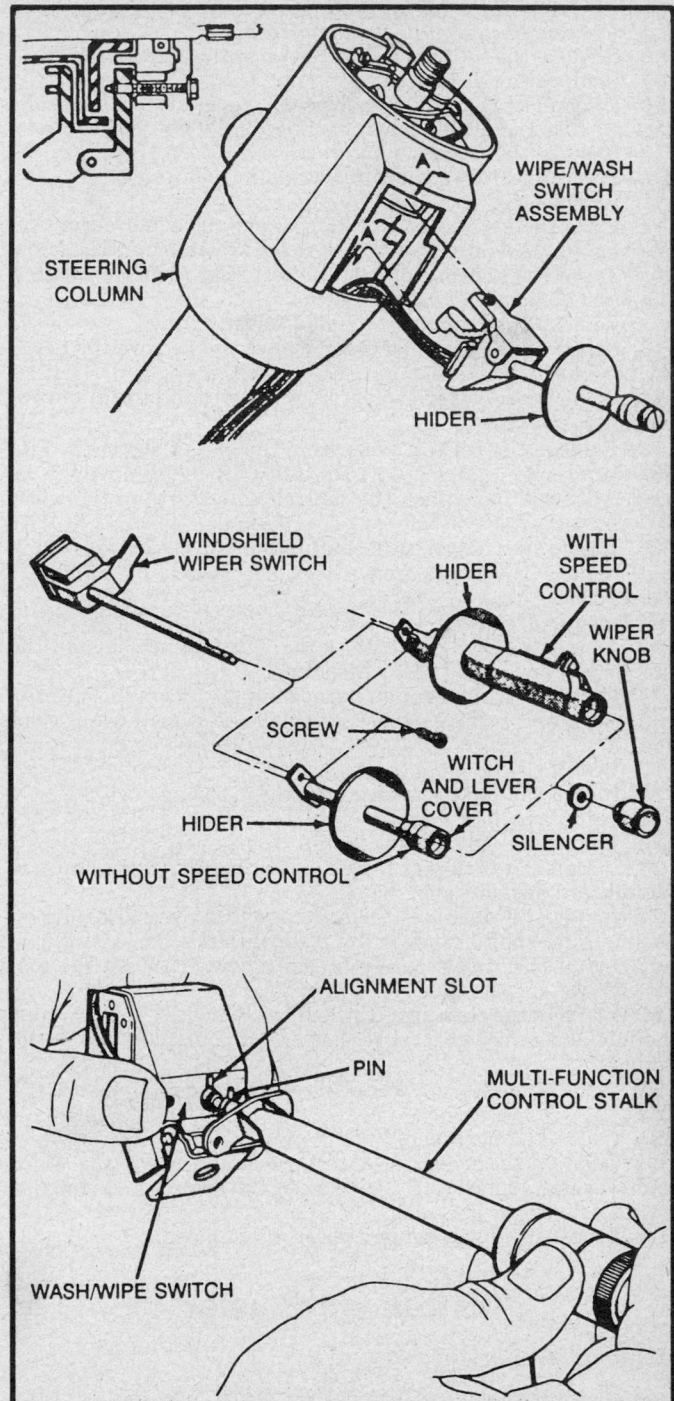

Removing the wiper switch—except tilt wheel

2. Remove the lower steering column cover, if equipped and remove the plastic wiring channel from the underside of the steering column.
3. Remove the horn pad mounting screws from behind the steering wheel and remove the horn pad.
4. Remove the steering wheel nut, matchmark the steering wheel to the shaft and remove the steering wheel with a suitable puller.
5. Depress the lock plate with the proper depressing tool, re-

move the retaining ring from its groove and remove the tool, ring, lock plate, cancelling cam and spring.

6. Remove the switch stalk actuator screw and arm.

7. Remove the hazard switch knob.

8. Disconnect the turn signal switch, wiper switch, intermittent module and cruise control connectors, if equipped.

9. Remove the 3 screws and remove the turn signal switch. Tape the connector to the wires to aid in removal.

10. Remove the ignition key lamp.

11. Place the key in the **LOCK** position and remove the key. Insert a thin tool into the slot next to the switch mounting screw boss, depress the spring latch at the bottom of the slot releasing the lock. Remove the lock cylinder.

12. Remove the buzzer switch and wedge spring.

13. Remove the 3 housing cover screws and remove the housing cover.

14. Remove the wiper switch pivot pin with a punch and remove the switch.

15. Remove the control knob from the end of the stalk. Pull the round nylon hider up the control stalk and remove the revealed screws that attach the control stalk sleeve to the wiper switch.

16. Rotate the control stalk shaft to the full clockwise position and remove the shaft from the wiper switch by pulling it straight out.

To install:

17. Install the control shaft to the wiper switch, install the screws, the hider and the control knob.

18. Run the wiring through the opening and down the steering column, position the switch and install the wiper switch pivot pin.

19. Install the housing cover.

20. Install the buzzer switch and wedge spring.

21. Install the lock cylinder.

22. Install the ignition key lamp.

23. Install the turn signal switch, switch stalk actuator arm and hazard switch knob.

24. Install the spring, cancelling cam, lock plate and ring on the steering shaft. Depress the plate with the depressing tool and install the ring securely in the groove. Remove the tool slowly.

25. Connect the turn signal switch, wiper switch, intermittent module and cruise control connectors, if equipped. Install the trough.

26. Install the steering wheel torque the nut to 45 ft. lbs. (61 Nm).

27. Install the horn pad.

28. Connect the negative battery cable and check the wiper and washer, cruise control, turn signal switch and dimmer switch for proper operation.

29. Install the lower column cover, if equipped.

Instrument Cluster

Removal and Installation

1. Disconnect the negative battery cable.

2. Remove the instrument cluster bezel. Cluster removal is not necessary if just removing gauges.

3. When only removing gauge(s) or the speedometer, remove the trip odometer reset knob if equipped, remove the mask and lens assembly and remove the desired gauge from the cluster. Disconnect the speedometer cable if removing the speedometer.

4. If equipped with automatic transmission or transaxle, remove the lower column cover and disconnect the gear indicator cable.

5. Remove the screws attaching the cluster to the instrument panel.

6. Pull the cluster out and disconnect all wiring and the speedometer cable. Remove the cluster from the vehicle.

To install:

7. Postion the cluster and feed the gear indicator cable through its slot.

8. Connect all wiring and install the speedometer cable to the speedometer. Make sure it is securely clicked in place.

9. Install the cluster retaining screws. Connect the gearshift indicator cable.

10. Install the cluster bezel.

11. Connect the negative battery cable and check all gauges and the speedometer for proper operation. Kake sure the gearshift indicator is properly aligned.

Headlight Switch

CARAVAN, VOYAGER AND TOWN & COUNTRY

1. Disconnect the negative battery cable.

2. Remove the headlight and accessory switch trim bezel.

3. Remove the switch plate from the lower panel, pull the assembly out and disconnect the wiring.

4. Depress the spring button and remove the headlight switch knob and stem.

5. Remove the headlight switch retainer and remove the switch.

6. The installation is the reverse of the removal procedure.

DAKOTA

1. Disconnect the negative battery cable.

2. Remove the steering column cover and remove the instrument panel bezel. Two screws are hidden behind the steering column cover.

3. Remove the screws from the headlight switch bezel, pull the assembly out and disconnect the wiring.

4. Remove the nut retaining the bezel to the bracket. Depress the spring button on the right side of the switch and remove the headlight switch knob and stem.

5. Remove the spanner nut and remove the switch.

6. The installation is the reverse of the removal procedure.

Dimmer Switch

Removal and Installation

1. Disconnect the negative battery cable.

2. Remove the lower steering column cover, if equipped.

3. Unplug the switch.

4. Holding the actuating rod against its upper seat, remove the bolts that attach the switch to the column and remove the switch.

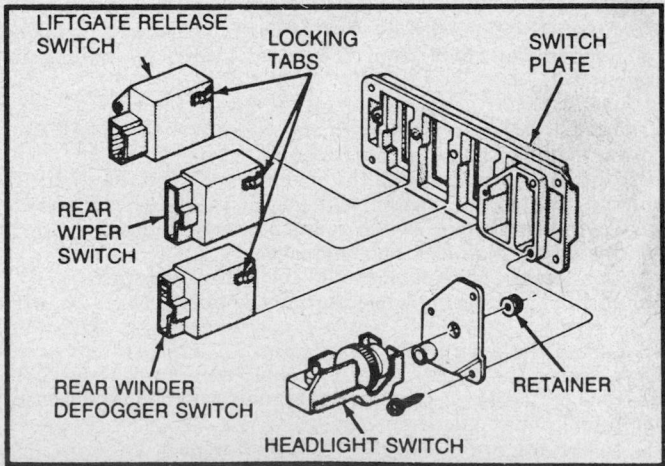

Headlight and accessory switch removal and Installation—Caravan, Voyager and Town & Country

5. The installation is the reverse of the removal procedure. Adjust the switch as required.

6. Connect the negative battery cable and check the switch for proper operation.

Turn Signal Switch

Removal and Installation

EXCEPT TILT COLUMN

1. Disconnect the negative battery cable.
2. Remove the lower steering column cover, if equipped.
3. Remove the horn pad mounting screws from behind the steering wheel and remove the horn pad.
4. Remove the steering wheel nut, matchmark the steering wheel to the shaft and remove the steering wheel with a suitable puller.
5. Remove the plastic wiring channel from the underside of the steering column and disconnect the turn signal switch connector.
6. Remove the hazard switch knob. Remove the slotted hex-head screw that attaches the wiper switch to the turn signal switch.
7. Remove the 3 screws and pull the turn signal switch out of the column.

To install:

8. Run the wiring through the opening and down the steering column, position the switch and install the hex-head screw. Make sure the dimmer switch rod is properly engaged.
9. Install the 3 screws and the hazard switch knob.
10. Connect the wires and install the wiring channel.
11. Install the steering wheel torque the nut to 45 ft. lbs. (61 Nm).
12. Install the horn pad.
13. Connect the negative battery cable and check the turn signal switch and dimmer switch for proper operation.
14. Install the lower column cover, if equipped.

TILT COLUMN

1. Disconnect the negative battery cable.
2. Remove the lower steering column cover, if equipped and remove the plastic wiring channel from the underside of the steering column.
3. Remove the horn pad mounting screws from behind the steering wheel and remove the horn pad.
4. Remove the steering wheel nut, matchmark the steering wheel to the shaft and remove the steering wheel with a suitable puller.
5. Depress the lock plate with the proper depressing tool, remove the retaining ring from its groove and remove the tool, ring, lock plate, cancelling cam and spring.
6. Remove the stalk actuator screw and arm.
7. Remove the hazard switch knob.
8. Disconnect the turn signal switch connector.
9. Remove the 3 screws and remove the turn signal switch. Tape the connector to the wires to aid in removal.

To install:

10. Run the wiring through the opening and down the steering column, install the turn signal switch, switch stalk actuator arm and hazard switch knob.
11. Install the spring, cancelling cam, lock plate and ring on the steering shaft. Depress the plate with the depressing tool and install the ring securely in the groove. Remove the tool slowly.
12. Connect the turn signal switch connector and install the channel.
13. Install the steering wheel torque the nut to 45 ft. lbs. (61 Nm).
14. Install the horn pad.

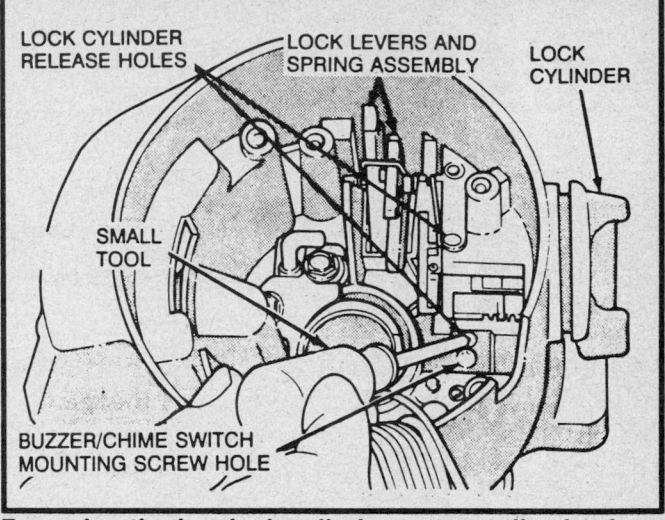

Removing the key lock cylinder – except tilt wheel

15. Connect the negative battery cable and check the turn signal switch and dimmer switch for proper operation.
16. Install the lower column cover, if equipped.

Ignition Lock

Removal and Installation

EXCEPT TILT COLUMN

1. Disconnect the negative battery cable.
2. Remove the horn pad mounting screws from behind the steering wheel and remove the horn pad.
3. Remove the steering wheel nut, matchmark the steering wheel to the shaft and remove the steering wheel with a suitable puller.
4. Remove the hazard switch knob. Remove the slotted hex-head screw that attaches the wiper switch to the turn signal switch.
5. Remove the 3 screws and pull the turn signal switch out of the column as far as it will go. Unplug it below if necessary.
6. Remove the ignition switch key lamp.
7. Place the key in the **LOCK** position and remove the key.
8. Insert 2 suitable small diameter tools into both release holes and push inward to release the spring loaded lock retainers while simultaneously pulling the key lock cylinder out of its bore.

To install:

9. Install the key cylinder.
10. Install the ignition switch key lamp.
11. Install the turn signal switch and hazard switch knob. Connect the wires if they were disconnected.
12. Install the steering wheel torque the nut to 45 ft. lbs. (61 Nm).
13. Install the horn pad.
14. Connect the negative battery cable and check the lock cylinder for proper operation.
15. Install the lower column cover, if equipped.

TILT COLUMN

1. Disconnect the negative battery cable.
2. Remove the horn pad mounting screws from behind the steering wheel and remove the horn pad.
3. Remove the steering wheel nut, matchmark the steering wheel to the shaft and remove the steering wheel with a suitable puller.
4. Depress the lock plate with the proper depressing tool, re-

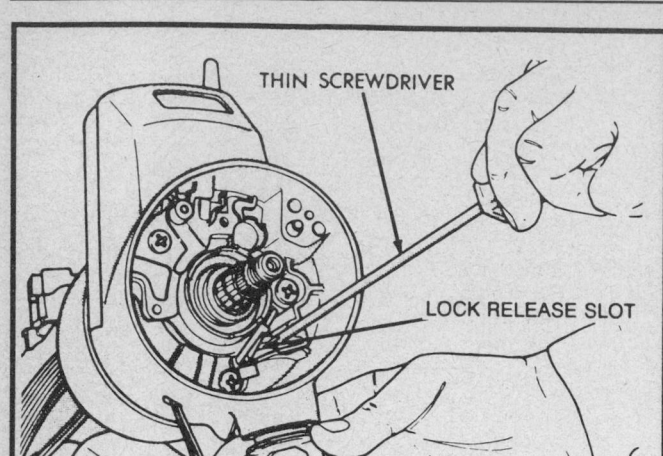

Removvng the key lock cylinder—tilt column

move the retaining ring from its groove and remove the tool, ring, lock plate, cancelling cam and spring.

5. Remove the stalk actuator screw and arm.
6. Remove the hazard switch knob.
7. Remove the 3 screws and pull the turn signal switch out of the column as far as it will go. Unplug it below if necessary.
8. Remove the ignition key lamp.
9. Place the key in the **LOCK** position and remove the key. Insert a thin tool into the slot next to the switch mounting screw boss, depress the spring latch at the bottom of the slot releasing the lock and remove the lock cylinder.

To install:
10. Install the lock cylinder.
11. Install the ignition key lamp.
12. Install the turn signal switch, switch stalk actuator arm and hazard switch knob.
13. Install the spring, cancelling cam, lock plate and ring on the steering shaft. Depress the plate with the depressing tool and install the ring securely in the groove. Remove the tool slowly.
14. Connect the wires if they were disconnected.
15. Install the steering wheel torque the nut to 45 ft. lbs. (61 Nm).
16. Install the horn pad.
17. Connect the negative battery cable and check the turn signal switch for proper operation.
18. Install the lower column cover, if it was removed.

Stoplight Switch

Removal and Installation

1. Disconnect the negative battery cable.
2. Remove the switch mounting bracket assembly from the brake pedal bracket.
3. Remove the switch from its bracket.
4. The installation is the reverse of the removal procedure.
5. Connect the negative battery cable and check the switch for proper operation.

Fuses and Circuit Breakers

Location

In all vehicles, the fuse block is located to the left of the steering column, covered by a removeable access panel.

ENGINE COOLING

Radiator

Removal and Installation

1. Disconnect the negative battery cable.
2. Open the radiator petcock and drain the antifreeze. Once the antifreeze has stopped draining, close the petcock.
3. Remove the upper hose and coolant reserve tank hose from the radiator.
4. If equipped with an electric cooling fan, remove the fan assembly.
5. If equipped with a belt driven fan, remove the shroud from the radiator and position it away from the radiator.
6. Raise the vehicle and support safely. Remove the lower hose from the radiator.
7. Disconnect the automatic transmission or transaxle cooler hoses, if equipped and plug them.
8. Remove the mounting screws and carefully lift the radiator out of the engine compartment.

To install:
9. Lower the radiator into position and install the mounting screws.
10. Raise the vehicle and support safely if necessary. Connect the automatic transmission or transaxle cooler lines, if they were removed.
11. Connect the lower hose.
12. Install the shroud or electric cooling fan.
13. Connect the upper hose and coolant reserve tank hose.
14. Fill the system with coolant.
15. Connect the negative battery cable, run the vehicle until the thermostat opens, fill the radiator completely and check the automatic transmission or transaxle fluid level, if equipped.
16. Once the vehicle has cooled, recheck the coolant level.

Electric Cooling Fan

Removal and Installation

1. Disconnect the negative battery cable.
2. Unplug the connector.
3. Remove the mounting screws.
4. Remove the fan assembly from the vehicle.
5. The installation is the reverse of the removal procedure.

Testing

──────────── CAUTION ────────────
Make sure the key is in the OFF position when checking the electric cooling fan. If not, the fan could turn on at any time, causing serious personal injury.
────────────────────────────────

1. Unplug the fan connector.
2. Using a jumper wire, connect the female terminal of the fan connector to the negative battery terminal.
3. The fan should come on when the other wire is connected to the positive battery terminal.
4. If not, the fan is defective and should be replaced.

Heater Core

Removal and Installation

CARAVAN AND VOYAGER
WITHOUT AIR CONDITIONING

1. Disconnect the negative battery cable. Drain the cooling system.
2. Remove the lower steering column cover.
3. Remove the lower reinforcement under the steering column, right side cowl and sill trim. Remove the bolt holding the right side instrument panel to the right cowl.
4. Loosen the 2 brackets supporting the lower edge of the heater housing. Remove the instrument panel trim covering and reinforcement. Remove the retaining screws from the right side to the steering column.
5. Disconnect the vacuum line at the brake booster.
6. Clamp off the heater hoses near the heater core and remove the hoses from the core tubes. Plug the hose ends and the core tubes to prevent spillage of coolant. Remove the heater assembly retaining nuts at the firewall.
7. Disconnect the blower motor wiring, resistor wiring and the temperature control cable. Disconnect the hanger strap from the package and rotate it out of the way.
8. Pull the right side of the instrument panel out as far as possible. Fold the carpeting and insulation back to provide a little more working room and to prevent spillage from staining the carpeting.
9. Pull the heater core assembly out from under instrument panel and remove it from the vehicle.
10. Disassemble the heater unit by removing the retaining screws from the cover. Remove the cover and the temperature control rod.
11. Remove the retaining screw from the heater core and remove the core from the housing assembly.

To install:

12. Clean out the inside of the housing. Wrap the heater core with foam tape and place it in position. Secure it with its screw.
13. Assemble the heater unit.
14. Install the assembly to the vehicle and install the nuts to the firewall. Fold the carpeting back into position.
15. Connect the hanger strap from the package and rotate it out of the way. Install the 2 brackets supporting the lower edge of the heater housing. Connect the blower motor wiring, resistor wiring and the temperature control cable.
16. Install the retaining screws from the right side to the steering column. Install the instrument panel trim covering and reinforcement.
17. Install the bolt holding the right side instrument panel to the right cowl. Install the lower reinforcement under the steering column, right side cowl and sill trim.
18. Install the heater hoses to the core tubes.
19. Connect the vacuum line at the brake booster.
20. Fill the cooling system.
21. Connect the negative battery cable and check the heater for proper operation and leaks.

CARAVAN, VOYAGER AND TOWN & COUNTRY
WITH AIR CONDITIONING

1. Disconnect the negative battery cable. Properly discharge the A/C system. Drain the cooling system.
2. Remove the lower steering column cover.
3. Remove the lower reinforcement under the steering column, right side cowl and sill trim. Remove the bolt holding the right side instrument panel to the right cowl.
4. Loosen the 2 brackets supporting the lower edge of the heater housing. Remove the instrument panel trim covering and reinforcement. Remove the retaining screws from the right side to the steering column.

5. Disconnect the vacuum lines at the brake booster and water valve.
6. Clamp off the heater hoses near the heater core and remove the hoses from the core tubes. Plug the hose ends and the core tubes to prevent spillage of coolant.
7. Disconnect the H-valve connection at the valve and remove the H-valve. Remove the retaining nuts from the package mounting studs at the firewall. Remove the condensation tube.
8. Disconnect the blower motor wiring, resistor wiring and the temperature control cable. Disconnect the vacuum harness at the connection at the top of the heater unit.
9. Disconnect the hanger strap from the package and rotate it out of the way.
10. Pull the right side of the instrument panel out as far as possible. Fold the carpeting and insulation back to provide a little more working room and to prevent spillage from staining the carpeting.
11. Remove the entire housing assembly from the dash panel and remove it from the vehicle.
12. To disassemble the housing assembly, remove the vacuum diaphragm and retaining screws from the cover and remove the cover.
13. Remove the retaining screw from the heater core and remove the core from the housing assembly.

To install:

14. Remove the temperature control door from the unit and clean the unit out with solvent. Lubricate the lower pivot rod and its well and install. Wrap the heater core with foam tape and place it in position. Secure it with its screw.
15. Assemble the unit, making sure all vacuum tubing is properly routed.
16. Install the assembly to the vehicle and connect the vacuum harness. Install the nuts to the firewall and install the condensation tube. Fold the carpeting back into position.
17. Connect the hanger strap from the package and rotate it out of the way. Install the 2 brackets supporting the lower edge of the heater housing. Connect the blower motor wiring, resistor wiring and the temperature control cable.
18. Install the retaining screws from the right side to the steering column. Install the instrument panel trim covering and reinforcement.
19. Install the bolt holding the right side instrument panel to the right cowl. Install the lower reinforcement under the steering column, right side cowl and sill trim.
20. Connect the vacuum lines at the brake booster and water valve.
21. Connect the heater hoses to the core tubes.
22. Using new gaskets, install the H-valve and connect the hose connection at the valve.
23. Evacuate and recharge the air conditioning system.
24. Fill the cooling system.
25. Connect the negative battery cable and check the entire climate control system for proper operation and leakage.

DAKOTA WITHOUT AIR CONDITIONING

1. Disconnect the negative battery cable. Drain the coolant.
2. Remove the steering column cover, intermittent wiper control, if equipped and the lower instrument panel module retaining screw to the right of the steering column.
3. Remove the center distribution duct retaining screws and panel support screw at the bottom of the module.
4. Remove the courtesy lamp at the lower right corner of the module and the screw near the ash tray.
5. Open the glovebox and remove the screws along the top edge.
6. Move the module out and down far enough to unclip the wiring harness and antenna cable and disconnect the speaker wire (if equipped with monaural radio) and glovebox light wire. Remove the module from the vehicle.
7. Remove the center air distribution duct.

8. Remove the antenna wire from retaining clip at the right end of the heater unit.

9. Disconnect the blower motor connector and remove the thermal insulator retainer from the heater unit.

10. Disconnect the demister hoses from the adaptor at the top of the heater unit.

11. Disconnect the vacuum feed line from the check valve.

12. Disconnect the temperature control cable flag retainer from the heater unit.

13. Remove the adjusting clip from the blend air door crank.

14. Disconnect the heater hoses from the core tubes and plug them.

15. Remove 4 heater unit attaching nuts from the rear engine compartment dash panel.

16. Remove the heater unit support attaching screw and rotate the brace out of the way.

17. Remove the heater unit from the vehicle.

18. To disassemble the housing assembly, vacuum diaphragm and retaining screws from the cover and remove the cover.

19. Remove the retaining screw from the heater core and remove the core from the housing assembly.

To install:

20. Remove the temperature control door from the unit and clean the unit out with solvent. Lubricate the lower pivot rod and its well and install. Wrap the heater core with foam tape and place it in position. Secure it with its screw.

21. Assemble the unit, making sure all vacuum tubing is properly routed.

22. Install the assembly to the vehicle and connect the vacuum harness. Install the nuts to the firewall. Install the support brace to the heater unit.

23. Connect the demister hoses to the adaptor at the top of the heater unit.

24. Connect the blower motor connector and install the thermal insulator retainer to the heater unit.

25. Connect the vacuum feed line to the check valve.

26. Connect the temperature control cable flag retainer to the heater unit and install the adjusting clip from the blend air door crank.

27. Install the center air distribution duct.

28. Install the antenna wire from retaining clip at the right end of the heater unit.

29. Install the instrument panel module and all related parts.

30. Connect the heater hoses to the core tubes.

31. Fill the cooling system.

32. Connect the negative battery cable and check the heater for proper operation and leakage.

DAKOTA WITH AIR CONDITIONING

1. Disconnect the negative battery cable. Properly discharge the air conditioning system. Drain the coolant.

2. Remove the steering column cover, intermittent wiper control and the lower instrument panel module retaining screw to the right of the steering column.

3. Remove the center distribution duct retaining screws and panel support screw at the bottom of the module.

4. Remove the courtesy lamp at the lower right corner of the module and the screw near the ash tray.

5. Open the glovebox and remove the screws along the top edge.

6. Move the module out and down far enough to unclip the wiring harness and antenna cable and disconnect the speaker wire (if equipped with monaural radio) and glovebox light wire. Remove the module from the vehicle.

7. Remove the center air distribution duct.

8. Remove the antenna wire from retaining clip at the right end of the heater unit.

9. Disconnect the blower motor connector and remove the thermal insulator retainer from the heater unit.

10. Disconnect the demister hoses from the adaptor at the top of the heater unit.

11. Disconnect the vacuum harness connector from the air conditioning control hose and vacuum feed line from the check valve.

12. Disconnect the temperature control cable flag retainer from the heater unit and remove the adjusting clip from the blend air door crank.

13. Disconnect the heater hoses from the core tubes and plug them.

14. Remove the condensation drain tube.

15. Remove 4 heater-A/C unit attaching nuts from the rear engine compartment dash panel.

16. Remove the heater-A/C unit support attaching screw and rotate the brace out of the way.

17. Remove the heater-A/C unit from the vehicle.

18. To disassemble the housing assembly, vacuum diaphragm and retaining screws from the cover and remove the cover.

19. Remove the retaining screw from the heater core and remove the core from the housing assembly.

To install:

20. Remove the temperature control door from the unit and clean the unit out with solvent. Lubricate the lower pivot rod and its well and install. Wrap the heater core with foam tape and place it in position. Secure it with its screw.

21. Assemble the unit, making sure all vacuum tubing is properly routed.

22. Install the assembly to the vehicle and connect the vacuum harness. Install the nuts to the firewall and install the condensation tube. Install the support brace to the heater-A/C unit.

23. Connect the demister hoses to the adaptor at the top of the heater unit.

24. Connect the blower motor connector and install the thermal insulator retainer to the heater unit.

25. Connect the vacuum harness connector to the air conditioning control hose and vacuum feed line to the check valve.

26. Connect the temperature control cable flag retainer to the heater unit and install the adjusting clip from the blend air door crank.

27. Install the center air distribution duct.

28. Install the antenna wire from retaining clip at the right end of the heater unit.

29. Install the instrument panel module and all related parts.

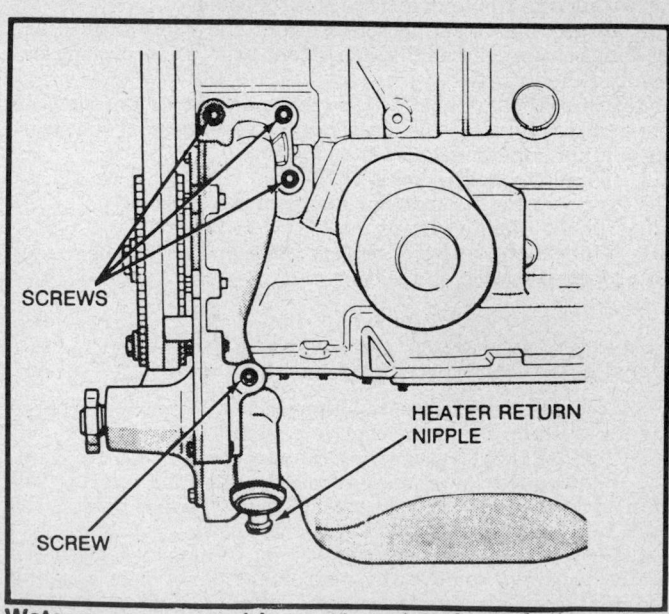

Water pump assembly—2.2L and 2.5L engines

30. Connect the heater hoses to the core tubes.

31. Using new gaskets, install the H-valve and connect the hose connection at the valve.

32. Evacuate and recharge the air conditioning system.

33. Fill the cooling system.

34. Connect the negative battery cable and check the entire climate control system for proper operation and leakage.

Water Pump

Removal and Installation

2.2L AND 2.5L ENGINES

1. Disconnect the negative battery cable.

2. Drain the cooling system.

3. If the vehicle is equipped with air conditioning, remove the compressor from the bracket and position it to the side.

4. Raise the vehicle and support safely, if necessary and remove the alternator and bracket. Remove the pulley from the water pump.

5. Disconnect the lower radiator hose and heater hose from the water pump.

6. Remove the water pump housing attaching screws and remove the assembly from the vehicle. Discard the O-ring.

7. Remove the water pump from the housing.

To install:

8. Using a new gasket or silicone sealer, install the water pump to the housing.

9. Install a new O-ring to the housing and install to the engine. Torque the bolts to 21 ft. lbs. (30 Nm).

10. Install the water pump pulley. Connect the radiator hose and heater hose to the water pump.

11. Install all items removed to gain access to the water pump and adjust the belts.

12. Remove the hex-head plug on the top of the thermostat housing (some carbureted engines have a vacuum switching valve at that location). Fill the radiator with coolant until the coolant comes out the plug hole. Install the plug or valve and continue to fill the radiator.

13. Connect the negative battery cable, run the vehicle until the thermostat opens, fill the radiator completely and check for leaks.

14. Once the vehicle has cooled, recheck the coolant level.

2.6L ENGINE

1. Disconnect the negative battery cable.

2. Drain the cooling system. Remove the air cleaner assembly.

3. Remove the radiator hose, bypass hose and heater hose from the water pump.

4. Remove the drive pulley shield.

5. Remove the locking screw and pivot screws.

6. Remove the water pump retaining bolts and remove the water pump from the engine. Discard the O-ring from the body.

7. Remove the pump from the pump body.

To install:

8. Using a new gasket, install the water pump to the pump body.

9. Install a new O-ring to the pump body and install to the engine.

10. Install the mounting screws finger tight. Adjust the belt tension and torque the bolts to 17 ft. lbs. (23 Nm).

11. Install the pulley shield.

12. Install the radiator hose, bypass hose and heater hose to the water pump.

13. Install the air cleaner assembly.

14. Fill the radiator with coolant. This cooling system has a self-bleeding thermostat, so system bleeding is not required.

15. Connect the negative battery cable, run the vehicle until the thermostat opens, fill the radiator completely and check for leaks.

16. Once the vehicle has cooled, recheck the coolant level.

3.0L ENGINE

1. Disconnect the negative battery cable.

2. Drain the cooling system.

3. Remove the timing cover If the same timing belt will be re-used, mark the direction of the timing belt's rotation, for installation in the same direction. Make sure the engine is positioned so the No. 1 cylinder is at the TDC of it's compression stroke and the sprockets timing marks are aligned with the engine's timing mark indicators.

4. Loosen the timing belt tensioner bolt and remove the belt. Position the tensioner as far away from the center of the engine

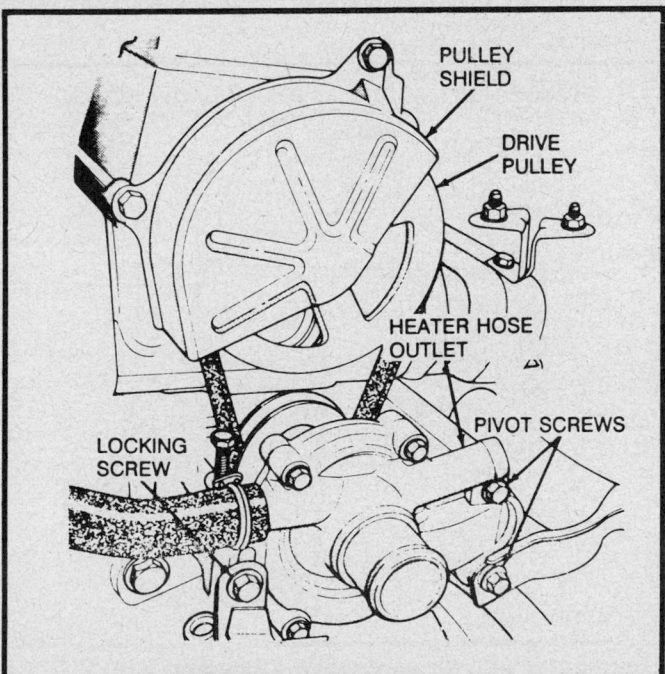

Water pump assembly—2.6L engine

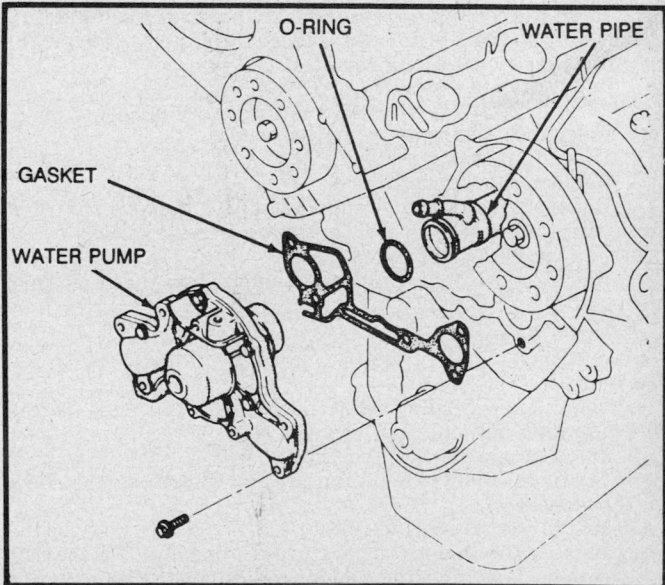

Water pump assembly—3.0L engine

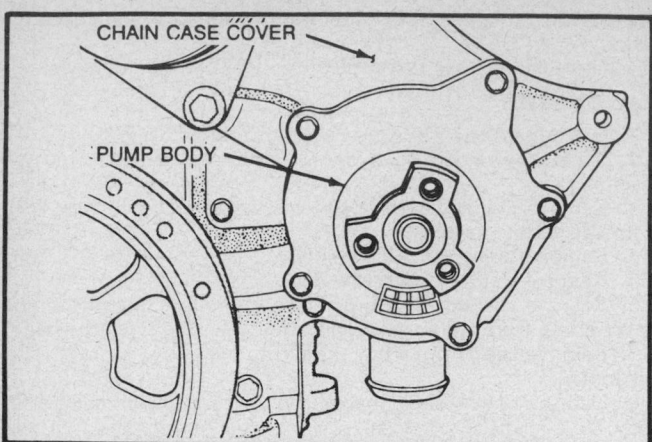

Water pump assembly – 3.3L engine

as possible and tighten the bolt. Remove the water pump mounting bolts, separate the pump from the water inlet pipe and remove the pump from the engine.

To install:

5. Install the pump with a new gasket to the engine. Torque the water pump mounting bolts to 20 ft. lbs. (27 Nm).

6. If not already done, position both camshafts so the marks line up with those on the alternator bracket (rear bank) and inner timing cover (front bank). Rotate the crankshaft so the timing mark aligns with the mark on the oil pump.

7. Install the timing belt on the crankshaft sprocket and while keeping the belt tight on the tension side (right side), install the belt on the front camshaft sprocket.

8. Install the belt on the water pump pulley, then the rear camshaft sprocket and the tensioner.

9. Rotate the front camshaft counterclockwise to tension the belt beween the front camshaft and the crankshaft. If the timing marks came out of line, repeat the procedure.

10. Install the crankshaft sprocket flange.

11. Loosen the tensioner bolt and allow the spring to tension the belt.

12. Turn the crankshaft 2 full turns in the clockwise direction only until the timing marks align again. Now that the belt is properly tensioned, torque the tensioner lock bolt to 21 ft. lbs. (29 Nm).

13. Refill the cooling system. This system uses a self-bleeding thermostat, so there is no need to bleed the system. Connect the negative battery cable and road test the vehicle.

3.3L ENGINE

1. Disconnect the negative battery cable.
2. Drain the cooling system.
3. Remove the serpentine belt.
4. Raise the vehicle and support safely. Remove the right front tire and wheel assembly and lower fender shield.
5. Remove the water pump pulley.
6. Remove the 5 mounting screws and remove the pump from the engine.
7. Discard the O-ring.

To install:

8. Using a new O-ring, install the pump to the engine. Torque the mounting bolts to 21 ft. lbs. (30 Nm).
9. Install the water pump pulley.
10. Install the fender shield and tire and wheel assembly. Lower the vehicle.
11. Install the serpentine belt.
12. Remove the engine temperature sending unit. Fill the radiator with coolant until the coolant comes out the sending unit hole. Install the sending unit and continue to fill the radiator.

13. Connect the negative battery cable, run the vehicle until the thermostat opens, fill the radiator completely and check for leaks.

14. Once the vehicle has cooled, recheck the coolant level.

3.9L ENGINE

1. Disconnect the negative battery cable. Drain the coolant.
2. Remove the shroud from the radiator and slide it over the fan.
3. Remove the radiator and lower hose.
4. Remove the fan blade, spacer or viscous drive unit, pully, bolts and shroud together. Remove the air pump belt and power steering pump belt.

NOTE: Do not place the viscous fan in an upright position because the silicone fluid in the drive could drain into the bearing and contaminate its lubricant.

5. Loosen the alternator mounting bolts and remove the alternator/air conditioning or idler pulley belts.

6. Remove the alternator bracket. On 1988–90 vehicles, this bracket also supports the air conditioning compressor or idler pulley, which will remain supported by its rear mount.

7. Remove the air pump. Remove the air pump bracket and unbolt the power steering pump bracket with the pump still attached and position it out of the way.

8. Disconnect the heater hose and bypass hose.

9. On 1987 vehicles with air conditioning, remove the air conditioning compressor pulley and field coil assembly, if necessary to remove the water pump to compressor front mount bolts and bracket.

10. Remove the remaining pump retaining bolts (if any) and remove the pump from the engine.

To install:

11. Clean and dry the pump mating surfaces. Install a new bypass hose to the engine.

12. Install a new gasket and install the water pump to the engine.

13. Install any bolts that do not retain a bracket. Tighten the bypass hose clamps. Install the heater hose.

14. Install the water pump to compressor front mount bolts and bracket, if it was removed.

15. Install all remaining brackets and components that were

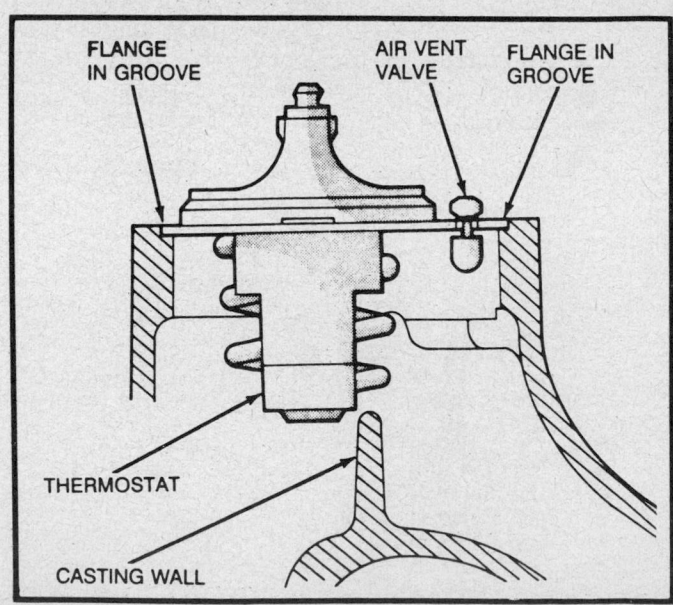

Thermostat with air vent valve – 2.6L and 3.0L engines

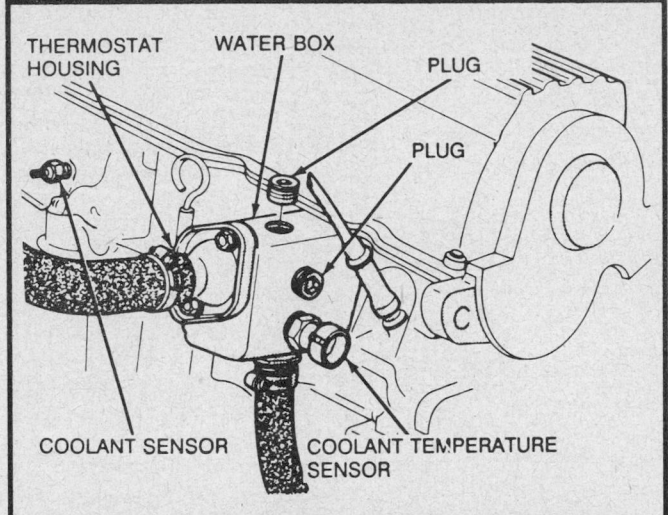

Cooling system bleed plug—2.2L and 2.5L engines

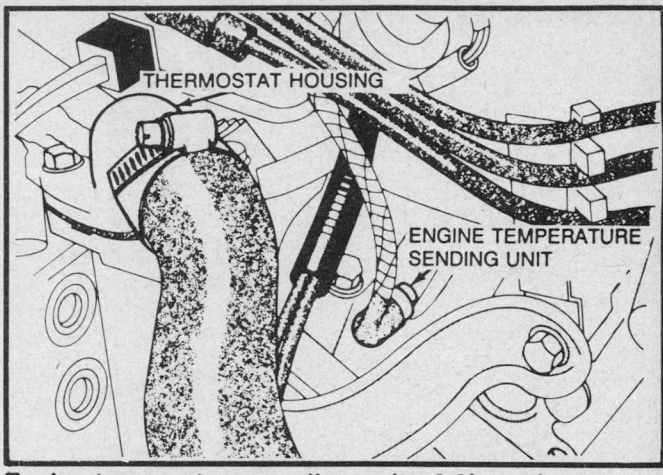

Engine temperature sending unit—3.3L engine

removed during the removal procedure. Torque all water pump retaining bolts that do not go through adjusting slots to 30 ft. lbs. (41 Nm).

16. Install the air conditioning compressor pulley and field coil assembly, if it was removed. Install and adjust the alternator/air conditioning or idler belts. Place the remaining belts over their components.

17. Install the fan blade, spacer or viscous drive unit, pully and bolts along with the shroud.

18. Install the radiator, lower hose and shroud.

19. Adjust all belts and torque the remaining water pump retaining bolts to 30 ft. lbs. (41 Nm).

20. Fill the radiator with coolant. This cooling system is self-bleeding, so system bleeding is not required.

21. Connect the negative battery cable, run the vehicle until the thermostat opens, fill the radiator completely and check for leaks.

22. Once the vehicle has cooled, recheck the coolant level.

Thermostat

Removal and Installation

1. Disconnect the negative battery cable. Drain the coolant down to thermostat level or below.

2. Remove the thermostat housing.

3. Remove the thermostat and discard the gasket.

4. Clean the housing mating surfaces and use a new gasket.

5. The installation is the reverse of the removal procedure.

6. On 2.2L and 2.5L engines, remove the hex-head plug or vacuum switching valve on the thermostat housing. Fill the radiator with coolant until the coolant comes out the plug hole. Install the plug or valve and continue to fill the radiator. On the 3.3L engine, remove the engine temperature sending unit. Fill the radiator with coolant until the coolant comes out the sending unit hole. Install the sending unit and continue to fill the radiator. All other engines are self-bleeding.

7. Connect the negative battery cable, run the vehicle until the thermostat opens, fill the radiator completely and check for leaks.

8. Once the vehicle has cooled, recheck the coolant level.

Cooling System Bleeding

The thermostat in the 2.6L and 3.0L engines is equipped with a small air vent valve that allows trapped air to bleed from the system during refilling. This valve negates the need for cooling system bleeding in those engines. The 3.9L engine cooling system is also self-bleeding and does not require bleeding when refilling.

To bleed air from the 2.2L and 2.5L engines, remove the 8mm hex-head plug on the top of the thermostat housing (some carbureted engines have a vacuum switching valve at that location). On the 3.3L engine, remove the engine temperature sending unit. Fill the radiator with coolant until the coolant comes out the hole. Install the plug, valve or switch and continue to fill the radiator. This will vent all trapped air from the engine.

FUEL SYSTEM

Fuel System Service Precaution

Relieving Fuel System Pressure

EXCEPT 3.9L ENGINE

1. Loosen the fuel filler cap to release fuel tank pressure.

2. Locate the fuel injector harness connector.

3. Connect a jumper wire from terminal No. 1 of the appropriate connector to ground.

4. Being careful not to allow contact between the jumper wire to terminal No. 2 of the connector and touch the other end of the jumper to the positive battery post for no longer than 5 seconds. This will relieve fuel pressure.

5. Remove the jumper wires and connect the connector.

3.9L ENGINE

1. Loosen the fuel filler cap to release fuel tank pressure.

2. Locate the fuel injector harness connector.

3. Connect a jumper wire from either of the end pins in the connector to ground.

4. Being careful not to allow contact between the jumper leads, connect a jumper wire to the pin next to the one that is grounded and touch the other end of the jumper to the positive battery post for no longer than 5 seconds. This will relieve fuel pressure.

5. Remove the jumper wires and connect the connector.

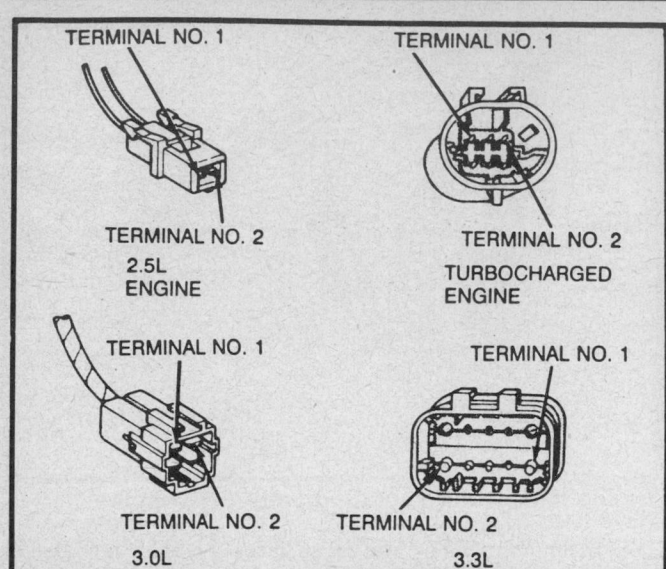

Fuel injector harness connector terminals—except 3.9L engine

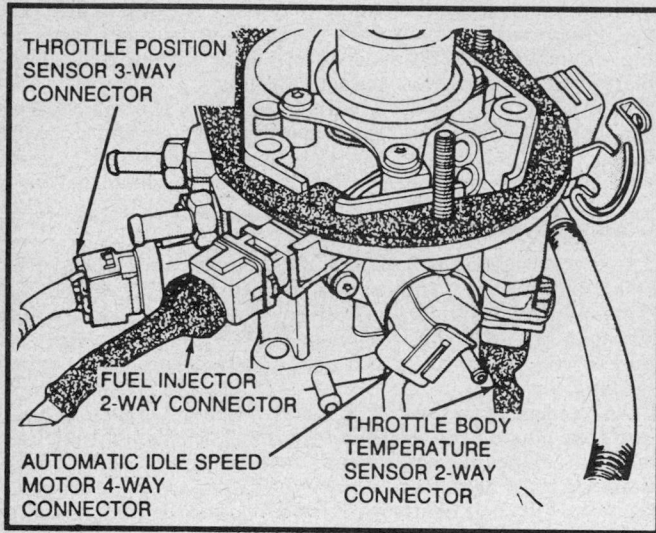

Fuel injector harness connector location—2.5L non-turbocharged engine

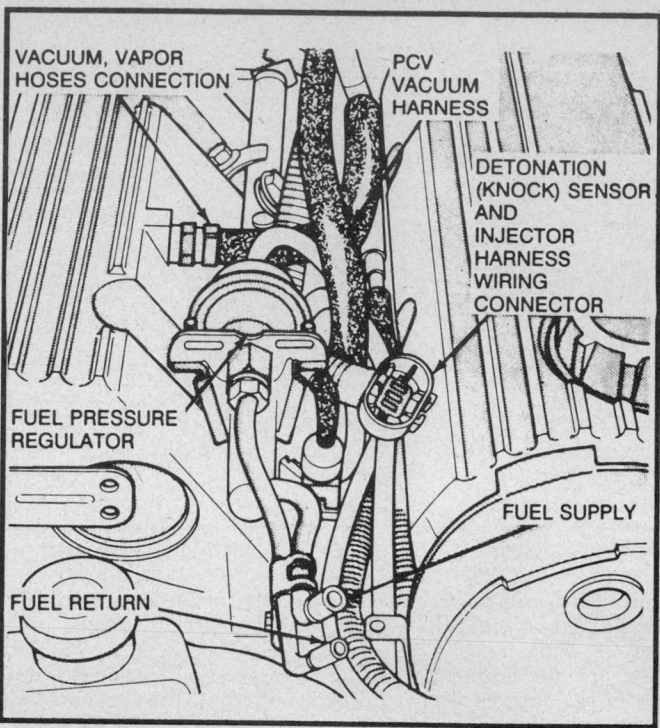

Fuel injector harness connector location—2.5L turbocharged engine

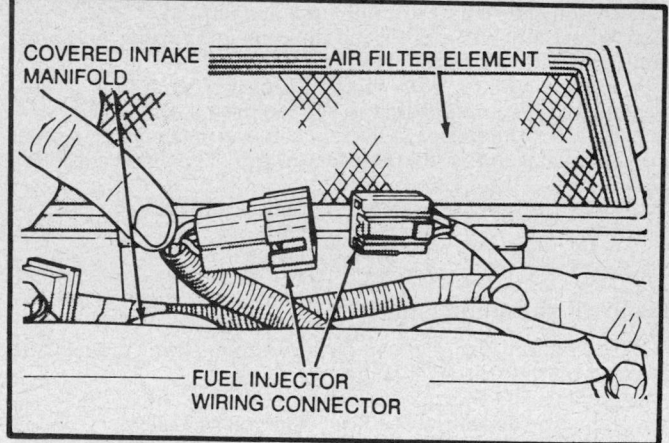

Fuel injector harness connector location—3.0L engine

Fuel Filter

Removal and Installation

CARBURETED ENGINE

1. Disconnect the negative battery cable.
2. Raise the vehicle and support safely, if necessary.
3. Remove the air cleaner assembly, if necessary. On 2.6L engine, remove the black carburetor bracket. Remove the fuel filter and any hoses that are included with the new filter kit.

NOTE: Some vehicles may be equipped with a field package designed to combat driveability problems associated with fuel foaming. Affected vehicles have a special replaceable filter/reservoir mounted either on a plate on the carburetor or near the thermostat. When the kit is installed on a 2.2L engine, the conventional filter is discarded. Do not install a conventional filter or conventional clamps or hoses in place of the special replacement parts; they are not compatible with the electronic fuel pump installed with the kit.

4. Install the new filter, hoses and clamps.
5. Connect the negative battery cable, start the engine and check for leaks.

FUEL INJECTED ENGINE

— CAUTION —

Do not use conventional fuel filters, hoses or clamps when servicing this fuel system. They are not compatible with the injection system and could

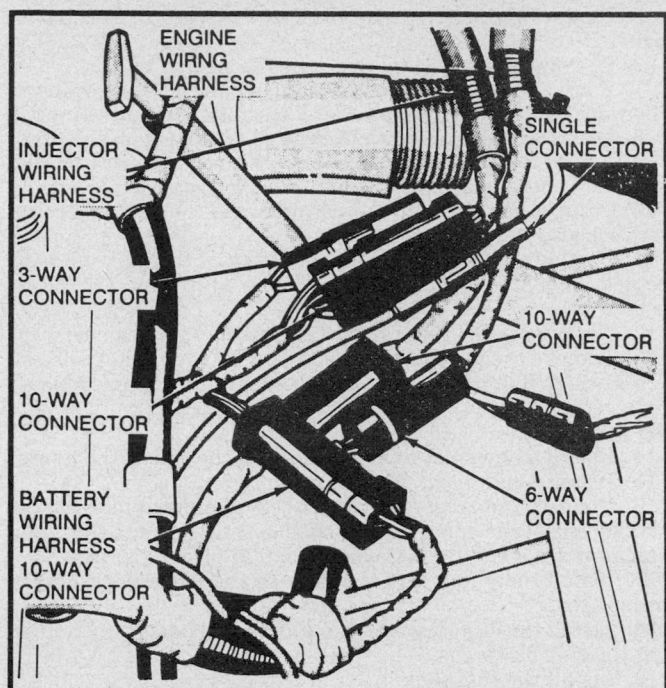

Fuel injector harness connector location—3.3L engine

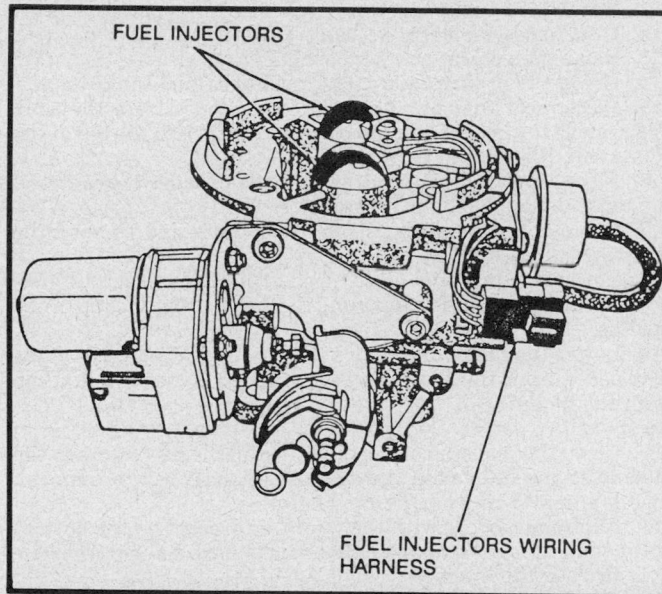

Injector wiring harness connector—3.9L engine

fail, causing personal injury or damage to the vehicle. Use only hoses and clamps specifically designed for fuel injection.

1. Relieve the fuel pressure.
2. Disconnect the negative battery cable.
3. The filter is located on the frame rail toward the rear of the vehicle. Raise the vehicle and support safely. Remove the filter retaining screw and remove the filter assembly from the mounting plate.
4. Loosen the outlet hose clamp on the filter and inlet hose clamp on the rear fuel tube.

5. Wrap a shop towel around the hoses to absorb fuel. Remove the hoses from the filter and fuel tube and discard the clamps and the filter.

To install:

6. Install the inlet hose on the fuel tube and tighten the new clamp to 10 inch lbs.
7. Install the outlet hose on the filter outlet fitting and tighten the new clamp to 10 inch lbs.
8. Position the filter assembly on the mounting plate and tighten the mounting screw to 75 inch lbs. (8 Nm).
9. Connect the negative battery cable, start the engine and check for leaks.

Mechanical Fuel Pump

Pressure Testing

1. Raise the vehicle and support safely.
2. Connect a pressure gauge (0–15 psi minimum range) to the fuel pump outlet fitting.
3. Crank the engine several times while observing the gauge.
4. The 2.2L and 2.6L engines should develop 4.5–6.0 psi. The 1987 3.9L engine should develop 5.75–7.25 psi. (1988–90 3.9L engines are equipped with an electric fuel pump). If the vehicle is equipped with the field package noted above, fuel pressure should be 13–15 psi.

Removal and Installation

1. Disconnect the negative battery cable.
2. Raise the vehicle and support safely, if necessary.
3. Disconnect the fuel lines from the pump and plug them.
4. Remove the fuel pump retaining bolts or nuts and remove the pump from the engine.
5. Clean and dry the mounting surfaces and bolt holes.
6. The installation is the reverse of the removal procedure. Use new gaskets and an insulator, if equipped.
7. Connect the negative battery cable, start the engine and check for leaks.

Electric Fuel Pump

Pressure Testing

1. Relieve the fuel pressure.
2. Properly connect the fuel system pressure tester:
   a. 2.5L non-turbocharged and 3.9L engines—special tool C–4799A, or equivalent is installed between the fuel supply hose and the engine fuel line assembly.
   b. 3.0L engine—special tool C–4799A and adaptor 6433, or equivalent is installed between the fuel supply hose and the engine fuel line assembly.
   c. 2.5L turbocharged and 3.3L engines—special tool C–4799A, or equivalent is installed to the fuel rail service valve.
3. With the key in the **RUN** position, put the DRB I or II in the activate auto shutdown relay mode; this will activate the fuel pump and pressurize the system.
4. If the pressure is within specifications, reinstall the fuel hose.
5. If fuel pressure is below specifications, install the tester in the fuel supply line between the tank and the filter and repeat the test.
6. If the pressure is 5 psi higher than in Step 5, replace the fuel filter. If no change is observed, squeeze the return hose. If pressure increases, replace the pressure regulator. If no change is observed, the problem is either a plugged in-tank sock filter or a defective pump.
7. If fuel pressure is above specifications, remove the fuel return line hose from the chassis line at the fuel tank and connect a 3 foot piece of fuel hose to the return line. Put the other end into a 2 gallon minimum capacity approved gasoline container.

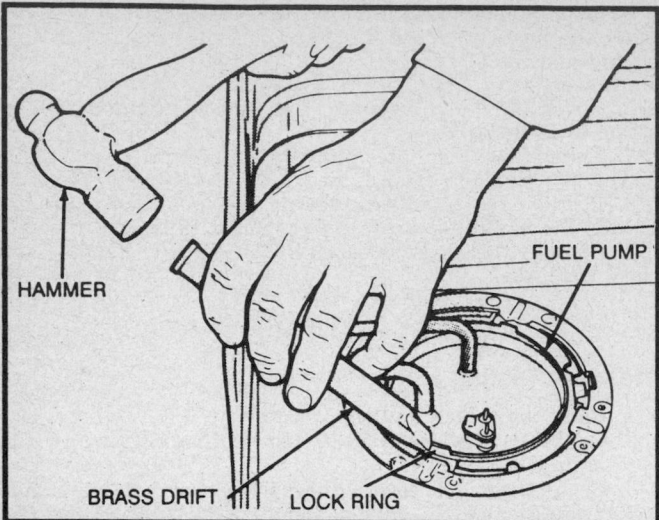

Removing the fuel pump from the tank—Caravan, Voyager and Town & Country

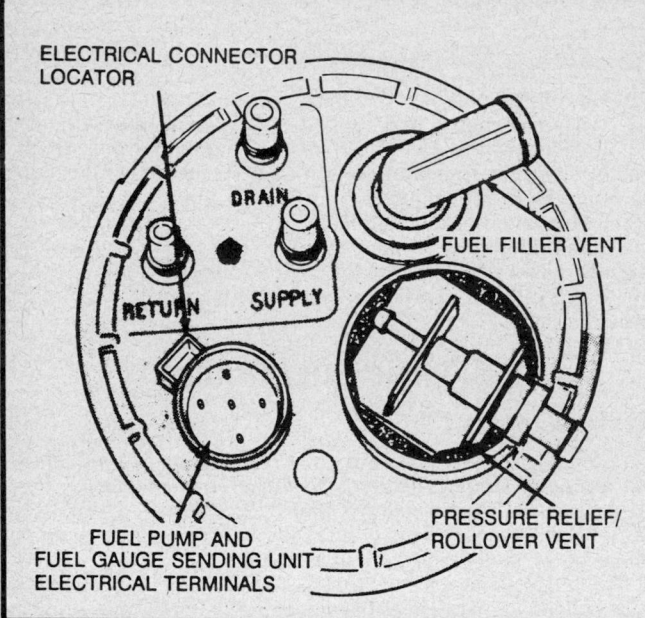

Top of the fuel pump module—Dakota

Repeat the test. If pressure is now correct, check the in-tank return hose for kinking. Replace the fuel pump assembly if the in-tank reservoir check valve or aspirator jet is obstructed.

8. If pressure is still above specifications, remove the fuel return hose from the throttle body. Connect a substitute hose to the throttle body return nipple and place the other end of the hose in a clean container. Repeat the test. If pressure is now correct, check for a restricted fuel return line. If no change is observed, replace the fuel pressure regulator.

Removal and Installation
CARAVAN, VOYAGER AND TOWN & COUNTRY

1. Relieve the fuel pressure.
2. Disconnect the negative battery cable.
3. Raise the vehicle and support safely.
4. Using the proper equipment, drain the fuel tank.

5. Remove the screws that hold the filler neck to the quarter panel.
6. Disconnect the wiring and hoses from the tank.
7. Place a transmission jack or equivalent under the center of the tank and apply slight pressure. Remove the tank straps.
8. Lower the tank and remove the filler tube from the tank.
9. Lower the tank and disconnect the vapor separator rollover valve hose and remove the fuel tank from the vehicle.
10. Using a hammer and a brass drift, tap the lock ring counterclockwise to release the pump.
11. Partially pull the pump assembly out of the tank until the return line hose connection is visible at the of the pump assembly.
12. Disconnect the fuel fitting by pressing in on the ears.
13. Remove the pump from the tank with the O-ring. Discard the O-ring, pump inlet filter and inlet seal. Disassemble as required.

To install:
14. Install a new inlet seal and filter on the end of the pump.
15. Install a new O-ring to the pump.
16. Connect the reservoir hose to the pump assembly at the suction end of the pump. Press the female fitting onto the pump assembly male end until the ears snap in place.
17. Install the pump into the tank so the fuel return hose is not kinked.
18. Install the lock ring with a hammer and brass punch turning the ring clockwise.
19. Install the fuel tank.
20. Connect the negative battery cable, start the engine and check for leaks.

DAKOTA
1. Relieve the fuel pressure.
2. Disconnect the negative battery cable.
3. Raise the vehicle and support safely.
4. Using the proper equipment, drain the fuel tank.
5. Disconnect the vent hoses and filler hose from the tank and remove the hoses from the bracket attached to the top of the frame rail, if equipped.
6. Place a transmission jack or equivalent under the center of the tank and apply slight pressure.
7. Remove the retaining strap J-bolt nuts and remove the straps.
8. Lower the tank enough to reach in and disconnect the electrical connector and the remaining fuel tubes from the top of the module.
9. Lower the tank and remove the module. When the module is released from the tank it will spring up. Remove the pump from the module.

To install:
10. Clean the seal area of the tank. Install the new pump to the module so the filter is in the same position as before removal. Install a new O-ring on the module.
11. Align the module with the retaining bracket on the bottom of the tank. It is normal for the module to have a slight interference fit with the bracket.
12. Push the module down and install the retaining clamp.
13. Install the fuel tank.
14. Connect the negative battery cable, start the engine and check for leaks.

Carburetor

Removal and Installation

1. Disconnect the negative battery cable. On 2.6L engine, drain the radiator because the choke control element is water activated.
2. Remove the air cleaner assembly.
3. Remove and install the fuel tank cap to relieve any pressure in the tank.

4. Matchmark all vacuum hoses and electrical connectors and remove them from the carburetor.

5. Disconnect the throttle, cruise control, choke and kickdown cables and linkages, if equipped.

6. Disconnect and plug the fuel inlet line.

7. Remove the mounting bolts and/or nuts and remove the carburetor from the intake manifold.

To install:

8. Clean the mounting surface of the manifold and install a new base gasket.

9. Install the mounting bolts and/or nuts and tighten them alternately to compress the base gasket evenly.

10. Connect the fuel line.

11. Connect the throttle, cruise control, choke and kickdown cables and linkages, if equipped.

12. Install all vacuum hoses and electrical connectors in their proper locations.

13. Install the air cleaner.

14. Connect the negative battery cable, start the engine and perform all necessary adjustments.

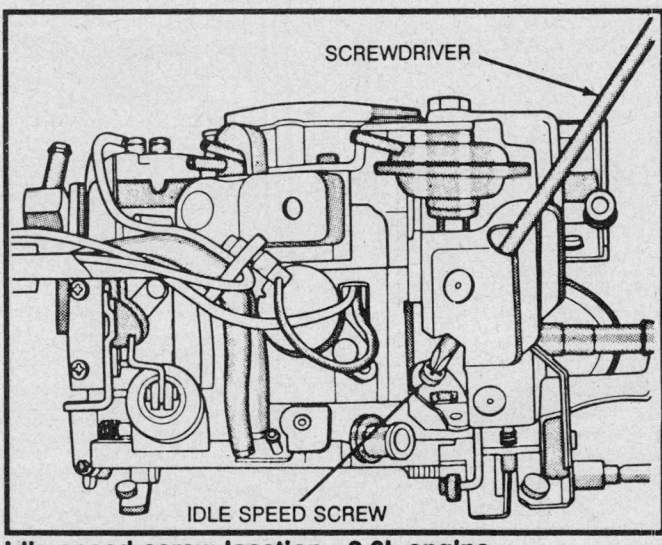

Idle speed screw location—2.6L engine

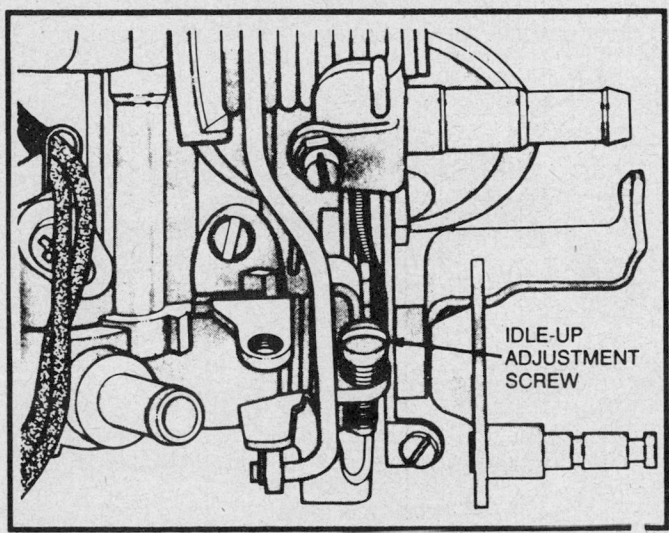

Idle-up adjustment screw—2.6L engine

Idle Speed Adjustment

2.2L ENGINE

1. Before checking or adjusting the idle speed, check ignition timing and adjust if necessary.

2. Disconnect and plug the vacuum connector at the coolant vacuum switch cold closed valve.

3. Unplug the connector at the radiator fan and install a jumper wire so the fan will run continuously.

4. Remove the PCV valve and allow it to draw underhood air.

5. Connect a tachometer to engine.

6. Ground the carburetor switch with a jumper wire.

7. Disconnect the oxygen system test connector located on left fender shield, if equipped.

8. Start and run the engine until normal operating temperature is reached.

9. If tachometer indicates rpm is not at specifications, turn the idle speed screw until correct idle speed is obtained. The screw is located on top of the solenoid mounted on the back of the carburetor.

10. Reconnect the PCV valve, oxygen connector and vacuum connector.

11. Remove jumper wire and reconnect the radiator fan.

12. After Steps 9 and 10 are completed, the idle speed may change slightly. This is normal and engine speed should not be readjusted.

13. Make sure the solenoid kicker moves the throttle blade adequately so the idle does not change when the air conditioning is working.

2.6L ENGINE

1. Start the engine and allow it to reach normal operating temperature. Before checking or adjusting the idle speed, check ignition timing and adjust if necessary.

2. Turn all lights and accessories **OFF**. Disconnect the radiator fan. Connect a tachometer to the engine.

3. Open the throttle and run at 2500 rpm for 10 seconds. Allow the engine to idle for 2 minutes.

4. Check the idle speed. If the tachometer indicates rpm is not at specifications, turn the idle speed screw until correct idle speed is obtained. The screw can be accessed through the hole in the front cover.

5. Once the idle speed is set, connect the radiator fan plug and turn the air conditioning on to its coldest position, if equipped.

6. With the compressor running, set the idle to 900 rpm by turning the idle-up screw. This screw can also be accessed through the hole in the front cover.

3.9L ENGINE

1. Start the engine and run until at normal operating temperature. Check and adjust the ignition timing. Turn the engine **OFF**.

2. Disconnect and plug the EGR hose. Disconnect the oxygen sensor, if equipped.

3. Disconnect and plug the 3/16 in. hose at the canister.

4. Remove the PCV hose from the valve cover and allow it to draw underhood air.

5. Ground the carburetor switch with a jumper wire, if equipped.

6. Disconnect the vacuum hose from the computer, if equipped and connect an auxiliary vacuum supply of 16 Hg in.

7. Make sure all accessories are off. Install a tachometer and start the engine.

8. Allow the engine to run for 2 minutes to stabilize. Turn the idle speed screw until the correct idle speed according to the Vehicle Emission Control Information label is reached.

9. Connect all wires and hoses that were previously disconnected. It is normal for the idle speed to vary after all hoses and wires are reconnected; do not readjust.

Idle Mixture Adjustment

1. Disconnect and plug the EGR hose. Disconnect the oxygen sensor, if equipped.
2. Disconnect and plug the 3/16 in. hose at the canister.
3. Remove the PCV hose from the valve cover and allow it to draw underhood air.
4. Ground the carburetor switch with a jumper wire, if equipped.
5. Disconnect the vacuum hose from the computer, if equipped and connect an auxiliary vacuum supply of 16 Hg in.
6. Remove the concealment plug. Disconnect the vacuum supply hose to the tee and install a propane supply hose in its place.
7. Make sure all accessories are off. Install a tachometer and start the engine. Allow the engine to run for 2 minutes to stabilize.
8. Open the main propane valve. Slowly open the propane metering valve until the maximum engine rpm is reached. When too much propane is added, the engine will begin to stumble; at this point back off until the engine stabilizes.
9. Adjust the idle rpm to obtain the specified propane rpm. Fine tune the metering valve to obtain the highest rpm again. If there has been a change to the maximum rpm, readjust the idle screw to the specified propane rpm.
10. Turn the main propane valve off and allow the engine to run for 1 minute to stabilize.
11. Adjust the mixture screw to obtain the smoothest idle at the specified idle rpm.
12. Open the main propane valve. Fine tune the metering valve to obtain the highest rpm. If the maximum engine speed is more that 25 rpm different than the specified propane rpm, repeat the procedure.
13. Turn the propane valves off and remove the propane canister. Reinstall the vacuum supply hose to the tee.
14. Perform the idle speed adjustment procedure.
15. Connect all wires and hoses that were previously disconnected.

Service Adjustments

For all carburetor service adjustment procedures and Specifications, please refer to "Carburetor Service" in the Unit Repair section.

Fuel Injection

Idle Speed Adjustment

EXCEPT 3.9L ENGINE

The idle speed is controlled by the automatic idle speed motor (AIS) which is controlled by the logic module. The logic module receives data from various sensors and switches in the system and adjusts the engine idle to a predetermined speed. Idle speed specifications can be found on the Vehicle Emission Control Information (VECI) label located in the engine compartment. If the idle speed is not within specifications and there are no problems with the system, the throttle body should be replaced.

3.9L ENGINE

1. Start the engine and allow it to reach normal operating temperature. If it is already hot, run it for 2 minutes.
2. Turn the engine off and allow 1 minute for the Idle Speed Control (ISC) actuator shaft to fully extend.
3. Disconnect the ISC actuator connector and the coolant temperature sensor.
4. Connect a tachometer to the engine and start the engine.
5. Adjust the extension screw on the actuator shaft until the rpm is within specifications.
6. Turn the engine off. Reconnect the ISC actuator connector and the coolant temperature sensor. Remove the tachometer.

Idle Mixture Adjustment

There is no idle mixture adjustment provided with any Chrysler fuel injection system.

Fuel Injector

Removal and Installation

2.5L NON-TURBOCHARGED ENGINE AND 3.9L ENGINE

1. Remove the air cleaner assembly.
2. Relieve the fuel pressure.
3. Disconnect the negative battery cable.

NOTE: On the 3.9L engine, there is a small spacer below the injector hold-down clamp. Take the proper precaution to prevent this spacer from falling into the throttle body.

4. Remove the injector hold-down Torx® screw, the hold-down and the spacer.
5. Using a small flat-tipped tool, lift the cap off of the injector.

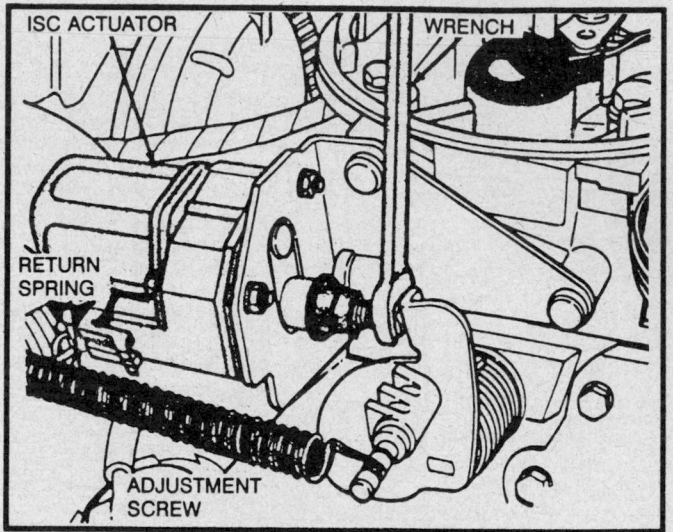

Adjusting the idle speed—3.9L engine

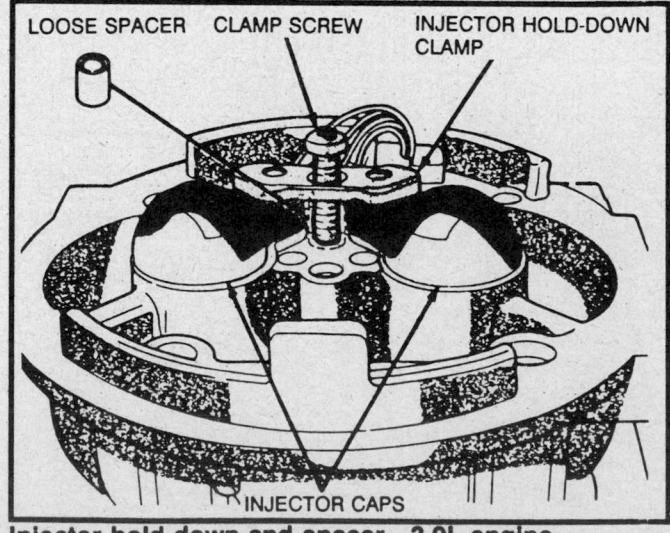

Injector hold-down and spacer—3.9L engine

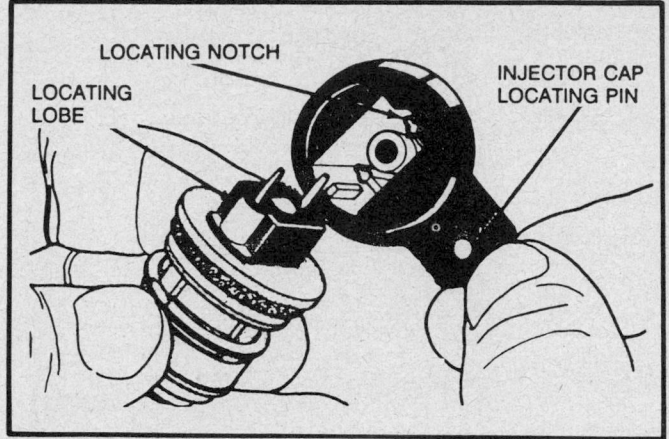

Installing the injector to the cap—2.5L non-turbocharged and 3.9L engines

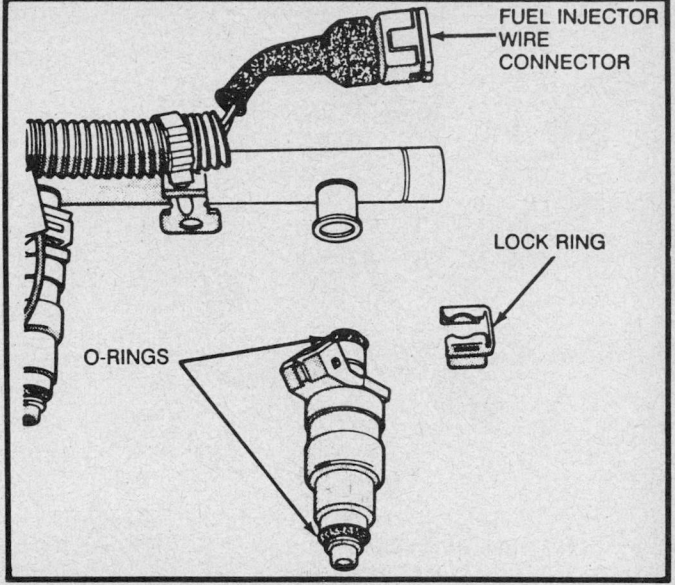

Fuel injector removal and installation—2.5L turbocharged engine

6. Using the same tool, gently pry the injector from its pod.
7. Remove the lower O-ring from the pod.

To install:

8. Install the new lower O-ring on the injector.
9. Align the injector terminal housing with the locating socket in the injector cap.
10. Press the injector cap so that the upper O-ring flange is flush with the lower surface of the cap.
11. Spray the inner surfaces of the injector pod with suitable carburetor parts cleaner to remove residual varnish and gasoline.
12. Lubricate the O-rings sparingly with unmedicated petroleum jelly.
13. Place the injector and cap into the injector pod and align the cap locating pin with the locating hole in the casting. On the 3.9L engine, the right side locating pin in 5mm in diameter and will not fit into the other hole. The left side pin is 4mm in diameter and will be loose in the other hole.
14. Press firmly on the injector cap until it is flush with the casting surface.
15. Install the spacer, if equipped and align the holes in the hold-down with the pins on the caps and install.
16. Push down on the caps, install the screw and torque to 35 inch lbs. (4 Nm).
17. Connect the negative battery cable and check for leaks using the DRB I or II to activate the fuel pump.
18. Install the air cleaner.

2.5L TURBOCHARGED ENGINE

1. Relieve the fuel pressure.
2. Disconnect the negative battery cable.
3. Disconnect the injector wiring connector from the injector.
4. Unbolt the fuel rail from the rear of the engine. Position the fuel rail assembly so the fuel injectors are easily accessible.
5. Remove the injector clip from the fuel rail and injector. Pull the injector straight out of the fuel rail receiver cup.
6. Check the injector O-ring for damage. If the O-ring is damaged, replace it. If the injector is being reused, install a protective cap on the injector tip to prevent damage.
7. Repeat the procedure for the remaining injectors.

To Install:

8. Before installing an injector the rubber O-ring should be lubricated with a drop of clean engine oil to aid in installation.
9. Install injector top end into fuel rail receiver cup.
10. Install injector clip by sliding the open end into top slot of the injector and onto the receiver cup ridge into the side slots of clip.
11. Repeat the steps for the remaining injectors.

12. Install the fuel rail.
13. Connect the negative battery cable and check for leaks using the DRB I or II to activate the fuel pump.

3.0L ENGINE

1. Relieve the fuel pressure.
2. Disconnect the negative battery cable.
3. Remove the air cleaner to throttle body hose.
4. Disconnect the throttle cable from the throttle body and disconnect the kickdown linkage. Remove the throttle cable bracket attaching bolts.
5. Disconnect the connectors to the throttle body.
6. Matchmark and carefully remove the vacuum hoses from the throttle body.
7. Remove the PCV and brake booster hoses from the air intake plenum.
8. Remove the ignition coil from the intake plenum, if it is mounted there.
9. Remove the EGR tube flange from the intake plenum, if equipped.
10. Unplug the coolant temperature sensor and charge temperature sensor, if equipped.
11. Remove the vacuum connection from the air intake plenum vacuum connector.
12. Remove the fuel hoses from the fuel rail and plug them.
13. Remove the air intake plenum to intake manifold bolts and remove the plenum and gaskets. Cover the intake manifold openings.
14. Remove the vacuum hoses from the fuel rail.
15. Disconnect the fuel injector wiring harness.
16. Remove the fuel rail attaching bolts and remove the fuel rail with the wiring harness from the vehicle. Position the rail on the bench upside down so the injectors are easily accessible.
17. Remove the small connector retainer clip and unplug the injector. Remove the injector clip off the fuel rail and injector. Pull the injector straight out of the rail.

To install:

18. Lubricate the rubber O-ring with clean oil and install to the rail receiver cap. Install the injector clip to the **TOP** slot of the injector, plug in the connector and install the connector clip.
19. Install the fuel rail to the vehicle and plug in the injector harness. Connect the vacuum hoses to the fuel rail.

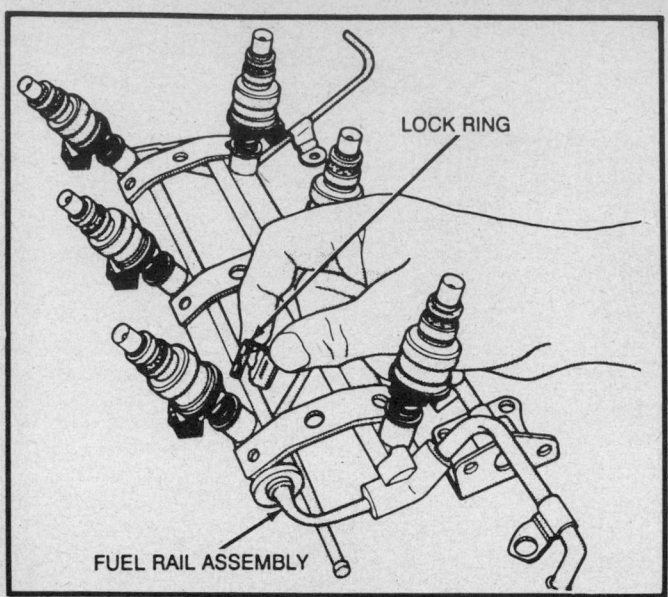

LOCK RING

FUEL RAIL ASSEMBLY

Fuel rail assembly – 3.0L engine

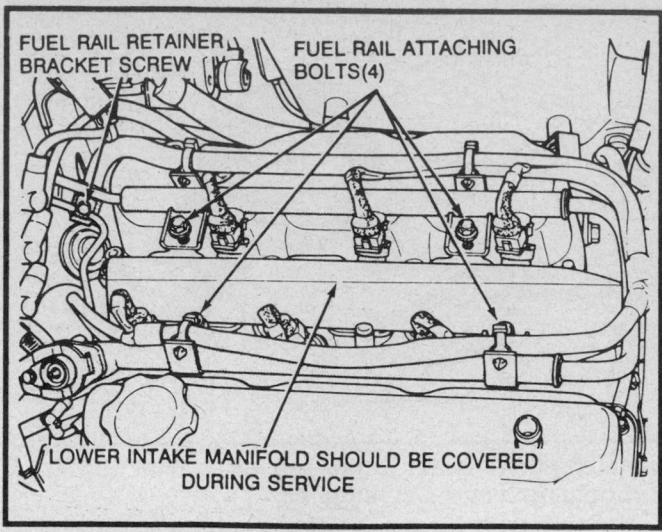

FUEL RAIL RETAINER BRACKET SCREW

FUEL RAIL ATTACHING BOLTS(4)

LOWER INTAKE MANIFOLD SHOULD BE COVERED DURING SERVICE

Fuel rail installed – 3.3 L engine

20. Install new intake plenum gaskets with the beaded sealer side up and install the intake plenum. Torque the attaching bolts and nuts to 115 inch lbs. (13 Nm).

21. Install the fuel hoses to the fuel rail.

22. Install or connect all items that were removed or disconnected from the intake plenum and throttle body.

23. Connect the negative battery cable and check for leaks using the DRB I or II to activate the fuel pump.

3.3L ENGINE

1. Relieve the fuel pressure.
2. Disconnect the negative battery cable.
3. Remove the air cleaner and hose assembly.
4. Disconnect the throttle cable. Remove the wiring harness from the throttle cable bracket and intake manifold water tube.
5. Remove the vacuum hose harness from the throttle body.
6. Remove the PCV and brake booster hoses from the air intake plenum.
7. Remove the EGR tube flange from the intake plenum, if equipped.
8. Unplug the charge temperature sensor and unplug all vacuum hoses from the intake plenum.
9. Remove the cylinder head to intake plenum strut.
10. Disconnect the MAP sensor and oxygen sensor connector. Remove the engine mounted ground strap.
11. Release the fuel hose quick disconnect fittings and remove the hoses from the fuel rail. Plug the hoses.
12. Remove the Direct Ignition System (DIS) coils and the alternator bracket to intake manifold bolt.
13. Remove the intake manifold bolts and rotate the manifold back over the rear valve cover. Cover the intake manifold.
14. Remove the vacuum harness from the pressure regulator.
15. Remove the fuel tube retainer bracket screw and fuel rail

attaching bolts. Spread the retainer bracket to allow for clearance when removing the fuel tube.

16. Remove the fuel rail injector wiring clip from the alternator bracket.

17. Disconnect the cam sensor, coolant temperature sensor and engine temperature sensor.

18. Remove the fuel rail.

19. Position the rail on the bench so the injectors are easily accessible.

20. Remove the small connector retainer clip and unplug the injector. Remove the injector clip off the fuel rail and injector. Pull the injector straight out of the rail.

To install:

21. Lubricate the rubber O-ring with clean oil and install to the rail receiver cap. Install the injector clip to the slot in the injector, plug in the connector and install the connector clip.

22. Install the fuel rail.

23. Connect the cam sensor, coolant temperature sensor and engine temperature sensor.

24. Install the fuel rail injector wiring clip to the alternator bracket.

25. Install the fuel rail attaching bolts and fuel tube retainer bracket screw.

26. Install the vacuum harness to the pressure regulator.

27. Install the intake manifold with a new gasket. Install the bolts only fingertight. Install the alternator bracket to intake manifold bolt and the cylinder head to intake manifold strut and bolts. Torque the intake manifold mounting bolts to 21 ft. lbs. (28 Nm) starting from the middle and working outward. Torque the bracket and strut bolts to 40 ft. lbs. (54 Nm).

28. Install or connect all items that were removed or disconnected from the intake manifold and throttle body.

29. Connect the fuel hoses to the rail. Push the fittings in until they click in place.

30. Install the air cleaner assembly.

31. Connect the negative battery cable and check for leaks using the DRB I or II to activate the fuel pump.

EMISSION CONTROLS

Please refer to "Professional Emission Component Application Guide".

Emission Warning Lamps

Resetting

1986–88 VEHICLES

1. Locate the EMR switch module. It is a plastic box located either on the lower portion of the steering column or to the left of the steering column.
2. Remove the 9 volt battery (under the small black panel) from the module. Some 1988 vehicles do not have the 9 volt battery.

3. Reset the switch by inserting a small rod into a hole in the case of the module, which closes a switch and turns the lamp off.
4. Install a new 9 volt battery, if equipped.

1989–90 VEHICLES

1. Connect the DRBII to the diagnostic connector.
2. Turn the ignition switch to the **RUN** position and access the Emissions EMR Tests on the DRBII.
3. Select EMR Memory Check.
4. Select Reset EMR Light. This will reset the EMR timing in the computer and turn the light off.
5. Disconnect the DRBII.

ENGINE MECHANICAL

NOTE: Disconnecting the negative battery cable on some vehicles may interfere with the functions of the on board computer systems and may require the computer to undergo a relearning process, once the negative battery cable is reconnected.

Engine

Removal and Installation

CARAVAN, VOYAGER AND TOWN & COUNTRY

2.2L and 2.5L Engines

1. If equipped with fuel injection, relieve the fuel pressure. Disconnect the negative battery cable and all engine ground straps.
2. Mark the hood hinge outline on the hood and remove the hood.
3. Drain the cooling system. Remove the radiator hoses, fan assembly, radiator shroud and radiator.
4. Remove the air cleaner, duct hoses and oil filter.
5. Unbolt the air conditioning compressor from its mount, if equipped and position it to the side.
6. Remove the power steering pump mounting bolts and position the pump to the side, without disconnecting any fluid lines.
7. Label and disconnect all electrical connectors from the engine, alternator and carburetor or fuel injection system.
8. Disconnect the fuel line, heater hoses and accelerator linkage.
9. Disconnect the air pump lines and remove the pump, if equipped.
10. Remove the alternator.
11. Disconnect the shift linkage(s), clutch linkage (as required) and speedometer cable.
12. Raise the vehicle and support safely. Disconnect the exhaust pipe from the manifold. Remove the right inner fender shield.
13. If equipped with a manual transaxle, remove the transaxle.
14. If equipped with an automatic transaxle, perform the following procedures:
    a. Remove the lower cover from the transaxle case.
    b. Remove the exhaust pipe-to-exhaust manifold bolts. Separate the pipe from the manifold.
    c. Remove the starter and set it aside.
    d. Matchmark the flex plate to the torque converter, for installation purposes.
    e. Remove the torque converter bolts. Separate the converter from the flex plate. Remove the lower bellhousing bolts.

15. Lower the vehicle and support the transaxle (if still in the vehicle) with a floor jack or equivalent. Attach an engine lifting device to the engine.
16. To lower the engine, separate the right side engine bracket from the yoke bracket. To raise the engine, remove the yoke/insulator long bolt.

NOTE: If removing the insulator-to-rail screws, first mark the position of the insulator on the side rail to insure proper alignment during reinstallation.

17. Remove the remaining bellhousing bolts. Remove the front engine mount nut/bolt and the left insulator through bolt or the insulator bracket-to-transaxle bolts.
18. Lift the engine from the vehicle and remove.

To Install:

19. Lower the engine into the engine compartment. Loosely install all of the mounting bolts. With all bolts installed, torque the:
    Engine to mount bolts to 40 ft. lbs.
    Engine to transaxle bolts to 70 ft. lbs.
    Torque converter bolts to 40 ft. lbs.
20. Connect or install all items disconnected or removed during the removal procedure. Fill the engine with the proper amount of engine oil.
21. Refill the cooling system. Start the engine, allow it to reach normal operating temperature. Check for leaks. Check the ignition timing and adjust if necessary. Adjust the idle speed/mixture (if possible) and the transaxle linkage.

2.6L, 3.0L and 3.3L Engines

1. If equipped with fuel injection, relieve the fuel pressure. Disconnect the negative battery cable.
2. Matchmark the hinge-to-hood position and remove the hood.
3. Drain the cooling system. Disconnect and label all engine electrical connections.
4. Remove the coolant hoses from the radiator and engine. Remove the radiator and cooling fan assembly.
5. Remove the air cleaner assembly. Disconnect the fuel lines from the engine. Disconnect the accelerator cable from the engine.
6. Raise the vehicle and support safely. Drain the engine oil.
7. Remove the air conditioning compressor mounting bolts, the drive belt(s) and position the compressor to the side. Disconnect the exhaust pipe from the exhaust manifold.
8. Remove the transaxle inspection cover, matchmark the converter to the flexplate and remove the torque converter bolts.

9. Remove the power steering pump mounting bolts and set the pump aside, upright, with the fluid lines attached.

10. Remove the lower bellhousing bolts. Disconnect and label the starter motor wiring and remove the starter motor from the engine.

11. Lower the vehicle. Disconnect and label the vacuum hoses and engine ground straps.

12. Support the transaxle with a floor jack or equivalent. Attach an engine lifting device to the engine.

13. Remove the upper transaxle-to-engine bolts.

14. To separate the engine mounts from the insulators, mark the right insulator-to-right frame support and remove the mounting bolts. Remove the front engine mount through bolt. Remove the left insulator through bolt, from inside the wheel housing. Remove the insulator bracket-to-transaxle bolts.

15. Lift and remove the engine from the vehicle.

To Install:

16. Lower the engine into the engine compartment. Align the engine mounts and install the bolts; do not tighten the bolts until all bolts have been installed. Torque the through bolts to 75 ft. lbs.

17. Install the upper transaxle-to-engine mounting bolts and torque to 75 ft. lbs. Remove the engine lifting fixture from the engine.

18. Raise the vehicle and support safely.

19. Align the converter marks, install the torque converter bolts.Install the transaxle inspection cover.

20. Connect the exhaust pipe to the exhaust manifold. Install the starter motor and connect the wiring.

21. Install the power steering pump and air conditioning compressor. Adjust the drive belt tension, if necessary.

22. Lower the vehicle. Reconnect all vacuum hoses and electrical connections to the engine.

23. Connect the fuel lines and accelerator cable.

24. Install the radiator and fan assembly. Connect the fan motor wiring. Connect the radiator hoses and refill the cooling system.

25. Refill the engine with the proper oil to the correct level.

26. Connect the engine ground straps. Install the hood and align the matchmarks. Connect the battery.

27. Start and run the engine until it reaches normal operating temperatures and check for leaks. Adjust the transaxle linkage, if necessary.

DAKOTA

1. Relieve the fuel pressure if the vehicle is equipped with fuel injection. Disconnect the negative battery cable from the battery and from the engine.

2. Remove the hood and the oil dipstick.

3. Raise the vehicle and support safely. Drain the engine oil and coolant. Remove the lower radiator hose.

4. Remove the starter. Remove the engine to transmission struts, if equipped.

5. Remove the exhaust pipe from the exhaust manifold(s).

6. If the vehicle is equipped with a manual transmission, remove the transmission and all related parts.

7. If the vehicle is equipped with an automatic transmission, remove the inspection plate, matchmark the flex plate to the converter, remove the torque converter bolts and push the torque converter backwards as far as it will go. Remove the lower bell housing bolts.

8. If the vehicle is 2WD, remove the engine mount lower nuts.

9. If the vehicle is equipped with 4WD:

   a. On the left side, remove the 2 bolts attaching the bracket to the transmission bellhousing and 2 bracket to pinion nose adaptor bolts. Separate the engine from the insulator by removing the upper nut washer assembly and through-bolt from the engine support bracket.

   b. On the right side, remove the 2 bracket to axle Discon-

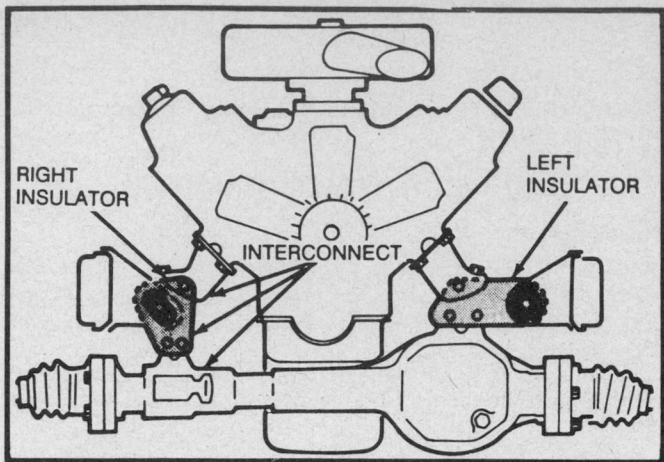

Interconnected motor mounts—Dakota with 4WD

nect housing bolts and 1 bracket to bellhouisng bolt. Separate the engine from the insulator by removing the upper nut washer assembly and the through-bolt from the engine support bracket.

10. Disconnect and plug the rubber fuel inlet and return hoses from the fuel lines at the front of the vehicle. Lower the vehicle.

11. Remove the air cleaner assembly and disconnect all linkages and cables. On the 3.9L engine, remove the carburetor or throttle body. Stuff a clean shop towel into the intake manifold opening to prevent foreign objects from entering.

12. Unbolt the compressor from the engine and position it to the side.

13. Remove the radiator and shroud. Remove the fan and all related parts.

14. Unbolt the power steering pump brackets from the engine and position it to the side.

15. Remove the alternator, air pump and all brackets. Disconnect the heater hoses.

16. Remove the distributor cap with all spark plug wires attached. Disconnect all remaining electrical connectors, vacuum hoses and check for any other items preventing engine removal.

17. Attach an engine removal device to the intake manifold or cylinder head.

18. If the vehicle is equipped with an automatic transmission, support the transmission with a floor jack, or equivalent. Remove the remaining bell housing bolts.

19. Remove the engine from the vehicle slowly and carefully.

To install:

20. Lower the engine into position and install the engine mount bolts on the 2.5L engine. Install the upper bell housing bolts. Remove the engine removal device. Install the oil dipstick.

21. Raise the vehicle and support safely.

22. On 3.9L engine, install the engine mount and interconnect nuts and bolts. Install the remaining bell housing bolts.

23. If the vehicle is equipped with a manual transmission, install the transmission and all related parts.

24. If the vehicle is equipped with an automatic transmission, align the torque converter and flex plate and install the bolts. Install the inspection plate, starter and the engine to transmission struts, if equipped.

25. Connect the rubber fuel inlet and return hoses to the fuel lines at the front of the vehicle.

26. Install the exhaust pipe to the exhaust manifold(s). Install the lower radiator hose. Lower the vehicle.

27. Connect the heater hoses.

28. Make sure the negative battery cable is not connected to the battery. Connect the engine side of the negative cable to the

engine. Install the alternator, air pump, power steering pump and all brackets.

29. Install the air conditioning compressor.

30. Install the throttle body or carburetor using a new base gasket and connect all linkages and cables. Connect all electrical connectors, vacuum hoses, etc. that were disconnected during the engine removal procedure.

31. Install the fan and all related parts. Adjust all belt tensions.

32. Install the radiator and shroud.

33. Install the distributor cap with all spark plug wires attached.

34. Install the air cleaner assembly.

35. Install the hood.

36. Fill the engine with the specified amount of oil and fill the radiator with coolant.

37. Connect the negative battery cable and set all adjustments to specification.

Cylinder Head

Removal and Installation

2.2L AND 2.5L ENGINES

1. Relieve the fuel pressure if equipped with fuel injection. Disconnect the negative battery cable and unbolt it from the head. Drain the cooling system. Remove the dipstick bracket nut from the thermostat housing.

2. Remove the air cleaner assembly. Remove the upper radiator hose and disconnect the heater hoses.

3. Disconnect and label the vacuum lines, hoses and wiring connectors from the manifold(s), carburetor or throttle body and from the cylinder head. Remove the air pump, if equipped.

4. Disconnect the all linkages and the fuel line from the carburetor or throttle body. Unbolt the cable bracket. Remove the ground strap attaching screw from the firewall.

5. If equipped with air conditioning, remove the upper compressor mounting bolts. The cylinder head can be remove with the compressor and bracket still mounted. Remove the upper part of the timing belt cover.

6. Raise the vehicle and support safely. Disconnect the converter from the exhaust manifold. Disconnect the water hose and oil drain from the turbocharger, if equipped.

7. Rotate the engine by hand, until the timing marks align (No. 1 piston at TDC). Lower the vehicle.

8. With the timing marks aligned, remove the camshaft sprocket. The camshaft sprocket can be suspended to keep the timing intact. Remove the spark plug wires from the spark plugs.

9. Remove the valve cover and curtain, if equipped. Remove the cylinder head bolts and washers, starting from the middle and working outward.

10. Remove the cylinder head from the engine.

NOTE: Before disassembling or repairing any part of the cylinder head assembly, identify factory installed oversized components. To do so, look for the tops of the bearing caps pained green and O/SJ stamped rearward of the oil gallery plug on the rear of the head. In addition, the barrel of the camshaft is painted green and O/SJ is stamped onto the rear end of the camshaft. Installing standard sized parts in an head equipped with oversized parts—or visa versa—will cause severe engine damage.

11. Clean the cylinder head gasket mating surfaces.

12. Using new gaskets and seals, install the head to the engine. Using new head bolts assembled with the old washers, torque the cylinder head bolts in sequence, to 45 ft. lbs. Repeating the sequence, torque the bolts to 65 ft. lbs. With the bolts at 65 ft. lbs., turn each bolt an additional ¼ turn.

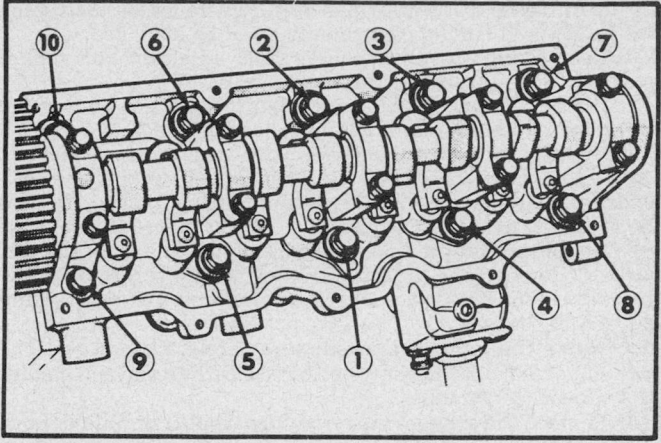

Cylinder head bolt torque sequence—2.2L and 2.5L engines

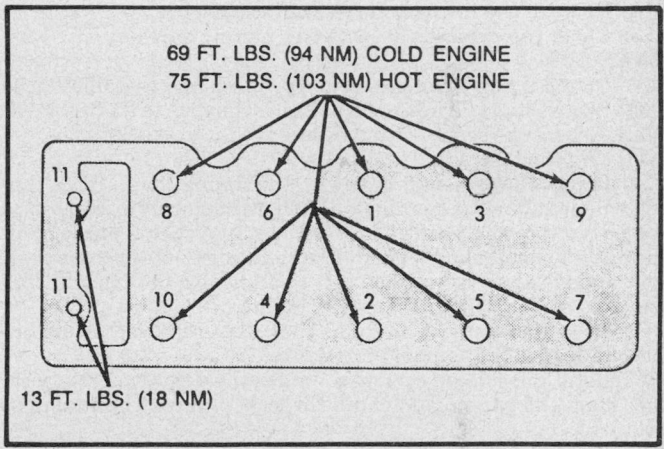

Cylinder head bolt torque sequence—2.6L engine

NOTE: Head bolt diameter for 1986-90 vehicles is 11mm. These bolts are identified with the number 11 on the head of the bolt. The 10mm bolts used on previous vehicles will thread into an 11mm bolt hole, but will permanently damage the cylinder block. Make sure the correct bolts are being used when replacing old head bolts.

13. Install the timing belt.

14. Install or connect all items that were removed or disconnected during the removal procedure.

15. Refill the cooling system. Connect the negative battery cable. Start the engine and check for leaks.

2.6L ENGINE

1. Disconnect the negative battery cable and unbolt if from the head.

2. Drain the cooling system. Remove the upper radiator hose and disconnect the heater hoses. Remove the air cleaner assembly.

3. Remove the dipstick bracket bolt from the thermostat housing.

4. Remove the carburetor to valve cover bracket. Remove the valve cover. Remove and plug the fuel lines to the carburetor.

5. Matchmark the distributor gear to its drive gear and remove the distributor. Remove the camshaft bolt and remove the distributor drive gear. Remove the camshaft gear with the chain installed from the camshaft and allow to rest on the holder just below it. This will not upset the valve timing. Do not crank the

engine until the distributor has been reinstalled or the timing will be lost and timing components could be damaged.

6. Remove the water pump drive pulley retaining bolt and remove the pulley from the camshaft.

7. Disconnect and label the vacuum lines, hoses and wiring connectors from the manifold(s), carburetor and cylinder head. Since some of the vacuum lines from the carburetor connect to a solenoid pack on the right side inner fender, unbolt the solenoids from the fender with the vacuum lines attached and fold the assembly over the carburetor.

8. Disconnect all the linkages and the fuel line from the carburetor. Remove the ground strap attaching screw from the firewall. Unbolt the power steering pump from the bracket and position to the side.

9. Raise the vehicle and support safely. Disconnect the vacuum hoses from the source below the carburetor and disconnect the air feeder tubes.

10. Remove the exhaust pipe from the exhaust manifold. Lower the vehicle.

11. Remove the small end bolts from the head first, then remove the remaining head bolts, starting from the outside and working inward.

12. Remove the cylinder head from the engine.

13. Clean the cylinder head gasket mating surfaces.

To install:

14. Install a new head gasket to the block and install all head bolts and washers. Torque the bolts in sequence to 34 ft. lbs. (40 Nm). Repeat the sequence increasing the torque to 69 ft. lbs. (94 Nm). Tighten the small end bolts to 13 ft. lbs. (18 Nm).

15. Install the camshaft gear with the timing chain. If the timing will not allow for gear installation, reach into the case with a long, thin tool and push the rubber foot into the oil pump to allow for more chain movement. Install the distributor drive gear, bolt and washer. Torque the bolt to 40 ft. lbs. (54 Nm). Install the distributor, aligning the matchmarks.

16. Install or connect all items that were removed or disconnected during the removal procedure.

17. Refill the cooling system. Connect the negative battery cable. Start the engine and check for leaks. Adjust the timing as required.

3.0L ENGINE

1. Relieve the fuel pressure. Disconnect the negative battery cable. Drain the cooling system.

2. Remove the drive belt and the air conditioning compressor from its mount and support it aside. Using a ½ in. drive breaker bar, insert it into the square hole of the serpentine drive belt tensioner, rotate it counterclockwise (to reduce the belt tension) and remove the belt. Remove the alternator and power steering pump from the brackets and move them aside.

3. Raise the vehicle and support safely. Remove the right front wheel assembly and the right inner splash shield.

4. Remove the crankshaft pulleys and the torsional damper.

5. Lower the vehicle. Using a floor jack and a block of wood positioned under the oil pan, raise the engine slightly. Remove the engine mount bracket from the timing cover end of the engine and the timing belt covers.

6. To remove the timing belt, perform the following procedures:

   a. Rotate the crankshaft to position the No. 1 cylinder on the TDC of its compression stroke; the crankshaft sprocket timing mark should align with the oil pan timing indicator and the camshaft sprockets timing marks (triangles) should align with the rear timing belt covers timing marks.

   b. Mark the timing belt in the direction of rotation for reinstallation purposes.

   c. Loosen the timing belt tensioner and remove the timing belt.

NOTE: When removing the timing belt from the camshaft sprocket, make sure the belt does not slip off of the

other camshaft sprocket. Support the belt so it can not slip off of the crankshaft sprocket and opposite side camshaft sprocket.

7. Remove the air cleaner assembly. Label and disconnect the spark plug wires and the vacuum hoses.

8. Remove the valve cover.

9. Install auto lash adjuster retainers (tool MD998443 or equivalent) on the rocker arms.

10. If removing the right cylinder head, matchmark the distributor rotor to the distributor housing and the housing to distributor extension locations. Remove the distributor and the distributor extension.

11. Remove the camshaft bearing assembly to cylinder head bolts (do not remove the bolts from the assembly). Remove the rocker arms, rocker shafts and bearing caps as an assembly, as required. Remove the camshafts from the cylinder head and inspect them for damage, if necessary.

12. Remove the intake manifold assembly.

13. Remove the exhaust manifold.

14. Remove the cylinder head bolts starting from the outside and working inward. Remove the cylinder head from the engine.

15. Clean the gasket mounting surfaces and check the heads for warpage; the maximum warpage allowed is 0.008 in. (0.20mm).

To install:

16. Install the new cylinder head gaskets over the dowels on the engine block.

17. Install the cylinder heads on the engine and torque the cylinder head bolts in sequence using 3 even steps, to 70 ft. lbs. (95 Nm).

18. Install or connect all items that were removed or disconnected during the removal procedure.

19. When installing the timing belt over the camshaft sprocket, use care not to allow the belt to slip off the opposite camshaft sprocket.

20. Make sure the timing belt is installed on the camshaft sprocket in the same position as when removed.

21. Refill the cooling system. Connect the negative battery cable. Start the engine and check for leaks using the DRB I or II to active the fuel pump. Adjust the timing as required.

3.3L ENGINE

1. Relieve the fuel pressure. Disconnect the negative battery cable. Drain the cooling system.

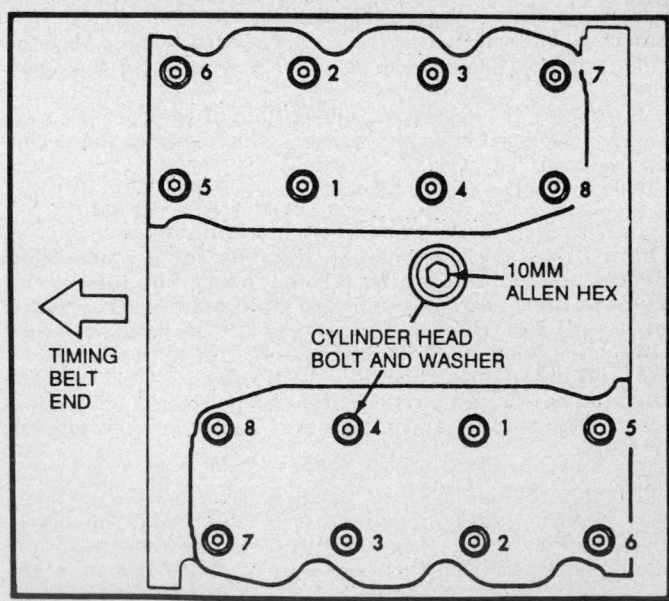

Cylinder head bolt torque sequence—3.0L engine

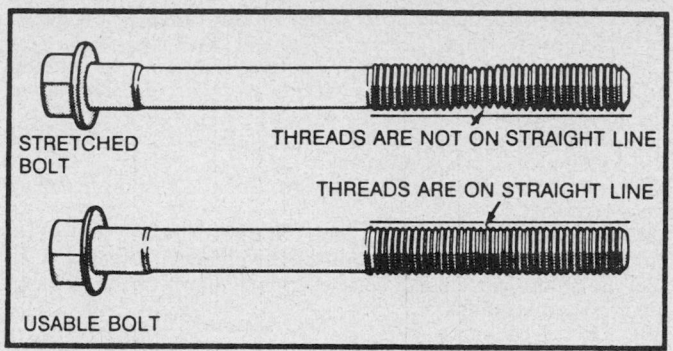

Checking the head bolt for stretching

STRETCHED BOLT

THREADS ARE NOT ON STRAIGHT LINE

THREADS ARE ON STRAIGHT LINE

USABLE BOLT

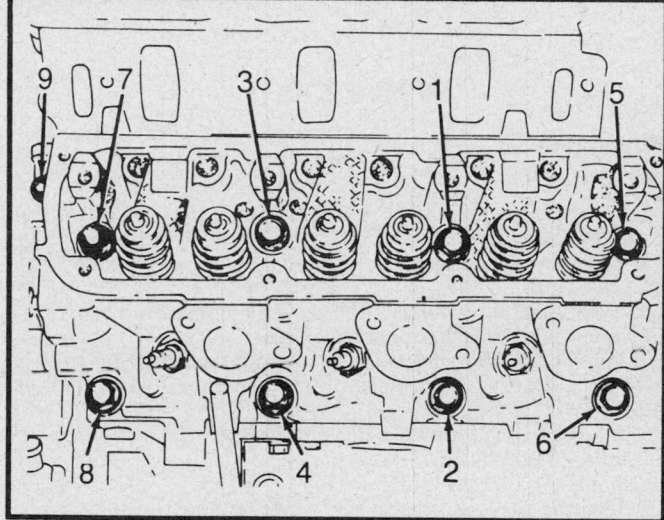

Cylinder head bolt torque sequence—3.3L engine

2. Remove the intake manifold with throttle body.

3. Disconnect the coil wires, sending unit wire, heater hoses and bypass hose.

4. Remove the closed ventilation system, evaporation control system and cylinder hear cover.

5. Remove the exhaust manifold.

6. Remove the rocker arm and shaft assemblies. Remove the pushrods and identify them in ensure installation in their original positions.

7. Remove the head bolts and remove the cylinder head from the block.

To install:

8. Clean the gasket mounting surfaces and install a new head gasket to the block.

9. Install the head to the block. Before installing the head bolts, inspect them for stretching. Hold a straight edge up to the threads. If the threads are not all on line, the bolt is stretched and should be replaced.

10. Torque the bolts in sequence to 45 ft. lbs. (61 Nm). Repeat the sequence and torque the bolts to 65 ft. lbs. (88 Nm). With the bolts at 65 ft. lbs., turn each bolt an additional ¼ turn.

11. Torque the lone head bolt to 25 ft. lbs. (33 Nm) after the other 8 bolts have been properly torqued.

12. Install the pushrods, rocker arms and shafts and torque the bolts to 21 ft. lbs. (12 Nm).

13. Place a drop of silicone sealer onto each of the 4 manifold to cylinder head gasket corners.

CAUTION

The intake manifold gasket is composed of very thin and sharp metal.

Handle this gasket with care or damage to the gasket or personal injury could result.

14. Install the intake manifold gasket and torque the end retainers to 105 inch lbs. (12 Nm).

15. Install the intake manifold and torque the bolts in sequence to 10 inch lbs. Repeat the sequence increasing the torque to 17 ft. lbs. (23 Nm) and recheck each bolt for 17 ft. lbs. of torque. After the bolts are torqued, inspect the seals to ensure that they have not become dislodged.

16. Lubricate the injector O-rings with clean oil and position the fuel rail in place. Install the rail mounting bolts.

17. Install the valve cover with a new gasket. Install the exhaust manifold.

18. Install or connect all remaining items that were removed or disconnected during the removal procedure.

19. Refill the cooling system. Connect the negative battery cable. Start the engine and check for leaks using the DRB I or II to activate the fuel pump.

3.9L ENGINE

1. Relieve the fuel pressure if the vehicle is equipped with fuel injection. Disconnect the negative battery cable from the battery and drain the cooling system.

2. Raise the vehicle and safely support. Disconnect the exhaust pipe from the manifolds.

3. Remove the alternator if the right head is being removed and the air pump and battery ground cable if the left head is being removed.

4. Remove the air cleaner assembly. Unbolt the air conditioning compressor and lay it to the side, if equipped. Remove the distributor cap with all wires attached.

5. Disconnect all wires, hoses, linkages and cables from the carburetor or throttle body. Disconnect and plug the fuel line.

6. Disconnect the ignition coil, coolant temperature sending unit wire and all other connectors along the wiring harness connected to items on the intake manifold.

7. Disconnect the heater hose, upper radiator hose and the lower bypass hose clamp.

8. Remove the valve covers.

9. Remove the intake manifold assembly. Remove the exhaust manifolds.

10. Remove the rocker arm and shaft assembly from the heads. Do not disassemble unless service is required.

11. Remove the pushrods and identify them to ensure installation in their original locations.

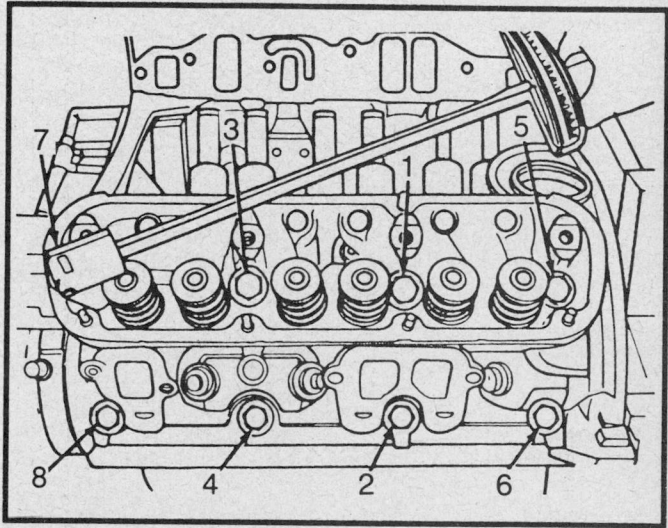

Cylinder head bolt torque sequence—3.9 L engine

12. Remove the head bolts and remove the cylinder head(s).

To install:

13. Clean and dry all gasket surfaces of the cylinder block and head. Inspect all surfaces with a straightedge. If the flatness exceeds 0.0075 times the length of the span measured (in any direction), replace or machine the head gasket surface.

14. Using no sealer whatsoever, install the new head gasket(s) to the block. Clean, dry and lightly oil all head bolts threads. Install the heads and install the head bolts.

15. Torque the head bolts in sequence to 50 ft. lbs. (68 Nm). Repeat the sequence retightening the bolts to a final torque of 105 ft. lbs. (143 Nm) and repeat the second step to ensure all bolts are accurately torqued.

16. Assemble the rocker shaft assembly, if it was serviced. Make sure all rocker arms with an **RH** stamped on them are installed to the right of those with an **LH**. Install the pushrods, rocker arms and shaft(s) with the notch on the end of the shaft pointing to the engine centerline and to the rear of the right bank or to the front of the left bank. Make sure the long stamped steel retainers are at the number 2 and 4 positions. Torque the bolts evenly and gradually to 17 ft. lbs. (23 Nm).

17. Clean and dry the intake manifold contact surfaces. Coat the intake manifold side gaskets very lightly with sealer and install the gaskets to the heads. Cutouts at the front of the gaskets differentiate the right and left sides.

18. Apply a thin uniform coat of quick dry cement to the front and rear intake manifold gaskets and mounting surfaces on the block and apply a thin bead of sealer to each of 4 the corners. Install the front and rear gaskets engaging the hole in the block and the tangs from the head gaskets. Apply a second thin bead of sealer above the gaskets in the 4 corners.

19. Carefully lower the intake manifold into position engaging the bypass hose; after it is satisfactorily in place, inspect the gaskets to make sure they have not become dislodged.

20. Install the intake manifold bolts and torque in sequence to 25 ft. lbs. (34 Nm). Repeat the sequence retightening the bolts to a final torque of 40 ft. lbs. (54 Nm) and repeat the second step to ensure all bolts are accurately torqued.

21. Install the exhaust manifold(s) and torque the bolts to 20 ft. lbs. (27 Nm). Torque the end nuts to 15 ft. lbs. (20 Nm).

22. Clean and dry the valve cover mating surfaces, bolts and bolt holes. Install the valve covers each with a new gasket.

23. Connect the heater hose, upper radiator hose and the lower bypass hose clamp.

24. Connect the ignition coil, coolant temperature sending unit wire and all other connectors that were disconnected along the wiring harness.

25. Install the air conditioning compressor, if equipped. Install the distributor cap and all spark plug wires.

26. Install the alternator, battery ground and air pump, if they were removed.

27. Connect all wires, hoses, cables and the fuel line to the carburetor or throttle body. Install the air cleaner assembly.

28. Raise the vehicle and safely support. Connect the exhaust pipe to the manifolds.

29. Fill the cooling system.

30. Connect the negative battery cable and set all adjustments to specification.

Valve Lash

Adjustment
2.6L ENGINE

1. Run the engine until at normal operating temperature. Remove the valve cover.

2. In sequence, check that the head bolts are torqued to 75 ft. lbs. (103 Nm).

3. Position the piston at TDC on the compression stroke.

4. Loosen the valve adjuster locknut.

5. Adjust the valve clearance by turning the adjusting screw a little at a time while measuring the clearance with a feeler gauge.

6. The specifications on a hot engine are:
Intake – 0.006 in. (0.15mm)
Exhaust – 0.010 in. (0.25mm)

7. Tighten the locknut securely while holding the adjustment screw stationary. Recheck the clearance after the locknut has been tightened.

8. Repeat the procedure for the remaining valves.

9. Install the valve cover with a new gasket.

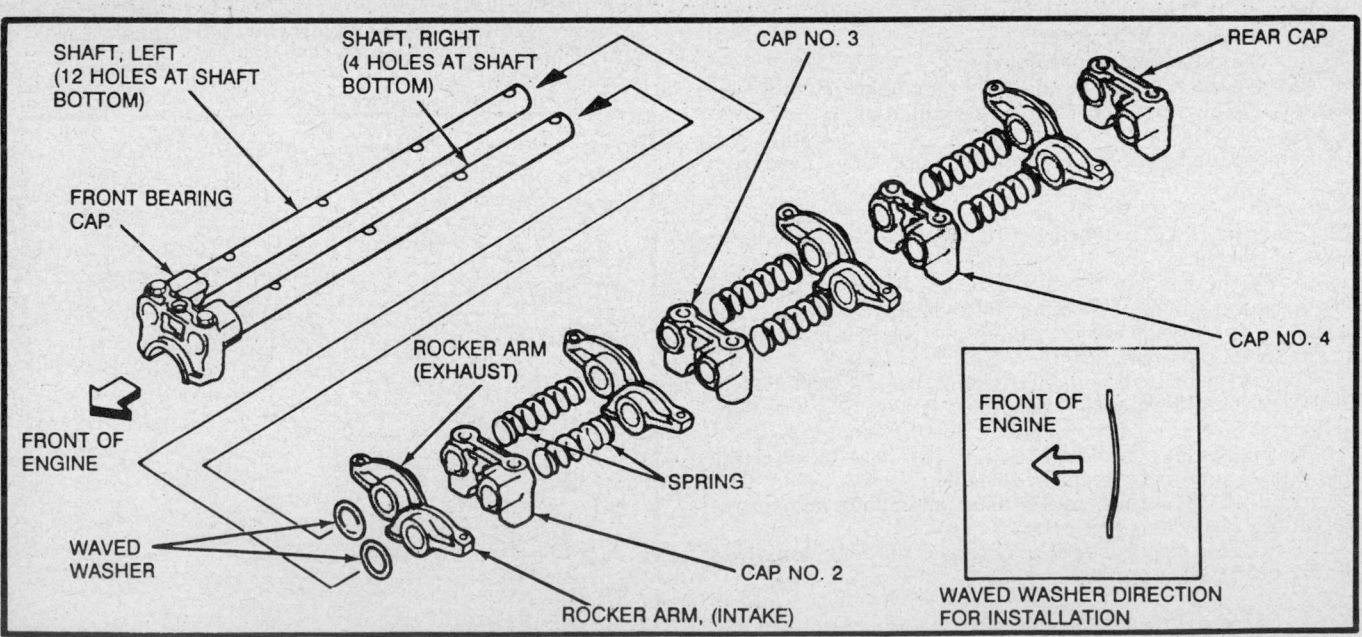

Rocker shafts/arms assembly – 2.6L engine

Rocker Arms and Shafts

Removal and Installation

2.2L AND 2.5L ENGINES

1. Disconnect the negative battery cable.
2. Remove the valve cover.
3. Rotate the crankshaft until the low point of the desired cam lobe is contacting the rocker arm.
4. Use the special valve spring compressor tool, or equivalent, depress the valve spring (without dislodging the keepers) and slide the rocker arm out.
5. The installation is the reverse of the removal procedure.

2.6L ENGINE

1. Disconnect the negative battery cable.
2. Remove the valve cover.
3. Tighten the water pump belt if it is loose. This will hold the camshaft in place while the rocker shafts and arms are removed.
4. Loosen the camshaft cap bolts but do not remove them from the caps. Remove the caps, arms, shafts and bolts all as an assembly.
5. Disassemble the unit keeping all parts in order and repair as required.
6. The installation is the reverse of the removal procedure. Make sure the arrows on the caps are all pointing to the front of the engine. Torque the cap bolts first to 85 inch lbs. (10 Nm), then to 175 inch lbs. (18 Nm) in the following order: No. 3 cap, No. 2 cap, No. 4 cap, Front cap, Rear cap.

3.0L ENGINE

1. Disconnect the negative battery cable. Remove the air cleaner assembly.

2. Remove the valve cover.
3. Using the auto lash adjuster retainer tools MD998443 or equivalent, install them on the rocker arms to keep the lash adjusters from falling out.
4. On the right side cylinder head, remove the distributor extension.
5. Have a helper hold the rear end of the camshaft down. If the rear of the camshaft cannot be held down, the belt will dislodge and the valve timing will be lost. Loosen the camshaft cap bolts but do not remove them from the caps. Remove the caps, arms, shafts and bolts all as an assembly.
6. Disassemble the unit keeping all parts in order and repair as required.
7. The installation is the reverse of the removal procedure. Apply a drop of sealant to the rear edge of the rear cap. Torque the cap bolts first to 85 inch lbs. (19 Nm), then to 180 inch lbs. (19 Nm) in the following order: No. 3 cap, No. 2 cap, No. 1 cap, No. 4 cap.

3.3L ENGINE

1. Disconnect the negative battery cable.
2. Remove the upper intake manifold assembly.
3. Remove the valve cover.
4. Remove the rocker shaft retaining bolts and retainers.
5. Remove the rocker shaft and arm assembly. Disassemble and repair as required.
6. The installation is the reverse of the removal procedure. Torque the retaining bolts gradually and evenly to 21 ft. lbs. (28 Nm).
7. Allow 20 minutes tappet bleed down time after rocker shaft installation before starting the engine.

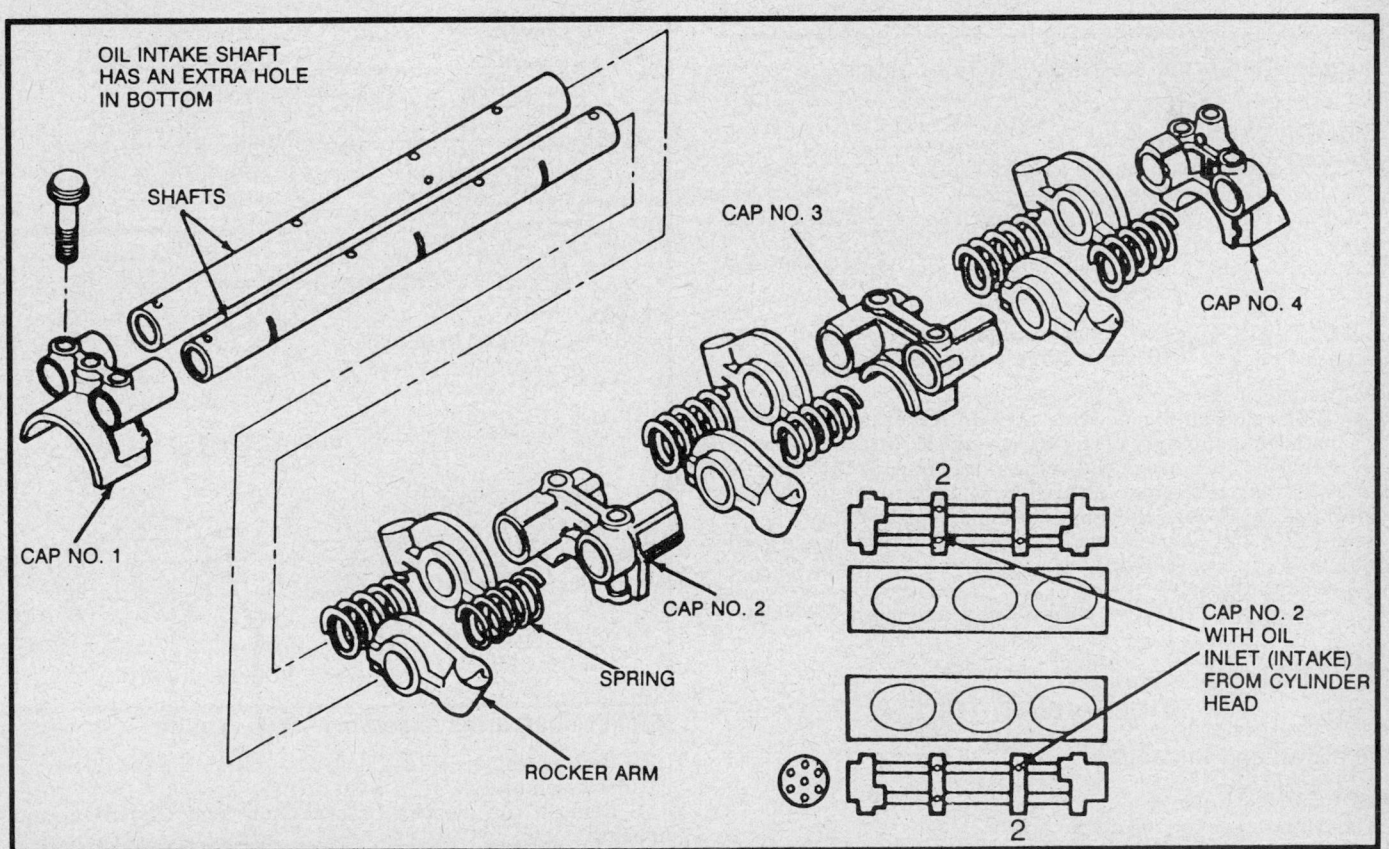

Rocker shafts/arms assembly—3.0L engine

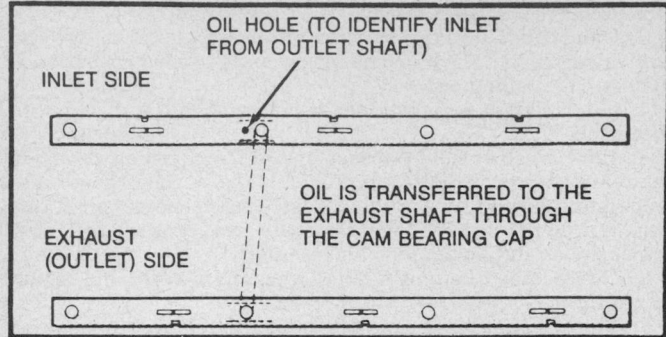

INLET SIDE

OIL HOLE (TO IDENTIFY INLET FROM OUTLET SHAFT)

OIL IS TRANSFERRED TO THE EXHAUST SHAFT THROUGH THE CAM BEARING CAP

EXHAUST (OUTLET) SIDE

Identifying the rocker shafts—3.0L engine

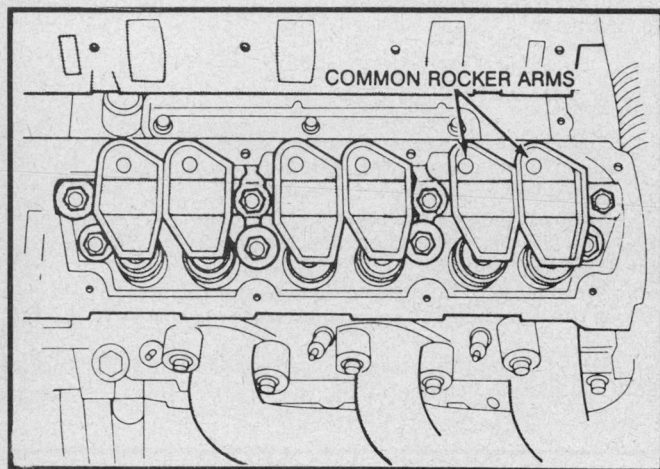

COMMON ROCKER ARMS

Rocker shaft/arms assembly—3.3L engine

3.9L ENGINE

1. Disconnect the negative battery cable.
2. Remove the valve cover and gasket.
3. Note the positioning of the oil notch and remove the rocker arms and shaft assembly from the head.
4. Disassemble the unit as required and replace all worn parts.

NOTE: On engines with exhaust valve rotators, the exhaust rocker arm must have relief for clearance.

To install:

5. Make sure all rocker arms with an **RH** stamped on them are installed to the right of those with an **LH**. Install the assembly with the notch on the end of the shaft pointing to the engine centerline and to the rear of the right bank or to the front of the left bank. Make sure the longer stamped steel retainers are at the number 2 and 4 positions. Torque the bolts evenly and gradually to 17 ft. lbs. (23 Nm).
6. Install the valve cover.
7. Connect the negative battery cable and check for leaks.

Intake Manifold

Removal and Installation

2.6L ENGINE

1. Disconnect the negative battery cable.
2. Drain the cooling system. Disconnect the hose from the water pump to the intake manifold.

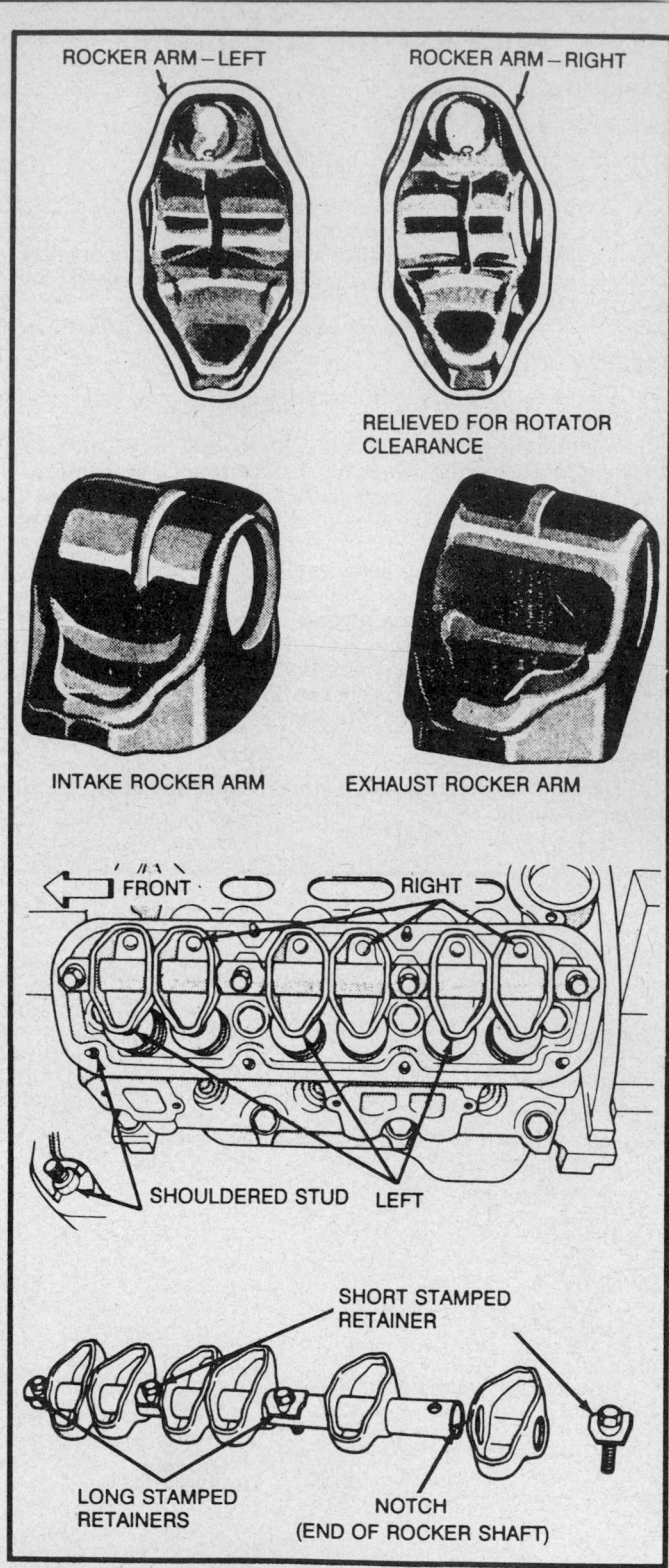

ROCKER ARM—LEFT ROCKER ARM—RIGHT

RELIEVED FOR ROTATOR CLEARANCE

INTAKE ROCKER ARM   EXHAUST ROCKER ARM

FRONT RIGHT

SHOULDERED STUD   LEFT

SHORT STAMPED RETAINER

LONG STAMPED RETAINERS

NOTCH (END OF ROCKER SHAFT)

Rocker shaft/arms assembly—3.9L engine

3. Remove the air intake hose along with the top of the air cleaner assembly.
4. Remove the dipstick bracket bolt from the thermostat housing.
5. Remove the carburetor to valve cover bracket. Remove and plug the fuel lines to the carburetor.

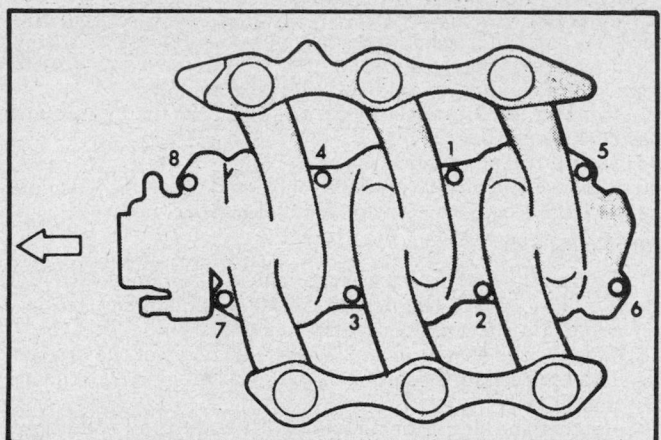

Intake manifold bolt torque sequence — 3.0L engine

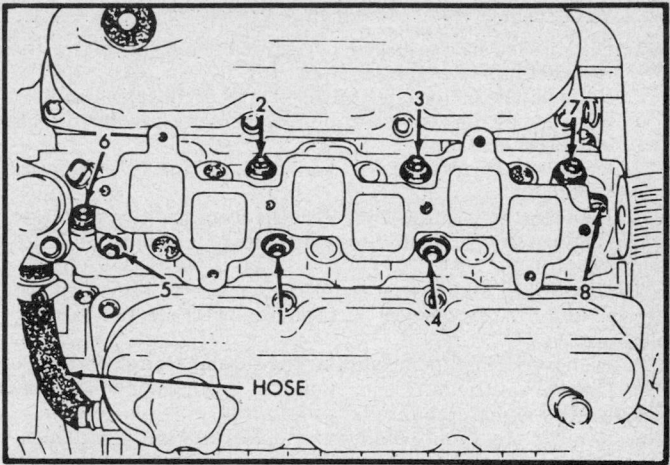

Intake manifold bolt torque sequence — 3.3L engine

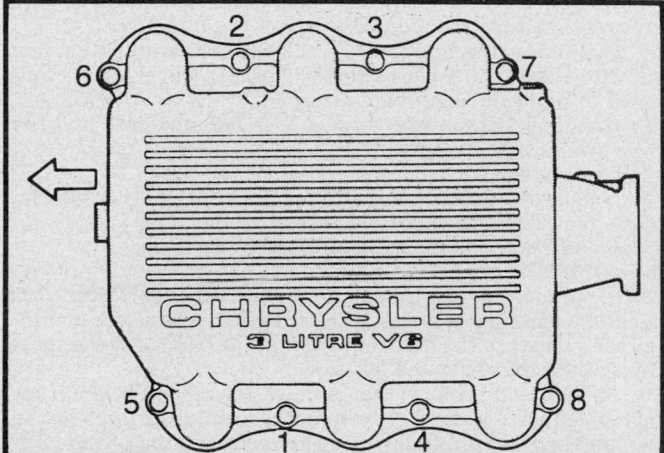

Air intake plenum bolt torque sequence — 3.0L engine

6. Disconnect and label the vacuum lines, hoses and wiring connectors from the manifolds and carburetor. Since some of the vacuum lines from the carburetor connect to a solenoid pack on the right side inner fender, unbolt the solenoids from the fender with the vacuum lines attached and fold the assembly over the carburetor.

7. Disconnect all the linkages and the fuel line from the carburetor.

8. Raise the vehicle and support safely. Disconnect the vacuum hoses from the source below the carburetor and disconnect the air feeder tubes.

9. Remove the manifold nuts and bolts and remove the manifold from the engine.

10. The installation is the reverse of the removal procedure. Torque the intake manifold nuts and bolts to 12 ft. lbs. (17 Nm).

3.0L ENGINE

1. Relieve the fuel system pressure. Disconnect the negative battery cable.

2. Drain the cooling system.

3. Remove the throttle body to air cleaner hose.

4. Remove the throttle body and transaxle kickdown linkage.

5. Remove the AIS motor and TPS wiring connectors from the throttle body.

6. Remove and label the vacuum hose harness from the throttle body.

7. From the air intake plenum, remove the PCV and brake booster hoses and the EGR tube flange.

8. Disconnect and label the charge and temperature sensor wiring at the intake manifold.

9. Remove the vacuum connections from the air intake plenum vacuum connector.

10. Remove the fuel hoses from the fuel rail.

11. Remove the air intake plenum mounting bolts and remove the plenum.

12. Remove the vacuum hoses from the fuel rail and pressure regulator.

13. Disconnect the fuel injector wiring harness from the engine wiring harness.

14. Remove the fuel pressure regulator mounting bolts and remove the regulator from the fuel rail.

15. Remove the fuel rail mounting bolts and remove the fuel rail from the intake manifold.

16. Separate the radiator hose from the thermostat housing and heater hoses from the heater pipe.

17. Remove the intake manifold mounting bolts and remove the manifold from the engine.

18. Clean the gasket mounting surfaces on the engine and intake manifold.

To Install:

19. Using new gaskets, position the intake manifold on the engine and install the mounting nuts and washers.

20. Torque the mounting nuts gradually and evenly, in sequence, to 15 ft. lbs. (20 Nm).

21. Make sure the injector holes are clean. Lubricate the injector O-rings with a drop of clean engine oil and install the injector assembly onto the engine.

22. Install and torque the fuel rail mounting bolts to 10 ft. lbs. (14 Nm).

23. Install the fuel pressure regulator onto the fuel rail.

24. Install the fuel supply and return tube and the vacuum crossover hold-down bolt.

25. Connect the fuel injection wiring harness to the engine wiring harness.

26. Connect the vacuum harness to the fuel pressure regulator and fuel rail assembly.

27. Remove the cover from the lower intake manifold and clean the mating surface.

28. Place the intake plenum gasket with the beaded sealant side up, on the intake manifold. Install the air intake plenum and torque the mounting bolts gradually and evenly, in sequence, to 10 ft. lbs. (14 Nm).

29. Connect or install all remaining items that were disconnected or removed during the removal procedure.

30. Refill the cooling system. Connect the negative battery cable and check for leaks using the DRB I or II to activate the fuel pump.

3.3L ENGINE

1. Disconnect the negative battery cable. Relieve the fuel pressure. Drain the cooling system.
2. Remove the air cleaner to throttle body hose assembly.
3. Disconnect the throttle cable and remove the wiring harness from the bracket.
4. Remove AIS motor and TPS wiring connectors from the throttle body.
5. Remove the vacuum hose harness from the throttle body.
6. Remove the PCV and brake booster hoses from the air intake plenum.
7. Disconnect the charge temperature sensor electrical connector. Remove the vacuum harness connectors from the intake plenum.
8. Remove the cylinder head to the intake plenum strut.
9. Disconnect the MAP sensor and oxygen sensor connectors. Remove the engine mounted ground strap.
10. Remove the fuel hoses from the fuel rail and plug them.
11. Remove the DIS coils and the alternator bracket to intake manifold bolt.
12. Remove the upper intake manifold attaching bolts and remove the upper manifold.
13. Remove the vacuum harness connector from the fuel pressure regulator.
14. Remove the fuel tube retainer bracket screw and fuel rail attaching bolts. Spread the retainer bracket to allow for clearance when removing the fuel tube.
15. Remove the fuel rail injector wiring clip from the alternator bracket.
16. Disconnect the cam sensor, coolant temperature sensor and engine temperature sensor.
17. Remove the fuel rail.
18. Remove the upper radiator hose, bypass hose and rear intake manifold hose.
19. Remove the intake manifold bolts and remove the manifold from the engine.
20. Remove the intake manifold seal retaining screws and remove the manifold gasket.
21. Clean out clogged end water passages and fuel runners.

To install:

22. Clean and dry all gasket mating surfaces.
23. Place a drop of silicone sealer onto each of the 4 manifold to cylinder head gasket corners.

----- CAUTION -----
The intake manifold gasket is composed of very thin and sharp metal. Handle this gasket with care or damage to the gasket or personal injury could result.

24. Install the intake manifold gasket and torque the end retainers to 10 ft. lbs. (12 Nm).
25. Install the intake manifold and torque the bolts in sequence to 10 inch lbs. Repeat the sequence increasing the torque to 17 ft. lbs. (23 Nm) and recheck each bolt for 17 ft. lbs. of torque. After the bolts are torqued, inspect the seals to ensure that they have not become dislodged.
26. Lubricat the injector O-rings with clean oil and position the fuel rail in place. Install the rail mounting bolts.
27. Connect the cam sensor, coolant temperature sensor and engine temperature sensor.
28. Install the fuel rail injector wiring clip to the alternator bracket.
29. Install the fuel rail attaching bolts and fuel tube retainer bracket screw.
30. Install the vacuum harness to the pressure regulator.
31. Install the upper intake manifold with a new gasket. Install the bolts only fingertight. Install the alternator bracket to intake manifold bolt and the cylinder head to intake manifold strut and bolts. Torque the intake manifold mounting bolts to

21 ft. lbs. (28 Nm) starting from the middle and working outward. Torque the bracket and strut bolts to 40 ft. lbs. (54 Nm).
32. Install or connect all items that were removed or disconnected from the intake manifold and throttle body.
33. Connect the fuel hoses to the rail. Push the fittings in until they click in place.
34. Install the air cleaner assembly.
35. Connect the negative battery cable and check for leaks using the DRB I or II to activate the fuel pump.

3.9L ENGINE

1. Relieve the fuel pressure if the vehicle is equipped with fuel injection. Disconnect the negative battery cable from the battery and drain the cooling system.
2. Remove the air pump and bracket. Removal of the bracket will allow for easier installation of the left front corner of the intake manifold.
3. Remove the air cleaner assembly. Unbolt the air conditioning compressor and lay it to the side, if equipped. Remove the distributor cap with all wires attached.
4. Disconnect all wires, hoses, linkages and cables from the carburetor or throttle body. Disconnect the fuel line.
5. Disconnect the ignition coil, coolant temperature sending unit wire and all other connectors along the wiring harness connected to items on the intake manifold.
6. Disconnect the heater hose, upper radiator hose and the lower bypass hose clamp.
7. Remove the valve covers.
8. Unbolt the intake manifold from the heads and remove the intake manifold assembly. Disassemble the manifold as required and clean out the exhaust crossover passages.

To install:

9. Clean and dry the intake manifold contact surfaces. Coat the intake manifold side gaskets very lightly with sealer and install the gaskets to the heads. Cutouts at the front of the gaskets differentiate the right and left sides.
10. Apply a thin uniform coat of quick dry cement to the front and rear intake manifold gaskets and mounting surfaces on the block and apply a thin bead of sealer to each of 4 the corners. Install the front and rear gaskets engaging the hole in the block and the tangs from the head gaskets. Apply a second thin bead of sealer above the gaskets in the 4 corners.
11. Carefully lower the intake manifold into position engaging

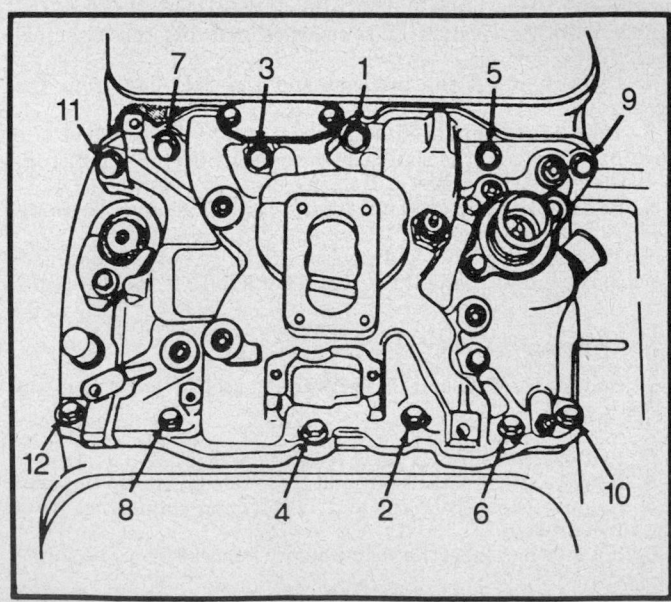

Intake manifold bolt torque sequence — 3.9L engine

the bypass hose; after it is satisfactorily in place, inspect the gaskets to make sure they have not become dislodged.

12. Install the intake manifold bolts with the aspirator tube, air pump bracket and kickdown linkage bracket in place, if equipped. Torque the bolts in sequence to 25 ft. lbs. (34 Nm). Repeat the sequence retightening the bolts to a final torque of 40 ft. lbs. (54 Nm) and repeat the second step to ensure all bolts are accurately torqued.

13. Clean and dry the valve cover mating surfaces, bolts and bolt holes. Install the valve covers with a new gasket. Torque the screws or nuts to 95 inch lbs. (11 Nm).

14. Connect the heater hose, upper radiator hose and the lower bypass hose clamp.

15. Connect the ignition coil, coolant temperature sending unit wire and all other connectors that were disconnected along the wiring harness.

16. Install the air conditioning compressor, if equipped. Install the distributor cap and all spark plug wires.

17. Install air pump.

18. Connect all wires, hoses, cables and the fuel line to the carburetor or throttle body. Install the air cleaner assembly.

19. Fill the cooling system.

20. Connect the negative battery cable. Use the DRBII to activate the fuel pump on fuel injected vehicles. Check for leaks.

Exhaust Manifold

Removal and Installation

2.6L ENGINE

1. Disconnect the negative battery cable.
2. Remove the air cleaner assembly.
3. Unbolt the power steering pump and postion it to the side.
4. Remove the heat cowl from the exhaust manifold.
5. Remove the bolts that attach the exhaust manifold to the after burn chamber below it.
6. Remove manifold mounting nuts and remove the manifold from the engine.
7. The installation is the reverse of the removal procedure. Replace the after burn chamber gasket and exhaust manifold gasket when installing. Torque the manifold mounting nuts to 13 ft. lbs. (18 Nm) starting from the middle and working outward.

3.0L ENGINE

1. Disconnect the negative battery cable. Raise and safely support the vehicle.
2. Disconnect the exhaust pipe from the rear exhaust manifold, at the articulated joint.
3. Disconnect the EGR tube from the rear manifold and the oxygen sensor wire.
4. Remove the crossover pipe to manifold bolts.
5. Remove the rear manifold to cylinder head nuts and the manifold.
6. Lower the vehicle and remove the heat shield from the manifold.
7. Remove the front manifold to cylinder head nuts and the manifold.
8. Clean the gasket mounting surfaces. Inspect the manifolds for cracks, flatness and/or damage.
9. The installation is the reverse of the removal procedure. When installing, the numbers 1–3–5 on the gaskets are used with the rear cylinders and 2–4–6 are on the gasket for the front cylinders. Torque the manifold to cylinder head nuts to 14 ft. lbs. (19 Nm).
10. Start the engine and check for exhaust leaks.

3.3L ENGINE

1. Disconnect the negative battery cable.
2. If removing the rear manifold, raise the vehicle and sup-

port safely. Disconnect the exhaust pipe at the articulated joint from the rear exhaust manifold.

3. Separate the EGR tube from the rear manifold and disconnect the oxygen sensor wire.
4. Remove the alternator/power steering support strut.
5. Remove the bolts attaching the crossover pipe to the manifold.
6. Remove the bolts attaching the manifold to the head and remove the manifold.
7. If removing the front manifold, remove the heat shield, bolts attaching the crossover pipe to the manifold and the nuts attaching the manifold to the head.
8. Remove the manifold from the engine.
9. The installation is the reverse of the removal procedure. Torque all exhaust manifold attaching bolts to 17 ft. lbs. (23 Nm).
10. Start the engine and check for exhaust leaks.

3.9L ENGINE

1. Disconnect the negative battery cable. Remove the hot air tube and heat shield, if necessary.
2. Raise the vehicle and support safely. Remove the exhaust pipe from the exhaust manifolds. Lower the vehicle.
3. Take note of all conical washer locations and remove the bolts, nuts and washers attaching the manifold to the head.
4. Remove the manifold.
To install:
5. If either of the end studs came out with the nuts, install a new stud using sealer on the coarse threads.

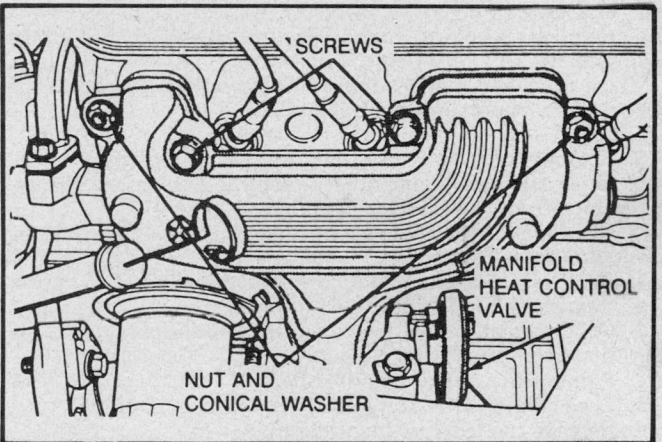

Exhaust manifold bolt installation—3.9L engine

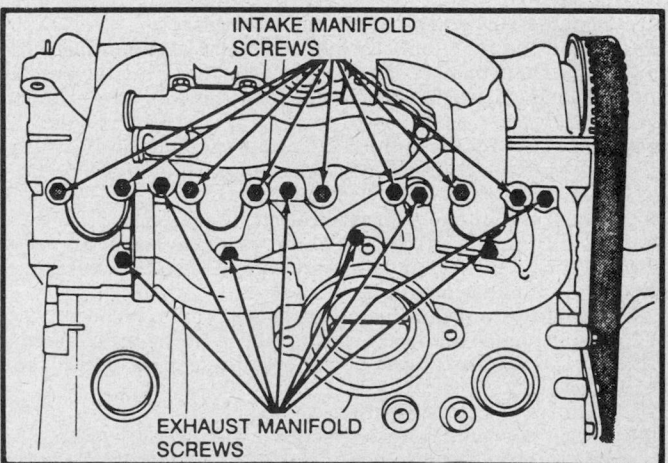

Combination manifold attaching nuts and bolts—2.2L and 2.5L non-turbocharged engine

6. Position the manifold on the end studs. Install conical washers and nuts on the studs.

7. Install the remaining bolts and washers in their proper locations. The inner bolts are not mounted with washers. Working outward from the center, torque the bolts to 20 ft. lbs. (27 Nm) and the nuts to 15 ft. lbs. (20 Nm).

8. Install the exhaust pipe to the manifolds.

9. Connect the negative battery cable and check for exhaust leaks.

Combination Manifold

Removal and Installation

2.2L AND 2.5L ENGINES

Without Turbocharger

NOTE: On some vehicles, some of the manifold attaching bolts are not accessible or too heavily sealed from the factory and cannot be removed on the vehicle. Head removal would be necessary in these situations.

1. Disconnect the negative battery cable.
2. Drain the cooling system.
3. Remove the air cleaner and disconnect all vacuum lines, electrical wiring and fuel lines from the carburetor or throttle body.
4. Disconnect the throttle linkage.
5. Loosen the power steering pump and remove the drive belt. On Dakota, remove the power steering and air pump support bracket.
6. Remove the power brake vacuum hose from the intake manifold.
7. On Canadian models, remove the coupling hose from the diverter valve to the exhaust manifold air injection tube assembly.
8. Remove the water hoses from the water crossover.
9. Raise and safely support the vehicle. Disconnect the exhaust pipe from the exhaust manifold.
10. On Caravan and Voyager, remove the power steering pump and set it aside.
11. Remove the intake manifold support bracket, if equipped.
12. Remove the EGR tube.
13. On Canadian models, remove the air injection tube bolts and the air injection tube assembly.
14. Remove the intake manifold bolts.
15. Lower the vehicle and remove the intake manifold.
16. Remove the exhaust manifold nuts.
17. Remove the exhaust manifold.

To install:

18. Install a new combination manifold gasket.
19. Install the manifold assembly. Install the mounting nuts and torque them to 13 ft. lbs. (18 Nm.) starting from the middle and working outward. Install the heat cowl to the exhaust manifold.
20. Install the intake manifold. Torque the bolts to 17 ft. lbs. (23 Nm.) starting from the middle and working outward.
21. Install the EGR tube.
22. Install the intake support bracket, if equipped.
23. Install the power steering pump, if it was removed.
24. Raise the vehicle and support safely. Install the exhaust pipe to the exhaust manifold.
25. Install the water hoses to the water crossover.
26. Install the power brake vacuum hose to the intake manifold. On Dakota, install the power steering and air pump support bracket.
27. Connect the throttle linkage.
28. Install all vacuum lines, electrical wiring and fuel lines to the carburetor or throttle body.
29. Install the air cleaner assembly.
30. Refill the cooling system.

31. Connect the negative battery cable and check manifolds for leaks.

With Turbocharger

NOTE: On some vehicles, some of the manifold attaching bolts are not accessible or too heavily sealed from the factory and cannot be removed on the vehicle. Head removal would be necessary in these situations.

1. Disconnect the negative battery cable. Drain the cooling system. Raise and safely support the vehicle.
2. Disconnect the exhaust pipe at the articulated joint. Disconnect the oxygen sensor at the electrical connection.
3. Remove the turbocharger to engine support bracket.
4. Loosen the oil drain back tube connector hose clamps. Move the tube down on the engine block fitting.
5. Disconnect the turbocharger coolant inlet tube from the engine block and disconnect the tube support bracket.
6. Remove the air cleaner assembly, including the throttle body adaptor, hose and air cleaner box with support bracket.
7. Disconnect the accelerator linkage, throttle body electrical connector and vacuum hoses.
8. Relocate the fuel rail assembly. Remove the bracket to intake manifold screws and the bracket to heat shield clips. Lift and secure the fuel rail (with injectors, wiring harness and fuel lines intact) up and out of the way.
9. Disconnect the turbocharger oil feed line at the oil sending unit Tee fitting.
10. Disconnect the upper radiator hose from the thermostat housing.
11. Remove the cylinder head, manifolds and turbocharger as an assembly.
12. With the assembly on a workbench, loosen the upper turbocharger discharge hose end clamp.

NOTE: Do not disturb the center deswirler retaining clamp.

13. Remove the throttle body to intake manifold screws and throttle body assembly. Disconnect the turbocharger coolant return tube from the water box. Disconnect the retaining bracket on the cylinder head.
14. Remove the heat shield to intake manifold screws and the heat shield.
15. Remove the turbocharger to exhaust manifold nuts and the turbocharger assembly.
16. Remove the intake manifold bolts and the intake manifold.
17. Remove the exhaust manifold nuts and the exhaust manifold.

To install:

18. Place a new 2-sided Grafoil type intake/exhaust manifold gasket; do not use sealant.
19. Position the exhaust manifold on the cylinder head. Apply anti-seize compound to threads, install and torque the retaining nuts, starting at center and progressing outward in both directions, to 17 ft. lbs. (23 Nm). Repeat this procedure until all nuts are at 17 ft. lbs. (23 Nm).
20. Position the intake manifold on the cylinder head. Install and torque the retaining screws, starting at center and progressing outward in both directions, to 19 ft. lbs. (26 Nm). Repeat this procedure until all screws are at 19 ft. lbs. (26 Nm).
21. Connect the turbocharger outlet to the intake manifold inlet tube. Position the turbocharger on the exhaust manifold. Apply anti-seize compound to threads and torque the nuts to 30 ft. lbs. (41 Nm). Torque the connector tube clamps to 30 inch lbs. (41 Nm).
22. Install the tube support bracket to the cylinder head.
23. Install the heat shield on the intake manifold. Torque the screws to 105 inch lbs. (12 Nm).
24. Install the throttle body air horn into the turbocharger inlet tube. Install and torque the throttle body to intake manifold

screws to 21 ft. lbs. (28 Nm). Torque the tube clamp to 30 inch lbs.

25. Install the cylinder head/manifolds/turbocharger assembly on the engine.

26. Reconnect the turbocharger oil feed line to the oil sending unit Tee fitting and bearing housing, if disconnected. Torque the tube nuts to 10 ft. lbs. (14 Nm).

27. Install the air cleaner assembly. Connect the vacuum lines and accelerator cables.

28. Reposition the fuel rail. Install and torque the bracket screws to 21 ft. lbs. (28 Nm). Install the air shield to bracket clips.

29. Connect the turbocharger inlet coolant tube to the engine block. Torque the tube nut to 30 ft. lbs. (41 Nm). Install the tube support bracket.

30. Install the turbocharger housing to engine block support bracket and the screws hand tight. Torque the block screw 1st to 40 ft. lbs. (54 Nm). Torque the screw to the turbocharger housing to 20 ft. lbs. (27 Nm).

31. Reposition the drain back hose connector and tighten the hose clamps. Reconnect the exhaust pipe.

32. Connect the upper radiator hose to the thermostat housing.

33. Refill the cooling system.

34. Connect the negative battery cable and check the manifolds for leaks.

Turbocharger

Removal and Installation

NOTE: On some vehicles, some of the turbocharger to exhaust manifold nuts are not accessible enough to loosen and cannot be removed on the vehicle. Head removal would be necessary in these situations.

1. Disconnect the negative battery cable. Drain the cooling system.

2. Disconnect the EGR valve tube at the EGR valve.

3. Disconnect the turbocharger oil feed at the oil sending unit hex and the coolant tube at the water box. Disconnect the oil/coolant support bracket from the cylinder head.

4. Remove the right intermediate shaft, bearing support bracket and outer driveshaft assemblies.

5. Remove the turbocharger to engine block support bracket.

6. Disconnect the exhaust pipe at the articulated joint. Disconnect the oxygen sensor at the electrical connection.

7. Loosen the oil drain-back tube connector clamps and move the tube hose down on the nipple.

8. Disconnect the coolant tube nut at the block outlet (below steering pump bracket) and tube support bracket.

9. Remove the turbocharger to exhaust manifold nuts. Carefully routing the oil and coolant lines, move the assembly down and out of the vehicle.

To Install:

NOTE: Before installing the turbocharger assembly, be sure it is first charged with oil. Failure to do this may cause damage to the assembly.

10. Position the turbocharger on the exhaust manifold. Apply an anti-seize compound, Loctite® 771–64 or equivalent, to the threads and torque the retaining nuts to 40 ft. lbs. (54 Nm).

11. Connect the coolant tube to engine block fitting. Torque the tube nut to 30 ft. lbs. (41 Nm).

12. Position the oil drain-back hose and torque the clamps to 30 inch lbs.

13. Install and torque the:
Turbocharger to engine support bracket block screw to 40 ft. lbs. (54Nm).
Turbocharger housing screw to 20 ft. lbs. (27 Nm).
Articulated joint shoulder bolts to 21 ft. lbs. (28 Nm).

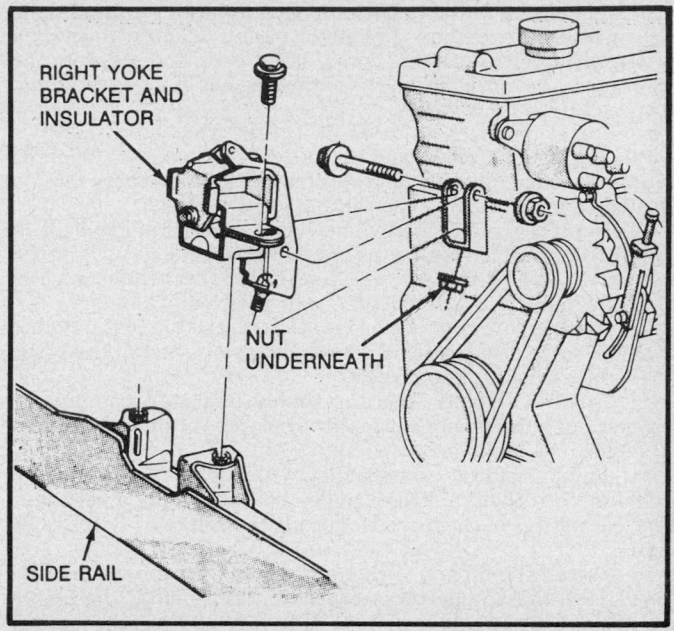

Right side motor mount – Caravan and Voyager with 2.6L engine

14. Install the right driveshaft assembly, the starter and the oil feed line at the sending unit hex. Torque the oil feed tube nut to 10 ft. lbs. (14 Nm) and the EGR tube to EGR valve nut to 60 ft. lbs. (81 Nm).

15. Refill the cooling system. Connect the negative battery cable and check the turbocharger for proper operation.

Timing Chain Case Cover

Removal and Installation

2.6L ENGINE

1. Disconnect the negative battery cable.

2. Drain the cooling system.

3. Loosen the power steering pump and air conditioning/alternator belts.

4. Remove the valve cover. Matchmark the distributor to its drive gear and remove the distributor. Remove the alternator.

5. Remove the two small front bolts from the cylinder head; these screw into and seal the top of the timing cover.

6. Support the vehicle safely and raise the vehicle slightly. Support the oil pan with a floor jack and remove the right side motor mount by removing the 2 bolts on either side of the mount, the through bolt and the 21mm nut from the underside of the mount. Remove all of the upper cover bolts that are accessible. Attach a suitable engine support device to the engine. Lower the engine slowly until its weight is supported by the engine support device.

7. Raise the vehicle and support safely. Remove the right wheel and tire assembly and the splash shield. Remove the crankshaft bolt and pull off the crankshaft pulley with the belts.

8. Unbolt the air conditioning compressor bracket from the cover and position it, with the compressor still bolted to it, to the side.

9. Drain the engine oil and remove the oil pan.

—————— **CAUTION** ——————

As soon as the timing cover gasket seal is broken, antifreeze will start pouring out from the water jacket extension in the cover. Stand back when breaking the cover seal, or personal injury may result, especially if the engine is hot.

10. Remove the remaining timing cover retaining bolts and the timing indicator. Remove the motor mount adaptor. Position a drainpan under the timing cover, stand back and separate the cover from the block. When the antifreeze has stopped draining, remove the chain cover.

To install:

11. Thoroughly clean and dry all gasket surfaces. Clean or sand the timing indicator and paint a white mark where the 7 is located to aid in setting the timing.

12. Replace the adjuster window gasket and crankshaft seal. Carefully pry the oil seal out of the cover without scratching the seal bore. Install a new seal with a seal driver or installer such as MD998376–01 and MB990938–01, or their equivalents.

13. Apply a thin coat of silicone sealer to the top of the timing chain cover to seal the head gasket extension. Install the cover to the block using new gaskets.

14. Install the bolts with the timing indicator, compressor bracket and motor mount adaptor in place. Torque the bolts to 13 ft. lbs. (18 Nm).

15. Install the crankshaft pulley with the belts. Thoroughly clean and dry the crankshaft pulley bolt and apply a very thin bead of Loctite® to the threads. Torque the bolt to 87 ft. lbs. (118 Nm).

16. Install the oil pan with a new gasket. Lower the vehicle.

17. Jack the engine up into position and install the motor mount. Torque the upper bolts to 21 ft. lbs. (29 Nm), the nut underneath to 75 ft. lbs. (102 Nm) and the through bolt and nut to 75 ft. lbs. (102 Nm). Remove the engine support device.

18. Thoroughly clean and dry the 2 end bolts that attach the chain cover to the head. Install them and torque to 13 ft. lbs. (18 Nm).

19. Install the alternator.

20. Install the distributor aligning the matchmarks.

21. Install the valve cover with a new gasket.

22. Adjust all belt tensions.

23. Refill the cooling system and fill the engine with oil.

24. Connect the negative battery cable, road test the vehicle and check for leaks.

3.3L ENGINE

1. Disconnect the negative battery cable. Drain the cooling system.

2. Support the engine with a suitable engine support device and remove th right side motor mount.

3. Raise the vehicle and support safely. Drain the engine oil and remove the oil pan.

4. Remove the right wheel and tire assembly and the splash shield.

5. Remove the drive belt.

6. Unbolt the air conditioning compressor and position it to the side. Remove the compressor mounting bracket.

7. Remove the crankshaft pulley bolt and remove the pulley using a suitable puller.

8. Remove the idler pulley from the engine bracket and remove the bracket.

9. Remove the cam sensor from the timing chain cover.

10. Unbolt and remove the cover from the engine. Make sure the oil pump inner rotor does not fall out. Remove the three O-rings from the coolant passages and the oil pump outlet.

To install:

11. Thoroughly clean and dry the gasket mating surfaces. Install new O-rings to the block.

12. Remove the crankshaft oil seal from the cover. The seal must be removed from the cover when installing to ensure proper oil pump engagement.

13. Using a new gasket, install the chain case cover to the engine.

14. Make certain that the oil pump is engaged onto the crankshaft before proceeding, or severe engine damage will result. Install the attaching bolts and torque to 20 ft. lbs. (27 Nm).

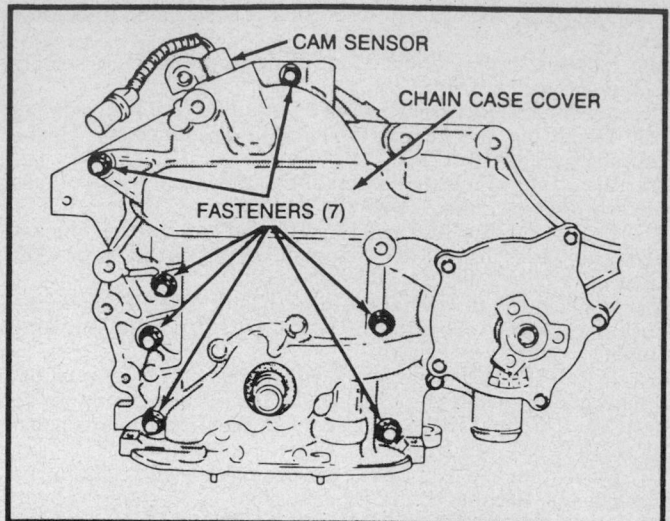

Timing chain cover—3.3L engine

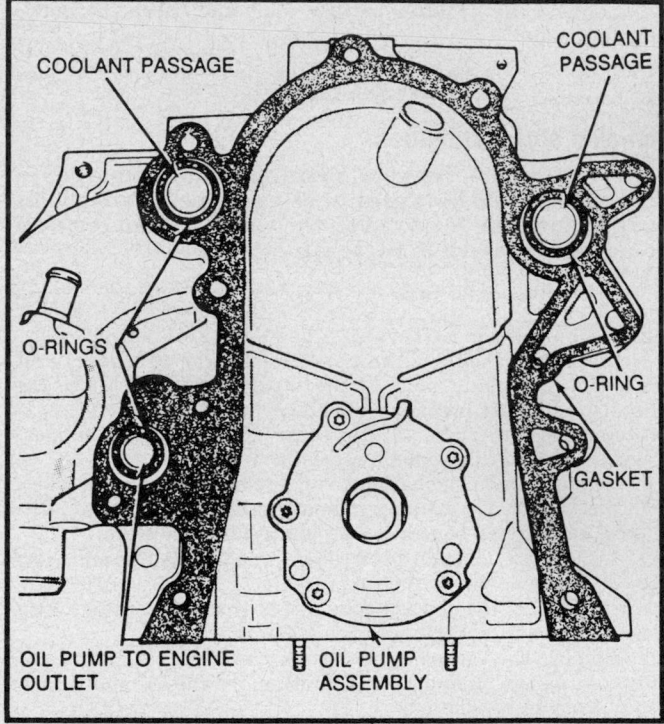

Timing chain cover removed—3.3L engine

15. Use tool C–4992 to install the crankshaft oil seal. Install the crankshaft pulley using a 5.9 in. suitable bolt and thrust bearing and washer plate L–4524. Make sure the pulley bottoms out on the crankshaft seal diameter. Install the bolt and torque to 40 ft. lbs. (54 Nm).

16. Install the engine bracket and torque the bolts to 40 ft. lbs. (54 Nm). Install the idler pulley to the engine bracket.

17. To install the cam sensor, first clean off the old spacer from the sensor face completely. Inspect the O-ring for damage and replace if necessary. A new spacer must be attached to the cam sensor prior to installation; if a new spacer is not used, engine performance will be adversely affected. Oil the O-ring lightly and push the sensor into its bore in the chain case cover until

contact is made with the cam timing gear. Hold in this position and tighten the bolt to 9 ft. lbs. (12 Nm).

18. Install the air conditioning compressor and bracket.
19. Install the drive belt.
20. Install the inner splash shield and the wheel and tire assembly.
21. Install the oil pan with a new gasket.
22. Install the motor mount.
23. Remove the engine temperature sensor and fill the cooling system until the level reaches the vacant sensor hole. Install the sensor and continue to fill the radiator. Fill the engine with the proper amount of oil.
24. Connect the negative battery cable and check for leaks.

3.9L ENGINE

1. Disconnect the negative battery cable.
2. Drain the cooling system.
3. Remove the radiator, fan and all related parts. Remove the water pump.
4. Remove the crankshaft pulley.
5. Remove the vibration damper using the proper puller.
6. Disconnect the fuel lines from the fuel pump, if equipped.
7. Remove the 2 front bolts from the oil pan.
8. Unbolt the chain cover from the block and remove, using caution to avoid damaging the oil pan gasket. Remove the fuel pump from the cover, if equipped.

To install:

9. Clean and dry the mating surfaces of the cover and block. Apply a thin bead of sealer to the oil pan gasket.
10. Install a new cover gasket and install the cover. Torque the bolts to to 30 ft. lbs. (41 Nm).
11. Install the water pump with a new gasket.
12. Install the vibration damper with tool C–3638, install the bolt and washer and torque to specification. Apply a small amount of sealer to the bolts and install the crankshaft pulley.
13. Install the fuel pump using a new gasket, if equipped and connect the fuel lines. Install the 2 oil pan bolts.
14. Install the radiator, fan and all related parts.
15. Fill the cooling system.
16. Connect the negative battery cable and check for leaks.

Front Cover Oil Seal

Removal and Installation

2.6L ENGINE

1. Disconnect the negative battery cable.
2. Loosen the power steering pump and air conditioning compressor.
3. Raise the vehicle and support safely. Remove the right front tire and wheel assembly and the inner splash shield.
4. Remove the crankshaft pulley with the belts.
5. Pry the seal from its bore using a suitable prying tool.

To install:

6. Install a new seal with a seal driver or installer such as MD998376–01 and MB990938–01, or their equivalents.
7. Install the crankshaft pulley with the belts. Thoroughly clean and dry the crankshaft pulley bolt and apply a very thin bead of Loctite® to the threads. Torque the bolt to 87 ft. lbs. (118 Nm).
8. Adjust the belt tensions.
9. Install the splash shield and the tire and wheel assembly.
10. Connect the negative battery cable and check for leaks.

3.3L ENGINE

1. Disconnect the negative battery cable.
2. Raise the vehicle and support safely. Remove the right front tire and wheel assembly and the inner splash shield.
3. Remove the drive belt.
4. Remove the crankshaft bolt. Using a suitable puller, remove the crankshaft pulley.

5. Use tool C–4991 to remove the seal.

To install:

6. Clean out the bore. Place the seal with the spring toward the engine. Install the new seal using tool C–4992 until it is flush with the cover.
7. Install the crankshaft pulley using a 5.9 in. suitable bolt and thrust bearing and washer plate L–4524. Make sure the pulley bottoms out on the crankshaft seal diameter. Install the bolt and torque to 40 ft. lbs. (54 Nm).
8. Install the drive belt.
9. Install the splash shield and the tire and wheel assembly.
10. Connect the negative battery cable and check for leaks.

3.9L ENGINE

1. Disconnect the negative battery cable.
2. Remove the belts from the crankshaft pulley.
3. Remove the fan and shroud from the vehicle.
4. Remove the crankshaft pulley.
5. Remove the vibration damper using the proper puller.
6. Using a suitable tool behind the lips of the oil seal, pry outward. Take care not to damage the crankshaft seal surface of the cover.

To install:

7. Install the new seal by installing the threaded shaft part of the special tool C–4251 into the threads of the crankshaft.
8. Place the seal into the opening with the spring toward the engine. Place the installing adapter C–4251–3 with the thrust bearing and nut on the shaft. Tighten the nut until the tool is flush with the timing chain cover. Remove the tool.
9. Install the damper with tool C–3638, install the bolt and washer and torque to specification.
10. Apply a small amount of sealer to the bolts and install the crankshaft pulley.
11. Install the fan and shroud.
12. Connect the negative battery cable and check for leaks.

Timing Chain and Gears

Removal and Installation

2.6L ENGINE

1. If possible, position the engine so that the No. 1 piston is at TDC on the compression stroke. Disconnect the negative battery cable. Drain the coolant.
2. Remove the timing chain case cover.
3. Remove the 3 silent shaft chain guides. Label each bolt as it is removed. The bolts are of different lengths and styles and must be replaced in the correct locations.
4. Remove the flange bolts from the the chain from the right silent shaft and oil pump gears and carefully remove the chain with all 3 gears. Watch for the aligning keys on the oil pump shaft and right silent shaft. If the chain is removed individually, remove the gears afterward.

NOTE: The 2 gears are identical, but the oil pump drive sprocket is installed with the concave side toward the engine while the right silent shaft sprocket has the concave side out.

5. The timing chain tensioner maintains constant spring pressure on the chain. To prevent it from popping out of the oil pump it must be fastened in place. Run a piece of wire around the plunger and the left side of the oil pump. Remove the remaining chain guides.
6. Remove the camshaft gear bolt and pry the distributor drive gear from the cam gear. Remove the gear from the camshaft and allow it to sit on the gear holder below it. Rotate the camshaft so the spring pin is at the 12 o'clock position.
7. Unbolt the holder and remove the chain with both gears. Remove the tensioner and spring from the oil pump.

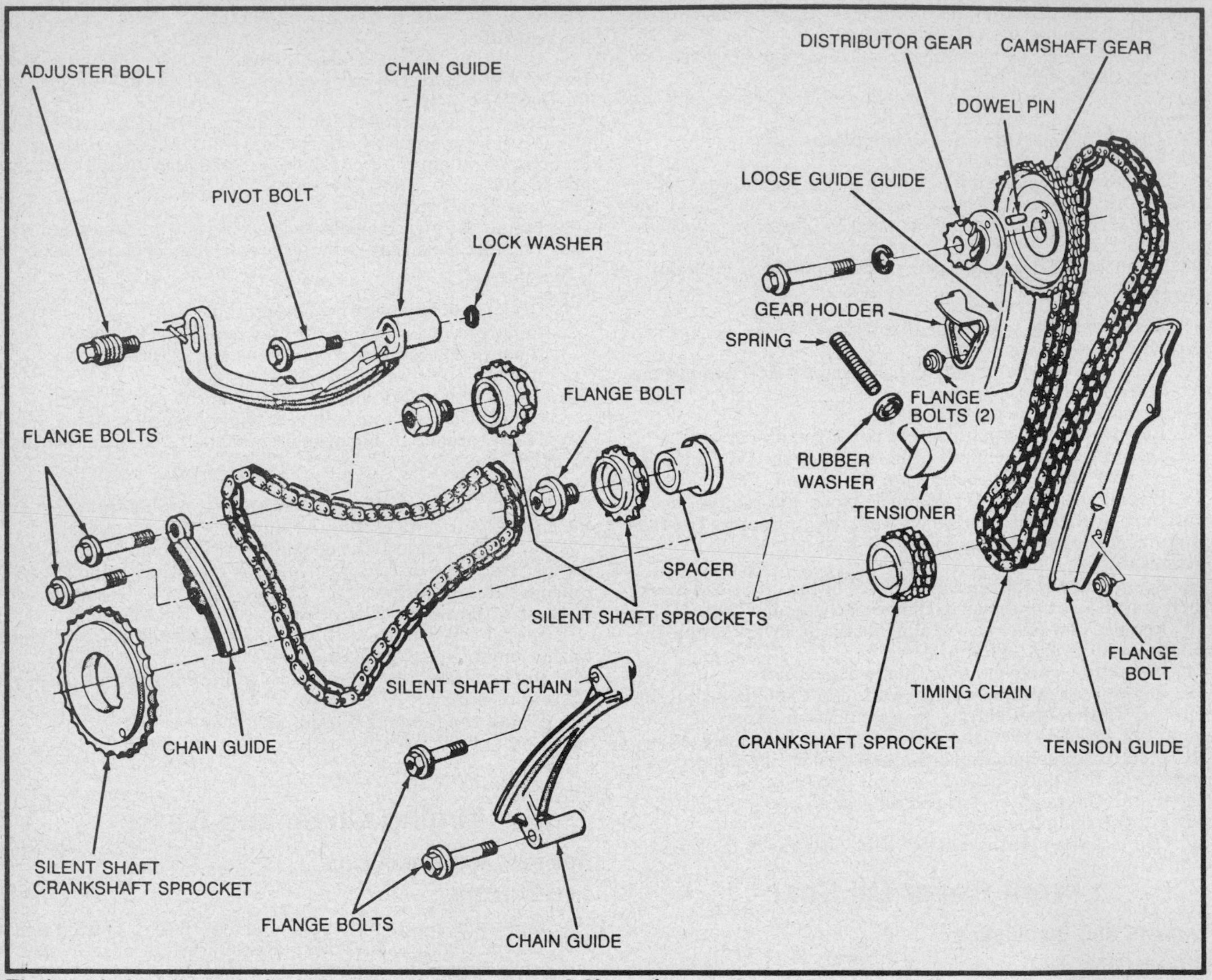

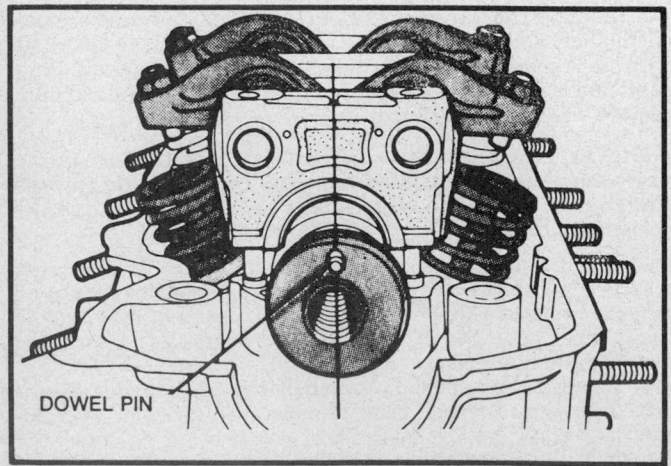

Timing chain, silent shaft chain and related parts — 2.6L engine

Camshaft position for chain installation — 2.6L engine

8. Inspect all gears for wear and replace as required.

To install:

9. Assemble the new timing chain with the gears. Both the crankshaft sprocket and the camshaft sprocket have a small dot on their faces. Assemble the chain and sprockets so that each dot aligns with the plated links on the chain. Both sets of marks and links must align.

10. Turn the crankshaft as required so that the installed positions of the respective gears are correct.

11. Install the new tensioner and spring in the bore of the oil pump and hold it down with a piece of wire.

12. Install the crankshaft gear to the crankshaft and install the cam gear holder while holding the gear up in place. Allow the cam gear to rest on the holder.

13. Lift the cam gear into place against the camshaft, install the distributor drive gear and install the bolt. Make certain the sprocket engages the guide pin correctly. Tighten the bolt to 40 ft. lbs.

14. Remove the wire holding the tensioner plunger and allow it to tension the chain. Install the left side guide.

15. Assemble the silent shaft gear, the oil pump gear and the silent shaft chain. Again, each sprocket is marked with a dot which must be aligned with the plated links on the chain. The

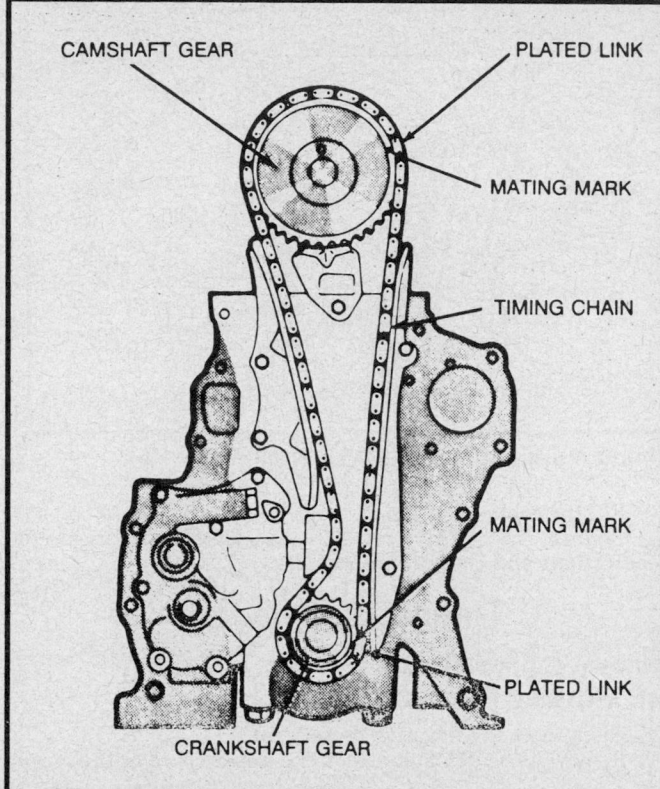

Timing chain installation—2.6L engine

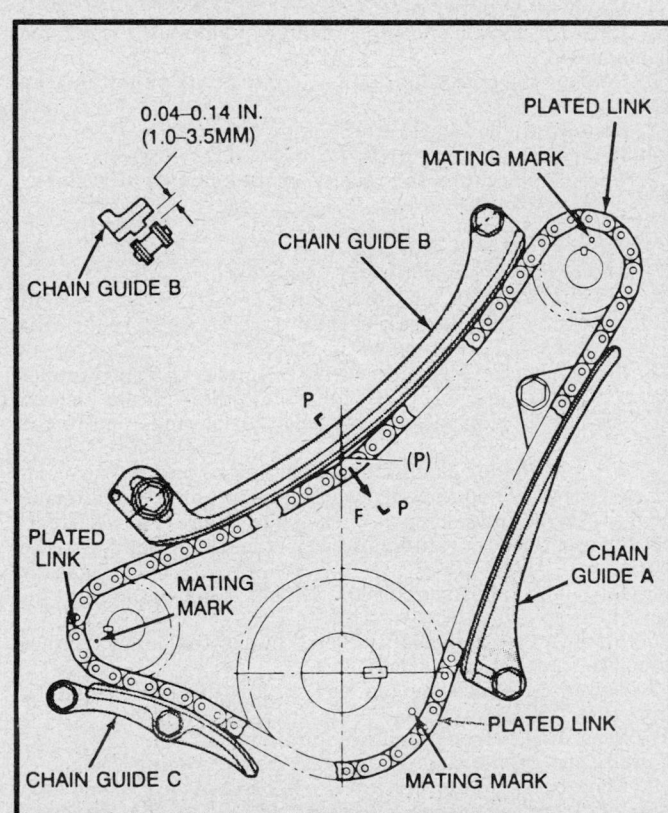

Silent shaft chain installion—2.6L engine

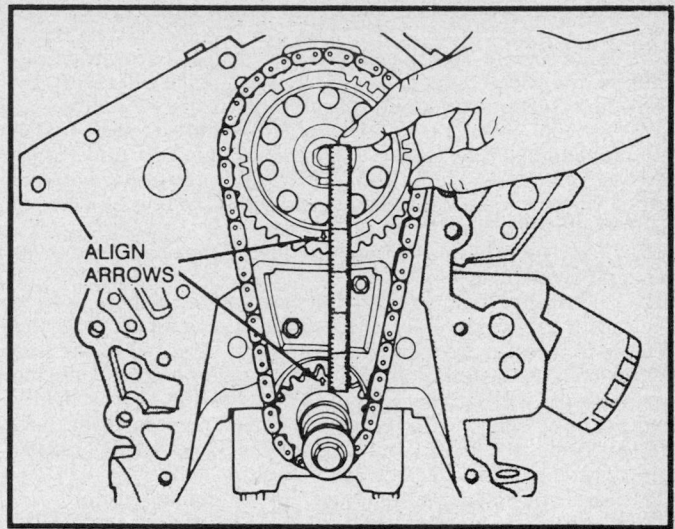

Timing mark alignment—3.3L engine

sprocket for the silent shaft mounts with the concave side facing out (away from the engine block) and the sprocket for the oil pump mounts with the concave side facing the engine block.

16. Install the silent chain with gears onto the shafts. Turn the oil pump shaft and right silent shaft as required to keep the marks aligned.

17. Install the chain guides. Make sure the lock washer is installed between the tensioner guide pivot bolt and the timing chain guide under it. Torque all 10mm flanged bolts to 13 ft. lbs. (18 Nm). Adjust the upper guide so that when the chain is pulled downward at the center, the clearance between the chain and the guide is 0.008–0.031 in. (0.20–0.80mm). Torque the tensioner guide locking bolt to 14 ft. lbs.

18. Install the gear retaining bolts to the oil pump and right silent shaft. Torque the bolts to 25 ft. lbs. (34 Nm).

19. Install the timing chain case cover and all related parts.

20. Refill the cooling system and fill the engine with oil.

21. Connect the negative battery cable, road test the vehicle and check for leaks.

3.3L ENGINE

1. If possible, position the engine so that the No. 1 piston is at TDC on the compression stroke. Disconnect the negative battery cable. Drain the coolant.

2. Remove the timing chain case cover.

3. Remove the camshaft gear attaching cup washer and remove the timing chain with both gears attached. Remove the timing chain snubber.

To install:

4. Assemble the timing chain and gears.

5. Turn the crankshaft and camshaft to line up with the keyway locations of the gears.

6. Slide both gears over their respective shafts and use a straightedge to confirm alignment.

7. Install the cup washer and camshaft bolt. Torque the bolt to 35 ft. lbs. (47 Nm).

8. Check camshaft endplay. The specification with a new plate is 0.002–0.006 in. (0.051–0.052mm) and 0.002–0.010 in. (0.51–0.254mm) with a used plate. Replace the thrust plate if not within specifications.

9. Install the timing chain snubber.

10. Thoroughly clean and dry the gasket mating surfaces.

11. Install new O-rings to the block.

12. Remove the crankshaft oil seal from the cover. The seal must be removed from the cover when installing to ensure proper oil pump engagement.

13. Using a new gasket, install the chain case cover to the engine.

14. Make certain that the oil pump is engaged onto the crankshaft before proceeding, or severe engine damage will result. Install the attaching bolts and torque to 20 ft. lbs. (27 Nm).

15. Use tool C–4992 to install the crankshaft oil seal. Install the crankshaft pulley using a 5.9 in. suitable bolt and thrust bearing and washer plate L-4524. Make sure the pulley bottoms out on the crankshaft seal diameter. Install the bolt and torque to 40 ft. lbs. (54 Nm).

16. Install all other parts removed during the chain case cover removal procedure.

17. To install the cam sensor, first clean off the old spacer from the sensor face completely. Inspect the O-ring for damage and replace if necessary. A new spacer must be attached to the cam sensor prior to installation; if a new spacer is not used, engine performance will be adversely affacted. Oil the O-ring lightly and push the sensor into its bore in the chain case cover until contact is made with the cam timing gear. Hold in this position and tighten the bolt to 10 ft. lbs. (12 Nm).

18. Refill the cooling system and fill the engine with oil.

19. Connect the negative battery cable, road test the vehicle and check for leaks.

3.9L ENGINE

1. If possible, crank the engine around so that the No. 1 cylinder is at TDC on the compression stroke. Remove the distributor cap to confirm and line the timing mark on the damper pulley with **0** on the timing scale. This will aid in aligning timing marks when installing the timing gears. Disconnect the negative battery cable.

2. Drain the cooling system.

3. Remove the radiator, fan and all related parts. Remove the water pump.

4. Remove the crankshaft pulley.

5. Remove the vibration damper using the proper puller.

6. Disconnect the fuel lines from the fuel pump, if equipped.

7. Remove the 2 front bolts from the oil pan.

8. Unbolt the chain cover from the block and remove, using caution to avoid damaging the oil pan gasket. Remove the fuel pump from the cover, if equipped.

9. Remove the camshaft gear retaining bolt, cup washer and fuel pump eccentric, if equipped. Remove the timing chain and gears.

To install:

10. Place both camshaft and crankshaft gears on the bench with the timing marks on the exact imaginary center line through both gear bores as they are installed on the engine. Place the timing chain around both sprockets.

11. Turn the crankshaft and camshaft so the keys line up with the keyways in the gears when the timing marks are in proper position.

12. Slide both gears over their respective shafts and use a straightedge to check timing mark alignment.

13. Install the fuel pump eccentric and cup washer, if equipped. Torque the camshaft gear retaining bolt to 35 ft. lbs. (47 Nm).

14. Clean and dry the mating surfaces of the timing chain cover and block. Apply a thin bead of sealer to the oil pan gasket.

15. Install a new cover gasket and install the cover. Torque the bolts to 30 ft. lbs.

16. Install the water pump with a new gasket, if it was removed.

17. Install the damper with tool C–3638, install the bolt and washer and torque to specification. Apply a small amount of sealer to the bolts and install the crankshaft pulley.

18. Install the fuel pump using a new gasket, if equipped and connect the fuel lines. Install the 2 oil pan bolts, if they were removed.

19. Install the radiator, fan and all related parts.

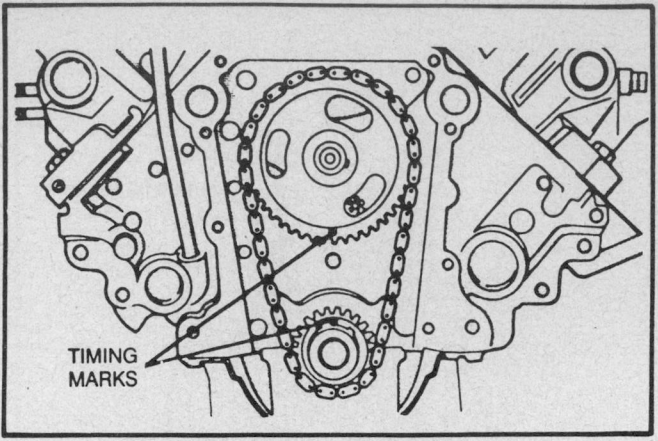

Timing mark alignment—3.9L engine

20. Fill the cooling system.

21. Connect the negative battery cable, set all adjustments to specifications and check for leaks.

Timing Belt Cover

Removal and Installation

2.2L AND 2.5L ENGINES

1. Disconnect the negative battery cable.

2. Remove the nuts that attach the upper cover to the valve cover.

3. Remove the bolt that attaches the upper cover to the lower cover.

4. Remove the upper cover.

5. Raise the vehicle and support safely. Remove the right side splash shield.

6. Remove the crankshaft pulley, water pump pulley and the belts.

7. Remove the lower cover attaching bolts.

8. Remove the lower cover.

9. The installation is the reverse of the removal procedure.

3.0L ENGINE

1. Disconnect the negative battery cable.

2. If equipped with air conditioning, loosen the adjustment pulley locknut, turn the screw counterclockwise to reduce the drive belt tension and remove the belt.

3. To remove the serpentine drive belt, insert a ½ in. breaker bar in to the square hole of the tensioner pulley, rotate it counterclockwise to reduce the drive belt tension and remove the belt.

4. Remove the air conditioning compressor and the air compressor bracket if equipped, power steering pump and alternator from the mounts; support them aside. Remove power steering pump/alternator automatic belt tensioner bolt and the tensioner.

5. Raise and safely support the vehicle. Remove the right inner fender splash shield.

6. Remove the crankshaft pulley bolt and the pulley/damper assembly from the crankshaft.

7. Lower the vehicle and place a floor jack under the engine to support it.

8. Separate the front engine mount insulator from the bracket. Raise the engine slightly and remove the mount bracket.

9. Remove the timing belt cover bolts and the upper and lower covers from the engine.

10. The installation is the reverse of the removal procedure. The engine mount through bolt must be torqued to 75 ft. lbs.

(102 Nm) on 1987–88 vehicles or 100 ft. lbs. (136 Nm) on 1989–90 vehicles with the engine support removed and the engine's weight on the mount.

Timing Belt and Tensioner

Adjustment

2.2L AND 2.5L ENGINES

1. Disconnect the negative battery cable.
2. Raise the vehicle and support safely. Remove the right front inner splash shield.
3. Remove the tensioner cover.
4. Place the special tensioning tool C–4703 on the hex of the tensioner so the weight is at about the 10 o'clock position and loosen the bolt.
5. The tensioner should drop down to the 9 o'clock position. Reposition the tool as required in order to have it end up at the 9 o'clock position (parallel to the ground, hanging to the left) plus or minus 15 degrees.
6. Hold the tool in position and tighten the bolt. Do not pull the tool past the 9 o'clock position; this will make the belt too tight and will cause it to howl or possibly break.
7. Install the cover and the splash shield.

3.0L ENGINE

1. Loosen the bolt that holds the timing belt tensioner in place. The bolt is located to the left of the accessory belt tensioner mounting.
2. Allow the spring to pull the tensioner in automatically.
3. Tighten the tensioner locking bolt.

Removal and Installation

2.2L AND 2.5L ENGINES

1. If possible, position the engine so that the No. 1 piston is at TDC. Disconnect the negative battery cable.
2. Remove the timing belt covers. Remove the timing belt tensioner and allow the belt to hang free.
3. On Caravan and Voyager, place a floor jack under the engine and separate the right motor mount.
4. Remove the air conditioning compressor belt idler pulley, if equipped and remove the mounting stud. Unbolt the compressor/alternator bracket and position it to the side.
5. Remove the timing belt from the vehicle.

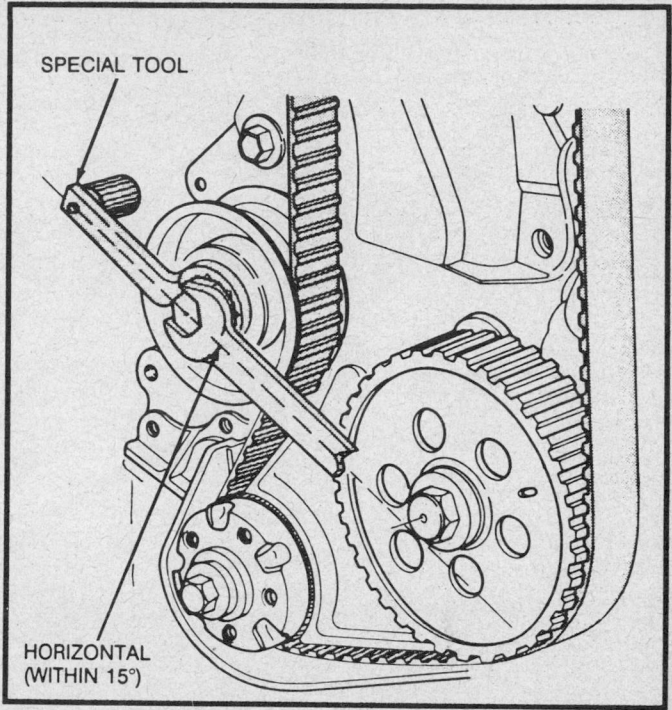
Adjusting the timing belt—2.2L and 2.5L engines

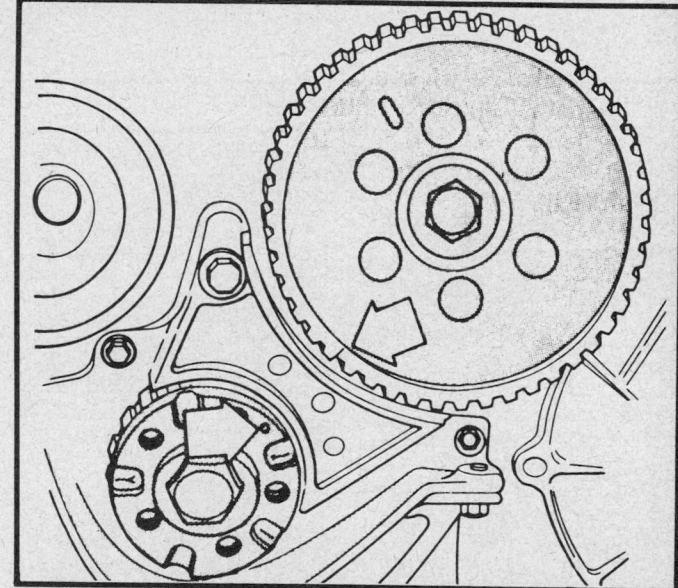
Alignment of the crankshaft sprocket and intermediate shaft sprocket—2.2L and 2.5L engines

To install:
6. Turn the crankshaft sprocket and intermediate shaft sprocket until the marks are in line. Use a straightedge from bolt to bolt to confirm alignment.
7. Turn the camshaft until the small hole in the sprocket is at the top and rows on the hub are in line with the camshaft cap to cylinder head mounting lines. Use a mirror to see the alignment so it is viewed straight on and not at an angle from above. Install the belt, but let at hang free at this point.
8. Install the air conditioning compressor/alternator bracket, idler pulley and motor mount. Remove the floor jack. Raise the vehicle and support safely. Have the tensioner at an arm's reach

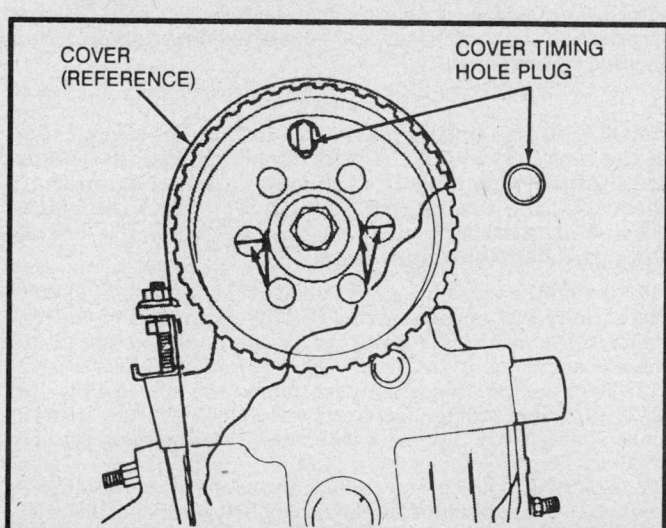
Alignment of the arrows on the camshaft sprocket with the camshaft cap to cylinder head mounting line

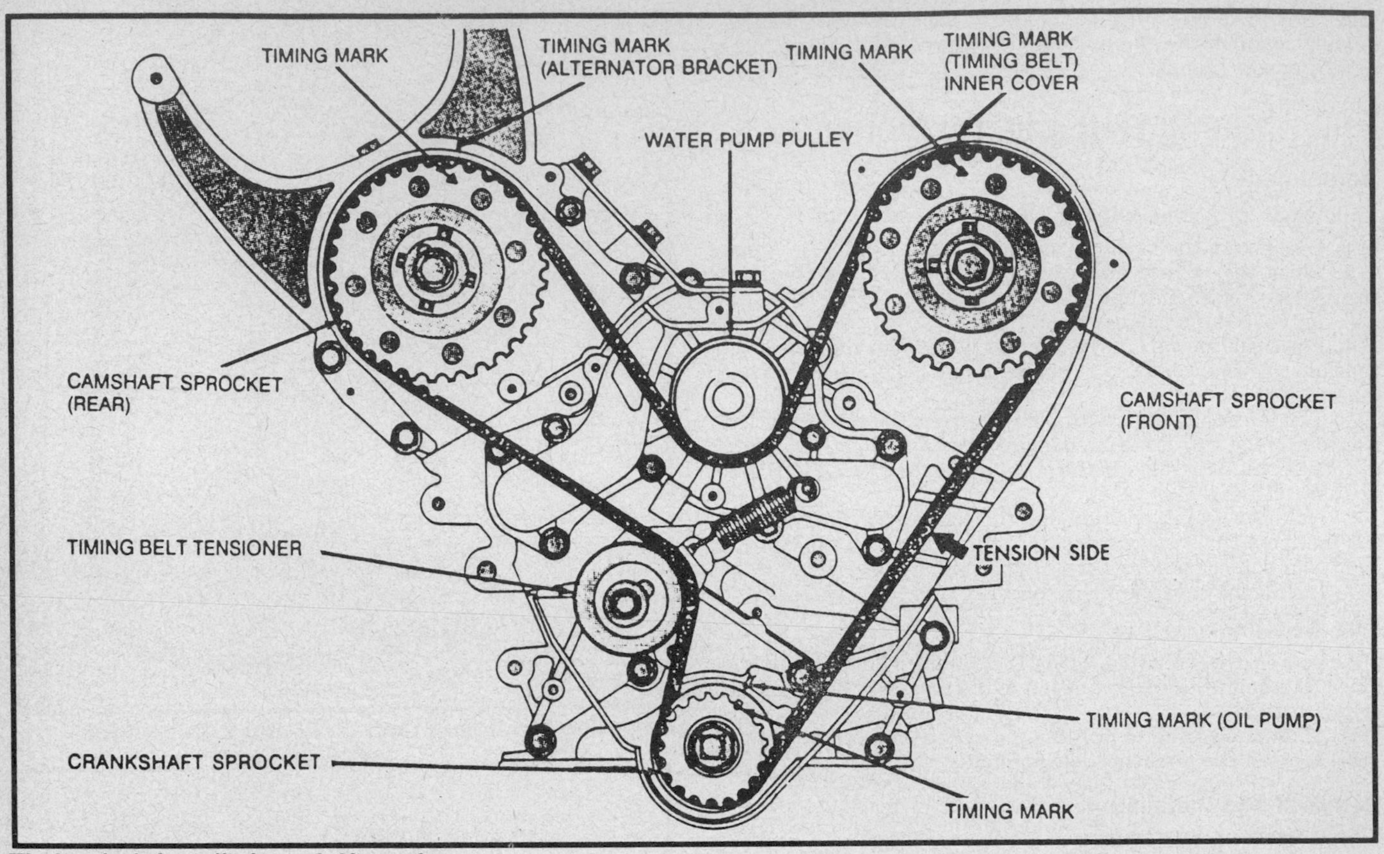

TIMING MARK   TIMING MARK (ALTERNATOR BRACKET)   TIMING MARK   TIMING MARK (TIMING BELT) INNER COVER

WATER PUMP PULLEY

CAMSHAFT SPROCKET (REAR)

CAMSHAFT SPROCKET (FRONT)

TIMING BELT TENSIONER

TENSION SIDE

TIMING MARK (OIL PUMP)

CRANKSHAFT SPROCKET

TIMING MARK

Timing belt installation—3.0L engine

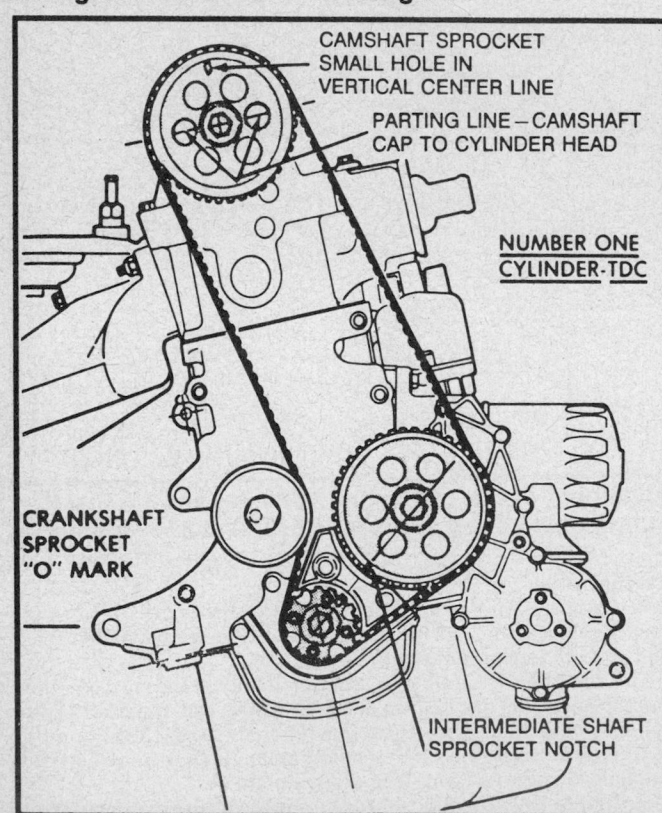

CAMSHAFT SPROCKET SMALL HOLE IN VERTICAL CENTER LINE

PARTING LINE—CAMSHAFT CAP TO CYLINDER HEAD

NUMBER ONE CYLINDER-TDC

CRANKSHAFT SPROCKET "O" MARK

INTERMEDIATE SHAFT SPROCKET NOTCH

Timing belt installation—2.2L and 2.5L engines

because the timing belt will have to be held in position with one hand.

9. To properly install the timing belt, reach up and engage it with the camshaft sprocket. Turn the intermediate shaft counterclockwise slightly, then engage the belt with the intermediate shaft sprocket. Hold the belt against the intermediate shaft sprocket and turn clockwise to take up all tension; if the timing marks are out of alignment, repeat until alignment is correct.

10. Using a 13mm wrench, turn the crankshaft sprocket counterclockwise slightly and wrap the belt around it. Turn the sprocket clockwise so there is no slack in the belt between sprockets; if the timing marks are out of alignment, repeat until alignment is correct.

NOTE: If the timing marks are in line but slack exists in the belt between either the camshaft and intermediate shaft sprockets or the intermediate and crankshaft sprockets, the timing will be incorrect when the belt is tensioned. All slack must be only between the crankshaft and camshaft sprockets.

11. Install the tensioner and install the mounting bolt loosely. Place the special tensioning tool C–4703 on the hex of the tensioner so the weight is at about the 9 o'clock position (parallel to the ground, hanging to the left) plus or minus 15 degrees.

12. Hold the tool in position and tighten the bolt to 45 ft. lbs. (61 Nm). Do not pull the tool past the 9 o'clock position; this will make the belt too tight and will cause it to howl or possibly break.

13. Lower the vehicle and recheck the camshaft sprocket positioning. If it is correct install the timing belt covers and all related parts.

14. Connect the negative battery cable and road test the vehicle.

3.0L ENGINE

1. If possible, position the engine so that the No. 1 cylinder is at TDC. Disconnect the negative battery cable. Remove the timing covers from the engine.

2. If the same timing belt will be reused, mark the direction of the timing belt's rotation, for installation in the same direction. Make sure the engine is positioned so the No. 1 cylinder is at the TDC of it's compression stroke and the sprockets timing marks are aligned with the engine's timing mark indicators.

3. Loosen the timing belt tensioner bolt and remove the belt. If not removing the tensioner, position it as far away from the center of the engine as possible and tighten the bolt.

4. If the tensioner is being removed, paint the outside of the spring to ensure that it is not installed backwards. Unbolt the tensioner and remove it along with the spring.

To install:

5. Install the tensioner, if removed and hook the upper end of the spring to the water pump pin and the lower end to the tensioner in exactly the same position as originally installed. If not already done, position both camshafts so the marks line up with those on the alternator bracket (rear bank) and inner timing cover (front bank). Rotate the crankshaft so the timing mark aligns with the mark on the oil pump.

6. Install the timing belt on the crankshaft sprocket and while keeping the belt tight on the tension side (right side), install the belt on the front camshaft sprocket.

7. Install the belt on the water pump pulley, then the rear camshaft sprocket and the tensioner.

8. Rotate the front camshaft counterclockwise to tension the belt between the front camshaft and the crankshaft. If the timing marks came out of line, repeat the procedure.

9. Install the crankshaft sprocket flange.

10. Loosen the tensioner bolt and allow the spring to tension the belt.

11. Turn the crankshaft 2 full turns in the clockwise direction only until the timing marks align again. Now that the belt is properly tensioned, torque the tensioner lock bolt to 21 ft. lbs. (29 Nm).

12. Install the timing belt covers and all related parts.

13. Connect the negative battery cable and road test the vehicle.

Timing Sprockets

Removal and Installation

2.2L AND 2.5L ENGINES

1. Disconnect the negative battery cable. Remove the timing belt.

2. Remove the crankshaft sprocket bolt. Using the puller tool C–4685 or equivalent and the button from tool L–4524 or equivalent, remove the crankshaft sprocket.

3. Using the tool C–4687 or equivalent, hold the camshaft and/or intermediate sprocket, remove the center bolt and the sprocket(s).

4. The installation is the reverse of the removal procedure. Torque the camshaft and intermediate sprocket bolts to 65 ft. lbs. (88 Nm) and the crankshaft sprocket bolt to 50 ft. lbs. (68 Nm).

3.0L ENGINE

1. Disconnect the negative battery cable.
2. Remove the timing belt.
3. To remove the camshaft sprocket, hold the sprocket with tool MB990775, or equivalent and remove the retaining bolt and washer.
4. To remove the crankshaft sprocket, remove the bolt and remove the sprocket from the crankshaft.
5. The installation is the reverse of the removal procedure. Torque the camshaft sprocket bolt to 70 ft. lbs. (95 Nm) while

holding the sprocket with the holding tool. Torque the crankshaft sprocket bolt. to 110 ft. lbs. (150 Nm).

Camshaft

Removal and Installation

2.2L AND 2.5L ENGINES

1. Disconnect the negative battery cable. Relieve the fuel pressure, if equipped with fuel injection.

2. Turn the crankshaft so the No. 1 piston is at the TDC of the compression stroke. Remove the upper timing belt cover. Remove the air pump pulley, if equipped.

3. Remove the camshaft sprocket bolt and the sprocket and suspend tightly so the belt does not lose tension. If it does, the belt timing will have to be reset.

4. Remove the valve cover.

5. If the rocker arms are being reused, mark them for installation identification and loosen the camshaft bearing bolts, evenly and gradually.

6. Using a soft mallet, rap the rear of the camshaft a few times to break the bearing caps loose.

7. Remove the bolts, bearing caps and the camshaft with seals.

NOTE: Before replacing the camshaft, identify factory installed oversized components. To do so, look for the tops of the bearing caps pained green and O/SJ stamped rearward of the oil gallery plug on the rear of the head. In addition, the barrel of the camshaft is painted green and 'O/SJ is stamped onto the rear end of the camshaft. Installing standard sized parts in an head equipped with oversized parts – or visa versa – will cause severe engine damage.

Also, take note of the color of the paint stripe on the rear camshaft seal. These stripes differentiate seal sizes. If a seal with a different color stripe is installed, a severe leak will develop if the seal is too small, or the cap will not be able to be fully installed if the seal is too big.

8. Check the oil passages for blockages and the parts for wear and damage and replace parts, as required. Clean the gasket mounting surfaces.

To Install:

9. Transfer the sprocket key to the new camshaft. New rocker arms and a new camshaft sprocket bolt are normally included with the camshaft package. Install the rocker arms, lubricate the camshaft and install with end seals installed.

10. Place the bearing caps with No. 1 at the timing belt end and No. 5 at the transaxle end. The camshaft bearing caps are numbered and have arrows facing forward. Torque the camshaft bearing bolts evenly and gradually to 18 ft. lbs. (24 Nm).

NOTE: Apply RTV silicone gasket material to the No. 1 and 5 bearing caps. Install the bearing caps before the seals are installed.

11. Mount a dial indicator to the front of the engine and check the camshaft endplay. Play should not exceed 0.006 in.

12. Install the camshaft sprocket and the new bolt. Install the air pump pulley, if equipped.

13. Install the valve cover with a new gasket.

14. Connect the negative battery cable and check for leaks.

2.6L ENGINE

1. Disconnect the negative battery cable.
2. Remove the valve cover.
3. Remove the camshaft gear retaining bolt and matchmark the distributor gear to its drive gear. Remove the distributor. Pry the distributor drive gear off of the cam gear.
4. Remove the cam gear from the camshaft and allow it to rest on the holder below it.

5. Remove the water pump pulley.

6. Remove the camshaft cap bolts evenly and gradually.

7. Remove the caps, shafts, rocker arms and bolts together as an assembly.

8. Remove the camshaft with the rear seal from the engine.

To install:

9. Install a new roll pin to the camshaft. Lubricate the camshaft and install with the rear seal in place. Install the camshaft in position so the hole in the gear will line up with the roll pin.

10. Install the rocker caps, shafts and arms assembly. Tighten the camshaft bearing cap bolts in the following order to 85 inch lbs. (10 Nm): No. 3, No. 2, No. 4, front cap, rear cap. Repeat the sequence increasing the torque to 175 inch lbs. (19 Nm).

11. Install the gear to the camshaft engaging the roll pin. Install the distributor drive gear and install the bolt and washer. Torque the bolt to 40 ft. lbs. (54 Nm). Install the distributor.

12. Install the valve cover and all related parts.

3.0L ENGINE

1. Disconnect the negative battery cable. Remove the air cleaner assembly and valve covers.

2. Install auto lash adjuster retainers MD998443 or equivalent on the rocker arms.

3. If removing the right side (front) camshaft, remove the distributor extension.

4. Remove the camshaft bearing caps but do not remove the bolts from the caps.

5. Remove the rocker arms, rocker shafts and bearing caps, as an assembly.

6. Remove the camshaft from the cylinder head.

7. Inspect the bearing journals on the camshaft, cylinder head and bearing caps.

To Install:

8. Lubricate the camshaft journals and camshaft with clean engine oil and install the camshaft in the cylinder head.

9. Align the camshaft bearing caps with the arrow mark (depending on cylinder numbers) and in numerical order.

10. Apply sealer at the ends of the bearing caps and install the assembly.

11. Torque the bearing cap bolts, in the following sequence: No. 3, No. 2, No. 1 and No. 4 to 85 inch lbs. (10 Nm).

12. Repeat the sequence increasing the torque to 175 inch lbs. (18 Nm).

13. Install the distributor extension, if it was removed.

14. Install the valve cover and all related parts.

3.3L ENGINE

1. Relieve the fuel pressure. Disconnect the negative battery cable.

2. Remove the engine from the vehicle. Remove the intake manifold, cylinder heads, timing chain cover and timing chain from the engine.

3. Remove the rocker arm and shaft assemblies.

4. Label and remove the pusrods and lifters.

5. Remove the camshaft thrust plate.

6. Install a long bolt into the front of the camshaft to facilitate its removal. Remove the camshaft being careful not to damage the cam bearings with the cam lobes.

To install:

7. Install the camshaft to within 2 in. of its final installation position.

8. Install the camshaft thrust plate and 2 bolts and torque to 10 ft. lbs. (12 Nm).

9. Place both camshaft and crankshaft gears on the bench with the timing marks on the exact imaginary center line through both gear bores as they are installed on the engine. Place the timing chain around both sprockets.

10. Turn the crankshaft and camshaft so the keys line up with the keyways in the gears when the timing marks are in proper position.

11. Slide both gears over their respective shafts and use a straightedge to check timing mark alignment.

12. Measure camshaft endplay. If not within specifications, replace the thrust plate.

13. If the camshaft was not replaced, lubricate and install the lifters in their original locations. If the camshaft was replaced, new lifters must be used.

14. Install the pushrods and rocker shaft assemblies.

15. Install the timing chain cover, cylinder heads and intake manifold.

16. Install the engine in the vehicle.

17. When everything is bolted in place, change the engine oil and replace the oil filter.

NOTE: If the camshaft or lifters have been replaced, add 1 pint of Mopar crankcase conditioner, or equivalent when replenishing the oil to aid in break in. This mixture should be left in the engine for a minimum of 500 miles and drained at the next normal oil change.

18. Fill the radiator with coolant.

19. Connect the negative battery cable, set all adjustments to specifications and check for leaks.

3.9L ENGINE

1. If possible, crank the engine around so that the No. 1 cylin-

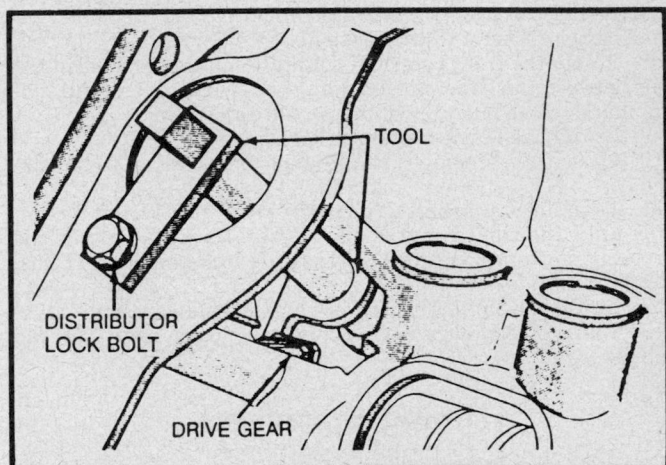

Installing the camshaft blocking tool—3.9L engine

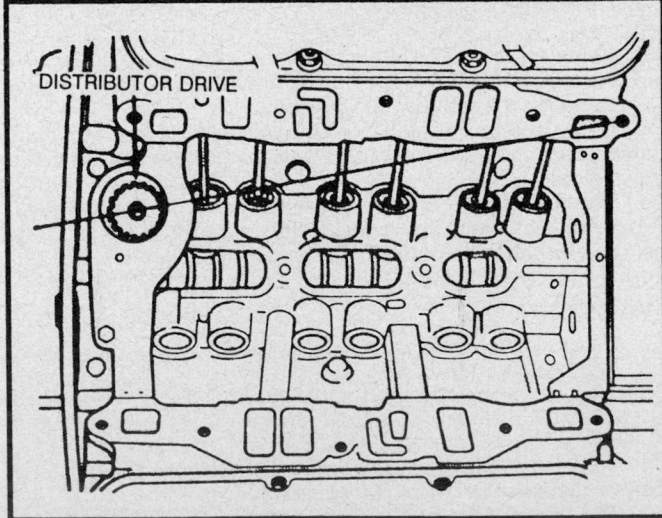

Installed distributor drive gear position—3.9L engine

der is at TDC on the compression stroke. Remove the distributor cap to confirm and line the timing mark on the damper pulley with **0** on the timing scale. This will aid in aligning timing marks when installing the timing gears.

2. If the vehicle is equipped with fuel injection, relieve the fuel pressure. Disconnect the negative battery cable. Drain the cooling system.

3. Remove the valve cover(s).

4. Remove the rocker shaft assemblies. Identify and remove the pushrods.

5. Remove the intake manifold. Identify and remove all lifters.

6. Remove the distributor.

7. Lift out the oil pump and distributor driveshaft.

8. Remove the radiator, fan and all related parts.

9. Remove the fuel pump, if equipped. Remove the timing chain cover, timing chain and gears.

10. Note the location of the oil tab and remove the camshaft thrust plate.

11. Install suitable long bolt into the front of the camshaft to facilitate removal. Remove the camshaft, being careful not to damage any of the cam bearings with the cam lobes.

To install:

12. Install the camshaft to within 2 in. of its final installation position.

13. Install the camshaft blocking tool C–3509 and bolt it in place with the distributor hold-down bolt. This will prevent the camshaft from being pushed in too far and knocking out the welch plug at the rear of the block. This tool should remain in place until the timing chain installation has been completed.

14. Install the camshaft thrust plate and chain oil tab. Make sure the tang of the oil tab enters the hole in the thrust plate at the lower right. Torque the bolts to 18 ft. lbs. (24 Nm). Make sure the top edge of the oil tab is flat against the thrust plate or it will not feed oil to the chain.

15. Place both camshaft and crankshaft gears on the bench with the timing marks on the exact imaginary center line through both gear bores as they are installed on the engine. Place the timing chain around both sprockets.

16. Turn the crankshaft and camshaft so the keys line up with the keyways in the gears when the timing marks are in proper position.

17. Slide both gears over their respective shafts and use a straightedge to check timing mark alignment.

18. Install the fuel pump eccentric and cup washer, if equipped. Torque the camshaft gear retaining bolt to 35 ft. lbs. (47 Nm). Remove the camshaft blocking tool, if it was installed.

19. Measure camshaft endplay, if applicable. Replace the thrust plate if not within specifications.

20. Coat the oil pump and distributor driveshaft with oil. Install the shaft so that when the gear spirals into place and drops into the oil pump, the slot in the top of the gear is pointing directly to the left front intake manifold bolt hole.

21. If the camshaft was not replaced, lubricate and install the lifters in their original locations. If the camshaft was replaced, new lifters must be used.

22. Install the pushrods and rocker shaft assemblies.

23. Install the intake manifold, if it was removed. Install the valve covers.

24. Install the distributor so the rotor points to the No. 1 spark plug wire position on the cap.

25. Install the timing chain cover and all related parts.

26. Install the fuel pump if equipped and radiator.

27. When everything is bolted in place, change the engine oil and replace the oil filter.

NOTE: If the camshaft or lifters have been replaced, add 1 pint of Mopar crankcase conditioner, or equivalent when replenishing the oil to aid in break in. This mixture should be left in the engine for a minimum of 500 miles and drained at the next normal oil change.

28. Fill the radiator with coolant.

29. Connect the negative battery cable, set all adjustments to specifications and check for leaks.

Intermediate Shaft

Removal and Installation

2.2L AND 2.5L ENGINES

1. Disconnect the negative battery cable.

2. Crank the engine around until the No. 1 piston is at TDC. Remove the timing belt covers to confirm that all timing marks are lined up.

3. Remove the fuel pump, if equipped. Remove the distribu-

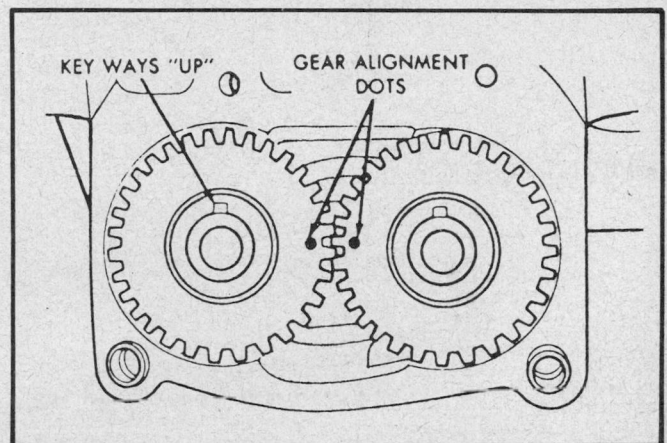

Alignment of balance shaft sprockets—2.5L engine

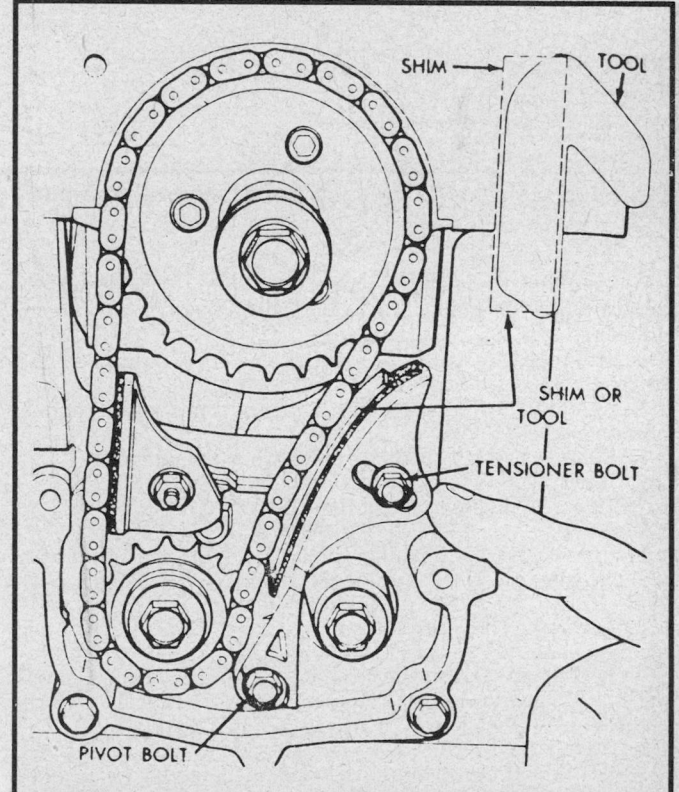

Adjusting the balance shaft chain tensioner—2.5L engine

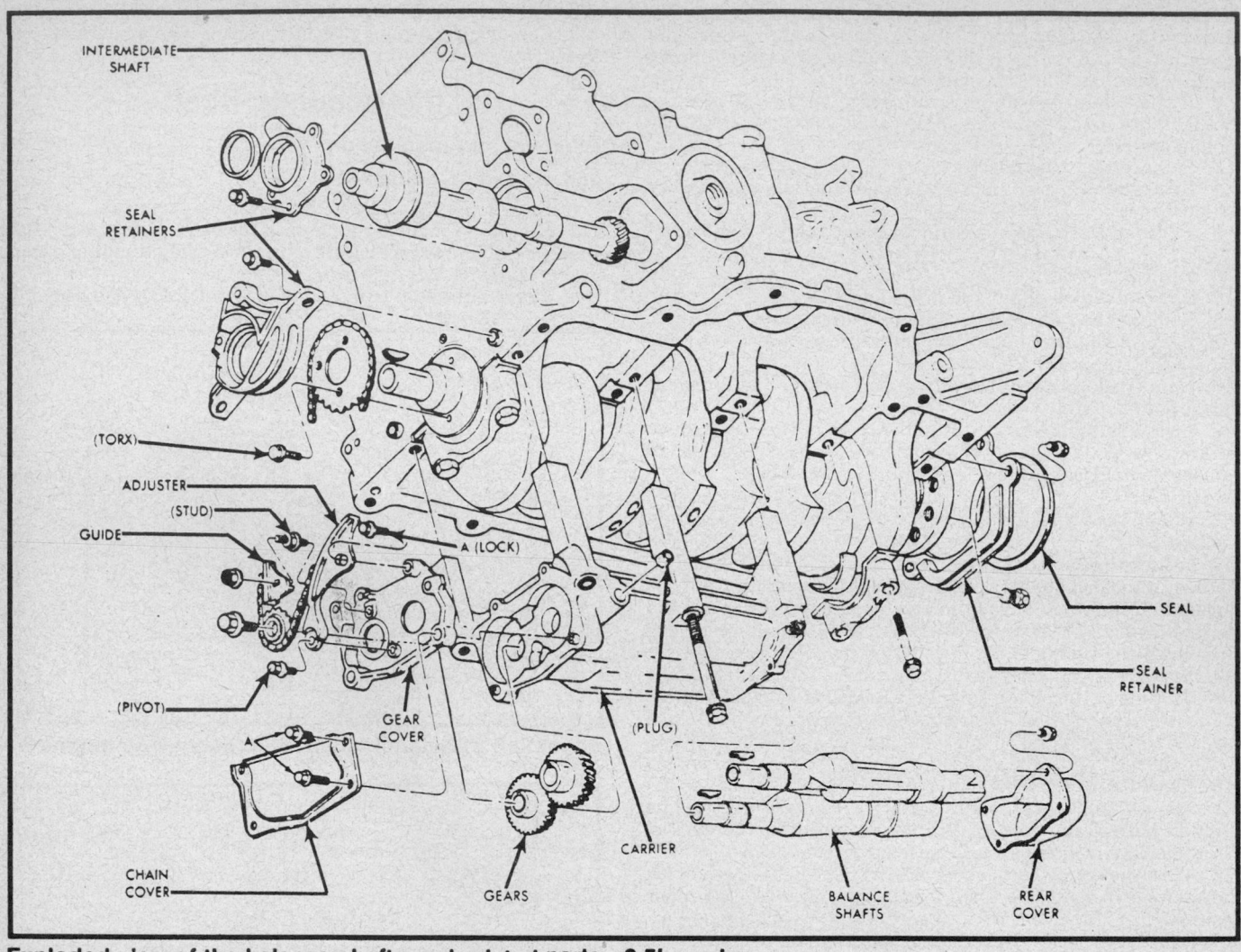

Exploded view of the balance shafts and related parts—2.5L engine

tor. Looking down at the oil pump, the slot in the shaft must be parallel with the center line of the crankshaft. Remove the oil pump.

4. Remove the timing belt and the intermediate shaft sprocket.

5. Remove the shaft retainer bolts and remove the retainer from the block.

6. Remove the intermediate shaft from the engine.

7. If necessary, remove the front bushing using tool C–4697–2 and the rear bushing using tool C–4686–2.

To install:

8. Install the front bushing using tool C–4697–1 until the tool is flush with the block. Install the rear bushing using tool C–4686–1 until the tool is flush with the block.

9. Lubricate the distributor drive gear and install the intermediate shaft.

10. Replace the seal in the retainer and apply silicone sealer to the mating surface of the retainer. Install the retainer to the block and torque the bolts to 10 ft. lbs. (12 Nm).

11. Install the intermediate shaft sprocket and the timing belt.

12. With the timing belt properly installed, install the oil pump so the slot is parallel to the center line of the crankshaft. Install the distributor so the rotor is aligned with the No. 1 spark plug wire tower on the cap.

13. Install the fuel pump, if equipped.

14. Connect the negative battery cable and road test the vehicle.

Balance Shafts

Removal and Installation

2.5L ENGINE

1. Disconnect the negative battery cable. Raise the vehicle and support safely.

2. Remove the timing belt. Remove the oil pan, the oil pickup, the crankshaft belt sprocket and the front crankshaft oil seal retainer.

3. Remove the balance shaft chain cover, the guide and the tensioner.

4. Remove the balance shaft sprocket to shaft bolt, the gear cover to balance shaft bolt and the crankshaft sprocket to crankshaft bolts, then the sprockets with the balance shaft chain.

5. Remove the front gear cover to carrier housing stud, the gear cover and the balance shaft drive gears.

6. Remove the rear gear cover to carrier housing bolts, the rear cover and the balance shafts from the rear of the carrier.

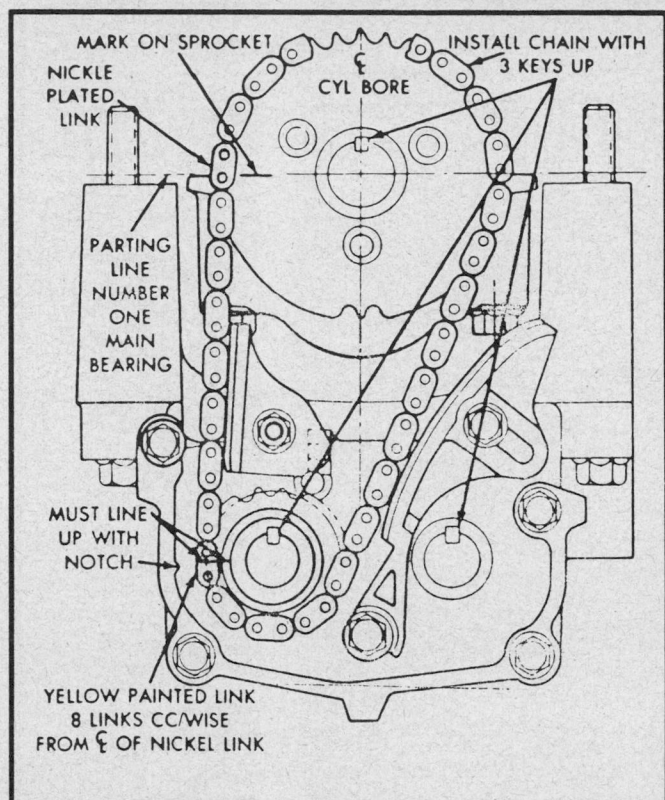

Timing the balance shaft sprocket with the crankshaft sprocket—2.5L engine

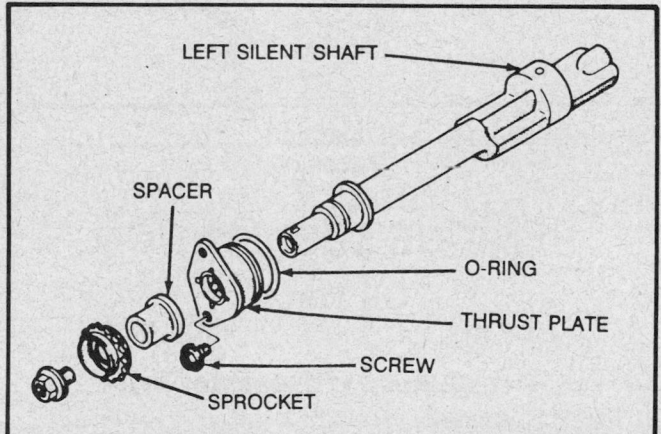

Left silent shaft and related parts—2.6L engine

7. If necessary, remove the carrier housing to crankcase bolts and the housing.

To install:

8. If the carrier housing is being installed, torque the carrier housing to crankcase bolts to 40 ft. lbs. (54 Nm).

9. Rotate the balance shafts until the keyways are facing upward (parallel to the vertical centerline of the engine).

10. Install the short hub gear on the sprocket driven shaft and the long hub gear on the gear driven shaft; make sure the gear timing marks are aligned (facing each other).

11. Install the front gear cover and torque the front gear cover to carrier housing stud bolt to 8.5 ft. lbs. (12 Nm).

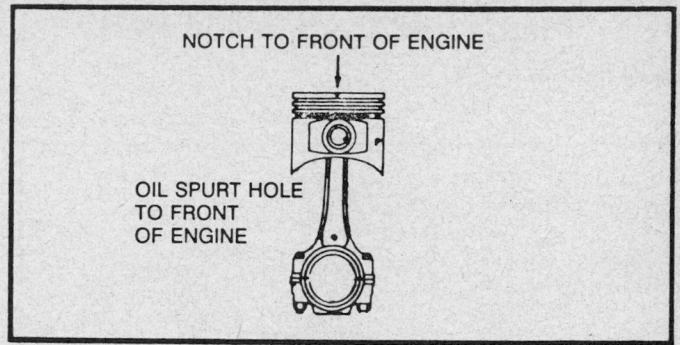

Piston positioning—2.2L and 2.5L engines

12. Install the balance chain sprocket and torque the sprocket to crankshaft bolts to 11 ft. lbs. (13 Nm).

13. Rotate the crankshaft to position the No. 1 cylinder on the TDC of the compression stroke; the timing marks on the chain sprocket should align with the parting line on the left side of the No. 1 main bearing cap.

14. Position the balance shaft sprocket into the balance chain so the sprocket (yellow dot) timing mark mates with the yellow link on the chain.

15. Install the balance chain/sprocket assembly onto the crankshaft and the balance shaft. Torque the sprocket to shaft bolts to 21 ft. lbs. (28 Nm). If necessary to secure the crankshaft while tightening the bolts, place a block of wood between the crankcase and the crankshaft counterbalance.

16. Loosely install the chain tensioners and place a shim (0.039 in. × 2.75 in.) between the chain and the tensioner. Apply firm pressure (to reduce the chain slack) to the tensioner shoe. Torque the tensioner to front gear cover bolts to 8.5 ft. lbs. (12 Nm).

17. Install the chain cover and the rear cover to the carrier housing and torque the bolts to 8.5 ft. lbs. (12 Nm).

18. Replace the crankshaft retainer seal, apply silicone sealer to the mating surface and install the retainer.

19. Install the oil pickup and oil pan.

20. Install the crankshaft sprocket and the timing belt.

21. Connect the negative battery cable and road test the vehicle.

Silent Shafts

Removal and Installation

2.6L ENGINE

1. Disconnect the negative battery cable.

2. Matchmark the silent chain to the gears and remove the chain.

3. Remove the oil pump. The right silent shaft will come out with the pump. To remove the shaft from the pump, remove the retaining bolt from the pump and remove the shaft from the pump.

4. Remove the left silent shaft gear and spacer. Remove the thrust plate retaining screws and remove the thrust plate by installing two $\frac{1}{32}$ in. screws into the threaded holes and pulling the plate out.

5. Remove the silent shaft.

6. Install a new O-ring to the thrust plate.

7. The installation is the reverse of the removal procedure. Torque the silent shaft retaining bolts to 25 ft. lbs. (34 Nm).

8. Connect the negative battery cable and road test the vehicle.

Piston and Connecting Rod

Positioning

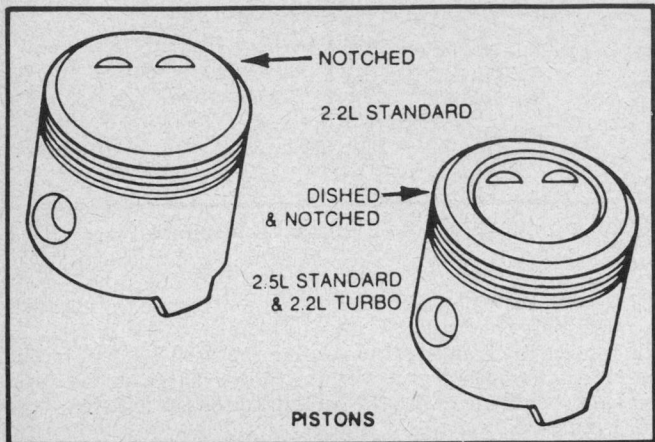

2.2L and 2.5L engines—piston differences

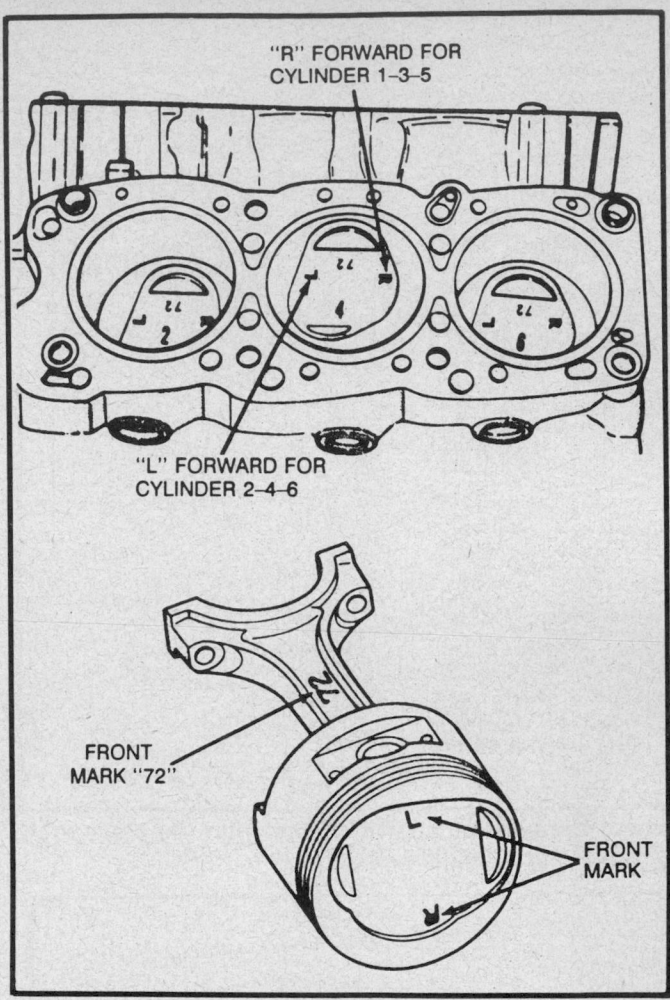

Piston positioning—3.0L engine

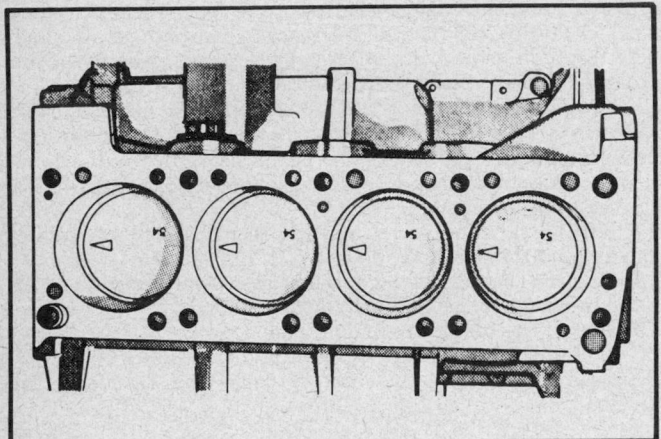

Piston positioning—2.6L engine

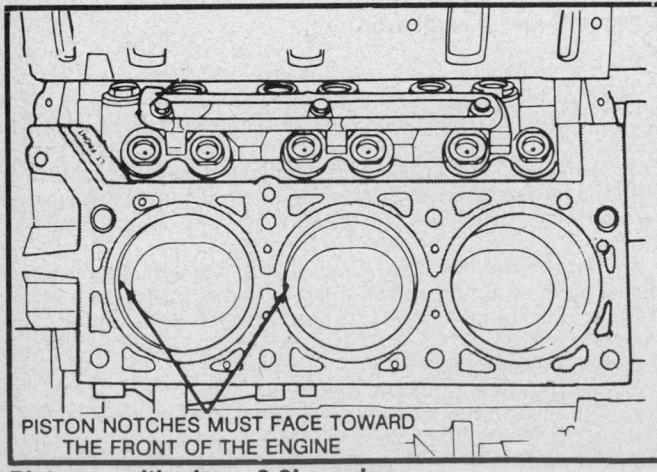

Piston positioning—3.3L engine

ENGINE LUBRICATION

Oil Pan

Removal and Installation

CARAVAN, VOYAGER AND TOWN & COUNTRY

2.2L and 2.5L Engines

1. Disconnect the negative battery cable. Remove the oil dipstick.
2. Raise the vehicle and support safely.
3. Drain the engine oil.
4. Remove the engine to transaxle struts, if equipped.
5. Remove the torque converter or clutch inspection cover, if equipped.
6. Remove the oil pan retaining screws and remove the oil pan and the side seals.

To install:

7. Thoroughly clean and dry all sealing surfaces, bolts and bolt holes.
8. Apply silicone sealer to the 4 end seal to block corners and install the end seals making sure the corners are not twisted.
9. Apply silicone to the 4 pan to block corners. Install a new pan gasket or apply silicone sealer to the sealing surface of the

pan and install to the engine making sure not to dislodge the end seals.

10. Install the retaining screws and torque to 17 ft. lbs. (23 Nm).

11. Install the torque converter inspection cover and engine to transaxle struts, if equipped. Lower the vehicle.

12. Install the dipstick. Fill the engine with the proper amount of oil.

13. Connect the negative battery cable and check for leaks.

2.6L, 3.0L and 3.3L Engines

1. Disconnect the negative battery cable.
2. Raise the vehicle and support safely.
3. Remove the torque converter bolt access cover, if equipped.
4. Drain the engine oil.
5. Remove the oil pan retaining screws and remove the oil pan and gasket.

To install:

6. Thoroughly clean and dry all sealing surfaces, bolts and bolt holes.

7. Apply silicone sealer to the chain cover to block mating seam and the rear main seal retainer to block seam, if equipped.

8. Install a new pan gasket or apply silicone sealer to the sealing surface of the pan and install to the engine.

9. Install the retaining screws and torque to 50 inch lbs. (6 Nm) on 2.6L and 3.0L engines and 13 ft. lbs. (17 Nm) on 3.3L engine.

10. Install the torque converter bolt access cover, if equipped. Lower the vehicle.

11. Install the dipstick. Fill the engine with the proper amount of oil.

12. Connect the negative battery cable and check for leaks.

DAKOTA

2.2L and 2.5L Engines

1. Disconnect the negative battery cable. Remove the oil dipstick.

2. Disconnect the air pump relief valve upper hose. Raise the vehicle and support safely.

3. Remove the clutch housing to engine strut and clutch inspection cover.

4. Remove the lower radiator hose support bracket.

5. Slightly loosen the right motor mount through bolt just enough to relieve the tension.

6. Using the proper equipment, support the weight of the engine. Loosen the left motor mount through bolt enough to clear the bracket.

7. Raise the left side of the engine about 2 inches.

8. Remove the oil pan retaining screws and remove the oil pan and gasket.

To install:

9. Thoroughly clean and dry all sealing surfaces, bolts and bolt holes.

10. Apply silicone sealer to the 4 end seal to block corners and install the end seals making sure the corners are not twisted.

11. Apply silicone to the 4 pan to block corners. Install a new pan gasket or apply silicone sealer to the sealing surface of the pan and install to the engine making sure not to dislodge the end seals.

12. Install the pan retaining screws and torque to 17 ft. lbs. (23 Nm).

13. Lower the engine. Torque the motor mount through bolts to 50 ft. lbs. (68 Nm).

14. Install the clutch inspection cover and housing to engine strut. Install the lower radiator hose support bracket. Lower the vehicle.

15. Install the dipstick and air pump hose. Fill the engine with the proper amount of oil.

16. Connect the negative battery cable and check for leaks.

3.9L Engine With 2WD

1. Disconnect the negative battery cable. Remove the oil dipstick. Disengage the distributor cap and remove it away from the firewall.

2. Raise the vehicle and support safely. Drain the engine oil.

3. Remove the exhaust crossover.

4. Loosen the motor mount bolts. Using the proper equipment, raise the engine. When the engine is high enough, install replacement bolts (similar in size to the motor mount bolts), in the engine mount attaching points on the frame brackets. Lower the engine so the bottom of the motor mounts rest on the 2 replacement bolts. Remove the torque converter inspection cover, if equipped.

5. Remove the oil pan retaining screws and remove the oil pan and gaskets.

To install:

6. Thoroughly clean and dry all sealing surfaces, bolts and bolt holes.

7. Place a drop of silicone sealer to the timing chain cover to block mating seam.

8. Install the new gaskets to the engine and add a drop of silicone sealer to the corners where the rubber and cork meet. Install the rubber seals to the pan.

9. Install the pan to the engine and torque the retaining screws to 17 ft. lbs. (23 Nm). Install the torque converter inspection cover, if equipped.

10. Reinstall the engine to the mount and install the exhaust crossover. Lower the vehicle.

11. Install the distributor cap.

12. Install the dipstick. Fill the engine with the proper amount of oil.

13. Connect the negative battery cable and check for leaks.

3.9L Engine With 4WD

1. Disconnect the negative battery cable. Remove the oil dipstick.

2. Raise the vehicle and support safely.

3. Using the proper equipment, support the weight of the engine. Remove the front driving axle.

4. Remove the exhaust crossover and the lower transmission cover.

5. Remove the oil pan retaining screws and remove the oil pan and gaskets.

To install:

6. Thoroughly clean and dry all sealing surfaces, bolts and bolt holes.

7. Place a drop of silicone sealer to the timing chain cover to block mating seam.

8. Install the new gaskets to the engine and add a drop of silicone sealer to the corners where the rubber and cork meet. Install the rubber seals to the pan.

9. Install the pan to the engine and torque the retaining screws to 17 ft. lbs. (23 Nm). Install the lower transmission cover, if equipped.

10. Install the exhaust crossover.

11. Install the front driving axle. Lower the vehicle.

12. Install the dipstick. Fill the engine with the proper amount of oil.

13. Connect the negative battery cable and check for leaks.

Oil Pump

Removal and Installation

2.2L AND 2.5L ENGINES

1. Crank the engine around so that the No. 1 piston is at TDC. Disconnect the negative battery cable.

2. Matchmark the rotor to the block and remove the distributor to confirm that the slot in the oil pump shaft is parallel to the

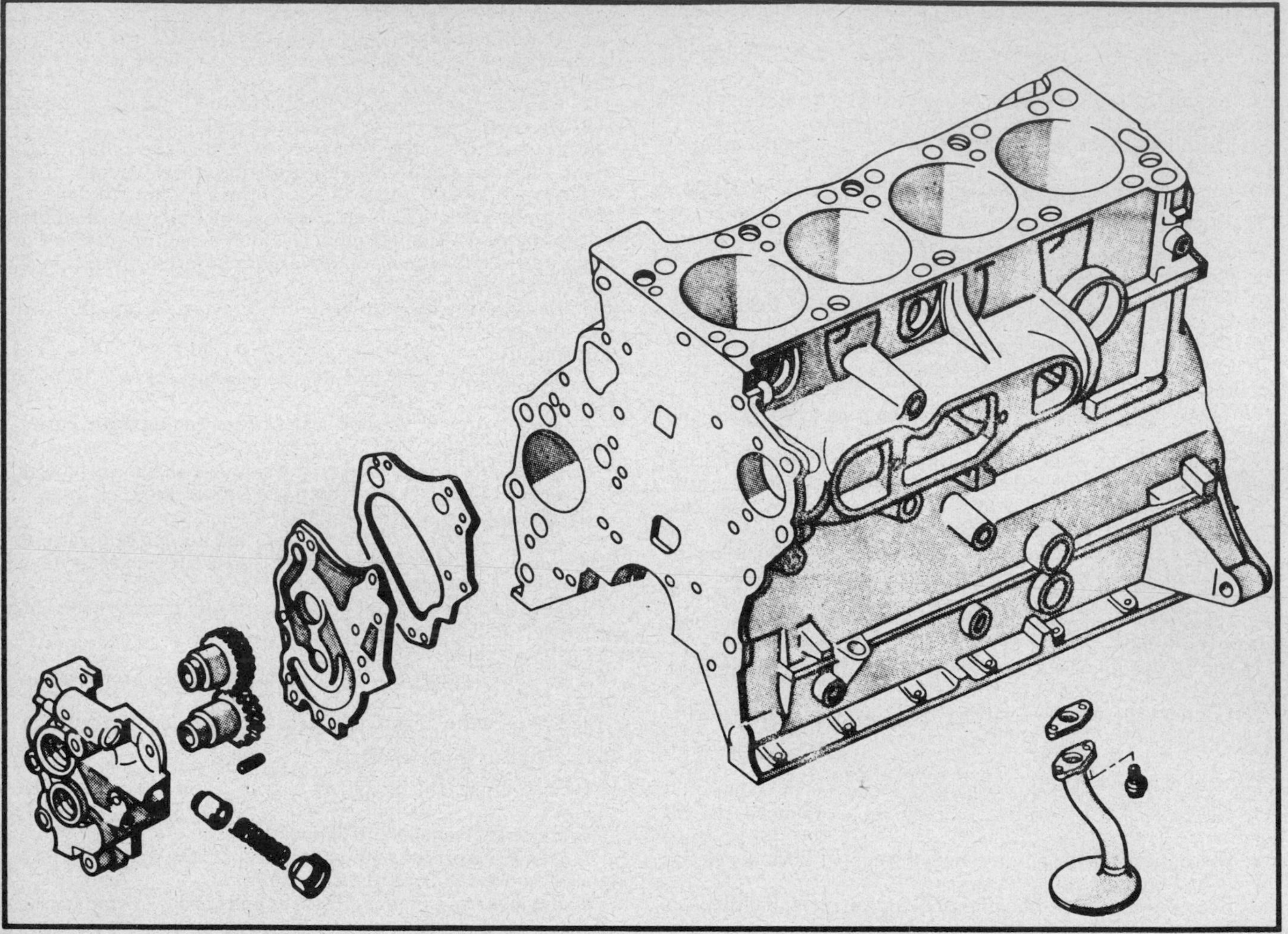

Oil pump and pickup assemblies—2.6L engine

PARALLEL TO CENTER LINE OF CRANKSHAFT

OIL FILTER

Aligning the slot in the oil pump shaft—2.2L and 2.5L engines

centerline of the crankshaft. Matchmark the slot to the distributor bore, if desired.

3. Remove the dipstick. Raise the vehicle and support safely. Drain the engine oil and remove the pan.

4. Remove the oil pickup.

5. Remove the 2 mounting bolts and remove the oil pump from the engine.

To install:

6. Prime the pump by pouring fresh oil into the pump intake and turning the driveshaft until oil comes out the pressure port. Repeat a few times until no air bubbles are present.

7. Apply sealer (Loctite® 515, or equivalent) to the pump body to block machined surface interface. Lubricate the oil pump and distributor driveshaft.

8. Align the slot so it will be in the same position as when it was removed. If it is not, the distributor will not be timed correctly. Install the pump fully and rotate back and forth to ensure proper positioning between the pump mounting surface and the machined surface of the block.

9. Install the mounting bolts fingertight and lower the vehicle to confirm proper slot positioning. If the slot is not properly positioned, raise the vehicle and move the gear as required. If the slot is correct, hold the pump firmly against the block and torque the mounting bolts to 17 ft. lbs. (23 Nm).

10. Clean out the oil pickup or replace as required. Replace the oil pickup O-ring and install the pickup to the pump.

11. Install the oil pan using new gaskets. Lower the vehicle.

12. Install the distributor.

13. Install the dipstick. Fill the engine with the proper amount of oil.

14. Connect the negative battery cable, check the timing and check the oil pressure.

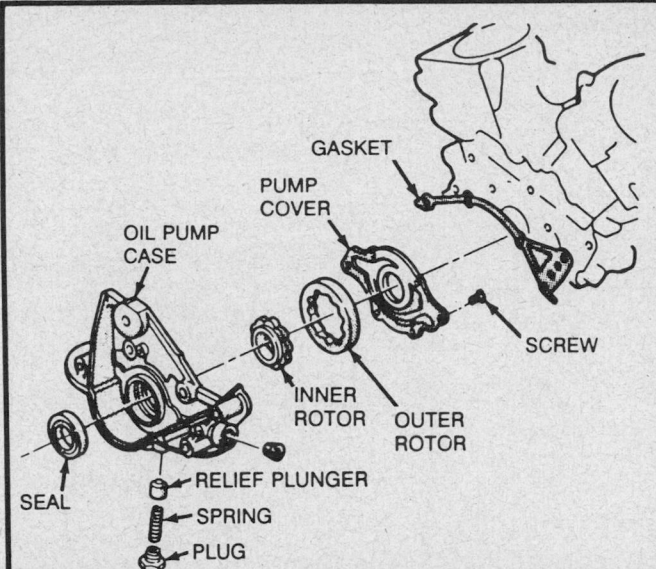

Exploded view of the oil pump—3.0L engine

2.6L ENGINE

1. Disconnect the negative battery cable. Remove the dipstick.

2. Drain the engine coolant and oil. Remove the oil pan and timing chain cover. Rotate the engine until all 3 silent chain gear marks are in a position to matchmark them to the corresponding chain link. Using different color paint, matchmark the chain to the gears. Remove the silent shaft chain. The lower guide bolts are also oil pump mounting bolts.

3. Remove the oil pump mounting bolts and remove the pump with the timing chain tensioner and the right side silent shaft.

4. Remove the silent shaft and its key from the oil pump.

To install:

5. Remove the gasket material from the block.

6. Prime the pump by pouring fresh oil into the pump intake and turning the driveshaft until oil comes out the pressure port. Repeat a few times until no air bubbles are present.

7. Install the silent shaft key to the oil pump and install the silent shaft itself to the pump.

8. Install the timing chain tensioner and spring to its bore it the pump. Make sure the rubber washer is installed on the tensioner and is not damaged. If it is, the timing chain will make noise.

9. Install the new gasket to the pump and install the pump to the block engaging the tensioner with the timing chain. Make sure the dowels are seated in their bores. Torque the mounting bolts to 13 ft. lbs. (18 Nm)

10. Install the silent shaft chain aligning the matchmarks.

11. Remove the oil pickup and clean or replace, as required. Reinstall with a new gasket.

12. Install the timing chain cover, oil pan and all related parts.

13. Install the dipstick. Fill the engine with the proper amount of oil.

14. Connect the negative battery cable and check the oil pressure.

3.0L ENGINE

1. Disconnect the negative battery cable. Remove the dipstick.

2. Raise the vehicle and support safely. Remove the timing belt, drain the engine oil and remove the oil pan from the engine. Remove the oil pickup.

3. Remove the oil pump mounting bolts and remove the pump from the front of the engine. Note the different length bolts and their position in the pump for installation.

To install:

4. Clean the gasket mounting surfaces of the pump and engine block.

5. Prime the pump by pouring fresh oil into the pump and turning the rotors or, using petroleum jelly, pack the inside of the oil pump. Using a new gasket, install the oil pump on the engine and torque all bolts to 11 ft. lbs. (15 Nm).

6. Install the balancer and crankshaft sprocket to the end of the crankshaft.

7. Clean out the oil pickup or replace as required. Replace the oil pickup gasket ring and install the pickup to the pump.

8. Install the timing belt, oil pan and all related parts.

9. Install the dipstick. Fill the engine with the proper amount of oil.

10. Connect the negative battery cable and check the oil pressure.

3.3L ENGINE

1. Disconnect the negative battery cable. Remove the dipstick.

2. Raise the vehicle and support safely. Drain the oil and remove the oil pan.

3. Remove the oil pickup.

4. Remove the chain case cover.

5. Disassemble the oil pump as required.

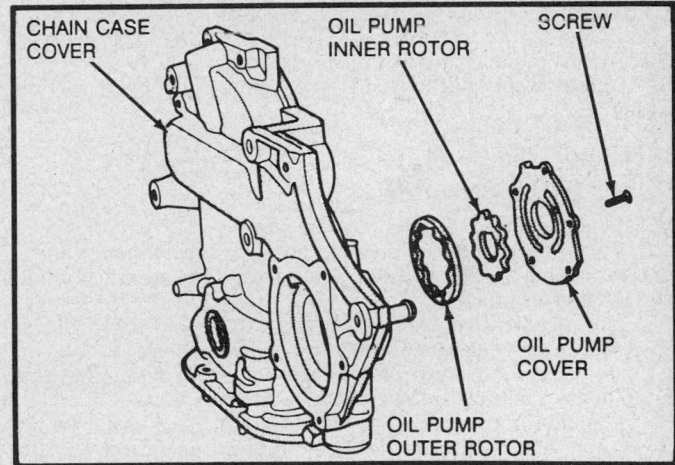

Oil pump components—3.3L engine

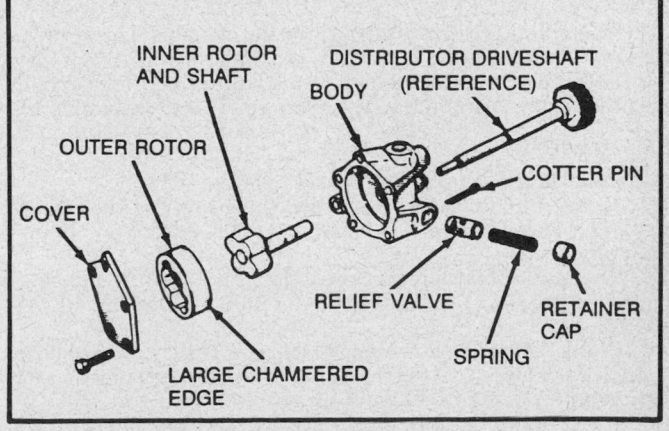

Exploded view of the oil pump—3.9L engine

To install:

6. Assemble the pump. Torque the cover screws to 10 ft. lbs. (12 Nm).

7. Prime the oil pump by filling the rotor cavity with fresh oil and turning the rotors until oil comes out the pressure port. Repeat a few times until no air bubbles are present.

8. Install the chain case cover.

9. Clean out the oil pickup or replace as required. Replace the oil pickup O-ring and install the pickup to the pump.

10. Install the oil pan.

11. Install the dipstick. Fill the engine with the proper amount of oil.

12. Connect the negative battery cable and check the oil pressure.

3.9L ENGINE

1. Disconnect the negative battery cable.

2. Raise the vehicle and support safely. Drain the oil and remove the oil pan.

3. Remove the screen.

4. Unbolt the oil pump from the rear main bearing cap and remove it from the vehicle.

To install:

5. Prime the pump by pouring fresh oil into the pump intake and turning the driveshaft until oil comes out the pressure port. Repeat a few times until no air bubbles are present. Install the oil pump with a rotating motion to ensure proper pump driveshaft engagement.

6. Hold the pump flush against the main cap and finger tighten the attaching bolts.

7. Torque the bolts to 30 ft. lbs. (41 Nm).

8. Install the screen.

9. Install the oil pan with a new gasket.

10. Connect the negative battery cable and check the oil pressure.

Checking

2.2L AND 2.5L ENGINES

1. Remove the cover from the oil pump.

2. Check endplay of the inner rotor using a feeler gauge and a straight edge placed across the pump body. The specification is 0.001–0.004 in. (0.03–0.09mm).

3. Measure the clearance between the inner and outer rotors. The maximum clearance is 0.008 in. (0.20mm).

4. Measure the clearance between the outer rotor and the pump body. The maximum clearance is 0.014 in. (0.35mm).

5. The minimum thickness of the outer rotor is 0.944 in. (23.96mm). The minimum diameter of the outer rotor is 2.77 in. (62.70mm). The minimum thickness of the inner rotor is 0.943 in. (23.95mm).

6. Check the cover for warpage. The maximum allowable is 0.003 in. (0.076mm).

7. Check the pressure relief valve for damage. The spring's freelength specification is 1.95 in. (49.50mm).

8. Assemble the outer rotor with the larger chamfered edge in the pump body. Torque the cover screws to 10 ft. lbs. (12 Nm).

2.6L ENGINE

1. Remove the cover from the oil pump.

2. Measure the clearance between the gears and their bearings. The specification for both is 0.0008–0.0020 in. (0.02–0.05mm).

3. Check the clearance between the gears and the housing. The specification for both gears is 0.004–0.006 in. (0.11–0.15mm).

4. Check endplay of the gears using a feeler gauge and a straight edge placed across the pump body. The specification for both is 0.002–0.004 in. (0.04–0.11mm).

5. Check the pressure relief valve for damage. The spring's freelength specification is 1.85 in. (47.00mm).

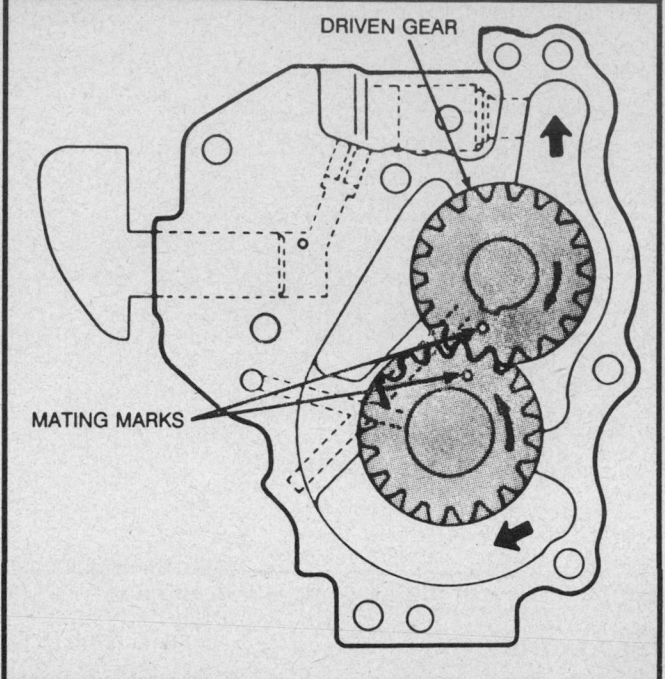

Alignment of the oil pump gear mating marks—2.6L engine

6. If the gears were removed from the body, install them with the mating aligned. If they are not aligned properly, the silent shaft will be out of time.

7. Torque the cover screws to 13 ft. lbs. (18 Nm).

3.0L ENGINE

1. Remove the rear cover.

2. Remove the pump rotors and inspect the case for excessive wear.

3. Measure the diameter of the inner rotor hub that sits in the case. Measure the inside diameter of the inner rotor hub bore. Subtract the first measurement from the second; if the result is over 0.006 in. (0.15mm), replace the oil pump assembly.

4. Measure the clearance between the outer rotor and the case. The specification is 0.004–0.007 in. (0.10–0.18mm).

5. Check the side clearance of the rotors using a feeler gauge and a straightedge placed across the case. The specification is 0.0015–0.0035 in. (0.04–0.09mm).

6. Check the relief plunger and spring for damage and breakage.

7. Install the rear cover to the case.

3.3L ENGINE

1. Thoroughly clean and dry all parts. The mating surface of the chain case cover should be smooth. Replace the pump cover if it is scratched or grooved.

2. Lay a straightedge across the pump cover surface. If a 0.003 in. (0.076mm) feeler gauge can be inserted between the cover and straightedge, the cover should be replaced.

3. The minimum thickness of the outer rotor is 0.301 in. (7.63mm). The minimum diameter of the outer rotor is 3.14 in. (79.78mm). The minimum thickness of the inner rotor is 0.301 in. (7.64mm).

4. Install the outer rotor onto the chain case cover, press to one side and measure the clearance between the rotor and case. If the measurement exceeds 0.022 in. (56mm) and the rotor is good, replace the chain case cover.

5. Install the inner rotor to the chain case cover and measure the clearance between the rotors. If the clearance exceeds 0.008 in. (0.203mm), replace both rotors.

6. Place a straightedge over the chain case cover between bolt holes. If a 0.004 in. (0.102mm) thick feeler gauge can be inserted under the straightedge, reolace the pump assembly.

7. Inspect the relief valve plunger for scoring and freedom of movement. Small marks may be removed with 400-grit wet or dry sandpaper.

8. The relief valve spring should have a freelength of 1.95 in.

9. Assemble the pump using new parts where necessary.

3.9L ENGINE

1. Disassemble the pump.

2. Replace the pump assembly if the cover is scratched or grooved or if the cover is warped more than 0.0015 in. (0.038mm).

3. The minimum thickness of the outer rotor is 0.825 in. (20.96mm). The minimum diameter of the outer rotor is 2.469 in. (62.70mm). The minimum thickness of the inner rotor is 0.825 in. (20.96mm). If any of the above measurements are not within specifications, replace the shaft and both rotors.

4. The maximum clearance between the outer rotor and the pump body is 0.014 in. (0.356mm). Replace the pump assembly if not within specifications.

5. Install the inner rotor and place a straightedge across the bolt holes. If a feeler gauge of 0.004 in. (0.101mm) or more fits, replace the pump assembly.

6. The maximum clearance between the rotors is 0.010 in. (0.254mm). Replace the shaft and both rotors if not within specifications.

7. Inspect the relief valve plunger for scoring. Small marks may be removed with 400-grit wet or dry sandpaper.

8. The relief valve spring should have a freelength of about 2 in. Replace the spring if it fails to meet specifications.

9. Assemble the pump using new parts where necessary.

Rear Main Bearing Oil Seal

Removal and Installation

EXCEPT 3.9L ENGINE

1. Disconnect the negative battery cable.

2. Remove the transmission or transaxle. Remove the flywheel or flexplate.

3. If there is any leakage coming from the rear seal retainer, drain the engine oil and remove the oil pan, if necessary. Remove the rear main oil seal retainer.

4. Remove the seal from the retainer.

To install:

5. Lightly coat the seal outer diameter with Loctite® Stud N' Bearing Mount, or equivalent.

6. Install the seal to the retainer.

7. If the retainer was removed, thoroughly clean and dry the retainer to block sealing surfaces and install a new gasket or apply silicone sealer and install the retainer. Install the pan, if it was removed.

8. Install the flywheel or flexplate and the transmission or transaxle.

9. Connect the negative battery cable and check for leaks.

3.9L ENGINE

1. Raise the vehicle and support safely. Drain the engine oil. Remove the oil pan and oil pump.

2. Remove the rear main bearing cap.

3. Remove the lower seal from the cap.

4. To remove the upper rope seal, use oil seal remover and installer kit KD–492, or equivalent, following the instructions provided with the tool.

To install:

5. Wipe the crankshaft surface clean and coat it lightly with oil.

6. Use oil seal remover and installer kit KD–492, or equivalent to install the upper rope seal. Trim the ends of the upper seal to eliminate frayed ends.

7. Install the lower rope seal in the main cap so that both ends protrude. Use tool C–3511 to seat the seal in its groove. Cut of the portions of the seal that extend above the cap on both sides and install the end seals to the cap.

8. Install the main cap to the block and torque the bolts to 85 ft. lbs. (115 Nm).

9. Install the pan and fill the engine with the proper amount of oil.

10. Connect the negative battery cable and check for leaks.

MANUAL TRANSMISSION

For further information, please refer to "Professional Transmission Manual".

Transmission Assembly

Removal and Installation

1. Disconnect the negative battery cable.

2. Shift the transmission into Neutral and remove the upper shift lever.

3. Raise the vehicle and support safely. Remove the skid plate(s), if equipped. Drain the transmission lubricant.

4. Matchmark and remove the driveshaft(s).

5. Disconnect the wires from the distance sensor, if equipped. Then loosen the sensor coupling and remove the sensor from the speedometer adaptor.

6. Disconnect the reverse light switch. Remove the transfer case, if equipped.

7. Install engine support fixture C–3487–A, or equivalent to support the engine while the transmission is out of the vehicle. Raise the engine slightly with the support fixture.

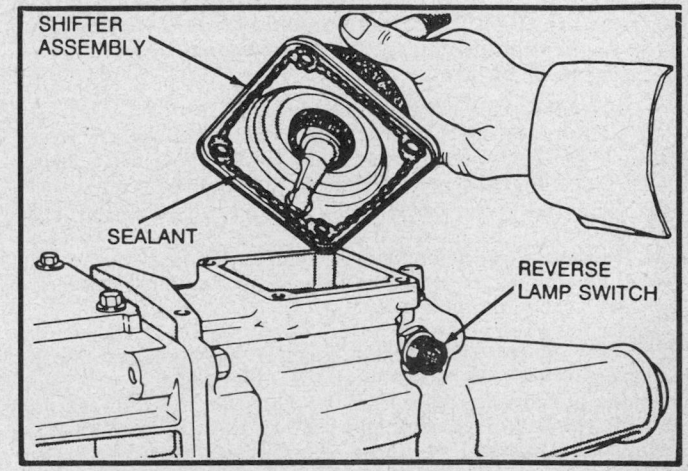

Removing or installing the shifter assembly – Dakota with NP–2500 transfer case

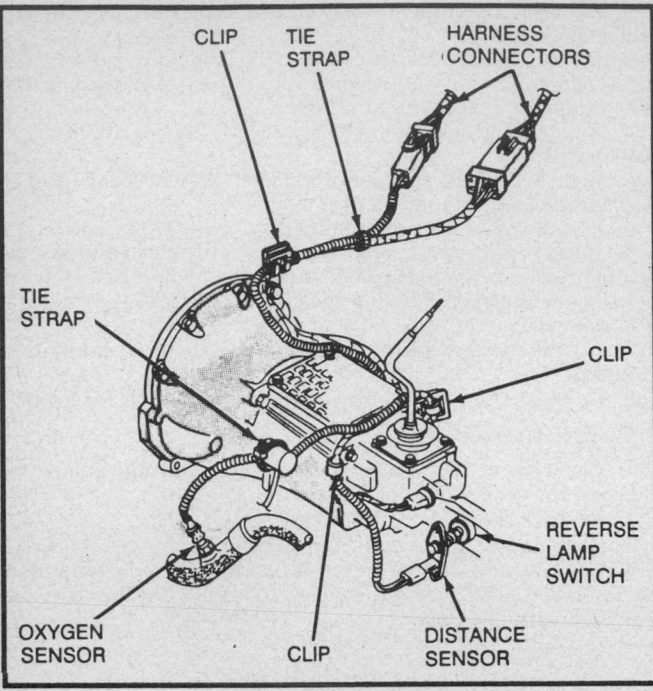

Manual transmission wiring harness routing—NP-2500 transfer case

8. Disconnect the insulator from the extension housing.
9. Using the proper equipment, support the transmission and remov ethe crossmember.

10. Remove the transmission to clutch housing bolts.
11. Slide the transmission rearward until the input shaft clears the clutch disc.
12. Pull the transmission completely away from the clutch housing and remove the transmission from the vehicle.

To install:
13. Lubricate the pilot bushing and input shaft splines very lightly with high temperature lubricant.
14. Mount the transmission securely on a suitable transmission jack and lift it in place until the input shaft is centered in the clutch housing opening. Roll the transmission forward until the input shaft splines fully engage with the clutch disc.
15. Install the transmission to clutch housing bolts. Torque the bolts to 50 ft. lbs. (68 Nm).
16. Install the transmission crossmember. Remove the transmission and engine support fixtures.
17. Install the transfer case, if equipped and connect all linkage, electrical connectors and vacuum lines to the transfer case.
18. Connect the reverse light switch connector and clip all wiring to the transmission case.
19. Connect speedometer cable and distance sensor, if equipped.
20. Install the driveshaft(s).
21. Fill the transmission with the proper amount of 10W-30 engine oil with an API classification SG/CD. Fill the transfer case, if equipped, with the proper amount of Dexron®II lubricant.
22. Apply silicone sealer to the perimeter of the shifter base and install the shifter assembly.
23. Install the skid plate(s), if equipped.
24. Connect the negative battery cable and check the transmission for proper operation.

MANUAL TRANSAXLE

For further information, please refer to "Professional Transmission Manual".

Transaxle Assembly

Removal and Installation

NOTE: If the vehicle is going to be rolled while the transaxle is out of the vehicle, obtain 2 outer CV joints to install to the hubs. If the vehicle is rolled without the proper torque applied to the front wheel bearings, the bearings will be destroyed.

1. Disconnect the negative battery cable.
2. Remove the air cleaner assembly if it is preventing access to the upper bell housing bolts. Remove the upper bell housing bolts. Disconnect the reverse light switch and the ground wire.
3. Remove the starter attaching nut and bolt at the top of the bell housing.
4. Raise the vehicle and support safely. Remove the tire and wheel assemblies. Remove the axle end cotter pins, nut locks, spring washers and axle nuts.
5. Remove the ball joint retaining bolts and pry the control arm from the steering knuckle. Position a drainpan under the transaxle where the axles enter the differential or extension housing. Remove the axles from the transaxle or center bearing. Unbolt the center bearing and remove the intermediate axle from the transaxle, if equipped.
6. Remove the anti-rotation link from the crossmember. Disconnect the shifter cables from the transaxle and unbolt the cable bracket.

7. Remove the speedometer cable adaptor bolt and remove the adaptor from the transaxle.
8. Remove the rear mount from the starter, unbolt the starter and position it to the side.
9. Using the proper equipment, support the weight of the engine.
10. Remove the front motor mount and bracket.
11. Position a suitable transaxle jack under the transaxle.
12. Remove the lower bell housing bolts.
13. Remove the left side splash shield. Remove the transaxle mount bolts.
14. Carefully pry the transaxle from the engine.
15. Slide the transaxle rearward until the input shaft clears the clutch disc.
16. Pull the transaxle completely away from the clutch housing and remove from the vehicle.
17. To prepare the vehicle for rolling, support the engine with a suitable support or reinstall the front motor mount to the engine. Then reinstall the ball joints to the steering knuckle and install the retaining bolt. Install the obtained outer CV joints to the hubs, install the washers and torque the axle nuts to 180 ft. lbs. (244 Nm). The vehicle may now be safely rolled.

To install:
18. Lubricate the pilot bushing and input shaft splines very lightly with high temperature lubricant.
19. Mount the transaxle securely on a suitable jack and and install the left side mount bolts. Lift it in place until the input shaft is centered in the clutch housing opening. Roll the trans-

axle forward until the input shaft splines fully engage with the clutch disc.

20. Install the transaxle to clutch housing bolts.

21. Jack the transaxle up and install the front motor mount and bracket.

22. Remove the engine and transaxle support fixtures.

23. Install the starter to the transaxle and install the lower bolt fingertight.

24. Install a new O-ring to the speedometer cable adaptor and install to the extension housing; make sure it snaps in place. Install the retaining bolt.

25. Install the shift cable bracket and snap the cable ends in place. Install the anti-rotation link.

26. Install the axles and center bearing, if equipped. Install the ball joints to the steering knuckles. Torque the axle nuts to 180 ft. lbs. (244 Nm) and install new cotter pins. Fill the transaxle with SAE 5W-30 engine oil. Install the splash shield and install the wheels. Lower the vehicle.

27. Install the upper bell housing bolts.

28. Install the starter attaching nut and bolt at the top of the bell housing. Raise the vehicle again and tighten the starter bolt from underneath the vehicle. Lower the vehicle.

29. Connect the reverse light switch and the ground wire.

30. Install the air cleaner assembly, if it was removed.

31. Connect the negative battery cable and check the transaxle for proper operation.

Cable Adjustment

1. Working over the left front fender, remove the lock pin from the transaxle selector shaft housing.

2. Reverse the lock pin (long end down) and insert it into the same threaded hole while pushing the selector shaft into the selector housing. A hole in the selector shaft will align with the lock pin, allowing the lock pin to be screwed into the housing. This operation locks the selector shaft in the neutral position between either 1st and 2nd gears or 3rd and 4th gears.

3. Remove the gearshift knob, the retaining nut and the pull-up ring from the gearshift lever.

4. If necessary, remove the shift lever boot and console to expose the gearshift linkage.

5. Fabricate 2 cable adjusting pins: $3/16$ in. diameter × 5 in. long with a $1/2$ in. 90 degrees bend at one end.

6. Place a pin in the hole provided at the right side and the other in the hole provided at the rear side of the shifting mechanism (make sure the alignment holes match). Torque the selector (right side) and the crossover (left side) adjusting bolts to 4–5 ft. lbs.

7. Remove the lock pin from the selector shaft housing and reinstall the lock pin (with the long end up) in the selector shaft housing. Torque the lock pin to 10 ft. lbs. (12 Nm).

8. Check the first/reverse shifting and blockout into reverse.

9. Reinstall the console, boot, pull-up ring, retaining nut and knob.

CLUTCH

Clutch Assembly

Removal and Installation

CARAVAN AND VOYAGER

1. Disconnect the negative battery cable. Remove the transaxle.

2. Matchmark the clutch/pressure plate cover and flywheel. Insert a suitable clutch plate alignment tool into the clutch disc hub.

3. Loosen the flywheel to pressure plate bolts gradually and evenly to avoid warpage.

4. Remove the pressure plate/clutch assembly from the flywheel.

5. Sand the flywheel or replace it if it is scored, cracked or heat damaged.

6. Sparingly apply anti-sieze compound to the input shaft and clutch disc splines. Install a new release bearing.

7. The installation is the reverse of the removal procedure. Use the clutch disc alignment tool when tightening the pressure plate bolts to center the disc. Torque the pressure plate/clutch assembly mounting bolts to the flywheel gradually and evenly to 21 ft. lbs. (28 Nm).

DAKOTA

1. Disconnect the negative battery cable.

2. Raise the vehicle and support safely.

3. Remove the transmission and transfer case, if equipped.

4. Remove the inspection cover at the bottom of the bell housing.

5. Rotating the engine with a flywheel turner, remove the clutch cover bolts gradually as they appear.

6. Remove the clutch cover and disc by lowering it through the opening at the bottom of the housing.

To install:

7. Sparingly apply anti-sieze compound to the input shaft and clutch disc splines. Install a new release bearing.

8. Raise the clutch cover and disc into place and use a suitable clutch aligning tool or spare input shaft to center the disc. Tighten all of the bolts finger tight.

9. The cover bolts must be turned gradually, evenly and to the proper torque to avoid distorting the cover. Torque the bolts to 21 ft. lbs. (28 Nm).

10. Install the transmission and transfer case, if equipped.

11. Install the inspection cover.

12. Connect the negative battery cable and check the clutch for proper operation.

Pedal Free-play Adjustment

NOTE: The Caravan and Voyager are equipped with a self-adjusting cable operated mechanism and no adjustment is provided. The Dakota has been equipped with a hydraulic clutch release system since its inception. There is no adjustment for free-play on this system.

Clutch Cable

Removal and Installation

1. Disconnect the negative battery cable.

2. Remove the clip from the cable mounting bracket on the shock tower and remove the cable from the bracket.

3. Remove the retainer from the clutch release lever on the transaxle.

4. Pry out the ball end of the cable from the position adjuster inside the pedal.

5. The installation is the reverse of the removal procedure. After installing, push the clutch pedal 2 or 3 times to allow the self-adjuster mechanism to function.

Clutch Master Cylinder and Slave Cylinder

The clutch master cylinder, remote reservoir, slave cylinder and connecting lines are all serviced as a complete assembly. The cylinders and connecting lines are sealed units. They are prefilled

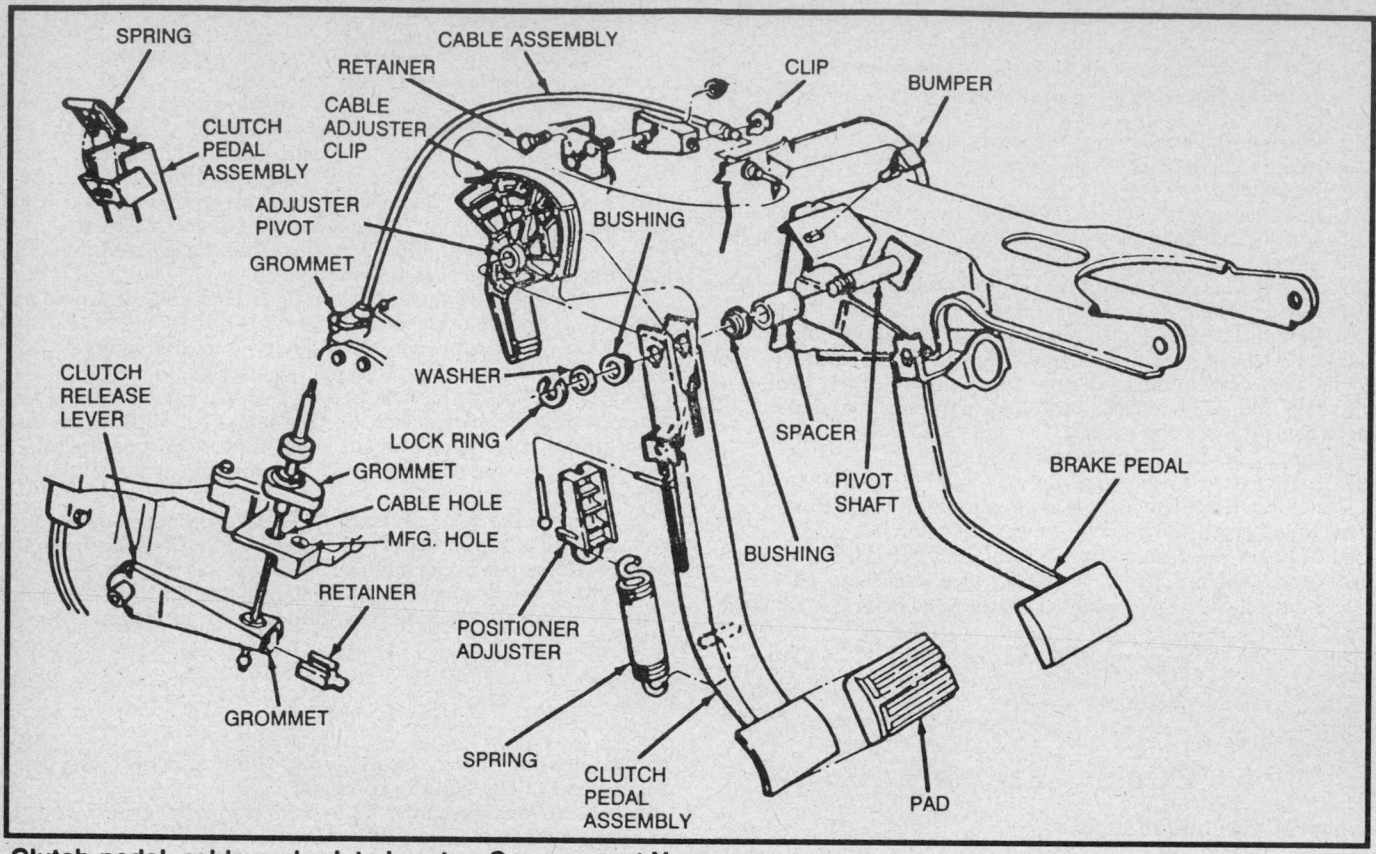

Clutch pedal, cable and related parts—Caravan and Voyager

with fluid from the factory and cannot be disassembled or serviced separately.

Removal and Installation

1. Disconnect the negative battery cable.
2. Raise the vehicle and support safely.
3. Remove the nuts attaching the slave cylinder to the bell housing.
4. Remove the slave cylinder and clip from the housing.
5. Lower the vehicle.
6. Remove the locating clip from the clutch master cylinder mounting bracket.
7. Remove the retaining ring, flat washer and wave washer that attach the clutch master cylinder pushrod to the clutch pedal. Slide the pushrod off of the pedal pin. Inspect the bushing on the pedal pin and replace if it is excessively worn.
8. Verify that the cap on the clutch master cylinder reservoir is tight so that fluid will not spill during removal.
9. Remove the screws attaching the reservoir and bracket to the dash panel and remove the reservoir.
10. Pull the clutch master cylinder rubber seal from the dash panel.
11. Rotate the clutch master cylinder 45 degrees to unlock it. Remove the cylinder from the dash panel.

12. Remove the clutch master cylinder, remote reservoir, slave cylinder and connecting lines from the vehicle.
To install:
13. Verify that the cap on the fluid reservoir is tight so that fluid will not spill during installation.
14. Position the components in the replacement kit in their places on the vehicle.
15. Insert the master cylinder in the dash. Rotate it 45 degrees to lock it in place.
16. Lubricate the rubber seal with a suitable lubricant to ease installation. Seat the seal around the cylinder in the dash.
17. Install the fluid reservoir and bracket, if equipped, to the dash panel.
18. Install the master cylinder pushrod to the clutch pedal pin. Secure the rod with the wave washer, flat washer and retaining ring. Install the locating clip. Do not remove the plastic shipping stop from the pushrod until the slave cylinder has been installed.
19. Raise the vehicle and support safely.
20. Insert the slave cylinder pushrod through the opening and make sure the cap on the end of the pushrod is securely engaged in the release lever before tightening the attaching nuts. Torque the nuts to 17 ft. lbs. (23 Nm).
21. Lower the vehicle. Remove the plastic shipping stop from the master cylinder pushrod.
22. Operate the clutch pedal a few times to verify proper operation of the system.
23. Connect the negative battery cable and road test the vehicle.

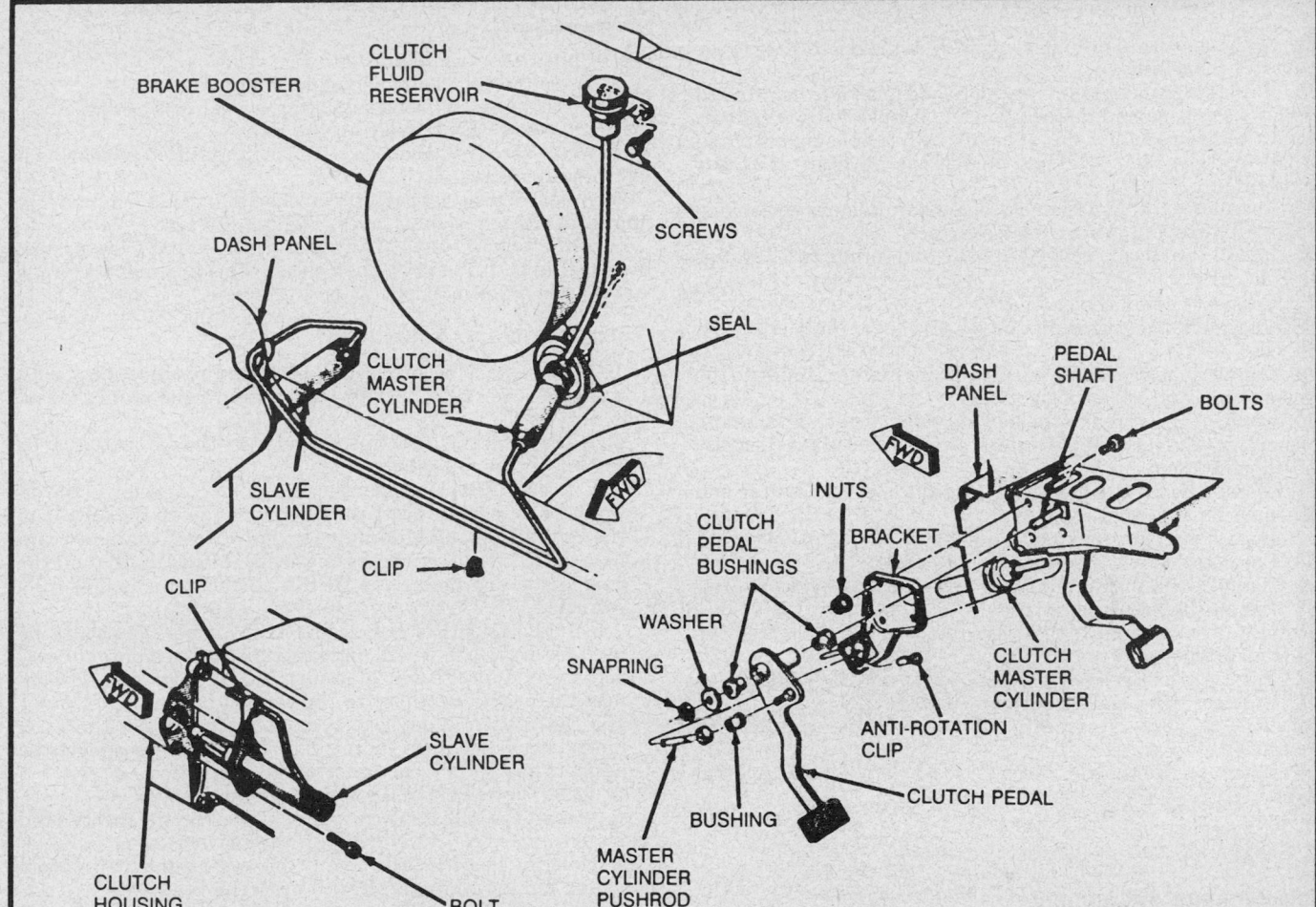

Clutch hydraulic linkage components—Dakota

AUTOMATIC TRANSMISSION

For further information, please refer to "Professional Transmission Manual".

Transmission Assembly

Removal and Installation

1. Disconnect the negative battery cable.
2. Raise the vehicle and support safely. Drain the transmission and transfer case, if equipped.
3. Remove the exhaust crossover pipe.
4. Remove the skid plates, if equipped.
5. Matchmark and remove the driveshaft(s).
6. Disconnect the distance sensor, if equipped and the speedometer cable.
7. If equipped with 4WD, disconnect all linkage, electrical connectors and vacuum lines from the transfer case. Using a suitable jack, support the transfer case, unbolt the transfer case from the transmission and slide it backwards to remove it from the vehicle.
8. Remove the engine to transmission struts.
9. Remove the starter and the fluid cooler lines bracket.

10. Remove the torque converter inspection cover.
11. Matchmark the converter to the flex plate. Remove the torque converter bolts.
12. Disconnect the wires to the neutral safety switch and lock-up solenoid, if equipped.
13. Disconnect and plug the oil cooler lines from the transmission.
14. Disconnect the gearshift rod and torque shaft assembly from the transmission.
15. Disconnect the throttle rod from the lever.
16. Unbolt the oil filler tube brace and lift the oil filler tube out of its bore.
17. Install an appropriate engine support fixture to hold the engine in place when the transmission is out of the vehicle.
18. Raise the transmission slightly using a suitable transmission jack.
19. Remove the transmission crossmember.
20. Remove the oil filter, if necessary. Remove all bell housing bolts and remove the transmission from the vehicle.

To install:
21. Install the transmission securely on the transmission jack.

Rotate the converter so it will align with the positioning of the flex plate.

22. Apply a coating of high temperature grease to the torque converter pilot hub.

23. Raise the transmission into place and push it forward until the dowels engage and the bell housing is flush with the block.

24. Install the oil filler tube. Install the bell housing bolts and torque to 30 ft. lbs. (41 Nm). Install the oil filter, if it was removed.

25. Install the transmission crossmember. Remove the engine support fixture and the transmission jack.

26. Install the torque converter bolts and torque to 23 ft. lbs. (31 Nm).

27. Connect the oil cooler lines.

28. Connect the throttle rod to the lever and adjust if necessary.

29. Connect the gearshift rod and torque shaft assembly to the transmission and adjust if necessary.

30. Connect the wires to the neutral safety switch and lockup solenoid, if equipped. Make sure all wires are routed correctly and clipped in place.

31. Install the torque converter inspection cover, starter and transmission struts.

32. Install the transfer case, if equipped.

33. Connect the distance sensor, if equipped.

34. Connect the speedometer cable.

35. Install the driveshaft(s).

36. Install exhaust parts that were removed in order to remove the transmission.

37. Fill the transfer case, if equipped. Lower the vehicle.

38. Connect the negative battery cable.

39. Fill the transmission with the proper amount of Dexron®II.

40. Road test the vehicle, check for leaks and recheck the fluid level.

Shift Linkage Adjustment

NOTE: Do not attempt to adjust the linkage if any of th parts are excessively worn. If any rods are removed from the plastic grommets, new grommets should be installed. Pry only where the grommet and rod attach, not on the rod itself. Use pliers to snap the rod into the new grommet.

1. Shift the transmission into **P**.
2. Raise the vehicle and support safely.
3. Loosen the shift rod adjusting swivel lock screw. Make sure the swivel turns freely on the rod.
4. Make sure the valve body is in the **P** position by moving it all the way rearward.
5. Adjust the swivel position on the shift rod to obtain a free pin fit in the toque shaft lever. Tighten the lock screw.
6. If the vehicle starts in any gear other than **P** or **N**, or does not start in both **P** and **N**, then either the adjustment is wrong or another problem exists.

Throttle Linkage Adjustment

1. If the vehicle is carbureted, perform the adjustment with the engine at normal operating temperature and off of the fast idle cam.
2. If the vehicle is fuel injected, retract the ISC actuator by doing one of the following:

   a. If the DRBII is available, connect its connector to the diagnostic connector. Start the engine and place the DRBII in the "Throttle Body Minimum Air Flow Test" mode. Disconnect the electrical connector on the ISC actuator. Shut off the engine and disconnect the DRBII; the actuator is now fully retracted.

   b. If the DRBII is not available, 2 jumper wires may be used. With the engine off, disconnect the connector to the ISC actuator. Connect a pair of jumper wires to the battery. Connect the negative jumper to the top pin of the ISC actuator and the positive jumper to the other pin. Do not leave the jumpers connected for more than 5 seconds. Disconnect the jumpers and the ISC actuator is fully retracted.
3. Raise the vehicle and support safely.
4. Loosen the adjustable swivel lock screw on the throttle rod enough so the rod travels freely in the swivel.
5. Hold the throttle lever firmly forward against its internal stop and tighten the lock screw. Lower the vehicle.
6. Reconnect the ISC actuator, if equipped.
7. If equipped with fuel injection, turn the ignition key to the **RUN** position for at least 5 seconds, but do not start the engine. Turn the key to the **OFF** position.
8. Start the engine and road test the vehicle.

AUTOMATIC TRANSAXLE

For further information, please refer to "Professional Transmission Manual".

Transaxle Assembly

Removal and Installation

NOTE: If the vehicle is going to be rolled while the transaxle is out of the vehicle, obtain 2 outer CV joints to install to the hubs. If the vehicle is rolled without the proper torque applied to the front wheel bearings, the bearings will be destroyed.

1. Disconnect the negative battery cable. If equipped with 3.0L or 3.3L engine, drain the coolant. Remove the dipstick.
2. Remove the air cleaner assembly if it is preventing access to the upper bell housing bolts. Remove the upper bell housing bolts and water tube, where applicable. Unplug all electrical connectors from the transaxle.
3. If equipped with a 2.2L or 2.5L engine, remove the starter attaching nut and bolt at the top of the bell housing.

4. Raise the vehicle and support safely. Remove the tire and wheel assemblies. Remove the axle end cotter pins, nut locks, spring washers and axle nuts.
5. Remove the ball joint retaining bolts and pry the control arm from the steering knuckle. Position a drainpan under the transaxle where the axles enter the differential or extension housing. Remove the axles from the transaxle or center bearing. Unbolt the center bearing and remove the intermediate axle from the transaxle, if equipped.
6. Drain the transaxle. Disconnect and plug the fluid cooler hoses. Disconnect the shifter and kickdown linkage from the transaxle, if equipped.
7. Remove the speedometer cable adaptor bolt and remove the adaptor from the transaxle.
8. Remove the starter. Remove the torque converter inspection cover, matchmark the torque converter to the flexplate and remove the torque converter bolts.
9. Using the proper equipment, support the weight of the engine.
10. Remove the front motor mount and bracket.
11. Position a suitable transaxle jack under the transaxle.

12. Remove the lower bell housing bolts.

13. Remove the left side splash shield. Remove the transaxle mount bolts.

14. Carefully pry the transaxle from the engine.

15. Slide the transaxle rearward until dowels disengage from the mating holes in the transaxle case.

16. Pull the transaxle completely away from the engine and remove from the vehicle.

17. To prepare the vehicle for rolling, support the engine with a suitable support or reinstall the front motor mount to the engine. Then reinstall the ball joints to the steering knuckle and install the retaining bolt. Install the obtained outer CV joints to the hubs, install the washers and torque the axle nuts to 180 ft. lbs. (244 Nm). The vehicle may now be safely rolled.

To install:

18. Install the transmission securely on the transmission jack. Rotate the converter so it will align with the positioning of the flex plate.

19. Apply a coating of high temperature grease to the torque converter pilot hub.

20. Raise the transaxle into place and push it forward until the dowels engage and the bell housing is flush with the block.

20. Install the transaxle to bell housing bolts.

21. Jack the transaxle up and install the left side mount bolts. Install the torque converter bolts and torque to 55 ft. lbs. (74 Nm).

22. Install the front motor mount and bracket. Remove the engine and transaxle support fixtures.

23. Install the starter to the transaxle. Install the bolt finger tight if equipped with a 2.2L or 2.5L engine.

24. Install a new O-ring to the speedometer cable adaptor and install to the extension housing; make sure it snaps in place. Install the retaining bolt.

25. Connect the shifter and kickdown linkage to the transaxle, if equipped.

26. Install the axles and center bearing, if equipped. Install the ball joints to the steering knuckles. Torque the axle nuts to 180 ft. lbs. (244 Nm) and install new cotter pins. Install the splash shield and install the wheels. Lower the vehicle. Install the dipstick.

27. Install the upper bell housing bolts and water pipe, if removed.

28. If equipped with 2.2L or 2.5L engine, install the starter attaching nut and bolt at the top of the bell housing. Raise the vehicle again and tighten the starter bolt from underneath the vehicle. Lower the vehicle.

29. Connect all electrical wiring to the transaxle.

30. Install the air cleaner assembly, if it was removed. Fill the transaxle with the proper amount of Dexron®II.

31. Connect the negative battery cable and check the transaxle for proper operation.

Upshift and Kickdown Learning Procedure

A-604 ULTRADRIVE TRANSAXLE

In 1989, the A-604 4 speed, electronic transaxle was introduced; it is the first to use fully adaptive controls. The controls perform their functions based on real time feedback sensor information.

Although, the transaxle is conventional in design, its functions are controlled by the ECM.

Since the A-604 is equipped with a learning function, each time the battery cable is disconnected, the ECM memory is lost. In operation, the transaxle must be shifted many times for the learned memory to be reinputed in the ECM; during this period, the vehicle will experience rough operation. The transaxle must be at normal operating temperature when learning occurs.

1. Maintain constant throttle opening during shifts. Do not move the accelerator pedal during upshifts.

2. Accelerate the vehicle with the throttle ⅛–½ open.

3. Make 15 to 20 1/2, 2/3 and 3/4 upshifts. Accelerating from a full stop to 50 mph each time at the aforementioned throttle opening is sufficient.

4. With the vehicle speed below 25 mph, make 5 to 8 wide open throttle kickdowns to 1st gear from either 2nd or 3rd gear. Allow at least 5 seconds of operation in 2nd or 3rd gear prior to each kickdown.

5. With the vehicle speed greater than 25 mph, make 5 to part throttle to wide open throttle kickdowns to either 3rd or 2nd gear from 4th gear. Allow at least 5 seconds of operation in 4th gear, preferably at road load throttle prior to performing the kickdown.

Shift Linkage Adjustment

1. Place the shifter in the **P** detent.

2. Loosen the clamp bolt on the gearshift cable bracket.

3. Pull the shift lever all the way to the front detent position and tighten the lock screw.

4. Check for proper neutral safety switch operation.

Throttle Pressure Cable Adjustment

1. Run the engine until it reaches normal operating temperature.

2. Loosen the cable mounting bracket lock screw.

3. Position the bracket so that both alignment tabs are touching the transaxle case surface and tighten the lock screws.

4. Release the cross lock on the cable assembly by pulling the cross lock up.

5. To ensure proper adjustment, the cable must be free to slide all the way toward the engine against its stop after the cross lock is released.

6. Move the transaxle throttle control lever fully clockwise and press the cross lock down until it snaps into position.

7. Road test the vehicle and check the shift points.

Throttle Pressure Rod Adjustment

1. Run the engine until it reaches normal operating temperature.

2. Loosen the adjustment swivel lock screw.

3. To ensure proper adjustment, the swivel must be free to slide along the flat end of the throttle rod. Disassembly, clean and lubricate as required.

4. Hold the transaxle throttle control lever firmly toward the engine and tighten the swivel screw.

5. Road test the vehicle and check the shift points.

TRANSFER CASE

Transfer Case Assembly

Removal and Installation

1. Disconnect the negative battery cable.

2. Raise the vehicle and support safely.

3. Remove the skid plates, if equipped. Drain the transfer case fluid.

4. Disconnect the distance sensor, if equipped and disconnect the speedometer cable from the transfer case.

5. Matchmark and remove the driveshafts.

6. Disconnect the PTO, if equipped.

7. Disconnect the linkage, electrical connectors and vacuum lines from the transfer case. Using a suitable jack, support the transfer case and remove the crossmember.

8. Unbolt the transfer case from the transmission and slide it backwards to remove it from the vehicle.

9. The installation is the reverse of the removal procedure. Torque the transfer case to transmission case nuts to 26 ft. lbs. (35 Nm). Fill the transfer case with Dexron®II.

Linkage Adjustment

1. Move the transfer case shift lever boot aside for access to the shift lever and gate.

2. Move the shift lever into the **2H** position on 1987 vehicles or the **4H** position on 1988–90 vehicles. Make sure the lever is against the appropriate gate. Insert a ⅛ inch spacer between the shift lever and gate and secure the lever with tape.

3. Raise the vehicle and support safely.

4. Loosen the shift rod clamp screw until the shift rod is free to slide in the swivel.

5. Verify that the lever is in the **2H** or **4H** (depending on year); position and move it if it has moved out of position.

6. Tighten the clamp screw.

7. Check the smoothness of operation of the transfer case.

DRIVE AXLE

Halfshaft

Removal and Installation

1. Disconnect the negative battery cable.

2. Raise the vehicle and support safely.

3. Remove the tire and wheel assembly.

4. Remove the cotter pin from the end of the halfshaft. Remove the nut lock, spring washer, axle nut and washer.

5. Remove the ball joint retaining bolt and pry the control arm down to release the ball stud from the steering knuckle.

6. Position a drainpan under the transaxle where the halfshaft enters the differential or extension housing. Remove the halfshaft from the transaxle or center bearing. Unbolt the center bearing from the block and remove the intermediate shaft from the transaxle, if equipped.

To install:

7. Install the halfshaft or intermediate shaft to the transaxle, being careful not to damage the side seals. Make sure the inner joint clicks into pace inside the differential. Install the center bearing retaining bolts, if equipped. Install the outer shaft to the center bearing if equipped.

8. Pull the front strut out and insert the outer joint into the front hub.

9. Turn the ball joint stud, if necessary to position the bolt retaining indent to the inside of the vehicle. Install the ball joint stud into the steering knuckle. Install the retaining bolt and nut.

10. Install the axle nut washer and nut and torque the nut to 180 ft. lbs. (244 Nm). Install the spring washer, nut lock and a new cotter pin.

11. Install the tire and wheel assembly.

Driveshaft and U-Joints

Removal and Installation

1. Raise the vehicle and support safely.

2. Matchmark the driveshaft and the rear axle drive pinion gear shaft yoke. Unbolt the support collar from the frame, if equipped.

3. Remove the rear U-joint attaching bolts and both strap clamps from the rear axle drive pinion gear shaft yoke.

4. Fluid may run from the rear of the extension housing or transfer case when the shaft is removed, so position a suitable drain pan under the area.

5. Remove the driveshaft from the transmission or transfer case.

6. The installation is the reverse of the removal procedure. Torque the clamp bolts to 14 ft. lbs. (19 Nm) and the support collar bolts to 50 ft. lbs. (68 Nm).

Front Axle Shaft, Seal and Bearing

Removal and Installation

LEFT SIDE SHAFT

1. Raise the vehicle and support safely.

2. Disconnect the left CV driveshaft from the axle shaft flange.

3. Remove the differential housing cover. Rotate the differential case so that the differential pinion mate gear shaft lock screw is accessible. Remove the lock screw and the pinion mate gear shaft from the differential case.

4. Force the left axle shaft toward the center of the vehicle and remove the shaft C-clip lock from the recessed groove in the axle shaft.

5. Remove the axle shaft from the differential housing. Inspect the axle shaft bearing contact surface for brinelling, spalling and pitting. If any of these conditions exist, replace the axle shaft and bearing.

6. Remove the axle shaft seal from the end of the housing bore with a suitable pry bar. Remove the axle shaft bearing only if it is being replaced; do not reinstall used bearings. Use removal tool C–4167 and slide hammer tool C–637 to remove the bearing.

To install:

7. Thoroughly clean and dry the bearing bore in the differential housing.

8. Insert the new bearing into the pilot of bearing installation tool C–4198 and attach to the handle. Insert the bearing to the housing until it is seated against the bore shoulder.

9. Install the new seal using tool C–4203 with the flat side of

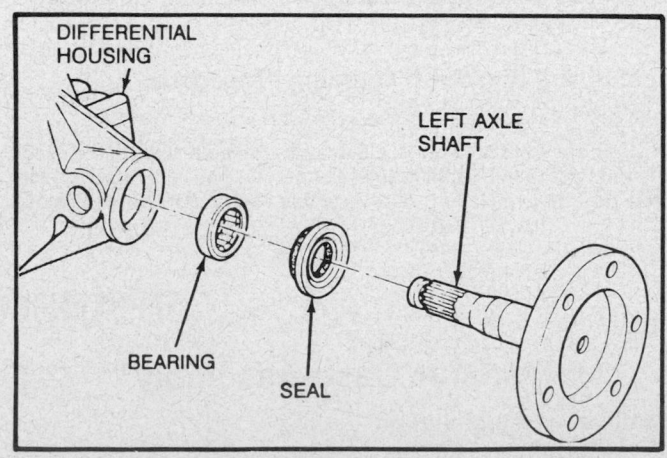

Left side axle shaft assembly

the tool facing the seal. When the installation tool contacts the housing flange face, the seal is installed to the correct depth.

10. Lubricate the bearing bore and seal lip, insert the axle shaft into the housing and engage the splines. With the shaft in place, install the C-clip lock and push the shaft outward to seal the lock.

11. Install the mate shaft, align the hole in the shaft with the lock screw hole in the differential case and install the lock screw. Torque the lock screw to 8 ft. lbs. (11 Nm).

12. Thoroughly clean and dry the case cover, mating surface, bolts and bolt holes. Apply silicone sealer to the cover and install.

13. Connect the CV driveshaft.

14. Level the vehicle and fill the differential with multi-purpose gear lubricant.

15. Road test the vehicle and check for leaks and correct front axle operation.

RIGHT SIDE AND INTERMEDIATE SHAFT

1. Raise the vehicle and support safely.
2. Remove the tire and wheel assembly.
3. Remove the cotter pin, nut lock and spring washer from the stub shaft. Remove the hub nut and washer.
4. Remove the bolts that attach the inner CV joint to the axle shaft flange.
5. Separate the stub shaft splines from the hub bearing splines and remove the CV joint shaft.
6. Remove the differential housing cover.
7. Disconnect the 4WD indicator lamp switch and the vacuum tube from the shift motor. Remove the shift motor, housing cover and gasket from the shift motor housing.
8. Remove the bearing seal/retainer attaching screws accessible via the holes in the axle shaft flange.
9. Remove the outer axle shaft from the differential housing.
10. Remove the snapring and the splined gear from the outer axle shaft. Separate the bearing and seal from the outer axle shaft.
11. Remove the shift collar from the shift motor housing.
12. Rotate the differential case so that the differential pinion mate gear shaft lock screw is accessible. Remove the lock screw and the pinion mate gear shaft from the differential case.
13. Force the intermediate shaft toward the center of the vehicle and remove the shaft C-clip lock from the recessed groove in the axle shaft. Remove the intermediate shaft from the differential housing and tube.

To install:

14. Insert the axle shaft into the tube and housing and engage the splines. With the shaft in place, install the C-clip locka dn push the shaft outward to seal the lock.

15. Install the mate shaft, align the hole in the shaft with the lock screw hole in the differential case and install the lock screw. Torque the lock screw to 8 ft. lbs. (11 Nm).

16. Install the shift collar to the intermediate shaft.

17. Install a new seal to the seal retainer and install to the outer shaft. Press on the new bearing, install the splined gear and the snapring.

18. Insert the outer axle shaft into the shift motor housing. Torque the attaching screws to 17 ft. lbs. (23 Nm).

19. Install the shift motor housing cover and gasket. Ensure that the shift fork is correctly engaged in the collar groove. Install the cover bolts. Connect the vacuum tubes to the shift motor and the connector to the 4WD lamp switch.

20. Thoroughly clean and dry the case cover, mating surface, bolts and bolt holes. Apply silicone sealer to the cover and install.

21. Lubricate the contact surface area of the CV driveshaft wear sleeve with grease and install the CV driveshaft. Torque the hub nut to 190 ft. lbs (258 Nm). Install the spring washer, nut lock and a new cotter pin.

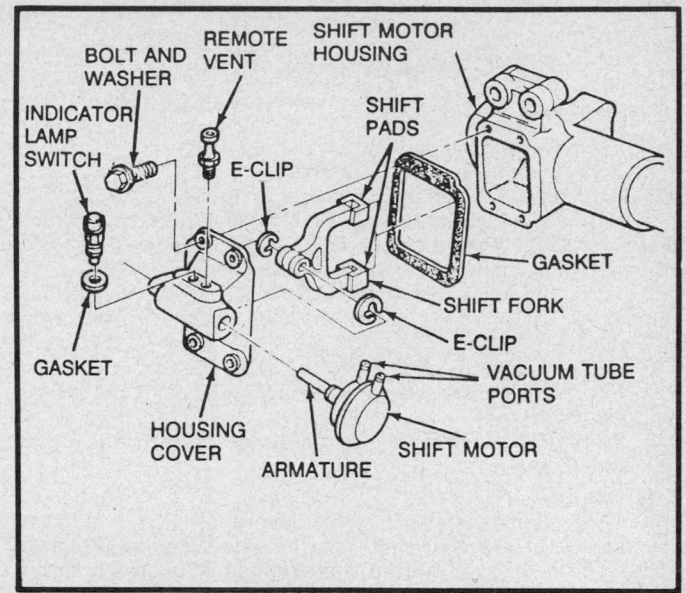
Shift motor and related parts

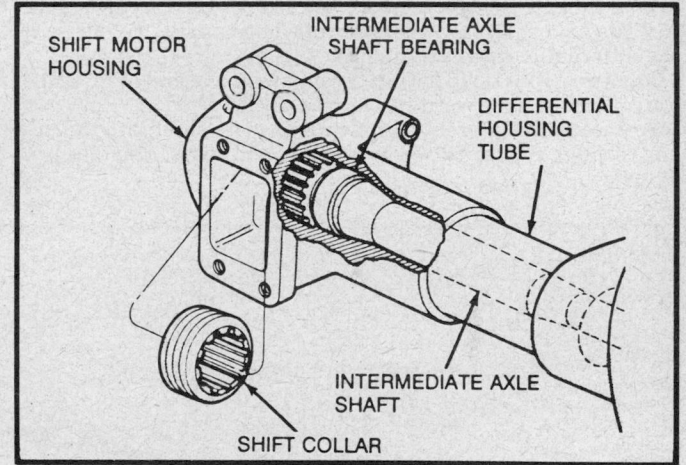
Shift collar and related parts

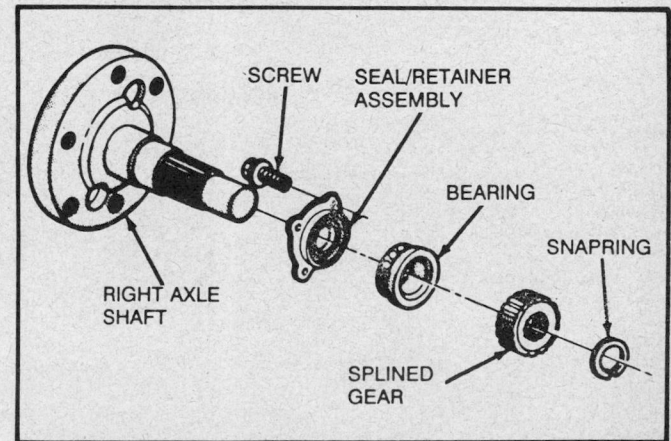
Right side axle shaft assembly

21. Level the vehicle and fill the differential with multi-purpose gear lubricant.

22. Road test the vehicle and check for leaks and correct front axle operation.

Rear Axle Shaft, Bearing and Seal

Removal and Installation

1. Raise the vehicle and support safely.
2. Remove the wheel and brake drum.
3. Remove the differential housing cover.
4. Rotate the differential case so that the differential pinion mate gear shaft lock screw is accessible. Remove the lock screw and the pinion mate gear shaft from the differential case.
5. Force the axle shaft toward the center of the vehicle and remove the axle shaft C-clip lock from the recessed groove in the axle shaft.
6. Remove the axle shaft from the axle housing.
7. Pry the axle shaft seal from the end of the axle tube using a suitable pry bar.
8. To remove the bearing, use tool C–4167 attached to a suitable slide hammer.

To install:

9. Clean the bearing bore in the axle tube.
10. Insert the new axle shaft bearing onto the pilot of tool C–4198. The bearing is fully installed when it is seated firmly against the shoulder in the axle tube.
11. Install the new seal to the axle tube.
12. Lubricate the bearing bore and seal lip with grease and insert the axle shaft into the axle tube engaging its splines with the differential side gear splines.
13. Install the C–clip lock in the groove at the end of the shaft. Force the shaft outward to seat the C–clip.
14. Insert the differential pinion gear mate shaft into the case and through the thrust washers and pinion gears. Align the hole in the shaft with the lock screw hole in the differential case and install the lock screw. Torque the screw to 14 ft. lbs. (19 Nm).
15. Thoroughly clean and dry the case cover, mating surface, bolts and bolt holes. Apply silicone sealer to the cover and install.
16. Install the drum and wheel.
17. Fill the differential with the proper lubricant.
18. Road test the vehicle and check for leaks.

Front Wheel Hub, Knuckle and Bearings

Removal and Installation

CARAVAN, VOYAGER AND TOWN & COUNTRY

1. Raise the vehicle and support safely.
2. Remove the tire and wheel assembly. Remove the brake caliper from the adaptor and remove the adaptor. Remove the brake disc.
3. Remove the halfshaft.
4. Disconnect the tie rod from the knuckle.
5. Remove the 2 strut clamp bolts and remove the knuckle from the vehicle.
6. Attach the hub removal tool C–4811 or equivalent and the triangular adapter, to the 3 rear threaded holes of the steering knuckle housing with the thrust button inside the hub bore.
7. Tighten the bolt in the center of the tool, to press the hub from the steering knuckle. Remove the removal tools.
8. Remove the bolts and bearing retainer from the outside of the steering knuckle.
9. Carefully pry the bearing seal from the machined recess of the steering knuckle and clean the recess.

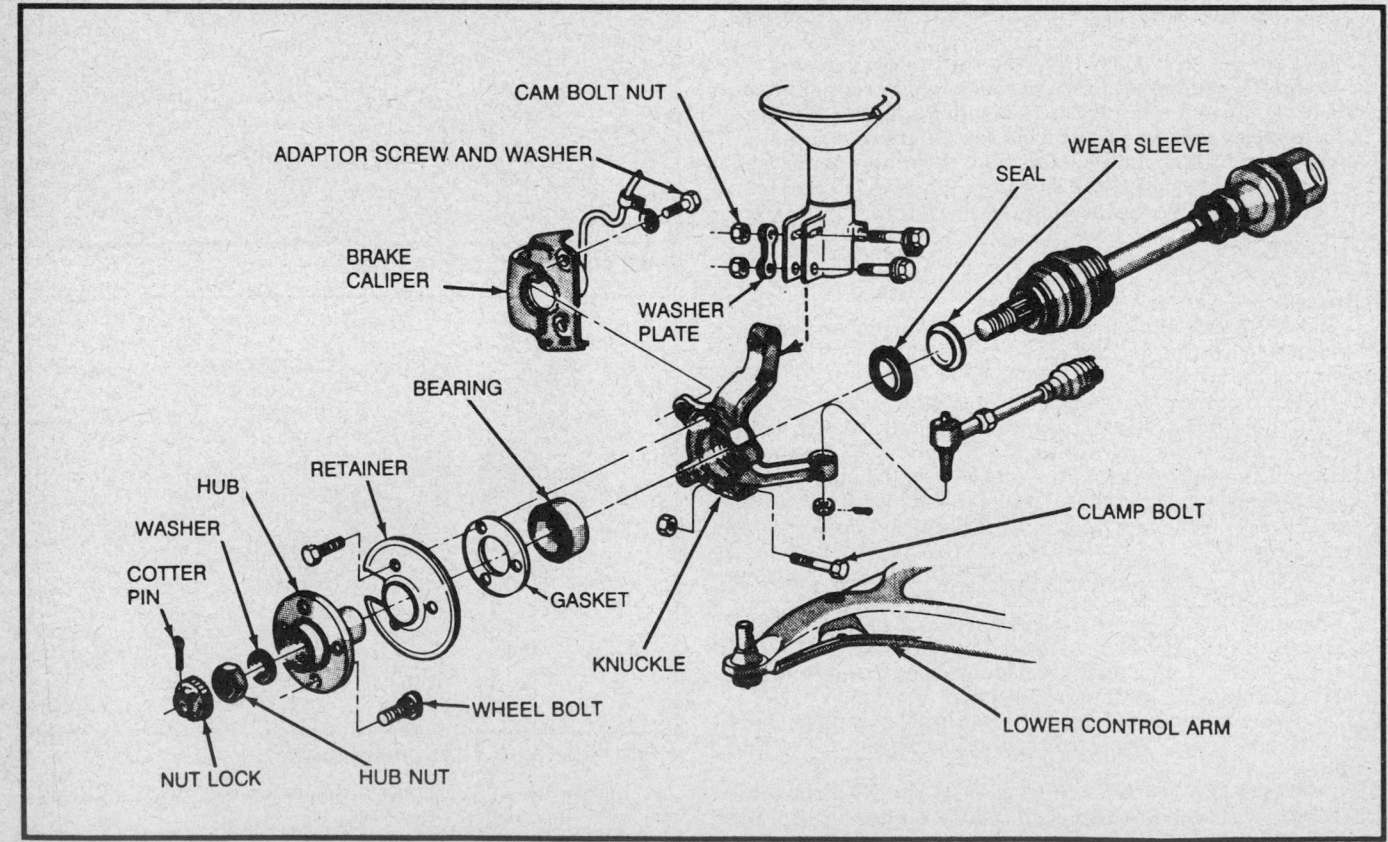

Front suspension components—Caravan, Voyager and Town & Country

10. Insert the tool C–4811 or equivalent, through the hub bearing and install bearing removal adapter to the outside of the steering knuckle. Tighten the tool to press the hub bearing from the steering knuckle. Discard the bearing and the seal.

To Install:

11. Use tool C–4811 or equivalent and the bearing installation adapter to press in the hub bearing into the steering knuckle.

12. Install a new seal, the bearing retainer and the bolts to the steering knuckle. Torque the bearing retainer bolts to 20 ft. lbs.

13. Use the tool C–4811 or equivalent and the hub installation adapter, to press the hub into the hub bearing.

14. Using the bearing installation tool C–4698 or equivalent, drive the new dust seal into the rear of the steering the hub and bearing from the knuckle as required.

15. The installation of the knuckle is the reverse of the removal procedure. Torque the tie rod nut to 35 ft. lbs. (47 Nm).

16. Align the front end.

DAKOTA WITH 2WD

1. Raise the vehicle and support safely.
2. Remove the tire and wheel assembly.
3. Remove the brake caliper and rotor with from the steering knuckle.
4. Disconnect the tie rod end from the steering knuckle.
5. Disconnect both ball joints from the steering knuckle.
6. Remove the steering knuckle from the vehicle. Remove the splash shield and the steering arm from the knuckle.
7. The installation is the reverse of the removal procedure. Torque the steering arm to knuckle nuts to 217 ft. lb.s (294 Nm).

DAKOTA WITH 4WD

1. Raise the vehicle and support safely. Remove the tire and wheel assembly.
2. Remove the cotter pin, nut lock and spring washer from the end of the CV driveshaft. Remove the hub nut and washer.
3. Remove the brake caliper and the rotor from the hub.
4. Remove the bolts that attach the wheel hub to the steering knuckle.
5. Remove the wheel hub from the steering knuckle and the stub shaft.
6. Disconnect the tie rod end from the knuckle.
7. Remove the torsion bar. Remove the lower shock absorber attaching bolt.

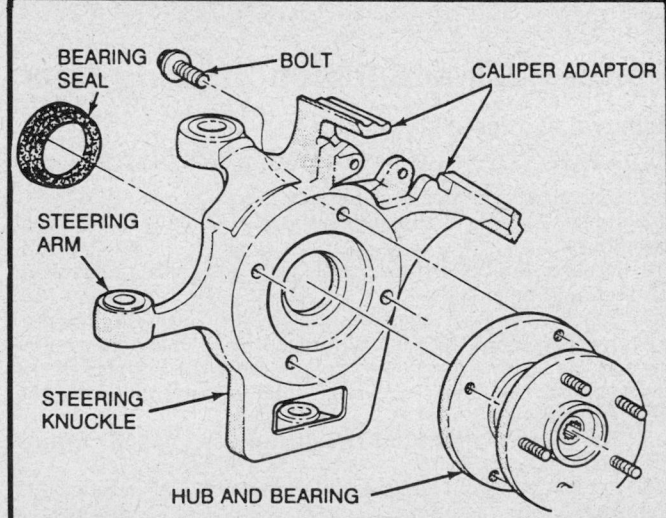

Front wheel hub removal and installation – Dakota with 4WD

8. Disconnect the stabilizer bar from the lower suspension arm.
9. Disconnect both ball joints from the steering knuckle.
10. Remove the steering knuckle from the vehicle and remove the bearing seal from the knuckle.

To install:

11. Install the wheel hub on the steering knuckle and torque the retaining bolts to 110 ft. lbs. (149 Nm)./.

12. Fill the cavity between the seal lip and the knuckle with multi-purpose lubricant. Position the new seal in the bore at the inner side of the knuckle and seat it with tool C–4698.

13. Lubricate the contact surface area of the CV driveshaft wear sleeve with grease and install the steering knuckle, engaging the splines of the CV driveshaft with those in the wheel hub. Torque the upper ball stud nut to 105 ft. lbs. (142 Nm) and the lower nut to 120 ft. lbs. (163 Nm).

14. Install the torsion bar.

15. Install the stabilizer bar and shock bolt.

16. Install the tie rod to the steering knuckle and torque the nut to 40 ft. lbs. (54 Nm).

17. Torque the hub nut to 190 ft. lbs (258 Nm). Install the spring washer, nut lock and a new cotter pin.

18. Install the tire and wheel assembly.

19. Set the front suspension height so that the difference between the distance from the surface that the tires are on to the lower suspension arm inner pivot and the distance that the tires are on to the outer end of the arm is 1–1½ in.

20. Align the front end.

21. Road tst the vehicle.

Pinion Seal

Removal and Installation

1. Raise the vehicle and support safely.
2. Matchmark and remove the driveshaft.
3. Remove the rear wheel and brake drums to prevent any drag.
4. Using an inch lb. torque wrench, measure the pinion bearing preload. Read the torque while the handle of the wrench is moving through several complete revolutions.
5. Using the proper tools, hold the companion flange and remove the drive pinion nut and washer.
6. Remove the companion flange. Lower the rear of the vehicle to prevent fluid loss.
7. Using a seal remover tool, remove the seal from the carrier and clean the seal seat.

To install:

8. The outside diameter of the seal is precoated with a special sealer so no sealing compound is required for installing. The seal is properly installed when the flange contacts the housing flange face.

9. Install the companion flange and the washer with the convex side out.

10. Tighten the pinion nut to 210 ft. lbs. (285 Nm) and check the pinion bearing preload. If the preload is less than the original preload measured, continue tightening the nut in very small increments until the proper preload is reached.

11. Install the driveshaft, drums and rear wheels.

12. Refill the differential with the proper lubricant.

13. Road test the vehicle and check for leaks.

Differential Case

Removal and Installation

CARAVAN, VOYAGER AND TOWN & COUNTRY

NOTE: The differential case can be removed from some vehicles with the transaxle installed. To do so, remove the halfshafts, remove the 2 K-frame mounting

nuts and 2 bolts and lower the K-frame to provide enough room to pull the differential case out of its housing and over the lowered frame.

1. Remove the right side extension housing.
2. Remove the differential cover.
3. Remove the bolts and remove the right side differential bearing retainer using tool L–4435, or equivalent.
4. Remove the differential case from the transaxle.
5. Use new seals and gasket material when assembling. The installation is the reverse of the removal procedure. Torque the extension housing and bearing retainer bolts to 21 ft. lbs. (28 Nm).

DAKOTA

1. Raise the vehicle and support safely.
2. Remove the wheels and the brake drums.
3. Remove the housing cover and drain the lubricant.
4. Remove the rear wheel anti-lock brake sensor, if equipped.
5. Remove both axle shafts.
6. Matchmark the bearing caps to the differential housing.
7. Remove the differential bearing threaded adjuster lock from each cap.
8. Loosen but do not remove the bearing caps.
9. Loosen the side adjusters using tool C–4164.
10. Remove the bearing caps, the threaded adjusters and the differential case.

To install:

11. Position the assembled differential case in the housing.

12. Install the bearing caps in their original positions according to the matchmarks made during the disassembly.
13. Torque the upper bolts to 10 ft. lbs. (14 Nm) and finger tighten the bottom bolts.
14. Tighten the side adjusters until the proper side play specifications are reached.
15. Torque the bearing caps bolts to 45 ft. lbs. (61 Nm) for 7¼ in. rear or 100 ft. lbs. (136 Nm) for 8¼ in. rears.
16. Install both axle shafts.
17. Install the rear wheel anti-lock brake sensor, if equipped.
18. Install the housing cover and fill with the proper lubricant.
19. Install the drums and wheels.
20. Road test the vehicle.

Axle Housing

Removal and Installation

1. Disconnect the negative battery cable. Raise vehicle and support safely.
2. Remove the rear wheel anti-lock brake sensor, if equipped.
3. Remove the rear wheels.
4. Disconnect the brake hose at the T-fitting.
5. Disconnect the parking brake cables.
6. Remove the driveshaft.
7. Support the weight of the assembly with the proper equipment. Disconnect the shock absorbers and remove the leaf spring nuts and U-bolts.
8. Remove the assembly from vehicle.
9. The installation is the reverse of the removal procedure.

STEERING

Steering Wheel

Removal and Installation

1. Disconnect the negative battery cable.
2. Remove the horn pad.
3. Remove the steering wheel hold-down nut. Matchmark the steering wheel to the shaft.
4. Using a suitable steering wheel puller, pull the steering wheel off of the shaft.
5. The installation is the reverse of the removal procedure.

Manual Rack and Pinion Steering Gear

Removal and Installation

CARAVAN AND VOYAGER

1. Disconnect the negative battery cable.
2. Raise the vehicle and support safely. Remove the front wheel assemblies.
3. Remove the cotter pins, castle nuts and tie rod ends from the steering knuckles.
4. Remove the steering column to steering gear coupling pin.
5. If equipped, remove the the air diverter valve bracket, from the left side of the crossmember. The lower universal joint is removed with the steering gear.
6. Remove the front suspension crossmember attaching bolts and nuts.
7. Lower the crossmember.
8. Remove the axle boot shield, if equipped.
9. Remove the boot shields.
10. Remove the steering gear bolts from the front suspension crossmember.
11. Remove the steering gear from the left side of the vehicle.
12. The installation is the reverse of the removal procedure.

The right rear crossmember bolt is a pilot bolt that correctly locates the crossmember, tighten it first. Torque the crossmember bolts to 90 ft. lbs. and the steering gear attaching bolts to 21 ft. lbs.

DAKOTA WITH 2WD

1. Disconnect the negative battery cable.
2. Remove the tie rod ends from the steering knuckle.
3. Remove the coupling pin.
4. Remove the bolts attaching the rack to the crossmember.
5. Remove the gear from the vehicle.
6. The installation is the reverse of the removal procedure. Torque the mounting bolts to 150 ft. lbs. (203 Nm).

Power Rack and Pinion Steering Gear

Removal and Installation

CARAVAN, VOYAGER AND TOWN & COUNTRY

1. Disconnect the negative battery cable.
2. Raise the vehicle and support safely. Remove front wheel assemblies.
3. Remove the cotter pins, castle nuts and tie rod ends from the steering knuckles.
4. Remove the steering column to steering gear coupling pin. If equipped, remove the anti-rotational link from the crossmember and the air diverter valve bracket, from the left side of the crossmember. he lower universal joint is removed with the steering gear.
5. Disconnect and plug the oil lines from the rack, if equipped.
6. Remove the front suspension crossmember attaching bolts and nuts.
7. Lower the crossmember.
8. Remove the axle boot shield, if equipped.
9. Remove the boot shields.

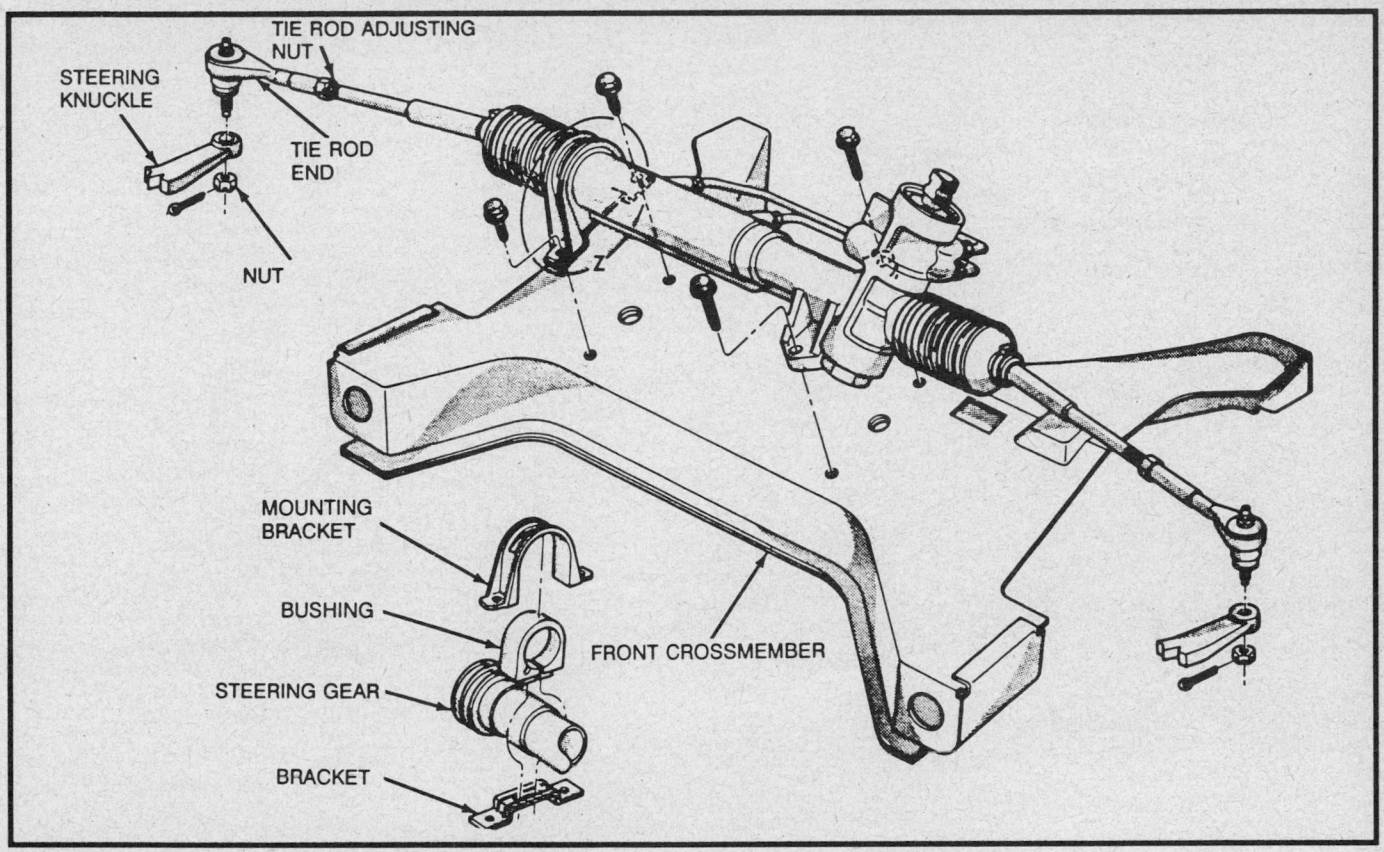

Rack and pinion steering gear mounting—Caravan, Voyager and Town & Country

10. Remove the steering gear bolts from the front suspension crossmember.
11. Remove the steering gear from the left side of the vehicle.
12. The installation is the reverse of the removal procedure. The right rear crossmember bolt is a pilot bolt that correctly locates the crossmember, tighten it first. Torque the crossmember bolts to 90 ft. lbs. and the steering gear attaching bolts to 21 ft. lbs. Refill the power steering pump.

DAKOTA WITH 2WD

1. Disconnect the negative battery cable.
2. Remove the tie rod ends from the steering knuckle.
3. Disconnect and plug the power steering fluid lines.
3. Remove the coupling pin.
4. Remove the bolts attaching the rack to the crossmember.
5. Remove the gear from the vehicle.
6. The installation is the reverse of the removal procedure. Torque the mounting bolts to 150 ft. lbs. (203 Nm).
7. Refill the power steering pump.

Power Steering Gear

Removal and Installation
DAKOTA WITH 4WD

1. Disconnect the negative battery cable.
2. Raise the vehicle and support safely. Center the steering.
3. Disconnect the pitman arm from the center link.
4. Disconnect and plug the pressure and return hoses.
5. Disconnect the steering gear to shaft coupling.
6. Remove the steering gear mount bolts and remove the gear from the vehicle.

7. Matchmark and remove the pitman arm from the sector shaft.
8. The installation is the reverse of the removal procedure. Torque the pitman arm nut to 175 ft. lbs. (237 Nm) and the mount bolts to 100 ft. lbs. (136 Nm).
9. Refill the power steering pump.

Adjustment

1. If the vehicle wanders of the steering has too much play, the sector shaft can be adjusted.
2. Loosen the adjusting screw locknut and turn the screw all the down.
3. Back the screw off ¼–½ turn.
4. Tighten the locknut.
5. Road test the vehicle. If the steering wheel does not return easily after a turn, back the screw off until the wheel returns easily.

Power Steering Pump

Removal and Installation

1. Disconnect the negative battery cable.
2. Position a drain pan under the power steering pump.
3. Disconnect the fluid hoses from the pump and plug them.
4. Remove the front bracket attaching bolts and remove the belt from the pulley.
5. Remove the rear pump to bracket nut and remove the pump.
6. Remove the bracket from the pump.
7. Remove the pulley from the pump with the proper puller. Install the pulley on the new pump using the special installation tools.

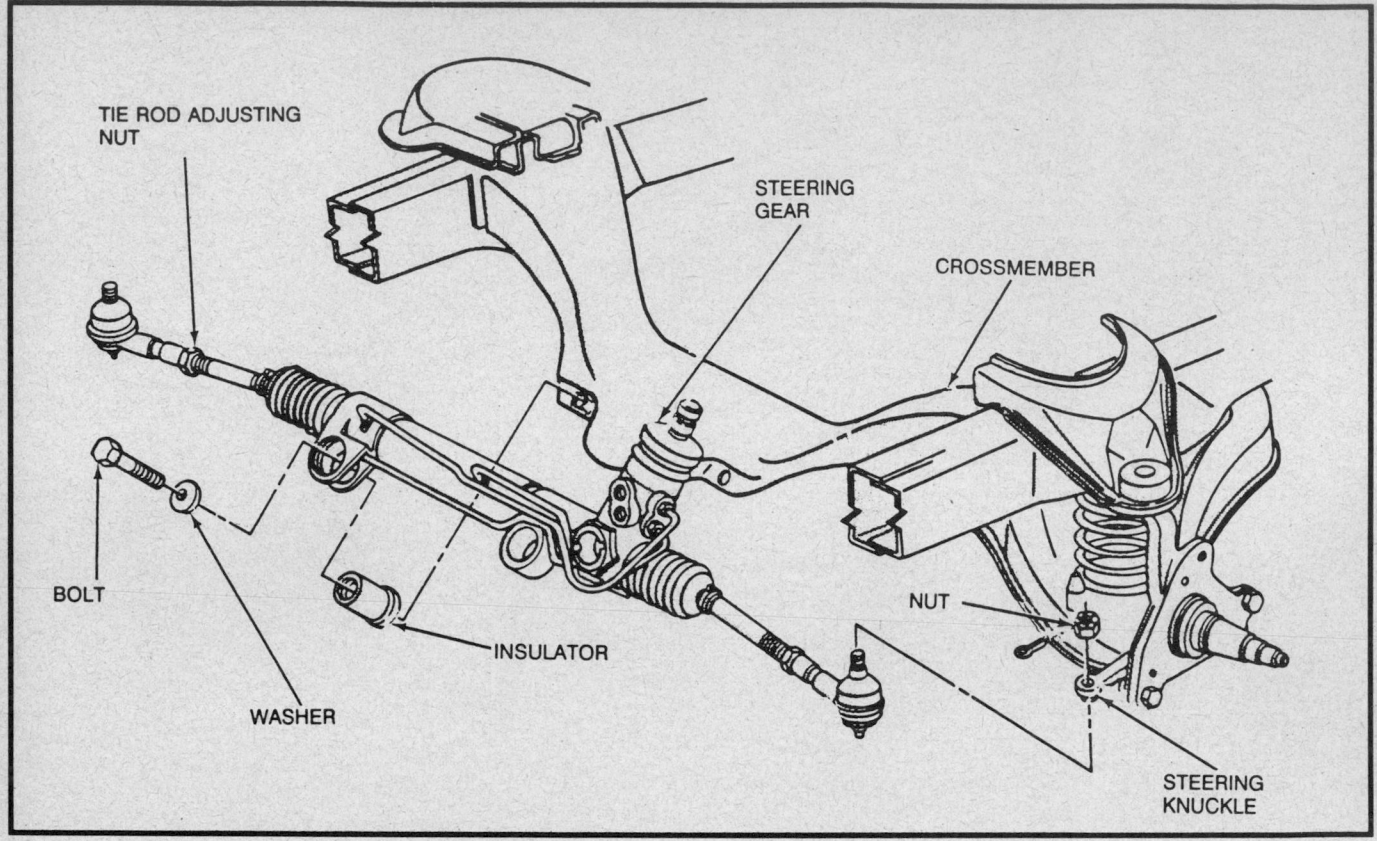

Rack and pinion steering gear mounting—Dakota

8. The installation is the reverse of the removal procedure.

Belt Adjustment

NOTE: The belt tension is automatically adjusted by a dynamic tensioner on the 3.0L and 3.3L engines. Adjustment is not possible.

1. Loosen the bracket mounting bolts.
2. Using a ½ in. drive breaker bar in the square hole provided in the bracket, move the pump away from the engine. Do not pry against the fluid reservoir.
3. With the pump moved enough so that the belt deflects about ¼–½ in. under a 10 lb. load, tighten the bolts.

System Bleeding

1. Fill the reservoir with power steering fluid.
2. Turn the wheels to the full left turn position and add fluid until the reservoir is full.
3. Start the engine and add fluid to bring the level to the correct level.

4. To purge the system of air, turn the steering wheel from side to side without contacting the stops.
5. Return the wheel to the straight ahead position and operate the engine for 2 minutes before road testing. This should bleed the system completely.

Tie Rod Ends

Removal and Installation

1. Raise the vehicle and support safely.
2. Remove the cotter pin and nut from the tie rod end.
3. Using a suitable puller, remove the tie rod from the steering knuckle or center link, if equipped.
4. Loosen the sleeve clamp nut and bolt, if equipped and unscrew the tie rod end from the sleeve or inner tie rod.
5. The installation is the reverse of the removal procedure. Torque the stud nuts to 45 ft. lbs. (61 Nm) and install a new cotter pin.
6. Perform a front end alignment as required.

BRAKES

For all brake system repair and service procedure not detained below, please refer to "Brakes" in the Unit Repair section.

Master Cylinder

Removal and Installation

1. Disconnect the negative battery cable.

2. Disconnect and plug the brake lines from the master cylinder.
3. Remove the nuts attaching the master cylinder to the power booster.
4. Remove the master cylinder from the mounting studs.
5. Remove the fluid reservoir from the cylinder.

To install:
6. Bench bleed the master cylinder.

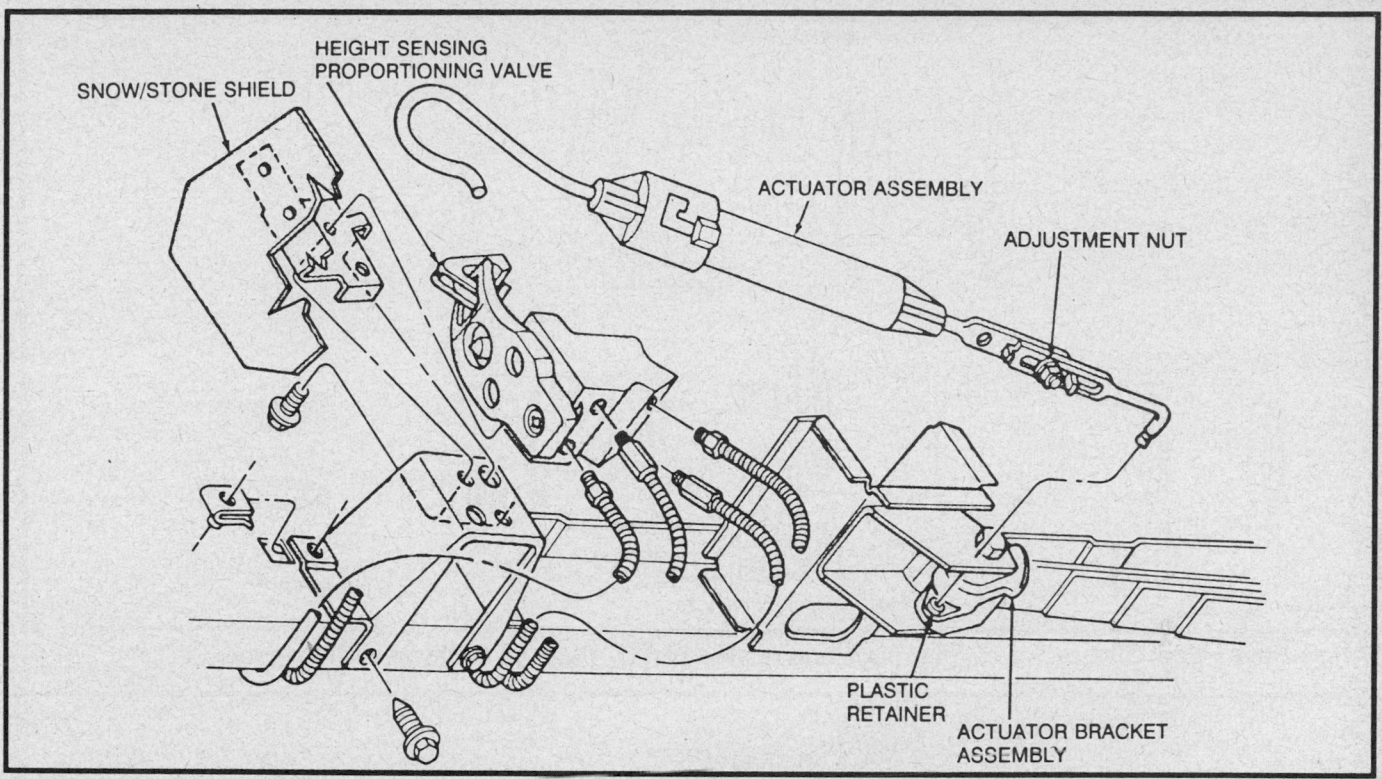

Height sensing proportioning valve — Caravan, Voyager and Town & Country

7. Install to the studs and install the nuts.
8. Install the brake lines to the master cylinder.

Combination Valve

Removal and Installation

1. Disconnect the negative battery cable.
2. Raise the vehicle and support safely.
3. Tag and disconnect the brake lines from the valve.
4. Disconnect the wires to the pressure switch.
5. Remove the combination valve from the frame bracket.
6. The installation is the reverse of the removal procedure.
7. Bleed the brakes in the following order:
   a. Rear wheel anti-lock valve, if equipped
   b. Right rear wheel cylinder
   c. Left rear wheel cylinder
   d. Right front caliper
   e. Left front caliper

Height Sensing Proportioning Valve Assembly

Removal and Installation

CARAVAN, VOYAGER AND TOWN & COUNTRY

1. Remove the snow/stone shield.
2. Remove the actuator assembly.
3. Tag and disconnect the brake lines from the valve.
4. Remove the valve from the frame bracket.
5. The installation is the reverse of the removal procedure.

Adjustment

1. With the vehicle lifted so that the rear suspension is hanging free, disconnect the shock absorbers.

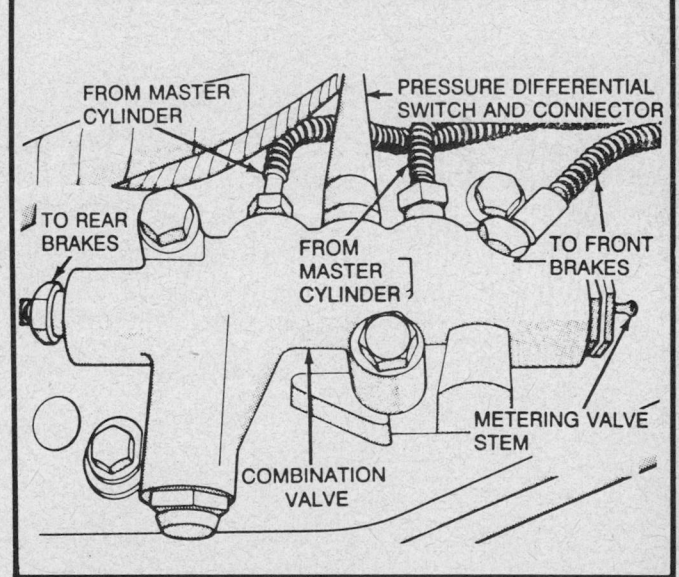

Combination switch — Dakota

2. Remove the rear tire and wheel assemblies and loosen both front spring hanger pivot bolts.
3. Make sure the actuator hook is properly seated on the valve lever. Loosen the adjustment nut on the actuator assembly.
4. Pull the actuator assembly toward the spring hanger until the valve lever bottoms on the valve body and hold the position.
5. Tighten the adjustment nut to 25 inch lbs. This will complete the adjustment.
6. Tighten the spring bolts, install the shocks and wheels and road test the vehicle.

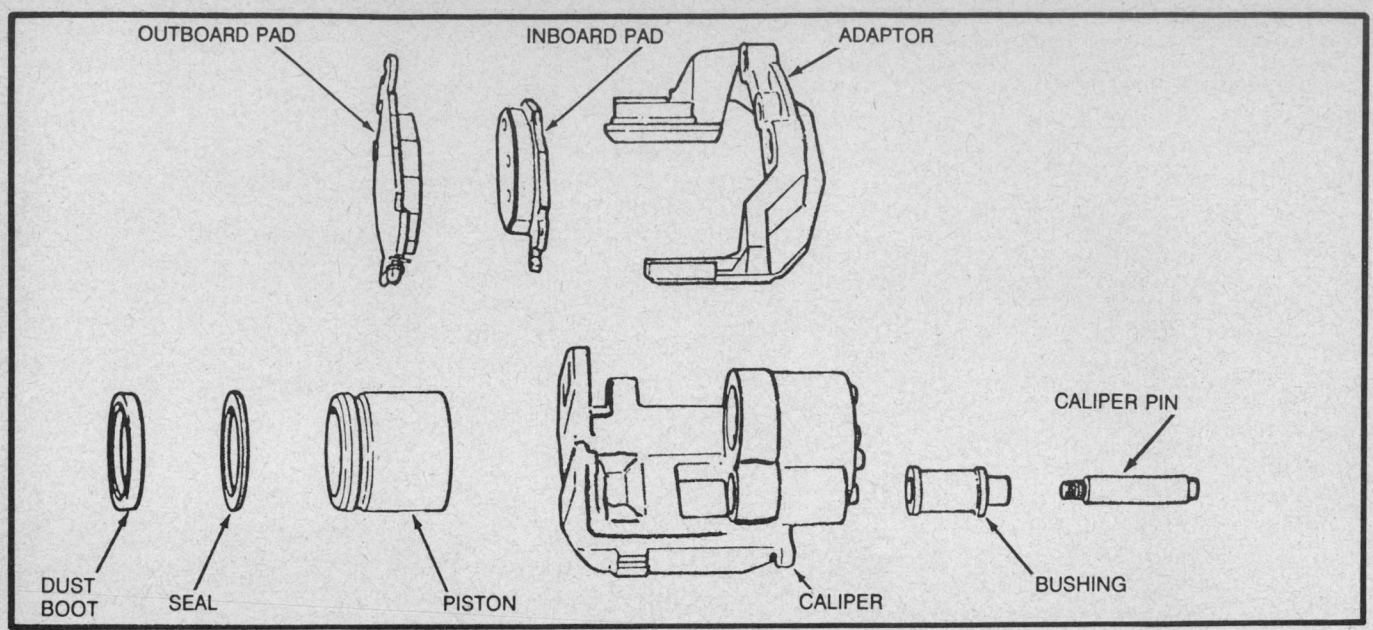

Kelsey-Hayes front disc brake caliper, pads and related parts—1986–88 Caravan and Voyager

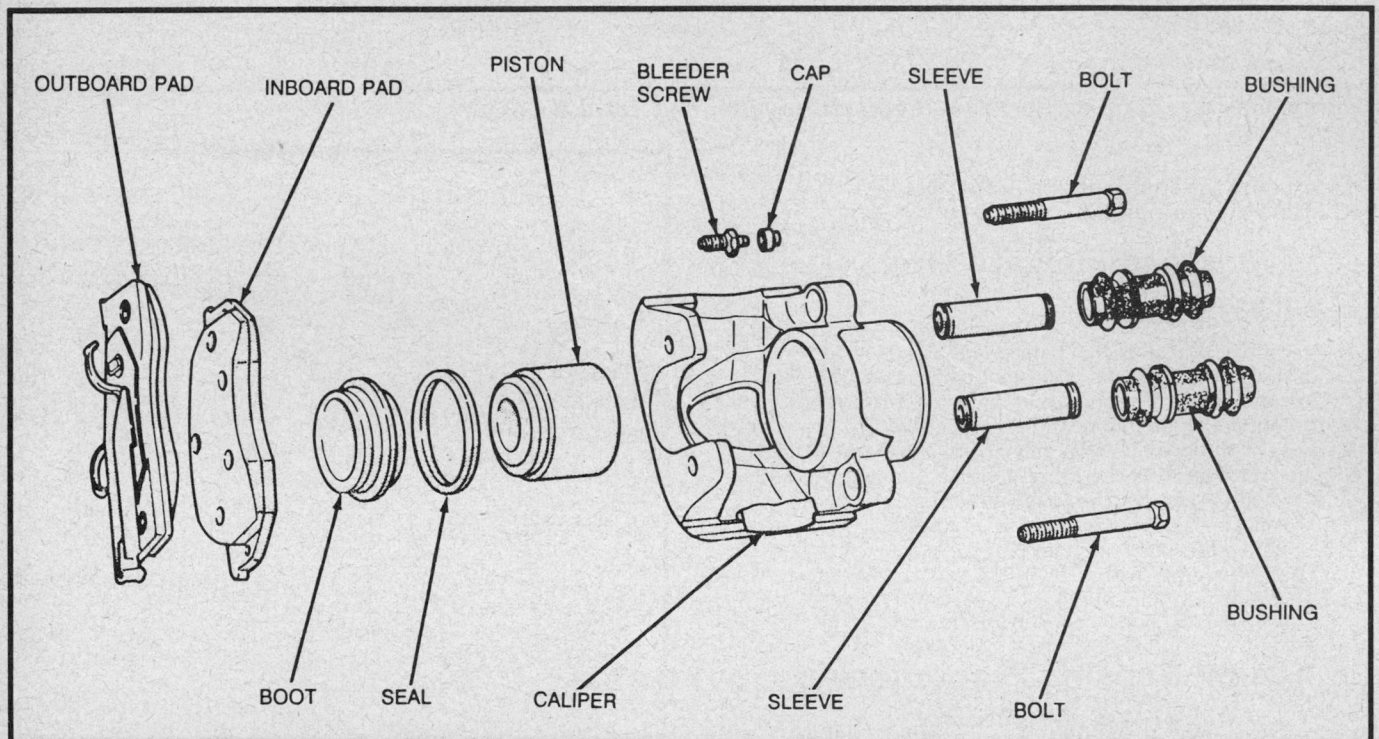

ATE front disc brake caliper, pads and related parts—1988–90 Caravan, Voyager and Town & Country

Power Brake Booster

Removal and Installation

1. Disconnect the negative battery cable. Disconnect the vacuum hose(s) from the booster.
2. Remove the nuts attaching the master cylinder to the booster and move the master cylinder to the side.
3. From inside of the vehicle, remove the clip that secures the booster pushrod to the brake pedal.
4. Remove the nuts that attach the booster to the dash panel and remove it from the vehicle.
5. Transfer the check valve to the new booster.
6. The installation is the reverse of the removal procedure.

Brake Caliper

Removal and Installation

1. Raise the vehicle and support safely.

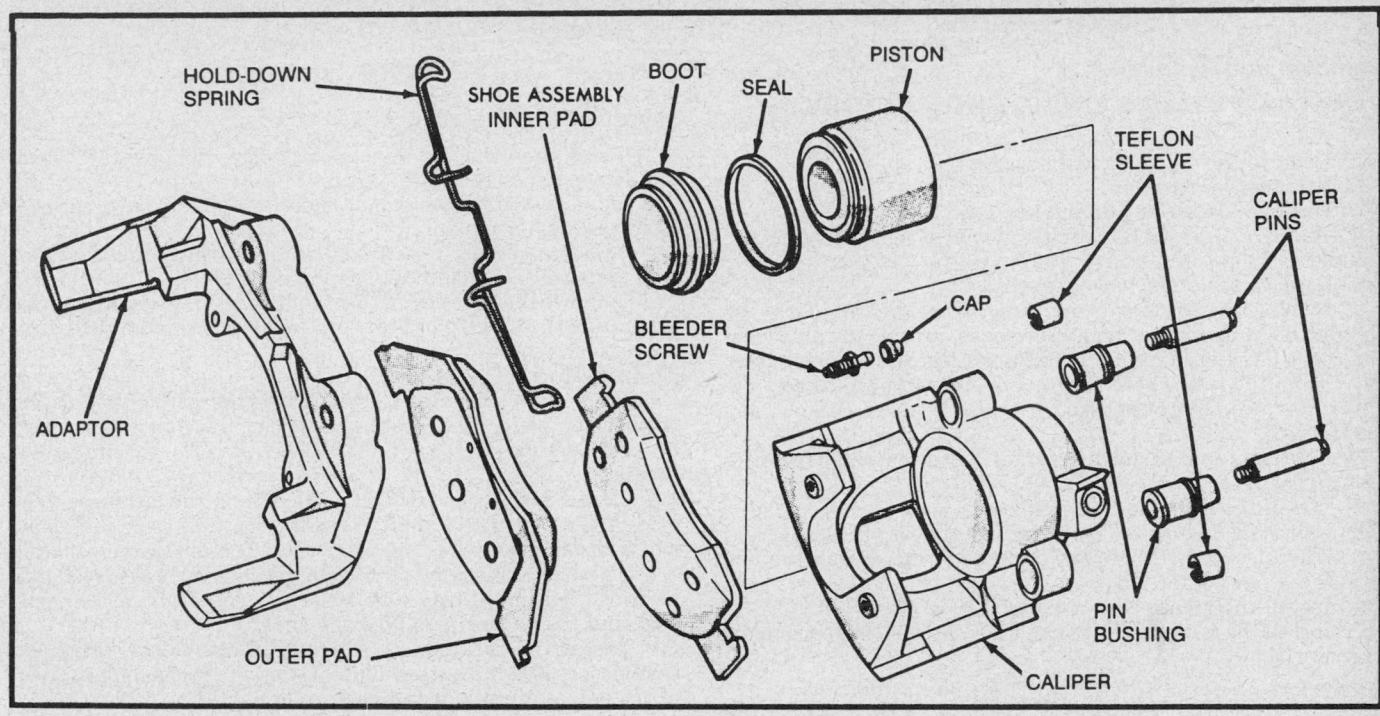

Kelsey-Hayes front disc brake caliper, pads and related parts—Dakota

2. Remove the tire and wheel assembly. Remove the hold-down spring on Dakota.
3. Remove the caliper mounting pin(s).
4. Lift the caliper off of the rotor. Remove the outer pad from the caliper.
5. Remove the brake hose retaining bolt from the caliper.

To install:
6. Install the brake hose to the caliper using new copper washers.
7. Position the caliper over the rotor so the caliper engages the adaptor correctly. Install the mounting pin(s). Install the hold-down spring, if equipped.
8. Fill the master cylinder and bleed the brakes.

Disc Brake Pads

Removal and Installation

1. Remove some of the fluid from the master cylinder.
2. Raise the vehicle and support safely. Remove the tire and wheel assemblies.
3. Remove the hold-down spring on Dakota. Remove the caliper and remove the outer pad from the caliper.
4. Remove the inner pad from the adaptor.
To install:
5. Use a large C-clamp to compress the piston back into the caliper bore.
6. Install the inner pad to the adaptor.
7. Position the caliper over the rotor so the caliper engages the adaptor correctly and install the retainer pin(s).
8. Install the hold-down spring, if equipped.
9. Refill the master cylinder.

Brake Rotor

Removal and Installation
CARAVAN, VOYAGER AND TOWN & COUNTRY

1. Raise the vehicle and support safely. Remove the tire and wheel assembly.
2. Remove the caliper and brake pads.
3. Remove the factory installed clips, if equipped. It is not necessary to reinstall these clips.
4. Remove the rotor from the hub.
5. The installation is the reverse of the removal procedure.

DAKOTA

1. Raise the vehicle and support safely.
2. Remove the wheel and tire assembly.
3. Remove the caliper and disc brake pads.
4. Remove the dust cap.
5. Remove the cotter pin, nut lock, wheel bearing nut and washer from the spindle.
6. Remove the outer wheel bearing.
7. Remove the rotor with the inner wheel bearing from the spindle. Remove the grease seal.

To install:
8. Lubricate and install the inner wheel bearing. Install a new grease seal.
9. Install the rotor to the spindle.
10. Lubricate and install the outer wheel bearing, washer and nut. When the bearing preload is properly set, install the nut lock and a new cotter pin.
11. Install the grease cap.
12. Install the brake pads and caliper.
13. Install the wheel and tire assembly.

Brake Drums

Removal and Installation

CARAVAN, VOYAGER AND TOWN & COUNTRY

1. Raise the vehicle and support safely.
2. Remove the wheel and tire assembly.
3. Remove the dust cap.
4. Remove the cotter pin and nut lock.
5. Remove the wheel bearing nut and washer from the spindle.
6. Remove the outer wheel bearing.
7. Remove the drum with the inner wheel bearing from the spindle. If the drum is difficult to remove, remove the plug from the rear of the backing plate and push the self adjuster lever away from the star wheel. Rotate the star wheel to retract the shoes. Remove the grease seal.

To install:

8. Lubricate and install the inner wheel bearing. Install a new grease seal.
9. Install the drum to the spindle.
10. Lubricate and install the outer wheel bearing, washer and nut. When the bearing preload is properly set, install the nut lock and a new cotter pin.
11. Install the grease cap.
12. Install the wheel and tire assembly. Adjust the rear brakes as required.

DAKOTA

1. Raise the vehicle and support safely.
2. Remove the wheel.
3. Remove the factory clips from the wheel studs, if equipped. It is not necessary to reinstall these clips.
4. Remove the drum. If the drum is difficult to remove, remove the plug from the rear of the backing plate and push the self adjuster lever away from the star wheel. Rotate the star wheel to retract the shoes.
5. The installation is the reverse of the removal procedure.

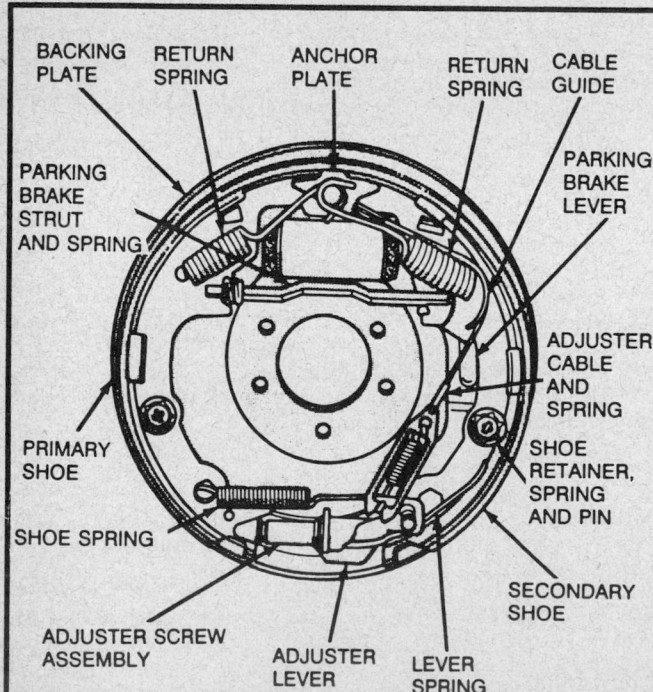

Typical rear brake shoe assembly

(Labels: BACKING PLATE, RETURN SPRING, ANCHOR PLATE, RETURN SPRING, CABLE GUIDE, PARKING BRAKE STRUT AND SPRING, PARKING BRAKE LEVER, PRIMARY SHOE, ADJUSTER CABLE AND SPRING, SHOE SPRING, SHOE RETAINER, SPRING AND PIN, SECONDARY SHOE, ADJUSTER SCREW ASSEMBLY, ADJUSTER LEVER, LEVER SPRING)

6. Adjust the rear brakes as required.

Brake Shoes

Removal and Installation

1. Raise the vehicle and support safely. Remove the wheel and tire assemblies and the drums.
2. Remove the primary and secondary shoe return springs from the anchor pin.
3. Lift the adjuster lever and disconnect the actuator cable.
4. Remove the shoe retainers and springs.
5. Remove the shoes (held together by the lower spring) while separating the parking brake actuating lever from the shoe with a twisting motion.

To install:

6. Thoroughly clean and dry the backing plate. To prepare the backing plate, lubricate the bosses, anchor pin and parking brake actuating lever pivot surface lightly with lithium based grease.
7. Remove, clean and dry all parts still on the old shoes. Lubricate the star wheel shaft threads with anti-sieze lubricant and transfer all parts to their proper locations on the new shoes.
8. Spread the shoes apart, engage the parking brake lever and position them on the backing plate so the wheel cylinder pins engage and the anchor pins hold the shoes.
9. Install the parking brake strut and hold-down spring assemblies. Install the anchor plate. Lubricate the sliding surface of the actuator cable plate lightly and install the cable.
10. Install the shoe return spring opposite the cable, then install the remaining cable.
11. Adjust the star wheel.
12. Remove any grease from the linings and install the drum.
13. Complete the brake adjustment with the wheels installed.

Wheel Cylinder

Removal and Installation

1. Raise the vehicle and support safely.
2. Remove the wheel, drum and brake shoes.
3. Remove the brake line from the wheel cylinder.
4. Remove the wheel cylinder bolts and remove the cylinder from the backing plate.

To install:

5. Apply a very thin coating of silicone sealer to the cylinder mounting surface, install the cylinder to the backing plate and install the retaining bolts.
6. Connect the brake line to the wheel cylinder.
7. Install all brake parts that were removed.
8. Install the tire and wheel assembly.
9. Bleed the brakes.

Front Parking Brake Cable

Removal and Installation

1. Raise the vehicle and support safely.
2. Remove the front cable adjusting nut.
3. Remove the clip securing the cable to the anchor bracket, if equipped and slide the cable out of the bracket.
4. Remove the retainer attaching the cable to the pedal assembly frame. Disengage the cable from the pedal clevis.
5. Remove the cable grommet from the floor pan and remove the cable.
6. The installation is the reverse of the removal procedure.

Intermediate Parking Brake Cable

Removal and Installation

1. Raise the vehicle and support safely.

2. Loosen the parkiing brake adjuster nut enough so the cable is slack.

3. Disengage the adjuster hook from the frame rail.

4. Disengage the intermediate cable from the connectors and the right side cable guide.

5. Remove the cable.

6. The installation is the reverse of the removal procedure.

Rear Parking Brake Cable

Removal and Installation

1. Release the parking brakes fully.

2. Raise the vehicle and support safely.

3. Remove the adjusting nut from the front cable.

4. Remove the brake drums. Remove the shoes, if necessary. Disconnect the cable from the lever and compress the cable retainer tabs and remove the cable from the backing plate.

5. Remove the cable from the guides and connectors or equalizer and remove the retaining clips from the frame bracket.

6. The installation is the reverse of the removal procedure.

Adjustment

1. Release the parking brakes fully.

2. Raise the vehicle and support safely.

3. Adjust the rear brakes.

4. Loosen the nut on the front cable until there is slack in all the cables.

5. Rotate the rear wheels and tighten the cable adjusting nut until there is a slight drag at the wheels.

6. Continue to rotate the rear wheels and loosen the nut until all drag is eliminated.

7. Back off the nut an additional 2 turns.

8. Apply and release the parking brake several times. Upon the least release, verify that there is no drag at the wheels.

9. To check the operation, make sure the parking brake holds on an incline.

FRONT SUSPENSION

Shock Absorbers

Removal and Installation

1. Support the vehicle safely and raise enough to so there is room to get to the upper shock mount.

2. Remove the upper shock nut, washer and bushing. Raise the vehicle fully.

3. Remove the lower mounting bolts and remove the shock from the vehicle.

4. The installation is the reverse of the removal procedure.

MacPherson Strut

Removal and Installation

1. Remove the 3 mounting nuts from the shock tower under the hood.

2. Raise the vehicle and support safely.

3. Remove the brake hose bracket screw from the strut.

4. Remove the strut to knuckle bolts, nuts and nut washer.

5. The installation is the reverse of the removal procedure. Torque the upper mounting nuts to 20 ft. lbs. (27 Nm).

6. Perform a front end alignment. Torque the strut to knuckle nuts to 75 ft. lbs. (100 Nm) plus ¼ turn.

Coil Spring

Removal and Installation

CARAVAN, VOYAGER AND TOWN & COUNTRY

1. Raise the vehicle and support safely. Remove the MacPherson strut from the vehicle.

2. Compress the coil spring using tool C-4838, or a suitable MacPherson spring compressor.

3. Remove the upper assembly retaining nut.

4. Remove the damper assembly and plastic strut tube, if equipped.

To install:

5. Install the compressed spring to the strut, making sure the spring end is seated in the recess.

6. Install the damper assembly to the strut rod.

7. Align the alignment notch or tab with the lower bracket.

8. Tighten the upper assembly retaining nut to 60 ft. lbs. (81

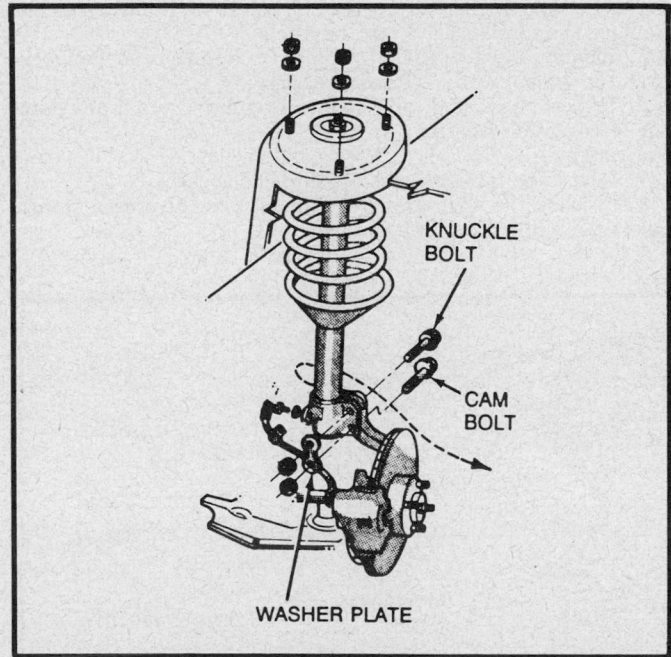

KNUCKLE BOLT

CAM BOLT

WASHER PLATE

MacPherson strut assembly

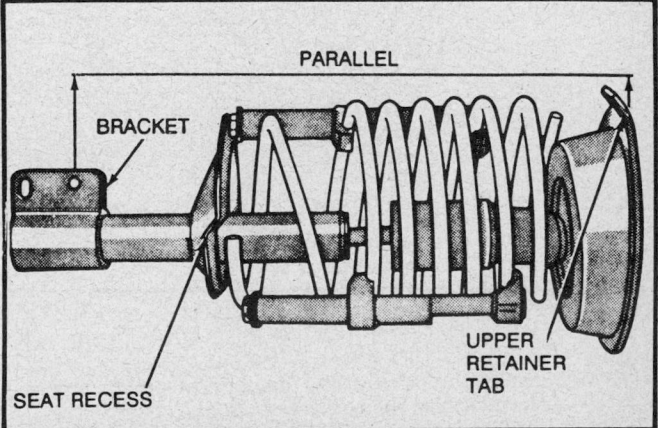

PARALLEL

BRACKET

SEAT RECESS

UPPER RETAINER TAB

Installing and aligning the damper assembly— 1986 Caravan and Voyager

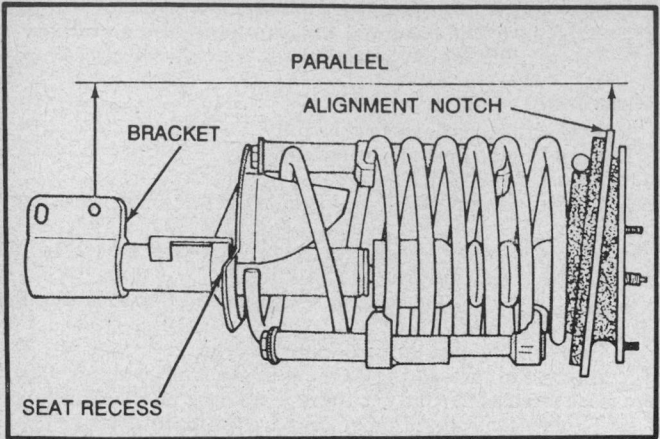

Installing and aligning the damper assembly— 1987–90 Caravan, Voyager and Town & Country

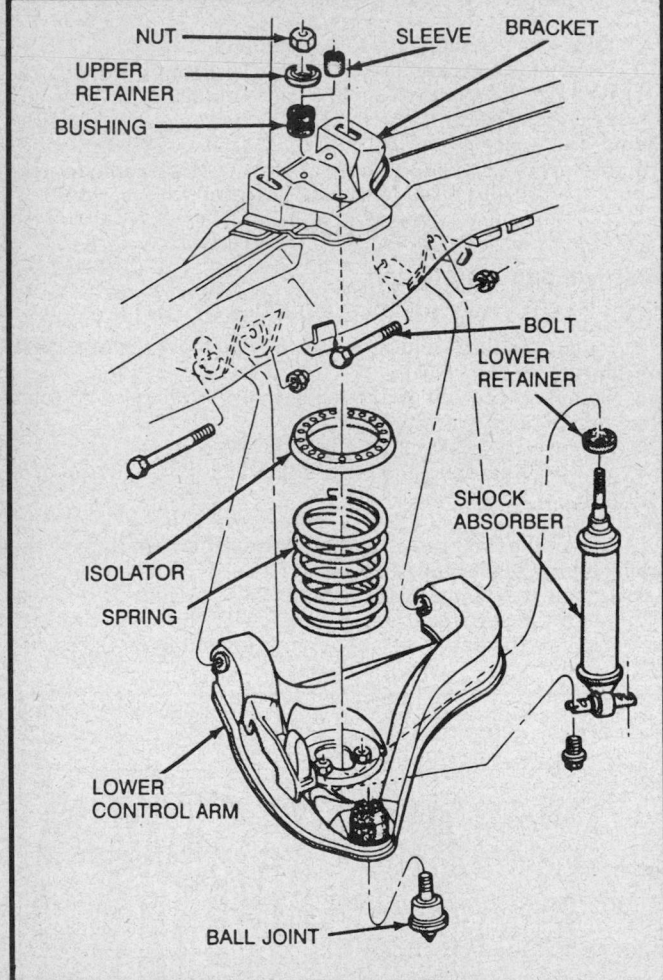

Front Suspension—Dakota with 2WD

Nm). Make sure the spring and damper assembly are still aligned before releasing the compressor tool.

9. Release the compressor tool.
10. Install the strut to the vehicle.
11. Perform a front end alignment.

DAKOTA WITH 2WD

1. Raise the vehicle and support safely.
2. Remove the shock absorber.
3. Disconnect the sway bar from the lower control arm, if equipped.
4. Install spring compressor tool DD–1278, or equivalent to the coil spring and tighten the nut finger tight, then back off half a turn.
5. Remove the cotter pin and lower ball joint nut.
6. Release the lower ball joint taper using ball stud loosening tool C–3564–A, or equivalent.
7. Remove the tool and remove the ball stud from the control arm. Release the compressor tool from the coil spring.
8. Pull the arm down and remove the spring with the rubber isolation pad from the vehicle.

To install:

9. Install the spring with the rubber isolator. Install the compressor tool and compress it enough so the lower ball joint can be inserted through the knuckle.
10. Torque the lower ball joint nut to 135 ft. lbs. (183 Nm). Install a new cotter pin. Remove the spring compressor.
11. Connect the sway bar to the lower control arm, if equipped.
12. Install the shock absorber.

Torsion Bar

Removal and Installation

DAKOTA WITH 4WD

NOTE: The left and right side torsion bars are not interchangeable. The bars are identified by the letter R or L stamped into one end of the bar. The bars do not have a front or rear, though and can be installed with either end facing foward.

1. Remove the upper control arm jounce bumper.
2. Raise the vehicle with the front suspension hanging free and support safely.
3. Release the load from the torsion bar by turning the adjustment bolt counterclockwise.
4. Remove the adjustment bolt from the swivel and then remove the torsion bar and the anchor together from the vehicle. Remove the torsion bar from the anchor.
5. Remove any dirt, rust or pebbles from the hex shaped socket in the anchor and lower control arm.
6. Inspect the anchor and bolt and replace them if any damage or corrosion exists.

To install:

7. Insert the torsion bar ends into the sockets.
8. Position the anchor and the bushing in the crossmember, insert the adjustment bolt and thread it into the swivel.

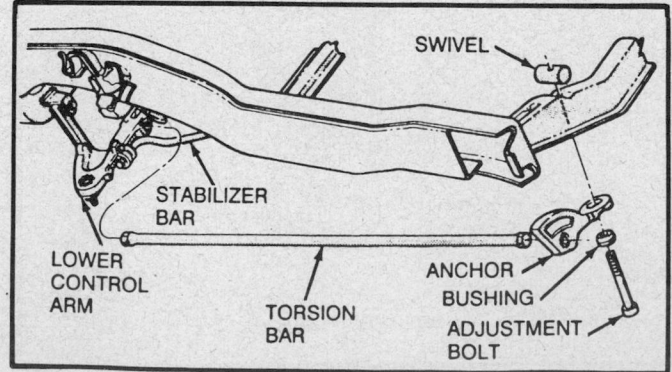

Torsion Bar assembly—Dakota with 4WD

9. Turn the adjustment bolt clockwise to apply a load on the bar.

10. Lower the vehicle.

11. Set the front suspension height so that the difference between the distance from the surface that the tires are on to the lower control arm inner pivot and the distance that the tires are on to the outer end of the arm is 1–1½ in.

12. Install the upper control arm jounce bumper.

Upper Ball Joint

Inspection

To inspect the ball joints, unload the suspension. Upper ball joints on 2WD vehicles and any ball joint on 4WD vehicles should be replaced if any play exists at all.

Removal and Installation

DAKOTA WITH 2WD

1. Raise the vehicle and support safely.

2. Position a support at the outer end of the lower control arm and lower the vehicle so that the support compresses the coil spring.

3. Remove the tire and wheel assembly.

4. Release the upper ball joint taper using ball stud loosening tool C–3564–A, or equivalent.

5. Unthread the ball joint from the control arm with tool C–3561, or equivalent.

6. Torque the ball joint itself to 125 ft. lbs. (169 Nm).

7. Torque the upper ball stud nut to 135 ft. lbs (183 Nm) and install a new cotter pin.

8. The installation is the reverse of the removal procedure.

DAKOTA WITH 4WD

1. Raise the vehicle and support safely.

2. Remove the CV driveshaft from the vehicle.

3. Turn the torsion bar adjustment nut counterclockwise to relieve all tension from the torsion bar.

4. Remove the cotter pin from the upper ball stud.

5. Release the upper ball joint taper using ball stud loosening tool C–3564–A, or equivalent. Remove the tool.

6. Remove the upper ball stud seal.

7. Force the ball joint from the arm using the ball stud removal and installation tool C–4212.

To install:

8. Install the new ball joint using the ball stud removal and installation tool C–4212.

9. Install the ball stud seal.

10. Insert the upper ball stud in the steering knuckle arm bore and install the nut. Torque the nut to 105 ft. lbs. (142 Nm) and install a new cotter pin.

11. Turn the torsion bar adjustment nut clockwise to apply a load on the bar.

12. Install the CV driveshaft and all related parts.

13. Lower the vehicle.

14. Set the front suspension height so that the difference between the distance from the surface that the tires are on to the lower control arm inner pivot and the distance that the tires are on to the outer end of the arm is 1–1½ in.

Lower Ball Joint

Inspection

To inspect the ball joints on Caravan, Voyager and Town & Country, grasp the grease fitting by hand with the vehicle on the ground. If the grease fitting can be moved at all by hand, the ball joint should be replaced.

To inspect the lower ball joints on Dakota, unload the suspen-

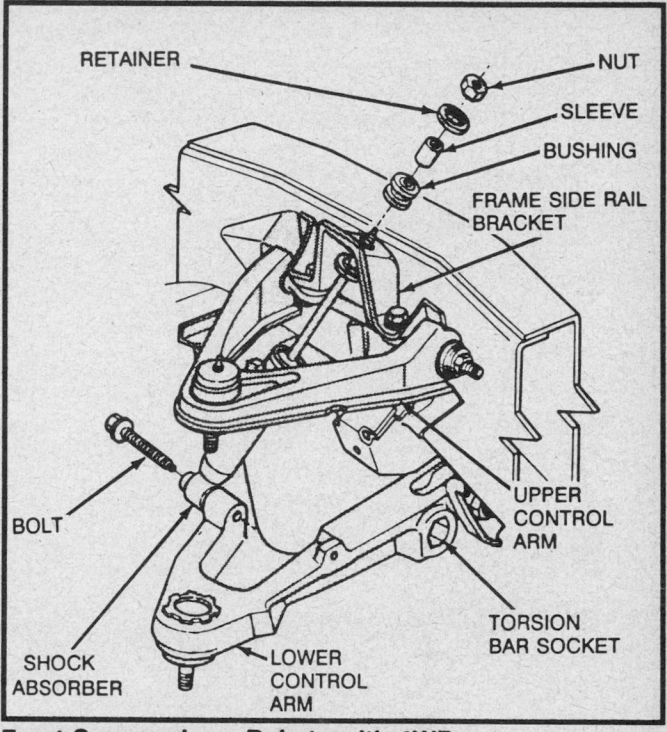

Front Suspension—Dakota with 4WD

sion. Lower ball joints on 2WD vehicles should be replaced if the have more than 0.020 in. play. Any ball joint on 4WD vehicles should be replaced if any play exists.

Removal and Installation

CARAVAN, VOYAGER AND TOWN & COUNTRY

On Caravan, Voyager and Town & Country, the ball joints are welded to the lower control arms. This necessitates replacement of the control arm assembly. Do not attempt to replace ball joints that are welded to the control arm; replacement control arms are equipped a new ball joint.

DAKOTA WITH 2WD

1. Raise the vehicle and support safely.

2. Remove the shock absorber.

3. Disconnect the sway bar from the lower control arm, if equipped.

4. Install spring compressor tool DD–1278, or equivalent to the coil spring and tighten the nut finger tight, then back off half a turn.

5. Remove the cotter pin and lower ball joint nut.

6. Release the lower ball joint taper using ball stud loosening tool C–3564–A, or equivalent.

7. Remove the tool and remove the ball stud from the control arm. Release the compressor tool from the coil spring.

8. Pull the arm down and remove the spring with the rubber isolation pad from the vehicle. Remove the ball joint boot. Use tool C–4212, or an appropriate ball joint press to remove the ball joint from the arm.

To install:

9. Use the remover tool to press the ball joint into the arm. Install a new rubber boot. Install the spring with the rubber isolators. Install the compressor tool and compress it enough so the lower ball joint can be inserted through the knuckle.

10. Torque the lower ball joint nut to 135 ft. lbs. (183 Nm). Install a new cotter pin. Remove the spring compressor.

11. Connect the sway bar to the lower control arm, if equipped.

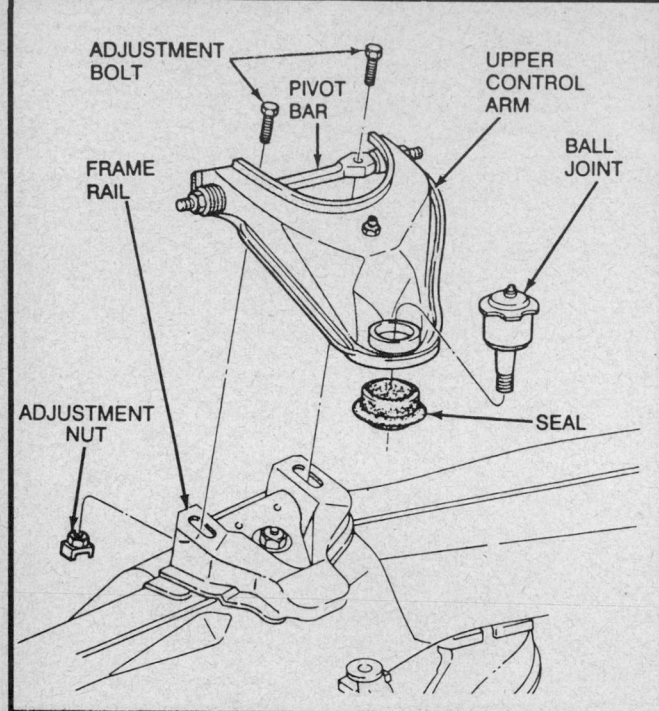

Upper control arm—Dakota with 2WD

12. Install the shock absorber.

DAKOTA WITH 4WD

1. Raise the vehicle and support safely.
2. Remove the CV driveshaft.
3. Remove the torsion bar.
4. Remove the shock absorber lower attaching bolt.
5. Disconnect the stabilizer bar from the lower control arm.
6. Remove the cotter pin and the nut from the lower ball stud. Separate the lower ball stud from the steering knucle.
7. Pry the peened ball joint retainer sections upward from the lower control arm and remove the ball joint from the arm.
To install:
8. Install the new ball joint in the control arm. Peen the ball joint housing retainer over to secure the ball joint.
9. Install the grease seal.
10. Insert the ball stud into the steering knuckle bore. Install the nut, torque to 120 ft. lbs. (163 Nm) and install a new cotter pin.
11. Attach the stabilizer bar to the control arm and install the shock mount bolt.
12. Install the torsion bar and turn the adjustment bolt clockwise to apply a load to the bar.
13. Install the CV driveshaft and all related parts.
14. Lower the vehicle.
15. Set the front suspension height so that the difference between the distance from the surface that the tires are on to the lower control arm inner pivot and the distance that the tires are on to the outer end of the arm is 1–1½ in.
16. Perform a front end alignment.

Upper Control Arm

Removal and Installation
DAKOTA WITH 2WD

1. Raise the vehicle and support safely.
2. Remove the shock absorber.

3. Disconnect the sway bar from the lower control arm, if equipped.
4. Install spring compressor tool DD–1278, or equivalent to the coil spring and tighten the nut finger tight, then back off half a turn.
5. Remove the cotter pin and upper ball joint nut. Suspend the rotor assembly with a wire so there is not excessive pull on the brake hose.
6. Release the upper ball joint taper using ball stud loosening tool C–3564–A, or equivalent.
7. Remove the tool and remove the ball stud from the control arm.
8. Remove the pivot bar retaining bolts and remove the arm from the vehicle.
To install:
9. Install the arm to the frame rail bracket and install the retaining bolts.
10. Torque the ball joint nut to 135 ft. lbs. (183 Nm). Install a new cotter pin. Remove the spring compressor.
11. Connect the sway bar from the lower control arm, if equipped.
12. Install the shock absorber.
13. Align the front end. When all settings are at specifications, torque the pivot bar retaining bolts to 155 ft. lbs. (210 Nm).

DAKOTA WITH 4WD

1. Raise the vehicle and support safely.
2. Remove the CV driveshaft from the vehicle.
3. Turn the torsion bar adjustment nut counterclockwise to relieve all tension from the torsion bar. Remove the screws that attach the brake hose bracket to the upper arm. Remove the shock absorber.
4. Remove the cotter pin from the upper ball stud.
5. Release the upper ball joint taper using ball stud loosening tool C–3564–A, or equivalent. Remove the tool. Remove the ball stud from the steering knuckle.
6. Remove the pivot bar retaining bolts.
7. Remove the arm from the vehicle.
To install:
8. Position the arm at the frame rail bracket.
9. Install the pivot arm nuts and bolts.
10. Insert the upper ball stud in the steering knuckle arm bore and install the nut. Torque the nut to 105 ft. lbs. (142 Nm) and install a new cotter pin. Install the shock absorber and attach the brake hose bracket.
11. Turn the torsion bar adjustment nut clockwise to apply a load on the bar.
12. Install the CV driveshaft and all related parts.
13. Lower the vehicle.
14. Set the front suspension height so that the difference between the distance from the surface that the tires are on to the lower control arm inner pivot and the distance that the tires are on to the outer end of the arm is 1–1½ in.

Lower Control Arm

Removal and Installation
CARAVAN, VOYAGER AND TOWN & COUNTRY

1. Raise the vehicle and support safely. Remove the tire and wheel assembly.
2. Remove the sway bar.
3. Remove the ball joint stud retaining bolt and nut.
4. Pry the lower control arm from the steering knuckle.
5. Remove the control arm to crossmember bolts, nuts bushings and retainers.
6. Remove the control arm from the vehicle.
7. Transfer all reusable parts to the new control arm and lubricate.

8. The installation is the reverse of the removal procedure. Torque the front pivot bolt to 120 ft. lbs. (163 Nm) and the rear mounting nut to 70 ft. lbs. (95 Nm).

9. Perform a front end alignment as required.

DAKOTA WITH 2WD

1. Raise the vehicle and support safely.
2. Remove the shock absorber.
3. Disconnect the sway bar from the lower control arm, if equipped.
4. Install spring compressor tool DD–1278, or equivalent to the coil spring and tighten the nut finger tight, then back off half a turn.
5. Remove the cotter pin and lower ball joint nut.
6. Release the lower ball joint taper using ball stud loosening tool C–3564–A, or equivalent.
7. Remove the tool and remove the ball stud from the control arm. Release the compressor tool from the coil spring.
8. Pull the arm down and remove the spring with the rubber isolation pad from the vehicle. Remove the lower control arm pivot bolts from the crossmember and remove the arm from the vehicle.

To install:

9. Install the arm to the crossmember finger tight. Install the spring with the rubber isolators. Install the compressor tool and compress it enough so the lower ball joint can be inserted through the knuckle.
10. Torque the lower ball joint nut to 135 ft. lbs. (183 Nm). Install a new cotter pin. Remove the spring compressor.
11. Connect the sway bar from the lower control arm, if equipped.
12. Install the shock absorber.
13. Lower the vehicle completely. When the weight of the vehicle is off of the lifting apparatus, torque the front lower arm pivot bolt to 130 ft. lbs. (176 Nm) and the rear nut to 80 ft. lbs. (108 Nm).
14. Align the front end as required.

DAKOTA WITH 4WD

1. Raise the vehicle and support safely.
2. Remove the CV driveshaft.
3. Remove the torsion bar.
4. Remove the shock absorber lower attaching bolt.
5. Disconnect the stabilizer bar from the lower control arm.
6. Remove the cotter pin and the nut from the lower ball stud. Separate the lower ball stud from the steering knucle.
7. Remove the pivot bolts and remove the arm from the vehicle.

To install:

8. Install the new control arm to the vehicle.
9. Install the pivot bolts.
10. Insert the ball stud into the steering knuckle bore. Install the nut, torque to 120 ft. lbs. (163 Nm) and install a new cotter pin.
11. Attach the stabilizer bar to the control arm and install the shock mount bolt.

12. Install the torsion bar and turn the adjustment bolt clockwise to apply a load to the bar.
13. Install the CV driveshaft and all related parts.
14. Lower the vehicle so the weight of the vehicle is completely off of the lifting apparatus.
15. Torque the front pivot nut to 80 ft. lbs. (108 Nm) and the rear nut to 130 ft. lbs. (176 Nm).
16. Set the front suspension height so that the difference between the distance from the surface that the tires are on to the lower control arm inner pivot and the distance that the tires are on to the outer end of the arm is 1–1½ in.
17. Perform a front end alignment.

Sway Bar

Removal and Installation

1. Raise the vehicle and support safely.
2. Remove the front sway bar brackets and retainers.
3. Remove the sway bar support brackets and bushings from the lower control arm. Remove the sway bar from the vehicle.
4. The installation is the reverse of the removal procedure.

Front Wheel Bearings

Removal and Installation

1. Raise the vehicle and support safely.
2. Remove the tire and wheel assembly.
3. Remove the caliper and disc brake pads.
4. Remove the dust cap.
5. Remove the cotter pin, castelated nut lock, wheel bearing nut and washer from the spindle.
6. Remove the outer wheel bearing.
7. Remove the rotor with the inner wheel bearing from the spindle. Remove the grease seal.

To install:

8. Lubricate and install the inner wheel bearing. Install a new grease seal.
9. Install the rotor to the spindle.
10. Lubricate and install the outer wheel bearing, washer and nut. When the bearing preload is properly set, install the nut lock and a new cotter pin.
11. Install the grease cap.
12. Install the brake pads and caliper.
13. Install the wheel.

Adjustment

1. Tighten the wheel bearing nut to 20–25 ft. lbs. (27–34 Nm) while turning the rotor.
2. Loosen the wheel bearing adjusting nut completely.
3. Tighten the nut finger tight.
4. Check the wheel bearing endplay. The specification is 0.0001–0.003 in.
5. Install the nut lock and cotter pin.

REAR SUSPENSION

Shock Absorber

Removal and Installation

1. Raise the vehicle and support safely.
2. Remove the bolts that attach the shock to the frame or bracket.
3. Remove the shock from the vehicle.
4. The installation is the reverse of the removal procedure.

Leaf Springs

Removal and Installation

CARAVAN, VOYAGER AND TOWN & COUNTRY

1. Raise the vehicle and support safely.
2. Disconnect the actuator valve for the height sensing proportional valve.
3. Disconnect the shock absorbers from the axle brackets.

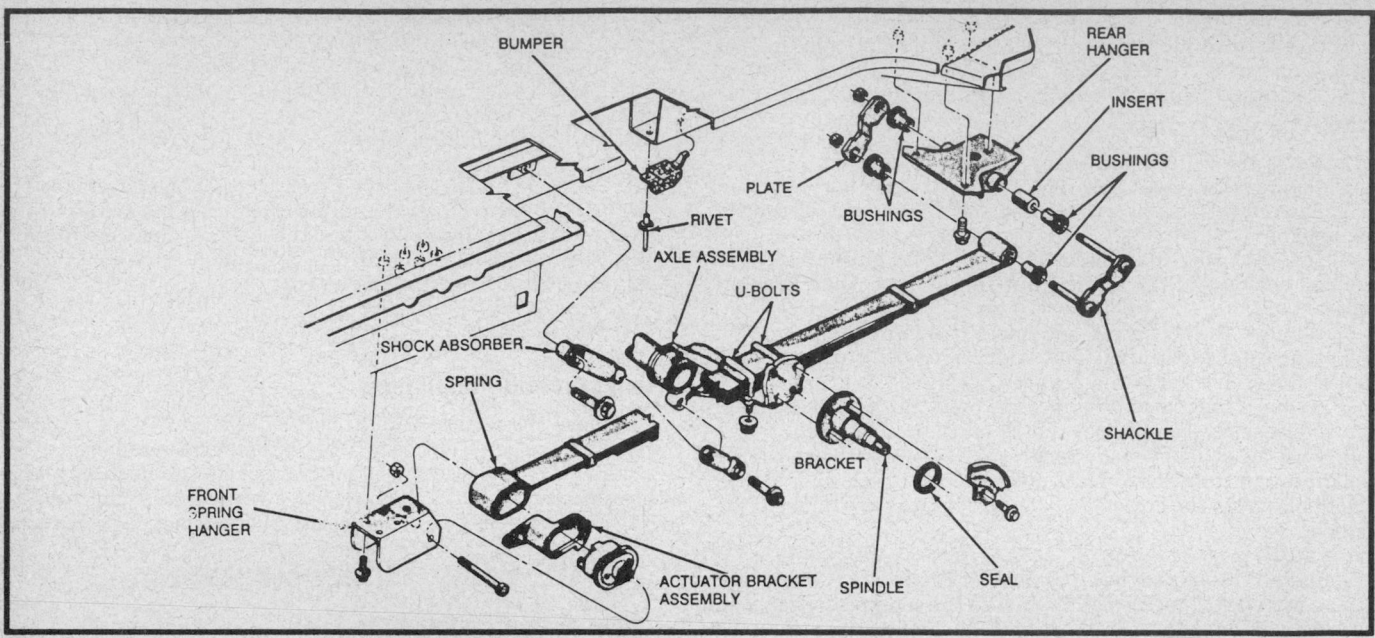

Rear suspension—Caravan, Voyager and Town & Country

4. Remove the U-bolt nuts and washers and remove the U-bolts.

5. Lower the rear axle assembly allowing the spring to hang free.

6. Remove the bolts from the front hanger.

7. Remove the rear spring shackle nuts and plate and remove the shackle from the spring.

8. Remove the front pivot bolt from the front spring hanger and remove the springs from the vehicle.

To install:

9. Assembly the shackle bushings and plate on the rear of the spring and ear spring hanger and start the shackle bolts.

10. Assembly the front spring hanger to the front of the spring eye and install the pivot bolt and nut. The pivot bolt must face inboard to prevent structural damage during installation.

11. Raise the front of the spring to the vehicle and install the 4 hanger bolts and torque to 45 ft. lbs. (61 Nm). Connect the actuator assembly for the height sensing proportioning valve.

12. Raise the axle assembly to the correct position with the axle centered under the spring center bolt.

13. Install the U-bolts, washers and nuts and torque the nuts to 60 ft. lbs. (81 Nm).

14. Install the shock absorbers.

15. Lower the vehicle so the full weight of the vehicle is off of the lifting apparatus.

16. Torque the front pivot bolts to 105 ft. lbs. (142 Nm).

17. Torque the shackle nuts to 35 ft. lbs. (47 Nm).

18. Adjust the height sensing proportioning valve.

DAKOTA

1. Raise the vehicle and support safely.

2. Using the proper equipment, support the weight of the axle.

3. Remove the nuts, washers and U-bolts attaching the springs to the axle housing. Remove the spacer.

4. Remove the spring shackle bolts, shackle and spring front bolt.

5. Remove the springs and auxiliary spring, if equipped, from the vehicle.

6. The installation is the reverse of the removal procedure.

Rear Wheel Bearings

Removal and Installation

CARAVAN, VOYAGER AND TOWN & COUNTRY

1. Raise the vehicle and support safely.

2. Remove the tire and wheel assembly.

3. Remove the dust cap.

4. Remove the cotter pin, nut lock and nut.

5. Remove the thrust washer and the outer wheel bearing.

6. Remove the drum with the inner wheel bearing and the grease seal.

7. Remove the grease seal and remove the inner bearing.

To install:

8. Lubricate the inner bearing and install to the drum.

9. Install a new grease seal.

10. Install the drum to the vehicle.

11. Lubricate and install the outer wheel bearing to the spindle.

12. Install the thrust washer.

13. Install and tighten the wheel bearng nut to 20–25 ft. lbs. (27–34 Nm) while rotating the drum.

14. Back off the adjusting nut ¼ turn then tighten it finger tight.

15. Install the nut lock and a new cotter pin.

Rear Axle Assembly

Removal and Installation

CARAVAN, VOYAGER AND TOWN & COUNTRY

1. Raise the vehicle and support safely.

2. Disconnect the brake hose connection from the axle tube.

3. Unclip the brake tubes from the axle housing.

4. Support the axle tube with jack stands.

5. Unbolt the shock absorbers from the axle.

6. Unbolt the axle tube from the leaf springs.

7. Remove the axle from the vehicle.

8. The installation is the reverse of the removal procedure.

SPECIFICATIONS

VEHICLE IDENTIFICATION CHART

It is important for servicing and ordering parts to be certain of the vehicle and engine identification. The VIN (vehicle identification number) is a 17 digit number visible through the windshield on the driver's side of the dash and contains the vehicle and engine identification codes. The tenth digit indicates model year and the eighth digit indicates engine code. It can be interpreted as follows:

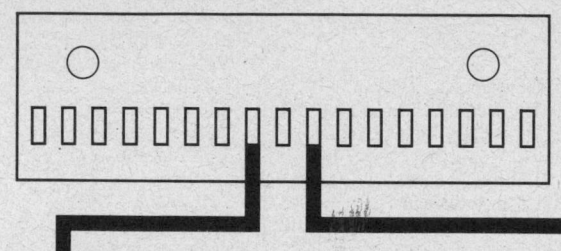

Engine Code

Code	Cu. In.	Liters	Cyl.	Fuel Sys.	Eng. Mfg.
Y (86)	300	4.9	6	1bbl	Ford
Y (87–90)	300	4.9	6	EFI	Ford
N	302	5.0	8	EFI	Ford
H (86–87)	351 (HD)	5.8	8	4bbl	Ford
H (88–90)	351	5.8	8	EFI	Ford
I	420	6.9	8	Diesel	International Harvester ①
M	445	7.3	8	Diesel	Navistar
G	460	7.5	8	EFI	Ford
L	460	7.5	8	4bbl	Ford

① Navistar—1987

Model Year

Code	Year
G	1986
H	1987
J	1988
K	1989
L	1990

ENGINE IDENTIFICATION

Year	Model	Engine Displacement cu. in. (liter)	Engine Series Identification (VIN)	No. of Cylinders	Engine Type
1986	Bronco	300 (4.9)	Y	6	OHV
	Bronco	302 (5.0)	N	8	OHV
	Bronco	351 (5.8)	H	8	OHV
	E-150	300 (4.9)	Y	6	OHV
	E-150	302 (5.0)	N	8	OHV
	E-150	351 (5.8)	H	8	OHV
	E-250	300 (4.9)	Y	6	OHV
	E-250	302 (5.0)	N	8	OHV
	E-250	351 (5.8)	H	8	OHV
	E-250	420 (6.9)	I	8	Diesel
	E-250	460 (7.5)	L	8	OHV
	E-350	300 (4.9)	Y	6	OHV
	E-350	351 (5.8)	H	8	OHV
	E-350	420 (6.9)	I	8	Diesel

ENGINE IDENTIFICATION

Year	Model	Engine Displacement cu. in. (liter)	Engine Series Identification (VIN)	No. of Cylinders	Engine Type
	E-350	460 (7.5)	L	8	OHV
	F-150	300 (4.9)	Y	6	OHV
	F-150	302 (5.0)	N	8	OHV
	F-150	351 (5.8)	H	8	OHV
	F-250	300 (4.9)	Y	6	OHV
	F-250	302 (5.0)	N	8	OHV
	F-250	351 (5.8)	H	8	OHV
	F-250	420 (6.9)	I	8	Diesel
	F-250	460 (7.5)	L	8	OHV
	F-350	300 (4.9)	Y	6	OHV
	F-350	351 (5.8)	H	8	OHV
	F-350	420 (6.9)	I	8	Diesel
	F-350	460 (7.5)	L	8	OHV
1987	Bronco	300 (4.9)	Y	6	OHV
	Bronco	302 (5.0)	N	8	OHV
	Bronco	351 (5.8)	H	8	OHV
	E-150	300 (4.9)	Y	6	OHV
	E-150	302 (5.0)	N	8	OHV
	E-150	351 (5.8)	H	8	OHV
	E-250	300 (4.9)	Y	6	OHV
	E-250	302 (5.0)	N	8	OHV
	E-250	351 (5.8)	H	8	OHV
	E-250	420 (6.9)	I	8	Diesel
	E-250	460 (7.5)	L	8	OHV
	E-350	300 (4.9)	Y	6	OHV
	E-350	351 (5.8)	H	8	OHV
	E-350	420 (6.9)	I	8	Diesel
	E-350	460 (7.5)	L	8	OHV
	F-150	300 (4.9)	Y	6	OHV
	F-150	302 (5.0)	N	8	OHV
	F-150	351 (5.8)	H	8	OHV
	F-250	300 (4.9)	Y	6	OHV
	F-250	302 (5.0)	N	8	OHV
	F-250	351 (5.8)	H	8	OHV
	F-250	420 (6.9)	I	8	Diesel
	F-250	460 (7.5)	L	8	OHV
	F-350	300 (4.9)	Y	6	OHV
	F-350	351 (5.8)	H	8	OHV
	F-350	420 (6.9)	I	8	Diesel
	F-350	460 (7.5)	L	8	OHV
1988	Bronco	300 (4.9)	Y	6	OHV
	Bronco	302 (5.0)	N	8	OHV
	Bronco	351 (5.8)	H	8	OHV
	E-150	300 (4.9)	Y	6	OHV

ENGINE IDENTIFICATION

Year	Model	Engine Displacement cu. in. (liter)	Engine Series Identification (VIN)	No. of Cylinders	Engine Type
1988	E-150	302 (5.0)	N	8	OHV
	E-150	351 (5.8)	H	8	OHV
	E-250	300 (4.9)	Y	6	OHV
	E-250	302 (5.0)	N	8	OHV
	E-250	351 (5.8)	H	8	OHV
	E-250	445 (7.3)	M	8	Diesel
	E-250	460 (7.5)	G	8	OHV
	E-350	300 (4.9)	Y	6	OHV
	E-350	351 (5.8)	H	8	OHV
	E-350	445 (7.3)	M	8	Diesel
	E-350	460 (7.5)	G	8	OHV
	F-150	300 (4.9)	Y	6	OHV
	F-150	302 (5.0)	N	8	OHV
	F-150	351 (5.8)	H	8	OHV
	F-250	300 (4.9)	Y	6	OHV
	F-250	302 (5.0)	N	8	OHV
	F-250	351 (5.8)	H	8	OHV
	F-250	445 (7.3)	M	8	Diesel
	F-250	460 (7.5)	G	8	OHV
	F-350	300 (4.9)	Y	6	OHV
	F-350	351 (5.8)	H	8	OHV
	F-350	445 (7.3)	M	8	Diesel
	F-250	460 (7.5)	G	8	OHV
	F-350	300 (4.9)	Y	6	OHV
	F-350	351 (5.8)	H	8	OHV
	F-350	445 (7.3)	M	8	Diesel
	F-350	460 (7.5)	G	8	OHV
1989	Bronco	300 (4.9)	Y	6	OHV
	Bronco	302 (5.0)	N	8	OHV
	Bronco	351 (5.8)	H	8	OHV
	E-150	300 (4.9)	Y	6	OHV
	E-150	302 (5.0)	N	8	OHV
	E-150	351 (5.8)	H	8	OHV
	E-250	300 (4.9)	Y	6	OHV
	E-250	302 (5.0)	N	8	OHV
	E-250	351 (5.8)	H	8	OHV
	E-250	445 (7.3)	M	8	Diesel
	E-250	460 (7.5)	G	8	OHV
	E-350	300 (4.9)	Y	6	OHV
	E-350	351 (5.8)	H	8	OHV
	E-350	445 (7.3)	M	8	Diesel
	E-350	460 (7.5)	G	8	OHV
	F-150	300 (4.9)	Y	6	OHV
	F-150	302 (5.0)	N	8	OHV

ENGINE IDENTIFICATION

Year	Model	Engine Displacement cu. in. (liter)	Engine Series Identification (VIN)	No. of Cylinders	Engine Type
1989	F-150	351 (5.8)	H	8	OHV
	F-250	300 (4.9)	Y	6	OHV
	F-250	302 (5.0)	N	8	OHV
	F-250	351 (5.8)	H	8	OHV
	F-250	445 (7.3)	M	8	Diesel
	F-250	460 (7.5)	G	8	OHV
	F-350	300 (4.9)	Y	6	OHV
	F-350	351 (5.8)	H	8	OHV
	F-350	445 (7.3)	M	8	Diesel
	F-350	460 (7.5)	G	8	OHV
	F-Super Duty	445 (7.3)	M	8	Diesel
	F-Super Duty	460 (7.5)	G	8	OHV
	Motor Home Chassis	460 (7.5)	G	8	OHV
1990	Bronco	300 (4.9)	Y	6	OHV
	Bronco	302 (5.0)	N	8	OHV
	Bronco	351 (5.8)	H	8	OHV
	E-150	300 (4.9)	Y	6	OHV
	E-150	302 (5.0)	N	8	OHV
	E-150	351 (5.8)	H	8	OHV
	E-250	300 (4.9)	Y	6	OHV
	E-250	302 (5.0)	N	8	OHV
	E-250	351 (5.8)	H	8	OHV
	E-250	445 (7.3)	M	8	Diesel
	E-250	460 (7.5)	G	8	OHV
	E-350	300 (4.9)	Y	6	OHV
	E-350	351 (5.8)	H	8	OHV
	E-350	445 (7.3)	M	8	Diesel
	E-350	460 (7.5)	G	8	OHV
	F-150	300 (4.9)	Y	6	OHV
	F-150	302 (5.0)	N	8	OHV
	F-150	351 (5.8)	H	8	OHV
	F-250	300 (4.9)	Y	6	OHV
	F-250	302 (5.0)	N	8	OHV
	F-250	351 (5.8)	H	8	OHV
	F-250	445 (7.3)	M	8	Diesel
	F-250	460 (7.5)	G	8	OHV
	F-350	300 (4.9)	Y	6	OHV
	F-350	351 (5.8)	H	8	OHV
	F-350	445 (7.3)	M	8	Diesel
	F-350	460 (7.5)	G	8	OHV

FORD MOTOR COMPANY
F SERIES (PICK-UP) • BRONCO • E SERIES (VAN)

GENERAL ENGINE SPECIFICATIONS

Year	VIN	No. Cylinder Displacement cu. in. (liter)	Fuel System Type	Net Horsepower @ rpm	Net Torque @ rpm (ft. lbs.)	Bore × Stroke (in.)	Compression Ratio	Oil Pressure @ rpm
1986	Y	6-300 (4.9)	1bbl	125 @ 3200	245 @ 1800	4.00 × 3.98	8.0:1	50 @ 2000
	N	8-302 (5.0)	EFI	150 @ 3600	249 @ 2600	4.00 × 3.00	8.4:1	50 @ 2000
	H	8-351 (5.8)	4bbl	210 @ 4000	304 @ 2800	4.00 × 3.50	8.3:1	52 @ 2000
	I	8-420 (6.9)	Diesel	170 @ 3300	315 @ 1400	4.00 × 4.18	20.7:1	50 @ 2000
	L	8-460 (7.5)	4bbl	226 @ 4400	365 @ 2800	4.36 × 3.85	8.0:1	52 @ 2000
1987	Y	6-300 (4.9)	EFI	150 @ 3400	260 @ 2000	4.00 × 3.98	8.8:1	50 @ 2000
	N	8-302 (5.0)	EFI	185 @ 3800	270 @ 2400	4.00 × 3.00	9.0:1	50 @ 2000
	H	8-351 (5.8)	4bbl	190 @ 4000	285 @ 2600	4.00 × 3.50	8.3:1	52 @ 2000
	I	8-420 (6.9)	Diesel	170 @ 3300	315 @ 1400	4.00 × 4.18	21.5:1	55 @ 2000
	L	8-460 (7.5)	4bbl	245 @ 4200	380 @ 2600	4.36 × 3.85	8.0:1	48 @ 2000
1988	Y	6-300 (4.9)	EFI	145 @ 3400 ④	265 @ 2000 ⑤	4.00 × 3.98	8.8:1	50 @ 2000
	N	8-302 (5.0)	EFI	185 @ 3800	270 @ 2400	4.00 × 3.00	9.0:1	50 @ 2000
	H	8-351 (5.8)	EFI	210 @ 3800	315 @ 2800 ①	4.00 × 3.50	8.8:1	50 @ 2000
	M	8-445 (7.3)	Diesel	180 @ 3300 ②	345 @ 1400 ③	4.11 × 4.18	21.5:1	55 @ 3300
	G	8-460 (7.5)	EFI	230 @ 3600	390 @ 2000	4.36 × 3.85	8.5:1	52 @ 2000
1989–90	Y	6-300 (4.9)	EFI	145 @ 3400 ④	265 @ 2000 ⑤	4.00 × 3.98	8.8:1	50 @ 2000
	N	8-302 (5.0)	EFI	185 @ 3800	270 @ 2400	4.00 × 3.00	9.0:1	50 @ 2000
	H	8-351 (5.8)	EFI	210 @ 3800	315 @ 2800 ①	4.00 × 3.50	8.8:1	50 @ 2000
	M	8-445 (7.3)	Diesel	180 @ 3300 ②	345 @ 1400 ③	4.11 × 4.18	21.5:1	55 @ 3300
	G	8-460 (7.5)	EFI	230 @ 3600	390 @ 2000	4.36 × 3.85	8.5:1	52 @ 2000

① 310 @ 2800 rpm on models over 8500 lbs. GVWR
② 160 @ 3300 rpm high altitude applications
③ 305 @ 1400 rpm high altitude applications
④ 150 @ 3400 rpm except Bronco, E-150 and F-150
⑤ 260 @ 2000 rpm except Bronco, E-150 and F-150

GASOLINE ENGINE TUNE-UP SPECIFICATIONS

Year	VIN	No. Cylinder Displacement cu. in. (liter)	Spark Plugs Type	Gap (in.)	Ignition Timing (deg.) MT	AT	Compression Pressure (psi)	Fuel Pump (psi)	Idle speed (rpm) MT	AT	Valve Clearance ① In.	Ex.
1986	Y	6-300 (4.9)	R84TS	.044	10	10	NA	5–7	600 ②	550 ②	Hyd.	Hyd.
	N	8-302 (5.0)	R42TS	.044	10	10	NA	35–45	775	675	Hyd.	Hyd.
	H	8-351 (5.8)	R42TS	.044	—	10	NA	6–8	—	650	Hyd.	Hyd.
	L	8-460 (7.5)	ASF-42	.044	8	8	NA	6–8	800	650	Hyd.	Hyd.
1987	Y	6-300 (4.9)	R84TS	.044	10	10	NA	35–45	675	575	Hyd.	Hyd.
	N	8-302 (5.0)	R42TS	.044	10	10	NA	35–45	775	675	Hyd.	Hyd.
	H	8-351 (5.8)	R42TS	.044	—	10 ③	NA	6–8	—	600	Hyd.	Hyd.
	L	8-460 (7.5)	ASF-42	.044	8	8	NA	6–8	800	650	Hyd.	Hyd.
1988	Y	6-300 (4.9)	R84TS	.044	10	10	NA	50–60	675	575	Hyd.	Hyd.
	N	8-302 (5.0)	R42TS	.044	10	10	NA	35–45	775	675	Hyd.	Hyd.
	H	8-351 (5.8)	R42TS	.044	10	10	NA	35–45	775	675	Hyd.	Hyd.
	G	8-460 (7.5)	ASF-42	.044	8	8	NA	40	800	650	Hyd.	Hyd.

GASOLINE ENGINE TUNE-UP SPECIFICATIONS

Year	VIN	No. Cylinder Displacement cu. in. (liter)	Spark Plugs Type	Spark Plugs Gap (in.)	Ignition Timing (deg.) MT	Ignition Timing (deg.) AT	Com- pression Pressure (psi)	Fuel Pump (psi)	Idle speed (rpm) MT	Idle speed (rpm) AT	Valve Clearance ① In.	Valve Clearance ① Ex.
1989–90	Y	6-300 (4.9)	R84TS	.044	10	10	NA	50–60	675	575	Hyd.	Hyd.
	N	8-302 (5.0)	R42TS	.044	10	10	NA	35–45	775	675	Hyd.	Hyd.
	H	8-351 (5.8)	R42TS	.044	10	10	NA	35–45	775	675	Hyd.	Hyd.
	G	8-460 (7.5)	ASF-42	.044	8	8	NA	40	800	650	Hyd.	Hyd.

①Shorter or longer pushrods are available for service to provide a means of compensating for dimensional changes in the valve mechanism.
②Not adjustable—electronically controlled
③High altitude—14° BTDC

DIESEL ENGINE TUNE-UP SPECIFICATIONS

Year	VIN	No. Engine Displacement cu. in. (liter)	Valve Clearance Intake (in.)	Valve Clearance Exhaust (in.)	Intake Valve Opens (deg.)	Injection Pump Setting (deg.)	Injection Nozzle Pressure (psi) New	Injection Nozzle Pressure (psi) Used	Idle Speed (rpm)	Cranking Compression Pressure (psi)
1986	I	8-420 (6.9)	Hyd.	Hyd.	—	1.5 ②	1875	1425	①	195–440
1987	I	8-420 (6.9)	Hyd.	Hyd.	—	1.5 ②	1875	1425	①	195–440
1988	M	8-445 (7.3)	Hyd.	Hyd.	—	6.5 ③	1875	1425	①	195–440
1989–90	M	8-445 (7.3)	Hyd.	Hyd.	—	8.5 ③	1875	1425	①	195–440

①Curb idle speed is specified on the Vehicle Emissions Control Information Decal
②ATDC @ 1400 rpm fuel cetane value of 47 or greater
③BTDC @ 2000 rpm

CAPACITIES

Year	Model	VIN	No. Cylinder Displacement cu. in (liter)	Engine Crankcase with Filter	Engine Crankcase without Filter	Transmission (pts.) 4-Spd	Transmission (pts.) 5-Spd	Transmission (pts.) Auto.	Drive Axle (pts.)	Fuel Tank (gal.)	Cooling System (qts.)
1986	Bronco	Y	6-300 (4.9)	6	5	7①	7	27	5.5	32	14
	Bronco	N	8-302 (5.0)	6	5	7①	7	27	5.5	32	14
	Bronco	H	8-351 (5.8)	6	5	7①	7	27	5.5	32	15
	E-150	Y	6-300 (4.9)	6	5	7①	7	24	6②	22	17.5
	E-150	N	8-302 (5.0)	6	5	7①	7	24	6②	22	③
	E-150	H	8-351 (5.8)	6	5	7①	7	24	6②	22	④
	E-250	Y	6-300 (4.9)	6	5	7①	7	24	6②	22	17.5
	E-250	N	8-302 (5.0)	6	5	7①	7	24	6②	22	③
	E-250	H	8-351 (5.8)	6	5	7①	7	24	6②	22	④
	E-250	I	8-420 (6.9)	10	9	7①	7	24	6②	22	31
	E-250	L	8-460 (7.5)	6	5	7①	7	24	6②	22	28
	E-350	Y	6-300 (4.9)	6	5	7①	7	24	6②	22	17.5
	E-350	H	8-351 (5.8)	6	5	7①	7	24	6②	22	④
	E-350	I	8-420 (6.9)	10	9	7①	7	24	6②	22	31
	E-350	L	8-460 (7.5)	6	5	7①	7	24	6②	22	28
	F-150	Y	6-300 (4.9)	6	5	7①	7	24 ⑤	6②	19	14
	F-150	N	8-302 (5.0)	6	5	7①	7	24 ⑤	6②	19	14

FORD MOTOR COMPANY
F SERIES (PICK-UP) • BRONCO • E SERIES (VAN)

CAPACITIES

Year	Model	VIN	No. Cylinder Displacement cu. in (liter)	Engine Crankcase with Filter	Engine Crankcase without Filter	Transmission (pts.) 4-Spd	Transmission (pts.) 5-Spd	Transmission (pts.) Auto.	Drive Axle (pts.)	Fuel Tank (gal.)	Cooling System (qts.)
1986	F-150	H	8-351 (5.8)	6	5	7 ①	7	24 ⑤	6 ②	19	15
	F-250	Y	6-300 (4.9)	6	5	7 ①	7	24 ⑤	6 ②	19	14
	F-250	N	8-302 (5.0)	6	5	7 ①	7	24 ⑤	6 ②	19	14
	F-250	H	8-351 (5.8)	6	5	7 ①	7	24 ⑤	6 ②	19	15
	F-250	I	8-420 (6.9)	10	9	7 ①	7	24 ⑤	6 ②	19	31
	F-250	L	8-460 (7.5)	6	5	7 ①	7	24 ⑤	6 ②	19	16
	F-350	Y	6-300 (4.9)	6	5	7 ①	7	24 ⑤	6 ②	19	17.5
	F-350	H	8-351 (5.8)	6	5	7 ①	7	24 ⑤	6 ②	19	15
	F-350	I	8-420 (6.9)	10	9	7 ①	7	24 ⑤	6 ②	19	31
	F-350	L	8-460 (7.5)	6	5	7 ①	7	24 ⑤	6 ②	19	16
1987	Bronco	Y	6-300 (4.9)	6	5	7 ①	7	27	5.5	32	14
	Bronco	N	8-302 (5.0)	6	5	7 ①	7	27	5.5	32	14
	Bronco	H	8-351 (5.8)	6	5	7 ①	7	27	5.5	32	14
	E-150	Y	6-300 (4.9)	6	5	7 ①	7	24	6 ③	22	17.5
	E-150	N	8-302 (5.0)	6	5	7 ①	7	24	6 ③	22	③
	E-150	H	8-351 (5.8)	6	5	7 ①	7	24	6 ③	22	④
	E-250	Y	6-300 (4.9)	6	5	7 ①	7	24	6 ②	22	17.5
	E-250	N	8-302 (5.0)	6	5	7 ①	7	24	6 ③	22	③
	E-250	H	8-351 (5.8)	6	5	7 ①	7	24	6 ②	22	④
	E-250	I	8-420 (6.9)	10	9	7 ①	7	24	6 ②	22	31
	E-250	L	8-460 (7.5)	6	5	7 ①	7	24	6 ②	22	28
	E-350	Y	6-300 (4.9)	6	5	7 ①	7	24	6 ②	22	17.5
	E-350	H	8-351 (5.8)	6	5	7 ①	7	24	6 ②	22	④
	E-350	I	8-420 (6.9)	10	9	7 ①	7	24	6 ②	22	31
	E-350	L	8-460 (7.5)	6	5	7 ①	7	24	6 ②	22	28
	F-150	Y	6-300 (4.9)	6	5	7 ①	7	24 ⑤	6 ②	19	14
	F-150	N	8-302 (5.0)	6	5	7 ①	7	24 ⑤	6 ③	19	14
	F-150	H	8-351 (5.8)	6	5	7 ①	7	24 ⑤	6 ②	19	15
	F-250	Y	6-300 (4.9)	6	5	7 ①	7	24 ⑤	6 ②	19	14
	F-250	N	8-302 (5.0)	6	5	7 ①	7	24 ⑤	6 ②	19	14
	F-250	H	8-351 (5.8)	6	5	7 ①	7	24 ⑤	6 ②	19	15
	F-250	I	8-420 (6.9)	10	9	7 ①	7	24 ⑤	6 ②	19	31
	F-250	L	8-460 (7.5)	6	5	7 ①	7	24 ⑤	6 ②	19	16
	F-350	Y	6-300 (4.9)	6	5	7 ①	7	24 ⑤	6 ②	19	17.5
	F-350	H	8-351 (5.8)	6	5	7 ①	7	24 ⑤	6 ②	19	15
	F-350	I	8-420 (6.9)	10	9	7 ①	7	24 ⑤	6 ②	19	31
	F-350	L	8-460 (7.5)	6	5	7 ①	7	24 ⑤	6 ②	19	16
1988	Bronco	Y	6-300 (4.9)	6	5	7	7	28	6	32	14
	Bronco	N	8-302 (5.0)	6	5	7	7	28	6	32	14
	Bronco	H	8-351 (5.8)	6	5	7	7	28	6	32	16
	E-150	Y	6-300 (4.9)	6	5	7	7	24	6	22	18
	E-150	N	8-302 (5.0)	6	5	7	7	24	6	22	18.5
	E-150	H	8-351 (5.8)	6	5	7	7	24	6	22	21

CAPACITIES

Year	Model	VIN	No. Cylinder Displacement cu. in (liter)	Engine Crankcase with Filter	Engine Crankcase without Filter	Transmission (pts.) 4-Spd	Transmission (pts.) 5-Spd	Transmission (pts.) Auto.	Drive Axle (pts.)	Fuel Tank (gal.)	Cooling System (qts.)
1988	E-250	Y	6-300 (4.9)	6	5	7	7	24	6	22	18
	E-250	N	8-302 (5.0)	6	5	7	7	24	6	22	18.5
	E-250	H	8-351 (5.8)	6	5	7	7	24	6	22	21
	E-250	M	8-445 (7.3)	10	9	7	7	24	6	22	31
	E-250	G	8-460 (7.5)	6	5	7	7	24	6	22	18
	E-350	Y	6-300 (4.9)	6	5	7	7	24	6	22	18
	E-350	H	8-351 (5.8)	6	5	7	7	24	6	22	21
	E-350	M	8-445 (7.3)	10	9	7	7	24	6	22	31
	E-350	G	8-460 (7.5)	6	5	7	7	24	6	22	28
	F-150	Y	6-300 (4.9)	6	5	7	7	24 ⑤	6	19	15
	F-150	N	8-302 (5.0)	6	5	7	7	24 ⑤	6	19	15
	F-150	H	8-351 (5.8)	6	5	7	7	24 ⑤	6	19	17
	F-250	Y	6-300 (4.9)	6	5	7	7	24 ⑤	6	19	15
	F-250	N	8-302 (5.0)	6	5	7	7	24 ⑤	6	19	15
	F-250	H	8-351 (5.8)	6	5	7	7	24 ⑤	6	19	17
	F-250	M	8-445 (7.3)	10	9	7	7	24 ⑤	6	19	29
	F-250	G	8-460 (7.5)	6	5	7	7	24 ⑤	6	19	18
	F-350	Y	6-300 (4.9)	6	5	7	7	24 ⑤	6	19	15
	F-350	H	8-351 (5.8)	6	5	7	7	24 ⑤	6	19	17
	F-350	M	8-445 (7.3)	10	9	7	7	24 ⑤	6	19	29
	F-350	G	8-460 (7.5)	6	5	7	7	24 ⑤	6	19	18
1989–90	Bronco	Y	6-300 (4.9)	6	5	7	7	24	6	32	15
	Bronco	N	8-302 (5.0)	6	5	7	7	24	6	32	15
	Bronco	H	8-351 (5.8)	6	5	7	7	24	6	32	17
	E-150	Y	6-300 (4.9)	6	5	7	7	24	6	22	18
	E-150	N	8-302 (5.0)	6	5	7	7	24	6	22	18.5
	E-150	H	8-351 (5.8)	6	5	7	7	24	6	22	21
	E-250	Y	6-300 (4.9)	6	5	7	7	24	6	22	18
	E-250	N	8-302 (5.0)	6	5	7	7	24	6	22	18.5
	E-250	H	8-351 (5.8)	6	5	7	7	24	6	22	21
	E-250	M	8-445 (7.3)	10	9	7	7	24	6	22	31
	E-350	G	8-460 (7.5)	6	5	7	7	24	6	22	28
	E-350	Y	6-300 (4.9)	6	5	7	7	24	6	22	18
	E-350	H	8-351 (5.8)	6	5	7	7	24	6	22	21
	E-350	M	8-445 (7.3)	10	9	7	7	24	6	22	31
	E-350	G	8-460 (7.5)	6	5	7	7	24	6	22	28
	F-150	Y	6-300 (4.9)	6	5	7	7	24 ⑤	6	19	15
	F-150	N	8-302 (5.0)	6	5	7	7	24 ⑤	6	19	15
	F-150	H	8-351 (5.8)	6	5	7	7	24 ⑤	6	19	17
	F-250	Y	6-300 (4.9)	6	5	7	7	24 ⑤	6	19	15
	F-250	N	8-302 (5.0)	6	5	7	7	24 ⑤	6	19	15
	F-250	H	8-351 (5.8)	6	5	7	7	24 ⑤	6	19	17
	F-250	M	8-445 (7.3)	10	9	7	7	24 ⑤	6	19	29

CAPACITIES

Year	Model	VIN	No. Cylinder Displacement cu. in (liter)	Engine Crankcase with Filter	Engine Crankcase without Filter	Transmission (pts.) 4-Spd	Transmission (pts.) 5-Spd	Transmission (pts.) Auto.	Drive Axle (pts.)	Fuel Tank (gal.)	Cooling System (qts.)
1989-90	F-250	G	8-460 (7.5)	6	5	7	7	24 ⑤	6	19	18
	F-350	Y	6-300 (4.9)	6	5	7	7	24 ⑤	6	19	15
	F-350	H	8-351 (5.8)	6	5	7	7	24 ⑤	6	19	17
	F-350	M	8-445 (7.3)	10	9	7	7	24 ⑤	6	19	29
	F-350	G	8-460 (7.5)	6	5	7	7	24 ⑤	6	19	18

① Ford overdrive 4.5 pts.
② Heavy duty 7.5 pts.
③ Manual transmission 17½ pts. Automatic transmission 18½ pts.
④ Manual transmission 15 pts. Automatic transmission 21 pts.
⑤ 4WD vehicles—27 pts.

FIRING ORDERS

NOTE: To avoid confusion, always replace spark plug wires one at a time.

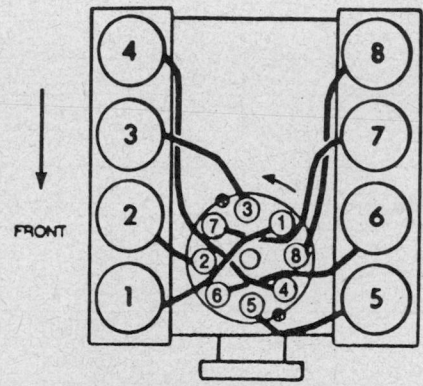

351 (5.8L) V8 engine
Firing order: 1–3–7–2–6–5–4–8

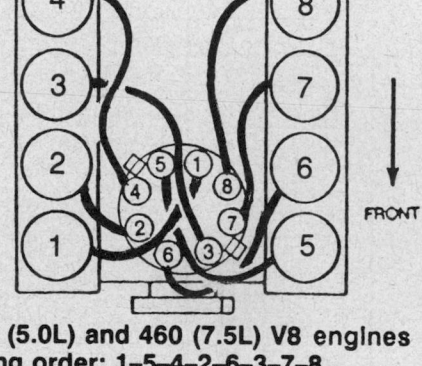

302 (5.0L) and 460 (7.5L) V8 engines
Firing order: 1–5–4–2–6–3–7–8
Distributor rotation: counterclockwise

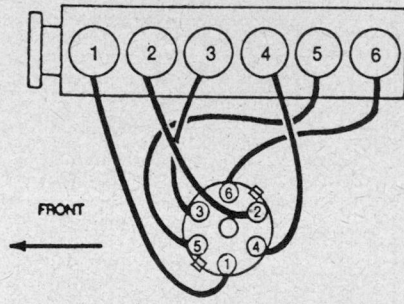

300 (4.9L) 6 cylinder engine
Firing order: 1–5–3–6–2–4
Distributor rotation: clockwise

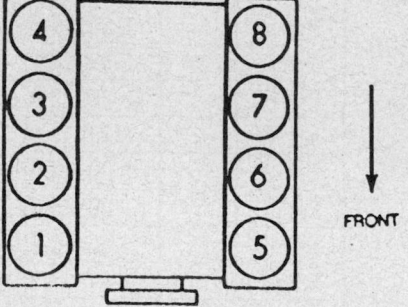

420 (6.9L) and 445 (7.3L) Diesel engines
Firing order: 1–2–7–3–4–5–6–8

CAMSHAFT SPECIFICATIONS

Year	VIN	No. Cylinder Displacement cu. in. (liter)	Journal Diameter 1	Journal Diameter 2	Journal Diameter 3	Journal Diameter 4	Journal Diameter 5	Lobe Lift In.	Lobe Lift Ex.	Bearing Clearance	Camshaft End Play
1986	Y	6-300 (4.9)	2.017–2.018	2.017–2.018	2.017–2.018	2.017–2.018	—	0.249–0.247	0.249–0.247	0.001–0.003	0.001–0.007
	N	8-302 (5.0)	2.080	2.065	2.050	2.035	2.020	0.237	0.247	0.001–0.003	0.001–0.007
	H	8.351 (5.8)	2.081	2.066	2.051	2.036	2.021	0.260	0.260	0.001–0.003	0.001–0.007

CAMSHAFT SPECIFICATIONS

Year	VIN	No. Cylinder Displacement cu. in. (liter)	Journal Diameter 1	2	3	4	5	Lobe Lift In.	Ex.	Bearing Clearance	Camshaft End Play
	I	8-420 (6.9)	2.099–2.100	2.099–2.100	2.099–2.100	2.099–2.100	2.099–2.100	NA	NA	0.001–0.005	0.001–0.009
	L	8-460 (7.5)	2.124–2.125	2.124–2.125	2.124–2.125	2.124–2.125	2.124–2.125	0.252	0.278	0.001–0.003	0.001–0.006
1987	Y	6-300 (4.9)	2.017–2.018	2.017–2.018	2.107–2.018	2.017–2.018	—	0.249–0.247	0.249–0.247	0.001–0.003	0.001–0.007
	N	8-302 (5.0)	2.080	2.065	2.050	2.035	2.020	0.237	0.247	0.001–0.003	0.001–0.007
	H	8-351 (5.8)	2.081	2.066	2.051	2.036	2.021	0.260	0.260	0.001–0.003	0.001–0.007
	I	8-420 (6.9)	2.099–2.100	2.099–2.100	2.099–2.100	2.099–2.100	2.099–2.100	NA	NA	0.002–0.006	0.001–0.009
	L	8-460 (7.5)	2.124–2.125	2.124–2.125	2.124–2.125	2.124–2.125	2.124–2.125	0.252	0.278	0.001–0.003	0.001–0.006
1988	Y	6-300 (4.9)	2.017–2.018	2.017–2.018	2.017–2.018	2.017–2.018	—	0.249–0.247	0.249–0.247	0.001–0.003	0.001–0.007
	N	8-302 (5.0)	2.080	2.065	2.050	2.035	2.020	0.237	0.247	0.001–0.003	0.001–0.007
	H	8-351 (5.8)	2.081	2.065	2.051	2.036	2.021	0.260	0.260	0.001–0.003	0.001–0.007
	M	8-445 (7.3)	2.099–2.100	2.099–2.100	2.099–2.100	2.099–2.100	2.099–2.100	NA	NA	0.001–0.003	0.002–0.009
	G	8-460 (7.5)	2.124–2.125	2.124–2.125	2.124–2.125	2.124–2.125	2.124–2.125	0.252	0.278	0.001–0.003	0.001–0.006
1989–90	Y	6-300 (4.9)	2.017–2.018	2.017–2.018	2.017–2.018	2.017–2.018	—	0.249–0.247	0.249–0.247	0.001–0.003	0.001–0.007
	N	8-302 (5.0)	2.080	2.065	2.050	2.035	2.020	0.237	0.247	0.001–0.003	0.001–0.007
	H	8-351 (5.8)	2.081	2.066	2.051	2.036	2.021	0.278	0.283	0.001–0.003	0.001–0.007
	M	8-445 (7.3)	2.099–2.100	2.099–2.100	2.099–2.100	2.099–2.100	2.099–2.100	NA	NA	0.001–0.003	0.002–0.009
	G	8-460 (7.5)	2.124–2.125	2.124–2.125	2.124–2.125	2.124–2.125	2.124–2.125	0.252	0.278	0.001–0.003	0.001–0.006

CRANKSHAFT AND CONNECTING ROD SPECIFICATIONS

All measurements are given in inches.

Year	VIN	No. Cylinder Displacement cu. in. (liter)	Crankshaft Main. Brg. Journal Dia.	Main Brg. Oil Clearance	Shaft End-play	Thrust on No.	Connecting Rod Journal Diameter	Oil Clearance	Side Clearance
1986	Y	6-300 (4.9)	2.3982–2.3990	0.0009–0.0028	0.004–0.008	5	2.1228–2.1236	0.0009–0.0027	0.006–0.013
	N	8-302 (5.0)	2.2482–2.2490	0.0008–0.0015	0.004–0.008	3	2.1228–2.1236	0.0008–0.0015	0.010–0.020
	H	8-351 (5.8)	2.9994–3.0002	0.0008–0.0015	0.004–0.008	3	2.3103–2.3111	0.0008–0.0026	0.010–0.020
	I	8-420 (6.9)	3.1228–3.1236	0.0018–0.0036	0.001–0.009	3	2.6905–2.6910	0.0011–0.0026	0.008–0.020

CRANKSHAFT AND CONNECTING ROD SPECIFICATIONS

All measurements are given in inches.

Year	VIN	No. Cylinder Displacement cu. in. (liter)	Crankshaft Main. Brg. Journal Dia.	Crankshaft Main Brg. Oil Clearance	Crankshaft Shaft End-play	Thrust on No.	Connecting Rod Journal Diameter	Connecting Rod Oil Clearance	Connecting Rod Side Clearance
	L	8-460 (7.5)	2.9994–3.0002	0.0008–0.0015	0.004–0.008	3	2.4992–2.5000	0.0008–0.0015	0.010–0.020
1987	Y	6-300 (4.9)	2.3982–2.3990	0.0009–0.0028	0.004–0.008	5	2.1228–2.1236	0.0009–0.0027	0.006–0.013
	N	8-302 (5.0)	2.2482–2.2490	0.0008–0.0015	0.004–0.008	3	2.1228–2.1236	0.0008–0.0015	0.010–0.020
	H	8-351 (5.8)	2.9994–3.0002	0.0008–0.0015	0.004–0.008	3	2.3103–2.3111	0.0008–0.0026	0.010–0.020
	I	8-420 (6.9)	3.1228–3.1236	0.0018–0.0036	0.001–0.009	3	2.6905–2.6910	0.0011–0.0026	0.008–0.020
	L	8-460 (7.5)	2.9994–3.0002	0.0008–0.0015	0.004–0.008	3	2.4992–2.5000	0.0008–0.0015	0.010–0.020
1988	Y	6-300 (4.9)	2.3982–2.3990	0.0010–0.0028	0.004–0.008	5	2.1228–2.1236	0.0007–0.0024	0.006–0.013
	N	8-302 (5.0)	2.2482–2.2490	0.0008–0.0015	0.004–0.008	3	2.1228–2.1236	0.0008–0.0015	0.010–0.020
	H	8-351 (5.8)	2.9994–3.0002	0.0008–0.0015	0.004–0.008	3	2.3103–2.3111	0.0008–0.0026	0.010–0.020
	M	8-445 (7.3)	3.1228–3.1236	0.0018–0.0046	0.0025–0.0085	3	2.4980–2.4990	0.0011–0.0036	0.012–0.024
	G	8-460 (7.5)	2.9994–3.0002	0.0008–0.0026	0.004–0.008	3	2.4992–2.5000	0.0008–0.0025	0.010–0.020
1989–90	Y	6-300 (4.9)	2.3982–2.3990	0.0010–0.0028	0.004–0.008	5	2.1228–2.1236	0.0007–0.0024	0.006–0.013
	N	8-302 (5.0)	2.2482–2.2490	0.0008–0.0015	0.004–0.008	3	2.1228–2.1236	0.0008–0.0015	0.010–0.020
	H	8-351 (5.8)	2.9994–3.0002	0.0008–0.0015	0.004–0.008	3	2.3103–2.3111	0.0008–0.0026	0.010–0.020
	M	8-445 (7.3)	3.1228–3.1236	0.0018–0.0046	0.0025–0.0085	3	2.4980–2.4990	0.0011–0.0036	0.012–0.024
	G	8-460 (7.5)	2.9994–3.0002	0.0008–0.0026	0.004–0.008	3	2.4992–2.5000	0.0008–0.0025	0.010–0.020

VALVE SPECIFICATIONS

Year	VIN	No. Cylinder Displacement cu. in. (liter)	Seat Angle (deg.)	Face Angle (deg.)	Spring Test Pressure (lbs.)	Spring Installed Height (in.)	Stem-to-Guide Clearance (in.) Intake	Stem-to-Guide Clearance (in.) Exhaust	Stem Diameter (in.) Intake	Stem Diameter (in.) Exhaust
1986	Y	6-300 (4.9)	45	44	175 ⑨	①	0.0010–0.0027	0.0010–0.0027	0.3420	0.3415
	N	8-302 (5.0)	45	44	②	③	0.0010–0.0027	0.0015–0.0032	0.3420	0.3415
	H	8-351 (5.8)	45	44	200 ⑩	④	0.0010–0.0027	0.0015–0.0032	0.3420	0.3415
	I	8-420 (6.9)	⑤	⑤	60 ⑪	—	0.0012–0.0029	0.0012–0.0029	0.3720	0.3720
	L	8-460 (7.5)	45	44	229 ⑧	1 13/16	0.0010–0.0027	0.0010–0.0027	0.3420	0.3420

VALVE SPECIFICATIONS

Year	VIN	No. Cylinder Displacement cu. in. (liter)	Seat Angle (deg.)	Face Angle (deg.)	Spring Test Pressure (lbs.)	Spring Installed Height (in.)	Stem-to-Guide Clearance (in.) Intake	Exhaust	Stem Diameter (in.) Intake	Exhaust
1987	Y	6-300 (4.9)	45	44	175 ⑨	①	0.0010–0.0027	0.0010–0.0027	0.3420	0.3415
	N	8-302 (5.0)	45	44	②	③	0.0010–0.0027	0.0015–0.0032	0.3420	0.3415
	H	8-351 (5.8)	45	44	200 ⑩	④	0.0010–0.0027	0.0015–0.0032	0.3420	0.3415
	I	8-420 (6.9)	⑤	⑤	80 ⑥	—	0.0012–0.0029	0.0012–0.0029	0.3720	0.3720
	L	8-460 (7.5)	45	44	229 ⑧	1¹³/₁₆	0.0010–0.0027	0.0010–0.0027	0.3420	0.3420
1988	Y	6-300 (4.9)	45	44	175 ⑨	①	0.0010–0.0027	0.0010–0.0027	0.3420	0.3415
	N	8-302 (5.0)	45	44	②	③	0.0010–0.0027	0.0015–0.0032	0.3420	0.3415
	H	8-351 (5.8)	45	44	200 ⑩	④	0.0010–0.0027	0.0015–0.0032	0.3420	0.3415
	M	8-445 (7.3)	⑤	⑤	80 ⑥	⑦	0.0055	0.0055	0.3716–0.3723	0.3716–0.3723
	G	8-460 (7.5)	45	44	229 ⑧	1⁵¹/₆₄	0.0010–0.0027	0.0010–0.0027	0.3415–0.3423	0.3415–0.3423
1989–90	Y	6-300 (4.9)	45	44	175 ⑨	①	0.0010–0.0027	0.0010–0.0027	0.3420	0.3415
	N	8-302 (5.0)	45	44	②	③	0.0010–0.0027	0.0015–0.0032	0.3420	0.3415
	H	8-351 (5.8)	45	44	200 ⑩	4	0.0010–0.0027	0.0015–0.0032	0.3420	0.3415
	M	8-445 (7.3)	⑤	⑤	80 ⑥	⑦	0.0055	0.0055	0.3716–0.3723	0.3716–0.3723
	G	8-460 (7.5)	45	44	220 ⑧	1⁵¹/₆₄	0.0010–0.0027	0.0010–0.0027	0.3415–0.3423	0.3415–0.3423

① Intake 1.64
  Exhaust 1.47
② Intake 204 @ 1.36 in.
  Exhaust 200 @ 1.20 in.
③ Intake 1.68 in.
  Exhaust 1.59 in.
④ Intake 1.78 in.
  Exhaust 1.59 in.
⑤ Intake 30
  Exhaust 37.5
⑥ @ 1.83 Inches
⑦ Intake 1.767 and Exhaust 1.833
⑧ 1.33 In.
⑨ @ 1.24 in.
⑩ @ 1.20 in.
⑪ @ 1.79 in.

PISTON AND RING SPECIFICATIONS
All measurements are given in inches.

Year	VIN	No. Cylinder Displacement cu. in. (liter)	Piston Clearance	Ring Gap Top Compression	Ring Gap Bottom Compression	Ring Gap Oil Control	Ring Side Clearance Top Compression	Ring Side Clearance Bottom Compression	Ring Side Clearance Oil Control
1986	Y	6-300 (4.9)	0.0001–0.0018	0.0100–0.0200	0.0100–0.0200	0.0100–0.0350	0.0016–0.0037	0.0016–0.0037	SNUG
	N	8.302 (5.0)	0.0018–0.0026	0.0100–0.0200	0.0100–0.0200	0.0150–0.0350	0.0020–0.0040	0.0020–0.0040	SNUG
	H	8-351 (5.8)	0.0022–0.0030	0.0100–0.0200	0.0100–0.0200	0.0150–0.0350	0.0019–0.0036	0.0020–0.0040	SNUG
	I	8-420 (6.9)	0.0055–0.0075	0.0140–0.0240	0.0100–0.0240	0.0600–0.0700	0.0020–0.0040	0.0020–0.0040	0.0010–0.0030
	L	8-460 (7.5)	0.0014–0.0022	0.0100–0.0200	0.0100–0.0200	0.0150–0.0350	0.0019–0.0036	0.0020–0.0040	SNUG
1987	Y	6-300 (4.9)	0.0010–0.0018	0.0100–0.0200	0.0100–0.0200	0.0100–0.0350	0.0019–0.0036	0.0020–0.0040	SNUG
	N	8-302 (5.0)	0.0018–0.0026	0.0100–0.0200	0.0100–0.0200	0.0150–0.0350	0.0020–0.0040	0.0020–0.0040	SNUG
	H	8-351 (5.8)	0.0022–0.0030	0.0100–0.0200	0.0100–0.0200	0.0150–0.0350	0.0019–0.0036	0.0020–0.0040	SNUG
	I	8-420 (6.9)	0.0055–0.0075	0.0140–0.0240	0.0100–0.0240	0.0600–0.0700	0.0020–0.0040	0.0020–0.0040	0.0010–0.0030
	L	8-460 (7.5)	0.0014–0.0022	0.0100–0.0200	0.0100–0.0200	0.0150–0.0350	0.0019–0.0036	0.0020–0.0040	SNUG
1988	Y	6-300 (4.9)	0.0010–0.0018	0.0100–0.0200	0.0100–0.0200	0.0100–0.0350	0.0019–0.0036	0.0020–0.0040	SNUG
	N	8-302 (5.0)	0.0018–0.0026	0.0100–0.0200	0.0100–0.0200	0.0150–0.0350	0.0020–0.0040	0.0020–0.0040	SNUG
	H	8-351 (5.8)	0.0022–0.0030	0.0100–0.0200	0.0100–0.0200	0.0150–0.0350	0.0019–0.0036	0.0020–0.0040	SNUG
	M	8-445 (7.3)	0.0055–0.0085	0.0130–0.0450	0.0600–0.0850	NA	0.0020–0.0040	0.0020–0.0040	0.0010–0.0030
	G	8-460 (7.5)	0.0022–0.0030	0.0100–0.0200	0.0100–0.0200	0.0100–0.0350	0.0025–0.0045	0.0025–0.0045	SNUG
1989-90	Y	6-300 (4.9)	0.0010–0.0018	0.0100–0.0200	0.0100–0.0200	0.0150–0.0550	0.0019–0.0036	0.0020–0.0040	SNUG
	N	8-302 (5.0)	0.0013–0.0030	0.0100–0.0200	0.0100–0.0200	0.0150–0.0550	0.0013–0.0033	0.0020–0.0040	SNUG
	H	8-351 (5.8)	0.0018–0.0026	0.0100–0.0200	0.0100–0.0200	0.0150–0.0550	0.0013–0.0033	0.0020–0.0040	SNUG
	M	8-445 (7.3)	0.0055–0.0085	0.0130–0.0450	0.0600–0.0850	NA	0.0020–0.0040	0.0020–0.0040	0.0010–0.0030
	G	8-460 (7.5)	0.0022–0.0030	0.0100–0.0200	0.0100–0.0200	0.0100–0.0350	0.0025–0.0045	0.0025–0.0045	SNUG

TORQUE SPECIFICATIONS

All readings in ft. lbs.

Year	VIN	No. Cylinder Displacement cu. in. (liter)	Cylinder Head Bolts	Main Bearing Bolts	Rod Bearing Bolts	Crankshaft Pulley Bolts	Flywheel Bolts	Manifold Intake	Manifold Exhaust	Spark Plugs
1986	Y	6-300 (4.9)	85 ①	60–70	40–45	130–150	75–85	22–32	22–32	10–15
	N	8-302 (5.0)	65–72 ②	60–70	19–24	70–90	75–85	23–25	18–24	10–15
	H	8-351 (5.8)	105–112 ③	95–105	40–45	70–90	75–85	23–25	18–24	10–15
	I	8-420 (6.9)	④	⑤	⑥	90	47	24	35	—
	L	8-460 (7.5)	⑦	95–105	45–50	70–90	75–85	22–32	28–33	5–10
1987	Y	6-300 (4.9)	85 ①	60–70	40–45	130–150	75–85	22–32	22–32	10–15
	N	8-302 (5.0)	65–72 ②	60–70	19–24	70–90	75–85	23–25	18–24	10–15
	H	8-351 (5.8)	105–112 ③	95–105	40–45	70–90	75–85	23–25	18–24	10–15
	I	8-420 (6.9)	④	⑤	⑥	90	47	24	35	—
	L	8-460 (7.5)	⑦	95–105	45–50	70–90	75–85	22–32	28–33	5–10
1988	Y	6-300 (4.9)	85 ①	60–70	40–45	130–150	75–85	22–32	22–32	10–15
	N	8-302 (5.0)	65–72 ②	60–70	19–24	70–90	75–85	23–25	18–24	10–15
	H	8-351 (5.8)	105–112 ③	95–105	40–45	70–90	75–85	23–25	18–24	10–15
	M	8-445 (7.3)	⑧	⑤	⑥	90	47	24	35	—
	G	8-460 (7.5)	⑦	95–105	45–50	70–90	75–85	22–35	22–30	5–10
1989–90	Y	6-300 (4.9)	85 ①	60–70	40–45	130–150	75–85	22–32	22–32	10–15
	N	8-302 (5.0)	65–72 ②	60–70	19–24	70–90	75–85	23–25	18–24	10–15
	H	8-351 (5.8)	105–112 ③	95–105	40–45	70–90	75–85	23–25	18–24	10–15
	M	8-445 (7.3)	⑧	⑤	⑥	90	47	24	35	—
	G	8-460 (7.5)	⑦	95–105	45–50	70–90	75–85	22–35	22–30	5–10

① Torque in 3 steps 55 ft. lbs., 60 ft. lbs. and 85 ft. lbs.
② Torque in 2 steps 55–65 ft. lbs. and 65–72 ft. lbs.
③ Torque in 3 steps 85, 95 ft. lbs. and 105–112 ft. lbs.
④ Torque to 40 ft. lbs. then 70 ft. lbs. and then to 80 ft. lbs. then torque to 80 ft. lbs. again in sequence
⑤ Torque in 2 steps 75 ft. lbs. then 95 ft. lbs.
⑥ Torque in 2 steps 38 ft. lbs. then to 49–54 ft. lbs.
⑦ Torque in 3 steps 80–90 ft. lbs., 100–110 ft. lbs. then to 130–140 ft. lbs.
⑧ Torque 65 ft. lbs. then to 90 ft. lbs. then 100 ft. lbs.

BRAKE SPECIFICATIONS

All measurements in inches unless noted

Year	Model	Lug Nut Torque (ft. lbs.)	Master Cylinder Bore	Brake Disc Minimum Thickness	Brake Disc Maximum Runout	Standard Brake Drum Diameter	Minimum Lining Thickness Front	Minimum Lining Thickness Rear
1986	Bronco	90–100	NA	1.120	0.003	11.03	.030	.030
	Bronco	90–100	NA	1.120	0.003	11.03	.030	.030
	Bronco	90–100	NA	1.120	0.003	11.03	.030	.030
	E-150	90–100	NA	1.120	0.003	11.03	.030	.030
	E-150	90–100	NA	1.120	0.003	11.03	.030	.030
	E-150	90–100	NA	1.120	0.003	11.03	.030	.030
	E-250	140	NA	1.180	0.003	12.00	.030	.030
	E-250	140	NA	1.180	0.003	12.00	.030	.030
	E-250	140	NA	1.180	0.003	12.00	.030	.030

BRAKE SPECIFICATIONS
All measurements in inches unless noted

Year	Model	Lug Nut Torque (ft. lbs.)	Master Cylinder Bore	Brake Disc Minimum Thickness	Brake Disc Maximum Runout	Standard Brake Drum Diameter	Minimum Lining Thickness Front	Minimum Lining Thickness Rear
1986	E-250	140	NA	1.180	0.003	12.00	.030	.030
	E-250	140	NA	1.180	0.003	12.00	.030	.030
	E-350	140	NA	1.180	0.003	12.00	.030	.030
	E-350	140	NA	1.180	0.003	12.00	.030	.030
	E-350	140	NA	1.180	0.003	12.00	.030	.030
	E-350	140	NA	1.180	0.003	12.00	.030	.030
	F-150	90–100	NA	1.120	0.003	11.03	.030	.030
	F-150	90–100	NA	1.120	0.003	11.03	.030	.030
	F-150	90–100	NA	1.120	0.003	11.03	.030	.030
	F-250	140	NA	1.120	0.003	12.00	.030	.030
	F-250	140	NA	1.180	0.003 ①	12.00	.030	.030
	F-250	140	NA	1.180	0.003 ①	12.00	.030	.030
	F-250	140	NA	1.180	0.003 ①	12.00	.030	.030
	F-250	140	NA	1.180	0.003 ①	12.00	.030	.030
	F-350	140	NA	1.180	0.003 ①	12.00	.030	.030
	F-350	140	NA	1.180	0.003 ①	12.00	.030	.030
	F-350	140	NA	1.180	0.003 ①	12.00	.030	.030
	F-350	140	NA	1.180	0.003 ①	12.00	.030	.030
1987	Bronco	90–100	NA	1.120	0.003 ①	11.03	.030	.030
	Bronco	90–100	NA	1.120	0.003	11.03	.030	.030
	Bronco	90–100	NA	1.120	0.003	11.03	.030	.030
	E-150	90–100	NA	1.120	0.003	11.03	.030	.030
	E-150	90–100	NA	1.120	0.003	11.03	.030	.030
	E-150	90–100	NA	1.120	0.003	11.03	.030	.030
	E-250	140	NA	1.180	0.003	12.00	.030	.030
	E-250	140	NA	1.180	0.003	12.00	.030	.030
	E-250	140	NA	1.180	0.003	12.00	.030	.030
	E-250	140	NA	1.180	0.003	12.00	.030	.030
	E-250	140	NA	1.180	0.003	12.00	.030	.030
	E-350	140	NA	1.180	0.003	12.00	.030	.030
	E-350	140	NA	1.180	0.003	12.00	.030	.030
	E-350	140	NA	1.180	0.003	12.00	.030	.030
	E-350	140	NA	1.180	0.003	12.00	.030	.030
	F-150	90–100	NA	1.120	0.003	11.03	.030	.030
	F-150	90–100	NA	1.120	0.003	11.03	.030	.030
	F-150	90–100	NA	1.120	0.003	11.03	.030	.030
	F-250	140	NA	1.180	0.003 ①	12.00	.030	.030
	F-250	140	NA	1.180	0.003 ①	12.00	.030	.030
	F-250	140	NA	1.180	0.003 ①	12.00	.030	.030
	F-250	140	NA	1.180	0.003 ①	12.00	.030	.030
	F-250	140	NA	1.180	0.003 ①	12.00	.030	.030
	F-350	140	NA	1.180	0.003 ①	12.00	.030	.030

BRAKE SPECIFICATIONS
All measurements in inches unless noted

Year	Model	Lug Nut Torque (ft. lbs.)	Master Cylinder Bore	Brake Disc Minimum Thickness	Brake Disc Maximum Runout	Standard Brake Drum Diameter	Minimum Lining Thickness Front	Minimum Lining Thickness Rear
1987	F-350	140	NA	1.180	0.003 ①	12.00	.030	.030
	F-350	140	NA	1.180	0.003 ①	12.00	.030	.030
	F-350	140	NA	1.180	0.003 ①	12.00	.030	.030
1988	Bronco	90–100	NA	1.120	0.003	11.03	.030	.030
	Bronco	90–100	NA	1.120	0.003	11.03	.030	.030
	Bronco	90–100	NA	1.120	0.003	11.03	.030	.030
	E-150	90–100	NA	1.120	0.003	11.03	.030	.030
	E-150	90–100	NA	1.120	0.003	11.03	.030	.030
	E-150	90–100	NA	1.120	0.003	11.03	.030	.030
	E-250	140	NA	1.180	0.003	12.00	.030	.030
	E-250	140	NA	1.180	0.003	12.00	.030	.030
	E-250	140	NA	1.180	0.003	12.00	.030	.030
	E-250	140	NA	1.180	0.003	12.00	.030	.030
	E-250	140	NA	1.180	0.003	12.00	.030	.030
	E-350	140	NA	1.180	0.003	12.00	.030	.030
	E-350	140	NA	1.180	0.003	12.00	.030	.030
	E-350	140	NA	1.180	0.003	12.00	.030	.030
	E-350	140	NA	1.180	0.003	12.00	.030	.030
	F-150	90–100	NA	1.120	0.003	12.00	.030	.030
	F-150	90–100	NA	1.120	0.003	12.00	.030	.030
	F-150	90–100	NA	1.120	0.003	12.00	.030	.030
	F-250	140	NA	1.180	0.003 ①	12.00	.030	.030
	F-250	140	NA	1.180	0.003 ①	12.00	.030	.030
	F-250	140	NA	1.180	0.003 ①	12.00	.030	.030
	F-250	140	NA	1.180	0.003 ①	12.00	.030	.030
	F-250	140	NA	1.180	0.003 ①	12.00	.030	.030
	F-350	140	NA	1.180	0.003 ①	12.00	.030	.030
	F-350	140	NA	1.180	0.003 ①	12.00	.030	.030
	F-350	140	NA	1.180	0.003 ①	12.00	.030	.030
	F-350	140	NA	1.180	0.003 ①	12.00	.030	.030
1989–90	Bronco	90–100	NA	1.120	0.003	11.03	.030	.030
	Bronco	90–100	NA	1.120	0.003	11.03	.030	.030
	Bronco	90–100	NA	1.120	0.003	11.03	.030	.030
	E-150	90–100	NA	1.120	0.003	11.03	.030	.030
	E-150	90–100	NA	1.120	0.003	11.03	.030	.030
	E-150	90–100	NA	1.120	0.003	11.03	.030	.030
	E-250	140	NA	1.180	0.003	12.00	.030	.030
	E-250	140	NA	1.180	0.003	12.00	.030	.030
	E-250	140	NA	1.180	0.003	12.00	.030	.030
	E-250	140	NA	1.180	0.003	12.00	.030	.030
	E-250	140	NA	1.180	0.003	12.00	.030	.030
	E-350	140	NA	1.180	0.003	12.00	.030	.030

BRAKE SPECIFICATIONS
All measurements in inches unless noted

Year	Model	Lug Nut Torque (ft. lbs.)	Master Cylinder Bore	Brake Disc Minimum Thickness	Brake Disc Maximum Runout	Standard Brake Drum Diameter	Minimum Lining Thickness Front	Minimum Lining Thickness Rear
1989–90	E-350	140	NA	1.180	0.003	12.00	.030	.030
	E-350	140	NA	1.180	0.003	12.00	.030	.030
	E-350	140	NA	1.180	0.003	12.00	.030	.030
	F-150	90–100	NA	1.120	0.003	11.03	.030	.030
	F-150	90–100	NA	1.120	0.003	11.03	.030	.030
	F-150	90–100	NA	1.120	0.003	11.03	.030	.030
	F-250	140	NA	1.180	0.003 ①	12.00	.030	.030
	F-250	140	NA	1.180	0.003 ①	12.00	.030	.030
	F-250	140	NA	1.180	0.003 ①	12.00	.030	.030
	F-250	140	NA	1.180	0.003 ①	12.00	.030	.030
	F-250	140	NA	1.180	0.003 ①	12.00	.030	.030
	F-350	140	NA	1.180	0.003 ①	12.00	.030	.030
	F-350	140	NA	1.180	0.003 ①	12.00	.030	.030
	F-350	140	NA	1.180	0.003 ①	12.00	.030	.030
	F-350	140	NA	1.180	0.003 ①	12.00	.030	.030

① 4WD vehicles

WHEEL ALIGNMENT

Year	Model	Caster Range (deg.)	Caster Preferred Setting (deg.)	Camber Range (deg.)	Camber Preferred Setting (deg.)	Toe-in (in.)	Steering Axis Inclination (deg.)
1986	Bronco	①	①	①	①	1/32	NA
	E-150	⑤	⑤	⑤	⑤	1/32	NA
	E-250	⑦	⑦	⑦	⑦	1/32	NA
	E-350	⑦	⑦	⑦	⑦	1/32	NA
	F-150	①③	①③	①③	①③	1/32	NA
	F-250	⑨⑩	⑨⑩	⑨⑩	⑨⑩	1/32 ⑪	NA
	F-350	⑨⑩	⑨⑩	⑨⑩	⑨⑩	1/32 ⑪	NA
1987	Bronco	①	①	①	①	1/32	NA
	E-150	⑤	⑤	⑤	⑤	1/32	NA
	E-250	⑦	⑦	⑦	⑦	1/32	NA
	E-350	⑦	⑦	⑦	⑦	1/32	NA
	F-150	①③	①③	①③	①③	1/32	NA
	F-250	⑨⑩	⑨⑩	⑨⑩	⑨⑩	1/32 ⑪	NA
	F-350	⑨⑩	⑨⑩	⑨⑩	⑨⑩	1/32 ⑪	NA
1988	Bronco	①	①	①	①	1/32	NA
	E-150	⑤	⑤	⑤	⑤	1/32	NA
	E-250	⑦	⑦	⑦	⑦	1/32	NA
	E-350	⑦	⑦	⑦	⑦	1/32	NA
	F-150	①③	①③	①③	①③	1/32	NA
	F-250	⑨⑩	⑨⑩	⑨⑩	⑨⑩	1/32 ⑪	NA
	F-350	⑨⑩	⑨⑩	⑨⑩	⑨⑩	1/32 ⑪	NA
1988–89	Bronco	②	②	②	②	1/32	NA
	E-150	⑥	⑥	⑥	⑥	1/32	NA

WHEEL ALIGNMENT

Year	Model	Caster Range (deg.)	Caster Preferred Setting (deg.)	Camber Range (deg.)	Camber Preferred Setting (deg.)	Toe-in (in.)	Steering Axis Inclination (deg.)
1989–90	E-250	⑧	⑧	⑧	⑧	1/32	NA
	E-350	⑧	⑧	⑧	⑧	1/32	NA
	F-150	②④	②④	②④	②④	1/32	NA
	F-250	⑨⑩	⑨⑩	⑨⑩	⑨⑩	1/32 ⑪	NA
	F-350	⑨⑩	⑨⑩	⑨⑩	⑨⑩	1/32 ⑪	NA

① 4WD
Ride Height: 3¼–3½ Caster 6–8   Camber − 1¾ to − ¼
Ride Height: 3½–3¾ Caster 5–7   Camber − ¾ to ¾
Ride Height: 4–4¼   Caster 4–6   Camber ¼ to 1¾
Ride Height: 4¼–4½ Caster 3–5   Camber 1¼ to 2¾

② 4WD
Ride Height: 3¼–3½ Caster 5⅛–7¾ Camber − 1⅝ to 1
Ride Height: 3½–3¾ Caster 4½–7⅛ Camber − 1 to 1½
Ride Height: 3¼–6½ Caster 3¼–6½ Camber 0 to 2¾
Ride Height: 4¼–4½ Caster 2½–5¼ Camber ¾ to 3½

③ 2WD
Ride Height: 3¼–3½ Caster 5–7   Camber − ¾ to ¾
Ride Height: 3½–4   Caster 4–6   Camber − ¼ to 1¼
Ride Height: 4–4¼   Caster 3¼–5¼ Camber ½ to 2
Ride Height: 4¼–4¾ Caster 2½–4½ Camber 2 to 3½
Ride Height: 4¾–5   Caster 1½–3½ Camber 3 to 4½

④ 2WD
Ride Height: 3¾–4   Caster 5¾–8¼ Camber − 1⅝ to 1
Ride Height: 4–4¼   Caster 4¾–7¾ Camber − 1 to 1½
Ride Height: 4¼–4½ Caster 5–7½   Camber 0 to 2½
Ride Height: 4½–4¾ Caster 4½–7   Camber ½ to 3
Ride Height: 4¾–5   Caster 4–6½   Camber 1 to 3½
Ride Height: 5–5¼   Caster 3½–6   Camber 1½ to 4

⑨ 4WD
Ride Height: 5–5¼   Caster 3–5   Camber − 1¾ to − ¼
Ride Height: 5½–5¾ Caster 3⅛–5⅛ Camber − ¾ to ¾
Ride Height: 6–6¼   Caster 3¼–5¼ Camber ½ to 2
Ride Height: 6¼–6½ Caster 3⅜–5⅜ Camber 1½ to 3

Ride Height: 4¼–4½ Caster 4–6¾   Camber − ½ to 2
Ride Height: 4½–4¾ Caster 3½–6   Camber 0 to 2¾
Ride Height: 4¾–5   Caster 2¾–4½ Camber ¾ to 3½
⑤ Ride Height: 4–4½ Caster 7½–9½ Camber − 1¼ to ¼
Ride Height: 4½–5   Caster 6¼–8¼ Camber − ⅛ to 1¼
Ride Height: 5–5½   Caster 5–7   Camber ⅞ to 2¼
Ride Height: 5½–5¾ Caster 3¼–5¼ Camber 1¾ to 3¼
⑥ Ride Height: 3½–3¾ Caster 7–9½ Camber − 2 to ½
Ride Height: 3¾–4   Caster 6½–9   Camber − 1½ to 1
Ride Height: 4–4¼   Caster 6–8½   Camber − 1 to 1½
Ride Height: 4¼–4½ Caster 5½–8   Camber − ½ to 2
Ride Height: 4½–4¾ Caster 5–7½   Camber 0 to 2½
Ride Height: 5–5¼   Caster 4–6½   Camber 1½ to 4
⑦ Ride Height: 3¾–4 Caster 7⅝–9⅝ Camber − ¾ to ½
Ride Height: 4¼–4½ Caster 6¼–8¼ Camber ¼ to 1½
Ride Height: 4¾–5   Caster 5 −7   Camber 1¼ to 2½
Ride Height: 5¼–5½ Caster 3¾–5¾ Camber 2¼ to 3½
⑧ Ride Height: 3¾–4 Caster 6–8½   Camber − 1 to 1½
Ride Height: 4–4¼   Caster 5½–8   Camber − ½ to 2
Ride Height: 6¾–7   Caster 3½–5½ Camber 2½ to 4
⑩ 2WD
Ride Height: 5¾–7¾ Caster 5¾–7¾ Camber − 1 to 1
Ride Height: 3¾–4   Caster 4½–6½ Camber ¼ to 1¾
Ride Height: 4¼–4½ Caster 3¼–5¼ Camber 1½ to 3
Ride Height: 4¾–5   Caster 2¼–4¼ Camber 2½ to 4
Ride Height: 5¼–5¾ Caster 1–3   Camber 3¾ to 5¼
⑪ 2WD
Models toe-in ³/₃₂ inch

ENGINE ELECTRICAL

NOTE: Disconnecting the negative battery cable on some vehicles may interfere with the functions of the on board computer systems and may require the computer to undergo a relearning process, once the negative battery cable is reconnected.

Distributor

Removal and Installation

DURASPARK II SYSTEM

1. Disconnect the negative battery cable. Remove the distributor cap and position the cap and ignition wires to the side.
2. Disconnect and plug the vacuum hose(s) from the vacuum diaphragm assembly.
3. Disconnect the wire harness plug from the distributor connector.
4. Rotate the engine to align the stator pole and armature pole.
5. Scribe a mark on the distributor body and engine block to indicate the position of the rotor tip and position of the distributor in the engine.
6. Remove the holddown bolt and clamp located at the base of the distributor.
7. Remove the distributor from the engine. Do not rotate the engine while the distributor is removed.

To install:

8. Position the distributor in the engine with the rotor aligned to the marks made on the distributor, or to the place the rotor pointed when the distributor was removed.

9. Install the mounting bolt and clamp, but do not tighten so the distributor can be turned for ignition timing purposes.

10. If the engine was rotated while the distributor was removed, rotate the engine (in normal direction of rotation) until No. 1 piston is on TDC (Top Dead Center) of the compression stroke. The TDC mark on the crankshaft pulley and the pointer should align. Rotor tip pointing at No. 1 spark plug wire position on distributor cap upon installation.

11. Engage the oil pump intermediate shaft and insert the distributor until fully seated on the engine, if the distributor does not fully seat, turn the engine slightly to fully engage the intermediate shaft.

NOTE: The oil pump intermediate shaft may be turned with a tool to align the shaft with the distributor.

12. Rotate the distributor in block if necessary to align armature and stator assembly poles. Install the distributor holddown bolt but do not fully tighten.

13. Check that No. 1 piston is on compression stroke and timing marks and rotor are aligned in the correct position.

14. Connect distributor to wiring harness connection.

15. Install the distributor cap and wires in the correct position.

16. Set the initial timing to specifications as shown on the Vehicle Emission Control Information Decal.

17. Tighten the distributor holddown bolt to 17–25 ft. lbs. Recheck the inital timing and readjust if necessary. Connect the diaphragm assembly hose(s).

TFI-IV SYSTEM (THICK FILM INTEGRATED)

1. Disconnect the negative battery cable. Disconnect the primary wiring connector from the distributor.

2. Remove the distributor cap and adapter and position it and the attached wires out of the way.

NOTE: Before removing the distributor cap, mark the position of the No. 1 wire tower on the distributor base for installation purposes.

3. Remove the rotor. Remove the TFI connector.

4. Remove the distributor holddown bolt (some engines may be equipped with security-type holddown bolt) and clamp.

5. Avoid turning the engine, if possible, while the distributor is removed. If the engine is turned from TDC position, TDC timing marks will have to be reset.

To install:

6. Rotate the distributor in the engine block to align the leading edge of the vane and the vane switch (vane should be centered in the vane switch stator assembly).

7. Check that No. 1 piston is on compression stroke and timing marks and rotor (rotor tip pointing at No. 1 spark plug wire position on distributor cap) are aligned in the correct position.

8. After the distributor has been fully seated on the block, install the hold down bracket and bolt. Do not fully tighten at this time.

9. Connect the distributor TFI and primary wiring harnesses.

10. Install the distributor rotor and cap adapter. Tighten the attaching screws to 2.1–2.9 ft. lbs.

11. Install the distributor cap and wires in the correct position.

12. Set the initial timing to specifications as shown on the Vehicle Emission Control Information Decal.

13. Tighten the distributor holddown bolt to 17–25 ft. lbs. Recheck the inital timing and readjust if necessary.

Ignition Timing

Adjustment

The procedure below is for setting inital timing only. This procedure is to be used under normal circumstances. If problems are

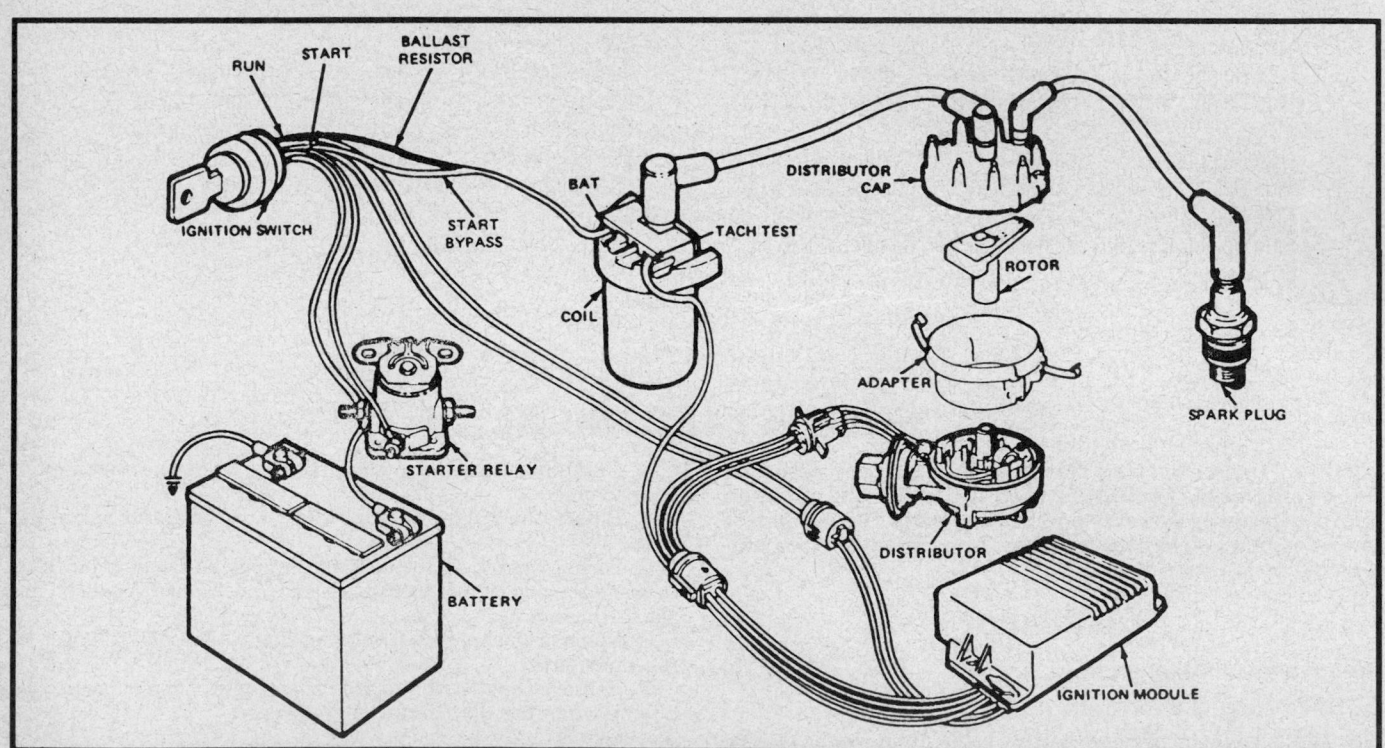

Duraspark II Ignition system

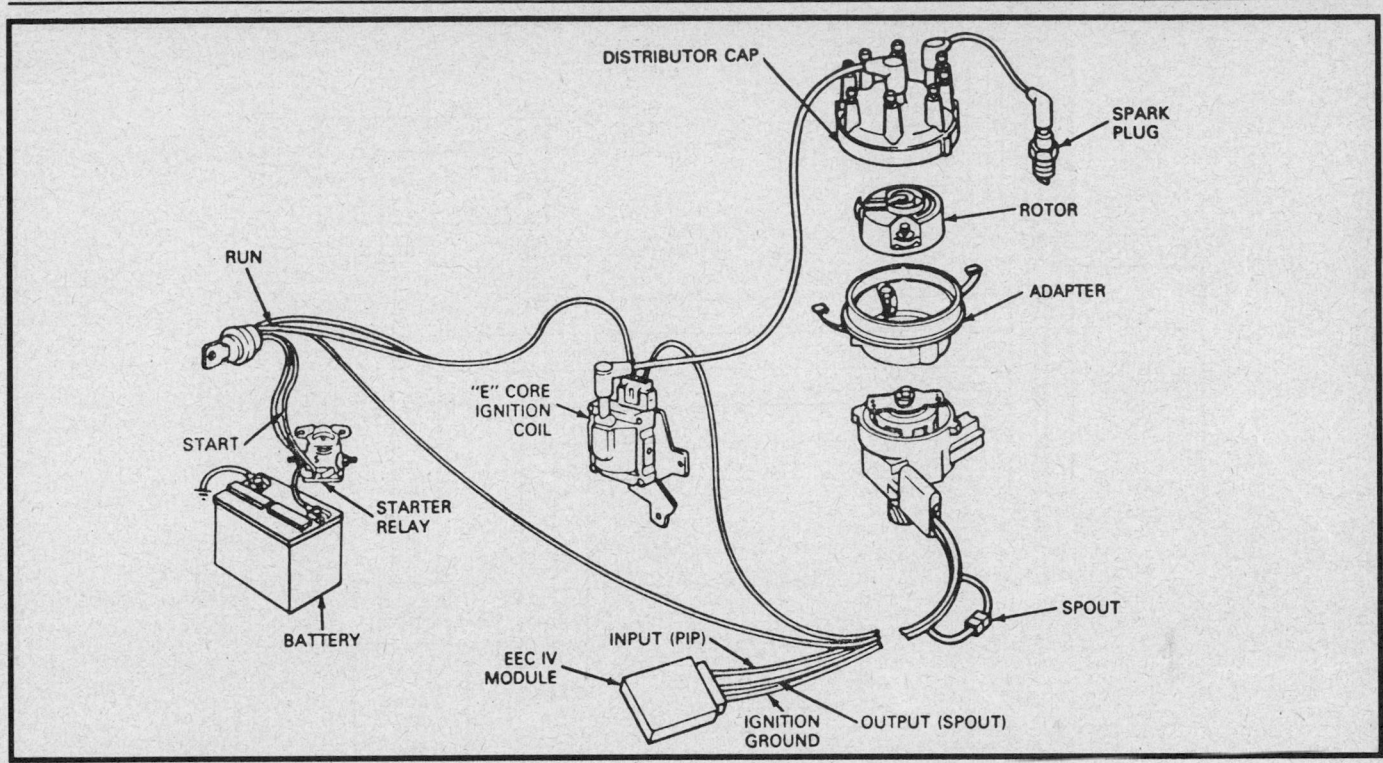

Thick film integrated (TFI) ignition system with universal distributor

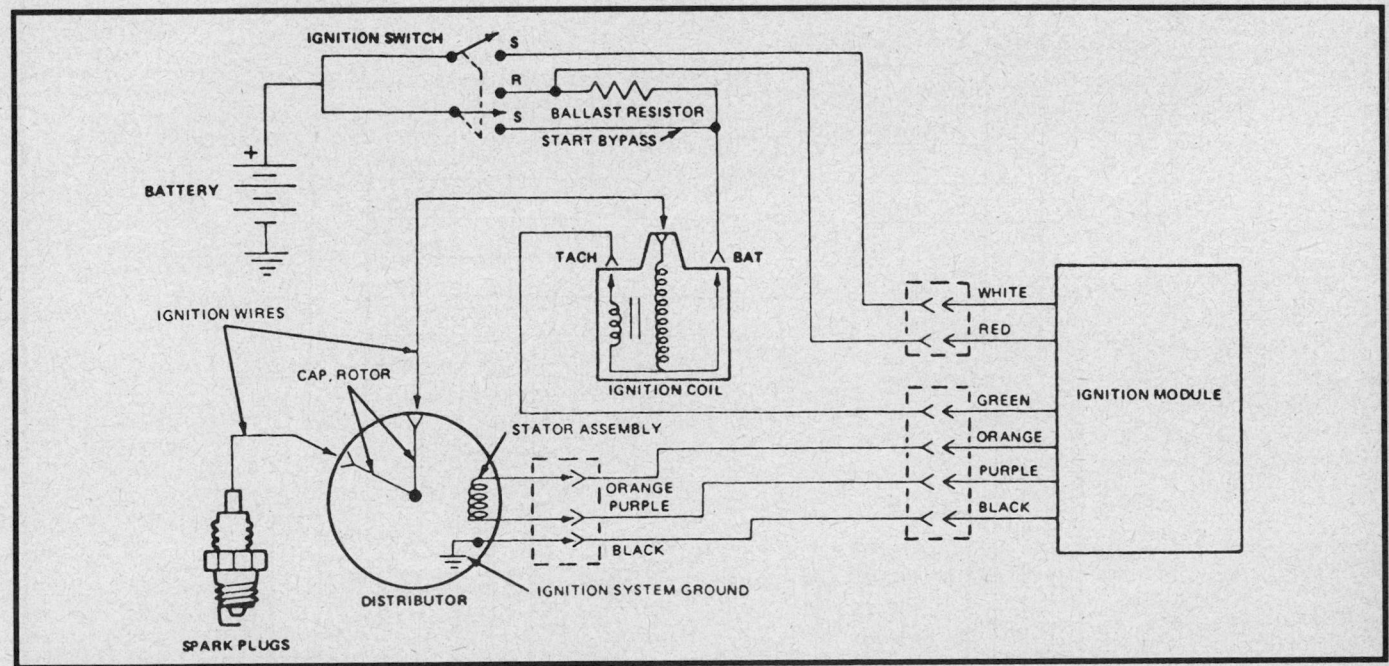

Typical schematic or Duraspark II ignition system

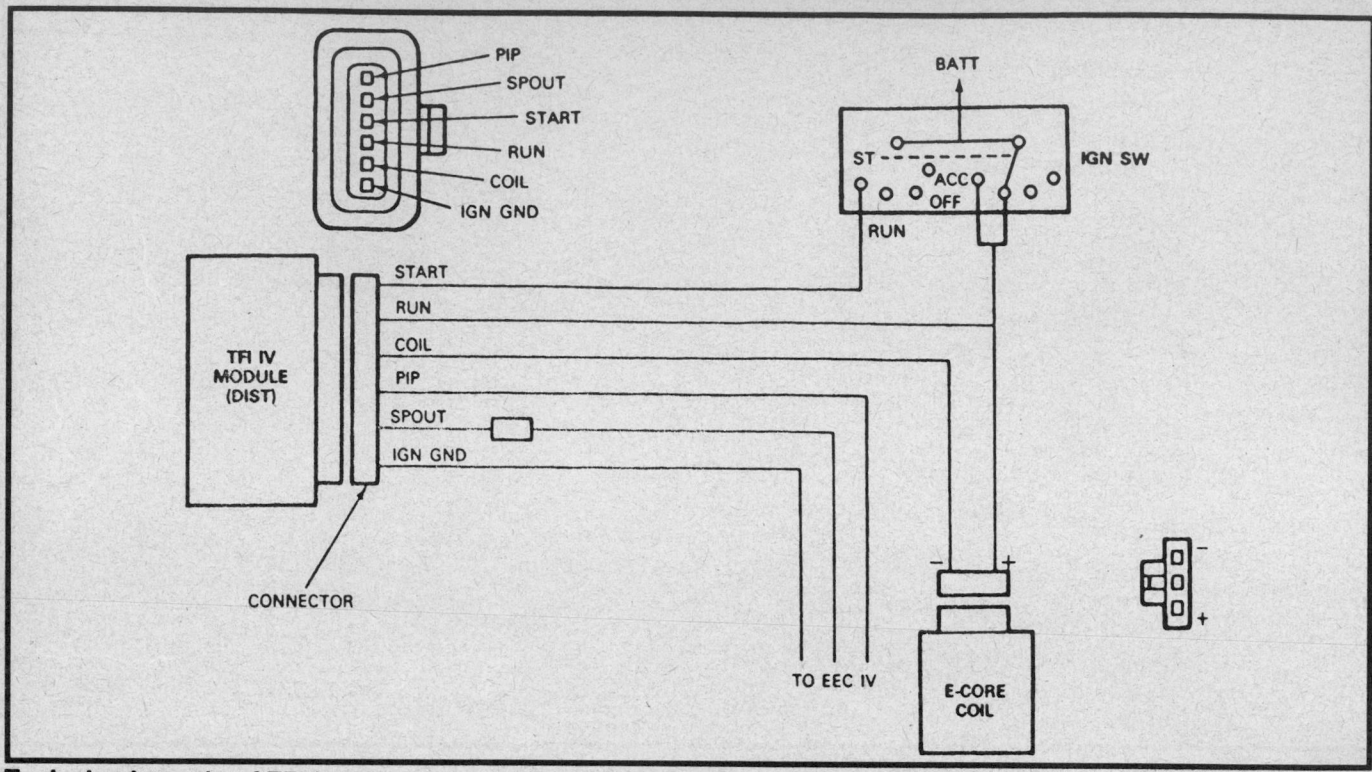

Typical schematic of TFI ignition system with universal distributor

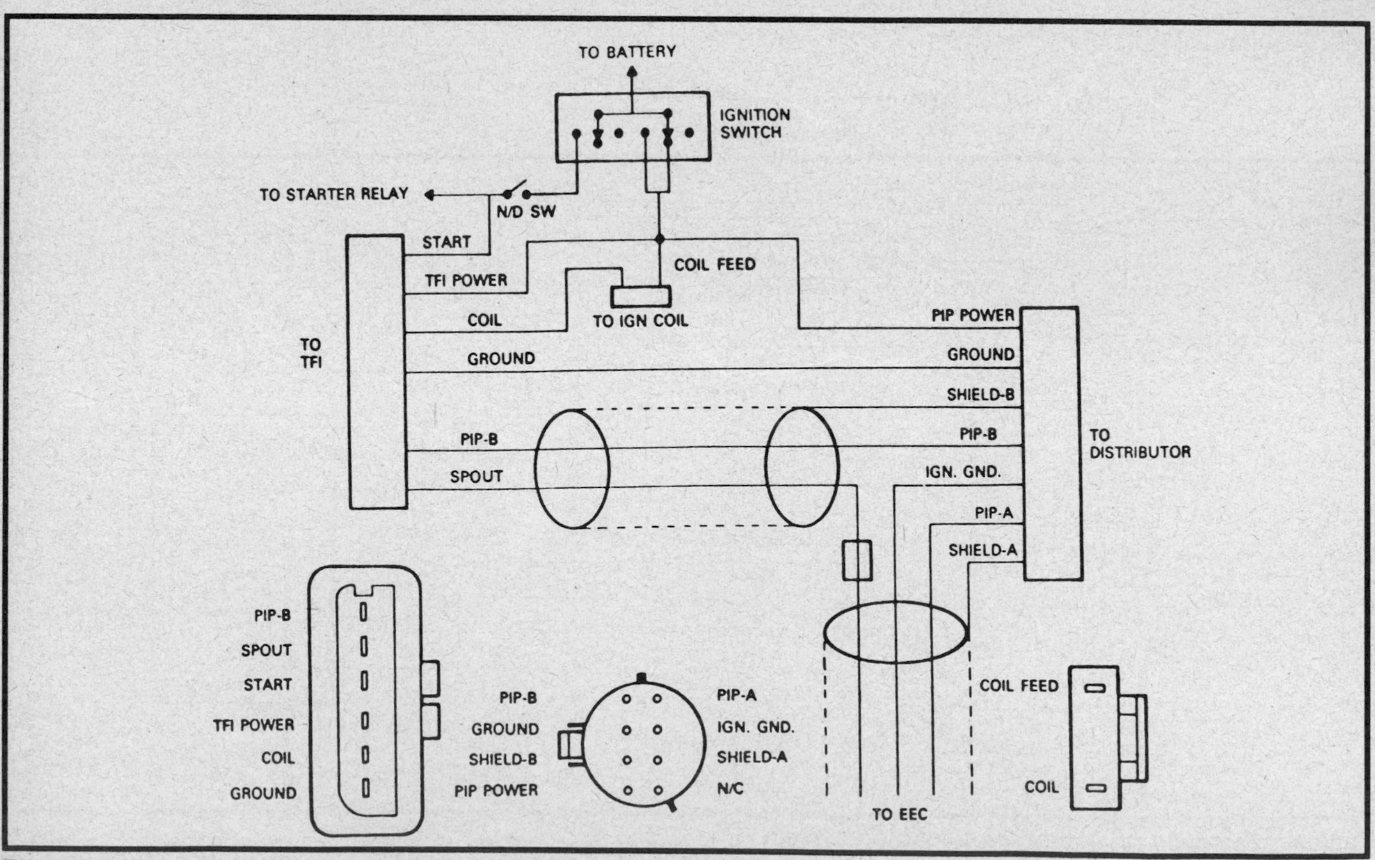

Typical schematic of TFI system with closed bowl distributor

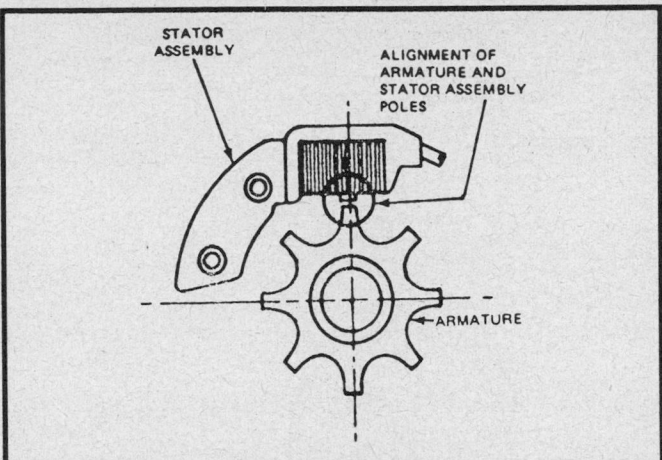

Armature/stator assembly alignment

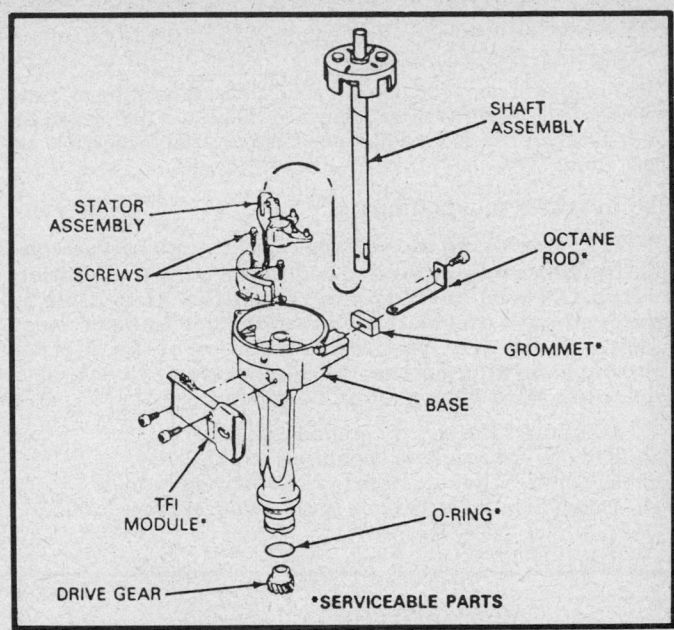

Exploded view universal distributor

encountered setting inital timing using this procedure than further diagnosis is necessary.

1. Place the transmission in **P** or **N**. Turn the air conditioner and heater to the **OFF** position.

2. Remove the vacuum hoses from the distributor vacuum advance connection at the distributor and plug the hoses on Non-EEC systems.

3. Connect inductive timing light and tachometer (Non-EEC systems).

4. Disconnect the single wire in-line spout connector (near the distributor) or remove the shorting bar from the double spout connector on EEC-IV systems.

5. If the vehicle is equipped on Non-EEC systems with a barometric pressure switch disconnect it from the ignition module. Install a jumper wire across the pins at the ignition module connector (yellow and black wires).

6. Start the engine and allow it to reach normal operating temperture.

7. With the engine at the timing rpm if specified, check inital timimg.

Alternator

Belt Tension Adjustment

MANUALLY TENSIONED BELT

1. Loosen alternator adjustment and pivot bolts.

2. Pry on alternator housing using a suitable tool to attain correct belt tension. Use caution not to damage alternator housing.

3. Tighten adjustment bolt and release pressure on tool.

4. Tighten pivot bolt and check belt tension.

5. The belt tension measurement specifications are if belt span is less than 12 inches the deflection should be ⅛–¼ in. If belt span is more than 12 inches the deflection should be ⅛–⅜ in.

AUTOMATICALLY TENSIONED BELT

The automatic belt tensioner will maintain correct belt tension if the correct length belt is used on the engine. To verfiy that the tensioner is working properly check to see that the belt length indicator mark on the tensioner is between the maximum and minimum marks. The belt tensioner has no provision for adjustment and will be damaged if forced to travel beyond the normal operating range.

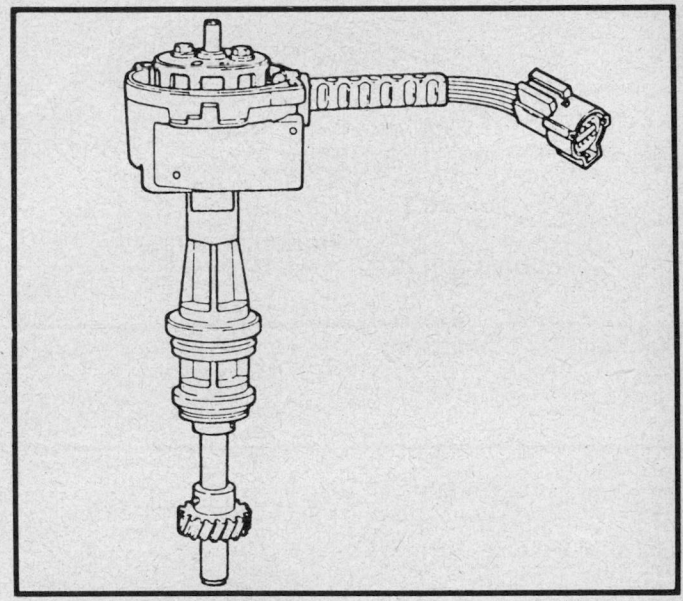

Closed bowl distributor

Removal and Installation

1. Disconnect battery ground cable(s).

2. Remove all electrical connectors from the alternator.

3. Loosen the alternator mounting bolts and remove the adjustment arm to alternator attaching bolt.

4. Disengage the alternator belt.

5. Remove the alternator mounting bolt and alternator. Remove the alternator fan shield if so equipped.

6. Installation is the reverse of the removal procedure.

Voltage Regulator

For further information, please refer to "Electrical" in the Unit Repair section.

Adjustment

EXTERNAL REGULATOR

These regulators are 100 percent solid state, consisting of transistors, diodes and resistors. They are calibrated and preset by the manufacturer. No readjustment is required or possible on these units.

Removal and Installation

NOTE: Removing the voltage regulator electrical connector from an ungrounded regulator with the ignition switch ON will destroy the regulator. If vehicle is equipped with an electric choke, be sure to disconnect electric choke wire from stator terminal of the alternator when working on the charging system. Check electric choke wire for a ground condition.

1. Disconnect the battery ground cable(s).
2. Remove the regulator mounting screws.
3. Disconnect the regulator from the wiring harness.
4. Installation is the reverse of the removal procedure.

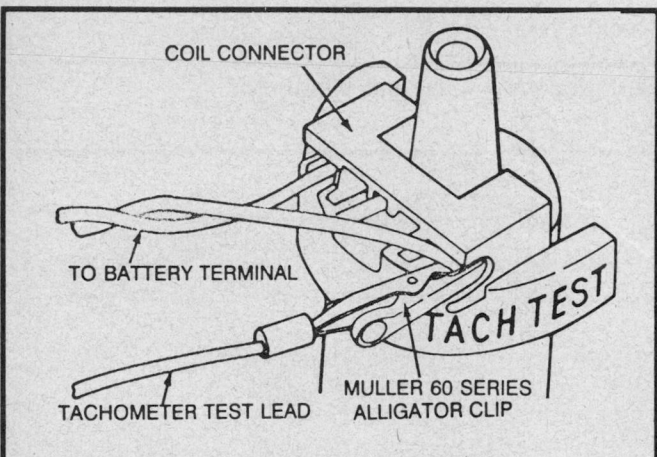

Tachometer connection

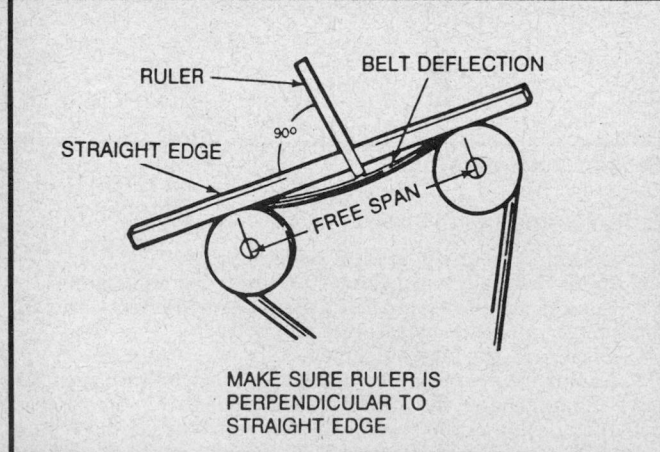

Manual belt deflection method

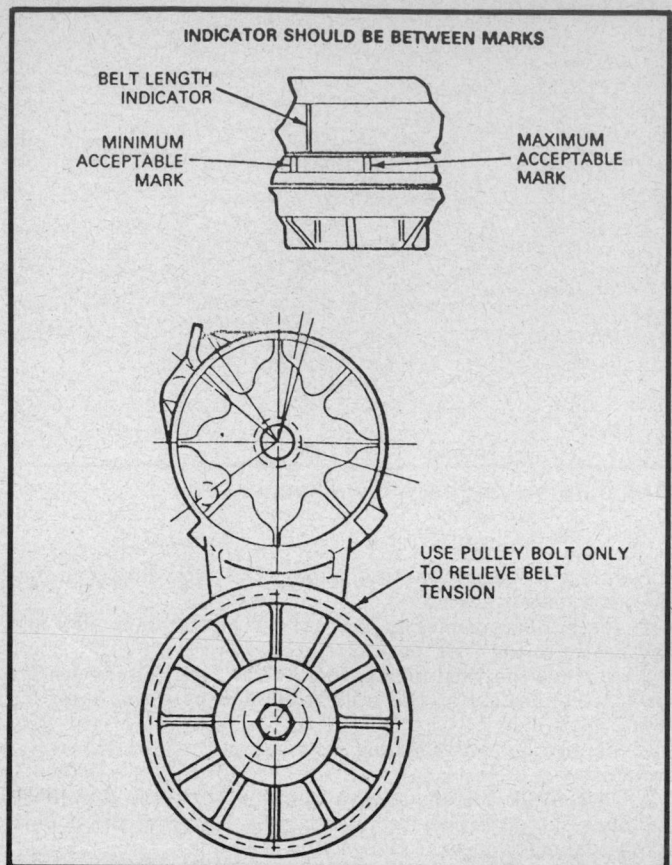

Typical automatic belt tensioner

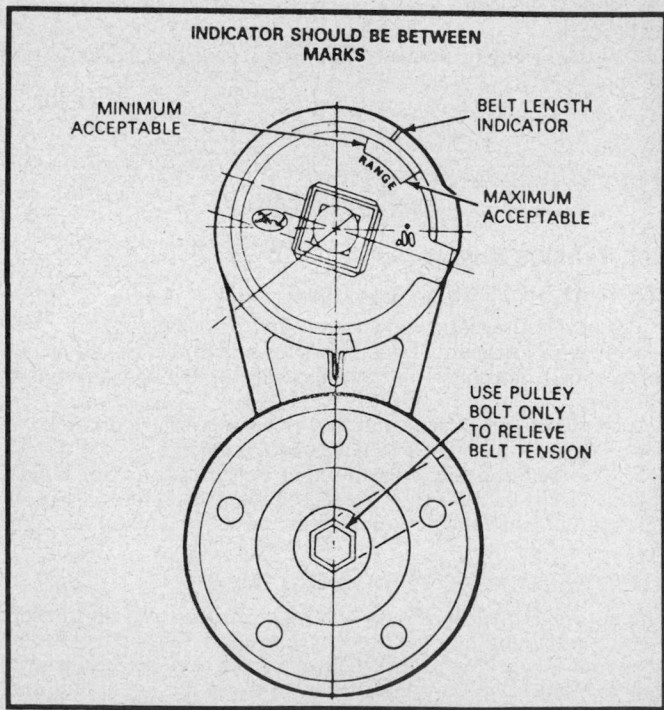

Typical automatic belt tensioner

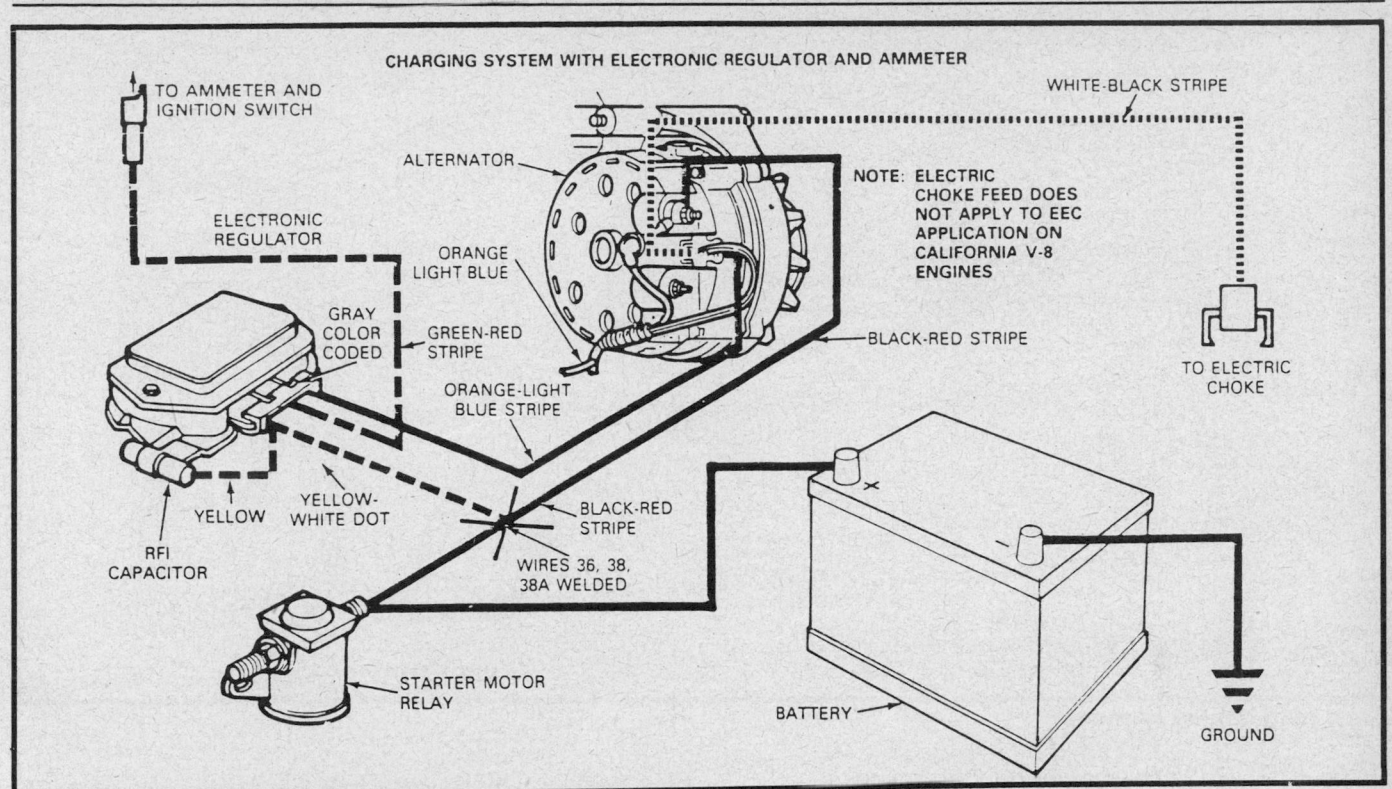

CHARGING SYSTEM WITH ELECTRONIC REGULATOR AND AMMETER

TO AMMETER AND IGNITION SWITCH

WHITE-BLACK STRIPE

ALTERNATOR

NOTE: ELECTRIC CHOKE FEED DOES NOT APPLY TO EEC APPLICATION ON CALIFORNIA V-8 ENGINES

ELECTRONIC REGULATOR

ORANGE LIGHT BLUE

GREEN-RED STRIPE

GRAY COLOR CODED

ORANGE-LIGHT BLUE STRIPE

BLACK-RED STRIPE

TO ELECTRIC CHOKE

YELLOW

YELLOW-WHITE DOT

BLACK-RED STRIPE

WIRES 36, 38, 38A WELDED

RFI CAPACITOR

STARTER MOTOR RELAY

BATTERY

GROUND

Charging system with electronic regulator and ammeter

COVER

COVER SCREW

GASKET

LEVER ASSEMBLY

SPRING

STARTING MOTOR CONTACT POINT ASSEMBLY

PIN

STARTER FRAME

SCREW POLE PIECE

DRIVE END HOUSING

GROMMET

SEAL

SPRING BRUSH

BRUSH HOLDER

BRUSH HOLDER INSULATOR

BUSHING

WASHER

BRUSH

FIELSD COILS

BRUSH

STARTER DRIVE END HOUSING

RING

STARTER BRUSH

BUSHING STARTER DRIVE END PLATE

THRU BOLT

RETAINER

FLANGE

SLEEVE

PLATE ASSEMBLY BRUSH END

STARTER MOTOR DRIVE

ARMATURE

POLE PIECE

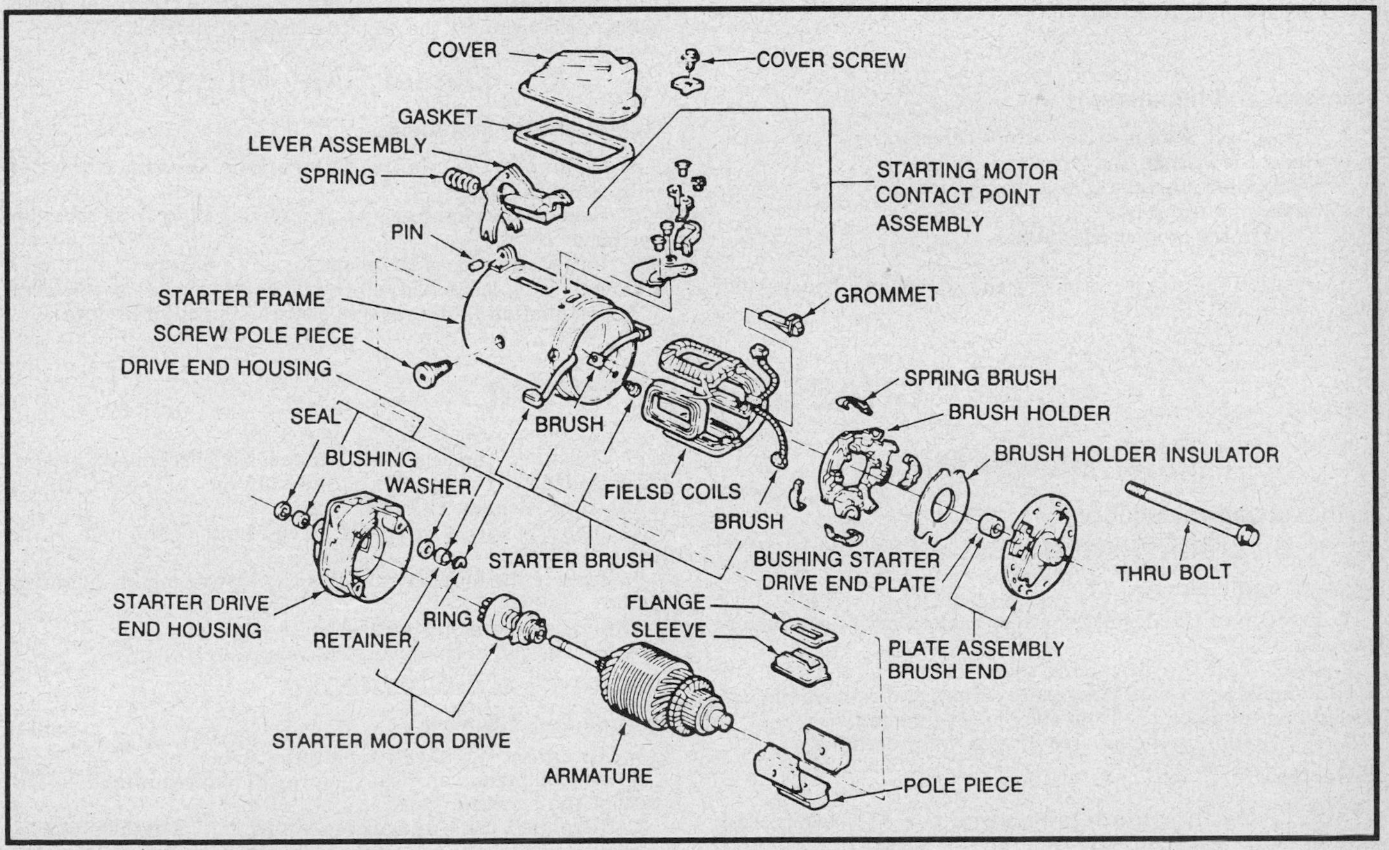

Exploded view of typical starter

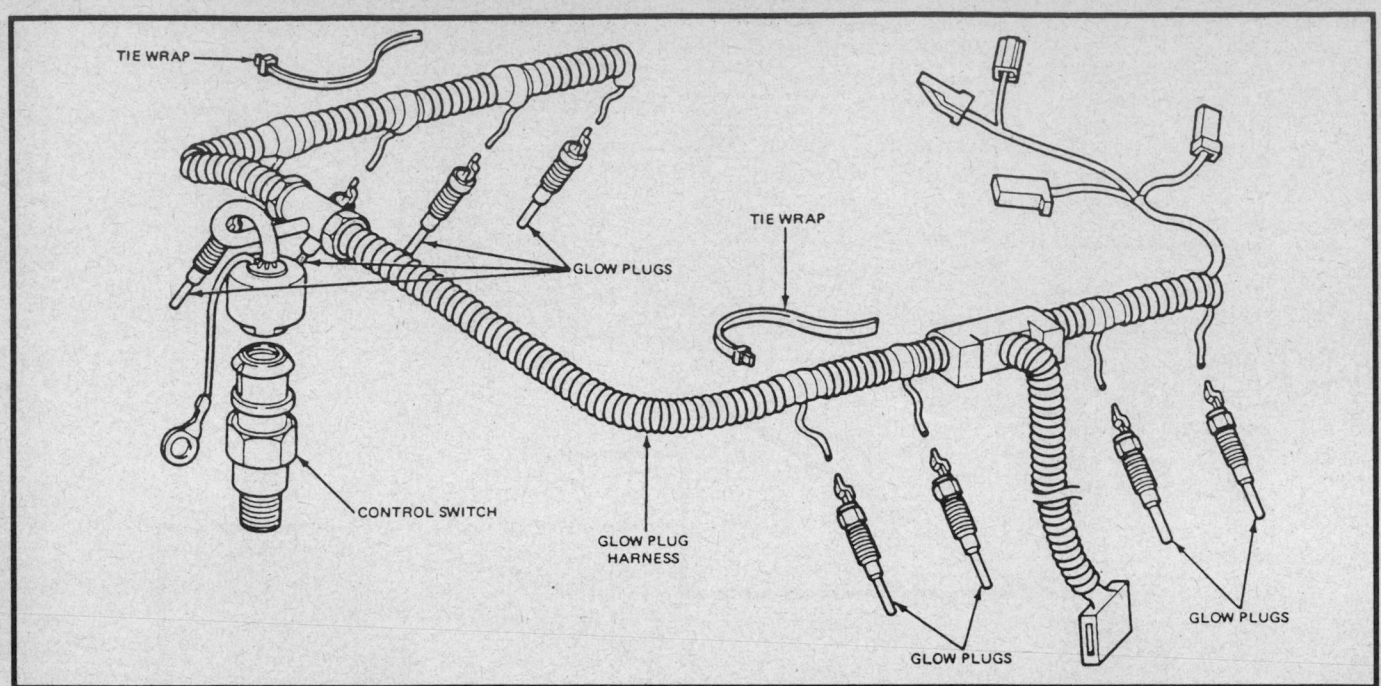

Glow plug engine harness

Starter

For further information, please refer to "Electrical" in the Unit Repair section.

Removal and Installation

1. Disconnect the negative battery cable(s).
2. Raise the vehicle and support it safely.
3. Disconnect starter cable at the starter terminal. Remove the starter mounting bolts.
4. Remove the starter assembly.

To install:

5. Position the starter assembly to the flywheel housing and start the mounting bolts.

6. Snug all the bolts while holding the starter squarely against its mounting surface and fully inserted into the pilot hole. Tighten the bolts to 15–20 ft. lbs.
7. Reconnect the starter cable at the starter terminal. Lower the vehicle. Connect the negative battery cable(s).

Diesel Glow Plugs

Removal and Installation

1. Disconnect the negative battery cable. Disconnect the glow plug electrical leads.
2. Remove the glow plugs by unscrewing them from the cylinder head.
3. Inspect the tips of the plugs for any evidence of melting. If a glow plug tip looks bad, all the glow plugs must be replaced.
4. Installation is the reverse of the removal procedure.

CHASSIS ELECTRICAL

Heater Blower Motor

Removal and Installation

WITH AIR CONDITIONING

Bronco and F Series

1. Disconnect the negative battery cable. Disconnect the motor connector.
2. Disconnect the air cooling tube from the motor.
3. Remove the 4 mounting plate screws and remove the motor and wheel assembly from the blower housing.
4. Installation is the reverse of removal procedure.

E Series

NOTE: On late models remove the blower motor mounting plate from the evaporator case then remove the blower motor from evaporator case.

1. Disconnect the negative battery cable. Disconnect the electrical leads from the resistor on the front face of the A/C blower scroll cover. Remove the scroll cover.
2. Push the wiring grommet forward out of the hole in the blower housing.
3. Remove the four screws from the blower motor mounting plate.
4. Remove the motor and wheel assembly.
5. Installation is the reverse of removal procedure.

WITHOUT AIR CONDITIONING

Bronco and F Series

1. Disconnect the negative battery cable(s).
2. On California vehicles, remove the emission module forward of the blower motor.
3. Disconnect the wire harness connection from the motor by pushing down on the tab while pulling the connector off at the motor.

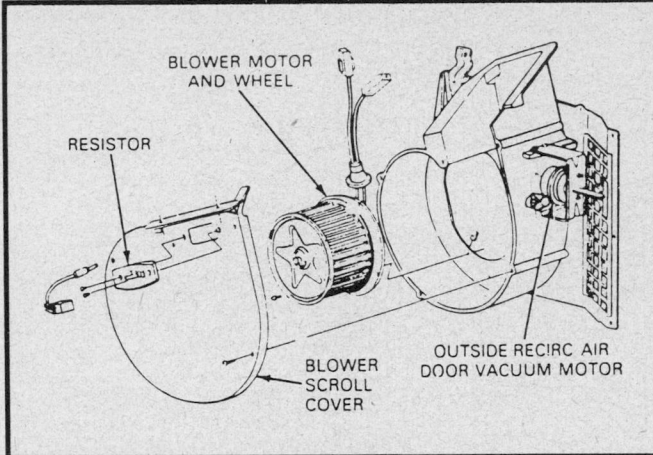

4. Disconnect the cooling tube from the blower motor.
5. Remove the blower motor retaining screws.
6. Position the cooling tube aside, pull the motor and wheel assembly from the blower housing.
7. Installation is the reverse of removal procedure.

E Series

1. Disconnect the negative battery cable. Disconnect the lead wire (orange/black) at the wiring harness.
2. Remove the ground wire (black) mounting from the heater blower assembly.
3. Remove the 3 mounting plate screws and remove the motor and wheel assembly.
4. Install in reverse order.

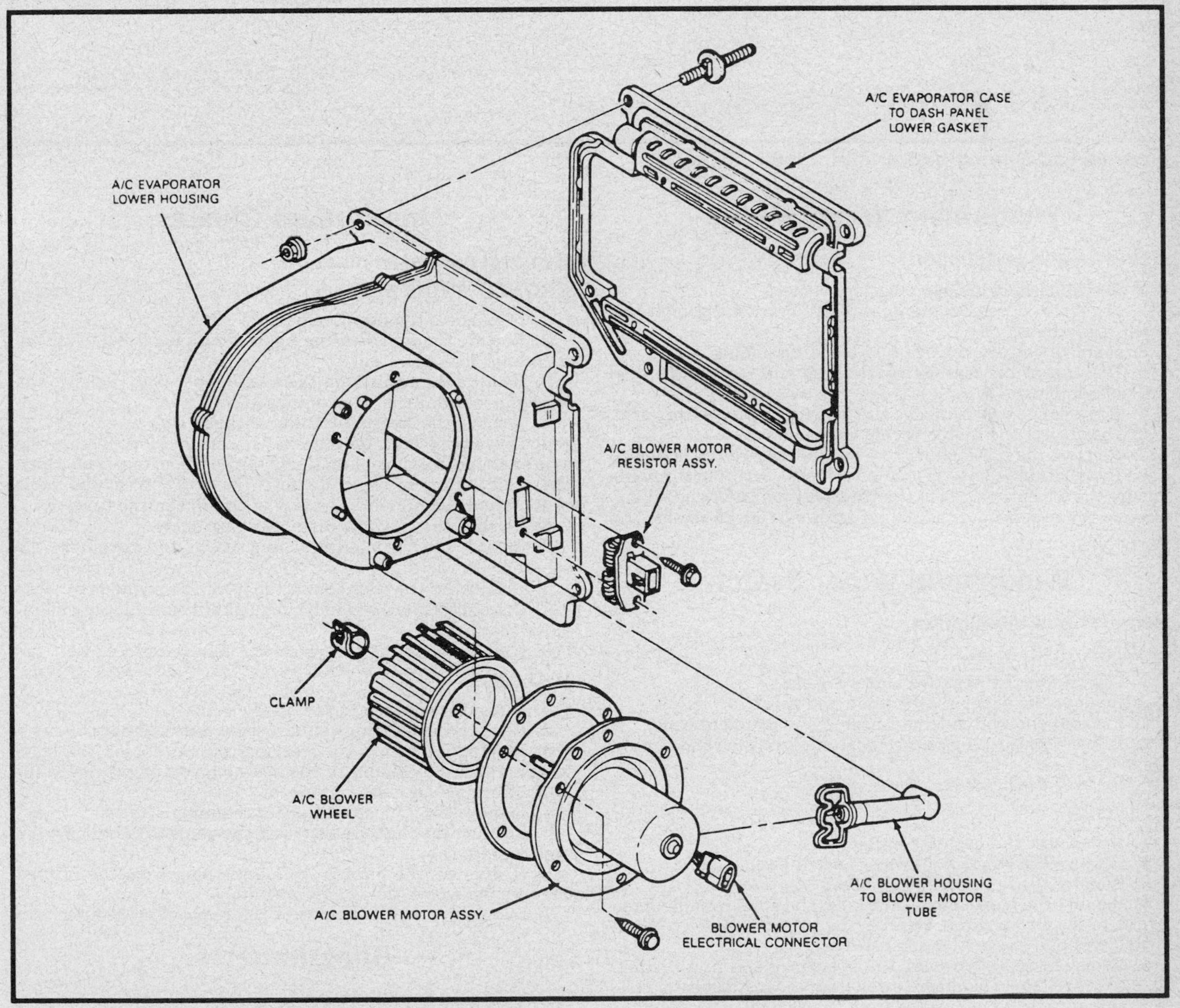

E series blower motor installation

E series blower motor installation hi-output system

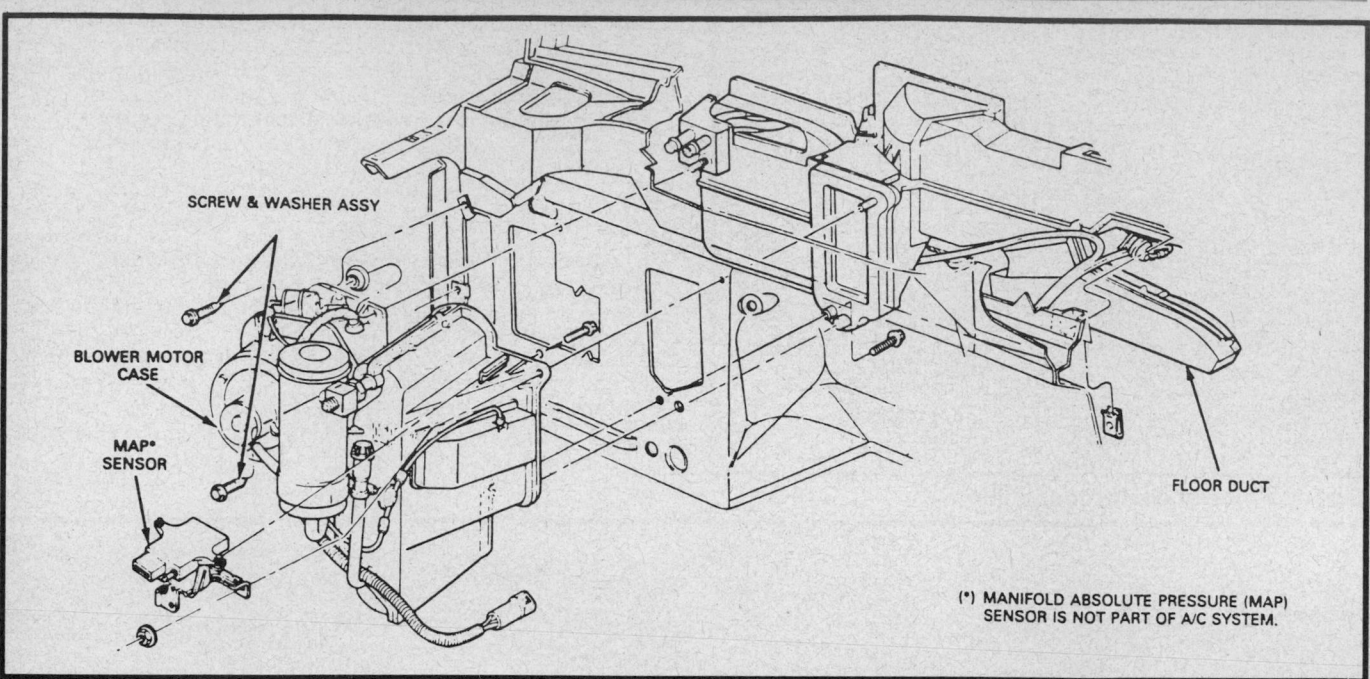

SCREW & WASHER ASSY

BLOWER MOTOR CASE

MAP* SENSOR

FLOOR DUCT

(*) MANIFOLD ABSOLUTE PRESSURE (MAP) SENSOR IS NOT PART OF A/C SYSTEM.

F series and Bronco blower motor installation

Windshield Wiper Motor

Removal and Installation

1. Disconnect the negative battery cable(s).
2. On E series, remove the fuse panel, bracket assembly and cover assemblies.
3. Remove both wiper arm and blade assemblies.
4. Disconnect the washer nozzle hose and remove the cowl grille assembly.
5. Remove the wiper linkage clip from the motor output arm.
6. Disconnect the motor wiring connector.
7. Remove the 3 attaching screws and remove the motor.
8. Installation is the reverse of removal procedure. Always ensure the wiper motor is in the park position before installing. Torque the wiper motor retaining screws to 60–85 in. lbs.

Windshield Wiper Switch

Removal and Installation

BRONCO AND F SERIES

1. Disconnect the negative battery cable(s).
2. Remove the wiper switch knob and bezel.
3. Pull out the switch from under the instrument panel.
4. Disconnect the plug connector from the switch and remove the switch.
5. Reverse the procedure for installation.

E SERIES

1. Disconnect the negative battery cable(s).
2. Remove the windshield wiper switch knob.
3. Remove the ignition switch bezel.
4. Remove the headlamp switch knob and shaft by pulling the switch to the **ON** position. Depress the button on the top of the switch and pull the knob and shaft out.
5. Remove the 2 screws at the bottom of the finish panel, then pry the 2 upper retainers away from the instrument panel.
6. Disconnect the connector from the switch.
7. Remove the attaching screws and remove the switch.
8. Reverse the procedure for installation.

Instrument Cluster

Removal and Installation

BRONCO AND F SERIES

1. Disconnect the negative battery cable(s).
2. Remove the wiper/washer knob using a hook tool to release each knob lock tab.
3. Remove the knob from the headlamp switch. Remove the fog lamp switch knob, if so equipped.
4. Remove the steering column shroud.
5. If equipped with an automatic transmission, remove the loop on the indicator cable assembly from the retainer pin. Open the cable retaining clips. Remove the screw from the cable bracket and slide the bracket out of the slot in the tube.
6. Remove the cluster finish panel assembly.
7. Remove the 4 cluster attaching screws and disconnect the speedometer cable.
8. Disconnect the wire connector from the printed circuit.
9. Disconnect the 4WD indicator light, if so equipped and remove the cluster.
10. Installation is the reverse of the removal procedure.

E SERIES

1. Disconnect the negative battery cable(s).
2. Remove the steering column shroud if necessary.
3. If equipped with a tilt steering column, loosen the bolts which attach the column to the band support to provide sufficient clearance for cluster removal.
4. Remove the 7 cluster to panel retaining screws.
5. Position the cluster away from the panel to disconnect the speedometer cable.
6. Disconnect the harness connector plug from the printed circuit and remove the cluster assembly.
7. Installation is the reverse of the removal procedure.

Speedometer

Removal and Installation

1. Disconnect the negative battery cable. Remove the instrument cluster.

2. Remove the lens and mask from the cluster.
3. Remove the 2 speedometer attaching screws and remove the speedometer cable.
4. Remove the speedometer.
5. Reverse the procedure for installation. If a new speedometer head is being installed, examine the square drive hole for suffient lubrication.

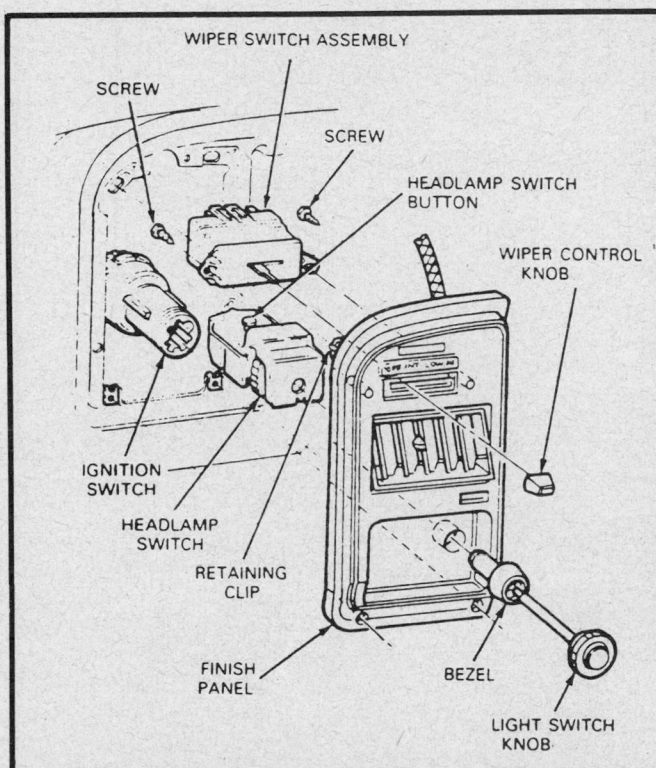

Windshield wiper control switch installation—E series

Headlight Switch

Removal and Installation
BRONCO AND F SERIES

1. Disconnect the negative battery cable(s).
2. Remove the wiper/washer and headlamp switch knobs using a hook tool to release each knob lock tab.
3. Remove the fog lamp switch knob if so equipped.
4. Remove the steering column shroud and the cluster finish panel.
5. Remove the switch from the instrument panel then the wiring connector from the switch.
6. Installation is the reverse of the removal procedure.

E SERIES

1. Disconnect the negative battery cable(s).
2. Pull the headlamp switch knob to the full **ON** position. Depress the shaft release button and remove the knob and shaft assembly.
3. Remove the instrument panel finish panel.
4. Unscrew the mounting nut. Remove the switch, then remove the wiring connector from the switch.
5. Installation is the reverse of the removal procedure.

Dimmer Switch

Removal and Installation

1. Disconnect the negative battery cable(s).
2. Pull back floor mat or carpet in the area of the switch. Remove the dimmer switch retaining screws.
3. Disconnect the electrical connection from the switch.
4. Installation is the reverse of the removal procedure.

Turn Signal Switch

Removal and Installation

1. Disconnect the negative battery cable(s).
2. Remove the horn switch.
3. Remove the steering wheel.
4. Unscrew the turn signal switch lever from the steering column.
5. Remove the steering column shroud and the opening cover if so equipped.
6. Disconnect the switch wiring connector.
7. Remove the screws that secure the switch to the column.
8. Vehicles equipped with a fixed column, remove the switch by lifting it out of the column and guiding the connector plug through the opening in the shift socket. On E series with automatic transmission, also remove the PRNDL lamp assembly from the shift socket.
9. Vehicles equipped with a tilt column require disassembly of the turn signal switch harness plug before removing the switch from the column. On E series with automatic transmission, remove the PRNDL lamp wire from the turn signal switch harness sheath.
10. Reverse the procedure for installation. Tighten turn signal lever to 10–20 in. lbs. Install steering wheel retaining nut to 30–40 ft. lbs.

Ignition Switch

Removal and Installation

1. Disconnect the negative battery cable(s).
2. Remove the steering column shroud and lower the steering column.
3. Disconnect the switch wiring at the multiple plug.
4. Remove the 2 nuts that hold the switch to the steering column.
5. Lift the switch upward to disengage the actuator rod and remove the switch.
6. To install the switch, the locking mechanism at the top of the column and the switch must be in the **LOCK** position for correct adjustment.
7. To hold the parts of the column in the **LOCK** position, move the shift lever into **P** (with automatic transmission) or **R** (with manual transmission), turn the key to the **LOCK** position and remove the key. New replacement switches are already pinned in the **LOCK** position.
8. Reverse the removal procedure for installation. Tighten the ignition switch retaining screws to 40–65 inch lbs. Check system in each range for proper operation.

Stoplight Switch

Removal and Installation

1. Disconnect the negative battery cable. Disconnect electrical connection from the switch. Locking tab must be lifted before connector can be removed.
2. Remove the hairpin retainer. Slide switch, master cylinder

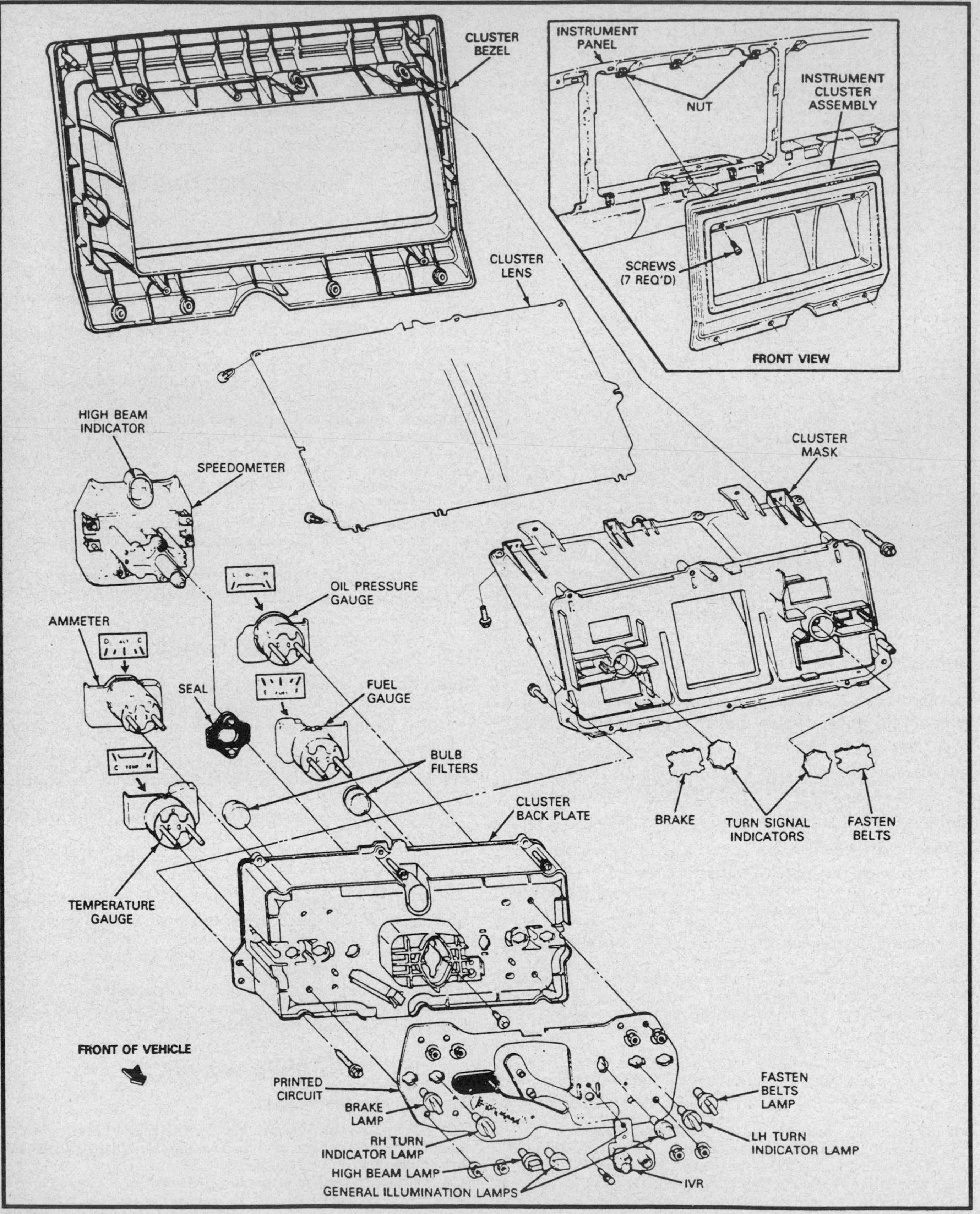

CLUSTER BEZEL

INSTRUMENT PANEL

NUT

INSTRUMENT CLUSTER ASSEMBLY

SCREWS (7 REQ'D)

FRONT VIEW

CLUSTER LENS

HIGH BEAM INDICATOR

SPEEDOMETER

CLUSTER MASK

OIL PRESSURE GAUGE

AMMETER

SEAL

FUEL GAUGE

BULB FILTERS

CLUSTER BACK PLATE

BRAKE

TURN SIGNAL INDICATORS

FASTEN BELTS

TEMPERATURE GAUGE

FRONT OF VEHICLE

PRINTED CIRCUIT

BRAKE LAMP

RH TURN INDICATOR LAMP

HIGH BEAM LAMP

GENERAL ILLUMINATION LAMPS

FASTEN BELTS LAMP

LH TURN INDICATOR LAMP

IVR

Instrument cluster–E series

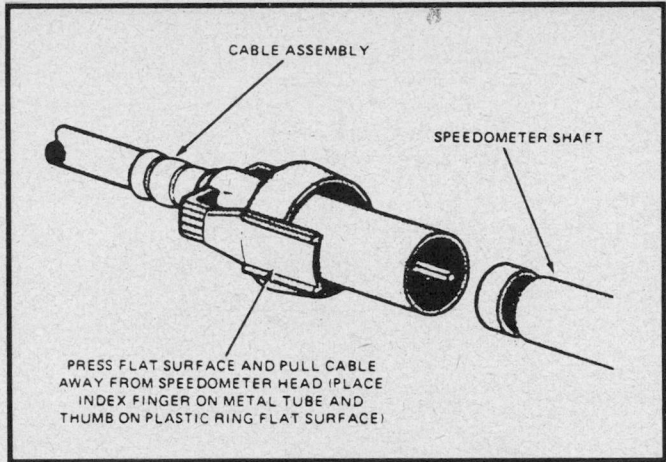

Speedometer cable quick connect

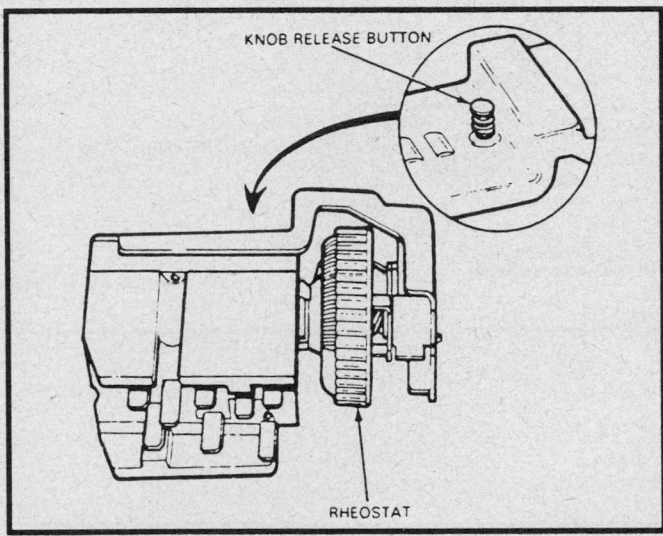

Typical headlamp switch

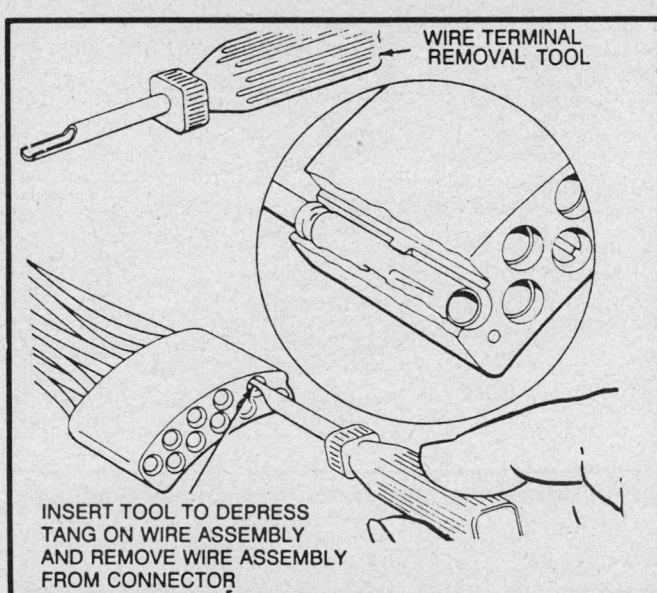

Wire terminal removal-tilt wheel only

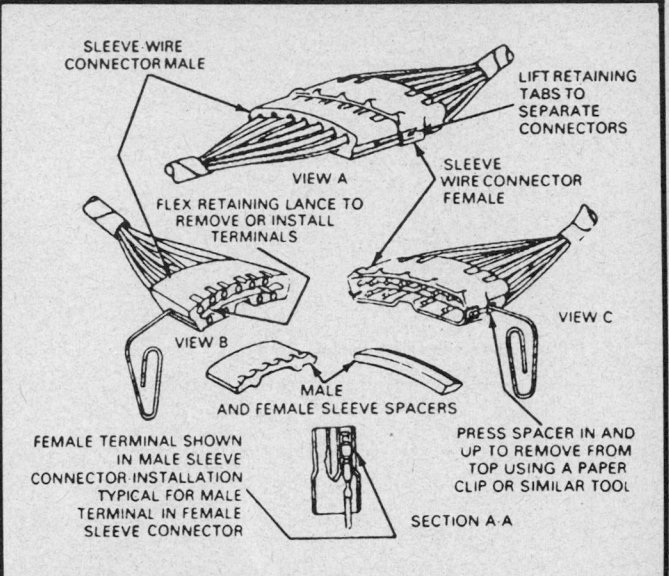

Wire connector removal

pushrod, nylon washer and bushing away from the pedal. Remove the washer, then switch by sliding switch up or down.

To install:

3. Position switch so that U-shaped side is nearest the pedal and directly over/under the pin. Then slide switch up/down installing the master cylinder pushrod and bushing between the switch side plates.

4. Push switch and pushrod assembly toward brake pedal arm. Install outside plastic washer to pin. Install the hairpin retainer (do not substitute for this retainer-use only factory supplied retainer) to entire assembly.

5. Install electrical connection to switch. Make sure switch wire harness has sufficient length to travel with switch during full stroke of brake pedal. Check switch for proper operation.

Clutch Switch

Removal and Installation

BRONCO AND F SERIES

1. Disconnect the negative battery cable. Disconnect the wiring harness from the switch.

2. Pull down on the orientation clip to separate it from the tab on the switch.

3. Rotate the switch to expose the plastic retainer.

4. Push the tabs together to allow the retainer to slide rearward and seperate from the switch.

5. Remove the switch from the clutch master cylinder pushrod.

6. Installation is the reverse of the removal procedure.

E SERIES

1. Disconnect the negative battery cable. Remove the nut and bolt attaching switch to bracket.

2. Disconnect the switch connector.

3. Installation is the reverse of the removal procedure.

Fuses And Circuit Breakers

Location

The fuse panel for the Bronco and F series vehicles is located on the firewall under the instrument panel left of the steering column. The fuse panel for the E series vehicles is located on the mounting bracket under the instrument panel left of the steering column. Circuit breakers are located in the fuse panel.

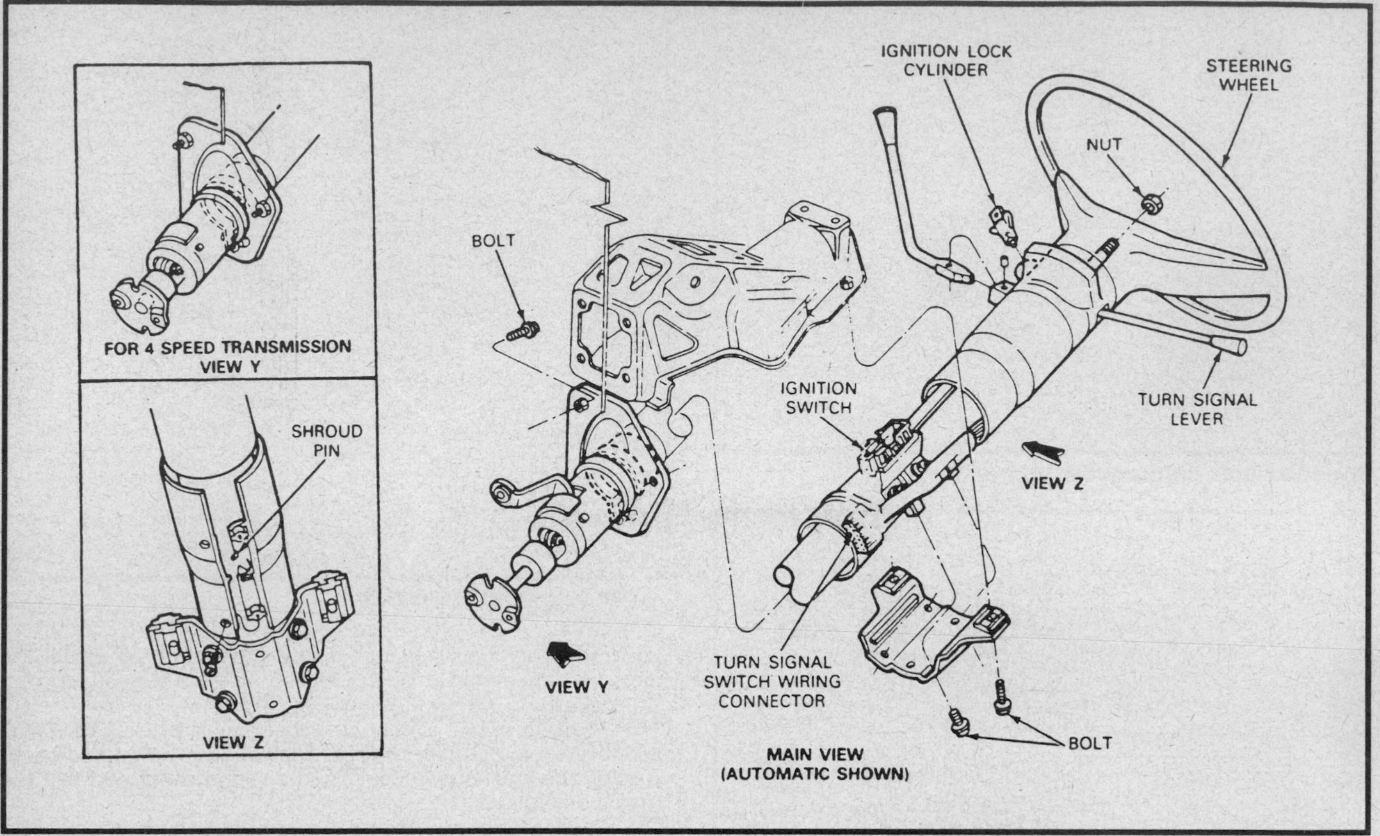

IGNITION LOCK
CYLINDER

STEERING
WHEEL

NUT

BOLT

FOR 4 SPEED TRANSMISSION
VIEW Y

SHROUD
PIN

IGNITION
SWITCH

TURN SIGNAL
LEVER

VIEW Z

VIEW Z

VIEW Y

TURN SIGNAL
SWITCH WIRING
CONNECTOR

BOLT

MAIN VIEW
(AUTOMATIC SHOWN)

Ignition switch installation

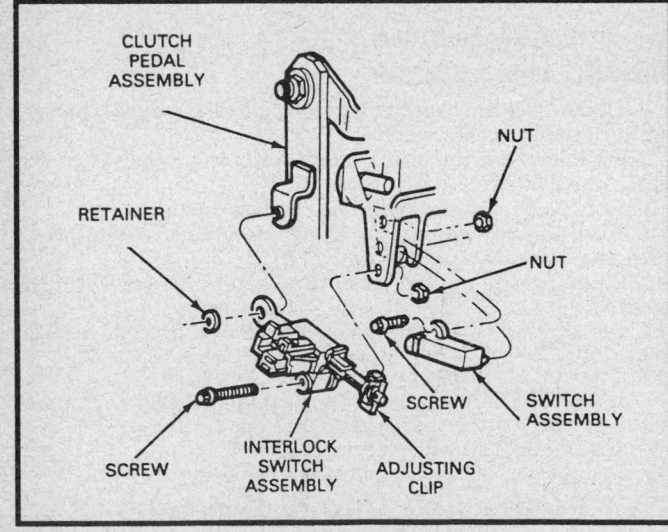

CLUTCH
PEDAL
ASSEMBLY

NUT

RETAINER

NUT

SCREW

SWITCH
ASSEMBLY

SCREW

INTERLOCK
SWITCH
ASSEMBLY

ADJUSTING
CLIP

Clutch/starter interlock switch–E series

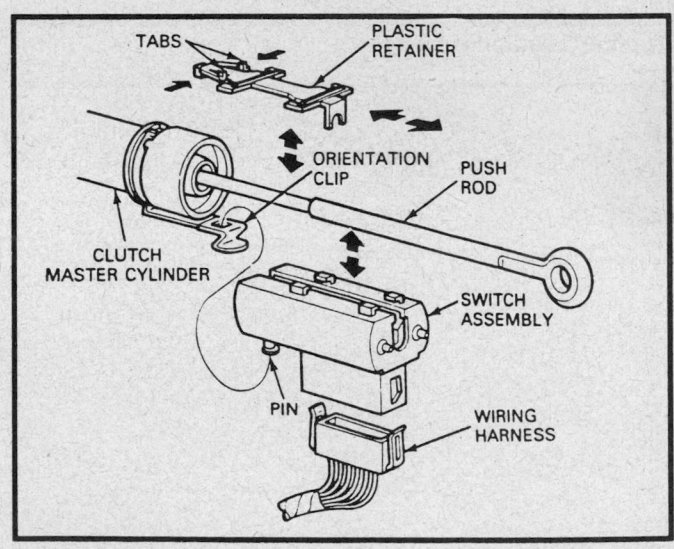

TABS

PLASTIC
RETAINER

ORIENTATION
CLIP

PUSH
ROD

CLUTCH
MASTER CYLINDER

SWITCH
ASSEMBLY

PIN

WIRING
HARNESS

Clutch/starter interlock switch–Bronco and F series

ENGINE COOLING

Radiator

Removal and Installation

1. Disconnect the negative battery cable. Drain the cooling system by removing the cap and opening the drain cock located at the lower rear corner of the radiator.
2. Remove the overflow tube from the coolant recovery bottle and shroud as necessary.
3. Remove the radiator shroud retaining bolts and position it out of the way.
4. Remove all water hoses from the radiator.
5. Disconnect the automatic transmission oil cooling lines if equipped.
6. Remove the radiator retaining bolts and tilt the radiator back to clear radiator support for removal from the vehicle.
7. Installation is the reverse of the removal procedure.

Heater Core

Removal and Installation
WITH AIR CONDITIONING
1986–90 Bronco and F Series

1. Disconnect the negative battery cable(s). Disconnect the heater hoses from the heater core tubes and plug the hoses.
2. Remove the glove compartment liner.
3. Remove 8 screws attaching the heater core cover to the ple-num and remove the cover. Remove and tag all vacuum lines.
4. Remove the heater core from the plenum.
5. Installation is the reverse of removal.

1986–87 E Series

1. Disconnect the negative battery cable(s). Disconnect the resistor electrical leads on the front of the blower cover inside the vehicle. Detach the vacuum line from the vacuum motor. Remove the blower cover.
2. Remove the nut and push washer from the air door shaft. Remove the control cable from the bracket and the air door shaft.
3. Remove the blower motor housing and the air door housing.
4. Drain the coolant and detach the heater hoses.
5. Remove the heater core retaining brackets. Remove the core and seal assembly.
6. Reverse the procedure for installation.

1988–90 E Series

1. Disconnect the negative battery cable(s). Disconnect and plug heater hoses from the heater core.
2. Remove the modesty panel from underside of instrument panel.
3. Remove the 4 screws from the heater core cover located on the left side of the heater case underneath the instrument panel.
4. Remove the heater core cover.
5. Remove heater core retaining bracket from assembly.

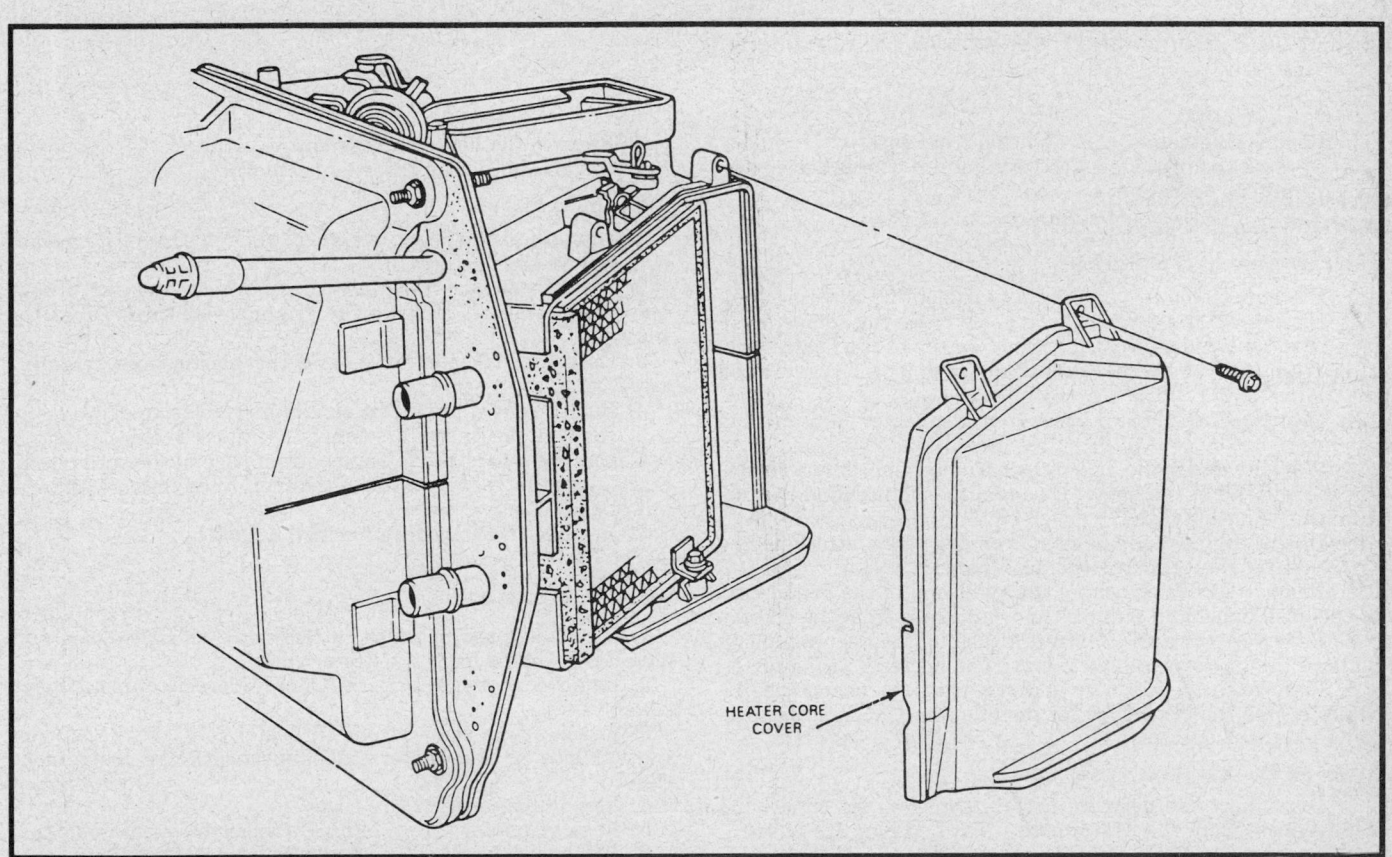

HEATER CORE COVER

Heater core–E series with air conditioning 1988–90

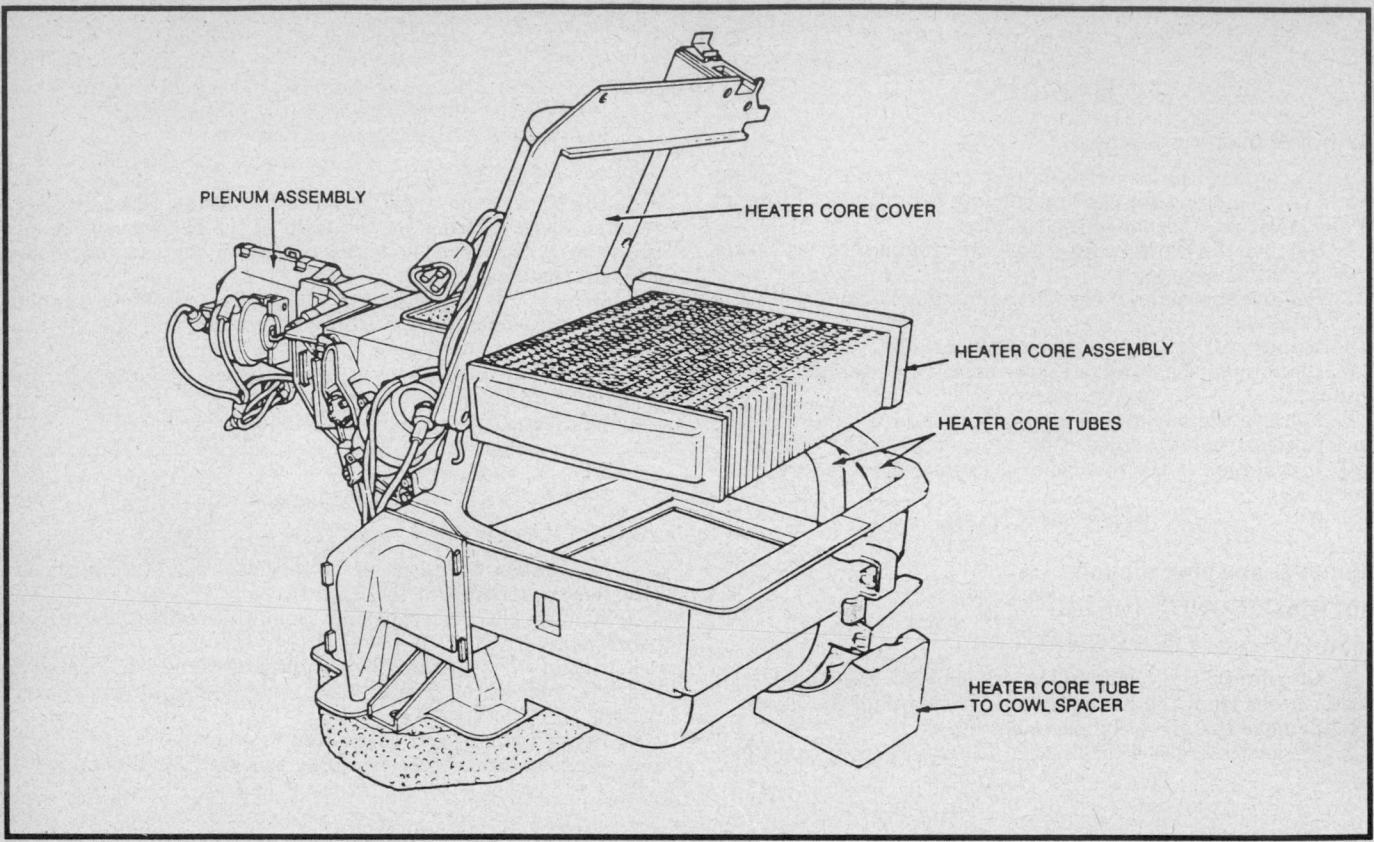

PLENUM ASSEMBLY

HEATER CORE COVER

HEATER CORE ASSEMBLY

HEATER CORE TUBES

HEATER CORE TUBE TO COWL SPACER

Heater core—Bronco and F series with air conditioning

6. Remove the heater core and seal from case.

7. Reverse the procedure for installation. Check heater system for proper operation.

WITHOUT AIR CONDITIONING

1986 Bronco and F Series

1. Disconnect the negative battery cable(s).

2. Disconnect the temperature cable from the temperature blend door and the mounting bracket on top of the heater case.

3. Disconnect the wires from the blower motor resistor and the blower motor.

4. Disconnect the heater hoses from the heater core and plug the hoses.

5. Working under the instrument panel, remove nuts retaining the left end of the heater case and the right end of the plenum to the dash panel.

6. In the engine compartment, remove screw attaching the top center of the heater to the dash panel.

7. Remove screws attaching the right end of the heater case to the dash panel and remove the heater case from the vehicle.

8. Remove screws and bolt/nut attaching the heater housing plate to the heater case and remove the heater housing plate.

9. Remove the heater core and seal from the heater case.

10. Reverse the procedure for installation. Check heater system for proper operation.

1987–90 Bronco and F Series

1. Disconnect the negative battery cable(s). Disconnect the heater hoses from the heater core tubes and plug the hoses.

2. Remove the glove compartment liner.

3. Remove 8 screws attaching the heater core cover to the plenum and remove the cover. Remove and tag all vacuum lines.

4. Remove the heater core from the plenum.

5. Installation is the reverse of removal.

1986–87 E Series

1. Disconnect the negative battery cable(s). Drain the coolant and remove the battery.

2. Disconnect the resistor wiring harness and the orange blower motor lead. Remove the ground wire screw from the firewall.

3. Detach the heater hoses and the plastic hose retaining strap.

4. Remove the 5 mounting screws inside the vehicle.

5. Remove the heater assembly.

6. Cut the seal at the top and bottom edge of the core retainer. Remove the 2 screws and the retainer. Slide the core and seal out of the case.

7. Reverse the procedure for installation.

1988–90 E Series

1. Disconnect the negative battery cable(s). Disconnect and plug heater hoses from the heater core.

2. Remove the modesty panel from underside of instrument panel.

3. Remove the 4 screws from the heater core cover located on the left side of the heater case underneath the instrument panel.

4. Remove the heater core cover.

5. Remove heater core retaining bracket from assembly.

6. Remove the heater core and seal from case.

7. Reverse the procedure for installation. Check heater system for proper operation.

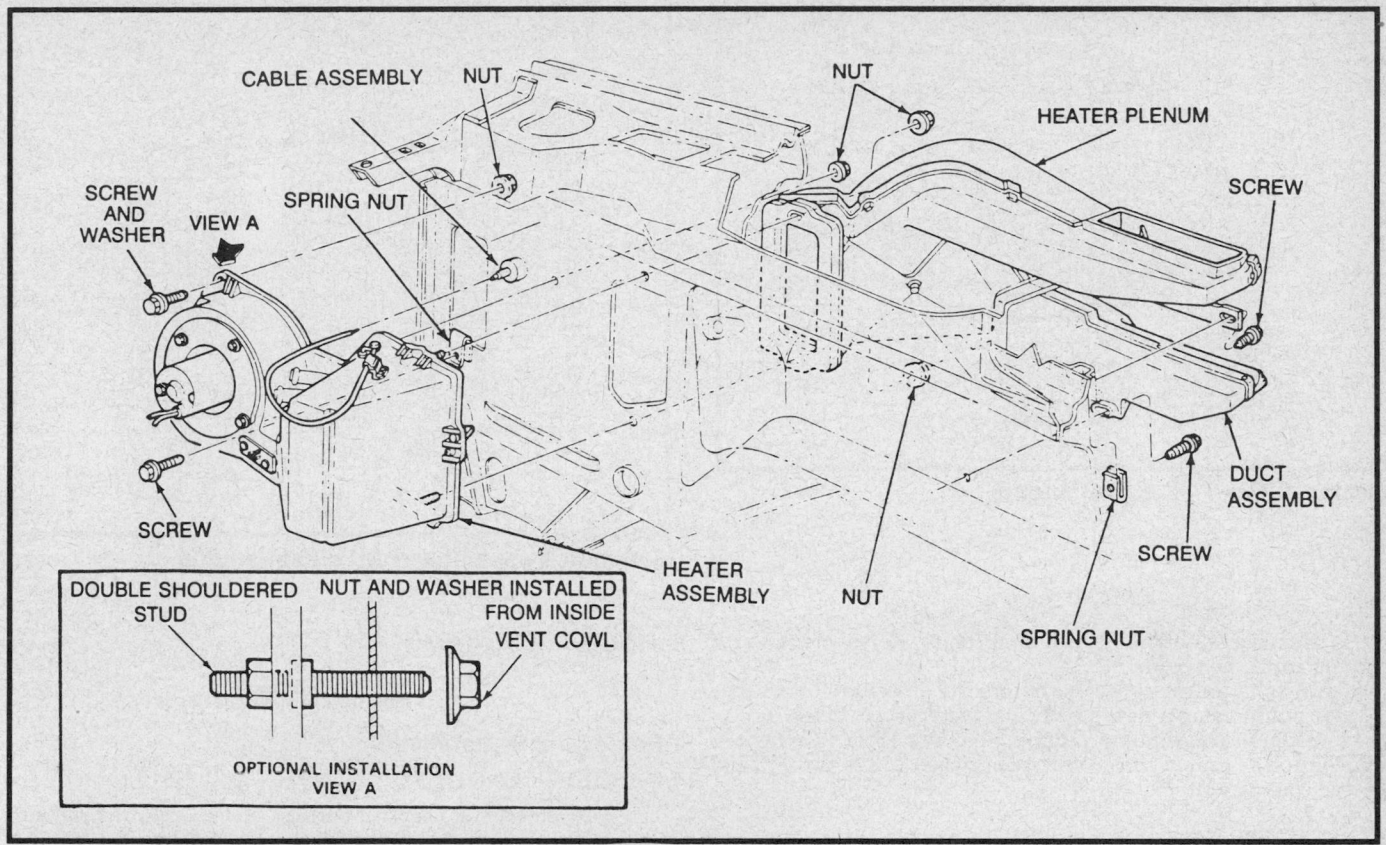

CABLE ASSEMBLY NUT NUT HEATER PLENUM

SCREW AND WASHER VIEW A SPRING NUT SCREW

SCREW DUCT ASSEMBLY

SCREW HEATER ASSEMBLY NUT SCREW

SPRING NUT

DOUBLE SHOULDERED STUD   NUT AND WASHER INSTALLED FROM INSIDE VENT COWL

OPTIONAL INSTALLATION VIEW A

Heater core–Bronco and F series without air conditioning 1986

Water Pump

Removal and Installation

4.9L ENGINE

1. Disconnect the negative battery cable. Drain cooling system.
2. Disconnect radiator lower hose and heater hose at the water pump.
3. Remove fan belt, fan and water pump pulley. Remove the air pump and alternator belts.
4. On vehicles equipped with air conditioning, remove the belt as required.
5. Remove water pump retaining bolts, then remove pump and gasket.

To install:

6. Clean mating gasket surfaces of pump body and engine block.
7. If a new water pump is being installed, remove the fittings from the old pump and install them on the new pump.
8. Coat new gasket with water-resistant sealer on both sides and install gasket and pump on engine. Tighten mounting bolts to 12–18 ft. lbs.
9. Install water pump pulley, fan and fan belt and adjust fan belt tension.
10. If so equipped, install air compressor belt.
11. Connect radiator and heater hoses.
12. Fill and bleed cooling system. Check for leaks and recheck coolant level.

5.0L AND 5.8L ENGINES

1. Disconnect the negative battery cable. Drain the cooling

system. On E series remove the air cleaner and intake duct assembly.
2. Remove the bolts securing the fan shroud to the radiator, if so equipped and position the shroud over the fan. On E series remove the radiator assembly.
3. Disconnect the lower radiator hose, heater hose and by-pass hose at the water pump. Remove the drive belts, fan, fan spacer and pulley. Remove the fan shroud, if so equipped.
4. Loosen the alternator pivot bolt and the bolt attaching the alternator adjusting arm to the water pump.
5. Remove the bolts securing the water pump to the timing chain cover and remove the water pump.
6. Installation is the reverse of removal procedure. Tighten water pump bolts to 12–18 ft. lbs on installation. Fill and bleed cooling system. Check for leaks and recheck coolant level.

6.9L AND 7.3L ENGINES

1. Disconnect the negative battery cable(s). Drain the cooling system and remove the fan shroud halves.

NOTE: Fan and clutch assembly has a left hand thread. Remove by turning nut clockwise.

2. Remove the fan and clutch assembly.
3. Remove all drive belts and water pump pulley.
4. Disconnect heater hose and hose fitting from the water pump.
5. Remove alternator adjusting arm and arm bracket.
6. Remove the air conditioning compressor attaching bolts and secure the compressor out of the way.
7. Remove the air conditioning compressor brackets.
8. Remove the power steering pump and bracket position out of the way.

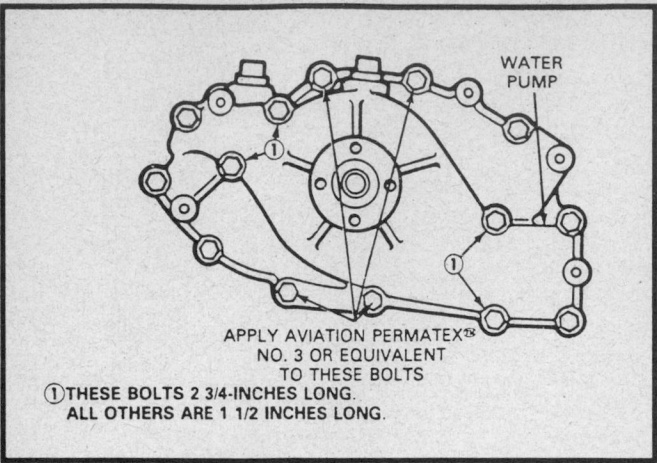

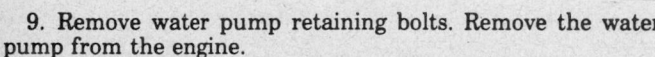

Water pump—7.3L diesel engine

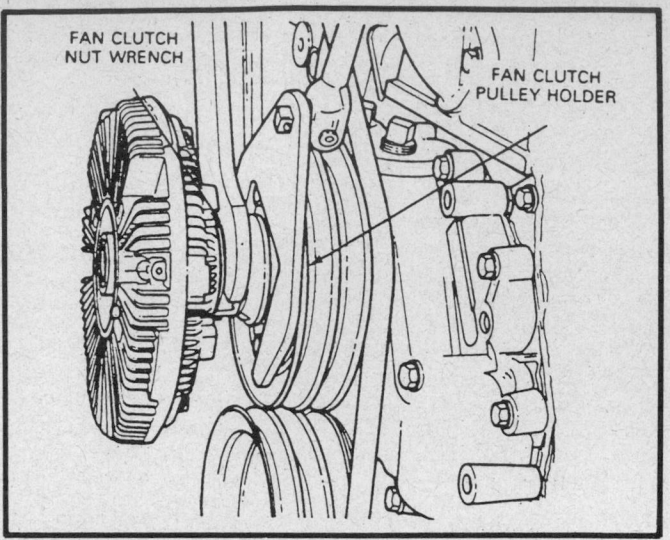

Fan clutch assembly—7.3L diesel engine

9. Remove water pump retaining bolts. Remove the water pump from the engine.

10. Installation is the reverse of removal procedure. Install the water pump using a new gasket and waterproof sealer.

11. Tighten water pump retaining bolts to 15 ft. lbs. Tighten fan clutch assembly bolt (counterclockwise) 163 ft. lbs. Fill and bleed cooling system.

7.5L ENGINE

1. Disconnect the negative battery cable. Drain the cooling system and remove the fan shroud attaching bolts.

2. Remove the fan assembly attaching screws and remove the shroud and fan.

3. Loosen the power steering pump attaching bolts.

4. If the vehicle is equipped with air conditioning, loosen the compressor attaching bolts and remove the air conditioning compressor and power steering pump drive belts.

5. Loosen the alternator pivot bolt. Remove the 2 attaching bolts and spacer. Remove the drive belt, then rotate the bracket out of the way.

6. Remove the 3 air conditioning compressor attaching bolts and secure the compressor out of the way.

7. Remove the power steering pump attaching bolts and position the pump to one side.

8. Remove the air conditioner bracket attaching bolts and remove the bracket.

9. Disconnect the lower radiator hose and heater hose from the water pump.

10. Loosen the bypass hose clamp at the water pump.

11. Remove the water pump attaching bolts and remove the pump from the front cover. Remove the separator plate from the pump. Discard the gaskets.

12. Remove all gasket material from all of the mating surfaces.

13. Install the water pump in the reverse order of removal, using a new gasket and waterproof sealer.

14. Tighten water pump retaining bolts to 15–21 ft. lbs. Fill and bleed cooling system.

Thermostat

Removal and Installation

GASOLINE ENGINE

1. Disconnect the negative battery cable. Drain the radiator so that the coolant level is below the thermostat.

2. If equipped with a V8 engine, disconnect the bypass hoses at the water pump and the intake manifold. Remove the bypass tube.

3. Remove the water outlet housing attaching bolts and pull the housing away from the engine to gain access to the thermostat.

4. Installation is the reverse of removal procedure. Fill and bleed cooling system as necessary.

DIESEL ENGINE

1. Disconnect ground cables from both batteries.

2. Drain the radiator so that the coolant level is below the thermostat.

3. Remove the alternator and vacuum pump drive belts.

4. Remove the alternator, vacuum pump and position out of the way.

5. Remove the water outlet housing attaching bolts and pull the housing away from the engine to gain access to the thermostat.

6. Installation is the reverse of removal procedure. Fill and bleed cooling system as necessary.

Cooling System Bleeding

To bleed cooling system disconnect the heater outlet hose at the water pump to bleed or release trapped air in the system. When the coolant begins to escape, connect the heater outlet.

GASOLINE FUEL SYSTEM

Fuel Service Precautions

Always disconnect the negative battery cable if possible. Never smoke, carry lighted tobacco, open flame and keep a Class B dry chemical fire extinguisher available. Always relieve the fuel pressure before working on any fuel system component.

Relieving Fuel System Pressure

1. Open hood and install protective covers.

2. Disconnect battery ground cable.

3. Remove the fuel cap from the gas tank. A valve at the fuel injection rail can be bleed for this purpose.

4. Alternate method is to remove the fuel pump relay or disconnect the electrical connection to the high pressure fuel pump.

5. Crank engine for approximately 10 seconds. If engine runs wait till engine stalls and crank engine an additional 5 seconds then disconnect the negative battery cable.

Fuel Filter

Removal and Installation
CARBURATED VEHICLE

1. Disconnect the negative battery cable. Remove the air cleaner.

2. Loosen (hold filter with backup wrench) and remove the fuel tube from the filter.

3. Remove the filter from the carburetor. If a inlet type fuel filter is used remove the fuel inlet fitting then remove the gasket, filter and spring.

4. Installation is the reverse of removal procedure. Always hand start filter threads before tightening with wrench.

FUEL INJECTED VEHICLE

NOTE: If vehicle has in-line reservoir fuel filter type relieve fuel pressure. Unscrew the lower canister using a flexible type oil filter wrench and slide filter and canister out from the frame rail.

1. Relieve fuel pressure. Disconnect the battery ground cable.

2. Raise and suport the vehicle safely.

3. Loosen screw clamp slide filter forward. Remove fuel lines from the filter. Some late models have push type connection fittings.

4. Remove fuel fiter from mounting bracket.

5. Installation is the reverse of removal procedure. Always hand start filter gas line threads before tightening with wrench.

Fuel Pump

Pressure Testing

1. Remove the air cleaner. Connect a suitable pressure gauge to carburetor end of the fuel line.

2. Start the engine and read the fuel pressure after 10 seconds. The fuel pressure should be 5–7 psi on 4.9L engine. On the 5.0L, 5.8L and 7.5L engines the pressure should be 6–8 psi with the fuel return line closed, if equipped.

3. Reconnect the fuel line and install the air cleaner.

Removal and Installation

1. Disconnect the negative battery cable. Loosen the threaded connections and then retighten them snugly. Do not remove the lines at this time.

2. Loosen the mounting bolts about 2 turns and loosen the fuel pump from the engine.

3. Rotate the engine until the fuel pump cam lobe is near its low position.

4. Disconnect the fuel pump inlet, outlet (wrap shop towel around fitting) and vapor return line, if so equipped.

5. Remove the fuel pump attaching bolts and remove the fuel pump and gasket.

6. Installation is the reverse of removal procedure. Install the fuel pump with a new mounting gasket and torque the retaining bolts to evenly to 19–27 ft. lbs. on 5.0L, 5.8L and 7.5L engines and 12–18 ft. lbs. on 4.9L engine.

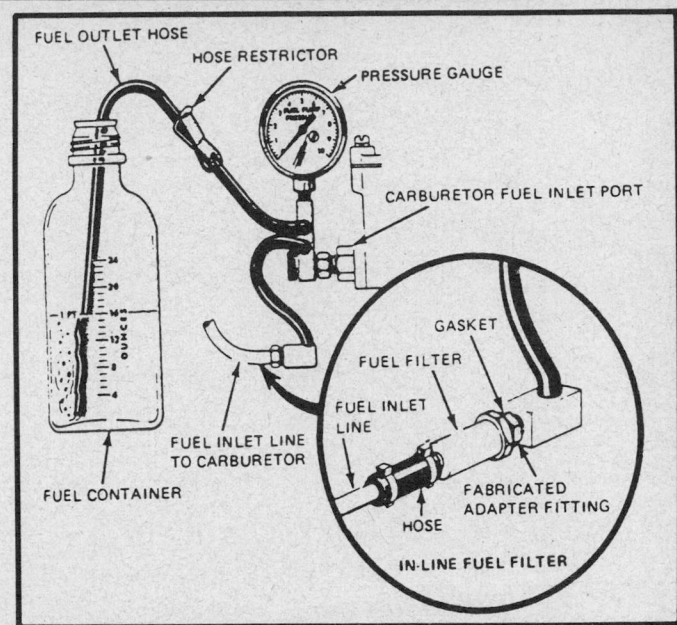

Testing mechanical pump

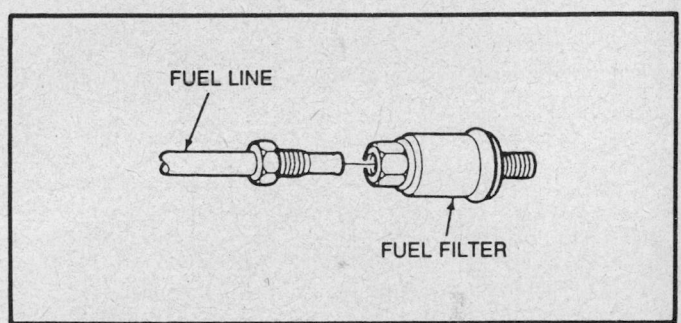

Typical fuel filter

Electric Fuel Pump

Removal and Installation
IN-TANK PUMP

1. Disconnect the negative battery cable.

2. Depressurize the system and drain as much gas from the tank by pumping out through the filler neck.

3. Raise the vehicle and safely support it.

4. Disconnect and plug the fuel supply, return and vent lines as necessary.

5. Disconnect the wiring harness to the fuel pump.

6. Support the gas tank, loosen and remove the mounting straps. Remove the gas tank.

7. Disconnect the lines and harness at the pump flange.

8. Clean the outside of the mounting flange and retaining ring. Turn the fuel pump lock ring counterclockwise and remove.

9. Remove the fuel pump.

10. Clean the mount faces. Put a light coat of grease on the mounting sufaces and on the new sealing ring. Install the new fuel pump.

11. Installation is in the reverse order of removal. Fill the tank with at least 10 gallons of gas. Turn the ignition key **ON** for 3 seconds. Repeat 6 or 7 times until the fuel system is pressurized. Check for any fitting leaks. Start the engine and check for leaks.

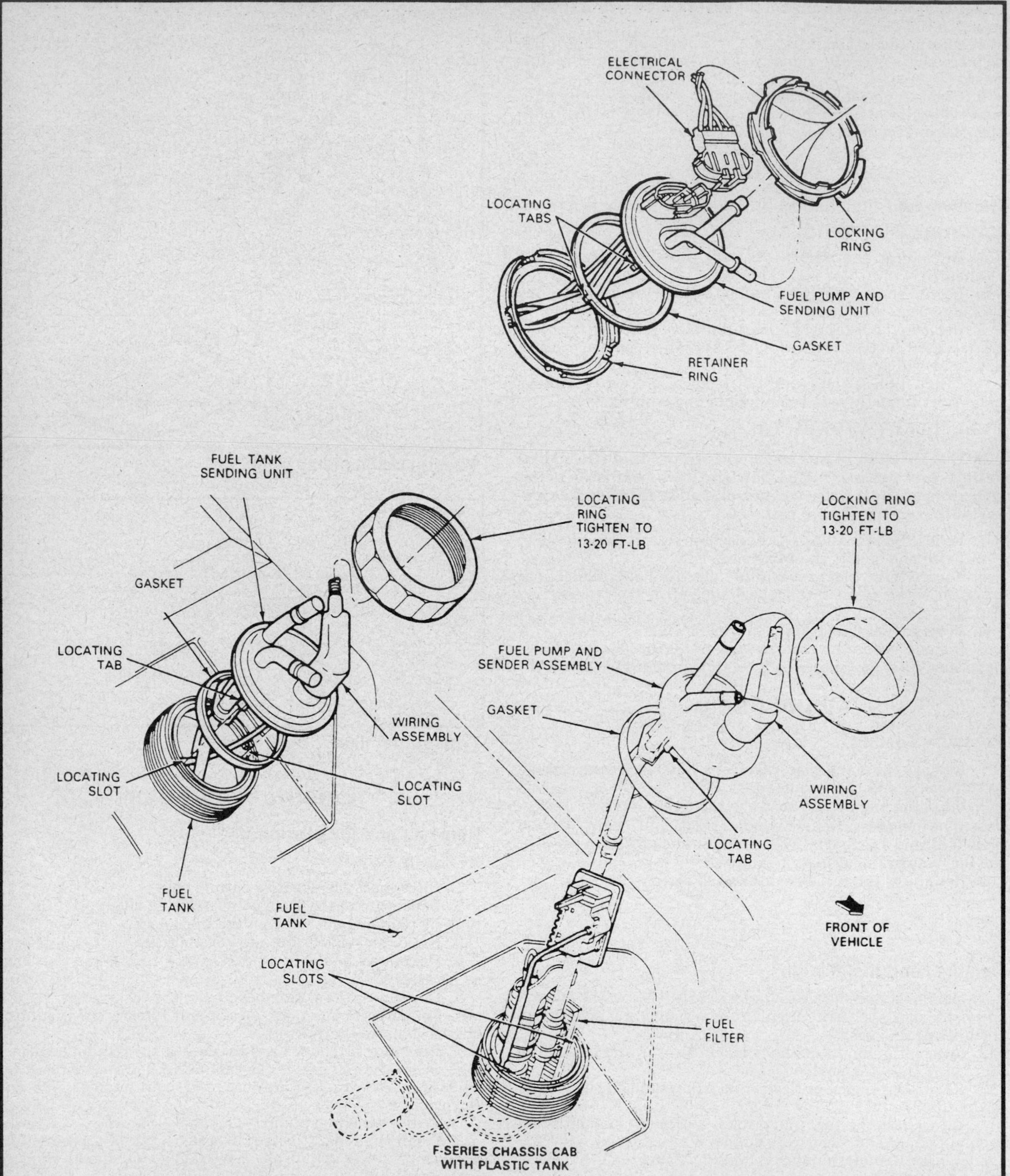

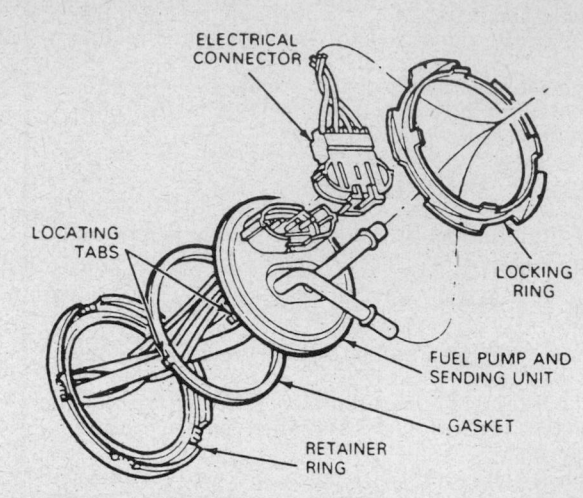

ELECTRICAL
CONNECTOR

LOCATING
TABS

LOCKING
RING

FUEL PUMP AND
SENDING UNIT

GASKET

RETAINER
RING

FUEL TANK
SENDING UNIT

GASKET

LOCATING
TAB

LOCATING
SLOT

FUEL
TANK

LOCATING
RING
TIGHTEN TO
13-20 FT-LB

WIRING
ASSEMBLY

LOCATING
SLOT

LOCKING RING
TIGHTEN TO
13-20 FT-LB

FUEL PUMP AND
SENDER ASSEMBLY

GASKET

WIRING
ASSEMBLY

LOCATING
TAB

FRONT OF
VEHICLE

FUEL
TANK

LOCATING
SLOTS

FUEL
FILTER

**F-SERIES CHASSIS CAB
WITH PLASTIC TANK**

Typical low pressure fuel pump

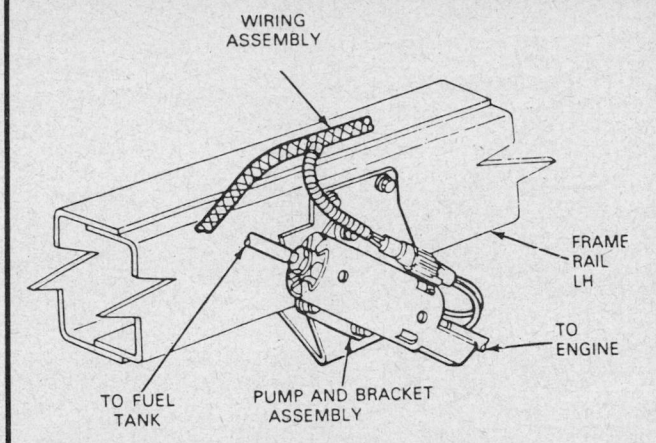

Typical high pressure fuel pump

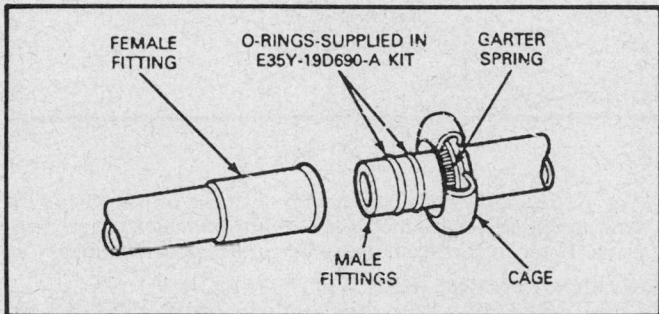

Gas line spring lock coupling

EXTERNAL PUMP

NOTE: The high pressure fuel pump is frame mounted and can be serviced from under the vehicle.

1. Disconnect the negative battery cable.
2. Depressurize the fuel system.
3. Raise and support the vehicle safely.
4. Disconnect and plug the inlet and outlet fuel lines.
5. Remove the pump from the mounting bracket.
6. Install in reverse order, make sure the pump is indexed correctly in the mounting bracket insulator. Always start fuel line threads by hand before tightening with wrench.

Carburetor

Removal and Installation

1. Disconnect the negative battery cable. Remove the air cleaner and duct assembly.
2. Remove the throttle cable or rod from the throttle lever. Disconnect the distributor vacuum line, EGR vacuum line, if so equipped, the inline fuel filter and the choke heat tube at the carburetor.
3. Disconnect the choke clean air tube from the air horn. Disconnect the choke actuating cable, if so equipped. Disconnect the electric choke wire at the connector, if so equipped. Disconnect the governor throttle control lines and governor wire connector at the carburetor, if so equipped.
4. Remove the carburetor retaining nuts, then remove the carburetor. Remove the carburetor mounting gasket, spacer and the lower gasket from the intake manifold.
5. Installation is the reverse of the removal procedure. Adjust the carburetor to specification, as required. Torque the carburetor mounting nuts to 14–20 ft. lbs.

Idle Speed Adjustment

4.9L ENGINE WITH YFA 1-V FB AND IDLE SPEED CONTROL CARBURETOR

1. Block drive wheels, apply parking brake and bring engine to normal operating temperature.
2. Remove the air cleaner and plug vacuum lines at air cleaner.
3. Turn off all accessories.
4. Perform closed throttle plate speed adjustment (kill speed) as follows:
   a. With the engine **OFF**, locate SELF-TEST connector and SELF-TEST INPUT (STI) connector. These 2 connectors are located on the passengener side of the engine compartment.
   b. Connect a jumper wire betwwen the STI connector and the signal return pin on the SELF-TEST connector.
   c. Turn ignition key to the run position. Do not start the engine.
   d. The ISC plunger wiil retract. Wait about 10 seconds and shut off key. Remove the jumper wire.
   e. Start the engine verify that the anti-diesel setting (when ISC motor is retracted the throttle should rest against anti-diesel screw) is at or below 500 rpm in **N**.
   f. Reset the anti-diesel screw as required. Reconnect the ISC electrical connection.
5. Perform maximum extension speed adjustment as follows:
   a. With engine in **P** or **N** and all accessories off, warm engine to normal operating temperture.
   b. Shut engine **OFF**. Disconnect engine coolant temperature sensor (ECT) connector.

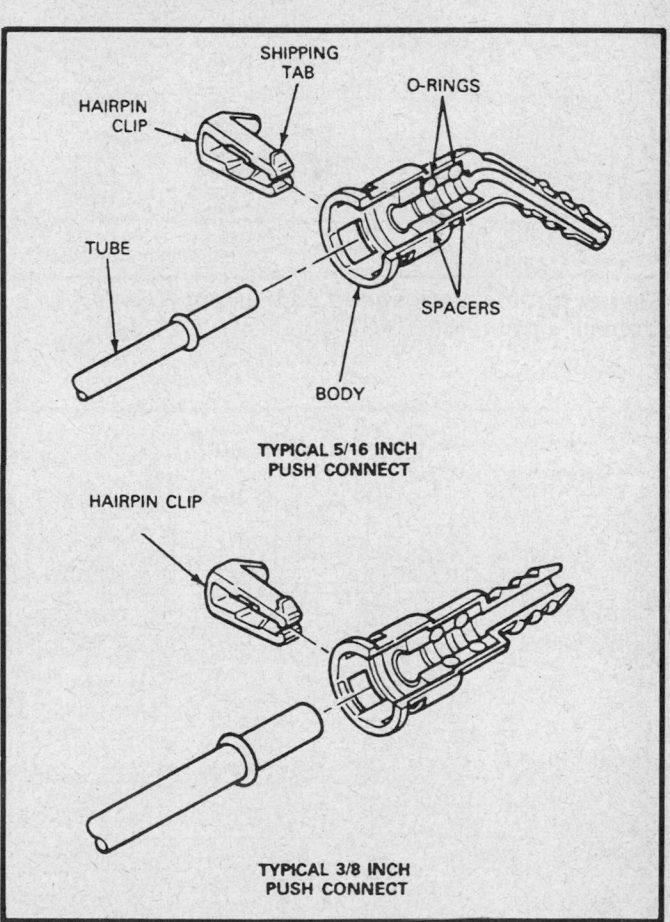

Gas line push connectors

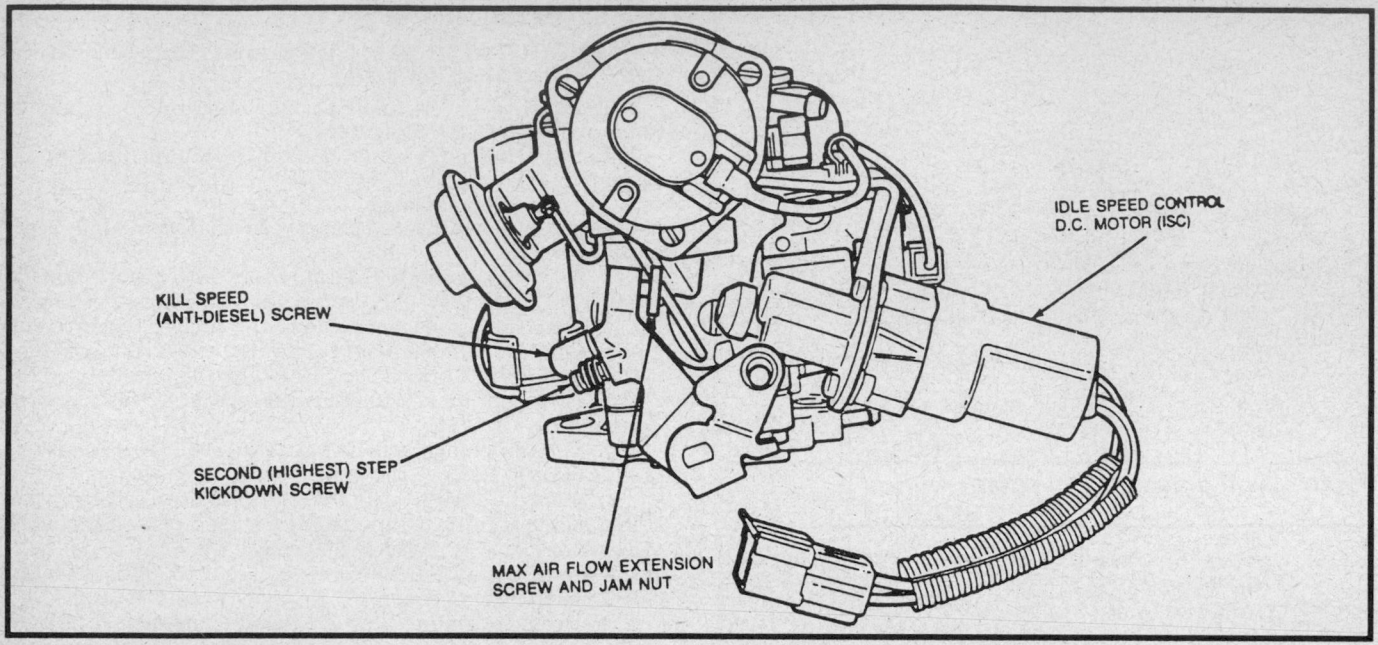

YFA-IV feeback carburetor

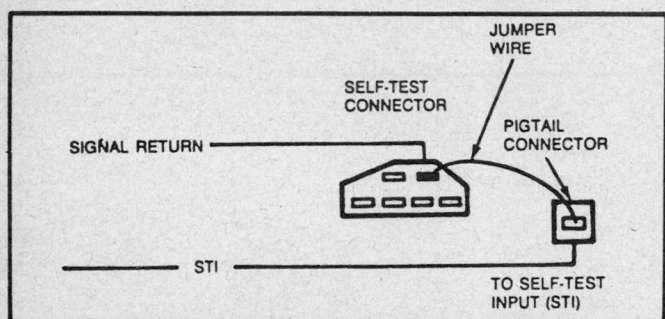

Closed throttle plate speed adjustment–YFA-IV feeback carburetor

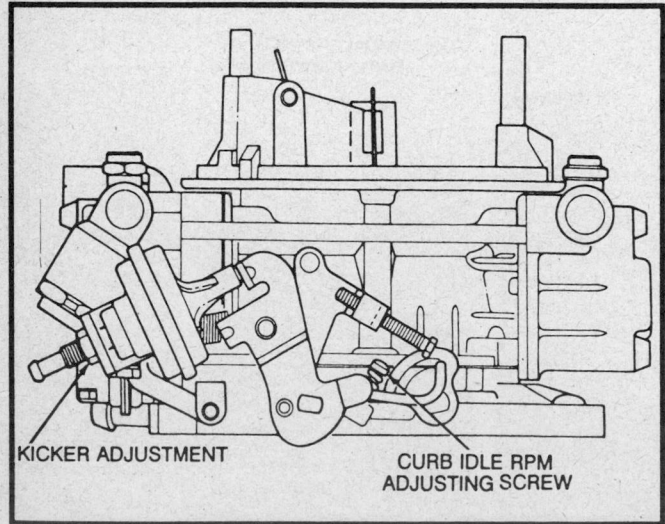

Curb idle adjustment–4180C 4-V carburetor

c. Start engine and open throttle 3 times. Adjust (using Allen wrench) idle speed motor maximum extension to specifications. Refer to Emission decal for correct specifications.

5.8L AND 7.5L ENGINES WITH 4180-C 4-V CARBURRETOR

1. Block drive wheels, apply parking brake and bring engine to normal operating temperature.
2. Place the transmission in **N** or **P** and turn off all accessories.
3. Disconnect and plug vacuum hoses at air bypass valve, EGR valve and purge control valve.
4. Adjust the curb idle speed screw as required. Refer to Emission decal for correct specifications.

Idle Mixture Adjustment
PROPANE ENRICHMENT METHOD

NOTE: Remove the air cleaner when necessary to perform adjustments. Use this service and adjustment procedure as a guide.

1. Bring the engine to normal operation temperature and connect a tachometer.
2. Disconnect the evaporative emission purge hose from the air cleaner. Disconnect the PCV closure hose from the air cleaner and plug the hose.
3. Adjust the curb idle speed to specifications.
4. If vehicle is equipped with thermactor system, revise the dump valve vacuum hoses as follows:
   a. For dump valves with 2 vacuum fittings, disconnect and plug the hose(s).
   b. For dump valves with 1 fitting, remove the hose at the dump valve and plug it. Connect a slave hose from the dump valve vacuum fitting to an intake manifold vacuum fitting.
5. Place the special gas tool into the air cleaner evaporative purge nipple. With the engine idling, slowly open the propane valve until the engine speed reaches a maximum and then begins to drop. Note the maximum speed increase. If the speed will not drop, check the bottle gas supply. If necessary, repeat the operation with a new bottle gas supply.
   a. If the speed increase is within specifications, but not

zero rpm, proceed to Step 6. If the speed increase is zero and minus specification is zero, proceed to Step 5d.

b. If the speed increase is higher than specification; enrich the mixture without propane by turning the mixture limiter screws counterclockwise in equal amounts until the rpm increases as necessary. Example: If the increase was 80 rpm and the desired reset is 50 rpm, the mixture screws should be richened to attain a 30 rpm increase. Repeat Steps 3 and 5.

c. If the speed increase is lower than specifications proceed as follows; lean the mixture without propane by turning the mixture screws clockwise in equal amounts until the rpm decreases as necessary. Example: If the increase was zero rpm and the desired reset increase is 20 rpm, the mixture screws should be leaned to attain a 20 rpm decrease. Repeat Steps 3 and 5.

d. If the speed increase is zero rpm and the minimum speed gain specification is zero, perform the following speed drop test; Turn the mixture limiters counterclockwise to the maximum rich position. (If the limiters have been removed, do not enrich; assume the mixture screws are already set at the maximum rich position.) Lean the idle fuel mixture by turning the screws clockwise equally as specified. Note the drop in engine rpm.

e. If the speed drop is equal to or greater than the specified minimum speed drop, return the mixture limiters to the maximum rich position or the mixture screws to the "assumed" maximum rich position. If the engine speed before mixture adjustment was 650 rpm and the speed drop specification is 100 rpm minimum, proceed to Step 6 if the engine speed drops to at least 550 rpm or stalls.

f. If the speed drop is less than the specified minimum speed drop, leave the mixture limiters or screws in the adjusted position and repeat Steps 3 and 5.

6. If the idle limiters were removed, install new blue service limiters at the maximum rich stop. Check the speed increase after installation of the limiters to be certain that the settings were not disturbed. If the setting is within specification, proceed to Step 7, if not correct as required.

7. Remove the gas tool from the nipple and connect all system components that were removed.

8. Set the curb idle speed to specification if Step 3 required an idle speed adjustment.

9. Turn off the engine and disconnect the tachometer. Remove the limiter caps with appropriate tool if required. Road test the vehicle for proper operation.

Service Adjustments

For all carburetor sevice adjustments procedures and Specifications, please refer to "Carburetor Service" in the Unit Repair section.

Fuel Injection

Idle Speed Adjustment

4.9L, 5.0L, 5.8L AND 7.5L EFI ENGINES

1. With engine **OFF** install feeler gauge between throttle plate stop screw and throttle lever. On 4.9L use 0.050 in. feeler gauge, 5.0L use 0.050 in. automatic transmission and 0.030 on manual transmission and on 5.8L use 0.030 in. on automatic and manual transmissions. This step of the procedure is not necessary on the 7.5L engine.

2. Unplug spout connector and verify timing is base plus or minus 2 degrees BTDC.

3. Disconnect idle speed control-air bypass solenoid on all engines.

4. With transmission in **N** or **P** race engine for 30 seconds at 2500 rpm then let engine idle for 2 minutes.

5. Adjust idle speed by turning the throttle plate stop screw as necessary.

4.9L, 5.0L and 5.8L engines EFI throttle body

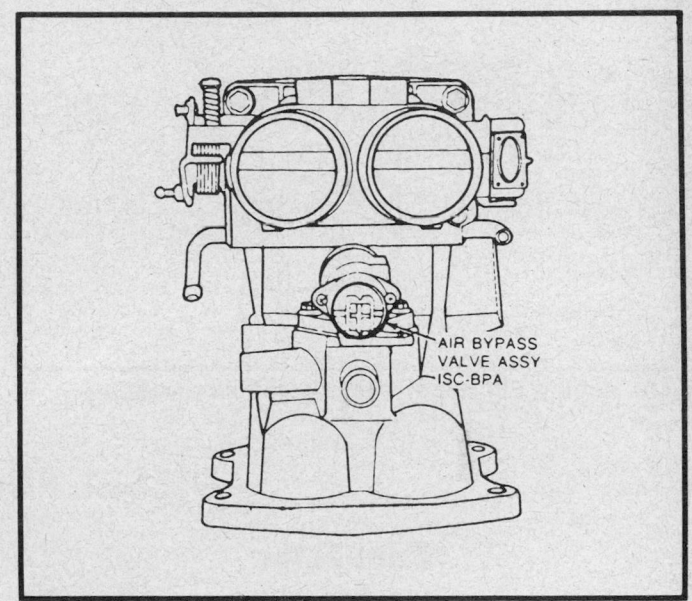

7.5L engine EFI throttle body

6. Repeat Steps 5 and 6. Turn engine to **OFF** position and disconnect battery for 3 minutes on 4.9L and 5.0L engines.

7. Remove the feeler gauge and reconnect the spout connector.

8. Start engine and let engine stabilize for 2 minutes. Road test the vehicle to check for proper operating conditions.

Fuel Injector

Removal and Installation

1. Disconnect the negative battery cable.

2. Release the pressure from the fuel system.

3. Remove the upper intake manifold as follows:

a. Disconnect the electrical connectors at the air bypass valve, throttle position sensor and EGR position sensor.

b. Disconnect the throttle linkage at the throttle ball and the AOD transmission linkage if so equipped from the throttle body.

c. Disconnect all vacuum lines to the upper intake, EGR valve and the fuel pressure regulator.

d. Disconnect the PCV system hose from the rear of the up-

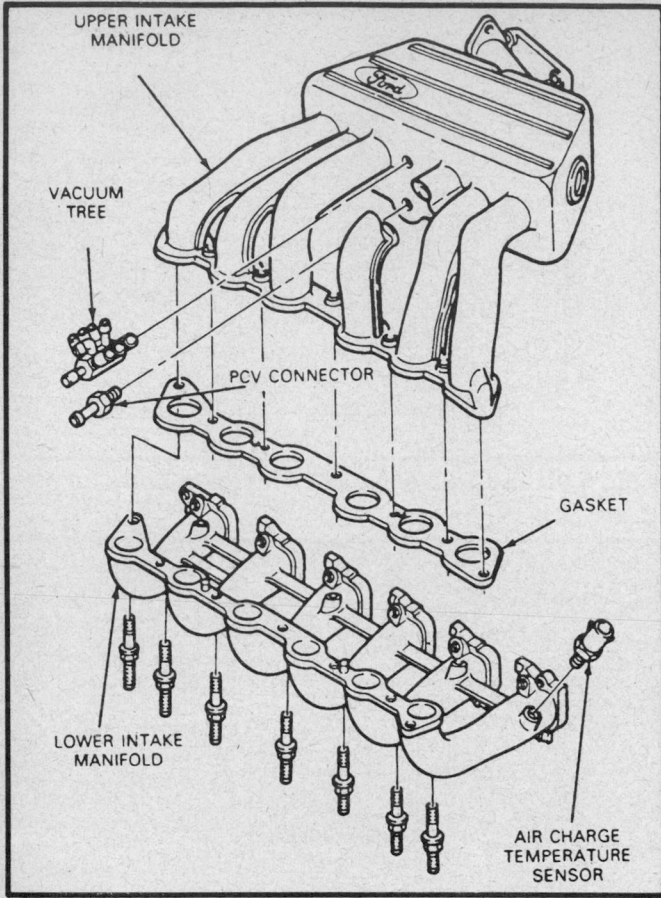

UPPER INTAKE MANIFOLD

VACUUM TREE

PCV CONNECTOR

GASKET

LOWER INTAKE MANIFOLD

AIR CHARGE TEMPERATURE SENSOR

4.9L engine EFI upper intake manifold assembly

per manifold.

e. Remove the canister purge lines and the water heater lines from the fittings on the throttle body.

f. Disconnect the EGR tube from the valve by removing the flange nut.

g. Remove the upper intake manifold retaining bolts and remove it and the throttle body as an assembly.

4. Remove the fuel supply manifold as follows:

a. Disconnect the fuel chassis inlet and outlet fuel hoses from the fuel supply manifold.

b. Disconnect the fuel supply and the return line connections.

c. Remove the manifold retaining bolts. Disengage the manifold from the injectors and remove it.

5. Remove the electrical harness connectors from the injectors and remove the injectors.

6. Installation is the reverse of the removal procedure. Never use silicone grease on injector O-rings it may clog the injectors. Torque the upper manifold retaining bolts to 12–18 ft. lbs.

DIESEL FUEL SYSTEM

Fuel Filter

Replacement

1. Disconnect the battery ground cables from both batteries.
2. Drain fuel from the fuel filter.
3. Remove the water drain tube from the bottom of the filter assembly.
4. Unscrew water separator drain bowl and remove. Remove the filter element.
5. Installation is the reverse of the removal procedure. Screw filter element onto filter base until seal contacts then tighten filter ½–1 turn additional.

Draining Water From The System

1. Turn ignition to the **OFF** position.
2. Place container under fuel filter/water separator drain tube.
3. Open drain valve. Allow drain valve to remian open approximately 15 seconds or until clear diesel fuel flows from the drain tube.
4. Close drain valve. Start engine Check Water In Fuel Lamp the lamp should not glow.

Diesel Injection Pump

Removal and Installation

1. Disconnect the negative battery cable(s).
2. Remove the engine cover (doghouse cover) on E250 and E350 series.
3. Remove the adapter housing cover plate.
4. Remove bolts attaching injection pump to drive gear.
5. Disconnect all electrical connections to injection pump.
6. Remove the fast idle solenoid bracket assembly to provide access to injection pump mounting nuts.
7. Disconnect accelerator cable and speed control cable from throttle lever, if so equipped.
8. Remove air cleaner and install suitable cover.
9. Remove accelerator cable bracket from intake manifold.
10. On E series vehicles, disconnect fuel inlet line from the fuel filter and cap all lines.
11. On E series vehicles, disconnect fuel return line from fuel filter and cap all lines.
12. On E series vehicles, remove fuel filter bracket attaching bolts and remove fuel filter and bracket as an assembly.
13. Remove fuel return hose and clip from the 90 degree elbow at the governor cover. Always cap all disconnected fuel lines.

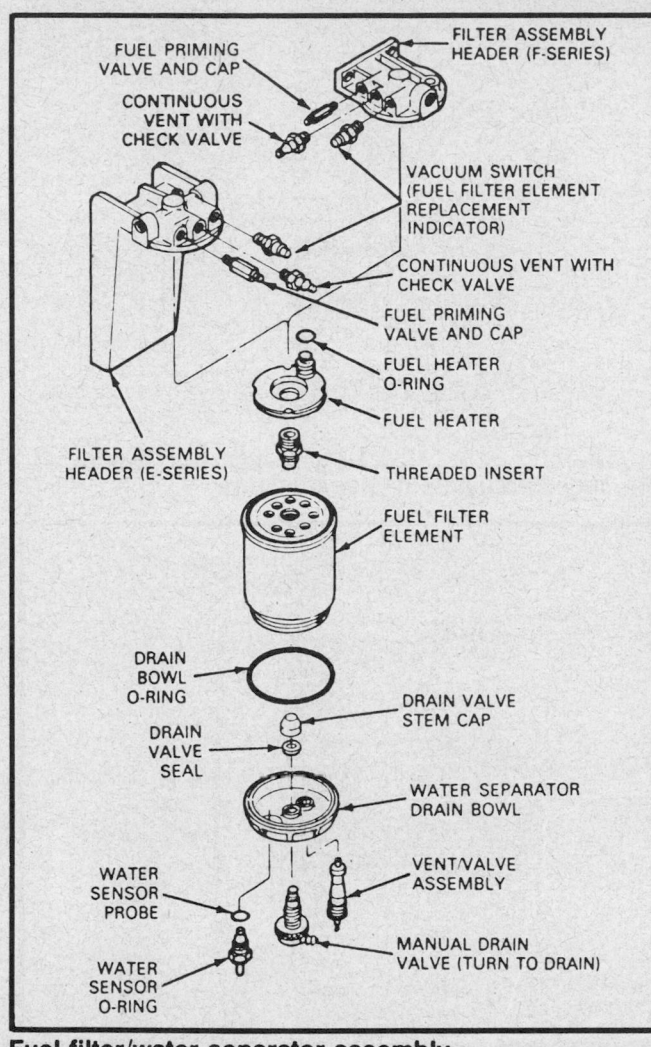

Fuel filter/water separator assembly

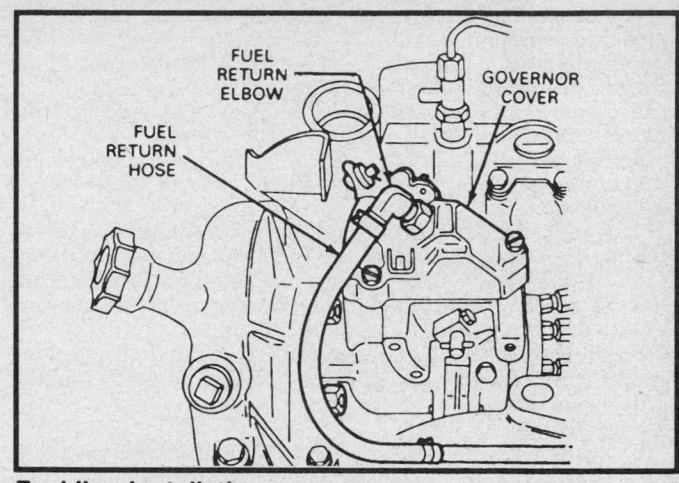

Fuel line installation

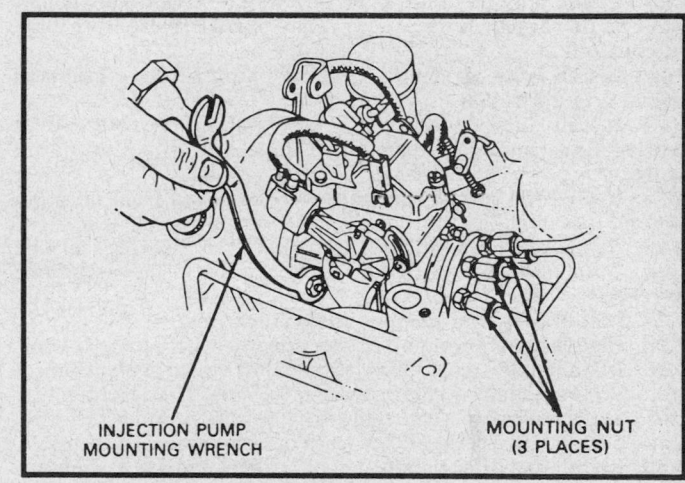

Injection pump mounting

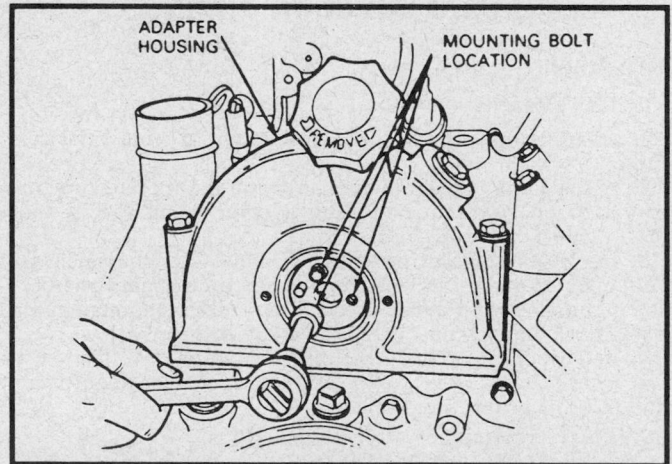

Injection pump drive gear attaching bolts

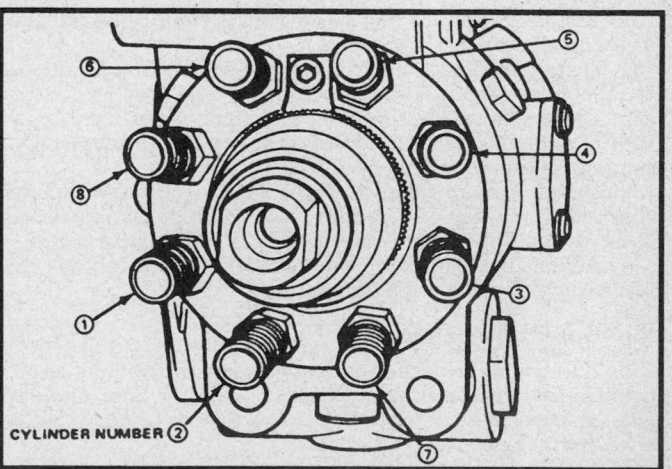

Injection pump cylinder sequence

14. Remove fuel filter to injection pump fuel line. It is not necessary to remove injection lines from injection pump to remove injection pump. If lines are to be removed, loosen injection line fittings at injection pump before removing it from engine.

15. Remove fuel injection lines from nozzles and cap lines and nozzles to prevent entry of dirt into the system.

16. Remove retaining nuts attaching injection pump to injection pump drive gear cover using special wrench T86T–9000–C or equivalent.

17. If injection pump is to be replaced, loosen injection line retaining clips and injection nozzle fuel lines and cap all fittings.

18. On F series vehicles remove injection pump, with nozzle lines attached, up and out of engine compartment. Do not carry injection pump by injection nozzle fuel lines.

19. On E series vehicles, remove injection pump through passenger compartment. Do not carry injection pump by injection nozzle fuel lines.

To install:

20. Position new O–ring onto drive gear end of injection pump.

21. On F series, install injection pump down and into position. On E series, install injection pump from passenger compartment.

22. Install alignment dowel on injection pump into alignment hole on drive gear. If necessary, rotate pump driveshaft to align drive slot.

23. Install bolts attaching injection pump to drive gear and tighten to 25 ft. lbs.

24. Install nuts attaching injection pump to adapter. Align scribe lines on injection pump flange and injection pump adapter.

25. If injection nozzle fuel lines were removed from injection pump, install at this time.

26. Remove protective caps from fuel lines. Install fuel line nuts onto nozzles and tighten to 22 ft. lbs. using a suitable wrench.

27. Install fuel inlet line and fuel return line.

28. Install injection pump fitting adapter with a new O-ring.

29. Install elbow (coat elbow threads with pipe sealant) in injection pump adapter and tighten to 6 ft. lbs. Then tighten further, if necessary, to align elbow with injection pump fuel inlet line, but do not exceed 360 degrees of rotation or 10 ft. lbs.

30. Install fuel filter to injection pump fuel line. On E series install fuel filter and bracket as an assembly.

31. Install fuel filter return line and inlet line as necessary.

32. Install accelerator cable bracket to intake manifold and air cleaner.

33. Install accelerator and speed control cable, if so equipped, to throttle lever.

34. Install fast idle solenoid bracket assembly. Reconnect electrical connectors on injection pump.

35. Clean adapter housing cover plate sealing surfaces. Apply a bead of sealant in adapter housing grooves. Install adapter cover tighten retaining bolts to 14 ft. lbs.

36. Install ground cables to both batteries. Start engine and check for fuel leaks. If necessary, bleed high pressure fuel lines of air by loosening connection ½ turn and cranking engine.

37. Adjust injection pump timing. Check idle speed and road test vehicle for proper operation.

Idle Speed Adjustment

1. Run engine to normal operating temperature. Idle speed is determined with manual transmission in **N** and automatic transmission in **D**.

2. Set transmission in **N** or **P**.

3. Check that curb idle adjusting screw is against the stop correct if necessary.

4. Check idle speed, using tachometer or equivalant test equipment. Idle speed is specified on the Vehicle Emissions Control Information decal. Adjust to specification using idle speed adjusting screw.

5. Road test to check for proper operation of the vehicle.

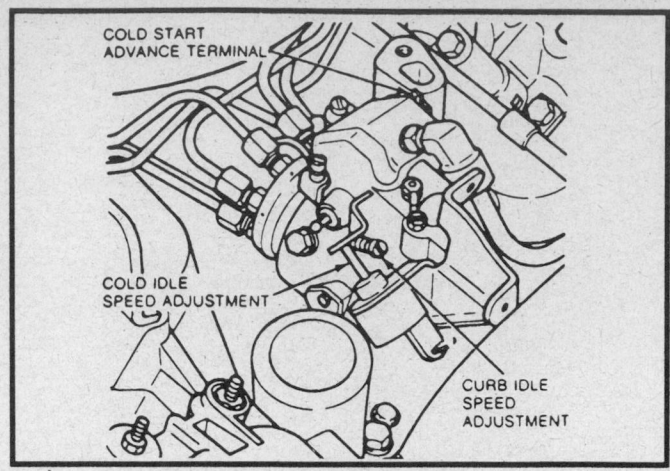

Idle speed adjustment–diesel engine

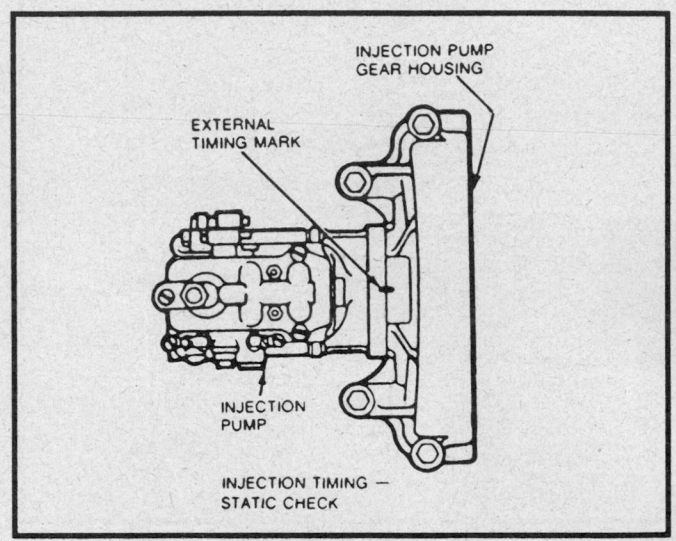

Injection pump timing marks

Diesel Injection Timing

Adjustment

STATIC TIMING

1. Remove fast idle bracket and solenoid from injection pump.

2. Break torque (keeping nuts snug) on 3 nuts attaching injection pump to pump mounting adapter using special tool T86T–9000–C or equivalent.

3. Install special rotating tool T83T–9000–C or equivalent on front of pump and rotate injection to align timing mark on injection pump mounting flange with timing mark on pump mounting adapter, to with plus or minus 0.030 inch.

4. Remove rotating tool and tighten nuts to 25 ft. lbs.

5. Check timing to verify that timing marks are aligned. Install fast idle bracket and solenoid.

DYNAMIC TIMING

6.9L Engine

1. Bring engine up to normal operating temperature. When checking or setting dynamic injection timing it is mandatory that the engine be stabilized at normal operating temperature. This temperature is needed to ensure proper fuel ignition in the precombustion chambers.

2. Obtain fuel sample and check cetane valve using special tester or equivalent.

3. Install special tool dynamic timing meter Rotunda 078–00200 or equivalent, by placing magnetic pickup in timing pointer probe hole. Insert pickup until it almost touches vibration damper.

4. Remove No. 1 glow plug. Install luminosity probe and tighten to 12 ft. lbs. Install photocell over probe.

5. Connect dynamic timing meter to battery and dial in minus 20 degrees offset on meter. Disconnect cold start advance solenoid connector from solenoid terminal.

6. With transmission in **N** and rear wheels raised off the ground, start engine. Using throttle control tool D83T–9000–E or equivalent, set engine speed to 1400 rpm with no accessory load. Observe injection timing on dynamic timing meter.

7. Apply battery voltage to cold start advance solenoid terminal to activate it. Activating cold start advance solenoid can result in engine speed increase. Adjust throttle control to attain 1400 rpm, if necessary.

8. Check timing at 1400 rpm. The timing should be advanced at least 2.5 degrees before the timing obtained in Step 9 of this procedure.

9. If dynamic timing is not with plus or minus 2 degrees of specification, adjustment of pump timing is necessary.

10. Turn engine off. Note timing mark alignment. Remove fast idle bracket and solenoid from injection pump. Break torque (keeping nuts snug) on nuts attaching injection pump to pump mounting adapter.

11. Install special rotating tool, T83T–9000–C or equivalent, on front of pump. Rotate clockwise (when viewed from front of engine) to retard and counterclockwise to advance timing, by lightly tapping tool with a rubber mallet. A 2 degree movement of dynamic timing is approximately 0.030 inch of timing mark movement.

12. Remove rotating tool and tighten nuts to 25 ft. lbs. Start engine and recheck timing.

13. Turn engine off. Remove dynamic timing components. Install glow plug and electrical connection. Install fast idle bracket and solenoid.

7.3L Engine

1. Bring engine up to normal operating temperature. When checking or setting dynamic injection timing it is mandatory that the engine be stabilized at normal operating temperature. This temperature is needed to ensure proper fuel ignition in the precombustion chambers.

2. Stop engine and install special tool dynamic timing meter Rotunda 078–00200 or equivalent, by placing magnetic pickup in timing pointer probe hole. Insert pickup until it almost touches vibration damper.

3. Install clamp from timing meter adapter Rotunda 078–00201 or equivalent, to the line pressure sensor on No. 1 injector nozzle (F series) and No. 4 injector nozzle (E series) and connect to timing meter.

4. Connect dynamic timing meter to battery and dial in minus 20 degrees offset on meter. Disconnect cold start advance solenoid connector from solenoid terminal.

5. With transmission in **N** and rear wheels raised off the ground, start engine. Using throttle control tool D83T–9000–E or equivalent, set engine speed to 2000 rpm with no accessory load. Observe injection timing on dynamic timing meter. Injection timing should be 8.5 degrees BTDC at 2000 rpm.

6. Apply battery voltage to cold start advance solenoid terminal to activate it. Activating cold start advance solenoid can result in engine speed increase. Adjust throttle control to attain 2000 rpm, if necessary.

7. Check timing at 2000 rpm. The timing should be advanced at least 1 degree before the timing obtained in Step 5. If the advance is less than 1 degree, replace fuel injection pump top cover assembly.

8. If dynamic timing is not with plus or minus 2 degrees of

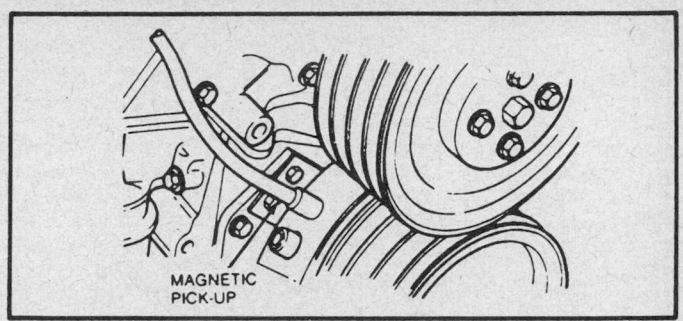
Magnetic pickup–dynamic timing

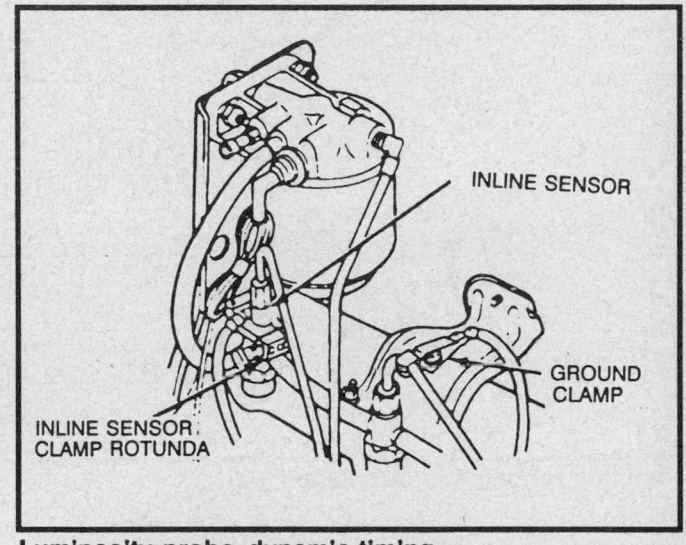
Luminosity probe–dynamic timing

specification, adjustment of pump timing is necessary.

9. Turn engine off. Note timing mark alignment. Remove fast idle bracket and solenoid from injection pump. Break torque (keeping nuts snug) on nuts attaching injection pump to pump mounting adapter.

10. Install special rotating tool, T83T–9000–C or equivalent, on front of pump. Rotate clockwise (when viewed from front of engine) to retard and counterclockwise to advance timing, by lightly tapping tool with a rubber mallet. A 2 degree movement of dynamic timing is approximately 0.030 inch of timing mark movement.

11. Remove rotating tool and tighten nuts to 25 ft. lbs. Start engine and recheck timing.

12. Turn engine off. Remove dynamic timing components. Install fast idle bracket and solenoid.

Fuel Nozzles

Removal and Installation

NOTE: Before removing nozzle assemblies, clean exterior of each nozzle assembly and the surrounding area with solvent to prevent entry of dirt into engine when nozzle assemblies are removed. Always cap all open fuel lines to prevent dirt from entering system.

1. Disconnect the negative battery cable. Disconnect nozzle fuel inlet (high pressure) and fuel leak off tees from each nozzle assembly.

2. Remove fuel leak off lines as an assembly.

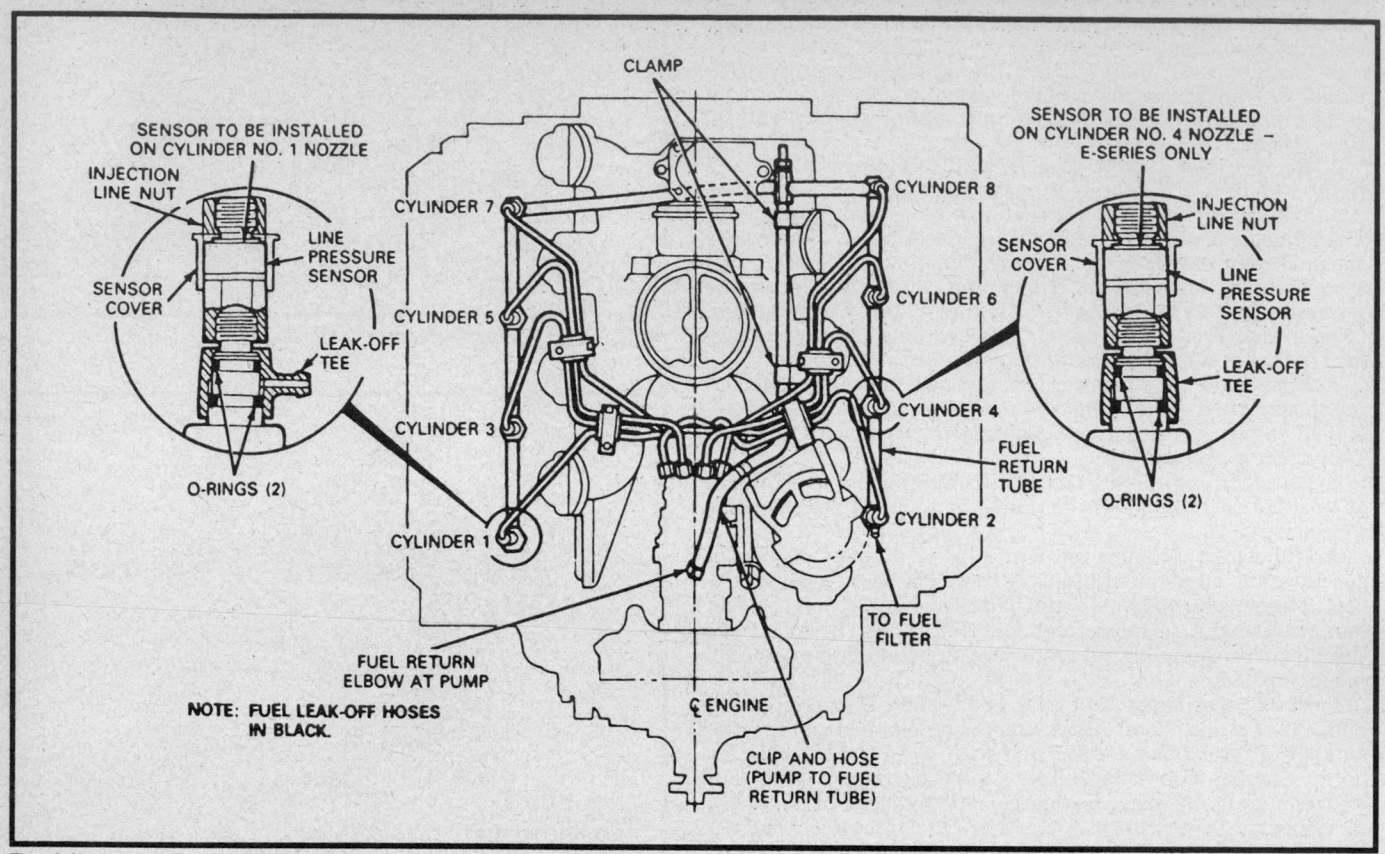

Fuel line routing and installation

3. Remove injection nozzles by turning counterclockwise. Pull nozzle assembly with copper washer from engine. Be careful not to strike nozzle tip against any hard surface during removal.

4. Installation is the reverse of the removal procedure. Thoroughly clean nozzle bore in cylinder head before reinserting nozzle assembly. Tighten nozzle assembly to 35 ft. lbs. Bleed fuel system if necessary.

EMISSION CONTROLS

Please refer to "Professional Emission Component Application Guide".

Emission Warning Lamps

Resetting

NOTE: The Emission Maintenance Warning (EMW) light system consists of an instrument panel mounted amber lens light that is electrically connected to a sensor module located under the instrument panel.

1. Turn the key switch to the **OFF** position.
2. Lightly push a tool through the 0.2 in. diameter hole with the sticker labeled "RESET" and press down and hold.

3. While pressing the tool, turn the keyswitch to the **RUN** position. The Emission Maintenance Warning (EMW) lamp will then light and remain lit for as long as the tool is pressed down.

4. Hold the tool down for 5 seconds. Remove the tool. The lamp should go out within 2 to 5 seconds indicating a reset has occurred.

5. Turn the keyswitch to the **OFF** position then turn the keyswitch to the **RUN** position. The EMW lamp will light for 2–5 seconds and will then go out. This verifies that a proper reset of the module has been accomplished.

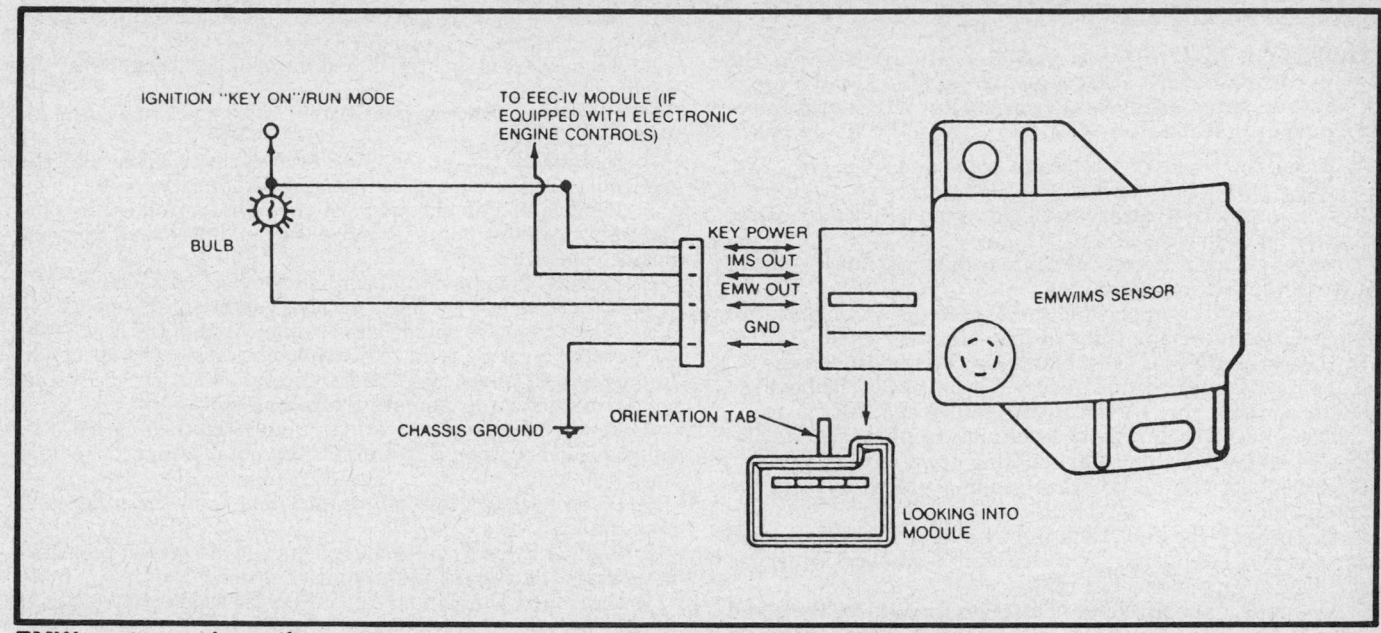

EMW system schematic

GASOLINE ENGINE MECHANICAL

Engine

Removal and Installation

BRONCO AND F SERIES

4.9L Engine

NOTE: On fuel injected vehicles always relieve the fuel pressure before starting this repair. Always mark all vacuum lines, electrical connection wires and hoses for correct installation.

1. Drain the cooling system and the crankcase. Remove (mark the hood hinges for correct installation) the hood and the air cleaner. Disconnect the negative battery cable.
2. Disconnect the heater hose from the water pump and coolant outlet housing.
3. Disconnect the flexible fuel line from the fuel pump. Remove the throttle body inlet tubes if so equipped.
4. Evacuate the air conditioning system. Remove the air conditioner compressor and the condenser.
5. Remove the radiator. Remove the fan, water pump pulley and fan belt.
6. Disconnect the accelerator cable at the carburetor or throttle body. Remove the throttle return spring.
7. On vehicles equipped with power brakes, disconnect the brake booster vacuum hose at the intake manifold. On vehicles with automatic transmission, disconnect the transmission kickdown rod at the bellcrank assembly or the cable at the throttle body.
8. Disconnect the exhaust pipe from the exhaust manifold. Disconnect the body ground strap and the battery ground cable from the engine. Disconnect the Electronic Engine Control (EEC) harness from all sensors if so equipped.
9. Disconnect the engine wiring harness at the ignition coil, the coolant temperature sending unit and the oil pressure send-

ing unit. Position the wiring harness out of the way.
10. Remove the alternator mounting bolts and position the alternator out of the way.
11. On a vehicle equipped with power steering, remove the power steering pump from the mounting brackets and move it to one side, leaving the lines attached.
12. Raise and safely support the vehicle.
13. Remove the starter and automatic transmission filler tube bracket, if so equipped. Also, remove the rear engine plate upper right bolt.
14. On manual transmission equipped vehicles, remove the flywheel housing lower attaching bolts and disconnect the clutch return spring.
15. On automatic transmission equipped vehicles, remove the converter housing access cover assembly and remove the flywheel-to-converter attaching nuts. Secure the converter in the housing. Remove the transmission oil cooler lines from the retaining clip at the engine. Remove the lower converter housing-to-engine attaching bolts.
16. Remove the nut from each of the 2 front engine mounts.
17. Lower the vehicle and position a jack under the transmission and support it. Remove the remaining bellhousing-to-engine attaching bolts.
18. Attach the engine lifting device and raise the engine slightly and carefully pull it from the transmission. Lift the engine out of the vehicle.
19. Installation is the reverse of the removal procedure.
20. Torque all bolts to specifications. Fill the cooling system. Fill the crankcase.

21. Start the engine and check for leaks. Bleed the cooling system. Adjust the clutch pedal free-play or the automatic transmission control linkage.

5.0L and 5.8L Engines

NOTE: On fuel injected vehicles always relieve the fuel pressure before starting this repair. Always mark all vacuum lines, electrical connection wires and hoses for correct installation.

1. Drain the cooling system and crankcase. Remove (mark the hinges for correct installation) the hood.
2. Disconnect the battery cable first and alternator cables from the cylinder block.
3. Remove the air cleaner and intake duct assembly, plus the crankcase ventilation hose.
4. Disconnect the upper and lower radiator hoses and if so equipped, the automatic transmission oil cooler lines.
5. Discharge the A/C system and remove the condenser.
6. Remove the fan shroud and lay it over the fan. Remove the radiator and fan, shroud, fan spacer, pulley and belt.
7. Disconnect the alternator leads and the alternator adjusting bolts. Allow the alternator to swing down out of the way.
8. Disconnect the oil pressure sending unit lead from the sending unit.
9. Disconnect the fuel tank-to-pump fuel line at the fuel pump and plug the line. For EFI, disconnect the chassis fuel line quick disconnects at the fuel rails.
10. Disconnect the accelerator linkage. Disconnect the speed control linkages. Disconnect the automatic transmission kickdown rod and remove the return spring, if so equipped.
11. Disconnect the power brake booster vacuum hose.
12. For EFI, after disconnecting the accelerator and the TV cable from the throttle body, disconnect the throttle bracket from the upper intake manifold and swing out of the way with the cables still attached to the bracket.
13. Disconnect the heater hoses from the water pump and intake manifold. Disconnect the temperature sending unit wire from the sending unit.
14. Remove the upper bellhousing-to-engine attaching bolts.
15. Disconnect the primary wire from the coil. Remove the wiring harness from the left rocker arm cover and position the wires out of the way. Disconnect the ground strap from the cylinder block.
16. Raise and safely support the vehicle and disconnect the starter cable from the starter. Remove the starter.
17. Disconnect the exhaust pipe from the exhaust manifolds.
18. Disconnect the engine mounts from the brackets on the frame.
19. On vehicles with automatic transmission, remove the converter inspection plate and remove the torque converter-to-flywheel attaching bolts.
20. Remove the remaining bellhousing-to-engine attaching bolts.
21. Lower the vehicle and support the transmission with a jack.
22. Install an engine lifting device.
23. Raise the engine slightly and carefully pull it out from the transmission. Lift the engine out of the engine compartment.
24. Install the engine in the reverse order of removal procedure. Make sure that the dowels in the engine block engage the holes in the bellhousing through the rear cover plate.
25. Torque all bolts to specifications. Fill the cooling system. Fill the crankcase.
26. Start the engine and check for leaks. Bleed the cooling system. Adjust the clutch pedal free-play or the automatic transmission control linkage as necessary.

7.5L Engine

NOTE: On fuel injected vehicles always relieve the fuel pressure before starting this repair. Always mark all vacuum lines, electrical connection wires and hoses for correct installation.

1. Mark the hood hinges for correct installation then remove the hood.
2. Drain the cooling system and the cylinder block. Drain the engine oil.
3. Disconnect the negative battery cable and remove the air cleaner assembly.
4. Disconnect the upper and lower radiator hoses and the transmission oil cooler lines from the radiator.
5. Remove the fan shroud from the radiator and remove the fan from the water pump. Remove the fan and shroud from the engine compartment.
6. Remove the upper support and remove the radiator.
7. If the vehicle is equipped with air conditioning, remove the compressor from the engine and position it out of the way. If the compressor must be removed completely, loosen the air conditioning service valves (disconnect) carefully to discharge the air conditioning system. Remove the compressor.
8. Remove the power steering pump from the engine, if so equipped and position it to one side. Do not disconnect the fluid lines.
9. Disconnect the fuel pump inlet line from the pump and plug the line.
10. Remove the alternator drive belts and disconnect the alternator from the engine, positioning it aside.
11. Disconnect the ground cable from the right front corner of the engine.
12. Disconnect the heater hoses.
13. Remove the transmission fluid filler tube attaching bolt from the right-side valve cover and position the tube out of the way.
14. Disconnect all vacuum lines at the rear of the intake manifold.
15. Disconnect the speed control cable at the carburetor, if so equipped. Disconnect the accelerator rod and the transmission kickdown rod and secure them out of the way.
16. Disconnect the engine wiring harness at the connector on the fire wall.
17. Raise and support the vehicle safely. Disconnect the exhaust pipes at the exhaust manifolds.
18. Disconnect the starter cable and remove the starter. Bring the starter forward and rotate the solenoid outward to remove the assembly.
19. Remove the access cover from the converter housing and remove the flywheel-to-converter attaching nuts. Remove the lower converter housing-to-engine attaching bolts.
20. Remove the engine mount through-bolts attaching the rubber insulators to the frame brackets.
21. Lower the vehicle and place a jack under the transmission to support it.
22. Remove the converter housing-to-engine block attaching bolts (left-side).
23. Disconnect the coil wire and remove the coil and bracket assembly from the intake manifold.
24. Attach the engine lifting device and carefully lift the engine from the engine compartment.
25. Install the engine in the reverse order of removal procedure.
26. Torque all bolts to specifications. Fill the cooling system. Fill the crankcase.
27. Start the engine and check for leaks. Bleed the cooling system. Adjust the clutch pedal free-play or the automatic transmission control linkage as necessary.

E SERIES

4.9L Engine

NOTE: On fuel injected vehicles always relieve the fuel pressure before starting this repair. Always mark all vacuum lines, electrical connection wires and hoses for correct installation.

1. Take off the engine cover (doghouse cover), drain the coolant, remove the air cleaner and disconnect the battery.
2. Remove the bumper, grille and gravel deflector.
3. Remove the upper radiator hose at the engine. Remove the alternator splash shield and detach the lower hose at the radiator. Remove the radiator and shroud, if equipped.
4. Disconnect the engine heater hoses and the alternator wires. Remove the power steering pump and support. If vehicle is equipped with air conditioning, discharge the system and remove the air conditioning compressor.
5. Disconnect and plug the fuel line at the pump.
6. Disconnect the Electronic Engine Control (EEC) harness from all sensors, if so equipped.
7. Detach from the engine: distributor and gauge sending unit wires, brake booster hose, accelerator cable and bracket.
8. Disconnect the automatic transmission kickdown linkage at the bellcrank. With fuel injection, disconnect the cable at the throttle body.
9. Remove the exhaust manifold heat deflector and unbolt the pipe from the manifold.
10. Disconnect the automatic transmission vacuum line from the intake manifold and from the junction. Remove the transmission dipstick tube support bolt at the intake manifold.
11. Raise and safely support the vehicle. Remove the upper engine-to-transmission bolts.
12. Remove the starter. Remove the flywheel inspection cover. Remove the automatic transmission torque converter retaining nuts, then remove the front engine support nuts. Drain the engine oil and remove the oil filter.
13. Remove the rest of the transmission-to-engine fasteners, then lift the engine out from the engine compartment with a floor crane.
14. Installation is the reverse of the removal procedure.
15. Check all fluid levels. Start the engine and check for leaks. Bleed the cooling system. Adjust the clutch pedal free-play or the automatic transmission control linkage as necessary.

5.0L, 5.8L and 7.5L Engines

NOTE: On fuel injected vehicles always relieve the fuel pressure before starting this repair. Always mark all vacuum lines, electrical connection wires and hoses for correct installation.

1. Take off the engine cover (doghouse cover), drain the coolant, remove the air cleaner and disconnect the battery. Remove the bumper, grille and gravel deflector. Remove the upper grille support bracket, hood lock support and air conditioning condenser upper mounting brackets.
2. With air conditioning, the system must be discharged to remove the condenser. Disconnect the lines at the compressor.
3. Remove the accelerator cable bracket and the heater hoses. Detach the radiator hoses and the automatic traransmission shift rod.
7. Disconnect the fuel and choke lines, detach the vacuum lines and remove the carburetor and spacer on vehicles so equipped.
8. Raise the vehicle and safely support as necessary. Drain oil and remove the oil finsmission cooler lines, if any. Remove the fan shroud, fan and radiator.
4. Pivot the alternator in and detach the wires.
5. Remove the air cleaner, duct and valve, exhaust manifold shroud and flex tube.
6. Disconnect the automatic tlter. Detach the exhaust pipe from the manifold. Unbolt the automatic transmission tube bracket from the cylinder head. Remove the starter.
9. Remove the engine mount bolts. With automatic, remove the converter inspection cover and unbolt the converter from the flex plate.
10. Unbolt the engine ground cable and support the transmission.

11. Remove the power steering front bracket. Detach only one vacuum line at the rear of the intake manifold. Disconnect the engine wiring loom. Remove the speed control servo from the manifold. Detach the compressor clutch wire.
12. Install a lifting bracket and attach a floor crane. Remove the transmission-to-engine bolts, making sure the transmission is supported. Remove the engine.
13. Installation is the reverse of the removal procedure.
14. Check all fluid levels. Start the engine and check for leaks. Bleed the cooling system. Adjust the clutch pedal free-play or the automatic transmission control linkage as necessary.

Cylinder Head

Removal and Installation

4.9L ENGINE

1. Drain the cooling system. Remove the air cleaner. Remove the oil filler tube. Disconnect the negative battery cable.
2. Relieve fuel pressure and throttle body inlet tubes if so equipped. Disconnect the muffler inlet pipe at the exhaust manifold. Pull the muffler inlet pipe down. Remove the gasket.
3. Disconnect the accelerator rod or cable retracting spring. Disconnect the choke control cable and the accelerator rod at the carburetor if so equipped.
4. Disconnect the transmission kickdown rod. Disconnect the accelerator linkage at the bellcrank assembly.
5. Disconnect the fuel inlet line at the fuel filter hose and the distributor vacuum line at the carburetor if so equipped. Disconnect other vacuum lines as necessary for accessibility and identify them for proper connection.
6. Remove the radiator upper hose at the coolant outlet housing.
7. Disconnect the distributor vacuum line at the distributor. Disconnect the carburetor if so equipped fuel inlet line at the fuel pump. Remove the lines as an assembly.
8. Disconnect the spark plug wires at the spark plugs and the temperature sending unit wire at the sending unit.
9. Grasp the PCV vent hose near the PCV valve and pull the valve out of the grommet in the valve rocker arm cover. Disconnect the PCV vent hose at the hose fitting in the intake manifold spacer and remove the vent hose and PCV valve.
10. Disconnect the carburetor if so equipped air vent tube and remove the valve rocker arm cover.
11. Remove the valve rocker arm shaft assembly. Remove the pushrods in sequence so that they can be identified and reinstalled in their original positions.
12. Remove the cylinder head bolts and remove the cylinder head. Do not pry between the cylinder head and the block as the gasket surfaces may be damaged.
13. Installation is the reverse of the removal procedure. Coat the threads of the cylinder head bolts with engine oil. Tighten the bolts in numerical sequence and tighten in 3 steps. The 1st

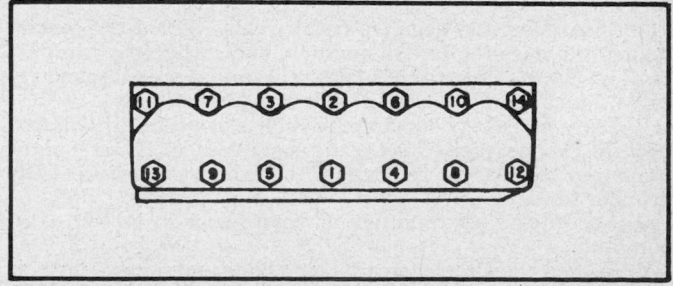

Cylinder head bolts tightening sequence—4.9L engine

step 50–55 ft. lbs., 2nd step 60–65 ft. lbs. and 3rd step 70–85 ft. lbs. It is not necessary to retorque cylinder head bolts after extended operation.

5.0L AND 5.8L ENGINES

1. Disconnect the negative battery cable. Drain the cooling system. Remove the intake manifold and carburetor as an assembly. On fuel injected vehicles relieve fuel pressure and remove intake manifold and throttle body as assembly.

2. Remove rocker arm cover.

3. To remove right cylinder head, loosen alternator adjusting arm bolt and remove the alternator mounting bracket bolt and spacer. Swing alternator down out of the way. On some vehicles it may be necessary to remove the coil and air cleaner inlet duct from the right head. To remove left cylinder head, remove accelerator shaft fastening bolts at the front of the head. On some later models, it may be necessary to remove the air conditioning compressor bracket.

4. Raise and safely support the vehicle. Disconnect exhaust pipe from the manifold.

5. Loosen rocker arm stud nuts and twist rocker arms so that the pushrods may be removed. Identify the pushrods when removing so that they may be reinstalled in their original locations.

6. Remove the cylinder head retaining bolts and remove the assembly from the vehicle.

To install:

7. Clean all gasket surfaces of block, head and rocker cover. Position new head gasket over the dowels onto the block (do use sealer on this composition gasket). Install the cylinder head on the engine block.

8. On 5.0L engine, install head bolts and tighten in 2 steps. The 1st step 55–65 ft. lbs. and the 2nd step 65–72 ft. lbs. On 5.8L engine, install head bolts and tighten in 3 steps. The 1st step 85 ft. lbs., 2nd step 95 ft. lbs. and 3rd step 105–112 ft. lbs. It is not necessary to retorque cylinder head bolts after extended operation.

9. Clean pushrods, blowing out oil passage and check them for straightness. Lubricate pushrod ends, valve stem tips and rocker arm cups, fulcrum sets and followers. Install pushrods in their original locations.

10. Connect the exhaust pipe to the manifold, using new gasket and torque nuts to 25–38 ft. lbs.

11. On right cylinder head, position the alternator and install the attaching bolt and spacer, ignition coil and air cleaner inlet duct. Adjust drive belt tension. On left cylinder head, install accelerator shaft assembly and air conditioning compressor bracket.

12. Install rocker cover using new gasket and tightening cover bolts to 3–5 ft. lbs.

13. Install intake manifold/carburetor assembly or intake manifold/throttle body as assembly.

14. Install the thermactor air supply assembly where necessary. Check all fluid levels and road test the vehicle for proper operation.

7.5L ENGINE

1. Disconnect the negative battery cable. Drain the cooling system. Remove the intake manifold and carburetor as an assembly. On fuel injected vehicles relieve fuel pressure and remove intake manifold and throttle body as assembly.

2. Raise and safely support the vehicle as necessary. Disconnect the exhaust pipe from the exhaust manifold. Some applications may require the removal of the exhaust manifold at the cylinder heads.

3. Loosen the air conditioning compressor drive belt, if so equipped.

4. Loosen the alternator attaching bolts and remove the bolt attaching the alternator bracket to the right cylinder head.

5. Disconnect the air conditioning compressor from the engine and move it aside, out of the way. Do not discharge the air conditioning system, if possible.

6. Remove the bolts securing the power steering reservoir bracket to the left cylinder head. Position the reservoir and bracket out of the way. Remove air brake and thermactor brackets as necessary.

7. Remove the valve rocker arm covers. Remove the rocker arm bolts, rocker arms, oil deflectors, fulcrums and pushrods in sequence so that they can be reinstalled in their original positions.

8. Remove the cylinder head bolts and lift the head and exhaust manifold off the engine. If necessary, pry at the forward corners of the cylinder head against the casting bosses provided on the cylinder block. Do not damage the gasket mating surfaces of the cylinder head and block by prying against them.

9. Remove all gasket material from the cylinder head and block. Clean all gasket material from the mating surfaces of the intake manifold. If the exhaust manifold was removed, clean the mating surfaces of the cylinder head exhaust port areas and install the exhaust manifold.

10. Position the 2 long cylinder head bolts in the 2 rear lower bolt holes of the left cylinder head. Place a long cylinder head bolt in the rear lower bolt hole of the right cylinder head. Use rubber bands to keep the bolts in position until the cylinder heads are installed on the cylinder block.

11. Position new cylinder head gaskets on the cylinder block dowels. Do not apply sealer to the gaskets, heads, or block.

12. Place the cylinder heads on the block, guiding the exhaust pipe connections. Install the remaining cylinder head bolts. The longer bolts go in the lower row of holes.

13. Tighten all the cylinder head attaching bolts in the proper sequence in 3 steps. The 1st step 80–90 ft. lbs., 2nd step 100–110 ft. lbs. and 3rd step 130–140 ft. lbs. It is not necessary to retorque cylinder head bolts after extended operation.

Valve Lash

Adjustment

4.9L ENGINE

A 0.060 in. shorter or longer pushrod is available for service to provide a means of adjustment in the valve mechanism. Use the following service prodcedure to determine wheter a shorter or longer pushrod is necessary.

1. Install an auxilary starter switch or equivalent.

2. Make 2 marks on the crankshaft damper. Space the marks 120 degress apart so that with timing mark the damper is divided into 3 equal parts.

3. With No. 1 piston on TDC at the end of the compression stroke, tighten the rocker arm bolts of the No. 1 intake and exhaust valve to 17–23 ft. lbs.

4. Slowly apply pressure to bleed down the tappet until the plunger is completely bottomed. Hold the tappet in this position and chech the available clearance between the rocker arm and the valve stem tip with a feeler gauge.

5. Repeat this procedure for the rest of the valves, turning the crankshaft one-third turn at a time in the direction of rotation. Adjust the valves in the firing order sequence 1–5–3–6–2–

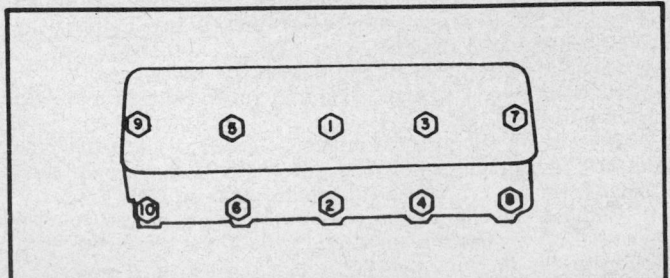

Cylinder head bolt tightening sequence—5.0L, 5.8L and 7.5L engines

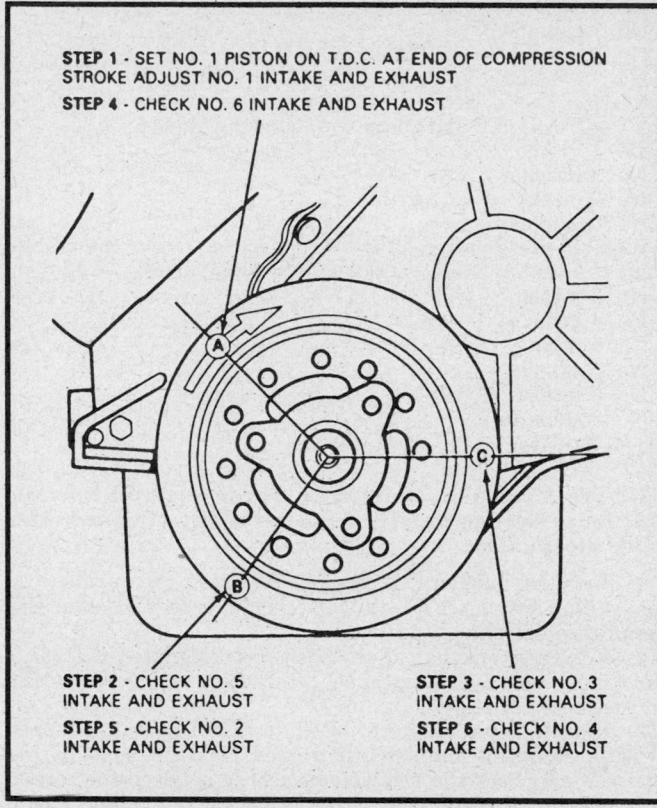

STEP 1 - SET NO. 1 PISTON ON T.D.C. AT END OF COMPRESSION STROKE ADJUST NO. 1 INTAKE AND EXHAUST

STEP 4 - CHECK NO. 6 INTAKE AND EXHAUST

STEP 2 - CHECK NO. 5 INTAKE AND EXHAUST

STEP 5 - CHECK NO. 2 INTAKE AND EXHAUST

STEP 3 - CHECK NO. 3 INTAKE AND EXHAUST

STEP 6 - CHECK NO. 4 INTAKE AND EXHAUST

4.9L engine–valve clearance adjustment

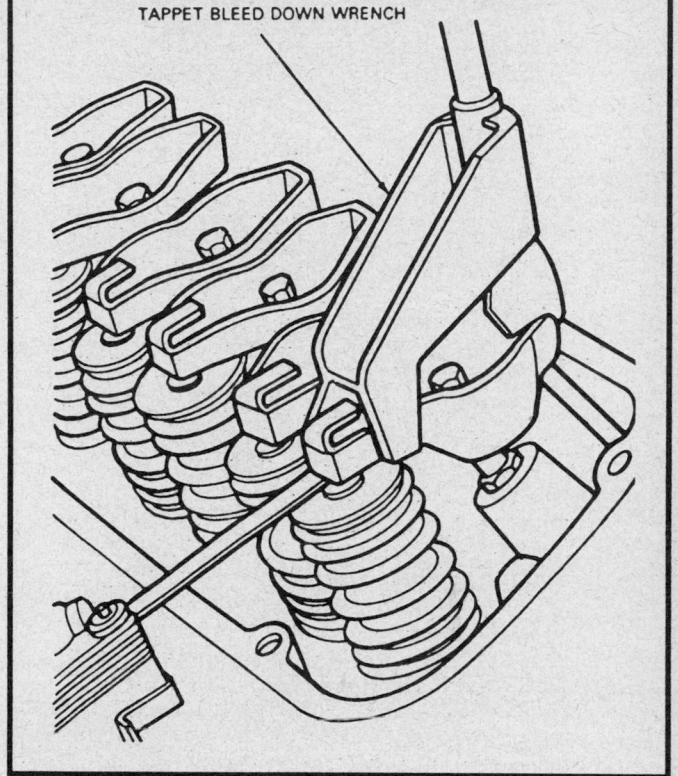

TAPPET BLEED DOWN WRENCH

Checking valve clearance

5.0L ENGINE

NOTE: A 0.060 in. shorter or longer pushrod is available for service to provide a means of adjustment in the valve mechanism.

1. Install an auxiliary starter switch. Crank the engine with the ignition switch OFF until No. 1 piston is on TDC after the compression stroke.

2. With the crankshaft in the positions designated in Steps 5, 6 and 7, position a hydraulic tappet compressor tool or equivalent on the rocker arm.

3. Slowly apply pressure to bleed down the hydraulic tappet until the plunger is completely bottomed. Hold the tappet in this position and check the available clearance between the rocker arm and the valve stem tip with a feeler gauge.

4. If the clearance is less than specification (0.060 in.), install a shorter pushrod. If clearance is greater than specification (0.060 in.), install a longer pushrod.

5. With the No. 1 piston on TDC at the end of the compression stroke, Position 1 on the crankshaft pulley, check the following valves:

No. 1 intake
No. 1 exhaust
No. 7 intake
No. 5 exhaust
No. 8 intake
No. 4 exhaust

6. After these valves have been checked, rotate the crankshaft to Position 2 and check the following valves:

No. 5 intake
No. 2 exhaust
No. 4 intake
No. 6 exhaust

7. After these valves have been checked, rotate the crankshaft to Position 3 and check the following valves:

No. 2 intake
No. 7 exhaust
No. 3 intake
No. 3 exhaust
No. 6 intake
No. 8 exhaust

5.8L ENGINE

NOTE: A 0.060 in. shorter or longer pushrod is available for service to provide a means of adjustment in the valve mechanism.

1. Disconnect the brown lead (I terminal) and the red and blue leads (S terminal) at the starter relay. Install an auxiliary starter switch between the battery and the S terminals of the starter relay. Crank the engine with the ignition switch OFF until No. 1 piston is on TDC after the compression stroke.

2. With the crankshaft in the positions designated in Steps 5, 6 and 7, position a hydraulic tappet compressor tool or equivalent on the rocker arm.

3. Slowly apply pressure to bleed down the hydraulic tappet until the plunger is completely bottomed. Hold the tappet in this position and check the available clearance between the rocker arm and the valve stem tip with a feeler gauge.

4. If the clearance is less than specification (0.060 in.), install a shorter pushrod. If clearance is greater than specification (0.060 in.), install a longer pushrod.

5. With the No. 1 piston on TDC at the end of the compression stroke, Position 1 on the crankshaft pulley, check the following valves:

No. 1 intake
No. 1 exhaust

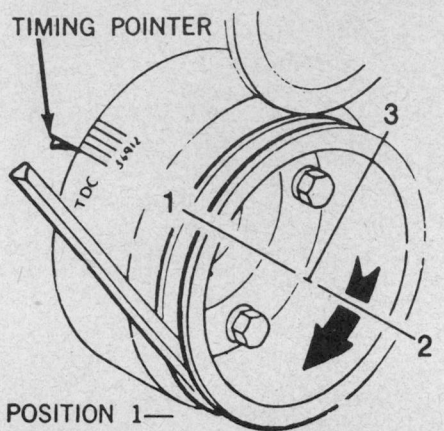

WITH NO. 1 AT TDC AT THE END OF THE COMPRESSION STROKE MAKE A CHALK MARK AT POINTS 2 AND 3 APPROXIMATELY 90 DEGREES APART.

TIMING POINTER

POSITION 1—
NO. 1 AT TDC AT THE END OF THE COMPRESSION STROKE

POSITION 2—
ROTATE THE CRANKSHAFT 180 DEGREES (ONE HALF REVOLUTION) CLOCKWISE FROM POSITION 1

POSITION 3—
ROTATE THE CRANKSHAFT 270 DEGREES (THREE QUARTER REVOLUTION CLOCKWISE FROM POSITION 2

5.0L and 5.8L engines–valve clearance adjustment

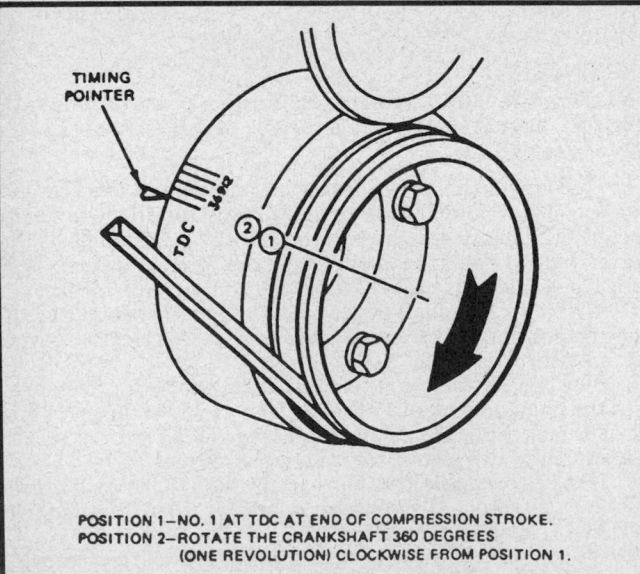

TIMING POINTER

POSITION 1–NO. 1 AT TDC AT END OF COMPRESSION STROKE.
POSITION 2–ROTATE THE CRANKSHAFT 360 DEGREES (ONE REVOLUTION) CLOCKWISE FROM POSITION 1.

7.5L engine–valve clearance adjustment

No. 4 intake
No. 3 exhaust
No. 8 intake
No. 7 exhaust

6. After these valves have been checked, rotate the crankshaft to Position 2 and check the following valves:
No. 3 intake
No. 2 exhaust
No. 7 intake
No. 6 exhaust

7. After these valves have been checked, rotate the crankshaft to Position 3 and check the following valves:
No. 2 intake
No. 4 exhaust
No. 5 intake
No. 5 exhaust
No. 6 intake
No. 8 exhaust

7.5L ENGINE

NOTE: A 0.060 in. shorter or longer pushrod is available for service to provide a means of adjustment in the valve mechanism.

1. Install an auxiliary starter switch. Crank the engine with the ignition switch **OFF** until No. 1 piston is on TDC after the compression stroke.

2. With the crankshaft in the positions designated in Steps 5 and 6, position a hydraulic tappet compressor tool or equivalent on the rocker arm.

3. Slowly apply pressure to bleed down the hydraulic tappet until the plunger is completely bottomed. Hold the tappet in this position and check the available clearance between the rocker arm and the valve stem tip with a feeler gauge.

4. If the clearance is less than specification (0.060 in.), install a shorter pushrod. If clearance is greater than specification (0.060 in.), install a longer pushrod.

5. With the No. 1 piston on TDC at the end of the compression stroke, Position 1 on the crankshaft pulley, check the following valves:
No. 1 intake
No. 1 exhaust
No. 3 intake
No. 4 exhaust
No. 7 intake
No. 5 exhaust
No. 8 intake
No. 8 exhaust

6. After these valves have been checked, rotate the crankshaft 360 degrees to Position 2 and check the following valves:
No. 2 intake
No. 2 exhaust
No. 4 intake
No. 3 exhaust
No. 5 intake
No. 6 exhaust
No. 6 intake
No. 7 exhaust

Rocker Arms/Shaft

Removal and Installation

4.9L ENGINE

1. Disconnect the negative battery cable. Remove the inlet air hose at the oil fill cap and air cleaner. On fuel injected engines remove the inlet air hose and throttle body inlet tubes.

2. Disconnect the accelerator cable at the carburetor or throttle body. Remove the cable retracting spring. Remove the accelerator cable bracket from the cylinder head and position the ca-

ble and bracket assembly out of the way.

3. On fuel injected engines relieve the fuel pressure and remove the fuel line from the fuel rail. Remove the upper intake and throttle body asembly.

4. Remove the PCV valve from the valve rocker arm cover. Remove the cover bolts and remove the valve rocker arm cover.

5. Remove (keep all parts in order for correct installation) the valve rocker arm stud nut, fulcrum seat and rocker arm.

6. Installation is the reverse of the removal procedure. Adjust the valve clearance as required. Tighten the valve cover retaining bolts starting in the middle and working toward the ends to 4–7 ft. lbs.

5.0L, 5.8L AND 7.5L ENGINES

1. Disconnect the negative battery cable. Remove air cleaner and intake duct assembly.

2. Remove crankcase ventilation hose from rocker cover. Remove the coil and the solenoid brackets.

3. For removal of the right side rocker cover, remove the lifting eye and the thermactor tube.

4. Remove the oil filler pipe hose from the left side rocker arm cover, if so equipped.

5. Disconnect spark plug leads and remove leads from bracket on the valve rocker cover.

6. Remove the vacuum harness and the electrical connectors to the vacuum solenoids mounted on the rocker arm covers and position out of the way.

7. Disconnect the choke tubes at the carburetor if so equipped and position out of the way.

8. Disconnect the evaporative system hoses from the canister and position out of the way.

9. Remove the thermactor air supply hose.

10. Remove the rocker cover bolts and remove the covers.

11. Remove the valve rocker arm bolt, fulcrum seat and rocker arm.

12. For installation, reverse the removal procedure. Install the fulcrum guide, valve rocker arm, fulcrum seat and bolt. Tighten the rocker arm bolts to 18–25 ft. lbs. and the valve cover retaining bolts to 10 ft. lbs. Adjust the valve clearance as required.

Intake Manifold

Removal and Installation

FUEL INJECTED ENGINE

5.0L and 5.8L Engines

1. To remove the upper manifold: Disconnect the negative battery cable and relieve fuel pressure. Remove the air cleaner. Disconnect the electrical connectors at the air bypass valve, throttle position sensor and EGR position sensor.

2. Disconnect the throttle linkage at the throttle ball and the transmission linkage from the throttle body. Remove the bolts that secure the bracket to the intake and position the bracket and cables out of the way.

3. Disconnect the upper manifold vacuum fitting connections by removing all the vacuum lines at the vacuum tree (label lines for position identification). Remove the vacuum lines to the EGR valve and fuel pressure regulator.

4. Disconnect the PCV system by disconnecting the hose from the fitting at the rear of the upper manifold.

5. Remove the 2 canister purge lines from the fittings at the throttle body.

6. Disconnect the EGR tube from the EGR valve by loosening the flange nut.

7. Remove the bolt from the upper intake support bracket to upper manifold. Remove the upper manifold retaining bolts and remove the upper intake manifold and throttle body as an assembly.

8. Position a new mounting gasket on the lower intake mani-

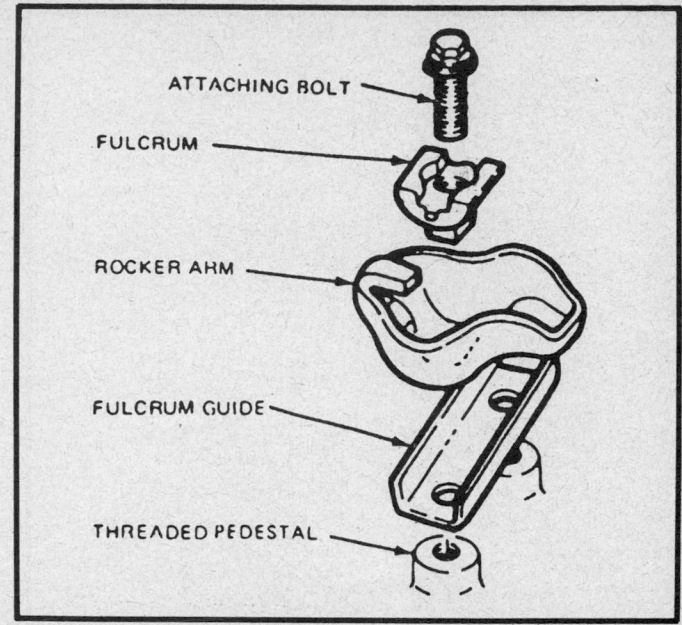

Rocker arm assembly

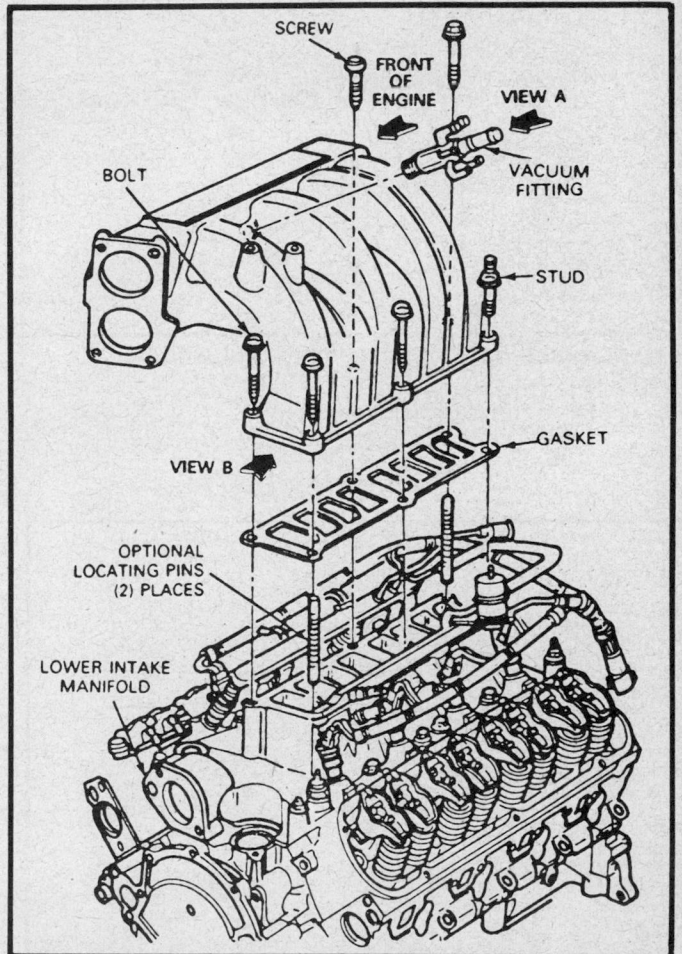

Upper intake manifold assembly–5.0L and 5.8L engines

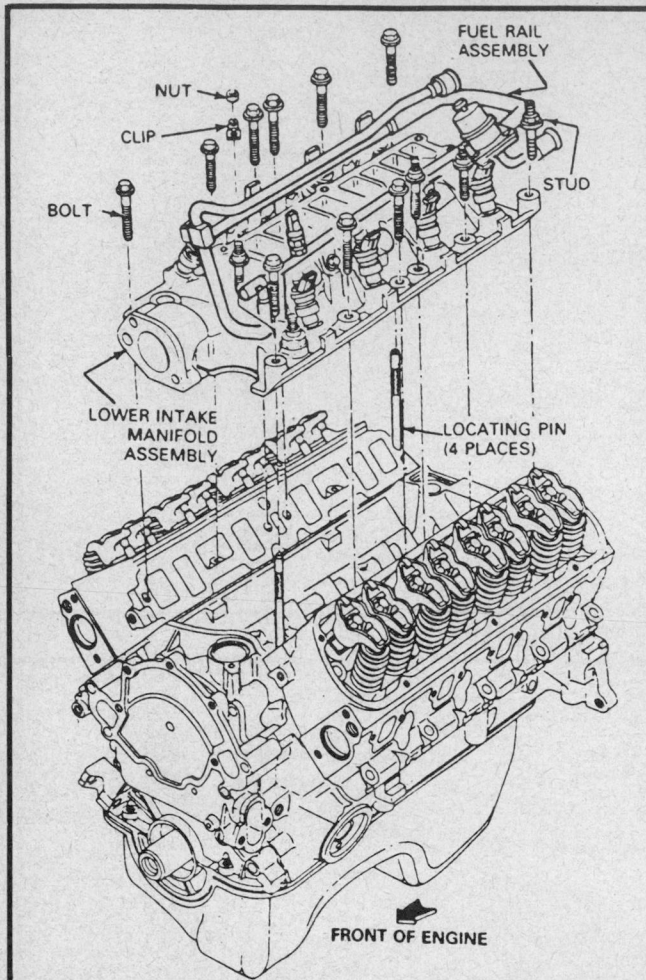

Lower intake manifold assembly–5.0L and 5.8L engines

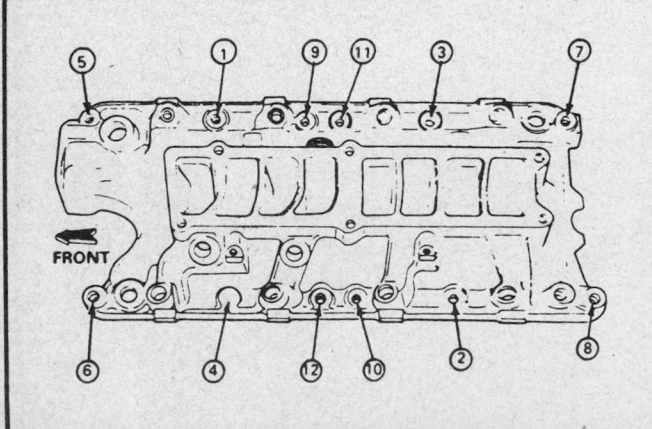

Lower manifold installation torque sequence–5.0L and 5.8L engines

fold and install the upper manifold in the reverse order of removal. Tighten the upper manifold retaining bolts to 12–18 ft. lbs.

9. To remove the lower intake manifold: Upper manifold and throttle body must be removed first.

10. Disconnect the negative battery cable. Drain the cooling system.

11. Remove the distributor assembly, cap and wires.

12. Disconnect the electrical connectors at the engine coolant temperature sensor and sending unit, at the air charge temperature sensor and at the knock sensor.

13. Disconnect the injector wiring harness from the main harness assembly. Remove the ground wire from the intake manifold stud. The ground wire must be installed at the same position it was removed from.

14. Relieve the fuel pressure. Disconnect the fuel supply and return lines from the fuel rails.

15. Remove the upper radiator hose from the thermostat housing. Remove the bypass hose. Remove the heater outlet hose at the intake manifold.

16. Remove the air cleaner mounting bracket. Remove the intake manifold mounting bolts and studs. Pay attention to the location of the bolts and studs for reinstallation. Remove the lower intake manifold assembly.

17. Installation is the reverse of the removal procedure. Tighten the upper manifold retaining bolts to 12–18 ft. lbs. and lower manifold retaining bolts in sequence to 22–32 ft. lbs.

7.5L Engine

1. Disconnect the battery cable. Drain the cooling system and remove the air cleaner assembly.

2. Disconnect the upper radiator hose at the engine.

3. Disconnect the heater hoses at the intake manifold and the water pump. Position them out of the way. Loosen the water pump bypass hose clamp at the intake manifold.

4. Disconnect the PCV valve and hose at right valve cover. Disconnect all of the vacuum lines at the rear of the intake manifold and tag them for proper reinstallation.

5. Disconnect the wires at the spark plugs and remove the wires from the brackets on the valve covers. Disconnect the high-tension wire from the coil and remove the distributor cap and wires as an assembly.

6. Remove the distributor.

7. Disconnect the accelerator linkage at the throttle body. Remove the speed control linkage bracket, if so equipped, from the manifold and throttle body.

8. Remove the bolts holding the accelerator linkage bellcrank and position the linkage and return springs out of the way.

9. Relieve the fuel pressure. Disconnect the fuel line at the fuel rail.

10. Disconnect the wiring harness from the main wiring harness. Remove lower intake manifold and wiring as an assembly.

11. Remove the throttle body heater hose. Remove the intake manifold attaching bolts and lift the manifold and throttle body from the engine as an assembly. It may be necessary to pry the manifold away from the cylinder heads. Do not damage the gasket sealing surfaces.

12. Install the manifold and related equipment in reverse order of removal. Tighten the upper manifold (if removed) retaining bolts to 12–18 ft. lbs. Using 3 steps, torque the lower intake manifold retaining nuts and bolts in sequence to 22–35 ft. lbs.

CARBURATED ENGINE
5.0L and 5.8L Engines

1. Disconnect the negative battery cable. Drain the cooling system. Remove the air cleaner and the intake duct assembly.

2. Disconnect the accelerator rod from the carburetor and remove the accelerator retracting spring. Disconnect the automatic transmission kick-down rod at the carburetor, if so equipped.

3. Disconnect the high tension lead and all other wires from

the ignition coil.

4. Disconnect the spark plug wires from the spark plugs by grasping the rubber boots and twisting and pulling at the same time. Remove the wires from the brackets on the rocker covers. Remove the distributor cap and spark plug wire assembly.

5. Remove the carburetor fuel inlet line and the distributor vacuum line from the carburetor.

6. Remove the distributor lock bolt and remove the distributor and vacuum line, as required.

7. Disconnect the upper radiator hose from the coolant outlet housing and the water temperature sending unit wire at the sending unit. Remove the heater hose from the intake manifold.

8. Loosen the clamp on the water pump bypass hose at the coolant outlet housing and slide the hose off the outlet housing.

9. Disconnect the PCV hose at the rocker cover.

10. If the engine is equipped with the thermactor exhaust emission control system, remove the air pump to cylinder head air hose at the air pump and position it out of the way. Also remove the air hose at the backfire suppressor valve. Remove the air hose bracket from the valve rocker arm cover and position the air hose out of the way. Remove the intake manifold retaining bolts.

11. Remove the intake manifold and carburetor as an assembly. It may be necessary to pry the intake manifold from the cylinder head. Remove all traces of the intake manifold to cylinder head gaskets and the 2 end seals from both the manifold and the other mating surfaces of the engine.

To install:

12. Clean the mating surfaces of the intake manifold, cylinder heads and block with laquer thinner or similar solvent. Apply a ⅛ in. bead of silicone rubber RTV sealant in the correct location.

13. Install new seals on the block and press the seal locating extensions into the holes in the mating surfaces.

14. Apply a ¹⁄₁₆ in. bead of sealer to the outer end of each manifold seal for the full length of the seal (4 places).

NOTE: This sealer sets in about 15 minutes, depending on brand, so work quickly but carefully. Do not drop any sealer into the manifold cavity. It will form, set and plug the oil gallery.

15. Position the manifold gasket onto the block and heads with the alignment notches under the dowels in the heads. Be sure gasket holes align with head holes.

16. Install the manifold and related equipment in reverse order of removal procedure. Torque the intake manifold retaining bolts in sequence to 23–25 ft. lbs. The torque sequence pattern is the same as the one used on the fuel injected engines.

7.5L ENGINE

1. Disconnect the battery cable. Drain the cooling system and remove the air cleaner assembly.

2. Disconnect the upper radiator hose at the engine.

3. Disconnect the heater hoses at the intake manifold and the water pump. Position them out of the way. Loosen the water pump by-pass hose clamp at the intake manifold.

4. Disconnect the PCV valve and hose at right valve cover. Disconnect all of the vacuum lines at the rear of the intake manifold and tag them for proper reinstallation.

5. Disconnect the wires at the spark plugs and remove the wires from the brackets on the valve covers. Disconnect the high-tension wire from the coil and remove the distributor cap and wires as an assembly.

6. Disconnect all of the distributor vacuum lines at the carburetor and vacuum control valve and tag them for proper installation. Remove the distributor and vacuum lines as an assembly.

7. Disconnect the accelerator linkage at the carburetor. Remove the speed control linkage bracket, if so equipped, from the manifold and carburetor.

8. Remove the bolts holding the accelerator linkage bellcrank

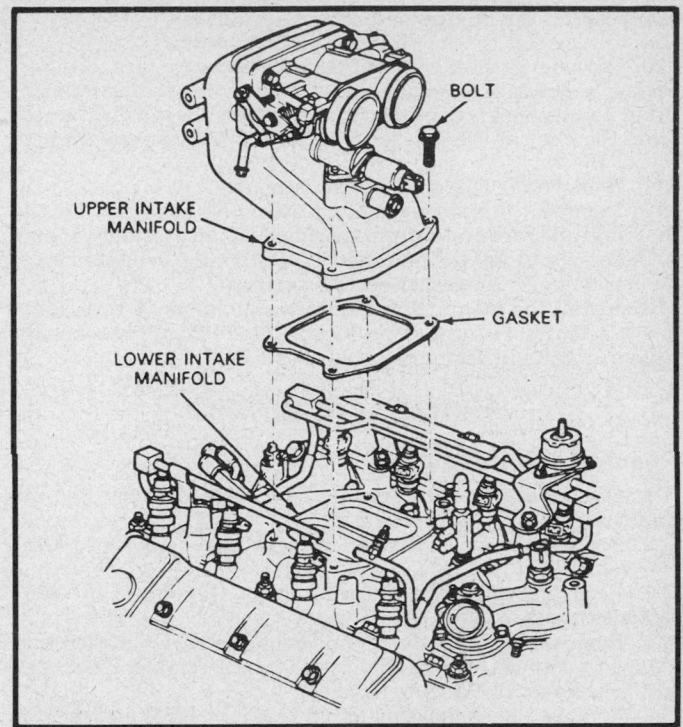

Intake manifold assembly–7.5L engine

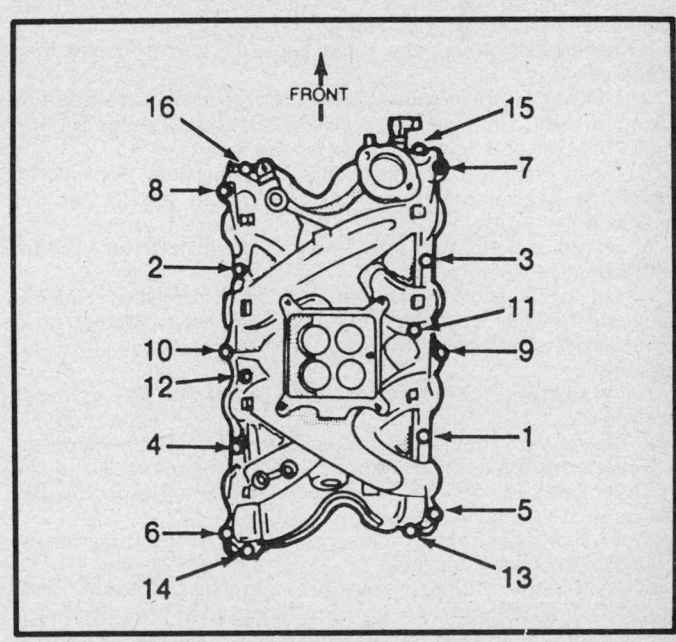

Intake manifold torque sequence–7.5L engine

and position the linkage and return springs out of the way.

9. Disconnect the fuel line at the carburetor.

10. Disconnect the wiring harness at the coil battery terminal, engine temperature sending unit, oil pressure sending unit and other connections as necessary. Disconnect the wiring harness from the clips at the left valve cover and position the harness out of the way.

11. Remove the coil and bracket assembly.

12. Remove the intake manifold attaching bolts and lift the manifold and carburetor from the engine as an assembly. It may be necessary to pry the manifold away from the cylinder heads. Do not damage the gasket sealing surfaces.

13. Install the manifold and related equipment in reverse order of removal. Using 3 steps, torque intake manifold retaining nuts and bolts in sequence to 22–35 ft. lbs.

Exhaust Manifold

Removal and Installation

1. Disconnect the negative battery cable. Remove the air cleaner and intake duct assembly.

2. Remove the air cleaner inlet duct retaining bolts on E series vehicles.

3. Raise and safely support the vehicle. Disconnect the muffler inlet pipes.

4. Remove the exhaust manifold heat shields, On the left side exhaust manifold remove oil dipstick tube assembly, speed control bracket and heat control valve.

5. Remove the exhaust manifold retaining bolts and remove the manifold from the vehicle.

6. Install the exhaust manifold in the reverse order of removal procedure. Tighten the attaching bolts to specifications, starting from the center and working to both ends alternately.

Combination Manifold

Removal and Installation

4.9L ENGINE

1. Disconnect the negative battery cable. Remove the air cleaner and on fuel injected engines remove the throttle body air inlet hoses. Disconnect the choke cable at the carburetor if so equipped.

2. Disconnect the accelerator cable or rod at the carburetor or throttle body. Remove the accelerator retracting spring. Remove bracket and position it out of the way.

3. On a vehicle with automatic transmission, remove the kickdown rod retracting spring. Remove the accelerator rod bellcrank assembly.

4. Disconnect the fuel inlet line and the distributor vacuum line from the carburetor.

5. On fuel injected vehicles relieve the fuel pressure and remove the fuel line from the fuel rail. Disconnect all vacuum lines and remove the upper intake manifold and throttle body as an assembly.

6. Disconnect the muffler inlet pipe from the exhaust manifold.

7. Disconnect the power brake vacuum line, if so equipped.

8. Remove the bolts and nuts attaching the manifolds to the cylinder head. Lift the manifold assemblies from the engine. Remove and discard the gaskets.

9. To separate the manifolds, remove the nuts joining the intake and exhaust manifolds.

10. Installation is the reverse of the removal procedure. Place the manifold assembly in position against the cylinder head. Make sure that the new gaskets have not become dislodged. Install the attaching washers, bolts and nuts. Tighten the attaching nuts and bolts in the proper sequence to 22–32 ft. lbs.

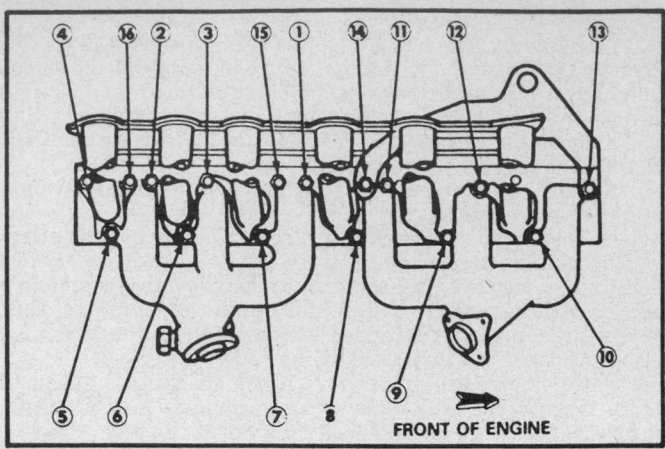

Combination manifold torque sequence—4.9L engine

Timing Chain Front Cover

Removal and Installation

NOTE: On E series vehicles raise and safely support the vehicle to aid in this service repair. On all vehicles, it may be necessary to remove the complete oil pan assembly to gain clearance to remove front cover.

1. Disconnect the negative battery cable. Drain the cooling system.

2. Remove all necessary hoses and vacuum lines. Remove the the shroud and radiator.

3. Remove the drive belt(s), power steering bracket, fan and pulleys.

4. Remove the screw and washer from the end of the crankshaft and remove the vibration damper using a suitable tool.

5. Remove the oil pan (loosen the first 6 bolts on each side and push down) and front cover attaching bolts. Remove the front cover.

6. Installation is the reverse of the removal procedure. Tighten oil pan retaining bolts to 10–15 ft. lbs. and front cover retaining bolts 12–18 ft. lbs.

Front Cover Oil Seal

Removal and Installation

NOTE: On E series vehicles raise and safely support the vehicle to aid in this service repair.

1. Disconnect the negative battery cable.

2. Remove the fan clutch assembly and the shroud.

3. Loosen the accessory drive belts.

4. Remove the crankshaft pulley.

5. Remove the crankshaft damper using a suitable tool.

6. Pry the seal from the front cover using care to prevent damage to front cover and the crankshaft.

7. Installation is the reverse of the removal procedure. Lubricate the seal lip with clean engine oil before installing. Tighten the crankshaft pulley bolt to specifications.

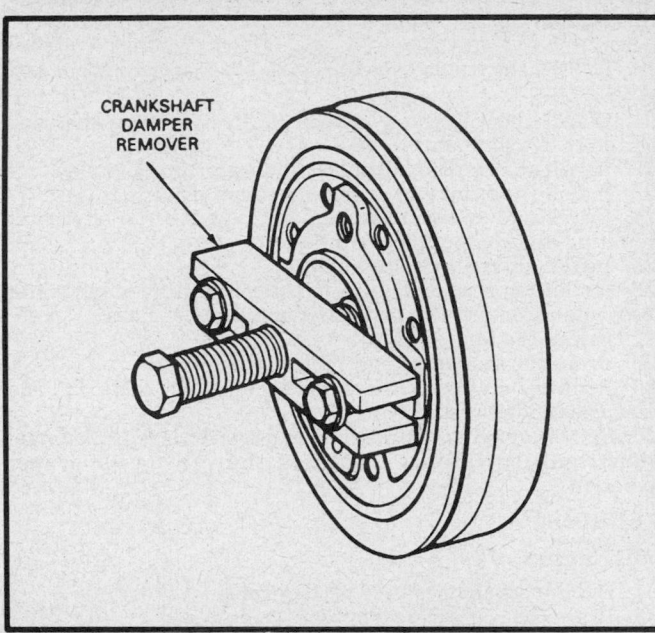

CRANKSHAFT
DAMPER
REMOVER

Removing crankshaft damper

Timing Chain and Gears

Removal and Installation

BRONCO AND F SERIES

4.9L Engine

1. Disconnect the negative battery cable.
2. Drain the cooling system.
3. Remove the front cover assembly.
4. Crank the engine until the timing marks are in the correct position.
5. Install a camshaft gear puller or equivalent and remove the camshaft and crankshaft gears.
6. Installation is the reverse of the removal procedure. Make sure that the camshaft gear key spacer and thrust plate are properly installed and timing marks are in the correct position. Drain the crankcase and replace the oil filter. Refill all fluid levels.

5.0L and 5.8L Engines

1. Bring the engine to No. 1 cylinder at TDC (top dead center) on the compression stroke. Disconnect the negative battery cable. Drain the cooling system.
2. Remove the fan shroud to radiator attaching bolts. Position the shroud over the fan.
3. Disconnect the radiator lower hose, heater hose and bypass hose at the water pump. Remove the drive belt(s), fan, fan spacer and pulley.
4. Remove the fan shroud.
5. Loosen the alternator pivot bolt and bolt attaching the alternator adjusting arm to the water pump.
6. Remove the crankshaft pulley from the crankshaft vibration damper. Remove the damper attaching bolt and washer. Install a puller or equivalent on the vibration damper and remove the damper.
7. Relieve fuel system pressure. Disconnect the fuel pump outlet line from the fuel pump. Remove the fuel pump to one side with the flexible fuel line still attached on vehicles equipped with a carburetor.
8. Remove the oil dipstick and the bolt attaching the dipstick

to the exhaust manifold as required.

9. Remove the oil pan to cylinder front cover attaching bolts. Cut the oil pan gasket flush with the cylinder block face prior to separating the cover from the cylinder block. Remove the cylinder front cover and water pump as an assembly.
10. Discard the cylinder front cover gasket. Remove the crankshaft front oil slinger.
11. Ensure that the timing marks on the sprockets are correctly aligned.
12. Remove the camshaft sprocket capscrew, washers and fuel pump eccentric. Slide both sprockets and the timing chain forward and remove the chain and sprockets as an assembly.
13. Position the sprockets and timing chain on the camshaft. Be sure that the timing marks are properly aligned.
14. Install the fuel pump, eccentric, washers and camshaft sprocket capscrew. Tighten the capscrew to 40–45 ft. lbs.
15. Install the crankshaft front oil slinger.
16. Clean the cylinder front cover, oil pan and block gasket surfaces. Clean the oil pan gasket surface where the oil pan and front cover fasten.
17. Install a new crankshaft front oil seal.
18. Lubricate the timing chain and fuel pump eccentric with a heavy engine oil.
19. Coat the gasket surface of the oil pan with sealer, then cut and position the required sections of a new gasket on the oil pan and apply sealer at the corners. Install the pan seal as required. Coat the gasket surfaces of the block and cover with sealer and position a new gasket on the block.
20. Position the cylinder front cover (with new front oil seal installed) on the cylinder block. Use care when installing the cover to avoid seal damage or possible gasket dislocation.
21. Install the cylinder front cover. It may be necessary to force the cover downward to slightly compress the pan gasket. This operation can be facilitated by using a suitable tool at the front cover attaching hole locations.
22. Coat the threads of the attaching bolts with a oil-resistant sealer and install the bolts. Tighten the oil pan to cover attaching bolts to 12–18 ft. lbs. Tighten the cover to block attaching bolts to 12–18 ft. lbs.
23. Apply Lubriplate or equivalent to the oil seal rubbing surface of the vibration damper inner hub to prevent damage to the seal.
24. Line up the crankshaft vibration damper keyway with the key on the crankshaft. Install the vibration damper on the crankshaft. Install the capscrew and washer and tighten to 70–90 ft. lbs. Install the crankshaft pulley.

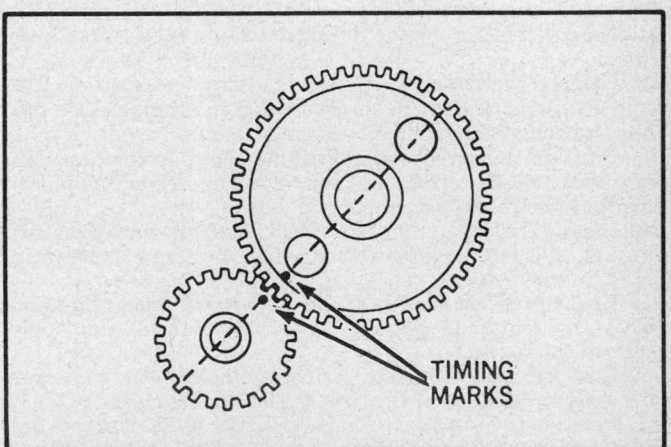

TIMING
MARKS

Timing mark alignment—4.9L engine

25. Lubricate the fuel pump lever with heavy engine oil and install the pump using a new gasket. Connect the fuel pump outlet pipe as required.

26. Install the alternator pivot bolt and bolt attaching the alternator adjusting arm to the water pump.

27. Position the fan shroud over the water pump. Install the pulley, spacer and fan. Install and adjust the drive belts. Connect the radiator, heater and bypass hoses. Position the fan shroud on the radiator and install the attaching bolts.

28. Fill and bleed the cooling system. Drain the crankcase and replace the oil filter.

29. Connect the battery cable. Run the engine and check for coolant and oil leaks. Check the coolant level. Check and adjust the ignition timing.

30. Install the air cleaner and intake duct assembly including the crankcase ventilation hose.

30. Road test the vehicle for proper operation.

7.5L Engine

1. Bring the engine to No. 1 piston at TDC (top dead center) on the compression stroke. Disconnect the negative battery cable. Drain the cooling system.

2. Remove the radiator shroud and fan.

3. Disconnect the upper and lower radiator hoses and the automatic transmission oil cooler lines from the radiator if so equipped.

4. Remove the radiator upper support and remove the radiator.

5. Remove the alternator splash shield. Loosen the alternator attaching bolts and air conditioning compressor idler pulley and remove the drive belts with the water pump pulley. Remove the bolts attaching the compressor support to the water pump and remove the bracket (support), if so equipped.

6. Remove the crankshaft pulley from the vibration damper. Remove the bolt and washer attaching the crankshaft damper and remove the damper with a puller. Remove the Woodruff key from the crankshaft.

7. Loosen the bypass hose at the water pump and disconnect the heater return tube at the water pump.

8. Relieve fuel system pressure. Disconnect and plug the fuel inlet and outlet lines at the fuel pump and remove the fuel pump on vehicles equipped with a carburetor.

9. Remove the bolts attaching the front cover to the cylinder block. Cut the oil pan seal flush with the cylinder block prior to separating the cover from the cylinder block. Remove the front cover and water pump as an assembly. Discard the front cover gasket and oil pan seal.

10. Clean all of the gasket sealing surfaces on both the front cover and the cylinder block.

11. Ensure that the engine timing marks on the sprockets are aligned.

12. Remove the camshaft sprocket capscrew, washer and fuel pump eccentric. Slide both sprockets and the timing chain forward and remove them as an assembly.

13. Position the sprockets and timing chain on the camshaft and crankshaft. Be certain that the timing marks on the sprockets are correctly aligned.

14. Install the fuel pump eccentric, washers and camshaft sprocket capscrew. Tighten the camshaft capscrew to 40–45 ft. lbs.

15. Coat the gasket surface of the oil pan with sealer. Cut and position the required sections of a new seal on the oil pan. Apply sealer to the corners.

16. Coat the gasket surfaces of the cylinder block and cover with sealer and position the new gasket on the block.

17. Position the front cover on the cylinder block. Use care not to damage the seal and gasket.

18. Coat the front cover attaching screws with sealer and install them. It may be necessary to force the front cover downward to compress the oil pan seal in order to install the front cover attaching bolts.

19. Tighten the oil pan to front cover attaching bolts to 9–11 ft. lbs.

20. Tighten the front cover to engine block attaching bolts to 15–21 ft. lbs.

21. Install the vibration damper capscrew and washer and tighten to 70–90 ft. lbs.

22. Install the crankshaft pulley and water pump pulley.

23. Install the front end engine accessory drive hardware.

24. Install and adjust all drive belts. Tighten the alternator mounting and compressor idler pulley.

25. Install alternator splash shield.

26. Install radiator and support assemblies. Install all water hoses and reconnect the transmission oil cooler lines.

27. Install the fan assembly.

28. Drain the crankcase and replace the oil filter.

29. Refill the crankcase. Reconnect the battery cable. Fill and bleed the cooling system.

30. Start the engine, check for oil and coolant leaks. Check and adjust ignition timing. Road test the vehicle for proper operation.

E SERIES

4.9L Engine

1. Disconnect the negative battery cable.

2. Drain the cooling system.

3. Remove the front cover assembly.

4. Crank the engine until the timing marks are in the correct position.

5. Install a camshaft gear puller or equivalent and remove the camshaft and crankshaft gears.

6. Installation is the reverse of the removal procedure. Make sure that the camshaft gear key spacer and thrust plate are properly installed and timing marks are in the correct position.7. Drain the crankcase and replace the oil filter. Refill all fluid levels.

5.0L and 5.8L Engines

1. Bring engine to No. 1 cylinder at TDC (top dead center) on the compression stroke. Disconnect the negative battery cable at the battery. Drain the radiator and remove the radiator from the vehicle. Disconnect and plug transmission lines if equipped with automatic transmission.

2. Remove the air conditioning idler pulley, bracket and drive belt if equipped.

3. Remove the upper radiator hose from the engine block. Remove the fan and shroud as an assembly. Raise and support the vehicle safely.

4. Loosen the thermactor and alternator drive belts.

5. Disconnect the lower radiator hose at the water pump. Relieve fuel system pressure. Disconnect the fuel line at the fuel pump and remove the pump on vehicles equipped with a carburetor. Lower the vehicle.

6. Remove the bypass hose. Remove the power steering pump drive belt if equipped. Remove the water pump pulley and disconnect the heater hose at the water pump.

7. Remove the air conditioning compressor upper bracket and the power steering pump mount.

8. Remove the crankshaft pulley. Remove the oil pan to front cover bolts. Remove the front cover.

9. Ensure that engine timing marks on the sprockets are correctly aligned.

10. Remove the camshaft sprocket capscrew, washers and fuel pump eccentric. Slide both sprockets and the timing chain forward and remove the chain and sprockets as an assembly.

11. Install the sprockets and timing chain on the camshaft. Be sure that the timing marks are properly aligned.

12. Install the fuel pump, eccentric, washers and camshaft sprocket capscrew. Tighten the capscrew to 40–45 ft. lbs.

13. Clean the front cover, fuel pump and damper. Clean the gasket surface at the pan and trim the gasket. Clean the front

cover gasket surface at the block.

14. Replace the oil seal in the front cover. Position the gasket on the front cylinder cover. Apply a silicone sealer to the oil pan and cylinder block. Cut the pan gasket and position on pan and front cover.

15. Install the front cover, fuel pump and vibration damper.

16. Tighten the oil pan to front cover attaching bolts to 12–18 ft. lbs.

17. Tighten the front cover to engine block attaching bolts to 12–18 ft. lbs.

18. Install the vibration damper capscrew and washer and tighten to 70–90 ft. lbs.

19. Install the power steering pump and water pump bypass hose. Connect the heater hose at the water pump.

20. Install the air conditioning compressor upper bracket, water pump pulley and power steering drive belt.

21. Install the alternator belt, thermactor belt and fan/shroud assembly.

22. Adjust the power steering belt.

23. Install the air conditioning drive belt idler pulley and bracket. Install the air conditioning drive belt and adjust.

24. Install the upper radiator hose.

25. Raise and safely support the vehicle. Install the fuel pump with a new gasket and connect the fuel line on vehicles equipped with a carburetor.

26. Install the lower radiator hose. Adjust the alternator and air injection pump drive belts.

27. Drain the crankcase and replace the oil filter as necessary. Lower the vehicle.

28. Connect the battery cable. Fill the crankcase and cooling system.

29. Start the engine, check for oil and coolant leaks. Check and adjust ignition timing. Road test the vehicle for proper operation.

7.5L Engine

1. Bring the engine to No. 1 piston at TDC (top dead center) on the compression stroke. Disconnect the negative battery cable. Drain the cooling system.

2. Remove the radiator shroud and fan.

3. Disconnect the upper and lower radiator hoses and the automatic transmission oil cooler lines from the radiator if so equipped.

4. Remove the radiator upper support and remove the radiator.

5. Remove the alternator splash shield. Loosen the alternator attaching bolts and air conditioning compressor idler pulley and remove the drive belts with the water pump pulley. Remove the

bolts attaching the compressor support to the water pump and remove the bracket (support), if so equipped.

6. Remove the crankshaft pulley from the vibration damper. Remove the bolt and washer attaching the crankshaft damper and remove the damper with a puller. Remove the Woodruff key from the crankshaft.

7. Loosen the bypass hose at the water pump and disconnect the heater return tube at the water pump.

8. Relieve the fuel system pressure. Disconnect and plug the fuel inlet and outlet lines at the fuel pump and remove the fuel pump on vehicles equipped with a carburetor.

9. Remove the bolts attaching the front cover to the cylinder block. Cut the oil pan seal flush with the cylinder block prior to separating the cover from the cylinder block. Remove the front cover and water pump as an assembly. Discard the front cover gasket and oil pan seal.

10. Clean all of the gasket sealing surfaces on both the front cover and the cylinder block.

11. Ensure that the engine timing marks on the sprockets are aligned.

12. Remove the camshaft sprocket capscrew, washer and fuel pump eccentric. Slide both sprockets and the timing chain forward and remove them as an assembly.

13. Position the sprockets and timing chain on the camshaft and crankshaft. Be certain that the timing marks on the sprockets are correctly aligned.

14. Install the fuel pump eccentric, washers and camshaft sprocket capscrew. Tighten the camshaft capscrew to 40–45 ft. lbs.

15. Coat the gasket surface of the oil pan with sealer. Cut and position the required sections of a new seal on the oil pan. Apply sealer to the corners.

16. Coat the gasket surfaces of the cylinder block and cover with sealer and position the new gasket on the block.

17. Position the front cover on the cylinder block. Use care not to damage the seal and gasket.

18. Coat the front cover attaching screws with sealer and install them. It may be necessary to force the front cover downward to compress the oil pan seal in order to install the front cover attaching bolts.

19. Tighten the oil pan to front cover attaching bolts to 9–11 ft. lbs.

20. Tighten the front cover to engine block attaching bolts to 15–21 ft. lbs.

21. Install the vibration damper capscrew and washer and tighten to 70–90 ft. lbs.

22. Install the crankshaft pulley and water pump pulley.

23. Install the front end engine accessory drive hardware.

24. Install and adjust all drive belts. Tighten the alternator mounting and compressor idler pulley.

25. Install alternator splash shield.

26. Install radiator and support assemblies. Install all water hoses and reconnect the transmission oil cooler lines.

27. Install the fan assembly.

28. Drain the crankcase and replace the oil filter.

29. Refill the crankcase. Reconnect the battery cable. Fill and bleed the cooling system.

30. Start the engine, check for oil and coolant leaks. Check and adjust ignition timing. Road test the vehicle for proper operation.

Camshaft

Removal and Installation

4.9L ENGINE

1. Drain the cooling system. Disconnect the negative battery cable. Remove the radiator shroud and radiator.

2. Remove the front cover.

3. Remove air cleaner and crankcase vent tube at the rocker

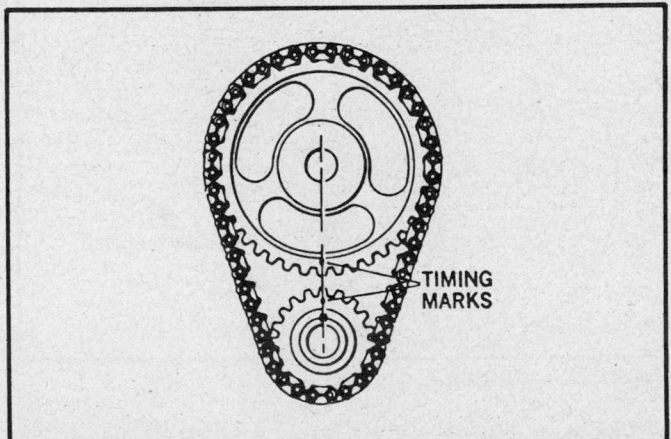

Timing mark alignment–5.0L, 5.8L and 7.5L engines

cover.

4. Disconnect accelerator cable, choke cable and hand throttle cable if so equipped. Remove accelerator cable retracting spring.

5. If applicable, remove air conditioning compressor and power steering belts.

6. Disconnect oil filler hose from rocker cover.

7. Remove distributor cap and wiring as an assembly, then disconnect vacuum line and primary wire and remove distributor (mark distributor for correct installation).

8. Remove fuel pump on vehicles equipped with carburetor.

9. Remove valve rocker arm cover, loosen rocker arm stud nuts and move rocker arms to one side. Remove pushrods, identifying each so that they may be installed in their original locations.

10. Remove pushrod cover and valve lifters, identifying the position of each.

11. Turn crankshaft to align timing marks, remove camshaft thrust plate bolts and carefully pull camshaft and gear from block.

12. To install camshaft reverse the removal procedures.

13. Oil journals and apply Lubriplate to lobes, then carefully install camshaft, spacer, thrustplate and gear as an assembly, making sure timing marks are aligned, then tightening thrustplate bolts to 9–12 ft. lbs.

14. Measure the camshaft endplay. If the endplay is more than 0.009 in., replace the thrust plate.

15. Do not rotate crankshaft until distributor is installed. Drain the crankcase replace oil filter. Refill all fluid levels. Check and adjust timing as necessary.

5.0L, 5.8L AND 7.5L ENGINES

1. Disconnect the negative battery cable. Drain the cooling system. Remove all required components to gain access to the intake manifold. On fuel injected vehicles relieve the fuel pressure. Remove the intake manifold assembly and valley pan, if so equipped.

2. Remove the radiator and front grille assembly as required. If equipped with A/C discharge the system then remove the condenser if necessary to gain clearance to remove the camshaft.

3. Remove the rocker covers and either remove the rocker arm shafts or loosen the rockers on their pivots. Remove the pushrods. The pushrods must be reinstalled in their original positions.

4. Remove the valve lifters in sequence with a magnet or equivalent. They must be replaced in their original positions.

5. Remove the timing cover and timing chain and sprockets.

6. Remove the camshaft thrust plate attaching screws and carefully slide the camshaft out of its bearing bores. Use extra caution not to scratch the bearing journals with the camshaft lobes.

7. Install the camshaft in the reverse order of removal. Coat the camshaft with engine oil liberally before installing it. Slide the camshaft into the engine very carefully so as not to scratch the bearing bores with the camshaft lobes. Install the camshaft thrust plate and tighten the attaching screws to 9–12 ft. lbs. Measure the camshaft endplay. If the endplay is more than 0.009 in., replace the thrust plate. Assemble the remaining components in the reverse order of removal.

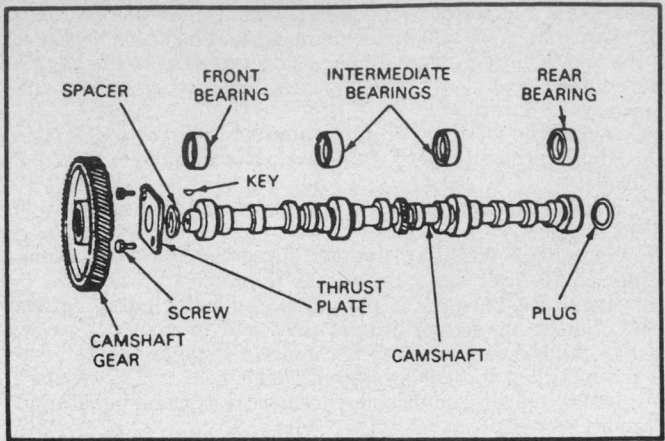

Camshaft assembly–4.9L engine

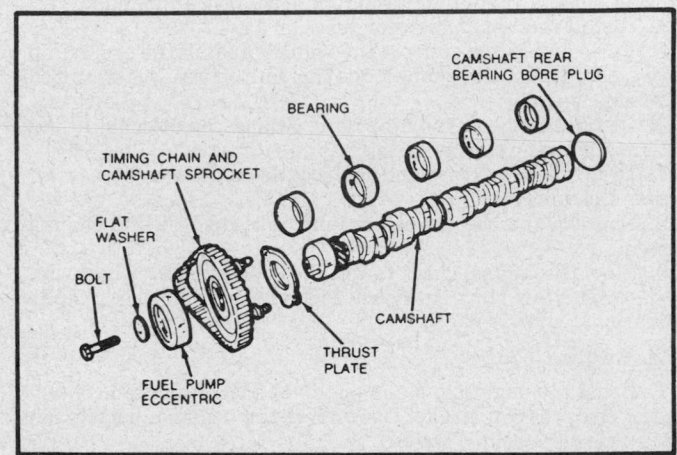

Typical camshaft assembly–8 cylinder engines

Piston and Connecting Rod

Positioning

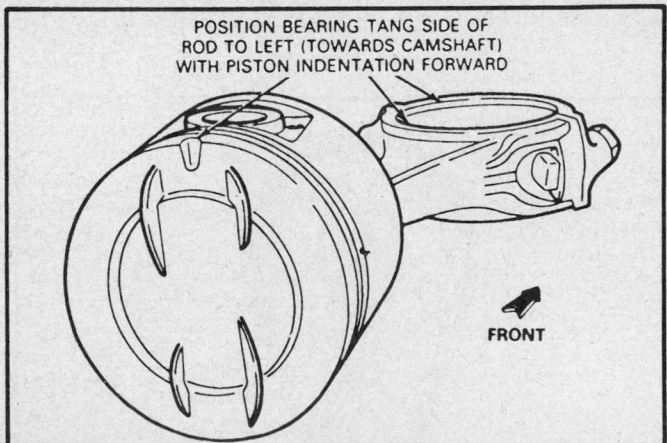

Piston–4.9L engine

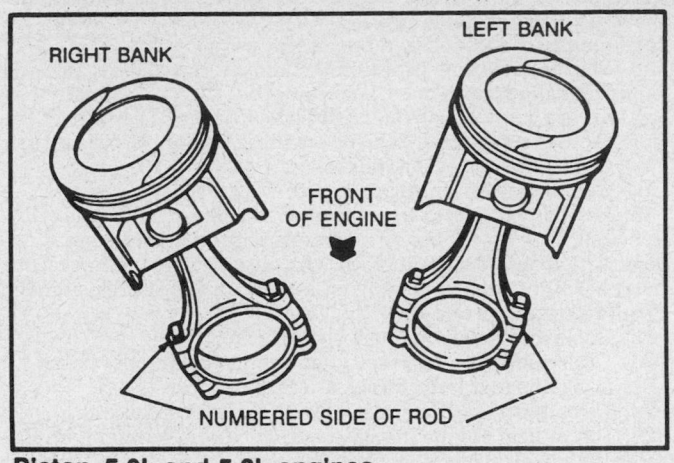

Piston–5.0L and 5.8L engines

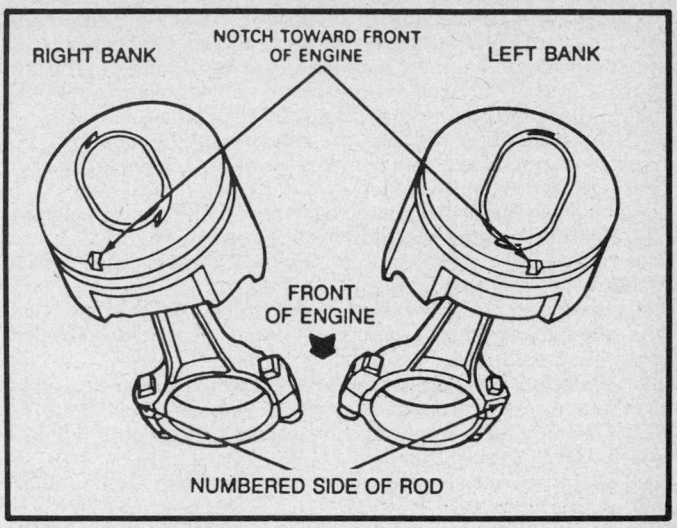

Piston–7.5L engine

DIESEL ENGINE MECHANICAL

Engine

Removal and Installation

F SERIES

1. Disconnect battery ground cables from both batteries.
2. Scribe alignment marks at hood hinges and remove hood.
3. Drain cooling system.
4. Remove air cleaner and intake duct assembly. Install intake manifold cover over air intake opening.
5. Remove radiator fan shroud halves.
6. Remove fan and clutch assembly. Left-hand thread. Remove by turning nut clockwise.
7. Disconnect radiator upper and lower hoses from radiator.
8. Disconnect and plug automatic transmission oil cooler lines at radiator, if so equipped.
9. Remove radiator.
10. Loosen A/C compressor, if so equipped and remove drive belt.
11. Remove A/C compressor from its mounting, if so equipped and position it on radiator upper support.
12. Loosen power steering pump and remove drive belt. Remove power steering pump and position out of the way on left side of engine compartment.
13. Disconnect fuel supply line heater and alternator wires at alternator. Disconnect oil pressure sending unit wire at sending unit. Remove oil pressure sender from dash panel and lay on engine.
14. Disconnect accelerator cable from injection pump. Disconnect speed control cable from injection pump, if so equipped. Remove accelerator cable bracket with cables attached, from intake manifold and position out of the way.
15. Disconnect transmission kickdown rod from injection pump, if so equipped. Disconnect main wiring harness connector from right side of engine. Disconnect engine ground strap from rear of engine. Disconnect fuel return hose from left rear of engine. Remove the vacuum supply hose from the vacuum pump.

16. Remove upper transmission-to-engine attaching bolts.
17. Disconnect heater hoses from water pump and right cylinder head. Disconnect water temperature sender wire from sender on left front of engine block. Disconnect water temperature overheat light switch wire from switch on top of left cylinder head. Position wires out of the way.
18. Raise and safely support the vehicle.
19. Disconnect both battery ground cables from lower front of engine.
20. Disconnect and cap fuel inlet line at fuel supply pump.
21. Disconnect starter cables at starter motor.
22. Disconnect muffler inlet pipe at exhaust manifold.
23. Disconnect engine insulators from No. 1 crossmember. Remove flywheel inspection plate. Remove converter-to-flywheel attaching nuts, if so equipped. Lower vehicle.
24. Support transmission with a floor jack. Remove lower transmission to engine attaching bolts.
25. Attach engine lifting sling and chain hoist. Raise engine high enough to clear number 1 crossmember and pull forward.
26. Rotate the front of the engine approximately 45 degrees to the left and lift it out of the engine compartment.
27. When installing the engine; lower engine into engine compartment. Use care not to damage windshield wiper motor when installing engine in vehicle.
28. Start transmission main shaft into clutch disc. It may be necessary to adjust position of transmission in relation to engine if main shaft binds or will not enter clutch disc. If engine hangs up after main shaft enters clutch disc, rotate crankshaft slowly (transmission in gear) until mainshaft splines mesh with clutch disc splines. Align convertor to flywheel studs, if so equipped.
29. Lower into engine insulator brackets on the number 1 crossmember.
30. Install lower transmission to engine attaching bolts and tighten. Remove engine lifting sling. Raise and safely support the vehicle.
31. Install converter to flywheel attaching nuts, if so equipped. Install flywheel inspection plate.

32. Install engine insulator support to crossmember bracket attaching nuts and washers. Connect muffler inlet pipes to exhaust manifolds. Connect both battery ground cables to the lower front of the engine. Connect starter cables to starter. Install fuel pump inlet line on fuel pump. Lower vehicle.

33. Connect water temperature sender wire to sender on left front of engine block. Connect wire to water temperature overheat light switch on top of left cylinder head. Install heater hoses on right cylinder head and water pump and tighten clamps.

34. Connect engine ground strap at rear of engine. Connect fuel return hose at left rear of engine. Connect transmission kickdown rod, if so equipped.

35. Install accelerator cable bracket on intake manifold. Connect accelerator cable to injection pump. Connect speed control cable, if so equipped, to injection pump.

36. Install oil pressure sender on dash panel. Connect oil pressure gauge sender wire to oil pressure sender.

37. Connect fuel supply line heater and alternator wires to alternator.

38. Install power steering pump and drive belt. Do not adjust belt at this time.

39. Install A/C compressor and drive belt. Adjust A/C compressor and power steering pump drive belts.

40. Install radiator. Connect automatic transmission oil cooler lines at radiator, if so equipped. Connect upper and lower radiator hoses to radiator and tighten hose clamps. Fill and bleed the cooling system.

41. Install fan and clutch assembly. Turn nut counterclockwise to tighten.

42. Install radiator fan shroud halves.

43. Remove intake manifold cover and install air cleaner. Install intake duct assembly.

44. Install hood using scribe marks drawn on hood at removal.

45. Connect battery ground cables at both batteries. Check the engine oil level and fill as required. Run engine and check for fuel, oil and coolant leaks.

E SERIES

1. Remove the engine (doghouse) cover. Remove the air cleaner assembly and inlet duct.

2. Disconnect battery ground cables from both batteries.

3. Drain cooling system.

4. Remove the front bumper, grille assembly and gravel deflector.

5. Remove the speed control servo bracket and position out of the way.

6. Mark the location and remove the hood latch and cable assembly from the grille upper support bracket. Remove the upper support bracket.

7. Evacuate the air conditioning system. Disconnect the A/C lines from the condensor and remove the condensor.

8. Disconnect automatic transmission oil cooler lines at radiator, if so equipped.

9. Remove the radiator cooling fan (left hand thread is used on fan/clutch assembly) and clutch. Remove the shroud.

10. Disconnect radiator upper and lower hoses from radiator. Remove radiator.

11. Loosen and remove the vacuum pump and drive belt. Disconnect vacuum hoses from the transmission shift modulator tube if so equipped. Loosen A/C compressor, if so equipped and remove drive belt.

12. Remove A/C compressor from its mounting, if so equipped and position it on radiator upper support.

13. Loosen power steering pump and remove drive belt. Remove power steering pump and position out of the way on left side of engine compartment.

14. Disconnect fuel supply line heater and alternator wires at alternator. Disconnect oil pressure sending unit wire at sending unit.

15. Disconnect accelerator cable from injection pump. Disconnect speed control cable from injection pump, if so equipped. Remove accelerator cable bracket with cables attached, from intake manifold and position out of the way.

16. Disconnect transmission kickdown rod from injection pump and all vacuum lines, if so equipped. Disconnect main wiring harness connector from right side of engine. Disconnect engine ground strap from rear of engine. Disconnect fuel return hose from left rear of engine.

17. Remove upper transmission-to-engine attaching bolts.

18. Disconnect heater hoses from water pump and right cylinder head. Disconnect water temperature sender wire from sender on left front of engine block. Disconnect water temperature overheat light switch wire from switch on top of left cylinder head. Position wires out of the way.

19. Raise and safely support the vehicle.

20. Disconnect and cap fuel inlet line at fuel supply pump.

21. Disconnect starter cables at starter motor.

22. Disconnect muffler inlet pipe at exhaust manifold.

23. Disconnect engine insulators from No. 1 crossmember. Remove flywheel inspection plate. Remove converter-to-flywheel attaching nuts, if so equipped. Lower vehicle.

24. Support transmission with a floor jack. Remove lower transmission to engine attaching bolts.

25. Attach engine lifting sling and floor crane. Raise engine up and out of vehicle from the driver/cargo compartment.

26. Lower engine into driver/cargo compartment. Install engine to transmission.

27. Install transmission to engine attaching bolts and tighten.

28. To complete the rest of the installation reverse the removal procedure. Connect battery ground cables at both batteries. Check the engine oil level and fill as required. Run engine and check for fuel, oil and coolant leaks.

Cylinder Head

Removal and Installation

1. Disconnect battery ground cables from both batteries.

2. Drain cooling system.

3. Remove the radiator fan shroud.

4. Remove the radiator cooling fan (left hand thread is used on fan/clutch assembly) and clutch assembly.

5. Disconnect all wiring from alternator and fuel filter/water separator.

6. Remove the alternator belt and alternator.

7. Remove the vacuum pump drive belt and vacuum pump.

8. Disconnect and cap all fuel lines. Remove alternator and vacuum pump mounting bracket. On F series remove fuel filter with bracket as an assembly.

9. Remove the heater hose from the cylinder head.

10. Remove the injection pump.

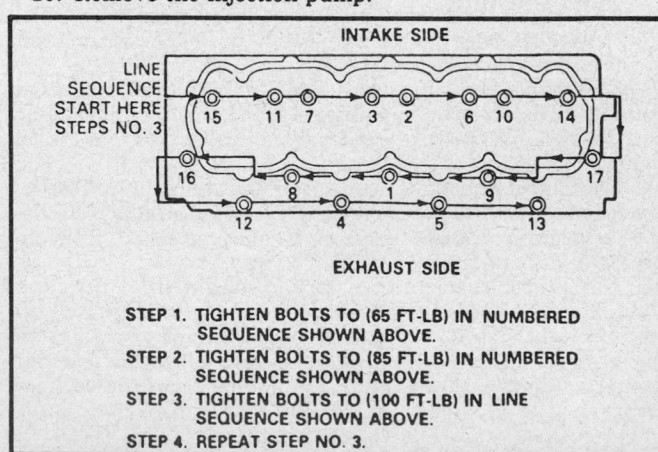

Cylinder head bolt tightening sequence—6.9L and 7.3L engines

11. Remove the intake manifold and valley cover.
12. Raise and safely support the vehicle.
13. Disconnect the muffler inlet pipe from the exhaust manifold.
14. On right side cylinder head, remove bolt holding the transmission dipstick and engine oil dipstick tube assembly (fasteners).
15. Lower the vehicle.
16. Remove the exhaust manifolds from the engine.
17. Remove the valve cover, rocker arm and pushrods.
18. Remove the injection nozzles and glow pugs.
19. Remove the cylinder head bolts. Attach a suitable lifting device and lift cylinder head from the engine. Pre chambers may fall out of cylinder head upon removal.
20. Installation is the reverse of the removal procedure. Always install new cylinder head gasket. Tighten intake manifold, exhaust manifold and cylinder head retaining bolts in sequence and to the correct specifications. Refill and bleed cooling and fuel system as required.

Rocker Arms/Shaft

Removal and Installation

1. Disconnet ground cables from both batteries.
2. On E series, remove fan shroud and engine (doghouse) cover.

NOTE: The following service procedure Steps 3–7 apply to the right side valve cover removal on E series only.

3. Remove engine oil dipstick tube fasteners and remove dipstick, tube assembly and valve cover bracket.
4. Remove transmission filler tube fasteners and remove filler tube and dipstick.
5. Raise vehicle and safely support the vehicle.
6. Remove nuts attaching right engine mount insulator (motor mount) to frame. Slightly raise right side of the engine until fuel filter header touches vehicle sheet metal. Install suitable wood block between insulator and frame. Lower engine on block.
7. Lower the vehicle.
8. Remove valve cover retaining bolts and remove covers. Remove valve rocker arm post mounting bolts. Remove valve rocker arms, posts and pushrods in order and identify so they are installed in the correct positions.
9. Install pushrods in correct positions, making sure they are fully seated in tappet pushrod seats. Install copper colored end of pushrod toward rocker arm.
10. Install valve rocker arms and posts in corrct position. Install valve rocker arm post attaching bolts.
11. Turn engine over by hand until timing mark is at 11 o'clock position as viewed from front of engine. Install all rocker arm post attaching bolts and tighten to 20 ft. lbs. Install valve covers on with new gaskets on cylinder heads.

NOTE: The following service procedure Steps 12–15 apply to the right side valve cover installation on E series only.

12. Raise and safely support the vehicle. Raise engine, remove wood block and lower engine onto crossmember.
13. Install insulator (motor mount) attaching washers and nuts.
14. Lower vehicle. Install transmission filler tube and transmission oil dipstick.
15. Install engine oil dipstick tube and valve cover bracket. Install engine oil dipstick.
16. Install radiator fan shroud halves. Install ground cables to both batteries.
17. Start the engine and inspect for oil leaks.

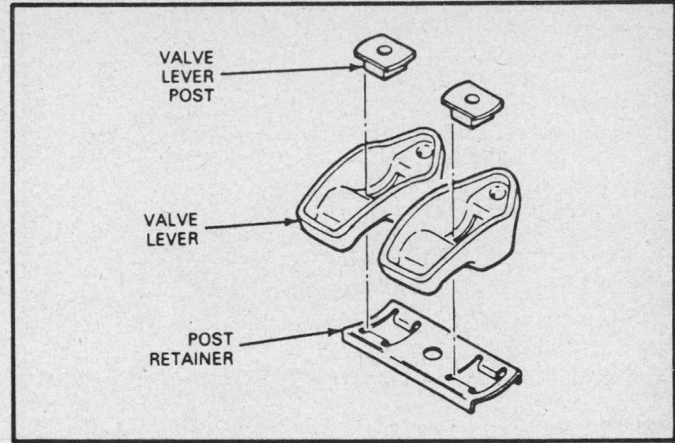

Rocker arm assembly–6.9L and 7.3L engines

Intake Manifold

Removal and Installation

1. Disconnect ground cables from both batteries.
2. On E series, remove engine (doghouse) cover.
3. Remove air cleaner and install intake manifold cover or equivalent.
4. On E series disconnect fuel inlet line and fuel return line from fuel filter. Remove fuel filter bracket attaching bolts and remove fuel filter and bracket as an assembly.
5. Remove injection pump assembly.
6. On F series, remove fuel return hoses from No. 7 and No. 8 rear nozzles and remove return hose to fuel tank.
7. Remove glow plug harness and controller. Remove engine wiring harness from engine. Remove engine harness ground cable from back of left cylinder head.
8. Remove intake manifold retaining bolts and remove intake manifold.

To install:

9. Clean cylinder block gasket surfaces of silicone rubber sealant or oil. Apply a ⅛ inch bead of Silicone Rubber Sealant D6AZ–19562–A or equivalent, to each end of the cylinder block.
10. Install intake manifold and tighten to specifications using the correct service procedure.
11. Install engine wiring harness on engine. Connect engine wiring harness ground wire to rear of left cylinder head.
12. Install glow plug controller and harness.
13. On E series, install fuel filter and bracket as as assembly. Install fuel filter return line and fuel filter inlet fuel line.
14. Install injection pump.
15. Reconnect fuel tank return hose and No. 7 and No. 8 nozzle fuel return hoses.
16. Remove intake manifold cover and install air cleaner. Install engine (doghouse) cover on E series.
17. Connect ground cables to both batteries. Start engine. Check for oil and fuel leaks. Bleed fuel system as required.
18. Road test the vehicle for proper operation.

Exhaust Manifold

Removal and Installation

F SERIES

1. Disconnect ground cables from both batteries.
2. Raise vehicle and safely support the vehicle as needed.
3. Disconnect muffler inlet pipe from exhaust manifolds.
4. Remove exhaust manifold attaching bolts and manifold.
5. Installation is ther revese of the removal procedure. Apply

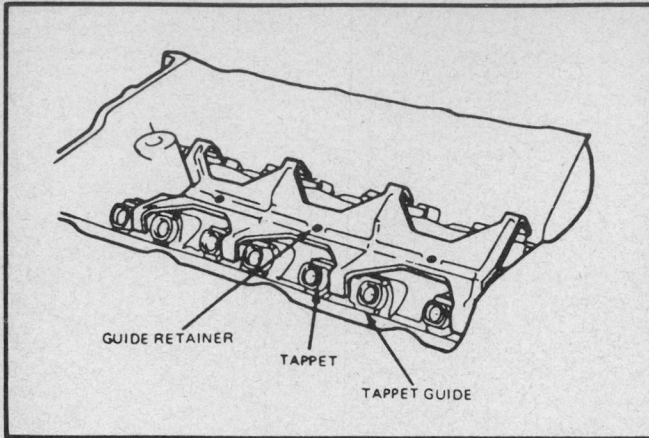

Valley pan—6.9L and 7.3L engines

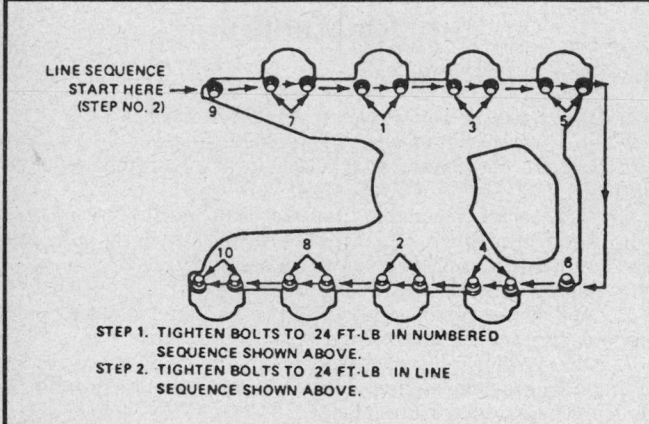

Intake manifold torque sequence—6.9L and 7.3L engines

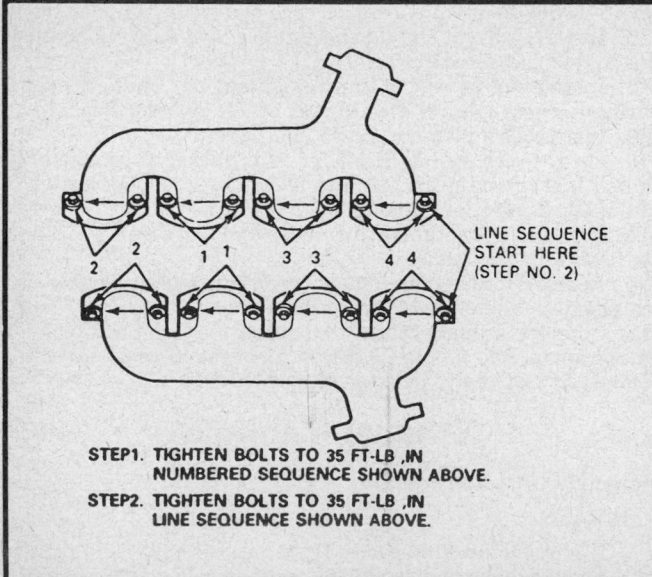

Exhaust manifold torque sequence—6.9L and 7.3L engines

anti-seize compound on exhaust manifold bolt threads and install manifold with new gasket. Tighten bolts (in 2 steps), in the proper sequence to 35 ft. lbs.

E SERIES

1. Remove engine (doghouse) cover. Disconnect battery ground cables from both batteries.
2. For right side only, remove radiator fan shroud halves.
3. For right side removal only, remove engine oil dipstick tube fasteners. Remove dipstick and tube. Remove transmission filler tube fasteners. Remove filler tube and dipstick.
4. Raise vehicle and safely support the vehicle.
5. For right side only, remove nuts attaching engine mount insulator to frame. Slightly raise right side of the engine until fuel filter header touches vehicle sheet metal. Install suitable wood block between insulator and frame. Lower engine on block.
6. Remove muffler inlet pipe from exhaust manifolds. Lower vehicle.
7. Remove exhaust manifold retaining bolts and exhaust manifold.
8. Installation is the reverse of the removal procedure. Apply anti-seize compound on exhaust manifold bolt threads and install manifold with new gasket. Tighten bolts (in 2 steps), in the proper sequence to 35 ft. lbs.

Engine Front Cover

Removal and Installation

1. Disconnect ground cables from both batteries. Drain cooling system.
2. Remove air cleaner and install intake air opening cap intake manifold cover or equivalent.
3. Remove radiator fan shroud.
4. Remove fan and clutch assembly. Left hand thread is used on the fan clutch assembly. Remove by turning nut clockwise.
5. Remove injection pump.
6. Remove injection pump adapter.
7. Remove water pump and components.
8. Raise vehicle and safely support the vehicle.
9. Remove crankshaft pulley and vibration damper using suitable tools.
10. Remove ground cables at front of engine. Remove bolts attaching front cover to engine block and oil pan.
11. Lower vehicle. Remove bolts attaching engine front cover to engine block and remove front cover.
12. Remove old gasket material and clean all sealing surfaces. Install fabricated alignment dowels if necessary on engine block and oil pan to align front cover and gaskets.
13. Apply a ⅛ inch bead of silicone sealer or equivalent, to rear corners of oil pan and apply a ¼ in. bead of silicone sealer or equivalent on oil pan.
14. Install engine front cover in position, on oil pan dowels and install retaining attaching bolts. Remove engine front cover alignment dowels if required. Install and hand tighten remaining front cover bolts.
15. Install water pump gasket and water pump. Remove alignment dowels if required and install remaining attaching bolts. Tighten (with sealer around threads) all water pump bolts to 14 ft lbs.
16. Tighten engine front cover bolts. Install injection pump adapter and injection pump.
17. Reconnect all cooling hoses. Raise and safely support the vehicle.
18. Lubricate damper seal nose with clean engine oil and install crankshaft vibration damper. Add silicone rubber sealant, to engine side of retaining bolt washer to prevent oil leakage past keyway. Install vibration damper attaching bolt and tighten to 90 ft. lbs.
19. Install crankshaft pulley. Install both battery ground ca-

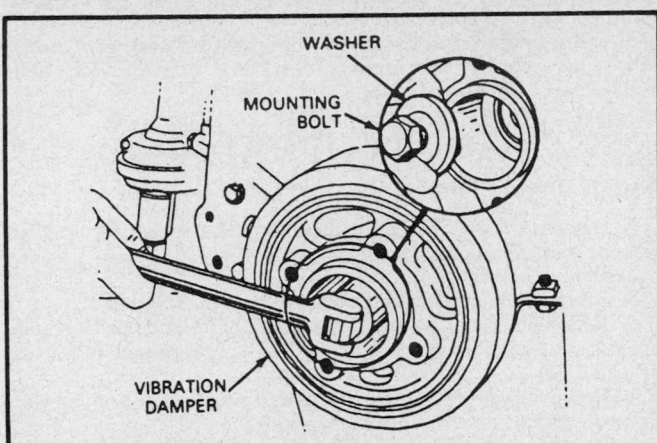

Removing vibration damper

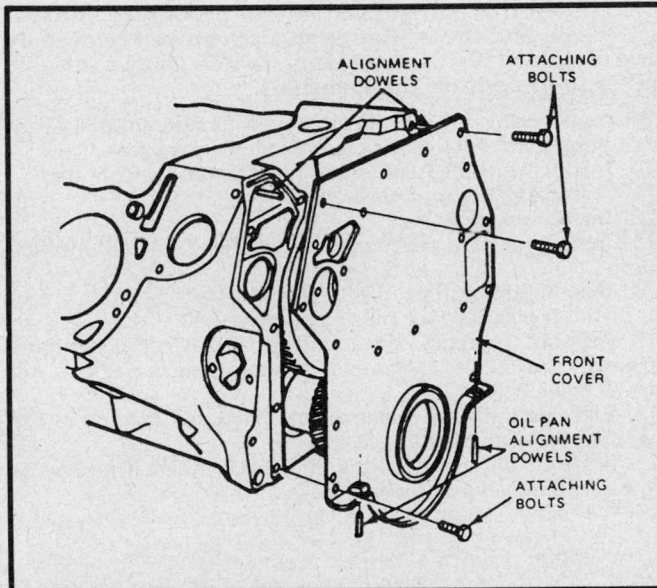

Front cover dowel positioning

bles on front of engine. Lower vehicle.

20. Install alternator adjusting arm bracket and water pump pulley.

21. Install power steering pump bracket, power steering pump and drive belt.

22. Install A/C compressor bracket, compressor and drive belt.

23. Install alternator adjusting arm, alternator and vacuum pump drive belts. Adjust all drive belts.

24. Install fan and clutch assembly. Install radiator fan shroud halves.

25. Remove intake manifold cover. Install air cleaner and re-connect ground cables to both batteries.

26. Fill and bleed cooling system. Start engine and inspect for coolant and oil leaks.

Front Cover Oil Seal

Removal and Installation

1. Disconnect battery ground cables from both batteries. Re-move radiator fan shroud.

2. Remove fan and clutch assembly. A left hand thread is used to retain the assembly. Remove by turning nut clockwise.

3. Remove all drive belts. Raise and safely support the vehicle.

4. Remove crankshaft pulley. Remove bolt attaching damper to crankshaft.

5. Install a suitable puller and remove crankshaft vibration damper.

6. Pry out front oil seal from the front cover.

7. Installation is the reverse of the removal procedure. Add silicone rubber sealant to engine side of washer (in area of key-way only), to prevent oil leakage past keyway. Install bolt at-taching vibration damper to crankshaft and tighten to 90 ft. lbs. Adjust all drive belts.

Crankshaft Drive Gear

Removal and Installation

1. Disconnect ground cables from both batteries. Remove air filter and install intake manifold cover on intake manifold opening.

2. Drain cooling system. Remove radiator fan shroud.

3. Remove fan and clutch assembly. A left hand thread is used on this assembly. Turn nut clockwise to remove.

4. Remove alternator and vacuum pump belts.

5. Remove A/C compressor and position out of the way. Re-move A/C mounting bracket.

6. Remove power steering pump and position out of the way. Remove power steering pump bracket.

7. Remove water pump pulley and water pump.

8. Remove engine front cover assembly.

9. Install a suitable puller remove crankshaft gear.

10. Install crankshaft gear and aligning crankshaft drive gear timing mark.

11. Clean all sealing surfaces. Install engine front cover.

12. Install crankshaft vibration damper. Apply silicone rubber sealant to engine side of washer (in area of keyway only), to pre-vent oil leakage past keyway. Install crankshaft vibration damp-er attaching bolt and tighten to 90 ft. lbs.

13. Install crankshaft pulley and water pump.

14. Install injection pump adapter and injection pump.

15. Install all cooling hoses.

16. Install power steering pump bracket, power steering pump and drive belt.

17. Install A/C compressor bracket, compressor and drive belt.

18. Install alternator adjusting arm. Install alternator and vacuum pump drive belts.

19. Adjust all drive belts. Check and set injection pump timing.

20. Install radiator fan and clutch assembly and radiator fan shroud halves. Fill and bleed cooling system.

21. Remove intake manifold cover. Install air cleaner assembly and connect ground cables to both batteries. Start engine and inspect for oil and coolant leaks.

Injection Pump Drive Gear

Removal and Installation

1. Disconnect ground cables from both batteries. Remove en-gine (doghouse) cover on E series.

2. Remove air cleaner and install intake opening cover.

3. Remove injection pump.

4. Remove bolts attaching injection pump drive gear cover to engine block and remove cover.

5. Turn engine over by hand to TDC (compression stroke) of No. 1 piston. Remove glow plugs, to facilitate turning engine over by hand.

6. To determine that No. 1 piston is at TDC (compression stroke), position injection pump drive gear dowel at 4 o'clock po-sition. The scribe line in vibration damper should be at TDC.

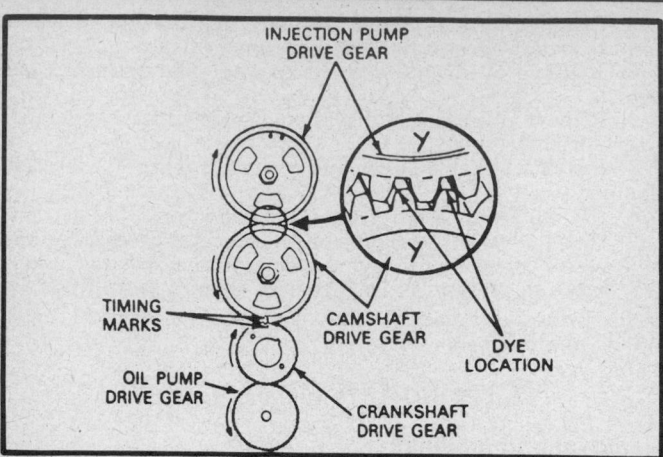

Timing marks–6.9L and 7.3L engines

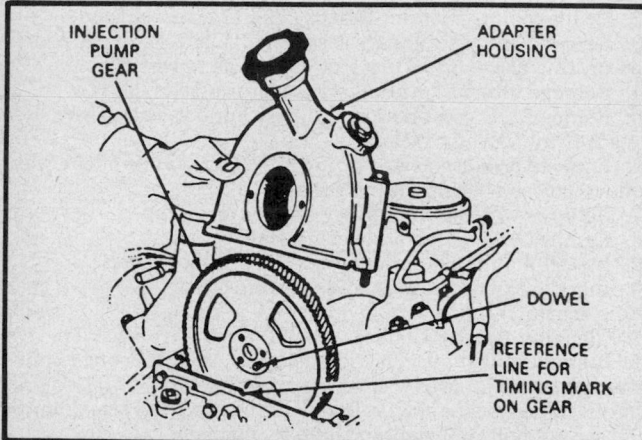

Injection pump drive gear cover

7. To aid aligning the timing marks, the pump drive gear and the camshaft gear are marked with "Y" timing marks. The crankshaft and camshaft gears are marked with "o" (dot) alignment marks. With engine at TDC compression for No. 1 cylinder, the "Y" marks should be aligned.

8. Slide injection pump gear back (do not remove) to expose top of camshaft gear when looking down into the front cover. In addition to the "Y", the gear teeth adjacent to the "Y" on the camshaft gear are permanently dyed.

9. Remove injection pump drive gear.

10. Clean all gasket and sealing surface.

NOTE: To determine that No. 1 piston is at TDC of compression stroke, position injection pump drive gear dowel at 4 o'clock position. The scribe line in vibration damper should be at TDC.

11. With drawn line on drive gear at 6 o'clock position, install gear and align all drive gear timing marks. Use extreme care to avoid disturbing injection pump drive gear, once it is in position.

12. Apply 1/8 inch bead of silicone sealant, along bottom surface of injection pump drive gear cover.

13. Install injection pump drive gear cover and tighten retaining bolts to 14 ft. lbs. Apply perfect seal sealing compound or equivalent, to bolt threads before assembly. With injection pump drive gear cover installed, the injection pump drive gear cannot jump timing.

14. Remove intake manifold cover. Install air cleaner and

ground cables to both batteries.

15. Start engine and bleed cooling and fuel system if necessary. Check for oil, fuel and coolant leaks. Install engine (doghouse) cover on E series.

Camshaft Drive Gear

Removal and Installation

1. Disconnect ground cables from both batteries. Remove air cleaner and install intake manifold cover.

2. Drain cooling system.

3. Remove alternator and vacuum pump drive belts.

4. Remove A/C compressor mounting bolts and position compressor out of the way. Remove A/C compressor mounting bracket.

5. Remove power steering pump and position out of the way. Remove power steering pump bracket.

6. Remove water pump pulley and water pump.

7. Remove engine front cover. Remove camshaft Allen screw and washer.

8. Install suitable gear puller and remove gear.

NOTE: At this point of the service procedure, the fuel pump cam and thrust flange spacer can be removed by first removing the the fuel pump then by using a suitable puller to press it off the camshaft.

9. Install camshaft drive gear against fuel pump cam, aligning timing mark with mark on crankshaft drive gear.

10. Install camshaft Allen screw and tighten to 15 ft. lbs.

11. Install engine front cover.

12. Install water pump.

13. Install injection pump gear and adapter. Install injection pump.

14. Install water pump pulley and power steering pump bracket. Install power steering pump and drive belt.

15. Install A/C compressor mounting bracket, compressor and drive belt. Install alternator and vacuum pump drive belts. Adjust all drive belts.

16. Reconnect ground cables to both batteries. Remove intake manifold cover and install air cleaner.

17. Start engine bleed cooling and fuel systems if necessary. Check for fuel, oil and coolant leaks.

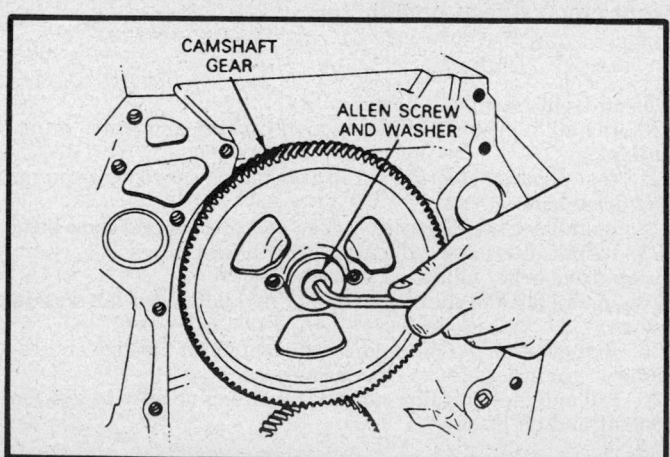

Camshaft drive gear assembly

Camshaft

Removal and Installation

1. Remove engine from vehicle.
2. Position engine in a suitable engine work stand.
3. Remove injection pump and adapter.
4. Remove intake manifold and valve lifters, engine front cover and fuel pump.
5. Remove camshaft drive gear, fuel supply pump cam, spacer and thrust plate from the camshaft assembly.
6. Remove camshaft. Use care to avoid damaging camshaft bearings.
7. Coat camshaft lobes with multi-purpose grease or equivalent and lubricate journals with engine oil before installation. Carefully slide camshaft through bearings. Install camshaft thrust plate onto cylinder block.
8. Install spacer and fuel pump cam against camshaft thrust flange using suitable tools.
9. Install camshaft drive gear against fuel pump cam, aligning timing mark with timing mark on crankshaft drive gear.
10. Install camshaft allen screw and tighten to 15 ft. lbs.
11. Install fuel pump assembly. Install new crankshaft oil seal in engine front cover. Install engine front cover.
12. Install water pump.
13. Install injection pump adapter. Lubricate the valve lifters and their bores with clean engine oil. Install the valve lifters in their original positions. Install the valve lifter guides. Install the valve lifter guide retainer.
14. Install pushrods, copper colored ends toward rocker arms making sure they are seated fully in pushrod seats. Install rocker arms and valve covers.
15. Install intake manifold and injection pump assemblies.
16. Install engine into vehicle. Check and fill all fluid levels. Start engine, bleed cooling and fuel system if necessary and check for leaks. Check injection pump timing and road test the vehicle for proper operation.

Piston and Connecting Rod

Positioning

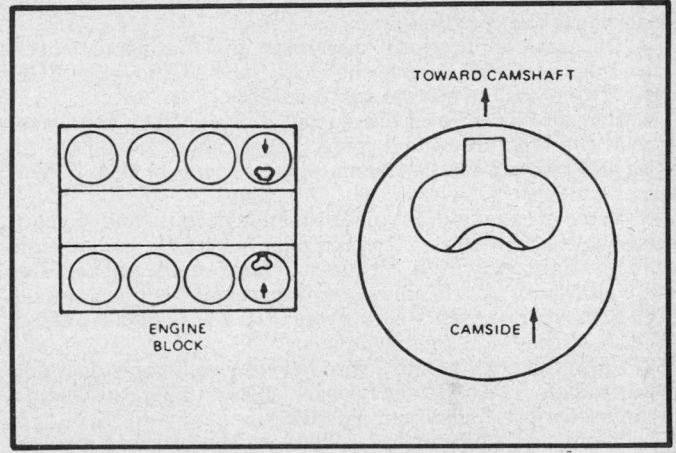

Piston orientation–6.9L and 7.3L engines

ENGINE LUBRICATION

Oil Pan

Removal and Installation

BRONCO AND F SERIES

4.9L Engine

1. Disconnect the negative battery cable. Drain the crankcase and the cooling system.
2. On some applications, it may be necessary to remove the radiator and shroud assembly.
3. Remove the upper intake and throttle body on fuel injected vehicles only.
4. Raise and safely support the vehicle. Disconnect the starter cable and remove the starter assembly.
5. Remove engine front support insulator to support bracket nuts and washers. Use a transmission jack or equivalent to raise the front of the engine (make sure fan clutch assembly does not break radiator shroud) then install wood blocks or equivalent between the front support insulators and support brackets. Lower engine onto blocks and remove jack.
6. Remove the attaching bolts and oil pan. It may be necessary to remove the oil pump inlet tube and screen assembly in order to free the pan (drop oil pump assembly in pan).
7. Installation is the reverse of the removal procedure. Tighten the oil pump inlet tube assembly screws to 10–15 ft. lbs. and nut to 22–32 ft. lbs. Tighten the oil pan retaining bolts working from the center to the end after securing the corner bolts to 10–15 ft. lbs. Refill all fluid levels and bleed cooling system.

5.0L and 5.8L Engines

1. Disconnect the negative battery cable. Remove the oil dipstick (on pan entry models only). Remove the bolts attaching the fan shroud to the radiator and position the shroud over the fan.
2. On fuel injected vehicles, remove the upper intake manifold.
3. Remove the nuts and lockwashers attaching the engine support insulators to the chassis bracket.
4. Disconnect the oil cooler lines, if equipped with automatic transmission.
5. Raise the engine (make sure fan clutch assembly does not break radiator shroud) and place wood blocks under the engine supports. Drain the crankcase.
6. Remove the oil pan bolts and lower the oil pan onto the crossmember.
7. Remove the oil pump pick-up tube and screen. Lower this assembly into the oil pan. Remove the oil pan.
8. Installation is the reverse of the removal procedure. Tighten the oil pump pick-up tube assembly screws to 10–15 ft. lbs. Tighten the oil pan retaining bolts working from the center to the end after securing the corner bolts to 9–11 ft. lbs. Refill all fluid levels.

7.5L Engine

1. Disconnect the battery ground cable. Disconnect the radiator shroud and position it over the fan.
2. Raise and support the vehicle. Drain the crankcase. Remove the oil filter.
3. Remove the through bolt from each engine support. Place a floor jack under the front edge of the oil pan, with a block of wood between the jack and the oil pan. Raise the engine (make sure fan clutch assembly does not break radiator shroud) just high enough to insert blocks of wood between the insulators and the brackets. Remove the floor jack.
4. Remove the oil pan bolts and remove the oil pan. It may be necessary to rotate the crankshaft to provide clearance between the pan and the crankshaft counterweights.
5. Installation is the reverse of the removal procedure. Tighten the oil pump pick-up tube assembly screws to 12–18 ft. lbs.

and nut to 22–32 ft. lbs. Tighten the oil pan retaining bolts working from the center to the end after securing the corner bolts to 8–11 ft. lbs. Refill all fluid levels.

E SERIES

4.9L Engine

1. Disconnect the negative battery cable. Remove the engine (doghouse) cover. Remove the air cleaner and the carburetor. On fuel injected engines remove air cleaner and air inlet tubes from the throttle body.
2. If equipped with air conditioning, discharge the system and remove the compressor.
3. On some applications, disconnect the thermactor check valve inlet hose and remove the check valve. Remove the EGR valve. Drain cooling system and crankcase.
4. Remove the radiator hoses and transmission cooling lines. Unbolt the fan shroud and correctly position it on the fan. If equipped with automatic transmission, disconnect the oil filler tube.
5. Remove exhaust inlet pipe at manifold. Raise and support the vehicle safely. Disconnect and plug fuel pump inlet line on vehicles equipped with a carburetor. Remove the starter. Remove alternator splash shield and front engine support nuts.
6. Remove the power steering return line clip which is located in front of the No. 1 crossmember.
7. Raise the engine (make sure fan clutch assembly does not break radiator shroud) and wooden blocks under the engine mounts. Remove the oil pan dipstick tube.
8. Remove the oil pan bolts. Remove the pickup tube and screen from the oil pump (lay in oil pan). Remove the oil pan.
9. Installation is the reverse of the removal procedure. Tighten the oil pump pickup tube assembly screws to 10–15 ft. lbs. and nut to 22–32 ft. lbs. Tighten the oil pan retaining bolts working from the center to the end after securing the corner bolts to 10–15 ft. lbs. Refill all fluid levels and bleed cooling system.

5.0L and 5.8L Engines

1. Disconnect the battery and remove engine (doghouse) cover. Remove the air cleaner. Drain the cooling system.
2. If equipped with power steering remove the pump and position it out of the way. If so equipped, remove the air conditioning compressor retainer and position the compressor out of the way.
3. Disconnect the radiator hoses. Remove the fan shroud bolts and oil filler tube. Remove the oil dipstick bolt. Raise and safely support the vehicle.
4. Remove the alternator splash shield. If equipped, disconnect the automatic transmission cooler lines at the radiator.
5. Disconnect and plug the fuel line at the fuel pump on vehicles equipped with a carburetor.
6. Remove the engine mount retaining nuts. Drain the engine oil. Remove the dipstick tube.
7. Disconnect the muffler inlet pipe from the exhaust manifolds.
8. If equipped, remove the automatic transmission dipstick and tube. Disconnect the manual linkage at the transmission. Remove the center driveshaft support and remove the driveshaft (mark the position of the driveshaft for correct installation) from the transmission.
9. Place a transmission jack or equivalent under the oil pan and insert a wooden block between the pan and jack. The engine and transmission assembly will pivot around the rear engine mount. The engine assembly must be raised 4 inches (measured from the front motor mounts). The engine must remain centered in the engine compartment to obtain this much lift.
10. Raise the engine (make sure fan clutch assembly does not break radiator shroud) and transmission assembly. Insert wooden blocks to support the engine.
11. Remove the oil pan bolts and lower the oil pan. Remove the

oil pump and the oil pickup tube and lay them in the oil pan. Remove the oil pan from the vehicle.
12. Installation is the reverse of the removal procedure. Tighten the oil pump pickup tube assembly screws to 10–15 ft. lbs. and oil pump retaining bolts to 22–32 ft. lbs. Tighten the oil pan retaining bolts working from the center to the end after securing the corner bolts to 9–11 ft. lbs. Refill all fluid levels and bleed cooling system.

7.5L Engine

1. Remove the engine (doghouse) cover, disconnect the battery and drain the cooling system.
2. Remove the air inlet tube and the air cleaner assembly. Disconnect the throttle and transmission linkage at the carburetor or throttle body. Disconnect the power brake vacuum lines.
3. Disconnect the fuel line, choke lines and remove the carburetor air cleaner adaptor from the carburetor. On fuel injected vehicles relieve the fuel pressure and remove fuel lines from the fuel rails. Disconnect air tubes at the throttle body.
4. Disconnect the radiator hoses. If equipped, disconnect the oil cooler lines. Remove the fan/shroud assembly and remove the radiator. If equipped, remove the power steering pump and position it aside.
5. Remove the front engine mount attaching bolts. Remove the engine oil dipstick tube from the exhaust manifold. Remove the oil filler tube and bracket.
6. If so equipped, rotate the air conditioning lines (at the rear of the compressor) down to clear the dash or remove them (evacuate the system as required).
7. Remove the upper intake manifold and throttle body as an assembly on fuel injected vehicles.
8. Raise and support the vehicle safely. Drain the crankcase and remove the oil filter.
9. Remove the muffler inlet pipe assembly. Disconnect the manual and kickdown linkage from the transmission. Remove the driveshaft (mark for correct installation) and coupling shaft assembly. Remove the transmission tube assembly.
10. Remove the dipstick and tube from the oil pan. Place a transmission jack or equivalent under the engine oil pan. Insert a wood block between the jack surface and the oil pan. Jack the engine upward, pivoting on the rear mount until the transmission contacts the floor. Block the engine in position. The engine must remain centralized to obtain the maximum height. The engine must be raised 4 inches at the mounts to remove the oil pan.
11. Remove the oil pan bolts and lower the oil pan. Remove the oil pump and pick up tube attachments and drop them into the oil pan. Remove the oil pan rearward from the vehicle. The oil pump must be removed when removing the oil pan.
12. Installation is the reverse of the removal procedure. Tighten the oil pump pickup tube assembly nut to 12–18 ft. lbs. Tighten the oil pan retaining bolts working from the center to the end after securing the corner bolts to 14 ft. lbs. Refill all fluid levels and bleed cooling system.

E AND F SERIES

6.9L and 7.3L Engines

1. Disconnect both battery ground cables.
2. Remove the engine oil dipstick and automatic transmission if so equipped level dipstick.
3. Remove the air cleaner and install intake opening cover or equivalent.
4. Remove the fan clutch asembly. A left hand thread is used to retain the fan clutch assemnbly.
5. Drain the cooling system and remove the automatic transmission cooling (cap lines after removal) lines if so equipped.
6. Disconnect the lower radiator hose. Remove the power steering return hose from the power steering pump.
7. Disconnect all electrical wiring at alternator.

8. Raise and safely support the vehicle.

9. Disconnect the fuel inlet line. Drain crankcase and remove the oil filter.

10. Remove the transmission filler tube assembly. Remove the front pipe from the exhaust manifold and muffler. Exhaust manifold upper right mounting stud may have to be removed to gain necessary clearance when motor is lifted.

11. Remove the attaching bolts at No. 1 crossmember. Lower the vehicle.

12. Using a suitable engine sling or lifting hooks and a floor crane raise the engine until transmission housing contacts body.

13. Install wood blocks between engine mounts and crossmember. Lower engine onto blocks.

14. Raise and safely support the vehicle. Remove the flywheel inspection plate and position any fuel lines out of the way.

15. Remove oil pan retaining bolts. Remove oil pump and pick-up tube from engine and lay in oil pan if necessary.

16. Remove the oil pan. Crankshaft may have to be turned to reposition counterweights to aid in removal of the oil pan.

17. Installation is the reverse of the removal procedure. Tighten the oil pump pickup tube assembly nut to 12–18 ft. lbs. Tighten the oil pan retaining bolts working from the center to the end after securing the corner bolts to 14 ft. lbs. Refill all fluid levels and bleed cooling system.

Oil Pump

Removal and Installation

1. Disconnect the negative battery cable(s). Raise and safely support the vehicle. Drain the engine oil. Remove the oil pan.

2. Remove the oil pump mounting bolts and remove the oil pump from the cylinder block.

To install:

3. Prime the pump by filling the inlet port with new engine oil. Rotate the pump shaft to distribute oil within the pump body. Install the distributor intermediate shaft in the oil pump rotor shaft.

4. Insert the intermediate shaft into the distributor shaft hex bore. Make certain that the intermediate shaft is properly seated. Do not force the pump into position if it will not seat readily. The intermediate shaft hex may be misaligned with the distributor shaft. To align, rotate the intermediate shaft until it can be seated.

NOTE: To align the distributor shaft use a long tool to turn the shaft to the proper position.

5. Install the oil pump to the cylinder block. Install the oil pan and other related parts.

Checking

Thoroughly clean all parts in solvent and dry with compressed air. Check the inside of the pump housing for obvious wear or scoring. Check mating surfaces of pump cover and rotors, replace the cover if it is scored or grooved.

Measure the inner rotor tip clearance. With the rotor assembly installed in the housing, place a straightedge over the rotor assembly and the housing. Measure the clearance (rotor endplay) between the straightedge and the rotor and outer race. Measure the driveshaft to housing clearance by comparing shaft outer diameter to housing bearing inner diameter. Inspect relief valve spring for collapsed or worn condition. Check the spring tension. Check relief valve piston and bore for scores and free operation.

The inner to outer rotor tip clearance is 0.012 maximum and rotor assembly endplay clearance is 0.004 maximum. If any part of the oil pump requires replacement, replace the complete pump assembly.

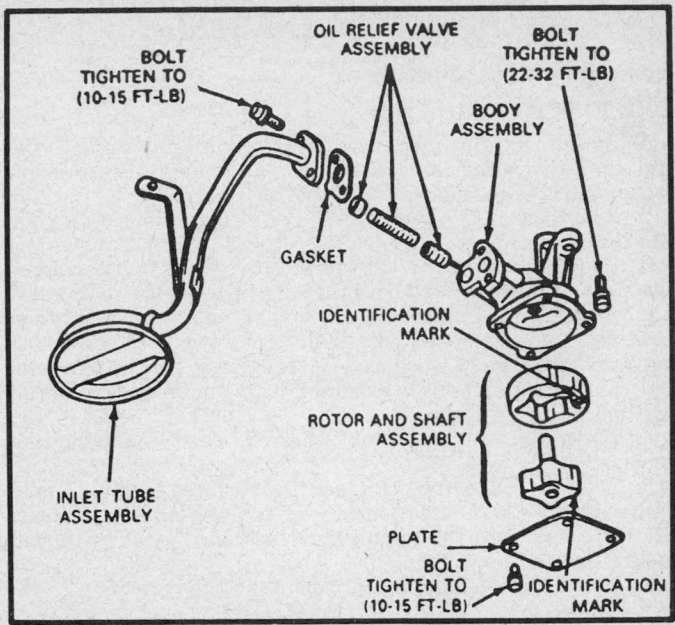

Typical oil pump assembly–V8 engine

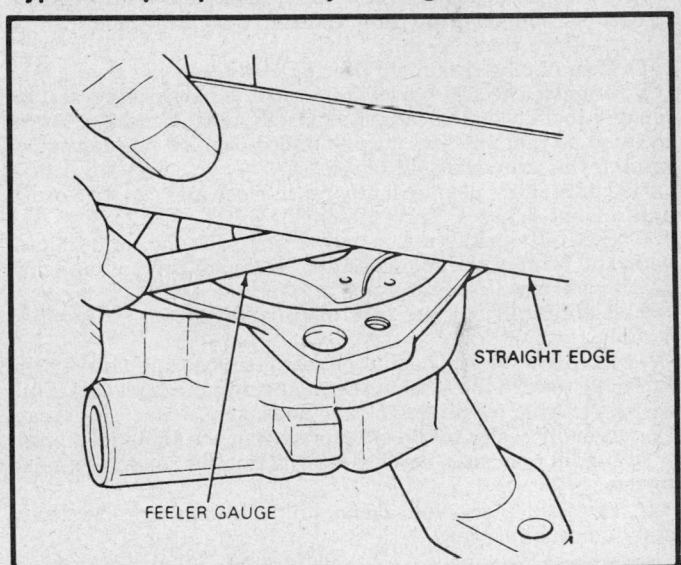

Checking rotor endplay

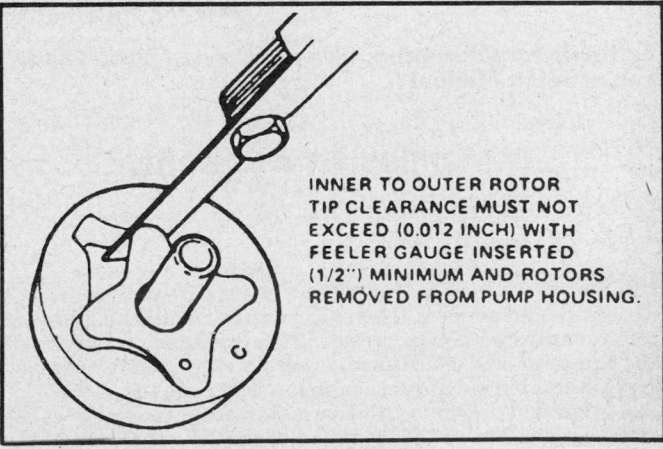

INNER TO OUTER ROTOR TIP CLEARANCE MUST NOT EXCEED (0.012 INCH) WITH FEELER GAUGE INSERTED (1/2'') MINIMUM AND ROTORS REMOVED FROM PUMP HOUSING.

Checking inner rotor tip clearance

Rear Main Oil Seal

Removal and Installation
ONE PIECE SEAL

1. Disconnect the negative battery cable and remove the starter. Remove the transmission and on manual transmission equipped vehicles remove the clutch assembly.

2. Remove the flywheel. Lower the oil pan if necessary for working room.

3. Use an awl or equivalent to punch two small holes on opposite sides of the seal just above the split between the main bearing cap and engine block. Install a sheet metal screw in each hole. Use two small pry bars and pry evenly on both screws using 2 small blocks of wood as a fulcrum point for the pry bars. Use caution throughout to avoid scratching or damage to the oil seal mounting surfaces.

4. When the seal has been removed, clean the mounting recess.

5. Coat the seal and block mounting surfaces with oil. Apply white lube to the contact surface of the seal and crankshaft. Start the seal into the mounting recess and install with seal mounting tool.

6. Install the remaining components in the reverse.

SPLIT SEAL

1. Disconnect the negative battery cable. Remove the oil pan. Loosen all main bearing caps, lowering the crankshaft slightly, but not more than $\frac{1}{32}$ in.

2. Remove the rear main bearing cap.

3. Remove the seal halves from cap and block. Use a seal removing tool on the block half or install a small metal screw in one end so that the seal may be pulled out. Do not damage or scratch the crankshaft seal surfaces.

4. Thoroughly clean seal grooves in block and cap with brush and solvent. Dip seal halves in engine oil.

5. Carefully install upper half of seal with the lip facing toward the front of the engine until $\frac{3}{8}$ in. is left protruding below parting surface. Be careful not to scrape seal.

6. Tighten all but the rear main bearing caps to specified torque.

7. Install lower seal half in the rear main bearing cap with the lip facing toward the front of the engine. Apply a light coat of oil-resistant sealer to the rear of the top mating surface of the cap. Do not apply sealer to the area forward of the side seal groove.

8. Install rear main bearing cap and tighten bolts to specified torque.

9. Install oil pump and oil pan. Fill crankcase and operate engine to check for leaks.

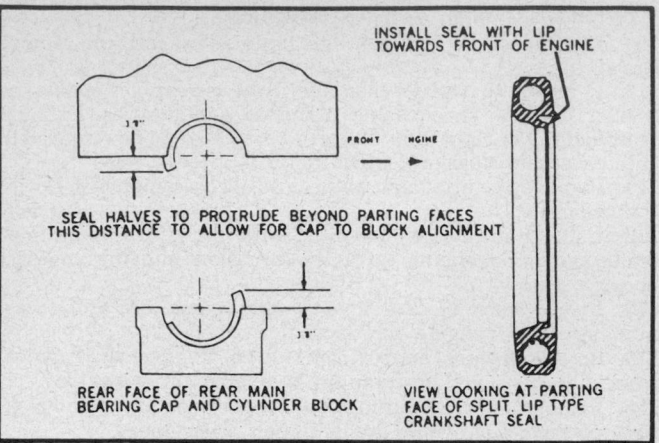

Installing split–type crankshaft rear oil seal

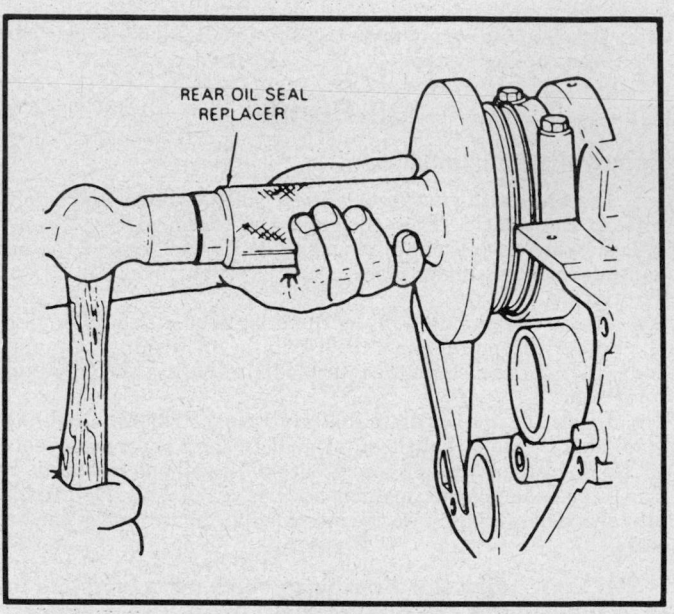

Installing one–piece crankshaft rear oil seal

MANUAL TRANSMISSION

For further information, please refer to "Professional Transmission Manual".

Transmission Assembly

Removal and Installation
FORD 3.03 THREE SPEED
E SERIES

1. Raise and support the vehicle safely. Drain the lubricant from the transmission by removing the drain plug if the vehicle is so equipped. For models without drain plugs, remove the lower extension housing-to-transmission bolt.

2. Mark and disconnect the driveshaft from the flange at the transmission. Secure the front end of the driveshaft out of the way with mechanic's wire or equivalent.

3. Disconnect the speedometer cable from the extension housing and disconnect the gear shift rods from the transmission shift levers.

4. Position a transmission jack under the transmission. Secure the transmission to the jack.

5. Raise the transmission slightly and remove the bolts retaining the transmission support crossmember to the frame side rails. Remove the bolt retaining the transmission extension housing to the crossmember.

6. Remove the 4 transmission-to-flywheel housing bolts.

7. Position engine support bar tool T65E–6000–J or equivalent (floor jack) to the frame.

8. Lower the transmission.

To install:

9. Make certain that the machined surfaces of the transmission case and the flywheel housing are free of dirt, paint and burrs.

10. Install a guide pin in each lower mounting bolt hole.
11. Start the input shaft through the release bearing. Align the splines on the input shaft with the splines in the clutch disc. Move the transmission forward on the guide pins until the input shaft pilot enters the bearing or bushing in the crankshaft. If the transmission front bearing retainer binds up on the clutch release bearing hub, work the release bearing lever until the hub slides onto the transmission front bearing retainer. Install the 2 transmission-to-flywheel housing upper mounting bolts and lockwashers. Remove the 2 guide pins and install the lower mounting bolts and lockwashers.
12. Raise the jack slightly and remove the engine support bar or equivalent.
13. Position the support crossmember on the frame side rails and install the retaining bolts. Install the extension housing-to-crossmember retaining bolt.
14. Connect the gear shift rods and the speedometer cable.
15. Install the driveshaft and torque the attaching bolts to 42–50 ft. lbs..
16. Fill the transmission to the bottom of the filler hole with the recommended lubricant.
17. Adjust the clutch pedal free travel and shift linkage as required.

F Series

1. Raise and support the vehicle safely. Support the engine with a jack and wood block placed under the oil pan.
2. Drain the transmission lubricant by removing the drain plug if the vehicle is so equipped. For models without drain plugs, remove the lower extension housing-to-transmission bolt.
3. Position a transmission jack under the transmission.
4. Disconnect the gear shift linkage at the transmission. Mark and disconnect the driveshaft from the vehicle.
5. Disconnect the speedometer cable and reverse light wiring from the transmission.

6. Remove the transmission-to-clutch housing attaching bolts.
7. Move transmission to the rear until the input shaft clears the clutch housing and lower the transmission. Do not depress the clutch pedal while the transmission is removed.
8. Before installing the transmission, apply a light film of lubricant to the clutch disc splines, release bearing inner hub surfaces, release lever fulcrum and fork and the transmission front bearing retainer. Exercise care to avoid contaminating the clutch disc with excessive grease.
9. Place the transmission on a transmission jack. Raise the transmission until the input shaft splines are in line with the

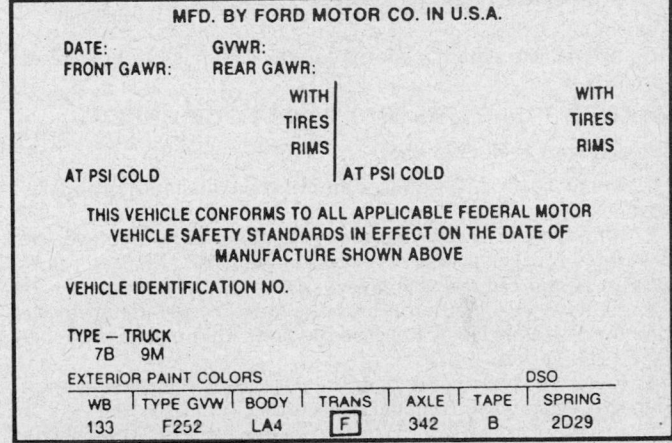

Typical identification code label–attached to drivers door lock pillar

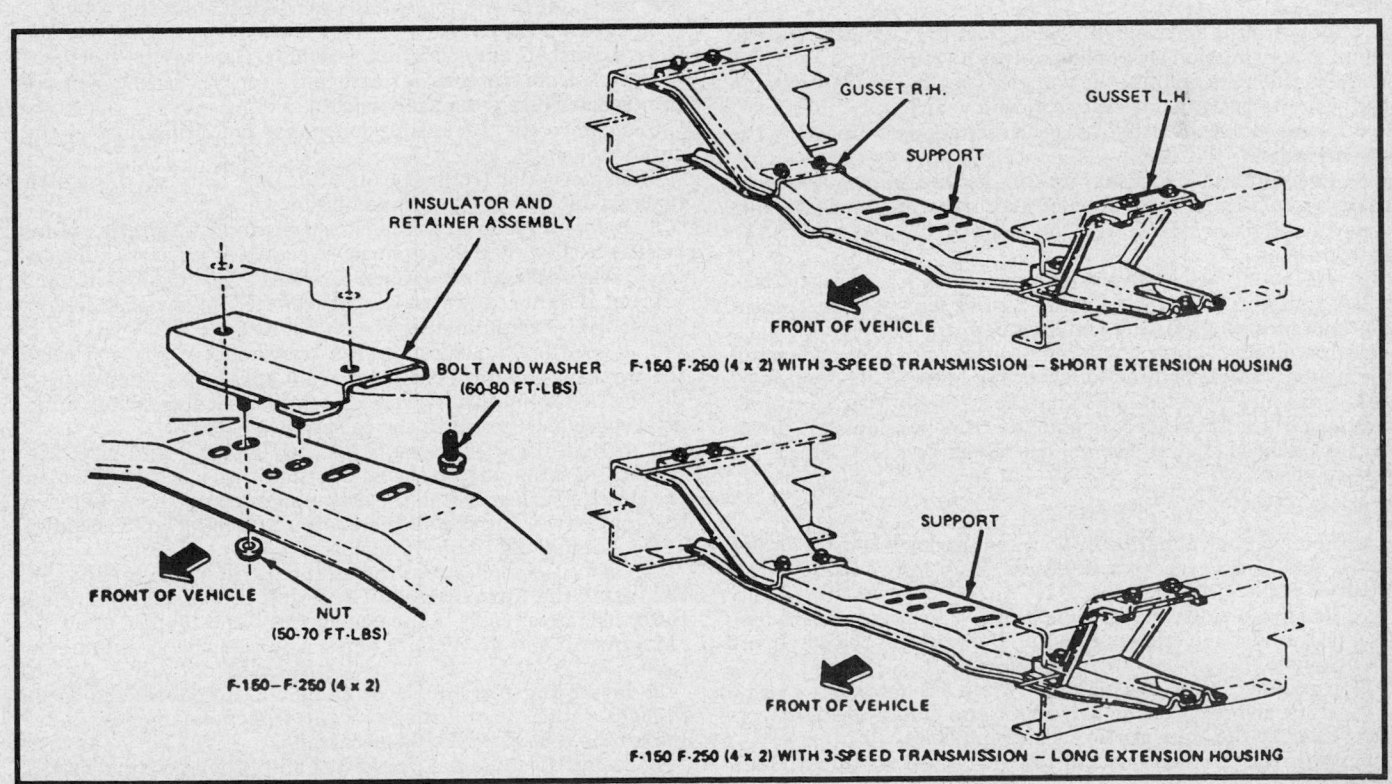

Typical transmission rear support

clutch disc splines. The clutch release bearing and hub must be properly positioned in the release lever fork.

10. Install a guide stud in each lower clutch housing-to-transmission case mounting bolt and align the splines on the input shaft with the splines on the clutch disc.

11. Slide the transmission forward on the guide studs until it contacts the clutch housing.

12. Install the 2 transmission to flywheel housing upper mounting bolts and nuts. Remove the 2 guide studs and install the lower mounting bolts. Tighten all retaining bolts to 42–50 ft. lbs.

13. Connect the speedometer cable. Install the driveshaft.

14. Connect each shift rod to its respective lever on the transmission.

15. Fill the transmission to the proper level with an approved lubricant.

16. Adjust the clutch pedal free travel and shift linkage as required.

WARNER T-18, T-19A AND T-19C FOUR SPEED

Bronco and F Series 4WD

1. Remove the shift knobs. Remove the transmission shift lever boot assembly.

2. Remove the screws holding the floor mat. Remove the screws holding the access cover to the floor pan. Place the shift lever in **R** and remove the cover.

3. Remove the insulator and the dust cover. Remove the transfer case shift lever. Remove the bolts holding the shift cover and the gasket.

4. Cover the shift cover opening to protect the transmission from dirt during the removal procedure.

5. Raise and support the vehicle safely. Drain the transmission.

6. Mark and disconnect the front and the rear driveshaft from the transfer case and wire them out of the way. Remove the cotter pin that holds the shift link in place and remove the shift link.

7. Remove the speedometer cable from the transfer case. Position a transmission jack or equivalent under the transfer case. Remove the bolts holding the transfer case to the transmission and remove the transfer case from the vehicle.

8. Remove the bolts that hold the rear support bracket to the transmission.

9. Position a transmission jack under the transmission and remove the rear support bracket and brace. Remove the bolts that hold the transmission to the bell housing and remove the transmission.

10. To install, place the transmission on a transmission jack and install it in the vehicle. Install 2 guide pins in the bell housing top holes, to guide the transmission in place.

11. Install the 2 lower bolts, remove the guide pins and install the upper 2 bolts. Tighten all retaining bolts to 35–50 ft. lbs.

12. Continue the installation in the reverse order of the removal. Fill the transfer case and the transmission with lubricant as reqired. Lower the vehicle. Road test the vehicle for proper operation.

F Series 2WD

1. Remove the rubber boot, floor mat and the body floor pan cover and remove the transmission shift lever. Remove the weather pad and pad retainer.

2. Raise and support the vehicle safely. Position a transmission jack under the transmission and disconnect the speedometer cable.

3. Disconnect the back-up light switch assembly.

4. Mark and remove the driveshaft and clutch linkage.

5. Remove the transmission attaching bolts.

6. Move the transmission to the rear until the input shaft clears the clutch housing and lower the transmission.

NOTE: Before installing the transmission, apply a light film of lubricant to the clutch disc splines, release bearing inner hub surfaces, release lever fulcrum and fork and the transmission front bearing retainer. Care must be exercised to avoid excessive grease from contaminating the clutch disc.

7. Place the transmission on a transmission jack and raise the transmission until the input shaft splines are aligned with the clutch disc splines. The clutch release bearing and hub must be properly positioned in the release lever fork.

8. Install guide studs in the clutch housing and slide the transmission forward on the guide studs until it is in position on the clutch housing. Install the attaching bolts and nuts. Remove the guide studs and install the 2 lower attaching bolts. Tighten all retaining bolts to 35–50 ft. lbs.

9. Connect the speedometer cable, electrical connection for reverse lights and shift linkage.

10. Install the driveshaft assembly.

11. Install the shift lever, boot and shift ball. Install the weather pad and pad retainer. Install the floor pan cover and floor mat.

12. Road test the vehicle for proper operation.

NEW PROCESS 435 FOUR SPEED

Bronco and F Series 2WD and 4WD

1. Remove the floor mat. Remove the shift lever, boot and ball as an assembly. On 4WD vehicles remove the transfer case shift lever, boot and ball as an assembly.

2. Remove the floor pan transmission cover plate. It may be necessary first to remove the seat assembly.

3. Remove the gearshift lever assembly from the housing. Disconnect the back-up light switch located in the rear of the gearshift housing cover.

4. Raise and support the vehicle safely. Position a transmission jack under the transmission and disconnect the speedometer cable. Mark and remove the driveshaft from the vehicle.

5. On 4WD appplications drain the transfer case. Remove the front driveshaft and shift link assembly. Remove the speedometer cable from the transfer case and support bracket. Remove the transfer case from the vehicle.

6. Remove the 2 transmission upper mounting nuts at the clutch housing.

7. Remove the transmission attaching bolts at the clutch housing and remove the transmission.

8. Before installing the transmission, apply a light film of lubricant to the clutch disc splines, release bearing inner hub surfaces, release lever fulcrum and fork and the transmission front bearing retainer. Care must be exercised to avoid excessive grease from contaminating the clutch disc.

9. Place the transmission on a transmission jack and raise the transmission until the input shaft splines are aligned with the clutch disc splines. The clutch release bearing and hub must be properly positioned in the release lever fork.

10. Install guide studs in the clutch housing and slide the transmission forward on the guide studs until it is in position on the clutch housing. Install the attaching bolts and nuts. Remove the guide studs and install the 2 lower attaching bolts. Tighten all retaining bolts to 35–50 ft. lbs.

11. On 4WD appplications install the transfer case to the vehicle. Install the front driveshaft and shift link assembly. Install the speedometer cable to the transfer case and support bracket.

12. Install the driveshaft and reconnect the speedometer cable.

13. Install the gearshift lever assembly. Reconnect the back-up light switch. Install the floor pan transmission cover plate. Install the seat assembly as necessary.

14. Install the floor mat. Install the shift lever, boot and ball as an assembly. On 4WD vehicles Install the transfer case shift le-

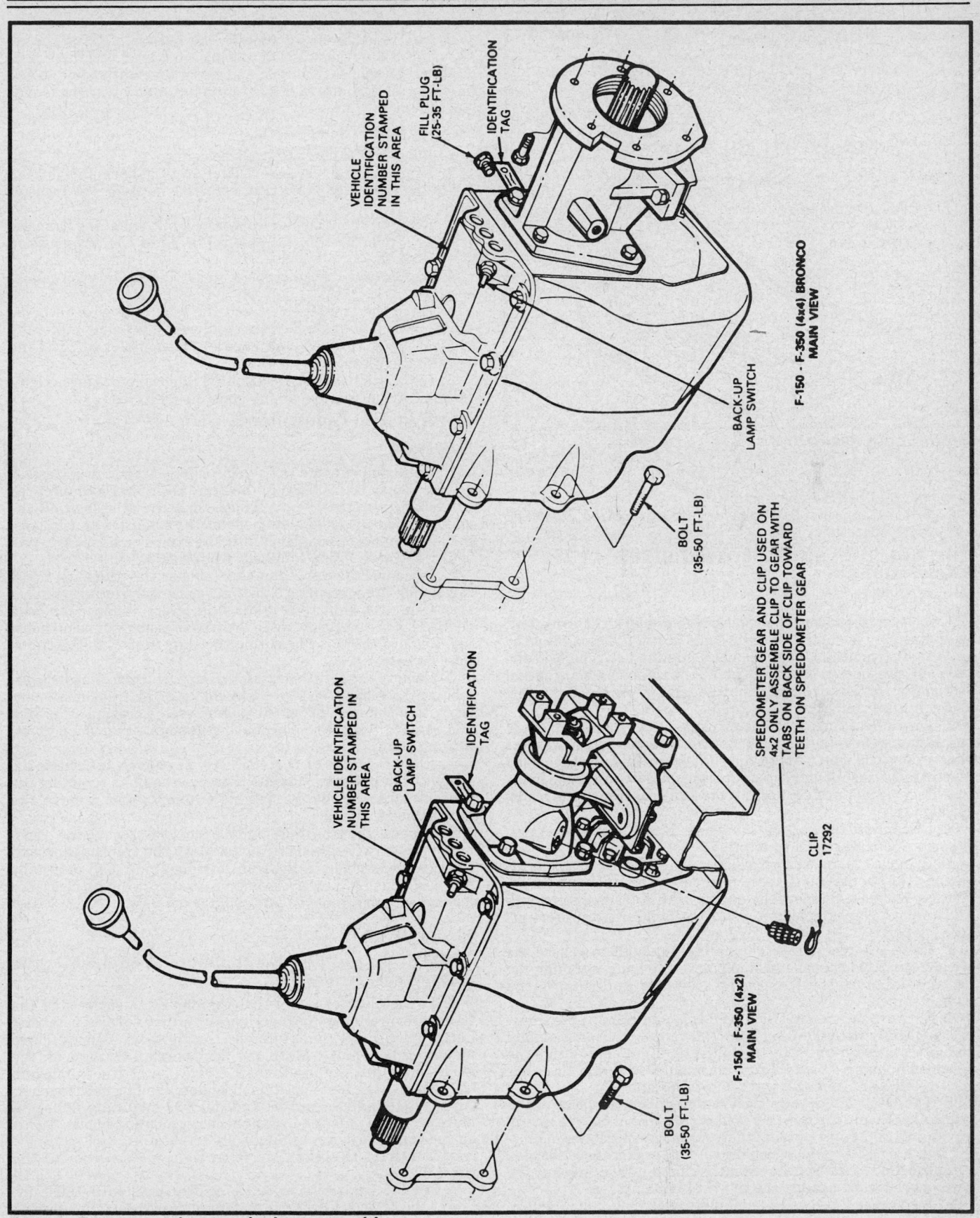

VEHICLE IDENTIFICATION NUMBER STAMPED IN THIS AREA

FILL PLUG (25-35 FT-LB)

IDENTIFICATION TAG

F-150 - F-350 (4x4) BRONCO MAIN VIEW

BACK-UP LAMP SWITCH

BOLT (35-50 FT-LB)

SPEEDOMETER GEAR AND CLIP USED ON 4x2 ONLY ASSEMBLE CLIP TO GEAR WITH TABS ON BACK SIDE OF CLIP TOWARD TEETH ON SPEEDOMETER GEAR

CLIP 17292

VEHICLE IDENTIFICATION NUMBER STAMPED IN THIS AREA

BACK-UP LAMP SWITCH

IDENTIFICATION TAG

F-150 - F-350 (4x2) MAIN VIEW

BOLT (35-50 FT-LB)

Warner T-18 manual transmission assembly

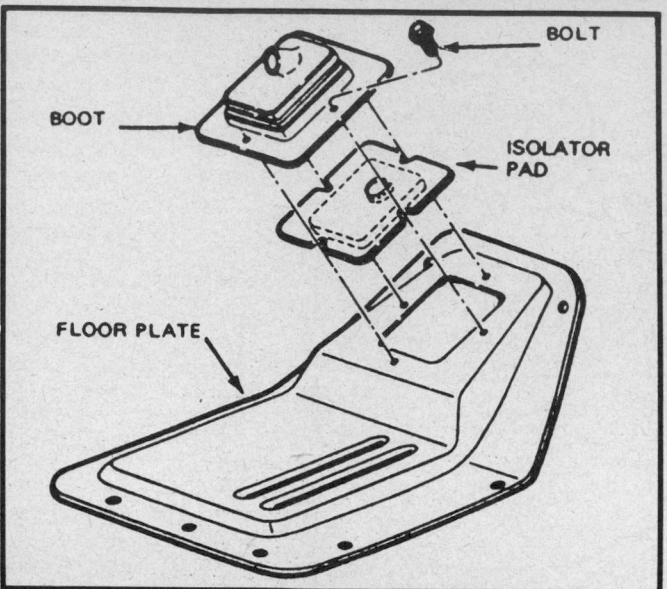

Shifter boot assembly

ver, boot and ball as an assembly.

15. Fill transmission and transfer case as required. Road test for proper operation.

TOP MOUNTED SHIFTER OVERDRIVE TRANSMISSION

F Series 2WD

1. Raise and support the vehicle safely. Mark the driveshaft so that it may be installed in the same position. Disconnect the driveshaft from the U-joint flange. Slide the driveshaft off the transmission output shaft and install the extension housing seal installation tool into the extension housing to prevent the transmission lubricant from leaking out.

2. Disconnect the speedometer cable at the extension housing. Remove the retaining clips, flat washers and spring washers that secure the shift rods to the shift levers. Remove the bolts connecting the shift control to the transmission extension housing. Remove the nut connecting the shift control to the transmission case.

3. Disconnect the back-up lamp switch and high gear switch if so equipped electrical connections.

4. Remove the rear transmission support connecting bolts attaching the support on the crossmember to the transmission extension housing. Support the engine with a transmission jack and remove the extension housing-to-engine rear support attaching bolts.

5. Raise the rear of the engine high enough to relieve the weight from the crossmember. Remove the bolts retaining the crossmember to the frame side supports and remove the crossmember.

6. Support the transmission on a jack and remove the transmission-to-flywheel housing bolts. Move the transmission and the jack rearward until the transmission input shaft clears the flywheel housing. Lower the engine enough to obtain clearance for transmission removal and remove the unit.

7. To install, make sure that the mounting surfaces of the transmission and the flywheel housing are free of dirt, paint and burrs. Install 2 guide pins in the flywheel housing lower mounting bolt holes. Move the transmission forward on the guide pins until the input shaft splines enter the clutch hub splines and the case is positioned against the flywheel housing.

8. Install the 2 upper transmission mounting bolts, remove the guide pins and install the lower mounting bolts. Tighten all

retaining bolts to 35–50 ft. lbs.

9. Continue the installation in the reverse order of the removal. Fill the transmission to the proper level with lubricant. Lower the vehicle. Road test and check the shift and crossover motion for full shift engagement and smooth crossover operation.

Bronco and F Series 4WD

1. Raise and support the vehicle safely.

2. Drain the transfer case. Disconnect the back-up light and 4WD indicator light electrical connections from the transfer case.

3. Remove the transfer case assembly from the transfer adapter. Slide the transfer case rearward of the transmission output shaft.

4. Support the transmission remove the transmission retaining bolts.

5. Move the transmission and the jack rearward until the transmission input shaft clears the flywheel housing. Lower the engine enough to obtain clearance for transmission removal and remove the unit.

6. Installation is the reverse of the removal procedure. Tighten the transmission retaining bolts 35–50 ft. lbs.

FOUR SPEED OVERDRIVE

E Series

1. Raise and support the vehicle safely. Mark the driveshaft so that it may be installed in the same position. Disconnect the driveshaft from the U-joint flange. Slide the driveshaft off the transmission output shaft and install the extension housing seal installation tool or equivalent into the extension housing to prevent the transmission lubricant from leaking out.

2. Disconnect the speedometer cable at the extension housing. Remove the retaining clips, flat washers and spring washers that secure the shift rods to the shift levers. Remove the bolts connecting the shift control to the transmission extension housing. Remove the nut connecting the shift control to the transmission case.

3. Remove the rear transmission support connecting bolts attaching the support on the crossmember to the transmission extension housing. Support the engine with a transmission jack and remove the extension housing-to-engine rear support attaching bolts.

4. Raise the rear of the engine high enough to relieve the weight from the crossmember. Remove the bolts retaining the crossmember to the frame side supports and remove the crossmember.

5. Support the transmission on a jack and remove the transmission-to-flywheel housing bolts. Move the transmission and the jack rearward until the transmission input shaft clears the flywheel housing. Lower the engine enough to obtain clearance for transmission removal and remove the unit.

NOTE: Do not depress the clutch pedal while the transmission is removed.

6. To install, make sure that the mounting surfaces of the transmission and the flywheel housing are free of dirt, paint and burrs. Install two guide pins in the flywheel housing lower mounting bolt holes. Move the transmission forward on the guide pins until the input shaft splines enter the clutch hub splines and the case is positioned against the flywheel housing.

7. Install the two upper transmission mounting bolts, remove the guide pins and install the lower mounting bolts. Tighten the transmission retaining bolts to 35–50 ft. lbs.

8. Continue the installation in the reverse order of the removal.

9. Fill the transmission to the proper level with lubricant. Lower the vehicle. Check the shift and crossover motion for full shift engagement and smooth crossover operation.

MAZDA M50D FIVE SPEED
Bronco, F and E Series 2WD

1. Shift the transmission into the **N** position. Disconnect the negative battery cable.
2. Remove the carpet or floor mat. Remove the shifter boot retainer screws and slide the boot up the shift lever shaft. Remove the shift lever retaining bolt and remove the shift lever.
3. Raise and support the vehicle safely. Disconnect the speedometer cable. Disconnect the backup lamp switch located at the top left hand side of the transmission.
4. Remove the drain plug from the transmission and drain the transmission fluid into a suitable drain pan. Position a suitable transmission jack under the transmission.
5. Disconnect the driveshaft from the transmission and wire it to one side. Disconnect the clutch hydraulic line.
6. Remove the transmission rear insulator and lower retainer. Remove the crossmember.
7. Remove the bolts that retain the transmission to the engine block. Move the transmission to the rear until the input shaft clears the engine flywheel. Lower the transmission from the vehicle.
8. With the transmission on a suitable transmission jack, install the guide studs into the engine block and raise the transmission up until the input shaft splines are aligned with the clutch disc splines.
9. Slide the transmission forward onto the guide studs until the transmission is in the correct position. Install the transmission retaining bolts and torque to 40–50 ft. lbs.
10. Installation is the reverse of the removal procedure. Fill the transmission to the proper level with lubricant. Lower the vehicle. Check the shift and crossover motion for full shift engagement and smooth crossover operation.

Bronco, F and E Series 4WD

1. Shift the transmission into the **N** position. Disconnect the negative battery cable.
2. Remove the carpet or floor mat. Remove the shifter boot retainer screws and slide the boot up the shift lever shaft. Remove the shift lever retaining bolt and remove the shift lever.
3. Raise and support the vehicle safely. Disconnect the driveshaft from the transmission and wire it to one side.
4. Disconnect the front driveshaft from the transfer case and wire it out of the way.
5. Disconnect the speedometer cable. Disconnect the backup lamp switch located at the top left hand side of the transmission. If equipped, remove the skid pad from underneath the transfer case.
6. Remove the drain plug from the transmission and drain the transmission fluid into a suitable drain pan. Position a suitable transmission jack under the transmission.
7. Support the transfer case, using a suitable transmission jack or equivalent. Remove the 6 bolts holding the transfer case to the transmission and carefully lower the transfer case from the vehicle, using care to ensure that the transfer case shift lever clears the opening in the floor pan.
8. Remove the transmission rear insulator and lower retainer. Remove the crossmember.
9. Remove the bolts that retain the transmission to the engine block. Move the transmission to the rear until the input shaft clears the engine flywheel. Lower the transmission from the vehicle.
10. With the transmission on a suitable transmission jack, install the guide studs into the engine block and raise the transmission up until the input shaft splines are aligned with the clutch disc splines.
11. Slide the transmission forward onto the guide studs until

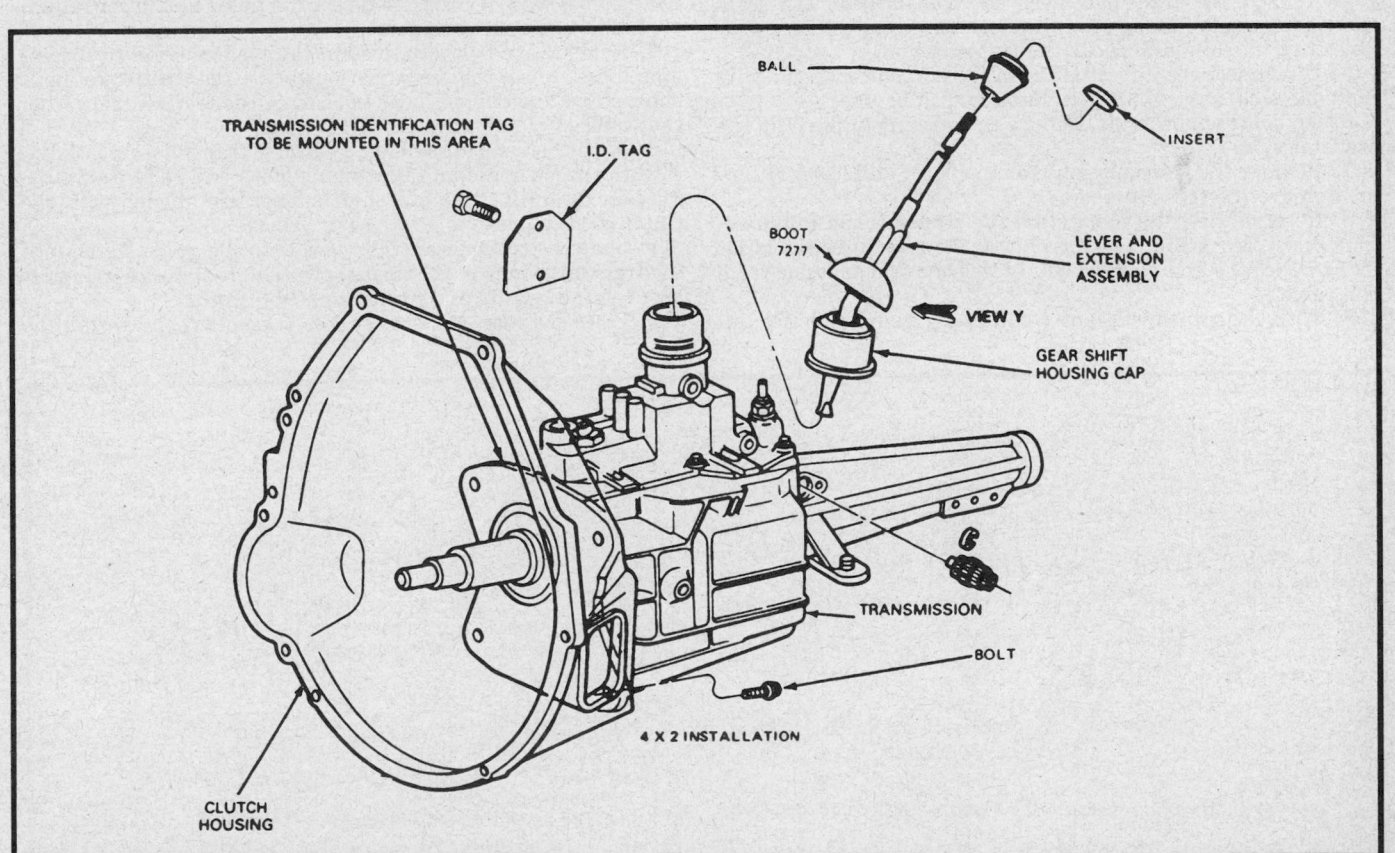

Top mounted shifter-manual transmission

the transmission is in the correct position. Install the transmission retaining bolts and torque to 40–50 ft. lbs.

12. Place the rear support bracket in position and install the retaining bolts. Install the crossmember. Position the insulator between the transmission and crossmember. Remove the transmission jack.

13. Position the transfer case on the transmission jack. Position the transfer case onto the transmission, using care to guide the transfer case shift lever through the opening in the floor pan. Install the gasket and 6 retaining bolts 24–34 ft. lbs.

14. Connect the speedometer cable and driven gear. Connect the backup lamp switch.

15. Install the driveshaft to the transmission.

16. Connect the rear driveshaft to the transfer case. Fill the transmission with the recommended transmission fluid to the proper level. Lower the vehicle.

17. Install the shift lever retaining bolt and tighten the retaining bolts. Slide the shifter boot into position on the shifter shaft and install the boot retaining screws.

18. Install the isolator pad assembly. Install the floor pan cover and floor mat. Install the shift ball on the transfer case shift lever.

S5–42 ZF FIVE SPEED

Bronco, F and E Series 2WD

1. Shift the transmission into the **N** position. Disconnect the negative battery cable.

2. Remove the carpet or floor mat. Remove the ball from the upper shift lever. Remove the boot and bezel from the transmission. Remove the upper shift lever from the lower shift lever.

3. Raise and support the vehicle safely. Disconnect the speedometer cable. Disconnect the backup lamp switch located at the top left hand side of the transmission.

4. Remove the drain plug from the transmission and drain the transmission fluid into a suitable drain pan. Position a suitable transmission jack under the transmission.

5. Disconnect the driveshaft from the transmission and wire it to one side. Disconnect the clutch hydraulic line.

6. On some applications, remove the parking brake from the transmission.

7. Remove the transmission rear insulator and lower retainer. Remove the crossmember.

8. Remove the bolts that retain the transmission to the engine block. Move the transmission to the rear until the input shaft clears the engine flywheel. Lower the transmission from the vehicle.

9. With the transmission on a suitable transmission jack, in-stall the guide studs into the engine block and raise the transmission up until the input shaft splines are aligned with the clutch disc splines.

10. Slide the transmission forward onto the guide studs until the transmission is in the correct position. Install the transmission retaining bolts and torque to 40–50 ft. lbs.

11. Installation is the reverse of the removal procedure. Fill the transmission to the proper level with lubricant. Lower the vehicle. Check the shift and crossover motion for full shift engagement and smooth crossover operation.

Bronco, F and E Series 4WD

1. Shift the transmission into the **N** position. Disconnect the negative battery cable.

2. Remove the carpet or floor mat. Remove the ball from the upper shift lever. Remove the boot and bezel from the transmission. Remove the upper shift lever from the lower shift lever.

3. Raise and support the vehicle safely. Disconnect the driveshaft from the transmission and wire it to one side.

4. Disconnect the front driveshaft from the transfer case and wire it out of the way.

5. Disconnect the speedometer cable. Disconnect the backup lamp switch located at the top left hand side of the transmission. If equipped, remove the skid pad from underneath the transfer case.

6. Remove the drain plug from the transmission and drain the transmission fluid into a suitable drain pan. Position a suitable transmission jack under the transmission.

7. Support the transfer case, using a suitable transmission jack or equivalent. Remove the 6 bolts holding the transfer case to the transmission and carefully lower the transfer case from the vehicle, using care to ensure that the transfer case shift lever clears the opening in the floor pan.

8. Remove the transmission rear insulator and lower retainer. Remove the crossmember.

9. Remove the bolts that retain the transmission to the engine block. Move the transmission to the rear until the input shaft clears the engine flywheel. Lower the transmission from the vehicle.

10. With the transmission on a suitable transmission jack, in-stall the guide studs into the engine block and raise the transmission up until the input shaft splines are aligned with the clutch disc splines.

11. Slide the transmission forward onto the guide studs until the transmission is in the correct position. Install the transmission retaining bolts and torque to 40–50 ft. lbs.

12. Place the rear support bracket in position and install the

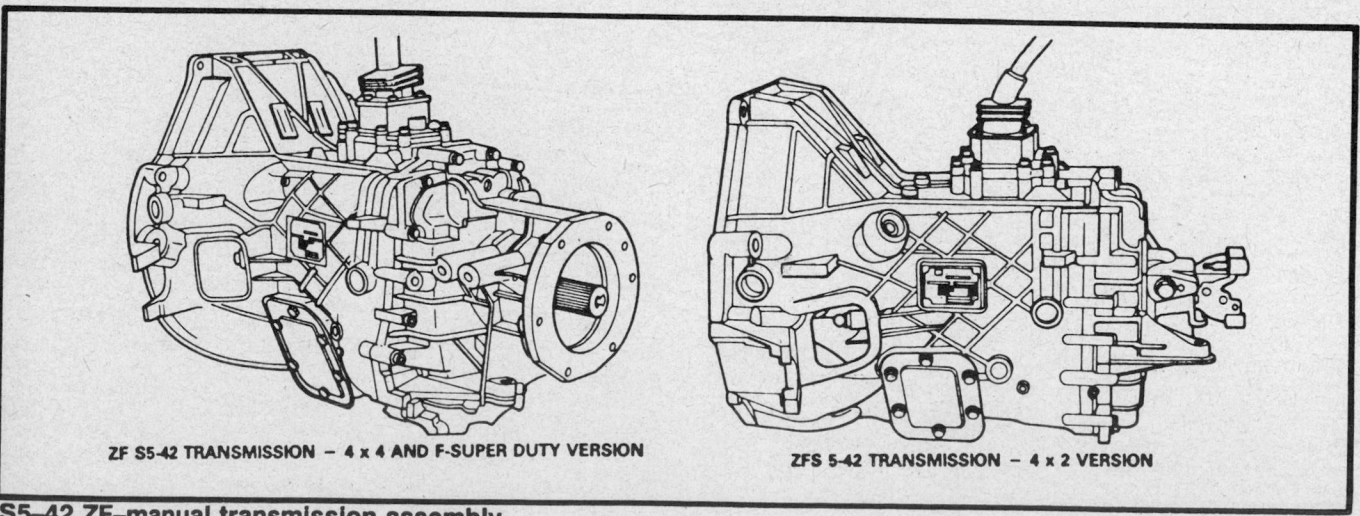

ZF S5-42 TRANSMISSION – 4 x 4 AND F-SUPER DUTY VERSION   ZFS 5-42 TRANSMISSION – 4 x 2 VERSION

S5–42 ZF–manual transmission assembly

retaining bolts. Install the crossmember. Position the insulator between the transmission and crossmember. Remove the transmission jack.

13. Position the transfer case on the transmission jack. Position the transfer case onto the transmission, using care to guide the transfer case shift lever through the opening in the floor pan. Install the gasket and 6 retaining bolts 24–34 ft. lbs.

14. Connect the speedometer cable and driven gear. Connect the backup lamp switch.

15. Install the driveshaft to the transmission. Connect the rear driveshaft to the transfer case. Fill the transmission with the recommended transmission fluid to the proper level. Lower the vehicle.

16. Install the shift lever retaining bolt and tighten the retaining bolts. Slide the shifter boot into position on the shifter shaft and install the boot retaining screws.

17. Install the isolator pad assembly. Install the floor pan cover and floor mat. Install the shift ball on the transfer case shift lever.

18. Road test the vehicle for proper shift operation.

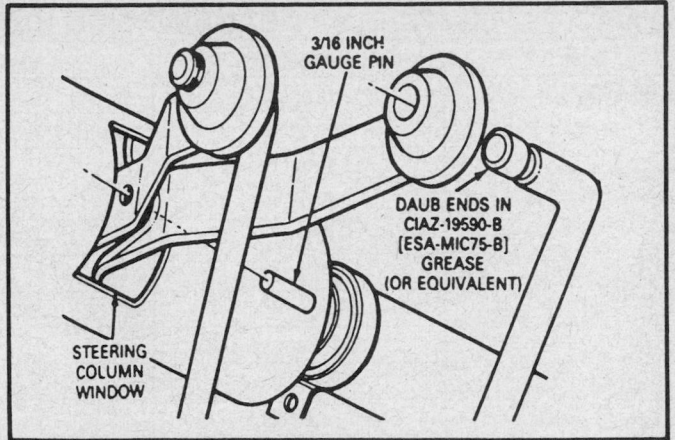

Linkage adjustment—Ford 3.03 transmission

Linkage Adjustment

FORD 3.03 THREE SPEED

NOTE: Always use new retaining rings and insulators when making linkage adjustments. The plastic grommets should be replaced when excessive wear or looseness is noted shift linkage.

1. Place the shifter in the **N** position and insert a gauge pin ($^3/_{16}$ in. diameter) through the locating hole in the steering column shift levers and the plastic spacer.

2. If the shift rods at the transmission are equipped with threaded sleeves, adjust the sleeves so that they enter the shift levers on the transmission easily with the shift levers in the **N** position. Now lengthen the rods 7 turns of the sleeves and insert them into the shift levers.

3. If the shift rods, are slotted, loosen the attaching nut, make sure that the transmission shift levers are in the **N** position, then retighten the attaching nuts.

4. Remove the gauge pin and check the operation of the shift linkage.

FOUR SPEED OVERDRIVE

1. Disconnect the 3 shift rods from the shifter assembly.

2. Insert a ¼ in. diameter pin through the alignment hole in the shifter assembly. Make sure the levers are in the **N** position.

3. Align the 3 transmission levers as follows: forward lever (3rd–4th lever) in the mid-position (neutral), rearward lever (1st–2nd lever) in the mid-position (neutral) and middle lever (reverse lever) rotate counterclockwise to the neutral position.

4. Rotate the output shaft to assure that the transmission is in neutral.

5. Shift the reverse lever (middle) clockwise to the reverse position. This causes the interlock system to align 1–2 and 3–4 rails in the neutral position.

6. Position the 1–2 and 3–4 shift rods to the correct transmission levers. Install and tighten the locknuts to 15–20 ft. lbs.

7. Rotate the reverse lever counterclockwise back to the neutral position. Install the reverse shift rod and tighten the locknut to 15–20 ft. lbs.

8. Remove the alignment pin. Check for proper operation.

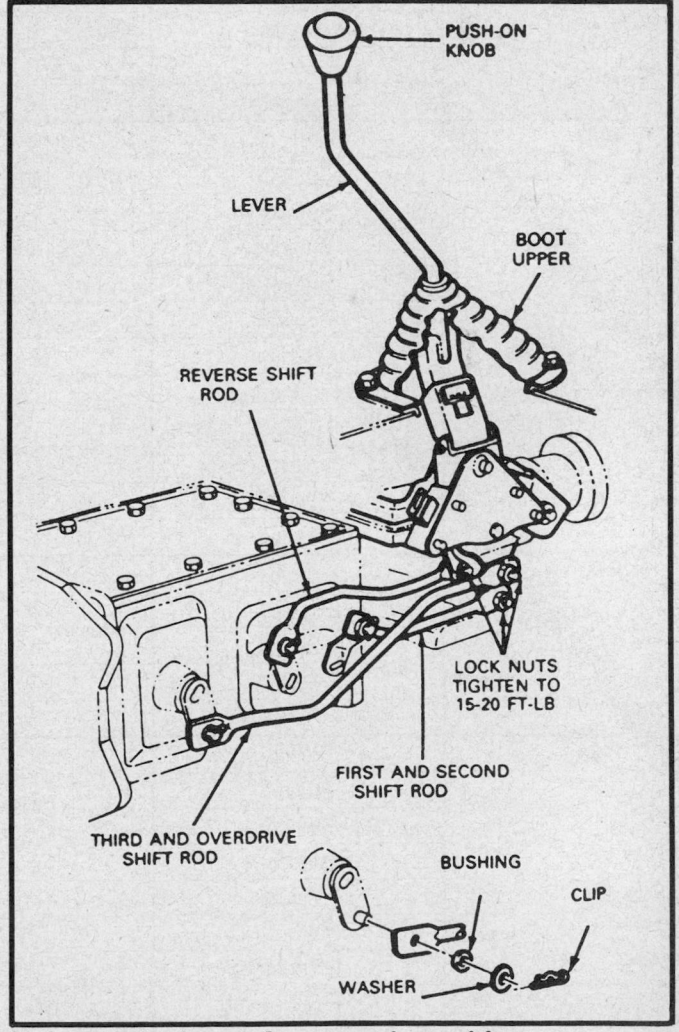

Linkage adjustment—four speed overdrive

TRANSMISSION IDENTIFICATION CODES

Year	Model	Code	Type
1986	Bronco	A	Manual—4-Speed New Process 435
	Bronco	B	Manual—4-Speed Overdrive
	Bronco	F	Manual—4-Speed Warner
	Bronco	K	Automatic—C6
	Bronco	T	Automatic—AOD
	F-Series	A	Manual—4-Speed New Process 435
	F-Series	B	Manual—4-Speed Overdrive
	F-Series	F	Manual—4-Speed Warner T-18
	F-Series	P	Manual—4-Speed Warner T-19
	F-Series	C	Manual—3-Speed Ford 3.03
	F-Series	K	Automatic—C6
	F-Series	T	Automatic—AOD
	F-Series	W	Automatic—C5
	E-Series	C	Manual—3-Speed 3.03
	E-Series	A	Manual—4-Speed New Process 435
	E-Series	F	Manual—4-Speed Warner
	E-Series	B	Manual—4-Speed Overdrive (SROD)
	E-Series	G	Automatic—C6
	E-Series	T	Automatic—4-Speed AOD
1987	Bronco	A	Manual—4-Speed New Process 435
	Bronco	B	Manual—4-Speed Overdrive
	Bronco	F	Manual—4-Speed Warner
	Bronco	K	Automatic—C6
	Bronco	T	Automatic—AOD
	F-Series	A	Manual—4-Speed New Process 435
	F-Series	B	Manual—4-Speed Overdrive
	F-Series	F	Manual—4-Speed Warner T-18
	F-Series	P	Manual—4-Speed Warner T-19
	F-Series	C	Manual—3-Speed Ford 3.03
	F-Series	K	Automatic—C6
	F-Series	T	Automatic—AOD
	F-Series	W	Automatic—C5
	E-Series	A	Manual—4-Speed New Process 435
	E-Series	B	Manual—4-Speed Overdrive (SROD)
	E-Series	G	Automatic—C6
	E-Series	T	Automatic 4-Speed AOD
1988	Bronco	K	Manual—5-Speed Overdrive (M50D)
	Bronco	T	Manual—5-Speed HD Overdrive (M50D-HD)
	Bronco	M	Automatic—C6
	Bronco	Z	Automatic—AOD
	F-Series	K	Manual—5-Speed Overdrive (M50D)
	F-Series	T	Manual—5-Speed HD Overdrive (M50D-HD)
	F-Series	M	Automatic—C6
	F-Series	Z	Automatic—AOD
	E-Series	K	Manual—5-Speed Overdrive (M50D)

TRANSMISSION IDENTIFICATION CODES

Year	Model	Code	Type
	E-Series	T	Manual—5-Speed HD Overdrive (M50D-HD)
	E-Series	M	Automatic—C6
	E-Series	Z	Automatic—AOD
1989-90	Bronco	K	Manual—5-Speed Overdrive (M50D)
	Bronco	T	Manual—5-Speed HD Overdrive (M50D-HD)
	Bronco	M	Manual—4-Speed
	Bronco	Z	Automatic—C6
	Bronco	F	Automatic—AOD
	F-Series	K	Manual—4-Speed
	F-Series	T	Manual—5-Speed Close Ratio
	F-Series	E	Manual—5-Speed Overdrive (M50D)
	F-Series	F	Manual—5-Speed HD Overdrive (M50D-HD)
	F-Series	C	Automatic—C6
	F-Series	M	Automatic—AOD
	F-Series	Z	Automatic—E40D
	E-Series	G	Manual—5-Speed Overdrive (M50D)
	E-Series	T	Manual—5-Speed HD Overdrive (M50D-HD)
	E-Series	E	Automatic—C6
	E-Series	M	Automatic 4-Speed AOD
	E-Series	Z	Automatic—E40D

CLUTCH

Clutch Assembly

Removal and Installation

1. Disconnect the negative battery cable. Raise and safely support the vehicle. Remove clutch slave cylinder or the hydraulic line as necessary.
2. Remove the dust cover and clutch release lever if so equipped.
3. Remove the transmission from the vehicle.
4. Mark the pressure plate and cover assembly and the flywheel, so that the parts can be reinstalled in the same position.
5. Loosen the pressure plate attaching bolts evenly and remove the clutch/preesure plate assembly. Do not remove the pilot bearing unless it is to be replaced.

To install:

6. Position the disc on the flywheel and install a pilot tool or spare transmission spline shaft.
7. Install the pressure plate assembly over the aligning tool and align the specifications. On a 10 in. clutch plate assembly tighten the retaining bolts to 15–20 ft. lbs. On a 11 inch clutch plate assembly tighten the retaining bolts to 20–29 ft. lbs.
8. Remove pilot tool and apply a light coat of lithium-base grease to the hub splines of the clutch disc.
9. Install the release lever onto the pivot stud if so equipped. Push inward to the lever snaps into position.

NOTE: Some vehicles use a concentric slave cylinder/ release bearing assembly. This assembly is installed on the transmission input shaft.

10. Reinstall the manual transmission. Install the clutch slave cylinder or the hydraulic line as necessary.
11. Connect negative battery cable and bleed the hydraulic system. Road test the vehicle for proper operation.

Pedal Height/Free Play Adjustment

The hydraulic clutch system provides automatic adjustment. No adjustment of clutch linkage or pedal position is required.

Clutch Master Cylinder

Removal and Installation

1. Disconnect the negative battery cable. Disconnect the master cylinder pushrod by prying the retainer bushing and the pushrod off the shaft. Disconnect any electrical connection.
2. Remove the line to the slave cylinder and plug the line to prevent entry of dirt.
3. Remove the master cylinder and reservoir from the engine compartment (rotate assembly as necessary).
4. Install in the reverse order of removal procedure. Bleed the hydraulic system.

Clutch Slave Cylinder

Removal and Installation

EXTERNAL TYPE

NOTE: For vehicles equipped with external slave cylinders, prior to any vehicle service that requires removal of the slave cylinder, the master cylinder pushrod must be disconnected from the clutch pedal. If not disconnected, permanent damage to the slave cylinder will occur if the clutch pedal is depressed while the slave cylinder is disconnected.

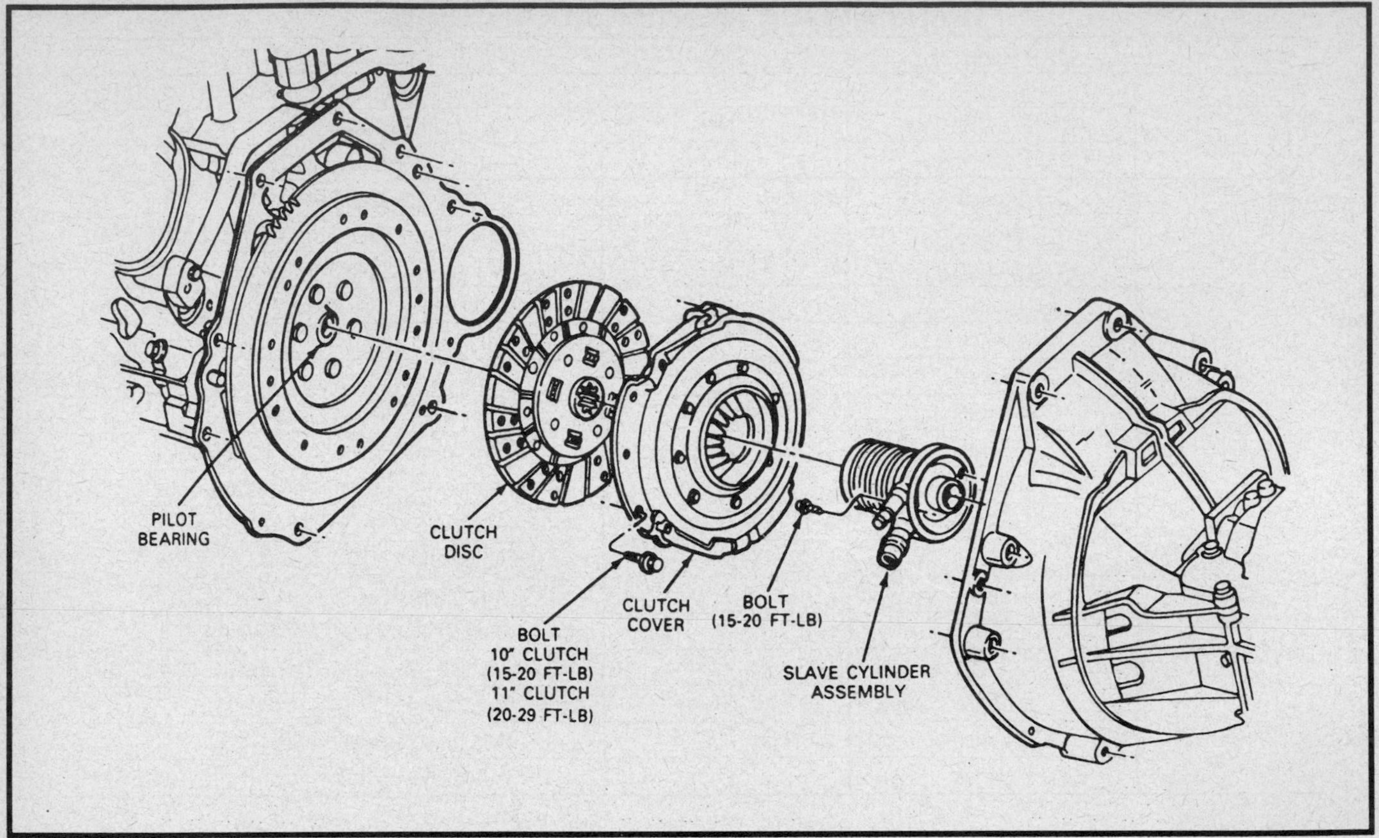

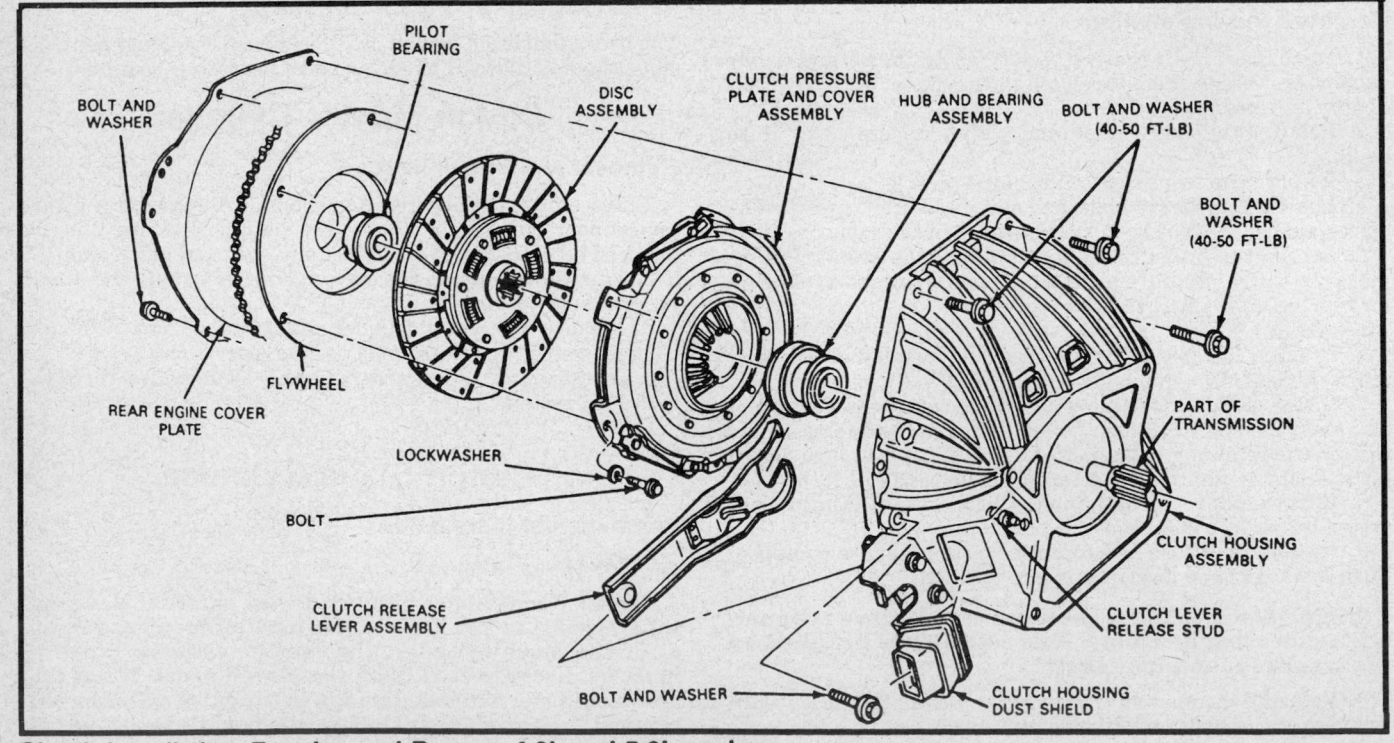

PILOT BEARING

CLUTCH DISC

CLUTCH COVER

BOLT
10" CLUTCH
(15-20 FT-LB)
11" CLUTCH
(20-29 FT-LB)

BOLT
(15-20 FT-LB)

SLAVE CYLINDER ASSEMBLY

Clutch installation with concentric slave cylinder—E series, F series and Bronco—4.9L, 5.0L and 5.8L engines

BOLT AND WASHER

PILOT BEARING

DISC ASSEMBLY

CLUTCH PRESSURE PLATE AND COVER ASSEMBLY

HUB AND BEARING ASSEMBLY

BOLT AND WASHER (40-50 FT-LB)

BOLT AND WASHER (40-50 FT-LB)

REAR ENGINE COVER PLATE

FLYWHEEL

LOCKWASHER

BOLT

CLUTCH RELEASE LEVER ASSEMBLY

BOLT AND WASHER

CLUTCH HOUSING DUST SHIELD

PART OF TRANSMISSION

CLUTCH HOUSING ASSEMBLY

CLUTCH LEVER RELEASE STUD

Clutch installation—F series and Bronco—4.9L and 5.0L engines

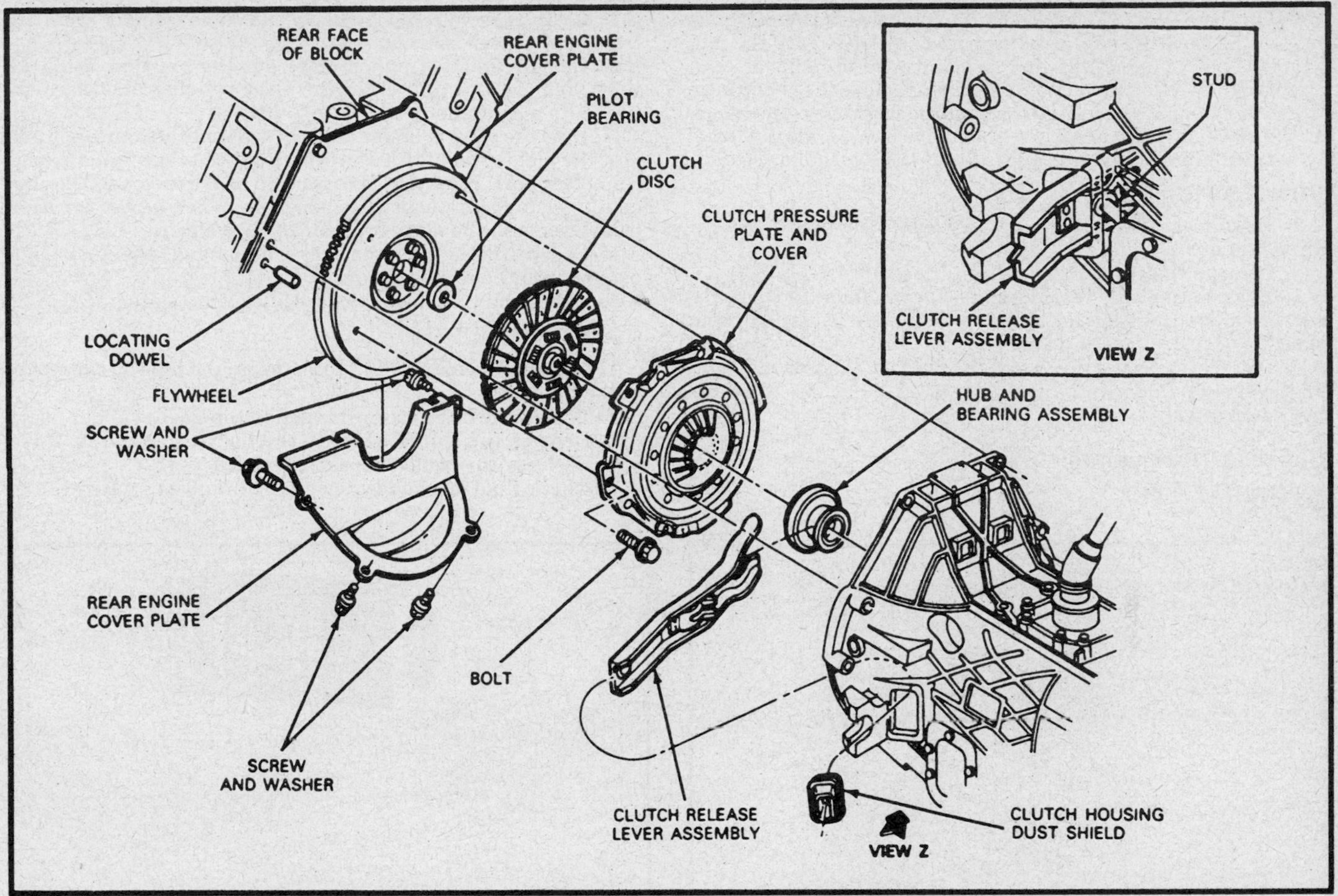

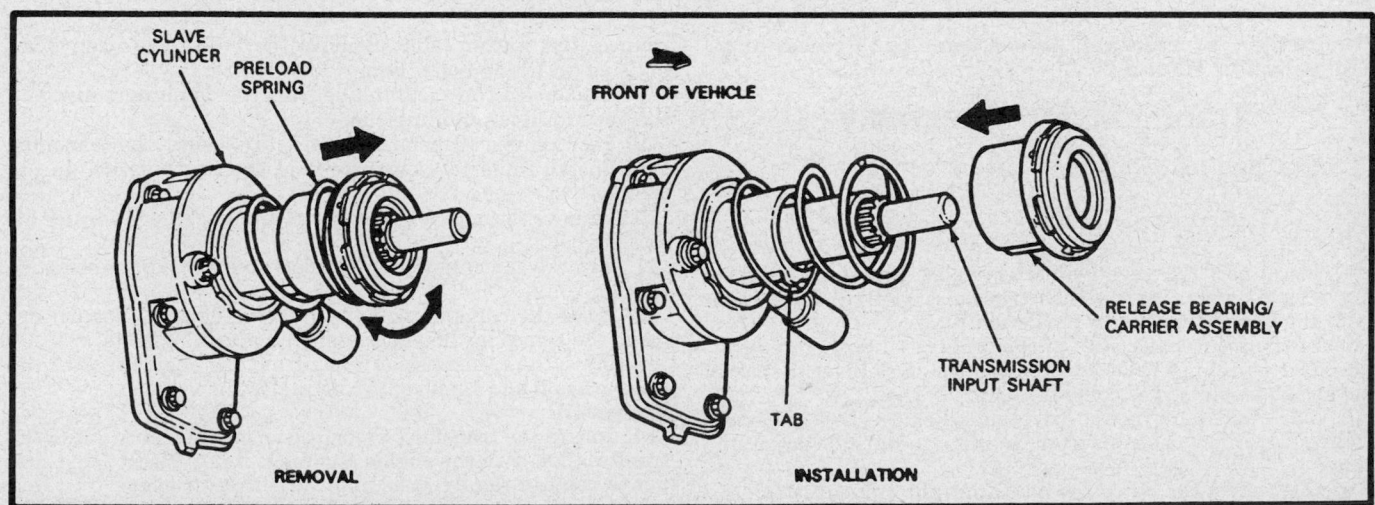

Clutch installation–F series–7.3L and 7.5L engines

Clutch release bearing removal–concentric slave cylinder

1. On the 6.9L, 7.3L and the 7.5L engines, lift the retaining tabs of the slave cylinder retaining bracket. Disengage the tabs from the bell housing lugs and slide outward to remove.

2. On the 4.9L, 5.0L and 5.8L engines remove the C-clip from the slave cylinder. Disengage the pushrod from the release lever as the slave cylinder is removed. Remove the slave cylinder.

3. Install in the reverse order. Bleed the hydraulic system.

CONCENTRIC TYPE

1. Disconnect the negative battery cable. Disconnect the hydraulic line.

2. Remove the transmission from the vehicle.

3. Remove the bolts retaining the slave cylinder to transmission. Remove the slave cylinder from the transmission input shaft.

4. Installation is the reverse of the removal procedure. Tighten the slave cylinder retaining bolts to 15–20 ft. lbs. Bleed the hydraulic system.

Bleeding The Hydraulic System
EXTERNAL TYPE

1. Clean reservoir cap. Remove the slave cylinder from the transmission bell housing.

2. Using a suitable punch drive out the pin that holds the tube. Remove the tube from the slave cylinder and place the tube into a container.

3. Hold the slave cylinder assembly so that the connector port is at the highest point. Fill the cylinder with brake fluid through connector port. It may be necessary to shake the cylinder while gently pushing on pushrod to expel air. When all the air is expelled reinstall the slave cylinder to the vehicle.

4. Gravity fill the clutch master cylinder and tube. Install end of tube into the slave cylinder body.

5. Check fluid level add the specified fluid as required.

CONCENTRIC TYPE

1. Clean reservoir cap. Fill reservoir to the top with approved brake fluid.

2. Loosen the bleed screw (located in the slave cylinder body).

3. Depress the clutch pedal to the floor and hold for 2 seconds. Release the pedal. Repeat 10 times.

4. Check fluid level add the specified fluid as required.

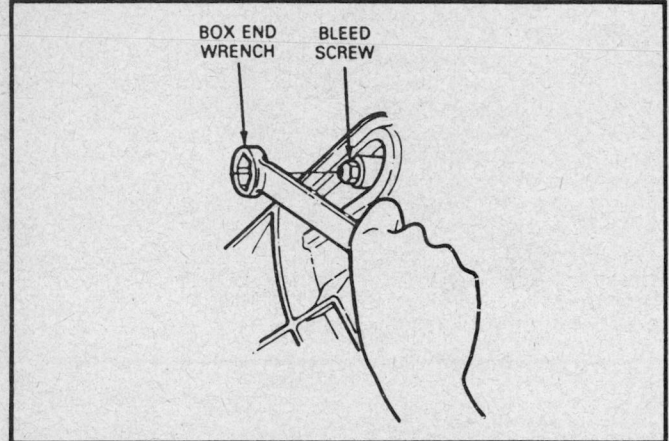

Bleeding the concentric slave cylinder

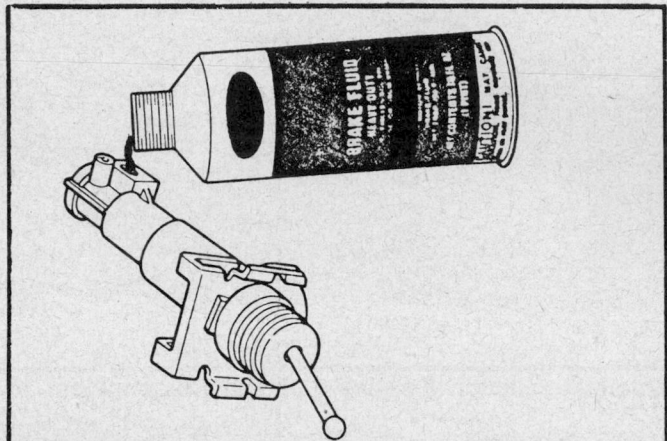

Bleeding external slave cylinder

AUTOMATIC TRANSMISSION

For further information, please refer to "Professional Transmission Manual".

Transmission Assembly

Removal and Installation
FORD C5
F Series

1. Disconnect the negative battery cable. Raise and support the vehicle safely. Remove the transmission fluid filler tube from the pan. Drain the transmission fluid.

2. At the front lower edge of the converter housing, remove the cover attaching bolts and remove the dust cover. Remove the splash shield at the control levers.

3. Mark and remove the driveshaft. Remove the converter drain plug. Allow the converter to drain and install the drain plug.

4. Disconnect the oil cooler lines from the transmission.

5. Disconnect the manual and downshift linkage rods from the transmission control levers.

6. Remove the speedometer gear from the extension housing.

7. Remove the 4 converter to flywheel attaching nuts. Dis-

connect the starter cable. Remove the 3 starter to converter housing attaching bolts. Remove the starter.

8. Disconnect the vacuum line from the diaphragm unit and the vacuum line retaining clip.

9. Position the transmission jack to support the transmission. Install the safety chain to hold the transmission on the jack.

10. Remove the engine rear support crossmember-to-frame attaching bolts.

11. Remove the engine rear support-to-extension housing attaching bolts.

12. Raise the transmission and remove the rear support. Remove the converter housing-to-engine attaching bolts.

13. Move the transmission away from the engine. Lower the transmission and remove it from under the vehicle.

To install:

14. Secure the transmission on a transmission jack. Align the transmission with the engine and move it into place, using care not to damage the flywheel and the converter pilot.

NOTE: The converter must rest squarely against the flywheel. This indicates that the converter pilot is not binding in the crankshaft.

15. Install the converter housing-to-engine attaching bolts and torque to 40–50 ft. lbs. Install the converter-to-flywheel attaching nuts torque to 20–34 ft. lbs.

16. Install the rear support. Install the rear support-to-extension housing attaching bolts.

17. Position the starter into the converter housing and install the attaching bolts. Install the starter cable.

18. Remove the transmission jack.

19. Connect the transmission filler tube to the transmission pan. Connect the oil coolers lines to the transmission.

20. Install the speedometer driven gear in the extension housing.

21. Connect the transmission linkage rods to the transmission control levers.

NOTE: When making transmission control attachments, new retaining rings and grommets should be used.

22. Install the driveshaft.

23. Install the vacuum line in the retaining clip. Connect the vacuum line to the diaphragm unit.

24. At the front lower area of the converter housing, install the lower cover and the control lever dust shield. Install the attaching bolts.

25. Secure the fluid filler tube to the pan.

26. Lower the vehicle and reconnect the negative battery cable.

27. Fill the transmission to the proper level.

28. Raise the vehicle and check for transmission fluid leakage. Lower the vehicle and adjust the throttle and manual linkage.

FORD C6

Bronco and F Series

1. Disconnect the negative battery cable. Raise and support the vehicle safely.

2. Remove the converter housing-to-engine bolts.

3. Remove the bolt securing the fluid filler tube to the engine cylinder head.

4. Drain the fluid from the transmission and converter.

5. Disconnect the coupling shaft (4WD applications) or driveshaft from the transmission companion flange and position it out of the way.

6. Disconnect the speedometer cable from the bearing retainer.

7. Disconnect the throttle and manual linkage rods from the levers at the transmission and all electrical connections if so equipped.

8. Disconnect the oil cooler lines from the transmission.

9. Remove the vacuum hose from the vacuum unit. Remove the vacuum line retaining clip.

10. Disconnect the cable from the terminal on the starter motor. Remove the attaching bolts and remove the starter motor.

11. Remove the 4 flywheel attaching nuts. Place a wrench on the crankshaft pulley attaching bolt to turn the converter to gain access to the nuts.

12. Drain and remove the transfer case, if equipped.

13. Remove the engine rear support crossmember-to-frame attaching bolts.

14. Remove the engine rear support-to-extension housing attaching bolts.

15. Remove the bolts securing the No. 2 crossmember to the frame side rails.

16. Raise the transmission with a transmission jack and remove both crossmembers.

17. Secure the transmission to the jack with the safety chain.

18. Remove the remaining converter housing-to-engine attaching bolts.

19. Move the transmission away from the engine. Lower the transmission and remove it from under the vehicle.

To install:

20. Tighten the converter drain plug. Position the converter on the transmission making sure the converter drive flats are fully engaged in the pump gear.

21. With the converter properly installed, place the transmission on the jack. Secure the unit to the jack with a chain.

22. Rotate the converter so that studs and drain plug are in alignment with those in the flywheel.

23. Move the transmission toward the cylinder block until they are in contact.

NOTE: The converter must rest squarely against the flywheel. This indicates that the converter pilot is not binding in the engine crankshaft.

24. Install the converter housing-to-engine bolts. On gasoline engines tighten the the retaining bolts to 40–50 ft. lbs. On diesel engines tighten the retaining bolts to 50–65 ft. lbs.

25. Remove the transmission jack safety chain from around the transmission.

26. Position the No. 2 crossmember to the frame side rails. Install the attaching bolts.

27. If equipped, install the transfer case.

28. Position the engine rear support crossmember to the frame side rails. Install the rear support to extension housing mounting bolts.

29. Lower the transmission and remove the jack.

30. Secure the engine rear support crossmember to the frame side rails with the attaching bolts.

31. Connect the vacuum line to the vacuum diaphragm making sure that the metal tube is secured in the retaining clip.

32. Connect the oil cooler lines to the transmission.

33. Connect the throttle and manual linkage rods to their respective levers on the transmission and all electrical connections.

34. Connect the speedometer cable to the bearing retainer.

35. Secure the starter motor in place with the attaching bolts. Connect the cable to the terminal on the starter.

36. Install a new O-ring on the lower end of the transmission filler tube and insert the tube in the case.

37. Secure the converter-to-flywheel attaching nuts. Use a wrench on the crankshaft pulley attaching nut to rotate the flywheel. Do not use a wrench on the converter attaching nuts to rotate it.

38. Install the converter housing dust shield and secure it with the attaching bolts.

39. Connect the coupling shaft (4WD applications) or driveshaft.

40. Adjust the shift linkage.

41. Install the transmission fluid filler tube to the cylinder head and secure with the attaching bolt. Lower the vehicle.

43. Fill the transmission and transfer case if so equipped to the correct level with the specified lubricant. Start the engine and shift the transmission through all ranges, then re-check the fluid level.

E Series

1. Disconnect the negative battery cable. Remove the engine (doghouse) cove from inside the vehicle.

2. Disconnect the neutral start wires at the plug connector.

3. If the vehicle is equipped with V8 engine, remove the flex hose from the air cleaner heat tube.

4. Remove the upper converter housing to engine attaching bolts. Remove the bolt securing the filler tube to the engine.

5. Raise the vehicle and support it safely.

6. Drain the transmission fluid pan loosening the bolts from the rear first and work toward the front of the pan.

7. Remove the converter cover from the flywheel housing.

8. Remove the coverter to flywheel attaching nuts. Use a wrench on the crankshaft pulley bolt to turn the converter to gain access to the nuts then turn the converter to gain access to

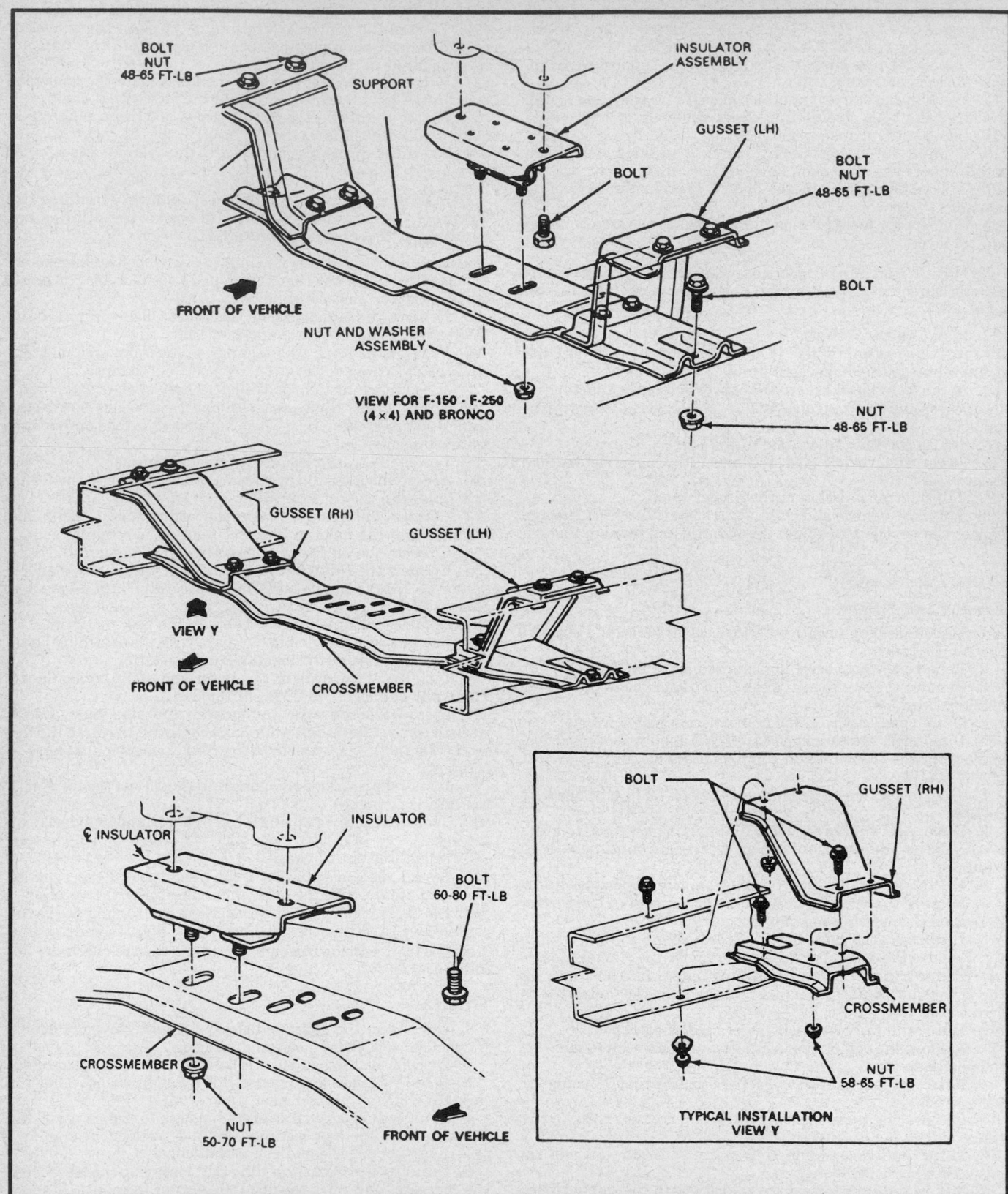

Typical crossmember installation

the drain plug and drain the converter.

9. Disconnect the driveshaft. Remove the fluid filler tube.

10. Disconnect the starter cable at the starter and remove the starter from the converter housing.

11. Disconnect the cooler lines from the transmission. Disconnect the vacuum line from the modulator.

12. Remove the speedometer driven gear from the extension housing.

13. Disconnect the manual and downshift linkage rods or cable from the control levers.

14. Support the engine. Position a jack under the transmission. Install the safety chain to hold the transmisson.

15. Remove the bolts and nuts securing the rear mount to the crossmember. Disconnect the crossmember from the side rails. Raise the transmission with the jack and remove the crossmember.

16. Remove the remaining converter housing to engine attaching bolts. Lower the jack and remove the converter and transmission assembly from under the vehicle.

17. Install in the reverse order of removal procedure. On gasoline engines tighten the the retaining bolts to 40–50 ft. lbs. On diesel engines tighten the retaining bolts to 50–65 ft. lbs.

18. Adjust shift linkage as required. Fill the transmission to the correct level with the specified lubricant. Start the engine and shift the transmission through all ranges, then re-check the fluid level.

FORD AOD

Bronco, F and E Series

1. Disconnect the negative battery cable. On E series remove the engine (doghouse) cover. Raise the vehicle and support it safely.

2. Place the drain pan under the transmission fluid pan. Starting at the rear of the pan and working toward the front, loosen the attaching bolts and allow the fluid to drain. Finally remove all of the pan attaching bolts except 2 at the front, to allow the fluid to further drain. With fluid drained, install 2 bolts on the rear side of the pan to temporarily hold it in place.

3. Remove the converter drain plug access cover from the lower end of the converter housing.

4. Remove the converter-to-flywheel attaching nuts. Place a wrench on the crankshaft pulley attaching bolt to turn the converter to gain access to the nuts.

5. Place a drain pan under the converter to catch the fluid. With the wrench on the crankshaft pulley attaching bolt, turn the converter to gain access to the converter drain plug and remove the plug. After the fluid has been drained, reinstall the plug.

6. Mark and disconnect (for proper installation) the driveshaft from the rear axle and slide shaft rearward from the transmission. Install a seal installation tool or equivalent in the extension housing to prevent fluid leakage.

7. Disconnect the cable from the terminal on the starter motor. Remove the attaching bolts and remove the starter motor. Disconnect the neutral start switch wires at the plug connector.

8. Remove the rear mount-to-crossmember attaching bolts and the crossmember-to-frame attaching bolts.

9. Remove the engine rear support-to-extension housing attaching bolts.

10. Disconnect the TV linkage rod from the transmission TV lever. Disconnect the manual rod from the transmission manual lever at the transmission.

11. Remove the bolts securing the bellcrank bracket to the converter housing.

12. On 4WD vehicles, drain and remove the transfer case from the vehicle.

13. Raise the transmission with a transmission jack to provide clearance to remove the crossmember. Remove the rear mount from the crossmember and remove the crossmember from the side supports.

14. Lower the transmission to gain access to the oil cooler lines.

15. Disconnect each oil line from the fittings on the transmission.

16. Disconnect the speedometer cable from the extension housing.

17. Remove the bolt that secures the transmission fluid filler tube to the cylinder block. Lift the filler tube and the dipstick from the transmission.

18. Secure the transmission to the jack with the chain.

19. Remove the converter housing-to-cylinder block attaching bolts.

20. Carefully move the transmission and converter assembly away from the engine and, at the same time, lower the jack to clear the underside of the vehicle.

21. Remove the converter and tighten the converter drain plug.

22. Position the converter on the transmission, making sure the converter drive flats are fully engaged in the pump gear by rotating the converter.

23. With the converter properly installed, place the transmission on the jack. Secure the transmission to the jack with a chain.

24. Rotate the converter until the studs and drain plug are in alignment with the holes in the flywheel.

25. Move the converter and transmission assembly forward into position, using care not to damage the flywheel and the converter pilot. The converter must rest squarely against the flywheel. This indicates that the converter pilot is not binding in the engine crankshaft.

26. Install and tighten the converter housing-to-engine attaching bolts to 40–50 ft. lbs. The remainder of the installation is the revese of the removal procedure.

27. Adjust the shift and throttle linkage as required. Fill the transmission to the correct level. Start the engine and shift the transmission through all ranges, then re-check the fluid level.

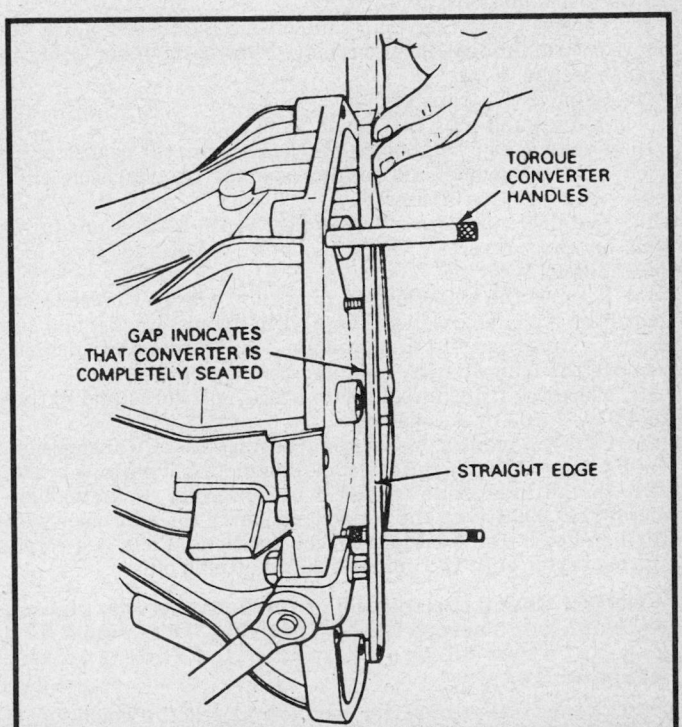

Installing converter–E4OD automatic transmission

FORD E4OD

Bronco, F and E Series

1. Disconnect negative battery cable at the battery. Remove the transmission dipstick. On E series remove the engine (doghouse) cover.
2. Place transmission selector in **N** position. Raise and safely support the vehicle.
3. On 4WD models, remove the front driveshaft. Remove the rear driveshaft. On F-Super Duty vehicles, remove the transmission mounted parking brake.
4. Disconnect the shift linkage. On 4WD model, remove the shift linkage from transfer case shift lever.
5. Remove the manual lever position sensor connector by squeezing connector tabs and pulling on connector.

NOTE: Do not attempt to pry tab with pry bar. Remove the heat shield from the transmission before attempting to remove the connector.

6. Remove the solenoid body connector heat shield.
7. Remove the solenoid body connector by pushing on the center tab and pulling on the wire harness.
8. On 4WD models, remove the 4WD drive switch connector from the transfer case. Use care not to overextend tabs.
9. Remove the wire harness locator from the extension housing wire bracket. On 4WD models, remove the wire harness locators from left hand side of the crossmember.
10. Remove the speedometer cable and the lower converter bolts.
11. Remove the rear engine cover plate bolts. Remove the starter.
12. Using a $^{15}/_{16}$ socket or equivalent, rotate the crankshaft bolt to gain access to converter nuts. Remove the 4 converter mounting nuts and discard the nuts.
13. Place a transmission stand fixture tool 014–00763 or equivalent on a universal transmission jack and position under the transmission. Use a safety strap to secure the transmission to the transmission stand fixture.
14. Loosen the 2 rear transmission mounting pad nuts. Remove the retaining bolts and remove the crossmember from the transmission.
15. Remove the transmission cooling lines from the case. Cap cooling lines and plug fittings at transmission.
16. Remove the 6 bell housing bolts. Back out the converter pilot from the flywheel and gently lower the transmission while observing for obstructions.
17. Install torque converter handles, T81P-8902-C or equivalent on the converter with handles in the 6 and 12 o'clock positions.
18. Remove the transmission filler tube. On 4WD models, remove the transfer case vent hose form detent bracket and the transfer case from the transmission. On F-Super Duty models, remove the transmission mounted parking brake.
19. Place the transmission onto a transmission stand fixture tool 014–4–763 or equivalent.
20. On 4WD models, install the transfer case to transmission. On F-Super Duty, install transmission mounted parking brake.
21. Install the torque converter using torque converter handles T81P–7902–C or the equivalent. Carry the converter with the handles in the 6 and 12 o'clock positions. Push and rotate the converter onto the pump until it bottoms out.

NOTE: Check the seating of the converter by placing a straightedge across the bell housing. There must be a gap between the converter pilot face and the straightedge.

22. Remove the converter handles. Check the condition of filler tube O-ring, if damaged or worn replace the O-ring. Install the filler tube.
23. Rotate the converter studs to align with flywheel mounting holes. Raise transmission into position while observing for any obstructions. Do not allow converter drive flats to disengage from pump gear. Use rubber converter drain plug cover or equivalent to aid in the alignment of the converter studs.

NOTE: Use care not to damage the flywheel and convert pilot. The converter must rest squarely against the flywheel. This indicates that the converter pilot is not binding in the engine crankshaft.

24. Alternately snug up the bell housing bolts and final torque to 40–50 ft. lbs.
25. Install the rubber converter drain plug cover and transmission cooling lines.
26. Install the crossmember and the transmission retaining bolts. Remove the safety strap and the universal high lift transmission jack.
27. Rotate the crankshaft to gain access to converter studs. Install new stud nuts and torque to 20–30 ft. lbs.
28. Install the starter motor, rear engine plate cover and lower dust cover.
29. Install the speedometer cable.
30. Completely seat the solenoid body connector into solenoid valve body recepticle. An audible click sound indicates proper installation.
31. Install the solenoid body connector heat shield with offset bending inward.
32. On 4WD models, install wire harness locators into crossmember.
33. Install the wire harness locator into extension housing wire bracket.
34. On 4WD models, install the 4WD drive switch connector and connect the transfer case shift linkage.
35. Install the manual lever position sensor connector. An audible click sound indicates proper installation.
36. Install the shift linkage. On 4WD models, install the shift rod to transfer case shift lever.
37. Install the rear driveshaft and install the front driveshaft on 4WD models.
38. Lower the vehicle, connect the negative battery cable and refill the transmission. Start the engine and check the fluid level.
39. Road test vehicle for proper operation and correct shift patterns.

Shift Linkage Adjustment
BRONCO, E AND F SERIES

1. Position the selector lever in the Drive (D) position for C5 and C6 transmissions and in the Overdrive (OD) position for AOD and E40D transmissions. Hold it against the stop by applying an 8 pound weight to the selector lever knob.
2. Loosen the shift rod adjusting nut.
3. Shift the manual lever at the transmission into the Drive (D) or Overdrive (OD) position, by moving the lever all the way rearward, then forward 2 detents.
4. With the selector lever and the manual lever in position, tighten the nut at the bell housing to 12–18 ft. lbs.
5. Remove the 8 pound wieght from the steering column selector lever knob.
6. Check the selector lever in all detent positions with engine running to ensure correct adjustment.

Throttle Valve Control Cable Adjustment
AUTOMATIC OVERDRIVE TRANSMISSION
4.9L and 5.0L Engines

1. Set the parking brake and put selector in the **N** range. Remove the protective cover over the the cable linkage if so equipped. (Do not put selector in **P**).
2. Verify that the throttle lever is at the idle stop. Do not at-

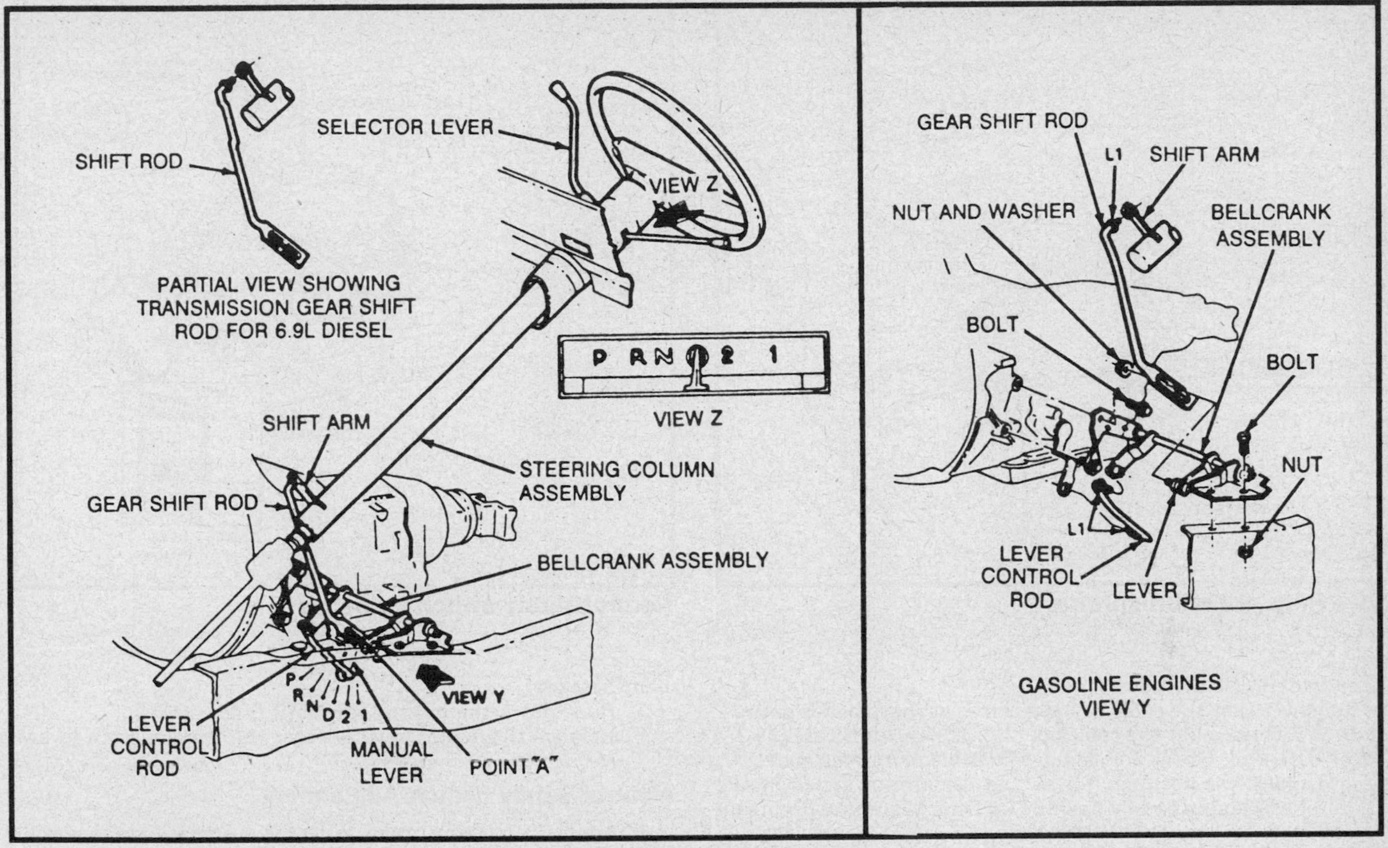

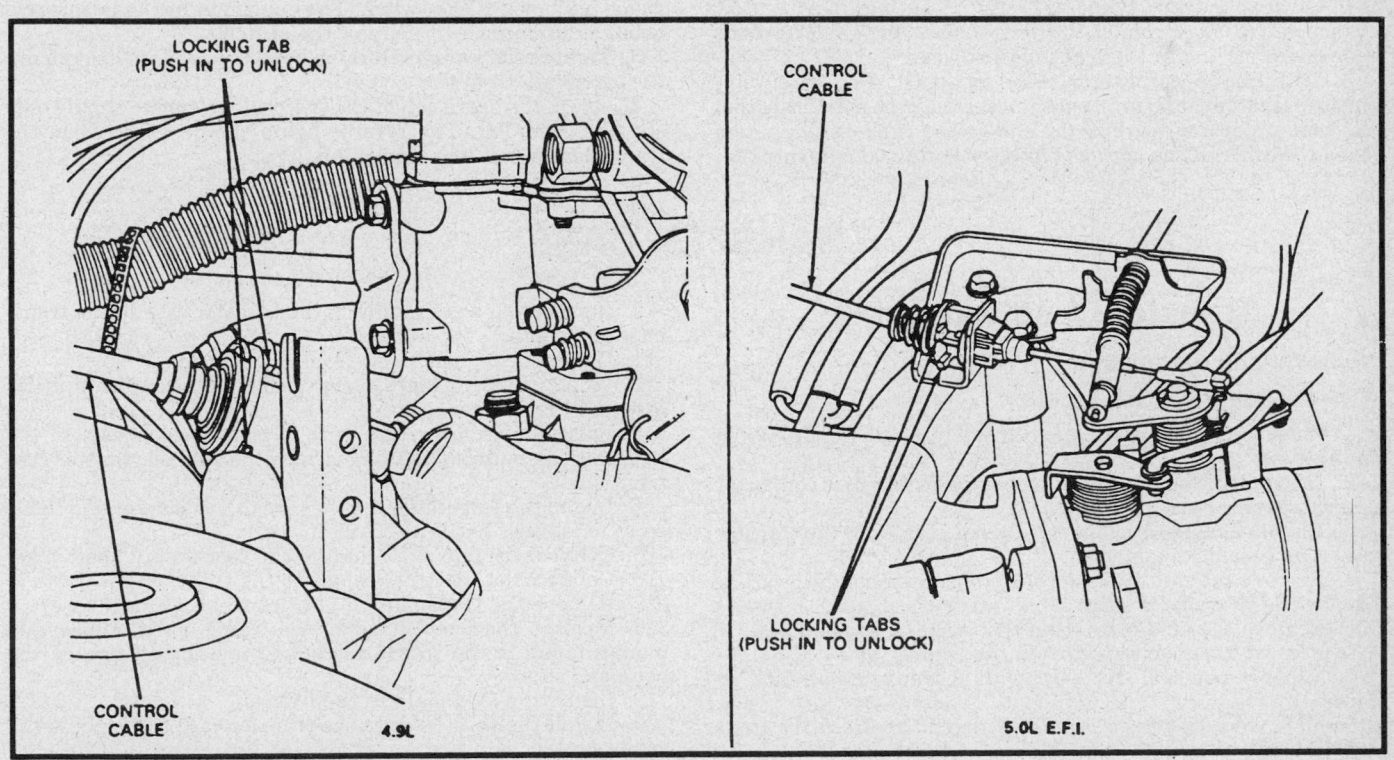

SHIFT ROD

SELECTOR LEVER

VIEW Z

PARTIAL VIEW SHOWING
TRANSMISSION GEAR SHIFT
ROD FOR 6.9L DIESEL

P R N D 2 1

VIEW Z

SHIFT ARM

GEAR SHIFT ROD

STEERING COLUMN
ASSEMBLY

BELLCRANK ASSEMBLY

P R N D 2 1

VIEW Y

LEVER CONTROL ROD

MANUAL LEVER

POINT "A"

GEAR SHIFT ROD

L1   SHIFT ARM

NUT AND WASHER

BELLCRANK ASSEMBLY

BOLT

BOLT

NUT

L1

LEVER CONTROL ROD

LEVER

GASOLINE ENGINES
VIEW Y

Shift linkage adjustment-C5 and C6 transmission F series and Bronco

LOCKING TAB
(PUSH IN TO UNLOCK)

CONTROL CABLE

CONTROL CABLE

4.9L

LOCKING TABS
(PUSH IN TO UNLOCK)

5.0L E.F.I.

TV control cable locking tabs

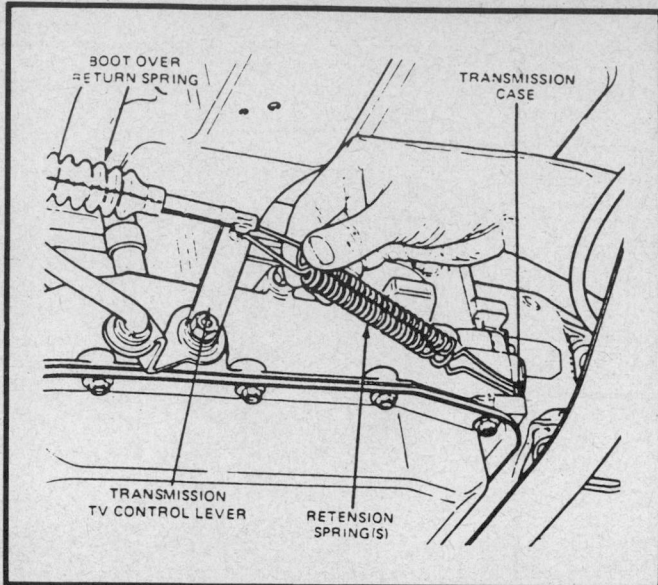

Installing retention springs

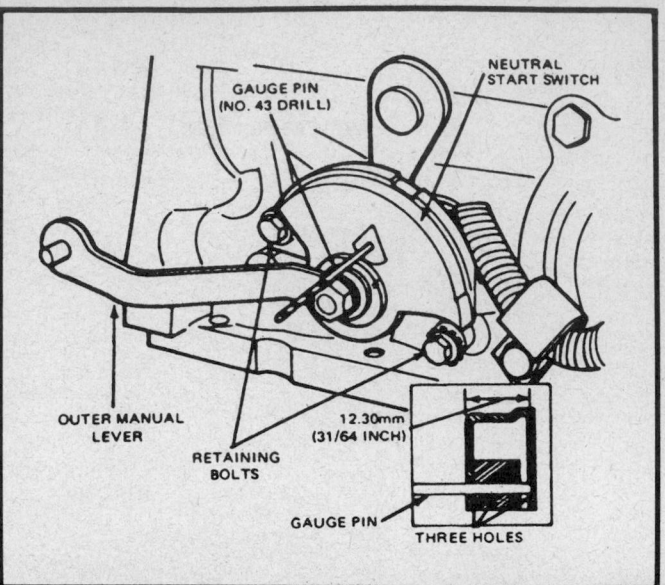

Neutral safety switch adjustment

tempt to adjust the idle stop.

3. Verify that the cable routing is free of sharp bends or pressure points and that the cable operates freely. Lubricate the TV lever ball stud. Check for damage to cable or rubber boot.

4. Unlock the locking tab at the carburetor/upper intake manifold assembly end by pushing up from below and prying up the rest of the way to free the cable.

5. A retention spring must be installed on the TV control lever, to hold it in the idle position (as far to rear as the lever will travel) with about 10 pounds of force. If a suitable single spring is not available, two 8 cylinder TV return springs may be used. Attach retention spring(s) to the transmission TV lever hook rear end of spring to the transmission case.

6. **De-cam the carburetor if so equipped.** The carburetor throttle lever must be in the anti-diesel idle position. Verify that the take-up spring (carburetor end of the cable properly tensions the cable. If the spring is loose or bottomed out, check for

bent brackets.

7. Push down the locking tab until flush.

8. Remove the detent springs from the transmission lever.

Neutral Safety Switch Adjustment

1. Apply the parking brake. With the automatic transmission linkage properly adjusted, loosen the 2 switch retaining bolts.

2. Place the transmission lever in **N** position. Rotate the switch and insert the gauge pin (drill No.43 shank end) into the gauge pin holes of the switch. The gauge pin has to be inserted about ½ in. into the 3 holes of the switch.

3. Tighten the switch retaining bolts to 55–75 in. lbs. remove the gauge pin from the switch.

4. Check the operation of the switch. The engine should only start in **N** and **P**. The reverse lights should work when the transmission is in the **R** position.

TRANSFER CASE

Transfer Case Assembly

Removal and Installation

NEW PROCESS MODEL 208

1. Raise the vehicle and support it safely. Drain the fluid from the transfer case.

2. Disconnect the 4WD drive indicator switch wire connector at the transfer case.

3. Disconnect the speedometer driven gear from the transfer case rear bearing retainer.

4. Remove the nut retaining the transmission shift lever assembly to the transfer case.

5. Remove the skid plate from the frame, if so equipped.

6. Remove the heat shield from the frame.

7. Support the transfer case with a transmission jack or equivalent.

8. Mark and disconnect the front driveshaft from the front output shaft yoke.

9. Mark and disconnect the rear driveshaft from the rear output shaft yoke.

10. Remove the bolts retaining the transfer case to the transmission adapter.

11. Lower the transfer case from the vehicle.

12. When installing place a new gasket between the transfer case and the adapter.

13. Raise the transfer case with a transmission jack so the transmission output shaft aligns with the splined transfer case input shaft.

14. Install the bolts retaining the case to the adapter and tighten to (crisscross pattern) 20–25 ft. lbs.

15. Connect the rear driveshaft to the rear output shaft yoke.

16. Connect the front driveshaft to the front output yoke.

17. Remove the transmission jack from the transfer case.

18. Position the heat shield to the frame crossmember and mounting lug to the transfer case and install and tighten the bolts and screw.

19. Install the skid plate to the frame.

20. Install the shift lever to the transfer case and tighten the retaining nut.

21. Install the speedometer driven gear to the transfer case.

22. Connect the 4WD indicator switch wire to the transfer

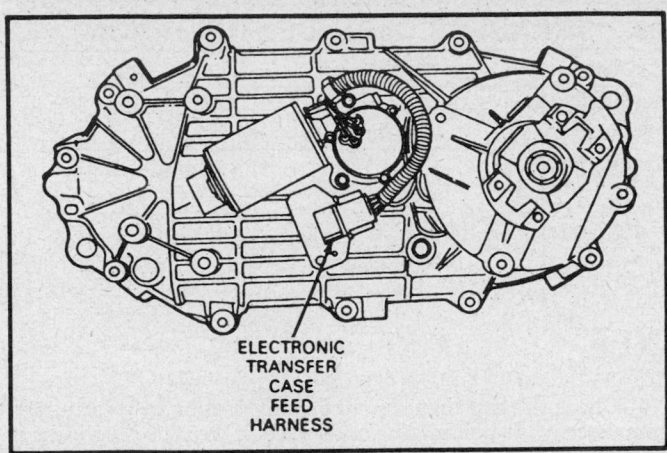

Borg Warner model 1356 electronic shift

case.

23. Install the drain plug. Remove the filler plug and install 9 pints of Dexron®II or equivalent type transmission fluid.

24. Lower the vehicle.

BORG WARNER MODEL 1345

1. Raise the vehicle and support it safely.
2. Drain the fluid from the transfer case.
3. Disconnect the 4WD indicator switch wire connector at the transfer case.
4. Remove the skid plate from the frame, if so equipped.
5. Mark and disconnect the front driveshaft from the front output yoke.
6. Mark and disconnect the rear driveshaft from the rear output shaft yoke.
7. Disconnect the speedometer driven gear from the transfer case rear bearing retainer.
8. Remove the retaining rings and shift rod from the transfer case shift lever.
9. Disconnect the vent hose from the transfer case.
10. Remove the heat shield from the frame.
11. Support the transfer case with a transmission jack.
12. Remove the bolts retaining the transfer case to the transmission adapter.

13. Lower the transfer case from the vehicle.
14. When installing place a new gasket between the transfer case and the adapter.
15. Raise the transfer case with the transmission jack so that the transmission output shaft aligns with the splined transfer case input shaft. Install the bolts retaining the transfer case to the adapter and tighten the bolts (crisscross pattern) to 25–43 lbs.
16. Remove the transmission jack from the transfer case.
17. Connect the rear driveshaft to the rear output shaft yoke.
18. Install the shift lever to the transfer case and install the retaining nut.
19. Connect the speedometer driven gear to the transfer case.
20. Connect the 4WD indicator switch wire connector at the transfer case.
21. Connect the front driveshaft to the front output yoke.
22. Position the heat shield to the frame crossmember and the mounting lug on the transfer case. Install and tighten the retaining bolts.
23. Install the skid plate to the frame.
24. Install the drain plug. Remove the filler plug and install 6.5 pints of Dexron®II type transmission fluid or equivalent.
25. Lower the vehicle.

BORG WARNER MODEL 1356 ELECTRONIC AND MANUAL SHIFT

1. Raise the vehicle and support it safely.
2. Remove the nuts, bolts and skid plate from the frame, if so equipped.
3. Remove the plug and drain the fluid from the transfer case.
4. Remove the wire connector from the feed wire harness at the rear of the transfer case on electronic shift type. On manual shift type remove the 4WD indicator light.
5. Mark and disconnect the front driveshaft from the front output shaft yoke.
6. Mark and disconnect the rear driveshaft from the transfer case rear output shaft yoke.
7. Disconnect the speedometer driven gear from the transfer case rear cover.
8. Disconnect the vent hose from the mounting bracket. On manual shift type remove the shift rod assembly.
9. Support the transfer case with a jack. Remove the bolts retaining the transfer case to the transmission and the extension

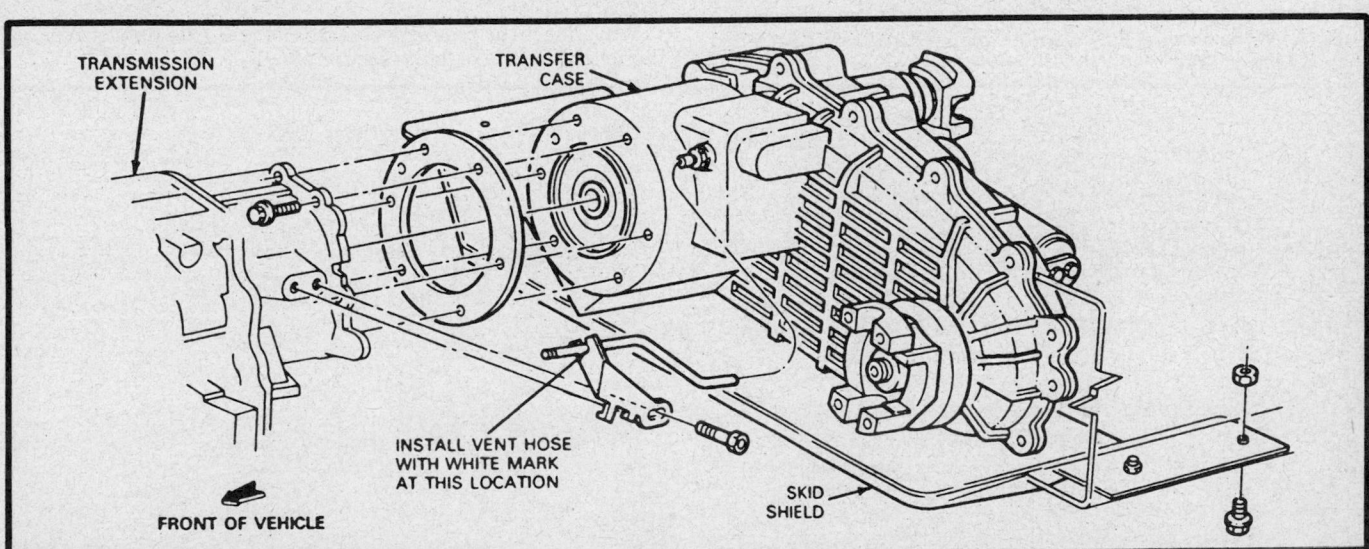

Typical transfer case installation

housing.

10. Slide the transfer case rearward off the transmission output shaft and lower the transfer case from the vehicle.

11. Install in the reverse order of removal. Tighten the transfer case retaining bolts (crisscross pattern) to 25–43 ft. lbs. Remove the filler plug and install 4.0 pints of Mercon® type transmission fluid or equivalent.

Linkage Adjustment

No adjustment is possible or necessary on these transfer case units.

TRANSFER CASE IDENTIFICATION

Year	Vehicle	Type
1986-87	F-150, F-250 and Bronco	New Process 208
1986-90	F-150, F-250 and F-350	Borg Warner 1345
1987-90	F-150, F, 250, F-350 and Bronco	Borg Warner 1356

DRIVE AXLE

Driveshaft and U-Joints

Removal and Installation

DRIVESHAFT

1. Raise and safely support the vehicle. If the alignment marks are not visible, mark the relationship of the rear driveshaft yoke and the drive pinion flange of the axle in line with the driveshaft so that they may be re-installed in the same position.

2. Disconnect the rear U-joint from the companion flange. Wrap tape or equivalent around the loose bearing caps to prevent them from falling off the spider. Pull the driveshaft toward the rear of the vehicle until the slip yoke clears the transmission extension housing and the seal. Install the appropriate tool in the housing to prevent the lubricant or fluid from leaking.

3. To install, reverse the removal procedure, taking note that if either the rubber seal on the output shaft or the seal in the end of the transmission extension housing is damaged it must be replaced. Also if the lugs on the axle pinion flange are shaved or distorted so that the bearings slide, replace the flange.

4. Install the U-bolts and torque the nuts to 8–15 ft. lbs. Mark the relationship of the rear driveshaft yoke and axle pinion flange before disassembly, to maintain driveline balance. If a vibration should exist, the driveshaft should be disconnected from the axle, rotated 180 degrees and re-installed.

CENTER BEARING

1. Remove the driveshafts.

2. Remove the center support bearing attaching bolts and remove the assembly from the vehicle.

3. Do not immerse the sealed bearing in any type of cleaning fluid. Wipe the bearing and cushion clean with a cloth dampened with cleaning fluid.

4. Check the bearing for wear or rough action by rotating the inner race while holding the outer race. If wear or roughness is evident, replace the bearing. Examine the rubber cushion for evidence of hardening, cracking, or deterioration. Replace it if it is damaged in any way.

5. Place the bearing in the rubber support and the rubber support in the U-shaped support and install the bearing in the reverse order of removal.

SINGLE TYPE U-JOINT

1. Disconnect the driveshaft from the rear axle flange.

2. If vehicle has a coupling shaft, slide the driveshaft off the coupling splines.

3. Working from the center support nearest to the rear of the vehicle, remove the attaching bolts and support the bearing.

4. On a vehicle with more than one coupling shaft, disconnect the rear shaft from the front one.

5. Remove the remaining center support attaching bolts and support the bearing.

6. Remove the transmission coupling shaft flange attaching nuts and remove the shaft and center bearing(s) as an assembly.

7. Thoroughly clean all driveshaft components before installing.

To install:

8. Connect the front flange or joint to the transmission flange.

9. Secure the center bearing to the frame bracket, tightening the bracket attaching bolts securely.

10. If vehicle has more than one coupling shaft, connect the rear shaft to the forward one, then install the remaining center support.

11. Connect the rear universal to the rear axle flange, tightening (evenly) nuts or bolts securely.

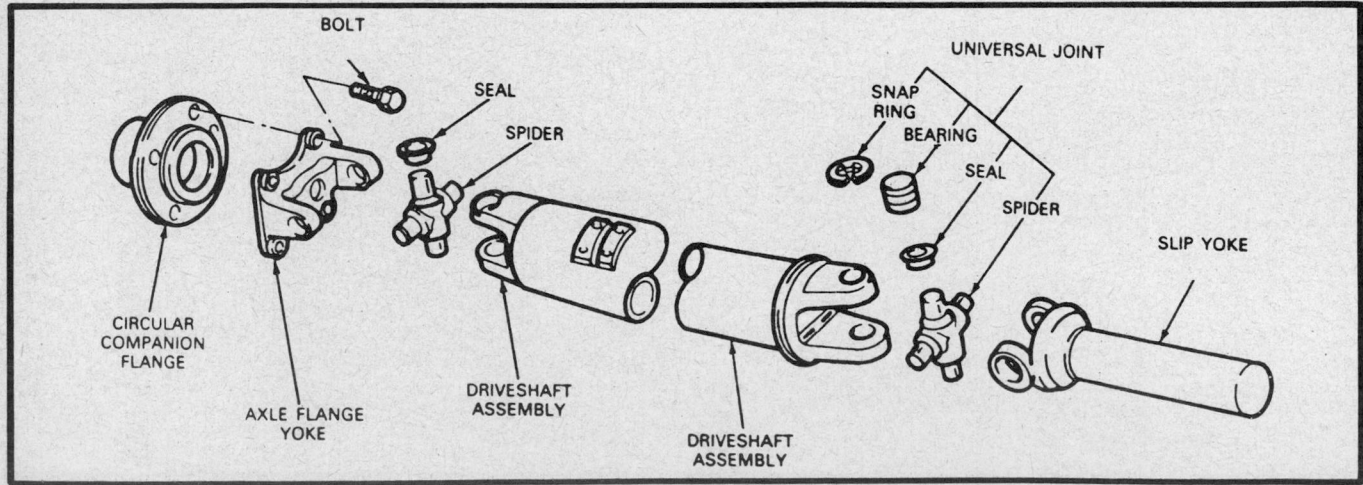

Single type U-joint assembly

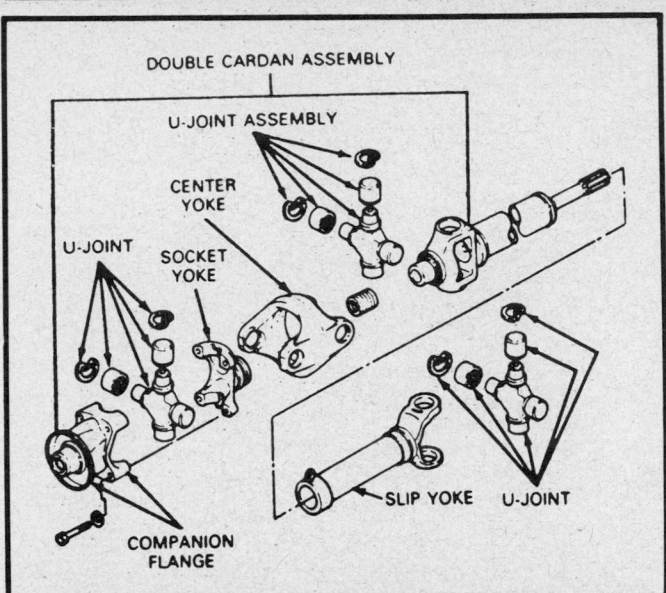

Double Cardan type U-joint assembly

DOUBLE CARDAN TYPE U-JOINT

1. To remove the front or rear driveshaft, disconnect the double cardan joint from the flange at the transfer case.
2. Disconnect the single U-joint from the flange at the axle. Remove the driveshaft.
3. To install, position the single U-joint end of the driveshaft to the axle, before the cardan end. Install and tighten (evenly) all U-bolts, nuts, bolts and lockwashers.

Front Axle Shaft, Bearing and Seal

Removal and Installation
DANA MODEL 60 MONOBEAM

1. Raise the vehicle and support it safely. Remove the front wheel.
2. Remove the disc brake caliper and wire it to the frame.
3. Remove the cap (Allen head screws) from the hub body. Remove the snapring that retains the axle shaft in the hub body.
4. Remove the lock ring seated in the groove of the hub body.

Remove the body from the hub.
5. Remove the outer locknut, lockwasher and the inner locknut from the spindle. Remove the hub and rotor.
6. Remove the nuts retaining the spindle to the knuckle. Remove the splash shield and the caliper support from the knuckle.
7. Pull the axle shaft out of the steering knuckle. If required remove the caged needle bearing from the spindle and remove the seal.
8. Install in the reverse order of removal. Pack the wheel bearing with suitable grease. Also pack the thrust face of the seal in the spindle bore and the V-seal on the axle shaft with grease.

DANA MODELS 44 AND 50

1. Raise the vehicle and support it safely. Remove the front wheel.
2. Remove the disc brake caliper and wire it to the frame.
3. Remove the hub locks, wheel bearings and locknuts.
4. Remove the rotor and the outer wheel bearing.
5. Remove the grease seal and the inner wheel bearing from the rotor. Remove the inner and the outer races from the rotor.
6. Remove the spindle from the steering knuckle. Remove the splash shield.
7. On the right side of the vehicle, remove the shaft and joint by pulling the assembly out of the carrier. On the right side of the carrier, remove the clamp from the shaft and joint.
8. Slide the rubber boot onto the stub shaft and pull the shaft and joint from the splines of the stub shaft.
9. If required remove the needle bearing from the spindle and remove the seal from the shaft.
10. Install in the reverse order of removal. Pack the bearing with (wheel bearing) multi-purpose grease. Also pack the thrust face of the seal in the spindle bore and the V-seal on the axle shaft with grease.

Rear Axle Shaft, Bearing and Seal

Removal and Installation
REMOVABLE CARRIER

1. Raise and support the vehicle and remove the wheel/tire assembly from the brake drum.
2. Remove the nuts which secure the brake drum to the axle flange, then remove the drum from the flange.
3. Working through the hole provided in each axle shaft flange, remove the nuts which secure the wheel bearing retainer plate.
4. Using an axle puller, pull the axle shaft assembly out of the axle housing.

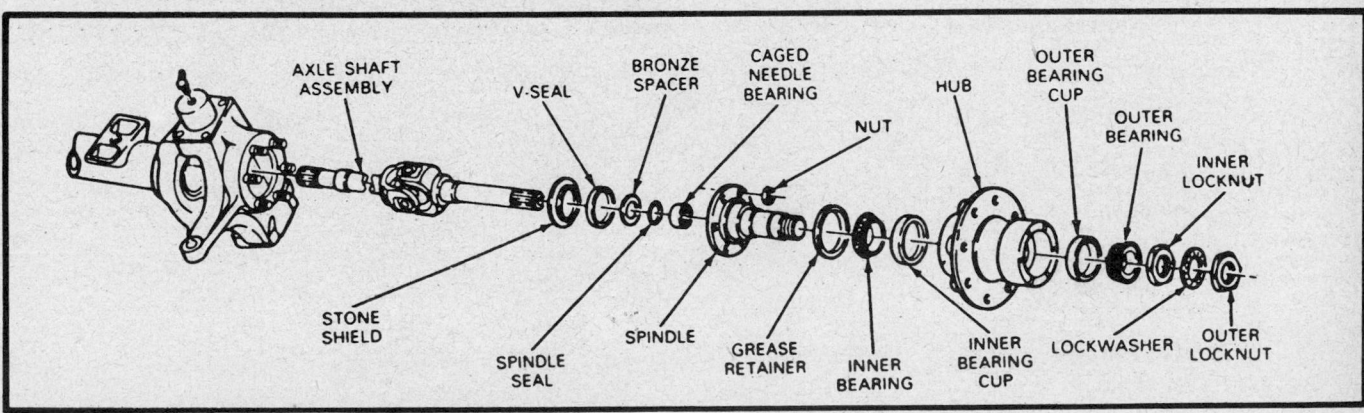

Dana model 60 Monobeam front drive axle assembly

SHAFT (RH)

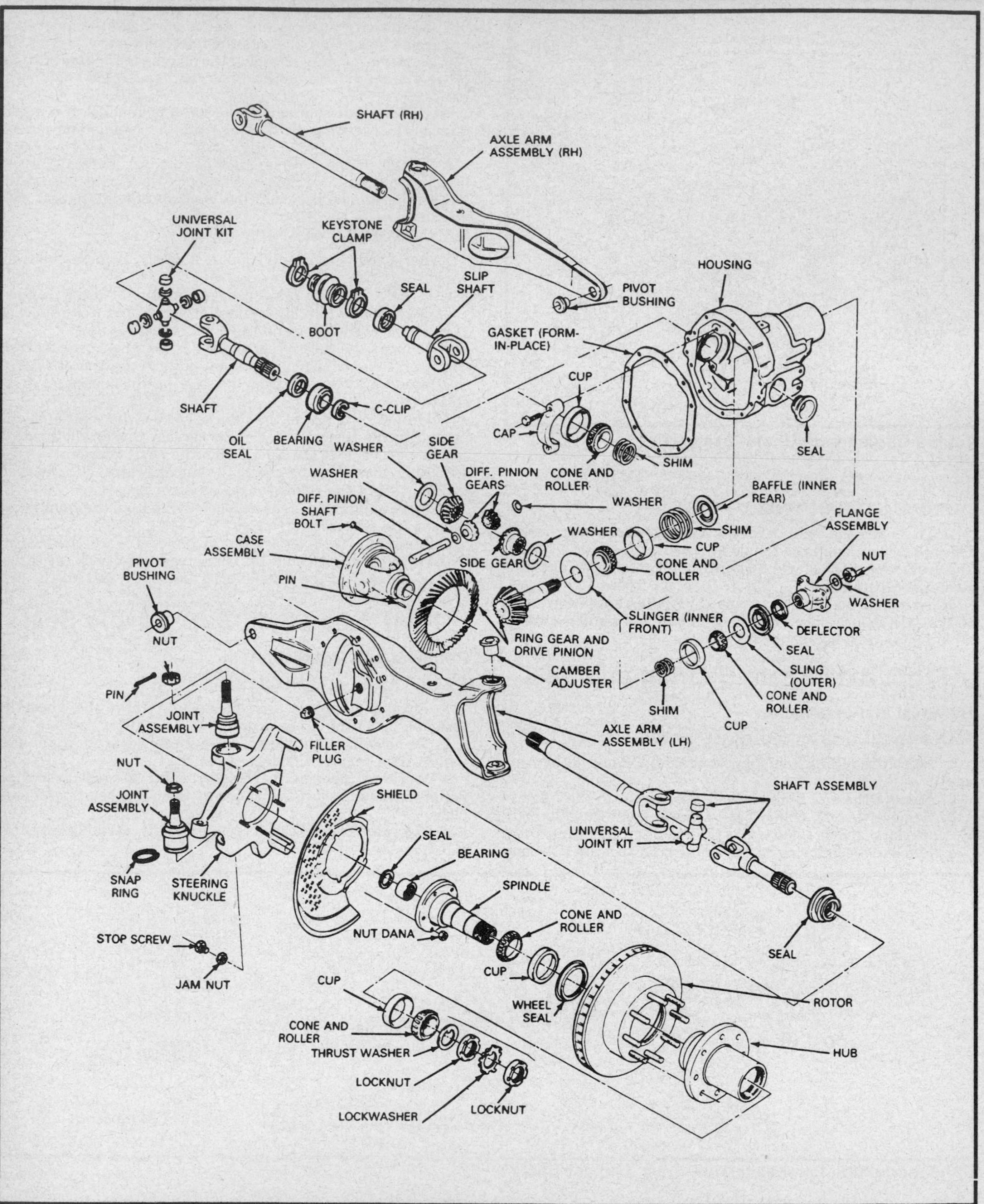

AXLE ARM ASSEMBLY (RH)

UNIVERSAL JOINT KIT

KEYSTONE CLAMP

SEAL

SLIP SHAFT

BOOT

PIVOT BUSHING

HOUSING

SHAFT

OIL SEAL

BEARING

WASHER

C-CLIP

SIDE GEAR

GASKET (FORM-IN-PLACE)

CUP

CAP

SHIM

SEAL

WASHER

WASHER

DIFF. PINION GEARS

CONE AND ROLLER

WASHER

BAFFLE (INNER REAR)

DIFF. PINION SHAFT BOLT

CASE ASSEMBLY

WASHER

SHIM

CUP

FLANGE ASSEMBLY

NUT

PIVOT BUSHING

PIN

SIDE GEAR

CONE AND ROLLER

WASHER

NUT

RING GEAR AND DRIVE PINION

SLINGER (INNER FRONT)

DEFLECTOR

PIN

CAMBER ADJUSTER

SEAL

JOINT ASSEMBLY

FILLER PLUG

SHIM

SLING (OUTER) CONE AND ROLLER

NUT

CUP

JOINT ASSEMBLY

AXLE ARM ASSEMBLY (LH)

SHAFT ASSEMBLY

SNAP RING

STEERING KNUCKLE

SHIELD

SEAL

BEARING

SPINDLE

UNIVERSAL JOINT KIT

STOP SCREW

NUT DANA

CONE AND ROLLER

SEAL

JAM NUT

CUP

CUP

WHEEL SEAL

ROTOR

CONE AND ROLLER

THRUST WASHER

HUB

LOCKNUT

LOCKNUT

LOCKWASHER

Exploded view Dana model 50–front drive axle assembly

NOTE: The brake backing plate must not be dislodged. Install a nut to hold the plate in place after the axle shaft is removed.

5. If the axle has ball bearings: Loosen the bearing retainer ring by nicking it in several places with a cold chisel, then slide it off the axle shaft. On vehicles equipped with a thick retaining ring, drill a ¼–½ inch hole part way through the ring, then break it with a cold chisel. A hydraulic press is needed to press the bearing off and to press the new one on. Press the new bearing and the new retainer ring on separately. Use a slide hammer to pull the old seal out of the axle housing. Carefully drive the new seal evenly into the axle housing, preferably with a seal driver tool.

6. If the axle has tapered roller bearings, use a slide hammer to remove the bearing cup from the axle housing. Drill a ¼–½ inch hole part way through the bearing retainer ring, then break it with a cold chisel. A hydraulic press is needed to press the bearing off and remove the seal. Press on the new seal and bearing, then the new retainer ring. Do not press the bearing and ring on together. Put the cup on the bearing, not in the housing and lubricate the outer diameter of the cup and seal.

7. With ball bearings: Place a new gasket between the housing flange and backing plate. Carefully slide the axle shaft into place. Turn the shaft to start the splines into the side gear and push it in.

8. With tapered roller bearing: Move the seal out toward the axle shaft flange so there is at least ³⁄₃₂ in. between the edge of the outer seal and the bearing cup, to prevent snagging on installation. Carefully slide the axle shaft into place. Turn the shaft to start the splines into the side gear and push it in.

9. Install the bearing retainer plate.

10. Install the brake drum and the wheel/tire assembly.

INTEGRAL CARRIER TYPE

1. Raise the vehicle and support it safely.

2. Remove the wheel/tire assembly and the brake drums.

3. Place a drain pan under the housing and drain the lubricant. Remove the housing cover and gasket, if used.

4. Remove the differential pinion mate shaft lockscrew. Discard lockscrew and replace with a new screw upon installation.

5. Lift out the differential pinion mate shaft. Shaft is a slip fit design and may be removed by hand.

6. Push the axle shafts inward and remove the C-locks from the inner end of the axle shafts. Temporarily replace the shaft and lockbolt to retain the differential gears in position.

7. Remove the axle shafts. Be sure the seal is not damaged by the splines on the axle shaft.

8. Remove the bearing and oil seal from the housing. Inspect the axle shaft housing and axle shafts for burrs or damage.

9. Lightly coat the bearing assembly rollers with axle lubricant. Install the bearings in the axle housing until the bearing seats firmly against the shoulder.

10. Wipe all lubricant from the oil seal bore, before installing the seal. Install the oil seal.

11. Remove the lock screw and pinion shaft. Carefully slide the axle shafts into place. Be careful that you do not damage the seal with the splined end of the axle shaft. Engage the splined end of the shaft with the differential side gears.

12. Install the axle shaft C-locks on the inner end of the axle shafts and seat the C-locks in the counterbore of the differential side gears.

13. Rotate the differential pinion gears until the differential pinion shaft can be installed. Install the differential pinion shaft lockscrew. Tighten to 20–25 ft. lbs.

14. Install the brake drum and wheel/tire assemblies.

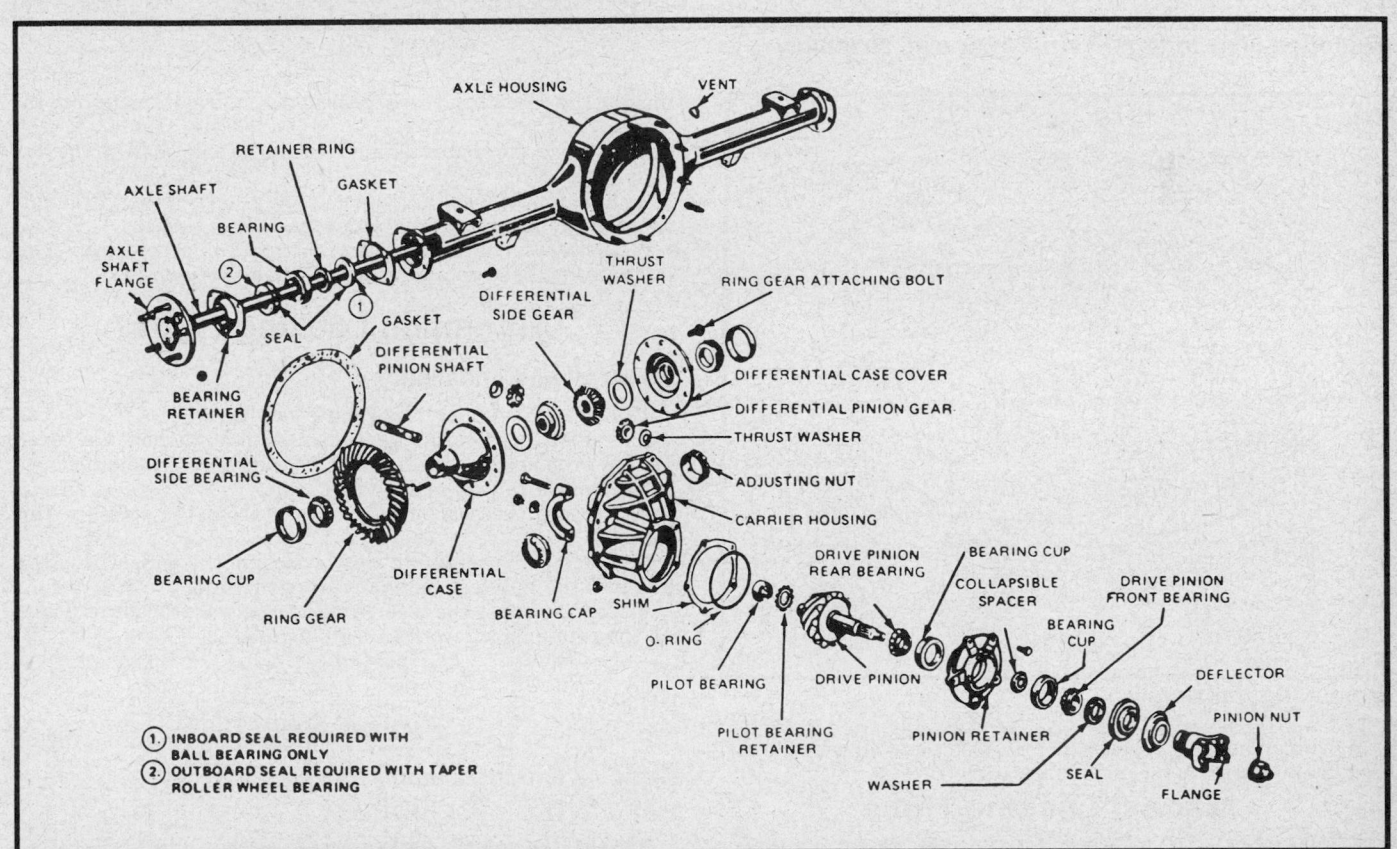

Exploded view removable carrier-rear axle assembly

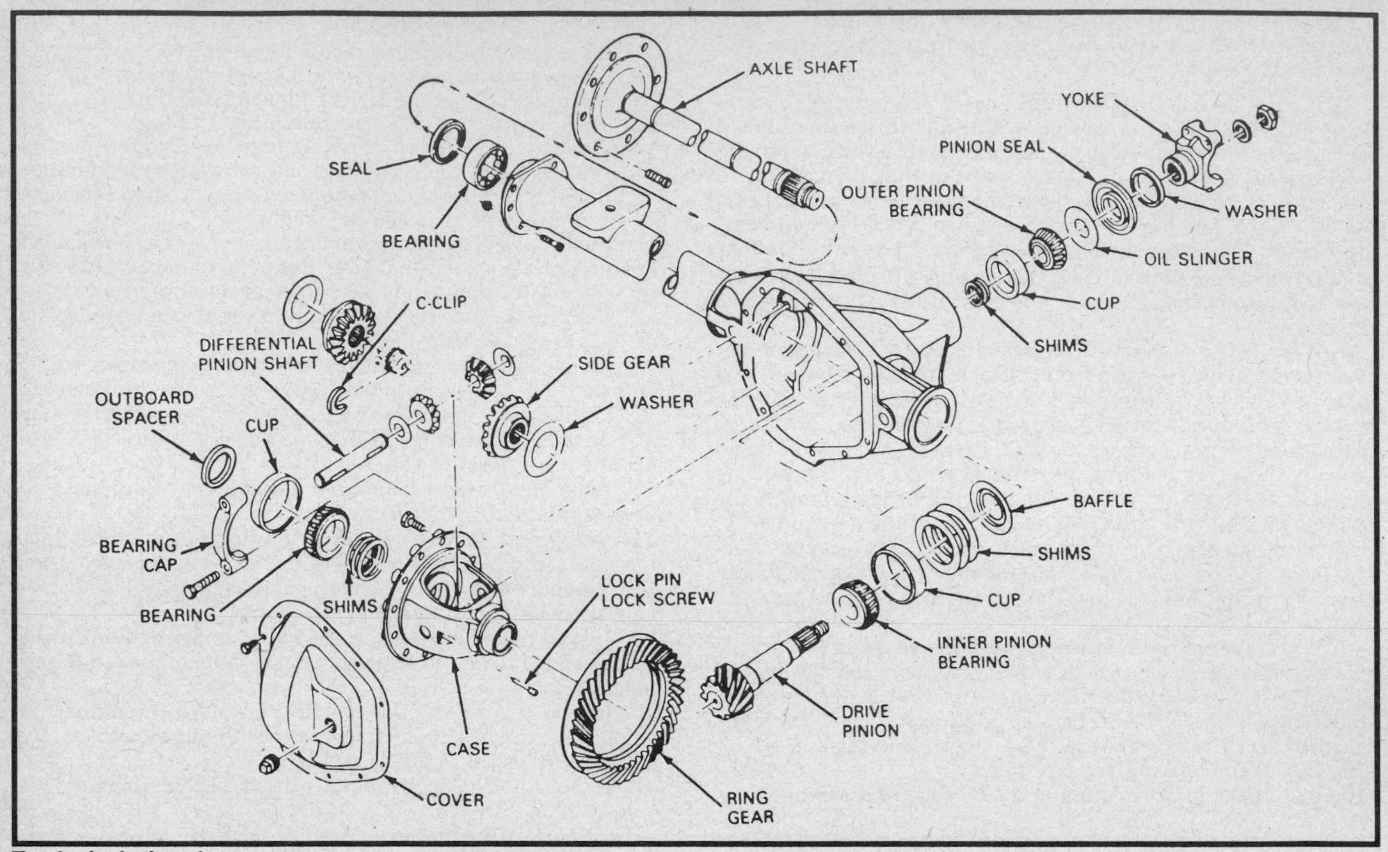

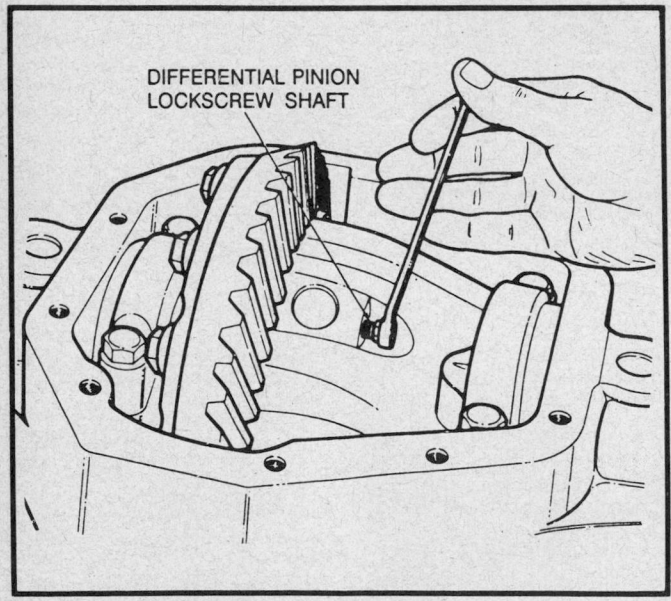

Exploded view intergal carrier-rear axle assembly

Removing lockscrew

15. Install housing cover with new gasket and fill with the correct amount of the specified lubricant.

Manual Locking Hubs

Removal and Installation

1. Raise and support the vehicle safely.
2. Seperate the cap asembly from the body assembly by re-

moving the Aleen head capscrews and remobve the cap from the body.
3. Remove the snapring that retains the axle shaft in the hub body assembly.
4. Remove the lock ring seated in the groove of the wheel hub. Remove the body assembly from the hub.
5. Installation is the reverse of the removal procedure. Tighten the Allen head retaining screws to 40–60 inch lbs.

Automatic Locking Hubs

Removal and Installation

1. Raise and support the vehicle safely.
2. Remove capscrews from body assembly. Remove the cover. Do not drop spring, ball bearing, bearing race or retainer.
3. Remove rubber seal.
4. Remove the seal bridge retainer from the retainer ring spacer.
5. Remove the retaining ring by closing the ends with a tool and pull the hub lock assembly from the hub.
6. Installation is the reverse of the removal procedure. Tighten the retaining screws to 40–50 inch lbs.

Pinion Seal

Removal and Installation

DANA INTEGRAL CARRIER

1. Raise the vehicle and support it safely.
2. Mark the driveshaft axle end flange and the axle companion flange for correct installation. Remove the driveshaft.
3. Using a suitable tool, hold the pinion flange. Remove the

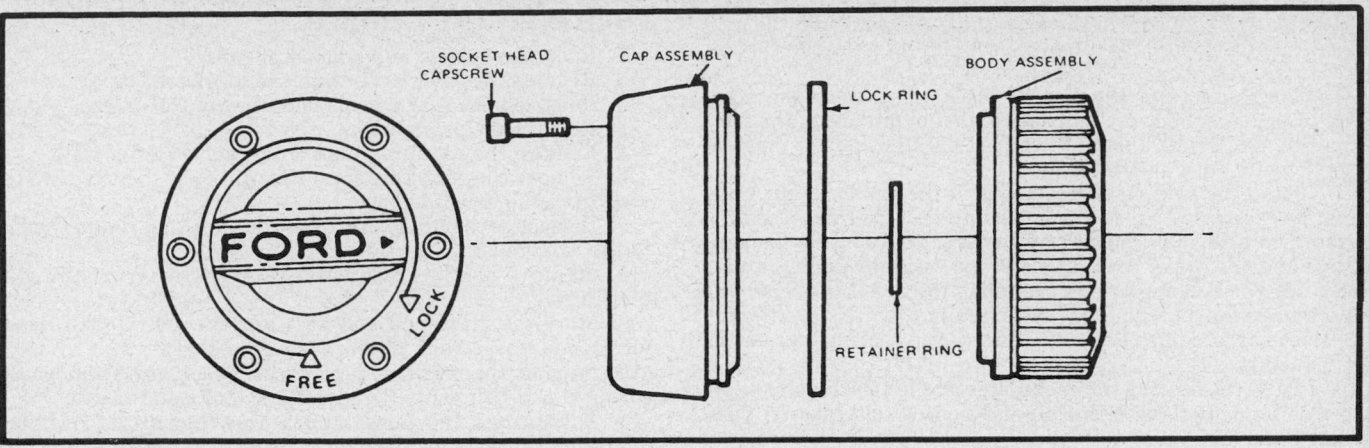

Manual locking hubs

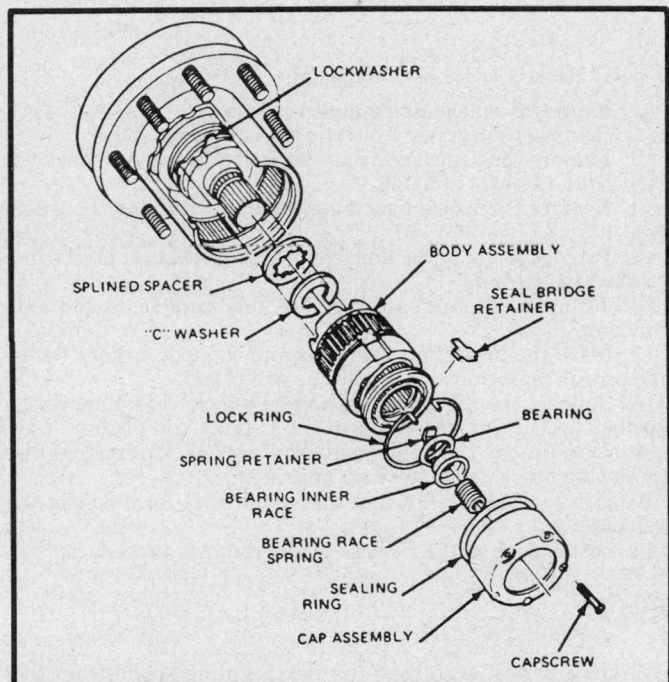

Automatic locking hubs

pinion shaft nut.

4. Remove the pinion flange. To remove the seal, pry it out of the carrier.

5. Installation is the reverse of the removal procedure. The pinion flange must never be hammered on or installed with power tools. Tighten the pinion nut 250–270 ft. lbs. on the Dana models 60, 61 and 70. Tighten the pinion nut 440–500 ft. lbs. on the Dana model 80.

FORD INTEGRAL CARRIER AND FORD REMOVABLE CARRIER

NOTE: This service procedure disturbs the pinion bearing preload and this preload must be carefully reset when assembling.

1. Raise the vehicle and support it safely.
2. Remove the wheels and the brake drums.
3. Mark the driveshaft axle end flange and the axle companion flange for correct installation. Remove the driveshaft.
4. Using an inch pound torque wrench on the pinion nut,

record the torque required for rotation of the pinion through several revolutions.

5. Remove the pinion nut. Mark the companion flange in relation to the pinion for reinstallation.
6. Remove the rear axle companion flange. To remove the seal, pry it out of the carrier.
7. Installation is the reverse of the removal procedure. Tighten the pinion nut to a minimum torque of 160 ft. lbs., rotating the pinion to insure proper bearing seating. Take frequent drive pinion bearing torque preload readings unti the original recorded preload reading is obtained.

Differential Carrier

Removal and Installation

FORD REMOVABLE CARRIER

1. Raise the vehicle and support it safely. Remove the rear wheel/tire assemblies.
2. Remove the brake drums from the axle shaft flange studs.
3. Working through the hole provided in each axle shaft flange, remove the nuts that secure the rear wheel bearing retainer plate. Pull each axle shaft assembly out of the axle housing. Care must be exercised to prevent damage to oil seal. Install a nut on one of the brake carrier plate attaching bolts to hold the plate to the axle housing after the shaft has been removed. Whenever a rear axle shaft is replaced, the wheel bearing oil seals must be replaced. Remove the seals.
4. Scribe marks on the driveshaft end yoke and the axle U-joint flange to insure proper position at assembly. Disconnect the driveshaft at the rear axle U-joint, remove the driveshaft from the transmission extension housing. Install a suitable tool in the housing to prevent transmission leakage.
5. Place a drain pan under the carrier and housing, remove the carrier attaching nut and drain the axle. Remove the carrier assembly from the axle housing.
6. Synthetic wheel bearing seals must not be cleaned, soaked or washed in cleaning solvent. Clean the axle housing and shafts using kerosene and swabs. To avoid contamination of the grease in the sealed ball bearings, do not allow any quantity of solvent directly on the wheel bearings. Clean the matting surfaces of the axle housing and carrier.
7. Position the differential carrier on the studs in the axle housing using a new gasket between carrier and housing. Install the carrier-to-housing attaching nuts and tighten to 25–40 ft. lbs.
8. Remove the tool from extension housing. Position the driveshaft so that the front U-joint slip yoke splines to the transmission output shaft.
9. Connect the driveshaft to the axle U-joint flange, aligning

the scribe marks made on the driveshaft end yoke and the axle U-joint flange during the removal procedure. Install the U-bolts and nuts.

10. Wipe a small amount of an oil-resistant sealer on the outer edge of each seal before it is installed. Do not put any of the sealer on the sealing lip. Install the oil seals in the ends of the rear axle housing with a suitable tool.

11. Install the axle shaft assemblies in the axle housing. Care must be exercised to prevent damage to the oil seals. When installing an axle shaft, place a new gasket between the housing flange and the brake backing plate and carefully slide the axle shaft into the housing so that the rough forging of the shaft will not damage the oil seal. Start the axle splines into the differential side gear and push the shaft in until the bearing bottoms in the housing.

12. Install the bearing retainer plates on the attaching bolts on the axle housing flanges. Install and tighten (alternately) nuts to 20–40 ft. lbs.

13. Install the rear brake drums and wheel/tire assemblies. Fill the rear axle with lubricant.

Axle Housing

Removal and Installation
DANA INTEGRAL CARRIER

1. Loosen the wheel stud nuts and the axle shaft retaining bolts.

2. Disconnect the rear shock absorbers from the spring seat caps. Then raise the rear end of the vehicle frame until the weight is off the rear springs. Place safety stands under the frame in this position.

3. Disconnect the flexible hydraulic line at the frame and disconnect the axle vent hose at the axle connection.

4. Disconnect the parking brake cable if so equipped at the equalizer and remove the cables from the cable support brackets.

5. Mark and disconnect the driveshaft from the rear U-joint flange.

6. Remove the nuts from the spring clips (U-bolts) and remove the spring seat caps.

7. Roll the axle from under the vehicle and drain the lubricant. Remove the wheels. Installation is the reverse of the removal procedure.

FORD INTEGRAL CARRIER

1. Raise the vehicle and support it safely.
2. Remove the cover and drain the lubricant.
3. Remove both rear wheels and remove the drums.
4. Remove the axle shafts.
5. Remove the retaining nuts from each backing plate.
6. Remove the vent hose from the vent tube then remove the vent from the axle housing.
7. Disengage the brake line from the clips that retain the line to the axle housing.
8. Remove the hydraulic brake T-fitting from the axle housing.
9. Mark the driveshaft end yoke and the axle U-joint flange for proper reassembly. Remove the driveshaft.
10. Support the rear axle housing on a jack, then remove the spring clip U-bolt nuts. Remove the U-bolts and plates.
11. Disconnect the lower shock absorber studs from the mounting brackets on the axle housing.
12. Lower the axle housing and remove it from under the vehicle.
13. Installation is the reverse of the removal procedure.

FORD REMOVABLE CARRIER

1. Raise the vehicle and support it safely.
2. Remove the carrier from the axle housing.
3. Remove the vent hose from the vent tube then remove the vent from the axle housing.
4. Remove the brake backing plate and wire it to the frame rail.
5. Disengage the brake line from the clips that retain the line to the axle housing.
6. Remove the hydraulic brake T-fitting from the axle housing.
7. Mark the driveshaft end yoke and the axle U-joint flange for proper reassembly. Remove the driveshaft.
8. Support the rear axle housing on a jack, then remove the spring clip U-bolt nuts. Remove the U-bolts and plates.
9. Disconnect the lower shock absorber studs from the mounting brackets on the axle housing.
10. Lower the axle housing and remove it from under the vehicle.
11. Installation is the reverse of the removal procedure.

STEERING

Steering Wheel

Removal and Installation

1. Park the vehicle in a straight head position. Note position of the steering wheel. Disconnect the negative battery cable.

2. Remove the screw underside each steering wheel spoke and lift the horn switch assembly from the steering wheel.

3. Remove all electrical connections and remove horn switch assembly.

4. Remove steering wheel retaining nut. Using a suitable puller remove the steering wheel from the steering shaft. Do not hammer or use knock off type puller on steering wheel.

5. Installation is the reverse of the removal procedure. Install the steering wheel in the noted position. Tighten the steering wheel retaining nut to 30–42 ft. lbs.

Manual Steering Gear

Removal and Installation

1. Raise the vehicle and support it safely with the front wheels in the straight ahead position.

2. On F series, disengage the flex coupling shield from the steering gear input shaft shield and slide it up the intermediate shaft.

3. Disconnect the flex (rag joint) coupling from the steering shaft flange by removing the attaching nuts.

4. Disconnect the drag link from the sector shaft pitman arm.

5. Mark and remove the pitman arm from the gear sector shaft using proper pulling tools.

NOTE: Do not hammer on the end of the sector shaft or the tool, this will damage the steering gear.

6. While supporting the steering gear, disconnect it from the frame side rail. Lower the gear assembly from the vehicle.

7. Install in the reverse order of removal. Before installing the gear, rotate the input shaft from stop to stop counting the total number of turns. Then turn back exactly half way, placing the gear on center. Make sure that the flat on the gear input shaft is facing straight up and aligns with the flat on the flex coupling. Tighten steering gear mounting bolts to 70 ft. lbs. and pitman arm retaining nut to 230 ft. lbs.

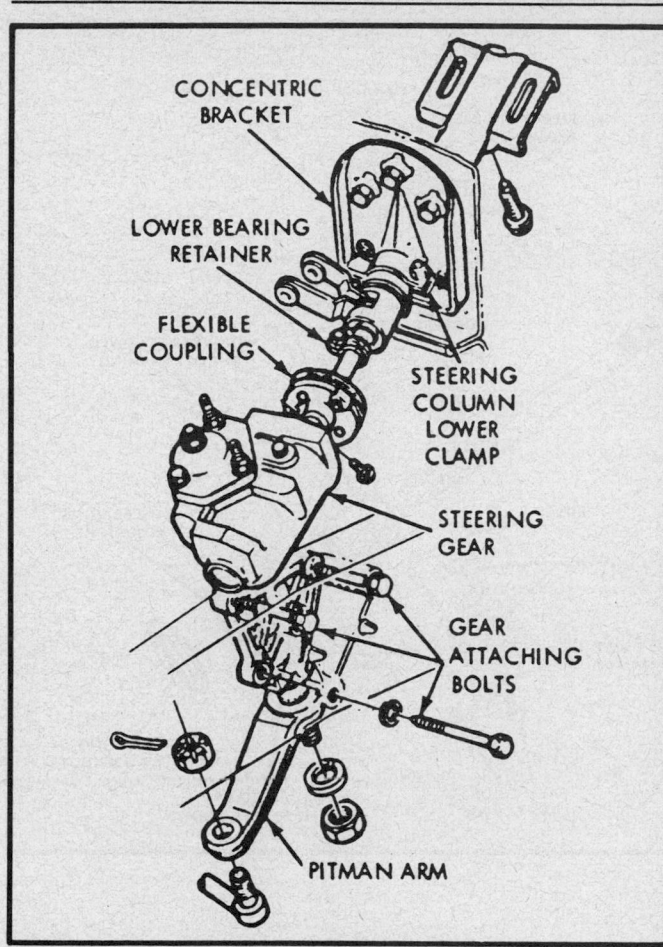

Manual steering gear installation—F series

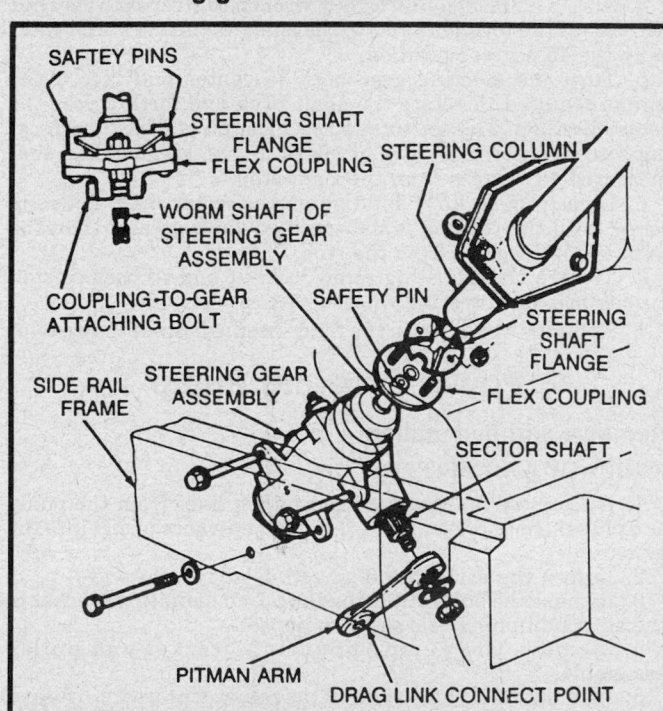

Manual steering gear installation—E series

Adjustment

PRELOAD AND MESHLOAD CHECK–IN VEHICLE

1. Make sure that the steering column is properly aligned and that the intermediate shaft flex coupling is not distorted.
2. Disconnect the pitman arm at the ball stud.
3. Lubricate the wormshaft seal with a drop of automatic transmission fluid.
4. Remove the horn pad assembly from the steering wheel and turn the wheel to one stop.
5. Using a torque wrench on the steering wheel nut, measure the torque (preload) required to rotate the steering wheel at a constant speed for approximately 1½ turns.
6. If the gear preload is not within 5–9 inch lbs. the preload must be readjusted. Gear must be removed to adjust worm preload.
7. With the torque wrench still on the steering wheel nut, observe the highest reading (meshload) by rotating the steering shaft 90 degrees either way across center. The meshload must be within 9–14 inch lbs. and at least 2 inch lbs. over the preload. Meshload can be adjusted in the vehicle.

PRELOAD AND MESHLOAD ADJUSTMENT–GEAR REMOVED

1. Tighten the selector cover bolts to 40 ft. lbs. Loosen preload adjuster locknut and tighten the worm bearing adjuster nut until all endplay has been removed.
2. Using a torque wrench and socket on wormshaft turn the wormshaft all the way to the right. Measure the left turn torque (preload) required to rotate the wormshaft at a constant speed for approximately 1½ turns.
3. Tighten or loosen the adjuster locknut until the correct preload (7–9 in. lbs.) is obtained. Torque locknut to 187 ft. lbs.
4. Rotate the wormshaft from stop to stop, counting the total number of turns, turn back halfway placing the gear on the center position.
5. With the torque wrench still on wormshaft, observe the highest reading (meshload) by rotating the wormshaft 90 degress either way across center. The meshload must be within 12–14 inch lbs. and at least 4 inch lbs. over the preload.
6. Turn the selector shaft adjusting screw as required. hold the sector shaft adjusting screw and tighten locknut to 25 ft. lbs.

Power Steering Gear

Removal and Installation

1. Disconnect the negative battery cable. Disconnect the pressure and return lines from the gear. Plug the lines and the ports in the gear to prevent entry of dirt.
2. If equipped, remove the splash shield from the flex coupling. Disconnect the flex coupling at the steering gear.
3. Raise the vehicle and support it safely. Remove the pitman arm from the sector shaft.
4. Support the steering gear and remove the attaching bolts. Work the steering gear free from the flex coupling and remove the gear from the vehicle.
5. Install in the reverse order of removal procedure. Bleed power steering system if necesaary.

Adjustment

FORD INTERGAL GEAR TYPE

1. Make sure that the steering column is correctly aligned and remove the steerring wheel cover. Disconnect the pitman arm from the sector shaft.
2. Disconnect the fluid reservoir return line and cap the reservoir return line tube. Place the end of the return line in a clean container and turn the steering wheel back and forth several times to empty the steering gear.
3. Turn the steering wheel to 45 degrees from the right stop.

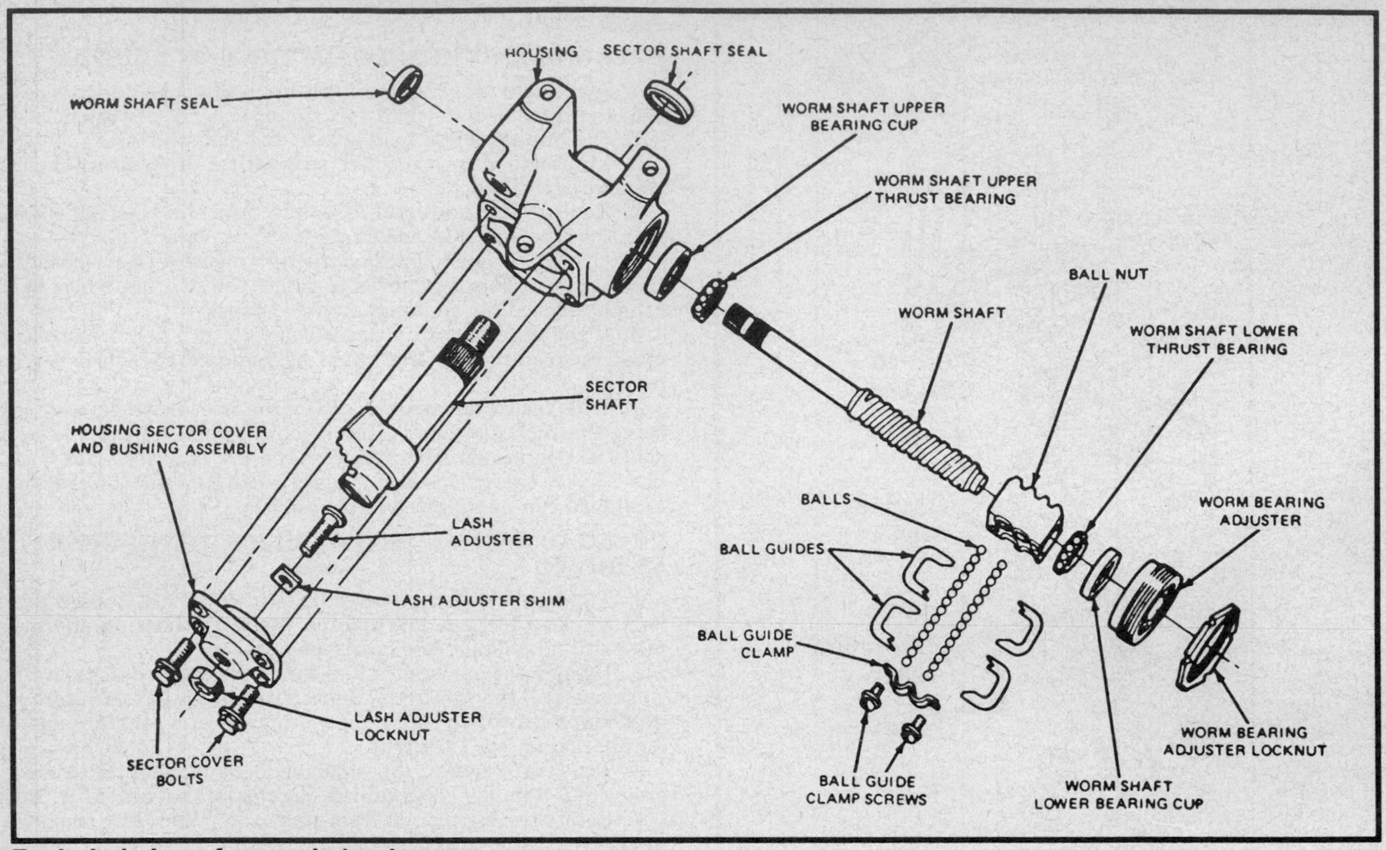

WORM SHAFT SEAL
HOUSING
SECTOR SHAFT SEAL
WORM SHAFT UPPER BEARING CUP
WORM SHAFT UPPER THRUST BEARING
BALL NUT
WORM SHAFT
WORM SHAFT LOWER THRUST BEARING
SECTOR SHAFT
HOUSING SECTOR COVER AND BUSHING ASSEMBLY
BALLS
WORM BEARING ADJUSTER
BALL GUIDES
LASH ADJUSTER
BALL GUIDE CLAMP
LASH ADJUSTER SHIM
LASH ADJUSTER LOCKNUT
WORM BEARING ADJUSTER LOCKNUT
SECTOR COVER BOLTS
BALL GUIDE CLAMP SCREWS
WORM SHAFT LOWER BEARING CUP

Exploded view of manual steering gear

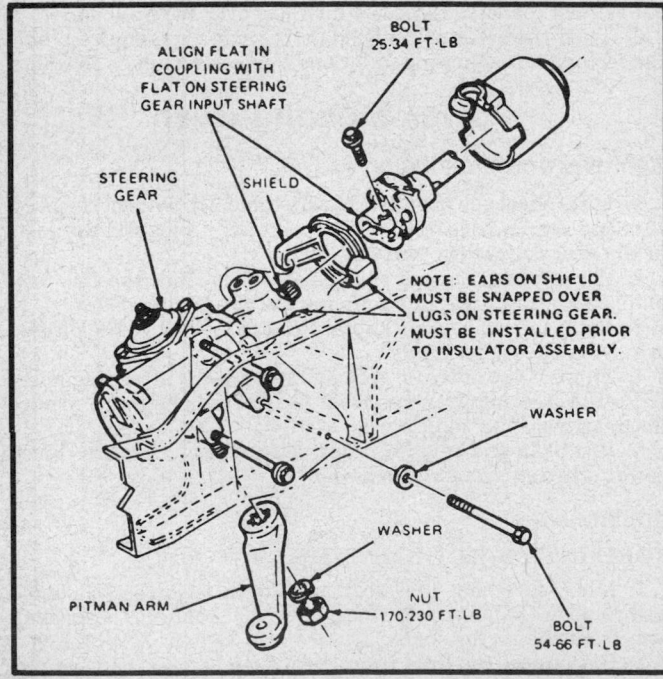

ALIGN FLAT IN COUPLING WITH FLAT ON STEERING GEAR INPUT SHAFT
BOLT 25-34 FT·LB
STEERING GEAR
SHIELD
NOTE: EARS ON SHIELD MUST BE SNAPPED OVER LUGS ON STEERING GEAR. MUST BE INSTALLED PRIOR TO INSULATOR ASSEMBLY.
WASHER
WASHER
PITMAN ARM
NUT 170-230 FT·LB
BOLT 54-66 FT·LB

Power steering installation—Bronco and F series

4. Attach an inch pound torque wrench to steering wheel nut and record the torque to rotate the shaft ⅛ turn toward center from the 45 degreee position.

5. Turn the steering gear back to center and record the torque required to rotate the shaft back and forth across the center position. The set torque specification is measured rocking across center to a valve of 10–14 in. lbs. greater than that measured 45 degress from the right stop.

6. Loosen the locknut and tighten the sector shaft adjusting screw until the reading is the specified valve greater than the torque at 45 degress from the stop.

7. Tighten the adjusting screw locknut and recheck. Install pitman arm and steering wheel cover.

8. Refill the system with the fluid specified. Bleed the system.

Power Steering Pump

Removal and Installation
SAGINAW AND ZF TYPE

1. Disconnect the pressure and return lines from the pump and plug them to prevent loss of fluid or entrance of dirt into the system.

2. Loosen the belt tension adjusting bolt all the way.

3. Remove the bolts attaching the pump mounting bracket to the air conditioning bracket if equipped.

4. Remove the pump, mounting bracket and pulley asssembly.

5. Installation is the reverse of the removal procedure. Adjust belt tension. Refill and bleed system if necessary.

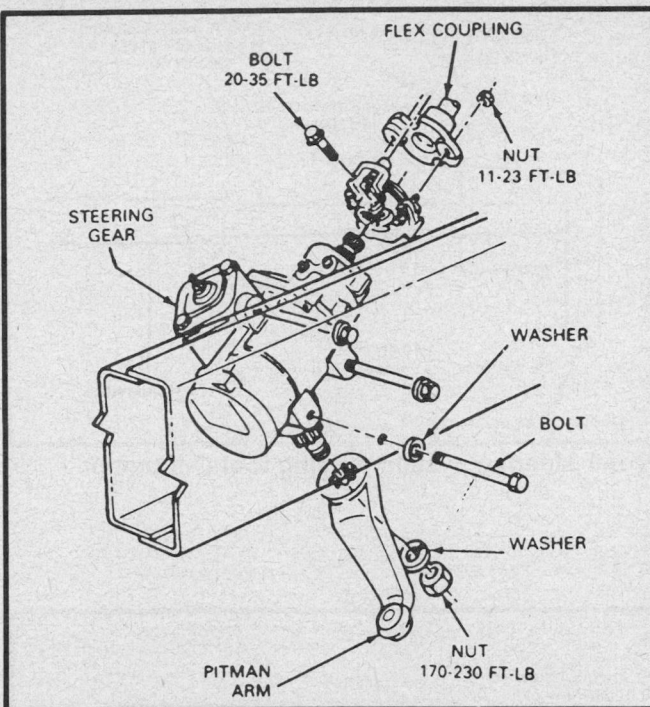

Power steering installation–E series

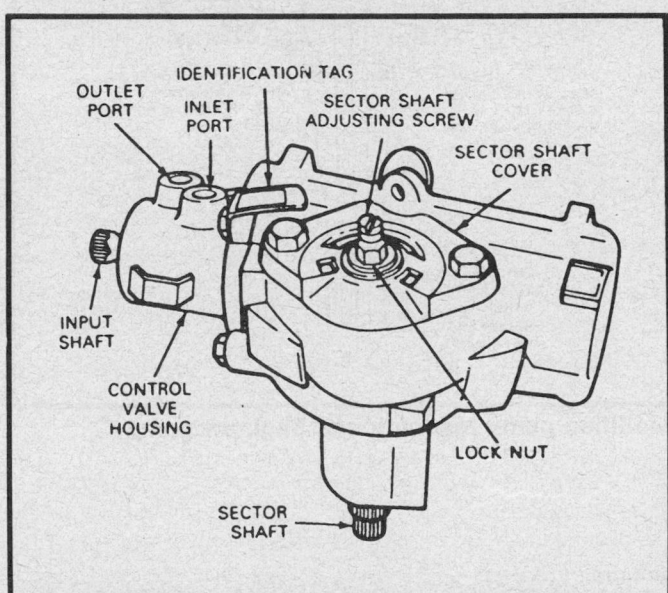

Ford intergal power steering gear

C-II TYPE

NOTE: The C-II pump is equipped with a fiberglas reservoir and can be identified by the reservoir. Never pry against the fiberglass, as damage will occur.

1. Disconnect the negative battery cable. Remove the power steering fluid from the pump reservoir, disconnect the fluid return hose at the reservoir and drain the fluid into a container. Remove the pressure hose from the pump.
2. Remove the bolts from the pump adjustment bracket.

Loosen the pump sufficiently to remove the belt off the pulley. Remove the pump (still attached to the adjustment bracket) from the support bracket.

3. Remove the pulley from the pump if required.
4. Remove the bolts attaching the adjustment bracket to the pump and remove the pump.
5. Place the adjustment bracket on the pump. Install the pulley on the pump if removed.
6. Place the pump with adjustment bracket and pulley on the support bracket. Install the bolts connecting the support bracket to the adjustment bracket.
7. Place the belt on the pulley and adjust belt tension. Tighten bolts on adjustment bracket.
8. Install the pressure hose to the pump fitting. Connect the return hose to the pump and tighten the clamp.
9. Fill the reservoir with power steering fluid, start the engine and turn the steering wheel from stop to stop to remove air from the system. Check for leaks and recheck the fluid level. Add fluid if necessary.

Belt Adjustment
CONVENTIONAL BELT

1. Check belt tension with a belt tension gauge. New belt tension is 120–150 lbs. and used belt tension is 90–120 lbs.
2. On vehicles equipped with pivot type adjustment brackets, loosen the pivot bolts. Insert a tool in adjustment slot, raise upward and tighten pivot bolts.
3. On vehicles equipped with slider type adjustment bracket, loosen the bolts in the slider slots. Insert a tool to pry against pump to obtain the correct belt tension. Tighten all bolts.
4. Recheck and adjust belt if necessary.

AUTOMATICALLY TENSIONED BELT

The automatic belt tensioner will maintain correct belt tension if the correct length belt is used on the engine. To verfiy that the tensioner is working properly check to see that the belt length indicator mark on the tensioner is between the maximum and minimum marks. The belt tensioner has no provision for adjustment and will be damaged if forced to travel beyond the normal operating range.

System Bleeding
CONVENTIONAL METHOD

1. Check and fill the power steering pump reservoir oil level to the correct level.
2. Run engine. Turn the steering wheel, approximately 5 times, one full cycle (without hitting the stops). This will help remove air trapped in the system.
3. Check fluid level add fluid as necessary.

DEVAC METHOD

NOTE: A fabricated Devac purging tool must be used for this service procedure.

1. Check the pump reservoir oil level (must be at correct level).
2. Insert the rubber stopper end of an air evacuator assembly into the filler tube tightly.
3. Connect a length of hose from the other end of the evacuator to a distributor machine or an air conditioner vacuum pump. Do not use engine vacuum.
4. Let the engine idle for 15 minutes. Turn the steering wheel one full cycle (without hitting the stops) every five minutes. This will help remove air trapped in the system.
5. Disconnect and remove the evacuator and reinstall the filler tube dipstick.

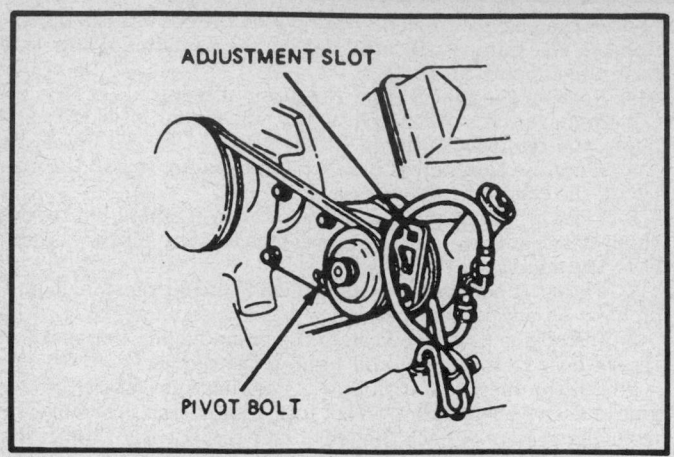

Power steering belt adjustment-conventional belt

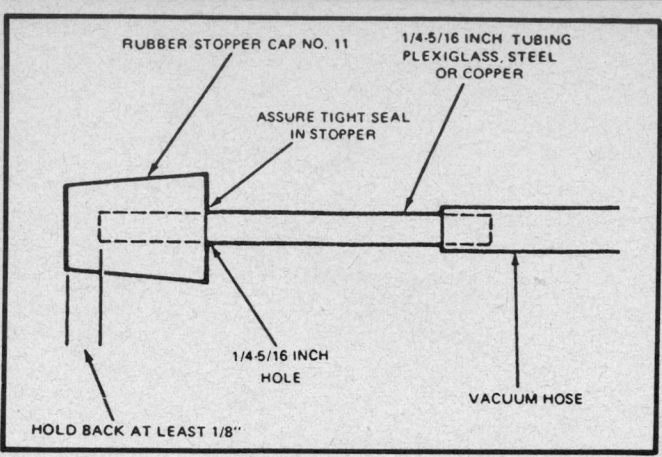

Power steering system purging tool C-II pump

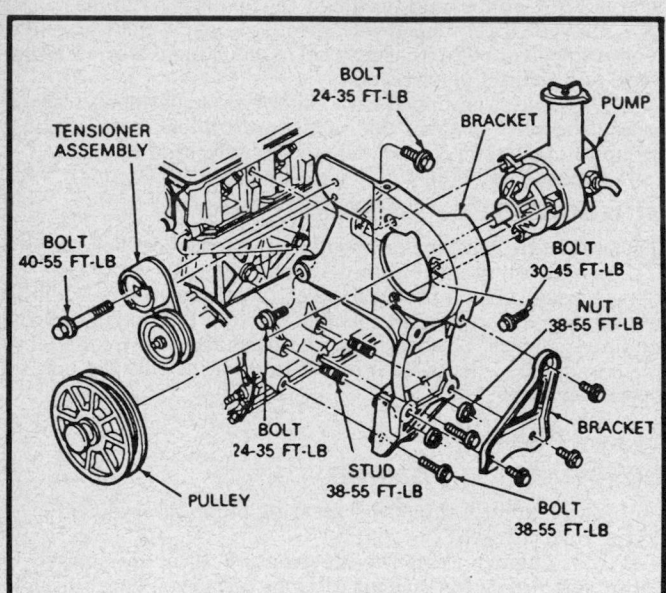

C-II power steering pump installation-typical

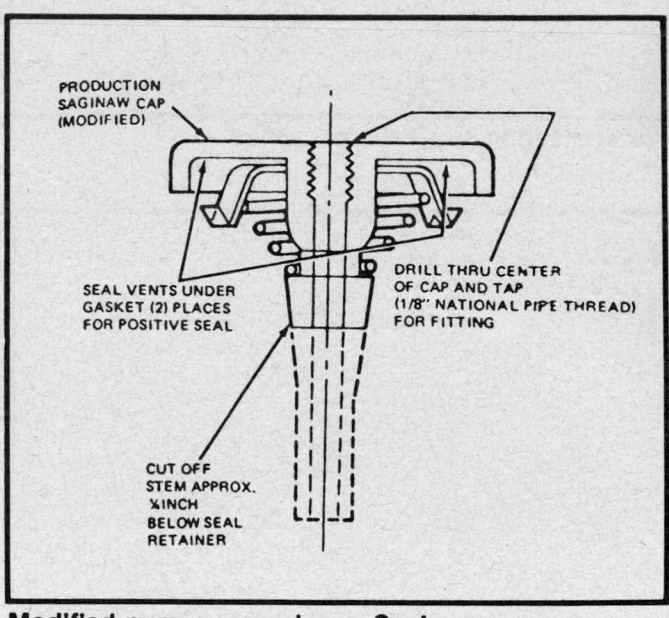

Modified pump reservoir cap Saginaw pump

Tie Rod Ends

Removal and Installation

NOTE: Replace the drag link or tie rod if a ball stud is excessively loose or if the drag link or tie rod is bent. Do not attempt to straighten a drag link or tie rod.

1. Disconnect the negative battery cable. Remove the cotter pin and nut from the tie rod ball studs.
2. Using suitable tools, remove tie rod ball studs from spindle and drag link.
3. If replacing just one tie rod end remove the end from the the adjusting sleeve. Always record the number of turns to remove the tie rod end from sleeve. When installing this will provide approxmate toe in setting.

4. Installation is the reverse of the removal procedure. Always position adjusting sleeve clamp towards engine (nut faces front of engine). Tighten ball stud nut to 50–75 ft. lbs., use new cotter pins and check front end alignment.

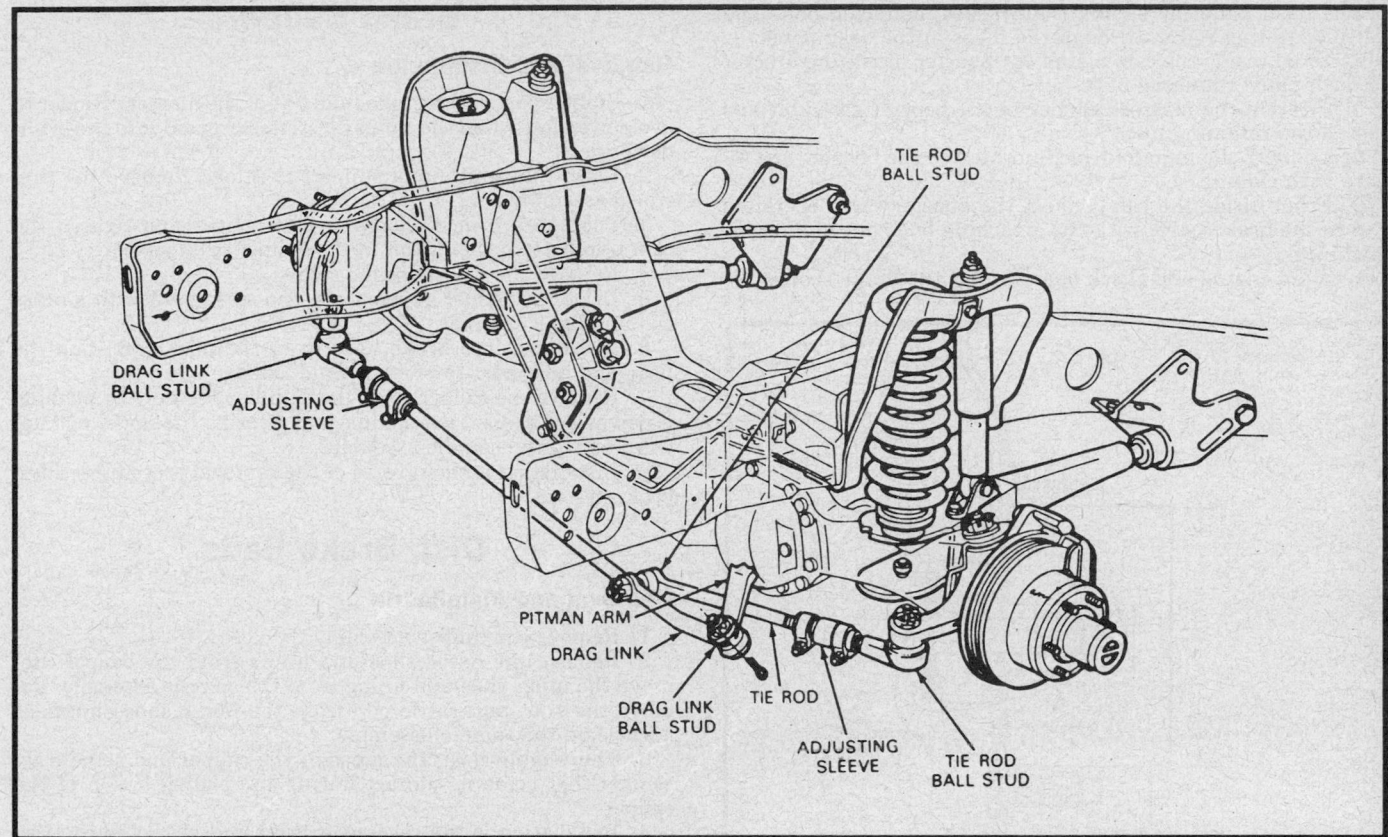

Steering linkage– F–150 and Bronco

BRAKES

For all brake system repair and service procedure not detailed below, please refer to "Brakes" in the Unit repair section.

Master Cylinder

Removal and Installation

1. Disconnect the negative battery cable. Disconnect fluid level indicator switch connector from the master cylinder.
2. Disconnect the hydraulic lines from the master cylinder.
3. Remove the brake booster to master cylinder retaining nuts. Remove the master cylinder from the brake booster.
4. Installation is the reverse of the removal procedure. Before installing the master cylinder, check the distance from the outer end of the booster assembly pushrod, to the front face of the brake asssembly. The service specification (Bendix booster) is 0.995 in. Bleed brake system as required.

Height Sensing Brake Proportioning Valve

Removal and Installation

1. Raise and safely support the vehicle (rear suspension should hang at fully extended position).
2. Remove the linkage arm from the height sensing valve.
3. Remove the flow bolt holding the brake hose to valve.
4. Disconnect the brake line from the valve.
5. Remove bolts securing valve to mounting bracket. Remove valve.
6. Installation is the reverse of the removal procedure. Bleed brake system as required.

Power Brake Boosters

Removal and Installation

1. Disconnect the negative battery cable. Remove retaining nuts and master cylinder from booster.
2. Loosen hose clamp and remove manifold vacuum hose from booster.
3. From inside the cab, remove the attaching bolt, nut and plastic bushings and disconnect the booster pushrod from the brake pedal.
4. Remove nuts that retain the booster mounting bracket to the dash panel.
5. Remove the booster assembly from engine compartment.
To install:
6. Mount the booster and bracket assembly to the engine side

of the dash panel by sliding the bracket mounting bolts and valve operating rod in through the holes in the dash panel.

7. From inside the cab, install the booster mounting bracket to dash panel retaining nuts.

8. Position the master cylinder to the booster assembly and install the retaining nuts.

9. Connect the manifold vacuum hose to the booster and secure with clamp.

10. From inside the cab connect the booster valve operating rod to the brake pedal with the attaching bolt, nut and plastic bushings.

11. Start engine and check operation of the brake system.

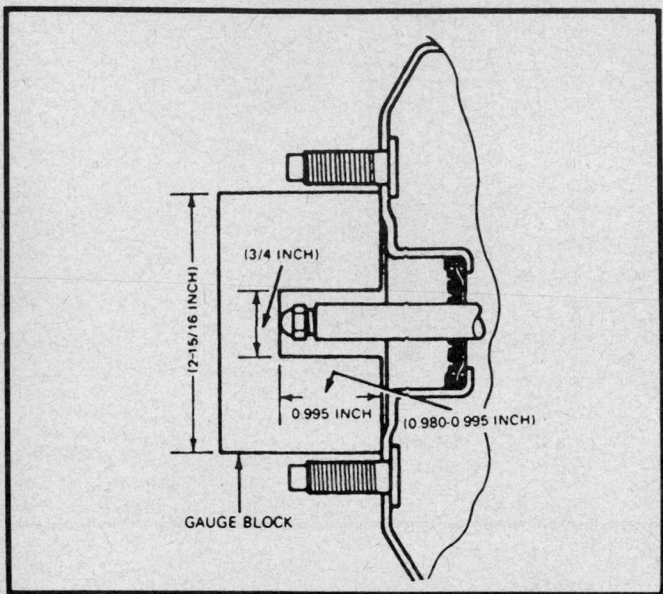

Bendix booster pushrod gauge dimemsions and adjustment

Brake Caliper

Removal and Installation

1. Siphon part of the brake fluid out of the master cylinder to avoid overflow when the caliper piston is pressed into the cylinder bore.

2. Raise the vehicle and support it safely. Remove the tire/wheel assembly.

3. Position a 8 in. C-clamp on the caliper and tighten the clamp to bottom the piston in the caliper cylinder bore.

4. Remove the key retaining screw.

5. Drive the caliper support key and spring out with a brass rod and light hammer.

6. Disconnect the brake hose from the inlet port. Cap the hose and inlet port to prevent fluid leakage.

7. Remove the caliper from the spindle assembly by pushing it downward against the spindle and rotating the upper end upward out of the spindle assembly.

8. Installation is the reverse of the removal procedure. Bleed brake system.

Disc Brake Pads

Removal and Installation

1. Remove the caliper assembly.

2. Remove the outer shoe and lining from the caliper. Remove the inner shoe and lining from the spindle assembly. Remove the shoe anti-rattle clip from the lower shoe abutment surface on the spindle assembly.

3. Thoroughly clean the areas of the caliper and spindle assembly that come in contact during the sliding action of the caliper.

4. Installation is the reverse of the removal procedure. Use new components as required. Bleed the system as required.

Brake Rotor

Removal and Installation

1. Raise and safely support the vehicle. Remove the wheel.

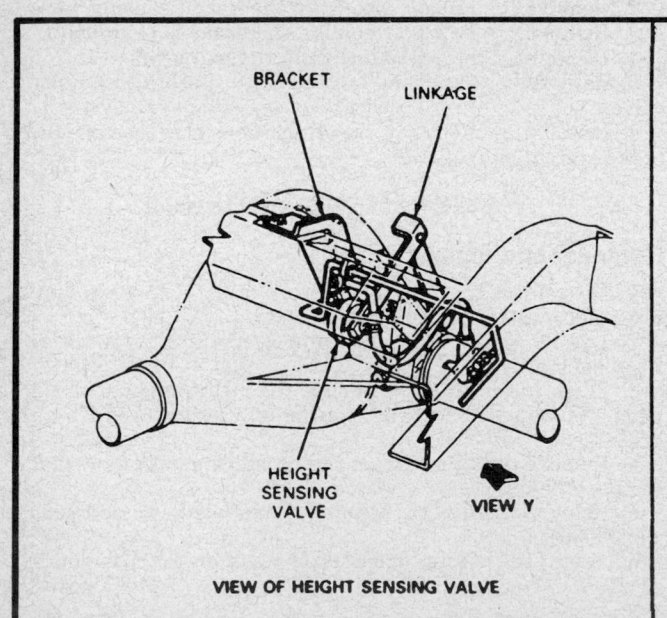

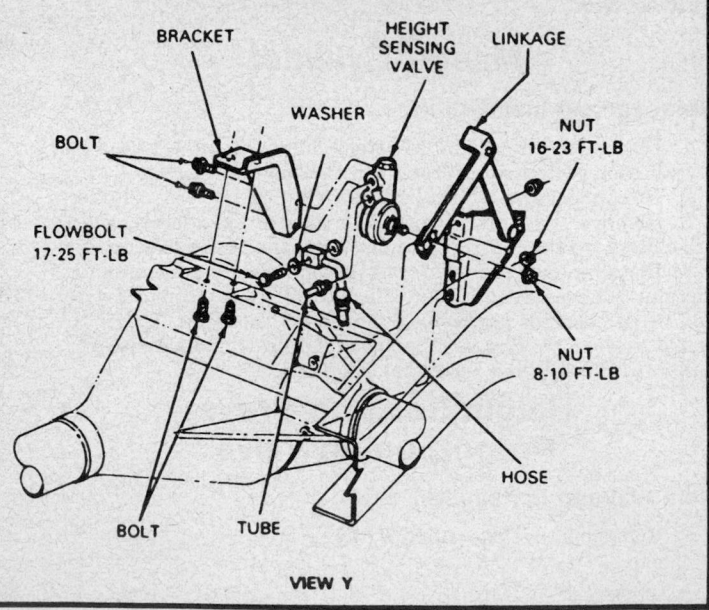

Height sensing brake proportioning valve installation- E series

2. Remove the caliper assembly from the rotor and support it out of the way with wire or equivalent.

3. Remove the dust cap, cotter pin, nut, washer and outer bearing and remove the rotor from the spindle.

4. On 4WD vehicles, the locking hub assembly must also be removed.

5. Install in the reverse order of removal procedure. Adjust wheel bearings. If replacing rotor assembly, always replace the grease seal for inner bearing.

Brake Drum

Removal and Installation

1. Raise and safely support the vehicle. Remove the wheel.
2. Remove the spring retaining nuts if equipped and remove the brake drum.
3. Install in the reverse order of removal procedure. If brake drum will not come off, insert a narrow tool through the brake adjusting hole in the backing plate and disengage the adjusting lever while loosening the brake adjusting screw.

Brake Shoe

Removal and Installation

NOTE: Before removing brake shoes record color and position of all brake springs they must be installed in their original position.

1. Raise and safely support the vehicle. Remove the brake drum.
2. Install a brake cylinder clamp around wheel cylinder to stop it from expanding.
3. Remove the bottom brake adjuster retaining spring. Remove the self-adjusting cable from the lever.
4. Remove the primary shoe to anchor spring.
5. Remove the secondary shoe to anchor spring. Remove the cable guide from the secondary shoe.
6. Remove the left and right shoe hold down spring.
7. Remove the brake adjuster assembly.
8. Remove the parking brake link and spring (note position for correct installation). Disconnect the parking brake cable from the brake lever.
9. Remove the brake shoes. Remove the parking brake lever from the secondary shoe by removing the retaining clip and spring washer.
10. Installation is the reverse of the removal procedure. The primary shoe (short shoe) always is installed toward the front of the vehicle. The secondary shoe (long shoe) is installed toward the rear of the vehicle. Replace all brake springs as necessary. Lube with white brake grease where the brake shoes touch the backing plate. Check the brake fluid and adjust the brake system.

Wheel Cylinder

Removal and Installation

1. Raise and safely support the vehicle. Remove the wheel, drum and brake shoes.
2. Remove the cylinder to shoe connecting pins.
3. Disconnect the brake line from the wheel cylinder.
4. Remove the wheel cylinder retaining bolts and remove the cylinder from the brake backing plate.
5. Installation is the reverse of the removal procedure. Adjust the brakes and bleed the system as required.

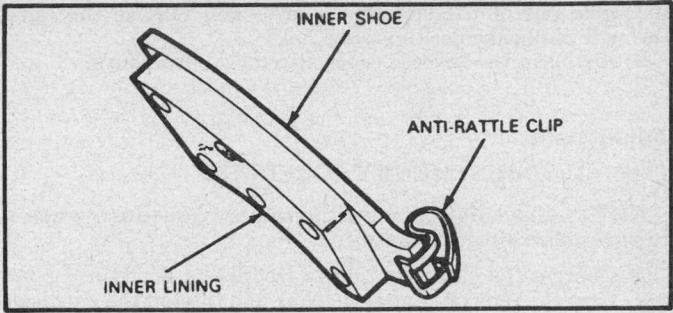

Installing anti-rattle clip on inner pad

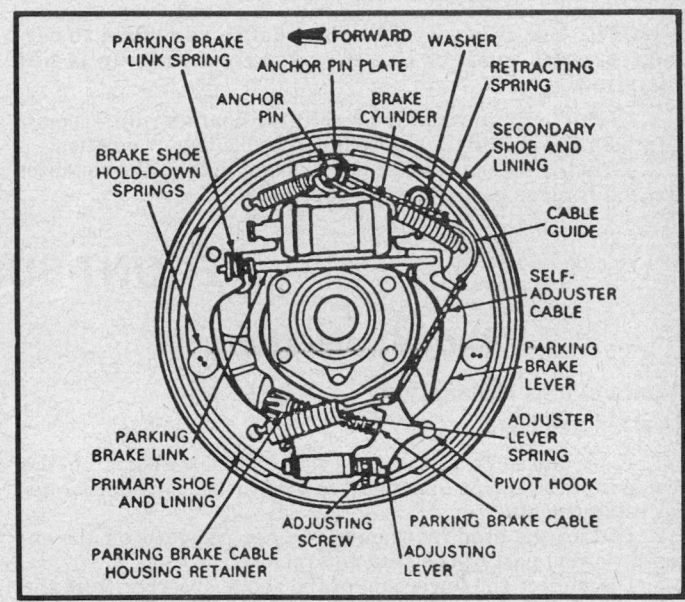

Typical rear brake shoe assembly

Parking Brake Cable

Removal and Installation

EQUALIZER TO CONTROL ASSEMBLY

1. Raise the vehicle and support it safely.
2. Back off the equalizer nut and remove slug of front cable from the tension limiter.
3. Remove the parking brake cable from the bracket or crossmember. Lower the vehicle.
4. Remove the forward ball end of the parking brake cable from the control clevis.
5. Remove the cable from the control by compressing the conduit end fitting prongs.
6. Using a cord attached to the control lever end of the cable, remove the cable from the vehicle.
7. Install in the reverse order of removal procedure.

EQUALIZER TO REAR WHEEL

1. Raise the vehicle and support it safely.
2. Remove the wheel, tension limiter and brake drum.
3. Remove the locknut on the threaded rod and disconnect the cable from the equalizer.
4. Working on the wheel side, compress the prongs on the cable retainer so they can pass through the hole in the brake backing plate.
5. With the spring tension off of the parking brake lever, lift

the cable out of the slot in the lever and remove the cable through the brake backing plate hole.

6. Install in the reverse order of removal procedure.

Adjustment
INITIAL ADJUSTMENT PROCEDURE

NOTE: Use this service adjustment procedure when a new tension limiter installed.

1. Depress the parking brake to last detent position.
2. Grip the tension limiter housing and tighten the equalizer nut 3 in. up the rod.
3. Check to make sure cinch strap has 1½ in. remaining.

FIELD ADJUSTMENT PROCEDURE

NOTE: Use this service adjustment procedure to correct a slack system if a new tension limiter is not installed.

1. Vehicle drums must be cold for correct adjustment. Depresss the parking brake to last possible detent position.
2. Grip the tension limiter housing and tighten the equalizer nut 6 full turns past the original position.

3. Using a cable tension guide or equivalent the tension should be 350 lbs. If tension is low repeat Step 2.
4. Release parking brake and check for rear wheel drag. There should be no brake drag.

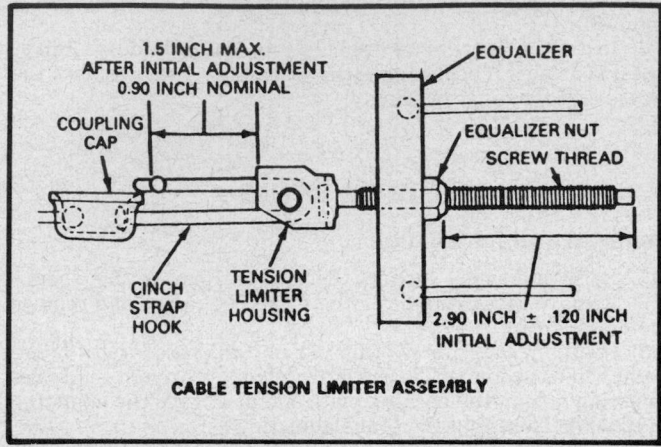

CABLE TENSION LIMITER ASSEMBLY

Tension limiter assembly

FRONT SUSPENSION

Shock Absorbers

Removal and Installation
2WD VEHICLES

1. Raise and safely support the vehicle. Insert a tool from the rear side of the spring upper seat to hold the shock absorber upper retaining nut.
2. Loosen the stud by turning the hex provided on the exposed (lower) part of the stud and remove the nut.
3. Disconnect the lower end of the shock absorber from the lower bracket by removing the nut and bolt.
4. Compress the shock absorber and remove it from the vehicle.
5. Installation is the reverse of the removal procedure.

4WD VEHICLES

1. Raise and safely support the vehicle. Remove the nut and bolt that retains the shock absorber to the upper shock bracket.
2. Disconnect the lower end of the shock absorber from the U-bolt plate.
3. Compress the shock absorber and remove it.
4. Reverse the removal procedure for installation.

Coil Springs

Removal and Installation

1. Raise the front of the vehicle and support it safely. Also put a jack under the axle.
2. Disconnect the shock absorber from the lower bracket.
3. Remove the spring lower retainer attaching nuts from inside of the spring coil and remove the retainer.
4. Remove the spring upper retainer attaching screws and remove the retainer.
5. Slowly lower the axle and remove the spring.
6. Installation is the reverse of the removal procedure.

Leaf Springs

Removal and Installation

1. Raise the vehicle frame until the weight is off the front spring and the wheels stil touching the floor.
2. Disconnect the lower end of the shock absorber from the U-bolt spacer. Remove the U-bolts, cap and the spacer.
3. On vehicles equipped with a Dana Model 60 Monobeam axle, remove the 2 bolts that retain the tracking bar to the right spring cap and tracking bar mounting bracket.
4. Remove the nut from the hanger bolt retaining the spring at the rear. Drive out the hanger bolt.
5. Remove the nut connecting the front shackle and the spring eye. Drive out the shackle bolt and remove the spring.
6. Installation is the reverse of the removal procedure.

Upper Ball Joints

Inspection

NOTE: Always adjust the wheel bearings before ball joint inspection service procedure.

1. Raise the vehicle and place safety stands under the I-Beam axle beneath the spring.
2. Move the (upper part) wheel in and out. Observe the upper spindle arm and the upper part of the axle jaw.
3. A ⅟₃₂ in. or greater movement between the upper part of the axle jaw and the upper spindle arm indicates that the upper ball joint must be replaced.

Removal and Installation

1. Raise and safely support the vehicle. Remove the front wheel assembly. Remove the spindle. Remove the snapring from the upper ball joint if so equipped.
2. Assemble the C-frame tool T74P-4635-C and reciever cup tool D81T-3010-A or equivalent on the upper ball joint.
3. Turn the forcing screw clockwise until the ball joint is removed from the spindle.
4. Installation is the reverse of the removal procedure. Do not heat the ball joint or the spindle to aid in removal.

Lower Ball Joints

Inspection

NOTE: Always adjust the wheel bearings before ball joint inspection service procedure.

1. Raise the vehicle and place safety stands under the I-Beam axle beneath the spring.
2. Move the (lower part) wheel in and out. Observe the lower spindle arm and the lower part of the axle jaw.
3. A $\frac{1}{32}$ in. or greater movement between the lower part of the axle jaw and the lower spindle arm indicates that the lower ball joint must be replaced.

Removal and Installation

1. Raise and safely support the vehicle. Remove the front wheel assembly. Remove the spindle. Remove the snapring from the lower ball joint.
2. Assemble the C-frame tool T74P–4635–C and reciever cup tool D81T–3010–A or equivalent on the lower ball joint.
3. Turn the forcing screw clockwise until the ball joint is removed from the spindle.
4. Installation is the reverse of the removal procedure. Do not heat the ball joint or the spindle to aid in removal.

Stabilizer Bar

Removal and Installation

E AND F SERIES

1. Disconnect the left and right ends of the bar from the link assembly attached to the I-Beam bracket.
2. Disconnect the retainer bolts and remove the stabilizer bar.
3. Disconnect the link assemblies by looosening the right and left locknuts from their I-Beam brackets.
4. Install in the reverse order of removal.

NOTE: The link must be installed with the bend facing forward on E series. On F series, right and left link assemblies are stamped with an "R" or an "L" to identify them.

BRONCO AND F 150 4WD

1. Disconnect the stabilizer bar from the connecting links. Remove the nuts and bolts of the stabilizer bar retainer.
2. Remove stabilizer bar retainer.
3. Remove the stabilizer bar and insulator. The stud does not have to be removed.
4. Installation is the reverse of the removal procedure.

F 250 4WD

1. Remove the bolts, washers and the nuts securing the links to the spring seat caps. If equipped with a Dana Model 60 Monobeam front axle, the links are secured to the mounting brackets.
2. Disconnect the links from the stabilizer bar and remove them.
3. Remove the retainers from the mounting bracket. Remove the stabilizer bar.
4. Installation is the reverse of the removal procedure.

King Pin and Bushings

Removal and Installation

1. Raise and support the vehicle safely.
2. Remove the wheel/tire assembly.
3. Remove the caliper assembly. It is not necessary to disconnect the brake fluid hose. Wire the caliper to a suspension part to remove the weight of the caliper from the hose. Disconnect the steering linkage from the spindle arm.
4. Disconnect the steering linkage from the integral spindle and spindle arm.
5. Remove the nut and lockwasher from the locking pin and remove the locking pin.
6. Remove the upper and lower spindle bolt plugs and drive the spindle bolt out from the top of the axle. Remove the spindle and bearing. Knock out the seal.
7. Make sure that the spindle bolt hole in the axle is free of nicks, burrs and dirt. Install a new seal and coat the spindle bolt bushings and bolt hole with oil.
8. Place the spindle in position on the axle.
9. Pack the spindle thrust bearing with chassis lubricant and insert the bearing into the spindle with the open end of the bearing seal facing down into the spindle.
10. Install the spindle pin in (T stamped end faces up) the spindle with the locking pin notch in the spindle bolt aligned with the locking pin hole in the axle. Drive the spindle bolt through the axle from the top side until the spindle bolt locking pin notch is aligned with the locking pin hole.
11. Install a new locking pin. Install the locking pin lockwasher and nut. Tighten the nut to 40–55 ft. lbs. Install the spindle bolt plugs at the top and bottom of the spindle bolt.
12. Install the cailper assembly and connect the steering linkage to spindle. Install the wheel/tire assembly.
13. Grease the spindle assembly. Check and adjust, if necessary, the toe-in adjustment.

Twin I-Beam Axle

Removal and Installation

1. Raise and safely support the vehicle as necessary. Remove the front wheel spindle, the front spring and the stabilizer bar if so equipped.
2. Remove the spring lower seat from the radius arm and then remove the bolt and nut that attaches the stabilizer bar bracket and radius arm to the front axle.
3. Remove the axle to frame pivot bracket bolt and nut. Remove the axle assembly.

To install:

4. Position the axle to the frame pivot bracket and install the bolt and nut finger tight.
5. Position the opposite end of the of the axle to the radius arm, install the attaching bolt from underneath through the bracket, the radius arm and the axle. Install the nut and tighten to 120–150 ft. lbs.
6. Install the spring lower seat on the radius arm so that the hole in the seat indexes over the arm to axle bolt. Install the front spring.
7. Install the front wheel spindle.
8. Lower the vehicle on its wheels or support the vehicle on the front springs. Tighten the axle to frame pivot bracket bolt.

Front Wheel Bearings

Removal and Installation

1. Raise the vehicle. Support the vehicle safely and remove the wheel.
2. Remove the brake caliper and wire it to the underbody to prevent damage to the brake hose.
3. Remove the grease cap, cotter pin, retainer adjusting nut and washer. Remove the outer bearing.
4. Pull the hub and rotor off the spindle. Remove and discard the grease seal.
5. Remove the inner bearing from the hub. Remove all traces of old lubricant from the bearings, hub and spindle with solvent and dry thoroughly.
6. Inspect the bearing races for scratches, pits or cracks. If the races are worn or damaged, remove them with a drift.

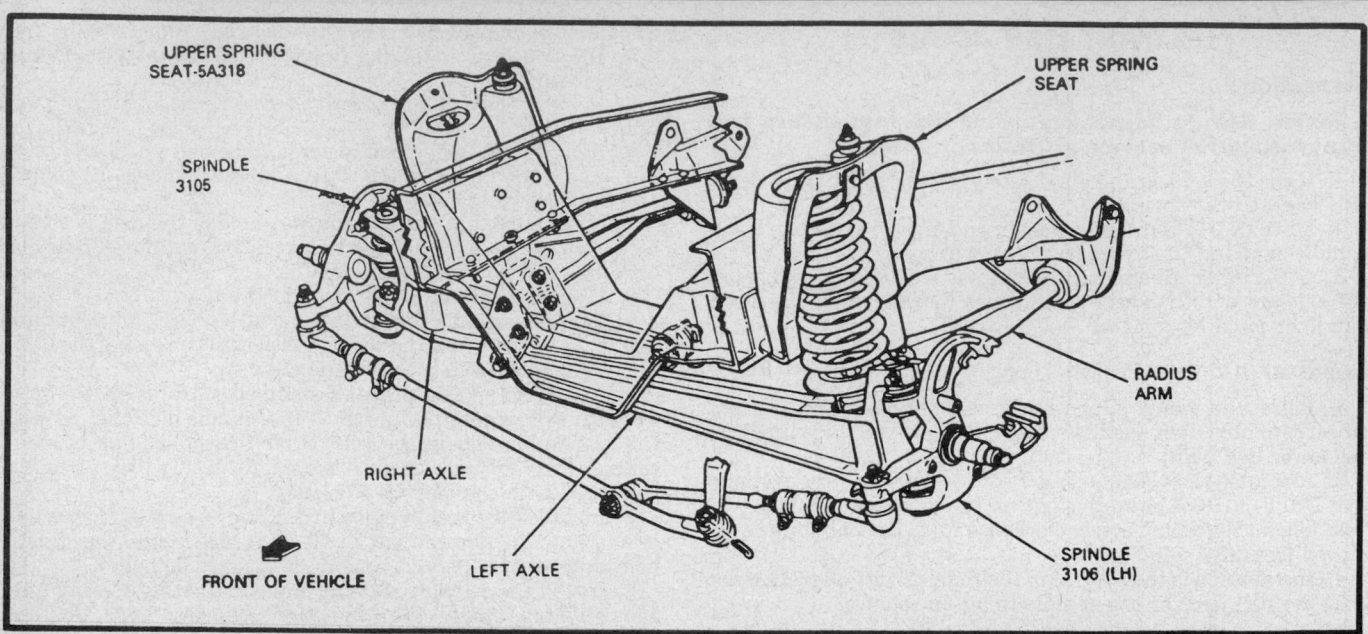

Twin I-Beam axle with ball joints

7. If the inner or outer bearing races were removed, replace them in the hub with the proper tool. The races will be properly seated when they are fully bottomed.

8. Replace the grease retainer. Pack the inside of the hub with lithium base grease, high temperature multi-purpose long life lubricant. Fill the hub until the grease is flush with the inside diameters of both bearing races.

9. Pack the bearings with wheel bearing grease, working as much lubricant as possible between the rollers and the cages.

10. For installation reverse the removal procedure. Adjust the wheel bearings.

Adjustment

2WD VEHICLES

1. Raise the vehicle and support it safely.

2. Remove the wheel cover and the grease cap from the hub. Remove the cotter pin and the locknut. Loosen the adjusting nut 3 turns.

3. Remove the caliper. While rotating the wheel, tighten the adjusting nut to 22–25 ft. lbs. to seat the bearings.

4. Back off the adjusting nut 1/8 turn and install the retainer and new cotter pin without additional movement of the adjusting nut.

5. Check the wheel rotation. The bearing endplay is 0.001–0.010 in. Reinstall the grease cap and the wheel cover.

4WD VEHICLES

1. Raise the vehicle and support it safely.

2. For Bronco and F series (manual locking hubs) with Dana 44IFS front axle, use the following:

    a. Remove the hub lock assembly.

    b. Using a torque wrench and a locknut wrench, apply inward pressure to unlock the adjusting nut locking splines and turn the nut clockwise to tighten to 50–60 ft. lbs. while rotating the wheel back and forth.

    c. Apply inward pressure to the locknut wrench to disengage the adjusting nut locking splines and back off the adjusting nut 180 degress.

    d. Retighten the adjusting nut to 15 ft. lbs. The final endplay on the wheel on the spindle is 0.00–0.006 in. Remove the tools and install the hub lock.

3. For F series (automatic hubs) with Dana 50IIFS and Dana 60 Monobeam front axle, use the following:

    a. Remove the hub lock assembly.

    b. Remove the outer locknut and lockwasher.

    c. Using a locknut wrench, tighten the inner locknut to 50 ft. lbs. to seat the bearing.

    d. Back off the inner locknut and retighten to 31–39 ft. lbs.

    e. While rotating the wheel, back off the locknut 135°–150°. Install the lockwasher. Install the outer locknut and tighten to 160–205 ft. lbs. Install the hub locks.

4. Lower the vehicle. The final endplay on the wheel on the spindle is 0.00–0.006 inch.

REAR SUSPENSION

Shock Absorber

Removal and Installation

BRONCO AND E SERIES

1. Raise the vehicle and support it safely.

2. Remove the shock absorber lower attaching nut and bolt and swing the lower end free of the mounting bracket on the axle housing.

3. Remove the attaching nut from the upper mounting stud and remove the shock absorber.

To install:

4. Position the shock absorber with the rubber bushings and steel washers to the upper mounting bolt.

5. Swing the lower end of the shock absorber into the mounting bracket on the axle housing. Install the attaching washers, mounting bolt and self-locking nut.

6. Install the self-locking nut on the upper mounting bolt.

7. Lower the vehicle.

F SERIES

1. Raise and safely support as necessary. Remove the self-locking nut, steel washer and rubber bushings at the upper and lower ends of the shock absorber.
2. Remove the unit from the vehicle.
3. To install, position the shock absorber on the mounting brackets with the large diameter at the top.
4. Install the rubber bushing, steel washer and self-locking nut.

Leaf Spring

Removal and Installation
E SERIES

1. Raise the rear end of the vehicle and support the chassis with safety stands. Support the rear axle with a floor jack or hoist.
2. Disconnect the lower end of the shock absorber from the bracket on the axle housing.
3. Remove the spring clips (U-bolts) and the spring clip cap.
4. Lower the axle and remove the spring front bolt from the hanger.
5. Remove the 2 attaching bolts from the rear of the spring. Remove the spring and the shackle.
6. Assemble the upper end of the shackle to the spring with the attaching bolt.
7. Connect the front of the spring to the front bracket with the attaching bolt.
8. Assemble the spring and shackle to the rear bracket with the attaching bolt.
9. Place the spring clip plate over the head of the center bolt.
10. Raise the axle with a jack and guiding it so that the center bolt enters the pilot hole in the pad on the axle housing.
11. Install the spring clips, cap and attaching nuts. Tighten the nuts snugly.
12. Connect the lower end of the shock absorber to the lower bracket.
13. Tighten the spring front mounting bolt and nut, the rear shackle nuts and spring clip nuts.
14. Remove the safety stands and lower the vehicle.

F SERIES 2WD

1. Raise the vehicle frame, until the weight is off the rear spring, with the tires still touching the floor.
2. Remove the nuts from the spring U-bolts and drive the U-bolts from the U-bolt plate. If so equipped, remove the auxiliary spring and the spacer.

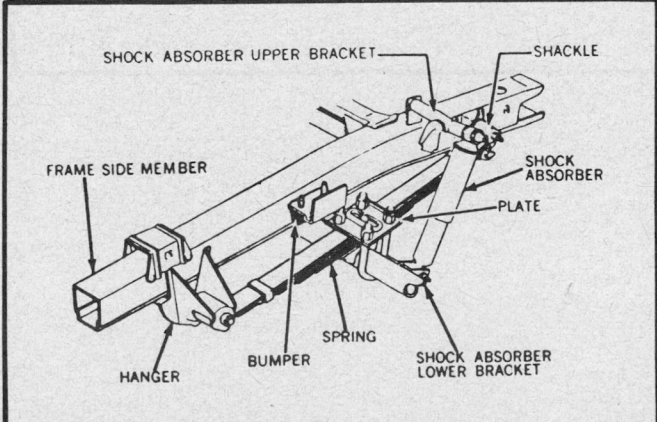

SHOCK ABSORBER UPPER BRACKET — SHACKLE
FRAME SIDE MEMBER
SHOCK ABSORBER
PLATE
SPRING
BUMPER
HANGER
SHOCK ABSORBER LOWER BRACKET

Typical rear suspension

3. Remove the spring-to-bracket nut and bolt at the front of the spring.
4. Remove the shackle upper and lower nuts and bolts at the rear of the spring. Remove the spring and shackle assembly from the rear shackle bracket.
5. If the bushings in the spring or shackle are worn or damaged, replace them.

To install:

6. Position the spring in the shackle and install the upper shackle-to-spring bolt and nut with the bolt head facing outboard.
7. Position the front end of the spring in the bracket and install. Position the shackle in the rear bracket and install.
8. Position the spring on top of the axle with the spring tie bolt centered in the hole provided in the seat. If equipped, install the auxiliary spring and spacer.
9. Install the spring U-bolt plate and nuts. Lower the vehicle. Tighten the spring U-bolt nuts. Tighten the front spring bolt and nut and the rear shackle bolts and nuts.

F SERIES 4WD

1. Raise the vehicle frame until the weight is off the rear springs with the wheels still touching the floor.
2. Remove the nuts from the spring U-bolts.
3. Drive the U-bolts out of the shock absorber lower bracket and the spring cap and remove the U-bolts.
4. Remove the spacer from the top of the spring.
5. If equipped with auxiliary springs, remove the auxiliary spring and spacer.
6. Remove the shackle to bracket bolt and nut from the rear of the spring.
7. Remove the spring-to-hanger bolt and nut from the front of the spring and remove the spring.
8. Remove the shackle-to-spring bolt and nut and remove the shackle from the spring.
9. Position the shackle to the spring and install the attaching bolt and nut. The bolt must be installed so the nut is away from the frame.
10. Position the spring to the spring front hanger and install the attaching bolt and nut.
11. Position the shackle to the bracket and install the attaching bolt and nut.
12. Align the spring toe bolt with the pilot hole in the axle spring seat and, if so equipped, install the auxiliary spring and spacer.
13. Position the spacer on top of the spring and install the U-bolts over the spacer, spring and axle.
14. Position the spring cap and shock lower bracket to the axle and U-bolts. Install the U-bolt attaching nuts.
15. Lower the vehicle and tighten the front spring bracket bolt and nut and the rear shackle bolts and nuts.

BRONCO

1. Raise the vehicle by the axles and install safety stands under the frame.
2. Disconnect the shock absorber from the axle.
3. Remove the U-bolt attaching nuts and remove the U-bolts and the spring clip plate.
4. Lower the axle to relieve spring tension and remove the nut from the spring front attaching bolt.
5. Remove the spring front attaching bolt from the spring and hanger with a drift.
6. Remove the nut from the shackle to hanger attaching bolt and drive the bolt from the shackle and hanger with a drift and remove the spring from the vehicle.
7. Remove the nut from the spring rear attaching bolt. Drive the bolt out of the spring and shackle with a drift.
8. Position the shackle (closed section facing toward front of vehicle) to the spring rear eye and install the bolt and nut.
9. Position the spring front eye and bushing to the spring

front hanger and install the attaching bolt and nut.

10. Position the spring rear eye and bushing to the shackle and install the attaching bolt and nut.

11. Raise the axle to the spring and install the U-bolts (when an axle cap is not used, the U-bolt shank should contact the leaf edges) and spring clip plate. Align the spring leaves.

12. Tighten the U-bolt nuts and the spring front and rear attaching bolt nuts. The U-bolts should contact the spring assembly edges or axle seat.

13. Connect the shock absorber to the axle and tighten the nut.

14. Remove the safety stands and lower the vehicle.

Rear Wheel Bearings

Removal and Installation

DANA FULL FLOATING AXLE

1. Loosen the axle shaft attaching bolts.

2. Raise the rear wheels off the floor and place jackstands under the rear axle housing so that the axle is parallel with the floor.

3. Remove the axle shaft attaching bolts.

4. Remove brake drum, axle shaft and gaskets.

5. With the axle shaft removed, remove the gasket from the axle shaft flange studs.

6. Remove the wheel bearing hub adjusting nuts.

7. Remove the outer bearing cone and pull the wheel straight off the axle.

8. With a suitable tool that will clear the outer bearing cup, drive the inner bearing cone and inner seal out of the wheel hub.

9. Wash all the old grease or axle lubricant out of the wheel hub, using a suitable solvent.

10. Wash the bearing cups and rollers and inspect them for pitting, galling and uneven wear patterns. Inspect the roller for end wear.

11. If the bearing cups are to be replaced, drive them out with a drift. Install the new cups with a block of wood and hammer or press them in.

12. If the bearing cups are properly seated, a 0.0015 in. feeler gauge will not fit between the cup and the wheel hub.

13. Pack each bearing cone and roller with a bearing packer or equivalent.

14. Place the inner bearing cone and roller assembly in the wheel hub. Install a new inner seal in the hub.

15. Install the hub assembly (with hub tab and keyway aligned) and outer bearing.

16. Install and tighten the bearing adjusting nut to 65–75 ft. lbs. while rotating the wheel.

17. Back off (loosen) the adjusting nut ¼ of a turn then tighten to 15–20 ft. lbs.

18. Install axle shafts with new axle flange gaskets.

19. Install drum and tire/wheel assembly. Tighten the axle shaft retaining bolts to 40–50 ft. lbs.

Adjustment

DANA FULL FLOATING AXLE

1. Tighten the bearing adjusting nut to 65–75 ft. lbs. while rotating the wheel.

2. Back off the adjusting nut ¼ of a turn then retorque to 15–20 ft. lbs.

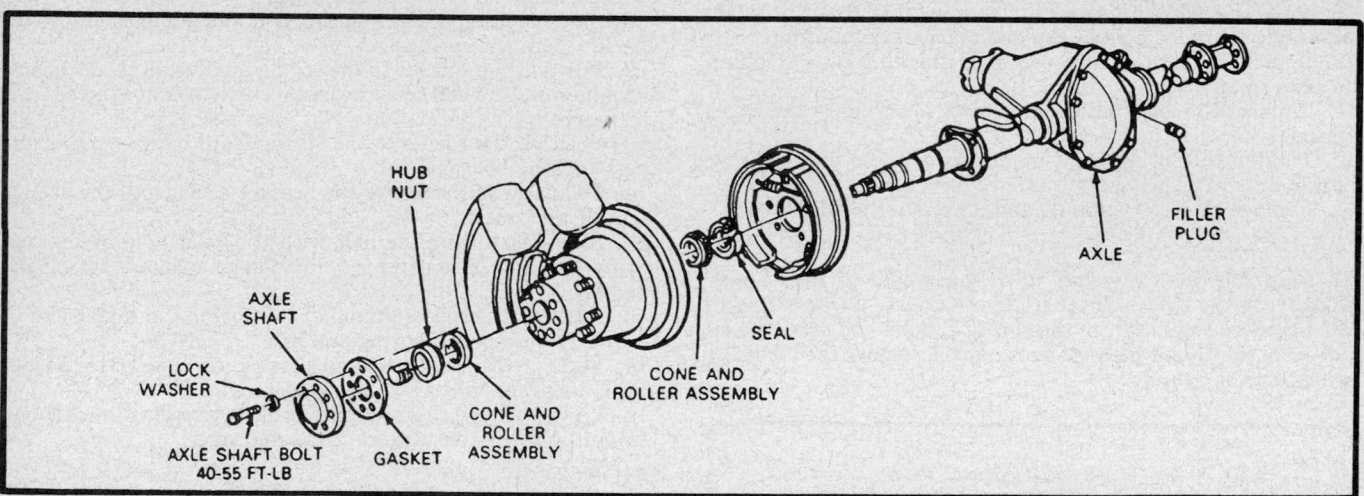

Dana full floating axle rear wheel hub assembly

SPECIFICATIONS

VEHICLE IDENTIFICATION CHART

It is important for servicing and ordering parts to be certain of the vehicle and engine identification. The VIN (vehicle identification number) is a 17 digit number visible through the windshield on the driver's side of the dash and contains the vehicle and engine identification codes. The tenth digit indicates model year and the eighth digit indicates engine code. It can be interpreted as follows:

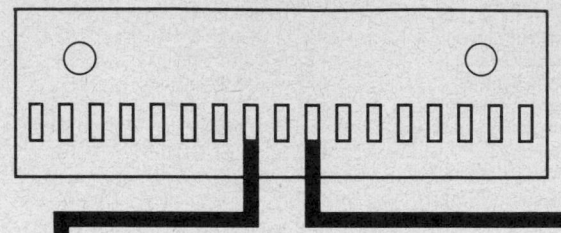

Engine Code

Code	Cu. In.	Liters	Cyl.	Fuel Sys.	Eng. Mfg.
C	122	2.0	4	Carb.	Ford
A	140	2.3	4	EFI	Ford
E	140	2.3	4	(Turbo Diesel)	Mitsubishi
S	171	2.8	6	Carb.	Ford
T	177	2.9	6	EFI	Ford
U	183	3.0	6	EFI	Ford
X	244	4.0	6	EFI	Ford

Model Year

Code	Year
G	1986
H	1987
J	1988
K	1989
L	1990

ENGINE IDENTIFICATION

Year	Model	Engine Displacement cu. in. (liter)	Engine Series Identification (VIN)	No. of Cylinders	Engine Type
1986	Aerostar	140 (2.3)	A	4	OHC
	Aerostar	171 (2.8)	S	6	OHV
	Aerostar	183 (3.0)	U	6	OHV
	Bronco II	177 (2.9)	T	6	OHV
	Ranger	122 (2.0)	C	4	OHC
	Ranger	140 (2.3)	A	4	OHC
	Ranger	140 (2.3)	E	4	OHC ①
	Ranger	177 (2.9)	T	6	OHV
1987	Aerostar	140 (2.3)	A	4	OHC
	Aerostar	171 (2.8)	S	6	OHV
	Aerostar	183 (3.0)	U	6	OHV
	Bronco II	177 (2.9)	T	6	OHV
	Ranger	122 (2.0)	C	4	OHC
	Ranger	140 (2.3)	A	4	OHC
	Ranger	140 (2.3)	E	4	OHC ①
	Ranger	177 (2.9)	T	6	OHV

ENGINE IDENTIFICATION

Year	Model	Engine Displacement cu. in. (liter)	Engine Series Identification (VIN)	No. of Cylinders	Engine Type
1988	Aerostar	183 (3.0)	U	6	OHV
	Bronco II	177 (2.9)	T	6	OHV
	Ranger	122 (2.0)	C	4	OHC
	Ranger	140 (2.3)	A	4	OHC
	Ranger	177 (2.9)	T	6	OHV
1989	Aerostar	183 (3.0)	U	6	OHV
	Bronco II	177 (2.9)	T	6	OHV
	Ranger	140 (2.3)	A	4	OHC
	Ranger	177 (2.9)	T	6	OHV
1990	Aerostar	183 (3.0)	U	6	OHV
	Aerostar	244 (4.0)	X	6	OHV
	Bronco II	177 (2.9)	T	6	OHV
	Ranger	140 (2.3)	A	4	OHC
	Ranger	177 (2.9)	T	6	OHV
	Ranger	244 (4.0)	X	6	OHV

① Turbo Diesel

GENERAL ENGINE SPECIFICATIONS

Year	VIN	No. Cylinder Displacement cu. in. (liter)	Fuel System Type	Net Horsepower @ rpm	Net Torque @ rpm (ft. lbs.)	Bore × Stroke (in.)	Compression Ratio	Oil Pressure @ rpm
1986	C	4-122 (2.0)	1 bbl	73 @ 4000	107 @ 2400	3.52 × 3.13	9.0:1	50 @ 2000
	A	4-140 (2.3)	EFI	90 @ 4000	130 @ 1800	3.78 × 3.13	9.0:1	50 @ 2000
	E	4-140 (2.3)	Diesel	86 @ 4200	134 @ 2000	3.59 × 3.54	21.0:1	11.4 @ 750
	S	6-171 (2.8)	2 bbl.	115 @ 4600	150 @ 2600	3.65 × 2.70	8.7:1	50 @ 2000
	T	6-177 (2.9)	EFI	140 @ 4600	170 @ 2600	3.66 × 2.83	9.0:1	50 @ 2000
	U	6-183 (3.0)	EFI	145 @ 4800	165 @ 3600	3.50 × 3.14	9.3:1	50 @ 2500
1987	C	4-122 (2.0)	2 bbl	80 @ 4200	106 @ 2600	3.52 × 3.13	9.0:1	50 @ 2000
	A	4-140 (2.3)	EFI	90 @ 4000	134 @ 2000	3.78 × 3.13	9.5:1	50 @ 2000
	E	4-140 (2.3)	Diesel	86 @ 4200	134 @ 2000	3.59 × 3.54	21.0:1	11.4 @ 750
	S	6-171 (2.8)	2 bbl.	115 @ 4600	150 @ 2600	3.65 × 2.70	8.7:1	50 @ 2000
	T	6-177 (2.9)	EFI	140 @ 4600	170 @ 2600	3.66 × 2.83	9.0:1	50 @ 2000
	U	6-183 (3.0)	EFI	145 @ 4800	165 @ 3600	3.50 × 3.14	9.3:1	50 @ 2500
1988	C	4-122 (2.0)	2 bbl	80 @ 4200	106 @ 2600	3.52 × 3.13	9.0:1	50 @ 2000
	A	4-140 (2.3)	EFI	90 @ 4000	134 @ 2000	3.78 × 3.13	9.5:1	50 @ 2000
	T	6-177 (2.9)	EFI	140 @ 4600	170 @ 2600	3.66 × 2.83	9.0:1	50 @ 2000
	U	6-183 (3.0)	EFI	145 @ 4800	165 @ 3600	3.50 × 3.14	9.3:1	50 @ 2500
1989–90	A	4-140 (2.3)	EFI	90 @ 4000	134 @ 2000	3.78 × 3.13	9.5:1	50 @ 2000
	T	6-177 (2.9)	EFI	140 @ 4600	170 @ 2600	3.66 × 2.83	9.0:1	50 @ 2000
	U	6-183 (3.0)	EFI	145 @ 4800	165 @ 3600	3.50 × 3.14	9.3:1	50 @ 2500

GASOLINE ENGINE TUNE-UP SPECIFICATIONS

Year	VIN	No. Cylinder Displacement cu. in. (liter)	Spark Plugs Type	Gap (in.)	Ignition Timing (deg.) MT	AT	Compression Pressure (psi)	Fuel Pump (psi)	Idle Speed (rpm) MT	AT	Valve Clearance In.	Ex.
1986	C	4-122 (2.0)	AWSF-52C	.044	6	—	NA	5–7	800 ①	—	Hyd.	Hyd.
	A	4-140 (2.3)	AWSF-44C	.044	10	10	NA	40	650 ①	700 ①	Hyd.	Hyd.
	S	6-171 (2.8)	AWSF-42C	.044	10	10	NA	5–7	850 ①	750 ①	0.014	0.016
	T	6-177 (2.9)	AWSF-42C	.044	10	10	NA	40	850 ①	800 ①	Hyd.	Hyd.
	U	6-183 (3.0)	AWSF-32P	.044	—	10	NA	40	—	650 ①	Hyd.	Hyd.
1987	C	4-122 (2.0)	AWSF-52C	.044	6	—	NA	5–7	800	—	Hyd.	Hyd.
	A	4-140 (2.3)	AWSF-44C	.044	10	10	NA	39	720	720	Hyd.	Hyd.
	S	6-171 (2.8)	AWSF-42C	.044	10	10	NA	5–7	850 ①	750 ①	0.014	0.016
	T	6-177 (2.9)	AWSF-42C	.044	10	10	NA	40	850	800	Hyd.	Hyd.
	U	6-183 (3.0)	AWSF-32P	.044	10	10	NA	40	800	700	Hyd.	Hyd.
1988	C	4-122 (2.0)	AWSF-32P	.044	6	—	NA	5–7	800	—	Hyd.	Hyd.
	A	4-140 (2.3)	AWSF-44C	.044	10	10	NA	40	720	720	Hyd.	Hyd.
	T	6-177 (2.9)	AWSF-42C	.044	10	10	NA	40	850	800	Hyd.	Hyd.
	U	6-183 (3.0)	AWSF-32P	.044	10	10	NA	40	800	700	Hyd.	Hyd.
1989–90	A	4-140 (2.3)	AWSF-44C	.044	10	10	NA	40	720	720	Hyd.	Hyd.
	T	6-177 (2.9)	AWSF-42C	.044	10	10	NA	40	720	720	Hyd.	Hyd.
	U	6-183 (3.0)	AWSF-32P	.044	10	10	NA	40	720	720	Hyd.	Hyd.

① Electronically controlled—not adjustable

DIESEL ENGINE TUNE-UP SPECIFICATIONS

Year	VIN	No. Engine Displacement cu. in. (liter)	Valve Clearance Intake (in.)	Exhaust (in.)	Intake Valve Opens (deg.)	Injection Pump Setting (deg.)	Injection Nozzle Pressure (psi) New	Used	Idle Speed (rpm)	Cranking Compression Pressure (psi)
1986	E	4-140 (2.3)	0.010	0.010	20° BTDC	5° ①	—	③	750	384 ②
1987	E	4-140 (2.3)	0.010	0.010	20° BTDC	5° ①	—	③	750	384 ②

① Static timing
② At 250 rpm
③ 1707–1849 PSI

FIRING ORDERS

NOTE: To avoid confusion, always replace spark plug wires one at a time.

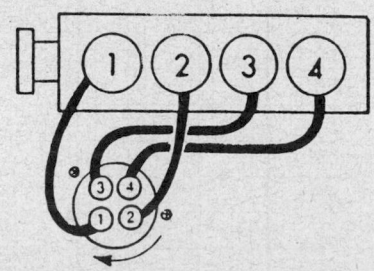

122 (2.0L) and 140 (2.3L) 4 cylinder
Engine firing order: 1–3–4–2
Distributor rotation: clockwise

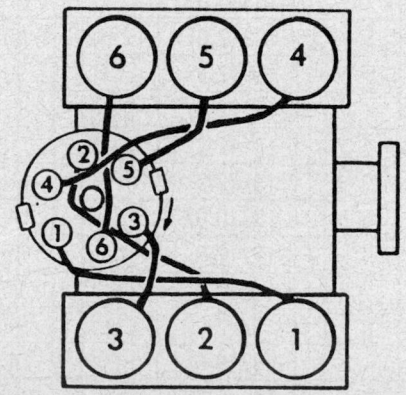

171 (2.8L), 177 (2.9L) and 183 (3.0L) V6 engines
Firing order: 1–4–2–5–3–6
Distributor rotation: clockwise

CAPACITIES

Year	Model	VIN	No. Cylinder Displacement cu. in (liter)	Engine Crankcase with Filter	Engine Crankcase without Filter	Transmission (pts.) 4-Spd	Transmission (pts.) 5-Spd	Transmission (pts.) Auto.	Drive Axle (pts.)	Fuel Tank (gal.)	Cooling System (qts.)
1986	Aerostar	A	4-140 (2.3)	5	4	—	3	19	5	17	7
	Aerostar	S	6-171 (2.8)	5	4	—	3	19	5	17	8
	Aerostar	U	6-183 (3.0)	5	4	—	3	19	5	17	8
	Bronco II	T	6-177 (2.9)	5	4	3	3	16	②	23	7.8
	Ranger	C	4-122 (2.0)	5	4	—	①	18	②	15	7.8
	Ranger	A	4-140 (2.3)	6.5	5.5	—	①	18	②	15	7.2
	Ranger	E	4-140 (2.3)	6.8	6.8	3.1	—	—	②	15	13
	Ranger	T	6-177 (2.9)	5	4	3	3	16	②	15	13
1987	Aerostar	A	4-140 (2.3)	5	4	—	3	19	5	17	③
	Aerostar	S	6-171 (2.8)	5	4	—	3	19	5	17	8
	Aerostar	U	6-183 (3.0)	5	4	—	3	19	5	17	8
	Bronco II	T	6-177 (2.9)	5	4	3	3	16	②	23	7.8
	Ranger	C	4-122 (2.0)	5	4	—	①	18	②	15	7.8
	Ranger	A	4-140 (2.3)	6.5	5.5	—	①	18	②	15	7.2
	Ranger	E	4-140 (2.3)	6.8	6.8	3.1	—	—	②	15	13
	Ranger	T	6-177 (2.9)	5	4	3	3	16	②	15	13
1988	Aerostar	U	6-183 (3.0)	5	4	—	3	19	5	17 ④	12
	Bronco II	T	6-177 (2.9)	5	4	3	3	16	②	23	7.8
	Ranger	C	4-122 (2.0)	5	4	—	①	18	②	15	7.8
	Ranger	A	4-140 (2.3)	6.5	5.5	—	①	18	②	15	7.2
	Ranger	T	6-177 (2.9)	5	4	3	3	16	②	15	13
1989–90	Aerostar	U	6-183 (3.0)	5	4	—	3	19	5	17 ④	12
	Bronco II	T	6-177 (2.9)	5	4	3	3	16	②	23	7.8
	Ranger	A	4-140 (2.3)	6.5	5.5	—	①	18	②	15	7.2
	Ranger	T	6-177 (2.9)	5	4	3	3	16	②	15	13

① Mazda trans. 3 pts.
  Mitsubishi trans. 4.8 pts.
② 6³/₄" ring gear 3 pts.
  7¹/₂" ring gear 5 pts.
③ w/Manual 6.8
  w/Automatic 7.6
④ Extended Van 21.0 gal.

CAMSHAFT SPECIFICATIONS

All measurements given in inches.

Year	VIN	No. Cylinder Displacement cu. in. (liter)	Journal Diameter 1	Journal Diameter 2	Journal Diameter 3	Journal Diameter 4	Journal Diameter 5	Lobe Lift In.	Lobe Lift Ex.	Bearing Clearance	Camshaft End Play
1986	C	4-122 (2.0)	1.7713–1.7720	1.7713–1.7720	1.7713–1.7720	1.7713–1.7720	—	0.238	0.238	0.001–0.003	0.001–0.007
	A	4-140 (2.3)	1.7713–1.7720	1.7713–1.7720	1.7713–1.7720	1.7713–1.7720	—	0.238	0.238	0.001–0.003	0.001–0.007
	E	4-140 (2.3)	1.181	1.181	1.181	1.181	—	NA	NA	0.002–0.004	NA

FORD MOTOR COMPANY
RANGER • BRONCO II • AEROSTAR

CAMSHAFT SPECIFICATIONS
All measurements given in inches.

Year	VIN	No. Cylinder Displacement cu. in. (liter)	Journal Diameter					Lobe Lift		Bearing Clearance	Camshaft End Play
			1	2	3	4	5	In.	Ex.		
1986	S	6-171 (2.8)	1.7285–1.7293	1.7135–1.7143	1.6985–1.6992	1.6835–1.6842	—	0.255	0.255	0.001–0.003	0.001–0.004
	T	6-177 (2.9)	1.7285–1.7293	1.7135–1.7143	1.6985–1.6992	1.6835–1.6842	—	0.359	0.370	0.001–0.003	0.001–0.004
	U	6-183 (3.0)	2.0074–2.0084	2.0074–2.0084	2.0074–2.0084	2.0074–2.0084	—	0.260	0.260	0.001–0.003	①
1987	C	4-122 (2.0)	1.7713–1.7720	1.7713–1.7720	1.7713–1.7720	1.7713–1.7720	—	0.238	0.238	0.001–0.003	0.001–0.007
	A	4-140 (2.3)	1.7713–1.7720	1.7713–1.7720	1.7713–1.7720	1.7713–1.7720	—	0.238	0.238	0.001–0.003	0.001–0.007
	E	4-140 (2.3)	1.181	1.181	1.181	1.181	—	NA	NA	0.002–0.004	NA
	S	6-171 (2.8)	1.7285–1.7293	1.7135–1.7143	1.6985–1.6992	1.6835–1.6842	—	0.255	0.255	0.001–0.003	0.001–0.004
	T	6-177 (2.9)	1.7285–1.7293	1.7135–1.7143	1.6985–1.6992	1.6835–1.6842	—	0.359	0.370	0.001–0.003	0.001–0.004
	U	6-183 (3.0)	2.0074–2.0084	2.0074–2.0084	2.0074–2.0084	2.0074–2.0084	—	0.260	0.260	0.001–0.003	①
1988	C	4-122 (2.0)	1.7713–1.7720	1.7713–1.7720	1.7713–1.7720	1.7713–1.7720	—	0.238	0.238	0.001–0.003	0.001–0.007
	A	4-140 (2.3)	1.7713–1.7720	1.7713–1.7720	1.7713–1.7720	1.7713–1.7720	—	0.238	0.238	0.001–0.003	0.001–0.007
	T	6-177 (2.9)	1.7285–1.7293	1.7135–1.7143	1.6985–1.6992	1.6835–1.6842	—	0.359	0.370	0.001–0.003	0.001–0.004
	U	6-183 (3.0)	2.0074–2.0084	2.0074–2.0084	2.0074–2.0084	2.0074–2.0084	—	0.260	0.260	0.001–0.003	0.007
1989–90	A	4-140 (2.3)	1.7713–1.7720	1.7713–1.7720	1.7713–1.7720	1.7713–1.7720	—	0.238	0.238	0.001–0.003	0.001–0.007
	T	6-177 (2.9)	1.7285–1.7293	1.7135–1.7143	1.6985–1.6992	1.6835–1.6842	—	0.359	0.370	0.001–0.003	0.001–0.004
	U	6-183 (3.0)	2.0074–2.0084	2.0074–2.0084	2.0074–2.0084	2.0074–2.0084	—	0.260	0.260	0.001–0.003	0.007

① No endplay specification—camshaft is retained by spring

CRANKSHAFT AND CONNECTING ROD SPECIFICATIONS

All measurements are given in inches.

Year	VIN	No. Cylinder Displacement cu. in. (liter)	Crankshaft Main Brg. Journal Dia.	Main Brg. Oil Clearance	Shaft End-play	Thrust on No.	Connecting Rod Journal Diameter	Oil Clearance	Side Clearance
1986	C	4-122 (2.0)	2.3982–2.3990	0.0008–0.0015	0.0040–0.0080	3	2.0472	0.0008–0.0015	0.0035–0.0105
	A	4-140 (2.3)	2.3982–2.3990	0.0008–0.0015	0.0040–0.0080	3	2.0472	0.0008–0.0015	0.0035–0.0105
	E	4-140 (2.3)	2.598	0.0008–0.0020	0.0008–0.0020	3	2.087	0.0008–0.0024	0.0008–0.0020
	S	6-171 (2.8)	2.2441	0.0008–0.0015	0.012	3	2.1260	0.0006–0.0016	0.0040–0.0110
	T	6-177 (2.9)	2.2433–2.2441	0.0008–0.0015	0.0040–0.0080	3	2.1252–2.1260	0.0006–0.0016	0.0040–0.0110
	U	6-183 (3.0)	2.5190–2.5198	0.0010–0.0014	0.0040–0.0080	3	2.1253–2.1261	0.0010–0.0014	0.0060–0.0140
1987	C	4-122 (2.0)	2.3982–2.3990	0.0008–0.0015	0.0040–0.0080	3	2.0472	0.0008–0.0015	0.0035–0.0105
	A	4-140 (2.3)	2.3982–2.3990	0.0008–0.0015	0.0040–0.0080	3	2.0472	0.0008–0.0015	0.0035–0.0105
	E	4-140 (2.3)	2.598	0.0008–0.0020	0.0008–0.0020	3	2.087	0.0008–0.0024	0.0008–0.0020
	S	6-171 (2.8)	2.2441	0.0008–0.0015	0.012	3	2.1260	0.0006–0.0016	0.0040–0.0110
	T	6-177 (2.9)	2.2433–2.2441	0.0008–0.0015	0.0040–0.0080	3	2.1252–2.1260	0.0006–0.0016	0.0040–0.0110
	U	6-183 (3.0)	2.5190–2.5198	0.0010–0.0014	0.0040–0.0080	3	2.1253–2.1261	0.0010–0.0014	0.0060–0.0140
1988	C	4-122 (2.0)	2.3982–2.3990	0.0008–0.0015	0.0040–0.0080	3	2.0472	0.0008–0.0015	0.0035–0.0105
	A	4-140 (2.3)	2.3982–2.3990	0.0008–0.0015	0.0040–0.0080	3	2.0472	0.0008–0.0015	0.0035–0.0105
	T	6-177 (2.9)	2.2433–2.2441	0.0008–0.0015	0.0040–0.0080	3	2.1252–2.1260	0.0006–0.0016	0.0040–0.0110
	U	6-183 (3.0)	2.5190–2.5198	0.0010–0.0014	0.0040–0.0080	3	2.1253–2.1261	0.0010–0.0014	0.0060–0.0140
1989–90	A	4-140 (2.3)	2.3982–2.3990	0.0008–0.0015	0.0040–0.0080	3	2.0472	0.0008–0.0015	0.0035–0.0105
	T	6-177 (2.9)	2.2433–2.2441	0.0008–0.0015	0.0040–0.0080	3	2.1252–2.1260	0.0006–0.0016	0.0040–0.0110
	U	6-183 (3.0)	2.5190–2.5198	0.0010–0.0014	0.0040–0.0080	3	2.1253–2.1261	0.0010–0.0014	0.0060–0.0140

VALVE SPECIFICATIONS

Year	VIN	No. Cylinder Displacement cu. in. (liter)	Seat Angle (deg.)	Face Angle (deg.)	Spring Test Pressure (lbs.)	Spring Installed Height (in.)	Stem-to-Guide Clearance (in.) Intake	Stem-to-Guide Clearance (in.) Exhaust	Stem Diameter (in.) Intake	Stem Diameter (in.) Exhaust
1986	C	4-122 (2.0)	45	44	149	1.49	0.0010–0.0027	0.0015–0.0032	0.3420	0.3415
	A	4-140 (2.3)	45	44	149	1.49	0.0010–0.0027	0.0015–0.0032	0.3420	0.3415
	E	4-140 (2.3)	45	44	149	1.49	0.0010–0.0027	0.0015–0.0032	0.3420	0.3415
	S	6-171 (2.8)	45	44	144	1.58	0.0008–0.0025	0.0018–0.0035	0.3163	0.3133
	T	6-177 (2.9)	45	44	144	1.58	0.0008–0.0025	0.0018–0.0035	0.3163	0.3133
	U	6-183 (3.0)	45	44	185	1.85	0.0010–0.0027	0.0015–0.0032	0.3135	0.3125
1987	C	4-122 (2.0)	45	44	149	1.49	0.0010–0.0027	0.0015–0.0032	0.3420	0.3415
	A	4-140 (2.3)	45	44	149	1.49	0.0010–0.0027	0.0015–0.0032	0.3420	0.3415
	E	4-140 (2.3)	45	44	149	1.49	0.0010–0.0027	0.0015–0.0032	0.3420	0.3415
	S	6-171 (2.8)	45	44	144	1.58	0.0008–0.0025	0.0018–0.0035	0.3163	0.3133
	T	6-177 (2.9)	45	44	144	1.58	0.0008–0.0025	0.0018–0.0035	0.3163	0.3133
	U	6-183 (3.0)	45	44	185	1.85	0.0010–0.0027	0.0015–0.0032	0.3135	0.3125
1988	C	4-122 (2.0)	45	44	149	1.49	0.0010–0.0027	0.0015–0.0032	0.3420	0.3415
	A	4-140 (2.3)	45	44	149	1.49	0.0010–0.0027	0.0015–0.0032	0.3420	0.3415
	T	6-177 (2.9)	45	44	144	1.58	0.0008–0.0025	0.0018–0.0035	0.3163	0.3133
	U	6-183 (3.0)	45	44	185	1.85	0.0010–0.0027	0.0015–0.0032	0.3135	0.3125
1989–90	A	4-140 (2.3)	45	44	149	1.49	0.0010–0.0027	0.0015–0.0032	0.3420	0.3415
	T	6-177 (2.9)	45	44	144	1.58	0.0008–0.0025	0.0018–0.0035	0.3163	0.3133
	U	6-183 (3.0)	45	44	185	1.85	0.0010–0.0027	0.0015–0.0032	0.3135	0.3125

PISTON AND RING SPECIFICATIONS
All measurements are given in inches.

Year	VIN	No. Cylinder Displacement cu. in. (liter)	Piston Clearance	Ring Gap Top Compression	Bottom Compression	Oil Control	Ring Side Clearance Top Compression	Bottom Compression	Oil Control
1986	C	4-122 (2.0)	0.0014–0.0022	0.0100–0.0200	0.0100–0.0200	0.0150–0.0550	0.0020–0.0040	0.0020–0.0040	Snug
	A	4-140 (2.3)	0.0014–0.0022	0.0100–0.0200	0.0100–0.0200	0.0150–0.0550	0.0020–0.0040	0.0020–0.0040	Snug
	E	4-140 (2.3)	0.0016–0.0024	0.0100–0.0160	0.0100–0.0160	0.0100–0.0180	0.0010–0.0020	0.0010–0.0030	0.0010–0.0030
	S	6-171 (2.8)	0.0011–0.0019	0.0150–0.0230	0.0150–0.0230	0.0150–0.0550	0.0020–0.0033	0.0020–0.0033	Snug
	T	6-177 (2.9)	0.0011–0.0019	0.0150–0.0230	0.0150–0.0230	0.0150–0.0550	0.0020–0.0033	0.0020–0.0033	Snug
	U	6-183 (3.0)	0.0012–0.0023	0.0100–0.0200	0.0100–0.0200	0.0100–0.0490	0.0016–0.0037	0.0016–0.0037	Snug
1987	C	4-122 (2.0)	0.0014–0.0022	0.0100–0.0200	0.0100–0.0200	0.0150–0.0550	0.0020–0.0040	0.0020–0.0040	Snug
	A	4-140 (2.3)	0.0014–0.0022	0.0100–0.0200	0.0100–0.0200	0.0150–0.0550	0.0020–0.0040	0.0020–0.0040	Snug
	E	4-140 (2.3)	0.0016–0.0024	0.0100–0.0160	0.0100–0.0160	0.0100–0.0180	0.0010–0.0020	0.0010–0.0030	0.0010–0.0030
	S	6-171 (2.8)	0.0011–0.0019	0.0150–0.0230	0.0150–0.0230	0.0150–0.0550	0.0020–0.0033	0.0020–0.0033	Snug
	T	6-177 (2.9)	0.0011–0.0019	0.0150–0.0230	0.0150–0.0230	0.0150–0.0550	0.0020–0.0033	0.0020–0.0033	Snug
	U	6-183 (3.0)	0.0012–0.0023	0.0100–0.0200	0.0100–0.0200	0.0100–0.0490	0.0016–0.0037	0.0016–0.0037	Snug
1988	C	4-122 (2.0)	0.0014–0.0022	0.0100–0.0200	0.0100–0.0200	0.0150–0.0550	0.0020–0.0040	0.0020–0.0040	Snug
	A	4-140 (2.3)	0.0014–0.0022	0.0100–0.0200	0.0100–0.0200	0.0150–0.0550	0.0020–0.0040	0.0020–0.0040	Snug
	T	6-177 (2.9)	0.0011–0.0019	0.0150–0.0230	0.0150–0.0230	0.0150–0.0550	0.0020–0.0033	0.0020–0.0033	Snug
	U	6-183 (3.0)	0.0012–0.0023	0.0100–0.0200	0.0100–0.0200	0.0100–0.0490	0.0016–0.0037	0.0016–0.0037	Snug
1989–90	A	4-140 (2.3)	0.0014–0.0022	0.0100–0.0200	0.0100–0.0200	0.0150–0.0550	0.0020–0.0040	0.0020–0.0040	Snug
	T	6-177 (2.9)	0.0011–0.0019	0.0150–0.0230	0.0150–0.0230	0.0150–0.0550	0.0020–0.0033	0.0020–0.0033	Snug
	U	6-183 (3.0)	0.0012–0.0023	0.0100–0.0200	0.0100–0.0200	0.0100–0.0490	0.0016–0.0037	0.0016–0.0037	Snug

TORQUE SPECIFICATIONS

All readings in ft. lbs.

Year	VIN	No. Cylinder Displacement cu. in. (liter)	Cylinder Head Bolts	Main Bearing Bolts	Rod Bearing Bolts	Crankshaft Pulley Bolts	Flywheel Bolts	Manifold Intake	Manifold Exhaust	Spark Plugs
1986	C	4-122 (2.0)	①	①	⑦	100–120	56–64	20	23	10
	A	4-140 (2.3)	①	①	⑦	100–120	56–64	20	23	10
	E	4-140 (2.3)	②	55–61	33–34	123–137	94–101	15	15	—
	S	6-171 (2.8)	③	65–75	19–24	85–96	47–52	18	25	18
	T	6-177 (2.9)	④	65–75	19–24	85–96	47–52	18	25	18
	U	6-183 (3.0)	⑤	65–81	⑧	141–169	54–64	18	25	10
1987	C	4-122 (2.0)	①	①	⑦	100–120	56–64	20	23	10
	A	4-140 (2.3)	①	①	⑦	100–120	56–64	20	23	10
	E	4-140 (2.3)	②	55–61	33–34	123–137	94–101	15	15	—
	S	6-171 (2.8)	③	65–75	19–24	85–96	47–52	18	25	18
	T	6-177 (2.9)	④	65–75	19–24	85–96	47–52	18	25	18
	U	6-183 (3.0)	⑤	65–81	⑧	141–169	54–64	18	25	10
1988	C	4-122 (2.0)	①	①	⑦	100–120	56–64	20	23	10
	A	4-140 (2.3)	①	①	⑦	100–120	56–64	20	23	10
	T	6-177 (2.9)	④	65–75	19–24	85–96	47–52	18	25	18
	U	6-183 (3.0)	⑤	65–81	⑧	107	59	18	19	10
1989–90	A	4-140 (2.3)	①	①	⑦	100–120	56–64	20	23	10
	T	6-177 (2.9)	④	65–75	19–24	85–96	47–52	18	25	18
	U	6-183 (3.0)	⑥	66	26	107	59	18	19	10

① Torque in 2 steps:
  A. 50–60
  B. 80–90
② Cold 76–83
  Hot 84–90

③ Torque in 3 steps:
  A. 29–40
  B. 40–51
  C. 70–85

④ Torque in 3 steps:
  A. 22
  B. 51–55
  C. Then turn 90°

⑤ Torque in 2 steps:
  A. 48–54
  B. 63–80
⑥ Torque in 2 steps:
  A. 37
  B. 68

⑦ Torque in 2 steps:
  A. 25–30
  B. 30–36
⑧ Torque in 3 steps:
  A. 20–28
  B. Back off a minimum of 2 turns
  C. 20–25

BRAKE SPECIFICATIONS

All measurements in inches unless noted

Year	Model	Lug Nut Torque (ft. lbs.)	Master Cylinder Bore	Brake Disc Minimum Thickness	Brake Disc Maximum Runout	Standard Brake Drum Diameter	Minimum Lining Thickness Front	Minimum Lining Thickness Rear
1986	Aerostar	85–115	N/A	0.810	0.003	9.000 ①	0.030	0.030
	Bronco II	85–115	0.9375	0.810	0.003	9.000 ②	0.030	0.030
	Ranger	85–115	0.9375	0.810	0.003	9.000 ②	0.030	0.030
1987	Aerostar	85–115	N/A	0.810	0.003	9.000 ①	0.030	0.030
	Bronco II	85–115	0.9375	0.810	0.003	9.000 ②	0.030	0.030
	Ranger	85–115	0.9375	0.810	0.003	9.000 ②	0.030	0.030
1988	Aerostar	85–115	N/A	0.810	0.003	9.000 ①	0.030	0.030
	Bronco II	85–115	0.9375	0.810	0.003	9.000 ②	0.030	0.030
	Ranger	85–115	0.9375	0.810	0.003	9.000 ②	0.030	0.030
1989–90	Aerostar	85–115	N/A	0.810	0.003	9.000 ①	0.030	0.030
	Bronco II	85–115	0.9375	0.810	0.003	9.000 ②	0.030	0.030
	Ranger	85–115	0.9375	0.810	0.003	9.000 ②	0.030	0.030

① Option w/10″ rear brakes—10.000
② 4WD Models use 10″ rear brakes—10,000

WHEEL ALIGNMENT

Year	Model	Caster Range (deg.)	Caster Preferred Setting (deg.)	Camber Range (deg.)	Camber Preferred Setting (deg.)	Toe-in (in.)	Steering Axis Inclination (deg.)
1986	Aerostar	3–5	4	5/16N to 11/16P	3/16	1/32	N/A
	Bronco II	①	—	①	—	①	N/A
	Ranger 2WD	②	—	②	—	②	N/A
	Ranger 4WD	①	—	①	—	①	N/A
1987	Aerostar	3–5	4	5/16N to 11/16P	3/16	1/32	N/A
	Bronco II	①	—	①	—	①	N/A
	Ranger 2WD	②	—	②	—	②	N/A
	Ranger 4WD	①	—	①	—	①	N/A
1988	Aerostar	2½–4½	3½	5/16N to 11/16P	3/16	1/32	N/A
	Bronco II	①	—	①	—	①	N/A
	Ranger 2WD	②	—	②	—	②	N/A
	Ranger 4WD	①	—	①	—	①	N/A
1989–90	Aerostar	2½–4½	3½	3/4N to 3/4P	0	1/32	N/A
	Bronco II	④	—	④	—	④	N/A
	Ranger 2WD	③	—	③	—	③	N/A
	Ranger 4WD	④	—	④	—	④	N/A

① Ride Height

Ride Height	Caster		Camber		Toe-In
2¾–3	5½	8½	2N	½N	1/32
3¼–3½	4	7	1N	½	1/32
3½–3¾	3	6	0	1½	1/32
4–4¼	2	5	1	2½	1/32
4¼–4½	1	4	2	3½	1/32

② Ride Height

w/Forged Axle

Ride Height	Caster		Camber		Toe-In
3¼–3½	5¼	8¼	2N	½N	1/32
3½–3¾	4½	7½	1⅝N	⅛	1/32
3¾–4	3½	6½	½N	1	1/32
4–4¼	3	6	¼	1¾	1/32
4½–4¾	1⅞	4⅞	1¼	2¾	1/32

w/Stamped Axle

Ride Height	Caster		Camber		Toe-In
3–3¼	5¼	8¼	2N	½N	1/32
3¼–3½	4½	7½	1⅝N	⅛	1/32
3½–3¾	3½	6½	½N	1	1/32
3¾–4	3	6	¼	1¾	1/32
4¼–4½	1⅞	4⅞	1¼	2¾	1/32

③ Ride Height

Ride Height	Caster		Camber		Toe-In
3¼–3½	6⅛	8¾	1½N	1	0
3½–3¾	5½	8⅛	1N	1¾	0
3¾–4	4⅝	7½	¼N	2⅜	0
4–4¼	3¾	6⅝	⅜	3	0
4¼–4½	3¼	5¾	1	4	0
4½–4¾	2½	5¼	2	4⅝	0

④ Ride Height

Ride Height	Caster		Camber		Toe-In
2¾–3	5¼	8	2N	½	0
3¼–3½	4	6½	⅞N	1¾	0
3½–3¾	3¼	6	¼N	2⅜	0
3¾–4	2⅝	5¼	⅜	2⅞	0
4–4½	1⅞	4⅝	⅞	3½	0
4¼–4½	1⅛	3⅞	1½	4¼	0

N—Negative
P—Positive

ENGINE ELECTRICAL

NOTE: Disconnecting the negative battery cable on some vehicles may interfere with the functions of the on board computer systems and may require the computer to undergo a relearning process, once the negative battery cable is reconnected.

Distributor

Removal and Installation

DURASPARK II IGNITION SYSTEM

1. Disconnect the negative battery cable. Remove the distributor cap and position the cap and ignition wires to the side.
2. Disconnect and plug the vacuum hose(s) from the vacuum diaphragm assembly
3. Disconnect the wire harness plug from the distributor connector.
4. Rotate the engine to align the stator pole and any armature pole.
5. Scribe a mark on the distributor body and engine block to indicate the position of the rotor tip and position of the distributor in the engine.
6. Remove the holddown bolt and clamp located at the base of the distributor.
7. Remove the distributor from the engine. Do not rotate the engine while the distributor is removed.

To install:

8. Position the distributor in the engine with the rotor aligned to the marks made on the distributor, or to the place the rotor pointed when the distributor was removed.
9. Install the mounting bolt and clamp, but do not tighten so the distributor can be turned for ignition timing purposes.
10. If the engine was rotated while the distributor was removed, rotate the engine (in normal direction of rotation) until No. 1 piston is on TDC (Top Dead Center) of the compression stroke. The TDC mark on the crankshaft pulley and the pointer should align. Rotor tip pointing at No. 1 spark plug wire position on distributor cap upon installation.
11. Engage the oil pump intermediate shaft and insert the distributor until fully seated on the engine, if the distributor does not fully seat, turn the engine slightly to fully engage the intermediate shaft.

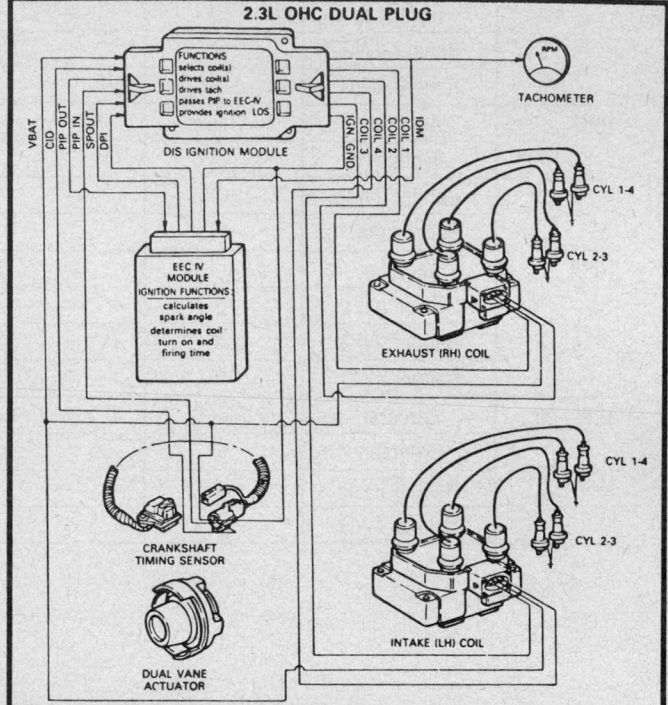

Distributorless Ignition system

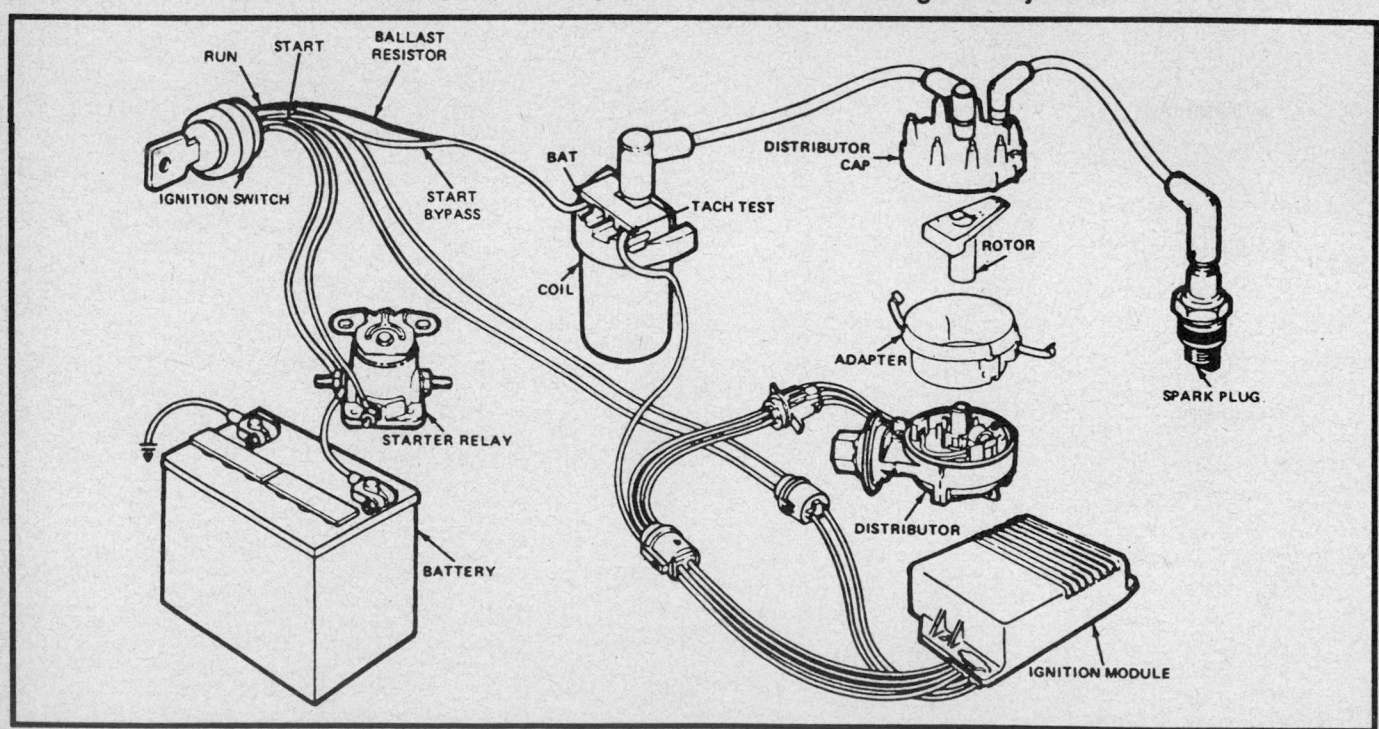

Dura Spark II ignition system

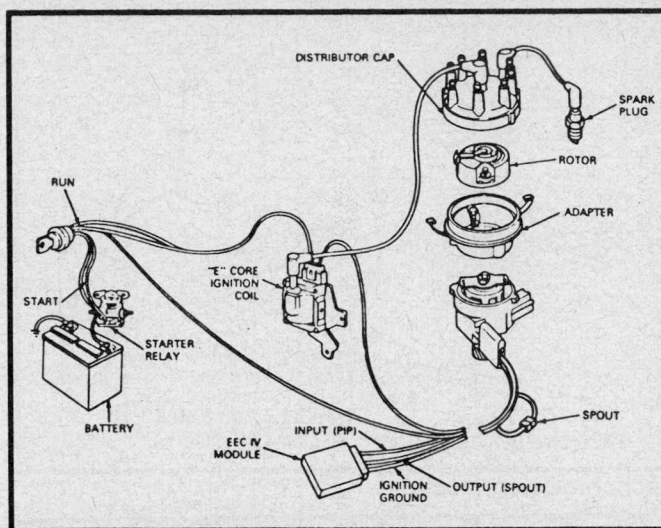

Thick Film Integrated (TFI) ignition system with universal distributor

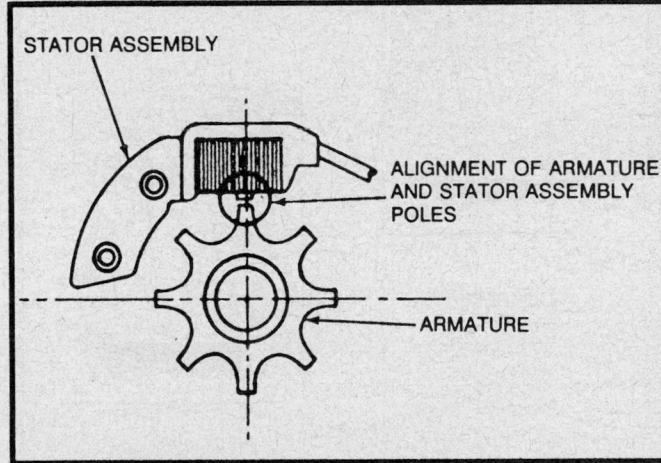

Armature/stator assembly alignment

NOTE: The oil pump intermediate shaft may be turned with a tool to align the shaft with the distributor.

12. Rotate the distributor in block if necessary to align armature and stator assembly poles. Install the distributor holddown bolt but do not fully tighten.

13. Check that No. 1 piston is on compression stroke and timing marks and rotor are aligned in the correct position.

14. Connect distributor to wiring harness connection.

15. Install the distributor cap and wires in the correct position.

16. Reconnect the negative battery cable. Set the initial timing to specifications as shown on the Vehicle Emission Control Information Decal.

17. Tighten the distributor holddown bolt to 17–25 ft. lbs. Recheck the inital timing and readjust if necessary. Connect the diaphragm assembly hose(s).

TFI-IV SYSTEM (THICK FILM INTEGRATED) IGNITION SYSTEM

1. Disconnect the negative battery cable. Disconnect the primary wiring connector from the distributor.

2. Remove the distributor cap and adapter and position it and the attached wires out of the way.

NOTE: Before removing the distributor cap, mark the position of the No. 1 wire tower on the distributor base for installation purposes.

3. Remove the rotor. Remove the TFI connector.

4. Remove the distributor holddown bolt (some engines may be equipped with security type holddown bolt) and clamp.

5. Avoid turning the engine, if possible, while the distributor is removed. If the engine is turned from TDC position, TDC timing marks will have to be reset before the distributor is installed.

6. Rotate the distributor in the engine block to align the leading edge of the vane and the vane switch (vane should be centered in the vane switch stator assembly).

7. Check that No. 1 piston is on compression stroke and timing marks and rotor (rotor tip pointing at No. 1 spark plug wire position on distributor cap) are aligned in the correct position.

8. After the distributor has been fully seated on the block, install the hold down bracket and bolt. Do not fully tighten at this time.

9. Connect the distributor TFI and primary wiring harnesses.

10. Install the distributor rotor and cap adapter. Tighten the attaching screws to 2.1–2.9 ft. lbs.

11. Install the distributor cap and wires in the correct position. Reconnect the negative battery cable.

12. Set the initial timing to specifications as shown on the Vehicle Emission Control Information Decal.

13. Tighten the distributor holddown bolt to 17–25 ft. lbs. Recheck the inital timing and readjust if necessary.

DISTRIBUTORLESS IGNITION SYSTEM

All engine timing and spark distribution is handled electronically with no moving parts. During basic operation the EEC IV module determines the ignition timing required by the engine and DIS module determines which ignition coil to fire.

The distributorless ignition system for the 2.3L (twin spark plug) engine consists of a crankshaft timing sensor, DIS module, 2 ignition coil packs and a spark angle portion of the EEC IV module.

Crankshaft Timing Sensor Assembly

1. Disconnect the negative battery cable.

2. Disconnect the sensor electrical connectors from the engine wiring harness.

3. Remove the large electrical connector from the crankshaft timing sensor assembly by prying out the red retaining clip and removing the 4 wires.

4. Remove the crankshaft pulley assembly by removing the accessory drive belts and then the 4 bolts that retain the crankshaft pulley hub assembly. Remove the timing belt outer cover.

5. Rotate the crankshaft so that the keyway is at the 10 o'clock position. This will place the vane window of both the inner and outer vane cups over the crankshaft sensor timing assembly.

NOTE: The vane cups are attached to the crankshaft pulley hub assembly.

6. Remove the 2 crankshaft timing sensor retaining bolts and the plastic wire harness retainer which secures the crankshaft sensor to its mounting bracket.

7. Remove the crankshaft timing sensor assembly, sliding the wires out from behind the inner timing belt cover.

To install:

8. Remove the large electrical connector from the new crankshaft timing sensor assembly.

9. Position the crankshaft timing sensor assembly. First slide the electrical wires behind the inner timing belt cover, now hold the sensor assembly loosely in place with the retaining bolts but do not tighten the bolts at this time.

10. Install the large electrical connector onto the crankshaft timing sensor assembly.

NOTE: Be sure that the 4 wires to the large electrical connector are installed in the proper locations. The sensor will not function properly if the wires are installed incorrectly.

11. Reconnect both of the crankshaft timing sensor electrical connectors to the engine harness.

12. Rotate the crankshaft so that the outer vane on the crankshaft pulley hub assembly engages both sides of the crankshaft Hall Effect sensor positioner tool T89P–6316–A or equivalent and tighten the sensor assembly retaining bolts to 22–31 inch lbs.

13. Rotate the crankshaft so that the vane on the crankshaft pulley hub is no longer engaged in the crankshaft sensor positioner tool and remove the tool.

14. Install a new plastic wire harness retainer to secure the crankshaft timing sensor harness to its mounting bracket and trim off the excess.

15. Install the timing belt outer cover.

16. Install the crankshaft pulley assembly and tighten the 4 attaching bolts to 12–18 ft. lbs.

17. Install the drive belts and adjust as necessary. Reconnect the negative battery cable and perform a vehicle road test.

Ignition Module Assembly

1. Disconnect the negative battery cable.

2. Disconnect each electrical connector of the DIS ignition module assembly by pushing down the connector locking tabs where it is stamped **PUSH** and then pull it away from the module.

3. Remove the 3 retaining screws, remove the ignition module assembly from the lower intake manifold.

To install:

4. Apply an even coat (approximately $\frac{1}{32}$ in.) of a suitable silicone dielectric compound to the mounting surface of the DIS module.

5. Mount the DIS module assembly onto the intake assembly and install the retaining screws. Torque the screws to 22–31 inch lbs.

6. Install the electrical connectors to the DIS ignition module assembly. Reconnect the negative battery cable.

Ignition Coil Assemblies

1. Disconnect the negative battery cable.

2. Disconnect the electrical harness connector from the ignition coil pack.

3. Remove the spark plug wires by squeezing the locking tabs to release the coil boot retainers.

4. Remove the coil pack mounting screws and remove the coil pack. On vehicle equipped with power steering it may be necessary to remove the intake (left side) coil and bracket as an assembly.

To install:

5. Install the coil pack and the retaining screws. Torque the retaining screws to 40–62 inch lbs.

6. Connect the spark plug wires and connect the electrical connector to the coil pack.

7. Reconnect the negative battery cable. Be sure to place some dielectric compound into each spark plug boot prior to installation of the spark plug wire.

Ignition Timing

Adjustment

The procedure below is for setting inital timing only. This procedure is to be used under normal circumstances. If problems are encountered setting inital timing using this procedure further diagnosis is necessary.

NOTE: On the distributorless ignition system timing is preset and is not adjustable.

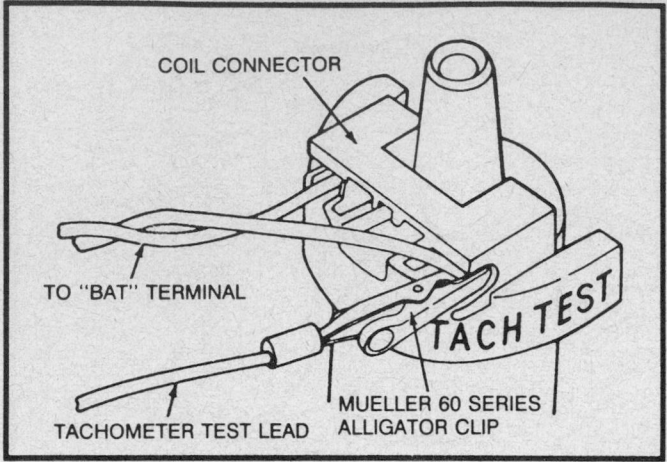

Tachometer connection

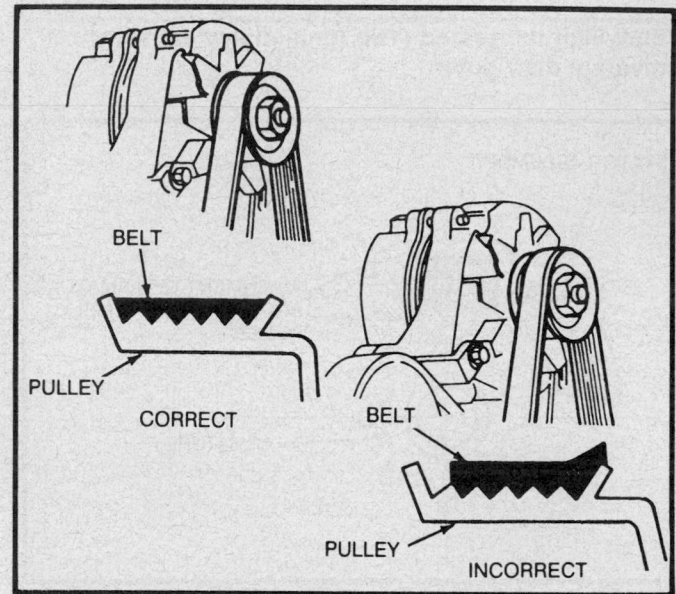

Alternator belt installation

1. Place the transmission in **P** or **N**. Turn the air conditioner and heater to the **Off** position.

2. Remove the vacuum hoses from the distributor vacuum advance connection at the distributor and plug the hoses on non EEC systems.

3. Connect inductive timing light and tachometer (non EEC systems).

4. Disconnect the single wire in line spout connector (near the distributor) or remove the shorting bar from the double spout connector on EEC-IV systems.

5. If the vehicle is equipped on non EEC systems with a barometric pressure switch disconnect it from the ignition module. Install a jumper wire across the pins at the ignition module connector (yellow and black wires).

6. Start the engine and allow it to reach normal operating temperture.

7. With the engine at the timing rpm if specified, check inital timimg.

Alternator

Belt Tension Adjustment

1. Disconnect the negative battery cable. Loosen alternator adjustment and pivot bolts.

2. Position alternator housing using a suitable tool to attain correct belt tension. Use caution not to damage alternator housing.

3. Tighten adjustment bolt and release pressure on tool.

4. Tighten pivot bolt and check belt tension using belt tension gauge T63L–8620A or equivalent. The gauge should be positioned at mid-point between 2 pulleys.

5. The belt tension measurement specification parameters are (new belt) 50–190 lbs. (used belt) 40–160 lbs. and the allowable minimum is 40–90 lbs. Use the parameters as a guideline, and the larger the engine displacement the more tension required for belt adjustment. The smaller the engine displacement the less belt tension required. Reconnect the negative battery cable.

Removal and Installation

1. Disconnect battery ground cable(s).
2. Remove all electrical connectors from the alternator.
3. Loosen the alternator mounting bolts and remove the adjustment arm to alternator attaching bolt.
4. Disengage the alternator belt.
5. Remove the alternator mounting bolt and alternator. Remove the alternator fan shield if so equipped.
6. Installation is the reverse of the removal procedure.

Starter

For further information, please refer to "Electrical" in the Unit Repair section.

Removal and Installation

1. Disconnect the negative battery cable(s).
2. Raise the vehicle and support it safely.
3. Disconnect starter cable at the starter terminal.
3. Remove the starter mounting bolts.
4. Remove the starter assembly.

To install:

5. Position the starter assembly to the flywheel housing and start the mounting bolts.
6. Snug all the bolts while holding the starter squarely against its mounting surface and fully inserted into the pilot hole. Tighten the bolts to 15–20 ft. lbs.

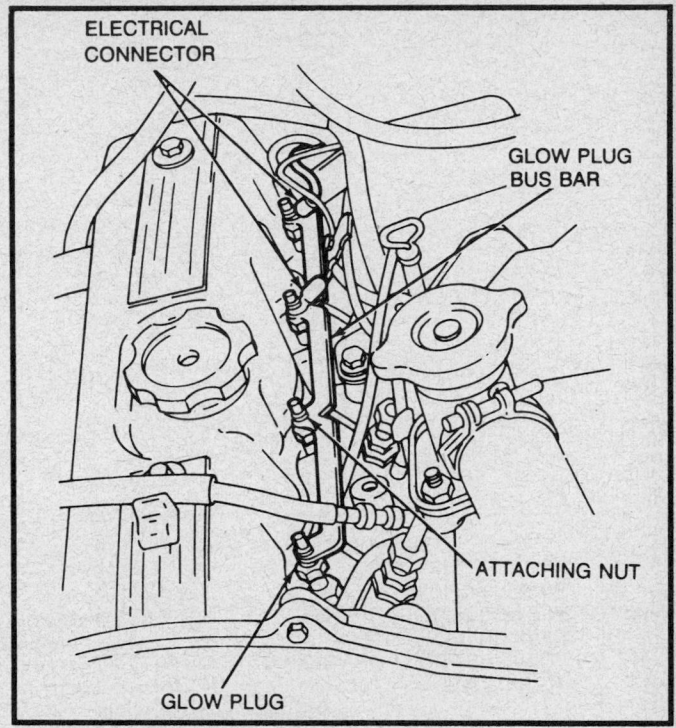

Glow plug installation

7. Reconnect the starter cable at the starter terminal. Lower the vehicle. Connect the negative battery cable(s).

Diesel Glow Plugs

Removal and Installation

1. Disconnect the negative battery cables.
2. Remove the nuts attaching bus bar to glow plugs. Remove glow plugs from the cylinder head.
3. Installation is the reverse of the removal procedure. Tighten the glow plugs to 11–14 ft. lbs. and bus bar attaching nuts to 9–12 inch lbs.

CHASSIS ELECTRICAL

Heater Blower Motor

Removal and Installation
WITH AIR CONDITIONING

1. Disconnect the negative battery cable(s).
2. In the engine compartment, disconnect the wire harness connection from the motor by pushing down on the tab while pulling the connector off at the motor.
3. Remove the solenoid box cover, if so equipped.
4. Remove the air cleaner or the air inlet duct as necessary.
5. Disconnect the cooling tube from the blower motor.
6. Remove the mounting plate screws and remove the motor and wheel assembly from the evaporator assembly housing.
7. Installation is the reverse of removal procedure.

WITHOUT AIR CONDITIONING

1. Disconnect the negative battery cable(s). On California vehicles, remove the emission module forward of the blower motor.
2. On Aerostar, remove the air cleaner and duct as necessary. Remove the vacuum reservoir from the blower.
3. Disconnect the wire harness connection from the motor by pushing down on the tab while pulling the connector off at the motor.
4. Disconnect the cooling tube from the blower motor. Remove the mounting plate screws.
5. Holding the cooling tube aside, pull the motor and wheel assembly from heater blower housing.
6. Installation is the reverse of removal procedure.

Windshield Wiper Motor

Removal and Installation

1. Turn the wiper switch on. Turn the ignition switch **ON** un-

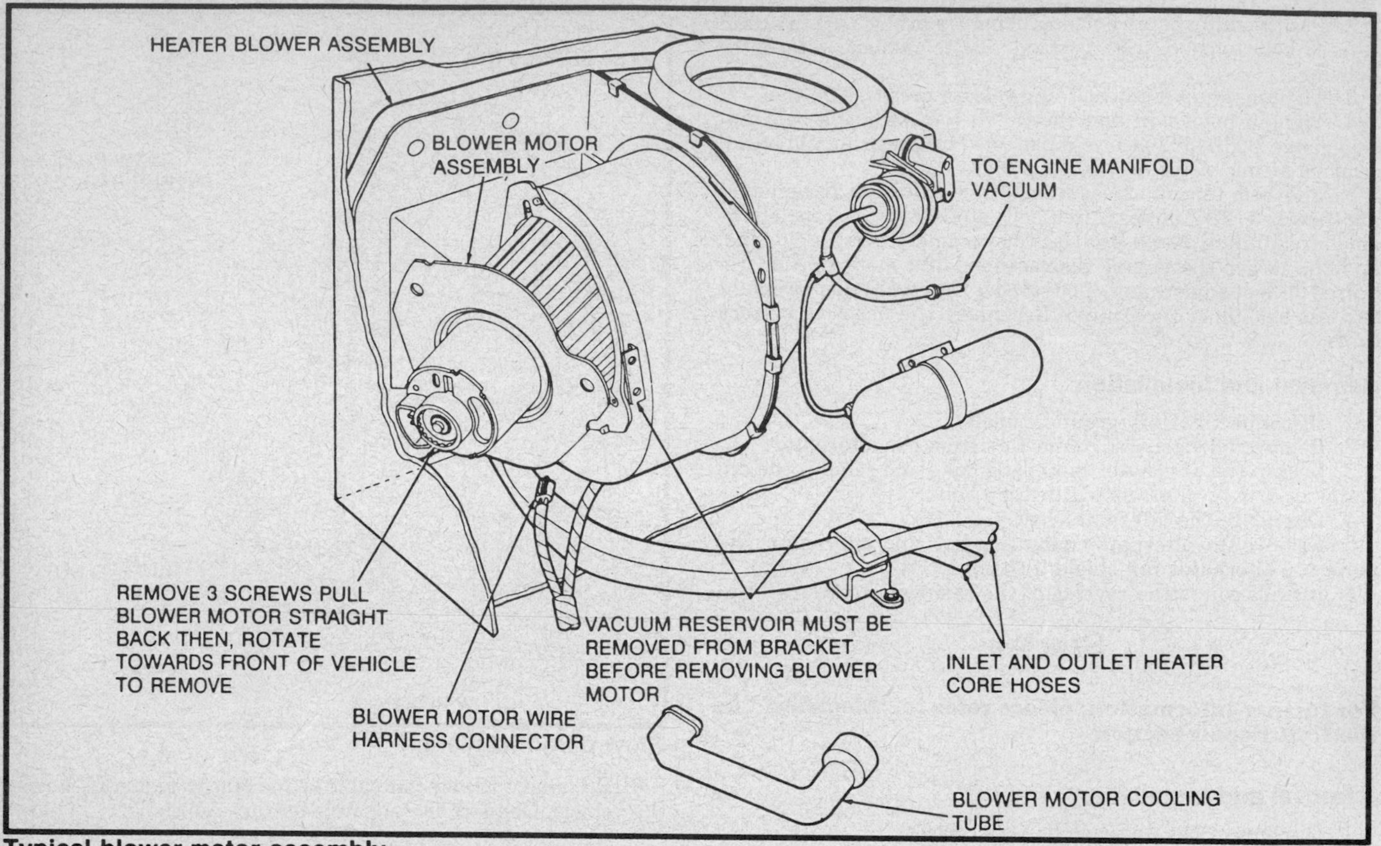

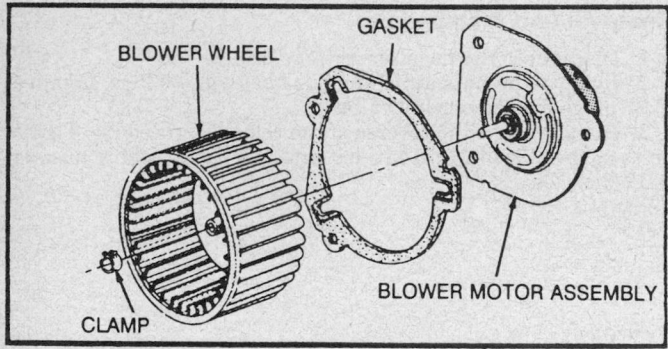

HEATER BLOWER ASSEMBLY

BLOWER MOTOR ASSEMBLY

TO ENGINE MANIFOLD VACUUM

REMOVE 3 SCREWS PULL BLOWER MOTOR STRAIGHT BACK THEN, ROTATE TOWARDS FRONT OF VEHICLE TO REMOVE

VACUUM RESERVOIR MUST BE REMOVED FROM BRACKET BEFORE REMOVING BLOWER MOTOR

INLET AND OUTLET HEATER CORE HOSES

BLOWER MOTOR WIRE HARNESS CONNECTOR

BLOWER MOTOR COOLING TUBE

Typical blower motor assembly

BLOWER WHEEL

GASKET

CLAMP

BLOWER MOTOR ASSEMBLY

Blower motor assembly components

til the blades are straight up. Then turn the ignition switch **OFF** to keep them there.

2. Disconnect the negative battey cable(s). Disconnect the wiper motor wiring connector.

3. Remove the right hand wiper arm and blade. On the Aerostar, remove both wiper arms and the cowl grille.

4. Remove the right hand pivot nut and allow the linkage to drop into the cowl.

5. Remove the linkage access cover, located on the right side of the dash panel near the wiper motor.

6. Reach through the access cover opening and unsnap the wiper motor clip.

7. Push the clip away from the linkage until it clears the crank pin, then push it off of the linkage.

8. Remove the wiper linkage from the motor crank pin. Remove the attaching screws and remove the motor.

9. Installation is the reverse of the removal procedure.

Windshield Wiper Switch

Removal and Installation
AEROSTAR

NOTE: The switch handle is an integral part of the switch and cannot be removed seperately.

1. Disconnect the negative battery cable.
2. Remove the cluster finish panel retaining screws.
3. Remove the 3 left control pod retaining screws.
4. Remove the wiring connector from the switch.
5. Remove the 2 lamp switch to control pod retaining screws and remove the switch.
6. Installation is the reverse of the removal procedure.

BRONCO II AND RANGER

NOTE: The switch handle is an integral part of the switch and cannot be removed seperately.

1. Disconnect the negative battery cable(s).
2. Remove the trim shrouds.
3. Disconnect the electrical connector.
4. Peel back the foam sight shield.
5. Remove the screws holding the switch and remove the switch.
6. Installation is the reverse of the removal procedure.

Instrument Cluster

Removal and Installation
AEROSTAR

1. Disconnect the negative battery cable.
2. Remove the cluster housing.
3. Remove the cluster mounting screws.

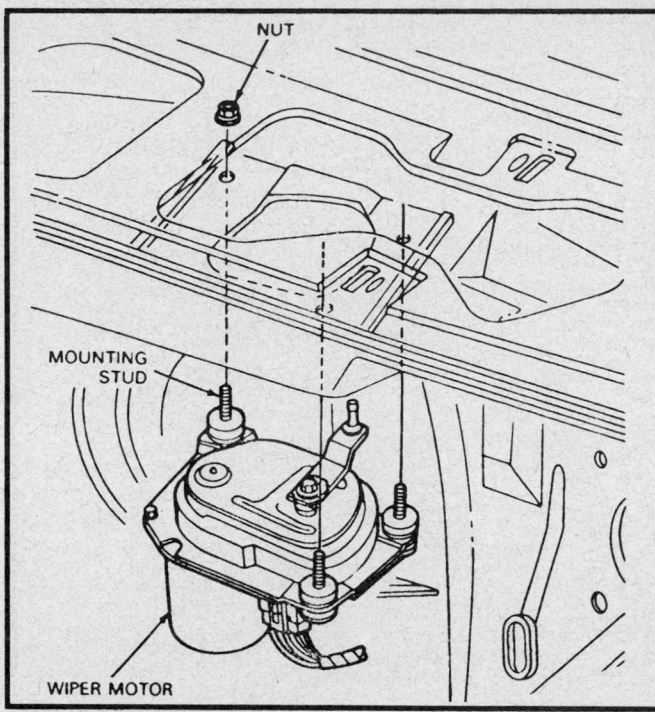

Wiper motor–Aerostar

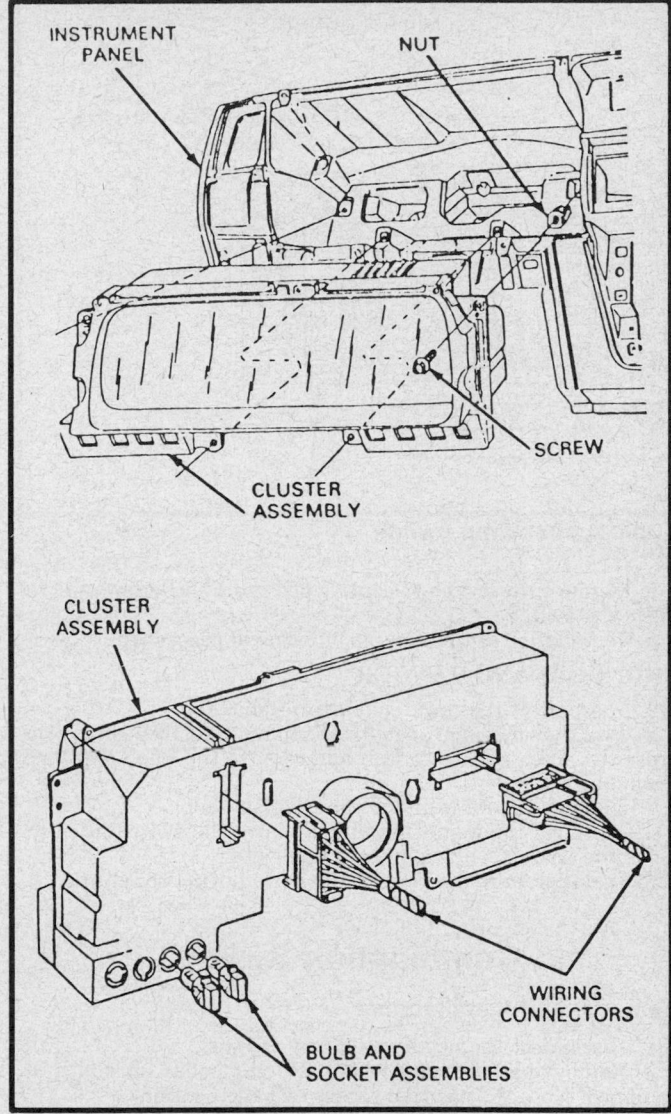

Instrument cluster–Bronco II/Ranger

4. Disconnect the wiring harness connectors from the printed circuit.

5. Disconnect the speedometer cable and remove the cluster assembly.

6. If equipped with an electronic cluster, pull the top toward the steering wheel. Reach behind the cluster and unplug the connectors. Swing the bottom of the cluster out and remove it.

7. Installation is the reverse of removal procedure.

BRONCO II AND RANGER

1. Disconnect the negative battery cable(s).
2. Remove the steering column shroud.
3. If equipped with a tilt steering column, loosen the bolts which attach the column to the band support to provide sufficient clearance for cluster removal.
4. Remove the cluster to panel retaining screws.
5. Position the cluster away from the panel to disconnect the speedometer cable.
6. Disconnect the harness connector plug from the printed circuit and remove the cluster assembly.
7. Installation is the reverse of removal procedure.

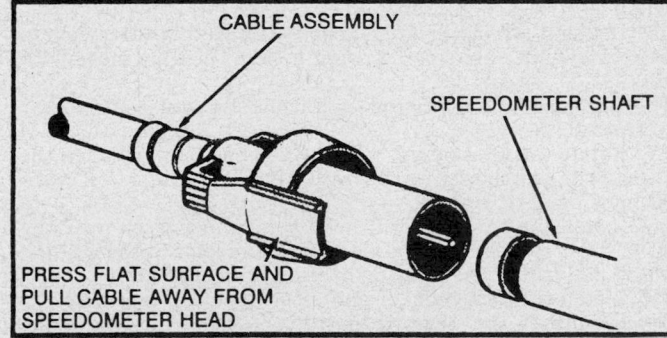

Speedometer cable quick connect

Speedometer

Removal and Installation

1. Disconnect the negative battery cable(s). Remove the instrument cluster.
2. Remove the lens and mask from the cluster.
3. Remove the 2 speedometer attaching screws and remove the speedometer head assembly.
4. Reverse the procedure for installation.

Headlight Switch

Removal and Installation

AEROSTAR

1. Disconnect the negative battery cable.
2. Remove the cluster finish panel assembly retaining screws.
3. Remove the left control pad retaining screws.
4. Remove the wiring connector from the switch.

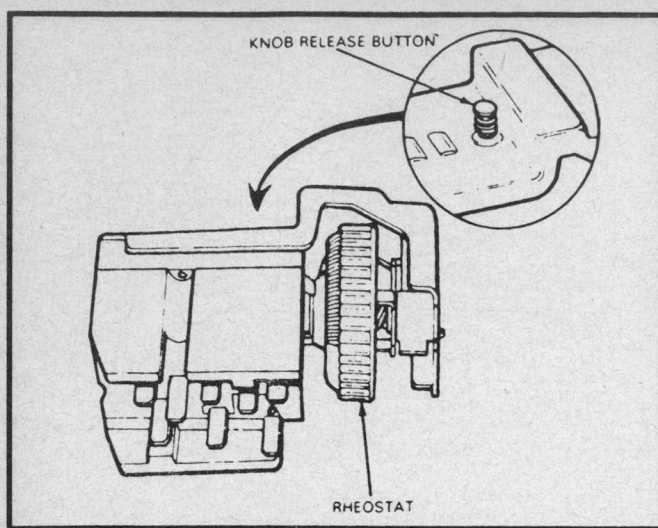
Typical headlamp switch

5. Remove the switch to control pod retaining screws and remove the switch.
6. Installation is the reverse of removal procedure.

BRONCO II AND RANGER

1. Disconnect the negative battery cable(s).
2. Pull the headlamp switch knob to the full **ON** position. Depress the shaft release button and remove the knob and shaft assembly.
3. Remove the instrument panel finish panel.
4. Unscrew the mounting nut. Remove the switch, then remove the wiring connector from the switch.
5. Installation is the reverse of the removal procedure.

Combination Switch

Removal and Installation

1. Disconnect the negative battery cable(s).
2. Remove the steering wheel and tilt collar shroud if so equipped. Note the position for correct installation.
3. On Aerostar remove the lock assembly.

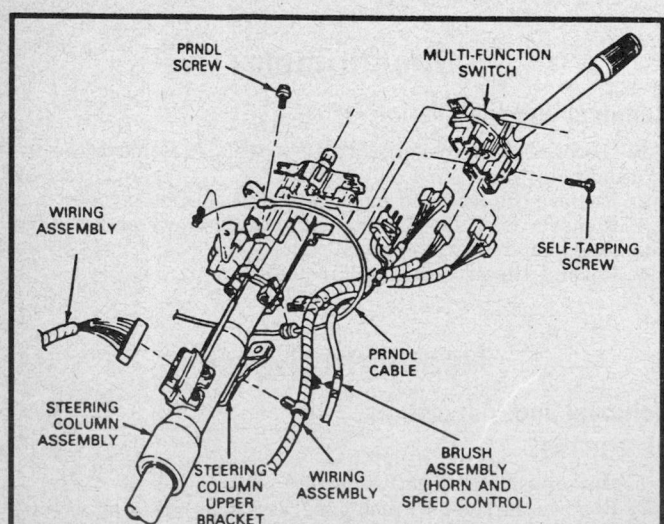
Multi-function switch–late model Bronco II

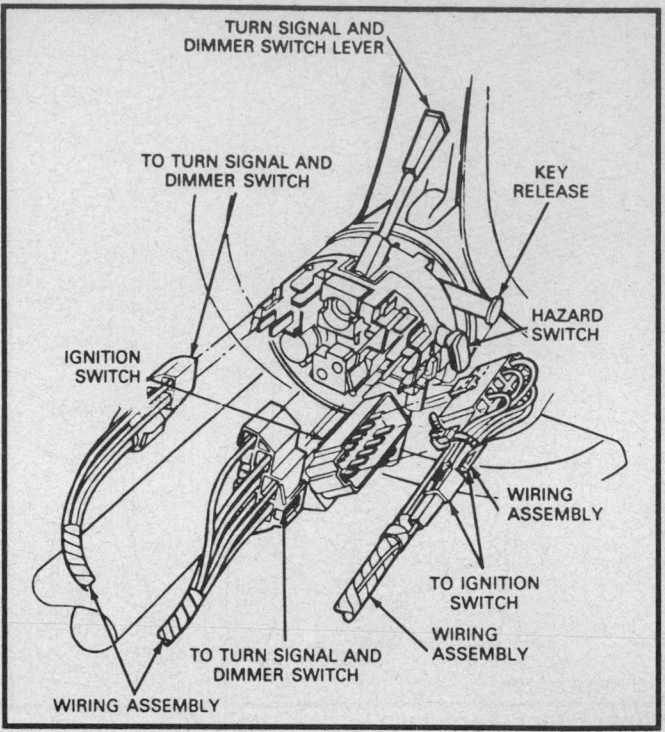
Turn signal switch assembly

4. Remove the switch lever by pulling it straight out from the switch.
5. Remove the steering column shroud(s).
6. Peel back the foam sight shield from the turn signal switch.
7. Remove the 2 self tapping screws that attach the switch to the lock cylinder housing and disengage the switch from the housing.
8. Disconnect the electrical connectors.
9. For installation reverse the removal procedure.

Ignition Switch

Removal and Installation

1. Rotate the lock cylinder to the **LOCK** position. Disconnect the negative battery cable(s).
2. Remove the steering wheel.
3. On tilt wheel applications, remove the upper extension shroud by squeezing it at the top and bottom positions and popping it free of the retaining plate at the right.
4. Remove the 2 trim shroud halves. Disconnect the ignition switch electrical connector.
5. Drill out the break off head bolts connecting the switch to the lock cylinder housing by using a ⅛ in. drill. Remove both bolts.
6. Disengage the ignition switch from the actuator pin.
To install:
7. Rotate the ignition key to the **RUN** position and align the holes in the switch casting base with the holes in the lock cylinder housing.
8. Install the new break off head bolts and tighten until the heads shear off. Connect the electrical connector to the ignition switch and install the steering column trim shrouds.
9. Install the lock cylinder and steering wheel assembly.
10. Reconnect the negative battery cable(s) and check the switch for proper operation.

Stoplight Switch

Removal and Installation

1. Disconnect the negative battery cable(s). Disconnect electrical connection from the switch. Locking tab must be lifted before connector can be removed.
2. Remove the hairpin retainer. Slide switch, master cylinder pushrod, nylon washer and bushing away from the pedal. Remove the washer, then switch by sliding switch up or down.

To install:

3. Position switch so that U-shaped side is nearest the pedal and directly over/under the pin. Then slide switch up/down installing the master cylinder pushrod and bushing between the switch side plates.
4. Push switch and pushrod assembly toward brake pedal arm. Install outside plastic washer to pin. Install the hairpin retainer (do not substitute for this retainer use only factory supplied retainer) to entire assembly.
5. Install electrical connection to switch and reconnect battery cable. Make sure switch wire harness has sufficient length to travel with switch during full stroke of brake pedal. Check switch for proper operation.

Clutch Switch

Removal and Installation

1. Disconnect the negative battery cable(s). Disconnect the wiring harness from the switch.
2. Pull down on the orientation clip to separate it from the tab on the switch.
3. Rotate the switch to expose the plastic retainer.

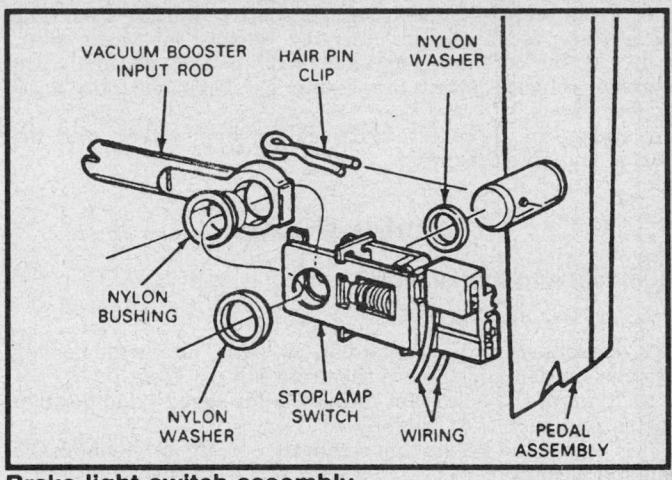

Brake light switch assembly

4. Push the tabs together to allow the retainer to slide rearward and seperate from the switch.
5. Remove the switch from the clutch master cylinder pushrod.
6. Installation is the reverse of the removal procedure.

Fuses And Circuit Breakers

Location

The fuse panel is located on the dash panel under the instrument panel left of the steering column. Circuit breakers are located in the fuse panel.

ENGINE COOLING

Radiator

Removal and Installation

1. Disconnect the negative battery cable. Drain the cooling system.
2. Remove the overflow tube from the coolant recovery bottle and shroud, as necessary.
3. Remove the radiator shroud retaining bolts and position it out of the way.
4. Remove all water hoses from the radiator.
5. Disconnect and plug the auotmatic transmission oil cooling lines, if equipped.
6. Remove the radiator retaining bolts and tilt the radiator back to clear radiator support for removal from the vehicle.
7. Installation is the reverse of the removal procedure.

Heater Core

Removal and Installation

NOTE: On vehicles equipped with air conditioning care should be exercised when removing heater core assembly.

1. Disconnect the negative battery cable(s). Allow the engine to cool down completely. Drain the cooling system to a point that is below the heater hoses.
2. Disconnect the heater hoses from the heater core tubes. Plug the core tubes.

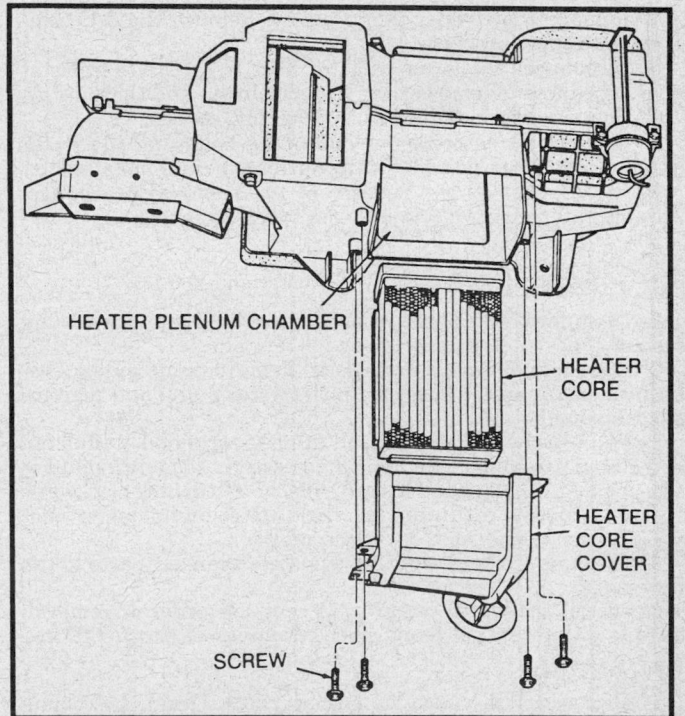

Heater core assembly

3. From under the dash, remove the screws that attach the access cover to the plenum assembly. Remove the access cover.

4. Pull the core down and out of the plenum assembly. On Aerostar vehicles depress the retainer bracket at the top of heater core.

5. Install in the reverse order. Fill cooling system, start the engine and check for leaks.

Water Pump

Removal and Installation

2.0L AND 2.3L ENGINES

1. Disconnect the negative battery cable. Drain the cooling system. Loosen and remove the drive belt.

2. Remove the bolts that retain the fan shroud and position the shroud back over the fan.

3. Remove the 4 bolts that retain the cooling fan. Remove the fan and shroud.

4. Loosen and remove the power steering and A/C compressor drive belts, if so equipped.

5. Remove the water pump pulley and the vent hose to the emissions canister.

6. Remove the heater hose at the water pump.

7. Remove the cam belt cover. Remove the lower radiator hose from the water pump.

8. Remove the water pump mounting bolts and the water pump. Clean all gasket mounting surfaces.

9. Install the water pump in the reverse order of removal. Coat the threads of the mounting bolts with sealer before installation and torque retaining bolts to 14–21 ft. lbs.

2.3L TURBOCHARGED DIESEL ENGINE

1. Disconnect the negative battery cables. Drain the cooling system.

2. Remove the fan and shroud assembly.

3. Remove the A/C compressor and power steering pump belt tensioner.

4. Remove thew water pump pulley. Remove the A/C compressor support bracket.

5. Disconnect the lower radiator hose from the thermostat housing adapter. Remove thermostat housing and thermostat.

6. Remove upper and lower front timing covers.

7. Remove the water pump mounting bolts and the water pump. Clean all gasket mounting surfaces before installation.

8. Installation is the reverse of the removal procedure. Torque water pump retaining bolts to 14–21 ft. lbs.

2.8L ENGINE

1. Disconnect the negative battery cable. Drain the cooling system.

2. Loosen and remove drive belts. Remove pump pulley. Disconnect all the water hoses from the water pump and thermostat housing.

3. Remove the radiator shroud (if necessary) and cooling fan and clutch assembly. The fan clutch assembly mounting nut is equipped with a left hand thread, remove by turning clockwise.

4. Remove the mounting bolts and water pump, water inlet and thermostat housing as an assembly.

5. Clean all gasket mounting surfaces. Transfer parts to the new pump.

6. Install the water pump in the reverse order of removal. Torque water pump to front cover retaining bolts to 7–9 ft. lbs.

2.9L ENGINE

1. Disconnect the negative battery cable. Drain the cooling system.

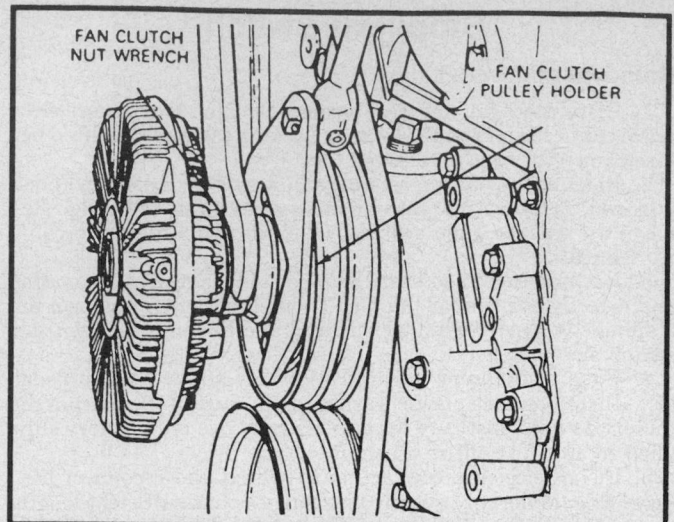

Typical fan clutch assembly

2. Remove the lower radiator hose and the heater return hose from the pump.

3. Remove the fan and clutch assembly. The fan clutch assembly mounting nut is equipped with a left hand thread, remove by turning clockwise.

4. Loosen the alternator mounting bolts and remove the belt. Equipped with A/C, remove the alternator and the bracket.

5. Remove the water pump pulley.

6. Remove the water pump attaching bolts and remove the pump assembly.

7. Installation is the reverse of removal. Torque water pump to front cover retaining bolts to 7–9 ft. lbs.

3.0L ENGINE

NOTE: The fan clutch assembly mounting nut is equipped with a left hand thread, remove by turning clockwise.

1. Disconnect the negative battery cable. Drain the cooling system.

2. Loosen the accessory drive belt idler and remove the belts.

3. Remove the idler bracket to the engine.

4. Disconnect the heater hose at the water pump.

5. Remove the pulley to pump hub bolts. The pulley will remain loose on the hub due to insufficient clearance between the body and the pump restricting removal.

6. Remove the water pump to engine attaching bolts (always mark or note location of bolts for correct installation) and remove the pump.

7. Installation is the reverse of removal. Torque small retaining bolts to 7 ft. lbs and long retaining bolts to 19 ft. lbs.

Thermostat

Removal and Installation

NOTE: To prevent incorrect installation of the thermostat, the water outlet casting contains a locking recess into which the thermostat is turned and locked.

1. Disconnect the negative battery cable(s). Drain the radiator so that the coolant level is below the thermostat.

2. Disconnect all water hoses at the thermostat housing.

3. Remove the water outlet housing attaching bolts and pull the housing away from the engine to gain access to the thermostat.

4. Installation is the reverse of removal procedure. Fill and bleed cooling system as necessary.

Cooling System Bleeding

To bleed cooling system disconnect the heater outlet hose at the water pump to bleed or release trapped air in the system. When the coolant begins to escape, connect the heater outlet.

GASOLINE FUEL SYSTEM

Fuel Service Precautions

Always disconnect the negative battery cable if possible. Never smoke, carry lighted tobacco, open flame and keep a Class B dry chemical fire extinguisher available. Always relieve the fuel pressure before working on any fuel system component.

Relieving Fuel System Pressure

1. Disconnect battery ground cable.

2. Remove the fuel cap from the fuel tank. Use tool T80L–9974 or equivalent attached to the pressure measuring port on the engine fuel rail.

3. Direct drain hose to a suitable container and depress the pressure relief button.

4. An alternate method is disconnect the inertia switch electrical connection and crank engine for approximately 20 seconds.

Fuel Filter

Removal and Installation

CARBURETED VEHICLE

1. Disconnect the negative battery cable. Remove the air cleaner.

2. Loosen (hold filter with back up wrench) and remove the fuel tube from the filter.

3. Remove the filter from the carburetor. If a inlet type fuel filter is used remove the fuel inlet fitting then remove the gasket, filter and spring.

4. Installation is the reverse of removal procedure. Always hand start filter threads before tightening with wrench.

FUEL INJECTED VEHICLE

NOTE: On Aerostar vehicles, a second fuel filter is located on the in-tank fuel pump. Remove the fuel pump from the tank to service this filter.

1. Relieve fuel pressure. Disconnect the battery ground cable.

2. Raise and suport the vehicle safely.

3. Loosen screw clamp slide filter forward. Remove fuel lines from the filter. Some vehicles have push type connection fittings.

4. On reservior type fuel filter remove the filter from from retainer. Note the direction of the flow arrow.

5. Remove fuel fiter from mounting bracket.

6. Installation is the reverse of removal procedure. Always hand start filter gas line threads before tightening with wrench.

Mechanical Fuel Pump

Pressure Testing

1. Remove the air cleaner. Connect a suitable pressure gauge to carburetor end of the fuel line.

2. Start the engine and read the fuel pressure after 10 seconds. The fuel pressure should be 5–7 psi.

3. Reconnect the fuel line and install the air cleaner.

Removal and Installation

1. Disconnect the negative battery cable. Loosen the threaded connections and then retighten them snugly. Do not remove the lines at this time.

2. Loosen the mounting bolts about 2 turns and loosen the fuel pump from the engine.

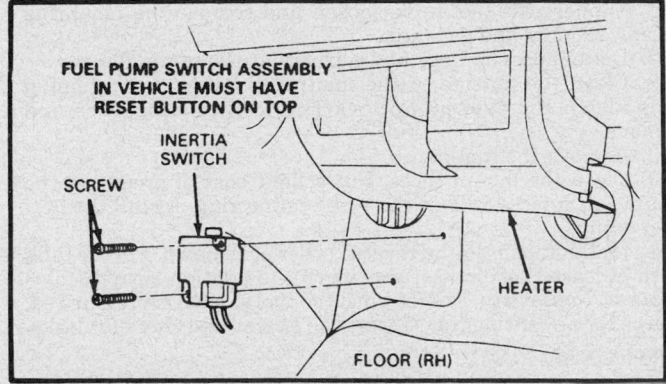

Typical location of inertia switch

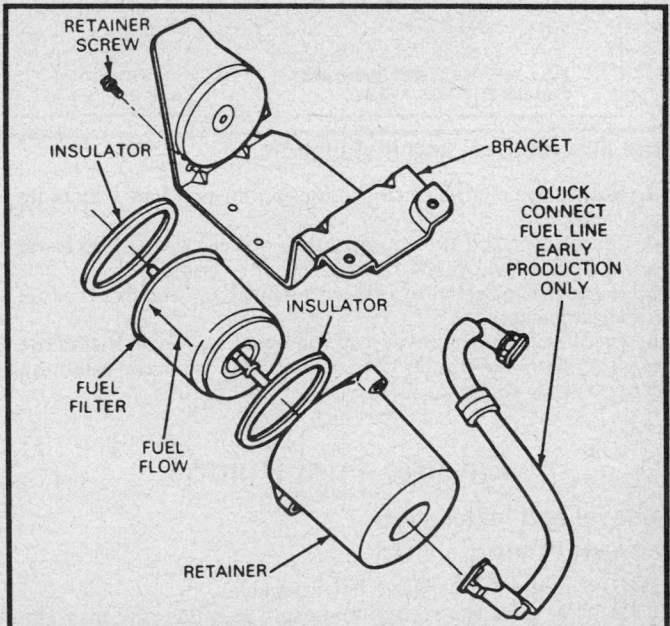

Reservoir type fuel filter

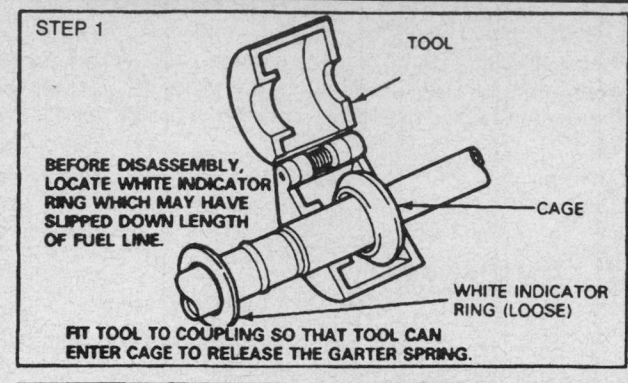

STEP 1

BEFORE DISASSEMBLY, LOCATE WHITE INDICATOR RING WHICH MAY HAVE SLIPPED DOWN LENGTH OF FUEL LINE.

TOOL

CAGE

WHITE INDICATOR RING (LOOSE)

FIT TOOL TO COUPLING SO THAT TOOL CAN ENTER CAGE TO RELEASE THE GARTER SPRING.

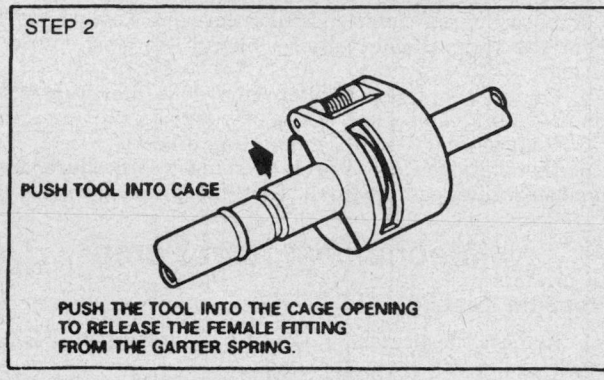

STEP 2

PUSH TOOL INTO CAGE

PUSH THE TOOL INTO THE CAGE OPENING TO RELEASE THE FEMALE FITTING FROM THE GARTER SPRING.

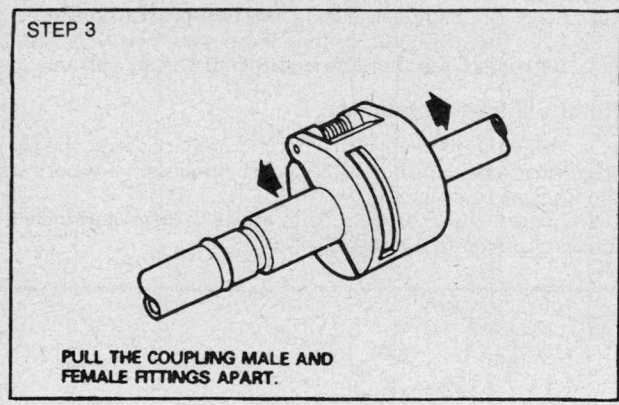

STEP 3

PULL THE COUPLING MALE AND FEMALE FITTINGS APART.

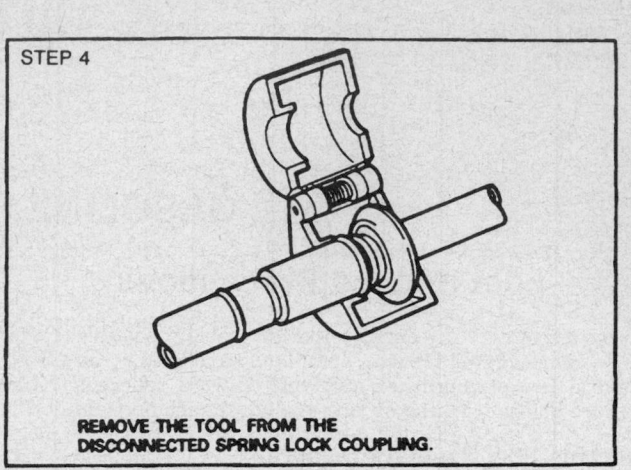

STEP 4

REMOVE THE TOOL FROM THE DISCONNECTED SPRING LOCK COUPLING.

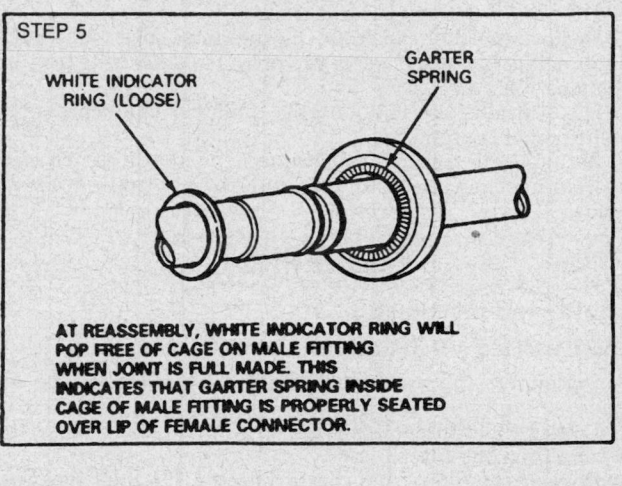

STEP 5

WHITE INDICATOR RING (LOOSE)

GARTER SPRING

AT REASSEMBLY, WHITE INDICATOR RING WILL POP FREE OF CAGE ON MALE FITTING WHEN JOINT IS FULL MADE. THIS INDICATES THAT GARTER SPRING INSIDE CAGE OF MALE FITTING IS PROPERLY SEATED OVER LIP OF FEMALE CONNECTOR.

Fuel line removal and installation

3. Rotate the engine until the fuel pump cam lobe is near its low position.

4. Disconnect the fuel pump inlet, outlet (wrap shop towel around fitting) and vapor return line, if so equipped.

5. Remove the fuel pump attaching bolts and remove the fuel pump and gasket.

6. Installation is the reverse of removal procedure. Install the fuel pump with a new mounting gasket and torque the retaining bolts to evenly to 14–21 ft. lbs.

Electric Fuel Pump

Removal and Installation

IN-TANK PUMP

1. Disconnect the negative battery cable.

2. Depressurize the system and drain as much fuel from the tank by pumping out through the filler neck.

3. Raise the vehicle and safely support it.

4. Disconnect the fuel supply, return and vent lines and plug as necessary.

5. Disconnect the wiring harness to the fuel pump.

6. Support the fuel tank, loosen and remove the mounting straps. Remove the gas tank.

7. Disconnect the lines and harness at the pump flange.

8. Clean the outside of the mounting flange and retaining ring. Turn the fuel pump lock ring counterclockwise and remove.

9. Remove the fuel pump.

10. Clean the mount faces. Put a light coat of grease on the mounting sufaces and on the new sealing ring. Install the new fuel pump.

11. Installation is in the reverse order of removal. Fill the tank with at least 10 gallons of gas. Turn the ignition key **ON** for 3 seconds. Repeat 6 or 7 times until the fuel system is pressurized. Check for any fitting leaks. Start the engine and check for leaks.

EXTERNAL PUMP

NOTE: The high pressure fuel pump is frame mounted and can be serviced from under the vehicle.

1. Disconnect the negative battery cable.
2. Depressurize the fuel system.
3. Raise and support the vehicle safely.
4. Disconnect the inlet and outlet fuel lines and plug as necessary.
5. Remove the pump from the mounting bracket.
6. Install in reverse order, make sure the pump is indexed correctly in the mounting bracket insulator. Always start fuel line threads by hand before tightening with wrench.

Carburetor

Removal and Installation

1. Disconnect the negative battery cable. Remove the air cleaner and duct assembly.
2. Remove the throttle cable or rod from the throttle lever. Disconnect the distributor vacuum line, EGR vacuum line, if so equipped, the inline fuel filter and the choke heat tube at the carburetor.
3. Disconnect the choke clean air tube from the air horn. Disconnect the choke actuating cable, if so equipped. Disconnect the electric choke wire at the connector, if so equipped. Disconnect the governor throttle control lines and governor wire connector at the carburetor, if so equipped.
4. Remove the carburetor retaining nuts, then remove the carburetor. Remove the carburetor mounting gasket, spacer and the lower gasket from the intake manifold.
5. Installation is the reverse of the removal procedure. Adjust the carburetor to specification, as required. Torque the carburetor mounting nuts to 14–20 ft. lbs.

Idle Speed Adjustment

2.0L ENGINE WITH YFA-IV AND YFA-IV FB CARBURETORS

1. Block the wheels and apply the parking brake. Place the transmission in **N** or **P**.
2. Bring the engine to normal operating temperature.
3. Turn **OFF** the ignition key and place the A/C selector in the **OFF** position.
4. Disconnect the vacuum hose at the EGR valve and plug it.
5. Place the fast idle rpm adjusting screw on the specified step of the fast idle cam (see the underhood sticker).
6. Start the engine without touching the accelerator pedal check/adjust the fast idle rpm to specifications.
7. Reconnect the EGR vacuum hose.
8. Place the transmission in the specified position (see the underhood sticker) and check/adjust the curb idle rpm.
9. If adjustment is required, turn the hex head adjustment at the rear of the TSP housing.
10. If curb idle rpm adjustment was required and the carburetor is equipped with a dashpot, adjust the dashpot clearance as follows:
    a. Turn the key to the **ON** position.
    b. Open the throttle to allow the TSP solenoid plunger to extend to the curb idle position.
    c. Collapse the dashpot plunger to the maximum extent. Measure the clearance between the tip of the plunger and the extension pad on the throttle vent lever.
    d. If required, adjust to specifications and tighten the dashpot locknut
11. If curb idle adjustment was required, check/adjust the bowl vent setting as follows:
    a. Turn ignition key to the **ON** position to activate the TSP (engine not running). Open throttle to allow the TSP solenoid plunger to extend to the curb idle position.
    b. Secure the choke plate in the wide open position.
    c. Open throttle so that the throttle vent lever does not touch the bowl vent rod. Close the throttle to the idle set posi-

tion and measure the travel of the fuel bowl vent rod from the open throttle position.
    d. Travel of the bowl vent rod should be within specification (0.100–0.150 in.).
    e. If out of specification, bend the throttle vent lever at notch to obtain required travel.
10. Remove all test equipment and reinstall air cleaner assembly. Tighten the holddown bolt.

2.8L ENGINE WITH 2150 2VFB CARBURETOR

1. Set parking brake and block wheels.
2. Put the transmission in **P**.
3. Bring the engine to normal operating temperature.
4. Disconnect the electric connector on the EVAP purge solenoid.
5. Disconnect and plug the vacuum hose to the VOTM kicker.
6. Place the transmission in **D** position.
7. Check/adjust curb idle rpm, if adjustment is required:
    a. Use the curb idle speed screw.
    b. Use the saddle bracket adjusting screw.
8. Place the transmission in **N** or **P**. Rev the engine momentarily. Place the transmission in **D** position and recheck curb idle rpm. Readjust if required.
9. Remove the plug from the vacuum hose to the VOTM kicker and reconnect.
10. Reconnect the electrical connector on the EVAP purge solenoid. Remove all test equipment and road test to check for proper operation.

Idle Mixture Adjustment
PROPANE ENRICHMENT METHOD

NOTE: Remove the air cleaner when necessary to perform adjustments. Use this service and adjustment procedure as a guide.

1. Bring the engine to normal operation temperature and connect a tachometer.
2. Disconnect the evaporative emission purge hose from the air cleaner. Disconnect the PCV closure hose from the air cleaner and plug the hose.
3. Adjust the curb idle speed to specifications.
4. If vehicle is equipped with thermactor system, revise the dump valve vacuum hoses as follows:
    a. For dump valves with 2 vacuum fittings, disconnect and plug the hose(s).
    b. For dump valves with 1 fitting, remove the hose at the dump valve and plug it. Connect a slave hose from the dump valve vacuum fitting to an intake manifold vacuum fitting.
5. Place the special gas tool into the air cleaner evaporative purge nipple. With the engine idling, slowly open the propane valve until the engine speed reaches a maximum and then begins to drop. Note the maximum speed increase. If the speed will not drop, check the bottle gas supply. If necessary, repeat the operation with a new bottle gas supply.
    a. If the speed increase is within specifications, but not zero rpm, proceed to Step 6. If the speed increase is zero and minus specification is zero, proceed to Step 5d.
    b. If the speed increase is higher than specification; enrich the mixture without propane by turning the mixture limiter screws counterclockwise in equal amounts until the rpm increases as necessary. Example: If the increase was 80 rpm and the desired reset is 50 rpm, the mixture screws should be richened to attain a 30 rpm increase. Repeat Steps 3 and 5.
    c. If the speed increase is lower than specifications proceed as follows; lean the mixture without propane by turning the mixture screws clockwise in equal amounts until the rpm decreases as necessary. Example: If the increase was zero rpm and the desired reset increase is 20 rpm, the mixture screws should be leaned to attain a 20 rpm decrease. Repeat Steps 3 and 5.

d. If the speed increase is zero rpm and the minimum speed gain specification is zero, perform the following speed drop test; Turn the mixture limiters counterclockwise to the maximum rich position. (If the limiters have been removed, do not enrich; assume the mixture screws are already set at the maximum rich position.) Lean the idle fuel mixture by turning the screws clockwise equally as specified. Note the drop in engine rpm.

e. If the speed drop is equal to or greater than the specified minimum speed drop, return the mixture limiters to the maximum rich position or the mixture screws to the "assumed" maximum rich position. If the engine speed before mixture adjustment was 650 rpm and the speed drop specification is 100 rpm minimum, proceed to Step 6 if the engine speed drops to at least 550 rpm or stalls.

f. If the speed drop is less than the specified minimum speed drop, leave the mixture limiters or screws in the adjusted position and repeat Steps 3 and 5.

6. If the idle limiters were removed, install new blue service limiters at the maximum rich stop. Check the speed increase after installation of the limiters to be certain that the settings were not disturbed. If the setting is within specification, proceed to Step 7, if not correct as required.

7. Remove the gas tool from the nipple and connect all system components that were removed.

8. Set the curb idle speed to specification if Step 3 required an idle speed adjustment.

9. Turn off the engine and disconnect the tachometer. Remove the limiter caps with appropriate tool if required. Road test the vehicle for proper operation.

Service Adjustments

For all carburetor sevice adjustments procedures and specifications, please refer to "Carburetor Service" in the Unit Repair section.

Fuel Injection

Idle Speed Adjustment

1. Disconnect idle speed control air bypass solenoid.
2. With transmission in **N** or **P** race engine for 30 seconds at 2500 rpm then let engine idle for 2 minutes.
3. Place automatic transmission in **D** and manual transmission in **N**. Check/adjust idle speed by turning the throttle plate stop screw as necessary.
4. Repeat Steps 2 and 3. Turn engine to **OFF** position and disconnect battery for 3 minutes on 2.9L and 3.0L engines.
5. With engine **OFF** reconnect idle speed control air bypass solenoid. Verify that the throttle and linkage is operating properly.
6. Start engine and let engine stabilize for 2 minutes. Road test the vehicle to check for proper operating conditions.

Fuel Injector

Removal and Installation

NOTE: To remove a injector grasp injector body, pull up while gently rocking injector from side to side. Use a light twisting pushing motion to install a injector.

1. Disconnect the negative battery cable.
2. Release the pressure from the fuel system.
3. Remove the upper intake manifold (air intake manifold) as follows:

a. Disconnect the electrical connectors at the air bypass valve, throttle position sensor, EGR position sensor and air charge temperature sensor.

b. Remove the air inlet tube from the air cleaner to throttle body.

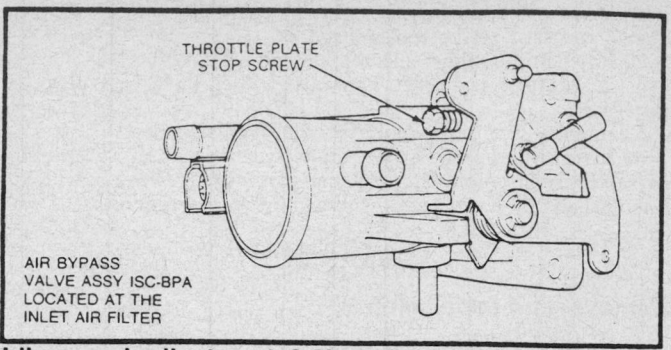

Idle speed adjustment–2.3L engine

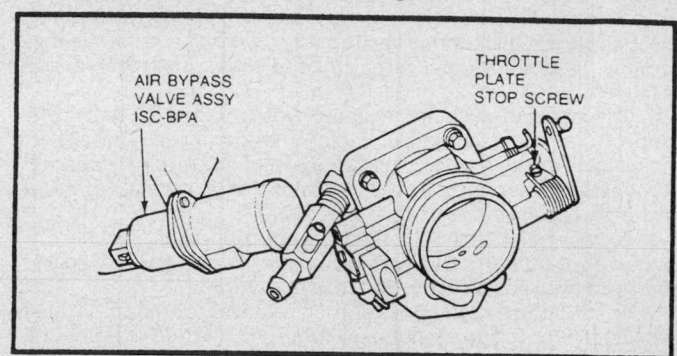

Idle speed adjustment–2.9L engine

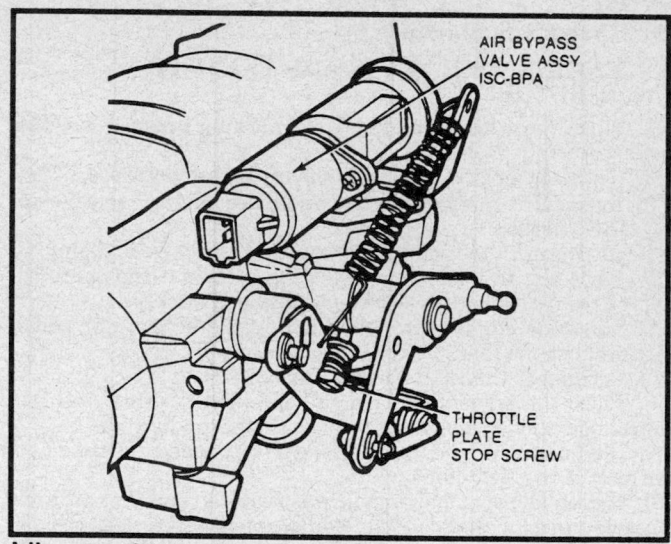

Idle speed adjustment–3.0L engine

c. Remove protective shield. Disconnect the throttle linkage at the throttle ball.

d. Disconnect all vacuum lines to the upper intake, EGR valve and the fuel pressure regulator.

e. Disconnect the PCV system hose from the rear of the upper manifold.

f. Remove the canister purge lines from the fitting near power steering pump. Disconnect the EGR tube from the valve by removing the flange nut. Remove A/C line retaining bolt clamp if so equipped.

g. Remove the upper intake manifold retaining bolts and remove it and the throttle body as an assembly.

4. Remove the fuel supply manifold as follows:

a. Disconnect the fuel chassis inlet and outlet fuel hoses from the fuel supply manifold.

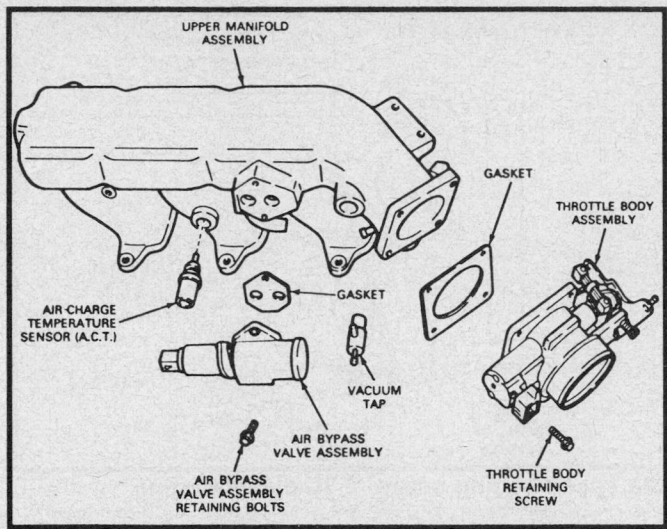

Upper intake manifold assembly–2.9L engine

b. Disconnect the fuel supply and the return line connections.

c. Remove the fuel supply manifold retaining bolts. Remove the fuel supply manifold electrical harness connectors from the injectors and remove the injector retaining clips. Remove the injectors.

6. Installation is the reverse of the removal procedure. Never use silicone grease on injector O-rings it may clog the injectors. Torque the upper manifold retaining bolts to 15–22 ft. lbs. on

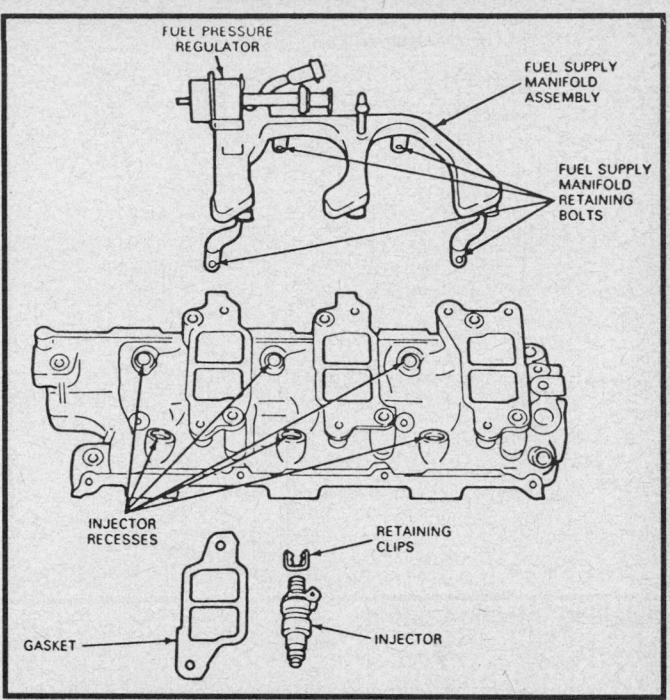

Fuel supply manifold assembly–2.9L engine

2.3L engine. Torque the upper manifold retaining bolts to 11–15 ft. lbs. on 2.9L engine. Torque the air intake manifold (upper manifold) retaining bolts to 19 ft. lbs. on 3.0L engine.

DIESEL FUEL SYSTEM

Fuel Filter

Replacement

1. Disconnect the battery ground cables from both batteries.
2. Remove the fuel filter rear bracket shield and all attaching components. Remove the fuel lines from the the filter element.
3. Remove the hold down clamps from rectangular filter element. Remove the filter element from base.
4. Installation is the reverse of the removal procedure.

Purging Air And Priming Fuel Filter

1. Turn ignition to the **ON** position.
2. Loosen the air vent plug on filter housing until fuel flows from the air vent plug hole free of bubbles.
3. Tighten air vent plug. Start ther engine and check for fuel leaks.

Diesel Injection Pump

Removal and Installation

1. Disconnect the negative battery cables.
2. Remove radiator fan and shroud.
3. Loosen and remove accessory drive belts.
4. Rotate crankshaft in direction of engine rotation to bring No. 1 piston to TDC on compression stroke.
5. Remove upper front timing cover.
6. Loosen and remove timing belt from injection pump.
7. Remove nut attaching sprocket to injection pump.

8. Install puller T77F–4220–B1, or equivalent and remove sprocket.
9. Disconnect throttle cable and speed control cables, if so equipped.
10. Disconnect coolant hoses from injection pump wax element.

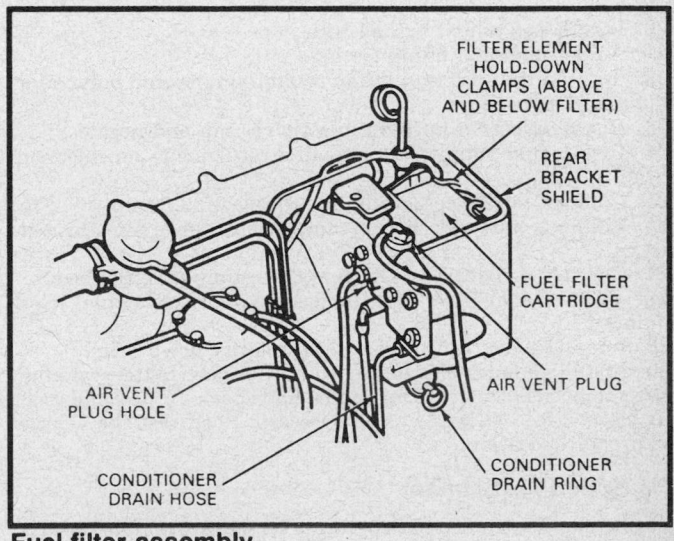

Fuel filter assembly

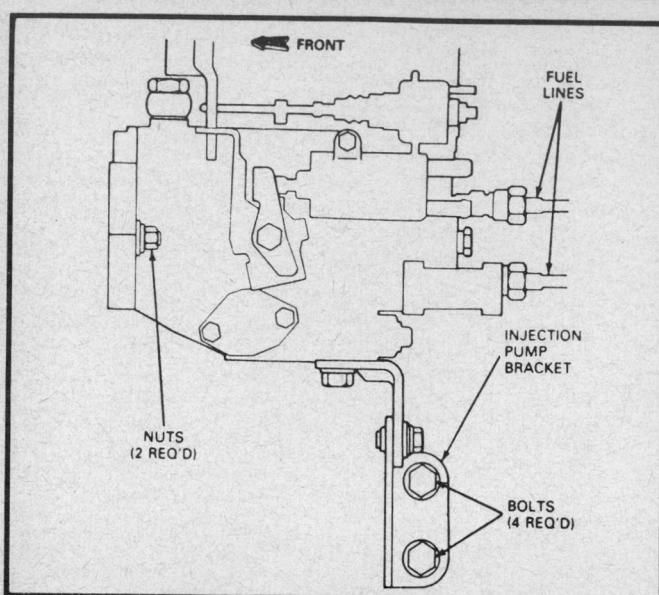

Installing injection pump

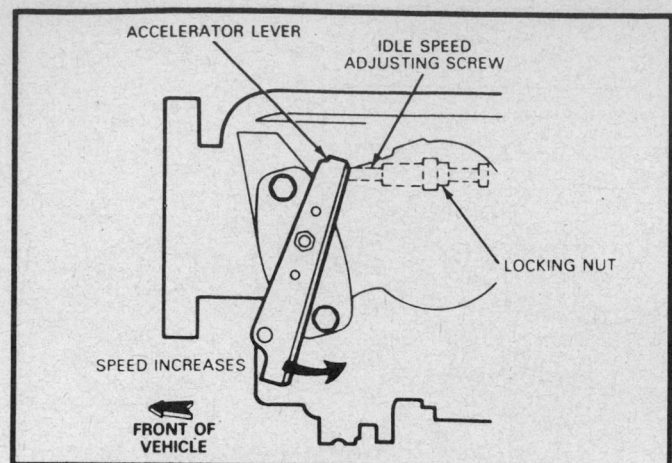

Idle speed setting screw–2.3L diesel engine

11. Disconnect hoses from boost compensator and A/C throttle kicker.

12. Disconnect fuel return line at injection pump from injection return pipe.

13. Disconnect chassis fuel return line from injection pump.

14. Disconnect and cap fuel supply line from fuel filter.

15. Disconnect and remove fuel lines at injection pump and nozzles. Cap all lines and fittings using protective cap set, T85T-9395-A or equivalent.

16. Remove 2 nuts attaching injection pump to rear front case. Remove 2 injection pump bracket-to-engine bracket bolts and 2 engine bracket-to-engine block bolts. Remove the injection pump.

To install:

17. Position injection pump on engine and install 2 nuts attaching injection pump to engine rear front cover. Position injection pump bracket-to-engine bracket on engine block and install 2 bolts.

18. Install 2 injection pump bracket-to-engine bracket bolts.

19. Install injection pump sprocket. Tighten nut to 40–50 ft. lbs.

20. Install and adjust timing belt.

21. Adjust injection pump timing.

22. Tighten the injection pump retaining nuts and bolts after adjustment procedure.

23. Install injection lines on injection pump and nozzles.

24. Install fuel supply line and fuel return line on injection pump.

25. Connect nozzle returning line to injection pump.

26. Connect hoses to boost compensator and A/C throttle kicker.

27. Connect coolant hoses to injection pump wax element.

28. Connect throttle cable and speed control cable, if so equipped.

29. Install upper front cover and accessory drive belts.

30. Install radiator fan and shroud. Connect battery ground cables to both batteries. Run engine and check for fuel and coolant leaks. Bleed all systems as necesary. Road test the vehicle for proper operation.

Idle Speed Adjustment

1. Run engine to normal operating temperature. Idle speed is determined with manual transmission in neutral position.

2. Check that curb idle adjusting screw is against the stop correct if necessary.

3. Check idle speed, using tachometer or equivalant test equipment. Idle speed is specified on the Vehicle Emissions Control Information decal. Adjust to specification using idle speed adjusting screw.

4. Roadtest to check for proper operation of the vehicle.

Diesel Injection Timing

Adjustment

1. Remove top timing belt cover.

2. Rotate engine until No. 1 piston is at TDC on the compression stroke. Verify by checking timing marks.

3. If engine temperature is below 122 degrees Fahrenheit the cold start mechanism as follows. Install a suitable tool and rotate the fast idle lever. Insert a spacer or a tool at least 7mm thick between cold start advance lever and the cold start device.

4. Loosen, but do not remove, the 2 mounting bolts and 2 nuts attaching the injection pump to the mounting bracket and front cover.

5. To prevent the delivery valve holders from turning with the fuel line nuts, loosen, but do not remove, the nuts securing the fuel lines to the injection pump using a backup wrench.

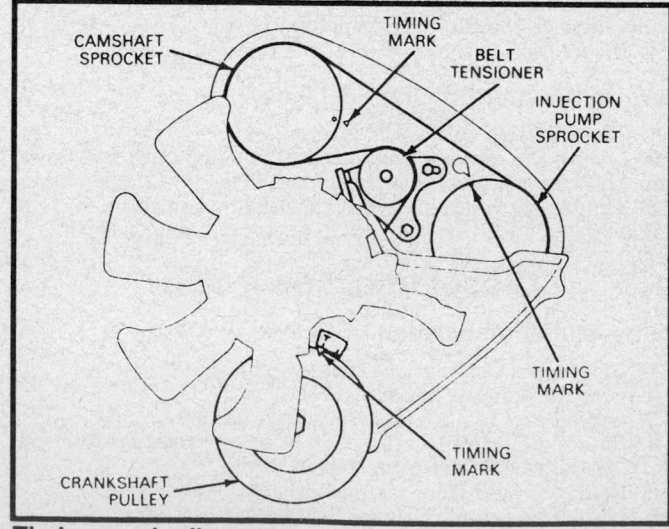

Timing mark alignment

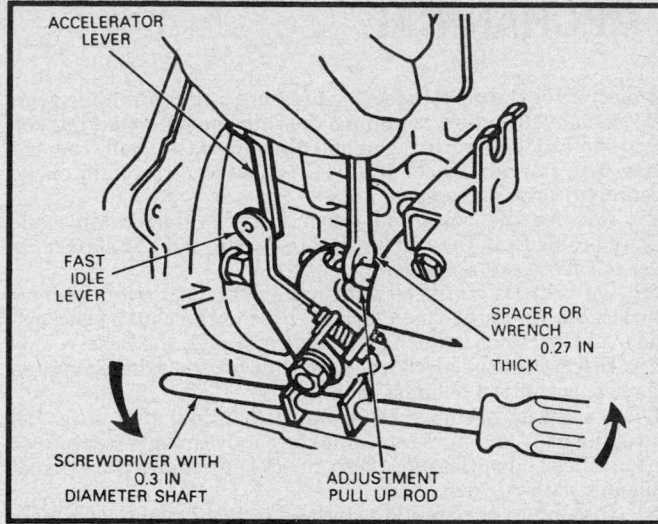

Bypass cold start device

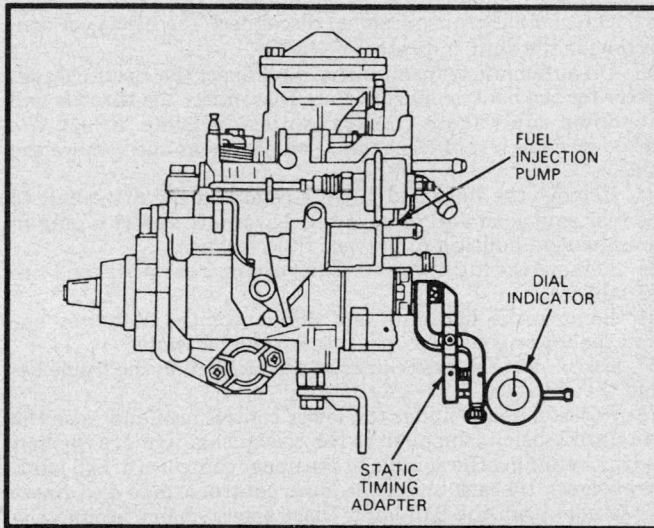

Timing adapter and dial indicator installation

6. Remove the timing plug bolt from the center of the fuel injection pump hydraulic head.

7. Install adapter Rotunda tool model 014–00303 or equivalent, into the port in the hydraulic head.

8. Mount tool D82L–1201–A or equivalent dial indicator, in timing adapter with a minimum preload of 0.010 in. (0.25mm).

9. Rotate the crankshaft approximately 30 degrees counter-clockwise. Position the dial indicator to zero.

10. Rotate the crankshaft clockwise to 5 degrees ATDC and check that the dial indicator indicates 0.0394 in. plus or minus 0.0011 in.

11. If the timing is out of specification, rotate the injection pump body until the dial indicator indicates specification. Rotate the pump clockwise if the reading is more than specification, or counterclockwise if less than specification. Tighten the injection pump mounting nuts to 11–15 ft. lbs. and tighten the bolts to 15–19 ft. lbs.

12. After tightening injection pump mounting bolts and nuts, repeat Steps 9 and 10 to ensure that the injection timing has not changed.

13. Tighten the fuel line nuts at the injection pump to 17–26 ft. lbs.

14. Using a new copper gasket, install the injection timing plug bolt and tighten to 10–14 ft. lbs.

15. Install the upper timing belt cover.

16. Run the engine and check for fuel leaks at the injection pump.

Fuel Nozzles

Removal and Installation

NOTE: **Before removing nozzle assemblies, clean exterior of each nozzle assembly and the surrounding area with solvent to prevent entry of dirt into engine when nozzle assemblies are removed. Always cap all open fuel lines to prevent dirt from entering system.**

1. Disconnect battery ground cables from both batteries.

2. Disconnect and remove injection lines from injection nozzles and injection pump. Cap all lines and fittings as required.

3. Remove fuel return pipe and gaskets.

4. Remove nozzles, using a 21mm deep well socket. Remove holder gasket and nozzles gasket, using a suitable tool.

To install:

5. Install new nozzle gasket and holder gasket in cylinder. Install nozzles.

7. Install fuel return pipe using new gaskets. Tighten nuts to 22–28 ft. lbs.

8. Install injection lines on nozzle and fuel injection pump and tighten line nuts.

9. Connect battery ground cables to both batteries.

10. Run engine and check for fuel leaks.

EMISSION CONTROLS

Please refer to "Professional Emission Component Application Guide".

Emission Warning Lamps

Resetting

NOTE: **The Emission Maintenance Warning (EMW) Light System consists of an instrument panel mounted amber lens light that is electrically connected to a sensor module located under the instrument panel near glove box.**

1. Turn the key switch to the **OFF** position.

2. Lightly push a tool through the 0.2 in. diameter hole with the sticker labeled "RESET" and press down and hold.

3. While pressing the tool down, turn the keyswitch to the **RUN** position. The Emission Maintenance Warning (EMW) lamp will then light and remain lit for as long as the tool is pressed down.

4. Hold the tool down for 5 seconds. Remove the tool. The lamp should go out within 2 to 5 seconds indicating a reset has occurred.

5. Turn the keyswitch to the **OFF** position then turn the keyswitch to the **RUN** position. The EMW lamp will light for 2–5 seconds and will then go out. This verifies that a proper reset of the module has been accomplished.

GASOLINE ENGINE MECHANICAL

Engine

Removal and Installation

AEROSTAR

2.3L Engine

NOTE: The engine removal procedure requires that the engine and front suspension subframe be removed from beneath the vehicle. Mark or tag all electrical and vacuum connections before disconnection to make installation easier.

1. Disconnect the negative battery cable.
2. Loosen the draincock and drain the coolant from the radiator.
3. Disconnect the air cleaner outlet tube at the throttle body and the idle speed control hose.
4. Remove the upper and lower hoses from the radiator and engine. Disconnect the lower intake manifold hose from the tee fitting in the heater hose.
5. Remove the bolts retaining the fan shroud to the radiator, remove the fan shroud.
6. Disconnect the electrical connectors to the alternator.
7. Remove the throttle linkage shield and disconnect the accelerator cable and cruise control (if equipped) from the throttle body. Unbolt the cables from the bracket and position them out of the way.
8. If equipped with air conditioning, discharge the system. After discharging, disconnect the suction and discharge hoses from the compressor. Disconnect the A/C compressor clutch electrical connector from the compressor.
9. From the lower left front of the engine, disconnect the electrical connector for the coil.
10. From beneath the lower intake manifold, disconnect the electrical connector for the TFI module on the distributor.
11. Disconnect the electrical connector from the knock sensor on the side of the upper intake manifold.
12. Tag and disconnect all hoses to the vacuum tree at the top of the upper intake manifold.
13. Disconnect the electrical connector and vacuum hose from the exhaust gas recirculation (EGR) valve at the rear of the upper intake manifold.
14. Remove the engine cover from inside the cab.
15. Disconnect the electrical connector for the throttle position sensor (TPS) at the rear of the throttle body.
16. Disconnect the electrical elbow connector for the oil pressure sender at the left rear of the engine.
17. Relieve the fuel system pressure. Disconnect the fuel return and supply lines.
18. Disconnect the electrical connector for the fuel injection wiring harness.
19. Disconnect the electrical connector for the air charge temperature (ACT) sensor at the rear side of the lower intake manifold.
20. Disconnect the electrical connector for the coolant temperature sensor at the center of the lower intake manifold.
21. Remove the nut and disconnect the ground strap from the right rear side of the engine below the lifting eye.
22. If equipped with manual transmission, place the shift lever in neutral position and remove the bolts retaining the shift lever to the floor. Remove the bolts retaining the shift lever assembly to the transmission and remove the lever assembly.
23. Raise the vehicle and safely support.
24. If equipped with automatic transmission, disconnect and plug the fluid lines at the radiator.
25. If equipped with power steering, disconnect the electrical

connector for the power steering pressure switch from the gear.
26. Remove the bolt retaining the intermediate steering column shaft to the steering gear and disconnect the shaft from the gear. The steering wheel and wheels should be straight ahead (centered) prior to removal.
27. Remove the bolts and disconnect the starter cable and ground cable from the starter. Route the ground and starter cables out from the crossmember.
28. On vehicles equipped with manual transmission, remove the lockpin retaining the hydraulic hose to the clutch slave cylinder in the clutch housing. Remove and plug the hose.
29. Disconnect the electrical connector for the exhaust gas oxygen sensor at the exhaust manifold.
30. Loosen and remove the exhaust manifold stud nuts. Remove the bolts and nuts retaining the catalytic converter pipe to the muffler and outlet pipe. Disconnect and remove the exhaust pipe and catalytic converter.
31. Disconnect the speedometer and/or tachometer cable from the transmission. Disconnect the electrical connector from the backup lamp switch.
32. On manual transmissions, disconnect the electrical connector for the shift indicator sender.
33. On automatic transmissions, disconnect the electrical connector for the neutral start switch. Disconnect the throttle and kickdown cable from the transmission lever. Route the kickdown cable out of the engine compartment and remove the cable.
34. Remove the nuts and U-bolts retaining the driveshaft to the rear axle yoke and remove the driveshaft. Insert a plug in the extension housing to prevent fluid leakage.
35. Remove the lug nuts and remove both front wheel and tire assemblies.
36. Remove the bar nuts and disconnect the stabilizer bar from the lower control arms. Discard the bar nuts.
37. Disconnect the brake lines at the bracket on the frame behind the spindles.
38. Position a jack under the lower control arm and raise the arm until tension is applied to the coil spring. Remove the bolt and nut retaining the spindle to the upper control arm ball joint. Slowly lower the jack under the lower control arm to disconnect the spindle from the ball joint. Place safety chains around the lower arms and spring upper seat.
39. Position a jack under the transmission and slightly raise the transmission. Remove the nuts and bolts retaining the crossmember to the frame and the nuts retaining the transmission to the crossmember. Remove the crossmember.
40. If required, remove the transmission. The engine may be removed with the transmission removed or attached.
41. Position a suitable dolly under the crossmember and engine assembly.
42. Slowly lower the vehicle until the crossmember rests on the dolly. Place wood blocks under the front crossmember and the rear of the engine block (or transmission, if installed) to keep the engine and crossmember assembly level. Install safety chains around the engine and dolly.
43. With the engine and crossmember securely supported on the dolly, remove the three nuts from the bolts that retain the engine and crossmember assembly to the frame on each side of the vehicle.
44. Slowly raise the body off the engine and crossmember assembly on the dolly. Make sure that any wiring or hoses do not interfere with the removal process.
45. With the engine and crossmember assembly clear of the vehicle, roll the dolly out from under the van.
46. Connect a lifting chain to the lifting eyes on the right rear and front left portions of the engine. Attach the chain to a suitable chain hoist or shop crane.

47. If equipped with power steering, disconnect the hoses from the pump and plug them to prevent the entry of dirt.

48. With lifting tension applied, remove the nuts retaining the engine to the crossmember assembly, then lift the engine off the crossmember.

49. Remove the required components to attach the engine assembly to a suitable engine stand if required.

To install:

50. Attach a lifting chain and shop crane to the engine. Remove the bolts retaining the engine to the engine stand and lift the engine with the shop crane.

51. With the front crossmember securely positioned on a dolly, slowly lower the engine until the motor mount studs are piloted in the crossmember holes. Install the remaining nuts and tighten them to 45–65 ft. lbs.

52. Install wood blocks under the oil pan and/or transmission and crossmember, then remove the lifting chain and shop crane.

53. If equipped with power steering, connect the hoses to the power steering pump.

54. Position the support dolly under the vehicle. Make sure the van body is securely supported. Align the dolly so that the engine/subframe assembly is correctly lined up with the 3 mounting bolts on each side of the frame. The bolts should align with the holes in the crossmember.

55. Slowly lower the body so the bolts are piloted in the crossmember holes. Continue lowering until the crossmember is against the frame. Install the nuts retaining the crossmember to the frame and tighten them to 187–260 ft. lbs.

56. Raise the vehicle and remove the support dolly.

57. Install the transmission as required.

58. Position a transmission jack under the transmission and slightly raise the transmission to place the crossmember in position on the frame and transmission. Install the retaining nuts and bolts to the crossmember, then install the nut retaining the transmission mount and insulator to the crossmember and tighten to 71–94 ft. lbs.

59. Remove the safety chains from around the lower control arm and upper spring seat.

60. Install a floor jack under the lower control arms. Slowly raise the control arm until the coil spring is under tension. Continue to raise the arm until the spindle upper arm can be connected to the upper control arm ball joint. Install a new nut and bolt.

61. Connect the stabilizer bar to the lower control arms. Install new bar nuts.

62. Connect the front brake lines to the caliper hoses at the frame brackets.

63. Install the front wheels.

64. Connect the driveshaft to the transmission and rear axle yoke. Install the nuts and U-bolts retaining the driveshaft to the rear axle yoke.

65. On vehicles with automatic transmission, connect the throttle and kickdown cables to the transmission lever. Connect the electrical connector to the neutral start switch and route the kickdown cable into the engine compartment.

66. On manual transmissions, connect the electrical connector for the shift indicator sender.

67. Connect the speedometer and/or tachometer to the transmission, then connect the electrical connector for the backup lamp switch.

68. Install new gaskets on the exhaust manifold and catalytic converter. Place the assembly in position on the exhaust manifold, muffler and outlet pipe. Install the 2 nuts and bolts retaining the converter to the muffler and outlet pipe. Install the nuts retaining the pipe to the exhaust manifold and tighten alternately.

69. Connect the electrical connector for the exhaust gas oxygen sensor on the exhaust manifold.

70. On manual transmissions, attach the hydraulic hose to the slave cylinder in the clutch housing. Install the lockpin retaining the hose to the cylinder.

71. Position the ground cable on the starter and install and tighten the mounting bolt. Connect the starter cable to the motor and install the screw and washer. Route the starter and ground cables over the crossmember and into position in the engine compartment.

72. With the front wheels and steering wheel centered (straight ahead), connect the steering column lower shaft to the steering gear. Install the bolt and tighten it to 31–42 ft. lb.

73. If equipped with power steering, connect the power steering pressure switch at the gear.

74. If equipped with automatic transmission, connect the fluid lines at the radiator.

75. Lower the vehicle.

76. From inside the cab, if equipped with manual transmission, position the shift lever assembly on the transmission. Make sure the transmission and shifter are in the neutral position. Install and tighten the retaining bolts to 6–9 ft. lbs. Position the boot over the lever assembly.

77. On the right rear side of the engine below the lifting eye, position the ground strap on the lifting eye, then install and tighten the retaining nut.

78. In the center of the lower intake manifold, connect the electrical connector for the coolant temperature sensor.

79. Connect the electrical connector for the air charge temperature (ACT) sensor at the rear side fo the lower intake manifold.

80. Connect the electrical connector for the fuel injection wiring harness.

81. Connect the hoses to the fuel return and fuel supply lines.

82. Connect the electrical connector for the oil pressure sender at the left rear side of the engine.

83. Connect the electrical connector for the throttle position sensor (TPS) at the rear of the throttle body.

84. Install the engine cover inside the cab.

85. Connect the electrical connector and vacuum hose for the EGR valve at the rear of the upper intake manifold.

86. Connect all vacuum hoses in their proper positions on the vacuum tree at the top of the upper intake manifold.

87. Connect the electrical connector for the knock sensor at the side of the upper intake manifold.

88. Connect the electrical connector for the Thick Film Ignition (TFI) module on the distributor, underneath the lower intake manifold.

89. Connect the electrical connector for the coil at the lower left front side of the engine.

90. If equipped with air conditioning, connect the A/C clutch compressor connector to the compressor. Connect the suction and discharge hoses to the compressor and recharge the A/C system.

91. Connect the accelerator cable and cruise control cable (if equipped) to the throttle body. Install the cables in the retaining bracket and install and tighten the bolt. Install the throttle linkage shield.

92. Connect the 2 electrical connections to the alternator.

93. Connect the electrical connector and vacuum hose to the manifold absolute pressure (MAP) sensor.

94. Position the fan shroud on the radiator, then install and tighten the retaining bolts.

95. Install the upper and lower radiator hoses and the heater hoses. Install the lower intake manifold hose to the tee in the heater hose.

96. Connect the air cleaner tube at the throttle body and the idle speed control hose. Install the ground cable on the negative battery terminal.

97. Fill the cooling system to the specified level with approved coolant. Check and adjust all fluid levels as required. Bleed the brake system.

98. Start the engine and check for leaks. Correct as required.

The front end alignment should be checked and adjusted as soon as possible.

2.8L and 3.0L Engines

NOTE: The engine removal procedures for the 2.8L and 3.0L are basically identical with the exception of the fuel system. The 2.8L engine uses a carburetor, while the 3.0L engine is equipped with fuel injection. The engine is removed from the bottom along with the subframe and front suspension.

1. Disconnect the negative battery cable.
2. Loosen the draincock and drain the coolant from the radiator.
3. Remove the air cleaner and intake duct assembly.
4. Disconnect the upper and lower hoses at the radiator.
5. Remove the fan shroud retaining bolts and remove the shroud.
6. On 2.8L engines, disconnect the manifold absolute pressure (MAP) sensor electrical connector from the sensor, located on the dash panel.
7. If equipped with air conditioning, disconnect the A/C clutch electrical connector from the compressor. On the 2.8L engine, loosen the idler pulley adjustment bolt to slacken drive belt tension and remove the belt from the compressor clutch pulley, then remove the compressor mounting bolts and position the compressor out of the way. On the 3.0L engine, discharge the A/C system and disconnect the compressor discharge and suction hoses from the compressor.
8. Disconnect the accelerator able and the transmission kickdown cable at the throttle lever ball stud or throttle body.
9. Disconnect the electrical connector for the idle speed control (ISC) motor on 2.8L engine or the idle air control (IAC) valve on 3.0L engine.
10. Disconnect the electrical connectors for the engine coolant temperature sensor and the water temperature sender switch, located in the thermostat housing.
11. Disconnect the vacuum hose from the exhaust gas recirculation (EGR) valve and the electrical connector from the EGR valve position sensor.
12. Disconenct the electrical connectors from the alternator.
13. On the 2.8L engine, tag and disconnect the electrical connectors for the throttle position sensor on the carburetor choke shield, canister purge valve solenoid and the solenoid valve carburetor bowl vent. Disconnect the electrical connector to the variable voltage choke cap. Disconnect the evaporative emission hose from the solenoid valve carburetor bowl vent to the vapor storage canister. Route the wiring harness out of the engine compartment.
14. Remove the engine cover from inside the cab.
15. On the 3.0L engine, tag and disconnect the evaporative emission line, fuel injector wiring harness (including 6 injectors), air charge temperature sensor, throttle position sensor and the radio frequency supressor, if equipped.
16. Remove the retaining bolt, then remove the bracket and accelerator cable and transmission kickdown linkage.
17. If equipped with cruise control, disconnect the cruise control cable from the throttle linkage.
18. Disconnect the electrical connector and supressor wire from the ignition coil.
19. On the 2.8L engine, disconnect the hose from the air control valve to the catalytic converter.
20. Disconnect the electrical connector for the Thick Film Ignition (TFI) module at the distributor. Disconnect the electrical connector for the knock sensor on the 3.0L engine.
21. On the 2.8L engine, disconnect the electrical connector for the feedback control solenoid at the rear of the carburetor.
22. Tag and disconnect all the hoses from the vacuum manifold fitting.
23. Disconnect the brake booster vacuum hose from the clip.

24. If equipped with manual transmission, place the shift lever in neutral and remove the bolts retaining the shift lever to the floor. Remove the bolts retaining the shift lever assembly to the transmission and remove the lever assembly.
25. Raise the vehicle and support it safely.
26. If equipped with automatic transmission, disconnect the fluid lines at the radiator.
27. Remove the heater hoses from the bracket underneath the engine at the front of the crossmember.
28. Make sure the steering wheel and front wheels are straight ahead (centered), then remove the bolt retaining the intermediate steering column shaft to the steering gear and disconnect the shaft from the gear.
29. Disconnect the elbow connector from the oil pressure sender beneath the fuel pump on the 2.8L engine, or the oil pressure sending switch connector on the 3.0L engine.
30. On the 2.8L engine, disconnect and plug the inlet hose on the fuel pump from the lines on the frame. On the 3.0L engine release the fuel system pressure. Disconnect the fuel delivery and return lines.
31. Remove the bolt retaining the ground strap to the engine and remove the strap.
32. Remove the bolts and disconnect the starter cable and ground cable from the starter. Route the ground and starter cables out from the crossmember.
33. On vehicles with manual transmission, remove the lockpin retaining the hydraulic hose to the slave cylinder in the clutch housing. Remove and plug the hose.
34. Disconnect the electrical connector for the exhaust gas oxygen sensor from the left exhaust manifold. Disconnect the electrical connector for the knock sensor from the engine block above the starter.
35. Loosen and remove the exhaust manifold stud nuts. On the 2.8L engine, disconnect the tube to the check valve on the managed thermactor air tube. Remove the bolts and nuts retaining the catalytic converter pipe to the muffler and outlet pipe. Disconnect and remove the exhaust pipe and catalytic converter.
36. Disconnect the speedometer cable from the transmission. Disconnect the electrical connector from the backup lamp switch.
37. On manual transmissions, disconnect the electrical connector for the shift indicator sender.
38. On automatic transmissions, disconnect the electrical connector for the neutral start switch. Disconnect the throttle and kickdown cable from the transmission lever. Route the kickdown cable out of the engine compartment and remove the cable.
39. Remove the nuts and U-bolts retaining the driveshaft to the rear axle and remove the driveshaft. Insert a plug in the extension housing to prevent fluid leakage.
40. Remove the front wheel assemblies.
41. Remove the bar nuts and disconnect the stabilizer bar from the lower control arms. Discard the bar nuts.
42. Disconnect and plug the brake lines at the bracket on the frame behind the spindles.
43. Position a jack under the lower control arm and raise the arm until tension is applied to the coil spring. Remove the bolt and nut retaining the spindle to the upper control arm ball joint. Slowly lower the jack under the lower control arm to disconnect the spindle from the ball joint. Place safety chains around the lower control arms and spring upper seat.
44. Position a transmission jack under the transmission and slightly raise the transmission. Remove the nuts and bolts retaining the crossmember to the frame and the nuts retaining the transmission to the crossmember. Remove the crossmember.
45. Remove the transmission as required.
46. Position a wheeled dolly under the crossmember and engine assembly.

47. Slowly lower the vehicle until the crossmember rests on the dolly. Place wood blocks under the front crossmember and the rear of the engine block (or transmission, if installed), to keep the engine and crossmember assembly level. Install safety chains around the crossmember and dolly.

48. With the engine and crossmember securely supported on the dolly, remove the 3 nuts from the bolts that retain the engine and crossmember assembly to the frame on each side of the vehicle.

49. Slowly raise the body off the engine and crossmember assembly on the dolly. Make sure that any wiring or hoses do not snag or interfere with the removal process.

50. When the engine and crossmember assembly are clear of the van body, roll the dolly out from under the vehicle.

51. Install lifting eyes on each side of the exhaust manifold, then connect a suitable chain to the lifting eyes and attach a shop crane or chain hoist.

52. If equipped with power steering, disconnect the power steering hoses from the pump to the gear and plug the hose ends.

53. With lifting tension applied, loosen the nuts retaining the motor mounts to the crossmember and lift the engine off the crossmember.

54. Remove the necessary components to attach the engine to a suitable engine stand. Make sure the engine is securely bolted to the stand before releasing tension on the hoist.

To install:

55. Attach a suitable shop crane or chain hoist and remove the engine from the work stand.

56. With the front crossmember securely attached to a wheeled dolly, slowly lower the engine until the motor mount studs are piloted in the crossmember holes. Install the retaining nuts and tighten them to 71–94 ft. lbs. Install wood blocks under the oil pan and crossmember to level the assembly, then detach the lifting chain and hoist. Remove the lifting eyes.

57. If equipped with power steering, attach the hoses to the pump and gear. Roll the dolly under the vehicle and make sure the 3 mounting bolts on each side of the frame are in alignment with the holes in the crossmember.

58. Slowly lower the body so the bolts are piloted in the crossmember holes. When the crossmember is against the frame, install the retaining nuts and tighten them to 187–260 ft. lbs. Raise the vehicle and remove the dolly.

59. If removed, install the transmission.

60. Position a transmission jack under the transmission and slightly raise the transmission. Place the crossmember in position in the frame and on the transmission, then install the nuts retaining the transmission mount and insulator to the crossmember. Tighten the retaining nuts to 71–94 ft. lbs.

61. Remove the safety chains from around the lower control arms and spring seat.

62. Install a jack under the lower control arms, then slowly raise the control arm until the coil spring is under tension. Continue to raise the arm until the spindle upper arm can be connected to the lower control arm ball joint. Install a new nut and bolt.

63. Connect the stabilizer bar to the lower control arms. Install new bar nuts.

64. Connect the front brake lines to the caliper hoses at the frame brackets.

65. Install the front wheels.

66. Connect the driveshaft to the rear axle and transmission. Install the nuts and bolts retaining the driveshaft to the rear axle end yoke.

67. If equipped with automatic transmission, connect the throttle and kickdown cables to the transmission lever. Connect the electrical connector for the neutral start switch and route the kickdown cable into the engine compartment.

68. On manual transmissions, connect the electrical connector for the shift indicator sender.

69. Connect the cable/electrical sender for the speedometer to the transmission. Connect the electrical connector for the back-up lamp switch.

70. Install new gaskets on the exhaust manifold and catalytic converter. Install the nuts and bolts retaining the converter to the muffler and outlet pipe. Install the nuts retaining the pipe to the exhaust manifold and tighten alternately.

71. Connect the electrical connectors for the exhaust gas oxygen sensor and the knock sensor.

72. On manual transmissions, attach the hydraulic hose to the slave cylinder in the clutch housing. Install the lockpin retaining the hose to the cylinder. Bleed the clutch hydraulic system.

73. Position the ground cable on the starter and tighten the mounting bolt. Connect the starter cable to the motor and install the screw and washer and tighten. Route the starter and ground cables over the crossmember and into position in the engine compartment.

74. Position the ground strap on the engine and install and tighten the bolt.

75. On the 2.8L engine, connect the fuel pump inlet hose to the line on the frame. On the 3.0L engine, reconnect the fuel return and delivery lines.

76. Connect the elbow connector to the oil pressure sender beneath the fuel pump.

77. With the front wheel and steering wheel straight ahead (centered), connect the steering column intermediate shaft to the steering gear. Install and tighten the bolt to 30–42 ft. lbs.

78. Install the heater hoses to the bracket underneath the engine at the front of the crossmember.

79. If equipped with automatic transmission, connect the fluid lines at the radiator.

80. Lower the vehicle.

81. From inside the cab, connect the brake vacuum booster hose to the vacuum manifold fitting on the rear of the engine. Connect the hose to the clip. If equipped with cruise control, connect the vacuum hose from the cruise control to the fitting. Make sure all hoses disconnected prior to engine removal are connected to their correct ports.

82. On the 2.8L engine, connect the electrical connector for the feedback control solenoid at the rear of the carburetor. On the 3.0L engine, connect the fuel injection wiring harness and all injectors.

83. Connect the electrical connector for the Thick Film Ignition (TFI) module at the distributor. On the 2.8L engine, connect the hose for the air control valve to the catalytic converter. Connect the electrical connector and supressor wire to the coil.

84. Connect the cruise control cable to the carburetor or throttle body assembly. Position the accelerator and kickdown cables in the bracket and install the bolt.

85. If equipped with manual transmission, position the shift lever assembly on the transmission. Make sure the transmission and shifter assembly are in neutral, then install and tighten the retaining bolts. Position the boot over the lever assembly.

86. Reconnect all remaining wiring connectors accessible from the top of the engine, then replace the engine cover in the cab.

87. Route the wiring into position in the engine compartment.

88. On the 2.8L engine, connect the electrical connectors for the throttle position sensor, canister purge valve solenoid and solenoid valve/carburetor bowl vent. Connect the elbow connector to the variable voltage choke cap, then connect the evaporative emission hose from the solenoid valve/carburetor bowl vent to the vapor storage canister.

89. Connect the electrical connectors to the alternator. Connect the vacuum hose to the exhaust gas recirculation (EGR) valve and the electrical connectors for the engine coolant temperature sender and the water temperature sensor.

90. On the 2.8L engine, connect the electrical connector for

the idle speed control (ISC) motor. Connect the accelerator and transmission kickdown cables to the throttle lever ball stud.

91. Position the A/C compressor in the engine brackets. Install the retaining bolts. On the 3.0L engine, connect the compressor suction and discharge hoses. Install the drive belt on the compressor clutch and idler pulley, if removed and adjust the drive belt tension. Connect the A/C compressor clutch electrical connector.

92. Connect the manifold absolute pressure (MAP) sensor electrical connector to the sensor on the dash panel.

93. Install the shroud over the fan and in position on the radiator, then install and tighten the retaining bolts. Connect the upper and lower radiator hoses.

94. Connect the ground cable to the battery and install the air cleaner and air intake duct assembly.

95. Refill the cooling system and check all fluid levels. Bleed the brakes and recharge the air conditioning system if the compressor hoses were disconnected during service.

96. Start the engine and check for leaks. The front end alignment should be checked and adjusted as soon as possible.

BRONCO II

2.9L Engine

1. Disconnect the battery ground cable and drain the cooling system.

2. Remove the hood after scribing hinge positions. Remove the air cleaner and intake duct assembly.

3. Remove or disconnect thermactors system parts that will interfere with removal or installation of the engine.

4. Disconnect the radiator upper and lower hoses at the radiator. Remove the fan shroud attaching bolts and position the shroud over the fan. Remove the radiator and shroud.

5. Remove the alternator and bracket. Position the alternator out of the way. Disconnect the alternator ground wire from the cylinder block.

6. Remove A/C compressor (do not discharge the system) and power steering and position out of way, if so equipped.

7. Disconnect the heater hoses at the block and water pump.

8. Remove the ground wires from the cylinder block.

9. Relieve the fuel pressure. Disconnect the fuel tank to fuel pump fuel line at the fuel pump. Plug the fuel tank line.

10. Disconnect the throttle cable linkage at the throttle body and intake manifold.

11. Disconnect the primary wires from the ignition coil. Disconnect the brake booster vacuum hose. Disconnect the wiring from the oil pressure and engine coolant temperature senders.

12. Raise and support the vehicle safely. Disconnect the muffler inlet pipes at the exhaust manifolds.

13. Disconnect the starter cable and remove the starter.

14. Remove the engine front support to crossmember attaching nuts or through bolts.

15. If equipped with automatic transmission, remove the converter inspection cover and disconnect the flywheel from the converter.

16. Remove the kickdown rod. Remove the converter housing to cylinder block bolts and the adapter plate to converter housing bolt.

17. On vehicles equipped with a manual transmission, remove the clutch linkage. Lower the vehicle.

18. Attach engine lifting sling and hoist to lifting brackets at exhaust manifolds.

19. Position a jack under the transmission. Raise the engine slightly and carefully pull it from the transmission. Carefully lift the engine out of the engine compartment so that the rear cover plate is not bent or components damaged.

20. Reverse the procedure for installation. Refill the cooling system and check all fluid levels. Start the engine and check for leaks, road test the vehicle.

RANGER

2.0L And 2.3L Engines

1. Raise the hood and install protective fender covers. Drain the coolant from the radiator. Remove the air cleaner and duct assembly.

2. Disconnect the battery ground cable at the engine and disconnect the battery positive cable at the battery and set aside.

3. Mark the location of the hood hinges and remove the hood.

4. Disconnect the upper and lower radiator hoses from the engine. Remove the radiator shroud screws. Remove the radiator upper supports.

5. Remove engine fan and shroud assembly. Remove the radiator. Remove the oil fill cap.

6. Disconnect the coil primary wire at the coil. Disconnect the oil pressure and the water temperature sending unit wires from the sending units.

7. Disconnect the alternator wire from the alternator, the starter cable from the starter and the accelerator cable from the carburetor. If so equipped, disconnect the transmission kickdown rod.

8. If so equipped, remove the A/C compressor from the mounting bracket and position it out of the way, leaving the refrigerant lines attached.

9. Disconnect the power brake vacuum hose. Relieve the fuel pressure. Disconnect the chassis fuel line from the fuel pump. Disconnect the heater hoses from the engine.

10. Remove the engine mount nuts. Raise and safely support the vehicle.

11. Drain engine oil from the crankcase. Remove the starter motor.

12. Disconnect the muffler exhaust inlet pipe at the exhaust manifold.

13. Remove the dust cover (manual transmission) or converter inspection plate (automatic transmission).

14. On vehicles with a manual transmission, remove the flywheel housing cover lower attaching bolts. On vehicles with automatic transmissions, remove the converter-to-flywheel bolts, then remove the converter housing lower attaching bolts.

15. Remove clutch slave cylinder (manual transmission). Lower the vehicle.

16. Support the transmission and flywheel or converter housing with a jack.

17. Remove the flywheel housing or converter housing upper attaching bolts.

18. Attach the engine lifting hooks to the existing lifting brackets. Carefully, so as not to damage any components, lift the engine out of the vehicle.

19. Installation is the reverse of the removal procedure. Check and fill all fluid levels. Road test the vehicle for proper operation.

2.9L Engine

1. Disconnect the battery ground cable and drain the cooling system.

2. Remove the hood after scribing hinge positions. Remove the air cleaner and intake duct assembly.

3. Remove or disconnect thermactors system parts that will interfere with removal or installation of the engine.

4. Disconnect the radiator upper and lower hoses at the radiator. Remove the fan shroud attaching bolts and position the shroud over the fan. Remove the radiator and shroud.

5. Remove the alternator and bracket. Position the alternator out of the way. Disconnect the alternator ground wire from the cylinder block.

6. Remove A/C compressor (do not discharge the system) and power steering and position out of way, if so equipped.

7. Disconnect the heater hoses at the block and water pump.

8. Remove the ground wires from the cylinder block.

9. Relieve the fuel pressure. Disconnect the fuel tank to fuel pump fuel line at the fuel pump. Plug the fuel tank line.

10. Disconnect the throttle cable linkage at the throttle body and intake manifold.

11. Disconnect the primary wires from the ignition coil. Disconnect the brake booster vacuum hose. Disconnect the wiring from the oil pressure and engine coolant temperature senders.

12. Raise and support the vehicle safely. Disconnect the muffler inlet pipes at the exhaust manifolds.

13. Disconnect the starter cable and remove the starter.

14. Remove the engine front support to crossmember attaching nuts or through bolts.

15. If equipped with automatic transmission, remove the converter inspection cover and disconnect the flywheel from the converter.

16. Remove the kickdown rod. Remove the converter housing to cylinder block bolts and the adapter plate to converter housing bolt.

17. On vehicles equipped with a manual transmission, remove the clutch linkage. Lower the vehicle.

18. Attach engine lifting sling and hoist to lifting brackets at exhaust manifolds.

19. Position a jack under the transmission. Raise the engine slightly and carefully pull it from the transmission. Carefully lift the engine out of the engine compartment so that the rear cover plate is not bent or components damaged.

20. Reverse the procedure for installation. Check and fill all fluid levels. Road test the vehicle for proper operation.

Cylinder Head

Removal and Installation

2.0L AND 2.3L ENGINES

1. Drain the cooling system. Disconnect the negative battery cable.

2. Remove the air cleaner, spark plugs and dipstick tube assembly.

3. Remove the valve cover. On vehicles with air conditioning, remove the mounting bolts and the drive belt and position the compressor with the hoses attached, out of the way. Remove the compressor upper mounting bracket from the cylinder head. If the compressor refrigerant lines do not have enough slack to permit repositioning of the compressor without first disconnecting the refrigerant lines, the air conditioning system will have to be evacuated.

4. Raise and safely support the vehicle as necessary. Remove the intake and exhaust manifolds from the head.

5. Remove the camshaft drive belt cover. Note the location of the belt cover attaching screws that have rubber grommets if so equipped.

6. Loosen the timing belt tensioner and remove the belt.

7. Remove the water outlet elbow from the cylinder head with the hose attached.

8. Remove the cylinder head attaching bolts.

9. Remove the cylinder head from the engine.

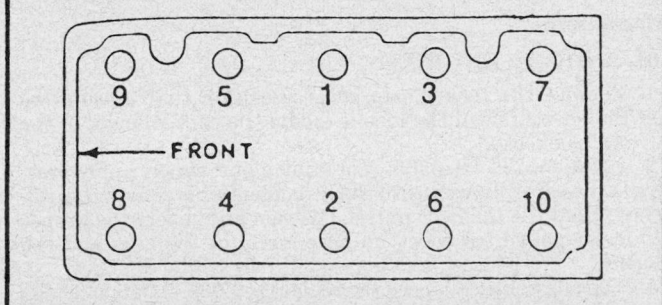

Cylinder head bolt torque sequence—2.0L and 2.3L engines

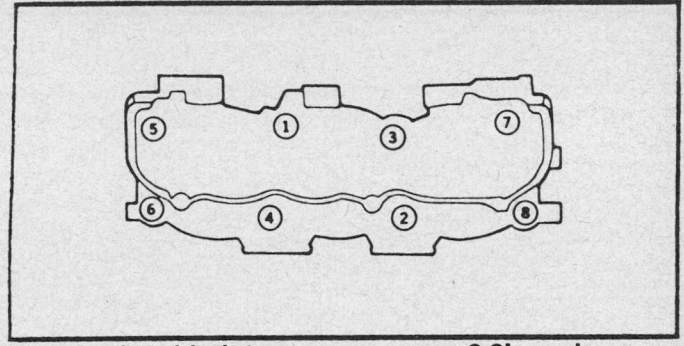

Cylinder head bolt torque sequence—2.8L engine

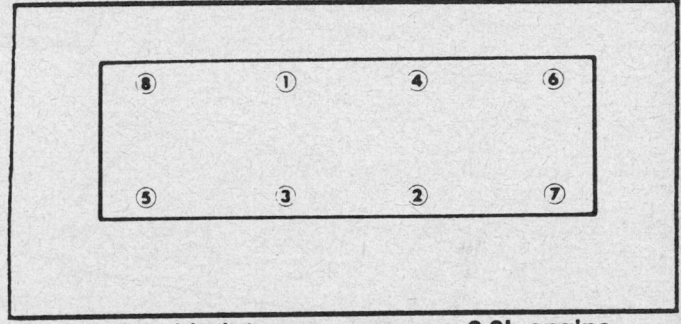

Cylinder head bolt torque sequence—2.9L engine

10. Clean all gasket material and carbon from the top of the cylinder block and pistons and from the bottom of the cylinder head.

11. Installation is the reverse of the removal procedure. Torque the cylinder head bolts in sequence in 2 steps. The 1st step in sequence to 50–60 ft. lbs. and the 2nd step in sequence to 80–90 ft. lbs.

2.8L AND 2.9L ENGINES

1. Disconnect the battery ground cable.

2. Drain the radiator coolant.

3. Remove the air cleaner from the carburetor and disconnect the throttle linkage on the 2.8L engine. Remove the intake tube from the throttle body and disconnect the throttle linkage and cover on the 2.9L engine.

4. Mark and remove the distributor.

5. Remove the radiator hose and the bypass hose from the thermostat housing and intake manifold.

6. Remove the rocker arm covers and the rocker arm shafts (keep all parts in order for correct installation).

7. Remove the fuel line from carburetor and remove the carburetor on the 2.8L engine. Relieve the fuel system pressure. Remove the fuel line from the fuel rail on the 2.9L engine.

8. Remove the intake manifold assembly.

9. Remove and label the pushrods in order to keep them in sequence for proper assembly.

10. Raise and safely support the vehicle as necessary. Remove the exhaust manifolds.

11. Remove the cylinder head attaching bolts. Remove the cylinder heads and discard the head gaskets.

To install:

12. Clean the cylinder heads, intake manifold, valve rocker arm cover and cylinder block gasket surfaces.

13. Place the cylinder head gaskets in position on the cylinder block.

NOTE: Gaskets are marked with the words FRONT and TOP for correct positioning. Left and right cylinder head gaskets are not interchangeable. Use new cylinder head bolts.

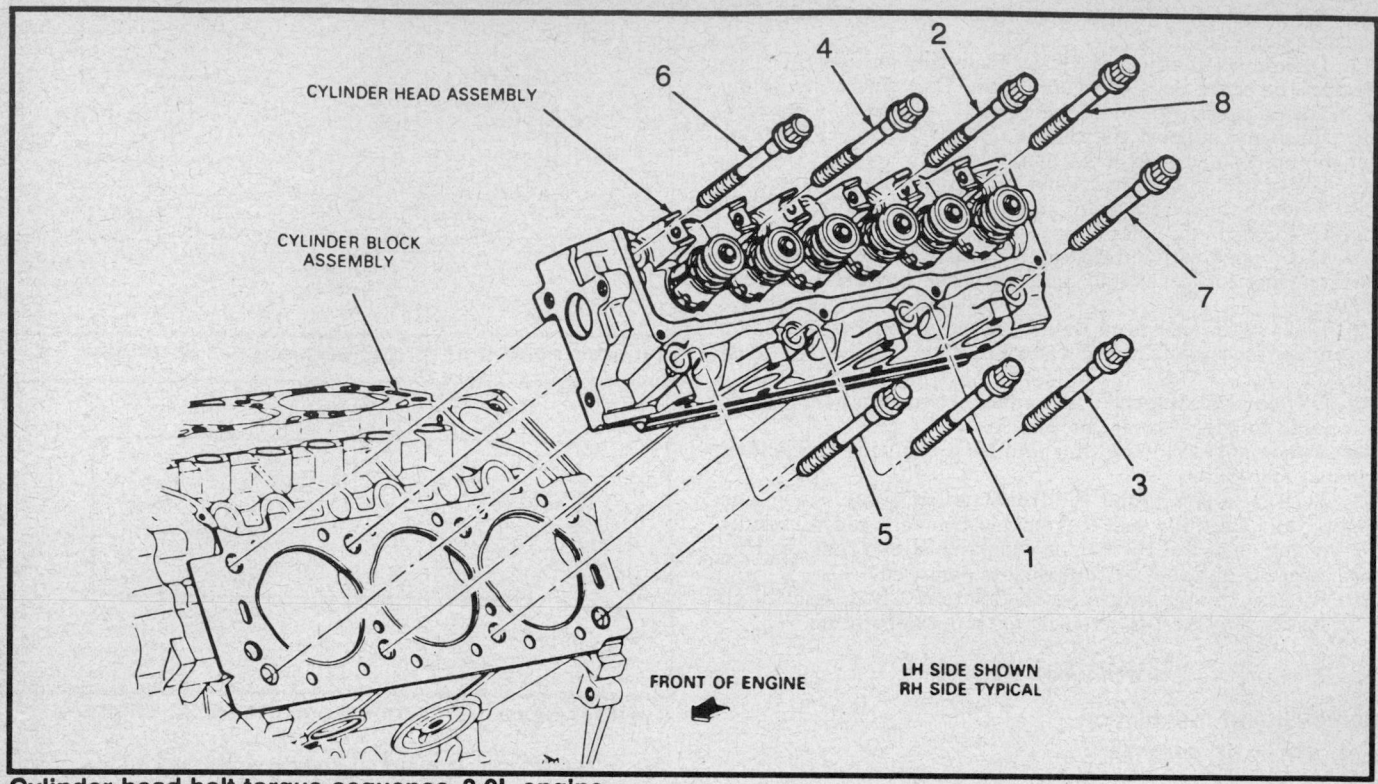

CYLINDER HEAD ASSEMBLY

CYLINDER BLOCK ASSEMBLY

FRONT OF ENGINE

LH SIDE SHOWN
RH SIDE TYPICAL

Cylinder head bolt torque sequence—3.0L engine

14. Install the fabricated alignment dowels in the cylinder block and install the cylinder head assemblies on the cylinder block.

15. Remove the alignment dowels and install the cylinder head attaching bolts. Tighten the bolts to specification following the torque sequence.

16. Install the intake manifold assembly.

17. Install the exhaust manifold assemblies.

18. Install the pushrods. Install oil baffles and rocker arms in the correct order.

19. Install the distributor. Adjust the valves. Install the rocker arm covers.

20. Install the carburetor and connect the fuel line to the carburetor on the 2.8L engine. Connect the fuel line to the fuel rail on the 2.9L engine.

21. Install the distributor cap and spark plug wires. Install the throttle linkage and the air cleaner or air cleaner intake tube.

22. Fill the cooling system and bleed the cooling system. Connect the battery ground cable.

23. Start the engine and check for oil, fuel and coolant leaks. Check and adjust if necessary the ignition timing and idle speed. Road test the vehicle for proper operation.

3.0L ENGINE

1. Disconnect the negative battery cable.
2. Drain the cooling system.
3. Remove the air cleaner and the necessary duct work.
4. Remove the drive belt for the accessories as required.
5. To remove the left cylinder head, remove the power steering pump brackets from the cylinder head and set aside in a position to avoid fluid leakage. Remove and set aside the A/C compressor (do not remove the refrigerant lines).
6. To remove the right cylinder head, disconnect the thermactor diverter valve and hose at the bypass valve and downstream air tube. Remove the assembly. Remove the accessory drive idler. Remove the alternator. Remove the thermactor

pump pulley. Remove the thermactor pump. Remove the alternator bracket. Remove the PCV valve.

7. Relieve the fuel pressure. Remove the intake manifold assembly.

8. Remove the rocker arm cover attaching screws and remove the valve covers.

9. Raise and safely support the vehicle as necessary. Remove the exhaust manifolds.

10. Loosen the rocker arm fulcrum attaching bolts enough to allow the rocker arms to be lifted off the pushrods and rotated to one side. Remove the pushrods, keeping them in order for correct installation.

11. Remove the cylinder head attaching bolts and carefully remove the cylinder head from the engine block.

12. To reassemble the cylinder heads to the engine block, reverse the removal procedures. Use new gaskets during the reassembly, along with new cylinder head bolts. Torque the cylinder head bolts in sequence to the proper specification.

Valve Lash

Adjustment

2.0L AND 2.3L ENGINES

1. Remove the rocker arm cover. Position the camshaft so that the base circle of the lobe is facing the cam follower of the valve to be checked.

2. Using tool T74P–6565–A or equivalent, slowly apply pressure to the cam follower until the lash adjuster is completely collapsed. Hold the follower in this position and insert the proper size feeler gauge between the base circle of the cam and the follower.

3. The allowable collapsed tappet gap is 0.035–0.055 in. at the camshaft. The desired collapsed tappet gap is 0.040–0.050 in. at the camshaft. If the clearance is excessive, replace the necessary components.

2.8L ENGINE

1. With engine **COLD** and valve covers removed, place a finger on the adjusting screw of the intake valve rocker arm for cylinder No. 5.

2. Use a remote starter switch or equivalent to rotate (bump) the engine over until you can just feel the valve begin to open. The cam is now in position to adjust the intake and exhaust valves on the No. 1 cylinder.

3. Adjust the No. 1 intake valve so that a 0.014 in. feeler gauge has a slight drag, while a 0.015 in. feeler gauge is a tight fit. To decrease lash, turn the adjusting screw clockwise; to increase lash, turn the adjusting screw counterclockwise. There are no lockbolts to tighten as the adjusting screws are self-tightening.

NOTE: Do not use a step-type, "go-no-go" feeler gauge. When checking lash, you must insert the feeler gauge and move it parallel with the crankshaft. Do not move it in and out perpendicular with the crankshaft as this will give an erroneous feel which will result in overtightened valves.

4. Adjust the exhaust valve the same way so that an 0.016 in. feeler gauge has a slight drag, while a 0.017 in. gauge is a tight fit.

5. The rest of the valves are adjusted in the same way, in their firing order (1–4–2–5–3–6), by positioning the cam according to the valve adjusting chart.

VALVE ADJUSTMENT CHART—2.8L ENGINE

Intake valve must be opening for cylinder no.	5	Adjust Intake and Exhaust for cylinder no.	1
"	3	"	4
"	6	"	2
"	1	"	5
"	4	"	3
"	2	"	6

2.9L ENGINE

1. Remove the valve cover assembly. On the cylinder to be adjusted, position the cams so that the tappets are on the base circle.

2. Loosen the adjusting screws until a lash between the roller arm pad and the valve tip end can be noticed.

3. Screw in the adjustment screws until the roller arms slightly touch the valves.

4. To achieve the nominal working position of the plunger, turn in the adjusting screw 1.5 turns, equivalent to 0.07 in. specification.

Rocker Arms/Shaft

Removal and Installation

2.0L AND 2.3L ENGINES

1. Disconnect the negative battery cable. Remove the valve cover and associated parts as required. On 2.3L engine relieve the fuel pressure. Remove the throttle linkage and throttle body assembly.

2. Rotate the camshaft so that the base circle of the cam is against the cam follower you intend to remove.

3. Remove the retaining spring from the cam follower, if so equipped.

4. Using special tool T74P–6565–B or a valve spring compressor tool, collapse the lash adjuster and/or depress the valve spring, as necessary and slide the cam follower over the lash adjuster and out from under the camshaft.

5. Install the cam follower in the reverse order of removal. Make sure that the lash adjuster is collapsed and released before rotating the cam shaft.

2.8L ENGINE

1. Disconnect the negative battery cable. Remove all necessary components to gain access to the rocker arm covers. Remove the rocker arm covers.

2. Remove rocker arm shaft stand retaining bolts by loosening the bolts 2 turns at a time, in sequence (center to end). Lift off rocker arm and shaft assembly and oil baffle.

To install:

3. Loosen the valve lash adjusting screws a few turns.

4. Apply engine oil to the assembly to provide initial lubrication.

5. Install oil baffle and rocker arm shaft assembly to the cylinder block and guide adjusting screws on to pushrods.

6. Install and tighten rocker arm stand attaching bolts to 43–50 ft. lbs. torque rocker arm stand attaching bolts 2 turns at a time in sequence-center to end.

7. Adjust valve lash to **COLD** specified setting.

8. Clean the valve rocker arm cover and cylinder head gasket surfaces. Install the valve cover, making sure the gasket seats evenly around the head. Tighten the cover attaching bolts.

9. Install all parts removed to gain access to rocker arm and shaft assemblies. Reconnect the battery ground cable. Run the engine and check for oil leaks.

2.9L ENGINE

1. Disconnect the negative battery cable. Mark and disconnect the spark plug wires.

2. Relieve the fuel pressure. Disconnect the fuel supply and return lines and position out of the way.

3. Remove the left hand lifting eye on vehicles equipped with A/C.

4. Remove the PCV valve hose and breather.

5. Remove the rocker arm attaching screws and the load distribution washers. Ensure the washers are installed in their original position.

6. Tap the rocker arm cover to break the seal and remove the covers.

7. Remove the rocker arm shaft stand attaching bolts by loosening the bolts 2 turns at a time, in sequence (center to end).

8. Lift off the rocker arm and shaft assembly and the oil baffle.

9. Reverse the removal procedure to install. Apply SF type engine oil to the assembly to provide initial lubrication. Torque the rocker arm shaft support bolt to 43–50 ft. lbs. in sequence (center to end). Adjust the valve lash.

3.0L ENGINE

1. Disconnect the negative battery cable. Disconnect the ignition wires from spark plugs (mark or label to ensure correct installation).

2. Remove the ignition wire separators from the the valve covers.

3. To remove the left side valve cover:
   a. Relieve fuel pressure as necessary. Remove the throttle body assembly.
   b. Remove the PCV valve.

4. To remove the right side valve cover:
   a. Remove the oil filler tube assembly.
   b. Disconnect closure system hose.

5. Remove the rocker cover bolts and remove the valve covers.

6. Remove the valve rocker arm bolt, fulcrum seat and rocker arm.

7. For installation, reverse the removal procedure. The fulcrums must be fully seated in cylinder heads and pushrods must be fully seated in rocker arm sockets prior to final torque. Install the fulcrum guide, valve rocker arm, fulcrum seat and bolt. Tighten to 18–26 ft. lbs. in 2 steps.

Intake Manifold

Removal and Installation

2.0L ENGINE

1. Raise and safely support the vehicle as necessary. Drain the cooling system. Remove the air cleaner and duct assembly. Disconnect the negative battery cable.

2. Disconnect the accelerator cable, vacuum hoses (as required) and the water hose at the manifold fitting. Be sure to identify all vacuum hoses for proper reinstallation.

3. Remove the engine oil dipstick. Disconnect the heat tube at the EGR (exhaust gas recirculation) valve. Disconnect the fuel line at the carburetor fuel fitting.

4. Remove the dipstick retaining bolt from the intake manifold.

5. Disconnect and remove the PCV at the engine and intake manifold.

6. Remove the distributor cap and position the cap and wires out of the way, after removing the plastic plug connector from the valve cover.

7. Remove the intake manifold retaining bolts. Remove the manifold from the engine.

8. Clean all gasket mounting surfaces.

9. Install a new mounting gasket and intake manifold on the engine. Torque the bolts in proper sequence in steps to correct

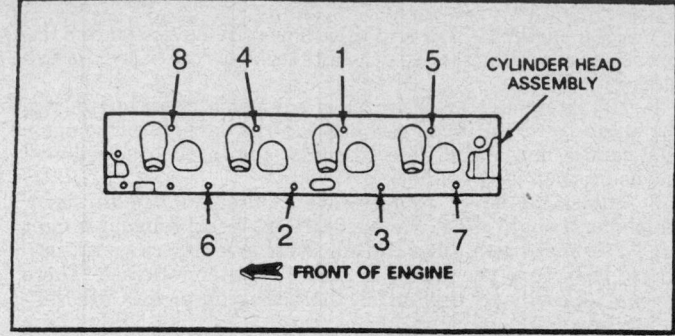

Intake manifold bolt torque sequence–2.0L and 2.3L engines

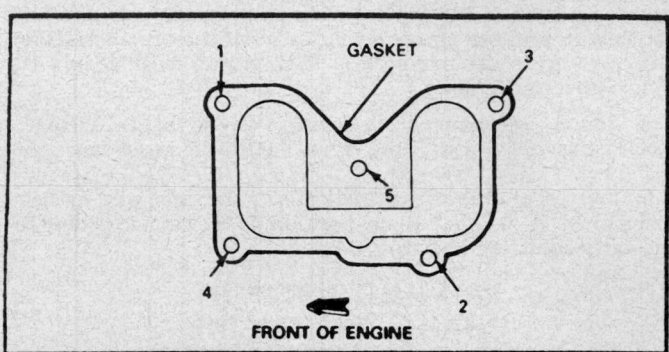

Upper intake to lower intake manifold bolt torque sequence–2.3L engine

specification. The rest of the installation procedure is in the reverse order of removal.

2.3L ENGINE

1. Disconnect the negative battery cable and drain cooling system. Raise the vehicle and support as necessary.

2. Release the pressure from the fuel system.

3. Disconnect the electrical connectors at, throttle position sensor, engine coolant, ignition control asembly, EGR position sensor and air charge temperature sensor.

4. Disconnect the injector wiring harness at main engine harness and at water temperture indicator sensor.

5. Disconnect all vacuum lines to the upper intake, EGR valve and the fuel pressure regulator.

6. Remove protective shield. Disconnect the throttle linkage, cruise control and kickdown cable if equipped. Position accelerator cable and bracket out of way.

7. Disconnect air intake hose and crankcase vent hose. Remove the PCV system hose from the rear of the upper manifold. Remove water bypass line at lower intake manifold.

8. Disconnect the EGR tube from the valve by removing the flange nut.

9. Remove the upper intake manifold retaining bolts (note location of bolts for correct installation) and remove it and the **throttle body as an assembly.**

10. Remove the engine oil dipstick bracket retaininig bolt. Remove all fuel line retaining clips and disconnect all fuel lines as required.

11. Disconnect the electrical connections from fuel injectors and position harness aside. Remove the fuel supply manifold retaining bolts. Remove fuel supply manifold and injectors.

12. Remove the upper and lower retaining bolts from lower manifold. Remove lower intake manifold assembly.

13. Installtion is the reverse of the removal procedure. Torque (always torque retaining bolts in steps) lower manifold to cylinder head and upper intake manifold in sequence to 15–22 ft. lbs.

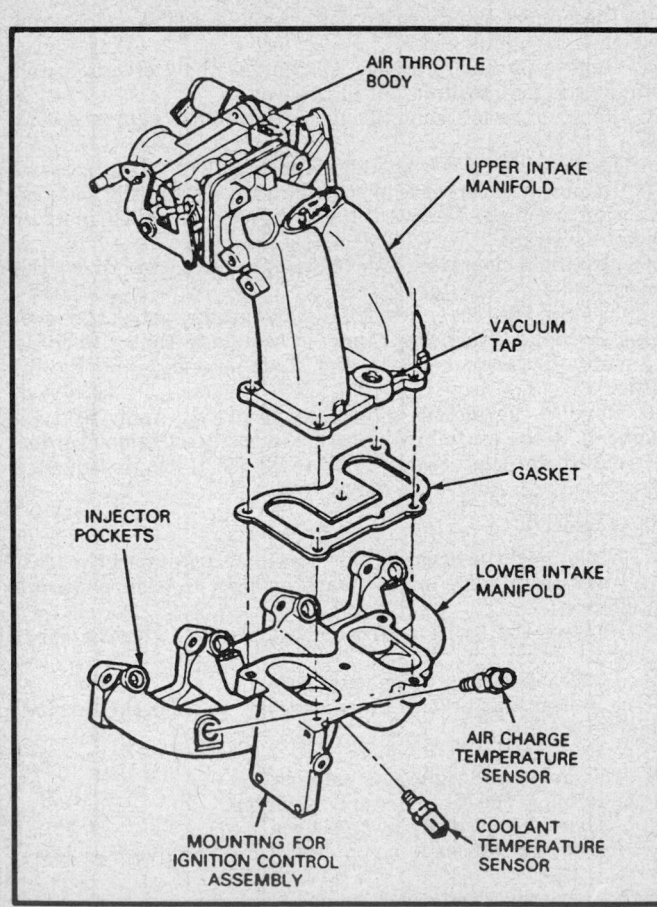

Intake manifold assembly–2.3L engine

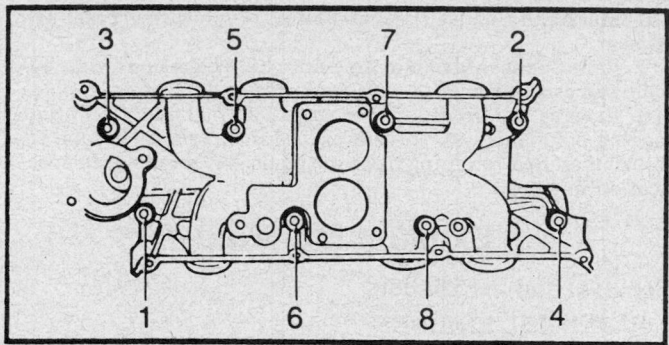

Intake manifold bolt torque sequence—2.8L engine

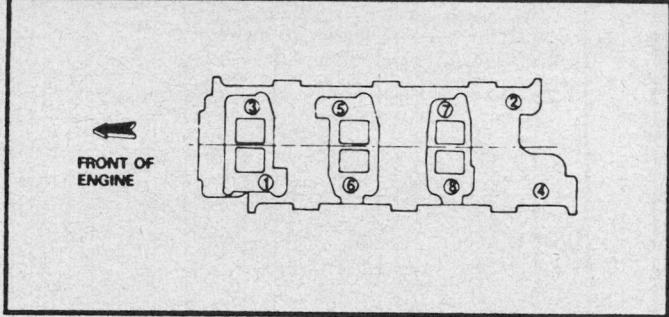

FRONT OF ENGINE

Intake manifold bolt torque sequence—2.9L engine

Torque the fuel supply manifold to 15–22 ft. lbs. Pressurize fuel system check for leaks. Check engine for correct idle.

2.8L ENGINE

1. Raise and safely support the vehicle as necessary. Drain the cooling system. Remove the air cleaner and duct assembly.
2. Disconnect the negative battery cable. Disconnect the accelerator cable from the carburetor linkage.
3. Disconnect and remove the upper radiator hose. Disconnect and remove the bypass hose from the intake manifold and thermostat housing.
4. Remove the distributor cap and spark plug wires as an assembly. Turn the engine till No. 1 piston is at TDC (top dead center) on the compression stroke. Mark and remove the distributor.
5. Remove the fuel line from the fuel filter. Remove carburetor and EGR spacer as required. Remove any vacuum lines and controls that will interfere with the intake manifold removal. Label all hoses for identification.
6. Remove both valve covers. Remove the manifold mounting (note location for correct installation) nuts and bolts. Remove the manifold.

To install:
7. Remove all old gasket material and sealing compound from the mounting surfaces.
8. Apply sealing compound to the joining surfaces. Place the intake mounting gasket into position. Make sure that the tab on the right bank head gasket fits into the cutout of the manifold gasket. Apply sealing compound to the intake manifold bolt bosses and install the intake manifold. Tighten (always torque retaining bolts in steps) the mounting nuts and bolts in the proper torque sequence to correct specification.
9. Install the distributor and the rest of the removed components in reverse order. Reconnect the negative battery cable.
10. Refill the cooling system, start the engine and check for coolant or oil leaks.
11. Check idle rpm and ignition timing. Adjust if necessary.

2.9L ENGINE

1. Raise and safely support the vehicle as necessary. Disconnect battery negative cable.
2. Remove air cleaner air intake duct from throttle body.
3. Disconnect throttle cable and bracket assembly.
4. Disconnect EGR tube at EGR valve.
5. Disconnect all vacuum hoses from fittings on upper intake manifold.
6. Disconnect electrical connections at throttle body, EGR pressure sensor, intake manifold upper and lower and distributor. Also disconnect fuel injector sub harness from main EEC harness.
7. Remove upper intake manifold (plenum) assembly.
8. Drain coolant. Disconnect and remove hose from water outlet to radiator and heat supply.
9. Remove distributor cap and spark plug wires as an assembly.

10. Observe and mark the location of the distributor rotor and housing so ignition timing can be maintained as reassembly. Remove distributor hold down screw and clamp and lift out distributor.
11. Remove rocker arm covers.
12. Remove intake manifold attaching bolts and nuts. Note length of manifold attaching bolts during removal so that they may be installed in their original positions. Remove intake manifold.
13. Remove all old gasket material and sealing compound.

To install:
14. Apply sealing compound to the joining surfaces. Place the intake manifold gasket in position. Ensure the tab on the right hand bank cylinder head gasket fits into the cutout of the manifold gasket.
15. Apply sealing compound to the attaching bolt bosses on the intake manifold and position the intake manifold. Follow the tightening sequence and tighten the bolts to specifications in 4 equal steps. Always recheck torque after normal operating temperature is reached.
16. Install distributor so that rotor and housing are in the same position marked at removal.
17. Install distributor clamp and attaching bolts.
18. Replace rocker arm cover gasket and install rocker arm valve covers.
19. Install distributor cap and spark plug wires. Connect distributor wiring harness.
20. Apply sealing compound, joining surfaces of upper and lower intake manifold. Install upper intake manifold gaskets.
21. Install upper intake manifold (plenum) assembly and torque retaining bolts in sequence (center to end) to 15–18 ft. lbs. in steps.
22. Connect all vacuum hoses to fittings on upper intake manifold.
23. Connect electrical connections at throttle body, EGR pressure sensor, intake manifolds sub harness to EEC main harness.
24. Install and adjust throttle linkage bracket assembly and cover as required.
25. Connect hoses from water outlet to radiator and bypass hose from thermostat housing rear cover to intake manifold.
26. Connect battery negative cable. Refill and bleed the cooling system.
27. Recheck ignition timing and reset engine idle speed to specification. Start engine and check for coolant and oil leaks.

3.0L ENGINE

1. Raise and safely support the vehicle as necessary. Disconnect the negative battery cable.
2. Drain the engine cooling system.
3. Relieve the fuel pressure. Remove the throttle body. Disconnect the fuel lines.
4. Remove the fuel injector wiring harness from the engine.
5. Disconnect the upper radiator hose and the water outlet heater hose.

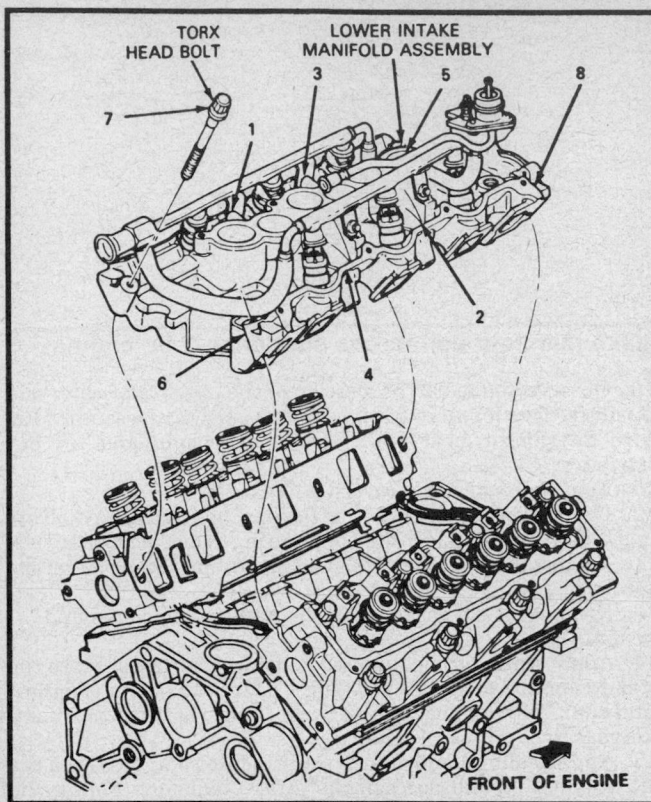

TORX
HEAD BOLT

LOWER INTAKE
MANIFOLD ASSEMBLY

FRONT OF ENGINE

Intake manifold bolt torque sequence—3.0L engine

6. Mark and remove the distributor. Remove the rocker arm covers.

7. Remove the intake manifold attaching bolts and studs. The manifold can be removed with fuel rails and injectors in place.

8. Reverse the procedure for installation. Lightly oil all attaching bolts and stud threads before installation. Torque the intake manifold retaining bolts in the proper sequence to specification in steps.

Exhaust Manifold

Removal and Installation

2.0L AND 2.3L ENGINES

1. Disconnect the negative battery cable. Raise and safely support the vehicle as necessary. Remove the air cleaner and duct assembly.

2. Remove the EGR line at the exhaust manifold. Loosen the EGR tube. Remove the check valve at the exhaust manifold and disconnect the hose at the end of the air bypass valve.

3. Remove the bracket attaching the heater hoses to the valve cover. Disconnect the exhaust pipe from the exhaust manifold.

4. Disconnect the EGO sensor. Remove the exhaust manifold mounting bolts/nuts. Remove the manifold.

5. Install the exhaust manifold in the reverse order. Torque bolts in sequence and to specification.

2.8L AND 2.9L ENGINES

1. Disconnect the negative battery cable. Raise and safely support the vehicle as necessary. Remove the air cleaner and duct assembly.

2. Remove the left side heat shroud from the exhaust manifold. Remove any thermactor system parts that will interfere with manifold removal. Disconnect the choke heat tube at the carburetor on the 2.8L engine.

3. Disconnect the exhaust pipes from the exhaust manifolds. Remove the mounting nuts from exhaust manifold studs. Remove the exhaust manifolds.

4. Install in the reverse order using new exhaust pipe to man-

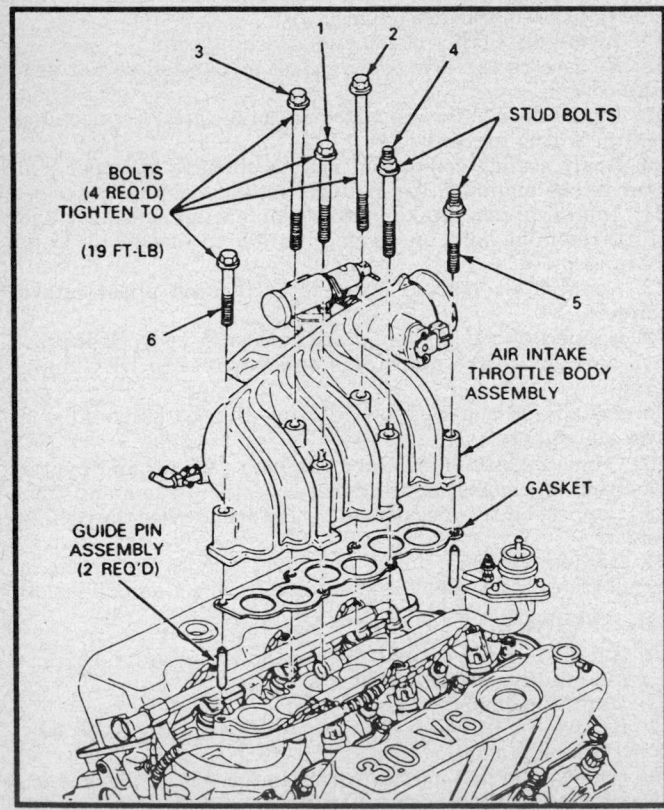

STUD BOLTS

BOLTS
(4 REQ'D)
TIGHTEN TO
(19 FT-LB)

AIR INTAKE
THROTTLE BODY
ASSEMBLY

GASKET

GUIDE PIN
ASSEMBLY
(2 REQ'D)

Air intake manifold bolt torque sequence—3.0L engine

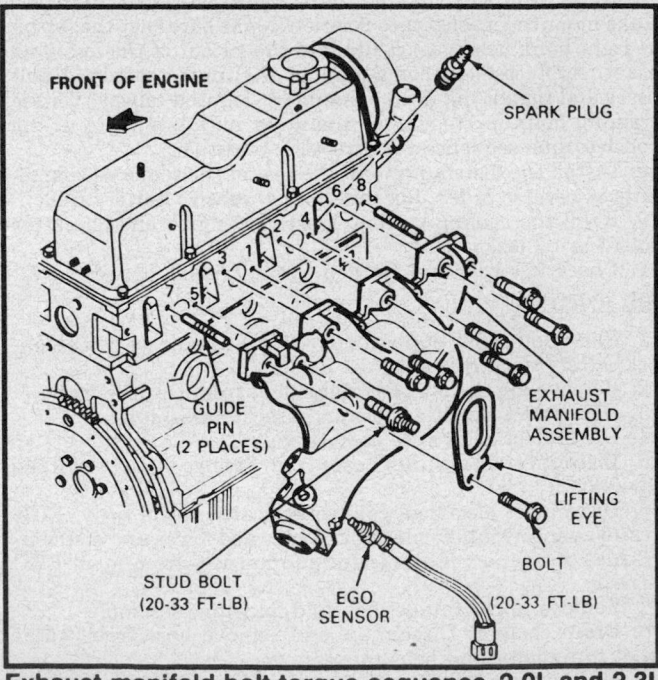

FRONT OF ENGINE

SPARK PLUG

GUIDE
PIN
(2 PLACES)

EXHAUST
MANIFOLD
ASSEMBLY

LIFTING
EYE

BOLT

STUD BOLT
(20-33 FT-LB)

EGO
SENSOR

(20-33 FT-LB)

Exhaust manifold bolt torque sequence—2.0L and 2.3L engines

ifold gaskets. Torque the retaining bolts to proper specification working from the center to the end of the manifold.

3.0L ENGINE

1. Disconnect the negative battery cable. Raise and support the vehicle as necessary. The following steps are for removal of the left side manifold.
   a. Remove the dipstick tube support bracket.
   b. Remove the power steering pump pressure and return hoses.
   c. Remove the manifold to exhaust pipe attaching nuts.
   d. Remove the exhaust manifold attaching bolts and remove the manifold.
2. The following steps are for removal of the right side manifold.
   a. Remove the heater hose support bracket.
   b. Disconnect the heater hoses.
   c. Remove the manifold to exhaust pipe attaching nuts.
   d. Remove the manifold attaching bolts and remove the manifold.
3. Install the manifolds in the reverse order of removal. Torque the retaining bolts to proper specification working from the center to the end of the manifold.

Timing Chain Front Cover

Removal and Installation

1. Disconnect the negative battery cable. Raise and safely support the vehicle as necessary. Drain the cooling system.
2. Drain engine oil. Remove the oil pan. Lower the vehicle. Remove all necessary hoses and vacuum lines. Remove the the shroud and radiator.
3. Remove the drive belt(s), power steering bracket and A/C compressor if so equipped, fan assembly.
4. Remove the water pump. Remove the drive pulley (and damper on 3.0L engine) from the crankshaft using a suitable tool.
5. Remove the front cover attaching bolts. Remove the front cover.
6. Installation is the reverse of the removal procedure. Tighten oil pan retaining bolts to 5–8 ft. lbs. and front cover retaining bolts 13–16 ft. lbs.

Front Cover Oil Seal

Removal and Installation

2.8L AND 2.9L ENGINES

NOTE: It is not necessary to remove the front cover for this service procedure.

1. Disconnect the negative battery cable. Raise and safely support the vehicle as necessary. Drain the coolant and remove the radiator.
2. Remove the crankshaft pulley and the water pump drive belt.
3. Remove the front cover oil seal with tool 1175–AC or equivalent and impact slide hammer T59L–100–B or equivalent.
4. Installation is the reverse of removal. Coat the new front seal with heavy SF engine oil before installing.

3.0L ENGINE

NOTE: It is not necessary to remove the front cover for this service procedure.

1. Disconnect the negative battery cable. Raise and safely support the vehicle as necessary. Remove drive belts.
2. Remove the crankshaft pulley.
3. Remove the damper bolt and washer. Remove the damper

from the crankshaft using tool T58P–6316–D and T82L–6316–B or equivalent.
4. Pry the seal from the timing cover with a flat bladed tool. Use care to prevent damage to the front cover and the crankshaft.
5. Installation is the reverse of removal. Lubricate the seal lip with clean engine oil before installing.

Timing Chain and Gears

Removal and Installation

2.8L ENGINE

1. Crank the engine until the timing marks are in the correct (aligned) position. Disconnect the negative battery cable. Raise and safely support the vehicle as necessary.
2. Drain the cooling system and crankcase.
3. Remove the oil pan and radiator.
4. Remove the front cover assembly.
5. Remove the camshaft gear.
6. Install a gear puller or equivalent and remove the crankshaft gear.
7. Installation is the reverse of the removal procedure. Check camshaft for endplay. Make sure that timing marks are in the correct position upon installation. Torque the camshaft gear bolt to 30–36 ft. lbs. Torque camshaft thrust plate to 13–16 ft.

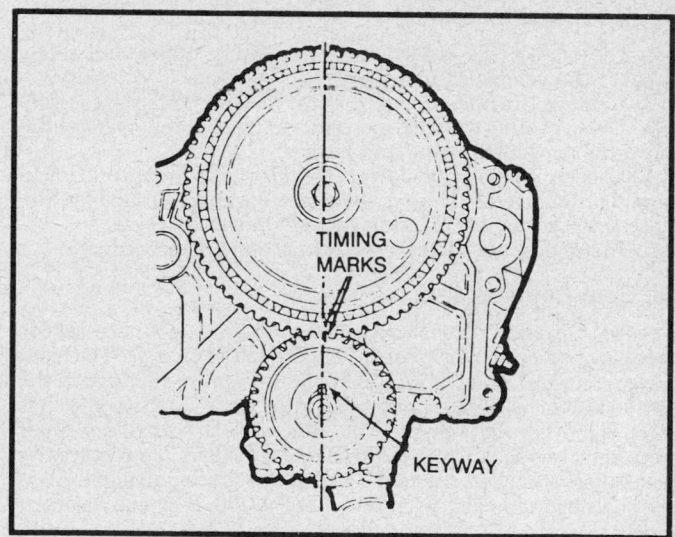

Timing marks–2.8L engine

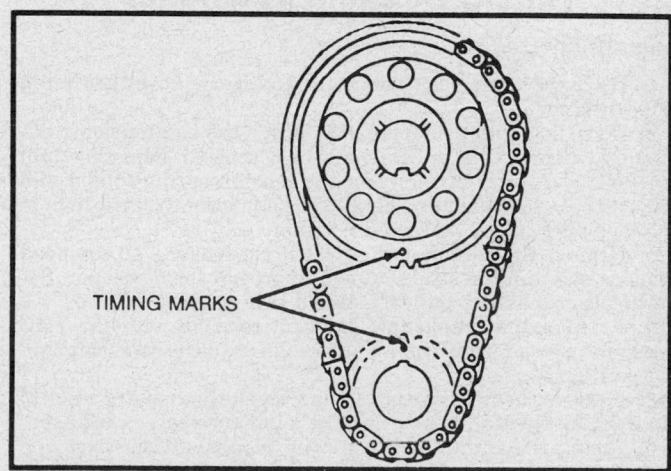

Timing marks–2.9L and 3.0L engines

lbs. Torque the crankshaft pulley retaining bolt to 85–96 ft. lbs. Replace the oil filter. Refill all fluid levels. Road test the vehicle for proper operation.

2.9L AND 3.0L ENGINES

1. Crank the engine until the timing marks are in the correct (aligned) position. Disconnect the negative battery cable. Raise and safely support the vehicle as necessary.

2. Remove the crankshaft pulley, damper if so equipped and front cover assemblies.

3. Remove the camshaft sprocket attaching bolt and washer. Slide both sprockets and timing chain forward and remove as assembly.

4. Installation is the reverse of the removal procedure. Torque the camshaft sprocket bolt to 19–28 ft. lbs. on the 2.9L engine and 46 ft. lbs. on the 3.0L engine. Torque the crankshaft pulley to 85–96 ft. lbs. on the 2.9L engine crankshaft damper bolt to 107 ft. lbs. on the 3.0L engine. Torque camshaft thrust plate to 13–16 ft. lbs. on the 2.9L engine and 7 ft. lbs on the 3.0L engine.

5. Start the engine, check for leaks. Check and adjust ignition timing. Replace the oil filter. Refill all fluid levels. Road test the vehicle for proper operation.

Timing Belt Outer Cover

Removal and Installation

1. Disconnect the negative battery cable. Raise and safely support the vehicle as necessary.

2. Remove the fan assembly. Remove drive belts as required.

3. Drain cooling system and remove upper radiator hose. Remove thermostat housing and gasket.

4. Loosen and position power steering pump mounting bracket aside. Remove the timing belt outer cover retaining bolt. Release the 8 cover interlocking tabs. Remove the cover.

5. Installation is the reverse of the removal procedure.

Oil Seal Replacement

The front oil seal has been designed so that it is not necessary to remove the front cover with the engine in the chassis. The front cover, camshaft and the auxiliary shaft seals are replaced in the same manner with the same tools after the respective gear has been removed. To remove the cam and the auxiliary shaft sprockets, use tool T74P–6256–B or equivalent. To remove the crankshaft sprocket, use tool T74P–6306–A or equivalent. All of the seals are removed with tool T74P–6700–B or equivalent.

Timing Belt and Tensioner

Adjustment

1. Disconnect the negative battery cable. Remove the timing belt outer cover.

2. If the belt timing is incorrect, loosen the belt tensioner adjustment screw. Place camshaft belt tension adjusting tool T74P–6254–A or equivalent on the tension spring rollpin and retract the belt tensioner. Tighten the adjustment screw to hold the tensioner in the retracted position.

3. Remove the bolts holding the timing sensor if so equipped in place and pull the sensor assembly free of the dowel pin. Remove the crankshaft pulley/hub and belt guide.

4. Position the crankshaft sprocket to align with the TDC mark and the camshaft sprocket to align with the camshaft timing pointer.

5. Remove the distributor cap and set the distributor rotor to No. 1 firing position by turning the auxiliary shaft as required.

6. Install the timing belt over the crankshaft sprocket and then counterclockwise over the auxiliary and camshaft sprockets. Align belt over sprockets.

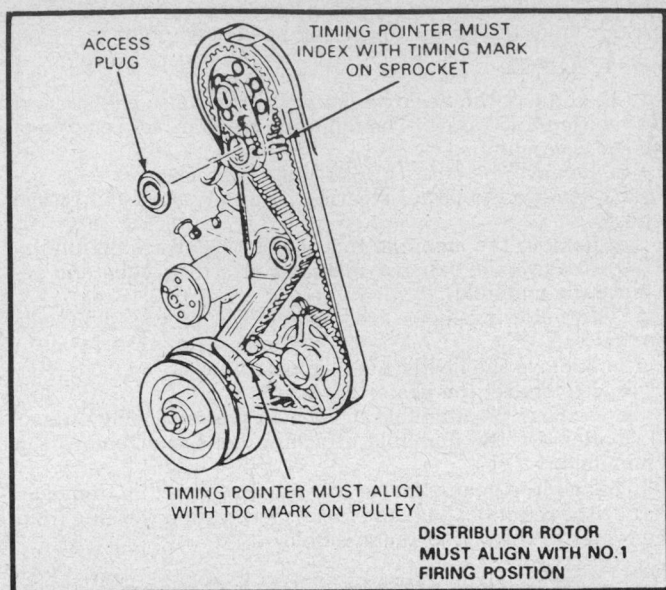

Timing marks–2.0L and 2.3L engines

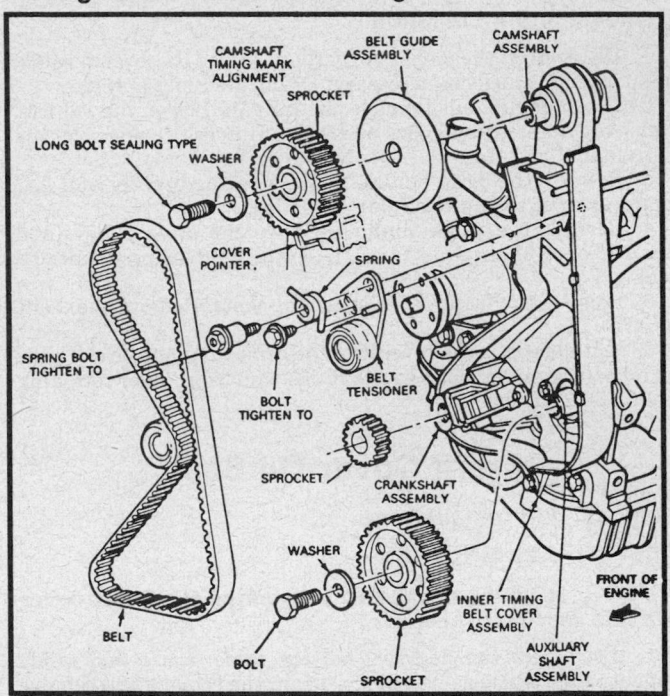

Timing belt assembly–2.3L engine

7. Loosen the tensioner adjustment bolt and allow the tensioner to move against the belt. Manually push the roller against the belt and tighten the bolt as necessary. The spring cannot be used to set belt tension. A tool must be used on the tensioner assembly.

8. To ensure the belt does not jump time during rotation, remove the spark plugs. Rotate the crankshaft 2 complete turns in normal rotation to remove the slack from the belt. Tighten tensioner adjustment bolt 14–21 ft. lbs. and pivot (spring) bolt to 28–40 ft. lbs. Check the alignment of the timing marks.

9. Install the crankshaft belt guide. Install the timing sensor if so equipped onto the dowel pin and tighten the 2 longer bolts.

10. To align the timing sensor if so equipped rotate the crankshaft 45 degrees (¼ turn) counterclockwise and install the crankshaft pulley/hub assembly and bolt.

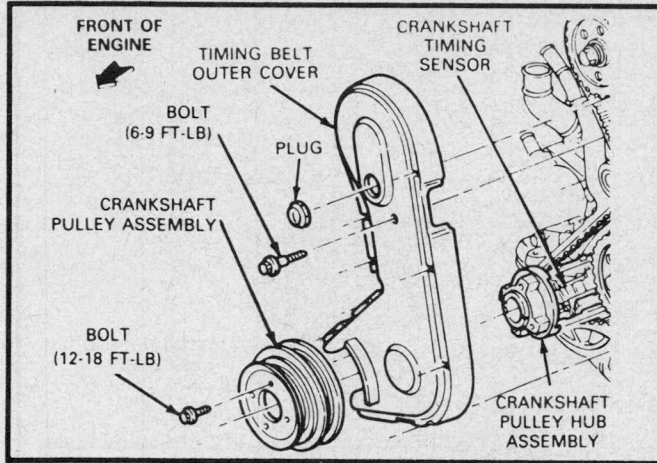

Timing cover assembly–2.3L engine (1989)

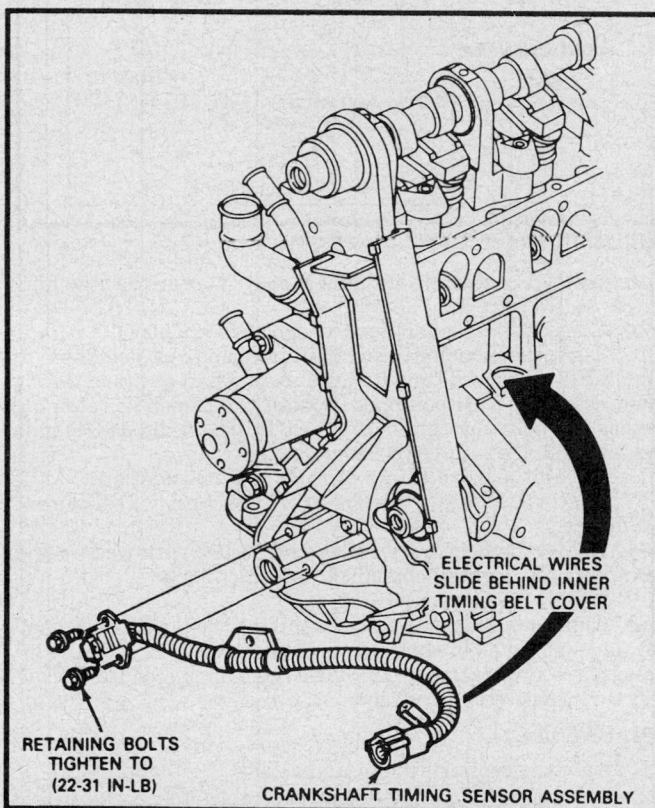

Crankshaft timing sensor–2.3L engine (1989)

11. Rotate the crankshaft 90 degrees (½ turn) clockwise so that the vane of the crankshaft pulley engages with the timing sensor positioner. Tighten the 2 shorter sensor bolts.

12. Rotate the crankshaft 90 degrees (½ turn) counterclockwise and remove the timing sensor positioner.

13. Rotate the crankshaft 90 degress (½ turn) clockwise and measure the outer vane to sensor air gap. The air gap must be 0.018–0.039 in.

14. Install the timing belt outer cover and the spark plugs. Reconnect the negative battery cable.

Removal and Installation

1. Disconnect the negative battery cable. Raise and safely support the vehicle as necessary.

2. Drain the cooling system. Lower the vehicle. Remove the alternator assembly as required.

3. Disconnect the upper radiator hose. Remove the water pump pulley.

4. Remove the crankshaft pulley. Remove the timing belt outer cover assembly.

5. Loosen belt tensioner pulley assembly and remove the timing belt.

To install:

6. Install new timing belt. Release timing belt tensioner pulley.

7. Set camshaft/crankshaft (distributor rotor No. 1 firing position) timing and belt adjustment. Install timing belt outer cover and retaining bolt.

8. Install water pump pulley. Install crankshaft pulley.

9. Install alternator as necessary. Adjust drive belt.

10. Connect upper radiator hose and battery cable. Refill the cooling system. Start the engine and inspect for leaks. Check/adjust timing as required.

Timing Sprockets

Removal and Installation

1. Disconnect the negative battery cable. Raise and safely support the vehicle as necessary.

2. Remove timing belt cover. Remove timing belt assembly.

3. Remove timing sprockets retaining bolt(s). Remove timing sprocket as necessary with a suitable puller or equivalent.

4. Installation is the reverse of the remove procedure.

Camshaft

Removal and Installation

2.0L AND 2.3L ENGINES

NOTE: The following procedure covers camshaft removal and installation with the cylinder head on or off the engine. If the cylinder head has been removed start at Step 9.

1. Drain the cooling system. Remove the air cleaner assembly and disconnect the negative battery cable. On 2.3L engine relieve the fuel pressure.

2. Remove the spark plug wires from the plugs, disconnect the retainer from the valve cover and position the wires out of the way. Disconnect vacuum lines as necessary.

3. Remove all drive belts. Remove the alternator mounting bracket-to-cylinder head mounting bolts, position bracket and alternator out of the way.

4. Disconnect and remove the upper radiator hose. Disconnect the radiator shroud.

5. Remove the fan blades and water pump pulley and fan shroud. Remove cam belt (timing belt) and valve cover.

6. Align engine timing marks at TDC. Remove cam drive (timing belt) belt.

7. Raise and support the vehicle safely as required. Remove the front motor mount bolts. Disconnect the lower radiator hose from the radiator. Disconnect and plug the automatic transmission cooler lines if so equipped.

8. Raise the engine carefully as far as it will go. Place blocks of wood between the engine mounts and crossmember pedestals.

9. Remove the rocker arms (camshaft followers).

10. Remove the camshaft drive gear guide using a suitable puller. Remove the front oil seal.

11. Remove the camshaft retainer located on the rear mounting stand by unbolting the 2 bolts.

12. Remove the camshaft by carefully withdrawing toward the front of the engine. Care should be used to prevent damage to cam bearings, lobes and journals.

13. Check the camshaft journals and lobes for wear. Inspect the cam bearings, replace as required. The cylinder head must be removed for new bearings to be installed.

14. Installation is in the reverse order of removal. Coat the camshaft with heavy SF oil before sliding it into the cylinder head. Install a new front seal. Set camshaft timing and belt adjustment. Adjust valve lash (collapsed tappet gap) as required.

2.8L AND 2.9L ENGINES

1. Disconnect the negative battery cable from the battery. Relieve the fuel pressure on the 2.9L engine. Drain the coolant and remove the radiator, fan, spacer, water pump pulley and the drive belt.

2. Remove the distributor cap with spark plug wires as an assembly. Remove the distributor vacuum line, distributor (mark for correct installation), alternator, thermactor, rocker arm covers, fuel line and filter, carburetor if so equipped, EGR tube and intake manifold. Remove the spark plug wire boots.

3. Remove the rocker arm and the shaft assemblies. Lift out the pushrods and mark so they can be reinstalled in the same location.

4. Raise and safely support the vehicle as necessary. Drain oil and remove the oil pan.

5. Remove the drive sprocket attaching bolt and slide the sprocket off the end of the shaft.

6. Remove the engine front cover and water pump as an assembly.

7. Remove the camshaft gear retaining bolt and slide the gear off the camshaft on 2.8L engines. Remove the camshaft gear and timing chain assembly on the 2.9L engine.

8. Remove the camshaft thrust plate and the screws.

9. Remove the valve lifters (lifters must be kept in order for correct installation).

10. Carefully remove the camshaft from the block, avoiding any damage to the camshaft bearings. Remove the camshaft gear key and spacer ring.

To install:

11. Oil the camshaft journals with gear oil or assembly lube and apply it to the cam lobes.

12. Install the camshaft in the block, carefully avoiding damage to the bearing surfaces.

13. Install the spacer ring with the chamfered side toward the camshaft. Insert the camshaft key and install the thrust

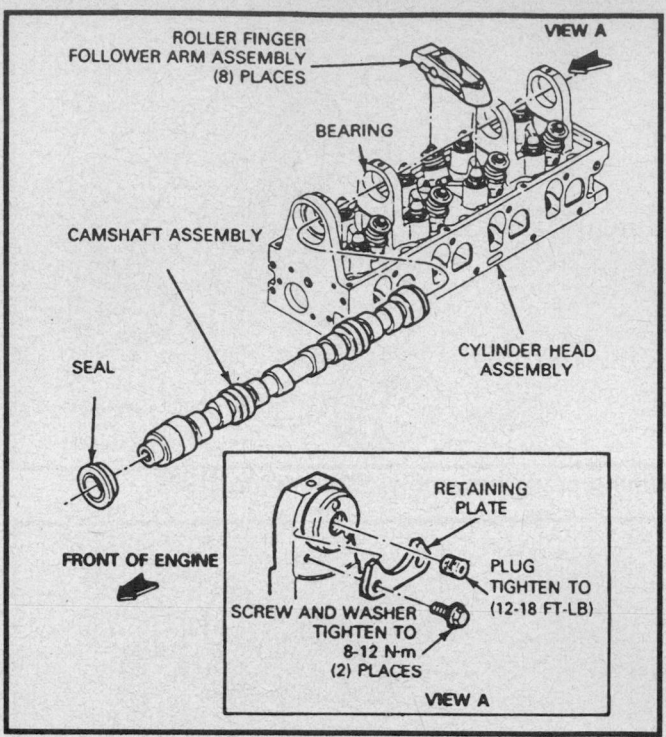

Camshaft assembly–2.3L engine

plate so that it covers the main oil gallery. Torque the attaching screws to 13–16 ft. lbs.

14. Check the camshaft for the specified endplay.

15. Turn the camshaft and the crankshaft as necessary to align the timing marks and install the camshaft gear and timing chain assembly if so equipped. Install the camshaft retaining washer and bolt and tighten to 30–36 ft. lbs on the 2.8L engine and 19–28 ft. lbs . on the 2.9L engine.

16. Install the valve lifters to their original locations.

17. Install the engine front cover and water pump assemblies.

18. Install the belt drive pulley and secure with washer and retaining bolt. Tighten the bolt to specifications.

19. Install the oil pan.

20. Apply a light grease to both ends of the pushrods. Install the valve pushrods in their original locations. Continue the installation in the reverse order of the removal procedure. Reconnect the negative battery cable.

3.0L ENGINE

1. Drain the cooling system and relieve the fuel pressure.

2. Disconnect the negative battery cable. Raise and safely support the vehicle as necessary. Drain engine oil. Remove the engine (this is a factory recommened procedure) from the vehicle and position in a engine stand or equivalent.

3. Remove the throttle body and intake manifold. Remove the timing cover assembly.

4. Position the rocker arm fulrum attaching bolts to one side. Remove the pushrods. Note location for correct installation.

5. Remove the valve lifters (must be installed in original location). If they are stuck in the bores from excessive varnish, use puller tool T70L–6500–A to remove them.

6. Check the camshaft endplay. If it is excessive, replace the thrust plate.

7. Remove the timing chain and the sprockets as an assembly.

8. Remove the camshaft thrust plate. Remove the camshaft by pulling it toward the front of the engine. Avoid damaging the bearings journals and the lobes.

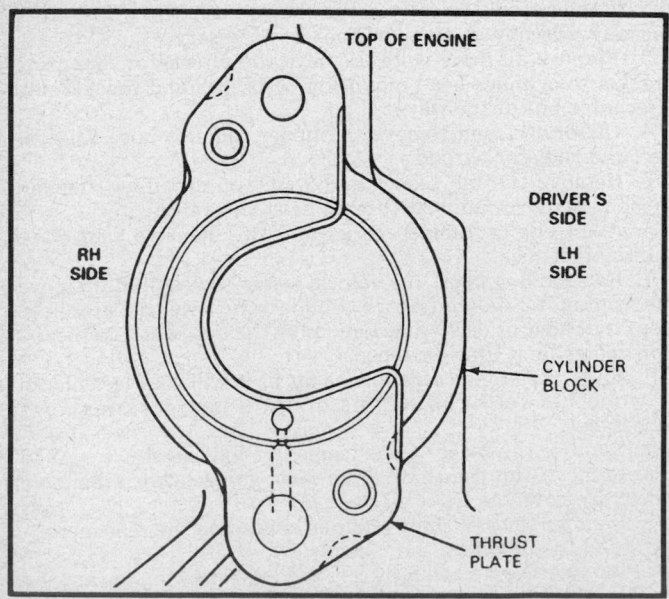

Camshaft thrust plate–2.9L engine

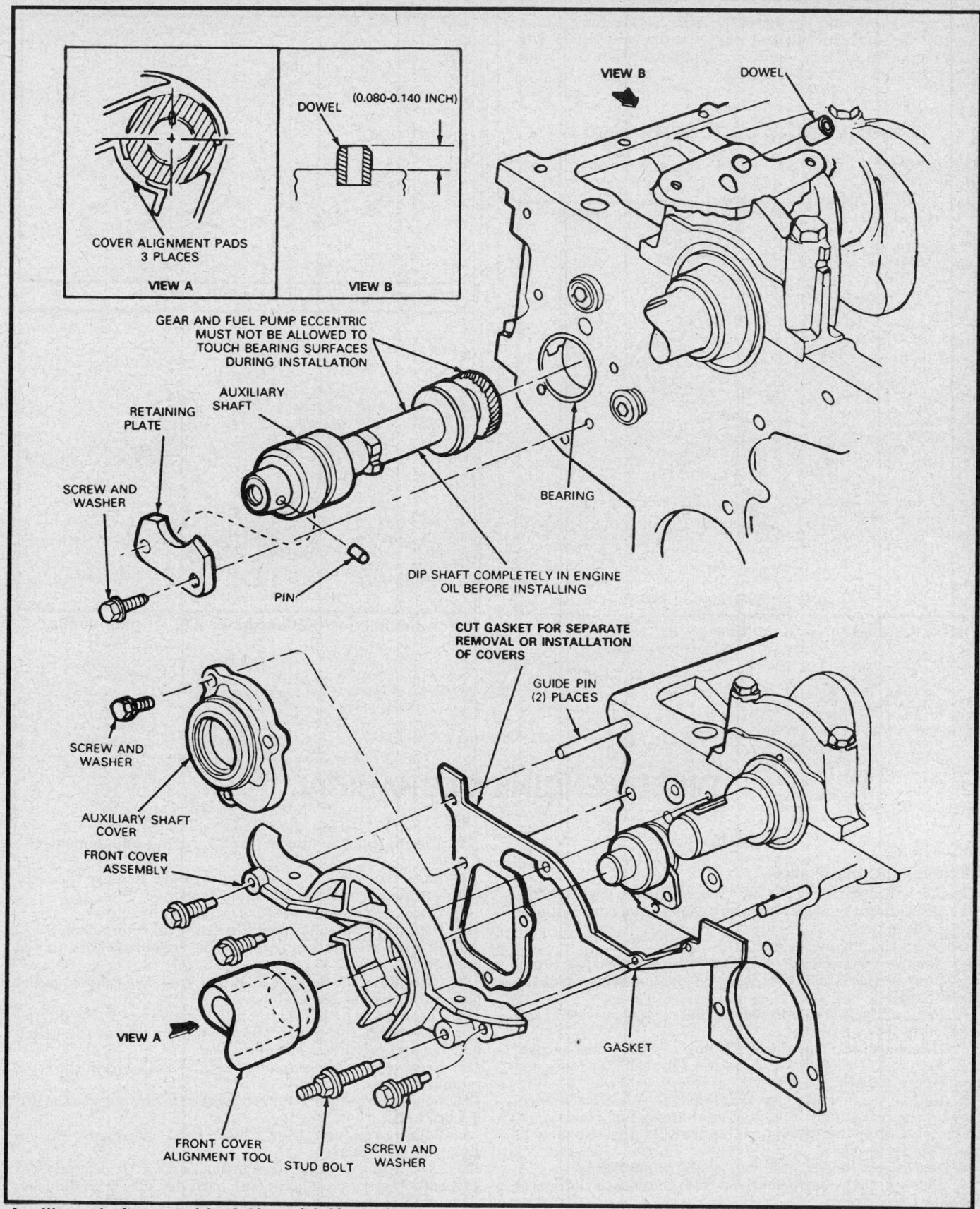

VIEW B

DOWEL

DOWEL   (0.080-0.140 INCH)

COVER ALIGNMENT PADS
3 PLACES

VIEW A

VIEW B

GEAR AND FUEL PUMP ECCENTRIC
MUST NOT BE ALLOWED TO
TOUCH BEARING SURFACES
DURING INSTALLATION

RETAINING
PLATE

AUXILIARY
SHAFT

SCREW AND
WASHER

BEARING

PIN

DIP SHAFT COMPLETELY IN ENGINE
OIL BEFORE INSTALLING

CUT GASKET FOR SEPARATE
REMOVAL OR INSTALLATION
OF COVERS

GUIDE PIN
(2) PLACES

SCREW AND
WASHER

AUXILIARY SHAFT
COVER

FRONT COVER
ASSEMBLY

VIEW A

GASKET

FRONT COVER
ALIGNMENT TOOL

STUD BOLT

SCREW AND
WASHER

Auxiliary shaft assembly–2.0L and 2.3L engines

9. Installation is the reverse of the removal procedure. Lubricate the camshaft journals and lobes and the valve lifters with heavy engine oil (SAE 50) before installation. Torque the thrust plate attaching bolts to 6–8 ft. lbs.

Piston and Connecting Rod

Positioning

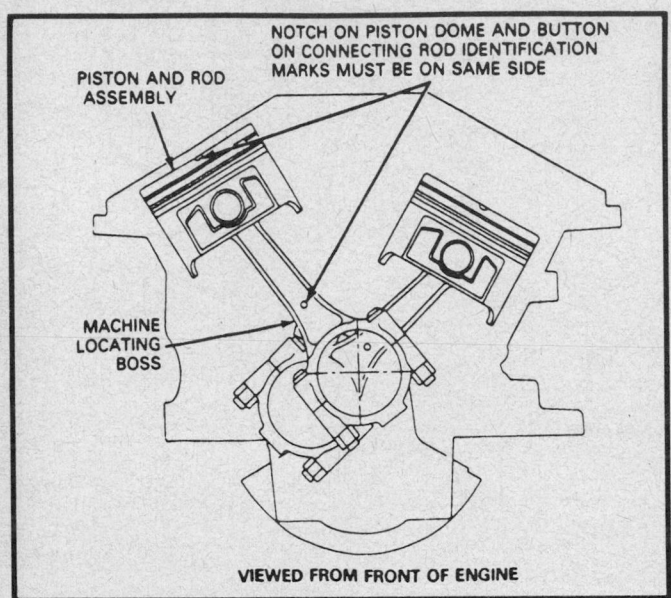

Piston installation–3.0L engine

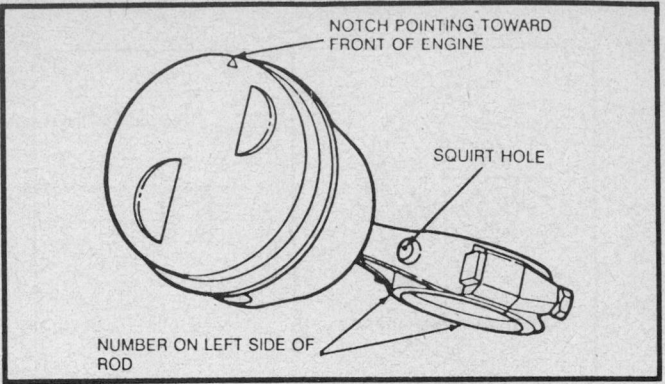

Piston installation–2.0L and 2.3L engines

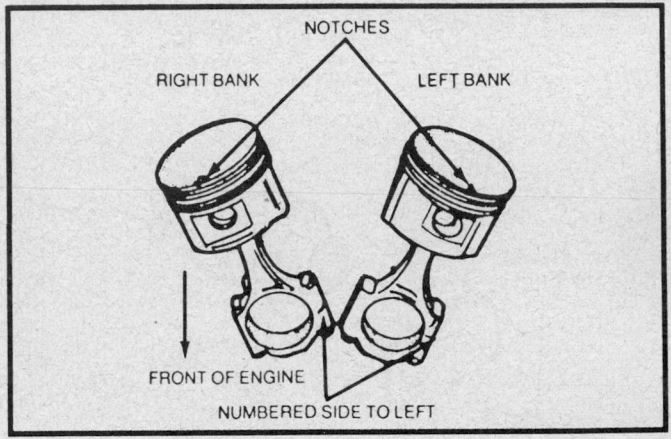

Piston installation–2.8L engine, 2.9L engine similar

DIESEL ENGINE MECHANICAL

Engine

Removal and Installation

1. Mark the location of the hood hinges and remove the hood.
2. Disconnect the negative battery cables from both batteries and at the engine.
3. Drain the engine coolant.
4. Remove the crankcase breather hose at the rocker cover.
5. Remove the intake hose between the air cleaner and the turbocharger.
6. Remove the A/C compressor (do not discharge system) and position it out of the way.
7. Disconnect and plug the heater hoses from the heater core.
8. Remove the cooling fan. Disconnect the radiator hoses and remove the radiator.
9. Relieve the fuel pressure. Disconnect the electrical connector and the fuel supply line (plug line) at the fuel conditioner. Disconnect (cap) the fuel return line and the throttle cable at the injection pump.
10. Disconnect the vacuum lines at the pump fitting.
11. Disconnect the engine harness from the chassis harness at the alternator bracket.
12. Disconnect the wires from the glow plug bus bar.
13. Disconnect the starter motor wiring and remove the starter.
14. Raise the vehicle and support it safely. Remove the right side wheel and the right side inner fender.
15. Disconnect the oil pressure switch wire.
16. Disconnect the oil filter lines at the oil filter adapter.
17. Remove the nuts attaching the engine mounts to the brackets.
18. Disconnect the muffler inlet pipe from the exhaust outlet pipe (turbocharger assembly).
19. Disconnect the power steering pump hoses at the pump.
20. Disconnect the clutch servo hydraulic line at the clutch housing and position it out of the way.
21. Remove the transmission attaching bolts, except the top 2 retaining bolts.
22. Lower the vehicle. Attach an engine lifting hoist to the lifting brackets.
23. Remove the top 2 transmission bolts and remove the engine from the vehicle.
24. Installation is the reverse of the removal procedure. Connect battery ground cables at both batteries. Check all fluid levels and fill as required. Run engine and check for fuel, oil and coolant leaks. Road test the vehicle for proper operation.

Cylinder Head

Removal and Installation

1. Disconnect battery ground cables from both batteries.
2. Mark location of hood hinges and remove hood.
3. Drain cooling system.
4. Disconnect breather hose from rocker cover.
5. Remove heater hose clamp from rocker cover and position hoses out of the way.
6. Remove cooling fan and shroud.
7. Remove accessory drive belts.
8. Remove upper front timing belt cover.
9. Loosen and remove camshaft/injection pump timing belt from camshaft sprocket.
10. Remove inlet hose between air cleaner and the turbocharger inlet.
11. Raise and safely support the vehicle. Disconnect muffler inlet pipe from turbocharger assembly exhaust fitting. Lower vehicle.
12. Remove fuel conditioner and bracket and position assembly out of the way.
13. Disconnect and remove fuel lines between injection pump and nozzles. Cap all lines and fittings using protective cap set T85L-9395-A or equivalent.
14. Disconnect heater hose from fitting on left hand rear of cylinder head.
15. Remove A/C compressor and mounting bracket.
16. Disconnect glow plug electrical leads from No. 2 and No. 3 glow plugs.
17. Disconnect coolant temperature switch wire.
18. Remove intake and exhaust manifold.
19. Remove rocker cover.
20. Remove cylinder head retaining bolts in correct sequence.
21. Remove cylinder head. Remove old head gasket.
22. Remove components as necessary.

To install:

23. Assemble components to head as necessary.
24. Clean gasket mating surfaces on cylinder head and engine block.
25. Position new cylinder head gasket on engine block.
26. Position cylinder head on engine block and install cylinder head bolts. Tighten bolts in sequence shown, as follows:
    a. Tighten bolts in sequence to 38–42 ft. lbs.
    b. Tighten bolts in sequence to 76–83 ft. lbs.
27. Install rocker cover. Ensure half moon gasket is installed in rear of cylinder.
28. Install intake and exhaust manifolds.
29. Connect coolant temperature switch connector.
30. Connect glow plug connectors to No. 3 and No. 4 glow plugs.
31. Install A/C compressor bracket and A/C compressor.
32. Connect heater hose to fitting on left hand rear of cylinder head.
33. Connect fuel lines to injection pump and nozzles.
34. Install fuel conditioner and bracket.
35. Raise vehicle and connect muffler inlet pipe to turbocharger assembly exhaust fitting. Lower vehicle.
36. Connect inlet hose between air cleaner and turbocharger inlet.
37. Install and adjust injection pump/camshaft timing belt.
38. Install upper timing belt cover. Install accessory drive belts.
39. Install heater hoses on rocker cover and install clamp.
40. Connect breather hose to rocker cover. Change engine oil and filter. Fill engine with specified quantity and quality of oil.
41. Fill and bleed cooling system. Connect battery ground cables to both batteries.
42. Run engine and check for oil, fuel and coolant leaks. Install hood.

Valve Lash

Adjustment

1. Warm engine to normal operating condition. Remove rocker cover.
2. Rotate the engine until No. 1 piston is at TDC of compression stroke. Check or adjust valve clearance of valves labeled A.
3. Rotate the engine (360 degrees) until No. 4 piston is at TDC of compression stroke. Check or adjust valve clearance of valves labeled B.
4. If valve clearance is not within specifications. Valve clearance on a hot engine is 0.010 in. for intake and exhaust valves. Loosen adjusting screw locknut. Rotate the adjust screw to the proper clearance. Hold adjusting screw and tighten locknut to 9–13 ft. lbs.
5. Install rocker cover.

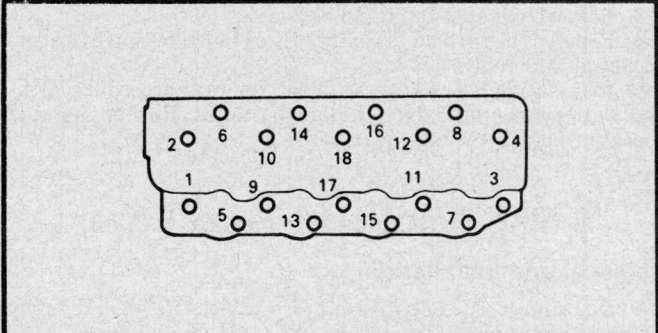

Cylinder head bolt removal sequence–2.3L diesel engine

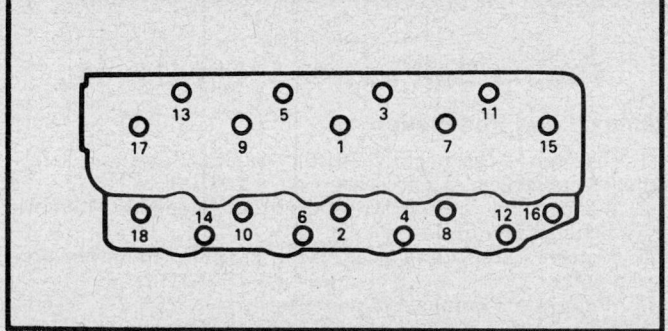

Cylinder head bolt installation sequence–2.3L diesel engine

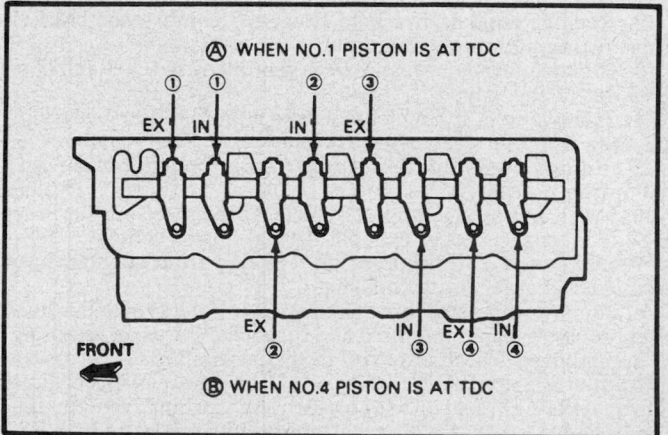

Valve clearance adjustment

Rocker Arms/Shaft

Removal and Installation

1. Disconnect ground cables from both batteries. Remove the valve cover.
2. Remove the bolts attaching the rocker shaft to the cylinder head, 1 turn at a time from the front to the rear and remove the rocker shaft.

To install:

3. Position the rocker shaft on the cylinder head. Be certain the end of the rocker shaft with the single oil hole is toward the front of the engine. Also, ensure the rocker shaft is installed with the oil holes down.
4. Install the rocker shaft retaining bolts and tighten one turn at a time from front to rear, repeating the sequence until all the bolts are seated. Tighten the bolts to 25–28 ft. lbs.
5. Adjust valve rocker arms. Install the valve cover.
6. Reconnect the ground cables. Run the engine and check for oil leaks.

Intake Manifold

Removal and Installation

1. Disconnect ground cables from both batteries.
2. Remove support braces from A/C compressor bracket, inlet fitting and intake manifold.
3. Remove A/C compressor from mounting bracket and position out of the way.
4. Remove inlet fitting from intake manifold.
5. Remove turbocharger oil feed line from cylinder head and turbocharger center housing. Remove oil line clamp bolt.
6. Loosen bolts attaching turbocharger heat shield to exhaust manifold. Remove top bolt and position shield out of the way.
7. Remove wastegate actuator from turbocharger and mounting bracket.
8. Remove 2 top actuator mounting bracket bolts. Loosen bottom bracket bolts and position bracket out of the way.
9. Remove remaining intake manifold bolts and nuts and remove intake manifold.
10. Installation is the reverse of the removal procedure. Torque all retaining bolts and nuts to specification in steps. Run engine and check for oil and intake air leaks. Road test the vehicle for proper operation.

Exhaust Manifold

Removal and Installation

1. Disconnect battery ground cable from both batteries.
2. Remove support brackets from A/C compressor bracket, inlet fitting and intake manifold.
3. Remove A/C compressor from mounting bracket and position out of the way.
4. Remove inlet fitting from intake manifold. Remove air inlet tube from air cleaner-to-turbocharger inlet.
5. Remove wastegate actuator from turbocharger and mounting bracket.
6. Raise and safely support vehicle. Disconnect muffler inlet pipe from turbocharger exhaust fitting. Lower vehicle.
7. Disconnect turbocharger oil feed line from cylinder head and turbocharger center housing.
8. Remove nuts attaching exhaust manifold to cylinder head and remove exhaust manifold and turbocharger as an assembly.
9. Remove turbocharger from exhaust manifold if necessary.
10. Installation is the reverse of the removal procedure. Torque all retaining bolts to specification working from the center to end in steps. Connect battery ground cables to both batteries. Run engine and check for oil and exhaust leaks.

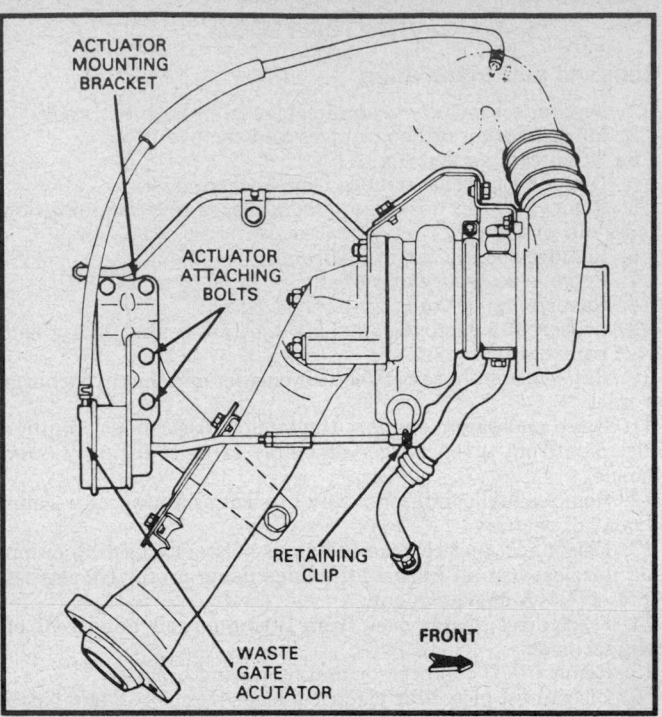

Turbocharger assembly

Turbocharger

Removal and Installation

1. Disconnect battery ground cable from both batteries.
2. Raise and safely support the vehicle as necessary.
3. Remove exhaust manifold assembly.
4. Remove the turbocharger mounting bolts. Remove the turbocharger assembly.
5. Installation is the reverse of the removal procedure. Connect battery ground cables to both batteries. Run engine and check for oil and exhaust leaks.

Timing Belt Upper Front Cover

Removal and Installation

1. Disconnect the negative battery cables. Raise and safely support the vehicle as necessary.
2. Remove drive belts as required.
3. Remove the 5 cover attaching bolts. Remove the upper front cover.
4. Installation is the reverse of the removal procedure.

Timing Belt Lower Front Cover

Removal and Installation

1. Disconnect the negative battery cables. Raise and safely support the vehicle as necessary.
2. Remove the cooling fan and shroud assembly. Remove drive belts as required.
3. Remove water pump pulley retaining bolts. Remove water pump pulley.
4. Remove the crankshaft pulley.
5. Remove the 5 cover attaching bolts. Remove the lower front cover.
6. Installation is the reverse of the removal procedure.

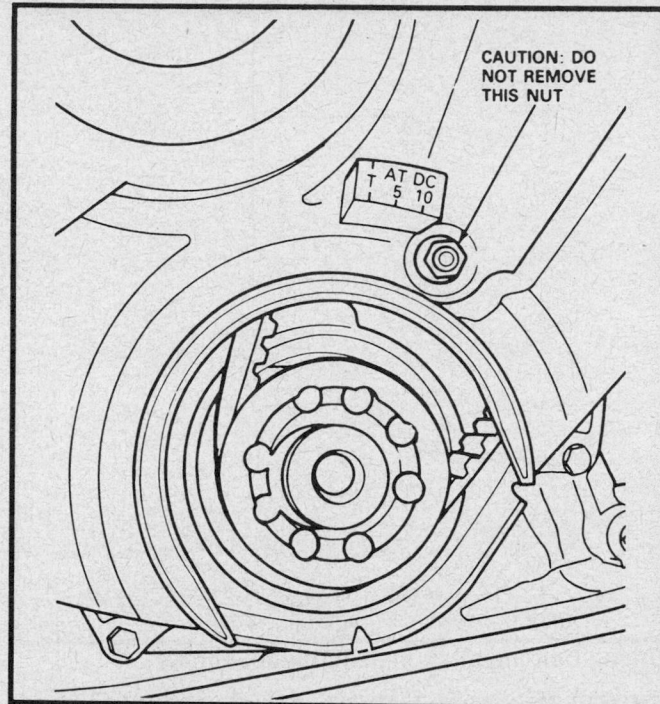

Timing belt lower cover

Oil Seal Replacement

1. Disconnect the negative battery cable. Raise and safely support the vehicle as necessary.
2. Remove the cooling fan and shroud assembly. Remove drive belts.
3. Remove the crankshaft pulley, upper and lower timing belt covers and timing belt.
4. Remove the crankshaft sprockets and timing plate.
5. Using a suitable tool remove the seal from engine assembly.
6. Installation is the reverse of the removal procedure. Torque the crankshaft pulley bolt to 123–137 ft. lbs.

Timing Belt and Tensioner

Adjustment

INJECTION PUMP/CAMSHAFT

1. Remove timing belt upper cover.
2. Rotate engine until No. 1 piston is at TDC on compression stroke.
3. Ensure crankshaft pulley, injection pump sprocket and camshaft sprocket are aligned with their timing marks.
4. Loosen top belt tensioner bolt 1 or 2 turns and loosen bottom bolt one complete turn. This allows tensioner spring to automatically adjust belt tension.
5. Rotate crankshaft clockwise to that alignment pointer on timing cover aligns with second tooth from alignment mark on camshaft sprocket.

NOTE: Rotate crankshaft smoothly by 2 camshaft sprocket teeth. Failure to do so will result in an incorrect belt tension and possible engine damage.

6. Tighten top belt tensioner mounting bolt to 16–21 ft. lbs, then tighten bottom bolt to 16–21 ft. lbs. Always tighten the top bolt first. Tighten bottom bolt first can cause tensioner to rotate and over-tension the timing belt.
7. Rotate crankshaft counterclockwise until timing marks

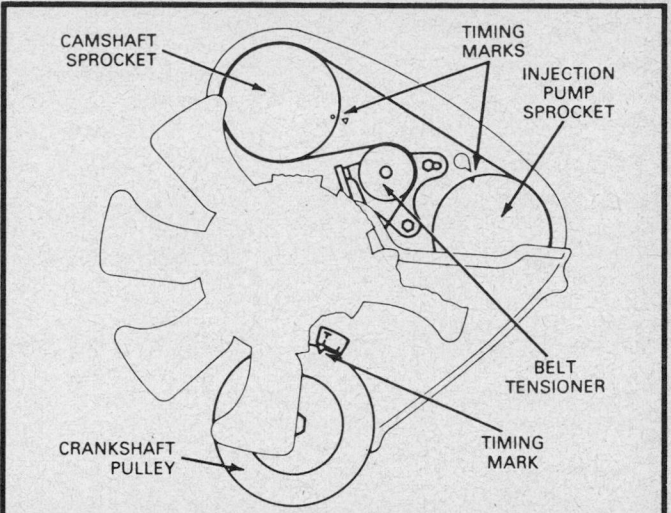

Timing marks belt adjustment–2.3L diesel engine

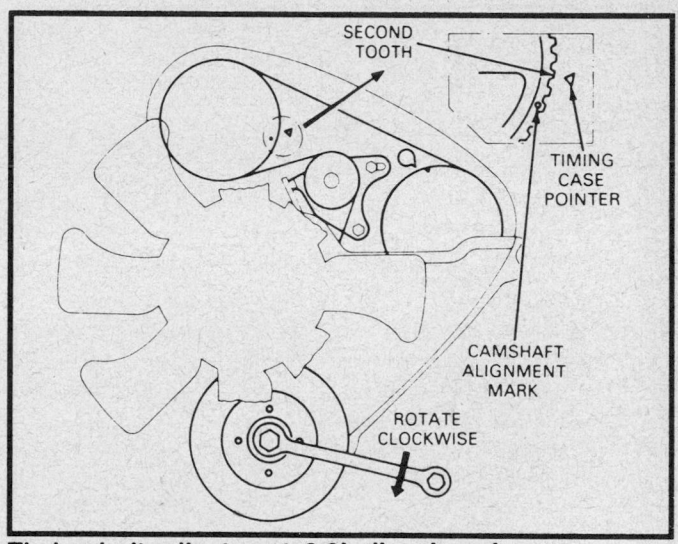

Timing belt adjustment–2.3L diesel engine

are aligned. Push belt down halfway between injection pump sprocket and camshaft sprocket and check deflection. If properly tensioned, belt should deflect 0.16–0.20 in.

SILENT SHAFT

1. Rotate crankshaft until No. 1 piston is at TDC on compression stroke.
2. Remove access cover for top belt tensioner bolt by inserting a suitable tool in slot and prying out.
3. Loosen top belt tension mounting bolt 1 complete turn. Then, loosen bottom bolt 1 to 2 turns. This allows tensioner spring to automatically adjust belt tension.
4. Tighten bottom tensioner bolt to 16–21 ft. lbs., then tighten top bolt to 15–19 ft. lbs. Always tighten bottom bolt first. Tighten top bolt first can cause tensioner to rotate and over-tension the timing belt.
5. Install access cover for top tensioner bolt by sliding down along 2 guide lines embossed on front lower cover.

Removal and Installation

1. Disconnect battery ground cables from both batteries.
2. Remove cooling fan and fan shroud.
3. Remove accessory drive belts.

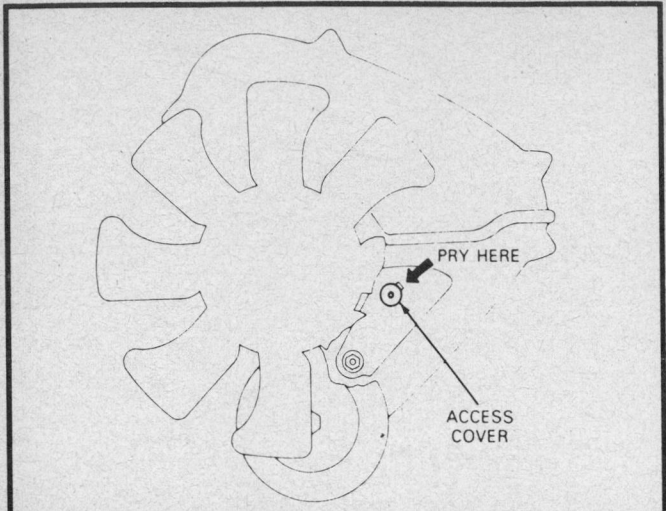

Silent shaft belt adjustment

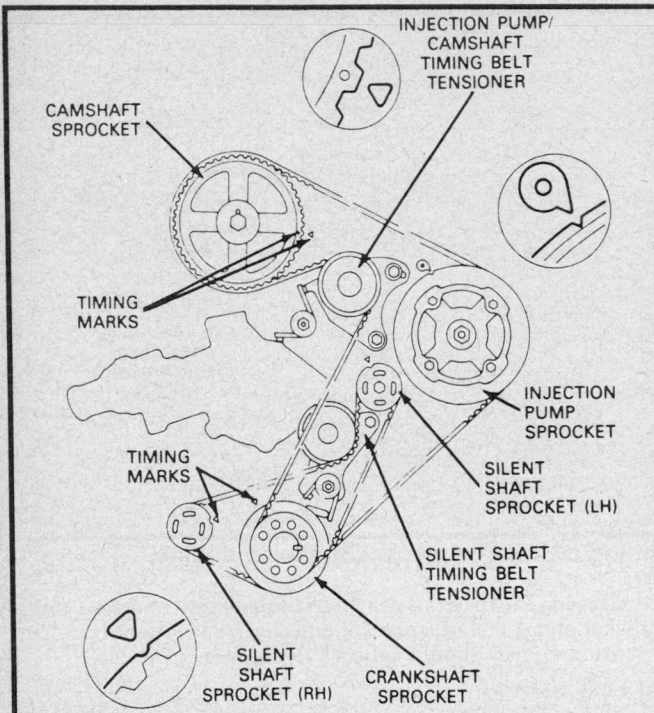

Timing marks for belt installation—2.3L diesel engine

4. Rotate crankshaft in direction of engine rotation to bring No. 1 piston to TDC of compression stroke.
5. Remove crankshaft pulley.
6. Remove upper and lower front covers.
7. Loosen belt tensioners from timing belts. Remove belt(s), as necessary.

To install:

8. Align crankshaft timing marks.
9. Align left hand and right hand silent shaft timing marks.
10. Install silent shaft belt.

NOTE: Install belt in original direction of rotation. For ease of installation, pry on tensioner spring to reduce load on tensioner.

11. Align camshaft timing marks.
12. Install injection pump/camshaft timing belt as follows:

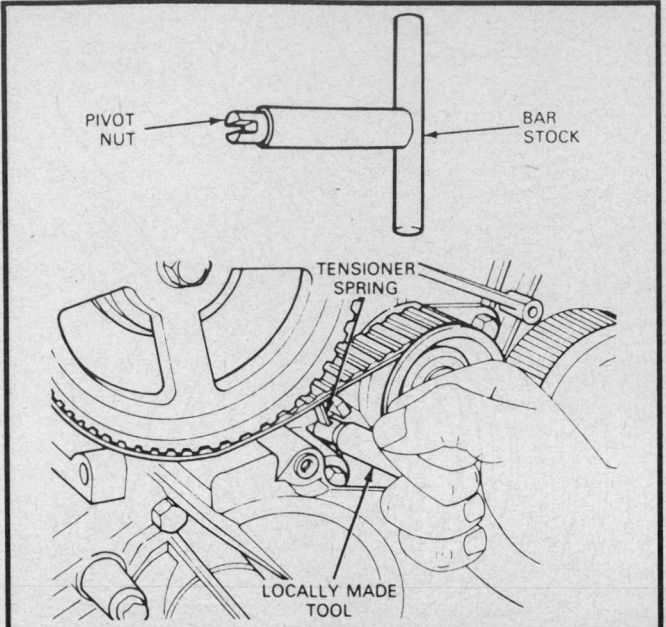

Timing belt installation—2.3L diesel engine

NOTE: To ease installation, locally manufacture the following tool. Using a pivot nut from a rear brake shoe adjuster, weld a piece of bar stock on the end.

a. Using the tensioner spring tool or equivalent, release the tension on the tension spring for the injection pump/camshaft timing belt.
b. After releasing spring tension, rotate tensioner toward water pump and tighten top bolt.
c. Install the belt (original direction of rotation).
d. Maintain tension on the belt to prevent the belt from slipping. After the belt is positioned, loosen the top tensioner bolt to tension the belt.

13. Adjust silent shaft belt and camshaft/injection pump belt tensions.
14. Install upper and lower front timing covers.
15. Install crankshaft pulley.
16. Install accessory drive belts.
17. Install cooling fan and fan shroud.
18. Connect battery ground cables to both batteries.

Timing Sprockets

Removal and Installation

1. Disconnect the negative battery cable. Raise and safely support the vehicle as necessary.
2. Remove timing belt covers. Remove timing belt(s).
3. Remove timing sprockets retaining bolt(s). Remove timing sprocket as necessary with a suitable puller or equivalent.
4. Installation is the reverse of the remove procedure.

Camshaft

Removal and Installation

1. Disconnect battery ground cables from both batteries.
2. Remove rocker cover.
3. Remove upper front timing cover.
4. Rotate crankshaft until No. 1 piston is at TDC on compression stroke.
5. Loosen camshaft/injection pump drive belt tensioner and remove timing belt from camshaft pulley.

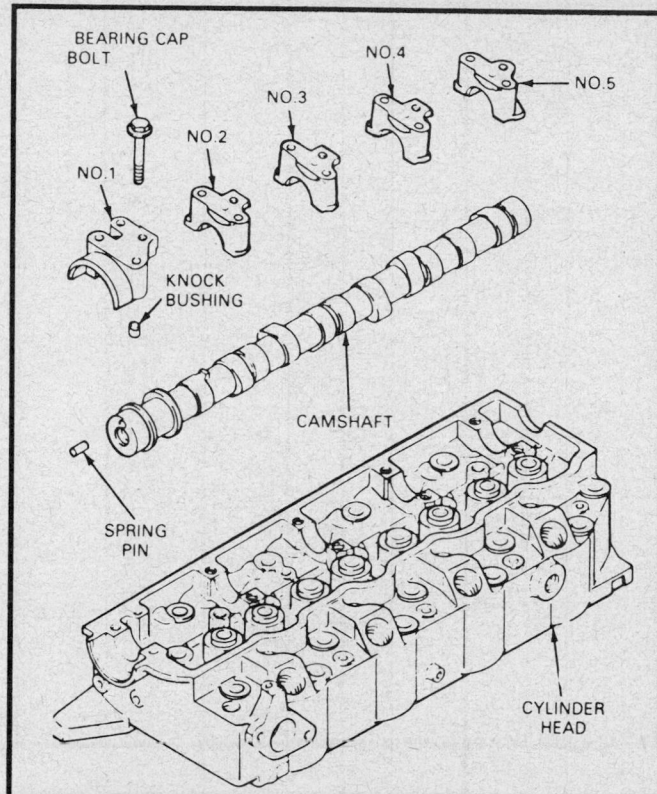

Camshaft assembly–2.3L diesel engine

6. Remove camshaft pulley bolt and remove pulley.
7. Remove rocker arm shaft.
8. Remove camshaft bearing caps (note location for correct installation) and remove camshaft.
9. Remove and discard camshaft oil seal.
10. Inspect camshaft and bearings.

To install:

11. Position camshaft on cylinder head and install bearing caps. Tighten bolts to 14–15 ft. lbs. Ensure bearing caps are installed in their original positions.
12. Coat sealing lip of new camshaft seal with engine oil and install seal using suitable tool. Ensure seal installer is positioned with hole over spring pin on camshaft.
13. Install rocker arm.
14. Install camshaft pulley.
15. Install camshaft/injection pump drive belt. Adjust drive belt.
16. Adjust valves. Install upper front timing cover and rocker cover.
17. Fill cooling system. Connect battery ground cable to both batteries. Run engine and check for oil leaks.

Auxiliary Shafts

Removal and Installation

RIGHT HAND SILENT SHAFT ASSEMBLY

1. Disconnect battery ground cables from both batteries.
2. Remove cooling fan and fan shroud.
3. Remove water pump pulley, crankshaft pulley, upper and lower timing belt covers, timing belts and crankshaft sprockets.
4. Raise and safely support the vehicle as necessary. Drain the engine oil and remove oil pan.
5. Remove pipe plug in right hand side of engine block, Insert cross point tool into hole to prevent right hand silent shaft from

rotating. Remove nut attaching silent shaft sprocket to drive gear and remove sprocket.
6. Remove bolts attaching front case to engine block (note location of bolts for correct installation).
7. Remove front case and gasket.
8. Remove silent shaft reverse rotation gear cover and remove silent shaft and gears.
9. Remove oil pump cover and remove oil pump drive gear and inner/outer gears (mark oil pump gears for correct installation).
10. Remove silent shaft reverse rotation drive gear oil seal using seal remover tool T58L–101–B or equivalent.
11. Remove crankshaft front oil seal.

To install:

12. Install silent shaft oil seal using a 21mm socket or equivalent.
13. Install silent shaft reverse rotation gears with marks aligned.
14. Install oil pump gears in front housing.

NOTE: Align marks on oil pump gears when installing.

15. Install oil pump gear cover.
16. Install silent shaft in reverse rotation drive gear. Position front cover and new gasket on engine block using care not to damage silent shaft bearing. Install bolts and tighten to 9–10 ft. lbs.
17. Install silent shaft sprocket. Insert suitable tool in hole in block to prevent silent shaft from rotating. Tighten sprocket nut to 25–28 ft. lbs.
18. Remove tool and install pipe plug.

NOTE: When installing silent shaft sprocket, ensure D flat on sprocket is aligned with D flat on shaft.

19. Install crankshaft front oil seal.
20. Install crankshaft sprocket.
21. Apply a bead of silicone sealant or equivalent along split lines between lower front case cover and rear oil seal retainer and engine block.
22. Install oil pan and retaining bolts tighten to 5–7 ft. lbs.
23. Install and adjust timing belts.
24. Install upper and lower timing belt covers.
25. Install crankshaft and water pump pulleys.
26. Install accessory drive belts, cooling fan and fan shroud.
27. Connect battery ground cables to both batteries. Run and check for oil leaks. Road test the vehicle for proper operation.

LEFT HAND SILENT SHAFT ASSEMBLY

1. Disconnect battery ground cables from both batteries.
2. Remove cooling fan and fan shroud.
3. Raise and safely support the vehicle as necessary. Remove accessory drive belts.
4. Remove alternator and bracket.
5. Remove water pump and crankshaft pulleys.
6. Remove upper and lower timing belt covers, timing belts and injection pump.
7. Remove access plate on left hand side of engine and insert a socket extension tool or equivalent in hole to prevent left hand silent shaft from rotating.
8. Remove bolt attaching sprocket to silent shaft and remove sprocket.
9. Remove bolts attaching front case to engine block and remove case.
10. Remove silent shaft.
11. Remove silent shaft seal using seal remover tool–1175–AC or equivalent.

To install:

12. Install a new silent shaft seal using an appropriate size socket or equivalent.
13. Install silent shaft.

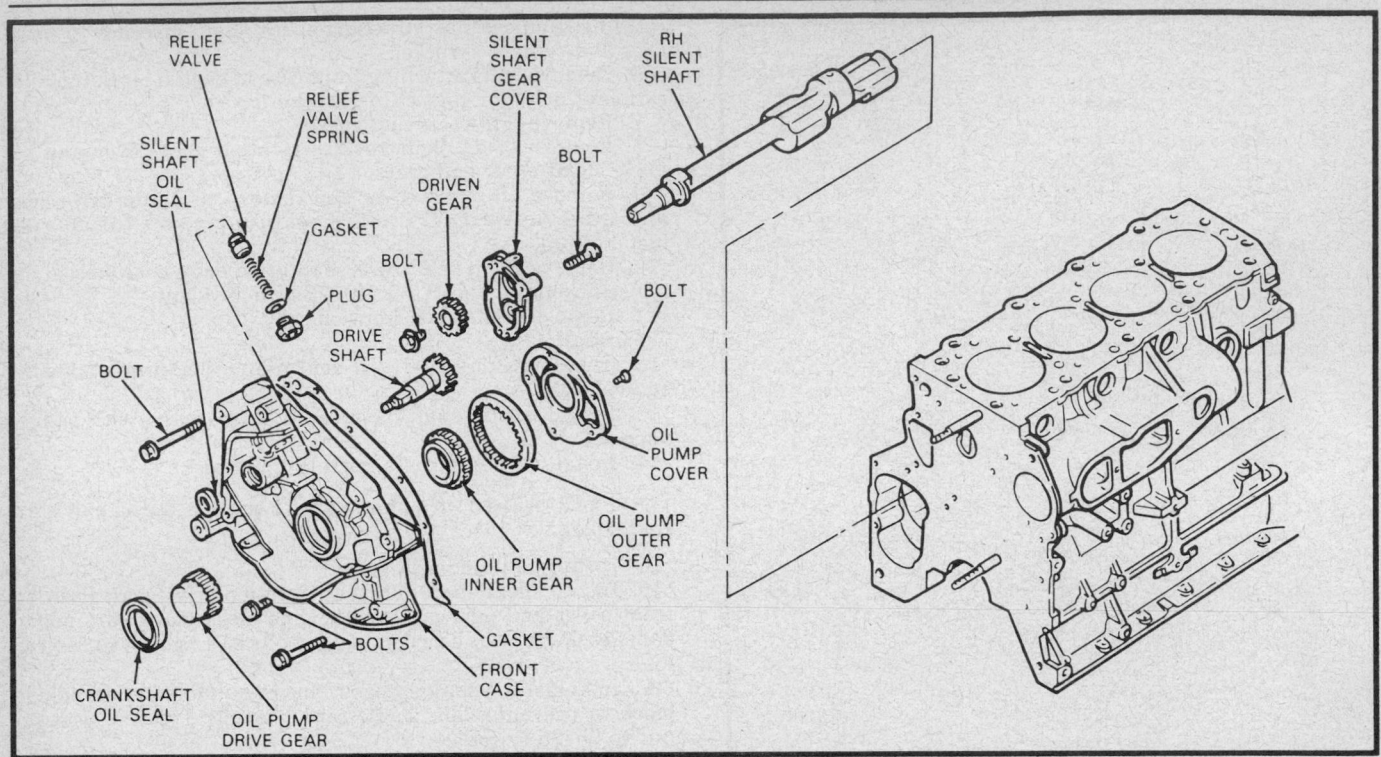

RELIEF VALVE

RELIEF VALVE SPRING

SILENT SHAFT OIL SEAL

GASKET

PLUG

BOLT

DRIVE SHAFT

BOLT

SILENT SHAFT GEAR COVER

DRIVEN GEAR

BOLT

RH SILENT SHAFT

BOLT

OIL PUMP COVER

OIL PUMP OUTER GEAR

OIL PUMP INNER GEAR

GASKET

FRONT CASE

BOLTS

CRANKSHAFT OIL SEAL

OIL PUMP DRIVE GEAR

Right hand silent shaft assembly

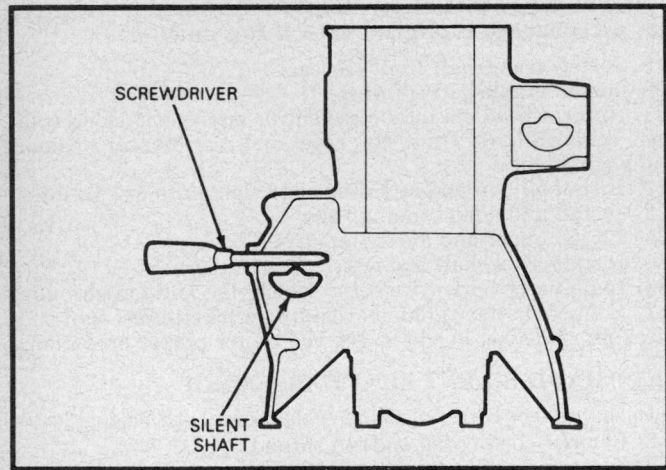

SCREWDRIVER

SILENT SHAFT

Right hand silent shaft removal

"D" FLATS

Silent shaft sprocket installation

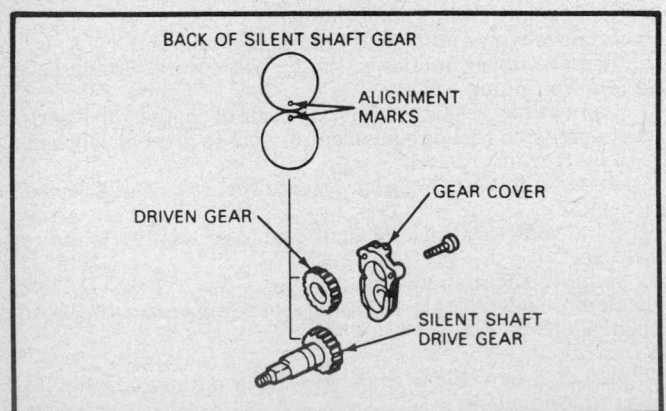

BACK OF SILENT SHAFT GEAR

ALIGNMENT MARKS

DRIVEN GEAR

GEAR COVER

SILENT SHAFT DRIVE GEAR

Right hand silent shaft installation

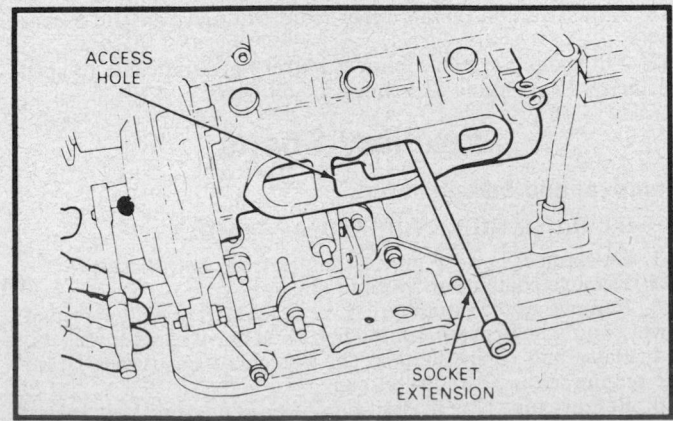

ACCESS HOLE

SOCKET EXTENSION

Left hand silent shaft removal

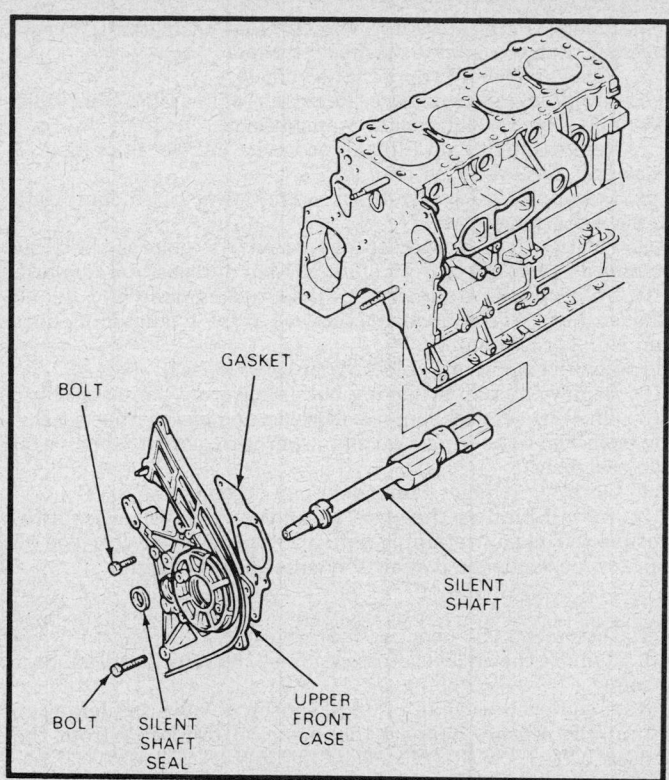

Left hand silent shaft assembly

Piston and Connecting Rod

Positioning

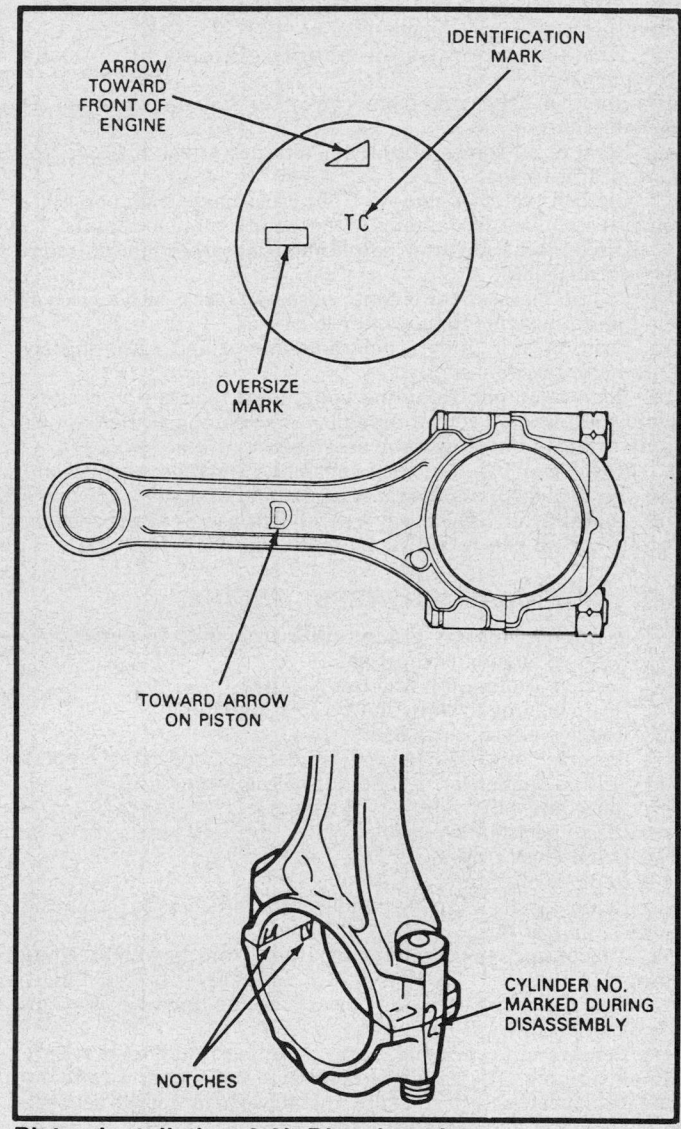

Piston installation–2.3L Diesel engine

14. Install front cover and new gasket on engine block. Note front cover bolts are different lengths.

15. Insert socket extension or equivalent in access hole in left hand side of engine.

16. Install silent shaft sprocket on silent shaft and tighten bolt to 25–28 ft. lbs. When installing silent shaft sprocket, ensure **D** flat on sprocket is aligned with **D** flat on shaft.

17. Remove extension from access hole and install cover.

18. Install crankshaft sprockets.

19. Install injection pump and sprocket.

20. Install and adjust timing belts.

21. Install upper and lower timing belt covers, water pump pulley and crankshaft pulley.

22. Install accessory drive belts.

23. Install cooling fan and shroud.

24. Connect battery ground cables to both batteries. Run engine and check for oil leaks. Road test the vehicle for proper operation.

ENGINE LUBRICATION

Oil Pan

Removal and Installation

2.0L AND 2.3L ENGINES

NOTE: Vehicles equipped with automatic transmission remove oil pan out the front of the engine compartment. Vehicles equipped with manual transmissions remove the oil pan out the rear of the engine compartment.

1. Disconnect the negative battery cable.

2. Remove air cleaner assembly on 2.0L engine. Remove air cleaner outlet tube at throttle body on 2.3L engine. Remove oil dipstick. Remove engine mount retaining nuts.

3. Remove oil cooler lines at the radiator, if so equipped. Remove bolts retaining the fan shroud to the radiator and remove shroud.

4. Remove radiator retaining bolts (automatic transmission). Position radiator upward and wire to the hood (automatic transmission).

5. Raise and safely support the vehicle.
6. Drain oil from crankcase.
7. Remove starter cable from starter and remove starter.
8. Disconnect the exhaust manifold tube to the inlet pipe bracket at the thermactor check valve. Disconnect the catalytic converter at the inlet pipe.
9. Remove transmission mount retaining nuts to the crossmember.
10. Remove bellcrank from converter housing (automatic transmission).
11. Remove oil cooler lines from retainer at the block (automatic transmission).
12. On 2WD vehicles remove front crossmember and on 4WD vehicles stabilizer bar assembly (automatic transmission).
13. Disconnect right front lower shock absorber mount (manual transmission).
14. Position jack under engine, raise and block with a piece of wood or equivalent. Remove jack.
15. Position jack under the transmission and raise slightly (automatic transmission).
16. Remove oil pan retaining bolts, lower pan to the chassis. Remove the low oil sensor assembly if so equipped. Remove oil pump drive and pick up tube assembly.
17. Remove oil pan (out the front for automatic transmission) (out the rear for manual transmission).
18. Installation is the reverse of the removal procedure. Torque the oil pan retaining bolts in steps to 7–10 ft. lbs.

2.3L TURBOCHARGED DIESEL ENGINE

1. Disconnect battery ground cable from both batteries.
2. Remove engine oil dipstick.
3. Remove cooling fan and fan shroud.
4. Drain cooling system and remove radiator.
5. Remove alternator belt.
6. Remove bolts securing A/C condenser to radiator support and position condenser up and out of the way.
7. Raise and safely support the vehicle.
8. Disconnect oil level switch wire.
9. Drain engine oil.
10. Remove oil filter.
11. Remove bolts securing stabilizer bar brackets to frame and lower stabilizer bar.
12. Disconnect power steering lines from power steering pump.
13. Remove clamp securing power steering line to crossmember; position line out of the way.
14. Remove nuts securing motor mounts to support brackets.
15. Position a jack under transmission housing and raise engine until it contacts dash panel. Install wooden wedges between motor mounts and crossmembers.
16. Remove oil pan bolts and let pan rest on crossmember.
17. Remove 2 bolts and 1 nut securing pickup tube to engine and lower pickup into oil pan.
18. Rotate crankshaft until crankshaft main bearing throws are parallel to bottom of engine to provide clearance to remove oil pan.
19. Remove oil pan through the front by first raising it up between the engine and radiator support. Then bring it out through the bottom.
20. Installation is the reverse of the removal procedure. Torque the retaining bolts to 5–7 ft. lbs. Connect battery ground cables to both batteries. Run engine and check for fluid leaks.

2.8L AND 2.9L ENGINES

1. Disconnect negative battery cable. Remove carburetor air cleaner assembly on 2.8L engine. Remove air intake tube on the 2.9L engine.
2. Remove fan shroud and position over fan.
3. Remove distributor cap, position forward of dash panel. Remove distributor and cover bore opening.

4. Remove nuts attaching engine front insulators to cross member. Remove engine oil dipstick tube.
5. Raise and safely support the vehicle.
6. Drain engine crankcase. Remove transmission fluid filler tube and plug pan hole (auto transmission).
7. Remove engine oil filter. Disconnect muffler inlet pipe(s), except on 2WD vehicles.
8. Disconnect oil cooler bracket and lower (if so equipped). Remove starter motor.
9. Position out of way, transmission oil cooler lines (if so equipped). Disconnect front stabilizer bar and position forward.
10. Position jack under engine and raise engine and install wooden blocks or equivalent between front insulator mounts and No. 2 crossmember.
11. Lower engine onto blocks and remove jack.
12. Remove oil pan attaching bolts. Lower oil pan assembly.
13. On 4WD vehicles remove oil pump and pickup tube assembly (attached to bearing cap) and lower into oil pan. Remove oil pan assembly.
14. On 2WD vehicles remove oil pan assembly.
15. Installation is the reverse of the removal procedure. Torque the oil pan retaining bolts in steps to 4–6 ft. lbs. The oil pan torque sequence is rear of engine to front inline.

3.0L ENGINE

1. Disconnect the negative battery cable.
2. Remove the oil level dipstick. Raise the vehicle and support it safely.
3. If equipped with an oil level sensor, remove the retaining clip at the sensor. Remove the electrical connector from the sensor.
4. Drain the crankcase. Remove the starter motor.
5. On 1986–88 vehicles remove the flywheel dust cover from the converter housing. Loosen the transmission bolts and slide the transmission ¼ in. rearward.
6. Remove the oil pan attaching bolts and remove the pan.
7. Installation is the reverse of removal. Torque the oil pan retaining bolts in steps to 6–8 ft. lbs.

Oil Pump

Removal and Installation

2.3L, 2.8L, 2.9L AND 3.0L ENGINES

1. Disconnect the negative battery cable. Raise and safely support the vehicle as necessary. Drain engine oil. Remove the oil pan.
2. Remove the oil pump inlet tube and screen assembly if necessary.
3. Remove the oil pump attaching bolts and remove the oil pump gasket and intermediate driveshaft.
To install:
4. Prime oil pump by filling the inlet and outlet port with clean engine oil and rotating the shaft of the pump to distribute it.
5. Position the intermediate driveshaft into the distributor socket.
6. Position the new gasket on the pump body and insert the intermediate driveshaft into the pump body.
7. Install the pump and intermediate driveshaft as an assembly. Do not force the pump if it does not seat readily. The driveshaft may be misaligned with the distributor shaft. To align it, rotate the intermediate driveshaft into a new position.
8. Install the oil pump attaching bolts. Install the oil pan. Reconnect the negative battery cable.

2.3L TURBOCHARGED DIESEL ENGINE

1. Disconnect battery ground cables from both batteries.
2. Remove cooling fan and fan shroud.
3. Remove water pump pulley, crankshaft pulley, upper and

lower timing belt covers, timing belts and crankshaft sprockets.

4. Raise and safely support the vehicle. Drain engine oil. Remove the oil pan.

5. Remove pipe plug in right hand side of engine block, Insert cross point tool into hole to prevent right hand silent shaft from rotating. Remove nut attaching silent shaft sprocket to drive gear and remove sprocket.

6. Remove bolts attaching front case to engine block and remove front case.

7. Remove front case and gasket.

8. Remove silent shaft reverse rotation gear cover and remove silent shaft and gears.

NOTE: Make alignment marks on oil pump components before removal for correct installation.

9. Remove oil pump cover and remove oil pump drive gear and inner and outer gears.

10. Installation is the reverse of the removal procedure. Connect battery ground cables to both batteries. Run again and check for oil leaks.

Checking

Thoroughly clean all parts in solvent and dry with compressed air. Check the inside of the pump housing for obvious wear or scoring.

Measure the inner rotor tip clearance. With the rotor assembly installed in the housing, place a straightedge over the rotor assembly and the housing. Measure the clearance (rotor endplay) between the straightedge and both the inner rotor and outer race. Measure the driveshaft to housing clearance by comparing shaft outer diameter to housing bearing inner diameter. Inspect relief valve spring for collapsed or worn condition. Check the spring tension. Check relief valve piston and bore for scores and free operation.

The inner to outer rotor tip clearance is 0.012 in. maximum (feeler gauge inserted ½ in.) and rotor assembly endplay clearance is 0.005 maximum. If any part of the oil pump requires replacement, replace the complete pump assembly.

Rear Main Bearing Oil Seal

Removal and Installation

ONE PIECE SEAL

1. Disconnect the negative battery cable. Raise and safely support the vehicle and remove the starter. Remove the transmission and on manual transmission equipped vehicles remove the clutch assembly.

2. Remove the flywheel. Lower the oil pan if necessary for working room.

3. Use an awl or equivalent to punch two small holes on opposite sides of the seal just above the split between the main bear-

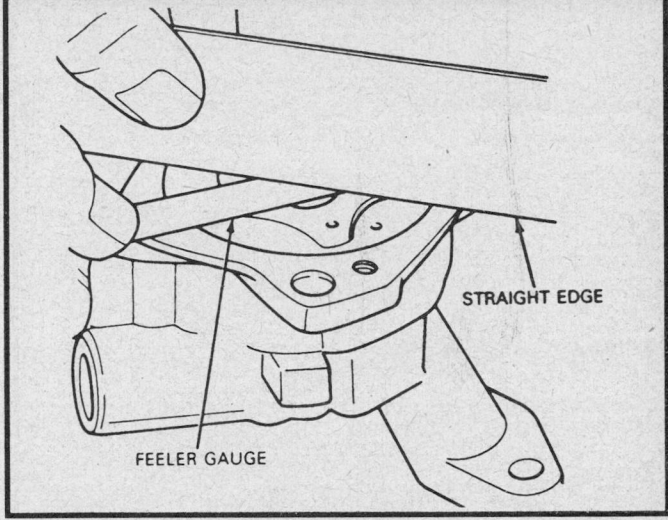
Measure rotor endplay

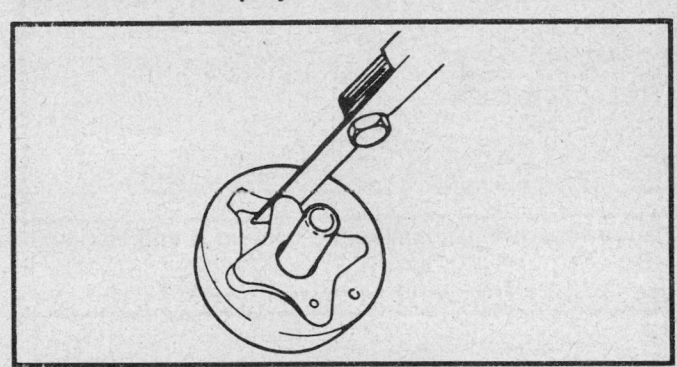
Measure inner rotor tip clearance

ing cap and engine block. Install a sheet metal screw in each hole. Use 2 small pry bars and pry evenly on both screws using two small blocks of wood as a fulcrum point for the pry bars. Use caution throughout to avoid scratching or damage to the oil seal mounting surfaces.

4. When the seal has been removed, clean the mounting recess.

5. Coat the seal and block mounting surfaces with oil. Apply white lube to the contact surface of the seal and crankshaft. Start the seal into the mounting recess and install with seal mounting tool.

6. Install the remaining components in the reverse order of removal.

MANUAL TRANSMISSION

For further information, please refer to "Professional Transmission Manual".

Transmission Assembly

Removal and Installation

1. Place the gearshift lever in neutral. Remove the boot retainer screws. Remove the bolts attaching the retainer (some ve-

hicles have 1 shifter retaining bolt) cover to the gearshift lever retainer. Disconnect the clutch master cylinder pushrod from the clutch pedal.

2. Pull the gearshift lever assembly, shim and bushing straight up and away from the gearshift lever retainer. Cover the shift tower opening in the extension housing with a cloth.

3. Disconnect the clutch hydraulic system master cylinder pushrod from the clutch pedal.

4. Disconnect the negative battery cable from the battery terminal.

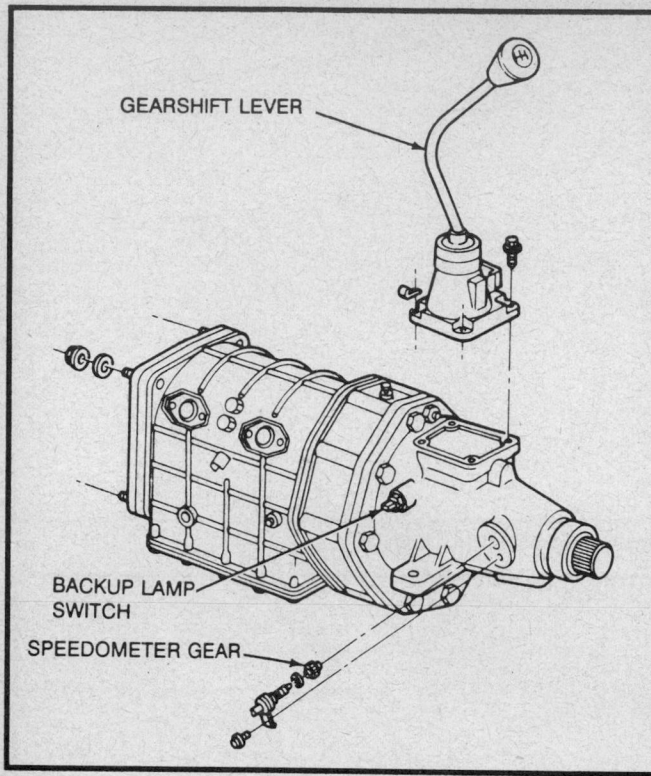

5 speed manual transmission–Bronco II and Ranger

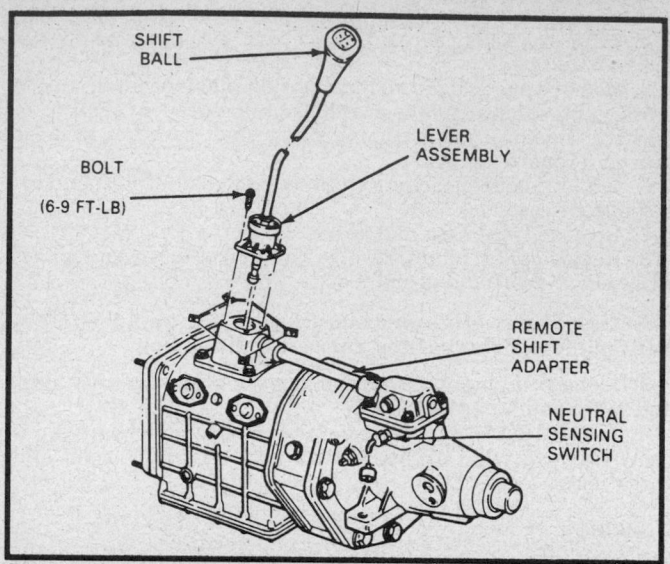

5 speed manual transmission–Aerostar

5. Raise and safely support the vehicle. Mark and disconnect the driveshaft at the rear. Pull the driveshaft rearward and disconnect from the transmission. Install a suitable plug in the extension housing to prevent lubricant leakage.

6. Remove the clutch housing dust shield and slave cylinder hydraulic line and secure it at one side.

7. Remove the speedometer cable from the extension housing.

8. Disconnect the starter motor and back-up lamp switch wires.

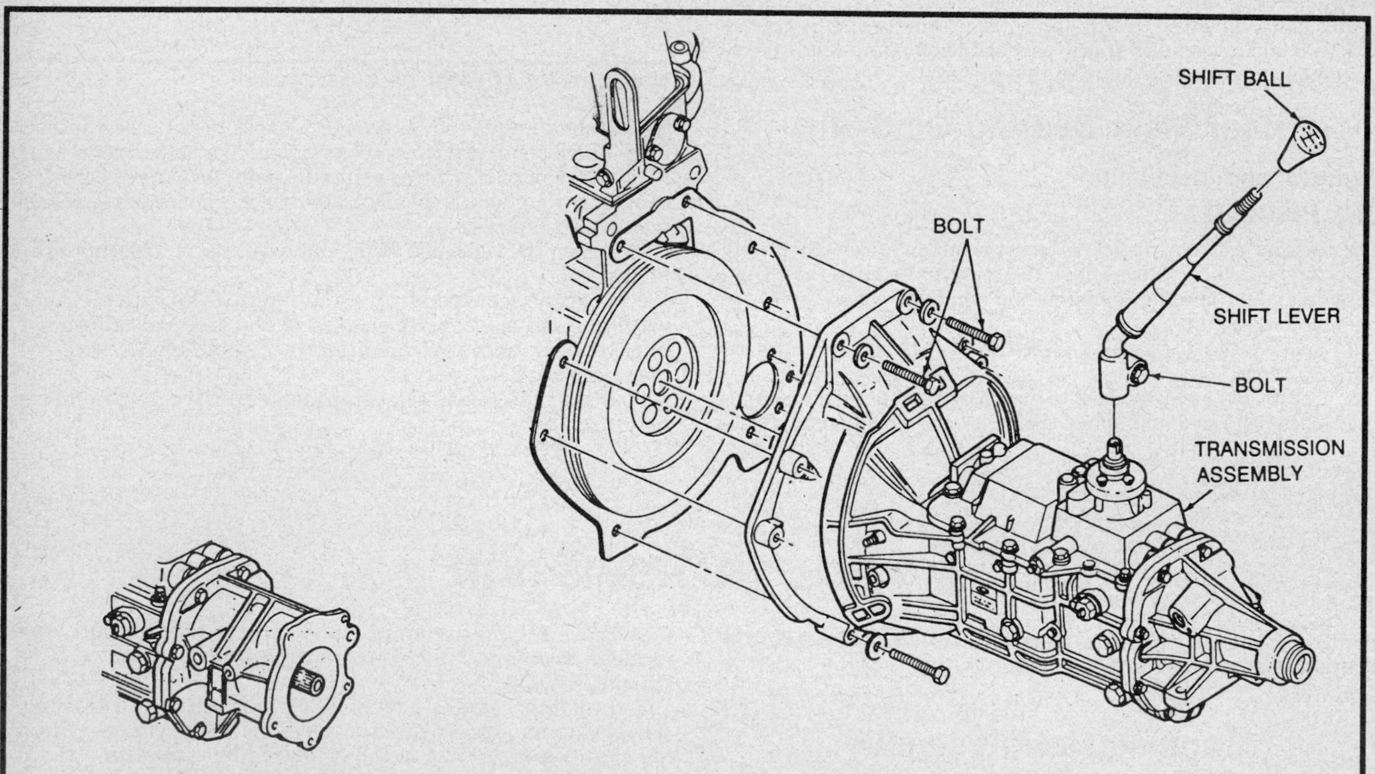

M50D manual transmission

9. Place a jack under the engine, protecting the oil pan with a wood block or equivalent.

NOTE: If vehicle is 4WD, remove the transfer case at this point of the service procedure.

10. Remove the starter motor. Position a suitable jack under the transmission.

11. Remove the bolts (note location of bolts for correct installation), lockwashers and flat washers attaching the transmission to the engine rear plate.

12. Remove the nuts and bolts attaching the transmission mount and damper to the crossmember.

13. Remove the nuts attaching the crossmember to the frame side rails and remove the crossmember.

14. Lower the engine jack. Work the clutch housing off the locating dowels and slide the transmission rearward until the input shaft spline clears the clutch disc. Remove the transmission from the vehicle.

15. Installation is the reverse of removal procedure. Always torque all retaining bolts in progressive steps.

Linkage Adjustment

No service adjustments are possible or necessary for these vehicles.

CLUTCH

Clutch Assembly

Removal and Installation

1. Disconnect the negative battery cable.

2. Disconnect the clutch hydraulic system master cylinder pushrod from the clutch pedal.

3. Raise and safely support the vehicle as necessary. Remove the starter.

4. Disconnect the hydraulic coupling at the transmission with a tool or depress the white retainer bushing while pulling on the the hydraulic line.

5. Remove the transmission from the vehicle.

6. Mark the pressure plate and cover assembly and the flywheel, so that the parts can be reinstalled in the same position.

7. Loosen the pressure plate attaching bolts evenly and remove the clutch/preesure plate assembly.

8. Remove the clutch/pressure plate assembly from the vehicle.

9. Installation is the reverse of the removal procedure. Connect negative battery cable and bleed the hydraulic system as necessary. Roadtest the vehicle for proper operation.

Pedal Height/Free Play Adjustment

The hydraulic clutch system provides automatic adjustment. No adjustment of clutch linkage or pedal position is required.

Clutch Master Cylinder

Removal and Installation

1. Disconnect the negative battery cable. Raise and safely support the vehicle as necessary.

2. Disconnect the master cylinder pushrod by prying the retainer bushing and the pushrod off the shaft. Disconnect any electrical connection.

3. Remove the hydraulic line to the slave cylinder and plug the line to prevent entry of dirt.

4. Remove the master cylinder and reservoir from the engine compartment (rotate assembly as necessary). On Aerostar vehicles slide the reservoir out of the relay bracket.

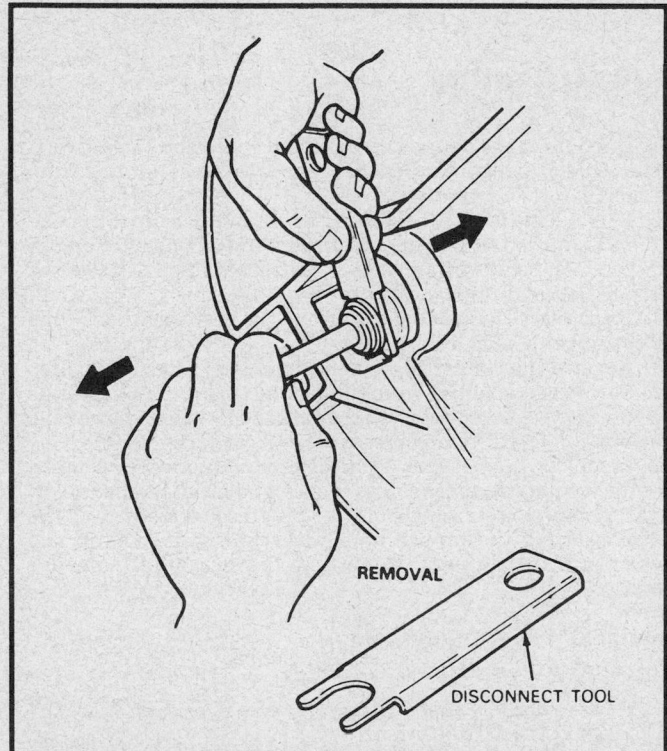

Hydraulic line removal

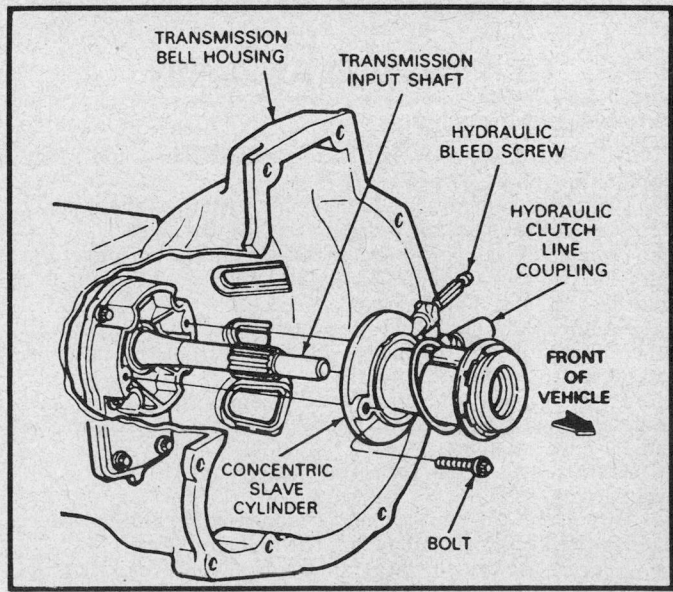

Concentric slave cylinder assembly

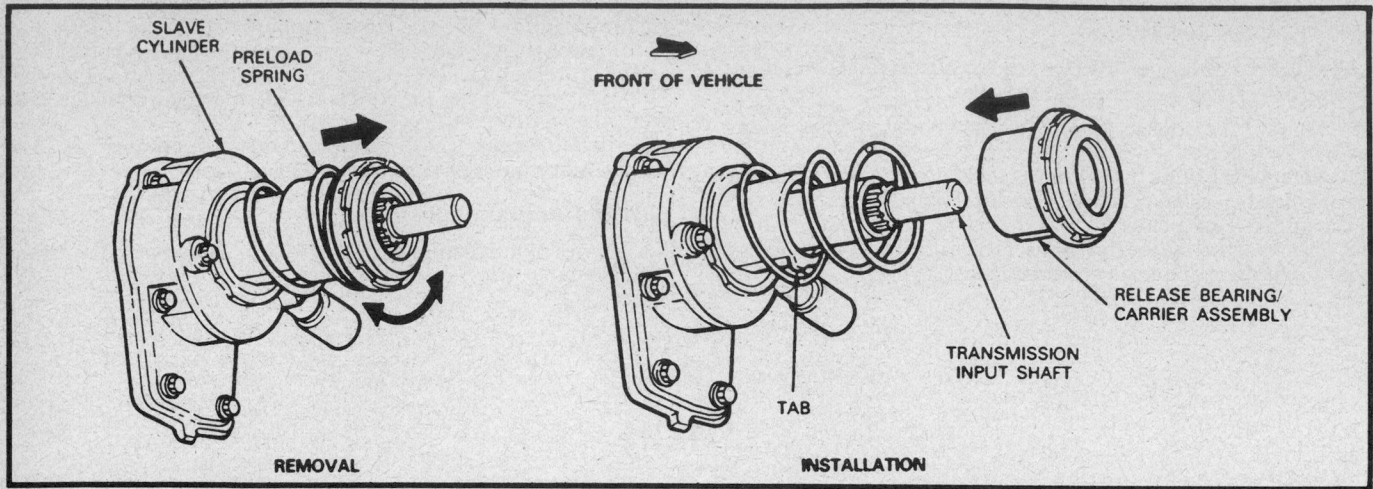

SLAVE CYLINDER
PRELOAD SPRING
FRONT OF VEHICLE
RELEASE BEARING/ CARRIER ASSEMBLY
TRANSMISSION INPUT SHAFT
TAB
REMOVAL
INSTALLATION

Clutch release bearing assembly

5. Install in the reverse order of removal procedure. Bleed the hydraulic system.

Clutch Slave Cylinder

Removal and Installation

1. Disconnect the negative battery cable. Disconnect the hydraulic line.
2. Raise and safely support the vehicle as necessary. Remove the manual transmission from the vehicle.
3. Remove the bolts retaining the slave cylinder to transmission. Remove the concentric type slave cylinder from the transmission input shaft.
4. Installation is the reverse of the removal procedure. Tighten the concentric type slave cylinder retaining bolts to 13–19 ft. lbs. Bleed the hydraulic system.

Bleeding The Hydraulic System

1. Clean reservoir cap. Fill reservoir to the top with approved brake fluid.
2. Raise and safely support the vehicle as necessary. Loosen the bleed screw (located in the slave cylinder body).
3. Depress the clutch pedal to the floor and hold for 2 seconds. Release the pedal. Repeat 10 times or as necessary. Close bleed screw.
4. Check fluid level add the specified fluid as required.

AUTOMATIC TRANSMISSION

For further information, please refer to "Professional Transmission Manual".

Transmission Assembly

Removal and Installation

1. Disconnect the negative battery cable. Raise and safely support the vehicle as necessary.
2. Drain the transmission fluid pan. Loosen the bolts starting at the rear of the pan and working toward the front.
3. Remove the converter access cover from the bottom of the engine oil pan on 2.0L and 2.3L engines and from the right side on 2.8L, 2.9L and 3.0L engines.
4. Remove the 4 flywheel to converter attaching nuts. Rotate the crankshaft pulley clockwise (as viewed from the front) to gain access to each of the nuts.
5. Scribe a mark indexing the driveshaft to the rear axle flange. Remove the driveshaft. On 4WD applications remove the transfer case assembly.
6. Remove the speedometer cable from the extension housing.
7. Disconnect the shift rod at the transmission manual lever. Remove the kickdown cable from the ball stud lever.
8. Depress the tab on the retainer and remove the kickdown cable from the bracket.
9. Remove the starter motor from the converter housing.

10. Disconnect the neutral start switch wires and the converter clutch solenoid connector. Disconnect the vacuum line from the modulator.
11. Remove the filler tube. Position a jack under the transmission and remove the rear mount to crossmember nut. Remove the crossmember to frame side rail attaching bolts. Raise the transmission and remove the crossmember.
12. Disconnect the oil cooler lines at the transmisslion. Plug the openings to keep dirt out.
13. Remove the converter housing to engine attaching bolts.
14. Move the transmission to the rear so that it disengages the dowl pins and the converter disengages the flywheel. Lower the transmission (A4LD transmission type)) from the vehicle.
15. Install in the reverse order of removal procedure. Make sure the torque converter rotates freely and is not bound up. Always tighten all retaining bolts in progressive steps. Fill the transmission to the proper level with the specified fluid and check for fluid leakage. Road test the vehicle for proper operation.

Manual Linkage Adjustment

AEROSTAR

1. Raise and safely support the vehicle as necessary. Place the shift lever in the **OD** position.
2. Loosen the adjustment screw on the shift cable and remove the end fitting from the manual lever ball stud.

3. Position the manual lever in the Overdrive position by moving the lever all the way rearward, then 3 detents forward.

4. Hold the shift lever against the rear stop. Connect the cable end fitting to the manual lever.

5. Tighten the adjustment screw to 45–60 inch lbs.

6. Check the selector lever in all detent positions with engine running to ensure correct adjustment.

BRONCO II AND RANGER

1. Raise and safely support the vehicle as necessary. Position the selector lever in the **D** position and loosen the trunnion bolt.

2. Position the manual lever in the **D** position by moving the bell crank lever all the way rearward, then forward 4 detents.

3. With the floor shifter selector lever and manual lever in the Drive position, apply light forward pressure to the floor shifter lower arm while tightening the trunnion bolt to 13–23 ft. lbs.

4. Check the selector lever in all detent positions with engine running to ensure correct adjustment.

TRANSFER CASE

Transfer Case Assembly

Removal and Installation

MECHANICAL SHIFT TYPE

1. Disconnect the negative battery cable. Raise and safely support the vehicle as necessary. Remove the skid plate from the frame if so equipped.

2. Remove the drain plug and drain fluid from the transfer case.

3. Disconnect the 4WD drive indicator switch wire connector at the transfer case.

4. Disconnect the front driveshaft from the axle input yoke.

5. Loosen the clamp retaining the front driveshaft boot to the transfer case and pull the driveshaft and front boot assembly out of the transfer case front output shaft.

6. Disconnect the rear driveshaft from the transfer case output shaft yoke.

7. Disconnect the speedometer driven gear from the transfer case rear cover. Disconnect the vent hose from the control lever.

8. Loosen or remove the large bolt and the small bolt retaining the shifter to the extension housing. Pull on the control lever until the bushing slides off the transfer case shift lever pin. If necessary, unscrew the shift lever from the control lever. Remove the heat shield from the transfer case if so equipped.

9. Support the transfer case with a suitable jack. Remove the 5 bolts retaining the transfer case to the transmission and the extension housing.

10. Slide the transfer case rearward off the transmission output shaft and lower the transfer case from the vehicle. Remove the gasket from between the transfer case and extension housing.

11. Installation is the reverse of removal procedure. Torque the transfer case to extension housing retaining bolts in sequence to 25–43 ft. lbs. Road test the vehicle in all ranges for correct operation.

ELECTRONIC SHIFT TYPE

1. Disconnect the negative battery cable. Raise and safely support the vehicle as necessary. Remove the skid plate from the frame if so equipped.

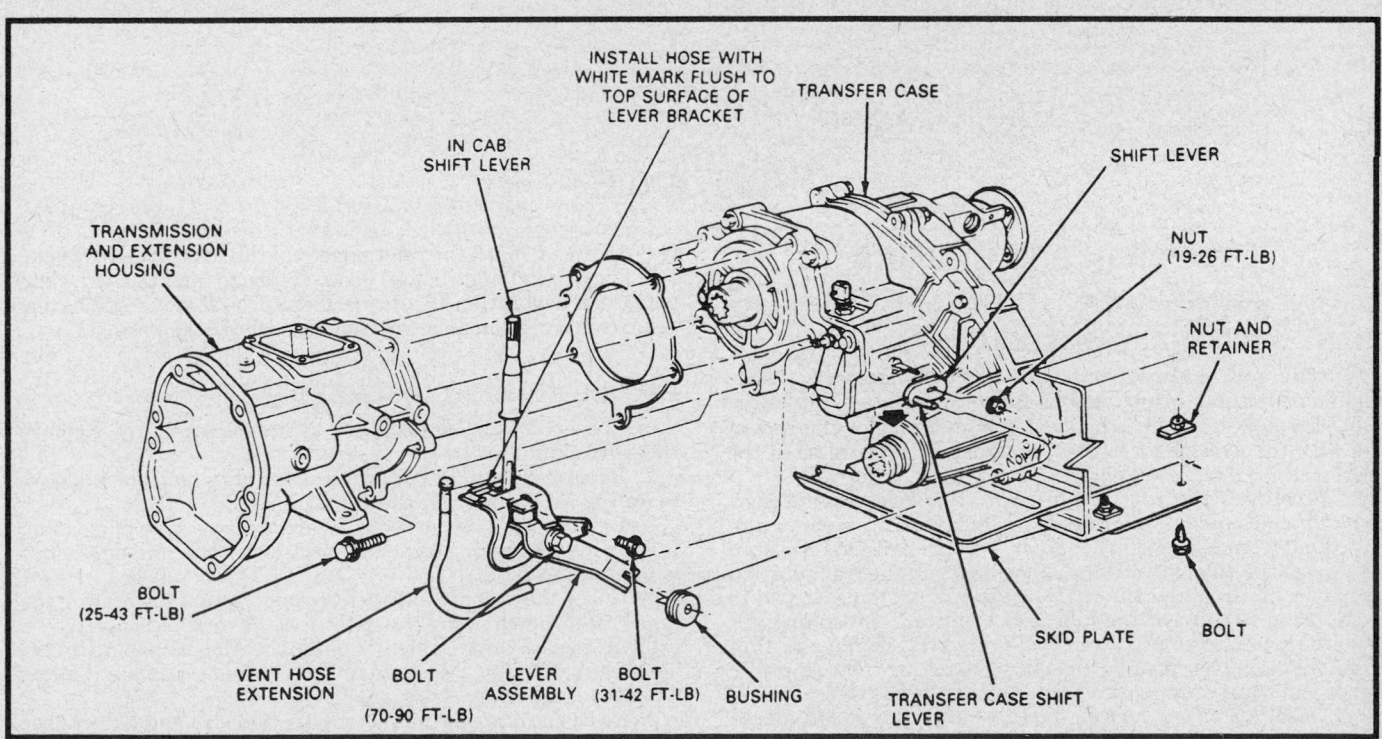

Transfer case—mechanical shift type

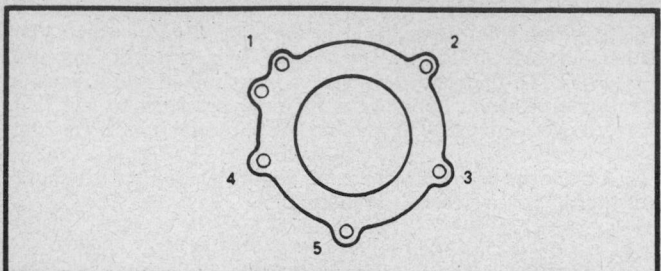

Transfer case to extension housing bolt torque sequence

2. Remove the drain plug and drain fluid from the transfer case.

3. Remove the wire connector from the feed wire harness at the rear of the transfer case. Do not pull directly on the wires pull outwardly on the locking tabs.

4. Disconnect the front driveshaft from the axle input yoke.

5. Pull the driveshaft and front boot assembly out of the transfer case front output shaft.

6. Disconnect the rear driveshaft from the transfer case output shaft flange.

7. Disconnect the speedometer driven gear from the transfer case rear cover. Disconnect the vent hose from the mounting bracket.

8. Support the transfer case with a suitable jack. Remove the 5 bolts retaining the transfer case to the transmission and the extension housing.

9. Slide the transfer case rearward off the transmission output shaft and lower the transfer case from the vehicle. Remove the gasket from between the transfer case and extension housing.

10. Installation is the reverse of removal procedure. Torque the transfer case to extension housing retaining bolts in sequence to 25–43 ft. lbs. Road test the vehicle in all ranges for correct operation.

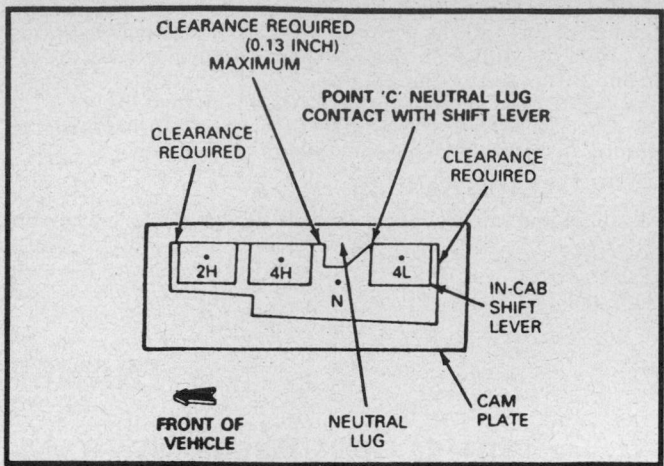

Transfer case shifter cam plate adjustment

Linkage Adjustment
MECHANICAL SHIFT TYPE

1. Raise the shift boot to expose the top surface of the cam plate.

2. Loosen the bolts on the control lever assembly approximately 2 turns. Move the transfer shift lever to the **4L** position.

3. Move the cam plate rearward until the bottom chamfered corner of the neutral lug just contacts the forward right edge of the shift lever.

4. Hold the cam plate in this position and tighten the 2 control lever bolts.

5. Move the in cab shift lever to all shift positions to check the positive engagement. There should be clearance (not to exceed 0.13 in.) between the shift lever and cam plate in **2H** (front) **4H** (rear) and **4L** shift positions.

6. Install the shift boot assembly.

DRIVE AXLE

Driveshaft and U-Joints

Removal and Installation
FRONT DRIVESHAFT ASSEMBLY

1. Raise and safely support the vehicle as necessary. If the alignment marks are not visible, mark the relationship of the rear driveshaft yoke and the drive pinion flange of the axle in line with the driveshaft so that they may be reinstalled in the same position.

2. Disconnect the rear U-joint from the companion flange. Wrap tape or equivalent around the loose bearing caps to prevent them from falling off the spider. Pull the driveshaft toward the rear of the vehicle until the slip yoke clears the transmission extension housing and the seal. Install the appropriate tool in the housing to prevent the lubricant or fluid from leaking.

3. To install, reverse the removal procedure, taking note that if either the rubber seal on the output shaft or the seal in the end of the transmission extension housing is damaged it must be replaced. Also if the lugs on the axle pinion flange are shaved or distorted so that the bearings slide, replace the flange.

4. Install the U-bolts and torque (progressive steps) the nuts to 8–15 ft. lbs. Mark the relationship of the rear driveshaft yoke and axle pinion flange before disassembly, to maintain driveline balance. If a vibration should exist, the driveshaft should be disconnected from the axle, rotated 180 degrees and reinstalled.

CENTER BEARING ASSEMBLY

1. Raise and safely support the vehicle as necessary. Remove the driveshaft.

2. Remove the center support bearing attaching bolts and remove the assembly from the vehicle.

3. Do not immerse the sealed bearing in any type of cleaning fluid. Wipe the bearing and cushion clean with a cloth dampened with cleaning fluid.

4. Check the bearing for wear or rough action by rotating the inner race while holding the outer race. If wear or roughness is evident, replace the bearing. Examine the rubber cushion for evidence of hardening, cracking, or deterioration. Replace it if it is damaged in any way.

5. Place the bearing in the rubber support and the rubber support in the U-shaped support and install the bearing in the reverse order of removal.

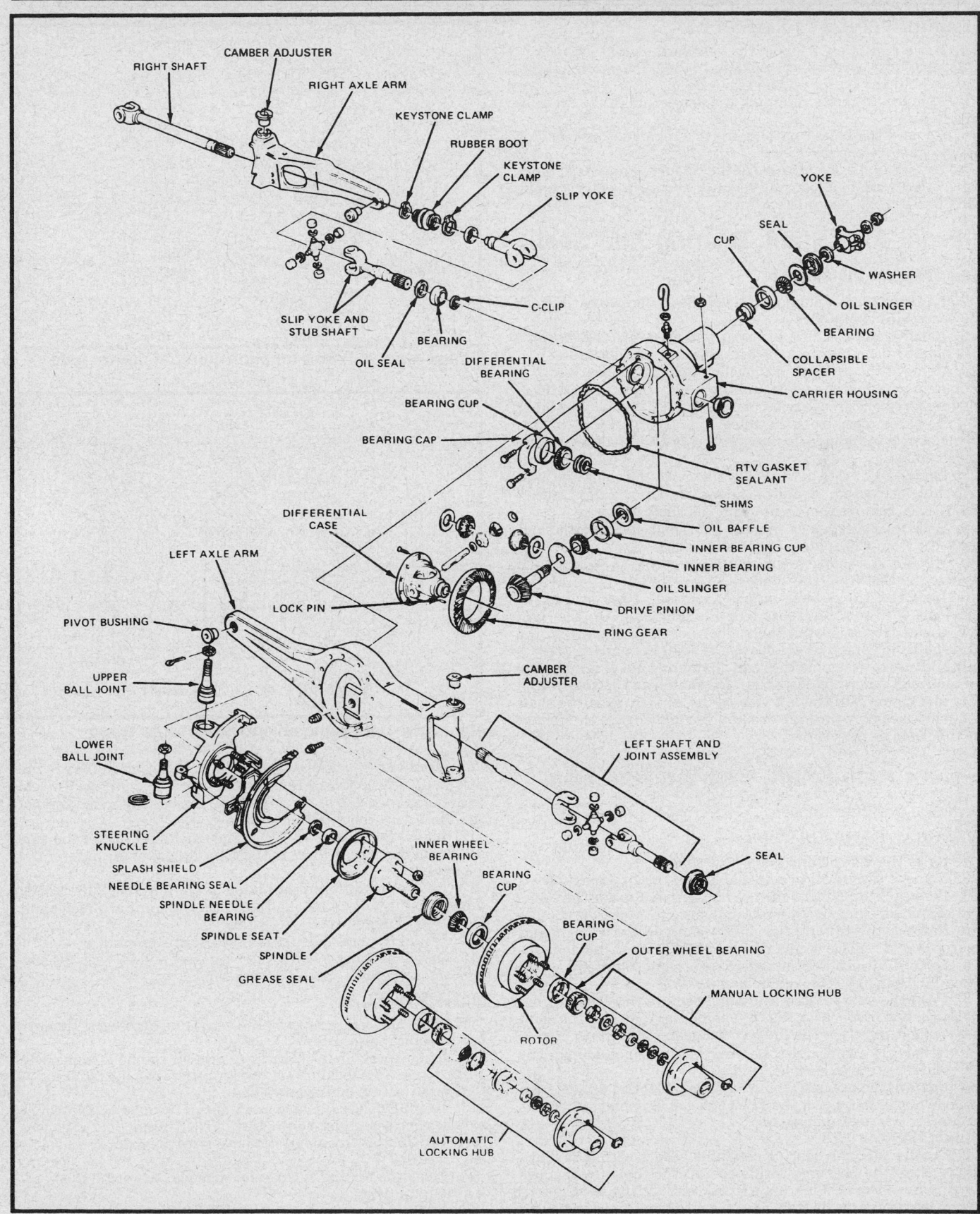

RIGHT SHAFT
CAMBER ADJUSTER
RIGHT AXLE ARM
KEYSTONE CLAMP
RUBBER BOOT
KEYSTONE CLAMP
SLIP YOKE
YOKE
SEAL
CUP
WASHER
OIL SLINGER
BEARING
COLLAPSIBLE SPACER
CARRIER HOUSING
SLIP YOKE AND STUB SHAFT
BEARING
C-CLIP
OIL SEAL
DIFFERENTIAL BEARING
BEARING CUP
BEARING CAP
RTV GASKET SEALANT
SHIMS
OIL BAFFLE
INNER BEARING CUP
INNER BEARING
OIL SLINGER
DRIVE PINION
RING GEAR
DIFFERENTIAL CASE
LEFT AXLE ARM
PIVOT BUSHING
UPPER BALL JOINT
LOCK PIN
CAMBER ADJUSTER
LEFT SHAFT AND JOINT ASSEMBLY
LOWER BALL JOINT
SEAL
STEERING KNUCKLE
SPLASH SHIELD
NEEDLE BEARING SEAL
SPINDLE NEEDLE BEARING
SPINDLE SEAT
SPINDLE
GREASE SEAL
INNER WHEEL BEARING
BEARING CUP
BEARING CUP
OUTER WHEEL BEARING
MANUAL LOCKING HUB
ROTOR
AUTOMATIC LOCKING HUB

Front drive axle assembly

REAR DRIVESHAFT ASSEMBLY

1. Raise and safely support the vehicle as necessary.
2. Mark the driveshaft in relation to the flange on the transfer case and the flange on the rear axle.
3. Remove the bolts retaining the driveshaft to the transfer case flange.
4. Remove the bolts retaining the driveshaft to the rear axle flange. Remove the driveshaft.
5. Installation is the reverse of the removal procedure. Index marks that were made during removal and torque all retaining bolts to 61–87 ft. lbs. in steps.

Front Axle Shaft, Bearing And Seal

Removal and Installation

1. Raise and safely support the vehicle as necessary. Remove the wheel/tire assemblies.
2. Remove the disc brake caliper and wire it to the frame.
3. Remove the hub locks, wheel bearings and locknuts.
4. Remove the hub, rotor and the outer wheel bearing.
5. Remove the grease seal and the inner wheel bearing from the rotor (replace grease seal upon assembly). Remove the inner and the outer races from the rotor.
6. Remove the spindle from the steering knuckle. Remove the splash shield.
7. On the right side of the vehicle, remove the shaft and joint by pulling the assembly out of the carrier. On the right side of the carrier, remove the clamp from the shaft and joint.
8. Slide the rubber boot onto the stub shaft and pull the shaft and joint from the splines of the stub shaft.
9. If required remove the needle bearing from the spindle and remove the seal from the shaft.
10. Install in the reverse order of removal. Pack all bearing and seals with multi-purpose long life lubricant. On the right side of the carrier, install the rubber boot and clamps on the stub shaft slip yoke. The splines on the shaft are phased, there is only one way to assemble the right shaft and joint assembly into the slip yoke. Align splines, slide right shaft into slip yoke install boot and clamp. On the left side of the carrier, slide the shaft and joint assembly through the knuckle and engage the splines on the shaft in the carrier.

Rear Axle Shaft, Bearing And Seal

Removal and Installation

INTEGRAL CARRIER TYPE

1. Raise the vehicle and support it safely.
2. Remove the wheel/tire assembly and the brake drums.
3. Place a drain pan under the housing and drain the lubricant. Remove the housing cover and gasket, if used.
4. Remove the differential pinion shaft lockscrew. Discard lockscrew and replace with a new screw (bolt) upon installation.
5. Lift out the differential pinion mate shaft. Shaft is a slip fit design and may be removed by hand.
6. Push the axle shafts inward and remove the C-locks from the inner end of the axle shafts. Temporarily replace the shaft and lockbolt to retain the differential gears in position.
7. Remove the axle shafts. Be sure the seal is not damaged by the splines on the axle shaft.
8. Remove the bearing (using suitable tools) and oil seal from the axle housing. Inspect the axle shaft housing and axle shafts for cracks, burrs or damage.
To install:
9. Lightly coat the bearing assembly rollers with axle lubricant. Install the bearings (using the proper tools) in the axle housing until the bearing seats firmly against the shoulder.
10. Wipe all lubricant from the oil seal bore, before installing the seal. Install the oil seal.

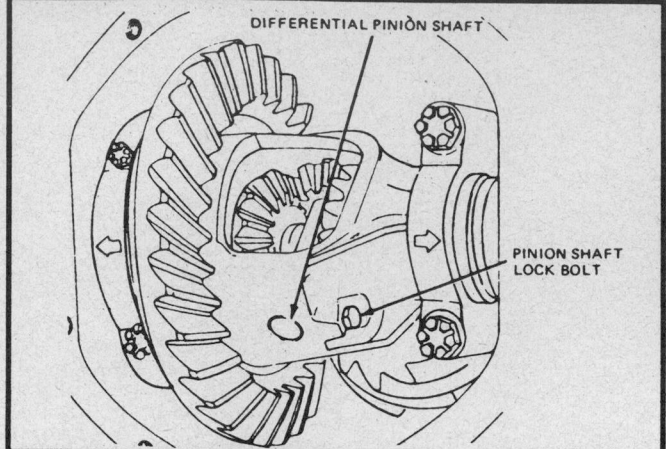

Pinion shaft lockbolt location–Integral carrier type

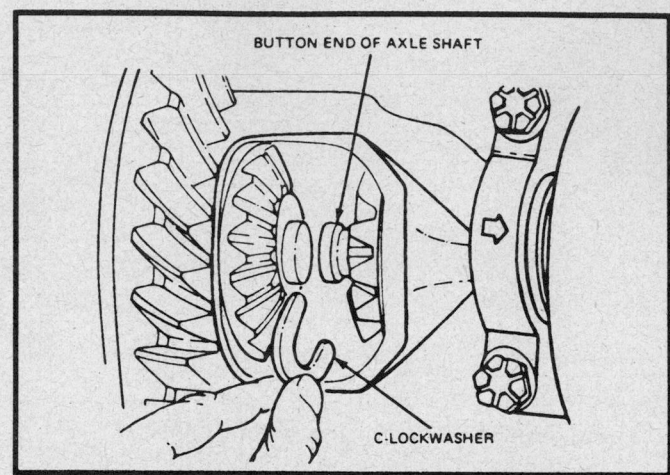

Rear axle shaft removal–Integral carrier type

11. Remove the lockscrew and pinion shaft. Carefully slide the axle shafts into place. Be careful that you do not damage the seal with the splined end of the axle shaft. Engage the splined end of the shaft with the differential side gears.
12. Install the axle shaft C-locks on the inner end of the axle shafts and seat the C-locks in the counterbore of the differential side gears.
13. Rotate the differential pinion gears until the differential pinion shaft can be installed. Install the differential pinion shaft lockscrew. Tighten to 15–20 ft. lbs.
14. Install the brake drum and wheel/tire assemblies.
15. Install housing cover with new gasket and fill with the correct amount of the specified lubricant.

DANA MODEL 30

1. Raise and safely support the vehicle as necessary. Remove the wheel/tire assembly.
2. Remove the drum. Working through the hole in the axle shaft, remove the lockbolts and lockwashers which hold the axle flange to the bearing retainer plate.
3. Carefully slide the axle shaft out of the axle housing. The axle bearing/seal must be pressed (spilt retainer ring as necessary) off shaft at this point of the service procedure.
To install:
4. Clean the mating surfaces of the axle flange and the bearing retainer assembly.
5. Position a new gasket on the axle flange (with new bearing/seal assembly pressed on) and carefully slide the axle shaft into

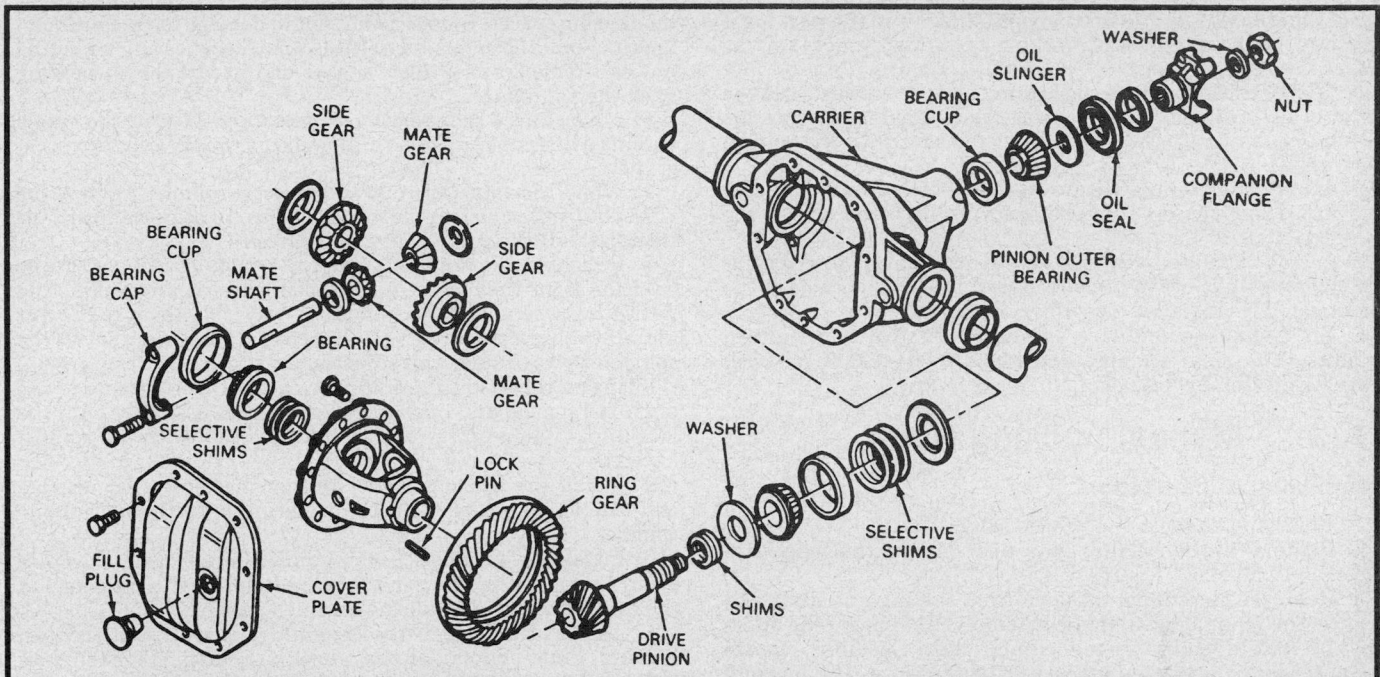

Rear axle assembly–Dana model 30

the axle housing. When the splined end of the axle shaft reaches the side gear, gently rotate the shaft until it is inserted into the side gear.

6. Position the gasket between the axle flange and the bearing retainer and install the lockbolts and lockwashers.

7. Torque the bearing retainer bolts to 25–35 ft. lbs. Install the brake drum and wheel/tire assembly.

8. Check and add lubricant through filler hole as required.

Front Wheel Hub and Bearings

Removal and Installation

1. Raise and safely support the vehicle. Remove the wheel/tire assemblies.

2. Remove the brake caliper and wire it to the underbody to prevent damage to the brake hose.

3. Remove the retainer washers and manual or automatic hub assemblies. Remove the snapring, axle shaft spacer, thrust bearing, thrust washer and locknut (adjusting nut) assembly.

4. Remove the outer bearing. Pull the hub and rotor off the spindle. Remove and discard the grease seal.

5. Remove the inner bearing from the hub. Remove all traces of old lubricant from the bearings, hub and spindle with solvent and dry thoroughly.

6. Inspect the bearing races for scratches, pits or cracks. If the races are worn or damaged, remove them with a drift. If the inner or outer bearing races were removed, replace them in the hub with the proper tool. The races will be properly seated when they are fully bottomed.

7. Replace the grease retainer. Pack the inside of the hub with lithium base grease, high temperature multi-purpose long life lubricant. Fill the hub until the grease is flush with the inside diameters of both bearing races.

8. Pack the bearings with wheel bearing grease, working as much lubricant as possible between the rollers and the cages.

9. For installation reverse the removal procedure. Adjust the wheel bearings.

Adjustment
MANUAL LOCKING HUBS

1. Raise and safely support the vehicle. Remove the wheel/tire assembly. Remove the retainer washers from the lug nut studs and remove the manual locking hub assembly from the spindle.

2. Remove the snapring from the end of the spindle shaft. Remove the axle shaft spacer, needle thrust bearing and the bearing spacer.

3. Remove the outer wheel bearing locknut and the washer from the spindle.

4. Loosen the inner wheel bearing locknut and then tighten to 35 ft. lbs. to seat the bearings.

5. Spin the rotor and back off the inner locknut ¼ turn. Retighten the inner locknut to 16 inch lbs.

6. Install the lockwasher and the outer wheel bearing locknut and tighten to 150 ft. lbs.

7. Install bearing thrust spacer, needle thrust bearing and axle shaft spacer. Install snapring onto the end of the spindle. Install hub assembly over the spindle. The final endplay should be 0.001–0.003 in. with wheel/tire assembly on spindle.

AUTOMATIC LOCKING HUBS

1. Raise and safely support the vehicle as necessary. Remove the wheel/tire assembly. Remove the retainer washers from the lug nut studs and remove the automatic locking hub assembly from the spindle. Remove the snapring from the end of the spindle shaft.

2. Remove the axle shaft spacer, needle thrust bearing and the bearing spacer.

3. Pull the plastic cam assembly off the wheel bearing adjusting nut and remove the thrust washer and needle thrust bearing from the adjusting nut.

4. Loosen the wheel bearing adjusting nut from the spindle. While rotating the hub and rotor, tighten the wheel bearing adjusting nut to 35 ft. lbs. to seat the bearings.

5. Spin the rotor and back off the nut ¼ turn (90 degrees). Retighten the nut to 16 inch lbs. using a torque wrench. Align the closest hole in the wheel bearing adjusting nut with the cen-

ter of the spindle keyway slot. Advance the nut to the next lug if required. Install the separate locking key in the spindle keyway under the adjusting nut.

6. Install the locknut needle bearing and thrust washer in the order of removal and push or press the cam assembly onto the locknut by lining up the key in the fixed cam with the spindle keyway.

7. Install the bearing thrust washer, needle thrust bearing and axle shaft spacer. Clip the snapring onto the end of the spindle.

8. Install the automatic locking hub assembly over the spindle by lining up 3 legs in the hub assembly with 3 pockets in the cam assembly. Install the retainer washers.

9. Install the wheel/tire assembly. Install and tighten lugnuts. The final endplay should be 0.001–0.003 in. with wheel/tire assembly on spindle.

Manual Locking Hubs

Removal and Installation

1. Raise and support the vehicle safely.
2. Remove the wheel lug nuts and remove the wheel/tire assembly.
3. Remove the retainer washers from the lug nut studs and remove the manual locking hub assembly. To remove the internal hub lock assembly from the outer body assembly, remove the outer lock ring seated in the hub body groove. The internal assembly, spring and clutch gear will now slide out of the hub body. Do not remove the screw from the plastic dial.
4. Rebuild the hub assembly in the reverse order of disassembly.
5. Adjust the wheel bearing if necessary. Install the manual locking hub assembly over the spindle and place the retainer washers on the lug nut studs.
6. Install the wheel/tire assembly.

Automatic Locking Hubs

Removal and Installation

1. Raise and support the vehicle safely. Remove the wheel lug nuts and remove the wheel/tire assembly.
2. Remove the retainer washers from the lug nut studs and remove the automatic locking hub assembly from the spindle.
3. Remove the snapring from the end of the spindle shaft.
4. Remove the axle shaft spacer, needle thrust bearing and

the bearing spacer. Being careful not to damage the plastic moving cam, pull the cam assembly off the wheel bearing adjusting nut and remove the thrust washer and needle thrust bearing from the adjusting nut.

5. Adjust the wheel bearing if necessary. Loosen the wheel bearing adjusting nut from the spindle using a 2 3/8 in. hex socket tool.

6. While rotating the hub and rotor assembly, tighten the wheel bearing adjusting nut to 35 ft. lbs. to seat the bearings, then back off the nut 1/4 turn 90 degrees.

7. Retighten the adjusting nut to 16 inch lb. using a torque wrench. Align the closest hole in the wheel bearing adjusting nut with the center of the spindle keyway slot. Advance the nut to the next lug if required. Install the separate locking key in the spindle keyway under the adjusting nut.

8. Install the locknut needle bearing and thrust washer in the order of removal and push or press the cam assembly onto the locknut by lining up the key in the fixed cam with the spindle keyway.

9. Install the bearing thrust washer, needle thrust bearing and axle shaft spacer. Clip the snapring onto the end of the spindle.

10. Install the automatic locking hub assembly over the spindle by lining up the 3 legs in the hub assembly with 3 pockets in the cam assembly. Install the retainer washers.

11. Install the wheel/tire assembly. Install and tighten lugnuts. Final endplay of the wheel on the spindle should be 0.001–0.003 in.

Pinion Seal

Removal and Installation

NOTE: **This service procedure disturbs the pinion bearing preload and this preload must be carefully reset when assembling.**

1. Raise the vehicle and support it safely.
2. Remove the wheels and the brake drums.
3. Mark the driveshaft axle end flange and the axle companion flange for correct installation. Remove the driveshaft.
4. Using an inch pound torque wrench on the pinion nut, record the torque required for rotation of the pinion through several revolutions.
5. While holding the companion flange remove the pinion nut. Mark the companion flange in relation to the pinion shaft for reinstallation.

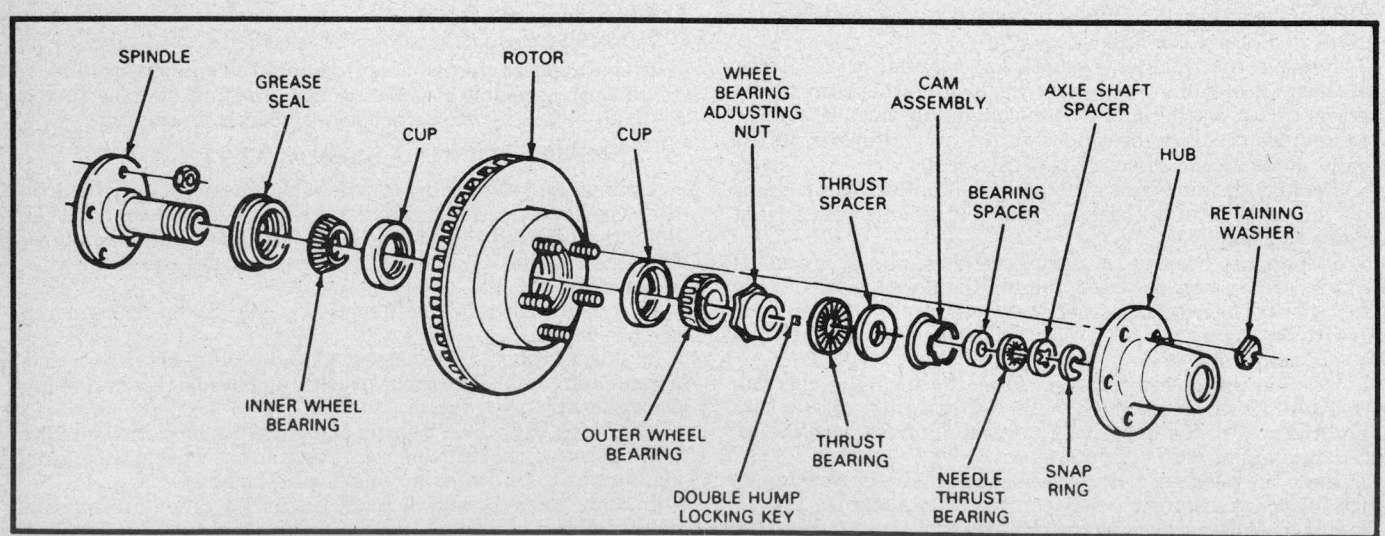

Automatic locking hub assembly

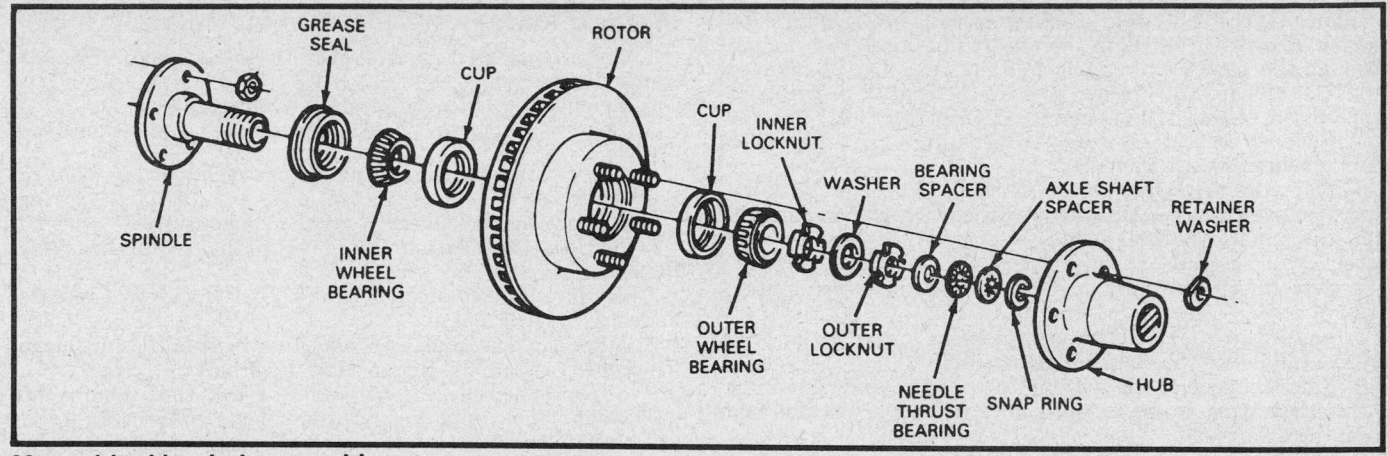

Manual locking hub assembly

6. Using a suitable puller remove the rear axle companion flange. To remove the seal, pry it out of the carrier.

7. Installation is the reverse of the removal procedure. Tighten the new pinion nut rotating the pinion to insure proper bearing seating. Take pinion bearing torque preload readings until the original recorded preload reading is obtained or 8–14 inch lbs. specification is reached. Under no circumstances should the pinion nut be backed off to reduce preload. If reduced preload is required, a new collapsible pinion spacer and pinion nut must be installed.

Front Drive Axle Housing

Removal and Installation

1. Raise the vehicle and support it safely under the radius arm brackets.

2. Disconnect the driveshaft from the front axle yoke. Remove the wheel/tire assembly.

3. Remove the disc brake calipers and support them on a frame rail as necessary.

4. Disconnect the steering linkage from the spindle.

5. Position a jack under the axle arm and slightly compress the coil spring. Remove the nut that retains the lower part of the spring to the axle arm. Lower the jack and remove the coil spring, spacer, seat and stud.

6. Disconnect the shock absorber from the radius arm bracket. Remove the bracket and radius arm from the axle arm.

7. Remove the pivot bolt that secures the right axle arm assembly to the crossmember.

8. Remove the clamps securing the axle shaft boot from the axle shaft slip yoke and axle shaft and slide the rubber boot over. Disconnect the right driveshaft from the slip yoke assembly. Lower the jack and remove the right axle arm assembly.

9. Position another jack under the differential housing. Remove the bolt that connects the left axle arm to crossmember. Lower the jacks and remove the left axle arm assembly.

10. Install in the reverse order of removal. Tighten the pivot bracket bolts to 120–150 ft. lbs. Tighten the radius arm to axle arm new stud to 190–230 ft. lbs. and the tie rod to ball joint nut to 50–75 ft. lbs.

Rear Drive Axle Housing

Removal and Installation

AEROSTAR

1. Raise and safely support the vehicle as necessary.

2. Release the parking brake cable tension by pulling rearward on the front cable. Clamp the cable behind the crossmember to release the tension on the rear cables.

3. On some vehicles release the parking brake cable tension

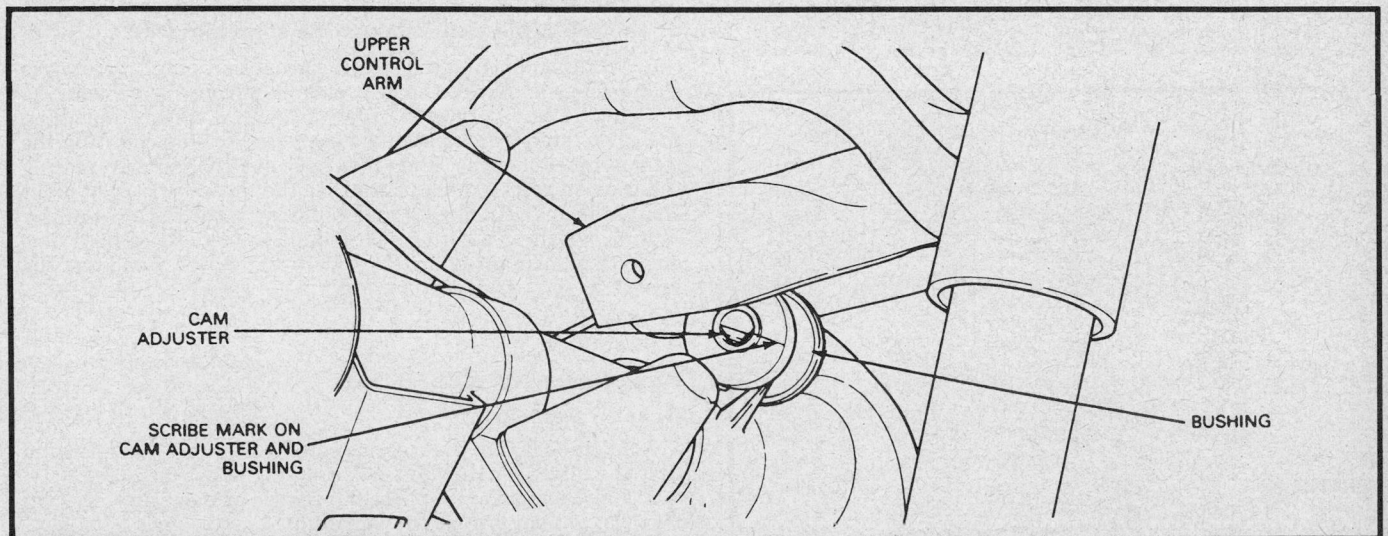

Rear axle assembly installation

by removing the boot cover from the parking brake control assembly. Place the control in the released position. Insert a pin through the pawl lock out pin hole the pin must be inserted from the inboard side (larger hole) of the control assembly to displace the self-adjusting pawl.

4. Remove the cables from the equalizer. Pull the cables through the rear crossmember.

5. Mark the driveshaft to the rear axle for correct installation. Remove the driveshaft. Remove the wheel/tire assemblies.

6. Disconnect the brake lines at the master cylinder rear tube.

7. Disconnect the shock absorbers from the lower control arm.

8. Lower the axle until the springs are no longer under compression. Remove the coil springs assembly.

9. Raise the axle to the normal load position and disconnect the control arms at the axle. Remove the upper control arm from the axle.

10. Mark the position of the cam adjuster in the axle bushing. Lower the axle from the vehicle.

11. Install in the reverse order of removal procedure.

BRONCO II AND RANGER

1. Raise the vehicle and support it safely under the rear frame crossmember.

2. Remove the cover and drain the lubricant.

3. Remove both rear wheel/tire assemblies and remove the drums.

4. Remove the 4 retaining nuts from each backing plate to underbody.

5. Remove the vent hose from the axle housing.

6. Remove the brake line from the clips that retain the line to the axle housing.

7. Remove the hydraulic brake T-fitting from the axle housing.

8. Mark the driveshaft end yoke and the axle U-joint flange for proper reassembly. Remove the driveshaft.

9. Support the rear axle housing on a jack, then remove the spring clip U-bolt nuts. Remove the U-bolts and plates.

10. Disconnect the lower shock absorber studs from the mounting brackets on the axle housing. Lower the axle housing and remove it from under the vehicle.

11. Installation is the reverse of the removal procedure.

STEERING

Steering Wheel

Removal and Installation

1. Position the vehicle in a straight head position. Note position of the steering wheel. Disconnect the negative battery cable(s).

2. Remove the screw underside each steering wheel spoke and lift the horn switch assembly from the steering wheel.

3. Remove all electrical connections and remove horn switch cover assembly.

4. Remove steering wheel retaining nut. Using a suitable puller remove the steering wheel from the steering shaft. Do not hammer or use knock off type puller on steering wheel.

5. Installation is the reverse of the removal procedure. Install the steering wheel in the noted position. Tighten the steering wheel retaining nut to 23–33 ft. lbs.

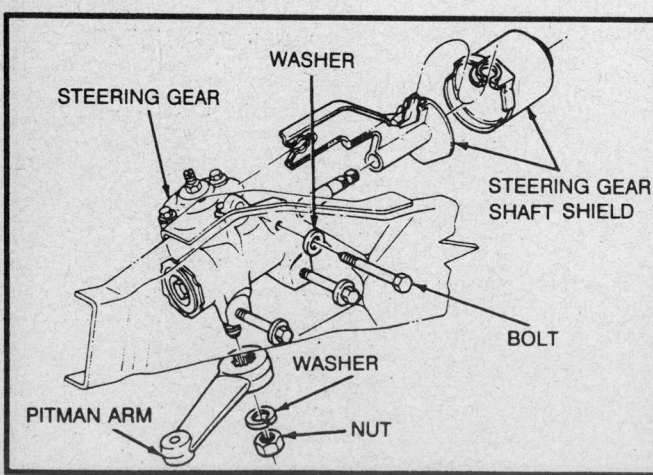

STEERING GEAR

WASHER

STEERING GEAR SHAFT SHIELD

BOLT

WASHER

PITMAN ARM

NUT

Typical manual steering gear installation

Manual Steering Gear

Removal and Installation

1. Raise the vehicle and support it safely with the front wheels in the straight ahead position.

2. Disengage the flex coupling shield from the steering gear input shaft shield and slide it up the intermediate shaft.

3. Disconnect the flex (rag joint) coupling from the steering shaft flange by removing the attaching nuts. Remove shaft shield if so equipped

4. Disconnect the pitman arm from the sector shaft.

5. Mark and remove the pitman arm from the gear sector shaft using proper pulling tools.

NOTE: Do not hammer on the end of the sector shaft or the tool, this will damage the steering gear.

6. While supporting the steering gear, disconnect it from the frame side rail. Lower the gear assembly from the vehicle.

7. Install in the reverse order of removal. Before installing the gear, rotate the input shaft from stop to stop counting the total number of turns. Then turn back exactly half way, placing the gear on center. Make sure that the flat on the gear input shaft is facing straight up and aligns with the flat on the flex coupling. Tighten steering gear mounting bolts to 54–66 ft. lbs. and pitman arm retaining nut to 170–230 ft. lbs. Road test the vehicle for proper operation.

Adjustment

PRELOAD AND MESHLOAD

Gear In Vehicle

1. Make sure that the steering column is properly aligned and that the intermediate shaft flex coupling is not distorted.

2. Raise and safely support the vehicle as necessary. Disconnect the pitman arm at the ball stud.

3. Lubricate the wormshaft seal with a drop of automatic transmission fluid.

4. Remove the horn pad assembly from the steering wheel and turn the wheel to one stop.

5. Using a torque wrench on the steering wheel nut, measure the torque (preload) required to rotate the steering wheel at a constant speed for approximately 1½ turns.

6. If the gear preload is not within 2–6 inch lbs. the preload must be readjusted. Gear must be removed to adjust worm preload.

7. Rotate the steering wheel from stop to stop counting the number of turns then back halfway, placing the steering gear in the center position.

8. Place a torque wrench on the steering wheel nut, observe the highest reading (meshload) by rotating the steering shaft 90 degrees either way across center. The meshload must be within 4–10 inch lbs. and at least 2 inch lbs. over the preload. Meshload can be adjusted in the vehicle.

Gear Removed

1. Tighten the selector cover bolts to 40 ft. lbs. Loosen preload adjuster locknut and tighten the worm bearing adjuster nut until all endplay has been removed.

2. Using a torque wrench and socket on wormshaft turn the wormshaft all the way to the right. Measure the left turn torque (preload) required to rotate the wormshaft at a constant speed for approximately 1½ turns.

3. Tighten or loosen the adjuster locknut until the correct preload (5–6 inch lbs.) is obtained. Torque locknut to 187 ft. lbs.

4. Rotate the wormshaft from stop to stop, counting the total number of turns, turn back halfway placing the gear on the center position.

5. With the torque wrench still on wormshaft, observe the highest reading (meshload) by rotating the wormshaft 90 degrees either way across center. The meshload must be within 9–11 inch lbs. and at least 4 inch lbs. over the preload.

6. Turn the selector shaft adjusting screw as required. Hold the sector shaft adjusting screw and tighten locknut to 25 ft. lbs.

Manual Rack and Pinion

Removal and Installation

1. Raise the vehicle and support it safely with the front wheels in the straight ahead position.

2. To center the steering gear, rotate the input shaft from stop to stop counting the total number of turns. Then turn back exactly half way placing the gear on center.

3. Remove the bolt retaining the intermediate steering column shaft to the steering gear pinion. Separate the shaft from the pinion.

4. Separate the tie rod ends from the spindle arms using a suitable puller.

5. Support the steering gear and disconnect it from the crossmember. Remove the gear from the vehicle.

6. Installation is the reverse of the removal procedure.

Adjustment

The gear preload on a manual rack and pinion steering gear is determined by the pinion plug torque valve and is preset at the factory.

Power Steering Gear

Removal and Installation

1. Disconnect the pressure and return lines from the gear. Plug the lines and the ports in the gear to prevent entry of dirt.

2. If equipped, remove the splash shield from the flex coupling. Disconnect the flex coupling at the steering gear.

3. Raise the vehicle and support it safely. Remove the pitman arm from the sector shaft.

4. Support the steering gear and remove the attaching bolts. Work the steering gear free from the flex coupling and remove the gear from the vehicle.

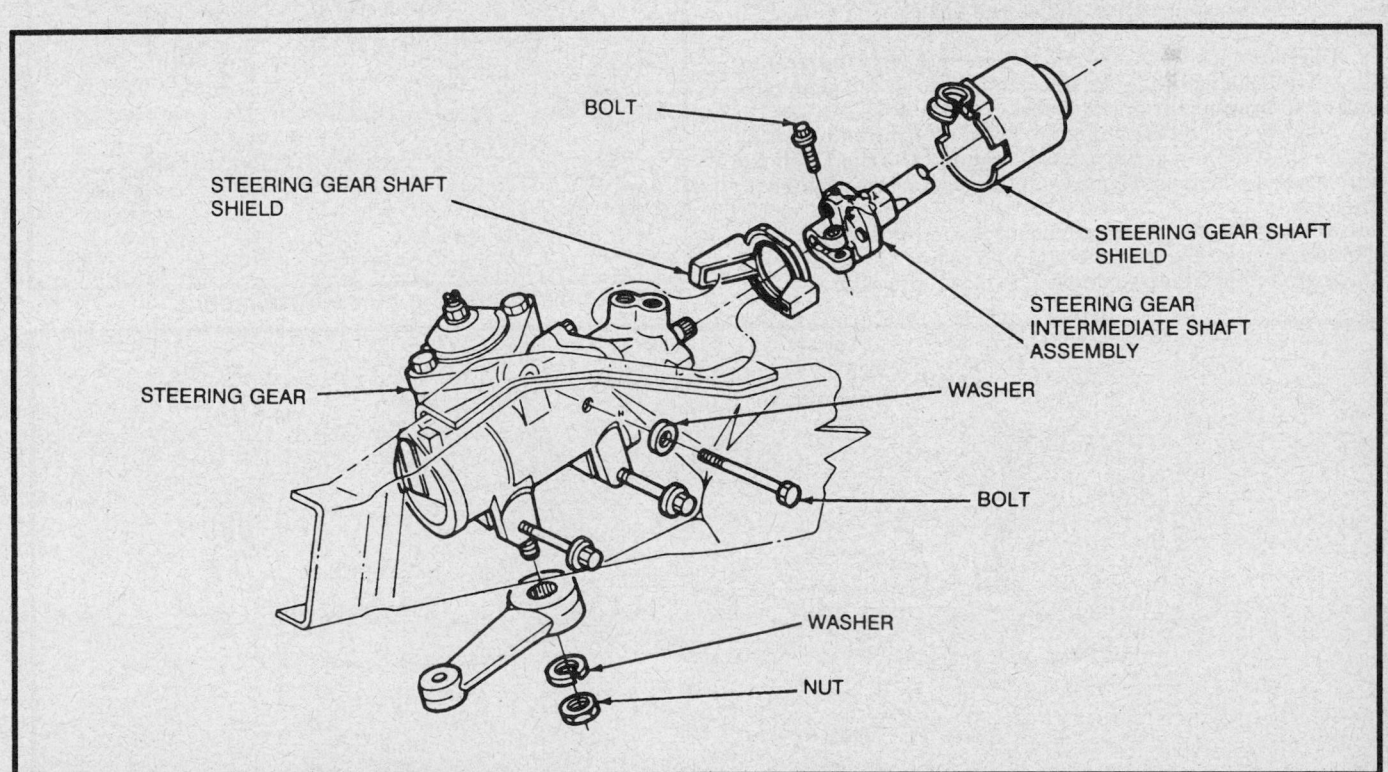

Typical power steering gear installation

5. Install in the reverse order of removal procedure. Bleed power steering system if necessary.

Adjustment

1. Make sure that the steering column is correctly aligned and remove the steerring wheel cover. Raise and safely support the vehicle as necessary. Disconnect the pitman arm from the sector shaft.

2. Disconnect the fluid reservoir return line and cap the reservoir return line tube. Place the end of the return line in a clean container and turn the steering wheel back and forth several times to empty the steering gear.

3. Turn the steering wheel to 45 degrees from the right stop.

4. Attach an inch pound torque wrench to steering wheel nut and record the torque to rotate the shaft ⅛ turn toward center from the 45 degreee position.

5. Turn the steering gear back to center and record the torque required to rotate the shaft back and forth across the center position. The set torque specification is measured rocking across center to a valve of 10–14 inch lbs. greater than that measured 45 degress from the right stop.

6. Loosen the locknut and tighten the sector shaft adjusting screw until the reading is the specified valve greater than the torque at 45 degress from the stop.

7. Tighten the adjusting screw locknut and recheck. Install pitman arm and steering wheel cover.

8. Refill the system with the fluid specified. Bleed the system.

Power Rack and Pinion

Removal and Installation

1. Place the steering system in the on center position by rotating the steering wheel from stop to stop, counting the number of turns. Divide the number by 2 to determine the half way point.

2. Disconnect the negative battery cable and leave the ignition key in the **ON** position. Raise the vehicle and support it safely.

3. Disconnect the pressure and return lines from the steering gear valve housing. Plug the lines and ports in the gear valve housing to prevent the entry of dirt.

4. Remove the bolt retaining the lower intermediate steering column shaft to the steering gear. Disconnect the shaft from the gear. Separate the tie rod ends from the spindle arms using suitable tools.

5. Support the steering gear and disconnect it from the crossmember. Remove the gear from the vehicle.

6. Install in the reverse order of removal procedure.

Adjustment

No service adjustments are necessary on this system.

Power Steering Pump

Removal and Installation
SAGINAW TYPE

1. Raise and safely support the vehicle as necessary. Disconnect the pressure and return lines from the pump and plug them to prevent loss of fluid or entrance of dirt into the system.

2. Loosen the belt tension adjusting bolt all the way.

3. Remove the bolts attaching the pump mounting bracket to the air conditioning bracket (if equipped).

4. Remove the pump, mounting bracket and pulley asssembly.

5. Installation is the reverse of the removal procedure. Adjust belt tension. Refill and bleed system if necessary.

C-II TYPE

NOTE: The C-II pump is equipped with a fiberglas reservoir and can be identified by the reservoir. Never pry against the fiberglass, as damage will occur.

1. Raise and safely support the vehicle as necessary. To remove the power steering fluid from the pump reservoir, discon-

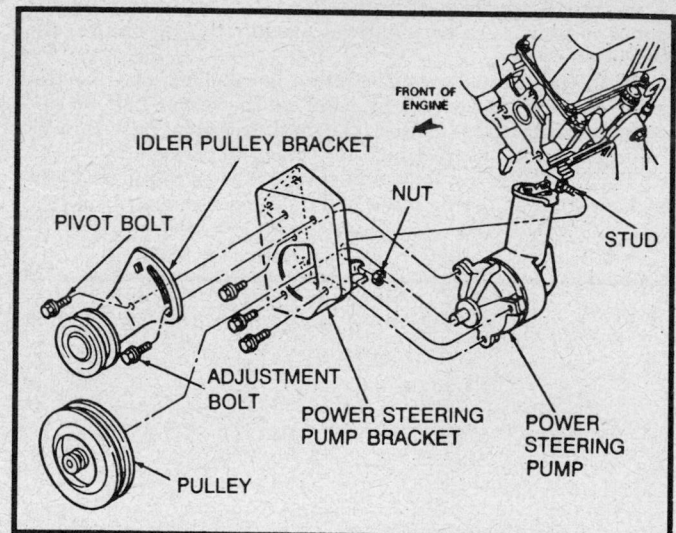

Typical power steering pump installation

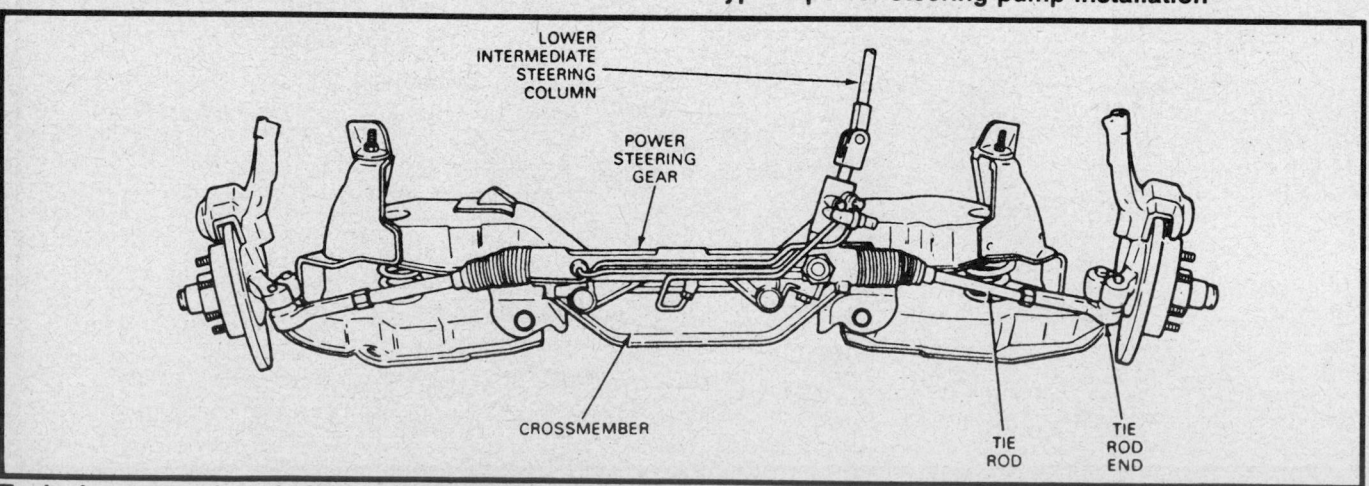

Typical power rack and pinion steering gear

4-66

nect the fluid return hose at the reservoir and drain the fluid into a container. Remove the pressure hose from the pump.

2. Loosen idler pulley assembly pivot and adjustment bolts or adjustment nut and slider bolt.

3. Remove the drive belt from the pulley and dipsitck tube if necessary. Remove support brace if so equipped.

4. Remove the power steering pump bracket retaining bolts. Remove the power steering pump with bracket and pulley from the vehicle.

5. Installation is the reverse of the removal procedure. Fill the reservoir with power steering fluid, start the engine and turn the steering wheel from stop to stop to remove air from the system. Check for leaks and recheck the fluid level. Add fluid if necessary.

Belt Adjustment

1. Check belt tension with a belt tension gauge. New belt tension is 100–190 lbs. and used belt tension is 80–160 lbs. Use the belt tension parameters as a guideline for belt adjustment.

2. On vehicles equipped with pivot type adjustment brackets, loosen the pivot bolts. Insert a tool in adjustment slot, raise upward and tighten pivot bolts.

3. On vehicles equipped with slider type adjustment bracket, loosen the bolts in the slider slots and position pump to obtain the correct belt tension. Tighten all bolts.

4. Recheck and adjust belt if necessary.

System Bleeding

CONVENTIONAL METHOD

1. Check and fill the power steering pump reservoir oil level to the correct level.

2. Run engine. Turn the steering wheel, approximately 5 times, a full cycle (without hitting the stops). This will help remove air trapped in the system.

3. Check fluid level add fluid as necessary.

DEVAC METHOD

NOTE: A fabricated Devac purging tool must be used for this service procedure.

1. Check the pump reservoir oil level (must be at correct level).

2. Insert the rubber stopper end of an air evacuator assembly into the filler tube tightly.

3. Connect a length of hose from the other end of the

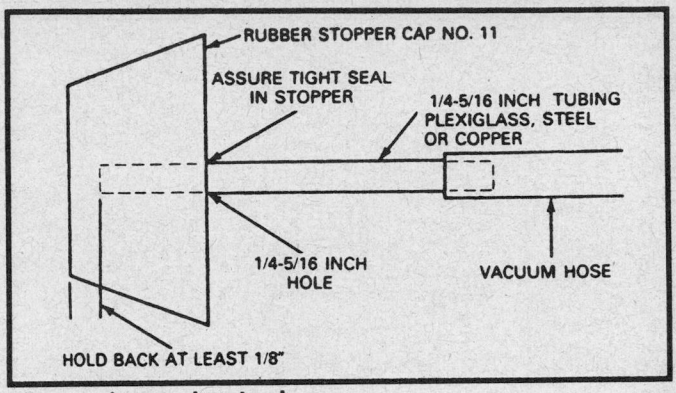

Devac air purging tool

evacuator to a distributor machine or an air conditioner vacuum pump. Do not use engine vacuum.

4. Let the engine idle for 15 minutes. Turn the steering wheel a full cycle (without hitting the stops) every 5 minutes. This will help remove air trapped in the system.

5. Disconnect and remove the evacuator and reinstall the filler tube dipstick.

Tie Rod Ends

Removal and Installation

NOTE: Replace the drag link or tie rod if a ball stud is excessively loose or if the drag link or tie rod is bent. Do not attempt to straighten a drag link or tie rod.

1. Raise and safely support the vehicle as necessary. Remove the cotter pin and nut from the tie rod ball studs.

2. Using suitable tools, remove tie rod ball studs from spindle and drag link. On Aerostar, remove tie rod ball stud from spindle and loosen tie rod jam nut.

3. If replacing just one tie rod end remove the end from the the adjusting sleeve. Always record the number of turns to remove the tie rod end from sleeve. When installing this will provide approxmate toe in setting.

4. Installation is the reverse of the removal procedure. Always position adjusting sleeve clamp towards engine (nut faces front of engine). Tighten ball stud nut to 50–75 ft. lbs., use new cotter pins and check front end alignment.

BRAKES

For all brake system repair and service procedure not detailed below, please refer to "Brakes" in the Unit repair section.

Master Cylinder

Removal and Installation

1. Disconnect the negative battery cable(s). Disconnect the brake warning lamp electrical connection from master cylinder.

2. Disconnect the hydraulic lines from the master cylinder.

3. Remove the brake booster to master cylinder retaining nuts. Remove the master cylinder from the brake booster.

4. Installation is the reverse of the removal procedure. Before installing the master cylinder, check the distance from the outer end of the booster assembly pushrod, to the front face of the

brake assembly. The service specification (Bendix booster) is 0.995 in. Bleed brake system as required.

Power Brake Booster

Removal and Installation

1. Disconnect the negative battery cable. Remove retaining nuts and master cylinder from booster.

2. Loosen hose clamp and remove manifold vacuum hose from booster.

3. From inside the cab, remove the hairpin retainer and plastic bushings and disconnect the booster pushrod from the brake pedal. The stoplight switch must be positioned off brake pedal arm.

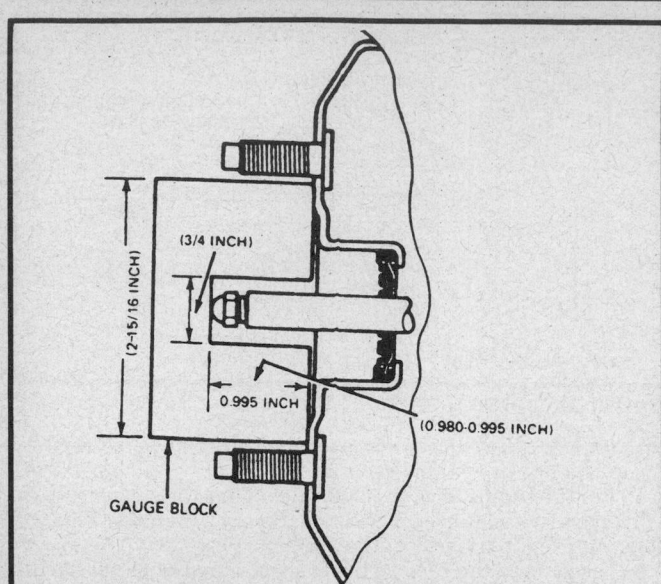

Checking distance of brake booster pushrod

4. Remove nuts that retain the booster mounting bracket to the dash panel.

5. Remove the booster assembly from engine compartment.

To install:

6. Mount the booster and bracket assembly to the engine side of the dash panel by sliding the bracket mounting bolts and valve operating rod in through the holes in the dash panel.

7. From inside the cab, install the booster mounting bracket to dash panel retaining nuts.

8. Position the master cylinder to the booster assembly and install the retaining nuts.

9. Connect the manifold vacuum hose to the booster and secure with clamp.

10. From inside the cab connect the booster valve operating rod to the brake pedal with the hairpin retainer and plastic bushings. Reposition the stoplight switch on the brake pedal arm and reconnect the battery cable. Start engine and check operation of the brake system.

Brake Caliper

Removal and Installation

1. Siphon part of the brake fluid out of the master cylinder to avoid overflow when the caliper piston is pressed into the cylinder bore.

2. Raise the vehicle and support it safely. Remove the wheel/tire assembly.

3. Position a 8 in. C-clamp on the caliper and tighten the clamp to bottom the piston in the caliper cylinder bore. Remove clamp.

4. Drive the upper caliper pin (compress pin tabs) out the caliper slide groove with a brass rod and light hammer.

5. Drive the lower caliper pin (compress pin tabs) out the caliper slide groove with a brass rod and light hammer.

6. Disconnect the brake hose from the inlet port. Cap the hose and inlet port to prevent fluid leakage.

7. Remove the caliper from the spindle assembly by pushing it downward against the spindle and rotating the upper end upward out of the spindle assembly.

8. Installation is the reverse of the removal procedure. The tabs on each end of the caliper pin must catch on the spindle face. Adjust rear brakes and bleed brake system as required.

Disc Brake Pad

Removal and Installation

1. Raise and safely support the vehicle. Remove the wheel/tire assembly. Remove the caliper assembly.

2. Remove the outer shoe and lining from the caliper. Remove the inner shoe and lining from the spindle assembly. Remove the shoe anti-rattle clip from the lower shoe abutment surface on the spindle assembly.

3. Thoroughly clean the areas of the caliper and spindle assembly that come in contact during the sliding action of the caliper.

4. Installation is the reverse of the removal procedure. Use new components as required. Adjust rear brakes and bleed the system as required.

Brake Rotor

Removal and Installation

1. Raise and safely support the vehicle. Remove the wheel/tire assembly.

2. Remove the caliper assembly from the rotor and support it out of the way with wire or equivalent.

3. Remove the dust cap, cotter pin, nut, washer and outer bearing and remove the rotor from the spindle.

4. On 4WD vehicles, the locking hub assembly must also be removed.

5. Install in the reverse order of removal procedure. Adjust wheel bearings. If replacing rotor assembly, always replace the grease seal for inner bearing.

Brake Drum

Removal and Installation

1. Raise and safely support the vehicle. Remove the wheel/tire assembly.

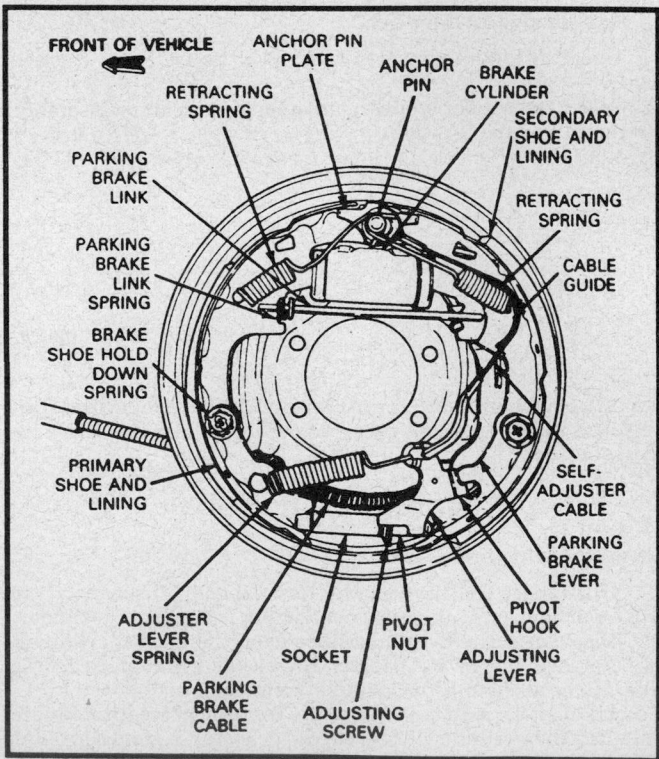

Rear brake shoe assembly

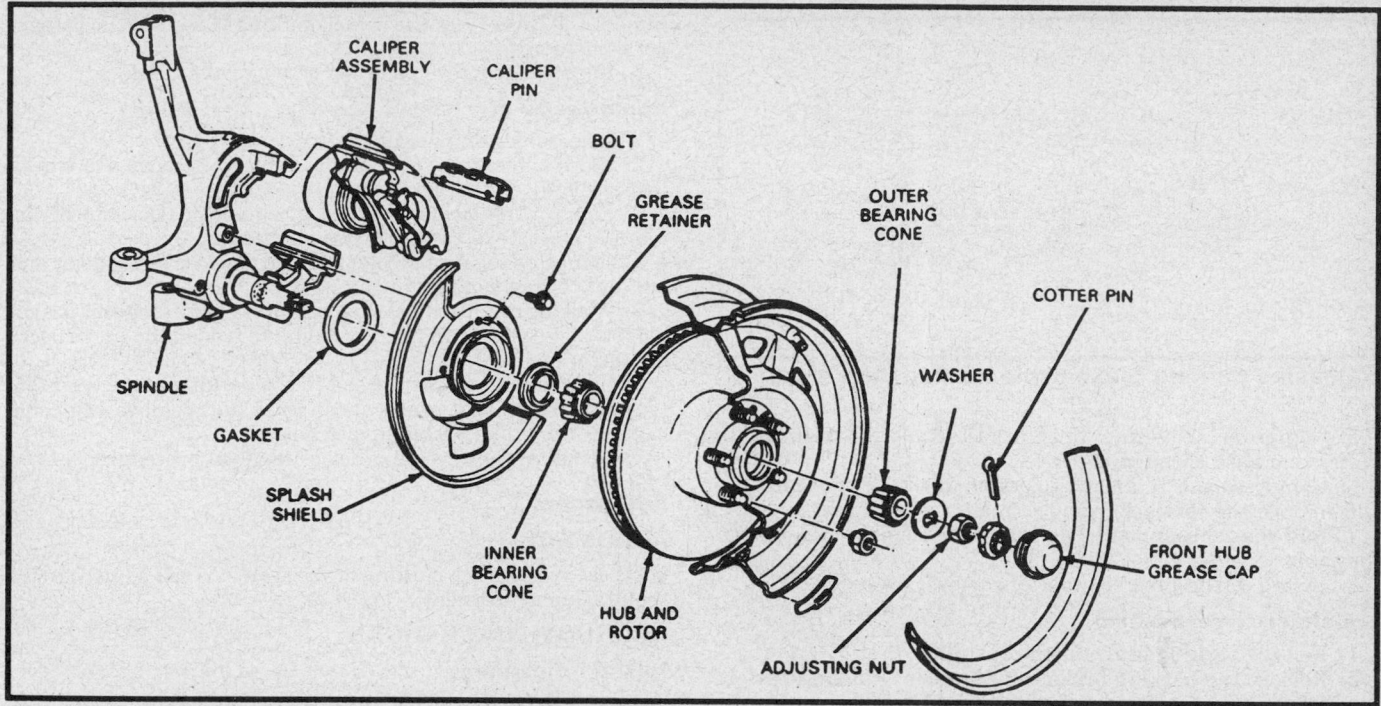

Spindle, wheel and caliper assembly–Aerostar

2. Remove the spring retaining nuts (if equipped) and remove the brake drum.

3. Install in the reverse order of removal procedure. If brake drum will not come off, insert a narrow tool through the brake adjusting hole in the backing plate and disengage the adjusting lever while loosening the brake adjusting screw.

Brake Shoe

Removal and Installation

NOTE: Before removing brake shoes record color and position of all brake springs they must be installed in their original position. Only service one side at a time so the other side may be used as a guide.

1. Raise and safely support the vehicle. Remove the wheel/tire assembly. Remove the brake drum.

2. Install a brake cylinder clamp around wheel cylinder to stop it from expanding.

3. Remove the bottom brake adjuster retaining spring. Remove the self-adjusting cable from the lever. Remove lever and brake adjuster.

4. Remove the primary shoe to anchor spring.

5. Remove the secondary shoe to anchor spring. Remove the cable guide and cable from the secondary shoe.

6. Remove the left and right shoe hold down spring.

7. Remove the parking brake link and spring assembly (note position for correct installation). Disconnect the parking brake cable from the brake lever.

8. Remove the brake shoes. Remove the parking brake lever from the secondary shoe by removing the retaining clip and spring washer.

9. Installation is the reverse of the removal procedure. The primary shoe (short shoe) always is installed toward the front of the vehicle. The secondary shoe (long shoe) is installed toward the rear of the vehicle. Replace all brake springs as necessary. Lube with white brake grease where the brake shoes touch the backing plate. Check the brake fluid and adjust the brake system.

Wheel Cylinder

Removal and Installation

1. Raise and safely support the vehicle. Remove the wheel, drum and brake shoes.

2. Remove the wheel cylinder to shoe connecting pins.

3. Disconnect the brake line from the wheel cylinder.

4. Remove the wheel cylinder retaining bolts and remove the cylinder from the brake backing plate.

5. Installation is the reverse of the removal procedure. Adjust the brakes and bleed the system as required.

Parking Brake Cable

Removal and Installation

AEROSTAR

Equalizer-to-control assembly

1. Place the parking brake hand control in the released position. Release the parking brake cable tension as follows:

   a. Remove the boot cover from the parking brake control assembly.

   b. Insert a steel pin through the pawl lockout pin hole. The pin must be inserted from the inboard side of the control at a upward and forward angle then moved downward and rearward to displace the self adjusting pawl to be inserted through the other hole. This locks out the self adjusting pawl.

   c. With a suitable tool rotate the spring loaded wheel (self adjuster mechanism) back as far as possible to release cable tension.

2. Raise and safely support the vehicle. Disconnect the rear parking brake cables from the equalizer. Remove the equalizer from front cable.

3. Remove the cover from the underbody reinforcemnet bracket. It may be necessary to loosen fuel tank straps and lower fuel tank to gain access to cover.

4. Remove the cable anchor pin from the pivot hole in the control ratchet plate. Guide the front cable from the control.

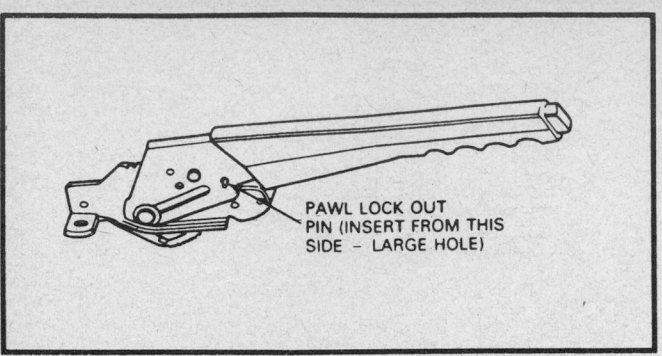

PAWL LOCK OUT
PIN (INSERT FROM THIS
SIDE – LARGE HOLE)

Releasing parking brake cable tension–Aerostar

5. Compress the retainer fingers of the cable and push the retainer rearward through the hole.

6. Compress the retainer fingers on the rear crossmember and remove the retainer from the rear crossmember.

7. Pull the cable ends through the crossmember and remove the cable.

8. Install in the reverse order of removal procedure.

Equalizer-to-rear wheel

1. Release parking brake hand control.

2. Release the parking brake cable tension. Raise and safely support the vehicle. Remove the wheel/tire assembly and brake drum.

3. Disconnect the rear parking brake cable from the equalizer.

4. Compress the prongs that retain cable to crossmember and pull out the cable and housing.

5. Working on the wheel side, compress the prongs on the cable retainer so they can pass through the hole in the brake backing plate.

6. Lift the cable out of the slot in the parking brake lever (attached to secondary brake shoe) lever and remove the cable through the brake backing plate hole.

7. Install in the reverse order of removal procedure.

BRONCO II AND RANGER
Equalizer-to-control assembly

1. Raise and safely support the vehicle. Release parking brake control.

2. Back off the equalizer nut and remove slug of front cable from the tension limiter.

3. Remove the parking brake cable from the bracket or crossmember.

4. Remove the forward ball end of the parking brake cable from the control clevis.

5. Remove the cable from the control assembly.

6. Using a cord attached to the control lever end of the cable,

remove the cable from the vehicle pulling it up into the passenger compartment.

7. Install in the reverse order of removal procedure.

Equalizer-to-rear wheel

1. Release parking brake control.

2. Raise and safely support the vehicle. Remove the wheel/tire assembly and brake drum.

3. Remove the locknut on rod at equalizer. Disconnect the rear parking brake cable from the equalizer.

4. Compress the prongs that retain cable to crossmember and pull out the cable and housing.

5. Working on the wheel side, compress the prongs on the cable retainer so they can pass through the hole in the brake backing plate.

6. Lift the cable out of the slot in the parking brake lever (attached to secondary brake shoe) lever and remove the cable through the brake backing plate hole.

7. Install in the reverse order of removal procedure.

Adjustment
AEROSTAR

On these vehicles the parking brake system is self adjusting and requires no adjustment.

BRONCO II AND RANGER
Initial Adjustment

NOTE: Use this service adjustment procedure when a new tension limiter installed. Adjust rear brakes before adjusting parking brake. Brake drums must be cold for correct adjustment.

1. Depress the parking brake to last detent position.

2. Raise and safely support the vehicle as necessary. Grip the tension limiter housing and tighten the equalizer nut 2½ in. up the rod.

3. Check to make sure cinch strap has 1⅜ in. remaining.

4. Release parking brake and check for proper operation.

Field Adjustment

NOTE: Use this service adjustment procedure to correct a slack system if a new tension limiter is not installed. Adjust rear brakes before adjusting parking brake.

1. Vehicle drums must be cold for correct adjustment. Depress the parking brake to last possible detent position.

2. Raise and safely support the vehicle as necessary. Grip the tension limiter housing and tighten the equalizer nut 6 full turns past the original position.

3. Using a cable tension guide or equivalent the tension should be 400–600 lbs. in front of the equalizer assembly. If tension is low repeat Step 2.

4. Release parking brake and check for rear wheel drag. There should be no brake drag.

FRONT SUSPENSION

Shock Absorbers

Removal and Installation

1. Raise and safely support the vehicle as necessary. Remove the nut and the washer that attaches the shock absorber to the spring seat.

2. Remove the nut and bolt that retain the shock absorber to the radius arm and lower shock bracket.

3. Slightly compress the shock and remove it from the vehicle.

4. On Aerostar remove the 2 bolts retaining the shock absorber to the bottom of the lower control arm. Remove the shock through the lower control arm.

5. Installation is the reverse of the removal procedure.

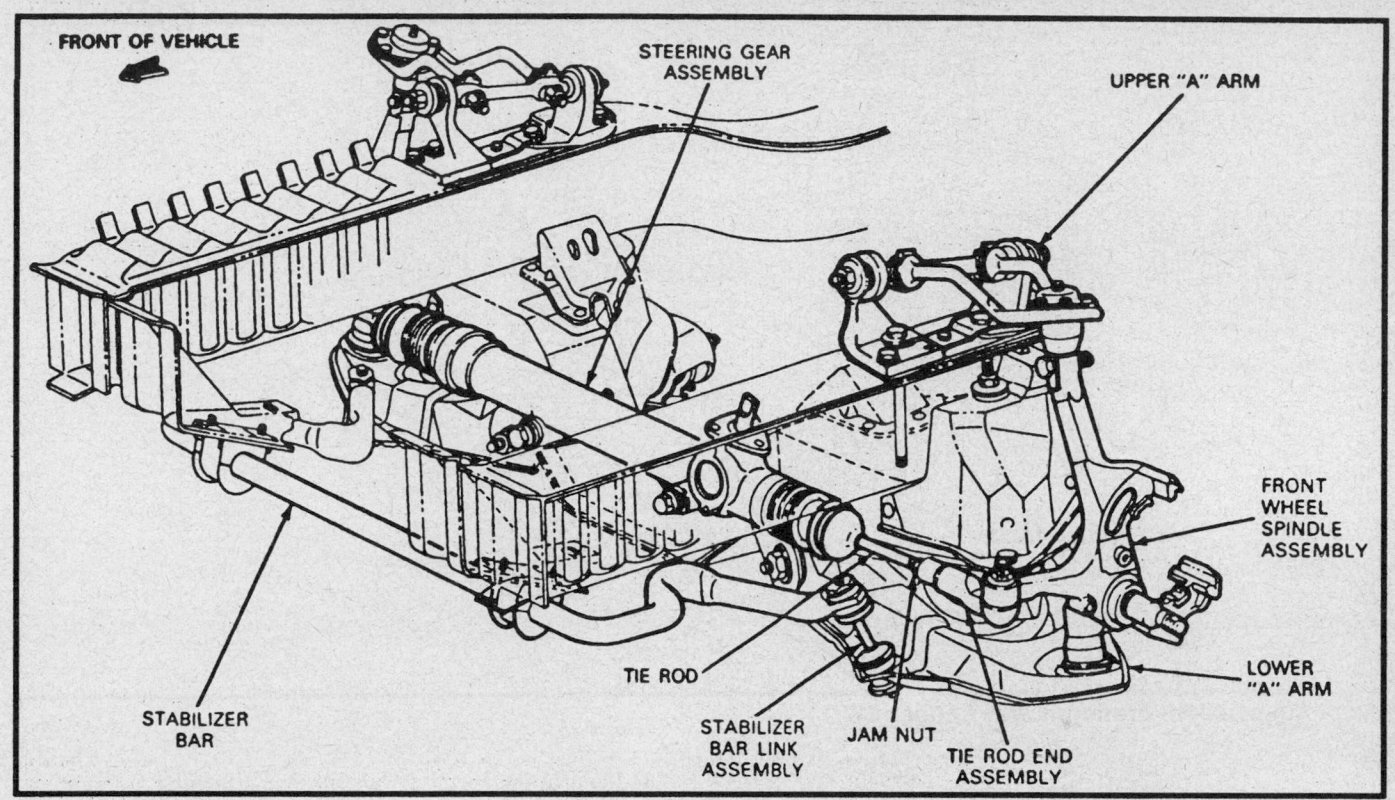

FRONT OF VEHICLE

STEERING GEAR ASSEMBLY

UPPER "A" ARM

FRONT WHEEL SPINDLE ASSEMBLY

LOWER "A" ARM

TIE ROD

STABILIZER BAR

STABILIZER BAR LINK ASSEMBLY

JAM NUT

TIE ROD END ASSEMBLY

Front suspension–Aerostar

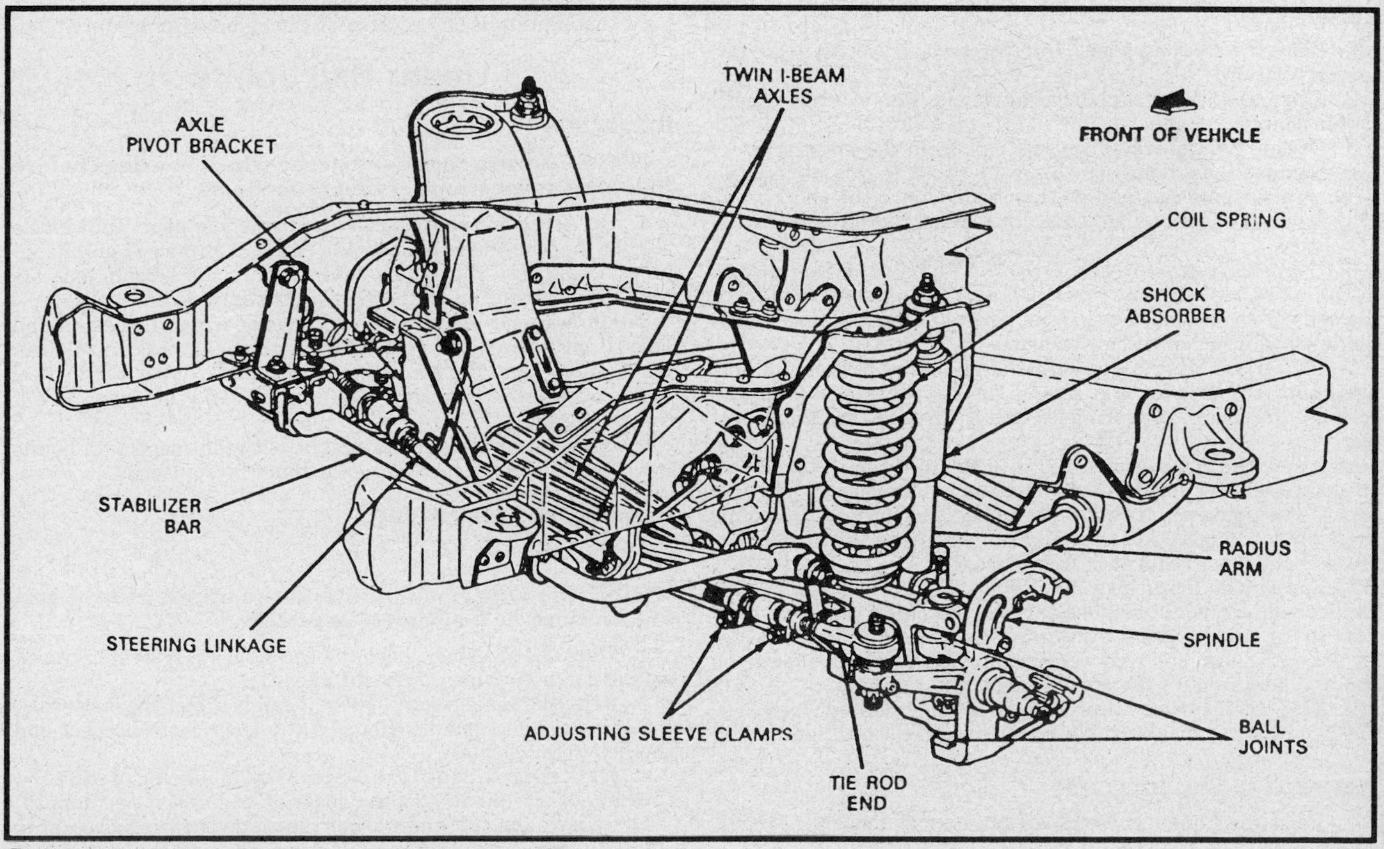

AXLE PIVOT BRACKET

TWIN I-BEAM AXLES

FRONT OF VEHICLE

COIL SPRING

SHOCK ABSORBER

STABILIZER BAR

RADIUS ARM

STEERING LINKAGE

SPINDLE

ADJUSTING SLEEVE CLAMPS

BALL JOINTS

TIE ROD END

Front suspension–Bronco II and Ranger 2WD

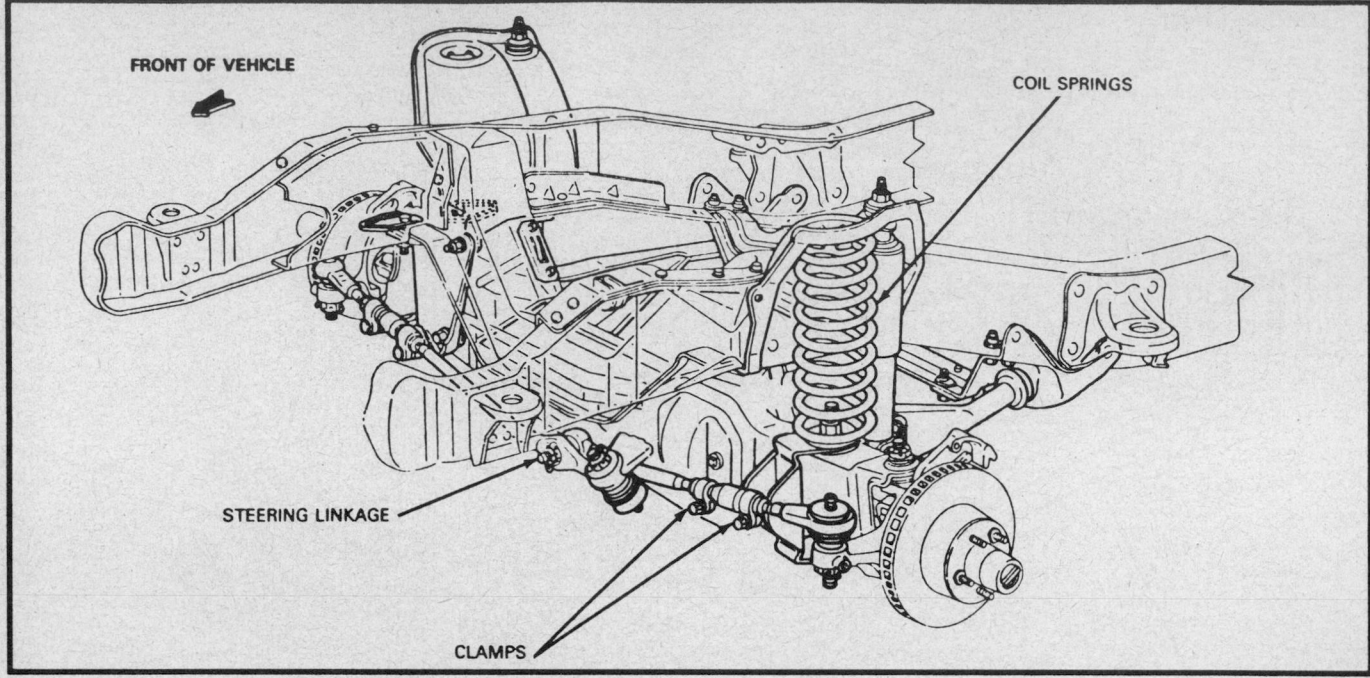

FRONT OF VEHICLE

COIL SPRINGS

STEERING LINKAGE

CLAMPS

Front suspension–Bronco II and Ranger 4WD

Coil Springs

Removal and Installation

AEROSTAR

1. Place the steering wheel and the steering system in the on center position.
2. Raise and safely support the vehicle. Remove the wheel/tire assembly.
3. Disconnect the stabilizer link bolt from the lower arm.
4. Remove the 2 bolts attaching the shock to the lower arm. Remove the upper nut and washer and remove the shock.
5. Remove the steering center link from the pitman arm if necessary.
6. Using spring compressor tool D78P–5310–A or equivalent, install one plate with the pivot ball seat facing downward into the coils of the spring. Rotate the plate so that it is flush with the upper surface of the lower arm.
7. Install the other plate with the pivot ball seat facing upward into the coils of the spring. Insert the upper ball nut through the coils of the spring, so that the nut rests in the upper plate.
8. Insert the compression rod into the opening in the lower arm, through the upper and lower plate and upper ball nut. Insert the securing pin through the upper ball nut and the compression rod. Tighten the forcing nut until the spring is compressed enough so that it is free in its seat.
9. Loosen the lower arm pivot bolts. Remove the cotter pin and loosen but do not remove the nut attaching the lower ball joint to the spindle. Loosen the lower ball joint nut. Support the lower control arm and remove the ball joint nut. Lower the control arm and remove the spring assembly.
10. Reverse the removal procedure for installation. Installed upper and lower insulator plates in the correct position.

BRONCO II AND RANGER

1. Raise the front of the vehicle and support it safely. Also put a jack under the axle.
2. Disconnect the shock absorber from the lower bracket.

3. Remove the spring lower retainer attaching nuts and remove the lower retainer.
4. Slowly lower the axle and remove the spring. Rotate the spring to clear upper spring retaininer.
5. Installation is the reverse of the removal procedure.

Upper Ball Joints

Inspection

NOTE: Always check/adjust the wheel bearings before ball joint inspection service procedure.

1. On Aerostar vehicles, raise and safely support the vehicle so that the wheel assemblies hang free. On Bronco II and Ranger vehicles, raise the vehicle and support the I-Beam axle beneath the coil spring so that spring is compressed.
2. On Aerostar vehicles, move the (upper part) wheel in and out. Observe the upper spindle arm and the upper control arm. On Bronco II and Ranger vehicles, move the (upper part) wheel in and out. Observe the upper spindle arm and the upper part of the axle jaw.
3. A $\frac{1}{32}$ in. or greater movement between inspection points indicates that the upper ball joint must be replaced.

Removal and Installation

AEROSTAR

NOTE: The upper ball joint and the upper control arm are serviced as a complete assembly.

1. Place the steering wheel and the steering system in the on center position (wheels straight ahead) .
2. Raise the vehicle and support it safely under the body rails.
3. Remove the spindle. Remove the cowl drain bracket and the bolt retainer plate.
4. Mark the position of the control arm mounting brackets on the flat plate. Note number and location of shims if so equipped.
5. Remove the bolt and washer retaining the front bracket to the flat plate.
6. From beneath the rail, remove the 3 nuts from the bolts re-

taining the 2 upper control arm mounting brackets to the body rail.

7. Remove the 3 long bolts retaining the mounting brackets to the body rail by rotating the upper control arm out of position in order to remove the bolts.

8. Remove the upper control arm, upper ball joint and mounting bracket assembly and flat plate from the vehicle.

9. Installation is the reverse of the removal procedure. Install shims (correct number) in the proper location. The torque required for the mounting bracket to body rails nuts and bolts is very important. The torque specification is 145–195 ft. lbs. Make sure the mounting brackets do not move from the marked position on the flat plate. Check/adjust the front end alignmemt as required.

BRONCO II AND RANGER

1. Raise and safely support the vehicle as necessary.
2. Remove the spindle/ball joint assembly from axle.
3. Remove the snapring from the upper ball joint if so equipped.
4. Assemble the C-frame tool T74P–4635–C and reciever cup tool D81T–3010–A or equivalent on the upper ball joint.
5. Turn the forcing screw until the ball joint is removed from the spindle assembly.
6. Installation is the reverse of the removal procedure. Do not heat the ball joint or the spindle to aid in removal. Always remove or install lower ball joint to spindle assembly first when servicing upper ball joint.

Lower Ball Joints

Inspection

NOTE: Always check/adjust the wheel bearings before ball joint inspection service procedure.

1. On Aerostar vehicles, raise and safely support the vehicle so that the wheel assemblies hang free. On Bronco II and Ranger vehicles, raise the vehicle and support the I-Beam axle beneath the coil spring so that spring is compressed.

2. On Aerostar vehicles, move the (lower part) wheel in and out. Observe the lower spindle jaw and the lower control arm. On Bronco II and Ranger vehicles, move the (lower part) wheel in and out. Observe the lower spindle arm and the lower part of the axle jaw.

3. A $\frac{1}{32}$ in. or greater movement between inspection points indicates that the lower ball joint must be replaced.

Removal and Installation

AEROSTAR

NOTE: The lower ball joint and the lower control arm are serviced as a complete assembly.

1. Place the steering and the steering system in the on center position (wheels straight ahead).
2. Raise the vehicle and support it safely under the frame.
3. Remove the coil spring.
4. Remove the bolts and nuts retaining the control arm to the No.1 crossmember. Remove the lower control arm.
5. Install in the reverse order of removal. Final torque is with vehicle in normal ride position. The lower control arm to crossmember torque specification is 100–140 ft. lbs.

BRONCO II AND RANGER

1. Raise and safely support the vehicle as necessary.
2. Remove the spindle/ball joint assembly from axle.
3. Remove the snapring from the lower ball joint if so equipped.
4. Assemble the C-frame tool T74P–4635–C and reciever cup tool D81T–3010–A or equivalent on the lower ball joint.

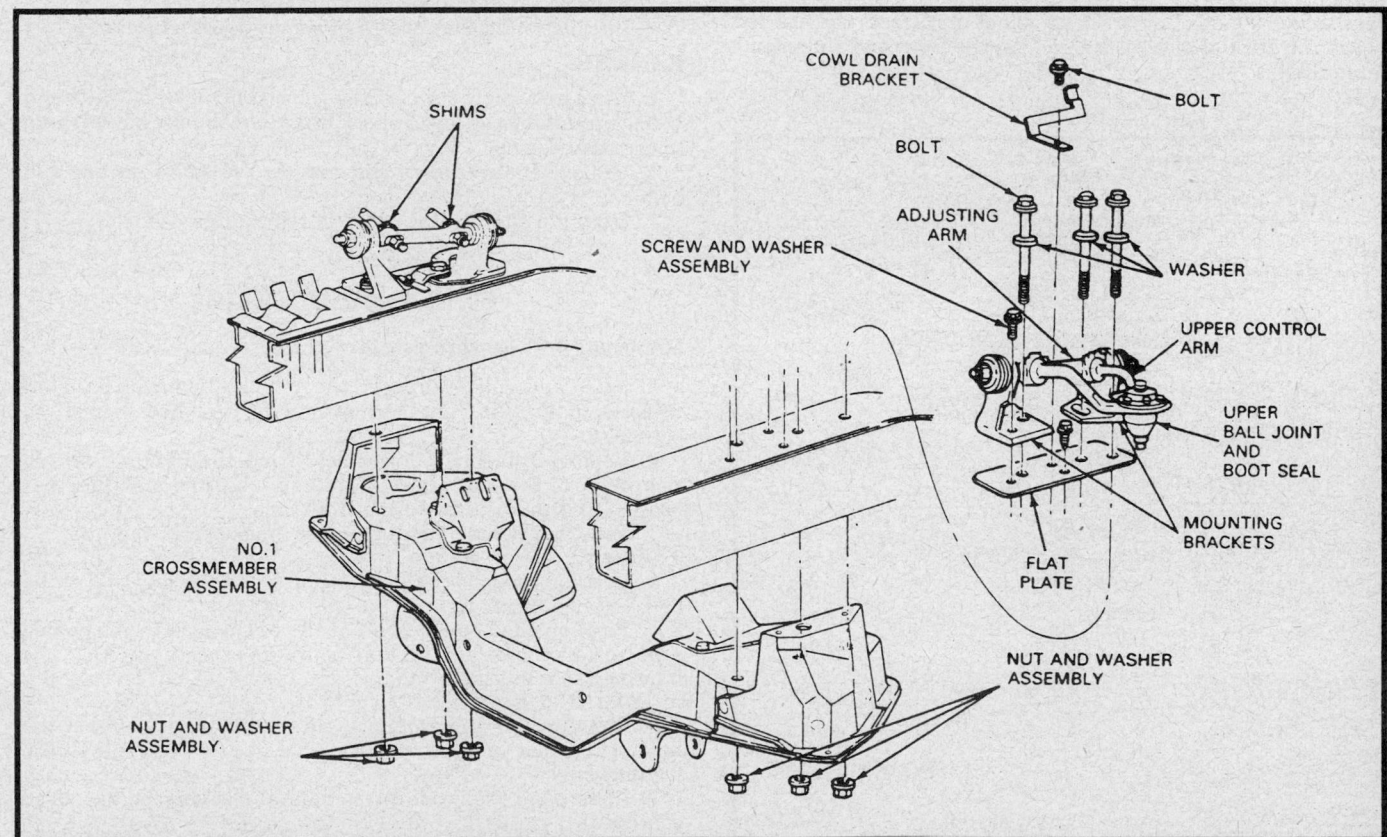

Front upper control arm assembly–Aerostar

5. Turn the forcing screw until the ball joint is removed from the spindle assembly.

6. Installation is the reverse of the removal procedure. Do not heat the ball joint or the spindle to aid in removal. Always remove or install lower ball to spindle assembly first.

Upper Control Arms

Removal and Installation
AEROSTAR

1. Place the steering wheel and the steering system in the on center position (wheels straight ahead).

2. Raise the vehicle and support it safely under the body rails.

3. Remove the spindle. Remove the cowl drain bracket and the bolt retainer plate.

4. Mark the position of the control arm mounting brackets on the flat plate. Note number and location of shims if so equipped.

5. Remove the bolt and washer retaining the front bracket to the flat plate.

6. From beneath the rail, remove the 3 nuts from the bolts retaining the 2 upper control arm mounting brackets to the body rail.

7. Remove the 3 long bolts retaining the mounting brackets to the body rail by rotating the upper control arm out of position in order to remove the bolts.

8. Remove the upper control arm, upper ball joint and mounting bracket assembly and flat plate from the vehicle.

9. Installation is the reverse of the removal procedure. Install shims (correct number) in the proper location. The torque required for the mounting bracket to body rails nuts and bolts is very important. The torque specification is 145–195 ft. lbs. Make sure the mounting brackets do not move from the marked position on the flat plate. Check/adjust the front end alignmemt as required.

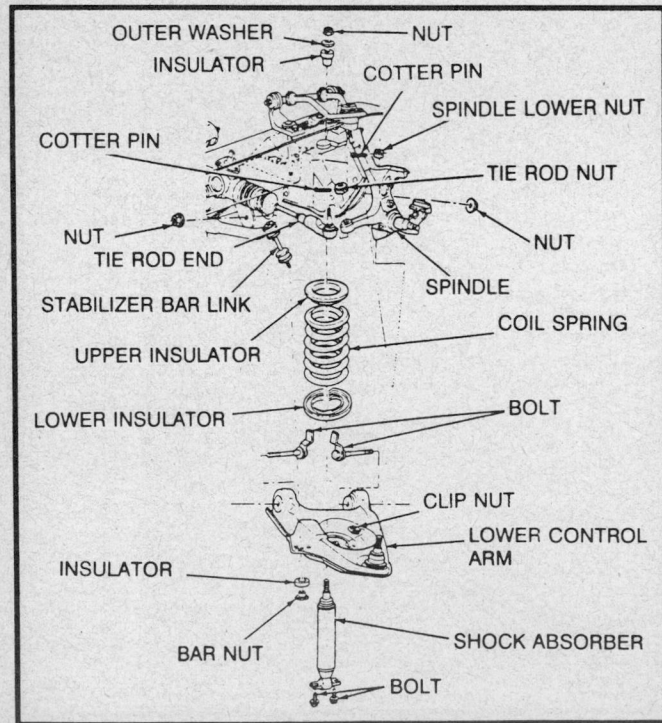

Front lower control arm assembly–Aerostar

Lower Control Arms

Removal and Installation
AEROSTAR

1. Place the steering and the steering system in the on center position (wheels straight ahead).

2. Raise the vehicle and support it safely under the frame.

3. Remove the coil spring.

4. Remove the bolts and nuts retaining the control arm to the No.1 crossmember. Remove the lower control arm.

5. Install in the reverse order of removal. Final torque is with vehicle in normal ride position. The lower control arm to crossmember torque specification is 100–140 ft. lbs.

Stabilizer Bar

Removal and Installation
AEROSTAR

1. Raise and safely support the vehicle. Remove the nuts retaining the stabilizer bar to the lower control arm link.

2. Remove the insulators and disconnect the bar from the links. If required, remove the links from the lower control arm.

3. Remove the bolts retaining the bar mounting bracket to the frame and remove the stabilizer bar.

4. Install in the reverse order of removal procedure.

BRONCO II

1. Raise and safely support the vehicle. Remove the bolts and the retainers from the center and the right hand end of the stabilizer bar.

2. Disconnect the stabilizer bar from the stabilizer link.

3. Remove the stabilizer bar and bushings.

4. Installation is the reverse of removal procedure.

RANGER

1. Raise and safely support the vehicle. Remove the nuts and U-bolts retaining the lower shock bracket/stabilizer bar bushing to the radius arm.

2. Remove the retainers and remove the stabilizer bar and bushing.

3. Install in the reverse order of removal procedure.

Twin I-Beam Axle

Removal and Installation

1. Raise and safely support the vehicle. Remove the front wheel spindle, the front spring and the stabilizer bar (if so equipped).

2. Remove the spring lower seat from the radius arm and then remove the bolt and nut that attaches the stabilizer bar bracket and radius arm to the front axle.

3. Remove the axle to frame pivot bracket bolt and nut.

To install:

4. Position the axle to the frame pivot bracket and install the bolt and nut finger tight.

5. Position the opposite end of the of the axle to the radius arm, install the attaching bolt from underneath through the bracket, the radius arm and the axle. Install the nut and tighten to 120–150 ft. lbs.

6. Install the spring lower seat on the radius arm so that the hole in the seat indexes over the arm to axle bolt. Install the front spring.

7. Install the front wheel spindle and stabilizer bar if so equipped.

8. Lower the vehicle (weight on suspension for final torque). Tighten the axle to frame pivot bracket bolts to 120–150 ft. lbs.

Front Wheel Bearings

Removal and Installation

1. Raise and safely support the vehicle. Remove the wheel/tire assemblies.
2. Remove the brake caliper and wire it to the underbody to prevent damage to the brake hose.
3. Remove the grease cap, cotter pin, retainer adjusting nut and washer.
4. Remove the outer bearing. Pull the hub and rotor off the spindle. Remove and discard the grease seal.
5. Remove the inner bearing from the hub. Remove all traces of old lubricant from the bearings, hub and spindle with solvent and dry thoroughly.
6. Inspect the bearing races for scratches, pits or cracks. If the races are worn or damaged, remove them with a drift. If the inner or outer bearing races were removed, replace them in the hub with the proper tool. The races will be properly seated when they are fully bottomed.
7. Replace the grease retainer. Pack the inside of the hub with lithium base grease, high temperature multi-purpose long life lubricant. Fill the hub until the grease is flush with the inside diameters of both bearing races.
8. Pack the bearings with wheel bearing grease, working as much lubricant as possible between the rollers and the cages.
9. For installation reverse the removal procedure. Adjust the wheel bearings.

Adjustment

1. Raise the vehicle and support it safely.
2. Remove the wheel cover and the grease cap from the hub. Remove the cotter pin and the locknut. Loosen the adjusting nut 3 turns.
3. Obtain running clearance (runnning clearance must be maintained throughout adjustment procedure) remove the brake caliper or equivalent. While rotating the wheel, tighten the adjusting nut to 17–25 ft. lbs. to seat the bearings.
4. Back off the adjusting nut ½ turn. Retighten the nut to 18–20 inch lbs. Install the retainer and new cotter pin without additional movement of the adjusting nut.
5. Check the wheel rotation. Reinstall the grease cap and the wheel cover.

REAR SUSPENSION

Shock Absorber

Removal and Installation

AEROSTAR

1. Raise and safely support the vehicle.
2. Remove load off shock absorber assembly with jack or equivalent. Remove the shock absorber lower attaching nut and bolt and swing the lower end free of the mounting bracket on the axle housing.
3. Remove the attaching nut from the upper mounting stud and remove the shock absorber.
4. Installation is the reverse of the removal procedure. Torque the upper and lower mounting bolts to 63 ft. lbs.

BRONCO II AND RANGER

1. Raise and safely support the vehicle.
2. Remove load off shock absorber assembly with jack or equivalent. Remove the self-locking nut, steel washer and rubber bushings if so equipped at the upper and lower ends of the shock absorber. Remove the shock assembly from the vehicle.
3. Installation is the reverse of the removal procedure. Torque the upper mounting bolt to 63 ft. lbs and lower mounting bolt to 73 ft. lbs.

Coil Spring

Removal and Installation

AEROSTAR

1. Raise and safely support the vehicle as necessary.
2. Place safety stands or equivalent on the frame rear lift points.
3. Disconnect the shock absorber from the axle mount on the lower control arm and disconnect it from the axle bracket.
4. Lower the rear axle until the coil springs are no longer under compression.
5. Mark and disconnect the lower spring retainer assembly from the control arm. Mark and disconnect the upper spring retainer assembly from the frame.
6. Remove the spring, retainers and insulators from vehicle.
7. Install in the reverse order of removal procedure. The small diameter spring coils face upward with upper pigtail (spring end) resting against the upper insulator rubber stop. Rotate the complete spring assembly until the lower pigtail (spring end) points in a 3 o'clock position. Torque the upper retainer bolt to 40 ft. lbs and lower retainer bolt 65 ft. lbs.

Leaf Spring

Removal and Installation

BRONCO II AND RANGER

1. Raise the vehicle frame (safely support) until the weight is off the rear spring, with the tires still touching the floor or equivalent.
2. Remove the nuts from the spring U-bolts and drive the U-bolts from the U-bolt plate.
3. Remove the spring-to-bracket nut and bolt at the front of the spring.
4. Remove the shackle upper and lower nuts and bolts at the rear of the spring. Remove the spring and shackle assembly from the rear shackle bracket.
5. If the bushings in the spring or shackle are worn or damaged, replace them.
To install:
6. Position the spring in the shackle and install the upper shackle-to-spring bolt and nut with the bolt head facing outboard.
7. Position the front end of the spring in the bracket and install. Position the shackle in the rear bracket and install.
8. Position the spring on top of the axle with the spring tie bolt centered in the hole provided in the seat.
9. Install the spring U-bolt plate and nuts. Lower the vehicle. Tighten the spring U-bolt nuts. Tighten the front spring bolt and nut and the rear shackle bolts and nuts.

Rear Upper Control Arm

Removal and Installation

AEROSTAR

1. Raise the vehicle and support it safely.

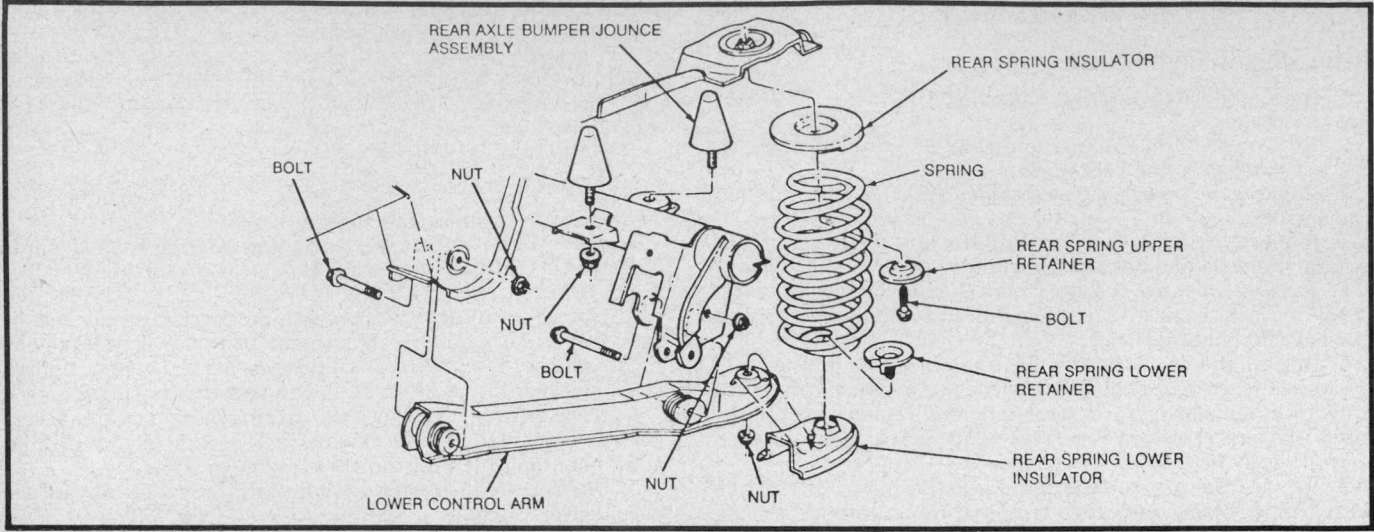

Rear lower control arm assembly–Aerostar

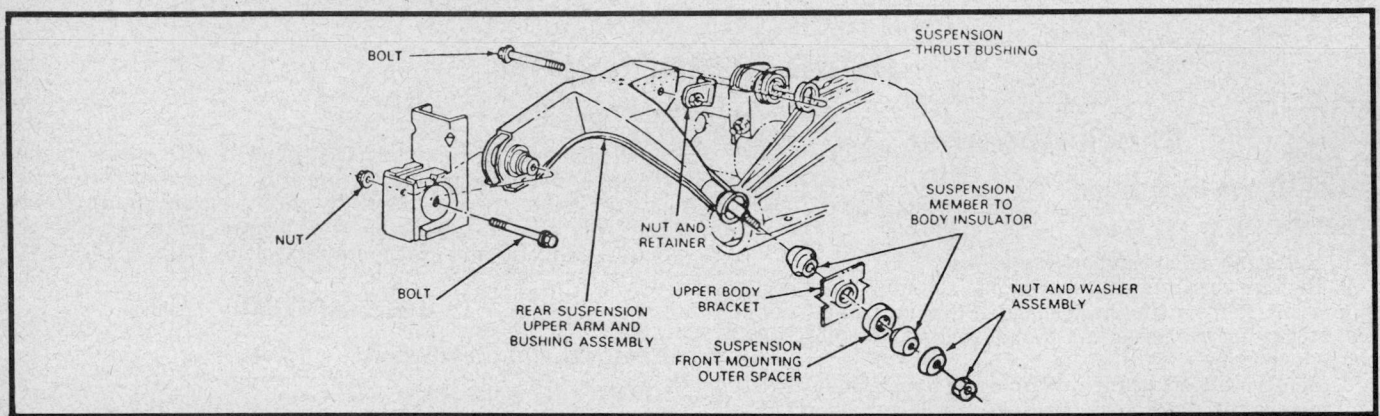

Rear upper control arm assembly–Aerostar

2. Place safety stands or equivalent on the frame rear lift points.

3. Disconnect the shock absorber from the axle mount on the lower control arm and disconnect it from the axle bracket.

4. Lower the rear axle assembly until the coil springs are no longer under compression.

5. Remove the bolt and nut retaining the upper control arm to the rear axle housing. Disconnect the upper control arm from the axle housing. Scribe a mark aligning the position of the cam adjuster in the axle bushing. The cam adjuster controls the rear axle pinion angle for driveline angularity.

6. Remove the bolt and nut retaining the upper control arm to the right frame bracket. Rotate the arm to disengage from the body bracket.

7. Remove the nut and washer retaining the upper control arm to the left frame bracket. Remove the outer insulator and spacer. Remove the control arm from the bracket. Remove the inner insulator from the control arm stud.

To install:

8. Position the inner insulator on the control arm stud. Install the control arm so the stud extends through the left frame bracket. Install the spacer and outer insulator over the stud. Install nut and washer assembly and tighten until snug. Do not torque at this time.

9. Position the upper control arm in the right frame bracket. Install bolt and nut assembly and tighten until snug. Do not torque at this time.

10. Align marks on cam adjuster and axle bushing. Install the

upper control arm to axle hosing. Install nut and bolt and tighten until snug. Do not torque at this time.

11. Raise the rear axle assembly and install shock absorber assembly. With the axle in the normal ride position tighten control arm to left frame bracket to 60–100 ft. lbs., control arm to right frame bracket to 100–145 ft. lbs. and control arm to center of axle housing to 100–145 ft. lbs.

12. Remove the safety stands and lower the vehicle.

Rear Lower Control Arms

Removal and Installation

AEROSTAR

1. Raise and safely support the vehicle. Place safety stands under the frame rear lift points.

2. Disconnect the shock absorber from the axle bracket. Swing the lower end of the shock free of the axle bracket.

3. Lower the rear axle until the coil springs are no longer under compression.

4. Disconnect the lower retainer from the control arm. Remove the insulator from the arm.

5. Remove the bolt and nut retaining the lower control arm to the axle housing.

6. Disconnect the lower control arm from the frame bracket. Remove the lower control arm.

7. Install in the reverse order of removal procedure. With the axle in the normal ride position tighten lower control arm to axle housing to 100–145 ft. lbs. and lower control arm to frame bracket to 100–145 ft. lbs.

SPECIFICATIONS

VEHICLE IDENTIFICATION CHART

It is important for servicing and ordering parts to be certain of the vehicle and engine identification. The VIN (vehicle identification number) is a 17 digit number visible through the windshield on the driver's side of the dash and contains the vehicle and engine identification codes. The tenth digit indicates model year and the eighth digit indicates engine code. It can be interpreted as follows:

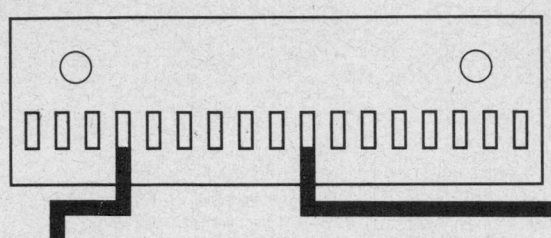

Engine Code						Model Year	
Code	Cu. In.	Liters	Cyl.	Fuel Sys.	Eng. Mfg.	Code	Year
N	262	4.3	6	4bbl.	Chev.	G	1986
Z	262	4.3	6	TBI	Chev.	H	1987
T	292	4.8	6	1bbl.	GM of Mexico	J	1988
F	305	5.0	8	4bbl.	Chev.	K	1989
H (1986)	305	5.0	8	4bbl.	Chev.	L	1990
H (1987–90)	305	5.0	8	TBI	Chev.		
L	350	5.7	8	4bbl.	Chev.		
M	350	5.7	8	4bbl.	Chev.		
K	350	5.7	8	TBI	Chev.		
C	379	6.2	8	Diesel	DDAD		
J	379	6.2	8	Diesel	DDAD		
W	454	7.4	8	4bbl.	Chev.		
N	454	7.4	8	TBI	Chev.		

DDAD—Detroit Diesel Allison Division

ENGINE IDENTIFICATION

Year	Model	Engine Displacement cu. in. (liter)	Engine Series Identification (VIN)	No. of Cylinders	Engine Type
1986	C10/1500 Pick-Up	262 (4.3)	N	6	OHV
	C10/1500 Pick-Up	305 (5.0)	H	8	OHV
	C10/1500 Pick-Up	379 (6.2)	C	8	OHV (Diesel)
	K10/1500 Pick-Up	262 (4.3)	N	6	OHV
	K10/1500 Pick-Up	305 (5.0)	F	8	OHV
	K10/1500 Pick-Up	305 (5.0)	H	8	OHV
	K10/1500 Pick-Up	350 (5.7)	L	8	OHV
	K10/1500 Pick-Up	379 (6.2)	C	8	OHV (Diesel)
	C20/2500 Pick-Up	262 (4.3)	N	8	OHV
	C20/2500 Pick-Up	292 (4.8)	T	6	OHV
	C20/2500 Pick-Up	305 (5.0)	H	8	OHV
	C20/2500 Pick-Up	350 (5.7)	L	8	OHV
	C20/2500 Pick-Up	350 (5.7)	M	8	OHV
	C20/2500 Pick-Up	379 (6.2)	C	8	OHV (Diesel)

ENGINE IDENTIFICATION

Year	Model	Engine Displacement cu. in. (liter)	Engine Series Identification (VIN)	No. of Cylinders	Engine Type
1986	C20/2500 Pick-Up	379 (6.2)	J	8	OHV (Diesel)
	C20/2500 Pick-Up	454 (7.4)	W	8	OHV
	K20/2500 Pick-Up	292 (4.8)	T	6	OHV
	K20/2500 Pick-Up	350 (5.7)	L	8	OHV
	K20/2500 Pick-Up	350 (5.7)	M	8	OHV
	K20/2500 Pick-Up	379 (6.2)	C	8	OHV (Diesel)
	K20/2500 Pick-Up	379 (6.2)	J	8	OHV (Diesel)
	C30/3500 Pick-Up	292 (4.8)	T	6	OHV
	C30/3500 Pick-Up	350 (5.7)	M	8	OHV
	C30/3500 Pick-Up	379 (6.2)	J	8	OHV (Diesel)
	C30/3500 Pick-Up	454 (7.4)	W	8	OHV
	K30/3500 Pick-Up	292 (4.8)	T	6	OHV
	K30/3500 Pick-Up	350 (5.7)	M	8	OHV
	K30/3500 Pick-Up	379 (6.2)	J	8	OHV (Diesel)
	K30/3500 Pick-Up	454 (7.4)	W	8	OHV
	C10/1500 Suburban	305 (5.0)	H	8	OHV
	C10/1500 Suburban	350 (5.7)	L	8	OHV
	C10/1500 Suburban	379 (6.2)	C	8	OHV (Diesel)
	K10/1500 Suburban	350 (5.7)	L	8	OHV
	K10/1500 Suburban	379 (6.2)	C	8	OHV (Diesel)
	C20/2500 Suburban	350 (5.7)	M	8	OHV
	C20/2500 Suburban	379 (6.2)	J	8	OHV (Diesel)
	C20/2500 Suburban	454 (7.4)	W	8	OHV
	G10/1500 Sport Van/Rally	262 (4.3)	N	6	OHV
	G10/1500 Sport Van/Rally	305 (5.0)	H	8	OHV
	G10/1500 Sport Van/Rally	350 (5.7)	L	8	OHV
	G20/2500 Sport Van/Rally	262 (4.3)	N	8	OHV
	G20/2500 Sport Van/Rally	305 (5.0)	H	8	OHV
	G20/2500 Sport Van/Rally	350 (5.7)	L	8	OHV
	G20/2500 Sport Van/Rally	379 (6.2)	C	8	OHV (Diesel)
	G30/3500 Sport Van/Rally	350 (5.7)	L	8	OHV
	G30/3500 Sport Van/Rally	350 (5.7)	M	8	OHV
	G30/3500 Sport Van/Rally	379 (6.2)	J	8	OHV (Diesel)
	G30/3500 Cutaway Van	350 (5.7)	M	8	OHV
	G30/3500 Cutaway Van	379 (6.2)	J	8	OHV (Diesel)
	G30/3500 Hi-Cube Van	350 (5.7)	M	8	OHV
	G30/3500 Hi-Cube Van	379 (6.2)	J	8	OHV (Diesel)
	G30/3500 RV Cutaway Van	350 (5.7)	M	8	OHV
	G30/3500 RV Cutaway Van	379 (6.2)	J	8	OHV (Diesel)
	K Blazer/Jimmy	305 (5.0)	H	8	OHV
	K Blazer/Jimmy	350 (5.7)	L	8	OHV
	K Blazer/Jimmy	379 (6.2)	C	8	OHV (Diesel)
1987	R10/1500 Pick-Up	262 (4.3)	Z	6	OHV
	R10/1500 Pick-Up	305 (5.0)	H	8	OHV

GENERAL MOTORS CORPORATION
C/K SERIES (PICK-UP) • R/V SERIES (PICK-UP) • BLAZER/JIMMY • SUBURBAN • G SERIES (VAN)

ENGINE IDENTIFICATION

Year	Model	Engine Displacement cu. in. (liter)	Engine Series Identification (VIN)	No. of Cylinders	Engine Type
1987	R10/1500 Pick-Up	350 (5.7)	K	8	OHV
	R10/1500 Pick-Up	379 (6.2)	C	8	OHV (Diesel)
	V10/1500 Pick-Up	262 (4.3)	Z	6	OHV
	V10/1500 Pick-Up	305 (5.0)	H	8	OHV
	V10/1500 Pick-Up	350 (5.7)	K	8	OHV
	V10/1500 Pick-Up	379 (6.2)	C	8	OHV (Diesel)
	R20/2500 Pick-Up	262 (4.3)	Z	6	OHV
	R20/2500 Pick-Up	305 (5.0)	H	8	OHV
	R20/2500 Pick-Up	350 (5.7)	K	8	OHV
	R20/2500 Pick-Up	379 (6.2)	C	8	OHV (Diesel)
	R20/2500 Pick-Up	379 (6.2)	J	8	OHV (Diesel)
	R20/2500 Pick-Up	454 (7.4)	N	8	OHV
	V20/2500 Pick-Up	350 (5.7)	K	8	OHV
	V20/2500 Pick-Up	379 (6.2)	C	8	OHV (Diesel)
	V20/2500 Pick-Up	379 (6.2)	J	8	OHV (Diesel)
	R30/3500 Pick-Up	350 (5.7)	K	8	OHV
	R30/3500 Pick-Up	379 (6.2)	J	8	OHV (Diesel)
	R30/3500 Pick-Up	454 (7.4)	N	8	OHV
	V30/3500 Pick-Up	350 (5.7)	K	8	OHV
	V30/3500 Pick-Up	379 (6.2)	J	8	OHV (Diesel)
	V30/3500 Pick-Up	454 (7.4)	N	8	OHV
	R20/2500 Chassis Cab	350 (5.7)	K	8	OHV
	R20/2500 Chassis Cab	379 (6.2)	J	8	OHV (Diesel)
	R20/2500 Chassis Cab	454 (7.4)	N	8	OHV
	R30/3500 Chassis Cab	350 (5.7)	K	8	OHV
	R30/3500 Chassis Cab	379 (6.2)	J	8	OHV (Diesel)
	R30/3500 Chassis Cab	454 (7.4)	N	8	OHV
	V30/3500 Chassis Cab	350 (5.7)	K	8	OHV
	V30/3500 Chassis Cab	379 (6.2)	J	8	OHV (Diesel)
	V30/3500 Chassis Cab	454 (7.4)	N	8	OHV
	R10/1500 Suburban	305 (5.0)	H	8	OHV
	R10/1500 Suburban	350 (5.7)	K	8	OHV
	R10/1500 Suburban	379 (6.2)	C	8	OHV (Diesel)
	V10/1500 Suburban	350 (5.7)	K	8	OHV
	V10/1500 Suburban	379 (6.2)	C	8	OHV (Diesel)
	R20/2500 Suburban	350 (5.7)	K	8	OHV
	R20/2500 Suburban	379 (6.2)	C	8	OHV (Diesel)
	V20/2500 Suburban	350 (5.7)	K	8	OHV (Diesel)
	V20/2500 Suburban	379 (6.2)	C	8	OHV (Diesel)
	G10/1500 Vandura	262 (4.3)	Z	6	OHV
	G10/1500 Vandura	305 (5.0)	H	8	OHV
	G20/2500 Vandura	262 (4.3)	Z	6	OHV
	G20/2500 Vandura	305 (5.0)	H	8	OHV
	G20/2500 Vandura	350 (5.7)	K	8	OHV

ENGINE IDENTIFICATION

Year	Model	Engine Displacement cu. in. (liter)	Engine Series Identification (VIN)	No. of Cylinders	Engine Type
1987	G20/2500 Vandura	379 (6.2)	C	8	OHV (Diesel)
	G30/3500 Vandura	262 (4.3)	Z	6	OHV
	G30/3500 Vandura	350 (5.7)	K	8	OHV
	G30/3500 Vandura	379 (6.2)	J	8	OHV (Diesel)
	G10/1500 Sport Van/Rally	262 (4.3)	Z	6	OHV
	G10/1500 Sport Van/Rally	305 (5.0)	H	8	OHV
	G10/1500 Sport Van/Rally	350 (5.7)	K	8	OHV
	G20/2500 Sport Van/Rally	262 (4.3)	Z	6	OHV
	G20/2500 Sport Van/Rally	305 (5.0)	H	8	OHV
	G20/2500 Sport Van/Rally	350 (5.7)	K	8	OHV
	G20/2500 Sport Van/Rally	379 (6.2)	C	8	OHV (Diesel)
	G30/3500 Sport Van/Rally	350 (5.7)	M	8	OHV
	G30/3500 Sport Van/Rally	379 (6.2)	J	8	OHV (Diesel)
	G30/3500 Cutaway Van	350 (5.7)	K	8	OHV
	G30/3500 Cutaway Van	350 (5.7)	M	8	OHV
	G30/3500 Cutaway Van	379 (6.2)	J	8	OHV (Diesel)
	G30/3500 Hi-Cube Van	350 (5.7)	K	8	OHV
	G30/3500 Hi-Cube Van	350 (5.7)	M	8	OHV
	G30/3500 Hi-Cube Van	379 (6.2)	J	8	OHV (Diesel)
	G30/3500 RV Cutaway Van	350 (5.7)	K	8	OHV
	G30/3500 RV Cutaway Van	350 (5.7)	M	8	OHV
	G30/3500 RV Cutaway Van	379 (6.2)	J	8	OHV (Diesel)
	V Blazer/Jimmy	305 (5.0)	H	8	OHV
	V Blazer/Jimmy	350 (5.7)	K	8	OHV
	V Blazer/Jimmy	379 (6.2)	C	8	OHV (Diesel)
1988	C10/1500 Pick-Up	262 (4.3)	Z	6	OHV
	C10/1500 Pick-Up	305 (5.0)	H	8	OHV
	C10/1500 Pick-Up	350 (5.7)	K	8	OHV
	K10/1500 Pick-Up	262 (4.3)	Z	6	OHV
	K10/1500 Pick-Up	305 (5.0)	H	8	OHV
	K10/1500 Pick-Up	350 (5.7)	K	8	OHV
	C20/2500 Pick-Up	262 (4.3)	Z	6	OHV
	C20/2500 Pick-Up	305 (5.0)	H	8	OHV
	C20/2500 Pick-Up	350 (5.7)	K	8	OHV
	C20/2500 Pick-Up	379 (6.2)	C	8	OHV (Diesel)
	K20/2500 Pick-Up	262 (4.3)	Z	6	OHV
	K20/2500 Pick-Up	305 (5.0)	H	8	OHV
	K20/2500 Pick-Up	350 (5.7)	K	8	OHV
	K20/2500 Pick-Up	379 (6.2)	C	8	OHV (Diesel)
	C30/3500 Pick-Up	350 (5.7)	K	8	OHV
	C30/3500 Pick-Up	379 (6.2)	J	8	OHV (Diesel)
	C30/3500 Pick-Up	454 (7.4)	N	8	OHV
	K30/3500 Pick-Up	350 (5.7)	K	8	OHV
	K30/3500 Pick-Up	379 (6.2)	J	8	OHV (Diesel)

ENGINE IDENTIFICATION

Year	Model	Engine Displacement cu. in. (liter)	Engine Series Identification (VIN)	No. of Cylinders	Engine Type
1988	K30/3500 Pick-Up	454 (7.4)	N	8	OHV
	R20/2500 Pick-Up	292 (4.8)	T	6	OHV
	R20/2500 Pick-Up	350 (5.7)	K	8	OHV
	R20/2500 Pick-Up	379 (6.2)	J	8	OHV (Diesel)
	R20/2500 Pick-Up	454 (7.4)	N	8	OHV
	R30/3500 Pick-Up	292 (4.8)	T	6	OHV
	R30/3500 Pick-Up	350 (5.7)	K	8	OHV
	R30/3500 Pick-Up	379 (6.2)	J	8	OHV (Diesel)
	R30/3500 Pick-Up	454 (7.4)	N	8	OHV
	V30/3500 Pick-Up	292 (4.8)	T	6	OHV
	V30/3500 Pick-Up	350 (5.7)	K	8	OHV
	V30/3500 Pick-Up	379 (6.2)	J	8	OHV (Diesel)
	V30/3500 Pick-Up	454 (7.4)	N	8	OHV
	C30/3500 Chassis Cab	350 (5.7)	K	8	OHV
	C30/3500 Chassis Cab	379 (6.2)	J	8	OHV (Diesel)
	C30/3500 Chassis Cab	454 (7.4)	N	8	OHV
	K30/3500 Chassis Cab	350 (5.7)	K	8	OHV
	K30/3500 Chassis Cab	379 (6.2)	J	8	OHV (Diesel)
	K30/3500 Chassis Cab	454 (7.4)	N	8	OHV
	R30/3500 Chassis Cab	292 (4.8)	T	6	OHV
	R30/3500 Chassis Cab	350 (5.7)	K	8	OHV
	R30/3500 Chassis Cab	350 (5.7)	K	8	OHV
	R30/3500 Chassis Cab	350 (5.7)	M	8	OHV
	R30/3500 Chassis Cab	379 (6.2)	J	8	OHV (Diesel)
	R30/3500 Chassis Cab	454 (7.4)	W	8	OHV
	R30/3500 Chassis Cab	454 (7.4)	N	8	OHV
	V30/3500 Chassis Cab	292 (4.8)	T	6	OHV
	V30/3500 Chassis Cab	350 (5.7)	K	8	OHV
	V30/3500 Chassis Cab	350 (5.7)	M	8	OHV
	V30/3500 Chassis Cab	379 (6.2)	J	8	OHV (Diesel)
	V30/3500 Chassis Cab	454 (7.4)	W	8	OHV
	V30/3500 Chassis Cab	454 (7.4)	N	8	OHV
	R10 Suburban	350 (5.7)	K	8	OHV
	R10 Suburban	379 (6.2)	C	8	OHV (Diesel)
	V10 Suburban	350 (5.7)	K	8	OHV
	V10 Suburban	379 (6.2)	C	8	OHV (Diesel)
	R20 Suburban	350 (5.7)	K	8	OHV
	R20 Suburban	379 (6.2)	J	8	OHV (Diesel)
	R20 Suburban	454 (7.4)	N	8	OHV
	V20 Suburban	350 (5.7)	K	8	OHV
	V20 Suburban	379 (6.2)	J	8	OHV (Diesel)
	G10/1500 Vandura	262 (4.3)	Z	6	OHV
	G10/1500 Vandura	305 (5.0)	H	8	OHV
	G20/2500 Vandura	262 (4.3)	Z	6	OHV

ENGINE IDENTIFICATION

Year	Model	Engine Displacement cu. in. (liter)	Engine Series Identification (VIN)	No. of Cylinders	Engine Type
1988	G20/2500 Vandura	305 (5.0)	H	8	OHV
	G20/2500 Vandura	350 (5.7)	K	8	OHV
	G20/2500 Vandura	379 (6.2)	C	8	OHV (Diesel)
	G30/3500 Vandura	262 (4.3)	Z	6	OHV
	G30/3500 Vandura	350 (5.7)	R	8	OHV
	G30/3500 Vandura	379 (6.2)	J	8	OHV (Diesel)
	G30/3500 Vandura	454 (7.4)	N	8	OHV
	G10/1500 Sport Van/Rally	262 (4.3)	Z	6	OHV
	G10/1500 Sport Van/Rally	305 (5.0)	H	8	OHV
	G10/1500 Sport Van/Rally	350 (5.7)	K	8	OHV
	G20/2500 Sport Van/Rally	262 (4.3)	Z	6	OHV
	G20/2500 Sport Van/Rally	305 (5.0)	H	8	OHV
	G20/2500 Sport Van/Rally	350 (5.7)	K	8	OHV
	G20/2500 Sport Van/Rally	379 (6.2)	C	8	OHV (Diesel)
	G30/3500 Sport Van/Rally	350 (5.7)	K	8	OHV
	G30/3500 Sport Van/Rally	379 (6.2)	J	8	OHV (Diesel)
	G30/3500 Sport Van/Rally	454 (7.4)	N	8	OHV
	G30/3500 Cutaway Van	350 (5.7)	K	8	OHV
	G30/3500 Cutaway Van	350 (5.7)	M	8	OHV
	G30/3500 Cutaway Van	379 (6.2)	J	8	OHV (Diesel)
	G30/3500 Cutaway Van	454 (7.4)	N	8	OHV
	G30/3500 Hi-Cube Van	350 (5.7)	K	8	OHV
	G30/3500 Hi-Cube Van	350 (5.7)	M	8	OHV
	G30/3500 Hi-Cube Van	379 (6.2)	J	8	OHV
	G30/3500 Hi-Cube Van	454 (7.4)	N	8	OHV
	G30/3500 RV Cutaway Van	350 (5.7)	K	8	OHV
	G30/3500 RV Cutaway Van	350 (5.7)	M	8	OHV
	G30/3500 RV Cutaway Van	379 (6.2)	J	8	OHV (Diesel)
	G30/3500 RV Cutaway Van	454 (7.4)	N	8	OHV
	V Blazer/Jimmy	350 (5.7)	K	8	OHV
	V Blazer/Jimmy	379 (6.2)	C	8	OHV
1989	C1500 Pick-Up	262 (4.3)	Z	6	OHV
	C1500 Pick-Up	305 (5.0)	H	8	OHV
	C1500 Pick-Up	350 (5.7)	K	8	OHV
	C1500 Pick-Up	379 (6.2)	C	8	OHV (Diesel)
	N1500 Pick-Up	262 (4.3)	Z	6	OHV
	K1500 Pick-Up	305 (5.0)	H	8	OHV
	K1500 Pick-Up	350 (5.7)	K	8	OHV
	K1500 Pick-Up	379 (6.2)	C	8	OHV (Diesel)
	C2500 Pick-Up	262 (4.3)	Z	6	OHV
	C2500 Pick-Up	305 (5.0)	H	8	OHV
	C2500 Pick-Up	350 (5.7)	K	8	OHV
	C2500 Pick-Up	379 (6.2)	C	8	OHV (Diesel)
	C2500 Pick-Up	379 (6.2)	J	8	OHV (Diesel)

ENGINE IDENTIFICATION

Year	Model	Engine Displacement cu. in. (liter)	Engine Series Identification (VIN)	No. of Cylinders	Engine Type
1989	K2500 Pick-Up	262 (4.3)	Z	6	OHV
	K2500 Pick-Up	305 (5.0)	H	8	OHV
	K2500 Pick-Up	350 (5.7)	K	8	OHV
	K2500 Pick-Up	379 (6.2)	C	8	OHV (Diesel)
	K2500 Pick-Up	379 (6.2)	J	8	OHV (Diesel)
	C3500 Pick-Up	350 (5.7)	K	8	OHV
	C3500 Pick-Up	379 (6.2)	J	8	OHV (Diesel)
	C3500 Pick-Up	454 (7.4)	N	8	OHV
	K3500 Pick-Up	350 (5.7)	K	8	OHV
	K3500 Pick-Up	379 (6.2)	J	8	OHV (Diesel)
	K3500 Pick-Up	454 (7.4)	N	8	OHV
	R2500 Pick-Up	350 (5.7)	K	8	OHV
	R2500 Pick-Up	379 (6.2)	J	8	OHV Pick-Up
	R2500 Pick-Up	454 (7.4)	N	8	OHV
	R3500 Pick-Up	350 (5.7)	K	8	OHV
	R3500 Pick-Up	379 (6.2)	J	8	OHV (Diesel)
	R3500 Pick-Up	454 (7.4)	N	8	OHV
	V3500 Pick-Up	350 (5.7)	K	8	OHV
	V3500 Pick-Up	379 (6.2)	J	8	OHV (Diesel)
	V3500 Pick-Up	454 (7.4)	N	8	OHV
	C2500 Chassis Cab	350 (5.7)	K	8	OHV
	C2500 Chassis Cab	379 (6.2)	J	8	OHV (Diesel)
	K2500 Chassis Cab	350 (5.7)	K	8	OHV
	K2500 Chassis Cab	379 (6.2)	N	8	OHV (Diesel)
	C3500 Chassis Cab	350 (5.7)	K	8	OHV
	C3500 Chassis Cab	379 (6.2)	J	8	OHV (Diesel)
	C3500 Chassis Cab	454 (7.4)	N	8	OHV
	K3500 Chassis Cab	350 (5.7)	K	8	OHV
	K3500 Chassis Cab	379 (6.2)	J	8	OHV (Diesel)
	K3500 Chassis Cab	454 (7.4)	N	8	OHV
	R30 Chassis Cab	350 (5.7)	K	8	OHV
	R30 Chassis Cab	379 (6.2)	J	8	OHV (Diesel)
	R30 Chassis Cab	454 (7.4)	N	8	OHV
	R30 Chassis Cab	454 (7.4)	W	8	OHV
	V30 Chassis Cab	350 (5.7)	K	8	OHV
	V30 Chassis Cab	379 (6.2)	J	8	OHV (Diesel)
	V30 Chassis Cab	454 (7.4)	N	8	OHV
	V30 Chassis Cab	454 (7.4)	W	8	OHV
	R1500 Suburban	350 (5.7)	K	8	OHV
	R1500 Suburban	379 (6.2)	C	8	OHV (Diesel)
	V1500 Suburban	350 (5.7)	K	8	OHV
	V1500 Suburban	379 (6.2)	C	8	OHV (Diesel)
	R2500 Suburban	350 (5.7)	K	8	OHV
	R2500 Suburban	379 (6.2)	J	8	OHV (Diesel)

ENGINE IDENTIFICATION

Year	Model	Engine Displacement cu. in. (liter)	Engine Series Identification (VIN)	No. of Cylinders	Engine Type
1989	R2500 Suburban	454 (7.4)	N	8	OHV
	V2500 Suburban	350 (5.7)	K	8	OHV
	V2500 Suburban	379 (6.2)	J	8	OHV (Diesel)
	G10/1500 Sport Van/Rally	262 (4.3)	Z	6	OHV
	G10/1500 Sport Van/Rally	305 (5.0)	H	8	OHV
	G10/1500 Sport Van/Rally	351 (5.7)	K	8	OHV
	G20/2500 Sport Van/Rally	262 (4.3)	Z	6	OHV
	G20/2500 Sport Van/Rally	305 (5.0)	H	8	OHV
	G20/2500 Sport Van/Rally	350 (5.7)	K	8	OHV
	G20/2500 Sport Van/Rally	379 (6.2)	C	8	OHV (Diesel)
	G30/3500 Sport Van/Rally	350 (5.7)	K	8	OHV
	G30/3500 Sport Van/Rally	379 (6.2)	J	8	OHV (Diesel)
	G10/1500 Vandura	262 (4.3)	Z	6	OHV
	G10/1500 Vandura	305 (5.0)	H	8	OHV
	G20/1500 Vandura	262 (4.3)	Z	6	OHV
	G20/2500 Vandura	305 (5.0)	H	8	OHV
	G20/2500 Vandura	350 (5.7)	K	8	OHV
	G20/2500 Vandura	379 (6.2)	C	8	OHV (Diesel)
	G30/3500 Vandura	262 (4.3)	Z	6	OHV
	G30/3500 Vandura	350 (5.7)	K	8	OHV
	G30/3500 Vandura	379 (6.2)	J	8	OHV (Diesel)
	G30/3500 Cutaway Van	350 (5.7)	K	8	OHV
	G30/3500 Cutaway Van	379 (6.2)	J	8	OHV (Diesel)
	G30/3500 Hi-Cube/Magnavan	350 (5.7)	K	8	OHV
	G30/3500 Hi-Cube/Magnavan	379 (6.2)	J	8	OHV (Diesel)
	G30/3500 RV Cutaway Van	350 (5.7)	K	8	OHV
	G30/3500 RV Cutaway Van	379 (6.2)	J	8	OHV (Diesel)
	V Blazer/Jimmy	350 (5.7)	K	8	OHV
	V Blazer/Jimmy	379 (6.2)	C	8	OHV (Diesel)
1990	C1500 Pick-Up	262 (4.3)	Z	6	OHV
	C1500 Pick-Up	305 (5.0)	H	8	OHV
	C1500 Pick-Up	350 (5.7)	K	8	OHV
	C1500 Pick-Up	379 (6.2)	C	8	OHV (Diesel)
	C1500 Pick-Up	454 (7.4)	N	8	OHV
	K1500 Pick-Up	262 (4.3)	Z	6	OHV
	K1500 Pick-Up	305 (5.0)	H	8	OHV
	K1500 Pick-Up	350 (5.7)	K	8	OHV
	K1500 Pick-Up	379 (6.2)	C	8	OHV (Diesel)
	C2500 Pick-Up	262 (4.3)	Z	6	OHV
	C2500 Pick-Up	305 (5.0)	H	8	OHV
	C2500 Pick-Up	350 (5.7)	K	8	OHV
	C2500 Pick-Up	379 (6.2)	C	8	OHV (Diesel)
	C2500 Pick-Up	379 (6.2)	J	8	OHV (Diesel)
	K2500 Pick-Up	262 (4.3)	Z	6	OHV

ENGINE IDENTIFICATION

Year	Model	Engine Displacement cu. in. (liter)	Engine Series Identification (VIN)	No. of Cylinders	Engine Type
1990	K2500 Pick-Up	305 (5.0)	H	8	OHV
	K2500 Pick-Up	350 (5.7)	K	8	OHV
	K2500 Pick-Up	379 (6.2)	C	8	OHV (Diesel)
	K2500 Pick-Up	379 (6.2)	J	8	OHV (Diesel)
	C3500 Pick-Up	350 (5.7)	K	8	OHV
	C3500 Pick-Up	379 (6.2)	J	8	OHV (Diesel)
	C3500 Pick-Up	454 (7.4)	N	8	OHV
	K3500 Pick-Up	350 (5.7)	K	8	OHV
	K3500 Pick-Up	379 (6.2)	J	8	OHV (Diesel)
	K3500 Pick-Up	454 (7.4)	N	8	OHV
	R3500 Pick-Up	350 (5.7)	K	8	OHV
	R3500 Pick-Up	379 (6.2)	J	8	OHV (Diesel)
	R3500 Pick-Up	454 (7.4)	N	8	OHV
	V3500 Pick-Up	350 (5.7)	K	8	OHV
	V3500 Pick-Up	379 (6.2)	J	8	OHV (Diesel)
	V3500 Pick-Up	454 (7.4)	N	8	OHV
	C2500 Chassis Cab	350 (5.7)	K	8	OHV
	C2500 Chassis Cab	379 (6.2)	J	8	OHV (Diesel)
	K2500 Chassis Cab	350 (5.7)	K	8	OHV
	K2500 Chassis Cab	379 (6.2)	J	8	OHV (Diesel)
	C3500 Chassis Cab	350 (5.7)	K	8	OHV
	C3500 Chassis Cab	379 (6.2)	J	8	OHV (Diesel)
	C3500 Chassis Cab	454 (7.4)	N	8	OHV
	K3500 Chassis Cab	350 (5.7)	K	8	OHV
	K3500 Chassis Cab	379 (6.2)	J	8	OHV (Diesel)
	K3500 Chassis Cab	454 (7.4)	N	8	OHV
	R3500 Chassis Cab	350 (5.7)	K	8	OHV
	R3500 Chassis Cab	379 (6.2)	J	8	OHV (Diesel)
	R3500 Chassis Cab	454 (7.4)	N	8	OHV
	V3500 Chassis Cab	350 (5.7)	K	8	OHV
	V3500 Chassis Cab	379 (6.2)	J	8	OHV (Diesel)
	V3500 Chassis Cab	454 (7.4)	N	8	OHV
	R1500 Suburban	350 (5.7)	K	8	OHV
	R1500 Suburban	379 (6.2)	C	8	OHV (Diesel)
	V1500 Suburban	350 (5.7)	K	8	OHV
	V1500 Suburban	379 (6.2)	C	8	OHV (Diesel)
	R2500 Suburban	350 (5.7)	K	8	OHV
	R2500 Suburban	379 (6.2)	J	8	OHV (Diesel)
	R2500 Suburban	454 (7.4)	N	8	OHV
	V2500 Suburban	350 (5.7)	K	8	OHV
	V2500 Suburban	379 (6.2)	J	8	OHV (Diesel)
	G10/1500 Vandura	262 (4.3)	Z	6	OHV
	G10/1500 Vandura	305 (5.0)	H	8	OHV
	G20/2500 Vandura	262 (4.3)	Z	6	OHV

ENGINE IDENTIFICATION

Year	Model	Engine Displacement cu. in. (liter)	Engine Series Identification (VIN)	No. of Cylinders	Engine Type
1990	G20/2500 Vandura	305 (5.0)	H	8	OHV
	G20/2500 Vandura	350 (5.7)	K	8	OHV
	G20/2500 Vandura	379 (6.2)	C	8	OHV (Diesel)
	G30/3500 Vandura	262 (4.3)	Z	6	OHV
	G30/3500 Vandura	350 (5.7)	K	8	OHV
	G30/3500 Vandura	379 (6.2)	J	8	OHV (Diesel)
	G30/3500 Vandura	454 (7.4)	N	8	OHV
	G10/1500 Sport Van/Rally	262 (4.3)	Z	6	OHV
	G10/1500 Sport Van/Rally	305 (5.0)	H	8	OHV
	G10/1500 Sport Van/Rally	350 (5.7)	K	8	OHV
	G20/2500 Sport Van/Rally	262 (4.3)	Z	6	OHV
	G20/2500 Sport Van/Rally	305 (5.0)	H	8	OHV
	G20/2500 Sport Van/Rally	350 (5.7)	K	8	OHV
	G20/2500 Sport Van/Rally	379 (6.2)	C	8	OHV (Diesel)
	G10/1500 Beauville/Rally	262 (4.3)	Z	6	OHV
	G10/1500 Beauville/Rally	305 (5.0)	H	8	OHV
	G10/1500 Beauville/Rally	350 (5.7)	K	8	OHV
	G20/2500 Beauville/Rally	262 (4.3)	Z	6	OHV
	G20/2500 Beauville/Rally	305 (5.0)	H	8	OHV
	G20/2500 Beauville/Rally	350 (5.7)	K	8	OHV
	G20/2500 Beauville/Rally	379 (6.2)	C	8	OHV (Diesel)
	G30/3500 Sport Van/Rally	350 (5.7)	K	8	OHV
	G30/3500 Sport Van/Rally	379 (6.2)	J	8	OHV (Diesel)
	G30/3500 Sport Van/Rally	454 (7.4)	N	8	OHV
	G30/3500 Beauville/Rally	350 (5.7)	K	8	OHV
	G30/3500 Beauville/Rally	379 (6.2)	J	8	OHV (Diesel)
	G30/3500 Beauville/Rally	454 (7.4)	N	8	OHV
	G30 Cutaway Van	350 (5.7)	K	8	OHV
	G30 Cutaway Van	379 (6.2)	J	8	OHV (Diesel)
	G30 Cutaway Van	454 (7.4)	N	8	OHV
	G30 RV Cutaway Van	350 (5.7)	K	8	OHV
	G30 RV Cutaway Van	379 (6.2)	J	8	OHV (Diesel)
	G30 RV Cutaway Van	454 (7.4)	N	8	OHV
	G30 Hi-Cube/Magnavan	350 (5.7)	K	8	OHV
	G30 Hi-Cube/Magnavan	379 (6.2)	J	8	OHV (Diesel)
	G30/Hi-Cube/Magnavan	454 (7.4)	N	8	OHV
	V Blazer/Jimmy	350 (5.7)	K	8	OHV
	V Blazer/Jimmy	379 (6.2)	C	8	OHV (Diesel)

GENERAL MOTORS CORPORATION
C/K SERIES (PICK-UP) • R/V SERIES (PICK-UP) • BLAZER/JIMMY • SUBURBAN • G SERIES (VAN)

GENERAL ENGINE SPECIFICATIONS

Year	VIN	No. Cylinder Displacement cu. in. (liter)	Fuel System type	Net Horsepower @ rpm	Net Torque @ rpm (ft. lbs.)	Bore × Stroke (in.)	Com-pression Ratio	Oil Pressure @ rpm
1986	N	6-262 (4.3)	Carb	145 @ 4000	225 @ 2400	4.00 × 3.48	8.3:1	50 ⑪
	Z	6-262 (4.3)	F.I.	145 @ 4000	230 @ 2400	4.00 × 3.48	9.3:1	35 ⑪
	T	6-292 (4.8)	Carb.	115 @ 3400	215 @ 1600	3.88 × 4.12	8.0:1	50 ⑪
	F	8-305 (5.0)	Carb.	150 @ 3800	240 @ 2400	3.74 × 3.48	8.5:1	45 ⑪
	H	8-305 (5.0)	Carb.	165 @ 4400	240 @ 2000	3.75 × 3.48	9.0:1	45 ⑪
	L	8-350 (5.7)	Carb.	165 @ 3800	275 @ 1600	4.00 × 3.48	8.3:1	45 ⑪
	M	8-350 (5.7)	Carb.	185 @ 4000	285 @ 2400	4.00 × 3.48	8.3:1	45 ⑪
	C	8-379 (6.2)	Diesel	230 @ 3600	240 @ 2000	3.98 × 3.80	21.0:1	35 ⑪
	J	8-379 (6.2)	Diesel	135 @ 3600	240 @ 2000	3.98 × 3.80	21.0:1	35 ⑪
	W	8-454 (7.4)	Carb.	240 @ 3800	375 @ 3200	4.25 × 4.00	8.0:1	40 ⑪
1987	Z	6-262 (4.3)	F.I.	145 @ 4000	230 @ 2400	4.00 × 3.48	9.3:1	35 ⑪
	T	6-292 (4.8)	Carb.	115 @ 3400	215 @ 1600	3.88 × 4.12	8.0:1	50 ⑪
	H	8-305 (5.0)	F.I.	165 @ 4400	240 @ 2000	3.75 × 3.48	9.0:1	45 ⑪
	L	8-350 (5.7)	Carb.	165 @ 3800	275 @ 1600	4.00 × 3.48	8.3:1	45 ⑪
	K	8-350 (5.7)	F.I.	—	—	4.00 × 3.48	8.5:1	45 ⑪
	M	8-350 (5.7)	Carb.	185 @ 4000	285 @ 2400	4.00 × 3.48	8.3:1	45 ⑪
	C	8-379 (6.2)	Diesel	130 @ 3600	240 @ 2000	3.98 × 3.80	21.0:1	35 ⑪
	J	8-379 (6.2)	Diesel	135 @ 3600	240 @ 2000	3.98 × 3.80	21.0:1	35 ⑪
	W	8-454 (2.4)	Carb.	240 @ 3800	375 @ 3200	4.25 × 4.00	8.0:1	40 ⑪
	N	8-454 (7.4)	F.I.	—	—	4.25 × 4.00	8.0:1	40 ⑪
1988	Z	8-262 (4.3)	F.I.	145 @ 4000	230 @ 2400	4.00 × 3.48	9.3:1	35 ⑪
	T	6-292 (4.8)	Carb.	115 @ 3400	215 @ 1600	3.88 × 4.12	8.0:1	50 ⑪
	H	8-305 (5.0)	F.I.	165 @ 4400	240 @ 2000	3.74 × 3.48	9.0:1	45 ⑪
	K	8-350 (5.7)	F.I.	—	—	4.00 × 3.48	8.5:1	45 ⑪
	M	8-350 (5.7)	Carb.	185 @ 4000	285 @ 2400	4.00 × 3.48	8.3:1	45 ⑪
	C	8-379 (6.2)	Diesel	130 @ 3600	240 @ 2000	3.98 × 3.80	21.0:1	35 ⑪
	J	8-379 (6.2)	Diesel	135 @ 3600	240 @ 2000	3.98 × 3.80	21.0:1	35 ⑪
	N	8-454 (7.4)	F.I.	—	—	4.25 × 4.00	8.0:1	40 ⑪
1989	Z	6-262 (4.3)	EFI	①	②	4.00 × 3.48	9.3:1	18 min. @ 2000
	H	8-305 (5.0)	EFI	170 @ 4000	270 @ 2400	3.74 × 3.48	9.3:1	30–55 @ 2000
	K	8-350 (5.7)	EFI	③	④	4.00 × 3.48	8.3:1	30–55 @ 2000
	J	8-379 (6.2)	Diesel	⑤	257–259 @ 2000	3.98 × 3.80	21.3:1	40–45 @ 2000
	C	8-379 (6.2)	Diesel	⑥	⑦	3.98 × 3.80	21.3:1	40–45 @ 2000
	N	8-454 (7.4)	EFI	230 @ 3600	385 @ 1600	4.25 × 4.00	7.9:1	40–60 @ 2000
	W	8-454 (7.4)	Carb.	230 @ 3800	370 @ 2800	4.25 × 4.00	7.9:1	40–60 @ 2000
1990	Z	6-262 (4.3)	EFI	⑧	⑨	4.00 × 3.48	9.3:1	18 min. @ 2000
	H	8-305 (5.0)	EFI	170 @ 4000	270 @ 2400	3.74 × 3.48	⑩	18 min. @ 2000
	K	8-350 (5.7)	EFI	③	④	4.00 × 3.48	8.2:1	18 min. @ 2000
	J	8-379 (6.2)	Diesel	⑤	257–259 @ 2000	3.98 × 3.80	21.3:1	40–45 @ 2000
	C	8-379 (6.2)	Diesel	⑥	⑦	3.98 × 3.80	21.3:1	40–45 @ 2000
	N	8-454 (7.4)	EFI	230 @ 3600	385 @ 1600	4.25 × 4.00	7.9:1	40–60 @ 2000

GENERAL ENGINE SPECIFICATIONS

① C-K Pick-Up: 160 @ 2400
   G Vans: 150 @ 2400
② C-K Pick-Ups: 235 @ 2400
   G Vans: 230 @ 2400
③ C-K Pick-Up:
   Up to 8500 lbs.—210 @ 4000
   8501 lbs. to 10,000 lbs.—190 @ 4000
   R-V Pick-Up: 190 @ 4000
   R-V and C-K Chassis Cab: 190 @ 4000
   V Blazer/Jimmy: 210 @ 4000
   R-V 1500 Suburban: 210 @ 4000
   R-V-2500 Suburban: 195 @ 4000
   G Vans:
      up to 8500 lbs.—195 @ 4000
      8501 lbs. to 10,000 lbs.—190 @ 4000
   Hi-Cube, Cutaway Vans: 190 @ 4000

④ C-K Pick-Up:
   Up to 8500 lbs.—300 @ 2800
   8501 lbs. to 10,000 lbs.—300 @ 2400
   R-V Pick-Up: 300 @ 2400
   R-V, C-K Chassis Cab: 300 @ 2400
   Suburban: 300 @ 2800
   Blazer/Jimmy: 300 @ 2800
   G Van/Vandura:
      Up to 8500 lbs.—290 @ 2400
      8600 lbs.—300 @ 2400
   Sport Van/Rally:
      Up to 8600 lbs.—290 @ 2400
      8600 lbs.—295 @ 2400
⑤ C-K Pick-Up: 143 @ 3600
   R-V Pick-Up: 148 @ 3600
   R-V, C-K Chassis Cab: 148 @ 3600
   Suburban: 148 @ 3600
   Sport Van/Rally: 148 @ 3600
   Vandura: 143 @ 3600

⑥ C-K Pick-Up: up to 8500 lbs.
   With manual transmission—126 @ 3600
   With automatic transmission—
      140 @ 3600
   Blazer, Suburban, Van: 130 @ 3600
⑦ C-K Pick-Up: up to 8500 lbs.
   With manual transmission—240 @ 2000
   With automatic transmission—
      247 @ 2000 Blazer, Suburban,
      Van: 240 @ 2000
⑧ C-K Pick-Ups:
   With standard engine—160 @ 2400
   With H.D. engine—155 @ 4000
   G Vans: 150 @ 2400
⑨ C-K Pick-Ups:
   With standard engine—235 @ 2400
   With H.D. engine—230 @ 2400
   G Vans: 230 @ 2400
⑩ Standard engine: 9.3:1, H.D. engine: 8.6:1
⑪ @ 2000 rpm

GASOLINE ENGINE TUNE-UP SPECIFICATIONS

Year	VIN	No. Cylinder Displacement cu. in. (liter)	Spark Plugs Type	Gap (in.)	Ignition Timing (deg.) MT	AT	Compression Pressure (psi)	Fuel Pump (psi)	Idle Speed (rpm) MT	AT	Valve Clearance In.	Ex.
1986	N	6-262 (4.3)	R43CTS	.040	0	0	NA	5.0	①	①	Hyd.	Hyd.
	T	6-292 (4.8)	R44T	.035	8	8	NA	5.0	700	700	Hyd.	Hyd.
	H	8-305 (5.0)	R45TS	.045	4	4	NA	8.0	700	700	Hyd.	Hyd.
	L	8-350 (5.7)	R45TS	.045	4	4	NA	8.0	700	700	Hyd.	Hyd.
	M	8-350 (5.7)	R45TS	.045	4	4	NA	8.0	700	700	Hyd.	Hyd.
	W	8-454 (7.4)	R44T	.045	4	4	NA	8.0	700	700	Hyd.	Hyd.
1987	Z	6-262 (4.3)	R43CTS	.040	0	0	NA	5.0	①	①	Hyd.	Hyd.
	T	6-292 (4.8)	R44T	.035	8	8	NA	5.0	700	700	Hyd.	Hyd.
	H	8-305 (5.0)	R45TS	.045	4	4	NA	40–47 ③	700	700	Hyd.	Hyd.
	L	8-350 (5.7)	R45TS	.045	4	4	NA	34–46 ③	700	700	Hyd.	Hyd.
	M	8-350 (5.7)	R45TS	.045	4	4	NA	34–46 ③	700	700	Hyd.	Hyd.
	K	8-350 (5.7)	R45TS	.045	4	4	NA	34–46 ③	700	700	Hyd.	Hyd.
	N	8-454 (7.4)	44T	.045	4	4	NA	34–46 ③	700	700	Hyd.	Hyd.
1988	Z	6-262 (4.3)	R43CTS	.040	0	0	NA	5.0	①	①	Hyd.	Hyd.
	T	6-292 (4.8)	R44T	.035	8	8	NA	5.0	700	700	Hyd.	Hyd.
	H	8-305 (5.0)	R45TS	.045	4	4	NA	40–47 ③	700	700	Hyd.	Hyd.
	M	8-350 (5.7)	R45TS	.045	4	4	NA	34–46 ③	700	700	Hyd.	Hyd.
	K	8-350 (5.7)	R45TS	.045	4	4	NA	34–46 ③	700	700	Hyd.	Hyd.
	N	8-454 (7.4)	R44T	.045	4	4	NA	34–46 ③	700	700	Hyd.	Hyd.
	W	8-454 (7.4)	44T	.045	4	4	NA	5.0	700	700	Hyd.	Hyd.
1989	Z	6-262 (4.3)	CR43TS	0.045	②	②	NA	4.5–6.0	②	②	Hyd.	Hyd.
	H	8-305 (5.0)	CR45TS	0.045	②	②	NA	7.5–9.0	②	②	Hyd.	Hyd.
	K	8-350 (5.7)	CR43TS	0.045	②	②	NA	7.5–9.0	②	②	Hyd.	Hyd.
	N	8-454 (7.4)	CR43TS	0.045	②	②	NA	7.5–9.0	②	②	Hyd.	Hyd.
	W	8-454 (7.4)	R44T	0.045	②	②	NA	7.5–9.0	②	②	Hyd.	Hyd.

GASOLINE ENGINE TUNE-UP SPECIFICATIONS

Year	VIN	No. Cylinder Displacement cu. in. (liter)	Spark Plugs Type	Spark Plugs Gap (in.)	Ignition Timing (deg.) MT	Ignition Timing (deg.) AT	Compression Pressure (psi)	Fuel Pump (psi)	Idle Speed (rpm) MT	Idle Speed (rpm) AT	Valve Clearance In.	Valve Clearance Ex.
1990	Z	6-262 (4.3)	CR43TS	0.045	②	②	NA	4.5–6.0	②	②	Hyd.	Hyd.
	H	8-305 (5.0)	CR43TS	0.045	②	②	NA	7.5–9.0	②	②	Hyd.	Hyd.
	K	8-350 (5.7)	CR43TS	0.045	②	②	NA	7.5–9.0	②	②	Hyd.	Hyd.
	N	8-454 (7.4)	CR43TS	0.045	②	②	NA	7.5–9.0	②	②	Hyd.	Hyd.

① Controlled By E.C.M.   ② See Underhood Sticker   ③ Fuel Injected

DIESEL ENGINE TUNE-UP SPECIFICATIONS

Year	VIN	No. Engine Displacement cu. in. (liter)	Valve Clearance Intake (in.)	Valve Clearance Exhaust (in.)	Intake Valve Opens (deg.)	Injection Pump Setting (deg.)	Injection Nozzle Pressure (psi) New	Injection Nozzle Pressure (psi) Used	Idle Speed (rpm)	Cranking Compression Pressure (psi)
1986–90	C	8-379 (6.2)	Hyd.	Hyd.	—	①	—	1500	550–575	380–400
	J	8-379 (6.2)	Hyd.	Hyd.	—	①	—	1500	550–575	380–400

① Scribe Mark

FIRING ORDERS

NOTE: To avoid confusion, always replace spark plug wires one at a time.

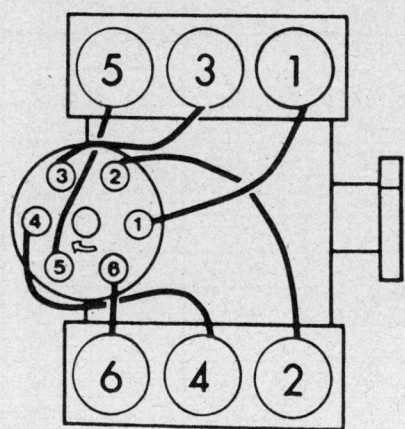

4.3L engine
Firing order: 1–6–5–4–3–2
Distributor rotation: clockwise

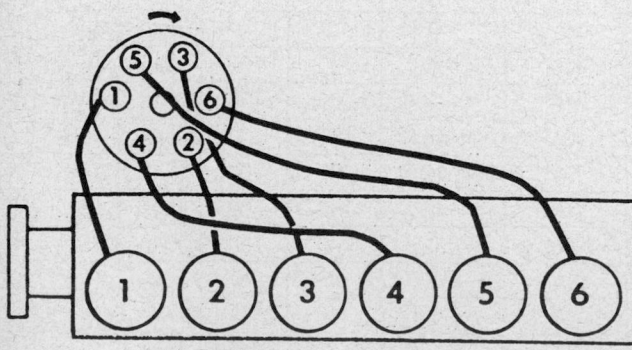

4.8L engine
Firing order: 1–5–3–6–2–4
Distributor rotation: clockwise

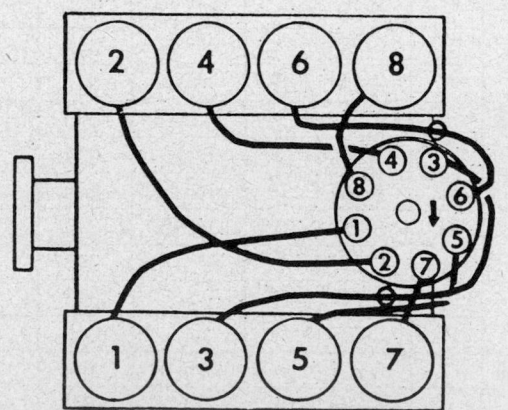

5.0L, 5.7L and 7.4L engines
Firing order: 1–8–4–3–6–5–7–2
Distributor rotation: clockwise

CAPACITIES

Year	Model	VIN	No. Cylinder Displacement cu. in. (liter)	Engine Crankcase with Filter	Engine Crankcase without Filter	Transmission (pts.) 4-Spd	5-Spd	Auto.	Drive Axle (pts.)	Fuel Tank (gal.)	Cooling System (qts.)
1986	C10/1500 Pick-Up	N	262 (4.3)	5	4	⑤	—	⑥	②	①	10.9
	C10/1500 Pick-Up	H	305 (5.0)	5	4	⑤	—	⑥	②	①	18.0
	C10/1500 Pick-Up	C	379 (6.2)	7	7	⑤	—	⑥	②	①	25.0
	K10/1500 Pick-Up	N	262 (4.3)	5	4	⑤	—	⑥	②③	①	10.9
	K10/1500 Pick-Up	F	305 (5.0)	5	4	⑤	—	⑥	②③	①	18.0
	K10/1500 Pick-Up	H	305 (5.0)	5	4	⑤	—	⑥	②③	①	18.0
	K10/1500 Pick-Up	L	350 (5.7)	5	4	⑤	—	⑥	②③	①	18.0
	K10/1500 Pick-Up	C	379 (6.2)	7	7	⑤	—	⑥	②③	①	25.0
	C20/2500 Pick-Up	N	262 (4.3)	5	4	⑤	—	⑥	②	①	10.9
	C20/2500 Pick-Up	T	292 (4.8)	6	5	⑤	—	⑥	②	①	16.0
	C20/2500 Pick-Up	H	305 (5.0)	5	4	⑤	—	⑥	②	①	18.0
	C20/2500 Pick-Up	M	350 (5.7)	5	4	⑤	—	⑥	②	①	18.0
	C20/2500 Pick-Up	L	350 (5.7)	5	4	⑤	—	⑥	②	①	18.0
	C20/2500 Pick-Up	C	379 (6.2)	7	7	⑤	—	⑥	②	①	25.0
	C20/2500 Pick-Up	J	379 (6.2)	7	7	⑤	—	⑥	②	①	25.0
	C20/2500 Pick-Up	W	454 (7.4)	7	6	⑤	—	⑥	②	①	24.5
	K20/2500 Pick-Up	T	292 (4.8)	6	5	⑤	—	⑥	②③	①	16.0
	K20/2500 Pick-Up	L	350 (5.7)	5	4	⑤	—	⑥	②③	①	18
	K20/2500 Pick-Up	M	350 (5.7)	5	4	⑤	—	⑥	②③	①	18.0
	K20/2500 Pick-Up	C	379 (6.2)	7	7	⑤	—	⑥	②③	①	25.0
	K20/2500 Pick-Up	J	379 (6.2)	7	7	⑤	—	⑥	②③	①	25.0
	C30/3500 Pick-Up	T	292 (4.8)	6	5	⑤	—	⑥	②	①	16.0
	C30/3500 Pick-Up	M	350 (5.7)	5	4	⑤	—	⑥	②	①	18.0
	C30/3500 Pick-Up	J	379 (6.2)	7	7	⑤	—	⑥	②	①	25.0
	C30/3500 Pick-Up	W	454 (7.4)	7	6	⑤	—	⑥	②	①	24.5
	K30/3500 Pick-Up	T	292 (4.8)	6	5	⑤	—	⑥	②④	①	16.0
	K30/3500 Pick-Up	M	350 (5.7)	5	4	⑤	—	⑥	②④	①	18.0
	K30/3500 Pick-Up	J	379 (6.2)	7	7	⑤	—	⑥	②④	①	25.0
	K30/3500 Pick-Up	W	454 (7.4)	6	5	⑤	—	⑥	②④	①	24.5
	C10/1500 Suburban	H	305 (5.0)	5	4	⑤	—	⑥	②	⑦	18.0
	C10/1500 Suburban	L	350 (5.7)	5	4	⑤	—	⑥	②	⑦	18.0
	C10/1500 Suburban	C	379 (6.2)	7	7	⑤	—	⑥	②	⑧	25.0
	K10/1500 Suburban	L	350 (5.7)	5	4	⑤	—	⑥	②③	⑦	18.0
	K10/1500 Suburban	C	379 (6.2)	7	7	⑤	—	⑥	②③	⑧	25.0
	C20/2500 Suburban	M	350 (5.7)	5	4	⑤	—	⑥	②③	⑦	18.0
	C20/2500 Suburban	J	379 (6.2)	7	7	⑤	—	⑥	②	⑧	25.0
	C20/2500 Suburban	W	454 (7.4)	7	6	⑤	—	⑥	②③	⑦	24.5
	G10/1500 Sport Van/Rally	N	262 (4.3)	5	4	⑤	—	⑥	②	⑪	11.1
	G10/1500 Sport Van/Rally	H	305 (5.0)	5	4	⑤	—	⑥	②	⑪	17.0
	G10/1500 Sport Van/Rally	L	350 (5.7)	5	4	⑤	—	⑥	②	⑪	17.0
	G20/2500 Sport Van/Rally	N	262 (4.3)	5	4	⑤	—	⑥	②	⑪	11.1
	G20/2500 Sport Van/Rally	H	305 (5.0)	5	4	⑤	—	⑥	②	⑪	17.0
	G20/2500 Sport Van/Rally	L	350 (5.7)	5	4	⑤	—	⑥	②	⑪	17.0

GENERAL MOTORS CORPORATION
C/K SERIES (PICK-UP) • R/V SERIES (PICK-UP) • BLAZER/JIMMY • SUBURBAN • G SERIES (VAN)

CAPACITIES

Year	Model	VIN	No. Cylinder Displacement cu. in. (liter)	Engine Crankcase with Filter	Engine Crankcase without Filter	Transmission (pts.) 4-Spd	Transmission (pts.) 5-Spd	Transmission (pts.) Auto.	Drive Axle (pts.)	Fuel Tank (gal.)	Cooling System (qts.)
1986	G20/2500 Sport Van/Rally	C	379 (6.2)	7	7	⑤	—	⑥	②	⑪	24.0
	G30/3500 Sport Van/Rally	L	350 (5.7)	5	4	⑤	—	⑥	②	⑪	17.0
	G30/3500 Sport Van/Rally	M	350 (5.7)	5	4	⑤	—	⑥	②	⑪	17.0
	G30/3500 Sport Van/Rally	J	379 (6.2)	7	7	⑤	—	⑥	②	⑪	25.6
	G30/3500 Cutaway Van	M	350 (5.7)	5	4	⑤	—	⑥	②	⑪	17.0
	G30/3500 Cutaway Van	J	379 (6.2)	7	7	⑤	—	⑥	②	⑪	25.6
	G30/3500 Hi-Cube Van	M	350 (5.7)	5	4	⑤	—	⑥	②	⑪	17.0
	G30/3500 Hi-Cube Van	J	379 (6.2)	7	7	⑤	—	⑥	②	⑪	25.6
	G30/3500 RV Cutaway Van	M	350 (5.7)	5	4	⑤	—	⑥	②	⑪	17.0
	G30/3500 RV Cutaway Van	J	379 (6.2)	7	7	⑤	—	⑥	②	⑪	25.6
	K Blazer/Jimmy	H	305 (5.0)	5	4	⑤	—	⑥	②③	⑨	18.0
	K Blazer/Jimmy	L	350 (5.7)	5	4	⑤	—	⑥	②③	⑨	18.0
	K Blazer/Jimmy	C	379 (6.2)	7	7	⑤	—	⑥	②③	⑩	25.0
1987	R10/1500 Pick-Up	Z	262 (4.3)	5	4	⑤	—	⑥	②	①	10.9
	R10/1500 Pick-Up	H	305 (5.0)	5	4	⑤	—	⑥	②	①	18.0
	R10/1500 Pick-Up	K	350 (5.7)	5	4	⑤	—	⑥	②	①	18.0
	R10/1500 Pick-Up	C	379 (6.2)	7	7	⑤	—	⑥	②③	20	25.0
	V10/1500 Pick-Up	Z	262 (4.3)	5	4	⑤	—	⑥	②③	①	10.9
	V10/1500 Pick-Up	H	305 (5.0)	5	4	⑤	—	⑥	②③	①	18.0
	V10/1500 Pick-Up	K	350 (5.7)	5	4	⑤	—	⑥	②③	①	18.0
	V10/1500 Pick-Up	C	379 (6.2)	7	7	⑤	—	⑥	②③	20	25.0
	R20/2500 Pick-Up	Z	262 (4.3)	5	4	⑤	—	⑥	②	①	10.9
	R20/2500 Pick-Up	H	305 (5.0)	5	4	⑤	—	⑥	②	①	18.0
	R20/2500 Pick-Up	K	350 (5.7)	5	4	⑤	—	⑥	②	①	18.0
	R20/2500 Pick-Up	C	379 (6.2)	7	7	⑤	—	⑥	②	20	25.0
	R20/2500 Pick-Up	J	379 (6.2)	7	7	⑤	—	⑥	②	20	25.0
	R20/2500 Pick-Up	N	454 (7.4)	6	5	⑤	—	⑥	②	①	24.5
	V20/2500 Pick-Up	K	350 (5.7)	5	4	⑤	—	⑥	②③	①	18.0
	V20/2500 Pick-Up	C	379 (6.2)	7	7	⑤	—	⑥	②③	20	25.0
	V20/2500 Pick-Up	J	379 (6.2)	7	7	⑤	—	⑥	②③	20	25.0
	R30/3500 Pick-Up	K	350 (5.7)	5	4	⑤	—	⑥	②	①	18.0
	R30/3500 Pick-Up	J	379 (6.2)	7	7	⑤	—	⑥	②	20	25.0
	R30/3500 Pick-Up	N	454 (7.4)	6	5	⑤	—	⑥	②	①	24.5
	V30/3500 Pick-Up	K	350 (5.7)	5	4	⑤	—	⑥	②④	20	18.0
	V30/3500 Pick-Up	J	379 (6.2)	7	7	⑤	—	⑥	②④	①	25.0
	V30/3500 Pick-Up	N	454 (7.4)	6	5	⑤	—	⑥	②④	①	24.5
	R20/2500 Chassis Cab	K	350 (5.7)	5	4	⑤	—	⑥	②	①	18.0
	R20/2500 Chassis Cab	J	379 (6.2)	7	7	⑤	—	⑥	②	20	25.0
	R20/2500 Chassis Cab	N	454 (7.4)	6	5	⑤	—	⑥	②	①	24.5
	R30/3500 Chassis Cab	K	350 (5.7)	5	4	⑤	—	⑥	②	①	18.0
	R30/3500 Chassis Cab	J	379 (6.2)	7	7	⑤	—	⑥	②	20	25.0
	R30/3500 Chassis Cab	N	454 (7.4)	6	5	⑤	—	⑥	②	①	24.5
	V30/3500 Chassis Cab	K	350 (5.7)	5	4	⑤	—	⑥	②④	①	18.0

CAPACITIES

Year	Model	VIN	No. Cylinder Displacement cu. in. (liter)	Engine Crankcase with Filter	Engine Crankcase without Filter	Transmission (pts.) 4-Spd	5-Spd	Auto.	Drive Axle (pts.)	Fuel Tank (gal.)	Cooling System (qts.)
1987	V30/3500 Chassis Cab	J	379 (6.2)	7	7	⑤	—	⑥	②④	20	25.0
	V30/3500 Chassis Cab	N	454 (7.4)	6	5	⑤	—	⑥	②④	①	24.5
	R10/1500 Suburban	H	305 (5.0)	5	4	⑤	—	⑥	②	⑦	18.0
	R10/1500 Suburban	K	350 (5.7)	5	4	⑤	—	⑥	②	⑦	18.0
	R10/1500 Suburban	C	379 (6.2)	7	7	⑤	—	⑥	②	⑧	25.0
	V10/1500 Suburban	K	350 (5.7)	5	4	⑤	—	⑥	②③	⑦	18.0
	V10/1500 Suburban	C	379 (6.2)	7	7	⑤	—	⑥	②③	⑧	25.0
	G10/1500 Vandura	Z	262 (4.3)	5	4	⑤	—	⑥	②	⑪	11.0
	G10/1500 Vandura	H	305 (5.0)	5	4	⑤	—	⑥	②	⑪	17.0
	G20/2500 Vandura	Z	262 (4.3)	5	4	⑤	—	⑥	②	⑪	11.0
	G20/2500 Vandura	H	305 (5.0)	5	4	⑤	—	⑥	②	⑪	17.0
	G20/2500 Vandura	K	350 (5.7)	5	4	—	—	⑥	②	⑪	17.0
	G20/2500 Vandura	C	379 (6.2)	7	7	⑤	—	⑥	②	⑪	25.5
	G30/3500 Vandura	Z	262 (4.3)	5	4	⑤	—	⑥	②	⑪	11.0
	G30/3500 Vandura	K	350 (5.7)	5	4	⑤	—	⑥	②	⑪	17.0
	G30/3500 Vandura	J	379 (6.2)	7	7	⑤	—	⑥	②	⑪	25.5
	G10/1500 Sport Van/Rally	Z	262 (4.3)	5	4	⑤	—	⑥	②	⑪	11.0
	G10/1500 Sport Van/Rally	H	305 (5.0)	5	4	⑤	—	⑥	②	⑪	17.0
	G10/1500 Sport Van/Rally	K	350 (5.7)	5	4	⑤	—	⑥	②	⑪	17.0
	G20/2500 Sport Van/Rally	Z	262 (4.3)	5	4	⑤	—	⑥	②	⑪	11.0
	G20/2500 Sport Van/Rally	H	305 (5.0)	5	4	⑤	—	⑥	②	⑪	17.0
	G20/2500 Sport Van/Rally	K	350 (5.7)	5	4	⑤	—	⑥	②	⑪	17.0
	G20/2500 Sport Van/Rally	C	379 (6.2)	7	7	⑤	—	⑥	②	⑪	25.5
	G30/3500 Sport Van/Rally	M	350 (5.7)	5	4	⑤	—	⑥	②	⑪	17.0
	G30/3500 Sport Van/Rally	J	379 (6.2)	7	7	⑤	—	⑥	②	⑪	17.0
	G30/3500 Cutaway Van	K	350 (5.7)	5	4	⑤	—	⑥	②	⑪	17.0
	G30/3500 Cutaway Van	M	350 (5.7)	5	4	⑤	—	⑥	②	⑪	17.0
	G30/3500 Cutaway Van	J	379 (6.2)	7	7	⑤	—	⑥	②	⑪	25.5
	G30/3500 Hi-Cube Van	K	350 (5.7)	5	4	⑤	—	⑥	②	⑪	17.0
	G30/3500 Hi-Cube Van	M	350 (5.7)	5	4	⑤	—	⑥	②	⑪	17.0
	G30/3500 Hi-Cube Van	J	379 (6.2)	7	7	⑤	—	⑥	②	⑪	25.5
	G30/3500 RV Cutaway Van	K	350 (5.7)	5	4	⑤	—	⑥	②	⑪	17.0
	G30/3500 RV Cutaway Van	M	350 (5.7)	5	4	⑤	—	⑥	②	⑪	17.0
	G30/3500 RV Cutaway Van	J	379 (6.2)	7	7	⑤	—	⑥	②	⑪	25.5
	V Blazer/Jimmy	H	305 (5.0)	5	4	⑤	—	⑥	②③	⑨	18.0
	V Blazer/Jimmy	K	350 (5.7)	5	4	⑤	—	⑥	②③	⑨	18.0
	V Blazer/Jimmy	C	379 (6.2)	7	7	⑤	—	⑥	②③	⑩	24.5
1988	C10/1500 Pick-Up	Z	262 (4.3)	5	4	⑮	3.6	⑥	②	⑫	10.9
	C10/1500 Pick-Up	H	305 (5.0)	5	4	⑮	3.6	⑥	②	⑫	18.0
	C10/1500 Pick-Up	K	350 (5.7)	5	4	⑮	3.6	⑥	②	⑫	18.0
	K10/1500 Pick-Up	Z	262 (4.3)	5	4	⑮	3.6	⑥	②③	⑫	10.9
	K10/1500 Pick-Up	H	305 (5.0)	5	4	⑮	3.6	⑥	②③	⑫	18.0
	K10/1500 Pick-Up	K	350 (5.7)	5	4	⑮	3.6	⑥	②③	⑫	18.0

GENERAL MOTORS CORPORATION
C/K SERIES (PICK-UP) • R/V SERIES (PICK-UP) • BLAZER/JIMMY • SUBURBAN • G SERIES (VAN)

CAPACITIES

Year	Model	VIN	No. Cylinder Displacement cu. in. (liter)	Engine Crankcase with Filter	without Filter	Transmission (pts.) 4-Spd	5-Spd	Auto.	Drive Axle (pts.)	Fuel Tank (gal.)	Cooling System (qts.)
1988	C20/2500 Pick-Up	Z	262 (4.3)	5	4	⑮	3.6	⑥	②	⑫	10.9
	C20/2500 Pick-Up	H	305 (5.0)	5	4	⑮	3.6	⑥	②	⑫	18.0
	C20/2500 Pick-Up	K	350 (5.7)	5	4	⑮	3.6	⑥	②	⑫	18.0
	C20/2500 Pick-Up	C	379 (6.2)	7	7	⑮	3.6	⑥	②	⑫	25.0
	K20/2500 Pick-Up	Z	262 (4.3)	5	4	⑮	3.6	⑥	②⑬	⑫	10.9
	K20/2500 Pick-Up	H	305 (5.0)	5	4	⑮	3.6	⑥	②⑬	⑫	18.0
	K20/2500 Pick-Up	K	350 (5.7)	5	4	⑮	3.6	⑥	②⑬	⑫	18.0
	K20/2500 Pick-Up	C	379 (6.2)	7	7	⑮	3.6	⑥	②⑬	⑫	25.0
	C30/3500 Pick-Up	K	350 (5.7)	5	4	⑮	3.6	⑥	②	⑫	18.0
	C30/3500 Pick-Up	J	379 (6.2)	5	4	⑮	3.6	⑥	②	⑫	25.0
	C30/3500 Pick-Up	N	454 (7.4)	6	5	⑮	3.6	⑥	②	⑫	25.0
	K30/3500 Pick-Up	K	350 (5.7)	5	4	⑮	3.6	⑥	②⑭	⑫	18.0
	K30/3500 Pick-Up	J	379 (6.2)	7	7	⑮	3.6	⑥	②⑭	⑫	25.0
	K30/3500 Pick-Up	N	454 (7.4)	6	5	⑮	3.6	⑥	②⑭	⑫	25.0
	R20/2500 Pick-Up	T	292 (4.8)	6	5	8.4	—	⑥	②	①	16.0
	R20/2500 Pick-Up	K	350 (5.7)	5	4	8.4	—	⑥	②	①	18.0
	R20/2500 Pick-Up	J	379 (6.2)	7	7	8.4	—	⑥	②	20	25.0
	R20/2500 Pick-Up	N	454 (7.4)	6	5	8.4	—	⑥	②	①	24.5
	R30/3500 Pick-Up	T	292 (4.8)	6	5	8.4	—	⑥	②	①	16.0
	R30/3500 Pick-Up	K	350 (5.7)	5	4	8.4	—	⑥	②	①	18.0
	R30/3500 Pick-Up	J	379 (6.2)	7	7	8.4	—	⑥	②	20	25.0
	R30/3500 Pick-Up	N	454 (7.4)	6	5	8.4	—	⑥	②	①	24.5
	V30/3500 Pick-Up	T	292 (4.8)	6	5	8.4	—	⑥	②④	①	16.0
	V30/3500 Pick-Up	K	350 (5.2)	5	4	8.4	—	⑥	②④	①	18.0
	V30/3500 Pick-Up	J	379 (6.2)	7	7	8.4	—	⑥	②④	20	25.0
	V30/3500 Pick-Up	N	454 (7.4)	6	5	8.4	—	⑥	②④	①	24.5
	C30/3500 Chassis Cab	K	350 (5.7)	5	4	8.4	—	⑥	②	①	18.0
	C30/3500 Chassis Cab	J	379 (6.2)	7	7	8.4	—	⑥	②	20	25.0
	C30/3500 Chassis Cab	N	454 (7.4)	6	5	8.4	—	⑥	②	①	24.5
	K30/3500 Chassis Cab	K	350 (5.7)	5	4	8.4	—	⑥	②⑭	①	18.0
	K30/3500 Chassis Cab	J	379 (6.2)	7	7	8.4	—	⑥	②⑭	20	25.0
	K30/3500 Chassis Cab	N	454 (7.4)	6	5	8.4	—	⑥	②⑭	①	24.5
	R30/3500 Chassis Cab	T	292 (4.8)	6	5	8.4	—	⑥	②	①	16.0
	R30/3500 Chassis Cab	K	350 (5.7)	5	4	8.4	—	⑥	②	①	18.0
	R30/3500 Chassis Cab	M	350 (5.7)	5	4	8.4	—	⑥	②	①	18.0
	R30/3500 Chassis Cab	J	379 (6.2)	7	7	8.4	—	⑥	②	20	25.0
	R30/3500 Chassis Cab	W	454 (7.4)	7	6	8.4	—	⑥	②	①	24.5
	R30/3500 Chassis Cab	N	454 (7.4)	6	5	8.4	—	⑥	②	①	24.5
	V30/3500 Chassis Cab	T	292 (4.8)	6	5	8.4	—	⑥	②④	①	16.0
	V30/3500 Chassis Cab	K	350 (5.7)	5	4	8.4	—	⑥	②④	①	18.0
	V30/3500 Chassis Cab	M	350 (5.7)	5	4	8.4	—	⑥	②④	①	18.0
	V30/3500 Chassis Cab	J	379 (6.2)	7	7	8.4	—	⑥	②④	20	25.0
	V30/3500 Chassis Cab	W	454 (7.4)	7	6	8.4	—	⑥	②④	①	24.5
	V30/3500 Chassis Cab	N	454 (7.4)	6	5	8.4	—	⑥	②④	①	24.5

CAPACITIES

Year	Model	VIN	No. Cylinder Displacement cu. in. (liter)	Engine Crankcase with Filter	Engine Crankcase without Filter	Transmission (pts.) 4-Spd	5-Spd	Auto.	Drive Axle (pts.)	Fuel Tank (gal.)	Cooling System (qts.)
1988	R10 Suburban	K	350 (5.7)	5	4	8.4	—	⑥	②	⑦	18.0
	R10 Suburban	C	379 (6.2)	7	7	8.4	—	⑥	②	⑧	25.0
	V10 Suburban	K	350 (5.7)	6	5	8.4	—	⑥	②③	⑦	18.0
	V10 Suburban	C	379 (6.2)	7	7	8.4	—	⑥	②③	⑧	25.0
	R20 Suburban	K	350 (5.7)	5	4	8.4	—	⑥	②	⑦	18.0
	R20 Suburban	J	379 (6.2)	7	7	8.4	—	⑥	②	⑧	25.0
	R20 Suburban	N	454 (7.4)	6	5	8.4	—	⑥	②	⑦	24.5
	V20 Suburban	K	350 (5.7)	5	4	8.4	—	⑥	②	⑦	18.0
	V20 Suburban	J	379 (6.2)	7	7	8.4	—	⑥	②③	⑧	25.0
	G10/1500 Vandura	Z	262 (4.3)	5	4	8.4	—	⑥	②③	⑪	11.0
	G10/1500 Vandura	H	305 (5.0)	5	4	8.4	—	⑥	②	⑪	17.0
	G20/2500 Vandura	Z	262 (4.3)	5	4	8.4	—	⑥	②	⑪	11.0
	G20/2500 Vandura	H	305 (5.0)	5	4	8.4	—	⑥	②	⑪	17.0
	G20/2500 Vandura	K	350 (5.7)	5	4	8.4	—	⑥	②	⑪	17.0
	G20/2500 Vandura	C	379 (6.2)	7	7	8.4	—	⑥	②	⑪	24.0
	G30/3500 Vandura	Z	262 (4.3)	5	4	8.4	—	⑥	②	⑪	11.0
	G30/3500 Vandura	K	350 (5.7)	5	4	8.4	—	⑥	②	⑪	17.0
	G30/3500 Vandura	J	379 (6.2)	7	7	8.4	—	⑥	②	⑪	25.0
	G30/3500 Vandura	N	454 (7.4)	6	5	8.4	—	⑥	②	⑪	17.0
	G10/1500 Sport Van/Rally	Z	262 (4.3)	5	4	8.4	—	⑥	②	⑪	11.0
	G10/1500 Sport Van/Rally	H	305 (5.0)	5	4	8.4	—	⑥	②	⑪	17.0
	G10/1500 Sport Van/Rally	K	350 (5.7)	5	4	8.4	—	⑥	②	⑪	17.0
	G20/2500 Sport Van/Rally	Z	262 (4.3)	5	4	8.4	—	⑥	②	⑪	11.0
	G20/2500 Sport Van/Rally	H	305 (5.0)	5	4	8.4	—	⑥	②	⑪	17.0
	G20/2500 Sport Van/Rally	K	350 (5.7)	5	4	8.4	—	⑥	②	⑪	17.0
	G20/2500 Sport Van/Rally	C	379 (6.2)	7	7	8.4	—	⑥	②	⑪	24.0
	G30/3500 Sport Van/Rally	K	350 (5.7)	5	4	8.4	—	⑥	②	⑪	17.0
	G30/3500 Sport Van/Rally	J	379 (6.2)	7	7	8.4	—	⑥	②	⑪	25.0
	G30/3500 Sport Van/Rally	N	454 (7.4)	6	5	8.4	—	⑥	②	⑪	17.0
	G30/3500 Cutaway Van	K	350 (5.7)	5	4	8.4	—	⑥	②	⑪	17.0
	G30/3500 Cutaway Van	M	350 (5.7)	5	4	8.4	—	⑥	②	⑪	17.0
	G30/3500 Cutaway Van	J	379 (6.2)	7	7	8.4	—	⑥	②	⑪	25.0
	G30/3500 Cutaway Van	N	454 (7.4)	6	5	8.4	—	⑥	②	⑪	17.0
	G30/3500 Hi-Cube Van	K	350 (5.7)	5	4	8.4	—	⑥	②	⑪	17.0
	G30/3500 Hi-Cube Van	M	350 (5.7)	5	4	8.4	—	⑥	②	⑪	17.0
	G30/3500 Hi-Cube Van	J	379 (6.2)	7	7	8.4	—	⑥	②	⑪	25.0
	G30/3500 Hi-Cube Van	N	454 (7.4)	6	5	8.4	—	⑥	②	⑪	17.0
	G30/3500 RV Cutaway Van	K	350 (5.7)	5	4	8.4	—	⑥	②	⑪	17.0
	G30/3500 RV Cutaway Van	M	350 (5.7)	5	4	8.4	—	⑥	②	⑪	17.0
	G30/3500 RV Cutaway Van	J	379 (6.2)	7	7	8.4	—	⑥	②	⑪	25.0
	G30/3500 RV Cutaway Van	N	454 (7.4)	5	4	8.4	—	⑥	②	⑪	17.0
	V Blazer/Jimmy	K	350 (5.7)	5	4	8.4	—	⑥	②③	⑨	18.0
	V Blazer/Jimmy	C	379 (6.2)	7	7	8.4	—	⑥	②③	⑩	25.0

CAPACITIES

Year	Model	VIN	No. Cylinder Displacement cu. in. (liter)	Engine Crankcase with Filter	Engine Crankcase without Filter	Transmission (pts.) 4-Spd	Transmission (pts.) 5-Spd	Transmission (pts.) Auto.	Drive Axle (pts.)	Fuel Tank (gal.)	Cooling System (qts.)
1989	C1500 Pick-Up	Z	262 (4.3)	5	4	⑮	3.6	⑥	②	⑫	10.9
	C1500 Pick-Up	H	305 (5.0)	5	4	⑮	3.6	⑥	②	⑫	18.0
	C1500 Pick-Up	K	350 (5.7)	5	4	⑮	3.6	⑥	②	⑫	18.0
	C1500 Pick-Up	C	379 (6.2)	7	7	⑮	3.6	⑥	②	⑫	25.0
	K1500 Pick-Up	Z	262 (4.3)	5	4	⑮	3.6	⑥	②⑬	⑫	10.9
	K1500 Pick-Up	H	305 (5.0)	5	4	⑮	3.6	⑥	②⑬	⑫	18.0
	K1500 Pick-Up	K	350 (5.7)	5	4	⑮	3.6	⑥	②⑬	⑫	18.0
	K1500 Pick-Up	C	379 (6.2)	7	7	⑮	3.6	⑥	②⑬	⑫	25.0
	C2500 Pick-Up	Z	262 (4.3)	5	4	⑮	3.6	⑥	②	⑫	10.9
	C2500 Pick-Up	H	305 (5.0)	5	4	⑮	3.6	⑥	②	⑫	18.0
	C2500 Pick-Up	K	350 (5.7)	5	4	⑮	3.6	⑥	②	⑫	18.0
	C2500 Pick-Up	C	379 (6.2)	7	7	⑮	3.6	⑥	②	⑫	25.0
	C2500 Pick-Up	J	379 (6.2)	7	7	⑮	3.6	⑥	②	⑫	25.0
	K2500 Pick-Up	Z	262 (4.3)	5	4	⑮	3.6	⑥	②⑬	⑫	10.9
	K2500 Pick-Up	H	305 (5.0)	5	4	⑮	3.6	⑥	②⑬	⑫	18.0
	K2500 Pick-Up	K	350 (5.7)	5	4	⑮	3.6	⑥	②⑬	⑫	18.0
	K2500 Pick-Up	C	379 (6.2)	7	7	⑮	3.6	⑥	②⑬	⑫	25.0
	K2500 Pick-Up	J	379 (6.2)	7	7	⑮	3.6	⑥	②⑬	⑫	25.0
	C3500 Pick-Up	K	350 (5.7)	5	4	⑮	3.6	⑥	②	⑫	18.0
	C3500 Pick-Up	J	379 (6.2)	7	7	⑮	3.6	⑥	②	⑫	25.0
	C3500 Pick-Up	N	454 (7.4)	6	5	⑮	3.6	⑥	②	⑫	24.5
	K3500 Pick-Up	K	350 (5.7)	5	4	⑮	3.6	⑥	②⑭	⑫	18.0
	K3500 Pick-Up	J	379 (6.2)	7	7	⑮	3.6	⑥	②⑭	⑫	25.0
	K3500 Pick-Up	N	454 (7.4)	6	5	⑮	3.6	⑥	②⑭	⑫	24.5
	R2500 Pick-Up	K	350 (5.7)	5	4	8.4	—	⑯	⑰	20	17.5
	R2500 Pick-Up	J	379 (6.2)	7	7	8.4	—	⑯	⑰	20	25.0
	R2500 Pick-Up	N	454 (7.4)	6	5	8.4	—	⑯	⑰	20	23.0
	R3500 Pick-Up	K	350 (5.7)	5	4	8.4	—	⑯	⑰	20	17.5
	R3500 Pick-Up	J	379 (6.2)	7	7	8.4	—	⑯	⑰	20	25.0
	R3500 Pick-Up	N	454 (7.4)	6	5	8.4	—	⑯	⑰	20	23.0
	U3500 Pick-Up	K	350 (5.7)	5	4	8.4	—	⑯	⑰④	20	17.5
	U3500 Pick-Up	J	379 (6.2)	7	7	8.4	—	⑯	⑰④	20	25.0
	U3500 Pick-Up	N	454 (7.4)	6	5	8.4	—	⑯	⑰④	20	23.0
	C2500 Chassis Cab	K	350 (5.7)	5	4	⑮	3.6	⑥	②	⑫	18.0
	C2500 Chassis Cab	J	379 (6.2)	7	7	⑮	3.6	⑥	②	⑫	25.0
	K2500 Chassis Cab	K	350 (5.7)	5	4	⑮	3.6	⑥	②⑬	⑫	18.0
	K2500 Chassis Cab	N	379 (6.2)	7	7	⑮	3.6	⑥	②⑬	⑫	25.0
	C3500 Chassis Cab	K	350 (5.7)	5	4	⑮	3.6	⑥	②	⑫	18.0
	C3500 Chassis Cab	J	379 (6.2)	7	7	⑮	3.6	⑥	②	⑫	25.0
	C3500 Chassis Cab	N	454 (7.4)	6	5	⑮	3.6	⑥	②	⑫	24.5
	K3500 Chassis Cab	K	350 (5.7)	5	4	⑮	3.6	⑥	②⑭	⑫	18.0
	K3500 Chassis Cab	J	379 (6.2)	7	7	⑮	3.6	⑥	②⑭	⑫	25.0
	K3500 Chassis Cab	N	454 (7.4)	6	5	⑮	3.6	⑥	②⑭	⑫	24.5

CAPACITIES

Year	Model	VIN	No. Cylinder Displacement cu. in. (liter)	Engine Crankcase with Filter	Engine Crankcase without Filter	Transmission (pts.) 4-Spd	5-Spd	Auto.	Drive Axle (pts.)	Fuel Tank (gal.)	Cooling System (qts.)
1989	R30 Chassis Cab	K	350 (5.7)	5	4	8.4	—	[16]	[17]	20	17.5
	R30 Chassis Cab	J	379 (6.2)	7	7	8.4	—	[16]	[17]	20	25.0
	R30 Chassis Cab	N	454 (7.4)	6	5	8.4	—	[16]	[17]	20	23.0
	R30 Chassis Cab	W	454 (7.4)	6	5	8.4	—	[16]	[17]	20	23.0
	U30 Chassis Cab	K	350 (5.7)	5	4	8.4	—	[16]	[17][4]	20	17.5
	U30 Chassis Cab	J	379 (6.2)	7	7	8.4	—	[16]	[17][4]	20	25.0
	U30 Chassis Cab	N	454 (7.4)	6	5	8.4	—	[16]	[17][4]	20	23.0
	U30 Chassis Cab	W	454 (7.4)	6	5	8.4	—	[16]	[17][4]	20	23.0
	R1500 Suburban	K	350 (5.7)	5	4	8.4	—	[16]	[17]	[18]	17.5
	R1500 Suburban	C	379 (6.2)	7	7	8.4	—	[16]	[17]	[19]	25.0
	V1500 Suburban	K	350 (5.7)	5	4	8.4	—	[16]	[17][3]	[18]	17.5
	V1500 Suburban	C	379 (6.2)	7	7	8.4	—	[16]	[17][3]	[19]	25.0
	R2500 Suburban	K	350 (5.7)	6	5	8.4	—	[16]	[17]	[18]	17.5
	R2500 Suburban	J	379 (6.2)	7	7	8.4	—	[16]	[17]	[19]	25.0
	R2500 Suburban	N	454 (7.4)	6	5	8.4	—	[16]	[17]	[18]	23.0
	U2500 Suburban	K	350 (5.7)	5	4	8.4	—	[16]	[17]	[18]	17.5
	U2500 Suburban	J	379 (6.2)	7	7	8.4	—	[16]	[17][3]	[19]	25.0
	G10/1500 Sport Van/Rally	Z	262 (4.3)	5	4	8.4	—	[16]	[17][3]	[11]	11.0
	G10/1500 Sport Van/Rally	H	305 (5.0)	5	4	8.4	—	[16]	[17]	[11]	17.0[20]
	G10/1500 Sport Van/Rally	K	350 (5.7)	5	4	8.4	—	[16]	[17]	[11]	17.0[20]
	G20/2500 Sport Van/Rally	Z	262 (4.3)	5	4	8.4	—	[16]	[17]	[11]	11.0
	G20/2500 Sport Van/Rally	H	305 (5.0)	5	4	8.4	—	[16]	[17]	[11]	17.0[20]
	G20/2500 Sport Van/Rally	K	350 (5.7)	5	4	8.4	—	[16]	[17]	[11]	17.0[20]
	G20/2500 Sport Van/Rally	C	379 (6.2)	7	7	8.4	—	[16]	[17]	[11]	24.0
	G30/3500 Sport Van/Rally	K	350 (5.7)	5	4	8.4	—	[16]	[17]	[11]	17.0[20]
	G30/3500 Sport Van/Rally	J	379 (6.2)	7	7	8.4	—	[16]	[17]	[11]	25.5
	G10/1500 Vandura	Z	262 (4.3)	5	4	8.4	—	[16]	[17]	[11]	11.0
	G10/1500 Vandura	H	305 (5.0)	5	4	8.4	—	[16]	[17]	[11]	17.0[20]
	G20/1500 Vandura	Z	262 (4.3)	5	4	8.4	—	[16]	[17]	[11]	11.0
	G20/2500 Vandura	H	305 (5.0)	5	4	8.4	—	[16]	[17]	[11]	17.0[20]
	G20/2500 Vandura	K	350 (5.7)	5	4	8.4	—	[16]	[17]	[11]	17.0[20]
	G20/2500 Vandura	C	379 (6.2)	7	7	8.4	—	[16]	[17]	[11]	24.0
	G30/3500 Vandura	Z	262 (4.3)	5	4	8.4	—	[16]	[17]	[11]	11.0
	G30/3500 Vandura	K	350 (5.7)	5	4	8.4	—	[16]	[17]	[11]	17.0[20]
	G30/3500 Vandura	J	379 (6.2)	7	7	8.4	—	[16]	[17]	[11]	25.5
	G30/3500 Cataway Van	K	350 (5.7)	5	4	8.4	—	[16]	[17]	[11]	17.0[20]
	G30/3500 Cataway Van	J	379 (6.2)	7	7	8.4	—	[16]	[17]	[11]	25.5
	G30/3500 Hi-Cube/Magnavan	K	350 (5.7)	5	4	8.4	—	[16]	[17]	[11]	17.0[20]
	G30/3500 Hi-Cube/Magnavan	J	379 (6.2)	7	7	8.4	—	[16]	[17]	[11]	25.5
	G30/3500 RV Cutaway Van	K	350 (5.7)	5	4	8.4	—	[16]	[17]	[11]	17.0[20]
	G30/3500 RV Cutaway Van	J	379 (6.2)	7	7	8.4	—	[16]	[17]	[11]	25.5
	V Blazer/Jimmy	K	350 (5.7)	5	4	8.4	—	[16]	[17][3]	[18]	17.5[20]
	V Blazer/Jimmy	C	379 (6.2)	7	7	8.4	—	[16]	[17][3]	[19]	25.0

GENERAL MOTORS CORPORATION
C/K SERIES (PICK-UP) • R/V SERIES (PICK-UP) • BLAZER/JIMMY • SUBURBAN • G SERIES (VAN)

CAPACITIES

Year	Model	VIN	No. Cylinder Displacement cu. in. (liter)	Engine Crankcase with Filter	Engine Crankcase without Filter	Transmission (pts.) 4-Spd	Transmission (pts.) 5-Spd	Transmission (pts.) Auto.	Drive Axle (pts.)	Fuel Tank (gal.)	Cooling System (qts.)
1990	C1500 Pick-Up	Z	262 (4.3)	5	4	⑮	3.6	⑥	②	⑫	10.9
	C1500 Pick-Up	H	305 (5.0)	5	4	⑮	3.6	⑥	②	⑫	18.0
	C1500 Pick-Up	K	350 (5.7)	5	4	⑮	3.6	⑥	②	⑫	18.0
	C1500 Pick-Up	C	379 (6.2)	7	7	⑮	3.6	⑥	②	⑫	25.0
	C1500 Pick-Up	N	454 (7.4)	6	5	⑮	3.6	⑥	②	⑫	24.5
	K1500 Pick-Up	Z	262 (4.3)	5	4	⑮	3.6	⑥	②⑬	⑫	10.9
	K1500 Pick-Up	H	305 (5.0)	5	4	⑮	3.6	⑥	②⑬	⑫	18.0
	K1500 Pick-Up	K	350 (5.7)	5	4	⑮	3.6	⑥	②⑬	⑫	18.0
	K1500 Pick-Up	C	379 (6.2)	7	7	⑮	3.6	⑥	②⑬	⑫	25.0
	C2500 Pick-Up	Z	262 (4.3)	5	4	⑮	3.6	⑥	②	⑫	10.9
	C2500 Pick-Up	H	305 (5.0)	5	4	⑮	3.6	⑥	②	⑫	18.0
	C2500 Pick-Up	K	350 (5.7)	5	4	⑮	3.6	⑥	②	⑫	18.0
	C2500 Pick-Up	C	379 (6.2)	7	7	⑮	3.6	⑥	②	⑫	25.0
	C2500 Pick-Up	J	379 (6.2)	7	7	⑮	3.6	⑥	②	⑫	25.0
	K2500 Pick-Up	Z	262 (4.3)	5	4	⑮	3.6	⑥	②⑬	⑫	10.9
	K2500 Pick-Up	H	305 (5.0)	5	4	⑮	3.6	⑥	②⑬	⑫	18.0
	K2500 Pick-Up	K	350 (5.7)	5	4	⑮	3.6	⑥	②⑬	⑫	18.0
	K2500 Pick-Up	C	379 (6.2)	7	7	⑮	3.6	⑥	②⑬	⑫	25.0
	K2500 Pick-Up	J	379 (6.2)	7	7	⑮	3.6	⑥	②⑬	⑫	25.0
	C3500 Pick-Up	K	350 (5.7)	5	4	⑮	3.6	⑥	②	⑫	18.0
	C3500 Pick-Up	J	379 (6.2)	7	7	⑮	3.6	⑥	②	⑫	25.0
	C3500 Pick-Up	N	454 (7.4)	6	5	⑮	3.6	⑥	②	⑫	24.5
	K3500 Pick-Up	K	350 (5.7)	5	4	⑮	3.6	⑥	②⑭	⑫	18.0
	K3500 Pick-Up	J	379 (6.2)	7	7	⑮	3.6	⑥	②⑭	⑫	25.0
	K3500 Pick-Up	N	454 (7.4)	6	5	⑮	3.6	⑥	②⑭	⑫	24.5
	R3500 Pick-Up	K	350 (5.7)	5	4	⑮	—	⑯	⑰	20	18.0
	R3500 Pick-Up	J	379 (6.2)	7	7	⑮	—	⑯	⑰	20	25.0
	R3500 Pick-Up	N	454 (7.4)	6	5	⑮	—	⑯	⑰	20	25.0
	V3500 Pick-Up	K	350 (5.7)	5	4	⑮	—	⑯	⑰④	20	18.0
	V3500 Pick-Up	J	379 (6.2)	7	7	⑮	—	⑯	⑰④	20	25.0
	V3500 Pick-Up	N	454 (7.4)	6	5	⑮	—	⑯	⑰④	20	25.0
	C2500 Chassis Cab	K	350 (5.7)	5	4	⑮	—	⑥	②	⑫	18.0
	C2500 Chassis Cab	J	379 (6.2)	7	7	⑮	—	⑥	②	⑫	25.0
	K2500 Chassis Cab	K	350 (5.7)	6	5	⑮	—	⑥	②⑬	⑫	18.0
	K2500 Chassis Cab	J	379 (6.2)	7	7	⑮	—	⑥	②⑬	⑫	25.0
	C3500 Chassis Cab	K	350 (5.7)	5	4	⑮	3.6	⑥	②	⑫	18.0
	C3500 Chassis Cab	J	379 (6.2)	7	7	⑮	3.6	⑥	②	⑫	25.0
	C3500 Chassis Cab	N	454 (7.4)	6	5	⑮	3.6	⑥	②	⑫	24.5
	K3500 Chassis Cab	K	350 (5.7)	5	4	⑮	3.6	⑥	②⑭	⑫	18.0
	K3500 Chassis Cab	J	379 (6.2)	7	7	⑮	3.6	⑥	②⑭	⑫	25.0
	K3500 Chassis Cab	N	454 (7.4)	6	5	⑮	3.6	⑥	②⑭	⑫	24.5
	R3500 Chassis Cab	K	350 (5.7)	5	4	⑮	—	⑥	⑰	20	18.0
	R3500 Chassis Cab	J	379 (6.2)	7	7	⑮	—	⑥	⑰	20	25.0

CAPACITIES

Year	Model	VIN	No. Cylinder Displacement cu. in. (liter)	Engine Crankcase with Filter	Engine Crankcase without Filter	Transmission (pts.) 4-Spd	Transmission (pts.) 5-Spd	Transmission (pts.) Auto.	Drive Axle (pts.)	Fuel Tank (gal.)	Cooling System (qts.)
1990	R3500 Chassis Cab	N	454 (7.4)	6	5	⑮	—	⑥	⑰	20	25.0
	U3500 Chassis Cab	K	350 (5.7)	5	4	⑮	—	⑥	⑰④	20	18.0
	U3500 Chassis Cab	J	379 (6.2)	7	7	⑮	—	⑥	⑰④	20	25.0
	U3500 Chassis Cab	N	454 (7.4)	6	5	⑮	—	⑥	⑰④	20	25.0
	R1500 Suburban	K	350 (5.7)	5	4	⑮	—	⑥	⑰	⑱	18.0
	R1500 Suburban	C	379 (6.2)	7	7	⑮	—	⑯	⑰	⑲	25.0
	V1500 Suburban	K	350 (5.7)	6	5	⑮	—	⑯	⑰③	⑱	18.0
	V1500 Suburban	C	379 (6.2)	7	7	⑮	—	⑯	⑰③	⑲	25.0
	R2500 Suburban	K	350 (5.7)	5	4	⑮	—	⑯	⑰	⑱	18.0
	R2500 Suburban	J	379 (6.2)	7	7	⑮	—	⑯	⑰	⑲	25.0
	R2500 Suburban	N	454 (7.4)	6	5	⑮	—	⑯	⑰	⑱	25.0
	U2500 Suburban	K	350 (5.7)	5	4	⑮	—	⑯	⑰③	⑱	18.0
	U2500 Suburban	J	379 (6.2)	7	7	⑮	—	⑯	⑰③	⑲	25.0
	G10/1500 Vandura	Z	262 (4.3)	5	4	⑮	—	⑯	⑰	⑪	10.9
	G10/1500 Vandura	H	305 (5.0)	5	4	⑮	—	⑯	⑰	⑪	18.0
	G20/2500 Vandura	Z	262 (4.3)	5	4	⑮	—	⑯	⑰	⑪	10.9
	G20/2500 Vandura	H	305 (5.0)	5	4	⑮	—	⑯	⑰	⑪	18.0
	G20/2500 Vandura	K	350 (5.7)	5	4	⑮	—	⑯	⑰	⑪	18.0
	G20/2500 Vandura	C	379 (6.2)	7	7	⑮	—	⑯	⑰	⑪	25.0
	G30/3500 Vandura	Z	262 (4.3)	5	4	⑮	—	⑯	⑰	⑪	10.9
	G30/3500 Vandura	K	350 (5.7)	5	4	⑮	—	⑯	⑰	⑪	18.0
	G30/3500 Vandura	J	379 (6.2)	7	7	⑮	—	⑯	⑰	⑪	25.0
	G30/3500 Vandura	N	454 (7.4)	6	5	⑮	—	⑯	⑰	⑪	25.0
	G10/1500 Sport Van/Rally	Z	262 (4.3)	5	4	⑮	—	⑯	⑰	⑪	10.9
	G10/1500 Sport Van/Rally	H	305 (5.0)	5	4	⑮	—	⑯	⑰	⑪	18.0
	G10/1500 Sport Van/Rally	K	350 (5.7)	5	4	⑮	—	⑯	⑰	⑪	18.0
	G20/2500 Sport Van/Rally	Z	262 (4.3)	5	4	⑮	—	⑯	⑰	⑪	10.9
	G20/2500 Sport Van/Rally	H	305 (5.0)	5	4	⑮	—	⑯	⑰	⑪	18.0
	G20/2500 Sport Van/Rally	K	350 (5.7)	5	4	⑮	—	⑯	⑰	⑪	18.0
	G20/2500 Sport Van/Rally	C	379 (6.2)	7	7	⑮	—	⑯	⑰	⑪	25.0
	G10/1500 Beauville/Rally	Z	262 (4.3)	5	4	⑮	—	⑯	⑰	⑪	10.9
	G10/1500 Beauville/Rally	H	305 (5.0)	5	4	⑮	—	⑯	⑰	⑪	18.0
	G10/1500 Beauville/Rally	K	350 (5.7)	5	4	⑮	—	⑯	⑰	⑪	18.0
	G20/2500 Beauville/Rally	Z	262 (4.3)	5	4	⑮	—	⑯	⑰	⑪	10.9
	G20/2500 Beauville/Rally	H	305 (5.0)	5	4	⑮	—	⑯	⑰	⑪	18.0
	G20/2500 Beauville/Rally	K	350 (5.7)	5	4	⑮	—	⑯	⑰	⑪	18.0
	G20/2500 Beauville/Rally	C	379 (6.2)	7	7	⑮	—	⑯	⑰	⑪	25.0
	G30/3500 Sport Van/Rally	K	350 (5.7)	5	4	⑮	—	⑯	⑰	⑪	18.0
	G30/3500 Sport Van/Rally	J	379 (6.2)	7	7	⑮	—	⑯	⑰	⑪	25.0
	G30/3500 Sport Van/Rally	N	454 (7.4)	6	5	⑮	—	⑯	⑰	⑪	25.0
	G30/3500 Sport Van/Rally	K	350 (5.7)	5	4	⑮	—	⑯	⑰	⑪	18.0
	G30/3500 Beauville/Rally	J	379 (6.2)	7	7	⑮	—	⑯	⑰	⑪	25.0
	G30/3500 Beauville/Rally	N	454 (7.4)	6	5	⑮	—	⑯	⑰	⑪	25.0

CAPACITIES

Year	Model	VIN	No. Cylinder Displacement cu. in. (liter)	Engine Crankcase with Filter	Engine Crankcase without Filter	Transmission (pts.) 4-Spd	Transmission (pts.) 5-Spd	Transmission (pts.) Auto.	Drive Axle (pts.)	Fuel Tank (gal.)	Cooling System (qts.)
1990	G30 Cutaway Van	K	350 (5.7)	5	4	⑮	—	⑯	⑰	⑪	18.0
	G30 Cutaway Van	J	379 (6.2)	7	7	⑮	—	⑯	⑰	⑪	25.0
	G30 Cutaway Van	N	454 (7.4)	6	5	⑮	—	⑯	⑰	⑪	25.0
	G30 RV Cutaway Van	K	350 (5.7)	5	4	⑮	—	⑯	⑰	⑪	18.0
	G30 RV Cutaway Van	J	379 (6.2)	7	7	⑮	—	⑯	⑰	⑪	25.0
	G30 RV Cutaway Van	N	454 (7.4)	6	5	⑮	—	⑯	⑰	⑪	25.0
	G30 Hi-Cube/Magnavan	K	350 (5.7)	5	4	⑮	—	⑯	⑰	⑪	18.0
	G30 Hi-Cube/Magnavan	J	379 (6.2)	7	7	⑮	—	⑯	⑰	⑪	25.0
	G30 Hi-Cube/Magnavan	N	454 (7.4)	6	5	⑮	—	⑯	⑰	⑪	25.0
	V Blazer/Jimmy	K	350 (5.7)	5	4	⑮	—	⑯	⑰③	⑱	18.0
	V Blazer/Jimmy	C	379 (6.2)	7	7	⑮	—	⑯	⑰③	⑲	25.0

① Short bed—16 gal.
  Long bed—20 gal.
  Dual tanks—16 gal. each tank, above 8600 GUWR; 20 gal. each
② 8½ in. ring gear—4.2 pts.
  9½ in. ring gear—6.5 pts.
  9¾ in. ring gear—6.0 pts.
  10½ in. ring gear—6.5 pts.
③ Front axle—2 qts., transfer case—5 qts.
④ Front axle—3 qts., transfer case—2½ qts.
⑤ 3 speed—3.2 pts.
  4 speed—4.2 pts.
⑥ 350c—6.3 pts.
  400—9.0 pts.
  700-R4—10.0 pts.
⑦ Standard—25 gals.
  Optional—31 gals. & 40 gals.
⑧ Standard—27 gals.
  Optional—32 gals. & 41 gals.
⑨ Standard—25 gals.
  Optional—31 gals.

⑩ Standard—27 gals.
  Optional—32 gals.
⑪ Standard—22 gals.
  Optional—33 gals.
⑫ Standard—26 gals.
  Deluxe tank (long bed)—34 gals.
⑬ Front axle—1.75 qts., transfer case—1.4 qts.
⑭ Front axle—2.2 qts., transfer case—2.75 qts.
⑮ 117 mm—8.4 pts.
  85 mm—3.6 pts.
⑯ 400/475—9 pts.
  700-R4—10 pts.
⑰ 8½ in. ring gear—4.2 pts.
  9½ in. ring gear—5.5 pts.
  9¾-10½ in. (DANA) ring gear—5.5 pts.
  10½ in. (Chevrolet) ring gear—7.2 pts.
⑱ Standard—31 gals.
  Optional—40 gals.
⑲ Standard—32 gals.
  Optional—41 gals.
⑳ With rear heater—20 qts.

CAMSHAFT SPECIFICATIONS
All measurements given in inches.

Year	VIN	No. Cylinder Displacement cu. in. (liter)	Journal Diameter 1	2	3	4	5	Lobe Lift In.	Lobe Lift Ex.	Bearing Clearance	Camshaft End Play
1986	N	6-262 (4.3)	1.8682–1.8692	1.8682–1.8692	1.8682–1.8692	1.8682–1.8692	—	0.357	0.390	—	0.004–0.012
	T	6-292 (4.8)	1.8677–1.8697	1.8677–1.8697	1.8677–1.8697	1.8677–1.8697	—	① 0.2315	① 0.2315	—	0.003–0.008
	H	8.305 (5.0)	1.8682–1.8692	1.8682–1.8692	1.8682–1.8692	1.8682–1.8692	1.8682–1.8692	0.2484	0.2667	—	0.004–0.002
	L	8-350 (5.7)	1.8682–1.8692	1.8682–1.8692	1.8682–1.8692	1.8682–1.8692	1.8682–1.8692	0.2600	0.2733	—	0.004–0.002
	M	8-350 (5.7)	1.8682–1.8692	1.8682–1.8692	1.8682–1.8692	1.8682–1.8692	1.8682–1.8692	0.2600	0.2733	—	0.004–0.012

CAMSHAFT SPECIFICATIONS
All measurements given in inches.

Year	VIN	No. Cylinder Displacement cu. in. (liter)	Journal Diameter					Lobe Lift		Bearing Clearance	Camshaft End Play
			1	2	3	4	5	In.	Ex.		
1986	C	8-379 (6.2)	2.1642–2.1633	2.1642–2.1633	2.1642–2.1633	2.1642–2.1633	2.0067–2.0089	2.808	2.808	②	0.002–0.012
	J	8-379 (6.2)	2.1642–2.1633	2.1642–2.1633	2.1642–2.1633	2.1642–2.1633	2.0067–2.0089	2.808	2.808	②	0.002–0.012
	W	8-454 (7.4)	1.9482–1.9492	1.9482–1.9492	1.9482–1.9492	1.9482–1.9492	1.9482–1.9492	① 0.2343	① 0.2530	—	—
1987	Z	6-262 (4.3)	1.8682–1.8692	1.8682–1.8692	1.8682–1.8692	1.8682–1.8692	—	0.357	0.390	—	0.004–0.012
	H	8.305 (5.0)	1.8682–1.8692	1.8682–1.8692	1.8682–1.8692	1.8682–1.8692	1.8682–1.8692	0.2484	0.2667	—	0.004–0.012
	K	8-350 (5.7)	1.8682–1.8692	1.8682–1.8692	1.8682–1.8692	1.8682–1.8692	1.8682–1.8692	0.2600	0.2733	—	0.004–0.012
	M	8-350 (5.7)	1.8682–1.8692	1.8682–1.8692	1.8682–1.8692	1.8682–1.8692	1.8682–1.8692	0.2600	0.2733	—	0.004–0.012
	J	8-379 (6.2)	2.1642–2.1633	2.1642–2.1633	2.1642–2.1633	2.1642–2.1633	2.0067–2.0089	2.808	2.808	②	0.002–0.012
	C	8-379 (6.2)	2.1642–2.1633	2.1642–2.1633	2.1642–2.1633	2.1642–2.1633	2.0067–2.0089	2.808	2.808	②	0.002–0.012
	N	8-454 (7.4)	1.9482–1.9492	1.9482–1.9492	1.9482–1.9492	1.9482–1.9492	1.9482–1.9492	① 0.2343	① 0.2530	—	—
1988	Z	6-262 (4.3)	1.8682–1.8692	1.8682–1.8692	1.8682–1.8692	1.8682–1.8692	—	0.357	0.390	—	0.004–0.012
	T	6-292 (4.8)	1.8677–1.8697	1.8677–1.8697	1.8677–1.8697	1.8677–1.8697	—	① 0.2315	① 0.2315	—	0.003–0.008
	H	8.305 (5.0)	1.8682–1.8692	1.8682–1.8692	1.8682–1.8692	1.8682–1.8692	1.8682–1.8692	0.2484	0.2667	—	0.004–0.012
	K	8-350 (5.7)	1.8682–1.8692	1.8682–1.8692	1.8682–1.8692	1.8682–1.8692	1.8682–1.8692	0.2600	0.2733	—	0.004–0.002
	M	8-350 (5.7)	1.8682–1.8692	1.8682–1.8692	1.8682–1.8692	1.8682–1.8692	1.8682–1.8692	0.2600	0.2733	—	0.004–0.002
	C	8-379 (6.2)	2.1642–2.1633	2.1642–2.1633	2.1642–2.1633	2.1642–2.1633	2.0067–2.0089	2.808	2.808	②	0.002–0.012
	J	8-379 (6.2)	2.1642–2.1633	2.1642–2.1633	2.1642–2.1633	2.1642–2.1633	2.0067–2.0089	2.808	2.808	②	0.002–0.012
	N	8-454 (7.4)	1.9482–1.9492	1.9482–1.9492	1.9482–1.9492	1.9482–1.9492	1.9482–1.9492	① 0.2343	① 0.2530	—	—
	W	8-454 (7.4)	1.9482–1.9492	1.9482–1.9492	1.9482–1.9492	1.9482–1.9492	1.9482–1.9492	① 0.2343	① 0.2530	—	—
1989	Z	6-262 (4.3)	1.8682–1.8692	1.8682–1.8692	1.8682–1.8692	1.8682–1.8692	—	0.357	0.390	—	0.004–0.012
	H	8.305 (5.0)	1.8682–1.8692	1.8682–1.8692	1.8682–1.8692	1.8682–1.8692	1.8682–1.8692	0.2484	0.2667	—	0.004–0.012
	K	8-350 (5.7)	1.8682–1.8692	1.8682–1.8692	1.8682–1.8692	1.8682–1.8692	1.8682–1.8692	0.2600	0.2733	—	0.004–0.012
	J	8-379 (6.2)	2.1642–2.1633	2.1642–2.1633	2.1642–2.1633	2.1642–2.1633	2.0067–2.0089	2.808	2.808	②	0.002–0.012
	C	8-379 (6.2)	2.1642–2.1633	2.1642–2.1633	2.1642–2.1633	2.1642–2.1633	2.0067–2.0089	2.808	2.808	②	0.002–0.012

CAMSHAFT SPECIFICATIONS
All measurements given in inches.

Year	VIN	No. Cylinder Displacement cu. in. (liter)	Journal Diameter 1	2	3	4	5	Lobe Lift In.	Ex.	Bearing Clearance	Camshaft End Play
1989	N	8-454 (7.4)	1.9482–1.9492	1.9482–1.9492	1.9482–1.9492	1.9482–1.9492	1.9482–1.9492	① 0.2343	① 0.2530	—	—
	W	8-454 (7.4)	1.9482–1.9492	1.9482–1.9492	1.9482–1.9492	1.9482–1.9492	1.9482–1.9492	① 0.2343	① 0.2530	—	—
1990	Z	6-262 (4.3)	1.8682–1.8692	1.8682–1.8692	1.8682–1.8692	1.8682–1.8692	—	0.357	0.390	—	0.004–0.012
	H	8.305 (5.0)	1.8682–1.8692	1.8682–1.8692	1.8682–1.8692	1.8682–1.8692	1.8682–1.8692	0.2484	0.2667	—	0.004–0.012
	K	8-350 (5.7)	1.8682–1.8692	1.8682–1.8692	1.8682–1.8692	1.8682–1.8692	1.8682–1.8692	0.2600	0.2733	—	0.004–0.012
	J	8-379 (6.2)	2.1642–2.1633	2.1642–2.1633	2.1642–2.1633	2.1642–2.1633	2.0067–2.0089	2.808	2.808	②	0.002–0.012
	C	8-379 (6.2)	2.1642–2.1633	2.1642–2.1633	2.1642–2.1633	2.1642–2.1633	2.0067–2.0089	2.808	2.808	②	0.002–0.012
	N	8-545 (7.4)	1.9482–1.9492	1.9482–1.9492	1.9482–1.9492	1.9482–1.9492	1.9482–1.9492	① 0.2343	① 0.2530	—	—

① ± 0.002
② Nos. 1, 2, 3, 4: 0.00098–0.0046
No. 5: 0.00078–0.0044

CRANKSHAFT AND CONNECTING ROD SPECIFICATIONS
All measurements are given in inches.

Year	VIN	No. Cylinder Displacement cu. in. (liter)	Crankshaft Main Brg. Journal Dia.	Main Brg. Oil Clearance	Shaft End-play	Thrust on No.	Connecting Rod Journal Diameter	Oil Clearance	Side Clearance
1986	N	6-262 (4.3)	①	②	.0020–.0060	4	2.2487–2.2497	.0020–.0030	.0070–.0150
	T	6-292 (4.8)	2.2979–2.2994	③	.0020–.0060	7	2.0990–2.1000	.0010–.0030	.0010–.0026
	H	8-305 (5.0)	①	④	.0020–.0060	5	2.0988–2.0998	.0013–.0035	.0080–.0140
	L	8-350 (5.7)	①	④	.0020–.0060	5	2.0988–2.0998	.0013–.0035	.0080–.0140
	M	8-350 (5.7)	①	④	.0020–.0060	5	2.0988–2.0998	.0013–.0035	.0080–.0140
	C	8-379 (6.2)	⑨	⑦	.0020–.0070	3	2.3980–2.3990	.0017–.0039	.0070–.0240
	J	8-379 (6.2)	⑨	⑦	.0020–.0070	3	2.3980–2.3990	.0017–.0039	.0070–.0240
	W	8-454 (7.4)	⑤	⑥	.0060–.0010	5	2.1990–2.2000	.0009–.0025	.0130–.0230
1987	Z	6-262 (4.3)	①	②	.0020–.0060	4	2.2487–2.2497	.0020–.0030	.0070–.0150
	H	8-305 (5.0)	①	④	.0020–.0060	5	2.0988–2.0998	.0013–.0035	.0080–.0140
	L	8-350 (5.7)	①	④	.0020–.0060	5	2.0988–2.0998	.0013–.0035	.0080–.0140

CRANKSHAFT AND CONNECTING ROD SPECIFICATIONS
All measurements are given in inches.

Year	VIN	No. Cylinder Displacement cu. in. (liter)	Crankshaft				Connecting Rod		
			Main Brg. Journal Dia.	Main Brg. Oil Clearance	Shaft End-play	Thrust on No.	Journal Diameter	Oil Clearance	Side Clearance
1987	K	8-350 (5.7)	①	④	.0020–.0060	5	2.0988–2.0998	.0013–.0035	.0080–.0140
	M	8-350 (5.7)	①	④	.0020–.0060	5	2.0988–2.0998	.0013–.0035	.0080–.0140
	C	8-379 (6.2)	⑨	⑦	.0020–.0070	3	2.3980–2.3990	.0017–.0039	.0070–.0240
	J	8-379 (6.2)	⑨	⑦	.0020–.0070	3	2.3980–2.3990	.0017–.0039	.0070–.0240
	N	8-454 (7.4)	⑤	⑥	.0060–.0010	5	2.1990–2.2000	.0009–.0025	.0130–.0230
1988	Z	6-262 (4.3)	①	②	.0020–.0060	4	2.2487–2.2497	.0020–.0030	.0070–.0150
	T	6-292 (4.8)	2.2979–2.2994	③	.0020–.0060	7	2.0990–2.1000	.0010–.0036	.0010–.0026
	H	8-305 (5.0)	①	④	.0020–.0060	5	2.0988–2.0998	.0013–.0035	.0080–.0014
	K	8-350 (5.7)	①	④	.0020–.0060	5	2.0988–2.0998	.0013–.0035	.0080–.0014
	M	8-350 (5.7)	①	④	.0020–.0060	5	2.0988–2.0998	.0013–.0035	.0080–.0014
	C	8-379 (6.2)	⑨	⑦	.0020–.0070	3	2.3480–2.3990	.0017–.0039	.0070–.0240
	J	8-379 (6.2)	⑨	⑦	.0020–.0070	3	2.3480–2.3990	.0017–.0039	.0070–.0240
	N	8-454 (7.4)	⑤	⑥	.0060–.0010	5	2.1990–2.2000	.0009–.0025	.0130–.0230
	W	8-434 (7.4)	⑤	⑥	.0060–.0100	5	2.1990–2.2000	.0009–.0025	.0130–.0230
1989	Z	6-262 (4.3)	①	⑧	.0020–.0060	4	2.2487–2.2497	.0013–.0035	.0060–.0140
	H	8-305 (5.0)	①	⑧	.0020–.0060	5	2.0988–2.0998	.0013–.0035	.0060–.0140
	K	8-350 (5.7)	①	⑧	.0020–.0060	5	2.0988–2.0998	.0013–.0035	.0060–.0140
	J	8-379 (6.2)	⑨	⑦	.0040–.0010	5	2.3981–2.3992	.0018–.0039	.0060–.0025
	C	8-379 (6.2)	⑨	⑦	.0040–.0010	5	2.3981–2.3992	.0018–.0039	.0060–.0250
	N	8-454 (7.4)	⑤	⑥	.0060–.0010	5	2.1990–2.2000	.0009–.0025	.0130–.0230
	W	8-454 (7.4)	⑤	⑥	.0060–.0010	5	2.1990–2.2000	.0009–.0025	.0130–.0230
1990	Z	6-262 (4.3)	①	⑧	.0020–.0060	4	2.2487–2.2497	.0013–.0035	.0060–.0140
	H	8-305 (5.0)	①	⑧	.0020–.0060	5	2.0988–2.0998	.0013–.0035	.0060–.0140
	K	8-350 (5.7)	①	⑧	.0020–.0060	5	2.0988–2.0998	.0013–.0035	.0060–.0140

GENERAL MOTORS CORPORATION
C/K SERIES (PICK-UP) • R/V SERIES (PICK-UP) • BLAZER/JIMMY • SUBURBAN • G SERIES (VAN)

CRANKSHAFT AND CONNECTING ROD SPECIFICATIONS
All measurements are given in inches.

Year	VIN	No. Cylinder Displacement cu. in. (liter)	Main Brg. Journal Dia.	Main Brg. Oil Clearance	Shaft End-play	Thrust on No.	Journal Diameter	Oil Clearance	Side Clearance
			Crankshaft				Connecting Rod		
1990	J	8-379 (6.2)	⑨	⑦	.0040–.0010	5	2.3981–2.3992	.0018–.0039	.0060–.0025
	C	8-379 (6.2)	⑨	⑦	.0040–.0010	5	2.3981–2.3992	.0018–.0039	.0060–.0250
	N	8-454 (7.4)	⑤	⑥	.0060–.0010	5	2.1990–2.2000	.0009–.0025	.0130–.0230

① Front—2.4484–2.4493
Inter.—2.4481–2.4490
Rear—2.4479–2.4488
② Front—.0010–.0015
Inter.—.0010–.0020
Rear—.0025–.0030
③ 1–6—.0010–.0024
7—.0016–.0035

④ 1—.0008–.0020
2–4—.0011–.0023
5—.0017–.0032
⑤ 1–4—2.7481–2.7490
5—2.7476–2.7486
⑥ 1–4—.0013–.0025
5—.0024–.0040

⑦ 1–4—.0045–.0083
5—.0055–.0093
⑧ 1—.0010–.0015
2–3—.0010–.0025
4—.0025–.0035
⑨ 1–4—2.9495–2.9504
5—2.9493–2.9502

VALVE SPECIFICATIONS

Year	VIN	No. Cylinder Displacement cu. in. (liter)	Seat Angle (deg.)	Face Angle (deg.)	Spring Test Pressure (lbs.)	Spring Installed Height (in.)	Stem-to-Guide Clearance (in.) Intake	Stem-to-Guide Clearance (in.) Exhaust	Stem Diameter (in.) Intake	Stem Diameter (in.) Exhaust
1986	N	6-260 (4.3)	46	45	220 @ 1.25	1.70	.0010–.0027	.0010–.0027	.3410–.3417	.3410–.3417
	T	6-292 (4.8)	46	46	175 @ 1.26	1.66	.0010–.0027	.0015–.0032	.3410–.3417	.3410–.3417
	H	8-305 (5.0)	46	45	200 @ 1.25	1.70	.0010–.0027	.0010–.0027	.3410–.3417	.3410–.3417
	L	8-350 (5.7)	46	45	200 @ 1.25	1.70	.0010–.0027	.0010–.0027	.3410–.3417	.3410–.3417
	M	8-350 (5.7)	46	45	200 @ 1.25	1.70	.0010–.0027	.0010–.0027	.3410–.3417	.3410–.3417
	C	8-379 (6.2)	46	45	230 @ 1.38	1.81	.0010–.0027	.0010–.0027	.3414	.3414
	J	8-379 (6.2)	46	45	230 @ 1.38	1.81	.0010–.0027	.0010–.0027	.3414	.3414
	W	8-454 (7.4)	46	45	220 @ 1.40	1.80	.0010–.0027	.0012–.0027	.3715–.3722	.3715–.3722
1987	Z	6-262 (4.3)	46	45	220 @ 1.25	1.70	.0010–.0027	.0010–.0027	.3410–.3417	.3410–.3417
	H	8-305 (5.0)	46	45	200 @ 1.25	1.70	.0010–.0027	.0010–.0027	.3410–.3417	.3410–.3417
	L	8-350 (5.7)	46	45	200 @ 1.25	1.70	.0010–.0027	.0010–.0027	.3410–.3417	.3410–.3417
	K	8-350 (5.7)	46	45	200 @ 1.25	1.70	.0010–.0027	.0010–.0027	.3410–.3417	.3410–.3417
	M	8-350 (5.7)	46	45	200 @ 1.25	1.70	.0010–.0027	.0010–.0027	.3410–.3417	.3410–.3417
	C	8-379 (6.2)	46	45	230 @ 1.38	1.81	.0010–.0027	.0010–.0027	.3414	.3414

VALVE SPECIFICATIONS

Year	VIN	No. Cylinder Displacement cu. in. (liter)	Seat Angle (deg.)	Face Angle (deg.)	Spring Test Pressure (lbs.)	Spring Installed Height (in.)	Stem-to-Guide Clearance (in.)		Stem Diameter (in.)	
							Intake	Exhaust	Intake	Exhaust
1987	J	8-379 (6.2)	46	45	230 @ 1.38	1.81	.0010–.0027	.0010–.0027	.3414	.3414
	N	8-454 (7.4)	46	45	220 @ 1.40	1.80	.0010–.0027	.0012–.0029	.3715–.3722	.3715–.3722
1988	Z	6-262 (4.3)	46	45	220 @ 1.25	1.70	.0010–.0027	.0010–.0027	.3410–.3417	.3410–.3417
	T	6-292 (4.8)	46	46	175 @ 1.26	1.66	.0010–.0027	.0015–.0032	.3410–.3417	.3410–.3417
	H	8-305 (5.0)	46	45	220 @ 1.25	1.70	.0010–.0027	.0010–.0027	.3410–.3417	.3410–.3417
	K	8-350 (5.7)	46	45	220 @ 1.25	1.70	.0010–.0027	.0010–.0027	.3410–.3417	.3410–.3417
	M	8-350 (5.7)	46	45	220 @ 1.25	1.70	.0010–.0027	.0010–.0027	.3410–.3417	.3410–.3417
	C	8-379 (6.2)	46	45	230 @ 1.38	1.81	.0010–.0027	.0010–.0027	.3414	.3414
	J	8-379 (6.2)	46	45	230 @ 1.38	1.81	.0010–.0027	.0010–.0027	.3414	.3414
	N	8-454 (7.4)	46	45	220 @ 1.40	1.80	.0010–.0027	.0012–.0027	.3715–.3722	.3715–.3722
	W	8-454 (7.4)	46	45	220 @ 1.40	1.80	.0010–.0027	.0012–.0027	.3715–.3722	.3715–.3722
1989	Z	6-262 (4.3)	46	45	220 @ 1.25	1.72	.0010–.0027	.0010–.0027	.3414	.3414
	H	8-305 (5.0)	46	45	200 @ 1.25	1.71	.0010–.0027	.0010–.0027	.3414	.3414
	K	8-350 (5.7)	46	45	200 @ 1.25	1.71	.0010–.0027	.0010–.0027	.3414	.3414
	J	8-379 (6.2)	46	45	230 @ 1.39	1.81	.0010–.0027	.0010–.0027	.3414	.3414
	C	8-379 (6.2)	46	45	230 @ 1.39	1.81	.0010–.0027	.0010–.0027	.3414	.3414
	N	8-454 (7.4)	46	45	220 @ 1.40	1.80	.0010–.0027	.0012–.0027	.3719	.3719
	W	8-454 (7.4)	46	45	220 @ 1.40	1.80	.0010–.0027	.0012–.0027	.3719	.3719
1990	Z	6-262 (4.3)	46	45	220 @ 1.25	1.70	.0010–.0027	.0010–.0027	.3414	.3414
	H	8-305 (5.0)	46	45	200 @ 1.25	1.70	.0010–.0027	.0010–.0027	.3414	.3414
	K	8-350 (5.7)	46	45	200 @ 1.25	1.70	.0010–.0027	.0010–.0027	.3414	.3414
	J	8-379 (6.2)	46	45	230 @ 1.39	1.81	.0010–.0027	.0010–.0027	.3414	.3414
	C	8-379 (6.2)	46	45	230 @ 1.39	1.81	.0010–.0027	.0010–.0027	.3414	.3414
	N	8-454 (7.4)	46	45	220 @ 1.40	1.80	.0010–.0027	.0012–.0029	.3719	.3719

GENERAL MOTORS CORPORATION
C/K SERIES (PICK-UP) • R/V SERIES (PICK-UP) • BLAZER/JIMMY • SUBURBAN • G SERIES (VAN)

PISTON AND RING SPECIFICATIONS
All measurements are given in inches.

Year	VIN	No. Cylinder Displacement cu. in. (liter)	Piston Clearance	Ring Gap Top Compression	Ring Gap Bottom Compression	Ring Gap Oil Control	Ring Side Clearance Top Compression	Ring Side Clearance Bottom Compression	Ring Side Clearance Oil Control
1986	N	6-262 (4.3)	.0017–.0017	.0100–.0250	.0100–.0250	.0150–.0550	.0012–.0032	.0012–.0032	.0020–.0070
	T	6-292 (4.8)	.0026–.0036	.0100–.0200	.0100–.0200	.0150–.0550	.0010–.0027	.0020–.0040	.0005–.0055
	H	8-305 (5.0)	.0007–.0017	.0100–.0200	.0100–.0250	.0150–.0550	.0012–.0032	.0012–.0032	.0020–.0070
	L	8-350 (5.7)	.0007–.0017	.0100–.0200	.0130–.0250	.0150–.0550	.0012–.0032	.0012–.0032	.0020–.0070
	M	8-350 (5.7)	.0007–.0017	.0100–.0200	.0130–.0250	.0150–.0550	.0012–.0032	.0012–.0032	.0020–.0070
	C	8-379 (6.2)	①	.0120–.0220	.0300–.0400	.0100–.0210	.0030–.0071	.0300–.0400	.0016–.0038
	J	8-379 (6.2)	①	.0120–.0220	.0300–.0400	.0100–.0210	.0030–.0071	.0300–.0400	.0016–.0038
	W	8-454 (7.4)	.0030–.0040	.0100–.0200	.0100–.0200	.0150–.0550	.0017–.0032	.0017–.0032	.0050–.0065
1987	Z	6-262 (4.3)	.0017–.0017	.0100–.0250	.0100–.0250	.0150–.0550	.0012–.0032	.0012–.0032	.0020–.0070
	H	8-305 (5.0)	.0007–.0017	.0100–.0200	.0100–.0250	.0150–.0550	.0012–.0032	.0012–.0032	.0020–.0070
	L	8-350 (5.7)	.0007–.0017	.0100–.0200	.0130–.0250	.0150–.0550	.0012–.0032	.0012–.0032	.0020–.0070
	K	8-350 (5.7)	.0007–.0017	.0100–.0200	.0130–.0250	.0150–.0550	.0012–.0032	.0012–.0032	.0020–.0070
	M	8-350 (5.7)	.0007–.0017	.0100–.0200	.0130–.0250	.0150–.0550	.0012–.0032	.0012–.0032	.0020–.0070
	C	8-379 (6.2)	①	.0120–.0220	.0300–.0400	.0100–.0210	.0030–.0071	.0300–.0400	.0016–.0038
	J	8-379 (6.2)	①	.0120–.0220	.0300–.0400	.0100–.0210	.0030–.0071	.0300–.0400	.0016–.0038
	N	8-454 (7.4)	.0030–.0040	.0100–.0200	.0100–.0200	.0150–.0550	.0017–.0032	.0017–.0032	.0050–.0065
1988	Z	6-262 (4.3)	.0017–.0017	.0100–.0250	.0100–.0250	.0150–.0550	.0012–.0032	.0012–.0032	.0020–.0070
	T	6-292 (4.8)	.0026–.0036	.0100–.0200	.0100–.0200	.0150–.0550	.0010–.0027	.0020–.0040	.0005–.0055
	H	8-305 (5.0)	.0007–.0017	.0100–.0200	.0100–.0250	.0150–.0550	.0012–.0032	.0012–.0032	.0020–.0070
	K	8-350 (5.7)	.0007–.0017	.0100–.0200	.0130–.0250	.0150–.0550	.0012–.0032	.0012–.0032	.0020–.0070
	M	8-350 (5.7)	.0007–.0017	.0100–.0200	.0130–.0250	.0150–.0550	.0012–.0032	.0012–.0032	.0020–.0070
	C	8-379 (6.2)	①	.0120–.0220	.0300–.0400	.0100–.0210	.0030–.0071	.0300–.0400	.0016–.0038
	J	8-379 (6.2)	①	.0120–.0220	.0300–.0400	.0100–.0210	.0030–.0071	.0300–.0400	.0016–.0038
	N	8-454 (7.4)	.0030–.0040	.0100–.0200	.0100–.0200	.0150–.0550	.0017–.0032	.0017–.0032	.0050–.0065

PISTON AND RING SPECIFICATIONS
All measurements are given in inches.

Year	VIN	No. Cylinder Displacement cu. in. (liter)	Piston Clearance	Ring Gap			Ring Side Clearance		
				Top Compression	Bottom Compression	Oil Control	Top Compression	Bottom Compression	Oil Control
1988	W	8-454 (7.4)	.0030–.0040	.0100–.0200	.0100–.0200	.0150–.0550	.0017–.0032	.0017–.0032	.0050–.0065
1989	Z	6-262 (4.3)	.0017–.0017	.0100–.0250	.0100–.0250	.0150–.0550	.0012–.0032	.0012–.0032	.0020–.0070
	H	8-305 (5.0)	.0007–.0017	.0100–.0200	.0100–.0250	.0150–.0550	.0012–.0032	.0012–.0032	.0020–.0070
	K	8-350 (5.7)	.0007–.0017	.0100–.0200	.0130–.0250	.0150–.0550	.0012–.0032	.0012–.0032	.0020–.0070
	M	8-350 (5.7)	.0007–.0017	.0100–.0200	.0130–.0250	.0150–.0550	.0012–.0032	.0012–.0032	.0020–.0070
	C	8-379 (6.2)	①	.0120–.0220	.0300–.0400	.0100–.0210	.0030–.0071	.0300–.0400	.0016–.0038
	J	8-379 (6.2)	①	.0120–.0220	.0300–.0400	.0100–.0210	.0030–.0071	.0300–.0400	.0016–.0038
	N	8-454 (7.4)	.0030–.0040	.0100–.0200	.0100–.0200	.0150–.0550	.0017–.0032	.0017–.0032	.0050–.0065
	W	8-454 (7.4)	.0030–.0040	.0100–.0200	.0100–.0200	.0150–.0550	.0017–.0032	.0017–.0032	.0050–.0065
1990	Z	6-262 (4.3)	.0017–.0017	.0100–.0250	.0100–.0250	.0150–.0550	.0012–.0032	.0012–.0032	.0020–.0070
	H	8-305 (5.0)	.0007–.0017	.0100–.0200	.0100–.0250	.0150–.0550	.0012–.0032	.0012–.0032	.0020–.0070
	K	8-350 (5.7)	.0007–.0017	.0100–.0200	.0130–.0250	.0150–.0550	.0012–.0032	.0012–.0032	.0020–.0070
	M	8-350 (5.7)	.0007–.0017	.0100–.0200	.0130–.0250	.0150–.0550	.0012–.0032	.0012–.0032	.0020–.0070
	C	8-379 (6.2)	①	.0120–.0220	.0300–.0400	.0100–.0210	.0030–.0071	.0300–.0400	.0016–.0038
	J	8-379 (6.2)	①	.0120–.0220	.0300–.0400	.0100–.0210	.0030–.0071	.0300–.0400	.0016–.0038
	N	8-454 (7.4)	.0030–.0040	.0100–.0200	.0100–.0200	.0150–.0550	.0017–.0032	.0017–.0032	.0050–.0065

① Bohn Pistons
  1–6—0.0035–0.0045
  7–8—0.0040–0.0050

Zollner Pistons
  1–6—0.0044–0.0054
  7–8—0.0049–0.0059

TORQUE SPECIFICATIONS
All readings in ft. lbs.

Year	VIN	No. Cylinder Displacement cu. in. (liter)	Cylinder Head Bolts	Main Bearing Bolts	Rod Bearing Bolts	Crankshaft Pulley Bolts	Flywheel Bolts	Manifold		Spark Plugs
								Intake	Exhaust	
1986	N	6-262 (6.2)	65	70	45	60	65	30	20	22
	T	6-292 (4.8)	95 ①	65	44	50	110	⑤	⑤	17–27
	H	8-305 (5.0)	65	④	45	60	60	35	⑥	17–27
	L	8-350 (5.7)	65	④	45	60	60	35	⑥	17–27
	M	8-350 (5.7)	65	④	45	60	60	35	⑥	17–27

GENERAL MOTORS CORPORATION
C/K SERIES (PICK-UP) ● R/V SERIES (PICK-UP) ● BLAZER/JIMMY ● SUBURBAN ● G SERIES (VAN)

TORQUE SPECIFICATIONS
All readings in ft. lbs.

Year	VIN	No. Cylinder Displacement cu. in. (liter)	Cylinder Head Bolts	Main Bearing Bolts	Rod Bearing Bolts	Crankshaft Pulley Bolts	Flywheel Bolts	Manifold Intake	Manifold Exhaust	Spark Plugs
1986	C	8-379 (6.2)	②	③	48	151	60	31	25	—
	J	8-379 (6.2)	②	③	48	151	60	31	25	—
	W	8-454 (7.4)	80	110	50	85	65	30	20	17–27
1987	Z	6-262 (4.3)	65	75	45	70	75	36	⑦	22
	H	8-305 (5.0)	65	④	45	60	60	35	⑥	17–27
	L	8-350 (5.7)	65	④	45	60	60	35	⑥	17–27
	K	8-350 (5.7)	65	④	45	60	60	35	⑥	17–27
	M	8-350 (5.7)	65	④	45	60	60	35	⑥	17–27
	C	8-379 (6.2)	②	③	48	151	60	31	25	—
	J	8-379 (6.2)	②	③	48	151	60	31	25	—
	N	8-454 (7.4)	80	110	50	85	65	30	20	17–27
1988	Z	6-262 (4.3)	65	80	45	70	75	36	⑦	22
	T	6-292 (4.8)	95 ①	65	44	50	110	⑤	⑤	17–27
	H	8-305 (5.0)	65	④	45	60	60	35	⑦	17–27
	K	8-350 (5.7)	65	④	45	60	60	35	⑦	17–27
	M	8-350 (5.7)	65	④	45	60	60	35	⑦	17–27
	C	8-379 (6.2)	②	③	48	151	60	31	25	—
	J	8-379 (6.2)	②	③	48	151	60	31	25	—
	N	8-454 (7.4)	80	110	50	85	65	30	20	17–27
	W	8-454 (7.4)	80	110	50	85	65	30	20	17–27
1989	Z	6-262 (4.3)	65	80	45	70	75	36	⑦	22
	H	8-305 (5.0)	65	④	45	60	60	35	⑦	17–27
	K	8-350 (5.7)	65	④	45	60	60	35	⑦	17–27
	M	8-350 (5.7)	65	④	45	60	60	35	⑦	17–27
	C	8-379 (6.2)	②	③	48	151	60	31	25	—
	J	8-379 (6.2)	②	③	48	151	60	31	25	—
	N	8-454 (7.4)	80	110	50	85	65	30	20	17–27
	W	8-454 (7.4)	80	110	50	85	65	30	20	17–27
1990	Z	6-262 (4.3)	65	80	45	70	75	36	⑦	22
	H	8-305 (5.0)	65	④	45	60	60	35	⑦	17–27
	K	8-350 (5.7)	65	④	45	60	60	35	⑦	17–27
	M	8-350 (5.7)	65	④	45	60	60	35	⑦	17–27
	C	8-379 (6.2)	②	③	48	151	60	31	25	—
	J	8-379 (6.2)	②	③	48	151	60	31	25	—
	N	8-454 (7.4)	80	110	50	85	65	30	20	17–27

① Left front bolt 85 ft. lbs.
② 1st step 20 ft. lbs.
   2nd step 50 ft. lbs.
   3rd ¼ turn ft. lbs.

③ Inner bolts 110 ft. lbs.
   Outer bolts 100 ft. lbs.
④ 2, 3, 4 bolts 70 ft. lbs.
   Other bolts 80 ft. lbs.

⑤ Intake manifold to exhaust manifold—44 ft. lbs.
   Manifold to cylinder head—38 ft. lbs.
⑥ Cast manifold—two center bolts—26 ft. lbs., all others 20 ft. lbs.
   Tubular stainless steel—26 ft. lbs.
⑦ Two center bolts—26 ft. lbs., all others—20 ft. lbs.

BRAKE SPECIFICATIONS
All measurements in inches unless noted.

Year	Model	Lug Nut Torque (ft. lbs.)	Master Cylinder Bore	Brake Disc Minimum Thickness	Brake Disc Maximum Runout	Standard Brake Drum Diameter	Minimum Lining Thickness Front	Minimum Lining Thickness Rear
1986	C10/1500 Pick-Up	100	—	0.980	0.004	11.00	③	③
	C20/2500 Pick-Up	120	—	1.230	0.004	11.15	③	③
	C20/2500 Pick-Up	120	—	1.230	0.004	13.00	③	③
	C30/3500 Pick-Up	120 ①	—	1.230	0.004	13.00	③	③
	K10/1500 Pick-Up	100 ②	—	0.980	0.004	11.15	③	③
	K20/2500 Pick-Up	120	—	0.980	0.004	11.15	③	③
	K20/2500 Pick-Up	120	—	1.230	0.004	13.00	③	③
	K30/3500 Pick-Up	120 ①	—	1.230	0.004	13.00	③	③
	C10/1500 Suburban	100	—	0.980	0.004	11.15	③	③
	C20/2500 Suburban	120	—	1.230	0.004	13.00	③	③
	K10/1500 Suburban	100 ②	—	0.980	0.004	11.15	③	③
	K20/2500 Suburban	120	—	1.230	0.004	13.00	③	③
	K10/1500 Blazer/Jimmy	100 ②	—	0.980	0.004	11.15	③	③
	G10/1500 Van	100	—	0.980	0.004	11.00	③	③
	G20/2500 Van	100	—	0.980	0.004	11.15	③	③
	G30/3500 Van	120	—	1.230	0.004	13.00	③	③
1987	R10/1500 Pick-Up	100	—	0.980	0.004	11.00	③	③
	R20/2500 Pick-Up	120	—	1.230	0.004	11.15	③	③
	R20/2500 Pick-Up	120	—	1.230	0.004	13.00	③	③
	R30/3500 Pick-Up	120 ①	—	1.230	0.004	13.00	③	③
	V10/1500 Pick-Up	100 ②	—	0.980	0.004	11.15	③	③
	V10/1500 Pick-Up	120	—	0.980	0.004	11.15	③	③
	V20/2500 Pick-Up	120	—	1.230	0.004	13.00	③	③
	V30/3500 Pick-Up	120 ①	—	1.230	0.004	13.00	③	③
	R10/1500 Suburban	100	—	0.980	0.004	11.15	③	③
	R20/2500 Suburban	120	—	1.230	0.004	13.00	③	③
	V10/1500 Blazer/Jimmy	100 ②	—	0.980	0.004	11.15	③	③
	G10/1500 Van	100	—	0.980	0.004	11.00	③	③
	G20/2500 Van	100	—	0.980	0.004	11.15	③	③
	G30/3500 Van	120	—	1.230	0.004	13.00	③	③
1988	C10/1500 Pick-Up	90	—	0.979	0.004	10.00	③	③
	C20/2500 Pick-Up	90	—	0.979	0.004	11.15	③	③
	C20/2500 Pick-Up	90	—	1.230	0.004	13.00	③	③
	C30/3500 Pick-Up	90 ④	—	1.230	0.004	13.00	③	③
	K10/1500 Pick-Up	90	—	0.979	0.004	10.00	③	③
	K20/2500 Pick-Up	90	—	0.979	0.004	11.15	③	③
	K30/3500 Pick-Up	90 ④	—	1.230	0.004	13.00	③	③
	R20/2500 Pick-Up	120	—	1.230	0.004	13.00	③	③
	R30/3500 Pick-Up	120	—	1.230	0.004	13.00	③	③
	V30/3500 Pick-Up	120	—	1.230	0.004	13.00	③	③
	R10/1500 Suburban	100	—	0.979	0.004	11.15	③	③
	R20/2500 Suburban	120	—	1.230	0.004	13.00	③	③
	V10/1500 Suburban	100 ②	—	0.979	0.004	11.15	③	③

BRAKE SPECIFICATIONS
All measurements in inches unless noted.

Year	Model	Lug Nut Torque (ft. lbs.)	Master Cylinder Bore	Brake Disc Minimum Thickness	Brake Disc Maximum Runout	Standard Brake Drum Diameter	Minimum Lining Thickness Front	Minimum Lining Thickness Rear
1988	V20/2500 Suburban	120	—	1.230	0.004	13.00	③	③
	V Blazer/Jimmy	100 ②	—	0.979	0.004	11.15	③	③
	G10/1500 Van	100	—	0.979	0.004	11.00	③	③
	G20/2500 Van	100	—	0.979	0.004	11.15	③	③
	G30/3500 Van	120	—	1.230	0.004	13.00	③	③
1989	C10/1500 Pick-Up	105	—	0.979	0.004	10.00	③	③
	C20/2500 Pick-Up	105	—	0.979	0.004	11.15	③	③
	C20/2500 Pick-Up	105	—	1.230	0.004	13.00	③	③
	C30/3500 Pick-Up	105 ④	—	1.230	0.004	13.00	③	③
	K10/1500 Pick-Up	105	—	0.979	0.004	10.00	③	③
	K20/2500 Pick-Up	105	—	0.979	0.004	11.15	③	③
	K30/3500 Pick-Up	105 ④	—	1.230	0.004	13.00	③	③
	R20/2500 Pick-Up	120	—	1.230	0.004	13.00	③	③
	R30/3500 Pick-Up	120	—	1.230	0.004	13.00	③	③
	V30/3500 Pick-Up	120	—	1.230	0.004	13.00	③	③
	R10/1500 Suburban	100	—	0.979	0.004	11.15	③	③
	R20/2500 Suburban	120	—	1.230	0.004	13.00	③	③
	V10/1500 Suburban	100 ②	—	0.979	0.004	11.15	③	③
	V20/2500 Suburban	120	—	1.230	0.004	13.00	③	③
	V Blazer/Jimmy	100 ②	—	0.979	0.004	11.15	③	③
	G10/1500 Van	100	—	0.979	0.004	11.00	③	③
	G20/2500 Van	100	—	0.979	0.004	11.15	③	③
	G30/3500 Van	120	—	1.230	0.004	13.00	③	③
1990	C10/1500 Pick-Up	105	—	0.979	0.004	10.00	③	③
	C20/2500 Pick-Up	105	—	0.979	0.004	11.15	③	③
	C20/2500 Pick-Up	105	—	1.230	0.004	13.00	③	③
	C30/3500 Pick-Up	105 ④	—	1.230	0.004	13.00	③	③
	K10/1500 Pick-Up	105	—	0.979	0.004	10.00	③	③
	K20/2500 Pick-Up	105	—	0.979	0.004	11.15	③	③
	K30/3500 Pick-Up	105 ④	—	1.230	0.004	13.00	③	③
	R20/2500 Pick-Up	120	—	1.230	0.004	13.00	③	③
	R30/3500 Pick-Up	120	—	1.230	0.004	13.00	③	③
	V30/3500 Pick-Up	120	—	1.230	0.004	13.00	③	③
	R10/1500 Suburban	100	—	0.979	0.004	11.15	③	③
	R20/2500 Suburban	120	—	1.230	0.004	13.00	③	③
	V10/1500 Suburban	100 ②	—	0.979	0.004	11.15	③	③
	V20/2500 Suburban	120	—	1.230	0.004	13.00	③	③
	V Blazer/Jimmy	100 ②	—	0.979	0.004	11.15	③	③
	G10/1500 Van	100	—	0.979	0.004	11.00	③	③

BRAKE SPECIFICATIONS
All measurements in inches unless noted.

Year	Model	Lug Nut Torque (ft. lbs.)	Master Cylinder Bore	Brake Disc Minimum Thickness	Brake Disc Maximum Runout	Standard Brake Drum Diameter	Minimum Lining Thickness Front	Minimum Lining Thickness Rear
1990	G20/2500 Van	100	—	0.979	0.004	11.15	③	③
	G30/3500 Van	120	—	1.230	0.004	13.00	③	③

① Dual wheels—140 ft. lbs.
② Aluminum wheels—100 ft. lbs., Steel wheels—88 ft. lbs.
③ Within 1/32 inch of rivet head or shoe
④ Dual wheels—125 ft. lbs.

NOTE—Minimum lining thickness is as recommended by the manufacturer. Because of variations in state inspection regulations, the minimum allowable thickness may be different than recommended by the manufacturer.

WHEEL ALIGNMENT

Year	Model	Caster Range (deg.)	Caster Preferred Setting (deg.)	Camber Range (deg.)	Camber Preferred Setting (deg.)	Toe-in (in.)	Steering Axis Inclination (deg.)
1986	C10/1500 Pick-Up	—	②	0–1⅜P	11/16	3/16 ± 1/8	—
	K10/1500 Pick-Up	—	③	¾P–2P	1½	0 ± 1/8	—
	C20/2500 Pick-Up	—	④	½N–1P	¼	3/16 ± 1/8	—
	K20/2500 Pick-Up	—	③	¾P–2P	1½	0 ± 1/8	—
	C30/3500 Pick-Up	—	④	½N–1P	¼	3/16 ± 1/8	—
	K30/3500 Pick-Up	—	③	¾P–2P	1½	0 ± 1/8	—
	C10/1500 Suburban	—	②	0–1⅜P	11/16	3/16 ± 1/8	—
	K10/1500 Suburban	—	③	¾P–2P	1½	0 ± 1/8	—
	C20/2500 Suburban	—	④	½N–1P	¼	3/16 ± 1/8	—
	K20/2500 Suburban	—	③	¾P–2P	1½	0 ± 1/8	—
	K Blazer/Jimmy	—	③	¾P–2P	1½	0 ± 1/8	—
	G10/1500 Van	—	⑤	¼N–1¼P	½	3/16	—
	G20/2500 Van	—	⑤	¼N–1¼P	½	3/16	—
	G30/3500 Van	—	⑤	½N–1P	¼	3/16	—
1987	R10/1500 Pick-Up	—	②	0–1⅜P	11/16	3/16 ± 1/8	—
	V10/1500 Pick-Up	—	③	¾P–2P	1½	0 ± 1/8	—
	R20/2500 Pick-Up	—	④	½N–1P	¼	3/16 ± 1/8	—
	V20/2500 Pick-Up	—	③	¾P–2P	1½	0 ± 1/8	—
	R30/3500 Pick-Up	—	④	½N–1P	¼	3/16 ± 1/8	—
	V30/3500 Pick-Up	—	③	¾P–2P	1½	0 ± 1/8	—
	R10/1500 Suburban	—	②	0–1⅜P	11/16	3/16 ± 1/8	—
	V10/1500 Suburban	—	③	¾P–2P	1½	0 ± 1/8	—
	R20/2500 Suburban	—	④	½N–1P	¼	3/16 ± 1/8	—
	V20/2500 Suburban	—	③	¾P–2P	1½	0 ± 1/8	—
	K Blazer/Jimmy	—	③	¾P–2P	1½	0 ± 1/8	—
	G10/1500 Van	—	⑤	¼N–1¼P	½	3/16	—
	G20/2500 Van	—	⑤	¼N–1¼P	½	3/16	—
	G30/3500 Van	—	⑤	½N–1P	¼	3/16	—

GENERAL MOTORS CORPORATION
C/K SERIES (PICK-UP) • R/V SERIES (PICK-UP) • BLAZER/JIMMY • SUBURBAN • G SERIES (VAN)

WHEEL ALIGNMENT

Year	Model	Caster		Camber		Toe-in (in.)	Steering Axis Inclination (deg.)
		Range (deg.)	Preferred Setting (deg.)	Range (deg.)	Preferred Setting (deg.)		
1988	C10/1500 Pick-Up	2¾P–4¾P ①	3¾	0–1P	½	⅛	—
	K10/1500 Pick-Up	3P–5P ①	4	¹³/₃₂P–¹³/₃₂P	²⁹/₃₂	¹/₁₆	—
	C20/2500 Pick-Up	2¾P–4¾P ①	3¾	0–1P	½	⅛	—
	K20/2500 Pick-Up	3P–5P ①	4	¹³/₃₂P–1¹³/₃₂P	²⁹/₃₂	¹/₁₆	—
	C30/3500 Pick-Up	2¾P–4¾P ①	3¾	0–1P	½	⅛	—
	K30/3500 Pick-Up	3P–5P ①	4	¼P–1¼P	¾	¹/₁₆	—
	R20/2500 Pick-Up	—	④	½N–1P	¼	³/₁₆	—
	R30/3500 Pick-Up	—	④	½N–1P	¼	³/₁₆	—
	U30/3500 Pick-Up	—	④	¾–2	1½	⅛	—
	R10 Suburban	—	⑥	0–1⅜P	¹¹/₁₆	³/₁₆	—
	V10 Suburban	—	③	¾–2P	1½	⅛	—
	R20 Suburban	—	④	½N–1P	¼	³/₁₆	—
	V20 Suburban	—	③	¾P–2P	1½	⅛	—
	V Blazer/Jimmy	—	③	¾P–2P	1½	⅛	—
	G10/1500 Van	—	⑤	¼N–1¼	½	³/₁₆	—
	G20/2500 Van	—	⑤	¼N–1¼	½	³/₁₆	—
	G30/3500 Van	—	⑤	½N–1P	¼	³/₁₆	—
1989	C1500 Pick-Up	2¾P–4¾P ①	3¾	0–1P	½	⅛	—
	K1500 Pick-Up	2P–4P ①	3	⁵/₃₂P–1⁵/₃₂P	²¹/₃₂	⅛	—
	C2500 Pick-Up	2¾P–4¾P ①	3¾	0–1P	½	⅛	—
	K2500 Pick-Up	2P–4P ①	3	⁵/₃₂P–1⁵/₃₂P	²¹/₃₂	⅛	—
	C3500 Pick-Up	2¾P–4¾P ①	3¾	0–1P	½	⅛	—
	K3500 Pick-Up	2P–4P ①	3	¼–1¼P	¾	¹/₁₆	—
	R2500 Pick-Up	—	④	½N–1P	¼	³/₁₆	—
	R3500 Pick-Up	—	④	½N–1P	¼	³/₁₆	—
	V3500 Pick-Up	—	③	¾P–2P	1½	⅛	—
	R1500 Suburban	—	⑥	0–1⅜P	¹¹/₁₆	³/₁₆	—
	V1500 Pick-Up	—	③	¾–2	1½	⅛	—
	R2500 Suburban	—	④	½N–1P	¼	³/₁₆	—
	V2500 Suburban	—	③	¾–2P	1½	⅛	—
	V Blazer/Jimmy	—	③	¾–2P	1½	⅛	—
	G10/1500 Van	—	⑤	¼N–1¼P	½	³/₁₆	—
	G20/2500 Van	—	⑤	¼N–1¼P	½	³/₁₆	—
	G30/3500 Van	—	⑤	½N–1P	¼	³/₁₆	—
1990	C1500 Pick-Up	2¾P–4¾P ①	3¾	0–1P	½	⅛	—
	K1500 Pick-Up	2P–4P ①	3	⁵/₃₂P–1⁵/₃₂P	²¹/₃₂	⅛	—
	C2500 Pick-Up	2¾P–4¾P ①	3¾	0–1P	½	⅛	—
	K2500 Pick-Up	2P–4P ①	3	⁵/₃₂P–1⁵/₃₂P	²¹/₃₂	⅛	—
	C3500 Pick-Up	2¾P–4¾P ①	3¾	0–1P	½	⅛	—
	K3500 Pick-Up	2P–4P ①	3	¼–1¼P	¾	¹/₁₆	—
	R2500 Pick-Up	—	④	½N–1P	¼	³/₁₆	—
	R3500 Pick-Up	—	④	½N–1P	¼	³/₁₆	—
	V3500 Pick-Up	—	③	¾P–2P	1½	⅛	—

WHEEL ALIGNMENT

Year	Model	Caster Range (deg.)	Caster Preferred Setting (deg.)	Camber Range (deg.)	Camber Preferred Setting (deg.)	Toe-in (in.)	Steering Axis Inclination (deg.)
1990	R1500 Suburban	—	⑥	0–1 3/8P	11/16	3/16	—
	V1500 Suburban	—	⑥	3/4–2P	1 1/2	1/8	—
	R2500 Suburban	—	④	1/2N–1P	1/4	3/16	—
	V2500 Suburban	—	③	3/4–2P	1 1/2	1/8	—
	V Blazer/Jimmy	—	③	3/4–2P	1 1/2	1/8	—
	G10/1500 Van	—	⑤	1/4N–1 1/4P	1/2	3/16	—
	G20/2500 Van	—	⑤	1/4N–1 1/4P	1/2	3/16	—
	G30/3500 Van	—	⑤	1/2N–1P	1/4	3/16	—

① Caster/camber adjustment kit must be installed to make adjustments
② If ride height is 2 1/2, caster should be 3 5/8
If ride height is 3, caster should be 3 1/8
If ride height is 3 1/2, caster should be 2 5/8
If ride height is 3 3/4, caster should be 2 3/8
If ride height is 4, caster should be 2
③ If ride height is 2 1/2 to 4, caster should be 8
④ If ride height is 2 1/2, caster should be 1 1/2
If ride height is 3, caster should be 15/16
If ride height is 3 1/2, caster should be 5/16
If ride height is 3 3/4, caster should be 1/8
If ride height is 4, caster should be 0
⑤ If ride height is 1 1/2, caster should be 3 3/8
If ride height is 2, caster should be 3
If ride height is 2 1/2, caster should be 2 11/16
If ride height is 3, caster should be 2 5/16
If ride height is 3 1/2, caster should be 2
If ride height is 3 3/4, caster should be 1 13/16
If ride height is 4, caster should be 1 11/16
⑥ If ride height is 2 1/2, caster should be 3 5/8
If ride height is 3, caster should be 3 1/8
If ride height is 3 1/2, caster should be 2 5/8
If ride height is 3 3/4, caster should be 2 3/8
If ride height is 4, caster should be 2 1/8

ENGINE ELECTRICAL

NOTE: Disconnecting the negative battery cable on some vehicles may interfere with the functions of the on board computer systems and may require the computer to undergo a relearning process, once the negative battery cable is reconnected.

Distributor

Removal and Installation

1. Disconnect the negative battery cable.
2. Remove all necessary components in order to gain access to the distributor assembly.
3. Disconnect the distributor electrical connectors. If equipped, disconnect the vacuum line. Mark and remove the spark plug wires.
4. Remove the distributor cap. Position the engine at TDC. Matchmark the rotor and the distributor body. Matchmark the distributor assembly and the engine block.
5. Remove the distributor retaining bolt. Carefully remove the distributor from the vehicle.

NOTE: As the distributor is removed from the engine, the rotor will turn counterclockwise. Observe and mark the start and finish rotation of the rotor. When reinstalling, position the rotor at the last mark and set the distributor into the engine. As the distributor drops into place, the rotor should turn to its original position, providing the engine crankshaft had not been rotated with the distributor out.

6. Installation is the reverse of the removal procedure.

Ignition Timing

Connect the timing light per manufacturers instructions to the engine. Be sure to time the engine on No.1 cylinder. Connect the tachometer to the engine per manufacturers instructions. If the vehicle is equipped with a diesel engine, a special timing light and a digital tachometer must be used. Some engines incorporate a bracket and hole which are cast into the timing case cover for the use of a magnetic timing probe, which is connected to a special electronic timing meter for precise ignition timing. If using this type of timing equipment, be sure to follow the manufacturers instructions.

Adjustment

EXCEPT MAGNETIC TIMING

1. Locate the timing marks on the crankshaft pulley and the front of the timing case cover.
2. Clean off the timing marks.
3. Use chalk or white paint to color the mark on the scale that will indicate the correct timing, when aligned with the mark on the pulley or the pointer.
4. Attach a tachometer to the engine. Attach a timing light to the engine.
5. On some engines, it is necessary to disconnect the EST connector to set the timing. See the underhood sticker for details.
6. Disconnect and plug the vacuum lines to the distributor, if equipped. Loosen the distributor lockbolt just enough so that the distributor can be turned with a little resistance.
7. Adjust the idle to the correct specification.

8. With the timing light aimed at the pulley and the marks on the engine, turn the distributor in the direction of rotor rotation to retard the spark, and in the opposite direction of rotor rotation to advance the spark. Align the marks on the pulley and the engine with the flashes of the timing light.

MAGNETIC TIMING

A bracket and hole are cast into the timing case cover for the use of a magnetic timing probe, which is connected to a special electronic timing meter for precise ignition timing. The probe is inserted into the hole of the bracket until the vibration damper is touched. When the engine is started, the probe is automatically spaced away from the damper by the dampers eccentricity, or being slightly out of center. The probe senses a milled slot on the damper and compensating for the brackets top dead center position, registers the reading on the timing meter. Any necessary corrections can then be made to the ignition timing. Do not use the probe bracket and hole to check the ignition timing when using a conventional timing light.

Alternator

For further information, please refer to "Electrical" in the Unit Repair section.

Belt Tension Adjustment

V-BELT

1. Place a belt tension gauge at the center of the greatest span of a warm not hot drive belt and measure the tension.
2. If the belt is below the specification, loosen the component mounting bracket and adjust to specification.
3. Run the engine at idle for 15 minutes to allow the belt to reseat itself in the pulleys.
4. Allow the drive belt to cool and re-measure the tension. Adjust as necessary to meet the following specifications:
    a. On the 4.3L, 5.0L, 5.7L, 7.4L engines—old belt-90 ft. lbs. (400 N), new belt-135 ft. lbs.(600 N).
    b. On the 4.8L engine—old belt-90 ft. lbs. (400 N), new belt-169 ft. lbs.(750 N).
    c. On the 6.2L diesel engine—old belt-67 ft. lbs. (300 N), new belt-146 ft. lbs.(650 N).

Serpentine Belts

Serpentine belts use an automatic tensioner which is spring activated and can be turned to the left or the right to apply or release the pulley tension.

Removal and Installation

1. Disconnect the negative battery cable. Disconnect the electrical connectors at the alternator.
2. Remove the necessary components in order to gain access to the alternator assembly.
3. Remove the alternator belt. Remove the alternator retaining bolts. Remove the alternator from the vehicle.
4. Installation is the reverse of the removal procedure. Adjust the alternator belt, as required.

Starter

For further information, please refer to "Electrical" in the Unit Repair section.

Removal and Installation

1. Disconnect the negative battery cable. As required, raise and support the vehicle safely.
2. Remove the flywheel cover. Remove the exhaust crossover pipe, as required.

3. Disconnect the electrical wiring harness and battery leads at solenoid terminals.
4. Remove the starter mounting bolts and retaining nuts. Remove the starter assembly from the vehicle.
5. Installation is the reverse of the removal procedure. Install any shims that were removed with the starter.

Diesel Glow Plugs

Removal and Installation

1. Disconnect the negative battery cable.
2. Disconnect the electrical connection at the glow plug.
3. Using a suitable tool remove the glow plug.
4. Installation is the reverse of removal. Torque the glow plugs to 12 ft. lbs.

Testing

INHIBIT SWITCH

Check the temperature controlled switch to make sure it is closed at low temperatures and open at high temperatures.

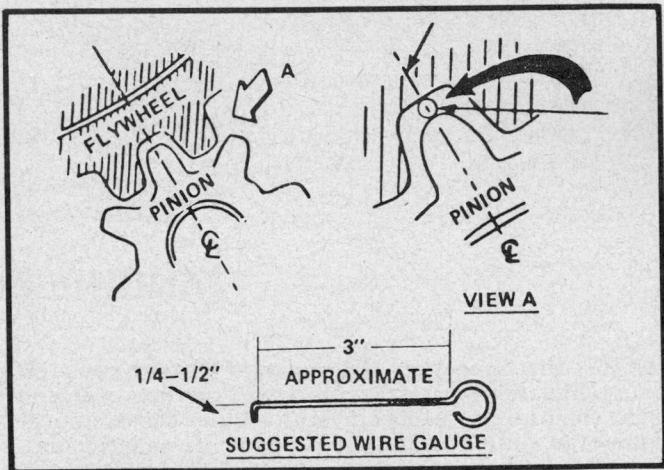

Flywheel to starter pinion clearance during starter installation

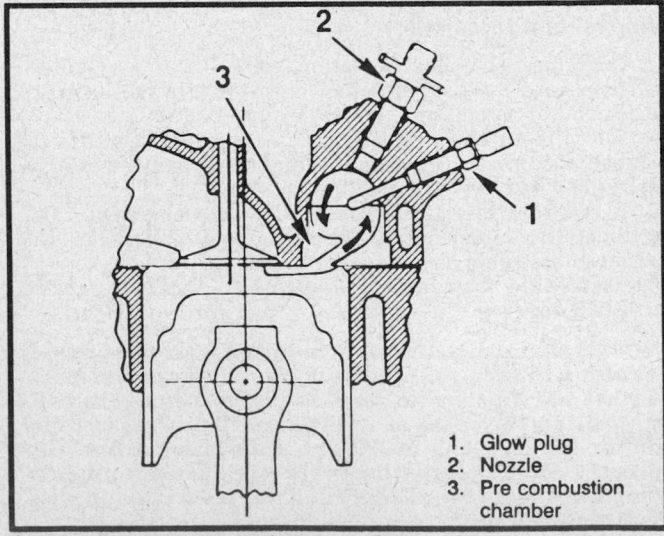

Diesel engine glow plug location

1. Glow plug
2. Nozzle
3. Pre combustion chamber

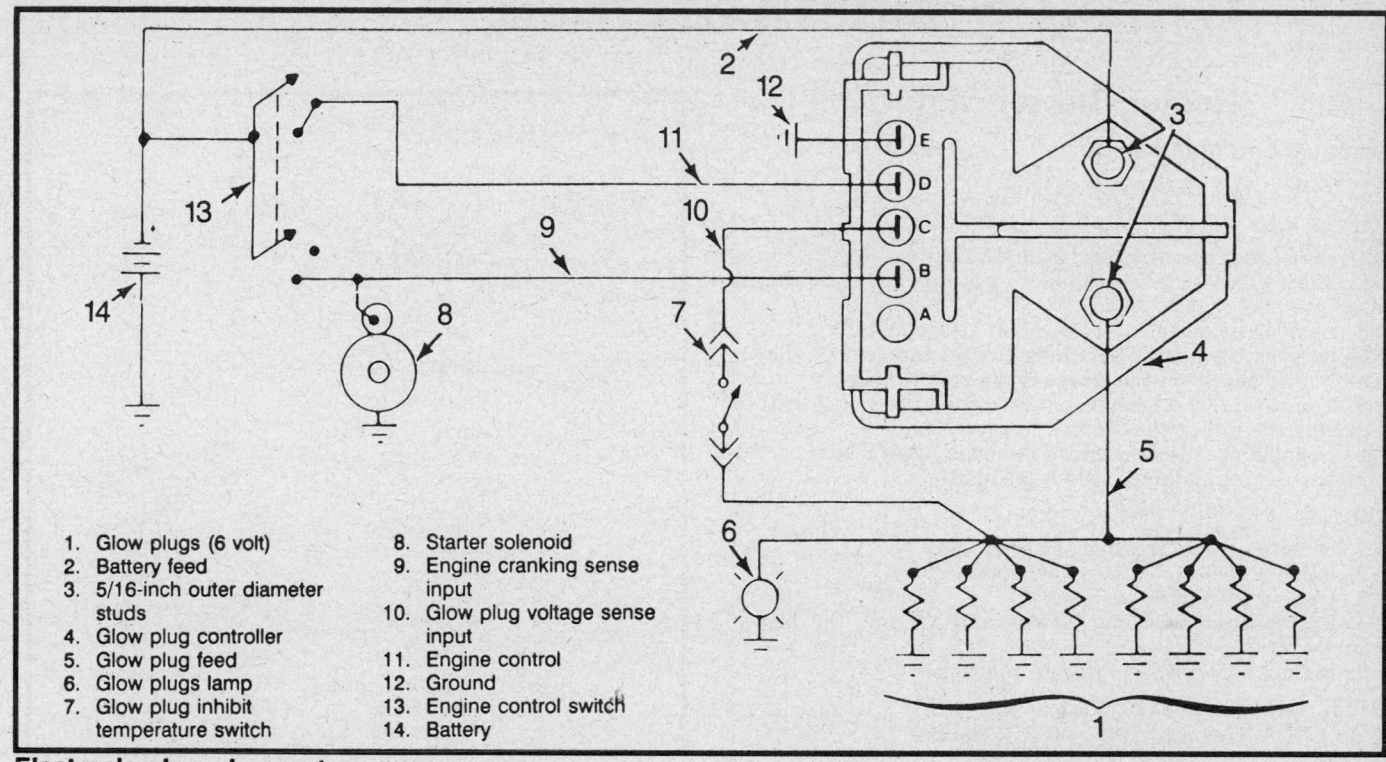

1. Glow plugs (6 volt)
2. Battery feed
3. 5/16-inch outer diameter studs
4. Glow plug controller
5. Glow plug feed
6. Glow plugs lamp
7. Glow plug inhibit temperature switch
8. Starter solenoid
9. Engine cranking sense input
10. Glow plug voltage sense input
11. Engine control
12. Ground
13. Engine control switch
14. Battery

Electronic glow plug system

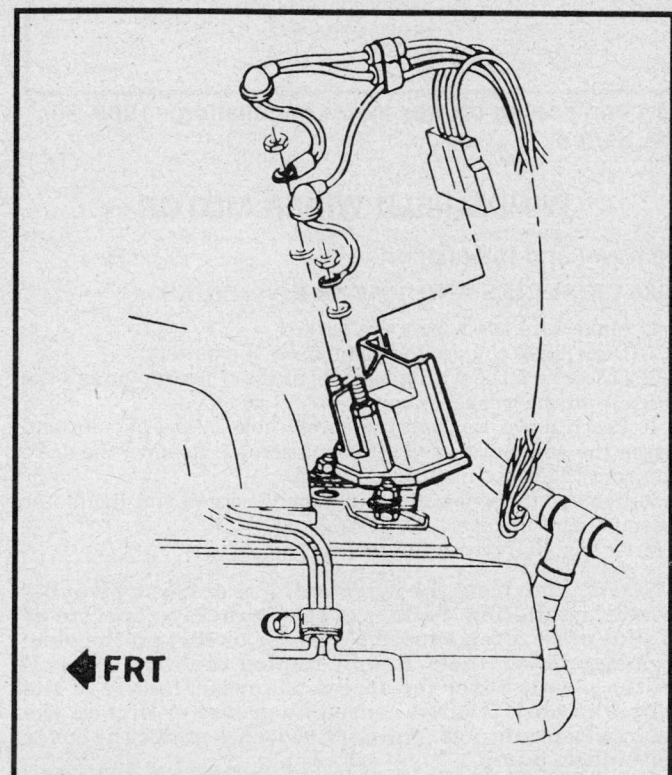

◄FRT

Glow plug controller

1. Remove the connector from the inhibit switch when the engine temperature is below 100°F.

2. Set the ohmmmeter on a low range or use a self powered test lamp.

3. Test across the terminals. The switch should be closed (test lamp on or a reading of less than 0.1 ohm on the meter).

4. Test terminals to ground with a test lamp or the ohmmeter on a high range. The lamp should be off or the meter show greater than 1.0 megaohm.

5. Replace the switch if it test open across the terminals or if either terminal is closed to the ground.

6. Disconnect the plug from the switch terminals when the engine is above 125 degrees F.

7. Set the ohmmeter on the highest scale or use a self powered test lamp and test across the terminals. Test across each terminal to ground.

8. The switch should be open (test lamp off or high ohm reading of greater than 1 megohm on the meter).

9. Replace the switch if it is closed. Use a socket wrench when installing the switch and torque to 17 ft. lbs.

Controller

The glow plug controller provides glow plug operation after starting a cold engine.

1. With the engine cold 80 °F, turn the engine control switch to the **RUN** position and let the glow plugs cycle.

2. After 2 minutes crank the engine for 1 second. (It is not important that the engine starts.) Return the engine control switch to **RUN**. The glow plugs should cycle at least once after cranking.

3. If the the plugs do not turn on, disconnect the controller connector and check terminal B with a grounded 12 volt test lamp. The lamp should be off with the engine control switch in **RUN**, and on when the engine is cranked.

4. If the lamp does not operate as described, repair a short or open in the engine harness purple wire.

5. If the lamp works right but the afterstart glow plug feature does not, replace the controller.

CHASSIS ELECTRICAL

Heater Blower Motor

Removal and Installation

WITHOUT AIR CONDITIONING

Except Van

1. Disconnect the negative battery terminal.
2. Mark the position of the blower motor in relation to its case.
3. Remove the electrical connection at the motor.
4. Remove the blower attaching screws and remove the assembly. Pry gently on the flange if the sealer sticks.
5. The blower wheel can be removed from the motor shaft by removing the nut at the center.
6. Installation is the reverse of removal. Apply a bead of sealer to the mounting flange before installation.

Van

1. Disconnect the negative battery cable.
2. Remove the coolant overflow bottle.
3. Unplug the motor wiring.
4. Remove the attaching screws and lift out the blower motor.
5. Installation is the reverse of removal.

WITH AIR CONDITIONING

1986 C/K Series and 1987–90 R/V Series

1. Disconnect the negative battery terminal.
2. Remove the attaching bolts and nuts and on the diesel engine, remove the insulating shield from the case.
3. Mark the position of the blower motor in relation to its case.
4. Remove the electrical connection at the motor.
5. Disconnect the blower motor cooling tube.
6. Remove the blower attaching screws and remove the assembly. Pry gently on the flange if the sealer sticks.
7. The blower wheel can be removed from the motor shaft by removing the nut at the center.
8. Installation is the reverse of removal. Apply a bead of sealer to the mounting flange before installation.

1988–90 C/K Series

1. Disconnect the negative battery terminal.
2. Remove the electrical connection at the motor.
3. Remove the blower attaching screws and remove the assembly. Pry gently on the flange if the sealer sticks.
4. The blower wheel can be removed from the motor shaft by removing the nut at the center.
5. Installation is the reverse of removal. Apply a bead of sealer to the mounting flange before installation.

1986–89 Van

1. Disconnect the negative battery cable.
2. Remove the power antenna, if so equipped.
3. Remove the coolant overflow bottle.
4. Unplug the motor wiring.
5. Remove the attaching screws and lift out the blower motor.
6. Installation is the reverse of removal.

1990 Van

1. Disconnect the negative battery terminal.
2. Remove the coolant overflow bottle.
3. Unplug the motor wiring.
4. Remove the attaching screws and lift out the blower motor.
5. Installation is the reverse of removal.

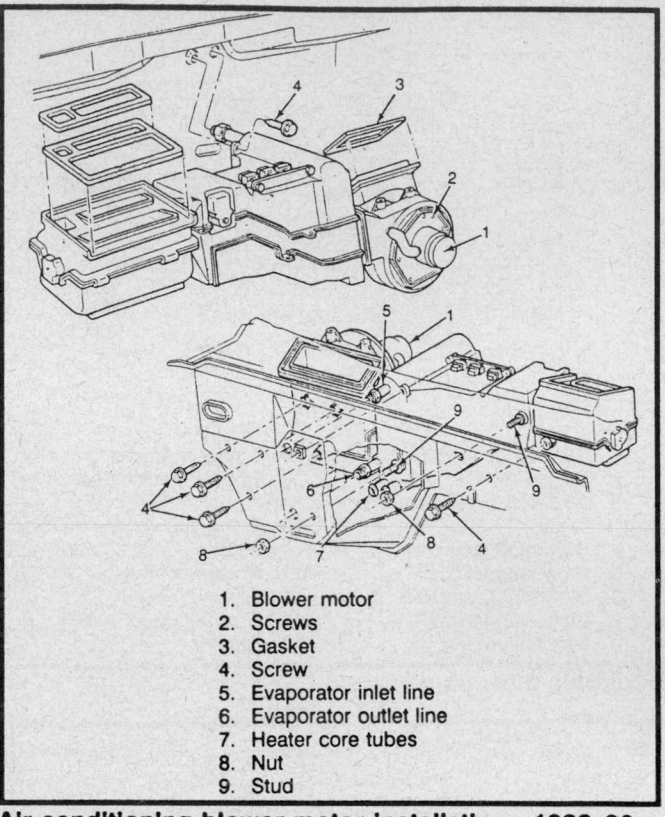

1. Blower motor
2. Screws
3. Gasket
4. Screw
5. Evaporator inlet line
6. Evaporator outlet line
7. Heater core tubes
8. Nut
9. Stud

Air conditioning blower motor installation—1988–90 C/K Series

WINDSHIELD WIPER MOTOR

Removal and Installation

1986 CK SERIES AND 1987–90 R/V SERIES

1. Make sure the wipers are parked.
2. Disconnect the ground cable from the battery.
3. Disconnect the wiring harness at the wiper motor and the hoses from the washer pump.
4. Reach down through the access hole in the plenum and loosen the wiper drive rod attaching screws. Remove the drive rod from the wiper motor crank arm.
5. Remove the wiper motor attaching screws and the motor assembly and linkage.
6. To install, reverse the removal procedure.

NOTE: Lubricate the wiper motor crank arm pivot before reinstallation. Failure of the washers to operate or to shut off is often caused by grease or dirt on the electromagnetic contacts. Simply unplug the wire and pull off the plastic cover for access. Likewise, failure of the wipers to park is often caused by grease or dirt on the park switch contacts. The park switch is under the cover behind the pump.

1988–90 C/K SERIES

1. Disconnect the battery ground cable.
2. Pivot the wiper arm away from the windshield, move the latch to the open position and lift the wiper arm off of the driveshaft.

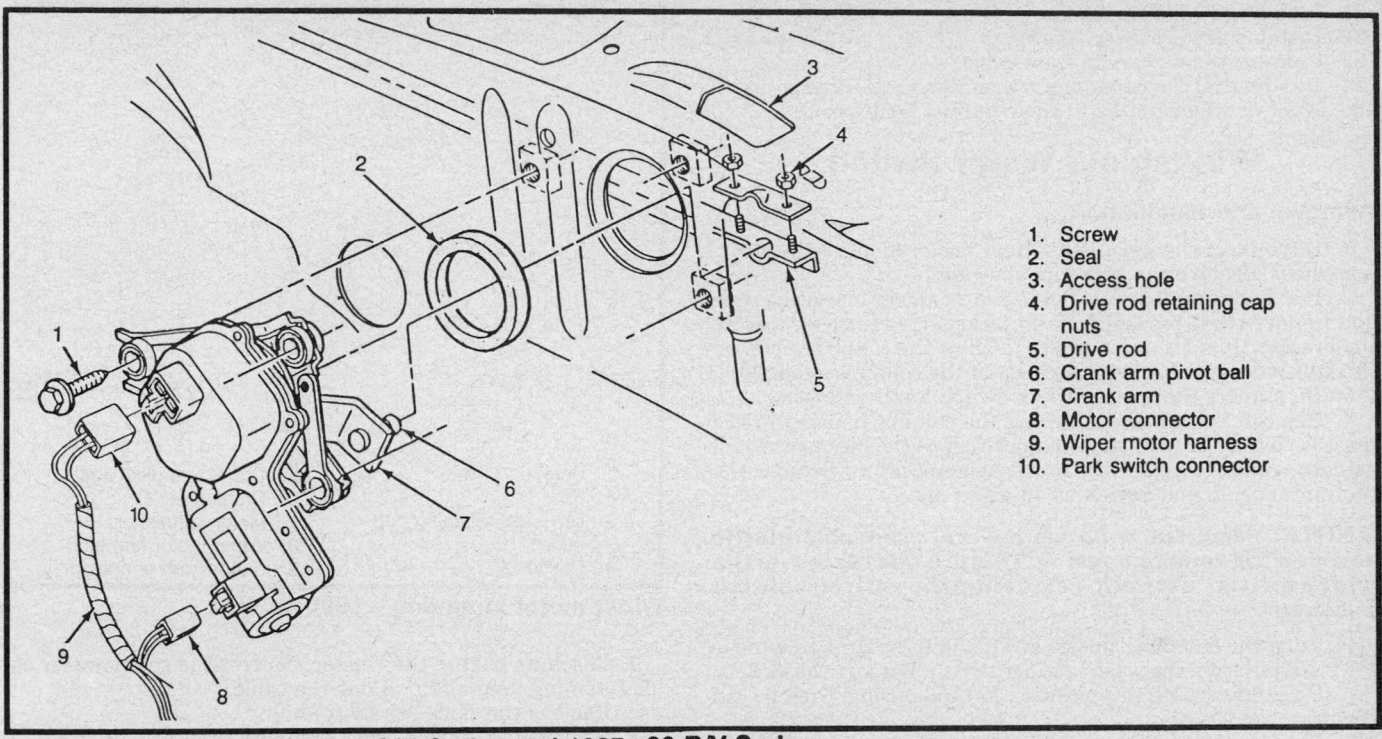

1. Screw
2. Seal
3. Access hole
4. Drive rod retaining cap nuts
5. Drive rod
6. Crank arm pivot ball
7. Crank arm
8. Motor connector
9. Wiper motor harness
10. Park switch connector

Wiper motor mounting—1986 C/K Series and 1987– 90 R/V Series

3. Remove the cowl vent grille.
4. Unplug the wiring from the motor.
5. Remove the drive link-to-crank arm screws and slide the links from the arm.
6. Remove the motor mounting bolts and lift the motor out.
7. Installation is the reverse of removal.

VAN

1. Make sure the wipers are parked. The wiper arms should be in their normal **OFF** position.
2. Open the hood and disconnect the battery ground cable.
3. Remove the exposed cowl cover screws with the hood up.
4. Remove the wiper arms. This can be done by pulling the wiper arms away from the glass to release the clip underneath. The wiper arms are splined to the shafts and can be pulled off.
5. Remove the remaining screws securing the cowl panel and remove it.
6. Loosen the nuts holding the transmission linkage to the wiper motor crank arm.
7. Disconnect the power feed to the wiper arm at the connector next to the radio.
8. Remove the flex hose from the left defroster outlet to gain access to the wiper motor screws.
9. Remove the screw holding the left hand heater duct to the engine shroud and move the heater duct down and out.
10. Remove the windshield washer hoses from the pump.
11. Remove the 3 screws holding the wiper motor to the cowl and lift the wiper motor out from under the dash.

To install:
12. Position the wiper motor in the park position.
13. Position the wiper motor under the dash.
14. Install the 3 screws holding the wiper motor to the cowl.
15. Install the windshield washer hoses at the pump.
16. Install the screw holding the left hand heater duct to the engine.
17. Install the flex hose at the left defroster outlet.
18. Connect the power feed to the wiper arm at the connector next to the radio.

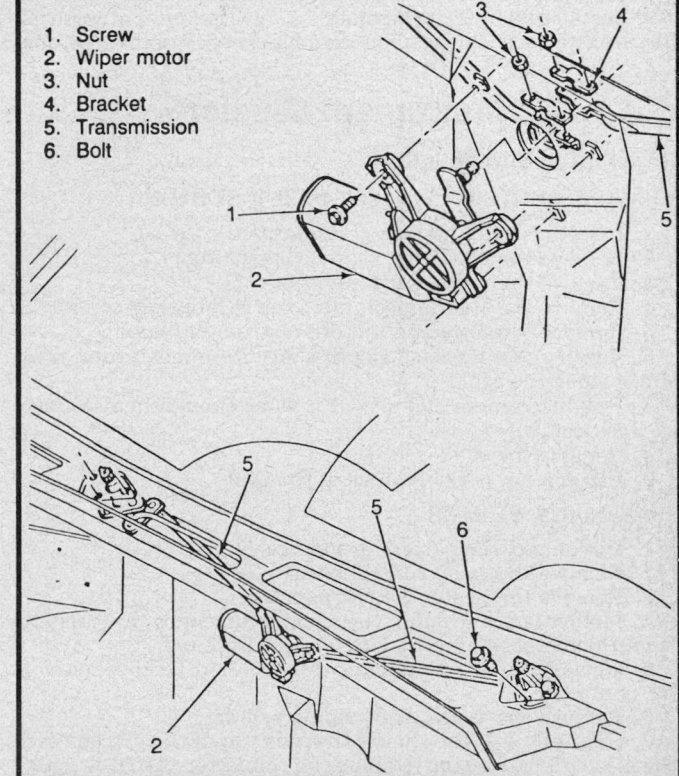

1. Screw
2. Wiper motor
3. Nut
4. Bracket
5. Transmission
6. Bolt

Wiper motor mounting—1988–90 C/K Series

19. Tighten the nuts holding the transmission linkage to the wiper motor crank arm.
20. Install the cowl panel.

21. Install the wiper arms.
22. Install the cowl cover screws.
23. Connect the battery ground cable.
24. Be sure that the wiper motor arm is in the parked position. The wiper arms should be in their normal **OFF** position.

Windshield Wiper Switch

Removal and Installation

1. Disconnect the negative battery cable. Remove the steering wheel. Remove the turn signal switch.
2. It may be necessary to loosen the 2 column mounting nuts and remove the 4 bracket to mast jacket screws, then separate the bracket from the mast jacket to allow the connector clip on the ignition switch to be pulled out of the column assembly.
3. Disconnect the washer/wiper switch lower connector.
4. Remove the screws attaching the column housing to the mast jacket. Be sure to note the position of the dimmer switch actuator rod for reassembly in the same position. Remove the column housing and switch as an assembly.

NOTE: Some tilt columns have a removable plastic cover on the column housing. This provides access to the wiper switch without removing the entire column housing.

5. Turn the assembly upside down and use a drift to remove the pivot pin from the washer/wiper switch. Remove the switch.
6. Place the switch into position in the housing, then install the pivot pin.
7. Position the housing onto the mast jacket and attach by installing the screws. Install the dimmer switch actuator rod in the same position as noted earlier. Check switch operation.
8. Reconnect lower end of switch assembly.
9. Install remaining components in reverse order of removal. Be sure to attach column mounting bracket in original position.

Instrument Cluster

Removal and Installation

1986 C/K SERIES AND 1987-90 R/V SERIES

1. Disconnect the battery ground cable.
2. Remove the headlamp switch control knob.
3. Remove the radio control knobs.
4. Remove the steering column cover 4 retaining screws.
5. Remove 8 screws and remove instrument bezel.
6. Reach under the dash, depress the speedometer cable tang, and remove the cable.
7. Pull instrument cluster out just far enough to disconnect all lines and wires.
8. Remove the cluster.
9. Installation is the reverse of removal.

1988-90 C/K SERIES

1. Disconnect the battery ground cable.
2. Remove the radio control head.
3. Remove the heater control panel.
4. Momentarily ground the cluster assembly by jumping from the metal retaining plate to a good ground.
5. On vehicles with automatic transmission, remove the cluster trim plate.
6. Remove the 4 cluster retaining screws.
7. Carefully pull the cluster towards you until you can reach the electrical connector. Unplug the connector. Avoid touching the connector pins.
8. Installation is the reverse of removal.

VAN

1. Disconnect the battery ground cable.

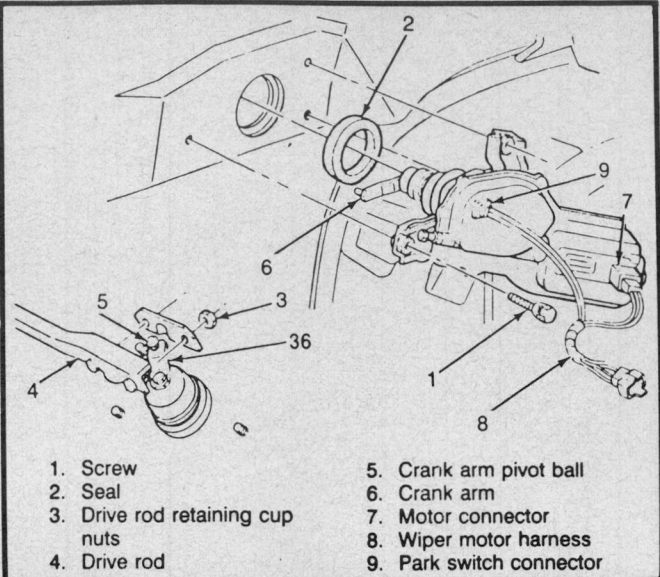

1. Screw
2. Seal
3. Drive rod retaining cup nuts
4. Drive rod
5. Crank arm pivot ball
6. Crank arm
7. Motor connector
8. Wiper motor harness
9. Park switch connector

Wiper motor mounting — 1986-90 Van

2. Reach up behind the cluster, depress the speedometer cable retaining tang and pull out the cable.
3. Remove the clock set stem knob.
4. Remove the cluster bezel retaining screws.
5. Remove the cluster bezel.
6. Remove the 2 lower cluster retaining screws.
7. Pull the top of the cluster away from the panel and lift out the bottom of the cluster. Pull the cluster out just far enough to unplug the wiring and remove the cluster.
8. Installation is the reverse of removal.

Speedometer

Removal and Installation

1986 C/K SERIES AND 1987-90 R/V SERIES

1. Disconnect the negative battery cable.
2. Remove the headlamp switch knob assembly.
3. Remove the radio control knobs.
4. Remove the clock adjuster stem.
5. Remove the instrument cluster bezel.
6. Remove the steering column cover.
7. Remove the instrument cluster lens.
8. Remove the transmission shift indicator.
9. Remove the cluster retainer.
10. Depress the spring clip and disconnect the speedometer cable.
11. Remove the speedometer.
12. Installation is the reverse of removal.

1988-90 C/K SERIES

1. Disconnect the negative battery cable.
2. Remove the cluster.
3. Remove the speedometer mounting screws.
4. Carefully pull the speedometer from the circuit board. Avoid touching any of the circuit board pins.
5. Installation is the reverse of removal.

VAN

1. Disconnect the negative battery cable.
2. Remove the cluster.
3. Remove the speedometer dial retaining screws.
4. Remove the 2 hex head screws and rubber grommets that hold the speedometer assembly to the cluster cover.

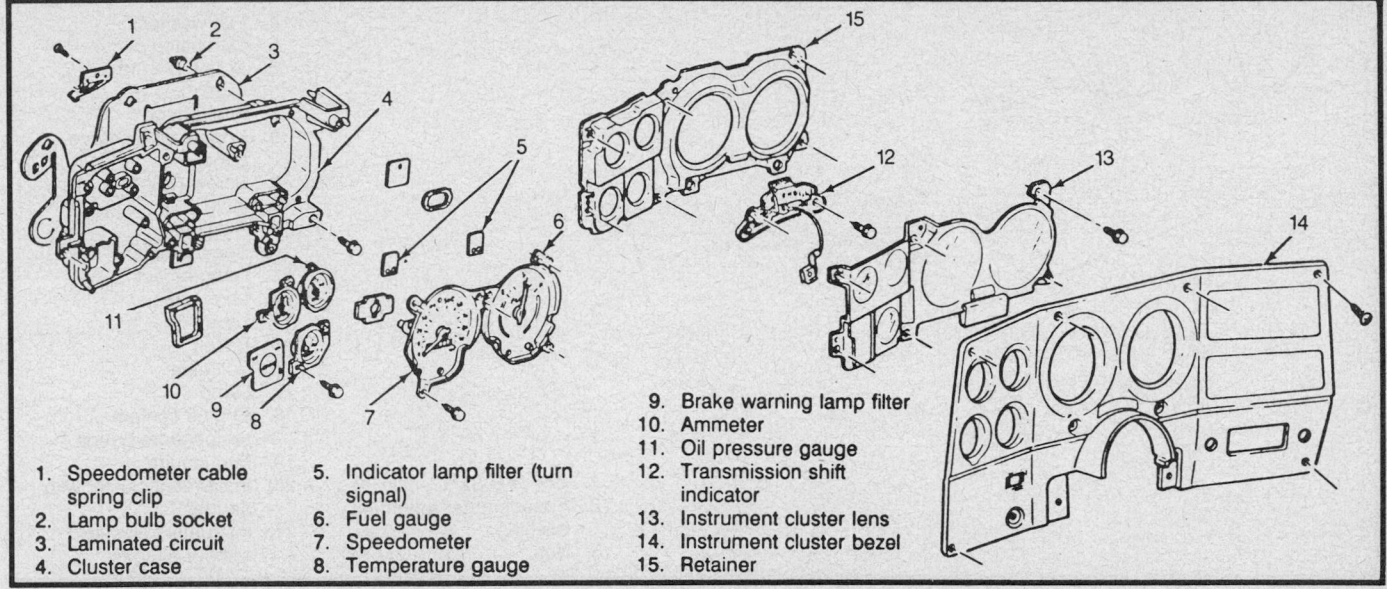

1. Speedometer cable spring clip
2. Lamp bulb socket
3. Laminated circuit
4. Cluster case
5. Indicator lamp filter (turn signal)
6. Fuel gauge
7. Speedometer
8. Temperature gauge
9. Brake warning lamp filter
10. Ammeter
11. Oil pressure gauge
12. Transmission shift indicator
13. Instrument cluster lens
14. Instrument cluster bezel
15. Retainer

Exploded view of the cluster assembly — 1986 C/K Series and 1987–90 R/V Series

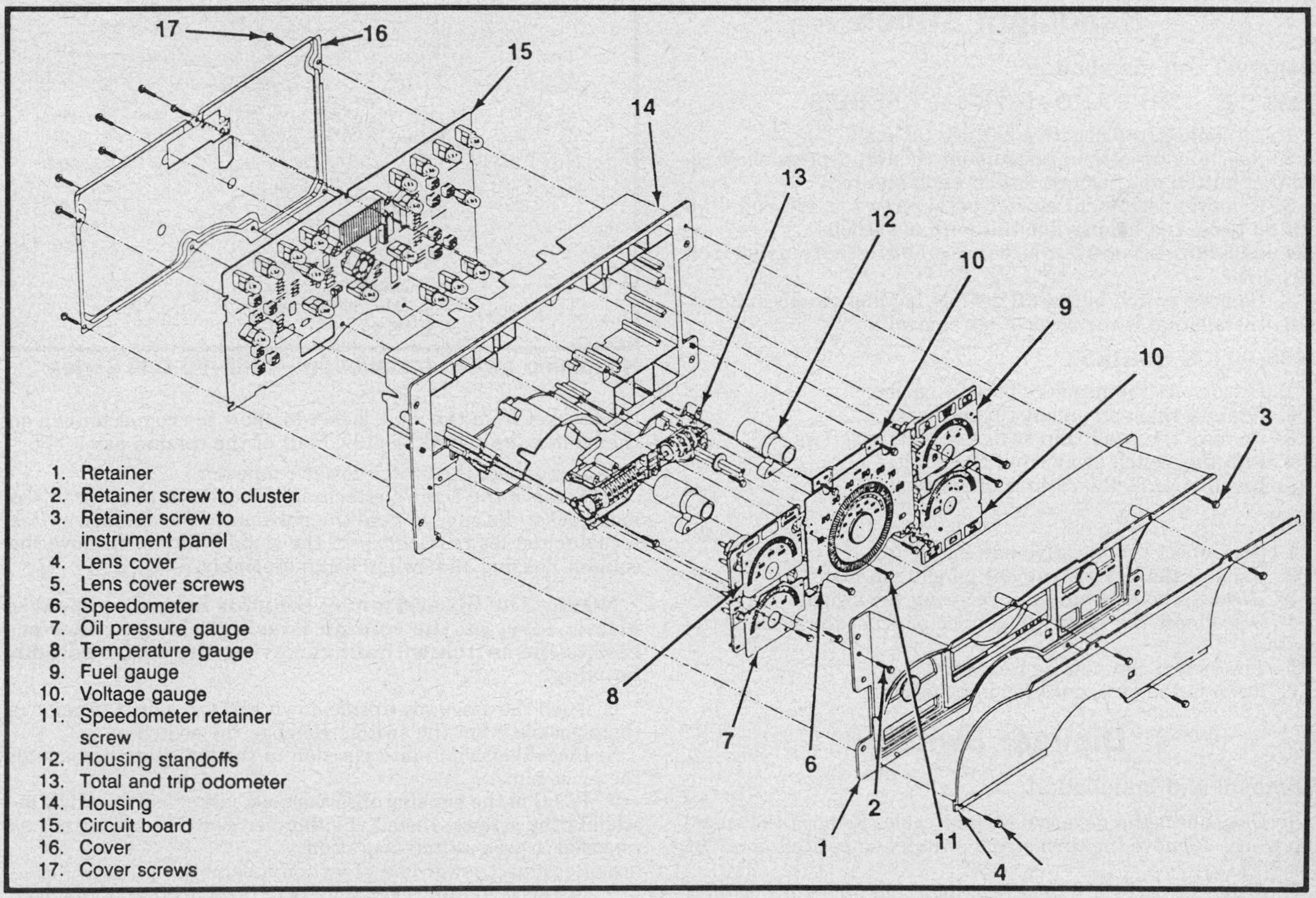

1. Retainer
2. Retainer screw to cluster
3. Retainer screw to instrument panel
4. Lens cover
5. Lens cover screws
6. Speedometer
7. Oil pressure gauge
8. Temperature gauge
9. Fuel gauge
10. Voltage gauge
11. Speedometer retainer screw
12. Housing standoffs
13. Total and trip odometer
14. Housing
15. Circuit board
16. Cover
17. Cover screws

Exploded view of the cluster assembly — 1988–90 C/K Series

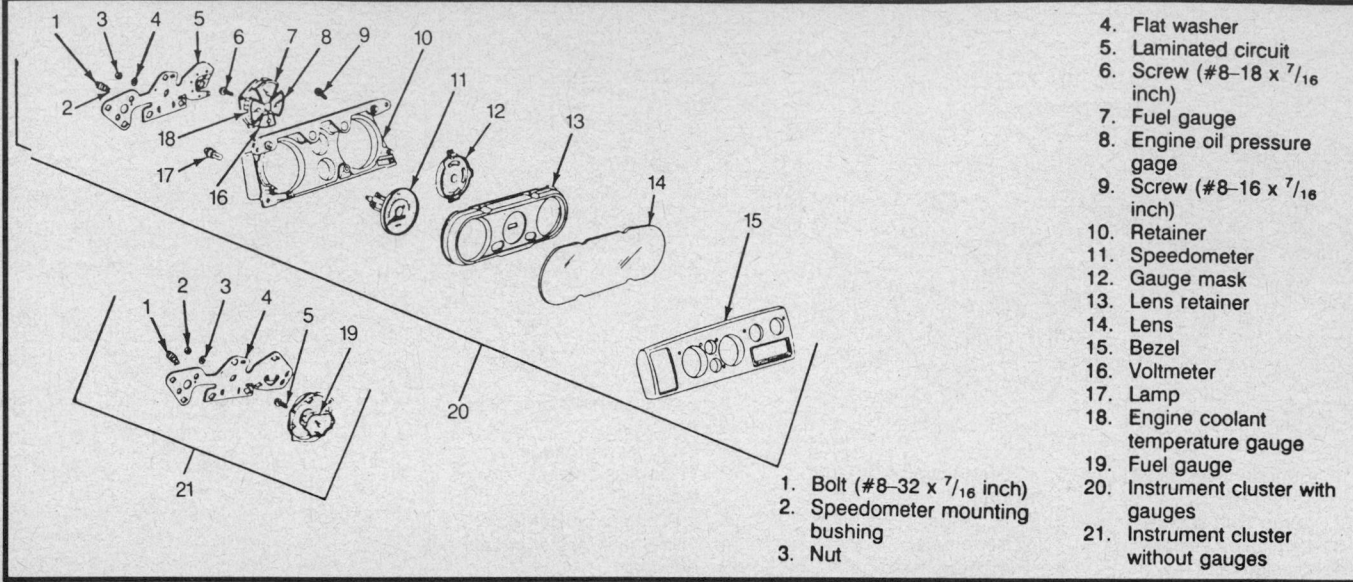

4. Flat washer
5. Laminated circuit
6. Screw (#8–18 x 7/16 inch)
7. Fuel gauge
8. Engine oil pressure gage
9. Screw (#8–16 x 7/16 inch)
10. Retainer
11. Speedometer
12. Gauge mask
13. Lens retainer
14. Lens
15. Bezel
16. Voltmeter
17. Lamp
18. Engine coolant temperature gauge
19. Fuel gauge
20. Instrument cluster with gauges
21. Instrument cluster without gauges

1. Bolt (#8–32 x 7/16 inch)
2. Speedometer mounting bushing
3. Nut

Exploded view of the cluster assembly—1986–90 Van

5. Disconnect the speedometer cable from the speedometer and remove the speedometer.
6. Installation is the reverse of removal.

HeadLight Switch

Removal and Installation

1986 C/K SERIES AND 1987–90 R/V SERIES

1. Disconnect the negative battery cable.
2. Reaching up behind instrument cluster, depress shaft retaining button and remove switch knob and rod.
3. Remove instrument cluster bezel screws on left end. Pull out on bezel and hold switch nut with a wrench.
4. Disconnect multiple wiring connectors at switch terminals.
5. Remove switch by rotating while holding switch nut.
6. Installation is the reverse of removal.

1988–90 C/K SERIES

1. Disconnect the negative battery cable.
2. Remove the instrument cluster bezel.
3. Remove the headlamp switch retaining screws.
4. Pull the switch away from the bezel.
5. Installation is the reverse of removal.

VAN

1. Disconnect the negative battery cable.
2. Remove the left instrument panel trim plate.
3. Remove the retaining nut securing the switch.
4. Disconnect the electrical connector from the back of the switch.
5. The switch can now be removed.
6. Reverse the procedure for installation.

Dimmer Switch

Removal and Installation

1. Disconnect the negative battery cable. Remove the steering wheel. Remove the turn signal switch and position it out of the way.
2. It may be necessary to loosen the 2 column mounting nuts and remove the 4 bracket to mast jacket screws, then separate

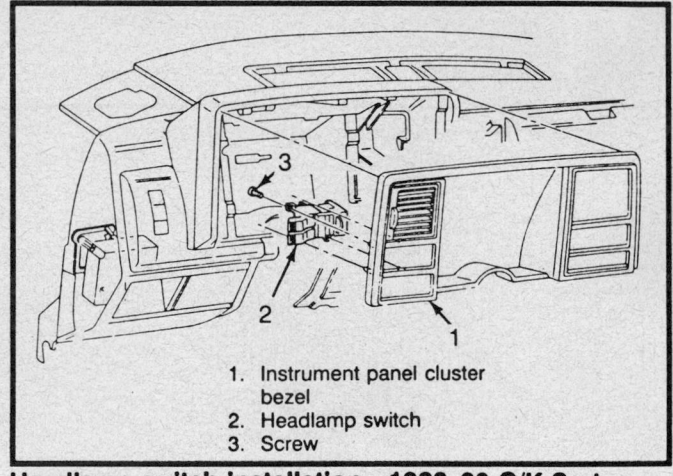

1. Instrument panel cluster bezel
2. Headlamp switch
3. Screw

Headlamp switch installation—1988–90 C/K Series

the bracket from the mast jacket to allow the connector clip on the ignition switch to be pulled out of the column assembly.

3. Disconnect the switch lower connector.
4. Remove the screws attaching the column housing to the mast jacket. Be sure to note the position of the dimmer switch actuator rod for reassembly in the same position. Remove the column housing and switch as an assembly.

NOTE: The tilt and travel columns have a removable plastic cover on the column housing. This provides access to the switch without removing the entire column housing.

5. Turn the assembly upside down and use a drift to remove the pivot pin from the switch. Remove the switch.
6. Place the switch into position in the housing, then install the pivot pin.
7. Position the housing onto the mast jacket and attach by installing the screws. Install the dimmer switch actuator rod as required. Check switch operation.
8. Reconnect lower end of switch assembly.
9. Install remaining components in reverse order of removal. Be sure to attach column mounting bracket in original position.

Turn Signal Switch

Removal and Installation

STANDARD STEERING COLUMN

1. Disconnect the negative battery cable.
2. Remove the steering wheel.
3. Insert a suitable tool into the lockplate and remove the lockplate cover assembly.
4. Install a spring compressor onto the steering shaft. Tighten the tool to compress the lockplate and the spring. Remove the snapring from the groove in the shaft.
5. Remove the lockplate and slide the turn signal cam and the upper bearing preload spring and the thrust washer off the upper steering shaft.
6. Remove the steering column lower cover.
7. Remove the turn signal lever from the column.
8. On vehicles equipped with cruise control, disconnect the cruise control wire from the harness near the bottom of the column. Remove the harness protector from the cruise control wire. Remove the turn signal lever. Do not remove the wire from the column.
9. Remove the vertical bolts at the steering column upper support. Remove the shim packs. Keep the shims in order for reinstallation.
10. Remove the screws securing the column upper mounting bracket to the column. Remove the bracket.
11. Disconnect the turn signal wiring and remove the wires from the plastic protector.
12. Remove the turn signal switch mounting screws.
13. Slide the switch connector out of the bracket on the steering column.
14. If the switch is known to be bad, cut the wires and discard the switch. Before cutting the wires, verify that the wire codes are the same. Tape the connector of the new switch to the old wires, and pull the new harness down through the steering column while removing the old wires.
15. If the original switch is to be reused, wrap tape around the wire and connector and pull the harness up through the column. It may be helpful to attach a length of wire to the harness connector before pulling it up through the column to facilitate installation.
16. After freeing the switch wiring protector from its mounting, pull the turn signal switch straight up and remove the switch, switch harness, and the connector from the column.

17. Installation is the reverse of the removal procedure.

TILT STEERING COLUMN

1. Disconnect the negative battery cable. Remove the steering wheel.
2. Remove the rubber sleeve bumper from the steering shaft.
3. Remove the plastic retainer and disengage the tabs on the retainer from the C-ring.
4. Compress the upper steering shaft preload spring with a spring compressor and remove the C-ring. When installing the spring compressor, pull the upper shaft up about one inch and turn the ignition to the **LOCK** position to hold the shaft in place.
5. Remove the spring compressor and remove the upper steering shaft lockplate, horn contact carrier and the preload spring.
6. Remove the steering column lower cover. Unscrew and remove the turn signal lever.
7. If equipped with cruise control, disconnect the cruise control wire from the harness near the bottom of the steering column. Slide the protector off the cruise control wire. Remove the lever attaching screw and carefully pull the lever out enough to allow the removal of the turn signal switch.
8. Remove the nuts and shim packs from the upper column support. Keep the shims together as a unit for reinstallation.
9. Remove the bracket from the steering column by removing the two attaching screws from each side.
10. Disconnect the turn signal wiring harness and remove the wires from the plastic protector.
11. Remove the turn signal switch retaining screws and pull the switch up out of the steering column.
12. If the switch is to be replaced, cut the wires from the switch and tape the new switch connector to the old wires. Verify that the wire codes are the same, before cutting the wires. Carefully pull the new harness down through the column as the old wires are removed.
13. If the old switch is to be reused, tape the connector to the wires and carefully pull the harness up out of the column.
14. Feed the wiring harness down through the steering column to replace the old switch.
15. Secure the switch in the steering column.
16. Install the upper shaft preload spring.
17. Install the lockplate and carrier assembly. Make sure that the flat on the lower end of the steering shaft is pointing up and that the small plastic tab on the carrier is up or nearest the top

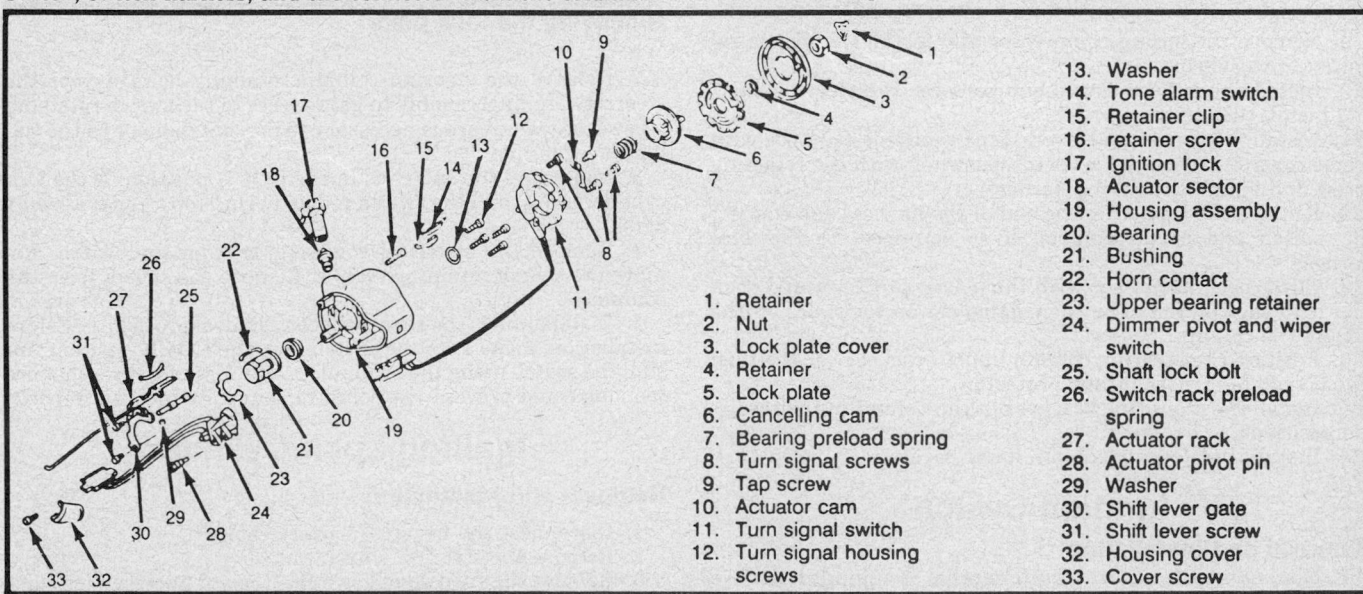

1. Retainer
2. Nut
3. Lock plate cover
4. Retainer
5. Lock plate
6. Cancelling cam
7. Bearing preload spring
8. Turn signal screws
9. Tap screw
10. Actuator cam
11. Turn signal switch
12. Turn signal housing screws
13. Washer
14. Tone alarm switch
15. Retainer clip
16. retainer screw
17. Ignition lock
18. Acuator sector
19. Housing assembly
20. Bearing
21. Bushing
22. Horn contact
23. Upper bearing retainer
24. Dimmer pivot and wiper switch
25. Shaft lock bolt
26. Switch rack preload spring
27. Actuator rack
28. Actuator pivot pin
29. Washer
30. Shift lever gate
31. Shift lever screw
32. Housing cover
33. Cover screw

Turn signal switch location — except 1988–90 C/K Series with tilt wheel

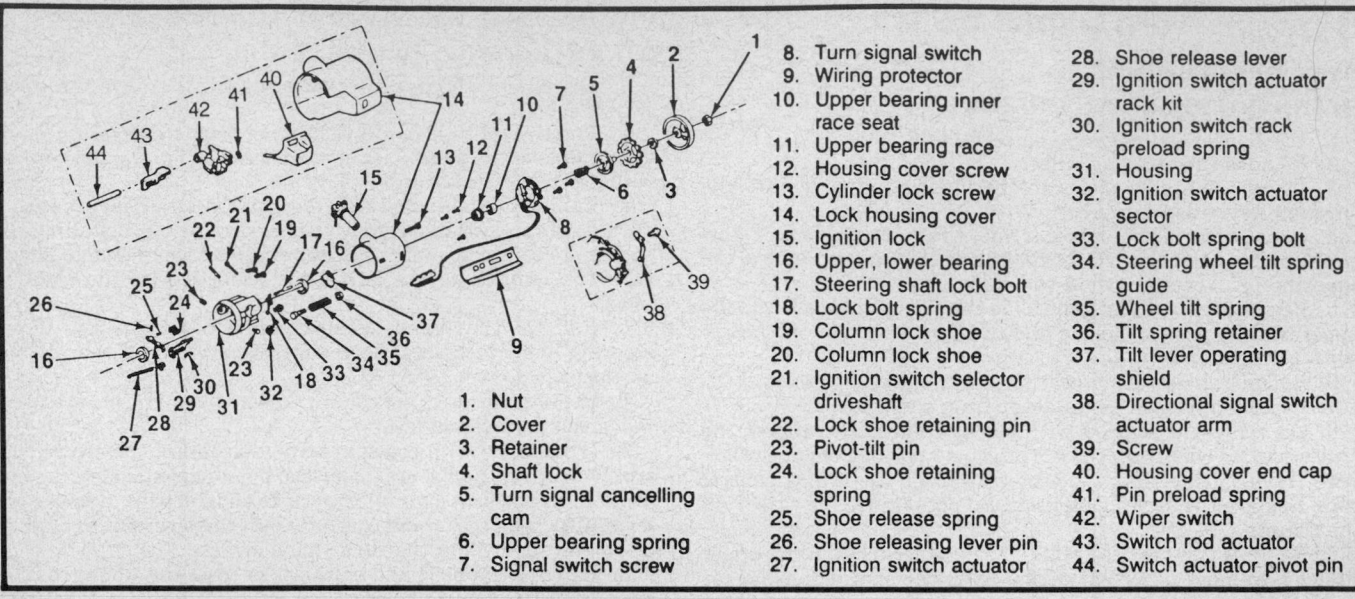

8. Turn signal switch
9. Wiring protector
10. Upper bearing inner race seat
11. Upper bearing race
12. Housing cover screw
13. Cylinder lock screw
14. Lock housing cover
15. Ignition lock
16. Upper, lower bearing
17. Steering shaft lock bolt
18. Lock bolt spring
19. Column lock shoe
20. Column lock shoe
21. Ignition switch selector driveshaft
22. Lock shoe retaining pin
23. Pivot-tilt pin
24. Lock shoe retaining spring
25. Shoe release spring
26. Shoe releasing lever pin
27. Ignition switch actuator

28. Shoe release lever
29. Ignition switch actuator rack kit
30. Ignition switch rack preload spring
31. Housing
32. Ignition switch actuator sector
33. Lock bolt spring bolt
34. Steering wheel tilt spring guide
35. Wheel tilt spring
36. Tilt spring retainer
37. Tilt lever operating shield
38. Directional signal switch actuator arm
39. Screw
40. Housing cover end cap
41. Pin preload spring
42. Wiper switch
43. Switch rod actuator
44. Switch actuator pivot pin

1. Nut
2. Cover
3. Retainer
4. Shaft lock
5. Turn signal cancelling cam
6. Upper bearing spring
7. Signal switch screw

Turn signal switch location—1988–90 C/K Series with tilt wheel

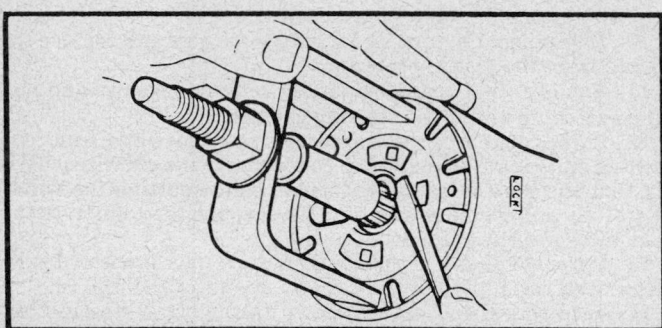

Removing the lock plate retaining ring

of the column. The flat surface of the lockplate must be installed facing down against the turn signal switch.

18. Install the spring compressor, compress the preload spring and lockplate and install the C-ring with the wide side toward the keyway.

19. Remove the spring compressor and install the plastic retainer on the C-ring.

20. Install the rubber sleeve bumper over the steering shaft and install the steering wheel.

21. Install the turn signal lever. If the vehicle is equipped with cruise control, secure the lever to the switch with the retaining screw and install the wiring harness.

22. Remove the tape from the end of the harness and connect the switch and cruise control, if so equipped, to the wire harness.

23. Cover both harnesses with the plastic protector and position it to the column. The turn signal connector slides on the tabs of the column.

24. Position the steering column upper bracket over the turn signal switch harness plastic protector.

25. Install the mounting bracket nuts and shims in their original positions.

26. Install the steering column lower cover.

Ignition Switch

Removal and Installation

1. Disconnect the negative battery cable. If equipped, remove the lower trim panel.

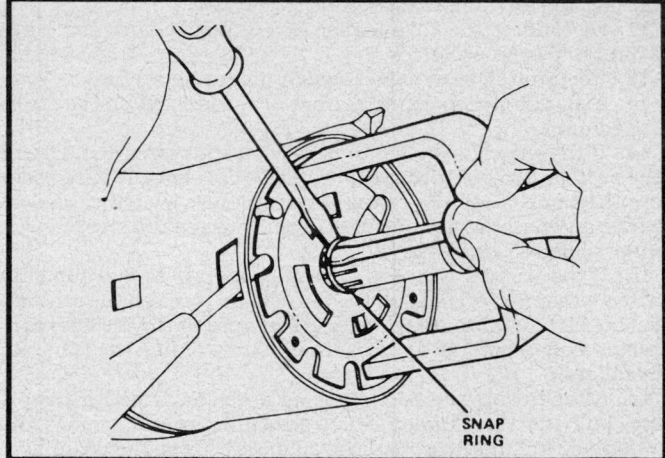

Removing the lock plate

2. Remove the steering column retaining bolts. Lower the steering column assembly to gain access to the switch retaining screws. Extreme care is necessary to prevent damage to the collapsible column.

3. Make sure the switch is in the **LOCK** position. If the lock cylinder is out, pull the switch rod up to the stop, then go down 1 detent.

4. Remove the electrical connections from the switch. Remove the switch retaining screws. Remove the switch from the column.

5. Installation is the reverse of the removal procedure. Before installation, make sure the switch is in the **LOCK** position. Install the switch using the original screws. Use of screws that are too long could prevent the column from collapsing on impact.

Ignition Lock Cylinder

Removal and Installation

1. Disconnect the negative battery cable.
2. Remove the steering wheel.
3. Remove the turn signal switch. It is not necessary to completely remove the switch from the column. Pull the switch

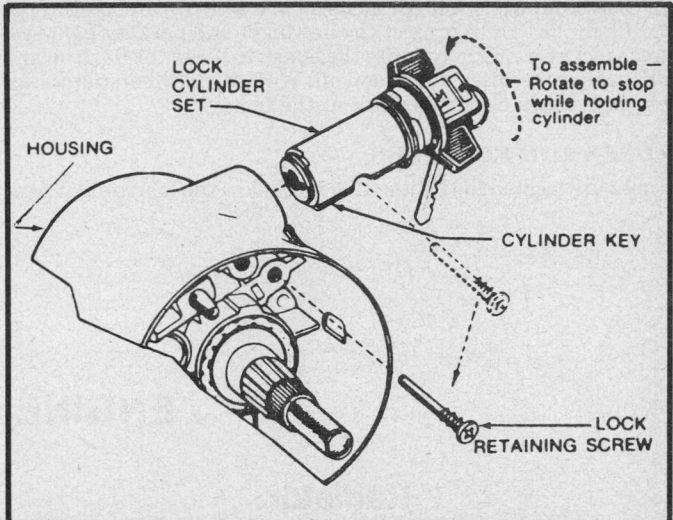

Ignition switch shown in the LOCK position for removal

rearward far enough to slip it over the end of the shaft, but do not pull the harness out of the column.

4. Turn the lock to **RUN**.
5. Remove the lock retaining screw and remove the lock cylinder.

NOTE: If the retaining screw is dropped on removal, it may fall into the column, requiring complete disassembly of the column to retrieve the screw.

6. To install, rotate the key to the stop while holding onto the cylinder.
7. Push the lock all the way in.
8. Install the screw. Tighten the screw to 40 inch lbs. for regular columns, 22 inch lbs. for adjustable columns.
9. Install the turn signal switch and the steering wheel.

Stoplight Switch

Removal and Installation

1. Disconnect the negative battery cable.
2. Disconnect the switch electrical connections. Remove the switch assembly from its mounting.
3. Installation is the reverse of the removal procedure. Adjust the switch, as required.

Adjustment

EXCEPT 1988–90 C/K SERIES

1. Depress the brake pedal and press the switch in until it is firmly seated in its mounting.
2. Pull the brake pedal against the pedal stop until the switch does not make any noise.
3. Electrical contact should be made when the brake pedal is depressed from its fully released position.

1988–90 C/K SERIES

1. Depress the brake pedal fully.
2. Pull the lever on the brake switch back to its stop.
3. Pull the brake pedal back to its stop position.

Fuses and Circuit Breakers

Location

FUSIBLE LINKS

In addition to circuit breakers and fuses, the wiring harness incorporates fusible links to protect the wiring. Links are used rather than a fuse, in wiring circuits that are not normally fused, such as the ignition circuit. Fusible links are color coded red in the charging and load circuits to match the color of the circuits they protect. Each link is four gauges smaller than the cable it protects, and is marked on the insulation with the gauge

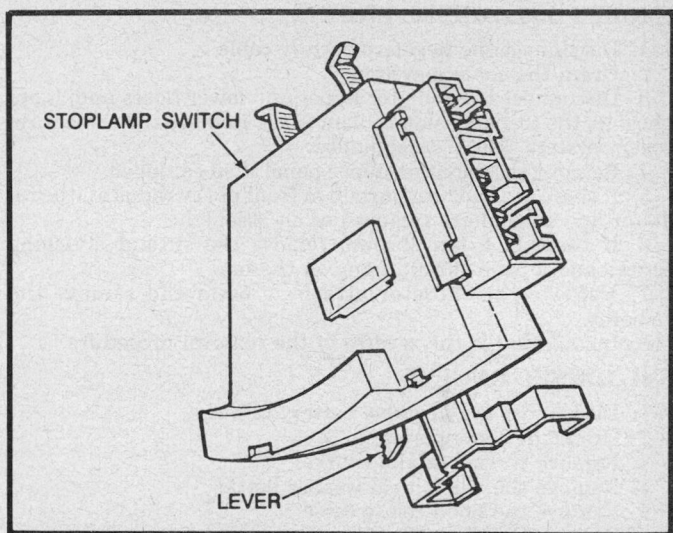

Ignition lock cylinder removal and installation

Stoplamp switch adjustment lever — 1988–90 C/K Series

size because the insulation makes it appear heavier than it really is.

The engine compartment wiring harness has several fusible links. The same size wire with a special hypalon insulation must be used when replacing a fusible link. The links are located in the following areas:

1. A molded splice at the starter solenoid BAT terminal, a 14 gauge red wire.
2. A 16 gauge red fusible link at the junction block to protect the unfused wiring of 12 gauge or larger wire. This link stops at the bulkhead connector.
3. The alternator warning light and field circuitry is protected by a 20 gauge red wire fusible link used in the battery feed to voltage regular No. 1 terminal. The link is installed as a molded splice in the circuit at the junction block.
4. The ammeter circuit is protected by two 20 gauge fusible links installed as molded splices in the circuit at the junction block and battery to starter circuit.

CIRCUIT BREAKERS

A circuit breaker is an electrical switch which breaks the circuit

in case of an overload. All models have a circuit breaker in the headlight switch to protect the headlight and parking light systems. An overload may cause the lamps to flicker or flash on and off, or in some cases, to remain off. Windshield wiper motors are protected by a circuit breaker at the motor.

FUSES AND FLASHERS
Fuses are located in the junction box below the instrument pan-el to the left of the steering column. The turn signal flasher and the hazard/warning flasher also plug into the fuse block. Each fuse receptacle is marked as to the circuit it protects and the correct amperage of the fuse. Inline fuses are also used on the underhood lamp and air conditioning.

NOTE: A special heavy duty turn signal flasher is required to properly operate the turn signals when a trailer's lights are connected to the system.

ENGINE COOLING

Radiator

Removal and Installation
EXCEPT 6.2L DIESEL ENGINE
1. Disconnect the negative battery cable.
2. Drain the cooling system.
3. Disconnect the radiator upper and lower hoses and, if applicable, the transmission coolant lines. Remove the coolant recovery system line, if so equipped.
4. Remove the radiator upper panel if so equipped.
5. If there is a radiator shroud in front of the radiator, the radiator and shroud are removed as an assembly.
6. If there is a fan shroud, remove the shroud attaching screws and let the shroud hang on the fan.
7. Remove the radiator attaching bolts and remove the radiator.
8. Installation is the reverse of the removal procedure.

6.2L DIESEL ENGINE
1. Disconnect the negative battery cables.
2. Drain the cooling system.
3. Remove the air intake snorkel.
4. Remove the windshield washer bottle.
5. Remove the hood relase cable.
6. Remove the upper fan shroud.
7. Disconnect the upper radiator hose.
8. Disconnect the transmission cooler lines.
9. Disconnect the low coolant sensor wire.
10. Disconnect the overflow hose.
11. Disconnect the engine oil cooler lines.
12. Disconnect the lower radiator hose.
13. On the Van, remove the brake master cylinder from the booster.
14. Unbolt and remove the radiator.
To install:
15. Install the radiator.
16. On the Van, install the brake master cylinder on the booster.
17. Connect the lower radiator hose.
18. Connect the engine oil cooler lines.
19. Connect the overflow hose.
20. Connect the low coolant sensor wire.
21. Connect the transmission cooler lines.
22. Connect the upper radiator hose.
23. Install the upper fan shroud.
24. Install the hood relase cable.
25. Install the windshield washer bottle.
26. Install the air intake snorkel.
27. Fill the cooling system.

Auxiliary Electric Cooling Fan

Removal and Installation
1. Disconnect the negative battery cable.
2. Remove the grille.
3. Unplug the fan harness connector.
4. Remove the fan-to-brace bolts and lift out the fan.
5. Installation is the reverse of removal. Torque the bolts to 53 ft. lbs.

Heater Core

Removal and Installation
WITHOUT AIR CONDITIONING
1986 C/K Series and 1987–90 R/V Series
1. Disconnect the battery ground cable.
2. Disconnect the heater hoses at the core tubes and drain the engine coolant. Plug the core tubes to prevent spillage.
3. Remove the nuts from the distributor air ducts in the engine compartment.
4. Remove the glove compartment and door.
5. Disconnect the air-defrost and temperature door cables.
6. Remove the floor outlet and remove the defroster duct-to-heater distributor screw.
7. Remove the heater distributor-to-instrument panel screws. Pull the assembly rearward to gain access to the wiring harness and disconnect the wires attached to the unit.
8. Remove the heater distributor from the vehicle.
9. Remove the heater core retaining straps and remove the core from the vehicle.
10. Installation is the reverse of removal. Be sure that the core-to-core and case-to-dash panel sealer is intact. Fill the cooling system and check for leaks.

1988–90 C/K Series
1. Disconnect the battery ground cable.
2. Remove the coolant overflow bottle.
3. Drain the cooling system.
4. Disconnect the heater hoses at the core tubes.
5. In the engine compartment, remove the heater case-to-firewall screws.
6. Disconnect the antenna cable at the mast.
7. Remove the glove box.
8. Disconnect the wiring harness at the engine's Electronic Control Module (ECM).
9. Remove the ECM and bracket.
10. Remove the right side kick panel.
11. Remove the right side lower dash panel bolt and nut.
12. Remove the heater case mounting bolts.

13. While lifting the instrument panel slightly, remove the case assembly.

14. Lift the core from the case.

To install:

15. Lower the core into the case.

16. Position the case assembly against the firewall.

17. Install the heater case mounting bolts.

18. Install the right side lower dash panel bolt and nut.

19. Install the right side kick panel.

20. Install the ECM and bracket.

21. Connect the ECM wiring harness.

22. Install the glove box.

23. Connect the antenna cable at the mast.

24. Install the heater case-to-firewall screws.

25. Connect the heater hoses at the core tubes.

26. Fill the cooling system.

27. Install the coolant overflow bottle.

28. Connect the battery ground cable.

1986–90 Van

1. Disconnect the negative battery cable.

2. Remove the coolant recovery bottle.

3. Place a pan under the Van and disconnect the heater intake and outlet hoses. Quickly remove and plug the hoses and support them in an upright position. Drain the coolant from the heater core into the pan.

4. Remove the heater distributor duct-to-case attaching screws and the duct-to-engine cover screw. Remove the duct.

5. Remove the engine cover.

6. Remove all the instrument panel attaching screws.

7. Carefully lower the steering column. Raise and support the right side of the instrument panel.

8. Remove the defroster duct-to-case attaching screws and the 2 screws attaching the distributor to the heater case.

9. Disconnect the temperature door cable. Carefully fold the cable back and out of the way.

10. Remove the 3 nuts from the engine compartment side of the distributor case and the screw from the passenger compartment side.

11. Remove the heater case and core assembly.

12. Remove the core retaining straps and remove the core.

To install:

13. Install the core.

14. Install the core retaining straps.

15. Install the heater case and core assembly.

16. Install the 3 nuts on the engine compartment side of the distributor case and the screw on the passenger compartment side.

17. Connect the temperature door cable.

18. Install the defroster duct-to-case attaching screws and the 2 screws attaching the distributor to the heater case.

19. Install the steering column.

20. Install all the instrument panel attaching screws.

21. Install the engine cover.

22. Install the duct. Install the heater distributor duct-to-case attaching screws and the duct-to-engine cover screw.

23. Connect the heater intake and outlet hoses.

24. Fill the cooling system.

25. Install the coolant recovery bottle.

26. Connect the negative battery cable.

WITH AIR CONDITIONING

1986 C/K and 1987–90 R/V Series

1. Disconnect the battery ground cable.

2. Disconnect the heater hoses at the core tubes and drain the engine coolant. Plug the core tubes to prevent spillage.

3. Remove the glove compartment and door.

4. Disconnect the center duct from the defroster outlet duct.

5. Disconnect the center, lower air distributor and the center air outlet ducts.

6. Disconnect the temperature door cable.

7. Remove the nuts from the 3 selector duct studs that project into the engine compartment.

8. Remove the outlet duct-to-instrument panel screws. Pull the assembly rearward to gain access to the wiring harness and disconnect the wires and vacuum tubes attached to the unit.

9. Remove the heater distributor from vehicle vehicle.

10. Remove the heater core retaining straps and remove the core from the case.

11. Installation is the reverse of removal. Be sure that the core-to-core and case-to-dash panel sealer is intact. Fill the cooling system and check for leaks.

1988–90 C/K Series

1. Disconnect the battery ground cable.

2. Drain the cooling system.

3. Discharge the system.

4. Remove the coolant overflow tank.

5. Disconnect the heater hoses at the core tubes.

6. Disconnect and cap the refrigerant lines at the evaporator.

7. Unplug the electrical connector at the temperature actuator.

8. Remove the 7 attaching screws and remove the heater case bottom plate.

9. Remove the screws and brackets that hold the heater core to the case and lift the core from the case.

To install:

10. Install the heater core in the case.

11. Install the heater case bottom plate.

12. Connect the electrical connector at the temperature actuator.

13. Connect the refrigerant lines at the evaporator. Always use a back-up wrench. Use new O-rings coated with clean refrigerant oil. Tighten the inlet line to 30 ft. lbs.; the outlet line to 18 ft. lbs.

14. Connect the heater hoses at the core tubes.

15. Install the coolant overflow tank.

16. Evacuate and charge the system.

17. Fill the cooling system.

18. Connect the battery ground cable.

1986–90 Van

1. Disconnect the battery ground cable.

2. Remove the engine cover.

3. Remove the steering column to instrument panel bolts. Lower the column carefully.

4. Remove the upper and lower instrument panel attaching screws. Remove the radio support bracket screw.

5. Raise and support the right side of the instrument panel.

6. Remove the lower right instrument panel bracket.

7. Remove the vacuum actuator from the kick panel.

8. Disconnect the temperature cable and vacuum hoses at the case. Remove the heater distributor duct from over the engine hump.

9. Remove the 2 defroster duct to firewall attaching screws below the windshield.

10. Under the hood, disconnect and plug the heater hoses at the firewall.

11. Remove the three nuts and one screw (inside) holding the heater case to the firewall.

12. Remove the case from the vehicle. Remove the gasket for access to the screws holding the case together. Remove the temperature cable support bracket. Remove the screws and separate the case. Remove the heater core.

To install:

13. Install the heater core.

14. Install the screws and separate the case.

15. Install the temperature cable support bracket.

16. Install the gasket.

17. Install the case in the vehicle.

18. Install the three nuts and one screw (inside) holding the heater case to the firewall.

19. Connect and plug the heater hoses at the firewall.

20. Install the two defroster duct-to-firewall attaching screws below the windshield.

21. Install the heater distributor duct.

22. Connect the temperature cable and vacuum hoses at the case.

23. Install the vacuum actuator at the kick panel.

24. Install the lower right instrument panel bracket.

25. Install the radio support bracket screw.

26. Install the upper and lower instrument panel attaching screws.

27. Install the steering column to instrument panel bolts.

28. Install the engine cover.

29. Connect the battery ground cable.

30. Refill the cooling system as necessary.

Water Pump

Removal and Installation

EXCEPT 6.2L DIESEL ENGINE

1. Disconnect the negative battery cable.

2. Drain the radiator.

3. Loosen the alternator and other accessories at their adjusting points, and remove the fan belts from the fan pulley.

4. Remove the fan and pulley.

5. Remove any accessory brackets that might interfere with water pump removal.

6. Disconnect the hose from the water pump inlet and the heater hose from the nipple on the pump. Remove the bolts, pump assembly and old gasket from the timing chain cover.

7. Check the pump shaft bearings for endplay or roughness in operation. Water pump bearings usually emit a squealing sound with the engine running when the bearings need to be replaced. Replace the pump if the bearings are not in good shape or have been noisy.

To install:

8. Make sure the gasket surfaces on the pump and timing chain cover are clean.

9. Install the pump assembly with a new gasket. On all except the 4.8 L engine, tighten the bolts to 30 ft. lbs. On the 4.8 L engine, tighten the bolts to 15 ft. lbs.

10. Connect the hose between the water pump inlet and the nipple on the pump.

11. Install any accessory brackets.

12. Install the fan and pulley.

13. Install and adjust the alternator and other accessories.

14. Install the fan belts from the fan pulley.

15. Fill the cooling system.

16. Connect the battery.

6.2L DIESEL ENGINE

1. Disconnect the negative battery cables.

2. Remove the fan and fan shroud.

3. Drain the radiator.

4. If the vehicle is equipped with air conditioning, remove the air conditioning hose bracket nuts.

5. Remove the oil filler tube.

6. Remove the alternator pivot bolt and remove the generator belt.

7. Remove the alternator lower bracket.

8. Remove the power steering belt and secure it out of the way.

9. Remove the air conditioning belt if equipped.

10. Disconnect the bypass hose and the lower radiator hose.

11. Remove the water pump bolts. Remove the water pump plate and gasket and water pump. If the pump gasket is to be replaced, remove the plate attaching bolts to the water pump and remove (and replace) the gasket.

To install:

12. When installing the pump, the flanges must be free of oil. Apply an anaerobic sealer (GM part No.1052357 or equivalent).

NOTE: The sealer must be wet to the touch when the bolts are torqued.

13. Attach the water pump and plate assembly. Torque the bolts to 35 ft. lbs.

14. Connect the bypass hose and the lower radiator hose.

15. Install the air conditioning belt if equipped.

16. Install the power steering belt.

17. Install the alternator lower bracket.

18. Install the alternator pivot bolt.

19. Install the alternator belt.

20. Install the oil filler tube.

21. If the vehicle is equipped with air conditioning, install the air conditioning hose bracket nuts.

22. Fill the radiator.

23. Install the fan and fan shroud.

24. Connect the batteries.

Thermostat

Removal and Installation

EXCEPT 6.2L DIESEL ENGINE

1. Disconnect the negative battery cable.

2. Drain the radiator until the level is below the thermostat level (below the level of the intake manifold).

3. Remove the water outlet elbow assembly from the engine. Remove the thermostat from inside the elbow.

4. Install new thermostat in the reverse order of removal, making sure the spring side is inserted into the elbow. Clean the gasket surfaces on the water outlet elbow and the intake manifold. Use a new gasket when installing the elbow to the manifold. On the 4.8L engine, torque the thermostat housing bolts to 28 ft. lbs. and on all other engines to 20 ft. lbs.

5. Refill the cooling system.

6.2L DIESEL ENGINE

1. Disconnect the negative battery cables.

2. Remove the upper fan shroud.

3. Drain the cooling system to a point below the thermostat.

4. Remove the engine oil dipstick tube brace and the oil fill brace.

5. Remove the upper radiator hose.

6. Remove the water outlet.

7. Remove the thermostat and gasket.

8. Installation is the reverse of removal. Use a new gasket coated with sealer, Make sure that the spring end of the thermostat is in the engine. Torque the bolts to 35 ft. lbs.

GASOLINE FUEL SYSTEM

Fuel System Service Precaution

When working with the fuel system certain precautions should be taken; always work in a well ventilated area, keep a dry chemical (Class B) fire extinguisher near the work area. Always disconnect the negative battery cable and do not make any repairs to the fuel system until all the necessary steps for repair have been reviewed.

Relieving Fuel System Pressure

The 220 TBI unit used on the V6 and V8 engines has a constant bleed in the pressure regulator to relieve pressure any time the engine is turned off, however a small amount of fuel may be released when the fuel line is disconnected. As a precaution, cover the fuel line with a cloth and dispose of properly. Also, loosen the fuel filler cap to relieve tank vapor pressure.

Fuel Filter

Removal and Installation
CARBURETED ENGINE

Filter In Carburetor

1. Disconnect the negative battery cable.
2. Disconnect the fuel line connecting at the intake fuel filter nut. Plug the opening to prevent loss of fuel.
3. Remove the intake fuel filter nut from the carburetor.
4. Remove the filter element and spring.
5. Check the element for restrictions by blowing on the cone end. Air should pass freely.
6. Clean or replace the element, as necessary.
7. Install the element spring, then the filter element in the carburetor. Bronze filters should have the small section of the cone facing out.
8. Install a new gasket on the intake fuel nut. Install the nut in the carburetor body and tighten securely.
9. Install the fuel line and tighten the connector.

Inline Filter

Some vehicles may have an inline filter. This is a can shaped device located in the fuel line between the pump and the carburetor. It may be made of either plastic or metal. To replace the filter:
1. Disconnect the negative battery cable.
2. Place some absorbent rags under the filter.
3. Use a pair of pliers to expand the clamp on one end of the filter, then slide the clamp down past the point to which the filter pipe extends in the rubber hose. Do the same with the other clamp.
4. Gently twist and pull the hoses free of the filter pipes. Remove and discard the old filter.

NOTE: Most replacement filters come with new hoses that should be installed with a new filter.

4. Install the new filter into the hoses, slide the clamps back into place, and check for leaks with the engine idling.

FUEL INJECTED ENGINE

The inline filter is found along the frame rail.
1. Disconnect the negative battery cable.
2. Release the fuel system pressure.
3. Raise and support the vehicle safely.
4. Disconnect the fuel lines.
5. Remove the fuel filter from the retainer or mounting bolt.
6. To install, reverse the removal procedures. Start the engine and check for leaks.

NOTE: The filter has an arrow (fuel flow direction) on the side of the case, be sure to install it correctly in the system, the with arrow facing away from the fuel tank.

Mechanical Fuel Pump

Testing

Fuel pumps should always be tested on the vehicle. The larger line between the pump and tank is the suction side of the system and the smaller line, between the pump and carburetor, is the pressure side. A leak in the pressure side would be apparent because of dripping fuel. A leak in the suction side is usually only apparent because of a reduced volume of fuel delivered to the pressure side.

1. Tighten any loose line connections and look for any kinks or restrictions.
2. Disconnect the fuel line at the carburetor. Disconnect the distributor-to-coil primary wire. Place a container at the end of the fuel line and crank the engine a few revolutions. If little or no fuel flows from the line, either the fuel pump is inoperative or the line is plugged. Blow through the lines with compressed air and try the test again. Reconnect the line.
3. If fuel flows in good volume, check the fuel pump pressure to be sure.
4. Attach a pressure gauge to the pressure side of the fuel line. On vehicles equipped with a vapor return system, squeeze off the return hose.
5. Run the engine at idle and note the reading on the gauge. Stop the engine and compare the reading to the specification. If the pump is operating properly, the pressure will be as specified and will be constant at idle speed. If pressure varies sporadically or is too high or low, the pump should be replaced.
6. Remove the pressure gauge.

Removal and Installation

1. Disconnect the negative battery cable.
2. Disconnect the fuel intake and outlet lines at the pump and plug the pump intake line.
3. You can remove the upper bolt from the right front engine mounting boss (on the front of the block) and insert a long bolt (³⁄₈ in.-16 × 2 in.) to hold the fuel pump pushrod.
4. Remove the 2 pump mounting bolts and lockwashers; remove the pump and its gasket.
5. If the rocker arm pushrod is to be removed, remove the 2 adapter bolts and lockwashers and remove the adapter and its gasket.
6. Install the fuel pump with a new gasket reversing the removal procedure. Heavy grease can be used to hold the fuel pump pushrod up when installing the pump, if you didn't install the long bolt in Step 2. Coat the mating surfaces with sealer.
7. Connect the fuel lines an check for leaks.

Electric Fuel Pump

Testing

1. Secure 2 sections of ³⁄₈ in. × 10 in. (steel tubing), with a double-flare on 1 end of each section.
2. Install a flare nut on each section of tubing, then connect each of the sections into the flare nut-to-flare nut adapter, while care included in the gauge adapter tool J–29658–82.
3. Attach the pipe and the adapter assembly to the gauge tool J–29658.
4. Raise and support the vehicle safely.
5. Remove the air cleaner and plug the THERMAC vacuum port on the TBI.

6. Disconnect the fuel feed hose between the fuel tank and the filter, then secure the other ends of the ⅜ in. tubing into the fuel hoses with hose clamps.

7. Start the engine, check for leaks and observe the fuel pressure, it should be 9–13 psi.

8. Depressurize the fuel system, remove the testing tool, remove the plug from the THERMAC vacuum port, reconnect the fuel line, start the engine and check for fuel leaks.

Removal and Installation

1. With the engine turned off, relieve the fuel pressure at the pressure regulator.

2. Disconnect the negative battery cable.

3. Raise and support the rear of the vehicle safely.

4. Drain the fuel tank, then remove it.

5. Using a hammer and a drift punch, drive the fuel lever sending device and pump assembly locking ring (located on top of the fuel tank) counterclockwise, lift the assembly from the tank and remove the pump from the fuel lever sending device.

6. Pull the pump up into the attaching hose while pulling it outward away from the bottom support. Be careful not to damage the rubber insulator and strainer during removal. After the pump assembly is clear of the bottom support, pull it out of the rubber connector.

7. To install, reverse the removal procedures.

Carburetor

Removal and Installation

1. Disconnect the negative battery terminal. Remove the air cleaner assembly and gasket.

2. Disconnect the electrical connectors from the choke and idle stop solenoid.

3. Disconnect and tag the vacuum hoses.

4. Disconnect the accelerator linkage, downshift cable and cruise control linkage, if so equipped.

5. Disconnect and plug the fuel line connection at the fuel inlet nut.

6. Remove the carburetor attaching bolts and the carburetor with the flange insulator.

7. Install the carburetor with a new flange gasket. It is good shop practice to fill the carburetor float bowl before installing the carburetor. This reduces the strain on starting motor and battery and reduces the possibility of backfiring while attempting to start the engine. Operate the throttle several times and check the discharge from pump jets before installing the carburetor.

8. Install the carburetor attaching bolts and torque them to 12 ft. lbs. (16 Nm). Be sure to torque the bolts in a criss-cross pattern.

9. Install the fuel line to the fuel inlet nut, cruise control cable, if so equipped, downshift cable, accelerator linkage, vacuum hoses, electrical connectors to the choke and idle stop solenoid, air cleaner assembly with gasket and the negative battery terminal.

NOTE: After servicing the carburetor, tighten the mounting bolts in a clockwise direction to 12 ft. lbs. (16 Nm). When tightening the carburetor at recommended maintenance intervals, check the bolt torque. If less than 5 ft. lbs. (7 Nm), retighten to 8 ft. lbs. (11 Nm); but if greater than 5 ft. lbs. (7 Nm), do not retighten.

Idle Speed and Mixture Adjustment

In case of a major carburetor overhaul, throttle body replacement, or high idle CO (when indicated by an emissions inspection), the idle mixture may be adjusted. Adjusting the mixture by other than the following method may violate Federal and/or state laws. Idle mixture needle socket J–29030–B or equivalent is required for this adjustment.

1. Set the parking brake and block the drive wheels.

2. Remove the carburetor from the engine.

3. Drain the fuel from the the carburetor into a container. Dispose of the fuel in an approved container.

4. Remove the idle mixture needle plugs as follows:

   a. Invert the carburetor and support it to avoid damaging external components.

   b. Make 2 parallel hacksaw cuts in the throttle body, between the locator points near one idle mixture needle plug. The distance between the cuts depends on the size of the punch to be used.

   c. Cut down to the plug, but not more than ⅛ in. beyond the locator point.

   d. Place a flat punch at a point near the ends of the saw marks. Hold the punch at a 45° angle and drive it into the throttle body until the casting breaks away, exposing the steel plug.

   e. Use a center punch to break the plug apart, uncover idle mixture needle. Remove all loose pieces of plug.

   f. Repeat the previous steps for the other needle plug.

5. Use idle mixture needle socket J–29030–B or equivalent to lightly seat the idle mixture needles, then back them out 3 turns.

6. Reinstall the carburetor on the engine.

7. Place the transmission in **P** (automatic transmission) or neutral (manual transmission).

8. Start the engine and bring it to a normal operating temperature, choke valve open, and air conditioning off.

9. Connect a known accurate tachometer to the engine.

10. Check ignition timing, and adjust if necessary, by following the procedure described on the emission control information label located under the hood on the vehicle.

11. Use idle mixture needle socket J–29030–B or equivalent to turn the mixture needles equally (⅛ turn at a time), in or out, to obtain the highest rpm (best idle).

12. Adjust the idle speed screw (throttle stop) to obtain the base idle speed specified on the underhood emission control information label.

13. Again try to readjust mixture needles to obtain the highest idle rpm. The adjustment is correct when the highest rpm (best idle) is reached with the minimum number of mixture needle turns from the seated position.

14. If necessary, readjust the idle speed screw (throttle stop) to obtain the specified base idle speed.

15. Check and if necessary, adjust the idle speed solenoid activated speed and fast idle speed. Refer to the underhood emission control information label.

16. Check the throttle kicker and adjust if necessary.

17. Turn off the engine, remove all test equipment and remove the block from the drive wheels.

Service Adjustments

For all carburetor service adjustment procedures and specifications, please refer to "Carburetor Service" in the Unit Repair section

Fuel Injection

Idle Speed Adjustment

Only if parts of the throttle body have been replaced should this procedure be performed; the engine should be at operating temperature.

1. Remove the air cleaner, adapter and gaskets. Discard the gaskets. Plug any vacuum line ports, as necessary.

2. Leave the idle air control (IAC) valve connected and ground the diagnostic terminal (ALDL connector).

3. Turn the ignition switch to the **ON** position, do not start the engine. Wait for at least 30 seconds (this allows the IAC valve pintle to extend and seat in the throttle body).

4. With the ignition switch still in the **ON** position, disconnect IAC electrical connector.

5. Remove the ground from the diagnostic terminal and start the engine. Let the engine reach normal operating temperature.

6. Apply the parking brake and block the drive wheels. Remove the plug from the idle stop screw by piercing it first with a suitable tool, then applying leverage to the tool to lift the plug out.

7. With the engine in the drive position adjust the idle stop screw to obtain the following specifications:

500–550 rpm in **D** on models equipped with automatic transmissions.

600–650 rpm in neutral on models equipped with manual transmissions.

8. Turn the ignition off and reconnect the IAC valve connector. Unplug any plugged vacuum line ports and install the air cleaner, adapter and new gaskets.

Removing the fuel injector on the TBI 220

Fuel Injector

Removal and Installation

NOTE: When removing the injectors, be careful not to damage the electrical connector pins (on top of the injector), the injector fuel filter and the nozzle. The fuel injector is serviced as a complete assembly only. The injector is an electrical component and should not be immersed in any kind of cleaner.

1. Disconnect the negative battery cable.

2. Remove the air cleaner. Relieve the fuel pressure.

3. At the injector connector, squeeze the 2 tabs together and pull straight up.

4. Remove the fuel meter cover and leave the cover gasket in place.

5. Using a small pry bar or tool No. J–26868, carefully lift the injector until it is free from the fuel meter body.

6. Remove the small O-ring from the nozzle end of the injector. Carefully rotate the injector's fuel filter back and forth to remove it from the base of the injector.

7. Discard the fuel meter cover gasket.

8. Remove the large O-ring and back-up washer from the top of the counterbore of the fuel meter body injector cavity.

9. To install, lubricate the O-rings with automatic transmission fluid and reverse the removal procedures.

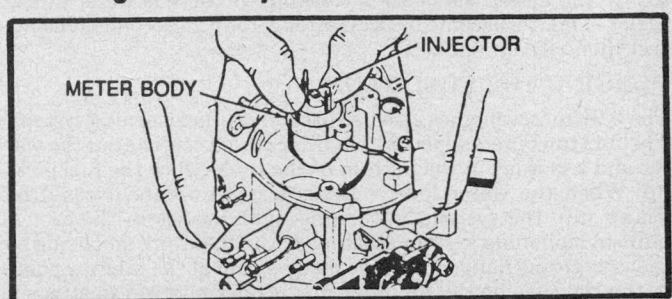
Replacing the fuel injector on the TBI 220

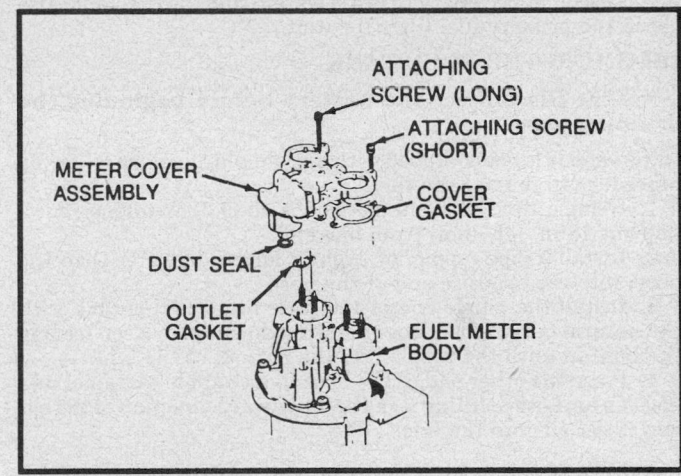
Replacing the fuel meter cover on the TBI 220

DIESEL FUEL SYSTEM

Fuel Filter

Removal and Installation

1. Drain the fuel from the fuel filter by opening both the air bleed and the water drain valve allowing the fuel to drain out into an appropriate container.

2. Remove the fuel tank cap to release any pressure or vacuum in the tank.

3. Unstrap both bail wires with a suitable tool and remove the filter.

4. Before installing the new filter, insure that both filter mounting plate fittings are clear of dirt.

5. Install the new filter, snap into place with the bail wires.

6. Close the water drain valve and open the air bleed valve.

Connect a ⅛ in. (3mm) I.D. hose to the air bleed port and place the other end into a suitable container.

7. Disconnect the fuel injection pump shut off solenoid wire.

8. Crank the engine for 10–15 seconds, then wait 1 minute for the starter motor to cool. Repeat until clear fuel is observed coming from the air bleed.

NOTE: If the engine is to be cranked, or starting attempted with the air cleaner removed, care must be taken to prevent dirt from being pulled into the air inlet manifold which could result in engine damage.

9. Close the air bleed valve, reconnect the injection pump solenoid wire and replace the fuel tank cap.

10. Start the engine, allow it to idle for 5 minutes and check the fuel filter for leaks.

Draining Water From The System

Water is the worst enemy of the diesel fuel injection system. The injection pump, which is designed and constructed to extremely close tolerances, and the injectors can be easily damaged if enough water if forced through them in the fuel. Engine performance will also be drastically affected, and engine damage can occur.

Diesel fuel is much more susceptible than gasoline to water contamination. Diesel engine vehicles are equipped with an indicator lamp system that turns on an instrument panel lamp if water (1–2½ gallons) is detected in the fuel tank. The lamp will come on for 2–5 seconds each time the ignition is turned on, assuring the driver the lamp is working. If there is water in the fuel, the light will come back on after a 15 to 20 second off delay, and then remain on.

PURGING THE FUEL TANK

The 6.2L diesel engines also use a water-in-fuel warning system. The fuel tank is equipped with a filter which screens out the water and lets it lay in the bottom of the tank below the fuel pick-up. When the water level reaches a point where it could be drawn into the system, a warning light flashes in the cab. A built-in siphoning system starting at the fuel tank and going to the rear spring hanger on some models, and at the midway point of the right frame rail on other models permits you to attach a hose at the shut-off and siphon out the water.

If it becomes necessary to drain water from the fuel tank, also check the primary fuel filter for water.

DRAINING THE FUEL TANK

NOTE: Disconnect the battery before beginning the draining operation.

If the vehicle is not equipped with a drain plug, use the following procedure to remove the fuel.

1. Using a 10 ft. (305cm) piece of ⅜ in. (9.525mm) hose cut a flap slit 18 in. (457mm) from one end.
2. Install a pipe nipple, of slightly larger diameter than the hose, into the opposite end of the hose.
3. Install the nipple end of the hose into the fuel tank with the natural curve of the hose pointing downward. Keep feeding the hose in until the nipple hits the bottom of the tank.
4. Place the other end of the hose in a suitable container and insert a air hose pointing it in the downward direction of the slit and inject air into the line.

NOTE: If the vehicle is to be stored, always drain the fuel from the complete fuel system including, fuel pump supply, fuel injection pump, fuel lines, and tank.

Removal and Installation

1. Disconnect the negative battery cable.
2. Drain the tank.
3. Raise and support the vehicle safely.
4. Remove the clamp on the filler neck and the vent tube hose.
5. Remove the gauge hose which is attached to the frame.
6. While supporting the tank securely, remove the support straps.
7. Lower the tank until the gauge wiring can be removed.
8. Remove the tank.
9. Install the unit by reversing the removal procedure. Make certain that the anti-squeak material is replaced during installation.
10. Lower the vehicle.

Diesel Injection Pump

Removal and Installation

1. Disconnect both batteries.

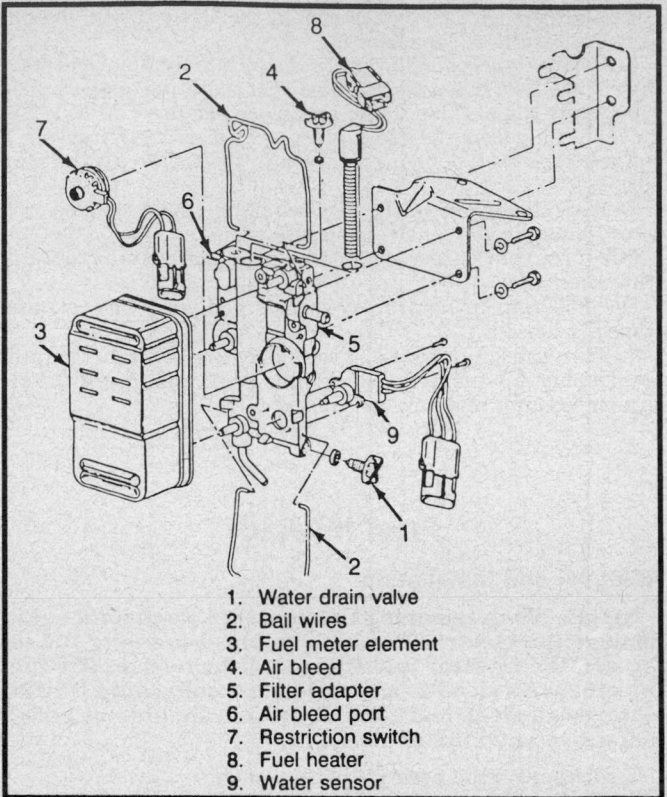

1. Water drain valve
2. Bail wires
3. Fuel meter element
4. Air bleed
5. Filter adapter
6. Air bleed port
7. Restriction switch
8. Fuel heater
9. Water sensor

Diesel engine fuel filter

2. Remove the fan and fan shroud.
3. Remove the intake manifold.
4. Remove the fuel lines.
5. Disconnect the alternator cable at the injection pump, and the detent cable where applicable.
6. Tag and disconnect the necessary wires and hoses at the injection pump.
7. Disconnect the fuel return line at the top of the injection pump.
8. Disconnect the fuel feed line at the injection pump.
9. Remove the air conditioning hose retainer bracket if equipped with A/C.
10. Remove the oil fill tube, including the crankcase depression valve vent hose assembly.
11. Remove the grommet.
12. Scribe or paint a matchmark on the front cover and on the injection pump flange.
13. The crankshaft must be rotated in order to gain access to the injection pump drive gear bolts through the oil filler neck hole.
14. Remove the injection pump-to-front cover attaching nuts. Remove the pump and cap all open lines and nozzles.
To install:
15. Replace the gasket. This is important.
16. Align the locating pin on the pump hub with the slot in the injection pump driven gear. At the same time, align the timing marks.
17. Attach the injection pump to the front cover, aligning the timing marks before torquing the nuts to 30 ft. lbs.
18. Install the drive gear to injection pump bolts, torquing the bolts to 20 ft. lbs.
19. Install the remaining components in the reverse order of removal. Torque the fuel feed line at the injection pump to 20 ft. lbs. Start the engine and check for leaks.

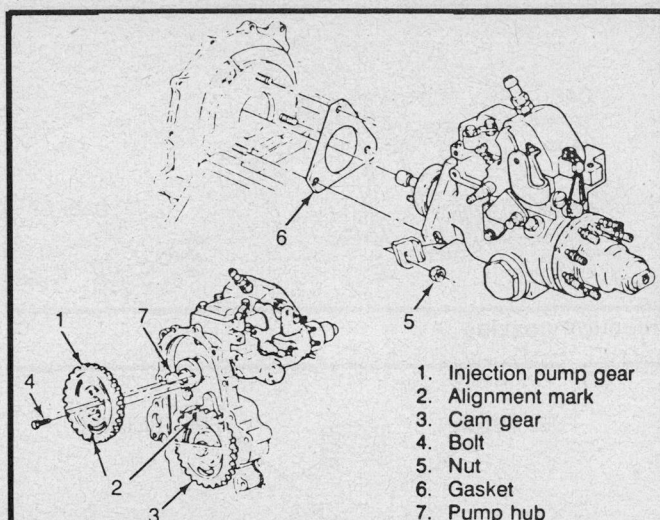

1. Injection pump gear
2. Alignment mark
3. Cam gear
4. Bolt
5. Nut
6. Gasket
7. Pump hub

Diesel injection pump mounting

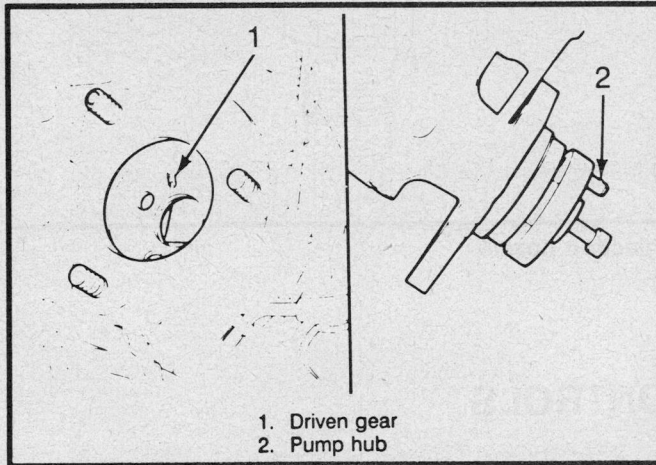

1. Driven gear
2. Pump hub

Diesel injection pump locating pin

Injection Pump Fuel Lines

Removal and Installation

NOTE: When the fuel lines are to be removed, clean all fuel line fittings thoroughly before loosening. Immediately cap the lines, nozzles and pump fittings to maintain cleanliness.

1. Disconnect both batteries.
2. Disconnect the air cleaner bracket at the valve cover.
3. Remove the crankcase ventilator bracket and move it aside.
4. Disconnect the secondary filter lines.
5. Remove the secondary filter adapter.
6. Loosen the vacuum pump hold-down clamp and rotate the pump in order to gain access to the intake manifold bolt. Remove the intake manifold bolts. The injection line clips are retained by the same bolts.
7. Remove the intake manifold. Install a protective cover so no foreign material falls into the engine.
8. Remove the injection line clips at the loom brackets.
9. Remove the injection lines at the nozzles and cover the nozzles with protective caps.
10. Remove the injection lines at the pump and tag the lines for later installation.

11. Remove the fuel line from the injection pump.
12. Install all components in the reverse order of removal.

Idle Speed Adjustment

NOTE: A special tachometer suitable for diesel engines must be used. A gasoline engine type tach will not work with the diesel engine.

1. Set the parking brake and block the drive wheels.
2. Run the engine up to normal operating temperature. The air cleaner must be mounted and all accessories turned off.
3. Install the diesel tachometer as per the manufacturer's instructions.
4. Adjust the low idle speed screw on the fuel injection pump to 650 rpm in neutral for manual transmission equipped vehicles or **P** for automatic transmission equipped vehicles.

NOTE: All idle speeds are to be set within 25 rpm of the specified values.

5. Adjust the fast idle speed as follows:
   a. Remove the connector from the fast idle solenoid. Use an insulated jumper wire from the battery positive terminal to the solenoid terminal to energize the solenoid.
   b. Open the throttle momentarily to ensure that the fast idle solenoid plunger is energized and fully extended.
   c. Adjust the extended plunger by turning the hex-head screw to an engine speed of 800 rpm in neutral.
   d. Remove the jumper wire and reinstall the connector to the fast idle solenoid.
6. Disconnect and remove the tachometer.

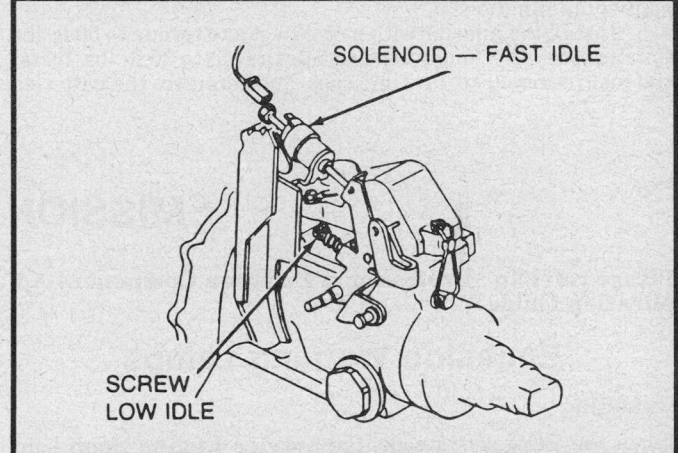

SOLENOID — FAST IDLE

SCREW LOW IDLE

Diesel injection pump idle adjustment locations

Injection Timing Adjustment

For the engine to be properly timed, the lines on the top of the injection pump adapter and the flange of the injection pump must be aligned.
1. The engine must be off for resetting the timing.
2. Loosen the 3 pump retaining nuts with tool J–26987, an injection pump intake manifold wrench, or its equivalent.
3. Align the mark on the injection pump with the marks on the adapter and tighten the nuts. Torque to 35 ft. lbs. Use a ¾ in. open-end wrench on the boss at the front of the injection pump to aid in rotating the pump to align the marks.
4. Adjust the throttle rod.

Fuel Injector

Removal and Installation

1. Disconnect both batteries.

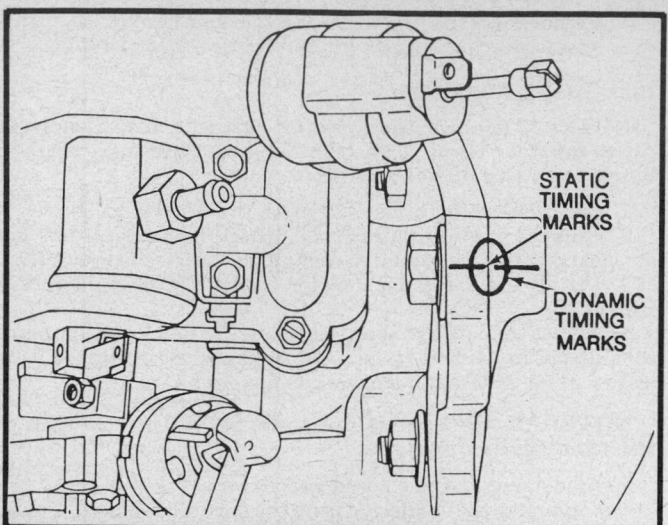

Diesel injection timing alignment marks

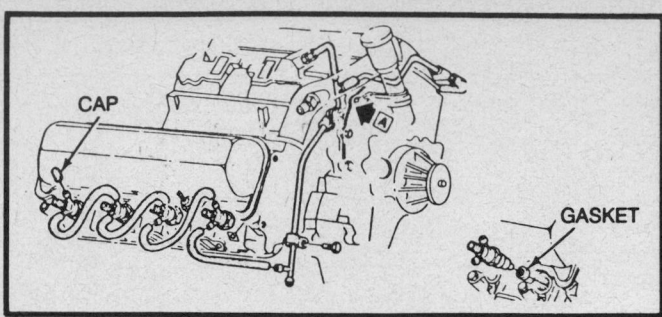

Injection nozzles

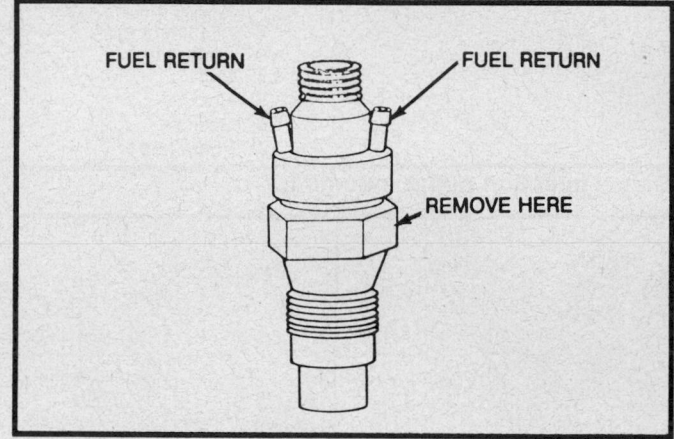

Injection nozzle

2. Disconnect the fuel line clip, and remove the fuel return hose.

3. Remove the fuel injection line.

4. Using GM special tool J-29873, remove the injector. Always remove the injector by turning the 30mm hex protion of the injector; turning the round portion will damage the injector. Always cap the injector and fuel lines when disconnected, to prevent contamination.

5. Install the injector with new gasket and torque to 50 ft. lbs. Connect the injection line and torque the nut to 20 ft. lbs. Install the fuel return hose, fuel line clips, and connnect the batteries.

EMISSION CONTROLS

Please refer to "Professional Emission Component Application Guide".

Emission Warning Lamps

Resetting

When the ECM sets a code, the **Service Engine Soon** light will come **ON** and a code will be stored in memory. If the problem is intermittent, the light will go out after 10 seconds when the fault goes away. However the code will stay in the memory for 50 starts or until the battery voltage to the ECM is removed. Removing battery voltage for 30 seconds will clear all stored codes. On 1988–90 vehicles, the ECM B fuse can also be used to clear codes on all vehicles except the C/K series which has a fuse link.

NOTE: To prevent damage to the ECM, the key must be OFF when disconnecting or connecting power to the ECM.

GASOLINE ENGINE MECHANICAL

NOTE: Disconnecting the negative battery cable on some vehicles may interfere with the functions of the on board computer systems and may require the computer to undergo a relearning process, once the negative battery cable is reconnected.

Engine

Removal and Installation
1986 C/K SERIES AND 1987–90 R/V SERIES
4.8L Engine

1. Disconnect the negative battery cable. Remove the battery, as required. Matchmark and remove the hood. Drain the cooling system.

2. Disconnect the accelerator cable from the carburetor throttle lever. As required, remove the detent cable from the throttle lever.

3. Remove air cleaner assembly. Disconnect all necessary electrical wiring from the engine. Disconnect all necessary vacuum hoses from the engine.

4. Remove the radiator hoses from the radiator. Remove the heater hoses from the engine. Remove the radiator. Remove the fan assembly and water pump pulley.

5. Properly relieve the fuel pump pressure. Disconnect and plug the fuel line at the fuel pump.

6. Raise the vehicle and support it safely. Drain the engine oil. Remove the starter. Remove the flywheel cover. Disconnect the exhaust pipe from the exhaust manifold.

7. Properly support the engine and remove the engine mount through bolts. If equipped with an automatic transmission, remove the flex plate bolts. If equipped with 4WD, remove the strut rods at the engine mounts. Remove the bell housing to engine retaining bolts.

8. **Properly support the transmission assembly. Using the proper lifting device, carefully remove the engine from the vehicle.**

9. Installation is the reverse of the removal procedure.

4.3L, 5.0L, 5.7L and 7.4L Engines

1. Matchmark and remove the hood. Disconnect the negative battery cable. As required, remove the battery. Drain the cooling system.

2. Remove the air cleaner assembly. Remove the fan assembly and the water pump pulley.

3. Disconnect the upper and lower radiator hoses at the engine. Disconnect the heater hoses at the engine. If equipped with automatic transmission, disconnect and plug the cooler lines at the radiator. Remove the radiator and shroud assembly.

4. Disconnect the accelerator linkage. As required, disconnect the detent cable. If equipped with air conditioning, remove the compressor and position it aside.

5. If equipped with power steering, remove the pump from the engine and position it aside. Remove the engine wiring harness from the engine components.

6. Properly relieve the fuel line pressure. Disconnect the fuel line at the engine. Disconnect all necessary vacuum lines.

7. Raise the vehicle and support it safely. Drain the engine oil. Disconnect the exhaust pipe from the exhaust manifold.

8. On 4WD vehicles equipped with automatic transmission, remove the strut rods from the engine mounts. Remove the flywheel cover.

9. Disconnect the wiring along the right pan rail and the gas gauge wire. Remove the starter. If equipped with automatic transmission, remove the converter to flex plate attaching bolts.

10. Properly support the transmission. Remove the bell housing to engine bolts, leaving 1 or more loose to support the weight of the asssembly. Remove the lower engine mount bracket to frame bolts. Lower the vehicle.

11. Attach a lifting device to the engine, remove the remaining bell housing bolts. Carefully remove the engine from the vehicle.

12. Installation is the reverse of the removal procedure.

1988–90 C/K SERIES

4.3L, 5.0L and 5.7L Engines

1. Disconnect the negative battery cable.
2. Remove the hood.
3. Drain the cooling system.
4. Remove the air cleaner.
5. Remove the accessory drive belt, fan and water pump pulley.
6. Remove the radiator and shroud.
7. Disconnect the heater hoses at the engine.
8. Disconnect the accelerator, cruise control and detent linkage if used.
9. Disconnect the air conditioning compressor, if used, and lay aside.
10. Remove the power steering pump, if used, and lay aside.
11. Disconnect the engine wiring from the engine.
12. Release the fuel system pressure as required. Disconnect the fuel line.
13. Disconnect the vacuum lines from the intake manifold.
14. Raise the vehicle and support it safely.
15. Drain the engine oil.
16. Disconnect the exhaust pipes from the manifold.

17. Disconnect the strut rods at the engine mountings, if used.
18. Remove the flywheel or torque converter cover.
19. Disconnect the wiring along the oil pan rail.
20. Remove the starter.
21. Disconnect the wire for the fuel gauge.
22. On vehicles equipped with automatic transmission, remove the converter to flex plate bolts.
23. Lower the vehicle and suitably support the transmission. Attach a suitable lifting fixture to the engine.
24. Remove the bell housing to engine bolts.
25. Remove the rear engine mounting to frame bolts and the front through bolts and remove the engine.

To install:
26. Raise the vehicle and support it safely.
27. Lower the engine and install the engine mounting bolts. Torque the rear engine mounting to frame bolts or nuts to 45 ft. lbs., the front through bolts to 70 ft. lbs. and the front nuts to 50 ft. lbs.
28. Install the bell housing to engine bolts and torque to 35 ft. lbs.
29. Install the converter to flex bolts and torque to 35 ft. lbs.
30. Install the fuel gauge wiring and starter.
31. Install the flywheel or torque converter cover.
32. Connect the strut rods at the engine mountings, if used.
33. Install the exhaust pipes at the manifold.
34. Lower the vehicle.
35. Connect the vacuum lines to the intake manifold.
36. Install the fuel line.
37. Connect the engine wiring harness.
38. Install the power steering pump, if used.
39. Connect the air conditioning compressor, if used.
40. Connect the accelerator, cruise control and detent linkage.
41. Connect the heater hoses.
42. Install the radiator and shroud.
43. Install the accessory drive belts.
44. Install the hood.
45. Install the proper quantity and grade of coolant and engine oil.
46. Connect the negative battery cable.

7.4L Engine

1. Remove the hood.
2. Disconnect the negative battery cable.
3. Remove the air cleaner.
4. Remove the radiator and fan shroud.
5. Disconnect and tag all necessary engine wiring.
6. Disconnect the accelerator, cruise control and TVS linkage.
7. Properly relieve the fuel system pressure as required and disconnect the fuel supply lines.
8. Disconnect all necessary vacuum wires.
9. Disconnect the air conditioning compressor, if used, and lay aside.
10. Remove the power steering pump, if used, and lay aside.
11. Raise the vehicle and support it safely.
12. Disconnect the exhaust pipes from the manifold.
13. Remove the starter.
14. Remove the flywheel or torque converter cover.
15. On vehicles equipped with automatic transmission, remove the converter to flex plate bolts.
16. Lower the vehicle and suitably support the transmission. Attach a suitable lifting fixture to the engine.
17. Remove the bell housing to engine bolts.
18. Remove the rear engine mounting to frame bolts and the front through bolts and remove the engine.

To install:
19. Lower the engine and install the engine mounting bolts. Torque the rear engine mounting to frame bolts or nuts to 45 ft. lbs., the front through bolts to 70 ft. lbs. and the front nuts to 50 ft. lbs.

20. Install the bell housing to engine bolts and torque to 35 ft. lbs.
21. Remove the engine lifting fixture and transmission jack.
22. Raise the vehicle and support it safely.
23. Install the converter to flex bolts and torque to 35 ft. lbs.
24. Install the fuel gauge wiring and starter.
25. Install the flywheel or torque converter cover.
26. Install the starter.
27. Install the exhaust pipes at the manifold.
28. Lower the vehicle.
29. Install the power steering pump.
30. Install the air conditioning compressor.
31. Install all vacuum hoses.
32. Install the fuel supply line.
33. Connect the accelerator, cruise control and TVS linkage.
34. Connect the engine wiring.
35. Install the radiator and fan shroud.
36. Install the air cleaner.
37. Install the hood.
38. Connect the negative battery cable.
39. Install the proper quantity and grade of coolant.

VAN

4.3L Engine

1. Disconnect the battery cables.
2. Remove the glove box.
3. Drain the cooling system.
4. Remove the engine cover.
5. Remove the outside air duct.
6. Remove the power steering reservoir.
7. Remove the hood release cable.
8. Remove the upper fan shroud bolts.
9. Remove the fan and pulley.
10. Remove the air cleaner.
11. Remove the cruise control servo, servo bracket and transducer.
12. Tag and disconnect all vacuum hoses.
13. Disconnect the accelerator linkage and TVS cables.
14. Properly relieve the fuel system pressure and remove the TBI unit.
15. Remove the distributor cap.
16. Disconnect the heater hoses at the engine.
17. Remove the PCV valve.
18. Discharge the air conditioning system using the proper equipment and remove the airconditioning vacuum reservoir.
19. Remove the air conditioning compressor and bracket.
20. Remove the upper half of the engine dipstick tube.
21. Remove the oil filler tube.
22. Remove the transmission dipstick tube and the accelerator cable at the tube.
23. Remove the fuel line at the fuel pump.
24. Remove the power steering pump.
25. Remove the head light bezels and the grille.
26. Remove the upper radiator support.
27. Remove the lower fan shroud and filler panel.
28. Remove the hood latch support.
29. Remove the condenser. Cap all openings.
30. Raise and support the vehicle safely.
31. Drain the engine oil.
32. Disconnect the exhaust pipes at the manifolds.
33. Remove the strut rods at the torque converter or flywheel underpan.
34. Remove the torque converter or flywheel cover.
35. Remove the starter.
36. Remove the flex plate-to-torque converter bolts (automatic transmissions).
37. Remove the bell housing-to-engine bolts.
38. Remove the engine mounting through bolts.
39. Lower the Van support the transmission using the proper equipment.

40. Attach an engine crane to the engine, pull the engine forward and upward and remove it from the Van.

To install:
41. Raise the engine into position.
42. Install the engine mount through bolts. Torque the bolts to 75 ft. lbs.
43. Install the bellhousing-to-engine bolts. Torque the bolts to 50 ft. lbs.
44. Install the flex plate-to-torque converter bolts (automatic transmissions). Torque the bolts to 40 ft. lbs.
45. Install the starter.
46. Install the torque converter or flywheel cover.
47. Install the strut rods at the torque converter or flywheel underpan.
48. Connect the exhaust pipes at the manifolds.
49. Install the fuel line at the fuel pump.
50. Install the condenser.
51. Install the hood latch support.
52. Install the lower fan shroud and filler panel.
53. Install the transmission dipstick tube and the accelerator cable at the tube.
54. Install the PCV valve.
55. Install the distributor cap.
56. Install the cruise control servo, servo bracket and transducer.
57. Install the oil filler pipe and the engine dipstick tube.
58. Install the thermostat housing.
59. Connect the heater hoses at the engine.
60. Connect the engine wiring harness from the firewall connection.
61. Install the air conditioning compressor mounting bracket.
62. Install the radiator and the shroud.
63. Install the radiator support bracket.
64. Install the TBI unit.
65. Connect the accelerator linkage and TVS cable.
66. Install the windshield wiper jar and bracket.
67. Install the air conditioning compressor.
68. Install the air conditioning vacuum reservoir.
69. Charge the air conditioning system, using the proper equipment.
70. If the Van is equipped with an automatic transmission, install the fluid cooler lines at the radiator.
71. Install the power steering reservoir.
72. Install the hood release cable.
73. Connect the radiator hoses at the radiator.
74. Install the head light bezels and the grille.
75. Install the air cleaner.
76. Install the outside air duct.
77. Install the engine cover.
78. Fill the cooling system.
79. Fill the crankcase.
80. Connect the battery cables.
81. Install the glove box.

5.0L and 5.7L Engines

1. Disconnect the negative battery cable, then the positive battery cable, at the battery.
2. Drain the cooling system.
3. Remove the radiator coolant reservoir bottle.
4. Remove the upper radiator support.
5. Remove the grille and the lower grille valance.
6. Discharge the air conditioning system using the proper equipment and remove the air conditioning vacuum reservoir.
7. Remove the air conditioning condenser from in front of the radiator.
8. If the Van is equipped with an automatic transmission, remove the fluid cooler lines from the radiator.
9. Disconnect the radiator hoses at the radiator.
10. Remove the radiator support bracket and remove the radiator and the shroud.

11. Remove the engine cover.
12. Remove the air cleaner.
13. Disconnect the accelerator linkage.
14. Disconnect all hoses and wires at the carburetor or TBI unit.
15. Relieve the fuel system pressure and remove the carburetor or TBI unit.
16. Disconnect the engine wiring harness from the firewall connection.
17. Tag and disconnect all vacuum lines.
18. Remove the power steering pump. It's not necessary to disconnect the hoses; just lay it aside.
19. Disconnect the heater hoses at the engine.
20. Remove the thermostat housing.
21. Remove the oil filler tube.
22. Raise and support the vehicle safely.
23. Remove the cruise control servo, servo bracket and transducer.
24. Drain the engine oil.
25. Disconnect the exhaust pipes at the manifolds.
26. Remove the driveshaft and plug the end of the transmission.
27. Disconnect the transmission shift linkage and the speedometer cable.
28. Remove the fuel line from the fuel tank and at the fuel pump.
29. Remove the transmission mounting bolts.
30. Lower the Van, support the transmission and engine.
31. Remove the engine mount bracket-to-frame bolts.
32. Remove the engine mount through bolts.
33. Raise the engine slightly and remove the engine mounts. Support the engine with wood between the oil pan and the crossmember.
34. Remove the manual transmission and clutch as follows:
  a. Remove the clutch housing rear cover.
  b. Remove the bolts attaching the clutch housing to the engine and remove the transmission and clutch as a unit.

NOTE: Support the transmission as the last bolt is being removed to prevent damaging the clutch.

  c. Remove the starter and clutch housing rear cover.
  d. Loosen the clutch mounting bolts a little at a time to prevent distorting the disc until spring pressure is released. Remove all of the bolts, the clutch disc and the pressure plate.
35. Remove the automatic transmission as follows:
  a. Lower the engine and support it on blocks.
  b. Remove the starter and converter housing underpan.
  c. Remove the flywheel-to-converter attaching bolts.
  d. Support the transmission on blocks.
  e. Disconnect the detent cable on the Turbo Hydra-Matic.
  f. Remove the transmission-to-engine mounting bolts.
  g. Remove the blocks from the engine only and glide the engine away from the transmission.

To install:
36. Raise the engine slightly and install the engine mounts. Torque the bolts to 40 ft. lbs.
37. Install the manual transmission and clutch as follows:
  a. Install the clutch disc and the pressure plate. Tighten the clutch mounting bolts a little at a time to prevent distorting the disc.
  b. Install the starter and clutch housing rear cover.
  c. Install the bolts attaching the clutch housing to the engine and install the transmission and clutch as a unit. Torque the bolts to 40 ft. lbs.
  d. Install the clutch housing rear bolts.
38. Install the automatic transmission as follows:
  a. Position the transmission.
  b. Install the transmission-to-engine mounting bolts.
  c. Connect the throttle linkage and detent cable.

  d. Install the flywheel-to-converter attaching bolts. Torque the bolts to 40 ft. lbs.
  e. Install the starter and converter housing underpan.
39. Install the engine mount through bolts. Torque the bolts to 40 ft. lbs.
40. Install the engine mount bracket-to-frame bolts. Torque the bolts to 40 ft. lbs.
41. Install the clutch cross-shaft.
42. Install the transmission mounting bolts. Torque the bolts to 40 ft. lbs.
43. Connect the transmission shift linkage and the speedometer cable.
44. Install the driveshaft.
45. Install the condenser.
46. Install the hood latch support.
47. Install the lower fan shroud and filler panel.
48. Install the transmission dipstick tube and the accelerator cable at the tube.
49. Install the coolant hose at the intake manifold and the PCV valve.
50. Install the distributor cap.
51. Install the cruise control servo, servo bracket and transducer.
52. Install the oil filler pipe and the engine dipstick tube.
53. Install the thermostat housing.
54. Connect the heater hoses at the engine.
55. Connect the engine wiring harness from the firewall connection.
56. Install the radiator and the shroud.
57. Install the radiator support bracket.
58. Install the carburetor or TBI unit.
59. Connect the accelerator linkage.
60. Install the windshield wiper jar and bracket.
61. Install the air conditioning condenser.
62. Install the air conditioning vacuum reservoir.
63. Charge the air conditioning system using the proper equipment.
64. If the Van is equipped with an automatic transmission, install the fluid cooler lines at the radiator.
65. Install the radiator coolant reservoir bottle.
66. Connect the radiator hoses at the radiator.
67. Install the upper radiator support the grille and the lower grille valance.
68. Install the air cleaner.
69. Install the air stove pipe.
70. Install the engine cover.
71. Fill the cooling system.
72. Connect the battery cables.

7.4L Engine
1. Disconnect the battery cables.
2. Drain the cooling system.
3. Remove the engine cover.
4. Remove the air cleaner.
5. Remove the cruise control servo, servo bracket and transducer.
6. Remove the grille and lower grille valance.
7. Remove the upper radiator support.
8. Discharge the air conditioning system using the proper equipment and remove the air conditioning vacuum reservoir.
9. Remove the air conditioning condenser from in front of the radiator. Cap all openings at once!
10. Disconnect the radiator hoses at the radiator.
11. Remove the fluid cooler lines from the radiator.
12. Remove the radiator coolant reservoir bottle.
13. Remove the radiator support bracket and remove the radiator and the shroud.
14. Remove the power steering pump.
15. Remove the air conditioning compressor and cap all openings.

16. Disconnect the wiring fuel lines and linkage at the TBI unit.

17. Properly relieve the fuel system pressure and remove the TBI unit.

18. Disconnect the engine wiring harness from the firewall connection.

19. Disconnect the starter wires.

20. Disconnect the alternator wires.

21. Disconnect the temperature sensor wire.

22. Disconnect the oil pressure sender.

23. Disconnect the distributor and coil wiring.

24. Disconnect and plug the fuel supply and vapor lines.

25. Tag and disconnect all vacuum hoses.

26. Disconnect the heater hoses at the engine.

27. Remove the thermostat housing.

28. Remove the windshield wiper jar and bracket.

29. Remove the oil filler pipe and the engine dipstick tube.

30. Raise and support the vehicle safely.

31. Disconnect the exhaust pipes at the manifolds.

32. Remove the driveshaft and plug the end of the transmission.

33. Disconnect the transmission shift linkage and the speedometer cable.

34. Drain the engine oil.

35. Support the engine with a floor jack. Do not position the jack under the oil pan, crankshaft pulley or any sheet metal!

36. Attach an engine crane to the engine and take up its weight.

37. Remove the transmission mounting bolts.

38. Raise the engine slightly and remove the engine mounts. Support the engine with wood between the oil pan and the crossmember.

39. Lower the Van.

40. Raise the engine as necessary and maneuver the engine/transmission assembly from the Van.

41. Separate the engine and transmission as follows:
   a. Support the engine on blocks.
   b. Remove the starter and converter housing underpan.
   c. Remove the flywheel-to-converter attaching bolts.
   d. Support the transmission on blocks.
   e. Disconnect the detent cable.
   f. Remove the transmission-to-engine mounting bolts.
   g. Remove the blocks from the engine only and guide the engine away from the transmission.

42. Mount the engine on a work stand.

To install:

43. Install the automatic transmission as follows:
   a. Position the transmission.
   b. Install the transmission-to-engine mounting bolts. Torque the bolts to 40 ft. lbs.
   c. Connect the throttle linkage detent cable on the Turbo Hydra-Matic.
   d. Install the flywheel-to-converter attaching bolts. Torque the bolts to 40 ft. lbs.
   e. Install the starter and converter housing underpan.

44. Raise the engine/transmission and guide the assembly into position in the Van.

45. Raise the engine slightly and install the engine mounts. Torque the mount-to-block bolts to 36 ft. lbs.

46. Install the engine mount through bolts. Torque the bolts to 75 ft. lbs.

47. Install the engine mount bracket-to-frame bolts. Torque the front mount bolts to 30 ft. lbs.; the rear mount bolts to 40 ft. lbs.

48. Install the transmission mounting bolts. Torque the nuts to 36 ft. lbs.

49. Connect the transmission shift linkage and the speedometer cable.

50. Install the driveshaft.

51. Connect the exhaust pipes at the manifolds.

52. Install the oil filler pipe and the engine dipstick tube.

53. Install the windshield wiper jar and bracket.

54. Install the thermostat housing.

55. Connect the heater hoses at the engine.

56. Connect all vacuum hoses.

57. Connect the fuel supply and vapor lines.

58. Connect the distributor and coil wiring.

59. Connect the oil pressure sender.

60. Connect the temperature sensor wire.

61. Connect the alternator wires.

62. Connect the starter wires.

63. Connect the engine wiring harness at the firewall connection.

64. Install the TBI unit.

65. Connect the wiring, fuel lines and linkage at the TBI unit.

66. Install the air conditioning compressor.

67. Install the power steering pump.

68. Install the radiator and the shroud.

69. Install the radiator support bracket.

70. Install the radiator coolant reservoir bottle.

71. Install the fluid cooler lines at the radiator.

72. Connect the radiator hoses at the radiator.

73. Install the air conditioning condenser.

74. Install the air conditioning vacuum reservoir.

75. Charge the air conditioning system using the proper equipment.

76. Install the upper radiator support.

77. Connect the radiator hoses at the radiator.

78. Install the grille and the lower grille valance.

79. Install the cruise control servo, servo bracket and transducer.

80. Fill the crankcase.

81. Install the air cleaner.

82. Install the engine cover.

83. Fill the cooling system.

84. Connect the battery cables.

Cylinder Head

Removal and Installation

4.3L ENGINE

1. Disconnect the negative battery cable.

2. Remove the engine cover and drain the cooling system.

3. Relieve the fuel system pressure and remove the intake manifold.

4. Remove the exhaust manifold.

5. Remove the air pipe at the rear of the head (right cylinder head).

6. Remove the alternator mounting bolt at the cylinder head (right cylinder head).

7. Remove the power steering pump and brackets from the cylinder head, and lay them aside (left cylinder head).

8. Remove the air conditioner compressor, and lay it aside (left cylinder head).

9. Remove the rocker arm cover.

10. Remove the spark plugs.

11. Remove the rocker arms and pushrods.

12. Remove the cylinder head bolts.

13. Remove the cylinder head.

To install:

14. Clean all gasket mating surfaces, install a new gasket and reinstall the cylinder head.

15. Install the cylinder heads using new gaskets. Install the gaskets with the head up.

NOTE: Coat a steel gasket on both sides with sealer. If a composition gasket is used, do not use sealer.

16. Clean the bolts, apply sealer to the threads, and install them hand tight.

Cylinder head bolt torque sequence—4.3L engine

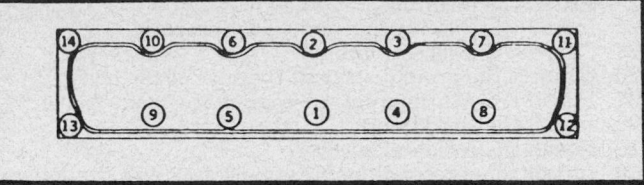

Cylinder head bolt torque sequence—4.8L engine

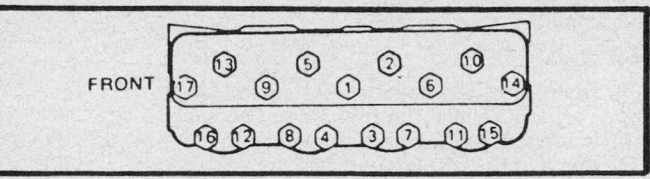

Cylinder head bolt torque sequence—5.0L and 5.7L engines

17. Tighten the head bolts a little at a time to the proper sequence and the proper torque specifications.
18. Install the intake and exhaust manifolds.
19. Install the rocker arms and pushrods.
20. Adjust the rocker arms.
21. Install the spark plugs.
22. Install the rocker arm cover.
23. Install the air conditioner compressor.
24. Install the power steering pump and brackets.
25. Install the alternator mounting bolt at the cylinder head.
26. Install the air pipe at the rear of the head.
27. Install the exhaust manifold.
28. Install the intake manifold.
29. Install the engine cover.
30. Connect the negative battery cable.

4.8L ENGINE

1. Disconnect the negative battery cable. Drain cooling system. Remove air cleaner assembly.
2. Properly relieve the fuel pump pressure. Disconnect the fuel line at the carburetor. Disconnect the accelerator and transmission linkages. Disconnect all required electrical and vacuum lines.
3. Remove the combination manifold assembly retaining bolts. Remove the combination manifold from the engine.
4. Remove the valve cover. Remove the rocker arms and pushrods. Keep them in order for reinstallation.
5. If equipped, disconnect the AIR injection hose at the check valve. Disconnect the upper radiator hose at the thermostat housing. Remove the battery ground strap.
6. Remove the cylinder head retaining bolts. Remove the cylinder head from the engine.
7. Installation is the reverse of the removal procedure. Be sure that the cylinder bolt threads in the block and threads on the bolts are cleaned, as dirt will affect bolt torque.
8. Coat the threads of the cylinder head bolts with sealing compound 1052080 or equivalent.
9. Position the new gasket over the dowel pins. Torque the cylinder head bolts a little at a time, to specification, and in the proper sequence.

5.0L AND 5.7L ENGINES

1. Disconnect the negative battery cable.
2. Properly relieve the fuel system pressure.
3. Drain the cooling system.
4. Remove the intake manifold.
5. Remove the exhaust manifolds and tie out of the way.
6. If the vehicle is equipped with air conditioning, remove the air conditioning compressor and the forward mounting bracket and lay the compressor aside. Do not disconnect any of the refrigerant lines.
7. Remove the valve covers. Back off the rocker arm nuts and pivot the rocker arms out of the way so that the pushrods can be removed. Identify the pushrods so that they can be installed in their original positions.
8. Remove the cylinder head bolts and remove the heads.
9. Install the cylinder heads using new gaskets. Install the gaskets with the word **HEAD** up.

NOTE: Coat a steel gasket on both sides with sealer. If a composition gasket is used, do not use sealer.

10. Clean the bolts, apply sealer to the threads, and install them hand tight.
11. Tighten the head bolts a little at a time to the proper sequence and torque specifications.
12. Install the intake and exhaust manifolds.
13. Adjust the rocker arms.

7.4L ENGINE

Right Side

1. Disconnect the negative battery cable.
2. Properly relieve the fuel system pressure.
3. Drain the cooling system.
4. Remove the intake manifold.
5. Remove the exhaust manifolds.
6. Remove the alternator on 1986 C/K series and 1987–90 R/V series.
7. Remove the power steering pump and lay it aside on the Van.
8. Remove the AIR pump and brackets.
9. If the vehicle is equipped with air conditioning, remove the air conditioning compressor and the forward mounting bracket and lay the compressor aside. Do not disconnect any of the refrigerant lines.
10. Remove the idler pulley and A/C compressor rear bracket on the Van.
11. Remove the rocker arm cover.
12. Remove the spark plugs.
13. Remove the AIR pipes at the rear of the head.
14. Disconnect the ground strap at the rear of the head.
15. Disconnect the sensor wire.
16. Back off the rocker arm nuts and pivot the rocker arms out of the way so that the pushrods can be removed. Identify the pushrods so that they can be installed in their original positions.
17. Remove the cylinder head bolts and remove the heads.

To install:

18. Thoroughly clean the mating surfaces of the head and block. Clean the bolt holes thoroughly.
19. Install the cylinder heads using new gaskets. Install the gaskets with the word **HEAD** up.

NOTE: Coat a steel gasket on both sides with sealer. If a composition gasket is used, do not use sealer.

20. Clean the bolts, apply sealer to the threads, and install them hand tight.
21. Tighten the head bolts a little at a time to the proper sequence and to the proper torque specifications.
22. Install the intake and exhaust manifolds.

23. Install the pushrods.
24. Install the rocker arms and adjust properly.
25. Connect the sensor wire.
26. Connect the ground strap at the rear of the head.
27. Install the AIR pipes at the rear of the head.
28. Install the spark plugs.
29. Install the rocker arm cover.
30. Install the air conditioning compressor and the forward mounting bracket.
31. Install the AIR pump.
32. Install the alternator.

Left Side

1. Disconnect the negative battery cable.
2. Properly relieve the fuel system pressure.
3. Drain the cooling system.
4. Remove the intake manifold.
5. Remove the exhaust manifolds.
6. Remove the alternator and brackets on the 1988–90 C/K series and the Van.
7. Remove the power steering pump and brackets and lay it to one side on the 1988–90 C/K series.
8. Remove the rocker arm cover.
9. Remove the spark plugs.
10. Remove the AIR pipes at the rear of the head.
11. Disconnect the ground strap at the rear of the head.
12. Disconnect the sensor wire.
13. Back off the rocker arm nuts and pivot the rocker arms out of the way so that the pushrods can be removed. Identify the pushrods so that they can be installed in their original positions.
14. Remove the cylinder head bolts and remove the heads.

To install:

15. Thoroughly clean the mating surfaces of the head and block. Clean the bolt holes thoroughly.
16. Install the cylinder heads using new gaskets. Install the gaskets with the word **HEAD** up.

NOTE: Coat a steel gasket on both sides with sealer. If a composition gasket is used, do not use sealer.

17. Clean the bolts, apply sealer to the threads, and install them hand tight.
18. Tighten the head bolts a little at a time to the proper sequence and torque specifications.
19. Install the intake and exhaust manifolds.
20. Install the pushrods.
21. Install the rocker arms.
22. Connect the sensor wire.
23. Connect the ground strap at the rear of the head.
24. Install the AIR pipes at the rear of the head.
25. Install the spark plugs.
26. Install the rocker arm cover.
27. Install the air conditioning compressor and the forward mounting bracket.
28. Install the alternator and power steering pump.

Valve Lash

ADJUSTMENT

All engines use hydraulic lifters, which require no periodic adjustment. In the event of cylinder head removal or any operation that requires disturbing the rocker arms, the rocker arms will have to be adjusted.
1. Remove the rocker covers and gaskets.
2. Adjust the valves on V6 and V8 engines as follows:
  a. Crank the engine until the mark on the damper aligns with the **TDC** or **0** mark on the timing tab and the engine is in No. 1 firing position. This can be determined by placing the fingers on the No. 1 cylinder valves as the marks align. If the valves do not move, it is in No. 1 firing position. If the valves

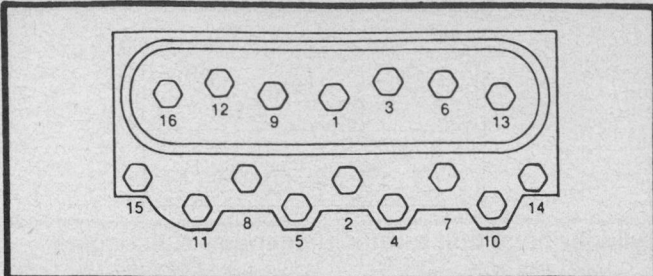

Cylinder head bolt torque sequence—7.4L engine

move, it is in No. 6 firing position (No. 4 on the V6) and the crankshaft should be rotated 1 more revolution to the No. 1 firing position.
  b. The adjustment is made in the same manner as 6 cylinder engines.
  c. With the engine in No. 1 firing position, the following valves can be adjusted:
V6 Engine
  Exhaust—1, 5, 6
  Intake—1, 2, 3
V8 Engine
  Exhaust—1, 3, 4, 8
  Intake—1, 2, 5, 7
  d. Crank the engine 1 full revolution until the marks are again in alignment. This is No. 6 firing position (No. 4 on the V6). The following valves can now be adjusted:
V6 Engine
  Exhaust—2, 3, 4
  Intake—4, 5, 6
V8 Engine
  Exhaust—2, 5, 6, 7
  Intake—3, 4, 6, 8
3. Reinstall the rocker arm covers using new gaskets.
4. Install the distributor cap and wire assembly.

Rocker Arm

Removal and Installation

1. Disconnect the negative battery cable. On Van, remove the engine cover.
2. Remove all the necessary components in order to gain access to the engine valve covers. As required, properly relieve the fuel system pressure before disconnecting any fuel lines.
3. Remove the valve cover retaining bolts. Remove the valve cover from the engine.
4. Remove the rocker arm assemblies. Keep them in order for reinstallation.
5. Installation is the reverse of the removal procedure. Be sure to use new gaskets or RTV sealant, as necessary.

Valve Arrangement

4.8L ENGINE

E–I–I–E–E–I–I–E–E–I–I–E

4.3L ENGINE

Left Side E–I–E–I–I–E
Right Side E–I–I–E–I–E

5.0L AND 5.7L ENGINE

E–I–I–E–E–I–I–E

7.4L ENGINE

E–I–E–I–E–I–E–I

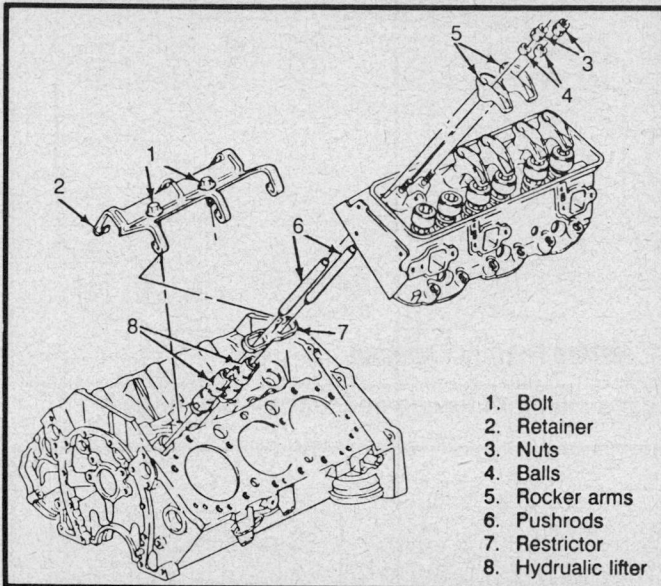

1. Bolt
2. Retainer
3. Nuts
4. Balls
5. Rocker arms
6. Pushrods
7. Restrictor
8. Hydrualic lifter

Cylinder head and components — 4.3L engine

Intake Manifold

Removal and Installation
1986 C/K SERIES AND 1987–90 R/V SERIES
4.3L, 5.0L, 5.7L and 7.4L Engines

1. Disconnect the negative battery cable.
2. Drain the cooling system.
3. Remove the air cleaner assembly.
4. Remove the thermostat housing and the bypass hose. It is not necessary to remove the top radiator hose from the thermostat housing.
5. Disconnect the heater hose at the rear of the manifold.
6. Disconnect all electrical connections and vacuum lines from the manifold. Remove the EGR valve if necessary.
7. On vehicles equipped with power brakes remove the vacuum line from the vacuum booster to the manifold.
8. Remove the distributor.
9. Move the air conditioning compressor to one side, if necessary.
10. Relieve the fuel system pressure.
11. Remove the fuel line to the carburetor or TBI unit.
12. Remove the carburetor linkage.
13. Disconnect the electrical connections at the TBI unit.
14. Remove the carburetor or TBI unit, if necessary.
15. Remove the intake manifold bolts. Remove the manifold and the gaskets. Remember to reinstall the O-ring seal between the intake manifold and timing chain cover during assembly, if so equipped.
16. Reconnect all wires, hoses and linkage. Use plastic gasket retainers to prevent the manifold gasket from slipping out of place, if so equipped.

Make sure all gasket mating surfaces are thoroughly clean and on all except the 7.4L engine, place a $\frac{3}{16}$" bead of RTV type silicone sealer on the front and rear ridges of the cylinder block-to-manifold mating surfaces. Extend the bead ½" up each cylinder head to seal and retain the manifold side gaskets. Torque the manifold bolts in the proper sequence and to the proper specification.

1988–90 C/K SERIES
4.3L, 5.0L and 5.7L Engines

1. Disconnect the negative battery cable. Drain the cooling system.

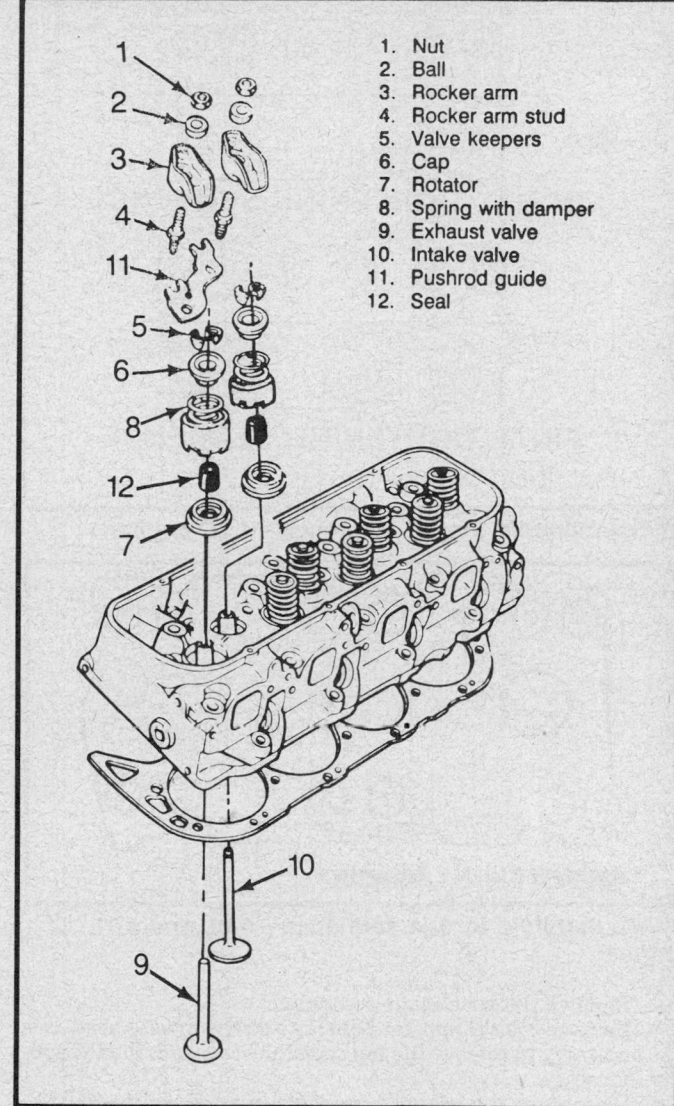

1. Nut
2. Ball
3. Rocker arm
4. Rocker arm stud
5. Valve keepers
6. Cap
7. Rotator
8. Spring with damper
9. Exhaust valve
10. Intake valve
11. Pushrod guide
12. Seal

Cylinder head and components — 7.4L engine

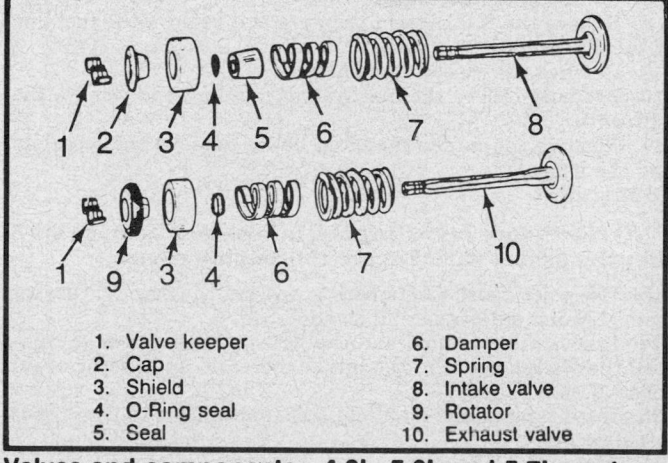

1. Valve keeper
2. Cap
3. Shield
4. O-Ring seal
5. Seal
6. Damper
7. Spring
8. Intake valve
9. Rotator
10. Exhaust valve

Valves and components — 4.3L, 5.0L and 5.7L engines

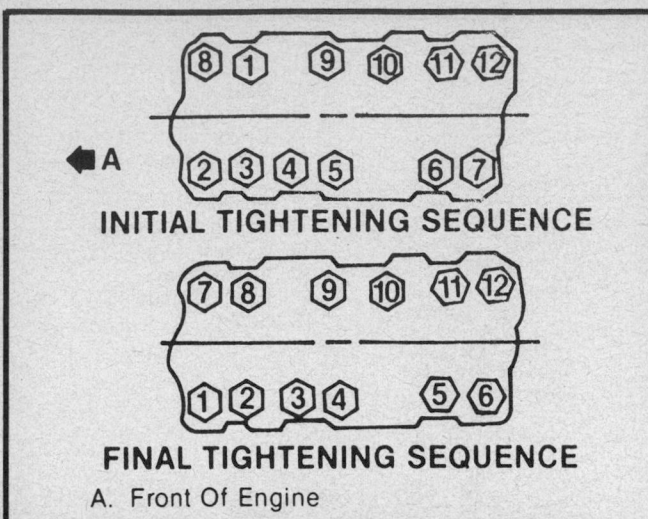

INITIAL TIGHTENING SEQUENCE

FINAL TIGHTENING SEQUENCE

A. Front Of Engine

Intake manifold torque sequence—4.3L engine

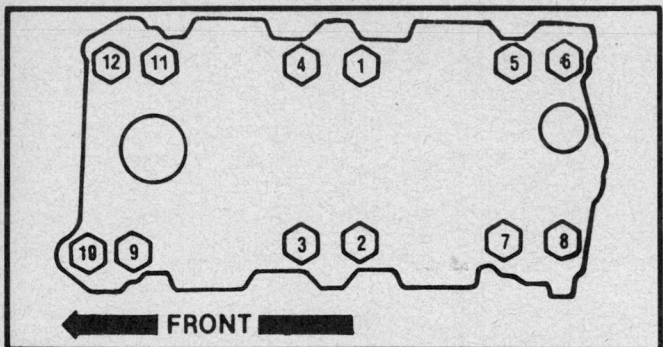

Intake manifold torque sequence—5.0L and 5.7L engine

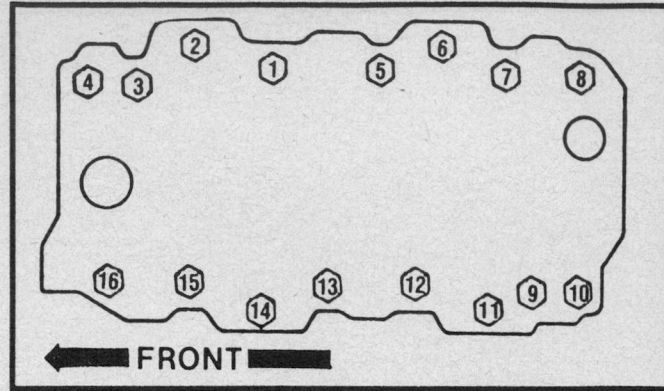

Intake manifold torque sequence—7.4L engine

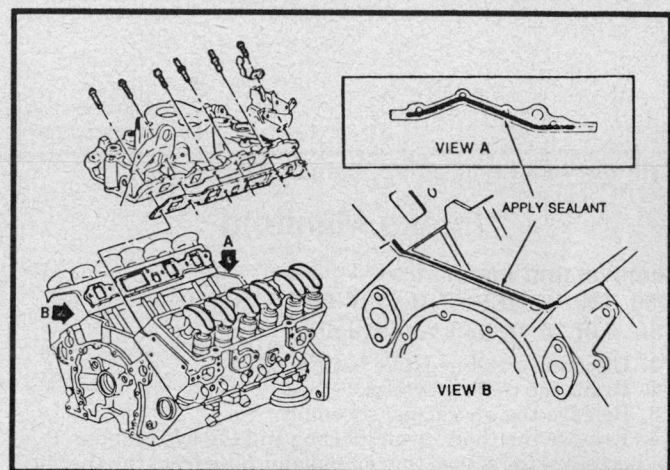

Intake manifold installation—4.3L engine

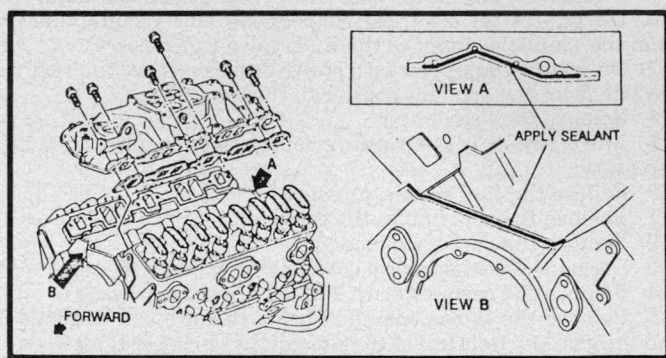

Intake manifold installation—5.0L and 5.7L engines

2. Remove the air cleaner assembly.

3. Remove the thermostat housing and the bypass hose. It is not necessary to remove the top radiator hose from the thermostat housing.

4. Disconnect the heater hose at the rear of the manifold.

5. Disconnect all electrical connections and vacuum lines from the manifold. Remove the EGR valve if necessary.

6. Remove the power brake vacuum line from the vacuum booster to the manifold.

7. Remove the distributor.

8. Relieve the fuel system pressure and remove the fuel line at the TBI unit.

9. Remove the accelerator linkage.

10. Properly relieve the fuel system pressure and remove the TBI unit.

11. Remove the intake manifold bolts. Remove the manifold and the gaskets.

To install:

NOTE: Before installing the intake manifold, be sure that the gasket surfaces are thoroughly clean.

13. Use plastic gasket retainers to prevent the manifold gasket from slipping out of place, if so equipped.

14. Install the manifold and the gaskets. Remember to reinstall the O-ring between the intake manifold and timing chain cover, if so equipped.

15. Install the intake manifold bolts and torque to the proper specification.

16. Install the TBI unit.

17. Install the TBI linkage.

18. Install the fuel line.

19. Install the distributor.

20. Install the vacuum line between the vacuum booster and manifold.

21. Connect all electrical connections and vacuum lines at the manifold. Install the EGR valve if necessary.

22. Connect the heater hose at the rear of the manifold.

23. Install the thermostat housing and the bypass hose.

24. Install the air cleaner assembly.

25. Fill the cooling system.

7.4L Engine

1. Disconnect the negative battery cable.

2. Drain the cooling system.
3. Remove the air cleaner assembly.
4. Remove the upper radiator hose, thermostat housing and the bypass hose.
5. Disconnect the heater hose and pipe.
6. Tag and disconnect all electrical connections and vacuum lines from the manifold.
7. Disconnect the accelerator linkage.
8. Disconnect the cruise control cable.
9. Disconnect the TVS cable.
10. Properly relieve the fuel system pressure. Remove the fuel line at the TBI unit.
11. Remove the TBI unit.
12. Remove the distributor.
13. Remove the cruise control transducer.
14. Disconnect the ignition coil wires.
15. Remove the EGR solenoid and bracket.
16. Remove the MAP sensor and bracket.
17. Remove the air conditioning compressor rear bracket.
18. Remove the front alternator/AIR pump bracket.
19. Remove the intake manifold bolts.
20. Remove the manifold and the gaskets and seals.

To install:

NOTE: Before installing the intake manifold, be sure that the gasket surfaces are thoroughly clean. Remember to reinstall the O-ring between the intake manifold and timing chain cover during assembly, if so equipped.

21. Install the manifold and the gaskets and seals.
22. Install the intake manifold bolts. Torque the bolts to 30 ft. lbs.
23. Install the front alternator/AIR pump bracket.
24. Install the air conditioning compressor rear bracket.
25. Install the MAP sensor and bracket.
26. Install the EGR solenoid and bracket.
27. Connect the ignition coil wires.
28. Install the cruise control transducer.
29. Install the distributor.
30. Install the TBI unit.
31. Install the fuel line at the TBI unit.
32. Connect the TVS cable.
33. Connect the cruise control cable.
34. Connect the accelerator linkage.
35. Connect all electrical connections and vacuum lines at the manifold.
36. Connect the heater hose and pipe.
37. Install the upper radiator hose, thermostat housing and the bypass hose.
38. Install the air cleaner assembly.
39. Fill the cooling system.
40. Connect the battery.

VAN
4.3L, 5.0L and 5.7L Engines

1. Disconnect the negative battery cable. Drain the cooling system.
2. Remove the air cleaner assembly.
3. Remove the thermostat housing and the bypass hose. It is not necessary to remove the top radiator hose from the thermostat housing.
4. Disconnect the heater hose at the rear of the manifold.
5. Disconnect all electrical connections and vacuum lines from the manifold. Remove the EGR valve if necessary.
6. Remove the vacuum line from the vacuum brake booster to the manifold.
7. Remove the distributor.
8. Reliese the fuel system pressure and remove the fuel line at the TBI unit.
9. Remove the accelerator linkage.
10. Remove the TBI unit.

11. Remove the intake manifold bolts. Remove the manifold and the gaskets. Remember to reinstall the O-ring between the intake manifold and timing chain cover during assembly, if so equipped.

To install:

NOTE: Before installing the intake manifold, be sure that the gasket surfaces are thoroughly clean.

13. Use plastic gasket retainers to prevent the manifold gasket from slipping out of place, if so equipped.
14. Install the manifold and the gaskets. Remember to reinstall the O-ring between the intake manifold and timing chain cover, if so equipped.
15. Install the intake manifold bolts and torque to the proper specification and the proper sequence.
16. Install the TBI unit.
17. Install the TBI linkage.
18. Install the fuel line.
19. Install the distributor.
20. Install the vacuum line between the vacuum brake booster and manifold.
21. Connect all electrical connections and vacuum lines at the manifold. Install the EGR valve if necessary.
22. Connect the heater hose at the rear of the manifold.
23. Install the thermostat housing and the bypass hose.
24. Install the air cleaner assembly.
25. Fill the cooling system.

7.4L Engine

1. Disconnect the negative battery cable.
2. Drain the cooling system.
3. Remove the air cleaner assembly.
4. Remove the upper radiator hose, thermostat housing and the bypass hose.
5. Disconnect the heater hose and pipe.
6. Tag and disconnect all electrical connections and vacuum lines from the manifold.
7. Disconnect the accelerator linkage.
8. Disconnect the cruise control cable.
9. Disconnect the TVS cable.
10. Relieve the fuel system pressure and remove the fuel line at the TBI unit.
11. Remove the TBI unit.
12. Remove the distributor.
13. Remove the cruise control transducer.
14. Disconnect the ignition coil wires.
15. Remove the EGR solenoid and bracket.
16. Remove the MAP sensor and bracket.
17. Remove the air conditioning compressor rear bracket.
18. Remove the front alternator/AIR pump bracket.
19. Remove the intake manifold bolts.
20. Remove the manifold and the gaskets and seals. Remember to reinstall the O-ring between the intake manifold and timing chain cover during assembly, if so equipped.

To install:

NOTE: Before installing the intake manifold, be sure that the gasket surfaces are thoroughly clean.

21. Install the manifold and the gaskets and seals.
22. Install the intake manifold bolts. Torque the bolts to 30 ft. lbs.
23. Install the front alternator/AIR pump bracket.
24. Install the air conditioning compressor rear bracket.
25. Install the MAP sensor and bracket.
26. Install the EGR solenoid and bracket.
27. Connect the ignition coil wires.
28. Install the cruise control transducer.
29. Install the distributor.
30. Install the TBI unit.
31. Install the fuel line at the TBI unit.

32. Connect the TVS cable.
33. Connect the cruise control cable.
34. Connect the accelerator linkage.
35. Connect all electrical connections and vacuum lines at the manifold.
36. Connect the heater hose and pipe.
37. Install the upper radiator hose, thermostat housing and the bypass hose.
38. Install the air cleaner assembly.
39. Fill the cooling system.
40. Connect the battery.

Exhaust Manifold

Removal and Installation

EXCEPT VAN

4.3L, 5.0L and 5.7L Engines

Tab locks are used on the front and rear pairs of bolts on each exhaust manifold. When removing the bolts, straighten the tabs from beneath the vehicle using a suitable tool. When installing the tab locks, bend the tabs against the sides of the bolt, not over the top of the bolt.

1. Disconnect the negative battery cable. Remove the air cleaner.
2. Remove the hot air shroud, if so equipped.
3. On some vehicles it may be necessary to loosen the alternator and remove its lower bracket.
4. On some vehicles it may be necessary to remove A/C compressor rear bracket on the manifold left side and the diverter valve and bracket on the right side.

NOTE: On models with air conditioning it may be necessary to remove the compressor, and tie it out of the way. Do not disconnect the compressor lines.

5. Disconnect the oxygen sensor wire, if so equipped.
6. On 1988–90 C/K series, disconnect the power steering pump rear bracket on the manifold left side and the AIR hose at the check valve.
7. Raise and support the vehicle safely.
8. Disconnect the crossover pipe from both manifolds.
9. Remove the manifold bolts and remove the manifold(s). Some models have lock tabs on the front and rear manifold bolts which must be bent with a drift pin.
10. Installation is the reverse of removal. Torque the bolts to the proper specification and in the proper sequence.

7.4L Engine

RIGHT SIDE

1. Disconnect the negative battery cable.
2. Remove the heat stove pipe.
3. Remove the dipstick tube.
4. Disconnect the AIR hose at the check valve.
5. Remove the spark plugs.
6. Raise and support the vehicle safely. Disconnect the exhaust pipe at the manifold.
7. Lower the vehicle and remove the manifold bolts and spark plug heat shields.
8. Remove the manifold.

To install:

9. Clean the mating surfaces.
10. Clean the stud threads.
11. Install the manifold and bolts. Tighten the bolts to 40 ft. lbs. starting from the center bolts and working towards the outside.
12. Connect the exhaust pipe at the manifold.
13. Install the spark plugs.
14. Connect the AIR hose at the check valve.

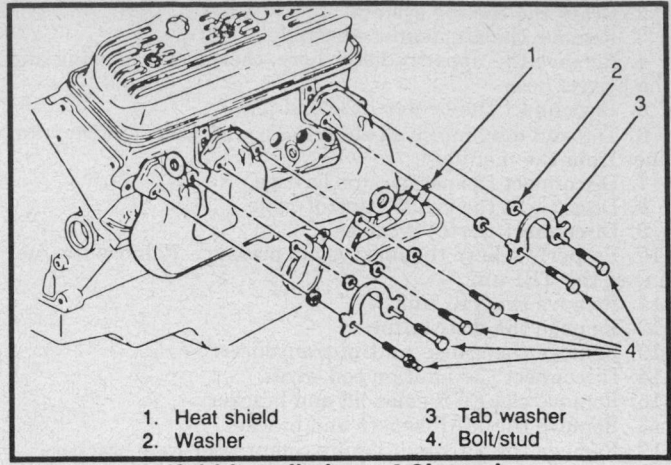

1. Heat shield	3. Tab washer
2. Washer	4. Bolt/stud

Exhaust manifold installation – 4.3L engine

15. Install the dipstick tube.
16. Install the heat stove pipe.
17. Connect the battery.

LEFT SIDE

1. Disconnect the negative battery cable.
2. Disconnect the oxygen sensor wire.
3. Disconnect the AIR hose at the check valve.
4. Remove the spark plugs.
5. Raise and support the vehicle safely. Disconnect the exhaust pipe at the manifold.
6. Lower the vehicle and remove the manifold bolts and spark plug heat shields.
7. Remove the manifold.

To install:

8. Clean the mating surfaces.
9. Clean the stud threads.
10. Install the manifold and bolts. Tighten the bolts to 40 ft. lbs. starting from the center bolts and working towards the outside.
11. Connect the exhaust pipe at the manifold.
12. Install the spark plugs.
13. Connect the AIR hose at the check valve.
14. Connect the oxygen sensor wire.
15. Connect the battery.

VAN

4.3L, 5.0L and 5.7L Engines

Tab locks are used on the front and rear pairs of bolts on each exhaust manifold. When removing the bolts, straighten the tabs from beneath the Van using a suitable tool. When installing the tab locks, bend the tabs against the sides of the bolt, not over the top of the bolt.

1. Disconnect the negative battery cable. Remove the air cleaner.
2. Remove the hot air shroud, if so equipped.
3. Loosen the alternator and remove its lower bracket.
4. On some vehicles it may be necessary to remove the power steering pump rear bracket on the left manifold and the dipstick tube bracket on the right side.
5. Disconnect the oxygen sensor wire, if so equipped.
6. Raise and support the vehicle safely.
7. Disconnect the crossover pipe from both manifolds.

NOTE: On models with air conditioning it may be necessary to remove the compressor, and tie it out of the way. Do not disconnect the compressor lines.

8. Lower the vehicle, remove the manifold bolts and remove the manifold(s). Some models have lock tabs on the front and

rear manifold bolts which must be removed before removing the bolts. These tabs can be bent with a drift pin.

9. Installation is the reverse of removal. Torque the bolts to the proper specification and in the proper sequence.

7.4L Engine

RIGHT SIDE

1. Disconnect the negative battery cable.
2. Remove the heat stove pipe.
3. Remove the dipstick tube.
4. Disconnect the AIR hose at the check valve.
5. Remove the spark plugs.
6. Raise and support the vehicle safely and disconnect the exhaust pipe at the manifold.
7. Lower the vehicle and remove the manifold bolts and spark plug heat shields.
8. Remove the manifold.

To install:

9. Clean the mating surfaces.
10. Clean the stud threads.
11. Install the manifold and bolts. Tighten the bolts to 40 ft. lbs. starting from the center bolts and working towards the outside.
12. Connect the exhaust pipe at the manifold.
13. Install the spark plugs.
14. Connect the AIR hose at the check valve.
15. Install the dipstick tube.
16. Install the heat stove pipe.
17. Connect the battery.

LEFT SIDE

1. Disconnect the negative battery cable.
2. Disconnect the oxygen sensor wire.
3. Disconnect the AIR hose at the check valve.
4. Remove the spark plugs.
5. Raise and support the vehicle safely and disconnect the exhaust pipe at the manifold.
6. Lower the vehicle and remove the manifold bolts and spark plug heat shields.
7. Remove the manifold.

To install:

8. Clean the mating surfaces.
9. Clean the stud threads.
10. Install the manifold and bolts. Tighten the bolts to 40 ft. lbs. starting from the center bolts and working towards the outside.
11. Connect the exhaust pipe at the manifold.
12. Install the spark plugs.
13. Connect the AIR hose at the check valve.
14. Connect the oxygen sensor wire.
15. Connect the battery.

Combination Manifold

Removal and Installation

1986 C/K SERIES

4.8L Engine

1. Disconnect the negative battery cable.
2. Remove the air cleaner.
3. Disconnect the throttle controls at the bellcrank.
4. Remove the carburetor, if necessary.
5. Disconnect the fuel and vacuum lines from the manifold.
6. Remove the AIR pump and bracket.
7. Disconnect the PCV hose.
8. Disconnect the exhaust pipe.
9. Remove the manifold heat stove.
10. Remove the clamps, bolts and washers and remove the combination manifold.

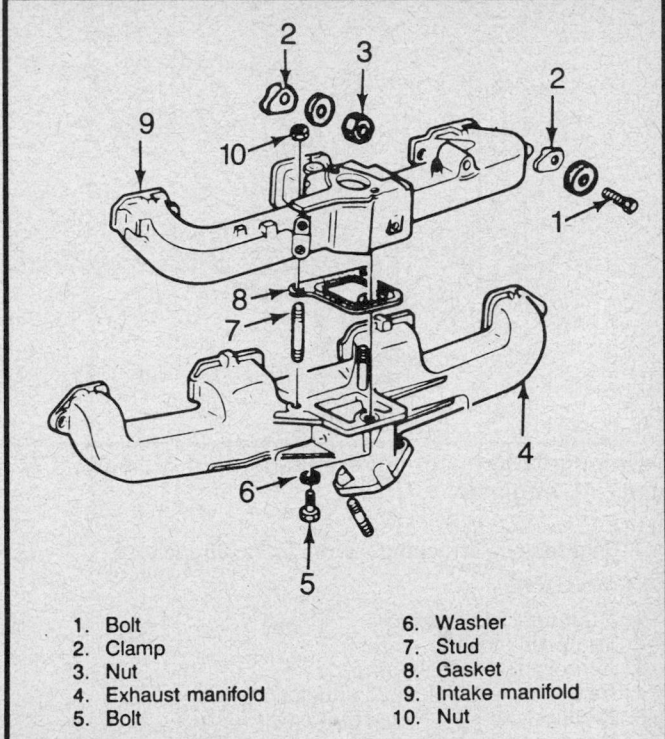

1.	Bolt	6.	Washer
2.	Clamp	7.	Stud
3.	Nut	8.	Gasket
4.	Exhaust manifold	9.	Intake manifold
5.	Bolt	10.	Nut

Combination manifolds — 4.8L engine

11. Separate the manifolds by removing the bolts and nuts.

To install:

12. Clean the mating surfaces.
13. Clean the stud threads.
14. Assemble the manifolds with a new gasket and leave the nuts finger tight.
15. Install a new gasket over the manifold studs on the cylinder head and install the manifold assembly.
16. Install the bolts, clamps and nuts.

NOTE: Always tighten the manifold to cylinder head bolts and nuts (38 ft. lbs.) before tightening the manifold center bolts and nuts (44 ft. lbs.).

17. The remainder of the installation is the reverse of removal.

Timing Chain Cover and Oil Seal

Removal and Installation

4.3L, 5.0L AND 5.7L ENGINES

1. Disconnect the negative battery cable. Drain the cooling system.
2. Remove the crankshaft pulley and damper. Remove the water pump. Remove the screws holding the timing case cover to the block and remove the cover and gaskets.
3. Use a suitable tool to pry the old seal out of the front face of the cover.
4. Install the new seal so that the open end is toward the inside of the cover.

NOTE: Coat the lip of the new seal with oil prior to installation.

5. Check that the timing chain oil slinger is in place against the crankshaft sprocket.
6. Apply sealer to the front cover. Install the cover carefully onto the locating dowels.

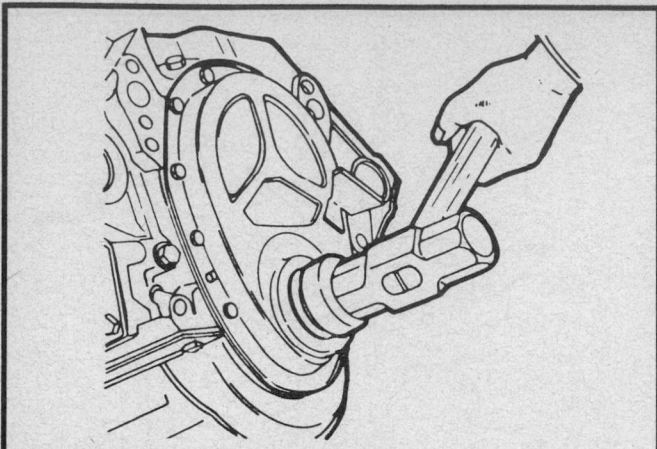

Seal installation with cover installed—4.3L, 5.0L, 5.7L and 7.4L engines

7. Tighten the attaching screws to 72–96 inch lbs.

4.8L ENGINE

1. Disconnect the battery.
2. Drain the cooling system.
3. Remove the water pump.
4. Remove the crankshaft pulley and damper.
5. Remove the oil pan-to-front cover bolts.
6. Remove the screws holding the timing case cover to the block, pull the cover forward enough to cut the front oil pan seal. Cut the seal flush with the block on both sides.
7. Pull off the cover and gaskets.
8. Use a suitable tool to pry the old seal out of the front face of the cover.

To install:

9. Lubricate the new seal lip with engine oil and using a seal centering tool and installer J–23042, or equivalent, press the new seal into place. Leave the tool in position on the seal.
10. Install a new front pan seal, cutting the tabs off.
11. Coat a new cover gasket with adhesive sealer and position it on the block.
12. Apply a ⅛ in. bead of RTV gasket material to the front cover. Install the cover carefully in place with the centering tool still atttached.
13. Tighten the timing gear cover to block bolts to 80 inch lbs.
14. Tighten the cover-to-pan bolts to 45 inch lbs.
15. Install the damper.
16. Install the water pump.
17. Connect the battery cables.
18. Fill the cooling system.

7.4L ENGINE

1. Disconnect the negative battery cable.
2. Drain the cooling system.
3. Remove the water pump.
4. Remove the crankshaft pulley and damper.
5. Remove the oil pan-to-front cover bolts.
6. Remove the screws holding the timing case cover to the block, pull the cover forward enough to cut the front oil pan seal. Cut the seal flush with the block on both sides.
7. Pull off the cover and gaskets.
8. Use a suitable tool to pry the old seal out of the front face of the cover.

To install:

9. Using seal driver J–22102, or equivalent, install the new seal so that the open end is toward the inside of the cover.

NOTE: Coat the lip of the new seal with oil prior to installation.

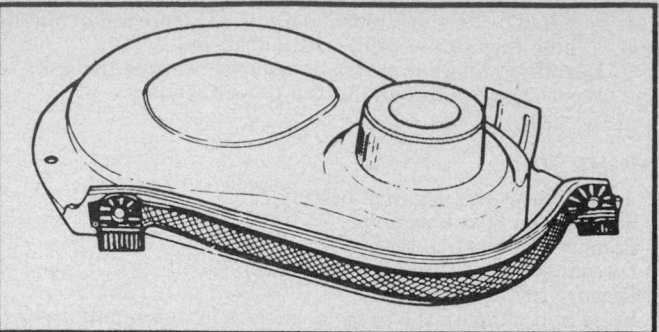

Installing the timing gear cover and seal—4.8L engine

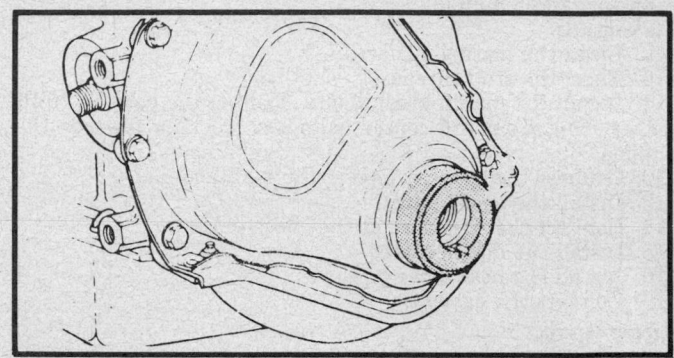

Installing the timing gear cover and seal—4.8L engine

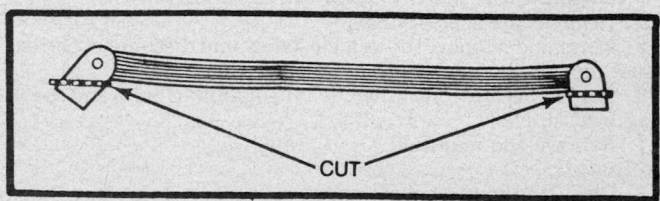

Cut these portions off the front cover to pan seal—4.8L engine

10. Install a new front pan seal, cutting the tabs off.
11. Coat a new cover gasket with adhesive sealer and position it on the block.
12. Apply a ⅛ in. bead of RTV gasket material to the front cover. Install the cover carefully onto the locating dowels.
13. Tighten the attaching screws to 96 inch lbs.
14. Tighten the cover-to-pan bolts to 70 inch lbs.
15. Install the damper.
16. Install the water pump.
17. Connect the battery cables.
18. Fill the cooling system.

Timing Chain and Sprockets

Removal and Installation

4.3L, 5.0L, 5.7L AND 7.4L ENGINES

1. Disconnect the negative battery cable. Remove the radiator, water pump, the harmonic balancer and the crankcase front cover. This will allow access to the timing chain.
2. Crank the engine until the timing marks on both sprockets are nearest each other and in line between the shaft centers.
3. Take out the 3 bolts that hold the camshaft gear to the camshaft. This gear is a light press fit on the camshaft and will

come off easily. It is located by a dowel. The chain comes off with the camshaft gear.

NOTE: A gear puller will be required to remove the crankshaft gear.

4. Without disturbing the position of the engine, mount the new crankshaft gear on the shaft, and mount the chain over the camshaft gear. Arrange the camshaft gear in such a way that the timing marks will line up between the shaft centers and the camshaft locating dowel will enter the dowel hole in the cam sprocket.

5. Place the cam sprocket, with its chain mounted over it, in position on the front of the vehicle and pull up with the 3 bolts that hold it to the camshaft.

6. After the gears are in place, turn the engine 2 full revolutions to make certain that the timing marks are in correct alignment between the shaft centers.

Endplay of the camshaft is zero.

Camshaft Timing Gear

Removal and Installation

4.8L ENGINE

The camshaft on these engines is gear driven, unlike the chain driven V6 and V8 engines. The camshaft must be removed to replace the gear.

1. Disconnect the negative battery cable. Remove the camshaft and place in an arbor press.

NOTE: Support the camshaft gear not the thrust plate.

2. Press the gear off of the camshaft and remove the thrust plate and the spacer.

To install:

3. Support the camshaft at the front journal with tool J–22912–01 or equivalent, and mount the camshaft in a press.

4. Lubricate the thrust plate with engine oil.

5. Install the key if removed.

6. Install the spacer making sure the chamfer in the spacer faces toward the journal radius.

7. Install the thrust plate.

8. Install the camshaft gear on with the timing mark to the outside and press the gear on until it bottoms on the spacer.

9. Remove the camshaft from the press.

NOTE: The clearance between the camshaft and thrust plate should be 0.003–0.008 in.

Camshaft

Removal and Installation

4.3L ENGINE

1986 C/K Series and 1987 R/V Series

1. Disconnect the negative battery cable and properly relieve the fuel system pressure.

2. Remove the fan, shroud and drain and remove the radiator.

3. Remove the fuel pump.

4. Remove the air cleaner.

5. Remove the alternator belt, loosen the alternator bolts and move the alternator to the side.

6. Remove the rocker arm covers.

7. Disconnect the fuel line.

8. Remove the water pump.

9. Remove the torsional damper.

10. Remove the front cover.

11. Disconnect the electrical and vacuum connections.

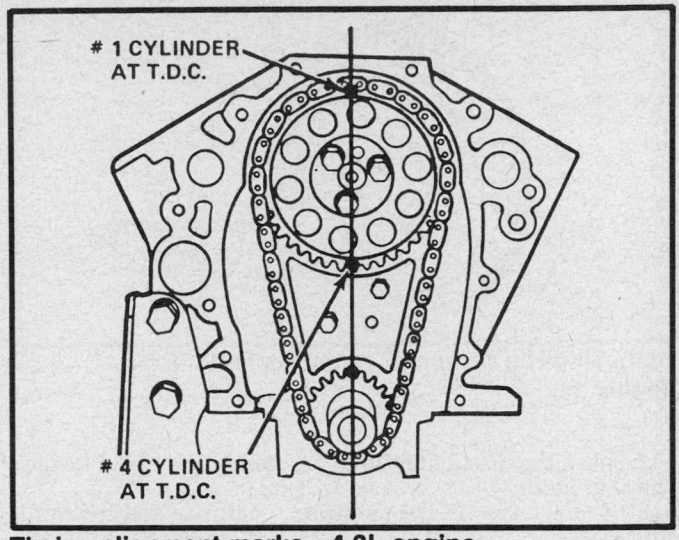

Timing alignment marks—4.3L engine

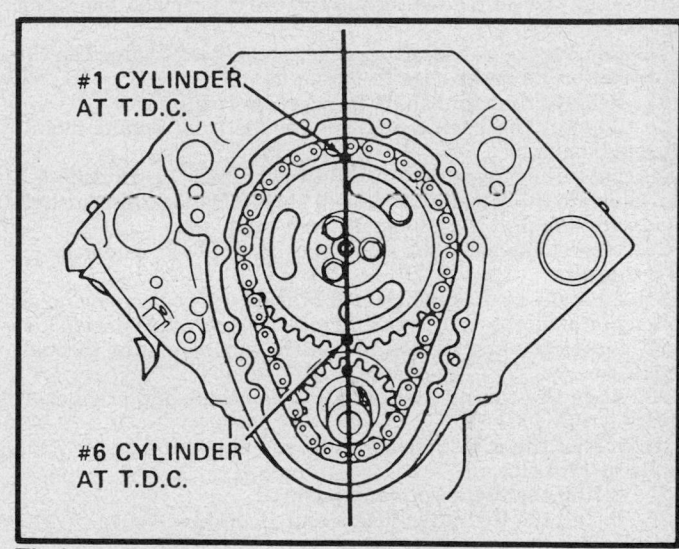

Timing alignment marks—5.0L, 5.7L and 7.4L engines

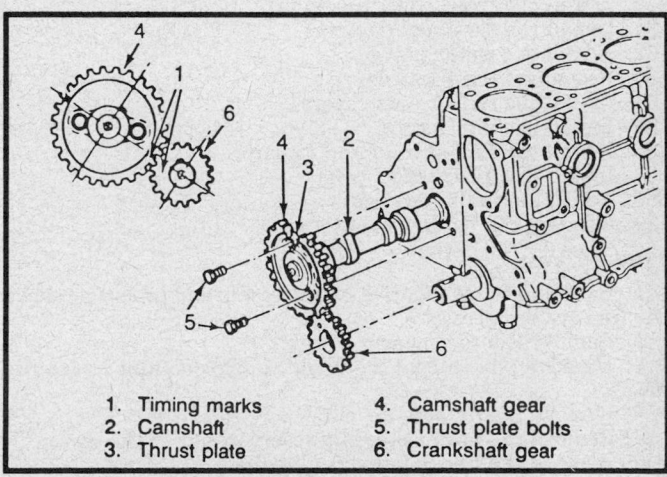

1. Timing marks
2. Camshaft
3. Thrust plate
4. Camshaft gear
5. Thrust plate bolts
6. Crankshaft gear

Camshaft and components installation and alignment—4.8L engine

Removing the camshaft thrust plate bolts—4.8L engine

12. Mark the distributor as to location in the block. Remove the distributor.

13. Remove the intake manifold, pushrods and hydraulic lifters.

14. Remove the fuel pump pushrod.

15. Align the timing marks and remove the camshaft sprocket bolts.

16. Remove the camshaft sprocket and timing chain. Tap the sprocket on its lower edge to loosen it.

17. Remove the crankshaft sprocket, as required.

18. Support the engine and remove the front engine mount through bolts.

19. Raise the engine and install two or three $^5/_{16}$–18 bolts 4–5 in. long into the camshaft threaded holes to handle the camshaft and carefully pull the camshaft from the block.

20. Inspect the shaft for signs of excessive wear or damage.

To install:

21. Liberally coat camshaft and bearing with heavy engine oil or engine assembly lubricant and insert the cam into the engine.

22. Lower the engine and install the engine mount through bolts.

23. Align the timing marks on the camshaft and crankshaft gears.

24. Install the camshaft sprocket and chain and tighten the bolts to 18 ft. lbs.

25. Install the fuel pump and pushrod.

26. Install the hydraulic lifters and pushrods.

27. Adjust the valves.

28. Install the intake manifold.

29. Install the distributor.

30. Install the front cover assembly.

31. Install the torsional damper.

32. Install the water pump.

33. Reconnect the fuel line.

34. Install the rocker arm covers.

35. Install the alternator.

36. Install the fan, shroud and radiator.

37. Install the air cleaner.

38. Refill the cooling system.

39. Connect the battery cable.

1986–87 Van

1. Disconnect the negative battery cable and properly relieve the fuel system pressure.

2. Remove the rocker arm covers.

3. Remove the intake manifold, pushrods and hydraulic lifters.

4. Remove the outside air duct.

5. Remove the power steering reservoir out of the way.

6. Remove the upper fan shroud bolts.

7. Drain and remove the radiator.

8. Disconnect the hood release cable at the latch.

9. Remove the upper fan shroud.

10. Remove the AIR pump, generator, air conditioning compressor, and power steering pump belts.

11. Remove the AIR pump and bracket.

12. Remove the water pump.

13. Remove the torsional damper.

14. Remove the front cover.

15. Remove the fuel pump and pushrod.

16. Align the timing marks on the timing gears.

17. Remove the camshaft sprocket and timing chain. Tap the sprocket on its lower edge to loosen it.

18. Remove the crankshaft sprocket, as required.

19. Support the engine and remove the front engine mount through bolts.

20. Install two or three $^5/_{16}$–18 bolts 4–5 in. long into the camshaft threaded holes to handle the camshaft and carefully pull the camshaft from the block.

21. Inspect the shaft for signs of excessive wear or damage.

To install:

22. Liberally coat camshaft and bearing with heavy engine oil or engine assembly lubricant and insert the cam into the engine.

23. Lower the engine and install the engine mount through bolts.

24. Align the timing marks on the camshaft and crankshaft gears.

25. Install the camshaft sprocket and chain and tighten the bolts to 18 ft. lbs.

26. Install the fuel pump and pushrod.

27. Install the front cover assembly.

28. Install the water pump.

29. Install the AIR pump and bracket.

31. Remove the AIR pump, generator, air conditioning compressor, and power steering pump belts.

32. Install the torsional damper.

33. Place into position the upper fan shroud.

34. Install the hood release cable.

35. Install the radiator.

36. Install the upper fan shroud bolts.

37. Install the power steering reservoir.

38. Install the outside air ducts.

39. Install the hydraulic lifters and pushrods and adjust the valves.

40. Install the rocker arm covers.

41. Connect the battery negative cable.

1988–90 R/V Series and 1988–90 Van

1. Disconnect the negative battery cable and properly relieve the fuel system pressure.

2. Remove the rocker arm covers.

3. Remove the intake manifold, pushrods and hydraulic lifters.

4. Remove the outside air duct.

5. Remove the power steering reservoir out of the way.

6. Remove the upper fan shroud bolts.

7. Drain and remove the radiator.

8. Disconnect the hood release cable at the latch.

9. Remove the upper fan shroud.

10. Remove the water pump.

11. Remove the torsional damper.

12. Remove the front cover.

13. Align the timing marks and remove the camshaft sprocket bolts.

14. Remove the camshaft sprocket and timing chain. Tap the sprocket on its lower edge to loosen it.

15. Remove the crankshaft sprocket, as required.

16. Support the engine and remove the front engine mount through bolts.

17. Install two or three $^5/_{16}$–18 bolts 4–5 in. long into the camshaft threaded holes to handle the camshaft and carefully pull the camshaft from the block.

18. Inspect the shaft for signs of excessive wear or damage.

To install:

19. Liberally coat camshaft and bearing with heavy engine oil or engine assembly lubricant and insert the cam into the engine.

20. Lower the engine and install the engine mount through bolts.

21. Align the timing marks on the camshaft and crankshaft gears.

22. Install the camshaft sprocket and chain and tighten the bolts to 21 ft. lbs.

23. Install the front cover assembly.

24. Install the torsional damper.

25. Install the water pump.

26. Install the fan shroud and radiator.

27. Connect the hood release cable at the latch.

28. Install the outside air duct.

29. Install the hydraulic lifters and pushrods.

30. Adjust the valves.

31. Install the rocker arm covers.

32. Install the intake manifold.

33. Refill the cooling system.

34. Connect the battery cable.

1988–90 C/K Series

1. Disconnect the negative battery cable and properly relieve the fuel system pressure.

2. Remove the air cleaner.

3. Remove the fan, shroud and drain and remove the radiator.

4. Remove the rocker arm covers.

5. Remove the water pump.

6. Remove the torsional damper.

7. Remove the front cover.

8. Mark the distributor as to location in the block. Remove the distributor.

9. Remove the intake manifold, pushrods and hydraulic lifters.

10. Align the timing marks and remove the camshaft sprock bolts.

11. Remove the camshaft sprocket and timing chain. Tap the sprocket on its lower edge to loosen it.

12. Remove the screws and the thrust plate.

13. Remove the crankshaft sprocket, as required.

14. Install two or three $^5/_{16}$–18 bolts 4–5 in. long into the camshaft threaded holes to handle the camshaft and carefully pull the camshaft from the block.

15. Inspect the shaft for signs of excessive wear or damage.

To install:

16. Liberally coat camshaft and bearing with heavy engine oil or engine assembly lubricant and insert the cam into the engine.

17. Install the screws and the thrust plate.

18. Install the crankshaft sprocket, as required.

19. Align the timing marks on the camshaft and crankshaft gears.

20. Install the camshaft sprocket and chain and tighten the bolts to 23 ft. lbs.

21. Install the hydraulic lifters and pushrods.

22. Adjust the valves.

23. Install the intake manifold.

24. Install the front cover assembly.

25. Install the torsional damper.

26. Install the water pump.

27. Install the rocker arm covers.

28. Install the fan, shroud and radiator.

29. Install the air cleaner.

30. Refill the cooling system.

31. Connect the battery cable.

4.8L ENGINE

1986 C/K Series

1. Remove the engine assembly and mount in a suitable stand.

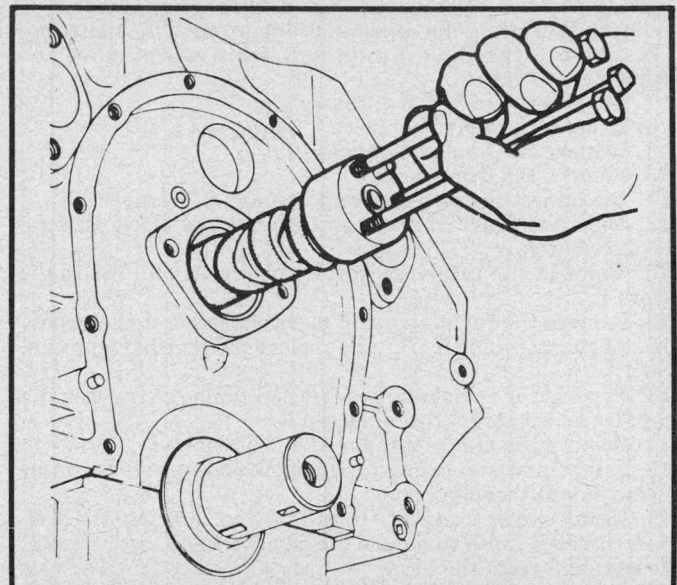

Install two or three $^5/_{16}$–18 bolts 4–5 inches long into the camshaft threaded holes to handle the camshaft—4.3L, 5.0L, 5.7L and 7.4L engines

2. Remove the hydraulic lifters.

3. Remove the timimg gear cover.

4. Remove the fuel pump.

5. Remove the distributor.

6. Align the timing marks on the camshaft and crankshaft gears.

7. Remove the thrust plate bolts.

8. Support and carefully remove the camshaft.

9. If either the camshaft or the camshaft gear is being renewed, the gear must be pressed off the camshaft. The replacement parts must be assembled in the same way. When placing the gear on the camshaft, press the gear onto the shaft until it bottoms against the gear spacer ring. The end clearance of the thrust plate should be 0.003–0.008 in.

10. Pre-lube the camshaft lobes with clean engine oil and then install the camshaft assembly in the engine. Be careful not to damage the Bearings.

11. Turn the crankshaft and the camshaft gears so that the timing marks align. Push the camshaft into position and install and torque the thrust plate bolts to 80 inch lbs.

12. Check camshaft and crankshaft gear runout with a dial indicator. Camshaft gear runout should not exceed 0.004 inches and crankshaft gear run-out should not be above 0.003 inches.

13. Using a dial indicator, check the backlash at several points between the camshaft and crankshaft gear teeth. Backlash should be 0.004–0.006 inches.

14. Install the timing gear cover.

15. Install the distributor.

16. Install the fuel pump.

17. Install the valve lifters and the pushrods.

18. Install the engine.

5.0L AND 5.7L ENGINES

All Series

1. Disconnect the negative battery cable, Drain the cooling system and properly relieve the fuel system pressure before disconnecting fuel lines.

2. On the Van, remove the engine cover.

3. Remove the air cleaner.

4. On the Van, remove the grille.

5. On the Van, remove the air conditioning condenser, if equipped, and swing the condenser forward from its mounting.

6. Remove the fan, shroud and drain and remove the radiator.

7. Remove the rocker arm covers.

8. Remove the water pump.

9. Remove the torsional damper.

10. Remove the front cover.

11. Disconnect the electrical and vacuum connections.

12. Mark the distributor as to location in the block. Remove the distributor.

13. Remove the intake manifold, pushrods and hydraulic lifters.

14. Remove the fuel pump and pushrod, carbureted engines.

15. Align the timing marks and remove the camshaft sprocket bolts.

16. Remove the camshaft sprocket and timing chain. Tap the sprocket on its lower edge to loosen it.

17. Remove the crankshaft sprocket, as required.

18. Safely raise and support the engine and remove the front engine mount through bolts.

19. Install two or three $5/16$–18 bolts 4–5 in. long into the camshaft threaded holes to handle the camshaft and carefully pull the camshaft from the block.

20. Inspect the shaft for signs of excessive wear or damage.

To install:

21. Liberally coat camshaft and bearing with heavy engine oil or engine assembly lubricant and insert the cam into the engine.

22. Lower the engine and install the engine mount through bolts.

23. Align the timing marks on the camshaft and crankshaft gears.

24. Install the camshaft sprocket and chain and tighten the bolts to 18 ft. lbs.

25. Install the fuel pump and pushrod (carbureted engines).

26. Install the hydraulic lifters and pushrods and adjust the valves.

27. Install the distributor.

28. Install the front cover.

29. Install the torsional damper.

30. Install the water pump.

31. Install the rocker arm covers.

32. Install the fan, shroud and radiator.

33. On the Van, install the air conditioning condenser, if equipped.

34. On the Van, install the grille.

35. Install the air cleaner.

36. On the Van, install the engine cover.

37. Connect the battery cable and fill the cooling system.

7.4L ENGINE

All Series

1. Disconnect the negative battery cable. Properly relieve the fuel system pressure before disconnecting fuel lines.

2. Remove the air cleaner.

3. Remove the grille.

4. Properly discharge the air conditioning system. Remove the air conditioning condenser.

5. Drain the cooling system.

6. Remove the fan shroud and radiator.

7. Remove the alternator belt, loosen the alternator bolts and move the alternator to one side.

8. Remove the valve covers.

9. Disconnect the hoses from the water pump.

10. Remove the water pump.

11. Remove the harmonic balancer and pulley.

12. Remove the engine front cover.

13. Mark the distributor as to location in the block. Remove the distributor.

14. Remove the intake manifold.

15. Mark the lifters, pushrods, and rocker arms as to location so that they may be installed in the same position. Remove these parts.

16. Rotate the camshaft so that the timing marks align.

17. Remove the camshaft sprocket bolts.

18. Pull the camshaft sprocket and timing chain off. The sprocket is a tight fit, so you have to tap it loose with a plastic mallet.

19. Install two $5/16$–18 bolts in the holes in the front of the camshaft and carefully pull the camshaft from the block.

To install:

20. Liberally coat camshaft and bearing with heavy engine oil or engine assembly lubricant and insert the cam into the engine.

21. Align the timing marks on the camshaft and crankshaft gears.

22. Install the camshaft sprocket and chain and tighten the bolts to 20 ft. lbs.

23. Install the lifters and pushrods and adjust the valves.

24. Install the intake manifold.

25. Install the distributor using the locating marks made during removal.

26. Install the engine front cover.

27. Install the harmonic balancer and pulley.

28. Install the water pump.

29. Connect the hoses at the water pump.

30. Install the valve covers.

31. Install the alternator.

32. Install the fan shroud and radiator.

33. Fill the cooling system.

34. Install the air conditioning condenser.

35. Install the grille.

36. Install the air cleaner.

37. Connect the battery.

Piston and Conncecting Rod

Positioning

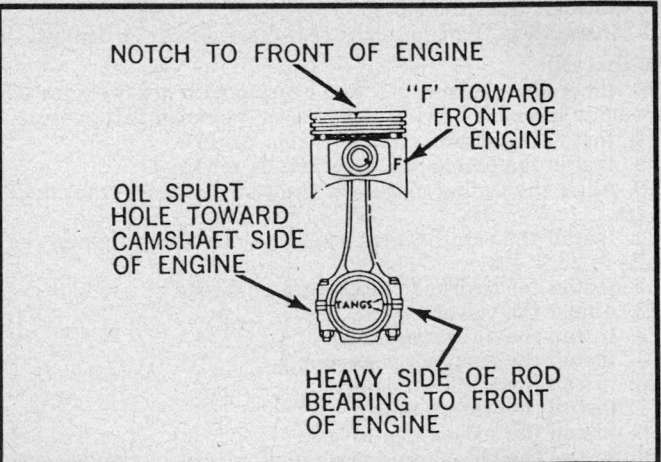

Correct relationship of the piston and rod—4.8L engine

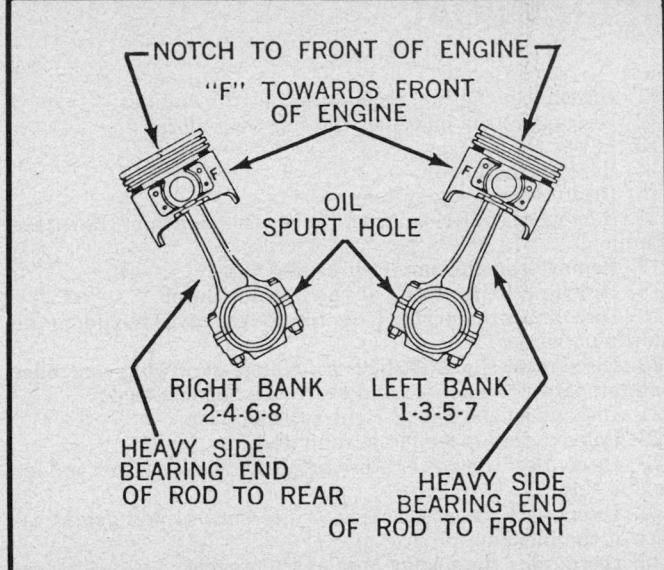

Correct relationship of the piston and rod—5.0L, 5.7L engines

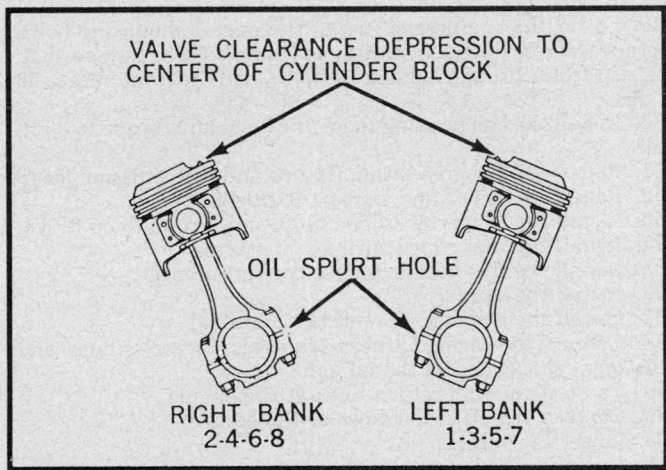

Correct relationship of the piston and rod—7.4L engine

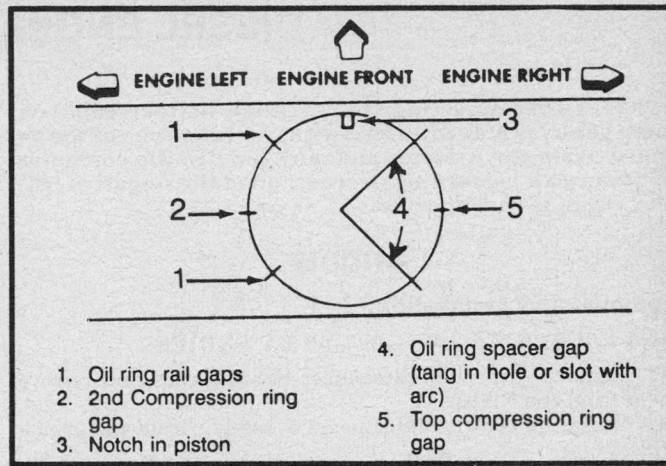

1. Oil ring rail gaps
2. 2nd Compression ring gap
3. Notch in piston
4. Oil ring spacer gap (tang in hole or slot with arc)
5. Top compression ring gap

Piston ring gap locations—4.3L, 5.0L, 5.7L engines

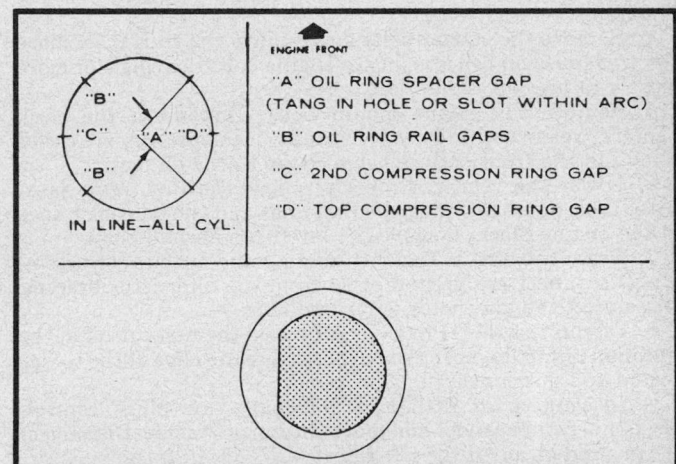

"A" OIL RING SPACER GAP (TANG IN HOLE OR SLOT WITHIN ARC)

"B" OIL RING RAIL GAPS

"C" 2ND COMPRESSION RING GAP

"D" TOP COMPRESSION RING GAP

Piston ring gap locations—4.8L engine

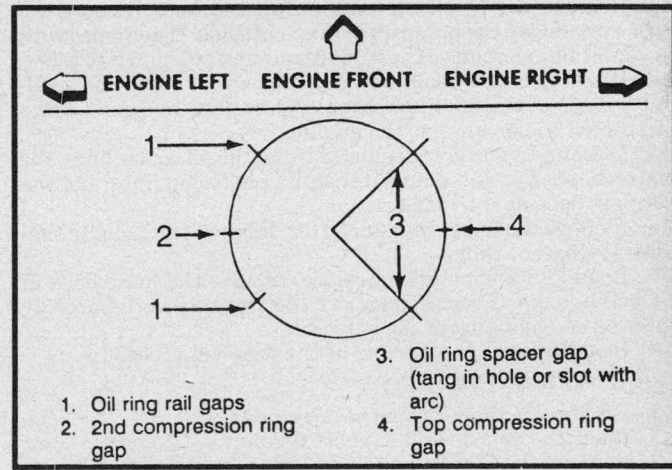

1. Oil ring rail gaps
2. 2nd compression ring gap
3. Oil ring spacer gap (tang in hole or slot with arc)
4. Top compression ring gap

Piston ring gap locations—7.4L engine

DIESEL ENGINE MECHANICAL

NOTE: Disconnecting the negative battery cable on some vehicles may interfere with the functions of the on board computer systems and may require the computer to undergo a relearning process, once the negative battery cable is reconnected.

Engine

Removal and Installation

1986 C/K SERIES AND 1987–90 RV SERIES

1. Remove the hood. Disconnect the batteries and remove them from the vehicle.
2. Raise the vehicle and support it safely. Drain the engine oil.
3. Remove the flywheel cover. Disconnect the torque converter from the flexplate. Disconnect the exhaust pipes from the manifolds.
4. Remove the starter bolts and remove the starter. Remove the transmission bell housing to engine bolts, leaving 1 or more loosely to prevent separation.
5. Remove the engine mount bolts. Disconnect the block heaters, remove the wiring harness, transmission oil cooler lines and the front battery cable clamp at the oil pan.
6. Lower the vehicle. Properly relieve the fuel pump pressure. Disconnect and plug the fuel lines and the oil cooler lines at the engine block. Remove the lower fan shroud bolts.
7. Drain the engine coolant. Remove the air cleaner assembly. Disconnect the ground cable from the alternator bracket. Disconnect the alternator wires and clips.
8. Disconnect the TPS, EGR–EPR and the fuel cut-off at the injection pump. Remove the harness from the clips at the rocker covers and disconnect the glow plugs.
9. Disconnect the EGR–EPR solenoids, glow plugs, controller, temperature sender and move the harness aside. Disconnect the ground strap on the left side.
10. Remove the fan assembly. Remove the upper radiator hoses at the engine. Remove the fan shroud.
11. Remove the power steering pump and belt. Remove the reservoir and lay the pump and reservoir aside. If equipped with air conditioning, remove the compressor and position it to aside.
12. Disconnect the vacuum lines at the cruise servo and accelerator cable at the injection pump. Disconnect the heater hoses and the oil cooler lines at the engine.
13. Disconnect the lower radiator hose, the oil cooler lines, the heater hose, the automatic transmission cooler lines and the overflow hose at the radiator.
14. Remove the upper radiator cover. Remove the radiator. Remove the detent cable.
15. Install an engine lifting device, remove the loose bolts in the bell housing. Properly support the transmission. Carefully remove the engine from the vehicle.
17. Installation is the reverse of the removal procedure.

1988–90 C/K SERIES

1. Disconnect the negative battery cable.
2. Raise the vehicle and support it safely.
3. Remove the flywheel or torque converter cover.
4. On vehicles equipped with automatic transmission, remove the converter to flex plate bolts.
5. Disconnect the exhaust pipes from the manifold.
6. Remove the starter.
7. Remove the bell housing bolts.
8. Remove the engine mounting through bolts.
9. Disconnect the block heater wiring.
10. Disconnect the wiring harness, transmission cooler lines, and a battery cable clamp at the oil pan.

11. Disconnect the fuel return lines at the engine.
12. Disconnect the oil cooler lines at the engine.
13. Lower the vehicle.
14. Remove the hood.
15. Drain the cooling system.
16. Remove the air cleaner and cover the mouth of the intake manifold.
17. Remove the alternator wires and clips.
18. Disconnect the wiring at the injector pump.
19. Disconnect the wiring from the rocker cover including the glow plug wires.
20. Disconnect the EGR-EPR solenoids, glow plug controller and temperature solenoid and move the harness aside.
21. Disconnect the left or right ground strap.
22. Remove the upper fan shroud and fan.
23. Disconnect the power steering pump and reservoir and lay to one side.
24. Disconnect the accelerator, cruise control and detent cables at the injection pump.
25. Disconnect the heater hose at the engine.
26. Remove the radiator.
27. Support the transmission with a suitable jack.
28. Remove the engine.

To install:

29. Lower the engine and install the engine mounting bolts. Torque the rear engine mounting to frame bolts or nuts to 45 ft. lbs., the front through bolts to 70 ft. lbs. and the front nuts to 50 ft. lbs.
30. Install the bell housing to engine bolts and torque to 30 ft. lbs.
31. Remove the engine lifting fixture and transmission jack.
32. Raise the vehicle and support it safely.
33. Install the converter to flex bolts and torque to 35 ft. lbs.
34. Install the fuel gauge wiring and starter.
35. Install the flywheel or torque converter cover.
36. Install the starter.
37. Install the exhaust pipes at the manifold.
38. Connect the wiring harness, transmission cooler lines, and a battery cable clamp at the oil pan.
40. Connect the fuel return lines at the engine.
42. Connect the oil cooler lines at the engine.
38. Lower the vehicle.
40. Install the radiator.
41. Install the heater hose to the engine.
42. Connect the accelerator, cruise control and detent cables at the injection pump.
43. Connect the power steering pump and reservoir.
44. Install the fan and the upper fan shroud.
45. Install the ground strap.
46. Connect the wiring to the rocker cover including the glow plug wires.
47. Connect the EGR-EPR solenoids, glow plug controller and temperature solenoid harness.
48. Connect the alternator wires and clips.
49. Connect the wiring at the injector pump.
50. Install the air cleaner.
51. Install the hood.
52. Connect the negative battery cable.
53. Install the proper quantity and grade of coolant.

VAN

1. Disconnect the negative battery cable, then the positive battery cable, at the battery. Properly relieve the fuel system pressure.
2. Remove the upper radiator support.
3. Remove the grille.
4. Remove the bumper.

5. Remove the lower grille valance.
6. Remove the hood latch.
7. Drain the cooling system.
8. Remove the radiator coolant reservoir bottle.
9. Remove the radiator support bracket.
10. Remove the radiator and the fan shroud.
11. Remove the engine cover.
12. Remove the air cleaner.
13. Properly discharge the air conditioning system.
14. Remove the air conditioning condenser and cap all openings.
15. Disconnect the air cleaner bracket at the valve cover.
16. Remove the crankcase ventilator bracket and move it aside.
17. Disconnect the secondary fuel filter lines.
18. Remove the secondary fuel filter adapter.
19. Loosen the vacuum pump holddown clamp and rotate the pump in order to gain access to the intake manifold bolt.
20. Remove the intake manifold bolts. The injection line clips are retained by the same bolts.
21. Remove the injection line clips at the loom brackets.
22. Remove the injection lines at the nozzles and cover the nozzles with protective caps.
23. Remove the injection lines at the pump and tag the lines for later installation.
24. Remove the fuel line from the injection pump.
25. Disconnect the alternator cable at the injection pump, and the detent cable where applicable.
26. Tag and disconnect the necessary wires and hoses at the injection pump.
27. Remove the air conditioning hose retainer bracket if equipped with air conditioning.
28. Remove the oil fill tube, including the crankcase depression valve vent hose assembly.
29. Remove the grommet.
30. Scribe or paint a matchmark on the front cover and on the injection pump flange.
31. The crankshaft must be rotated in order to gain access to the injection pump drive gear bolts through the oil filler neck hole.
32. Remove the injection pump-to-front cover attaching nuts.
33. Remove the pump and cap all open lines and nozzles.
34. Remove the intake manifold.
35. Raise and support the vehicle safely.
36. Disconnect the exhaust pipes at the manifolds.
37. Lower the vehicle. Disconnect the radiator hoses at the radiator.
38. If the vehicle is equipped with an automatic transmission, remove the fluid cooler lines from the radiator.
39. Remove the windshield wiper jar and bracket.
40. Disconnect the engine wiring harness from the firewall connection.
41. Disconnect the heater hoses at the engine.
42. Remove the oil filler pipe.
43. Remove the engine dipstick tube.
44. Remove the cruise control servo, servo bracket and transducer.
45. Remove the glow plug relay.
46. **Remove the alternator upper bracket.**
47. Remove the coolant crossover/thermostat assembly.
48. Disconnect the block heater wires.
49. Remove the coolant hose at the intake manifold.
50. Remove the transmission dipstick tube and the accelerator cable.
51. Remove the air conditioning idler pulley.
52. Remove the lower fan shroud and filler panel.
53. Raise the vehicle and support it safely.
54. Drain the engine oil.
55. Remove the fuel line from the fuel tank and at the fuel pump.

56. Remove the driveshaft and plug the end of the transmission.
57. Disconnect the transmission shift linkage.
58. Disconnect the speedometer cable.
59. Remove the transmission mounting bolts.
60. Remove the engine mount bracket-to-frame bolts.
61. Remove the engine mount through bolts.
62. Raise the engine slightly and remove the engine mounts. Support the engine with wood between the oil pan and the crossmember.
63. Remove the engine and transmission as 1 unit.
64. Remove the manual transmission and clutch as follows:
    a. Remove the clutch housing rear bolts.
    b. Remove the bolts attaching the clutch housing to the engine and remove the transmission and clutch as a unit.

NOTE: Support the transmission as the last bolt is being removed to prevent damaging the clutch.

    c. Remove the starter and clutch housing rear cover.
    d. Loosen the clutch mounting bolts a little at a time to prevent distorting the disc until spring pressure is released. Remove all of the bolts, the clutch disc and the pressure plate.
65. Remove the automatic transmission as follows:
    a. Lower the engine and support it on blocks.
    b. Remove the starter and converter housing underpan.
    c. Remove the flywheel-to-converter attaching bolts.
    d. Support the transmission on blocks.
    e. Disconnect the throttle linkage and the detent cable on the Turbo Hydra-Matic.
    f. Remove the transmission-to-engine mounting bolts.
    g. Remove the blocks from the engine only and glide the engine away from the transmission.

To install:
66. Raise the engine into position.
67. Raise the engine slightly and install the engine mounts. Torque the bolts to 36 ft. lbs.
68. Install the manual transmission and clutch as follows:
    a. Install the clutch disc and the pressure plate. Tighten the clutch mounting bolts a little at a time to prevent distorting the disc.
    b. Install the starter and clutch housing rear cover.
    c. Install the bolts attaching the clutch housing to the engine and install the transmission and clutch as a unit. Torque the bolts to 30 ft. lbs.
    d. Install the clutch housing rear bolts.
69. Install the automatic transmission as follows:
    a. Position the transmission.
    b. Install the transmission-to-engine mounting bolts. Torque the bolts to 30 ft. lbs.
    c. Connect the throttle linkage and the detent cable on the Turbo Hydra-Matic.
    d. Install the flywheel-to-converter attaching bolts. Torque the bolts to 40 ft. lbs.
    e. Install the starter and converter housing underpan.
70. Install the engine mount through bolts. Torque the bolt to 75 ft. lbs.
71. Install the engine mount bracket-to-frame bolts. Torque the bolts to 40 ft. lbs. and the nuts to 30 ft. lbs.
72. Install the clutch cross-shaft.
73. Install the transmission mounting bolts. Torque the bolts to 36 ft. lbs.
74. Connect the transmission shift linkage.
75. Connect the speedometer cable.
76. Install the driveshaft.
77. Install the condenser.
78. Install the hood latch support.
79. Install the lower fan shroud and filler panel.
80. Install the air conditioning idler pulley.
81. Install the transmission dipstick tube and the accelerator cable.

82. Replace the injection pump gasket.

83. Align the locating pin on the pump hub with the slot in the injection pump driven gear. At the same time, align the timing marks.

84. Attach the injection pump to the front cover, aligning the timing marks before torquing the nuts to 30 ft. lbs.

85. Install the drive gear to injection pump bolts, torquing the bolts to 20 ft. lbs.

86. The crankshaft must be rotated in order to gain access to the injection pump drive gear bolts through the oil filler neck hole.

87. Install the air conditioning hose retainer bracket if equipped with air conditioning.

88. Connect the fuel feed line at the injection pump. Torque the fuel feed line at the injection pump to 20 ft. lbs.

89. Connect the fuel return line at the top of the injection pump.

90. Connect the necessary wires and hoses at the injection pump.

91. Connect the alternator cable at the injection pump, and the detent cable where applicable.

92. Install the intake manifold.

93. Install the fuel line at the injection pump.

94. Install the injection lines at the pump.

95. Install the injection lines at the nozzles.

96. Install the injection line clips at the loom brackets.

97. Install the secondary fuel filter adapter.

98. Connect the secondary fuel filter lines.

99. Install the crankcase ventilator bracket.

100. Connect the air cleaner bracket at the valve cover.

101. Connect the coolant hose at the intake manifold.

102. Install the cruise control servo, servo bracket and transducer.

103. Install the oil filler pipe.

104. Install the engine dipstick tube.

105. Install the glow plug relay.

106. Install the alternator upper bracket.

107. Install the coolant crossover/thermostat assembly.

108. Connect the block heater wires.

109. Connect the heater hoses at the engine.

110. Connect the engine wiring harness at the firewall connection.

111. Install the radiator and the shroud.

112. Install the radiator support bracket.

113. Install the windshield wiper jar and bracket.

114. Install the air conditioning vacuum reservoir.

115. Properly charge the air conditioning system.

116. If the vehicle is equipped with an automatic transmission, install the fluid cooler lines at the radiator.

117. Install the radiator coolant reservoir bottle.

118. Connect the radiator hoses at the radiator.

119. Install the upper radiator support.

120. Install the grille.

121. Install the lower grille valance.

122. Install the air cleaner.

123. Install the engine cover.

124. Fill the cooling system.

125. Connect the battery cables.

Cylinder Head

Removal and Installation

RIGHT SIDE

1. Disconnect the negative battery cable, relieve the fuel system pressure and drain the coolant system. Remove the intake manifold.

2. Remove the fuel injection lines.

3. Remove the cruise control transducer.

4. Remove the upper fan shroud.

5. Remove the air conditioning compressor belt.

6. Remove the exhaust manifold.

7. Disconnect and label the glow plug wiring.

8. Remove the oil dipsticke tube.

9. Remove the oil fill tube upper bracket.

10. Remove the rocker arm cover(s), after removing any accessory brackets which interfere with cover removal.

11. Remove the rocker arm assemblies. It is a good practice to number or mark the parts to avoid interchanging them.

12. Remove the pushrods. Keep them in order.

13. Remove the air cleaner resonator and bracket.

14. Remove the automatic transmission dipstick and tube.

15. Drain the cooling system.

16. Disconnect the heater hoses at the head.

17. Disconnect the upper radiator hose.

18. Disconnect the bypass hose.

19. Remove the alternator upper bracket.

20. Remove the coolant crossover pipe and thermostat.

21. Remove the head bolts.

22. Remove the cylinder head.

To install:

23. Clean the mating surfaces of the head and block thoroughly.

24. Install a new head gasket on the engine block. Do not coat the gaskets with any sealer on either engine. The gaskets have a special coating that eliminates the need for sealer. The use of sealer will interfere with this coating and cause leaks. Install the cylinder head onto the block.

25. Clean the head bolts thoroughly. The left rear head bolt must be installed into the head prior to head installation. Coat the threads and heads of the head bolts with sealing compound GM part No. 1052080 or equivalent, before installation. Tighten the head bolts to 20 ft. lbs. in the proper sequence, next tighten all bolts to 50 ft. lbs in the proper sequence, and finally tighten all bolts an additional 90 degrees (¼ turn).

26. Install the coolant crossover pipe and thermostat.

27. Install the alternator upper bracket.

28. Connect the bypass hose.

29. Connect the upper radiator hose.

30. Connect the heater hoses at the head.

31. Install the automatic transmission dipstick and tube.

32. Install the air cleaner resonator and bracket.

33. Install the pushrods.

34. Install the rocker arm assemblies.

35. Adjust the valves.

36. Install the rocker arm cover.

37. Install the oil fill tube upper bracket.

38. Install the oil dipsticke tube.

39. Connect the glow plug wiring.

40. Install the exhaust manifold.

41. Install the air conditioning compressor belt.

42. Install the upper fan shroud.

43. Install the cruise control transducer.

44. Install the fuel injection lines.

45. Install the intake manifold.

46. Fill the cooling system.

LEFT SIDE

1. Remove the intake manifold.

2. Remove the fuel injection lines.

3. Remove the cruise control transducer.

4. Remove the upper fan shroud.

5. Remove the air conditioning compressor belt.

6. Remove the exhaust manifold.

7. Remove the power steering pump lower adjusting bolts.

8. Disconnect and label the glow plug wiring.

9. Remove the air conditioning compressor and position it out of the way. Do not disconnect any refrigerant lines.

10. Remove the power steering pump and position it out of the way. Do not disconnect the fluid lines.

11. Remove the oil dipsticke tube.

12. Disconnect the transmission detent cable.
13. Remove the glow plug controller and bracket.
14. Remove the rocker arm cover(s), after removing any accessory brackets which interfere with cover removal.
15. Remove the rocker arm assemblies. It is a good practice to number or mark the parts to avoid interchanging them.
16. Remove the pushrods. Keep them in order.
17. Remove the air cleaner resonator and bracket.
18. Remove the automatic transmission dipstick and tube.
19. Drain the cooling system.
20. Remove the alternator upper bracket.
21. Remove the coolant crossover pipe and thermostat.
22. Remove the head bolts.
23. Remove the cylinder head.

To install:

24. Clean the mating surfaces of the head and block thoroughly.
25. Install a new head gasket on the engine block. Do NOT coat the gaskets with any sealer on either engine. The gaskets have a special coating that eliminates the need for sealer. The use of sealer will interfere with this coating and cause leaks. Install the cylinder head onto the block.
26. Clean the head bolts thoroughly. The left rear head bolt must be installed into the head prior to head installation. Coat the threads and heads of the head bolts with sealing compound (GM part #1052080 or equivalent) before installation. Tighten the head bolts as explained in the Torque Specifications Chart.
27. Install the coolant crossover pipe and thermostat.
28. Install the alternator upper bracket.
29. Install the automatic transmission dipstick and tube.
30. Install the air cleaner resonator and bracket.
31. Install the pushrods.
32. Install the rocker arm assemblies.
33. Adjust the valves.
34. Install the rocker arm cover(s).
35. Install the oil fill tube upper bracket.
36. Install the oil dipsticke tube.
37. Connect the glow plug wiring.
38. Install the compressor.
39. Install the power steering pump.
40. Install the glow plug controller.
41. Install the exhaust manifold.
42. Connect the detent cable.
43. Install the air conditioning compressor belt.
44. Install the upper fan shroud.
45. Install the cruise control transducer.
46. Install the fuel injection lines.
47. Install the intake manifold.
48. Fill the cooling system.

Valve Lash

ADJUSTMENT

All engines use hydraulic lifters, which require no periodic adjustment.

Rocker Arm

Removal and Installation

1. Disconnect the negative battery cables. On the Van, remove the engine cover.
2. Remove all the necessary components in order to gain access to the engine valve covers. As required, properly relieve the fuel system pressure before disconnecting any fuel lines.
3. Remove the valve cover retaining bolts. Remove the valve cover from the engine.
4. Remove the rocker arm assemblies. Keep them in order for reinstallation.
5. Installation is the reverse of the removal procedure. Be sure to use new gaskets or RTV sealant, as necessary.

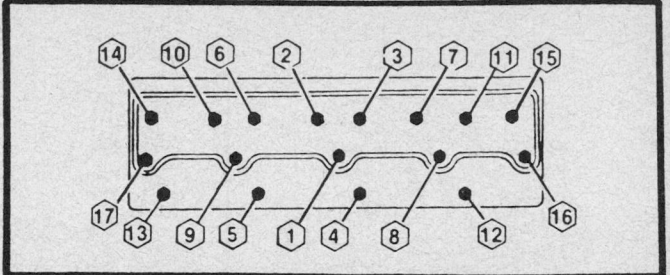

Cylinder head bolt torque sequence—6.2L diesel engine

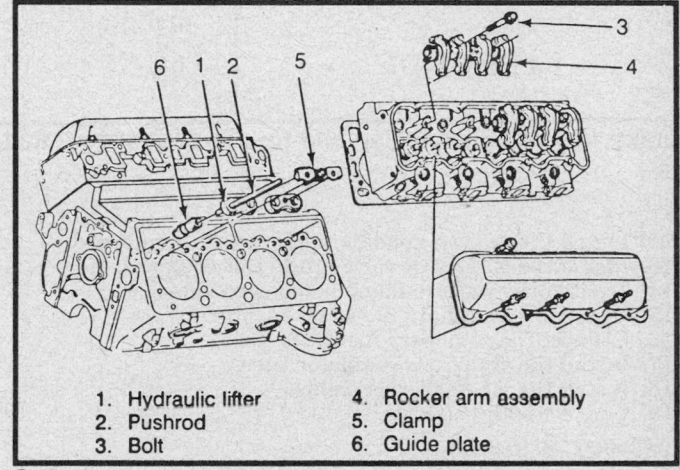

1. Hydraulic lifter	4. Rocker arm assembly
2. Pushrod	5. Clamp
3. Bolt	6. Guide plate

Cylinder head and components—6.2L diesel engine

Intake Manifold

Removal and Installation

1986 C/K SERIES AND 1987–90 R/V SERIES

1. Disconnect both batteries.
2. Drain the cooling system and properly relieve the fuel system pressure. Remove the air cleaner assembly.
3. Remove the crankcase ventilator tubes, and disconnect the secondary fuel filter lines. Remove the secondary filter and adaptor.
4. Loosen the vacuum pump holddown clamp and rotate the pump to gain access to the nearest manifold bolt.
5. Remove the EPR/EGR valve bracket, if equipped.
6. Remove the rear air conditioning bracket, if equipped.
7. Remove the intake manifold bolts. The injection line clips are retained by these bolts.
8. Remove the intake manifold.

NOTE: If the engine is to be further serviced with the manifold removed, install protective covers over the intake ports.

To install:

9. Clean the manifold gasket surfaces on the cylinder heads and install new gaskets before installing the manifold.

NOTE: The gaskets have an opening for the EGR valve on light duty installations. An insert covers this opening on heavy duty installations.

10. Install the manifold. Torque the bolts in the proper sequence and to the correct specification.
11. The secondary filter must be filled with clean diesel fuel before it is reinstalled.

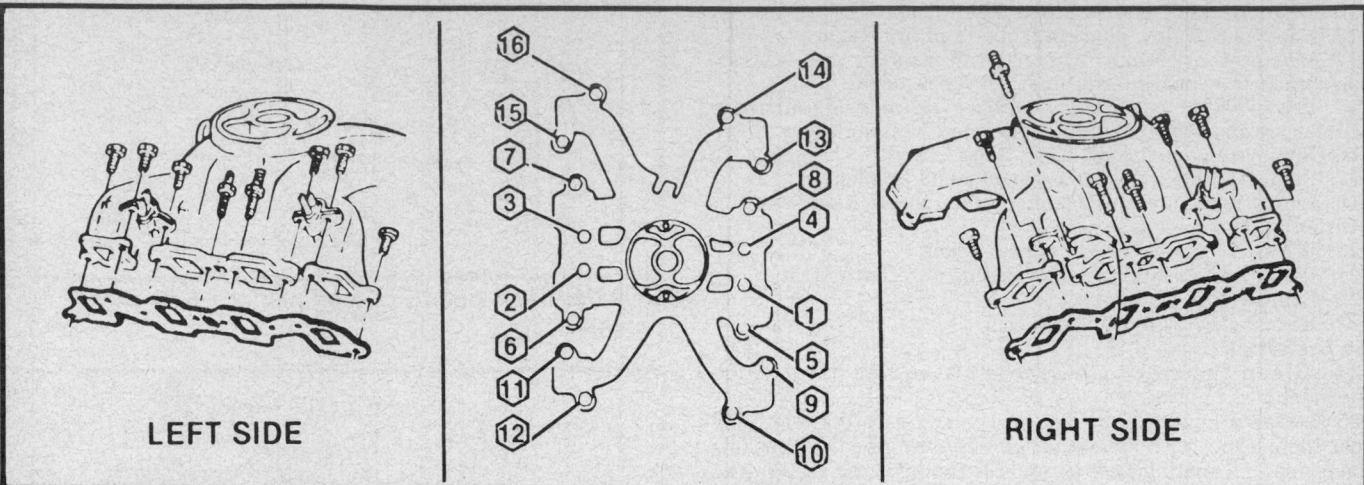

LEFT SIDE   RIGHT SIDE

Intake manifold installation and torque sequence— 6.2L diesel engine

12. Install the rear air conditioning bracket, if equipped.
13. Install the EPR/EGR valve bracket, if equipped.
14. Tighten the vacuum pump holddown clamp.
15. Install the secondary filter and adaptor.
16. Connect the secondary fuel filter lines.
17. Install the crankcase ventilator tubes.
18. Install the air cleaner assembly.
19. Connect both batteries.

1988–90 C/K SERIES

1. Disconnect both batteries.
2. Drain the cooling system and properly relieve the fuel system pressure. Remove the air cleaner assembly.
3. Remove the crankcase ventilator tubes, and disconnect the secondary fuel filter lines. Remove the secondary filter and adaptor.
4. Loosen the vacuum pump holddown clamp and rotate the pump to gain access to the nearest manifold bolt.
5. Remove the EPR/EGR valve bracket, if equipped.
6. Remove the rear air conditioning bracket, if equipped.
7. Remove the intake manifold bolts. The injection line clips are retained by these bolts.
8. Remove the intake manifold.

NOTE: If the engine is to be further serviced with the manifold removed, install protective covers over the intake ports.

To install:
9. Clean the manifold gasket surfaces on the cylinder heads and install new gaskets before installing the manifold.

NOTE: The gaskets have an opening for the EGR valve on light duty installations. An insert covers this opening on heavy duty installations.

10. Install the manifold. Torque the bolts in the proper sequence and to the correct specification.
11. The secondary filter must be filled with clean diesel fuel before it is reinstalled.
12. Install the rear air conditioning bracket, if equipped.
13. Install the EPR/EGR valve bracket, if equipped.
14. Tighten the vacuum pump holddown clamp.
15. Install the secondary filter and adaptor.
16. Connect the secondary fuel filter lines.
17. Install the crankcase ventilator tubes.
18. Install the air cleaner assembly.
19. Connect both batteries.

VAN

1. Disconnect both batteries.
2. Drain the cooling system and properly relieve the fuel system pressure. Remove the air cleaner assembly.
3. Remove the crankcase ventilator tubes, and disconnect the secondary fuel filter lines. Remove the secondary filter and adaptor.
4. Loosen the vacuum pump holddown clamp and rotate the pump to gain access to the nearest manifold bolt.
5. Remove the EPR/EGR valve bracket, if equipped.
6. Remove the rear air conditioning bracket, if equipped.
7. Remove the intake manifold bolts. The injection line clips are retained by these bolts.
8. Remove the intake manifold.

NOTE: If the engine is to be further serviced with the manifold removed, install protective covers over the intake ports.

To install:
9. Clean the manifold gasket surfaces on the cylinder heads and install new gaskets before installing the manifold.

NOTE: The gaskets have an opening for the EGR valve on light duty installations. An insert covers this opening on heavy duty installations.

10. Install the manifold. Torque the bolts in the proper sequence and to the correct specification.
11. The secondary filter must be filled with clean diesel fuel before it is reinstalled.
12. Install the rear air conditioning bracket, if equipped.
13. Install the EPR/EGR valve bracket, if equipped.
14. Tighten the vacuum pump holddown clamp.
15. Install the secondary filter and adaptor.
16. Connect the secondary fuel filter lines.
17. Install the crankcase ventilator tubes.
18. Install the air cleaner assembly.
19. Connect both batteries.

Exhaust Manifold

Removal and Installation

1686 C/K SERIES AND 1987–90 R/V SERIES

Right Side

1. Disconnect the batteries.

2. Raise and support the vehicle safely.

3. Disconnect the exhaust pipe from the manifold flange and lower the vehicle.

4. Disconnect the glow plug wires.

5. Remove the air cleaner duct bracket.

6. Remove the glow plug wires.

7. Remove the manifold bolts and remove the manifold.

8. To install, reverse the above procedure and torque the bolts to specifications.

Left Side

1. Disconnect the batteries.

2. Remove the dipstick tube nut, and remove the dipstick tube.

3. Disconnect the glow plug wires.

4. Remove the air conditioner compressor rear bracket, if so equipped.

5. Raise and support the vehicle safely.

6. Disconnect the exhaust pipe at the manifold flange.

7. Remove the manifold bolts. Remove the manifold from underneath the vehicle.

8. Reverse the above procedure to install. Start the manifold bolts while the vehicle is raised. Torque the bolts to specifications.

1988–90 C/K SERIES
Right Side

1. Disconnect the batteries.

2. Raise and support the vehicle safely.

3. Disconnect the exhaust pipe from the manifold flange and lower the vehicle.

4. Disconnect the glow plug wires.

5. Remove the air cleaner duct bracket.

6. Remove the glow plug wires.

7. Remove the manifold bolts and remove the manifold.

8. To install, reverse the above procedure and torque the bolts to 26 ft. lbs.

Left Side

1. Disconnect the batteries.

2. Remove the dipstick tube nut, and remove the dipstick tube.

3. Disconnect the glow plug wires.

4. Raise and support the vehicle safely.

5. Disconnect the exhaust pipe at the manifold flange.

6. Remove the manifold bolts. Remove the manifold from underneath the vehicle.

7. Reverse the above procedure to install. Start the manifold bolts while the vehicle is raised. Torque the bolts to 26 ft. lbs.

VAN

1. Disconnect the batteries.

2. Raise and support the vehicle safely.

3. Disconnect the exhaust pipe from the manifold flange and lower the vehicle.

4. Remove the engine cover and disconnect the glow plug wires.

5. Remove the air cleaner duct bracket.

6. Remove the glow plug wires.

7. Remove the air conditioner compressor rear bracket, if so equipped.

8. Remove the manifold bolts and remove the manifold.

9. To install, reverse the above procedure and torque the bolts to 26 ft. lbs.

Timing Chain Cover and Front Oil Seal

Removal and Installation

1. Disconnect both negative battery cables. Drain the cooling system.

2. Remove the water pump.

3. Rotate the crankshaft to align the marks on the injection pump driven gear and the camshaft gear.

4. Scribe a mark aligning the injection pump flange and the front cover.

5. Remove the crankshaft pulley and torsional damper.

6. Remove the front cover-to-oil pan bolts (4).

7. Remove the 2 fuel return line clips.

8. Remove the injection pump gear.

9. Remove the injection pump retaining nuts from the front cover.

10. Remove the baffle. Remove the remaining cover bolts, and remove the front cover.

11. If the front cover oil seal is to be replaced, it can now be pried out of the cover with a suitable prying tool. Press the new seal into the cover evenly.

NOTE: The oil seal can also be replaced with the front cover installed. Remove the torsional damper first, then pry the old seal out of the cover using a suitable prying tool. Use care not to damage the surface of the crankshaft. Install the new seal evenly into the cover and install the damper.

12. To install the front cover, first clean both sealing surfaces until all traces of old sealer are gone. Apply a 2mm bead of sealant (GM sealant No. 1052357 or equivalent) to the sealing surface. Apply a bead of RTV type sealer to the bottom portion of the front cover which attached to the oil pan. Install the front cover.

13. Install the baffle.

14. Install the injection pump, making sure the scribe marks on the pump and front cover are aligned. Tighten the nuts to 31 ft. lbs.

15. Install the injection pump driven gear, making sure the marks on the cam gear and pump are aligned. Be sure the dowel pin and the three holes on the pump flange are also aligned. Torque the injection pump gear bolts to 17 ft. lbs.

16. Install the fuel line clips, the front cover-to-oil bolts, and the torsional damper and crankshaft pulley. Torque the pan bolts to 4–7 ft. lbs., and the damper bolt to 200 ft. lbs.

Timing Chain

Removal and Installation

1. Disconnect the negative battery cables. Remove the front cover.

2. Remove the bolt and washer attaching the camshaft gear. Remove the injection pump gear.

3. Remove the camshaft sprocket, timing chain and crankshaft sprocket as a unit.

To install:

4. Install the cam sprocket, timing chain and crankshaft sprocket as a unit, aligning the timing marks on the sprockets.

5. Rotate the crankshaft 360 degrees so that the camshaft gear and the injection pump gear are aligned.

6. Install the front cover. The injection pump must be retimed since the timing chain assembly was removed.

Camshaft

Removal and Installation

1986 C/K Series and 1987–90 R/V Series

1. Disconnect the battery cables.

2. Drain the cooling system.

3. Remove the radiator shrouds and fan.

4. Remove the vacuum pump.

5. Remove the power steering pump.

6. Remove the alternator.

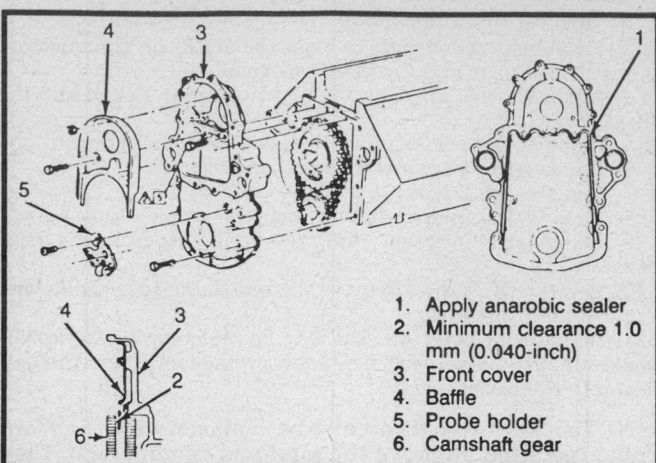

1. Apply anarobic sealer
2. Minimum clearance 1.0 mm (0.040-inch)
3. Front cover
4. Baffle
5. Probe holder
6. Camshaft gear

Front cover and components—6.2L diesel engine

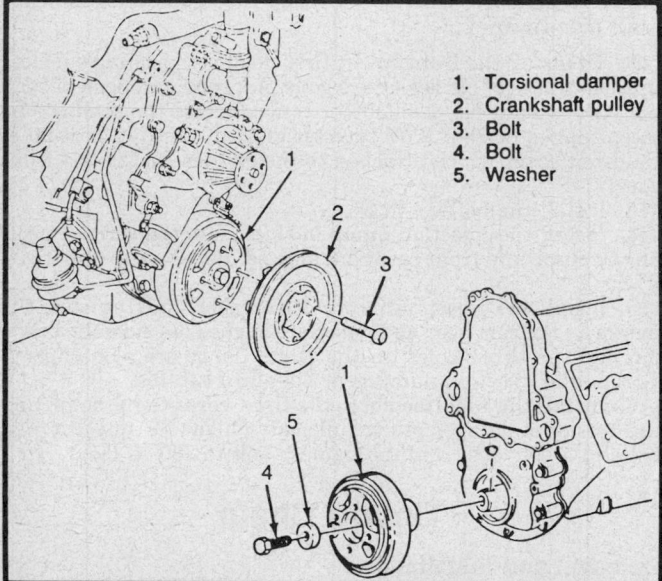

1. Torsional damper
2. Crankshaft pulley
3. Bolt
4. Bolt
5. Washer

Torsioner damper and crankcase pulley installation—6.2L diesel engine

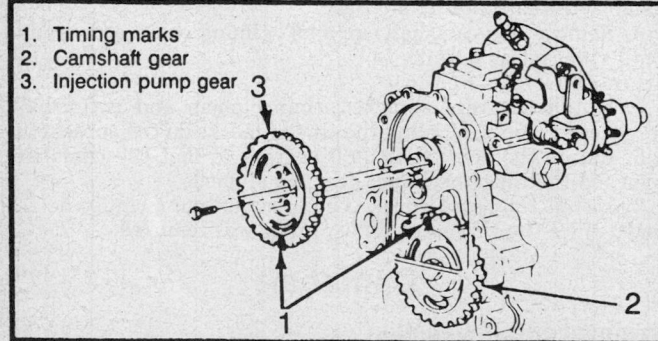

1. Timing marks
2. Camshaft gear
3. Injection pump gear

Injection pump gear and timing marks—6.2L diesel engine

7. Remove the air conditioning compresser without disconnecting the freon hoses and position to one side.
8. Remove the rocker arm covers.
9. Remove the rocker arm assemblies and pushrods. Mark them so they can be returned to their original position.

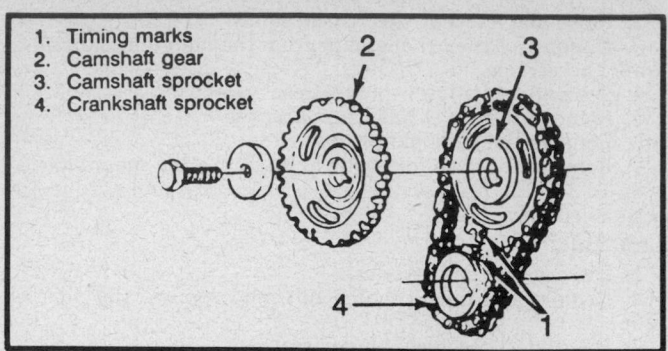

1. Timing marks
2. Camshaft gear
3. Camshaft sprocket
4. Crankshaft sprocket

Camshaft and sprockets—6.2L diesel engine

10. Remove the hydraulic lifters and keep them in order so they can be returned to their original bore.
11. Remove the front cover.
12. Remove the fuel pump.
13. Disconnect the air conditioning condenser mounting bolts and lift the condenser out of the way.
14. Remove the timing chain and camshaft sprocket.
15. Raise the engine and suppport it safely.
16. Remove the front engine mounting through bolts.
17. Remove the bolts and thrust plate.
18. Carefully remove the camshaft from the block.
19. Remove the spacer, if necessary.

To install:

20. Install the spacer with the ID chamfer toward the camshaft.

NOTE: It is recommended that the engine oil, oil filter and hydraulic lifters be replaced when installing a new camshaft.

21. Coat the camshaft lobes with Molykote, or equivalent.
22. Lubricate the camshaft journals with engine oil.
23. Insert the camshaft carefully into the block, install the thrust plate and bolts and torque to 17 ft. lbs.
24. Lower the engine and install the engine through mounting bolts.
25. Align the timing marks and install the timing chain and sprockets.
26. Install the air conditioner condensor, if so equipped.
27. Install the fuel pump.
28. Install the front cover.
29. Install the hydraulic lifters in the same bore as they were removed.
30. Install the rocker arm assemblies and pushrods in their original locations.
31. Install the rocker arm covers.
32. Install the air conditioner compressor.
33. Install the alternator.
34. Install the power steering pump.
35. Install the vacuum pump.
36. Install the fan, radiator and shrouds.
37. Install the battery cables.
38. Fill the cooling system.

1988–90 C/K Series

1. Disconnect the battery cables and relieve the fuel system pressure.
2. Drain the cooling system.
3. Remove the radaitor shrouds and fan.
4. Remove the grille and parking lamp assembly.
5. Remove the hood latch and brace.
6. Remove the oil pump drive.
7. Remove the power steering pump, alternator and air conditioner compressor and move to one side out of the way.
8. Remove the rocker arm covers.

9. Remove the rocker arm assemblies and pushrods. Mark them so they can be returned to their original position.

10. Remove the hydraulic lifters and keep them in order so they can be returned to their original bore.

11. Remove the front cover.

14. Remove the timing chain and camshaft sprocket.

15. Remove the fuel pump.

16. Raise the engine and suppport it safely.

17. Remove the front engine mounting through bolts.

18. Remove the air conditioner condensor mounting bolts and lift the condensor out.

19. Remove the bolts and thrust plate.

20. Carefully remove the camshaft from the block.

21. Remove the spacer, if necessary.

To install:

22. Install the spacer with the ID chamfer toward the camshaft.

NOTE: It is recommended that the engine oil, oil filter and hydraulic lifters be replaced when installing a new camshaft.

23. Coat the camshaft lobes with Molykote, or equivalent.

24. Lubricate the camshaft journals with engine oil.

25. Insert the camshaft carefully into the block, install the thrust plate and bolts and torque to 17 ft. lbs.

26. Lower the engine and install the engine through mounting bolts.

27. Align the timing marks and install the timing chain and sprockets.

28. Install the air conditioner condensor, if so equipped.

29. Install the fuel pump.

30. Install the front cover.

31. Install the hydraulic lifters in the same bore as they were removed.

32. Install the rocker arm assemblies and pushrods in their original locations.

33. Install the rocker arm covers.

34. Install the power steering pump, alternator and air conditioner compressor.

35. Install the oil pump drive.

36. Install the hood latch and brace.

37. Install the grille and parking lamp assembly.

38. Install the radaitor shrouds and fan.

39. Fill the cooling system.

40. Connect the battery cables.

Van

1. Disconnect the battery cables and relieve the fuel system pressure.

2. Remove the headlight bezels.

3. Remove the grille, bumper and lower valence panel.

4. Remove the hood latch.

5. Remove the coolant recovery bottle.

6. Remove the upper tie bar.

7. Remove the air conditioner compressor.

8. Drain the cooling system and remove the radiator and fan.

9. Remove the oil pump drive.

10. Remove the cylinder heads.

11. Remove the alternator lower bracket.

12. Remove the water pump.

13. Remove the tortional damper.

14. Remove the front cover.

15. Remove the fuel pump.

16. Remove the rocker arm covers.

17. Remove the rocker arm assemblies and pushrods. Mark them so they can be returned to their original position.

18. Remove the hydraulic lifters and keep them in order so they can be returned to their original bore.

19. Remove the timing chain and camshaft sprocket.

20. Remove the bolts and thrust plate.

21. Carefully remove the camshaft from the block.

22. Remove the spacer, if necessary.

To install:

23. Install the spacer with the ID chamfer toward the camshaft.

NOTE: It is recommended that the engine oil, oil filter and hydraulic lifters be replaced when installing a new camshaft.

24. Coat the camshaft lobes with Molykote, or equivalent.

25. Lubricate the camshaft journals with engine oil.

26. Insert the camshaft carefully into the block, install the thrust plate and bolts and torque to 17 ft. lbs.

27. Align the timing marks and install the timing chain and sprockets.

28. Install the hydraulic lifters in the same bore as they were removed.

29. Install the rocker arm assemblies and pushrods in their original locations.

30. Install the rocker arm covers.

31. Install the fuel pump.

32. Install the front cover.

33. Install the tornsional damper and water pump.

34. Install the alternator lower bracket.

35. Install the cylinder head.

36. Install the oil pump drive.

37. Install the radiator and fan.

38. Install the air conditioner compressor.

39. Install the upper tie bar.

40. Install the coolant recovery bottle.

41. Install the hood latch.

42. Install the grille, bumper and lower valence panel.

43. Install the headlight bezels.

44. Install the battery cables.

45. Fill the cooling system.

46. Evacuate and charge the air conditioner system.

Piston and Conncecting Rod

Positioning

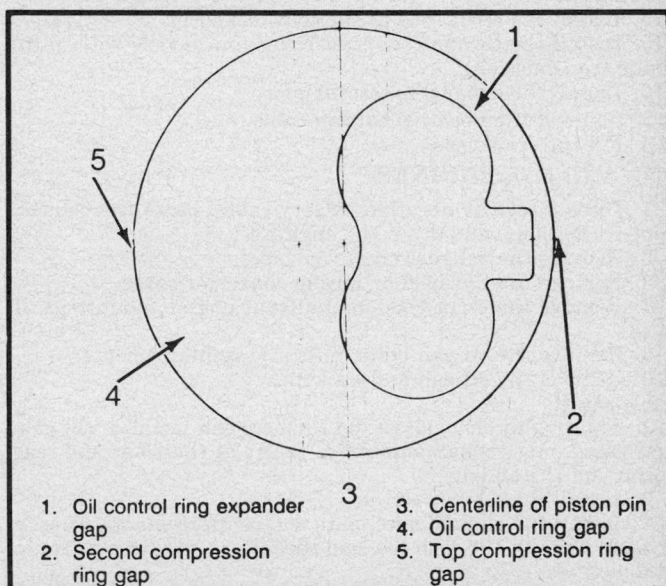

1. Oil control ring expander gap
2. Second compression ring gap
3. Centerline of piston pin
4. Oil control ring gap
5. Top compression ring gap

Piston ring gap locations – 6.2L diesel engine

ENGINE LUBRICATION

Oil Pan

Removal and Installation

4.8L ENGINE

1. Disconnect the negative battery cable. Raise the vehicle and support it safely. Drain the engine oil.
2. Remove the flywheel cover. Remove the starter assembly.
3. Remove the engine mount through bolts from the engine front mounts. Raise the engine enough to remove the oil pan.
4. Remove the oil pan retaining bolts. Remove the oil pan from the engine.
5. Installation is the reverse of the removal procedure. Use new gaskets or RTV sealant, as required. Torque the pan to front cover bolts to 45 inch lbs. Torque the 1/4 in. pan to block bolts to 80 in. lbs. and the 5/16 in. bolts to 165 inch lbs.

4.3L ENGINE

A one piece type oil pan gasket is used.

1. Disconnect the negative battery cable. Raise the vehicle, support it safely, and drain the engine oil.
2. Remove the exhaust crossover pipe.
3. Remove the torque converter cover (on models with automatic transmission).
4. Remove the strut rods at the flywheel cover.
5. Remove the strut rod brackets at the front engine mountings.
6. Remove the starter.
7. Remove the oil pan bolts, nuts and reinforcements.
8. Remove the oil pan and gaskets.

To install:

9. Thoroughly clean all gasket surfaces and install a new gasket, using only a small amount of sealer at the front and rear corners of the oil pan.
10. Install the oil pan and new gaskets.
11. Install the oil pan bolts, nuts and reinforcements. Torque the pan bolts to 100 inch lbs. and the oil pan nuts at corners to 200 inch lbs.
12. Install the starter.
13. Install the strut rod brackets at the front engine mountings.
14. Install the strut rods at the flywheel cover.
15. Install the torque converter cover (on models with automatic transmission).
16. Install the exhaust crossover pipe.
17. Connect the negative battery cable.
18. Fill the crankcase.

5.0L AND 5.7L ENGINES

1. Disconnect the negative battery cable. Raise the vehicle, support it safely, and drain the engine oil.
2. Remove the exhaust crossover pipe.
3. Remove the flywheel or torque converter cover.
4. Remove the strut rods at the front engine mountings, if used.
5. Remove the oil pan bolts, nuts and reinforcements.
6. Remove the oil pan and gaskets.

To install:

7. Thoroughly clean all gasket surfaces and install a new gasket, using only a small amount of sealer at the front and rear corners of the oil pan.
8. Install the oil pan and new gaskets.
10. Install the oil pan bolts, nuts and reinforcements. Torque the pan bolts to 100 inch lbs. and the oil pan nuts at corners to 200 inch lbs.
11. Install the strut rods at the front engine mountings.
12. Install the torque converter or flywheel cover.

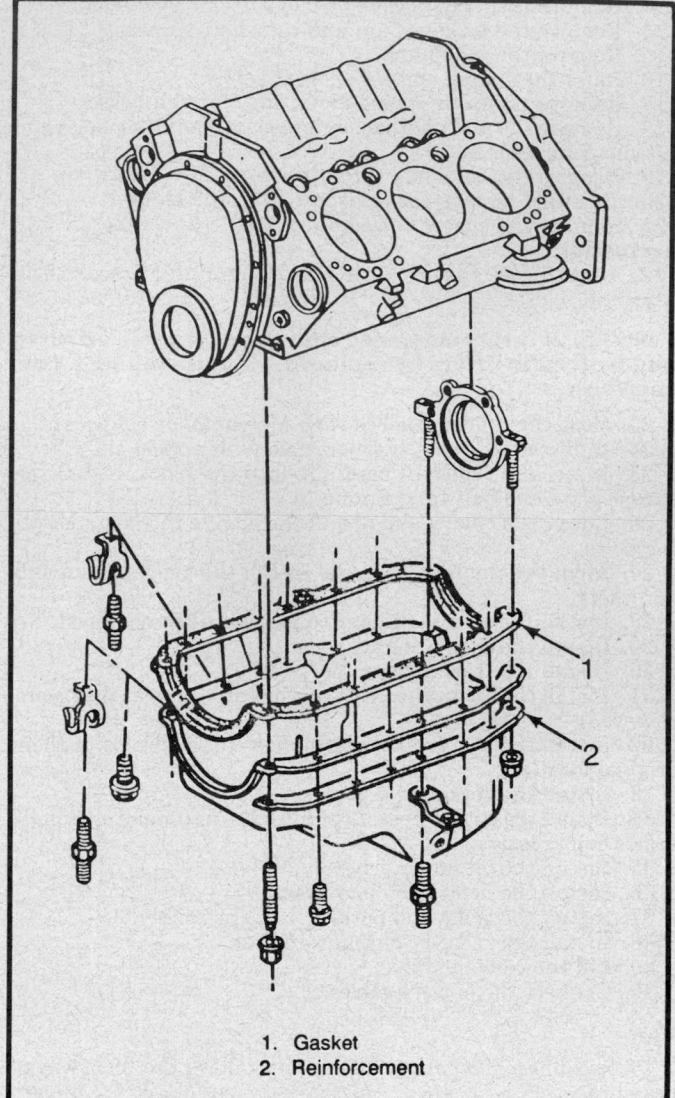

1. Gasket
2. Reinforcement

Oil pan assembly — 4.3L engine

13. Install the exhaust crossover pipe.
14. Connect the negative battery cable.
15. Fill the crankcase.

6.2L DIESEL ENGINE

1986 C/K Series and 1987–90 R/V Series

1. Disconnect the battery cables.
2. Raise the vehicle and support it safely.
3. Drain the engine oil.
4. Remove the flywheel cover.
5. Raise the engine and remove the left engine mounting through bolt.
6. Remove the oil pan bolts and remove the oil pan.
7. Remove the oil pan rear seal.
8. To install clean the old RTV sealant from the oil pan and block.
9. Apply a 3/16 in. bead of RTV sealant to the oil pan sealing surface, inboard of the bolt holes. The sealant must be wet to the touch when the oil pan is to be installed.

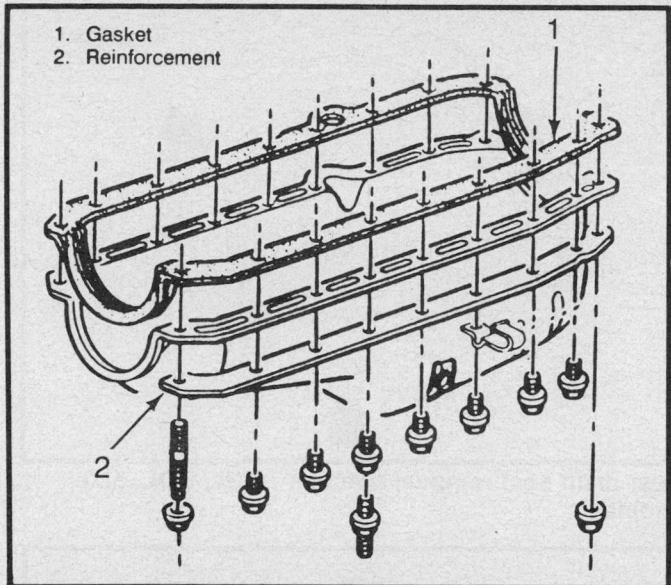

1. Gasket
2. Reinforcement

Oil pan assembly —5.0L, 5.7L engines

10. Install the oil pan rear seal.
11. Install the oil pan to the engine and install the retaining bolts. Torque all except the rear 2 bolts to 84 inch lbs. Torque the rear 2 bolts to 17 ft. lbs.

NOTE: Be sure to connect the oil dipstick.

12. Lower the engine.
13. Install the engine mounting through bolt and nut.
14. Install the flywheel cover and lower the vehicle.
15. Refill with the proper grade and quanity of oil.
16. Install the battery cables.

1988–90 C/K Series

1. Disconnect the battery cables.
2. Raise the vehicle and support it safely.
3. Drain the engine oil.
4. Remove the flywheel cover.
5. Disconnect the exhaust pipes from the manifolds.
6. Raise the engine and remove the front engine mounting through bolts.
7. Remove the oil pan bolts and remove the oil pan.
8. Remove the oil pan rear seal.
9. To install clean the old RTV sealant from the oil pan and block.
10. Apply a $^3/_{16}$ in. bead of RTV sealant to the oil pan sealing surface, inboard of the bolt holes. The sealant must be wet to the touch when the oil pan is to be installed.
11. Install the oil pan rear seal.
12. Install the oil pan to the engine and install the retaining bolts. Torque all except the rear 2 bolts to 84 inch lbs. Torque the rear 2 bolts to 17 ft. lbs.
13. Lower the engine.
14. Install the engine mounting through bolt and nut.
15. Install the exhaust pipes to the manifolds.
16. Install the flywheel cover and lower the vehicle.
17. Refill with the proper grade and quanity of oil.
18. Install the battery cables.

Van

1. Disconnect the battery cables.
2. Remove the engine cover.
3. Remove the engine oil dipstick.
4. Remove the engine oil dipstick tube at the rocker cover.
5. Raise the vehicle and support it safely.

6. Disconnect the transmission.
7. Drain the engine oil.
8. Disconnect the oil cooler lines at the block.
9. Remove the starter.
10. Remove the oil pan bolts and remove the oil pan and oil pan rear seal.

To install:
11. Apply a $^3/_{16}$ in. bead of RTV sealant to the oil pan sealing surface, inboard of the bolt holes. The sealant must be wet to the touch when the oil pan is to be installed.
12. Install the oil pan rear seal.
13. Install the oil pan to the engine and install the retaining bolts. Torque all except the rear 2 bolts to 84 inch lbs. Torque the rear 2 bolts to 17 ft. lbs.
14. Install the starter.
15. Install the engine oil cooler lines.
16. Connect the transmission.
17. Lower the vehicle.
18. Install the engine oil dipstick tube at the rocker cover.
19. Install the engine oil dipstick.
20. Install the engine cover.
21. Refill with the proper grade and quanity of oil.
22. Install the battery cables.

7.4L ENGINE

1. Disconnect the negative battery cable.
2. Remove the fan shroud.
3. Remove the air cleaner.
4. Remove the distributor cap.
5. Raise and support the vehicle safely.
6. Drain the engine oil.
7. Remove the converter housing pan.
8. Remove the oil filter.
9. Remove the oil pressure line.
10. Support the engine with a floor jack.
11. Remove the engine mounting through bolts.
12. Raise the engine just enough to remove the pan.
13. Remove the oil pan and discard the gaskets.

To install:
14. Clean all mating surfaces thoroughly.
15. Apply RTV gasket material to the front and rear corners of the gaskets.
16. Coat the gaskets with adhesive sealer and position them on the block.
17. Install the rear pan seal in the pan with the seal ends mating with the gaskets.
18. Install the front seal on the bottom of the front cover, pressing the locating tabs into the holes in the cover.
19. Install the oil pan.
20. Install the pan bolts, clips and reinforcements. Torque the pan-to-cover bolts to 70 inch lbs.; the pan-to-block bolts to 13 ft. lbs.
21. Lower the engine onto the mounts.
22. Install the engine mount through-bolts.
23. Install the oil pressure line.
24. Install the oil filter.
25. Install the converter housing pan.
26. Install the distributor cap.
27. Install the air cleaner.
28. Install the fan shroud.
29. Connect the battery.
30. Fill the crankcase.

Oil Pump

Removal and Installation

4.8L ENGINE

1. Raise and support the vehicle safely.
2. Remove the oil pan.

SECTION 5

GENERAL MOTORS CORPORATION
C/K SERIES (PICK-UP) • R/V SERIES (PICK-UP) • BLAZER/JIMMY • SUBURBAN • G SERIES (VAN)

3. Remove the oil pump tube bracket main bearing cap nut.

4. Remove the oil pump bolts and the oil pump.

To install:

5. Position the oil pump to he engine and align the slot in the oil pump shaft with the tang on the distributor shaft. The oil pump should slide easily in place.

6. Install the oil pump bolts and tighten to 115 inch lbs.

7. Install the oil pump pick-up tube to the main bearing cap nut and tighten to 25 ft. lbs.

8. Install the oil pan.

4.3L, 5.0L, 5.7L AND 7.4L ENGINES

1. Raise and support the vehicle safely and remove the oil pan.

2. Remove the bolt attaching the pump to the rear main bearing cap. Remove the pump and the extension shaft, which will come out behind it.

3. If the pump has been disassembled, is being replaced, or for any reason oil has been removed from it, it must be primed. It can either be filled with oil before installing the cover plate (and oil kept within the pump during handling), or the entire pump cavity can be filled with petroleum jelly.

NOTE: If the pump is not primed, the engine could be damaged before it receives adequate lubrication when the engine is started.

4. Engage the extension shaft with the oil pump shaft. Align the slot on the top of the extension shaft with the drive tang on the lower end of the distributor driveshaft, and then position the pump at the rear main bearing cap so the mounting bolt can be installed. Install the bolt, torquing to 65 ft. lbs.

5. Install the oil pan.

6.2L DIESEL ENGINE

1. Raise and support the vehicle safely. Drain the oil.

2. Lower the oil pan enough to gain access to the pump.

2. Rotate the crankshaft so that the forward crankshaft throw and Nos. 1 and 2 connecting rod journals are up.

3. Remove the bolt retaining the pump to the main bearing cap. Let the pump and extension shaft fall into the pan.

To install:

4. Maneuver the pan, pump and extension shaft into position.

5. Position the pump on the bearing cap.

6. Align the extension shaft with the oil pump drive or vacuum pump. The pump should push easily into place. Install the pump and tighten the bolt to 65 ft. lbs.

7. Install the pan.

Rear Main Bearing oil Seal

Removal and Installation

4.3L, 5.0L AND 5.7L ENGINES

1. Raise and support the vehicle safely and remove the transmission from the vehicle.

2. Remove the oil pan bolts. Lower the oil pan.

3. Remove the screws and remove the seal retainer assembly.

4. Remove the gasket.

5. Insert a suitable tool into the notches provided in the seal retainer and pry the seal out.

NOTE: Whenever the retainer is removed a new retainer gasket and rear main seal must be installed.
Care should be taken when removing the seal so as not to nick the crankshaft sealing surface.

6. Before installation lubricate the new seal with clean engine oil.

7. Install the seal on tool J–35621 or equivalent. Thread the tool into the rear of the crankshaft. Tighten the screws snugley.

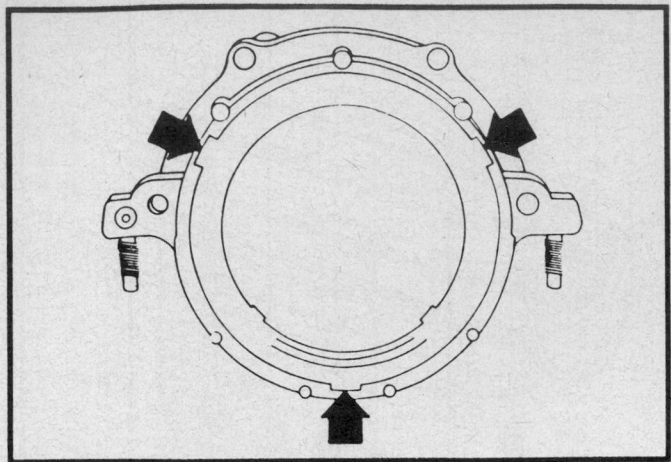

Rear main seal removal notches—4.3L, 5.0L, 5.7L engines

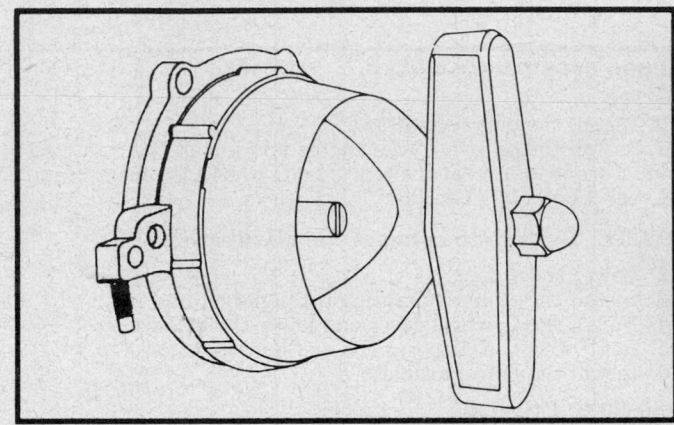

Rear main seal installation—4.3L, 5.0L, 5.7L engines

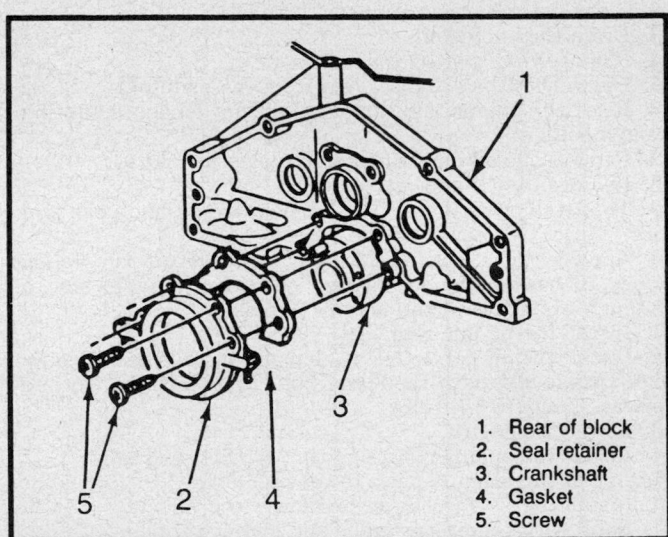

1. Rear of block
2. Seal retainer
3. Crankshaft
4. Gasket
5. Screw

Rear main seal retainer installation—4.3L, 5.0L, 5.7L engines

This is to insure that the seal will be installed squarely over the crankshaft. Tighten the tool wing nut until it bottoms.

8. Remove the tool from the crankshaft.

9. Install the transmission.

4.8L ENGINE

The rear main bearing oil seal, both halves, can be removed without removal of the crankshaft. Always replace the upper and lower halves together.

1. Raise and support the vehicle safely, drain the oil and remove the oil pan.

2. Remove the rear main bearing cap.

3. Remove the old oil seal from its groove in the cap, prying from the bottom using a suitable tool.

4. Coat a new seal half completely with clean engine oil, and insert it into the bearing cap groove. Keep oil off of the parting line surface, as this surface is treated with glue. Gradually push the seal with a hammer handle until the seal is rolled into place.

5. To remove the upper half of the old seal, use a small hammer and a soft, blunt punch to tap one end of the oil seal out until it protrudes far enough to be removed with needlenosed pliers. Push the new seal into place with the lip toward the front of the engine.

6. Install the bearing cap and torque the bolts to a loose fit — do not final torque. With the cap fitted loosely, move the crankshaft first to the rear and then to the front with a rubber mallet. This will properly position the thrust bearing. Torque the bearing cap to a final torque of 65 ft. lb. Install the oil pan.

6.2L DIESEL ENGINE

The crankshaft need not be removed to replace the rear main bearing upper oil seal. The lower seal is installed in the bearing cap.

NOTE: Engines are originally equipped with a rope-type seal. This should be replaced with the lip-type seal available as a service replacement.

1. Raise and support the vehicle safely. Drain the crankcase oil and remove the oil pan and rear main bearing cap.

2. Using a special main seal tool or a tool that can be made from a dowel, drive the upper seal into its groove on each side until it is tightly packed. This is usually ¼–¾ in. (6.35–19.05mm).

3. Measure the amount the seal was driven up on one side. Add 1/16 in. (1.5875mm) and cut another length from the old seal. Use the main bearing cap as a holding fixture when cutting the seal as illustrated. Carefully trim protruding seal.

4. Work these two pieces of seal up into the cylinder block on each side with two nailsets or small screwdrivers. Using the packing tool again, pack these pieces into the block, then trim the flush with a razor blade or hobby knife as shown. Do not scratch the bearing surface with the razor.

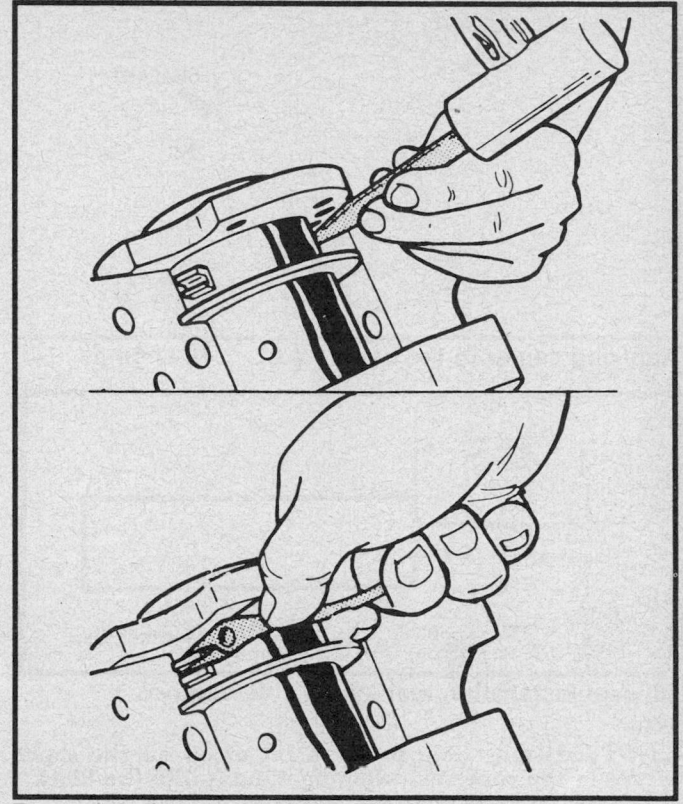

Removing the upper oil seal half — 4.8L, 7.4L engines

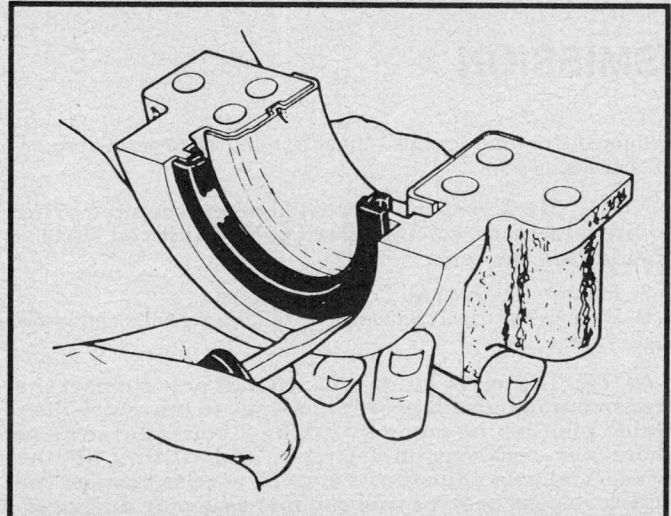

Removing the lower oil seal half — 4.8L, 7.4L engines

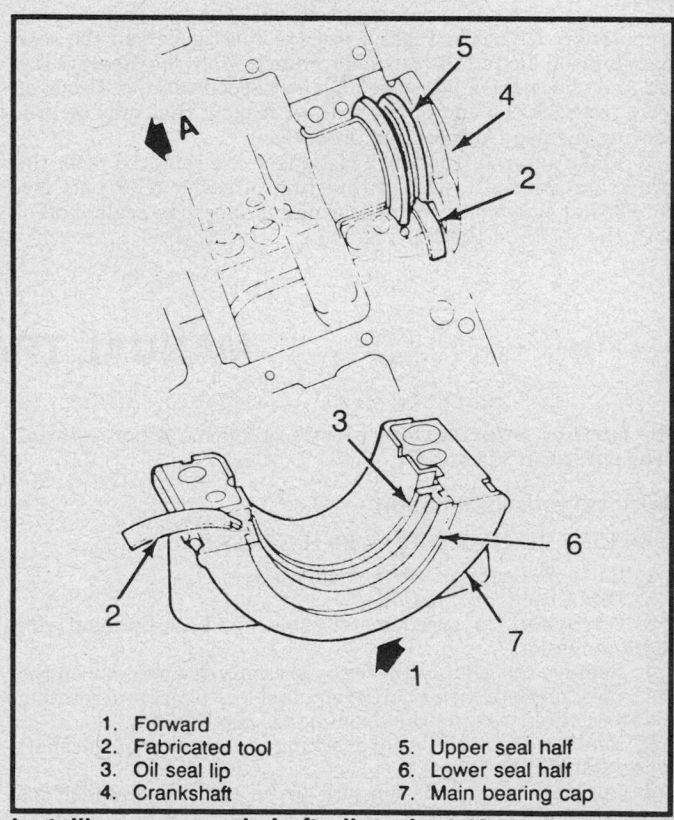

1. Forward
2. Fabricated tool
3. Oil seal lip
4. Crankshaft
5. Upper seal half
6. Lower seal half
7. Main bearing cap

Installing rear crankshaft oil seal — 4.8L, 7.4L engines

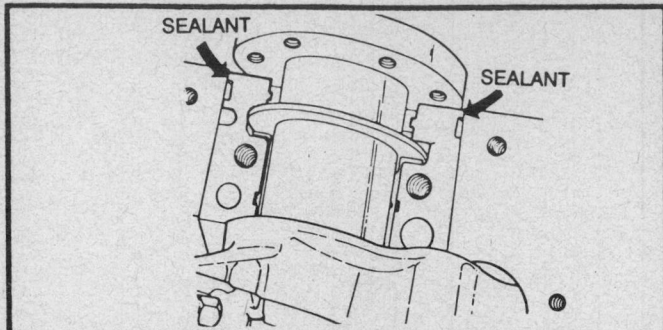

Applying sealer to the block—4.8L, 7.4L engines

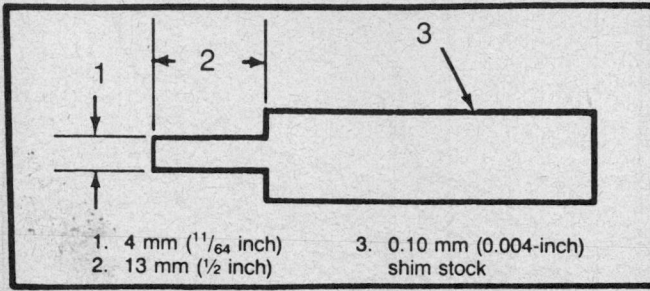

| 1. 4 mm ($^{11}/_{64}$ inch) | 3. 0.10 mm (0.004-inch) |
| 2. 13 mm (½ inch) | shim stock |

Oil seal installation tool—4.8L, 7.4L engines

NOTE: It may help to use a bit of oil on the short pieces of the rope seal when packing it into the block.

5. Apply Loctite® No. 496 sealer or equivalent to the rear main bearing cap and install the rope seal. Cut the ends of the seal flush with the cap.

6. Check to see if the rear main cap with the new seal will seat properly on the block. Place a piece of Plastigage® on the rear main journal, install the cap and torque to 70 ft. lbs. Remove the cap and check the Plastigage® against specifications. If out of specs, recheck the end of the seal for fraying that may be preventing the cap from seating properly.

7. Make sure all traces of Plastigage® are removed from the crankshaft journal. Apply a thin film of sealer (GM part No. 1052357 or equvalent) to the bearing cap. Keep the sealant off of both the seal and the bearing.

8. Just before assembly, apply a light coat of clean engine oil on the crankshaft surface that will contact the seal.

9. Install the bearing cap and torque to specification.

10. Install the oil pump and oil pan.

7.4L ENGINE

The rear main bearing oil seal, both halves, can be removed without removal of the crankshaft. Always replace the upper and lower halves together.

1. Raise and support the vehicle safely, drain the oil and remove the oil pan.

2. Remove the oil pump and the rear main bearing cap.

3. Using a small pry bar, pry the oil seal from the rear main bearing cap.

4. Using a small hammer and a brass pin punch, drive the top half of the oil seal from the rear main bearing. Drive it out far enough, so it may be removed with a pair of pliers.

5. Using a non-abrasive cleaner, clean the rear main bearing cap and the crankshaft.

6. Fabricate an oil seal installation tool from 0.004" shim stock, shape the end to ½ in. long by $^{11}/_{64}$ in. wide.

7. Coat the new oil seal with engine oil; do not coat the ends of the seal.

8. Position the fabricated tool between the crankshaft and the seal seat in the cylinder case.

9. Position the new half seal between the crankshaft and the top of the tool, so that the seal bead contacts the tip of the tool.

NOTE: Make sure that the seal lip is positioned toward the front of the engine.

10. Using the fabricated tool as a shoe horn, to protect the seal's bead from the sharp edge of the seal seat surface in the cylinder case, roll the seal around the crankshaft. when the seal's ends are flush with the engine block, remove the installation.

11. Using the same manner of installation, install the lower half onto the lower half of the rear main bearing cap.

12. Apply sealant to the cap-to-case mating surfaces and install the lower rear main bearing half to the engine; keep the sealant off of the seal's mating line.

13. Install the rear main bearing cap bolts and torque to 10–12 ft.lb. Using a lead hammer, tap the crankshaft forward and rearward, to line up the thrust surfaces. Torque the main bearing bolts to 110 ft.lb. on 1986 C/K series and 1986–90 R/V series and 100 ft. lbs. on 1988–90 C/K series. Reverse the removal procedures. Refill the crankcase.

MANUAL TRANSMISSION

For further information, please refer to "Professional Transmission Manual".

Removal and Installation

1986 C SERIES AND 1987–90 R SERIES

1. Raise and support the vehicle safely.

2. Drain the transmission.

3. Disconnect the speedometer cable, and back-up lamp wire at transmission.

4. Remove the gearshift lever by pressing down firmly on the slotted collar plate with a pair of channel lock pliers and rotating counterclockwise. Plug the opening to keep out dirt.

5. Remove driveshaft after marking the position of the shaft to the flange.

6. Position a transmission jack or its equivalent under the transmission to support it.

7. Remove the crossmember. Visually inspect to see if other equipment, brackets or lines, must be removed to permit removal of transmission.

NOTE: Mark position of crossmember when removing to prevent incorrect installation. The tapered surface should face the rear.

8. Remove the flywheel housing underpan.

9. Remove the top 2 transmission to housing bolts and insert 2 guide pins.

NOTE: The use of guide pins will not only support the transmission but will prevent damage to the clutch disc. Guide pins can be made by taking 2 bolts, the same as those just removed only longer, and cutting off the heads. Make an adjustment slot. Be sure to support the clutch release bearing and support assembly during removal of the transmission. This will prevent the release from falling out of the flywheel housing.

10. Remove two remaining bolts and slide transmission straight back from engine. Use care to keep the transmission drive gear straight in line with clutch disc hub.

11. Remove the transmission from beneath your vehicle.

To install:

12. Place the transmission in 4th gear.

13. Coat the input shaft splines with high temperature grease.

14. Raise the transmission into position.

15. Install the guide pins in the top 2 bolt holes.

16. Roll the transmission forward and engage the clutch splines. Keep pushing the transmission forward until it mates with the engine.

17. Install the bolts, removing the guide pins. Torque the bolts to 75 ft. lbs.

18. Install the flywheel housing underpan.

19. Install the crossmember. Torque the crossmember-to-frame bolts to 55 ft. lbs.; the crossmember-to-transmission bolts to 40 ft. lbs.

20. Remove the transmission jack.

21. Install the driveshaft.

22. Install the gearshift lever.

23. Connect the speedometer cable, and back-up lamp wire at transmission.

24. Fill the transmission.

NOTE: Do not force the transmission into the clutch disc hub. Do not let the transmission hang unsupported in the splined portion of the clutch disc.

1986 K SERIES AND 1987–90 V SERIES

1. Raise and support the vehicle safely.

2. Drain the transmission.

3. Disconnect the speedometer cable, and back-up lamp wire at transmission.

4. Remove the gearshift lever by pressing down firmly on the slotted collar plate with a pair of channel lock pliers and rotating counterclockwise. Plug the opening to keep out dirt.

5. Remove driveshaft after marking the position of the shaft to the flange.

6. Remove the transfer case.

7. Remove the exhaust pipes.

8. Position a transmission jack or its equivalent under the transmission to support it.

9. Remove the crossmember. Visually inspect to see if other equipment, brackets or lines, must be removed to permit removal of transmission.

NOTE: Mark position of crossmember when removing to prevent incorrect installation. The tapered surface should face the rear.

10. Remove the flywheel housing underpan.

11. Remove the top 2 transmission to housing bolts and insert 2 guide pins.

NOTE: The use of guide pins will not only support the transmission but will prevent damage to the clutch disc. Guide pins can be made by taking 2 bolts, the same as those just removed only longer, and cutting off the heads. Make an adjustment slot. Be sure to support the clutch release bearing and support assembly during removal of the transmission. This will prevent the release from falling out of the flywheel housing.

12. Remove two remaining bolts and slide transmission straight back from engine. Use care to keep the transmission drive gear straight in line with clutch disc hub.

13. Remove the transmission from beneath the vehicle.

To install:

14. Place the transmission in 4th gear.

15. Coat the input shaft splines with high temperature grease.

16. Raise the transmission into position.

17. Install the guide pins in the top 2 bolt holes.

18. Roll the transmission forward and engage the clutch splines. Keep pushing the transmission forward until it mates with the engine.

19. Install the bolts, removing the guide pins. Torque the bolts to 75 ft. lbs.

20. Install the flywheel housing underpan.

21. Install the crossmember. Torque the crossmember-to-frame bolts to 55 ft. lbs.; the crossmember-to-transmission bolts to 40 ft. lbs.

22. Install the transfer case.

23. Remove the transmission jack.

24. Install the exhaust system.

25. Install the driveshaft.

26. Install the gearshift lever.

27. Connect the speedometer cable, and back-up lamp wire at transmission.

28. Fill the transmission.

NOTE: Do not force the transmission into the clutch disc hub. Do not let the transmission hang unsupported in the splined portion of the clutch disc.

1988–90 C SERIES

1. Raise and support the vehicle safely.

2. Drain the transmission.

3. Remove driveshaft after marking the position of the shaft to the flange.

4. Remove the exhaust pipes.

5. Disconnect the wiring harness at the transmission.

6. Remove the gearshift lever.

7. Remove the clutch slave cylinder and support it out of the way.

8. On the 85mm transmission, remove the flywheel housing inspection cover.

9. Position a transmission jack or its equivalent under the transmission to support it.

10. Remove the crossmember. Visually inspect to see if other equipment, brackets or lines, must be removed to permit removal of transmission.

NOTE: Mark position of crossmember when removing to prevent incorrect installation. The tapered surface should face the rear.

11. Remove the top 2 transmission to housing bolts and insert two guide pins.

NOTE: The use of guide pins will not only support the transmission but will prevent damage to the clutch disc. Guide pins can be made by taking two bolts, the same as those just removed only longer, and cutting off the heads. Make an adjustment slot. Be sure to support the clutch release bearing and support assembly during removal of the transmission. This will prevent the release from falling out of the flywheel housing.

11. Remove the remaining bolts and slide transmission straight back from engine. Use care to keep the transmission drive gear straight in line with clutch disc hub.

12. Remove the transmission from beneath the vehicle.

To install:

13. Place the transmission in 4th gear.

14. Coat the input shaft splines with high temperature grease.

15. Raise the transmission into position.

16. Install the guide pins in the top 2 bolt holes.

17. Roll the transmission forward and engage the clutch splines. Keep pushing the transmission forward until it mates with the engine.

18. Install the bolts, removing the guide pins. Torque the bolts to 75 ft. lbs. on the 117mm transmission and 37 ft. lbs on the 85mm transmission.

19. Install the crossmember. Torque the crossmember-to-

frame bolts to 55 ft. lbs.; the crossmember-to-transmission bolts to 40 ft. lbs.

20. Remove the transmission jack.
21. Install the slave cylinder.
22. Install the driveshaft.
23. Install the exhaust system.
24. Install the inspection cover on the 85mm transmission.
25. Install the gearshift lever.
26. Connect the wiring harness at the transmission.
27. Fill the transmission.

NOTE: Do not force the transmission into the clutch disc hub. Do not let the transmission hang unsupported in the splined portion of the clutch disc.

1988–90 K SERIES

1. Raise and support the vehicle safely.
2. Drain the transmission.
3. Remove driveshaft after making the position of the shaft to the flange.
4. Remove the transfer case.
5. Remove the exhaust pipes.
6. Disconnect the wiring harness at the transmission.
7. Remove the gearshift lever.
8. Remove the clutch slave cylinder and support it out of the way.
9. Remove the flywheel housing inspection cover.
10. Position a transmission jack or its equivalent under the transmission to support it.
11. Remove the crossmember. Visually inspect to see if other equipment, brackets or lines, must be removed to permit removal of transmission.

NOTE: Mark position of crossmember when removing to prevent incorrect installation. The tapered surface should face the rear.

12. Remove the top 2 transmission to housing bolts and insert two guide pins.

NOTE: The use of guide pins will not only support the transmission but will prevent damage to the clutch disc. Guide pins can be made by taking 2 bolts, the same as those just removed only longer, and cutting off the heads. Make an adjustment slot for a screwdriver. Be sure to support the clutch release bearing and support assembly during removal of the transmission. This will prevent the release from falling out of the flywheel housing.

13. Remove the remaining bolts and slide transmission straight back from engine. Use care to keep the transmission drive gear straight in line with clutch disc hub.
14. Remove the transmission from beneath the vehicle.

To install:
15. Place the transmission in 4th gear.
16. Coat the input shaft splines with high temperature grease.
17. Raise the transmission into position.
18. Install the guide pins in the top 2 bolt holes.
19. Roll the transmission forward and engage the clutch splines. Keep pushing the transmission forward until it mates with the engine.
20. Install the bolts, removing the guide pins. Torque the bolts to 37 ft. lbs.
21. Install the crossmember. Torque the crossmember-to-frame bolts to 55 ft. lbs.; the crossmember-to-transmission bolts to 40 ft. lbs.
22. Install the transfer case.
23. Remove the transmission jack.
24. Install the slave cylinder.
25. Install the driveshaft.
26. Install the exhaust system.

27. Install the gearshift lever.
28. Install the inspection cover.
29. Connect the wiring harness at the transmission.
30. Fill the transmission.

NOTE: Do not force the transmission into the clutch disc hub. Do not let the transmission hang unsupported in the splined portion of the clutch disc.

VAN

1. Raise and support the vehicle safely.
2. Drain the transmission.
3. Disconnect the speedometer cable, back-up light and TCS switch.
4. Remove the shift controls from the transmission.
5. Disconnect the driveshaft and remove it from the vehicle.
6. Support the transmission using the proper equipment.
7. Inspect the transmission to be sure that all necessary components have been removed or disconnected.
8. Mark the front of the crossmember to be sure that it is installed correctly.
9. Support the clutch release bearing to prevent it from falling out of the flywheel housing when the transmission is removed.
10. Remove the flywheel housing under pan and transmission mounting bolts.
11. Move the transmission slowly away from the engine, keeping the mainshaft in alignment with the clutch disc hub. Be sure that the transmission is supported.
12. Remove the transmission from under the vehicle.

To install:
13. Lightly coat the mainshaft with high temperature grease. Do not use much grease, since, under normal operation, the grease will be thrown onto the clutch, causing it to fail.
14. Raise the transmission into position under the vehicle.
15. Roll the unit forward, engaging the spline of the mainshaft with the splines in the clutch hub. Continue pushing forward until the transmission mates with the bellhousing.
16. Install and tighten the transmission-to-bellhousing bolts to 75 ft. lbs.
17. Install the flywheel housing under pan.
18. Install the crossmember. Torque the bolts to 50 ft. lbs.
19. Inspect the transmission to be sure that all necessary components have been installed or connected.
20. Connect the driveshaft.
21. Install the shift controls.
22. Connect the speedometer cable.
23. Connect the back-up light switch.
24. Connect the TCS switch.
25. Fill the transmission with lubricant.
26. Road test the vehicle.

Linkage Adjustment

3 SPEED COLUMN SHIFT

The gearshift linkage should be adjusted each time it is disturbed or removed.

The 1st/reverse rod must be adjusted before the 2nd/3rd rod.
1. Loosen the shift rod-to-transmission lever bolt.
2. Move the 1st/reverse transmission lever to the front detent, or, the 2nd/3rd transmission lever to the front detent, then back 1 detent.
3. Put the 1st/reverse column lever into reverse and lock the column, or, put the 2nd/3rd column lever into neutral.
4. Using a ¼ in. drill bit as a gauge pin, place the bit through the holes in the column levers and the relay lever. All should align.
5. Hold the shift rod down tightly in the swivel and tighten the bolt. Remove the gauge pin.

CLUTCH

Mechanical Clutch Assembly

Removal and Installation

VAN

1. Raise and support the vehicle safely and remove the transmission.

2. Disconnect the clutch fork pushrod and spring. Remove the clutch housing.

3. Remove the clutch fork by pressing it away from the ball mounting with a suitable tool until the fork snaps loose from the ball or remove the ball stud from the clutch housing. Remove the throwout bearing from the clutch fork.

4. Install a pilot tool to hold the clutch while you are removing it.

NOTE: Before removing the clutch from the flywheel, mark the flywheel, clutch cover and pressure plate lug, so that these parts may be assembled in their same relative positions.

5. Loosen the clutch attaching bolts a turn at a time to prevent distortion of the clutch cover until the tension is released.

6. Remove the clutch pilot tool and the clutch from the vehicle.

7. Check the pressure plate and flywheel for signs of wear, scoring, overheating, etc. If the clutch plate, flywheel, or pressure plate is oil-soaked, inspect the engine rear main seal and the transmission input shaft seal, and correct leakage as required. Replace any damaged parts.

8. Install the pressure plate in the cover assembly, aligning the notch in the pressure plate with the notch in the cover flange. Install pressure plate retracting springs, lock washers and drive strap to pressure plate bolts. Tighten to 11 ft. lbs. The clutch is now ready to be installed.

9. Turn the flywheel until the **X** mark is at the bottom.

10. Install the clutch disc, pressure plate and cover, using an aligning tool.

11. Turn the clutch until the **X** mark or painted white letter on the clutch cover aligns with the **X** mark on the flywheel.

12. Install the attaching bolts and tighten them a little at a time in a crossing pattern until the spring pressure is taken up.

13. Remove the aligning tool.

14. Pack the clutch ball fork seat with a small amount of high temperature grease and install a new retainer in the groove of the clutch fork.

NOTE: Be careful not to use too much grease. Excessive amounts will get on the clutch fingers and cause clutch slippage.

15. Install the retainer with the high side up with the open end on the horizontal.

16. If the clutch fork ball was removed, reinstall it in the clutch housing and snap the clutch fork onto the ball.

17. Lubricate the inside of the throwout bearing collar and the throwout fork groove with a small amount of graphite grease.

18. Install the throwout bearing. Install the clutch housing.

19. Install the transmission.

20. Further installation is the reverse of removal. Adjust the clutch.

Hydraulic Clutch Assembly

Removal and Installation

EXCEPT VAN

NOTE: Before removing the bellhousing, the engine must be supported. This can be done by placing a hydraulic jack, with a board on top, under the oil pan.

1. Raise and support the vehicle safely and remove the transmission.

2. Remove the slave cylinder.

3. Remove the bellhousing cover.

4. Remove the bellhousing from the engine.

5. Remove the throwout spring and fork.

6. Remove the ballstud from the bellhousing.

7. Install a pilot tool to hold the clutch while you are removing it.

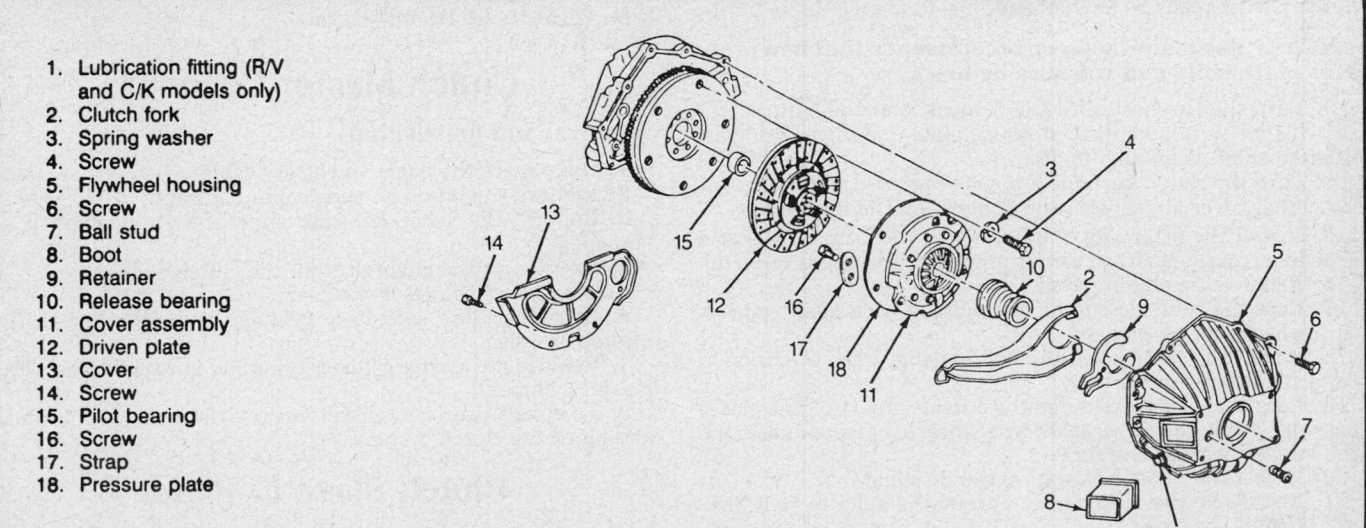

1. Lubrication fitting (R/V and C/K models only)
2. Clutch fork
3. Spring washer
4. Screw
5. Flywheel housing
6. Screw
7. Ball stud
8. Boot
9. Retainer
10. Release bearing
11. Cover assembly
12. Driven plate
13. Cover
14. Screw
15. Pilot bearing
16. Screw
17. Strap
18. Pressure plate

Exploded view of the clutch assembly—except 1988– 90 C/K Series

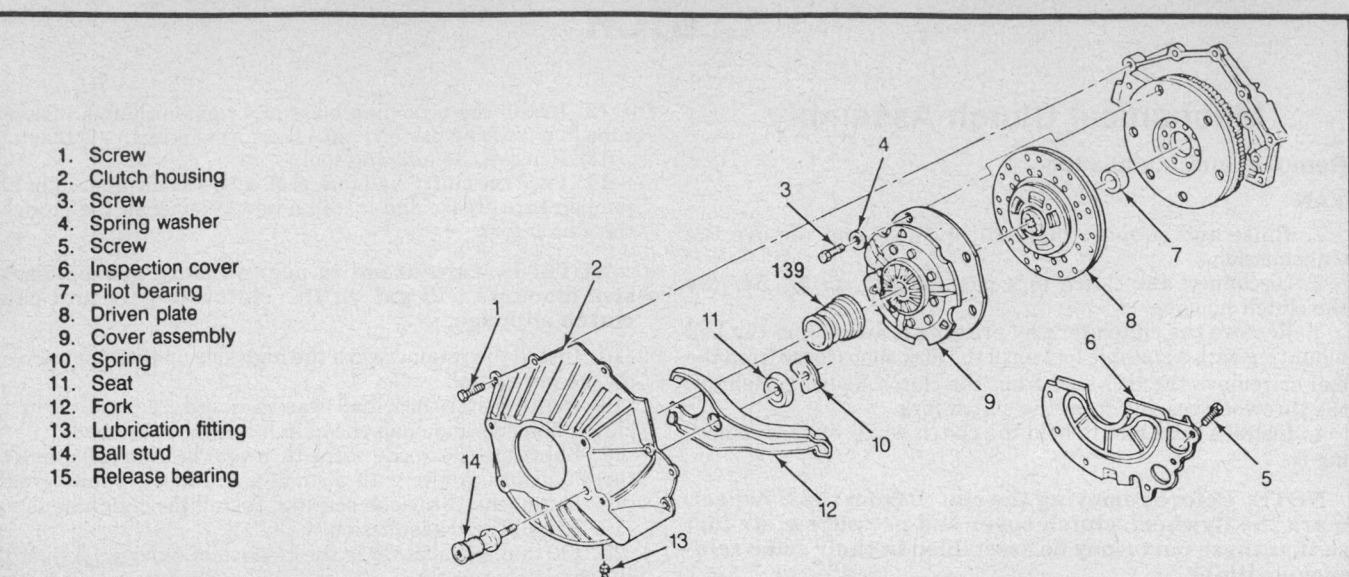

1. Screw
2. Clutch housing
3. Screw
4. Spring washer
5. Screw
6. Inspection cover
7. Pilot bearing
8. Driven plate
9. Cover assembly
10. Spring
11. Seat
12. Fork
13. Lubrication fitting
14. Ball stud
15. Release bearing

Exploded view of the clutch assembly — 1988–90 C/K Series

NOTE: Before removing the clutch from the flywheel, mark the flywheel, clutch cover and one pressure plate lug, so that these parts may be assembled in their same relative positions. They were balanced as an assembly.

8. Loosen the clutch attaching bolts one turn at a time to prevent distortion of the clutch cover until the tension is released.
9. Remove the clutch pilot tool and the clutch from the vehicle.
10. Check the pressure plate and flywheel for signs of wear, scoring, overheating, etc. If the clutch plate, flywheel, or pressure plate is oil-soaked, inspect the engine rear main seal and the transmission input shaft seal, and correct leakage as required. Replace any damaged parts.

To install:
11. Install the pressure plate in the cover assembly, aligning the notch in the pressure plate with the notch in the cover flange. Install pressure plate retracting springs, lockwashers and drive strap-to-pressure plate bolts. Tighten to 11 ft. lbs. The clutch is now ready to be installed.

NOTE: The manufacturer recommends that new pressure plate bolts and washers be used.

12. Turn the flywheel until the **X** mark is at the bottom.
13. Install the clutch disc, pressure plate and cover, using an old mainshaft as an aligning tool.
14. Turn the clutch until the **X** mark or painted white letter on the clutch cover aligns with the **X** mark on the flywheel.
15. Install the attaching bolts and tighten them a little at a time in a crossing pattern until the spring pressure is taken up.
16. Remove the aligning tool.
17. Coat the rounded end of the ballstud with high temperature wheel bearing grease.
18. Install the ballstud in the bellhousing. Pack the ballstud from the lubrication fitting.
19. Pack the inside recess and the outside groove of the release bearing with high temperature wheel bearing grease and install the release bearing and fork.
20. Install the relase bearing seat and spring.
21. Install the clutch housing. Torque the bolts to 55 ft. lbs.
22. Install the cover.
23. Install the slave cylinder. Torque the bolt to 13 ft. lbs.
24. Install the transmission.
25. Bleed the hydraulic system.

Free Pedal Travel Adjustment
MECHANICAL CLUTCH

This adjustment is for the amount of clutch pedal free travel before the throwout bearing contacts the clutch release fingers. It is required periodically to compensate for clutch lining wear. Incorrect adjustment will cause gear grinding and clutch slippage or wear.

1. Raise and support the vehicle safely. Disconnect the clutch fork return spring at the fork on the clutch housing.
2. Loosen the outer locknut on the adjusting rod.
3. Move the clutch fork back until clutch spring pressure is felt.
4. Hold the clutch pedal against its bumper and turn the inner adjusting nut until it is 0.28 in. (7.1mm) from the cross lever.
5. Tighten the locknut against the cross lever.
6. Install the return spring.
7. Check the free travel at the pedal and readjust as necessary. It should be 1⅜ in. (34mm).

Clutch Master Cylinder

Removal and Installation
1. Disconnect the negative battery cable.
2. Remove the lower steering column covers.
3. Remove the lower left side air conditioning duct, if so equipped.
4. Disconnect the pushrod from the clutch pedal.
5. Disconnect the reservoir hose.
6. Disconnect the secondary cylinder hydraulic line to the master cylinder.
7. Remove the master cylinder retaining nuts and remove the master cylinder.
8. To install, use a new gasket, reverse the removal procedure and bleed the clutch system.

Clutch Slave Cylinder

Removal and Installation
1. Disconnect the negative battery cable.
2. Raise the vehicle and support it safely.

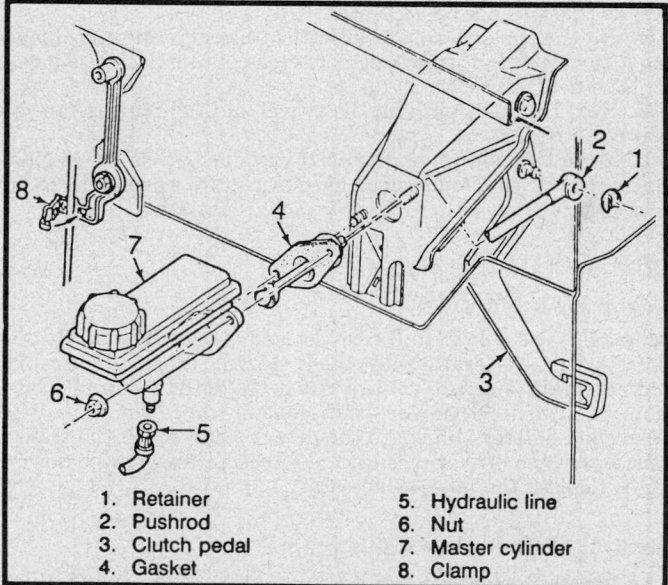

1. Retainer
2. Washer
3. Pushrod
4. Wave washer
5. Reservoir
6. Gasket
7. Hydraulic line, secondary cylinder
8. Nut
9. Master cylinder
10. Reservoir hose
11. Screw

Master cylinder and reservoir—except 1988–90 C/K Series

1. Retainer
2. Pushrod
3. Clutch pedal
4. Gasket
5. Hydraulic line
6. Nut
7. Master cylinder
8. Clamp

Master cylinder and reservoir—1988–90 C/K Series

3. Disconnect the hydraulic line from the secondary cylinder.

4. Disconnect the hydraulic line from ther master cylinder.

5. On all models except the 1988–90 C/K series, remove the nut retaining the hydraulic line and the speedometer cable to the cowl, than install the nut to hold the speedometer cable in place.

6. Cover all hydraulic lines to prevent dirt and moisture from entering the system.

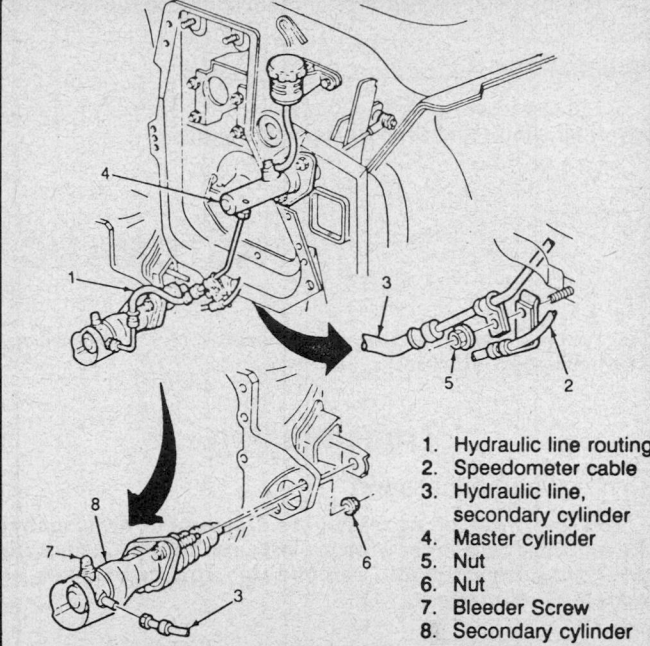

1. Hydraulic line routing
2. Speedometer cable
3. Hydraulic line, secondary cylinder
4. Master cylinder
5. Nut
6. Nut
7. Bleeder Screw
8. Secondary cylinder

Secondary (slave) cylinder and hydraulic line— except 1988–90 C/K Series

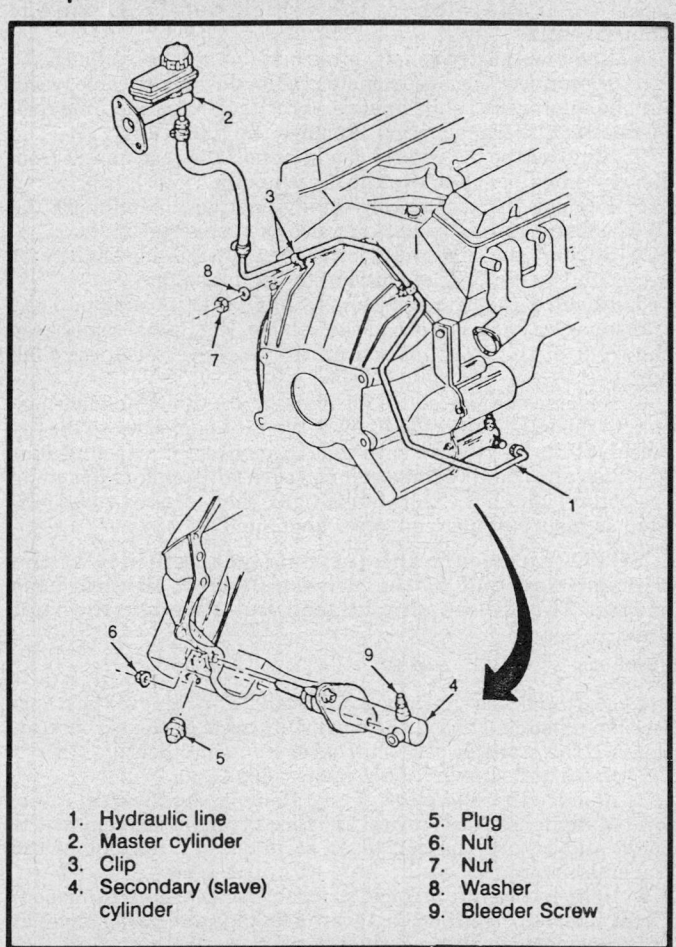

1. Hydraulic line
2. Master cylinder
3. Clip
4. Secondary (slave) cylinder
5. Plug
6. Nut
7. Nut
8. Washer
9. Bleeder Screw

Secondary (slave) cylinder and hydraulic line—1988–90 C/K Series

7. Installation is the reverse of removal. Bleed the clutch hydraulic system.

Bleeding The Hydraulic Clutch System

1. Fill the clutch master cylinder with the proper grade and type fluid. Raise and support the vehicle safely.

2. Remove the slave cylinder retaining bolts. Hold the cylinder about 45 degrees with the bleeder at the highest point.

3. Fully depress the clutch pedal and open the bleeder screw. Repeat until all air is expelled from the system.

4. Be sure that the fluid level remains full in the clutch master cylinder throughout the bleeding procedure.

AUTOMATIC TRANSMISSION

For further information, please refer to "Professional Transmission Manual".

Transmission

Removal and Installation

NOTE: It may be necessary to disconnect and remove the exhaust crossover pipe on V8s, and to disconnect the catalytic converter and remove its support bracket, on models so equipped.

2WD

1. Disconnect the battery ground cable. Disconnect the detent cable at the carburetor.

2. Raise and support the vehicle safely. Drain the transmission.

3. Remove the driveshaft, after matchmarking its flanges.

4. Disconnect the speedometer cable, downshift cable, vacuum modulator line, shift linkage, throttle linkage and fluid cooler lines at the transmission. Remove the filler tube.

5. Support the transmission and unbolt the rear mount from the crossmember. Remove the crossmember.

6. Remove the torque converter underpan, matchmark the flywheel and converter, and remove the converter bolts.

7. Support the engine and lower the transmission slightly for access to the upper transmission to engine bolts.

8. Remove the transmission to engine bolts and pull the transmission back and out of the vehicle. Rig up a strap or keep the front of the transmission up so the converter doesn't fall out.

9. Reverse the procedure for installation. Bolt the transmission to the engine first (34 ft. lbs.), then the converter to the flywheel (50 ft. lbs.). Make sure that the converter attaching lugs are flush and that the converter can turn freely before installing the bolts. Tighten the bolts finger tight, then torque to specification, to insure proper converter alignment.

NOTE: Lubricate the internal yoke splines at the transmission end of the driveshaft with lithium base grease. The grease should seep out through the vent hole.

4WD

1. Disconnect the battery ground cable and remove the transmission dipstick. Detach the downshift cable at the carburetor. Remove the transfer case shift lever knob and boot.

2. Raise and support the vehicle safely.

3. Remove the skid plate, if any. Remove the flywheel cover.

4. Matchmark the flywheel and torque converter, remove the bolts, and secure the converter so it doesn't fall out of the transmission.

5. Detach the shift linkage, speedometer cable, vacuum modulator line, downshift cable, throttle linkage and cooler times at the transmission. Remove the filler tube.

6. Remove the exhaust crossover pipe to manifold bolts.

7. Unbolt the transfer case adapter from the crossmember.

Support the transmission and transfer case. Remove the crossmember.

8. Move the exhaust system aside. Detach the driveshafts after matchmarking their flanges. Disconnect the parking brake cable.

9. Unbolt the transfer case from the frame bracket. Support the engine. Unbolt the transmission from the engine, pull the assembly back, and remove.

10. Reverse the procedure for installation. Bolt the transmission to the engine first (34 ft. lbs.), then the converter to the flywheel (50 ft. lbs.). Make sure that the converter attaching lugs are flush and that the converter can turn freely before installing the bolts.

Shift Linkage Adjustment

1. Raise and support the vehicle safely.

2. Loosen the shift lever bolt or nut at the transmission lever so that the lever is free to move on the rod.

3. Set the column shift lever to the neutral gate notch, by rotating it until the shift lever drops into the neutral gate. Do not use the indicator pointer as a reference to position the shift lever, as this will not be accurate.

4. Set the transmission lever in the neutral position by moving it clockwise to the park detent, then counterclockwise 2 detents to neutral.

5. Hold the rod tightly in the swivel and tighten the nut or bolt to 17 ft. lbs.

6. Move the column shifter to **P** and check that the engine starts. Check the adjustment by moving the selector to each gear position.

Downshift Control Relay

Turbo Hydra-Matic 400

All models use a downshift relay located on the firewall. By depressing the accelerator fully, the ECM will recognize the rapid increase in MAP sensor voltage, due to the drop in manifold vacuum, and turn on the downshift control relay. The relay will then send battrey voltage to the detent solenoid, in the transmission, which opens an orfice and forces a transmission downshift. Replace the relay as necessary.

Neutral Start Switch Adjustment

This switch prevents the engine from being started unless the transmission is in Neutral or Park. It is located on the steering column. This switch also activates the back-up lights.

NOTE: The manual transmission back-up light switch is on the rear of the transmission.

1. Move the switch housing all the way toward the low gear position.

2. Move the gear selector to the **PARK** position. The main housing and housing back should ratchet, providing proper switch adjustment.

Throttle Valve Cable Adjustment

THM 700R4

The adjustment is made at the engine end of the cable with the engine off, by rotating the throttle lever by hand. Do not use the accelerator pedal to rotate the throttle lever.

  1. Remove the air cleaner.

  2. Depress and hold down the metal adjusting tab at the end of the cable.

  3. Move the slider until it stops against the fitting.

  4. Release the adjusting tab.

  5. Rotate the throttle lever to the full extent of it travel.

  6. The slider must move towards the lever when the lever is at full travel. Make sure that the cable moves freely.

NOTE: The cable may appear to function properly with the engine cold. Recheck it with the engine hot.

  7. Road test the vehicle.

TRANSFER CASE

Transfer Case Assembly

Removal and Installation

1986 K SERIES AND 1987–90 V SERIES

Model 205

  1. Disconnect the negative battery cable. Raise and support the vehicle safely.

  2. Drain the fluid from the transfer case. Disconnect the speedometer cable. Remove the skid plate and the crossmember supports, as required.

  3. Matchmark the transfer case front output shaft yoke and driveshaft for reassembly. Disconnect the driveshaft from the transfer case.

  4. Matchmark the rear axle yoke and the driveshaft for reassembly. Remove the driveshaft. Disconnect the shift lever rod from the shift rail link.

  5. Properly support the transfer case assembly. Remove the transfer case retaining bolts.

  6. Remove the transfer case from the vehicle.

  7. Installation is the reverse of the removal procedure.

Model 208

  1. Disconnect the negative battery cable. Shift the transfer case into the 4HI position.

  2. Raise and support the vehicle safely. Drain the fluid from the transfer case. Remove the cotter pin from the shift lever swivel.

  3. Matchmark the transfer case front output shaft yoke and driveshaft for reassembly. Disconnect the driveshaft from the transfer case.

  4. Matchmark the rear axle yoke and the driveshaft for reassembly. Remove the driveshaft.

  5. Disconnect the speedometer cable. Disconnect the vacuum harness and all electrical connections at the transfer case.

  6. Disconnect the parking brake cable guide from the pivot on the right frame rail, as required.

  7. If the vehicle is equipped with automatic transmission, remove the right strut rod from the transfer case assembly.

  8. Properly support the transfer case assembly. Remove the transfer case retaining bolts.

  9. Remove the transfer case from the vehicle.

  10. Installation is the reverse of the removal procedure.

1988–90 K SERIES

  1. Disconnect the negative battery cable. Shift the transfer case into the 4HI position.

  2. Raise and support the vehicle safely. Drain the fluid from the transfer case. Remove the the shift lever swivel. Disconnect the speed sensor electrical wire. Disconnect the indicator switch electrical wire.

  3. Matchmark the transfer case front output shaft yoke and driveshaft for reassembly. Disconnect the driveshaft from the transfer case.

  4. Matchmark the rear axle yoke and the driveshaft for reassembly. Remove the driveshaft.

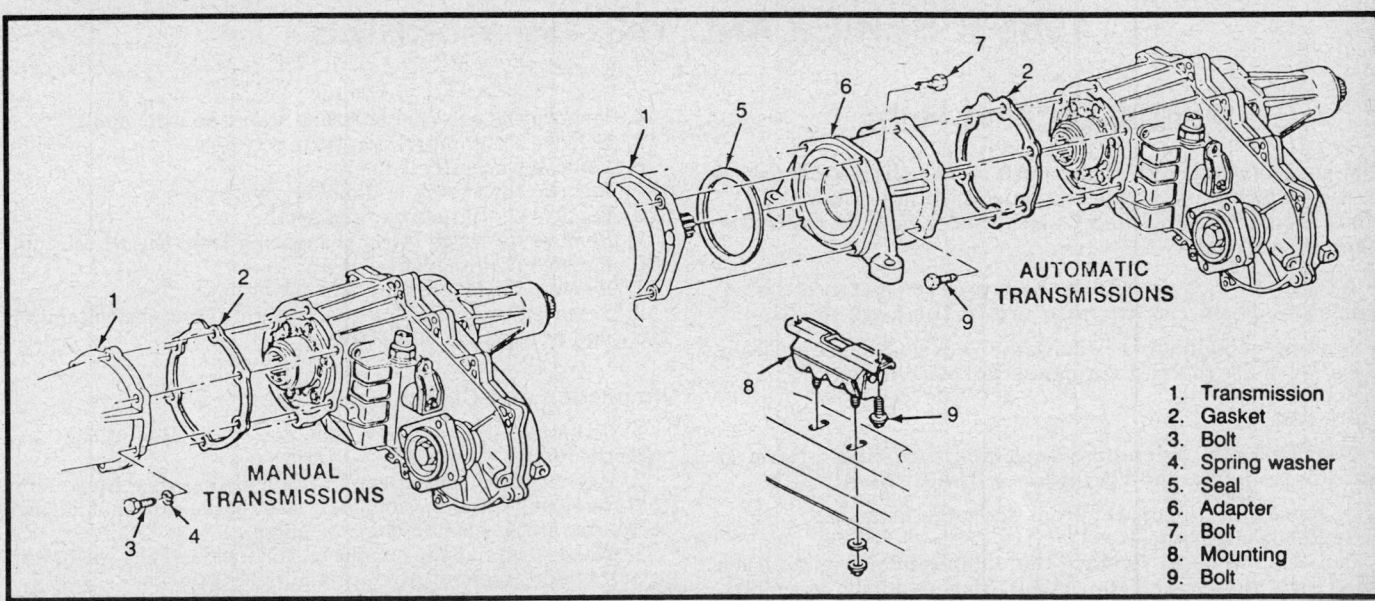

1. Transmission
2. Gasket
3. Bolt
4. Spring washer
5. Seal
6. Adapter
7. Bolt
8. Mounting
9. Bolt

Transfer case installation – except 1988–90 C/K Series

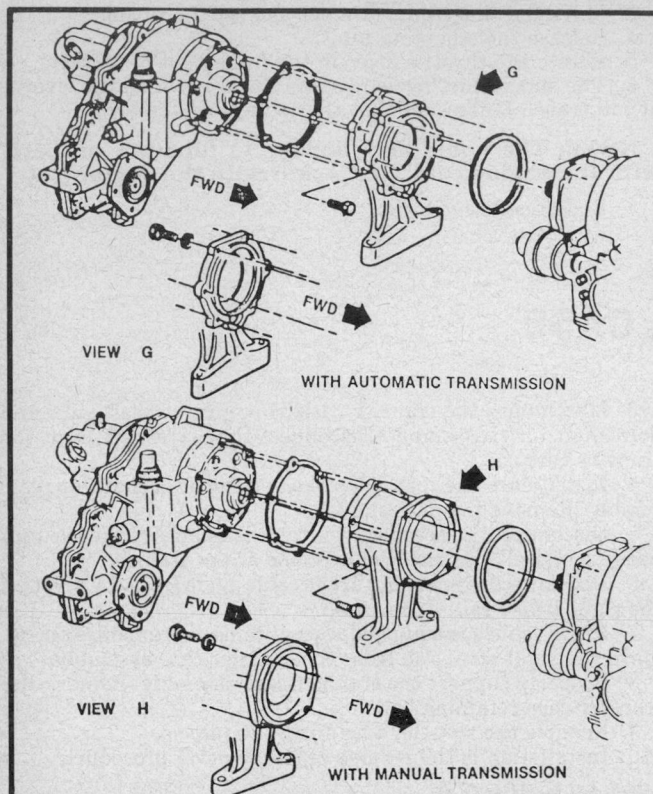

Transfer case installation—1988–90 C/K Series

5. Disconnect the parking brake cable guide from the pivot on the right frame rail, as required.

6. Properly support the transfer case assembly. Remove the transfer case retaining bolts.

7. Remove the skid shield and plate. Remove the transfer case from the vehicle.

8. Installation is the reverse of the removal procedure.

Linkage

Adjustment

MODEL 208

1. Position the transfer case lever in the 4HI detent. Push the lower shift lever forward to the 4HI stop.

2. Install the swivel rod in the shift lever hole. Hang a 0.200 in. gauge rod behind the swivel.

3. Install the rear rod nut against the gauge with the shifter against the 4HI stop.

4. Remove the gauge tool. Push the rear of the swivel rearward against the nut.

5. Tighten the front rod nut against the swivel. Check for proper operation.

MODEL 205

1. Raise and support the vehicle safely. Remove the swivel from the transfer case shift lever.

2. Turn the swivel inward or outward to determine the correct shift detent.

3. Reinstall the swivel to the shift lever.

MODEL 1370

1. Position the transfer case lever in the 4HIposition.
2. Raise and support the vehicle safely.
3. Disconnect the linkage rod from the console shift lever.
4. Shift the transfer case into the 4HI position (transfer shift lever in the forward detent).
5. Adjust the swivel to align with the hoile in the console shift lever.
6. Lower the vehicle.

MODEL NP241

No adjustments are necessary on this model

FRONT DRIVE AXLE
1986 K SERIES AND 1987–90 V SERIES

Manual Locking Hubs

The engagement and disengagement of the hubs is a manual operation which must be performed at each hub assembly. The hubs should be placed fully in either Lock or Free position or damage will result.

NOTE: Do not use place the transfer case in either 4-wheel mode unless the hubs are in the Lock position!

Locking hubs should be run in the Lock position periodically for a few miles to assure proper differential lubrication.

Removal

NOTE: This procedure requires snapring pliers. It cannot be performed properly without them!

1. Raise and support the front end on jackstands.
2. Remove the wheels.
3. Lock the hubs. Remove the outer retaining plate Allen head bolts and take off the plate, O-ring, and knob assembly.

NOTE: These bolts may have washers.

4. Remove the external snapring from the axle shaft.
5. Remove the compression spring.
6. Remove the clutch cup.
7. Remove the O-ring and dial screw.
8. Remove the clutch nut and seal.
9. Remove the large internal snapring from the wheel hub.
10. Remove the inner drive gear.
11. Remove the clutch ring and spring.
12. Remove the smaller internal snapring from the clutch hub body and remove the hub body.

Inspection and Cleaning

1. Clean all hub parts in a safe, non-flammable solvent and wipe them dry.
2. Inspect each component for wear or damage. Make sure that the springs are functional and stiff. Make sure that all gear teeth are intact, with no chips or burrs.
3. Make sure that the splines on the inside of the wheel hub are clean and free of dirt, chips and burrs.
4. Surface irregularities can be cleaned up with light filing or emery paper.

5. Prior to assembly, coat all parts with the same wheel bearing grease you've used on the wheel bearings.

Installation

1. Install the hub body. Install the smaller internal snapring in the clutch hub body.
2. Install the clutch ring and spring.
3. Install the inner drive gear.
4. Install the large internal snapring in the wheel hub.
5. Install the external snapring on the axle shaft. If the snapring groove is not completely visible, reach around, inside the knuckle and push the axle shaft outwards.
6. Install the clutch nut and seal.
7. Install the O-ring and dial screw.
8. Install the clutch cup.
9. Install the compression spring.
10. Place the hub dial in the Lock position.
11. Coat the hub dial assembly O-ring with wheel bearing grease and position the hub dial and retainer on the hub.
12. Install the allen head bolts. Make sure that you used any washers that were there originally. Tighten these bolts to 45 inch lbs.
13. Rotate the hub dial to the Free position and turn the wheel hubs to make sure that the axle is free.
14. Install the wheels.

Automatic Locking Hubs

Removal and Installation

The following procedure covers removal and installation only, for the hub assembly. The hub should be disassembled ONLY if overhaul is necessary. In that event, an overhaul kit will be required. Follow the instructions in the overhaul kit to rebuild the hub.

1. Remove the capscrews and washer from the hub cap.
2. Remove the hub cap and spring.
3. Remove the bearing race, bearing and retainer.
4. Remove the keeper from the outer clutch housing.
5. Remove the large snapring to release the locking unit. The snapring is removed by squeezing the ears of the snapring with needle-nose pliers.
6. Remove the locking unit from the hub. You can make this job easier by threading 2 hub cap screws into the outer clutch housing and hold these to pull out the unit.

To install:

7. Wipe clean all parts and check for wear or damage.
8. Coat all parts with the same wheel bearing grease you've used on the bearings.
9. Position the locking unit in the hub and install the large snapring. Pull outward on the unit to make sure the snapring is fully seated in its groove.
10. Install the keepers.
11. Install the bearing retainer, bearing and race. Make sure that the bearing is fully pack with grease.
12. Coat the hub cap O-ring with wheel bearing grease and install the hub cap.
13. Install the capscrews and washers. Torque the screws to 45 inch lbs.

Wheel Hub and Bearing

NOTE: Sodium-based grease is not compatible with lithium-based grease. Be careful not to mix the 2 types. If there is any doubt as to the type of grease used, completely clean the old grease from the bearing and hub before replacing.

Removal

1. Raise and support the vehicle safely.

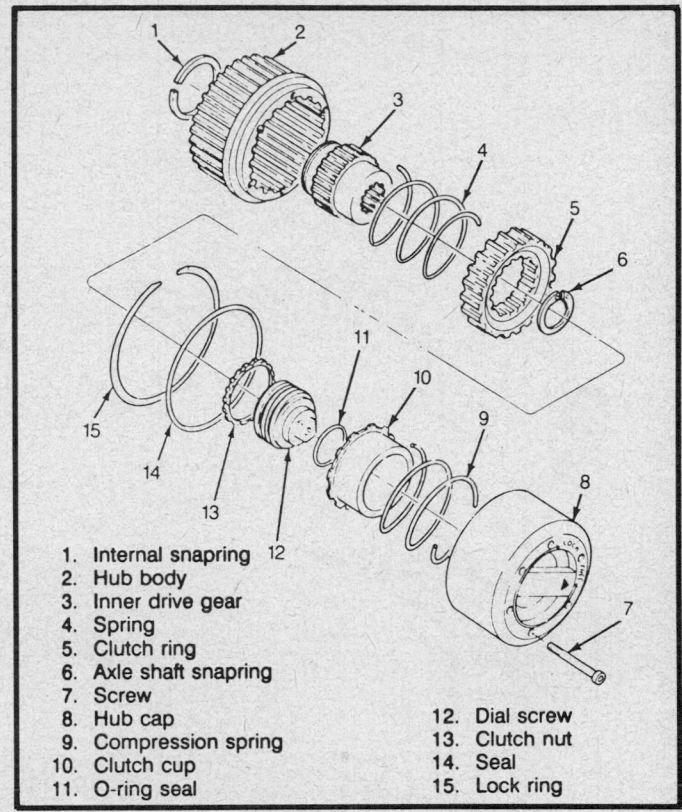

1. Internal snapring	12
2. Hub body	
3. Inner drive gear	
4. Spring	
5. Clutch ring	
6. Axle shaft snapring	
7. Screw	
8. Hub cap	12. Dial screw
9. Compression spring	13. Clutch nut
10. Clutch cup	14. Seal
11. O-ring seal	15. Lock ring

Manual hub components—except 1988–90 C/K Series

2. Remove the wheels.
3. Remove the hubs.
4. Wipe the inside of the hub to remove as much grease as possible.
5. Using your bearing nut socket, remove the locknut from the spindle.
6. With the locknut off you'll be able to see the locking ring on the adjusting nut. Remove the locking ring. A tool such as a dental pick will make this easier.
7. Using the special socket, remove the bearing adjusting nut.

NOTE: The adjusting nut and the locknut are almost identical. The difference is, the adjusting nut has a small pin on one side which indexes with a hole in the locking ring. Do not confuse the two nuts.

8. Dismount the brake caliper and suspend it out of the way, without disconnecting the brake line.
9. Pull the hub off of the spindle. The outer bearing will tend to fall out as soon as it clears the spindle, so have a hand ready to catch it.

Disassembly

1. If you are going to reuse the outer bearing, place it on a clean surface.
2. Position the hub, face up, on 2 wood blocks placed under opposite sides of the rotor. Have a paper towel positioned under the hub.
3. Using a hardened wood dowel or a hammer handle, drive out the inner bearing and seal. If your are going to reuse the inner bearing, move it to a clean area. Discard the seal.
4. If the bearings are being replaced, you'll have to replace the races. The races are pressed into the hub, but you can drive them out.
5. With the hub in position on the blocks, use a long drift and

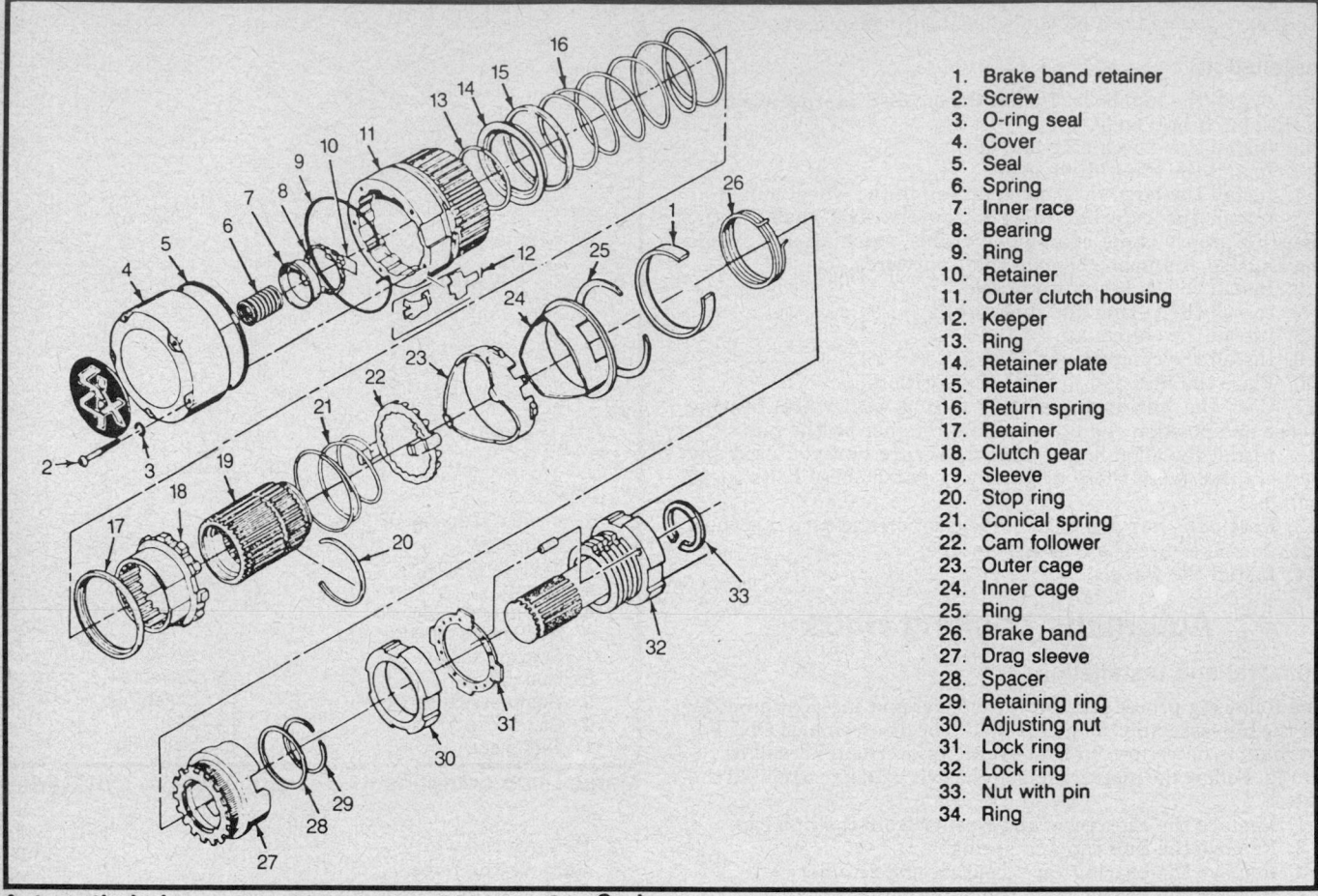

1. Brake band retainer
2. Screw
3. O-ring seal
4. Cover
5. Seal
6. Spring
7. Inner race
8. Bearing
9. Ring
10. Retainer
11. Outer clutch housing
12. Keeper
13. Ring
14. Retainer plate
15. Retainer
16. Return spring
17. Retainer
18. Clutch gear
19. Sleeve
20. Stop ring
21. Conical spring
22. Cam follower
23. Outer cage
24. Inner cage
25. Ring
26. Brake band
27. Drag sleeve
28. Spacer
29. Retaining ring
30. Adjusting nut
31. Lock ring
32. Lock ring
33. Nut with pin
34. Ring

Automatic hub components — except 1988–90 C/K Series

hammer evenly around the outside diameter of the inner bearing race until it is free. Discard the race.

6. Turn the hub over and repeat this procedure for the outer bearing race.

Inspection

1. If reusing the bearings, wash them in a non-flammable solvent and let them air-dry. Never use compressed air to spin-dry the bearings.

2. If either bearing shows any sign of damage, rust, heat blueing or excessive looseness, both bearings in that hub must be replaced as a set. If bearings are replaced, the races must be replaced also.

NOTE: If the bearings show signs of heat blueing, wipe the spindle clean and check for heat blueing on the spindle surface. If the spindle shows large areas of heat blueing, it should be replaced.

3. If reusing the bearings, wash out the hub with solvent and wipe it clean. Check the races. If they show signs of wear, pitting, cracking, rusting or heat blueing, they, along with the bearings, must be replaced.

Installation

1. If new races are being installed, coat the race and its bore in the hub with high temperature wheel bearing grease.

2. Position the race in the bore and start gently tapping it into place. There are drivers made for this purpose. Just tap evenly around the race as it is driven into place so that it doesn't

cock in the bore. Drive the race in until it is fully seated against the shoulder in the bore. It's fully seated in 2 ways:

   a. The hammer blows will sound differently when the race seats against the shoulder.

   b. The grease applied to the bore will be squeezed out below the race as the race seats against the shoulder.
Either race can be installed first.

3. Pack the bearings thoroughly with high temperature wheel bearing grease.

4. Place the inner bearing in its race and position a new seal in the hub bore. Gentlty tap around the outer diameter of the seal with a plastic mallet until the seal is flush with the end of the bore.

5. Carefully place the hub assembly on the spindle. Take care to avoid damaging the seal on the spindle threads. Make sure the hub is all the way on the spindle.

6. Place the outer bearing on the spindle and slide it into place in its race.

7. Thread the adjusting nut on the spindle until it contacts the outer bearing.

NOTE: Make sure the adjusting nut is used. Remember, it has a small pin on one side. That pin must face outwards.

8. Using the special socket and the torque wrench:

   a. Tighten the adjusting nut to 50 ft. lbs. while rotating the hub.

   b. Back off the adjusting nut until it is loose.

   c. While rotating the hub, tighten the adjusting nut to 35

ft. lbs. for automatic locking hubs or 50 ft. lbs. for manual locking hubs.

    d. Back off the adjusting nut ¼ to ⅜ of a turn for automatic hubs or ⅙ to ¼ turn for manual hubs.

9. Coat the locking ring with wheel bearing grease. Place the locking rin on the spindle. There is a tab on the inner diameter of the ring which must fit in the slot on the top of the spindle. Slide the locking ring in until it contacts the adjusting nut. The pin on the adjusting nut must enter one of the holes in the locking ring. If the locking ring is seated properly the grease on the ring will be pushed out of one of the holes by the pin, and the ring will not rock from side-to-side when pressed on either side. If the locking ring and pin don't index, take note of how far off they are, pull the ring off the spindle and turn the nut, either by hand or with the socket, just enough for a good fit. Try the locking ring again.

10. When the locking ring engages the adjusting nut pin properly, your bearing adjustment is set. Thread the locknut onto the spindle until it contacts the locking ring.

11. Tighten the locknut to *at least* 160 ft. lbs. This locknut ensures that the locking ring and adjusting nut don't move. Overtightening the locknut has no effect on the bearing adjustment.

12. Install the locking hub.

13. Install the caliper.

15. Install the wheel.

Axle Shaft

Removal and Installation

1. Raise and support the vehicle safely.
2. Remove the wheel.
3. Remove the locking hub.
4. Remove the hub and bearing assembly.
5. Remove the nuts and remove the caliper mounting bracket and splash shield.
6. Tap the end of the spindle with a plastic mallet to break it loose from the knuckle. If tapping won't break it loose, proceed as follows:

    a. Thread the bearing locknut part way onto the spindle.

    b. Position a 2- or 3-jawed pull with the jaws grabbing the locknut and the screw bearing in the end of the axle shaft.

    c. Tighten the puller until the spindle breaks free. It will be very helpful to spray Liquid Wrench®, WD-40® or similar solvent around the spindle mating area and around the bolt holes. As the puller is tightened, tap the spindle with the plastic mallet. This often helps break the spindle loose.

7. Pull out the axle shaft assembly.

To install:

8. Place the spacer and a new seal on the axle shaft.

NOTE: The spacer's chamfer points towards the oil deflector.

9. Pack the spindle bearing with wheel bearing grease.
10. Slide the axle shaft into the housing. When installing the axle shaft, turn the shaft slowly to align the splines with the differential.
11. Place the spindle on the knuckle. Be sure the seal and oil deflector are in place.
12. Install the caliper bracket and splash shield.
13. Using new washers, install the nuts and torque them to 65 ft. lbs.
14. Install the hub and rotor assembly. Adjust the wheel bearings.
15. Install the locking hubs.
16. Install the caliper.
17. Install the wheel.

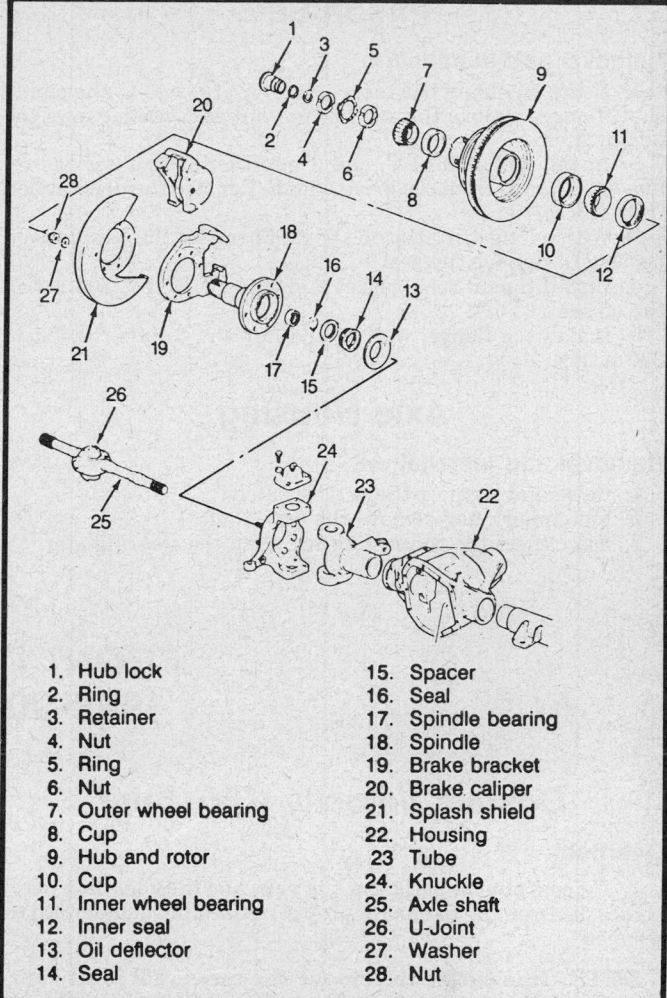

1.	Hub lock	15.	Spacer
2.	Ring	16.	Seal
3.	Retainer	17.	Spindle bearing
4.	Nut	18.	Spindle
5.	Ring	19.	Brake bracket
6.	Nut	20.	Brake caliper
7.	Outer wheel bearing	21.	Splash shield
8.	Cup	22.	Housing
9.	Hub and rotor	23.	Tube
10.	Cup	24.	Knuckle
11.	Inner wheel bearing	25.	Axle shaft
12.	Inner seal	26.	U-Joint
13.	Oil deflector	27.	Washer
14.	Seal	28.	Nut

Front driving axle components—except 1988–90 C/K Series

Axle Shaft U-Joint

Overhaul

1. Raise and support the vehicle safely and remove the axle shaft.
2. Squeeze the ends of the trunnion bearings in a vise to relieve the load on the snaprings. Remove the snaprings.
3. Support the yoke in a vise and drive on one end of the trunnion bearing with a brass drift enough to drive the opposite bearing from the yoke.
4. Support the other side of the yoke and drive the other bearing out.
5. Remove the trunnion.
6. Clean and check all parts. You can buy U-joint repair kits to replace all the worn parts.
7. Lubricate the bearings with wheel bearing grease.
8. Replace the trunnion and press the bearings into the yoke and over the trunnion hubs far enough to install the lock rings.
9. Hold the trunnion in one hand and tap the yoke lightly to seat the bearings against the lock rings.
10. The axle slingers can be pressed off the shaft.

NOTE: Always replace the slingers if the spindle seals are replaced.

11. Replace the shaft.

Pinion Seal

Removal and Installation

1. Using a holding bar tool J–8614–1, attached to the pinion shaft flange, remove the self locking nut and washer from the pinion shaft.
2. Install tool J–8614–2, and 3 into the holding bar and remove the flange from the drive pinion. Remove the drive pinion from the carrier.
3. With a long drift, tap on the inner race of the outer pinion bearing to remove the seal.
4. Install the oil seal, gasket and using Tool J-22804 install the oil seal.
5. Install the flange, washer and nut and torque the nut to 270 ft. lbs.

Axle Housing

Removal and Installation

1. Raise and support the vehicle safely.
2. Matchmark and remove the driveshaft.
3. Disconnect the connecting rod from the steering arm.

4. Disconnect the brake caliper and position it out of the way, without disconnecting the brake line.
5. Disconnect the shock absorbers from the axle brackets.
6. Remove the front stabilizer bar.
7. Disconnect the axle vent tube clip at the differential housing.
8. Take up the weight of the axle assembly using a suitable jack.
9. Remove the nuts, washers, U-bolts and plates from the axle and separate the axle from the springs. Remove the axle assembly from the vehicle.

To install:

10. Position the axle under the vehicle.
11. Install the plates, U-bolts, washers, and nuts. Tighten the nuts to 150 ft. lbs.
12. Remove the jack.
13. Connect the axle vent tube clip at the differential housing.
14. Install the front stabilizer bar.
15. Connect the shock absorbers at the axle brackets. Torque the bolts to 65 ft. lbs.; 88 ft. lbs. with quad shocks.
16. Install the brake caliper
17. Connect the connecting rod at the steering arm.
18. Install the driveshaft.

FRONT DRIVE AXLE
1988–90 K SERIES

Costant Velocity (CV) Joint

Overhaul

1. Using a punch, mark the link yoke and the adjoining yokes before disassembly to ensure proper reassembly and driveshaft balance.

NOTE: It is easier to remove the universal joint bearings from the flange yoke first. The first pair of flange yoke universal joint bearings to be removed is the pair in the link yoke.

2. With the driveshaft in a horizontal position, solidly support the link yoke (a 1⅞ in. pipe will do).
3. Apply force to the bearing cup on the opposite side with a 1⅛ in. pipe or a socket the size of the bearing cup. Use a vise or press to apply force. Force the cup inward as far as possible.

NOTE: In the absence of a press, a heavy vise may be used, but make sure that the universal to be removed is at a right angle to the jaws of the vise. Do not cock the bearing cups in their bores.

4. Remove the pieces of pipe and complete the removal of the protruding bearing cup by tapping around the circumference of the exposed portion of the bearing with a small hammer.
5. Reverse the position of the pieces of pipe and apply force to the exposed journal end. This will force the other bearing cup out of its bore and allow removal of the flange.

NOTE: There is a ball joint located between the two universals. The ball portion of this joint is on the inner end of the flange yoke. The ball, as well as the ball seat parts, is replaceable. Care must be taken not to damage the ball. The ball portion of this joint is on the driveshaft. To remove the seat, pry the seal out with a screwdriver.

6. To remove the journal from the flange, use steps two through five.

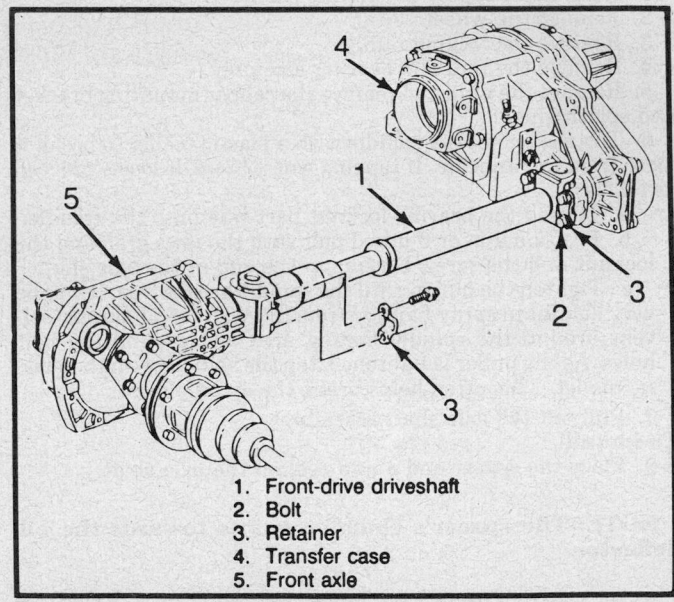

1. Front-drive driveshaft
2. Bolt
3. Retainer
4. Transfer case
5. Front axle

Front drive driveshaft – 1988–90 C/K Series

7. Remove the universal joint bearings from the driveshaft using the steps from two through five. The first pair of bearing caps that should be removed is the pair in the link yoke.
8. Examine the ball stud seat and ball stud for scores or wear. Worn seats can be replaced with a kit. A worn ball, however, requires the replacement of the entire shaft yoke and flange assembly. Clean the ball seat cavity and fill it with grease. Install the spring, washer, ball seats, and spacer, if removed.
9. Install the universal joints opposite the order in which they were disassembled.
10. Install a bearing ¼ of the way into one side of the yoke.

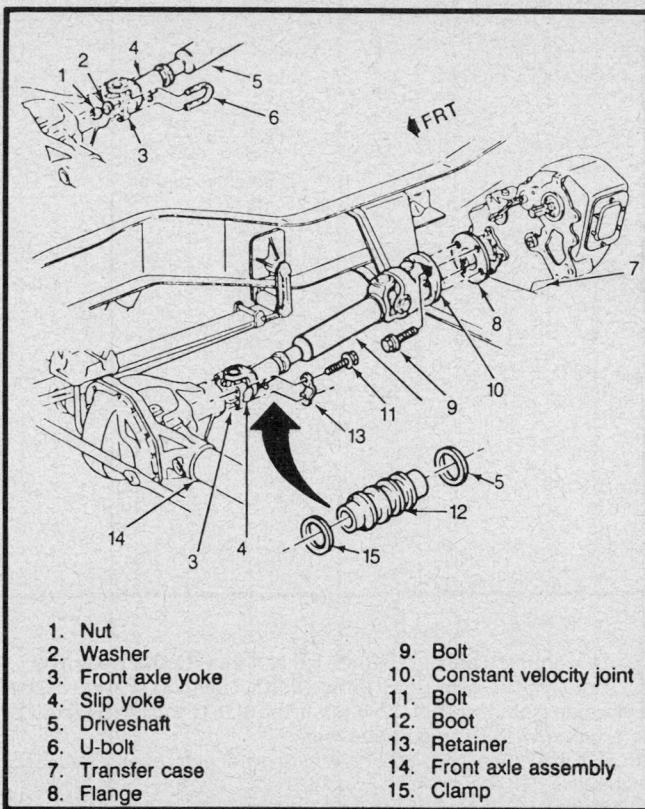

1. Nut
2. Washer
3. Front axle yoke
4. Slip yoke
5. Driveshaft
6. U-bolt
7. Transfer case
8. Flange
9. Bolt
10. Constant velocity joint
11. Bolt
12. Boot
13. Retainer
14. Front axle assembly
15. Clamp

Front drive driveshaft—except 1988–90 C/K Series

11. Insert the journal into the yoke so that an arm of the journal seats into the bearing.
12. Press the bearing in the remaining distance and install its snapring.
13. Install the opposite bearing. Do not allow the bearing rollers to jam. Continually check for free movement of the journal in the bearings as they are pressed into the yoke.
14. Install the rest of the bearings in the same manner.

NOTE: The flange yoke should snap over center to the right or left and up or down by the pressure of the ball seat spring.

Indicator Switch

Replacement
1. Remove the skid plate.
2. Unplug the electrical connector.
3. Unscrew the switch.
4. Installation is the reverse of removal. Coat the threads of the switch with sealer. Torque the switch to 15 ft. lbs. and the skid plate bolts to 25 ft. lbs.

Thermal Actuator

Replacement
1. Remove the skid plate.
2. Unplug the electrical connector.
3. Unscrew the actuator.
4. Installation is the reverse of removal. Coat the threads of the actuator with sealer. Torque the actuator to 16 ft. lbs.

Left Side Axle Shaft, Hub and Bearing

Removal and Installation
1. Raise and support the vehicle safely.
2. Remove the wheel.
3. Remove the skid plate.
4. Remove the left stabilizer bar clamp.
5. Remove the left stabilizer bar bolt, spacer and bushings at the lower control arm.
6. Disconnect the left inner tie rod end from the steering relay rod.
7. Remove the hub nut and washer. Insert a long drift or dowel through the vanes in the brake rotor to hold the rotor in place.
8. Remove the axle shaft inner flange bolts.
9. Using a puller, force the outer end of the axle shaft out of the hub. Remove the shaft.

NOTE: Never allow the vehicle to rest on the wheels with the axle shaft removed.

To install:
10. Position the shaft in the hub and install the washer and hub nut. Leave the drift in the rotor vanes and tighten the hub nut to 175 ft. lbs.
11. Install the flange bolts. Tighten them to 59 ft. lbs. Remove the drift.
12. Connect the left inner tie rod end at the steering relay rod. Torque the nut to 35 ft. lbs.
13. Install the left stabilizer bar bolt, spacer and bushings at the lower control arm. Torque the bolt to 24 ft. lbs.
14. Install the left stabilizer bar clamp. Torque the bolts to 12 ft. lbs.
15. Install the skid plate.

Right Side Axle Shaft, Hub and Bearing

Removal and Installation
1. Raise and support the vehicle safely.
2. Remove the wheel.
3. Remove the skid plate.
4. Remove the right stabilizer bar clamp.
5. Remove the right stabilizer bar bolt, spacer and bushings at the lower control arm.
6. Disconnect the right inner tie rod end from the steering relay rod.
7. Remove the hub nut and washer. Insert a long drift or dowel through the vanes in the brake rotor to hold the rotor in place.
8. Remove the axle shaft inner flange bolts.
9. Using a puller, force the outer end of the axle shaft out of the hub. Remove the shaft.

NOTE: Never allow the vehicle to rest on the wheels with the axle shaft removed!

To install:
10. Position the shaft in the hub and install the washer and hub nut. Leave the drift in the rotor vanes and tighten the hub nut to 175 ft. lbs.
11. Install the flange bolts. Tighten them to 59 ft. lbs. Remove the drift.
12. Connect the right inner tie rod end at the steering relay rod. Torque the nut to 35 ft. lbs.
13. Install the right stabilizer bar bolt, spacer and bushings at the lower control arm. Torque the bolt to 12 ft. lbs.
14. Install the right stabilizer bar clamp. Torque the bolts to 24 ft. lbs.

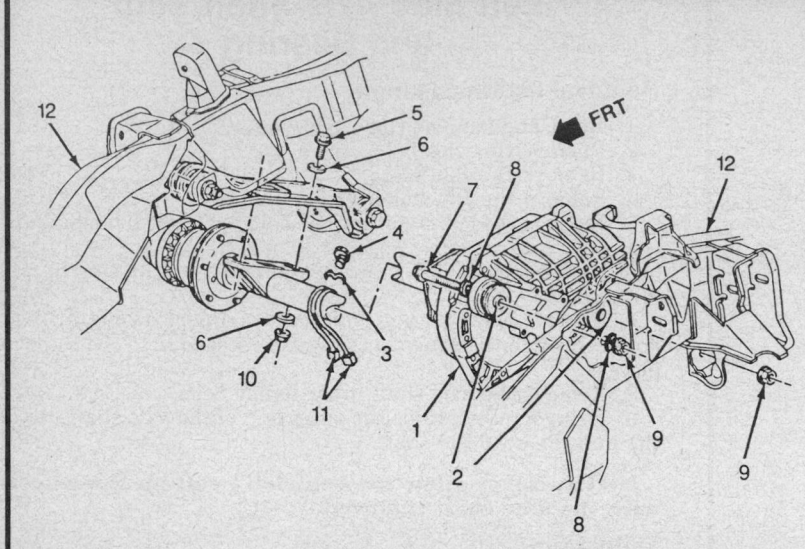

1. Differential carrier
2. Bushing
3. Clamp
4. Screw
5. Screw
6. Washer
7. Screw
8. Washer
9. Nut
10. Nut
11. Connectors
12. Frame

Differential carrier mounting—1988–90 C/K Series

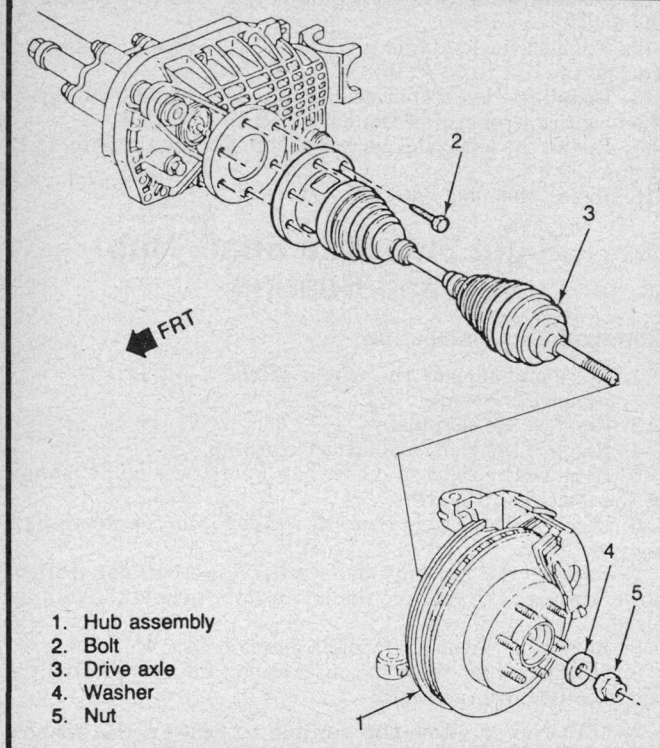

1. Hub assembly
2. Bolt
3. Drive axle
4. Washer
5. Nut

Drive axle—1988–90 C/K Series

15. Install the skid plate.

Axle Tube Assembly

Removal

1. Raise and support the vehicle safely.
2. Remove the right wheel.
3. Position a drain pan under the axle.
4. Remove the stabilizer bar.
5. Remove the skid plate.

6. Disconnect the right inner tie rod end at the relay rod.
7. Remove the axle shaft flange bolts, turn the wheel to loosen the axle from the axle tube, push the axle towards the front of the truck and tie it out of the way.
8. Unplug the indicator switch and actuator electrical connectors.
9. Remove the drain plug and drain the fluid from the case.
10. Remove the axle tube-to-frame mounting bolts.
11. Remove the axle tube-to-carrier bolts.
12. Remove the axle tube/shaft assembly. Keep the open end up.

Disassembly

1. Position the axle tube, open end up, in a vise by clamping on the mounting flange.
2. Remove the snapring, sleeve, connector and thrust washer from the shaft end.
3. Tap out the axle shaft with a plastic mallet.
4. Turn the tube, outer end up, and pry out the deflector and seal.
5. Using a slide hammer and bearing remover adapter, remove the bearing.
6. Clean all parts in a non-flammable solvent and inspect them for wear or damage. Clean off all old gasket material.

Assembly

1. Using a bearing driver, install the new bearing in the tube.
2. Coat the lips of a new seal with wheel bearing grease and tap it into place in the tube.
3. Install the deflector.
4. Insert the axle shaft into the tube.
5. Coat the thrust washer with grease to hold it in place and position it on the tube end. Make sure the tabs index the slots.
6. Install the sleeve, connector and snapring.

Installation

1. Position a new gasket, coated with sealer, on the carrier. Raise the tube assembly into position and install the tube-to-carrier bolts. Torque the bolts to 30 ft. lbs.
2. Install the axle shaft flange bolts and torque them to 59 ft. lbs.
3. Install the axle tube-to-frame bolts.

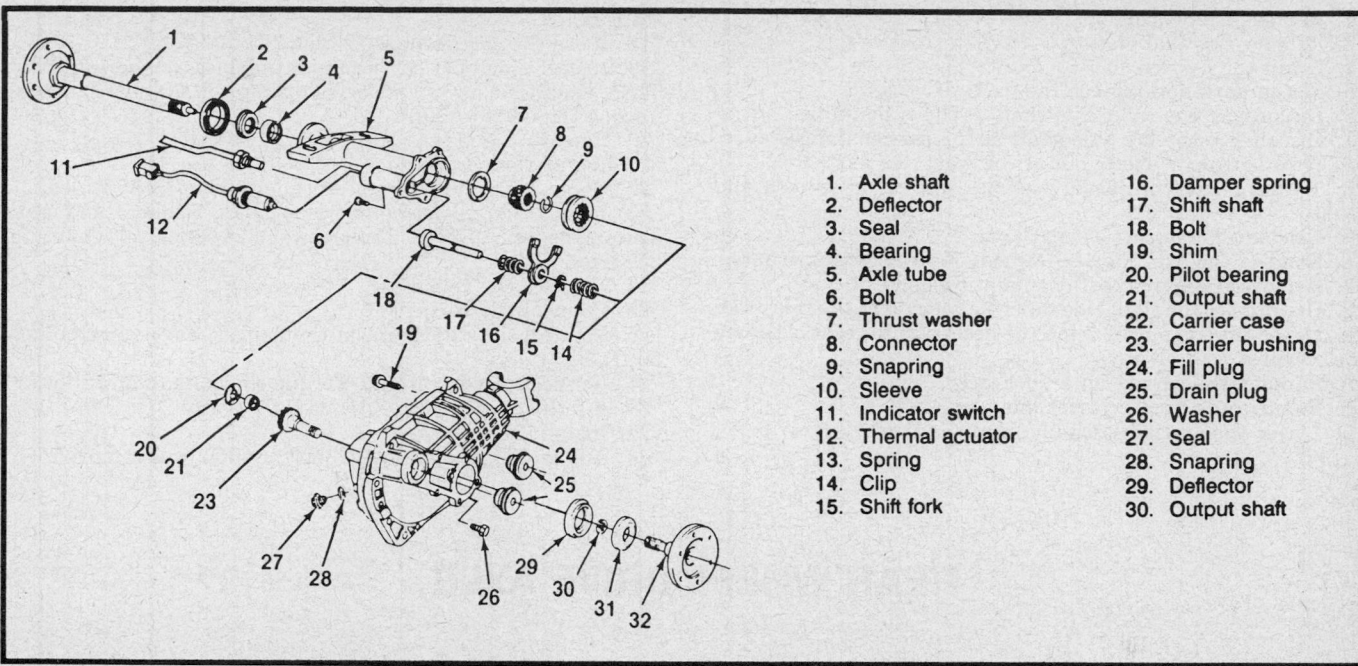

1.	Axle shaft	16.	Damper spring
2.	Deflector	17.	Shift shaft
3.	Seal	18.	Bolt
4.	Bearing	19.	Shim
5.	Axle tube	20.	Pilot bearing
6.	Bolt	21.	Output shaft
7.	Thrust washer	22.	Carrier case
8.	Connector	23.	Carrier bushing
9.	Snapring	24.	Fill plug
10.	Sleeve	25.	Drain plug
11.	Indicator switch	26.	Washer
12.	Thermal actuator	27.	Seal
13.	Spring	28.	Snapring
14.	Clip	29.	Deflector
15.	Shift fork	30.	Output shaft

Front axle components — 1988–90 C/K Series

4. Connect the tie rod end to the relay rod. Torque the nut to 35 ft. lbs.

5. Install the stabilizer bar. Torque the brackets to 24 ft. lbs.; the links to 12 ft. lbs.

6. Connect the actuator and switch.

7. Install the drain plug. Tighten it to 24 ft. lbs.

8. Fill the axle and tighten the filler plug to 24 ft. lbs.

9. Install the skid plate. Tighten the bolts to 25 ft. lbs.

Output Shaft

Removal and Installation

1. Raise and support the vehicle safely.
2. Drain the axle.
3. Remove the left side axle shaft.
4. Remove the lower carrier mounting bolt.
5. Carefully pry against the lower part of the carrier to provide clearance for the output shaft removal. While prying, insert a prybar between the output shaft flange and the carrier case. Pry the output shaft free. Be careful, as possible damage to the carrier may result.
6. Remove the deflector and seal from the carrier.

To install:
1. Lubricate the lips of a new seal with wheel bearing grease and drive it into place.
2. Install the deflector.
3. Pry against the case and position the output shaft in the carrier. Tap it into place with a plastic mallet.
4. Install the lower carrier mounting bolt, washer and nut. Torque the bolt to 80 ft. lbs.
5. Install the left axle shaft.
6. Fill the axle.

Pinion Seal

Replacement

1. Raise and support the vehicle safely.
2. Matchmark and disconnect the front driveshaft at the carrier.

3. Remove the wheels.
4. Dismount the calipers and wire them up, out of the way.
5. Position an inch pound torque wrench on the pinion nut. Measure the torque needed to rotate the pinion one full revolution. Record the figure.
6. Matchmark the pinion flange, shaft and nut. Count and record the number of exposed threads on the pinion shaft.
7. Hold the flange and remove the nut and washer.
8. Using a puller, remove the flange.
9. Carefully pry the seal from its bore. Be careful to avoid scratching the seal bore.
10. Remove the deflector from the flange.

To install:
11. Clean the seal bore thoroughly.
12. Remove any burrs from the deflector staking on the flange.
13. Tap the deflector onto the flange and stake it in three places.
14. Position the new seal in the carrier bore and drive it into place until flush. Coat the seal lips with wheel bearing grease.
15. Coat the outer edge of the flange neck with wheel bearing grease and slide it onto the pinion shaft.
16. Place a new nut and washer onto the pinion shaft and tighten it to the position originally recorded. That is, the alignment marks are aligned, and the recorded number of threads are exposed on the pinion shaft.

NOTE: Never hammer the flange onto the pinion.

17. Measure the rotating torque of the pinion. Compare this to the original torque. Tighten the pinion nut, in small increments, until the rotating torque is 3 inch lbs. greater than the original torque.
18. Install the driveshaft.
19. Install the calipers.
20. Install the wheels.

Differential Carrier

Removal and Installation

1. Raise and support the vehicle safely.

5 SECTION

GENERAL MOTORS CORPORATION
C/K SERIES (PICK-UP) • R/V SERIES (PICK-UP) • BLAZER/JIMMY • SUBURBAN • G SERIES (VAN)

2. Remove the wheels.
3. Remove the skid plate.
4. Drain the carrier.
5. Matchmark and remove the front driveshaft.
6. Disconnect the right axle shaft at the tube flange.
7. Disconnect the left axle shaft at the carrier flange.
8. Wire both axle shafts out of the way.
9. Unplug the connectors at the indicator switch and actuator.
10. Disconnect the carrier vent hose.
11. Remove the axle tube-to-frame bolts, washers and nuts.
12. Remove the lower carrier mounting bolt.
13. Disconnect the right side inner tie rod end at the relay rod.
14. Depending on model, it may be necessary to remove the engine oil filter.
15. Support the carrier on a floor jack
16. Remove the upper carrier mounting bolt.
17. Lower the carrier assembly from the truck.

To install:
18. Raise the carrier into position.
19. Install the upper carrier mounting bolt, washers and nut. Then, install the lower carrier mounting bolt, washers and nut. Torque the bolts to 80 ft. lbs.
20. Remove the jack.
21. Install the oil filter.
22. Connect the tie rod end. Torque the nut to 35 ft. lbs.
23. Install the axle tube-to-frame bolts, washers and nuts. Torque the nuts to 75 ft. lbs. for 15 and 25 series; 107 ft. lbs. for 35 series.
24. Connect the vent hose.
25. Connect the wiring.
26. Connect the axle shafts at the flanges. Torque the bolts to 59 ft. lbs.
27. Connect the driveshaft. Torque the bolts to 15 ft. lbs.
28. Fill the carrier with SAE 85W-90 gear oil.
29. Install the wheels.
30. Add any engine oil lost when the filter was removed.

REAR WHEEL DRIVE AXLE

Driveshaft and U-Joints

Tubular driveshafts are used on all models, incorporating needle bearing U-joints. An internally splined sleeve at the forward end compensates for variation in distance between the rear axle and the transmission.

The number of driveshafts used is determined by the length of the wheelbase. On vehicles that use 2 driveshafts there is a center support incorporating a rubber cushioned ball bearing mounted in a bracket attached to the frame crossmember. The ball bearing is permanently sealed and lubricated.

Extended lift U-joints have been incorporated on most models and can be identified by the absence of a lubrication fitting.

Rear Driveshaft

Removal and Installation
ALL MODELS

1. Raise and support the vehicle safely.
2. Scribe alignment marks on the driveshaft and flange of the rear axle, and transfer case or transmission. If the vehicle is equipped with a two piece driveshaft, be certain to also scribe marks at the center joint near the splined connection. When reinstalling driveshafts, it is necessary to place the shafts in the same position from which they were removed. Failure to reinstall the driveshaft properly will cause driveline vibrations and reduced component life.
3. Disconnect the rear universal joint by removing U-bolts or straps. Tape the bearings into place to avoid losing them.
4. If there are U-bolts or straps at the front end of the shaft, remove them. Tape the bearings into place. For vehicles with 2 piece shafts, remove the bolts retaining the bearing support to the frame crossmember. Compress the shaft slightly and remove it.
5. If there are no fasteners at the front end of the transmission, there will only be a splined fitting. Slide the shaft forward slightly to disengage the axle flange, lower the rear end of the shaft, then pull it back out of the transmission. Most 2WD vehicles are of this type. For vehicles with 2 piece driveshafts, remove the bolts retaining the bearing support to the frame crossmember.
6. Reverse the procedure for installation. It may be tricky to get the scribed alignment marks to match up on vehicles with two piece driveshafts. For those models only, the following instructions may be of some help. First, slide the grease cap and gasket onto the rear splines.
7. Models with 32 splines have an alignment key. The driveshaft cannot be replaced incorrectly. Simply match up the key with the keyway.
8. On 2WD automatic transmission models, lubricate the internal yoke splines at the transmission end of the shaft with lithium base grease. The grease should seep out through the vent hole.

NOTE: A thump in the rear driveshaft sometimes occurs when releasing the brakes after braking to a stop, especially on a downgrade. This is most common with automatic transmission. It is often caused by the driveshaft splines binding and can be cured by removing the driveshaft, inspecting the splines for rough edges, and carefully lubricating. A similar thump may be caused by the clutch plates in Positraction limited slip rear axles binding. If this isn't caused by wear, it can be cured by draining and refilling the rear axle with the special lubricant and adding Positraction additive, both of which are available from dealers and aftermarket suppliers.

U-Joints

Overhaul

There are 2 types of U-joints used in these vehicles. The first is held together by wire snaprings in the yokes. The second type is held together with injection molded plastic retainer rings. This type cannot be reassembled with the same parts, once disassembled. However, repair kits are available. end of the front driveshaft.

SNAPRING TYPE

1. Remove the driveshaft(s) from the vehicle.
2. Remove the lockrings from the yoke and remove the lubrication fitting.
3. Support the yoke in a bench vise. Never clamp the driveshaft tube.
4. Use a soft drift pin and hammer to drive against one trunnion bearing to drive the opposite bearing from the yoke.

NOTE: The bearing cap cannot be driven completely out.

5. Grasp the cap and work it out.

6. Support the other side of the yoke and drive the other bearing cap from the yoke and remove as in Steps 4 and 5.

7. Remove the trunnion from the driveshaft yoke.

8. If equipped with a sliding sleeve, remove the trunnions bearings from the sleeve yoke in the same manner as above. Remove the seal retainer from the end of the sleeve and pull the seal and washer from the retainer.

To remove the bearing support:

9. Remove the dust shield, or, if equipped with a flange, remove the cotter pin and nut and pull the flange and deflector assembly from the shaft.

10. Remove the support bracket from the rubber cushion and pull the cushion away from the bearing.

11. Pull the bearing assembly from the shaft. If equipped, remove the grease retainers and slingers from the bearing.

Assemble the bearing support as follows:

12. Install the inner deflector on the driveshaft and punch the deflector on 2 opposite sides to be sure that it is tight.

13. Pack the retainers with special high melting grease. Insert a slinger (if used) inside one retainer and press this retainer over the bearing outer race.

14. Start the bearing and slinger on the shaft journal. Support the driveshaft and press the bearing and inner slinger against the shoulder of the shaft with a suitable pipe.

15. Install the second slinger on the shaft and press the second retainer on the shaft.

16. Install the dust shield over the shaft (small diameter first) and depress it into position against the outer slinger or, if equipped with a flange, install the flange and deflector. Align the centerline of the flange yoke with the centerline of the driveshaft yoke and start the flange straight on the splines of the shaft with the end of the flange against the slinger.

17. Force the rubber cushion onto the bearing and coat the outside diameter of the cushion with clean brake fluid.

18. Force the bracket onto the cushion.

Assemble the trunnion bearings:

19. Repack the bearings with grease and replace the trunnion dust seals after any operation that requires disassembly of the U-joint. But be sure that the lubricant reservoir at the end of the trunnion is full of lubricant. Fill the reservoirs with lubricant from the bottom.

20. Install the trunnion into the driveshaft yoke and press the bearings into the yoke over the trunnion hubs as far as it will go.

21. Install the lockrings.

22. Hold the trunnion in one hand and tap the yoke slightly to seat the bearings against the lockrings.

23. On the rear driveshafts, install the sleeve yoke over the trunnion hubs and install the bearings in the same manner as above.

MOLDED RETAINER TYPE

1. Remove the driveshaft.

2. Support the driveshaft in a horizontal position. Place the U-joint so that the lower ear of the shaft yoke is supported by a 1⅛ in. socket. Press the lower bearing cup out of the yoke ear. This will shear the plastic retaining the lower bearing cup.

NOTE: Never clamp the driveshaft tubing in a vise.

3. If the bearing cup is not completely removed, lift the cross, insert a spacer and press the cup completely out.

4. Rotate the driveshaft, shear the opposite plastic retainer, and press the other bearing cup out in the same manner.

5. Remove the cross from the yoke. Production U-joints cannot be reassembled. There are no bearing retainer grooves in the cups. Discard all parts that we removed and substitute those in the overhaul kit.

6. Remove the sheared plastic bearing retainer. Drive a small

pin or punch through the injection holes to aid in removal.

7. If the front U-joint is serviced, remove the bearing cups from the slip yoke in the manner previously described.

8. Be sure that the seals are installed on the service bearing cups to hold the needle bearings in place for handling. Grease the bearings if they aren't pregreased.

9. Install one bearing cup partway into one side of the yoke and turn this ear to the bottom.

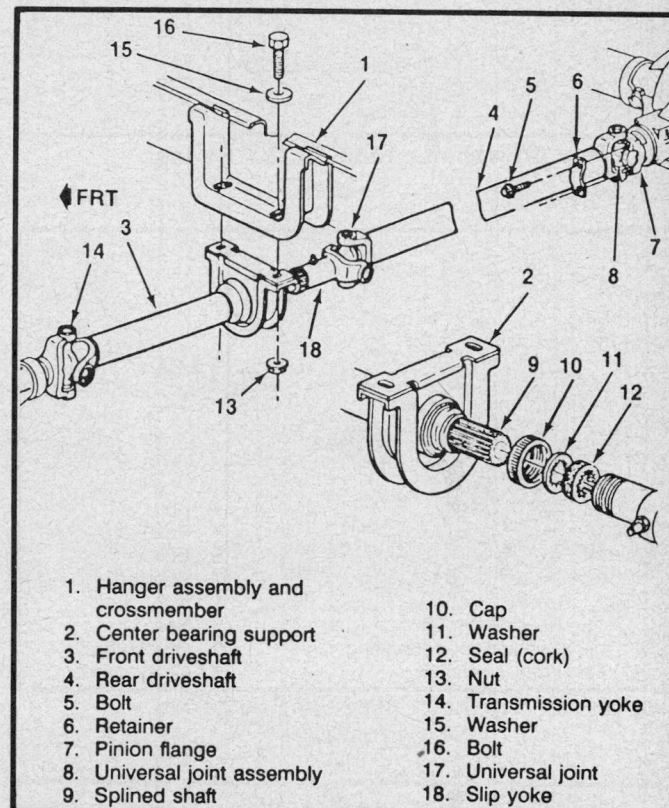

1. Hanger assembly and crossmember
2. Center bearing support
3. Front driveshaft
4. Rear driveshaft
5. Bolt
6. Retainer
7. Pinion flange
8. Universal joint assembly
9. Splined shaft
10. Cap
11. Washer
12. Seal (cork)
13. Nut
14. Transmission yoke
15. Washer
16. Bolt
17. Universal joint
18. Slip yoke

Center bearing and driveshaft—except 1988–90 C/K Series

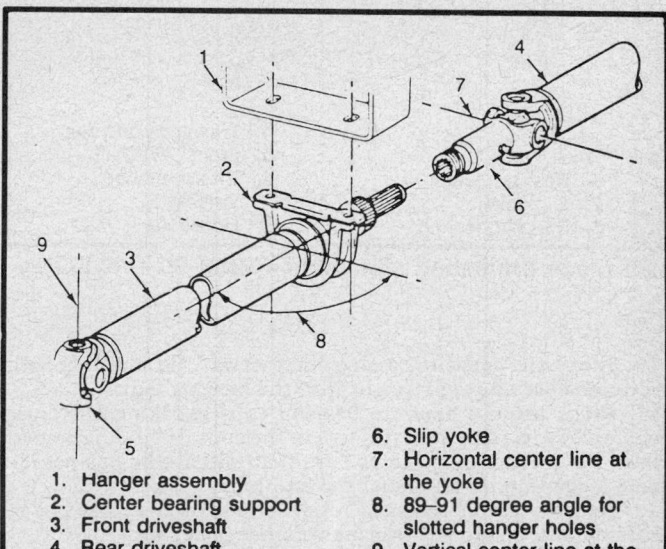

1. Hanger assembly
2. Center bearing support
3. Front driveshaft
4. Rear driveshaft
5. Transmission yoke
6. Slip yoke
7. Horizontal center line at the yoke
8. 89–91 degree angle for slotted hanger holes
9. Vertical center line at the yoke

Multiple driveshaft alignment—except 1988–90 C/K Series

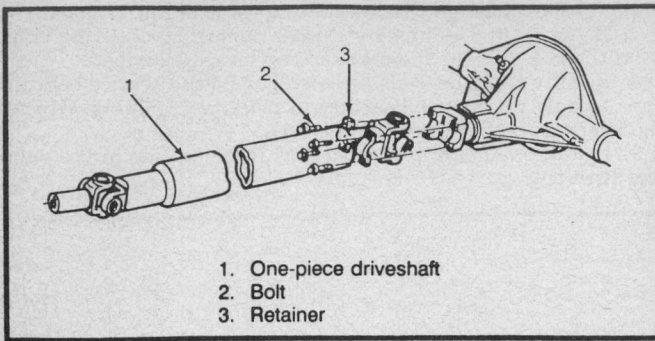

1. One-piece driveshaft
2. Bolt
3. Retainer

One piece driveshaft — 1988–90 C/K Series

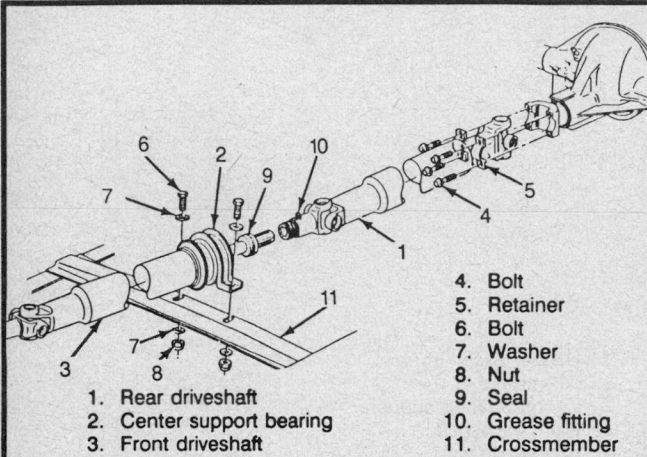

6. Bolt	4. Bolt
2. (Center support bearing)	5. Retainer
1. Rear driveshaft	6. Bolt
2. Center support bearing	7. Washer
3. Front driveshaft	8. Nut
	9. Seal
	10. Grease fitting
	11. Crossmember

Two piece driveshaft — 1988–90 C/K Series

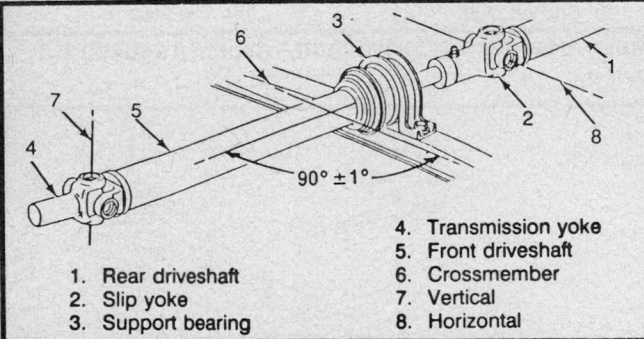

90° ± 1°

1. Rear driveshaft
2. Slip yoke
3. Support bearing
4. Transmission yoke
5. Front driveshaft
6. Crossmember
7. Vertical
8. Horizontal

Two piece driveshaft alignment — 1988–90 C/K Series

10. Insert the opposite bearing cup partway. Be sure that both trunnions are started straight into the bearing cups.

11. Press against opposite bearing cups, working the cross constantly to be sure that it is free in the cups. If binding occurs, check the needle rollers to be sure that one needle has not become lodged under an end of the trunnion.

12. As soon as one bearing retainer groove is exposed, stop pressing and install the bearing retainer snapring.

13. Continue to press until the opposite bearing retainer can be installed. If difficulty installing the snaprings is encountered, rap the yoke with a hammer to spring the yoke ears slightly.

14. Assemble the other half of the U-joint in the same manner.

Axle Shaft

Removal and Installation

CHEVROLET 8½ AND 9½ INCH WITHOUT EATON LOCKING DIFFERENTIAL

1. Raise and support the vehicle safely. Remove the tire and wheel assembly. Remove the brake drums.

2. Remove the carrier cover retaining bolts. Remove the carrier cover.

3. Remove the rear axle pinion shaft lock screw and the rear axle pinion shaft. Discard the lock screw.

4. Push the flanged end of the axle shaft toward the center of the vehicle. Remove the C lock clip from the button end of the shaft.

5. Remove the axle shaft from the housing. Be careful not to damage the oil seal.

6. When removing the axle shaft on vehicles equipped with the 9½ inch ring gear, be sure that the thrust washer in the differential case does not slide out.

7. Installation is the reverse of the removal procedure. Be sure to use a new carrier gasket or RTV, as required. Fill the axle housing to within ⅜ in. of the filler hole.

CHEVROLET 8½ AND 9½ INCH WITH EATON LOCKING DIFFERENTIAL

1. Raise and support the vehicle safely. Remove the tire and wheel assembly. Remove the brake drums.

2. Remove the carrier cover retaining bolts. Remove the carrier cover.

3. Rotate the case so that the thrust block and the pinion shaft are upward. Support the pinion shaft so that it cannot fall into the case. Remove the lock screw.

4. Carefully withdraw the pinion shaft part way out of its mounting. Rotate the case until the case just touches the housing.

5. Using a suitable tool, reach into the case and rotate the C lock until its open points directly inward. The axle shaft cannot be pushed inward until the C lock is properly positioned.

6. When the C lock is positioned to pass through the end of the thrust block, push the axle shaft inward. Remove the C lock.

7. Remove the axle shaft from the vehicle.

8. Installation is the reverse of the removal procedure. Be sure to use a new carrier gasket or RTV, as required. Fill the axle housing to within ⅜ in. of the filler hole.

CHEVROLET 10½ AND DANA 9¾ AND 10½ INCH

1. Raise and support the vehicle safely. Remove the tire and wheel assembly.

2. Remove the bolts that retain the axle shaft flange to the wheel hub.

3. Tap the flange with a suitable hammer and loosen the axle shaft.

4. Twist the shaft assembly and remove it from the axle tube.

5. Installation is the reverse of the removal procedure.

6. Place a new gasket or apply RTV sealant over the axle shaft. Position the shaft in the housing so that the shaft splines enter the differential side gear.

Axle Shaft Seal

Removal and Installation

CHEVROLET 8½ AND 9½ INCH

1. Raise and support the vehicle safely. Remove the tire and wheel assembly. Remove the brake drum.

2. Remove the carrier cover retaining bolts. Remove the carrier cover.

3. Remove the rear axle pinion shaft lock screw and the rear axle pinion shaft. Discard the lock screw.

4. Push the flanged end of the axle shaft toward the center of

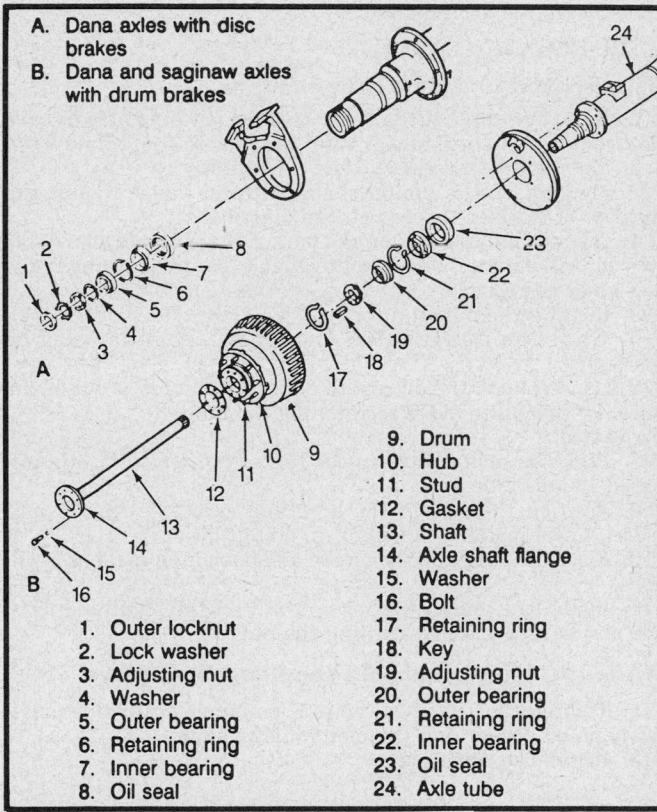

1. Drum
2. Bolt
3. Shaft
4. Lock
5. Seal
6. Bearing
7. Housing
8. Clip
9. Bolt
10. Carrier cover
11. Backing plate
12. Bolt

Axle shaft and housing components

A. Dana axles with disc brakes
B. Dana and saginaw axles with drum brakes

1. Outer locknut
2. Lock washer
3. Adjusting nut
4. Washer
5. Outer bearing
6. Retaining ring
7. Inner bearing
8. Oil seal
9. Drum
10. Hub
11. Stud
12. Gasket
13. Shaft
14. Axle shaft flange
15. Washer
16. Bolt
17. Retaining ring
18. Key
19. Adjusting nut
20. Outer bearing
21. Retaining ring
22. Inner bearing
23. Oil seal
24. Axle tube

Full floating axle and components

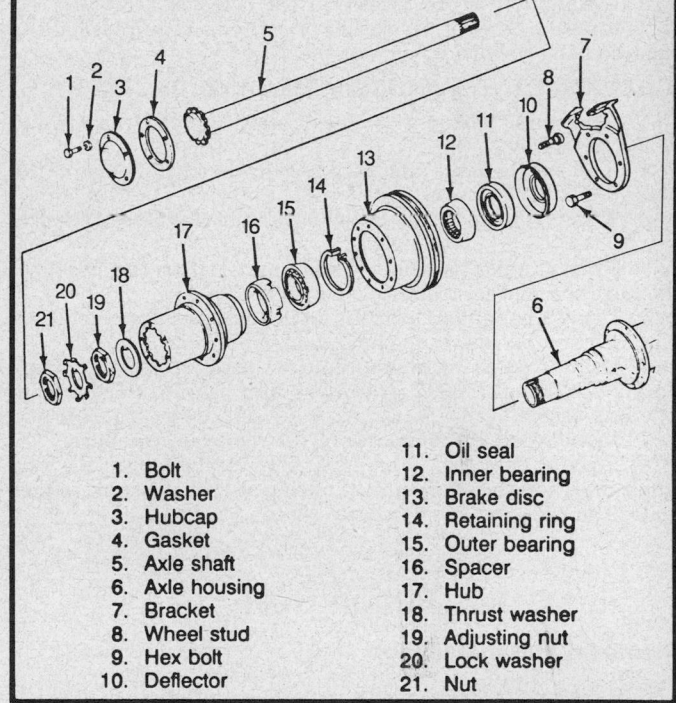

1. Bolt
2. Washer
3. Hubcap
4. Gasket
5. Axle shaft
6. Axle housing
7. Bracket
8. Wheel stud
9. Hex bolt
10. Deflector
11. Oil seal
12. Inner bearing
13. Brake disc
14. Retaining ring
15. Outer bearing
16. Spacer
17. Hub
18. Thrust washer
19. Adjusting nut
20. Lock washer
21. Nut

Rockwell 12 inch ring gear axle and hub components

the vehicle. Remove the C lock clip from the button end of the shaft.

5. Remove the axle shaft from the housing.

6. When removing the axle shaft on vehicles equipped with the 9½ inch ring gear, be sure that the thrust washer in the differential case does not slide out.

7. Using the proper removal tool, remove the seal from its mounting.

8. Installation is the reverse of the removal procedure. Be sure to use a new carrier gasket or RTV, as required. Fill the axle housing to within ⅜ in. of the filler hole.

CHEVROLET 10½ AND DANA 9¾ AND 10½ INCH

1. Raise and support the vehicle safely. Remove the tire and wheel assembly.

2. Remove the bolts that retain the axle shaft flange to the wheel hub.

3. Tap the flange with a suitable hammer and loosen the axle shaft.

4. Twist the shaft assembly and remove it from the axle tube. Remove the oil seal from its mounting.

5. Installation is the reverse of the removal procedure.

6. Place a new gasket or apply RTV sealant over the axle shaft. Position the shaft in the housing so that the shaft splines enter the differential side gear.

Axle Shaft Bearings

Removal and Installation

CHEVROLET 8½ AND 9½ INCH

1. Raise and support the vehicle safely. Remove the tire and wheel assembly. Remove the brake drum.

2. Remove the carrier cover retaining bolts. Remove the carrier cover.

3. Remove the rear axle pinion shaft lock screw and the rear axle pinion shaft. Discard the lock screw.

4. Push the flanged end of the axle shaft toward the center of the vehicle. Remove the C-lock clip from the button end of the shaft.

5. Remove the axle shaft from the housing.

6. When removing the axle shaft on vehicles equipped with the 9½ inch ring gear, be sure that the thrust washer in the differential case does not slide out.

7. Using the proper removal tool, remove the seal from its mounting.

8. Insert tool J-23689 into the bore so that the tool grasps behind the bearing. Slide the washer against the outside of the seal. Turn the nut finger tight. Using a slide hammer remove the bearing and seal.

9. On vehicles equipped with the 9½ inch ring gear, use tool J-29712. Insert the tool into the axle tube so that it grasps behind the bearing. Center the receiver on the axle tube and tighten the nut. Back off the nut and remove the bearing and seal from the tool.

10. Installation is the reverse of the removal procedure. Be sure to use a new carrier gasket or RTV, as required. Fill the axle housing to within ⅜ in. of the filler hole.

CHEVROLET 10½ AND DANA 9¾ AND 10½ INCH

1. Raise and support the vehicle safely. Remove the tire and wheel assembly.

2. Remove the bolts that retain the axle shaft flange to the wheel hub.

3. Tap the flange with a suitable hammer and loosen the axle shaft.

4. Twist the shaft assembly and remove it from the axle tube. Remove the oil seal from its mounting.

5. Using a hammer and a long drift pin, knock the inner bearing, cup and oil seal from the hub assembly.

6. Using a snapring pliers, remove the outer bearing. Using tool J-24426 and J-8092, drive the outter bearing and cup from the hub assembly.

7. Installation is the reverse of the removal procedure.

8. Place a new gasket or apply RTV sealant over the axle shaft. Position the shaft in the housing so that the shaft splines enter the differential side gear.

Pinion Seal

Removal and Installation

SEMI-FLOATING AXLES

1. Raise and support the vehicle safely. It would help to have the front end slightly higher than the rear to avoid fluid loss.

2. Matchmark and remove the driveshaft.

3. Release the parking brake.

4. Remove the rear wheels. Rotate the rear wheels by hand to make sure that there is absolutely no brake drag. If there is brake drag, remove the drums.

5. Using a torque wrench on the pinion nut, record the force needed to rotate the pinion.

6. Matchmark the pinion shaft, nut and flange. Count the number of exposed threads on the pinion shaft.

7. Install a holding tool on the pinion. A very large adjustable wrench will do, or, if one is not available, put the drums back on and set the parking brake as tightly as possible.

8. Remove the pinion nut.

9. Slide the flange off of the pinion. A puller may be necessary.

10. Centerpunch the oil seal to distort it and pry it out of the bore. Be careful to avoid scrratching the bore.

To install:

11. Pack the cavity between the lips of the seal with lithium-based chassis lube.

12. Position the seal in the bore and carefully drive it into place.

13. Pack the cavity between the end of the pinion splines and the pinion flange with Permatex No.2® sealer, or equivalent non-hardening sealer.

14. Place the flange on the pinion and push it on as far as it will go.

15. Install the pinion washer and nut on the shaft and force the pinion into place by turning the nut.

NOTE: Never hammer the flange into place.

16. Tighten the nut until the exact number of threads previously noted appear and the matchmarks align.

17. Measure the rotating torque of the pinion under the same circumstances as before. Compare the two readings. As necessary, tighten the pinion nut in very small increments until the torque necessary to rotate the pinion is 3 inch lbs. higher than the originally recorded torque.

18. Install the driveshaft.

FULL FLOATING AXLE

With 9¾ and 10½ Inch Ring Gear

1. Raise and support the vehicle safely. It would help to have the front end slightly higher than the rear to avoid fluid loss.

2. Matchmark and remove the driveshaft.

3. Matchmark the pinion shaft, nut and flange. Count the number of exposed threads on the pinion shaft.

4. Install a holding tool on the pinion. A very large adjustable wrench will do, or, if one is not available, set the parking brake as tightly as possible.

5. Remove the pinion nut.

6. Slide the flange off of the pinion. A puller may be necessary.

7. Centerpunch the oil seal to distort it and pry it out of the bore. Be careful to avoid scrratching the bore.

To install:

8. Pack the cavity between the lips of the seal with lithium-based chassis lube.

9. Position the seal in the bore and carefully drive it into place. A seal installer is helpful in doing this.

10. Place the flange on the pinion and push it on as far as it will go.

11. Install the pinion washer and nut on the shaft and force the pinion into place by turning the nut.

WARNING: Never hammer the flange into place!

12. Tighten the nut until the exact number of threads previously noted appear and the matchmarks align.

13. Install the driveshaft.

Differential Carrier

Removal and Installation

DANA 9¾ AND 10½ INCH

1. Raise and support the vehicle safely. Allow the rear axle assembly to hang freely. Remove the tire and wheel assemblies. Drain the lubricant.

2. Remove the axle shaft to hub retaining nuts. Rap the axle shaft to loosen it from the hub. Remove the shafts.

3. Remove the cap screws and lock washers retaining the cover to the carrier. Remove the carrier cover and gasket.

4. Mark one side of the carrier and matching cap for reassembly in the same position. Remove the bearing caps.

5. Using a spreader tool and a dial indicator gauge, spread the carrier assembly to a maximum of .015 in.

6. Remove the dial indicator tool. Use a prybar and remove the differential case from the carrier.

7. Record the dimension and location of the side bearing shims. Remove the spreader tool.

8. Installation is the reverse of the removal procedure.

Axle Housing Assembly

Removal and Installation

ALL SERIES

1. Raise and support the vehicle safely.

2. For the 9¾ in. ring gear and the 10½ in. ring gear axles, place jackstands under the frame side rails for support.

3. Drain the lubricant from the axle housing and remove the driveshaft.

4. Remove the wheel, the brake drum or hub and the drum assembly.

5. Disconnect the parking brake cable from the lever and at the brake flange plate.

6. Disconnect the hydraulic brake lines from the connectors.

7. Disconnect the shock absorbers from the axle brackets.

8. Remove the vent hose from the axle vent fitting (if used).

9. Disconnect the height sensing and brake proportional valve linkage (if used).

10. Support the stabilizer shaft assembly with a hydraulic jack and remove (if used).

11. Remove the nuts and washers from the U-bolts.

12. Remove the U-bolts, spring plates and spacers from the axle assembly.

13. Lower the jack and remove the axle assembly.

To install:

14. Raise the axle assembly into position.

15. Install the U-bolts, spring plates and spacers.

16. Install the nuts and washers on the U-bolts. Torque the nuts to 130 ft. lbs. for 30/3500 series; 120 series for all other models.

17. Install the stabilizer shaft.

18. Connect the height sensing and brake proportional valve linkage.

19. Install the vent hose at the axle vent fitting.

20. Connect the shock absorbers at the axle brackets. Torque the nuts to 80 ft. lbs.

21. Connect the hydraulic brake lines.

22. Connect the parking brake cable.

23. Install the wheels.

24. Install the driveshaft.

25. Fill the axle housing.

STEERING

Steering Wheel

Removal and Installation

1. Disconnect the battery ground cable.

2. Remove the horn button cap. On some models, it may be necessary to disconnect the horn wire.

3. Mark the steering wheel-to-steering shaft relationship.

4. Remove the snapring from the steering shaft.

5. Remove the nut and washer from the steering shaft.

6. Remove the steering wheel with a puller.

7. Installation is the reverse of removal. The turn signal control assembly must be in the Neutral position to prevent damaging the canceling cam and control assembly. Torque the nut to 30 ft. lbs.

Manual Steering Gear

Removal and Installation

1986 C/K SERIES, 1987–90 R/V SERIES AND VAN

1. Set the front wheels in straight ahead position by driving vehicle a short distance on a flat surface.

2. Raise and support the vehicle safely, as required.

4. Matchmark the relationship of the universal yoke to the wormshaft.

5. Remove the universal yoke pinch bolt.

6. Mark the relationship of the pitman arm to the pitman shaft.

7. Remove the pitman shaft nut and then remove the pitman arm from the pitman shaft, using puller J–6632.

8. Remove the steering gear to frame bolts and remove the gear assembly.

To install:

7. Place the steering gear in position, guiding the steering gear shaft into the universal yoke.

8. Install the steering gear to frame bolts and torque to 75 ft. lbs.

9. Install the yoke pinch bolt. Torque the pinch bolt to 45 ft. lbs.

10. Install the pitman arm onto the pitman shaft, lining up the marks made at removal. Install the pitman shaft nut torque to 185 ft. lbs.

1988–90 C/K SERIES

1. Set the front wheels in straight ahead position by driving vehicle a short distance on a flat surface. Raise and support the vehicle safely.

2. Remove the shield.

3. Remove the adapter nut and washer and remove the adapter.

4. Mark the relationship of the pitman arm to the pitman shaft.

5. Remove the pitman shaft nut and washer then remove the pitman arm from the pitman shaft, using a puller.

6. Remove the steering gear to frame bolts.

7. Disconnect the the flexible coupling from the steering shaft and remove the gear assembly.

To install:

8. Align the flat of the flexible coupling with the flat on the shaft. Push the coupling onto the shaft until the wormshaft bottoms on the coupling reinforcement.

9. Install the steering gear to the frame and tighten the bolts to 100 ft. lbs.

10. Install the pinch bolt. Make sure the bolt passes through the shaft undercut. Tighten the pinch bolt to 22 ft. lbs.

11. Install the adapter to the steering box, install the washer and nut and tighten to 5.3 inch lbs.

12. Install the shield to the adapter.

13. Install the pitman arm onto the pitman shaft, lining up the marks made at removal. Install the pitman shaft nut and torque to 185 ft. lbs.

Adjustment

Before any steering gear adjustments are made, it is recom-

5 GENERAL MOTORS CORPORATION
C/K SERIES (PICK-UP) • R/V SERIES (PICK-UP) • BLAZER/JIMMY • SUBURBAN • G SERIES (VAN)

SECTION

mended that the front end of the vehicle be raised and supported safely and a thorough inspection be made for stiffness or lost motion in the steering gear, steering linkage and front suspension. Worn or damaged parts should be replaced, since a satisfactory adjustment of the steering gear cannot be obtained if bent or badly worn parts exist.

It is also very important that the steering gear be properly aligned in the vehicle. Misalignment of the gear places a stress on the steering worm shaft, therefore a proper adjustment is impossible. To align the steering gear, loosen the steering gear-to-frame mounting bolts to permit the gear to align itself. Check the steering gear to frame mounting seat. If there is a gap at any of the mounting bolts, proper alignment may be obtained by placing shims where excessive gap appears. Tighten the steering gear-to-frame bolts. Alignment of the gear in the van is very important and should be done carefully so that a satisfactory, trouble-free gear adjustment may be obtained.

The steering gear is of the recirculating ball nut type. The ball nut, mounted on the worm gear, is driven by means of steel balls which circulate in helical grooves in both the worm and nut. Ball return guides attached to the nut serve to recirculate the two sets of balls in the grooves. As the steering wheel is turned to the right, the ball nut moves upward. When the wheel is turned to the left, the ball nut moves downward.

Before doing the adjustment procedures given below, ensure that the steering problem is not caused by faulty suspension components, bad front end alignment, etc. Then, proceed with the following adjustments.

Bearing Drag

1. Disconnect the pitman arm from the gear.
2. Disconnect the battery ground cable.
3. Remove the horn cap.
4. Turn the steering wheel gently to the left stop, then back ½ turn.
5. Position an inch-pound torque wrench on the steering wheel nut and rotate it through a 90 degree arc. Note the torque. Proper torque is 5–8 inch lbs.
6. If the torque is incorrect, loosen the adjuster plug locknut and back off the plug ¼ turn, then tighten the plug to give the proper torque.
7. Hold the plug and tighten the adjuster plug locknut to 85 ft. lbs.

Overcenter Preload

1. Turn the steering wheel lock-to-lock counting the total number of turns. Turn the wheel back ½ the total number of turns to center it.
2. Turn the lash (sector shaft) adjuster screw clockwise to remove all lash between the ball nut and sector teeth. Tighten the locknut to 22 ft. lbs.
3. Using a torque wrench on the steering wheel nut, observe the highest reading while the gear is turned through the center position. It should be 16 inch lbs. or less.
4. If necessary repeat adjust the preload with the adjuster screw. Tighten the locknut to 22 ft. lbs.

Power Steering Gear

Removal and Installation

1986 C/K SERIES AND 1987–90 R/V SERIES

1. Set the front wheels in straight ahead position by driving vehicle a short distance on a flat surface. Raise and support the vehicle safely as required.
2. Place a drain pan below the steering gear.
3. Disconnect the negative battery cable.
4. Disconnect the fluid lines. Cap the openings.
5. Remove the flexible coupling to the steering shaft flange bolts.

6. Mark the relationship of the pitman arm to the pitman shaft.
7. Remove the pitman shaft nut and then remove the pitman arm from the pitman shaft, using puller J–6632.
8. Remove the steering gear to frame bolts and remove the gear assembly.
9. Align the flat of the flexible coupling with the flat on the shaft. Push the coupling onto the shaft until the wormshaft bottoms against the end of the shaft.
10. Install the pinch bolt. Make sure the bolt passes through the shaft undercut. Tighten the pinch bolt to 31 ft. lbs.
11. Place the steering gear into position, guiding the coupling bolts into the proper holes in the shaft flange.
12. Install the Install the steering gear to frame bolts and torque to 75 ft. lbs.
13. Install the coupling flange nuts and washers. Make sure the coupling alignment pins are centered in the flange slots. Tighten the nuts to 20 ft. lbs. Maintain a coupling to flange dimension of 0.250–0.375 inches.
14. Install the pitman arm.
15. Install the hoses.

1988–90 C/K SERIES

1. Set the front wheels in straight ahead position by driving vehicle a short distance on a flat surface. Raise and support the vehicle safely, as required.
2. Place a drain pan below the steering gear.
3. Disconnect the negative battery cable.
4. Disconnect the fluid lines. Cap the openings.
5. Remove the shield draw alignment marks on the clamp and the steering shaft and remove the lower clamp bolt. Remove the clamp from the shaft.
6. Remove the pitman shaft nut and then remove the pitman arm from the pitman shaft, using puller J–6632.
7. Remove the steering gear to frame bolts and remove the gear assembly.
To install:
8. Install the steering gear to the frame using the bolts and washers and tighten to 69 ft. lbs.
9. Install the pitman arm.
10. Make sure the alignment marks line up and install the clamp and tighten the bolt to 30 ft. lbs.
11. Install the hoses and tighten the hose coupling to 45 ft. lbs. Bleed the system.

VAN

1. Set the front wheels in straight ahead position by driving vehicle a short distance on a flat surface. Raise and support the vehicle safely, as required.
2. Place a drain pan below the steering gear.
3. Disconnect the negative battery cable.
4. Disconnect the fluid lines. Cap the openings.
5. Matchmark the relationship of the universal yoke to the stubmshaft.
6. Remove the universal yoke pinch bolt.
5. Mark the relationship of the pitman arm to the pitman shaft.
6. Remove the pitman shaft nut and then remove the pitman arm from the pitman shaft, using puller J–6632.
7. Remove the steering gear to frame bolts and remove the gear assembly.
To install:
8. Place the steering gear in position, guiding the steering gear shaft into the universal yoke.
9. Install the steering gear to frame bolts and torque to 75 ft. lbs.
10. Install the yoke pinch bolt. Torque the pinch bolt to 45 ft. lbs.
11. Install the pitman arm onto the pitman shaft, lining up the marks made at removal. Install the pitman shaft nut torque to 185 ft. lbs.

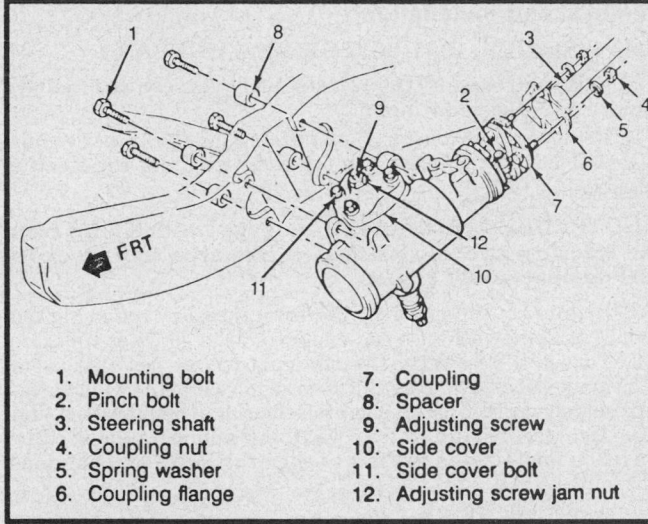

1. Mounting bolt
2. Spring washer
3. Pinch bolt
4. Steering shaft
5. Coupling nut
6. Spring washer
7. Coupling flange
8. Coupling
9. Adjusting screw
10. Side cover
11. Side cover bolt
12. Adjusting screw jam nut

Power steering gear installation—1986 C Series and 1987–90 R Series

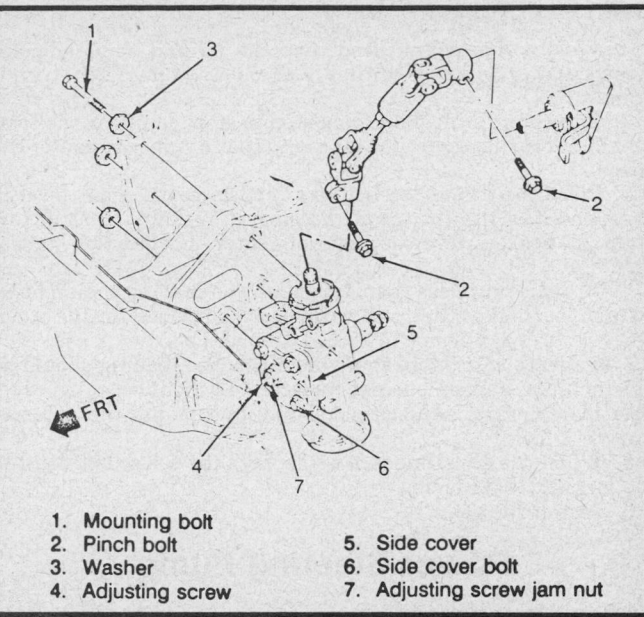

1. Mounting bolt
2. Pinch bolt
3. Washer
4. Adjusting screw
5. Side cover
6. Side cover bolt
7. Adjusting screw jam nut

Power steering gear installation—1986–90 Van

1. Mounting bolt
2. Pinch bolt
3. Steering shaft
4. Coupling nut
5. Spring washer
6. Coupling flange
7. Coupling
8. Spacer
9. Adjusting screw
10. Side cover
11. Side cover bolt
12. Adjusting screw jam nut

Power steering gear installation—1986 K Series and 1987–90 V Series

12. Connect the fluid lines and refill the reservoir. Bleed the system.

Adjustments

For proper adjustment, remove the gear from the vehicle and drain all the fluid from the gear and place the gear in a vise.

It is important that the adjustments be made in the order given.

Worm Bearing Preload

1. Remove the adjuster plug locknut.
2. Turn the adjuster plug in clockwise until firmly bottomed. Then, tighten it to 20 ft. lbs.
3. Place an index mark on the gear housing in line with one of the holes in the adjuster plug.
4. Measure counterclockwise from the mark about ¼ inch and make another mark on the housing.
5. Rotate the adjuster plug counterclockwise until the hole is aligned with the second mark.
6. Install the locknut. Hold the plug and tighten the locknut to 81 ft. lbs.
7. Place an inch pound torque wrench and 12-point deep socket on the stub shaft and measure the stub shaft rotating

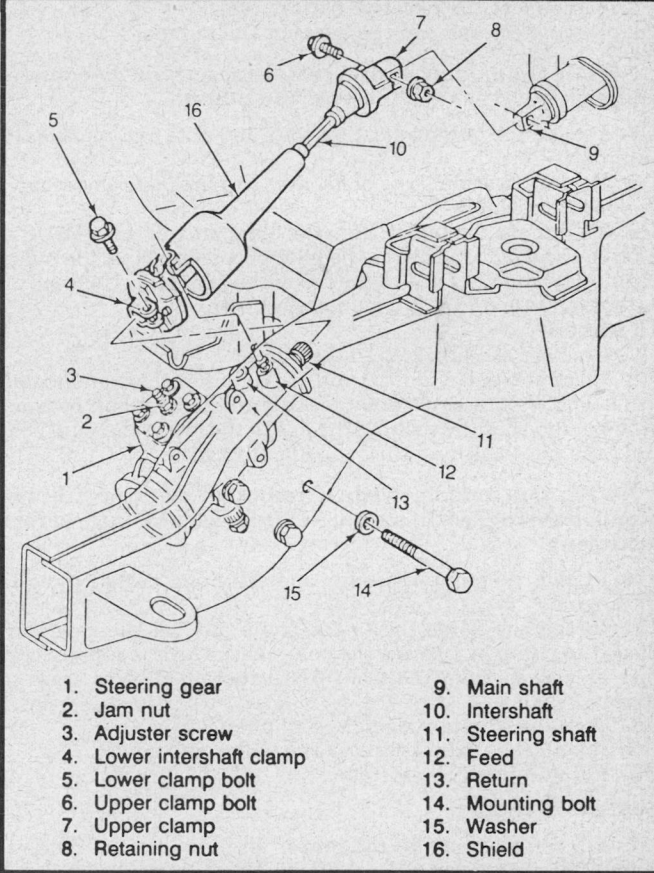

1. Steering gear
2. Jam nut
3. Adjuster screw
4. Lower intershaft clamp
5. Lower clamp bolt
6. Upper clamp bolt
7. Upper clamp
8. Retaining nut
9. Main shaft
10. Intershaft
11. Steering shaft
12. Feed
13. Return
14. Mounting bolt
15. Washer
16. Shield

Power steering gear installation—1988–90 C/K Series

torque, starting with the torque wrench handle in a vertical position to a point ¼ turn to either side. Note your reading. The proper torque should be 4–10 inch lbs. If the reading is incorrect, wither your adjustment was done incorrectly or there is gear damage.

Overcenter Preload

1. Loosen the locknut and turn the pitman shaft adjuster screw counterclockwise until it is all the way out. Then, turn it in ½ turn.

2. Rotate the stub shaft from stop to stop, counting the total number of turns, then turn it back ½ that number to center the gear.

3. Place the torque wrench in a vertical position on the stub shaft and measure the torque necessary to rotate the shaft to a point 45 degrees to either side of center. Record the highest reading.

On gears with less than 400 miles, the reading should be 6–10 inch lbs. higher than the worm bearing preload torque previously recorded, but not to exceed 18 inch lbs..

On gears with more than 400 miles, the reading should be 4–5 inch lbs. higher, but not to exceed 14 inch lbs.

4. If necessary, adjust the reading by turning the adjuster screw.

5. When the adjustment is made, hold the screw and tighten the locknut to 32 ft. lbs.

6. Install the gear.

Power Steering Pump

Removal and Installation

1. Place a drain pan under the pump.
2. Disconnect the negative battery cable.
3. Disconnect and cap the hoses at the pump.

NOTE: On models with a remote reservoir disconnect and cap the reservoir hose at the pump.

4. Loosen the pump adjusting bolts and nuts and remove the pump belt.

5. Remove the adjusting bolts, nuts and brackets and remove the pump assembly.

6. To remove the pulley from the pump install tool J–29785–A or equivalent. Make sure the pilot bolt bottoms in the pump shaft by turning the nut to the top of the pilot bolt. Hold the pilot bolt and turn the nut counterclockwise.

To install:

7. Connect the brackets to the pump.

8. Place the pulley on the end of the pump shaft and install tool J–25033–B or equivalent. Make sure the pilot bolt bottoms in the pump shaft by turning the nut to the top of the pilot bolt. Hold the pilot bolt and turn the nut clockwise.

NOTE: On models with a remote reservoir fill the pump housing with as much fluid as possible before mounting.

9. Install the pump assembly and attaching parts loosely to the engine.

10. Install the hoses the to the pump and fill the reservoir. Bleed the pump by turning the pulley backwards (counterclockwise as viewed from the front) until the air bubbles cease to appear.

11. Tighten all retaining bolts and nuts.

12. Install the pump belt over the pulley and adjust.

13. Fill and bleed the system.

System Bleeding

1. Fill the reservoir to the proper level and let the fluid remain undisturbed for at least 2 minutes.

2. Start the engine and run it for only about 2 seconds.

3. Add fluid as necessary.

4. Repeat Steps 1–3 until the level remains constant.

5. Raise the front of the vehicle so that the front wheels are off the ground. Set the parking brake and block both rear wheels front and rear. Manual transmissions should be in neutral; automatic transmissions should be in **PARK**.

6. Start the engine and run it at approximately 1500 rpm.

7. Turn the wheels (off the ground) to the right and left, lightly contacting the stops.

8. Add fluid as necessary.

9. Lower the vehicle and turn the wheels right and left on the ground.

10. Check the level and refill as necessary.

11. If the fluid is extremely foamy, let the vehicle stand for a few minutes with the engine off and repeat the procedure. Check the belt tension and check for a bent or loose pulley. The pulley should not wobble with the engine running.

12. Check that no hoses are contacting any parts of the vehicle, particularly sheet metal.

13. Check the oil level and refill as necessary. This step and the next are very important. When willing, follow Steps 1–10 above

14. Check for air in the fluid. Aerated fluid appears milky. If air is present, repeat the above operation. If it is obvious that the pump will not respond to bleeding after several attempts, a pressure test may be required.

Tie Rod Ends

Removal and Installation

1986 C SERIES, 1987–90 R SERIES AND VAN

1. Raise and support the vehicle safely. As required, remove the tire and wheel assembly.

2. Remove the cotter pins and nuts. Using the proper removal tool, J–6627A, separate the outer tie rod from the steering knuckle.

NOTE: Do not attempt to disengage the ball joint from the steering knuckle using a wedge type tool, because seal damage could result.

3. Disconnect the inner tie rod from the relay rod using tool J–6627A. Remove the tie rod ends from the adjuster tubes.

4. To install, grease the threads and turn the new tie rod end in as many turns as were needed to remove it. This will give approximately correct toe-in. Tighten the clamp bolts to 14 ft. lbs.

5. Tighten the stud nuts to 45 ft. lbs. and install new cotter pins. You may tighten the nut to align the cotter pin, but don't loosen it.

6. Adjust the toe-in.

1986 K SERIES AND 1987–90 V SERIES

1. Raise and support the vehicle safely. As required, remove the tire and wheel assembly.

2. Remove the cotter pins and nuts from the rod assembly. Disconnect the shock absorber from the tie rod assembly.

3. Using the proper removal tool, J–6627A, separate the outer tie rod from the steering knuckle.

NOTE: Do not attempt to disengage the ball joint from the steering knuckle using a wedge type tool, because seal damage could result.

4. Disconnect the tie rod end bodies. Count the number of turns needed to remove the end bodies. Remove the tie rod ends from the adjuster tibe.

5. For reinstallation note the position of the adjuster tube and the direction from which the bolts are installed.

6. Installation is the reverse of removal. When installing the tie rod ends, turn them in until the same number of threads previously visible are achieved. Tighten the locknuts.

7. Install the tie rod assembly in the knuckles and tighten the castellated nuts to 40 ft. lbs. Always advance the nut to align the cotter pin hole. Never back it off.

8. Tighten the tie rod end locknuts to 175 ft. lbs.

9. Adjust the front alignment, as required.

1988–90 C/K SERIES

1. Raise and support the vehicle safely.

2. Remove the nut from the knuckle end ball stud. Discard the nut.

3. Using a screw-type ball joint tool, separate the tie rod ball stud from the knuckle.

4. Remove the nut from the relay rod end ball stud.

5. Using a screw-type ball joint tool, separate the tie rod ball stud from the relay rod.

6. Clean the threaded parts of the tie rod ends thoroughly and count the exact number of threads exposed on each tie rod end. Measure the overall length of the tie rod assembly.

7. Loosen the clamp nuts, spread the clamps and unscrew each tie rod end.

To install:

8. Coat the threaded parts of the new tie rod ends with chassis grease. Screw the tie rod ends into the sleeve until the exact number of threads is exposed on each tie rod end. Check the

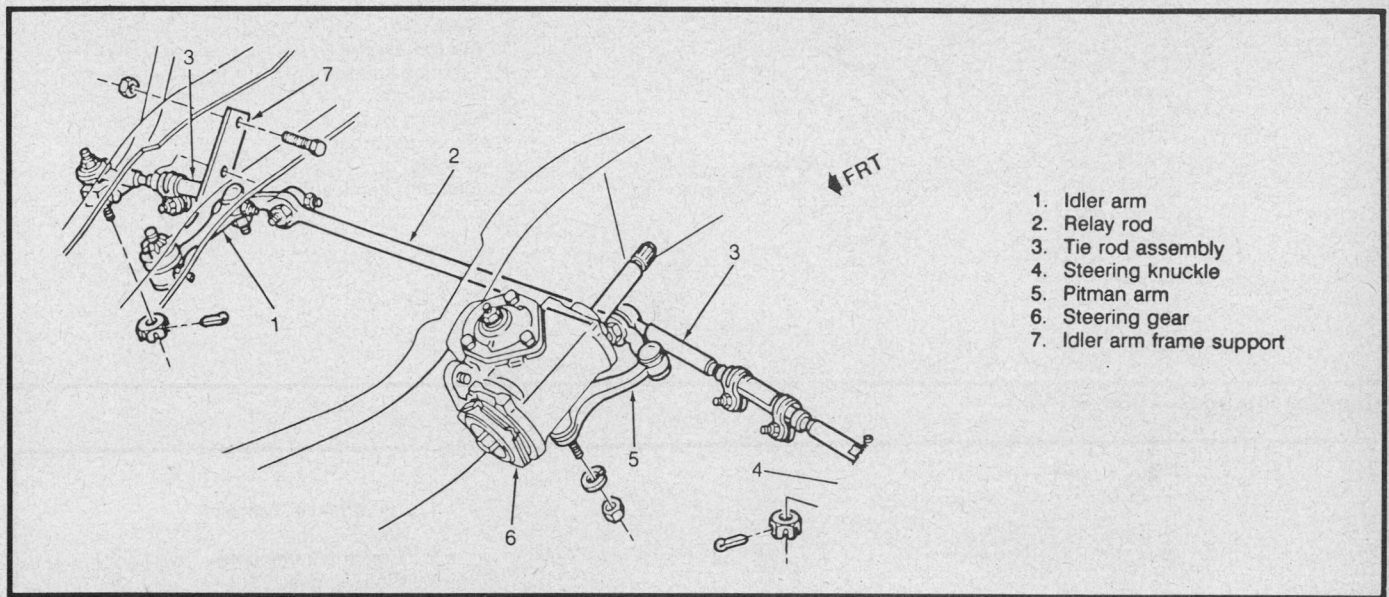

◄ FRT

1. Idler arm
2. Relay rod
3. Tie rod assembly
4. Steering knuckle
5. Pitman arm
6. Steering gear
7. Idler arm frame support

Steering linkage – 1986 C Series and 1987–90 R Series

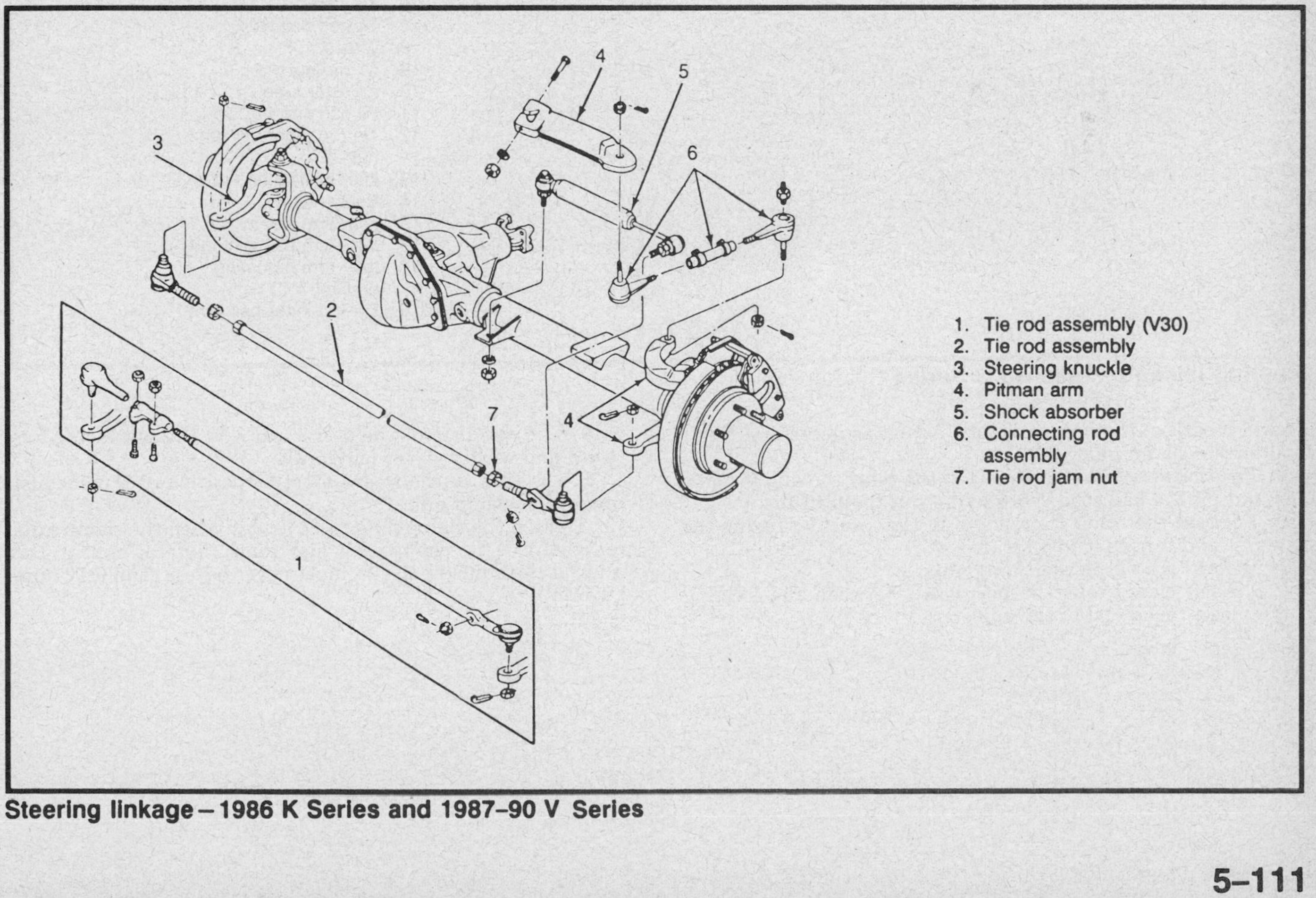

1. Tie rod assembly (V30)
2. Tie rod assembly
3. Steering knuckle
4. Pitman arm
5. Shock absorber
6. Connecting rod assembly
7. Tie rod jam nut

Steering linkage – 1986 K Series and 1987–90 V Series

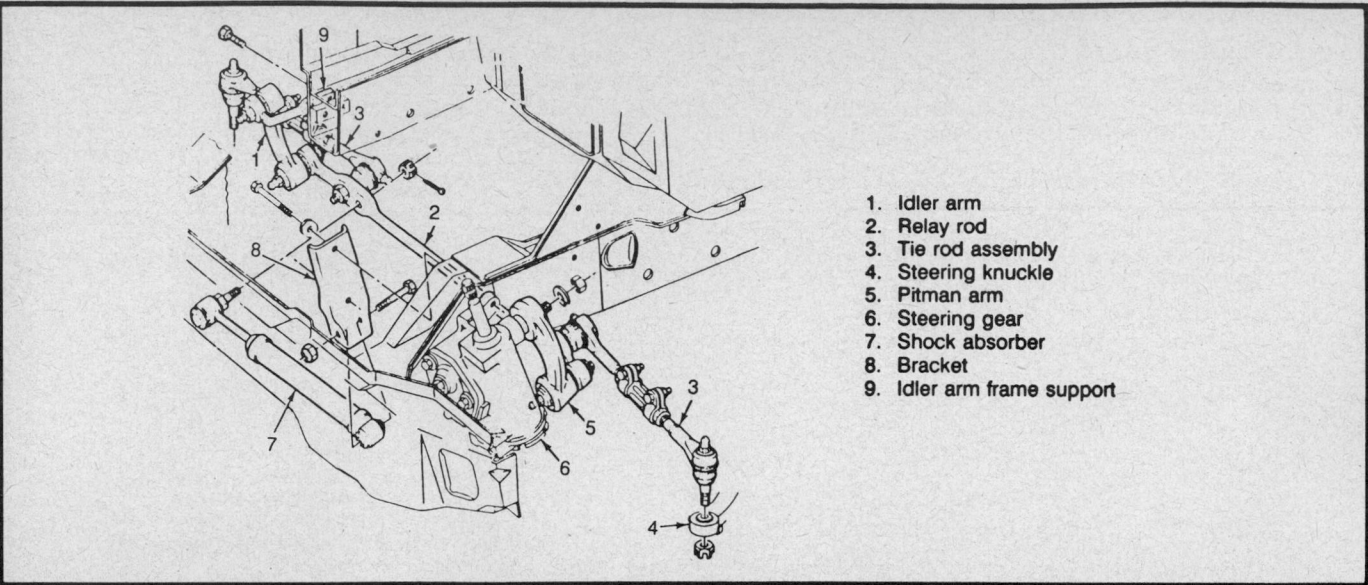

1. Idler arm
2. Relay rod
3. Tie rod assembly
4. Steering knuckle
5. Pitman arm
6. Steering gear
7. Shock absorber
8. Bracket
9. Idler arm frame support

Steering linkage – 1986–90 Van

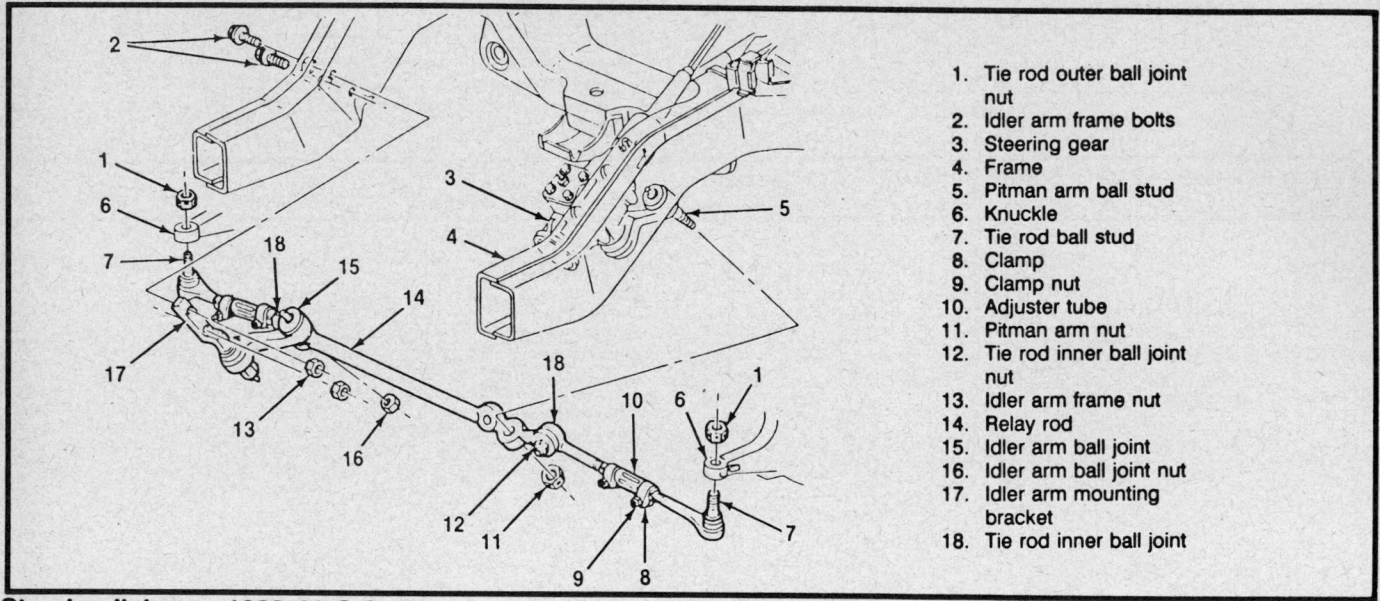

1. Tie rod outer ball joint nut
2. Idler arm frame bolts
3. Steering gear
4. Frame
5. Pitman arm ball stud
6. Knuckle
7. Tie rod ball stud
8. Clamp
9. Clamp nut
10. Adjuster tube
11. Pitman arm nut
12. Tie rod inner ball joint nut
13. Idler arm frame nut
14. Relay rod
15. Idler arm ball joint
16. Idler arm ball joint nut
17. Idler arm mounting bracket
18. Tie rod inner ball joint

Steering linkage – 1988–90 C Series

overall length of the new assembly. Adjust as necessary. Don't tighten the clamp nuts yet.

9. Position the tie rod assembly in the relay rod and install a new nut on the ball stud. Torque the nut to 40 ft. lbs.

10. Position the other tie rod end in the knuckle. Install the new nut and torque it to 40 ft. lbs.

11. Before tightening the clamp nuts:

a. Each clamp must be positioned between the locating dimples at each end of the adjuster.

b. The clamps must be positioned with the nut facing forward and within 45° of horizontal.

c. The split in the sleeve must be position at a point just above the clamp nut.

12. Tighten the clamp nuts to 14 ft. lbs. When the clamp nuts are tightened, the clamp ends may touch, but the split in the clamp, at the adjuster sleeve, must never be less than 0.127mm (0.005 in.).

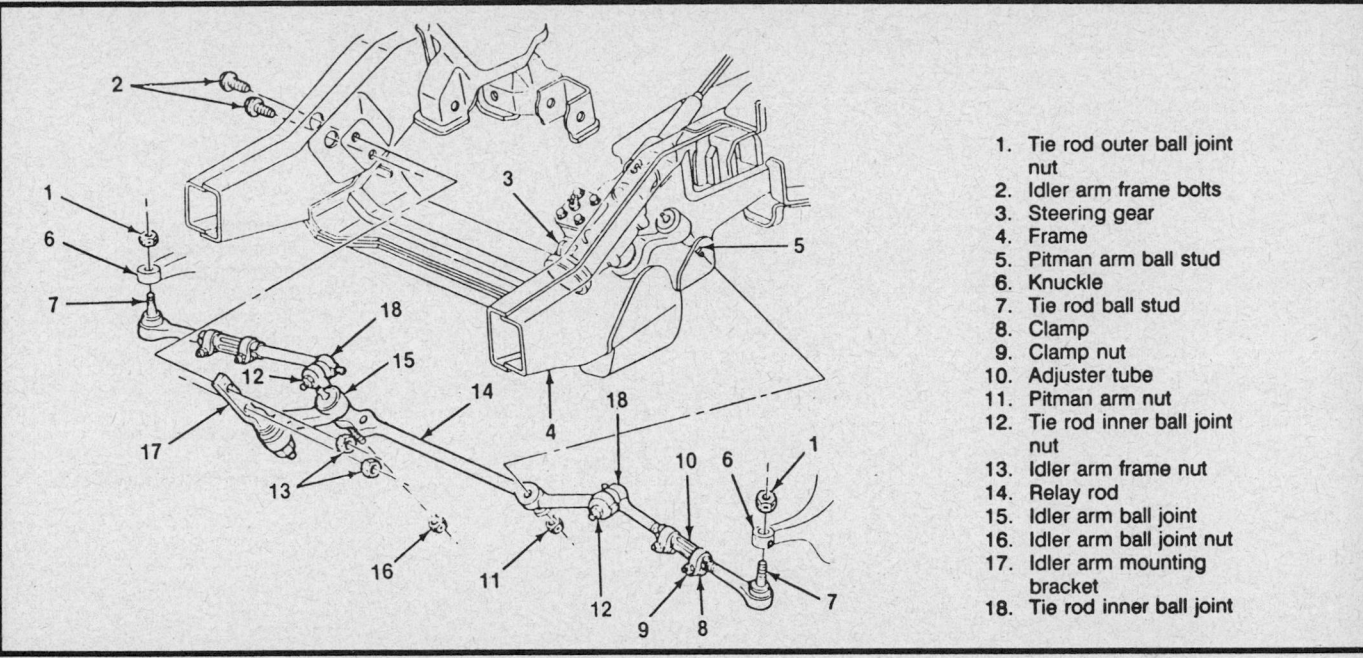

1. Tie rod outer ball joint nut
2. Idler arm frame bolts
3. Steering gear
4. Frame
5. Pitman arm ball stud
6. Knuckle
7. Tie rod ball stud
8. Clamp
9. Clamp nut
10. Adjuster tube
11. Pitman arm nut
12. Tie rod inner ball joint nut
13. Idler arm frame nut
14. Relay rod
15. Idler arm ball joint
16. Idler arm ball joint nut
17. Idler arm mounting bracket
18. Tie rod inner ball joint

Steering linkage – 1988–90 K Series

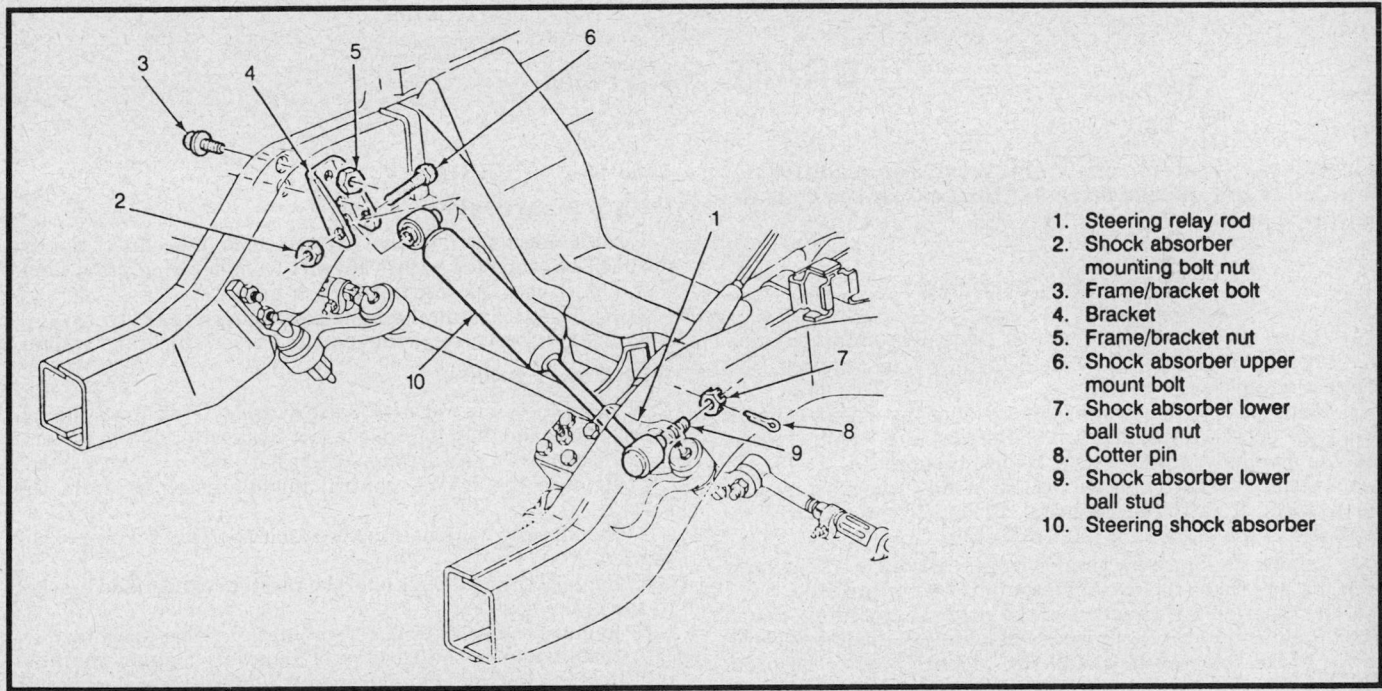

1. Steering relay rod
2. Shock absorber mounting bolt nut
3. Frame/bracket bolt
4. Bracket
5. Frame/bracket nut
6. Shock absorber upper mount bolt
7. Shock absorber lower ball stud nut
8. Cotter pin
9. Shock absorber lower ball stud
10. Steering shock absorber

Steering shock absorber – 1988–90 C Series

1. Steering relay rod
2. Shock absorber mounting bolt nut
3. Bracket
4. Shock absorber upper mount bolt
5. Shock absorber lower ball stud nut
6. Cotter pin
7. Shock absorber lower ball stud
8. Steering shock absorber

Steering shock absorber—1988–90 K Series

BRAKE SYSTEM

For all brake system repair and service procedures not detailed below, please refer to "Brakes" in the Unit Repair section.

Master Cylinder

1. Disconnect the negative battery cable. Disconnect any electrical connections from the master cylinder, as required. Disconnect and plug the fluid lines.
2. If equipped with power brakes, remove the master cylinder to power booster retaining bolts. Remove the RAWL control module assembly, 1988–90 C/K Series, if equipped.
3. If equipped with manual brakes, remove the master cylinder pushrod from the brake pedal. Remove the RAWL control module assembly, on 1988–90 C/K Series.
4. Remove the master cylinder from the vehicle. If equipped with power brakes remove the vacuum booster pushrod.
5. Installation is the reverse of the removal procedure. Bench bleed the master cylinder prior to installation. If equipped with power brakes be sure to install the vacuum booster pushrod. Bleed the system, as required.

Proportioning Valve

Removal and Installation

1986 C/K SERIES, 1987–90 R/V SERIES AND VAN

1. Disconnect the negative battery cable. Disconnect the hydraulic lines and plug to prevent dirt from entering the system.
2. Disconnect the warning switch harness.
3. Remove the retaining bolts and remove the valve.
4. Install in reverse of removal and bleed the brake system.

1988–90 C/K SERIES

With Manual Brakes

1. Disconnect the negative battery cable. Disconnect the hydraulic lines and plug to prevent dirt from entering the system.
2. Disconnect the warning switch harness.
3. Remove the retaining bolts and remove the valve.
4. Install in reverse of removal and bleed the brake system.

With Power Brakes

1. Disconnect the negative battery cable. Disconnect the hydraulic lines and plug to prevent dirt from entering the system.
2. Disconnect the warning switch harness.
3. Remove the RAWL control module assembly from the bracket.
4. Remove the bolts holding the Isolation/Dump Valve to the bracket.
5. Remove the nuts that hold the master cylinder and bracket to the brake booster.
6. Remove the bracket and combination valve assembly.
7. Installation is the reverse of removal. Tighten the nuts that hold the master cylinder and bracket to the brake booster to 20 ft. lbs. and the bolts holding the Isolation/Dump Valve to the bracket to 21 ft. lbs.

Power Brake Boosters

Removal and Installation

VACUUM BOOSTER

1. Disconnect the negative battery cable. Apply the parking brakes.
2. Support the master cylinder and remove the master cylinder mounting nuts.

3. Disconnect the vacuum hose from the check valve.

4. Disconnect the booster pushrod.

5. Remove the booster mounting nuts from inside the vehicle and remove the booster.

6. Installation is the reverse of removal.

HYDRAULIC BOOSTER (HYDRA-BOOST)

1. Disconnect the negative battery cable. Apply the parking brakes.

2. Disconnect the hydraulic lines from the booster.

3. Support the master cylinder and remove the master cylinder mounting nuts.

4. Disconnect the booster pushrod.

5. Remove the booster mounting nuts from inside the vehicle and remove the booster.

6. Installation is the reverse of removal. Bleed the brake system, as required.

7. To bleed the hydro boost system, fill the power steering pump to the proper level. Allow the fluid to remain undisturbed for a few minutes.

8. Start the engine and add fluid until the level is constant with the engine running.

9. Raise and support the vehicle safely. Start the engine and turn the wheels from stop to stop, add fluid as required. Turn the engine off and lower the vehicle.

10. Start the engine and depress the brake pedal several times while rotating the steering wheel from stop to stop. Turn the engine off and pump the brake pedal 4 or 5 times.

11. If the power steering fluid is extremely foamy, allow the vehicle to sit for a short time and then perform step nine again.

Brake Caliper

Removal and Installation

1986 C/K SERIES, 1987–90 R/V SERIES AND VAN

Delco Type

1. Remove the cover on the master cylinder and siphon enough fluid out of the reservoirs to bring the level to ⅓ full. This step prevents spilling fluid when the piston is pushed back.

2. Raise and support the vehicle safely. Remove the front wheels and tires.

3. Push the brake piston back into its bore using a C-clamp to pull the caliper outward.

4. Remove the 2 bolts which hold the caliper and then lift the caliper off the disc.

NOTE: Do not let the caliper assembly hang by the brake hose.

5. Remove the inboard and outboard shoe.

NOTE: If the pads are to be reinstalled, mark them inside and outside.

6. Remove the pad support spring from the piston.

7. Remove the 2 sleeves from the inside ears of the caliper and the 4 rubber bushings from the grooves in the caliper ears.

8. Remove the hose from the steel brake line and tape the fittings to prevent foreign material from entering the line or the hoses.

9. Remove the retainer from the hose fitting.

10. Remove the hose from the frame bracket and pull off the caliper with the hose attached.

11. Check the inside of the caliper for fluid leakage; if so, the caliper should be overhauled.

NOTE: Do not use compressed air to clean the inside of the caliper as this may unseat the dust boot.

12. Connect the brake line to start re-installaiton. Lubricate the sleeves, rubber bushings, bushing grooves, and the end of the mounting bolts using silicone lubricant.

13. Install new bushing in the caliper ears along with new sleeves. The sleeve should be replaced so that the end toward the shoe is flush with the machined surface of the ear.

14. Position the support spring and the inner pad into the center cavity of the piston. The outboard pad has ears which are bent over to keep the pad in position while the inboard pad has ears on the top end which fit over the caliper retaining bolts. A spring which is inside the brake piston hold the bottom edge of the inboard pad.

15. Push down on the inner pad until it lays flat against the caliper. It is important to push the piston all the way into the caliper if new linings are installed or the caliper will not fit over the rotor.

16. Position the outboard pad with the ears of the pad over the caliper ears and the tab at the bottom engaged in the caliper cutout.

17. With the 2 pads in position, place the caliper over the brake disc and align the holes in the caliper with those of the mounting bracket.

NOTE: Make certain that the brake hose is not twisted or kinked.

18. Install the mounting bracket bolts through the sleeves in the inboard caliper ears and through the mounting bracket, making sure that the ends of the bolts pass under the retaining ears on the inboard pad.

19. Tighten the mounting bolts to 35 ft. lbs. Pump the brake pedal to seat the pad against the rotor. Don't do this unless both calipers are in place. Use a pair of channel lock pliers to bend over the upper ears of the outer pad so it isn't loose.

20. Install the front wheel and lower the vehicle.

21. Add fluid to the master cylinder reservoirs so that they are ¼ in. (6.35mm) from the top.

22. Test the brake pedal by pumping it to obtain a hard pedal. Check the fluid level again and add fluid as necessary. Do not move the vehicle until a hard pedal is obtained.

Bendix Type

1. Remove approximately ⅓ of the brake fluid from the master cylinder. Discard the used brake fluid.

2. Raise and support the front of the vehicle safely. Remove the wheel.

3. Push the piston back into its bore. This can be done by suing a C-clamp.

4. Remove the bolt at the caliper support key. Use a brass drift pin to remove the key and spring.

5. Rotate the caliper up and forward from the bottom and lift it off the caliper support.

6. Unscrew the brake line at the caliper. Plug the opening. Discard the copper washer. Be careful not to damage the brake line.

7. Remove the outer shoe from the caliper.

To install:

8. Using a new copper washer, connect the brake line at the caliper. Torque the connector to 32 ft. lbs.

9. Lubricate the caliper support and support spring with silicone.

10. Position the outboard shoe in the caliper with the ears at the top of the shoe over the caliper ears and the tab at the bottom of the shoe engaged in the caliper cutout. If assembly is difficult, a C-clamp may be used. Be careful not to mar the lining.

11. Position the caliper over the brake disc, top edge first. Rotate the caliper downward onto the support.

12. Place the spring over the caliper support key, install the assembly between the support and lower caliper groove. Tap into place until the key retaining screw can be installed.

13. Install the screw and torque to 12–18 ft. lbs. The boss must fit fully into the circular cutout in the key.

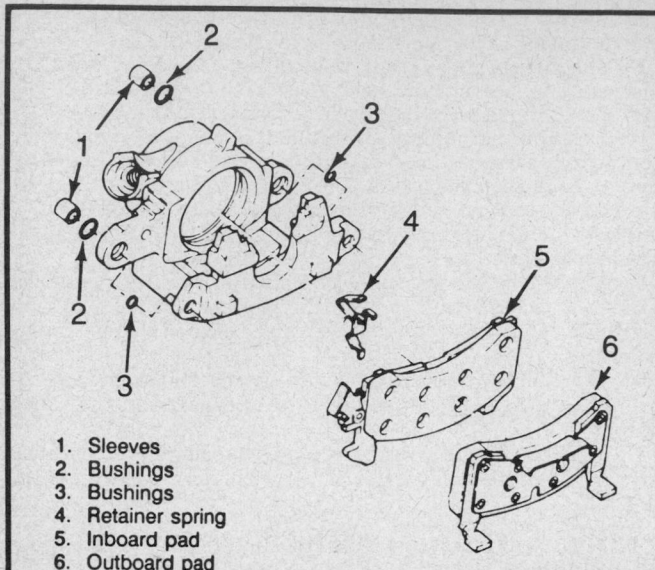

1. Sleeves
2. Bushings
3. Bushings
4. Retainer spring
5. Inboard pad
6. Outboard pad

Replacing the disc brake pads—Delco type—except 1988–90 C/K Series

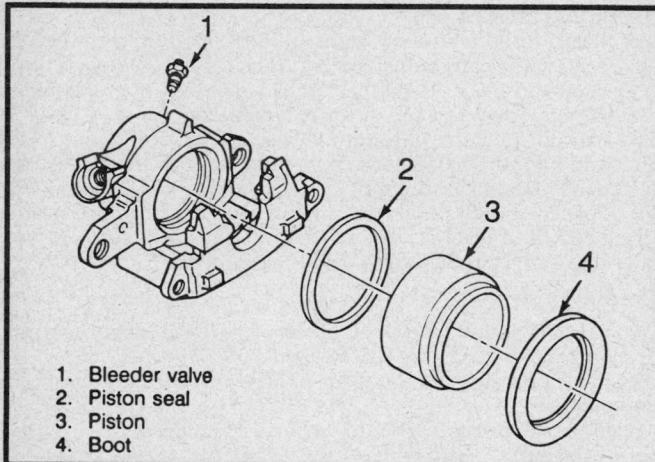

1. Bleeder valve
2. Piston seal
3. Piston
4. Boot

Caliper components—Delco type—except 1988–90 C/K Series

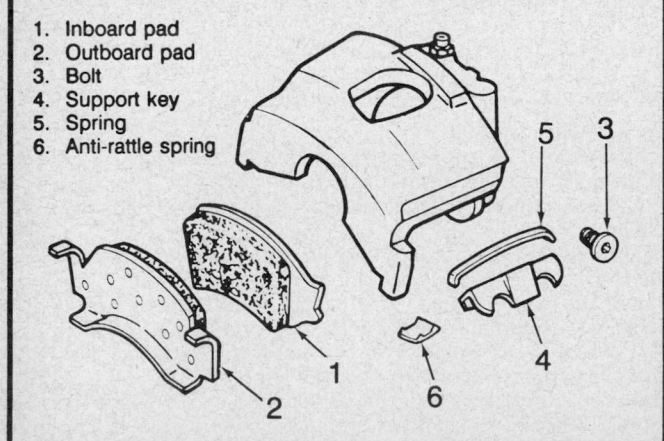

1. Inboard pad
2. Outboard pad
3. Bolt
4. Support key
5. Spring
6. Anti-rattle spring

Replacing the disc brake pads—Bendix type—except 1988–90 C/K Series

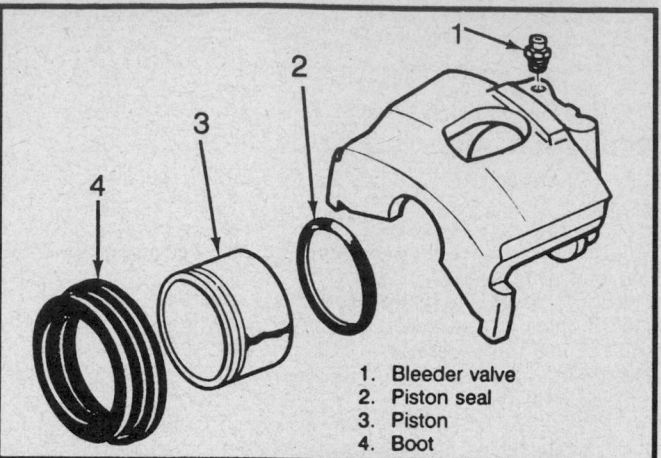

1. Bleeder valve
2. Piston seal
3. Piston
4. Boot

Caliper components—Bendix type—except 1988–90 C/K Series

14. Install the wheel and and add brake fluid as necessary.

1988–90 C/K SERIES

1. Remove approximately ⅓ of the brake fluid from the master cylinder. Discard the used brake fluid.
2. Raise and support the front of the vehicle safely.
3. Remove the front wheels and reinstall 2 lug nuts to retain the rotor.
4. Remove the brake hose from the caliper by removing the inlet fitting bolt.
5. Use 12 inch adjustable pliers over the inboard brake shoe and the flange on the caliper housing to bottom the piston into the caliper bore.
6. Remove the 2 mounting bolt and sleeve assemblies.
7. Remove the caliper from the rotor and mounting bracket.

NOTE: Do not let the caliper assembly hang by the brake hose.

8. Remove the inboard and outboard shoe.

NOTE: If the pads are to be reinstalled, mark them inside and outside.

9. Remove the bolt boots.
10. Remove the mounting bolt seals from the bolt holes in the caliper.
11. Remove the bushings from the grooves in the mounting bolt holes.

To install:
12. Install new, lubricated bushings in the grooves in the mounting bolt holes.
13. Install new bolt boots.
14. Install the inboard shoe and lining by snaping the retainer spring into the piston. The shoe must lay flat against the piston.
15. Install the outboard shoe and lining with the wear sensor at the leading edge of the shoe during forward wheel rotation. The back of the shoe must lay flat against the caliper.
16. Install the caliper over the rotor and in the mounting bracket. Liberally fill both cavities between the bushings in the housing with silicone grease.
17. Install the mounting bolt and sleeve assemblies and torque to 28 ft. lbs.
18. Install the brake hose and torque to 33 ft. lbs. Remove the 2 lug nuts and install the wheels.
19. Pump the brake pedal until a firm pedal is obtained.

Disc Brake Pads

Removal and Installation

1986 C/K SERIES, 1987–90 R/V SERIES AND VAN

Delco Type

1. Remove the cover on the master cylinder and siphon out ⅔ of the fluid. This step prevents spilling fluid when the piston is pushed back.
2. Raise and support the front end of the vehicle safely.
3. Remove the wheels.
4. Push the brake piston back into its bore using a C-clamp to pull the caliper outward.
5. Remove the 2 bolts which hold the caliper and then lift the caliper off the disc.

NOTE: Do not let the caliper assembly hang by the brake hose.

6. Remove the inboard and outboard shoe.

NOTE: If the pads are to be reinstalled, mark them inside and outside.

7. Remove the pad support spring from the piston.

To install:

8. Position the support spring and the inner pad into the center cavity of the piston. The outboard pad has ears which are bent over to keep the pad in position while the inboard pad has ears on the top end which fit over the caliper retaining bolts. A spring which is inside the brake piston hold the bottom edge of the inboard pad.
9. Push down on the inner pad until it lays flat against the caliper. It is important to push the piston all the way into the caliper if new linings are installed or the caliper will not fit over the rotor.
10. Position the outboard pad with the ears of the pad over the caliper ears and the tab at the bottom engaged in the caliper cutout.
11. With the two pads in position, place the caliper over the brake disc and align the holes in the caliper with those of the mounting bracket.

NOTE: Make certain that the brake hose is not twisted or kinked.

12. Install the mounting bracket bolts through the sleeves in the inboard caliper ears and through the mounting bracket, making sure that the ends of the bolts pass under the retaining ears on the inboard pad.
13. Tighten the mounting bolts to 35 ft. lbs. Pump the brake pedal to seat the pad against the rotor. Don't do this unless both calipers are in place. Use a pair of channel lock pliers to bend over the upper ears of the outer pad so it isn't loose.
14. Install the front wheel and lower the vehicle.
15. Add fluid to the master cylinder reservoirs so that they are ¼ in. (6.35mm) from the top.
16. Test the brake pedal by pumping it to obtain a hard pedal. Check the fluid level again and add fluid as necessary. Do not move the vehicle until a hard pedal is obtained.

Bendix

1. Remove approximately ⅓ of the brake fluid from the master cylinder. Discard the used brake fluid.
2. Raise and support the vehicle safely and remove the wheel.
3. Push the piston back into its bore. This can be done by suing a C-clamp.
4. Remove the bolt at the caliper support key. Use a brass drift pin to remove the key and spring.

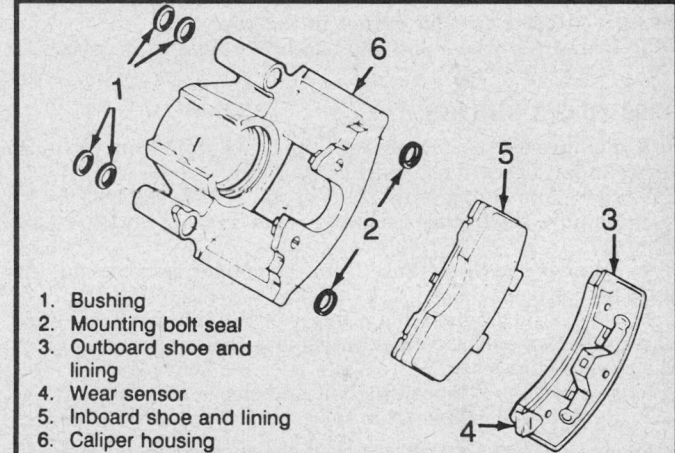

1. Bushing
2. Mounting bolt seal
3. Outboard shoe and lining
4. Wear sensor
5. Inboard shoe and lining
6. Caliper housing

Replacing the disc brake pads—1988–90 C/K Series

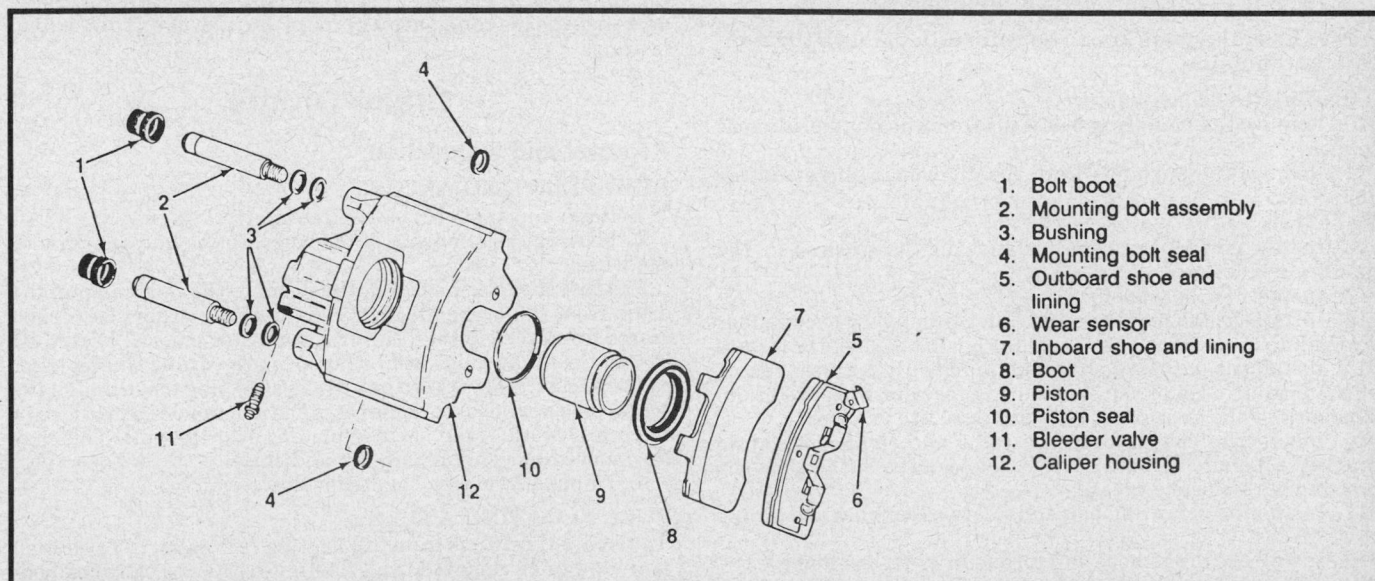

1. Bolt boot
2. Mounting bolt assembly
3. Bushing
4. Mounting bolt seal
5. Outboard shoe and lining
6. Wear sensor
7. Inboard shoe and lining
8. Boot
9. Piston
10. Piston seal
11. Bleeder valve
12. Caliper housing

Caliper components—1988–90 C/K Series

5. Rotate the caliper up and forward from the bottom and lift it off the caliper support.

6. Tie the caliper out of the way with a piece of wire. Be careful not to damage the brake line.

7. Remove the inner shoe from the caliper support. Discard the inner shoe clip.

8. Remove the outer shoe from the caliper.

To install:

9. Lubricate the caliper support and support spring, with silicone.

10. Install a new inboard shoe clip on the shoe.

11. Install the lower end of the inboard shoe into the groove provided in the support. Slide the upper end of the shoe into position. Be sure the clip remains in position.

10. Position the outboard shoe in the caliper with the ears at the top of the shoe over the caliper ears and the tab at the bottom of the shoe engaged in the caliper cutout. If assembly is difficult, a C-clamp may be used. Be careful not to mar the lining.

11. Position the caliper over the brake disc, top edge first. Rotate the caliper downward onto the support.

12. Place the spring over the caliper support key, install the assembly between the support and lower caliper groove. Tap into place until the key retaining screw can be installed.

13. Install the screw and torque to 12–18 ft. lbs. The boss must fit fully into the circular cutout in the key.

14. Install the wheel and and add brake fluid as necessary.

1988–90 C/K SERIES

1. Remove approximately ⅓ of the brake fluid from the master cylinder. Discard the used brake fluid.

2. Raise and support the front of the vehicle safely.

3. Remove the front wheels and reinstall 2 lug nuts to retain the rotor.

4. Remove the brake hose from the caliper by removing the inlet fitting bolt.

5. Use 12 inch adjustable pliers over the inboard brake shoe and the flange on the caliper housing to bottom the piston into the caliper bore.

6. Remove the 2 mounting bolt and sleeve assemblies.

7. Remove the caliper from the rotor and mounting bracket.

NOTE: Do not let the caliper assembly hang by the brake hose.

8. Remove the inboard and outboard shoe.

NOTE: If the pads are to be reinstalled, mark them inside and outside.

9. Remove the bolt boots.

10. Remove the mounting bolt seals from the bolt holes in the caliper.

11. Remove the bushings from the grooves in the mounting bolt holes.

To install:

12. Install new, lubricated bushings in the grooves in the mounting bolt holes.

13. Install new bolt boots.

14. Install the inboard shoe and lining by snaping the retainer spring into the piston. The shoe must lay flat against the piston.

15. Install the outboard shoe and lining with the wear sensor at the leading edge of the shoe during forward wheel rotation. The back of the shoe must lay flat against the caliper.

16. Install the caliper over the rotor and in the mounting bracket. Liberally fill both cavities between the bushings in the housing with silicone grease.

17. Install the mounting bolt and sleeve assemblies and torque to 28 ft. lbs.

18. Install the brake hose and torque to 33 ft. lbs. Remove the 2 lug nuts and install the wheels.

19. Pump the brake pedal until a firm pedal is obtained.

Brake Rotor

Removal and Installation

1986 C/K SERIES, 1987–90 R/V SERIES AND VAN

2WD

1. Raise and support the vehicle safely.
2. Remove the brake caliper.
3. Remove the outer wheel bearing.
4. Remove the rotor from the spindle.
5. Reverse procedure to install.

4WD

1. Raise and support the vehicle safely.
2. Remove the locking hubs.
3. Remove the wheel bearing outer locknut, retainer and and wheel bearing inner adjusting nut.
4. Remove the hub and disc assembly and outer wheel bearing.
5. Remove the oil seal and inner bearing cone from the hub using a brass drift and tapping with a hammer. Discard the oil seal.
6. Remove the inner and outer bearing cups using a brass drift and a hammer.
7. Clean, inspect and lubricate all parts as require with a high speed grease.

NOTE: Lubrication must be applied to prevent deterioration before the unit is placed in service.

7. Assemble the outer wheel bearing cup into the wheel hub using a bearing driver tool.
8. Assemble the inner wheel bearing cup into the wheel hub using a bearing driver tool.
9. Pack the wheel bearing cone with a high melting point type wheel bearing grease and insert the cone into the cup.
10. Install thje hub and disc and wheel bearings to the spindle.
11. Adjust the wheel bearings.

1988–90 C/K SERIES

1. Raise and support the vehicle safely.
2. Remove the brake caliper.
3. Remove the cap, cotter pin nut and washer and remove hub and disc from the spindle.
4. Installation is the reverse of removal. Pack the wheel bearing cone with a high melting point type wheel bearing grease and insert the cone into the cup. Adjust the front wheel bearings.

Brake Drums

Removal and Installation

SEMI-FLOATING AXLES

1. Raise and support the vehicle safely.
2. Mark the relationship of the wheel to the hub and remove the wheel.
3. Mark the relationship of the drum to the hub and pull the drum from the brake assembly. If the brake drums have been scored from worn linings, the brake adjuster must be backed off so that the brake shoes will retract from the drum. The adjuster can be backed off by inserting a brake adjusting tool through the access hole provided. In some cases the access hole is provided in the brake drum. A metal cover plate is over the hole. This may be removed by using a hammer and chisel.
4. To install, reverse the removal procedure.

FULL FLOATING AXLES

To remove the drums from full floating rear axles, the axle shaft will have to be removed. Full floating rear axles can readily be identified by the bearing housing protruding through the center of the wheel.

1. Raise and support the vehicle safely.
2. Remove the wheel.
3. Remove the axle shaft.
4. Remove the retaining ring, key and adjusting nut.
5. Remove the hub and drum.

To install:

6. Install the hub and drum to the tube.
7. Install the adjusting nut and torque to 50 ft. lbs. while turning the hub.
8. Install the key and retaining ring.
9. Install the axle shaft and wheel.

Brake Shoes

Removal and Installation

1. Raise the vehicle and support it safely.
2. Loosen the parking brake equalizer enough to remove all tension on the brake cable.
3. Remove the brake drums.

NOTE: The brake pedal must not be depressed while the drums are removed.

4. Using a brake tool, remove the shoe springs.
5. Remove the self-adjuster actuator spring.
6. Remove the link from the secondary shoe by pulling it from the anchor pin.
7. Remove the holddown pins. These are the brackets which run though the backing plate. They can be removed with a pair of pliers. Reach around the rear of the backing plate and hold the back of the pin. Turn the top of the pin retainer 45° with the plier. This will align the elongated tang with the slot in the retainer. Be careful, as the pin is spring loaded and may fly off when released. Use the same procedure for the other pin assembly.
8. Remove the adjuster actuator assembly.

NOTE: Since the actuator, pivot, and override spring are considered an assembly it is not recommended that they be disassembled.

9. Remove the shoes from the backing plate. Make sure that you have a secure grip on the assembly as the bottom spring will still exert pressure on the shoes. Slowly let the tops of the shoes come together and the tension will decrease and the adjuster and spring may be removed.

NOTE: If the linings are to be reused, mark them for identification.

10. Remove the rear parking brake lever from the secondary shoe. Using a pair of plier, pull back on the spring which surrounds the cable. At the same time, remove the cable from the notch in the shoe bracket. Make sure that the spring does not snap back or injury may result.
11. Use a brake cleaning fluid to remove dirt from the brake drum. Check the drums for scoring and cracks. Have the drums checked for out-of-round and service the drums as necessary.
12. Check the wheel cylinders by carefully pulling the lower edges of the wheel cylinder boots away from the cylinders. If there is excessive leakage, the inside of the cylinder will be moist with fluid. If there is any leakage at all, a cylinder overhaul is in order. Do not delay, as a brake failure could result.

NOTE: A small amount of fluid will be present to act as a lubricant for the wheel cylinder pistons.

13. Check the flange plate, which is located around the axle, for leakage of differential lubricant. This condition cannot be overlooked as the lubricant will be absorbed into the brake linings and brake failure will result. Replace the seals as necessary.

NOTE: If new linings are being installed, check them against the old units for length and type.

14. Check the new linings for imperfections.

NOTE: It is important to keep your hands free of dirt and grease when handling the brake shoes. Foreign matter will be absorbed into the linings and result in unpredictable braking.

15. Lightly lubricate the parking brake and cable and the end of the parking brake lever where it enters the shoe. Use high temperature, waterproof, grease or special brake lube.
16. Install the parking brake lever into the secondary shoe with the attaching bolt, spring washer, lockwasher, and nut. It is important that the lever move freely before the shoe is attached. Move the assembly and check for proper action.
17. Lubricate the adjusting screw and make sure that it works freely. Sometimes the adjusting screw will not move due to lack of lubricant or dirt contamination and the brakes will not adjust. In this case, the adjuster should be disassembled, thoroughly cleaned, and lubricated before installation.
18. Connect the brake shoe spring to the bottom portion of both shoes. Make certain that the brake linings are installed in the correct manner, the primary and secondary shoe in the correct position. If you are not sure remove the other brake drum and check it.
19. Install the adjusting mechanism below the spring and separate the top of the shoes.

Make the following checks before installation:

    a. Be certain that the right hand thread adjusting screw is on the left hand side of the vehicle and the left hand screw is on the right hand side of the vehicle.

    b. Make sure that the star adjuster is aligned with the adjusting hole.

    c. The adjuster should be installed with the starwheel nearest the secondary shoe and the tension spring away from the adjusting mechanism;

    d. If the original linings are being reused, put them back in their original locations.

20. Install the parking brake cable.
21. Position the primary shoe (the shoe with the short lining) first. Secure it with the holddown pin and with its spring by pushing the pin through the back of the backing plate and, while holding it with one hand, install the spring and the retainer using a pair of needlenose pliers. Install the adjuster actuator assembly.
22. Install the parking brake strut and the strut spring by pulling back the spring with pliers and engaging the end of the cable onto the brake strut and then releasing the spring.
23. Place the small metal guide plate over the anchor pin and position the self-adjuster wire cable eye.

NOTE: The wire should not be positioned with the conventional brake installation tool or damage will result. It should be positioned on the actuator assembly first and then placed over the anchor pin stud by hand with the adjuster assembly in full downward position.

24. Install the actuator return spring. Do not pry the actuator lever to install the return spring. Position it using the end of a screwdriver or another suitable tool.

NOTE: If the return springs are bent or in any way distorted, they should be replaced.

25. Using the brake installation tool, place the brake return springs in position. Install the primary spring first over the anchor pin and then place the spring from the secondary show over the wire link end.
26. Pull the brake shoes away from the backing plate and apply a thin coat of high temperature, waterproof, grease or special brake lube in the brake shoe contact points.

NOTE: Only a small amount is necessary. Keep the lubricant away from the brake linings.

27. Once the complete assembly has been installed, check the operation of the self-adjusting mechanism by moving the actuating lever by hand.

28. Adjust the brakes.

a. Turn the star adjuster until the drum slides over the brakes shoes with only a slight drag.

b. With the drum and wheel installed turn the adjusting screw until the wheel can be just be turned by hand. The brake drag should be equal at both wheels.

c. Back of the adjusting screw 33 notches. The brakes should have no drag after the screw has been backed off about 15 notches.

NOTE Avoid overtightening the lug nuts to prevent damage to the brake drum. Alloy wheels can also be cracked by overtightening. Use of a torque wrench is highly recommended.

d. If the adjusting hole in the drum has been punched out, make certain that the insert has been removed from the inside of the drum. Install a rubber hole cover to keep dirt out of the brake assembly. Also, be sure that the drums are installed in the same position as they were when removed, with the locating tang in line with the locating hole in the axle shaft flange.

e. Make the final adjustment by backing the vehicle and pumping the brakes until the self-adjusting mechanisms adjust to the proper level and the brake pedal reaches satisfactory height.

29. Adjust the parking brake.

Wheel Cylinders

REMOVAL AND INSTALLATION

1. Raise and support the vehicle safely.

2. Remove the wheel.

3. Back off the brake adjustment if necessary and remove the drum.

4. Disconnect and plug the brake line.

5. Remove the brake shoe pull-back springs and shoes as necessary.

6. Remove the bolts securing the wheel cylinder to the backing plate.

7. Disengage the wheel cylinder pushrods from the brake shoes and remove the wheel cylinder.

8. Installation is the reverse of removal. Bleed the system.

Parking Brake Cable

Removal and Installation

Front Cable

1. Raise and support the vehicle safely.

2. Remove adjusting nut from equalizer.

3. Remove retainer clip from rear portion of front cable at frame and from lever arm.

4. Disconnect front brake cable from parking brake pedal or lever assemblies. Remove front brake cable. On some models, it may assist installation of new cable if a heavy cord is tied to other end of cable in order to guide new cable through proper routing.

5. Install cable by reversing removal procedure.

6. Adjust parking brake.

Center Cable

1. Raise and support the vehicle safely.

2. Remove adjusting nut from equalizer.

3. Unhook connector at each end and disengage hooks and guides.

4. Install new cable by reversing removal procedure.

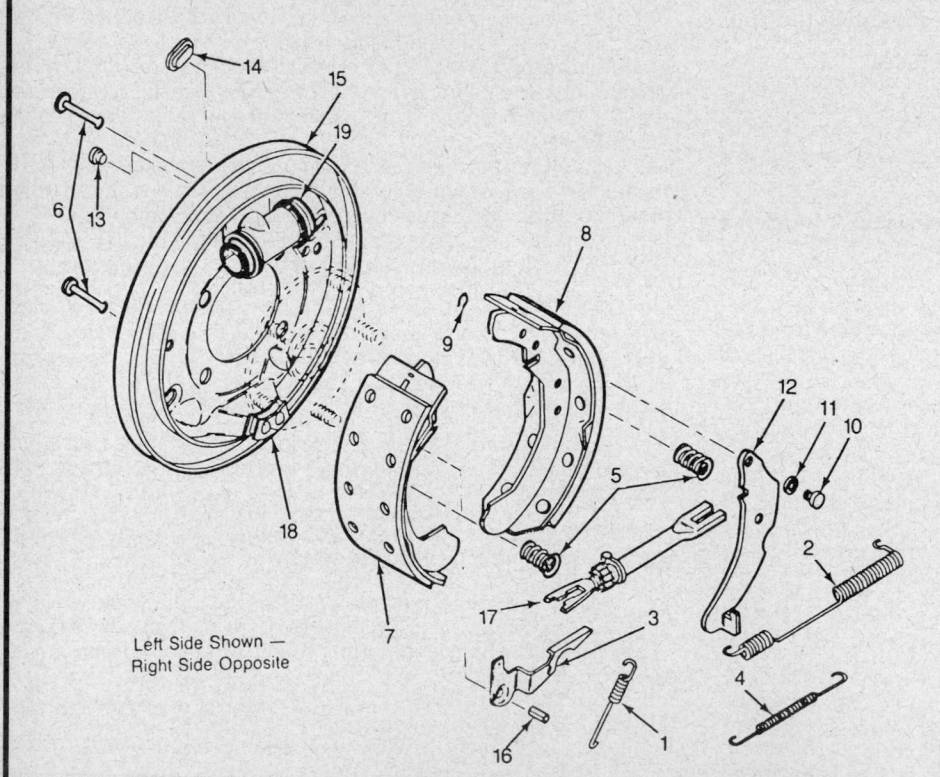

1. Actuator spring
2. Upper return spring
3. Adjuster actuator
4. Lower return spring
5. Hold-down spring assembly
6. Hold-down pin
7. Adjuster shoe and lining
8. Shoe and lining
9. Retaining ring
10. Pin
11. Spring washer
12. Park brake lever
13. Access hole plug
14. Inspection cover
15. Backing plate assembly
16. Adjuster pin
17. Adjusting screw assembly
18. Anchor plate
19. Wheel cylinder assembly

Left Side Shown — Right Side Opposite

Exploded view of the rear drum brake assembly — Leading/Trailing type

1. Hold-down pins
2. Backing plate
3. Parking brake lever
4. Washer
5. Secondary shoe
6. Retaining ring
7. Shoe guide
8. Parking brake strut
9. Strut spring
10. Actuator lever
11. Actuator link
12. Return spring
13. Return spring
14. Hold down spring
15. Lever pivot
16. Lever return spring
17. Adjusting screw assembly
18. Adjusting screw spring
19. Primary shoe

Exploded view of the rear drum brake assembly – Duo-Servo type

5. Adjust parking brake.
6. Apply parking brake 3 times with heavy pressure and repeat adjustment.

Rear Cable

1. Raise and support the vehicle safely.
2. Remove rear wheel and brake drum.
3. Loosen adjusting nut at equalizer.
4. Disengage rear cable at connector.
5. Bend retainer fingers.
6. Disengage cable at brake shoe operating lever.
7. Install new cable by reversing removal procedure.
8. Adjust parking brake.

Adjustment

The rear brakes serve a dual purpose. They are used as service brakes and as parking brakes. To obtain proper adjustment of the parking brake, the service brakes must first be properly adjusted as outlined earlier.

1986 C/K SERIES, 1987–90 R/V SERIES AND VAN

Foot Pedal Type

1. Apply the parking brake 4 notches from the fully released position.
2. Raise and support the vehicle.
3. Loosen the jam nut at the equalizer.
4. Tighten or loosen the adjusting nut until a light drag is felt when the rear wheels are rotated forward.
5. Tighten the check nut.
6. Release the parking brake and rotate the rear wheels. No drag should be felt. If even a light drag is felt, readjust the parking brake.
7. Lower the vehicle.

NOTE: If a new parking brake cable is being installed, pre-stretch it by applying the parking brake hard about three times before making adjustments.

Lever Type

1. Raise and support the vehicle safely. Turn the adjusting knob on the parking brake lever counterclockwise until it stops.
2. Apply the parking brake. Loosen the equalizer nut.
3. Tighten the equalizer nut until light drag is felt while rotating the rear wheels in the forward motion.

4. Adjust the knob on the parking brake lever until a definite snap over center is felt.
5. Release the parking brake. Rotate the rear wheels in the forward motion. There should be no brake drag.

Driveshaft Type

1. Raise and support the vehicle safely. Remove the clevis pin connecting the pull rod and the relay lever.
2. Rotate the brake drum to align the access hole with the adjusting screw. If the vehicle is equipped with manual transmission the access hole is located at the bottom of the backing plate. If the vehicle is equipped with automatic transmission the access hole is located at the top of the shoe.
3. For first time adjustment it will be necessary to remove the driveshaft and the drum in order to remove the lanced area from the drum and clean out the metal shavings.
4. Adjust the screw until the drum cannot be rotated by hand. Back off the adjusting screw ten notches, the drum should rotate freely.
5. Position the parking brake lever in the fully released position. Take up the slack in the cable to overcome spring tension.
6. Adjust the clevis of the pull rod to align with the hole in the relay lever. Install the clevis pin. Install a new cover in the drum access hole.

1988–90 C/K SERIES

1. Raise and support the vehicle safely. Matchmark the wheel to the axle flange. Remove the tire and wheel assembly.
2. Matchmark the drum to the axle flange. Remove the brake drum.
3. Using tool J–21177A, or equivalent, measure and record the brake drum inside diameter.
4. Turn the adjuster nut and adjust the shoe and lining to a diameter 0.010–0.020 in. less than the measured inside diameter of the brake drum.
5. Be sure that the stops on the parking brake levers are against the edge of the brake shoe web. If not, loosen the parking brake cable adjustment.
6. Tighten the parking brake cable at the adjuster nut until the lever stops begin to move off of the shoe webs. Loosen the adjustment nut until the lever stops move back, barely touching the shoe webs. The final clearance between the stops and either web should be 0.5mm.
7. Install the drums and wheels. Align the assemblies with the matchmarks made during removal.

5–121

8. Apply and release the service brake pedal 30–35 times using normal pedal force. Pause about one second between each pedal application.

9. Depress the parking brake six clicks. Check the rear wheels they should not rotate.

10. Release the parking brake lever. Check for free wheel rotation.

FRONT SUSPENSION

Shock Absorbers

Removal and Installation

1986 C SERIES, 1987–90 R SERIES AND VAN

1. Raise and support the vehicle safely. Properly support the lower control arm assembly, as required. Remove the tire and wheel assembly.
2. Remove the upper shock absorber retaining bolt. Remove the lower shock absorber retaining bolt. Vehicles equipped with quad shocks have a spacer between them.
3. Remove the shock absorber from the vehicle.
4. Installation is the reverse of the removal procedure. On the R series vehicle, torque the upper end nut to 140 ft. lbs.; the lower end bolt to 59 ft. lbs. On the Van, torque the bolts to 80 ft. lbs.

1986 K SERIES, 1987–90 V SERIES

1. Raise and support the vehicle safely.
2. Remove the nuts and eye bolts securing the upper and lower shock absorber eyes. Quad shocks have a spacer between the lower end bushings.
3. Remove the shock absorber(s) and inspect the rubber eye bushings. If these are defective, replace the shock absorber assembly.
4. Installation is the reverse of removal. Make sure that the spacer is installed at the bottom end on quad shocks. Torque the upper end nut to 65 ft. lbs. On dual shocks, torque the lower end to 65 ft. lbs. On quad shocks, torque the lower end to 89 ft. lbs.

1988–90 C SERIES

1. Remove the upper shock absorber retaining bolt. Raise and support the vehicle safely.
2. Properly support the lower control arm, as required. Remove the lower shock absorber retaining bolt.
3. Remove the shock absorber from the vehicle.
4. Installation is the reverse of removal. Tighten the upper nut to 8 ft. lbs. (96 inch lbs.); tighten the lower mounting bolts to 20 ft. lbs.

1988–90 K SERIES

1. Raise and support the vehicle safely.
2. Remove the upper end bolt, nut and washer.
3. Remove the lower end bolt, nut and washer.
4. Remove the shock absorber and inspect the rubber bushings. If these are defective, replace the shock absorber assembly.
5. Installation is the reverse of removal. Torque the both nuts to 48 ft. lbs. Make sure that the bolts are inserted in the proper direction. The bolt head on the upper end should be forward; the bottom end bolt head is rearward.

Coil Springs

Removal and Installation

1986 C SERIES, 1987–90, R SERIES AND VAN

1. Raise and support the vehicle safely under the frame rails. The control arms should hang freely.
2. Remove the wheel.

3. Disconnect the shock absorber at the lower end and move it aside.
4. Disconnect the stabilizer bar from the lower control arm.
5. Support the lower control arm and install a spring compressor on the spring, or chain the spring to the control arm as a safety precaution.

NOTE: On vehicles with an air cylinder inside the spring, remove the valve core from the cylinder and expel the air by compressing the cylinder with a prybar. With the cylinder compressed, replace the valve core so that the cylinder will stay in the compressed position. Push the cylinder as far as possible towards the top of the spring.

6. Raise the jack to remove the tension from the lower control arm cross-shaft and remove the two U-bolts securing the cross-shaft to the crossmember.

NOTE: The cross-shaft and lower control arm keeps the coil spring compressed. Use care when lowering the assembly.

7. Slowly release the jack and lower the control arm until the spring can be removed. Be sure that all compression is relieved from the spring.
8. If the spring was chained, remove the chain and spring. If you used spring compressors, remove the spring and slowly release the compressors.
9. Remove the air cylinder, if so equipped.
To install:
10. Install the air cylinder so that the protector plate is towards the upper control arm. The schrader valve should protrude through the hole in the lower control arm.
11. Install the chain and spring. If you used spring compressors, install the spring and compressors.
12. Slowly raise the jack and lower the control arm. Line up the indexing hole in the shaft with the crossmember attaching studs.
13. Install the two U-bolts securing the cross-shaft to the crossmember. Torque the nuts to 65 ft. lbs on the Van and 85 ft. lbs on all others.
14. Remove the jack.
15. Connect the stabilizer bar to the lower control arm. Torque the nuts to 24 ft. lbs.
16. Connect the shock absorber at the lower end. Torque the bolt to 80 ft. lbs. on the Van and 59 ft. lbs. on all others.
17. If equipped with air cylinders, inflate the cylinder to 60 psi.
18. Install the wheel.
19. Lower the vehicle. Once the weight of the vehicle is on the wheels, reduce the air cylinder pressure to 50 psi.
20. Check the alignment checked.

1988–90 C SERIES

1. Raise and support the vehicle safely. Allow the control arms to hang free. Remove the tire and wheel assembly. Remove the shock absorber assembly, as required.
2. With the vehicle supported so that the control arms hang free, install tool J–23028. Secure the tool using a suitable jack. Install a safety chain around the spring and through the lower control arm.

3. Remove the stabilizer shaft from the lower control arm. Raise the jack and remove the tension on the lower control arm bolts.

4. Remove the lower control arm rear bolt, than remove the other retaining bolt.

5. Lower the jack and allow the lower control arm to hang free. Remove the spring assembly from the vehicle.

To install:

6. Install the chain and spring. If you used spring compressors, install the spring and compressors.

   a. Make sure that the insulator is in place.

   b. Make sure that the tape is at the lower end. New springs will have an identifying tape.

   c. Make sure that the gripper notch on the top coil is in the frame bracket.

   d. Make sure that on drain hole in the lower arm is covered by the bottom coil and the other is open.

7. Slowly raise the jack and lower the control arm. Guide the control arm into place with a prybar.

8. Install the pivot shaft bolts, front one first. The bolts must be installed with the heads towards the front of the vehicle. Remove the safety chain or spring compressors.

NOTE: Do not torque the bolts yet. The bolts must be torque with the vehicle at its proper ride height.

9. Remove the jack.

10. Connect the stabilizer bar to the lower control arm. Torque the nuts to 13 ft. lbs.

11. Install the shock absorber.

12. Install the wheel.

13. Lower the vehicle. Once the weight of the vehicle is on the wheels:

   a. Lift the front bumper about 38mm and let it drop.

   b. Repeat this procedure 2 or 3 more times.

   c. Draw a line on the side of the lower control arm from the centerline of the control arm pivot shaft, dead level to the outer end of the control arm.

   d. Measure the distance between the lowest corner of the steering knuckle and the line on the control arm. Record the figure.

   e. Push down about 38mm on the front bumper and let it return. Repeat the procedure 2 or 3 more times.

   f. Re-measure the distance at the control arm.

   g. Determine the average of the 2 measurements. The average distance should be 73.6mm ± 6mm.

   h. If the figure is correct, tighten the control arm pivot nuts to 96 ft. lbs.

   i. If the figure is not correct, tighten the pivot bolts to 96 ft. lbs. and have the front end alignment corrected.

Leaf Spring

Removal and Installation

1986 K SERIES AND 1987–90 V SERIES

1. Raise and support the vehicle safely so that all tension is taken off of the front suspension.

2. Remove the shackle retaining bolts, nuts and spacers.

3. Remove the front spring-to-frame bracket bolt, washer and nut.

4. On the 10/1500 and 20/2500 both sides and the 30/3500 left side: remove the U-bolt nuts, washers, U-bolts, plate and spacers.

5. On the 30/3500 right side: remove the inboard spring plate bolts, U-bolt nuts, washers, U-bolt, plate and spacers.

To replace the bushing, place the spring in a press or vise and press out the bushing. Press in the new bushing. The new bushing should protrude evenly on both sides of the spring.

6. Installation is the reverse of removal. Coat all bushings with silicone grease prior to installation. Install all bolts and nuts finger-tight. When all fasteners are installed, torque the bolts. Torque the U-bolt nuts, inclusind the inboard right side 30/3500 series bolts, in the crisscross pattern shown, to 150 ft. lbs. Torque the shackle nuts to 50 ft. lbs. Torque the front eye bolt nut to 90 ft. lbs.

Torsion Bar

Removal and Installation

1988 K SERIES

1. Raise and support the vehicle safely.

2. Remove the torsion bar adjusting screw. Record the number of turns on the adjusting bolt for reinstallation.

3. Remove the support retainer retaining bolts.

4. Slide the torsion bar forward in the lower control arm until the torsion bar clears the support. Pull down on the bar and remove it from the control arm.

5. Remove the required components and remove the torsion bar from the vehicle.

6. Installation is the reverse of the removal procedure. The gap between the torsion bar adjusting arm and the support assembly should not exceed 1.3 in.

7. Tighten the bolts to 35 ft. lbs. and the bolt/screw to 33 ft. lbs. Check and adjust front alignment, as required.

1989–90 K SERIES

1. Raise and support the vehicle safely.

2. Remove the wheels.

3. Support the lower control arm with a floor jack.

4. Matchmark the both torsion bar adjustment bolt positions.

5. Using tool J-36202, increase the tension on the adjusting arm.

6. Remove the adjustment bolt and retaining plate.

7. Move the tool aside.

8. Slide the torsion bars forward.

9. Remove the adjusting arms.

10. Remove the nuts and bolts from the torsion bar support crossmember and slide the support crossmember rearwards.

11. Matchmark the position of the torsion bars and note the markings on the front end of each bar. They are not interchangeable. Remove the torsion bars.

12. Remove the support crossmember.

13. Remove the retainer, spacer and bushing from the support crossmember.

To install:

14. Assemble the retainer, spacer and bushing on the support.

15. Position the support assembly on the frame, out of the way.

16. Align the matchmarks and install the torsion bars, sliding them forward until they are supported.

17. Install the adjuster arms on the torsion bars.

18. Bolt the support crossmember into position. Torque the center nut to 18 ft. lbs.; the edge nuts to 46 ft. lbs.

19. Install the adjuster retaining plate and bolt on each torsion bar.

20. Using tool J-36202, increase tension on both torsion bars.

21. Install the adjustment retainer plate and bolt on both torsion bars.

22. Set the adjustment bolt to the marked position.

23. Release the tension on the torsion bar until the load is take up by the adjustment bolt.

24. Remove the tool.

25. Install the wheels.

26. Check the front end alignment.

Upper Ball Joint

Removal and Installation

1986 C SERIES, 1987–90, R SERIES AND VAN

1. Raise and support the vehicle safely. Properly support the

lower control arm, using the necessary equipment. The control arm must be supported so that the spring and the control arm remain intact.

2. Remove the wheel assembly. Remove the brake caliper and position it to the side.

3. Remove the cotter pin and the upper ball joint retaining bolt. Using the proper tool separate the upper joint from its mounting. Support the knuckle assembly so that its weight will not damage the brake hose.

4. Remove the rivets from the ball joint assembly, using the proper tools. Remove the ball joint from the upper control arm.

To install:

5. Start the new ball joint into the control arm. Position the bleed vent in the rubber boot facing inward.

6. Turn the screw until the ball joint is seated in the control arm.

7. Lower the upper arm and match the steering knuckle to the lower ball stud.

8. Install the brake caliper, if removed.

9. Install the ball stud nut and torque it to 80-100 ft. lbs. plus the additional torque necessary to align the cotter pin hole. Do not exceed 130 ft. lbs. or back the nut off to align the holes with the pin.

10. Install a new lube fitting and lubricate the new joint.

11. Install the tire and wheel.

12. Lower the vehicle.

1986 K SERIES AND 1987–90 V SERIES

1. Raise and support the vehicle safely. Remove the tire and wheel assembly.

2. Remove the hub and rotor assembly. Remove the spindle.

3. Remove the steering knuckle assembly. If removing the left axle yoke ball joints, remove the steering arm. Position the steering knuckle assembly in a suitable vise.

4. The lower ball joint must be removed before service can be performed on the upper ball joint. first. Press the lower ball joint from the knuckle assembly, using the proper tools.

5. Press the upper ball joint from the knuckle assembly, using the proper tools.

6. Installation is the reverse of the removal procedure. Check and adjust front alignment, as required.

1988–90 C SERIES

1. Raise and support the vehicle safely. Properly support the lower control arm, using the necessary equipment. The control arm must be supported so that the spring and the control arm remain intact.

2. Remove the tire and wheel assembly. Remove the brake caliper and position it to the side.

3. Remove the cotter pin and the upper ball joint retaining bolt. Using the proper tool separate the upper joint from its mounting. Support the knuckle assembly so that its weight will not damage the brake hose.

4. Remove the rivets from the ball joint assembly, using the proper tools. Remove the ball joint from the upper control arm.

To Install:

5. Install the replacement ball joint in the control arm, using the bolts and nuts supplied. Torque the nuts to 17 ft. lbs. for 15 and 25 Series; 52 ft. lbs. for 35 Series.

6. Position the ball stud in the knuckle. Make sure it is sqaurely seated. Torque the ball stud nut to 90 ft. lbs.

7. Install a new cotter pin.

8. Install a new lube fitting and lubricate the new joint.

9. If removed, install the brake caliper.

10. Install the wheel and lower the vehicle.

Inspection

1. Raise and support the vehicle so that the control arms hang free.

2. Remove the wheel.

3. Support the lower control arm with a jackstand and disconnect the upper ball stud from the steering knuckle.

4. The upper ball joint is spring loaded in its socket. If it has any perceptible lateral shake or can be twisted in its socket, it should be replaced.

1988–90 K SERIES

1. Raise and support the vehicle safely.

2. Remove the wheel.

3. Unbolt the brake hose braket from the control arm.

4. Using a $\frac{1}{8}$ in. drill bit, drill a pilot hole through each ball joint rivet.

5. Drill out the rivets with a $\frac{1}{2}$ in. drill bit. Punch out any remaining rivet material.

6. Remove the cotter pin and nut from the ball stud.

7. Support the lower control arm with a floor jack.

8. Using a screw-type forcing tool, separate the ball joint from the knuckle.

To install:

9. Position the new ball joint on the control arm.

NOTE: Service replacement ball joints come with nuts and bolts to replace the rivets.

10. Install the bolts and nuts. Tighten the nuts to 17 ft. lbs. for 15 and 25 Series; 52 ft. lbs. for 35 Series.

NOTE: The bolts are inserted from the bottom.

11. Start the ball stud into the knuckle. Make sure it is squarely seated. Install the ball stud nut and pull the ball stud into the knuckle with the nut. Don't final-torque the nut yet.

12. Install the wheel.

13. Lower the vehicle. Once the weight of the vehicle is on the wheels:

   a. Lift the front bumper about 38mm and let it drop.

   b. Repeat this procedure 2 or 3 more times.

   c. Draw a line on the side of the lower control arm from the centerline of the control arm pivot shaft, dead level to the outer end of the control arm.

   d. Measure the distance between the lowest corner of the steering knuckle and the line on the control arm. Record the figure.

   e. Push down about 38mm on the front bumper and let it return. Repeat the procedure 2 or 3 more times.

   f. Re-measure the distance at the control arm.

   g. Determine the average of the 2 measurements. The average distance should be 73.6mm ± 6mm.

   h. If the figure is correct, tighten the control arm pivot nuts to 94 ft. lbs.

   i. If the figure is not correct, tighten the pivot bolts to 94 ft. lbs. and have the front end alignment corrected.

Lower Ball Joint

Removal and Installation

1986 C SERIES, 1987–90, R SERIES AND VAN

1. Raise and support the vehicle safely. Properly support the lower control arm, using the necessary equipment. The control arm must be supported so that the spring and the control arm remain intact.

2. Remove the tire and wheel assembly. As required, remove the brake caliper and position it to the side.

3. Remove the cotter pin and the lower ball joint retaining bolt. Using the proper tool separate the ball joint from its mounting. Support the knuckle assembly so that its weight will not damage the brake hose.

4. Press the ball joint out of the lower control arm, using the proper tools.

To install:

5. Start the new ball joint into the control arm. Position the bleed vent in the rubber boot facing inward.

6. Turn the screw until the ball joint is seated in the control arm.

7. Lower the upper arm and match the steering knuckle to the lower ball stud.

8. Install the brake caliper, if removed.

9. Install the ball stud nut and torque it to 80-100 ft. lbs. plus the additional torque necessary to align the cotter pin hole. Do not exceed 130 ft. lbs. or back the nut off to align the holes with the pin.

10. Install a new lube fitting and lubricate the new joint.

11. Install the tire and wheel.

12. Lower the vehicle.

1988–90 C SERIES

1. Raise and support the vehicle safely. Properly support the lower control arm, using the necessary equipment. The control arm must be supported so that the spring and the control arm remain intact.

2. Remove the tire and wheel assembly. As required, remove the brake caliper and position it to the side.

3. Remove the cotter pin and the lower ball joint retaining bolt. Using the proper tool separate the ball joint from its mounting. Support the knuckle assembly so that its weight will not damage the brake hose.

4. Remove the rivets from the ball joint assembly, using the proper tools. Remove the ball joint from the control arm.

To install:

5. Start the new ball joint into the control arm.

6. Force the ball joint into position using a screw-type forcing tool. The ball joint will bottom in the control arm. The grease seal should face inboard.

7. Start ball stud into the knuckle. Install the nut and tighten it to 90 ft. lbs. Advance the nut to align the cotter pin hole and insert the new cotter pin. Never back off the nut to align the cotter pin hole; always advance it!

8. Install the brake caliper, if removed.

9. Install a new lube fitting and lubricate the new joint.

10. Install the wheel.

11. Lower the vehicle.

12. Check the front end alignment.

Inspection

1. Support the weight of the control arm at the wheel hub.

2. Measure the distance between the tip of the ball joint stud and the grease fitting below the ball joint.

3. Move the support to the control arm and allow the hub and drum to hang free. Measure the distance again. If the variation between the 2 measurements exceeds $3/32$ in. (2.38mm) the ball joint should be replaced.

1988–90 K SERIES

1. Raise and support the vehicle safely.

2. Remove the wheel.

3. Remove the splash shield from the knuckle.

4. Disconnect the the inner tie rod end from the relay rod using a ball joint separator.

5. Remove the hub nut and washer. Insert a long drift or dowel through the vanes in the brake rotor to hold the rotor in place.

6. Remove the axle shaft inner flange bolts.

7. Using a puller, force the outer end of the axle shaft out of the hub. Remove the shaft.

8. Using a $1/8$ in. drill bit, drill a pilot hole through each ball joint rivet.

9. Drill out the rivets with a $1/2$ in. drill bit. Punch out any remaining rivet material.

10. Remove the cotter pin and nut from the ball stud.

11. Support the lower control arm with a floor jack.

12. Matchmark the both torsion bar adjustment bolt positions.

13. Using tool J-36202, increase the tension on the adjusting arm.

14. Remove the adjustment bolt and retaining plate.

15. Move the tool aside.

16. Slide the torsion bars forward.

17. Using a screw-type forcing tool, separate the ball joint from the knuckle.

To install:

18. Position the new ball joint on the control arm.

NOTE: Service replacement ball joints come with nuts and bolts to replace the rivets.

19. Install the bolts and nuts. Tighten the nuts to 45 ft. lbs.

NOTE: The bolts are inserted from the bottom.

20. Start the ball stud into the knuckle. Make sure it is squarely seated. Install the ball stud nut and pull the ball stud into the knuckle with the nut. Don't final-torque the nut yet.

21. Using tool J-36202, increase tension on both torsion bars.

22. Install the adjustment retainer plate and bolt on both torsion bars.

23. Set the adjustment bolt to the marked position.

24. Release the tension on the torsion bar until the load is take up by the adjustment bolt.

25. Remove the tool.

26. Position the shaft in the hub and install the washer and hub nut. Leave the drift in the rotor vanes and tighten the hub nut to 175 ft. lbs.

27. Install the flange bolts. Tighten them to 59 ft. lbs. Remove the drift.

28. Connect the inner tie rod end at the steering relay rod. Torque the nut to 35 ft. lbs.

29. Install the splash shield.

30. Install the wheel.

31. Lower the vehicle. Once the weight of the vehicle is on the wheels:

   a. Lift the front bumper about 38mm and let it drop.

   b. Repeat this procedure 2 or 3 more times.

   c. Draw a line on the side of the lower control arm from the centerline of the control arm pivot shaft, dead level to the outer end of the control arm.

   d. Measure the distance between the lowest corner of the steering knuckle and the line on the control arm. Record the figure.

   e. Push down about 38mm on the front bumper and let it return. Repeat the procedure 2 or 3 more times.

   f. Re-measure the distance at the control arm.

   g. Determine the average of the 2 measurements. The average distance should be 73.6mm ± 6mm.

   h. If the figure is correct, tighten the control arm pivot nuts to 94 ft. lbs.

   i. If the figure is not correct, tighten the pivot bolts to 94 ft. lbs. and have the front end alignment corrected.

Upper and Lower Ball Joint

Removal and Installation

1986 K SERIES AND 1987–90 V SERIES

1. Raise and support the vehicle safely.

2. Remove the wheels.

3. Remove the locking hubs.

4. Remove the spindle.

5. Disconnect the tie rod end from the knuckle.

6. Remove the knuckle-to-steering arm nuts and adapters.

7. Remove the steering arm from the knuckle.

8. Remove the cotter pins and nuts from the upper and lower ball joints.

NOTE: Do not remove the adjusting ring from the knuckle. If it is necessary to loosen the ring to remove the knuckle, don't loosen it more than 2 threads. The non-hardened threads in the yoke can be easily damaged by the hardened threads in the adjusting ring if caution is not used during knuckle removal

9. Insert the wedge-shaped end of the heavy prybar, or wedge-type ball joint tool, between the lower ball joint and the yoke. Drive the prybar in to break the knuckle free.

10. Repeat the procedure at the upper ball joint.

11. Lift off the knuckle.

12. Secure the knuckle in a vise.

13. Remove the snapring from the lower ball joint. Using tools J-9519-30, J-23454-1 and J-23454-4, or their equivalent screw-type forcing tool, force the lower ball joint from the knuckle.

14. Using tools J-9519-30, J-23454-3 and J-23454-4, or their equivalent screw-type forcing tool, force the upper ball joint from the knuckle.

To install:

15. Position the lower ball joint (the one without the cotter pin hole) squarely in the knuckle. Using tools J-9519-30, J-23454-2 and J-23454-3, or their equivalent screw-type forcing tool, force the lower ball joint into the knuckle until it is fully seated.

16. Install the snapring.

17. Position the upper ball joint (the one with the cotter pin hole) squarely in the knuckle. Using tools J-9519-30, J-23454-2 and J-23454-3, or their equivalent screw-type forcing tool, force the upper ball joint into the knuckle until it is fully seated.

18. Position the knuckle on the yoke.

19. Start the ball joints into their sockets. Place the nuts onto the ball studs. The nut with the cotter pin slot is the upper nut. Tighten the lower nut to 30 ft. lbs., for now.

20. Using tool J-23447, tighten the adjusting ring to 50 ft. lbs.

21. Tighten the upper nut to 100 ft. lbs. Install a new cotter pin. Never loosen the nut to align the cotter pin hole; always tighten it.

22. Tighten the lower nut to 70 ft. lbs.

23. Attach the steering arm to the knuckle using adapters and new nuts. Torque the nuts to 90 ft. lbs.

24. Connect the tie rod end to the knuckle.

25. Install the spindle.

26. Install the hub/rotor assembly and wheel bearings. Adjust the bearings.

27. Install the locking hubs.

28. Install the wheel.

29. Check the front end alignment.

Upper Control Arm

Removal and Installation

1986 C SERIES, 1987–90 R SERIES AND VAN

1. Note and record the amount of shims. These shims must be installed in the same location as removed. Remove the nuts and the shims.

2. Raise and support the vehicle safely. Properly support the lower control arm, using the necessary equipment. The control arm must be supported so that the spring and the control arm remain intact.

3. Remove the tire and wheel assembly. Remove the brake caliper assembly and position it to the side. Loosen the upper ball joint from the steering knuckle, using the proper tool. Support the hub assembly.

4. Remove the upper control arm retaining bolts. Remove the upper control arm from the vehicle.

To install:

5. Place the control arm in position and install the nuts. Before tightening the nuts, insert the caster and camber shims in the same order as when installed.

6. Install the nuts securing the control arm shaft studs to the crossmember bracket. Tighten the nuts to 70 ft. lbs. for 10/1500 and 20/2500 series; 105 ft. lbs. for 30/3500 series.

7. Install the ball stud nut. Torque the nut to 90 ft. lbs. for 10/1500 series and 20/2500 series; 130 ft. lbs. for 30/3500 series.

8. Install the cotter pin. Never back off the nut to install the cotter pin. Always advance it.

9. Install the brake caliper. Remove the spring compressor.

10. Install the wheel.

11. Check the front end alignment.

1988–90 C/K SERIES

1. Raise and support the vehicle safely.

2. Support the lower control arm with a floor jack.

3. Remove the wheel.

4. Unbolt the brake hose bracket from the control arm.

5. Remove the air cleaner extension.

6. Remove the cotter pin from the upper control arm ball stud and loosen the stud nut until the bottom surface of the nut is slightly below the end of the stud.

7. Install a spring compressor on the coil spring for safety.

8. Using a screw-type forcing tool, break loose the ball joint from the knuckle.

9. Remove the nuts and bolts securing the control arm to the frame brackets.

10. Tape the shims and spacers together and tag for proper reassembly. The 35 Series bushings are replaceable. The 15/25 Series bushings are welded in place.

To install:

11. Place the control arm in position and install the shims, bolts and new nuts. Both bolt heads must be inboard of the control arm brackets. Tighten the nuts finger tighte for now.

NOTE: Do not torque the bolts yet. The bolts must be torque with the vehicle at its proper ride height.

12. Install the ball stud nut. Torque the nut to 90 ft. lbs. Install the cotter pin. Never back off the nut to install the cotter pin. Always advance it.

13. Install the brake caliper.

14. Remove the spring compressor or safety chain.

15. Install the wheel.

16. Install the brake hose.

17. Install the air cleaner extension.

18. Install the battery ground cable.

19. Lower the vehicle. Once the weight of the vehicle is on the wheels:

   a. Lift the front bumper about 38mm and let it drop.

   b. Repeat this procedure 2 or 3 more times.

   c. Draw a line on the side of the lower control arm from the centerline of the control arm pivot shaft, dead level to the outer end of the control arm.

   d. Measure the distance between the lowest corner of the steering knuckle and the line on the control arm. Record the figure.

   e. Push down about 38mm on the front bumper and let it return. Repeat the procedure 2 or 3 more times.

   f. Re-measure the distance at the control arm.

   g. Determine the average of the 2 measurements. The average distance should be 73.6mm ± 6mm.

   h. If the figure is correct, tighten the control arm pivot nuts to 88 ft. lbs.

   i. If the figure is not correct, tighten the pivot bolts to 88 ft. lbs. and check the front end alignment.

Lower Control Arm

Removal and Installation

1986 C SERIES, 1987–90 R SERIES AND VAN

1. Raise and support the vehicle safely. Properly support the

lower control arm assembly. Remove the tire and wheel assembly. Remove the brake caliper and position it to the side.

2. Remove the coil spring. Remove the lower ball joint cotter pin and retaining nut. Using the proper tool, separate the lower ball joint from the steering knuckle.

3. Remove the lower control arm from the vehicle.

To install:

4. Install the lower control arm. Torque the U-bolts to 85 ft. lbs.

5. Install the ball stud nut. Torque the nut to 90 ft. lbs. for 10/1500 series and 20/2500 series; 130 ft. lbs. for 30/3500 series. Install the cotter pin. Never back off the nut to install the cotter pin. Always advance it.

6. Install the brake caliper.

7. Install the spring.

1988–90 C SERIES

1. Raise and support the vehicle safely. Remove the tire and wheel assembly. Properly support the lower control arm assembly. Remove the coil spring.

2. Remove the lower ball joint cotter pin and retaining nut. Using the proper tool, seperate the lower ball joint from the steering knuckle.

3. Remove the lower control arm from the vehicle.

To install:

4. Slowly raise the jack and lower the control arm. Guide the control arm into place with a prybar.

5. Install the pivot shaft bolts, front one first. The bolts must be installed with the heads towards the front of the vehicle. Remove the safety chain or spring compressors.

NOTE: Do not torque the bolts yet. The bolts must be torque with the vehicle at its proper ride height.

6. Remove the jack.

7. Connect the stabilizer bar to the lower control arm. Torque the nuts to 13 ft. lbs.

8. Install the shock absorber.

9. Install the wheel.

10. Lower the vehicle. Once the weight of the vehicle is on the wheels:

    a. Lift the front bumper about 38mm and let it drop.

    b. Repeat this procedure 2 or 3 more times.

    c. Draw a line on the side of the lower control arm from the centerline of the control arm pivot shaft, dead level to the outer end of the control arm.

    d. Measure the distance between the lowest corner of the steering knuckle and the line on the control arm. Record the figure.

    e. Push down about 38mm on the front bumper and let it return. Repeat the procedure 2 or 3 more times.

    f. Re-measure the distance at the control arm.

    g. Determine the average of the 2 measurements. The average distance should be 73.6mm ± 6mm.

    h. If the figure is correct, tighten the control arm pivot nuts to 96 ft. lbs.

    i. If the figure is not correct, tighten the pivot bolts to 96 ft. lbs. and have the front end alignment corrected.

1988–90 K SERIES

1. Raise and support the vehicle safely.

2. Remove the wheel.

3. Remove the splash shield from the knuckle.

4. Disconnect the stabilizer bar from ther control arm.

5. Remove the shock absorber.

6. Disconnect the tie rod end from the relay rod.

7. Remove the hub nut and washer. Insert a long drift or dowel through the vanes in the brake rotor to hold the rotor in place.

8. Remove the axle shaft inner flange bolts.

9. Using a puller, force the outer end of the axle shaft out of the hub. Remove the shaft.

10. Support the lower control arm with a floor jack.

11. Matchmark the both torsion bar adjustment bolt positions.

12. Using tool J-36202, increase the tension on the adjusting arm.

13. Remove the adjustment bolt and retaining plate.

14. Move the tool aside.

15. Slide the torsion bars forward.

16. Remove the adjusting arm.

17. Remove the cotter pin from the lower ball stud and loosen the nut.

18. Loosen the lower ball stud in the steering knuckle using a ball joint stud removal tool. When the stud is loose, remove the nut from the stud. It may be necessary to remove the brake caliper and wire it to the frame to gain clearance.

19. Remove the control arm-to-frame bracket bolts, nuts and washers.

20. Remove the lower control arm and torsion bar as a unit.

21. Separate the control arm and torsion bar.

22. On 15 and 25 Series, the bushings are not replaceable. If they are damaged, the control arm will have to be replaced. On 35 Series, proceed as follows:

    a. FRONT BUSHING: Unbend the crimps with a punch. Force out the bushings with tools J-36618-2, J-9519-23, J-36618-4 and 36618-1.

    b. REAR BUSHING: Force out the bushings with tools J-36618-5, J-9519-23, J-36618-3 and J-36618-2. There are no crimps.

To install:

23. On 35 Series, install a new front bushings, then a new rear bushing using the removal tools.

24. Assemble the control arm and torsion bar.

25. Raise the control arm assembly into position. Insert the front leg of the control arm into the crossmember first, then the rear leg into the frame bracket.

26. Install the bolts, front one first. The bolts must be installed with the front bolt head heads towards the front of the vehicle and the rear bolt head towards the rear of the vehicle!

NOTE: Do not torque the bolts yet. The bolts must be torque with the vehicle at its proper ride height.

27. Start the ball joint into the knuckle. Make sure it is squarely seated. Tighten the nut to 96 ft. lbs. and install a new cotter pin. Always advance the nut to align the cotter pin hole. Never back it off.

28. Install the adjuster arm.

29. Using tool J-36202, increase tension on both torsion bars.

30. Install the adjustment retainer plate and bolt on both torsion bars.

31. Set the adjustment bolt to the marked position.

32. Release the tension on the torsion bar until the load is take up by the adjustment bolt.

33. Remove the tool.

34. Position the shaft in the hub and install the washer and hub nut. Leave the drift in the rotor vanes and tighten the hub nut to 175 ft. lbs.

35. Install the flange bolts. Tighten them to 59 ft. lbs. Remove the drift.

36. Connect the inner tie rod end at the steering relay rod. Torque the nut to 35 ft. lbs.

37. Install the splash shield.

38. Connect the stabilizer bar to the lower control arm. Torque the nuts to 13 ft. lbs.

39. Install the shock absorber.

40. Install the wheel.

41. Lower the vehicle. Once the weight of the vehicle is on the wheels:

    a. Lift the front bumper about 38mm and let it drop.

    b. Repeat this procedure 2 or 3 more times.

c. Draw a line on the side of the lower control arm from the centerline of the control arm pivot shaft, dead level to the outer end of the control arm.

d. Measure the distance between the lowest corner of the steering knuckle and the line on the control arm. Record the figure.

e. Push down about 38mm on the front bumper and let it return. Repeat the procedure 2 or 3 more times.

f. Re-measure the distance at the control arm.

g. Determine the average of the 2 measurements. The average distance should be 73.6mm ± 6mm.

h. If the figure is correct, tighten the control arm nuts to 135 ft. lbs.

i. If the figure is not correct, tighten the pivot bolts to 135 ft. lbs. and have the front end alignment corrected.

Steering Knuckle

Removal and Installation

1986 C SERIES, 1987–90 R SERIES AND VAN

1. Raise and support the vehicle safely.
2. Remove the wheels.
3. Dismount the caliper and suspend it out of the way without disconnecting the brake lines.
4. Remove the hub/rotor assembly.
5. Unbolt the splash shield and discard the old gasket.
6. Using a ball joint separator, disconnect the tie rod end from the knuckle.
7. Position a floor jack under the lower control arm, near the spring seat. Raise the jack until it just takes up the weight of the suspension, compressing the spring. Safety-chain the coil spring to the lower arm.
8. Remove the upper and lower ball joint nuts.
9. Using tool J-23742, or equivalent, break loose the upper ball joint from the knuckle.
10. Raise the upper control arm just enough to disconnect the ball joint.
11. Using the afore-mentioned tool, break loose the lower ball joint.
12. Lift the knuckle off of the lower ball joint.
13. Inspect and clean the ball stud bores in the knuckle. Make sure that there are no cracks or burrs. If the knuckle is damaged in any way, replace it.
14. Check the spindle for wear, heat discoloration or damage. If at all damaged, replace it.

To install:

15. Maneuver the knuckle onto both ball joints.
16. Install both nuts. On 10/1500 series and 20/2500 series, torque the upper nut to 50 ft. lbs. and the lower nut to 90 ft. lbs. On 30/3500 series, torque both nuts to 90 ft. lbs.
17. Install the cotter pins. Always advance the nut to align the cotter pin hole. Never back it off. On the upper nut which was originally torque to 50 ft. lbs., don't exceed 90 ft. lbs. when aligning the hole. On nuts torqued originally to 90 ft. lbs., don't exceed 130 ft. lbs. to align the hole.
18. Remove the floor jack.
19. Install a new gasket and the splash shield. Torque the bolts to 10 ft. lbs.
20. Connect the tie rod end.
21. Install the hub/rotor assembly.
22. Install the caliper.
23. Adjust the wheel bearings.
24. Install the wheels.
25. Check the alignment.

1986 K SERIES, 1987–90 V SERIES

10/1500 and 20/2500 Series

1. Raise and support the vehicle safely.
2. Remove the wheels.

3. Remove the locking hubs.
4. Remove the spindle.
5. Disconnect the tie rod end from the knuckle.
6. Remove the knuckle-to-steering arm nuts and adapters.
7. Remove the steering arm from the knuckle.
8. Remove the cotter pins and nuts from the upper and lower ball joints.

NOTE: Do not remove the adjusting ring from the knuckle. If it is necessary to loosen the ring to remove the knuckle, don't loosen it more than 2 threads. The non-hardened threads in the yoke can be easily damaged by the hardened threads in the adjusting ring if caution is not used during knuckle removal!

9. Insert the wedge-shaped end of the heavy prybar, or wedge-type ball joint tool, between the lower ball joint and the yoke. Drive the prybar in to break the knuckle free.
10. Repeat the procedure at the upper ball joint.
11. Lift off the knuckle.

To install:

12. Position the knuckle on the yoke.
13. Start the ball joints into their sockets. Place the nuts onto the ball studs. The nut with the cotter pin slot is the upper nut. Tighten the lower nut to 30 ft. lbs., for now.
14. Using tool J-23447, tighten the adjusting ring to 50 ft. lbs.
15. Tighten the upper nut to 100 ft. lbs. Install a new cotter pin. Never loosen the nut to align the cotter pin hole; always tighten it.
16. Tighten the lower nut to 70 ft. lbs.
17. Attach the steering arm to the knuckle using adapters and new nuts. Torque the nuts to 90 ft. lbs.
18. Connect the tie rod end to the knuckle.
19. Install the spindle.
20. Install the hub/rotor assembly and wheel bearings. Adjust the bearings.
21. Install the locking hubs.
22. Install the wheel.

30/3500 Series

1. Raise and support the vehicle safely.
2. Remove the wheel.
3. Remove the hub/rotor/bearings assembly.
4. Remove the locking hubs.
5. Remove the spindle. See the procedure above.
6. Remove the upper cap from the right side knuckle and/or steering arm from the left side knuckle, by loosening the bolts (right side) and/or nuts (left side) a little at a time in an alternating pattern. This will safely relieve spring pressure under the cap and/or arm. Once spring pressure is relieved, remove the bolts and/or nuts, washers and cap and/or steering arm.
7. Remove the gasket and compression spring.
8. Remove the bolts and washers and remove the lower bearing cap and the lower kingpin.
9. Remove the upper kingpin bushing by pulling it out through the knuckle.
10. Remove the knuckle from the axle yoke.
11. Remove the retainer from the knuckle.
12. Using a large breaker bar and adapter J-26871, remove the upper kingpin from the axle yoke by applying 500-600 ft. lbs. of torque to the kingpin to break it free.
13. Using a hammer and blunt drift, drive out the retainer, race bearing and seal from the axle yoke. These are driven out all at once.

To install:

14. Using tool J-7817, install a new retainer and race in the axle yoke.
15. Fill the recessed area in the retainer and race with the same grease used on the wheel bearings.
16. Completely pack the upper yoke roller bearing with wheel bearing grease. A cone-type bearing packer is preferable, but the

bearing may be packed by hand. See the Wheel Bearing PAcking procedure.

17. Install the bearing and a new seal in the upper axle yoke, using a bearing driver such as J-22301. Don't distort the seal. It should protrude slightly above the yoke when fully seated.
18. Using adapter tool J-28871, install the upper kingpin. The kingpin must be torque to 550 ft. lbs.
19. Position the knuckle in the yoke. Working through the knuckle, install a new felt seal over the kingpin and position the knuckle on the kingpin.
20. Install the bushing over the kingpin.
21. Install the compression spring, gasket, bearing cap and/or steering arm and bolts and/or nut and washer. Torque the bolts and/or nuts, in an alternating pattern, to 80 ft. lbs.
22. Install the lower bearing cap and kingpin. Torque the bolts to 80 ft. lbs. in an alternating pattern.
23. Thoroughly lube both king pins through the grease fittings.
24. Install the spindle.
25. Install the hub/rotor/bearing assembly. Adjust the bearings.
27. Install the locking hubs.
28. Install the wheel.
29. Check the front end alignment.

1988–90 C SERIES

1. Raise and support the vehicle safely. Let the control arms hang freely.
2. Remove the wheels.
3. Disconnect the tie rod end from the knuckle.
4. Dismount the caliper and suspend it out of the way without disconnecting the brake lines.
5. Remove the hub/rotor assembly.
6. Unbolt the splash shield from the knuckle and discard the old gasket.
7. If a new knuckle is being installed, remove the knuckle seal carefully, without damaging it.
8. Position a floor jack under the lower control arm, near the spring seat. Raise the jack until it *just* takes up the weight of the suspension, compressing the spring. Safety-chain the coil spring to the lower arm.
9. Remove the upper and lower ball joint nuts.
10. Using tool J-23742, or equivalent, break loose the upper ball joint from the knuckle.
11. Raise the upper control arm just enough to disconnect the ball joint.
12. Using the afore-mentioned tool, break loose the lower ball joint.
13. Lift the knuckle off of the lower ball joint.
14. Inspect and clean the ball stud bores in the knuckle. Make sure that there are no cracks or burrs. If the knuckle is damaged in any way, replace it.
15. Check the spindle for wear, heat discoloration or damage. If at all damaged, replace it.
To install:
16. Maneuver the knuckle onto both ball joints.
17. Install both nuts. Torque the nuts to 90 ft. lbs.
18. Install new cotter pins. Always advance the nut to align the cotter pin hole. Never back it off.
19. Install the knuckle seal.
20. Remove the floor jack.
21. Install a new gasket and the splash shield. Torque the bolts to 12 ft. lbs.
22. Connect the tie rod end.
23. Install the hub/rotor assembly.
24. Install the caliper.
25. Adjust the wheel bearings.
26. Install the wheels.
27. Have the alignment checked.

1988–90 K SERIES

1. Disconnect the negative battery cable.
2. Remove ⅔ of the brake fluid from the reservoir.
3. Raise and support the vehicle safely.
4. Remove the wheel, caliper and brake disc.
5. Remove the drive axle nut and washer.
6. Remove the tie rod nut and remove the tie rod end from the end of the washer.
7. Remove the hub and bearing assembly, using a puller.
8. Remove the drive axle.
9. Remove the splash shield.
10. Remove the splash shield bolts and splash shield.
11. Support the lower control arm, using suitable equipment.
12. Remove the upper ball joint nut and remove the upper ball joint.
13. Remove the knuckle and the knuckle seal, as requiered.
To install:
14. Install the seal into the knuckle, using tool J–36605, or equivalent.
15. Install the knuckle to the upper and lower ball joints and tighten the nuts to 94 ft. lbs. Tighten the nuts to align the new cotter pin, but do not tighten more than $1/6$ turn. Bend the pin ends against the nut flats.
17. Install the splash shield and tighten the bolts to 12 ft. lbs.
18. Install the drive axle.
19. Install the hub and bearing assembly. Align the threaded holes and tighten the bolts to 66 ft. lbs.
20. Install the tie rod end to the knuckle, and tighten the tie rod nut to 35 ft. lbs.
21. Install the washer and axle nut and torque to 173 ft. lbs.
22. Install the brake disc and caliper.
23. Install the axle joint cover.
24. Install the wheel and torque the wheel nuts to 90 ft. lbs for all except the K300 with dual wheels. For the K300 with dual wheels, torque to 120 ft. lbs.
25. Lower the vehicle and check the front end alignment.

Stabilizer Bar

Removal and Installation

1986 C SERIES, 1987–90 R SERIES AND VAN

1. Raise and support the vehicle safely. As required, remove the tire and wheel assemblies.
2. Properly support the stabilizer bar assembly. Remove the stabilizer shaft bushing retaining bolts. Remove the stabilizer link bushing nuts and bolts.
3. Remove the stabilizer bar from the vehicle.
4. Installation is the reverse of removal. Note, the split in the bushing faces forward. Coat the bushings with silicone grease prior to installation. Install all fasteners finger-tight. When all the fasteners are in place torque all of them to 24 ft. lbs.

1986 K SERIES AND 1987–90 V SERIES

1. Raise and support the vehicle safely.
2. Remove the wheels.
3. Remove the stabilizer bar-to-frame clamps.
4. Remove the stabilizer bar-to-spring plate bolts.
5. Remove the stabilizer bar and bushings.
6. Check the bushings for wear or splitting. Replace any damaged bushings.
7. Installation is the reverse of removal. Note, the split in the bushing faces forward. Coat the bushings with silicone grease prior to installation. Install all fasteners finger-tight. When all the fasteners are in place torque the stabilizer bar-to-frame nuts to 52 ft. lbs. Torque the stabilizer bar-to-spring plate bolts to 133 ft. lbs.

1988–90 C SERIES

NOTE: The end link bushings, bolts and spacers are not interchangeable from left to right, so keep them separate.

1. Raise and support the vehicle safely.
2. Remove the nuts from the end link bolts.
3. Remove the bolts, bushings and spacers.
4. Remove the bracket bolts and remove the stabilizer bar.
5. Inspect the bushings for wear or damage. Replace them as necessary.
6. Installation is the reverse of removal. Coat the bushings with silicone grease prior to assembly. The slit in the bushings faces the front of the vehicle. Torque the frame bracket bolts to 24 ft. lbs.; the end link nuts to 13 ft. lbs.

1988–90 K SERIES

NOTE: The end link bushings, bolts and spacers are not interchangeable from left to right, so keep them separate.

1. Raise and support the vehicle safely.
2. Remove the nuts, bolts, spacer and clamp from the ends.
3. Remove the stabilizer bar and remove the insulator.
4. Inspect all parts for wear or damage and replace them as necessary.
5. Installation is the reverse of removal.
6. Unload the torsion bar using tool J–36202, as noted in torsion bar removal.
7. Coat the bushings with silicone grease prior to assembly. Torque the frame bracket bolts to 24 ft. lbs.; the end link nuts to 12 ft. lbs.

King Pins

Removal and Installation

V30/3500 AND K30/3500 SERIES

1. Remove the hub and spindle as previously outlined. Check the bronze spacer between the axle shaft joint assembly and bearing, if worn it must be replaced.

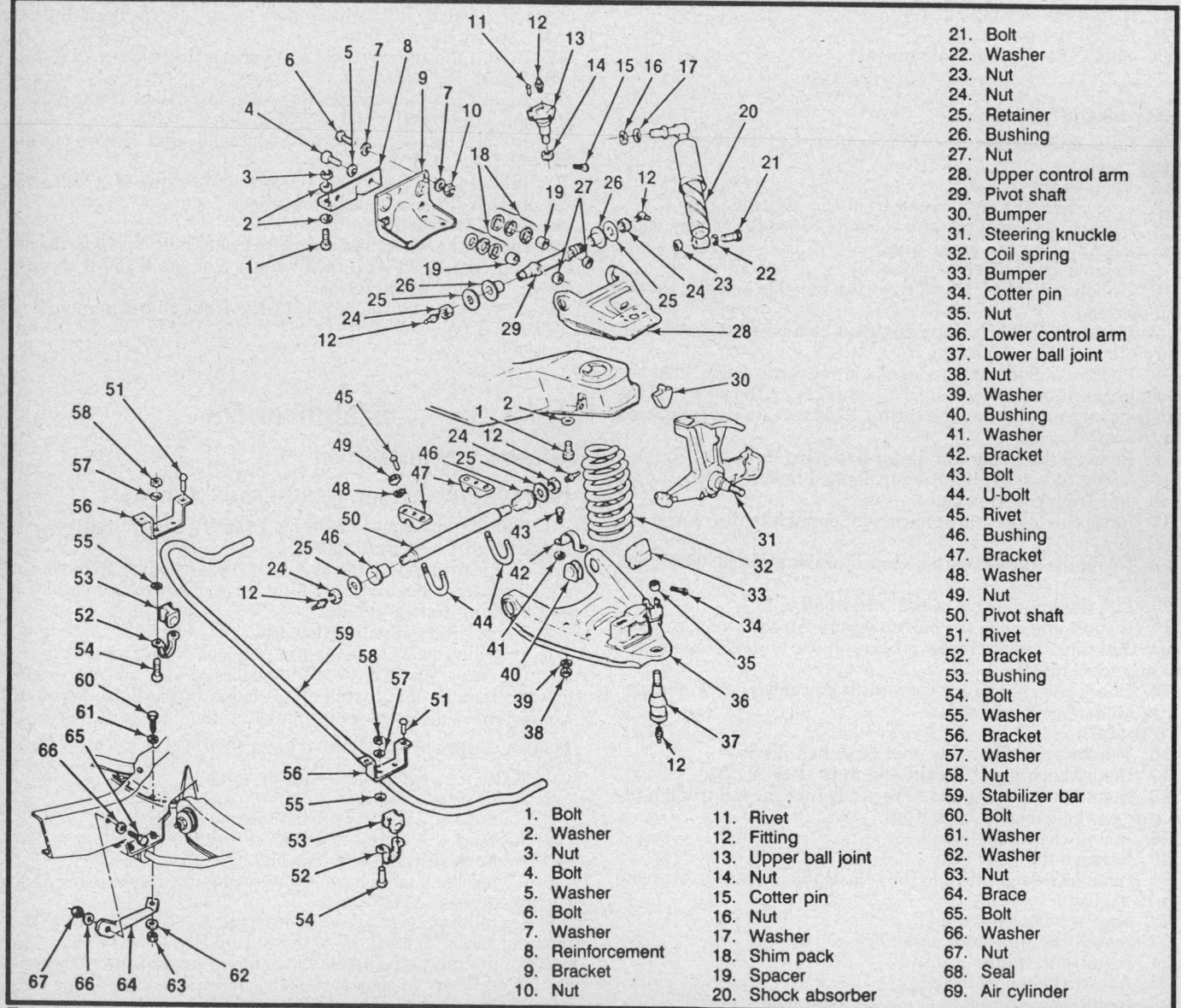

21. Bolt		
22. Washer		
23. Nut		
24. Nut		
25. Retainer		
26. Bushing		
27. Nut		
28. Upper control arm		
29. Pivot shaft		
30. Bumper		
31. Steering knuckle		
32. Coil spring		
33. Bumper		
34. Cotter pin		
35. Nut		
36. Lower control arm		
37. Lower ball joint		
38. Nut		
39. Washer		
40. Bushing		
41. Washer		
42. Bracket		
43. Bolt		
44. U-bolt		
45. Rivet		
46. Bushing		
47. Bracket		
48. Washer		
49. Nut		
50. Pivot shaft		
51. Rivet		
52. Bracket		
53. Bushing		
54. Bolt		
55. Washer		
56. Bracket		
57. Washer		
58. Nut		
59. Stabilizer bar		
60. Bolt		
61. Washer		
62. Washer		
63. Nut		
64. Brace		
65. Bolt		
66. Washer		
67. Nut		
68. Seal		
69. Air cylinder		

1. Bolt	11. Rivet
2. Washer	12. Fitting
3. Nut	13. Upper ball joint
4. Bolt	14. Nut
5. Washer	15. Cotter pin
6. Bolt	16. Nut
7. Washer	17. Washer
8. Reinforcement	18. Shim pack
9. Bracket	19. Spacer
10. Nut	20. Shock absorber

Front suspension assembly—1986 C Series and 1987–90 R Series

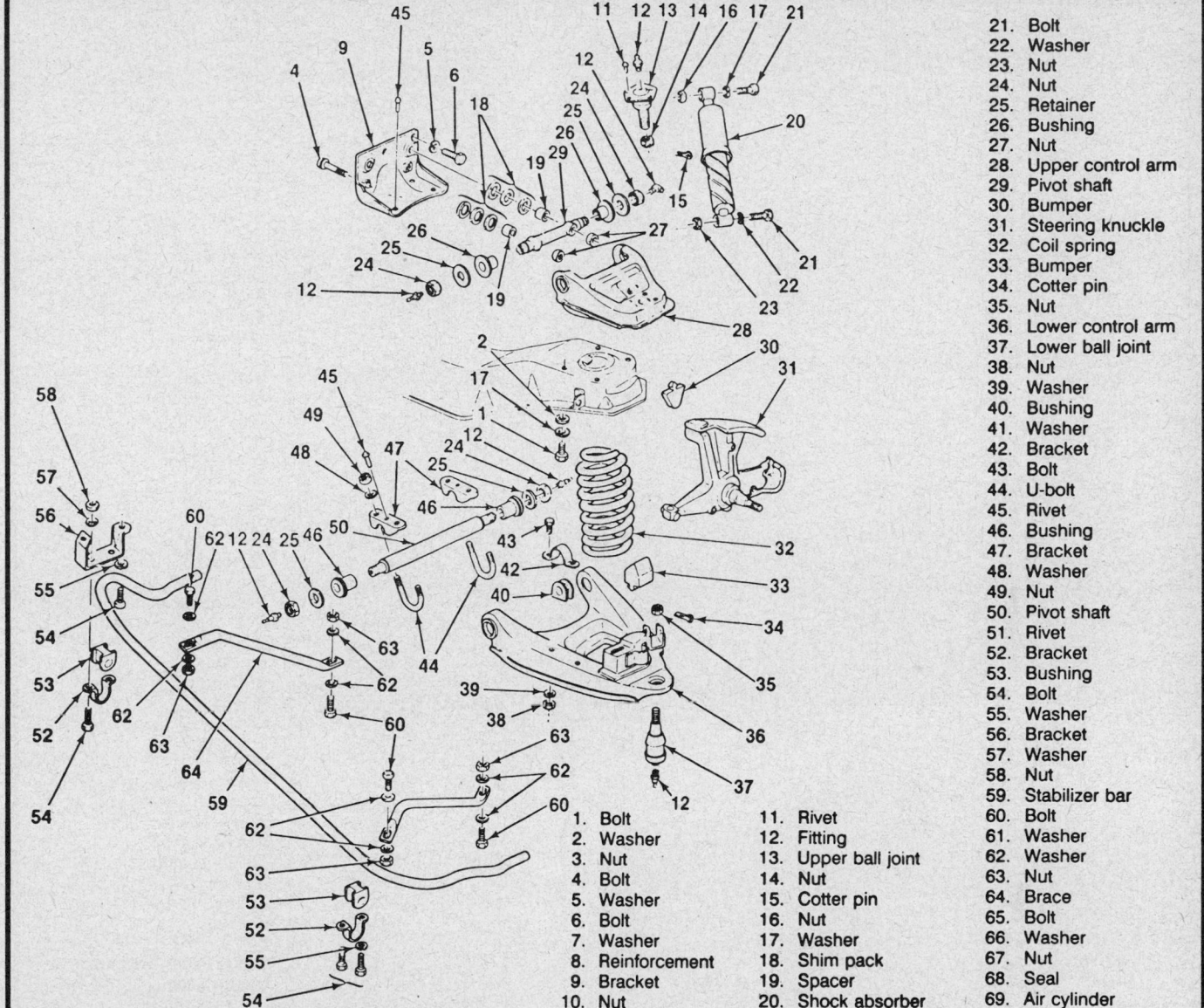

21.	Bolt
22.	Washer
23.	Nut
24.	Nut
25.	Retainer
26.	Bushing
27.	Nut
28.	Upper control arm
29.	Pivot shaft
30.	Bumper
31.	Steering knuckle
32.	Coil spring
33.	Bumper
34.	Cotter pin
35.	Nut
36.	Lower control arm
37.	Lower ball joint
38.	Nut
39.	Washer
40.	Bushing
41.	Washer
42.	Bracket
43.	Bolt
44.	U-bolt
45.	Rivet
46.	Bushing
47.	Bracket
48.	Washer
49.	Nut
50.	Pivot shaft
51.	Rivet
52.	Bracket
53.	Bushing
54.	Bolt
55.	Washer
56.	Bracket
57.	Washer
58.	Nut
59.	Stabilizer bar
60.	Bolt
61.	Washer
62.	Washer
63.	Nut
64.	Brace
65.	Bolt
66.	Washer
67.	Nut
68.	Seal
69.	Air cylinder

1.	Bolt	11.	Rivet	
2.	Washer	12.	Fitting	
3.	Nut	13.	Upper ball joint	
4.	Bolt	14.	Nut	
5.	Washer	15.	Cotter pin	
6.	Bolt	16.	Nut	
7.	Washer	17.	Washer	
8.	Reinforcement	18.	Shim pack	
9.	Bracket	19.	Spacer	
10.	Nut	20.	Shock absorber	

Front suspension assembly – 1986–90 Van

2. Remove the upper king pin cap nuts alternately, as the spring pressure will be forcing the cap up.

3. Remove the cap, compression spring, and gasket. Discard the gasket.

4. Remove the four cap screws from the lower king pin bearing cap. Remove the gearing cap and king pin.

5. Remove the upper king pin tapered bushing and knuckle from the yoke. Remove the felt seal and remove the knuckle.

6. Remove the upper king pin from the yoke with a large breaker bar.

7. Remove the lower king pin bearing cup, cone, grease retainer, and seal. Discard the seal. If the grease retainer is damaged, replace it.

To install:

8. Install the new grease retainer and lower king pin bearing cup using special tool J–7817 or its equivalent.

9. Fill the grease retainer, grease the bearing and install. Install the lower seal using tool J22301 or its equivalent.

NOTE: Do not distort the oil seal. It will protrude slightly from the surface of the yoke when installed.

10. Install the upper king pin using tool J18871 or its equal. Torque to 500–600 ft. lbs.

11. Install the felt seal on the king pin.

12. Install the knuckle and tapered bushing over the king pin.

13. Install the lower bearing cap and king pin. Torque the cap screws to 80 ft. lbs.

14. Place the compression spring on the upper king pin bush-

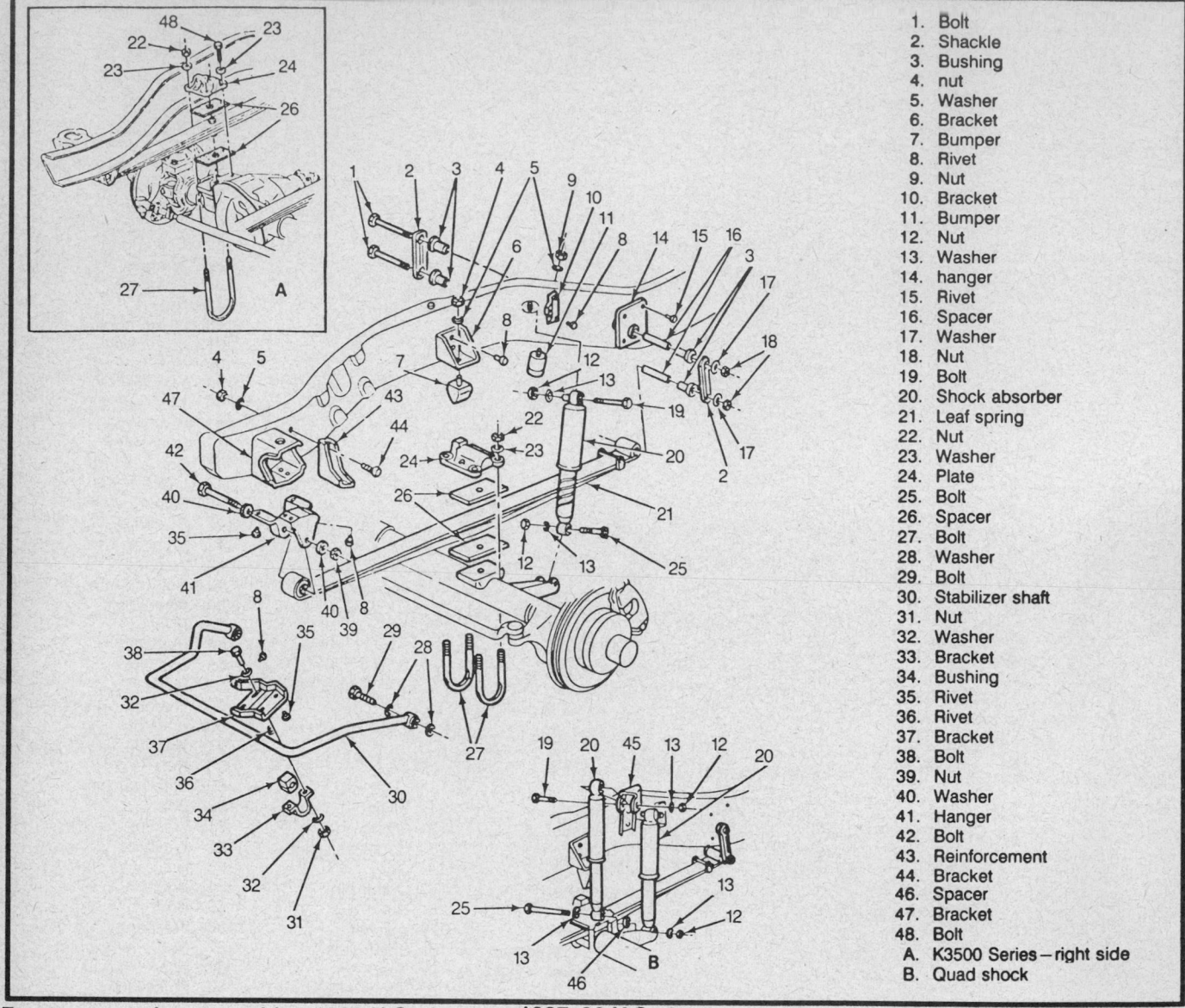

1. Bolt
2. Shackle
3. Bushing
4. nut
5. Washer
6. Bracket
7. Bumper
8. Rivet
9. Nut
10. Bracket
11. Bumper
12. Nut
13. Washer
14. hanger
15. Rivet
16. Spacer
17. Washer
18. Nut
19. Bolt
20. Shock absorber
21. Leaf spring
22. Nut
23. Washer
24. Plate
25. Bolt
26. Spacer
27. Bolt
28. Washer
29. Bolt
30. Stabilizer shaft
31. Nut
32. Washer
33. Bracket
34. Bushing
35. Rivet
36. Rivet
37. Bracket
38. Bolt
39. Nut
40. Washer
41. Hanger
42. Bolt
43. Reinforcement
44. Bracket
46. Spacer
47. Bracket
48. Bolt
A. K3500 Series – right side
B. Quad shock

Front suspension assembly—1986 K Series and 1987–90 V Series

ing. Install the bearing cap with a new gasket. Torque the nuts to 80 ft. lbs.

Front Wheel Bearings

NOTE: For 4WD vehicles, refer to Drive Axle removal and installation procedures.

Removal and Installation

2WD

1. Raise and support the vehicle safely. Remove the tire and wheel assembly.
2. Remove the brake caliper and position it to the side. Remove the dust cover, cotter pin, washer and spindle nut.
3. Remove the outer wheel bearing assembly. Remove the brake rotor. Remove the inner wheel bearing assembly.

4. Installation is the reverse of the removal procedure. When installing new bearings be sure to install new bearing races inside the rotor, using the proper removal and installation tools.
5. Pack new bearings, with the proper grade and type wheel bearing grease. Adjust wheel bearings, as required.

Adjustment

2WD

1. Raise and support the vehicle safely. Remove the dust cap and cotter pin.
2. Tighten the spindle nut to 12 ft. lbs. while turning the tire and wheel assembly. Back off the nut to the just loose position.
3. Hand tighten the spindle nut. Loosen the nut until the cotter pin can be installed in the spindle slot.
4. End play should be 0.001–0.005 inches (except 1988–90 C/K Series) and 0.001–0.008 inches (1988–90 C/K Series).

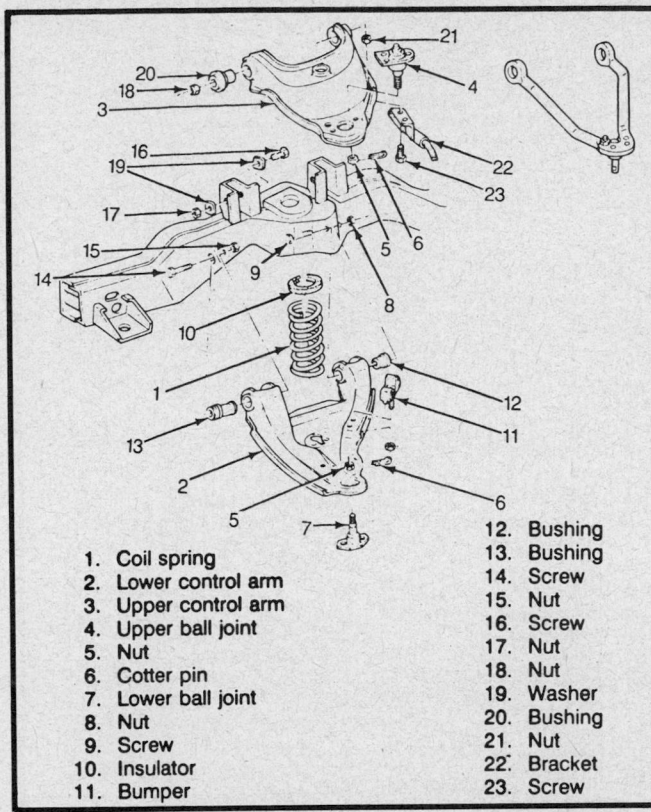

1.	Coil spring	12.	Bushing
2.	Lower control arm	13.	Bushing
3.	Upper control arm	14.	Screw
4.	Upper ball joint	15.	Nut
5.	Nut	16.	Screw
6.	Cotter pin	17.	Nut
7.	Lower ball joint	18.	Nut
8.	Nut	19.	Washer
9.	Screw	20.	Bushing
10.	Insulator	21.	Nut
11.	Bumper	22.	Bracket
		23.	Screw

Front suspension assembly – 1988 – 90 C Series

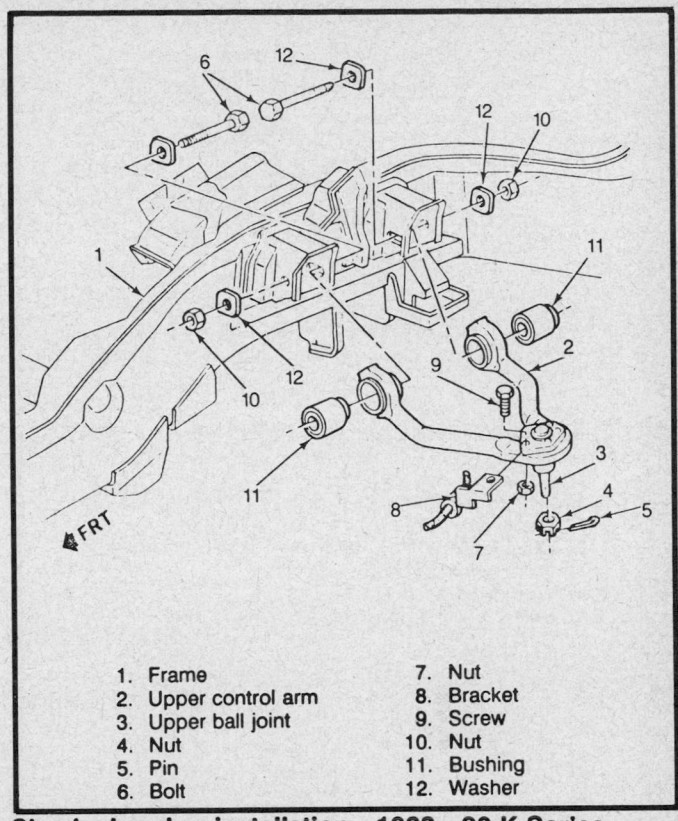

1.	Frame	7.	Nut
2.	Upper control arm	8.	Bracket
3.	Upper ball joint	9.	Screw
4.	Nut	10.	Nut
5.	Pin	11.	Bushing
6.	Bolt	12.	Washer

Shock absorber installation – 1988 – 90 K Series

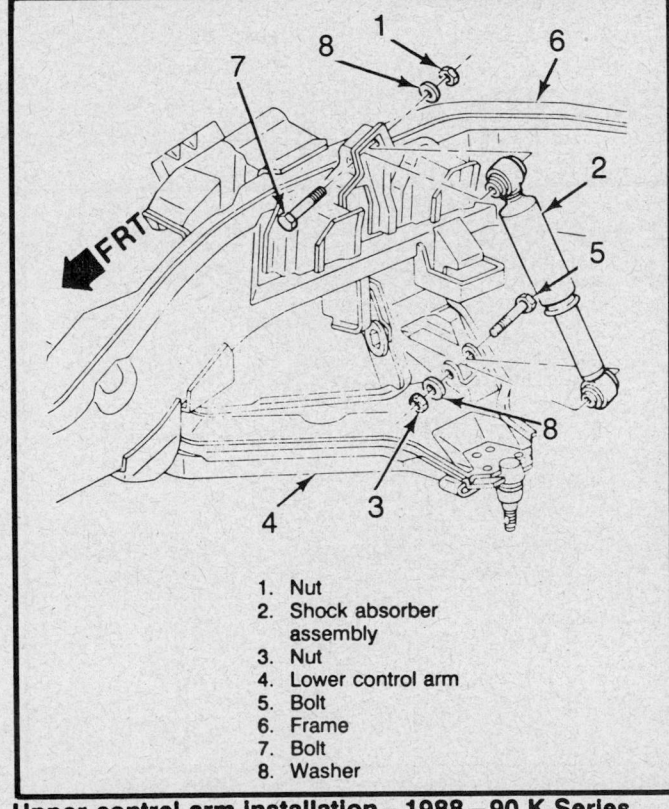

1.	Nut
2.	Shock absorber assembly
3.	Nut
4.	Lower control arm
5.	Bolt
6.	Frame
7.	Bolt
8.	Washer

Upper control arm installation – 1988 – 90 K Series

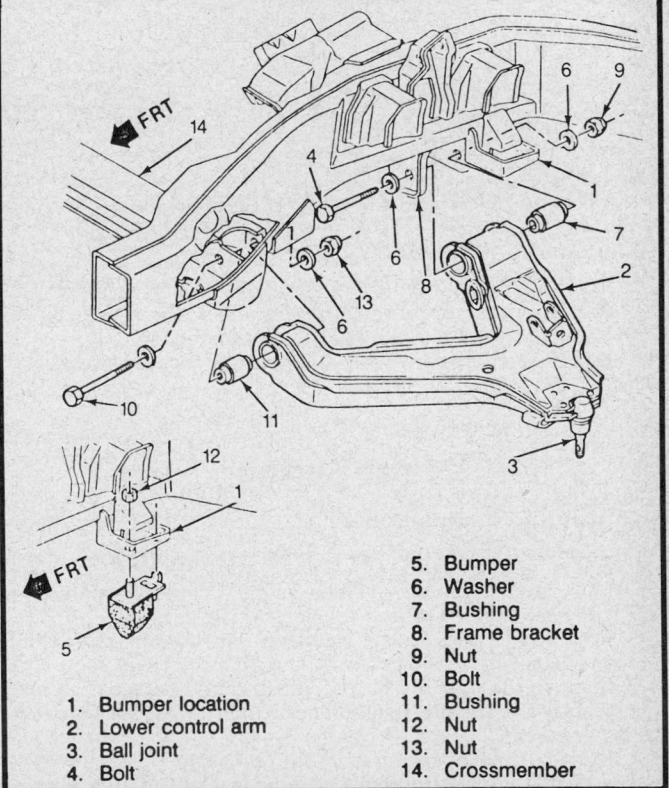

1.	Bumper location	5.	Bumper
2.	Lower control arm	6.	Washer
3.	Ball joint	7.	Bushing
4.	Bolt	8.	Frame bracket
		9.	Nut
		10.	Bolt
		11.	Bushing
		12.	Nut
		13.	Nut
		14.	Crossmember

Lower control arm installation – 1988 – 90 K Series

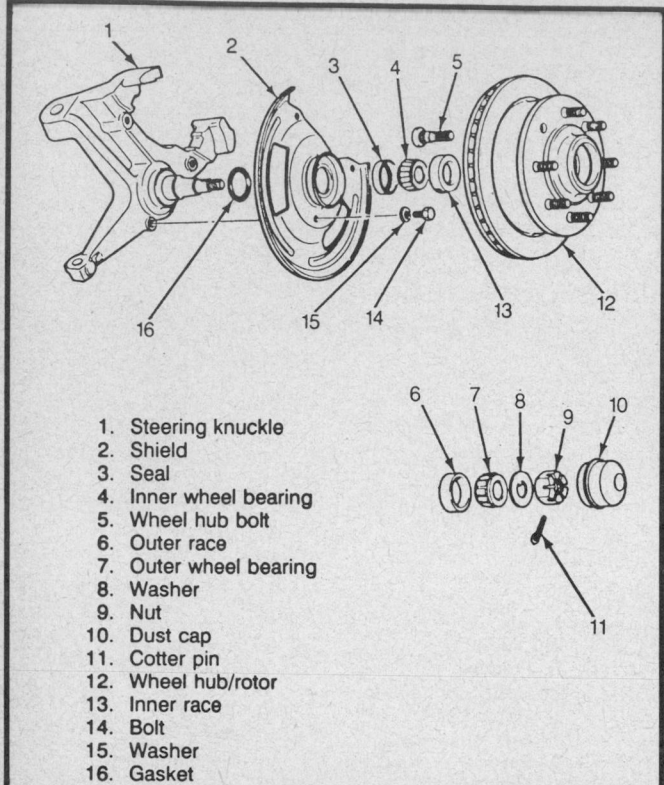

1. Steering knuckle
2. Shield
3. Seal
4. Inner wheel bearing
5. Wheel hub bolt
6. Outer race
7. Outer wheel bearing
8. Washer
9. Nut
10. Dust cap
11. Cotter pin
12. Wheel hub/rotor
13. Inner race
14. Bolt
15. Washer
16. Gasket

Hub and bearing assembly—except 1988–90 C/K Series

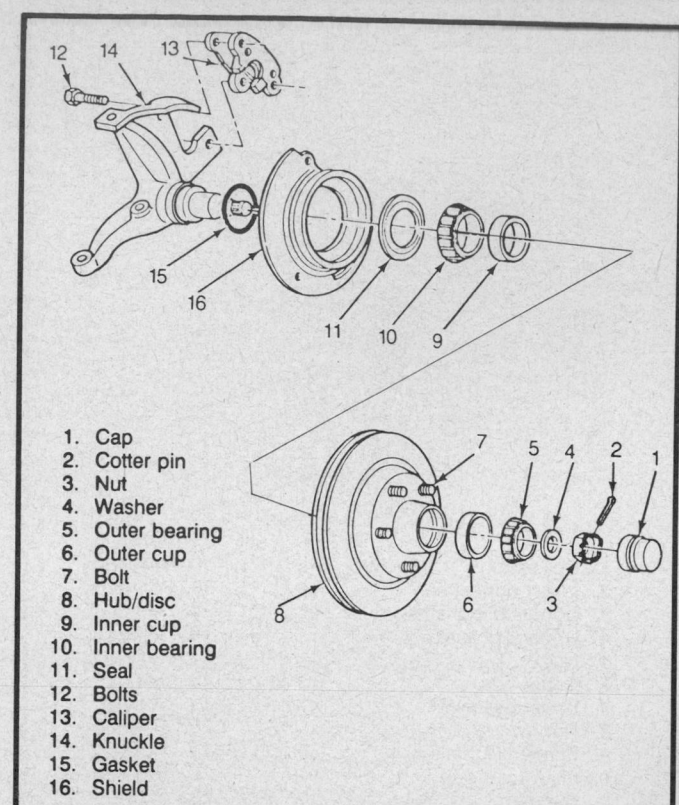

1. Cap
2. Cotter pin
3. Nut
4. Washer
5. Outer bearing
6. Outer cup
7. Bolt
8. Hub/disc
9. Inner cup
10. Inner bearing
11. Seal
12. Bolts
13. Caliper
14. Knuckle
15. Gasket
16. Shield

Hub and bearing assembly—1988–90 C/K Series

REAR SUSPENSION

Shock Absorbers

Removal and Installation

1. Raise and support the vehicle safely. Properly support the rear axle assembly. Remove the lower shock absorber bolt.
3. Remove the shock absorber from the vehicle.
4. Installation is the reverse of the removal procedure.

Leaf Spring

Removal and Installation

1986 C/K SERIES, 1987–90 R/V SERIES AND VAN

1. Raise and support the vehicle safely. Properly support the rear axle assembly to relieve tension on the springs.
2. If equipped, remove the stabilizer bar. Loosen, but do not remove the spring to shackle nut and bolt.
3. Remove the nut and bolt securing the shackle to the rear hanger. Remove the nut and bolt securing the leaf spring to the front hanger.
4. Remove the leaf spring from the front hanger. Remove the nut and bolt securing the shackle to the leaf spring. Remove the shackle.

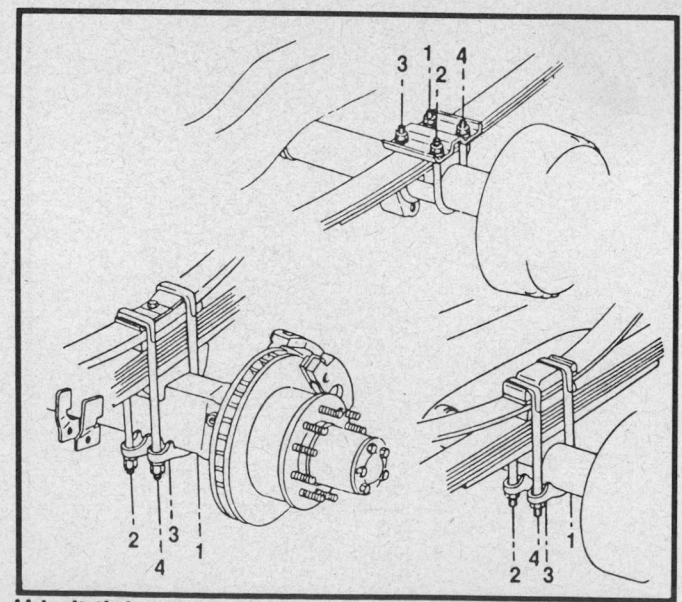

U-bolt tightening sequence—except 1988–90 C/K Series

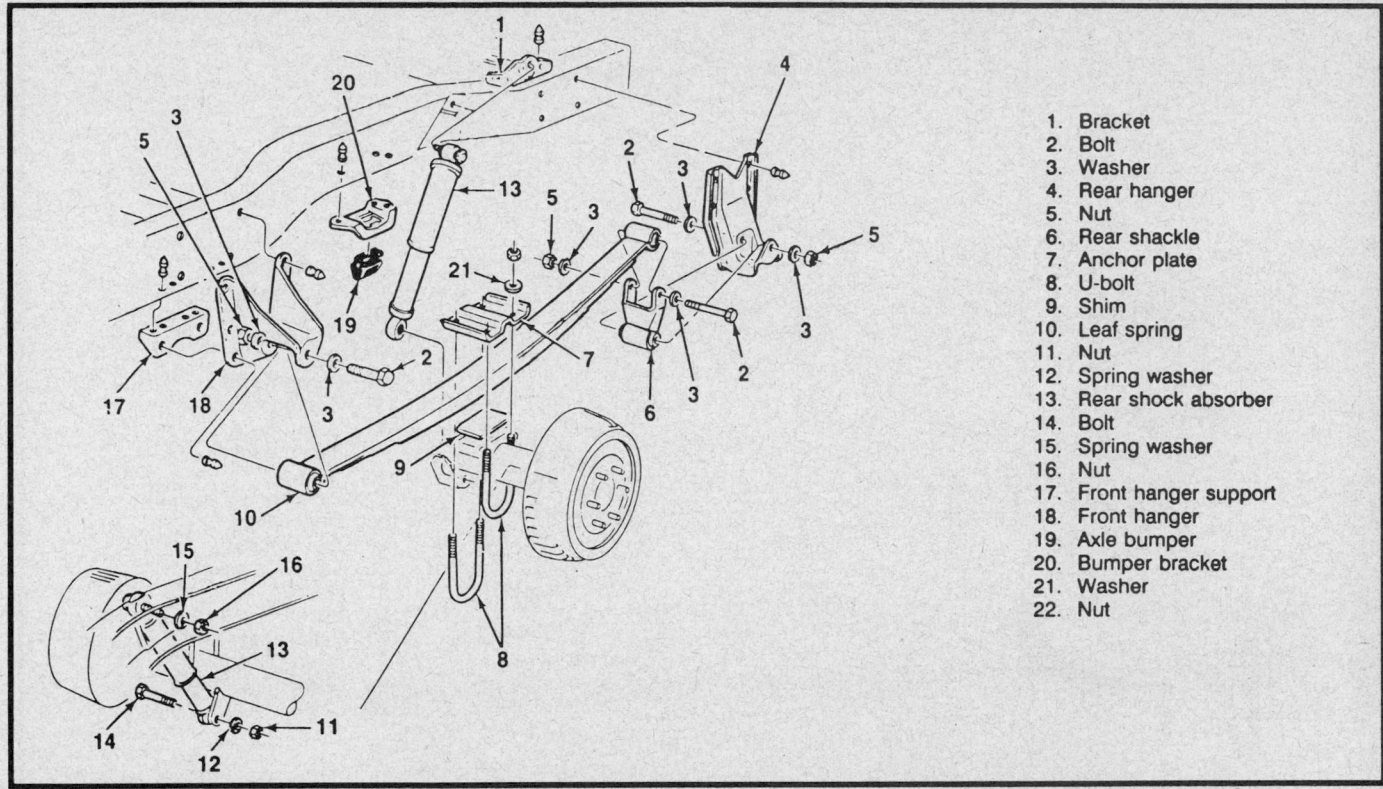

1. Bracket
2. Bolt
3. Washer
4. Rear hanger
5. Nut
6. Rear shackle
7. Anchor plate
8. U-bolt
9. Shim
10. Leaf spring
11. Nut
12. Spring washer
13. Rear shock absorber
14. Bolt
15. Spring washer
16. Nut
17. Front hanger support
18. Front hanger
19. Axle bumper
20. Bumper bracket
21. Washer
22. Nut

Rear suspension assembly – 1986 C/K 10/1500, 20/2500 Series and 1987–90 R/V 10/1500, 20/2500 Series

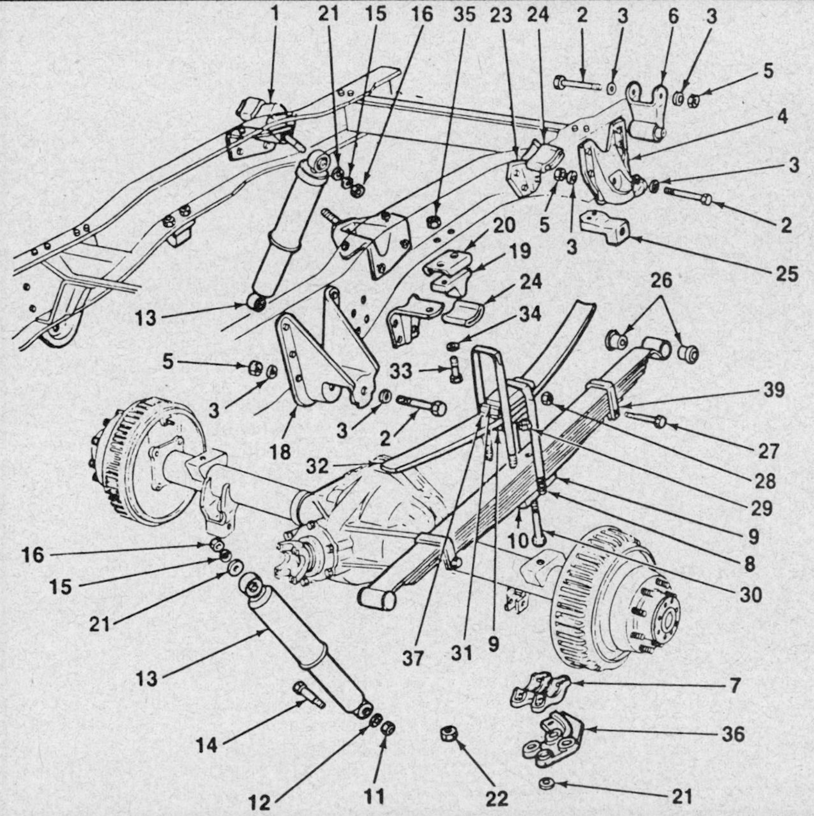

6. Rear shackle
7. Anchor plate
8. U-bolt
9. Shim
10. Leaf spring
11. Nut
12. Spring washer
13. Rear shock absorber
14. Bolt
15. Spring washer
16. Nut
17. Front hanger
18. Axle bumper
19. Bumper bracket
20. Washer
21. Nut
22. Bracket
23. Cushion
24. Rear hanger reinforcement
25. Leaf spring eye bushing
26. Bolt
27. Nut
28. Nut
29. Bolt
30. Spacer
31. Optional rear auxiliary spring
32. Bolt
33. Washer
34. Nut
35. Stabilizer bar anchor
36. Spacer
37. Spring clip

1. Bracket
2. Bolt
3. Washer
4. Rear hanger
5. Nut

Rear suspension assembly – 1986 C/K 30/3500 Series and 1987–90 R/V 30/3500 Series

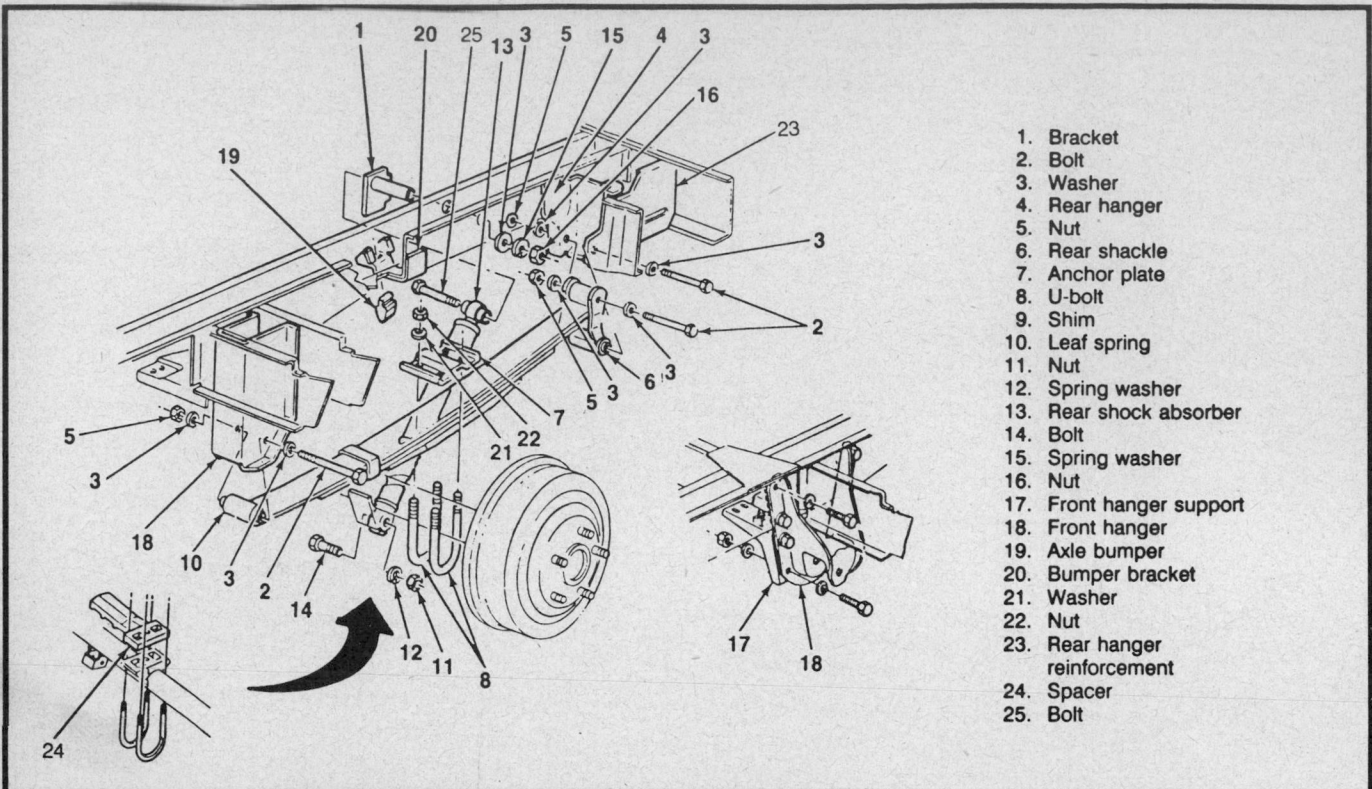

1. Bracket
2. Bolt
3. Washer
4. Rear hanger
5. Nut
6. Rear shackle
7. Anchor plate
8. U-bolt
9. Shim
10. Leaf spring
11. Nut
12. Spring washer
13. Rear shock absorber
14. Bolt
15. Spring washer
16. Nut
17. Front hanger support
18. Front hanger
19. Axle bumper
20. Bumper bracket
21. Washer
22. Nut
23. Rear hanger
    reinforcement
24. Spacer
25. Bolt

Rear suspension assembly—1986–90 G10/1500–30/ 3500 Series van

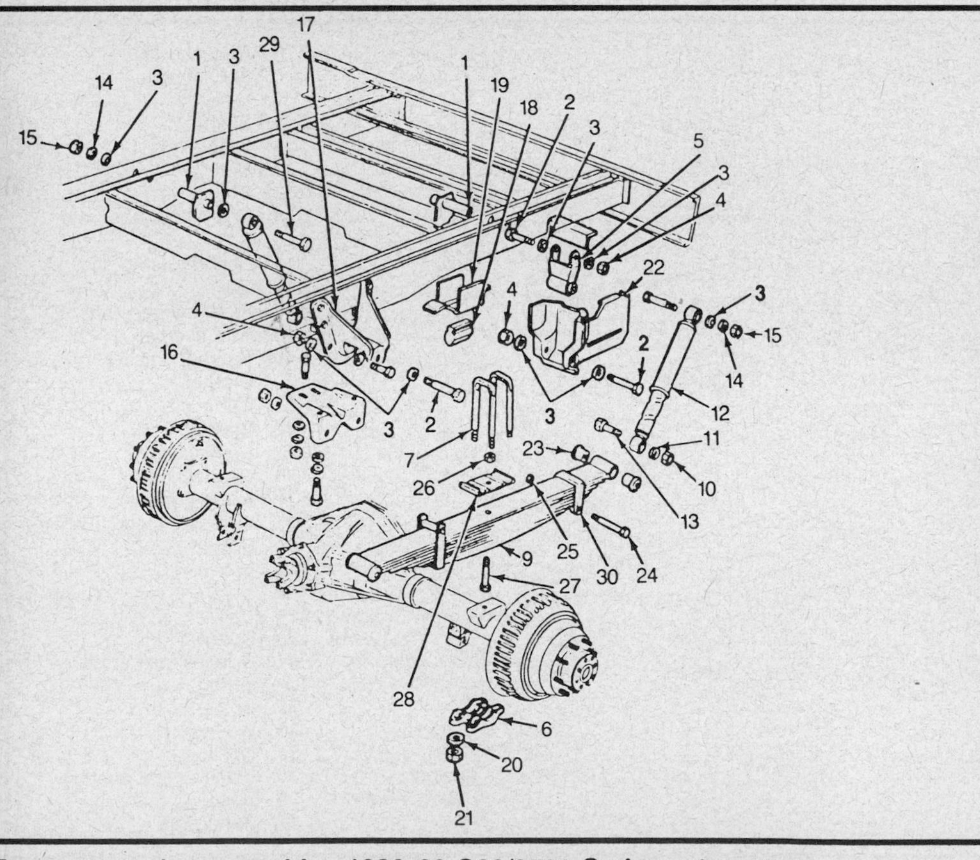

1. Bracket
2. Bolt
3. Washer
4. Nut
5. Rear shackle
6. Anchor plate
7. U-bolt
8. Shim
10. Nut
11. Spring washer
12. Rear shock absorber
13. Bolt
14. Spring washer
15. Nut
16. Front hanger support
17. Front hanger
18. Axle bumper
19. Bumper bracket
20. Washer
21. Nut
22. Rear hanger
    reinforcement
23. Leaf spring eye bushing
24. Bolt
25. Nut
26. Nut
27. Bolt
28. Spacer
29. Bolt
30. Spring clip

Rear suspension assembly—1986–90 G30/3500 Series cutaway van

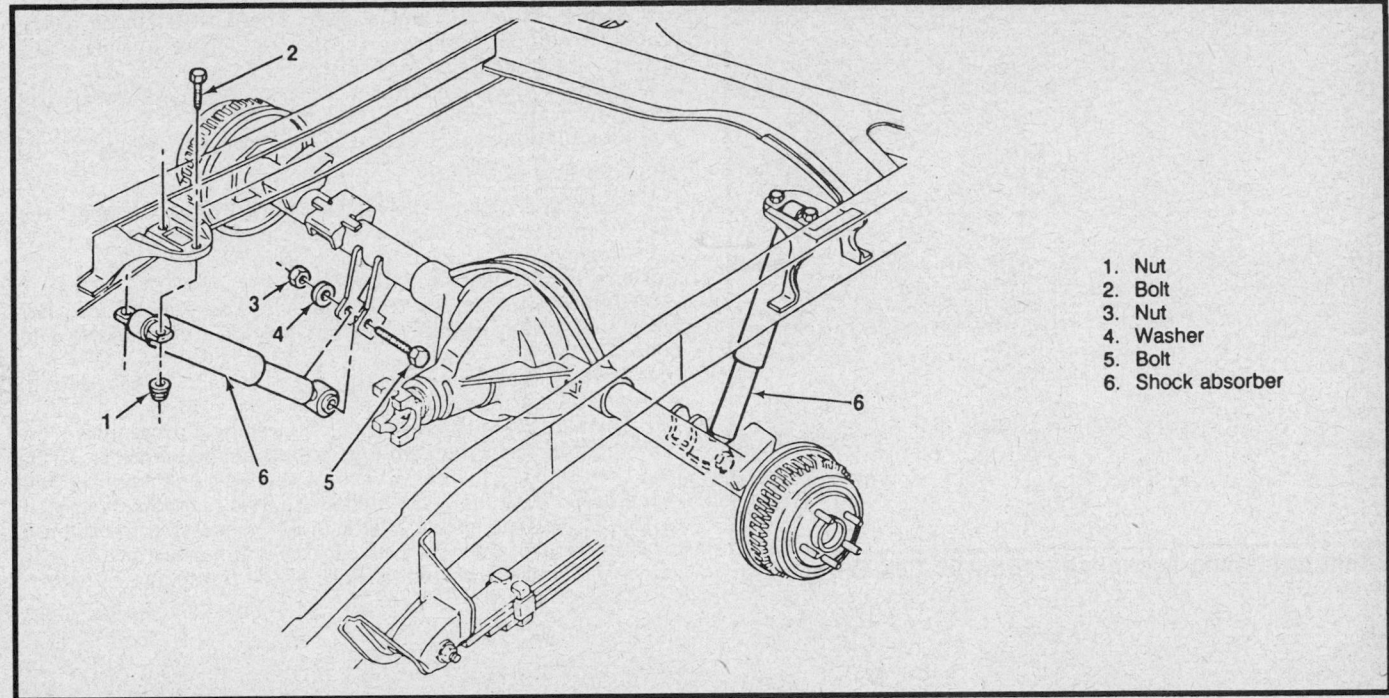

1. Nut
2. Bolt
3. Nut
4. Washer
5. Bolt
6. Shock absorber

Rear shock absorber installation — 1988—90 C/K Series

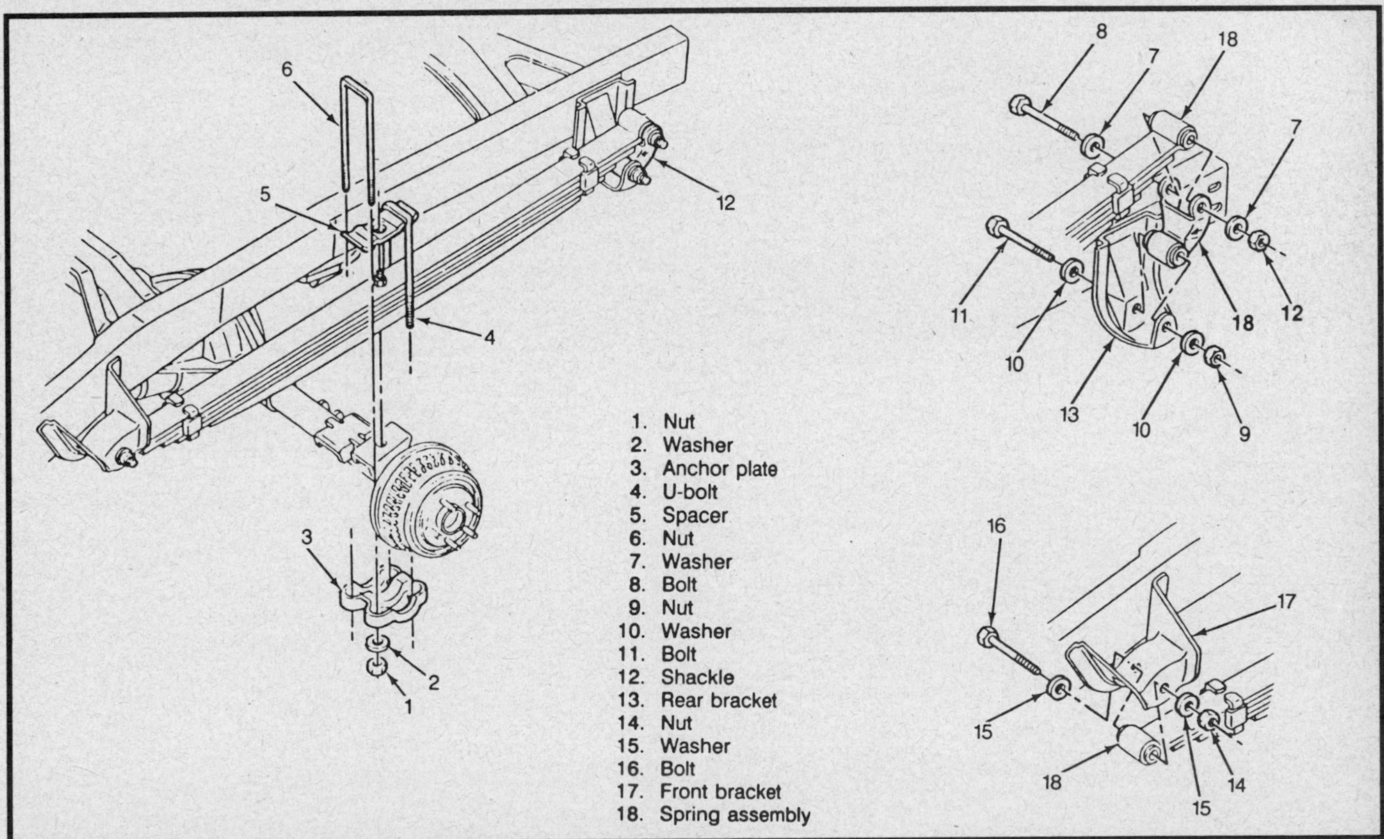

1. Nut
2. Washer
3. Anchor plate
4. U-bolt
5. Spacer
6. Nut
7. Washer
8. Bolt
9. Nut
10. Washer
11. Bolt
12. Shackle
13. Rear bracket
14. Nut
15. Washer
16. Bolt
17. Front bracket
18. Spring assembly

Rear leaf spring and cmponents — 1988—90 C/K Series

SECTION 5

GENERAL MOTORS CORPORATION
C/K SERIES (PICK-UP) • R/V SERIES (PICK-UP) • BLAZER/JIMMY • SUBURBAN • G SERIES (VAN)

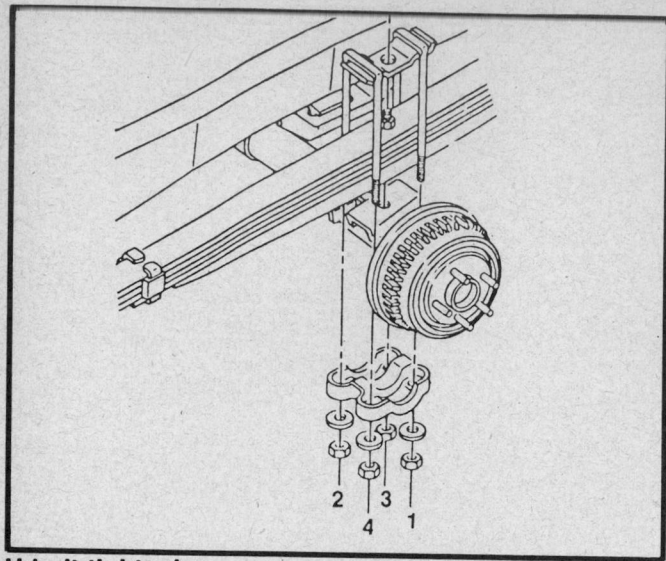

U-bolt tightening sequence—1988–90 C/K Series

5. Remove the nuts and washers holding the spring to the frame. If equipped, remove the rear stabilizer anchor plate, spacers, shims and auxiliary spring.

6. Remove the U bolts from the assembly. Remove the leaf spring from the vehicle.

7. Installation is the reverse of the removal procedure.

1988–90 C/K SERIES

1. Raise and support the vehicle safely. Properly support the rear axle assembly to relieve tension on the springs.

2. Remove the shock absorber. Remove the U bolt nuts, washers, anchor plate and U bolt.

3. Remove the shackle to frame bolt, washers and nut. Remove the spring assembly to front bracket nut, washers and bolt.

4. Remove the spring assembly from the vehicle. As required, separate the spring from the shackle.

5. Installation is the reverse of the removal procedure.

6. Tighten the U-bolt nuts in a diagonal sequence to 15 ft. lbs., then to 81 ft lbs. for all except the 7.4L engine with dual rear wheels. With the 7.4L engine with dual rear wheels tighten to 109 ft. lbs. The spring height must be adjusted to obtain a measurement of 7.17 in. between the top surface of the axle jounce pad and the bottom surface of the frame jounce pad.

SPECIFICATIONS

VEHICLE IDENTIFICATION CHART

It is important for servicing and ordering parts to be certain of the vehicle and engine identification. The VIN (vehicle identification number) is a 17 digit number visible through the windshield on the driver's side of the dash and contains the vehicle and engine identification codes. The tenth digit indicates model year and the eighth digit indicates engine code. It can be interpreted as follows:

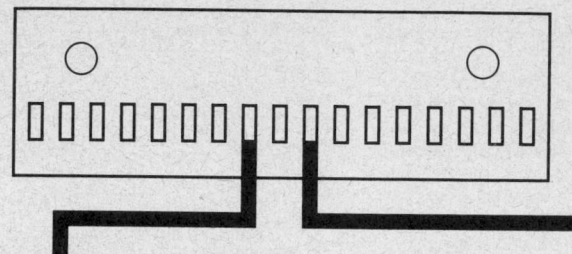

		Engine Code					Model Year	
Code	Cu. In.	Liters	Cyl.	Fuel Sys.	Eng. Mfg.		Code	Year
E	151	2.5	4	EFI	Pontiac		G	1986
R	173	2.8	6	EFI	Chevrolet		H	1987
D	189	3.1	6	EFI	Chevrolet		J	1988
Z	262	4.3	6	EFI	Chevrolet		K	1989
							L	1990

ENGINE IDENTIFICATION

Year	Model	Engine Displacement cu. in. (liter)	Engine Series Identification (VIN)	No. of Cylinders	Engine Type
1986	S10/15 Pick-Up 2WD	151 (2.5)	E	4	OHC
	S10/15 Pick-Up 2WD	173 (2.8)	R	6	OHC
	S10/15 Pick-Up 4WD	151 (2.5)	E	4	OHC
	S10/15 Pick-Up 4WD	173 (2.8)	R	6	OHC
	S10/15 Blazer/Jimmy 2WD	151 (2.5)	E	4	OHC
	S10/15 Blazer/Jimmy 2WD	173 (2.8)	R	6	OHC
	S10/15 Blazer/Jimmy 4WD	151 (2.5)	E	4	OHC
	S10/15 Blazer/Jimmy 4WD	173 (2.8)	R	6	OHC
	S10/15 Cab-Chassis	151 (2.5)	E	4	OHC
	S10/15 Cab-Chassis	173 (2.8)	R	6	OHC
	Astro/Safari	151 (2.5)	E	4	OHC
	Astro/Safari	262 (4.3)	Z	6	OHC
1987	S10/15 Pick-Up 2WD	151 (2.5)	E	4	OHC
	S10/15 Pick-Up 2WD	173 (2.8)	R	6	OHC
	S10/15 Pick-Up 4WD	151 (2.5)	E	4	OHC
	S10/15 Pick-Up 4WD	173 (2.8)	R	6	OHC

ENGINE IDENTIFICATION

Year	Model	Engine Displacement cu. in. (liter)	Engine Series Identification (VIN)	No. of Cylinders	Engine Type
1987	S10/15 Blazer/Jimmy 2WD	151 (2.5)	E	4	OHC
	S10/15 Blazer/Jimmy 2WD	173 (2.8)	R	6	OHC
	S10/15 Blazer/Jimmy 4WD	151 (2.5)	E	4	OHC
	S10/15 Blazer/Jimmy 4WD	173 (2.8)	R	6	OHC
	S10/15 Cab-Chassis	151 (2.5)	E	4	OHC
	S10/15 Cab-Chassis	173 (2.8)	R	6	OHC
	Astro/Safari	151 (2.5)	E	4	OHC
	Astro/Safari	262 (4.3)	Z	6	OHC
1988	S10/15 Pick-Up 2WD	151 (2.5)	E	4	OHC
	S10/15 Pick-Up 2WD	173 (2.8)	R	6	OHC
	S10/15 Pick-Up 4WD	151 (2.5)	E	4	OHC
	S10/15 Pick-Up 4WD	173 (2.8)	R	6	OHC
	S10/15 Blazer/Jimmy 2WD	151 (2.5)	E	4	OHC
	S10/15 Blazer/Jimmy 2WD	173 (2.8)	R	6	OHC
	S10/15 Blazer/Jimmy 4WD	173 (2.8)	R	6	OHC
	S10/15 Blazer/Jimmy 4WD	262 (4.3)	Z	6	OHC
	S10/15 Cab-Chassis	173 (2.8)	R	6	OHC
	Astro/Safari	151 (2.5)	E	4	OHC
	Astro/Safari	262 (4.3)	Z	6	OHC
1989	S10/15 Plck-Up 2WD	151 (2.5)	E	4	OHC
	S10/15 Pick-Up 2WD	173 (2.8)	R	6	OHC
	S10/15 Pick-Up 4WD	173 (2.8)	R	6	OHC
	S10/15 Pick-Up 4WD	262 (4.3)	Z	6	OHC
	S10/15 Blazer/Jimmy 2WD	151 (2.5)	E	4	OHC
	S10/15 Blazer/Jimmy 2WD	173 (2.8)	R	6	OHC
	S10/15 Blazer/Jimmy 2WD	262 (4.3)	Z	6	OHC
	S10/15 Blazer/Jimmy 4WD	173 (2.8)	R	6	OHC
	S10/15 Blazer/Jimmy 4WD	262 (4.3)	Z	6	OHC
	Astro/Safari	151 (2.5)	E	4	OHC
	Astro/Safari	262 (4.3)	Z	6	OHC
1990	S10/15 Pick-Up 2WD	151 (2.5)	E	4	OHC
	S10/15 Pick-Up 2WD	173 (2.8)	R	6	OHC
	S10/15 Pick-Up 2WD	262 (4.3)	Z	6	OHC
	S10/15 Pick-Up 4WD	262 (4.3)	Z	6	OHC
	S10/15 Blazer/Jimmy 2WD	262 (4.3)	Z	6	OHC
	S10/15 Blazer/Jimmy 4WD	262 (4.3)	Z	6	OHC
	Astro/Safari 2WD	151 (2.5)	E	4	OHC
	Astro/Safari 2WD	262 (4.3)	Z	6	OHC
	Astro/Safari 4WD	262 (4.3)	Z	6	OHC
	Lumina APV	189 (3.1)	D	6	OHC
	Silhouette	189 (3.1)	D	6	OHC
	Trans Sport	189 (3.1)	D	6	OHC

GENERAL ENGINE SPECIFICATIONS

Year	VIN	No. Cylinder Displacement cu. in. (liter)	Fuel System Type	Net Horsepower @ rpm	Net Torque @ rpm (ft. lbs.)	Bore × Stroke (in.)	Compression Ratio	Oil Pressure @ rpm
1986	E	4-151 (2.5)	EFI	92 @ 4400	134 @ 2800	4.00 × 3.00	9.0:1	45 @ 2000
	R	6-173 (2.8)	EFI	125 @ 4800	150 @ 2200	3.56 × 3.04	8.5:1	50 @ 2000
	Z	6-262 (4.3)	EFI	145 @ 4000	230 @ 2400	4.00 × 3.48	9.3:1	30 @ 2000
1987	E	4-151 (2.5)	EFI	92 @ 4400	134 @ 2800	4.00 × 3.00	9.0:1	45 @ 2000
	R	6-173 (2.8)	EFI	125 @ 4800	150 @ 2200	3.56 × 3.04	8.5:1	50 @ 2000
	Z	6-262 (4.3)	EFI	145 @ 4000	230 @ 2400	4.00 × 3.48	9.3:1	30 @ 2000
1988	E	4-151 (2.5)	EFI	92 @ 4400	130 @ 3200	4.00 × 3.00	8.3:1	41 @ 2000
	R	6-173 (2.8)	EFI	125 @ 4800	150 @ 2400	3.56 × 3.04	8.9:1	50 @ 2000
	Z	6-262 (4.3)	EFI	150 @ 4000	230 @ 2400	4.00 × 3.48	9.3:1	30 @ 2000
1989	E	4-151 (2.5)	EFI	92 @ 4400	130 @ 3200	4.00 × 3.00	8.3:1	41 @ 2000
	R	6-173 (2.8)	EFI	125 @ 4800	150 @ 2400	3.56 × 3.04	8.9:1	50 @ 2000
	Z	6-262 (4.3)	EFI	160 @ 4000	230 @ 2800	4.00 × 3.48	9.3:1	18 @ 2000
1990	E	4-151 (2.5)	EFI	92 @ 4400	130 @ 3200	4.00 × 3.00	8.3:1	41 @ 2000
	R	6-173 (2.8)	EFI	125 @ 4800	150 @ 2200	3.56 × 3.04	8.9:1	50 @ 2000
	D	6-189 (3.1)	EFI	120 @ 4200	175 @ 2200	3.50 × 3.40	8.5:1	50 @ 1200
	Z	6-262 (4.3)	EFI	160 @ 4000	230 @ 2800	4.00 × 3.48	9.3:1	18 @ 2000

GASOLINE ENGINE TUNE-UP SPECIFICATIONS

Year	VIN	No. Cylinder Displacement cu. in. (liter)	Spark Plugs Type	Gap (in.)	Ignition Timing (deg.) MT	AT	Compression Pressure (psi)	Fuel Pump (psi)	Idle speed (rpm) MT	AT	Valve Clearance In.	Ex.
1986	E	4-151 (2.5)	R43TS6	.060	①	①	②	9–13	①	①	Hyd.	Hyd.
	R	6-173 (2.8)	R43TSK	.040	①	①	②	9–13	①	①	Hyd.	Hyd.
	Z	6-262 (4.3)	R43TS	.040	①	①	②	9–13	①	①	Hyd.	Hyd.
1987	E	4-151 (2.5)	R43TS6	.060	①	①	②	9–13	①	①	Hyd.	Hyd.
	R	6-173 (2.8)	R43TSK	.040	①	①	②	9–13	①	①	Hyd.	Hyd.
	Z	6-262 (4.3)	R43TS	.040	①	①	②	9–13	①	①	Hyd.	Hyd.
1988	E	4-151 (2.5)	R43TS6	.060	①	①	②	9–13	①	①	Hyd.	Hyd.
	R	6-173 (2.8)	R43TSK	.040	①	①	②	9–13	①	①	Hyd.	Hyd.
	Z	6-262 (4.3)	R43TS	.040	①	①	②	9–13	①	①	Hyd.	Hyd.
1989	E	4-151 (2.5)	R43TS6	.060	①	①	②	9–13	①	①	Hyd.	Hyd.
	R	6-173 (2.8)	R43TSK	.040	①	①	②	9–13	①	①	Hyd.	Hyd.
	Z	6-262 (4.3)	R43TS	.040	①	①	②	9–13	①	①	Hyd.	Hyd.
1990	E	4-151 (2.5)	R43TS6	.060	①	①	②	9–13	①	①	Hyd.	Hyd.
	R	6-173 (2.8)	R43TSK	.040	①	①	②	9–13	①	①	Hyd.	Hyd.
	D	6-189 (3.1)	R43TS	.040	①	①	②	9–13	①	①	Hyd.	Hyd.
	Z	6-262 (4.3)	R43TS	.040	①	①	②	9–13	①	①	Hyd.	Hyd.

① See Underhood Sticker.
② Check all cylinders, should be within 50 psi of each other.

FIRING ORDERS

NOTE: To avoid confusion, always replace spark plug wires one at a time.

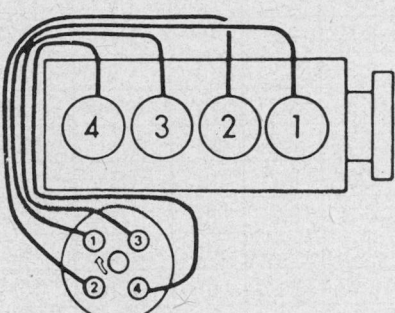

2.5L engine
Engine firing order: 1–3–4–2
Distributor rotation: clockwise

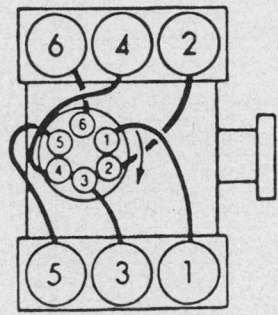

2.8L engine
Engine firing order: 1–2–3–4–5–6
Distributor rotation: counterclockwise

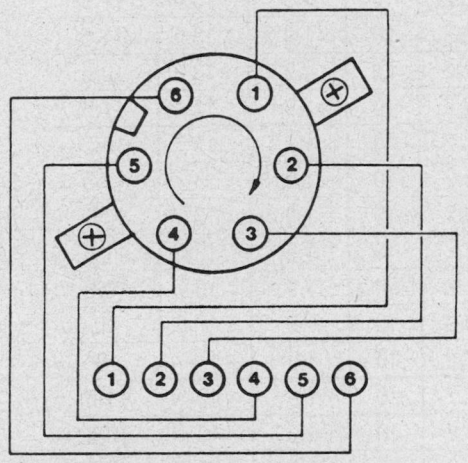

3.1L engine
Engine firing order: 1–2–3–4–5–6
Distributor rotation: clockwise

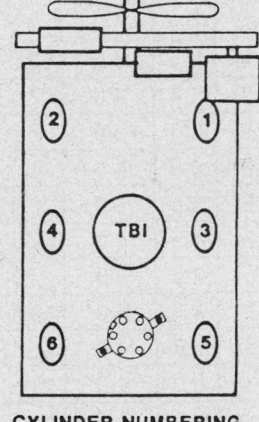

CYLINDER NUMBERING

◀ FRT

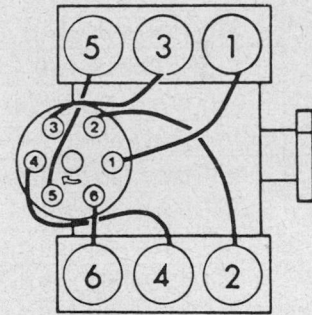

4.3L engine
Engine firing order: 1–6–5–4–3–2
Distributor rotation: clockwise

CAPACITIES

Year	Model	VIN	No. Cylinder Displacement cu. in (liter)	Engine Crankcase with Filter	Engine Crankcase without Filter	Transmission (pts.) 4-Spd	Transmission (pts.) 5-Spd	Transmission (pts.) Auto.	Drive Axle (qts.)	Fuel Tank (gal.)	Cooling System (qts.)
1986	S10/15 Pick-Up 2WD	E	4-151 (2.5)	3.5	3.0	2.5	2.2	10	1.9	13 ①	11.5
	S10/15 Pick-Up 2WD	R	6-173 (2.8)	4.5	4.0	2.5	2.2	10	1.9	13 ①	10.5
	S10/15 Pick-Up 4WD	E	4-151 (2.5)	3.5	3.0	2.5	2.2	10	1.9 ③	13 ①	11.5
	S10/15 Pick-Up 4WD	R	6-173 (2.8)	4.5	4.0	2.5	2.2	10	1.9 ③	13 ①	10.5
	S10/15 Blazer/Jimmy 2WD	E	4-151 (2.5)	3.5	3.0	2.5	2.2	10	1.9	13 ①	11.5
	S10/15 Blazer/Jimmy 2WD	R	6-173 (2.8)	4.5	4.0	2.5	2.2	10	1.9	13 ①	10.5
	S10/15 Blazer/Jimmy 4WD	E	4-151 (2.5)	3.5	3.0	2.5	2.2	10	1.9 ③	13 ①	11.5
	S10/15 Blazer/Jimmy 4WD	R	6-173 (2.8)	4.5	4.0	2.5	2.2	10	1.9 ③	13 ①	10.5
	S10/15 Cab-Chassis	E	4-151 (2.5)	3.5	3.0	2.5	2.2	10	1.9	13 ①	11.5
	S10/15 Cab-Chassis	R	6-173 (2.8)	4.5	4.0	2.5	2.2	10	1.9	13 ①	10.5
	Astro/Safari	E	4-151 (2.5)	5.0	4.0	2.5	2.2	10	1.9	17 ②	10
	Astro/Safari	Z	6-262 (4.3)	5.0	4.0	2.5	2.2	10	1.9	17 ②	10
1987	S10/15 Pick-Up 2WD	E	4-151 (2.5)	3.5	3.0	2.5	2.2	10	1.9	13 ①	11.5
	S10/15 Pick-Up 2WD	R	6-173 (2.8)	4.5	4.0	2.5	2.2	10	1.9	13 ①	10.5
	S10/15 Pick-Up 4WD	E	4-151 (2.5)	3.5	3.0	2.5	2.2	10	1.9 ③	13 ①	11.5
	S10/15 Pick-Up 4WD	R	6-173 (2.8)	4.5	4.0	2.5	2.2	10	1.9 ③	13 ①	10.5
	S10/15 Blazer/Jimmy 2WD	E	4-151 (2.5)	3.5	3.0	2.5	2.2	10	1.9	13 ①	11.5
	S10/15 Blazer/Jimmy 2WD	R	6-173 (2.8)	4.5	4.0	2.5	2.2	10	1.9	13 ①	10.5
	S10/15 Blazer/Jimmy 4WD	E	4-151 (2.5)	3.5	3.0	2.5	2.2	10	1.9 ③	13 ①	11.5
	S10/15 Blazer/Jimmy 4WD	R	6-173 (2.8)	4.5	4.0	2.5	2.2	10	1.9 ③	13 ①	10.5
	S10/15 Cab-Chassis	E	4-151 (2.5)	3.5	3.0	2.5	2.2	10	1.9	13 ①	11.5
	S10/15 Cab-Chassis	R	6-173 (2.8)	4.5	4.0	2.5	2.2	10	1.9	13 ①	10.5
	Astro/Safari	E	4-151 (2.5)	5.0	4.0	2.5	2.2	10	1.9	17 ②	10
	Astro/Safari	Z	6-262 (4.3)	5.0	4.0	2.5	2.2	10	1.9	17 ②	10
1988	S10/15 Pick-Up 2WD	E	4-151 (2.5)	3.5	3.0	—	2.2	10	1.9	13 ①	11.5
	S10/15 Pick-Up 2WD	R	6-173 (2.8)	4.5	4.0	—	2.2	10	1.9	13 ①	10.5
	S10/15 Pick-Up 4WD	E	4-151 (2.5)	3.5	3.0	—	2.2	10	1.9 ④	13 ①	11.5
	S10/15 Pick-Up 4WD	R	6-173 (2.8)	4.5	4.0	—	2.2	10	1.9 ④	13 ①	10.5
	S10/15 Blazer/Jimmy 2WD	E	4-151 (2.5)	3.5	3.0	—	2.2	10	1.9	13 ①	11.5
	S10/15 Blazer/Jimmy 2WD	R	6-173 (2.8)	4.5	4.0	—	2.2	10	1.9	13 ①	10.5
	S10/15 Blazer/Jimmy 4WD	R	6-173 (2.8)	4.5	4.0	—	2.2	10	1.9 ④	13 ①	10.5
	S10/15 Blazer/Jimmy 4WD	Z	6-262 (4.3)	5.0	4.0	—	2.2	10	1.9 ④	13 ①	13.5
	S10/15 Cab-Chassis	R	6-173 (2.8)	4.5	4.0	—	2.2	10	1.9	13 ①	10.5
	Astro/Safari	E	4-151 (2.5)	3.5	3.0	—	2.2	10	1.9	17 ②	10 ⑤
	Astro/Safari	Z	6-262 (4.3)	5.0	4.0	—	2.2	10	1.9	17 ②	13.5 ⑥
1989	S10/15 Pick-Up 2WD	E	4-151 (2.5)	3.5	3.0	—	2.2	10	1.9	13 ①	11.5
	S10/15 Pick-Up 2WD	R	6-173 (2.8)	4.5	4.0	—	2.2	10	1.9	13 ①	10.5
	S10/15 Pick-Up 4WD	R	6-173 (2.8)	4.5	4.0	—	2.2	10	1.9 ④	13 ①	10.5
	S10/15 Pick-Up 4WD	Z	6-262 (4.3)	5.0	4.0	—	2.2	10	1.9 ④	13 ①	13.5
	S10/15 Blazer/Jimmy 2WD	E	4-151 (2.5)	3.5	3.0	—	2.2	10	1.9	13 ①	11.5
	S10/15 Blazer/Jimmy 2WD	R	6-173 (2.8)	4.5	4.0	—	2.2	10	1.9	13 ①	10.5
	S10/15 Blazer/Jimmy 2WD	Z	6-262 (4.3)	5.0	4.0	—	2.2	10	1.9	13 ①	13.5
	S10/15 Blazer/Jimmy 4WD	R	6-173 (2.8)	4.5	4.0	—	2.2	10	1.9 ④	13 ①	10.5

CAPACITIES

Year	Model	VIN	No. Cylinder Displacement cu. in. (liter)	Engine Crankcase with Filter	Engine Crankcase without Filter	Transmission (pts.) 4-Spd	5-Spd	Auto.	Drive Axle (qts.)	Fuel Tank (gal.)	Cooling System (qts.)
1989	S10/15 Blazer/Jimmy 4WD	Z	6-262 (4.3)	5.0	4.0	—	2.2	10	1.9	13 ①	13.5
	S10/15 Cab-Chassis	R	6-173 (2.8)	4.5	4.0	—	2.2	10	1.9	13 ①	10.5
	Astro/Safari	E	4-151 (2.5)	3.5	3.0	—	2.2	10	1.9	17 ②	10 ⑤
	Astro/Safari	Z	6-262 (4.3)	5.0	4.0	—	2.2	10	1.9	17 ②	13.5 ⑥
1990	S10/15 Pick-Up 2WD	E	4-151 (2.5)	3.5	3.0	—	2.2	10	1.9	13 ①	11.5
	S10/15 Pick-Up 2WD	R	6-173 (2.8)	4.5	4.0	—	2.2	10	1.9	13 ①	10.5
	S10/15 Pick-Up 4WD	R	6-173 (2.8)	4.5	4.0	—	2.2	10	1.9 ④	13 ①	10.5
	S10/15 Pick-Up 4WD	Z	6-262 (4.3)	5.0	4.0	—	2.2	10	1.9 ④	13 ①	13.5
	S10/15 Blazer/Jimmy 2WD	E	4-151 (2.5)	3.5	3.0	—	2.2	10	1.9	13 ①	11.5
	S10/15 Blazer/Jimmy 2WD	R	6-173 (2.8)	4.5	4.0	—	2.2	10	1.9	13 ①	10.5
	S10/15 Blazer/Jimmy 2WD	Z	6-262 (4.3)	5.0	4.0	—	2.2	10	1.9	13 ①	13.5
	S10/15 Blazer/Jimmy 4WD	R	6-173 (2.8)	4.5	4.0	—	2.2	10	1.9 ④	13 ①	10.5
	S10/15 Blazer/Jimmy 4WD	Z	6-262 (4.3)	5.0	4.0	—	2.2	10	1.9	13 ①	13.5
	Astro/Safari	Z	6-262 (4.3)	5.0	4.0	—	2.2	10	1.9	27	16.5
	Astro/Safari 4WD	Z	6-262 (4.3)	5.0	4.0	—	2.2	10	1.9	27	16.5
	Lumina APV	D	6-189 (3.1)	4.5	4.0	—	—	8	—	18	13.4
	Silhouette	D	6-189 (3.1)	4.5	4.0	—	—	8	—	18	13.4
	Trans Sport	D	6-189 (3.1)	4.5	4.0	—	—	8	—	18	13.4

① 20 gallon tank optional
② 27 gallon tank optional
③ 2.5 qts. front axle
④ 1.3 qts. front axle
⑤ 13 qts. with rear heater
⑥ 16.5 qts. with rear heater

CAMSHAFT SPECIFICATIONS
All measurements given in inches.

Year	VIN	No. Cylinder Displacement cu. in. (liter)	Journal Diameter 1	2	3	4	5	Lobe Lift In.	Ex.	Bearing Clearance	Camshaft End Play
1986	E	4-151 (2.5)	1.869	1.869	1.869	—	—	0.398	0.398	0.0007–0.0027	0.0015–0.0050
	R	6-173 (2.8)	1.897–1.899	1.897–1.899	1.897–1.899	1.897–1.899	—	0.234	0.266	0.0010–0.0040	—
	Z	6-262 (4.3)	1.868–1.869	1.868–1.869	1.868–1.869	1.868–1.869	—	0.357	0.390	0.0010–0.0030	0.0004–0.0012
1987	E	4-151 (2.5)	1.869	1.869	1.869	—	—	0.398	0.398	0.0007–0.0027	0.0015–0.0050
	R	6-173 (2.8)	1.897–1.899	1.897–1.899	1.897–1.899	1.897–1.899	—	0.234	0.266	0.0010–0.0040	—
	Z	6-262 (4.3)	1.868–1.869	1.868–1.869	1.868–1.869	1.868–1.869	—	0.357	0.390	0.0010–0.0030	0.0004–0.0012

CAMSHAFT SPECIFICATIONS

All measurements given in inches.

Year	VIN	No. Cylinder Displacement cu. in. (liter)	Journal Diameter 1	2	3	4	5	Lobe Lift In.	Ex.	Bearing Clearance	Camshaft End Play
1988	E	4-151 (2.5)	1.869	1.869	1.869	—	—	0.398	0.398	0.0007–0.0027	0.0015–0.0050
	R	6-173 (2.8)	1.897–1.899	1.897–1.899	1.897–1.899	1.897–1.899	—	0.234	0.266	0.0010–0.0040	—
	Z	6-262 (4.3)	1.868–1.869	1.868–1.869	1.868–1.869	1.868–1.869	—	0.357	0.390	0.0010–0.0030	0.0004–0.0012
1989	E	4-151 (2.5)	1.869	1.869	1.869	—	—	0.232	0.232	0.0007–0.0027	0.0015–0.0050
	R	6-173 (2.8)	1.897–1.899	1.897–1.899	1.897–1.899	1.897–1.899	—	0.266	0.277	0.0010–0.0040	—
	Z	6-262 (4.3)	1.868–1.869	1.868–1.869	1.868–1.869	1.868–1.869	—	0.357	0.390	0.0010–0.0030	0.0004–0.0012
1990	E	4-151 (2.5)	1.869	1.869	1.869	—	—	0.232	0.232	0.0007–0.0027	0.0015–0.0050
	R	6-173 (2.8)	1.897–1.899	1.897–1.899	1.897–1.899	1.897–1.899	—	0.266	0.277	0.0010–0.0040	—
	D	6-189 (3.1)	1.867–1.881	1.867–1.881	1.867–1.881	1.867–1.881	—	.230	.261	0.0010–0.0040	—
	Z	6-262 (4.3)	1.868–1.869	1.868–1.869	1.868–1.869	1.868–1.869	—	0.357	0.390	0.0010–0.0030	0.0004–0.0012

CRANKSHAFT AND CONNECTING ROD SPECIFICATIONS

All measurements are given in inches.

Year	VIN	No. Cylinder Displacement cu. in. (liter)	Crankshaft Main Brg. Journal Dia.	Main Brg. Oil Clearance	Shaft End-play	Thrust on No.	Connecting Rod Journal Diameter	Oil Clearance	Side Clearance
1986	E	4-151 (2.5)	2.3000	0.0005–0.0022	0.0035–0.0085	5	2.000	0.0005–0.0026	0.0060–0.0220
	R	6-173 (2.8)	①	0.0016–0.0032	0.0020–0.0070	3	1.9983–1.9993	0.0014–0.0035	0.0063–0.0173
	Z	6-262 (4.3)	②	③	0.0020–0.0060	3	2.2487–2.2497	0.0013–0.0035	0.0060–0.0140
1987	E	4-151 (2.5)	2.3000	0.0005–0.0022	0.0035–0.0085	5	2.000	0.0005–0.0026	0.0060–0.0220
	R	6-173 (2.8)	①	0.0016–0.0032	0.0020–0.0070	3	1.9983–1.9993	0.0014–0.0035	0.0063–0.0173
	Z	6-262 (4.3)	②	③	0.0020–0.0060	3	2.2487–2.2497	0.0013–0.0035	0.0060–0.0140
1988	E	4-151 (2.5)	2.3000	0.0005–0.0022	0.0035–0.0085	5	2.000	0.0005–0.0026	0.0060–0.0220
	R	6-173 (2.8)	①	0.0016–0.0032	0.0020–0.0070	3	1.9983–1.9993	0.0014–0.0035	0.0063–0.0173
	Z	6-262 (4.3)	②	③	0.0020–0.0060	3	2.2487–2.2497	0.0013–0.0035	0.0060–0.0140

CRANKSHAFT AND CONNECTING ROD SPECIFICATIONS

All measurements are given in inches.

Year	VIN	No. Cylinder Displacement cu. in. (liter)	Crankshaft Main Brg. Journal Dia.	Main Brg. Oil Clearance	Shaft End-play	Thrust on No.	Connecting Rod Journal Diameter	Oil Clearance	Side Clearance
1989	E	4-151 (2.5)	2.3000	0.0005–0.0022	0.0035–0.0085	5	2.000	0.0005–0.0026	0.0060–0.0220
	R	6-173 (2.8)	①	0.0016–0.0032	0.0020–0.0070	3	1.9983–1.9993	0.0014–0.0035	0.0063–0.0173
	Z	6-262 (4.3)	②	③	0.0020–0.0060	3	2.2487–2.2497	0.0013–0.0035	0.0060–0.0140
1990	E	4-151 (2.5)	2.3000	0.0005–0.0022	0.0035–0.0085	5	2.000	0.0005–0.0026	0.0060–0.0220
	R	6-173 (2.8)	①	0.0016–0.0032	0.0020–0.0070	3	1.9983–1.9993	0.0014–0.0035	0.0063–0.0173
	D	6-189 (3.1)	2.6473–2.6483	0.0012–0.0027	0.0024–0.0083	3	1.9994–1.9983	0.0011–0.0032	0.0014–0.0267
	Z	6-262 (4.3)	②	③	0.0020–0.0060	3	2.2487–2.2497	0.0013–0.0035	0.0060–0.0140

① Journals 1, 2, 4: 2.5336–2.5345 Journal 3: 2.5332–2.5340
② Journal 1: 2.4484–2.4493 Journal 2, 3: 2.4481–2.4490
Journal 4: 2.4479–2.4488
③ Journal 1: 0.0008–0.0020 Journal 2, 3: 0.0011–0.0023 Journal 4: 0.0017–0.0032

VALVE SPECIFICATIONS

All measurements given in inches.

Year	VIN	No. Cylinder Displacement cu. in. (liter)	Seat Angle (deg.)	Face Angle (deg.)	Spring Test Pressure (lbs.)	Spring Installed Height (in.)	Stem-to-Guide Clearance (in.) Intake	Exhaust	Stem Diameter (in.) Intake	Exhaust
1986	E	4-151 (2.5)	46	46	175 @ 1.26	1.69	0.0010–0.0025	0.0013–0.0030	0.3430–0.3420	0.3420–0.3430
	R	4-173 (2.8)	46	46	175 @ 1.26	1.94	0.0010–0.0002	0.0010–0.0002	0.3410–0.3420	0.3410–0.3420
	Z	4-262 (4.3)	46	46	194 @ 1.25	1.39	0.0010–0.0027	0.0010–0.0027	0.3410–0.3420	0.3410–0.3420
1987	E	4-151 (2.5)	46	46	175 @ 1.26	1.69	0.0010–0.0025	0.0013–0.0030	0.3430–0.3420	0.3420–0.3430
	R	6-173 (2.8)	46	46	175 @ 1.26	1.94	0.0010–0.0002	0.0010–0.0002	0.3410–0.3420	0.3410–0.3420
	Z	6-262 (4.3)	46	46	194 @ 1.25	1.39	0.0010–0.0027	0.0010–0.0027	0.3410–0.3420	0.3410–0.3420
1988	E	4-151 (2.5)	46	46	175 @ 1.26	1.69	0.0010–0.0025	0.0013–0.0030	0.3430–0.3420	0.3420–0.3430
	R	6-173 (2.8)	46	46	175 @ 1.26	1.94	0.0010–0.0002	0.0010–0.0002	0.3410–0.3420	0.3410–0.3420
	Z	6-262 (4.3)	46	46	194 @ 1.25	1.39	0.0010–0.0027	0.0010–0.0027	0.3410–0.3420	0.3410–0.3420

VALVE SPECIFICATIONS

All measurements given in inches.

Year	No. VIN	Cylinder Displacement cu. in. (liter)	Seat Angle (deg.)	Face Angle (deg.)	Spring Spring Test Pressure (lbs.)	Stem-to-Guide Installed Height (in.)	Clearance (in.) Intake	Clearance (in.) Exhaust	Stem Diameter (in.) Intake	Stem Diameter (in.) Exhaust
1989	E	4-151 (2.5)	46	46	175 @ 1.26	1.69	0.0010–0.0025	0.0013–0.0030	0.3430–0.3420	0.3420–0.3430
	R	6-173 (2.8)	46	46	175 @ 1.26	1.94	0.0010–0.0002	0.0010–0.0002	0.3410–0.3420	0.3410–0.3420
	Z	6-262 (4.3)	46	46	194 @ 1.25	1.39	0.0010–0.0027	0.0010–0.0027	0.3410–0.3420	0.3410–0.3420
1990	E	4-151 (2.5)	46	46	175 @ 1.26	1.69	0.0010–0.0025	0.0013–0.0030	0.3430–0.3420	0.3420–0.3430
	R	6-173 (2.8)	46	46	175 @ 1.26	1.94	0.0010–0.0002	0.0010–0.0002	0.3410–0.3420	0.3410–0.3420
	D	6-189 (3.1)	46	46	191 @ 1.18	1.57	0.0010–0.0027	0.0010–0.0027	0.3410–0.3420	0.3410–0.3420
	Z	6-262 (4.3)	46	46	194 @ 1.25	1.39	0.0010–0.0027	0.0010–0.0027	0.3410–0.3420	0.3410–0.3420

PISTON AND RING SPECIFICATIONS

All measurements are given in inches.

Year	VIN	No. Cylinder Displacement cu. in. (liter)	Piston Clearance	Ring Gap Top Compression	Ring Gap Bottom Compression	Ring Gap Oil Control	Ring Side Clearance Top Compression	Ring Side Clearance Bottom Compression	Ring Side Clearance Oil Control
1986	E	4-151 (2.5)	0.0014–0.0022	0.0100–0.0200	0.0100–0.0200	0.0200–0.0600	0.0020–0.0030	0.0010–0.0030	0.0150–0.0550
	R	6-173 (2.8)	0.0007–0.0017	0.0100–0.0220	0.0100–0.0220	0.0200–0.0550	0.0012–0.0027	0.0015–0.0037	0.0078
	Z	6-262 (4.3)	0.0007–0.0017	0.0100–0.0200	0.0100–0.0250	0.0150–0.0550	0.0012–0.0032	0.0012–0.0032	0.0020–0.0070
1987	E	4-151 (2.5)	0.0014–0.0022	0.0100–0.0200	0.0100–0.0200	0.0200–0.0600	0.0020–0.0030	0.0010–0.0030	0.0150–0.0550
	R	6-173 (2.8)	0.0007–0.0017	0.0100–0.0220	0.0100–0.0220	0.0200–0.0550	0.0012–0.0027	0.0015–0.0037	0.0078
	Z	6-262 (4.3)	0.0007–0.0017	0.0100–0.0200	0.0100–0.0250	0.0150–0.0550	0.0012–0.0032	0.0012–0.0032	0.0020–0.0070
1988	E	4-151 (2.5)	0.0014–0.0022	0.0100–0.0200	0.0100–0.0200	0.0200–0.0600	0.0020–0.0030	0.0010–0.0030	0.0150–0.0550
	R	6-173 (2.8)	0.0007–0.0017	0.0100–0.0220	0.0100–0.0220	0.0200–0.0550	0.0012–0.0027	0.0015–0.0037	0.0078
	Z	6-262 (4.3)	0.0007–0.0017	0.0100–0.0200	0.0100–0.0250	0.0150–0.0550	0.0012–0.0032	0.0012–0.0032	0.0020–0.0070
1989	E	4-151 (2.5)	0.0010–0.0022	0.0100–0.0200	0.0100–0.0200	0.0200–0.0600	0.0020–0.0030	0.0010–0.0030	0.0150–0.0550
	R	6-173 (2.8)	0.0007–0.0017	0.0100–0.0220	0.0100–0.0220	0.0200–0.0550	0.0012–0.0027	0.0015–0.0037	0.0078
	Z	6-262 (4.3)	0.0007–0.0017	0.0100–0.0200	0.0100–0.0250	0.0150–0.0550	0.0012–0.0032	0.0012–0.0032	0.0020–0.0070

PISTON AND RING SPECIFICATIONS

All measurements are given in inches.

Year	VIN	No. Cylinder Displacement cu. in. (liter)	Piston Clearance	Ring Gap			Ring Side Clearance		
				Top Compression	Bottom Compression	Oil Control	Top Compression	Bottom Compression	Oil Control
1990	E	4-151 (2.5)	0.0010–0.0022	0.0100–0.0200	0.0100–0.0200	0.0200–0.0600	0.0020–0.0030	0.0010–0.0030	0.0150–0.0550
	R	6-173 (2.8)	0.0007–0.0017	0.0100–0.0220	0.0100–0.0220	0.0200–0.0550	0.0012–0.0027	0.0015–0.0037	0.0078
	D	6-189 (3.1)	0.0009–0.0022	0.0010–0.0200	0.0200–0.0280	0.0100–0.0300	0.0020–0.0035	0.0020–0.0035	0.0080
	Z	6-262 (4.3)	0.0007–0.0017	0.0100–0.0200	0.0100–0.0250	0.0150–0.0550	0.0012–0.0032	0.0012–0.0032	0.0020–0.0070

TORQUE SPECIFICATIONS

All readings in ft. lbs.

Year	VIN	No. Cylinder Displacement cu. in. (liter)	Cylinder Head Bolts	Main Bearing Bolts	Rod Bearing Bolts	Crankshaft Pulley Bolts	Flywheel Bolts	Manifold		Spark Plugs
								Intake	Exhaust	
1986	E	4-151 (2.5)	90	70	32	160	55	30	①	7–15
	R	6-173 (2.8)	70	70	39	70	52	23	25	22
	Z	6-262 (4.3)	65	75	45	70	75	35	②	21
1987	E	4-151 (2.5)	90	70	32	160	55	30	①	7–15
	R	6-173 (2.8)	70	70	39	70	52	23	25	22
	Z	6-262 (4.3)	65	75	45	70	75	35	②	21
1988	E	4-151 (2.5)	③	70	32	160	55 ④	30	①	7–15
	R	6-173 (2.8)	⑤	70	39	70	52	23	25	22
	Z	6-262 (4.3)	65	80	45	70	75	35	②	22
1989	E	4-151 (2.5)	③	70	32	160	55 ④	30	①	7–15
	R	6-173 (2.8)	⑤	70	39	70	52	23	25	22
	Z	6-262 (4.3)	65	80	45	70	75	35	②	22
1990	E	4-151 (2.5)	③	65	30	160	55 ④	25	①	15
	R	6-173 (2.8)	⑤	70	39	70	52	23	25	22
	D	6-189 (3.1)	⑤	72	39	85	52	19	19	25
	Z	6-262 (4.3)	65	80	45	70	75	35	②	22

① Inner bolts: 36 ft. lbs.
   Outer bolts: 32 ft. lbs.
② Center Bolts: 26 ft. lbs.
   Outer bolts: 20 ft. lbs.
③ Tighten in 3 stages:
   1st to 18 ft. lbs.
   2nd to 26 ft. lbs. (except studs—tighten to 18 ft. lbs.)
   3rd an additional 90 degrees (¼ turn)
④ With manual transmission 65 ft. lbs.
⑤ Tighten in 2 stages:
   1st to 40 ft. lbs.
   2nd an additional 90 degrees (¼ turn)

GENERAL MOTORS CORPORATION
S/T SERIES (PICK-UP) • S10 BLAZER/S15 JIMMY • ASTRO/SAFARI

BRAKE SPECIFICATIONS
All measurements in inches unless noted

Year	Model	Lug Nut Torque (ft. lbs.)	Master Cylinder Bore	Brake Disc Minimum Thickness	Brake Disc Maximum Runout	Standard Brake Drum Diameter	Minimum Lining Thickness Front	Minimum Lining Thickness Rear
1986	S10/15 Pick-Up 2WD	90	NA	0.965	0.004	9.500	0.030	0.030
	S10/15 Pick-Up 4WD	90	NA	0.965	0.004	9.500	0.030	0.030
	S10/15 Blazer/Jimmy 2WD	90	NA	0.965	0.004	9.500	0.030	0.030
	S10/15 Blazer/Jimmy 4WD	90	NA	0.965	0.004	9.500	0.030	0.030
	S10/15 Cab-Chassis	90	NA	0.965	0.004	9.500	0.030	0.030
	Astro/Safari	90	NA	0.965	0.004	9.500	0.030	0.030
1987	S10/15 Pick-Up 2WD	90	NA	0.965	0.004	9.500	0.030	0.030
	S10/15 Pick-Up 4WD	90	NA	0.965	0.004	9.500	0.030	0.030
	S10/15 Blazer/Jimmy 2WD	90	NA	0.965	0.004	9.500	0.030	0.030
	S10/15 Blazer/Jimmy 4WD	90	NA	0.965	0.004	9.500	0.030	0.030
	S10/15 Cab-Chassis	90	NA	0.965	0.004	9.500	0.030	0.030
	Astro/Safari	90	NA	0.965	0.004	9.500	0.030	0.030
1988	S10/15 Pick-Up 2WD	90	NA	0.965	0.004	9.500	0.030	0.030
	S10/15 Pick-Up 4WD	90	NA	0.965	0.004	9.500	0.030	0.030
	S10/15 Blazer/Jimmy 2WD	90	NA	0.965	0.004	9.500	0.030	0.030
	S10/15 Blazer/Jimmy 4WD	90	NA	0.965	0.004	9.500	0.030	0.030
	S10/15 Cab-Chassis	90	NA	0.965	0.004	9.500	0.030	0.030
	Astro/Safari	90	NA	0.965	0.004	9.500	0.030	0.030
1989	S10/15 Pick-Up 2WD	90	NA	0.965	0.004	9.500	0.030	0.030
	S10/15 Pick-Up 4WD	90	NA	0.965	0.004	9.500	0.030	0.030
	S10/15 Blazer/Jimmy 2WD	90	NA	0.965	0.004	9.500	0.030	0.030
	S10/15 Blazer/Jimmy 4WD	90	NA	0.965	0.004	9.500	0.030	0.030
	Astro/Safari	90	NA	0.965	0.004	9.500	0.030	0.030
1990	S10/15 Pick-Up 2WD	73 ①	NA	0.965	0.004	9.500	0.030	0.030
	S10/15 Pick-Up 4WD	73 ①	NA	0.965	0.004	9.500	0.030	0.030
	S10/15 Blazer/Jimmy 2WD	73 ①	NA	0.965	0.004	9.500	0.030	0.030
	S10/15 Blazer/Jimmy 4WD	73 ①	NA	0.965	0.004	9.500	0.030	0.030
	Astro/Safari	90	NA	0.965	0.004	9.500	0.030	0.030
	Astro/Safari 4WD	90			0.004	9.500	0.030	0.030
	Lumina APV	100	0.944	0.957	0.004	8.863	0.030	0.030
	Silhouette	100	0.944	0.957	0.004	8.863	0.030	0.030
	Trans Sport	100	0.944	0.957	0.004	8.863	0.030	0.030

① Steel wheels, aluminum wheels: 90 ft. lbs.

WHEEL ALIGNMENT

Year	Model	Caster Range (deg.)	Caster Preferred Setting (deg.)	Camber Range (deg.)	Camber Preferred Setting (deg.)	Toe-in (in.)	Steering Axis Inclination (deg.)
1986	S10/15 Pick-Up 2WD	1P–3P	2P	0–1⅝P	¹³/₁₆P	⅛	NA
	S10/15 Pick-Up 4WD	1P–3P	2P	0–1⅝P	¹³/₁₆P	⅛	NA
	S10/15 Blazer/Jimmy 2WD	1P–3P	2P	0–1⅝P	¹³/₁₆P	⅛	NA
	S10/15 Blazer/Jimmy 4WD	1P–3P	2P	0–1⅝P	¹³/₁₆P	⅛	NA
	S10/15 Cab-Chassis	1P–3P	2P	0–1⅝P	¹³/₁₆P	⅛	NA
	Astro/Safari	1¹¹/₁₆P–3¹¹/₁₆P	2¹¹/₁₆P	0–1¹⁹/₃₂P	¹³/₁₆P	³/₃₂	NA
1987	S10/15 Pick-Up 2WD	1P–3P	2P	0–1⅝P	¹³/₁₆P	⅛	NA
	S10/15 Pick-Up 4WD	1P–3P	2P	0–1⅝P	¹³/₁₆P	⅛	NA
	S10/15 Blazer/Jimmy 2WD	1P–3P	2P	0–1⅝P	¹³/₁₆P	⅛	NA
	S10/15 Blazer/Jimmy 4WD	1P–3P	2P	0–1⅝P	¹³/₁₆P	⅛	NA
	S10/15 Cab-Chassis	1P–3P	2P	0–1⅝P	¹³/₁₆P	⅛	NA
	Astro/Safari	1¹¹/₁₆P–3¹¹/₁₆P	2¹¹/₁₆P	0–1¹⁹/₃₂P	¹³/₁₆P	³/₃₂	NA
1988	S10/15 Pick-Up 2WD	1P–3P	2P	0–1⅝P	¹³/₁₆P	⅛	NA
	S10/15 Pick-Up 4WD	1P–3P	2P	0–1⅝P	¹³/₁₆P	⅛	NA
	S10/15 Blazer/Jimmy 2WD	1P–3P	2P	0–1⅝P	¹³/₁₆P	⅛	NA
	S10/15 Blazer/Jimmy 4WD	1P–3P	2P	0–1⅝P	¹³/₁₆P	⅛	NA
	S10/15 Cab-Chassis	1P–3P	2P	0–1⅝P	¹³/₁₆P	⅛	NA
	Astro/Safari	1¹¹/₁₆P–3¹¹/₁₆P	2¹¹/₁₆P	0–1¹⁹/₃₂P	¹³/₁₆P	³/₃₂	NA
1989	S10/15 Pick-Up 2WD	1P–3P	2P	0–1⅝P	¹³/₁₆P	⅛	NA
	S10/15 Pick-Up 4WD	1P–3P	2P	0–1⅝P	¹³/₁₆P	⅛	NA
	S10/15 Blazer/Jimmy 2WD	1P–3P	2P	0–1⅝P	¹³/₁₆P	⅛	NA
	S10/15 Blazer/Jimmy 4WD	1P–3P	2P	0–1⅝P	¹³/₁₆P	⅛	NA
	Astro/Safari	1¹¹/₁₆P–3¹¹/₁₆P	2¹¹/₁₆P	0–1¹⁹/₃₂P	¹³/₁₆P	³/₃₂	NA
1990	S10/15 Pick-Up 2WD	1P–3P	2P	0–1⅝P	¹³/₁₆P	⅛	NA
	S10/15 Pick-Up 4WD	1P–3P	2P	0–1⅝P	¹³/₁₆P	⅛	NA
	S10/15 Blazer/Jimmy 2WD	1P–3P	2P	0–1⅝P	¹³/₁₆P	⅛	NA
	S10/15 Blazer/Jimmy 4WD	1P–3P	2P	0–1⅝P	¹³/₁₆P	⅛	NA
	Astro/Safari	1¹¹/₁₆P–3¹¹/₁₆P	2¹¹/₁₆P	0–1¹⁹/₃₂P	¹³/₁₆P	³/₃₂	NA
	Lumina APV	¹²/₁₆P–2P	1¹²/₁₆P	0–½P	0	0	NA
	Silhouette	¹²/₁₆P–2P	1¹²/₁₆P	0–½P	0	0	NA
	Trans Sport	¹²/₁₆P–2P	1¹²/₁₆P	0–½P	0	0	NA

ENGINE ELECTRICAL

Distributor

Removal and Installation

1. Disconnect the negative battery cable.
2. Remove all necessary components in order to gain access to the distributor assembly.
3. Disconnect the distributor electrical connectors. Mark and remove the spark plug wires.
4. Remove the distributor cap. Position the engine at TDC. Matchmark the rotor and the distributor body. Matchmark the distributor assembly and the engine block.

5. Remove the distributor retaining bolt. Carefully remove the distributor from the vehicle.

NOTE: As the distributor is removed from the engine, the rotor will turn counterclockwise. Observe and mark the start and finish rotation of the rotor. When reinstalling, position the rotor at the last mark and set the distributor into the engine. As the distributor drops into place, the rotor should turn to its original position, providing the engine crankshaft had not been rotated with the distributor out.

6. Installation is the reverse of the removal procedure.

Ignition Timing

Adjustment

1. Locate and clean off the timing marks.
2. Use chalk or white paint to color the mark on the scale that will indicate the correct timing, when aligned with the mark on the pulley or the pointer.
3. Attach a tachometer to the engine. Attach a timing light to the engine.
4. On some engines, it is necessary to disconnect the EST connector to set the timing. See the underhood sticker.
5. Adjust the idle to the correct specification.
6. Loosen the distributor lock bolt just enough so that the distributor can be turned with a little resistance.
7. With the timing light aimed at the pulley and the marks on the engine, turn the distributor in the direction of rotor rotation to retard the spark, and in the opposite direction of rotor rotation to advance the spark. Align the marks on the pulley and the engine with the flashes of the timing light.

Alternator

For further information, please refer to "Electrical" in the Unit Repair section.

Removal and Installation

1. Disconnect the negative battery cable. Disconnect the electrical connectors at the alternator.
2. Remove the necessary components in order to gain access to the alternator assembly. On Astro and Safari, remove the upper radiator fan shroud.
3. Remove the alternator belt. On models so equipped relieve the tension on the serpentine drive belt and remove the serpentine drive belt.
4. Remove the alternator retaining bolts and remove the alternator from the vehicle.
5. Installation is the reverse of the removal procedure. Adjust the alternator belt, as required.

Belt Tension Adjustment

STANDARD BELT

1. Run the engine at idle for a minimum of 15 minutes. This allows the belt to reseat itself in the pulleys.
2. Allow the drive belt to cool, warm to the touch but not hot.
3. Place a belt tension gauge at the center of the greatest belt span. The tension should be between 67–90 ft. lbs. (300–400 Nm).

SERPENTINE DRIVE BELT

The serpentine belt grooves must match the grooves in the pulleys. The tensioner is spring loaded. After removing the belt the tensioner will return the tension position.

1. Insert a ½ in. breaker bar into the tensioner pulley.
2. Rotate the tensioner to the left (counterclockwise) and remove the belt.
3. Route the new belt over all the pulleys except the water pump.
4. Insert a ½ in. breaker bar into the tensioner pulley.
5. Rotate the tensioner pulley to the left (counterclockwise).
6. Install the belt over the water pump pulley.
7. Check the belt for correct V groove tracking.

Starter

For further information, please refer to "Electrical" in the Unit Repair section.

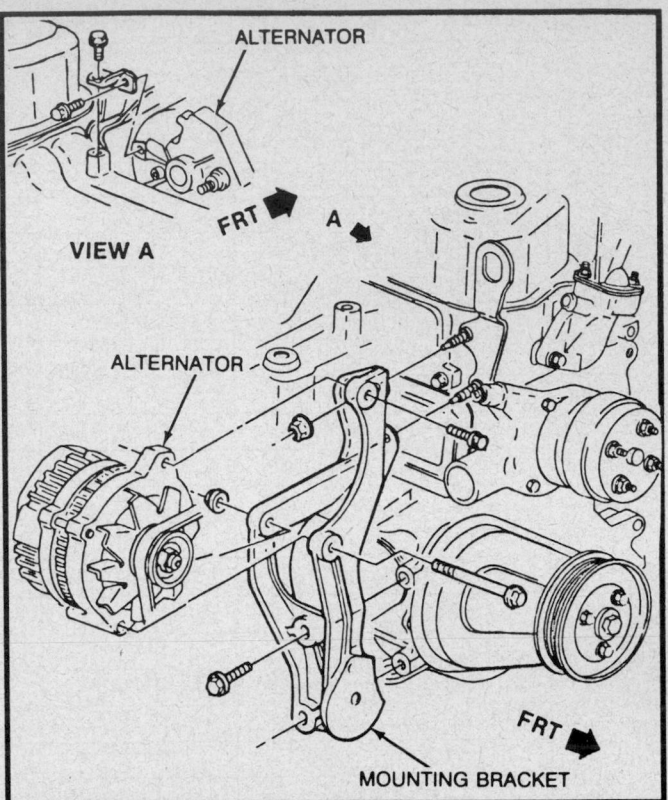

Alternator mounting—2.5L engine

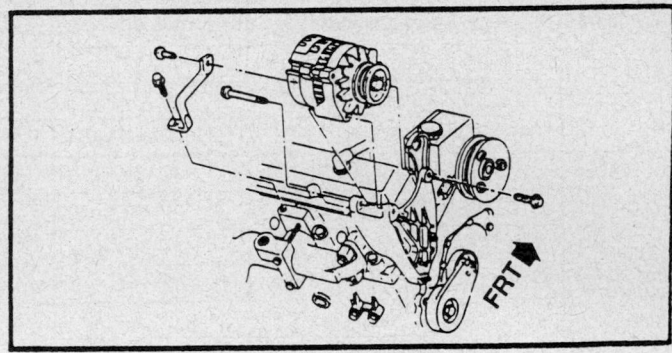

Alternator mounting—3.1L engine

Removal and Installation

PICK-UP, BLAZER AND JIMMY

2WD Vehicle

1. Disconnect the negative battery cable.
2. Raise and support the vehicle safely.
3. Disconnect the solenoid wiring.
4. On the 2.5L engine, disconnect the brush end mounting bracket and wiring.
5. Remove the 2 bolts and washers and remove the starter and the shim.
6. Installation is the reverse of removal. Install the shim and torque the mounting bolts to 31 ft. lbs. (2.5L engine), 30 ft. lbs. (2.8L and 4.3L engines).

4WD Vehicle

1. Disconnect the negative battery cable.
2. Raise and support the vehicle safely.

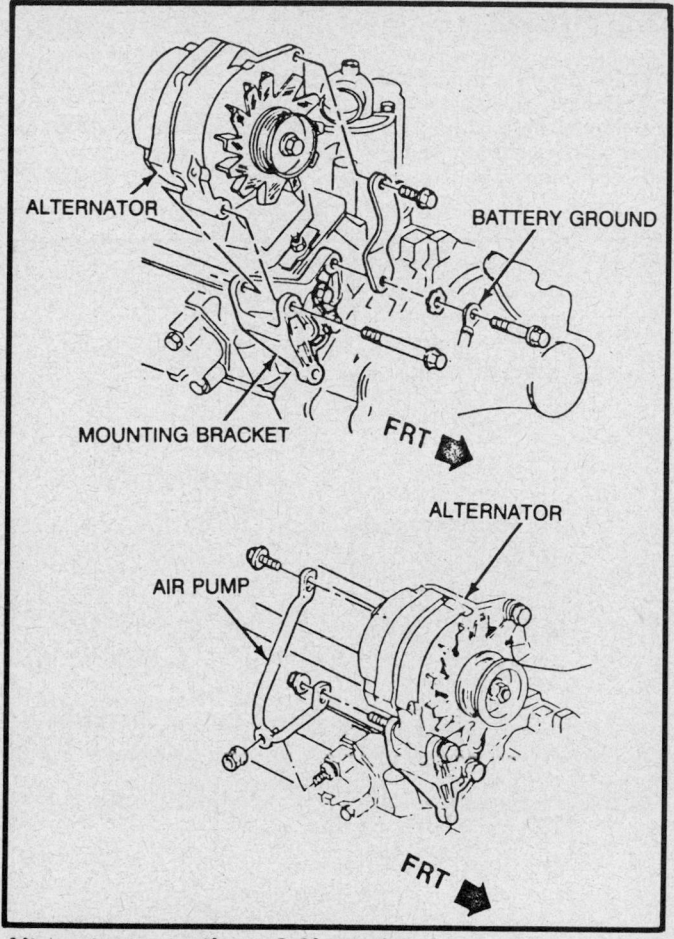

Alternator mounting—2.8L engine

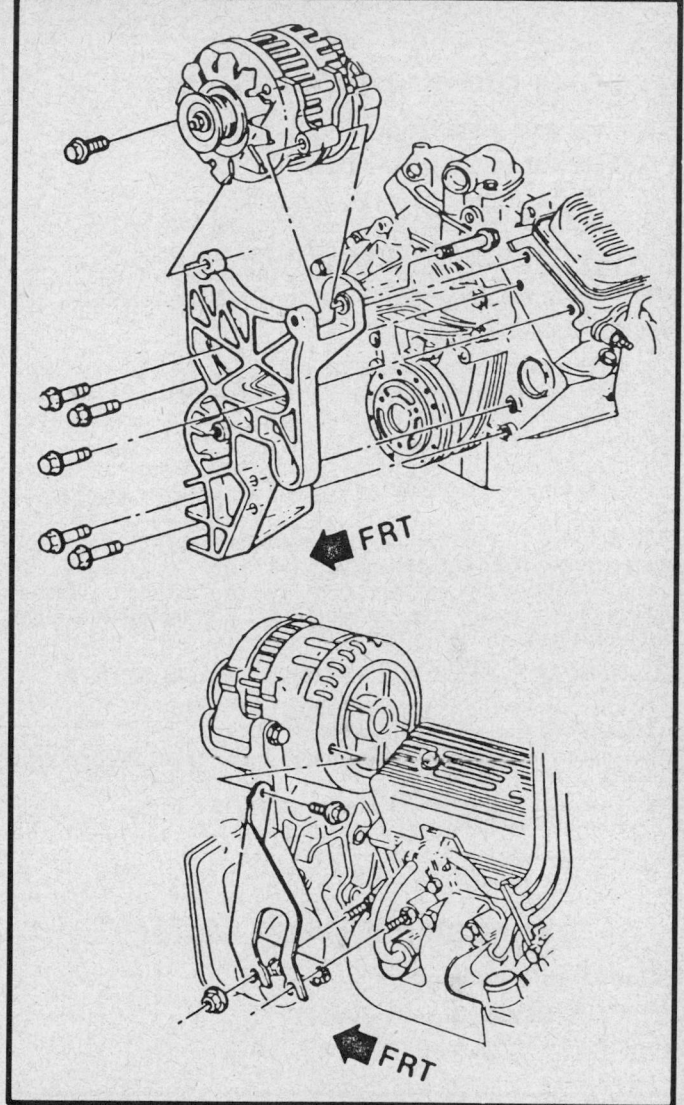

Alternator mounting—4.3L engine

3. Disconnect the solenoid wiring.
4. On the 2.5L engine, disconnect the brush end mounting bracket and wiring.
5. remove the 4 bolts on the skid plate, if so equipped and remove the skid plate.
6. Remove the bolts and 2 brackets holding the brake line to the crossmember.
7. Remove the 3 bolts on each side and remove the crossmember.
8. Remove the bracket holding the transmission cooler lines to the flywheel housing, brace rod to the flywheel housing, and the flywheel housing as necessary.
9. Remove the 2 bolts and washers and remove the starter and the shim.
6. Installation is the reverse of removal. Install the shim and torque the mounting bolts to 31 ft. lbs. (2.5L engine), 30 ft. lbs. (2.8L and 4.3L engines).

ASTRO AND SAFARI

1. Disconnect the negative battery cable.
2. Raise and support the vehicle safely.
3. Disconnect the solenoid wiring.
4. Remove the 2 bolts and washers and remove the starter and the shim.

5. Installation is the reverse of removal. Install the shim (if used) and torque the mounting bolts to 31 – 32 ft. lbs. (2.5L engine), 28 ft lbs. (1986–87 4.3L engine) and 35 ft. lbs. (1988–90 4.3L engine).

LUMINA APV, SILHOUETTE AND TRANS SPORT

1. Disconnect the negative battery cable.
2. As necessary, raise and support the vehicle safely.
3. Disconnect the oil pressure sensor electrical connector.
4. Disconnect the oil pressure sensor.
5. Disconnect the solenoid wiring.
6. Remove the 2 bolts and washers and remove the starter and the shim.
7. Installation is the reverse of removal. Install the shim, if used and torque the mounting bolts to 32 ft. lbs.

CHASSIS ELECTRICAL

Heater Blower Motor

Removal and Installation

PICK-UP, BLAZER AND JIMMY

1. Disconnect the battery ground cable.
2. Disconnect the blower motor electrical connections.
3. Remove the blower motor attaching screws.
4. Remove the blower motor from the vehicle.
5. Installation is the reverse of the removal procedure.

ASTRO AND SAFARI

1. Disconnect the negative battery cable.
2. Remove the engine coolant bottle. Remove the 2 bolts from the windshield washer bottle and position the assembly out of the way.
3. Disconnect the electrical connections from the heater blower assembly. Remove the blower motor relay bracket, as required.
4. Remove the blower motor retaining screws. Remove the heater motor from the vehicle.
5. Installation is the reverse of the removal procedure. Transfer the blower motor cage, as required. Upon installation align the motor assembly with the alignment pin.

LUMINA APV, SILHOUETTE AND TRANS SPORT

1. Disconnect the negative battery cable.
2. Remove the engine air cleaner.
3. Disconnect the left windshield wiper transmission arm linkage.
4. Disconenct the blower motor electrical harness.
5. Remove the blower motor retaining screws and remove the blower motor assembly.
6. Installation is the reverse of removal.

Windshield Wiper Motor

Removal and Installation

PICK-UP, BLAZER AND JIMMY

1. Disconnect the negative battery cable.

2. Remove the windshield wiper arms.
3. Remove the cowl screen, as required.
4. Mark the position of the wiper motor arm. Remove the wiper motor arm nut and remove the arm.
5. Disconnect the electrical wiring from the motor assembly.

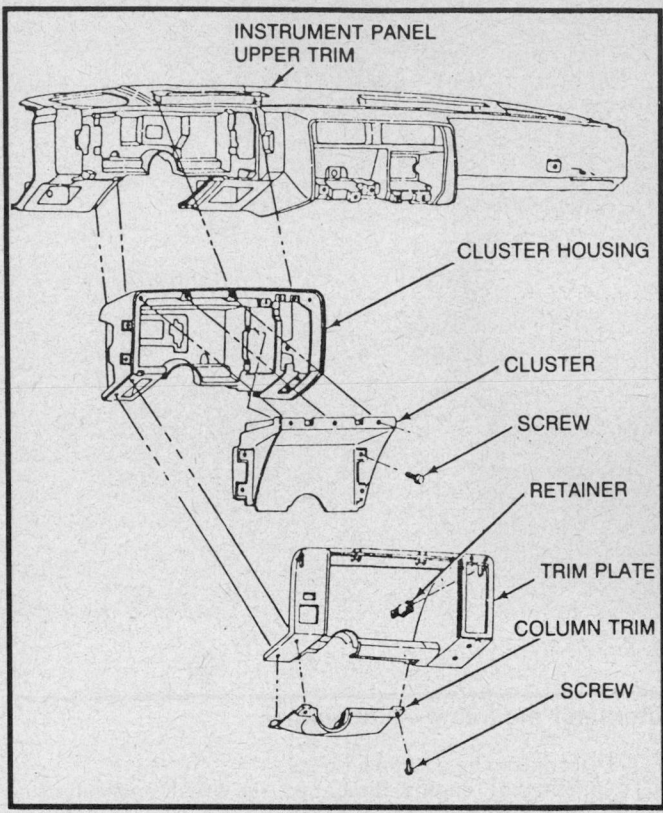

Instrument cluster assembly—Astro and Safari

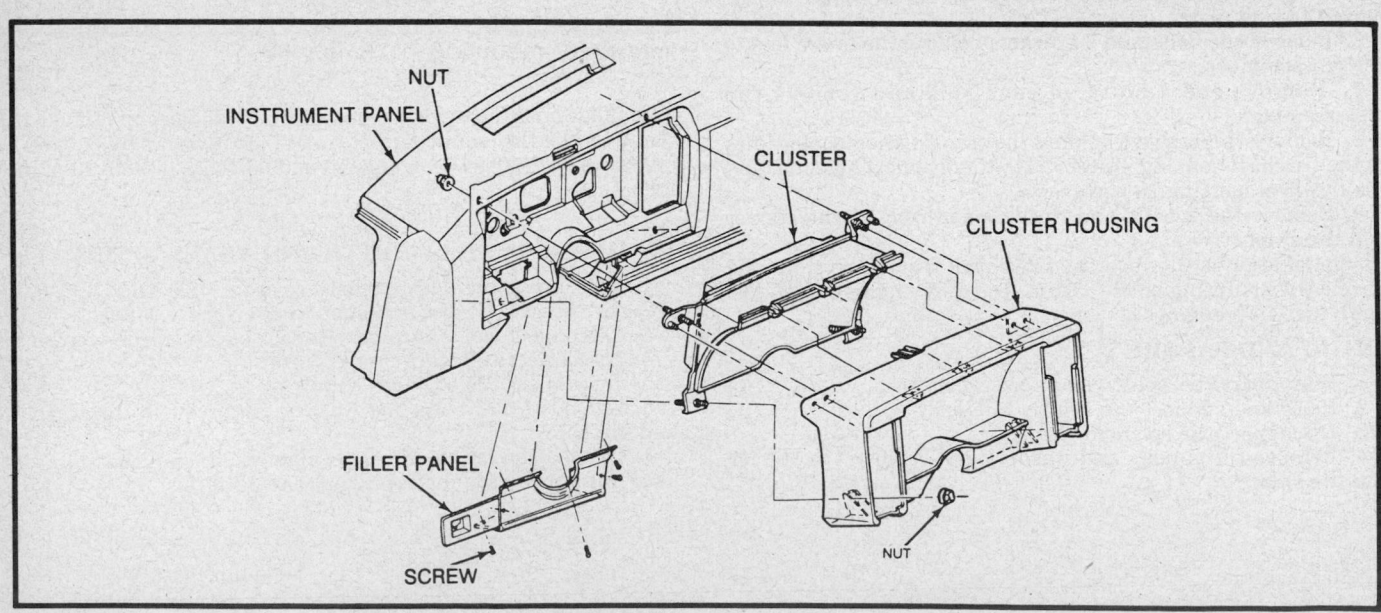

Instrument cluster assembly—Pick-Up, Blazer and Jimmy

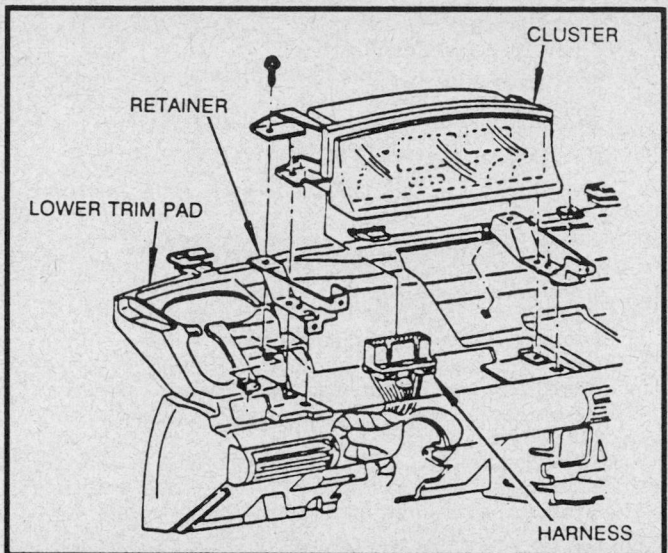

Instrument cluster assembly—Silhouette

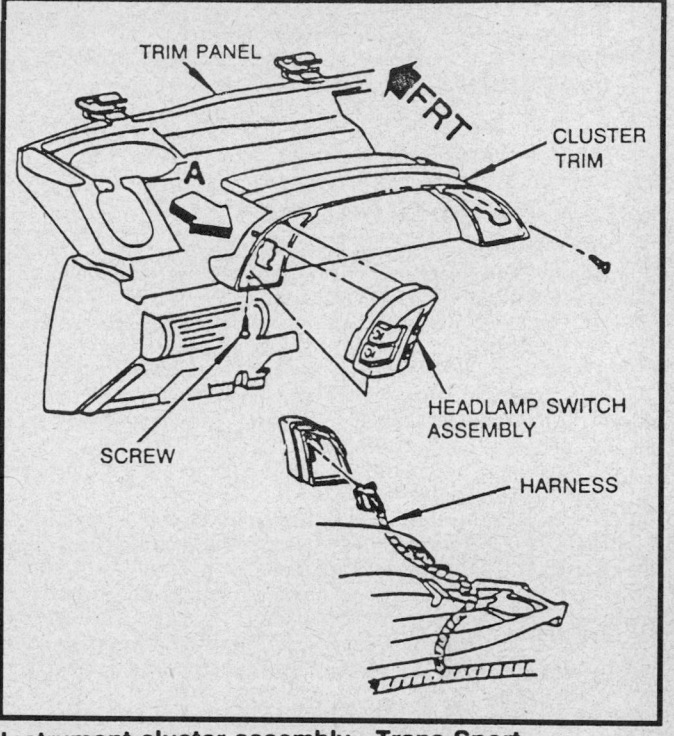

Instrument cluster assembly—Trans Sport

6. Remove the motor retaining screws. Remove the windshield wiper motor while guiding it through the hole.

7. Installation is the reverse of the removal procedure. Install the arm in alignment with the previously made mark.

ASTRO AND SAFARI

1. Disconnect the negative battery cable.
2. Disconnect the transmission link from the crank arm on the motor by pulling or prying it toward the rear of the vehicle.
3. Remove the wiper arm bolts and remove the wiper arm.
4. Remove the motor mounting bolts and remove the motor.
5. Installation is the reverse of removal.

LUMINA APV, SILHOUETTE AND TRANS SPORT

1. Run the wipers to the park position.
2. Disconnect the negative battery cable.
3. Disconnect the washer hoses.
4. Remove the nut from each wiper arm.
5. Lift each wiper arm and insert a suitable pin completely through the 2 holes located next to the pivot of the arm, then using tool J-22888 or equivalent, remove the arms from the drive shafts.
6. Remove the air cleaner.
7. Disconnect the wiring harness from the wiper motor.
8. Using a Torx® bit, remove the 2 wiper housing bolts.
9. Remove the 3 mounting nuts and washers and and remove the module from the vehicle.
10. Loosen the 2 crank arm socket screw and lockwashers until the socket releases from the crank arm ball.

NOTE: Do not remove the crank arm from the motor.

11. Remove the 3 wiper motor retaining screws and remove the wiper motor from the frame.
11. Make sure the wiper motor is in the park position and reverse the removal procedure.

Windshield Wiper Switch

Removal and Installation

PICK-UP, BLAZER, JIMMY, ASTRO, SAFARI AND LUMINA APV

The wiper switch on these vehicles is part of the multifunction switch on the column.

1. Disconnect the negative battery cable.
2. Remove the wiring protector cover underneath the column.
3. Disconnect the multi-function switch.
4. Disconnect the cruise control wire.
5. Remove the switch.
6. Installation is the reverse of removal. Feed the cruise control wire into the column using piano wire or something similar.

TRANS SPORT AND SILHOUETTE

1. Disconnect the negative battery cable.
2. Grip the pod and carefully pull the wiper switch out to release the 2 spring retaining clips.
3. Disconnect the electrical connector and remove the switch.
4. Installation is the reverse of removal.

Instrument Cluster

Removal and Installation

PICK-UP, BLAZER AND JIMMY

1. Disconnect the negative battery cable.
2. Remove the lamp switch trim plate screws and remove the trim plate.
3. Disconnect the lamp switch harness.
4. Remove the air conditioner and heater control assembly retaining screws and remove the control assembly.
5. Disconnect the air conditioner and heater control assembly harness.
6. Remove the filler panel screws and remove the filler panel.
7. Remove the instrument cluster housing nuts and remove the instrument cluster housing.
8. Remove the instrument cluster nuts and remove the instrument cluster.
9. Disconnect the speedometer drive cable and the cluster harness.
10. Installation is the reverse of removal.

ASTRO AND SAFARI

1. Disconnect the negative battery cable.
2. Remove the instrument panel cluster trim plate screws.
3. Remove the instrument panel cluster screws.
4. Disconnect the instrument panel cluster harness connectors.
5. Remove the instrument panel cluster.
6. Installation is the reverse of removal.

LUMINA APV AND TRANS SPORT

1. Disconnect the negative battery cable.
2. Remove the 4 screws securing the instrument panel pad to the instrument panel lower trim pad.
3. On Canadian models so equipped, disconnect the daytime running lights sensor attached to the pad under the front left hand speaker grille.
4. Lift the instrument panel trim pad up and pull the pad rearward to disengage the pad from the 4 slots in the lower trim pad and remove the pad assembly.
5. Grip the pod and carefully pull the wiper switch out to release the 2 spring retaining clips.
6. Disconnect the electrical connector and remove the switch.
7. Remove the 2 cluster housing screws attaching the trim to the instrument panel lower trim pad.
8. Feed the instrument panel harness through the switch pod openings in the housing.
9. Lift the housing up while pulling rearward to release the 2 tabs on the pad from the slots in the housing and remove the cluster housing.
10. Remove the 4 bolts securing the cluster to the right and left hand retainers.
11. Disconnect the instrument panel harness connector and remove the cluster.
12. Installation is the reverse of removal.

SILHOUETTE

1. Disconnect the negative battery cable.
2. Open the glove box door to access the 2 screws securing the lower instrument panel trim pad assembly to the instrument panel pad assembly.
3. Remove the 2 screws securing the instrument cluster trim panel to the instrument panel pad.
4. Remove the screw retaining the headlamp switch pod to the cluster trim panel and remove the headlamp switch pod. Disconnect the wiring harness to the pod.
5. Remove the screw retaining the windshield wiper switch pod to the cluster trim panel and remove the wiper switch pod. Disconnect the wiring harness to the pod.
6. Remove the 2 screws behind each switch pod securing the cluster trim panel to the left and right instrument cluster mounting brackets.
7. Remove the steering column opening filler.
8. Disconenct the **PNDRL** cable clip.
9. Disconnect the instrument panel harness connector to the instrument cluster.
10. Remove the 2 screws on each side from the left and right cluster retainer brackets and remove the instruments cluster.
11. Installation is the reverse of removal.

Speedometer

Removal and Installation
PICK-UP, BLAZER AND JIMMY

1. Remove the instrument cluster.
2. Remove the cluster case retaining screws.
3. Remove the speedometer to cluster case retaining screws.
4. Remove the cluster panel from the cluster case.
5. remove the speedometer mounting screws and remove the speedometer.
6. Installation is the reverse of removal.

ASTRO AND SAFARI

1. Remove the instrument cluster.
2. Remove the speedometer head retaining screws and remove the speedometer head.
3. Installation is the reverse of removal.

LUMINA APV, SILHOUETTE AND TRANS SPORT

On these vehicles the speedometer is part of the instrument cluster.

Turn Signal Switch

Removal and Installation

1. Disconnect the negative battery cable.
2. Remove the steering wheel.
3. If necessary, remove the instrument panel trim cover.
4. Insert a suitable tool in the slot in the lock plate cover and remove the cover.
5. Use lock plate compressing tool J–23653–A or equivalent on the steering shaft and compress the lock plate. Pry the retaining ring off of the shaft and remove the lock plate.

NOTE: If the column is being disassembled on a bench, the shaft could slide out of the end of the mast jacket when the snapring is removed.

6. Remove the turn signal lever screw and lever.
7. Press the hazzard warning knob inward and then unscrew.
8. Remove the turn signal switch mounting screws. Pull the switch straight up, guiding the wiring harness and cover through the column housing.
9. Installation is the reverse of removal.

Ignition Lock Cylinder

Removal and Installation

1. Disconnect the negative battery cable.
2. Place the lock cylinder in the **RUN** position.
3. Remove the steering wheel.
4. Remove the turn signal switch. Pull the switch rearward far enough to slip it over the shaft. Do not pull the harness out of the column.
5. Remove the retaining screw and remove the lock cylinder.
To install:
6. Align the cylinder and key with the keyway in the housing, rotate clockwise and push all the way in.
7. Install the retaining screw.
8. On the Pick-Up, Blazer, Jimmy, Astro and Safari, tighten the screw to 40 inch lbs. (non-tilt columns) and 22 inch lbs. (tilt columns).
9. On the Lumina APV, Silhouette and Trans Sport tighten the screw to 22 inch lbs.
10. Install the turn signal switch and steering wheel.

Ignition and Dimmer Switch

Removal and Installation

1. Disconnect the negative battery cable. If equipped, remove the lower trim panel.
2. Remove the steering column retaining bolts. Lower the steering column assembly to gain access to the switch retaining screws. Extreme care is necessary to prevent damage to the collapsible column.
3. Make sure the switch is in the **LOCK** position. If the lock cylinder is out, pull the switch rod up to the stop, then go down one detent.
4. Remove the electrical connections from the switches. Remove the switch retaining screws. Remove the either from the column.

5. Installation is the reverse of the removal procedure. Before installation, make sure the ignition switch is in the **LOCK** position.

6. To adjust the dimmer switch, depress the switch slightly to allow insertion of a $^3/_{32}$ in. drill bit into the hole above the actuator rod. Force the switch upward then tighten the screw.

7. Install the switch using the original screws. Use of screws that are too long could prevent the column from collapsing on impact.

Combination Switch

Removal and Installation

1. Disconnect the negative battery cable.
2. Remove the wiring protector cover underneath the column.
3. Disconnect the multi-function switch.
4. Disconnect the cruise control wire.
5. Remove the switch.
6. Installation is the reverse of removal. Feed the cruise control wire into the column using piano wire or something similar.

Stoplight Switch

Removal and Installation

1. Disconnect the negative battery cable. Remove the under dash trim panel.
2. Disconnect the switch electrical connections. Remove the switch assembly from its mounting.
3. Installation is the reverse of the removal procedure. Adjust the switch, as required.

Adjustment

1. Depress the brake pedal and press the switch in until it is firmly seated in its mounting.
2. Pull the brake pedal against the pedal stop until the switch does not make any noise.
3. Electrical contact should be made when the brake pedal is depressed from its fully released position.

Clutch Start Switch

Removal and Installation

PICK-UP, BLAZER, JIMMY, ASTRO AND SAFARI

1. Disconnect the negative battery cable. Remove the under dash hush panel.
2. Disconnect the switch electrical connections.
3. Remove the switch retaining screw and remove the switch from the clutch pedal.
To install:
4. Move the slider to the rear of the shaft.
5. Push the clutch pedal to the floor.
6. Move the slider down the shaft.
7. Release the clutch pedal.
8. Install the electrical connector.
9. Install the hush panel.
10. Reconnect the battery.

Fuses and Circuit Breakers

Location

PICK-UP, BLAZER, JIMMY, ASTRO AND SAFARI

The fuse block is located at the far left side of the instrument panel.

The convenience center is located at the far left side of the instrument panel. The hazard flasher, horn relay and alarm module or buzzers are mounted on the convenience center.

LUMINA APV, SILHOUETTE AND TRANS SPORT

The fuse panel is inside the glove compartment.

The convenience center is mounted to a bracket behind the glove compartment. It can be reached by removing the right sound insulator panel. It contains the hazard warning flasher, horn relay and circuit breakers, which can be removed by pulling straight out. It also contains the chime module and A/C low fan relay. To remove the chime module first release the locking tab.

ENGINE COOLING

Radiator

Removal and Installation

PICK-UP, BLAZER, JIMMY, ASTRO AND SAFARI

1. Disconnect the negative battery cable.
2. Drain the coolant from the radiator.
3. Remove the overflow hose.
4. Remove the upper fan shroud.
5. Disconnect the hoses.
6. Disconnect and plug the transmission fluid cooler lines, if equipped.
7. Disconnect and plug the engine oil cooler lines, if equipped.
8. Remove the radiator retaining bolts and remove the radiator.
9. Installation is the reverse of the removal procedure.

LUMINA APV, SILHOUETTE AND TRANS SPORT

1. Disconnect the negative battery cable.
2. Drain the coolant from the radiator.
3. Disconnect the engine forward strut bracket at the radiator, loosen the bolt at the other end and swing the strut rearward.

4. Disconnect the forward lamp harness from the fan frame and unplug the fan connector.
5. Remove the fan attaching bolts and remove the fan and frame assembly.
6. Scribe the latch location then remove the hood latch from the radiator support.
7. Disconnect the coolant hoses from the radiator and the coolant recovery tank hose from the radiator neck.
8. Disconnect and plug the transaxle oil cooler lines.
9. Remove the radiator to support attaching bolts and clamps and remove the radiator from the vehicle.
10. Installation is the reverse of removal.

Electric Cooling Fan

Removal and Installation

LUMINA APV, SILHOUETTE AND TRANS SPORT

1. Disconnect the negative battery cable.
2. Disconnect the engine forward strut bracket from the radiator frame and swing it rearward.
3. Disconnect the forward lamp harness from the fan frame.
4. Remove the fan attaching bolts.

5. Disconnect the fan wiring.
6. Remove the fan and frame assembly from the vehicle.
7. Installation is the reverse of the removal procedure.

Heater Core

Removal and Installation

PICK-UP, BLAZER AND JIMMY

1. Disconnect the negative battery cable.
2. Drain the cooling system.
3. Remove and plug the heater hoses at the heater core.
4. Remove the heater core cover attaching screws and remove the cover.
5. Remove the screw retainers at the end of the heater core.
6. Remove the core from under the dash assembly.
7. Installation is the reverse of the removal procedure.

ASTRO AND SAFARI

1. Disconnect the negative battery cable. Drain the engine coolant.
2. Remove the engine coolant bottle. Remove the bolts from the windshield washer bottle and position it to the side. Remove and plug the heater hoses at the heater core.
3. Remove the instrument panel lower right filler panel. Remove the air distributor duct. Remove the engine cover as needed.
4. Remove the air duct. Remove vacuum lines and control cables as required.
5. Remove the heater core assembly retaining screws. Remove the heater core assembly from the vehicle.
6. Remove the heater core cover plate. Remove the heater core.
7. Installation is the reverse of the removal procedure.

LUMINA APV, SILHOUETTE AND TRANS SPORT

1. Disconnect the negative battery cable.
2. Drain the cooling system.
3. Disconnect the heater hoses.
4. Remove the right side sound insulator from under the instrument panel.
5. Remove the glove box.
6. Disconnect the vacumm hoses and wiring from in front of the heater core cover.
7. Remove the heater core cover and remove the heater core.
8. Installation is the reverse of the removal procedure.

Water Pump

Removal and Installation

1. Disconnect the negative battery cable. Drain the coolant. Remove the fan shroud, as necessary. Remove the drive belts. Remove the fan and pulley assembly.
2. Remove the necessary components in order to gain access to the water pump retaining bolts.
3. Remove the water pump retaining bolts. Remove the water pump assembly from the engine.
4. Installation is the reverse of the removal procedure. Use a new gasket as required.
5. Before installation clean the mounting surface on water pump and engine block.
6. Torque the mounting bolts on the Lumina APV, Silhouette

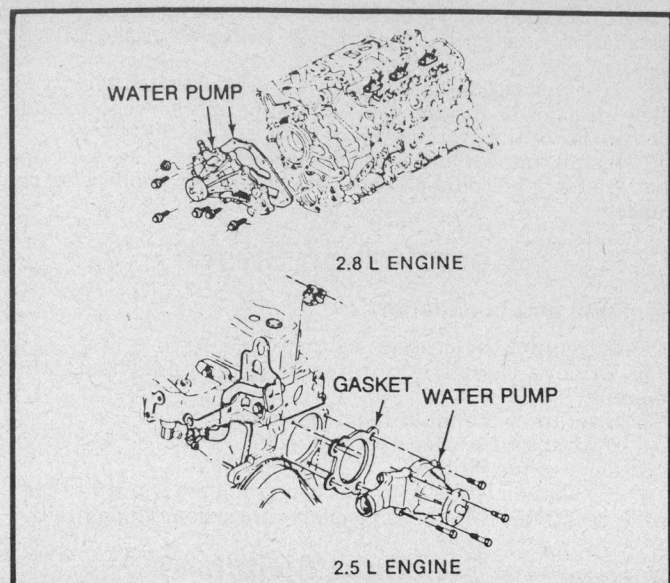

Water pump assembly mounting—2.5L and 2.8L engines

and Trans Sport to 89 inch lbs. and on the Pick-Up, Blazer, Jimmy, Astro and Safari to 22 ft. lbs.

Thermostat

Removal and Installation

1. Disconnect the negative battery cable.
2. Drain the engine coolant.
3. Disconnect the upper radiator hose from the thermostat outlet.
4. Remove the thermostat housing bolts and remove the housing.
5. Remove the thermostat from the housing.
6. Installation is the reverse of the removal procedure. Torque the housing bolts to 18 ft. lbs.
7. Bleed the cooling system.

Cooling System Bleeding

1. To bleed the system, start with the system cool, the radiator cap off and the radiator filled to about an inch below the filler neck.
2. Start the engine and run it at slightly above normal idle speed. If air bubbles appear and the coolant level drops, fill the system with an antifreeze/water mixture to bring the level back to the proper level.
3. Run the engine this way until the thermostat opens, coolant will move abruptly across the top of the radiator and the temperature of the radiator will suddenly rise.
4. At this point, air is often expelled and the level may drop quite a bit. Keep refilling the system until the level is near the top of the radiator and remains constant.
5. Fill the radiator right up to the filler neck. Replace the radiator filler cap.

FUEL SYSTEM

Fuel System Service Precaution

Relieving Fuel System Pressure

The fuel injection system used with the 2.8L, 3.1L and 4.3L engines has a built in bleed feature and requires no pressure relief before servicing. The fuel injection system used with the 2.5L engine does require pressure relief before servicing system components.

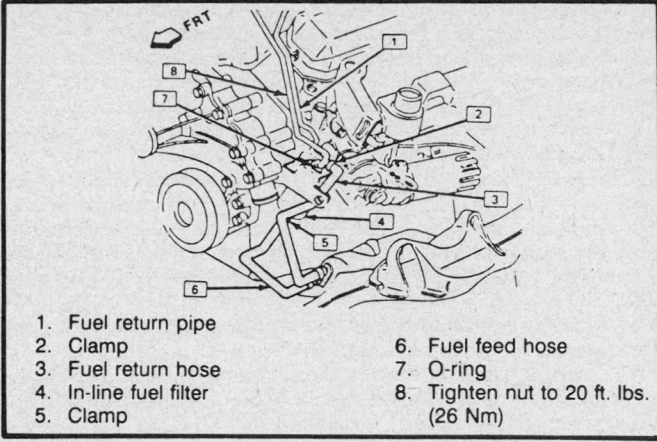

1. Fuel return pipe
2. Clamp
3. Fuel return hose
4. In-line fuel filter
5. Clamp
6. Fuel feed hose
7. O-ring
8. Tighten nut to 20 ft. lbs. (26 Nm)

Fuel filter removal and installation—2.8L engine

2.5L ENGINE

1. Place the transmission selector in the **P** position (neutral on vehicles with a manual transmission).
2. Set the parking brake and block the drive wheels.
3. Loosen the fuel filler cap. Raise and safely support the vehicle. Disconnect the electrical connector at the fuel tank.
4. Start the engine and allow it to run for a few seconds until it stalls.
5. Engage the starter a few times to bleed off any remaining pressure.
6. Disconnect the negative battery cable.
7. Service the system as required. When servicing is complete, reconnect the electrical connector at the fuel tank.

Fuel Filter

Removal and Installation

2.5L ENGINE

The fuel filter is located on the drivers side of the engine.
1. Relieve the fuel system pressure.
2. Disconnect the negative battery cable.
3. Remove the fuel line connections from the filter.
4. Remove the filter mounting clamp bolt and remove the filter.
5. Installation is the reverse of the removal procedure. Tighten the fuel line couplings to 20 ft. lbs.

2.8L AND 3.1L ENGINES

The fuel filter is located on the front drivers side of the engine.
1. Disconnect the negative battery cable.
2. Remove the fuel line connections from the filter.
3. Remove the filter mounting clamp bolt and remove the filter.
4. Installation is the reverse of the removal procedure. Tighten the fuel line couplings to 20 ft. lbs.

4.3L ENGINE

The fuel filter is located along the right rear frame rail of the vehicle.
1. Disconnect the negative battery cable.
2. Raise and safely support the vehicle.
3. Remove the fuel line connections from the filter.
4. Remove the filter mounting clamp bolt and remove the filter.
5. Installation is the reverse of the removal procedure. Tighten the fuel line couplings to 20 ft. lbs.
6. Lower the vehicle.

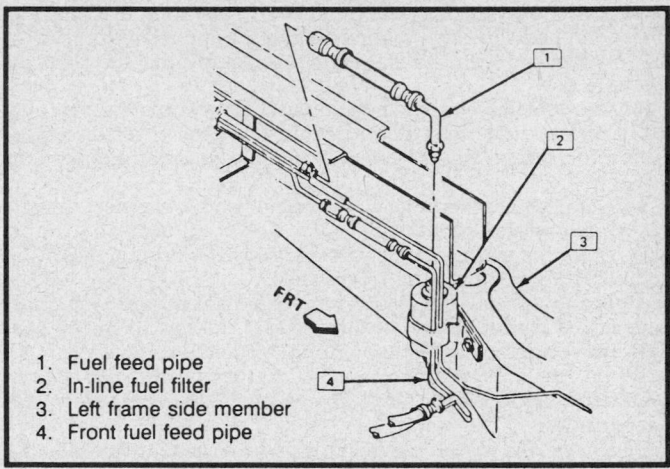

1. Fuel feed pipe
2. In-line fuel filter
3. Left frame side member
4. Front fuel feed pipe

Fuel filter removal and installation—4.3L engine

Electric Fuel Pump

Pressure Testing

1. Turn the engine **OFF** and relieve the fuel system pressure.
2. Disconnect the negative battery cable. Plug the Thermac vacuum port.
3. Disconnect the fuel supply line in the engine compartment. Install a suitable pressure gauge and T in the fuel line.
4. Connect the negative battery cable.
5. Start the engine and observe the pressure reading. The fuel pressure should be 9–13 psi.
6. If the fuel pressure is not to specification, the fuel system must be completetly checked.

Removal and Installation

1. Properly relieve the fuel system pressure, as required.
2. Disconnect the negative battery cable.
3. Drain the fuel from the vehicle, into a suitable container.
4. Raise and safely support the vehicle.
5. Disconnect the fuel lines from the fuel tank. Disconnect the electrical leads from the fuel tank.
6. Disconnect the fuel filler neck from the tank.
7. Remove the tank mounting bolts and carefully lower the tank from the vehicle.
8. Remove the pump and pick-up assembly retaining ring and remove the pump from the tank.
9. Installation is the reverse of the removal procedure. Torque the tank retaining bolts to 26 ft. lbs.

Fuel Injection

Idle Speed Adjustment

2.5L ENGINE

The throttle stop screw that is used to adjust the idle speed of the vehicle, is adjusted to specifications at the factory. The throttle stop screw is then covered with a steel plug to prevent the unnecessary readjustment in the field. If it is necessary to gain access to the throttle stop screw, the following procedure will allow access to the throttle stop screw without removing the TBI unit from the manifold.
1. Using a small punch or equivalent mark over the center line of the throttle stop screw. Drill a $5/32$ in. diameter hole through the casting of the hardened steel plug.
2. Using a $1/16$ in. diameter punch or equivalent punch out the steel plug.
3. With the transmission in the **P** (for automatic transmis-

sion equipped vehicles) positionor neutral (manual transmission equipped vehicles), the parking brake applied and the drive wheels blocked, remove the air cleaner and plug the thermac vacuum port.

4. On vehicles equipped with automatic transmsission, remove the transmission detent cable from the throttle control bracket in order to gain access to the minimum air adjustment screw.

5. Connect a tachometer to the engine and disconnect the idle air control motor connector.

6. Start the engine and let the engine reach normal operating temperature and the rpm to stabilize.

7. Install special tool J-33047 or equivalent in the idle air passage of the throttle body. Be sure to seat the tool in the air passage until it is bottomed our and no air leaks exist.

8. On the 2.5L engine, use a No. 20 torx head bit or equivalent, turn the throttle stop screws until the rpm is within specification.

9. If removed install the isolator. Install the transmission detent cable, as required.

10. Shut down the engine and remove the special tool or equivalent from the throttle body.

11. Reconnect the idle air control motor connector and seal the hole drilled through the throttle body housing with silicone sealant or equivalent.

12. Check the throttle position sensor voltage as required. Install the air cleaner and Thermac vacuum line.

2.8L, 3.1L AND 4.3L ENGINES

1. Remove the air cleaner, adapter and gaskets. Discard the gaskets. Plug any vacuum line ports, as necessary.

2. Leave the idle air control (IAC) valve connected and ground the diagnostic terminal (ALDL connector).

3. Turn the ignition switch to the **ON** position, do not start the engine. Wait for at least 30 seconds (this allows the IAC valve pintle to extend and seat in the throttle body).

4. With the ignition switch still in the **ON** position, disconnect IAC electrical connector.

5. Remove the ground from the diagnostic terminal and start the engine. Let the engine reach normal operating temperature.

6. Apply the parking brake and block the drive wheels. Remove the plug from the idle stop screw by piercing it first with a suitable tool, then applying leverage to the tool to lift the plug out.

7. With the engine in the proper shifter selector range adjust the idle stop screw to secification.

8. Turn the ignition **OFF** and reconnect the IAC valve connector. Unplug any plugged vacuum line ports and install the air cleaner, adapter and new gaskets.

Fuel Injector

Removal and Installation

1. Relieve the fuel system pressure. Disconnect the negative battery cable. Remove the air cleaner assembly.

2. Remove the fuel injector wire. Remove the fuel injector retainer clip screws. Remove the fuel injector retainer clip.

3. Using a small pair of pliers, gently grasp the center collar of the injector, between the electrical terminals and carefully remove the injector using a lifting and twisting motion.

4. Discard the upper and lower O-rings. Note that the back up ring fits over the upper O-ring.

5. Installation is the reverse of the removal procedure. Lubricate both O-rings with light oil before installation.

EMISSION CONTROLS

Please refer to "Professional Emission Component Application Guide".

Emission Warning Lamps

These vehicles are equipped with an "Service Engine Soon" light. This will illuminate only when a malfunction in the compute command control system occurs. The light can not be reset until the malfunction is corrected and the ECM memory is cleared of the fault.

ENGINE MECHANICAL

NOTE: Disconnecting the battery cable on some vehicles may interfere with the functions of the on board computer systems and may require the computer to undergo a relearning process, once the negative battery cable is disconnected.

Engine

Removal and Installation
PICK-UP, BLAZER AND JIMMY

1. Disconnect the negative battery cable. Matchmark the hood hinges and remove the hood.

2. Drain the cooling system and disconnect the upper radiator hose at the radiator. Disconnect the coolant overflow hose.

3. Remove the upper fan shroud and disconnect the oil cooler lines.

4. Remove the radiator and the cooling fan. Disconnect the heater hoses.

5. Remove the air cleaner assembly and disconnect the vacuum hoses. Disconnect all necessary wires at the bulkhead and all of the main feed wires.

6. Disconnect the throttle cable and cruise control cable (if equipped). Remove the distributor cap.

7. Raise and safely support the vehicle. Disconnect the converter-to-exhaust pipe bolts. Remove the front drive shaft on 4WD vehicles.

8. Disconnect the exhaust pipes at the manifolds. Disconnect the strut rods at the bell housing. Remove the flywheel cover.

9. Remove the torque converter bolts on automatic transmission equipped vehicles. Remove the second crossmember on 4WD vehicles.

10. Remove the rear catalytic converter shield and disconnect the converter hanger at the exhaust pipe.

11. Remove the lower fan shroud and disconnect the fuel lines. Remove the 2 outer air dam bolts.

12. Remove the 2 left body mount bolts and, using a suitable

jack, raise the body slightly. Remove the engine-to-transmission bolts.

13. Lower the body and remove the lower motor mount bolts. Lower the vehicle.

14. Remove the air conditioning compressor and power steering pump with their brackets from the engine. Do not disconnect the fluid or refrigerant lines.

15. Support the tranmission with a suitable jack. Attach a suitable lifting device to the engine and remove the engine from the vehicle.

To install:

16. Carefully lower the engine into position in the vehicle.

17. Remove the transmission support. Raise and safely support the vehicle. Install the motor mount bolts, tighten to 52 ft. lbs. (70 Nm). Install the lower bell housing bolts. Tighten to 32 ft. lbs. (44 Nm).

18. Raise the body and install the upper bell housing bolts. Tighten to 32 ft. lbs. (44 Nm).

19. Lower the body and install the body mount bolts. Install the outer air dam bolts. Connect the fuel lines and install the lower fan shroud.

20. Connect the converter hanger at the exhaust pipe and install the shield at the converter. Install the torque converter bolts and install the flywheel cover.

21. Connect the strut rods at the bell housing. Connect the exhaust pipes to the manifolds. Connect the converter to the exhaust pipes.

22. Lower the vehicle. Install the air conditioning compressor and power steering pump. Install the distributor cap.

23. Connect the throttle cable and cruise control cable. Connect all electrical wires and vacuum hoses.

24. Install the air cleaner and connect the heater hoses. Install the fan and radiator. Connect the oil cooler lines. Install the upper fan shroud.

25. Connect the overflow hose and the radiator hose. Fill the cooling system.

26. Install the hood. Connect the negative battery cable and run the engine. Bleed the cooling system.

ASTRO AND SAFARI

1. Disconnect the negative battery cable.

2. Drain the cooling system.

3. Raise and safely support the vehicle. Disconnect the exhaust pipes at the manifolds.

4. Disconnect the strut rods at the flywheel housing. Remove the flywheel cover. Remove the torque converter bolts. Drain the engine oil.

5. Remove the starter and oil filter. Disconnect the wires at the transmission. Disconnect the fuel lines.

6. Disconnect the oil cooler lines. Remove the lower fan shroud. Remove the motor mount bolts.

7. Lower the vehicle. Remove the headlight bezels and grille. Remove the radiator close out panel and the radiator support brace. Remove the lower tie bar.

8. Remove the hood latch mechanism. Remove the master cylinder and the upper fan shroud.

9. Remove the upper radiator core support and the radiator. If equipped, properly discharge the air conditioning system.

10. Remove the radiator filler panels. Remove the engine cover. Remove the air conditioning hose at the accumulator and remove the air conditioning compressor.

11. Remove the power steering pump. Disconnect the vacuum hoses at the intake manifold and the wiring at the bulkhead.

12. Remove the right kickpanel. Disconnect the harness at the ESC module and it through the bulkhead.

13. Remove the distributor cap. Remove the air conditioning accumulator, if equipped.

14. Disconnect the fuel lines. Remove the diverter valve. Remove the transmission dipstick tube.

15. Disconnect the heater hoses at the heater core. Remove the

horn and remove the AIR system check valves. Remove the engine-to-transmission bolts.

16. Attach a suitable lifting device to the engine and remove the engine from the vehicle.

To install:

17. Install the engine into the vehicle. Install the bell housing bolts.

18. Install the AIR system check valves. Install the horn and connect the heater hoses, Install the transmission dipstick tube.

19. Install the diverter valve and connect the fuel lines. Install the accumulator and install the distributor cap.

20. Connect the harness to the ESC module. Install the right kick panel.

21. Connect the bulkhead wiring and the vacuum hoses. Install the power steering pump and the air conditioning compressor.

22. Connect the refrigerant line to the accumulator. Install the engine cover.

23. Install the radiator filler panel and the radiator. Install the radiator supports and the upper fan shroud.

24. Install the hood latch and the master cylinder. Install the lower tie bar. Install the lower radiator close out panel.

25. Install the grille and headlight bezels. Raise and safely support the vehicle.

26. Install the engine mount bolts and tighten to 75 ft. lbs (100 Nm). Connect the oil cooler lines. Connect the fuel hoses and the wires at the transmission.

27. Install the oil filter and the starter. Install the torque converter bolts. Install the flywheel cover.

28. Install the strut rods at the flywheel housing. Connect the exhaust pipes. Lower the vehicle.

29. Connect the negative battery cable. Fill the cooling system and the crankcase. Charge the air conditioning system. Fill and bleed the brake system.

LUMINA APV, SILHOUETTE, TRANS SPORT

1. Disconnect the negative battery cable.

2. Drain the cooling system. Disconnect the air flow tube from the air cleaner.

3. Disconnect the electrical connector from the ECM and push it through to the engine compartment. Disconnect the harness from the clips on the body and lay it across the engine.

4. Disconnect the engine harness at the bulkhead connector. Disconnect the throttle and TV cables.

5. Disconnect the fuel lines. Disconnect the transaxle shift linkage.

6. Disconnect the cooler lines at the radiator. Disconnect the radiator and heater hoses.

7. Remove the air conditioning compressor from the bracket and support it out of the way. Remove the upper engine support strut.

8. Raise and safely support the vehicle. Remove the front wheel and tire assemblies.

9. Remove the stabilizer bar. Disconnect the tie rod ends and the lower control arm ball joints.

10. Disconnect the halfhsafts and support them out of the way. Disconnect the steering shaft pinch bolt.

11. Remove the starter.

12. Disconnect the exhaust pipe at the manifold. Support the engine and sub-frame with a suitable jack.

13. Remove the sub-frame bolts and lower the engine/transaxle and subframe from the vehicle.

To install:

14. Raise the engine assembly into position and install the subframe bolts. Tighten to 35 ft. lbs.

15. Connect the exhaust pipe at the rear manifold. Install the starter.

16. Connect the steering shaft and install the pinch bolt. Connect the halfshafts to the transaxle.

17. Connect the lower control arm ball joints to the steering knuckles.

18. Install the stabilizer bar. Install the upper engine strut.

19. Install the wheel and tire assemblies. Lower the vehicle. Install the radiator and heater hoses.

20. Install the shift linkage. Connect the fuel lines and the throttle and TV cables.

21. Connect the harness to bulkhead connector. Connect the ECM harness to the ECM.

22. Connect the air cleaner hose and the radiator upper support.

23. Fill the cooling system. Install the air conditioning compressor.

24. Connect the negative battery cable.

Cylinder Head

Removal and Installation

2.5L ENGINE

1. Disconnect the negative battery cable. Drain the cooling system. On Astro and Safari vehicles, remove the engine cover. Remove the air cleaner assembly.

2. Remove the air conditioning compressor and position it to the side. Remove the rocker arm cover. Remove the rocker arms and pushrods. Keep them in order for reinstallation.

3. Properly relieve the fuel system pressure. Disconnect the fuel line from the TBI unit. Disconnect all necessary electrical and vacuum lines.

4. Disconnect the accelerator cable, the cruise control cable and the TV cables. Remove the alternator and brackets.

5. Remove the water pump bypass hose. Disconnect the heater hoses at the intake manifold. Remove the upper radiator hose.

6. Disconnect the exhaust pipe from the exhaust manifold. Remove the fuel filter and filter brackets at the rear of the cylinder head assembly.

7. Remove the coil wire and spark plug wires. Disconnect the oxygen sensor electrical wire.

8. Remove the cylinder head retaining bolts. Remove the cylinder head along with the intake and exhaust manifold assembly.

9. Installation is the reverse of the removal procedure. Be sure that the cylinder bolt threads in the block and threads on the bolts are cleaned, as dirt will affect bolt torque.

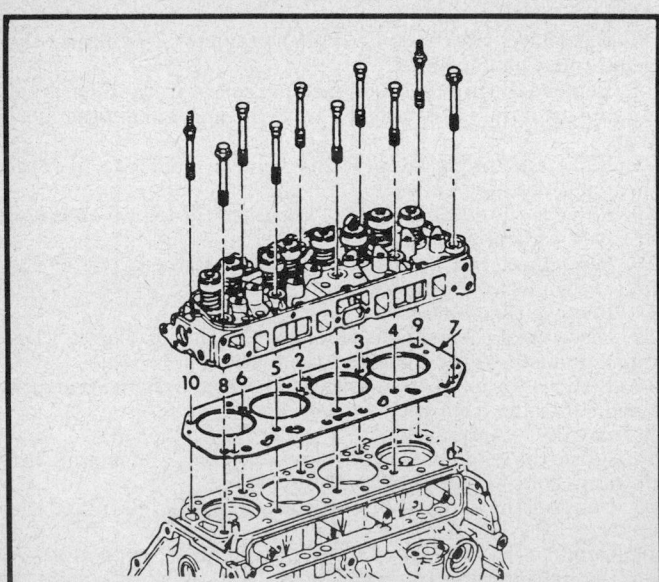

Cylinder head bolt torque sequence—2.5L engine

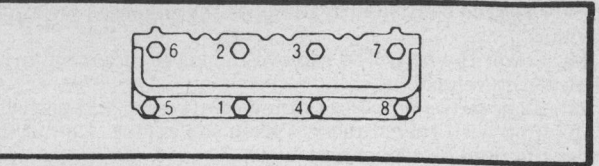

Cylinder head bolt torque sequence—2.8L and 3.1L engines

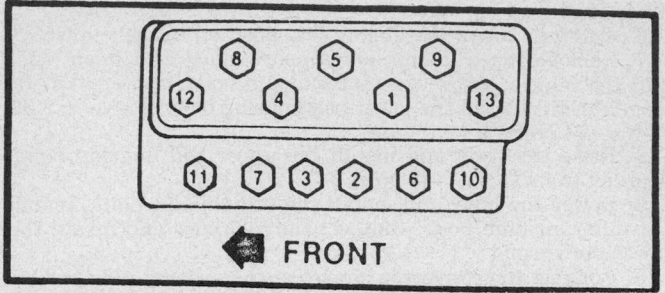

Cylinder head bolt torque sequence—4.3L engine

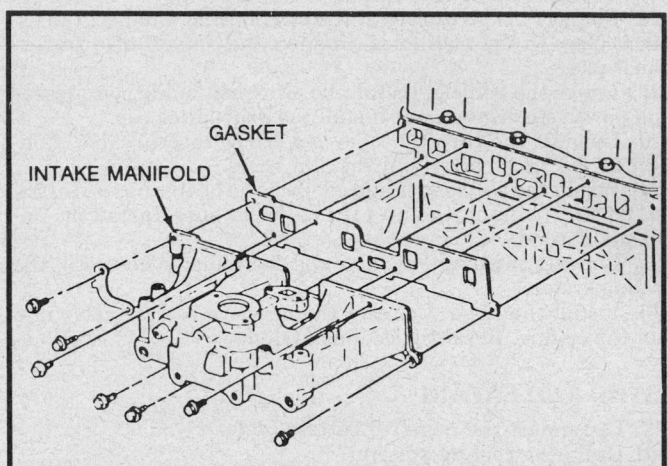

Intake manifold mounting—2.5L engine

10. Coat the threads of the 2 cylinder head bolts that use studs on top of the bolt head with sealing compound 1052080 or equivalent.

11. Position the new gasket over the dowel pins. Torque the cylinder head bolts a little at a time, to specification, and in the proper sequence.

2.8L, 3.1L AND ENGINES

1. Disconnect the negative battery cable. Drain the radiator. Remove the intake manifold.

2. Remove the valve covers. Remove the rocker arms and pushrods. Keep them in order for reinstallation.

3. Raise and support the vehicle safely. Disconnect the exhaust manifolds from the exhaust pipes. On the left side disconnect the dipstick tube attachment. On the right side remove the alternator bracket. Lower the vehicle.

4. Remove the cylinder head retaining bolts. Remove the cylinder head from the engine along with the exhaust manifold.

5. Installation is the reverse of the removal procedure. Be sure that the cylinder bolt threads in the block and threads on the bolts are cleaned, as dirt will affect bolt torque.

6. Coat the threads of the cylinder head bolts with sealing compound 1052080 or equivalent.

7. Position the new gasket over the dowel pins with THIS

SIDE UP showing. Torque the cylinder head bolts a little at a time, to specification, and in the proper sequence.

4.3L ENGINE

1. Disconnect the negative battery cable. Remove the engine cover. Drain the radiator. Remove the intake manifold. Remove the required electrical and vacuum connections.

2. Remove the valve covers. Remove the rocker arms and pushrods. Keep them in order for reinstallation. Remove the spark plugs.

3. Raise and support the vehicle safely. Remove the exhaust manifolds. On the left side, disconnect the dipstick tube attachment. On the right side, remove the alternator bracket. Lower the vehicle.

4. Remove the cylinder head retaining bolts. Remove the cylinder head from the engine.

5. Installation is the reverse of the removal procedure. Be sure that the cylinder bolt threads in the block and threads on the bolts are cleaned, as dirt will affect bolt torque.

6. If a steel gasket is used, be sure to coat both sides with sealer. Coat the threads of the cylinder head bolts with sealing compound 1052080 or equivalent.

7. Position the new gasket over the dowel pins. Torque the cylinder head bolts a little at a time, to specification and in the proper sequence.

Valve Lash

Adjustment

2.8L AND 4.3L ENGINES

1. On Astro and Safari vehicles, remove the engine cover. Remove the rocker covers.

2. Crank the engine until the mark on the damper aligns with the **0** on the timing tab and the engine is in the No. 1 firing position.

3. With the engine in the No. 1 firing position, the following valves may be adjusted on the 2.8L engine:
   a. Exhaust—1, 2, 3
   b. Intake—1, 5, 6

4. With the engine in the No. 1 firing position, the following valves may be adjusted on the 4.3L engine:
   a. Exhaust—1, 5, 6
   b. Intake—1, 2, 3

5. Back out the adjusting nut until lash is felt at the pushrod then turn in the nut until all lash is removed. When all lash has been removed, turn the adjusting nut in 1½ turns more.

6. Crank the engine until the mark on the damper aligns with the **0** mark on the timing tab. This is the No. 4 firing position.

7. With the engine in the No. 4 timing position, the following valves can be adjusted on the 2.8L engine:
   a. Exhaust—4, 5, 6
   b. Intake—2, 3, 4

8. With the engine in the No. 4 timing position, the following valves can be adjusted on the 4.3L engine:
   a. Exhaust—2, 3, 4
   b. Intake—4, 5, 6

9. Back out the adjusting nut until lash is felt at the pushrod then turn in the nut until all lash is removed. When all lash has been removed, turn the adjusting nut in 1½ turns more.

10. After all valves are adjusted, install the valve covers.

Rocker Arms

Removal and Installation

1. Disconnect the negative battery cable. On Astro and Safari, remove the engine cover.

2. Remove all the necessary components in order to gain access to the engine valve covers. On the 2.5L engine, properly re-

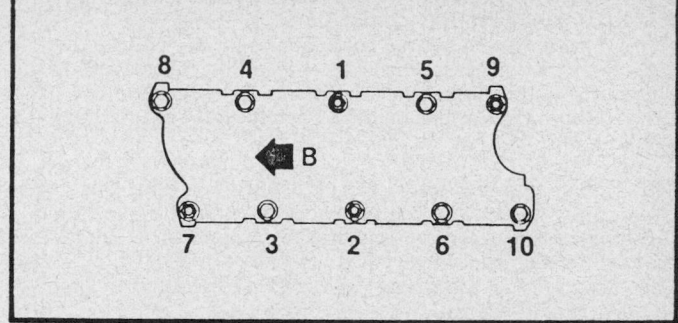

Intake manifold bolt torque sequence—2.8L engine

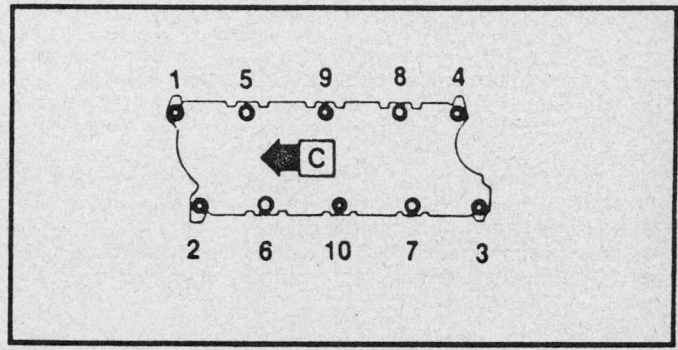

Intake manifold bolt torque sequence—3.1L engine

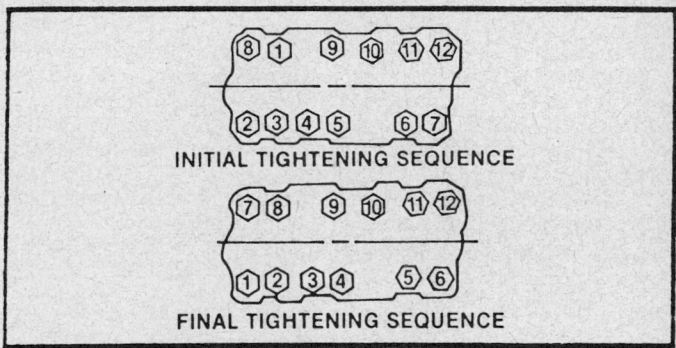

INITIAL TIGHTENING SEQUENCE

FINAL TIGHTENING SEQUENCE

Intake manifold bolt torque sequence—4.3L engine

lieve the fuel system pressure before disconnecting any fuel lines.

3. Remove the valve cover retaining bolts. Remove the valve cover from the engine.

4. Remove the rocker arm assemblies. Keep them in order for reinstallation.

5. Installation is the reverse of the removal procedure. Be sure to use new gaskets or RTV sealant.

Intake Manifold

Removal and Installation

2.5L ENGINE

1. Disconnect the negative battery cable. Remove the air cleaner assembly.

2. Drain the cooling system. Disconnect the vacuum pipe rail at the exhaust and thermostat housing.

3. Disconnect the electrical and vacuum connections, as required.

4. Disconnect the accelerator cable at the TBI unit.

5. Properly relieve the fuel pressure. Disconnect and plug the fuel lines at the intake manifold.

6. Disconnect the heater hoses at the intake manifold.

7. Remove the alternator bracket retaining bolts. Remove the alternator and position it aside. Remove the ignition coil.

8. Remove the intake manifold retaining bolts. Remove the intake manifold.

To install:

9. Install the manifold and gasket into position. Install the retaining bolts and tighten in sequence to the correct torque.

10. Install the alternator and bracket. Connect the heater hoses, vacuum and fuel lines.

11. Connect the accelerator cable. Install the air cleaner assembly. Install the coil.

12. Connect the negative battery cable. Fill the cooling system. Run the engine, check the idle speed and check for leaks.

2.8L AND 3.1L ENGINES

1. Disconnect the negative battery cable. Drain the cooling system. If equipped, remove the AIR pump and bracket.

2. Remove the distributor. Remove the heater and radiator hoses from the intake manifold. Remove the power brake vacuum hose.

3. Disconnect and label all vacuum hoses. Remove the EFE pipe from the rear of the manifold. Remove the accelerator linkage. Disconnect and plug the fuel line.

4. As required, remove the TBI unit. Remove the intake manifold retaining bolts. Remove the intake manifold from the engine.

To install:

5. The gaskets are marked for right and left side installation. Do not interchange them. Clean the sealing surface of the engine block and apply a $^3/_{16}$ in. bead of silicone sealer to each ridge.

6. Install the new gaskets onto the heads. The gaskets will have to be cut slightly to fit past the center pushrods. Do not cut any more material than necessary. Hold the gaskets in place by extending the ridge bead of sealer ¼ in. onto the gasket ends. Install the manifold and tighten the bolts in sequence to the correct torque.

7. When the intake manifold is installed the area between the ridges and the manifold should be completely sealed.

8. The remainder of the installation is the reverse of the removal procedure.

4.3L ENGINE

1. Disconnect the negative battery cable. Remove the engine cover assembly. Remove the air cleaner assembly.

2. Drain the cooling system. Remove the distributor cap and ignition wires.

3. Disconnect the ESC connector and remove the distributor.

4. Remove the detent and accelerator cables. If equipped, remove the air conditioning compressor rear brace.

5. Remove the transmission and engine oil filler tubes at the alternator brace. Remove the cruise control transducer, if equipped.

6. If equipped, remove the air conditioning idler pulley at the alternator brace. Remove the alternator brace.

7. Disconnect the fuel lines. Remove the necessary vacuum hoses and electrical wires.

8. Remove the AIR hoses and brackets. If necessary, remove the upper radiator hose. Remove the heater hose at the manifold. As required, remove the carburetor. As required remove the TBI unit.

9. Remove the intake manifold retaining bolts. Remove the intake manifold from the engine.

To install:

10. The gaskets are marked for right and left side installation. Do not interchange them. Clean the sealing surface of the engine block and apply a $^3/_{16}$ in. bead of silicone sealer to each ridge.

11. Install the new gaskets onto the heads. The gaskets will have to be cut slightly to fit past the center pushrods. Do not cut any more material than necessary. Hold the gaskets in place by extending the ridge bead of sealer ¼ in. onto the gasket ends. Install the manifold and tighten the bolts in sequence to the correct torque.

12. When the intake manifold is installed the area between the ridges and the manifold should be completely sealed.

13. The remainder of the installation is the reverse of the removal procedure.

Exhuast Manifold

Removal and Installation

2.5L ENGINE

1. Disconnect the negative battery cable.

2. Remove the exhaust stove pipe at the manifold. Disconnect the oxygen sensor wire.

3. Raise and safely support the vehicle. Disconnect the exhaust pipe at the exhaust manifold.

4. Remove the rear air conditioning compressor bracket.

5. Remove the exhaust manifold retaining bolts. Remove the manifold from the engine.

6. Installation is the reverse of the removal procedure. Torque the manifold to the correct specification.

Exhaust manifold bolt torque sequence—2.5L engine

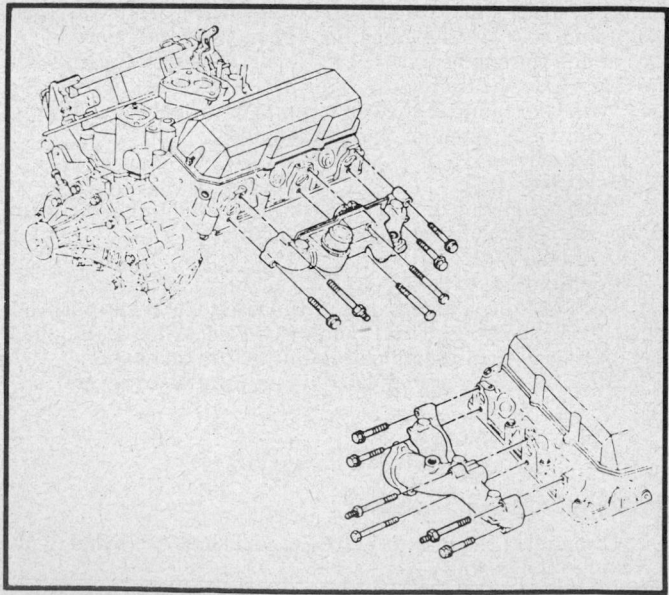

Exhaust manifold mounting—2.8L engine

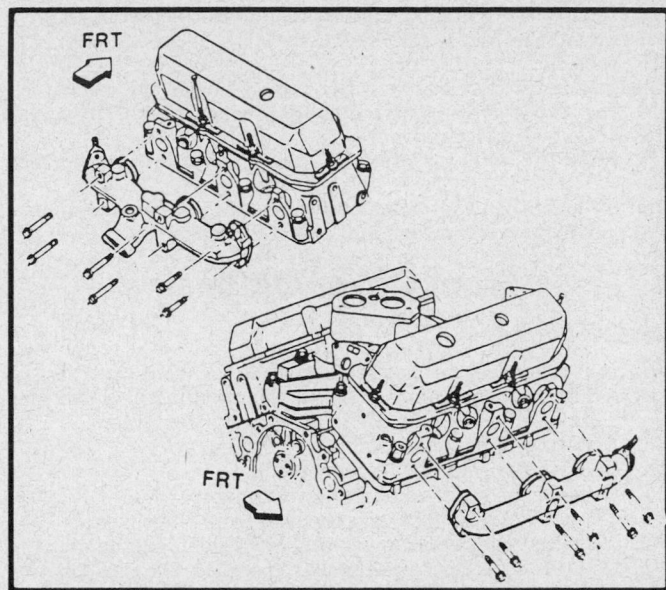

Exhaust manifold mounting—3.1L engine

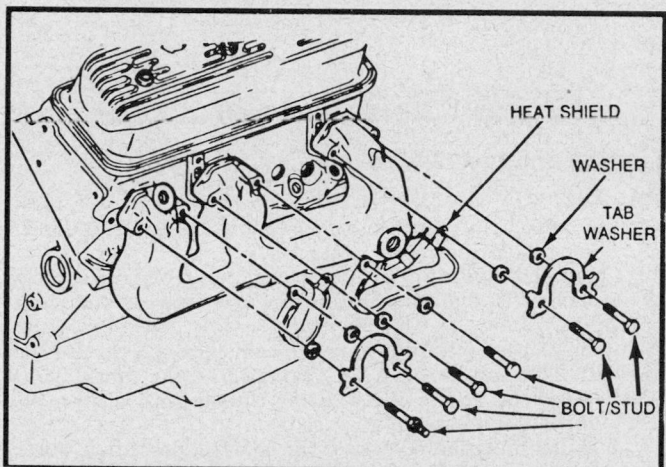

Exhaust manifold mounting—4.3L engine

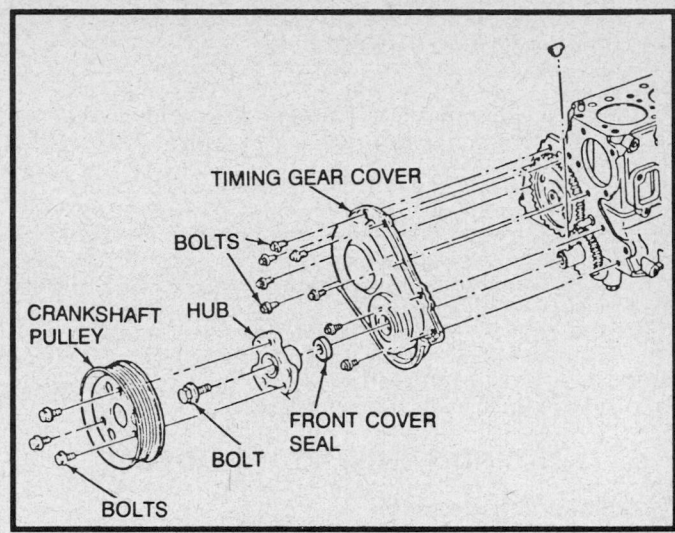

Front cover assembly 2.5L engine—exploded view

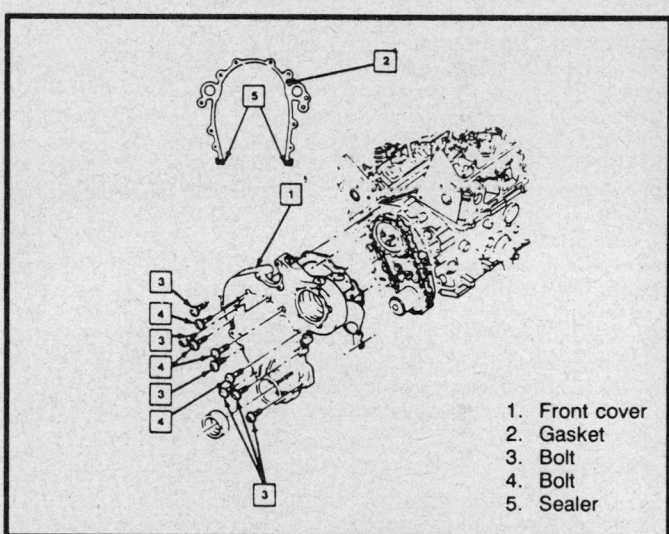

1. Front cover
2. Gasket
3. Bolt
4. Bolt
5. Sealer

Front cover assembly 3.1L engine—exploded view

2.8L AND 3.1L ENGINES

1. Disconnect the negative battery cable. Disconnect the exhaust pipe from the manifold.
2. Raise and support the vehicle safely. Remove the rear manifold retaining bolts.
3. Remove the air management hoses and electrical connections. Lower the vehicle. Remove the accessory drive belt.
4. If equipped, remove the power steering bracket when removing the left manifold.
5. Remove the remaining manifold attaching bolts. Remove the manifold from the engine.
6. Installation is the reverse of the removal procedure.

4.3L ENGINE

1. Disconnect the negative battery cable. On Astro and Safari, remove the engine cover. Raise and support the vehicle safely.
2. Disconnect the exhaust pipes from the exhaust manifolds. Lower the vehicle.
3. To remove the right manifold, disconnect the heat stove pipe and the dipstick tube bracket.

4. To remove the left manifold, disconnect the oxygen sensor wire.
5. Disconnect the power steering bracket at the manifold, if equipped. Disconnect the alternator bracket at the manifold.
6. Remove the AIR hoses at the check valve. Remove the exhaust manifold retaining bolts. Remove the manifold from the engine.
7. Installation is the reverse of the removal procedure.

Timing Gear Front Cover

Removal and Installation

2.5L ENGINE

1. Disconnect the negative battery cable. Drain the cooling system.
2. Remove the power steering fluid reservoir from its mounting and support it aside.
3. Remove the upper fan shroud. Remove the accessory drive belt.
4. Disconnect the wiring from the alternator. Remove the alternator and its mounting brackets.

5. Remove the crankshaft pulley and hub. Disconnect the lower radiator hose at the water pump.

6. Remove the cover retaining bolts and remove the cover.

To install:

7. Lubricate the crankshaft seal with clean oil. Apply a 10mm bead of RTV sealer to oil pan lips. Apply a 6mm wide bead of RTV to the timing cover.

8. Install the cover in position on the engine. Tighten the retaining bolts to 90 inch lbs.

9. Install the crankshaft pulley and hub. Connect the lower radiator hose to the water pump.

10. Install the alternator and its mounting brackets. Install the accessory drive belt.

11. Install the fan shroud and the power steering reservoir.

12. Refill the cooling system and connect the negative battery cable.

13. Run the engine and check for leaks.

Timing Chain Front Cover

Removal and Installation

2.8L AND 4.3L ENGINES

1. Disconnect the negative battery cable.
2. Drain the cooling system.
3. Remove the accessory drive belt.
4. Remove the water pump. Remove the power steering pump bracket.
5. Remove the crankshaft pulley and damper.
6. Disconnect the lower radiator hose. Remove the front cover retaining bolts.
7. Remove the front cover. Remove the old gasket material from the engine and the cover.

To install:

8. Install a new gasket in position. Install the front cover and tighten the retaining bolts to 18 ft. lbs. (24 Nm).
9. Install the water pump. Connect the lower radiator hose.
10. Install the crankshaft damper and pulley. Install the power steering mounting bracket.
11. Refill the cooling system to the correct level.
12. Connect the negative battery cable and bleed the cooling system.

3.1L ENGINE

1. Disconnect the negative battery cable.
2. Drain the cooling system.
3. Remove the accessory drive belt and tensioner.
4. Remove the power steering pump.
5. Raise and safely support the vehicle. Remove the splash shield.
6. Drain the engine oil. Remove the crankshaft pulley and damper. Remove the starter and support it to the side.
7. Place a suitable jack under the engine-to-transaxle mount.
8. Remove the engine mount bolts and the engine mount. Raise the engine slightly.
9. Remove the lower front cover bolts and lower the oil pan. Remove the radiator hose at the water pump.
10. Remove the heater hose at the cooling system fill pipe. Remove the bypass and overflow hoses.
11. Remove the remaining front cover bolts and remove the front cover.

To install:

12. Clean all gasket mating surfaces. Install a new gasket in position on the engine block.
13. Apply sealer to the lower edges of the front cover. Install the front cover in position on the engine block. Tighten the upper bolts to 20 ft. lbs. (27 Nm).
14. Install the oil pan in position. Install the lower cover bolts and tighten to 28 ft. lbs. (38 Nm).
15. Install the engine mount to the engine and lower the engine into position.

16. Install the crankshaft damper and pulley. Install the flywheel cover and inner splash shield.

17. Install the starter. Connect the heater bypass hose an the slower radiator hose to the water pump. Lower the vehicle.

18. Install the power steering pump bracket. Install the accessory drive belt and tensioner.

19. Refill the cooling system and the crankcase to the correct levels.

20. Connect the negative battery cable. Run the engine to normal operating temperature and check for leaks.

Front Cover Oil Seal

Replacement

The front cover seal can be replaced while the front cover is still on the vehicle. It is recommended by the manufacturer that the seal be replaced whenever the front cover is removed.

1. Disconnect the negative battery cable.
2. Remove the accessory drive belt.
3. Remove the crankshaft pulley and damper.
4. Using a suitable tool, pry the seal from the cover.
5. Lubricate the replacement seal with clean engine oil.
6. Using a suitable seal installer, position the seal on the crankshaft.
7. Install the crankshaft damper and pulley.
8. install the accessory drive belt.
9. Connect the negative battery cable.

Timing Chain and Sprockets

Removal and Installation

2.8L, 3.1L AND 4.3L ENGINES

1. Disconnect the negative battery cable. Drain the coolant.
2. Remove the front cover assembly.
3. Crank the engine until the marks punched on both sprockets are closest to one another and in line between the shaft centers.
4. Remove the bolts that hold the camshaft sprocket to the camshaft. This sprocket is a light press fit on the camshaft.
4. Remove the timing chain. Using the proper tools remove the crankshaft sprocket, as required.
5. Installation is the reverse of the removal procedure. After the sprockets are in place, turn the engine 2 full revolutions to make certain that the timing marks are in correct alignment between the shaft centers.

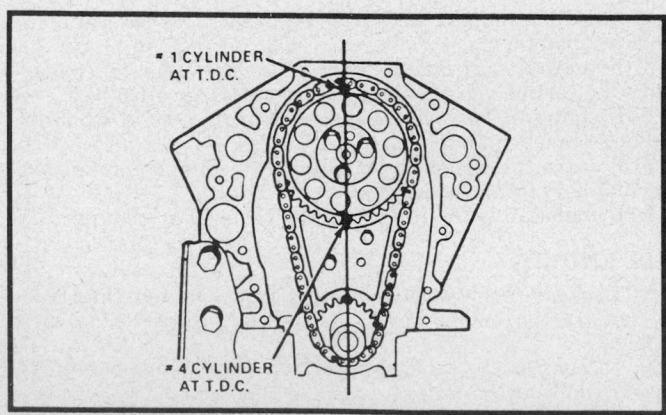

Timing mark alignment—2.8L and 3.1L engines

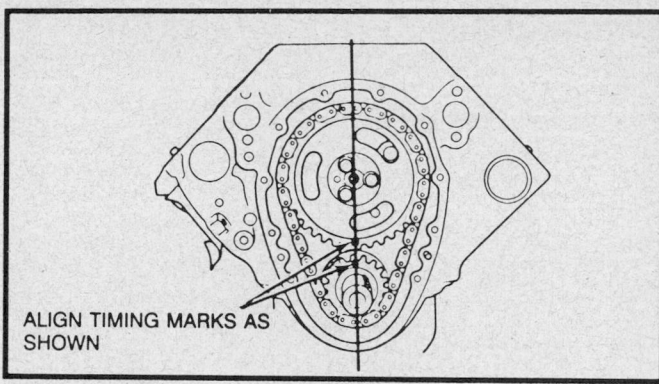

Timing mark alignment — 4.3L engine

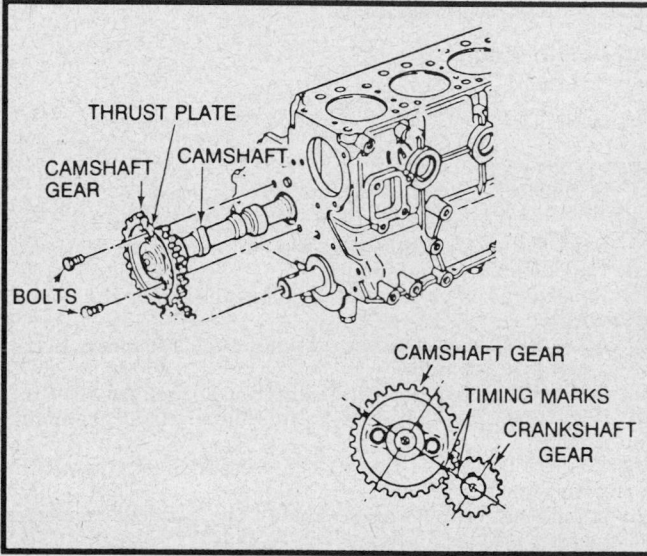

Timing gear assembly and timing mark alignment — 2.5L engine

Camshaft and Timing Gear

Removal and Installation

2.5L ENGINE

1. Disconnect the negative battery cable. Drain the cooling system. Remove the radiator.

2. Remove the engine side cover. Remove the air cleaner assembly. Remove the EGR valve.

3. Disconnect the power steering reservoir and position it to the side. Remove the drive belts and pulleys. Remove the upper fan shroud. Remove the front cover.

4. Rotate the crankshaft until the timing marks are in alignment. Remove the distributor assembly. Remove the oil pump drive shaft cover and drive shaft.

5. Remove the rocker cover. Remove the rockers and pushrods. Keep them in order for reinstallation. Remove the valve lifters. Keep them in order for reinstallation.

6. If equipped with air conditioning, it may be necessary to reposition the condenser in order to withdraw the camshaft from the engine. If the condenser must be removed, properly discharge the system before condenser removal.

7. Remove the headlight bezel and grille assembly.

8. Remove the camshaft thrust plate bolts. Carefully remove the camshaft from the vehicle.

To install:

9. Lubricate the camshaft lobes with Molykote or equivalent before installation.

10. Install the camshaft into the block, use care not to damage the bearings. Align the timing marks on the camshaft gear and the crankshaft gear.

11. Install the thrust plate bolts and tighten to 90 inch lbs.

12. Install the front cover. Install the distributor and the oil pump shaft cover.

13. Install the lifters, pushrods, rocker arms and the engine side cover.

14. Install the remaining components in the reverse order of removal.

15. Refill the cooling system and connect the negative battery cable.

Camshaft

Removal and Installation

2.8L AND 4.3L ENGINES

1. Disconnect the negative battery cable.

2. Drain the cooling system.

3. Remove the upper fan shroud.

4. Remove the radiator.

5. Remove the valve cover and the valve train components. Remove the intake manifold assembly.

6. Remove the front cover assembly.

7. Remove the timing chain and sprocket.

8. Remove the camshaft from the block by pulling it out. Use care not to damge the bearings.

To install:

9. Lubricate the camshaft with Molykote or equivalent, before installation.

10. Install the camshaft into the cylinder block, use care not to damage the bearings.

11. Install the timing chain and sprocket. Make sure that the timing marks align correctly.

12. Install the front cover assembly.

13. Install the intake manifold assembly. Install the valve train components and the valve cover.

14. Install the radiator and the fan shroud.

15. Fill the cooling system to the correct level and connect the negative battery cable.

3.1L ENGINE

1. Disconnect the negative battery cable.

2. Drain the cooling system.

3. Remove the engine from the vehicle and support it in a suitable holding fixture.

4. Remove the intake manifold. Remove the valve cover and the valve train components.

5. Remove the front cover assembly.

6. Remove the timing chain and sprocket.

7. Remove the camshaft from the block by pulling it out. Use care not to damage the bearings.

To install:

8. Lubricate the camshaft with Molykote or equivalent, before installation.

9. Install the camshaft into the cylinder block, use care not to damage the bearings.

10. Install the timing chain and sprocket. Make sure that the timing marks align correctly.

11. Install the front cover assembly.

12. Install the intake manifold assembly. Install the valve train components and the valve cover.

13. Install the engine into the vehicle.

14. Fill the cooling system to the correct level and connect the negative battery cable.

Piston and Connecting Rod

Positioning

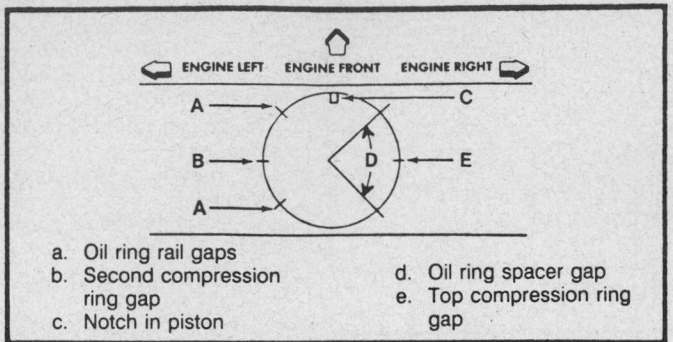

a. Oil ring rail gaps
b. Second compression ring gap
c. Notch in piston
d. Oil ring spacer gap
e. Top compression ring gap

Piston and ring positioning

ENGINE LUBRICATION

Oil Pan

Removal and Installation

2WD VEHICLES

1. Disconnect the negative battery cable.
2. Remove the power steering reservoir and support it aside.
3. Remove the radiator shroud.
4. Raise and safely support the vehicle.
5. Drain the engine oil.
6. Disconnect the strut rods. Disconnect the exhaust pipes at the manifolds.
7. Remove the catalytic converter and exhaust pipe.
8. Remove the flywheel cover. Remove the starter and brace.
9. Remove the brake lines from the crossmember. Remove the front engine mounting bolts.

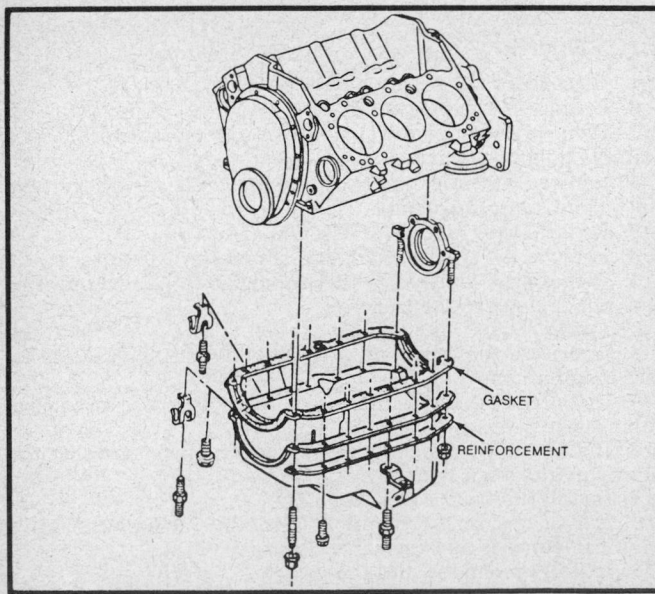

Oil pan assembly—4.3L engine

10. Raise the engine slightly, with a suitable lifting device and insert wooden blocks to hold it.
11. Remove the oil pan retaining bolts and remove the oil pan.
To install:
12. Apply RTV sealant to the oil pan flange and block. Install the oil pan into position.
13. Install the oil pan bolts and tighten to 90 inch lbs. (10 Nm).
14. Remove the blocks and lower the engine. Install the engine mount bolts.
15. Connect the brake line at the crossmember. Install the starter and brace.
16. Install the flywheel cover. Install the catalytic converter and the exhaust pipe.
17. Install the strut rods. Lower the vehicle. Install the radiator shroud.
18. Install the power steering reservoir. Refill the crankcase with the correct level of oil.
19. Connect the negative battery cable.

4WD VEHICLES

1. Disconnect the negative battery cable.
2. Remove the power steering pump from the fan shroud and remove the fan shroud.
3. Remove the crankcase dipstick. Raise and safely support the vehicle.
4. Drain the engine oil. Remove the brake line from the clips at the crossmember. Remove the crossmember.
5. Remove the transmission cooler lines at the flywheel cover bracket, if equipped.
6. Disconnect the exhaust pipe at the manifold. Remove the catalytic converter hanger.
7. Remove the flywheel cover. Remove the driveshaft splash shield.
8. Disconnect the idler arm assembly. Remove the steering gear retaining bolts and pull the gear and linkage forward.
9. Place a suitable support under the front differential housing and remove the differential support bracket bolts.
10. Move the differential assembly forward.
11. Remove the starter and brace.
12. Disconnect the front driveshaft at the pinion. Remove the engine mount through bolts.
13. Raise the engine slightly, using a suitable jack.
14. Remove the oil pan retaining bolts and remove the oil pan.

To install:

15. Clean all sealant from the block and the oil pan.

16. Apply a bead of RTV to the oil pan flange and to the sealing surfaces of the block.

17. Install the oil pan in position and install the retaining bolts. Tighten to 90 inch .lbs.

18. Lower the engine and install the engine mount through bolts. Connect the front driveshaft at the drive pinion.

19. Install the starter and brace. Pull the differential back into position and install the retaining bolts.

20. Install the steering gear and idler arm assembly mounting bolts.

21. Install the driveshaft shield and the flywheel cover.

22. Insall the catalytic converter hanger and the connect the exhaust pipe at the manifold.

23. Reconnect the transmission cooler lines to the clips at the flywheel housing.

24. Install the crossmember and reposition the brake lines. Lower the vehicle.

25. Install the dipstick. Refill the crankcase with oil. Install the upper fan shroud.

26. Install the power steering fluid reservoir. Connect the negative battery cable.

LUMINA APV, SILHOUETTE AND TRANS SPORT

1. Disconnect the negative battery cable. Remove the accessory drive belt.

2. Raise and safely support the vehicle.

3. Remove the crankshaft damper and pulley.

4. Drain the engine oil. Remove the flywheel shields.

5. Remove the starter. Support the engine with a suitable jack.

6. Remove the engine mounting bolts.

7. Raise the engine slightly.

8. Remove the oil pan bolts and the oil pan.

To install:

9. Install a new oil pan gaket and install the oil pan. Tighten M8 oil pan bolts to 19 ft. lbs. (25 Nm) and the M6 oil pan bolts to 7 ft. lbs. (10 Nm).

10. Lower the engine and install the engine mounting bolts.

11. Install the starter and flywheel shields.

12. Install the crankshaft damper and pulley.

13. Lower the vehicle and install the accessory drive belt.

14. Refill the crankcase and connect the negative battery cable.

Oil Pump

Removal and Installation

1. Disconnect the negative battery cable.

2. Raise and safely support the vehicle.

3. Drain the engine oil. Remove the oil pan.

4. Remove the oil pump retaining bolt and lower the pump from the block.

5. Remove the pump shaft.

6. Install the pump in position on the block with the retainer facing the rear of the block.

7. Install the pump retaining bolt and tighten to 30 ft. lbs. (41 Nm).

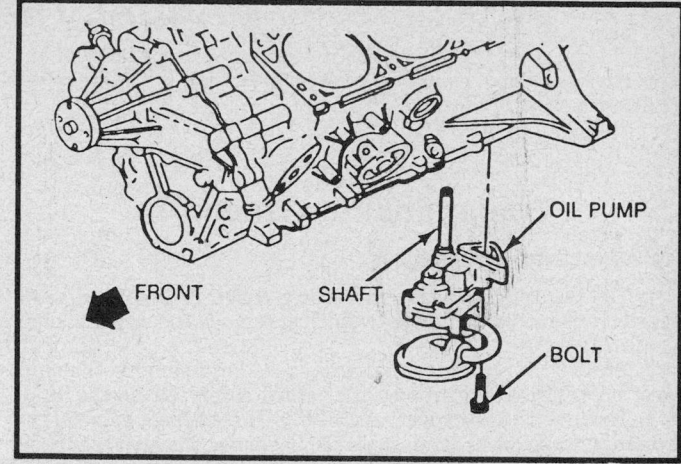

Oil pump mounting—2.8L, 3.1L and 4.3L engines

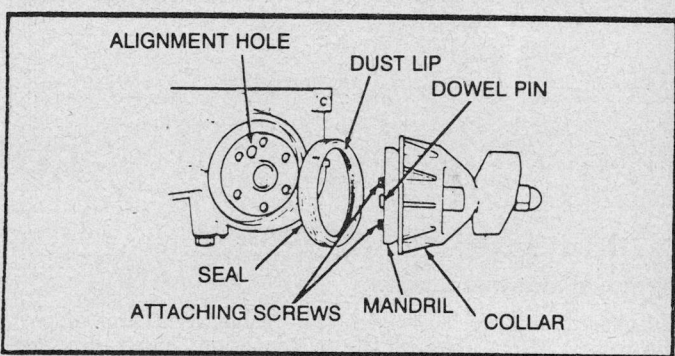

One piece rear main seal installation

8. Install the oil pan.

9. Lower the vehicle. Refill the crankcase with oil.

10. Connect the negative battery cable.

Rear Main Oil Seal

Removal and Installation

1. Disconnect the negative battery cable.

2. Raise and safely support the vehicle.

3. Remove the transmission from the vehicle.

4. Remove the flywheel (and clutch on manual transmission equipped vehicles).

5. Remove the oil seal by prying it out with a suitable tool.

6. Coat the seal lips with oil and install it on a suitable seal installer tool.

7. Using the tool, install it in the block. Make sure it is fully seated.

8. Install the flywheel. Install the transmission.

9. Lower the vehicle. Connect the negative battery cable.

MANUAL TRANSMISSION

For further information, please refer to "Professional Transmission Manual".

Transmission Assembly

Removal and Installation

1. Disconnect the negative battery cable. As required, on 4 speed transmission equipped vehicles, remove the upper starter mounting screw.

2. Shift the transmission into neutral and remove the shift lever boot. Raise and support the vehicle safely. Drain the fluid.

3. Remove the shift lever assembly. If equipped, remove the parking brake lever and controls. Remove the driveshaft. If equipped, drain and remove the transfer case.

4. Disconnect the speedometer cable at the transmission. Disconnect all electrical wires, as required.

5. Disconnect and remove exhaust components, as required. Properly support the transmission assembly. Remove the clutch slave cylinder from its mounting.

6. Remove the transmission assembly retaining bolts. Remove the transmission crossmember retaining bolts. Remove the transmission mount retaining bolts. Remove the crossmember from the vehicle.

7. As required, on 4 speed transmission equipped vehicles, remove the lower starter bolt and starter assembly. Properly support the clutch release bearing. Remove the engine-to-transmission bolts.

8. As required, on vehicles equipped with 4 speed transmission, remove the left body mounting bolts and loosen the radiator support screw. Raise and support the left side of the body.

9. Properly support the engine assembly. Carefully remove the transmission assembly from the vehicle.

10. Installation is the reverse of the removal procedure. Fill the transmission with the proper grade and type fluid. As adjust linkages, as required.

CLUTCH

Clutch Assembly

Removal and Installation

1. Disconnect the negative battery cable. Raise and support the vehicle safely. Remove the transmission. As required, remove the flywheel cover.

2. Remove the slave cylinder retaining bolts. Remove the slave cylinder from its mounting.

3. Remove the bell housing retaining bolts. Remove the bell housing from the vehicle.

4. Slide the clutch fork from the ball stud. Inspect the ball stud and replace as required.

5. Install the clutch removal tool and support the clutch assembly. Matchmark the clutch and pressure plate for reassembly.

6. Loosen the clutch plate retaining bolts slowly and evenly one at a time until all pressure is released from the pressure plate assembly.

7. Remove the clutch, pressure plate and removal tool from the vehicle. Check the flywheel for damage, repair or replace, as required.

8. Installation is the reverse of the removal procedure. Adjust the clutch, as required. Bleed the hydraulic clutch system.

Clutch Master Cylinder

Removal and Installation

1. Disconnect the negative battery cable. Remove the under dash hush panel. Remove the lower steering column cover, as required. Remove the left side air conditioning duct work.

2. Disconnect the pushrod from the clutch pedal. Disconnect the clutch master cylinder retaining nuts.

3. Disconnect and plug the reservoir hose at the clutch master cylinder assembly.

4. Disconnect and plug the fluid line to the slave cylinder at the clutch master cylinder assembly.

5. Remove the clutch master cylinder from the vehicle.

6. Installation is the reverse of the removal procedure. Bleed the hydraulic clutch system.

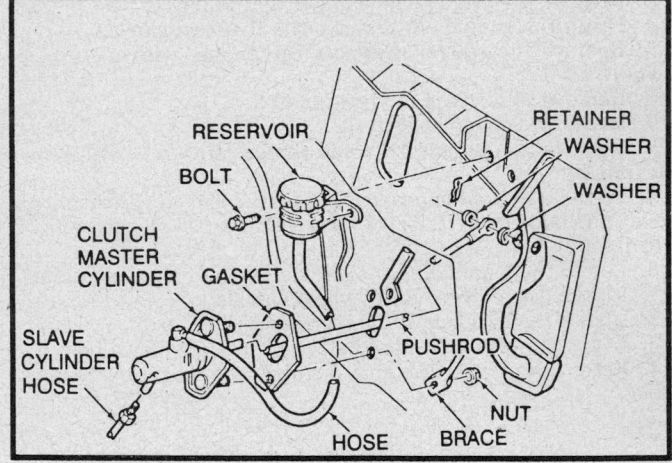

Clutch master cylinder mounting

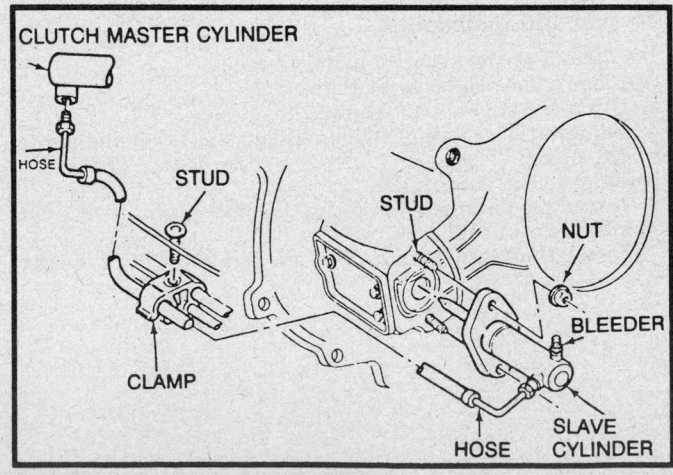

Clutch slave cylinder mounting

Clutch Slave Cylinder

Removal and Installation

1. Disconnect the negative battery cable.
2. Raise and support the vehicle safely. Disconnect and plug the fluid line at the slave cylinder.
3. Remove the slave cylinder retaining bolts. Remove the slave cylinder from the vehicle.
4. Installation is the reverse of the removal procedure. Bleed the system, as required.

Bleeding the Hydraulic Clutch System

1. Fill the clutch master cylinder with the proper grade and type fluid. Raise and support the vehicle safely.
2. Remove the slave cylinder retaining bolts. Hold the cylinder at about a 45 degree angle with the bleeder at the highest point.
3. Fully depress the clutch pedal and open the bleeder screw. Repeat until all air is expelled from the system.
4. Be sure that the fluid level remains full in the clutch master cylinder throughout the bleeding procedure.

AUTOMATIC TRANSMISSION

For further information, please refer to "Professional Transmission Manual".

Transmission Assembly

Removal and Installation

1. Disconnect the negative battery cable. Remove the air cleaner assembly. Disconnect the throttle valve cable and the throttle linkage.
2. Raise and support the vehicle safely.
3. Drain the transmission fluid. Disconnect the shift linkage. On some vehicles equipped with the 2.5L engine, it will be necessary to remove the upper starter bolt.
4. Remove the driveshaft. If equipped with a transfer case, disconnect the front driveshaft.
5. Disconnect and remove all required exhaust system components. Support the transmission using the proper equipment.
6. Remove the crossmember retaining bolts. Remove the transmission mount retaining bolts. Remove the crossmember from the vehicle.
7. Remove the transmission dipstick tube. Disconnect the speedometer cable. If equipped, disconnect the vacuum modulator line.
8. Disconnect all electrical connections from the transmission assembly. Disconnect and plug the fluid cooler lines.
9. If equipped, remove the transfer case assembly. Remove the damper and support, as required. Remove the flywheel housing cover.
10. Properly support the engine assembly. Removing the transmission to engine retaining bolts. Carefully remove the automatic transmission from the vehicle.
To install:
11. Install the transmission in position in the vehicle. Make sure the converter is proerly seated.

12. Install the engine-to-transmission bolts and tighten to 50 ft. lbs. (68 Nm).
13. Install the converter housing cover. Install the damper and support.
14. Connect all electrical leads to the transmission and connect the speedometer cable.
15. Install the dipstick tube. Install the crossmember and install the transmission mount retaining bolts.
16. Connect all exhaust system components. Install the front driveshaft on 4WD vehicles.
17. Connect the shift linkage and install the skid plate, if equipped. Lower the vehicle.
18. Connect the TV cable and throttle linkage.
19. Install the air cleaner assembly. Connect the negative battery cable.
20. Check the operation of the transmission.

Shift Linkage Adjustment

1. As required, raise and support the vehicle safely.
2. Loosen the linkage rod retaining nut. Note the position of any washers, spacers and insulators. Position the transmission selector lever in the **N** position.
3. Do not use the indicator to determine the **N** position. Check the transmission shift lever bracket to determine that the transmission is in the **N** position.
4. Hold the selector rod and tighten the swivel to 17 ft. lbs. Position the selector lever in the **P** detent.
5. Check the adjustment. The selector lever must go into all positions. The engine must only start in the **P** or **N** position. Align the selector indicator, as required.

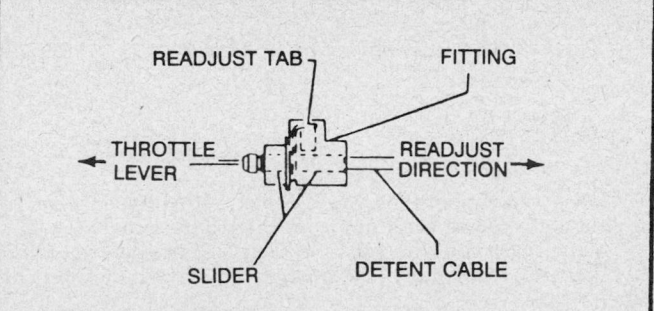

TV cable adjustment points

TV Cable Adjustment

1. As required, remove the air cleaner assembly.
2. Depress and hold down the metal readjust tab at the engine end of the throttle valve cable.
3. Move the slider until it stops against the fitting. Release the readjustment tab.
4. Rotate the throttle lever to its full travel position. The slider must move toward the lever when the lever is rotated to its full travel position.
5. Check for proper operation. When the engine is cold, the cable may appear to be functioning properly, check the cable when the engine is hot.
6. Road test the vehicle.

AUTOMATIC TRANSAXLE

For further information, please refer to "Professional Transmission Manual".

Transaxle Assembly

The automatic transaxle in the Lumina APV, Silhouette and Trans Sport, can only be removed by removing the engine and transaxle/sub-frame as an assembly.

Removal and Installation

1. Disconnect the negative battery cable.
2. Drain the cooling system. Disconnect the air flow tube from the air cleaner.
3. Disconnect the electrical connector from the ECM and push it through to the engine compartment. Disconnect the harness from the clips on the body and lay it across the engine.
4. Disconnect the engine harness at the bulkhead connector. Disconnect the throttle and TV cables.
5. Disconnect the fuel lines. Disconnect the transaxle shift linkage.
6. Disconnect the cooler lines at the radiator. Disconnect the radiator and heater hoses.
7. Remove the air conditioning compressor from the bracket and support it out of the way. Remove the upper engine support strut.
8. Raise and safely support the vehicle. Remove the front wheel and tire assemblies.
9. Remove the stabilizer bar. Disconnect the tie rod ends and the lower control arm ball joints.
10. Disconnect the halfhsafts and support them out of the way. Disconnect the steering shaft pinch bolt.
11. Remove the starter.
12. Disconnect the exhaust pipe at the manifold. Support the engine and sub-frame with a suitable jack.
13. Remove the sub-frame bolts and lower the engine/transaxle and subframe from the vehicle.

To install:
14. Raise the engine assembly into position and install the subframe bolts. Tighten to 35 ft. lbs.
15. Connect the exhaust pipe at the rear manifold. Install the starter.
16. Connect the steering shaft and install the pinch bolt. Connect the halfshafts to the transaxle.
17. Connect the lower control arm ball joints to the steering knuckles.
18. Install the stabilizer bar. Install the upper engine strut.
19. Install the wheel and tire assemblies. Lower the vehicle. Install the radiator and heater hoses.
20. Install the shift linkage. Connect the fuel lines and the throttle and TV cables.
21. Connect the harness to bulkhead connector. Connect the ECM harness to the ECM.
22. Connect the air cleaner hose and the radiator upper support.

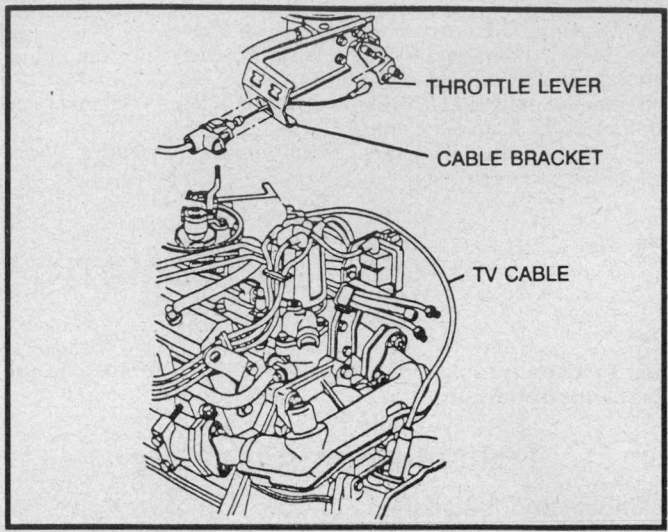

TV cable routing

23. Fill the cooling system. Install the air conditioning compressor.
24. Connect the negative battery cable.

TV Cable Adjustment

1. As required, remove the air cleaner assembly.
2. Depress and hold down the metal readjust tab at the engine end of the throttle valve cable.
3. Move the slider until it stops against the fitting. Release the readjustment tab.
4. Rotate the throttle lever to its full travel position. The slider must move toward the lever when the lever is rotated to its full travel position.
5. Check for proper operation. When the engine is cold, the cable may appear to be functioning properly, check the cable when the engine is hot.
6. Road test the vehicle.

Neutral Safety Switch Adjustment

1. Place the transaxle in the **N** position.
2. Loosen the switch attaching screws.
3. Rotate the switch on the shifter assembly to align the service hole in the switch with the hole in the carrier.
4. Insert a $^3/_{32}$ in. gauge pin into the hole then tighten the mounting bolts.
5. Remove the gauge pin and check the operation of the switch.
6. The vehicle should only start in **N** or **P**.

TRANSFER CASE

Transfer Case Assembly

Removal and Installation

PICK-UP, BLAZER, JIMMY, ASTRO AND SAFARI

1. Disconnect the negative battery cable. Shift the transfer case into the **4HI** position.

2. Raise and support the vehicle safely. If equipped, remove the skid plate. Drain the fluid from the transfer case.
3. Matchmark the transfer case front output shaft yoke and driveshaft for reassembly. Disconnect the driveshaft from the transfer case.
4. Matchmark the rear axle yoke and the driveshaft for reassembly. Remove the driveshaft.

5. Disconnect the speedometer cable. Disconnect the vacuum harness and all electrical connections at the transfer case. Remove the catalytic converter hanger bolts at the converter assembly.

6. Raise the transmission and transfer case assembly. Remove the transmission mount retaining bolts. Remove the mount and the catalytic converter hanger. Lower the transmission and transfer case assembly.

7. Properly support the transfer case assembly. Remove the transfer case retaining bolts.

8. On vehicles equipped with automatic transmission, it will be necessary to remove the shift lever bracket mounting bolts from the transfer case adapter in order to remove the upper left transfer case retaining bolt.

9. Separate the transfer case from its mounting and remove it from the vehicle.

To install:

10. Install a new gasket to the transmission. Install the transfer case into the vehicle.

11. Tighten the transfer case mounting bolts to 23 ft. lbs. (31 Nm).

12. Install the shift lever bracket bolts. Suport the transmission, raise the transmission slightly.

13. Install the converter mounting bracket. Install the rear transmission mounting bolts.

14. Connect the transfer case linkage. Connect the speedometer cable.

15. Install the driveshafts. Install the skid plate if equipped.

16. Fill the transfer case to the correct level.

17. Lower the vehicle. Connect the negative battery cable.

Linkage Adjustment

1. Loosen the selector lever retaining bolt. Loosen the shifter pivot bolt.

2. Shift the transfer case into the **4HI** position. Remove the console assembly. Raise the shifter boot out of the way.

3. Install a $5/16$ in. gauge pin through the shifter and into the bracket. Install a service bolt at the transfer case shift lever. This will lock the transfer case in the **4HI** position.

4. Tighten the selector lever retaining bolt 25–35 ft. lbs. Tighten the shifter pivot bolt 88–103 ft. lbs.

5. Remove the service bolt. Remove the gauge pin. Install removed parts.

6. Check for proper operation.

DRIVE AXLE

Halfshaft

Removal and Installation

PICK-UP, BLAZER, JIMMY, ASTRO AND SAFARI

1. Raise and support the vehicle safely. Remove the tire and wheel assemblies.

2. Remove the brake calipers and flex hose at their retaining brackets.

3. Using the proper tools, remove the tie rods at the steering knuckles.

4. Remove the lower shock absorber retaining bolts and move the shock absorbers out of the way. As required, remove the skid plate.

5. Remove the halfshaft to axle tube bolts. Remove the halfshaft cotter pin, nut and washer.

6. Move the inner part of the halfshaft forward. Support it away from the frame. Using a suitable tool, remove the shaft from the hub and bearing assembly.

7. Remove the halfshaft from the vehicle.

To install:

8. Install the halfshaft into position. Push it into the hub.

9. Install the shaft retaining nut and washer. Tighten the halfshaft retaining nut to 160–200 ft. lbs. (220–270 Nm).

10. Install the cotter pin in the nut. Install the halfshaft-to-axle tube bolts and tighten to 60 ft. lbs. (80 Nm).

11. Install the lower shock absorber bolts. Connect the tie rods to the steeering knuckle.

12. Install the brake calipers and hoses. Install the skid plate, if equipped.

13. Install the wheel and tire assemblies. Lower the vehicle

LUMINA APV, SILHOUETTE AND TRANS SPORT

1. Raise and safely support the vehicle.

2. Remove the tire and wheel assemblies.

3. Remove the halfshaft retaining nut and washer.

4. Remove the brake caliper from the rotor and support it aside.

5. Remove the brake rotor from the hub.

6. Disconnect the stabilizer shaft from the control arm and disconnect the ball joint from the steering knuckle.

7. Remove the halfshaft from the transaxle using a suitable tool with a slide hammer attachment.

8. Remove the halfshaft from the hub and bearing assembly.

To install:

9. Install the halfshaft into the hub and bearing assembly.

10. Connect the lower ball joint to the steering knuckle.

11. Connect the stabilizer shaft to the control arm. Install the rotor.

12. Install the brake caliper. Install a new halfshaft nut and tighten the nut to 185 ft. lbs. (260 Nm).

13. Seat the halfshaft into the transaxle, by pushing it in firmly. Check that the shaft is seated by pulling on it.

14. Install the wheel and tire assemblies.

15. Lower the vehicle.

Driveshaft and U-Joints

Removal and Installation

FRONT 1 PIECE – EXCEPT ASTRO AND SAFARI

1. Raise and support the vehicle safely.

2. If equipped, remove the skid plate.

3. Matchmark the rear yoke of the driveshaft to the transfer case. Matchmark the front of the driveshaft to the differential housing.

4. Remove the bolts and retainers from the rear of the driveshaft. Remove the driveshaft from the vehicle.

5. Installation is the reverse of the removal procedure. Tighten the bolts to 15 ft. lbs. (20 Nm).

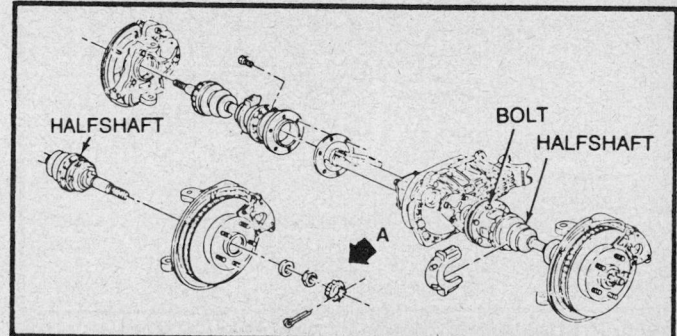

Front drive axle assembly – 4WD vehicles

FRONT 1 PIECE—ASTRO AND SAFARI

1. Raise and support the vehicle safely.
2. Matchmark the rear of the driveshaft to the transfer case. Matchmark the front of the driveshaft to the differential housing.
4. Remove the bolts from the rear flange of the driveshaft. Remove the bolts from the front flange of the driveshaft. Lower the driveshaft and remove it from the vehicle.
5. Installation is the reverse of the removal procedure. Tighten the front flange bolts to 53 ft. lbs. (72 Nm) and the rear falnge bolts to 92 ft. lbs. (125 Nm).

REAR 1 PIECE

1. Raise and support the vehicle safely.
2. If equipped, remove the skid plate.
3. Matchmark the front yoke of the driveshaft to the transmission. Matchmark the rear of the driveshaft to the differential housing.
4. Remove the bolts and retainers from the rear of the driveshaft. Remove the driveshaft from the vehicle.
5. Installation is the reverse of the removal procedure. Tighten the bolts to 15 ft. lbs. (20 Nm).

REAR 2 PIECE

1. Raise and support the vehicle safely.
2. As required, remove the skid plate.
3. Matchmark the front yoke of the driveshaft to the transmission. Matchmark the rear of the driveshaft to the differential housing.
4. Remove the center bearing bolts and washers. Remove the center bearing.
5. Remove the front driveshaft. Remove the rear driveshaft bolts and retainers. Remove the rear driveshaft.
6. Installation is the reverse of the removal procedure. When installing the center bearing, be sure to align it 90 degrees to the driveshaft center lines. Tighten the center bearing bolts to 25 ft. lbs. (34 Nm). and the driveshaft bolts to 15 ft. lbs. (20 Nm).

Rear Axle Shaft, Bearing and Seal

Removal and Installation

1. Raise and support the vehicle safely. Remove the tire and wheel assemblies. Drain the lubricant.
2. Remove the carrier cover retaining bolts. Remove the carrier cover.
3. Remove the rear axle pinion shaft lock screw and the rear axle pinion shaft. Discard the lock screw.

4. Push the flanged end of the axle shaft toward the center of the vehicle. Remove the C-lock clip from the button end of the shaft.
5. Remove the axle shaft from the housing. Be careful not to damage the oil seal. The bearing can be removed from the axle using an arbor press.

To install:
6. Slide the axle into position and install the C-lock clip, use care not to damage the oil seal.
7. Install the pinion shaft through the case and pinion.
8. Install a new pinion shaft lock bolt, tighten it to 25 ft. lbs. (34 Nm).
9. Install the carrier cover, using a new gasket. Tighten the cover bolts to 20 ft. lbs. (27 Nm).
10. Fill the differential to within $^3/_8$ in. of the filler opening.
11. Install the brake drum. Install the wheel and tire assembly.

Front Wheel Hub, Knuckle and Bearing

Removal and Installation

PICK-UP, BLAZER, JIMMY, ASTRO AND SAFARI

2WD Vehicles

1. Raise and safely support the vehicle.
2. Remove the wheel and tire assemblies.
3. Remove the brake caliper and remove the brake rotor. Use care not to drop the bearings from the rotor.
4. Remove the splash shield attaching bolts and remove the splash shield from the knuckle.
5. Remove the tie rod end from the knuckle. Remove the ball studs from the knuckle.
6. Remove the steering knuckle from the lower ball stud and the knuckle from the vehicle.
To install:
7. Install the upper and lower ball joint to the knuckle.
8. Attach the splash shield to the knuckle and tighten the bolts to 10 ft. lbs. (14 Nm).
9. Connect the tie rod end to the knuckle.
10. Install the rotor and bearings onto the spindle. Adjust the bearing.
11. Install the caliper. Install the wheel and tire assembly.
12. Lower the vehicle. Check the front end alignment.

4WD Vehicles

1. Raise and safely support the vehicle.
2. Remove the wheel and tire assembly.
3. Remove the brake caliper and support it aside.
4. Remove the brake rotor. Remove the halfshaft retaining nut.
5. Disconnect the tie rod end from the knuckle.

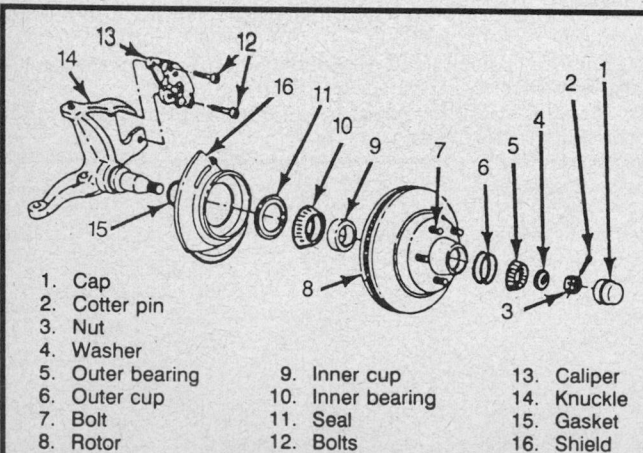

1. Cap	
2. Cotter pin	
3. Nut	
4. Washer	
5. Outer bearing	9. Inner cup
6. Outer cup	10. Inner bearing
7. Bolt	11. Seal
8. Rotor	12. Bolts

13. Caliper
14. Knuckle
15. Gasket
16. Shield

Rotor, knuckle and bearing assembly—2WD vehicles except Lumina APV, Silhouette and Trans Sport

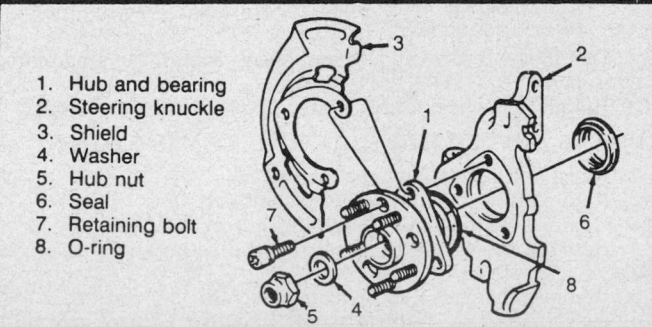

1. Hub and bearing
2. Steering knuckle
3. Shield
4. Washer
5. Hub nut
6. Seal
7. Retaining bolt
8. O-ring

Front hub and bearing assembly—Lumina APV, Silhouette and Trans Sport

6. Remove the hub and bearing assembly mounting bolts and remove the assembly from the steering knuckle.

7. Remove the splash shield from the knuckle. Remove the ball joints from the knuckle.

8. Remove the knuckle from the ball joints and remove the spacer from the knuckle.

To install:

9. Install the spacer on the knuckle. Install the knuckle in position on the ball joints.

10. Install the ball joint nuts and cotter pins. Install the splash shield to the knuckle.

11. Install the hub and bearing assembly to the knuckle. Tighten the hub mounting bolts to 86 ft. lbs. (116 Nm). Install the halfshaft retaining nut.

12. Connect the tie rod to the knuckle. Install the brake rotor and the brake caliper.

13. Install the wheel and tire assembly. Lower the vehicle.

14. Check the front end alignment.

LUMINA APV, SILHOUETTE AND TRANS SPORT

1. Raise and safely support the vehicle.

2. Remove the wheel and tire assembly.

3. Remove the brake caliper and support it aside.

4. Remove the brake rotor. Remove the halfshaft retaining nut.

5. Disconnect the tie rod end from the knuckle.

6. Remove the hub and bearing assembly mounting bolts and remove the assembly from the steering knuckle.

7. Remove the strut mounting bolts from the knuckle. Remove the splash shield from the knuckle. Remove the ball joint from the knuckle.

8. Remove the knuckle from the ball joint and remove the knuckle from the vehicle. Pull it off of the halfshaft.

To install:

9. Install the knuckle in position on the ball joint. Slide the knuckle onto the halfshaft.

10. Install the ball joint nut and cotter pin. Install the splash shield to the knuckle.

11. Install the hub and bearing assembly to the knuckle. Tighten the hub mounting bolts to 86 ft. lbs. (116 Nm). Install the halfshaft retaining nut.

12. Connect the tie rod to the knuckle. Install the brake rotor and the brake caliper.

13. Install the wheel and tire assembly. Lower the vehicle.

14. Check the front end alignment.

Pinion Seal

Removal and Installation

1. Raise and support the vehicle safely. Matchmark the driveshaft and the pinion flange.

2. Disconnect the driveshaft from the rear differential. Support the driveshaft out of the way.

3. Mark the position of the pinion flange, pinion shaft and nut. Remove the pinion flange nut and washer.

4. Remove the pinion flange. Position a drain pan under the assembly to catch any excess lubricant.

5. Using the proper tool, remove the seal from its mounting.

6. Installation is the reverse of the removal procedure. Refill the differential to the correct level.

Differential Carrier

Removal and Installation

1. Raise and support the vehicle safely. Allow the rear axle assembly to hang freely. Remove the tire and wheel assemblies. Drain the lubricant.

2. Remove the differential cover. Remove the brake drum. Remove the axle shafts.

3. Mark one side of the carrier and matching cap for reassembly in the same position. Remove the bearing caps.

4. Using a spreader tool and a dial indicator gauge, spread the carrier assembly to a maximum of 0.015 in.

5. Remove the dial indicator tool. Use a prybar and remove the differential case from the carrier.

6. Record the dimension and location of the side bearing shims. Remove the spreader tool.

7. Installation is the reverse of the removal procedure.

Axle Housing

Removal and Installation

FRONT

1. Raise and support the vehicle safely. Remove the wheel and tire assemblies.

2. Remove the bolt securing the steering stabilizer to the frame. Remove the idle arm retaining bolts.

3. Push the steering linkage toward the front of the vehicle. Remove the axle vent hose from the carrier fitting.

4. Disconnect the right halfshaft from the carrier. Disconnect the left hand halfshaft from the carrier by removing the retaining bolts. Keep the shaft from turning by inserting a drift through the opening in the top of the brake caliper into a corresponding vane of the brake rotor.

5. Disconnect the front driveshaft. Properly support the carrier assembly. Remove the carrier to frame retaining bolts.

6. Remove the differential carrier assembly from the vehicle.

7. Installation is the reverse of the removal procedure.

REAR

1. Raise and support the vehicle safely. Remove the tire and wheel assemblies. Properly support the rear axle assembly.

2. Disconnect the shock absorbers from the anchor plate. Matchmark the driveshaft and the pinion flange. Remove the driveshaft and support it aside.

3. Remove the brake line junction block from the axle housing. Disconnect and cap the brake lines at the junction block.

4. Remove the U bolts and anchor plates. Lower the axle assembly and remove the lower spring shackle bolts.

5. Disconnect the brake lines from the axle housing clips. Remove the backing plates.

6. Disconnect the lower control arms from the axle housing. Remove the axle housing from the vehicle.

7. Installation is the reverse of the removal procedure. Fill and bleed the brake system.

STEERING

Steering Wheel

Removal and Installation

1. Disconnect the negative battery cable.

2. Remove the horn pad retaining screws. Remove the horn pad and disconnect the electrical lead.

3. Matchmark the steering wheel and the shaft.

4. Remove the steering wheel retaining nut.

5. Remove the steering wheel, using a suitable puller.

6. Installation is the reverse of removal. Align the matchmarks made during removal and tighten the steering wheel retaining nut to 30 ft. lbs. (40 Nm).

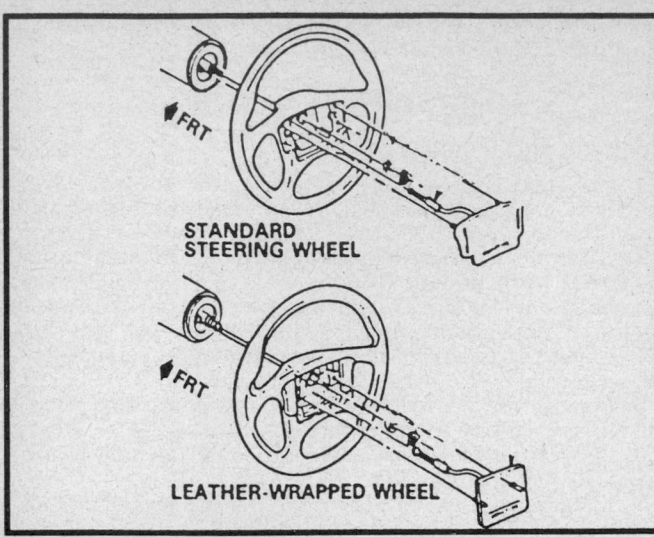

Steering wheel removal

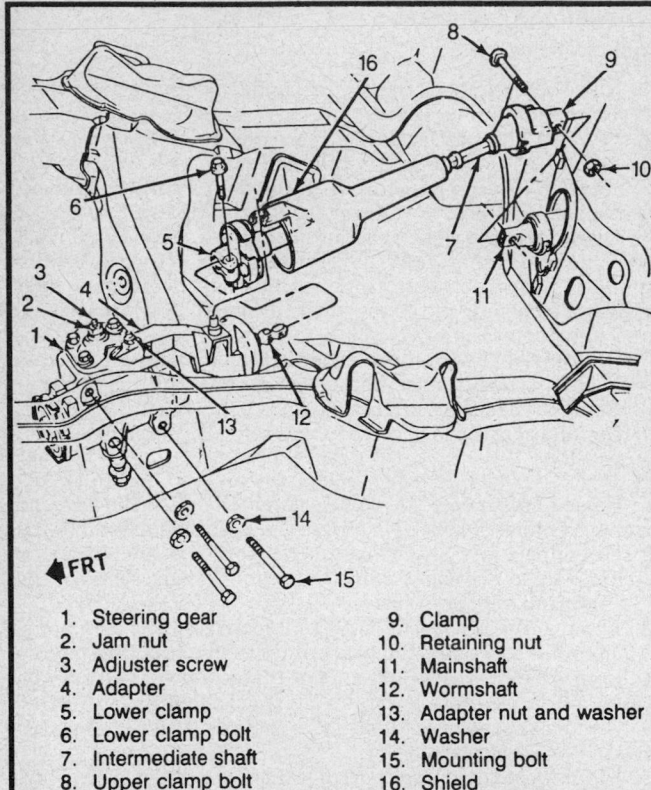

1. Steering gear
2. Jam nut
3. Adjuster screw
4. Adapter
5. Lower clamp
6. Lower clamp bolt
7. Intermediate shaft
8. Upper clamp bolt
9. Clamp
10. Retaining nut
11. Mainshaft
12. Wormshaft
13. Adapter nut and washer
14. Washer
15. Mounting bolt
16. Shield

Steering gear mounting—Pick-Up, Blazer, Jimmy, Astro and Safari

Manual Steering Gear

Removal and Installation

1. Disconnect the negative battery cable. Raise and support the vehicle safely. Position the wheels in the straight position. Be sure that the steering wheel is in the right position.
2. If equipped, remove the steering gear coupling shield. Remove the steering gear coupling bolt. On some vehicles it may be necessary to separate the coupling at the 2 flange bolts.
3. Matchmark the pitman arm to the steering gear. Remove the pitman arm retaining nut and washer. Using the proper tool, separate the pitman arm from the steering gear assembly.
4. Remove the steering gear retaining bolts. Remove the steering gear from the vehicle.

To install:
5. Install the steering gear in position in the vehicle.
6. Install the mounting bolts. Tighten the mounting bolts to 55 ft. lbs.
7. Connect the steering gear coupling at the flange bolts.
8. Connect the pitman arm to the steering gear. Tighten the pitman arm retaiing bolt to 185 ft. lbs. (250 Nm).
9. Install the coupling shield. Lower the vehicle
10. Connect the negative battery cable.

Adjustment

1. Raise and safely support the vehicle.
2. Remove the coupling shield. Remove the pitman arm nut and washer.
3. Matchmark the pitman arm to the pitman shaft.
4. Remove the pitman arm, using a suitable puller.
5. loosen the adjuster nut on the steering gear, then back out the adjust ¼ turn.
6. Lower the vehicle, keeping it just above the ground.
7. Remove the horn pad. Check the thrust bearing preload as follows:
   a. Tighten the adjuster plug until the proper preload is achieved, 5–8 inch lbs. (0.6–1.0 Nm).
   b. Tighten the adjuster nut to 85 ft. lbs.
   c. Turn the steering wheel to check the adjustment. The gear should turn smoothly with no stops, from lock to lock.
8. To check the overcenter preload:
   a. Turn the steering wheel from lock to lock counting the total number of turns.
   b. Turn the wheel bcak to exactly the ½ way point.
   c. Turn the over center adjuster screw clockwise, to take out all of the lash between the ball nut and the pitman shaft sector teeth and jam nut.
   d. Tighten the jam nut to 22 ft. lbs. (30 Nm).
   e. Check the torque at the steering wheel, taking the highest reading as the wheel is turned.
   f. Tighten the adjuster plug to 4–10 inch lbs. (0.5–1.2 Nm).

To install:
9. Install the pitman arm onto the pitman shaft, aligning the match marks made during disassembly.
10. Install the pitman arm washer and nut. Install the coupling shield.
11. Lower the vehicle completely and install the horn pad.
12. Connect the negative battery cable.

Power Steering Gear

Removal and Installation

1. Disconnect the negative battery cable. Raise and support the vehicle safely. Position the wheels in the straight position.
2. Disconnect and cap the fluid lines.
3. If equipped, remove the steering gear coupling shield. Remove the steering gear coupling bolt. On some vehicles it may be necessary to separate the coupling at the 2 flange bolts.
4. Matchmark the pitman arm to the steering gear. Remove the pitman arm retaining nut and washer. Using the proper tool, separate the pitman arm from the steering gear assembly.
5. Remove the steering gear retaining bolts. Remove the steering gear from the vehicle.

To install:
6. Install the steering gear in position in the vehicle.
7. Install the mounting bolts. Tighten the mounting bolts to 55 ft. lbs.
8. Connect the steering gear coupling at the flange bolts.

9. Connect the pitman arm to the steering gear. Tighten the pitman arm retaining bolt to 185 ft. lbs. (250 Nm).

10. Connect the fluid lines. Install the coupling shield. Lower the vehicle.

11. Connect the negative battery cable. Fill and bleed the power steering system.

Worm Bearing Preload Adjustment

1. With the steering gear removed from the vehicle, remove the adjuster plug nut.

2. Turn the adjuster plug in until it bottoms. Tighten the adjuster plug to 20 ft. lbs. (27 Nm).

3. Place an index mark on the housing, even with one of the holes in the adjuster plug.

4. Measure 13mm counterclockwise from the index mark and put a second mark on the housing.

5. Rotate the adjuster plug counterclockwise, until the hole in the plug is aligned with the second mark.

6. Install the adjuster plug nut (be sure the adjuster does not turn with the nut).

Power Steering Rack and Pinion

Removal and Installation

1. Disconnect the negative battery cable.

2. Remove the air cleaner assembly.

3. Remove the dust boot from the steering gear.

4. Remove the intermediate shaft lower pinch bolt and disconnect the intermediate shaft from the lower stub shaft.

5. Remove the fluid line retaining clips at the pump and disconnect the lines.

6. Raise and safely support the vehicle.

7. Remove the wheel and tire assemblies. Disconnect the tie rod ends at the steering knuckle.

8. Remove the remaining brackets and clips at the crossmember. Support the body safely with the appropriate equipment, to allow lowering of the subframe.

9. Remove the rear subframe mounting bolts and carefully lower the rear of the subframe approxiamtely 5 in.

10. Remove the rack and pinion mounting bolts and remove the rack through the left wheel opening.

To install:

11. Install the rack and pinion throught the left wheel opening.

12. Install the rack and pinion mounting nuts, tighten to 70 ft. lbs. (95 Nm).

13. Raise the subframe assembly and install the rear mounting bolts.

14. Remove any supports and install the brackets and clips to the crossmember.

15. Install the wheel and tire assemblies. Lower the vehicle.

16. Connect the fluid lines at the pump and tighten to 18 ft. lbs. (25 Nm).

17. Install the line retaining clips. Connect the intermediate shaft to the stub shaft.

18. Install the dust boot over the steering gear.

19. Install the air cleaner assembly and connect the negative battery cable.

20. Fill and bleed the steering system.

Power Steering Pump

Removal and Installation

1. Disconnect the negative battery cable. Disconnect and cap the power steering pump hoses. Remove the accessory drive belt.

2. Remove the power steering pump pulley using a suitable puller tool or equivalent.

3. Remove the pump mounting bolts. Remove the pump from the vehicle.

4. Installation is the reverse of the removal procedure. Tighten the pump mounting bolts to 20 ft. lbs (27 Nm) on the 2.5L engine, 36 ft. lbs. (50 Nm) on the 2.8L, 3.1L and 4.3L engine. Bleed the power steering system.

System Bleeding

1. Fill the fluid reservoir to the proper level.

2. Start the engine and let it run for at least 2 minutes. Turn the engine off.

3. Add fluid if necessary, then run the engine again. Repeat this until the fluid level remains constant.

4. Raise the front of the vehicle slightly, until the front wheels are just off the ground.

5. Start the engine and slowly turn the steering wheel from lock to lock, until the wheel contacts the stop.

6. Add fluid if necessary. Lower the vehicle to the ground.

7. Start the engine and again move the wheels side to side. Check the fluid level.

Tie Rod Ends

Removal and Installation

1. Raise and support the vehicle safely. Remove the tire and wheel assemblies.

2. Remove the cotter pins and nuts. Using the proper removal tool, separate the outer tie rod from the steering knuckle.

3. Disconnect the inner tie rod from the relay rod using the proper tool. Remove the tie rod ends from the adjuster tubes.

4. Installation is the reverse of the removal procedure. Tighten the inner tie rod ball stud nut to 35 ft. lbs. (47 Nm). Tighten the outer tie rod ball stud to the steering knuckle to 35 ft. lbs. (47 Nm). The number of threads on both the inner and outer tie rod ends must be equal within 3 threads.

5. Adjust the front end alignment, as required.

BRAKES

For all brake system repair and service procedures not detailed below, please refer to "Brakes" in the Unit Repair section.

Master Cylinder

Removal and Installation

1. Disconnect the negative battery cable.

2. Disconnect the electrical connections from the master cylinder. Disconnect and plug the fluid lines.

NOTE: On Lumina APV, Silhouette and Trans Sport, the master cylinder reservoir can be removed to ease master cylinder removal.

3. Remove the master cylinder to power booster retaining bolts. Remove the RWAL control module assembly, if equipped with anti-lock brakes.

3. Remove the master cylinder from the vehicle. Remove the vacuum booster pushrod.

4. Install the master cylinder in position on the booster. Connect the booster pushrod.

5. Install the master cylinder retaining bolts and tighten to 20 ft. lbs. (27 Nm).

6. Connect the fluid lines to the master cylinder. Connect the RWAL control unit, if equipped with anti-lock brakes, to the bracket.

7. Connect the negative battery cable. Refill the master cylinder and bleed the brake system.

Combination Valve

Removal and Installation

PICK-UP, BLAZER, JIMMY, ASTRO AND SAFARI

The combination valve is mounted on the master cylinder bracket. On vehicles with anti-lock brakes, the combination valve is replaced with a dump/isolation valve. It is removed in the same manner.

1. Disconnect the negative battery cable.
2. Disconnect the brake lines from the combination valve.
3. Remove the mounting bolts and remove the valve from the bracket.
4. Installation is the reverse of the removal procedure. Bleed the brake system.

Proportioning Valve

Removal and Installation

LUMINA APV, SILHOUETTE AND TRANS SPORT

1. Disconnect the negative battery cable.
2. Remove the electrical connector from the master cylinder.
3. Drain and remove the master cylinder reservoir.
4. Remove the proportioning valve caps from the master cyinder.
5. Remove the O-rings, springs and the valve pistons. Use care not to scratch the valves in any way.
6. Remove the valve seals from the valve pistons.

To install:
7. Install new seals on the valve pistons. Lubricate the seals and the pistons with silicon grease.
8. Install the valve pistons and O-rings into the master cylinder.
9. Install the valve cap assemblies and tighten to 20 ft. lbs. (27 Nm).

10. Install the reservoir assembly. Connect the electrical leads.
11. Connect the negative battery cable. Bleed the brake system.

Power Brake Booster

Removal and Installation

1. Disconnect the negative battery cable. Do not disconnect the master cylinder fluid lines, unless there is a clearance problem. Remove the master cylinder and position it to the side.
2. Remove the vacuum booster pushrod. Disconnect the vacuum hose from the booster assembly.
3. From inside the vehicle, remove the mounting studs which secure the vacuum booster to the fire wall.
4. Pull the booster away from the cowl and remove it from the vehicle.
5. Installation is the reverse of the removal procedure. Be sure to properly install the vacuum booster pushrod. Bleed the system.

Brake Caliper

Removal and Installation

1. Remove $\frac{2}{3}$ of the brake fluid from the master cylinder reservoir.
2. Raise and support the vehicle safely. Remove the tire and wheel assembly.
3. Disconnect and plug the caliper fluid line. Remove the bolts retaining the caliper to the rotor. Remove the caliper from the rotor.

NOTE: If the caliper is being removed for brake pad replacement, the fluid line need not be disconnected.

4. Remove the disc brake pads from the caliper. Remove the disc brake pad retaining clips from inside the caliper.

To install:
5. Fill both of the cavities in the caliper housing between the bushings with silicon grease. Install the pads in the caliper.
6. Install the caliper in position over the rotor and install the mounting bolts. Tighten the mounting bolts to 38 ft. lbs. (51 Nm).

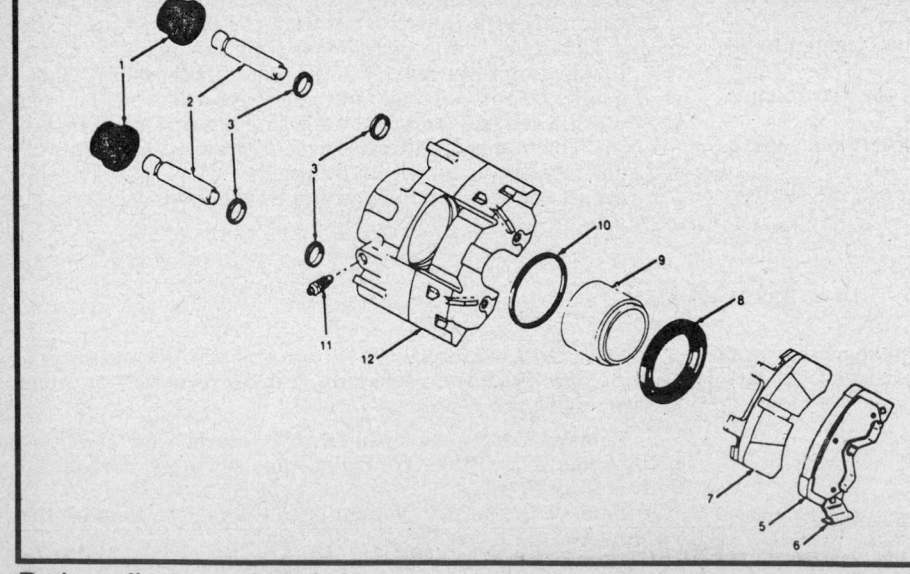

1. Bolt boot
2. Mounting bolt and sleeve
3. Bushing
5. Outboard shoe and lining
6. Wear sensor
7. Inboard shoe and lining
8. Boot
9. Piston
10. Piston seal
11. Bleeder valve
12. Caliper housing

Brake caliper—exploded view

7. Connect the fluid lines to the caliper, if disconnected, and tighten to 33 ft. lbs. (45 Nm).

8. Install the wheel and tire assembly.

9. Lower the vehicle and refill the master cylinder to the correct level. Bleed the brake system if the fluid lines were disconnected from the caliper.

Disc Brake Pads

Removal and Installation

1. Remove $2/3$ of the brake fluid rom the master cylinder.
2. Raise and safely support the vehicle.
3. Remove the brake caliper.
4. Remove the inboard pad and retaining spring from the caliper.
5. Remove the outboard pad and retaning spring from the caliper.
6. Remove the sleeves and bushings.

To install:

7. Lubricate the sleeves and bushing with silicon lubricant and install them in the caliper.
8. Clip the retaining sprig onto the inboard pad and install the pad in the caliper.
9. Install the outboard pad into the caliper.
10. Install the caliper in position over the rotor and install the mounting bolts. Bend the tabs, on the brake pads, over the caliper.
11. Install the wheel and tire assemblies.
12. Lower the vehicle and refill the master cylinder to the correct level.

Brake Rotor

Removal and Installation

PICK-UP, BLAZER, JIMMY, ASTRO AND SAFARI

2WD Vehicles

1. Remove $2/3$ of the brake fluid from the master cylinder.
2. Raise and support the vehicle safely. Remove the tire and wheel assembly.
3. Remove the bolts retaining the caliper to the rotor. Re-move the caliper from the rotor and position it to the side. Do not allow the caliper to hang unsupported.
4. Remove the dust cap, cotter pin, spindle nut, washer and outer wheel bearings.
5. Remove the rotor from the vehicle. On Astro and Safari with 4 wheel anti-lock brakes, remove the wheel speed sensor from behind the rotor.
5. Installation is the reverse of the removal procedure. Adjust the wheel bearings, as required.
6. Bleed the system. Start the vehicle and depress the brake pedal slowly, a few times, to seat the disc brakes on the rotor.

4WD Vehicles

1. Remove $2/3$ of the brake fluid from the master cylinder.
2. Raise and safely support the vehicle.
3. Remove the wheel and tire assemblies.
4. Remove the brake caliper from the rotor and support it aside. Do not disconnect the brake lines.
5. Remove the rotor from the hub.

To install:

6. Install the rotor on the hub. Install the brake caliper.
7. Install the wheel and tire assemblies.
8. Lower the vehicle and refill the master cylinder.

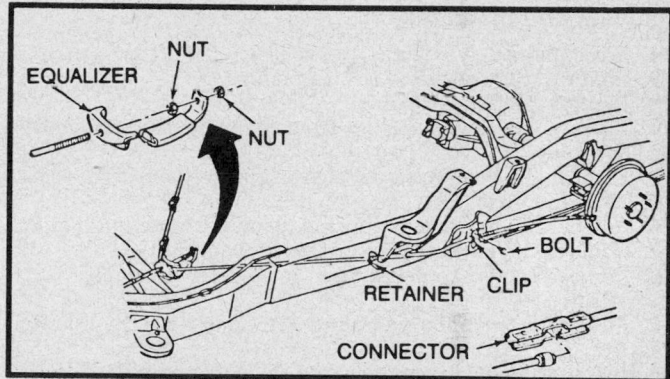

Parking brake cable routing—Pick-Up, Blazer, Jimmy, Astro and Safari

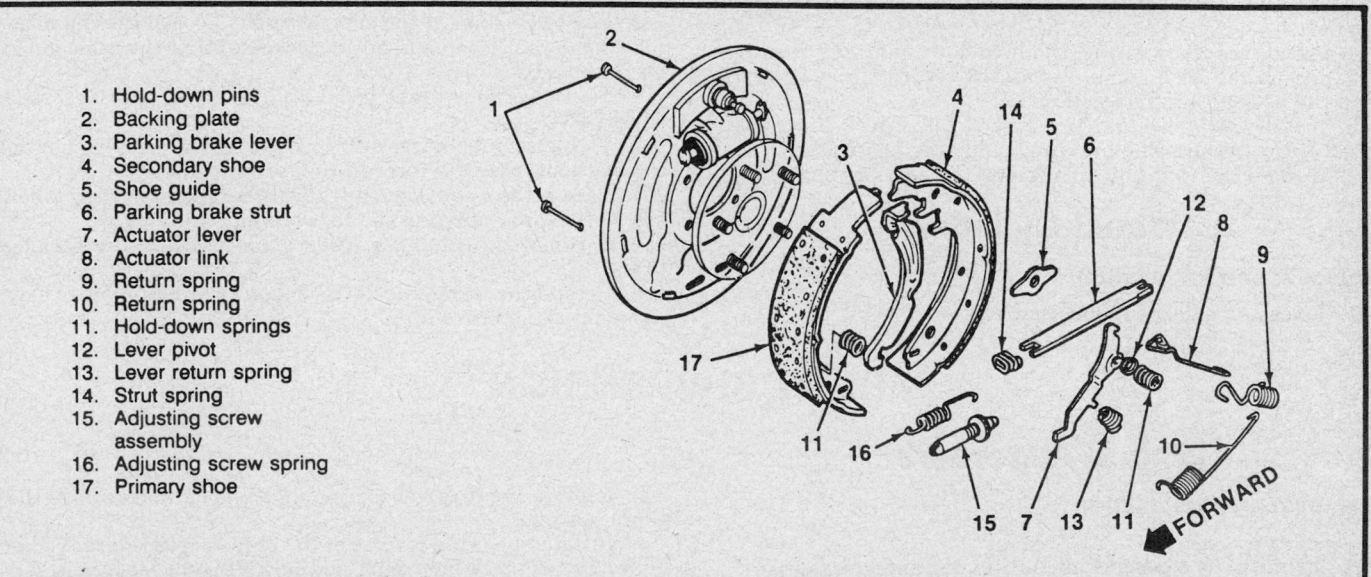

1. Hold-down pins
2. Backing plate
3. Parking brake lever
4. Secondary shoe
5. Shoe guide
6. Parking brake strut
7. Actuator lever
8. Actuator link
9. Return spring
10. Return spring
11. Hold-down springs
12. Lever pivot
13. Lever return spring
14. Strut spring
15. Adjusting screw assembly
16. Adjusting screw spring
17. Primary shoe

Drum brake assembly—exploded view

LUMINA APV, SILHOUETTE AND TRANS SPORT

1. Remove $^2/_3$ of the brake fluid from the master cylinder. Raise and safely support the vehicle.
2. Remove the wheel and tire assemblies.
3. Remove the brake caliper from the rotor and support it aside. Do not disconnect the brake lines.
4. Remove the rotor from the hub.

To install:

5. Install the rotor on the hub. Install the brake caliper.
6. Install the wheel and tire assemblies.
7. Lower the vehicle and refill the master cylinder.

Brake Drums

Removal and Installation

1. Raise and safely support the vehicle.
2. Remove the wheel and tire assembly.
3. Remove the brake drum from the vehicle. If the drum will not pull of of the axle, use a rubber mallet and tap it around the edge.
4. Install the drum on the axle and install the wheel and tire assembly.
5. Lower the vehicle.

Brake Shoes

Removal and Installation

1. Raise and safely support the vehicle.
2. Remove the wheel and tire assembly.
3. Remove the brake drum.
4. Remove the return springs from the brake shoes. Remove the shoe guide.
5. Remove the hold-down springs and pins. Remove the actuator lever and pivot.
6. Remove the lever return spring. Remove the actuator link.
7. Remove the parking brake strut and spring.
8. Remove the brake shoes and the adjuster assembly.

To install:

9. Lubricate the shoe pads and the adjuster with lithium grease.
10. Install the adjusting screw and spring assembly.
11. Install the shoe assembly onto the backing plate.
12. Install the parking brake lever, strut and strut spring.
13. Install the actuator lever and lever pivot. Install the actuator link.
14. Install the lever spring, the hold-down pins and springs.
15. Install the shoe guide. Install the return springs and install the brake drum in position.
16. Install the wheel and tire assemblies. Check the adjustment of the brakes. The brakes should drag just slightly.
17. If the wheel will not turn loosen the adjuster slightly.

Wheel Cylinder

Removal and Installation

1. Raise and safely support the vehicle.

2. Remove the wheel and tire assemblies.
3. Remove the brake drum and remove the brake shoes.
4. Disconnect the brake fluid line from the wheel cylinder.
5. Remove the wheel cylinder retaining bolt.
6. Remove the wheel cylinder from the backing plate.

To install:

7. Install the wheel cylinder in position on the backing plate.
8. Install the retaining bolt. Connect the brake line to the wheel cylinder.
9. Install the brake linings and the brake drum.
10. Install the wheel and tire assembly. Lower the vehicle.
11. Bleed the brake system.

Parking Brake Cable

Removal and Installation

REAR

1. Raise and support the vehicle safely. Remove the tire and wheel assembly. Remove the brake drum.
2. Loosen the equalizer and disconnect the cable at the center retainer.
3. Compress the plastic retainer fingers and remove the retainer from the frame bracket.
4. Remove the rear brake shoe assembly. Disconnect the parking brake cable. Remove the cable from the frame and from the brake backing plate.
5. Installation is the reverse of the removal procedure. Adjust the rear brakes, as required. Adjust the parking brake.

FRONT

1. Raise and support the vehicle safely. Loosen the adjuster nut and disconnect the front cable from the connector.
2. Compress the retainer fingers and loosen the assembly at the frame. Remove the supports.
3. Lower the vehicle. As required, remove dash trim panels to gain access to the parking brake pedal assembly.
4. Disconnect the cable from the parking brake pedal, compress the retainer fingers. Remove the cable from the vehicle.
5. Installation is the reverse of the removal procedure. Adjust the parking brake.

Adjustment

1. Raise and support the vehicle safely. Loosen the equalizer nut. Some vehicles may require the removal of the cable guide on the equalizer.
2. Set the parking brake pedal 2 clicks (2WD vehicles) and 3 clicks (4WD vehicles).
3. Tighten the equalizer nut until the rear wheels will not rotate without excessive force in the forward motion.
4. Back off the equalizer nut until there is light drag when the wheels are rotated in the forward motion.
5. If removed, install the cable guide. Release the parking brake.
6. Rotate the rear wheels in the forward motion. There should be no brake drag.

FRONT SUSPENSION

Shock Absorbers

Removal and Installation

1. Remove the top shock mounting nut and grommet.
2. Raise and safely support the vehicle.
3. Remove the wheel and tire assembly.

4. Remove the lower shock mounting bolts and remove the shock absorber.
5. Installation is the reverse of the removal procedure. Tighten the upper shock mounting nut on 2WD vehicles to 8 ft. lbs. (11 Nm) and the lower bolts to 20 ft. lbs. (27 Nm). On 4WD vehicles tighten the mounting bolts to 54 ft. lbs. (73 Nm).

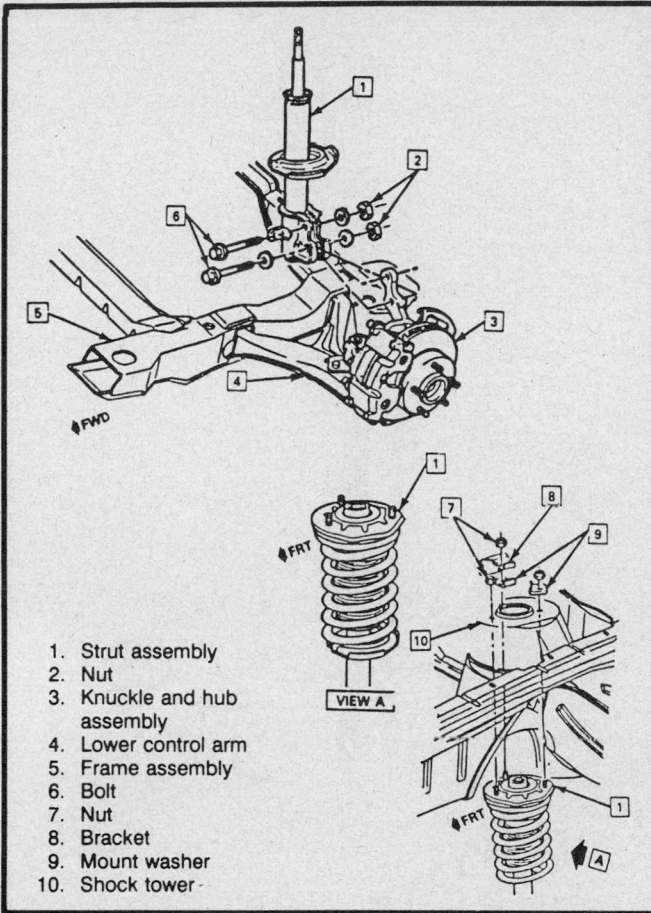

1. Strut assembly
2. Nut
3. Knuckle and hub assembly
4. Lower control arm
5. Frame assembly
6. Bolt
7. Nut
8. Bracket
9. Mount washer
10. Shock tower

Strut assembly mounting—Lumina APV, Silhouette and Trans Sport

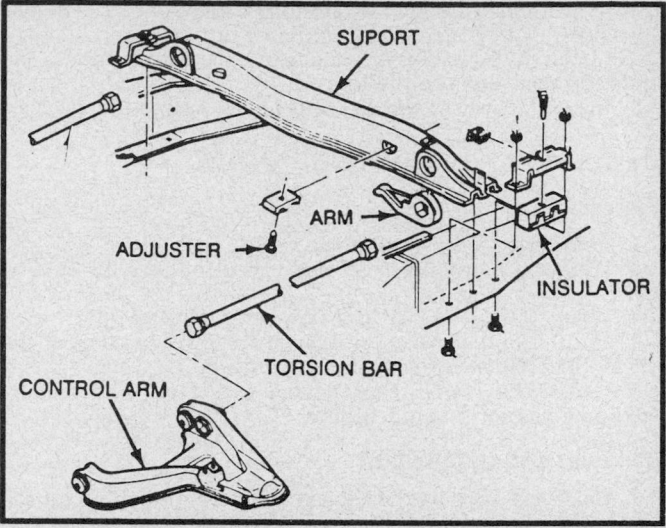

Torsion bar spring mountng—4WD Pick-Up, Blazer, Jimmy, Astro and Safari

MacPherson Strut

Removal and Installation

LUMINA APV, SILHOUETTE AND TRANS SPORT

1. Remove the 3 nuts that retain the top of the strut assembly.
2. Raise and safely support the vehicle.
3. Remove the wheel and tire assembly. Remove the brake line bracket from the strut mount.
4. Remove the lower strut mounting bolts.
5. Remove the strut from the vehicle.
6. Installation is the reverse of the removal procedure. Tighten the strut lower bolts to 140 ft. lbs. (190 Nm) and the upper mounting nuts to 18 ft. lbs. (25 Nm).

Coil Springs

Removal and Installation

PICK-UP, BLAZER, JIMMY, ASTRO AND SAFARI

2WD Vehicles

1. Raise and support the vehicle safely. Remove the wheel and tire assembly. Remove the shock absorber lower retaining bolts.
2. Push the shock absorber through the control arm and into the spring.
3. With the vehicle supported so that the control arms hang

free, install tool J–23028 or equivalent. Secure the tool using a suitable jack. Remove the stabilizer bar from the control arm.
4. Remove the stabilizer to lower control arm attachment. Raise the jack and remove the tension on the lower control arm bolts.
5. Install a safety chain around the spring and through the lower control arm. Remove the lower control arm rear bolt, than remove the other retaining bolt.
6. Lower the jack and allow the lower control arm to hang free. Remove the spring assembly from the vehicle.
7. Installation is the reverse of the removal procedure. When positioning the spring in the lower control arm, be sure that the spring insulator is in the proper position before lifting the control arm in place.
8. Check the front end alignment when complete.

Torsion Bars and Support

Removal and Installation

PICK-UP, BLAZER, JIMMY, ASTRO AND SAFARI

4WD Vehicles

1. Raise and safely support the vehicle. Remove the wheel and tire assemblies.
2. Remove the torsion bar adjusting bolt using tool J–36202 or equivalent. Count the number of tool turns required to remove the bolt.
3. Remove the torsion bar support retainer plate and insulator.
4. Remove the torsion bar by sliding it forward into the control arm and lowering it from the vehicle.
5. Remove the torsion bar support from the vehicle. Remove the adjusting arm and the adjusting arm bolt.

To install:

6. Install the adjusting arm to the support and loosely install the adjusting bolt.
7. Install the support to the frame and the insulator to the frame end.
8. Install the retainer to the support. Install the retainer mounting bolts and tighten to 26 ft. lbs. (35 Nm).
9. Tighten the center retainer bolt to 25 ft. lbs. (34 Nm).
10. Install the torsion bar to the lower control arm and raise and slide the torsion bar into the adjusting arm. The torsion bar should have 6mm clearance at the support.

11. Attach tool J–36202 to the support and tighten it against the adjusting arm the recorded number of turns.

12. Install the adjusting bolt and turn it in until it contacts the adjusting arm. Remove the tool.

13. Install the wheel and tire assemblies. Lower the vehicle.

Upper Ball Joint

Inspection

1. Raise and safely support the vehicle slightly.

2. Wipe the ball joint clean and check the seal for cuts or tears.

3. Check the wheel bearings for proper adjustment.

4. Position a dial indicator against the outside point of the wheel. Rock the wheel in and out.

5. Check the reading on the dial indicator. The reading should be no more than 3.18 mm.

Removal and Installation

1. Raise and support the vehicle safely. Properly support the lower control arm.

NOTE: The control arm must be supported so that the spring and the control arm remain intact.

2. Remove the tire and wheel assembly. As required, remove the brake caliper and position it to the side.

3. Remove the cotter pin and the upper ball joint retaining bolt. Using the proper tool separate the upper joint from its mounting. Support the knuckle assembly so that its weight will not damage the brake hose.

4. Remove the rivets from the ball joint assembly, using a drill with a ⅛ in. bit. Remove the ball joint from the upper control arm.

5. Installation is the reverse of the removal procedure. Be sure to use the nuts and bolts that are supplied with the replacement ball joint assembly. Tighten the replacement bolts to 17 ft. lbs. (23 Nm). Check and adjust the front end alignment, as required.

Lower Ball Joint

Inspection

1. Raise and safely support the vehicle.

2. The ball joint wear is indicated by the position of the grease fitting on the bottom of the joint.

3. The round portion of the grease nipple must protrude from the bottom of the joint. If the niple is flush wwith or inside of the joint, it must be replaced.

Removal and Installation

1. Raise and support the vehicle safely. Properly support the lower control arm.

NOTE: The control arm must be supported so that the spring and the control arm remain intact.

2. Remove the tire and wheel assembly. As required, remove the brake caliper and position it to the side.

3. Remove the cotter pin and the lower ball joint retaining bolt. Using the proper tool separate the ball joint from its mounting. Support the knuckle assembly so that its weight will not damage the brake hose.

4. Remove the rivets from the ball joint assembly, using a drill with a ⅛ in. bit. Remove the ball joint from the control arm.

5. Installation is the reverse of the removal procedure. Be sure to use the nuts and bolts that are supplied with the replacement ball joint assembly. Tighten the replacement bolts to 17 ft. lbs. (23 Nm). Check and adjust the front end alignment, as required.

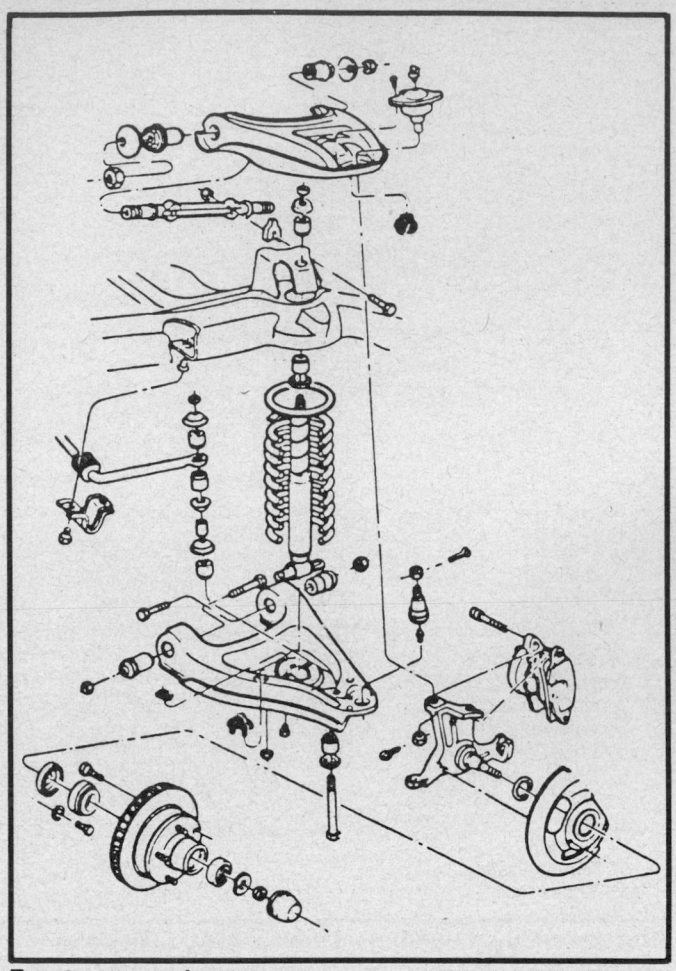

Front suspension components—2WD Pick-Up, Blazer, Jimmy, Astro and Safari

Upper Control Arms

Removal and Installation

1. Note and record the amount of shims used at the control arm retaining bolts. These shims must be installed in the same location as removed. Remove the nuts and the shims.

2. Raise and support the vehicle safely. Properly support the lower control arm. The control arm must be supported so that the spring and the control arm remain intact.

3. Remove the wheel and tire assembly. Loosen the upper ball joint from the steering knuckle, using the proper tool. Support the hub assembly.

4. Remove the upper control arm retaining bolts. Remove the upper control arm from the vehicle.

5. Installation is the reverse of the removal procedure. Tighten the upper control arm nuts to 65 ft. lbs. (88 Nm). Check and adjust the front end alignment, as required.

Lower Control Arms

Removal and Installation

PICK-UP, BLAZER, JIMMY, ASTRO AND SAFARI

2WD Vehicles

1. Raise and support the vehicle safely.

2. Remove the wheel and tire assemblies. Properly support the lower control arm assembly.

3. Remove the coil spring.

4. Remove the lower ball joint cotter pin and retaining nut.

5. Using the proper tool, separate the lower ball joint from the steering knuckle.

6. Remove the lower control arm from the vehicle.

7. Installation is the reverse of the removal procedure. Check and adjust front alignment, as required.

LUMINA APV, SILHOUETTE AND TRANS SPORT

1. Raise and safely support the vehicle so that the suspension hangs freely.

2. Remove the wheel and tire assemblies.

3. Remove the stabilizer shaft-to-control arm mounting bolt. Remove the lower ball joint pinch bolt.

4. Separate the steering knuckle from the lower ball joint.

5. Remove the lower control arm mounting bolts and remove the control arm from the vehicle.

To install:

6. Install the control arm in position on the vehicle frame. Do not tighten the control arm bolts at this time.

7. Install the stabilizer shaft to the control arm, do not tighten the bolts at this time.

8. Connect the steering knuckle to the control arm using a new pinch bolt. Tighte to 33 ft. lbs. (45 Nm). Lower the vehicle so that the weight is supported by the control arms.

9. Tighten the control arm bolts to 61 ft. lbs. (83 Nm). Tighten the stabilizer shaft bolts to 32 ft. lbs. (43 Nm).

10. Install the wheel and tire assemblies. Lower the vehicle completely.

Stabilizer Shaft

Removal and Installation

1. Raise and safely support the vehicle.

2. Remove the wheel and tire assembly.

3. Remove the left and right side stabilizer mounting bolts. Keep the sides separate for installation.

4. Remove the center stabilizer insulators and lower the stabilizer from the vehicle.

5. Install the stabilizer in position in the vehicle. Tighten the left and right mounting bolts to 24 ft. lbs. and the center bushing supports to 35 ft. lbs.

6. Install the wheel and tire assemblies and lower the vehicle.

Front Wheel Bearings

Removal and Installation

2WD PICK-UP, BLAZER, JIMMY, ASTRO AND SAFARI

1. Raise and support the vehicle safely. Remove the tire and wheel assembly.

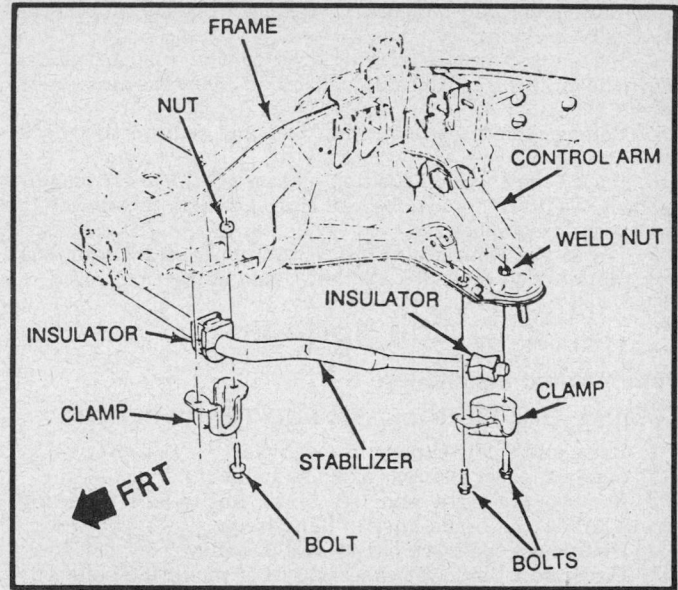

Stabilizer bar mounting—Pick-Up, Blazer, Jimmy, Astro and Safari

2. Remove the brake caliper and position it to the side. Remove the dust cover, cotter pin, washer and spindle nut.

3. Remove the outer wheel bearing assembly. Remove the brake rotor. Remove the inner wheel bearing assembly.

4. Installation is the reverse of the removal procedure. When installing new bearings, be sure to install new bearing races inside the rotor.

5. Pack new bearings with the proper grade and type wheel bearing grease. Adjust the wheel bearings.

Adjustment

1. Raise and safely support the vehicle.

2. Remove the brake caliper and the dust cap from the wheel hub.

3. Remove the cotter pin from the castle nut.

4. Tighten the castle nut to 12 ft. lbs. (16 Nm) while turning the rotor forward.

5. Loosen the castle nut, then tighten it, by hand to a just loose position.

6. Back the nut off slightly, until the hole in the spindle aligns with a slot in the nut. Do not back the nut off more than ½ of a flat.

7. Install a new cotter pin. Measure the rotor endplay at the castle nut, it should not exceed 0.0005 in. (0.13mm).

8. Install the bearing dust cover and install the wheel and tire assembly.

9. Lower the vehicle.

REAR SUSPENSION

Shock Absorbers

Removal and Installation

PICK-UP, BLAZER, JIMMY, ASTRO AND SAFARI

1. Raise and support the vehicle safely.

2. Properly support the rear axle assembly.

3. Remove the upper shock absorber retaining bolt.

4. Remove the lower shock absorber bolt.

5. Remove the shock absorber from the vehicle.

6. Install the shock in position and install the mounting bolts.

7. Tighten the top mounting bolts to 17 ft. lbs. (23 Nm) and the lower mounting bolts to 47 ft. lbs. (64 Nm).

8. Lower the vehicle.

LUMINA APV, SILHOUETTE AND TRANS SPORT

1. Open the lift gate and open the trim cover.

2. Remove the upper shock mounting nut and grommet.

3. Raise and safely support the vehicle. Properly support the rear axle assembly.

4. If equipped with electronic level control suspension, remove the air line from the shock absorber. Allow the air to bleed off.

5. Remove the lower mounting bolt and remove the shock from the vehicle.

6. Install the shock in position and install the lower mounting bolt. Tighten to 44 ft. lbs. (59 Nm). Connect the air line to the shock, if equipped.

7. Lower the vehicle and install the upper shock retaining nut, tighten it to 16 ft. lbs. (22 Nm). Install the trim cover.

Coil Springs

Removal and Installation

LUMINA APV, SILHOUETTE AND TRANS SPORT

1. Raise and safely support the vehicle.
2. Safely support the rear axle assembly.
3. Remove the right and left brake line-to-axle attaching screws. Allow the brake lines to hang freely.
4. Disconnect the track bar-to-axle attaching bolt.
5. Disconnect the lower shock absorber mounting bolts.
6. Slowly lower the rear axle and remove the springs and insulators.
7. Installation is the reverse of the removal procedure. Make sure the springs are fully seated in the pads.

Leaf Springs

Removal and Installation

PICK-UP, BLAZER, JIMMY, ASTRO AND SAFARI

1. Raise and support the vehicle safely. Properly support the rear axle assembly to relieve tension on the springs.
2. Remove the shock absorbers. Remove the U bolt nuts, washers, anchor plates and the U bolts.
3. Remove the shackle to frame bolt, washers and nut. Remove the spring assembly to front bracket nut, washers and bolt.
4. Remove the spring assembly from the vehicle. As required, separate the spring from the shackle.
5. Installation is the reverse of the removal procedure. Tighten the U bolts to 85 ft. lbs. (115 Nm) in 2 gradual steps. Tighten the front and rear shackle nuts to 92 ft. lbs. (125 Nm).

Rear Wheel Hub and Bearing Assembly

Removal and Installation

LUMINA APV, SILHOUETTE AND TRANS SPORT

1. Raise and safely support the vehicle.
2. Remove the wheel and tire assemblies.
3. Remove the brake drum.
4. Remove the hub and bearing assembly mounting bolts and remove it from the vehicle. Support the brake assembly with a wire.
5. Installation is the reverse of the removal procedure. Tighten the hub assembly mounting bolts to 45 ft. lbs. (60 Nm).

Track Bar

Removal and Installation

LUMINA APV, SILHOUETTE AND TRANS SPORT

1. Raise and safely support the vehicle.
2. Remove the track bar mounting bolts from the body and the axle.

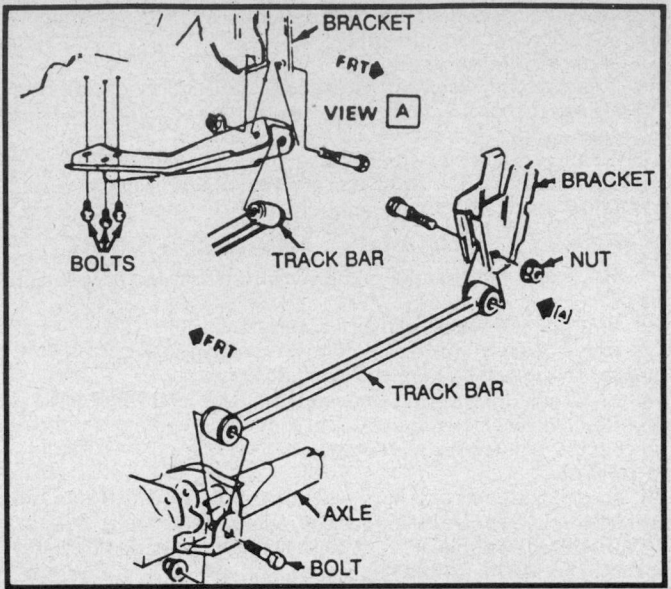

Rear track bar mounting—Lumina APV, Silhouette and Trans Sport

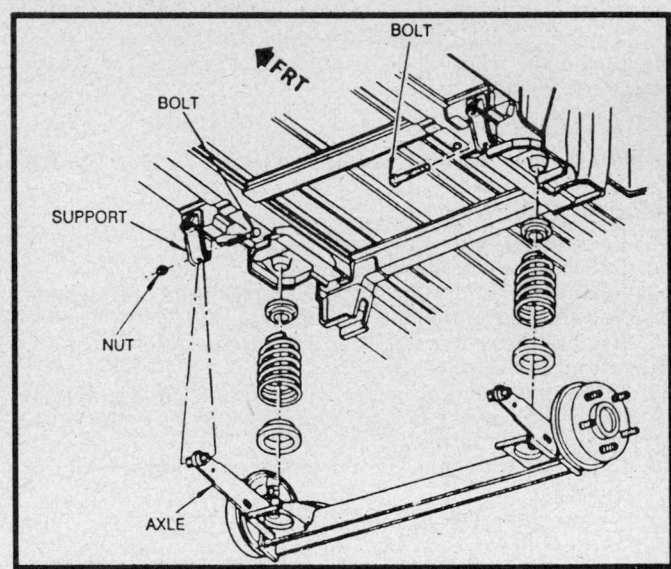

Rear axle assembly mounting—Lumina APV, Silhouette and Trans Sport

3. Lower the track bar from the vehicle.
4. Install the track bar at the axle, loosely install the bolt.
5. Connect the other end of the track bar at the frame.
6. Tighten the bolt at the axle to 44 ft. lbs. (60 Nm). and the track bar-to-frame bolt to 35 ft. lbs. (47 Nm).
7. Lower the vehicle.

Rear Axle Assembly

Removal and Installation

LUMINA APV, SILHOUETTE AND TRANS SPORT

1. Raise and safely support the vehicle.
2. Properly support the rear axle assembly.
3. Remove the wheel and tire assemblies. Remove the brake drums.

4. Disconnect the parking brake cable from the brake system.
5. Disconnect the brake line brackets from the axle assembly.
6. Disconnect the shock absorbers from the axle.
7. Disconnect the track bar bolt at the rear axle.
8. Lower the rear axle slightly and remove the coil springs and insulator.
9. Remove the hub and bearing assemblies, support the backing plate and brake assemblies with wire from the vehicle.

NOTE: Do not allow the backing plates to hang by the brake lines.

10. Remove the control arm to frame bracket attaching bolts and lower the axle assembly from the vehicle.

To install:

11. Raise the axle assembly to the vehicle and install the control arm bolts. Torque control arm bracket bolts to 84 ft. lbs. (115 Nm). Torque the control arm to bracket pivot bolts to 28 ft. lbs. (38 Nm).
12. Install the backing plate, hub and bearing assembly. Use car not to kink the brake lines.
13. Install the brake line brackets to the axle assembly. Connect the parking brake cable to the brake assembly.
14. Position the coil springs and insulators on the axle and raise the axle.
15. Connect the shock absorber lower bolts to the axle.
16. Connect the track bar to the rear axle.
17. Install the brake drums. Install the wheel and tire assemblies.
18. Lower the vehicle.

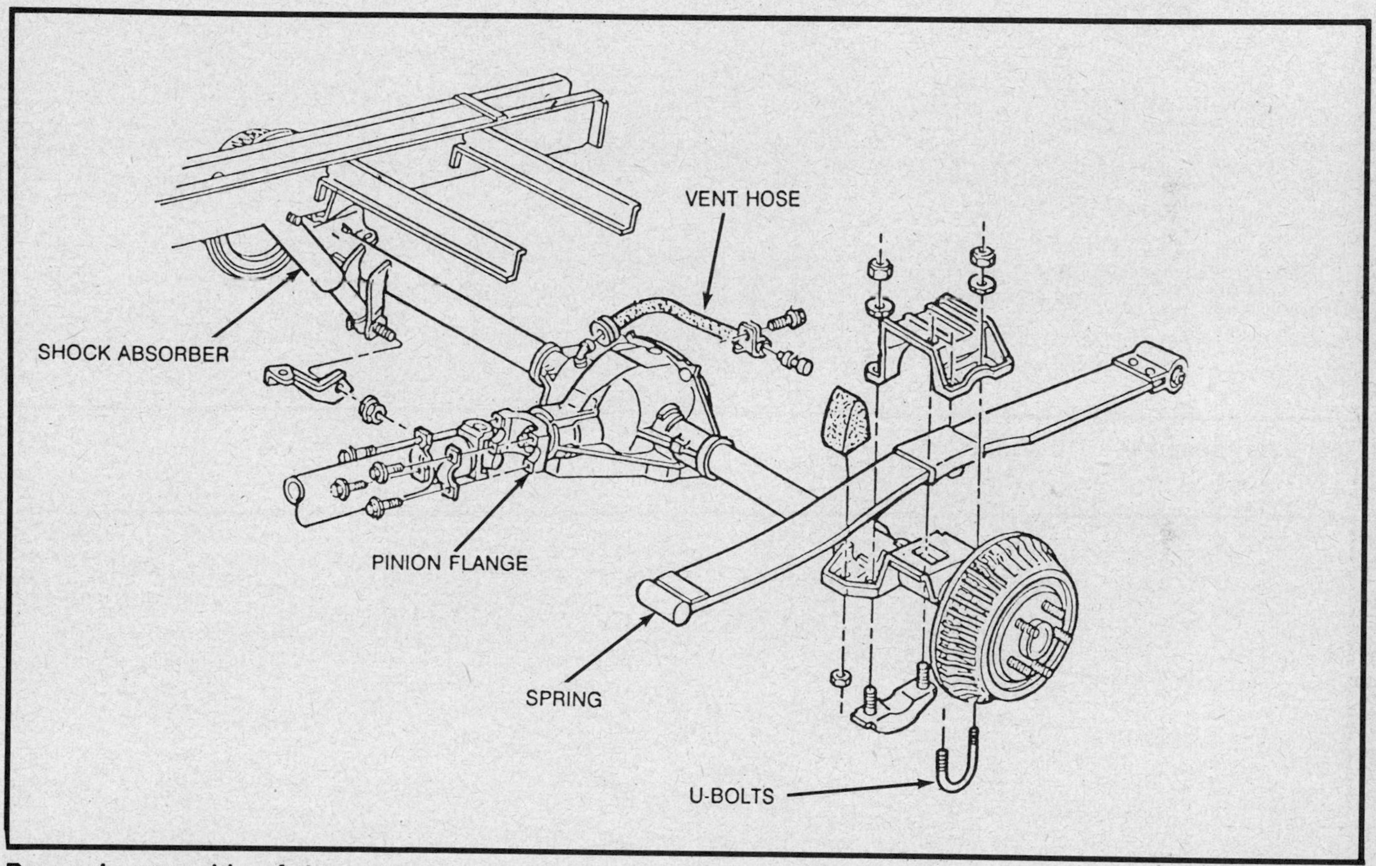

VENT HOSE

SHOCK ABSORBER

PINION FLANGE

SPRING

U-BOLTS

Rear axle assembly – Astro van

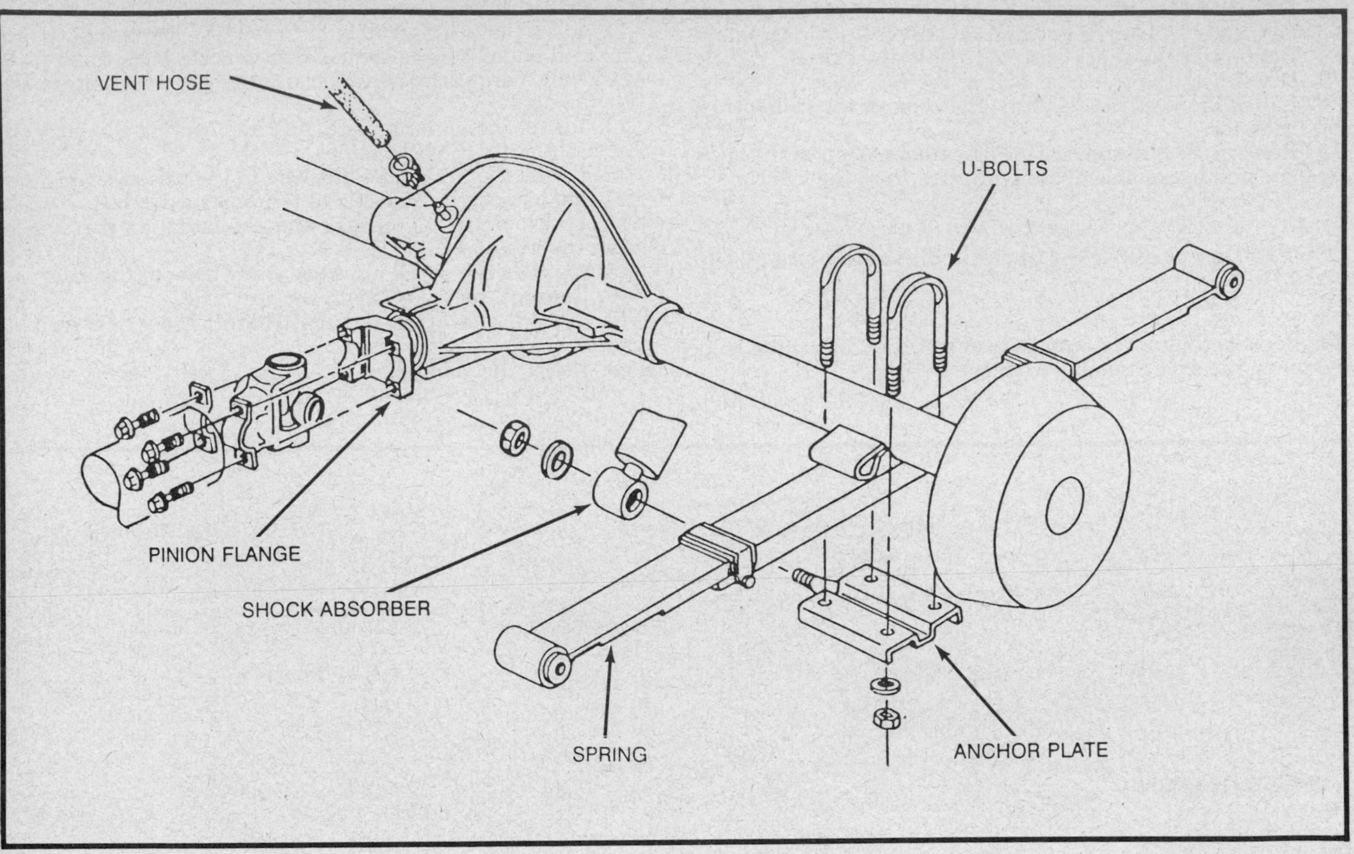

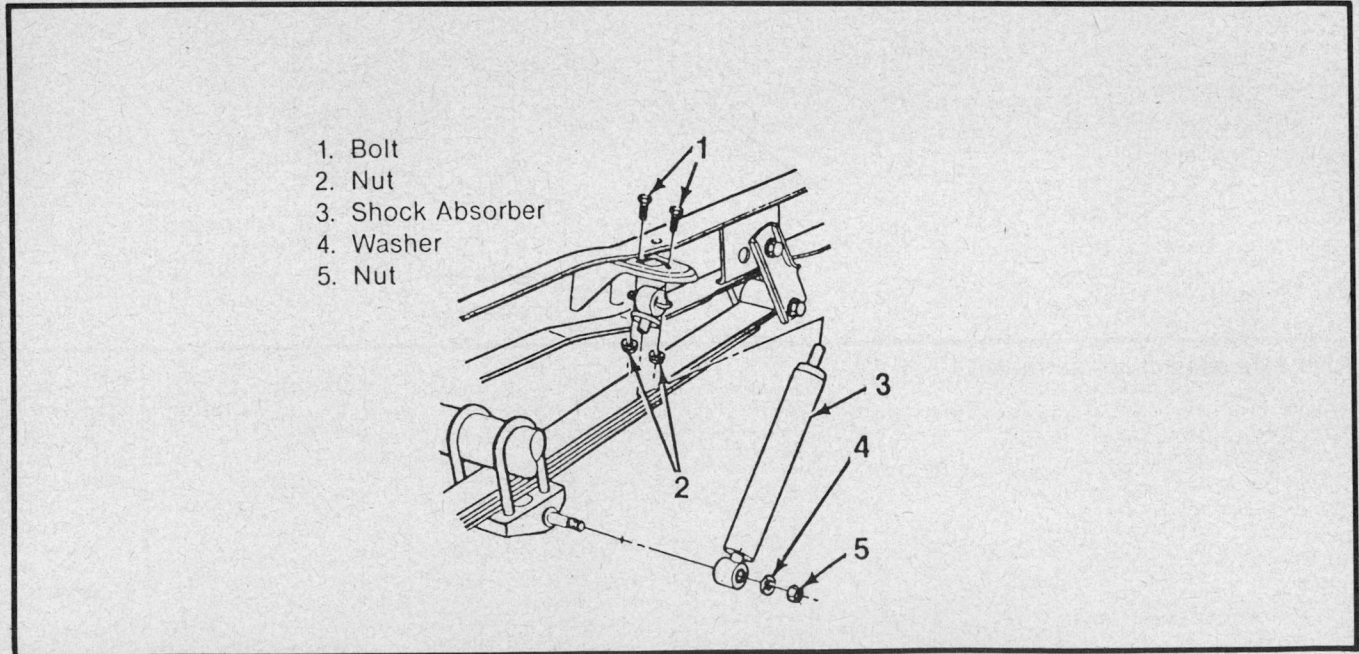

Rear axle assembly—S10 series

1. Bolt
2. Nut
3. Shock Absorber
4. Washer
5. Nut

Typical rear shock mounting

SPECIFICATIONS

VEHICLE IDENTIFICATION CHART

It is important for servicing and ordering parts to be certain of the vehicle and engine identification. The VIN (vehicle identification number) is a 17 digit number visible through the windshield on the driver's side of the dash and contains the vehicle and engine identification codes. The tenth digit indicates model year and the fourth digit indicates engine code. It can be interpreted as follows:

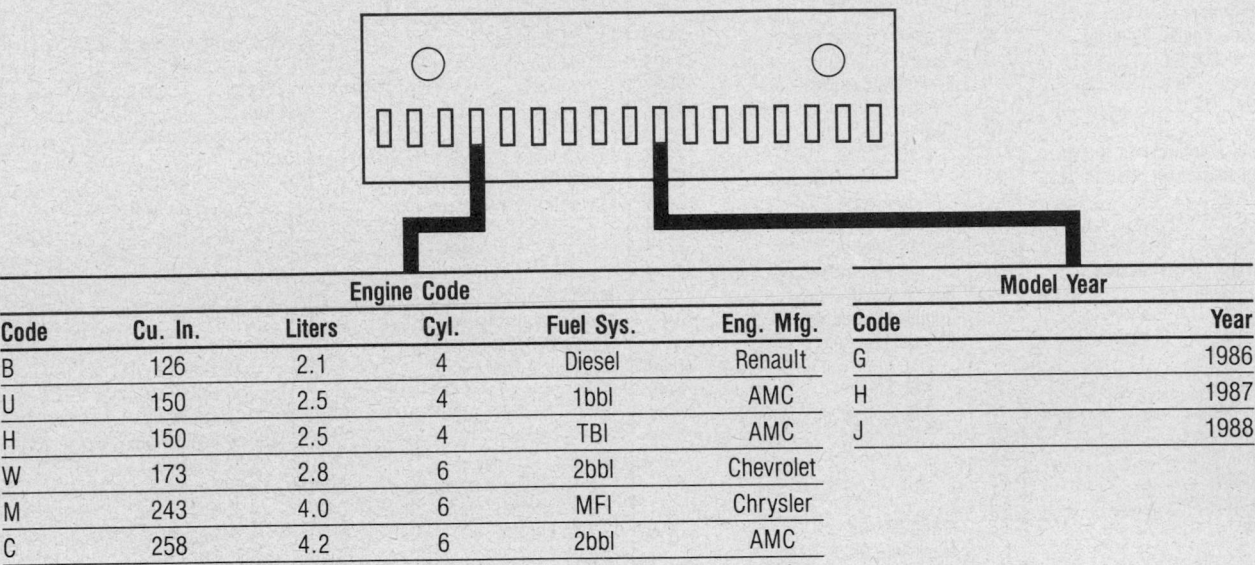

Engine Code						Model Year	
Code	Cu. In.	Liters	Cyl.	Fuel Sys.	Eng. Mfg.	Code	Year
B	126	2.1	4	Diesel	Renault	G	1986
U	150	2.5	4	1bbl	AMC	H	1987
H	150	2.5	4	TBI	AMC	J	1988
W	173	2.8	6	2bbl	Chevrolet		
M	243	4.0	6	MFI	Chrysler		
C	258	4.2	6	2bbl	AMC		
N	360	5.9	8	2bbl	AMC		

VEHICLE IDENTIFICATION CHART

It is important for servicing and ordering parts to be certain of the vehicle and engine identification. The VIN (vehicle identification number) is a 17 digit number visible through the windshield on the driver's side of the dash and contains the vehicle and engine identification codes. The tenth digit indicates model year and the eighth digit indicates engine code. It can be interpreted as follows:

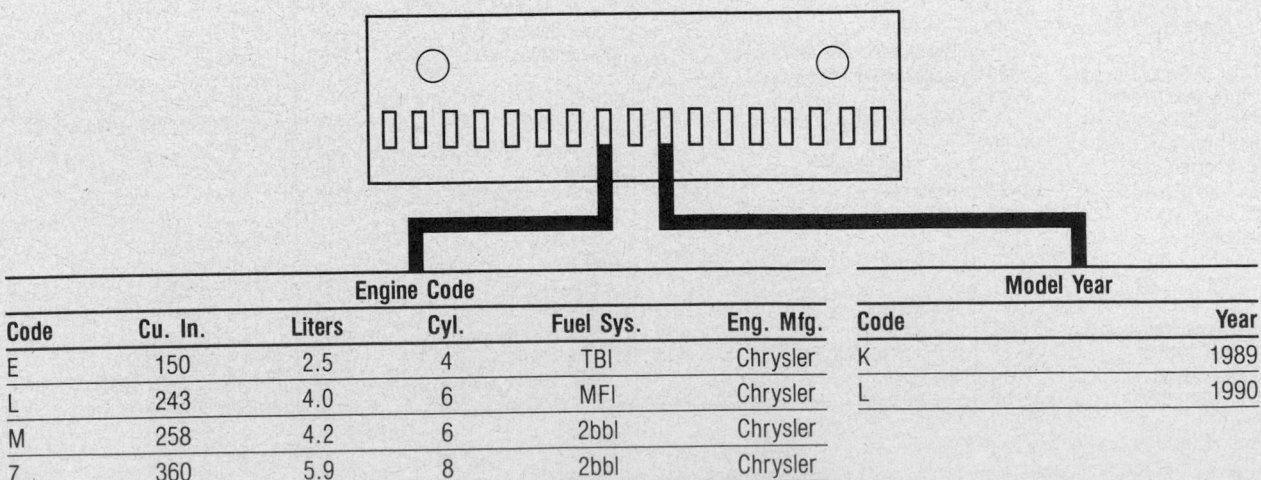

Engine Code						Model Year	
Code	Cu. In.	Liters	Cyl.	Fuel Sys.	Eng. Mfg.	Code	Year
E	150	2.5	4	TBI	Chrysler	K	1989
L	243	4.0	6	MFI	Chrysler	L	1990
M	258	4.2	6	2bbl	Chrysler		
7	360	5.9	8	2bbl	Chrysler		

ENGINE IDENTIFICATION

Year	Model	Engine Displacement cu. in. (liter)	Engine Series Identification (VIN)	No. of Cylinders	Engine Type
1986	Comanche	126 (2.1)	B	4	Turbo Diesel (OHV)
	Comanche	150 (2.5)	H	4	OHV
	Comanche	173 (2.8)	W	6	OHV
	CJ-7	150 (2.5)	U	4	OHV
	CJ-7	258 (4.2)	C	6	OHV
	Cherokee	126 (2.1)	B	4	Turbo Diesel (OHV)
	Cherokee	150 (2.5)	H	4	OHV
	Cherokee	173 (2.8)	W	6	OHV
	Wagoneer	126 (2.1)	B	4	Turbo Diesel (OHV)
	Wagoneer	150 (2.5)	H	4	OHV
	Wagoneer	173 (2.8)	W	6	OHV
	Grand Wagoneer	258 (4.2)	C	6	OHV
	Grand Wagoneer	360 (5.9)	N	8	OHV
	J10 Pick-Up	258 (4.2)	C	6	OHV
	J10 Pick-Up	360 (5.9)	N	8	OHV
	J20 Pick-Up	360 (5.9)	N	8	OHV
1987	Comanche	126 (2.1)	B	4	Turbo Diesel (OHV)
	Comanche	150 (2.5)	H	4	OHV
	Comanche	243 (4.0)	M	6	OHV
	Wrangler	150 (2.5)	U	4	OHV
	Wrangler	258 (4.2)	C	6	OHV
	Cherokee	126 (2.1)	B	4	Turbo Diesel (OHV)
	Cherokee	150 (2.5)	H	4	OHV
	Cherokee	243 (4.0)	M	6	OHV
	Wagoneer	126 (2.1)	B	4	Turbo Diesel (OHV)
	Wagoneer	150 (2.5)	H	4	OHV
	Wagoneer	243 (4.0)	M	6	OHV
	Grand Wagoneer	360 (5.9)	N	8	OHV
	J10 Pick-Up	258 (4.2)	C	6	OHV
	J10 Pick-Up	360 (5.9)	N	8	OHV
	J20 Pick-Up	360 (5.9)	N	8	OHV
1988	Comanche	150 (2.5)	H	4	OHV
	Comanche	243 (4.0)	M	6	OHV
	Wrangler	150 (2.5)	H	4	OHV
	Wrangler	258 (4.2)	C	6	OHV
	Cherokee	150 (2.5)	H	4	OHV
	Cherokee	243 (4.0)	M	6	OHV
	Wagoneer	243 (4.0)	M	6	OHV
	Grand Wagoneer	360 (5.9)	N	8	OHV
	J10 Pick-Up	258 (4.2)	C	6	OHV
	J10 Pick-Up	360 (5.9)	N	8	OHV
	J20 Pick-Up	360 (5.9)	N	8	OHV

ENGINE IDENTIFICATION

Year	Model	Engine Displacement cu. in. (liter)	Engine Series Identification (VIN)	No. of Cylinders	Engine Type
1989–90	Comanche	150 (2.5)	E	4	OHV
	Comanche	243 (4.0)	L	6	OHV
	Wrangler	150 (2.5)	E	4	OHV
	Wrangler	258 (4.2)	M	6	OHV
	Cherokee	150 (2.5)	E	4	OHV
	Cherokee	243 (4.0)	L	6	OHV
	Wagoneer	243 (4.0)	L	6	OHV
	Grand Wagoneer	360 (5.9)	7	8	OHV

GENERAL ENGINE SPECIFICATIONS

Year	VIN	No. Cylinder Displacement cu. in. (liter)	Fuel System Type	Net Horsepower @ rpm	Net Torque @ rpm (ft. lbs.)	Bore × Stroke (in.)	Compression Ratio	Oil Pressure @ rpm
1986	B	4-126 (2.1)	Diesel	85 @ 3750	132 @ 2750	3.358×3.503	21.5:1	43 @ 2000
	U	4-150 (2.5)	1bbl	83 @ 4200	116 @ 2600	3.876×3.188	9.2:1	40 @ 2000
	H	4-150 (2.5)	TBI	83 @ 4200	116 @ 2600	3.876×3.188	9.2:1	40 @ 2000
	W	6-173 (2.8)	2bbl	110 @ 4800	148 @ 2000	3.500×2.990	8.5:1	45 @ 2000
	C	6-258 (4.2)	2bbl	110 @ 3200	210 @ 1800	3.750×3.895	8.0:1	37 @ 2000
	N	8-360 (5.9)	2bbl	175 @ 4000	285 @ 2900	4.080×3.440	8.25:1	37 @ 2000
1987	B	4-126 (2.1)	Diesel	85 @ 3750	132 @ 2750	3.358×3.503	21.5:1	43 @ 2000
	U	4-150 (2.5)	1bbl	83 @ 4200	116 @ 2600	3.876×3.188	9.2:1	40 @ 2000
	H	4-150 (2.5)	TBI	83 @ 4200	116 @ 2600	3.876×3.188	9.2:1	40 @ 2000
	W	6-173 (2.8)	2bbl	110 @ 4800	148 @ 2000	3.500×2.990	8.5:1	45 @ 2000
	M	6-243 (4.0)	MPI	173 @ 4500	220 @ 2500	3.875×3.876	9.2:1	40 @ 2000
	C	6-258 (4.2)	2bbl	110 @ 3200	210 @ 1800	3.750×3.895	8.0:1	37 @ 2000
	N	8-360 (5.9)	2bbl	175 @ 4000	285 @ 2900	4.080×3.440	8.25:1	37 @ 2000
1988	H	4-150 (2.5)	TBI	83 @ 4200	116 @ 2600	3.876×3.188	9.2:1	40 @ 2000
	M	6-243 (4.0)	MPI	173 @ 4500	220 @ 2500	3.875×3.876	9.2:1	40 @ 2000
	C	6-258 (4.2)	2bbl	110 @ 3200	210 @ 1800	3.750×3.895	8.0:1	37 @ 2000
	N	8-360 (5.9)	2bbl	175 @ 4000	285 @ 2900	4.080×3.440	8.25:1	37 @ 2000
1989–90	E	4-150 (2.5)	TBI	121 @ 5250	141 @ 3250	3.876×3.188	9.2:1	37 @ 1600 ①
	L	6-242 (4.0)	MPI	177 @ 4500	224 @ 2500	3.880×3.440	9.2:1	37 @ 1600 ①
	M	6-258 (4.2)	2bbl	112 @ 3000	210 @ 2000	3.750×3.895	9.2:1	37 @ 1600 ①
	7	8-360 (5.9)	2bbl	144 @ 3200	280 @ 1500	4.080×3.440	8.25:1	37 @ 1600 ①

① Above 1600 rpm, pressure can vary to a maximum of 75 psi

GASOLINE ENGINE TUNE-UP SPECIFICATIONS

Year	VIN	No. Cylinder Displacement cu. in. (liter)	Spark Plugs Type	Gap (in.)	Ignition Timing (deg.) ② MT	AT	Compression Pressure (psi)	Fuel Pump (psi)	Idle Speed (rpm) MT	AT	Valve Clearance In.	Ex.
1986	U	4-150 (2.5)	RN14LY	0.035	12	12	①	6.5–8	750	750	Hyd.	Hyd.
	H	4-150 (2.5)	RN12LYC	0.035	12	12	①	14–15	750	750	Hyd.	Hyd.
	W	6-173 (2.8)	RUT2YC	0.040	10	10	①	5–7	750	750	③	③
	C	6-258 (4.2)	RFN14LY	0.035	8	12	①	4–5	700	600	Hyd.	Hyd.
	N	8-360 (5.9)	RN12Y	0.035	8	8	①	5–6.5	800	600	Hyd.	Hyd.
1987	U	4-150 (2.5)	RFN14LY	0.035	12	12	①	6.5–8	750	750	Hyd.	Hyd.
	H	4-150 (2.5)	RC12LYC	0.035	④	④	①	14–15	④	④	Hyd.	Hyd.
	W	6-173 (2.8)	RUT2YC	0.040	10	10	①	5–7	750	750	③	③
	M	6-243 (4.0)	RC9YC	0.035	④	④	①	31	④	④	Hyd.	Hyd.
	C	6-258 (4.2)	RFN14LY	0.035	9⑤	9⑤	①	4–5	700	600	Hyd.	Hyd.
	N	8-360 (5.9)	RN12Y	0.035	8	8	①	5–6.5	600	500	Hyd.	Hyd.
1988	H	04-150 (2.5)	RC12LYC	0.035	④	④	①	14–15	④	④	Hyd.	Hyd.
	M	6-243 (4.0)	RC9YC	0.035	④	④	①	31	④	④	Hyd.	Hyd.
	C	6-258 (4.2)	RFN14LY	0.035	9⑤	9⑤	①	4–5	700	600	Hyd.	Hyd.
	N	8-360 (5.9)	RN12Y	0.035	8	8	①	5–6.5	600	500	Hyd.	Hyd.
1989–90	E	4-150 (2.5)	RC12LYC	0.035	④	④	①	14–15	④	④	Hyd.	Hyd.
	L	6-242 (4.0)	RC9YC	0.035	④	④	①	31	④	④	Hyd.	Hyd.
	M	6-258 (4.2)	RFN14LY	0.035	9⑤	9⑤	①	4–5	700	600	Hyd.	Hyd.
	7	8-360 (5.9)	RN12Y	0.035	8	8	①	5–6.5	600	500	Hyd.	Hyd.

① Check all cylinders. Difference between all cylinders should be no more than 25%.
② BTDC
③ Hydraulic—Turn adjuster until lash is gone then tighten 1½ turns more
④ Not adjustable
⑤ At 1600 rpm: at high altitude—16 @ 1600 rpm

DIESEL ENGINE TUNE-UP SPECIFICATIONS

Year	VIN	No. Engine Displacement cu. in. (liter)	Valve Clearance Intake (in.)	Exhaust (in.)	Intake Valve Opens (deg.)	Injection Pump Setting (deg.)	Injection Nozzle Pressure (psi) New	Used	Idle Speed (rpm)	Cranking Compression Pressure (psi)
1986	B	4-126 (2.1)	0.008	0.010	14B	8B	1885	NA	800 ①	②
1987	B	4-126 (2.1)	0.008	0.010	14B	8B	1885	NA	800 ①	②

NA Not available
① Without solenoid. 1100 with solenoid
② Check all cylinders. The difference between cylinders should not be more than 25%.

FIRING ORDERS

NOTE: To avoid confusion, always replace spark plug wires one at a time.

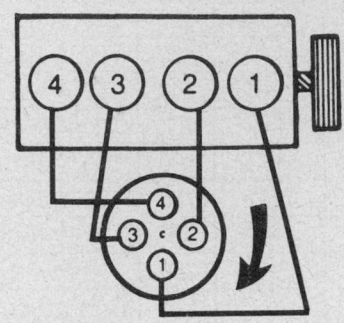

2.5L 4 cylinder
Firing order: 1–3–4–2
Distributor rotation: clockwise

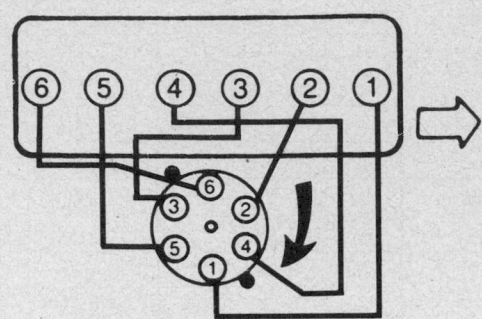

4.0L and 4.2L 6 cylinder
Firing order: 1–5–3–6–2–4
Distributor rotation: clockwise

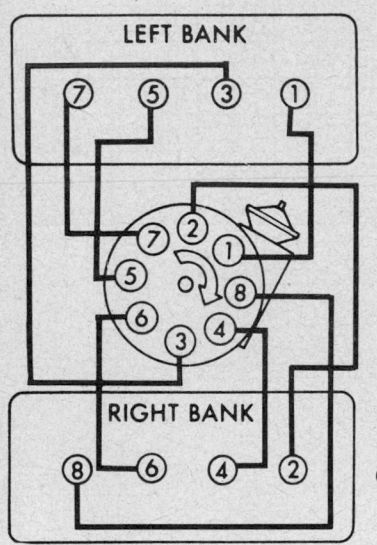

LEFT BANK

RIGHT BANK

FRONT ⇨

CLOCKWISE ROTATION
1-8-4-3-6-5-7-2

5.9L V8
Firing order: 1–8–4–3–6–5–7–2
Distributor rotation: clockwise

1-2-3-4-5-6

FRONT OF ENGINE

SCREWS (4)

2.8L V6
Firing order: 1–2–3–4–5–6
Distributor rotation: clockwise

CAPACITIES

Year	Model	VIN	No. Cylinder Displacement cu. in. (liter)	Engine Crankcase with Filter	Engine Crankcase without Filter	Transmission (pts.) 4-Spd	Transmission (pts.) 5-Spd	Transmission (pts.) Auto.	Drive Axle (pts.)	② Fuel Tank (gal.)	Cooling System (qts.)
1986	Comanche	B	4-126 (2.1)	6.3	6.3	4.0 ①	4.5	15.8	2.5	13.5 ②	9.0
	Comanche	H	4-150 (2.5)	4	4	4.0 ①	4.5	15.8	2.5	13.5 ②	9.0
	Comanche	W	6-173 (2.8)	5	5	4.0 ①	4.5	15.8	2.5	13.5 ②	9.0
	CJ-7	U	4-150 (2.5)	4	4	4.0	4.5	17.0	4.8	15	7.8
	CJ-7	C	6-258 (4.2)	6	6	3.5	—	17.0	4.8	15	10.5
	Cherokee	B	4-126 (2.1)	6.3	6.3	4.0 ①	4.5	15.8	2.5	13.5 ②	9.0
	Cherokee	H	4-150 (2.5)	4	4	4.0 ①	4.5	15.8	2.5	13.5 ②	9.0
	Cherokee	W	6-173 (2.8)	5	5	4.0 ①	4.5	15.8	2.5	13.5 ②	9.0

CAPACITIES

Year	Model	VIN	No. Cylinder Displacement cu. in. (liter)	Engine Crankcase with Filter	Engine Crankcase without Filter	Transmission (pts.) 4-Spd	Transmission (pts.) 5-Spd	Transmission (pts.) Auto.	Drive Axle (pts.)	Fuel Tank (gal.) ②	Cooling System (qts.)
1986	Wagoneer	B	4-126 (2.1)	6.3	6.3	4.0 ①	4.5	15.8	2.5	13.5 ②	9.0
	Wagoneer	H	4-150 (2.5)	4	4	4.0 ①	4.5	15.8	2.5	13.5 ②	9.0
	Wagoneer	W	6-173 (2.8)	5	5	4.0 ①	4.5	15.8	2.5	13.5 ②	9.0
	Grand Wagoneer	C	6-258 (4.2)	6	6	3.5	—	17.0	4.8	20	10.5
	Grand Wagoneer	N	8-360 (5.9)	5	5	—	—	17.0	4.8	20	15.0
	J-10 Pick-Up	C	6-258 (4.2)	6	6	3.5	—	15.8	4.8	18	10.5
	J-10 Pick-Up	N	8-360 (5.9)	5	5	—	—	15.8	4.8	18	15.0
	J-20 Pick-Up	N	8-360 (5.9)	5	5	—	—	17.0	6	18	15.0
1987	Comanche	B	4-126 (2.1)	6.3	6.3	4.0 ①	4.5	15.8	2.5	13.5 ②	9.0
	Comanche	H	4-150 (2.5)	4	4	4.0 ①	4.5	15.8	2.5	13.5 ②	9.0
	Comanche	M	6-243 (4.0)	6	6	3.9	4.5	15.8	2.5	13.5 ②	12.0
	Wrangler	U	4-150 (2.5)	4	4	4.0	4.5	17.0	2.5	15 ②	7.8
	Wrangler	C	6-258 (4.2)	6	6	3.5	—	17.0	2.5	15 ②	10.5
	Cherokee	B	4-126 (2.1)	6.3	6.3	4.0 ①	4.5	15.8	2.5	13.5 ②	9.0
	Cherokee	H	4-150 (2.5)	4	4	4.0 ①	4.5	15.8	2.5	13.5 ②	9.0
	Cherokee	M	6-243 (4.0)	6	6	3.9	4.5	15.8	2.5	13.5 ②	12.0
	Wagoneer	B	4-126 (2.1)	6.3	6.3	4.0 ①	4.5	15.8	2.5	13.5 ②	9.0
	Wagoneer	H	4-150 (2.5)	4	4	4.0 ①	4.5	15.8	2.5	13.5 ②	9.0
	Wagoneer	M	6-243 (4.0)	6	6	3.9	4.5	15.8	2.5	13.5 ②	12.0
	Grand Wagoneer	C	6-258 (4.2)	6	6	3.5	—	17.0	3.8	20	10.5
	Grand Wagoneer	N	8-360 (5.9)	5	5	—	—	17.0	3.8	20	15.0
	J-10 Pick-Up	C	6-258 (4.2)	6	6	3.5	—	15.8	4.8	18	10.5
	J-10 Pick-Up	N	8-360 (5.9)	5	5	—	—	15.8	4.8	18	15.0
	J-20 Pick-Up	N	8-360 (5.9)	5	5	—	—	17.0	6	18	15.0
1988	Comanche	H	4-150 (2.5)	4	4	4.0 ①	4.9	17.0	2.5	13.5 ②	9.0
	Comanche	M	6-243 (4.0)	6	6	4.0 ①	4.9	17.0	2.5	13.5 ②	12.0
	Wrangler	H	4-150 (2.5)	4	4	4.0 ①	4.9	17.0	2.5	15 ②	7.8
	Wrangler	C	6-258 (4.2)	6	6	4.0 ①	4.9	17.0	2.5	15 ②	10.5
	Cherokee	H	4-150 (2.5)	4	4	4.0 ①	4.9	17.0	2.5	13.5 ②	9.0
	Cherokee	M	6-243 (4.0)	6	6	4.0 ①	4.9	17.0	2.5	13.5 ②	12.0
	Wagoneer	M	6-243 (4.0)	6	6	3.5	4.9	17.0	2.5	13.5 ②	12.0
	Grand Wagoneer	N	8-360 (5.9)	5	5	—	—	17.0	3.8	20	15.0
	J-10 Pick-Up	C	6-258 (4.2)	6	6	3.5	—	17.0	4.8	18	10.5
	J-10 Pick-Up	N	8-360 (5.9)	5	5	3.5	—	17.0	4.8	18	15.0
	J-20 Pick-Up	N	8-360 (5.9)	5	5	—	—	15.8	6	18	15.0
1989–90	Comanche	E	4-150 (2.5)	4	4	4.0 ①	4.9	17.0	2.5	18.5	9.0
	Comanche	L	6-243 (4.0)	6	6	4.0 ①	4.9	17.0	2.5	18.5	12.0
	Wrangler	E	4-150 (2.5)	4	4	4.0 ①	4.9	17.0	2.5	20.0	7.8
	Wrangler	M	6-258 (4.2)	6	6	4.0 ①	4.9	17.0	2.5	20.0	10.5
	Cherokee	E	4-150 (2.5)	4	4	4.0 ①	4.9	17.0	2.5	20.0	9.0
	Cherokee	L	6-243 (4.0)	6	6	4.0 ①	4.9	17.0	2.5	20.0	12.0
	Wagoneer	L	6-243 (4.0)	6	6	3.5	4.9	17.0	2.5	20.0	12.0
	Grand Wagoneer	7	8-360 (5.9)	5	5	—	—	17.0	3.8	20.0	15.0

① Aisian Warner Transmission—7.4 pts.
② 1986–88 Cherokee, Comanche, Wrangler and Wagoneer had an optional 20 gallon fuel tank.

CAMSHAFT SPECIFICATIONS

Year	VIN	No. Cylinder Displacement cu. in. (liter)	Journal Diameter					Lobe Lift		Bearing Clearance	Camshaft End Play
			1	2	3	4	5	In.	Ex.		
1986	B	4-126 (2.1)	NA	NA	NA	NA	—	NA	NA	NA	0.001–0.005
	U	4-150 (2.5)	2.0300–2.0290	2.0200–2.0190	2.0100–2.0009	2.0000–1.9990	—	0.2650	0.2650	0.0010–0.0030	0
	H	4-150 (2.5)	2.0300–2.0290	2.0200–2.0190	2.0100–2.0009	2.0000–1.9990	—	0.2650	0.2650	0.0010–0.0030	0
	W	6-173 (2.8)	1.8690–1.8670	1.8690–1.8670	1.8690–1.8670	—	—	0.2311	0.2625	0.0010–0.0039	0
	C	6-258 (4.2)	2.0300–2.0290	2.0200–2.0190	2.0100–2.0090	2.0000–1.9990	—	0.2531	0.2531	0.0010–0.0030	0
	N	8-360 (5.9)	2.1195–2.1205	2.0895–2.0905	2.0595–2.0605	2.0295–2.0305	1.9995–2.0005	0.2660	0.2660	0.0010–0.0030	0
1987	B	4-126 (2.1)	NA	NA	NA	NA	—	NA	NA	NA	0.001–0.005
	U	4-150 (2.5)	2.0300–2.0290	2.0200–2.0190	2.0100–2.0009	2.0000–1.9990	—	0.2650	0.2650	0.0010–0.0030	0
	H	4-150 (2.5)	2.0300–2.0290	2.0200–2.0190	2.0100–2.0009	2.0000–1.9990	—	0.2650	0.2650	0.0010–0.0030	0
	W	6-173 (2.8)	1.8690–1.8670	1.8690–1.8670	1.8690–1.8670	—	—	0.2311	0.2625	0.0010–0.0039	0
	M	6-243 (4.0)	2.0300–2.0290	2.0200–2.0190	2.0100–2.0090	2.0000–1.9990	—	0.2530	0.2530	0.0010–0.0030	0
	C	6-258 (4.2)	2.0300–2.0290	2.0200–2.0190	2.0100–2.0090	2.0000–1.9990	—	0.2531	0.2531	0.0010–0.0030	0
	N	8-360 (5.9)	2.1195–2.1205	2.0895–2.0905	2.0595–2.0605	2.0295–2.0305	1.9995–2.0005	0.2660	0.2660	0.0010–0.0030	0
1988	H	4-150 (2.5)	2.0300–2.0290	2.0200–2.0190	2.0100–2.0009	2.0000–1.9990	—	0.2650	0.2650	0.0010–0.0030	0
	M	6-243 (4.0)	2.0300–2.0290	2.0200–2.0190	2.0100–2.0090	2.0000–1.9990	—	0.2530	0.2530	0.0010–0.0030	0
	C	6-258 (4.2)	2.0300–2.0290	2.0200–2.0190	2.0100–2.0090	2.0000–1.9990	—	0.2531	0.2531	0.0010–0.0030	0
	N	8-360 (5.9)	2.1195–2.1205	2.0895–2.0905	2.0595–2.0605	2.0295–2.0305	1.9995–2.0005	0.2660	0.2660	0.0010–0.0030	0
1989–90	E	4-150 (2.5)	2.0300–2.0290	2.0200–2.0190	2.0100–2.0009	2.0000–1.9990	—	0.2650	0.2650	0.0010–0.0030	0
	L	6-243 (4.0)	2.0300–2.0290	2.0200–2.0190	2.0100–2.0090	2.0000–1.9990	—	0.2530	0.2530	0.0010–0.0030	0
	M	6-258 (4.2)	2.0300–2.0290	2.0200–2.0190	2.0100–2.0090	2.0000–1.9990	—	0.2531	0.2531	0.0010–0.0030	0
	7	8-360 (5.9)	2.1195–2.1205	2.0895–2.0905	2.0595–2.0605	2.0295–2.0305	1.9995–2.0005	0.2660	0.2660	0.0010–0.0030	0

CRANKSHAFT AND CONNECTING ROD SPECIFICATIONS

All measurements are given in inches

Year	VIN	No. Cylinder Displacement cu. in. (liter)	Crankshaft Main Brg. Journal Dia.	Crankshaft Main Brg. Oil Clearance	Crankshaft Shaft End-play	Thrust on No.	Connecting Rod Journal Diameter	Connecting Rod Oil Clearance	Connecting Rod Side Clearance
1986	B	4-126 (2.1)	2.4750	0.0098	0.0050–0.0090	3	2.2163	0.0098	0.0120–0.0190
	U	4-150 (2.5)	2.4996–2.5001	0.0010–0.0025	0.0015–0.0065	2	2.0934–2.0955	0.0010–0.0025	0.0100–0.0190
	H	4-150 (2.5)	2.4996–2.5001	0.0010–0.0025	0.0015–0.0065	2	2.0934–2.0955	0.0010–0.0025	0.0100–0.0190
	W	6-173 (2.8)	2.4930–2.4940	0.0016–0.0030	0.0020–0.0060	3	1.9980–1.9990	0.0010–0.0030	0.0060–0.0170
	C	6-258 (4.2)	2.4996–2.5001	0.0010–0.0025	0.0015–0.0065	3	2.0934–2.0955	0.0010–0.0030	0.0100–0.0190
	N	8-360 (5.9)	2.7474–2.7489	0.0010–0.0020	0.0030–0.0080	3	2.0934–2.0955	0.0010–0.0030	0.0060–0.0180
1987	B	4-126 (2.1)	2.4750	0.0098	0.0050–0.0090	3	2.2163	0.0098	0.0120–0.0190
	U	4-150 (2.5)	2.4996–2.5001	0.0010–0.0025	0.0015–0.0065	2	2.0934–2.0955	0.0010–0.0025	0.0100–0.0190
	H	4-150 (2.5)	2.4996–2.5001	0.0010–0.0025	0.0015–0.0065	2	2.0934–2.0955	0.0010–0.0025	0.0100–0.0190
	W	6-173 (2.8)	2.4930–2.4940	0.0016–0.0030	0.0020–0.0060	3	1.9980–1.9990	0.0010–0.0030	0.0060–0.0170
	M	6-243 (4.0)	2.4996–2.5001	0.0010–0.0025	0.0015–0.0065	3	2.0934–2.0955	0.0010–0.0030	0.0100–0.0190
	C	6-258 (4.2)	2.4996–2.5001	0.0010–0.0025	0.0015–0.0065	3	2.0934–2.0955	0.0010–0.0030	0.0100–0.0190
	N	8-360 (5.9)	2.7474–2.7489	0.0010–0.0020	0.0030–0.0080	3	2.0934–2.0955	0.0010–0.0030	0.0060–0.0180
1988	H	4-150 (2.5)	2.4996–2.5001	0.0010–0.0025	0.0015–0.0065	2	2.0934–2.0955	0.0010–0.0025	0.0100–0.0190
	M	6-243 (4.0)	2.4996–2.5001	0.0010–0.0025	0.0015–0.0065	3	2.0934–2.0955	0.0010–0.0030	0.0100–0.0190
	C	6-258 (4.2)	2.4996–2.5001	0.0010–0.0025	0.0015–0.0065	3	2.0934–2.0955	0.0010–0.0030	0.0100–0.0190
	N	8-360 (5.9)	2.7474–2.7489	0.0010–0.0020	0.0030–0.0080	3	2.0934–2.0955	0.0010–0.0030	0.0060–0.0180
1989–90	E	4-150 (2.5)	2.4996–2.5001	0.0010–0.0025	0.0015–0.0065	2	2.0934–2.0955	0.0010–0.0025	0.0100–0.0190
	L	6-243 (4.0)	2.4996–2.5001	0.0010–0.0025	0.0015–0.0065	3	2.0934–2.0955	0.0010–0.0030	0.0100–0.0190
	M	6-258 (4.2)	2.4996–2.5001	0.0010–0.0025	0.0015–0.0065	3	2.0934–2.0955	0.0010–0.0030	0.0100–0.0190
	7	8-360 (5.9)	2.7474–2.7489	0.0010–0.0020	0.0030–0.0080	3	2.0934–2.0955	0.0010–0.0030	0.0060–0.0180

VALVE SPECIFICATIONS

Year	VIN	No. Cylinder Displacement cu. in. (liter)	Seat Angle (deg.)	Face Angle (deg.)	Spring Test Pressure (lbs. @ in.)	Spring Installed Height (in.)	Stem-to-Guide Clearance (in.) Intake	Stem-to-Guide Clearance (in.) Exhaust	Stem Diameter (in.) Intake	Stem Diameter (in.) Exhaust
1986	B	4-126 (2.1)	45	45	135 @ 1.173	1.547	0.0010–0.0030	0.0010–0.0030	0.3140	0.3140
	U	4-150 (2.5)	45	45	200 @ 1.216	1.640	0.0010–0.0030	0.0010–0.0030	0.3110–0.3120	0.3110–0.3120
	H	4-150 (2.5)	45	45	200 @ 1.216	1.640	0.0010–0.0030	0.0010–0.0030	0.3110–0.3120	0.3110–0.3120
	W	6-173 (2.8)	46	45	195 @ 1.180	1.570	0.0010–0.0027	0.0010–0.0027	0.3410–0.3416	0.3410–0.3416
	C	6-258 (4.2)	①	②	195 @ 1.411	1.786	0.0010–0.0030	0.0010–0.0030	0.3715–0.3725	0.3715–0.3725
	N	8-360 (5.9)	①	②	200 @ 1.356	1.786	0.0010–0.0030	0.0010–0.0030	0.3715–0.3725	0.3715–0.3725
1987	B	4-126 (2.1)	45	45	135 @ 1.173	1.547	0.0010–0.0030	0.0010–0.0030	0.3140	0.3140
	U	4-150 (2.5)	45	45	200 @ 1.216	1.640	0.0010–0.0030	0.0010–0.0030	0.3110–0.3120	0.3110–0.3120
	H	4-150 (2.5)	45	45	200 @ 1.216	1.640	0.0010–0.0030	0.0010–0.0030	0.3110–0.3120	0.3110–0.3120
	W	6-173 (2.8)	46	45	195 @ 1.180	1.570	0.0010–0.0027	0.0010–0.0027	0.3410–0.3416	0.3410–0.3416
	M	6-243 (4.0)	44.5	45	210 @ 1.200	1.625	0.0010–0.0030	0.0010–0.0030	0.3120	0.3120
	C	6-258 (4.2)	①	②	195 @ 1.411	1.786	0.0010–0.0030	0.0010–0.0030	0.3715–0.3725	0.3715–0.3725
	N	8-360 (5.9)	①	②	200 @ 1.356	1.786	0.0010–0.0030	0.0010–0.0030	0.3715–0.3725	0.3715–0.3725
1988	H	4-150 (2.5)	45	45	200 @ 1.216	1.640	0.0010–0.0030	0.0010–0.0030	0.3110–0.3120	0.3110–0.3120
	M	6-243 (4.0)	44.5	45	210 @ 1.200	1.625	0.0010–0.0030	0.0010–0.0030	0.3120	0.3120
	C	6-258 (4.2)	①	②	195 @ 1.411	1.786	0.0010–0.0030	0.0010–0.0030	0.3715–0.3725	0.3715–0.3725
	N	8-360 (5.9)	①	②	200 @ 1.356	1.786	0.0010–0.0030	0.0010–0.0030	0.3715–0.3725	0.3715–0.3725
1989–90	E	4-150 (2.5)	45	45	200 @ 1.216	1.640	0.0010–0.0030	0.0010–0.0030	0.3110–0.3120	0.3110–0.3120
	L	6-243 (4.0)	44.5	45	210 @ 1.200	1.625	0.0010–0.0030	0.0010–0.0030	0.3120	0.3120
	M	6-258 (4.2)	①	②	195 @ 1.411	1.786	0.0010–0.0030	0.0010–0.0030	0.3715–0.3725	0.3715–0.3725
	7	8-360 (5.9)	①	②	200 @ 1.356	1.786	0.0010–0.0030	0.0010–0.0030	0.3715–0.3725	0.3715–0.3725

① Intake: 30 degrees
   Exhaust: 44.5 degrees
② Intake: 29 degrees
   Exhaust: 44 degrees

PISTON AND RING SPECIFICATIONS
All measurements are given in inches

Year	VIN	No. Cylinder Displacement cu. in. (liter)	Piston Clearance	Ring Gap			Ring Side Clearance		
				Top Compression	Bottom Compression	Oil Control	Top Compression	Bottom Compression	Oil Control
1986	B	4-126 (2.1)	NA	NA	NA	NA	NA	NA	NA
	U	4-150 (2.5)	0.0013–0.0021	0.0100–0.0200	0.0100–0.0200	0.0150–0.0550	0.0010–0.0032	0.0100–0.0032	0.0010–0.0021
	H	4-150 (2.5)	0.0013–0.0021	0.0100–0.0200	0.0100–0.0200	0.0150–0.0550	0.0010–0.0032	0.0010–0.0032	0.0010–0.0021
	W	6-173 (2.8)	0.0006	0.0098–0.0196	0.0098–0.0196	0.0200–0.0550	0.0010–0.0027	0.0015–0.0037	0.0078
	C	6-258 (4.2)	0.0009–0.0017	0.0100–0.0200	0.0100–0.0200	0.0100–0.0250	0.0015–0.0030	0.0015–0.0030	0.0010–0.0080
	N	8-360 (5.9)	0.0012–0.0020	0.0100–0.0200	0.0100–0.0200	0.0150–0.0450	0.0015–0.0035	0.0015–0.0035	0.0010–0.0070
1987	B	4-126 (2.1)	NA	NA	NA	NA	NA	NA	NA
	U	4-150 (2.5)	0.0013–0.0021	0.0100–0.0200	0.0100–0.0200	0.0150–0.0550	0.0010–0.0032	0.0010–0.0032	0.0010–0.0021
	H	4-150 (2.5)	0.0013–0.0021	0.0100–0.0200	0.0100–0.0200	0.0150–0.0550	0.0010–0.0032	0.0010–0.0032	0.0010–0.0021
	W	6-173 (2.8)	0.0006	0.0098–0.0196	0.0098–0.0196	0.0200–0.0550	0.0010–0.0027	0.0015–0.0037	0.0078
	M	6-243 (4.0)	0.0009–0.0017	0.0100–0.0200	0.0100–0.0200	0.0100–0.0250	0.0017–0.0032	0.0017–0.0032	0.0010–0.0080
	C	6-258 (4.2)	0.0009–0.0017	0.0100–0.0200	0.0100–0.0200	0.0100–0.0250	0.0015–0.0030	0.0015–0.0030	0.0010–0.0080
	N	8-360 (5.9)	0.0012–0.0020	0.0100–0.0200	0.0100–0.0200	0.0150–0.0450	0.0015–0.0035	0.0015–0.0035	0.0010–0.0070
1988	H	4-150 (2.5)	0.0013–0.0021	0.0100–0.0200	0.0100–0.0200	0.0150–0.0550	0.0010–0.0032	0.0010–0.0032	0.0010–0.0021
	M	6-243 (4.0)	0.0009–0.0017	0.0100–0.0200	0.0100–0.0200	0.0100–0.0250	0.0017–0.0032	0.0017–0.0032	0.0010–0.0080
	C	6-258 (4.2)	0.0009–0.0017	0.0100–0.0200	0.0100–0.0200	0.0100–0.0250	0.0015–0.0030	0.0015–0.0030	0.0010–0.0080
	N	8-360 (5.9)	0.0012–0.0020	0.0100–0.0200	0.0100–0.0200	0.0150–0.0450	0.0015–0.0035	0.0015–0.0035	0.0010–0.0070
1989–90	E	4-150 (2.5)	0.0013–0.0021	0.0100–0.0200	0.0100–0.0200	0.0150–0.0550	0.0010–0.0032	0.0010–0.0032	0.0010–0.0021
	L	6-243 (4.0)	0.0009–0.0017	0.0100–0.0200	0.0100–0.0200	0.0100–0.0250	0.0017–0.0032	0.0017–0.0032	0.0010–0.0080
	M	6-258 (4.2)	0.0009–0.0017	0.0100–0.0200	0.0100–0.0200	0.0100–0.0250	0.0015–0.0030	0.0015–0.0030	0.0010–0.0080
	7	8-360 (5.9)	0.0012–0.0020	0.0100–0.0200	0.0100–0.0200	0.0150–0.0450	0.0015–0.0035	0.0015–0.0035	0.0010–0.0070

TORQUE SPECIFICATIONS

All readings in ft. lbs.

Year	VIN	No. Cylinder Displacement cu. in. (liter)	Cylinder Head Bolts	Main Bearing Bolts	Rod Bearing Bolts	Crankshaft Pulley Bolts	Flywheel Bolts	Manifold Intake	Manifold Exhaust	Spark Plugs
1986	B	4-126 (2.1)	①	69	48	96	44	15–20	15–20	—
	U	4-150 (2.5)	②	80	33	75–85	40	20–25	20–25	28
	H	4-150 (2.5)	②	80	33	75–85	40	20–25	20–25	28
	W	6-173 (2.8)	65–75	63–74	34–40	66–84	45–55	20–25	22–28	28
	C	6-258 (4.2)	85	75–85	30–35	75–85	100–110	20–25	③	28
	N	8-360 (5.9)	110	100	33	90	95	43	25	28
1987	B	4-126 (2.1)	①	69	48	96	44	15–20	15–20	—
	U	4-150 (2.5)	②	80	33	75–85	40	20–25	20–25	28
	H	4-150 (2.5)	②	80	33	75–85	40	20–25	20–25	28
	W	6-173 (2.8)	65–75	63–74	34–40	66–84	45–55	20–25	22–28	28
	M	6-243 (4.0)	④	80	30–35	80	100–110	20–25	⑤	28
	C	6-258 (4.2)	85	75–85	30–35	75–85	100–110	20–25	③	28
	N	8-360 (5.9)	110	100	33	90	95	43	25	28
1988	H	4-150 (2.5)	②	80	33	75–85	40	20–25	30	28
	M	6-243 (4.0)	④	80	30–35	80	100–110	20–25	⑤	28
	C	6-258 (4.2)	85	75–85	30–35	75–85	100–110	20–25	③	28
	N	8-360 (5.9)	110	100	33	90	95	43	25	28
1989–90	E	4-150 (2.5)	②	80	33	75–85	40	20–25	30	28
	L	6-243 (4.0)	④	80	30–35	80	100–110	20–25	⑤	28
	M	6-258 (4.2)	85	75–85	30–35	75–85	100–110	20–25	③	28
	7	8-360 (5.9)	110	100	33	90	95	43	25	28

① 1st Step—22 ft. lbs.
  2nd Step—37 ft. lbs.
  3rd Step—50–70 ft. lbs.
  4th Step—70–77 ft. lbs.
② Tighten bolts 1 thru 7; 9 and 10 to 110 ft. lbs.
  Tighten bolt 8 to 100 ft. lbs.

③ Tighten bolts 1 thru 11 to 23 ft. lbs.
  Bolts 12 and 13 to 50 ft. lbs.
④ Tighten bolts 1 thru 10 and 12 thru 14 to 110 ft. lbs.
  Bolt 11 to 100 ft. lbs.
⑤ Middle nuts to 30 ft. lbs.
  Outside nuts to 23 ft. lbs.

BRAKE SPECIFICATIONS

All measurements in inches unless noted.

Year	Model	Lug Nut Torque (ft. lbs.)	Master Cylinder Bore	Brake Disc Minimum Thickness	Brake Disc Maximum Runout	Standard Brake Drum Diameter	Minimum Lining Thickness Front	Minimum Lining Thickness Rear
1986	Comanche	75	0.937	0.815	0.004	10.00	0.031	0.031
	CJ-7	75	0.937	0.815	0.004	10.00	0.031	0.031
	Cherokee	75	0.937	0.815	0.004	10.00	0.031	0.031
	Wagoneer	75	0.937	0.815	0.004	10.00	0.031	0.031
	Grand Wagoneer	75	1.125	1.215	0.005	11.00	0.031	0.031
	J10 Pick-Up	75	1.125	1.215	0.005	11.00	0.031	0.031
	J20 Pick-Up	75	1.125	1.215	0.005	12.00	0.031	0.031

BRAKE SPECIFICATIONS

All measurements in inches unless noted.

Year	Model	Lug Nut Torque (ft. lbs.)	Master Cylinder Bore	Brake Disc Minimum Thickness	Brake Disc Maximum Runout	Standard Brake Drum Diameter	Minimum Lining Thickness Front	Minimum Lining Thickness Rear
1987	Comanche	75	0.937	0.815	0.004	10.00	0.031	0.031
	Wrangler	75	0.937	0.815	0.004	10.00	0.031	0.031
	Cherokee	75	0.937	0.815	0.004	10.00	0.031	0.031
	Wagoneer	75	0.937	0.815	0.004	10.00	0.031	0.031
	Grand Wagoneer	75	1.125	1.215	0.005	11.00	0.031	0.031
	J10 Pick-Up	75	1.125	1.215	0.005	11.00	0.031	0.031
	J20 Pick-Up	75	1.125	1.215	0.005	12.00	0.031	0.031
1988	Comanche	75	0.937	0.815	0.004	10.00	0.031	0.031
	Wrangler	75	0.937	0.815	0.004	10.00	0.031	0.031
	Cherokee	75	0.937	0.815	0.004	10.00	0.031	0.031
	Wagoneer	75	0.937	0.815	0.004	10.00	0.031	0.031
	Grand Wagoneer	75	1.125	1.215	0.005	11.00	0.031	0.031
	J10 Pick-Up	75	1.125	1.215	0.005	11.00	0.031	0.031
	J20 Pick-Up	75	1.125	1.215	0.005	12.00	0.031	0.031
1989–90	Comanche	75	0.937	0.815	0.004	10.00	0.031	0.031
	Wrangler	75	0.937	0.815	0.004	10.00	0.031	0.031
	Cherokee	75	0.937	0.815	0.004	10.00	0.031	0.031
	Wagoneer	75	0.937	0.815	0.004	10.00	0.031	0.031
	Grand Wagoneer	75	1.125	1.215	0.005	11.00	0.031	0.031

WHEEL ALIGNMENT

Year	Model	Caster Range (deg.)	Caster Preferred Setting (deg.)	Camber Range (deg.)	Camber Preferred Setting (deg.)	Toe-in (in.)	Steering Axis Inclination (deg.)
1986	Comanche	7P–8P	7½P	½N–½P	0	1/16P	NA
	CJ-7	NA	6	NA	0	3⅙P	10
	Cherokee	7P–8P	7½P	½N–½P	0	1/16P	NA
	Wagoneer	7P–8P	7½P	½N–½P	0	1/16P	NA
	Grand Wagoneer	3P–5P	4P	½N–½P	0	3/64P–3/32P	8½
	J10 Pick-Up	3P–5P	4P	½N–½P	0	3/64P–3/32P	8½
	J20 Pick-Up	3P–5P	4P	½N–½P	0	3/64P–3/32P	8½
1987	Comanche	7P–8P	7½P	½N–½P	0	1/16P	NA
	Wrangler	①	②	½N–½P	0	1/32P	NA
	Cherokee	7P–8P	7½P	½N–½P	0	1/16P	NA
	Wagoneer	7P–8P	7½P	½N–½P	0	1/16P	NA
	Grand Wagoneer	3P–5P	4P	½N–½P	0	3/64P–3/32P	8½
	J10 Pick-Up	3P–5P	4P	½N–½P	0	3/64P–3/32P	8½
	J20 Pick-Up	3P–5P	4P	½N–½P	0	3/64P–3/32P	8½

WHEEL ALIGNMENT

Year	Model	Caster Range (deg.)	Caster Preferred Setting (deg.)	Camber Range (deg.)	Camber Preferred Setting (deg.)	Toe-in (in.)	Steering Axis Inclination (deg.)
1988	Comanche	7P–8P	7½P	½N–½P	0	1/16P	NA
	Wrangler	①	②	½N–½P	0	1/32P	NA
	Cherokee	7P–8P	7½P	½N–½P	0	1/16P	NA
	Wagoneer	7P–8P	7½P	½N–½P	0	1/16P	NA
	Grand Wagoneer	3P–5P	4P	½N–½P	0	3/64P–3/32P	8½
	J10 Pick-Up	3P–5P	4P	½N–½P	0	3/64P–3/32P	8½
	J20 Pick-Up	3P–5P	4P	½N–½P	0	3/64P–3/32P	8½
1989–90	Comanche	7P–8P	7½P	½N–½P	0	1/16P	NA
	Wrangler	①	②	½N–½P	0	1/32P	NA
	Cherokee	7P–8P	7½P	½N–½P	0	1/16P	NA
	Wagoneer	7P–8P	7½P	½N–½P	0	1/16P	NA
	Grand Wagoneer	3P–5P	4P	½N–½P	0	3/64P–3/32P	8½

① With manual transmission 7½P–8½P
   With automatic transmission 6P–7P
② With manual transmission 8P
   With automatic transmission 6½P

ENGINE ELECTRICAL

NOTE: Disconnecting the battery cable on some vehicles may interfere with the functions of the on board computer systems and may require the computer to undergo a relearning process, once the negative battery cable is disconnected.

Distributor

Removal and Installation

1. Disconnect the negative battery cable.
2. Remove the electric cooling fan and shroud assembly, if equipped.
3. Scribe a mark on the distributor housing, below the left side of the No. 1 spark plug wire post on the distributor cap.
4. Remove the distributor cap. Turn the engine until the rotor points in the direction of the scribed mark.
5. Turn the engine until the timing mark on the damper aligns with the 0 on the timing scale.
6. Align the trailing edge of the rotor blade with the mark scribed on the distributor housing.
7. Remove the distributor hold down bolt and clamp. Remove the distributor.

To install:

8. If the engine has been turned while the distributor was removed, or if the marks were not drawn, it will be necessary to initially time the engine.
9. It is necessary to place the No. 1 cylinder in the firing position to correctly install the distributor.

10. Remove the No. 1 cylinder spark plug. Turn the engine until the piston in No. 1 cylinder is moving up on the compression stroke. This can be determined by placing a thumb over the spark plug hole and feeling the air being forced out of the cylinder.
11. Install the distributor, when the distributor shaft has reached the bottom of the hole, move the rotor back and forth slightly until the drive gears of the distributor and cam mesh and until the distributor assembly slides down into place.
12. Install the distributor hold down bolt and tighten to 9.5–14 ft. lbs. (13–19 Nm).
13. Install the cooling fan and shroud, if removed. Connect the negative battery cable.

Ignition Timing

Adjustment

NOTE: The ignition timing for the 4.0L engine is controlled by the ECU and is not adjustable.

2.5L, 2.8L, 4.2L AND 5.9L ENGINES

1. Locate the timing marks on the crankshaft pulley and the front of the timing case cover.
2. Clean off the timing marks.
3. Use chalk or white paint to color the mark on the scale that will indicate the correct timing, when aligned with the mark on the pulley or the pointer.
4. Attach a tachometer to the engine.
5. Attach a timing light to the engine.

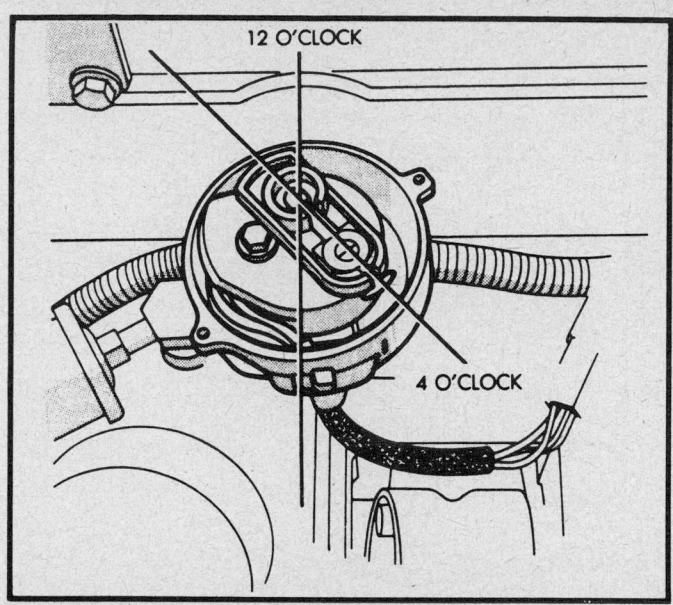

Distributor rotor alignment for installation

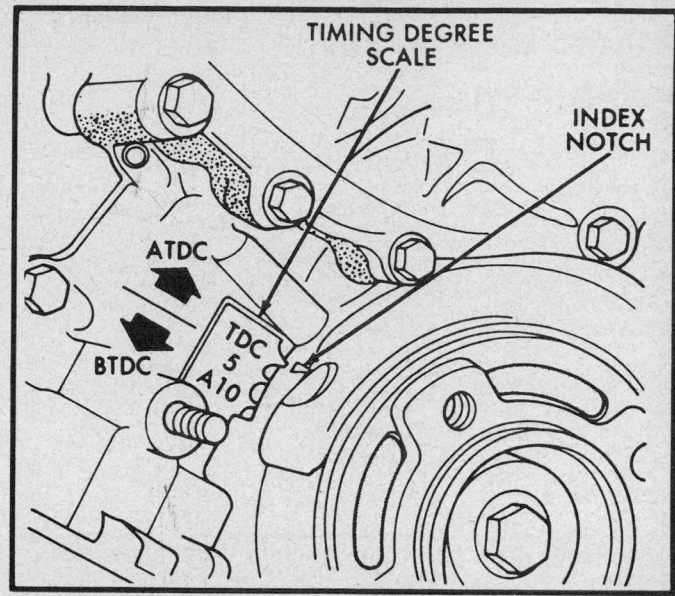

Timing mark location—5.9L engine

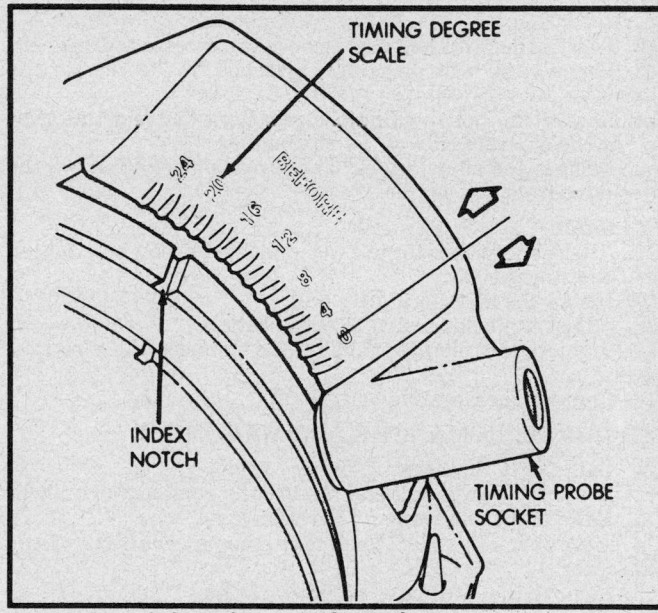

Timing mark location—4.2L engine

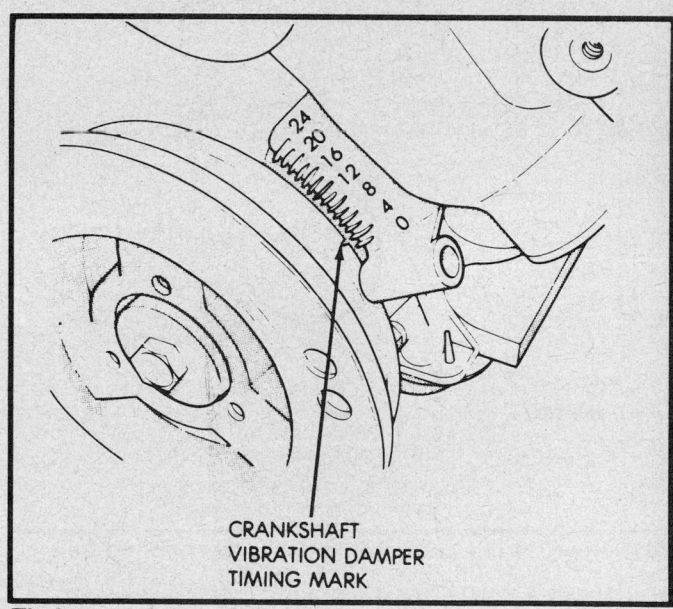

Timing mark location—4.0L engine

6. Disconnect and plug the vacuum lines to the distributor. Loosen the distributor lock bolt just enough so that the distributor can be turned with a little resistance.

7. Place the transmission in **P** and turn **OFF** all accessories.

8. Start the engine and check the idle, if necessary adjust it to the correct specification.

9. With the timing light aimed at the pulley and the marks on the engine, turn the distributor in the direction of rotor rotation to retard the spark, and in the opposite direction of rotor rotation to advance the spark. Align the marks on the pulley and the engine with the flashes of the timing light.

10. Tighten the holddown bolt and recheck the timing.

Alternator

For further information, please refer to "Electrical" in the Unit Repair section.

Belt Tension Adjustment

WITH V-BELTS

The belt tension should be checked using the gauge method. The gauge should be placed in the section of belt being checked. The correct specification for a new V-belt is 120–160 ft. lbs. (533–711 Nm) and the correct tension for a used V-belt is 90–115 ft. lbs. (400–511 Nm).

To adjust the belt tension:

1. On vehicles equipped with the 2.1L, 2.5L, 2.8L and 4.0L engines, loosen the power steering pump mounting bolts. On vehicles equipped with the 5.9L and 4.2L engines, loosen the alternator mounting bolts.

2. Pry the alternator (or power steering pump) away from the engine to tension the belt.

3. Tighten the mounting bolts to 20 ft. lbs. (27 Nm).

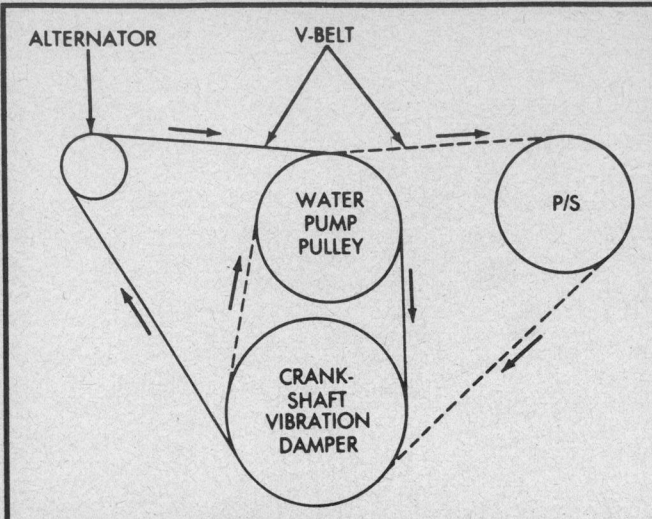

Accessory drive belt routing—with V-belts, except 5.9L

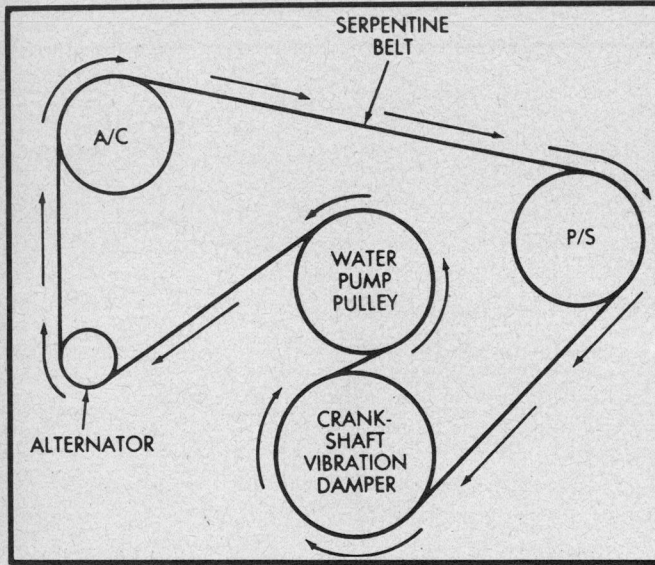

Accessory drive belt routing—with serpentine belt

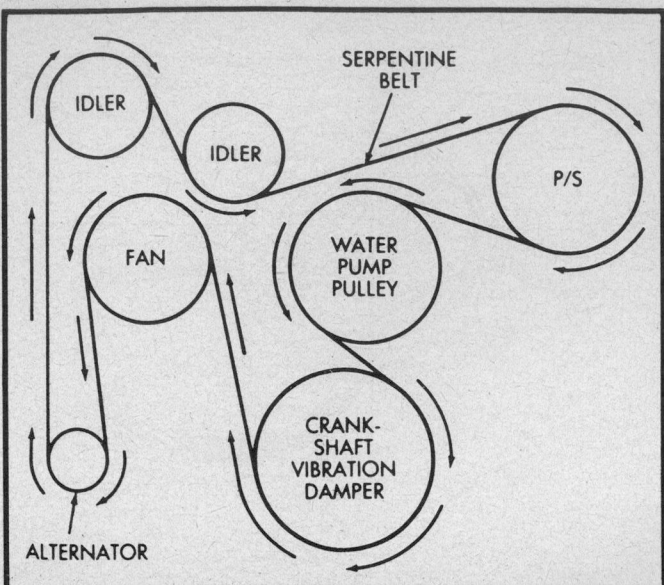

Accessory drive belt routing—5.9L engine with V-belts

WITH SERPENTINE BELT

The belt tension should be checked using the gauge method. The gauge should be placed in the section of belt being checked. The correct specification for a new serpentine belt is 180–200 ft. lbs (800–900 Nm) and the correct tension for a used serpentine belt is 140–160 ft. lbs. (623–712 Nm).

To adjust the belt tension:

1. On vehicles equipped with the 2.5L and 4.0L engines, loosen the power steering pump mounting bolts. On vehicles equipped with the 4.2L and engines, loosen the alternator mounting bolts.

2. Tighten the adjusting bolt to increase the belt tension and loosen it to release the belt tension.

3. Tighten the mounting bolts to 20 ft. lbs. (27 Nm).

Removal and Installation

GRAND WAGONEER, J10 PICK-UP, J20 PICK-UP, CJ-7 AND WRANGLER

1. Disconnect the negative battery cable.

2. Loosen the pivot bolt and remove the accessory drive belt.

3. Remove the wire terminals attached to the rear of the alternator.

4. Loosen the bolt holding the adjusting bar and the pivot bolt at the opposite side of the alternator.

5. Remove the adjusting bar and pivot bolts and remove the alternator from the engine.

To install:

6. Attach the alternator to the mounting bracket and tighten the bolts finger tight.

7. Install the accessory drive belt.

8. Adjust the belt tension to specification.

9. Tighten the mounting bolts and connect the electrical leads.

10. Connect the negative battery cable.

CHEROKEE, COMANCHE AND WAGONEER

1. Disconnect the negative battery cable.

2. Loosen the pivot bolt and remove the accessory drive belt.

3. Raise and safely support the vehicle.

4 Disconnect the electrical connector at the rear of the alternator.

5. Remove the alternator mounting bolts.

6. Remove the alternator from below the vehicle.

To install:

7. Attach the alternator to the mounting bracket and tighten the bolts to 28 ft. lbs. (38 Nm).

8. Connect the electrical leads and lower the vehicle.

9. Install the accessory drive belt.

10. Adjust the belt tension to specification.

11. Connect the negative battery cable.

Starter

For further information, please refer to "Electrical" in the Unit Repair section.

Removal and Installation

1. Disconnect the negative battery cable.

2. Raise and safely support the vehicle.

3. Disconnect the electrical leads from the starter.

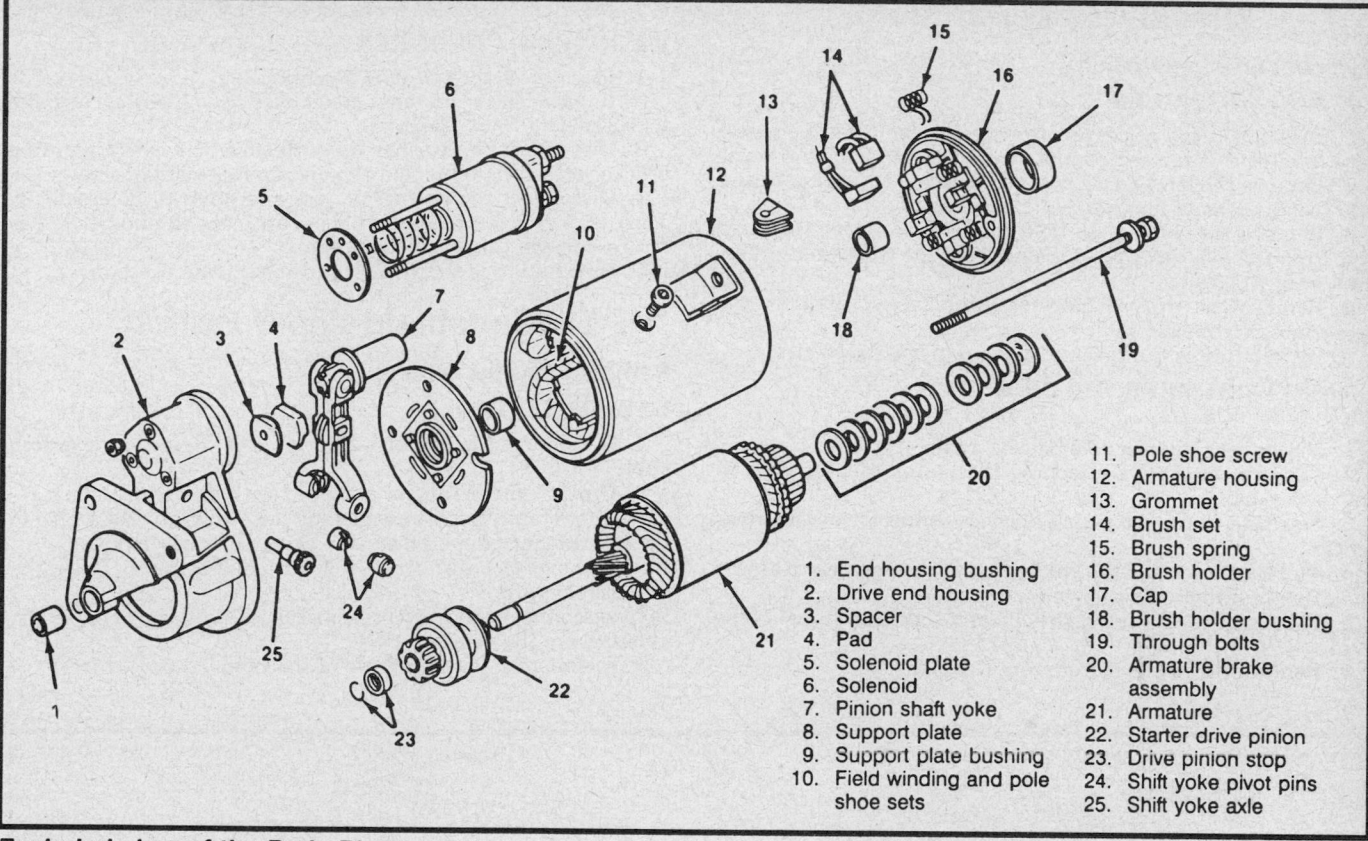

11. Pole shoe screw
12. Armature housing
13. Grommet
14. Brush set
15. Brush spring
16. Brush holder
17. Cap
18. Brush holder bushing
19. Through bolts
20. Armature brake assembly
21. Armature
22. Starter drive pinion
23. Drive pinion stop
24. Shift yoke pivot pins
25. Shift yoke axle

1. End housing bushing
2. Drive end housing
3. Spacer
4. Pad
5. Solenoid plate
6. Solenoid
7. Pinion shaft yoke
8. Support plate
9. Support plate bushing
10. Field winding and pole shoe sets

Exploded view of the Paris-Rhone starter

4. Remove the starter mounting bolts and remove the starter from the vehicle.

To install:

5. Install the starter in position.
6. Tighten the mounting bolts to 33 ft. lbs. (45 Nm).
7. Connect the electrical leads and lower the vehicle.

Diesel Glow Plugs

Removal and Installation

1. Disconnect the negative battery cable.
2. Disconnect the wire from the glow plug.

3. Unscrew the glow plug from the cylinder head.
4. Installation is the reverse of removal. Use a small amount of anti-seize compound on the glow plug threads. Torque the glow plug to 20 ft. lbs.

Testing

1. Remove the electrical lead from the glow plug.
2. Using a test light, connect the spring clip to the battery positive terminal. Touch the probe to each of the glow plugs.
3. If the light comes on, the glow plug is functioning. If the light does not come on, the glow plug is not working properly.

CHASSIS ELECTRICAL

Heater Blower Motor

Removal and Installation

1. Disconnect the negative battery cable. Remove the coolant overflow bottle.
2. If equipped with anti-lock brakes, remove the anti-lock brake pump and bracket and position it out of the way.
3. Remove the brake hose retaining bracket screw.
4. Unplug the blower motor wiring connector.

5. Remove the blower motor mounting screws and lift out the motor.

To install:

6. Install the blower motor into position and connect the electrical leads.
7. Connect the brake hose retaining bracket.
8. Install the anti-lock brake pump and bracket.
9. Install the coolant bottle and connect the negative battery cable.

Windshield Wiper Motor

Removal and Installation
CJ7 AND WRANGLER

1. Disconnect the negative battery cable. Remove the necessary hard or soft top components from the windshield frame.
2. Remove the left and right windshield holddown knobs and fold the windshield forward.
3. Remove the left access hole cover. Disconnect the drive link from the left wiper pivot. Disconnect the wiper motor harness from the switch.
4. Remove the wiper motor retaining screws. Remove the wiper motor from the vehicle.
5. Installation is the reverse of the removal procedure.

GRAND WAGONEER, J10 PICK-UP AND J20 PICK-UP

1. Disconnect the negative battery cable.
2. Remove the screws attaching the motor adapter plate to the dash panel.
3. Separate the wiper wiring harness connector at the wiper motor.
4. Pull the motor and the linkage out of the opening to expose the drive link to crank stud retaining clip.
5. Raise up the lock tab of the clip and slide the clip off of the stud.
6. Remove the wiper motor from the vehicle.

7. Installation is the reverse of the removal procedure.

WAGONEER, CHEROKEE AND COMANCHE

1. Disconnect the negative battery cable.
2. Remove the wiper arm assemblies. Remove the cowl and trim panel.
3. Disconnect the washer hose. Remove the cowl mounting bracket attaching bolts and the pivot pin attaching screws.
4. Disconnect the wiring harness and remove the assembly. The motor is protected by a rubber case, care should be used as not to damage this protective coat.
5. Installation is the reverse of the removal procedure.

Windshield Wiper Switch

Removal and Installation
DASH MOUNTED

1. Disconnect the negative battery cable. Remove the switch knob.
2. On CJ7 and Wrangler equipped with air conditioning, remove the retaining screws attaching the evaporator assembly to the instrument panel. Lower the evaporator assembly.
3. Remove the nut from the switch assembly. Push the switch rearward.
4. Disconnect the switch electrical connectors. Remove the switch from the vehicle.
5. Installation is the reverse of the removal procedure.

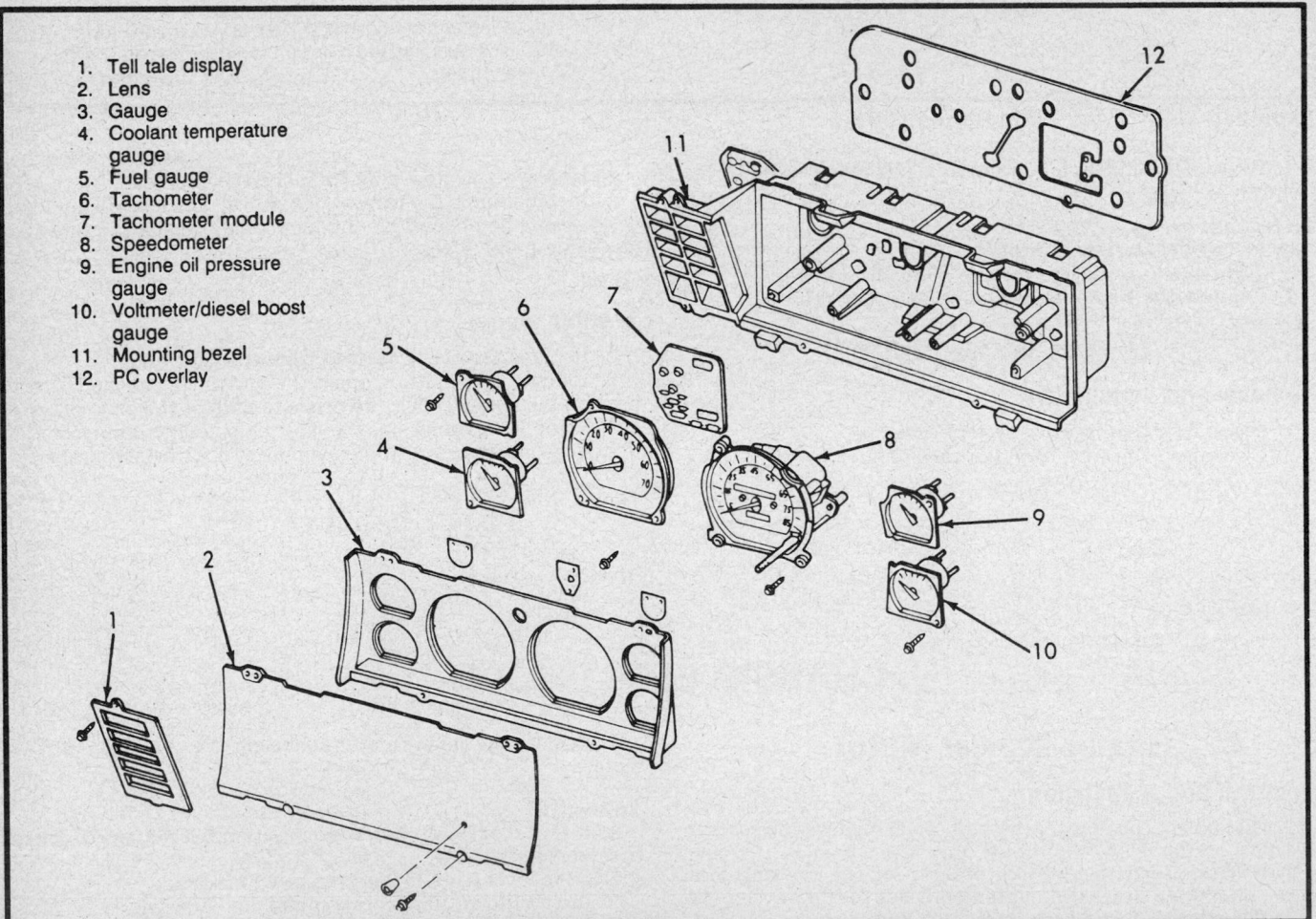

1. Tell tale display
2. Lens
3. Gauge
4. Coolant temperature gauge
5. Fuel gauge
6. Tachometer
7. Tachometer module
8. Speedometer
9. Engine oil pressure gauge
10. Voltmeter/diesel boost gauge
11. Mounting bezel
12. PC overlay

Instrument cluster assembly—Comanche, Cherokee and Wagoneer

Instrument Cluster

Removal and Installation

CJ7

1. Disconnect the negative battery cable.
2. Disconnect the speedometer cable from the back of the speedometer.
3. Remove the instrument cluster attaching screws and pull the cluster forward.
4. Disconnect the instrument cluster electrical connectors. Remove the cluster from the vehicle.
5. Installation is the reverse of the removal procedure.

WRANGLER

1. Disconnect the negative battery cable.
2. Remove the dash panel trim plate.
3. Remove the speedometer assembly retaining screws.
4. Pull the speedometer forward. Disconnect the electrical connectors, as required. Disconnect the speedometer cable.
5. Remove the speedometer from the vehicle.
6. Installation is the reverse of the removal procedure.

GRAND WAGONEER, J10 PICK-UP AND J20 PICK-UP

1. Disconnect the negative battery. Remove the cluster retaining screws.
2. Disconnect the speedometer cable.
3. Disconnect the cluster terminal pin plug. Disconnect the four terminal connector.
4. Mark the electrical connectors and hoses, disconnect them and the blend door air cable.
5. Remove the heater control panel lamps. Disconnect the heater temperature control wire from the lever. Remove the cluster.
6. Installation is the reverse of the removal procedure.

WAGONEER, CHEROKEE AND COMANCHE

1. Disconnect the negative battery cable.
2. Remove the instrument panel bezel screws and lift off the bezel. The bezel unsnaps.
3. Remove the cigarette lighter housing screws.
4. Remove the rocker switch housing screws.
5. Remove the cluster screws.
6. Disconnect the speedometer cable, pull the cluster out slowly and disconnect the electrical connectors at the cluster back. Remove the cluster.
7. Installation is the reverse of the removal procedure.

Speedometer

Removal and Installation

1. Disconnect the negative battery cable.
2. Remove the instrument cluster.
3. Remove the 2 attaching screws from the rear of the cluster.
4. Remove the screw from the front of the speedometer and pull it from the cluster. Pull the speedometer out of the circuit board carefully.
5. Install the speedometer in the reverse order of the removal procedure.

Headlight Switch

Removal and Installation
PULLOUT TYPE SWITCH

1. Disconnect the negative battery cable.
2. Pull the light switch control knob out as far as it will go. As required, remove the instrument panel trim plate.
3. From under the dash depress the headlight switch shaft

retainer button. Pull the shaft along with the knob from the headlight switch assembly.
4. Remove the headlight switch retaining nut. Disconnect the electrical connector from the switch.
5. Remove the headlight switch from the vehicle.
6. Installation is the reverse of the removal procedure.

ROCKER TYPE SWITCH

1. Disconnect the negative battery cable.
2. Remove the instrument cluster shroud.
3. Remove the 2 screws retaining the switch and remove the switch from the instrument panel.
4. Installation is the reverse of the removal procedure.

Dimmer Switch

Removal and Installation

1. Disconnect the negative battery cable.
2. On Comanche, Cherokee and Wagoneer, Remove the lower instrument panel trim cover.
3. On CJ7 and Wrangler, remove the 5 shroud screws and slide the shroud towards the steering wheel and apply slight upward pressure. Remove the shroud.
4. On the Wrangler, remove the evaporator housing mounting bolts and lower the housing.
5. On all models, disconnect the dimmer switch connector and remove the switch mounting screws. Remove the switch from the vehicle.
6. Installation is the reverse of the removal procedure.
7. To adjust the switch, depress the assembly slightly and insert a $3/32$ in. drill bit into the switch gauge adjusting hole. Move the switch toward the steering wheel. Once the slack is removed from the actuator rod tighten the switch retaining screws. Remove the drill bit.
8. Check the switch for proper operation.

Turn Signal Switch

Removal and Installation

1. Disconnect the negative battery cable.
2. Remove the column-to-dash bezel. Loosen the toe plate screws.
3. With tilt columns, place the column in the non-tilt position. Remove the steering wheel.
4. Remove the lock plate cover.
5. Compress the lock plate and unseat the steering shaft snapring. Remove the compressor and snapring.
6. Remove the lock plate, canceling cam and upper bearing preload spring.
7. Place the turn signal lever in the right turn position and remove the lever.
8. Remove the hazard warning knob. Press the knob inward and turn counterclockwise to remove it.
9. Remove the wiring harness protectors. Disconnect the wiring harness connectors.
10. Remove the turn signal switch attaching screws and lift out the switch.

To install:
11. Install the turn signal switch and attaching screws. Torque the screws to 35 inch lbs.
12. Connect the wiring harness connectors. Install the wiring harness protectors.
13. With the turn signal switch in the middle, install the hazard warning knob. Press the knob inward and turn clockwise to install it.
14. Install the lever. Torque the attaching screws to 35 inch lbs.
15. Install the upper bearing preload spring, canceling cam and lock plate.

16. Using the lock plate compressor, install the snapring and lock plate cover.

17. Install the steering wheel. Loosen the toe plate screws. Install the column-to-dash bezel.

18. Connect the negative battery cable.

Combination Switch

Removal and Installation

1. Disconnect the negative battery cable.

2. Disconnect the electrical harness connector from its mounting on the lower part of the steering column.

3. Remove the horn pad. Remove the steering wheel. Remove the lock plate cover.

4. Using a lock plate tool, compress the lock plate and remove the snapring.

5. Remove the lock plate tool, lock plate, canceling cam and upper bearing preload spring.

6. Position the combination lever in the right turn position. Remove the combination lever retaining screws.

7. Carefully pull the combination lever assembly upward and out of the steering column.

To install:

8. Install the combination lever into the steering column.

9. Using the appropriate tool, install the lock plate, canceling cam and upper bearing preload spring.

10. Install the lock plate cover and install the steering wheel.

11. Install the horn pad and connect the electrical leads at the bottom of the steering column.

12. Connect the negative battery cable.

Ignition Lock

Removal and Installation

1. Disconnect the negative battery cable.

2. Remove the turn signal switch.

3. Remove the wiper switch harness and any additional harnesses from the column.

4. Insert the key and turn it to the **ON** position.

5. Remove the key warning buzzer and clip.

6. Remove the lock cylinder retaining screw and pull the lock cylinder out of the column housing.

To install:

7. Before installation, insert the key into the cylinder. Hold the cylinder sleeve so it won't turn and rotate the key clockwise until it stops. This retracts the cylinder actuator.

8. Align the lock cylinder tab with the housing keyway.

9. Push the cylinder into the housing until it bottoms.

10. Install the cylinder retaining screw and torque it to 40 inch lbs.

11. Turn the key to **ON**.

12. Install the key warning buzzer switch and clip.

13. When installing the ignition switch, engage the actuator rod in the bottom of the switch. Install the switch on the column and tighten the screws.

14. Adjust the ignition switch as follows:

   a. Insert the key and turn the lock cylinder to the **OFF/UNLOCK** position.

   b. Loosen the switch mounting screws.

   c. Move the switch down the column to eliminate any play and tighten the screws to 35 inch lbs.

   d. Connect the wiring to the switch.

15. Engage the actuator rod in the dimmer switch and install the switch on the column.

16. Install the turn signal switch and attaching screws. Torque the screws to 35 inch lbs.

17. Connect the wiring harness connectors.

18. With the turn signal switch in the **N** position, install the

hazard warning knob. Press the knob inward and turn clockwise to install it.

19. Install the lever. Torque the attaching screws to 35 inch lbs.

20. Install the upper bearing preload spring. Install the canceling cam. Install the lock plate.

21. Using the compressor, install the snapring. Install the lock plate cover and install the steering wheel.

29. Loosen the toe plate screws. Install the column-to-dash bezel.

31. Connect the negative battery cable.

Ignition Switch

Removal and Installation

1. Disconnect the negative battery cable.

2. Position the key lock in the **OFF/LOCK** position.

3. Remove the lower trim panel, as required. Remove the ignition switch retaining screws.

4. Disconnect the ignition switch from the remote rod. Disconnect the electrical connectors from the switch assembly.

5. Remove the ignition switch from the vehicle.

To install:

6. With the actuator rod disconnected, position the switch to its mounting.

7. If the vehicle is equipped with a standard steering column, move the slider of the switch to the extreme left (**ACC**) position. The left side of the ignition switch is toward the steering wheel.

8. If the vehicle is equipped with a tilt steering column move the slider of the switch to the extreme right (**ACC**) position. The right side of the ignition switch is downward from the steering wheel.

9. Position the actuator rod in the slider hole. Install the switch to the steering column. Be sure not to move the slider out of the detent.

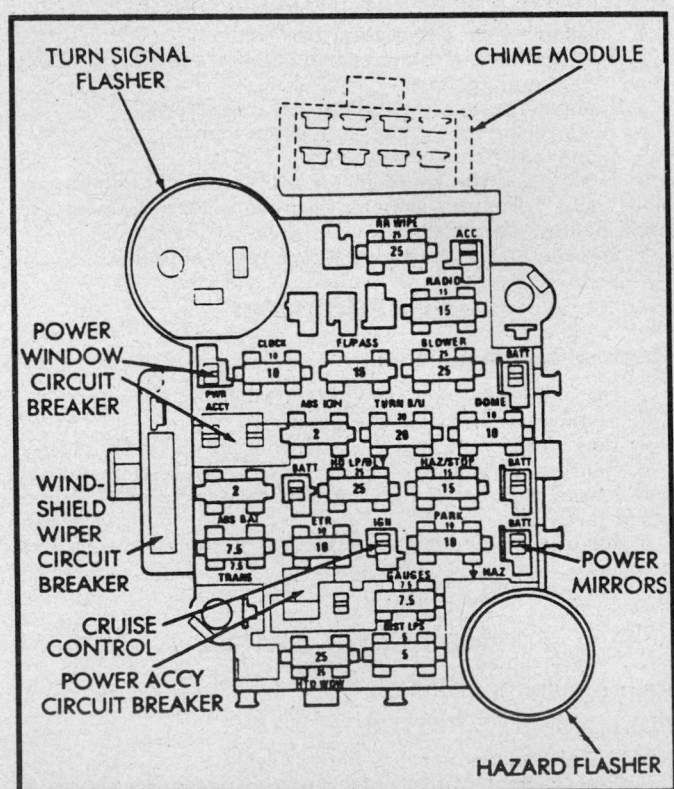

Typical fuse panel—Comanche, Cherokee and Wagoneer

10. Hold the ignition key in the **ACC** detent position and push the switch assembly down the steering column in order to remove the slack in the actuator rod.

11. Connect the switch electrical connectors. Check the switch for proper operation. Install the trim panel, as required.

12. Connect the negative battery cable.

Stoplight Switch

Removal and Installation

CJ7, WRANGLER, CHEROKEE, COMANCHE AND WAGONEER

NOTE: The stoplight switch is not adjustable.

1. Disconnect the negative battey cable.

2. Disconnect the wires from the switch, mounted at the brake pedal pushrod.

3. Remove the pushrod bolt and remove the switch from the pushrod. Note the position of the spacers for installation.

To install:

4. Install the bushings and spacers on the new switch.

5. Position the switch on the pushrod. Secure the pushrod to the pedal with the bolt and locknuts.

6. Tighten the inner nut to 25 ft. lbs. (34 Nm) and the outer nut to 75 inch lbs. (8.5 Nm).

7. Connect the switch wires and check the operation of the switch.

8. Connect the negative battery cable.

GRAND WAGONEER, J10 PICK-UP AND J20 PICK-UP

1. Disconnect the negative battery cable.

2. Disconnect the wires from the switch, mounted in the brake pedal bracket.

3. Unscrew the switch from the plastic retainer.

4. Install the new switch in position and adjust it by pulling the brake pedal back until a click is heard.

5. Connect the wires and connect the negative battery cable.

6. Check the operation of the switch and readjust if needed.

Fuses and Circuit Breakers

Location

A fuse panel is used to house the fuses and circuit breakers protecting the various components of the electrical system in the vehicle. The fuse panel is located under the instrument panel on the drivers side of the vehicle.

ENGINE COOLING

Radiator

Removal and Installation

1. Disconnect the negative battery cable.

2. Place a drain pan under the radiator and drain the radiator.

3. Remove the radiator upper and lower hoses.

4. Remove the alignment dowel E-clip from the lower radiator mounting bracket.

5. Disconnect the overflow tube from the radiator. Remove the fan shroud mounting bolts and pull the fan shroud back to the engine.

6. If equipped, disconnect the transmission cooler lines.

7. Remove the top radiator mounting bolts and remove the grille mounting screws. Remove the grille, if required.

8. If equipped, remove the condensor to radiator mounting bolts and pull the radiator out of the vehicle.

To install:

9. Slide the radiator into position behind the condensor, if equipped. Align the dowel pin with the bottom mounting bracket and install the E-clip.

10. Tighten the condenser-to-radiator bolts to 55 inch lbs. (6.2 Nm).

11. Install the grille. Install and tighten the radiator mounting bolts.

12. Connect the transmission cooler lines, if equipped. Install the fan shroud.

13. Connect the radiator hoses. Connect the negative battery cable.

14. Fill the cooling system to the correct level.

Electric Cooling Fan

Removal and Installation

1. Disconnect the negative battery cable.

2. Disconnect the electrical lead from the fan assembly.

3. Remove the fan mounting bolts and remove the fan assembly from the shroud and radiator.

4. Installation is the reverse of the removal procedure.

Testing

1. Remove the fan relay, mounted on the left inner fender panel.

2. Using a jumper wire, with an in-line 25 amp fuse, supply battery voltage to the the No. 4 terminal of the relay connector.

3. If the fan operates, the motor is good. If the motor does not operate, check the continuity between the No. 4 terminal and the body ground connections on the fender panel. If continuity exists, replace the fan motor. If there is no continuity, repair the open circuit and retest.

Heater Core

Removal and Installation

ALL EXCEPT CJ7 AND WRANGLER

1. Disconnect the negative battery cable. Drain the coolant.

2. Disconnect the heater hoses at the core tubes.

3. If equipped with air conditioning, discharge the refrigerant.

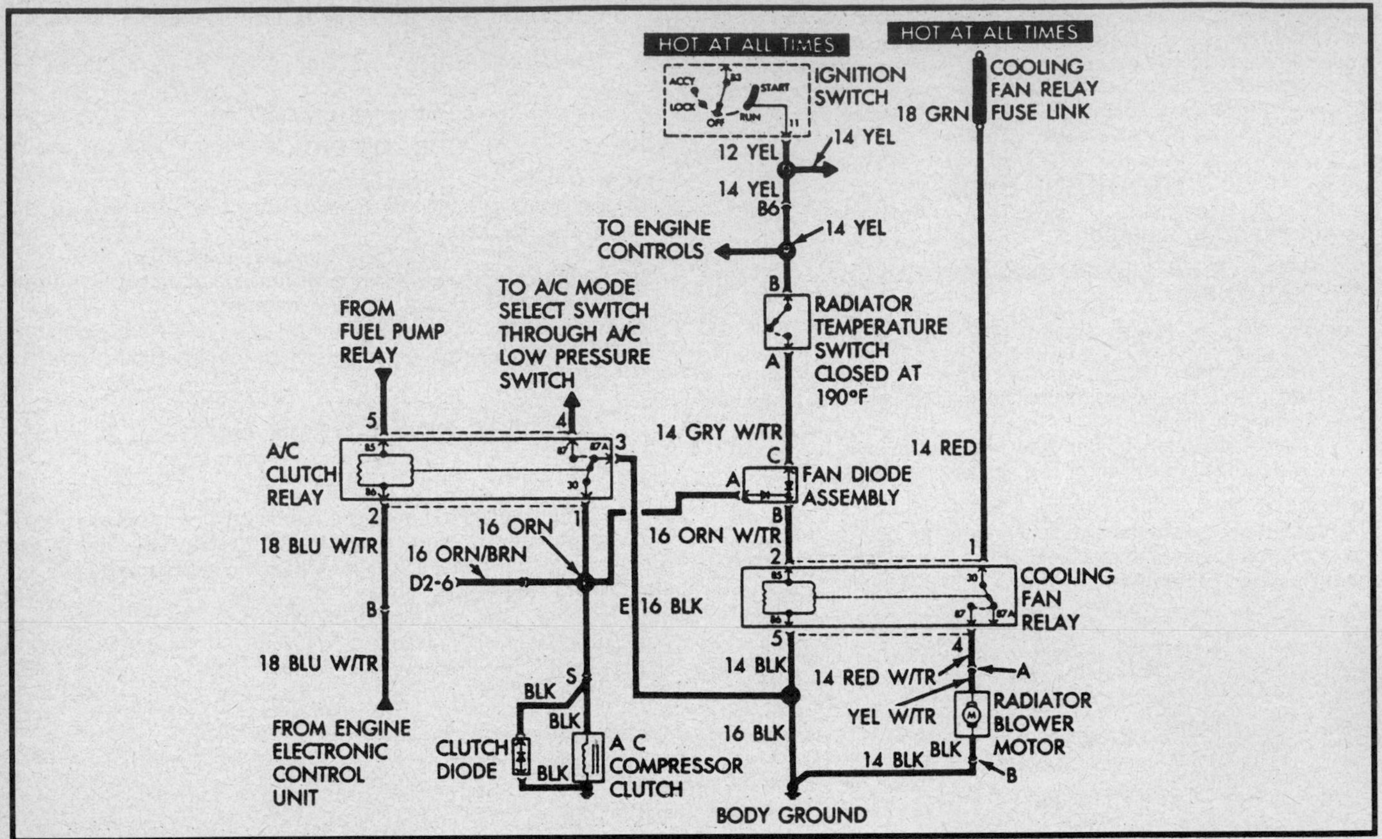

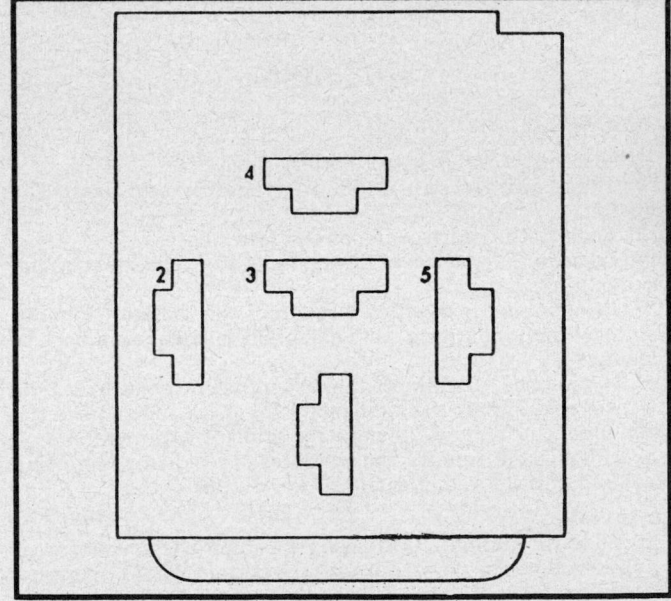

Auxiliary cooling fan system circuit

Auxiliary cooling fan connector

— CAUTION —

Use extreme caution when discharging the refrigerant. Refrigerant R–12 will freeze anything it comes in contact with, including skin and eyes.

4. Disconnect the air conditioning hose from the expansion valve and cap all openings. Always use a back-up wrench on the fitting.

5. Disconnect the blower motor wires and vent tube.

6. Remove the center console, if equipped.

7. Remove the lower half of the instrument panel.

8. Disconnect the wiring at the A/C relay, blower motor resistors and A/C thermostat. Disconnect the vacuum hoses at the vacuum motor.

9. Cut the plastic retaining strap that retains the evaporator housing to the heater core housing.

10. Disconnect and remove the heater control cable.

11. Remove the 3 clips at the rear blower housing flange and remove the retaining screws.

12. Remove the housing attaching nuts from the studs on the engine compartment side of the firewall.

13. Remove the evaporator drain tube.

14. Remove the right kick panel and the instrument panel support bolt.

15. Gently pull out on the right side of the dash and rotate the housing down and toward the rear to disengage the mounting studs from the firewall. Remove the housing.

16. Unbolt and remove the core from the housing.

To install:

17. Install the core in the housing.

18. Position the housing on the mounting studs on the firewall.

19. Install the right kick panel and the instrument panel support bolt.

20. Install the evaporator drain tube.

21. Install the housing attaching nuts from the studs on the engine compartment side of the firewall.

22. Install the 3 clips at the rear blower housing flange and install the retaining screws.

23. Connect the heater control cable.

24. Install a new plastic retaining strap that retains the evaporator housing to the heater core housing.

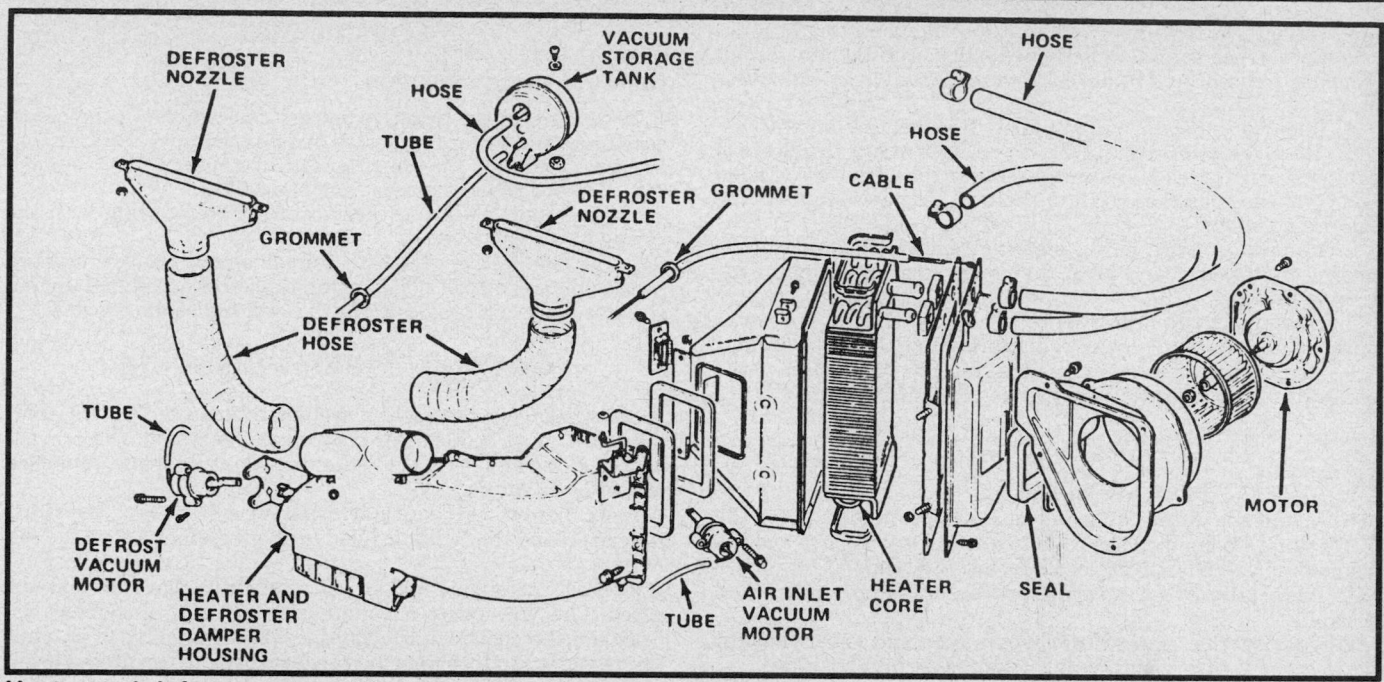

Heater and defroster assembly—typical Cherokee and Wagoneer

25. Connect the wiring at the A/C relay, blower motor resistors and A/C thermostat.
26. Connect the vacuum hoses at the vacuum motor.
27. Install the lower half of the instrument panel.
28. Install the center console, if equipped.
29. Connect the blower motor wires and vent tube.
30. Connect the air conditioning hose at the expansion valve. Always use a back-up wrench.
31. Connect the heater hoses at the core tubes.
32. Fill the cooling system.
33. Evacuate, charge and leak test the refrigerant system.

CJ7 AND WRANGLER

1. Disconnect the negative battery cable. Drain the radiator.
2. Disconnect the heater hoses. Disconnect the damper door control cables. Disconnect the blower motor wire.
3. Disconnect the defroster duct. Remove the heater core housing retaining nuts from inside the engine compartment.
4. Remove the heater core housing assembly from the vehicle.
5. Remove the heater core from the housing.
6. Installation is the reverse of the removal procedure.

Water Pump

Removal and Installation

2.1L ENGINE

1. Disconnect the negative battery cable. Drain the engine coolant.
2. Remove the coolant hose from the water pump.
3. Remove the drive belts.
4. Remove the fan and hub assembly.
5. It is not necessary to remove the timing belt tensioner. Use a long strap and clip in order to retain the timing belt tensioner plunger in place.
6. Remove the water pump retaining bolts. Remove the water pump assembly from the vehicle.

To install:
7. Clean the mating surfaces of all gasket material.
8. Do not use sealer on the new gasket. Position the gasket

and pump on the engine and install the bolts. Torque the bolts to 15 ft. lbs.
9. Check the timing belt tension.
10. Install the fan and hub.
11. Install the drive belts.
12. Install the coolant hoses.
13. Fill the cooling system.
14. Connect the negative battery cable.

2.5L, 4.0L AND 4.2L

NOTE: Some 2.5L engines with air conditioning are equipped with a serpentine drive belt and have a reverse rotating water pump coupled with a viscous fan drive assembly. The components are identified by the words REVERSE stamped on the cover of the viscous drive and on the inner side of the fan. The word REV is also cast into the body of the water pump.

1. Disconnect the negative battery cable. Drain the cooling system.
2. Disconnect the hoses at the pump.
3. Remove the drive belts.
4. Remove the power steering pump bracket.
5. Remove the fan and shroud.
6. Unbolt and remove the pump.

To install:
7. Clean the mating surfaces thoroughly.
8. Using a new gasket, install the pump and torque the bolts to 13 ft. lbs.
9. Reconnect the hoses at the pump and install accessory drive belt.
10. Install the power steering pump bracket. Install the fan and shroud.
11. Adjust the belt tension and fill the cooling system to the correct level.
12. Connect the negative battery cable.

2.8L AND 5.9L ENGINES

1. Disconnect the negative battery cable. Drain the cooling system.

2. Disconnect the upper radiator hoses at the radiator.

3. Loosen the accessory drive belts. Separate the fan shroud from the radiator and remove the fan assembly from the water pump.

4. Remove the water pump pulley. Remove the fan shroud.

5. Remove the alternator front mounting bracket. If equipped with air conditioning, remove the compressor bolts and pivot the compressor out of the way. Do not disconnect the compressor lines.

6. If equipped with power steering remove the stud/nut retaining the bracket and pivot the power steering/air pump assembly forward.

7. Disconnect the heater hose and bypass hose at the water pump. Disconnect the lower radiator hose at the water pump.

8. Remove the water pump mounting bolts and remove the pump from the engine.

To install:

9. Clean the gasket mating surfaces.

10. Install the water pump and gasket in position. Tighten the water pump-to-timing case bolts to 48 inch lbs. (5 Nm) and the water pump-to-block bolts to 28 ft. lbs. (38 Nm).

11. Install the power steering pump, air pump and bracket assembly.

12. Connect the heater hose, bypass hose and lower radiator hose. Pivot the air conditioning compressor into position.

13. Install the alternator front mounting brackets. Position the shroud against the engine and install the fan assembly.

14. Install the shroud to the radiator and install the accessory drive belts.

15. Connect the upper radiator hose. Connect the negative battery cable.

16. Fill the cooling system to the correct level and bleed the system.

Thermostat

Removal and Installation

1. Disconnect the negative battery cable. Remove the necessary hoses from the thermostat housing. Remove the 2 attaching screws and lift the housing from the engine.

2. Remove the thermostat and the gasket.

3. To install, place the thermostat in the housing with the spring inside the engine.

4. Install a new gasket with a small amount of sealing compound applied to both sides. Install the water outlet and tighten the attaching bolts to 30 ft. lbs. 5.Refill the cooling system.

Cooling System Bleeding

After working on the cooling system, even to replace the thermostat, it must be bled. Air trapped in the system will prevent proper filling and leave the radiator coolant level low, causing a risk of overheating.

1. To bleed the system, start with the system cool, the radiator cap off and the radiator filled to about an inch below the filler neck.

2. Start the engine and run it at slightly above normal idle speed. This will insure adequate circulation. If air bubbles appear and the coolant level drops, fill the system with an antifreeze/water mixture to bring the level back to the proper level.

3. Run the engine this way until the thermostat opens. When this happens, coolant will move abruptly across the top of the radiator and the temperature of the radiator will suddenly rise.

4. At this point, air is often expelled and the level may drop quite a bit. Keep refilling the system until the level is near the top of the radiator and remains constant.

5. If the vehicle has an overflow tank, fill the radiator right up to the filler neck. Replace the radiator filler cap.

GASOLINE FUEL SYSTEM

Fuel System Service Precaution

When working with the fuel system certain precautions should be taken; always work in a well ventilated area, keep a dry chemical (Class B) fire extinguisher near the work area. Always disconnect the negative battery cable and do not make any repairs to the fuel system until all the necessary steps for repair have been reviewed.

Relieving Fuel System Pressure

Fuel injection systems operate under high pressure, this makes it necessary to first relieve the system of pressure before servicing. The pressurized fuel when released may ignite or cause personal injury. the following outlined steps may be used for most fuel systems:

1. Disconnect the negative battery cable.

2. Remove the fuel tank filler cap.

3. Remove the cap from the pressure test port on the fuel rail in the engine compartment.

NOTE: Don't allow fuel to spray or spill on the engine or exhaust manifold. Place heavy shop towels under the pressure port to absorb any escaping fuel.

4. Using a suitable pressure gauge equipped with a pressure bleed valve, connect it to the test port valve to relieve fuel system pressure.

Fuel Filter

Removal and Installation
CARBURETED ENGINE

The fuel filter is located in the carburetor, at the inlet line.

1. Disconnect the negative battery cable.

2. Remove the fuel inlet line from carburetor.

3. Remove the large nut from the inlet port, use care not to loose the spring behind the nut.

4. Remove and clean or replace the filter.

5. Installation is the reverse of the removal procedure.

FUEL INJECTED ENGINE

The fuel filter for the fuel injected engines is located at the rear of the vehicle, on the drivers side frame rail.

1. Disconnect the battery ground cable.

2. Remove the fuel tank filler cap.

3. Relieve the fuel system pressure.

4. Raise and support the rear of the vehicle safely.
5. Remove the hoses and clamps from the filter.
6. Remove the filter strap bolt and remove the filter.

NOTE: The filter is marked for installation. IN goes towards the fuel tank; OUT towards the engine.

7. Place the new filter on the frame rail and tighten the strap bolt to 106 inch lbs.
8. Install and securely clamp the hoses.

Mechanical Fuel Pump

Pressure Testing

1. Disconnect the fuel inlet line at the carburetor.
2. Install a T-fitting on the open end of the fuel line and refit the line to the carburetor.
3. Plug a pressure gauge into the remaining opening of the T-fitting. The hose leading to the pressure gauge should not be any longer than 6 in. On pumps with a fuel return line, the line must be plugged.
4. Start the engine and allow it to idle. Fuel pressure readings should be as follows:
   a. 4 and 6 cylinder engines – 4.00–5.00 psi @ idle
   b. 8 cylinder engine – 6.00–7.50 psi @ idle

Removal and Installation

1. Disconnect the negative battery cable. Remove all the necessary components in order to gain access to the fuel pump. Disconnect the fuel lines.
2. Remove the attaching bolts that hold the fuel pump to the engine and lift the fuel pump off of the engine.
3. Before installing the fuel pump, make sure that all of the mating surfaces are clean.

To install:

4. Cement a new gasket to the mating surface of the fuel pump.
5. Position the fuel pump on the cylinder block so that the cam lever of the pump rests on the camshaft.
6. Secure the pump to the engine with the retaining bolts and lock washers.
7. Connect the fuel lines to the fuel pump.

Electric Fuel Pump

The fuel pump for fuel injected vehicles is located in the fuel tank attached to the fuel gauge sending unit.

Pressure Testing

THROTTLE BODY INJECTION

1. Remove the fuel pressure test port plug from the throttle body.
2. Install a pressure test fitting in the port.
3. Connect an 0–30 psi. gauge to the fitting.
4. Start the engine and allow it to idle.
5. The pressure gauge should read 14–15 psi. If the pressure is not in this range, adjust the pressure regulator to obtain the correct reading.
6. To adjust the pressure regulator, turn the screw at the bottom of the regulator in to increase the pressure and out to reduce the pressure.

MULTI-PORT FUEL INJECTION

1. Connect an 0–60 psi fuel pressure gauge to the test port pressure fitting on the fuel rail.
2. Remove the vacuum line from the fuel pressure regulator.
3. Start the engine and note the gauge reading.
4. The fuel pressure should be approximately 39 psi.

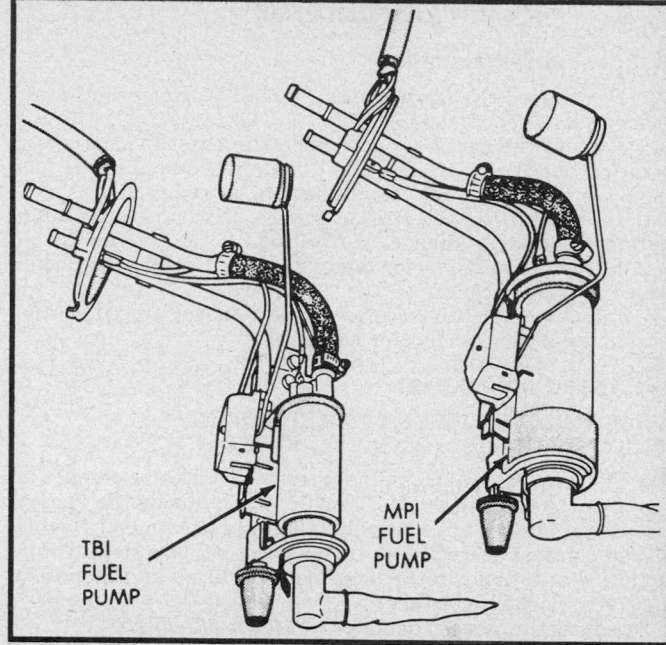

Electric fuel pumps—fuel injected vehicles

5. Reconnect the vacuum line to the pressure regulator, the fuel pressure should be approximately 31 psi.
6. If the fuel pressure is not approximately 8–10 psi higher with the vacuum line removed, check the line for kinks or pinches.
7. If the fuel pressure is below, momentarily pinch shut the hose section of the fuel line. If the pressure remains low, inspect the fuel supply system for blockage.

Removal and Installation

1. Disconnect the negative battery cable.
2. Remove the fuel tank filler cap.
3. Drain the fuel from the fuel tank.
4. Raise and safely support the rear of the vehicle.
5. Remove the fuel inlet and outlet hoses from the sending unit.
6. Remove the sending unit wires.
7. Using a brass punch and hammer, remove the sending unit retaining lock ring by tapping it counterclockwise.
8. Remove the sending unit, which incorporates the electric fuel pump, along with the O-ring seal from the fuel tank. Discard the O-ring.
9. Remove and discard the pump inlet filter.
10. Disconnect the fuel pump terminal wires.
11. Remove the pump outlet hose and clamp.
12. Remove the pump top mounting bracket nut and remove the pump.

To install:

13. Install a new inlet filter on the pump.
14. Assemble the pump and bracket. Connect the hose and wiring.
15. Install the unit and new O-ring in the tank. The rubber stopper on the end of the fuel return tube must be inserted into the cup in the fuel tank reservoir.
16. Install the lock ring. Carefully tap it into place until it seats against the stop on the tank.
17. Connect the hoses.
18. Connect the wiring.
19. Lower the vehicle, refill the fuel tank, run the engine and check for leaks.

Carburetor

Removal and Installation

1. Disconnect the negative battery cable. Remove the air cleaner assembly.
2. Remove the necessary components in order to gain access to the carburetor retaining bolts. Disconnect and plug the fuel line. Disconnect all electrical connectors, as required.
3. Disconnect the accelerator linkage. Disconnect the automatic transmission linkage, as required.
4. Remove the carburetor retaining bolts. Remove the carburetor from the vehicle.
5. Installation is the reverse of the removal procedure. Be sure to use a new carburetor base gasket.

Idle Speed Adjustment

2.5L ENGINE WITH YFA CARBURETOR, TRC(ANTI-DIESEL) AND CEC SYSTEM

The TRC (anti-diesel) adjustment screw is statically set at ¾ of turn from the throttle valve closed position during the factory assembly and does not normally require readjustment. Should this adjustment be required, turn the adjustment screw counterclockwise to the throttle plate closed position and then turn the screw clockwise ¾ turn.

To adjust the solevac actuator, proceed as follows;
1. Connect a tachometer to the ignition coil tach wire connector.
2. Place the transmission in the N position and depress the parking brake.
3. Start the engine and allow it to reach normal operating temperature.
4. Connect an external vacuum source to the solevac vacuum actuator and apply 10–15 in. Hg. Plug the engine vacuum hose.
5. Adjust the vacuum actuator to specification.
6. Remove the vacuum source from the vacuum actuator and retain the plug in the vacuum hose from the engine.
7. Adjust the curb idle speed to specification.
8. Stop the engine and connect the engine vacuum hose to the vacuum actuator.
9. Remove the tachometer from the engine.

2.8L ENGINE WITH 2SE CARBURETOR

1. Connect a tachometer to the ignition coil negative terminal or to the pigtail wire connector above the heater blower motor.
2. Disconnect and plug the vacuum hose at the distributor vacuum advance.
3. If necessary, adjust the ignition timing with the engine speed at or below specifications.
4. Reconnect the vacuum hose to the distributor vacuum advance unit.
5. Disconnect the deceleration valve hose and canister purge hose. Plug the hose and remove the air cleaner assembly.
6. If equipped with air conditioning, turn the control switch to the ON position and open the throttle momentarily to insure the solenoid armature is fully extended. Adjust the solenoid idle speed adjusting screw to obtain the specified engine curb idle speed rpm. Turn the air condition control switch to the OFF position.
7. If not equipped with air conditioning, adjust the engine idle speed rpm with the solenoid idle speed adjusting screw. Disconnect the solenoid wire and adjust the curb idle.
8. Install the air cleaner assembly. Connect all hoses and other connections.

2.8L ENGINE WITH E2SE CARBURETOR

NOTE: Some 1986 California models with the 2.8L engine, are equipped with a 2200 hour engine timer. The timer activates a solenoid to control operation of the carburetor secondary vacuum brake after 2200 hours of vehicle operation. The timer is not a serviceable component and must not be disassembled. In the event of a timer malfunction, the complete engine wiring harness must be replaced

1. Connect a tachometer to the ignition system. Start the engine and operate to normal operating temperature.
2. Turn OFF all accessories. Position manual transmission vehicles in N and automatic transmission vehicles in D with the parking brake locked and the wheels chocked.
3. Adjust the curb idle speed adjusting screw to obtain the specified rpm.
4. Disconnect the vacuum hose from the idle kick actuator and connect an outside vacuum source to the actuator. Apply 15 in. Hg of vacuum to the actuator.
5. Adjust the actuator hex head adjustment screw to 1200 rpm with the selector lever in the N position.
6. Stop the engine, remove the tachometer and vacuum pump. Install the vacuum hose to the actuator.

4.2L ENGINE WITH BBD CARBURETOR AND CEC SYSTEM

1. Run the engine until normal operating temperature is reached. Connect a tachometer to the ignition coil negative terminal. The carburetor choke and intake manifold heater must be OFF. This occurs when the engine coolant heats to approximately 160°F.
2. Remove the vacuum hose to the solevac vacuum actuator unit. Plug the vacuum hose. Disconnect the holding solenoid wire connector.
3. Adjust the curb idle speed screw to specification.
4. Apply a direct source of vacuum to the vacuum actuator, using a hand vacuum pump or its equivalent. When the solevac throttle positioner is fully extended, turn the vacuum actuator adjustment screw on the throttler lever until the specified engine rpm is obtained. Disconnect the vacuum source from the vacuum actuator.
5. With a jumper wire, apply battery voltage to energize the holding solenoid. The holding wire connector can be installed and either the rear window defroster or the air conditioner (with the compressor clutch wire disconnected) can be turned on to energize the holding solenoid.
6. Hold the throttle open manually to allow the throttle positioner to fully extend. Without the vacuum actuator, the throttle must be opened manually to allow the solevac throttle positioner to fully extend.
7. If the holding solenoid idle speed is not within specifications, adjust the idle using the ¼ in. hex head adjustment screw on the end of the solevac unit.
8. Disconnect the jumper wire from the solevac solenoid wire connector, if used. Connect the wire connector to the solevac unit, if not connected. Install the original vacuum hose to the vacuum actuator.
9. Remove the tachometer and if disconnected, connect the compressor clutch wire.

5.9L ENGINE WITH 2150 CARBURETOR

NOTE: If the vehicle is equipped with automatic transmission, lock the parking brake, block the wheels and place the selector lever in DRIVE before adjusting the idle speed.

1. Connect a tachometer to the ignition coil negative terminal.
2. Start the engine and allow it to reach normal operating temperature.
3. Turn the hex head adjustment screw on the solenoid carriage to obtain the correct engine speed.
4. Disconnect the solenoid wire connector and adjust the curb idle speed screw to specification.
5. Reconnect the solenoid wire connector and stop the engine.

6. If equipped with a dashpot, position the throttle at the curb idle position and depress the dashpot stem.

7. Measure the clearance between the stem and the throttle lever. A clearance of 0.032 in. should exist.

8. Adjust the clearance as required by loosening the locknut and turning the dashpot until the correct clearance is obtained. Tighten the dashpot locknut.

Idle Mixture Adjustment

2.5L ENGINE WITH YFA CARBURETOR AND CEC SYSTEM

The idle mixture is preset at the time of manufacture and should normally not require readjustment. To prevent easy access to the idle mixture screw, a tamper resistant plug is set into the carburetor assembly to cover the screw. Should adjustment be required due to system diagnosis, contamination, replacement of components or tampering, the following procedure may be used to bring the adjustment into compliance with specifications.

1. Connect a tachometer to the tach terminal of the ignition coil wire connector and a dwell meter to the mixture solenoid test terminals in the diagnosis connector (D2–14 and D2–7) and adjust the dwell meter to the 6 cylinder scale.

2. If the idle mixture screw tamper resistant plug has not been removed, the carburetor must be removed from the engine for access to the plug. With the carburetor off the engine, invert the carburetor and place it in a suitable holding device. Remove the plug by drilling a ⅛ in. hole in the center, installing a self tapping screw and pulling the plug from the carburetor.

3. Reinstall the carburetor on the engine, connect all lines and wires.

4. Place the transmission in the **N** position and apply the parking brake.

5. Disconnect and plug the canister purge vacuum hose at the charcoal canister.

6. Start the engine and operate at fast idle speed to bring the engine and coolant to normal operating temperature, thus allowing the CEC (feedback) system to operate in the closed loop mode of operation.

7. Return the engine to idle speed and adjust the carburetor for an idle speed of 700 rpm for automatic transmission vehicles in **D** and 750 rpm in **N** for manual transmission vehicles.

8. Adjust the idle mixture screw to obtain an average dwell reading of between 25–35 degrees, with 30 degrees preferred.

9. If the dwell is too low, turn the idle mixture screw counterclockwise. If the dwell is too high, turn the idle mixture screw clockwise. Allow time for the system to react and stabilize after each movement of the adjusting screw. The feedback system is very sensitive to adjustments.

10. Observe the final dwell indication with the adjusting tool removed. If the specified dwell cannot be obtained by adjustment, inspect the carburetor idle circuits for air leaks, restrictions and etc. Do any necessary repairs.

11. When the adjustment is complete, connect the canister purge hose and adjust the idle speed to specifications.

12. Stop the engine and remove the tachometer and dwell meter. Plug the idle mixture adjusting screw openings. Install the gasket and the air cleaner assembly on the carburetor.

2.8L ENGINE WITH E2SE CARBURETOR (FEEDBACK TYPE)

1. Remove the carburetor from the engine and remove the tamper resistant plug in order to gain access to the idle mixture adjusting screw.

2. Modify special Kent Moore tool J–29030–B or its equivalent, by grinding ⅛ in. off the rear and ¼ in. off the front of the tool. Place the modified tool onto the idle mixture adjusting screw.

3. Turn the idle mixture screw in until it is lightly seated and back out 4 turns. If the seal in the air horn concealing the idle

air bleed has been removed, replace the air horn. If the seal is still in place, do not remove the seal.

4. Remove the vent stack screen assembly to gain access to the lean mixture screw.

5. Turn the lean mixture screw in until lightly bottomed and then back out 2½ turns. Some resistance should be felt. If not, remove the screw and inspect for the presence of the spring.

6. Install the carburetor on the engine with the modified tool installed on the mixture adjusting screw. Do not install the air cleaner and gasket.

7. Disconnect the bowl vent line at the carburetor, disconnect the EGR valve hose and the canister purge hose at the carburetor. Cap the carburetor ports.

8. Refer to the vehicle emission control information label diagram, located under the vehicle hood, and locate the hose from port D on the carburetor to the temperature sensor and the secondary vacuum break thermal vacuum switch.

9. Disconnect the hose at the temperature sensor on the air cleanser and plug the hose.

10. Connect a dwell meter positive probe to the mixture control solenoid dwell test wire with a green connection.

11. Connect the negative probe to ground and set the meter at the 6 cylinder scale position.

12. Connect a tachometer to the ignition system, set the parking brake and chock the wheels.

13. Place the transmission in **P** for automatic or **N** for manual.

14. Start and operate the engine until normal operating temperature is reached and the electronic engine control system is in the closed loop mode of operation.

15. Operate the engine at 3000 rpm and adjust the lean mixture screw slowly in small increments, allowing time for the dwell to stabilize after turning the screw to obtain an average dwell of 35 degrees.

16. If the dwell is too low, back the screw out and if too high, turn the screw in. If unable to adjust to specifications, inspect the main metering system for leaks, restriction, etc.

17. Return the engine to idle speed. Allow the engine to stabilize before the dwell is recorded.

NOTE: The mixture control solenoid dwell is an indication of the ratio of ON to OFF time. The dwell of the mixture control solenoid is used to determine the calibration and is sensitive to changes in the fuel mixture caused by heat, air leaks, etc. While the engine is idling, it is normal for the dwell to increase and decrease fairly constant over a relativity narrow range, such as 5 degrees. However, it may occasionally vary as much as 10–15 degrees momentarily because of temporary mixture changes. The dwell specified is the average of the most consistant variations. The engine must be allowed to stabilize its self for a few minutes after returning the engine to idle in order to obtain a correct average.

18. Adjust the idle mixture screw with the modified tool J–29030–A or its equivalent, to obtain an average dwell of 25 degrees. If the dwell is too high, turn the screw in and if the dwell is too low, back the screw out. Allow time for the dwell to stabilize after each adjustment, because the adjustment is very sensitive. If unable to adjust to specifications, check for idle system air or vacuum leaks and restrictions.

19. Disconnect the mixture control solenoid and check for and engine speed change of at least 50 rpm. If the rpm does not change enough, inspect the idle air bleed circuit for restrictions, leaks, etc.

20. Increase the engine speed to 3000 rpm and operate for a few minutes. Note the dwell which should be varying with an average indications of 35 degrees.

21. If the average dwell is not at 25 degrees, adjust the lean mixture screw.

22. After adjusting the lean mixture screw, adjust the idle mixture screw to obtain 25 degrees dwell.

23. If at an average dwell of 25 degrees, remove the carburetor from the engine, remove the modified tool J–29030–A or equivalent from the idle mixture screw and seal the access hole.

24. Install the carburetor, connect all disconnected components and install the vent screen. Verify the idle speed is within specifications.

4.2L ENGINE WITH BBD CARBURETOR AND CEC SYSTEM

The idle mixture adjustment should only be performed if the adjustment screws were removed during a carburetor overhaul procedure. When the carburetor is mounted to the engine, it must be removed to gain access to the dowel pin locations, whose removal must be accomplished before any adjustment of the mixture screws can be made.

1. Connect a tachometer to the engine. Run the engine until normal operating temperature is reached.

2. Set the parking brake firmly and chock the wheels. Position the gear selector in the **N** for manual transmission and in **D** for automatic transmission. Adjust the idle speed.

3. Adjust the idle mixture screws clockwise (lean) until a loss of engine rpm is noted. Idle drop specification is 50 rpm for both automatic and manual transmission.

4. Turn the idle mixture screws counterclockwise (rich) until the highest engine rpm indication is obtained.

NOTE: Do not turn the screws any further than the point at which the highest engine rpm is first obtained. This is referred to as best lean mixture. The engine idle speed will increase above the curb idle speed by an amount that corresponds approximately to the idle drop specifications listed on the Emission Information Label.

5. Turn the mixture screws clockwise (lean) to obtain the specified drop in engine rpm. Turn both mixture screws in small, equal amounts until the specified idle drop is achieved.

6. If the final engine rpm differs more than 30 rpm plus or minus from the original curb idle rpm, adjust the curb idle speed to specifications and repeat the mixture adjustment procedure.

7. Install the dowel pins after completing the idle mixture adjustment. Use care not to disturb the mixture screw positions. It is necessary to remove the carburetor to gain access to the dowel pin locations. After the carburetor has been reinstalled, again check the idle speed specifications and correct as required.

5.9L ENGINE WITH 2150 CARBURETOR

NOTE: The idle mixture adjustment screws are concealed by tamper resistant caps. The idle mixture should be adjusted only if the mixture adjustment screws were removed or altered during major carburetor overhaul or tampering.

1. Connect a tachometer to the engine.

2. Start the engine and allow it to reach normal operating temperature.

3. Set the parking brake and chock the wheels. Position the automatic transmission in **D**.

4. Be sure choke is completely off and the idle speed is set to specifications.

5. Turn the idle mixture adjusting screws clockwise (leaner) until a perceptible loss of engine speed is noted on the tachometer.

6. Turn the idle mixture adjusting screws counterclockwise (richer) until the highest engine speed is obtained.

7. This position of the idle mixture adjusting screws is referred to as the lean best idle.

8. Turn both idle mixture adjusting screws clockwise in small, equal amounts until the specified idle speed drop is noted on the tachometer.

Service Adjustments

For all carburetor service adjustment procedures and specifications, please refer to "Carburetor Service" in the Unit Repair section.

Fuel Injection

Idle Speed and Mixture Adjustment

Idle speed and mixture adjustment are controlled by the ECU and are not adjustable.

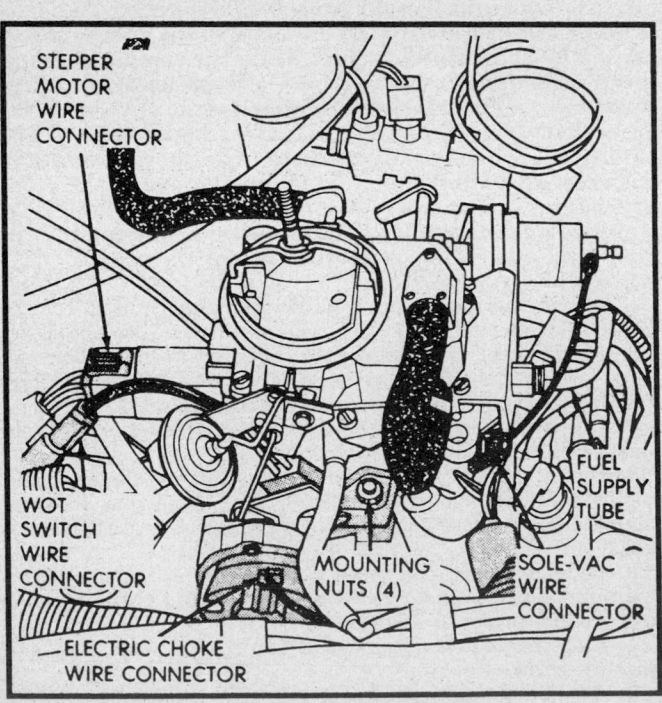

Carburetor mounting and connections

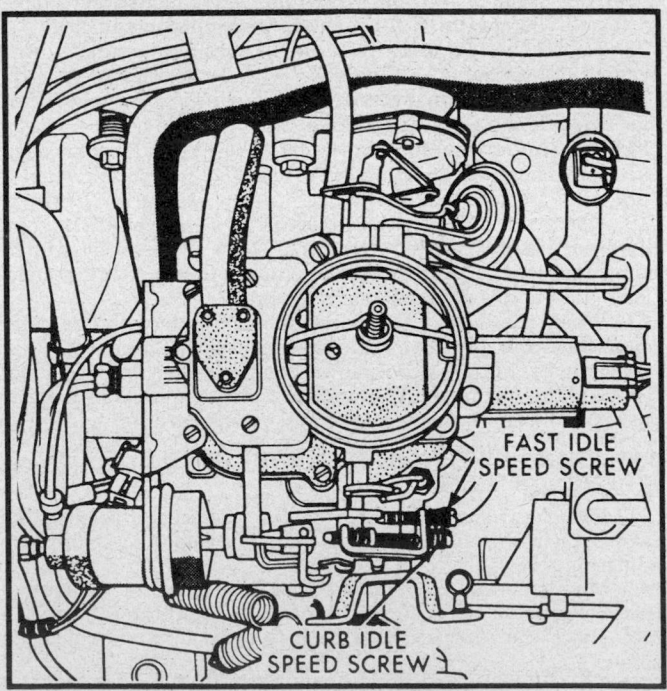

Carburetor adjustment screw locations

Fuel Injector

Removal and Installation

THROTTLE BODY INJECTION

1. Disconnect the negative battery cable. Remove the air cleaner and hose assembly. Relieve the fuel system pressure as necessary.
2. Remove the throttle body upper and lower covers.
3. Remove the fuel injector wire by compressing the tabs and pulling it upwards.
4. Remove the fuel injector retainer clip screws. Remove the fuel injector retainer clip.

NOTE: The injector has a small locating tab that fits into a slot in the bottom of the injector bore of the throttle body. Do not twist the injector during removal.

5. Using a small pair of pliers, gently grasp the center collar of the injector, between the electrical terminals, and carefully remove the injector using a lifting-rocking motion.
6. Discard the centering ring and the upper and lower O-rings. Never reuse these rings!
7. Installation is the reverse of the removal procedure. Lubricate both O-rings with light oil before installation. Align the tab on the injector with the slot in the throttle body.

MULTI-PORT FUEL INJECTION

1. Disconnect the negative battery cable. Relieve fuel system pressure.
2. Disconnect the fuel lines at the ends of the fuel rail assembly.
3. Mark and disconnect the injector wire harness connectors.
4. Remove the fuel rail retaining bolts.
5. Disconnect the vacuum line from the fuel pressure regulator.
6. Remove the fuel rail assembly from the engine.

NOTE: On models with automatic transmission, it may be necessary to remove the automatic transmission throttle pressure cable and bracket to remove the fuel rail assembly.

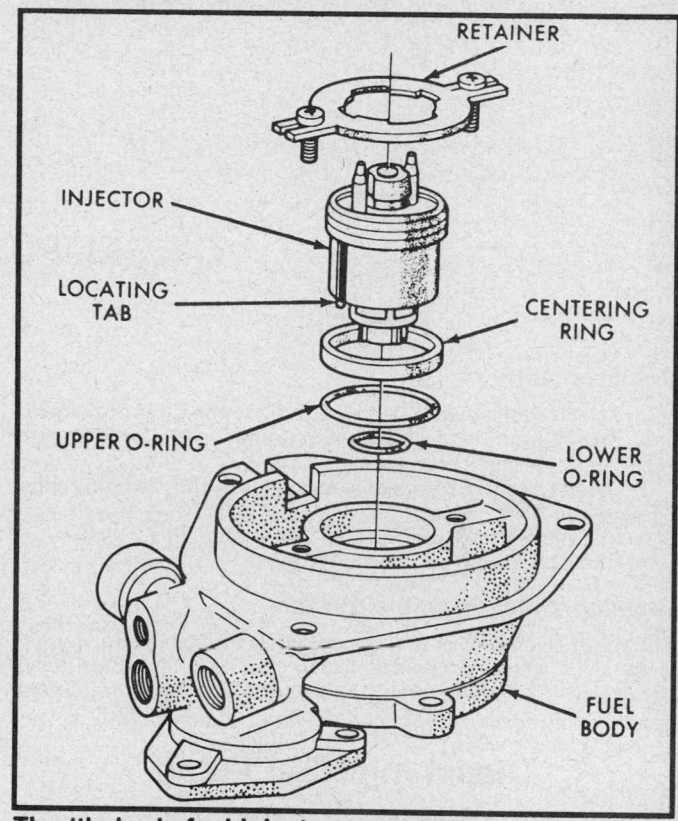

Throttle body fuel injector components

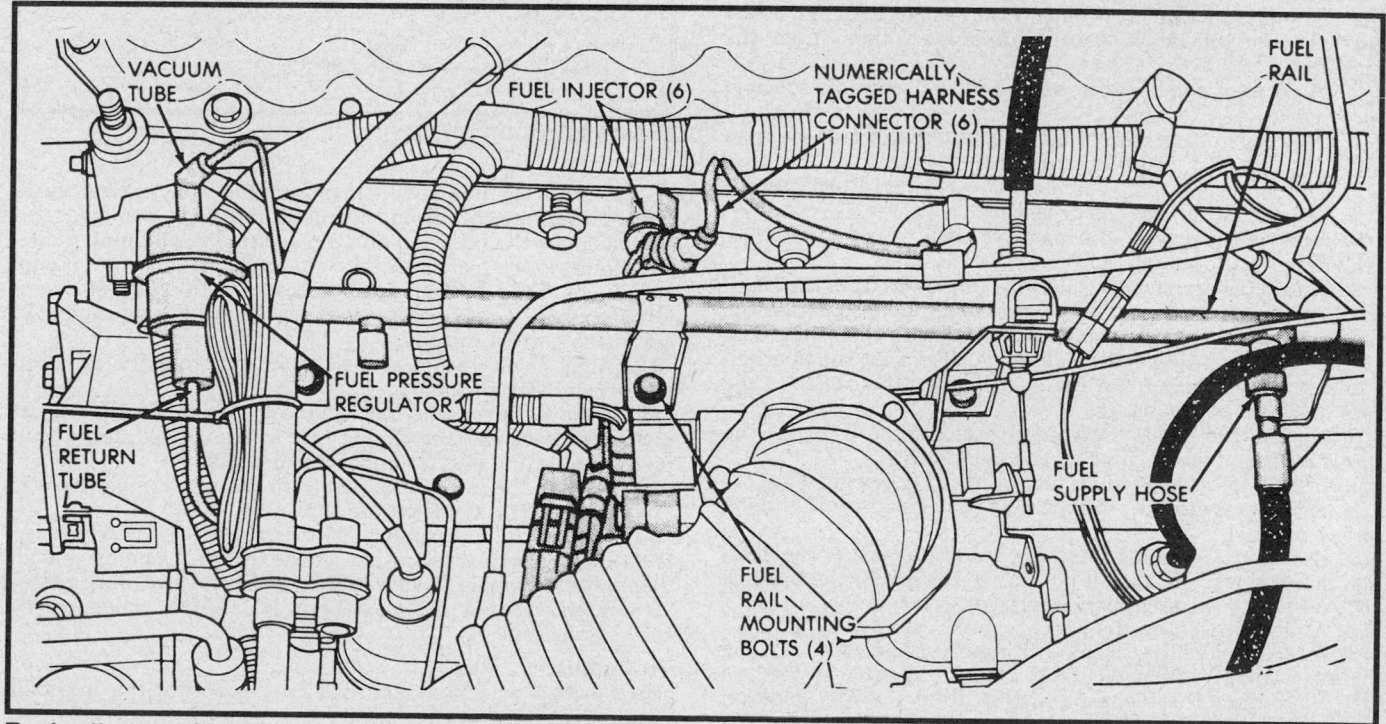

Fuel rail assembly location and mounting—4.0L engine

7. Remove the clips that retain the injectors to the fuel rail and remove the injectors. An O-ring kit is available which consists of 6 brown seals and 7 black seals. The brown seals fit on the injector tip area and seal the injector to the intake manifold. The black seals fit on the rail end of the injector to to seal the injector when it is installed into the fuel rail. The last black seal is for the fuel pressure regulator to seal the pressure regulator to the fuel rail. These seals cannot be interchanged.

8. Installation is the reverse of removal. Tighten the fuel rail mounting bolts to 20 ft. lbs. (27 Nm).

DIESEL FUEL SYSTEM

Fuel Filter

Replacement

1. Attach a long pice of flexible tubing to the filter drain cock.
2. Run the tubing to a suitable container, open the filter vent valve and open the drain cock.
3. Drain the filter completely and remove the retaining clips. Discard the filter.
4. Install the new filter into the retaining clips.
5. Run the engine and check for leaks.

Draining Water From the System

The water in the diesel fuel system must be drained during servicing. The water can be drained by placing a container under the drain valve and opening the valve. Allow fuel to drain out until it is uniform in color and no water is mixed with it.

Diesel Injection Pump

Removal and Installation

1. Disconnect the negative battery cable.
2. Using heavy clamps, clamp off the coolant inlet and outlet hoses at the cold start capsule, disconnect them from the capsule.
3. Disconnect the throttle cable and fuel shut-off solenoid wire.
4. If so equipped, disconnect the automatic transmission throttle cable, and cruise control cable.
5. Disconnect and plug the fuel delivery and return hoses.
6. Remove the alternator drive belt.
7. Remove the power steering drive belt.
8. Remove the timing belt cover.
9. Rotate the crankshaft clockwise, as viewed from the front, until No. 1 piston is at TDC compression. Make sure that the camshaft sprocket timing mark is aligned with the center boss on the cylinder head cover. Make sure, also, that the injection pump sprocket timing mark is aligned with the center of the boss on the injection pump.
10. Rotate the crankshaft counterclockwise, moving the sprocket timing marks by 3 timing belt teeth.
11. Install sprocket holding tool MOT–854, or equivalent. It may be necessary to turn the sprocket back and forth slightly to install the tool.
12. Loosen the sprocket retaining nut on the end of the injection pump shaft, and turn it out just to the end of the threads.
13. Assemble the appropriate sprocket removal tool.
14. Attach the tool to the injection pump sprocket.
15. Disconnect all the fuel pipe fittings from the injectors. Plug the injectors to prevent dirt from entering the fuel system.
16. Disconnect the fuel pipe fittings from the fuel injection pump. Plug the fittings to prevent dirt from entering the system.

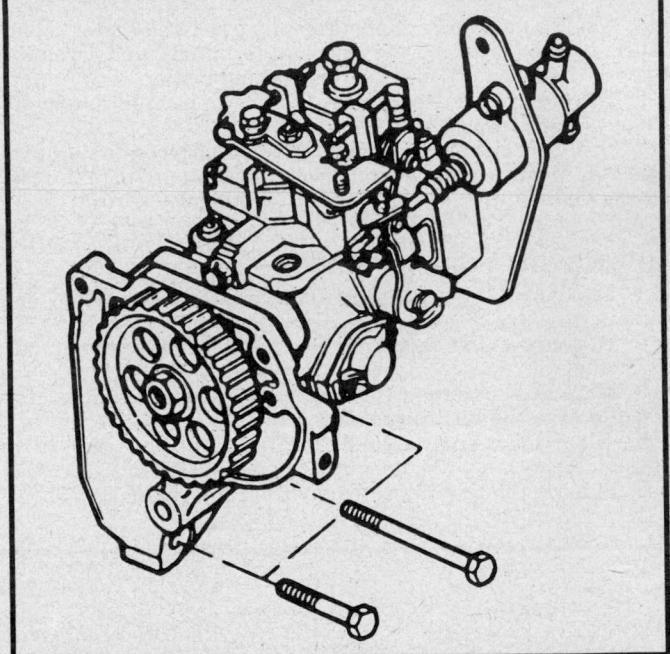

Diesel injection pump

17. Remove the fuel line fittings from the vehicle. Remove all hoses and connectors from the injection pump assembly.
18. Remove the injection pump rear bracket retaining nuts.
19. Remove the plastic shield from under the injection pump.
20. Remove the 3 retaining nuts located at the front of the injection pump. It may be necessary to remove the alternator to get to the bottom nut.
21. Using the sprocket removal tool, separate the injection pump from the sprocket.
22. Remove the removal tool and the sprocket nut. The sprocket holding tool and the timing belt will hold the sprocket in place, facilitating injection pump installation.
23. Remove the injection pump from the mounting brackets.
24. Remove the key from the shaft.
25. Remove the screw plug and copper washer located between the 4 high pressure fuel outlets, at the rear of the pump. Install dial indicator support tool Mot–856, or equivalent, in its place.
26. Install the stem of dial indicator Mot–LM, or equivalent, in the support tool.

To install:

27. Position a locknut and nut on the end of the injection pump driveshaft.
28. Tighten the locknut against the nut.

29. Loosen the control cable set screw on the clevis, move the levers back slightly and turn the clevis pin ¼ turn to disengage the cold start system.

30. Using the locknut, turn the pump driveshaft in the normal direction of rotation, to position the piston at bottom dead center. The dial indicator pointer will stop moving when the piston is at BTDC. Zero the pointer.

31. The pump driveshaft keyway should be located just before the centerline of the number 1 fuel outlet fitting.

32. Remove the nut and locknut.

33. Insert the key in its keyway.

34. Mount the injection pump in the sprocket, aligning the key.

35. Loosely install the washers and retaining nuts on the mounting bracket studs.

36. Install the sprocket washer and retaining nut on the pump driveshaft. Torque the nut to 37 ft. lbs.

37. Remove the sprocket holding tool.

38. Rotate the crankshaft in a clockwise direction at least 2 full revolutions. Check the timing belt tension as follows:

  a. Loosen the timing belt tensioner bolts ½ turn each, maximum.

  b. The belt tensioner should, automatically, place the proper tension on the belt.

  c. Using belt tension gauge ELE 346-04 or equivalent, at the straight, upper run, between the pump and camshaft sprockets, check belt deflection. Deflection should be 3-5mm when the gauge shoulder is flush with the plunger body.

39. Remove the threaded plug from the block, just behind the pump, and insert TDC rod Mot-861, or equivalent.

40. Slowly rotate the crankshaft clockwise until tool Mot-861 can be inserted into the TDC slot in the crankshaft counterweight.

41. At this point, the dial indicator pointer should indicate a piston travel distance of 0.82mm ± 0.02mm.

42. If the indicated travel is not within specifications, adjust it as follows:

  a. Rotate the pump toward, then away from the engine to increase travel, or

  b. Rotate the pump away from the engine to decrease lift.

NOTE: Adjustment should always be made by rotation away from the engine.

43. Tighten the injection pump mounting nuts.

44. Remove the TDC rod from the counterweight slot.

45. Observe the dial indicator and rotate the crankshaft clockwise 2 full revolutions until the rod can, once again, be installed into the counterweight hole. The dial indicator should return to 0, then move to 0.82mm ± 0.02mm. If so, injection pump static timing is correct.

46. Remove the TDC rod and install the plug.

47. Remove the dial indicator and install the washer and screw plug in the pump.

48. Connect the high pressure lines at the injectors.

49. Compress the timing control lever and install the clevis pin in the first position on the cable clamp.

50. With the lever against the clevis, tighten the setscrew.

51. Install and tighten the pump rear support bracket nuts.

52. Install all other parts in reverse order of removal.

NOTE: Don't mix the fuel delivery and return hose banjo bolts. The delivery banjo bolt has two 4mm diameter holes; the return banjo bolt has a calibrated orifice.

Idle Speed Adjustment

1. The idle speed is adjusted on the injection pump linkage.

2. Loosen the screw locknut, adjust the idle speed to 800 ± 50 rpm with the adjusting screw and tighten the locknut.

Diesel Injection Timing

Adjustment

1. Remove the injection pump.

2. Remove the key from the shaft.

3. Remove the screw plug and copper washer located between the 4 high pressure fuel outlets, at the rear of the pump. Install dial indicator support tool Mot-856, or equivalent in its place.

4. Install the stem of dial indicator Mot-LM, or equivalent in the support tool.

5. Position a locknut and nut on the end of the injection pump driveshaft.

6. Tighten the locknut against the nut.

7. Loosen the control cable set screw on the clevis, move the levers back slightly and turn the clevis pin ¼ turn to disengage the cold start system.

8. Using the locknut, turn the pump driveshaft in the normal direction of rotation, to position the piston at bottom dead center. The dial indicator pointer will stop moving when the piston is at BTDC. Zero the pointer.

9. The pump driveshaft keyway should be located just before the centerline of the number 1 fuel outlet fitting.

10. Remove the nut and locknut.

11. Insert the key in its keyway.

12. Mount the injection pump in the sprocket, aligning the key.

13. Loosely install the washers and retaining nuts on the mounting bracket studs.

14. Install the sprocket washer and retaining nut on the pump driveshaft. Torque the nut to 37 ft. lbs.

15. Remove the sprocket holding tool.

16. Rotate the crankshaft in a clockwise direction at least 2 full revolutions. Check the timing belt tension as follows:

  a. Loosen the timing belt tensioner bolts ½ turn each, maximum.

  b. The belt tensioner should, automatically, place the proper tension on the belt.

  c. Using a belt tension gauge, at the straight, upper run, between the pump and camshaft sprockets, check belt deflection. Deflection should be 3-5mm when the gauge shoulder is flush with the plunger body.

17. Remove the threaded plug from the block, just behind the pump, and insert TDC rod Mot-861, or equivalent.

18. Slowly rotate the crankshaft clockwise until tool Mot-861, or equivalent can be inserted into the TDC slot in the crankshaft counterweight.

19. At this point, the dial indicator pointer should indicate a piston travel distance of 0.82mm ± 0.02mm.

20. If the indicated travel is not within specifications, adjust it as follows:

  a. Rotate the pump toward, then away from the engine to increase travel, or

  b. Rotate the pump away from the engine to decrease lift.

NOTE: Adjustment should always be made by rotation away from the engine.

21. Tighten the injection pump mounting nuts.

22. Remove the TDC rod from the counterweight slot.

23. Observe the dial indicator and rotate the crankshaft clockwise 2 full revolutions until the rod can, once again, be installed into the counterweight hole. The dial indicator should return to 0, then move to 0.82mm ± 0.02mm. If so, injection pump static timing is correct.

24. Remove the TDC Rod and install the plug.

25. Remove the dial indicator and install the washer and screw plug in the pump.

26. Connect the high pressure lines at the injectors.

27. Compress the timing control lever and install the clevis pin in the first position on the cable clamp.

28. With the lever against the clevis, tighten the setscrew.
29. Install and tighten the pump rear support bracket nuts.
30. Install all other parts in reverse order of removal.

NOTE: Don't confuse the fuel delivery and return hose banjo bolts. The delivery banjo bolt has two 4mm diameter holes; the return banjo bolt has a calibrated orifice.

Fuel Injector

Removal and Installation

1. Disconnect the negative battery cable.
2. Remove the fuel return hoses and fittings from the injectors.

3. Remove the high pressure lines from the injectors.
4. Remove both injector clamp nuts and washers from each injector.
5. Remove the injector clamp.
6. Pull the injector from the head.
7. Remove the copper seal and the heat shield.

To install:

8. Clean the injector bore with a brass brush.
9. Install a new heat shield and a new copper seal.
10. Install the injector, high pressure fuel lines (finger tight at this time), clamps, washers and nuts.
11. Tighten the high pressure fuel lines.
12. Use new washers and install the fuel return lines. Tighten the fittings to 88 inch lbs.

EMISSION CONTROLS

Please refer to "Professional Emission Component Application Guide".

Emission Warning Lamps

The emission maintenance reminder light is connected to a timer, which will activate the light when PCV valve and oxygen sensor service is required. The interval for this light is 82,500 miles at hich time the timer module must be replaced as part of the emission service. There is no way to reset this lamp, except to replace the timer module.

The timer module is located under the instrument panel, above the parking brake assembly.

GASOLINE ENGINE MECHANICAL

NOTE: Disconnecting the battery cable on some vehicles may interfere with the functions of the on board computer systems and may require the computer to undergo a relearning process, once the negative battery cable is disconnected.

Engine

Removal and Installation

2.5L ENGINE

1. Disconnect the negative battery cable. As required, relieve the fuel system pressure.
2. Matchmark the hood and hinges, and remove the hood.
3. Remove the air cleaner. Drain the coolant and engine oil.
4. Remove the radiator hoses. Remove the fan shroud and transmission cooler lines.
5. Discharge the refrigerant. Remove the condenser and radiator.
6. Remove the fan and install a $5/16$ in. × ½ in. bolt through the pulley and into the water pump flange to maintain pulley alignment.
7. Disconnect the heater hoses.
8. Disconnect and tag all wires, hoses, and cables connected to the engine.

9. Remove the service ports from the air conditioning compressor and cap the openings.
10. Drain the power steering reservoir. Remove the power steering hoses at the gear.
11. Remove the check valve from the power brake vacuum hose.
12. Raise and safely support the vehicle.
13. Remove the starter. Disconnect the exhaust pipe at the manifold.
14. Remove the converter access plate, if equipped with an automatic transmission.
15. On vehicles equipped with automatic transmission, matchmark the torque converter and flywheel. Remove the attaching bolts.
16. Remove the upper flywheel housing-to-engine bolts; loosen the lower ones.
17. Lower the vehicle. Connect a suitable engine lift to the engine and remove the weight from the engine.
18. Remove the engine mount bolts. Raise the engine off the mounts.
19. Support the transmission with a floor jack.
20. Remove the remaining engine-to-flywheel housing bolts.
21. Move the engine forward to clear the transmission, and lift it from the vehicle.

To install:

22. Lower the engine into the vehicle.

NOTE: Be sure to align the engine with the mounts.

23. On vehicles with a manual trasnmission, engage the transmission input shaft with the clutch splines. Align the flywheel housing bolt holes and install the lower engine-to-transmission bolts finger tight.

24. On vehicles with an automatic transmission, align the torque converter housing and engine. Loosely install the 4 lower transmission-to-engine bolts.

25. Lower the engine onto the mounts. Remove the lifting device.

26. On vehicles equipped with an automatic transmission, install the torque converter-to-flywheel bolts. Torque the bolts to 40 ft. lbs.

27. Install the converter housing access plate.

28. Install the remaining engine-to-flywheel housing bolts. Torque the upper bolts to 27 ft. lbs.; the lower bolts to 43 ft. lbs.

29. Install the engine mount bolts. Torque the bolts to 48 ft. lbs.

30. Connect the exhaust pipe at the manifold. Torque the bolts to 23 ft. lbs.

31. Install the starter. Install the check valve on the power brake vacuum hose.

32. Install the power steering hoses at the gear. Fill the power steering reservoir.

33. Install the service ports on the air conditioning compressor.

34. Connect all wires, hoses, and cables to the engine.

35. Install the fan and pulley. Install the condenser and radiator.

36. Install the fan shroud and transmission cooler lines. Connect the radiator hoses.

37. Fill the cooling system and crankcase to the correct levels.

38. Install the air cleaner. Install the hood.

39. Connect the negative battery cable.

40. Evacuate, charge and leak test the refrigerant system.

2.8L ENGINE

1. Remove the negative battery cable. As required, relieve the fuel system pressure.

2. Remove the air cleaner. Scribe the location of the hood hinges and remove the hood.

3. Drain the cooling system. Remove the upper and lower radiator hoses.

4. Remove the fan shroud. Disconnect the automatic transmission cooler lines, if equipped.

5. Discharge the air conditioning refrigerant. Remove the radiator/condenser assembly.

6. Remove the fan. If equipped with a fan clutch, do not lay the fan on its back or front. This will cause the clutch to leak and be irreversibly damaged.

7. Remove the heater hoses. Disconnect and tag all remaining hoses attached to the engine.

8. Disconnect and tag all electrical leads attached to the engine.

9. Remove the power steering pump.

10. Disconnect the fuel pipe at the pump. Disconnect the refrigerant hoses at the compressor and cap the openings.

11. Raise and safely support the vehicle.

12. Disconnect the exhaust pipe at the converter flange. Remove the flywheel housing access plate.

13. On vehicles equipped with automatic transmission, matchmark the converter-to-flywheel and remove the bolts.

14. Remove the flywheel housing-to-engine bolts. Lower the vehicle.

15. Place a suitable jack under the transmission.

16. Attach a suitable lifting device to the engine lifting eyes. Remove the engine mount bolts and lift the engine from the vehicle.

To install:

17. Lower the engine into position in the vehicle, align the engine mounts while lowering the engine.

18. Install the flywheel housing-to-engine bolts finger tight.

19. Install the engine mount bolts. Torque the through-bolts to 92 ft. lbs.

20. Remove the lifting device and the transmission support.

21. On vehicles equipped with an automatic transmission, install the converter-to-flywheel bolts. Torque the bolts to 25 ft. lbs.

22. Install the flywheel housing access plate. Torque the engine-to-transmission bolts to 40 ft. lbs.

23. Connect the exhaust pipe at the converter flange. Connect the refrigerant hoses at the compressor.

24. Connect the fuel pipe at the pump. Install the power steering pump.

25. Connect all wires attached to the engine. Connect all electrical leads to the engine.

26. Connect all remaining hoses attached to the engine. Install the fan.

27. Install the radiator/condenser assembly. Connect the automatic transmission cooler lines. Install the fan shroud.

28. Install the upper and lower radiator hoses. Fill the cooling system.

29. Install the hood. Install the air cleaner and connect the negative battery cable.

30. Evacuate, charge and leak test the refrigerant system.

4.0L ENGINE

1. Disconnect the battery cables. Matchmark the hood and hinges and remove the hood.

2. Raise and safely support the vehicle. Drain the engine oil. Drain the cooling system. Lower the vehicle. Relieve the fuel system pressure.

3. Remove the battery and remove the air cleaner.

4. Remove the upper and lower radiator hoses.

5. Disconnect and cap the automatic transmission cooler lines, if equipped.

6. Remove the fan shroud and remove the radiator. Remove the electric cooling fan.

7. Disconnect the vacuum harness connector at the intake manifold.

8. Disconnect the electric fan switch. On vehicles with air conditioning, discharge the system, remove the compressor service valves and cap the ports.

9. Remove the radiator or radiator/condenser assembly. Disconnect the accelerator linkage. Disconnect the heater hoses at the engine.

10. Disconnect the cruise control cable, if equipped. Disconnect and tag all wires, hoses, cables, vacuum lines, etc., connected to the engine or in the way of engine removal.

11. Disconnect the injection system wiring harness at the firewall.

12. Disconnect the quick-connect fuel lines at the fuel rail and return line by squeezing the 2 tabs against the tube. Pull the fuel tube and retainer from the quick-connect fiting.

13. Remove the power brake vacuum check valve from the booster.

14. Disconnect the power steering hoses from the steering gear, drain the pump reservoir, and cap all openings.

15. Raise and safely support the vehicle. Remove the starter and disconnect the exhaust pipe at the support bracket and the manifold.

16. Disconnect the engine speed sensor wiring (2 screws). Remove the exhaust pipe support bracket.

17. On vehicles, equipped with an automatic transmission, remove the inspection cover. Matchmark the torque converter and flex plate. Turning the engine by hand, remove each torque converter-to-flex plate bolt.

18. Remove the upper flywheel housing-to-engine bolts and loosen the bottom bolts.

19. Remove the engine front support-to-frame nuts and lower the vehicle.

20. Take up the weight of the engine with a suitable lifting device. Support the transmission with a suitable jack.

21. Remove the lower engine-to-bellhousing bolts. Raise the engine, while guiding it forward and out of the vehicle.

To install:

22. Lower the engine into the vehicle.

NOTE: Be very careful to avoid damaging the trigger wheel on the flywheel on vehicles equipped with an automatic transmission.

23. On vehicles with a manual transmission, insert the input shaft into the clutch splines, align the flywheel housing with the engine and install the lower bolts finger tight.

24. On vehicles with an automatic transmission, align the engine and converter housing and install the 4 lower bolts finger tight.

25. Install the engine mount bolts finger tight.

26. Remove the transmission support and the engine lifting device.

27. Install the remaining flywheel housing-to-engine bolts and tighten all bolts to 28 ft. lbs. Raise and safely support the vehicle.

28. On vehicles equipped with an automatic transmission, turn the engine by hand and install each torque converter-to-flex plate bolt. Torque the bolts to 40 ft. lbs. Install the access cover.

29. Remove the exhaust pipe support bracket and connect the exhaust pipe.

30. Connect the engine speed sensor wiring (2 screws). Install the starter.

31. Connect the power steering hoses at the gear and fill the pump reservoir.

32. Install the power brake vacuum check valve at the booster.

33. Connect the quick-connect fuel lines at the fuel rail and return line.

34. Connect the injection system wiring harness at the firewall. Connect all wires, hoses, cables, vacuum lines, etc. Connect the cruise control cable.

35. Connect the accelerator linkage. Install the radiator or radiator/condenser assembly. On vehicles with air conditioning, install the compressor service valves.

36. Install the electric cooling fan and connect the electric fan switch.

37. Connect the vacuum harness connector at the intake manifold. Install the fan shroud.

38. Connect the automatic transmission cooler lines. Install the upper and lower radiator hoses. Install the air cleaner and the battery.

39. Refill the cooling system and the crankcase. Install the hood.

40. Evacuate, charge and leak test the refrigerant system.

4.2L ENGINE

1. Disconnect the negative battery cable. As required, relieve the fuel system pressure. Remove the air cleaner. Drain the cooling system and the engine oil.

2. Disconnect the upper and lower radiator hoses.

3. If equipped with an automatic transmission, disconnect the cooler lines from the radiator. Remove the radiator and the fan. If equipped with air onditioning, evacuate the system, remove the condenser and cap all openings immediately.

4. If so equipped, remove the power steering pump and the drive belt, and place the unit aside. Do not remove the power steering hoses.

5. If the vehicle has air conditioning, remove the compressor. Disconnect all wires, lines, linkage, and hoses that are connected to the engine. Remove the oil filter.

6. Remove both of the engine front support cushion-to-frame retaining nuts.

7. Disconnect the exhaust pipe at the support bracket and exhaust manifold.

8. Support the weight of the engine with a lifting device.

9. Remove the front support cushion and bracket assemblies from the engine.

10. Remove the transfer case shift lever boot and the transmission access cover.

11. If equipped with an automatic transmission, remove the upper bolts securing the transmission bell housing to the engine. If equipped with a manual transmission, remove the upper bolts that secure the clutch housing to the engine.

12. Remove the starter motor. If the vehicle is equipped with an automatic transmission:

   a. Remove the engine to transmission adapter plate inspection covers.

   b. Mark the assembled position of the converter and flex plate and remove the converter-to-flex plate retaining screws.

   c. Remove the remaining bolts securing the transmission bell housing to the engine.

13. If equipped with a manual transmission, remove the lower cover of the clutch housing and the remaining bolts that secure the clutch housing to the engine.

14. Support the transmission with a floor jack.

15. Attach a suitable lifting device to the engine and using a hoist, lift the engine upward and forward at the same time, removing it from the vehicle.

To install:

16. Lower the engine into the vehicle and slide it rearward to engage the transmission.

17. If equipped with an automatic transmission, install the upper bolts securing the transmission bell housing to the engine. Torque to 27 ft. lbs. If equipped with a manual transmission, install the upper bolts that secure the clutch housing to the engine. Torque to 27 ft. lbs.

18. If equipped with a manual transmission, install the lower cover of the clutch housing and the remaining bolts that secure the clutch housing to the engine. Torque the clutch housing spacer-to-bolts to 12–15 ft. lbs. Torque the clutch housing lower bolts to 43 ft. lbs.

19. If the vehicle is equipped with an automatic transmission:

   a. Install the remaining bolts securing the transmission bell housing to the engine. Torque the bell housing lower bolts to 43 ft. lbs.

   b. Mark the assembled position of the converter and flex plate and install the converter-to-flex plate retaining screws. Torque the bolts to 20–25 ft. lbs.

   c. Install the engine to transmission adapter plate inspection covers.

20. Install the starter motor. Torque the mounting bolts to 18 ft. lbs.

21. Install the transfer case shift lever boot and the transmission access cover.

22. Install the front support cushion and bracket assemblies from the engine.

23. Remove the lifting device.

24. Connect the exhaust pipe at the support bracket and exhaust manifold. Torque the nuts to 20 ft. lbs.

25. Install both of the engine front support cushion-to-frame retaining nuts. Torque to 35 ft. lbs.

26. Connect all wires, lines, linkage, and hoses that are connected to the engine. Install the oil filter.

27. If so equipped, install the power steering pump and the drive belt.

28. Install the radiator and the fan, and the condenser. Evacuate, charge and leak test the refrigerant system.

29. If equipped with an automatic transmission, connect the cooler lines to the radiator.

30. Connect the upper and lower radiator hoses and fill the cooling system.

31. Install the air cleaner. Connect the negative battery cable.

5.9L ENGINE

1. Disconnect the negative battery cable. Remove the air cleaner.

2. Drain the cooling system.

3. Disconnect the upper and lower radiator hoses.

4. If equipped with an automatic transmission, disconnect the cooler lines from the radiator.

5. Remove the radiator and the fan. If equipped with air conditioning, evacuate the system, remove the condenser and cap all openings immediately.

6. If so equipped, remove the power steering pump and the drive belt, place the unit aside. Do not remove the power steering hoses.

7. If the vehicle has air conditioning, remove the compressor.

8. Disconnect all wires, lines, linkage, and hoses that are connected to the engine. Rasie and safely support the vehicle.

9. Remove both of the engine front support cushion-to-frame retaining nuts.

10. Disconnect the exhaust pipes at the support bracket and exhaust manifold.

11. Support the weight of the engine with a lifting device.

12. Remove the front support cushion and bracket assemblies from the engine.

13. Remove the transfer case shift lever boot and the transmission access cover.

14. If equipped with an automatic transmission, remove the upper bolts securing the transmission bell housing to the engine. If equipped with a manual transmission, remove the upper bolts that secure the clutch housing to the engine.

15. Remove the starter motor.

16. If the vehicle is equipped with an automatic transmission:

   a. Remove the engine to transmission adapter plate inspection covers.

   b. Mark the assembled position of the converter and flex plate and remove the converter-to-flex plate retaining screws.

   c. Remove the remaining bolts securing the transmission bell housing to the engine.

17. If equipped with a manual transmission, remove the lower cover of the clutch housing and the remaining bolts that secure the clutch housing to the engine. Lower the vehicle.

18. Support the transmission with a suitable jack.

19. Attach a suitable lifting device to the engine and lift the engine upward and forward at the same time, removing it from the vehicle.

To install:

20. Lower the engine into the vehicle and slide it rearward to engage the transmission.

21. If equipped with an automatic transmission, install the upper bolts securing the transmission bell housing to the engine. Torque them to 27 ft. lbs. If equipped with a manual transmission, install the upper bolts that secure the clutch housing to the engine. Torque them to 27 ft. lbs.

22. If equipped with a manual transmission, install the lower cover of the clutch housing and the remaining bolts that secure the clutch housing to the engine. Torque the clutch housing spacer-to-bolts to 12–15 ft. lbs. Torque the clutch housing lower bolts to 43 ft. lbs.

23. If the vehicle is equipped with an automatic transmission:

   a. Install the remaining bolts securing the transmission bell housing to the engine. Torque the bell housing lower bolts to 43 ft. lbs.

   b. Mark the assembled position of the converter and flex plate and install the converter-to-flex plate retaining screws. Torque the bolts to 20–25 ft. lbs.

   c. Install the engine to transmission adapter plate inspection covers.

24. Install the starter motor. Torque the mounting bolts to 18 ft. lbs.

25. Install the transfer case shift lever boot and the transmission access cover.

26. Install the front support cushion and bracket assemblies from the engine.

27. Remove the lifting device.

28. Connect the exhaust pipes at the support bracket and exhaust manifold. Torque the nuts to 20 ft. lbs.

29. Install both of the engine front support cushion-to-frame retaining nuts. Torque them to 35 ft. lbs.

30. Connect all wires, lines, linkage, and hoses to the engine.

31. If so equipped, install the power steering pump and the drive belt.

NOTE: If the vehicle has air conditioning, mount and connect the air conditioning compressor.

32. Install the radiator, fan and the condenser.

33. Evacuate, charge and leak test the refrigerant system.

34. If equipped with an automatic transmission, connect the cooler lines to the radiator.

35. Connect the upper and lower radiator hoses.

36. Fill the cooling system and connect the negative battery cable.

37. Install the air cleaner.

Cylinder Head

Removal and Installation

2.5L ENGINE

1. Disconnect the negative battery cable. As required, relieve the fuel system pressure.

2. Drain the cooling system.

3. Disconnect the hoses at the thermostat housing.

4. Remove the air cleaner.

5. Remove the rocker arm cover. The cover seal is RTV sealer. Break the seal with a clean putty knife or razor blade. Don't attempt to remove the cover until the seal is broken. To remove the cover, pry where indicated at the bolt holes.

6. Remove the rocker arms and the pushrods. Keep them in their original order for installation.

7. Remove the power steering pump bracket. Suspend the pump out of the way.

8. Remove the intake and exhaust manifolds.

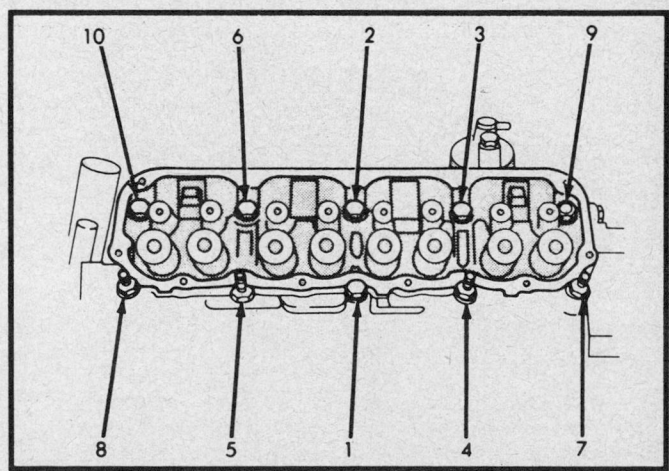

Cylinder head bolt torque sequence—2.5L engine

9. Remove the air conditioning compressor drive belt, if equipped.

10. Loosen the alternator drive belt. Remove the compressor/alternator bracket mounting bolt and unbolt the compressor. Suspend it out of the way without disconnecting the refrigerant lines.

11. Remove the spark plugs. Disconnect the temperature sending unit wire.

12. Remove the cylinder head bolts in the reverse order of the installation torque sequence.

13. Lift the head off the engine and remove the head gasket.

14. Thoroughly clean the gasket mating surfaces. Remove all traces of old gasket material. Remove all carbon deposits from the combustion chambers. Lay a straightedge across the head and check for flatness. Total deviation should not exceed 0.025mm.

To install:

15. Install the head gasket. Apply sealer to both sides of the new gasket. Place the head on the engine.

16. For carbureted engines, using the correct torque sequence, coat No.8 head bolt threads with Permatex No.2 sealant. Install the head bolts. Torque all the head bolts in sequence, in 3 even steps. The final step should be 110 ft. lbs. for all bolts except No. 8. That bolt is torqued to 100 ft. lbs.

17. Connect the temperature sending unit wire. Install the spark plugs.

18. Install the compressor/alternator bracket mounting bolt.

19. Install the accessory drive belt. Install the intake and exhaust manifolds. Install the power steering pump bracket.

20. Install the pushrods and rocker arms in their original positions.

21. Install the rocker arm cover. The cover gasket is RTV sealer. Thoroughly clean the mating surfaces of the head and rocker cover. Run a 1/8 in. bead of RTV sealer along the length of the sealing surface of the head. Position the cover on the head within 10 minutes of applying the sealer. Torque the cover bolts, in a crisscross pattern, to 55 inch lbs.

22. Install the air cleaner. Connect the hoses at the thermostat housing.

23. Fill the cooling system. Connect the negative battery cable.

24. Run the engine to normal operating temperature and check for leaks.

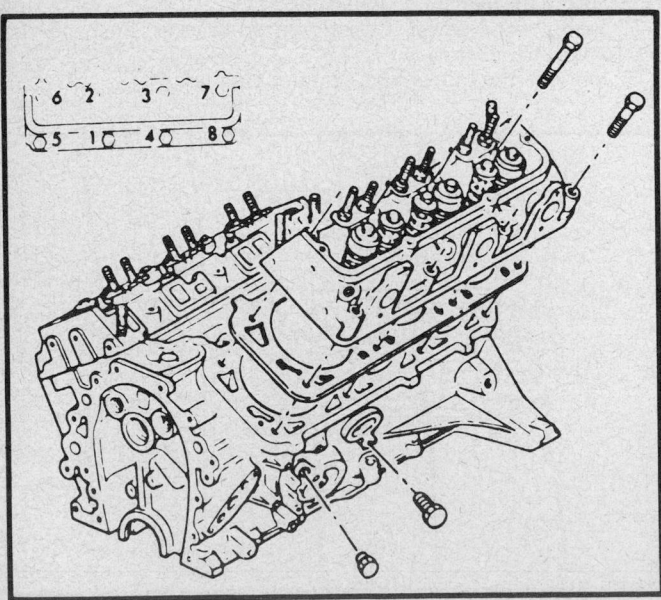

Cylinder head bolt torque sequence—2.8L engine

2.8L ENGINE

Left Side

1. Disconnect the negative battery cable. Raise and support the vehicle safely. Disconnect the exhaust pipe from the exhaust manifold.

2. Drain the coolant from the block and lower the vehicle.

3. Remove the intake manifold. Remove the exhaust manifold.

4. If equipped, remove the power steering pump and bracket. Remove the dipstick tube from the cylinder head.

5. Remove the rocker arm cover bolts and remove the cover. Loosen the rocker arm bolts and remove the pushrods. Keep the pushrods in the same order as removed.

6. Remove the cylinder head bolts in stages and in the reverse order of the tightening sequence.

7. Remove the cylinder head. Do not pry on the head to loosen it.

To install:

8. Thoroughly clean the head and block mating surfaces. All bolt holes must be free of foreign material.

9. Place a new head gasket on the block with the words "This Side Up", facing up.

10. Position the cylinder head on the block.

11. Coat the cylinder head bolts with RTV silicone sealant and install them. Torque the bolts, in sequence, to the correct torque in 3 equal stages.

12. Install the pushrods and rocker arms, keeping them in the same order as removed.

13. Install the dipstick tube. Install the power steering pump and bracket.

14. Install the exhaust manifold. Install the intake manifold.

15. Connect the exhaust pipe from the exhaust manifold.

16. Fill the cooling system. Connect the negative battery cable.

17. Run the engine to normal operating temperature and check for leaks.

Right Side

1. Disconnect the negative battery cable. Raise and support the vehicle safely. Drain the coolant from the block.

2. Disconnect the exhaust pipe and lower the vehicle.

3. If equipped, remove the cruise control servo bracket.

4. Remove the alternator and air pump bracket assembly.

5. Remove the intake manifold. Remove the rocker arm cover.

6. Loosen the rocker arm nuts and remove the pushrods. Keep the pushrods in the order in which they were removed.

7. Remove the cylinder head bolts in stages and in the reverse order of the tightening sequence.

8. Remove the cylinder head. Do not pry on the cylinder head to loosen it.

To install:

9. Thoroughly clean the head and block mating surfaces. All bolt holes must be free of foreign material.

10. Place a new head gasket on the block with the words "This Side Up", facing up.

11. Position the cylinder head on the block.

12. Coat the cylinder head bolts with RTV silicone sealant and install them. Torque the bolts, in sequence, to the correct torque.

13. Install the pushrods, keeping them in the same order as removed.

14. Install the rocker arms and the rocker arm cover.

15. Install the exhaust manifold. Install the intake manifold.

16. Connect the exhaust pipe from the exhaust manifold.

17. Fill the cooling system.

19. Connect the negative battery cable.

20. Run the engine to normal operating temperature and check for leaks.

4.0L AND 4.2L ENGINE

1. Disconnect the negative battery cable. Drain the cooling system and disconnect the hoses at the thermostat housing. As required, relieve the fuel system pressure.

2. Remove the cylinder head cover (valve cover), the gasket, the rocker arm assembly, and the pushrods.

NOTE: The pushrods must be replaced in their original positions.

3. Remove the intake and exhaust manifold from the cylinder head.

4. Disconnect the spark plug wires and the spark plugs to avoid damaging them.

5. Disconnect the temperature sending unit wire, ignition coil and bracket assembly from the engine.

6. Unbolt and set aside the power steering pump and bracket. Do not disconnect the hoses.

7. Remove the intake and exhaust manifold assembly.

8. Remove the air conditioning compressor drive belt pulley.

9. Loosen the serpentine belt tension.

10. Remove the alternator.

11. Unbolt the air conditioning compressor and set it aside. Don't disconnect the refrigerant lines.

12. Remove the ignition coil.

13. Remove the cylinder head bolts, the cylinder head and gasket from the block.

14. Discard the gasket. Thoroughly clean the head and block mating surfaces. Check them for warpage with a straightedge. Deviation should not exceed 0.002 in. in a 6 in. span.

To install:

15. Coat a new head gasket with sealer and place it on the block. Most replacement gaskets will have the word **TOP** stamped on them.

16. Install the cylinder head and bolts. The threads of bolt No. 11 must be coated with Loctite® 592 sealant before installation. Tighten the bolts in sequence, using the correct sequence, to 22 ft. lbs. Then, torque them to 45 ft. lbs. in sequence. When complete, check the torque at 45 ft. lbs. on all bolts in sequence. Then, torque all the bolts in sequence to 110 ft. lbs., except for No. 11, which is torqued to 100 ft. lbs.

17. Install the ignition coil.

18. Install the air conditioning compressor. Install the alternator.

19. Adjust the serpentine belt tension.

20. Install the air conditioning compressor drive belt pulley.

21. Install the intake and exhaust manifold assembly.

22. Install the power steering pump and bracket.

23. Connect the temperature sending unit wire, ignition coil and bracket.

24. Connect the spark plug wires.

25. Install the pushrods, rocker arm assembly, gasket, and cylinder head cover.

26. Connect the hoses at the thermostat housing.

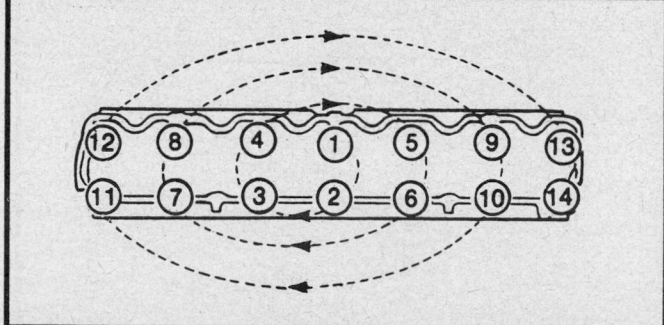

Cylinder head bolt torque sequence—4.0L and 4.2L engines

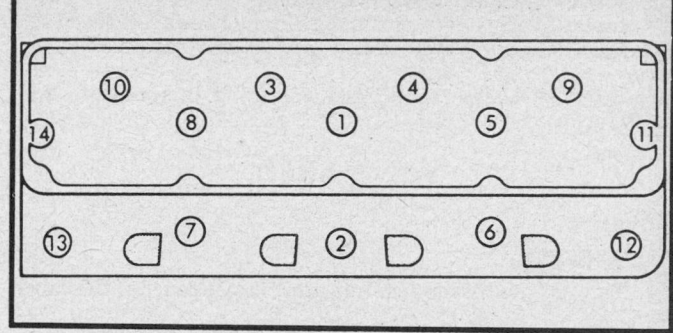

Cylinder head bolt torque sequence—5.9L engine

27. Fill the cooling system. Connect the negative battery cable.

28. Run the engine to normal operating temperature and check for leaks.

5.9L ENGINE

1. Disconnect the negative battery cable. Drain the cooling system.

2. When removing the right cylinder head, it may be necessary to remove the heater core housing from the firewall.

3. Remove the valve cover(s) and gasket(s).

4. Remove the rocker arm assemblies and the pushrods.

NOTE: The valve train components must be replaced in their original positions.

5. Remove the spark plugs to avoid damaging them.

6. Remove the intake manifold with the carburetor still attached.

7. Remove the exhaust pipes at the flange of the exhaust manifold. When replacing the exhaust pipes it is advisable to install new gaskets at the flange.

8. Loosen the accessory drive belts.

9. Disconnect the alternator bracket from the right cylinder head.

10. Disconnect the air pump and power steering pump brackets from the left cylinder head.

11. Remove the cylinder head bolts and lift the head(s) from the cylinder block.

12. Remove the cylinder head gasket from the head or the block.

13. Thoroughly clean the gasket mating surfaces. Remove all traces of old gasket material. Remove all carbon deposits from the combustion chambers. Lay a straightedge across the head and check for flatness. Total deviation should not exceed 0.001 in. (0.025mm).

To install:

14. Do not apply sealant to the head or block. Coat both sides of the gasket with sealer. The gasket should be stamped **TOP** for installation. Place the gasket on the block.

15. Install the head on the block. Insert the bolts and tighten, in sequence, to the proper torque.

16. Connect the air pump and power steering pump brackets to the left cylinder head.

17. Connect the alternator bracket to the right cylinder head.

18. Adjust all the accessory drive belts.

19. Install the exhaust pipes at the flange of the exhaust manifold. When replacing the exhaust pipes it is advisable to install new gaskets at the flange.

20. Install the intake manifold with the carburetor still attached.

21. Install the spark plugs.

22. Install the rocker arm assemblies and the pushrods.

NOTE: The valve train components must be replaced in their original positions.

23. Install the valve cover(s) and gasket(s).
24. Install the heater core housing on the firewall, if removed.
25. Fill the cooling system and connect the negative battery cable.
26. Run the engine to normal operating temperature and check for leaks.

Valve Lash

Adjustment

2.8L ENGINE

1. Tighten the rocker arm nut until it just touches the valve stem.
2. Rotate the engine until number one piston is at TDC of the compression stroke. The 0 on the timing scale should be aligned with the timing pointer and the rotor should be at the number one spark plug tower of the distributor cap.3. The following valves can now be adjusted:
   Exhaust valves—1–2–3
   Intake valves—1–5–6
4. Turn the adjusting nut until it backs off the stem slightly, then tighten until it just touches the stem. Then turn the nut 1½ turns more to center the tappet plunger.
5. Rotate the engine 1 complete revolution more. This will bring No. 4 piston to TDC on the compression stroke. At this point the following valves should be adjusted:
   Exhaust valves—4–5–6
   Intake valves—2–3–4

Rocker Arms and Shafts

Removal and Installation

2.5L, 4.0L AND 4.2L ENGINES

1. Disconnect the negative battery cable. As required, relieve the fuel system pressure. Remove the valve cover.
2. Remove the 2 capscrews at each bridge and pivot assembly.
3. Remove the bridges, pivots and rocker arms. Keep them in order as they must be installed in the same position as they were removed.

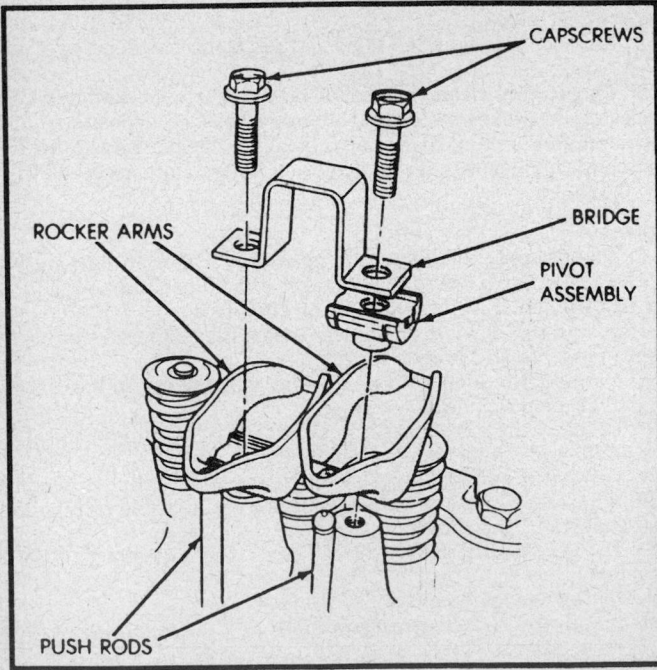

Typical rocker arm assembly

4. Installation is the reverse of the removal procedure. Torque the capscrews to 19 ft. lbs. Be sure to use new gaskets or RTV sealant as required.

2.8L ENGINE

1. Disconnect the negative battery cable. Remove the valve cover and gasket. Remove the rocker arm nut and ball.
2. Lift the rocker arm off the rocker arm stud, always keep the rocker arm, nut and ball together and always assemble them on the same stud.
3. Remove the pushrod from its bore. Make sure the pushrods are always installed in the same bore with the same end in the block.
4. Installation is the reverse of the removal procedure. As required, adjust the valves. Torque the rocker arm nut to 20 ft. lbs.

5.9L ENGINE

1. Disconnect the negative battery cable. Remove the valve cover and gasket.
2. Loosen the bridged pivot capscrews a turn at a time, so as not to break the bridge.
3. Remove the rocker arm and bridge assembly from the cylinder head. Keep these components in order and reinstall them in the same position as removed.
4. Installation is the reverse of the removal procedure. Torque the capscrews to 19 ft. lbs.

Intake Manifold

Removal and Installation

2.5L ENGINE

NOTE: It may be necessary to remove the carburetor or the throttle body from the intake manifold before the manifold is removed.

1. Disconnect the negative battery cable. As required, relieve the fuel system pressure. Drain the coolant.
2. Remove the air cleaner. Disconnect the fuel pipe. Remove the carburetor or the throttle body, as required.
3. Disconnect the coolant hoses from the intake manifold.
4. Disconnect the throttle cable from the bellcrank.
5. Disconnect the PCV valve vacuum hose from the intake manifold.
6. If equipped, remove the vacuum advance CTO valve vacuum hoses.
7. Disconnect the system coolant temperature sender wire connector (located on the intake manifold). Disconnect the air temperature sensor wire, if equipped.
8. Disconnect the vacuum hose from the EGR valve.
9. On vehicles equipped with power steering remove the power steering pump and its mounting bracket. Do not detach the power steering pump hoses.

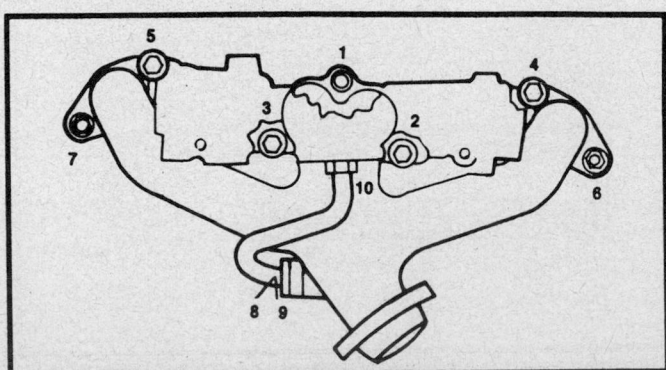

Intake manifold bolt torque sequence—2.5L engine

10. Disconnect the intake manifold electric heater wire connector, as required.

11. Disconnect the throttle valve linkage, if equipped with automatic transmission.

12. Disconnect the EGR valve tube from the intake manifold.

13. Remove the intake manifold attaching screws, nuts and clamps. Remove the intake manifold. Discard the gasket.

14. Clean the mating surfaces of the manifold and cylinder head.

NOTE: If the manifold is being replaced, ensure all fittings, etc., are transferred to the replacement manifold.

To install:

15. Clean the mating surfaces of the manifold and cylinder head.

16. Install the intake manifold, with a new gasket. Install the intake manifold attaching screws, nuts and clamps. Torque the nuts to 23 ft. lbs.

17. Connect the EGR valve tube. Connect the throttle valve linkage, if equipped with automatic transmission.

18. Connect the intake manifold electric heater wire connector, as required.

19. On vehicles equipped with power steering install the power steering pump and its mounting bracket.

20. Connect the vacuum hose to the EGR valve. Connect the system coolant temperature sender wire connector (located on the intake manifold).

21. Connect the air temperature sensor wire, if equipped. If equipped, install the vacuum advance CTO valve vacuum hoses.

22. Connect the PCV valve vacuum hose at the intake manifold. Connect the throttle cable at the bellcrank.

23. Connect the coolant hoses at the intake manifold.

24. Install the carburetor or the throttle body, as required. Torque the nuts to 14 ft. lbs.

25. Connect the fuel pipe. Install the air cleaner.

26. Connect the negative battery cable.

27. Fill the cooling system.

2.8L ENGINE

NOTE: It may be necessary to remove the carburetor from the intake manifold before the manifold is removed.

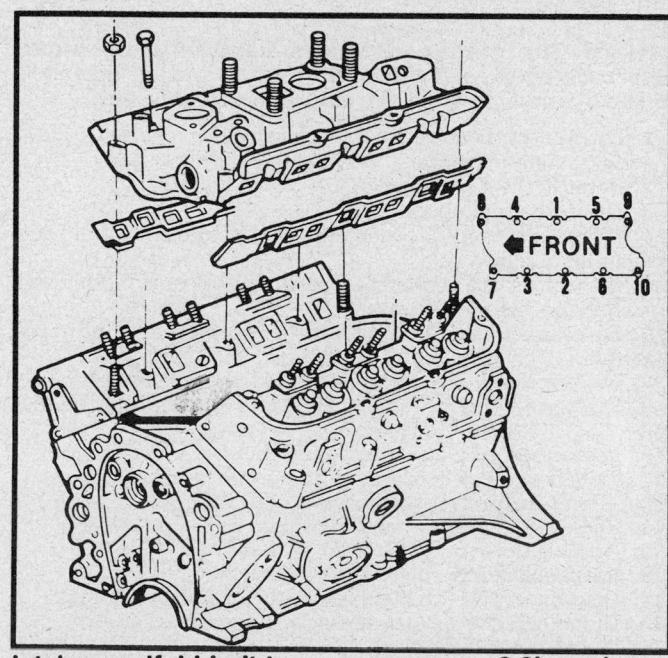

Intake manifold bolt torque sequence—2.8L engine

1. Disconnect the negative battery cable. Drain the radiator.

2. If equipped with air conditioning disconnect the compressor and move it aside. Disconnect the spark plug wires at the spark plugs. Disconnect the wires at the ignition coil.

3. If equipped, remove the air pump and bracket.

4. Remove the distributor cap. Mark the position of the ignition rotor in relation to the distributor body, and remove the distributor. Do not crank the engine with the distributor removed.

5. Remove the EGR valve. Remove the air hose. Disconnect the charcoal canister hoses. Remove the pipe bracket from the left cylinder head, if equipped.

6. Remove the diverter valve. Remove the power brake vacuum hose. Remove the heater and radiator hoses from the intake manifold.

7. Disconnect and label the vacuum hoses. If equipped, remove the EFE pipe from the rear of the manifold. Disconnect the coolant temperature switches.

8. Remove the carburetor linkage. Disconnect and plug the fuel line.

9. Remove the manifold retaining bolts and nuts.

10. Remove the intake manifold. Remove and discard the gaskets, and scrape off the old silicone seal from the front and rear ridges.

To install:

11. The gaskets are marked for right and left side installation; do not interchange them. Clean the sealing surface of the engine block, and apply a 5mm wide bead of silicone sealer to each ridge.

12. Install the new gaskets onto the heads. The gaskets will have to be cut slightly to fit past the center pushrods. Do not cut any more material than necessary. Hold the gaskets in place by extending the ridge bead of sealer ¼ in. onto the gasket ends.

13. Install the intake manifold. The area between the ridges and the manifold should be completely sealed.

14. Install the retaining bolts and nuts, and tighten in sequence to 23 ft. lbs. Do not overtighten the manifold.

15. Complete the installation in the reverse order of the removal procedures. Adjust the ignition timing after installation, and check the coolant level.

5.9L ENGINE

1. Disconnect the negative battery cable. Drain the coolant from the radiator.

2. Remove the air cleaner assembly.

3. Disconnect the spark plug wires. Remove the spark plug wire brackets from the valve covers, and the bypass valve bracket.

4. Disconnect the upper radiator hose and the bypass hose from the intake manifold. Disconnect the heater hose from the rear of the manifold.

5. Disconnect the ignition coil bracket and lay the coil aside.

6. Disconnect the TCS solenoid vacuum valve from the right side valve cover.

7. Disconnect all lines, hoses, linkages and wires from the carburetor and intake manifold and TCS components as required.

8. Disconnect the air delivery hoses at the air distribution manifolds.

9. Disconnect the air pump diverter valve and lay the valve and the bracket assembly, including the hoses, forward of the engine.

10. Remove the intake manifold retaining bolts and remove the intake manifold. Remove and discard the side gaskets and the end seals.

To install:

11. Clean the mating surfaces of the intake manifold and the cylinder head before replacing the intake manifold. Use new gaskets and tighten the bolts to the correct torque.

NOTE: There is no specified tighten sequence for this intake manifold. Start at the center bolts and work outward.

12. Connect the air pump diverter valve.
13. Connect the air delivery hoses at the air distribution manifolds.
14. Connect all lines, hoses, linkages and wires to the carburetor and intake manifold and TCS components as required.
15. Install the TCS solenoid vacuum valve to the right side valve cover.
16. Install the ignition coil bracket.
17. Connect the upper radiator hose and the by-pass hose to the intake manifold. Connect the heater hose to the rear of the manifold.
18. Connect the spark plug wires. Install the spark plug wire brackets on the valve covers, and the bypass valve bracket.
19. Install the air cleaner assembly.
20. Fill the cooling system. Connect the negative battery cable.

Exhaust Manifold

Removal and Installation

2.5L ENGINE

1. Disconnect the negative battery cable. Remove the intake manifold.
2. Disconnect the EGR tube.
3. Disconnect the exhaust pipe at the manifold.
4. Disconnect the oxygen sensor wire.
5. Support the manifold and remove the nuts from the studs.
6. If a new manifold is being installed, transfer the oxygen sensor. Torque the sensor to 35 ft. lbs.
7. Installation is the reverse of removal. Torque the nuts to 23 ft. lbs.

2.8L ENGINE

Left Side

1. Disconnect the negative battery cable. Remove the air cleaner. Remove the carburetor heat stove pipe.
2. Remove the air supply pipes from the exhaust manifold.
3. Raise and support the vehicle safely. Unbolt and remove the exhaust pipe at the manifold.
4. Unbolt and remove the manifold.
5. Clean the mating surfaces of the cylinder head and manifold. Install the manifold onto the head, and install the retaining bolts finger tight.
6. Tighten the manifold bolts in a circular pattern, working from the center to the ends, to 25 ft. lbs. in 2 stages.
7. Connect the exhaust pipe to the manifold.
8. The remainder of installation is the reverse of removal.

Right Side

1. Disconnect the negative battery cable. Raise and support the vehicle safely.
2. Disconnect the exhaust pipe from the exhaust manifold.
3. Lower the vehicle. Remove the spark plug wires from the plugs. Number them first if they are not already labeled. Remove the cruise control servo from the right inner fender panel, if equipped.
4. Remove the air supply pipes from the manifold. Remove the Pulsair bracket bolt from the rocker cover, on models so equipped, then remove the pipe assembly.
5. Remove the manifold retaining bolts and remove the manifold.
6. Clean the mating surfaces of the cylinder head and manifold. Position the manifold against the head and install the retaining bolts finger tight.
7. Tighten the bolts in a circular pattern, working from the center to the ends, to 25 ft. lbs. in 2 stages.

Intake manifold bolt torque sequence—4.0L engine

8. Install the air supply system. Install the spark plug wires. If equipped install the cruise control servo.
9. Raise and support the vehicle safely. Connect the exhaust pipe to the manifold. Lower the vehicle.

5.9L ENGINE

1. Disconnect the negative battery cable. Disconnect the spark plug wires. Disconnect the air delivery hose at the distribution manifold.
2. Remove the air distribution manifold and the injection tubes. Disconnect the exhaust pipe at the manifold.
3. Remove the exhaust manifold retaining bolts along with the spark plug shields. Remove the exhaust manifold from the vehicle.
4. Installation is the reverse of the removal procedure. Be sure to use a new gasket, as required. Torque the bolts to specification.

Combination Manifold

Removal and Installation

4.0L ENGINE

NOTE: The intake and exhaust manifold are mounted externally on the left side of the engine and are attached to the cylinder head. They are removed as a unit.

1. Disconnect the negative battery cable. As required, relieve the fuel system pressure.
2. Remove the air cleaner.
3. Drain the cooling system.
4. Disconnect the EGR tube nuts at the intake manifold and exhaust manifold.
5. Disconnect the accelerator cable, cruise control cable and transmission line pressure cable.
6. Disconnect the vacuum multi-connector at the intake manifold.
7. Disconnect all wiring connectors at the manifold.
8. Disconnect the fuel supply and return lines from the fuel rail.
9. Loosen the serpentine belt tensioner.
10. Unbolt the power steering pump and bracket and set it aside. Don't disconnect the hoses.
11. Remove the fuel rail and injectors.
12. Remove the intake manifold heat shield.
13. Raise and safely support the vehicle.
14. Disconnect the exhaust pipe at the exhaust manifold.
15. Disconnect the oxygen sensor wiring at the sensor.
16. Lower the vehicle.
17. Remove the manifold attaching bolts, nuts and clamps.

18. Separate the intake manifold and exhaust manifold from the engine as an assembly, and discard the gasket.

19. If either manifold is to be replaced, they should be separated.

20. Clean the mating surface of the manifolds and the cylinder head before replacing the manifolds.

To install:

21. If the manifolds were separated, install the EGR tube loosely. Don't tighten it until the manifold assembly is installed.

22. Install a new gasket over the alignment dowels on the head.

23. Position the manifold assemblies and loosely install the bolts. Tighten the bolts in sequence as follows:
   a. No. 1 – 30 ft. lbs.
   b. No. 2 through 11 – 23 ft. lbs.
   c. No. 12 and 13 (EGR tube) – 30 ft. lbs.

24. Connect the oxygen sensor wiring at the sensor.

25. Connect the exhaust pipe at the exhaust manifold.

26. Install the intake manifold heat shield.

27. Install the fuel rail and injectors.

28. Install the power steering pump and bracket.

29. Adjust the serpentine belt tensioner.

30. Connect the fuel supply and return lines at the fuel rail. Use new O-rings at the quick-connect fittings.

31. Connect all wiring connectors at the manifold.

32. Connect the vacuum multi-connector at the intake manifold.

33. Connect the accelerator cable, cruise control cable and transmission line pressure cable.

34. Connect the EGR tube nuts at the intake manifold and exhaust manifold.

35. Drain the cooling system.

36. Install the air cleaner.

37. Connect the negative battery cable.

4.2L ENGINE

1. Disconnect the negative battery cable. Remove the air cleaner and carburetor.

2. Disconnect the accelerator cable from the accelerator bellcrank.

3. Disconnect the PCS vacuum hose from the intake manifold.

4. Disconnect the distributor vacuum hose and electrical wires at the TCS solenoid vacuum valve.

5. Remove the TCS solenoid vacuum valve and bracket from the intake manifold. In some cases it might not be necessary to remove the TCS unit.

6. If so equipped, disconnect the EGR valve vacuum hoses.

7. Remove the power steering mounting bracket and pump and set it aside without disconnecting the hoses.

8. Remove the EGR valve, if so equipped.

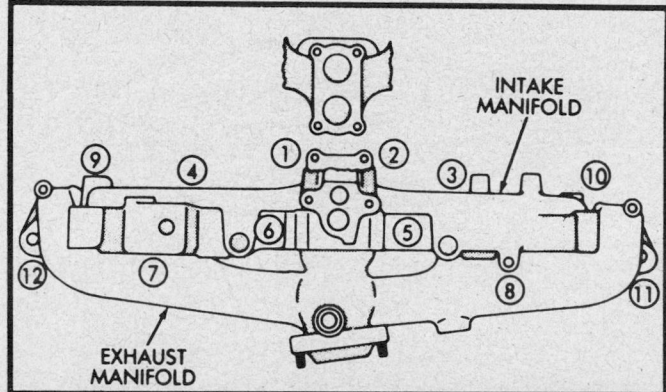

Intake manifold bolt torque sequence – 4.2L engine

9. Disconnect the exhaust pipe from the manifold flange. Disconnect the spark CTO hoses and remove the oxygen sensor.

10. Remove the manifold attaching bolts, nuts and clamps.

11. Separate the intake manifold and exhaust manifold from the engine as an assembly. Discard the gasket.

12. If either manifold is to be replaced, they should be separated at the heat riser area.

To install:

13. Clean the mating surfaces of the manifolds and the cylinder head before replacing the manifolds. Replace them in reverse order of the above procedure with a new gasket. Tighten the bolts and nuts to the specified torque in the proper sequence.

14. Connect the exhaust pipe to the manifold flange. Torque the nuts to 20 ft. lbs. Connect the spark CTO hoses and install the oxygen sensor.

15. Install the EGR valve, if so equipped.

16. Install the power steering mounting bracket and pump.

17. If so equipped, connect the EGR valve vacuum hoses.

18. Install the TCS solenoid vacuum valve and bracket to the intake manifold.

19. Connect the distributor vacuum hose and electrical wires at the TCS solenoid vacuum valve.

20. Connect the PCS vacuum hose to the intake manifold.

21. Connect the accelerator cable to the accelerator bellcrank.

22. Install the air cleaner and carburetor.

Timing Chain Front Cover and Seal

Removal and Installation

2.5L ENGINE

1. Disconnect the negative battery cable. Remove the drive belts and fan shroud.

2. Unscrew the vibration damper bolts and washer.

3. Using a puller, remove the vibration damper.

4. Remove the fan assembly. If the fan is equipped with a fan clutch, the fluid will leak out of the clutch and irreversibly damage the fan, if it is layed flat.

5. Remove the air conditioning compressor/alternator bracket assembly and lay it out of the way. Do not disconnect the refrigerant lines.

6. Unbolt the cover from the block and oil pan. Remove the cover and front seal.

7. Cut off the oil pan side gasket end tabs and oil pan front seal tabs.

8. Clean all gasket mating surfaces thoroughly.

9. Remove the seal from the cover.

To install:

10. Apply sealer to both sides of the new case cover gasket and position it on the block.

11. Cut the end tabs off the new oil pan side gaskets corresponding to those cut off the original gasket and attach the tabs to the oil pan with gasket cement.

12. Coat the front cover seal end tab recesses generously with RTV sealant and position the side seal in the cover.

13. Apply engine oil to the seal-to-pan contact surface.

14. Position the cover on the block.

15. Insert alignment tool J-22248 or equivalent, into the crankshaft opening in the cover.

16. Install the cover bolts. Tighten the cover-to-block bolts to 5 ft. lbs.; the cover-to-pan bolts to 11 ft. lbs.

17. Remove the alignment tool and position the new front seal on the tool with the seal lip facing outward. Apply a light film of sealer to the outside diameter of the seal. Lightly coat the crankshaft with clean engine oil.

18. Position the tool and seal over the end of the crankshaft and insert the draw screw J-9163-2, or equivalent, into the installation tool.

19. Tighten the nut until the tool just contacts the cover.

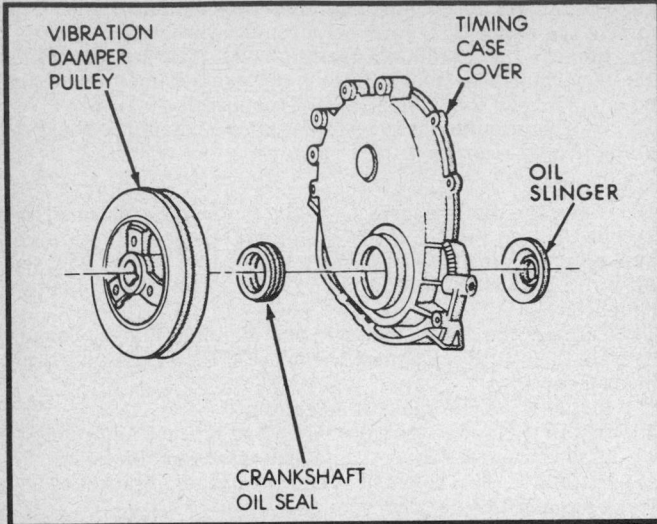

Timing case cover and components

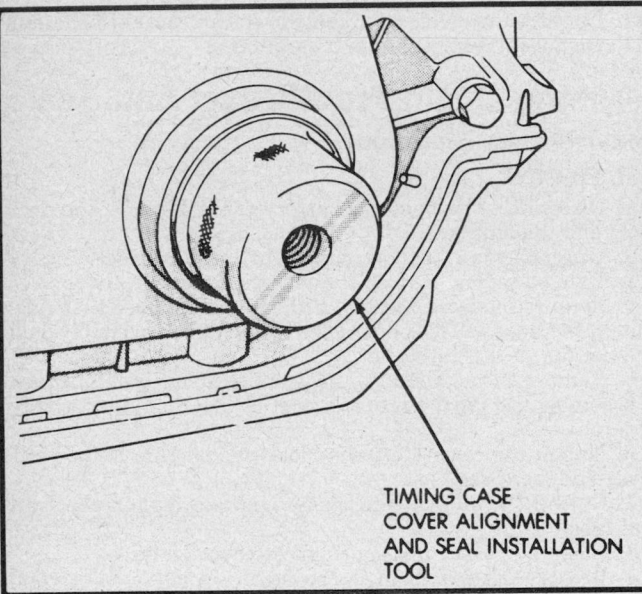

Timing case cover alignment and seal installation

20. Remove the tools and apply a light film of engine oil on the vibration damper hub contact surface of the seal.

21. With the key inserted in the keyway in the crankshaft, install the vibration damper, washer and bolt. Lubricate the bolt and tighten it to 108 ft. lbs.

22. Install the remaining components in the reverse order of removal.

2.8L ENGINE

1. Disconnect the negative battery cable.
2. Remove the drive belts.
3. Remove the fan shroud.
4. Remove the fan and pulley. If the fan is equipped with a fan clutch, the fluid will leak out and the fan clutch will have to be replaced, if the fan is layed flat.
5. Drain the cooling system.
6. Remove the air conditioning compressor and mounting bracket and position them out of the way, leave the refrigerant lines connected.
7. Remove the water pump.

8. Remove the vibration damper retaining bolt and, using a puller, remove the damper.

NOTE: On some vehicles the outer ring (weight) of the harmonic balancer is bonded to the hub with rubber. The balancer must be removed with a puller which acts on the inner hub only. Pulling on the outer portion of the balancer will break the rubber bond or destroy the tuning of the torsional damper.

9. Disconnect the lower radiator hose.
10. Unbolt and remove the cover. Pry out the seal.

To install:

11. Thoroughly remove all traces of gasket material from the mating surfaces.
12. Position a new seal in the cover with the open end of the seal facing outward.
13. Apply a $3/32$ in. bead of RTV silicone gasket material to the mating surfaces of the cover and block. Place the cover on the block and install the bolts. Torque the M8 × 1.25 bolts to 18 ft. lbs.; the M10 × 1.5 bolts to 30 ft. lbs. Tighten the bolts within 5 minutes, as the sealer will begin to set.
14. Install all other parts in reverse order of removal.

NOTE: Breakage may occur if the balancer is hammered back onto the crankshaft. A press or special installation tool is necessary.

4.0L AND 4.2L ENGINES

1. Disconnect the negative battery cable. Remove the drive belts, engine fan and hub assembly, the accessory pulley and vibration damper.
2. Unbolt the air conditioning compressor and bracket and set it aside. Don't disconnect the refrigerant lines.
3. Remove the oil pan to timing chain cover bolts and the bolts that attach the cover to the block.
4. Raise the timing chain cover just high enough to detach the retaining nibs of the oil pan neoprene seal from the bottom side of the cover. This must be done to prevent pulling the seal end tabs away from the tongues of the oil pan gaskets, which would cause a leak.
5. Remove the timing chain cover and gasket from the engine.

To install:

6. Use a razor blade to cut off the oil pan seal end tabs flush with the front face of the cylinder block and remove the seal.

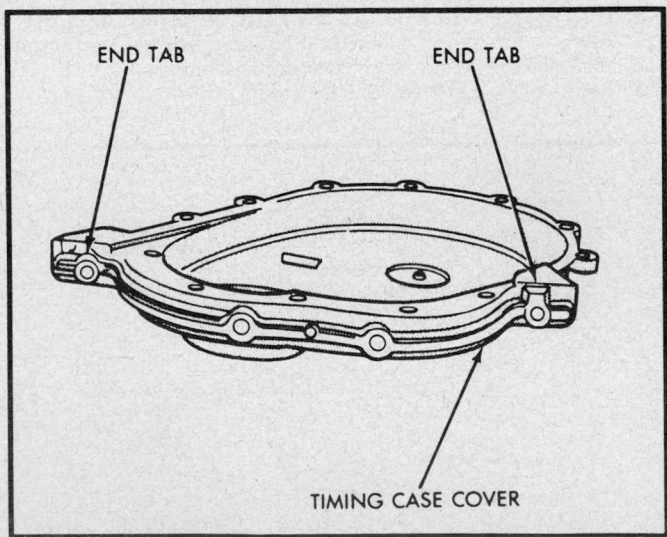

Timing case cover end tabs—4.0L and 4.2L engines

Clean the timing chain cover, oil pan, and cylinder block surfaces.

7. Remove the crankshaft oil seal from the timing chain cover. Thoroughly clean the mating surfaces.

8. Apply RTV gasket material to both sides of the new gasket and position the gasket on the block.

9. Cut the end tabs off of the replacement oil pan side gaskets, corresponding to those cut off of the original gasket. Cement the end tabs to the oil pan.

10. Coat the front cover end tab recesses with a generous amount of RTV gasket sealant and position the seal on the timing case cover. Apply a coat of clean engine oil to the seal-to-pan contact surfaces.

11. Position the case cover on the block.

12. Place cover alignment tool in the crankshaft opening of the cover.

13. Install the cover-to-block bolts and the oil pan-to-cover bolts. Torque the cover-to-block bolts to 62 inch lbs.; the cover-to-pan bolts to 11 ft. lbs.

14. Remove the alignment tool and position the seal on the tool with the lip facing outward.

15. Apply a light coat of sealer on the outside diameter of the seal.

16. Lightly coat the crankshaft with clean engine oil.

17. Position the tool and seal over the end of the crankshaft and insert a screw tool into the seal installation tool.

18. Tighten the nut against the tool until it contacts the cover.

19. Remove the tools and apply a light coating of engine oil on the vibration damper hub contact surface of the seal.

20. Install the damper.

21. Install the remaining components in reverse order of removal.

5.9L ENGINE

1. Disconnect the negative battery cable.

2. Drain the cooling system and disconnect the radiator hoses and bypass hose.

3. Remove all of the drive belts and the fan and spacer assembly.

4. Remove the alternator and the front portion of the alternator bracket as an assembly.

5. Disconnect the heater hose.

6. Remove the power steering pump and/or the air pump, and the mounting bracket as an assembly. Do not disconnect the power steering hoses.

7. Remove the distributor cap and note the position of the rotor. Remove the distributor.

8. Remove the fuel pump.

9. Remove the vibration damper and pulley.

10. Remove the front oil pan bolts and the bolts which secure the timing chain cover to the engine block.

NOTE: The timing gear cover retaining bolts vary in length and must be installed in the same locations from which they were removed.

11. Remove the cover by pulling forward until it is free of the locating dowel pins.

12. Clean the gasket surface of the cover and the engine block.

13. Pry out the original seal from inside the timing chain cover and clean the seal bore.

To install:

14. Drive the new seal into place from the inside with a block of wood until it contacts the outer flange of the cover.

15. Apply a light film of motor oil to the lips of the new seal.

16. Before reinstalling the timing gear cover, remove the lower locating dowel pin from the engine block. The pin is required for correct alignment of the cover and must either be reused or a replacement dowel pin installed after the cover is in position.

17. Cut both sides of the oil pan gasket flush with the engine block with a razor blade.

18. Trim a new gasket to correspond to the amount cut off at the oil pan.

19. Apply sealer to both sides of the new gasket and install the gasket on the timing case cover.

20. Install the new front oil pan seal.

21. Align the tongues of the new oil pan gasket pieces with the oil pan seal and cement them into place on the cover.

22. Apply a bead of sealer to the cutoff edges of the original oil pan gaskets.

23. Place the timing case cover into position and install the front oil pan bolts. Tighten the bolts slowly and evenly until the cover aligns with the upper locating dowel.

24. Install the lower dowel through the cover and drive it into the corresponding hole in the engine block.

25. Install the cover retaining bolts in the same locations from which they were removed. Tighten to 25 ft. lbs.

26. Assemble the remaining components in the reverse order of removal.

Timing Chain and Sprockets

Removal and Installation

2.5L ENGINE

1. Disconnect the negative battery cable. Remove the timing case cover.

2. Rotate the crankshaft so that the timing marks on the cam and crank sprockets align next to each other.

3. Remove the oil slinger from the crankshaft.

4. Remove the cam sprocket retaining bolt and remove the sprocket and chain. The crank sprocket may also be removed at this time. If the tensioner is to be removed, the oil pan must be removed, first.

5. Prior to installation, turn the tensioner lever to the unlock (down) position.

6. Pull the tensioner block toward the tensioner to compress the spring. Hold the block and turn the tensioner lever to the lock (up) position. The camshaft sprocket bolt should be torqued to 50 ft. lbs.

7. Install the sprockets and chain together, as a unit. Make sure the timing marks are aligned.

8. Install the oil pan, slinger and timing cover.

2.8L ENGINE

1. Disconnect the negative battery cable. Remove the timing cover.

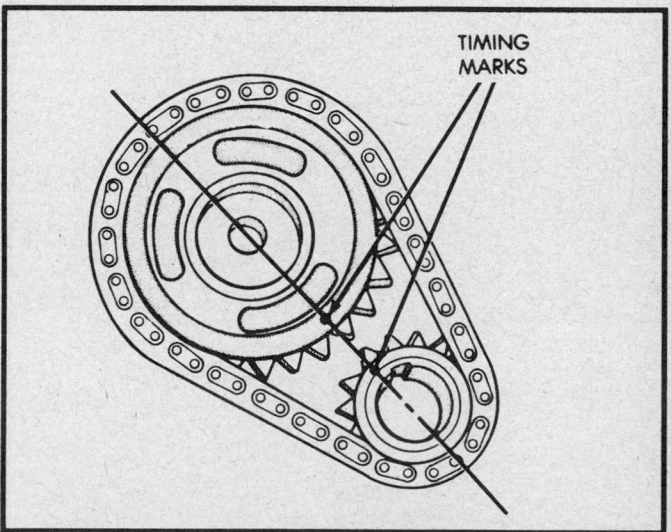

Timing mark alignment—2.5L engine

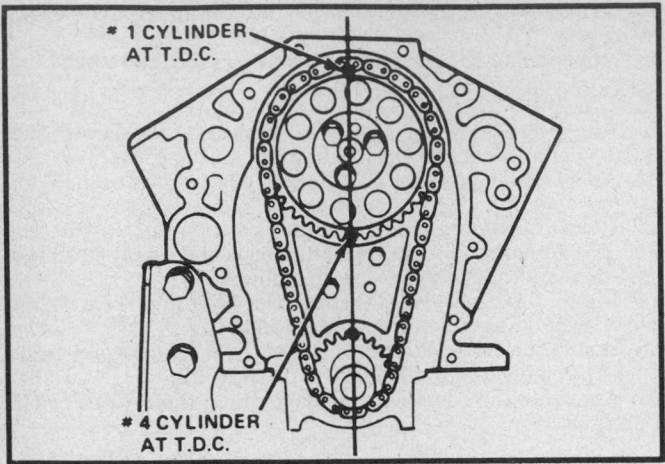

Timing mark alignment—2.8L engine

2. Turn the crankshaft to bring the No. 1 piston to TDC of its compression stroke. The timing marks on the crankshaft and camshaft sprockets should be aligned. With the camshaft sprocket timing mark at the 12 o'clock position, the engine will be in the No. 1 cylinder firing position. With the camshaft sprocket timing mark at the 6 o'clock position, the engine will be in the No. 4 cylinder firing position.

3. Unbolt and remove the camshaft sprocket and chain. If the sprocket is stuck, it can be removed by tapping it lightly with a plastic or wood mallet.

4. Lubricate the chain and sprockets with Molykote®, or equivalent. Install the cam sprocket and chain, with the marks aligned. Torque the cam sprocket bolts to 20 ft. lbs.

4.0L AND 4.2L ENGINES

1. Disconnect the negative battery cable. Remove the drive belts, engine fan and hub assembly, accessory pulley, vibration damper and timing chain cover.

2. Remove the oil seal from the timing chain cover.

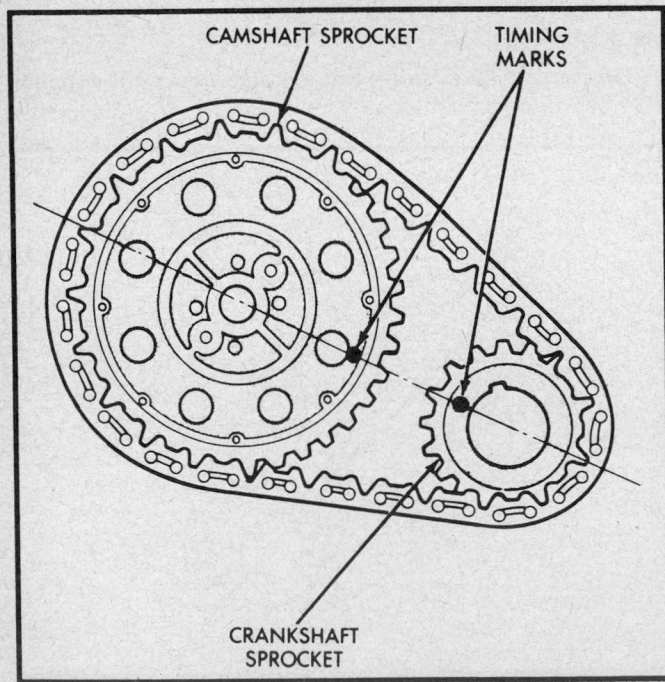

Timing mark alignment—4.0L and 4.2L engines

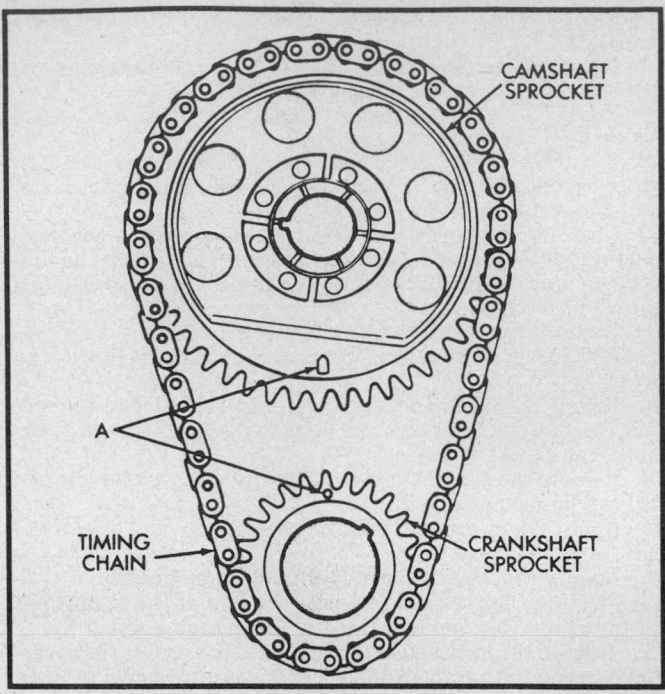

Timing mark alignment—5.9L engine

3. Remove the camshaft sprocket retaining bolt and washer.

4. Rotate the crankshaft until the timing mark on the crankshaft sprocket is closest to and in a center line with the timing pointer of the camshaft sprocket.

5. Remove the crankshaft sprocket, camshaft sprocket, and timing chain as an assembly. Disassemble the chain and sprockets.

6. Assemble the timing chain, crankshaft sprocket and camshaft sprocket with the timing marks aligned.

7. Install the assembly to the crankshaft and the camshaft. Double check the alignment by counting the number of links or pins with the sprockets positioned as illustrated. There must be 15 pins between the timing marks on both sprockets.

8. Install the camshaft sprocket retaining bolt and washer and tighten to 80 ft. lbs.

9. Install the timing chain cover and a new oil seal.

10. Install the vibration damper, accessory pulley, engine fan and hub assembly and drive belts. Tighten the belts to the proper tension.

5.9L ENGINE

1. Disconnect the negative battery cable. Remove the timing chain cover and gasket. Remove the crankshaft oil slinger.

2. Remove the camshaft sprocket retaining bolt and washer, distributor drive gear and fuel pump eccentric.

3. Rotate the crankshaft until the timing mark on the crankshaft sprocket is adjacent to, and on a center line with, the timing mark on the camshaft sprocket.

4. Remove the crankshaft sprocket, camshaft sprocket and timing chain as an assembly. Disassemble the chain and sprockets.

5. Assemble the timing chain, crankshaft sprocket and camshaft sprocket with the timing marks on both sprockets aligned. Install the assembly to the crankshaft and the camshaft.

6. Install the fuel pump eccentric. The fuel pump eccentric must be installed with the stamped word **REAR** facing the camshaft sprocket.

7. Install the distributor drive gear, washer and retaining bolt. Tighten the bolt to 25–35 ft. lbs.

8. Install the crankshaft oil slinger. Install the timing chain cover using a new gasket and oil seal.

Camshaft

Removal and Installation

2.5L ENGINE

1. Disconnect the negative battery cable. If equipped with air conditioning, properly discharge the system.
2. Drain the cooling system.
3. Remove the radiator and air conditioning condenser, if equipped.
4. Remove the fuel pump.
5. Matchmark the distributor and engine for installation. Note the rotor position by marking it on the distributor body. Unbolt and remove the distributor and wires.
6. Remove the rocker arm cover.
7. Remove the rocker arm assemblies.
8. Remove the pushrods.

NOTE: Keep all valve train components in order for installation.

9. Using tool J-21884, or equivalent, remove the hydraulic lifters.
10. Remove the timing case cover.

NOTE: If the camshaft sprocket appears to have been rubbing against the cover, check the oil pressure relief holes in the rear cam journal for debris.

11. Remove the timing chain and sprockets.
12. Slide the camshaft from the engine.
13. Installation is the reverse of removal. Inspect the camshaft for wear and damage.
14. Lubricate all moving parts with engine oil supplement. When installing the distributor, make sure that all matchmarks align.
15. Make sure that all camshaft timing marks align. It may be necessary to rotate the oil pump drive tang to facilitate installation of the distributor.
16. Torque the camshaft sprocket bolt to 50 ft. lbs.

2.8L ENGINE

1. Disconnect the negative battery cable. If equipped with air conditioning, properly discharge the system.
2. Drain the cooling system.
3. Remove the radiator and condensor.
4. Remove the intake manifold. Remove the fuel pump.
5. Remove the valve covers and remove the pushrods. Remove the lifters.
6. Remove the timing case cover. Remove the timing chain and sprockets.
7. Carefully slide the camshaft from the block.
8. Inspect the camshaft for wear or damage. If any journal is more than 0.025mm out of round, replace the camshaft.
9. Installation is the reverse of removal. Coat all parts with engine oil supplement, prior to installation. Whenever a new camshaft is installed, replace the oil filter and all the lifters. Torque the camshaft sprocket bolts to 20 ft. lbs.

4.0L AND 4.2L ENGINES

1. Disconnect the negative battery cable. Drain the cooling system and remove the radiator. As required, relieve the fuel system pressure.
2. Remove the condensor and receiver/drier as a charged unit.
3. Remove the valve cover and gasket, the rocker assemblies, pushrods, cylinder head and the lifters.

NOTE: The pushrods must be replaced in their original locations.

4. Remove the drive belts, cooling fan, fan hub assembly, vibration damper and the timing chain cover.

5. Remove the distributor assembly, including the spark plug wires.
6. Remove the cylinder head.
7. Remove the valve lifters. Keep them in order for installation.
8. Rotate the crankshaft until the timing mark of the crankshaft sprocket is adjacent to, and on a center line with, the timing mark of the camshaft sprocket.
9. Remove the crankshaft sprocket, camshaft sprocket, and the timing chain as an assembly.
10. Remove the front bumper or grille as required and carefully slide out the camshaft.

To install:

11. Lubricate the camshaft with an engine oil supplement.
12. Slide the camshaft into the block carefully to avoid damage to the bearings.
13. Install the crankshaft sprocket, camshaft sprocket, and the timing chain as an assembly.
14. Make sure the timing mark of the crankshaft sprocket is adjacent to, and on a center line with, the timing mark of the camshaft sprocket. Torque the camshaft sprocket bolt to 80 ft. lbs.
15. Install the valve lifters.
16. Install the cylinder head.
17. Install the distributor assembly.
18. Install the timing chain cover, vibration damper, fan hub, cooling fan and the drive belts.
19. Install the pushrods, the rocker assemblies, valve cover and gasket.
20. Install the condenser and receiver/drier as a charged unit.
21. Install the radiator. Recharge the air conditioning.
22. Fill the cooling system.

5.9L ENGINE

1. Disconnect the negative battery cable.
2. Drain the radiator and both banks of the block. Remove the lower hose at the radiator, the bypass hose at the pump, the thermostat housing and the radiator. If equipped with air conditioning, remove the condenser and receiver assembly.
3. Remove the distributor, all wires, and the coil from the manifold.
4. Remove the intake manifold as an assembly.
5. Remove the valve covers, rocker arms and pushrods.
6. Remove the lifters.

NOTE: The valve train components must be replaced in their original locations.

7. Remove the cooling fan and hub assembly, fuel pump, and heater hose at the water pump.
8. Remove the alternator and bracket as an assembly. Move it aside, do not disconnect the wiring.
9. Remove the crankshaft pulley and the damper. Remove the lower radiator hose at the water pump.
10. Remove the timing chain cover.
11. Remove the distributor/oil pump drive gear, fuel pump eccentric, sprockets and the timing chain.
12. Remove the grille.
13. Remove the camshaft carefully by sliding it forward out of the engine.

To install:

14. Coat all parts with engine oil supplement.
15. Slide the camshaft, carefully, into the engine.
16. Install the grille.
17. Install the distributor/oil pump drive gear, fuel pump eccentric, sprockets and the timing chain. Install the timing chain cover.
18. Install the crankshaft pulley and the damper.
19. Install the lower radiator hose at the water pump. Install the alternator and bracket as an assembly.
20. Install the cooling fan and hub assembly. Install the fuel pump.

21. Install the heater hose at the water pump. Install the lifters.

NOTE: The valve train components must be replaced in their original locations.

22. Install the valve covers, rocker arms and pushrods.
23. Install the intake manifold as an assembly.
24. Install the distributor, all wires, and the coil on the manifold.
25. Install the radiator.
26. If equipped with air conditioning, install the condenser and receiver assembly.
27. Install the thermostat and housing. Install the by-pass hose at the pump.
28. Install the lower hose at the radiator. Fill the cooling system.
29. Connect the negative battery cable.

Piston and Connecting Rod

Positioning

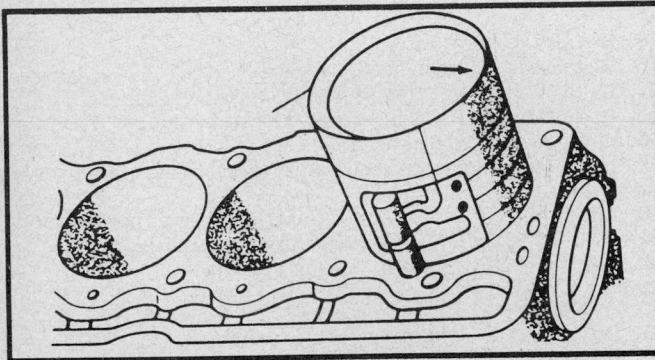

Piston positioning—all engines except 5.9L engine

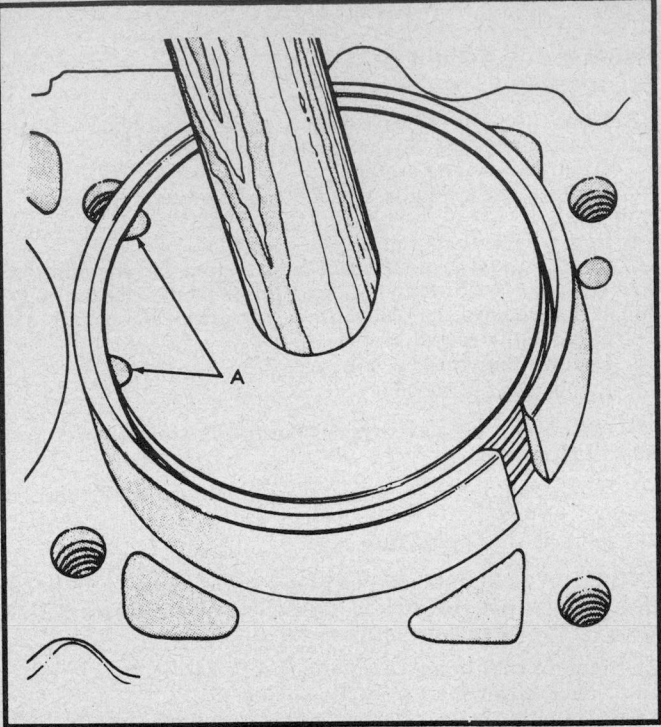

Piston positioning—5.9L engine

DIESEL ENGINE MECHANICAL

NOTE: Disconnecting the battery cable on some vehicles may interfere with the functions of the on board computer systems and may require the computer to undergo a relearning process, once the negative battery cable is disconnected.

Engine

Removal and Installation

2.1L ENGINE

1. Disconnect the battery cables and remove the battery. Remove the hood.
2. If equipped, remove the skid plate.
3. Drain the radiator. Remove the air cleaner assembly.
4. If equipped, discharge the air conditioning system.
5. Disconnect the radiator hoses and remove the E-clip from the bottom of the radiator.
6. Raise and support the vehicle safely. Drain the engine oil. If the vehicle is equipped with an automatic transmission, disconnect the oil cooler lines at the radiator.
7. Remove the splash shield from the oil pan. Lower the vehicle.

8. Loosen the radiator shroud and remove the radiator fan assembly. Remove the shroud and the splash shield.
9. Remove the radiator and the condenser assembly from the vehicle. Remove the inner cooler.
10. Remove the exhaust shield from the manifold. Disconnect the hoses at the remote oil filter. Remove the oil filter.
11. Tag and disconnect all vacuum hoses and electrical connections. Disconnect and plug the fuel inlet and outlet lines at the fuel pump.
12. If equipped with automatic transmission, remove the left motor mount through bolt retaining nut.
13. Remove the motor mount retaining bolts. Disconnect the accelerator cable. Raise and support the vehicle safely.
14. Disconnect and drain the power steering hoses at the power steering pump.
15. Disconnect the exhaust pipe at the exhaust manifold. Remove the motor mount retaining nuts.
16. Support the engine. Remove the left motor mount bolts. On automatic transmission equipped vehicles, remove the left motor mount.
17. Remove the starter.
18. If the vehicle is equipped with an automatic transmission, mark and remove the converter-to-drive plate bolts through the

starter opening. Install the left motor mount and retaining bolts finger tight. Install the motor mount cushion through bolt. Remove the engine support.

19. Remove the accessible transmission-to-engine retaining bolts.

20. Lower the vehicle. Remove the remaining engine-to-transmission retaining bolts.

21. Remove the power steering pump from the engine. Remove the oil separator and disconnect the hoses. Disconnect the heater hoses.

22. Remove the reference pressure regulator from the dash panel. Install the engine lifting device and position a jack under the transmission.

23. Remove the engine from the vehicle.

To install:

24. Lower the engine into the vehicle.

NOTE: It may be necessary to remove the engine mount cushions to ease alignment of the engine.

25. On vehicles with a manual transmission, slide the transmission input shaft into the clutch splines, align the flywheel housing bolt holes and install the lower bolts finger tight.

26. On vehicles with an automatic transmission, align the torque converter housing and engine and install the lower bolts finger tight.

27. Install all remaining bolts. Torque all bolts to 30 ft. lbs. Install any engine mount cushions previously removed.

28. Remove the engine lifting device.

29. If the vehicle is equipped with automatic transmission, install the converter-to-drive plate bolts through the starter opening. Torque the bolts to 40 ft. lbs.

30. Install the starter. Tighten all engine mount bolts to 30 ft. lbs.

31. Install the power steering pump. Tighten the rear bracket-to-block bolt to 20 ft. lbs.; all other bolts to 28 ft. lbs.

32. Connect the exhaust pipe at the exhaust manifold. Install the oil filter and lines.

33. Install the oil separator and connect the hoses. Connect the heater hoses.

34. Connect all vacuum hoses and electrical connections. Connect the fuel inlet and outlet lines at the fuel pump.

35. Install the reference pressure regulator from the dash panel.

36. Connect the accelerator cable. Install the exhaust shield at the manifold.

37. Install the radiator and the condenser assembly from the vehicle. Install the inner cooler.

38. Install the radiator fan assembly. Install the shroud and the splash shield. Install the splash shield on the oil pan.

39. If the vehicle is equipped with automatic transmission connect the oil cooler lines at the radiator.

40. Connect the radiator hoses and install the E-clip at the bottom of the radiator.

41. Install the air conditioning compressor. Evacuate, charge and leak test the air conditioning system.

42. Fill the cooling system. Install the air cleaner assembly. If equipped, install the skid plate. Install the battery.

43. Install the hood.

Cylinder Head

Removal and Installation

2.1L ENGINE

1. Disconnect the negative battery cable. Drain the engine coolant.

2. Remove the intake manifold. Remove the exhaust manifold.

3. Remove the valve cover. Remove the timing belt cover.

4. Install sprocket holding tool MOT–854 or equivalent and

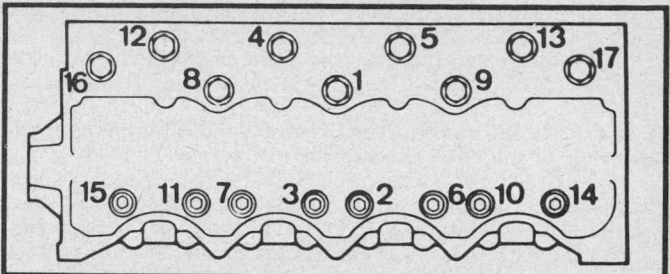

Cylinder head bolt torque sequence – 2.1L turbo diesel engine

remove the camshaft sprocket retaining bolt. Remove the special tool.

5. Loosen the bolts and move the tensioner away from the timing belt. Retighten the tensioner bolts.

6. Remove the timing belt from the sprockets.

NOTE: If it is necessary to remove the fuel injection pump sprocket use special tool BVI–28–01 or BVI–859, or their equivalents to accomplish this procedure.

7. Disconnect the fuel pipe fittings from the injectors. Plug them in order to prevent dirt from entering the system.

8. Disconnect the fuel pipe fittings from the fuel injection pump. Plug them in order to prevent dirt from entering the system.

9. Remove the fuel pipes from there mountings on the engine. Remove all hoses and connectors from the fuel injection pump.

10. Remove the injection pump retaining bolts. Remove the fuel injection pump and its mounting brackets, as an assembly, from the vehicle.

11. Remove the the retaining bolts and nuts from the cylinder head. Loosen pivot bolt but do not remove it. Remove the remaining cylinder head bolts.

12. Place a block of wood against the cylinder head and tap it with a hammer in order to loosen the cylinder head gasket. The pivot movement will be minimal due to the small clearance between the studs and the cylinder head. Remove the pivot bolt from the cylinder head.

13. Remove the retaining bolts and the rocker arm shaft assembly from the cylinder head.

NOTE: Do not lift the cylinder head from the cylinder block until the gasket is completely loosened from the cylinder liners. Otherwise, the liner seals could be broken.

14. Remove the cylinder head and the gasket from the engine block. While the head is off, install liner clamp tool Mot. 521–01 to hold the liners in place in the block.

To install:

15. Position cylinder head locating tool Mot–720 on the block to insure proper alignment.

16. Remove liner clamp tool Mot 521–01.

17. Position the cylinder head and the new gasket from the engine block. Be sure that the new cylinder head gasket is positioned properly on the cylinder head and that it is the correct thickness for piston protrusion. Whenever major components, such as pistons, liners, crankshaft, etc., have been replaced, the piston protrusion must be measured to determine proper replacement head gasket thickness. Measure the protrusion as follows:

a. Rotate the crankshaft one complete revolution clockwise and bring No. 1 piston to a point just below and before TDC.

b. Place thrust plate tool Mot. 252–01 on top of the piston.

c. Assemble dial indicator LM in block gauge Mot. 251–01 and place this assembly on one side of the thrust plate.

d. Zero the indicator with the stem on the cylinder block face.

e. Place the stem on the top of the piston and rotate the crankshaft clockwise to TDC of the piston. Record the psiton travel.

f. Repeat the procedure with the dial indicator on the opposite side of the block. Record the piston travel.

g. Add the figures together and divide by 2. Repeat the protrusion measurement for the 3 remaining pistons. The piston with the greatest protrusion should be the basis for determining gasket thickness. For example, if the amount of greatest piston protrusion is:

Less than 0.96mm, use a gasket 1.6mm thick
Between 0.96mm and 1.04mm, use a 1.7mm thick gasket
More than 1.04mm, use a 1.8mm thick gasket

18. Install the head bolts. Torque the cylinder head retaining bolts to 22 ft. lbs., then to 37 ft. lbs., then to 70–77 ft. lbs. Once all the bolts are tightened, recheck the torque.

NOTE: The cylinder head bolts must be retightened after the cylinder head is installed in the vehicle. Operate the engine for a minimum of 20 minutes. Allow the engine to cool for a minimum of 2½ hours. Loosen each cylinder head bolt in sequence about ½ turn. Then retighten in the proper sequence and torque to 70–77 ft. lbs. For the final tightening, tighten the bolts again, in sequence, without loosening them to 70–77 ft. lbs.

19. Remove tool Mot–720.
20. Install the rocker arm shaft assembly.
21. Install the fuel injection pump and its mounting brackets, as an assembly.
22. Install the fuel pipes on their mountings on the engine. Install all hoses and connectors on the fuel injection pump.
23. Connect the fuel pipe fittings to the fuel injection pump.
24. Connect the fuel pipe fittings from the injectors.
25. Install the timing belt. Retension the timing belt. Install the camshaft sprocket retaining bolt.
26. Install the valve cover. Install the timing belt cover. Install the intake manifold.
27. Install the exhaust manifold.
28. Fill the cooling system.
29. Connect the negative battery cable.

Valve Lash

Adjustment

1. Remove the valve cover.
2. Loosen the locknut and turn the adjustment screw as necessary.
3. As each adjustment screw is tightened, be sure that the bottom of the screw is aligned with the valve stem. If the adjustment screw is not aligned with the stem when tightened, the stem could bend. Tighten the locknut.
4. The exhaust valve adjustment specification is 0.25mm. The intake valve adjustment specification is 0.20mm.
5. Install the valve cover.

Rocker Arms/Shaft

Removal and Installation

2.1L ENGINE

1. Disconnect the negative battery cable.
2. Remove the cylinder head cover and gasket.
3. Remove the rocker shaft retaining bolts. Remove the rocker arm shaft assembly from the vehicle.
4. Installation is the reverse of the removal procedure. Be sure to use new gaskets and adjust the valves as required. Torque the bolts to 20 ft. lbs.
5. Be sure that the engine is cold before adjusting the valves.

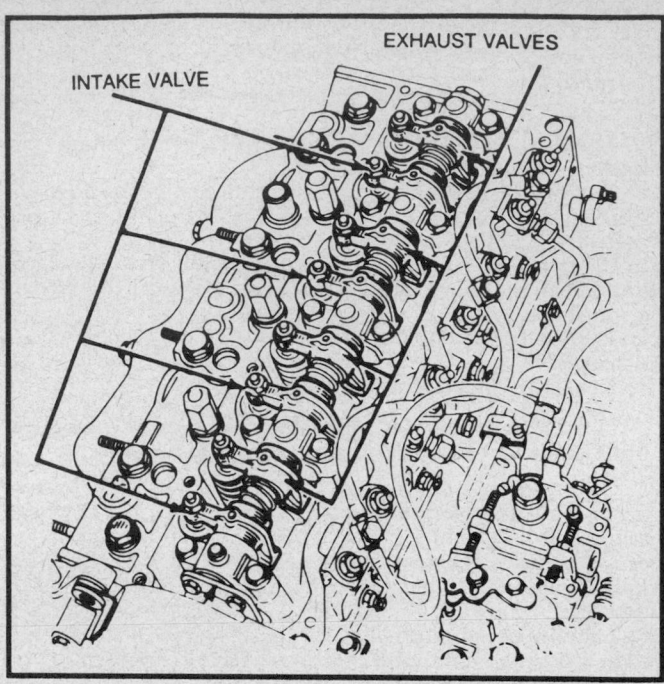

Rocker arm identification — used for clearance adjustment

6. Set number one cylinder to TDC on the compression stroke and check the valve clearance of No.1 and No.2 intake and No.1 and No.3 exhaust valves. Adjust as required.

7. Rotate the crankshaft 360 degrees and check the clearance of the No. 3 and No. 4 intake and No. 2 and No. 4 exhaust valves. Adjust as required.

NOTE: The No. 1 cylinder is located at the flywheel end of the engine.

8. To adjust, loosen the locknut and turn the adjustment screw as necessary. As each adjustment screw is tightened, be sure that the bottom of the screw is aligned with the valve stem. If the adjustment screw is not aligned with the stem when tightened, the stem could bend. Tighten the locknut.

9. The exhaust valve adjustment specification is 0.25mm. The intake valve adjustment specification is 0.20mm.

Intake Manifold

Removal and Installation

2.1L ENGINE

1. Disconnect the negative battery cable. Disconnect the air inlet hose at the intake manifold.
2. Tag and remove all hoses and/or wires as necessary in order to gain access to the intake manifold retaining bolts.
3. Tag and remove all vacuum hoses and electrical connections that are attached to the intake manifold.
4. Remove the intake manifold retaining bolts. Remove the assembly from the vehicle. Discard the intake manifold gaskets.
5. Installation is the reverse of removal.

Exhaust Manifold

Removal and Installation

2.1L ENGINE

1. Disconnect the negative battery cable. Remove the intake manifold.
2. Disconnect the exhaust pipe from the adapter.

3. Remove the oil supply pipe and the oil return hose from the turbocharger assembly.

4. Disconnect the turbocharger air inlet and outlet hoses.

5. Remove the turbocharger retaining bolts. Remove the turbocharger from the vehicle.

6. Remove the exhaust manifold retaining bolts. Remove the exhaust manifold and gasket. Discard the gasket.

7. Installation is the reverse of removal. Torque the bolts to specification.

Turbocharger

Removal and Installation

2.1L ENGINE

1. Disconnect the negative battery cable.

2. Remove all the necessary components in order to gain access to the turbocharger retaining bolts.

3. Disconnect the exhaust pipe flange. Remove the oil supply pipe. Remove the oil return hose.

4. Remove the turbocharger retaining bolts. Remove the turbocharger from the vehicle.

5. Installation is the reverse of removal. Torque the turbocharger support bracket bolts to 30 ft. lbs.

Timing Belt Cover

Removal and Installation

2.1L ENGINE

1. Disconnect the negative battery cable.

2. Remove all necessary components in order to gain access to the timing belt cover bolts.

3. Remove the timing belt cover retaining bolts. Remove the timing belt cover from the engine.

4. Installation is the reverse of removal.

Timing Belt and Tensioner

Removal and Installation

2.1L ENGINE

1. Disconnect the negative battery cable.

2. Remove the timing belt cover.

3. Install sprocket holding tool MOT–854 or equivalent and remove the camshaft sprocket retaining bolt. Remove the special tool.

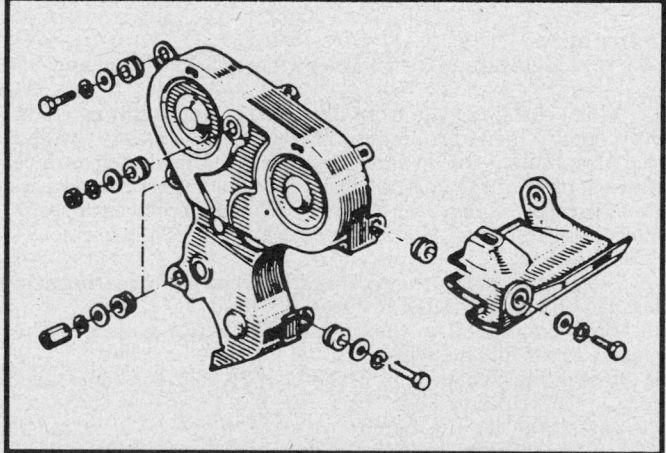
Timing gear cover – 2.1L turbo diesel engine

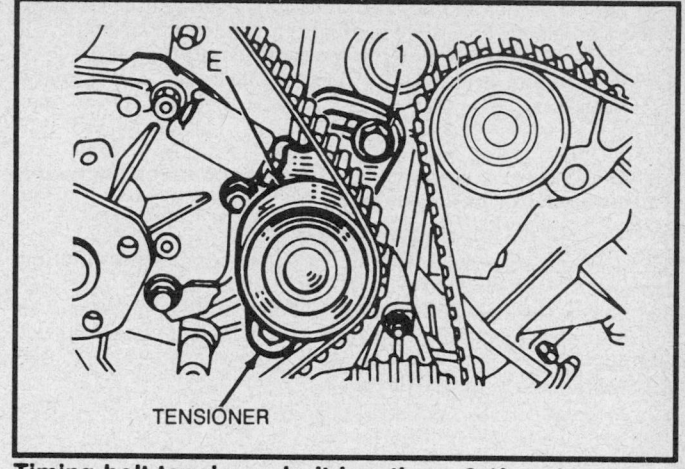
Timing belt tensioner bolt location – 2.1L turbo diesel

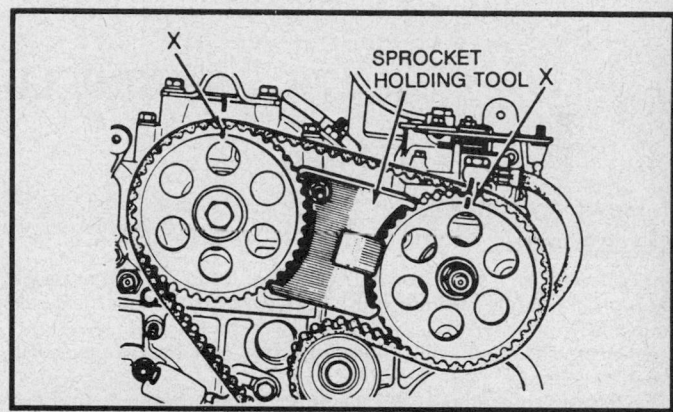
Camshaft and injection pump timing marks aligned – 2.1L turbo diesel

4. Loosen the bolts and move the chain tensioner away from the timing belt. Tighten the tensioner bolts.

5. Remove the timing belt from the sprockets. Inspect the belt for excess wear, splits or fraying.

6. If it is necessary to remove the fuel injection pump sprocket, use tools BVI–28–01 and BVI–859, or equivalent.

To install:

7. Remove the access plug in the block, on the left side, and install the holding tool, MOT–861 in the hole. Rotate the crankshaft slowly, clockwise, until the tool drops into the TDC locating slot in the crankshaft counterweight.

NOTE: Don't use this tool as a crankshaft holding tool. When tightening or loosening gear train fasteners, use a flywheel holding tool, such as tool Mot–582.

8. Install sprocket holding tool, MOT–854 to retain the camshaft and injection pump sprockets. Make sure that the timing marks are positioned correctly.

9. Install the timing belt. There should be a total of 19 belt teeth between the camshaft and injection pump timing marks.

10. Temporarily position the timing cover over the sprockets. The camshaft and injection pump timing marks must index with the pointers in the cover's timing slots.

11. Remove the cover.

12. Remove the holding tool, MOT–854.

13. Make sure that the timing belt tensioner bolts are ½ turn loose, maximum.

14. The tensioner should, automatically, bear against the belt, giving the proper belt tension. Tighten the tensioner bolts.

15. Remove the TDC locating tool and install the plug.

16. Rotate the crankshaft, slowly, clockwise, 2 complete revolutions.

NOTE: Never rotate the crankshaft counterclockwise while adjusting belt tension.

17. Loosen the tensioner bolts ½ turn, maximum, then tighten.

18. Check the belt deflection at a point midway between the camshaft and injection pump sprockets. The belt should deflect 3–5mm.

19. Install the timing belt cover.

Camshaft

Removal and Installation

2.1L ENGINE

1. Disconnect the negative battery cable.

2. Drain the cooling system. Remove the valve cover. Remove the timing belt cover.

3. Remove the cylinder head. Remove the rocker arm shaft. Remove the camshaft gear.

4. Remove the oil seal from the cylinder head by prying it out using a suitable tool. Remove the camshaft from the cylinder head.

5. Installation is the reverse of removal. Always use a new front seal. Hold the sprocket with holding tool Mot–855, or equivalent, while tightening the nut. Torque the nut to 37 ft. lbs.

ENGINE LUBRICATION

Oil Pan

Removal and Installation

2.1L ENGINE

1. Disconnect the negative battery cable. Raise and support the vehicle safely. Remove the converter housing shield, as required.

2. Drain the engine oil. This engine has 2 oil drain plugs, both must be opened.

3. Remove all the necessary components in order to gain access to the oil pan retaining bolts.

4. Remove the oil pan retaining bolts. Remove the oil pan from the engine.

5. Installation is the reverse of removal. Torque the bolts to 79 inch lbs.

2.5L ENGINE

1. Disconnect the negative battery cable.

2. Raise and support the vehicle safely.

3. Drain the oil.

4. Disconnect the exhaust pipe at the manifold.

5. Remove the starter.

6. Remove the bellhousing access plate.

7. Unbolt and remove the oil pan.

8. Clean the gasket surfaces thoroughly.

9. Install a replacement seal at the bottom of the timing case cover and at the rear bearing cap.

10. Using new gaskets coated with sealer, install the pan and torque the ¼-20 bolts to 84 inch lbs.; the 5/16-18 bolts to 11 ft. lbs.

11. Install the remaining components in the reverse order of removal.

2.8L ENGINE

1. Disconnect the negative battery cable.

2. Raise and safely support the vehicle.

3. Drain the oil.

4. Remove the bellhousing access cover.

5. Disconnect the left exhaust pipe at the manifold.

6. Remove the starter.

7. Disconnect the exhaust pipe at the converter flange.

8. Unbolt and remove the pan.

9. Remove all RTV gasket material.

To install:

10. Install a new rear pan seal.

11. Apply a 3mm bead of RTV gasket material all the way around the pan sealing surface.

12. Install the pan and torque the bolts to 12 ft. lbs.

13. Connect the exhaust pipe at the converter flange.

14. Install the starter.

15. Connect the left exhaust pipe at the manifold.

16. Install the bell housing access cover.

17. Refill the engine with oil and connect the negative battery cable.

4.0L, 4.2L AND 5.9L ENGINES

1. Disconnect the negative battery cable. Raise and safely support the vehicle.

2. Drain the engine oil.

3. Remove the starter motor.

4. Remove all of the oil pan attaching bolts and remove the oil pan.

5. Remove the oil pan front and rear oil seals and side gaskets.

To install:

6. Thoroughly clean the gasket surfaces of the oil pan and engine block.

7. When installing the front oil pan seal to the timing chain cover, apply a generous amount of Permatex® No. 2 to the end tabs. Also, cement the oil pan side gaskets to the mating surface on the bottom of the engine block. Coat the inside curved surface of the new oil pan rear seal with soap and apply a generous amount of Permatex® No. 2 to the gasket contacting surface of the seal end tabs.

8. Install the seal in the recess of the rear main bearing cap, making certain that it is fully seated.

9. Apply engine oil to the oil pan contacting surface of the front and rear oil pan seals.

10. Install the oil pan. Torque the ¼ × 20 bolts to 80 inch lbs.; the 5/16 × 18 bolts to 11 ft. lbs.

11. Install the starter motor.

12. Fill the crankcase with oil and connect the negative battery cable.

Oil Pump

Removal and Installation

2.1L ENGINE

1. Disconnect the negative battery cable.
2. Remove the vacuum pump along with the oil pump drive gear.
3. Remove the timing belt cover. Loosen the intermediate shaft drive sprocket using tool MOT–855 or equivalent.
4. Remove the intermediate shaft bolt, sprocket, cover, clamp plate and intermediate shaft.
5. Raise and support the vehicle safely. Drain the engine oil. Remove the oil pan.
6. Remove the piston skirt cooling oil jet assembly to oil pump pipe.
7. Remove the oil pump retaining bolts. Remove the oil pump.

To install:

8. Be sure that the oil pump locating dowels are in place on the pump.
9. Inspect the gears for abnormal wear, chips, looseness on the shafts, galling, and scoring.
10. Inspect the cover and cavity for breaks, cracks, distortion, and abnormal wear.
11. Install the gears into the pump cavity, and with the use of a straight edge and feeler gauge, check the gear to housing clearance.
12. Repair or replace defective components as required.
13. Installation is the reverse of the removal procedure. Be sure to use new gaskets and seals as required. Torque the pump mounting bolts to 33 ft. lbs.

2.5L ENGINE

1. Disconnect the negative battery cable. Raise and safely support the vehicle.
2. Drain the engine oil and remove the oil pan.
3. Unbolt and remove the pump assembly from the block. Discard the gasket.
4. Using a new gasket, install the pump on the block. Torque the short bolt to 10 ft. lbs. and the long bolt to 17 ft. lbs.
5. Install the oil pan.
6. Connect the negative battery cable.

2.8L ENGINE

1. Disconnect the negative battery cable. Rasie and safely support the vehicle.
2. Drain the engine oil and remove the oil pan.
3. Unbolt and remove the pump from the extension housing.
4. Using a new gasket, install the pump on the block. Torque the bolts to 25–30 ft. lbs.
5. Install the oil pan.
6. Connect the negative battery cable.

4.0L, 4.2L AND 5.9L ENGINE

1. Disconnect the negative battery cable. Rasie and safely support the vehicle.
2. Drain the oil and remove the oil pan.
3. Remove the oil pump retaining bolts and separate the oil pump and gasket from the engine block.

NOTE: Do not disturb the position of the oil pick-up tube and screen assembly in the pump body. If the tube is moved within the pump body, a new assembly must be installed to assure an airtight seal.

4. Using a new gasket, install the pump on the block. Torque the short bolt to 10 ft. lbs. and the long bolt to 17 ft. lbs.
5. Install the oil pan.
6. Connect the negative battery cable.

Gear to Body Clearance Check

1. With both oil pump gears in the body, check the clearance by inserting a feeler gauge between a gear tooth and the pump body.
2. Rotate the gears to measure each tooth to body clearance.
3. The correct tooth to body clearance is:
  a. 2.1L diesel engine – 0.0019–0.0047 in. (0.05–0.12 mm)
  b. 2.5L, 4.0L and 4.2L engine – 0.002–0.004 in. (0.051–0.102 mm)
  c. 5.9L engine – 0.0005–0.0025 in. (0.013–0.064 mm)

Rear Main Bearing Oil Seal

Removal and Installation

2.1L ENGINE

1. Remove the engine.
2. Remove the flywheel.

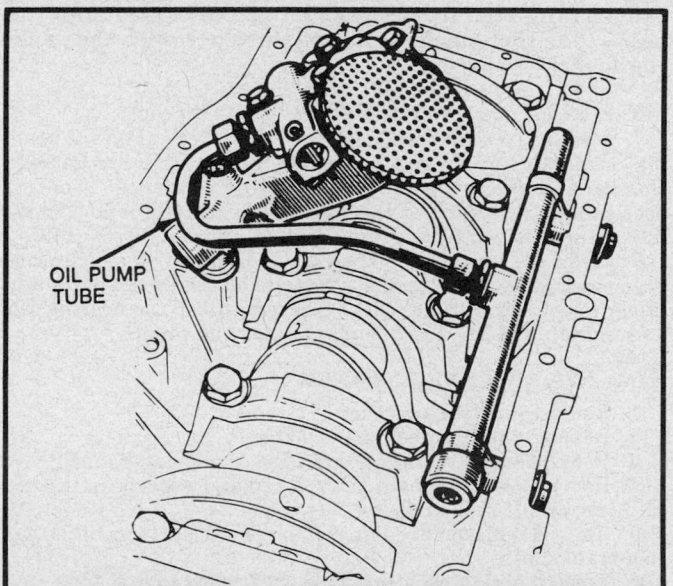

Oil pump and skirt cooling jet assembly mounting – 2.1L turbo diesel

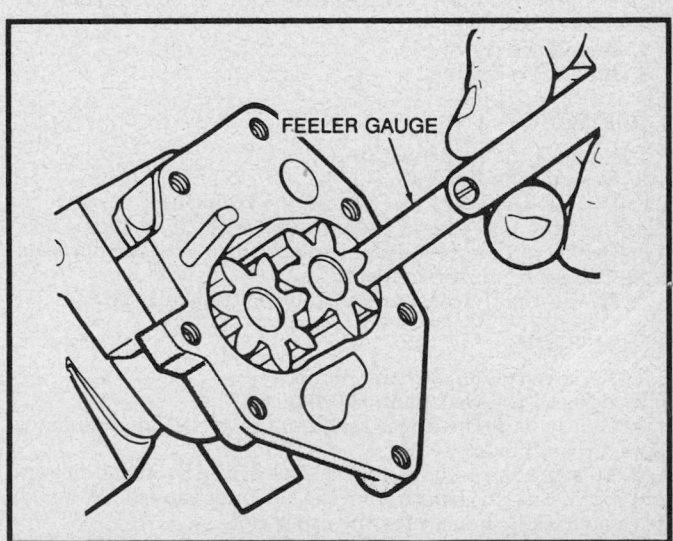

Checking oil pump gear tooth to body clearance

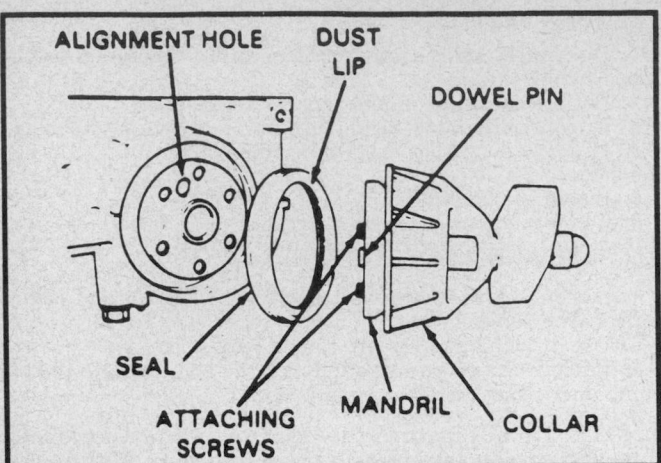

Rear main seal installation—2.5L engine

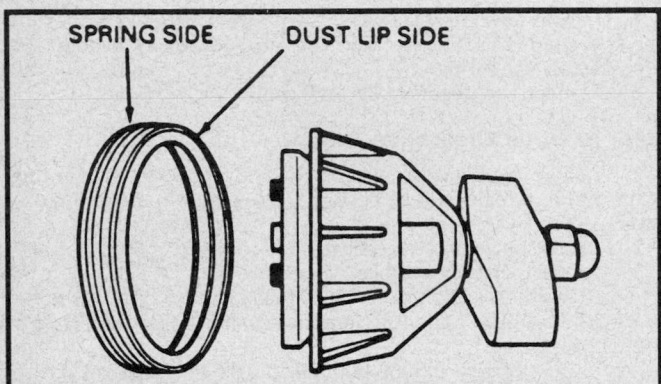

Installing the rear main seal on the installation tool—2.5L engine

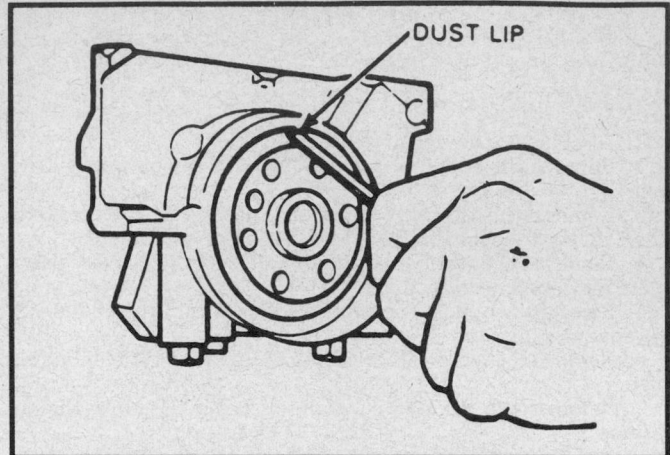

Removing the rear main seal 2.5L engine

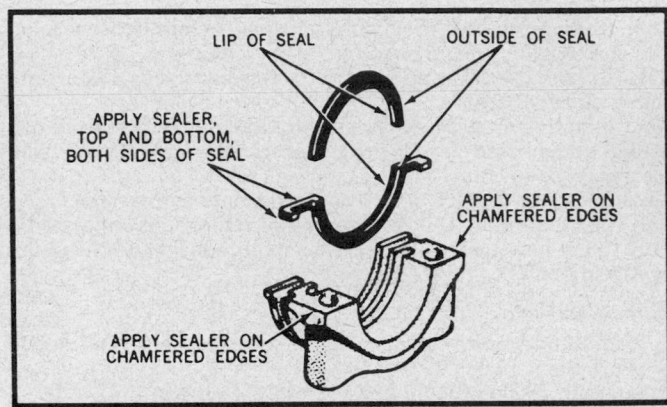

Two piece rear main seal installation

3. Using a sharp awl, punch a hole in the seal and pry it out of its bore.

4. Thoroughly clean the bore.

5. Coat the outer edge of the new seal with sealer and the inner sealing surface with clean engine oil.

6. Using a seal driver, such as Mot–788, or equivalent drive the new seal into place.

7. Install the flywheel.

8. Install the engine.

2.5L ENGINE

1. Remove the transmission.

2. Remove the flywheel.

3. Pry out the seal from around the crankshaft flange.

4. Coat the inner lip of the new seal with clean engine oil.

5. Gently tap the new seal into place, flush with the block, using a rubber or plastic mallet.

6. Install the flywheel and install the transmission.

2.8L ENGINE

1. Remove the oil pan and pump.

2. Remove the rear main bearing cap.

3. Gently pack the upper seal into the groove approximately ¼ in. on each side.

4. Measure the amount the seal was driven in on one side and add ¹⁄₁₆ in. Cut this length from the old lower cap seal. Be sure to get a sharp cut. Repeat for the other side.

5. Place the piece of cut seal into the groove and pack the seal into the block. Do this for each side.

NOTE: GM makes a guide tool (J–29114–1) which bolts to the block via an oil pan bolt hole, and a packing tool (J–29114–2) which are machined to provide a built-in stop for the installation of the short cut pieces. Using the packing tool, work the short pieces of seal onto the guide tool, then pack them into the block with the packing tool.

6. Install a new lower seal in the rear main cap.

7. Install a piece of Plastigage® or the equivalent on the bearing journal. Install the rear cap and tighten to 70 ft. lbs. Remove the cap and check the gauge for bearing clearance. If out of specification, the ends of the seal may be frayed or not flush, preventing the cap from proper sealing. Correct as required.

8. Clean the journal, and apply a thin film of RTV silione sealer to the mating surfaces of the cap and block. Do not allow any sealer to get onto the journal or bearing. Install the bearing cap and tighten to 70 ft. lbs. Install the pan and pump.

4.0L, 4.2L AND 5.9L ENGINES

1. Remove the transmission.

2. Remove the flywheel or flexplate.

3. Pry the seal out from around the crankshaft flange.

4. Remove the rear main bearing cap and wipe clean the cap and crankshaft seal surfaces.

5. Apply a thin coat of engine oil to the seal surfaces of the cap and crankshaft.

6. Coat the lip of each seal half with clean engine oil.

7. Position the upper seal half in the block. The lip of the seal faces the front of the engine.

8. Coat both side of the lower seal's end tabs with RTV silicone gasket material. Don't get any on the seal lip.

9. Coat the outer, curved surface of the lower seal with soap.

10. Seat the lower seal firmly in the bearing cap recess.

11. Coat both chamfered edges of the bearing cap with RTV silicone gasket material.

NOTE: Avoid getting and RTV material on the bearing cap-to-block mating surfaces. Doing so would change the bearing cleanace.

12. Install the bearing cap.

13. Torque all the main bearing caps to 80 ft. lbs.

MANUAL TRANSMISSION

For further information, please refer to "Professional Transmission Manual".

Transmission Assembly

Removal and Installation

2WD VEHICLES

1. Disconnect the negative battery cable. Raise the outer gearshift lever boot and remove the upper part of the console.

2. Remove the lower part of the console.

3. Remove the inner boot.

4. Remove the gearshift lever.

5. Raise and safely support the vehicle.

6. Drain the transmission oil.

7. Matchmark the driveshaft and yoke for installation alignment.

8. Unbolt and remove the driveshaft.

9. Position a suitable jack under the transmission and take the weight off the transmission slightly.

10. Unbolt and remove the rear crossmember.

11. Disconnect the speedometer cable.

12. Disconnect the back-up light switch.

13. Disconnect all linkage and hoses from the transmission.

14. Unbolt the transmission from the engine and lower the transmission while pulling it back.

To install:

15. Lightly grease the input shaft splines.

16. Raise the transmission into position.

17. Roll the transmission forward and engage the input shaft and clutch disc spline. Wiggle the output shaft yoke to get the splines to mesh. Once the splines mesh, push the trasmission forward all the way and align the bellhousing-to-engine bolt holes. Install the attaching bolts and torque them to 28 ft. lbs.

18. Connect all linkage and hoses at the transmission.

19. Connect the back-up light switch.

20. Connect the speedometer cable.

21. Install the rear crossmember. Torque the crossmember attaching bolt to 30 ft. lbs.; the transmission to crossmember bolts to 33 ft. lbs.

22. Remove the transmission jack.

23. Install the driveshaft. New strap bolts should be used whenever the driveshaft is disconnected. Torque the nuts to 14 ft. lbs.

24. Fill the transmission to the correct level with transmission oil.

25. Lower the vehicle.

26. Install the gearshift lever and install the inner boot. Install the lower part of the console. Install the upper part of the console.

27. Connect the negative battery cable.

4WD VEHICLES

1. Disconnnect the negative battery cable. Raise the outer gearshift lever boot and remove the upper part of the console.

2. Remove the lower part of the console.

3. Remove the inner boot.

4. Remove the gearshift lever.

5. Raise and safely support the vehicle.

6. Drain the transmission and transfer case.

7. Matchmark the rear driveshaft and yoke for installation alignment.

8. Unbolt and remove the rear driveshaft.

9. Position a suitable jack under the transmission and take up the weight slightly.

10. Unbolt and remove the rear crossmember.

11. Disconnect the speedometer cable.

12. Disconnect the back-up light switch.

13. Disconnect the transfer case vent hose at the case.

14. Disconnect all linkage and hoses from the transfer case and transmission.

15. Matchmark the front driveshaft and yoke.

16. Remove the front driveshaft.

17. Suuport the transmission to the jack.

18. Unbolt the transmission/transfer case assembly from the engine and lower the jack while pulling back.

To install:

19. If the transmission and transfer case were separated, torque the bolts to 26 ft. lbs.

20. Lightly grease the input shaft splines.

21. Raise the transmission into position.

22. Roll the transmission forward and engage the input shaft and clutch disc spline. Wiggle the output shaft yoke to get the splines to mesh. Once the splines mesh, push the trasmission forward all the way and align the bellhousing-to-engine bolt holes. Install the attaching bolts and torque them to 28 ft. lbs.

23. Install the front driveshaft. New strap bolts should be used every time the driveshaft is disconnected. Torque the strap bolt nuts to 14 ft. lbs.; the flange-to-transfer case bolts to 35 ft. lbs.

24. Connect all linkage and hoses at the transfer case and transmission.

25. Connect the transfer case vent hose at the case.

26. Connect the back-up light switch.

27. Connect the speedometer cable.

28. Install the rear crossmember. Torque the crossmember attaching bolts to 30 ft. lbs.; the transmission-to-crossmember bolts to 33 ft. lbs.

29. Remove the floor jack.

30. Install the rear driveshaft. Use new strap bolts. Torque the strap bolt nuts to 14 ft. lbs.; the flange-to-transfer case bolts to 35 ft. lbs.

31. Fill the transmission and transfer case.

32. Lower the vehicle.

33. Install the gearshift lever and the inner boot.

34. Install the lower part of the console and the upper part of the console.

35. Connect the negative battery cable.

CLUTCH

Clutch Assembly

Removal and Installation

1. Remove the transmission or transmission/transfer case assembly.
2. Matchmark the pressure plate and flywheel. Loosen the pressure plate bolts, a little at a time, in rotation, to avoid warpage.
3. Remove the pressure plate and clutch disc.
4. Remove the pilot bushing wick from the bushing bore. Soak the wick in clean engine oil.
5. Installation is the reverse of removal. A clutch aligning tool, either store-bought, or made from an old transmission input shaft, must be used to align the clutch properly for installation. The pressure plate bolts must be tightened a little at a time, in rotation, to avoid warpage. Torque the pressure plate bolts to:
   2.1L diesel engine: 16 ft. lbs.
   2.5L and 2.8L engine: 23 ft. lbs.
   4.0L, 4.2L and 5.9L engine: 40 ft. lbs.

Clutch Master Cylinder

Removal and Installation

1. Disconnect the hydraulic line at the master cylinder. Cap the line.
2. Disconnect the pushrod at the clutch pedal.
3. Unbolt the master cylinder from the firewall.
4. Installation is the reverse of removal. Torque the mounting nuts to 19 ft. lbs. Refill and bleed the system.

Clutch Slave Cylinder

Removal and Installation

1. Raise and safely support the vehicle.
2. Disconnect the hydraulic line at the cylinder. Cap the line.
3. Unbolt and remove the slave cylinder from the clutch housing.
4. Installation is the reverse of removal. Torque the mounting bolts to 16 ft. lbs. Refill and bleed the system.

Bleeding the Hydraulic Clutch System

1. Fill the clutch reservoir with clean brake fluid.
2. Raise and safely support the vehicle.
3. Remove the slave cylinder from the clutch housing, but do not disconnect the hydraulic line.
4. Remove the slave cylinder pushrod.
5. Using a wood dowel, compress the slave cylinder plunger.
6. Attach one end of a rubber hose to the slave cylinder bleeder screw and place the other end in a glass jar, filled halfway with clean brake fluid. Make sure that the hose will stay submerged.
7. Loosen the bleeder screw.
8. Have an assistant press and hold the clutch pedal to the floor. Tighten the bleeder screw with the pedal at the floor. Bubbles will have appeared in the jar when the pedal was depressed.
9. Release pedal, then perform the sequence again, until bubbles no longer appear in the jar.
10. Install the slave cylinder and lower the vehicle. Test the clutch.

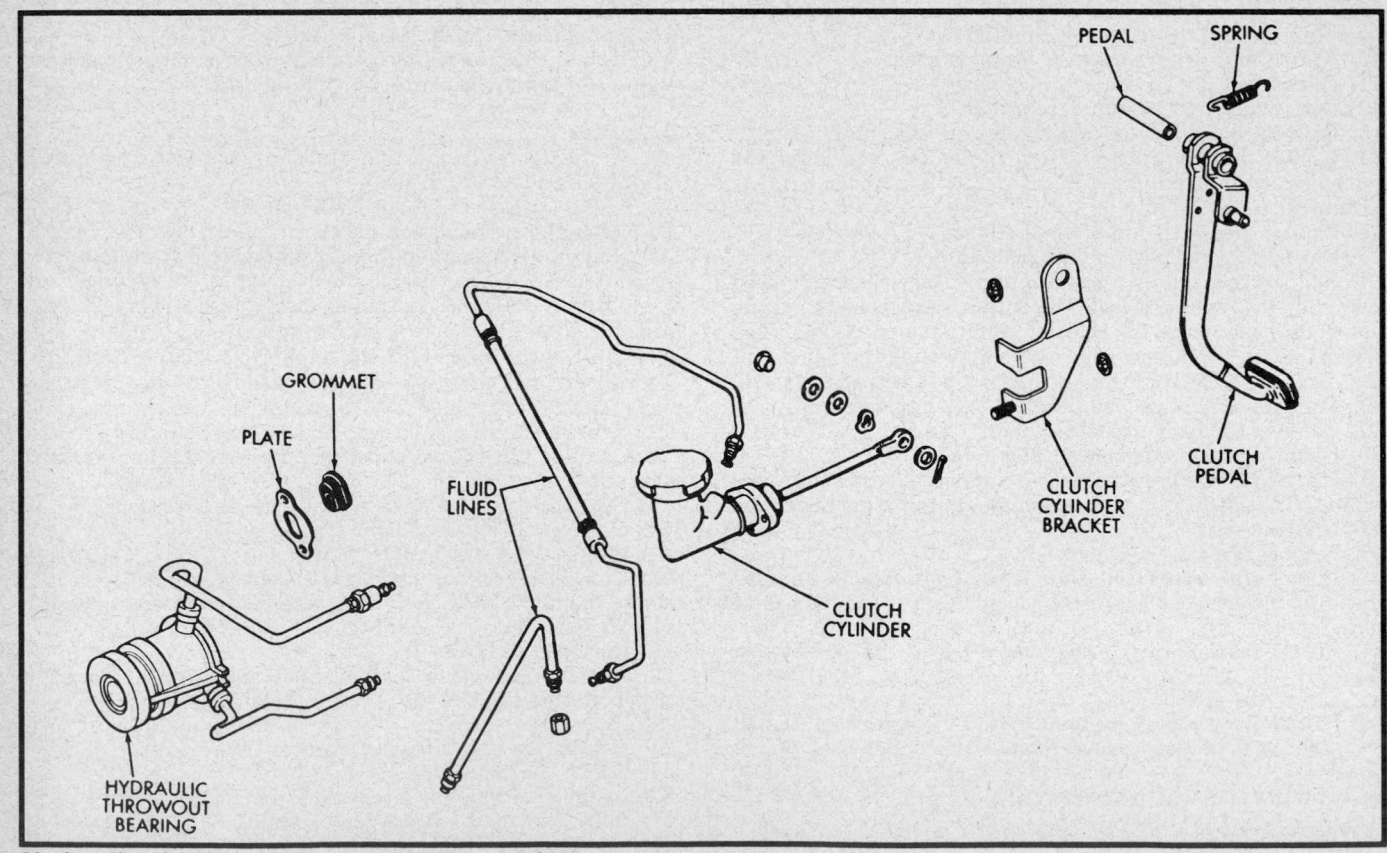

Hydraulic clutch system components—typical

AUTOMATIC TRANSMISSION

For further information, please refer to "Professional Transmission Manual".

Transmission Assembly

Removal and Installation

2WD VEHICLES

1. Disconnect the negative battery cable. Raise and support the vehicle safely.
2. Matchmark the rear driveshaft and yoke for reassembly. Disconnect and remove the rear driveshaft.
3. Remove the torque converter inspection cover. Mark the converter drive plate and converter assembly for reassembly.
4. Remove the bolts attaching the torque converter to the flex plate. Support the transmission assembly using a suitable jack.
5. Remove the bolts attaching the rear crossmember to the transmission side rail. Disconnect the exhaust pipe at the catalytic converter.
6. Lower the transmission slightly in order to disconnect the fluid cooler lines.
7. Disconnect the backup light switch wire and the speedometer cable. Disconnect the transmission linkage.
8. Remove the bolts attaching the transmission assembly to the engine. Move the transmission assembly and the torque converter rearward to clear the crankshaft.
9. Carefully lower the transmission assembly from the vehicle.

To install:

10. Carefully raise the transmission into position.
11. Install the bolts attaching the transmission assembly to the engine. Torque the bolts to 25 ft. lbs. for the 904. On the AW–4, torque the 10mm bolts to 25 ft. lbs.; the 12mm bolts to 42 ft. lbs.
12. Connect the backup light switch wire.
13. Connect the speedometer cable.
14. Connect the transmission linkage.
15. Connect the fluid cooler lines.
16. Install the rear crossmember. Torque the crossmember bolts to 30 ft. lbs.; the transmission-to-crossmember bolts to 33 ft. lbs.
17. Connect the exhaust pipe at the catalytic converter.
18. Install the bolts attaching the torque converter to the flex plate. Torque the bolts to 40 ft. lbs.
19. Remove the transmission jack.
20. Install the torque converter inspection cover.
21. Install the driveshaft. New strap bolts should be used everytime the driveshaft is disconnected. Torque the nuts to 14 ft. lbs.
22. Lower the truck.
23. Connect the negative battery cable.

4WD VEHICLES

1. Disconnect the negative battery cable. Raise and support the vehicle safely.
2. Matchmark the rear driveshaft and yoke for reassembly. Disconnect and remove the rear driveshaft.
3. Remove the torque converter inspection cover. Mark the converter drive plate and converter assembly for reassembly.
4. Remove the bolts attaching the torque converter to the flex plate. Support the transmission assembly with a jack.

NOTE: If the vehicle is equipped with a diesel engine, support the engine with a jack under the crankshaft damper, and remove the left motor mount and starter in order to gain access to the torque converter drive plate bolts through the starter opening.

5. Remove the bolts attaching the rear crossmember to the transmission side rail. Disconnect the exhaust pipe at the catalytic converter.
6. Lower the transmission slightly in order to disconnect the fluid cooler lines. Matchmark the front driveshaft assembly for installation. Disconnect the driveshaft at the transfer case and secure the assembly out of the way.
7. Disconnect the backup light switch wire and the speedometer cable. Disconnect the transfer case and the transmission linkage. Disconnect the vacuum lines and the vent hose.
8. Remove the bolts attaching the transmission assembly to the engine. Move the transmission assembly and the torque converter rearward to clear the crankshaft.
9. Carefully lower the transmission assembly from the vehicle. Remove the transfer case retaining bolts from the transmission assembly.

To install:

10. If the transmission and transfer case were separated, re-attach them and torque the bolts to 26 ft. lbs.
11. Carefully raise the transmission into position.
12. Install the bolts attaching the transmission assembly to the engine. Torque the bolts to 25 ft. lbs. for the 904. On the AW–4, torque the 10mm bolts to 25 ft. lbs.; the 12mm bolts to 42 ft. lbs.
13. Connect the backup light switch wire and the speedometer cable.
14. Connect the transfer case and the transmission linkage.
15. Connect the vacuum lines and the vent hose.
16. Connect the fluid cooler lines.
17. Connect the driveshaft at the transfer case. New strap bolts should be used whenever the driveshaft is disconnected. Torque the strap bolt nuts to 14 ft. lbs; the flange-to-case bolts to 35 ft. lbs.
18. Install the rear crossmember. Torque the crossmember attaching bolts to 30 ft. lbs.; the transmission-to-crossmember bolts to 33 ft. lbs.
19. Connect the exhaust pipe at the catalytic converter.
20. Install the bolts attaching the torque converter to the flex plate. Torque the bolts to 40 ft. lbs.
21. Remove the floor jack.
22. Install the torque converter inspection cover.
23. If the vehicle is equipped with a diesel engine, install the left motor mount and starter.
24. Install the rear driveshaft. Use new starp bolts. Torque the strap bolt nuts to 14 ft. lbs.; the flange bolts to 35 ft. lbs.
25. Lower the truck.
26. Connect the negative battery cable.

Shift Linkage Adjustment

1. Raise and safely support the vehicle.
2. Loosen the shift rod trunnion jamnuts.
3. Remove the lockpin that retains the shift rod trunnion to the bell crank. Disengage the trunnion and shift rod at the bell crank.
4. Place the gear shift lever in the **P** position and lock the steering column.
5. Move the transmission lever rearward into the **P** detent. Be sure the lever is as far rearward as it will go.
6. Check the engagement of the park detent by trying to rotate the driveshaft with the rear wheels off of the ground. The shaft will not rotate if the park detent is engaged.
7. Adjust the trunnion until it will fit in the bell crank arm freely. Tighten the jamnuts. Install the lock pin.
8. Check engine starting in **P** and **N**, be sure it will not start in any other gear.

Throttle Linkage Adjustment

2.5L ENGINE WITH CARBURETOR

1. Disconnect the throttle control rod spring at the carburetor.
2. Raise and support the vehicle safely.
3. Use the throttle control rod spring to hold the transmission throttle control lever forward against its stop.
4. Hook one end of a spring on the throttle control lever and the other end of the spring on the throttle linkage bellcrank bracket, which is attached to the torque converter housing.
5. Lower the vehicle. Block the choke in the open position. Set the carburetor throttle off the fast idle cam.
6. Turn the ignition key to the **ON** position in order to energize the solenoid.
7. Open the throttle halfway to allow the solenoid to lock. Return the carburetor to the idle position.
8. Loosen the retaining bolt on the throttle control adjusting link. Do not remove the spring clip and nylon washer.
9. Pull the end of the link to eliminate lash. Tighten the retaining bolt. Turn the ignition to the **OFF** position.
10. Raise and support the vehicle safely. Remove the throttle control rod spring from the linkage. Lower the vehicle. Install the spring on the throttle control rod.

2.5L ENGINE WITH TBI

NOTE: An idle speed assembly exerciser box is required in order to make this adjustment. The purpose of this special tool is to bypass the idle speed motor.

1. Be sure that the vehicle ignition key is in the **OFF** position. Raise and support the vehicle safely.
2. Hook one end of a spring on the throttle control lever and the other end of the spring on the throttle linkage bellcrank bracket, which is attached to the torque converter housing. Lower the vehicle.
3. Disconnect the idle speed actuator motor wire harness and connect the idle speed assembly exerciser box. Upon connection, the adjustment light should turn off and the ready light should turn on.
4. Loosen the retaining bolt on the throttle control adjusting link. Pull the end of the link in order to eliminate lash and tighten the link retaining bolt.
5. Press the extend button on the idle speed assembly exerciser box until the idle speed actuator motor ratchets.
6. Disconnect the idle speed assembly exerciser box and reconnect the idle speed actuator motor wiring harness.
7. Raise and safely support the vehicle. Remove the spring from the linkage. Lower the vehicle.

2.8L ENGINE

1. Remove the air cleaner assembly. Raise and support the vehicle safely.
2. Hold the throttle control lever rearward against its stop. Use a spring to hold the lever. Hook one end of the spring to the lever and the other end to a convenient mounting point.

3. Lower the vehicle. Block the choke open and set the carburetor linkage off of the fast idle cam.
4. Unlock the throttle control cable by releasing the T shaped cable adjuster clamp. Release the clamp by lifting it upward using a suitable tool.
5. Grasp the cable outer sheath and move the cable and sheath forward, this will remove any cable load on the throttle cable bellcrank.
6. Adjust the cable by moving the cable and sheath rearward until there is 0 lash between the plastic cable end and the bellcrank ball.
7. When this has been accomplished, lock the cable by pressing the T shaped adjuster clamp downward.
8. Install the air cleaner assembly. Raise and support the vehicle safely. Remove the spring from its mounting. Lower the vehicle.

4.2L ENGINE

1. Disconnect the throttle control return spring at the carburetor, if equipped. Raise and support the vehicle safely.
2. Use the throttle control rod spring to hold the throttle control lever forward against its stop, by hooking one end of the spring on the throttle control lever and the other end on the throttle linkage bell crank bracket which is attached to the transmission housing.
3. Block the choke plate open and move the throttle linkage off the fast idle cam.
4. On carburetors equipped with a throttle operated solenoid valve, turn the ignition **ON** to energize the solenoid, then open the throttle halfway to allow the solenoid to lock and return the carburetor to the idle position.
5. Loosen the retaining bolt on the throttle control adjusting link. Do not remove the spring clip and nylon washer.
6. Pull on the end of the link to eliminate play and tighten retaining bolt.
7. Remove the throttle control rod spring and install it on the control rod.

5.9L ENGINE

1. Disconnect the throttle control rod spring at the carburetor. Raise and support the vehicle safely.
2. Use the throttle control rod spring to hold the transmission throttle valve control lever against its stop.
3. Block the choke plate open and make sure the throttle linkage is off the fast idle cam.
4. On carburetors equipped with a throttle operated solenoid valve, turn the ignition to **ON** to energize the solenoid. Then turn the throttle halfway to allow the solenoid to lock and return the carburetor to idle.
5. Loosen the retaining bolt on the throttle control rod adjuster link. Remove the spring clip and move the nylon washer to the rear of the link.
6. Push on the end of the link to eliminate play and tighten the link retaining bolt. Install the nylon washer and spring clip.
7. Remove the throttle control rod spring and install it in its intended position.

TRANSFER CASE

Transfer Case Assembly

Removal and Installation

NEW PROCESS 207

1. Shift the case into **4H**.
2. Raise and safely support the vehicle.
3. Drain the transfer case.
4. Matchmark the rear driveshaft and remove it.
5. Disconnect the speedometer cable, vacuum hoses and vent hose from the case.
6. Support the transmission with a suitable transmission jack.
7. Remove the crossmember.
8. Matchmark the front driveshaft and remove it.
9. Disconnect the shift lever linkage rod at the case.
10. Remove the shift lever bracket bolts.
11. Support the transfer case with a suitable jack and remove the attaching bolts.
12. Pull the case out of the vehicle.

To install:

13. Raise the transfer case into position. Torque the attaching bolts to 26 ft. lbs.
14. Connect the shift lever linkage rod at the case.
15. Install the shift lever bracket bolts.
16. Install the front driveshaft. New strap bolts should be used. Torque the nuts to 14 ft. lbs. Torque the flange bolts to 35 ft. lbs.
17. Install the crossmember. Torque the bolts to 30 ft. lbs.
18. Remove the support jack.
19. Connect the speedometer cable, vacuum hoses and vent hose at the case.
20. Install the rear driveshaft. Use new strap bolts, torqued to 14 ft. lbs. Torque the flange bolts to 35 ft. lbs.
21. Fill the transfer case to the correct level.
22. Lower the vehicle.

NEW PROCESS 228

1. Raise and safely support the vehicle.
2. Drain the transfer case.
3. Disconnect the speedometer cable, vacuum hoses and vent hose from the case.
4. Disconnect the shift lever linkage rod at the case.
5. Support the transmission with a suitable jack. Remove the rear crossmember.
6. Matchmark the rear driveshaft and remove it.
7. Matchmark the front driveshaft and remove it.
8. Remove the shift lever bracket bolts.
9. Support the transfer case with a suitable jack and remove the attaching bolts.
10. Pull the case rearward out of the vehicle.

To install:

11. Position the transfer case in the vehicle. Torque the attaching bolts to 40 ft. lbs.
12. Install the shift lever bracket bolts.
13. Install the front and rear driveshafts. New strap bolts should be used. Torque the strap bolt nuts to 14 ft. lbs.; the flange nuts to 35 ft. lbs.
14. Install the rear crossmember. Torque the bolts to 30 ft. lbs.
15. Connect the shift lever linkage rod at the case.
16. Connect the speedometer cable, vacuum hoses and vent hose from the case.
17. Fill the transfer case to the correct level.
18. Lower the vehicle.

NEW PROCESS 229

1. Raise and safely support the vehicle.
2. Drain the transfer case.

3. Disconnect the speedometer cable and vent hose. Disconnect the shift lever link at the operating lever.
4. Support the transmission with a suitable jack.
5. Remove the rear crossmember.
6. Matchmark the driveshafts and remove them.
7. Disconnect the shift motor vacuum hoses.
8. Disconnect the shift linkage at the case.
9. Support the transfer case with a floor jack or transmission jack and remove the attaching bolts.
10. Pull the case rearward and remove it.
11. Clean the gasket mating surfaces and use new gasket material for installation.

To install:

12. Raise the transfer case into position. Make certain that the case and transmission are mated without binding, before torquing the attaching bolts. Torque the bolts to 26 ft. lbs.
13. Connect the shift linkage at the case.
14. Connect the shift motor vacuum hoses.
15. Install the driveshafts. New strap bolts should be used. Torque the nuts to 14 ft. lbs.; torque the flange nuts to 35 ft. lbs.
16. Install the rear crossmember. Torque the bolts to 30 ft. lbs.
17. Remove the transmission support jack.
18. Connect the speedometer cable and vent hose.
19. Connect the shift lever link at the operating lever.
20. Fill the transfer case.
21. Lower the vehicle.

NEW PROCESS 231

1. Shift the transfer case into **N**.
2. Raise and support the vehicle safely.
3. Drain the lubricant.
4. Matchmark and remove the front and rear driveshafts.
5. Support the transmission with a suitable jack.
6. Remove the rear crossmember.
7. Disconnect the speedometer cable.
8. Disconnect the linkage.

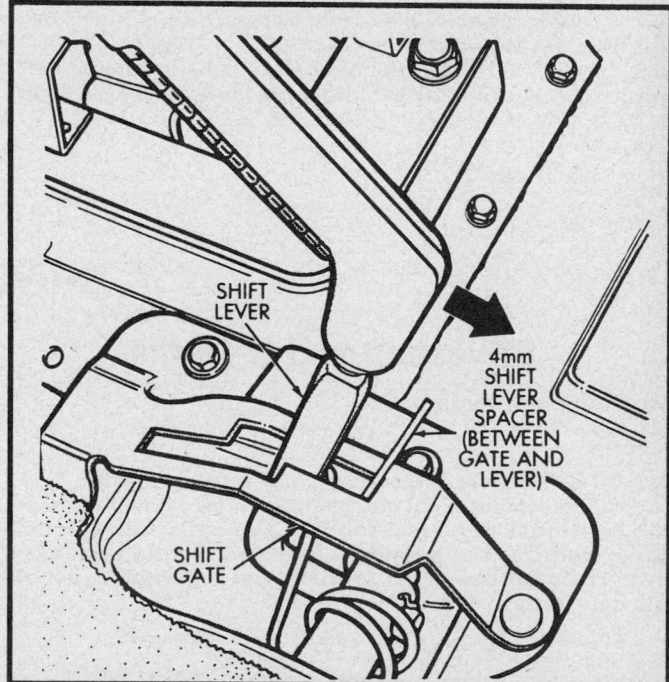

Installing the shift lever adjusting spacer

9. Disconnect the vent and vacuum hoses and the indicator wire.
10. Support the transfer case with a transmission jack.
11. Remove the transfer case-to-transmission bolts.
12. Pull the case rearward to disengage it and lower it from the truck.

To install:

13. Raise the transfer case into position. Make certain that the case and transmission are mated without binding, before torquing the attaching bolts. Torque the bolts to 26 ft. lbs.
14. Connect the shift linkage at the case.
15. Connect the vacuum hoses.
16. Install the driveshafts. New strap bolts should be used. Torque the nuts to 14 ft. lbs.; torque the flange nuts to 35 ft. lbs.
17. Install the rear crossmember. Torque the bolts to 30 ft. lbs.
18. Remove the transmission floor jack.
19. Connect the speedometer cable and vent hose.
20. Connect the shift lever link at the operating lever.
21. Fill the transfer case to the correct level.
22. Lower the vehicle.

NEW PROCESS 242

1. Shift the transfer case into **N**.
2. Raise and safely support the vehicle.
3. Drain the lubricant.
4. Matchmark and remove the front and rear driveshafts.
5. Support the transmission with a suitable jack.
6. Remove the rear crossmember.
7. Disconnect the speedometer cable.
8. Disconnect the linkage.
9. Disconnect the vent and vacuum hoses and the indicator wire.
10. Support the transfer case with a transmission jack.
11. Remove the transfer case-to-transmission bolts.
12. Pull the case rearward to disengage it and lower it from the truck.

To install:

13. Raise the transfer case into position. Make certain that the case and transmission are mated without binding, before torquing the attaching bolts. Torque the bolts to 26 ft. lbs.
14. Connect the shift linkage at the case.
15. Connect the vacuum hoses.
16. Install the driveshafts. New strap bolts should be used. Torque the nuts to 14 ft. lbs.; torque the flange nuts to 35 ft. lbs.

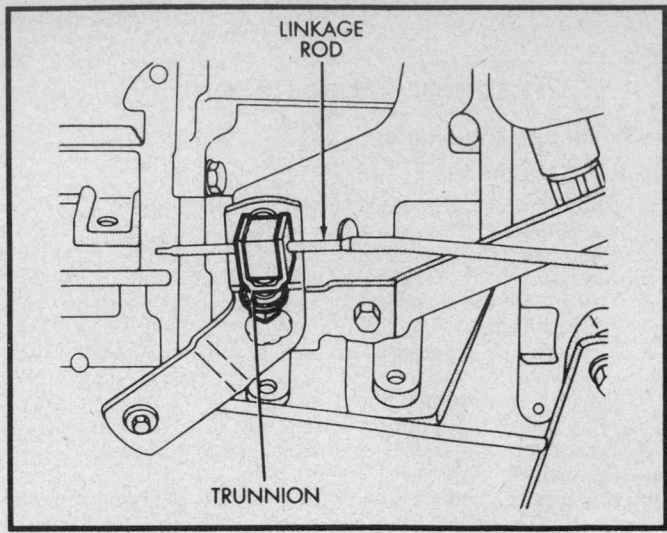

Shift linkage adjusting trunnion

17. Install the rear crossmember. Torque the bolts to 30 ft. lbs.
18. Remove the transmission floor jack.
19. Connect the speedometer cable and vent hose.
20. Connect the shift lever link at the operating lever.
21. Fill the transfer case.
22. Lower the vehicle.

Linkage Adjustment

1. Remove the shift lever boot.
2. Move the shift lever into the **4L** position.
3. Insert a 4mm (0.157 in.) spacer between the shift lever and the forward edge of the shift lever gate. Secure the lever and spacer with tape.
4. Raise and safely support the vehicle.
5. Loosen the trunnion lock bolt. The linkage rod should slide freely on the trunnion.
6. Position the linkage rod so that it is a free fit in the range lever, then tighten the trunnion locknut.
7. Lower the vehicle.
8. Remove the spacer and install the shift boot and bezel. Verify the operation of the shifter.

DRIVE AXLE

Driveshaft and U-Joints

Removal and Installation

FRONT

NOTE: These vehicles may come equipped with 2 different type front driveshafts. The first type has a conventional universal joint at the axle, but a double offset joint at the transfer case. The second type has a conventional universal joint at the axle and a double cardan joint at the transfer case.

1. Place the transmission and transfer case in **N**.
2. Raise and safely support the vehicle.
3. Matchmark the shaft ends, axle and transfer case.
4. Remove the U-joint strap bolts at the front axle yoke.

5. Remove the double offset joint flange nuts at the transfer case.
6. Installation is the reverse of removal.

REAR

NOTE: Two different driveshafts are used on these vehicles. With Command-Trac®, the driveshaft has welded yokes at each end. With Selec-Trac®, a welded yoke is used at the rear and a splined slip yoke is used at the front.

1. Place the transmission in **N**.
2. Raise and safely support the vehicle.
3. Matchmark the yokes and flanges.
4. On vehicles with Command-Trac®, the driveshaft may be removed by disconnecting it at the axle and sliding it from the

front yoke, leaving the front yoke attached to the transfer case. If done this way, matchmark the driveshaft and front yoke before separation.

5. On vehicles with Selec-Trac®, disconnect the yokes from the axle and transfer case. Remove the driveshaft.

6. Installation is the reverse of removal. Torque the U-joint strap nuts to 19 ft. lbs.

NOTE: New U-joint straps should be used.

Front Axle Shaft, Bearing and Seal

Removal and Installation

EXCEPT CJ7

1. Raise and support the vehicle safely.
2. Remove the wheels, calipers and rotors.
3. Remove the cotter pin, locknut and axle hub nut.
4. Remove the hub-to-knuckle attaching bolts.
5. Remove the hub and splash shield from the steering knuckle.
6. To remove the left shaft, remove the axle shaft from the housing.
7. To remove the right shaft:
   a. Disconnect the vacuum harness from the shift motor.
   b. Remove the shift motor from the housing.
   c. Remove the axle shaft from the housing.

To install:

8. To install the right axle shaft first be sure that the shift collar is in position on the intermediate shaft and that the axle shaft is fully engaged in the intermediate shaft end.
9. Install the shift motor, making sure that the fork engages with the collar. Tighten the bolts to 8 ft. lbs.
10. On the left side, install the axle shaft in the housing.
11. Partially fill the hub cavity of the knuckle with chassis lube and install the hub and splash shield.
12. Tighten the hub bolts to 75 ft. lbs.
13. Install the hub washer and nut. Torque the nut to 175 ft. lbs. Install the locknut. Install a new cotter pin.
14. Install the rotor, caliper and wheel.

CJ7

1. Raise and safely support the front of the vehicle. Remove the hub. Remove the brake caliper.
2. Remove the drive flange snapring.
3. Remove the rotor hub bolts, cover and gasket.
4. Release the locking lip of the lockwasher, and remove the outer nut, lockwasher, adjusting nut, and bearing lockwasher.
5. Remove the bearing and rotor.
6. Remove the backing plate adapter and splash shield.
7. Remove the spindle and spindle bushing.
8. Remove the axle shaft and universal joint assembly.

To install:

9. Clean all parts.
10. Insert the universal joint and axle shaft assembly into the axle housing, being careful not to knock out the inner seal. Insert the splined end of the axle shaft into the differential and push into place.
11. Install the wheel bearing spindle and bushing.
12. Install the backing plate adapter and splash shield.
13. Grease and assemble the wheel bearings and oil seal.
14. Install the rotor, hub, and caliper. Install the wheel bearing washer and adjusting nut. Tighten the nut to 50 ft. lbs., and back it off 1/6–1/4 turn while rotating the hub. Install the lockwasher and nut, tighten the nut to 50 ft. lbs. and then bend the lip of the lockwasher over onto the locknut.
15. Install the drive flange and gasket onto the hub and attach with 6 capscrews and lockwashers. Torque the capscrews to 30 ft. lbs. in an alternate and even pattern. Install the snapring onto the outer end of the axle shaft.
16. Install the hub cap or locking hub mechanism.
17. Install the wheel, lug nuts, and wheel disc.
18. Check the front wheel alignment, bleed the brakes and lubricate the front axle universal joints.

Rear Axle Shaft, Bearing and Seal

Removal and Installation

CJ7

1. Remove the cotter pins from the axle shaft nuts. Remove the axle shaft nuts. Raise the vehicle and support it safely.
2. Remove the rear wheels. Remove the brake drum retaining screws. Remove the brake drums.
3. Remove the axle hub using tool J–25109–01 or equivalent. Disconnect the brake lines at the wheel cylinders. Remove the support plates, oil seals and retainers and the endplay shims. Axle shaft endplay shims are installed on the left side of the axle only.
4. Remove the axle shafts using tool J–2498 or equivalent.
5. Installation is the reverse of the removal procedure. On vehicles equipped with a Trac-Loc differential, do not rotate the differential gears unless both axles are in position. If one shaft is removed and the other shaft rotated, the side gear splines will become misaligned and prevent installation of the replacement shaft.

WAGONEER, CHEROKEE AND COMANCHE

1. Raise and support the vehicle safely.
2. Remove the wheel, brake drum and brake support retaining nuts.
3. Pull the axle with a slide hammer.
4. Installation is the reverse of removal. Clean the bore in the axle housing and apply a thin coat of grease to the outer diameter of the bearing cup. Tighten the brake support nuts alternately and evenly to seat the bearing cup rib ring.

WRANGLER, GRAND WAGONEER, J10 PICK-UP AND J20 PICK-UP

1. Raise and support the vehicle safely. Remove the wheels. Remove the brake drum.
2. Remove the nuts attaching the support plate and retainer to the axle tube flange using the access hole in the axle shaft flange.
3. Position adapter tool J–21579, or equivalent and a slide hammer on the axle shaft flange. Remove the axle shaft from the rear axle assembly.
4. If the cup portion of the wheel bearing assembly remains in the axle assembly, remove it using tool J–2619–01 or J–26941.
5. Installation is the reverse of the removal procedure.

Steering Knuckle

Removal and Installation

1. Raise and safely support the vehicle. Remove the wheel assembly.
2. Remove the outer axle shaft.
3. Remove the caliper anchor plate from the knuckle.
4. Remove the knuckle-to-ball joint cotter pins and nuts.
5. Drive the knuckle out with a brass hammer.

NOTE: A split ring seat is located in the bottom of the knuckle. During installation, this ring seat must be set to a depth of 5.23mm. Measure the depth to the top of the ring seat.

6. Installation is the reverse of removal. Tighten the knuckle retaining nuts to 75 ft. lbs. and the caliper anchor bolts to 77 ft. lbs.

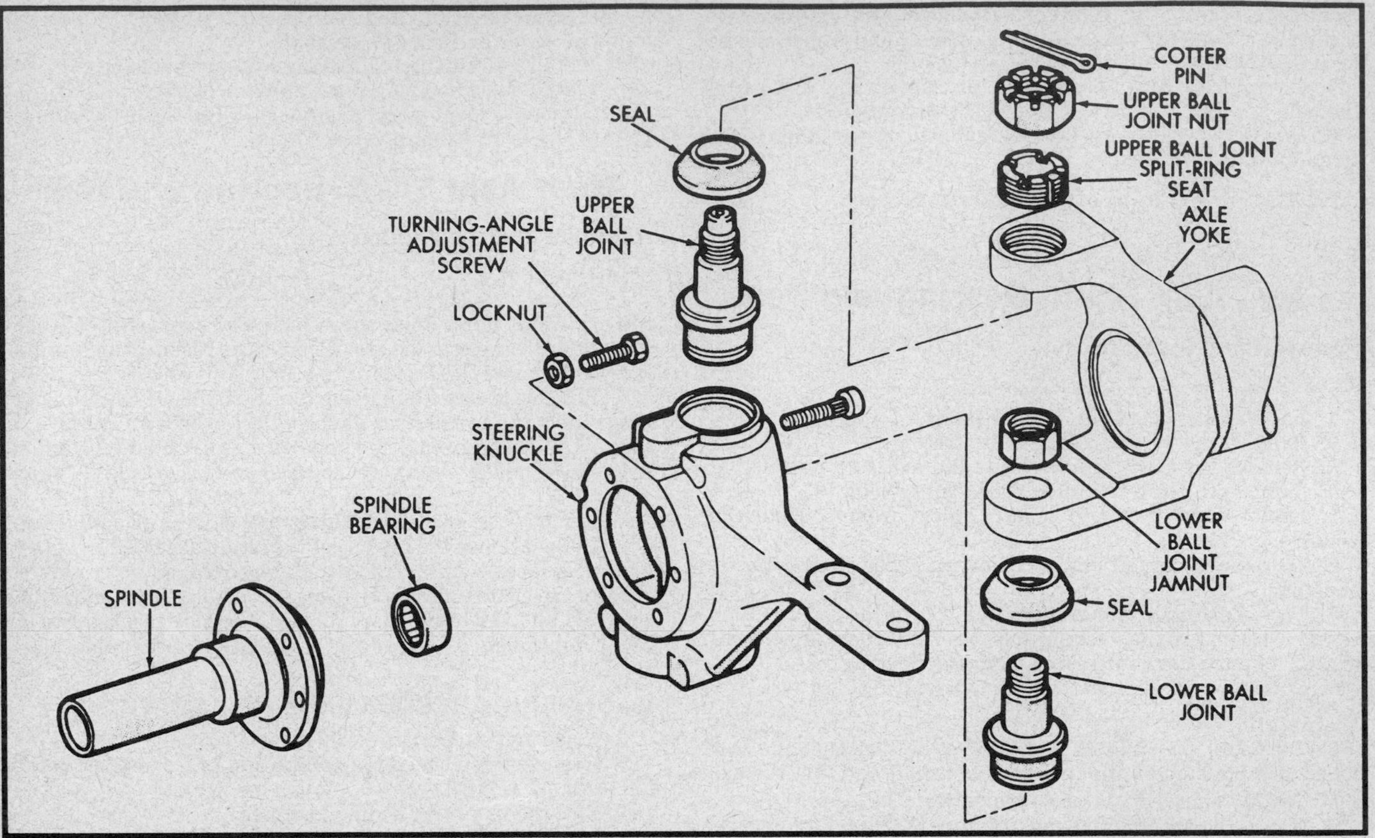

SEAL

TURNING-ANGLE ADJUSTMENT SCREW

UPPER BALL JOINT

LOCKNUT

STEERING KNUCKLE

SPINDLE BEARING

SPINDLE

COTTER PIN

UPPER BALL JOINT NUT

UPPER BALL JOINT SPLIT-RING SEAT

AXLE YOKE

LOWER BALL JOINT JAMNUT

SEAL

LOWER BALL JOINT

Steering knuckle assembly

Pinion Seal

Removal and Installation

1. Raise and support the vehicle safely.
2. Matchamrk and remove the driveshaft.
3. Using a holding tool and socket wrench, remove the pinion yoke nut and washer. Discard the nut.
4. Using a puller, remove the yoke.
5. Punch the seal with a pin punch and pry it from the seal bore.
6. Drive the new seal into place. A seal drive is helpful.
7. Install the yoke, washer and a new nut. Torque the nut to 210 ft. lbs.
8. Install the driveshaft. Torque the starp bolt nuts to 14 ft. lbs.

NOTE: New strap bolts should be used whenever the driveshaft is disconnected.

Differential Carrier

Removal and Installation

1. Raise the vehicle and support it safely. Remove the wheels and drums. Remove the axle shafts.
2. Drain the axle housing lubricant. Remove the axle housing cover. Mark the differential bearing caps for alignment during the assembly. Loosen the bearing cap bolts but do not remove.
3. Install an axle housing spreader tool on the axle housing and secure with the hold down clamps. Mount a dial indicator on the axle housing to measure the amount of spread. Zero the indicator dial.
4. Spread the axle housing no more than 0.020 in. Remove the differential bearing caps and the dial indicator from the

housing. Using 2 pry bars, remove the differential carrier from the axle housing.
5. Remove the spreader tool from the housing as soon as the differential carrier is removed to avoid the possibility of the axle housing taking a set.

To install:
6. Position the axle housing spreader tool on the axle housing

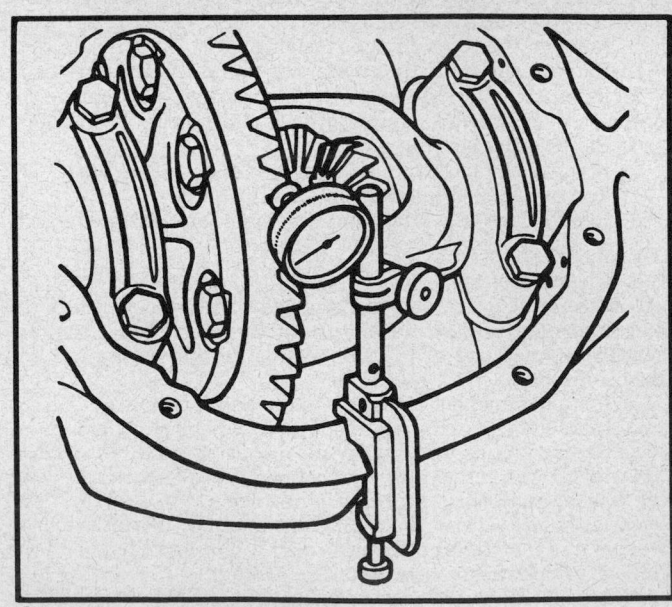

Checking ring gear endplay

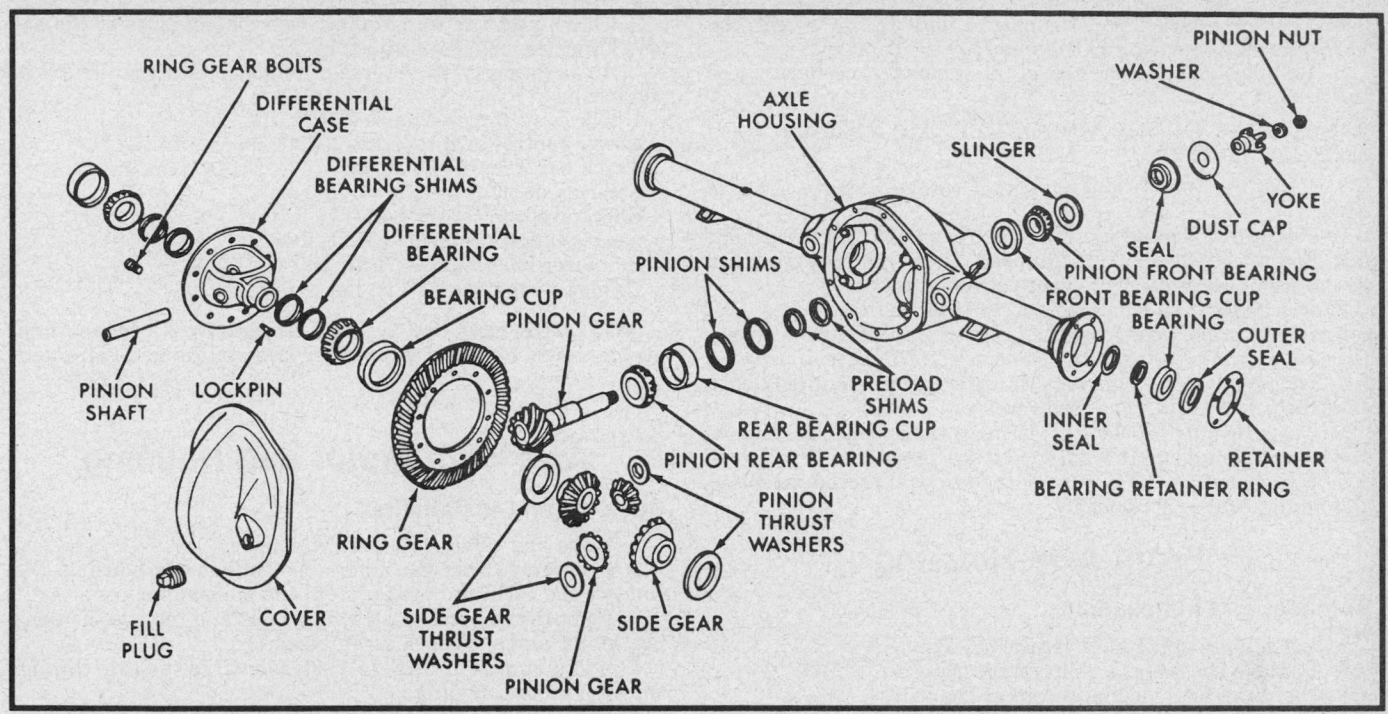

Exploded view of the Dana 44 axle

and secure it in place with the hold down clamps. Install a dial indicator and center the dial.

7. Spread the axle housing to a maximum of 0.020 in.. Remove the dial indicator. Lubricate the differential side bearings and install the differential carrier in the axle housing.

8. Prior shim fitting and bearing preload should be accomplished before differential carrier installation. Tap the unit in place with a soft faced hammer. Remove the axle housing spreader tool.

9. Install the bearing caps in their proper place and torque to 40 ft. lbs. on model 30 rear axle and to 80 ft. lbs. on models 44 and 60.

10. Install a dial indicator and recheck the ring gear backlash at 2 points. Correct as necessary. Complete the assembly in the reverse of the removal procedure.

Rear Axle Housing

Removal and Installation

CJ7

1. Remove the cotter pins from the axle shaft nuts. Remove the axle shaft nuts. Raise the vehicle and support it safely.

2. Remove the rear wheels. Remove the brake drum retaining screws. Remove the brake drums.

3. Remove the axle hub using tool J–25109–01 or equivalent. Disconnect the brake lines at the wheel cylinders. Remove the support plates, oil seals and retainers and the endplay shims. Axle shaft end play shims are installed on the left side of the axle only.

4. Remove the axle shafts using tool J–2498 or equivalent. Drain the lubricant and remove the axle housing cover. Disconnect the parking brake cables at the equalizer.

5. Mark the driveshaft for reinstallation. Disconnect the shaft at the axle yoke.

6. Disconnect the flexible brake hose at the body floorpan bracket. Disconnect the vent hose at the axle tube.

7. Properly support the rear axle assembly. Remove the

spring U-bolts, spring plates and spring clip plate, if the vehicle is equipped with a stabilizer bar.

8. Remove the rear axle from the vehicle.

9. Installation is the reverse of the removal procedure.

CHEROKEE, WAGONEER AND COMANCHE

1. Raise and support the vehicle safely. Remove the wheels and brake drums.

2. Disconnect the shock absorbers. Disconnect the brake hose at the frame rail. Disconnect the parking brake cables at the equalizer.

3. Mark the relation between the driveshaft and yoke and disconnect the driveshaft.

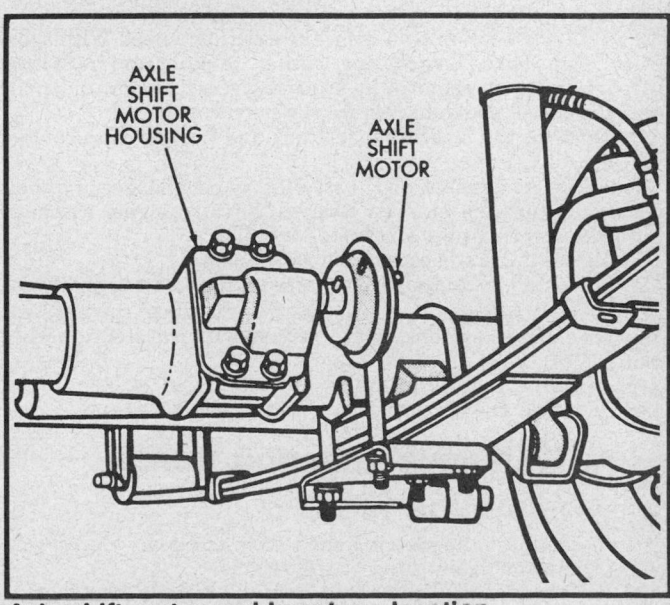

Axle shift motor and housing—location

4. Position a jack under the axle to take up the weight. Remove the axle to spring U-bolts and lower the axle.

5. Installation is the reverse of the removal procedure. Bleed the brakes.

WRANGLER, GRAND WAGONEER, J10 PICK-UP AND J20 PICK-UP

1. Raise the vehicle and support it safely. Remove the rear wheels.

2. Place an indexing mark on the rear yoke and driveshaft, and disconnect the shaft. If equipped, disconnect the track bar at the axle bracket and the vent tube at the axle.

3. Disconnect the shock absorbers from the axle tubes. Disconnect the brake hose from the tee fitting on the axle housing. Disconnect the parking brake cable at the frame mounting.

4. Remove U-bolts. On vehicles with spring mounted above axle, disconnect spring at rear shackle.

5. Properly support the axle. Remove the spring clips and remove the axle assembly from under the vehicle.

6. Installation is the reverse of the removal procedure. Bleed and adjust brakes accordingly.

Front Axle Housing

Removal and Installation

1. Raise and support the vehicle safely.
2. Remove the wheels, calipers and rotors.
3. Disconnect all vacuum hoses at the axle.
4. Mark the relation between the front driveshaft and yoke.
5. Disconnect the stabilizer bar, rod and center link, front driveshaft, shock absorbers, steering damper, track bar.
6. Support the front axle to take the weight off of it.

7. Disconnect the upper and lower control arms at the axle and lower the axle from the vehicle.

8. Installation is the reverse of removal. Observe the following torques:

   Upper control arm-to-axle — 55 ft. lbs.
   Lower control arm-to-axle — 133 ft. lbs.
   Track bar-to-axle — 74 ft. lbs.
   Steering damper-to-axle — 55 ft. lbs.
   Shock absorber lower bolt — 14 ft. lbs.
   Center link-to-knuckle — 35 ft. lbs.
   Stabilizer bar-to-axle — 70 ft. lbs.
   U-joint strap nuts — 14 ft. lbs.

NOTE: Discard the U-joint straps. New replacement straps must be used whenever the straps are removed.

Axle Shift Motor and Housing

Removal and Installation

1. Raise and safely support the vehicle.
2. Position a drain pan under the shift motor housing. Disconnect the vacuum harness from the shift motor.
3. Remove the housing attaching bolts and remove the housing, motor and shift fork as an assembly.
4. Add 5 ounces of SAE 75W–90 axle oil to the axle through the shift motor opening.
5. Install the motor housing into position adn tighten the mounting bolts to 101 inch lbs. (11 Nm).
6. Connect the vacuum harness and lower the vehicle.
7. Check the operation of the shift mechanism.

STEERING

Steering Wheel

Removal and Installation

1. Disconnect the negative battery cable.
2. Set the front tires in a straight ahead position.
3. Pull the horn button from the steering wheel. With sport wheel, remove the button, nut, washer, retainer and horn ring. It is necessary to remove the attaching screws from under the steering wheel spoke to remove the horn cover.
4. Remove the steering wheel nut and horn button contact cup.
5. Scribe a line mark on the steering wheel and steering shaft if there is not one already. Release the turn signal assembly from the steering post and install a puller.
6. Remove the steering wheel and spring.
7. To install, align the scribe marks on the steering shaft with the steering wheel and secure the steering wheel spring, steering wheel, and horn button contact cup with the steering wheel nut.
8. Install the horn button.
9. Connect the battery cable and test the horn.

Manual Steering Gear

Removal and Installation

1. Disconnect the steering shaft from the gear.
2. Raise and safely support the vehicle.
3. Disconnect the center link from the pitman arm.
4. Remove the front stabilizer bar.

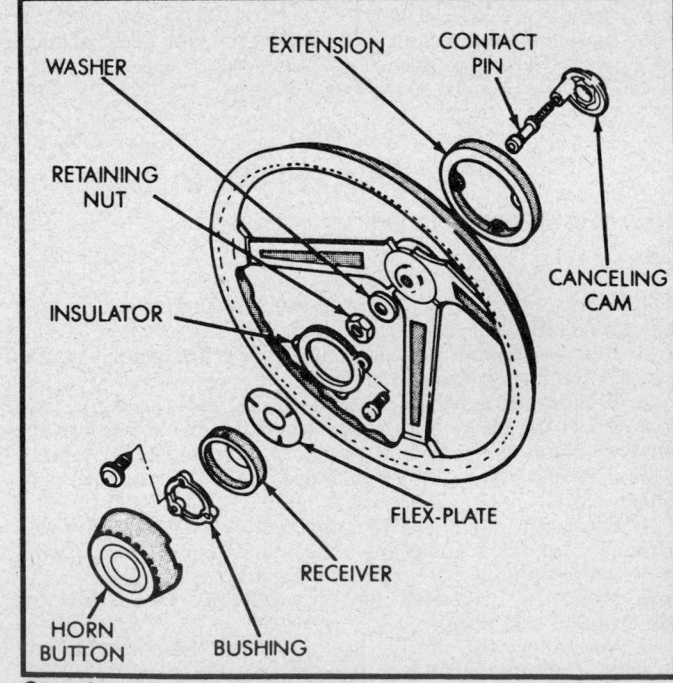

Steering wheel components

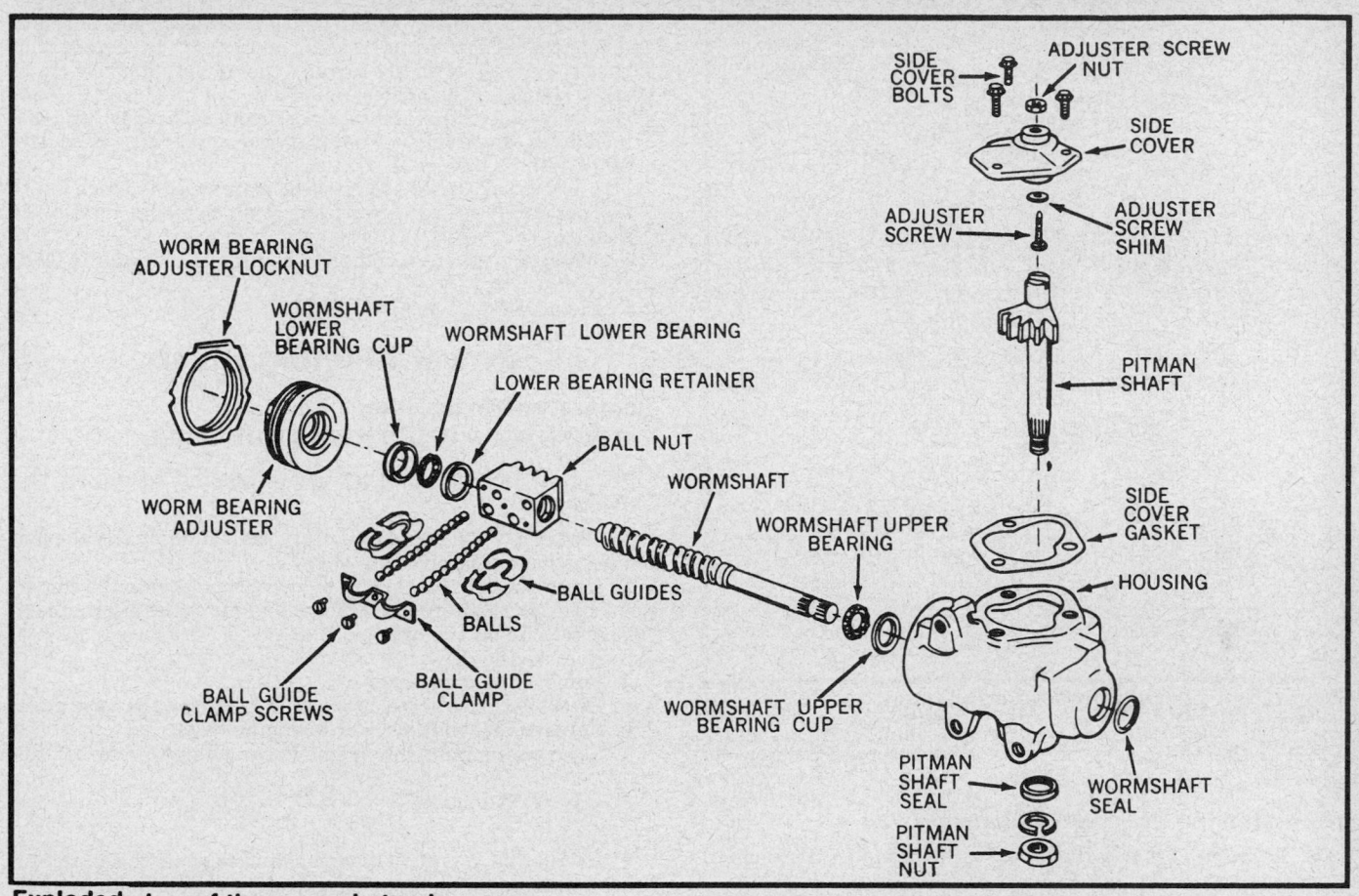

Exploded view of the manual steering gear

5. Remove the pitman arm nut, matchmark the arm and shaft, and remove the arm with a puller.
6. Unbolt and remove the gear.
7. Installation is the reverse of removal. The pitman arm nut must be securely staked. Observe the following torques:
   Steering gear-to-frame — 65 ft. lbs.
   Pitman arm-to-shaft — 185 ft. lbs.
   Stabilizer bar-to-frame — 55 ft. lbs.
   Stabilizer bar-to-link — 27 ft. lbs.
   Center link-to-pitman arm — 55 ft. lbs.

Adjustment

1. Raise and safely support the vehicle.
2. Check the steering gear mounting bolt torque.
3. Matchmark the pitman arm and shaft, and remove the pitman arm nut. Remove the arm with a puller.
4. Loosen the pitman adjusting screw locknut, then back off the adjusting screw 2–3 turns.
5. Remove the horn button and cover. Slowly turn the steering wheel in one direction as far as it will go, then back ½ turn.
6. Install a socket and torque wrench in the steering wheel nut. Measure the worm bearing preload by turning the wheel through a 90 degree arc (¼ turn) with the wrench. Preload should be 5–8 inch lbs.
7. If preload is not within specifications, turn the adjuster screw clockwise to increase, or counterclockwise to decrease, the preload.
8. When the desired preload is attained, tighten the adjuster locknut to 90 ft. lbs. and recheck the adjustment.
9. Rotate the steering wheel slowly from lock-to-lock, counting the number of turns. Turn the wheel back, ½ the number of turns to center the gear, then turn the wheel ½ turn off of center.
10. Install the torque wrench and socket on the steering wheel nut. Measure the torque required to turn the gear through the center point of travel. The drag should equal the worm bearing preload torque plus 4–10 inch lbs., but not exceed a total of 18 inch lbs.
11. If adjustment is required, loosen the pitman shaft screw locknut and turn the adjusting screw to obtain the desired torque. Tighten the locknut to 25 ft. lbs. and recheck the overcenter drag.
12. Install all parts and check steering wheel alignment.

Power Steering Gear

Removal and Installation

1. Disconnect the steering shaft from the gear.
2. Raise and safely support the vehicle.
3. Disconnect the center link from the pitman arm.
4. Remove the front stabilizer bar.
5. Remove the pitman arm nut, matchmark the arm and shaft, and remove the arm with a puller.
6. Disconnect and plug the power steering lines.
7. Unbolt and remove the gear.
8. Installation is the reverse of removal. The pitman arm nut must be securely staked. Observe the following torques:
   Steering gear-to-frame — 65 ft. lbs.
   Pitman arm-to-shaft — 185 ft. lbs.
   Stabilizer bar-to-frame — 55 ft. lbs.
   Stabilizer bar-to-link — 27 ft. lbs.
   Center link-to-pitman arm — 55 ft. lbs.

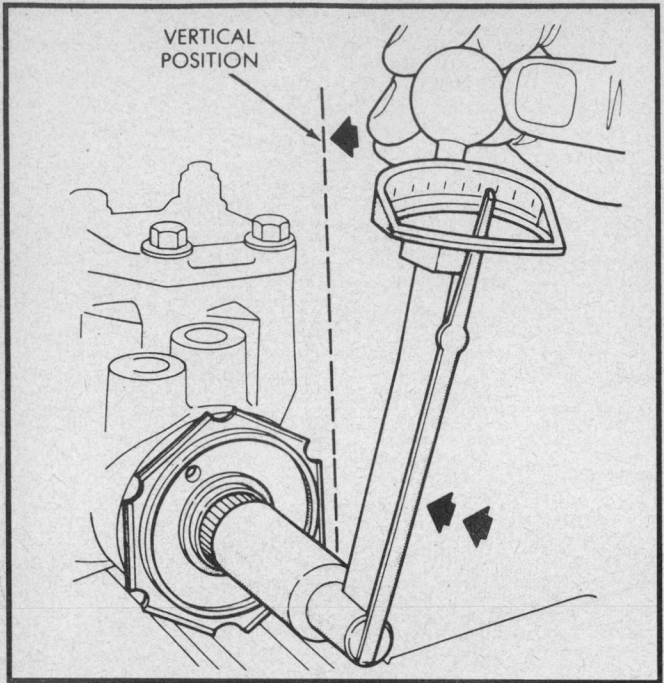

Wormshaft bearing preload adjustment

9. Fill the power steering system to the correct level and bleed the system.

Worm Bearing Preload Adjustment

1. Remove the steering gear and place in on a clean workbench.
2. Remove the adjuster plug locknut. Seat the adjuster plug firmly by applying about 20 ft. lbs. of torque.
3. Place an index mark on the gear housing, opposite one of the adjuster plug holes.
4. Going counterclockwise, make another mark $^3/_{16}$–$^1/_4$ in. from the first mark.
5. Turn the adjuster plug counterclockwise until the hole, which was aligned with the first mark, is now aligned with the second mark.
6. Install the adjuster plug locknut and torque it to 85 ft. lbs., making certain that the adjuster plug does not move.
7. Turn the stub shaft clockwise to its stop, then turn it back $^1/_4$ turn.
8. Using an inch pound (inch lbs.) torque wrench with a 50 inch lbs. scale and a 12 point deep socket on the stub shaft, take a reading of effort when the beam of the torque wrench passes the vertical point while turning. Torque at this point must be 4–10 inch lbs. If the reading is not correct, the adjuster plug is either not set correctly or moved while tightening the locknut, or, there is internal damage in the gear.

Pitman Shaft Overcenter Drag Torque

1. Turn the pitman shaft adjuster screw counterclockwise until it is fully extended, then, turn it back $^1/_2$ turn.
2. Rotate the stub shaft from stop to stop, counting the total number of full turns, then, turn it back $^1/_2$ the number of full turns. This is the center point of its travel. When the gear is centered, the flat on the stub shaft should face upward and be parallel with the side cover. The master spline on the pitman shaft should be aligned with the adjuster screw.
3. Place an inch pound torque wrench with a 50 inch lbs. scale, and a 12 point deep socket, on the stub shaft, with the torque wrench beam in the vertical position.

4. Rotate the torque wrench 45 degrees to each side of center and note the highest torque reading on or near the center point. Adjust the drag torque, by turning the adjusting screw clockwise, to the following values:
    a. New steering gears (used less than 400 miles), add 4–8 inch lbs. to the previously noted torque, but don't exceed a total of 18 inch lbs.
    b. Used gears (used 400 miles or more), add 4–5 inch lbs. to the previously noted torque, but don't exceed a total of 14 inch lbs.
5. When adjustment is complete, tighten the locknut to 20 ft. lbs.
6. Install the gear in the vehicle.

Power Steering Pump

Removal and Installation
ENGINES WITH SERPENTINE DRIVE BELT

NOTE: A belt tension gauge is needed to adjust the belt tension.

1. Disconnect the negative battery cable. Loosen the alternator adjustment and pivot bolts.
2. Insert the drive lug of a ½ in. drive ratchet into the adjustment hole in the alternator bracket and move the alternator to relieve tension on the belt.
3. Remove the drive belt.
4. Remove the air cleaner.
5. Disconnect the hoses at the pump and cap the hose ends.
6. Remove the front bracket-to-engine bolts.
7. Support the pump and remove the pump-to-rear bracket nuts.
8. Lift out the pump.

To install:
9. Install the pump in position and torque the pump-to-bracket nuts to 28 ft. lbs.; the bracket-to-engine bolts to 33 ft. lbs.
10. Install the drive belt. Using the ½ in. drive ratchet, move the alternator to put tension on the belt, tighten the alternator adjustment and pivot bolts and check the belt tension with a tension gauge at the mid-point of its longest straight run.
11. Belt tension should be 180–200 ft. lbs. for a new belt, or 140–160 ft. lbs. for a used belt.
12. When the tension is achieved, tighten the alternator pivot bolt to 28 ft. lbs.; the adjustment bolt to 18 ft. lbs.

ENGINES WITH V-TYPE DRIVE BELT

1. Disconnect the negative battery cable. Loosen the power steering pump adjustment and pivot bolts.
2. Insert the drive lug of a ½ in. drive ratchet into the adjustment hole in the pump rear bracket and move the pump to relieve tension on the belt.
3. Remove the drive belt.
4. Remove the air cleaner.
5. Disconnect the hoses at the pump and cap the hose ends.
6. Remove the front bracket-to-engine bolts.
7. Support the pump and remove the pump-to-rear bracket nuts.
8. Lift out the pump.
9. Install the pump into position and torque the pump-to-bracket nuts to 28 ft. lbs.; the bracket-to-engine bolts to 33 ft. lbs.
10. Install the drive belt. Using the ½ in. drive ratchet, move the pump to put tension on the belt, tighten the pump adjustment and pivot bolts and check the belt tension with a tension gauge at the mid-point of its longest straight run. Belt tension should be 120–160 ft. lbs. for a new belt, or 90–115 ft. lbs. for a used belt.
11. When the tension is achieved, tighten the pump pivot nut to 21 ft. lbs.; the adjustment bolt to 21 ft. lbs.

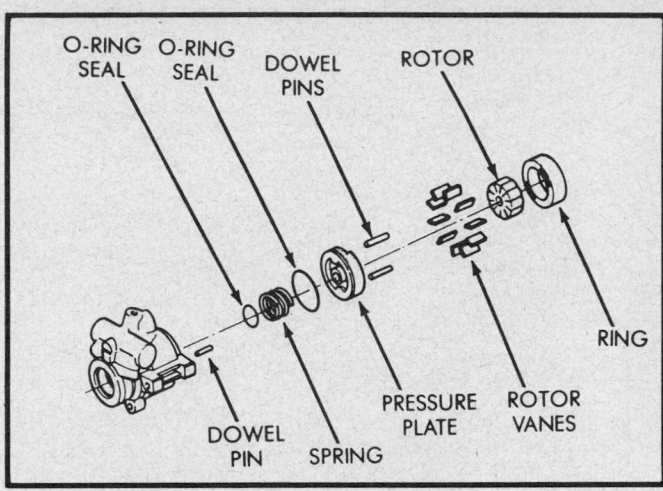

Power steering pump—exploded view

O-RING SEAL · O-RING SEAL · DOWEL PINS · ROTOR · RING · ROTOR VANES · PRESSURE PLATE · SPRING · DOWEL PIN

System Bleeding

1. Raise the front of the vehicle and support safely.
2. With the wheels turned all the way to the left, add power steering fluid to the **COLD** mark on the fluid level indicator.
3. Start the engine and check the fluid level at fast idle. Add fluid, if necessary to bring the level up to the **COLD** mark.
4. Bleed air from the system by turning the wheels from side-to-side without hitting the stops. Keep the fluid level just above the internal pump casting or at the **COLD** mark.
5. Return the wheels to the center position and continue running the engine for 2–3 minutes.
6. Road test the vehicle to check steering function and re-check the fluid level with the system at its normal operating temperature. Fluid should be at the **HOT** mark.

Tie Rod Ends

Removal and Installation

1. Raise and safely support the vehicle.
2. Remove the cotter pins and retaining nuts at both ends of the tie rod.
3. Remove the tie rod ends from the steering arm and center link.
4. Count the number of visible threads on the tie rod and unscrew the tie rod ends.
5. Installation is the reverse of removal. Install the tie rod ends, leaving the same number of threads exposed. Torque the retaining nuts to 35 ft. lbs.

BRAKES

For all brake system repair and service procedures not detailed below, please refer to "Brakes" in the Unit Repair section.

Anti-lock Brake System Pressure Relief

The anti-lock brake system operates under extremely high pressure. The pressure in the system must be relieved before any system repairs can be made.
1. Turn the ignition switch **OFF**.
2. Apply the brakes 45–50 times, until the pedal is firm, to reduce pressure in the accumulator, booster pump and lines.

Master Cylinder

Removal and Installation

EXCEPT ANTI-LOCK BRAKES

1. Disconnect the negative battery cable. Disconnect and plug the brake lines.
2. Disconnect the wires from the stoplight switch.
3. Remove all attaching bolts and nuts, and lift the assembly from the vehicle.
4. Prior to installation, fill the master cylinder and operate the pushrod until fluid squirts from the ports.
5. Installation is the reverse of removal. Torque the mounting nuts to 15–18 ft. lbs. Bleed the brake system.

ANTI-LOCK BRAKES

NOTE: **The master cylinder on the anit-lock brake system contains the system pressure accumulator and modulator.**

1. Disconnect the negative battery cable.
2. Remove the windshield washer fluid bottle.
3. Remove the air cleaner.
4. Disconnect the electronic control unit harness at the pressure modulator.
5. Disconnect the wiring at the proportioning valve.
6. Disconnect the brake line under the proportioning valve at the coupling.
7. Disconnect and cap the pressure line at the accumulator block.
8. Place a drain pan under the supply line and disconnect the supply line at the reservoir. Cap the openings. Discard the drained fluid.
9. Disconnect the low pressure switch wiring.
10. Disconnect the wiring at the modulator boost pressure and fluid level switches.
11. Disconnect the front brake lines at the outboard side of the pressure modulator.
12. Remove the instrument panel lower trim cover.
13. Disconnect the wiring at the brake light switch.
14. Remove the master cylinder pushrod bolt and disconnect the pushrod from the brake pedal. Discard the pushrod bolt nuts.
15. Remove the master cylinder mounting stud nuts.
16. In the engine compartment, pull the assembly and mounting bracket forward until the studs are clear of the firewall.
17. Lift the assembly out of the engine comaprtment.
To install:
18. Position the assembly in the firewall.
19. Install the master cylinder mounting stud nuts. Torque the nuts to 27 ft. lbs.
20. Connect the pushrod at the brake pedal. Torque the new nuts to 25 ft. lbs. for the inner locknut; 75 inch lbs. for the outer jam nut.

NOTE: **The pushrod must be installed with the bolt head on the left side of the pedal.**

21. Connect the wiring at the brake light switch.
22. Install the instrument panel lower trim cover.
23. Connect the front brake lines at the outboard side of the pressure modulator.

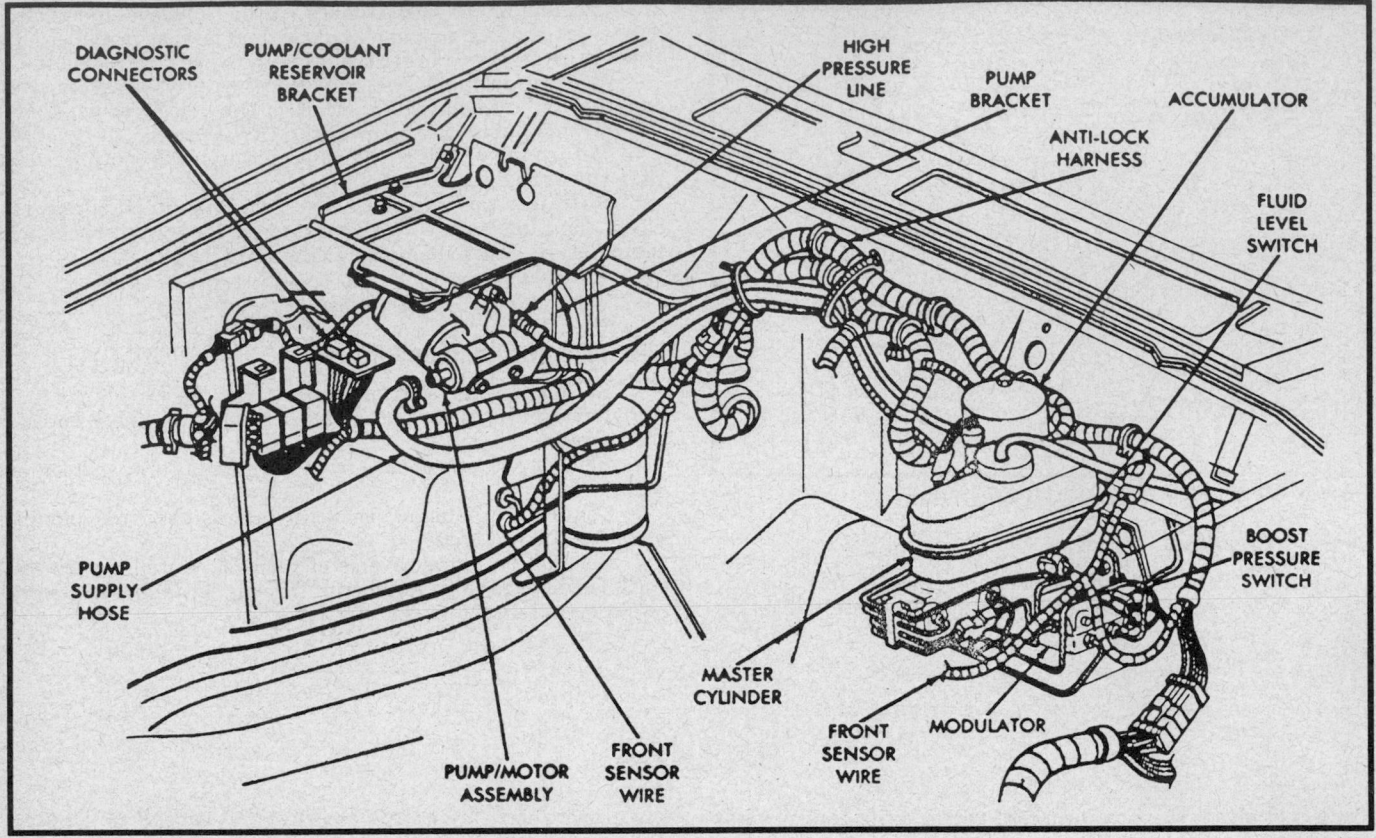

Anti-lock brake system component layout

24. Connect the wiring at the modulator boost pressure and fluid level switches.
25. Connect the low pressure switch wiring.
26. Connect the supply line at the reservoir.
27. Connect the pressure line at the accumulator block.
28. Connect the brake line under the proportioning valve at the coupling.
29. Connect the wiring at the proportioning valve.
30. Connect the electronic control unit harness at the pressure modulator.
31. Install the air cleaner.
32. Install the windshield washer bottle.
33. Connect the battery ground cable.
34. Clean the master cylinder cap area, remove the cap and, if necessary, fill the reservoir to the **MAX** line. Do not overfill.
35. Connect the battery and turn the ignition switch to **ON**. Listen for the sound of the pump running. An audible drop in pump rpm indicates that the system is pressurizing normally. If the pump rpm does not drop after 20 seconds, immediately turn the key **OFF** and check all line fittings for leaks.

NOTE: Letting the pump run for more than 20 seconds without system pressure will damage the pump.

36. Recheck the fluid level and bleed the brake system.

Proportioning Valve

Removal and Installation
STANDARD BRAKE SYSTEM
1. Disconnect the linkage and spring.
2. Disconnect and cap the brake lines.
3. Unbolt and remove the valve.
4. Installation is the reverse of removal. Torque the valve

bracket-to-frame bolts to 155 inch lbs.; the valve-to-bracket bolts to 118 inch lbs.

Adjustment
1. Remove the valve shaft nut and washer.
2. Disconnect the valve lever and remove the spring.
3. Remove and discard the bushing.
4. Rotate the valve shaft and install adjusting gauge tool J–35853–2, or equivalent.

NOTE: The gauge must be properly seated on the D shape of the shaft and the valve lower mounting bolt. All linkage components, except the spring, must be connected before installing the new bushing.

5. Place the bushing in the lever, and, using bushing aligning tool J–35853–1 or equivalent, press the bushing and lever onto the shaft.
6. Remove the lever and adjusting tool J–35853–2 or equivalent, and install the spring.
7. Install the lever, washer and nut. Tighten the nut to 100 inch lbs.
8. Connect the spring.

Power Brake Booster

Removal and Installation
STANDARD BRAKE SYSTEM
1. Disconnect the negative battery cable. Disconnect the power unit pushrod at the pedal.
2. Disconnect the vacuum line at the power unit check valve.
3. Unbolt the master cylinder from the power unit and move

it out of the way without disconnecting the brake lines. Be careful to avoid kinking the lines.

4. Unbolt and remove the power unit from the firewall.

5. Installation is the reverse of removal. Torque the power unit-to-firewall nuts to 30–35 ft. lbs.; the master cylinder-to-booster nuts to 15–18 inch lbs. Torque the pushrod nut to 35 ft. lbs.

Booster Pump and Motor

Removal and Installation

ANTI-LOCK BRAKE SYSTEM

1. Relieve the brake system pressure. Check the fluid level in the reservoir. It should have risen above the **MAX** fill line, but not overflowed. If overflowing occured, the system was overfilled to begin with.

2. Disconnect the negative battery cable.

3. Remove the coolant overflow bottle.

4. Remove the pump/motor mounting bracket bolts at the firewall and fender.

5. Rotate the pump/motor assembly to one side for access to the hoses and wires.

6. Unplug the wiring harness connector.

7. Slowly loosen the pressure line at the pump and allow any residual pressure to bleed off, then, disconnect the line.

8. Position a catch pan under the pump return line, loosen the clamp and disconnect the line. Discard any drined fluid.

9. Remove the pump/motor and bracket as an assembly. After removal, the units can be unbolted from the bracket.

To install:

10. Position the unit in the engine compartment.

11. Connect the pressure and return lines.

12. Connect the wiring harness.

13. Install the mounting bolts and torque to 30 ft. lbs.

14. Check the position of the lines. Make sure they are not kinked or touching any other component.

15. Clean the master cylinder cap area, remove the cap and, if necessary, fill the reservoir to the **MAX** line. Do not overfill it.

16. Connect the battery and turn the ignition switch to **ON**. Listen for the sound of the pump running. An audible drop in pump rpm indicates that the system is pressurizing normally. If the pump rpm does not drop after 20 seconds, immediately turn the key **OFF** and check all line fittings for leaks.

NOTE: Letting the pump run for more than 20 seconds without system pressure will damage the pump.

17. Recheck the fluid level.

Brake Caliper

Removal and Installation

1. Drain ⅔ of the brake fluid from the front reservoir. Use the bleeder screw at the front outlet port to drain the fluid. If equipped with anti-lock brakes, relieve the system pressure.

2. Raise and safely support the vehicle.

3. Remove the wheels.

4. Place a C-clamp on the caliper so that the solid end contacts the back of the caliper and the screw end contacts the metal part of the outboard brake pad.

5. Tighten the clamp until the caliper moves far enough to force the piston to the bottom of the piston bore. This will back the brake pads off of the rotor surface to facilitate the removal and installation of the caliper assembly.

6. Remove the C-clamp.

NOTE: Do not push down on the brake pedal or the piston and brake pads will return to their original positions up against the rotor.

7. Remove both of the allen head mounting bolts and lift the caliper off the rotor.

NOTE: If just the brake pads are being replaced, it is not necessary to remove the caliper assembly entirely from the vehicle. Do not remove the brake line. Rest the caliper on the front spring or other suitable support. Do not allow the brake hose to support the weight of the caliper.

8. If the caliper is being removed, it is necessary to disconnect the brake fluid hose. Clean the brake fluid hose-to-caliper connection thoroughly. Remove the hose-to-caliper bolt. Cap or tape the open ends to keep dirt out. Discard the copper gaskets.

9. Install the caliper in the reverse order of removal. Torque the mounting bolts to 35 ft. lbs.

NOTE: If the brake fluid hose was disconnected, it will be necessary to bleed the hydraulic system.

Disc Brake Pads

Removal and Installation

1. Raise and safely support the vehicle.

2. Drain ⅔ of the brake fluid from the front reservoir. Use the bleeder screw at the front outlet port to drain the fluid. If equipped with anti-lock brakes, relieve the system pressure.

3. Raise and support the vehicle safely.

4. Remove the wheels.

5. Place a C-clamp on the caliper so that the solid end contacts the back of the caliper and the screw end contacts the metal part of the outboard brake pad.

6. Tighten the clamp until the caliper moves far enough to force the piston to the bottom of the piston bore. This will back the brake pads off of the rotor surface to facilitate the removal and installation of the caliper assembly.

7. Remove the C-clamp.

NOTE: Do not push down on the brake pedal or the piston and brake pads will return to their original positions up against the rotor.

8. Remove both of the allen head mounting bolts and lift the caliper off the rotor.

9. Hold the anti-rattle clip against the caliper anchor plate and remove the outboard brake pad.

10. Remove the inboard pad and its anti-rattle clip.

11. Clean all the mounting holes and bushing grooves in the caliper ears. Clean the mounting bolts. Replace the bolts if they are corroded or if the threads are damaged. Wipe the inside of the caliper clean, including the exterior of the dust boot. Inspect the dust boot for cuts or cracks and for proper seating in the piston bore. If evidence of fluid leakage is noted, the caliper should be rebuilt.

NOTE: Do not use abrasives on the bolts in order not to destroy their protective plating. Do not use compressed air to clean the inside of the caliper, as it may unseat the dust boot seal.

12. Install the inboard anti-rattle clip on the trailing end of the anchor plate. The split end of the clip must face away from the rotor.

13. Install the inboard pad in the caliper. The pad must lay flat against the piston.

14. Install the outboard pad in the caliper while holding the anti-rattle clip.

15. With the pads installed, position the caliper over the rotor. Line up the mounting holes in the caliper and the support bracket and insert the mounting bolts. Make sure that the bolts pass under the retaining ears on the inboard shoes. Push the bolts through until they engage the holes of the outboard pad

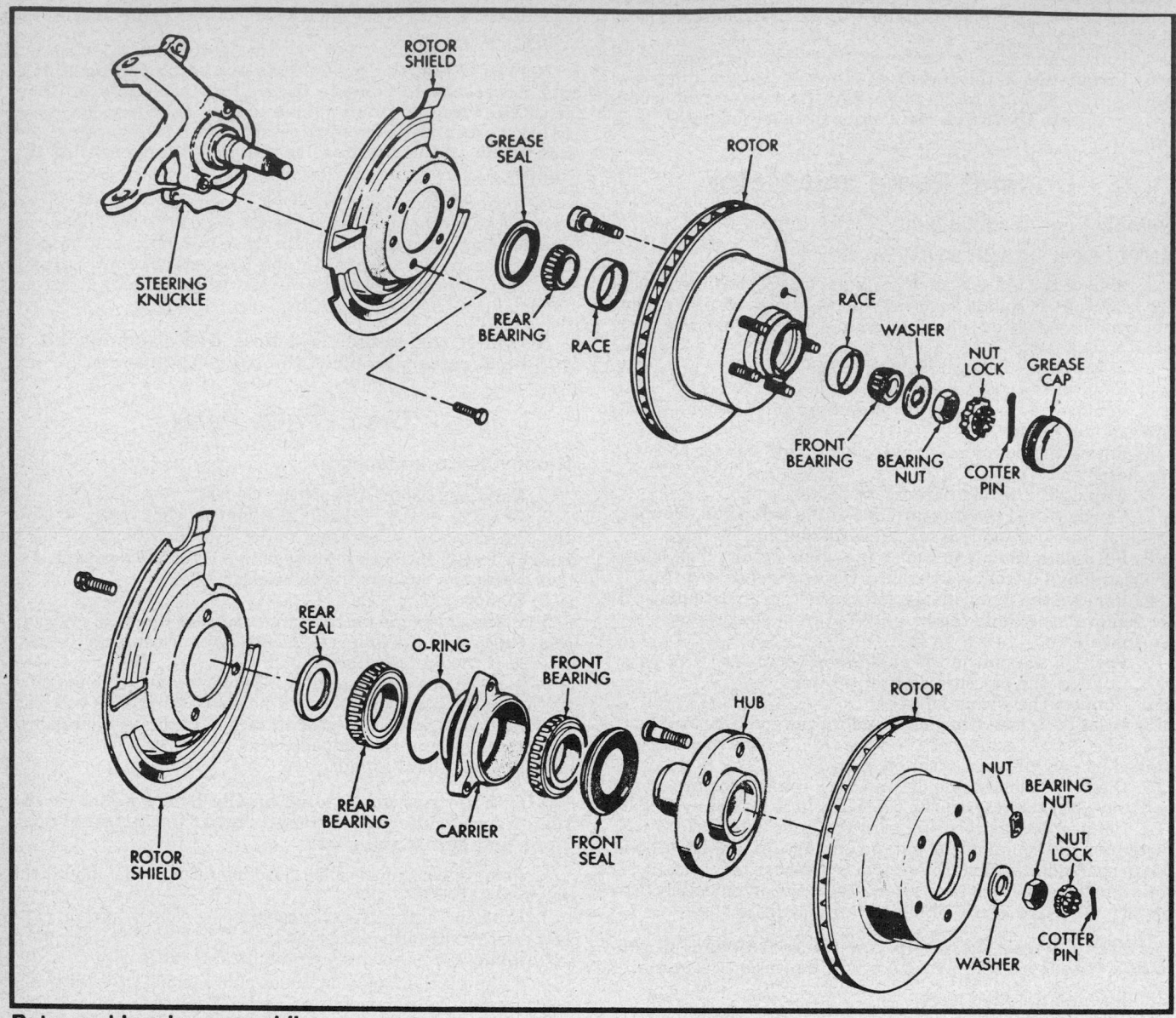

Rotor and bearing assemblies

and caliper ears. Thread the bolts into the support bracket and tighten them to 30 ft. lbs.

16. Fill the master cylinder with brake fluid and pump the brake pedal to seat the pads.

17. Install the wheel assembly and lower the vehicle. Check the level of the brake fluid in the master cylinder and fill as necessary. Test the operation of the brakes before taking the vehicle onto the road.

Brake Rotor

Removal and Installation

EXCEPT GRAND WAGONEER, J10 PICK-UP AND J20 PICK-UP

1. Loosen the lug nuts on the front wheels.
2. Raise and ssafely support the vehicle.
3. Remove the front wheels.

4. Remove the calipers, but don't disconnect the brake lines. Suspend the calipers out of the way.

5. Remove the rotor.

6. Installation is the reverse of removal.

GRAND WAGONEER, J10 PICK-UP AND J20 PICK-UP

1. Raise and safely support the vehicle.
2. Remove the wheels.
3. Remove the caliper without disconnecting the brake line. Suspend it out of the way.
4. Remove the grease cap, cotter pin, nut cap, nut, and washer from the spindle.
5. Pull slowly on the hub and catch the outer bearing as it falls.
6. Remove the hub and rotor. The inner bearing and seal can be removed by prying out and discarding the inner seal.

To install:

7. Clean and repack the hub and bearings, install the inner bearing and a new seal.

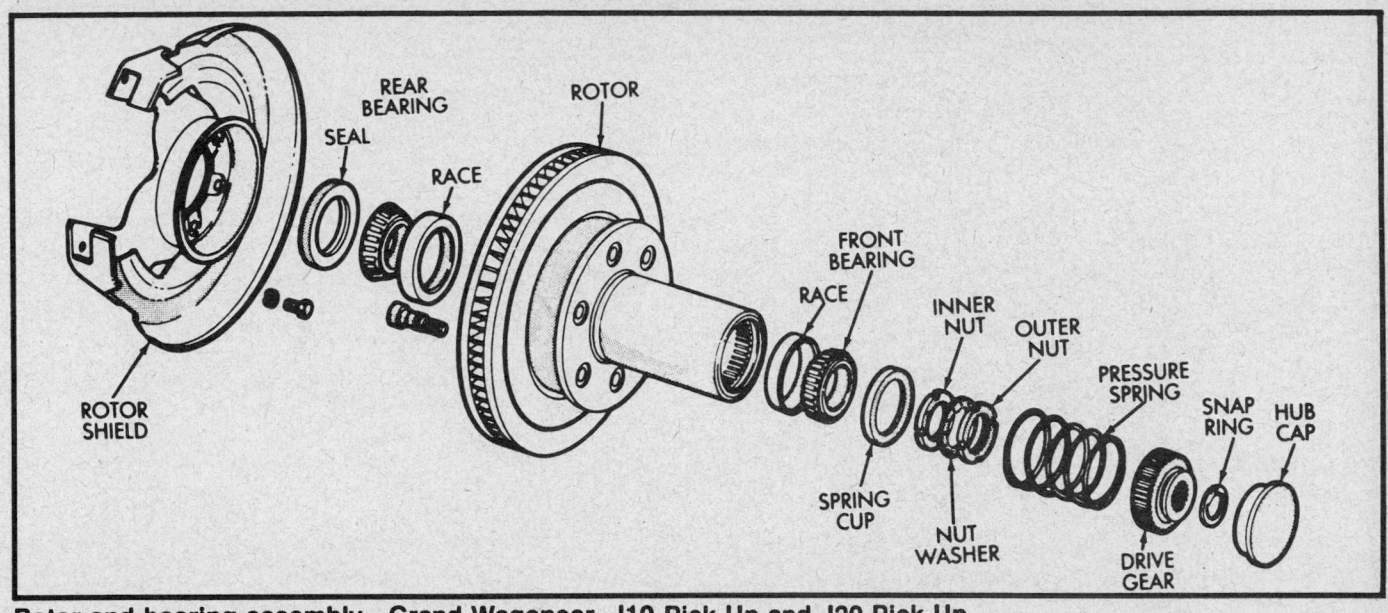

Rotor and bearing assembly—Grand Wagoneer, J10 Pick-Up and J20 Pick-Up

8. Position the hub and rotor on the spindle and install the outer bearing.

9. Install the washer and nut.

10. While turning the rotor, torque the nut to 25 ft. lbs. to seat the bearings.

11. Back off the nut ½ turn and, while turning the rotor, torque the nut to 19 inch lbs.

12. Install the nut cap and a new cotter pin. Install the grease cap.

13. Install the caliper.

14. Install the wheels.

Brake Drums

Removal and Installation

1. Raise and safely support the vehicle.

2. Remove the wheel.

3. Remove the spring nuts from the lug bolts and remove the drum from the vehicle.

NOTE: It may be necessary to back off the brake adjusters to remove the drum.

4. When placing the drum on the hub, make sure that the contacting surfaces are clean and flat.

5. Install the spring nuts on the lug bolts and install the wheel.

Brake Shoes

Removal and Installation

1. Raise and safely support the vehicle.

2. Turn the adjustment starwheel so that the brake shoes are retracted from the brake drum.

3. Remove the wheels and the drums to give access to the brake shoes.

4. Install wheel cylinder clamps to retain the wheel cylinder pistons in place and prevent leakage of brake fluid while replacing the shoes.

5. Remove the return springs with a brake spring remover tool.

6. Remove the adjuster cable, cable guide, adjuster lever and adjuster springs.

7. Remove the holddown washers and springs and remove the brake shoes.

8. Clean the backing plate with a brush or cloth. Place a dab of Lubriplate® on each spot where the brake shoes rub on the backing plate.

NOTE: Always replace brake linings in axle sets. Never replace linings on one side or on a single wheel.

9. Thoroughly clean the backing plate.

To install:

10. Apply a thin coat of multi-purpose chassis lube to the mounting pads on the backing plate.

11. Transfer the parking brake actuating lever to the new secondary shoe.

12. Position the brake shoes on the backing plate and install the holddown springs. Engage the parking brake lever with the cable.

13. Install the parking brake actuating bar and spring between the parking brake lever and primary shoe.

14. Install the self-adjusting cable, cable guide and upper return springs.

15. Thoroughly clean the starwheel and lightly lubricate the threads with lithium based grease.

16. Install the starwheel.

17. Install the self-adjusting cam and lower spring.

18. Check the surface of the brake shoes for any grease.

19. Install the drum and reach through the adjusting opening in the backing plate with a brake adjusting tool. Turn the starwheel outward so that the brakes lock the drum, then, holding the adjusting cam with a thin prybar, turn the starwheel back so that the drum is free and no drag is felt.

20. Once the wheels are on and the vehicle is lowered, back it up several times, applying the brakes to actuate the self-adjusters.

Wheel Cylinders

Removal and Installation

1. Raise and safely support the vehicle. If equipped with anti-lock brakes, relieve the system pressure.

2. Remove the wheel and remove the brake drum.

3. Disconnect the brake line at the wheel cylinder.

4. Remove the brake shoes.

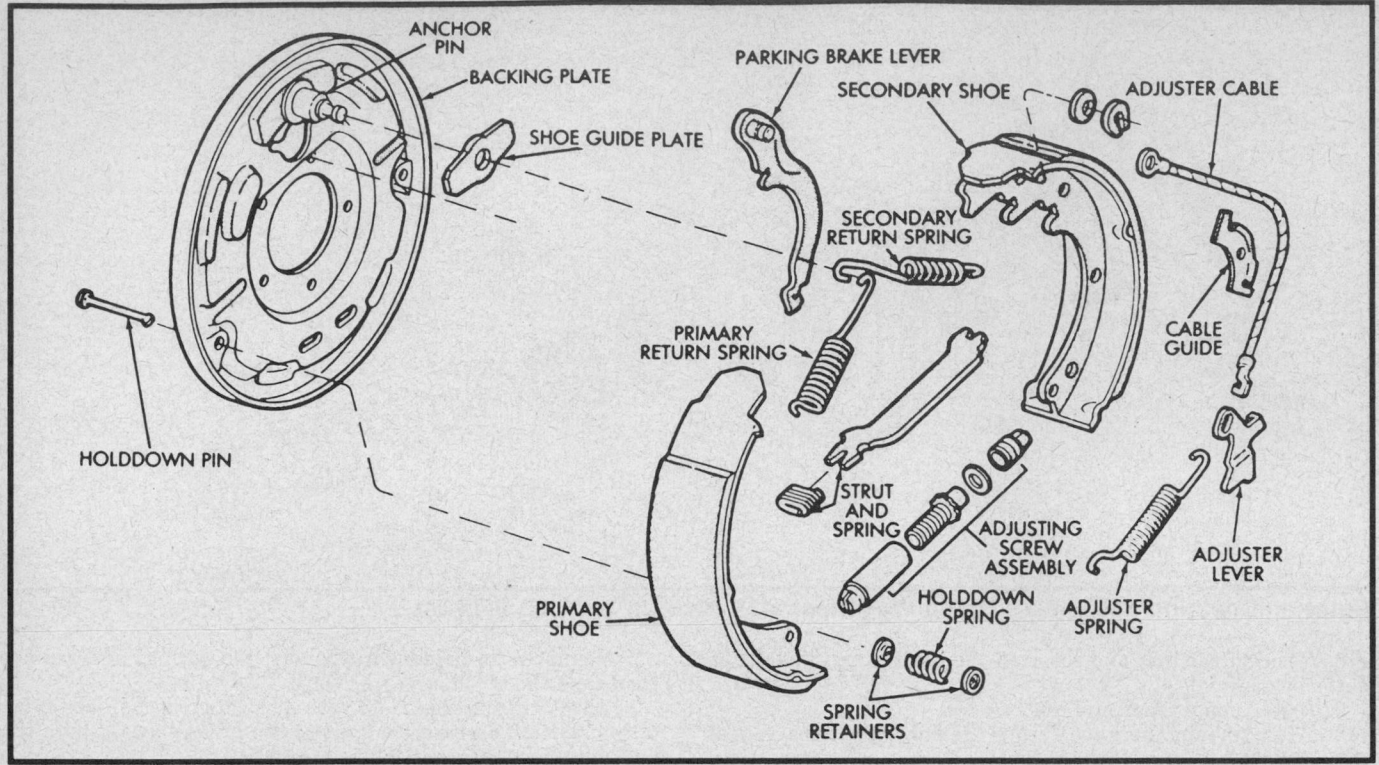

Drum brake assembly—exploded view

5. Remove the wheel cylinder attaching bolts and remove the wheel cylinder.

To install:

6. Position the wheel cylinder on the backing plate.

7. Connect the brake line to the cylinder fitting.

8. Install the wheel cylinder mounting bolts. On CJ7, Wrangler, Comanche, Cherokee and Wagoneer, tighten the bolts to 90 inch lbs. (10 Nm); Grand Wagoneer, J10 Pick-Up and J20 Pick-Up to 18 ft. lbs. (24 Nm).

9. Tighten the brake line fitting to 140 inch lbs. (16 Nm).

10. Install the brake shoes. Adjut the brake shoes.

11. Install the brake drum and wheel. Lower the vehicle.

12. Fill the brake system to the correct level and bleed the brakes.

Parking Brake Cable

Removal and Installation

1. Fully release the parking brake.

2. Raise and safely support the vehicle.

3. Remove the adjusting nut from the operating rod at the equalizer.

4. Disconnect the cable ends at the equalizer.

5. Unclip the cable from the frame bracket and unhook the locating spring from the cable.

6. Remove the rear wheels.

7. Remove the brake drums.

8. Remove the brake shoes.

9. Unhook the cable from the brake shoe actuating lever, compress the lock tabs at the backing plate and pull the cable out.

10. Installation is the reverse of removal.

Adjustment

1. Place the parking brake lever in the 5th notch.

2. Raise and safely support the vehicle.

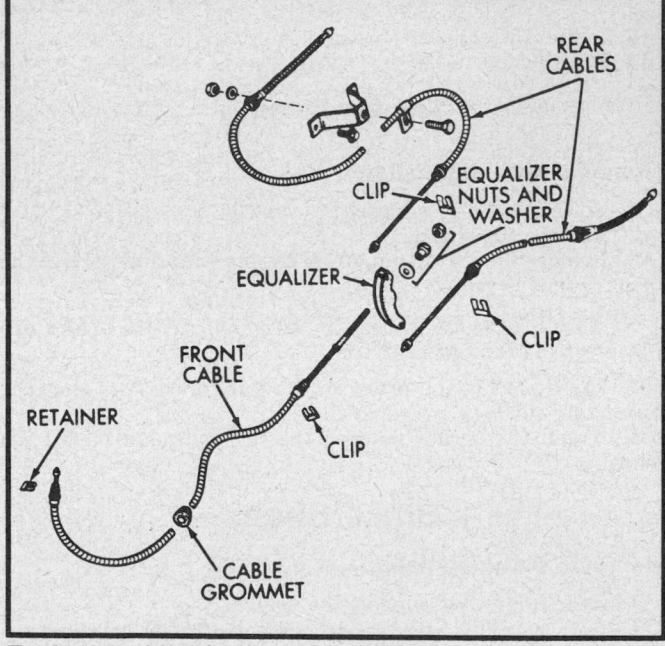

Typical parking brake cable layout

3. Using a torque wrench and adjustment adapter J–34651 or equivalent, apply a torque of 45–50 inch lbs.

4. Adjust the equalizer adjusting nut so that the gauge pointer is in the green band on the tool.

5. Apply and release the brake lever fully, 5 times, and recheck the adjustment.

6. When adjustment is correct, stake the adjusting nut.

FRONT SUSPENSION

Shock Absorbers

Removal and Installation

NOTE: Before installing new shocks, they should be purged of air. To do this, hold the shock upright and fully extend it, then invert and compress it. Do this several times.

1. Raise and safely support the front of the vehicle.
2. Remove the locknuts and washers.
3. Pull the shock absorber eyes and rubber bushings from the mounting pins.
4. Install the shocks in the reverse order of the removal procedure. Torque the upper end nut to 8 ft. lbs. and the lower end bolts to 14 ft. lbs.

Coil Springs

Removal and Installation

1. Raise and safely support the vehicle, allowing the front axle to hang.
2. Support the axle with a suitable jack.
3. Remove the wheels.
4. On 4WD vehicles, matchmark and disconnect the front driveshaft from the axle.
5. Disconnect the lower control arm at the axle.
6. Disconnect the stabilizer bar links and the shock absorbers at the axle.
7. Disconnect the track bar at the sill bracket.
8. Disconnect the tie rod at the pitman arm.
9. Lower the axle until tension is removed from the spring, then loosen the spring retainer and remove the spring.
10. Installation is the reverse of removal. Observe the following torques:

    control arm-to-axle — 133 ft. lbs.
    shock absorber-to-axle — 14 ft. lbs.
    stabilizer bar-to-axle — 70 ft. lbs.
    U-joint-to-axle — 14 ft. lbs.
    center link-to-pitman arm — 35 ft. lbs.
    track bar-to-frame rail — 35 ft. lbs.

Leaf Springs

Removal and Installation

1. Raise the vehicle and support it safely.
2. Position a suitable jack under the axle. Raise the axle to relieve the springs of the axle weight.
3. If equipped, disconnect the stabilizer bar. Remove the spring U-bolts and tie plates.
4. Remove the bolt attaching the spring front eye to the shackle. Remove the bolt attaching the spring rear eye to the shackle.
5. Remove the spring from its mounting.
6. Installation is the reverse of the removal procedure.

Front Stabilizer Bar

Removal and Installation

1. Raise and safely support the vehicle.
2. Remove the stabilizer bar-to-frame clamps and cushions.
3. Disconnect the stabilizer bar at the connecting links and remove the stabilizer bar. If necessary, disconnect the connecting links from the axle bracket.
4. Installation is the reverse of removal. Torque the clamp-to-frame bolts to 55 ft. lbs., the stabilizer bar-to-connecting link nuts to 27 ft. lbs., and the connecting link-to-axle bolts to 70 ft. lbs.

Track Bar

Removal and Installation

1. Raise and safely support the vehicle.
2. Remove the cotter pin and nut securing the track bar to the frame bracket.
3. Remove the bolt and nut securing the track bar to the axle.
4. Installation is the reverse of removal. Install both ends loosely, then torque the fasteners. Torque the frame-end nut to 35 ft. lbs.; the axle-end bolt to 55 ft. lbs.

Upper Ball Joint

Removal and Installation

1. Raise and safely support the vehicle. Remove the steering knuckle.
2. Position a ball joint removal tool J–34503–1 and 34503–3, or their equivalents, in a C-clamp and on the upper ball joint.
3. Tighten the clamp screw to remove the joint.
4. Use tools J–34503–5 and J–34503–12, or their equivalents, in a similar manner, to install the ball joint.
5. Install the knuckle.

Lower Ball Joint

Removal and Installation

1. Rasie and safely support the vehicle. Remove the steering knuckle.
2. Position a ball joint removal tool, J–34503–1 and J–34503–3 or their equivalents, on the lower ball joint.
3. Tighten the clamp screw to remove the joint.
4. Use tool J–34503–4 and J–34503–12 or their equivalents, to install the ball joint by reversing the removal procedure.
5. Install the knuckle.

Upper Control Arm

Removal and Installation

1. Raise and safely support the vehicle, allowing the suspension to hang freely.
2. On vehicles with the 2.8L engine, disconnect the right engine mount and raise the engine so that the rear bolt will clear the exhaust pipe.
3. Remove the wheels.
4. Remove the control arm-to-axle bolt.
5. Remove the control arm-to-frame bolt and remove the arm.
6. Installation is the reverse of removal. Torque the control arm bolts to 55 ft. lbs. at the axle; 66 ft. lbs. at the frame.

Lower Control Arm

Removal and Installation

1. Raise and safely support the vehicle, allowing the suspension to hang freely.
2. Disconnect the lower control arm at the axle and rear bracket. Remove the arm.
3. Installation is the reverse of removal. Torque the bolts to 133 ft. lbs.

Front Wheel Bearings

Removal and Installation
2WD VEHICLES

1. Loosen the lug nuts on the front wheels.
2. Raise and safely support the vehicle.
3. Remove the front wheels.
4. Remove the calipers, but don't disconnect the brake lines. Suspend the calipers out of the way.
5. Remove the dust cap, cotter pin, nut retainer, nut and thrust washer from the spindle.
6. Remove the rotor. Be ready to catch the outer bearing.
7. Carefully drive out the inner bearing and seal from the hub, using a wood block.
8. Inspect the bearing races for excessive wear, pitting or grooves. If they are cracked or grooved, or if pitting and excess wear is present, drive them out with a drift or punch.

To install:
9. Check the bearing for excess wear, pitting or cracks, or excess looseness.

NOTE: **If it is necessary to replace either the bearing or the race, replace both. Never replace just a bearing or a race. These parts wear in a mating pattern. If just one is replaced, premature failure of the new part will result.**

10. If the old parts are retained, thoroughly clean them in solvent and allow them to dry on a clean towel. Never spin dry them with compressed air.
11. Thoroughly clean the spindle.
12. Thoroughly clean the inside of the hub.
13. Pack the inside of the hub with EP wheel bearing grease. Add grease to the hub until it is flush with the inside diameter of the bearing cup.
14. Pack the bearing with the same grease.
15. If a new race is being installed, very carefully drive it into position until it bottoms all around, using a brass drift. Be careful to avoid scratching the surface.
16. Place the inner bearing in the race and install a new grease seal.
17. Position the hub and rotor on the spindle and install the outer bearing.
18. Install the washer and nut.
19. Install the nut cap and a new cotter pin. Install the grease cap.
20. Install the caliper.
21. Install the wheels.

Adjustment
CJ7

1. Raise and support the vehicle safely.
2. Remove the bolts attaching the front hub to the hub rotor. Remove the hub body and gasket.

3. Remove the snapring from the axle shaft and remove the hub clutch assembly.
4. Straighten the lip of the outer lock nut tabbed washer. Remove the outer locknut and tabbed washer.
5. Loosen and then tighten the inner locknut to 50 ft. lbs. Rotate the wheel while tightening the nut to seat the bearing properly.
6. Back off the inner locknut about $\frac{1}{6}$ of a turn while rotating the wheel. The wheel must rotate freely.
7. Install the tabbed washer and the outer locknut.
8. Torque the outer locknut to 50 ft. lbs.
9. Recheck the bearing adjustment. The wheel must rotate freely. Correct as required.

WRANGLER, CHEROKEE, COMANCHE AND WAGONEER

1. Raise and support the vehicle safely. Remove the tire and wheel. Remove the disc brake caliper as required. Remove the cotter pin, locknut and axle hub nut.
2. Tighten the hub bolts to 75 ft. lbs.
3. Install the hub washer and nut and tighten the hub nut to 175 ft. lbs. Install the locknut and new cotter pins.
4. Install the caliper, if removed. Install the wheel. Lower the vehicle.

GRAND WAGONEER, J10 PICK-UP AND J20 PICK-UP

1. Raise and support the vehicle safely.
2. If the vehicle is not equipped with front hubs, remove the wheel cover and hubcap. Remove the drive gear snapring. Remove the drive gear, pressure spring and spring cup.
3. If the vehicle is equipped with front hubs, Remove the socket head screws from the hub body and remove the body from the hub clutch assembly. Remove the large retaining ring from the hub. Remove the small retaining ring from the axle shaft. Remove the hub and clutch assembly. Remove the outer locknut and lock washer.
4. Seat the bearings by loosening and then tightening them to 50 ft. lbs. Back off the inner locknut about $\frac{1}{6}$ of a turn while rotating the wheel.
5. Install the lock washer. Align one of the lock washer holes with the peg on the inner locknut and install the washer on the nut.
6. Install and torque the outer locknut to 50 ft. lbs. Recheck the bearing adjustment. Correct as required.
7. On vehicles without front hubs, The spring cup must be installed so the recessed side faces the bearing and the flat side faces the pressure spring. The pressure spring should contact the flat side of the cup only.
8. Install the spring cup and the pressure spring. Install the drive gear and the drive gear snapring.
9. If the vehicle is equipped with front hubs, Install the clutch assembly. Install the small retaining ring on the axle shaft. Install the large retaining ring on the hub.
10. Install the hub body on the hub clutch. Install the socket head screws in the hub and torque them to 30 inch lbs.

REAR SUSPENSION

Shock Absorbers

Removal and Installation

NOTE: **Before installing new shocks, they should be purged of air. To do this, hold the shock upright and fully extend it, then invert and compress it. Do this several times.**

1. Raise and safely support the vehicle, support the rear axle with a suitable jack.
2. Remove the locknuts and washers.
3. Pull the shock absorber eyes and rubber bushings from the mounting pins.
4. Install the shocks in the reverse order of the removal procedure. Torque the upper end nut to 44 ft. lbs. and the lower end bolts to 44 ft. lbs.

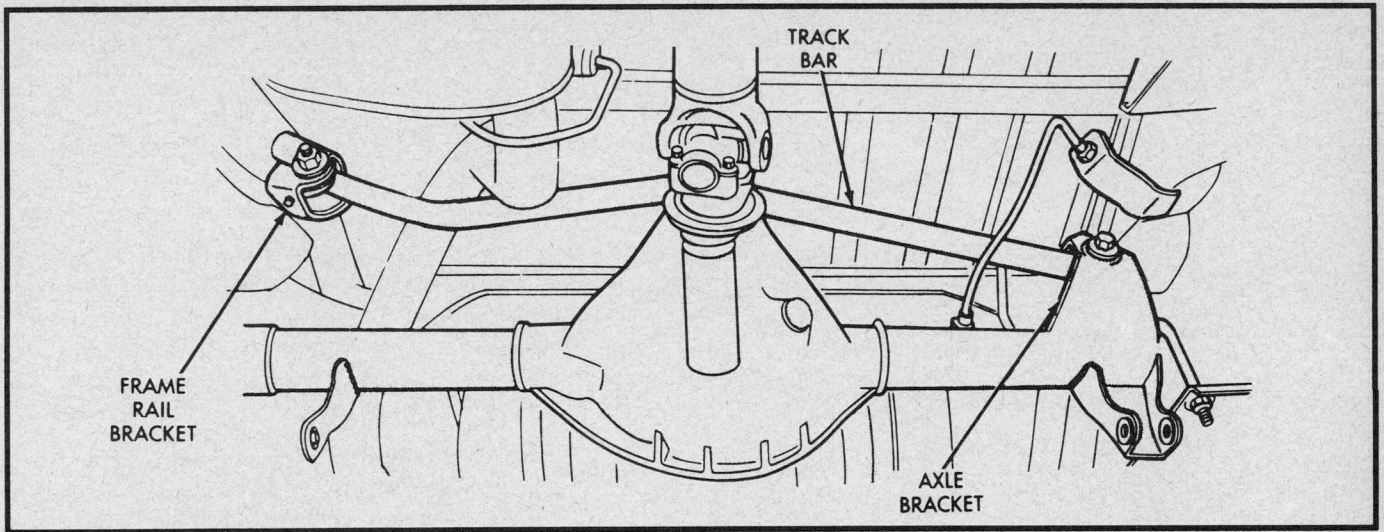

Rear track bar mounting

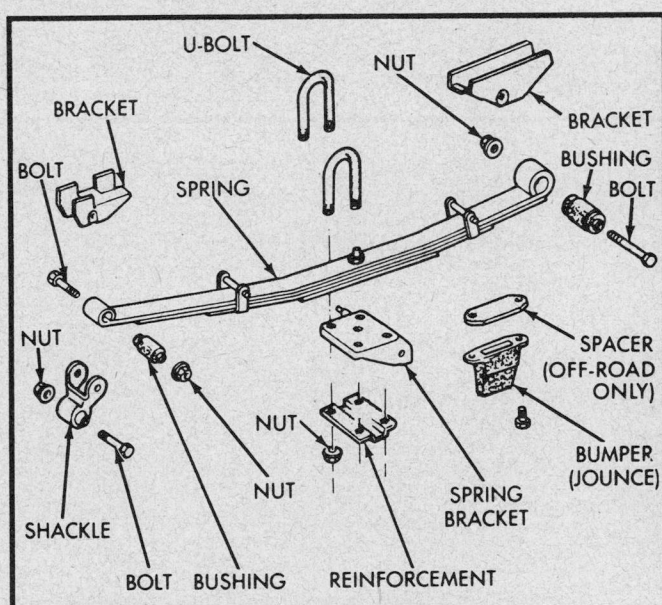

Rear spring mounting components

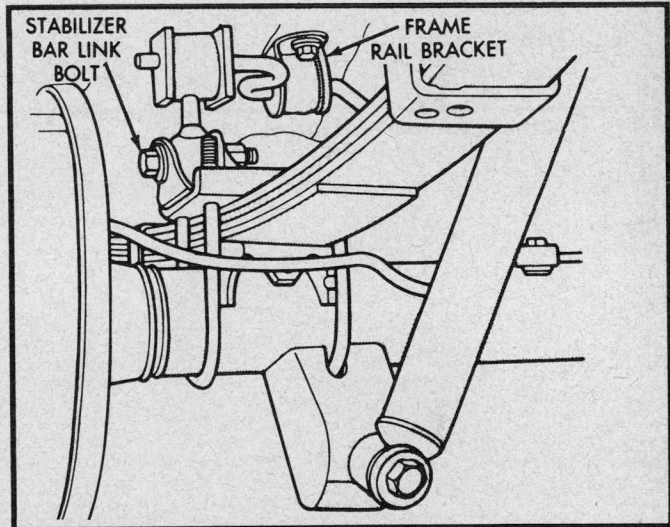

Rear stabilizer bar mounting

Leaf Springs

Removal and Installation

1. Raise and safely support the vehicle, allowing the suspension to hang freely.
2. Take up the weight of the axle with a suitable jack.
3. Disconnect the shock absorbers at the axle.
4. Remove the wheels.
5. Disconnect the stabilizer bar links at the spring plate.
6. Remove the U-bolts and spring plates.
7. Remove the rear spring-to-shackle bolt, then the front spring-to-shackle bolt.
8. Lower the axle and remove the spring.
9. Installation is the reverse of removal. Observe the following torques:
   a. Front and rear shackle bolts—111 ft. lbs.
   b. U-bolt nuts—52 ft. lbs.
   c. Shock absorber-to-axle nuts—44 ft. lbs.

Rear Track Bar

Removal and Installation

1. Raise and safely support the vehicle.
2. Remove the track bar attaching bolts at the frame and axle housing.
3. Remove the track bar.
4. Install the track bar into the brackets at the axle housing and the frame.
5. Tighten the attaching bolts to 105 ft. lbs. (168 Nm).
6. Lower the vehicle.

Rear Stabilizer Bar

Removal and Installation

1. Raise and safely support the vehicle.
2. Remove the stabilizer bar-to-frame clamps and cushions.
3. Disconnect the stabilizer bar connecting links at the spring tie plates and remove the stabilizer bar.
4. Installation is the reverse of removal. Torque the clamp bolts and the connecting link nuts to 55 ft. lbs.

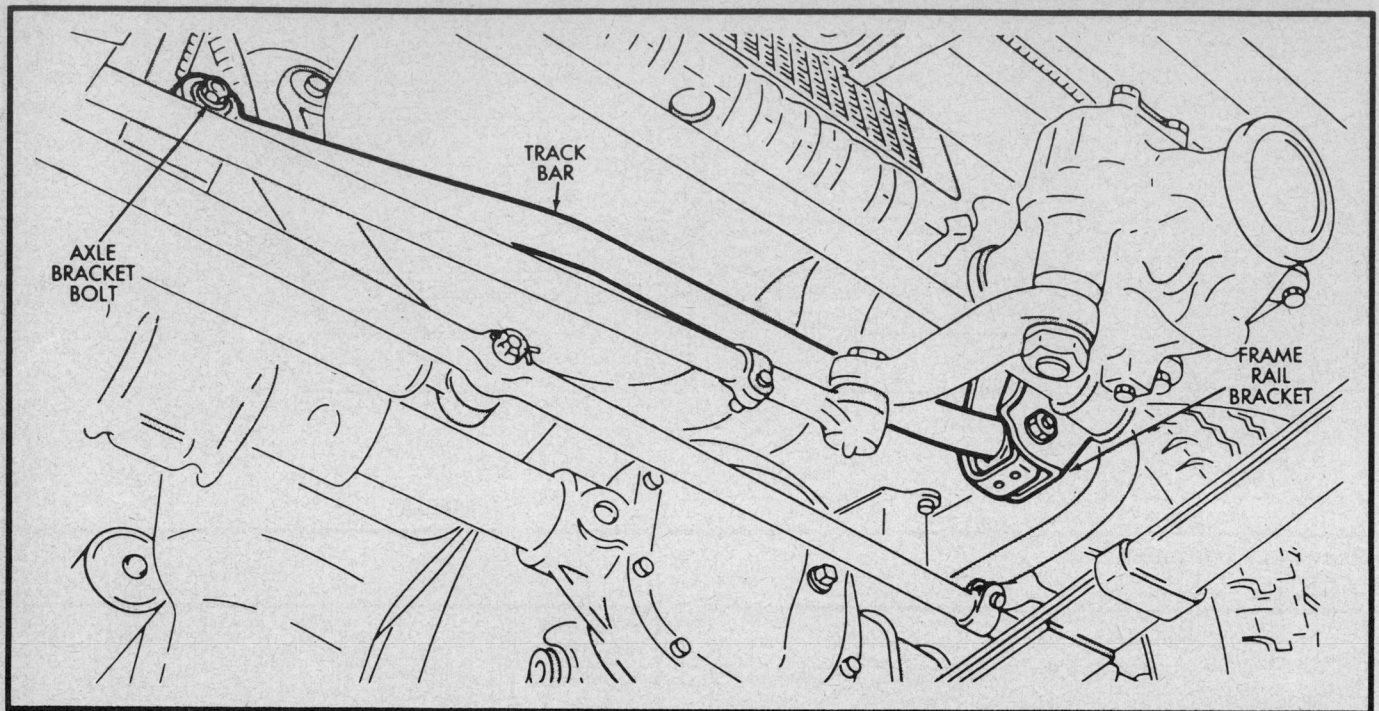

TRACK BAR

AXLE BRACKET BOLT

FRAME RAIL BRACKET

Front Track bar location—typical

ELECTRICAL DIAGNOSIS

To satisfy the growing trend toward organized engine diagnosis and tune-up, the following gauge and meter hook-ups, as well as diagnosis procedures are covered. The most sophisticated tune-up and diagnostic facilities are no more than a complex of the basic gauges and meters in common, everyday use. Therefore, to understand gauge and meter hook-ups, their applications and procedures, is to be equipped with the know how to perform the most exacting diagnosis.

KNOW YOUR INSTRUMENTS

OHMMETER

An ohmmeter is used to measure electrical resistance in a unit or circuit. The ohmmeter has a self contained power supply. In use, it is connected across (or in parallel with) the terminals of the unit being tested.

AMMETER

An ammeter is used to measure the amount of electricity flowing through a unit, or circuit. Ammeters are always connected in series with the unit or circuit being tested.

VOLTMETER

A voltmeter is used to measure voltage pushing the current through a unit, or circuit. The meter is connected across the terminals of the unit being tested.

ALTERNATORS AND REGULATORS

Diagnosis

The first step in diagnosing troubles of the charging system, is to identify the source of failure. Does the fault lie in the alternator or the regulator? The next move depends upon preference or necessity, either repair or replace the defective unit.

If the system is equipped with an external voltage regulator, it is easy to separate an alternator, electrically, from the regulator. Alternator output is controlled by the amount of current supplied to the field circuit of the system.

An alternator is capable of producing substantial current at idle speed. Higher maximum output is also a possibility. This presents a potential danger when testing. As a precaution, a field rheostat should be used in the field circuit when making the following isolation test. The field rheostat permits positive control of the amount of current allowed to pass through the field circuit during the isolation test. Unregulated alternator capacity could ruin the unit.

Most manufacturers of precision gauges offer special test connectors, in sets, that will adapt to the leads and connections of any charging system.

ALTERNATOR TEST PLANS

The following is a procedure pattern for testing the various alternators and their control systems.

There are certain precautionary measures that apply to alternator tests in general. These items are listed in detail to avoid repetition when testing each make of alternator and to encourage a habit of good test procedure.

1. Check alternator drive belt for condition and tension.
2. Disconnect the battery cables. Check physical, chemical and electrical condition of battery.

3. Be absolutely sure of polarity before connecting any battery in the circuit. Reversed polarity will ruin the diodes.
4. Never use a battery charger to start the engine.
5. Disconnect both battery cables when making a battery recharge hook-up.
6. Be sure of polarity hook-up when using a booster battery for starting.
7. Never ground the alternator output or battery terminal.
8. Never ground the field circuit between alternator and regulator.
9. Never run any alternator on an open circuit with the field energized.
10. Never try to polarize an alternator, unless directed by the manufacturer.
11. Do not attempt to motor an alternator.
12. When making engine idle speed adjustments, always consider potential load factors that influence engine rpm. To compensate for electrical load, switch **ON** the lights, radio, heater, air conditioner, etc.

Diagnosis

LOW OR NO CHARGING

1. Blown fuse
2. Broken or loose fan belt
3. Voltage regulator not working
4. Brushes sticking
5. Slip ring dirty
6. Open circuit
7. Faulty wiring connections
8. Faulty diode rectifier
9. High resistance in charging circuit
10. Grounded stator
11. May be open rectifiers (check all 3 phases)
12. If rectifiers are found or open, check capacitor

NOISY UNIT

1. Damaged rotor bearings
2. Poor alignment of unit
3. Broken or loose belt
4. Open diode rectifiers.

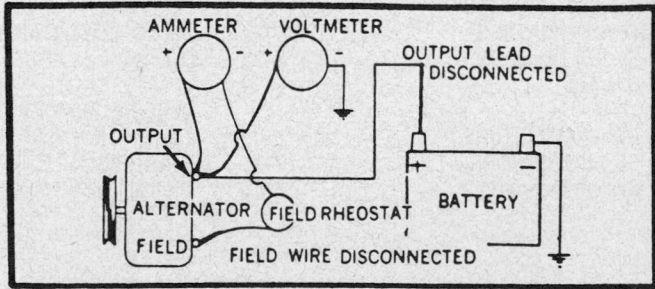

Checking field circuit current draw — as a precaution, a field rheostat should be used to control the amount of current allowed to pass through the circuit during isolation test

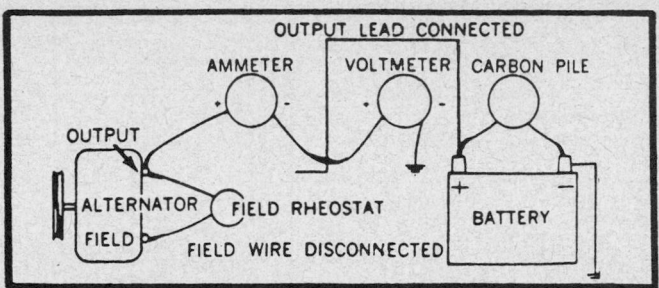

Checking current output of the charging system—if an overcharge of 10–15 amps is indicated, check for a faulty regulator

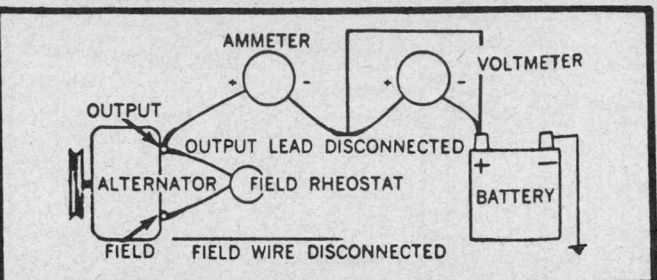

Checking charging system resistance to determine the amount of voltage drop between the alternator output terminal wire and the battery

CHRYSLER 60 AMP, 78 AMP AND 114 AMP ALTERNATOR WITH EXTERNAL REGULATOR

The 60 and 78 amp alternators are equipped with 6 built-in silicon rectifiers, while the 114 amp alternator is equipped with 12 built-in silicon rectifiers.

System Diagnosis

ON VEHICLE SERVICE

System Operation

NOTE: **If the current indicator is to give an accurate reading, the battery cables must be of the same gauge and length as the original equipment.**

1. With the engine running and all electrical systems **OFF**, place a current indicator over the positive battery cable.
2. If a charge of about 5 amps is recorded, the charging system is working. If a draw of about 5 amps is recorded the system is not working. The needle moves toward the battery when a charge condition is indicated and away from the battery when a draw condition is indicated. If a draw is indicated, proceed to the next testing procedure. If an overcharge of 10–15 amps is indicated, check for a faulty regulator.

Ignition Switch to Regulator Circuit Check

1. Disconnect the regulator wires at the regulator.
2. Turn the key **ON** but do not start the engine.
3. Using a voltmeter or test light check for voltage across the I and F terminals. If there is current present the circuit is good. If there is no current check for faulty connections, a faulty ballast resistor, a faulty ammeter, broken wires or a faulty ground at the alternator or voltage regulator. Also, check for voltage from the I wire to ground, current should be present. Check for voltage from the F terminal to ground, current should not be present.

Isolation Check

This test determines whether the regulator or alternator is faulty if everything else in the circuit was ok.

1. Disconnect, at the alternator, the wire that runs between 1 of the alternator field connections and the voltage regulator.
2. Run a jumper wire from the disconnected alternator terminal to ground.
3. Connect a voltmeter to the battery. The positive voltmeter

lead connects to the positive battery terminal and the negative lead goes to the negative terminal. Record the reading.
4. Make sure that all electrical systems are turned **OFF**. Start the engine. Do not race the engine.
5. Gradually increase engine speed to 1500–2000 rpm. There should be an increase of 1–2 volts on the voltmeter. If this is true the alternator is good and the voltage regulator should be repaired. If there is no voltage increase the alternator is faulty.

Charging Circuit Resistance Check

The purpose of this test is to determine the amount of voltage drop between the alternator output terminal wire and the battery.

1. Disconnect the battery ground cable and the BAT lead at the alternator output terminal.
2. Connect an ammeter with a scale to 100 amps in series between the alternator BAT terminal and the disconnected BAT wire.
3. Connect the positive lead of a voltmeter to the disconnected BAT wire. Connect the negative lead of the voltmeter to the negative post of the battery.
4. Disconnect the green colored regulator field wire from the alternator. Connect a jumper lead from the alternator field terminal to ground.
5. Connect a tachometer to the engine and reconnect the battery ground cable.
6. Connect a variable carbon pile rheostat to the battery cables. Be sure the carbon pile is in the **OPEN** or **OFF** position before connecting the leads to the battery terminals.
7. Start the engine and operate at idle.
8. Adjust the engine speed and carbon pile to maintain a flow of 20 amperes in the circuit. Observe the voltmeter reading which should not exceed 0.7 volts.
9. If a higher voltage reading is indicated inspect, clean and tighten all connections in the charging system.
10. If necessary a voltage drop test can be done at each connection until the excessive resistance is located.
11. If the charging system resistance is within specifications reduce the engine speed, turn **OFF** the carbon pile rheostat and stop the engine. Remove battery ground cable.
12. Remove the test instruments from the electrical system and reconnect the charging system wiring. Reconnect the battery ground cable.

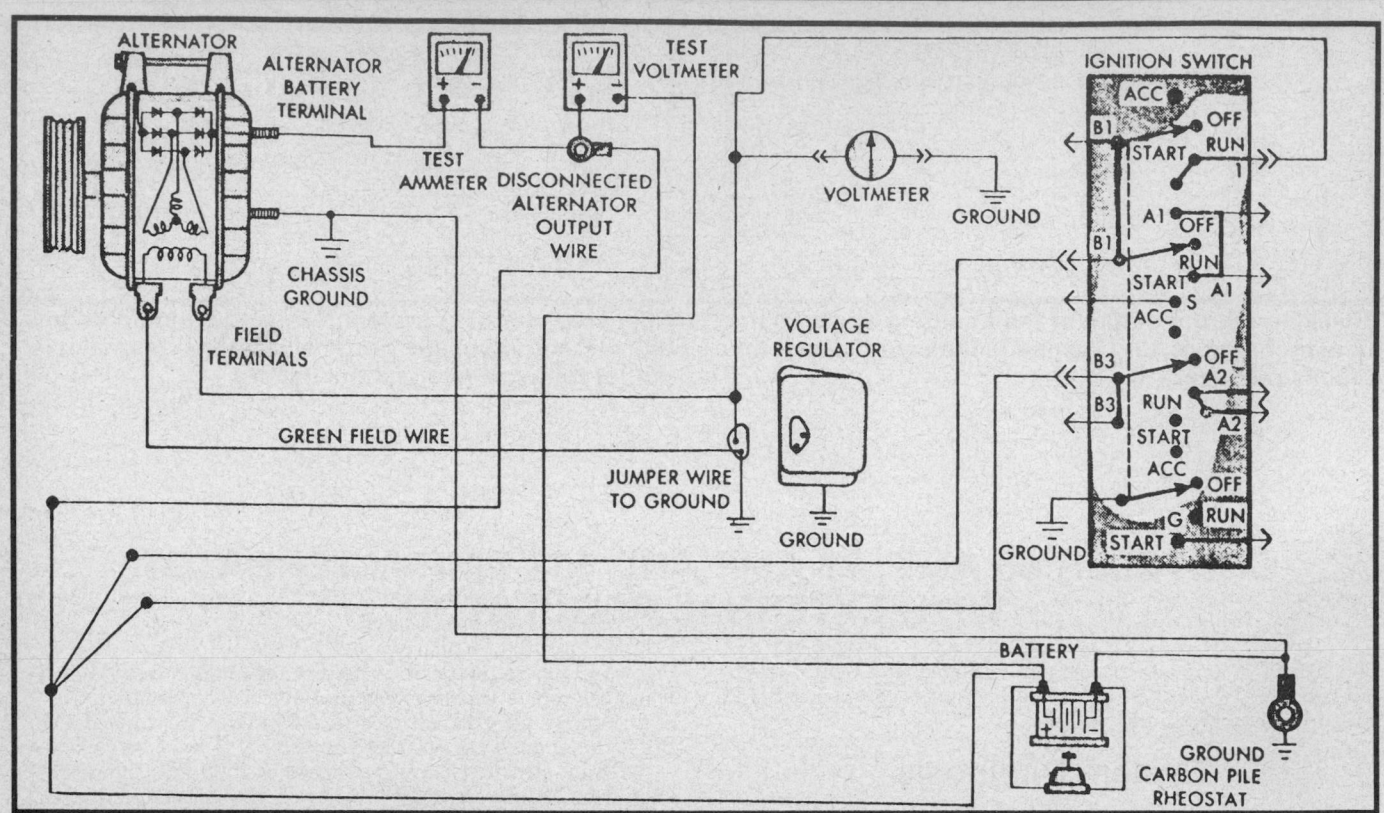

Chrysler 60, 78 and 114 amp alternators with external voltage regulator—charging system resistance test—adjust engine speed and carbon pile to maintain 20 amps, voltmeter reading should not exceed 0.5 volts

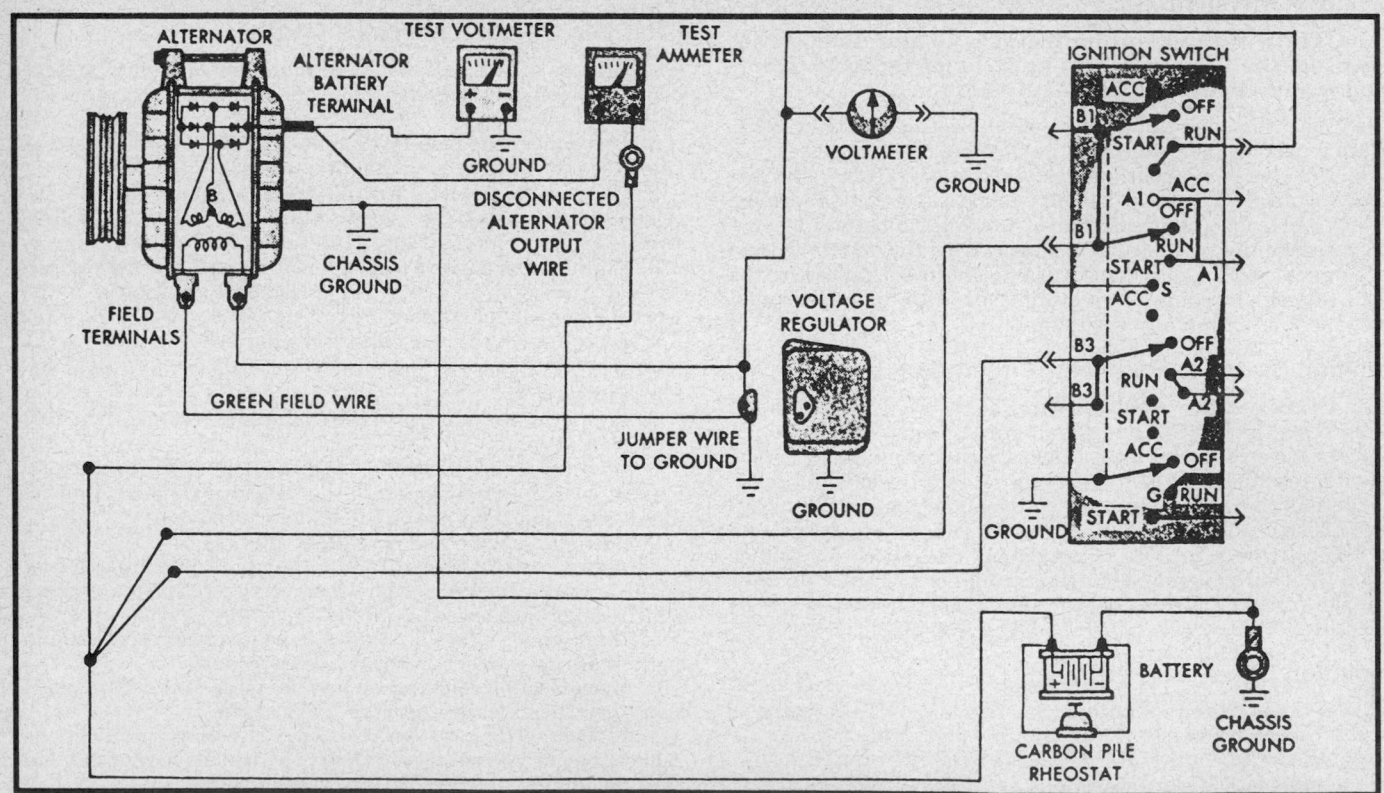

Chrysler 60, 78 and 144 amp alternators with external voltage regulator—current output test—adjust engine speed and carbon pile increments until an engine speed of 1250 rpm is reached, voltmeter reading should not exceed 15 volts

Current Rating	Identification	Current Output
60 amp	Blue, natural or yellow	47 amps min.
78 amp	Brown tag	58 amps min.
114 amp	Yellow	97 amps min.

Current rating chart

Current Output Check

This test determines if the alternator is capable of delivering its rated current output.

1. Disconnect the battery ground cable and the BAT lead wire at the alternator output terminal.
2. Connect an ammeter in series between the alternator output terminal and the disconnected BAT lead wire. The ammeter must have a scale of 100 amps.
3. Connect the positive lead of a voltmeter to the output terminal of the alternator and the negative lead to a good ground.
4. Disconnect the green colored wire at the voltage regulator and connect a jumper wire from the alternator field terminal to ground.
5. Connect a tachometer to the engine and reconnect the battery ground wire.
6. Connect a variable carbon pile rheostat between the positive and negative battery cables. Be sure the rheostat control is in the **OPEN** or **OFF** position before connecting the leads to the battery cables.
7. Start the engine and operate at idle. Adjust the carbon pile rheostat control and the engine speed in increments until the voltmeter reading is 15 volts (13 volts for the 114 amp alternators) and the engine speed is 1250 rpm (900 rpm for the 114 amp alternators). Do not allow the voltage to rise above 16 volts.
8. The ammeter readings must be within the following specifications.

NOTE: If measured at the battery, current output will be approximately 5 amperes lower than specified.

9. If the readings are less than specified, the alternator should be removed and checked during a bench test.
10. After the current output test is completed, reduce the engine speed, turn the carbon pile rheostat **OFF** and then stop the engine.
11. Disconnect the battery ground cable, remove the ammeter, voltmeter and carbon pile. Remove the jumper wire from the field terminal and reconnect the green colored wire to the alternator field terminal.
12. Reconnect the battery cable, if no further testing is to be done to the charging circuit.

Rotor Field Coil Draw Check

1. If on the vehicles remove the drive belt and wiring connections from the alternator.
2. Connect a jumper wire from the negative terminal of the battery to 1 of the field terminals of the alternator.
3. Connect the test ammeter positive lead to the other field terminal of the alternator and the negative ammeter lead to the positive battery terminal.
4. Connect a jumper wire between the alternator end shield and the battery negative terminal.
5. Slowly rotate the alternator pulley by hand and observe the ammeter reading.
6. The field coil draw should be 4.5–6.5 amperes at 12 volts. (4.75–6.0 amperes at 12 volts 114 amp alternators).

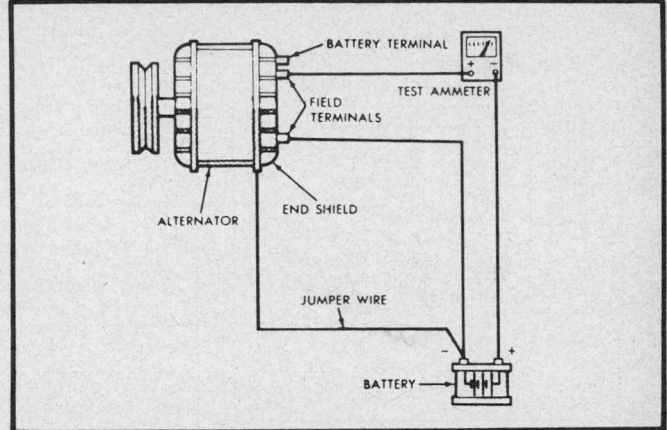

Chrysler alternator with external regulator—rotor field coil current draw test. Connect ammeter as shown, rotate alternator pulley slowly by hand and observe the field coil draw reading.

7. A low rotor coil draw is an indication of high resistance in the field coil circuit (brushes, slip-rings or rotor coil). A higher rotor coil draw indicates possible shorted rotor coil or grounded rotor. No reading indicates an open rotor or defective brushes.
8. Remove the test equipment and jumper leads.

Electronic Voltage Regulator Check

1. Make sure battery terminals are clean and battery is charged.
2. Connect the positive lead of a test voltmeter to ignition terminal No. 1 of the ballast resistor.
3. Connect the negative voltmeter lead to a good body ground.
4. Start engine and allow it to idle at 1250 rpm, all lights and accessories turned **OFF**. Voltage should be as indicated in the figure of the voltage regulator test.
5. If the voltage is below specification check the following. Voltage regulator ground check, voltage drop between regulator cover and ground. Harness wiring, disconnect regulator plug (ignition switch **OFF**), then turn **ON** ignition switch and check for battery voltage at the terminals having the red and green leads. Wiring harness must be disconnected from the regulator when checking individual leads. If no voltage is present in either lead the problem is in the wiring or alternator field.
6. If Step 5 tests showed no malfunctions, install a new regulator and repeat Step 4.
7. If voltage is above specifications (Step 4), or fluctuates, check the following. Ground between regulator and body, between body and engine. Ignition switch circuit between switch and regulator.
8. If voltage is still more than ½ volt above specifications install a new regulator and repeat Step 4.

OVERHAUL

Alternator disassembly, repair and assembly procedures are basically the same for all Chrysler alternators. Certain variations in design, or production modifications, could require slightly different procedures that should be obvious upon inspection of the unit being serviced.

Disassembly

To prevent damage to the brush assemblies (114 amp), they should be removed before proceeding with the disassembly of the alternator. The brushes are mounted in a plastic holder that positions the brushes vertically against the slip-rings.

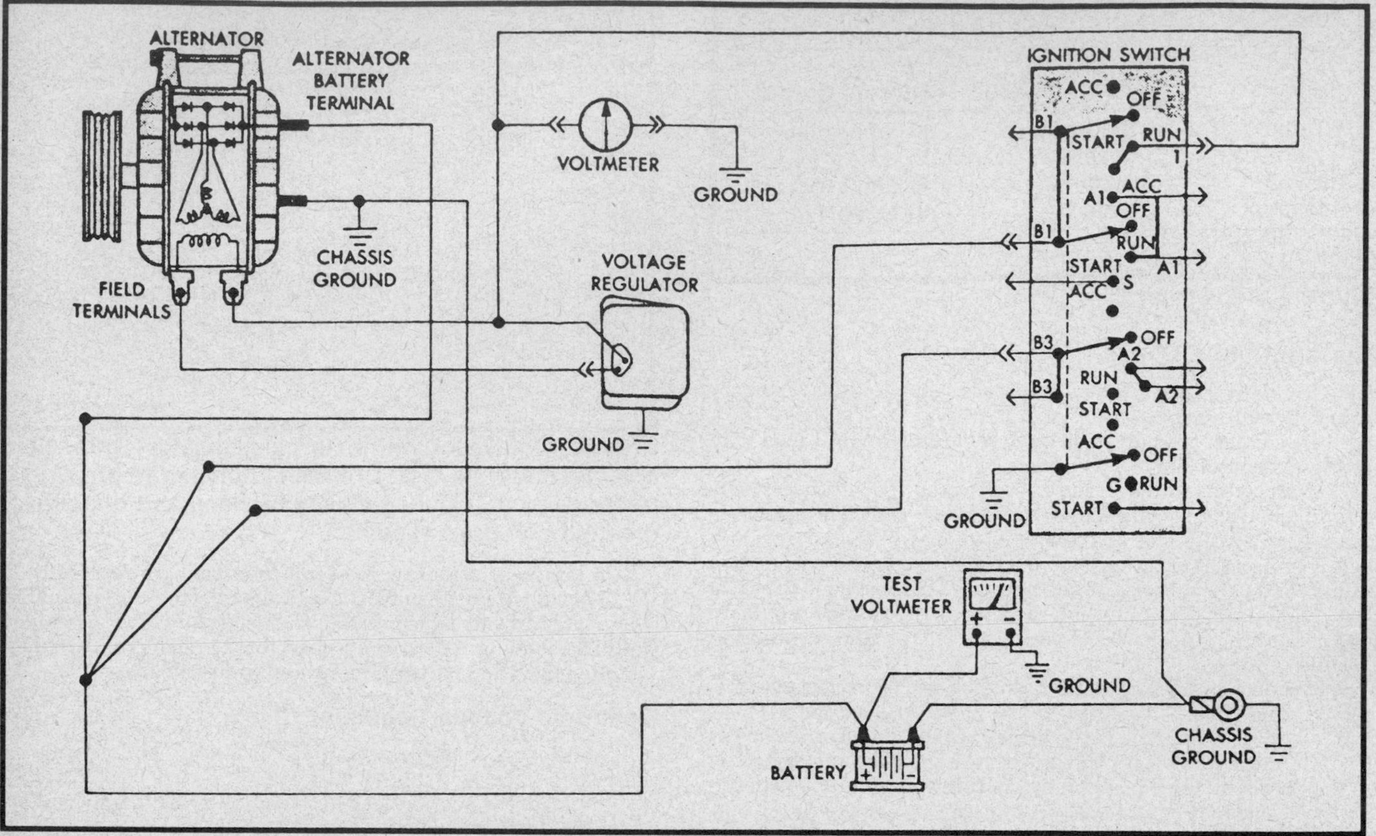

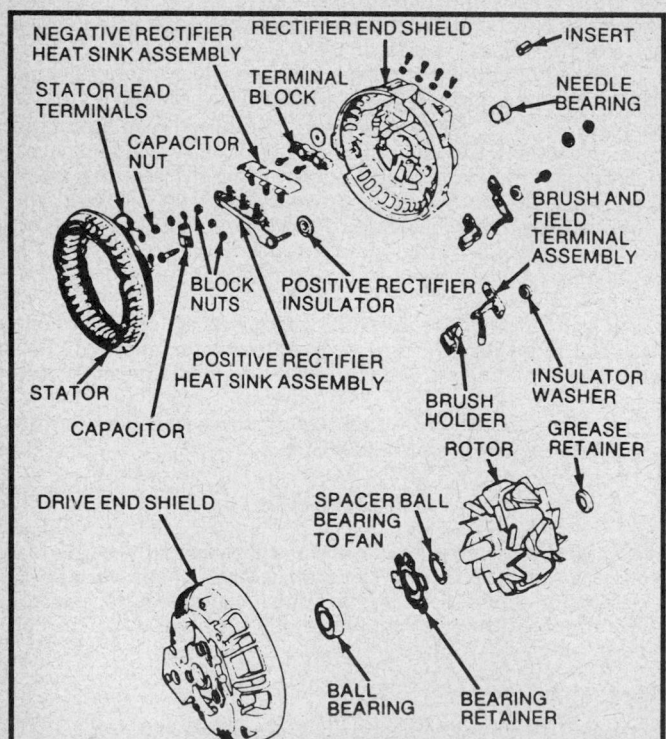

Chrysler 60, 78 and 114 amp alternators with external voltage regulator—voltage regulator test—idle engine at 1250 rpm with all lights and accessories off, voltmeter readings should equal shown in table

Typical Chrysler alternator—showing assembly sequence of components

1. Remove the retaining screw, flat washer, nylon washer and field terminal and carefully lift the plastic holder containing the spring and brush assembly from the end housing.

2. The ground brush (60 amp) is positioned horizontally against the slip-ring and is retained in the holder that is integral with the end housing. Remove the retaining screw and lift the clip, spring and brush assembly from the end housing. The stator is laminated so don't burr the stator or end housings.

3. Remove the through bolts and pry between the stator and drive end housing with a suitable tool. Carefully separate the drive end housing, pulley and rotor assembly from the stator and rectifier housing assembly.

4. The pulley is an interference fit on the rotor shaft. Remove with a puller and special adapters.

5. Remove the nuts and washers and, while supporting the end frame, tap the rotor shaft with a plastic hammer and separate the rotor and end housing.

6. The drive end ball bearing is an interference fit with the rotor shaft. Remove the bearing with puller and adapters.

NOTE: Further dismantling of the rotor is not advisable, as the remainder of the rotor assembly is not serviced separately.

7. Remove the DC output terminal nuts and washers and remove terminal screw and inside capacitor (on units so equipped).

8. Remove the insulator.

NOTE: Positive rectifiers are pressed into the heat sink and negative rectifiers in the end housing. When removing the rectifiers it is necessary to support the end housing and the heat sink in order to prevent damage to the castings. Do not subject the diode rectifiers to un-

necessary jolting. Heavy vibration or shock may ruin them. Cut rectifier wire at point of crimp. Support rectifier housing. The factory tool is cut away and slotted to fit over the wires and around the bosses in the housing. Be sure the bore of the tool completely surrounds the rectifier, then press the rectifier out of the housing. The roller bearing in the rectifier end frame is a press fit. To protect the end housing, it is necessary to support the housing with a tool when pressing out the bearing.

Inspection

RECTIFIERS OPEN IN ALL 3 PHASES

Testing with Ohmmeter

Disassemble the alternator and separate the wires at the Y-connection of the stator.

There are 6 diode rectifiers mounted in the back of the alternator (60 amp). Three of them are marked with a plus (+) and 3 are marked with a minus (−). These marks indicate diode case polarity. The 114 amp alternator has 12 silicon diodes; 6 positive and 6 negative.

To test, set ohmmeter to its lowest range. If case is marked positive (+), place positive meter probe to case and negative probe to the diode lead. Meter should read between 4–10 ohms. Now, reverse leads of ohmmeter, connecting negative meter probe to positive case and positive meter probe to wire of rectifier. Set meter on a high range. Meter needle should move very little, if any (infinite reading). Do this to all positive diode rectifiers.

The diode rectifiers with minus (−) marks on their cases are checked the same way as above. Only now the negative ohmmeter probe is connected to the case for a reading of 4–10 ohms. Reverse leads as above for the other part to test. If a reading of 4–10 ohms is obtained in 1 direction and no reading (infinity) is read on the ohmmeter in the other direction, diode rectifiers are good. If either infinity or a low resistance is obtained in both directions on a rectifier it must be replaced. If meter reads more than 10 ohms when ohmmeter positive probe is connected to positive on diode and negative probe to negative diode, replace diode rectifier.

NOTE: With this test it is necessary to determine the polarity of the ohmmeter probes. This can be done by connecting the ohmmeter to a DC voltmeter. The voltmeter will read up scale when the positive probe of the ohmmeter is connected to the positive side of the voltmeter and the negative probe of the ohmmeter is connected to the negative side of the voltmeter.

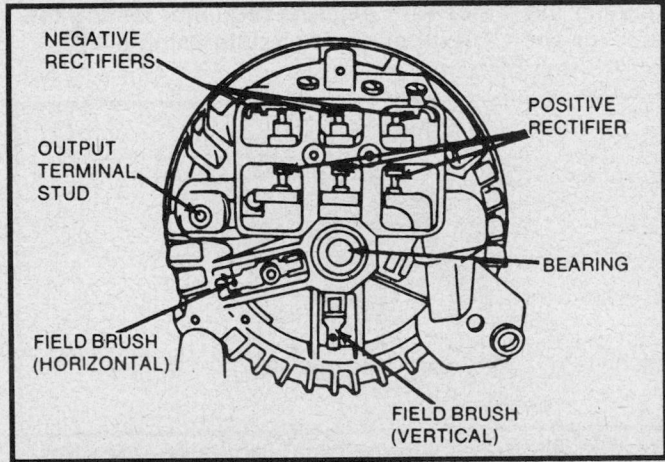

Chrysler alternator rear housing showing locations of rectifiers and field bushings

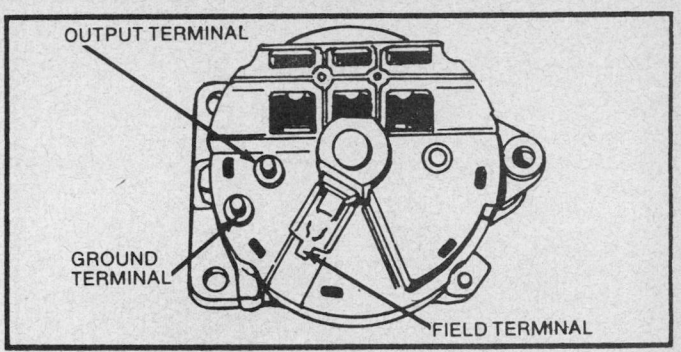

View of the rear housing terminal location—Chrysler alternator 114 amp

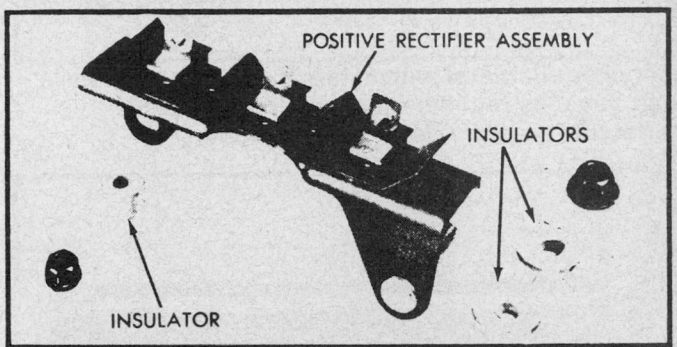

Positive rectifier assembly—114 amp alternator—note position of insulators. Positive rectifier is pressed into the heat sink

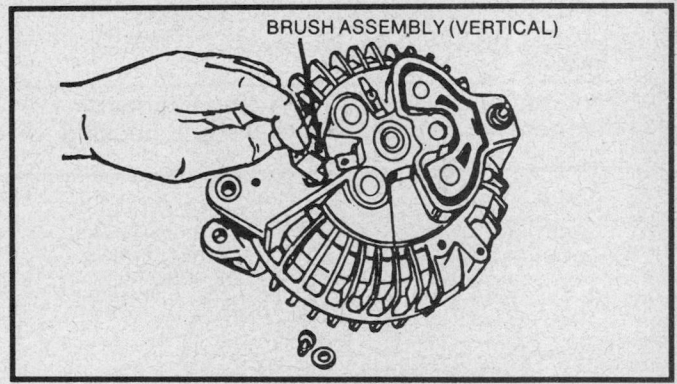

Chrysler alternator with external regulator removing alternator field brush (vertical)

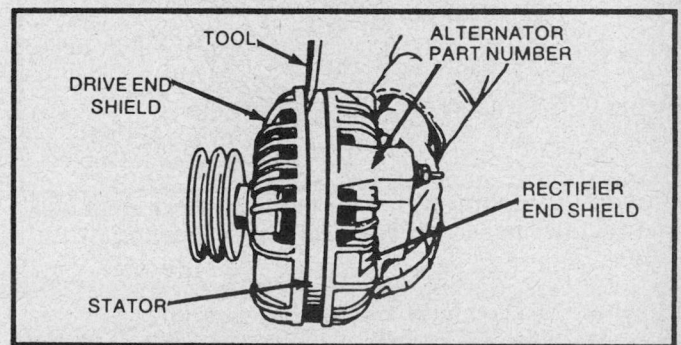

Chrysler alternator with external regulator— separating alternator drive end shield from stator, using a prybar

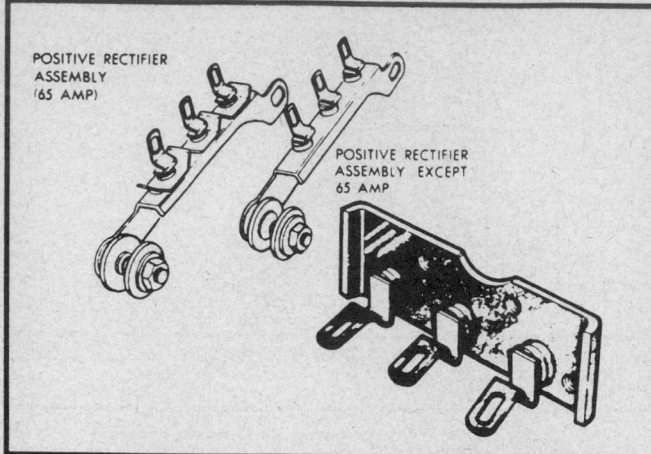

Chrysler alternator with external regulator—positive and negative rectifier identification—note the different types are not interchangeable

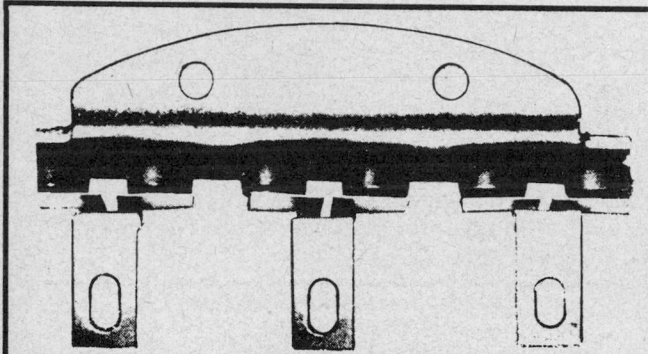

Negative rectifier assembly—114 amp alternator. Negative rectifier is pressed into the end housing

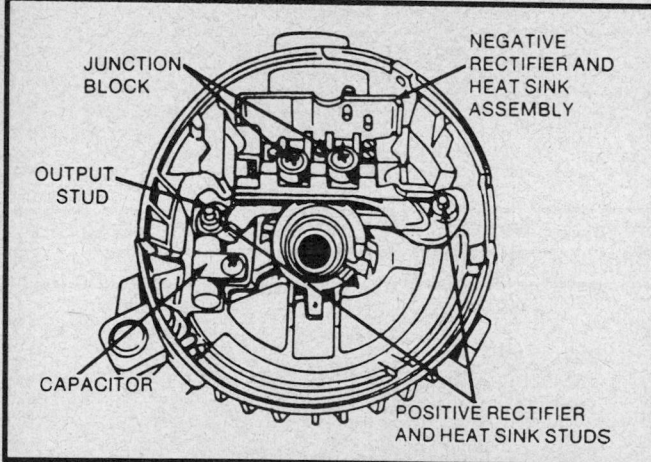

Chrysler alternator with external regulator—heat sink and rectifier assembly removal—note location of studs

Alternate Method with Test Lamp

Be sure that the lead from the center of the diode rectifiers is disconnected. To test rectifiers with positive cases, touch the positive probe of tester to case and the negative probe to lead wire of rectifier. Bulb should light if rectifier is good. If bulb does not light, replace rectifier. Now reverse tester probe connections to rectifier. Bulb should not light. If bulb does light, replace rectifier. For testing minus (−) marked cases follow the above procedure except that now bulb should light with negative probe of tester touching rectifier case and positive probe touching lead wire. Rectifier is good if the bulb lights when tester probes are connected one way and does not light when tester connections are reversed. Rectifier must be replaced if the bulb does not light either way. Also, replace rectifier if bulb lights both ways.

NOTE: The usual cause of an open diode or rectifier is a defective capacitor or a battery that has been installed in reverse polarity. If the battery is installed properly and the diodes are open, test the capacitor.

FIELD COIL DRAW TEST

1. Connect a jumper between one FLD terminal and the positive terminal of a fully charged 12 volt battery.
2. Connect the positive lead of a test ammeter to the other field (Fld) terminal and the negative test lead to the negative battery terminal.
3. Slowly rotate the rotor by hand and observe the ammeter. The proper field coil draw is 2.3–2.7 amps at 12 volts.

NOTE: Field coil draw for the 114 ampere alternators should be 4.75–6.0 amperes at 12 volts.

FIELD CIRCUIT GROUND TEST

1. Touch a test lead of a 110 volt AC test bulb to 1 of the alternator brush (field) terminals and the other test lead to the end shield.
2. If the lamp lights, remove the field brush assemblies and separate the end housing by removing the through bolts.

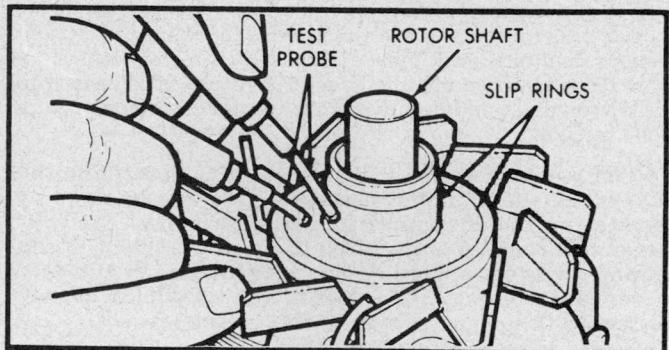

Chrysler alternator with external regulator testing the rotor for short circuit or open circuits using a 110 volt AC test bulb

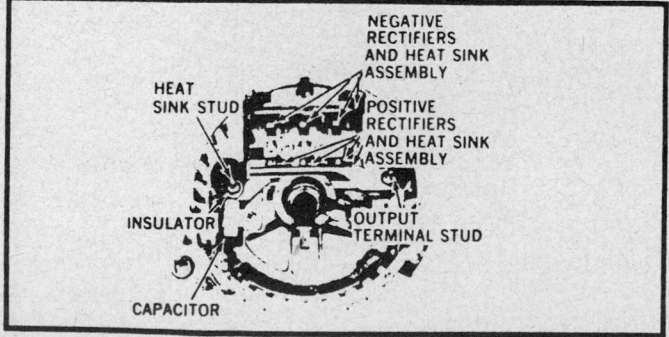

Chrysler alternator with external regulator—location of negative and positive rectifiers check part number of rectifier to be sure correct rectifier is being used

TROUBLESHOOTING
CHRYSLER ISOLATED FIELD ALTERNATOR
(WITH EXTERNAL ELECTRONIC REGULATOR)

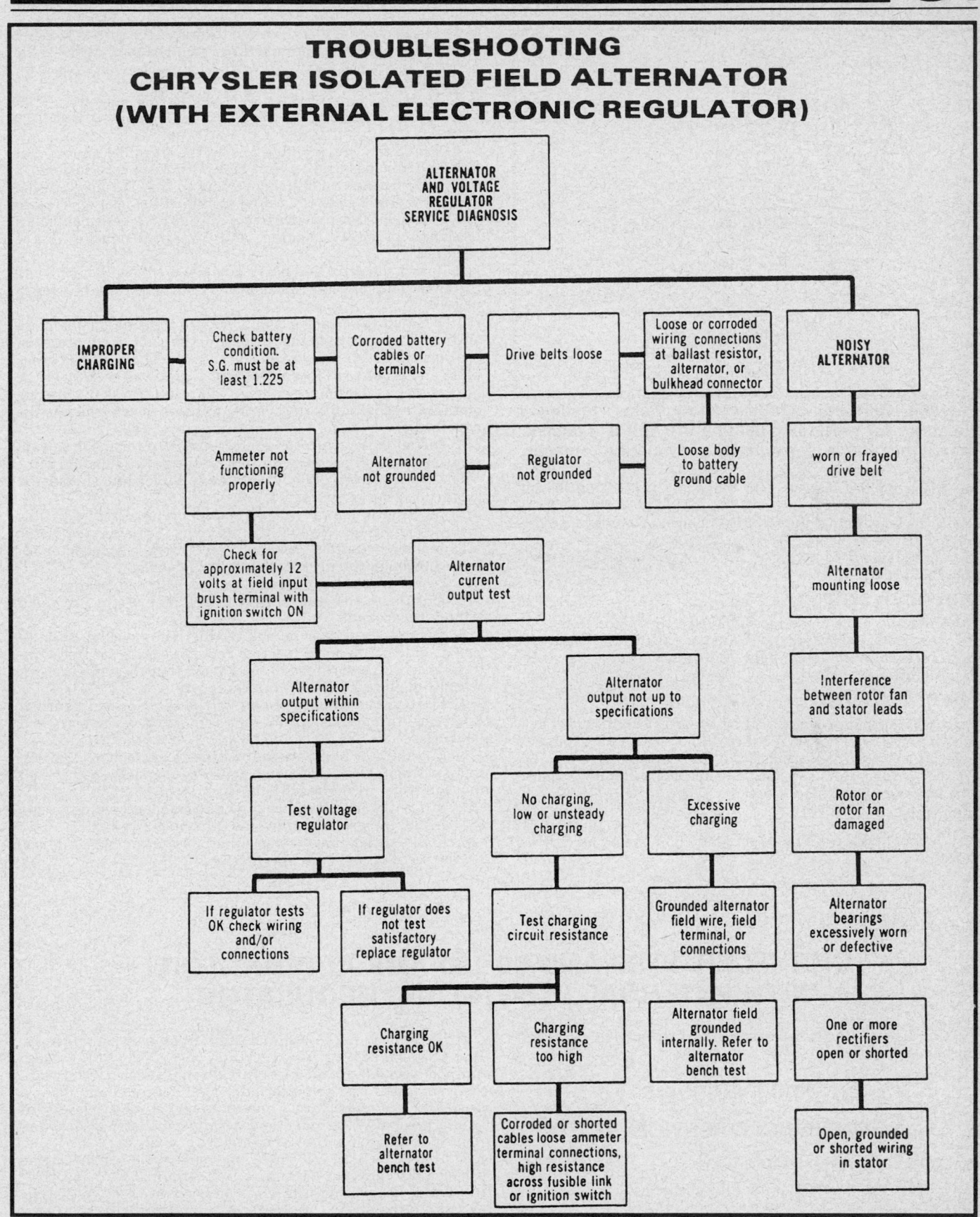

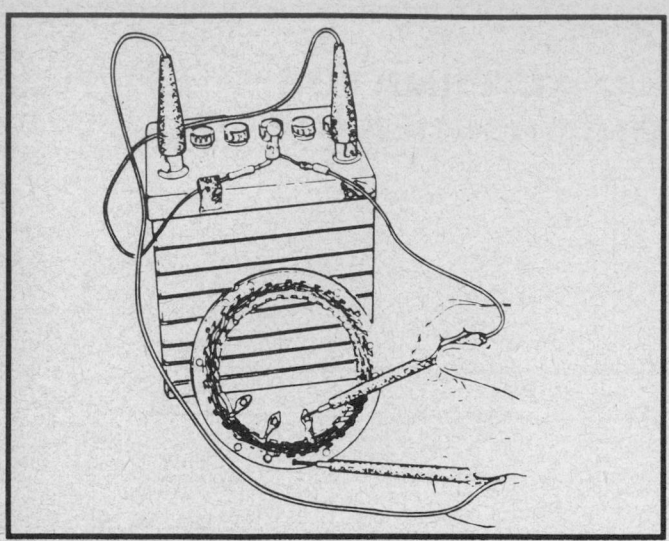

Chrysler alternator with external regulator—testing the stator for grounding using a 110 volt test lamp if lamp lights stator is grounded and must be replaced

3. Place one test lead on a slip-ring and the other on the end shield.
4. If the lamp lights, the rotor assembly is grounded internally and must be replaced.
5. If the lamp does not light, the cause of the problem was a grounded brush.

GROUNDED STATOR
1. Disconnect the diode rectifiers from the stator leads.
2. Test from stator leads to stator core, using a 110 volt test lamp. Test lamp should not light. If it does, the stator is grounded and must be replaced.

LOW OUTPUT TEST
About 50% output accompanied with a growl-hum caused by a shorted phase or a shorted rectifier. If the rectifiers are found to be within specifications replace the stator assembly.

If the rectifier tests satisfactorily, inspect the stator connections before replacing the stator.

Assembly
1. Support the heat sink or rectifier end housing on circular plate.

2. Check rectifier identification to be sure the correct rectifier is being used. The part numbers are stamped on the case of the rectifier. They are also marked red for positive and black for negative.
3. Start the new rectifier into the casting and press it in squarely. Do not start rectifier with a hammer or it will be ruined.
4. Crimp the new rectifier wire to the wires disconnected at removal or solder using a heat sink with rosin core solder.
5. Support the end housing on tool so that the notch in the support tool will clear the raised section of the heat sink, press the bearing into position with tool SP–3381, or equivalent. New bearings are prelubricated, additional lubrication is not required.
6. Insert the drive end bearing in the drive end housing and install the bearing plate, washers and nuts to hold the bearing in place.
7. Position the bearing and drive end housing on the rotor shaft and, while supporting the base of the rotor shaft, press the bearing and housing in position on the rotor shaft with an arbor press and arbor tool. Be careful that there is no cocking of the bearing at installation; or damage will result. Press the bearing on the rotor shaft until the bearing contacts the shoulder on the rotor shaft.
8. Install pulley on rotor shaft. Shaft of rotor must be supported so that all pressing force is on the pulley hub and rotor shaft. Do not exceed 6800 lbs. pressure. Pulley hub should just contact bearing inner race.
9. Some alternators will be found to have the capacitor mounted internally. Be sure the heat sink insulator is in place.
10. Install the output terminal screw with the capacitor attached through the heat sink and end housing.
11. Install insulating washers, lockwashers and locknuts.
12. Make sure the heat sink and insulator are in place and tighten the locknut.
13. Position the stator on the rectifier end housing. Be sure that all of the rectifier connectors and phase leads are free of interference with the rotor fan blades and that the capacitor (internally mounted) lead has clearance.
14. Position the rotor assembly in the rectifier end housing. Align the through bolt holes in the stator with both end housings.
15. Enter stator shaft in the rectifier end housing bearing, compress stator and both end housings manually and install through bolts, washers and nuts.
16. Install the insulated brush and terminal attaching screw.
17. Install the ground screw and attaching screw.
18. Rotate pulley slowly to be sure the rotor fan blades do not hit the rectifier and stator connectors.

CHRYSLER 40/90 AND 50/120 AMP ALTERNATOR WITH EXTERNAL ELECTRONIC REGULATOR

The 40/90 alternator is used as standard equipment. A 50/120 alternator is optional.

System Diagnosis

ON VEHICLE SERVICE

Charging Circuit Resistance Test
1. Be sure that the battery is fully charged.
2. Turn **OFF** ignition switch.
3. Disconnect negative battery cable.

4. Disconnect BAT terminal wire from alternator output BAT terminal post.
5. Connect a 0–100 amps minimum range scale DC test ammeter in series between alternator BAT terminal and disconnected BAT terminal wire. Connect ammeter positive lead wire to alternator BAT terminal and negative ammeter lead to disconnected alternator BAT terminal wire.
6. Connect a 0–18 volt minimum range scale test voltmeter between disconnected alternator BAT terminal wire and positive battery cable. Connect voltmeter positive lead to disconnected alternator BAT terminal wire and negative voltmeter lead to battery positive cable.

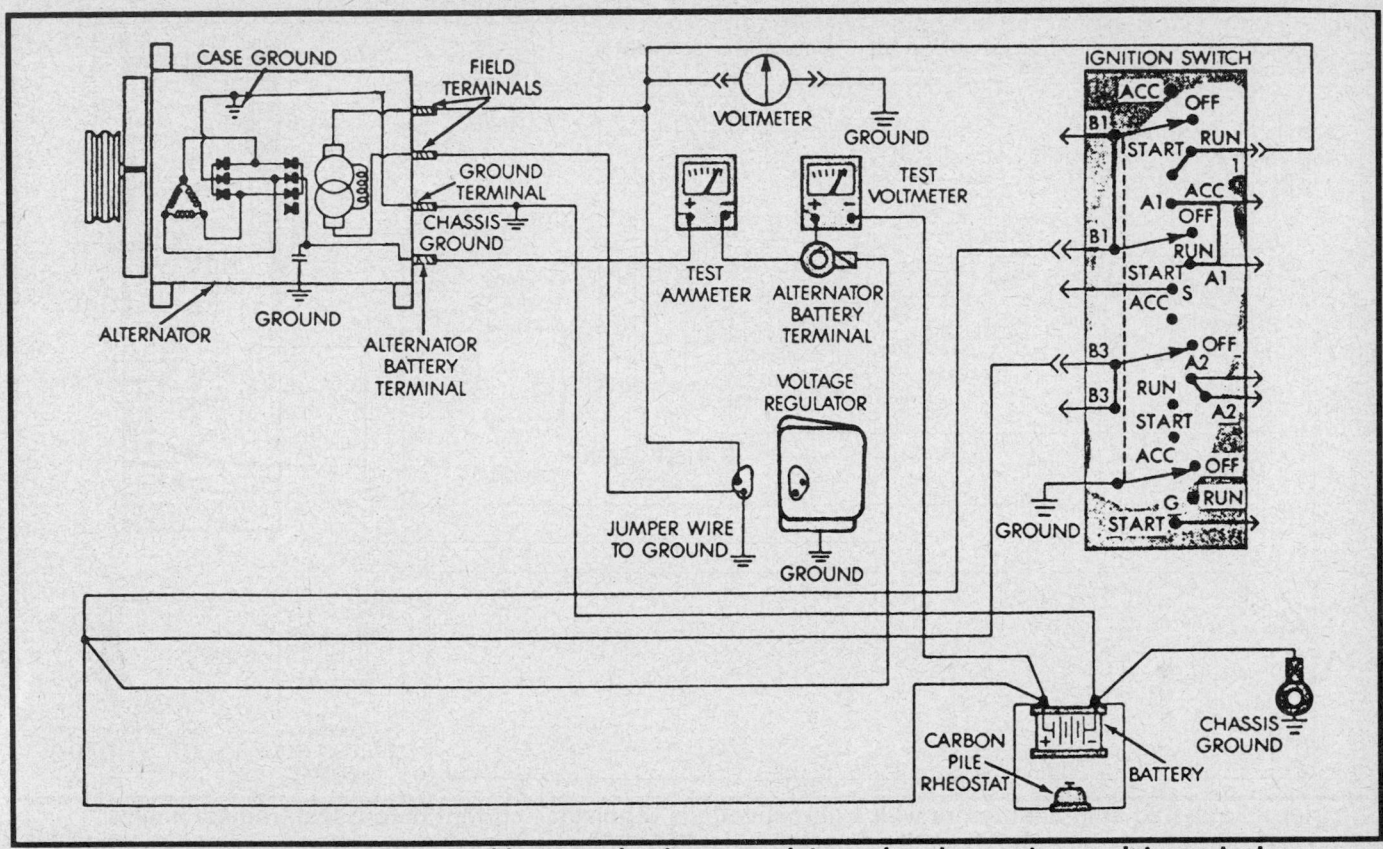

Chrysler 90 and 120 amp alternators with external voltage regulator—charging system resistance test—adjust engine speed and carbon pile to maintain 20 amps, voltmeter reading should not exceed 0.5 volts

7. Disconnect wiring harness connector from electronic voltage regulator on vehicle.

8. Connect a jumper wire from wiring harness connector green wire (outside terminal), to ground. Do not connect blue J2 lead of wiring connector to ground.

9. Connect an engine tachometer and reconnect negative battery cable. Connect a variable carbon pile rheostat to battery terminals. Be sure carbon pile is in **OPEN** or **OFF** position before connecting leads.

10. Start engine. Immediately after starting reduce engine speed to idle.

11. Adjust engine speed and carbon pile to maintain 20 amperes flowing in circuit. Observe voltmeter reading. Voltmeter reading should not exceed 0.5 volts.

NOTE: If a higher voltage drop is indicated, inspect, clean and tighten all connections in the charging circuit. A voltage drop test may be performed at each connection to locate connection with excessive resistance. If charging circuit resistance tested satisfactorily, reduce engine speed, turn OFF carbon pile and turn OFF ignition switch.

12. Disconnect negative battery cable.

13. Remove test ammeter, test voltmeter, variable carbon pile rheostat and engine tachometer.

14. Remove jumper wire connected between electronic voltage regulator wiring harness connector green wire terminal and ground.

15. Connect wiring harness connector to electronic voltage regulator.

16. Connect BAT terminal wire to alternator output BAT terminal.

17. Connect negative battery cable.

Current Output Test

1. Be sure that the battery is fully charged.

2. Turn **OFF** ignition switch.

3. Disconnect negative battery cable.

4. Disconnect the output wire from the alternator BAT terminal. Connect a 0-100 ammeter positive lead wire to alternator BAT terminal and negative ammeter lead to disconnected alternator BAT terminal wire.

5. Connect a 0–18 volt minimum range scale test voltmeter between alternator BAT terminal post and ground. Connect voltmeter positive lead to alternator BAT terminal post. Connect negative lead of test voltmeter to a good ground.

6. Disconnect wiring harness connector from electronic voltage regulator on vehicle.

7. Connect a jumper wire from wiring harness connector green wire (outside terminal) to ground. Do not connect blue J2 lead of wiring connector to ground.

8. Connect an engine tachometer and reconnect negative battery cable. Connect a variable carbon pile rheostat between battery terminals. Be sure the carbon pile is in **OPEN** or **OFF** position before connecting leads.

9. Start the engine. Immediately after starting reduce engine speed to idle.

10. Adjust carbon pile and engine speed in increments until a speed of 1250 rpm and voltmeter reading of 15 volts is obtained. Do not allow voltage meter to read above 16 volts.

11. Ammeter reading must be within the proper limits. If reading is less than specified alternator should be removed from vehicle and bench tested.

12. After current output test is completed reduce engine speed, turn **OFF** carbon pile and turn **OFF** ignition switch.

13. Disconnect negative battery cable.

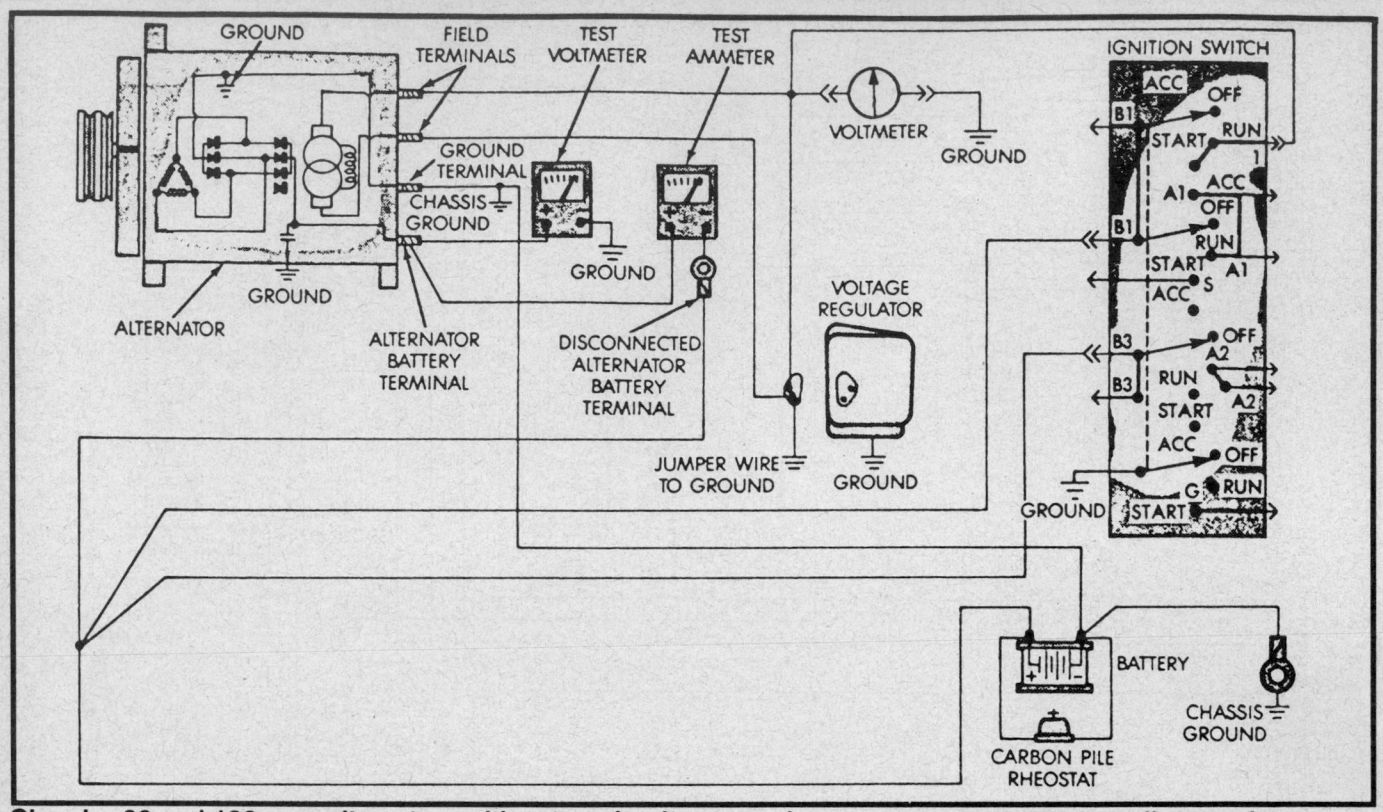

Chrysler 90 and 120 amp alternators with external voltage regulator—current output test—adjust engine speed and carbon pile increments until an engine speed of 1250 rpm is reached, voltmeter reading should not exceed 15 volts

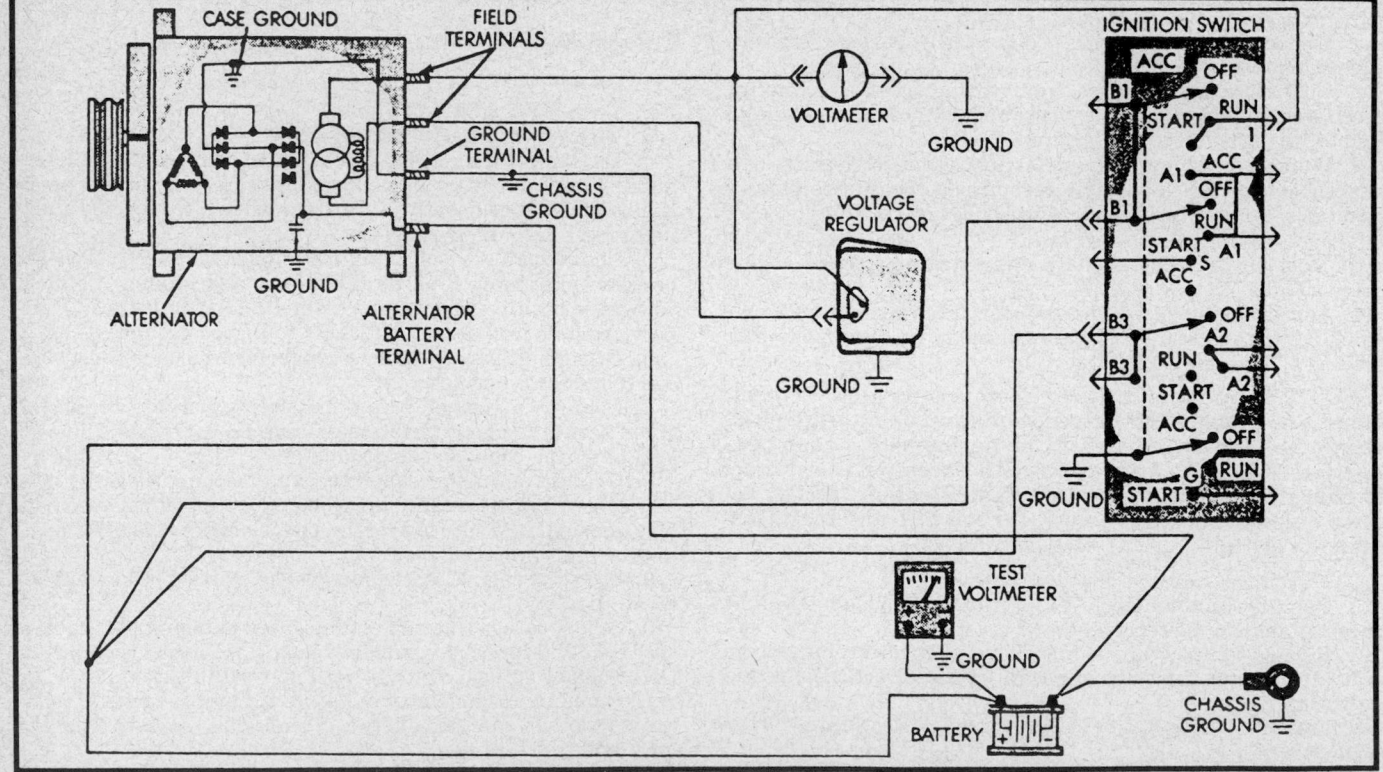

Chrysler 90 and 120 amp alternators with external voltage regulator—voltage regulator test—idle engine at 1250 rpm with all lights and accessories off, voltmeter readings should equal shown in table

14. Remove test ammeter, test voltmeter, tachometer and variable carbon pile rheostat.

15. Remove jumper wire connected between electronic voltage regulator wiring harness connector green wire terminal and ground.

16. Connect wiring harness connector to electronic voltage regulator.

17. Connect BAT terminal wire to alternator output BAT terminal.

18. Connect negative battery cable.

Voltage Regulator Test

1. Be sure that the battery is fully charged.
2. Turn **OFF** ignition switch.
3. Connect a 0–18 volts minimum range scale test voltmeter between vehicle battery and ground. Connect positive lead of voltmeter to positive battery cable terminal. Connect negative lead of voltmeter to a good vehicle body ground.
4. Connect a tachometer to engine.
5. Start engine and adjust engine speed to 1250 rpm with all lights and accessories turned **OFF**.
6. Check voltmeter, regulator is working properly if voltage readings are in accordance with the voltage chart.
7. If voltage is below limits or is fluctuating, proceed as follows. Check for a good voltage regulator ground. Voltage regulator ground is obtained through regulator case to mounting screws and to sheet metal of vehicle. This is ground circuit that is to be checked for opens.
8. Turn **OFF** ignition switch and disconnect voltage regulator wiring harness connector. Be sure terminals of connector have not spread open to cause an open or intermittant connection.
9. Do not start engine or distort terminals with voltmeter probe: turn **ON** ignition switch and check for battery voltage at voltage regulator wiring harness connector terminals. Both blue and green terminals should read battery voltage. Turn **OFF** ignition switch.
10. If satisfactory, replace the regulator and repeat the test.
11. If the voltage is above limits specification proceed as follows. Turn **OFF** ignition switch and disconnect voltage regulator wiring harness connector. Be sure terminals in connector have not spread open.
12. Do not start engine or distort terminals with voltmeter probe. Turn **ON** ignition switch and check for battery voltage at voltage regulator wiring harness connector terminals. Both blue and green terminals should read battery voltage. Turn **OFF** ignition switch.
13. If satisfactory, then replace regulator and repeat test. Remove test voltmeter and tachometer.

OVERHAUL

Disassembly

1. Remove the rectifier dust cover nut and separate the cover from the alternator.
2. Remove the brush holder bolts and separate it from the alternator.
3. Remove the stator lead, the rectifier and capacitor bolts. Separate the rectifier and insulator from the alternator.
4. If disassembling a 50/120 alternator rectifier, perform the following procedures:
   a. Remove the connecting strap from between the rectifiers.
   b. Remove the buss bar and insulator screws.
   c. Separate the insulators from the rectifier.
5. From the shield end, remove the through bolts.
6. From the drive end shield, separate the stator and rectifier end shield.
7. Separate the stator from the rectifier end shield.

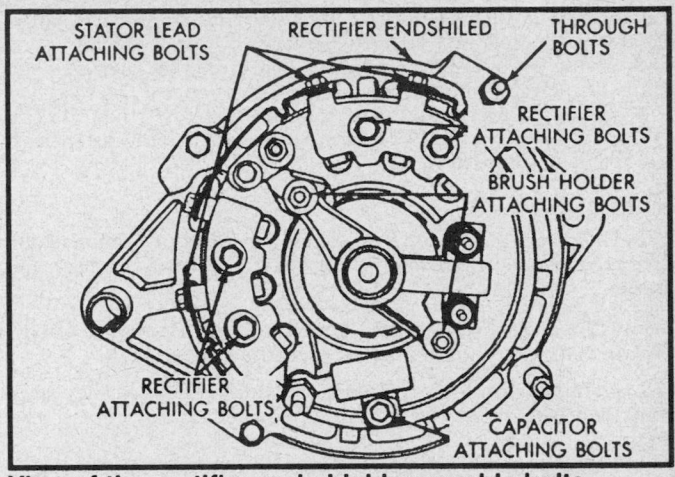

View of the rectifier end shield assembly bolts— Chrysler 90 and 120 amp alternator

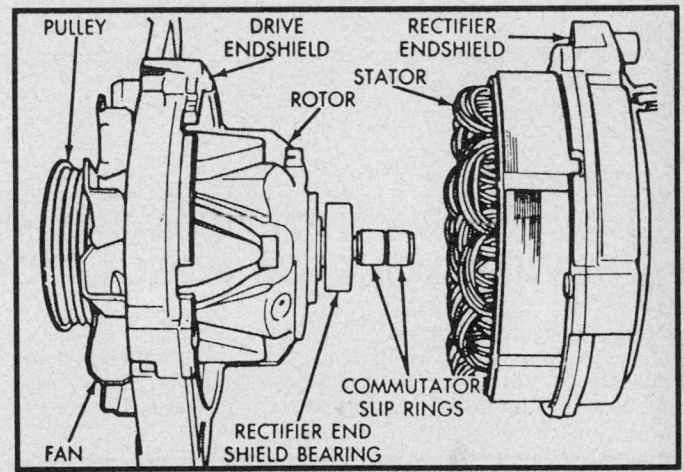

View of the stator and drive end shield assemblies— Chrysler 90 and 120 amp alternator

8. Remove the drive pulley nut, the washer, the pulley and the fan.
9. Press the rotor shaft from the drive end shield.

NOTE: If the bearing is defective, replace the drive end shield as an assembly.

10. If necessary to remove the rectifier end bearing from the rotor assembly, use a bearing puller to press the bearing from the rotor shaft.

Inspection

BRUSH HOLDER TESTS

1. Make sure the brushes move smoothly and return fully to the stops when released; if not, replace the brush holder assembly.
2. Using an ohmmeter, test inner brush-to-field terminals continuity; a field terminal should be open and the other closed. If not, replace the brush holder.
3. Using an ohmmeter, test outer brush-to-field terminals continuity; 1 field terminal should be open and the other closed. If not, replace the brush holder.

ROTOR TESTS

1. Check the field slip rings for excessive wear or roughness;

fine emery cloth may be used to repair minor damage. If the rings are excessively damaged, replace the rotor.

2. Using an ohmmeter, test for continuity between the slip rings; the circuit should be closed. If not, replace the rotor.

3. Using an ohmmeter, test for continuity between the slip rings and the rotor shaft or core; the circuit should be open. If not, replace the rotor.

STATOR TESTS

1. Check the stator for signs damage—weak or broken leads, distorted frame or burned windings; if necessary, replace the stator.

NOTE: Using a scraping device, clean a portion of the stator frame to assure good electrical contact.

2. Using an ohmmeter, test for continuity between the stator leads and frame; the circuit should be open. If not, replace the stator.

3. Using an ohmmeter, test for continuity between the stator leads; the circuit should be closed. If not, replace the stator.

RECTIFIER TESTS

1. Separate the positive diode leads from the negative diode leads.

2. Using an ohmmeter, test for continuity between the posi-

tive heat sink to each of the positive diode leads. Reverse the test probes and repeat the test; the diodes should show continuity in 1 direction. If not, replace the rectifier assembly.

3. Using an ohmmeter, test for continuity between the negative heat sink to each of the negative diode leads. Reverse the test probes and repeat the test; the diodes should show continuity in 1 direction. If not, replace the rectifier assembly.

Assembly

1. If the rectifier end bearing was removed, support the rotor assembly in a holding fixture and drive the bearing onto the rotor shaft with a bearing driver.

2. Press the drive end shield onto the rotor shaft and install the fan, the pulley, the washer and the drive pulley nut.

3. Assemble the stator to the rectifier end shield and the stator to the drive end shield. Install the through bolts.

4. If assembling a 50/120 alternator rectifier, perform the following procedures:
    a. Install the insulators on the rectifier.
    b. Install the insulator screws and the buss bar.
    c. Attach the connecting strap between the rectifiers.

5. Assemble the rectifier and insulator to the alternator. Install the capacitor, the rectifier and the stator lead bolts.

6. Install the brush holder and tighten the bolts.

7. Install the rectifier dust cover and nut.

CHRYSLER 40/90 AND 50/120 AMP ALTERNATOR WITH VOLTAGE REGULATOR IN ENGINE ELECTRONICS

The charging system consists of a battery, alternator, voltmeter and connecting wires. The 40/90 has 6 built-in silicon rectifiers, while the 50/120 has 12 built-in silicon rectifiers. The voltage regulator is built into the power and logic modules. The rectifi-

ers convert AC current into DC current. Current at the alternator battery terminal is DC. The alternator's main components are rotor, stator, capacitor, rectifiers, end shields, brushes, bearings, poly-vee drive pulley and fan.

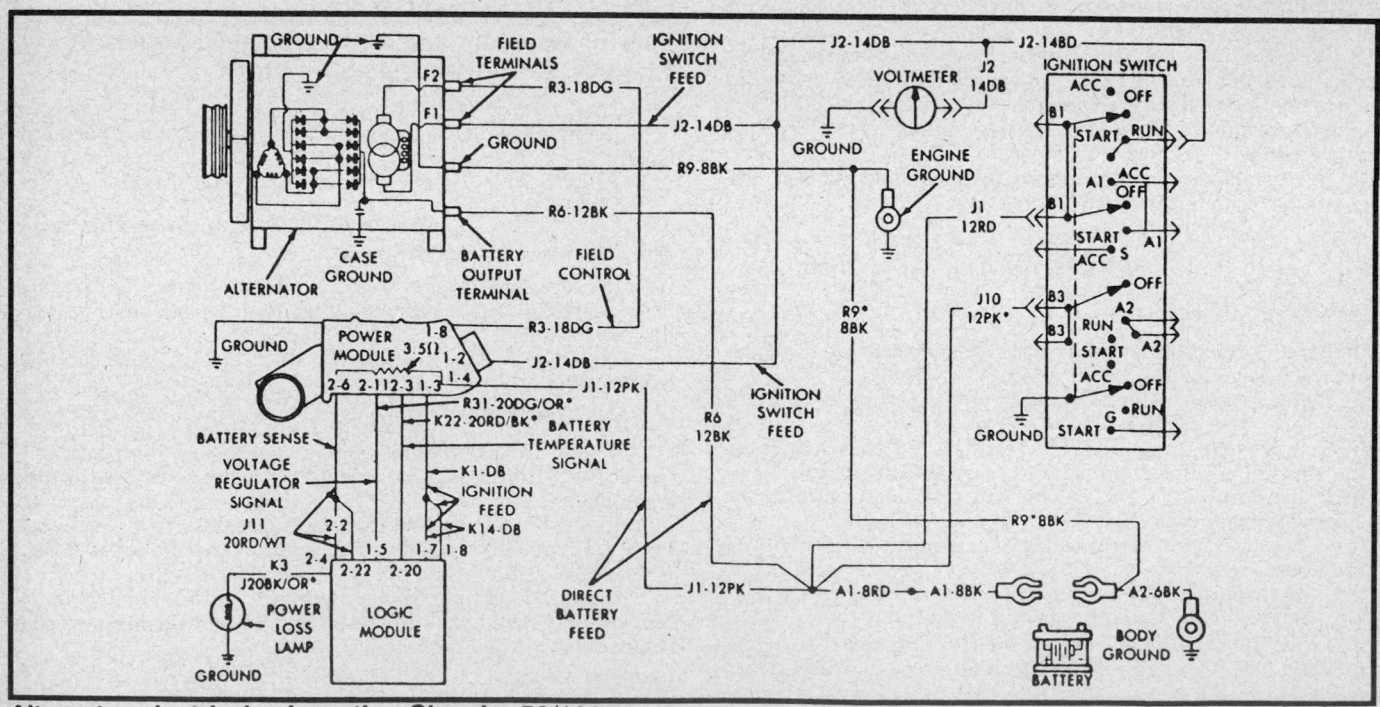

Alternator electrical schematic—Chrysler 50/120 amp

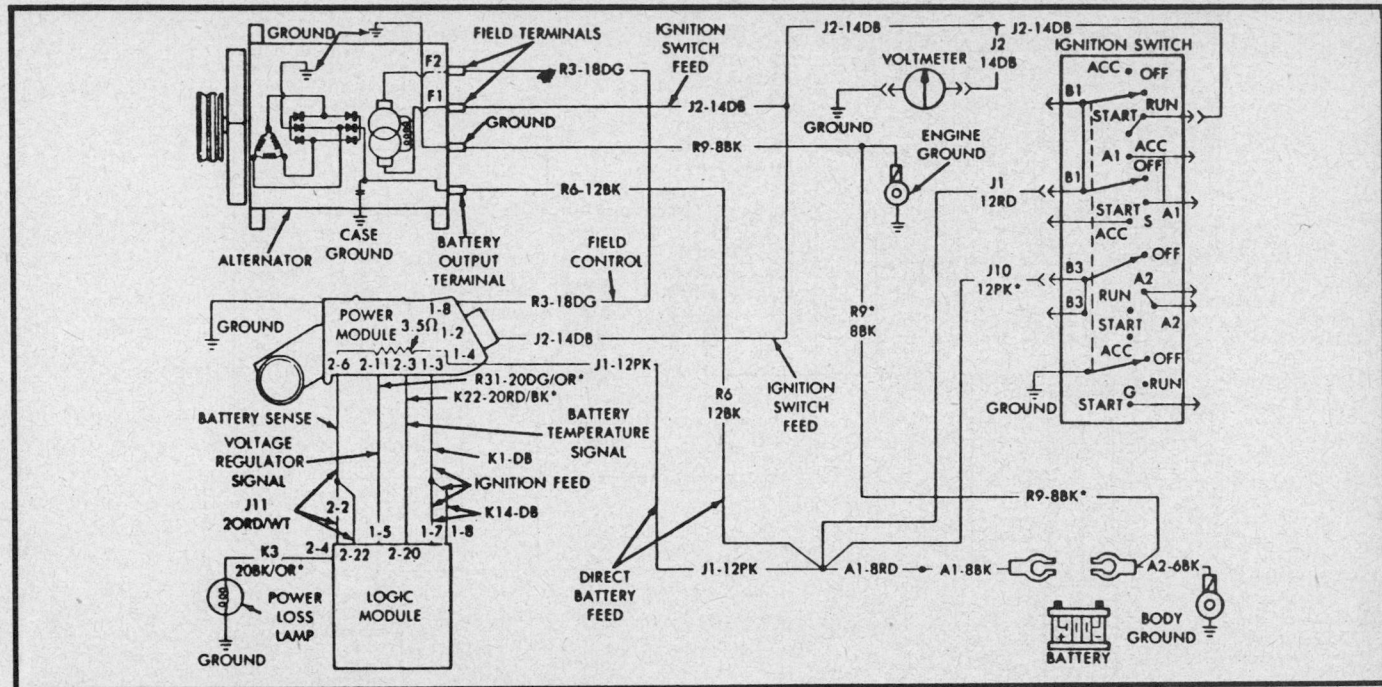

Alternator electrical schematic — Chrysler 40/90 amp

The electronic voltage regulator is contained within engine electronics power module and logic module. It is a device that regulates vehicle electrical system voltage by limiting output voltage that is generated by the alternator. This is accomplished by controlling amount of current that is allowed to pass through alternator field winding. The alternator field is turned **ON** by a driver in power module which is controlled by a predriver in the logic module. The logic module looks at battery temperature to determine control voltage. The field is then driven at a duty cycle proportional to the difference between battery voltage and desired control voltage. One important feature of the electronic regulator is the ability of its control circuit to vary regulated system voltage up or down as temperature changes. This provides varying charging conditions for battery throughout seasons of the year.

System Diagnosis

ON VEHICLE SERVICE

Resistance Test

Alternator output wire resistance test will show amount of voltage drop across alternator output wire between alternator BAT terminal and positive battery post.

1. Before starting test, make sure vehicle has a fully charged battery.
2. Turn **OFF** ignition switch.
3. Disconnect negative battery cable.
4. Disconnect alternator output wire from alternator output battery terminal.
5. Connect a 0–150 ampere scale DC ammeter in series between alternator BAT terminal and disconnected alternator output wire. Connect positive lead to alternator BAT terminal and negative lead to disconnected alternator output wire.
6. Connect positive lead of a test voltmeter (Range 0–18 volts minimum) to disconnected alternator output wire. Connect negative lead of test voltmeter to positive battery cable at positive post.

7. Remove air hose between power and module and air cleaner.
8. Connect an end of a jumper wire to ground and with other end probe green R3 lead wire on dash side of black 8-way connector.

NOTE: Do not connect the blue J2 lead of the 8-way connector to ground. Both R3 and J2 leads are green on the alternator side of the 8-way connector. At the dash end of the connector, R3 is green and J2 is blue.

9. Connect an engine tachometer and reconnect negative battery cable.
10. Connect a variable carbon pile rheostat between battery terminals. Be sure carbon pile is in **OPEN** or **OFF** position before connecting leads.
11. Start engine. Immediately after staring, reduce engine speed to idle. Adjust engine speed and carbon pile to maintain 20 amperes flowing in circuit. Observe voltmeter reading. Voltmeter reading should not exceed 0.5 volts.
12. If a higher voltage drop is indicated, inspect, clean and tighten all connections between alternator BAT terminal and positive battery post.
13. A voltage drop test may be performed at each connection to locate connection with excessive resistance. If resistance tested satisfactorily, reduce engine speed, turn **OFF** carbon pile and turn **OFF** ignition switch.
14. Disconnect negative battery cable. Remove test ammeter, voltmeter, carbon pile and tachometer. Remove jumper wire between 8-way black connector and ground.
15. Connect alternator output wire to alternator BAT terminal post. Tighten 45–75 inch lbs. Reconnect negative battery cable. Reconnect hose between power module and air cleaner.

Current Output Test

Current output test determines whether or not alternator is capable of delivering its rated current output.

1. Before starting any tests, make sure vehicle has a fully charged battery.
2. Disconnect negative battery cable.

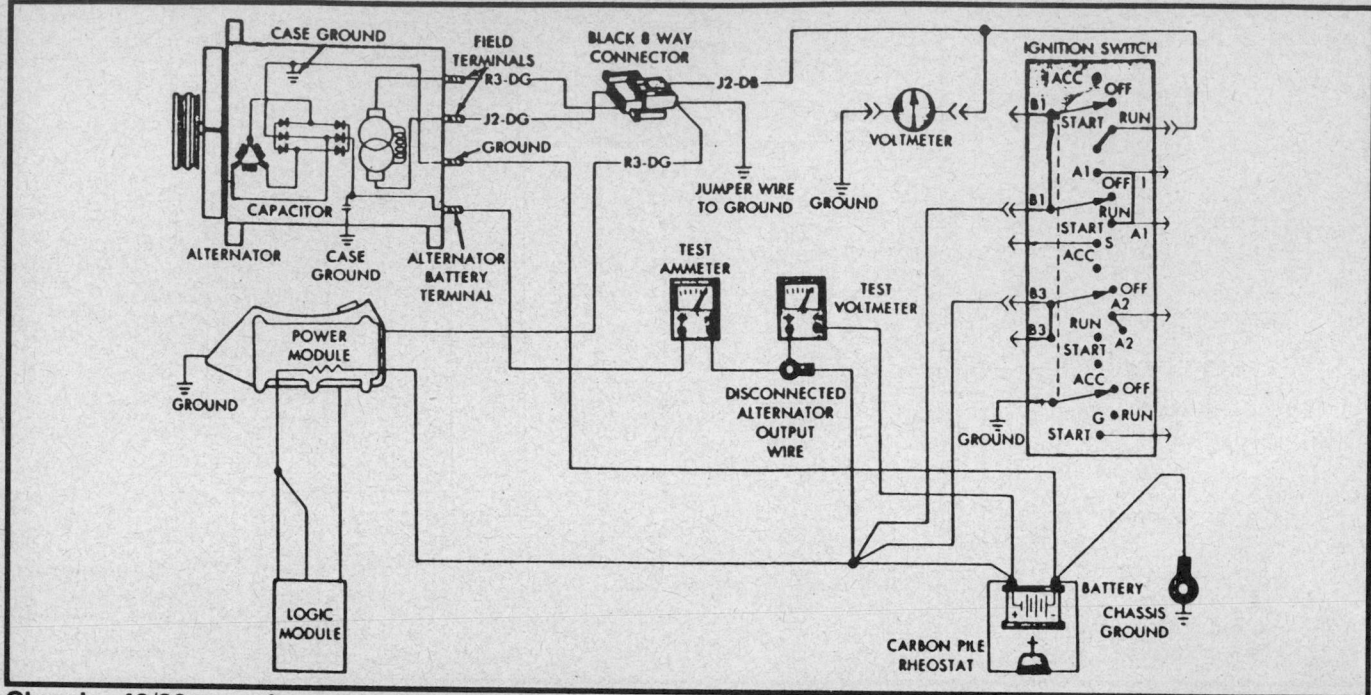

Chrysler 40/90 amp alternator with engine electronics — output wire resistance test

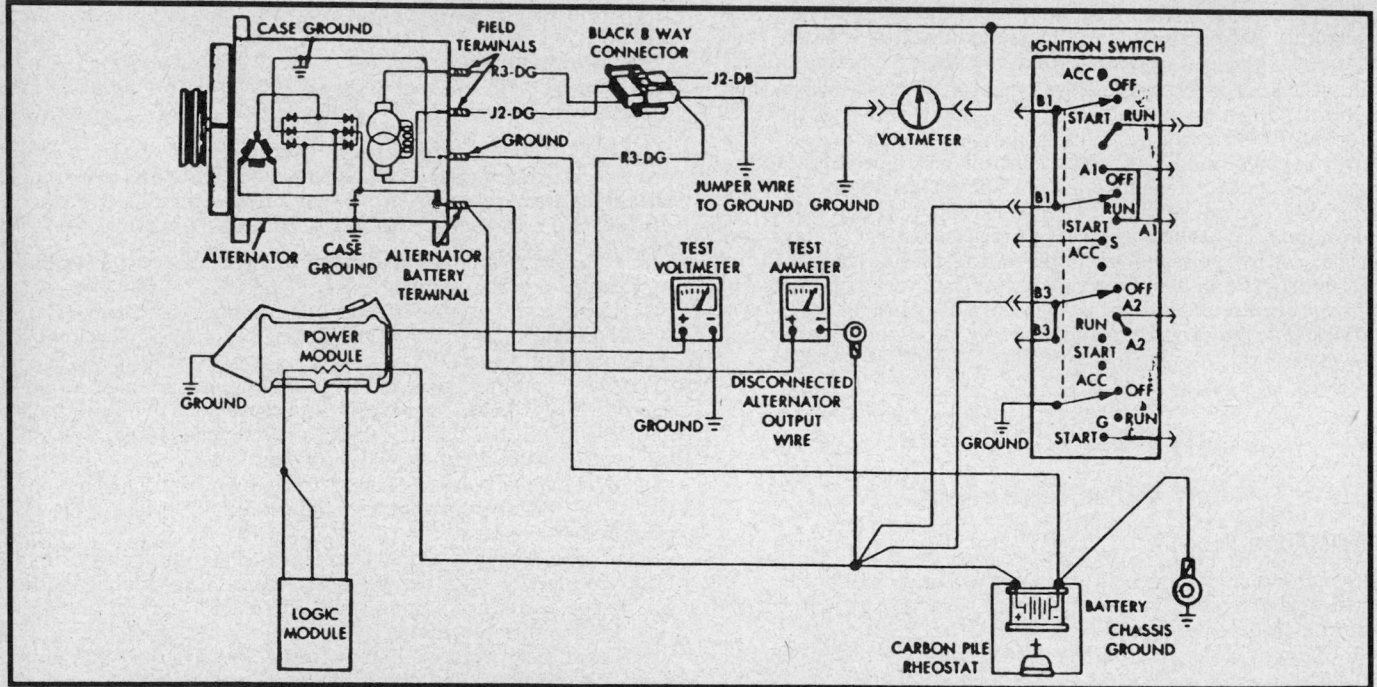

Chrysler 40/90 amp alternator with engine electronics — current output test

3. Disconnect alternator output wire at the alternator battery terminal.

4. Connect a 0–150 ampere scale DC ammeter in series between alternator BAT terminal and disconnected alternator output wire. Connect positive lead to alternator BAT terminal and negative lead to disconnected alternator output wire.

5. Connect positive lead of a test voltmeter (range 0–18 volts minimum) to alternator BAT terminal.

6. Connect negative lead of test voltmeter to a good ground.

7. Connect an engine tachometer and reconnect negative battery cable.

8. Connect a variable carbon pile rheostate between battery terminals. Be sure carbon pile is in **OPEN** or **OFF** position before connecting leads.

9. Remove air hose between power module and air cleaner.

10. Connect 1 end of a jumper wire to ground and with other end probe green R3 lead wire on dash side of Black 8-way connector.

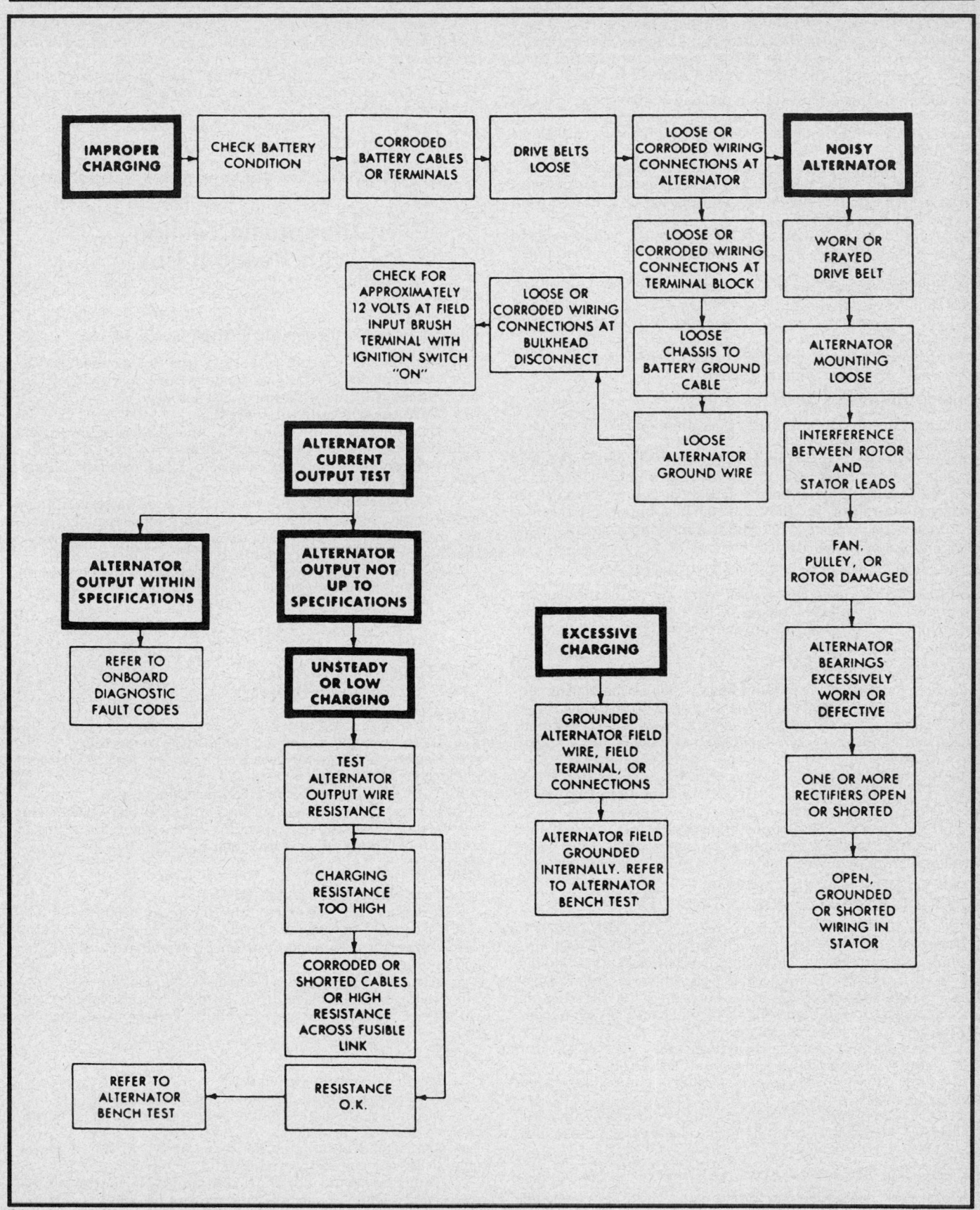

Alternator fault code chart—Chrysler 40/90 amp and 50/120 amp

NOTE: Do not connect the blue J2 lead of the 8-way connector to ground. Both R3 and J2 leads are green on the alternator side of the 8-way connector. At the dash end of the connector, R3 is green and J2 is blue.

11. Start engine. Adjust carbon pile and engine speed in increments until a speed of 1250 rpm and voltmeter reading of 15 volts is obtained. Do not allow the voltage meter to read above 16 volts.

12. The ammeter reading must be within the proper limits.

13. If reading is less than specified and alternator output wire resistance is not excessive alternator should be removed from vehicle and bench tested.

14. After current output test is completed, reduce engine speed, turn **OFF** carbon pile and ignition switch. Disconnect negative battery cable.

15. Remove test ammeter, voltmeter, tachometer and carbon pile. Remove jumper wire between 8-way black connector and ground. Disconnect alternator output wire to alternator BAT terminal post.

16. Reconnect negative battery cable. Reconnect air hose between power module and air cleaner.

Voltage Regulator Test

On board diagnostic fault codes play a major role in case of a charging system failure.

Fault codes are 2 digit numbers that identify which circuit is at fault. In most cases, they do not identify which component in a circuit is at fault. Therefore, a fault code is only a result, not necessarily a reason for the problem. It is important that the test procedure be followed in order to understand the fault codes of the on-board diagnostic system.

DIAGNOSTIC READOUT BOX OPERATION

The diagnostic readout box is used to put the on-board diagnostic system in 3 different modes of testing as called for in the driveability test procedure, only one of which is used in charging system diagnosis.

DIAGNOSTIC MODE

1. Connect diagnostic readout box C-4805 to the mating connector located in the wiring harness by right front shock tower.
2. Place read/hold switch on readout box in **READ** position.
3. Turn ignition switch **ON/OFF**, **ON/OFF**, on within 5 seconds.
4. Record all codes, displaying of codes may be stopped by moving read/hold button to **HOLD** position. Returning to **READ** position will continue displaying of codes.
5. If for some reason diagnostic readout box is not available, logic module can show fault codes by means of flashing power loss lamp on instrument cluster.

HOW TO USE POWER LOSS OR POWER LIMIT LAMP FOR CODES

To activate this function, turn ignition key **ON/OFF/ON/OFF/ON** within 5 seconds. The power loss lamp will turn **ON** for 2 seconds as a bulb check. Immediately following this it will display a fault code by flashing on and off. There is a short pause between flashes and a longer pause between digits. All codes displayed are 2 digit numbers with a 4 second pause between codes. An example of a code is as follows.

1. Lamp on for 2 seconds then turns off.
2. Lamp flashes 4 times, pauses and flashes once.
3. Lamp pauses for 4 seconds, flashes 4 times, pauses and flashes 7 times.
4. The 2 codes are 41 and 47. Any number of codes can be displayed as long as they are in memory. The lamp will flash until all of them are displayed.

CHARGING SYSTEM FAULT CODES

Perform test procedure categories using the following guide lines.

1. Each category is made up of many tests. Always start at the first test of a category. Starting at any other test will only give incorrect results.
2. Each test may have many steps. Only perform steps indicated under action required. It is not necessary to perform all steps in a test.
3. At the end of each test (not step) reconnect all wires and turn the engine **OFF** and reinstall any components that were removed for testing.
4. The vehicle being tested must have a fully charged battery.

Diagnostic Testing With Readout Box

TEST 1

Checking Battery Sensing Circuit Code 16

This test will check for direct battery feed to logic module. Circuit is also memory feed to logic module. Code 16 with lower battery voltage will turn **ON** power loss lamp.

1. Turn the ignition switch **OFF**.
2. Disconnect the (black on EFI, blue on turbocharged engines) connector from the logic module.
3. Connect a voltmeter to cavity No. 22 of logic module connector and ground.
4. Voltmeter should read within 1 volt of battery voltage. Voltage okay, replace logic module. Before replacing logic module, make sure the terminal in cavity No. 22 is not crushed so that it cannot touch logic module pin.
5. Zero volts, repair wire of cavity No. 22 for an open circuit to the wiring harness splice.

TEST 2

Fault Codes 41 and 46
Checking Charging System

STEP A

1. Disconnect the power module 10-way connector.
2. Connect a voltmeter between cavity No. 8 of 10-way connector and ground.
3. Turn ignition switch to **RUN** position.
4. Voltmeter should read within 1 volt of battery voltage. Not within 0–1 volts, repair alternator field circuit for short to ground. Voltage okay, perform Step B.

STEP B

1. Turn the ignition switch **OFF**.
2. Reconnect the power module 10-way connector.
3. Disconnect the power module 12-way connector.
4. Connect a voltmeter between F2 terminal on alternator and ground.
5. Turn the ignition switch to the **RUN** position.
6. Voltage should read within 1 volt of battery voltage. Not within 0–1 volt, replace power module. Voltage okay, perform Step C.

STEP C

1. Turn the ignition switch **OFF**.
2. With power module 12-way connector disconnected.
3. Disconnect the logic module (white on EFI, red on turbocharged engines) connector.
4. Connect an ohmmeter between cavity No. 11 of power module 12-way connector and ground.
5. Ommeter should not show continuity. No continuity, replace logic module. Continuity repair wire of cavity No. 11 for short circuit to ground.

TEST 3

Checking Codes 41 and 47

STEP A

1. Conenct a voltmeter between battery positive and ground.
2. Connect an end of jumper wire to a good engine ground.
3. Start the engine and note reading of voltmeter.
4. Very quickly touch other end of jumper wire to F2 terminal on alternator and watch voltmeter.
5. Voltmeter should show an increase in voltage. Voltage increases, this indicates alternator is operating correctly. Move on to Step B, for field circuit check. Voltage does not increase, this indicates alternator is not operating. If this is the case, perform Step E which checks for voltage to alternator field.

STEP B

1. Connect a voltmeter between cavity No. 2 of logic module (black on EFI, blue on turbocharged engines) connector and ground.
2. Connect an end of a jumper wire to cavity No. 5 of the logic module white connector.
3. Very quickly touch other end of jumper wire to logic module mounting stud and watch voltmeter.
4. Voltmeter should show an increase in voltage. If voltage increases, this indicates all components of system, except logic module, are operating correctly.
5. Before replacing the logic module, be sure that the terminal in cavity No. 5 is not crushed so that it cannot touch the logic module pin. If terminal in cavity 5 is not damaged, replace logic module. If no increase is indicated, move on to Step C.

STEP C

1. Turn the engine **OFF**.
2. Disconnect logic module (white on EFI, red on turbocharged engines) connector.
3. Connect a voltmeter between cavity No. 5 of logic module connector and ground.
4. Turn the ignition switch to **RUN** position. Voltmeter should read within 1 volt of battery voltage. Zero volts, disconnect power module 12-way and connect an ohmmeter between cavity 5 of logic module (white on EFI, red on turbocharged engines) connector and cavity 11 of power module. If open, repair wire or connector. If meter shows continuity replace power module. If voltage shown is within 1 volt of battery voltage, go on to Step D.

STEP D

1. Turn ignition switch **OFF**.
2. Disconnect 10-way connector from power module.
3. Connect a voltmeter between cavity No. 8 of 10-way connector and ground.
4. Turn ignition switch to **RUN** position. Voltmeter should read within 1 volt of battery voltage. If voltage shown is within 1 volt of battery voltage, replace power module.
5. Zero volts, turn ignition switch **OFF** and place an ohmmeter between cavity 8 of power module 10-way connector and F2 terminal of alternator. If open, repair wire or connector. If meter shows continuity, proceed to Step E.

STEP E

1. Turn ignition switch to **OFF** position.
2. Connect a voltmeter between F1 terminal of alternator and ground.
3. Turn ignition switch to **RUN** position.
4. Voltmeter should read within 1 volt of battery voltage. If voltage shown is within 1 volt of battery voltage, alternator is not functioning properly and must be removed form vehicle and repaired.
5. If no voltage is shown, this indicates an open circuit and

the wire from the F1 terminal to ignition switch must be repaired.

TEST 4

Checking Code 44

STEP A

1. Turn the ignition switch **OFF**.
2. Disconnect the logic module (black connector on EFI, blue connector on turbocharged engines).
3. Connect an ohmmeter between cavity No. 20 of logic module (black on EFI, blue on turbocharged engines) connector and ground.
4. Ohmmeter should show resistance, amount of resistance should be 8–29K ohms. Correct resistance, replace logic module. If 0 resistance, perform Step B. Open circuit, perform Step C.

STEP B

1. Ohmmter connected between cavity No. 20 of logic module (black on EFI, blue on turbocharged engines) connector and ground.
2. Disconnect power module 12-way connector.
3. Ohmmeter should show an open circuit. Open circuit, replace power module. If 0 resistance, repair wire of cavity No. 20 and cavity No. 3 of power module 12-way connector.

STEP C

1. Disconnect power module 12-way connector.
2. Connect an ohmmeter between pin 3 of power module 12-way and ground.
3. Ohmmeter should show resistance, amount of resistance should be between 8–29K ohms.
4. Correct resistance, repair wire in cavity No. 20 of logic module (black on EFI, blue on turbocharged engines) and cavity No. 3 of power module 12-way connector. Open circuit, replace power module.

OVERHAUL

Disassembly

1. Remove the dust cover mounting nut. Remove the dust cover.
2. Remove the brush holder assembly mounting screws. Remove the brush holder assembly.
3. Remove the stator to rectifier mounting screws. Remove the stator-to-rectifier assembly mounting screws. Remove the rectifier insulator. Remove the capacitor mounting screw. Remove the rectifier assembly.
4. Remove the through bolts. Carefully pry between the stator and the drive end shield, using a suitable tool and separate the end shields. The stator is laminated, do not burr the stator or the end shield.
5. Position the drive end of the alternator over the bosses of the holding fixture. Do not position the rotor plastic termination plate over the fixture boss or damage to the assembly will result.
6. Bolt the drive end of the assembly to shield fixture. Loosen the pulley mounting nut. Remove the pulley mounting nut. Remove the pulley washer.
7. Remove the poly-vee pulley. Remove the fan. Remove the front bearing spacer. Press the rotor assembly out of the drive end shield.
8. Remove the inner bearing spacer. Position the alternator bearing puller tool under the rear rotor bearing. Tighten the right puller bolt a ½ turn. Tighten the left puller bolt a ½ turn. Continue tightening the tool a ½ turn on each bolt until the rear rotor bearing is free. Remove the rear rotor bearing assembly from the rotor.

9. Position the rotor assembly in the holding fixture. Position the rear rotor bearing onto the rotor shaft.

10. Drive the rear rotor bearing onto the rotor until it bottoms. The rear rotor position is critical and must be installed using special tools C–4885 and C–4894.

11. Remove the front bearing retaining screws. Press the front bearing out of the drive end shield.

12. Carefully remove the stator from the rectifier end shield.

Inspection

ROTOR ASSEMBLY TEST

Check the outside circumference of slip-ring for dirtiness and roughness. Clean or polish with fine sandpaper, if required. A badly roughened slip-ring or a worn down slip-ring should be replaced.

Slip-rings are not serviced as a separate item. They are serviced with the rotor assembly.

ROTOR FIELD COILS FOR OPENS AND SHORTS TEST

To check for an open rotor field coil connect an ohmmeter between slip-rings. Ohmmeter readings should be between 1.5–2 ohms on rotor field coils at room ambient conditions. Resistance between 2.5–3.0 ohms would result from alternator rotor field coils that have been operated on vehicle at higher engine compartment temperatures. Readings about 3.5 ohms would indicate high resistance rotor field coils and further testing or replacement may be required.

To check for a shorted rotor field coil, connect an ohmmeter between both slip-rings. If the reading is below 1.5 ohms, the rotor field coil is shorted.

ROTOR FIELD COIL FOR GROUND TEST

To check for a grounded rotor field coil, connect an ohmmeter from each slip-ring to rotor shaft. Ohmmeter should be set for infinite reading when probes are apart and 0 when probes are shorted. The ohmmeter should read infinite. If the reading is 0 or low in value, rotor is grounded.

STATOR ASSEMBLY TEST

Stator Coil for Ground Test

1. Remove varnish from a spot on the stator frame.
2. Press an ohmmeter test probe firmly onto cleaned spot on frame. Be sure varnish has been removed from stator so that spot is bare.
3. Press the other ohmmeter test probe firmly to each of the 3 phase (stator) lead terminals 1 at a time. If ohmmeter reads 0 or low in value stator lead is grounded.
4. Replace stator if stator tested grounded.

Stator for Open or Short Circuit Test

The stator windings are delta wound. Therefore, they cannot be tested for opens or shorts with an ohmmeter. They can only be tested for these items with test equipment not common to automotive service test equipment. If stator is not grounded and all other electrical circuits and components of alternator test okay, it can be suspected that stator could possibly be open or shorted and must be replaced.

Rectifier Assemblies Test

When testing rectifiers with an ohmmeter, disconnect the 3 phase stator lead terminals from rectifier assembly. Pry stator lead terminals away from rectifier assembly.

Positive Rectifier Test

With an ohmmeter check for continuity between each positive (+) rectifier strap and positive (+) heat sink. Reverse test probes and retest. There should be continuity in one direction

only. If there is continuity in both directions, rectifier is short circuited. If there is no continuity in either direction, rectifier is open. If rectifier is shorted or open, replace rectifier assembly.

Negative Rectifier Test

With an ohmmeter, check for continuity between each negative (−) rectifier strap and negative (−) sink. Reverse test probes and retest. There should be continuity in one direction only. If there is continuity in both directions, rectifier is short circuited. If there is no continuity in either direction, rectifier is open. If rectifier is shorted or open, replace rectifier assembly. When installing a new rectifier assembly, apply 3 dabs (0.1 grams each) of heat sink compound to bottom of negative rectifier prior to mounting rectifier assembly to rectifier end shield.

Brushes and Brush Springs Continuity Test

When testing brushes and brush springs make sure that brushes move smoothly in brush holder. Sticking brushes require replacement of brush holder assembly.

Inner Brush Circuit Test

With an ohmmeter, touch a test probe to inner brush and another probe to field terminal. If there is no continuity, replace the brush assembly.

Outer Brush Circuit Test

With an ohmmeter, touch a test probe to outer brush and other probe to field terminal. If there is no continuity, replace brush assembly.

Cleaning Alternator Parts

Do not immerse stator field coil assembly, rotor assembly or rectifier assembly in cleaning solvent, as solvent will damage these parts.

Assembly

1. Be sure to repair or replace defective components as required.
2. To the front of the rotor, install the inner bearing spacer and press the drive end shield onto the rotor.

NOTE: The front drive end shield bearing must be replaced anytime the rotor or drive end shield is removed, for the front bearing is a press fit and may be damaged upon removal.

3. Position the drive end shield into a holding fixture so the fixture bosses do not contact the rotor plastic termination plate and tighten the holding bolt.
4. At the front of the drive end shield, install the pulley spacer (flat side up), the fan, the pulley, the washer and the pulley nut. Torque the pulley nut to 80–105 ft. lbs. (108–125 Nm).
5. Remove the drive end shield and rotor assembly from the holding fixture.
6. To assemble the rear end housing for the 40/90, perform the following procedures:
    a. Apply joint compound to the rectifier end shield surface, under the rectifier mounting position.
    b. Position the rectifier assembly to the rectifier drive end housing.
    c. Install the rectifier insulator, the insulator mounting screws and torque the screws to 36–46 inch lbs. (4–6 Nm).
    d. Install the capacitor terminal over the rectifier assembly battery terminal stud and torque the mounting screw to 36–48 inch lbs. (4–6 Nm).
    e. Install the alternator battery terminal nut and torque to 30–50 inch lbs. (3–6 Nm).
    f. Install the stator-to-rectifier screws and torque to 12–18 inch lbs. (1–2 Nm).

g. Slide the brushes into their cavity, Install the brush holder assembly and torque the screws to 12–18 inch lbs. (1–2 Nm).

h. Install the dust cover and torque the nut to 12–18 inch lbs. (1–2 Nm).

7. To assemble the rear end housing for the 50/120, perform the following procedures:

a. Apply joint compound to the rectifier end shield surface, under the rectifier mounting position.

b. Position the rectifier assemblies No. 1 and No. 2 to the rectifier drive end housing.

c. Install the rectifier insulators, the insulator mounting screws and torque to 36–46 inch lbs. (4–6 Nm).

d. Install the capacitor terminal over the rectifier assembly No. 2 battery terminal stud and torque the mounting screw to 36–48 inch lbs. (4–6 Nm).

e. Install the alternator battery terminal nut and torque to 30–50 inch lbs. (3–6 Nm).

f. Position a jumper strap between the rectifier assemblies No. 1 and No. 2.; torque the nut to 36–48 inch lbs. (4–6 Nm) and the screw to 15–35 inch lbs. (2–4 Nm).

g. Position the 3 buss bars to the rectifier assemblies and torque the screws to 12–18 inch lbs. (1–2 Nm).

h. Slide the brushes into their cavity, Install the brush holder assembly and torque the screws to 12–18 inch lbs. (1–2 Nm).

i. Install the dust cover and torque the nut to 12–18 inch lbs. (1–2 Nm).

8. Assemble the rear end housing to the drive end shield and rotor assemlby. Install the through bolts and torque to 48–72 inch lbs. (5–8 Nm).

9. Install the rear bearing oil seal.

BOSCH 35/75, 40/90, 75 HS, 90 HS AND 90 RS AMP ALTERNATORS

The alternators are alike, except, the 35/75 has 6 built-in silicon rectifiers and the 40/90 has 12 (1986–87) or 8 (1988–90) built-in silicon rectifiers.

The voltage regulator is built into the power and logic modules for 1986–88 or the Single Module Engine Controller (SMEC) for 1989–90.

System Diagnosis

ON VEHICLE SERVICE

Charging Circuit Resistance Test

1. Be sure that the battery is fully charged.
2. Disconnect negative battery cable.
3. Disconnect BAT lead at alternator output terminal.
4. Connect a 0–150 ampere scale DC ammeter in series between alternator output BAT terminal and disconnected BAT terminal wire. Connect positive lead to alternator output BAT terminal and negative lead to disconnected alternator BAT lead.
5. Connect positive lead of a test voltmeter (range 0–18 volts minimum) to alternator BAT terminal. Connect negative lead of test voltmeter to battery positive post.
6. Remove air hose between power module (1986–88) or single module engine controller (1989–90) and air cleaner.
7. Connect an end of a jumper wire to ground and with other end, probe the green R3 lead wire of black 8-way connector (1986–88) or back of the alternator (1989–90). Do not connect blue J2 lead of 8-way wiring connector (1986–88) or back of the atlernator (1989–90) to ground.

NOTE: On the 1986–88 vehicles, both R3 and J2 leads are green on alternator side of 8-way wiring connector. At dash end of 8-way connector, R3 is green and J2 is blue.

8. Connect an engine tachometer and reconnect negative battery cable.
9. Connect a variable carbon pile rheostat to the battery terminals. Be sure carbon pile is in **OPEN** or **OFF** position before connecting leads.
10. Start engine. Immediately after starting, reduce engine speed to idle.
11. Adjust engine speed and carbon pile to maintain 20 amperes flowing in circuit. Observe voltmeter reading. Voltmeter reading should not exceed 0.5 volts.

NOTE: If a higher voltage drop is indicated, inspect, clean and tighten all connections in charging circuit. A voltage drop test may be performed at each connection to locate connection with excessive resistance. If charging circuit resistance tested satisfactorily, reduce engine speed, turn OFF carbon pile and turn OFF ignition switch.

12. Disconnect negative battery cable.
13. Remove test ammeter, voltmeter, carbon pile and tachometer.
14. Remove jumper wire between 8-way black connector (1986–88) or the back of the alternator (1989–90) and ground.
15. Connect BAT lead to alternator output BAT terminal post.
16. Reconnect negative battery cable.
17. Reconnect hose between power module (1986–88) or single module engine controller (1989–90) and air cleaner.

Current Output Test

1. Be sure that the battery is fully charged.
2. Disconnect negative battery cable.
3. Disconnect the BAT lead wire at the alternator output terminal.
4. Connect a 0–150 ampere scale DC ammeter in series between alternator output BAT terminal and negative lead to disconnected BAT terminal.
5. Connect positive lead of a test voltmeter (range 0–18 volts minimum) to alternator output BAT terminal.
6. Connect negative lead of test voltmeter to a good ground.
7. Connect an engine tachometer and reconnect negative battery cable.
8. Connect a variable carbon pile rheostat tool between battery terminals. Be sure carbon pile is in **OPEN** or **OFF** position before connecting leads.
9. Remove air hose between power module (1986–88) or the single module engine controller (1989–90) and air cleaner.
10. Connect 1 end of a jumper wire to ground and with other end, probe the green R3 lead wire of black 8-way connector (1986–88) or at the back of the alternator (1989–90). Do not connect blue J2 lead of 8-way wiring connector (1986–88) or at the back of the alternator (1989–90) to ground.

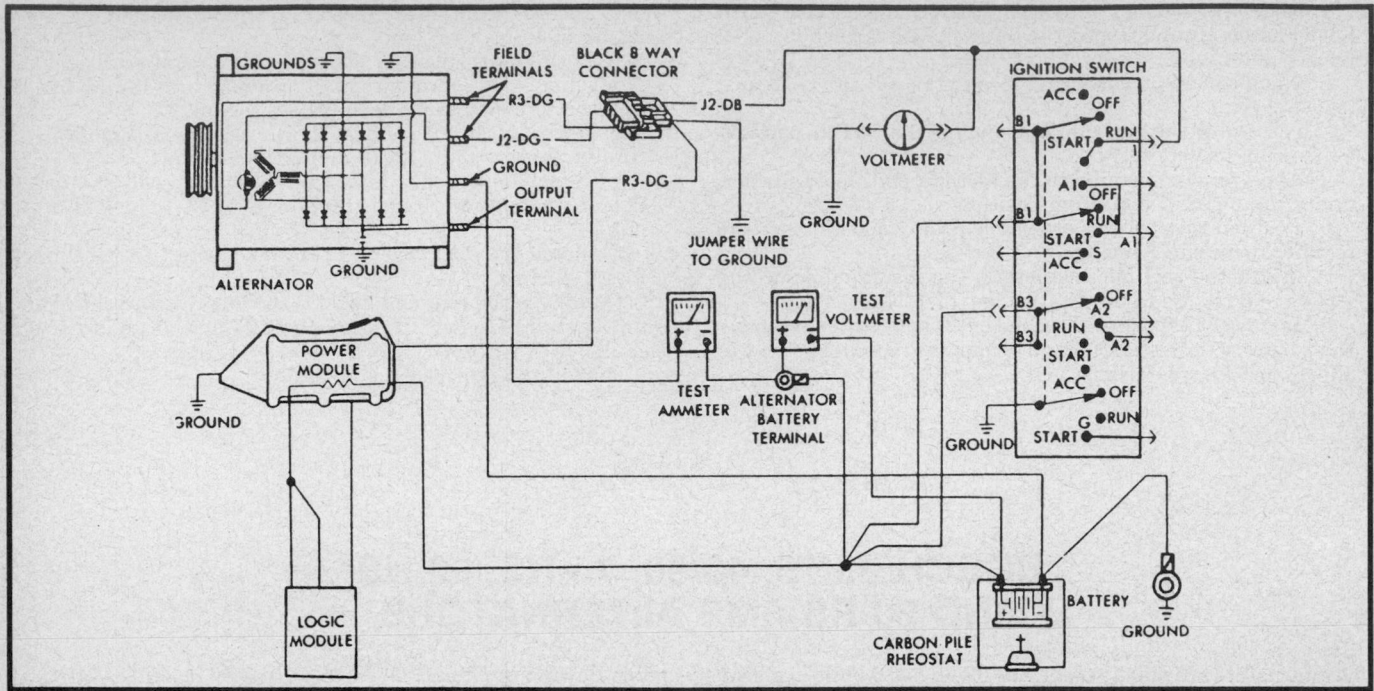

Bosch 40/90 amp alternator – charging resistance test – adjust engine speed and carbon pile to maintain 20 amps flowing in circuit. Voltmeter reading should not exceed 0.5 volts

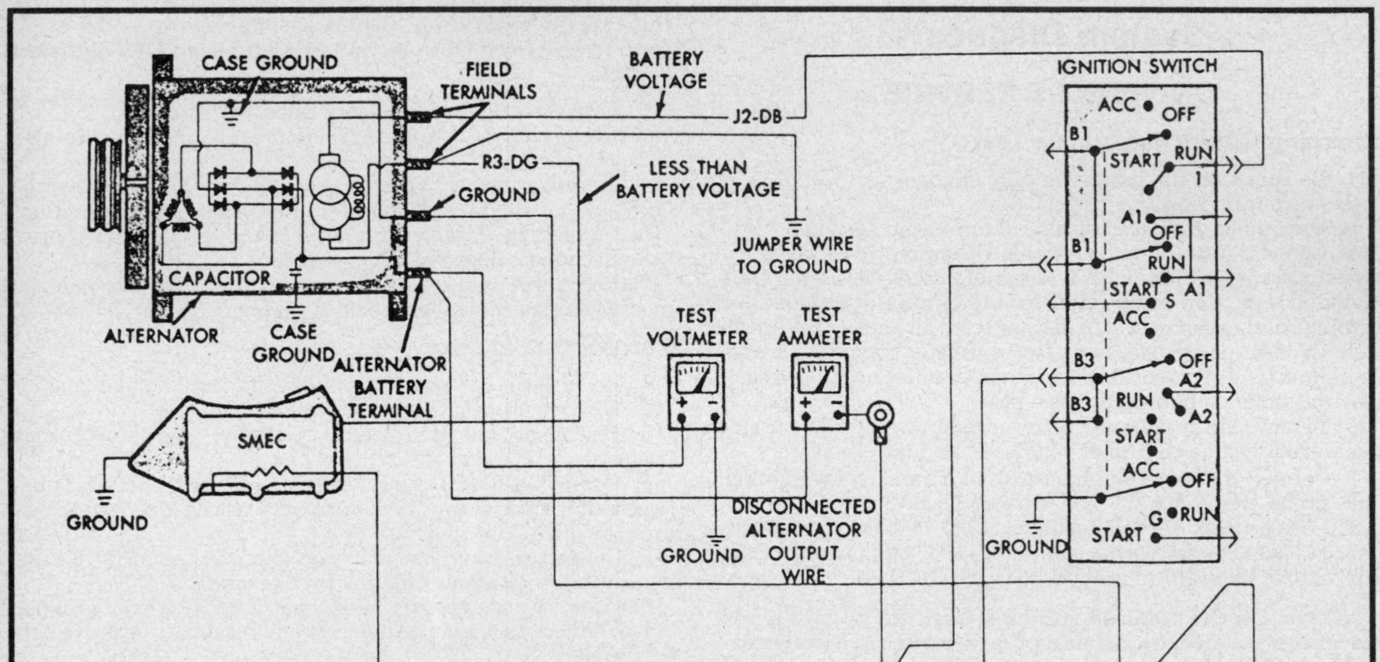

Bosch 90 RS amp alternator – charging system resistance test – adjust engine speed and carbon pile to maintain 20 amps, voltmeter reading should not exceed 0.5 volts

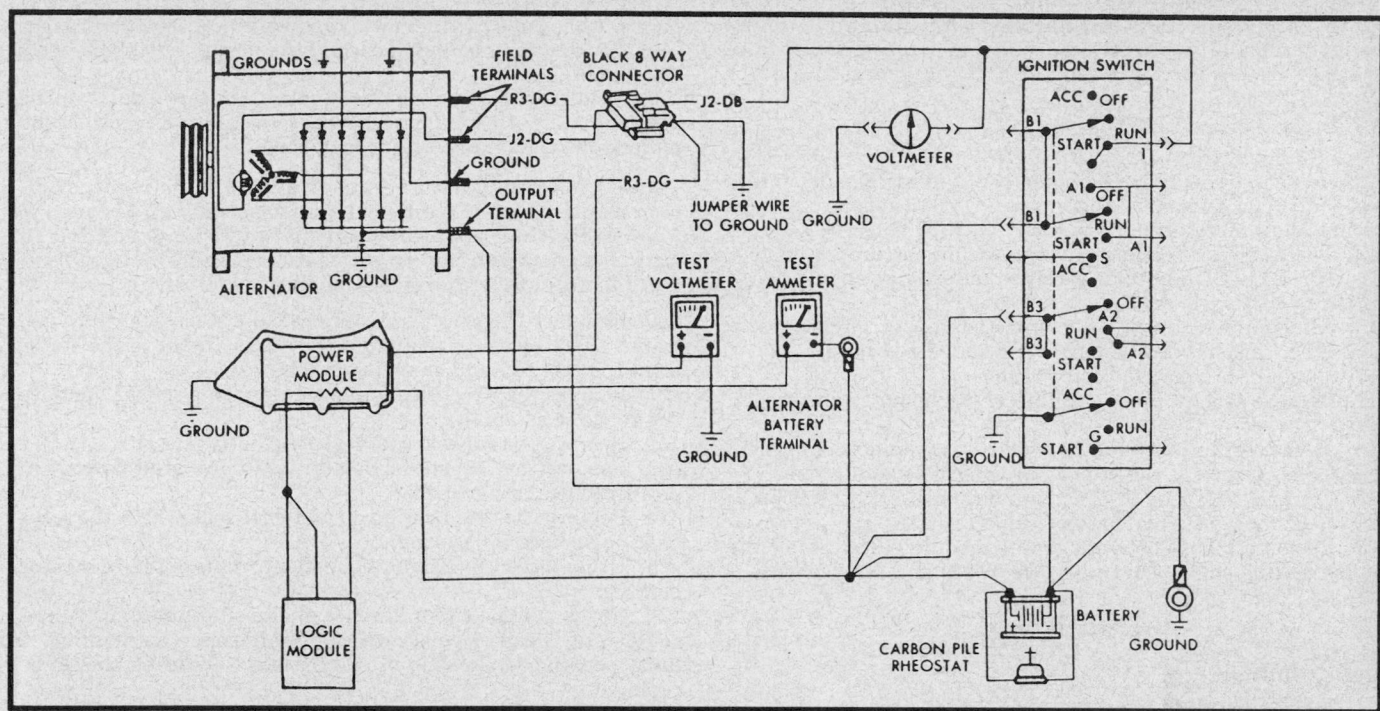

Bosch 40/90 amp alternator—current output test—adjust carbon pile and engine speed until a speed of 1250 rpm and voltmeter reading of 15 volts is obtained. The ammeter reading must be within proper limits

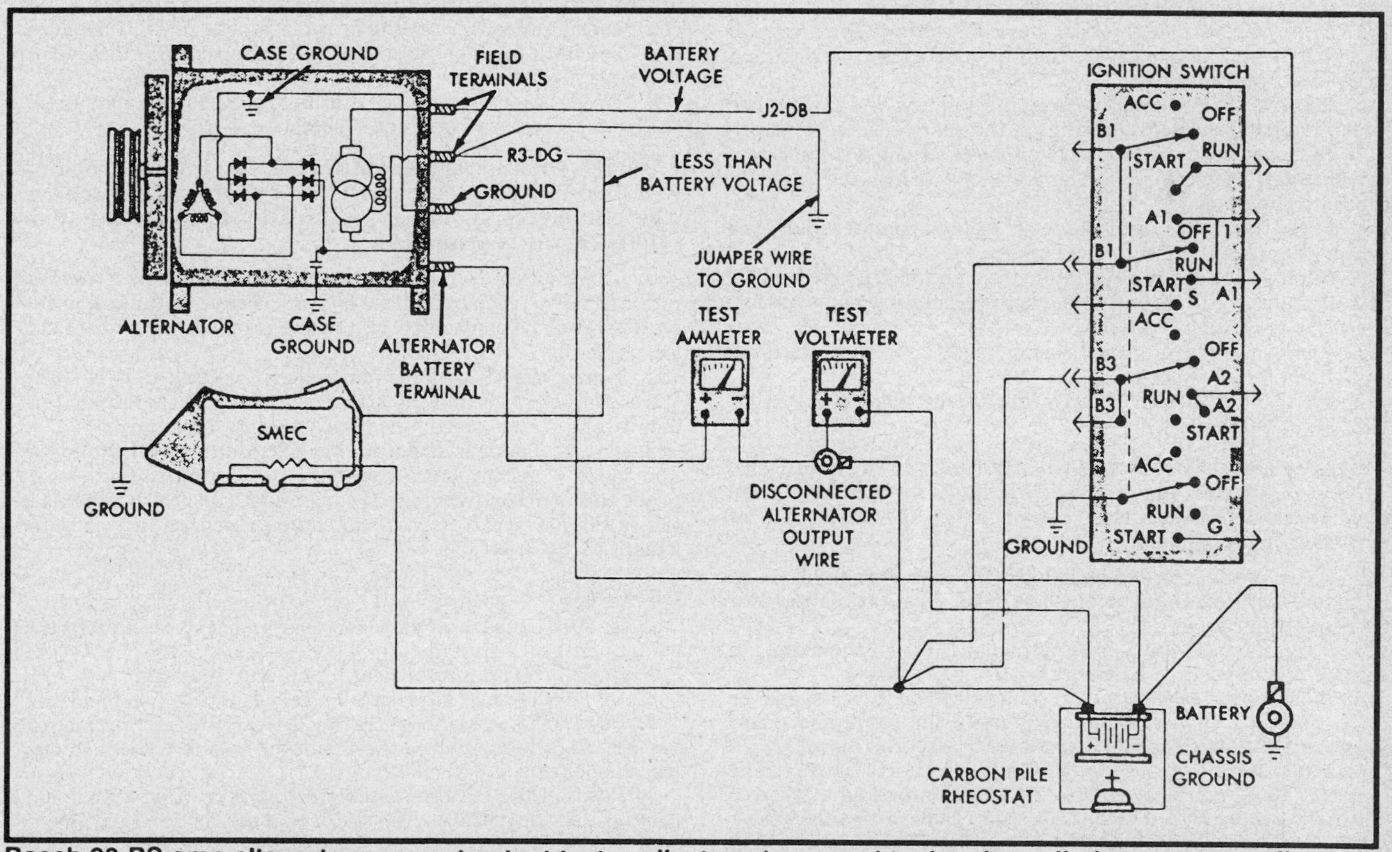

Bosch 90 RS amp alternator—current output test—adjust engine speed and carbon pile increments until an engine speed of 1250 rpm is reached, voltmeter reading should not exceed 15 volts

NOTE: On the 1986–88 vehicles, both R3 and J2 leads are green on alternator side of 8-way wiring connector. At dash end of 8-way connector, R3 is green and J2 is blue.

11. Start engine. Immediately after starting reduce engine speed to idle.

12. Adjust carbon pile and engine speed in increments until a speed of 1250 rpm and voltmeter reading of 15 volts is obtained. Do not allow voltage meter to read above 16 volts.

13. The ammeter reading must be within the proper limits.

14. If reading is less than specified, alternator should be removed from vehicle and bench tested.

15. After current output is completed reduce engine speed, turn **OFF** carbon pile and turn **OFF** ignition switch.

16. Disconnect negative battery cable.

17. Remove test ammeter, voltmeter, tachometer and carbon pile.

18. Remove jumper wire between 8-way black connector (1986–88) or back of the alternator (1989–90) and ground.

19. Connect BAT lead to alternator output BAT terminal post.

20. Reconnect negative battery cable.

21. Reconnect hose between power module (1986–88) or the single module engine controller (1989–90) and air cleaner.

OVERHAUL

Disassembly

1. Remove the alternator from the vehicle. Position the unit in a suitable holding fixture.

2. Remove the pulley nut and lockwasher. Remove the alternator pulley.

3. Remove the pulley to fan spacer and pulley fan.

4. Remove the Woodruff key from the rotor shaft.

5. From the rear of the alternator disconnect the electrical terminal from the capacitor. Remove the capacitor retaining screw and the capacitor.

6. Remove the brush holder retaining screw and remove the brush holder from its mounting on the rear of the alternator.

7. Remove the alternator through bolts. Using a suitable tool pry between the stator and the drive end shield and carefully separate the assembly.

8. Press the rotor out of the drive end shield and remove the spacer. Remove the pulley fan spacer.

9. Remove the front alternator drive end bearing screws.

10. Remove the drive end shield bearing retainer and press out the drive end shield bearing.

11. Remove the front drive bearing from the front of the drive end shield.

12. To test the positive and negative rectifiers use tool C–3929–A or equivalent.

NOTE: Do not break the plastic cases of the rectifiers. These cases are for protection against corrosion. Be sure to always touch the test probe to the metal pin of the nearest rectifier.

13. Position the rear end shield and the stator assembly on an insulated surface. Connect the test lead clip to the alternator battery output terminal.

14. Plug in tool C–3829–A or equivalent. Touch the metal pin of each of the positive rectifiers with the test probe.

15. Reading for satisfactory rectifiers will be 1¾ amperes or more. Reading should be approximately the same and meter needle must move in same direction for all 3 rectifiers.

16. When some rectifiers are good and 1 is shorted, the reading taken at good rectifiers will be low and the reading at shorted rectifiers will be zero. Disconnect stator lead to rectifiers reading zero and retest. Reading of good rectifiers will now be within satisfactory range.

17. When a rectifier is open it will read approximately 1 ampere and the good rectifiers will read within satisfactory range.

18. Touch the metal pin of each of the negative rectifiers with the test probe.

19. Test specifications are the same and the test results will be approximately same as for positive case rectifiers except that the meter will read on opposite side of scale.

NOTE: If a negative rectifier shows a shorted condition remove stator from rectifier assembly and retest. It is possible that a stator winding could be grounded to stator laminations or to an rectifier end shield, which would indicate a shorted negative rectifier.

20. Unsolder the stator to rectifier leads. Mark the stator coil frame, to aid in reinstallation of the stator. Remove the stator from the rectifier end shield assembly.

21. Remove the 3 rectifier assembly mounting screws. Remove the rectifier assembly.

22. Remove the inner battery (B+) stud insulator.

23. Remove the D+ stud insulator, stud nut, stud flatwasher and stud insulating washer.

24. Remove the rear bearing oil and dust seal. Check the rotor bearing surface for scoring.

25. Using puller C–4068 or equivalent, remove the rear rotor bearing.

26. Check outside circumference of slip-ring for dirtiness and roughness. Clean or polish with fine sandpaper, as required. A badly roughened slip-ring or a worn down slip-ring should be replaced.

27. To check for an open rotor field coil, connect an ohmmeter to slip-rings. Ohmmeter reading should be between 1.5–2 ohms on rotor coils at room ambient conditions. Resistance between 2.5–3.0 ohms would result from alternator rotors that have been operated on vehicle at higher engine compartment temperatures. Readings above 3.5 ohms would indicate high resistance rotor coils and further testing or replacement may be required.

28. To check for a shorted field coil connect an ohmmeter to slip-rings. If reading is below 1.5 ohms field coil is shorted.

29. To check for a grounded rotor field coil connect an ohmmeter from each slip-ring to rotor shaft.

NOTE: Ohmmeter should be set for infinite reading when probes are apart and 0 when probes are touching. The ohmmeter should read infinite. If reading is 0 or higher, rotor is grounded.

30. Check for continuity between leads of stator coil. Press test probe firmly to each of 3 phase (stator) lead terminals separately. If there is no continuity, stator coil is defective. Replace stator assembly.

31. To test the stator for ground check for continuity between the stator coil leads and the stator coil frame. If there is no continuity the stator is grounded and must be replaced.

32. To test the inner and outer brush circuit, use an ohmmeter and touch 1 test probe to the inner brush and the other test probe to the brush terminal. If continuity does not exist replace the brush assembly. Repeat the same procedure for the outer brush.

Assembly

1. Be sure to check all parts for wear and replace the defective components as required.

2. Install the rear rotor bearing oil and dust seal.

3. Install the inner alternator battery B+ terminal insulator.

4. Position the rectifier assembly. Install the rectifier mounting screws, the insulator, the insulator washer, the insulator lockwasher and the insulator nut.

5. Position the stator assembly into the rectifier end shield. Align the scribe marks on the stator and the rectifier end shield.

6. Solder the stator leads to the rectifier assembly; be sure to use needle nose pliers as a heat sink.

7. Position and press the front bearing into the drive end

shield. Install the bearing retainer and the pulley fan spacer onto the drive end shield.

8. Position the drive end shield and spacer over the rotor. Using a socket wrench, press the drive end shield onto the rotor.

9. Install the rectifier end shield and stator assembly into the drive end shield and rotor assembly. Install the through bolts and tighten.

10. Push the brushes into the brush holder and install the brush holder onto the alternator assembly.

11. Install the capacitor and terminal plug onto the alternator assembly.

12. Install the Woodruff key into the shaft and the fan over the shaft.

13. Install the drive pulley-to-fan spacer, the pulley, the lockwasher and the nut over the shaft. Secure the pulley and tighten the nut.

MITSUBISHI 75 AMP AND 90 AMP ALTERNATOR WITH INTERNAL REGULATOR

This integrated circuit alternator has 15 built-in rectifiers, that convert A.C. current into D.C. current at the alternator battery terminal. The main components of the alternator are the rotor, stator, rectifiers, end shields, pulley, fan and capacitor. The electronic voltage regulator is very compact and is built into the rectifier end shield of the alternator.

System Diagnosis

ON VEHICLE SERVICE

Charging Circuit Resistance Test

1. With the ignition switch in the **OFF** position, disconnect the negative battery cable and the output wire from the alternator battery cable.

2. Using a 0–100 amp DC ammeter, connect it in series between the alternator **BAT** terminal and the disconnected alternator output wire; connect the positive (+) wire to the alternator **BAT** terminal and the negative (−) wire to the disconnected alternator output wire.

3. Using a 0–18 volt voltmeter, connect its positive (+) lead to the disconnected alternator output wire and its negative (−) lead to the positive (+) battery post.

4. Install the tachometer to the engine.

5. Using a variable carbon pile rheostat, connect it between the battery posts; be sure the pile is in the **OPEN** or **OFF** position before connecting the leads.

6. Start the engine and allow it to idle.

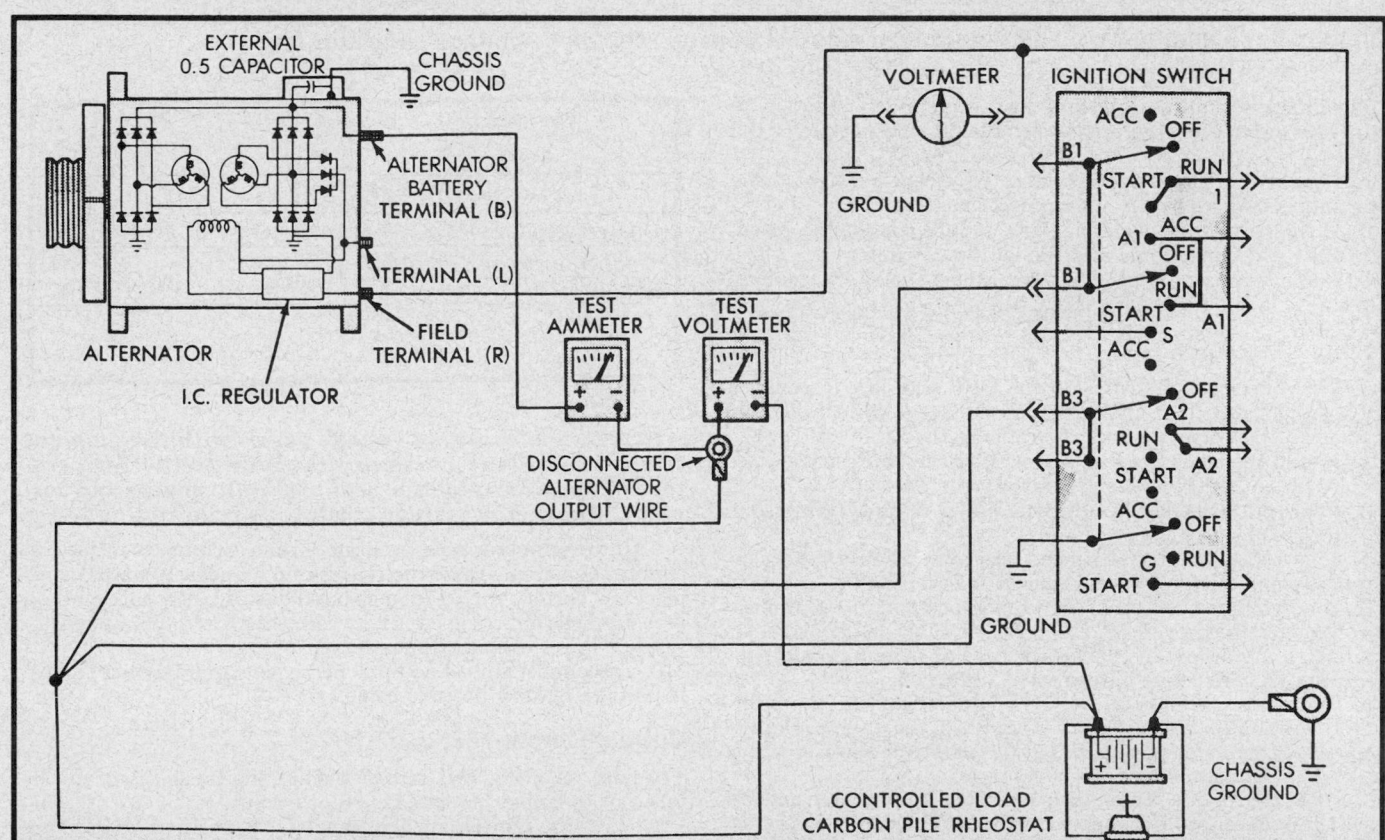

Mitsubishi 75 and 90 amp alternators with internal voltage regulator—charging system resistance test— adjust engine speed and carbon pile to maintain 20 amps, voltmeter reading should not exceed 0.5 volts

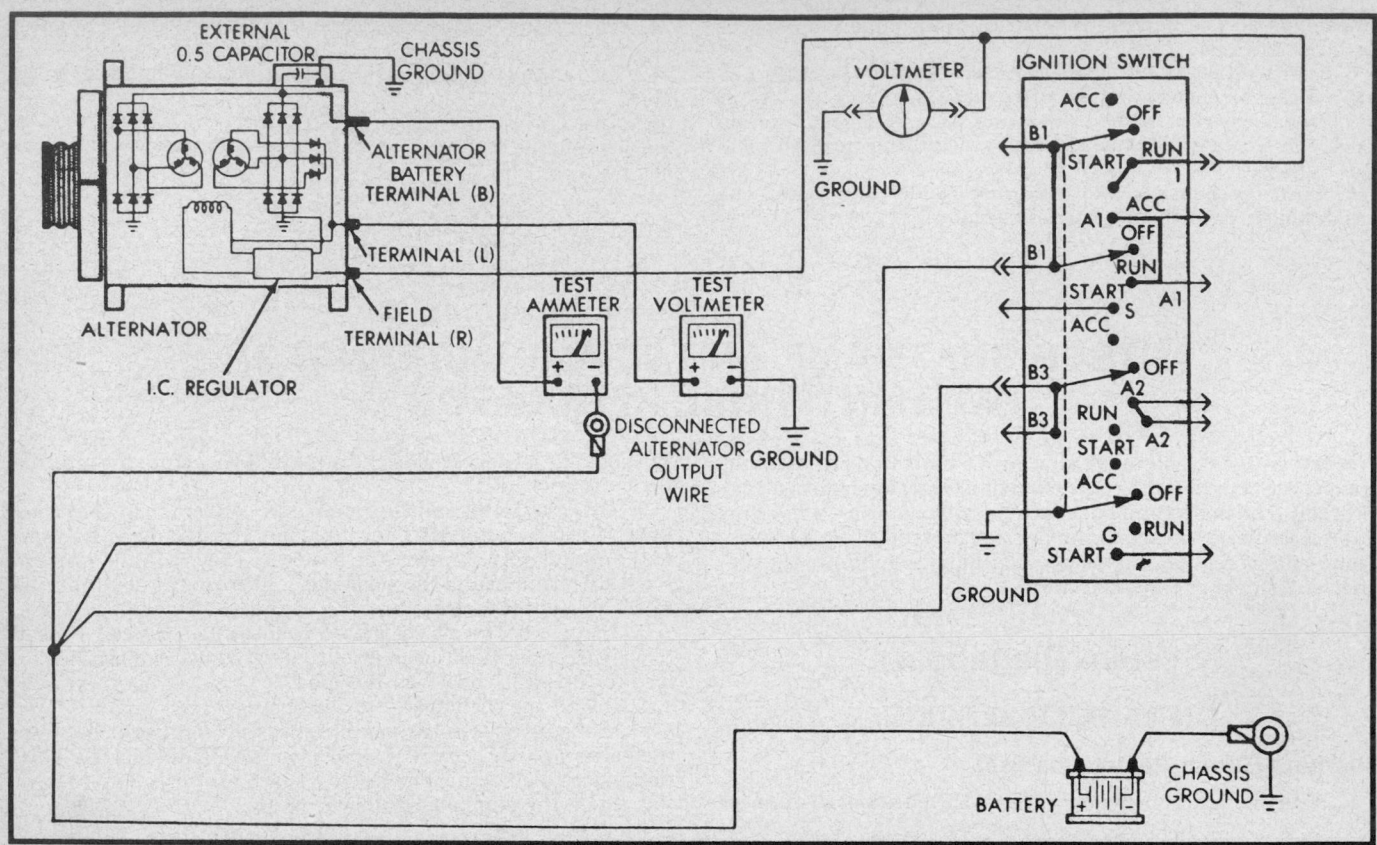

Mitsubishi 75 and 90 amp alternators with external voltage regulator—voltage regulator test

7. Adjust the engine speed and the carbon pile to maintain 20 amps flowing in the circuit; the voltmeter should not exceed 0.5 volts.

8. If a higher voltage drop is indicated, clean and tighten the alternator output wire circuit connections.

9. If the resistance is satisfactory, reduce the engine speed, turn **OFF** the carbon pile and the ignition switch.

10. Remove the test equipment. Reconnect the alternator output wire and the negative battery cable.

Voltage Regulator Test

1. With the ignition switch in the **OFF** position, disconnect the positive cable from the battery and place a knife switch on the battery post and connect the cable to the knife switch.

2. Install the leads from an ammeter to the knife switch connectors and open the switch-to-battery current.

3. Connect the leads of a voltmeter between the **L** terminal of the alternator and a good ground.

4. The voltage reading should be zero volts. Should voltage be present, a defective alternator or wiring is indicated.

5. If no voltage is present, turn the ignition switch **ON** position. The voltage present should be lower than battery voltage, by about 1 volt or less. If the voltage reading is higher or at battery voltage, a defective alternator is indicated.

6. Connect a tachometer to the engine and close the knife switch, mounted on the battery post. Start the engine. Do not apply any starting current through the ammeter when starting the engine. The ammeter can be ruined.

7. After the engine is operating, open the knife switch and increase the engine speed to approximately 2500 rpm and observe the ammeter reading.

8. If the ammeter reading is 10 amps or less, observe the voltage reading. This reading is the charging voltage.

VOLTAGE CHART	
Charging voltage	14.4 ± 0.3V at 20°C (68°F)
Temperature compensation gradient	−0.7 to .13V/10°C (50°F)

NOTE: The charging voltage varies with the ambient temperature. It is necessary to measure the temperature of the air around the rear of the alternator and correct the charging voltage reading as required.

9. If the ammeter reading is more than 10 amps, continue to charge the battery until the reading falls under 10 amps or replace the battery with a fully charged one. An alternate method is to limit the charging circuit by connecting a ¼ ohm (25 watt) resistor in series with the battery.

10. Disconnect all test equipment, remove knife switch and reinstall the battery positive cable.

Current Output Test

The purpose of this test is to determine the capability of the alternator to deliver its rated current output.

1. With the ignition switch in the **OFF** position, disconnect the battery ground cable.

2. Disconnect the **BAT** lead wire from the terminal of the alternator.

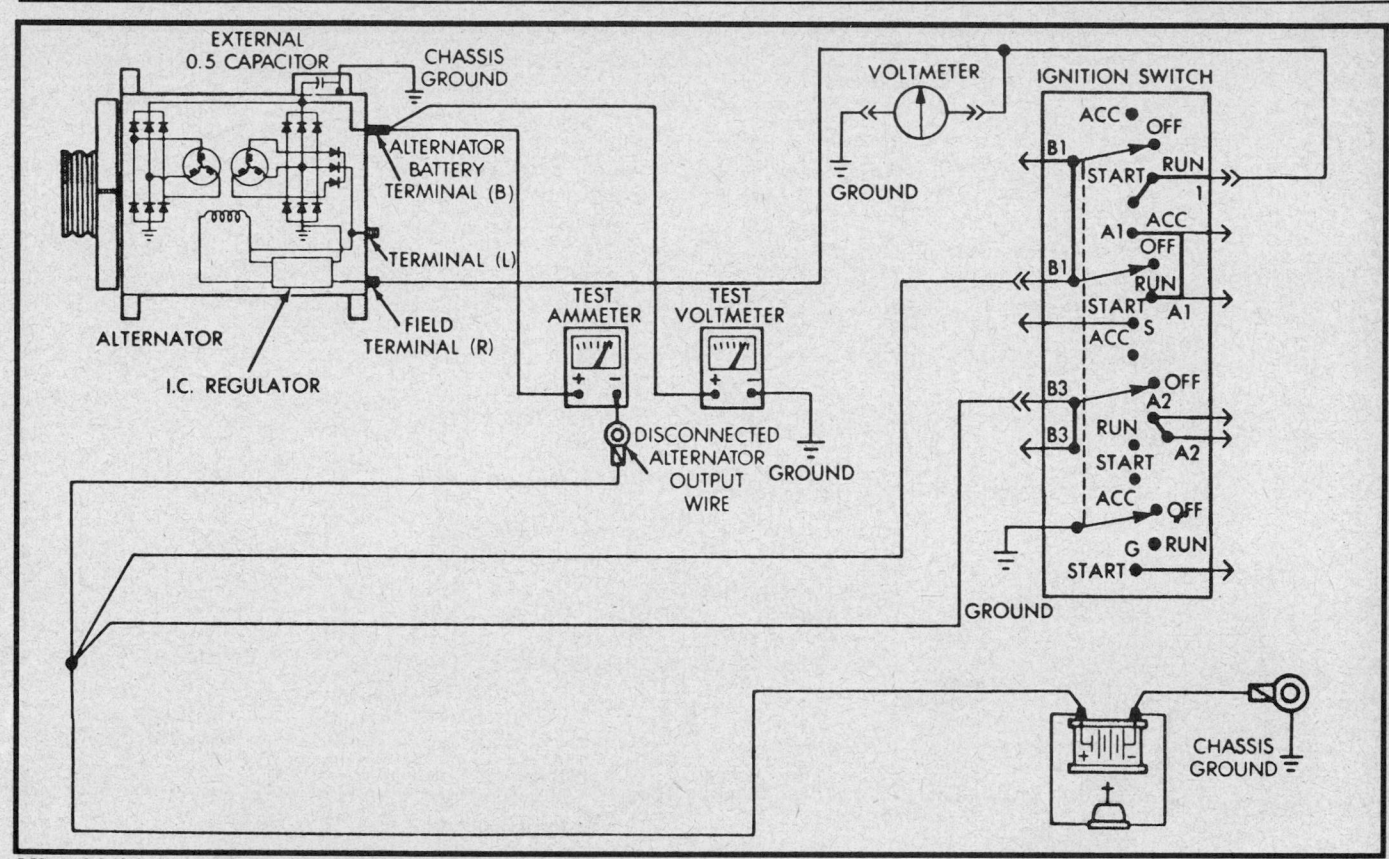

Mitsubishi 75 and 90 amp alternators with external voltage regulator—current output test

75 AMP CURRENT OUTPUT CHART	
Output current (Hot or Cold) at Engine RPM	44-51A at 13.0 Volts and 750 RPM
	64-72A at 13.0 Volts and 1000 RPM
	74-78A at 13.0 Volts and 2000 RPM

90 AMP CURRENT OUTPUT CHART	
Output current (Hot or Cold) at Engine RPM	58-71A at 13.0 Volts and 750 RPM
	80-91A at 13.0 Volts and 1000 RPM
	95-102A at 13.0 Volts and 2000 RPM

3. Connect a 0–100 scaled ammeter in series, between the **BAT** terminal and the **BAT** lead wire.

4. Connect the positive lead of a voltmeter to the **BAT** terminal of the alternator and ground the negative lead.

5. Disconnect the green field wire (to voltage regulator) at the alternator.

6. Connect a tachometer to the engine and reconnect the negative battery cable.

7. Connect a carbon pile rheostat between the battery terminals. Be sure the carbon pile is in the **OPEN** or **OFF** position before connecting the leads.

8. Start the engine and operate at idle.

9. Adjust the carbon pile and accelerate the engine to the specified speed and measure the output current. The current should be within specifications. Do not allow the voltage to increase over 16 volts.

10. The ammeter reading must be within the specified limits. If not the alternator should be removed and bench tested.

11. After the tests, disconnect the test equipment from the components.

OVERHAUL

Disassembly

1. Place the alternator in a vise or similar holding fixture, mark the body components and remove the through body bolts.

2. Pry between the stator and the drive end shield and carefully separate the drive end plate, the pulley and the rotor assembly from the stator and rectifier end shield assembly.

3. Carefully clamp the rotor and remove the pulley nut from the end of the shaft. Remove the pulley, the pulley fan, the pulley fan spacer and the alternator drive end shield from the rotor shaft.

4. The front bearing can be removed from the front drive housing by the removal of the dust seals, front and rear, the bearing retainer screws, the retainer, exposing the bearing so that it can be tapped from the drive housing.

5. To remove the stator assembly. The 6 stator leads must be unsoldered from the rectifiers, as per the manufacturer's recommendation.

6. Remove the rectifiers from the stator end shield housing.

7. Remove the brush holder and regulator retaining screw.

8. Remove the Bat terminal retaining nut and remove the capacitor from the terminal.

9. Remove the regulator and rectifier assembly. Unsolder 1 rectifier-to-regulator assembly and remove the other rectifier assembly by sliding the battery stud out of the regulator.

10. Inspect the rotor bearing surface for scores and make the necessary off vehicle test on the electrical components.

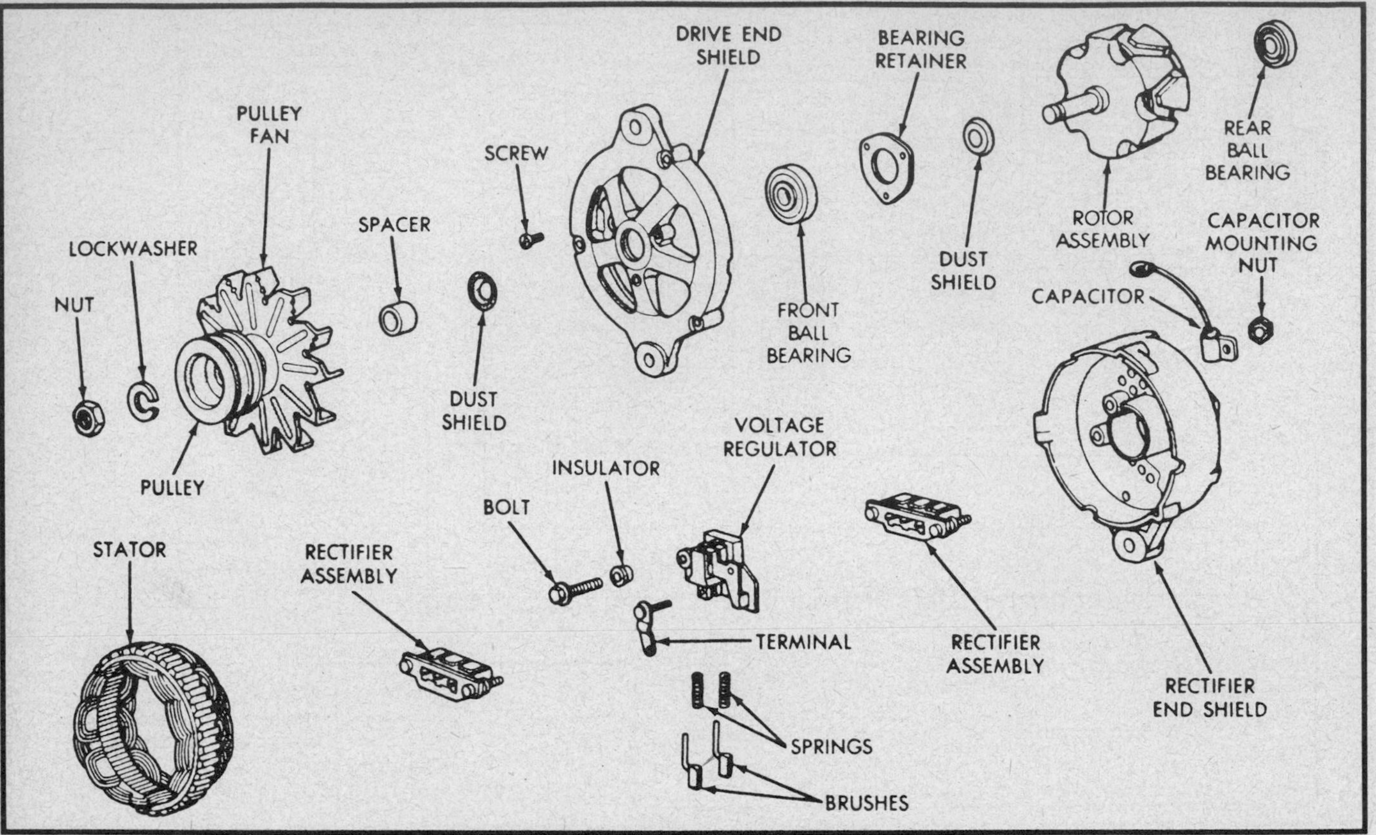

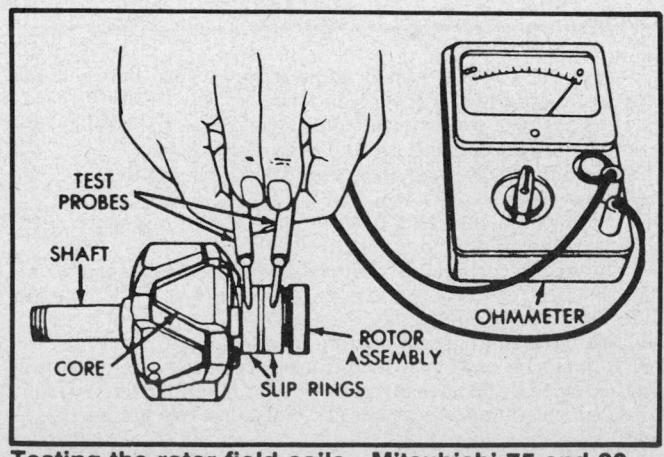

Exploded view of the alternator assembly—Mitsubishi 75 and 90 amp alternators

Inspection

ROTOR ASSEMBLY

1. Check the outside circumference of the slip ring for dirtiness and roughness. Clean or polish with fine sandpaper, if required. A badly roughened slip ring or a slip ring worn down beyond the service limit should be replaced.

2. Check for continuity between the field coil and slip ring. If there is no continuity, the field coil is defective. Replace the rotor assembly.

3. Check for continuity between the slip ring and shaft (or core). If there is continuity, the coil or slip ring is grounded. Replace the rotor assembly.

STATOR ASSEMBLY

Check for continuity between the leads of the stator coil. If there is no continuity the stator coil is defective. Replace the stator assembly.

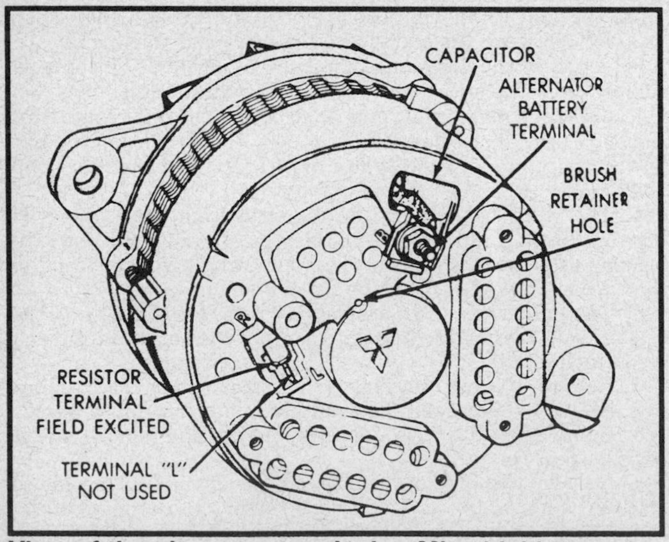

View of the alternator terminals—Mitsubishi 75 and 90 amp alternators

Testing the rotor field coils—Mitsubishi 75 and 90 amp alternators

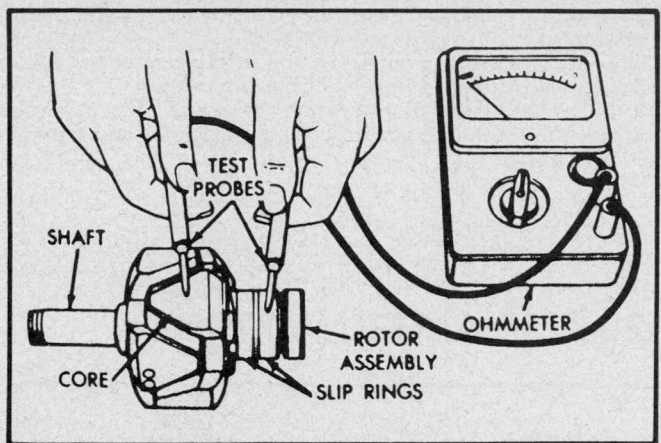

Testing the rotor for ground—Mitsubishi 75 and 90 amp alternators

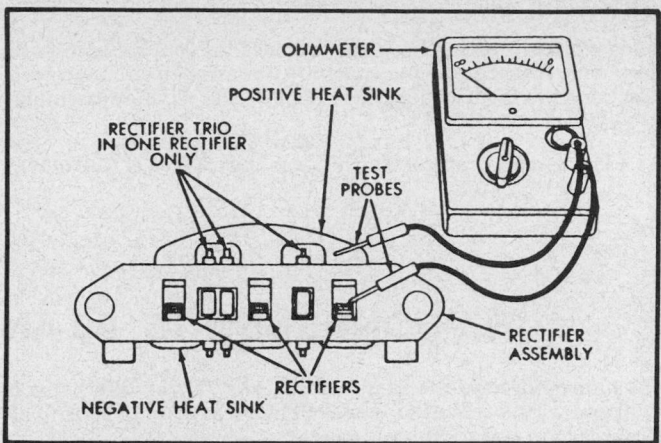

Testing the positive rectifiers—Mitsubishi 75 and 90 amp alternators

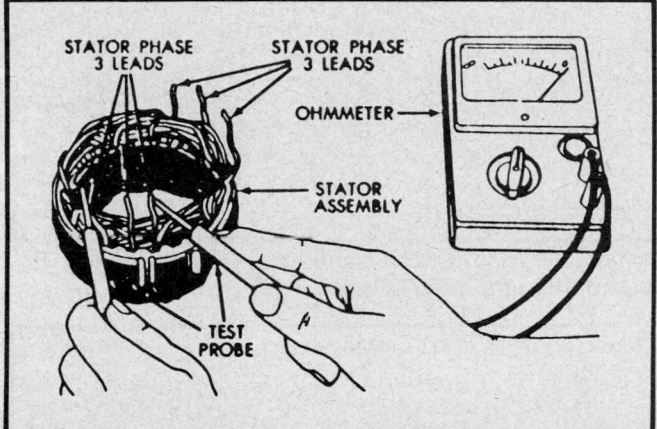

Stator coil continuity test—Mitsubishi 75 and 90 amp alternators

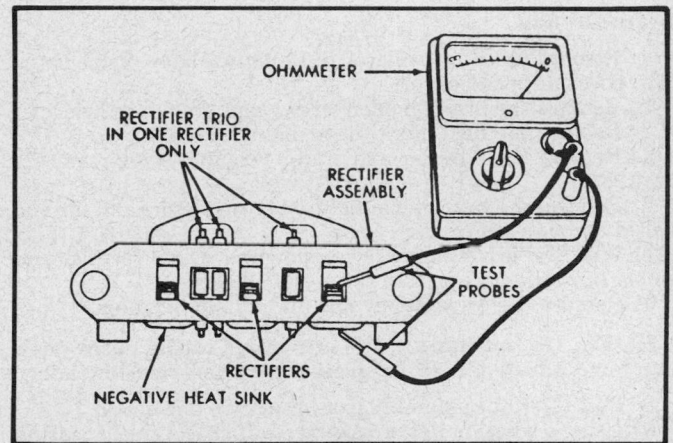

Testing the negative rectifiers—Mitsubishi 75 and 90 amp alternators

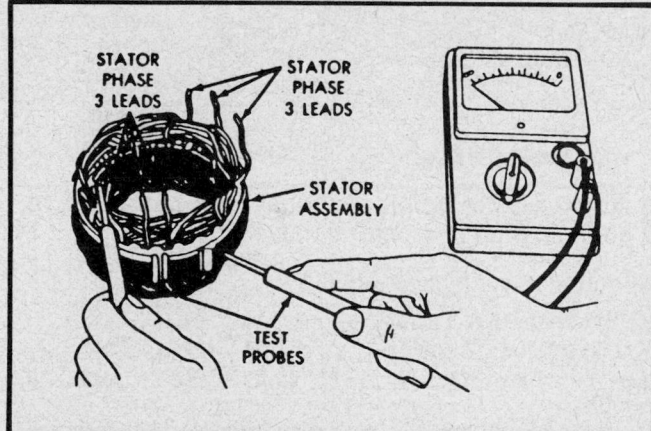

Stator coil ground test—Mitsubishi 75 and 90 amp alternators

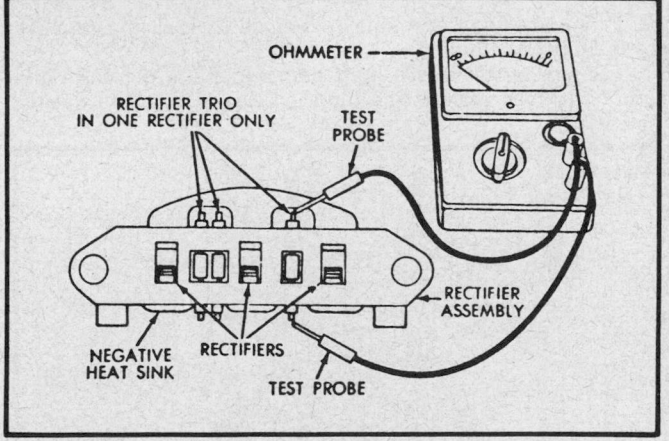

Testing the rectifier trio—Mitsubishi 75 and 90 amp alternators

RECTIFIER ASSEMBLY

Positive (+) Heat Sink Assembly

Check for continuity between the positive (+) heat sink and stator coil lead connection terminal with a continuity tester. If there is continuity in both directions the diode is short circuited. Replace the rectifier assembly.

Negative (–) Heat Sink Assembly

Check for continuity between the negative (–) heat sink and stator coil lead connection terminal. If there is continuity in both directions the diode is short circuited. Replace the rectifier assembly.

RECTIFIER TRIO TEST

Using a circuit tester check the 3 diodes for continuity in both directions. If there is either continuity or an open circuit in both directions the diode is defective. Replace the rectifier assembly.

Assembly

1. The assembly of the alternator is the reverse of the remov-

al procedure. Certain steps must be performed as the alternator is assembled.

2. Install the seals in the front and in the rear of the front bearing with the angled lip away from the bearing.

3. Push the brushes into the brush holder and insert a wire to hold them in the raised position. Install the rotor and remove the holding wire.

NIPPONDENSO 75, 90 AND 120 AMP ALTERNATORS

The alternators are the same, except, the 75 amp alternator is equipped with 3 sets of diodes and the 90 amp and 120 amp alternators are equipped with 4 sets.

OVERHAUL

Disassembly

1. Remove the B+ insulator nut and insulator. Remove the rear cover nuts and cover.
2. Remove the brush holder screws and the brush holder.
3. Remove the field block screws and the block.
4. Remove the rectifier and stator terminal screws and the rectifier.
5. Remove the stator terminal rubber insulators and the end shield through stud nuts.
6. With the drive pulley facing downward, tap rectifier end shield upward and separate the 2 end shields.
7. Remove the drive pulley nut and the drive pulley.

NOTE: Do not handle the slip rings of the rotor with the bare hands for oil or grease may restrict contact.

8. Pull the rotor assembly from the drive end shield.
9. Using a wheel puller, press the rectifier end shield bearing from the rotor shaft.

NOTE: When removing the bearing, be careful not to damage the slip rings.

10. From the drive end shield, remove the bearing retainer screws and the retainer.
11. Using a socket and a light hammer, place the drive end shield on a work surface and tap the bearing from the shield.

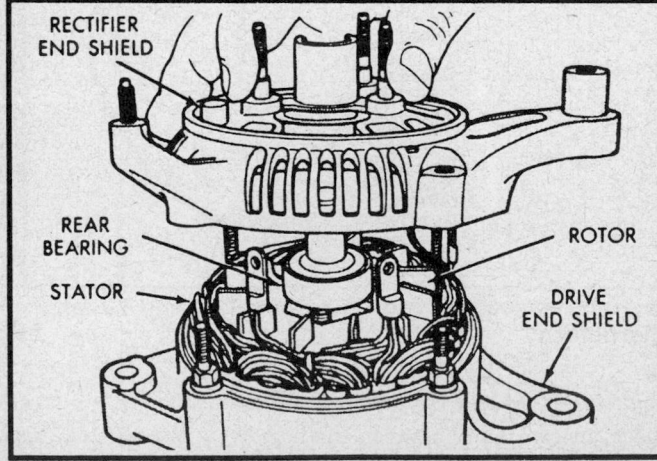

Separating the end shields—Nippondenso 75, 90 and 120 amp alternators

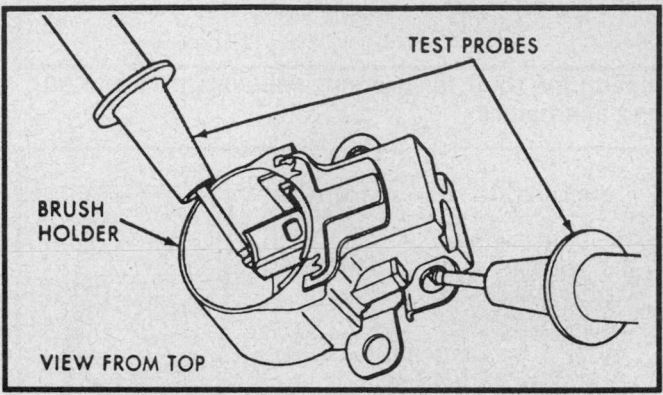

Testing the inner brush continuity—Nippondenso 75, 90 and 120 amp alternators

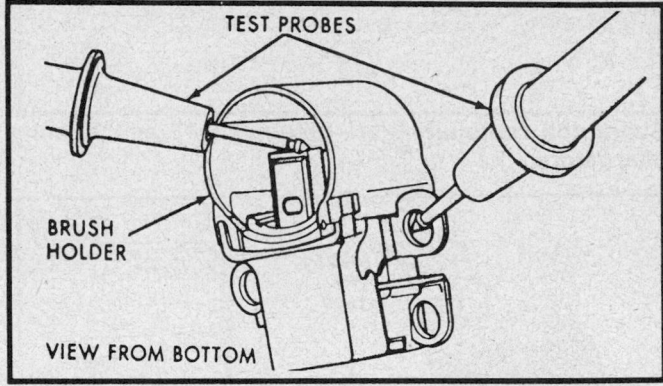

Testing the outer brush continuity—Nippondenso 75, 90 and 120 amp alternators

Inspection

BRUSH HOLDER TESTS

1. Make sure the brushes move smoothly and return fully to the stops when released; if not, replace the brush holder assembly.
2. Using an ohmmeter, test inner brush-to-field terminals continuity; 1 field terminal should be open and the other closed. If not, replace the brush holder.
3. Using an ohmmeter, test outer brush-to-field terminals continuity; a field terminal should be open and the other closed. If not, replace the brush holder.

FIELD BLOCK TESTS

1. Using an ohmmeter, test the outer brush terminal to R-3 field terminal for continuity; the circuit should be closed. If not, replace the field block.

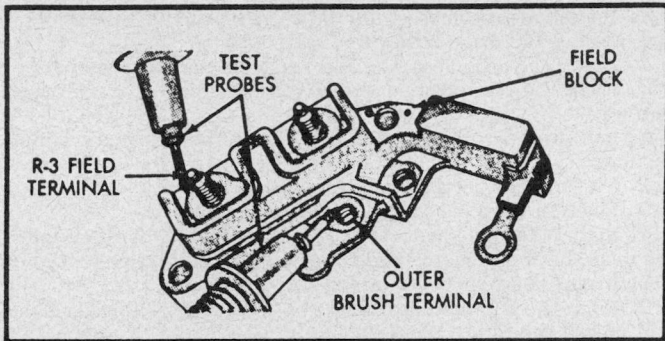

Testing the field block R-3 terminal—Nippondenso 75, 90 and 120 amp alternators

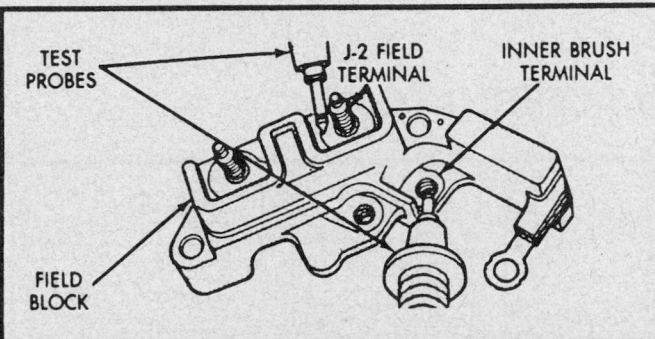

Testing the field block J-2 terminal—Nippondenso 75, 90 and 120 amp alternators

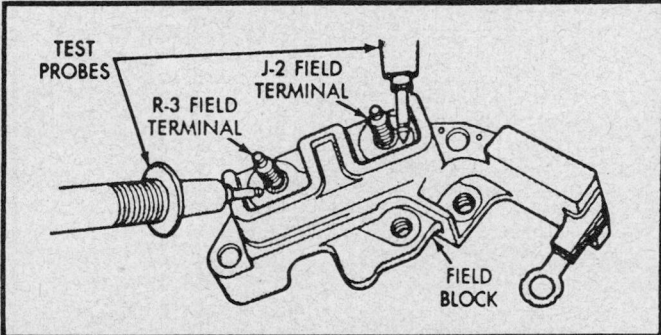

Testing the field block R-3 to J-2 terminals—Nippondenso 75, 90 and 120 amp alternators

2. Using an ohmmeter, test the inner brush terminal to J-2 field terminal for continuity; the circuit should be closed. If not, replace the field block.

3. Using an ohmmeter, test the R-3 field terminal to the J-2 terminal for continuity; the circuit should be open. If not, replace the field block.

4. Turn the field block over. Using an ohmmeter, test the radio supression capacitor terminals for continuity; the circuit should be open. If not, replace the field block.

ROTOR TESTS

1. Check the field slip rings for excessive wear or roughness; fine emery cloth may be used to repair minor damage. If the rings are excessively damaged, replace the rotor.

2. Using an ohmmeter, test for continuity between the slip rings; the circuit should be closed. If not, replace the rotor.

3. Using an ohmmeter, test for continuity between the slip rings and the rotor shaft or core; the circuit should be open. If not, replace the rotor.

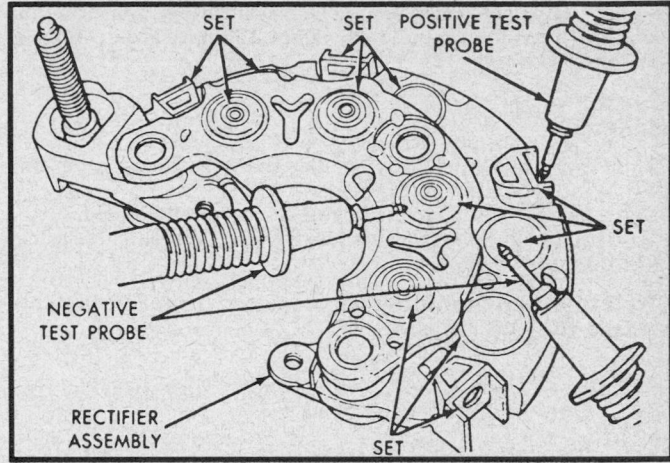

Testing the field block radio capacitor—Nippondenso 75, 90 and 120 amp alternators

STATOR TESTS

1. Check the stator for signs damage—weak or broken leads, distorted frame or burned windings; if necessary, replace the stator.

NOTE: Using a scraping device, clean a portion of the stator frame to assure good electrical contact.

2. Using an ohmmeter, test for continuity between the stator leads and frame; the circuit should be open. If not, replace the stator.

3. Using an ohmmeter, test for continuity between the stator leads; the circuit should be closed. If not, replace the stator.

RECTIFIER TESTS

1. Inspect the rectifier assembly for poor solder joints, cracks, loose terminals or signs of overheating.

2. At each diode location, scrape a small area of the coating to assure good electrical contact while testing.

NOTE: Using an analog ohmmeter or a digital volt ohmmeter, perform the following tests.

3. Position the negative test probe on the stator terminal and the positive test probe on a negative diode; the resistance should be 7–11 ohms or 0.4–0.6 volts. Position the positive test probe on a positive diode; there should be no continuity. Perform this procedure on each terminal to diode set. If failure is detected, replace the rectifier.

4. Position the positive test probe on the stator terminal and the negative test probe on a positive diode; the resistance should be 7–11 ohms or 0.4–0.6 volts. Position the negative test probe

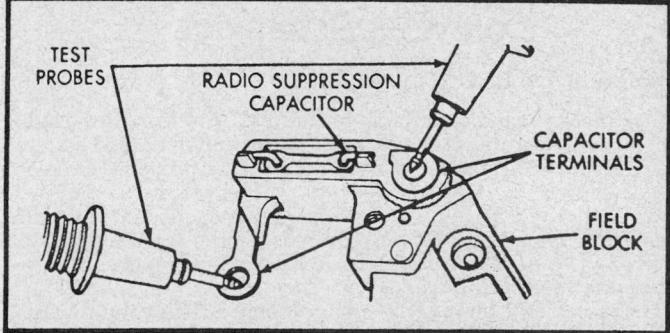

Testing the diodes—Nippondenso 75, 90 and 120 amp alternators

on a negative diode; there should be no continuity. Perform this procedure on each terminal to diode set. If failure is detected, replace the rectifier.

Assembly

1. Using a socket, slightly smaller than the bearing, tap the bearing into the drive end shield.
2. Install the bearing retainer in the drive end shield.
3. Using a shop press, press the rectifier end shield bearing onto the rotor shaft.

NOTE: When installing the bearing, be careful not to damage the slip rings.

4. Install the rotor assembly into the drive end shield.
5. Install the drive pulley and nut.
6. Using solvent, clean the slip rings on the rotor shaft.
7. Align the rectifier end shield and assemble it to the drive end shield.
8. Install the through stud nuts and the stator terminal insulators.
9. Position the rectifier and install the screws.
10. Position the field block and install the screws.
11. Retract the brushes into the brush holder, slide the assembly over the commutator rings and install the screws.
12. Install the rear cover and nuts.
13. Align the B+ insulator guide boss into the rear cover hole and install the nut.

GENERAL MOTORS SI ALTERNATORS

Delcotron alternators are available with different idle outputs and rated amp outputs.

All alternators incorporate a solid state voltage regulator which is mounted inside the alternator. The construction and operation of each alternator is basically the same. The Delcotron alternator consists of a forward and rear end frame assembly, a rotor, a stator, brushes, slip-rings and diodes. The rotor is supported in the drive end frame by ball bearings and in the slip-ring end frame by roller bearings. The bearings do not require periodic lubrication.

There are 2 brushes which carry current through the slip-rings to the field coil. The field coil is mounted on the rotor. The stator windings are assembled on the inside of a laminated core that is part of the alternator frame. The rectifier bridge which is connected to the stator windings contains 6 diodes, 3 of which are negative and 3 of which are positive. The positive and negative diodes are moulded into the assembly. The rectifier bridge changes stator AC voltage into DC voltage which appears at the output BAT terminal.

The blocking action of the diodes prevents the battery from discharging, back through the alternator. The need for a cutout relay is eliminated because of this blocking action. The alternator field current is supplied through a diode trio, which is connected to the stator windings. A capacitor is mounted in the end frame to protect the rectifier bridge and the 6 diodes from high voltage and radio interference. Periodic alternator adjustment or maintenance is not required. The voltage regulator is preset and needs no adjustment.

Typical Delcotron charging system wiring schematic

System Diagnosis

ON VEHICLE SERVICE

Indicator Lamp Operation Test

1. Check the indicator lamp for normal operation. If the indicator lamp operates properly, refer to the undercharged battery test. If the indicator lamp does not operate properly, proceed accordingly.
2. Switch **OFF**, lamp **ON**. Unplug the connector from the generator No. 1 and No. 2 terminals. If the lamp stays **ON**, there is a short between these 2 leads. If the lamp goes out, replace the rectifier bridge.
3. Switch **ON**, lamp **OFF**, engine stopped. This condition can be caused by the defects listed above or by an open in the circuit. To determine where an open exists proceed as follows. Check for a blown fuse, or fusible link, a burned out bulb, defective bulb

socket, or an open in No. 1 lead circuit between generator and ignition switch. If no defects have been found, proceed to undercharged battery test.
4. Switch **ON**, lamp **ON**, engine running. Check for a blown fuse, (where used), between indicator lamp and switch and also in A/C circuit.

Undercharged Battery Test

1. Be sure that the undercharged battery condition has not been caused by accessories that have been left **ON** for an extended period of time.
2. Check the alternator belt for proper belt tension. Inspect the battery for physical defects replace as required.
3. Inspect the wiring for defects. Check all connections for proper contact and cleanliness, including the slip connectors at the generator and baulkhead connections.
4. With ignition switch **ON** and all wiring harness leads con-

Delcotron Alternator Availability Chart

Alternator Type	Rated Amp Output
10SI	37, 42, 63
12SI	56, 66, 78, 94
15SI	70, 85
17SI	—
27SI	65, 80, 100

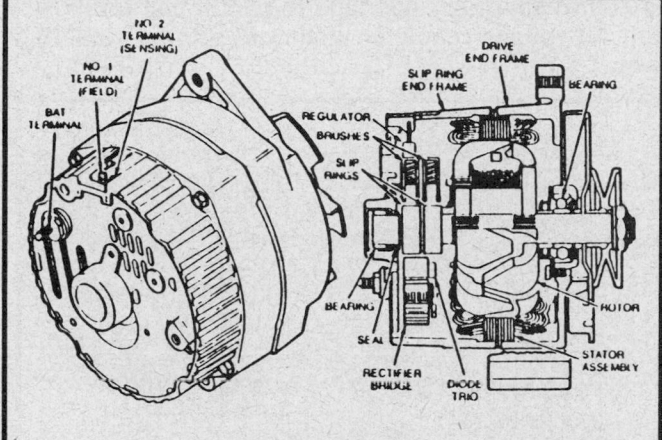

Delcotron alternator—showing location of components—typical

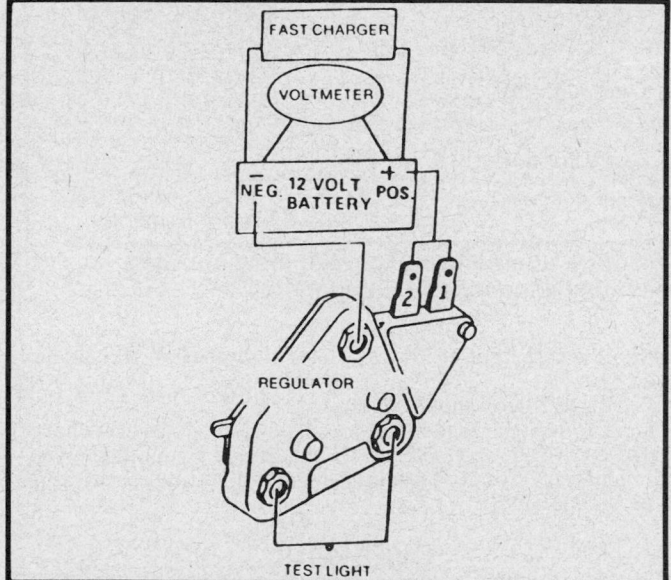

Delcotron alternator—voltage test

nected, connect a voltmeter from the generator BAT terminal to ground, from the generator No. 1 terminal to ground and from the generator No. 2 terminal to ground. A zero reading indicates an open circuit between voltmeter connection and battery.

5. Delcotron alternators have a built in feature, which prevents overcharge and accessory damage by preventing the alter-nator from turning on if there is an open circuit in the wiring harness connected to the No. 2 alternator terminal.

6. If Steps 1–5 check out okay, check the alternator as follows. Disconnect negative battery cable. Connect an ammeter or alternator tester in the circuit at the BAT terminal of the alternator. Reconnect negative battery cable.

7. Turn **ON** radio, windshield wipers, lights high beam and blower motor on high speed. Connect a carbon pile across the battery (or use alternator tester). Operate engine about 2000 rpm and adjust carbon pile as required, to obtain maximum current output. If ampere output is within 10 amperes of rated output as stamped on generator frame, alternator is not defective. Recheck Steps 1–5.

8. If ampere output is not within 10 percent of rated output, determine if test hole is accessible. Ground the field winding by inserting a suitable tool into the test hole. Tab is within ¾ in. of casting surface. Do not force suitable tool deeper than 1 in. into end frame to avoid damaging alternator.

9. Operate engine at moderate speed as required and adjust carbon pile as required to obtain maximum current output.

10. If output is within 10 amperes of rated output, check field winding, diode trio and rectifier bridge. Test regulator with an approved regulator tester.

11. If output is not within 10 amperes of rated output, check the field winding, diode trio, rectifier bridge and stator. If test hole is not accessible, disassemble alternator and repair as required.

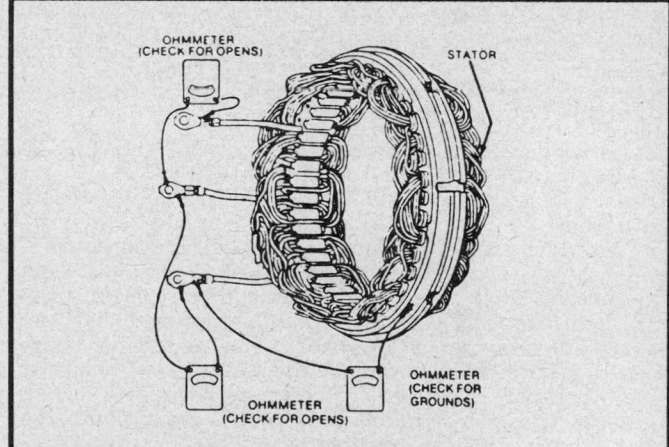

Testing Delcotron alternator stator—use an ohmmeter to check for opens or grounds

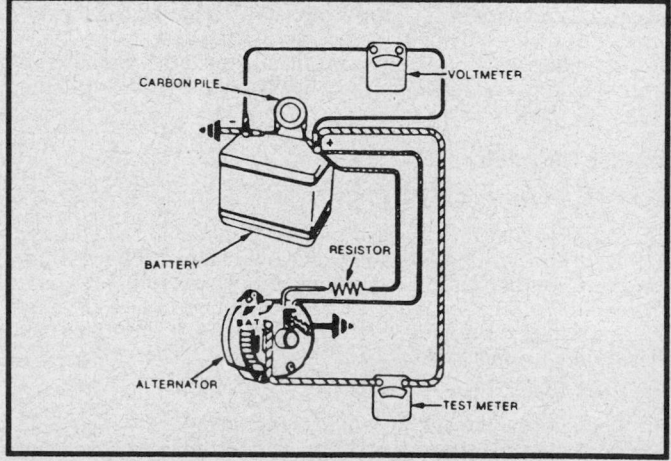

Bench test hook-up for testing the Delcotron alternator

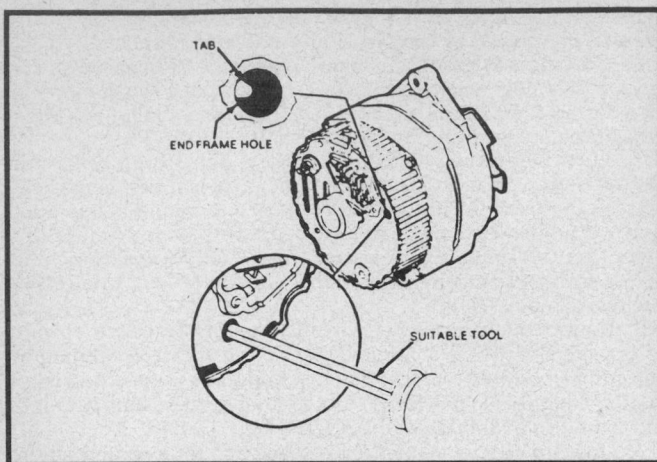

Delcotron alternator — if test hole is accessible, ground the field winding by inserting a suitable tool into the test hole (max. or 1 in.)

Overcharged Battery Test

1. Check the condition of the battery before any testing is done.
2. If an obvious overcharging condition exists, remove the alternator from the vehicle and check the field windings for grounds or shorts. If defective, replace the rotor. Test the regulator.

Alternator Diagnostic Tester (J–26290)

This special diagnostic tester is designed to determine if the alternator should be removed from the vehicle.

1. Install tester J–26290 according to manufacturers instructions.
2. With the engine **OFF** and all lights and accessories **OFF**, test the alternator as follows. Light flashes, go to Step 3. Light **ON**, indicates fault in tester which should be replaced. Light **OFF**, pull plug from generator. One flashing light, indicates that the alternator should be removed and the rectifier bridge replaced. Light **OFF**, indicates faulty tester or no voltage to tester. Check for 12 volts at No. 2 terminal of harness connector. Repair wiring or terminals if 12 volts is not available. Replace tester if 12 volts is available.
3. With the engine at fast idle and all accessories and lights **OFF**, test the alternator as follows. Light **OFF** indicates that the charging system good, do not remove alternator. Light **ON** indicates a component failure within the alternator. Remove alternator and check diode trio, rectifier bridge and stator. Light flashing indicates a problem within the alternator. Remove alternator and check regulator, rotor field coil, brushes and sliprings.

Voltage Regulator Test

ALTERNATOR ON VEHICLE

1. Connect a battery charger and a voltmeter to the battery.
2. Turn the ignition **ON** and slowly increase the charge rate. The alternator light in the vehicle will dim at the voltage regulator setting. Voltage regulator setting should be 13.5–16.0 volts. This test works if the rotor setting is good, even if the stator rectifier bridge or diode trio is bad.

ALTERNATOR OFF VEHICLE

1. Remove the alternator from the vehicle.
2. Disassemble the alternator and remove the voltage regualtor.
3. Connect a voltmeter and a fast charger to a 12 volt battery.

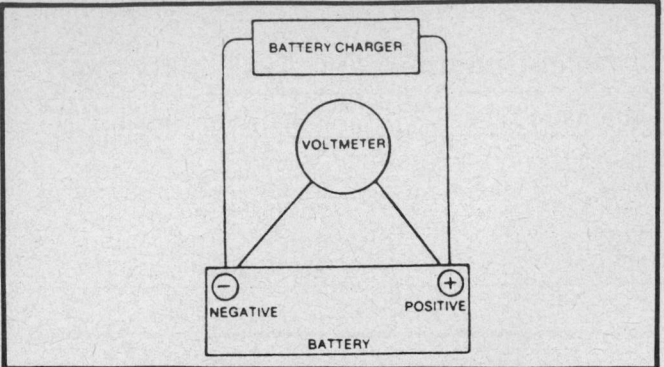

Delcotron alternator — voltage regulator test (on vehicle) voltage regulator setting should be 13.5–16.0 volts

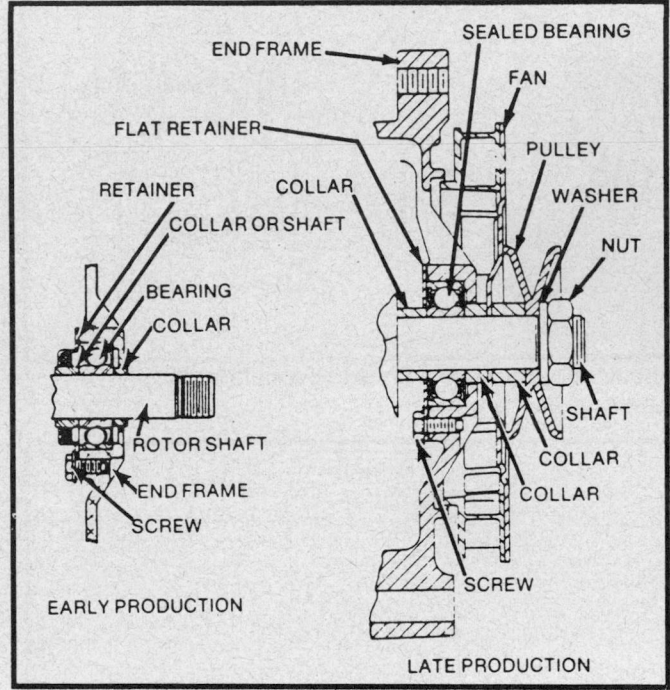

Delcotron alternator — exploded view showing assembly sequence of components

Connect a test light to the regulator and observe the battery polarity.

4. The test light should light.
5. Turn **ON** the fast charger and slowly increase the charge rate. Observe the voltmeter, the light should go out at the voltage regualtor setting. The voltage regulator setting specification is 13.5–16.0 volts.

OVERHAUL

Disassembly

1. Remove the alternator from the vehicle. Position the assembly in a suitable holding fixture.
2. Make scribe marks on the alternator case end frames to aid in reassembly.
3. Remove the through bolts that retain the assembly together. Separate the drive end frame assembly from the rectifier end frame assembly.

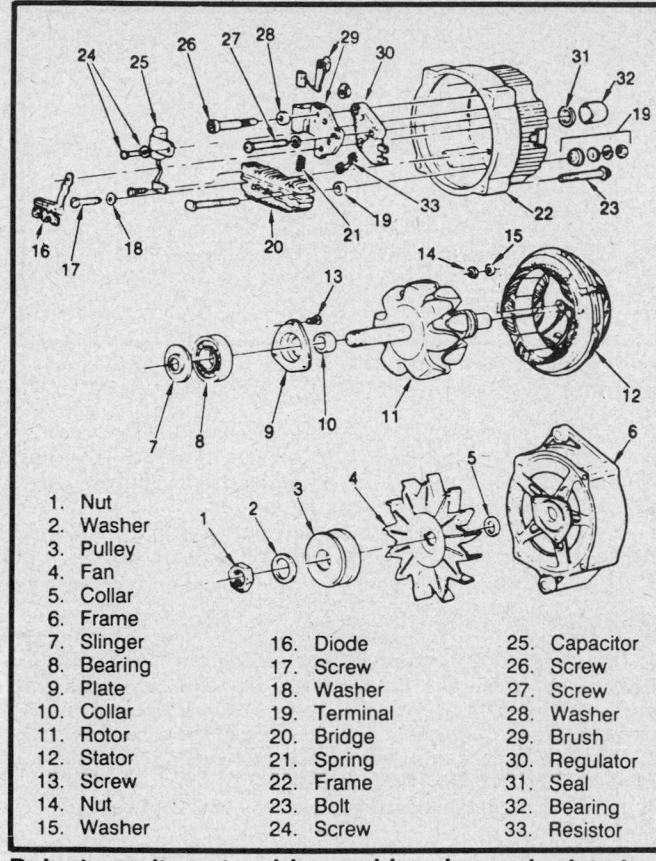

1.	Nut			
2.	Washer			
3.	Pulley			
4.	Fan			
5.	Collar			
6.	Frame			
7.	Slinger	16.	Diode	25. Capacitor
8.	Bearing	17.	Screw	26. Screw
9.	Plate	18.	Washer	27. Screw
10.	Collar	19.	Terminal	28. Washer
11.	Rotor	20.	Bridge	29. Brush
12.	Stator	21.	Spring	30. Regulator
13.	Screw	22.	Frame	31. Seal
14.	Nut	23.	Bolt	32. Bearing
15.	Washer	24.	Screw	33. Resistor

Delcotron alternator drive end bearing and related components

4. Remove the rectifier attaching nuts and the regulator attaching screws from the end frame assembly.

5. Separate the stator, diode trio and voltage regulator from the end frame assembly.

6. On the 10SI alternator, check the stator for opens using an ohmmeter. If high readings are obtained, replace the stator.

7. Check the stator for grounds using an ohmmeter. If readings are low, replace the stator.

8. Using an ohmmeter check the rotor for grounds. The ohmmeter reading should be very high. If not, replace the rotor.

9. Using an ohmmeter, check the rotor for opens. If the ohmmeter reading is not 2.4–3.5 ohms replace the rotor.

10. To check the diode trio connect the ohmmeter to the diode trio and then reverse the lead connections. The ohmmeter should read high and low if not replace the diode trio. Repeat the same test between the single connector and each of the other connectors.

11. Check rectifier bridge with ohmmeter connected from grounded heat sink to flat metal on terminal. Reverse leads. If both readings are the same replace rectifier bridge.

12. Repeat test between grounded heat sink and other 2 flat metal clips.

13. Repeat test between insulated heat sink and 3 flat metal clips.

14. Clean or replace the alternator brushes as required. Position the brushes in the brush holder and retain them in place using the brush retainer wire or equivalent.

15. To remove the rotor and drive end bearing, remove the shaft nut, washer and pulley, fan and collar. Push the rotor from the housing.

16. Remove the retainer plate from inside the drive end frame. Push the bearing out. Clean or replace parts as required.

Inspection
ALTERNATOR BENCH TEST

1. Remove the alternator from the vehicle. Position the unit in a suitable test stand.

2. Connect the alternator in series, but leave the carbon pile disconnected.

NOTE: Ground polarity of the battery must be the same as the alternator. Be sure to use a fully charged battery and a 10 ohm resistor rated at 6 watts or more between the alternator No. 1 terminal and the battery.

3. Increase the alternator speed slowly and observe the voltage.

4. If the voltage is uncontrolled with speed and increases above 15.5 volts, test regulator with an approved regulator tester and check field winding. If voltage is below 15.5 volts, connect the carbon pile.

5. Operate the alternator at moderate speed as required and

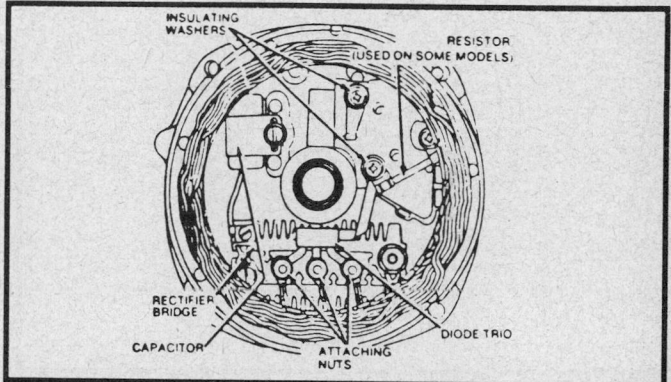

Delcotron alternator end frame—showing location of related components

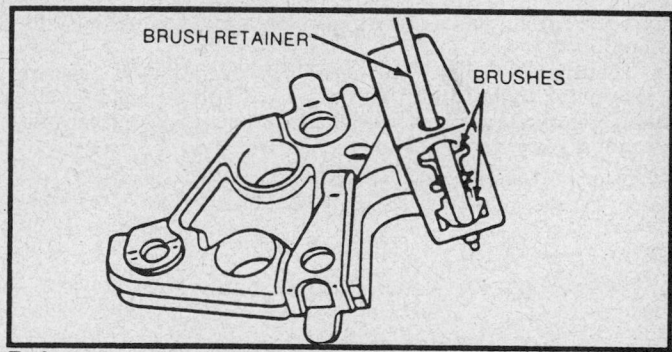

Delcotron alternator brush installation

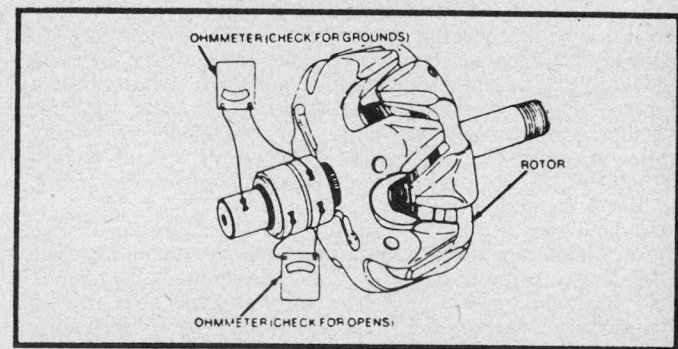

Delcotron alternator—rotor test use an ohmmeter to check for opens or grounds

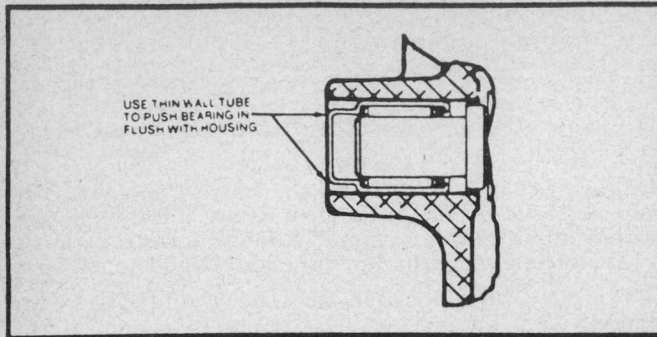

Delcotron alternator rectifier end bearing installation

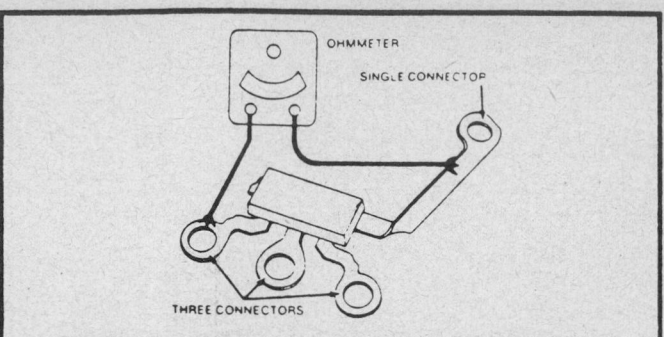

Testing Delcotron alternator diode trio using an ohmmeter

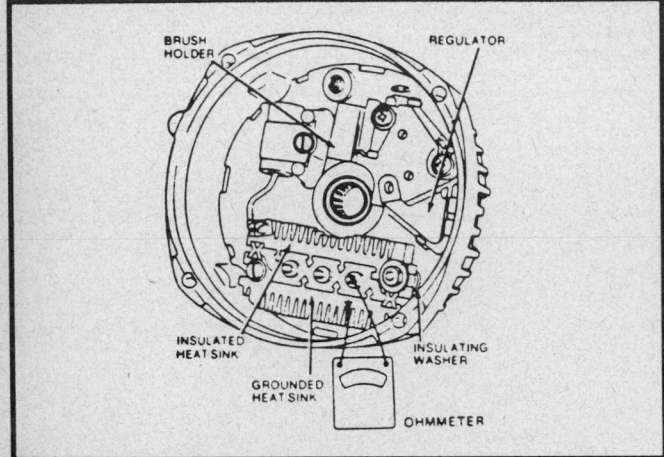

Testing Delcotron alternator rectifier bridge using an ohmmeter

adjust the carbon pile as required to obtain maximum current output.

6. If output is within 10 amperes of rated output as stamped on alternator frame, alternator is good. If output is not within 10 amperes of rated output, keep battery loaded with carbon pile and ground alternator field.

7. Operate alternator at moderate speed and adjust carbon pile as required to obtain maximum output. If output is within 10 amperes of rated output, test regulator with an approved regulator tester and check field winding.

8. If output is not within 10 amperes of rated output, check the field winding, diode trio, rectifier bridge and stator.

Assembly

1. Press against the outer bearing race to push the bearing in. On early production alternators it will be necessary to fill the bearing cavity with lubricant. Late production alternators use a sealed bearing and lubricant is not required for assembly.

2. Press rotor into end frame. Assemble collar, fan, pulley, washer and nut. Torque shaft nut 40–60 ft. lbs.

3. Push slip-ring end bearing out from outside toward inside of end frame.

4. On 10SI and 15SI, place flat plate over new bearing and press from outside toward inside until bearing is flush with end frame.

5. On 15SI alternators use the thin wall tube in the space between the grease cup and the housing to push the bearing in flush with the housing.

6. Assemble brush holder, regulator, resistor, diode trio, rectifier bridge and stator to slip-ring end frame.

7. Assemble end frames together with through bolts. Remove brush retainer wire.

GENERAL MOTORS CS ALTERNATORS

Another type of charging system is the CS charging system. There are 2 sizes of alternator available, 130 and 144, denoting the OD in mm of the stator laminations. CS alternators use a new type regulator a diode trio is not used. A delta stator, rectifier bridge and rotor with slip-rings and brushes are electrically similar to earlier alternators. A regular pulley and fan is used and, on the 130, an internal fan cools the slip-ring end frame, rectifier bridge and regulator.

Unlike 3 wire alternators, the 130 and 144 may be used with only 2 connections, the battery positive and an L terminal to the charge indicator bulb. Use of P, F and S terminals is optional. The P terminal is connected to the stator and may be connected externally to a tachometer or other device. The F terminal is connected internally to field positive and may be used as a fault indicator. The S terminal may be connected externally to a voltage, such as battery voltage, to sense voltage to be controlled.

As on other charging systems, the charge indicator lights when the switch is closed and goes out when the engine is running. If the charge indicator is **ON** with the engine running, a charging system defect is indicated. For all kinds of defects, the indicator will glow at full brilliance, not half lit. Also, the charge indicator will be **ON** with the engine running if system voltage is too high or too low. The regulator voltage setting varies with temperature and limits system voltage by controlling rotor field current.

This regulator switches rotor field current **ON** and **OFF** at a fixed frequency of about 400 cycles per second. By varying the **ON/OFF** time, correct average field current for proper system voltage control is obtained. At high speeds, the **ON** time may be 10% and the **OFF** time 90%. At low speeds, with high electrical loads, **ON/OFF** time may be 90% and 10% respectively. No periodic maintenance on the generator is required.

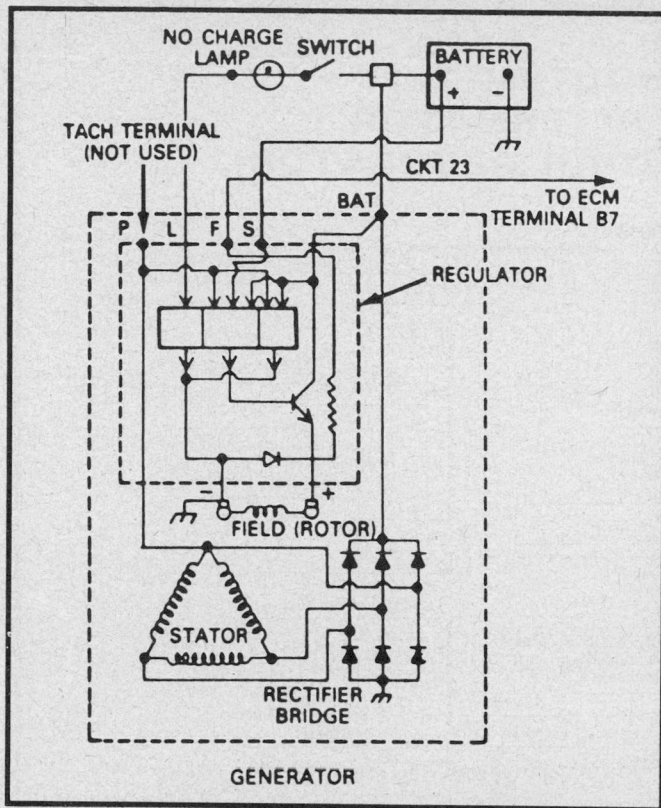

Schematic of the Delcotron CS series charging system

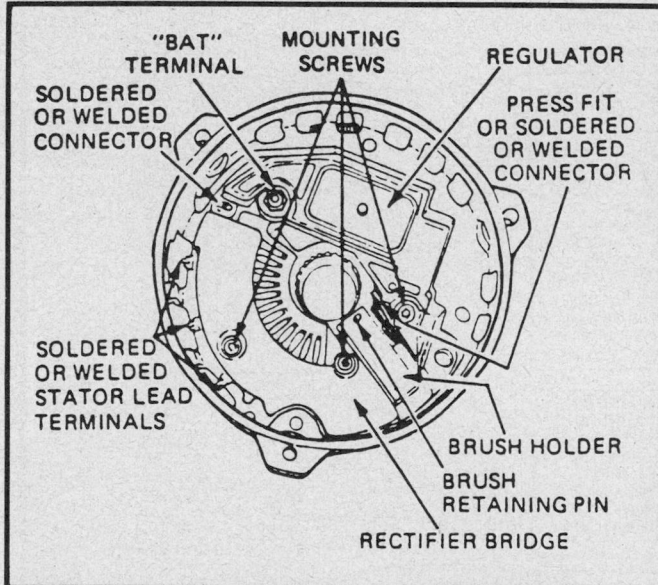

Location of the components—CS 130 alternator

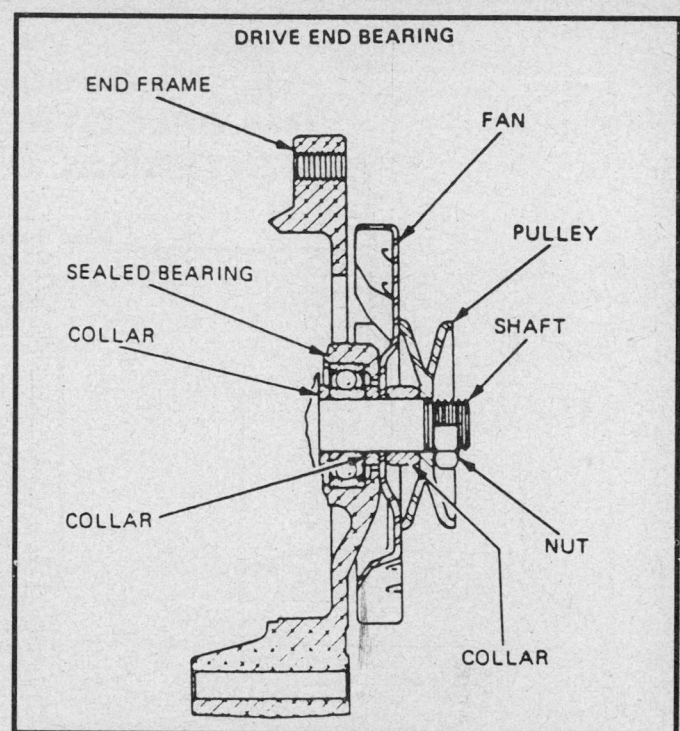

Cross-sectional view of the alternator drive end bearing assembly—Delcotron CS 130 alternator

System Diagnosis

ON VEHICLE SERVICE

When operating normally, the indicator lamp will illuminate when the ignition switch is turned **ON** and go out when the engine starts. If the lamp operates abnormally, or if an under-charged or overcharged battery condition occurs, the following procedure may be used to diagnose the charging system.

To diagnose the CS–130 and CS–144 charging systems, use the following procedure.

1. Visually check the belt and wiring.
2. For vehicles without charge indicator lamp, go to Step 5.
3. With switch **ON**, engine stopped, lamp should illuminate. If not, detach harness at generator and ground L terminal. If the lamp lights, repair or replace the generator. If the lamp does not light locate open circuit between grounding lead and ignition switch. Lamp may be open.
4. With switch **ON**, engine running at moderate speed, lamp should illuminate. If not, detach wiring harness at generator. If the lamp goes off, replace or repair generator. If the lamp stays on, check for grounded L terminal wire in harness.
5. Battery undercharged or overcharged. Detach wiring harness connector from generator. With switch **ON**, engine not running, connect voltmeter from ground to L terminal. Zero reading indicates open circuit between terminal and battery. Correct as required. Reconnect harness connector to generator, run engine at moderate speed. Measure voltage across battery. If above 16 volts, replace or repair generator.
6. Turn **ON** accessories, load battery with carbon pile to obtain maximum amperage. Maintain voltage at 13 volts or above. If within 15 amperes of rated output, generator is fine. If not within 15 amperes of rated output, repair or replace the generator.

OVERHAUL

Disassembly and Assembly

The alternator is serviced as an assembly only.

CS–144

1. Remove the alternator from the vehicle. Scribe marks on the end frames to facilitate assembly.
2. Remove the through bolts and separate the end frames.

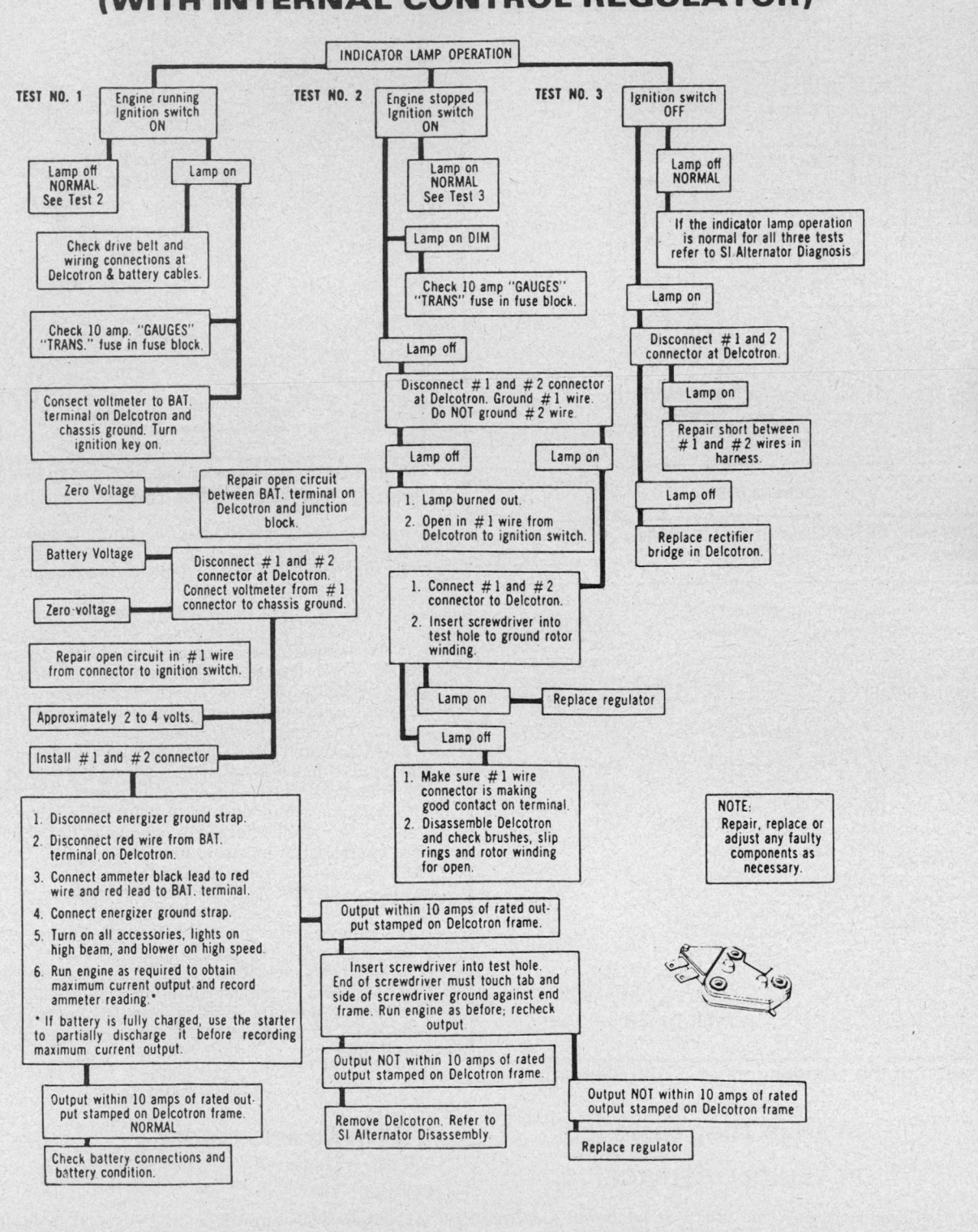

TROUBLESHOOTING GM DELCOTRON ALTERNATOR (WITH INTERNAL CONTROL REGULATOR)

INDICATOR LAMP OPERATION

TEST NO. 1 — Engine running Ignition switch ON

- Lamp off NORMAL. See Test 2
- Lamp on
  - Check drive belt and wiring connections at Delcotron & battery cables.
  - Check 10 amp. "GAUGES" "TRANS." fuse in fuse block.
  - Consect voltmeter to BAT. terminal on Delcotron and chassis ground. Turn ignition key on.
    - Zero Voltage → Repair open circuit between BAT. terminal on Delcotron and junction block.
    - Battery Voltage → Disconnect #1 and #2 connector at Delcotron. Connect voltmeter from #1 connector to chassis ground.
    - Zero voltage → Repair open circuit in #1 wire from connector to ignition switch.
    - Approximately 2 to 4 volts.
      - Install #1 and #2 connector
        1. Disconnect energizer ground strap.
        2. Disconnect red wire from BAT. terminal on Delcotron.
        3. Connect ammeter black lead to red wire and red lead to BAT. terminal.
        4. Connect energizer ground strap.
        5. Turn on all accessories, lights on high beam, and blower on high speed.
        6. Run engine as required to obtain maximum current output and record ammeter reading.*
        * If battery is fully charged, use the starter to partially discharge it before recording maximum current output.
          - Output within 10 amps of rated output stamped on Delcotron frame. NORMAL
            - Check battery connections and battery condition.

TEST NO. 2 — Engine stopped Ignition switch ON

- Lamp on NORMAL. See Test 3
- Lamp on DIM
  - Check 10 amp "GAUGES" "TRANS" fuse in fuse block.
- Lamp off
  - Disconnect #1 and #2 connector at Delcotron. Ground #1 wire. Do NOT ground #2 wire.
    - Lamp off
      1. Lamp burned out.
      2. Open in #1 wire from Delcotron to ignition switch.
    - Lamp on
      1. Connect #1 and #2 connector to Delcotron.
      2. Insert screwdriver into test hole to ground rotor winding.
        - Lamp on → Replace regulator
        - Lamp off
          1. Make sure #1 wire connector is making good contact on terminal.
          2. Disassemble Delcotron and check brushes, slip rings and rotor winding for open.
            - Output within 10 amps of rated output stamped on Delcotron frame.
              - Insert screwdriver into test hole. End of screwdriver must touch tab and side of screwdriver ground against end frame. Run engine as before; recheck output.
                - Output NOT within 10 amps of rated output stamped on Delcotron frame.
                  - Remove Delcotron. Refer to SI Alternator Disassembly.
                - Output NOT within 10 amps of rated output stamped on Delcotron frame
                  - Replace regulator

TEST NO. 3 — Ignition switch OFF

- Lamp off NORMAL
  - If the indicator lamp operation is normal for all three tests refer to SI Alternator Diagnosis.
- Lamp on
  - Disconnect #1 and 2 connector at Delcotron.
    - Lamp on
      - Repair short between #1 and #2 wires in harness.
    - Lamp off
      - Replace rectifier bridge in Delcotron.

NOTE:
Repair, replace or adjust any faulty components as necessary.

3. Check the rotor for grounds using an ohmmeter. The reading should be infinite, if not, replace the rotor.

4. Check the rotor for shorts and opens. Replace the rotor as required.

5. Remove the attaching nuts and the stator from the end frame.

6. Check the stator for grounds using an ohmmeter. If the reading is low replace the stator.

7. Unsolder the connections, remove the retaining screws and connector from the end frame. Separate the regulator and the brush holder from the end frame.

8. Check the rectifier bridge using an ohmmeter. Replace as required. Check the heat sink, using an ohmmeter. Replace as required. Clean the brushes. Replace them as required.

9. To remove the rotor and drive end bearing, Hold the rotor using a hex wrench in the shaft end while removing the nut. Push the rotor from the housing. Remove the plate and push the bearing out.

10. Assembly is the reverse of the disassembly procedure. Repair or replace defective components as required.

CS-130

1. Remove the alternator from the vehicle. Scribe marks on the end frames to facilitate assembly. Remove the through bolts and separate the end frames.

2. Remove the cover rivets or pins. Remove the cover on the slip-ring end frame.

3. Unsolder the stator leads at the 3 terminals on the rectifier bridge. Avoid excessive heat, as damage to the assembly will occur. Remove the stator.

4. Drive out the 3 baffle pins. Remove the baffle from inside of the slip-ring end frame.

5. Check the rotor for grounds using an ohmmeter. The reading should be infinite, if not, replace the rotor. Check the rotor for shorts and opens, the ohmmeter should read 1.7–2.3 ohms. Replace the rotor as required.

6. Check the stator for grounds using an ohmmeter. If the reading is low replace the stator.

7. Remove the brush holder screw. Disconnect the terminal and remove the brush holder assembly. Check and replace the brushes, as required.

8. Unsolder and pry open the terminal between the regulator and the rectifier bridge. Remove the terminal and the retaining screws. Remove the regulator and the rectifier bridge from the end frame.

9. To check the rectifier bridge, connect the proper (analog reading) ohmmeter, using the low scale, to a terminal and the heat sink, record the reading. Reverse the test leads and record the reading. If both readings are the same replace the rectifier bridge. Check the other diodes in the same manner.

10. To remove the rotor and drive end bearing, Hold the rotor using a hex wrench in the shaft end while removing the nut. Push the rotor from the housing. Remove the plate and push the bearing out.

11. Assembly is the reverse of the disassembly procedure. Repair or replace defective components as required.

Inspection

ALTERNATOR BENCH TEST

1. Make the proper connections but leave the carbon pile disconnected. The ground polarity of generator and battery must be the same. The battery must be fully charged. Use a 30–500 ohm resistor between battery and L terminal.

2. Slowly increase generator speed and observe voltage.

3. If the voltage is uncontrolled and increases above 16.0 volts, the rotor field is shorted, the regulator is defective or both. A shorted rotor field coil can cause the regulator to become defective. The battery must be fully charged when making this test.

4. If voltage is below 16.0 volts, increase speed and adjust carbon pile to obtain maximum amperage output. Maintain voltage above 13.0 volts.

5. If output is within 15 amperes of rated output, generator is good.

6. If output is not within 15 amperes of rated output, generator is faulty and requires repair or replacement.

GENERAL MOTORS ALTERNATOR WITH REAR VACUUM PUMP

The Delcotron alternator with rear vacuum pump, manufactured by Mitsubishi, is basically the same as the other Delcotron alternators, with the exception of a rear vacuum pump which is mounted on the back of the alternator assembly. The vacuum pump is driven by the alternator shaft and is used to provide vacuum to various control systems throughtout the vehicle.

OVERHAUL

Disassembly and Assembly

1. Remove the alternator from the vehicle. Position the unit in a suitable holding fixture.

2. Remove the vacuum pump retaining bolts. Remove the vacuum pump from the rear of the alternator while holding the center plate.

3. Remove the brush cover retaining bolts and brushes. Wrap the pump drive shaft spline with tape in order to protect the rear seal from damage.

4. Inspect the vacuum pump for wear and damage, replace defective components as required. Measure the length of the vanes, replace if not within specification (0.511–0.531 in.) Mea-

sure the inside diameter of the housing and replace if not within specification (2.440–2.441 in.).

5. Examine the check valve for damage. Apply light pressure to the valve and make sure the valve operates properly. Replace as required.

6. Check the inner face of the rear cover on the vacuum pump for oil leakage. Check the inner face of the oil seal for wear and damage. Replace the oil seal in the rear end housing of the vacuum pump as required.

7. Remove the alternator through bolts which hold the unit together. Matchmark the assembly to aid in reassembly. Separate the front end housing from the stator and rear end housing.

8. Remove the pulley nut, fan and front end housing from the rotor.

9. Remove the front bearing retainer screws. Remove the front bearing retainer and the bearing from the front end housing.

10. Remove the bolt and nuts retaining the stator, diodes and brush holder to the rear end housing. Note the position of the insulating washers for reassembly.

11. Separate the rear end housing from the stator and diode assembly.

12. Remove the diodes from the stator by melting the solder

from the terminals. Be sure to protect the diodes while melting the solder.

13. Remove the solder from the voltage regulator holder plate terminal. Remove the voltage regulator.

14. Check the slip-ring surfaces of the rotor for wear and damage, repair or replace as required.

15. Measure the outside diameter of the rotor slip-rings. If ring diameter is not 1.18–1.24 in., replace the rotor.

16. Connect the ohmmeter test leads to each slip-ring. Resistance should be 4.2 ohms at 68°F. If continuity does not exist the coil is open and the rotor must be replaced.

17. Connect the ohmmeter to either slip-ring and the rotor core. If continuity exists the coil is grounded and the rotor must be replaced.

18. Check the front and rear rotor bearings for wear and damage. Replace defective parts as required.

19. Check for continuity across the stator coils. If continuity does not exist in any 1 stator coil replace the stator assembly.

20. Check for continuity across any of the stator coils and the stator core. If continuity exists, 1 of the stator coils is grounded and the stator must be replaced.

21. Coil resistance should be 0.05 ohms at 68°F and should be measured from the coil lead to terminal N.

22. Inspect the alternator brush assembly for wear and damage. Replace defective components as required.

23. Check for continuity of positive diodes between each stator coil terminal and the battery terminal of rectifier assembly. Reverse the ohmmeter leads and recheck for continuity.

24. If continuity exists in both polarity directions or does not exist in both directions diode is defective and must be replaced.

25. Check for continuity of negative diodes between each stator lead and E terminal or rectifier assembly. Reverse ohmmeter leads and recheck for continuity. Continuity should exist in 1 direction only.

26. Assemble a test circuit using the following components: One 10 ohm 3 watt resistor (R_1) one 0–300 ohm 3 watt variable resistor (R_2), two 12 volt batteries (BAT_1 and BAT_2) and one 0–30 volt DC voltmeter.

27. Adjust variable resistor (R_2) until voltage at V_4 reads the same as voltage at V_3 (this should be all the way to 1 end of travel or 0 ohms).

28. Connect the test circuit to the integrated circuit regulator terminals. Measure voltage at V_1 and V_2. Voltage should measure 10–13 volts at V_1 and 0–2 volts at V_2.

29. Disconnect terminal S from circuit and measure voltage at V_3. Voltage at V_3 should be 20–26 volts. Reconnect terminal S.

30. Measure voltage at V_4 while increasing resistance at R_2 from 0 ohms. V_4 voltmeter reading should increase from 2 volts to 10–13 volts. Stop increasing R_2 when voltage reaches 10–13 volts.

31. If increase at V_4 is interrupted at any point up to 10–13 volts, while increasing resistance at R_2, regulator is defective.

32. Measure voltage at V_4 with R_2 at same setting as previous step that produced 10–13 volt reading at V_2. If V_4 not within 14–14.6 volts, regulator is defective.

33. Disconnect wire at terminal S. Connect it to terminal B. Repeat Step 30. If V_2 does not vary or V_4 is not within 14.5–16.6 volts, regulator is defective.

34. To assemble the alternator reverse the disassembly procedure. Be sure to check all parts for wear and damage. Replace defective components as required.

35. Insert the brushes into the brush holder and insert a wire to retain them in place. Install the rotor and remove the retaining wire.

FORD REAR TERMINAL ALTERNATOR

The Ford charging system is a negative ground system. It includes an alternator, electronic regulator, a charge indicator or an ammeter and a storage battery.

System Diagnosis

CHARGING SYSTEM OPERATION

NOTE: If the current indicator is to give an accurate reading, the battery cables must be of the same gauge and length as the original equipment.

1. With the engine running and all electrical systems turned **OFF**, position a current indicator over the positive battery cable.

2. If a charge of about 5 amps is recorded, the charging system is working. If a draw of about 5 amps is recorded, the system is not working. The needle moves toward the battery when a charge condition is indicated and away from the battery when a draw condition is indicated. If a draw is indicated continue to the next testing procedure. If an overcharge of 10–15 amps is indicated check for a faulty regulator or a bad ground at the regulator or the alternator.

Ignition Switch to Regulator Circuit Test

1. Disconnect the regulator wiring harness from the regulator.

2. Turn **ON** the key. Using a test light or voltmeter check for voltage between the I wire and ground. Check for voltage between the A wire and ground. If voltage is present at this part of the system the circuit is OK. If there is no voltage at the I wire check for a burned out charge indicator bulb, a burned-out resistor, or a break or short in the wiring. If there is no voltage present at the A wire check for a faulty connection at the starter relay or a break or short in the wire.

Isolation Test

This test determines whether the regulator or the alternator is faulty after the rest of the circuit is found to be in good working order.

1. Disconnect the regulator wiring harness from the regulator.

2. Connect a jumper wire from the A wire to the F wire in the wiring harness plug.

3. Connect a voltmeter to the battery. The positive voltmeter lead goes to the positive terminal and the negative lead to the negative terminal. Record the reading on the voltmeter.

4. Turn **OFF** all of the electrical systems and start the engine. Do not race the engine.

5. Gradually increase engine speed 1500–2000 rpm. The voltmeter reading should increase above the previously recorded battery voltage reading by at least 1–2 volts. If there is no increase the alternator is not working correctly. If there is an increase the voltage regulator needs to be replaced.

OVERHAUL

Disassembly

1. Matchmark both end housings for assembly.
2. Remove the housing through bolts.

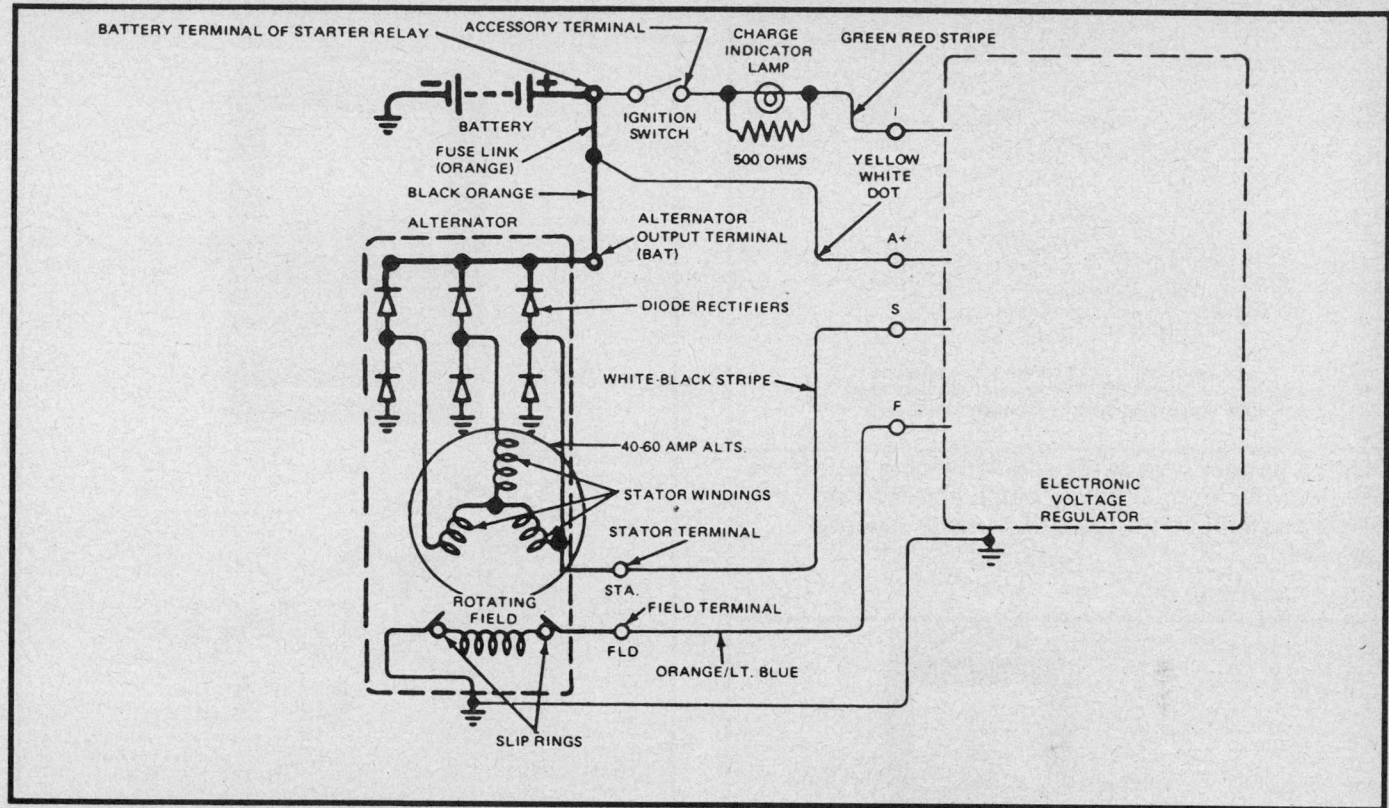

Ford alternator with external regulator—rear terminal alternator charging system schematic with indicator light—typical side terminal alternator

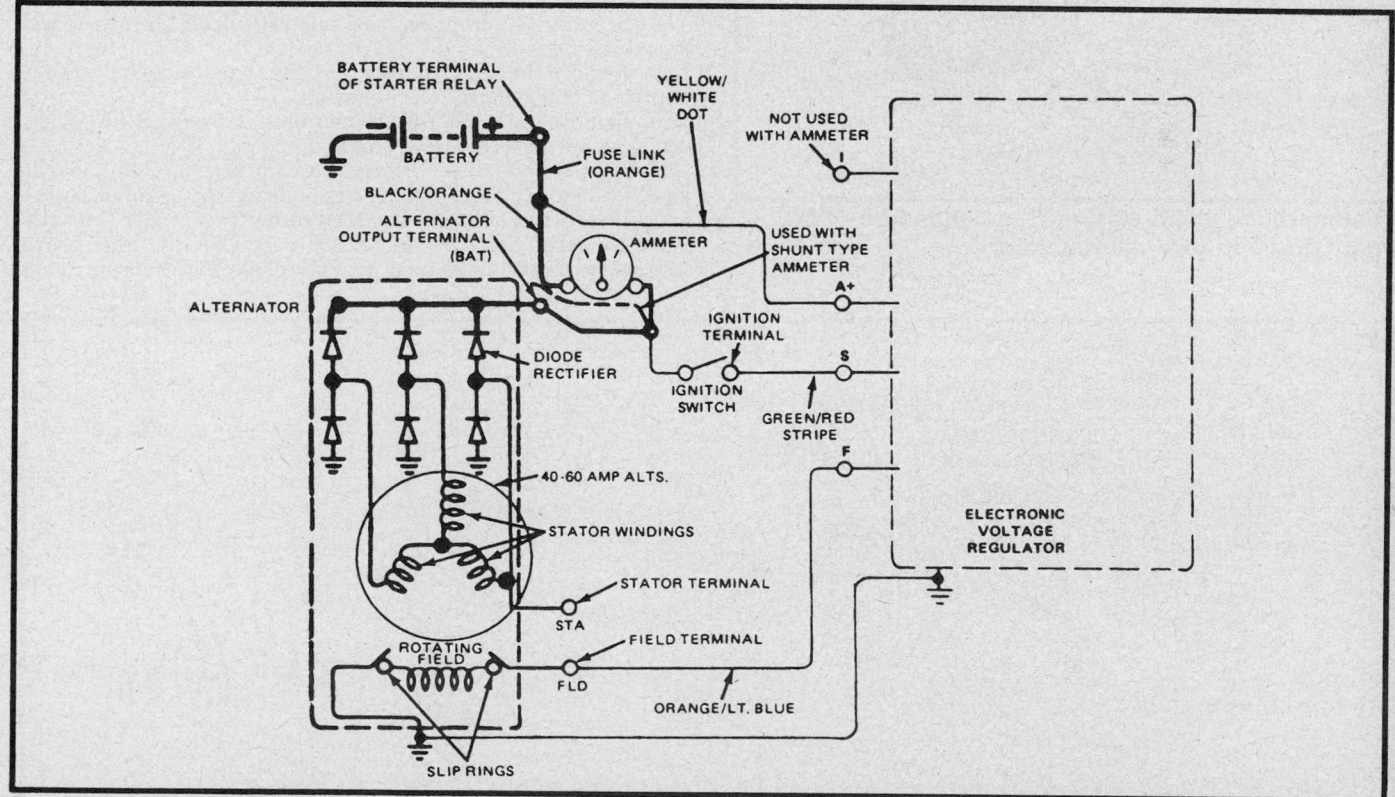

Ford alternator with external regulator—rear terminal alternator charging system schematic with ammeter—typical side terminal alternator

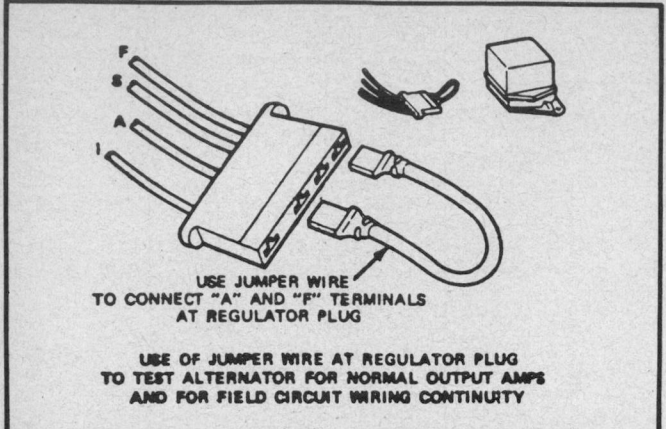

Using a jumper wire at the regulator plug to test the alternator for normal output amps and for field circuit wiring continuity—Ford alternator with external regulator

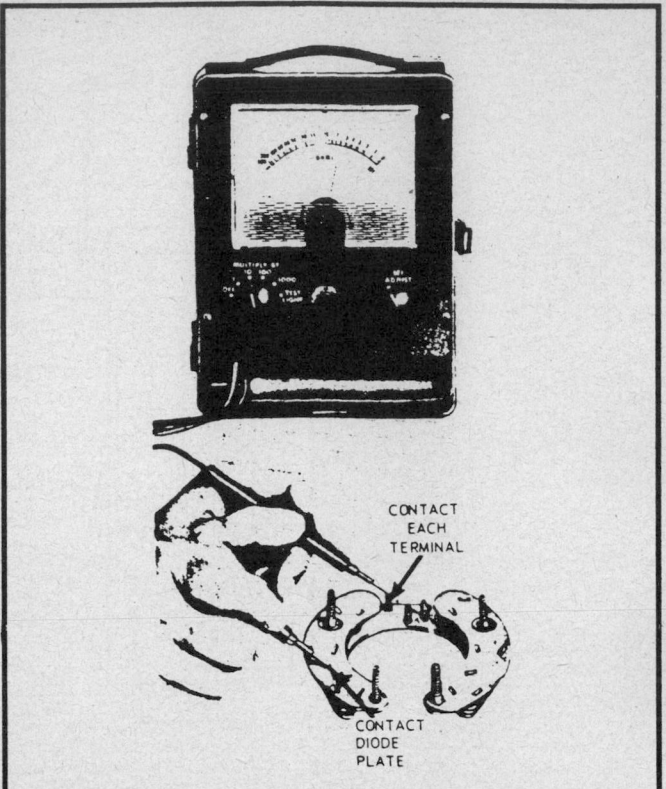

Testing diodes—Ford alternator with external regulator

3. Separate the front housing and rotor from the stator and rear housing.

4. Remove the nuts from the rectifier to rear housing mounting studs and remove rear housing.

5. Remove the brush holder mounting screws and the holder, brushes, springs, insulator and terminal.

6. If replacement is necessary press the bearing from the rear end housing while supporting the housing on the inner boss.

7. If rectifiers are to be replaced carefully unsolder the leads from the terminals. Use only a 100 watt soldering iron. Leave the soldering iron in contact with the diode terminals only long

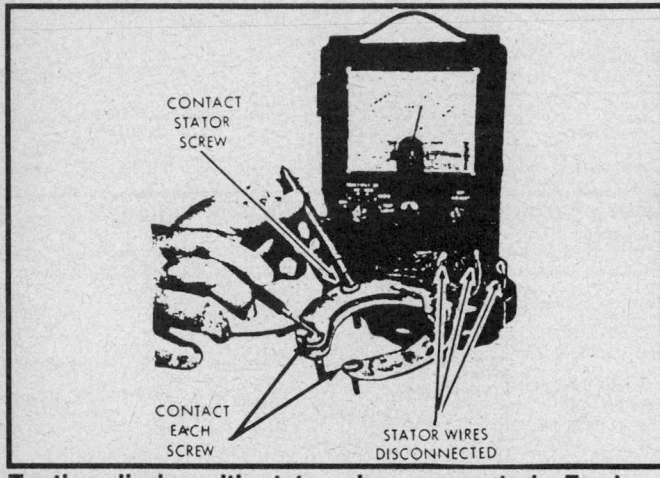

Testing diodes with stator wires connected—Ford alternator with external regulator

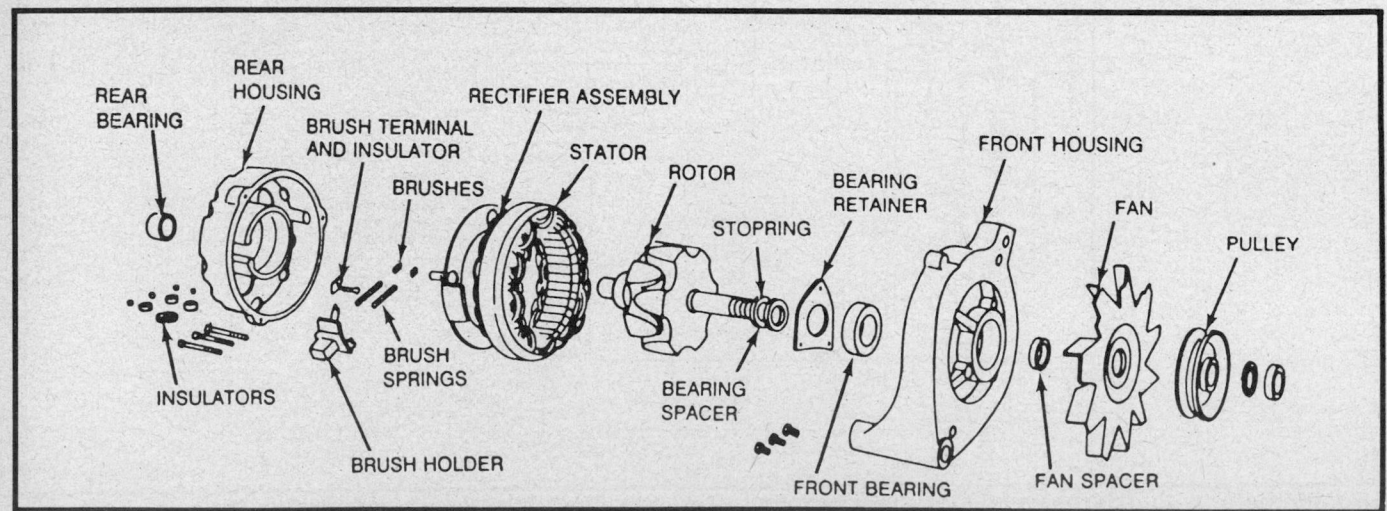

Exploded view of the rear terminal alternator with an external voltage regulator

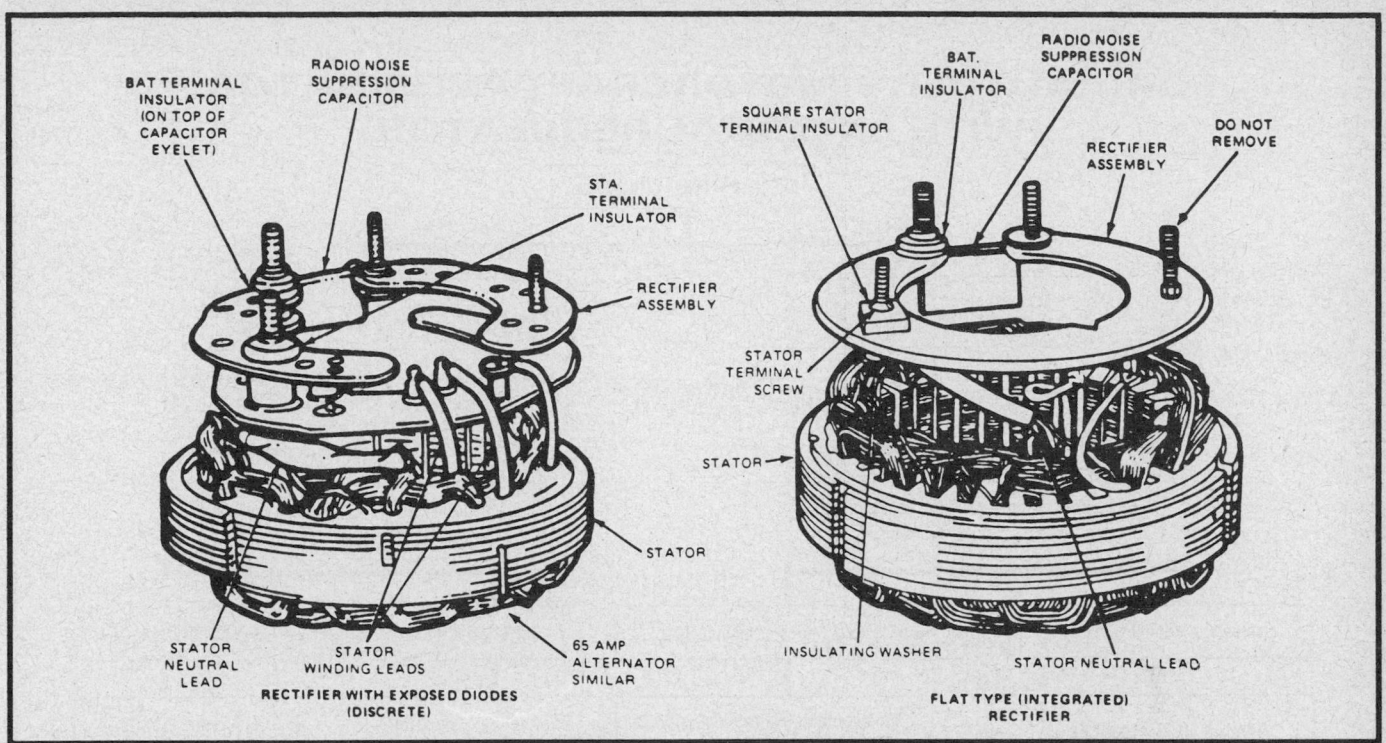

View of stator and rectifier assemblies and terminals—Ford alternator with external regulator

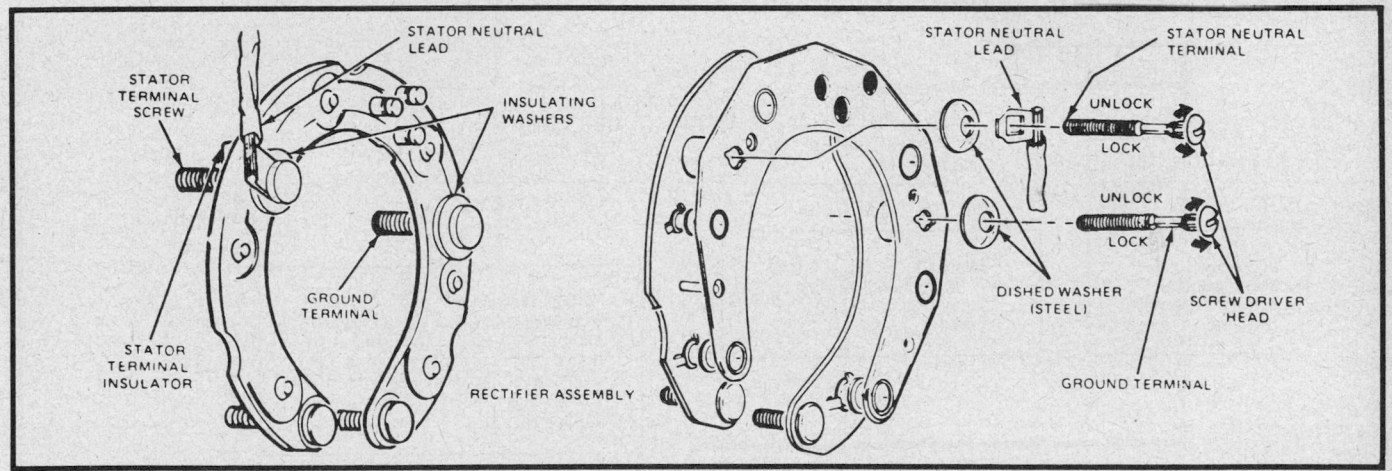

Rectifier assemblies and related components—Ford alternator with external regulator

enough to remove the wires. Use pliers as temporary heat sinks in order to protect the diodes.

8. There are various types of rectifier assembly circuit boards installed in production. One type has the circuit board spaced away from the diode plates and the diodes are exposed. Another type consists of a single circuit board with integral diodes; and still another has integral diodes with an additional booster diode plate containing 2 diodes.

9. This last type is used only on the 8 diode (61 amp) alternator. To disassemble use the following procedures. Exposed diodes remove the screws from the rectifier by rotating bolt heads ¼ turn clockwise to unlock and unscrewing. Integral diodes, press out the stator terminal screw, making sure not to twist it while doing this. Do not remove grounded screw. Booster diodes, press out the stator terminal screw about ¼ in., remove the nut from the end of the screw and lift screw from circuit board. Be sure not to twist it as it comes out.

10. Remove the drive pulley and fan. On alternator pulleys with threaded holes in the outer end of the pulley use a standard puller for removal.

11. Remove the front bearing retainer screws and the front housing. If the bearing is to be replaced press it from the housing.

Brush Replacement

1. Remove the brush holder and cover assembly from the rear housing.

2. Remove the terminal bolts from the brush holder and cover assembly. Remove the brush assemblies.

3. Position the new brush terminals on the terminal bolts and assemble the terminals, bolts, brush holder washers and nuts. The insulating washer mounts under the FLD terminal nut. The entire brush and cover assembly also is available for service.

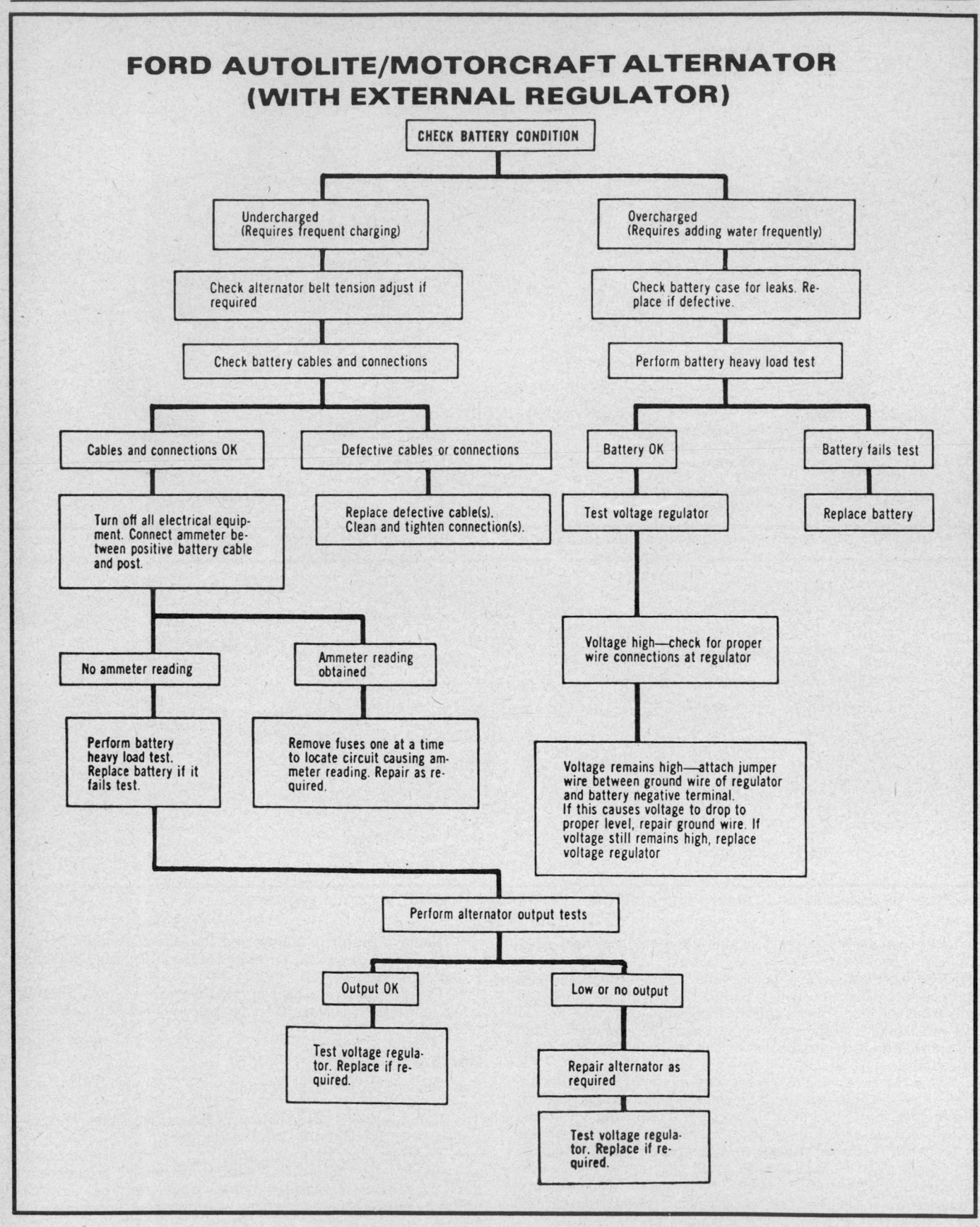

FORD AUTOLITE/MOTORCRAFT ALTERNATOR (WITH EXTERNAL REGULATOR)

CHECK BATTERY CONDITION

Undercharged (Requires frequent charging)

Overcharged (Requires adding water frequently)

Check alternator belt tension adjust if required

Check battery case for leaks. Replace if defective.

Check battery cables and connections

Perform battery heavy load test

Cables and connections OK

Defective cables or connections

Battery OK

Battery fails test

Turn off all electrical equipment. Connect ammeter between positive battery cable and post.

Replace defective cable(s). Clean and tighten connection(s).

Test voltage regulator

Replace battery

No ammeter reading

Ammeter reading obtained

Voltage high—check for proper wire connections at regulator

Perform battery heavy load test. Replace battery if it fails test.

Remove fuses one at a time to locate circuit causing ammeter reading. Repair as required.

Voltage remains high—attach jumper wire between ground wire of regulator and battery negative terminal. If this causes voltage to drop to proper level, repair ground wire. If voltage still remains high, replace voltage regulator

Perform alternator output tests

Output OK

Low or no output

Test voltage regulator. Replace if required.

Repair alternator as required

Test voltage regulator. Replace if required.

4. Depress the brush springs in the brush holder cavities and insert the brushes on top of the springs. Hold the brushes in position by inserting a stiff wire in the brush holder as shown. Position the brush leads as shown.

5. Install the brush holder and cover assembly into the rear housing. Remove the brush retracting wire and put a dab of silicone cement over the hole.

Inspection

1. The rotor, stator, diode rectifier assemblies and bearings are not to be cleaned with solvent. These parts are to be wiped off with a clean cloth. Cleaning solvent may cause damage to the electrical parts or contaminate the bearing internal lubricant. Wash all other parts in solvent and dry them.

2. Rotate the front bearing on the driveshaft. Check for any scraping noise, looseness or roughness that indicates that the bearing is excessively worn. As the bearing is being rotated look for excessive lubricant leakage. If any of these conditions exist replace the bearing. Check rear bearing and rotor shaft.

3. Place the rear end housing on the slip-ring end of the shaft and rotate the bearing on the shaft. Make a similar check for noise, looseness or roughness. Inspect the rollers and cage for damage. Replace the bearing if these conditions exist or if the lubricant is missing or contaminated.

4. Check both the front and rear housings for cracks.

5. Check all wire leads on both the stator and rotor assemblies for loose soldered connections and for burned insulation. Solder all poor connections. Replace parts that show burned insulation.

6. Check the slip-rings for damaged insulation and runout. If the slip-rings are more than 0.005 in. out of round, take a light cut (minimum diameter limit 1.220 in.) from the face of the rings to true them. If the slip-rings are badly damaged the entire rotor will have to be replaced as an assembly.

7. Replace any parts that are burned or cracked. Replace brushes that are worn to less than $^5/_{16}$ in. in length. Replace the brush spring if it has less than 7–12 oz. tension.

FIELD CURRENT DRAW TEST

1. Remove the alternator from the vehicle. Connect a test ammeter between the alternator frame and the positive post of a 12 volt test battery.

2. Connect a jumper wire between the negative test battery post and the alternator field terminal.

3. Observe the ammeter. Little or no current flow indicates high brush resistance, open field windings, or high winding resistance. Current in excess of specifications (approximately 2.9 amps for most models) indicates shorted or grounded field windings, or brush leads touching.

NOTE: The alternator, may produce current output at low engine speeds, but ceases to produce current at higher speeds. This can be caused by centrifugal force expanding the rotor windings to the point where they short to ground. Place in a test stand and check field current draw while spinning alternator.

DIODE TESTS

Disassemble the alternator. Disconnect diode assembly from stator and make tests. To test one set of diodes contact 1 ohmmeter probe to the diode plate and contact each of the 3 stator lead terminals with the other probe. Reverse the probes and repeat the test. All 6 tests (eight for 61 amp 8-diode models) should show a reading of about 60 ohms in one direction and infinite ohms in the other. If 2 high readings or 2 low readings are obtained after reversing probes, the diode is faulty and must be replaced.

STATOR TESTS

Disassemble the stator from the alternator assembly and rectifiers. Connect test ohmmeter probes between each pair of stator leads. If the ohmmeter does not indicate equally between each pair of leads the stator coil is open and must be replaced.

Connect test ohmmeter probes between one of the stator leads and the stator core. The ohmmeter should not show any reading. If it does show continuity the stator winding is grounded and must be replaced.

Assembly

1. Press the front bearing into the front housing boss by putting pressure on outer race only. Install bearing retainer.

2. If the stop ring on the driveshaft was damaged install a new stop ring. Push the new ring onto the shaft and into the groove.

3. Position the front bearing spacer on the driveshaft against the stop ring.

4. Place the front housing over the shaft with the bearing positioned in the front housing cavity.

5. Install fan spacer, fan, pulley, lockwasher and retaining nut and tighten nut 60–100 ft. lbs. while holding the driveshaft with an Allen key.

6. If rear bearing was removed, press a new one into rear housing.

7. Assemble brushes, springs, terminal and insulator in the brush holder, retract the brushes and insert a short length of $^1/_8$ in. rod or stiff wire through the hole in the holder to hold the brushes in the retracted position.

8. Position the brush holder assembly in the rear housing and install mounting screws. Position brush leads to prevent shorting.

9. Wrap the 3 stator winding leads around the circuit board terminals and solder them using only rosin core solder and a solder iron. Position the stator neutral lead eyelet on the stator terminal screw and install the screw in the rectifier assembly.

10. Exposed diodes, insert the special screws through the wire lug, dished washers and circuit board. Turn ¼ turn counterclockwise to lock in place. Integral diodes, insert the screws straight through the holes.

NOTE: The dished washers are to be used on the molded circuit boards only. Using these washers on a fiber board will result in a serious short circuit, as only a flat insulating washer between the stator terminal and the board is used on fiber circuit boards.

11. Booster diodes, position the stator wire terminal on the stator terminal screw, then position screw on rectifier. Position square insulator over the screw and into the square hole in the rectifier, rotate terminal screw until it locks, then press it in fingertight. Position the stator wire, then press the terminal screw into the rectifier and insulator with a vise.

12. Place the radio noise suppression condenser on the rectifier terminals. With molded circuit board and install the STA and BAT terminal insulators. With fiber circuit board place the square stator terminal insulator in the square hole in the rectifier assembly, then position BAT terminal insulator.

13. Position the stator and rectifier assembly in the rear housing, making sure that all terminal insulators are seated properly in the recesses. Position STA, BAT and FLD insulators on terminal bolts and install the nuts.

14. Clean the rear bearing surface of the rotor shaft with a rag and then position rear housing and stator assembly over rotor. Align matchmarks made during disassembly and install the through bolts. Remove brush retracting wire and place a dab of silicone sealer over the hole.

FORD ALTERNATOR WITH INTERNAL REGULATOR

The Ford alternator with internal regulator is manufactured by Motorcraft, which is a division of the Ford Motor Company. The field current is supplied from the alternator regulator which is mounted on the rear of the alternator, to the rotating field of the alternator through 2 brushes and 2 slip-rings.

The alternator produces power in the form of alternating current. The alternating current is rectified to direct current by 6 diodes. The alternator regulator automatically adjusts the alternator field current to maintain the alternator output voltage within prescribed limits to correctly charge the battery. The alternator is self current limiting.

The regulator voltage control circuit is turned on when the ignition switch is **ON** and voltage is applied to the regulator I terminal through a resistor in the I circuit. When the ignition switch is **OFF** the control circuit is turned off and no field current flows to the alternator.

On warning lamp equipped vehicles, the warning lamp is connected across the terminals of a 500 ohm resistor at the instrument cluster. Current passes through the warning lamp when the ignition switch is in the **RUN** position and there is no voltage at terminal S. When voltage at S rises to a preset value the regulator switching circuits stop the flow of current into terminal I and the lamp turns off.

System voltage is sensed and alternator field current is drawn through terminal A. The regulator switching circuits will turn the warning lamp on, indicating a system fault, if terminal A voltage is excessively high or low, or if the terminal S voltage signal is abnormal. A fusible link is included in the charging system wiring on all models. The fusible link is used to prevent damage to the wiring harness and alternator if the wiring harness should become grounded, or if a booster battery is connected to the charging system with the wrong polarity.

System Diagnostic
ON VEHICLE SERVICE

NOTE: **The following diagnostic tests are made with the alternator installed in the vehicle. Be sure that the battery is fully charged before any testing is done.**

Battery Voltage Test

1. Connect a voltmeter to the positive and negative battery terminals.
2. Record the battery voltage. If battery voltage is not within specification, correct as required.

Load Test

1. Be sure that the battery is fully charged before performing this test.
2. Connect the tachometer to the engine.
3. Start the engine. Turn the heater/air condition switch to the **HIGH** blower position. Turn **ON** the headlights with the high beams. Increase engine speed to 2000 rpm.
4. Voltmeter should indicate a minimum of a 0.5 volt increase over battery voltage.
5. If the system is working the above readings will be obtained. Be sure not to ground the A terminal of the voltage regulator.

No Load Test

1. Be sure that the battery is fully charged before performing this test.
2. Connect a tachometer to the engine. Start the engine and

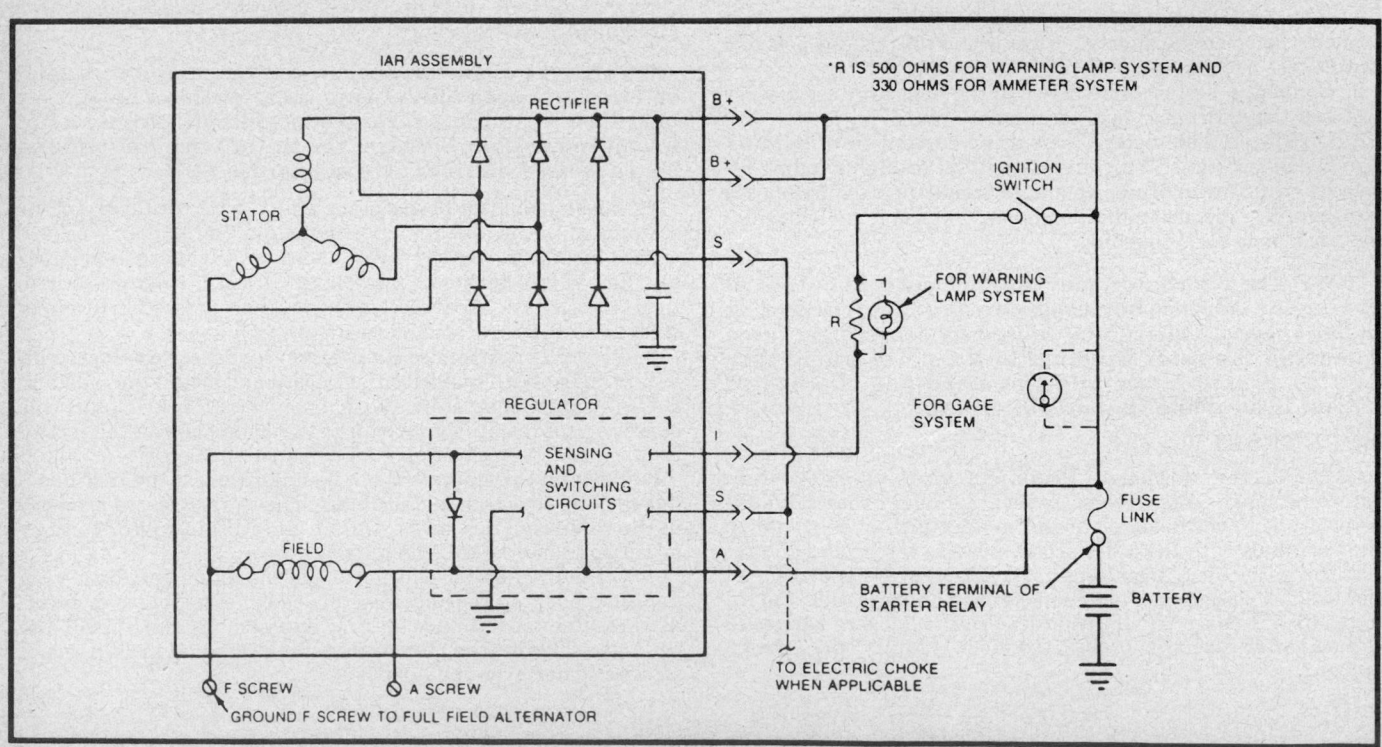

Schematic of the charging system—Ford alternator with internal regulator

increase the engine speed to 1500 rpm with no electrical load.

3. The voltmeter reading should be taken when the voltmeter needle stops moving. The voltmeter reading should be 1–2 volts above the voltage of the battery.

4. If the voltage increased properly proceed with another test.

High Voltage Test

1. Be sure that the battery is fully charged before performing this test.

2. Turn the ignition switch to the **ON** position. Connect the voltmeter negative lead to the rear of the alternator housing.

3. Connect voltmeter positive lead to alternator output terminal and record voltage. Connect voltmeter positive lead to the A terminal of regulator. Compare voltage difference recorded at alternator output terminal.

4. If voltage difference is greater than 0.5 volt, repair or replace wiring circuit to A terminal.

5. If high voltage condition still exists check ground connections at regulator to alternator, alternator to engine, firewall to engine and engine to battery.

6. If high voltage condition still exists connect voltmeter negative lead to rear of alternator housing. With ignition to **OFF** position connect voltmeter positive lead to A terminal of regulator and record reading. Connect voltmeter positive lead to F terminal of regulator.

7. Check if different voltage is present at A and F terminals. Different voltage readings indicate a defective regulator, grounded brush leads or grounded rotor coil.

8. If same voltage is present at both terminals and circuits tested in previous steps are good replace the regulator.

Low Voltage Test

1. Be sure that the battery is fully charged before performing this test.

2. Disconnect the wiring plug from the voltage regulator and install the ohmmeter between terminals A and F.

3. The ohmmeter reading should indicate more than 2.2 ohms. If the reading is less than 2.2 ohms, replace the voltage regulator and check the alternator for a shorted rotor or open field circuit. Repeat the load test. Do not replace the voltage regulator before a shorted rotor coil or field circuit has been determined not to be the problem. If not, damage to the new regulator could occur.

4. If the field circuit is okay, more than 2.2 ohms, reconnect the voltage regulator wiring plug and connect the voltmeter negative lead to the rear of the alternator. Connect the positive lead of the voltmeter to terminal A of the voltage regulator. Battery voltage should be present, if so go on. If not, repair wiring in circuit A.

5. With the ignition switch in the **OFF** position connect the positive lead of the voltmeter to the F terminal of the voltage regulator.

6. If battery voltage is present, go on. If not, replace the voltage regulator. Repeat the load test.

7. Turn the ignition switch to the **ON** position. The voltmeter should indicate 1.5 volts or less. If the reading is more than 1.5 volts, perform the regulator I circuit test. Repair the voltage regulator as required. Repeat the load test.

8. If the voltmeter reading is 1.5 volts or less, disconnect the alternator wiring plug and connect a 12 gauge jumper wire between the alternator plug terminal and the wiring harness connector.

9. Connect the positive lead of the voltmeter to 1 of the B terminals. Repeat the load test.

10. If the reading is 0.5 volt above battery voltage, repair the wiring harness from the alternator to the starter relay.

11. If the voltmeter reading is less than 0.5 volt above battery voltage, connect a jumper wire from the rear of the alternator housing to terminal F of the voltage regulator.

12. Repeat the load test. If the voltmeter reading is more than

0.5 volt, replace the voltage regulator. If the reading is less than 0.5 volt, repair the alternator.

Voltage Regulator Circuit I Test

1. Disconnect the voltage regulator wiring plug harness.

2. Connect the voltmeter negative lead to the battery ground. Connect the voltmeter positive lead to the harness side of terminal I.

3. With the ignition switch in the **OFF** position, voltage should not be present. If voltage is present repair the circuit as necessary.

4. With the ignition switch in the **ON** position, battery voltage should be present. If voltage is not present, check the wiring for an open or grounded circuit. Repair as required.

5. If the voltage readings are within specification, check the resistance of the I circuit resistor. If the vehicle is equipped with an indicator light the resistance is 500 ohms. If the vehicle is equipped with a gauge, the resistance is 300 ohms. If the specification obtained is not within plus or minus 50 ohms, replace the resistor. Repeat the load test.

6. Disconnect the voltage regulator wiring plug and remove the indicator light bulb, if equipped, before performing this test.

Field Circuit Drain Test

1. Connect the negative lead of the voltmeter to the rear of the alternator housing. Turn the ignition switch to the **OFF** position. Connect the positive lead of the voltmeter to the F terminal of the voltage regulator.

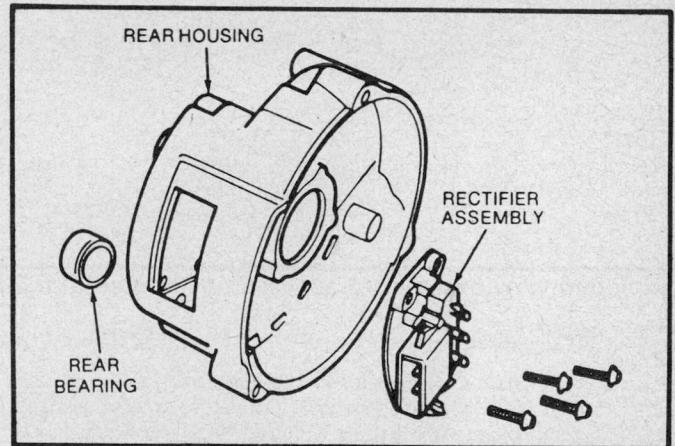

Ford alternator with internal regulator rear housing and related components.

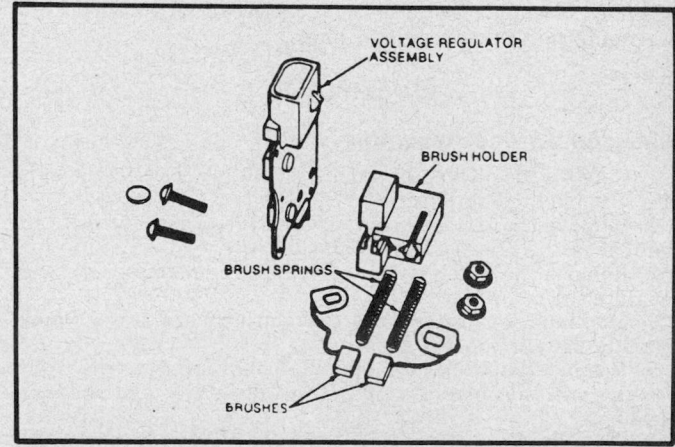

View of the voltage regulator and brush holder—Ford alternator with internal regulator

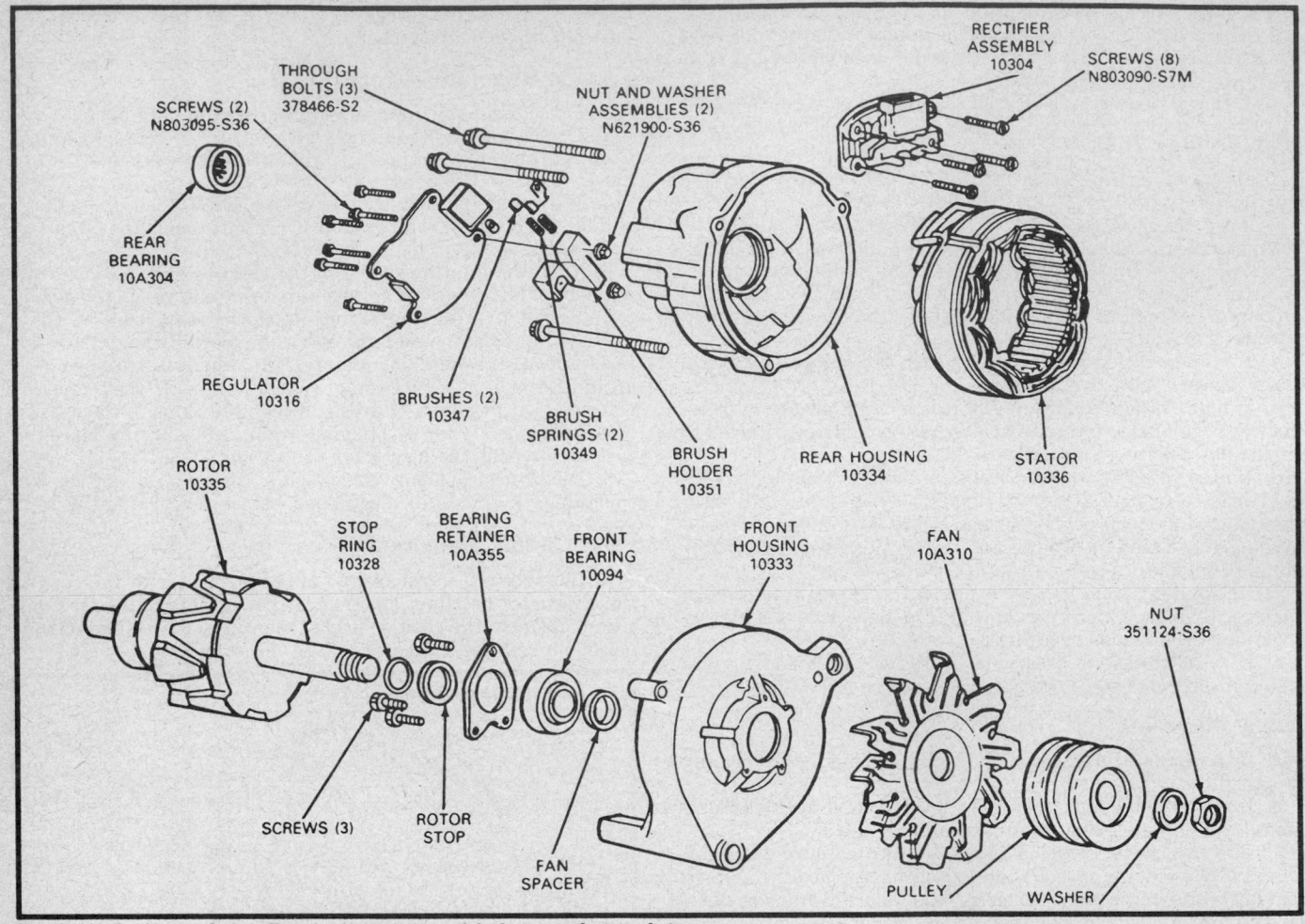

Exploded view of the Ford alternator with internal regulator

2. Battery voltage should be present. If no voltage is present, proceed.

3. If voltage is less than battery voltage, check I circuit. Disconnect regulator wiring harness. Connect voltmeter positive lead to S terminal of wiring plug. If voltage is present, proceed to Step 4. If no voltage is present replace regulator.

4. Disconnect wiring plug from alternator. Check S terminal for voltage. If no voltage is present, replace alternator rectifier assembly. If voltage is still present, replace or repair wiring between alternator and regulator plugs.

OVERHAUL

Disassembly and Assembly

1. Remove the alternator from the vehicle. Position the unit in a suitable holding fixture.

2. Remove the voltage regulator and the brush holder from the rear of the alternator assembly.

3. Remove the brush holder-to-voltage regulator screws and separate the components.

4. Matchmark the alternator end housings and stator frame to aid in installation.

5. Remove the alternator through bolts. Separate the front housing and the rotor assembly from the stator and the rear housing.

6. Unsolder the 3 stator leads from the rectifier assembly. Be careful that the rectifiers are not in contact with the solder iron, overheating them will cause damage.

7. Remove the rectifier assembly from the rear of the alternator housing. Press the rear alternator housing bearing from the rear housing.

8. From the front housing of the alternator remove the drive pulley nut from the rotor shaft.

9. Remove the lockwasher, drive pulley, fan and fan spacer from the rotor shaft.

10. Remove the rotor from the front housing. Remove the front bearing spacer from the rotor shaft. Do not remove the rotor stop ring unless it must be replaced.

11. Remove the front housing bearing retainer and bearing.

12. Assembly of the alternator is the reverse of the disassembly procedure. Be sure to clean and check all parts for wear and defects. Repair or replace defective components as required.

Inspection

NOTE: In performing the following tests, digital meters cannot be used.

STATOR GROUND TEST

1. Using an ohmmeter connect 1 test lead to the B terminal and the other test lead to the S terminal.

2. Reverse the test leads and repeat the test. The ohmmeter should read about 6.5 ohms in 1 direction and infinity when the test probes are reversed.

3. A reading in both directions indicates a faulty positive diode or a shorted radio suppression capacitor.

4. Perform the same test using the S terminal and the alternator rear housing.

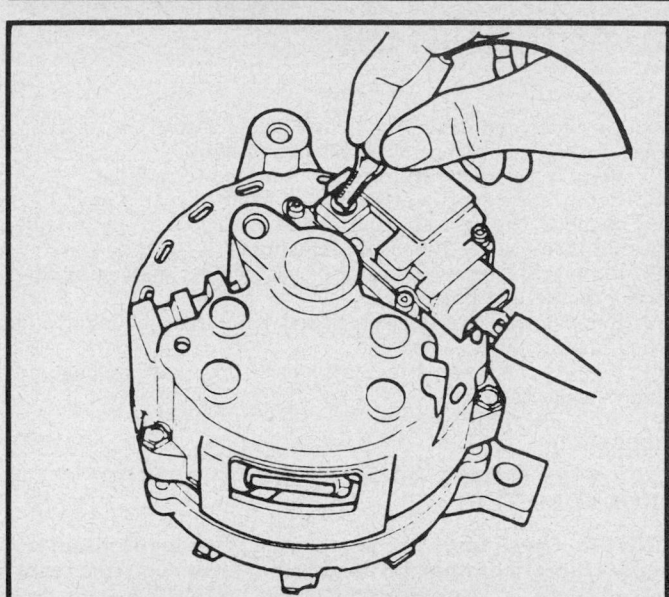

Ford alternator with external regulator

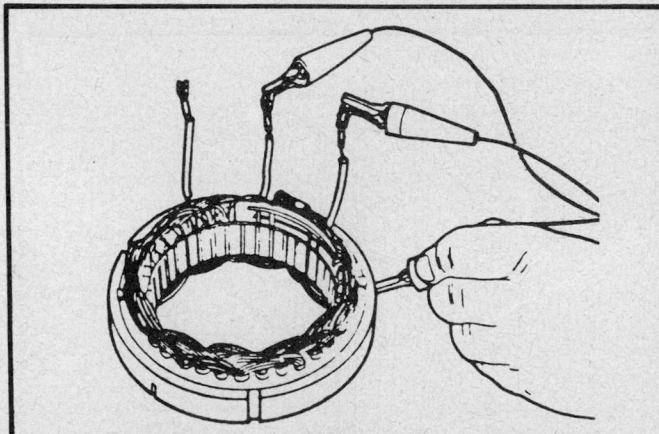

Stator coil open test, using an ohmmeter. If meter does not respond, an open is present and the stator should be replaced—Ford alternator with internal regulator

5. Readings in both directions indicate a faulty negative diode, grounded stator winding, grounded stator terminal or a shorted radio suppression capacitor.

6. If the ohmmeter needle does not move in 1 direction, or high resistance in the other direction exists, there is an open circuit in the rectifier assembly. Correct the problem as required.

FIELD OPEN OR SHORT CIRCUIT TEST

1. Using an ohmmeter connect 1 test lead to terminal A on the voltage regulator. Connect the other test lead to terminal F of the voltage regulator. Spin the alternator pulley. Reverse the ohmmeter connections and repeat the test.

2. In one test the ohmmeter should read between 2.2–100 ohms. The reading may fluctuate while the pulley is spinning.

3. In the other test the ohmmeter should read between 2.2–9 ohms.

4. An infinite reading in one test and a 9 ohm reading in the other test indicates an open brush lead, worn or stuck brushes, faulty rotor assembly or loose voltage regulator to brush holder retaining screws.

5. A reading of less than 2.2 ohms in both tests indicates a shorted rotor or a faulty voltage regulator.

6. A reading greater than 9 ohms in both tests indicates a defective voltage regulator or a loose F terminal screw.

7. Connect 1 ohmmeter test lead to the rear of the alternator. Connect the other test lead to terminal A of the voltage regulator and then to terminal F of the voltage regulator. The ohmmeter should read infinity at both points.

8. A test reading of less than infinity at both points indicates a grounded brush lead, grounded rotor or a faulty voltage regulator.

RECTIFIER ASSEMBLY TEST

1. Remove rectifier assembly from alternator. To test the positive set of diodes contact 1 ohmmeter test lead to B terminal and contact each of 3 stator lead terminals with other test lead.

2. Reverse the test leads and repeat test. All diodes should show readings of approximately 6.5 ohms in 1 direction and infinite readings with probes reversed.

3. Repeat test for negative set of diodes by connecting a test lead to rectifier assembly base plate and to other 3 terminals. If meter readings are not as specified replace rectifier assembly.

RADIO SUPPRESSION CAPACITOR TEST

NOTE: This is an open or shorted circuit test only and does not measure capacitance value.

1. Contact the ohmmeter test leads to the B terminal and the rectifier base plate assembly. Reverse the test leads while observing the indicator needle.

2. If the needle jumps momentarily and then returns to previous position, capacitor is okay. If needle does not jump replace rectifier assembly. Radio suppression capacitor must be replaced as a complete rectifier assembly.

STATOR COIL GROUND TEST

1. Remove the stator from the alternator.

2. Using an ohmmeter connect a test lead to a stator lead and the other test lead to the stator laminated core. The reading should be infinity.

3. If the meter needle moves then the stator winding is shorted to the core. Replace the stator. Repeat this test for each stator lead.

NOTE: Do not touch the metal test leads or the stator leads, an incorrect test reading will result.

STATOR COIL OPEN TEST

1. Disconnect the stator from the rectifier assembly.

2. Using an ohmmeter, connect a test lead to a stator lead and the other test lead to another stator lead.

3. If the meter does not respond, an open circuit is present and the stator should be replaced. Repeat the test with the other wire combinations. A single open phase cannot be detected on alternators using a delta connected stator.

ROTOR OPEN OR SHORT CIRCUIT TEST

1. Remove the rotor assembly from the alternator.

2. Using an ohmmeter contact each test lead to a rotor slip-ring. The ohmmeter should read 2.0–3.9 ohms.

3. If the readings are higher than specification it would indicate a damaged slip-ring solder connection or a broken wire.

4. If the readings are lower than specification it would indicate a shorted wire or slip-ring.

5. Replace the rotor if it is damaged. Connect an test lead of the ohmmeter to a rotor slip-ring and the other test lead to the rotor shaft.

6. The ohmmeter reading should be infinity. If this is not the case, the rotor is shorted to the shaft. Replace the rotor if the unit is shorted.

FORD SIDE TERMINAL ALTERNATOR

The warning lamp control circuit passes current to the warning lamp when the ignition switch is in the **RUN** position and there is no alternator voltage at terminal S. When the voltage at terminal S rises to a preset value, current is cut off to the warning lamp. This circuit is not included in the regulator for vehicles equipped with an ammeter rather than a warning lamp.

A 500 ohm, ¼ watt resistor is connected across the terminals of the lamp at the instrument cluster in vehicles equipped with an indicator warning lamp. The regulator switching circuit receives voltage from the ignition switch through the warning lamp at terminal I on vehicles equipped with an indicator warning lamp or through terminal S on vehicles equipped with an ammeter. With an input voltage present, the switching circuit turns on the voltage control circuit which, in turn, adjusts field current to control alternator output voltage.

Fuse links are included in the charging system wiring on all models. This fuse link is used to prevent damage to the wiring harness and alternator if the wiring harness should become grounded or if a booster battery is connected to the charging system with the wrong polarity.

System Diagnostic

OVERHAUL

Disassembly

1. Mark both end housings and stator with a scribe mark for assembly.
2. Remove housing through bolts and separate front housing and rotor from rear housing and stator. Slots are provided in front housing to aid in disassembly. Do not separate rear housing from stator at this time.
3. Remove drive pulley nut, lockwasher, pulley, fan and fan spacer from rotor shaft.
4. Pull rotor and shaft from front housing and remove spacer from rotor shaft.
5. Remove the screws retaining bearing to front housing. If bearing is damaged or has lost lubricant, remove bearing from housing. To remove bearing, support housing close to bearing boss and press bearing from housing.
6. Unsolder and disengage 3 stator leads from rectifier. Work quickly to prevent overheating rectifier.
7. Lift stator from rear housing.

8. Unsolder and disengage brush holder lead from rectifier. Work quickly to prevent overheating rectifier.
9. Remove screw attaching capacitor lead to rectifier.
10. Remove the screws attaching rectifier to rear housing.
11. Remove the terminal nuts and insulator from outside housing. Remove rectifier from housing.
12. Remove the screws attaching brush holder to housing. Remove brushes and holder.
13. Remove any sealing compound from rear housing and brush holder.
14. Remove the screw attaching capacitor to rear housing and remove capacitor.

Inspection

RECTIFIER SHORT GROUNDED AND STATOR GROUNDED TEST

NOTE: These tests are performed with an ohmmeter. Digital meters cannot be used to perform rectifier tests

1. Connect an ohmmeter probe to alternator BAT terminal (red insulator) and other probe to STA terminal (rear blade ter-

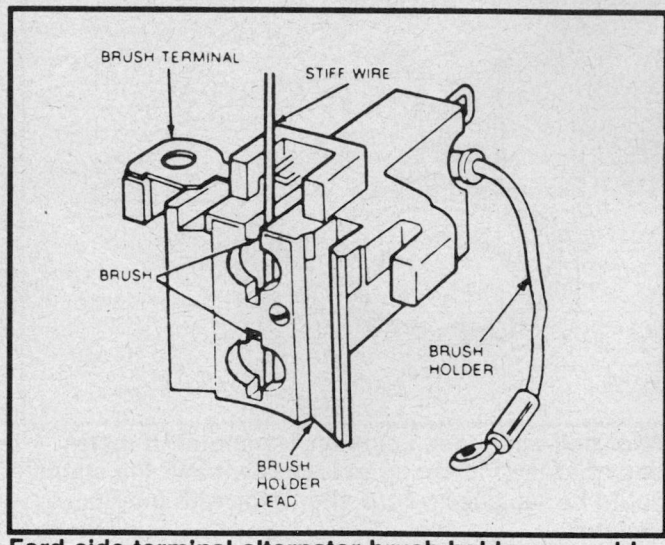

Ford side terminal alternator brush holder assembly

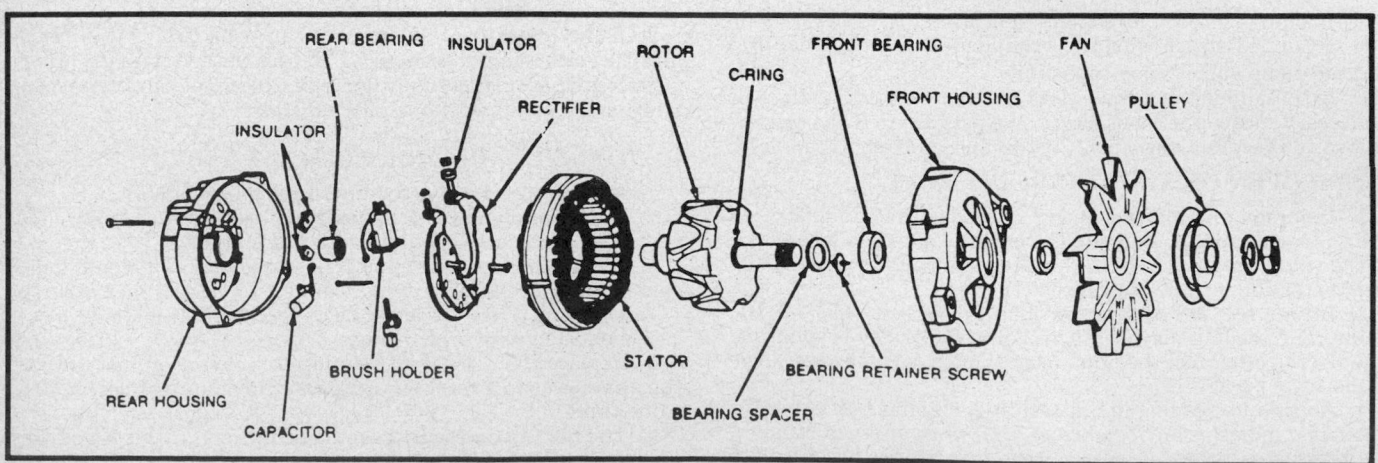

Exploded view of the Ford side terminal alternator

minal). Then reverse ohmmeter probes and repeat test. Normally, there will be no needle movement in one direction, indicating rectifier diodes are being checked in reverse current direction and are not shorted. A low reading with probes reversed indicates that rectifier positive diodes are being checked in forward current direction. Using referenced tester, low reading should be about 6 ohms, but may vary if another type of test is used. A reading in both directions indicates a damaged positive diode, a grounded positive diode plate, or a grounded BAT terminal.

2. Perform same test using STA and GND (ground) terminals of alternator. A reading in both directions indicates either a damaged negative diode, a grounded positive diode plate or a grounded BAT terminal.

3. If there is no needle movement with probes in 1 direction and no needle movement or high resistance (significantly over 6 ohms) in opposite direction, a faulty connection exists in stator circuit inside alternator.

FIELD OPEN OR SHORT CIRCUIT TEST

1. Using an ohmmeter, contact the alternator field terminal with 1 probe and ground terminal with other probe. Then, spin alternator pulley. Ohmmeter reading should be between 2.4–100 ohms and should fluctuate while pulley is turning.

2. An infinite reading (no meter movement) indicates a grounded brush lead, worn or stuck brushes or a worn or damaged rotor assembly.

3. An ohmmeter reading less than 2.4 ohms indicates a grounded brush assembly, a grounded field terminal or a worn or damaged rotor.

DIODE TEST

1. Remove the rectifier assembly from the alternator stator. To test a set of diodes, contact one probe to a terminal screw and contact each of 3 stator lead terminals with other probe. Reverse probes and repeat test. All diodes should show a low reading of about 6 ohms in one direction and an infinite reading (no needle movement) with probes reversed. Low reading may vary with type of ohmmeter used.

2. Repeat preceding tests for other set of diodes by contacting the other terminal screw and 3 stator lead terminals.

3. If meter readings are not as specified, replace rectifier assembly.

STATOR COIL GROUNDED TEST

1. Connect ohmmeter probes to a stator lead and to stator laminated core. Ensure that probe makes a good electrical connection with stator core. The meter should show an infinite reading (no meter movement).

2. If meter does not indicate an infinite reading (needle moves), stator winding is shorted to core and must be replaced.

3. Repeat this test for each stator lead. Do not touch the metal probes or stator leads with the hands. Such contact will result in an incorrect reading.

STATOR COIL OPEN TEST

NOTE: A single open phase will not be diagnosed by this test on a 100 amp alternator that has a delta connected stator.

1. Connect ohmmeter probe to a stator phase lead and touch other probe to another stator lead. Check meter reading.

2. Repeat this test with the other 2 stator lead combinations. If no meter movement occurs (infinite resistance) on a lead paired with either of the other phase leads, that phase is open and the stator should be replaced.

ROTOR OPEN OR SHORT CIRCUIT TEST

1. Contact each ohmmeter probe to a rotor slip-ring. The meter reading should be 2.3–2.5 ohms.

2. A higher reading indicates a damaged slip-ring solder connection or a broken wire.

3. A lower reading indicates a shorted wire or slip-ring. Replace rotor if it is damaged and cannot be serviced.

4. Contact an ohmmeter probe to a slip-ring and the other probe to rotor shaft. Meter reading should be infinite (no deflection).

5. A reading other than infinite indicates rotor is shorted to shaft. Inspect slip-ring soldered terminals to assure they are not bent and not touching rotor shaft, or that excess solder is not grounding rotor coil connections to shaft. Replace the rotor if it is shorted and cannot be serviced.

Assembly

1. If bearing replacement is necessary, support rear housing close to bearing boss and press bearing out of housing.

2. Wipe rotor, stator and bearings with a clean cloth. Do not clean these parts with solvent.

3. Rotate front bearing on drive end of rotor shaft. Check for any scraping noise, looseness or roughness. Look for excessive lubricant leakage. If any of these conditions exist, replace bearing.

4. Inspect rotor shaft rear bearing surface for roughness or sever chatter marks. Replace rotor assembly if shaft is not smooth.

5. Place rear bearing on slip-ring end of rotor shaft and rotate bearing. Make the same check for noise, looseness, or roughness as was made for front bearing. Inspect rollers and cage for damage. Replace bearing if these conditions exist, or if lubricant is lost or contaminated.

6. Check pulley and fan for excessive looseness on rotor shaft. Replace any pulley that is loose or bent out of shape.

7. Check both front and rear housing for cracks, particularly in webbed areas and at mounting ear. Replace damaged or cracked housing.

8. Check all wire leads on both stator and rotor assemblies for loose or broken soldered connections and for burned insulation. Resolder poor connections. Replace parts that show signs of burned insulation.

9. Check slip-rings for nicks and surface roughness. Nicks and scratches may be removed by turning down slip-rings. Do not go beyond minimum diameter of 1.220 in. If rings are badly damaged, replace rotor assembly.

10. Replace brushes if they are worn shorter than ¼ in.

12. If front housing bearing is being replaced, press new bearing in housing. Apply pressure on bearing outer race only. Install bearing retaining screws and tighten to 25–40 inch lbs.

13. Place inner spacer on rotor shaft and insert rotor shaft into front housing and bearing.

14. Install fan spacer, fan, pulley, lockwasher and nut on rotor shaft. Use the proper tool to tighten pulley nut.

15. If rear bearing is being replaced, press a new bearing in from inside housing until rear bearing face is flush with boss outer surface.

16. Position brush terminal on brush holder. Install springs and brushes in brush holder and insert a piece of stiff wire to hold brushes in place.

17. Brushes and springs are serviced as part of brush holder assembly. Position brush holder in rear housing and install attaching screws. Brush retaining wire must stick out enough to be grabbed and pulled from housing assembly.

18. Waterproof glue sealer may have to be pushed out of pin hole in housing. Push brush holder toward brush holder attaching screws. Reseal crack between brush holder and brush cavity in rear housing with caulking cord or equivalent body sealer. Do not use silicone base sealer for this application.

19. Position capacitor to rear housing and install attaching screw. Place 2 rectifier insulators on bosses inside housing.

20. Place insulator on BAT (large) terminal of rectifier and po-

sition rectifier in rear housing. Place outside insulator on BAT terminal and install nuts on BAT and Grd terminals fingertight. Install, but do not tighten, the rectifier attaching screws.

21. Tighten the BAT terminal nuts to 35–50 inch lbs. and GRD terminal nuts to 25–35 inch lbs. on outside of rear housing. Then, tighten rectifier attaching screws to 40–50 inch lbs.

22. Position capacitor lead to rectifier and install attaching screw.

23. Press brush holder lead on rectifier pin and solder securely. Work quickly to prevent overheating of rectifier.

24. Position stator in rear housing and align scribe marks.

Press 3 stator leads on rectifier pins and solder securely using resin core electrical solder. Work quickly to prevent overheating rectifier.

25. Position rotor and front housing into stator and rear housing. Align scribe marks and install through bolts. Tighten 2 opposing bolts and the remaining bolts.

26. Spin fan and pulley to be sure nothing is binding within alternator.

27. Remove brush retracting wire and place a daub of waterproof cement over hole to seal it. Do not use silicone sealer on hole.

JEEP DELCOTRON SI-SERIES

The charging system is an integrated AC generating system containing a built in voltage regulator. The regulator is mounted inside the slip ring end frame. All regulator components are enclosed in an epoxy molding and the regulator cannot be adjusted.

System Diagnosis

OVERHAUL

Disassembly

1. Remove the alternator from the vehicle. Position the assembly in a suitable holding fixture.

2. Make scribe marks on the alternator case end frames to aid in reassembly.

3. Remove the assembly through bolts and separate the drive end frame assembly from the rectifier end frame assembly.

4. Remove the rectifier nuts and the regulator screws from the end frame assembly.

5. Separate the stator, diode trio and voltage regulator from the end frame assembly.

6. Check the stator for opens using an ohmmeter. If high readings are obtained, replace the stator.

7. Check the stator for grounds, using an ohmmeter. If readings are low, replace the stator.

8. Using an ohmmeter, check the rotor for grounds. The ohmmeter reading should be very high. If not, replace the rotor.

9. Using an ohmmeter, check the rotor for opens. If the ohmmeter reading is not 2.4–3.5 ohms, replace the rotor.

10. To check the diode trio connect the ohmmeter to the diode trio and then reverse the lead connections. The ohmmeter should read high and low. If not, replace the diode trio. Repeat the same test between the single connector and each of the other connectors.

11. Check rectifier bridge with ohmmeter connected from grounded heat sink to flat metal on terminal. Reverse leads. If both readings are equal then replace rectifier bridge.

12. Repeat test between grounded heat sink and other 2 flat metal clips.

13. Repeat test between insulated heat sink and 3 flat metal clips.

14. Clean or replace the alternator brushes as required. Position the brushes in the brush holder and retain them in place using the brush retainer wire or equivalent.

15. To remove the rotor and drive end bearing, remove the shaft nut, washer and pulley, fan and collar. Push the rotor from the housing.

16. Remove the retainer plate from inside the drive end frame. Push the bearing out. Clean or replace parts as required.

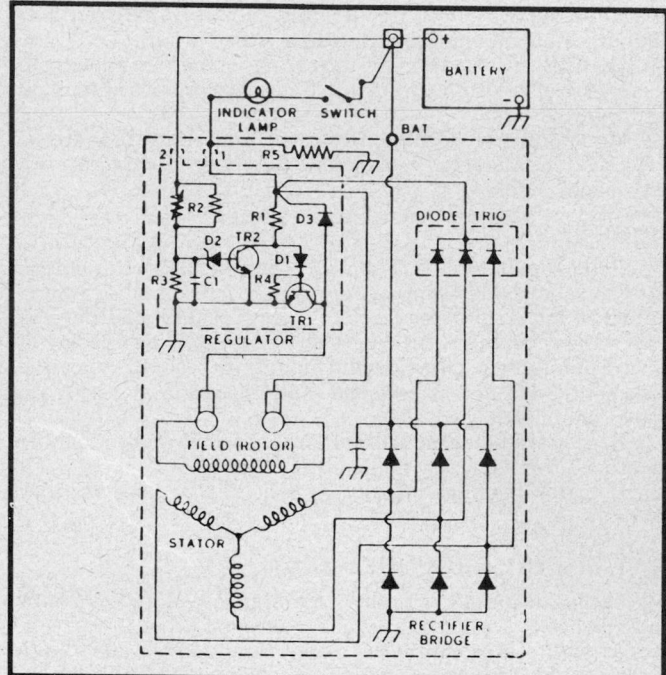

Schematic of the Delcotron charging system—Jeep

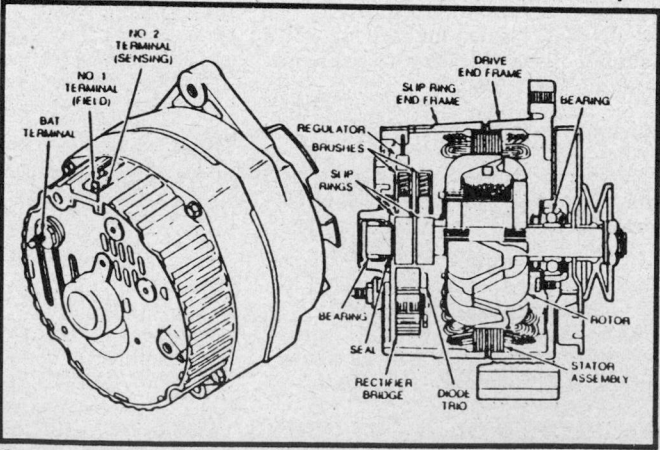

Cross-sectional view of the Delcotron alternator—Jeep

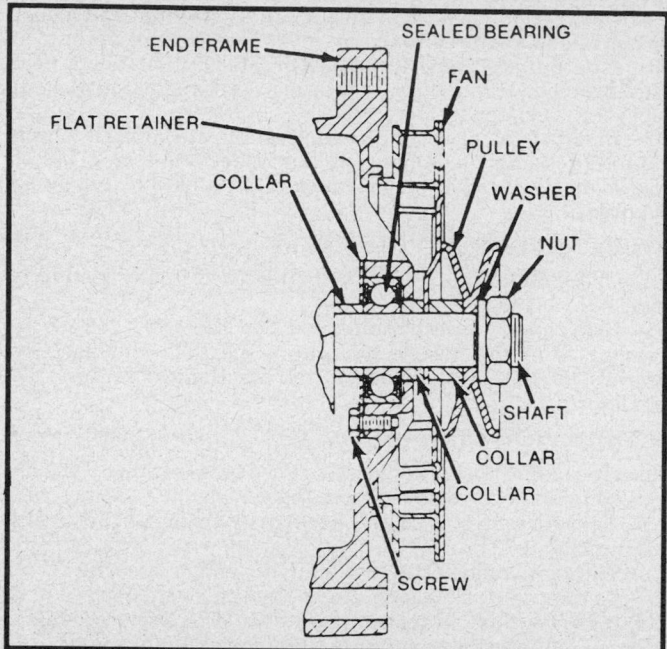

Exploded view of the end frame assembly—Delcotron alternator—Jeep

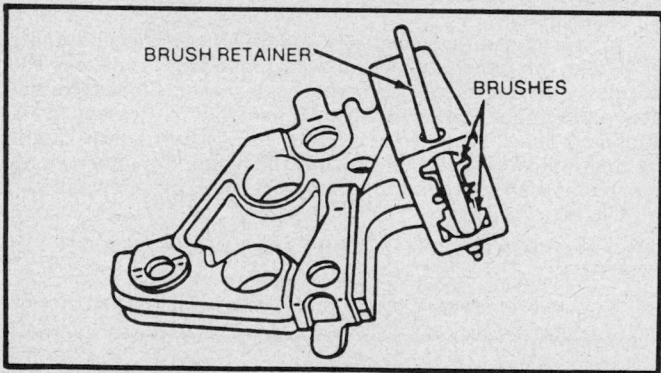

Installing the brushes into the holder—Delcotron alternator—Jeep

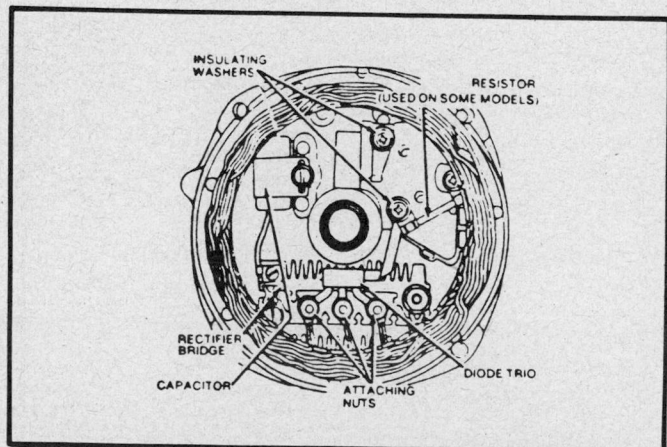

Location of the related end frame components—Delcotron alternator—Jeep

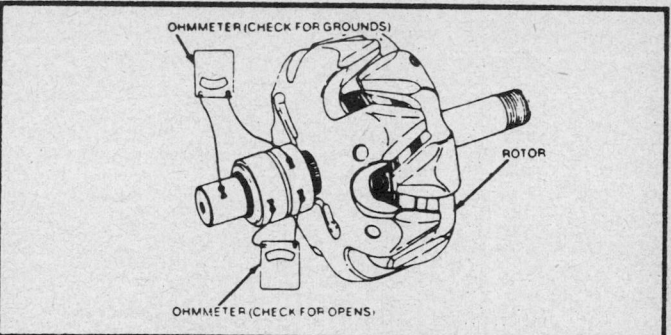

Using an ohmmeter to check the rotor for opens or grounds—Delcotron alternator—Jeep

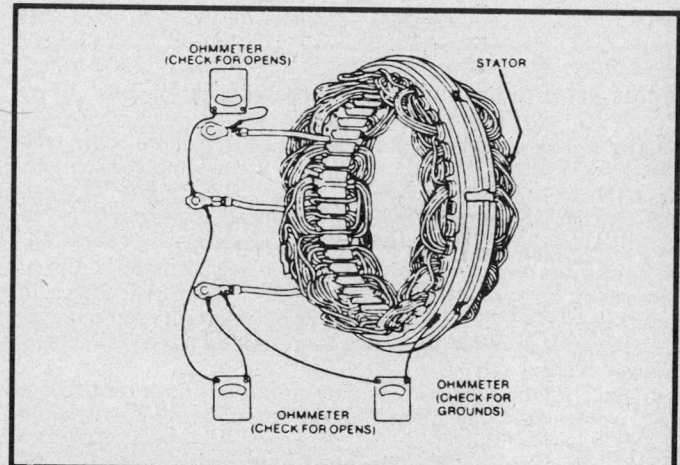

Using an ohmmeter to check the stator for opens or grounds—Delcotron alternator—Jeep

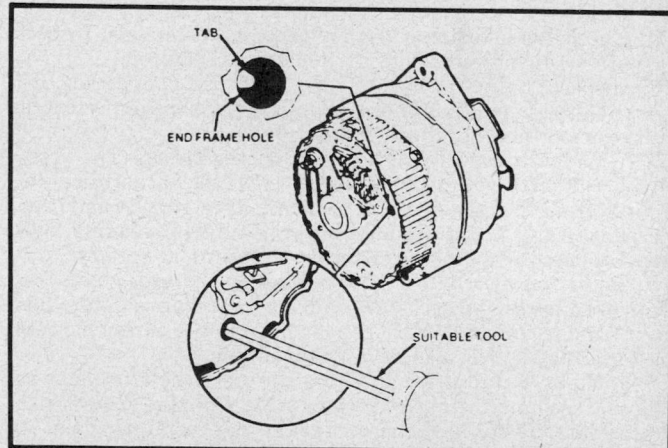

Grounding the field winding by inserting a tool into the test hole to a depth of 1 in.—Delcotron alternator—Jeep

Inspection

INDICATOR LAMP OPERATION TEST

1. Check the indicator lamp for normal operation. If the indicator lamp operates properly, refer to the undercharged battery test. If the indicator lamp does not operate properly, proceed with the following tests.
2. Switch **OFF**, lamp **ON**. Unplug the connector from the

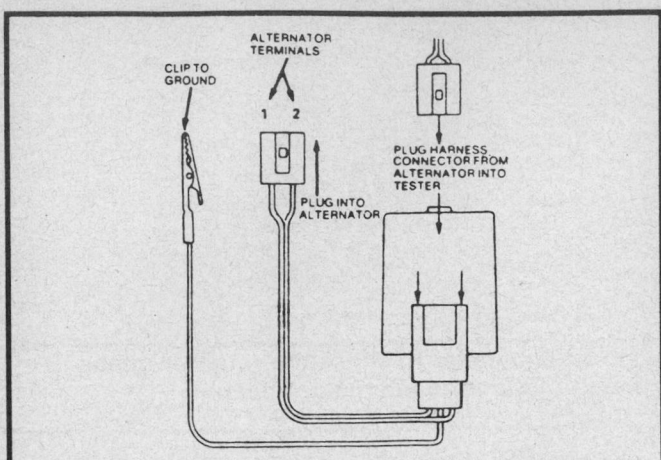

Delcotron alternator diagnostic tester (J-26290) use tester according to manufacturers instructions

generator No. 1 and No. 2 terminals. If the lamp stays **ON**, there is a short between these 2 leads. If the lamp goes out, replace the rectifier bridge.

3. Switch **ON**, lamp **OFF**, engine stopped. This condition can be caused by the defects listed above or by an open in the circuit. To determine where an open exists, proceed as follows. Check for a blown fuse or fusible link, a burned out bulb, defective bulb socket or an open in No. 1 lead circuit between generator and ignition switch. If no defects have been found, proceed to undercharged battery test.

4. Switch **ON**, lamp **ON**, engine running. Check for a blown fuse, (where used), between indicator lamp, ignition switch and also in A/C circuit.

UNDERCHARGED BATTERY TEST

1. Be sure the undercharged battery condition has not been caused by accessories that have been left **ON** for an extended period of time.

2. Check the alternator belt for proper belt tension. Inspect the battery for physical defects. Replace as required.

3. Inspect the wiring for defects. Check all connections for proper contact and cleanliness, including the slip connectors at the generator and bulkhead connections.

4. With ignition switch **ON** and all wiring harness leads connected, connect a voltmeter from the generator Bat terminal-to-ground, from the generator No. 1 terminal-to-ground and from the generator No. 2 terminal-to-ground. A zero reading indicates an open between voltmeter connection and battery.

5. Delcotron alternators have a built in feature which prevents overcharge and accessory damage by preventing the alternator from turning **ON** if there is an open in the wiring harness connected to the No. 2 alternator terminal.

6. If Steps 1 through 5 check out, inspect the alternator as follows. Disconnect negative battery cable. Connect an ammeter or alternator tester in the circuit at the Bat terminal of the alternator. Reconnect negative battery cable.

7. Turn **ON** radio, windshield wipers, lights (high beam) and blower motor on high speed. Connect a carbon pile across the battery (or use alternator tester). Operate engine about 2000 rpm and adjust carbon pile as required, to obtain maximum current output. If ampere output is within 10 amperes of rated output as stamped on generator frame, alternator is not defective. Recheck Steps 1 through 5.

8. If ampere output is not within 10 percent of rated output, determine if test hole is accessible. Ground the field winding by inserting a suitable tool into the test hole. Tab is within ¾ inch of casting surface. Do not force suitable tool deeper than an inch into end frame to avoid damaging alternator.

9. Operate engine at moderate speed as required and adjust carbon pile as required to obtain maximum current output.

10. If output is within 10 amperes of rated output, check field winding, diode trio and rectifier bridge. Test regulator with an approved regulator tested.

11. If output is not within 10 amperes of rated output, check the field winding, diode trio, rectifier bridge and stator. If test hole is not accessible, disassemble alternator and repair as required.

OVERCHARGED BATTERY TEST

1. Check the condition of the battery before any testing is done.

2. If an obvious overcharging condition exists, remove the alternator from the vehicle and check the field windings for grounds or shorts. If defective, replace the rotor. Test the regulator.

ALTERNATOR DIAGNOSTIC TESTER (J-26290)

This special diagnostic tester is designed to determine if the alternator should be removed from the vehicle.

1. Install tester J-26290 according to manufacturers instructions.

2. With the engine **OFF** and all lights and accessories **OFF**, test the alternator as follows. Light flashes, go to Step 3. Light **ON**, indicates fault in tester which should be replaced. Light **OFF**, pull plug from generator. A flashing light, indicates the alternator should be removed and the rectifier bridge replaced. Light **OFF**, indicates faulty tester or no voltage to tester. Check for 12 volts at No. 2 terminal of harness connector. Repair wiring or terminals if 12 volts is not available. Replace tester if 12 volts is available.

3. With the engine at fast idle and all accessories and lights **OFF**, test the alternator as follows. Light **OFF** indicates the charging system good, do not remove alternator. Light **ON** indicates a component failure within the alternator. Remove alternator and check diode trio, rectifier bridge and stator. Light flashing indicates a problem within the alternator. Remove alternator and check regulator, rotor field coil, brushes and slip rings.

VOLTAGE REGULATOR TEST (ALTERNATOR ON VEHICLE)

1. Connect a battery charger and a voltmeter to the battery.

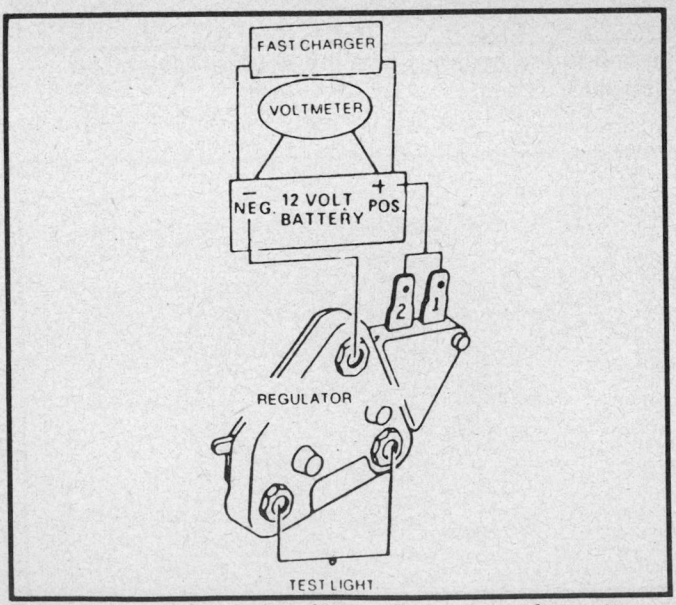

Testing the voltage regulator—Delcotron alternator—Jeep

2. Turn the ignition switch **ON** and slowly increase the charge rate. The alternator light in the vehicle will dim at the voltage regulator setting. Voltage regulator setting should be 13.5–16.0 volts. This test is performed to determine if the voltage regulator setting is within specifications. This test is accurate even if the stator rectifier bridge or diode trio is faulty.

VOLTAGE REGULATOR TEST (ALTERNATOR OFF VEHICLE)

1. Remove the alternator from the vehicle.
2. Disassemble the alternator and remove the voltage regualtor.
3. Connect a voltmeter and a fast charger to a 12 volt battery. Connect a test light to the regulator and observe the battery polarity.
4. The test light should light.
5. Turn **ON** the fast charger and slowly increase the charge rate. Observe the voltmeter, the light should go out at the voltage regulator setting. The voltage regulator setting specification is 13.5–16.0 volts.

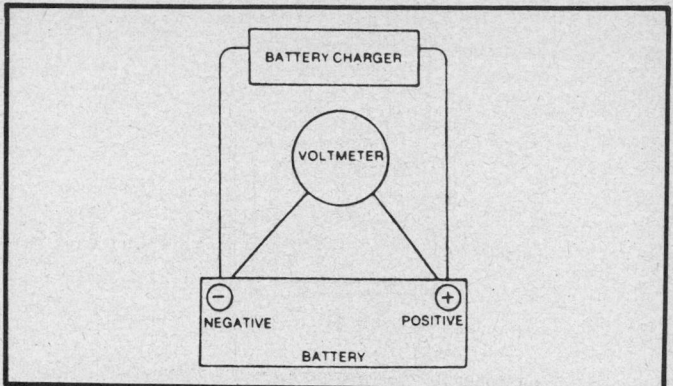

BATTERY CHARGER
VOLTMETER
NEGATIVE
POSITIVE
BATTERY

Voltage regulator test (on vehicle) voltage regulator setting should be 13.5–16.0 volts – Delcotron alternator – Jeep

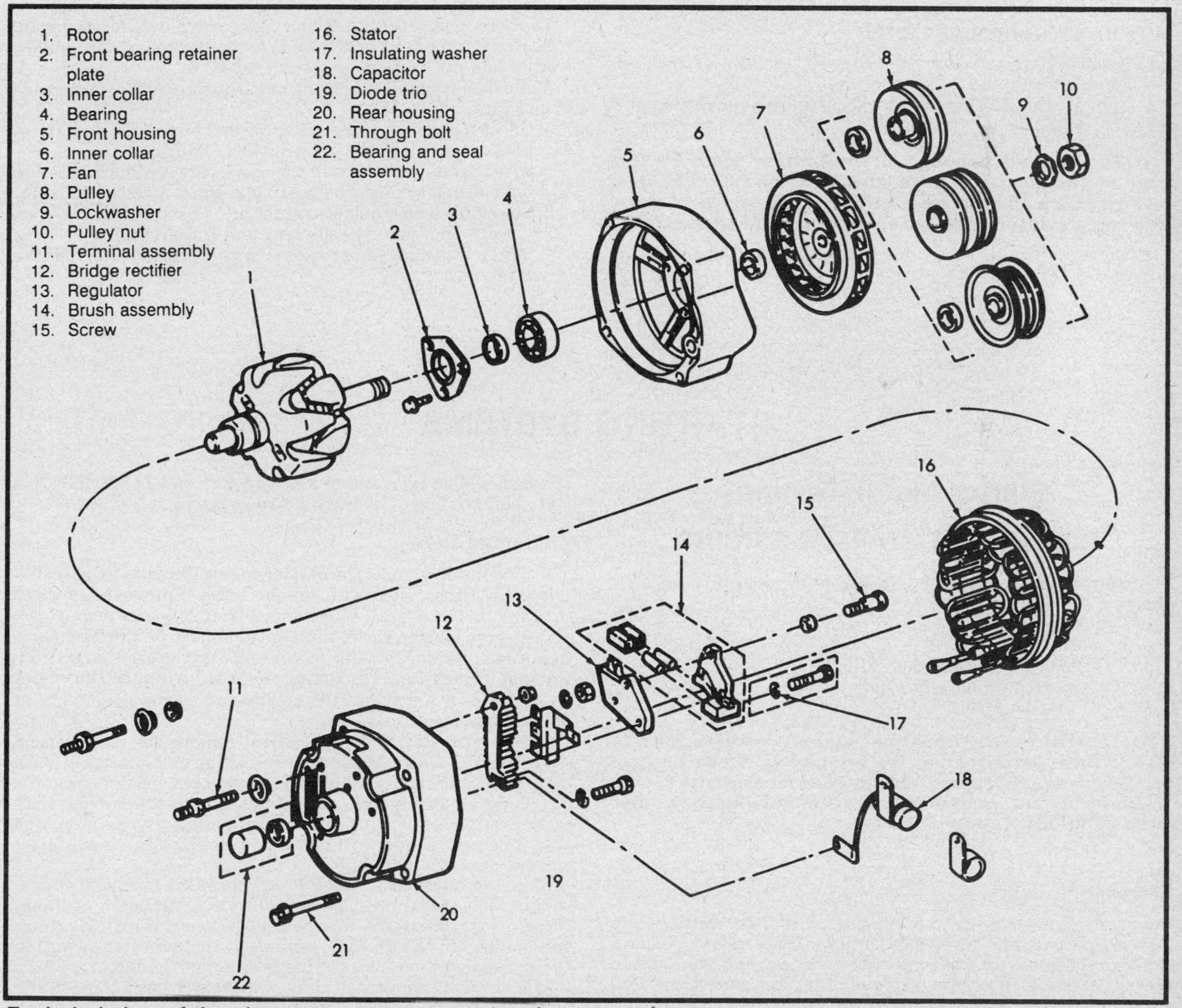

1. Rotor
2. Front bearing retainer plate
3. Inner collar
4. Bearing
5. Front housing
6. Inner collar
7. Fan
8. Pulley
9. Lockwasher
10. Pulley nut
11. Terminal assembly
12. Bridge rectifier
13. Regulator
14. Brush assembly
15. Screw
16. Stator
17. Insulating washer
18. Capacitor
19. Diode trio
20. Rear housing
21. Through bolt
22. Bearing and seal assembly

Exploded view of the alternator – Delcotron 15/81 alternator – Jeep

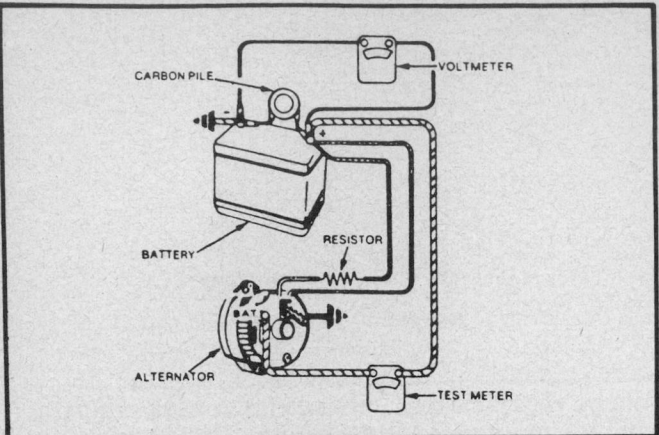

Bench test hook-up for testing — Delcotron alternator — Jeep

ALTERNATOR BENCH TEST

1. Remove the alternator from the vehicle. Position the unit in a suitable test stand.
2. Connect the alternator in series, but leave the carbon pile disconnected.

NOTE: Ground polarity of the battery must be the same as the alternator. Be sure to use a fully charged battery and a 10 ohm resistor rated at 6 watts or more between the alternator No. 1 terminal and the battery.

3. Increase the alternator speed slowly and observe the voltage.

4. If the voltage is uncontrolled with speed and increases above 15.5 volts on a 12 volt system or 31 volts on a 24 volt system, test regulator with an approved regulator tester and check field winding. If voltage is below 15.5 volts on a 12 volt system or 31 volts on a 24 volt system, connect the carbon pile.
5. Operate the alternator at moderate speed as required and adjust the carbon pile as required to obtain maximum current output.
6. If output is within 10 amperes of rated output as stamped on alternator frame, alternator is good. If output is not within 10 amperes of rated output, keep battery loaded with carbon pile and ground alternator field.
7. Operate alternator at moderate speed and adjust carbon pile as required to obtain maximum output. If output is within 10 amperes of rated output, test regulator with an approved regulator tester and check field winding.
9. If output is not within 10 amperes of rated output, check the field winding, diode trio, rectifier bridge and stator.

Assembly

1. Press against the outer bearing race to push the bearing in.
2. Press rotor into end frame. Assemble collar, fan, pulley, washer and nut. Torque shaft nut 40–60 ft. lbs.
3. Push slip ring end bearing out from outside toward inside of end frame.
4. Place flat plate over new bearing and press from outside toward inside until bearing is flush with end frame.
5. Use the thin wall tube in the space between the grease cup and the housing to push the bearing in flush with the housing.
6. Assemble brush holder, regulator, resistor, diode trio, rectifier bridge and stator-to-slip ring end frame.
7. Assemble end frames together with through bolts. Remove brush retainer wire.

STARTING SYSTEMS

Starter Motor Testing

TESTING THE STARTER CIRCUIT

The starter circuit should be divided and tested in 4 separate phases:
1. Cranking voltage check
2. Amperage draw
3. Voltage drop on grounded side
4. Voltage drop on battery side

NOTE: The battery must be in good condition for this test to have significance. To accurately check battery condition, use equipment designed to measure its capacity under a load. Instructions accompanying the equipment should be followed.

Cranking Voltage

Connect voltmeter leads to prods tapped into the battery posts (observe polarity and reverse meter leads if necessary). Remove the high tension wire from the distributor cap and ground it to prevent starting. With electronic ignition, disconnect the control box harness from the distributor. Now, turn the key. Observe both voltmeter reading and cranking speed. The cranking speed should be even and at a satisfactory rate of speed, with a voltmeter reading of at least 9.6 volts for 12 volt systems.

Amperage Draw

The amount of current the starter motor draws is usually (but not always) associated with the mechanical problems involved in cranking the engine. (Mechanical trouble in the engine, frozen or worn starter parts, misaligned starter or starter components, etc.) Because starter motor amperage draw is directly influenced by anything restricting the free turning of the engine or starter, it is important the engine and all components be at operating temperatures.

To measure starter current draw, remove the high tension wire from the center of the distributor cap and ground it. With electronic ignition, disconnect the control box harness from the distributor. A very simple and inexpensive starter current indicator is available at auto stores. This indicator is an induction type gauge and shows, without disconnecting any wires, starter current draw.

Place the yoke of the meter directly over the insulated starter supply cable (cable must be straight for a minimum of 2 in.). Close the starter switch for about 20 seconds, watch the meter dial and record the average reading. If the indicator swings in the wrong direction, reverse the position of the meter.

The cranking amperage draw can vary from 150–400 amperes, depending on the engine size, engine compression and starter type.

NOTE: When starter specifications are not available, average starter draw amperage can be derived from testing a like starter unit, known to be operating satisfactorily.

More accurate but complex equipment is available from many manufacturers. This equipment consists of a combination voltmeter, ammeter and carbon pile rheostat. When using this equipment, follow the equipment manufacturer's procedures and recommendations.

High amperage and lazy performance would suggest an excessively tight engine, friction in the starter or starter drive, grounded starter field or armature.

Normal amperage and lazy performance suggest high resistance or possibly poor connections somewhere in the starter circuit.

Low amperage and lazy or no performance suggest battery condition poor, bad cables or connections along the line.

Voltage Drop On Grounded Side

With a voltmeter on the 3 volt scale, without disconnecting any wires, connect negative test lead of the voltmeter to a prod secured in the grounded battery post. The positive test lead is connected to a cleaned, bare metal portion of the starter motor housing. Close the starter switch and note the voltmeter reading. If the reading is the same as battery reading, the ground circuit is open somewhere between the battery and the starter. In many cases the reading will be very small. The reading shown will indicate voltage drop (loss) between battery ground post and starter housing. The drop should not exceed 0.2 volts. If the voltage drop is above the specified amount, the next step is to isolate and correct the cause. It can be a bad cable or connection anywhere in the battery-to-starter ground circuit. A check of this type should progress along the various points of possible trouble, between the battery ground post and the starter motor housing, until the trouble spot has been located.

Voltage Drop On Battery Side

Bad starter cranking may result from poor connections or faulty components of the battery or hot phase of the starter motor circuit. To check this phase of the circuit, without disconnecting any wires, connect a lead of a voltmeter to a prod secured in the hot post of the battery and the other voltmeter lead to the field terminal of the starting motor. The meter should be set to the 16–20 volt scale. Before closing the starter switch, the voltmeter reading will be that of the battery. After closing the starter switch, change the selector on the voltmeter to the 3 volt scale. With a jumper wire between the relay battery terminal and the relay starter switch terminal, crank the engine. If the starting motor cranks the engine, the relay (solenoid) is operating.

While the engine is being cranked, watch the voltmeter. It should not register more than 0.5 volts. If more than this, check each part of the circuit for voltage drop to isolate the trouble, (high resistance).

Without disturbing the voltmeter-to-battery hook-up, move the free voltmeter lead to the battery terminal of the relay (solenoid) and crank the engine. The voltmeter should show no more than 0.1 volts.

If this reading is correct, move the same voltmeter lead to the starting motor terminal of the relay (solenoid). While the engine is being cranked, the voltmeter should show no more than 0.3 volts. If it does, the trouble lies in the relay.

If the reading is correct, the trouble is in the cable or connections between the relay and the starting motor.

DIAGNOSIS

Starter Won't Start Engine

1. Dead battery.
2. Open starter circuit, such as:
   a. Broken or loose battery cables
   b. Inoperative starter motor solenoid
   c. Broken or loose wire from starter switch-to-solenoid
   d. Poor solenoid or starter ground
   e. Faulty starter switch
3. Defective starter internal circuit, such as:
   a. Dirty or burned commutator
   b. Stuck, worn or broken brushes
   c. Open or shorted armature
   d. Open or grounded fields
4. Starter motor mechanical faults, such as:
   a. Jammed armature end bearings
   b. Faulty bearings, allowing armature to rub fields
   c. Bent shaft
   d. Broken starter housing
   e. Faulty starter worm or drive mechanism
   f. Faulty starter drive or flywheel driven gear
5. Engine hard or impossible to crank such as:
   a. Hydrostatic lock, water in combustion chamber
   b. Crankshaft seizing in bearings
   c. Piston or ring seizing
   d. Bent or broken connecting rod
   e. Seizing of connecting rod bearing
   f. Flywheel jammed or broken
6. Starter spins free, won't engage such as:
   a. Sticking or broken drive mechanism

CHRYSLER REDUCTION GEAR STARTER

OVERHAUL

Disassembly and Assembly

1. Support assembly in a soft jawed vise; be careful not to distort or damage the die cast aluminum.
2. Remove the through bolts and the end housing.
3. To disassemble the starter motor, perform the following procedures:
   a. Carefully pull the armature up and out of the gear housing and the starter frame and field assembly.
   b. Remove the steel and fiber thrust washer.
   c. Carefully pull the frame and field assembly up enough to expose the terminal screw and the solder connection of the shunt field at the brush terminal.
   d. Place 2 wood blocks between the starter frame and starter gear housing to facilitate removal of the terminal screw.
   e. Unsolder the shunt field wire at the brush terminal.

NOTE: The starting motors have the wire of the shunt field coil soldered to the brush terminal. A pair of brushes are connected to this terminal. Another pair of brushes are attached to the series field coils by means of a terminal screw.

4. Support the brush terminal with a finger behind terminal

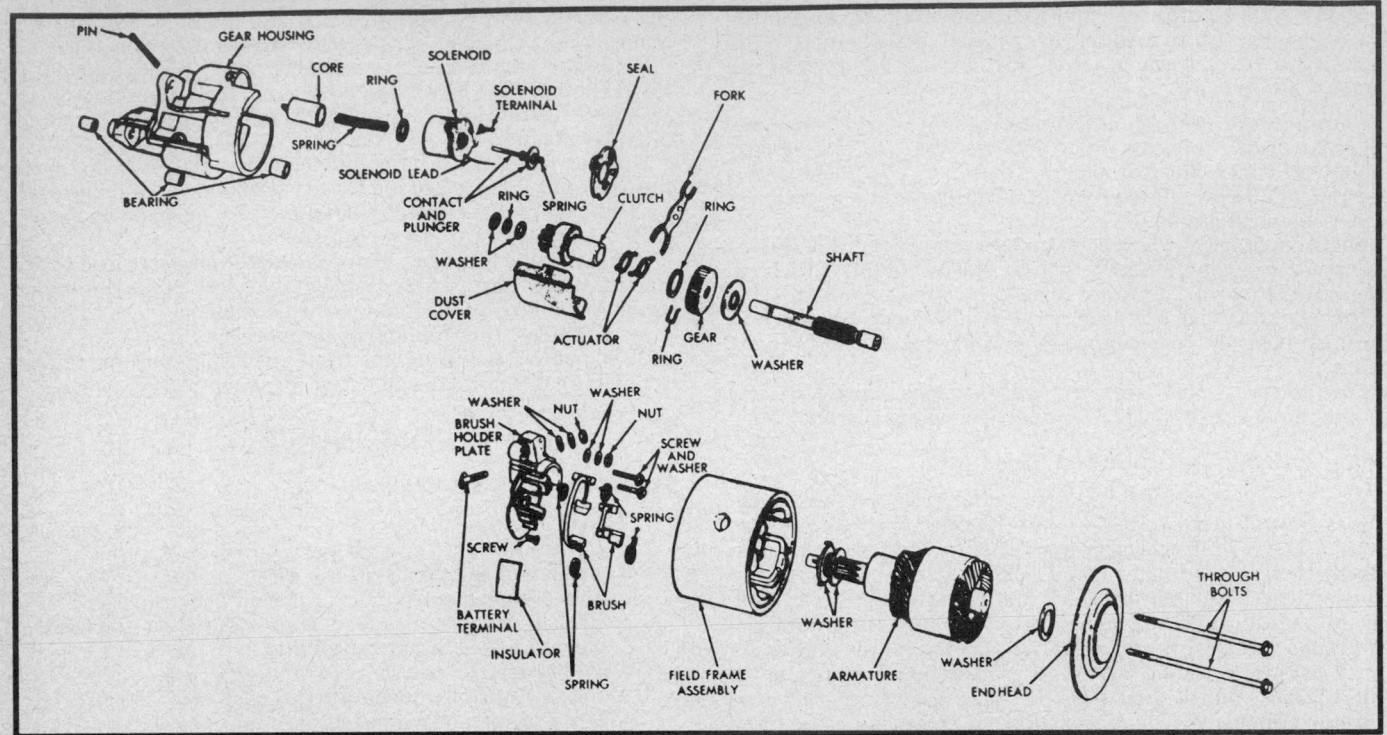

Exploded view of the reduction gear starter motor – Chrysler

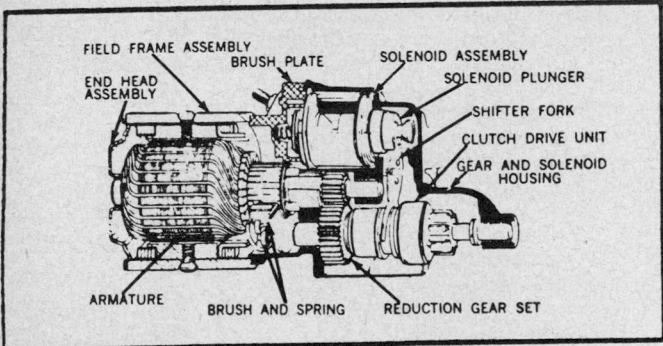

Cross-sectional view of the reduction gear starter motor – Chrysler

and remove the screw. Unsolder the shunt field coil lead from the brush terminal and housing.

5. The brush holder plate (with terminal contact) and brushes are serviced as an assembly. Clean all old sealer from around plate and housing.

6. Remove the brush holder screw. On the shunt type, unsolder the solenoid winding from the brush terminal.

7. Remove the $^{11}/_{32}$ in. nut, washer and insulator from solenoid terminal. Remove the brush holder plate with brushes as an assembly and the gear housing ground screw.

8. The solenoid assembly can be removed from the well. Remove the nut, washer and seal from starter battery terminal and the terminal from the plate.

9. Remove the solenoid contact and plunger from solenoid and the coil sleeve. Remove the solenoid return spring, coil retaining washer, retainer and the dust cover from the gar housing.

10. Release the snapring that locates the driven gear on pinion shaft. Release the front retaining ring.

11. Push the pinion shaft rearward and remove the snapring,

thrust washers, clutch/pinion and the 2 nylon shift fork actuators.

12. Remove the driven gear and friction washer. Pull the shifting fork forward and remove the moving core.

13. Remove the fork retaining pin and shifting fork assembly. The gear housing with bushings is serviced as an assembly.

14. Brushes that are worn to ½ the length of new brushes or oil soaked, should be replaced.

15. When resoldering the shunt field and solenoid lead, make a strong low resistance connection using a high temperature solder and resin flux; do not use acid or acid core solder. Be careful not to break the shunt field wire units when removing and installing the brushes.

16. Do not immerse the starter clutch unit in a cleaning solvent. The outside of the clutch and pinion must be cleaned with a cloth so the lubricant is not washed from inside the clutch.

17. Rotate the pinion. The pinion gear should rotate smoothly

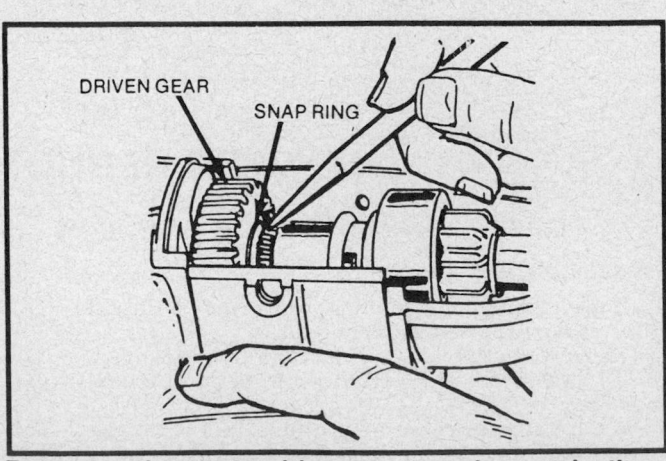

Removing the starter drive gear snapring – reduction gear starter motor – Chrysler

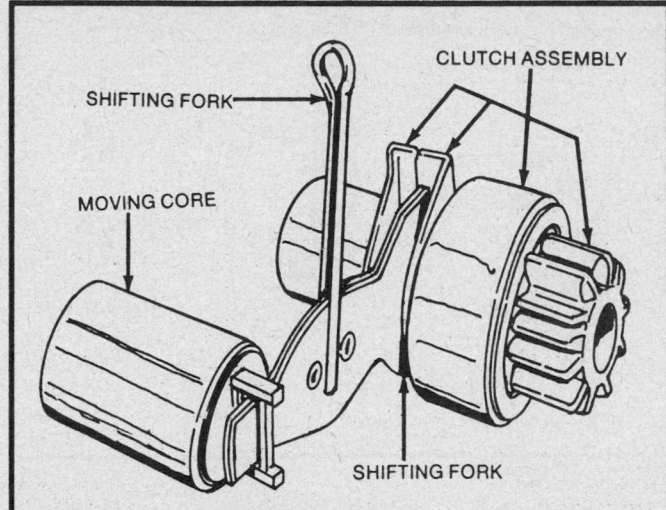

Shift fork and clutch arrangement—reduction gear starter motor—Chrysler

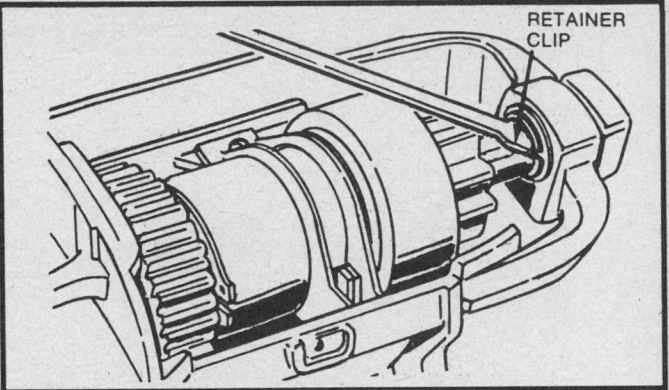

Removing the starter drive gear retaining ring—reduction gear starter motor—Chrysler

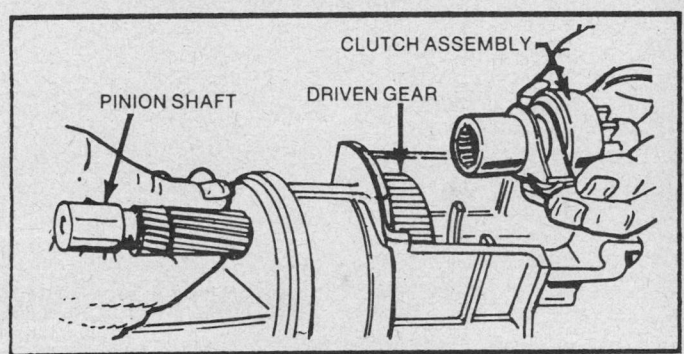

Removing the clutch assembly—reduction gear starter motor—Chrysler

and in 1 direction only. If the starter clutch unit does not function properly or the pinion is worn, chipped or burred, replace the starter clutch unit.

18. Inspect the commutator and the surface contacted by the brushes when the starter is assembled, for flat spots, out of roundness or excessive wear.

19. Reface the commutator, if necessary, removing only a sufficient amount of metal to provide a smooth even surface.

20. Using light pressure scrape the commutator grooves with a broken hacksaw blade; do not remove any metal or expand the grooves.

21. To assemble, lubricate the bushings and reverse the disassembly procedures. The shifter fork consists of 2 spring steel plates held together by 2 rivets. Before assembling the starter check the plates for side movement. After lubricating between the plates with a small amount of SAE 10 engine oil they should have about $\frac{1}{16}$ in. side movement to insure proper pinion gear engagement.

NIPPONDENSO/MITSUBISHI REDUCTION GEAR STARTER

OVERHAUL

Disassembly and Assembly

1. Position the assembly in a soft jawed vise. Remove the rubber boot from the field coil terminal, the nut from the field coil terminal stud and the field coil terminal from the stud.

2. Remove the through bolts and the splash shield. Remove the end shield screws from the brush plate and the end shield.

3. Slide the brushes from the holders. Pry the retaining springs back for access and remove the brush plate.

4. Slide the armature from the starter housing. Remove the starter housing from the gear housing and the solenoid terminal cover.

5. Remove the solenoid terminal nut/washer, the battery terminal nut/washer and the solenoid terminal assembly from the terminal posts.

6. Remove the solenoid terminal and the battery terminal from the insulator.

7. Remove the solenoid cover screws, the solenoid cover, the seal, the solenoid plunger from the housing and the plunger spring.

8. Remove the gear housing-to-solenoid screws and separate the gear housing from the solenoid housing.

9. Remove the reduction gear and clutch assembly from the gear housing.

10. Remove the reduction gear, pinion gear, retainer and roller assembly from the gear housing.

11. Inspect and clean all parts, as required. Repair or replace defective parts as required. Brushes that are worn less than ½ the length of new brushes or oil soaked should be replaced.

12. To assemble, reverse the disassembly procedures.

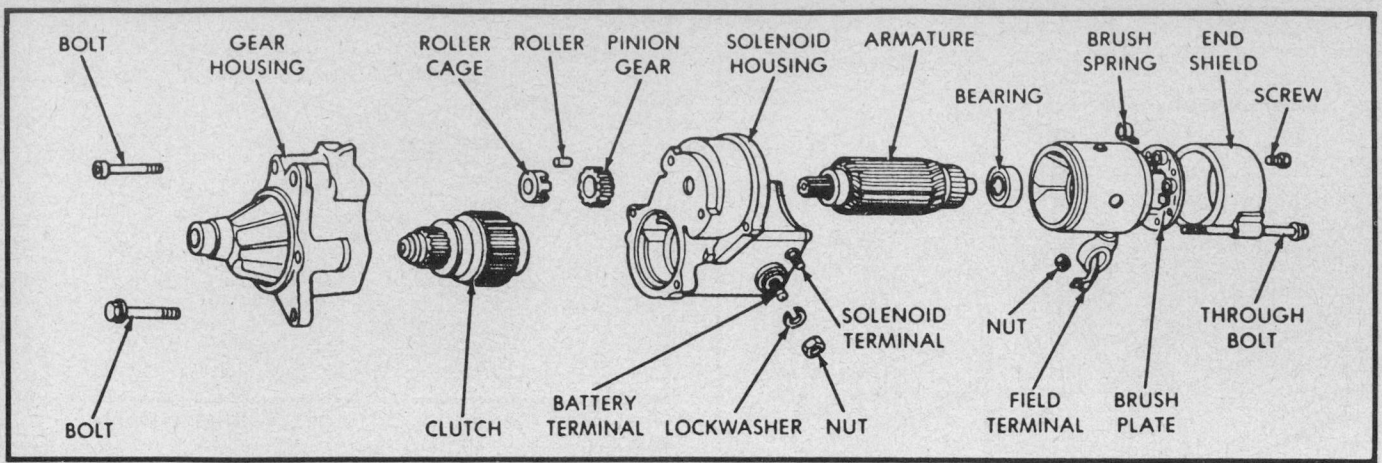

Exploded view of the Nippondenso reduction gear starter motor — Chrysler

BOSCH REDUCTION STARTER

OVERHAUL

Disassembly and Assembly

1. Position the assembly in a soft jawed vise. Remove the field terminal nut, the terminal and the washer.

2. Remove the solenoid-to-starter screws. Work the solenoid from the shift fork and remove the solenoid from the starter.

3. Remove the starter end shield bushing cap screws, the starter end shield bushing cap, the end shield bushing and C-washer.

4. Remove the starter end shield bushing washer and seal.

5. Remove the starter through bolts, the starter end shield and the brush plate.

6. Slide the field frame from the starter and over the arma-ture. Remove the armature assembly from the drive end housing.

7. Remove the rubber seal from the drive end housing. Remove the starter drive gear train.

8. Remove the dust plate. Press the stop collar from the snapring. Using snapring pliers, loosen the snapring.

9. Remove the output shaft snapring, the clutch stopring collar and the clutch assembly from the starter.

10. Remove the clutch shift lever bushing, the clutch shift lever and the C-clip retainer.

11. Remove the retaining washer, the sun and the planetary gears from the annulus gear.

12. To assemble, lubricate the necessary parts and reverse the disassembly procedures. Replace all defective components as required.

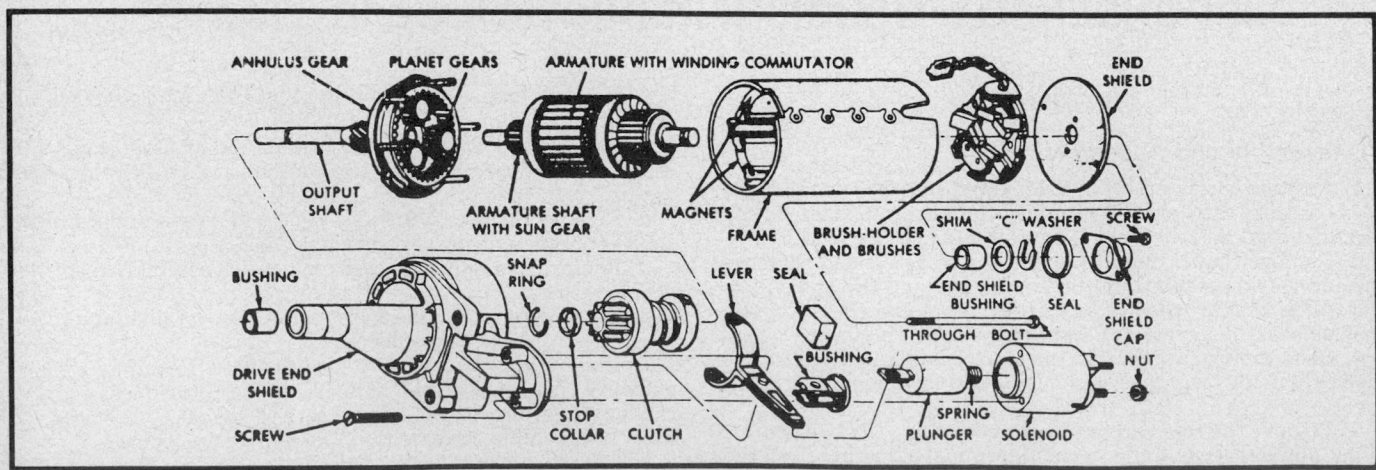

Exploded view of the Bosch reduction gear starter — Chrysler

FORD POSITIVE ENGAGEMENT STARTER

OVERHAUL

Disassembly and Assembly

1. Remove the starter from the vehicle. Position the unit in a soft jawed vise.

2. Remove the cover screw, the cover, through bolts, starter drive end housing and the starter drive plunger lever return spring.

3. Remove the pivot pin from the starter gear plunger lever, the lever and the armature. Remove the stopring retainer and the thrust washer from the armature shaft.

4. Remove the stopring from the groove in the armature

shaft and discard it. Remove the starter drive gear assembly, the brush end plate and insulator assembly.

5. Remove the brushes from the plastic brush holder and lift out the brush holder. Note the location of the holder in relation to the end terminal.

6. Remove the ground brush screws. Remove the sleeve and the retainer by bending up the edge of the sleeve which is inserted in the rectangular hole of the frame.

7. Using the tool 10044–A or equivalent, remove the pole retaining screws. An arbor press may have to be used in conjunction with the special tool.

8. Cut the positive brush leads from the coil fields as close to the field connection as possible.

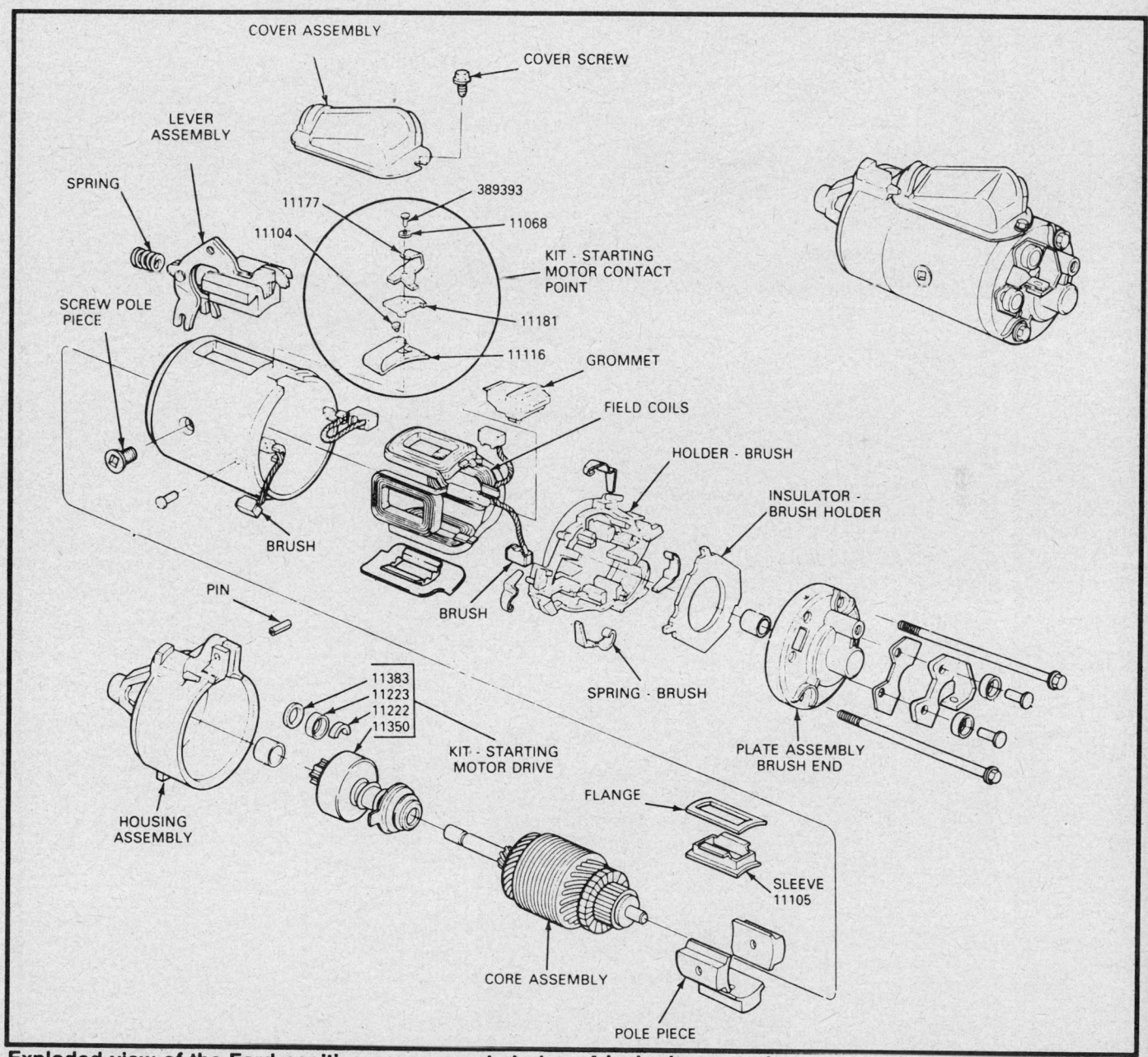

Exploded view of the Ford positive engagement starter — 4 inch plunger pole

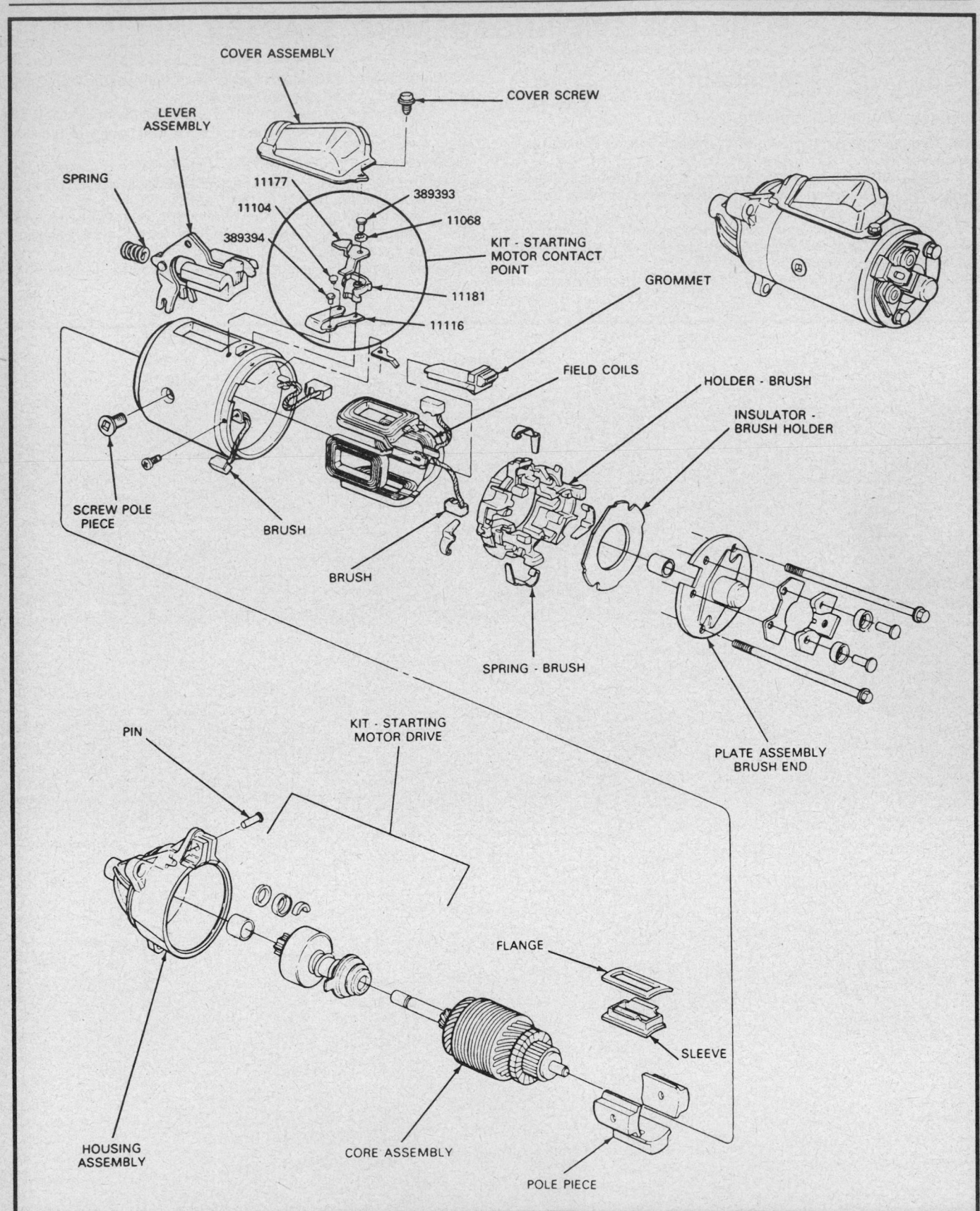

COVER ASSEMBLY

COVER SCREW

LEVER ASSEMBLY

SPRING

11177

11104

389394

389393

11068

11181

11116

KIT - STARTING MOTOR CONTACT POINT

GROMMET

FIELD COILS

HOLDER - BRUSH

INSULATOR - BRUSH HOLDER

SCREW POLE PIECE

BRUSH

BRUSH

SPRING - BRUSH

PLATE ASSEMBLY BRUSH END

PIN

KIT - STARTING MOTOR DRIVE

FLANGE

SLEEVE

HOUSING ASSEMBLY

CORE ASSEMBLY

POLE PIECE

Exploded view of the Ford positive engagement starter — 4½ inch plunger pole

9. Check the commutator for runout. If the commutator is rough, has flat spots or is more than 0.005 in. out of round, reface it.

10. Inspect the armature shaft and the bearings for scoring and excessive wear; replace it, if necessary. Inspect the starter drive; if the gear teeth are pitted, broken or excessively worn, replace the starter drive.

11. Lubricate the necessary parts and reverse the disassembly procedures.

12. Solder the field coil-to-starter switch terminal posts. Check for continuity and grounds in the assembled coils.

13. Position the ground brushes-to-starter frame and rivet securely.

14. Install the starter motor drive gear assembly onto the armature shaft. Install a new stopring, a new stopring retainer and thrust washer.

15. Install the armature.

16. Position the drive gear plunger lever to the frame and starter drive assembly. Fill the end housing bearing bore a ¼ full or grease. Position the drive end housing onto the frame and make sure the return spring engages the lever tang. Install the pivot pin.

17. Install the brush holder, the brushes and the brush springs; make sure the brushes are positioned properly to avoid grounding.

18. Install the brush end plate; be sure the end plate insulator is positioned correctly on the end plate.

19. Install the through bolts and torque to 55–80 inch lbs. (6–9 Nm).

20. Install the starter drive plunger ever cover and tighten the screw.

21. Check the starter no-load current draw; it should be 80 amps.

DELCO 42MT STARTER

OVERHAUL

Disassembly and Assembly

1. Remove the starter from the vehicle. Position the unit in a soft jawed vise.

2. Remove the field coil connector screw and the solenoid-to-starter screws. Rotate the solenoid 90 degrees and remove it along with the plunger return spring.

3. Remove the starter through bolts, the commutator end frame and washer.

4. Remove the field frame assembly from the drive gear housing.

5. If equipped, remove the center bearing screws. Remove the drive gear housing from the armature shaft.

6. To remove the overrunning clutch from the armature shaft, perform the following procedures:

   a. Remove the washer or collar from the armature shaft.

   b. Using a ⅝ in. deep socket, slide it over the shaft and against the retainer. Using the socket as a driving tool, tap it with a hammer to move the retainer of the snapring.

   c. Remove the snapring from the groove in the shaft; if the snapring is distorted, replace it.

d. Remove the retainer and the clutch assembly from the armature shaft.

7. If required, the shaft lever and the plunger can be disassembled by removing the roll pin.

8. To replace the starter brushes, remove the brush holder pivot pin which positions the insulated and the ground brushes. Remove the brush spring.

9. Inspect armature commutator, shaft and bushings, overrunning clutch pinion, brushes and springs for discoloration, damage or wear; replace the damaged parts.

10. Check fit of armature shaft in bushing in drive housing. The shaft should fit snugly in the bushing; if it is worn, replace it.

11. Inspect armature commutator. If commutator is rough, it should be refinished on a lathe. Do not undercut or turn to less than 1.650 in. O.D. Inspect the points where the armature conductors join the commutator bars to make sure they have a good connection. A burned commutator bar is usually evidence of a poor connection.

12. Using a growler and holding hacksaw blade over armature core while armature is rotated, inspect the armature for short circuits. If saw blade vibrates, armature is shorted.

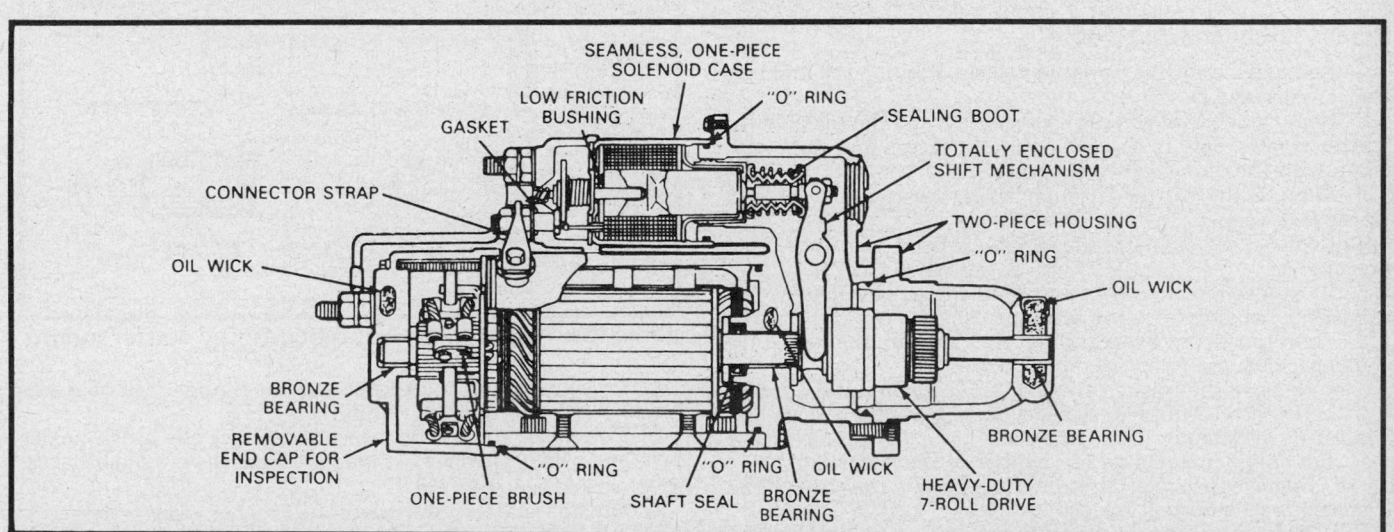

Cross-sectional view of the Delco 42 MT starter – Ford diesel engine

13. Using a test lamp place a lead on the shunt coil terminal and connect the other lead to a ground brush. The test should be made using both ground brushes to insure continuity through the brushes and leads. If the lamp fails to light, the field coil is open and will require replacement.

14. Using a test lamp place a lead on the series coil terminal and the other on the insulated brush. If the lamp fails to light the series coil is open and will require repair or replacement. The test should be made from each insulated brush to check brush and lead continuity.

15. If equipped with a shunt coil separate the series and shunt coil strap terminals during the test. Do not allow the strap terminals to touch case or other ground. Using a test lamp place a lead on the grounded brush holder and the other lead on either insulated brush. If the lamp lights a grounded series coil is indicated and must be repaired or replaced.

NOTE: If the solenoid has not been removed from the starter, the connector strap terminals must be removed before making the following tests. Complete the tests as fast as possible in order to prevent overheating the solenoid.

16. To check the starter winding, connect an ammeter in series with 12 volt battery and the switch terminal on the solenoid. Connect a voltmeter to the switch terminal and to ground. Connect a carbon pile across battery. Adjust the voltage to 10 volts and note the ammeter reading; it should be 14.5–16.5 amperes.

17. To check both windings, connect as for previous test and ground the solenoid motor terminal. Adjust the voltage to 10V and note the ammeter reading; it should be 41–47 amperes.

18. Current draw readings over specifications indicate shorted turns on a ground in the windings of the solenoid; the solenoid should be replaced. Current draw readings under specifications indicate excessive resistance. No reading indicates an open circuit. Check the connections and replace the solenoid (if necessary). Current readings will decrease as the windings heat up.

19. To assemble, reverse the disassembly procedures. Be sure to replace or repair all defective components as required.

NOTE: When the starter has been disassembled or the solenoid replaced, it is necessary to check the pinion clearance. Pinion clearance must be checked in order to prevent the buttons on the shift lever yoke from rubbing on the clutch collar during engine cranking.

20. To check the pinion clearance, perform the following procedures:

a. Disconnect the motor field coil connector from the solenoid motor terminal and insulate the terminal.

b. Connect the positive 12 volt battery lead to the solenoid switch terminal and the negative lead to the starter frame.

c. Touch a jumper lead momentarily from the solenoid motor terminal to the starter frame; this will shift the pinion into cranking position and remain there until the battery is disconnected.

d. Using a feeler gauge, push the pinion back as far as possible and check the clearance; the clearance should be 0.010–0.140 in.

e. Pinion clearance adjustment is not provided on the starter motor. If the clearance does not fall within limits check for improper installation and replace all worn parts.

GENERAL MOTORS DELCO 5MT, 10MT, 27MT AND 28MT STARTERS

NOTE: In 1989, the identification for the 5MT starter was converted to the SD200/SD250 starters and the 10MT was converted to the SD300 starter. The 28MT is used with the diesel engine.

OVERHAUL

Disassembly and Assembly

1. Remove the starter from the vehicle. Position the unit in a soft jawed vise.

2. Remove the field coil connector screw and the solenoid-to-starter screws. Rotate the solenoid 90 degrees and remove it along with the plunger return spring.

3. Remove the starter through bolts, the commutator end frame and washer.

4. Remove the field frame assembly from the drive gear housing.

5. If equipped, remove the center bearing screws. Remove the drive gear housing from the armature shaft.

6. To remove the overrunning clutch from the armature shaft, perform the following procedures:

a. Remove the washer or collar from the armature shaft.

b. Using a ⅝ in. deep socket, slide it over the shaft and against the retainer. Using the socket as a driving tool, tap it with a hammer to move the retainer of the snapring.

c. Remove the snapring from the groove in the shaft; if the snapring is distorted, replace it.

d. Remove the retainer and the clutch assembly from the armature shaft.

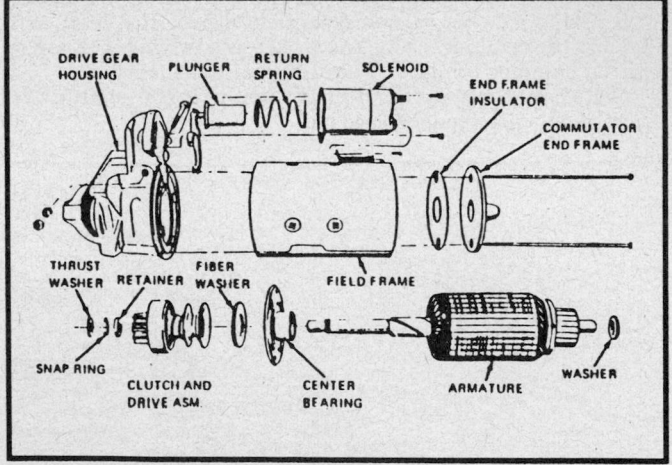

Exploded view of a typical Delco-Remy starter motor

7. If required, the shaft lever and the plunger can be disassembled by removing the roll pin.

8. To replace the starter brushes, remove the brush holder pivot pin which positions the insulated and the ground brushes. Remove the brush spring.

9. On 5MT starters, to replace the brushes remove the screw from the brush holder and separate the brushes from the holder.

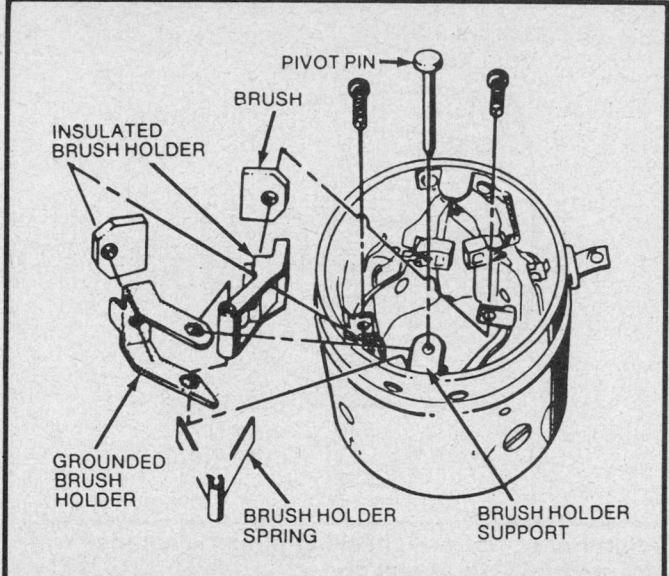

Delco-Remy starter brush replacement—all except 5MT starter

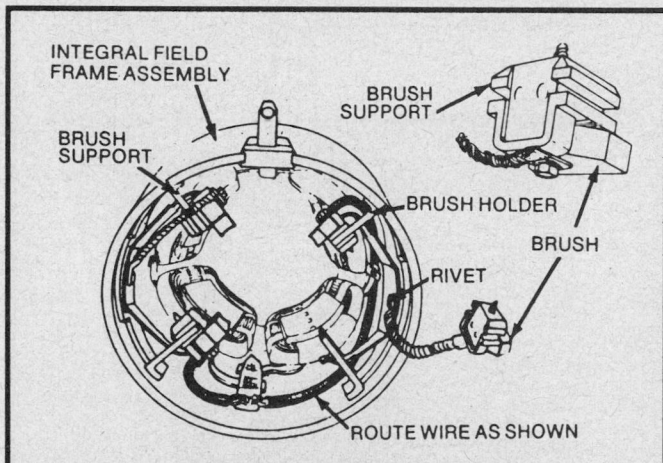

Delco-Remy 5MT starter-brush replacement

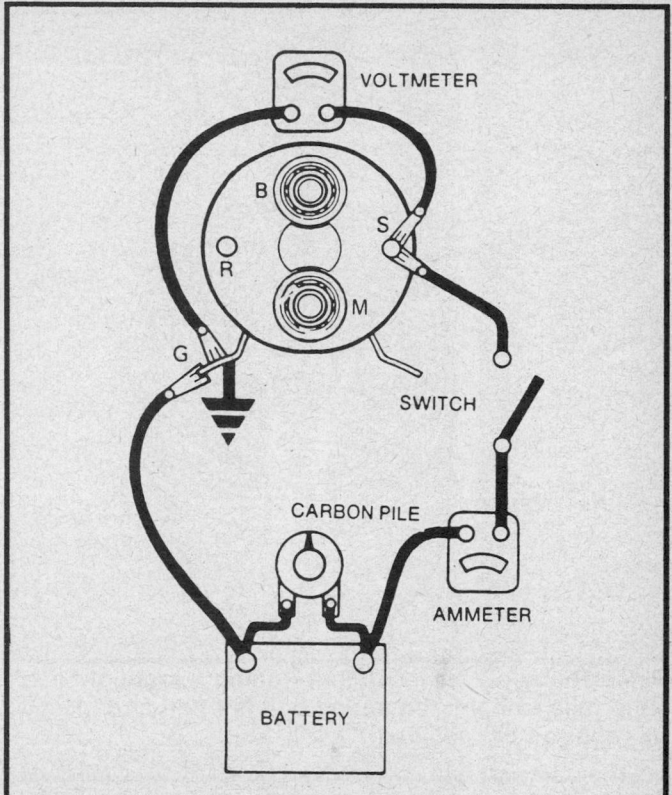

Delco-Remy starter—solenoid winding test—if solenoid is on vehicle, the connector strap must be removed before making test

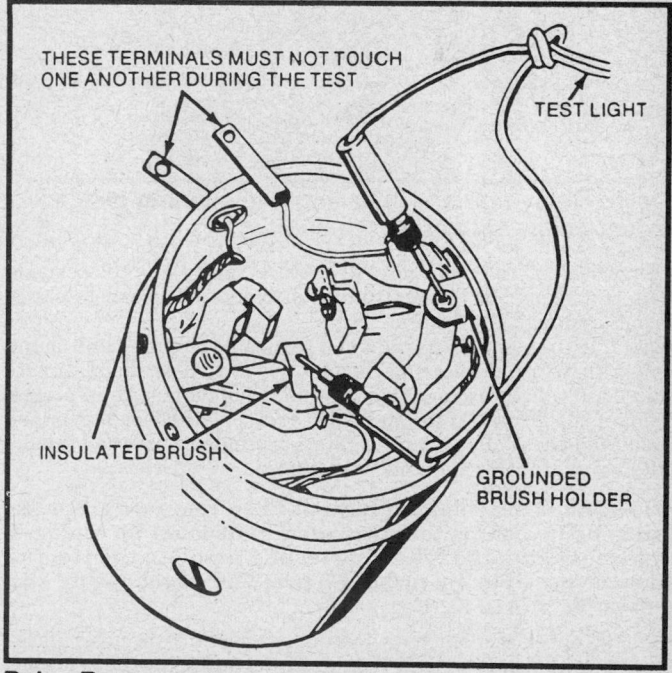

Delco-Remy starter—shunt coil test—using a test light do not let strap terminals touch case or other ground

10. Inspect armature commutator, shaft and bushings, overrunning clutch pinion, brushes and springs for discoloration, damage or wear; replace the damaged parts.

11. Check fit of armature shaft in bushing in drive housing. The shaft should fit snugly in the bushing; if it is worn, replace it.

12. Inspect armature commutator. If commutator is rough, it should be refinished on a lathe. Do not undercut or turn to less than 1.650 in. O.D. Inspect the points where the armature conductors join the commutator bars to make sure they have a good connection. A burned commutator bar is usually evidence of a poor connection.

13. Using a growler and holding hacksaw blade over armature core while armature is rotated, inspect the armature for short circuits. If saw blade vibrates, armature is shorted.

14. Using a test lamp place a lead on the shunt coil terminal and connect the other lead to a ground brush. The test should be made using both ground brushes to insure continuity through the brushes and leads. If the lamp fails to light, the field coil is open and will require replacement.

15. Using a test lamp place a lead on the series coil terminal and the other on the insulated brush. If the lamp fails to light

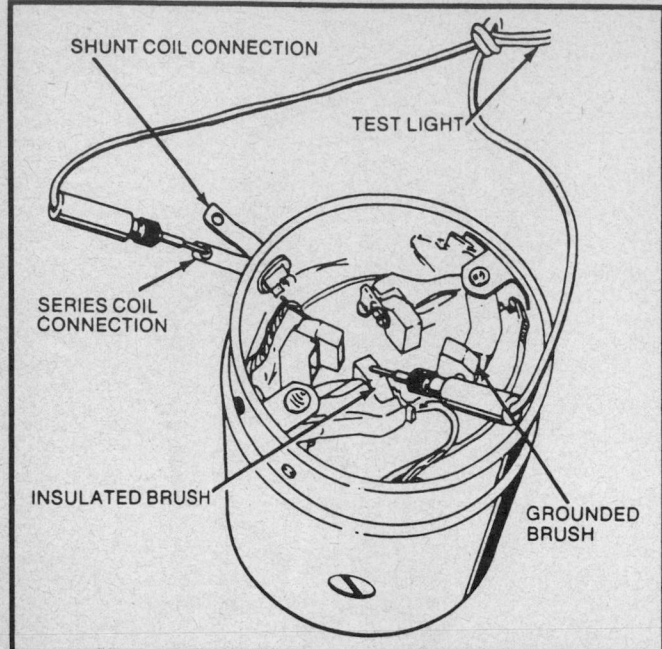

Delco-Remy starter—coil test—using a test light if lamp fails to light, the series coil is open and must be repaired or replaced

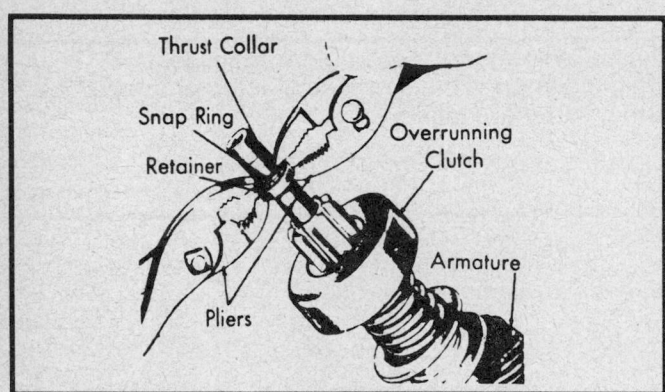

Delco-Remy starter—installing overrunning clutch thrust collar onto armature shaft

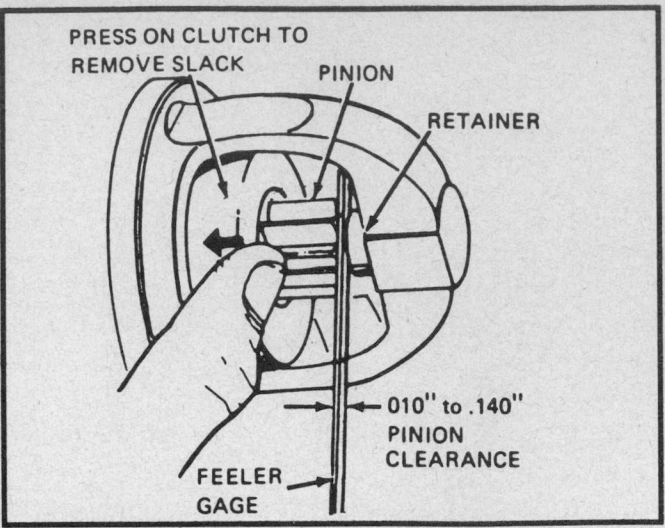

Delco-Remy starter—checking pinion clearance with solenoid only, in operation

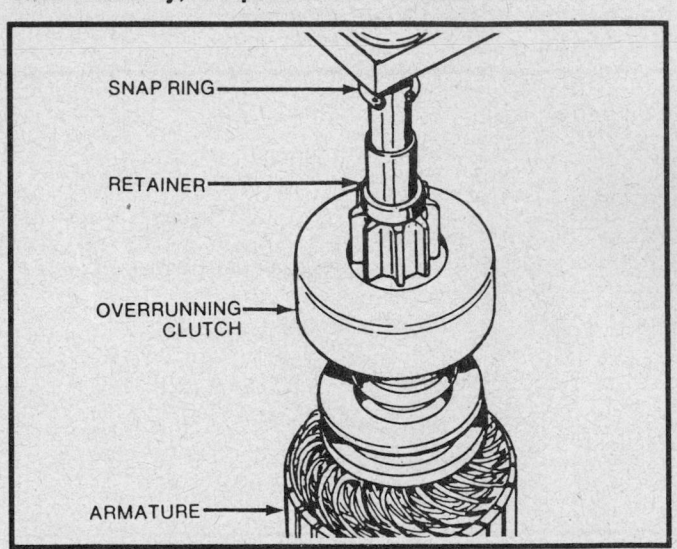

Delco-Remy starter—installing overrunning clutch thrust collar snapring onto armature shaft

the series coil is open and will require repair or replacement. The test should be made from each insulated brush to check brush and lead continuity.

16. If equipped with a shunt coil separate the series and shunt coil strap terminals during the test. Do not allow the strap terminals to touch case or other ground. Using a test lamp place a lead on the grounded brush holder and the other lead on either insulated brush. If the lamp lights a grounded series coil is indicated and must be repaired or replaced.

NOTE: If the solenoid has not been removed from the starter, the connector strap terminals must be removed before making the following tests. Complete the tests as fast as possible in order to prevent overheating the solenoid.

17. To check the starter winding, connect an ammeter in series with 12V battery and the switch terminal on the solenoid. Connect a voltmeter to the switch terminal and to ground. Connect a carbon pile across battery. Adjust the voltage to 10V and note the ammeter reading; it should be 14.5–16.5 amperes.

18. To check both windings, connect as for previous test and ground the solenoid motor terminal. Adjust the voltage to 10V and note the ammeter reading; it should be 41–47 amperes.

19. Current draw readings over specifications indicate shorted turns on a ground in the windings of the solenoid; the solenoid should be replaced. Current draw readings under specifications indicate excessive resistance. No reading indicates an open circuit. Check the connections and replace the solenoid (if necessary). Current readings will decrease as the windings heat up.

20. To assemble, reverse the disassembly procedures. Be sure to replace or repair all defective components as required.

NOTE: When the starter has been disassembled or the solenoid replaced, it is necessary to check the pinion clearance. Pinion clearance must be checked in order to prevent the buttons on the shift lever yoke from rubbing on the clutch collar during engine cranking.

21. To check the pinion clearance, perform the following procedures:
    a. Disconnect the motor field coil connector from the solenoid motor terminal and insulate the terminal.

b. Connect the positive 12 volt battery lead to the solenoid switch terminal and the negative lead to the starter frame.

c. Touch a jumper lead momentarily from the solenoid motor terminal to the starter frame; this will shift the pinion into cranking position and remain there until the battery is disconnected.

d. Using a feeler gauge, push the pinion back as far as possible and check the clearance; the clearance should be 0.010–0.140 in.

e. Pinion clearance adjustment is not provided on the starter motor. If the clearance does not fall within limits check for improper installation and replace all worn parts.

GENERAL MOTORS DELCO PERMANENT MAGNET GEAR REDUCTION (PMGR) STARTER

OVERHAUL

Disassembly and Assembly

1. Remove the starter from the vehicle. Position the unit in a soft jawed vise.

2. Remove the field coil screw, the field frame through bolts and separate the field frame assembly from the drive gear assembly. Separate the armature and the commutator end frame from the field frame.

3. Remove the solenoid screws and the solenoid from the drive housing.

4. Remove the retaining ring, shift lever shaft and housing through bolts. Separate the drive assembly, drive housing and gear assembly.

5. To remove the overrunning clutch from the armature shaft, perform the following procedures:

a. Remove the washer or collar from the armature shaft.

b. Using a ⅝ in. deep socket, slide it over the shaft and against the retainer. Use the socket as a driving tool, tap the socket with a hammer to move the retainer off of the snapring.

c. Remove the snapring from the groove in the shaft; if the snapring is distorted, replace it.

d. Remove the retainer and the clutch assembly from the armature shaft.

6. To replace the starter brushes, remove the brush holder pivot pin which positions the insulated and the ground brushes. Remove the brush spring.

7. Inspect armature commutator, shaft and bushings, overrunning clutch pinion, brushes and springs for discoloration, damage or wear; replace the damaged parts (if necessary). Check the armature shaft fit in drive housing bushing; the shaft should fit snugly in the bushing. If the bushing is worn, it should be replaced.

8. Inspect armature commutator. If commutator is rough, it should be refinished on a lathe; do not undercut or turn to less than 1.650 in. O.D. Inspect the points where the armature conductors join the commutator bars to make sure they have a good connection. A burned commutator is usually evidence of a poor connection.

9. Using a growler and holding hacksaw blade over armature core while armature is rotated, check the armature for short circuits; if the saw blade vibrates, the armature is shorted.

10. Using a test lamp, place a lead on the shunt coil terminal and the other lead to a ground brush. The test should be made from both ground brushes to insure continuity through both brushes and leads. If the lamp fails to light, the field coil is open and will require replacement.

11. Using a test lamp, place a lead on the series coil terminal and the other lead on the insulated brush. If the lamp fails to light, the series coil is open and will require repair or replacement. The test should be made from each insulated brush to check brush and lead continuity.

12. If equipped with a shunt coil, separate the series and shunt coil strap terminals during this test; do not allow the strap terminals to touch the case or other ground. Using a test lamp,

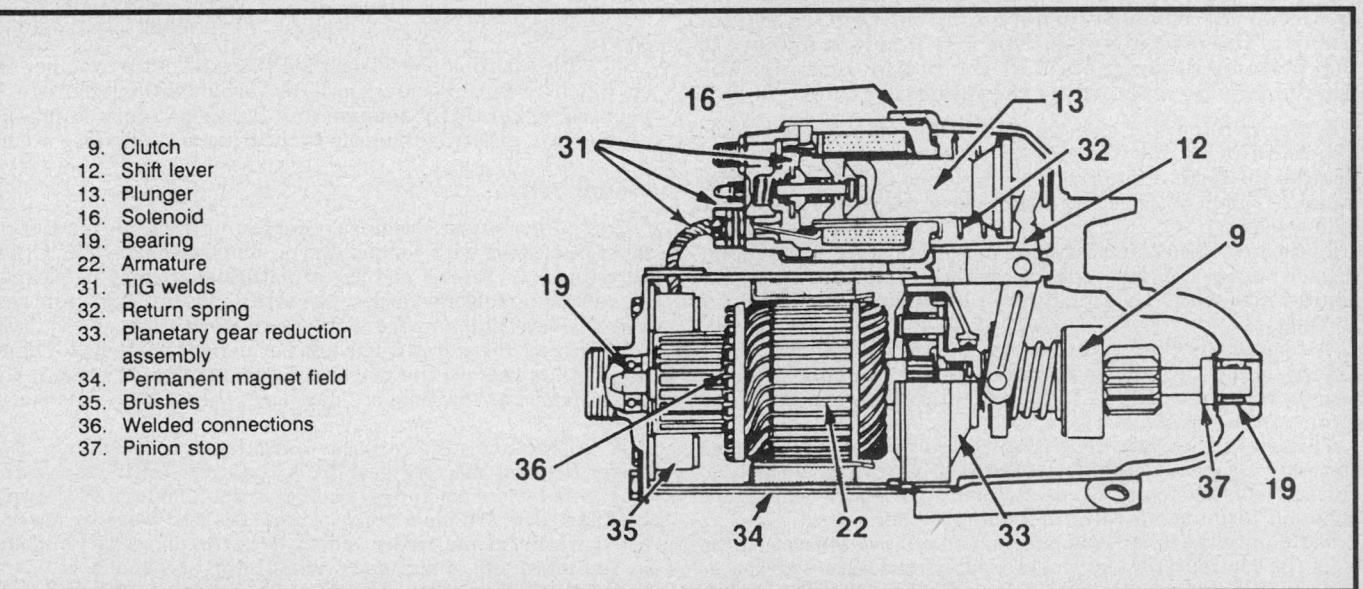

9. Clutch
12. Shift lever
13. Plunger
16. Solenoid
19. Bearing
22. Armature
31. TIG welds
32. Return spring
33. Planetary gear reduction assembly
34. Permanent magnet field
35. Brushes
36. Welded connections
37. Pinion stop

Cross-sectional view of the Permanent Magnet Gear Reduction (PMGR) starter

place a lead on the grounded brush holder and the other lead on either insulated brush. If the lamp lights, a grounded series coil is indicated and must be repaired or replaced.

NOTE: If the solenoid has not been removed from the starter, the connector strap terminals must be removed before making the following tests. Complete the tests as fast as possible in order to prevent overheating the solenoid.

13. To check the starter winding, connect an ammeter in series with a 12 volt battery, the switch terminal and to ground. Connect a carbon pile across the battery. Adjust the voltage to 10 volts and note the ammeter reading; it should be 14.5–16.5 amperes.

14. To check both windings, connect as for previous test. Ground the solenoid motor terminal, adjust the voltage to 10 volts and note the ammeter reading; it should be 41–47 amperes.

15. Current draw readings above specifications indicate shorted turns or a ground in the windings of the solenoid; the solenoid should be replaced. Current draw readings under specifications indicate excessive resistance. No reading indicates an open circuit. Check the connections and replace solenoid (if necessary). Current readings will decrease as windings heat up.

16. The roller bearing in the drive housing and the roller bearings in the gear housing must be replaced (if they are dry); do not lubricate or reuse the bearings.

17. To replace the gear housing bearing, use a tube or solid cylinder that just fits inside the housing to push bearing toward the armature side. In the opposite direction, use the tube or cylinder to press bearing flush with housing.

18. To replace the gear housing driveshaft bearing, use a tube or collar that just fits inside the housing and press bearing out; press against the open end of bearing. To install a new bearing, press against the closed end, using a thin wall tube or collar that fits in space between bearing and housing. Do not press against the flat end of the bearing; this will bend the thin metal of the bearing. As required, replace the drive housing bearing.

19. To assemble, reverse the disassembly procedures. Be sure to replace or repair all defective components as required.

NOTE: When the starter has been disassembled or the solenoid replaced, it is necessary to check the pinion clearance. The pinion clearance must be checked in order to prevent the buttons on the shift lever yoke from rubbing on the clutch collar during engine cranking.

20. To check the pinion clearance, perform the following procedures:

a. Disconnect the motor field coil connector from the solenoid motor terminal and insulate the terminal.

b. Connect the positive (+) 12 volt battery lead to the solenoid switch terminal and the other to the starter frame.

c. Touch a jumper lead momentarily from the solenoid motor terminal to the starter frame; this will shift the pinion into cranking position and retain it until the battery is disconnected.

d. Using a feeler gauge, push the pinion back as far as possible, to take up any movement, and check the clearance; the clearance should be 0.010–0.140 in.

e. Means for adjusting pinion clearance is not provided on the starter motor. If the clearance does not fall within limits, check for improper installation and replace worn parts.

JEEP BOSCH REDUCTION GEAR STARTER

OVERHAUL

Disassembly

NOTE: When performing disassembly procedures, do not stike the thin wall stator frame with a hammer or any other instrument. Do not clamp the thin wall stator frame in the jaws of a vise. This may result in damage to the permanent magnets and the stator housing. The starter may be clamped by the mounting flange only.

1. Position the starter motor assembly in a suitable holding fixture, ensuring that it is secured by the mounting flange only. Remove the field terminal nut. Remove the field coil wire (Terminal 45) from the solenoid switch terminal post. Remove the field washer.

2. Remove the solenoid switch mounting screws. Disengage the solenoid switch from the fork lever and withdraw the solenoid switch with the armature and return spring from the housing.

3. Loosen the closure cap screws, but do not remove them.

4. Remove the stator frame-to-shield housing hexagon screws, the stator frame with the cover plate, armature and commutator end shield.

5. Remove the cover plate from the surface of the drive end bearing ring gear. Carefully press the armature with the commutator end shield out of the stator frame. At the same time, push out terminal 45 with the sealing rubber.

6. Remove the closure cap screws and remove the closure cap from the commutator end shield. Remove the retaining washer and shims from the armature shaft and remove the commutator end shield.

7. Using the proper tool, remove the brush plate from the armature shaft.

8. Remove the sealing rubber from the bearing pedestal. Remove the planetary gear system with the overruning clutch and fork assembly from the drive end shield. Mount both assemblies onto a suitable mounting base in the verticle position.

9. Using the proper tool, drive the stop ring down the input shaft.

10. With snaping pliers, separate the ends of the retainer far enough to allow removal from the driveshaft without damage. If necessary, carefully remove any burrs or nicks from the ddriveshaft, otherwise damage to the drive bushing may occur.

Inspection

1. The armature windings, overrunning clutch, and relay must be cleaned with compressed air and a clean dry rag. Other parts, such as screws and the armature shaft may be cleaned with cleaning solvent. Inspect all parts, seals, bushings, and gaskets for wear and damage. Replace all worn parts as required.

2. Inspect the stator frame and permanent magnets for damage. Do not remove the magnets from the stator frame. If the stator frame or magnets are damaged, then replace the stator frame.

3. Loosen and remove the retainer from the planetary gear drive. Remove the ring gear from the driveshaft. Inspect the ring gear for cracks and wear. Check the bushings in the ring gear for excessive play, out of roundness and wear by moving the driveshaft from side-to-side. Check the driveshaft bushing in the drive end shield and commutator end shield with the proper tool. Inspect the driveshaft in the ring gear for wear or damage. Replace the shaft and ring gear, if worn.

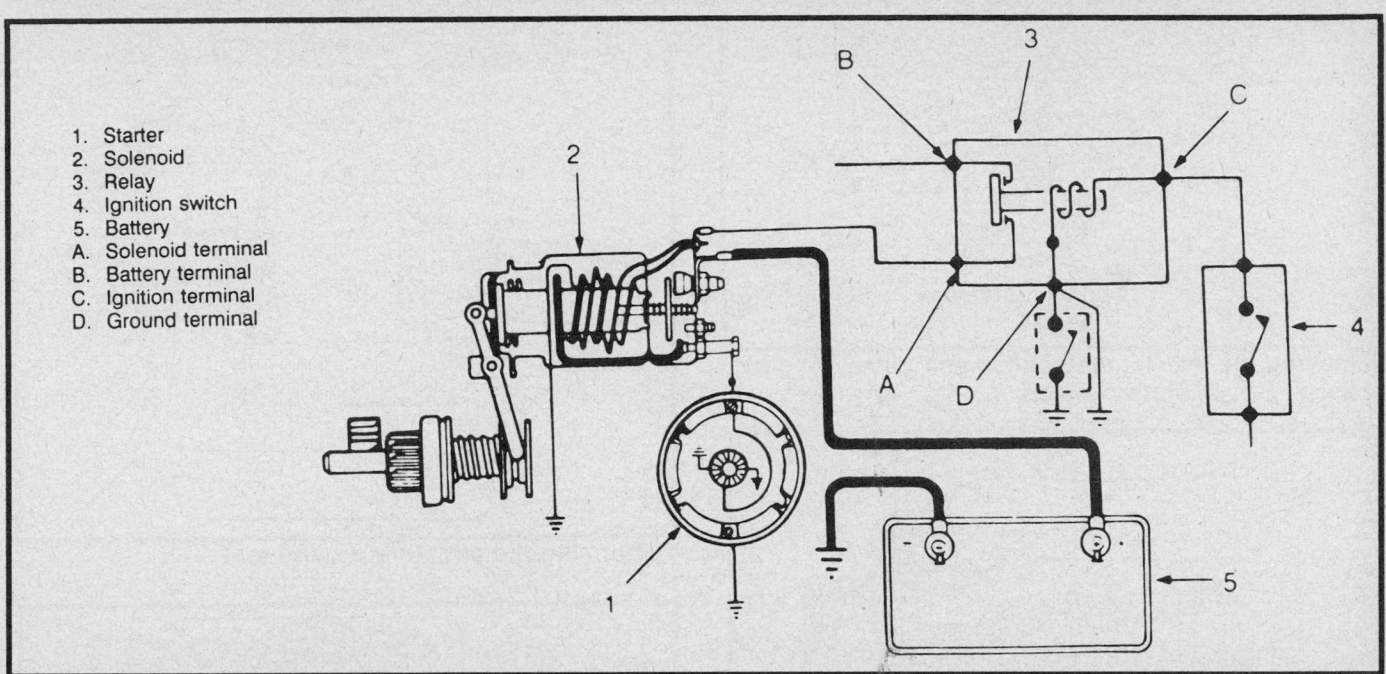

1. Starter
2. Solenoid
3. Relay
4. Ignition switch
5. Battery
A. Solenoid terminal
B. Battery terminal
C. Ignition terminal
D. Ground terminal

Schematic of the Bosch starter motor circuit—Jeep

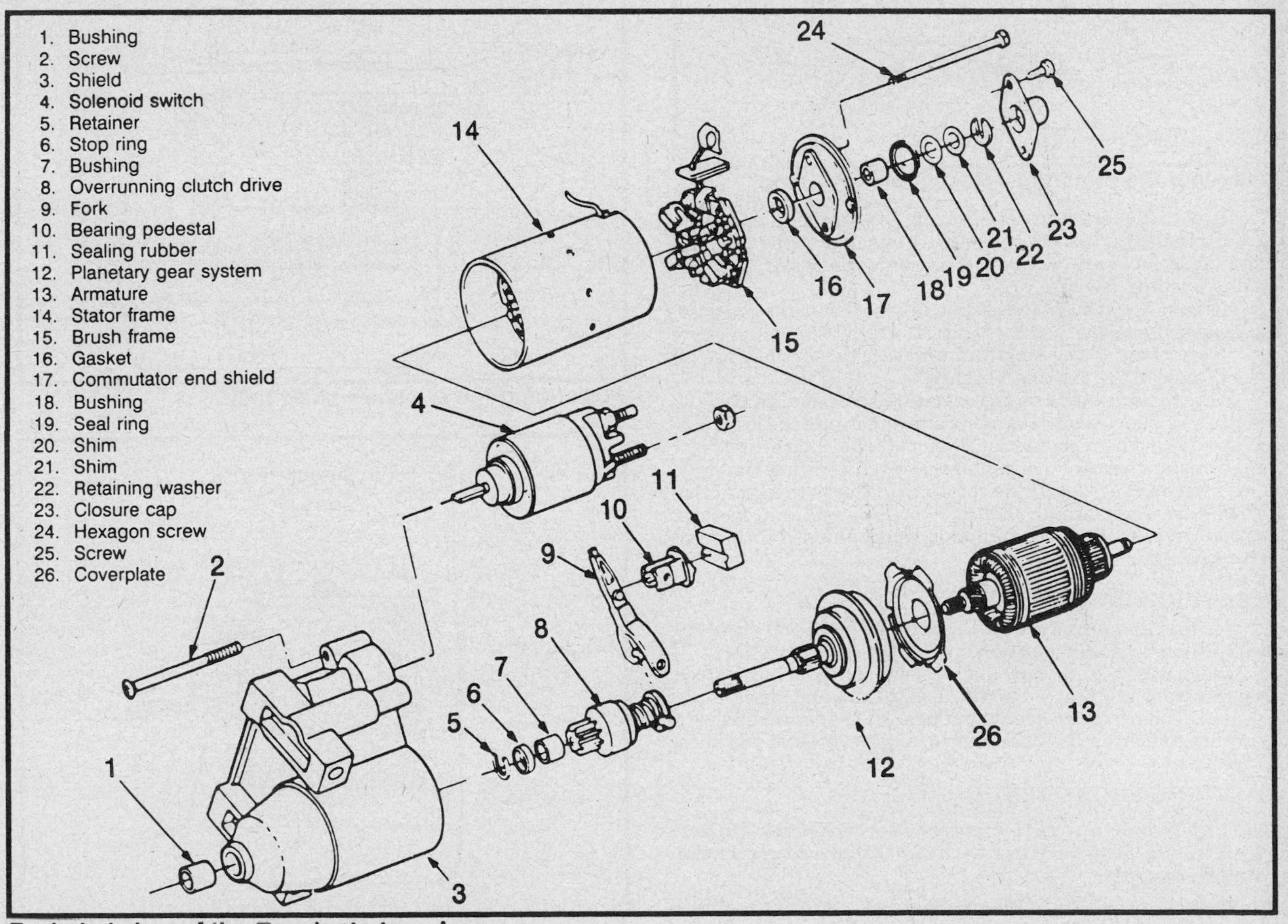

1. Bushing
2. Screw
3. Shield
4. Solenoid switch
5. Retainer
6. Stop ring
7. Bushing
8. Overrunning clutch drive
9. Fork
10. Bearing pedestal
11. Sealing rubber
12. Planetary gear system
13. Armature
14. Stator frame
15. Brush frame
16. Gasket
17. Commutator end shield
18. Bushing
19. Seal ring
20. Shim
21. Shim
22. Retaining washer
23. Closure cap
24. Hexagon screw
25. Screw
26. Coverplate

Exploded view of the Bosch starter—Jeep

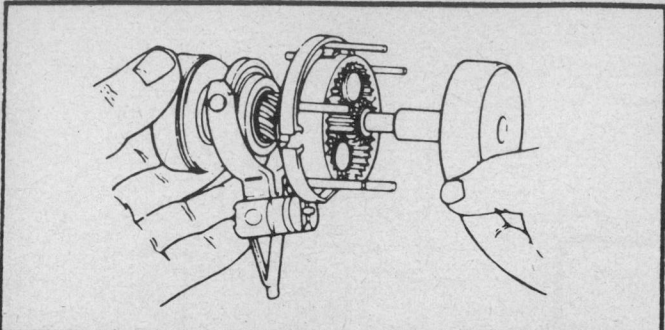

Removing the overrunning clutch and planetary gear system—Bosch starter—Jeep

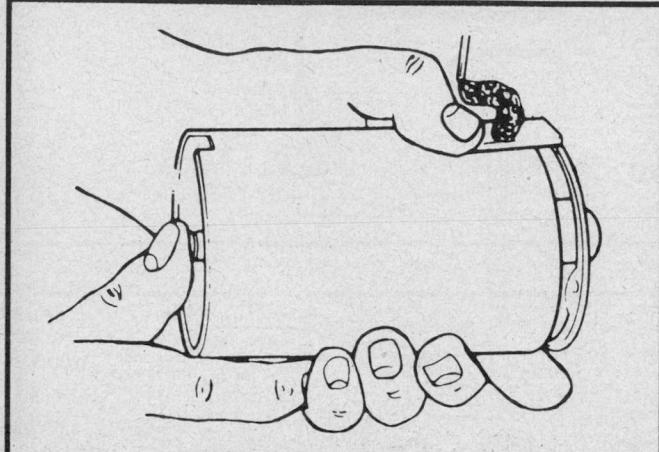

Removing the armature—Bosch starter—Jeep

4. Inspect the fork lever and bearing pedestal for damage, replace if necessary. Inspect the bearing bushing in the overrunning clutch for wear. Replace the overrunning clutch, if the bearing bushing is worn.

5. Remove and inspect the carbon brushes for excessive wear. The length of a new brush is $^{11}/_{16}$ in.. If the existing brushes are worn more than $\frac{1}{2}$ the length of a new brush or they are oil soaked, replace the existing brushes.

6. Place the drive unit on the armature shaft and support the armature by hand. Grasp the armature and rotate the drive pinion. The drive pinion should rotate smoothly in 1 direction only. Some resistance may be encountered when rotating the drive pinion; however, as long as the rotation is smooth then the drive unit is in good operating condition. If the clutch unit does not function properly or if the pinion is worn, chipped or burred, then replace the unit.

ARMATURE GROUND TEST

1. Position the armature in the growler jaws and turn the power switch-to-**TEST** position.

2. Touch a test probe-to-armature core (1). Touch the other test probe-to-commutator bar (2), 1 at a time and observe the test lamp. The test lamp should not light. If the test lamp lights on any bar, the armature has a short circuit-to-ground and must be replaced.

ARMATURE SHORT TEST

NOTE: Never operate the growler with the power switch in the Test position without the armature in the growler jaws.

1. Place the armature in the growler jaws and turn the power switch to the growler position.

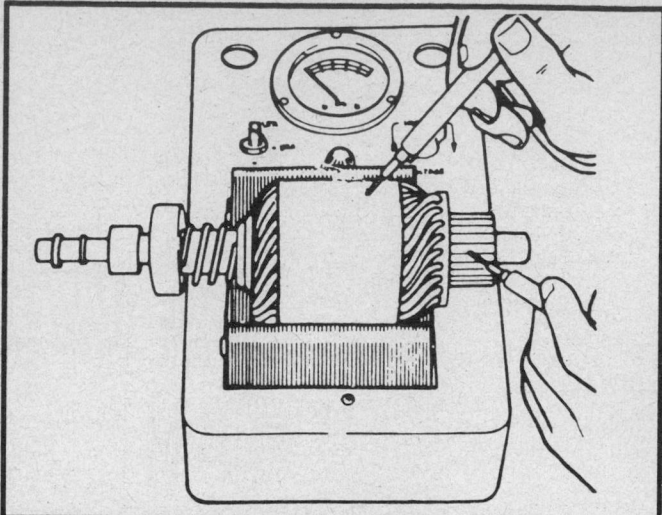

Performing the armature ground test

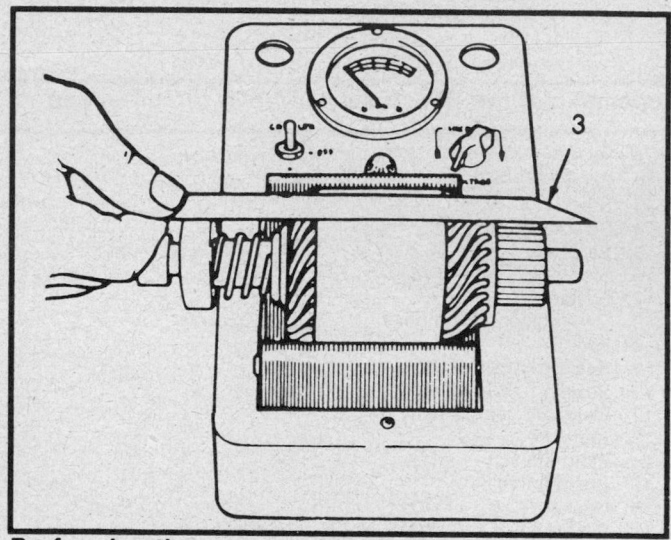

Performing the armature short test

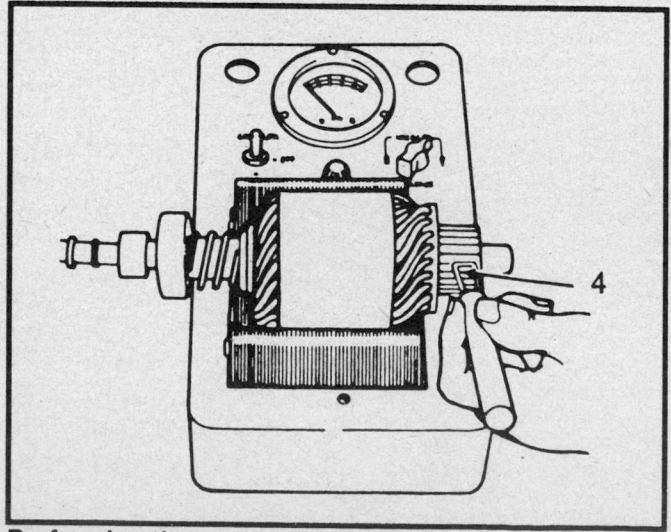

Performing the armature balance test

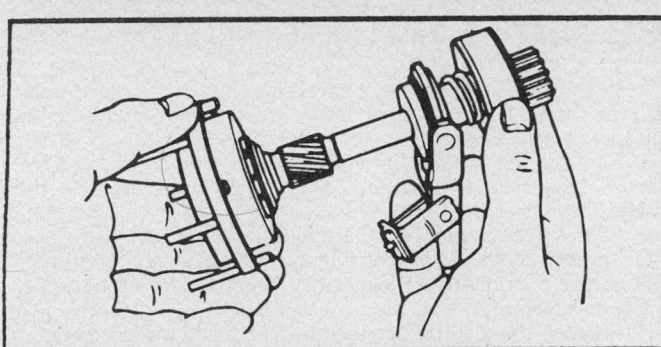

Assembling the overrunning clutch and planetary gear system

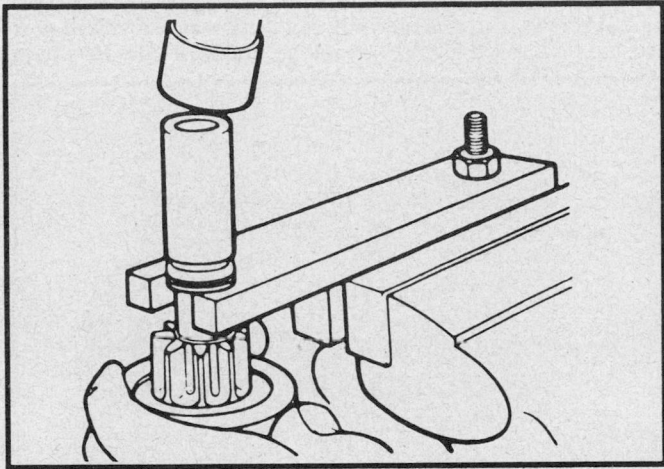

Seating the stop ring

2. Hold the steel blade parallel to and touching, the armature core (3). Slowly, rotate the armature 1 or more revolutions in the growler jaws. If the steel blade vibrates at any 1 area of the core, the windings have a short circuit and the armature must be replaced.

ARMATURE BALANCE TEST

1. Place the armature in the growler jaws and turn the power switch to the growler position.
2. Place the contact fingers of the meter test probe (4) across adjacent commutator bars at the side of the commutator.
3. Adjust the voltage control until the pointer indicates the highest voltage on the scale.
4. Test each commutator bar until all bars have been tested; 0 volts across any pair indicates a short circuit and requires the armature be replaced.

ARMATURE RUNOUT TEST

Check that the armature runout is within the range shown on the specifications chart. If the runout is not within tolerance, then replace the armature.

Assembly

1. Place a light film of 20W SAE oil onto the surface of the overrunning clutch pinion bearing surface.
2. Lightly grease the planetary gear spiral spline with Lubriplate grease.

3. Slide the overrunning clutch with the fork lever and bearing pedestal onto the driveshaft.
4. Slide the stop ring onto the armature shaft

NOTE: When installing the retainer, be careful not to scratch the armature shaft.

5. With snapring pliers, separate the ends of the retainer and carefully install onto the groove in the armature shaft.
6. Using the proper tool, seat the stop ring.
7. The planetary gear bearing is located forward of the planetary gears. Lubricate this bearing thoroughly, but lightly, with 20W SAE oil.
8. Insert the planetary gear train with the the pinion, overrunning clutch, fork lever, and bearing pedestal into the drive housing.
9. Install the rubber seal onto the pedestal bearing.
10. Position and install the cover plate on the surface of the ring gear, ensuring the recess in the cover plate mates with the lug machined in the surface of the ring gear.
11. Using the proper tool, position the brush plate onto the end of the commutator shaft. Slide the brush plate over the commutator, ensuring the brush holders are properly seated in the anchor point. After the are properly seated, remove the tool.
12. Place a light coat of 20W SAE oil onto the felt ring gasket and install the gasket on the commutator end of the armature shaft.
13. Place a light coat of Lithium-based lubricant onto the commutator end shield bushing and install the bushing onto the armature shaft.
14. Slide the commutator end shield onto the armature shaft.
15. Set the armature endplay by installing a shim and the retaining washer. After installing the shim, check the endplay with the appropriate feeler gauges. The endplay should be within the range of 0.002–0.016 in. Should additional shims be required, 3 sizes are available: 0.004 in., 0.047 in. and 0.055 in..
16. After setting the armature endplay, place a light coat of lubricant onto the retaining washer.
17. Position the seal ring against the commutator end shield and place the closure cap into installation position.
18. Install the closure cap screws far enough to hold the closure cap into place, but do not tighten at this time.
19. Support the stator frame by hand and slide the armature with the brush plate and commutator end shield carefully into the stator frame, ensuring that a sufficient gap is left to allow installation of the rubber seal.
20. Install the rubber seal onto terminal 45 and slide the rubber seal into the groove of the stator frame.
21. With moderate force, rotate the pinion gear until the armature spline meshes evenly with the planetary gears.

NOTE: When positioning the stator frame ensure the groove in the stator frame is aligned with and fits into the sealing rubber of the bearing pedestal.

22. Rotate the commutator end shield until the groove on the commutator end shield is aligned with the sealing rubber on the bearing pedestal.
23. When the proper alignment is achieved, install the stator frame-to-drive shield screws and torque to 2.0–2.6 ft. lbs.
24. Torque the closure cap screws to 1.0–1.5 ft. lbs..
25. Engage the solenoid switch armature with the fork lever and insert the armature return spring.
26. Install and tighten the solenoid switch housing screws.
27. Install the field washer and terminal wire (Terminal 45) onto the field terminal post. Install the field terminal nut.

MOTORCRAFT POSITIVE ENGAGEMENT STARTER MOTOR

The Motorcraft starting system, that is used with all Jeep 6 and 8 cylinder engines, consists of a lightweight positive engagement starter motor, a starter motor solenoid, an ignition/start switch, circuits protected by fusible links and the battery. Vehicles equipped with an automatic transmission also have a neutral safety switch to prevent operation of the starter if the selector lever is not in the **N** or **P** position. The Motorcraft starter motor has a moveable pole shoe and appropriate linkage to engage the drive mechanism. Inside the drive assembly, an overrunning clutch prevents the starter motor from being driven by the ring gear.

OVERHAUL

Disassembly

1. Remove the cover screw, cover, and through bolts.

2. Withdraw the pivot pin that retains the starter gear plunger lever. Remove the plunger lever, starter drive end housing and lever return spring.

3. Remove the stop ring retainer. Remove and discard the starter drive gear-to-armature shaft stop ring. Remove the starter drive gear assembly.

4. Remove the brush end plate and insulator assembly.

5. Remove the brushes from the plastic brush holder and lift out the brush holder. Note location of brush holder with respect to the end terminal.

6. Remove the ground brushes-to-frame screws or rivets.

7. Locate the field coil that operates the starter drive gear actuating lever. Bend the edges on the retaining sleeve of this field coil and remove the sleeve and retainer.

8. Position the starter frame in an arbor press and remove the coil screws. Cut the field coil connection at the switch post lead and remove the small diameter ground wire from the upper

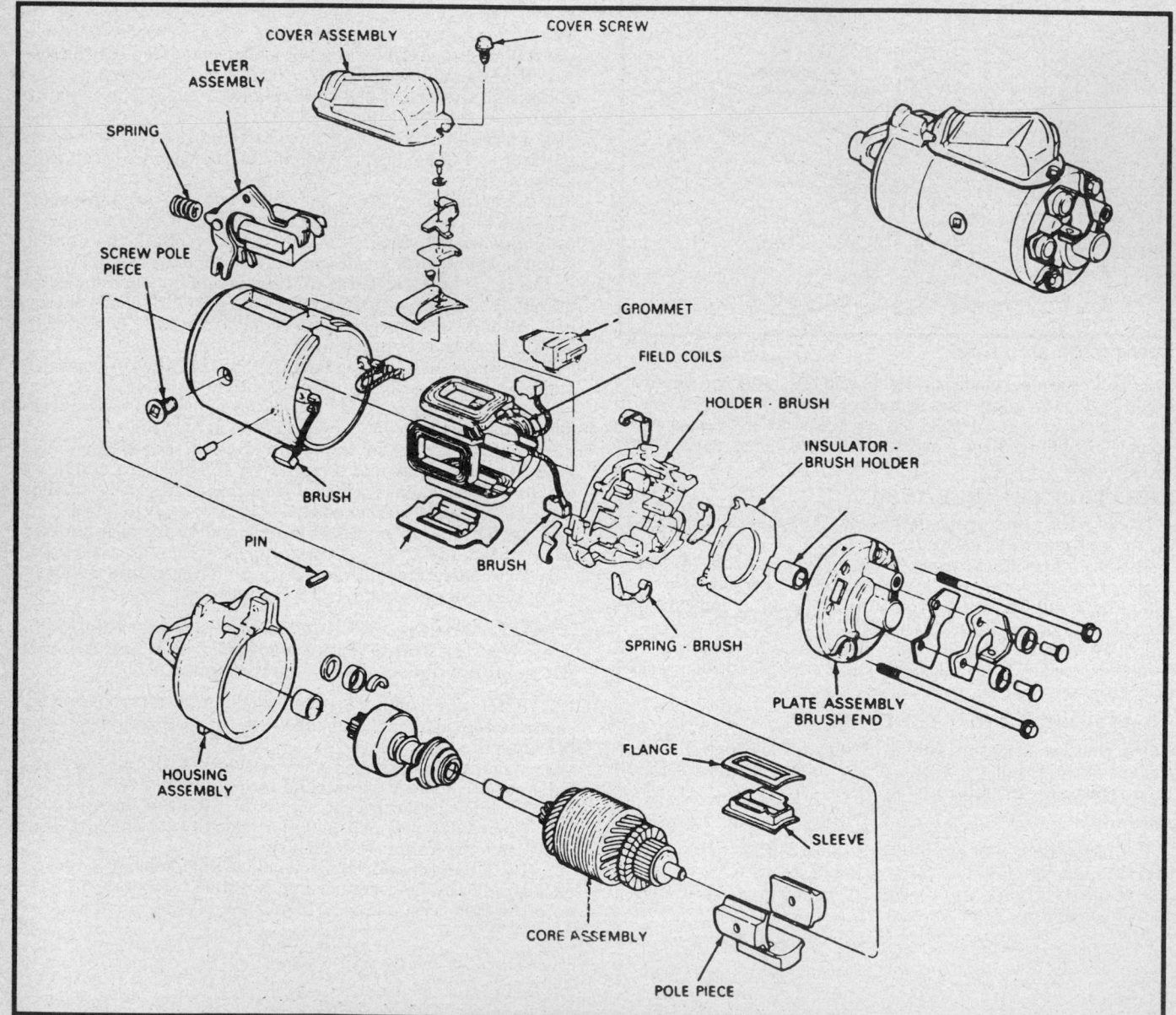

Exploded view of the Motorcraft positive engagement starter motor—Jeep

tab riveted to the frame. Remove the pole shoes and the coils from the frame.

9. Cut the positive brush leads from the the field coils as close to the field connection point as possible.

Inspection

1. Use a clean dry rag or compressed air to clean the field coils, armature, commutator, armature shaft, brush end plate and drive end housing. Wash all other parts in solvent and dry with a clean rag.

2. Inspect the armature windings for broken or burned insulation and unsoldered or open connections.

3. Check the plastic brush holder for cracks or broken mounting pads. Replace the brushes if worn to ¼ in. in length or if oil soaked.

4. Inspect the armature shaft and bushings for excessive wear and scoring. If necessary, lightly polish damaged surfaces.

5. Examine the wear pattern on the starter drive teeth. To eliminate premature starter and ring gear failure, the pinion teeth must penetrate to a depth greater than ½ the ring gear tooth depth.

6. Examine the starter drive gear for milled, pitted or broken teeth. Replace the starter drive if necessary.

7. Inspect the overrunning clutch by grasping and rotating the pinion gear. The pinion gear should rotate smoothly and freely in the clockwise direction and lock in the counterclockwise direction. Replace if necessary.

HOLD-IN COIL WINDING RESISTANCE TEST

1. Insert a piece of paper (1) between the contact points to insulate them.

2. With an ohmmeter, measure the resistance between the **S** terminal (2) and the starter motor frame. This will determine the resistance of the hold-in coil winding.

3. The resistance should be within the range of 2.0—3.5 ohms. If the resistance is not within this range, replace the field winding assembly.

SOLENOID CONTACT POINT CONNECTION TEST

1. With an ohmmeter, measure the resistance through solder joint (3). This will determine the integrity of the solder joint at the contacts.

2. A resistance reading greater than 0 ohms indicates the joint is faulty and must be repaired. If repair is required, resolder the joint.

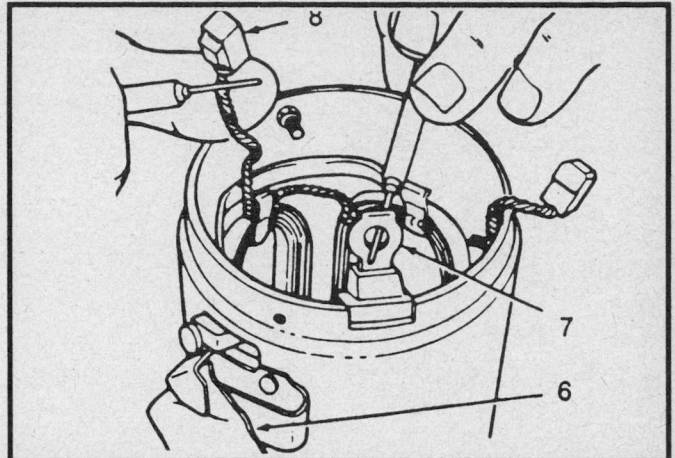

Performing the solenoid contact point connection test

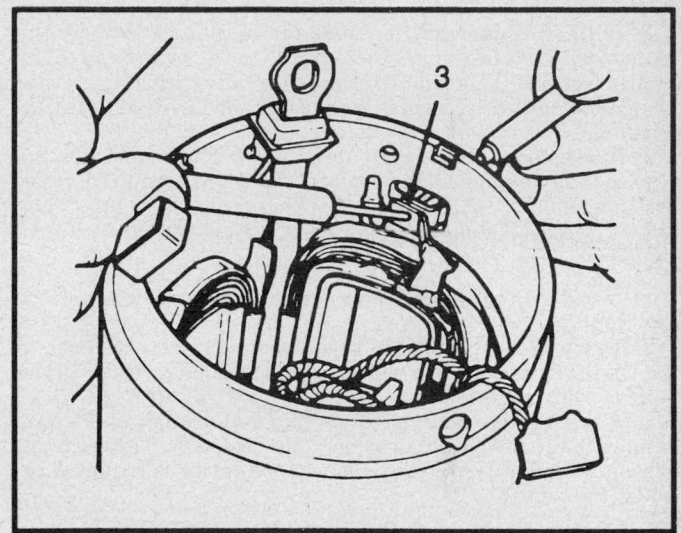

Performing the insulated brush connection test

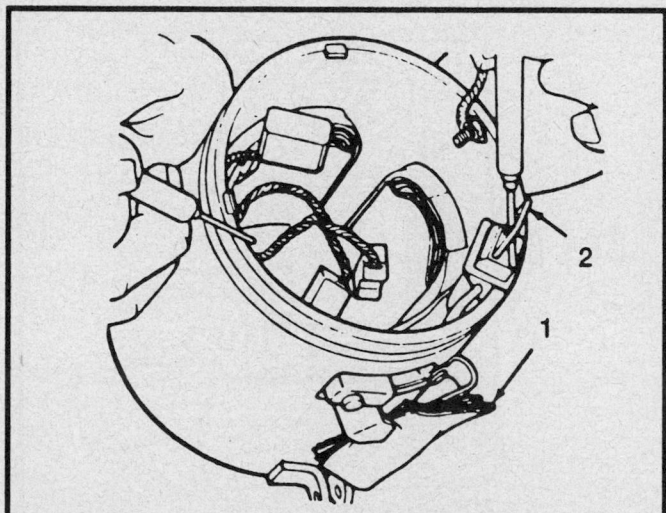

Performing the hold-in coil winding resistance test

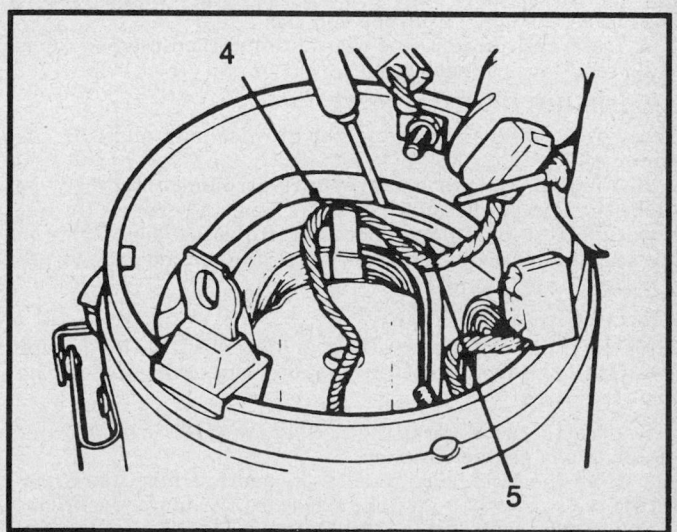

Performing the field winding terminal-to-brush continuity test

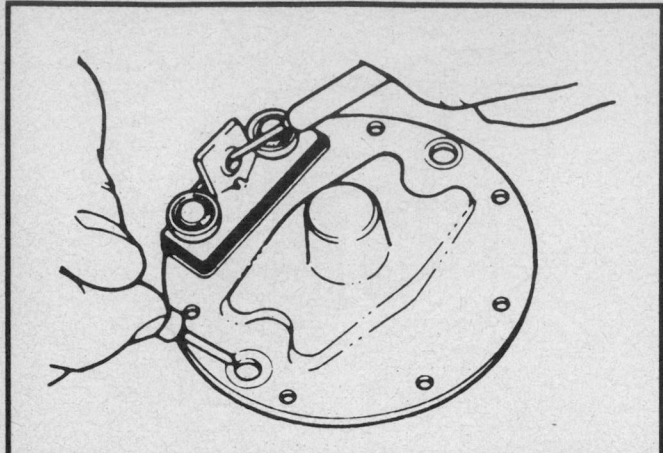

Performing the terminal bracket insulation test

INSULATED BRUSH CONNECTION TEST

1. With an ohmmeter, measure the resistance through the solder joint by touching the test probes to the brush and to the copper test bar. This will determine the integrity of the solder joint between the the insulated brush braided wire and the field windings.

2. A resistance reading greater than 0 ohms indicates the joint is faulty and must be repaired. If repair is required, resolder the joint.

FIELD WINDING TERMINAL TO BRUSH CONTINUITY TEST

1. Insert a piece of paper between the contact points to insulate them.

2. Touch the test probes to the field winding terminal and to the insulated brush. This will determine the integrity of all the field winding solder joints.

3. A resistance reading greater than 0 ohms indicates that 1 or more of the field winding solder joints is faulty. Test each solder joint to identify the faulty joint(s). If repair is required, resolder the joint(s).

TERMINAL BRACKET INSULATION TEST

1. With an ohmmeter, measure the resistance between the bracket and the cap. This will determine if the terminal bracket is properly insulated from the end cap.

2. If the resistance is less than infinite, then the end cap is faulty and must be replaced.

ARMATURE GROUND TEST

1. Position the armature in the growler jaws and turn the power switch to the test position.

2. Touch a test probe-to-armature core and the other test probe to each commutator bar, 1 at a time and observe the test lamp. The test lamp should not light. If the test lamp lights on any bar, the armature has a short circuit to ground and must be replaced.

ARMATURE SHORT TEST

NOTE: Never operate the growler with the power switch in the test position without the armature in the growler jaws.

1. Place the armature in the growler jaws and turn the power switch to the growler position.

2. Hold the steel blade parallel to, and touching, the armature core (3). Slowly, rotate the armature 1 or more revolutions in the growler jaws. If the steel blade vibrates at any 1 area of the core, the windings have a short circuit and the armature must be replaced.

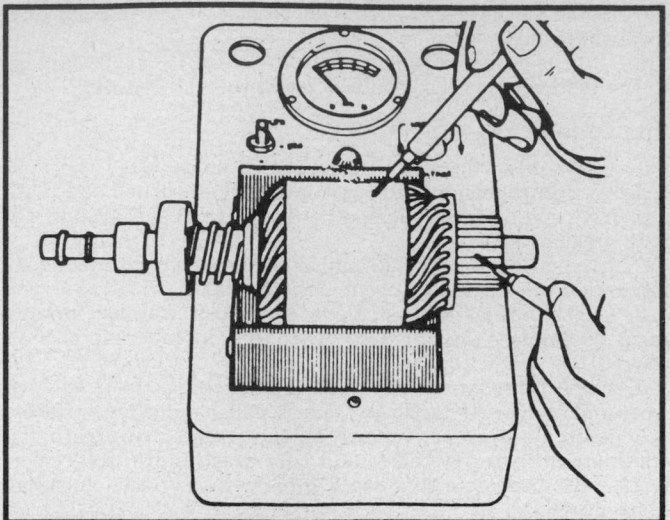

Performing the armature ground test

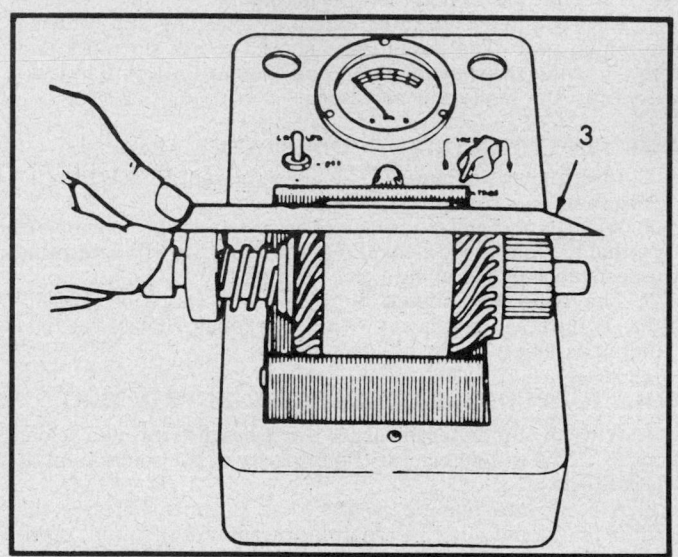

Performing the armature short test

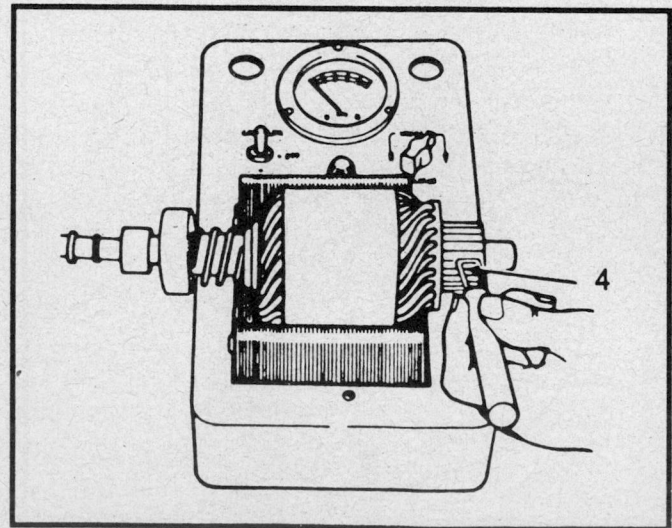

Performing the armature balance test

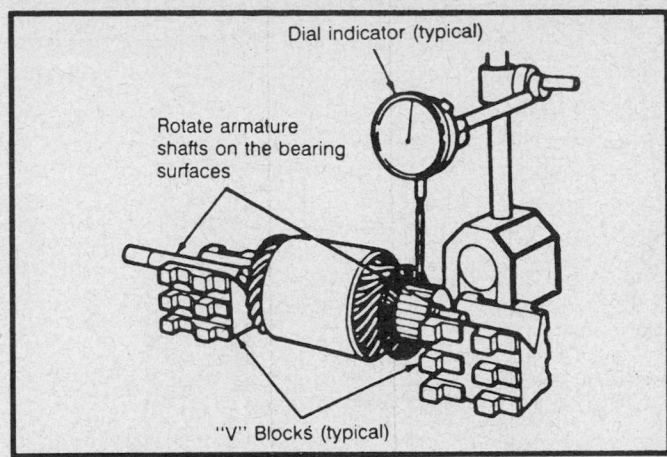

Performing the commutator runout check

ARMATURE BALANCE TEST

1. Place the armature in the growler jaws and turn the power switch to the growler position.
2. Place the contact fingers of the meter test probe (4) across adjacent commutator bars at the side of the commutator.
3. Adjust the voltage control until the pointer indicates the highest voltage on the scale.
4. Test each commutator bar until all bars have been tested; 0 volts across any pair indicates a short circuit and requires the armature be replaced.

ARMATURE RUNOUT TEST

1. Lightly polish the commutator with commutator cloth prior to measuring runout. Do not use emory cloth.
2. Measure the commutator runout. If the commutator is greater than 0.005 in. out-of-round or has insulation protruding from between the bars, turn it down on a lathe.

Assembly

1. Position 3 coils and pole pieces into the stator frame interior and support by hand. Install the pole piece screws.

2. Tighten the pole piece screws evenly and at regular intervals, tap the frame lightly with a soft-faced mallet. This will facilitate the alignment of the screws and the pole pieces.
3. Repeat procedures until the screws are securely fastened and the pole pieces are in proper alignment.
4. Install the remaining coil and retainer and bend the tabs to secure the coils to the frame.
5. Solder the field coils and solenoid wire to the starter terminal.
6. Check for continuity and grounds in the assembled coils.
7. Ground the coil, that is located in the area of the retaining sleeve, by positioning the small diameter wire leading from the coil under the copper tab, held by the rivet attaching the contact to the frame.
8. Attach the ground brushes to the starter frame with the screws or rivets.
9. Apply a thin coating of Lubriplate or equivalent, to the armature shaft splines. Install the starter motor drive gear assembly to the armature shaft and install a new retaining stop ring. Install a new stop retainer.
10. Install the armature assembly into the starter frame.
11. Fill the drive end housing bearing bore ¼ in. with lubricant. Position the starter drive gear plunger lever to the frame and starter drive assembly.
12. Position the starter drive plunger lever return spring and the drive end housing to the frame.
13. Install the brush holder and insert the brushes and springs into their respective positons. Position and install the brush holder insulator.

NOTE: When installing the endplate, do not to pinch or crimp the brush leads.

14. Position the end plate to the frame ensuring the plate locater is aligned with the frame slot. Install the thru-bolts and torque them to 55–75 inch lbs.. Install the pivot pin.
15. Thoroughly clean the sealing surface of the lever cover to remove any traces of existing gasket material. Apply rubber gasket compound or equivalent, to the sealing surface of the lever cover. Position the lever cover on the frame and secure with the attaching screw.
16. Check the starter no-load current draw.

MITSUBISHI REDUCTION GEAR STARTER

OVERHAUL

Disassembly and Assembly

NOTE: Do not place the stator frame in a vise or strike it with a hammer for damage to the permanent magnets could occur.

1. Disconnect the coil wire from the solenoid.
2. Remove the solenoid-to-front end frame screws and the solenoid.
3. Loosen, do not remove the commutator shield-to-brush holder screws.
4. Remove the through bolts, the rubber retainer (under solenoid) and the coin washer.

NOTE: When removing the output shaft assembly, do not loose the armature shaft ball.

5. Remove the stator frame, the commutator shield and output shaft assembly as a unit. Separate the clutch fork from the output shaft assembly.
6. From the stator frame, pull the output shaft assembly forward, then, push the armature and commutator shield to the rearward.
7. Remove the commutator shield-to-brush holder plate screws and the shield; do not remove the brush holder assembly.
8. Using a 22mm socket, slide it up against the commutator, slide the brush holder assembly onto the socket and position the socket/brush holder assembly aside.
9. To disassemble the output shaft assembly, perform the following procedures:
   a. Remove the rubber packing ring and the gears.
   b. Using a 17mm socket, position it into the armature end of the driveshaft and position the assembly in the vertical position, resting on the socket.
   c. Using a 12 point 14mm socket, position it against the stopring (on the clutch end). Using a hammer, strike the socket to unseat the stopring and expose the snapring.
   d. Remove the socket, the snapring and the stopring from the driveshaft.
   e. Using fine sandpaper, remove any burrs from the driveshaft. Remove the overruning clutch.
10. Using compressed air or dry cloths, clean the armature,

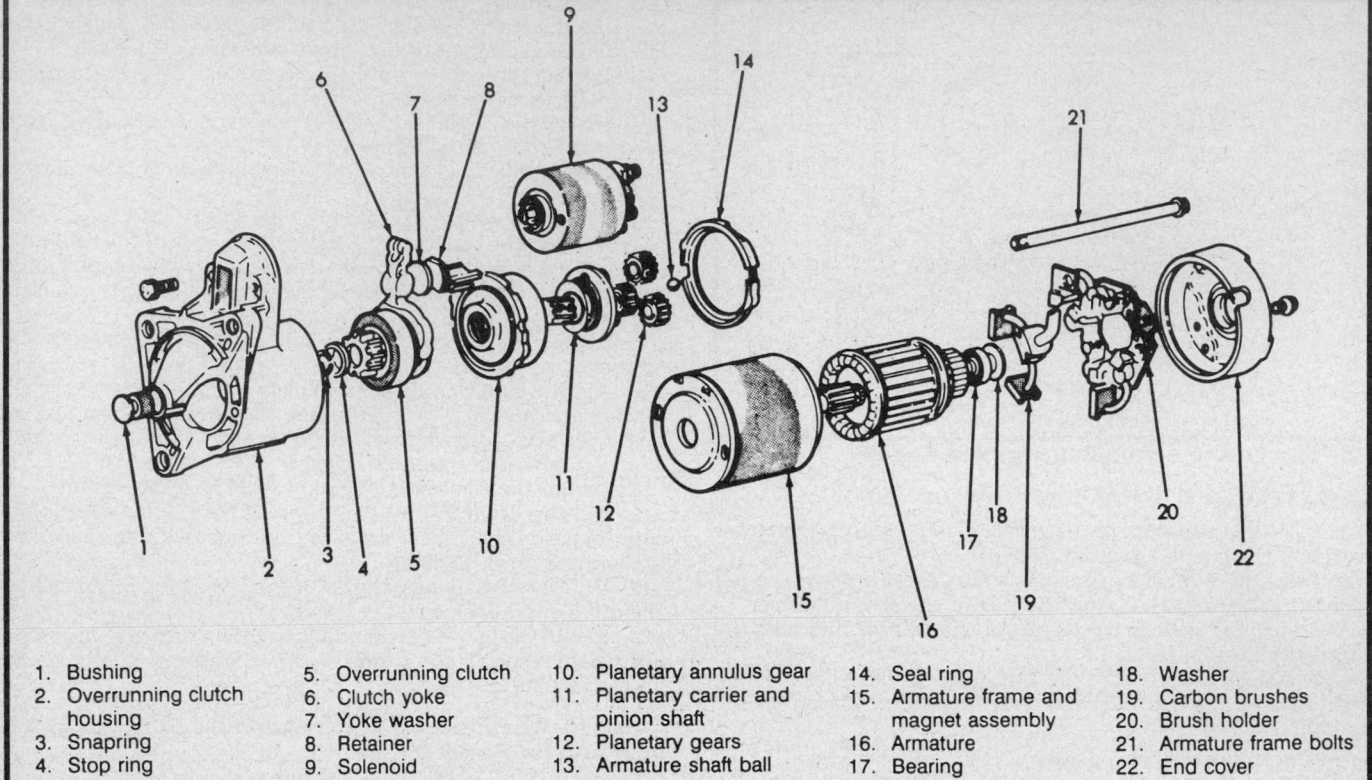

1. Bushing
2. Overrunning clutch housing
3. Snapring
4. Stop ring
5. Overrunning clutch
6. Clutch yoke
7. Yoke washer
8. Retainer
9. Solenoid
10. Planetary annulus gear
11. Planetary carrier and pinion shaft
12. Planetary gears
13. Armature shaft ball
14. Seal ring
15. Armature frame and magnet assembly
16. Armature
17. Bearing
18. Washer
19. Carbon brushes
20. Brush holder
21. Armature frame bolts
22. End cover

Exploded view of the Mitsubishi reduction gear starter—Jeep

the stator frame, the overrunning clutch, the solenoid and the brush holder. Using mineral spirits, clean all other components.

11. Inspect the following parts for damage and replace, if necessary:
   a. The stator frame and permanent magnets
   b. The driveshaft bushing (armature side)
   c. The planetary gear set and driveshaft
   d. The starter motor bushing and bearing
   e. The carbon brushes for cracks, distortion and wear below 0.354 in.

NOTE: When inspecting the brushes, do not remove the socket from the brush holder.

12. Using a growler and a hacksaw blade (placed on top of the armature), rotate the armature and check it for a shorted condition. If the hacksaw blade vibrates, a short exists; replace the armature.

13. Using a test light, place a lead on the armature's core and the other on each commutator segment, inspect the armature for a grounded condition. If a ground exists, the test light will turn **ON**; replace the armature.

14. Using a test light, place the leads on the adjacent commutator segments. If the test light turns **ON** between any 2 segments, the armature is shorted and must be replaced.

15. Inspect the commutator out-of-round, if it is more than 0.001 in., reface it on a lathe.

16. Using motor oil, lubricate the driveshaft and the overrunning clutch bushing. Using Lubriplate®, lubricate the overrunning clutch spiral cut splines.

17. Install the overrunning clutch on the driveshaft/planetary

gear assembly, followed by the stopring and the snapring; sure to seat the snapring in the shaft groove and crimp the it with a pair of pliers.

18. Using a battery terminal puller, attach it to the driveshaft tip and press the stopring over the snapring.

NOTE: When installing the stopring, be careful not to scratch the driveshaft.

19. Install the clutch fork, with the assembled planetary gear set, lubricated with lithium grease, into the front end housing; make sure the locating lugs are properly seated in the front end housing.

20. Install the coin washer and the rubber fork retainer.

21. Install the rubber backing ring by placing the largest rubber lug at the top.

22. Install the brush holder onto the armature's commutator; make sure the brushes and brush holders are seated in the holder. Inspect the flex washer and install the commutator shield onto the armature. Install the brush holder screws but do not tighten them.

23. Install the armature assembly into the stator frame and seat the wire grommet into the frame.

24. Be sure the armature spline gear is seated in the planetary gear seat with the armature shaft ball in place. Seat the armature shaft in the shaft bushing bore; rotate the stator frame to align the tabs on the drive housing frame.

25. Install the through bolts and torque to 28 inch lbs. Torque the brush holder screws to 18 inch lbs.

26. To complete the assembly, reverse the disassembly procedures.

CHRYSLER CORPORATION

Electronic Control Unit (ECU) Ignition System/Electronic Ignition System (EIS)

GENERAL INFORMATION

The system consists of battery, ignition switch, ignition resistor, control unit, coil, single or dual pick-up distributor, dual pick-up start/run relay, spark plugs and necessary components for routing of primary and secondary current.

The ECU/EIS system allows use of a dual pick-up distributor without electronic spark advance. Advance is applied mechanically through a vacuum advance unit on the side of the distributor.

The system is made up of 3 circuits. The primary, secondary and pick-up circuits. The primary circuit consists of battery, ignition switch, 1.2 ohm ignition resistor, primary windings of the ignition coil, power switching transistor of control unit, vehicle frame and dual pick-up start/run relay.

The secondary circuit consists of the coil secondary windings, distributor cap and rotor, spark plug cables, spark plugs and vehicle frame. On 5.9L engine, the ignition resistor is bypassed during starting, applying full battery voltage to the ignition coil.

The pick-up circuit is used to sense the proper timing for the control unit switching transistor. The reluctor, rotating with the distributor shaft, produces a voltage pulse in the magnetic pick-up each time a spark plug should be fired. This pulse is transmitted through the pick-up coil to the power switching transistor in the control unit. The transistor interrupts the current flow through the primary circuit. This break in the primary circuit induces a high voltage in the secondary coil circuit and fires the spark plug. The length of time that the switching transistor allows the flow of current in the primary circuit is determined by the circuitry within the ECU. Ignition maintenance is reduced to inspection of distributor cap, rotor, wiring and cleaning or replacing spark plugs as necessary.

The main relay in the EIS system is the dual pick-up/start run relay. The dual pick-up/start run relay allows the use of a dual pick-up distributor without the use of electronic spark advance. This has benefits of increased timing and improved fuel economy. During engine cranking, the dual pick-up start-run relay is energized through the starter solenoid circuit, which allows the start pick-up to adjust the timing for starting purposes only. As soon as the starter solenoid is de-energized, the start-run relay switches the sensing function back to the run pick-up.

IGNITION COIL

Testing

The ignition coil is designed to operate with an external resistor. When testing the coil for output, include the resistor in tests. Inspect the coil for external leaks and arcing. Test primary and secondary circuit resistances, replacing any coil or resistor not meeting manufacturer's specifications.

Every time an ignition coil is replaced because of a burned tower, carbon tracking or arcing, always replace coil secondary wire. Arcing will carbonize the nipple of wire; placing it on a new coil will usually cause the new coil to fail. Conversely, a coil which tests OK can be damaged by an old or worn coil wire.

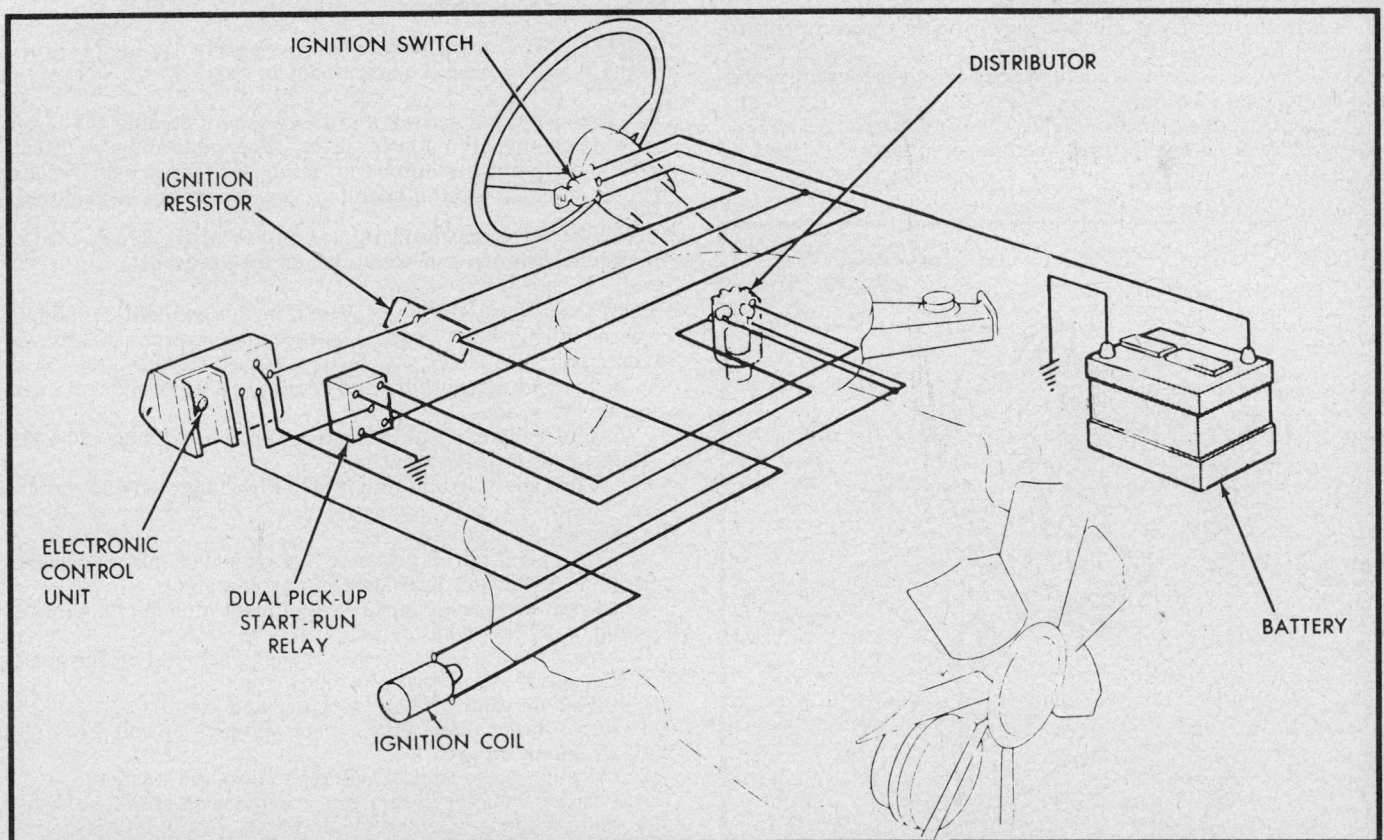

Ignition system diagram—Chrysler Corporation EIS

DISTRIBUTOR CAP AND ROTOR

Testing

The distributor cap and rotor must be inspected for flashover, cracking, burning and/or worn terminals. Check the carbon button in the cap for cracking. Light scale on terminals may be removed with a sharp knife, but heavy deposits on either cap terminals or the rotor require replacement of component.

A black silicone varnish covers tip (0.2–0.3 in.) of rotor electrode in place of silicone grease. Both types of coverage suppress magnetic radiation within the cap. The grease will darken with age, has an ash-like appearance and should not be removed. The ash formation on both types is normal and does not affect engine performance.

DUAL PICK–UP START/RUN RELAY

Testing

1. Remove the 2 way connector from pins No. 4 and No. 5 of dual pick-up start/run relay.
2. Using an ohmmeter, touch pins No. 4 and No. 5. The meter should read 20–30 ohms. If not, replace relay.

VACUUM ADVANCE

Testing

1. Connect timing light and adjust engine speed to 2500 rpm.
2. Check for advance by disconnecting and then reconnecting the vacuum hose at distributor and watching the advance or retard at crankshaft indicator.
3. For a more accurate determination of whether the vacuum advance mechanism is operating properly, remove vacuum hose from distributor and connect a hand vacuum pump.
4. Run the engine at idle and slowly apply vacuum pressure to check for advance.
5. If excessive advance is noted, look for a weak vacuum controller spring.
6. Insufficient advance or no advance could be caused by linkage problems or a ruptured vacuum diaphragm. Correct as necessary.

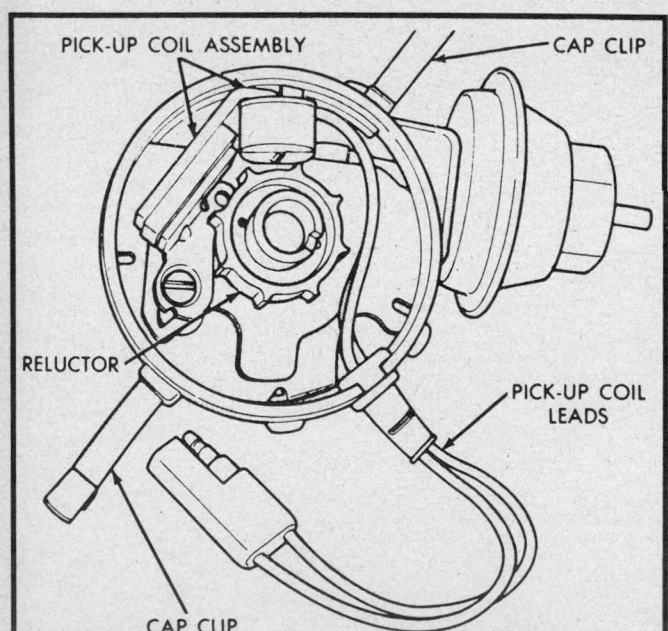

Chrysler Corporation EIS distributor components

DISTRIBUTOR

Shaft and Bushing Wear Test

1. Disconnect the negative battery cable. Remove the distributor cap. Remove the rotor. Use 2 small prybars under the upper part of rotor to pry off.
2. Remove the distributor and clamp it in a suitable holding fixture. Apply only enough pressure to restrict any movement of the distributor during test.
3. Attach a dial indicator to the distributor housing so indicator plunger arm rests against the reluctor.
4. Place an end of a wire loop around the reluctor sleeve just above the reluctor. Hook a spring scale to other end of wire loop.

NOTE: The wire loop must be down against the top of the reluctor to insure a straight pull. Be certain the wire loop does not interfere with the indicator or its holding bracket.

5. Apply 1½ lbs. of pull toward the dial indicator, then a 1 lb. pull away from indicator. Read the total movement of the shaft on indicator dial. If total indicated movement exceeds 0.006 in. (0.15mm), replace housing or shaft assembly.

Disassembly and Assembly

1. Disconnect the negative battery cable. Remove the distributor from the vehicle and remove the rotor from the shaft.
2. Remove the 2 screws and lockwashers attaching the vacuum control unit to distributor housing.
3. Disconnect the vacuum control arm from upper plate and remove vacuum control.
4. Remove the reluctor by carefully prying up from bottom of the reluctor with 2 small prybars. Be careful not to distort or damage teeth on reluctor.

NOTE: Maximum width for prybar is $^7/_{16}$ in. (11mm). Damage will occur if wider tool is used.

5. Remove the 2 screws and lockwashers holding the lower plate to housing; lift out lower plate, upper plate and pick-up coil as an assembly. Distributor cap clamp springs are held in place by peened metal around openings and should not be removed.

NOTE: Pick-up coil is not removable from plate; bothcomponents are serviced as an assembly.

6. If the side play in the shaft and bushing exceeds 0.006 in., replace housing, shaft, reluctor sleeve and governor weights as an assembly, as follows:
   a. Remove distributor shaft retaining pin and slide retainer off end of shaft.
   b. Use a file to clean burrs from around pin hole in shaft. Remove lower thrust washer.
   c. Push shaft up and remove shaft through top of distributor body.

To assemble:

7. Test operation of governor weights and inspect weight spring for distortion. Lubricate governor weights.
8. Inspect all bearing surfaces and pivot pins for roughness, binding or excessive looseness.
9. Lubricate and install upper thrust washer(s) on the shaft and slide shaft into distributor body.
10. Install distributor shaft retainer and pin.
11. Install lower plate, upper plate and pick-up coil assembly with attaching screws.
12. Install vacuum unit attaching screws and washers.
13. Position reluctor keeper pin into place on reluctor sleeve.
14. Slide reluctor down sleeve and press firmly into place.
15. Lubricate felt pad in top of reluctor sleeve with 1 drop light engine oil; install rotor.

Electronic Spark Control (ESC) System

GENERAL INFORMATION

The electronic spark control system consists of a Spark Control Computer (SCC), various sensors, a specially calibrated carburetor and a single or dual pick-up distributor. The system accurately controls the air/fuel mixture delivered to the engine.

The spark control computer controls the entire ignition system. It gives the capability of igniting the fuel mixture according to different engine conditions during the run drive cycle. It can deliver infinite electronic spark advance curves. The SCC has a built-in microprocessor which receives continuous input from the engine sensors. The computer electronically advances or retards the timing to provide even driveability.

During the crank-start period, the computer will provide a set amount of advanced timing to assure a quick, efficient start. The amount of electronic spark advance provided by the computer is determined by changes in coolant temperature, engine rpm and available manifold vacuum. The SCC also receives information from the oxygen sensor and the idle stop carburetor switch.

There are 2 functional modes of the computer, start and run. The start mode will only function during engine cranking and starting. The run mode only functions after the engine start and during engine operation. Both modes will never operate together.

For cranking and starting, the pick-up coil in the distributor feeds its signal to the computer. During this time the start mode is functioning and the run mode is bypassed. A fixed quantity of advance will be established in the ignition system because of the permanent position of the pick-up coil. The amount of advance in this mode will be determined by the position of the distributor.

After the engine starts and during engine operation, the pick-up coil (run pick-up on dual pick-up distributors) signal continues to feed into the computer. Now the run mode is functioning and the start mode is bypassed. The amount of advance will now be determined by the computer based on information received from all the sensors. If the run mode should fail during operation, the system will switch back to the start mode. The engine will keep running, but since timing in the start mode is fixed, performance and driveability will be below standard. This is also known as the "limp-in" or default mode. Should a failure of the pick-up coil(s) or the start mode of the computer occur, the engine will not start or run.

The pick-up coil signal is a reference signal. When the signal is received by the computer the maximum amount of timing advance is made available. Based on the data from all the sensors, the computer determines how much of this maximum advance is needed at that instant.

The amount of spark advance is determined by 2 factors, engine speed and engine vacuum. However, when it happens depends on the following conditions: Advance based on vacuum will be given by the computer when the carburetor switch is open. The amount is programmed into the computer and is proportioned to the amount of vacuum and engine rpm; Advance based on speed is given by the computer when the carburetor switch is open and is programmed to engine rpm.

IGNITION COIL

Testing

The ignition coil is designed to operate without an external igni-

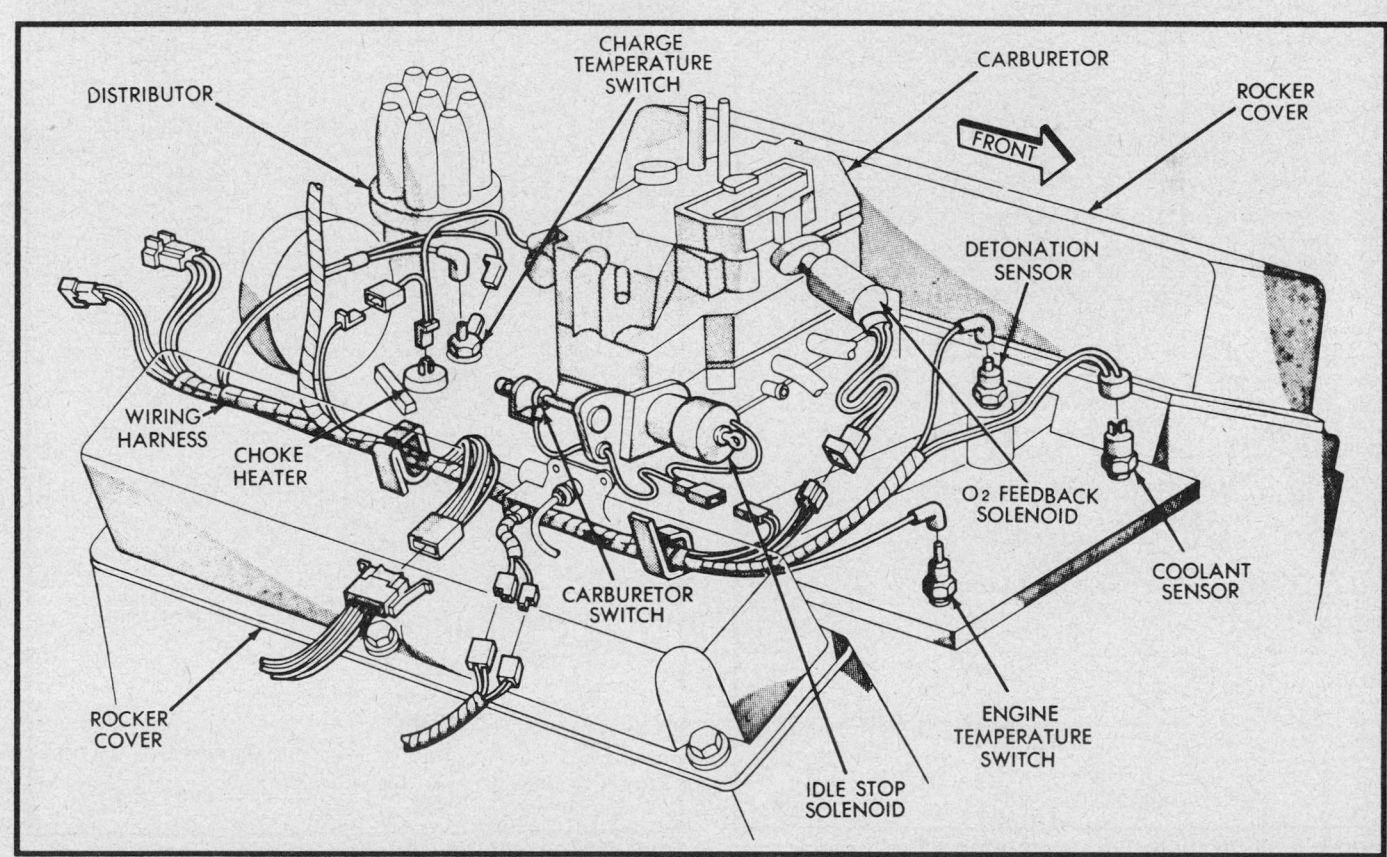

Ignition system diagram—Chrysler Corporation ESC

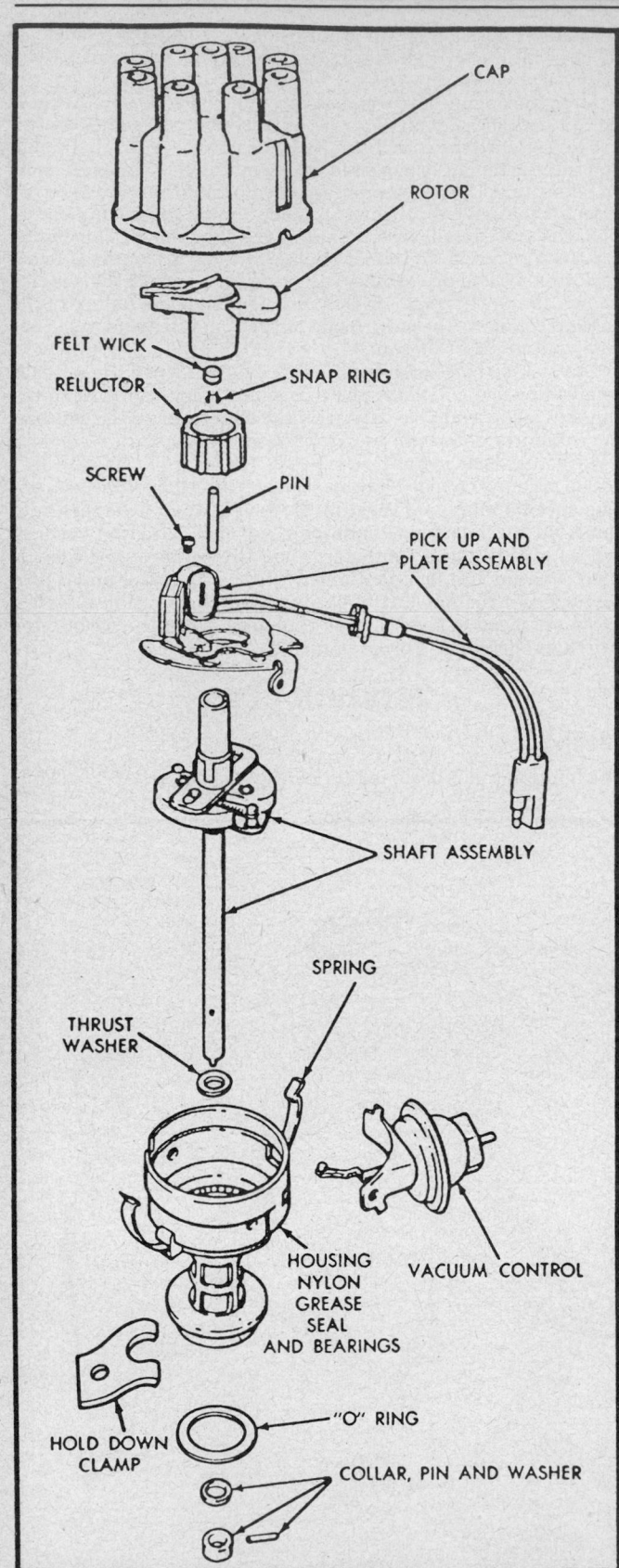

CAP

ROTOR

FELT WICK

RELUCTOR — SNAP RING

SCREW — PIN

PICK UP AND PLATE ASSEMBLY

SHAFT ASSEMBLY

SPRING

THRUST WASHER

HOUSING NYLON GREASE SEAL AND BEARINGS

VACUUM CONTROL

HOLD DOWN CLAMP

"O" RING

COLLAR, PIN AND WASHER

CAP

ROTOR

RELUCTOR

SCREW — PIN

PICK-UP AND PLATE ASSEMBLY

SHAFT ASSEMBLY

SPACER

THRUST WASHER

SPRING

HOUSING, NYLON GREASE SEAL AND BEARING

HOLD DOWN CLAMP

"O" RING

COLLAR, PIN AND WASHER

Single pick-up distributor components—Chrysler Corporation ignition systems

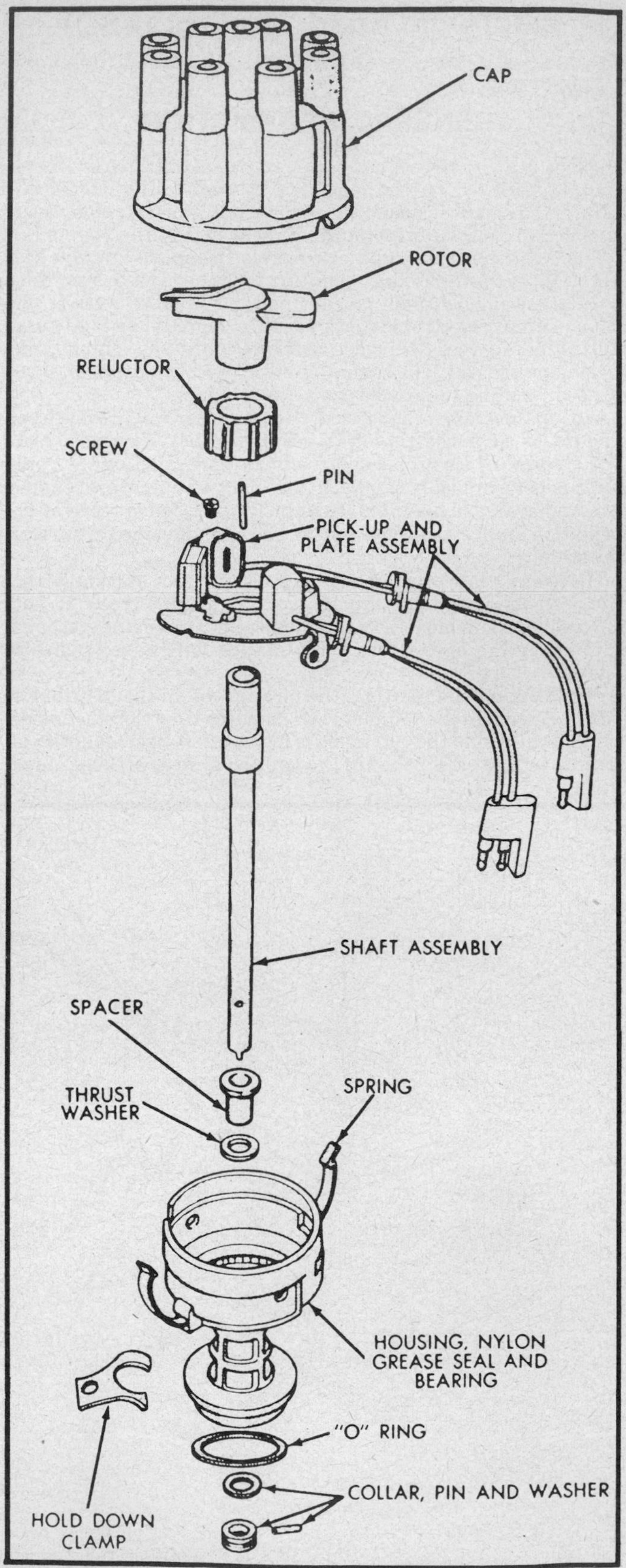

Dual pick-up distributor components—Chrysler Corporation ignition systems

tion resistor. Inspect coil for external leaks and arcing. Test primary and secondary circuit resistances, replacing any coil not meeting manufacturer's specifications.

Every time an ignition coil is replaced because of a burned tower, carbon tracking or arcing, always replace coil secondary wire. Arcing will carbonize nipple of wire; placing it on a new coil will usually cause the coil to fail. Conversely, a coil which tests OK can be damaged by an old or worn coil wire.

CAP AND ROTOR

Testing

The distributor cap and rotor must be inspected for flashover, cracking, burning and/or worn terminals. Check carbon button in cap for cracking. Light scale on terminals may be removed with a sharp knife, but heavy deposits on either cap terminals or rotor require replacement of component.

A black silicone varnish covers the tip (0.2–0.3 in.) of the rotor electrode in place of silicone grease. Both types of coverage suppress magnetic radiation within cap. The grease will darken with age, has an ash-like appearance and should not be removed. The ash formation on both types is normal and does not affect engine performance.

CHARGE TEMPERATURE SENSOR

Testing

1. Turn the ignition switch **OFF** and disconnect the wire from temperature sensor.
2. Connect a lead of an ohmmeter to a terminal of the sensor.
3. Connect the other lead of the ohmmeter to the remaining terminal of sensor.
4. Check for the following ohmmeter readings:
   a. Engine at room temperature (approximately 70°F): More than 6000 ohms. If not, replace switch.
   b. Hot engine (normal operating temperature, approx. 200°F): Less than 2500 ohms. If not, replace switch.

Removal and Installation

1. Disconnect electrical connector from sensor.
2. Remove the sensor from the engine.
3. Install the new sensor. Tighten to 20 ft. lbs. and reconnect the wiring.

SPARK CONTROL COMPUTER (SCC)

Testing

Incorporated within the digital microprocessor electronics are programmed spark advance schedules which occur during cold engine operation. These programmed advance schedules have been added to reduce engine emissions and improve driveability. Because they will be changing at different engine operating temperatures during warm-up, all spark advance testing should be done with engine at normal operating temperature and a temperature sensor that is connected and operating correctly.

The timing must be checked and adjusted as required. Perform the following procedures:

1. Place an insulator (piece of paper) between the curb idle adjusting screw and the carburetor switch, or be sure the screw is not touching the switch.
2. Remove and plug the vacuum line at vacuum transducer. Connect an auxiliary vacuum source to the vacuum transducer and set the vacuum at 16 in. Hg.
3. Increase the engine speed to 2000 rpm. Wait for approximately 1 minute and check the specifications. Advance specifications are in addition to basic timing.
4. On certain systems with an accumulator, the specified

time must elapse with the carburetor switch ungrounded before checking the specified spark advance schedule.
5. Should the computer fail to obtain specified settings the spark control computer should be replaced. Perform the same test on the replacement computer.

Removal and Installation

1. Disconnect the negative battery cable.
2. Remove the SCC cover on the air cleaner.
3. Remove the SCC mounting screws and remove it from the air cleaner.
4. The SCC is not serviceable and must be replaced as an unit.
5. Installation is the reverse of the removal procedure.

DISTANCE SENSOR

Removal and Installation

1. Disconnect the negative battery cable. Remove the electrical connector from sensor
2. Unscrew the sleeve and remove speedometer cable from sensor.
3. Install the new sensor and connect the speedometer cable, making sure cable is fully seated within housing. Tighten the cable sleeve.
4. Install the electrical connector. Connect the negative battery.

DISTRIBUTOR

Shaft and Bushing Wear Test

1. Disconnect the negative battery cable. Remove the distributor cap. Remove the rotor. Use 2 small prybars under the upper part of rotor to pry it off.
2. Remove the distributor. Clamp the distributor in a suitable holding fixture. Apply only enough pressure to restrict any movement of the distributor during test.
3. Attach a dial indicator to the distributor housing so the indicator plunger arm rests against reluctor.
4. Place an end of a wire loop around the reluctor sleeve just above the reluctor. Hook a spring scale to the other end of the wire loop.

NOTE: The wire loop must be down against top of reluctor to insure a straight pull. Be certain wire loop does not interfere with indicator or its holding bracket.

5. Apply 1½ lbs. of pull toward the dial indicator, then a 1 lb. pull away from the indicator. Read total movement of the shaft on the indicator dial. If total indicated movement exceeds 0.006 in. (0.15mm), replace housing or shaft assembly.

Disassembly and Assembly

1. Disconnect the negative battery cable. Remove the distributor from the engine and support it in a suitable holding fixture. Remove the rotor. Using 2 small pry bars, lift the reluctor out of the distributor. Be careful not to distort or damage teeth on reluctor.

NOTE: Maximum width for prybar is 7/16 in. (11mm). Damage will occur if wider tool is used.

2. Remove the 2 screws and lockwashers holding the plate to housing; lift out the plate and pick-up coil as an assembly. Distributor cap clamp springs are held in place by peened metal around the openings and should not be removed.

NOTE: Pick-up coil is not removable from plate; bothcomponents are serviced as an assembly.

3. If the distributor shaft side play exceeds 0.006 in., replace housing shaft and reluctor sleeve as follows:

a. Remove the distributor shaft retaining pin and slide the retainer off end of shaft.

b. Use a file to clean the burrs from around pin hole in shaft. Remove lower thrust washer.

c. Push shaft up and remove shaft through top of distributor body.

To install:

4. Lubricate and install the upper thrust washer(s) on shaft and slide shaft into distributor body.

5. Install the distributor shaft retainer and pin.

6. Install the plate and pick-up coil assembly with attaching screws.

7. Position the reluctor keeper pin into place on reluctor sleeve.

8. Slide the reluctor down the sleeve and press firmly into place. Install keeper pin.

Hall Effect Electronic Ignition System

GENERAL INFORMATION

The Hall Effect electronic ignition is used in conjunction with the Chrysler Spark Control Computer (SCC) controlling the entire ignition system. It consists of a sealed Spark Control Computer, specially calibrated carburetor and various engine sensors, such as the vacuum transducer, coolant switch, Hall Effect pick-up assembly, oxygen sensor and carburetor switch. A brief description of each follows:

Spark control computer—during cranking, an electrical signal is sent from the distributor to the computer. This signal will cause the computer to fire the spark plugs at a fixed amount of advance. Once the engine starts, the timing will then be controlled by the computer based on the information received from the various sensors.

There are essentially 2 modes of operation of the SCC: the start mode and the run mode. The start mode is only used during engine cranking. During cranking, only the Hall Effect pick-up signals the computer. These signals are interpreted to provide a fixed number of degrees of spark advance.

After the engine starts and during normal engine operation, the computer functions in the run mode. In this mode, the Hall Effect pick-up serves as only one of the signals to the computer. It is a reference signal of maximum possible spark advance. The computer then determines, from information provided by the other engine sensors, how much of this advance is necessary and delays the coil accordingly, firing the spark plug at the exact moment this advance (crankshaft position) is reached.

There is a third mode of operation which only becomes functional when the computer fails. This is the limp-in mode. This mode functions on signals from the pick-up only and results in very poor engine performance. However, it does allow the vehicle to be driven to a repair shop. If a failure occurs in the pick-up assembly or the start mode of the computer, the engine will neither start nor run.

Hall Effect pick-up—is located in the distributor assembly and supplies the engine rpm and ignition timing data to the SCC to advance or retard the ignition spark as required by current operating conditons.

Coolant temperature sensor—is located on the thermostat housing and provides the SCC with engine temperature data. The SCC uses this data to control various engine functions such as spark advance, fuel mixture, emission controls operation and radiator fan.

Vacuum sensor—is located on the SCC and informs the SCC as to the manifold vacuum during operation. The engine vacuum is one of the factors that will determine how the computer will advance/retard ignition timing and with the feedback carburetor, how the air/fuel ratio will be changed.

Carburetor switch—is located on the left side of the carburetor; it provides the SCC with throttle open or throttle closed signal.

Oxygen sensor—is located in the exhaust manifold and signals the computer how much oxygen is present in the exhaust gases. Since this amount is proportional to rich and lean mixtures, the computer will adjust the air/fuel ratio to a level which will maintain operating efficiency of the 3-way catalyst system and engine.

CARBURETOR SWITCH

Testing

1. With the ignition key **OFF**, disconnect the 10-way connector from the computer.

2. With the throttle completely closed, check for continuity between cavity 7 of the connector and a good ground.

3. If there is no continuity, check the the wire and the carburetor switch.

4. With the throttle open, check the continuity between cavity 7 of the connector and a good ground. There should be no continuity.

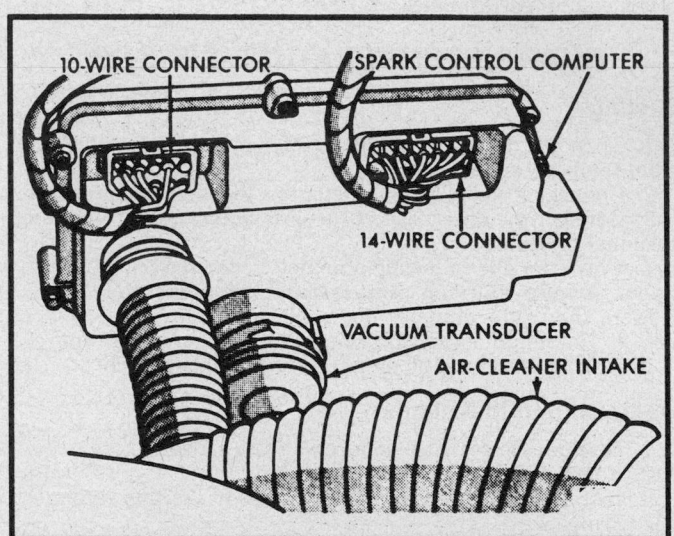

Spark computer connector locations—Chrysler Corporation SCC

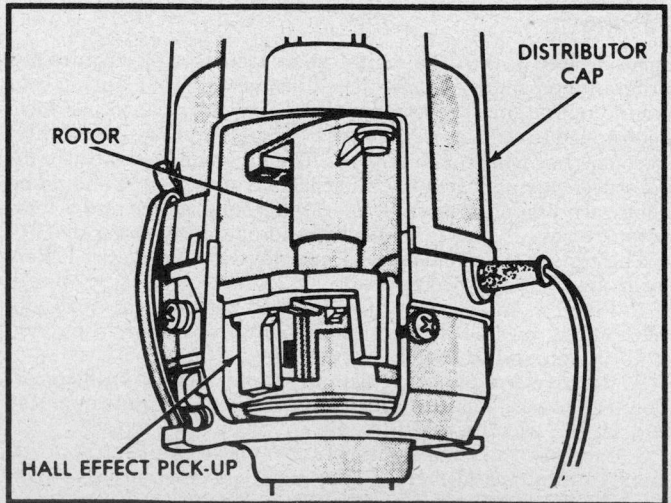

Hall Effect distributor—Chrysler Corporation SCC

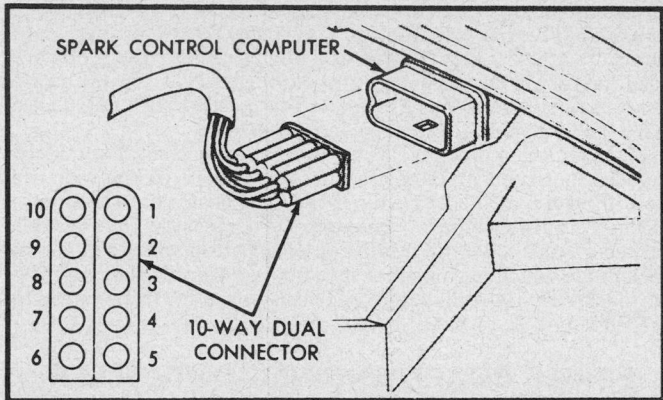

SPARK CONTROL COMPUTER

10-WAY DUAL CONNECTOR

Connector terminal locations—Chrysler Corporation SCC

Removal and Installation

The carburetor switch is replaced with its mounting bracket assembly. This requires the removal and disassembly of the carburetor.

COOLANT TEMPERATURE SENSOR

Test

1. With the key in the **OFF** position, disconnect the wire from the coolant sensor.
2. Connect a lead from the ohmmeter to terminal 1 of the coolant sensor. Connect the the other lead to terminal 2 (fan control circuit) of the sensor.
3. The resistance between the terminals should be:
   a. Temperature at 200°F — 700–800 ohms
   b. Temperature at approximately 70°F — 5000–6000 ohms

Removal and Installation

1. Disconnect the negative battery cable.
2. Disconnect the electrical lead from the sensor.
3. Remove the sensor from the engine.
4. Install the new sensor and tighten to 20 ft. lbs. Reconnect the electrical lead.
5. Connect the battery cable. Check the coolant level.

HALL EFFECT PICK-UP

Removal and Installation

1. Disconnect the negative battery cable. Remove the splash shield from the distributor and remove the distributor from the vehicle.
2. Pull straight up on the rotor and remove it.
3. Remove the pick-up assembly.
4. Install the new pick-up assembly into the distributor, use care to correctly route the leads.
5. Install the distributor cap and rotor.

DISTRIBUTOR

Disassembly and Assembly

1. Disconnect the negative battery cable.
2. Remove the distributor from the vehicle and support it in a suitable holding fixture.
3. Remove the distributor cap and rotor.
4. Remove the dust cover from the pick-up.
5. Remove the roll pin from the distributor shaft. Remove the gear from the shaft.
6. Pull the shaft from the body.

7. Remove the pick-up retaining screw and remove it from the distributor body.
To assemble:
8. Clean the distributor body and all of the components.
9. Install the pick-up in position.
10. Install the distributor shaft into position in the distributor body.
11. Install the distributor gear in position and install a new roll pin.
12. Install the dust cover, cap and rotor.
13. Install the distributor into the vehicle. Connect the negative battery cable.

Single Module Engine Controller (SMEC) System

GENERAL INFORMATION

The Hall Effect electronic ignition system is used in conjunction with the Single Module Engine Controller (SMEC). This system features improved decision making capabilities and offers almost infinite control of the fuel and spark advance. The system consists of the following components:

Single Module Engine Controller (SMEC) — the SMEC controls the entire ignition system. It gives the system the capability of igniting the fuel mixture according to different engine conditions during a run/drive period by constantly altering the electronic spark advance curves. The SMEC has a built in microprocessor that receives input from the engine monitoring sensors. The computer than advances or retards the ignition timing electronically to provide even driveability.

The amount of electronic spark advance provided is determined by 3 input factors, coolant temperature, engine rpm, and manifold vacuum. The SMEC also receives input from the oxygen sensor and adjusts the air/fuel mixture to assure efficient combustion.

Hall Effect pick-up — is located inside the distributor and supplies the engine rpm, ignition timing data to the SMEC.

Coolant temperature sensor — is mounted near the thermostat housing and provide the SMEC with the engine operating temperature.

Manifold Absolute Pressure (MAP) sensor — monitors manifold vacuum pressure. The SMEC uses this data to control the air/fuel mixture.

Automatic Shutdown (ASD) relay — inerrupts power to the electrical fuel pump, fuel injectors and ignition coil when there is no ignition signal present with the key in the **RUN** position.

SINGLE MODULE ENGINE CONTROLLER (SMEC)

Testing

The SMEC controls the fuel system as well as the ignition system, testing of the SMEC requires the use of its self diagnostic functions.

Removal and Installation

1. Disconnect the negative battery cable.
2. Remove the air cleaner duct from the SMEC.
3. Remove the SMEC mounting screws.
4. Carefully remove the 14 and 60 way connectors from the SMEC. Do not remove the grease from the connector cavities.
5. Remove the SMEC from the vehicle.
6. Install the SMEC in position, make sure there is at least a ¼ in. of grease in the connector openings.
7. Install the air cleaner duct and connect the negative battery cable.

COOLANT TEMPERATURE SENSOR

Testing

1. With the key in the **OFF** position, disconnect the electrical lead from the sensor.
2. Connect a lead from an ohmmeter to a terminal of the sensor.
3. Connect the other ohmmeter lead to the sensor. The ohmmeter should read:
   a. Coolant at operating temperature (200°F) – 700–1000 ohms
   b. Coolant at room temperature (70°F) – 7000–13000 ohms

Removal and Installation

1. Disconnect the negative battery cable.
2. Disconnect the electrical lead from the sensor.
3. Remove the sensor from the engine.
4. Install the new sensor and tighten to 20 ft. lbs. Reconnect the electrical lead.
5. Connect the battery cable. Check the coolant level.

HALL EFFECT PICK-UP

Removal and Installation

1. Disconnect the negative battery cable. Remove the splash shield from the distributor and remove the distributor from the vehicle.
2. Pull straight up on the rotor and remove it.
3. Remove the pick-up retaining screws. Remove the pick-up assembly.
4. Install the new pick-up assembly into the distributor, use care to correctly route the leads.
5. Install the distributor cap and rotor.

DISTRIBUTOR

Disassembly and Assembly

1. Disconnect the negative battery cable.
2. Remove the distributor from the vehicle and support it in a suitable holding fixture.
3. Remove the distributor cap and rotor.
4. Remove the dust cover from the Hall Efect pick-up.
5. Remove the roll pin from the distributor shaft. Remove the gear from the shaft.
6. Pull the shaft from the body.
7. Remove the pick-up retaining screw and remove it from the distributor body.

To assemble:
8. Clean the distributor body and all of the components.
9. Install the Hall Effect pick-up in position.
10. Install the distributor shaft into position in the distributor body.
11. Install the distributor gear in position and install a new roll pin.
12. Install the dust cover, cap and rotor.
13. Install the distributor into the vehicle. Connect the negative battery cable.

Optical Distributor System
GENERAL INFORMATION

The optical distributor system is based directly on the Chrysler Single Module Engine Controller (SMEC) system. The SMEC is replaced with the Single Board Engine Controller in the optical distributor system.

THe SBEC receives its engine speed and crankshaft signal from the optical distributor. The timing member in the distributor is a thin disk, driven at ½ the engine speed, from the left side camshaft. The disk has 2 sets of slots in it. The outer, high data rate slots are at 2 degree intervals of engine rotation. They are used for timing adjustment up to 1200 rpm. The low data rate set contains 6 slots that are related to crankshaft TDC. These are used to govern the fuel injection system.

Light emitting diodes (LEDs) and photo diodes are mounted in facing positions on opposite sides of the disk, in line with the slots. Masks over the LEDs focus the light beams onto the photo diodes. As each disk passes between the diodes, the light beam is turned on and off. This creates an alternating voltage in the in each diode which is converter into on and off pulses by an integrated circuit in the distributor. These pulses are transmitted to the SBEC.

SINGLE BOARD ENGINE CONTROLLER (SBEC)

Testing

The SBEC controls the fuel system as well as the ignition system, testing of the SBEC requires the use of its self diagnostic functions.

Removal and Installaion

1. Disconnect the negative battery cable.
2. Remove the air cleaner duct from the SBEC.
3. Remove the SBEC mounting screws.

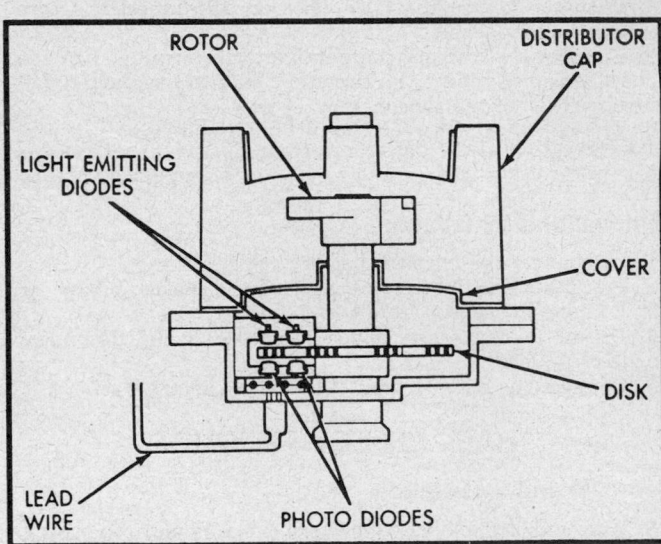

Optical distributor components – Chrysler Corporation optical distributor system

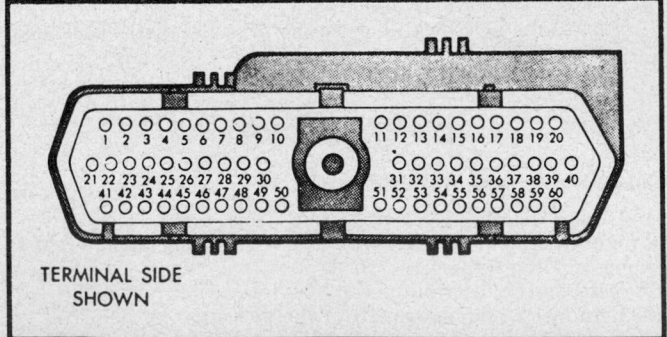

Connector terminal locations – Chrysler Corporation SBEC

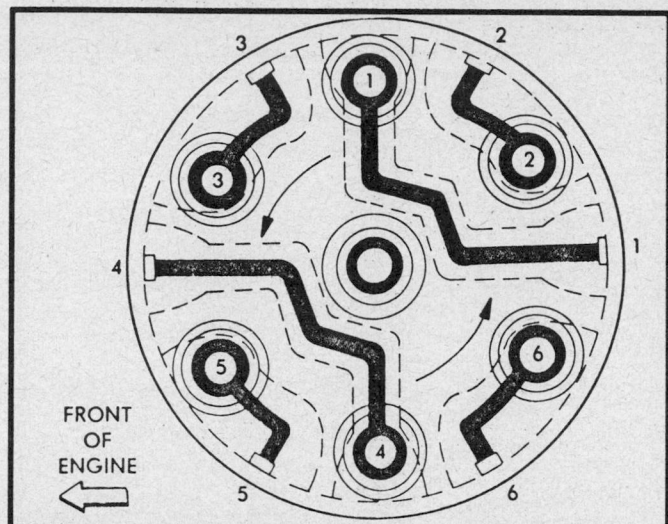

Distributor cap terminal routing—Chrylser optical distributor system

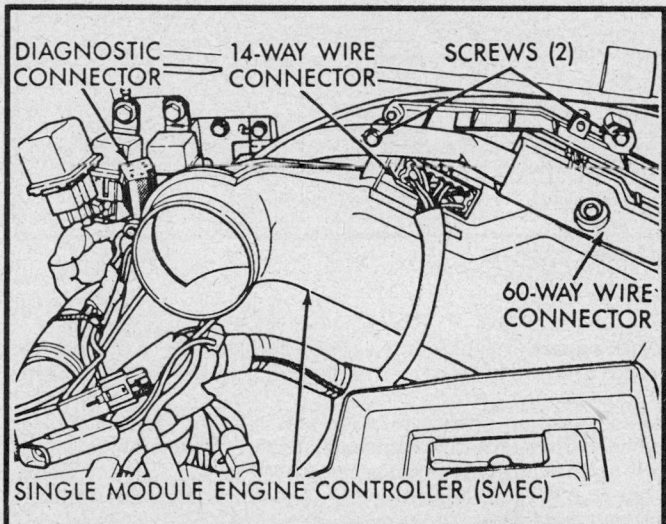

Connector locations—Chrysler Corporation optical distributor system

4. Carefully remove the 14 and 60 way connectors from the SBEC. Do not remove the grease from the connector cavities.

5. Remove the SBEC from the vehicle.

6. Install the SBEC in position, make sure there is at least a ¼ in. of grease in the connector openings.

7. Install the air cleaner duct and connect the negative battery cable.

COOLANT TEMPERATURE SENSOR

Testing

1. With the key in the **OFF** position, disconnect the electrical lead from the sensor.

2. Connect a lead from an ohmmeter to a terminal of the sensor.

3. Connect the other ohmmeter lead to the sensor. The ohmmeter should read:

   a. Coolant at operating temperature (200°F) — 700–1000 ohms

   b. Coolant at room temperature (70°F) — 7000–13000 ohms

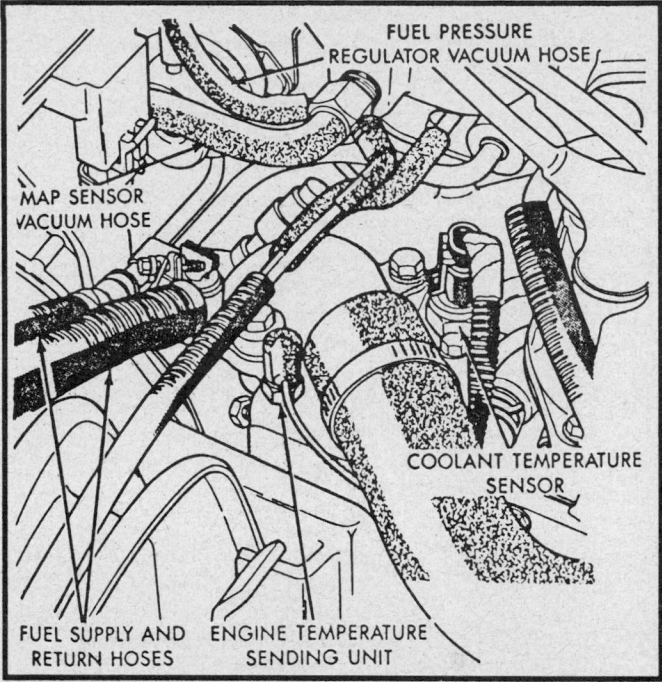

Coolant temperature sensor location—Chrysler Corporation SBEC

Removal and Installation

1. Disconnect the negative battery cable.

2. Disconnect the electrical lead from the sensor.

3. Remove the sensor from the engine.

4. Install the new sensor and tighten to 20 ft. lbs. Reconnect the electrical lead.

5. Connect the battery cable. Check the coolant level.

PHOTO OPTIC SENSING UNIT

Removal and Installation

1. Disconnect the negative battery cable. Remove the splash shield from the distributor and remove the distributor from the vehicle.

2. Pull straight up on the rotor and remove it.

3. Remove the photo optic sensing unit retaining screw. Remove the disc, bushing and photo sensing unit from the distributor.

4. Install the new photo sensing assembly into the distributor, use care to correctly route the leads.

5. Install the distributor cap and rotor.

DISTRIBUTOR

Disassembly and Assembly

1. Disconnect the negative battery cable. Remove the distributor from the vehicle and support it in a suitable holding fixture.

2. Remove the cap. Remove the rotor from the distributor shaft.

3. Remove the protective cover from the sensor unit.

4. Remove the lead in wire clamp screw and remove the wire.

5. Remove the optical disc spacers and the disc.

6. Remove the sensing unit screw and carefully remove the sensing unit.

7. Remove the bearing retaining screws from the distributor.

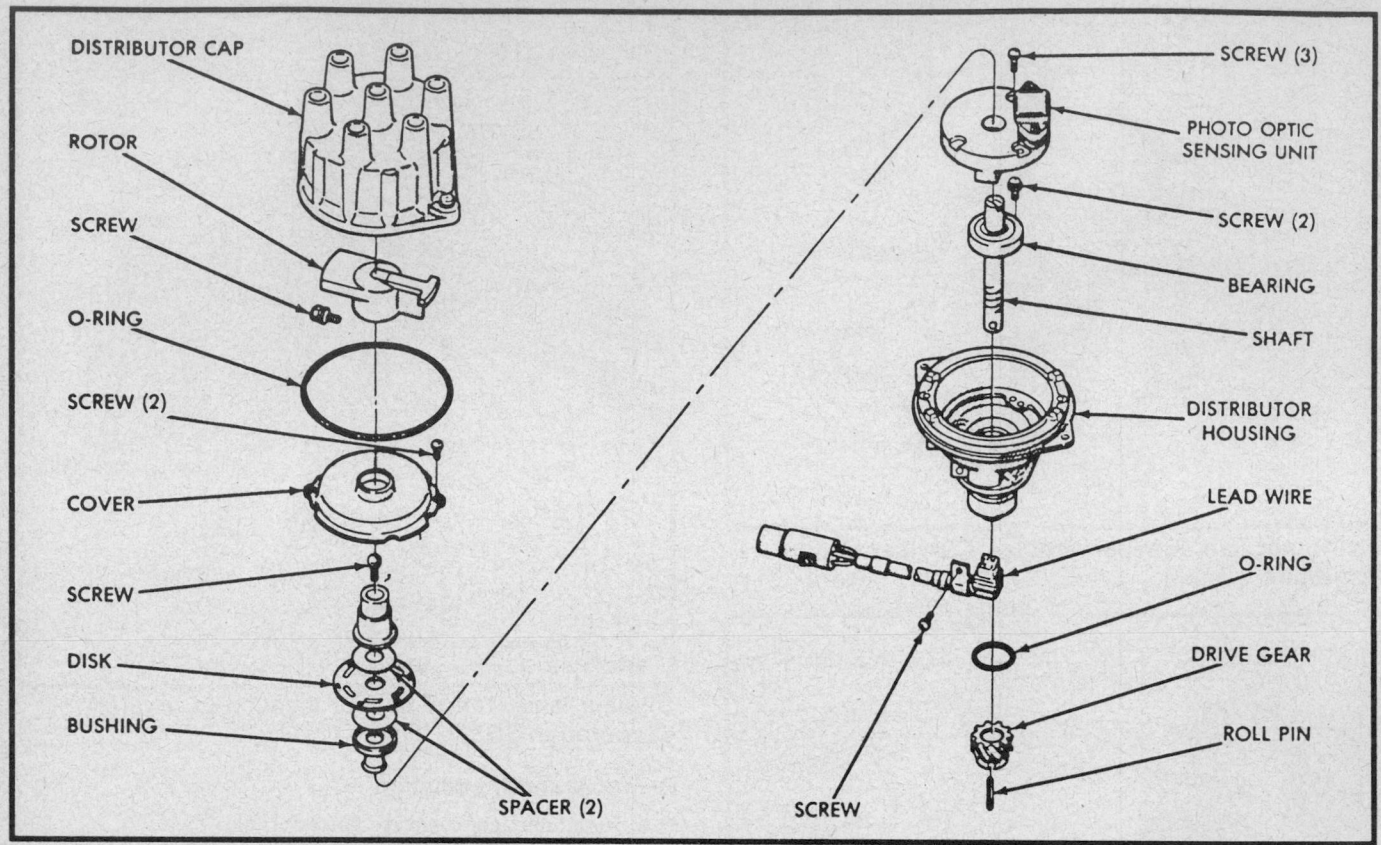

Distributor components—Chrysler Corporation optical distributor system

8. Using a punch, remove the roll pin from the drive gear and remove the gear from the shaft.

9. Pull the distributor shaft from the housing.

To assemble:

10. Install the shaft and bearing assembly into the distributor. Install the gear on the shaft and install a new roll pin.

11. Install the bearing retaining screws. Install the photo optic sensing unit and the bushing.

12. Install the disc and spacers. Install the disc assembly retaining screw.

13. Connect the lead in wire. Install the sensing unit cover.

14. Install the cap and rotor.

15. Install the distributor into the vehicle. Connect the negative battery cable.

Direct Ignition System (DIS)

GENERAL INFORMATION

The Direct Ignition System (DIS) is basically a Hall Effect system, with one exception, no distributor is used. The system is controlled by the Single Board Engine Controller (SBEC).

The SBEC receives the engine speed and crankshaft position signal from a Hall Effect pick-up, located on the transmssion housing. This crankshaft pick-up, senses slots located around the outer edge of an extension to the driveplate. A cam sensor, located on the timing chain case cover, supplies the cylinder identification information. The camshaft sensor, senses slots located on te cam timing gear.

The crankshaft sensor, senses 4 slots per cylinder, located 20 degrees apart. Basic timing is set by the position of the last slot in each group. This is a fixed basic timing system with no means of adjustment.

Fuel injection synchronization and cylinder identification is provided throught the camshaft sensor. The combination of slots on the camshaft timing gear is used by the SBEC to identify the cylinders to allow initiation of the fuel and spark, for start and run conditions.

The molded coil pack is mounted on the intake manifold. High tension leads route to each cylinder from the coil. The coil fires 2 spark plugs at the same time on every power stroke. One plug fires the cylinder under compression, the other fires a cylinder on the exhaust stroke. The SBEC determines which of the coils to charge and fire at the correct time.

A description of the system components follows:

Single Board Engine Controller (SBEC)—the SBEC controls the entire ignition system. It gives the system the capability of igniting the fuel mixture according to different engine conditions during a run/drive period by constantly altering the electronic spark advance curves. The SBEC has a built in microprocessor that receives input from the engine monitoring sensors. The computer than advances or retards the ignition timing electronically to provide even driveability.

Coolant temperature sensor—is mounted near the thermostat housing and provide the SMEC with the engine operating temperature.

Manifold Absolute Pressure (MAP) sensor—monitors manifold vacuum pressure. The SMEC uses this data to control the air/fuel mixture.

Automatic Shutdown (ASD) relay—inerrupts power to the electrical fuel pump, fuel injectors and ignition coil when there is no ignition signal present with the key in the **RUN** position.

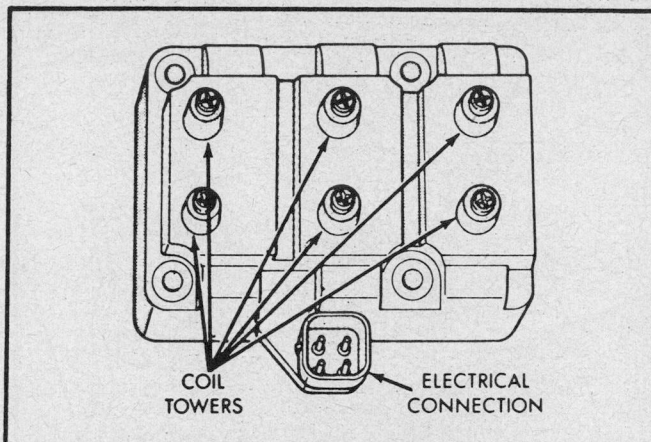

Ignition coil — Chrysler Corporation DIS

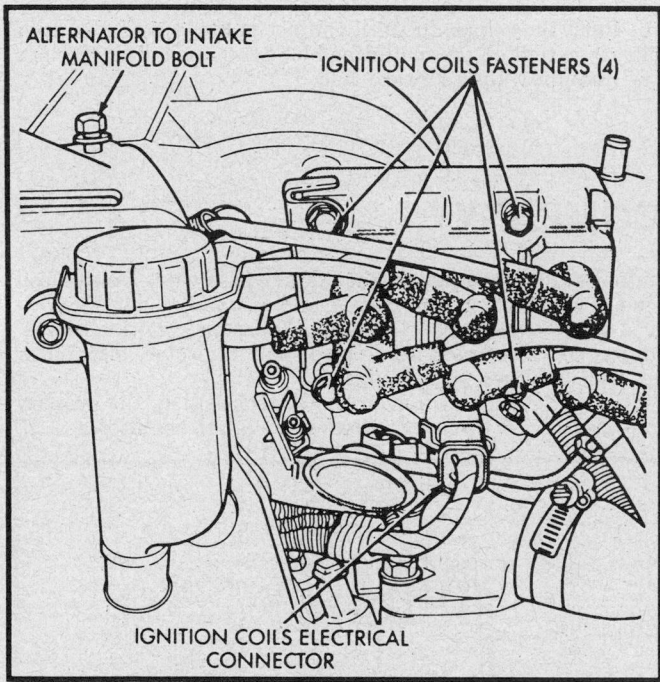

Ignition coil removal — Chrysler Corporation DIS

SINGLE BOARD ENGINE CONTROLLER (SBEC)

Testing

The SBEC controls the fuel system as well as the ignition system, testing of the SBEC requires the use of its self diagnostic functions.

Removal and Installtion

1. Disconnect the negative battery cable.
2. Remove the air cleaner duct from the SBEC.
3. Remove the SBEC mounting screws.
4. Carefully remove the 14 and 60 way connectors from the SBEC. Do not remove the grease from the connector cavities.
5. Remove the SBEC from the vehicle.
6. Install the SBEC in position, make sure there is at least a ¼ in. of grease in the connector openings.
7. Install the air cleaner duct and connect the negative battery cable.

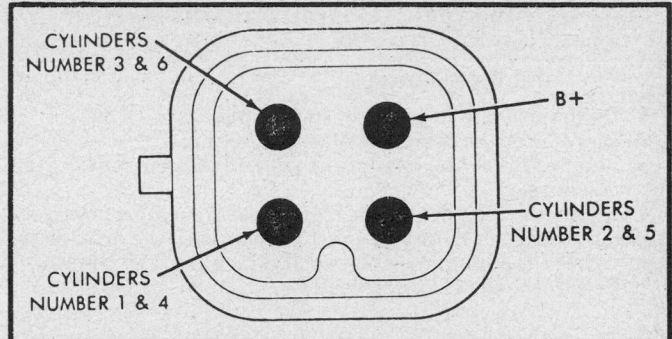

Ignition coil terminal identification — Chrysler Corporation DIS

IGNITION COIL PACK

Testing

NOTE: *Cylinders 1 and 4; 2 and 5; 3 and 6 are grouped together on the coil pack.*

1. Disconnect the ignition wires from the coil. Measure the resistance of the cables, the correct resistance should be 3,000–12,000 ohms per foot. Replace any cable out of range.
2. Disconnect the electrical connector from the coil. Measure the resistance between the B+ terminal and the terminal for each set of cylinders. The correct resistance should be 0.5–0.7 ohms.
3. Replace the coil if any of the cylinders are not within specification.
4. Measure the resistance between the towers of the grouped cylinders, resistance should be 7,000–12,000 ohms. Replace the coil if any are out of range.

Removal and installation

1. Disconnect the negative battery cable.
2. Remove the ignition cables from the coil.
3. Disconnect the electrical connector from the coil.
4. Remove the coil mounting bolts and remove the coil.
5. Install the replacement coil in position. Install the mounting bolts and connect the electrical leads. Tighten the mounting bolts to 105 inch lbs.
6. Connect the battery cable.

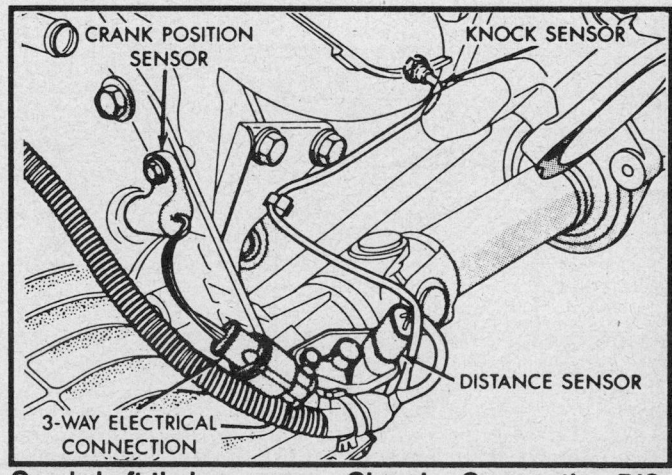

Crankshaft timing sensor — Chrysler Corporation DIS

CRANKSHAFT TIMING SENSOR

Removal and Installation

1. Disconnect the negative battery cable.
2. Disconnect the crankshaft sensor wiring.
3. Remove the sensor mounting bolt and pull the sensor from the transmission.
4. Install the sensor into the transmission, using a new spacer. Push the sensor in until contact is made with the drive plate, then tighten the mounting bolt to 105 inch lbs. (12 Nm).
5. Reconnect the electrical lead.

CAMSHAFT SENSOR

Removal and Installation

1. Disconnect the negative battery cable.
2. Disconnect the wiring from the sensor.
3. Loosen the sensor mounting bolt and slide the sensor out of position.
4. Install the sensor in position. Apply a few drops of engine oil to the O-ring before installing.

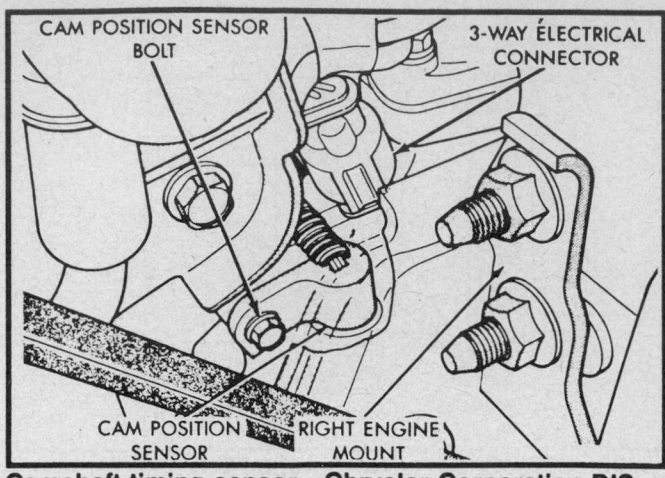

Camshaft timing sensor—Chrysler Corporation DIS

5. Push the sensor in until contact is made with the drive plate, then tighten the mounting bolt to 105 inch lbs. (12 Nm).
6. Reconnect the electrical lead.

FORD MOTOR COMPANY

Dura Spark Ignition System

GENERAL INFORMATION

The Dura Spark ignition system consists of the typical primary and secondary circuits. The primary circuit consists of; battery, ignition switch, ballast resistor start bypass wire, ignition coil primary winding, ignition module and distributor stator assembly. The secondary circuit consists of; battery, ignition switch, ignition coil secondary winding, distributor rotor, distributor cap, ignition wires, spark plugs.

With the ignition switch in the **RUN** position, the primary circuit is directed from the battery, through the ignition switch,

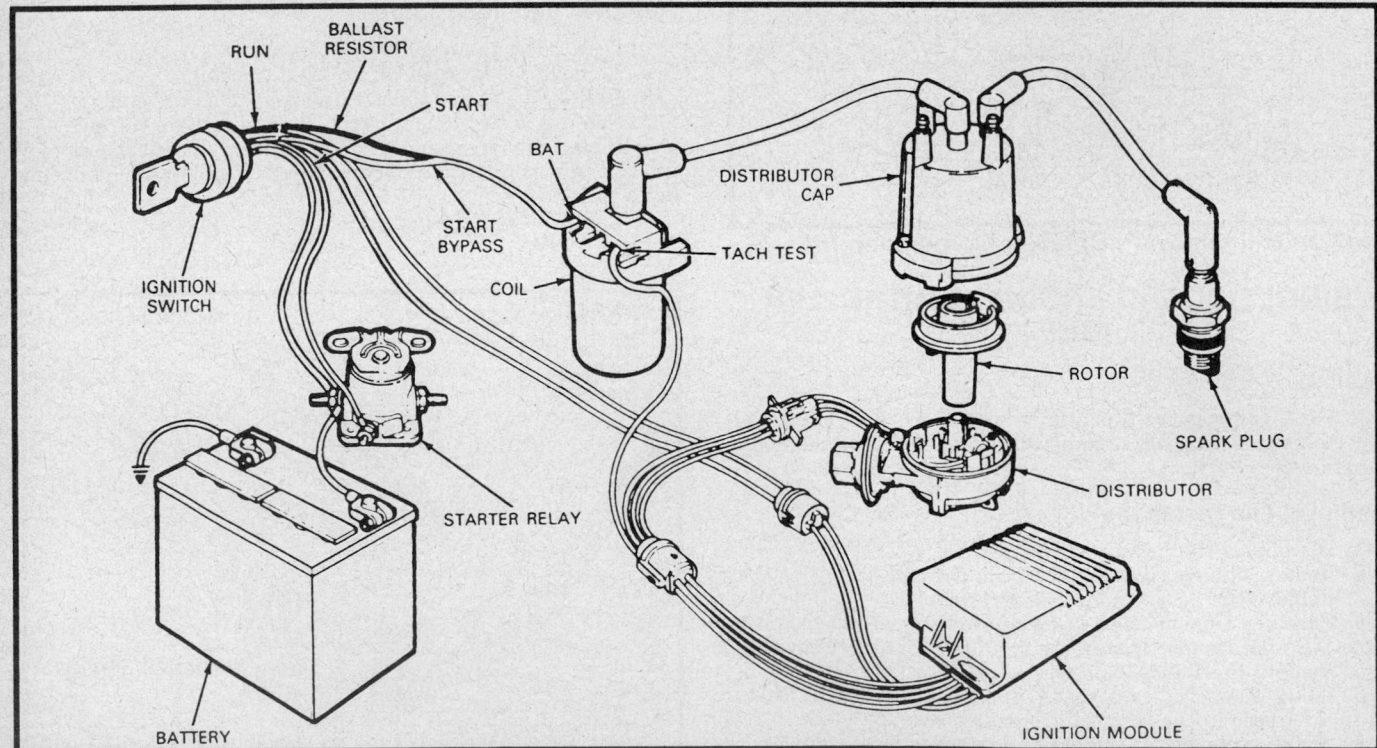

Ignition system diagram—Ford Dura-Spark

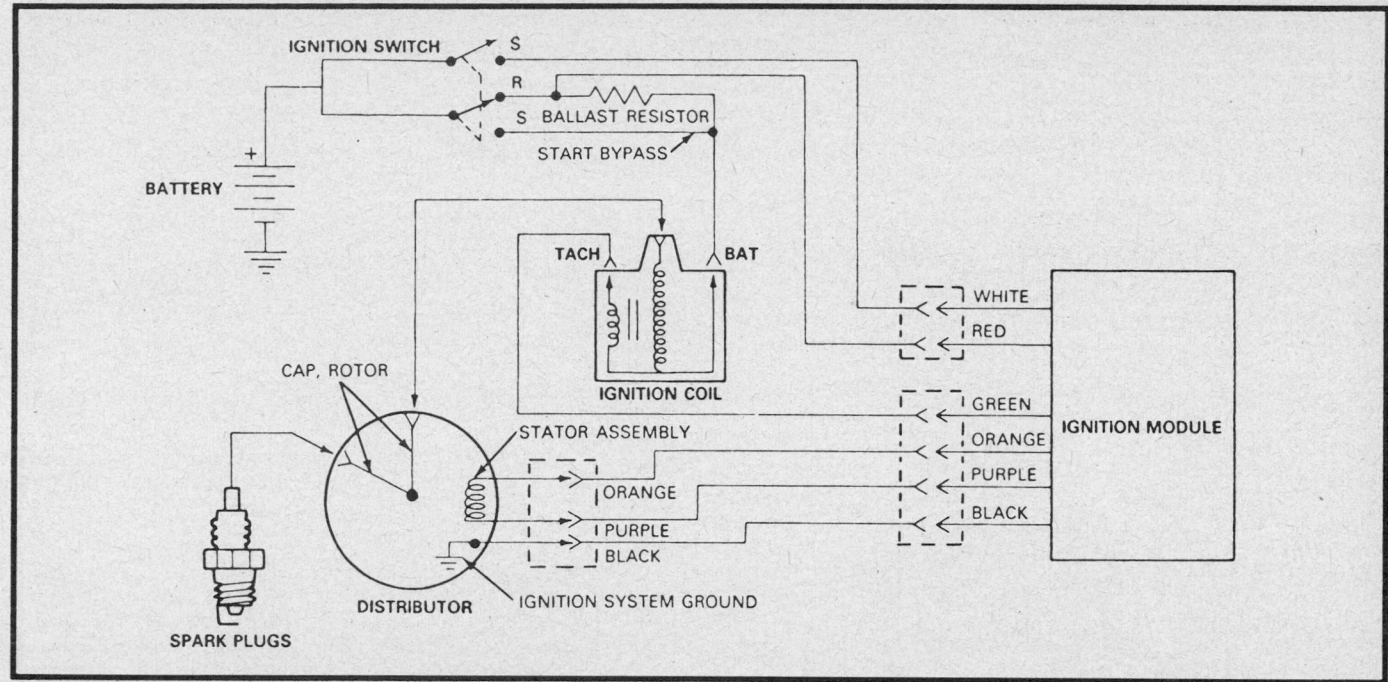

Ignition system schematic—Ford Dura-Spark

the ballast resistor, the ignition coil, the ignition module and back to the battery through the ignition system ground. This current flow causes a magnetic field to be built up in the ignition coil. When the poles on the armature and the stator assembly align, the ignition module turns the primary current flow off, collapsing the magnetic field in the ignition coil. The collapsing field induces a high voltage in the ignition coil secondary circuit. The ignition coil then conducts the high voltage to the distributor where the cap and rotor distribute it to the spark plugs.

A timing device in the ignition module turns the primary circuit back on after a very short period of time. High voltage is produced each time the magnetic field is built up and collapsed. A description of the system components follows:

Dura Spark ignition module—is equipped with an altitude sensor and an economy modulator. This module, when combined with the additional switches and sensors, varies the base engine timing according to altitude and engine load conditions. The module uses 3 wiring harness connectors. The module performs the function of turning off the current flow to the coil in response to a control signal. This signal comes from the stator in the distributor.

Distributor—the distributor provides a signal to the ignition module, which controls the timing of the spark at each plug. This signal is generated as the armature, attached to the distributor shaft, rotates past the stator assembly. The rotating armature causes fluctuations in a magnetic field produced by the stator assembly magnet. These fluctuations induce a voltage in the stator assembly pick-up coil. The occurence of the signal to the ignition module, in relation to the spark timing, is controlled by centrifugal and vacuum advance mechanisms.

Centrifugal spark advance mechanism—the centrifugal advance mechanism varies the relationship of the the armature to the stator assembly. The sleeve and plate assembly, on which the armature is mounted, rotates in relation to the distributor shaft. This rotation is caused by centrifugal weights moving in response to the engine rpm.

Vacuum spark control mechanism—also varies the armature to stator relationship. In this case the stator assembly position is changed by means of vacuum applied to the diaphragm assembly. This arrangement controls the rate of spark advance.

IGNITION COIL

Testing

The ignition coil must be diagnosed separately from the rest of the ignition system.

1. Primary resistance is measured between the 2 primary (low voltage) coil terminals, with the coil connector disconnected and the ignition switch **OFF**. Primary resistance must be 1.13–1.23 ohms.

2. The secondary resistance is measured between the BATT and high voltage (secondary) terminals of the ignition coil with the ignition **OFF** and the wiring from the coil disconnected. Secondary resistance must be 7700–9300 ohms on Dura Spark II systems.

3. If resistance tests are ok, but the coil is still suspected, test the coil on a coil tester by following the test equipment manufacturer's instructions for a standard coil. If the reading differs from the original test, check for a defective harness.

Removal and Installation

1. Disconnect the negative battery cable.
2. Remove the electrical leads from the coil.
3. Remove the coil mounting bolts and remove the coil from the vehicle.
4. Install the coil in position and connect the electrical leads.
5. Connect the negative battery cable.

STATOR ASSEMBLY

Removal and Installation

1. Disconnect the negative battery cable.
2. Remove the distributor cap and rotor.
3. Separate the distributor connector from the wiring harness.
4. Using a small gear puller or 2 suitable prybars, remove the armature from the sleeve and plate assembly. Use care not to loose the roll pin.
5. Remove the 2 screws retaining the lower plate assembly

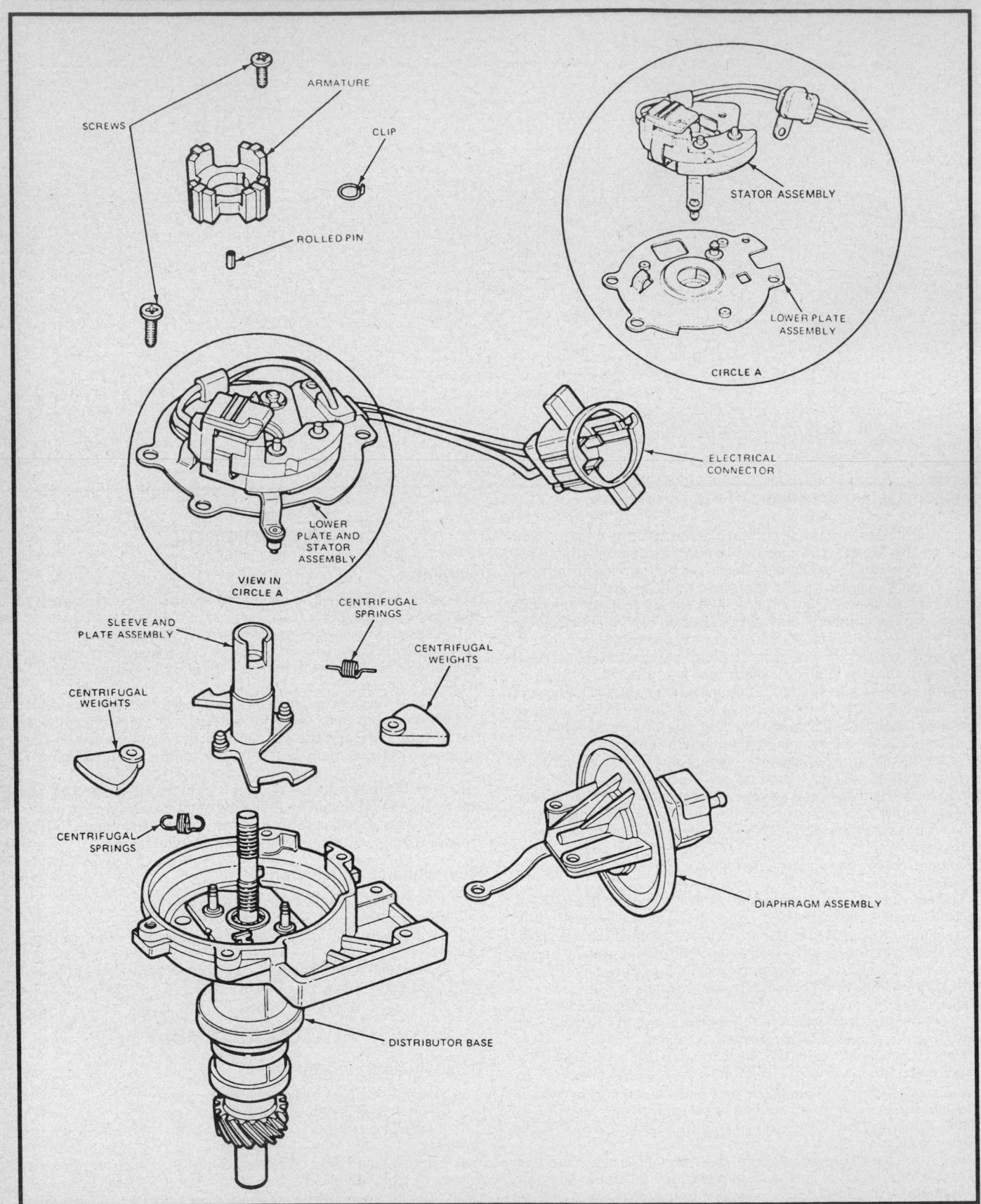

Distributor assembly—Ford Dura-Spark

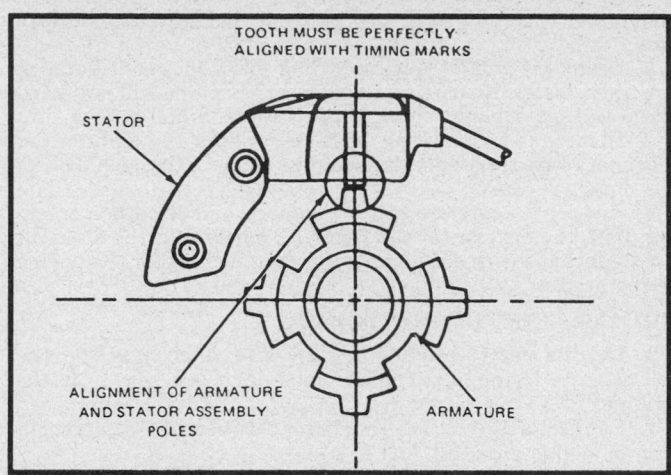

Stator assembly—Ford Dura-Spark

and stator assembly to the distributor base. Note that there are 2 different screws.

6. Remove the lower plate assembly and stator from the distributor.

7. Remove the C-clip, flatwasher and wave washer securing the stator assembly from the lower plate assembly. Note the position of the wave washer for installation.

To install:

8. Place the stator assembly on the lower plate assembly and install the wave washer, flat washer and C-clip.

9. Install the stator and lower plate assemblies on the distributor base. Engage the pin on the stator assembly with the diaphragm rod.

10. Install the 2 retaining screws and tighten to 15 inch lbs.

11. Install the aramature on the sleeve, noting the location of the notches. Install a new roll pin.

12. Connect the wiring harness. Install the distributor cap and rotor. Reconnect the ignition wires.

13. Connect the negative battery cable and check the ignition timing, adjust as needed.

DISTRIBUTOR

Disassembly and Assembly

1. Disconnect the negative battery cable.

2. Remove the distributor from the vehicle and support it in a suitable holding fixture.

3. Remove the distributor cap and rotor.

4. Using a small gear puller or 2 suitable prybars, remove the armature from the sleeve and plate assembly. Use care not to loose the roll pin.

5. Remove the 2 screws retaining the lower plate assembly and stator assembly to the distributor base. Note that there are 2 different screws.

6. Remove the lower plate assembly and stator from the distributor.

7. Remove the C-clip, flatwasher and wave washer securing the stator assembly from the lower plate assembly. Note the position of the wave washer for installation.

8. Remove the vacuum assembly from the distributor.

9. Remove the roll pin from the distributor drive gear and remove the drive gear.

10. Using a soft mallet, remove the distributor shaft from the housing.

To assemble:

11. Install the distributor shaft into the housing.

12. Install the distributor drive gear and install a new roll pin.

13. Install the vacuum assembly onto the housing.

14. Place the stator assembly on the lower plate assembly and install the wave washer, flat washer and C-clip.

15. Install the stator and lower plate assemblies on the distrib-

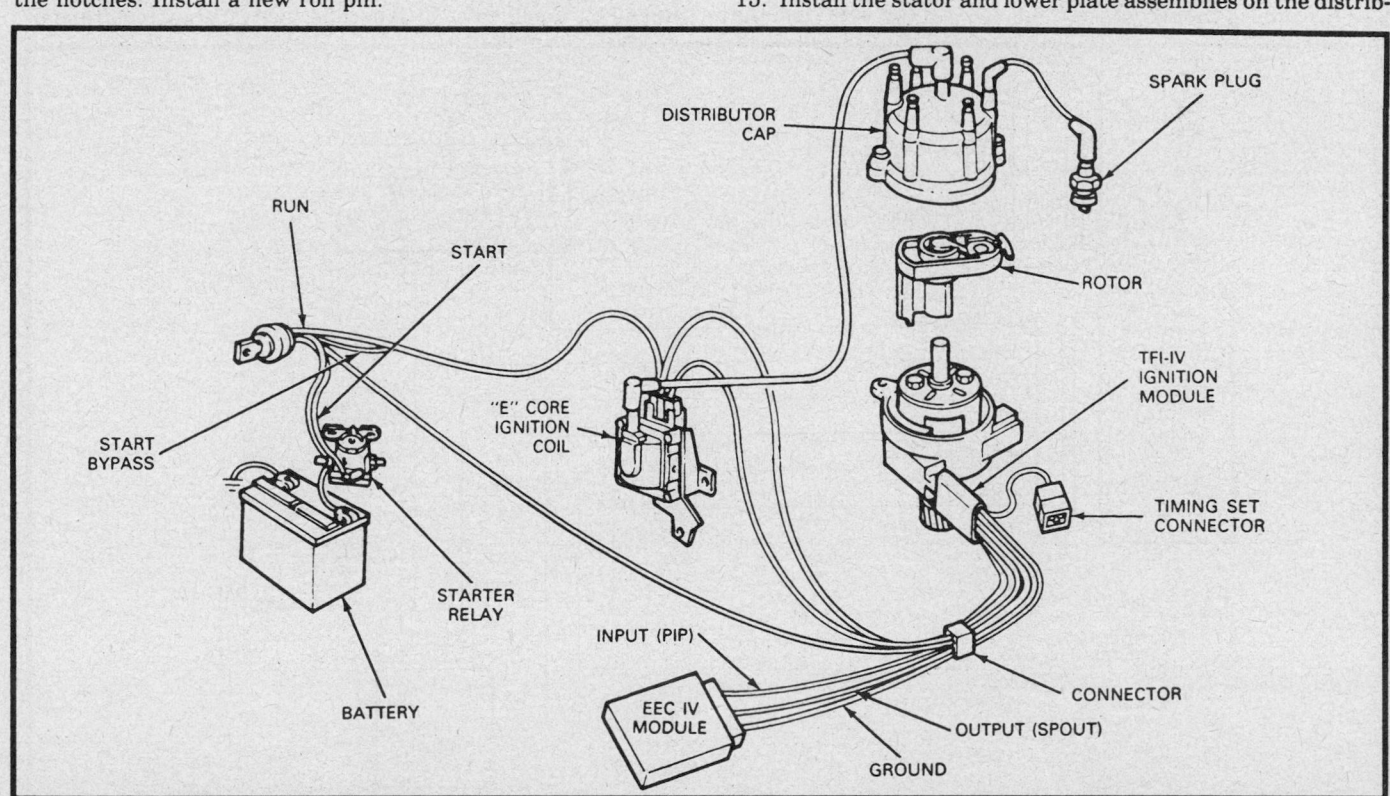

Ignition system diagram—Ford TFI

utor base. Engage the pin on the stator assembly with the diaphragm rod.

16. Install the 2 retaining screws and tighten to 15 inch lbs.

17. Install the armature on the sleeve, noting the location of the notches. Install a new roll pin.

18. Connect the wiring harness. Install the distributor cap and rotor. Reconnect the ignition wires.

19. Connect the negative battery cable and check the ignition timing, adjust as needed.

Thick Film Integrated (TFI) System

GENERAL INFORMATION

This system uses a universal distributor design which is gear driven and has a diecast base that incorporates an integrally mounted TFI-IV ignition module. The distributor also uses a Hall Effect vane switch stator assembly and has a provision for fixed octane adjustment. The new design eliminates the conventional centrifugal and vacuum advance mechanisms.

The ignition module is a thick film integrated design. The module is contained in moulded thermo plastic and is mounted on the distributor base. The TFI-IV module features a push start mode. This will allow push starting of the vehicle if it becomes necessary. The TFI-IV system uses an "E-Core" ignition coil, which replaces the oil-filled design used with previous ignition systems.

Provisions have been incorporated into the uiversal dstributor to allow fixed adjustment capability for octane needs. The adjustment is accomplished by replacing the standard 0 degree rod located in the distributor bowl.

IGNITION COIL

Testing

SECONDARY VOLTAGE

1. Disconnect the secondary (high voltage) coil wire from the distributor cap and install a spark tester between the coil wire and ground.

2. Crank the engine. A good, strong spark should be noted at the spark tester. If spark is noted, but the engine will not start, check the spark plugs, spark plug wiring and fuel system.

3. If there is no spark at the tester: Check the ignition coil secondary wire resistance; it should be no more than 5000 ohms per inch.

4. Inspect the ignition coil for damage and/or carbon tracking. With the distributor cap removed, verify that the distributor shaft turns with the engine; if it does not, repair the engine as required.

PRIMARY CIRCUIT SWITCHING

1. Insert a small straight pin in the wire which runs from the coil negative terminal to the TFI module, about 1 in. from the module.

2. Connect a 12 volt DC test lamp between the straight pin and an engine ground.

3. Crank the engine, noting the operation of the test lamp. If the test lamp flashes, check the coil resistance. If the test lamp lights but does not flash, test the wiring harness. If the test lamp does not light at all, check the primary circuit continuity.

IGNITION COIL RESISTANCE

The ignition coil must be diagnosed separately from the rest of the ignition system.

1. Primary resistance is measured between the 2 primary (low voltage) coil terminals, with the coil connector disconnected and the ignition switch **OFF**. Primary resistance must be 1.13–1.23 ohms.

2. The secondary resistance is measured between the BAT and high voltage (secondary) terminals of the ignition coil with the ignition **OFF** and the wiring from the coil disconnected. Secondary resistance must be 7700–9300 ohms on Dura Spark II systems.

3. If resistance tests are ok, but the coil is still suspected, test the coil on a coil tester by following the test equipment manu-

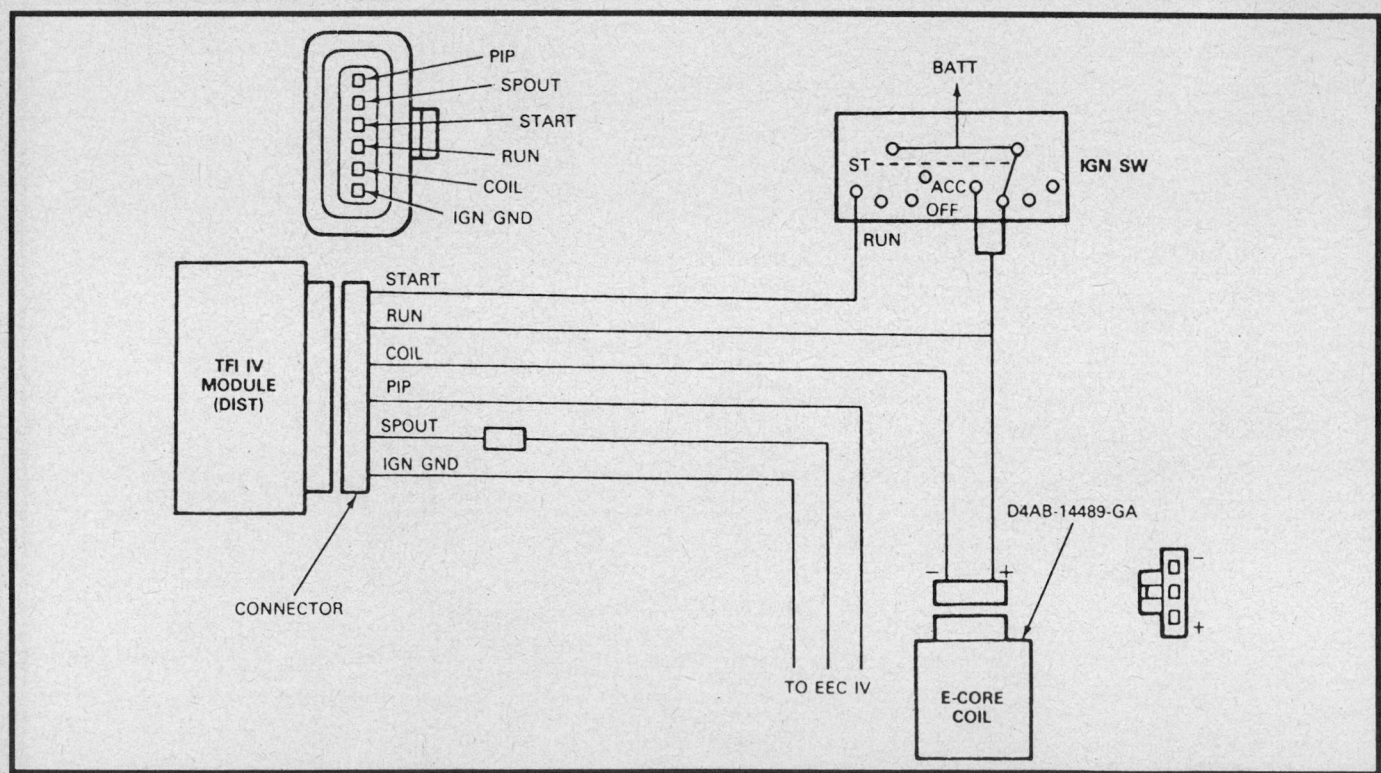

Ignition system schematic—Ford TFI

facturer's instructions for a standard coil. If the reading differs from the original test, check for a defective harness.

WIRING HARNESS

1. Disconnect the wiring harness connector from the TFI module; the connector tabs must be pushed to disengage the connector. Inspect the connector for damage, dirt and corrosion.

2. Attach the negative lead of a voltmeter to the base of the distributor. Attach the other voltmeter lead to a small straight pin. With the ignition switch in the **RUN** position, insert the straight pin into the No. 1 terminal of the TFI module connector.

3. Note the voltage reading. With the ignition switch in the **RUN** position, move the straight pin to the No. 2 connector terminal. Again, note the voltage reading.

4. Move the straight pin to the No. 3 connector terminal, then turn the ignition switch to the **START** position. Note the voltage reading then turn the ignition **OFF**.

5. The voltage readings should all be at least 90% of the available battery voltage.

6. If the readings are okay, proceed to the Stator Assembly and Module test. If any reading is less than 90% of the battery voltage, inspect the wiring, connectors and/or ignition switch for defects. If the voltage is low only at the No. 1 terminal, check the ignition coil primary voltage.

PRIMARY VOLTAGE

1. Attach the negative lead of a voltmeter to the distributor base.

2. Turn the ignition **ON** and connect the positive voltmeter lead to the negative ignition coil terminal. Note the voltage reading and turn the ignition **OFF**. If the voltmeter reading is less than 90% of the available battery voltage, inspect the wiring between the ignition module and the negative coil terminal, then proceed to the next test, which follows.

Supply Voltage

1. Attach the negative lead of a voltmeter to the distributor base.

2. Turn the ignition switch **ON** and connect the positive voltmeter lead to the positive ignition coil terminal Note the voltage reading, then turn the ignition **OFF**. If the voltage reading is at least 90% of the battery voltage, yet the engine will still not run; first, check the ignition coil connector and terminals for corrosion, dirt and/or damage; second, replace the ignition switch if the connectors and terminal are okay.

3. Connect any remaining wiring.

TFI IGNITION MODULE

Removal and Installation

1. Remove distributor cap and adapter. Position it and the attached wires aside.

2. Remove the TFI harness connector.

3. Remove the distributor from the engine.

4. Place the removed distributor in a suitable holding fixture. Remove the TFI module attachment screws.

5. Pull the right side of the module down the distributor mounting flange and then back up to disengage the module terminals for the connector in distributor base. The module may then be pulled toward flange and away from the distributor.

NOTE: Do not attempt to lift module from mounting surface prior to moving entire TFI module toward distributor flange as the pins at the distributor/module connector will break.

To install:

6. Coat the metal base plate of the TFI ignition module with silicone compound, approximately $\frac{1}{32}$ in. thick.

7. Place the TFI module on distributor base mounting flange.

8. Carefully position the TFI module assembly toward the distributor bowl and engage the distributor connector pins.

9. Install the TFI module mounting screws and tighten them 9–16 inch lbs.

10. Install the distributor on the engine.

11. Install the distributor cap and adapter and tighten adapter mounting screws.

12. Install the TFI harness connector.

13. Check the ignition timing.

OCTANE ROD

Removal and Installation

1. Remove the distributor cap, adapter and rotor.

2. Remove the octane rod 4mm retaining screw.

3. Slide the octane rod grommet out to a point where the rod can be disengaged from the stator retaining post and remove the octane rod. Retain the grommet for use with the new octane rod.

To install:

4. Install the grommet on the new octane rod.

5. Install the octane rod into the distributor, making sure it engages the stator retaining post.

6. Install the retaining screw and tighten to 15–35 inch lbs.

7. Install the rotor, adapter and cap.

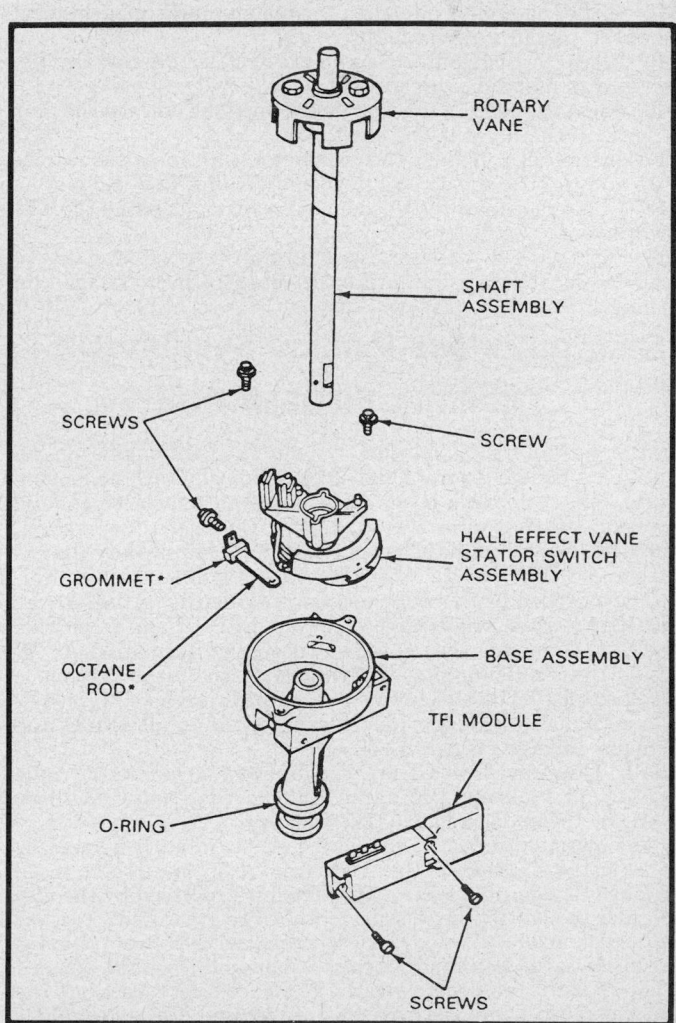

Distributor components—Ford TFI

STATOR

Removal and Installation

1. Disconnect the negative battery cable.
2. Remove the distributor from the vehicle and support it in a suitable holding fixture.
3. Remove the distributor cap and rotor. Remove the TFI module from the distributor.
4. Remove the screw retaining the armature and remove the armature.
5. Match mark the location of the stator with a felt tip pin. Remove the pins in the the stator gear and collar.
6. Using a suitable press, press the off the gear.
7. Remove the distributor shaft from the distributor body. Remove the octane rod.
8. Remove the stator mounting screws and remove the stator from the distributor body.

To install:

9. Install the stator in the distributor body. Press down on it to seat it in place.
10. Position the stator wires to the side and install the stator retaining bolts, tightening to 15–35 inch lbs. (1.7–4.0 Nm).
11. Install the octane rod in position. Tighten the retaining screws to 15–35 inch lbs. (1.7–4.0 Nm).
12. Apply a light coat of clean motor oil to the distributor shaft.
13. Insert the distributor shaft into the distributor body.
14. Install the collar and align the match marks made during removal. Install a new roll pin.
15. Place the distributor gear on the shaft and install the distributor in a suitable press.
16. Press the gear on the distributor until the holes in the gear align with the holes in the shaft.
17. Install the roll pin in the distributor gear. Install the armature and tighten the screws to 25–35 inch lbs. (2.8–4.0 Nm).
18. Check the shaft for freedom of movement. Install the TFI module onto the distributor.
19. Install the distributor cap and rotor.
20. Install the distributor into the vehicle. Check the ignition timing.

Distributorless Ignition System (DIS)

GENERAL INFORMATION

In the distributorless ignition system (DIS), all engine timing and spark distribution is handled electronically with no moving parts. This system has fewer parts that require replacement and provides a more accurately timed spark. During basic operation, the EEC-IV determines the ignition timing required by the engine and a DIS module determines which ignition coil to fire.

The purpose of the DIS module is to deliver a full energy spark at a crank angle targeted by the EEC-IV and to provide the EEC-IV module with speed and position information. An Ignition Diagnostic Monitor (IDM) Clean Tach Out (CTO) line is also provided. The DIS inputs and outputs are listed below;

a. Inputs – Variable Reluctance Sensor Input (VRS) and Spark Advance Word (SAW).

b. Outputs – Coil drivers, one for every 2 cylinders. Profile Ignition Pick-up (PIP) and Ignition Diagnostic Monitor (IDM) Clean Tach Out (CTO) line.

The Variable Reluctance Sensor (VRSA) input is derived by sensing the passage of the teeth from a 36 minus one tooth crankshaft mounted wheel. The signal is processed by the DIS in order to identify the missing tooth. Once the missing tooth is found, the module is said to be syncronized. Synchronization is essential to the DIS in order to ascertain and track the angular position of the crankshaft relative to a fixed reference. Since the missing tooth is indexed from top dead center (TDC) of the No. 1 cylinder, the cylinder pair of No. 1 and No. 4 is identified for 4 cylinder DIS. Cylinder pair indentification is a requirement for the Distributorless Ignition Systems (DIS) which fires a pair of simultaneous sparks (one on compression and one on exhaust).

A Profile Ignition Pick-Up (PIP) output is synthesized from the High Data Rate (HDR) VRTS signal and sent to the EEC-IV control module. This signal is a 50 percent duty cycle square wave with its rising edge at 10 degrees before top dead center of each cylinder event. The PIP signal is required by the EEC-IV control module to determine engine speed and position. Once the EEC-IV control module reconizes the the PIP signal, fuel and spark functions are enable. The Calculated spark target is sent to the DIS module as a pulse width modulated digital signal (SAW). This signal is sent once per cylinder event. It is then up to the DIS module to decode the SAW signal and to fire the next spark at the command spark target.

Coil firing is initiated by energizing the DIS coil in sequence referenced to the missing tooth (example 4 cylinder A-B) and firing at the command spark target. (default spark advance is 10 degrees BTDC). By energizing the primary side of the coils in proper sequence and by connecting the secondary wires in accordance with the engine firing order, a power stroke is achieved on each cylinder event with a wasted spark fired in the exhausting cylinder. In addition, an IDM/CTO signal is transmitted on each spark firing. This signal is intended to communicate diagnostic information by pulse width modulation and provide a clean buffered signal, proportional to engine speed, for tachometer operation. A brief description of the system components and their operation follows:

Variable Reluctance Sensor (VRS) – is a magnetic transducer with a pole piece wrapped with fine wire which , when exposed to a change in flux linkage will induce a differential voltage across the terminals of the wire windings. The output differential voltage of the transducer is a function of the sensor to tooth air gap (voltage increase with decreasing air gap), tooth and sensor pole piece width (fixed for a given design) and engine angular velocity (the voltage increases with increasing rpm).

When the VRS encounters a rotating timing wheel, the passing ferromagnetic teeth causes a change in the sensor reluctance. The varying reluctance alters the amount of magnetic flux linkage passing through the wire windings and induces a voltage proportional to both the rate of change in the magnetic flux and the number of coil windings. As a tooth approaches the pole piece of the sensor, a positive differential voltage is induced. This voltage is positive as long as the flux change is increasing. When the pole piece is in the center of the tooth there is no net change in the flux across the coil windings and the output voltage is zero. As the tooth moves away from the pole piece (increasing reluctance, decreasing flux), the output voltage swings negative.

The negative zero crossing of the differential VRS signal occurs when the pole piece of the sensor corresponds to the center of each physical tooth. The DIS module is sensitive only to this negative zero crossing and uses this transition to establish crankshaft position.

At normal engine running speeds, the VRS signal waveform is an approximation of a sine wave with increased amplitude adjacent to the missing tooth region. The variable reluctance sensor and wheel are designed to provide a nearly symetrical signal and meet the following specifications:

a. Minimum engine speed 30 rpm with a VRS output voltage of 150 milli-volts peak to peak.

b. Maximum engine speed 8000 rpm with a VRS output voltage of 300 volts peak to peak.

The DIS module will not operate if the polarity of the VRS signal is reversed. In addition, starting cables and other noise producing elements should be routed away from the VRS wires so as not to induce noise.

Profile Ignition Pick-Up (PIP) – the DIS synthetic PIP is not a hardware sensor output but rather a software driven signal. The PIP is generated in response to detection and recogni-

tion of VRS input signals corresponding to traditional PIP high and PIP low engine positions. The DIS module is hardware functionally compatible with the EEC-IV system. This compatibility minimizes the EEC-IV module complexity.

The PIP interface signal , historically has been generated by a magnetic Hall pick up sensor located in the distributor. The PIP output signal is synthesized from the VRS sensor and is the basic engine timing signal sent to the EEC-IV control module. The signal profile is a rising edge at 10 degrees BTDC of every cylinder event with a 50 percent duty cycle, i.e. (the falling edge is 90 degrees later on a 4 cylinder; 60 degrees later on a 6 cylinder and 45 degrees later on an 8 cylinder). This signal characteristic is a battery voltage square wave.

Spark Angle Word (SAW) — is a pulse width encoded spark advance word generated by the EEC-IV control module. In conventional TFI-IV systems, this signal line is called the Spout for spark out. The EEC-IV system hardware is identical for both of these systems.

In the conventional systems, a rising edge Spout corresponds to a spark firing event; the falling edge is used for dwell control. The EEC-IV control module is tasked with real time control for both spark placement and dwell. Additionally in the event of an EEC-IV control module failure, the EEC-IV system will enter a Limited Operation Strategy (LOS) mode which, among other things will put the Spout in a tri-state (i.e. high impedance state). This loss of Spout will by default force the TFI-IV to a 10 degrees BTDC fixed spark timing.

The DIS system utilizes a SAW signal. SAW is a pulse width modulated signal typically produced once per cylinder event. A SAW signal is required a minimum of once every 5 cylinder firings, but may by updated as often as every spark event. SAW may be transmitted at any time during the cylinder except at 10 degrees after top dead center (ATDC).

If the SAW value received is not within specification, the DIS module will target sparks to the last valid spark advance recognized. This spark timing will continue for 5 misinterpreted or unreceived SAW values. Additional SAW faults will invoke the 10 degrees BTDC default spark timing.

In EEC-IV LOS, the Spout line enters a tri-state mode, which results in a no SAW signal to the DIS module. This forces the DIS module to the 10 degrees BTDC timing after the criteria for 5 missing SAW pulses have been satisfied. Normal operation resumes when 3 consecutive valid SAW values have been recognized.

The SAW transfer function was designed to be compatible with 4, 6, and 8 cylinder DIS modules. To do this, it was required that the transfer function maximum pulse width be allowed enough time for transmission at a worse case DIS module for 8 cylinder at 800 rpm operating point. To insure a sufficient guard band, the SAW is specified to decrease in duration as spark advance is increased. At high rpm, the alotted time for SAW transmission is decreased; at the same time spark advance is typically increased. It is therefore desirable for the SAW pulse width to decrease as the spark target advances. A final constraint was to make the SAW easily decodeable. The following DIS SAW transfer function meets all of the described constraints SAW = 1540 - 25.6 spark advance. SAW is measured in micro-seconds and the valid spark advance is 57.5 degrees BTDC (+ 57.5 degrees: SAW-68 us) to 10 degrees ATDC (-10 degrees: SAW-1792 us). During respective spark, the SAW pulse width is increased by 2048 micro-seconds. This longer pulse width indicates to the DIS module that repetitive spark is desired.

Ignition Diagnostic Monitor (IDM) — is a signal line used to convey the DIS operating status to the EEC-IV system. The EEC-IV signal circuitry is identical to that used in the TFI-IV ignition system. The TFI-IV diagnostic line is referred to as the Ignition Diganostic Monitor (IDM).

In the DIS system, the IDM pulse is hardware triggered by the ignition coil flyback. The flyback voltage, which when inter-

nally sensed in the DIS module, indicates a pulse width encoded IDM output. The ignition diagnostic monitor is a battery voltage variable pulse width signal.

An additional function of the IDM line is to provide an optional method in which to drive a tachometer (TACH). In the DIS 4 cylinder system this signal is brought out on 2 pins, IDM and Clean Tach Out (CTO). The IDM and CTO driven tach lines may be used to provide a buffered TACH signal. This buffered tach signal eliminates radiated noise emissions associated with the high voltage IDM line signal harness.

Crankshaft Timing Sensor — besides the PIP signal there is another signal generated called the Cylinder Identification (CID). The CID signal is used to synchronize the ignition coils, due to the fact that the Ranger uses a 2 ignition coil pack DIS system.

The Dual Hall Effect crankshaft sensor contains 2 hall digital output devices (PIP and CID) in one package. The sensor is located on a bracket mounted near the crankshaft damper. Two rotary vane cups (or wheels) are mounted on the damper and used to trigger the Hall sensors.

When the window of the vane cup is between the magnet and the Hall Effect device, a magnetic flux field is completed from the magnet through the Hall Effect device back to the magnet the output signal will be low (0 volts). However, as the vane passes through the gap between the Hall Effect device and the magnet, the flux lines are shunted through the vane and back to the magnet and the output will change from a low voltage to a high voltage.

The PIP cup has 2 teeth resulting in a 2 positive going edges each revolution of the crankshaft, where as the CID cup has 1 tooth and generates a signal that is high half of the crankshaft revolution and low the other half. The CID is used by the DIS module to enable it to select the proper coils to fire. When the CID is high, coils 2 and 3 are enabled and when the CID is low 1 and 4 are enabled. The EEC-IV control module tells the DIS module when to fire but the DIS module has to select one of the 2 coils based on the CID (which 2 of 4 if in the DPI mode).

Ignition coil pack — there are 2 ignition coil packs used on the 2.3L dual plug engine. The 2 ignition coil packs are triggered by the DIS module and are timed by the EEC-IV control module. Each coil pack contains 2 separate ignition coils for a total of 4 ignition coils. Each ignition coil fires 2 spark plugs simultaneously, 1 spark plug on the compression stroke and 1 on the exhaust stroke. The spark plug fired on the exhaust stroke uses very little of the ignition coils stored energy and the majority of the ignition coils energy is used by the spark plug on the compression stroke. Since these 2 spark plugs are are connected in series, the firing voltage of one of the spark plugs will be negative with respect to ground, while the other one will be positive with respect to ground.

DIS module — the main function of the DIS module is to switch between the ignition coils and trigger the coils to spark. The DIS ignition module receives the PIP and the CID signals from the crankshaft timing sensor and the Spout (spark out) signal from the EEC-IV control module. During normal operation, the PIP signal is passed onto the EEC-IV control module and provides base timing and rpm information. The CID signal provides the DIS module with information required to switch between the coils for cylinders No. 1 and No. 4 and the coils for cylinders No. 2 and No. 3. The Spout signal (from the EEC-IV control module) contains the optimum spark timing and dwell time information. The spark angle is determined by the rising edge of the Spout while the falling edge of the Spout controls the coil current on or dwell time. The dwell time is controlled or varied by varying the duty cycle of the Spout signal.

This feature is called Computer Controlled Dwell (CCD). With the proper inputs of the PIP, CID and Spout the DIS module turns the ignition coils on and off in the proper sequence for spark control.

CRANKSHAFT TIMING SENSOR

Removal and Installation

1. Disconnect the negative battery cable.
2. Disconnect the sensor electrical connectors from the engine wiring harness.
3. Remove the large electrical connector from the crankshaft timing sensor assembly by prying out the red retaining clip and removing the 4 wires.
4. Remove the crankshaft pulley assembly by removing the accessory drive belts and then the 4 bolts that retaining the crankshaft pulley hub assembly. Remove the timing belt outer cover.
5. Rotate the crankshaft so that the keyway is at the 10 o'clock position. This will place the vane window of both the inner and outer vane cups over the crankshaft sensor timing assembly.

NOTE: The vane cups are attached to the crankshaft pulley hub assembly.

6. Remove the 2 crankshaft timing sensor retaining bolts and the plastic wire harness retainer which secures the crankshaft sensor to its mounting bracket.
7. Remove the crankshaft timing sensor assembly, sliding the wires out from behind the inner timing belt cover.

To install:

8. Remove the large electrical connector from the new crankshaft timing sensor assembly.
9. Position the crankshaft timing sensor assembly. First slide the electrical wires behind the inner timing belt cover, now hold the sensor assembly loosely in place with the retaining bolts but do not tighten the bolts at this time.
10. Install the large electrical connector onto the crankshaft timing sensor assembly.

NOTE: Be sure that the 4 wires to the large electrical connector are installed in the proper locations. The sensor will not function properly if the wires are installed incorrectly.

11. Reconnect both of the crankshaft timing sensor electrical connectors to the engine harness.
12. Rotate the crankshaft so that the outer vane on the crankshaft pulley hub assembly engages both sides of the crankshaft Hall Effect sensor positioner tool T89P-6316-A or equivalent and tighten the sensor assembly retaining bolts.
13. Rotate the crankshaft so that the vane on the crankshaft pulley hub is no longer engaged in the crankshaft sensor positioner tool and remove the tool.
14. Install a new plastic wire harness retainer to secure the crankshaft timing sensor harness to its mounting bracket and trim off the excess.
15. Install the timing belt outer cover.

16. Install the crankshaft pulley assembly and tighten the 4 attaching bolts to specifications.
17. Install the drive belts and adjust as necessary. Reconnect the negative battery cable and perform a vehicle road test.

DIS MODULE

Removal and Installation

1. Disconnect the negative battery cable.
2. Disconnect each electrical connector of the DIS ignition module assembly by pushing down the connector locking tabs where it is stamped **PUSH** and then pull it away from the module.
3. Remove the 3 retaining screws, remove the ignition module assembly from the lower intake manifold.

To install:

4. Apply an even coat (approximately $\frac{1}{32}$ in.) of a suitable silicone dielectric compound to the mounting surface of the DIS module.
5. Mount the DIS module assembly onto the intake assembly and install the retaining screws. Torque the screws to 22–31 inch lbs.
6. Install the electrical connectors to the DIS ignition module assembly. Reconnect the negative battery cable.

IGNITION COIL PACK

Removal and Installation

1. Disconnect the negative battery cable.
2. Disconnect the electrical harness connector from the ignition coil pack.
3. Remove the spark plug wires by squeezing the locking tabs to release the coil boot retainers.
4. Remove the coil pack mounting screws and remove the coil pack.

NOTE: On vehicle equipped with power steering it may be necessary to remove the intake (left hand) coil and bracket as an assembly.

To install:

5. Install the coil pack and the retaining screws. Torque the retaining screws to 40–62 inch lbs.
6. Connect the spark plug wires and connect the electrical connector to the coil pack.
7. Reconnect the negative battery cable.

NOTE: Be sure to place some dielectric compound into each spark plug boot prior to installation of the spark plug wire.

GENERAL MOTORS CORPORATION

High Energy Ignition (HEI) Systems
GENERAL INFORMATION

The Delco Remy High Energy Ignition (HEI) System is a breakerless, pulse triggered, transistor controlled, inductive discharge ignition system. There are only nine external electrical connections; the ignition switch feed wire and the eight spark plug leads. The ignition coil is located within the distributor cap, connecting directly to the rotor. All others have a separate coil. There are 2 basic systems that are used in conjunction with the basic high energy distributor, Electronic Spark Control (ESC) and Electronic Spark Timing (EST). Each uses an HEI system distributor with an increased number of sensors over the base HEI system.

The magnetic pick up assembly located inside the distributor contains a permanent magnet, a pole piece with internal teeth, and a pick-up coil. When the teeth of the rotating timer core and

pole piece align, an induced voltage in the pick-up coil signals the electronic module to open the coil primary circuit. As the primary current decreases, a high voltage is induced in the secondary windings of the ignition coil, directing a spark through the rotor and high voltage leads to fire the spark plugs. The dwell period is automatically controlled by the electronic module and is increased with increasing engine rpm. The HEI System features a longer spark duration which is instrumental in firing lean and EGR diluted fuel/air mixtures. The condenser (capacitor) located within the HEI distributor is provided for noise (static) suppression purposes only and is not a regularly replaced ignition system component.

Some engines use an Electronic Spark Timing (EST) distributor. This unit replaces vacuum and centrifugal advance units with an electronic actuator (Hall Effect stator). A vacuum sensor provides manifold vacuum information and a reference pulse is generated by a pulse generator located near the engine vibration damper. These signals are fed to an Electronic Control Module (ECM) which, in turn, sends a signal to the EST distributor for ignition timing determination.

Some engines also use an Electronic Spark Control (ESC) which responds to engine detonation with retardation of ignition timing. An engine block mounted sensor detects the presence of vibration generated by detonation and signals the ESC controller to process the signal and adjust the timing via the actuator on the distributor. The system gradually retards the spark until detonation has disappeared. A failed sensor would produce occasional detonation.

These ESC equipped engines also have a "tip in" vacuum switch. When the throttle is suddenly opened and manifold vacuum is suddenly decreased, the switch contacts close to send a signal to the ESC controller to arbitrarily retard the spark to prevent knock. Thus, if the engine knocks for a very short time after a rapid opening of the throttle, this switch may be at fault.

Vehicles equipped with the 2.5L engine have distributors that contain a Hall Effect Switch which provides a voltage signal to the ECM when the rotating iron vane blocks the magnetic flux between the permanent magnet and the switch circuit. On these

distributors, the **R** terminal on the module inside the distributor is not used.

The majority of system diagnosis is performed in conjunction with the computer command control system diagnosis and requires the reading of engine failure codes from the ECM.

IGNITION COIL

Testing

1. Remove the distributor cap.
2. Connect an ohmmeter to the distributor cap terminal C and ground.
3. The reading should be at or nearly 0. If not, replace the coil.
4. Connect an ohmmeter to the B+ terminal and high tension rotor contact in the center of the cap.
5. Use the ohmmeter on the high scale and measure the resistance. Reverse the leads and recheck the resistance.
6. If both readings are infinite, replace the coil.

Removal and Installation
INTEGRAL COIL

1. Disconnect the negative battery cable. Disconnect the feed and module wire terminal connectors from the distributor cap.
2. Remove the ignition set retainer.
3. Remove the 4 coil cover to distributor cap screws and the coil cover.
4. Remove the 4 coil to distributor cap screws.
5. Using a blunt drift, press the coil wire spade terminals up out of distributor cap.
6. Lift the coil up out of the distributor cap.
7. Remove and clean the coil spring, rubber seal washer and coil cavity of the distributor cap.
8. Installation is the reverse of the removal procedure.

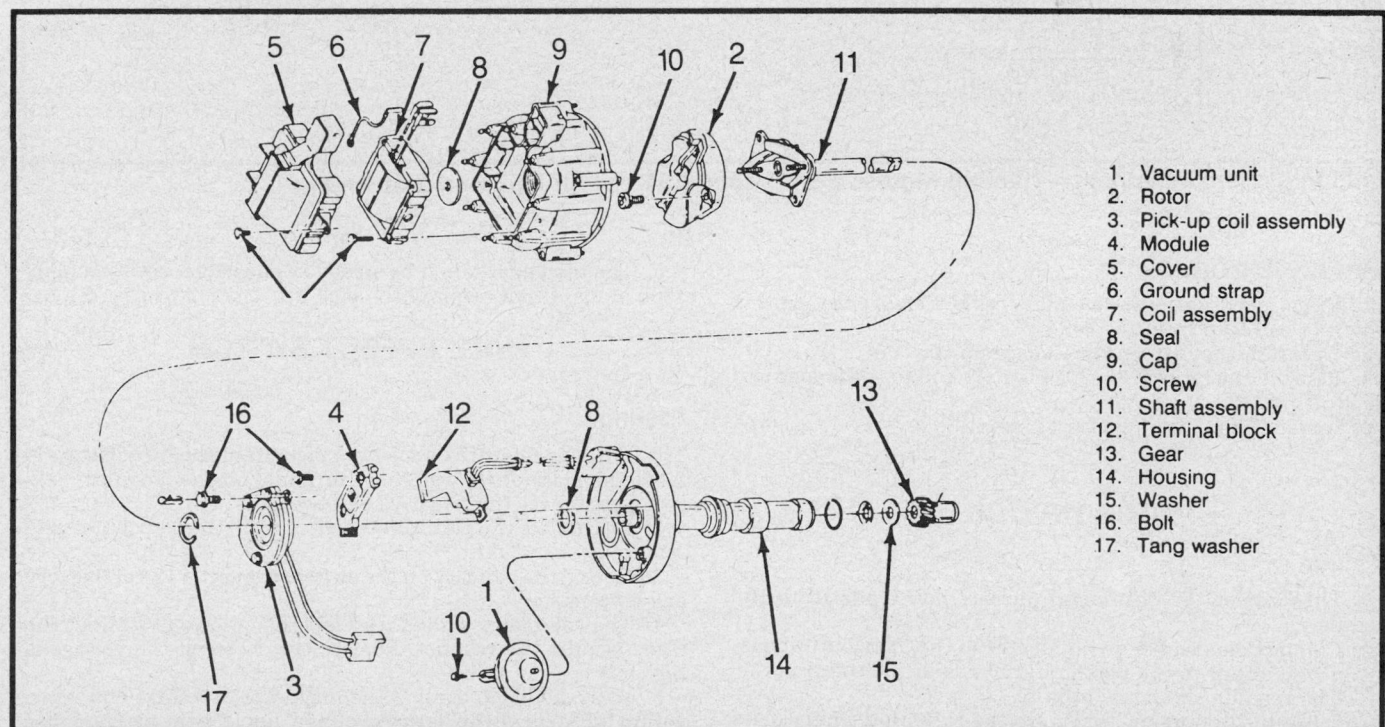

1. Vacuum unit
2. Rotor
3. Pick-up coil assembly
4. Module
5. Cover
6. Ground strap
7. Coil assembly
8. Seal
9. Cap
10. Screw
11. Shaft assembly
12. Terminal block
13. Gear
14. Housing
15. Washer
16. Bolt
17. Tang washer

Distributor assembly—General Motors Corporation HEI

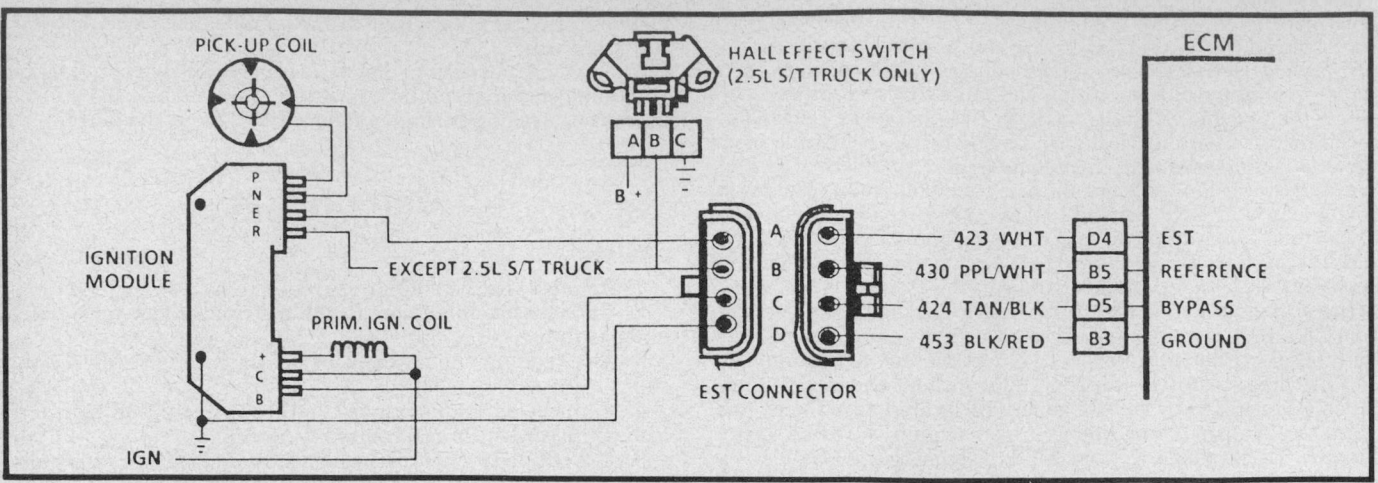

Ignition system schematic—General Motors Corporation 2.5L and 2.8L engine with EST

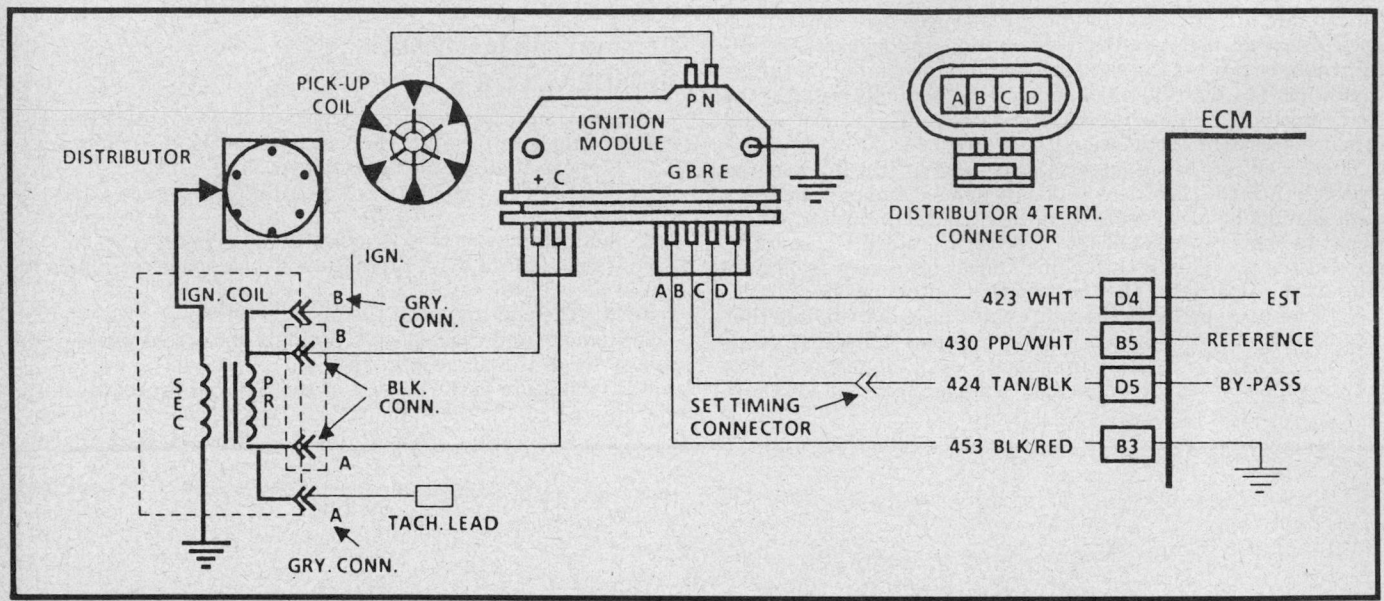

Ignition system schematic—General Motors Corporation EST except 2.5L and 2.8L engine

SEPARATE COIL

1. Disconnect the negative battery cable. Remove the ignition switch to coil lead from the coil.
2. Unfasten the distributor leads from the coil.
3. Remove the screws which secure the coil to the engine and lift it off.
4. Installation is the reverse of removal.

PICK-UP COIL

Testing

1. Disconnect the rotor and pick-up coil leads from the module.
2. Connect one lead of an ohmmeter to the distributor housing and the other to the pick-up terminals in the connector.
3. The reading should be infinite.
4. Place the ohmmeter leads into the pick-up terminals and measure the resistance.

5. The readings should be steady at one value, between 500–1500 ohms. If not, replace the pick-up.

HALL EFFECT SWITCH

Testing

The switch is mounted above the pick-up in the distributor, It takes the place of the reference terminal on the module.
1. Disconnect the negative battery cable.
2. Disconnect the Hall Effect switch from the distributor and remove it.
3. Noting the polarity on the switch, connect a 12 volt battery and a voltmeter.
4. The volt meter should read less than 0.5 volts without the blade against the magnet. Replace the switch if the voltage is higher.
5. With the blade against the magnet, the voltage should be within 0.5 volts of the battery voltage. Replace the switch if the voltage is low.

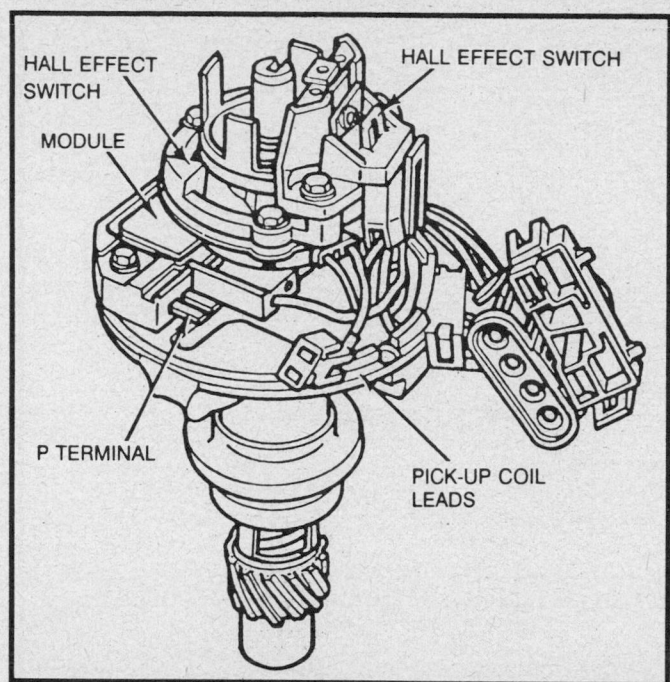

HALL EFFECT SWITCH

HALL EFFECT SWITCH

MODULE

P TERMINAL

PICK-UP COIL LEADS

Distributor components — General Motors Corporation EST with Hall Effect switch

DISTRIBUTOR

Removal and Installation

CAP

1. Disconnect the negative battery cable. Remove the feed and module wire terminal connectors from the distributor cap.
2. Remove the retainer and spark plug wires from the cap.
3. Depress and release the 4 distributor cap to housing retainers and lift off the cap assembly.
4. Remove the 4 coil cover screws and cover, on V8 engines.
5. Using a finger or a blunt drift, push the spade terminals up out of the distributor cap (V8 engines).
6. Remove all 4 coil screws and lift the coil, coil spring and rubber seal washer out of the cap coil cavity, V8 engines only.
7. Using a new distributor cap, reverse the above procedures to assemble.

ROTOR

1. Disconnect the feed and module wire connectors from the distributor.

2. Depress and release the 4 distributor cap to housing retainers and lift off the cap assembly.
3. Remove the 2 rotor attaching screws and rotor.
4. Reverse the above procedure to install.

VACUUM ADVANCE UNIT

1. Remove the distributor cap and rotor.
2. Disconnect the vacuum hose from the vacuum advance unit. Remove the module.
3. Remove the 2 vacuum advance retaining screws, pull the advance unit outward, rotate and disengage the operating rod from its tang.
4. Reverse the above procedure to install.

MODULE

1. Remove the distributor cap and rotor.
2. Disconnect the harness connector and pick-up coil spade connectors from the module (note their positions).
3. Remove the 2 screws and module from the distributor housing.
4. Coat the bottom of the new module with dielectric lubricant.
5. Reverse the removal procedure to install. Be sure that the leads are installed correctly.

DRIVEN GEAR

1. Disconnect the negative battery cable. Remove the distributor from the vehicle and support it in a suitable holding fixture. Use a $\frac{1}{8}$ in. pin punch and tap out the driven gear roll pin.
2. Hold the rotor end of shaft and rotate the driven gear to shear any burrs in the roll pin hole.
3. Remove the driven gear from the shaft.
4. Install the gear to the shaft and install a new roll pin.
5. Install the distributor into the vehicle.

MAINSHAFT

1. Disconnect the negative battery cable. Remove the distributor and support it in a suitable holding fixture. With the driven gear and rotor removed, gently pull the mainshaft out of the housing.
2. Remove the advance springs, weights and slide the weight base plate off the mainshaft.
3. Installation is the reverse of removal.

POLE PIECE, MAGNET OR PICK UP COIL

1. Disconnect the negative battery cable. Remove the distributor from the vehicle and support it in a suitable holding fixture. With the mainshaft out of its housing, remove the 3 retaining screws, pole piece and magnet and/or pick-up coil.
2. Reverse the removal procedure to install making sure that the pole piece teeth do not contact the timer core teeth by installing and rotating the mainshaft. Loosen the 3 screws and realign the pole piece as necessary.

JEEP CORPORATION

Solid State Ignition (SSI) System
GENERAL INFORAMTION

The Solid State Ignition (SSI) system is used on 4.2L and 5.9L engines. The SSI system consists of a Micro Computer Unit (MCU), electronic ignition control unit, ignition coil, resistance wire, distributor assembly, knock sensor, spark plugs and wires.

The MCU is a permanently sealed unit which is located in the engine compartment. The MCU cannot be serviced, and must be replaced as a unit.

The electronic ignition control unit is a solid state module. Its components are permanently sealed and cannot be serviced. If service is required, the module must be replaced.

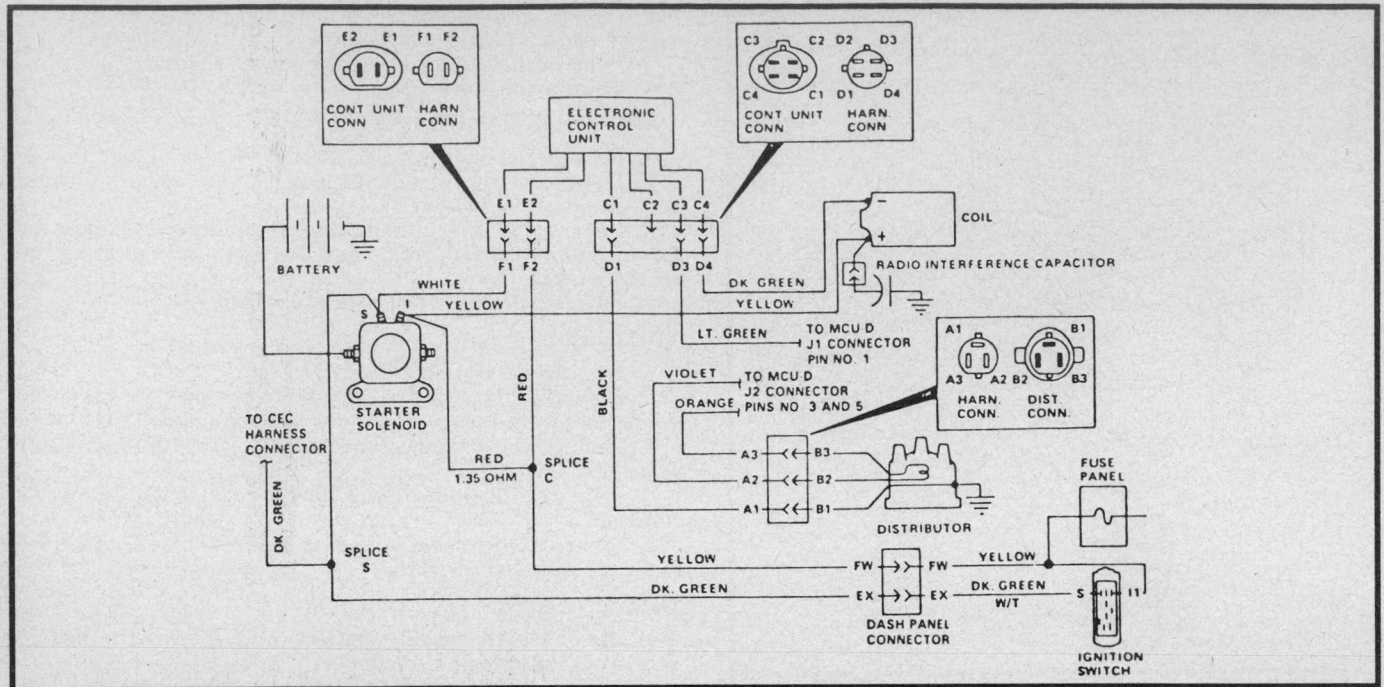

Jeep SSI system schematic — 4.2L engine

IGNITION COIL

Testing

PRIMARY WINDING RESISTANCE

1. Ensure ignition switch is **OFF**. Disconnect electrical connector from the positive and negative terminals of the ignition coil.
2. Set ohmmeter on low scale. Connect ohmmeter leads onto coil negative and positive terminals.
3. Resistance should read 1.13–1.23 ohms at 75°F. A difference of 1.5 ohms is acceptable if coil temperature is above 200°F.

SECONDARY WINDING RESISTANCE

1. Ensure ignition switch is **OFF**. Remove ignition wire from ignition coil.
2. Set ohmmeter on 1000x scale and adjust pointer to 0.
3. Connect ohmmeter leads to contact of ignition coil and onto either negative or positive terminal.
4. Resistance should read 7700–9300 ohms at 75°F. A difference of 12,000 ohms is acceptable if coil temperature is above 200°F.

CURRENT FLOW

1. Disconnect the electrical connector from ignition coil, then remove the positive and negative wires from the connector terminal.
2. Connect an ammeter onto the positive terminal of the coil and the disconnected positive wire, then a jumper wire from the coil negative terminal to ground.
3. Turn ignition switch to the **ON** position. Current flow should read approximately 7 amps and should exceed 7.6 amps. If current flow exceeds 7.6 amps, replace the ignition coil.
4. Remove jumper wire from coil, leaving the ammeter connected to the coil positive terminal.
5. Connect the coil green wire to the coil negative terminal. Current flow should read approximately 4 amps. If current flow is less than 3.5 amps, check for bad connections at the control unit, distributor and an insufficient ground at the ground screw

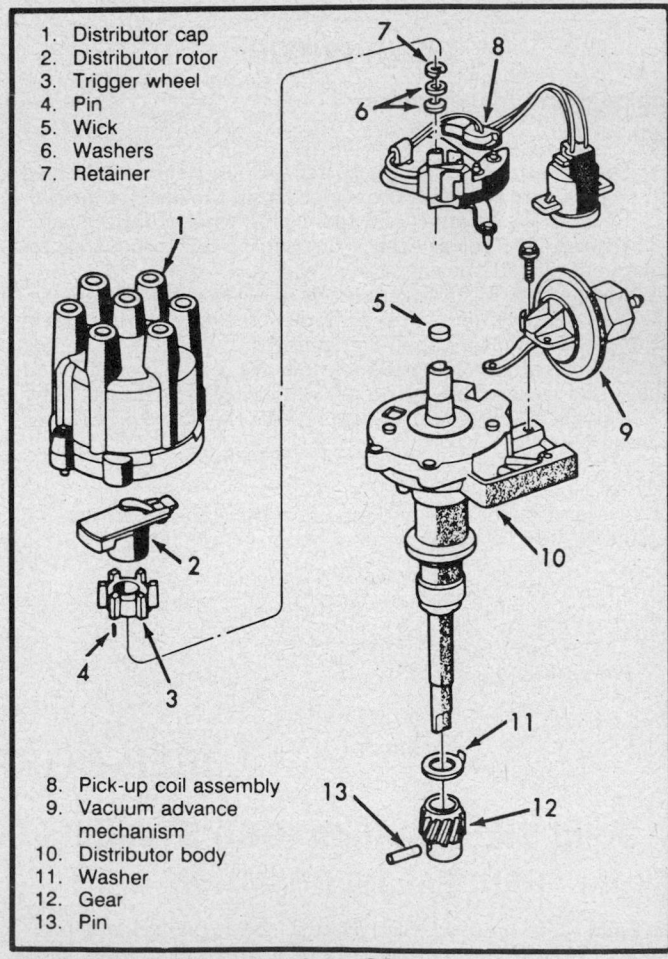

1. Distributor cap
2. Distributor rotor
3. Trigger wheel
4. Pin
5. Wick
6. Washers
7. Retainer
8. Pick-up coil assembly
9. Vacuum advance mechanism
10. Distributor body
11. Washer
12. Gear
13. Pin

Distributor assembly — Jeep SSI

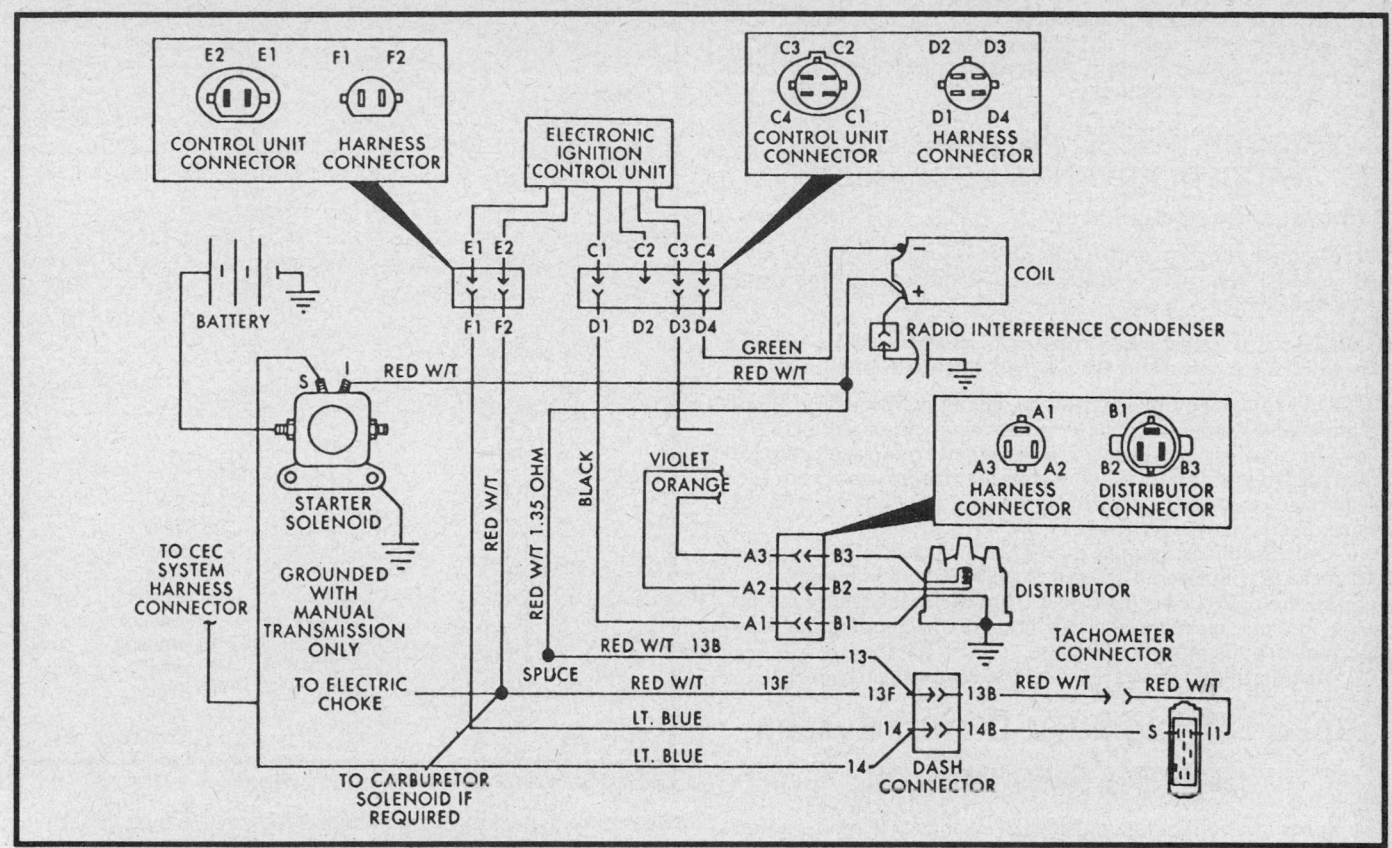

Jeep SSI system schematic—5.9L engine

inside the distributor. If current flow exceeds 5 amps, the ECU is defective and must be replaced.

6. Start engine. Normal current flow with engine operating should read 2.0–2.4 amps. If current flow is not within specifications, the ECU is defective and must be replaced.

OUTPUT

1. Connect a oscilloscope to the ignition coil.

NOTE: Do not operate engine for more than 30 seconds with spark plug wires disconnected. Damage to the catalytic converter could occur.

2. Disconnect any spark plug wire from the distributor cap. Note voltage applied to the spark plug wire on the oscilloscope. Minimum voltage should be 24,000 volts with a engine speed of 1000 rpm.

Removal and Installation

1. Disconnect the negative battery cable.
2. Disconnect the the high tension lead from the coil and disconnect the wiring connector from the coil.
3. Remove the coil mounting bolt and remove the coil from the vehicle.
4. Install the coil in position and connect the electrical leads.
5. Connect the negative battery cable.

DISTRIBUTOR

Testing

CENTRIFUGAL ADVANCE

1. Apply parking brake. On vehicles equipped with automatic transmission, position shift selector lever in the **P** position. On

vehicles equipped with manual transmissions, position shifter in the neutral position.

2. Start and allow engine to reach normal operating temperature. Ensure that air conditioning is **OFF**, if equipped.

3. With ignition switch **OFF**, disconnect the 3 pin connector from the 4 and 10 in. Hg. vacuum switch assembly on vehicles equipped with 4.2L engine.

4. Disconnect and plug the vacuum hose connected to the distributor advance.

5. Connect timing light to the No. 1 spark plug wire. Connect a calibrated scale tachometer to the coil negative terminal.

6. Start engine and slowly increase rpm while noting timing mark and index with timing light.

7. Ignition timing should increase smoothly as engine rpm increases. If not, check and repair centrifugal advance mechanism.

VACUUM ADVANCE

1. Apply parking brake. On vehicles equipped with automatic transmission, position shift selector lever in the **P** position. On vehicles equipped with manual transmission, position shifter in the **NEUTRAL** position.

2. Start and allow engine to reach normal operating temperature. Ensure that air conditioning is **OFF**, if equipped.

3. With ignition switch off, disconnect the 3 pin connector from the 4 and 10 in. Hg. vacuum switch assembly, on vehicles equipped with 4.2L engine.

4. Disconnect and plug vacuum hose connected to the vacuum advance mechanism.

5. Connect a hand operated vacuum pump to the distributor vacuum advance mechanism. Connect a timing light onto the No. 1 spark plug wire.

6. Connect a calibrated scale tachometer to the coil negative terminal, then start engine.

7. Increase engine rpm and apply 18 in. Hg. of vacuum. Note timing degrees and index with timing light.

8. Ignition timing should advance smoothly. If not, check MCU or ECU for malfunction.

TRIGGER WHEEL, PICK-UP COIL AND VACUUM ADVANCE MECHANISM

Removal and Installation

1. Remove the distributor cap, then the rotor.

2. Using trigger wheel puller tool J–28509, or equivalent, remove the trigger wheel.

NOTE: If trigger wheel puller is not available, trigger wheel can be removed by using 2 suitable pry bars.

3. On vehicles equipped with 4.2L engine, remove pick-up coil retainer and washers from the pivot pin on the base plate.

4. On vehicles equipped with 5.9L engine, remove pick-up coil snapring from the shaft. Remove retainer from vacuum advance mechanism-to-pick-up coil drive pin and position vacuum advance mechanism lever aside.

5. On all vehicles, remove pick-up coil plate attaching screws. Lift pick-up coil assembly from the distributor housing.

6. Disconnect the vacuum hose from vacuum advance mechanism. Remove attaching screws and lift mechanism out from distributor housing.

7. Installation is the reverse of the removal procedure.

Solid State Ignition (Renix) System

GENERAL INFORMATION

The Renix ignition system consists of a solid state Ignition Control Module (ICM), which is mounted inside the engine compartment just above the right strut tower, that supplies the voltage for spark plug firing; an Electronic Control Unit (ECU), which is located underneath the glove box, which sends input signals to ignite the ignition control module. The system also consists of spark plugs, a distributor and an ignition coil.

The ECU, located underneath the glove box, sends input signals to ignite the ignition control module. The system also consists of spark plugs, a distributor and an ignition coil.

The ICM is mounted to the ignition coil. The ECU triggers the ignition coil through the ICM. The ECU could advance or retard ignition timing by controlling the ignition coil through the ICM.

The ICM consists of a solid state ignition circuit, an integrated ignition circuit and an ignition coil that can be removed and serviced separately if necessary. The ECU sends an input signal to the ICM. The ICM has only 2 outputs: high voltage from the coil to distributor cap and a tach signal to the tachometer and diagnostic connector.

When the ignition switch is in the **START** or **RUN** positions, electrical current to the ICM is through terminal A of connector No. 1 on the control module. Terminal B of connector No. 1 is grounded at the oil dipstick bracket along with the ECU and oxygen sensor grounds.

The ICM tachometer output signal wire is connected to pin No. 1 of the D1 diagnostic connector. The tachometer signal wire is routed through the ECU, engine and instrument panel wiring harness, to the diagnostic connector. This routing of the tach wire eliminates any electrical interference from the various ECU system circuity.

Ignition signals from terminal No. 27 of the ECU are transmitted through terminal B of connector No. 2 on the ICM. The ignition signal from the ECU is received by the ICM. When the signal contacts the ignition circuitry in the ICM, the ICM charges the coil primary windings. The control module opens the primary windings, when coil saturation occurs, to collapse

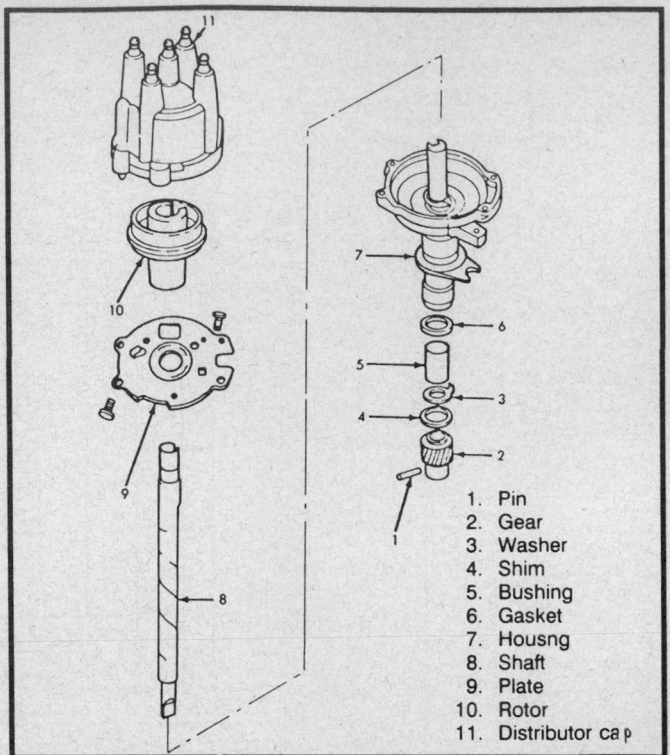

1. Pin
2. Gear
3. Washer
4. Shim
5. Bushing
6. Gasket
7. Housng
8. Shaft
9. Plate
10. Rotor
11. Distributor cap

Distributor components—Jeep Renix

the magnetic field in the windings. This creates high voltage in the coil secondary windings which is then sent to the spark plugs through the coil, distributor cap and rotor.

All system component diagnosis is done in conjunction with the fuel injection system diagnosis.

ELECTRONIC CONTROL UNIT (ECU)

Removal and Installation

1. Disconnect battery ground cable.
2. Remove the ECU attaching bolts, then the ground strap.
3. Remove the ECU from the vehicle and disconnect harness electrical connectors.
4. Install the ECU in position and reconnect the harness.
5. Connect the negative battery cable.

DISTRIBUTOR

Disassembly and Assembly

1. Disconnect the negative battery cable.
2. Remove the distributor from the vehicle and support it in a suitable holding fixture.
3. Remove the distributor cap.
4. Remove the rotor from the shaft.
5. Remove the plate retaining screws and remove the plate from the distributor housing.
6. Remove the roll pin from the distributor gear.
7. Remove the gear, bushing and gaskets from the shaft. Remove the shaft from the housing.

To install:

8. Install the shaft into the housing and position the gear, bushing and gaskets, at the bottom of the shaft.
9. Install a new roll pin in the gear.
10. Install the plate and rotor into the distributor housing.
11. Install the distributor cap and install the distributor into the vehicle.
12. Connect the negative battery cable.

HYDRAULIC BRAKE SYSTEM SERVICE

HYDRAULIC BRAKE SYSTEM TROUBLE DIAGNOSIS

Condition	Possible Cause	Correction
Insufficient brakes	1. Improper brake adjustment. 2. Worn lining. 3. Sticking brakes. 4. Brake valve pressure low. 5. Master cylinder low on brake fluid.	1. Adjust brakes. 2. Replace brake lining and adjust brakes. 3. Lubricate brake pivots and support platforms. 4. Inspect for leaks and obstructed brake lines. 5. Fill master cylinder and inspect for leaks.
Brakes apply slowly	1. Improper brake adjustment or lack of lubrication. 2. Excessive leakage with brakes applied. 3. Restriction in brake line or hose.	1. Adjust brakes and lubricate linkage. 2. Inspect all fittings and lines for leaks and repair as necessary. 3. Clean or replace brake line or hose.
Spongy pedal	1. Air in hydraulic system. 2. Swollen rubber parts due to contaminated brake fluid. 3. Improper brake shoe adjustment. 4. Brake fluid with low boiling point. 5. Brake drums ground excessively.	1. Fill and bleed hydraulic system. 2. Clean hydraulic system and recondition wheel cylinders and master cylinder. 3. Adjust brakes. 4. Flush hydraulic system and refill with proper brake fluid. 5. Replace brake drums.
Erratic brakes	1. Linings soaked with grease or brake fluid. 2. Primary and secondary shoes mounted in wrong position.	1. Correct the leak and replace brake lining. 2. Match the primary and secondary shoes and mount in proper position.
Chattering brakes	1. Improper adjustment of brake shoes. 2. Loose front wheel bearings. 3. Hard spots in brake drums. 4. Out-of-round brake drums. 5. Grease or brake fluid on lining.	1. Adjust brakes. 2. Clean, pack and adjust wheel bearings. 3. Grind or replace brake drums. 4. Grind or replace brake drums. 5. Correct leak and replace brake lining.
Squealing brakes	1. Incorrect lining. 2. Distorted brakedrum. 3. Bent brake support plate. 4. Bent brake shoes. 5. Foreign material embedded in brake lining. 6. Dust or dirt in brake drum. 7. Shoes dragging on support plate. 8. Loose support plate. 9. Loose anchor bolts. 10. Loose lining on brake shoes or improperly ground lining.	1. Install correct lining. 2. Grind or replace brake drum. 3. Replace brake support plate. 4. Replace brake shoes. 5. Replace brake shoes. 6. Use compressed air and blow out drums and support plate and shoes. 7. Sand support plate platforms and lubricate. 8. Tighten support plate attaching nuts. 9. Tighten anchor bolts. 10. Replace brake shoes and cam-grind lining.
Brakes fading	1. Improper brake adjustment. 2. Improper brake lining. 3. Improper type of brake fluid. 4. Brake drums ground excessively.	1. Adjust brakes correctly. 2. Replace brake lining. 3. Drain, flush and refill hydraulic system. 4. Replace brake drums.
Dragging brakes	1. Improper brake adjustment. 2. Distorted cylinder cups. 3. Brake shoe seized on anchor bolt. 4. Broken brake shoe return spring. 5. Loose anchor bolt.	1. Correct adjust brakes. 2. Recondition or replace cylinder. 3. Clean and lubricate anchor bolt. 4. Replace brake shoe return spring. 5. Adjust and tighten anchor bolt.

HYDRAULIC BRAKE SYSTEM TROUBLE DIAGNOSIS

Condition	Possible Cause	Correction
Dragging brakes	6. Distorted brake shoe. 7. Loose wheel bearings. 8. Obstruction in brake line. 9. Swollen cups in wheel cylinder or master cylinder. 10. Master cylinder linkage improperly adjusted.	6. Replace defective brake shoes. 7. Lubricate and adjust wheel bearings. 8. Clean or replace brake line. 9. Recondition wheel or master cylinder. 10. Correctly adjust master cylinder linkage.
Hard pedal	1. Incorrect brake lining. 2. Incorrect brake adjustment. 3. Frozen brake pedal linkage. 4. Restricted brake line or hose.	1. Install matched brake lining. 2. Adjust brakes and check fluid. 3. Free up and lubricate brake linkage. 4. Clean out or replace brake line hose.
Wheel locks	1. Loose or torn brake lining. 2. Incorrect wheel bearing adjustment. 3. Wheel cylinder cups sticking. 4. Saturated brake lining.	1. Replace brake lining. 2. Clean, pack and adjust wheel bearings. 3. Recondition or replace the wheel cylinder. 4. Reline front, rear or all four brakes.
Brakes fade (high speed)	1. Improper brake adjustment. 2. Distorted or out of round brake drums. 3. Overheated brake drums. 4. Incorrect brake fluid (low boiling temperature). 5. Saturated brake lining.	1. Adjust brakes and check fluid. 2. Grind or replace the drums. 3. Inspect for dragging brakes. 4. Drain, flush and refill and bleed the hydraulic brake system. 5. Reline brakes as necessary.

General Information

Servicing the hydraulic brake system is chiefly a matter of adjustments, replacement of worn or damaged parts and correcting the damage caused by grit, dirt or contaminated brake fluid. Always make sure the brake system is clean and tightly sealed when a brake job is completed and that only approved heavy duty brake fluid is used.

Approved heavy duty brake fluid keeps the correct consistency throughout the widest temperature range, will not affect rubber parts, helps protect metal parts and assures long, trouble free brake operation.

Never use brake fluid from a container that has been used for any other liquid. Mineral oil, alcohol, antifreeze or cleaning solvents, even in very small quantities, will contaminate brake fluid. Contaminated brake fluid will cause piston cups and the valve(s) in the master cylinder to swell and deteriorate.

Brake fluid will also absorb moisture from the air. Over time, brake fluid stored for long periods, and fluid inside the brake system will be affected by this moisture. Rust, corrosion and pitting of system components result. Some fleet managers change the brake fluid in their vehicles every year or two to avoid brake system problems caused by moisture.

Use extreme care when using brake fluid. It will damage painted surfaces.

The hydraulic braking system consists of a master cylinder, sometimes a power booster depending on application, hydraulic line and hoses, control valves and calipers and/or wheel cylinders. Newer models incorporate a computer controlled wheel antilock system. When the brake pedal is depressed, the master cylinder forces brake fluid to the calipers and/or cylinders. Sliding rubber seals contain the fluid and prevent leakage.

Return springs in the master cylinder help the brake pedal return to the unapplied position. Check valves, in most cases regulate the return flow of the fluid to the master cylinder. Other valves, such as the metering valve, proportioning valve, or combination valve, regulate the flow of fluid to the caliper/wheel cylinder, to achieve efficient braking.

Dual braking systems were introduced on many light trucks and vans during the late 1960's. The main difference is the use of a tandem master cylinder which is essentially two master cylinders in one. Two separate pistons share one bore and two fluid reservoirs are built into one housing. Dual brake lines split the calipers and/or wheel cylinders into two groups, each actuated by its own, separate master cylinder piston. In the event of failure of one of the dual systems, the other should provide enough braking to safely stop the vehicle. The development of dual braking systems is an improvement over the older single systems where a leak anywhere would allow the fluid to escape resulting in loss of braking.

The dual system usually includes some type of warning light on the instrument panel, activated by a pressure differential valve. The valve reacts to loss of hydraulic pressure that might result from failure on either side of the system.

Vehicles are generally equipped with either a front/rear wheel split or a diagonally split system. On front/rear systems, the front wheels are connected to one circuit while the rear wheels are connected to the other circuit. These systems are the most popular ever since front disc brakes were introduced. Since a greater amount of brake fluid is moved in a disc brake system, one chamber of the the master cylinder feeds the front discs, while the other chamber feeds the rear wheel cylinders.

Diagonally split systems have diagonally opposite wheels connected to each circuit.

Because of the differences in pressure and the amount of fluid required to operate disc brakes and drum brakes, a control valve, often called a proportioning valve or combination valve is installed between the master cylinder and the rest of the system. This valve has several sections and functions.

The metering, or hold off section of the valve limits the pressure to the front disc brakes until a predetermined front input pressure is reached, enough to overcome the rear shoe retractor springs. The is generally no restriction to the inlet pressures below about 3 psi to allow for pressure equalization during the no apply periods.

Another section of the valve proportions, or measures out the

outlet pressure to the rear brakes after a predetermined rear input pressure has been reached. This is done to prevent rear wheel lockup on vehicles with light rear wheel loads.

Yet another section of the valve is designed to constantly compare front and rear brake pressure from the master cylinder and will turn on a warning light in the event of a front or rear system malfunction. On some systems, after repairs are made, and the system properly bled, the valve will center itself and the warning lamp will shut off. On other systems, the switch will latch so the warning light will stay on until a repair is made, and the switch manually reset, generally be one or two firm brake applications.

These valves are also designed with a bypass feature which assures full system pressure to the rear brakes in the event of a front brake system malfunction, and full front pressure is retained in the event of a rear malfunction.

These valves are not to be disassembled for repair. Replace defective valves.

Most light trucks have some sort of height sensing valve. The vehicle braking force is distributed to the front and rear wheels as determined be either a light or heavy payload. The valve is usually mounted on the frame and a linkage connects the valve to a bracket mounted on the axle.

Adding suspension accessories or other equipment (such as load leveling kits, lift kits, extra springs, etc.) or making modifications that will change the distance between the axle and frame without changing the load will provide a false reading to the sensing valve. This could result in unsatisfactory brake performance which could result in an accident and possibly personal injury.

General Diagnosis

LOW PEDAL

Normal brake lining wear reduces pedal reserve. Low pedal reserve may also be caused by the lack of brake fluid in the master cylinder. This means a brake adjustment is required. Check fluid level in the master cylinder and add as required.

FLUID LOSS

If the master cylinde00requires constant addition of brake fluid, fluid may be leaking past the piston cups in the master cylinder, calipers or wheel cylinders, the brake lines or hoses, or through loose connections. Brake hoses often have copper sealing washers which may need to be replaced. Replace worn or damaged components, refill and bleed the system.

FLUID CONTAMINATION

To determine if contamination exists in the brake fluid as indicated by swollen, deteriorated rubber parts like wheel cylinder cups, the following tests can be made.

Place a small amount of the drained brake fluid into a clear glass bottle. Separation of the fluid into distinct layers will indicate mineral oil content. Be safe and discard the old brake fluid that has been bled from the system since it may contain dirt and other contamination and should not be reused.

BRAKE ADJUSTMENT

Self adjusting brakes usually do not require manual adjustment. When installing new brake shoes, it may be advisable to make the initial adjustment manually to speed up adjusting time.

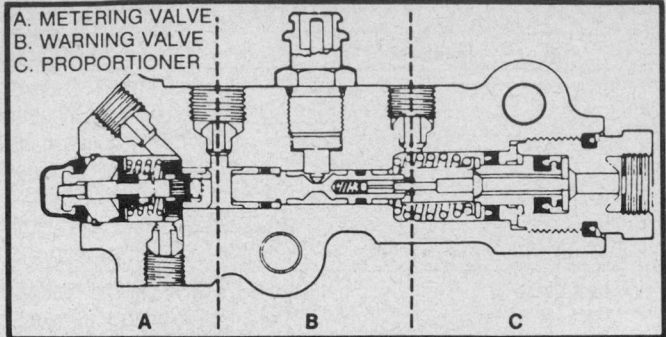

A. METERING VALVE
B. WARNING VALVE
C. PROPORTIONER

Brake proportioning valve—typical

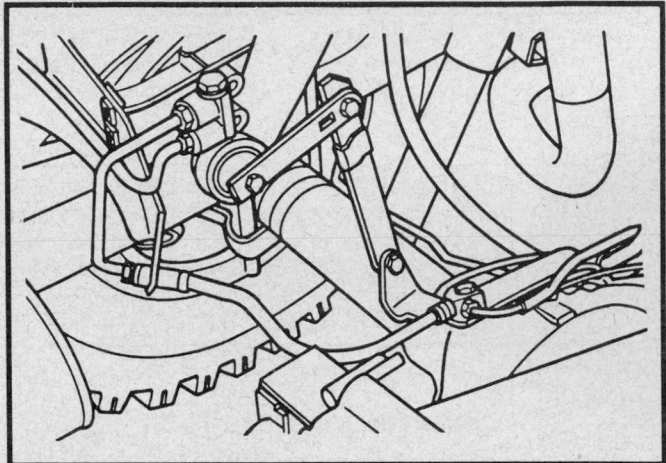

General Motors Corporation height sensing valve—typical

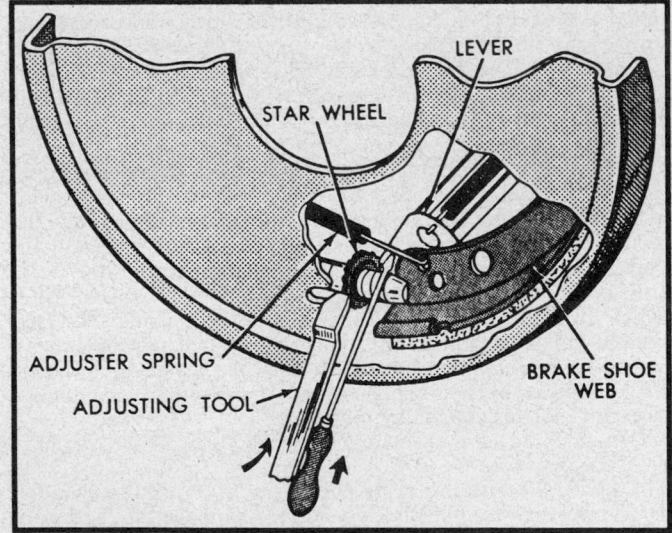

LEVER
STAR WHEEL
ADJUSTER SPRING
ADJUSTING TOOL
BRAKE SHOE WEB

Brake adjustment—typical

AUTOMATIC ADJUSTER CHECK

On most vehicles, drum brakes appear only on the rear axle. Brake adjustments are automatic and are made during reverse brake applications.

Raise and safely support the vehicle, have a helper in the driver's seat to apply brakes. Remove the plug from the adjustment slot to observe the star wheel (some models are adjusted

DIAGNOSIS OF THE BRAKE SYSTEM

Problem	Cause	Correction
Uneven brake action (brakes pull)	1. Incorrect tire pressure.	1. Inflate evenly on both sides to specifications.
	2. Front end out of alignment.	2. Check and align to specifications.
	3. Loose suspension parts.	3. Check all the suspension mountings.
	4. Worn out brake linings.	4. Replace with lining of the correct material.
	5. Incorrect lining material.	5. Replace with linings of the correct material.
	6. Malfunctioning caliper assembly.	6. Check for frozen or sluggish pistons and the lubrication of the retainer bolts. Caliper should slide.
	7. Loose calipers.	7. Check and torque.
	8. Contaminated brake linings.	8. Repair as necessary. Replace the linings in complete axle sets.
	9. Malfunctioning rear brakes.	9. Check for inoperative self adjusters. Weak return springs. Leaking wheel cylinders.
	10. Leaking wheel or piston cylinder seal.	10. Repair as necessary.
	11. Restricted brake tubes or hoses.	11. Check for collapsed rubber hoses or damaged lines. Repair as necessary.
	12. Unmatched tires on the same axle.	12. Same style tires with about the same tread should be used on the same axle.
Slow pedal return	Compensating (peripheral) holes in the quick take-up valve are clogged.	Replace the master cylinder.
Brakes squeak	1. Worn out linings.	1. Replace the linings.
	2. Glazed brake linings.	2. Replace the linings.
	3. Heat spotted rotors or drums.	3. Check per instructions. If within specifications, machine the rotor or drum.
	4. Weak or incorrect brake shoe retention springs.	4. Replace with new retention springs.
	5. Contaminated brake linings.	5. Repair as necessary. Replace the linings in complete axle sets.
	6. Incorrect lining material.	6. Replace with linings of correct material.
	7. Brake assembly attachments missing or loose.	7. Repair as necessary.
	8. Excessive brake lining dust.	8. Clean the dust from the brake assembly.
Brake pedal pulsates	1. Excessive rotor lateral runout.	1. Check per instructions. If within specifications, machine the rotor.
	2. Rear drums out of round.	2. Check per instructions. If within specifications, machine the drum.
	3. Heat spotted rotors or drums.	3. Check per instructions. If within specifications, machine the drum.
	4. Incorrect wheel bearing adjustments.	4. Repair as necessary.
	5. Out of balance wheel assembly.	5. Repair as necessary.
	6. Brake assembly attachments missing or loose.	6. Repair as necessary.
Excessive pedal effort	1. Leaking vacuum system.	1. Repair as necessary.
	2. Malfunctioning power brake unit.	2. Repair as necessary.
	3. Worn out linings.	3. Replace the linings.
	4. Malfunctioning proportioning valve.	4. Replace the combination valve.
	5. Incorrect lining material.	5. Replace with linings of the correct materials.
	6. Incorrect wheel cylinder.	6. Replace with the correct size wheel cylinder.

DIAGNOSIS OF THE BRAKE SYSTEM

Problem	Cause	Correction
	7. Center orifice in quick take-up valve clogged.	7. Replace the master cylinder.
Brakes drag	1. Malfunctioning caliper assembly.	1. Check for frozen or sluggish pistons and the lubrication of the retainer bolts. Caliper should slide.
	2. Contaminated or improper brake fluid.	2. Repair as necessary.
	3. Improperly adjusted parking brake.	3. Adjust as necessary.
	4. Restricted brake tube or hoses.	4. Check for collapsed rubber hoses or damaged lines. Repair as necessary.
	5. Malfunctioning proportioning valve.	5. Replace the combination valve.
	6. Malfunctioning self adjusters.	6. Repair as necessary.
	7. Malfunctioning master cylinder.	7. Repair as necessary.
	8. Improperly adjusted master cylinder pushrod.	8. Adjust pushrod length.
Brake warning light comes on	1. Air in the brake system.	1. Check the fluid level. Check for leaks in the lines, wheel cylinders, or master cylinder. Bleed the system.
	2. Malfunctioning master cylinder.	2. Check for malfunctioning or leaking metering valve. Repair as necessary.
	3. Contaminated or improper brake fluid.	3. Repair as necessary.
	4. Parking brake on or not fully released.	4. Check the parking brake. Repair as necessary.
	5. Worn out brake lining.	5. Replace the linings.
	6. Incorrect wheel bearing adjustment.	6. Repair as necessary.
	7. Malfunctioning self adjusters.	7. Repair as necessary.
	8. Brake assembly attachments missing or loose.	8. Replace or repair as necessary.
	9. Improperly adjusted master cylinder pushrod.	9. Adjust the pushrod length.
	10. RWAL system malfunction.	**10. Refer to REAR WHEEL ANTILOCK BRAKE SYSTEM**
Excessive pedal travel	1. Fluid level low in the master cylinder reservoir.	1. Fill the reservoir with approved brake fluid. Check for leaks and air in the system. Check the warning light.
	2. Air in the brake system.	2. Check for leaks in the lines, wheel cylinders, or master cylinder. Bleed the system.
	3. Malfunctioning self adjusters.	3. Repair as necessary.
	4. Master cylinder.	4. Replace or repair as necessary.
	5. Incorrect wheel bearing adjustment.	5. Repair as necessary.
	6. Improperly adjusted master cylinder pushrod.	6. Adjust the master cylinder pushrod.
	7. Fluid bypassing quick take-up valve to the reservoir.	7. Replace the master cylinder.
	8. Leaking brake line or connection.	8. Repair as necessary.
	9. Leaking wheel cylinder or caliper.	9. Repair as necessary.

through the face of the brake drum others through the backing plate). Tighten the adjusting star wheel screw until the wheel can just be turned by hand. The brake drag should be equal at both wheels. Back off the adjusting star wheel about 30-35 notches. The brakes should have no drag after the adjuster has been backed off about 15 notches. If heavy drag is present, the parking brake likely needs service and/or adjustment.

NOTE: It will be necessary to carefully insert a small, stiff wire or thin tool to hold the automatic adjustment lever away from the star wheel to allow backing off the

adjustment. Install adjusting hole cover in backing plate. Check parking brake adjustment.

HYDRAULIC LINE REPAIR

Steel tubing is used for the hydraulic lines, and special flexible hoses connect moving parts such as front calipers which turn with the steering, and the connection between the body and rear axle.

When replacing steel lines or flexible brake hose, use only exact replacements, in both size and quality.

NOTE: Never use copper tubing for hydraulic brake lines because copper is subject to fatigue cracking and corrosion which could result in brake failure. Use specially made steel brake lines only. Tighten all connections securely.

After replacement, bleed the brake system at each wheel and at the booster, if equipped with a bleeder screw.

Flexible hoses should be inspected for any signs of road damage, cracks or chafing any of which requires immediate hose replacement. Hoses feeding front brake calipers are often equipped with a copper washer for a seal. This should also be replaced when hoses are renewed. After hose installation, make sure the hose is not twisted. Many hoses have a painted stripe on them to help the technician determine if the hose is twisted.

If a length of steel brake line tubing must be replaced and the end flared, a special double flaring tool must be used. Always inspect newly formed flares for defects. Double lap flaring tools must be used. Single flares cannot hold the high pressures in the brake system and tend to crack. When bending brake tubing to fit the frame or rear axle contours, be careful not to crack or kink the tube. Always clean the inside of even new brake tube with clean isopropyl alcohol.

GENERAL MOTORS CORPORATION

Master Cylinder Service

In addition to standard master cylinder functions, a quick take-up feature in included on most models. This provides a large volume of fluid to the wheels at low pressure with the initial brake application. This large volume of fluid is needed to overcome the clearance created by the seals retracting the pistons into the front calipers and the spring retraction of the rear brake shoes.

NOTE: General Motors Corporation does not recommend honing the bores of either cast iron or composite master cylinders. When the brake master cylinder is overhauled, it is recommended that the cylinder body be replaced rather than attempting to clean up a scuffed cylinder by honing the bore. The master cylinder has a hard, highly polished surface which is produced by diamond boring followed by ball or roller burnishing under heavy pressure. Honing will destroy this surface which will cause rapid wear of rubber cups. Do not use kerosene, gasoline or other solvents for cleaning or flushing master cylinder and components. The use of these solvents or any other with a trace of mineral oil, will damage rubber parts.

DELCO CAST IRON MASTER CYLINDER

Disassembly and Assembly

1. Remove cover, rubber diaphragm and drain reservoir.
2. Remove snapring and primary piston assembly.
3. Plug rear port and apply low pressure air to front port. Secondary piston will pop out. Use shop cloth to catch piston. Use caution. The piston may come out with considerable force. Remove seals from secondary piston.
4. If tube seats must be replaced, thread in self-tapping screw into seat, remove with locking pliers.
5. Clean all metal parts in denatured alcohol, the rubber parts in brake fluid.
6. A stained or discolored bore may be cleaned with fine crocus cloth. Do not attempt to hone the bore.
7. Lube all seals and the bore with clean brake fluid. Install seals on pistons and assemble.
8. Push primary piston with smooth rounded end tool and install snapring.
9. If tube seats are replaced, seat with spare brake tube nut.
10. Install diaphragm into cover and install cover.

BENDIX MASTER CYLINDER

Disassembly and Assembly

1. Remove cover, rubber diaphragm and drain reservoir.

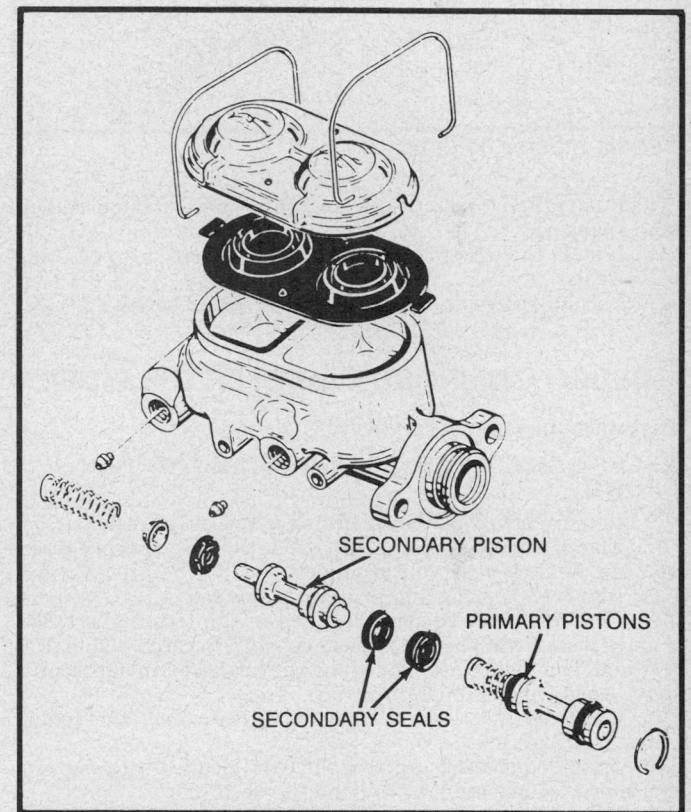

SECONDARY PISTON

PRIMARY PISTONS

SECONDARY SEALS

GM cast iron master cylinder

2. Locate and remove the reservoir to body bolts and remove reservoir.
3. Remove the seals, poppet valves and springs from cylinder body.
4. Remove snapring and primary piston.
5. Plug rear port and apply low pressure air to front port. Secondary piston will pop out. Use shop cloth to catch piston. Use caution. The piston may come out with considerable force. Remove seals from secondary piston.
6. Clean all metal parts in denatured alcohol, the rubber parts in brake fluid.
7. A stained or discolored bore may be cleaned with fine crocus cloth. Do not attempt to hone the bore.
8. Lube all seals and the bore with clean brake fluid. Install seals on pistons and assemble.

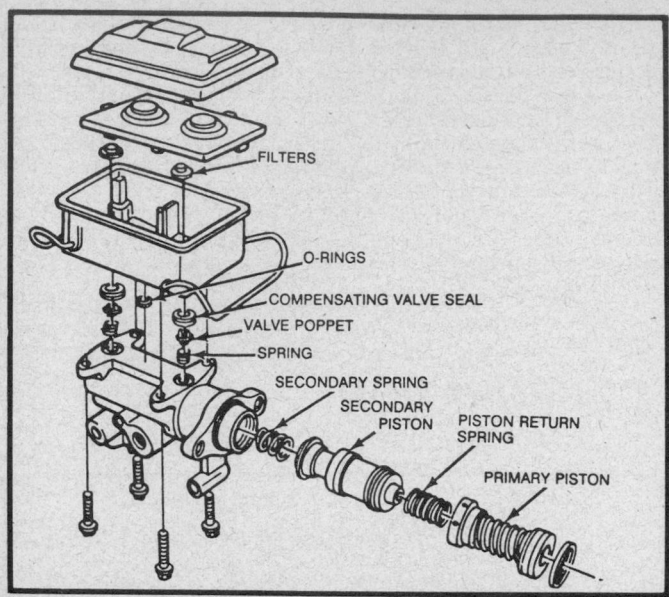

Bendix master cylinder

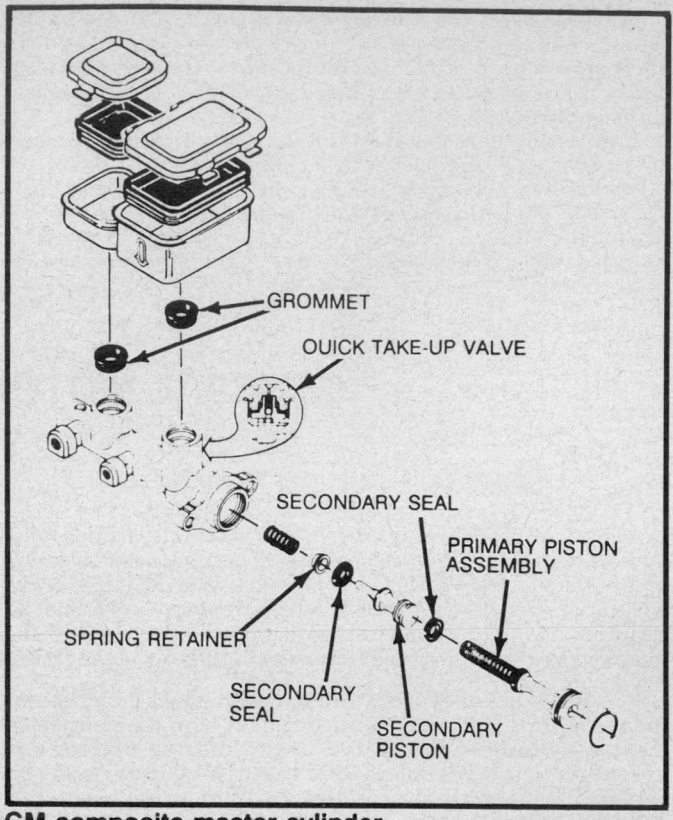

GM composite master cylinder

9. Push primary piston with smooth rounded end tool and install snapring.

10. Install O-ring, springs, valve poppets and compensating valve seals.

11. Bolt on reservoir, replace diaphragm and cover.

DELCO COMPOSITE MASTER CYLINDER

Disassembly and Assembly

EXCEPT LUMINA APV, SILHOUETTE AND TRANS SPORT

1. Remove cover, rubber diaphragm and drain reservoir.

2. Clamp mounting flange of cylinder in vise and pry reservoir off. Remove reservoir grommet.

3. Remove snapring and primary piston.

4. Plug rear port and apply low pressure air to front port. Secondary piston will pop out. Use shop cloth to catch piston. Use caution. The piston may come out with considerable force. Remove seals from secondary piston.

5. Clean all metal parts in denatured alcohol, the rubber parts in brake fluid.

6. A stained or discolored bore may be cleaned with fine crocus cloth. Do not attempt to hone the bore.

7. Lube all seals and the bore with clean brake fluid. Install seals on pistons and assemble.

8. Push primary piston with smooth rounded end tool and install snapring.

9. Install grommets and press reservoir on with rocking motion. Install diaphragm and cover.

LUMINA APV, SILHOUETTE AND TRANS SPORT

1. Remove cover, rubber diaphragm and drain reservoir.

2. Remove fluid level sensor switch using needle nose pliers to compress switch locking tabs at the inboard side of master cylinder.

3. Remove proportioner valve assemblies by unscrewing cap assemblies, removing the O-rings and springs. Remove pistons with needle nose pliers. Use care. Do not scratch piston stems.

3. Remove snapring and primary piston.

4. Apply low pressure air into upper outlet port at blind end of bore. Plug all other ports. Secondary piston will pop out. Use shop cloth to catch piston. Use caution. The piston may come

out with considerable force. Remove seals from secondary piston.

5. To remove reservoir, clamp flange (never the body) of master cylinder in vise. Drive out spring pins with 1/8 in. punch. Pull reservoir straight up and remove O-rings from grooves in reservoir.

6. Clean all metal parts in denatured alcohol, the rubber parts in brake fluid.

7. Inspect the bore for scoring or corrosion. If noted, replace master cylinder. No abrasives should be used in bore. Do not attempt to hone the bore.

8. Install new seals on reservoir, press into cylinder body and install spring pins.

9. Lube all seals and the bore with clean brake fluid. Install seals on pistons and assemble.

10. Push primary piston with smooth rounded end tool and install snapring.

11. Install proportioner valve assemblies and fluid level sensor, making sure locking tabs snap into place.

12. Install diaphragm and cover.

Brake Booster Service

Three types of brake boosters are used: a single diaphragm, a tandem diaphragm and a hydraulic booster (Hydro-Boost).

The vacuum boosters may have a vacuum switch to activate a brake warning light in case of low booster vacuum or vacuum pump malfunction. Under normal operating conditions, with brakes released, a vacuum suspended booster operates with vacuum on both sides of its diaphragm (or both diaphragms in a tandem diaphragm unit). When the brakes are applied, air at atmospheric pressure is admitted to one side of the diaphragm (or both diaphragms in a tandem diaphragm unit) to provide the power assist.

The hydraulic brake booster (Hydro-Boost) uses a hydraulic

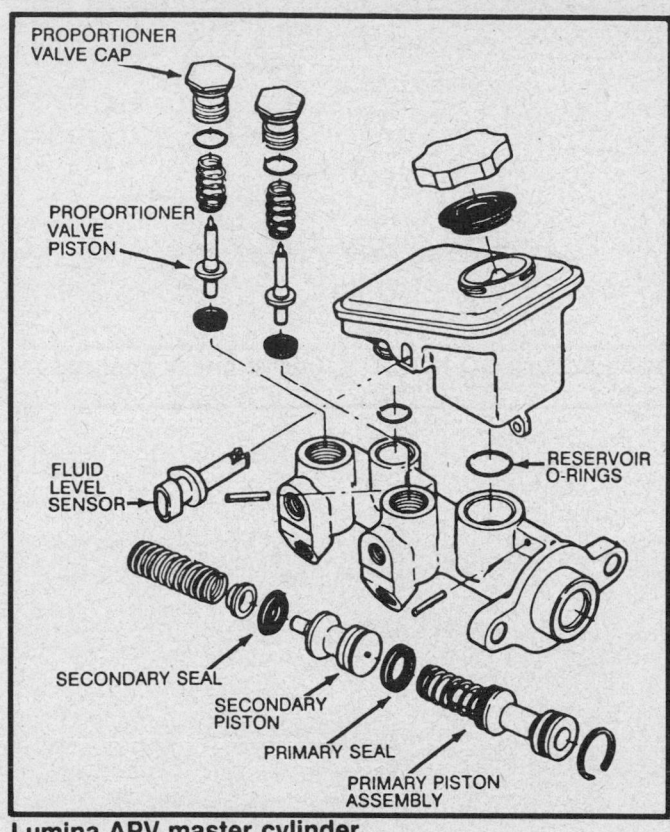

Lumina APV master cylinder

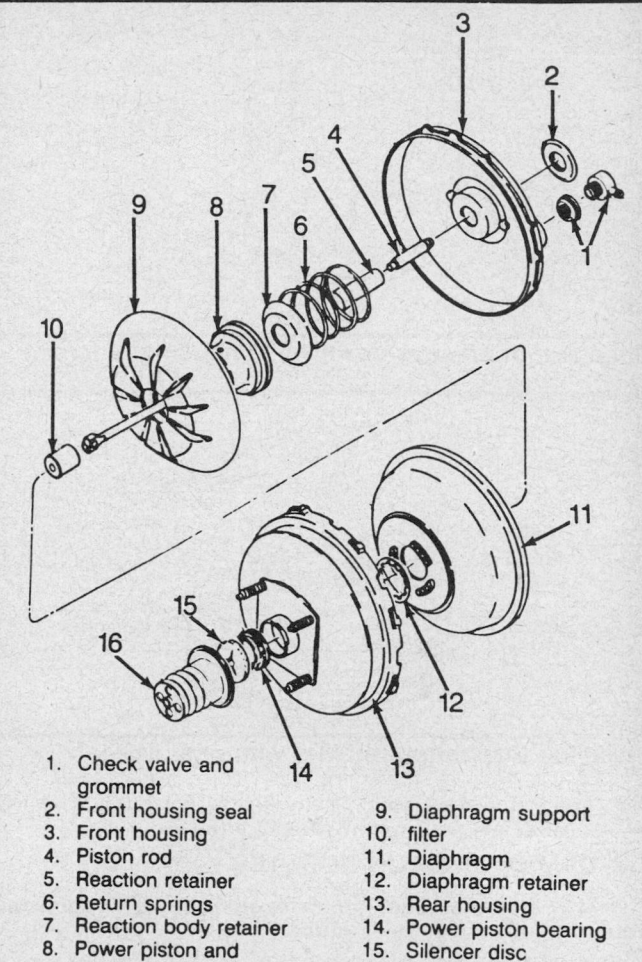

1. Check valve and grommet
2. Front housing seal
3. Front housing
4. Piston rod
5. Reaction retainer
6. Return springs
7. Reaction body retainer
8. Power piston and pushrod assembly
9. Diaphragm support
10. filter
11. Diaphragm
12. Diaphragm retainer
13. Rear housing
14. Power piston bearing
15. Silencer disc
16. Boot

GM Single Diaphragm Booster

pump to power the system and a pneumatic accumulator as a reserve system. In this system no special fluids are used. However, care must be taken to use the correct fluids. The master cylinder and brake system operate on standard brake fluid. The hydraulic pump, which is driven by pressure from the power steering pump, uses power steering fluid.

VACUUM DIAPHRAGM BRAKE BOOSTERS

Disassembly and Assembly

SINGLE DIAPHRAGM BOOSTER

NOTE: A special brake booster disassembly tool is recommended for this procedure.

1. With the booster unit off the vehicle, and the master cylinder removed from the booster, take off the boot and silencer disc from the booster's mounting (rear) side. Remove the vacuum check valve, grommet and the front housing seal from the face side.
2. Scribe a mark across the front and rear housings to aid assembly.
3. Clamp the base in a vise with the power section facing up. Separate the front and rear housings by pressing down (using the special disassembly tool, if available) and rotating the housing counterclockwise to the unlocked position. Loosen carefully as it is spring loaded.
4. Remove the large return spring and the power piston which will likely still have the pedal pushrod attached.
5. Remove the power piston bearing from the rear housing.
6. Remove the reaction body retainer, the master cylinder piston rod, and reaction retainer.
7. Remove the filter with an awl or similar tool.
8. Separate the power piston and pedal pushrod. To do this, grasp the outside edge of the diaphragm support and dia-

phragm. Hold the pushrod down against a hard surface and use slight force to dislodge the diaphragm retainer.
9. Remove the diaphragm from the diaphragm support.
10. Inspect all parts for corrosion, nicks, cracks, cuts, scoring, distortion or excessive wear. Replace as required. Clean all parts in denatured alcohol, but do not immerse the power piston and pushrod assembly in alcohol. Dry with compressed air.
11. Lubricate the inside diameter of the diaphragm lip with a thin layer of silicone grease and install the diaphragm into its support.
12. Install the diaphragm and support onto the power piston and pushrod assembly. Use a new retainer and install with a pipe-like driver.
13. Install filter, reaction retainer, piston rod, and reaction body retainer.
14. Install the reaction body retainer disc. Lubricate the inside and outside of the power piston bearing with silicone grease and install in rear housing.
15. Install power piston group into rear housing, put in the return spring and assemble front housing to rear housing. Align mating marks made before disassembly.
16. Apply pressure in clockwise direction to lock housings together. Stake the housing at two tabs 180 degrees apart. Do not stake a tab that has been previously staked.
17. Lubricate the check valve grommet with silicone grease and install it and the check valve in the front cover.
18. Install the front housing seal, silencer disc, and boot.

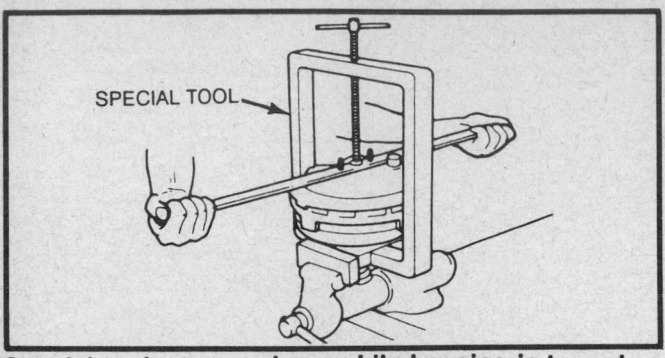
Special tool presses down while housing is turned

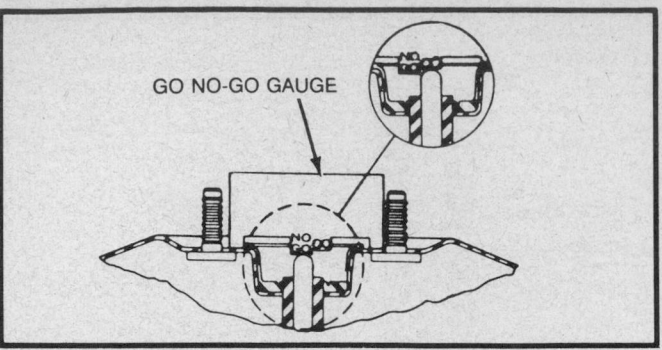
Using special GO NO-GO gauge to check pushrod

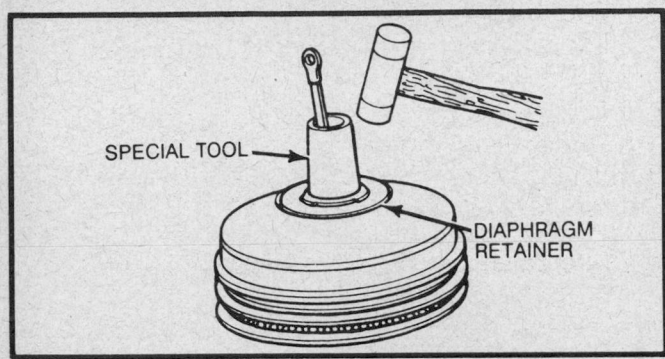
Installing diaphragm retainer with pipe driver

19. The piston rod should be checked with a special GO, NO-GO gauge. If not within limits, replace the rod.

TANDEM DIAPHRAGM BOOSTER

NOTE: A special brake booster disassembly tool is recommended for this procedure.

1. With the booster unit off the vehicle, and the master cylinder removed from the booster, take off the boot and silencer disc from the booster's mounting (rear) side. Remove the vacuum check valve, grommet and the front housing seal from the face side.

2. Scribe a mark across the front and rear housings to aid assembly.

3. Clamp the base in a vise with the power section facing up. Separate the front and rear housings by pressing down (using the special disassembly tool, if available) and rotating the housing counterclockwise to the unlocked position. Loosen carefully as it is spring loaded.

4. Remove the large return spring and the power piston which will likely still have the pedal pushrod attached.

5. Remove the power piston bearing from the rear housing.

6. Remove the piston rod, reaction retainer and power head silencer ring.

7. Remove the power piston assembly and pushrod. Grasp the assembly at the outside edge of the housing divider and both diaphragms. Hold the pushrod down against a hard surface. Tap to dislodge diaphragm retainer.

8. Remove the primary diaphragm (rear) and primary support plate from the housing divider and separate the primary diaphragm from its support plate.

9. Remove the secondary diaphragm (front) and secondary support plate from the housing divider. Remove the secondary piston bearing from the center of the housing divider and separate the secondary diaphragm from its support plate.

10. Remove the reaction plate retainer, reaction body, reaction disc, and reaction piston from the reaction body.

11. Remove the air valve spring and reaction bumper from the

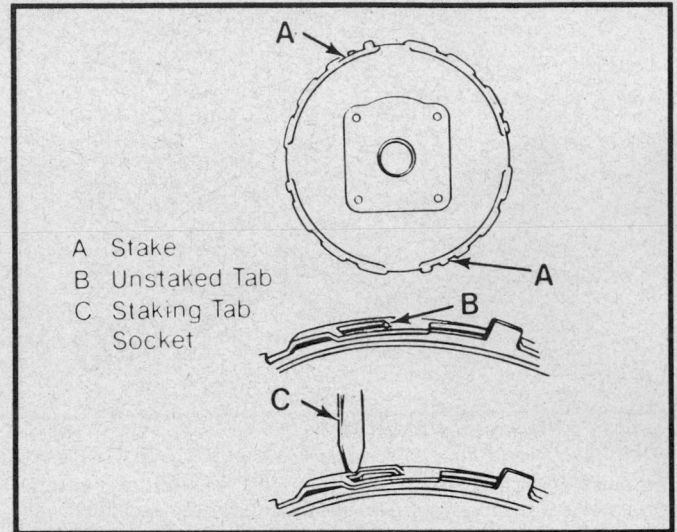
A   Stake
B   Unstaked Tab
C   Staking Tab
    Socket

Staking the booster tabs

end of the pushrod. Carefully remove the retaining ring from the pushrod, and remove the pushrod by inserting a suitable tool through the eyelet end and pulling straight out. Considerable force will be required.

12. Remove the filter, retainer and O-ring from the pushrod assembly.

13. Inpect all parts for corrosion, nicks, cracks, cuts, scoring, distortion or excessive wear. Replace as required. Clean all parts in denatured alcohol, but do not immerse the power piston and pushrod assembly in alcohol. Dry with compressed air.

14. Using silicone grease, lubricate the O-ring for the pushrod and install the pushrod into the power piston, then install the retainer and seat.

15. Install the filter over the pushrod eyelet and into the power piston and install the retaining ring.

16. Assemble the reaction bumber, air valve spring, reaction piston and reaction disc into the reaction body. Install the reaction body retainer.

17. Using silicone grease, lubricate the inside diameter of both the primary and secondary diaphragm as well as the secondary piston bearing.

18. Assemble the secondary diaphragm to its support plate and slide the assembly over the power piston/pushrod assembly.

19. Install the secondary piston bearing into the housing divider. The flat surface of the bearing goes on the same side as the six raised lugs on the divider. Install this assembly over the power piston/pushrod assembly.

20. Assemble the primary diaphragm to its support plate, by folding the diaphragm up, away from the support plate and slide the assembly over the power piston/pushrod assembly. Fold the

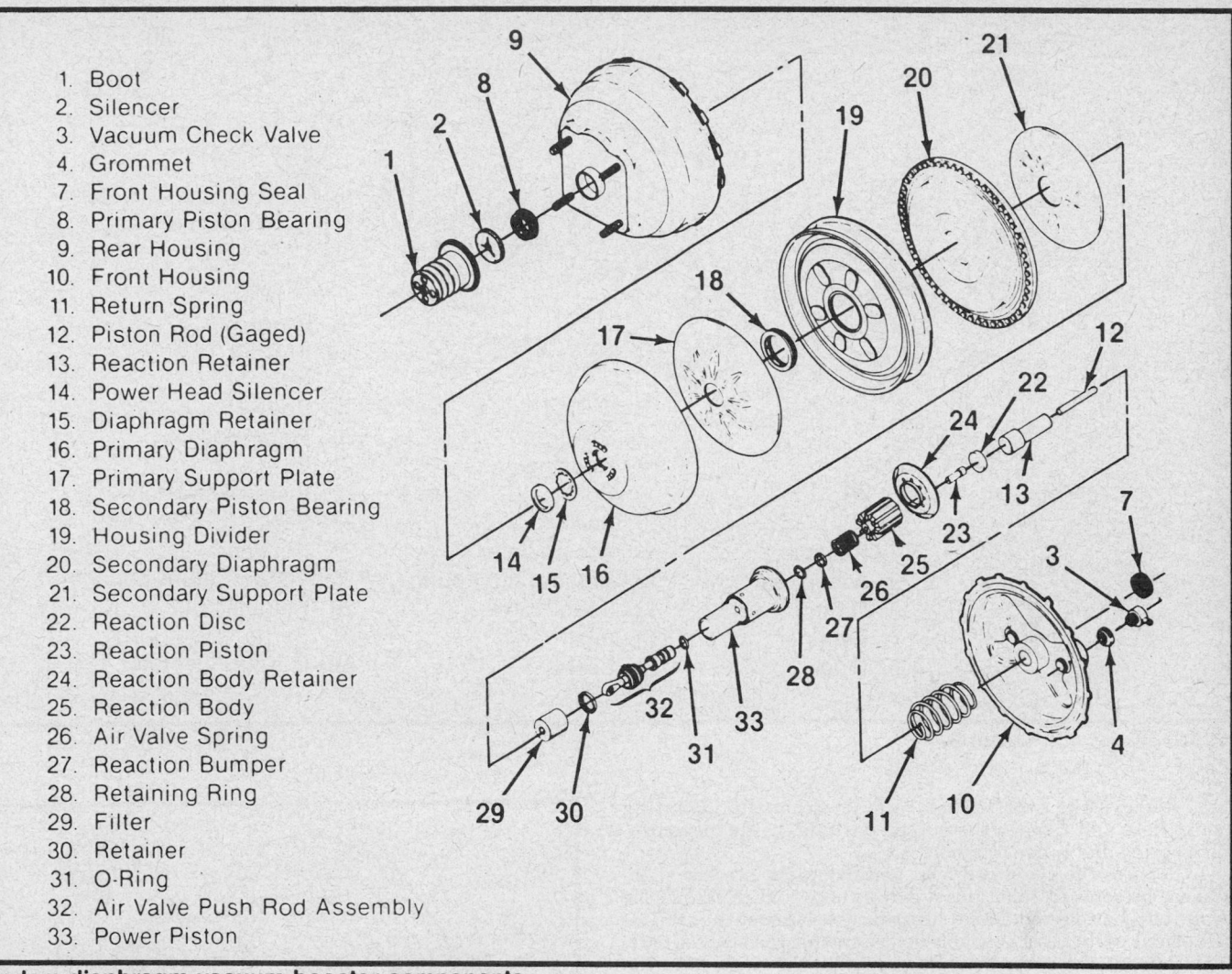

1. Boot
2. Silencer
3. Vacuum Check Valve
4. Grommet
7. Front Housing Seal
8. Primary Piston Bearing
9. Rear Housing
10. Front Housing
11. Return Spring
12. Piston Rod (Gaged)
13. Reaction Retainer
14. Power Head Silencer
15. Diaphragm Retainer
16. Primary Diaphragm
17. Primary Support Plate
18. Secondary Piston Bearing
19. Housing Divider
20. Secondary Diaphragm
21. Secondary Support Plate
22. Reaction Disc
23. Reaction Piston
24. Reaction Body Retainer
25. Reaction Body
26. Air Valve Spring
27. Reaction Bumper
28. Retaining Ring
29. Filter
30. Retainer
31. O-Ring
32. Air Valve Push Rod Assembly
33. Power Piston

Tandem diaphragm vacuum booster components

primary diaphragm back into position and pull the outside edge of the diaphragm over the formed flange of the housing divider.

NOTE: Check that the beads on the secondary diaphragm are seated evenly around the complete circumference.

21. Install a new diaphragm retainer and install with a pipe-like driver.
22. Install the silencer ring, reaction retainer and piston rod.
23. Lubricate the inside and outside diameters of the primary piston bearing with silicone grease and install into the rear housing.
24. Install the power piston assembly into the rear housing.
25. Install the return spring and assemble front housing to rear housing. Align mating marks made before disassembly.
26. Apply pressure in clockwise direction to lock housings together. Stake the housing at two tabs 180 degrees apart. Do not stake a tab that has been previously staked.
27. Lubricate the check valve grommet with silicone grease and install it and the check valve in the front cover.
28. Install the front housing seal, silencer disc, and boot.
29. The piston rod should be checked with a special GO, NO-GO gauge. If not within limits, replace the rod.

HYDRO-BOOST

The Bendix Hydro-Boost uses the hydraulic pressure supplied by the power steering pump to provide a power assist to brake application. It has identifying information stamped into the housing near the inlet line. When servicing this unit, there are some special tools that are recommended for these procedures.

Disassembly and Assembly

CAUTION

This system uses an accumulator that contains compressed gas. Do not apply heat to the accumulator. Use caution or personal injury may result. Do not attempt to repair a defective accumulator. Always replace with a new unit. Dispose of an inoperative accumulator by drilling a 1/16 in. diameter hole through the end of the accumulator can opposite the O-ring.

---

1. Remove the accumulator. Note that an adapter (a piece of strap metal with a hole drilled to accommodate a mounting stud) is used along with a C-clamp. Depress the accumulator with the C-clamp, insert a punch into the hole on the housing and remove the snaping retainer. Release the C-clamp, remove the accumulator and O-ring.
2. Remove the retainer from the small port above the mounting flange and remove the plug, O-ring and spring.

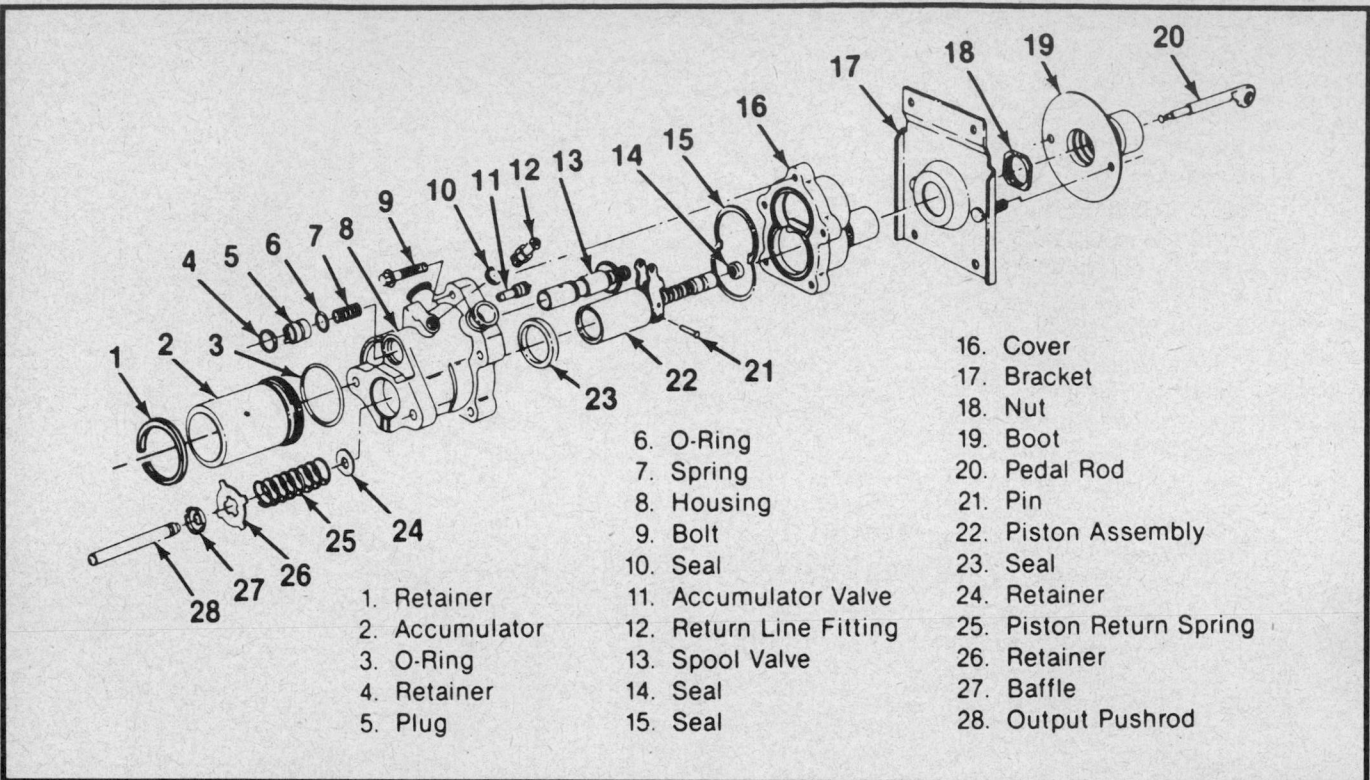

16. Cover
17. Bracket
18. Nut
19. Boot
20. Pedal Rod
21. Pin
22. Piston Assembly
23. Seal
24. Retainer
25. Piston Return Spring
26. Retainer
27. Baffle
28. Output Pushrod

6. O-Ring
7. Spring
8. Housing
9. Bolt
10. Seal
11. Accumulator Valve
12. Return Line Fitting
13. Spool Valve
14. Seal
15. Seal

1. Retainer
2. Accumulator
3. O-Ring
4. Retainer
5. Plug

Hydro-Boost components

3. Remove the star-shaped retainer from the mounting flange bore and remove the output pushrod, baffle, piston return spring and inner retainer.

4. Remove the pedal rod boot and mounting bracket, if installed. On some installations it may be necessary to saw off the eyelet of the pedal rod. Make sure exact replacements or the replacement parts kit is available before cutting the original part.

5. Remove the cover bolts and separate the cover from the housing. Remove the seals (a large figure-eight shaped seal and a smaller seal on the end of the piston assembly).

6. Remove the piston assembly and the O-ring seal on the housing side of the piston.

7. Remove the spool valve.

8. Remove the accumulator valve. It may be necessary to fish this small valve out with a thin wire hook.

9. Remove the return line fitting and seal.

10. Clean all parts in power steering fluid. Inspect the spool valve for corrosion, nicks and scoring. If found, replace the complete booster. Discoloration of the spool or bore is not harmful and is no cause for replacement. Check all components for damage or wear, especially the tube seat in the housing. This seat can be removed with a Easy-Out type remover, and its replacement installed by tapping gently into place.

11. Lubricate all seals and friction metal parts with power steering fluid.

12. Install the return line fitting and seal.

13. Install the accumulator valve and spool valve.

14. Install the seal and piston assembly, place the small seal on the piston assembly end and the figure eight shaped seal into the housing. Install the cover and torque the bolts to 22 ft. lbs.

15. Install the mounting bracket and pushrod boot.

16. On the master cylinder side of the unit, install the output pushrod, baffle, piston return spring and retainer.

17. Install the accumulator and O-ring using a large C-clamp as in disassembly procedure.

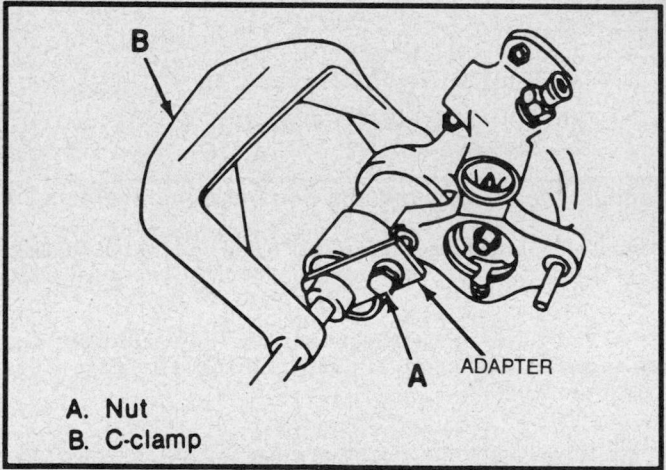

A. Nut
B. C-clamp

Removing the accumulator

18. Install the jam nut from the repair kit onto the pedal rod and install the eyelet onto the pedal rod.

Combination Valve

The combination valve (also called a proportioning valve) is made up of 3 sections, each serving a different function.

The metering or hold-off section of the valve limits the pressure to the front disc brakes until a predetermined front input pressure is reached, enough to overcome the rear shoe retractor springs. There is no restriction to the inlet pressures below 3 psi to allow for pressure equalization during no-apply periods.

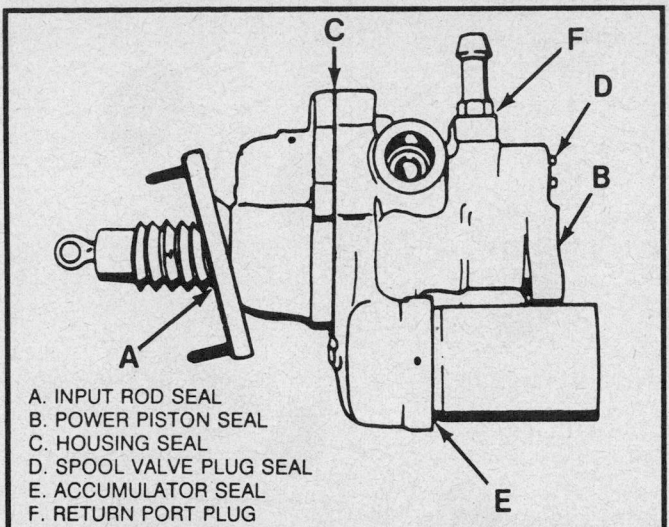

A. INPUT ROD SEAL
B. POWER PISTON SEAL
C. HOUSING SEAL
D. SPOOL VALVE PLUG SEAL
E. ACCUMULATOR SEAL
F. RETURN PORT PLUG

Hydro-Boost seal leak areas

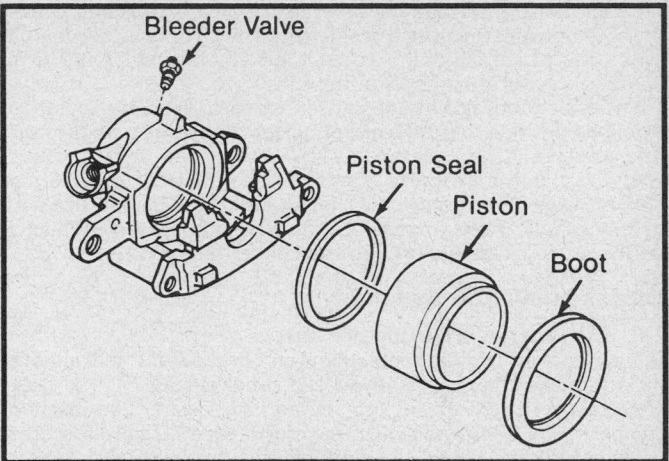

Caliper components—typical

The proportioning section of the combination valve proportions outlet pressure to the rear brakes after a predetermined rear input pressure has been reached. This is done to prevent rear wheel lockup on vehicles with light rear wheel loads.

The valve is designed to have a bypass feature which ensures full system pressure to the rear brakes in the event of a front brake system malfunction. Full front pressure is retained in the event of rear malfunction.

The pressure-differential warning switch is designed to constantly compare front and rear brake pressure from the master cylinder and energize the warning lamp on the instrument panel in the event of a front or rear system malfunction. The valve and switch are designed so the switch will latch in the warning postion once a malfunction has occurred. The only way the lamp can be turned off is to repair the malfunction and apply a pedal force required to develop about 450 psi line pressure (a firm brake application).

Valve Overhaul

The combination valve is not repairable and must be replaced as a complete assembly.

Caliper Service

The disc brake assembly consists of a caliper and piston assembly, rotor, linings, and an anchor plate. The caliper is mounted to the anchor plate, which allows the caliper to move laterally against the rotor. The caliper is a one-piece casting with the inboard side containing the piston bore. A square cut rubber seal is located in a groove in the piston bore which provides the hydraulic seal between the piston and the cylinder wall.

As the brake pedal is pressed, hydraulic pressure is applied against the piston. This pressure pushes the inboard brake lining against the inboard braking surface of the rotor. As the force increases against the rotor, the caliper assembly moves inboard and provides a clamping action on the rotor.

When brake pressure is released, the piston seal returns to its normal position, pulling the piston back into the caliper bore. This creates a running clearance between the inner brake lining and rotor.

Disassembly and Assembly

1. Drain all fluid from caliper.
2. Pad interior of caliper with clean shop towels and use just enough compressed air to ease the piston out of the bore.

CAUTION
Do not place fingers in front of piston to try to catch piston or protect it when applying compressed air. This could result in serious injury. Use just enough air to ease the piston out. If piston is blown out, even with padding, it may be damaged.

3. Remove boot, being careful not to scratch bore.
4. Remove square cut seal from caliper bore groove.
5. Remove bleeder valve.
6. Clean all parts with denatured alcohol, blow dry with compressed air. Inspect all parts for scoring, corrosion or damage to chrome plating on piston. Replace if damaged. Fine crocus cloth can be used to polish out any light corrosion.
7. Lubricate the new piston seal, caliper bore and piston with clean brake fluid and install the seal in the caliper bore groove. Make sure seal is not twisted.
8. Install the boot on the piston, slide the piston into the bore and gently tap the boot into the counterbore of the caliper housing using a suitable driver.
9. Install bleeder screw.

CAUTION
After the caliper has been installed and the system bled, before moving the vehicle, pump the brake pedal several times until the pedal is firm. Do not move the vehicle until a firm pedal is obtained. Check the fluid level in the master cylinder after pumping the brakes.

Wheel Cylinder Service

The drum brake assembly is a duo-servo design. Force which is applied by the wheel cylinder to the primary shoe is multiplied by the primary shoe friction to provide a large applied force to the secondary shoe. The torque from the brake shoes is transferred to the anchor pin and through the backing plate, the the axle flange. Brake adjustments are automatic and are made during reverse brake applications.

Wheel cylinders may need reconditioning or replacement whenever the brake shoes are replaced or when required to correct a leak condition. In some cases, the wheel cylinders can be disassembled without removing them from the backing plate. On others, the cylinder must be removed before being disassembled.

Leaks which coat the boot and the cylinder with fluid, or result in a dropped reservoir fluid level, or dampen and stain the brake linings are dangerous. Such leaks can cause the brakes to grab or fail and should be immediately corrected. A leakage, not immediately apparent, can be detected by pulling back the cylinder boot. A small amount of fluid seepage dampening the interi-

or of the boot is normal. However, a dripping boot is not. Unless other conditions causing a brake to pull, grab or drag become obvious, the wheel cylinder is suspect and should and should be included in general reconditioning.

Cylinder binding may be caused by rust, deposits, grime, or swollen cups due to fluid contamination, or by a cup wedged into an excessive piston clearance.

Hydraulic system parts should not be allowed to come into contact with oil or grease, neither should those be handled with greasy hands. Even a trace of any petroleum based product is sufficient to cause damage to the rubber parts.

Disassembly and Assembly

1. Remove the brake bleeder screw.
2. Remove the dust boots, allow any brake fluid to drain out.
3. Remove the pistons, seals and inner spring.
4. Inspect the bore for scoring and corrosion. The inside of the bore may be cleaned with fine crocus cloth. If bore is scored, replace cylinder. Clean the cylinder with brake fluid.
5. Lubricate the seals with brake fluid and install. Cup lips should always face inward. Install the spring assembly and seals.
6. Carefully install the pistons and dust boots.
7. Install the bleeder screw.

Anti-Lock Braking Systems

Despite advances in brake design over the years, even the best systems in use can still lock up during certain road conditions, such as wet road surfaces. When the brakes lock up, the driver can lose control of the vehicle, because a locked wheel cannot absorb any cornering or lateral forces, and steering is lost. It is impossible to brake to a maximum and at the same time steer the vehicle when the front wheels are locked. If the back wheels are locked the vehicle will become unstable and start to slide.

While many different ways have been tried over the years to solve this problem, mechanical sensors could not provide sufficient information about wheel rotation speed and mechanical control units could not operate the brakes fast enough to prevent brake lockup.

The growth of the electronics industry has allowed small computers (microprocessors) to be reduced in both size and cost. Coupled with fast reacting electronic sensors, anti-lock braking has become more reliable with widespread application.

REAR WHEEL ANTI-LOCK BRAKE SYSTEM

General Motors Corporation's system is called Rear Wheel Antilock System (RWAL) and its application is on selected 2WD models. It is designed to reduce the occurrence of the rear wheel lockup during a severe brake application.

The system functions by regulating the rear hydraulic brake line pressure. The pressure regulation is accomplished by a control valve which is located under the master cylinder. The control valve is made up of 2 valves, a dump valve which releases pressure into an accumulator, and an isolation valve which maintains rear brake pressure. The valve is controlled by a microcomputer which is part of the Electronic Control Unit (ECU). The ECU is mounted next to the master cylinder. In a severe brake application as pressure is applied to the brake pedal, the ECU is designed to permit the valve to do one of three functions or a combination of all three. The ECU will allow the valve to either maintain the same amount of hydraulic pressure, release hydraulic pressure through the dump valve into the accumulator, or increase the pressure by pulsing the isolation valve.

The ECU operates by receiving signals from the speed sensor which is located in the transmission and the brake lamp switch. The speed sensor sends its signal to the digital ratio adapter

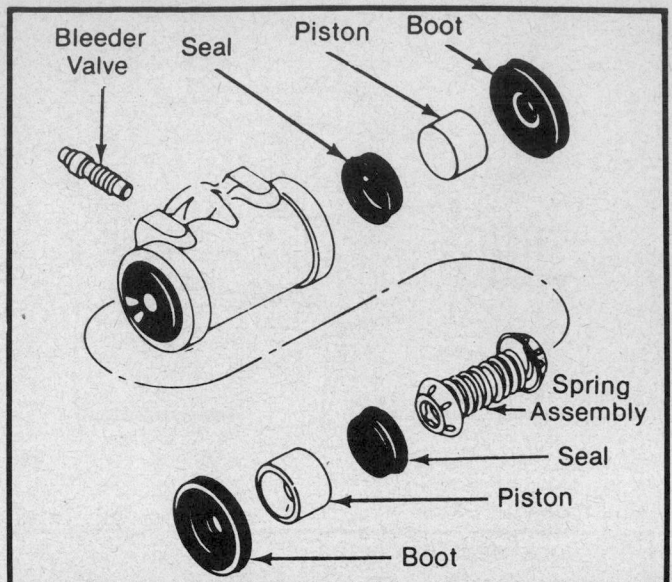

Wheel cylinder components — typical

which is part of the instrument cluster. If the axle ratio or tire size is changed, it will be necessary to recalibrate the digital ratio adapter.

The RWAL system is connected to the existing brake warning lamp located on the dash. An indication of the RWAL operation is a bulb check performed each time the ignition is turned ON. The warning lamp will remain on for about two seconds. A RWAL system malfunction is indicated by a brake warning lamp.

To aid in diagnosing problems, trouble codes are produced by the system. Trouble codes are available at the ALDL (Assembly Line Diagnostic Link) the twelve terminal connector wired to the Electronic Control Module and located under the instrument panel in the passenger compartment. These codes are read by jumping terminal A (which is ground) of the ALDL to terminal H of the ALDL and observing the flashing of the brake warning light. The terminals must be jumped for about 20 seconds before the code will begin to flash. In counting code pulses, count the number of short flashes starting from the long flash. Include the long flash as a count.

NOTE: Sometimes the first count sequence will be short. However, subsequent counts will be accurate. If there is more than one failure, only the first recognized failure code will be retained and flashed.

To clear trouble codes, with the ignition **OFF**, remove the brake fuse, wait five seconds, and then reinstall fuse.

Circuit Maintenance and Repair

All electrical connections must be kept clean and tight. Make sure that connectors are properly seated and all of the sealing rings on weather-proof connections are in place. With the low current and voltage levels found in some circuits, it is important that all connections be the best possible. Special tools are required for servicing GM's Weather-Pack connectors. This special tool is required to remove the pin and sleeve terminals. If removal is attempted with an ordinary pick, there is a good chance that the terminal will be bent or deformed. These terminals cannot be straightened once they are bent.

Use care when probing the connections or replacing terminals in them. It is possible to short between opposite terminals. If this happens to the wrong terminal part, it is possible to damage certain components. Always use jumper wires between connec-

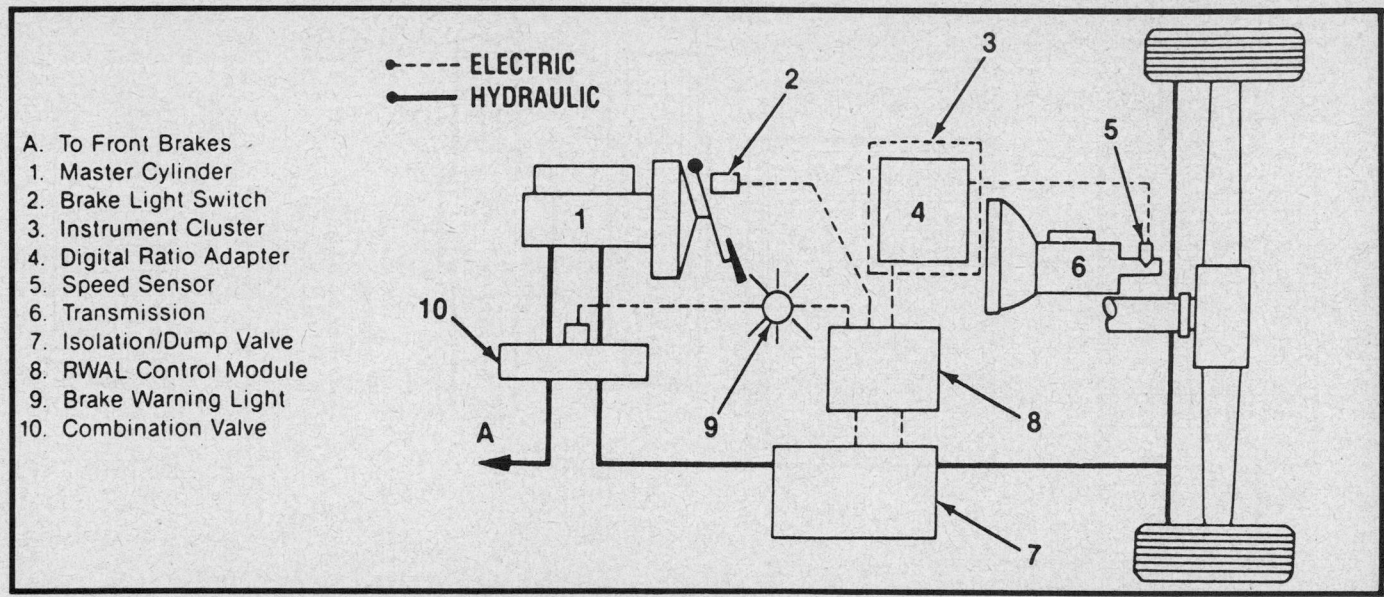

A. To Front Brakes
1. Master Cylinder
2. Brake Light Switch
3. Instrument Cluster
4. Digital Ratio Adapter
5. Speed Sensor
6. Transmission
7. Isolation/Dump Valve
8. RWAL Control Module
9. Brake Warning Light
10. Combination Valve

- - - - ● ELECTRIC
────── ● HYDRAULIC

General Motors Rear Wheel Antilock Brake System (RWAL)

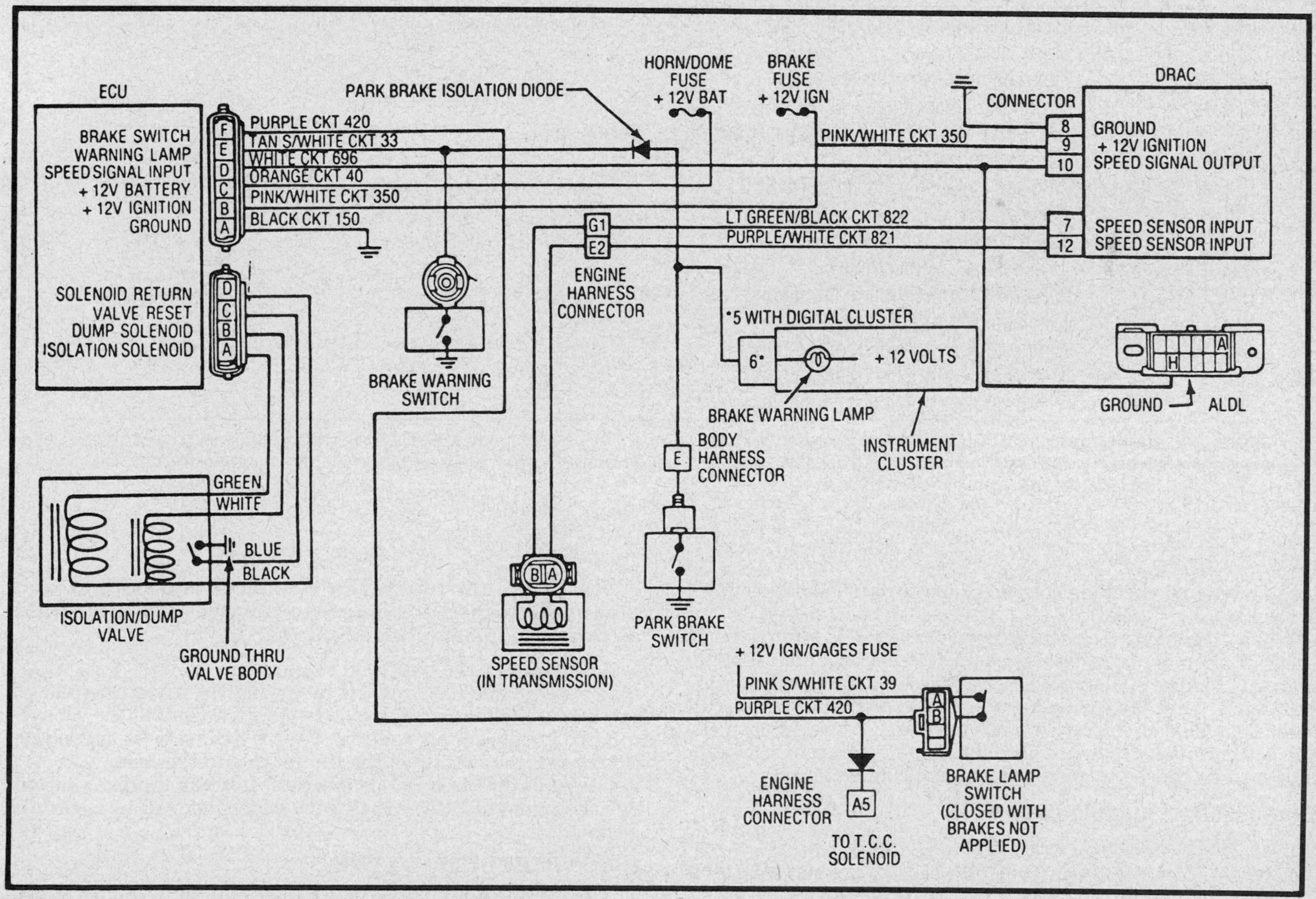

Rear wheel antilock braking system wiring diagram

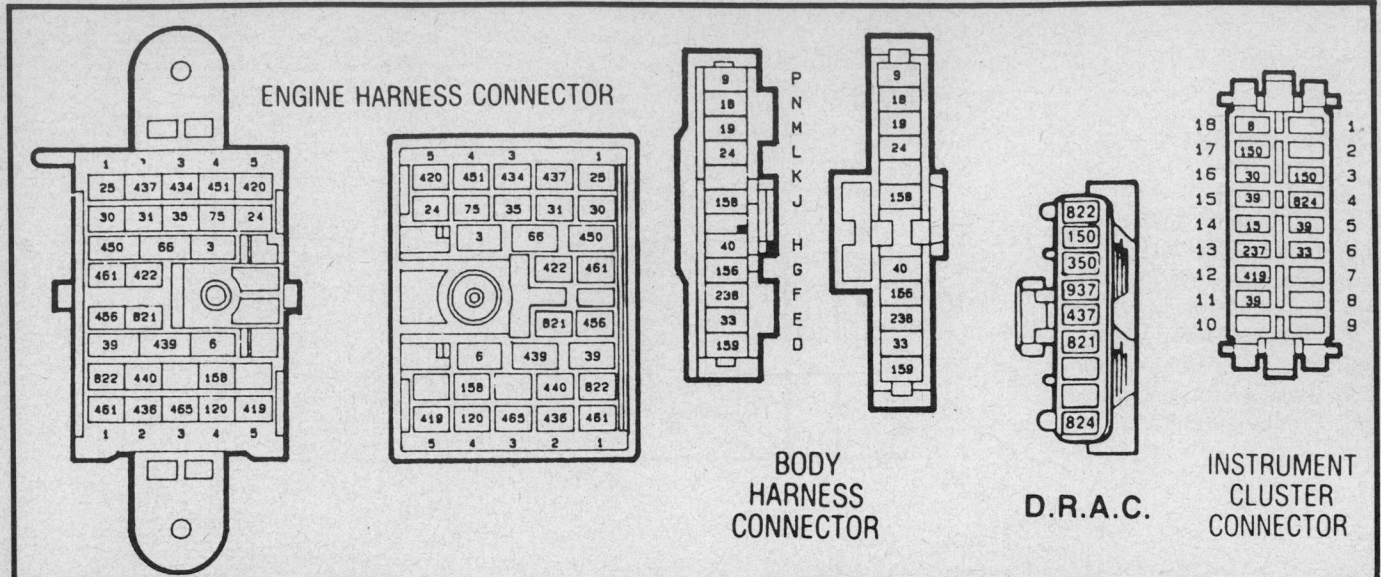

Rear wheel antilock connectors

REAR WHEEL ANTILOCK BRAKE SYSTEM DIAGNOSTIC CODES

CODE	SYSTEM PROBLEM
CODE 1	Electronic control unit malfunction
CODE 2	Open isolation valve or faulty ECU
CODE 3	Open dump valve or faulty ECU
CODE 4	Grounded antilock valve switch
CODE 5	Excessive actuations of dump valve during an antilock stop
CODE 6	Erratic speed signal
CODE 7	Shorted isolation valve or faulty ECU
CODE 8	Shorted dump valve or faulty ECU
CODE 9	Open circuit to the speed signal
CODE 10	Brake lamp switch circuit
CODE 11	Electronic control unit malfunction
CODE 12	Electronic control unit malfunction
CODE 13	Electronic control unit malfunction
CODE 14	Electronic control unit malfunction
CODE 15	Electronic control unit malfunction

Trouble codes are available at the ALDL (Assembly Line Diagnostic Link), the twelve terminal connector wired to the Electronic Control Module and located under the instrument panel in the passenger compartment. These codes are ready by jumping terminal A (which is ground) of the ALDL to terminal H of the ALDL and observing the flashing of the brake warning light.

tors for circuit checking. Never probe through Weather-Pack seals.

When diagnosing for possible open circuits, it is often difficult to locate them by sight because oxidation or terminal misalignment are hidden by the connectors. Merely wiggling a connector on a sensor or in the wiring harness may correct the open circuit condition. This should always be considered when an open circuit is indicated while troubleshooting. Intermittent problems may also be caused by oxidized or loose connections.

Removal and Installation

RWAL ELECTRONIC CONTROL UNIT

The RWAL Electronic Control Unit (ECU) is not serviceable. It should be replaced when diagnosis shows it to be malfunctioning.

NOTE: Do not touch the electrical connections and pins or allow them to come into contact with brake fluid as this will damage the RWAL ECU.

1. Disconnect the electrical connectors.
2. Remove the RWAL ECU by prying the tab at the rear of the ECU and pulling it forward toward the front of the vehicle.
3. To install, simply slide the RWAL ECU into its bracket on the master cylinder until the tab locks into the hole.
4. Install the electrical connectors. If brake fluid has gotten on the connectors, clean then with water followed by isopropyl alcohol.

ISOLATION/DUMP VALVE

The Isolation/Dump valve is not serviceable. It should be replaced when diagnosis shows it to be malfunctioning.

NOTE: Do not touch the electrical connections and pins or allow them to come into contact with brake fluid as this will damage the RWAL ECU.

1. Disconnect the brake line fittings and remove the bolts holding the valve to the bracket.

2. Disconnect the electrical connector from the RWAL ECU. Do not allow the valve to hang by the pigtail.

3. Remove the valve from the vehicle.

4. When installing replacement valve, torque bolts to 21 ft. lbs, brake line fittings to 18 ft. lbs.

5. Install the electrical connectors. If brake fluid has gotten on the connectors, clean them with water followed by isopropyl alcohol.

6. Bleed brake system.

SPEED SENSOR

The vehicle speed sensor is a permanent magnet signal generator located on the transmission output shaft housing. The vehicle speed sensor sends an analog signal proportional to the propeller shaft speed. This signal goes to the Digital Ratio Adapter Controller (DRAC) which is used to change the speed sensor signal to a digital signal for the electronic instrument cluster.

The speed sensor is not serviceable. It should be replaced when necessary. The sensor is located in the left rear of the transmission on 2WD models and on the transfer case of 4WD models.

The resistance of the speed sensor should be 900-2000 ohms.

1. Remove the electrical connector.

2. Most applications will use a bolt retainer which is removed. Pull the speed sensor out of transmission housing. Have container ready to catch transmission fluid.

3. Always use new O-ring seal when installing speed sensor. Coat the seal with a thin film of transmission fluid.

4. Install retainer bolt if used and connect electrical harness.

NOTE: The speedometer must recalibrated when rear axle ratio or tire size is changed.

FOUR WHEEL ANTI-LOCK BRAKE SYSTEM

In 1990, selected G.M. models with All Wheel Drive (AWD) could be equipped with a Four Wheel Antilock System (4WAL). It too is designed to to reduce wheel lockup during severe braking. Like the Rear Wheel Antilock system, it works by regulating hyrdaulic brake line pressure. An Electro-Hydraulic Control Unit valve (EHCU), located under the master cylinder, is made up of two types of valves. Isolation valves maintain pressure to each front wheel separately and to the rear wheels combined. Dump valves dump pressure to each front wheel separately and to the rear wheels combined. The valves are controlled by a microcomputer which is part of the EHCU valve. Under severe braking, the EHCU valve will allow the valves to either maintain the same hydraulic pressure, release hydraulic pressure through the dump valves into the accumulator, or increase pressure.

The EHCU valve operates by receiving signals from the speed sensors, located at each wheel and the brake lamp switch. The speed sensors are connected directly to the EHCU valve through the 8 pin connector.

The 4WAL system is connected to the ANTILOCK warning lamp in the instrument panel. An indication of 4WAL operation and a bulb check is performed each time the ignition is turned ON. The warning lamp will remain on for about 2 seconds. A 4WAL system malfunction is indicated by the ANTILOCK warning light.

To aid in diagnosing problems, trouble codes are produced by the system. Trouble codes are available at the Assembly Line Diagnostic Link (ALDL) the twelve terminal connector wired to the Electronic Control Module and located under the instrument panel in the passenger compartment. These codes are read

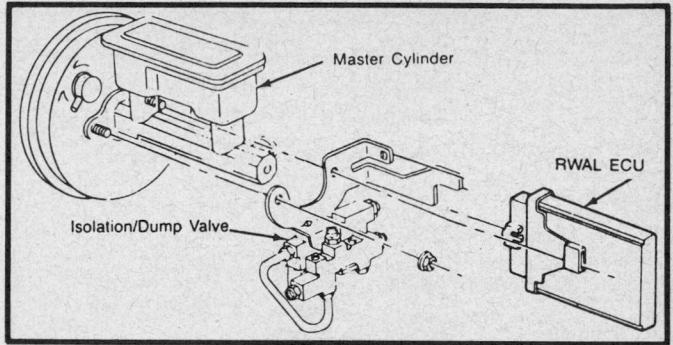

RWAL ECU and Isolation/Dump Valve

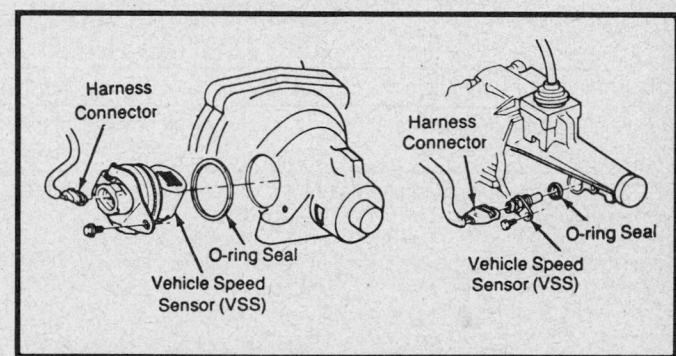

Transmission speed sensor installation

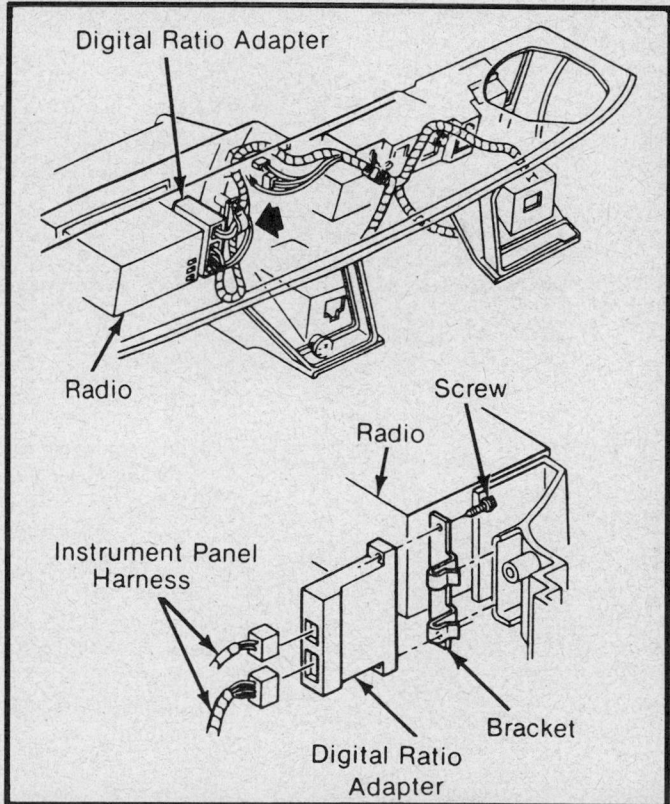

Digital ratio adapter controller mounting

by jumping terminal A of the ALDL to terminal H of the ALDL and observing the flashing of the ANTILOCK. The terminals must be jumped for a few seconds before the code will begin to flash. The ANTILOCK light will flash in a manner similar to the

TERMINAL IDENTIFICATION

A	GROUND	F	T.C.C. (IF USED)
B	DIAGNOSTIC TERMINAL	G	FUEL PUMP (CK)
C	A.I.R. (IF USED)	H	BRAKE SENSE SPEED INPUT (CK)
E	SERIAL DATA (V6/V8)	M	SERIAL DATA (L4)

ALDL Connector

SERVICE ENGINE SOON light for the fuel and emissions system.

In counting code pulses, count the number of short flashes starting from the long flash. Include the long flash as a count.

NOTE: Sometimes the first count sequence will be short. However, subsequent counts will be accurate. If there is more than one failure, only the first recognized failure code will be retained and flashed.

To clear trouble codes, turn the ignition switch to RUN. Use a jumper wire to ground the ALDL terminal H to A for two seconds. Remove the jumper wire for two seconds. Repeat the grounding and ungrounding 2 more times. Check that the memory is cleared by making a diagnostic request. Turn ignition OFF.

DIAGNOSIS OF THE VEHICLE SPEED SENSOR AND DIGITAL RATIO ADAPTER CONTROLLER

Problem	Possible Cause	Correction
Speedometer and odometer are inaccurate	Incorrect digital ratio adapter.	Check for the correct digital ratio adapter.
Speedometer and odometer do not operate properly	1. Inoperative digital ratio adapter.	1. Disconnect the digital ratio adapter, and place the ignition in run. Check for voltage between the pink/black wire in the harness and a good chassis ground. If the voltage is less than the battery voltage, check for an open or short in the pink/black wire.
	2. Poor ground path from the digital ratio adapter.	2. Check for voltage between the pink/black wire in the harness and the black/white wire. If the voltage is less than battery voltage, check for an open or short in the black/white wire.
	3. No signal from the vehicle speed sensor.	3. Raise and support the vehicle, start the engine, and place the transmission in drive. Check for AC voltage that changes with the engine rpm between the purple/white wire, and the light green/black wire at the digital ratio adapter. If there is not AC voltage at these wires, check for opens in the purple/white wire and the light green wire. If there are not shorts or opens, replace the vehicle speed sensor.
	4. Inoperative digital ratio adapter (speedometer output).	4. Raise and support the vehicle, start the engine, and place the transmission in drive. Check for AC voltage that changes with the engine rpm between the light blue/black and the black/white wires at the digital ratio adapter connector (connector attached) if AC voltage varies with RPM, replace the digital ratio adapter.
	5. Inoperative digital ratio adapter (cruise output).	5. Raise and support the vehicle, start the engine, and place the transmission in drive. Check for AC voltage that changes with the engine rpm between the yellow and the black/white wires at the digital ratio adapter connector (connector attached) if AC voltage varies with rpm, replace the digital ratio adapter.

G.M. FOUR WHEEL ANTILOCK BRAKE SYSTEM DIAGNOSTIC CODES

CODE	SYSTEM PROBLEM
CODE 21	Right front speed sensor or circuit open
CODE 22	Missing right front speed signal (set with vehicle in motion)
CODE 23	Erratic right front speed sensor
CODE 25	Left front speed sensor or circuit open
CODE 26	Missing left front speed signal (set with vehicle in motion)
CODE 27	Erratic left front speed sensor
CODE 28	Erratic speed sensor signal (two drop-outs above 20 mph)
CODE 29	Simultaneous drop-out of all four sensors (at speeds above 8 mph)
CODE 31	Right rear speed sensor or circuit open
CODE 32	Missing right rear speed signal (set with vehicle in motion)
CODE 33	Erratic right rear speed sensor
CODE 35	Left rear speed sensor or circuit open
CODE 36	Missing left rear speed signal (set with vehicle in motion)
CODE 37	Erratic left rear speed sensor
CODE 38	Wheel speed error (set with vehicle in motion)
CODES 41 thru 66 and 71 thru 74	4WAL control unit
CODE 67	Open motor circuit or shorted ECU output
CODE 68	Locked motor or shorted motor circuit
CODES 68, 43, 44, 47, 48, 53 and 54	Loss of power ground
CODE 81	Brake switch circuit shorted or open
CODE 85	Open antilock warning lamp
CODE 86	Shorted antilock warning lamp
CODE 88	Shorted brake warning lamp

Removal and Installation

ELECTRO-HYDRAULIC CONTROL UNIT (EHCU) VALVE

The EHCU valve is not serviceable. It should be replaced when diagnosis shows it to be malfunctioning.

1. Mark relationship between the intermediate steering shaft upper universal joint yoke to steering shaft and the lower yoke to steering gear wormshaft. Remove the upper and lower universal yoke pinch bolt.

2. Remove the steering gear frame bolts. Lower the steering gear. It is not necessary to disconnect the pitman arm from the steering gear pitman shaft.

3. Remove the intermediate steering shaft and universal joint assembly.

4. Remove the brake lines from the bottom of the combination valve. Remove the electrical connector.

5. Remove the master cylinder and combination valve assembly.

6. Remove the brake lines from the EHCU valve. Remove the electrical connectors from the EHCU valve.

7. Remove mounting bolt and nuts and remove EHCU from vehicle. Remove EHCU from its mounting bracket.

8. Install the EHCU valve to its mounting bracket. Tighten the 6 mounting bolts to only 60 inch lbs. Overtightening these bolts could result in excessive noise transfer from the EHCU valve.

9. Install the EHCU valve and bracket assembly into the vehicle and install the fasteners. Torque the bolt to 33 ft. lbs., the nuts to 20 ft. lbs.

10. Install the electrical connectors and the brake lines to the EHCU valve.

11. Install the master cylinder and combination valve assem-

9–19

FOUR WHEEL ANTILOCK WIRING DIAGRAM

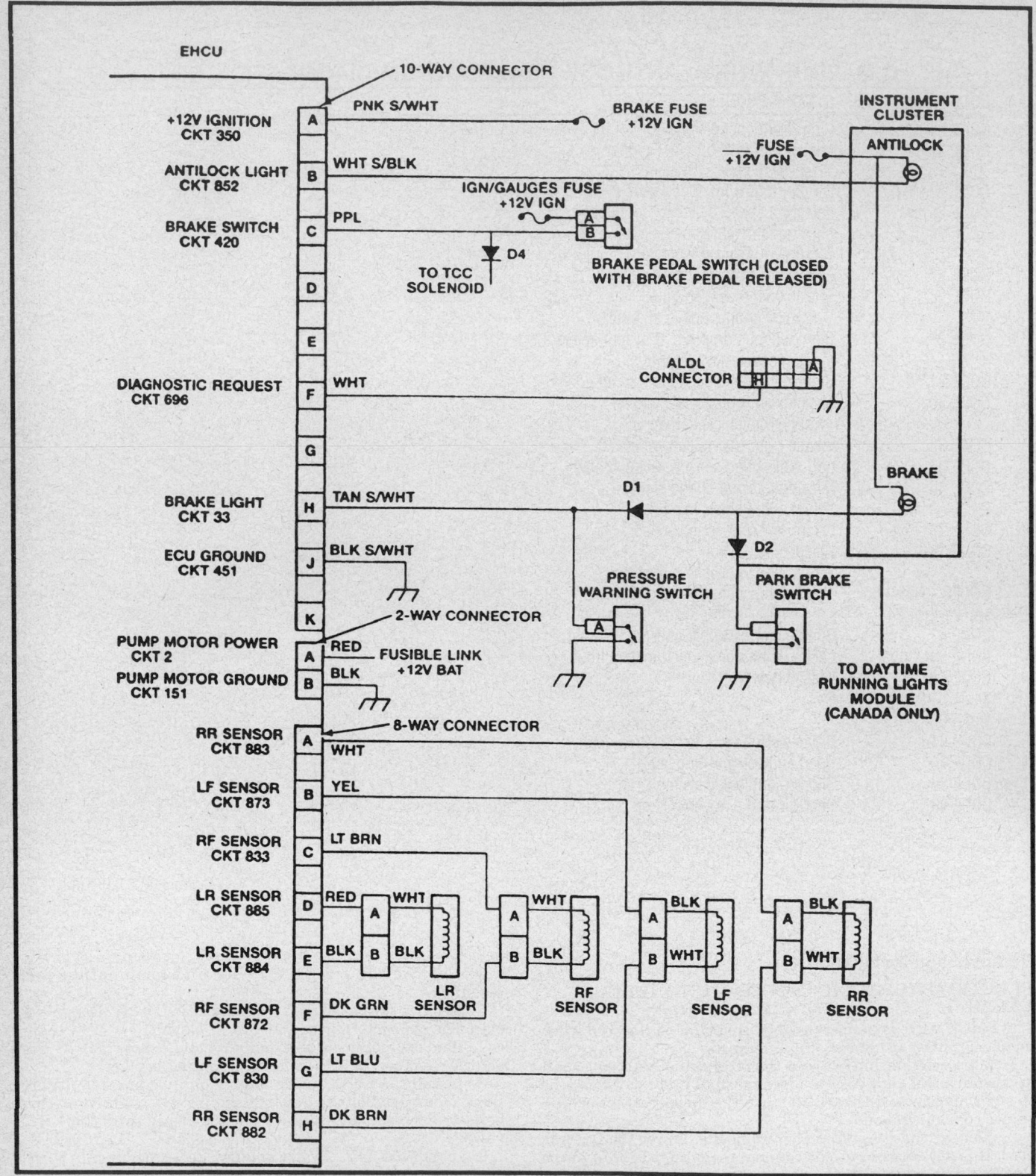

FOUR WHEEL ANTILOCK BRAKE SYSTEM

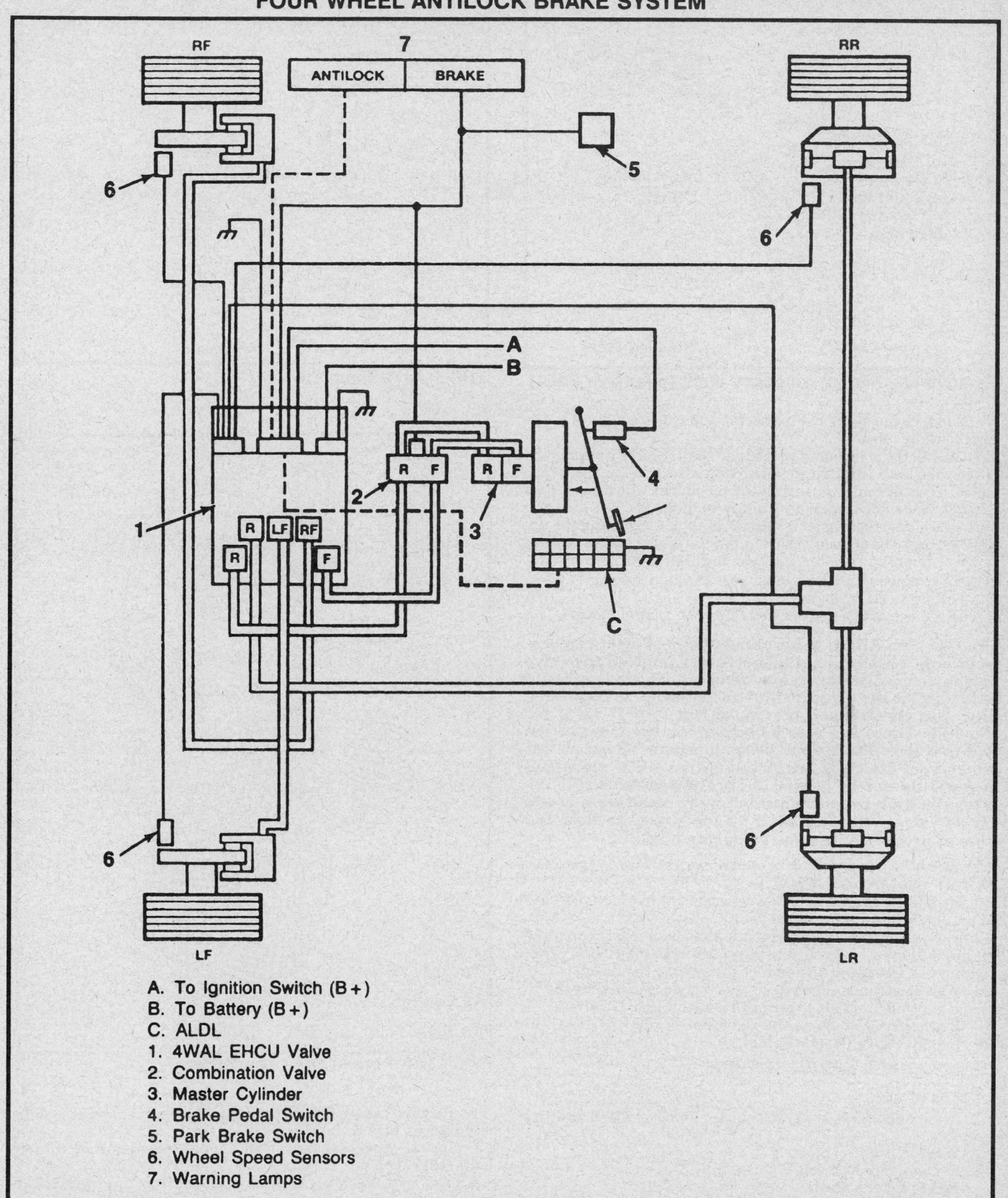

A. To Ignition Switch (B+)
B. To Battery (B+)
C. ALDL
1. 4WAL EHCU Valve
2. Combination Valve
3. Master Cylinder
4. Brake Pedal Switch
5. Park Brake Switch
6. Wheel Speed Sensors
7. Warning Lamps

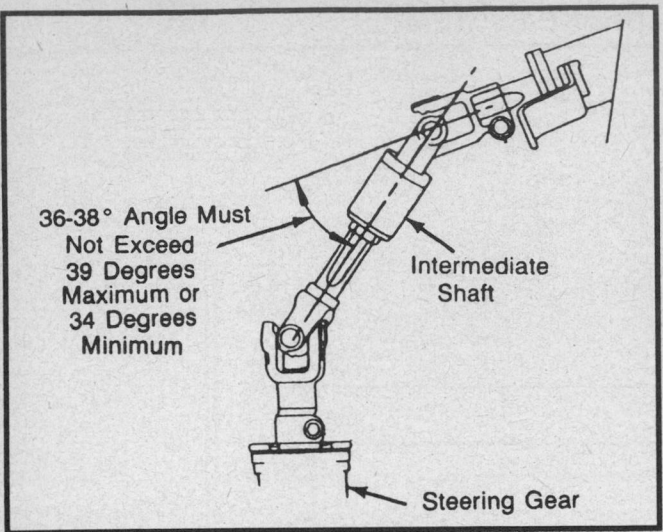

Remove steering intermediate shaft to remove EHCU

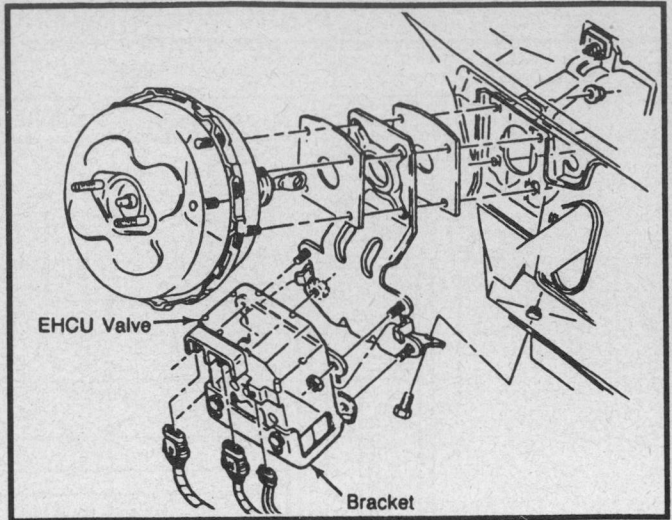

EHCU valve mounting

bly. Connect the electrical connector and the brake lines to the combination valve.

12. Install the steering intermediate shaft. Start by placing the lower yoke onto the steering gear wormshaft. Align the match marks made at removal. Install the pinch bolt which must pass through the shaft undercut. Torque to 30 ft. lbs.

13. Raise the steering gear into position while guiding the upper yoke onto the steering shaft. Align the match marks made at removal. Tighten the steering gear to frame bolts to 55 ft. lbs. Install the pinch bolt which must pass through the shaft undercut. Torque to 30 ft. lbs.

14. Bleed the brake system including the EHCU valve.

NOTE: The EHCU valve should be bled after replacement only. It should not be necessary to bleed the valve during normal brake system bleeding. The valve should be bled after the wheel cylinders and calipers have been bled. Use the 2 bleed screws on the EHCU valve for bleeding. There are also 2 bleeders on the front of the unit that look like normal brake bleeders. These are not the correct bleeders for bleeding the EHCU valve and they should not be turned. A special tool is used to depress the high pressure accumulator bleed stem of the EHCU valve. This is similar to tools used to hold the stem of proportioning valves during bleeding.

15. Bleed the wheel cylinders and calipers as usual (right rear, left rear, right front, left front).

16. Install the special hold-down tool on the left high pressure accumulator bleed stem of the EHCU valve.

17. Slowly depress brake pedal one time and hold. Loosen the left bleeder screw ¼–½ turn to purge air from the EHCU valve. Tighten the bleeder screw and slowly release the pedal.

18. Wait 15 seconds then repeat this sequence including the 15 second wait until all air is purged from the EHCU valve.

19. Repeat these steps on the right side of the EHCU valve.

20. Remove valve depressor tool.

FRONT WHEEL SPEED SENSOR

2 WD Vehicles

1. Raise and safely support vehicle. Remove wheel and tire assembly.

2. Remove brake caliper.

3. Remove hub and bearing assembly.

4. Remove rotor assembly.

5. Disconnect the sensor wire connector and unclip from upper control arm.

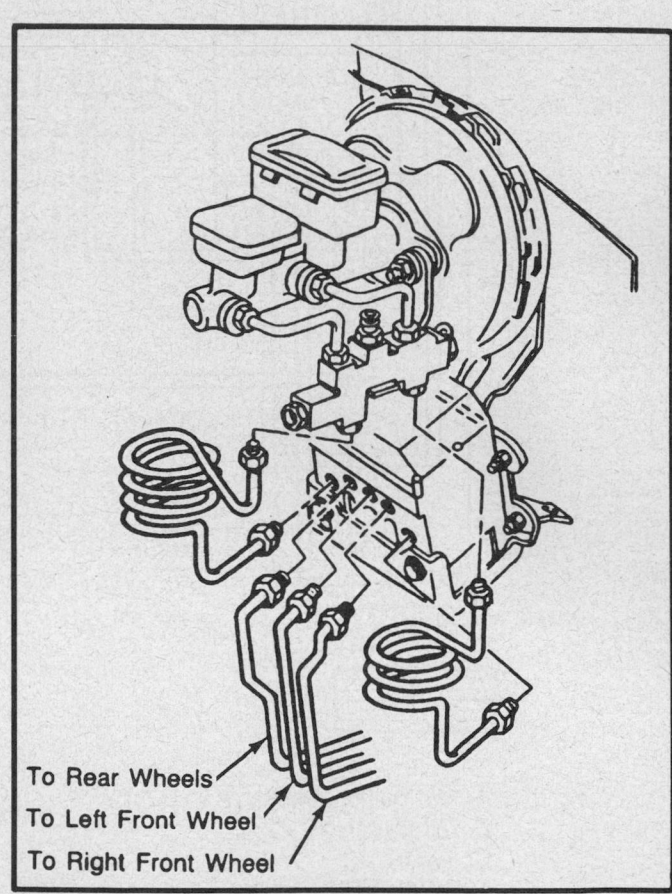

EHCU valve brake line connections

6. Remove bolts holding speed sensor/splash shield assembly and remove unit from vehicle.

7. Install speed sensor/splash shield assembly and torque bolts to 11 ft. lbs.

8. Clip wire to upper control arm and reconnect electrical connection.

9. Apply recommended lubricant to the spindle and inside of

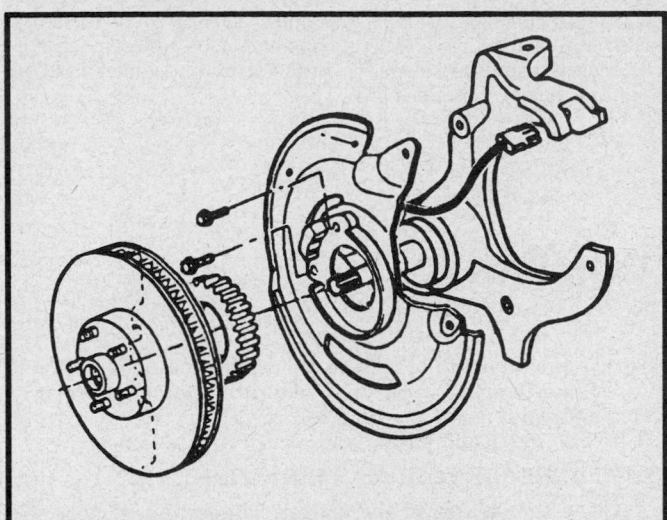

Front wheel speed sensor – 2 WD vehicles

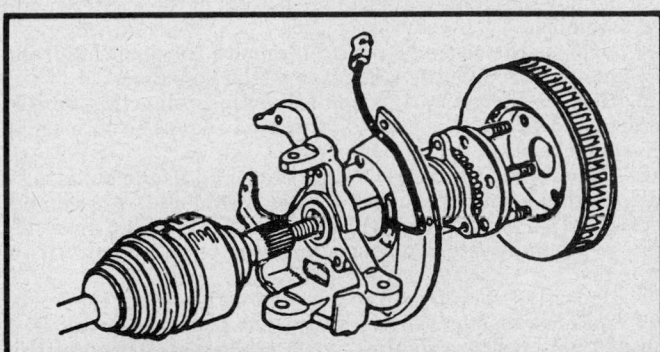

Front wheel speed sensor – 4 WD vehicles

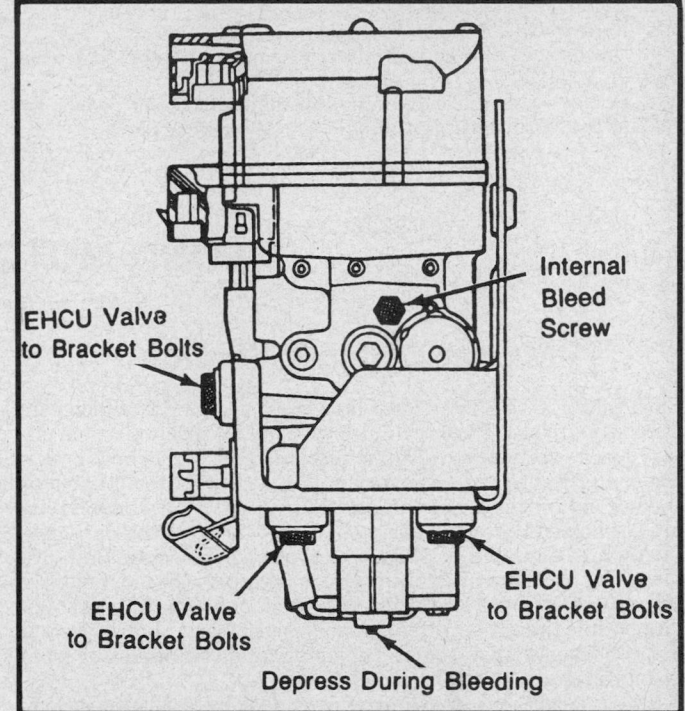

EHCU valve bleeders

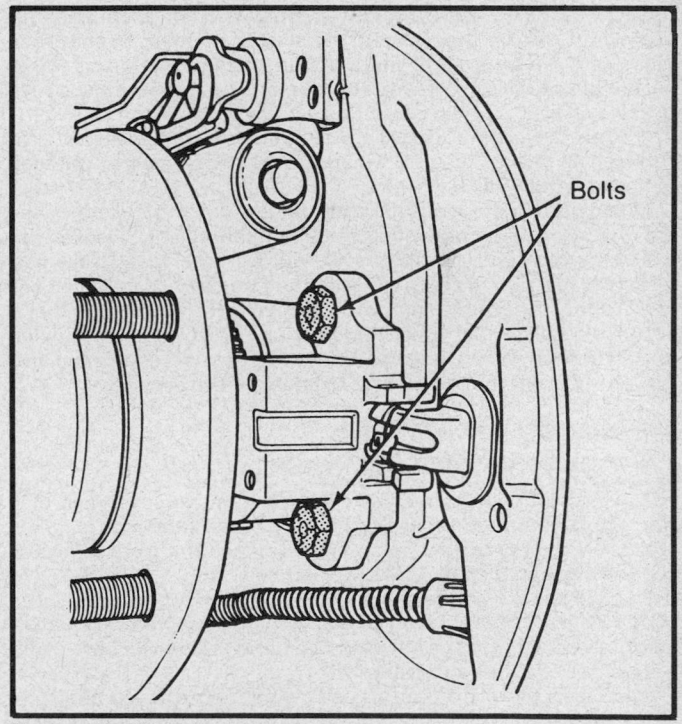

Rear wheel speed sensor

hub. Install hub and outer wheel bearing and washer with a generous amount of lubricant. Tighten nut to 12 ft. lbs. while turning the hub forward to seat the bearing. Back off the nut to the just loose position. Hand tighten nut, then back off until the hole in the spindle lines up with a slot on the nut. The nut should not be backed off more than ½ a flat. Install new cotter pin.

10. Install brake rotor.

11. Install caliper. Bushings should be lubricated with silicone grease. Make sure the brake line is not twisted.

12. Install wheel and tire assembly. Lower vehicle.

4 WD Vehicles

1. Raise and safely support vehicle. Remove wheel and tire assembly.

2. Remove brake caliper.

3. Remove brake rotor.

4. Remove hub and bearing assembly. On all-wheel drive models, remove the drive axle nut and washer. Use a puller to ease the hub from the drive axle.

5. Disconnect the sensor wire connector and unclip from upper control arm.

6. Remove bolts holding speed sensor/splash shield assembly and remove unit from vehicle.

7. Install speed sensor/splash shield assembly to the steering knuckle and torque the bolts to 11 ft. lbs.

8. Clip wire to upper control arm and reconnect electrical connection.

9. Install hub and bearing assembly, align threaded holes and tighten bolts to 66 ft. lbs.

10. Install outer axle washer and nut. Torque to 175 ft. lb.

11. Install brake rotor and caliper.

12. Install wheel and tire. Lower vehicle.

REAR WHEEL SPEED SENSOR
4WD Vehicles

1. Raise and safely support vehicle. Remove wheel and tire assembly.

2. Remove brake drum.

3. Remove the primary brake shoe.

4. Disconnect the sensor electric wire connector and wire from its axle clips.

5. Remove the retainer bolts and take out speed sensor by pulling the wire through the hole in the backing plate.

6. Install the speed sensor and bolts. Torque to 26 ft. lbs.

7. Install sensor wire to axle clips and hook up connector.

8. Install primary brake shoe, brake drum and wheel and tire assembly. Lower vehicle.

FORD MOTOR COMPANY

Master Cylinder Service

Ford Motor Company uses a dual master cylinder which contains a double hydraulic cylinder with 2 fluid reservoirs and primary and secondary hydraulic pistons. The rear wheel brakes are connected to the secondary outlet port and are actuated by the secondary piston piston assembly. The front wheel brakes are connected to the primary outlet port (nearest the dash panel) and are actuated by the primary piston assembly. Both primary and secondary pistons function together. On most models, the master cylinder is assisted by a vacuum booster. Both single and double diaphragm Bendix models are used. Hydraulic rear drum brakes with automatic adjusters and self-adjusting front disc brakes are standard on all models.

Two types of master cylinders were used by Ford Motor Company; 1) a cast iron master cylinder with built-in reservoir and separate proportioning valve and, 2) a master cylinder with a pressed on plastic see-through reservoir with the proportioning valve built into or integral with the master cylinder. In the event of a front brake system malfunction the proportioning valve with a bypass feature allows full hydraulic pressure to the rear brake system.

A Fluid Level Indicator (FLI) is built into the reservoir. It is serviced as part of the reservoir assembly. This master cylinder is found from 1987.

During normal operation, the fluid level in the master cylinder will rise during brake operation and fall during release. It is also expected that the fluid level will decrease with brake pad wear. In addition, a trace of brake fluid on the booster shell below the master cylinder mounting flange will often be found as a result of the normal lubricating action of the master cylinder bore and seal. All of these conditions are considered normal and are not indications the master cylinder needs service.

Disassembly and Assembly

CAST IRON MASTER CYLINDER

1. Clean outside of master cylinder, remove cover and diaphragm. Drain and discard remaining brake fluid.

2. Depress the primary piston and remove snapring at rear of the master cylinder bore.

3. Remove the primary piston and inspect for damage.

4. Remove the secondary piston assembly by directing a little compressed air into the outlet at the blind end of the bore while plugging the other outlet port.

5. Inspect the pistons, seals and cylinder bore for etching, pitting, scoring or other damage. If the bore is damaged, discard and replace with a new master cylinder. Do not attempt to hone the bore. If the bore is not damaged, use the proper repair kit to rebuild.

6. Clean the master cylinder body with isopropyl alcohol.

7. Dip the repair kit piston assemblies in clean heavy duty brake fluid to lubricate the seals. Carefully insert the complete secondary piston assembly into the master cylinder bore, followed by the primary piston assembly.

8. Depress the primary piston and install snapring. On man-

ual brake vehicle, install the push rod retainer onto the push rod and install into primary piston. Make sure retainer is properly seated and holding the pushrod securely.

9. Install cover and gasket and secure with retainer.

PLASTIC RESERVOIR MASTER CYLINDER

1. Clean the outside of the master cylinder and remove the cap and gasket. Drain and discard remaining brake fluid.

2. Remove the proportioning valve from the master cylinder.

3. Remove the stop-bolt from the bottom of the master cylinder assembly.

4. Depress the secondary piston, remove the snapring from the bore and remove the secondary piston assembly.

5. Remove the primary piston assembly by directing a little compressed air into the outlet at the blind end of the bore while plugging the other outlet port.

6. Inspect the pistons, seals and cylinder bore for etching, pitting, scoring or other damage. If bore is damaged, discard and replace with a new master cylinder. Do not attempt to hone the bore. If the bore is not damaged, use the proper repair kit to rebuild.

7. If plastic reservoir is to be removed, carefully pry the reservoir from the master cylinder body. The plastic reservoir is a push-fit with rubber grommets making the seal. Whenever the plastic reservoir is replaced, the grommets must also be replaced.

8. Dip the repair kit piston assemblies in clean heavy duty brake fluid to lubricate the seals. Carefully insert the complete primary piston assembly into the master cylinder bore, followed by the secondary piston assembly.

8. Depress the secondary piston and install snapring. Install the stop bolt in the bottom of the master cylinder bore.

9. Install the proportioning valve assembly in the master cylinder.

10. If the reservoir was removed, lubricate new retainer grommets with brake fluid and insert the grommets into the master cylinder body. Press the plastic reservoir into the grommets. The reservoir should snap into place indicating that it is secure. Make sure the fluid level indicator socket is facing the correct direction for the vehicle on which it is to be installed.

11. Install plastic cap on the master cylinder.

Brake Booster Service

Three types of brake boosters are used, a single diaphragm, a tandem diaphragm and a hydraulic booster (Hydro-Boost).

Under normal operating conditions, with brakes released, a vacuum suspended booster operates with vacuum on both sides of its diaphragm (or both diaphragms in a tandem diaphragm unit). When the brakes are applied, air at atmospheric pressure is admitted to one side of the diaphragm (or both diaphragms in a tandem diaphragm unit) to provide the power assist.

The hydraulic brake booster (Hydro-Boost) uses the power steering pump to power the system and a pneumatic accumulator as a reserve system. In this system no special fluids are used. However, care must be taken to use the correct fluids. The mas-

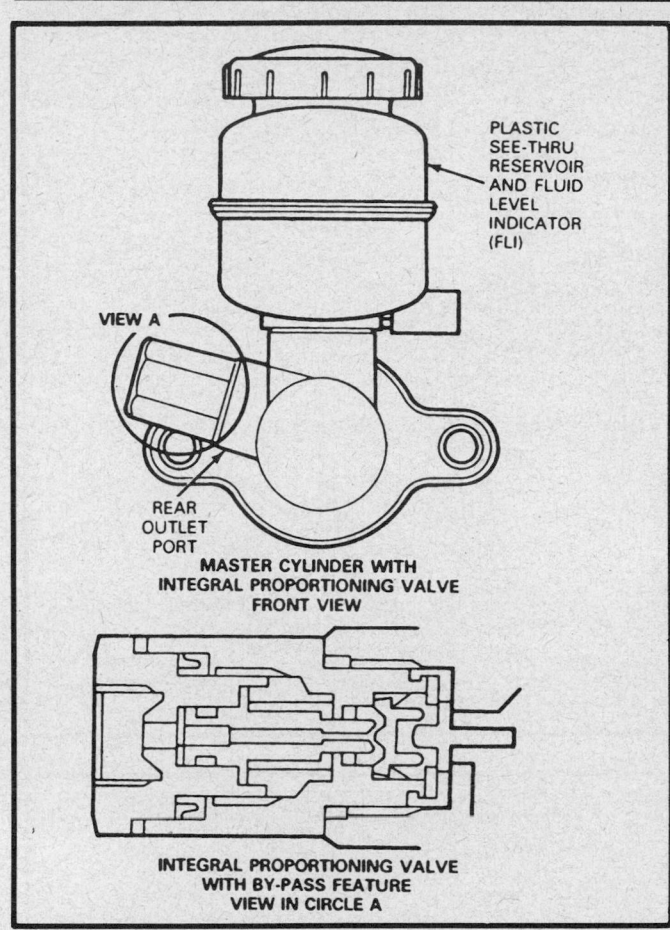

Ford master cylinder with see-through reservoir and integral proportioning valve

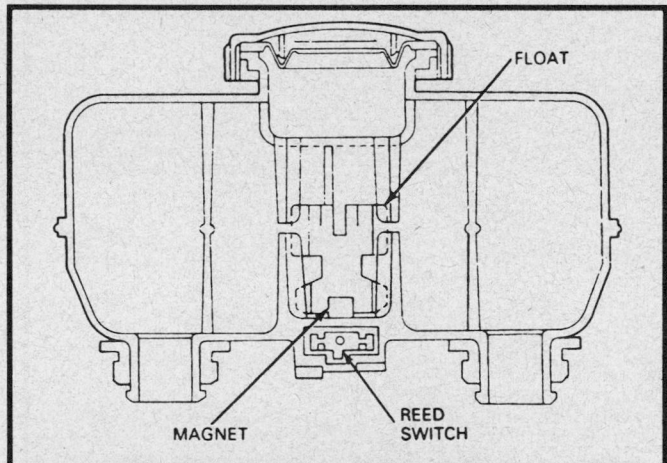

Plastic reservoir with fluid level indicator

ter cylinder and brake system operate on standard brake fluid. The hydraulic pump uses power steering fluid.

VACUUM DIAPHRAGM BRAKE BOOSTER

Both the Bendix single diaphragm and Bendix tandem diaphragm booster are not repairable and the booster must be replaced as a unit. The booster check valve is the only component which can be serviced on the booster assembly.

The Bendix Hydro-Boost uses the hydraulic pressure supplied by the power steering pump to provide a power assist to brake application. It has identifying information stamped into the housing near the inlet

The Hydro-Boost power brake booster is not to be disassembled and is to be serviced as a unit.

Brake Booster Vacuum Pump

On gasoline engine vehicles, engine vacuum is used to power the vacuum booster brake. On diesel engines, there is not enough vacuum available for vacuum booster brake operation.

On diesel engine vehicles, vacuum is supplied from a pump usually located on the top right side of the engine. It is usually driven by a single belt off the alternator.

Diesel engine equipped vehicles will also usually have a low-vacuum indicator switch which activates the BRAKE warning lamp when vacuum gets below a certain level. The switch senses vacuum through a fitting in the vacuum manifold (sometimes called a vacuum tree). Note that the BRAKE light will glow until vacuum builds up to normal level.

The low-vacuum switch for E Series is located to the left side fender panel. On F 250 – F 350 Series the switch is located on the right side of the engine compartment adjacent to the vacuum pump.

The vacuum pump is not to be disassembled. It is only serviced as a unit. The pulley is serviced as a separate item.

Caliper Service

Ford Motor Company uses several types of brake calipers, a Heavy Duty (HD) Pin Rail caliper, a Light Duty (LD) sliding brake caliper and a Light Duty (LD) Pin Rail caliper.

The HD caliper has 2 pistons on the same side of the rotor. Pin Rail type calipers slide on 2 pins that also attach the caliper to the spindle (or anchor plate on some F-Super Duty rear disc brakes). The caliper is a one-piece casting with the inboard side containing the piston bore(s). A square cut rubber seal is located in a groove in the piston bore which provides the hydraulic seal between the piston and the cylinder wall.

As the brake pedal is pressed, hydraulic pressure is applied against the piston(s). This pressure pushes the inboard brake lining against the inboard braking surface of the rotor. As the force increases against the rotor, the caliper assembly moves inboard and provides a clamping action on the rotor.

When brake pressure is released, the piston seal returns to its normal position, pulling the piston back into the caliper bore. This creates a running clearance between the inner brake lining and rotor.

NOTE: Some Ford trucks were available with four wheel disc brakes.

Disassembly and Assembly

1. Remove pads from caliper. Different types of anti-rattle springs have been used. Note their positions for reassembly. Drain all fluid from the caliper.
2. Pad interior of caliper with clean shop towels or soft wood block and slowly and carefully use just enough compressed air to ease the piston out of the bore.

─────────── **CAUTION** ───────────

Do not place fingers in front of piston to try to catch piston or protect it when applying compressed air. This could result in serious injury. Use just enough air to ease the piston out. If piston is blown out, even with padding, it may be damaged. If the piston is jammed or cocked and will not come out readily, release the air pressure and tap sharply on the end of the piston with a soft (brass) hammer or plastic mallet to straighten the piston. Do not use a sharp tool to pry the piston out of the bore.

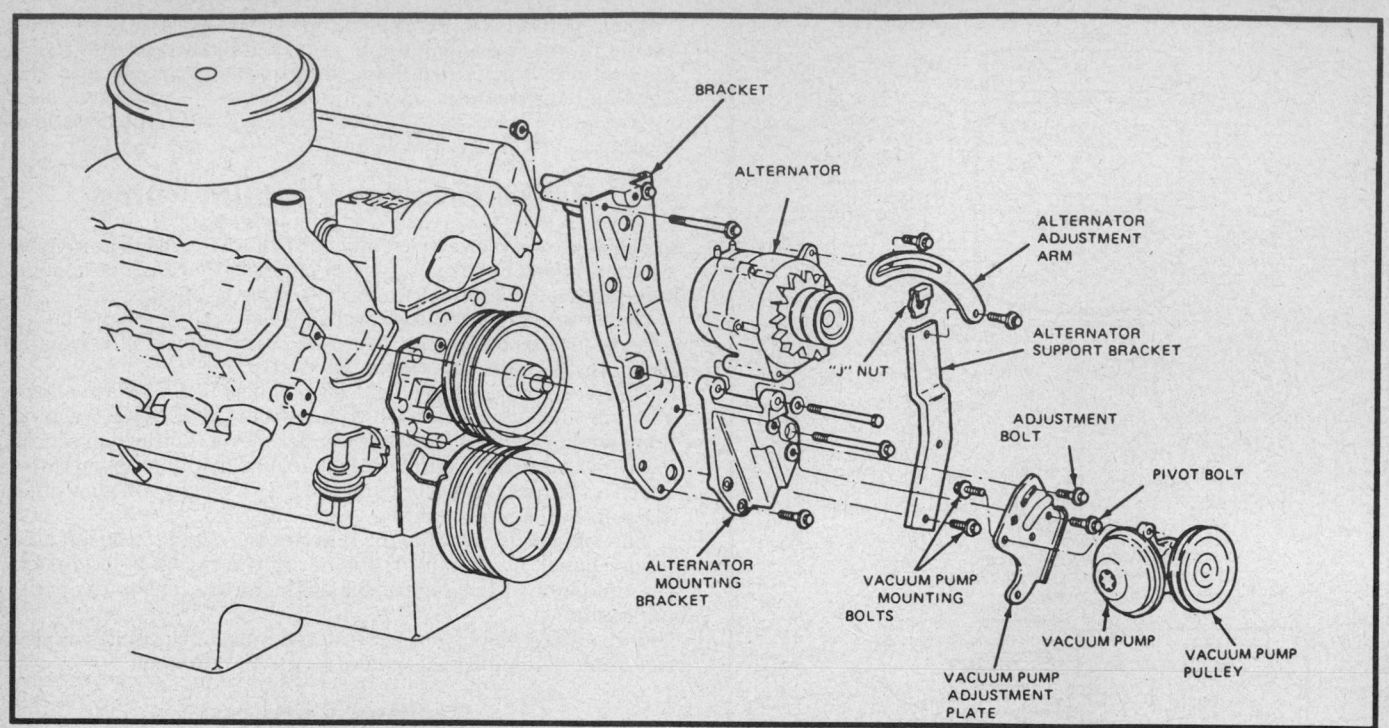

Vacuum pump installation—typical

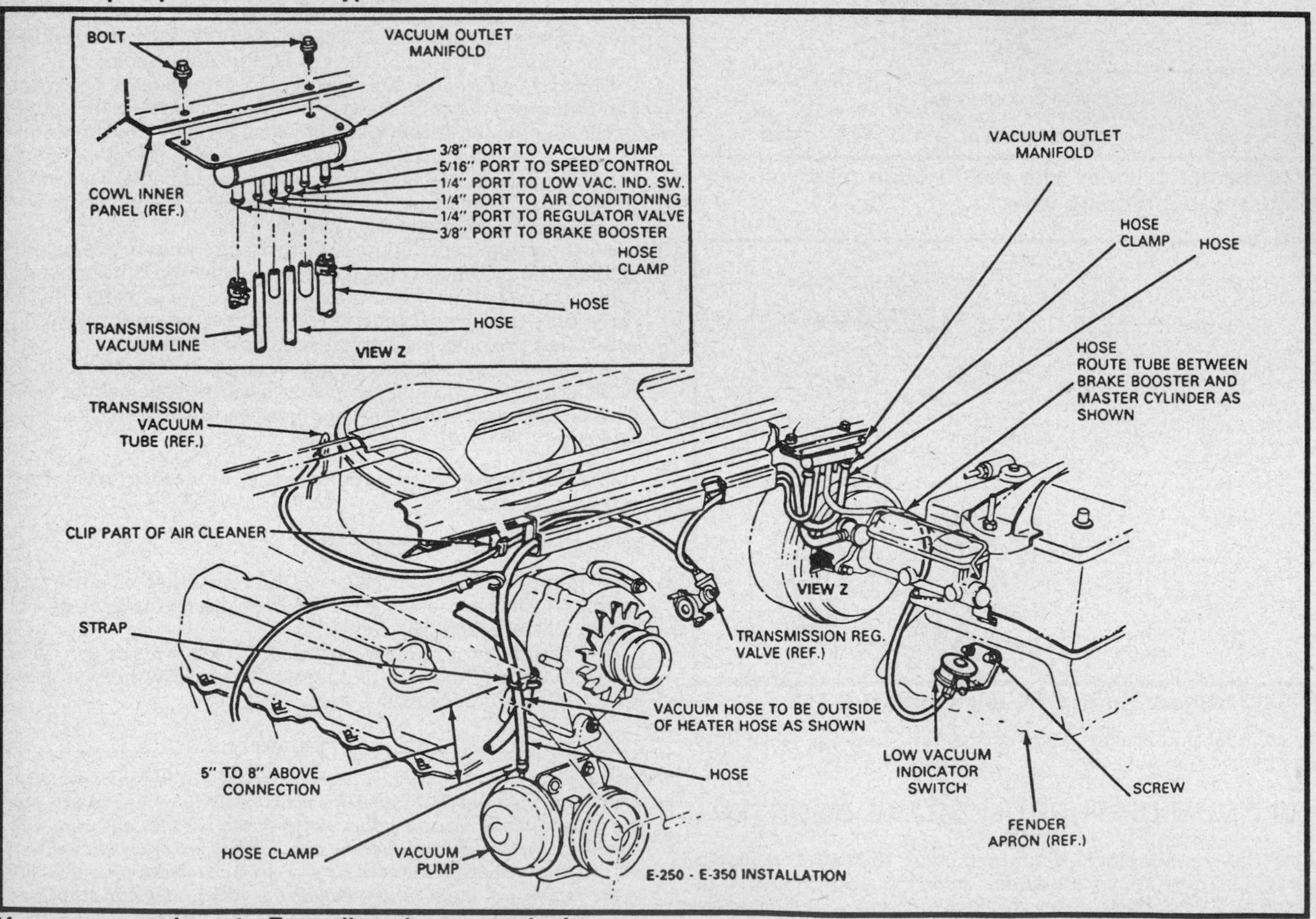

Labels in upper diagram:
- BRACKET
- ALTERNATOR
- ALTERNATOR ADJUSTMENT ARM
- ALTERNATOR SUPPORT BRACKET
- "J" NUT
- ADJUSTMENT BOLT
- PIVOT BOLT
- VACUUM PUMP PULLEY
- VACUUM PUMP
- VACUUM PUMP ADJUSTMENT PLATE
- VACUUM PUMP MOUNTING BOLTS
- ALTERNATOR MOUNTING BRACKET

Labels in lower diagram:
- BOLT
- VACUUM OUTLET MANIFOLD
- COWL INNER PANEL (REF.)
- 3/8" PORT TO VACUUM PUMP
- 5/16" PORT TO SPEED CONTROL
- 1/4" PORT TO LOW VAC. IND. SW.
- 1/4" PORT TO AIR CONDITIONING
- 1/4" PORT TO REGULATOR VALVE
- 3/8" PORT TO BRAKE BOOSTER
- HOSE CLAMP
- HOSE
- TRANSMISSION VACUUM LINE
- VIEW Z
- VACUUM OUTLET MANIFOLD
- HOSE CLAMP
- HOSE
- HOSE ROUTE TUBE BETWEEN BRAKE BOOSTER AND MASTER CYLINDER AS SHOWN
- TRANSMISSION VACUUM TUBE (REF.)
- CLIP PART OF AIR CLEANER
- STRAP
- VIEW Z
- TRANSMISSION REG. VALVE (REF.)
- VACUUM HOSE TO BE OUTSIDE OF HEATER HOSE AS SHOWN
- HOSE
- LOW VACUUM INDICATOR SWITCH
- SCREW
- FENDER APRON (REF.)
- 5" TO 8" ABOVE CONNECTION
- HOSE CLAMP
- VACUUM PUMP
- E-250 - E-350 INSTALLATION

Vacuum pump layout—Econoline shown—typical

BRAKE BOOSTER VACUUM PUMP TESTING—DIESEL ENGINES

TEST	PROCEDURE

Test 1	Isolating Problem
	A. Disconnect Low Vacuum Switch. Run engine at idle, apply brakes.
	    If brake warning light comes on, the problem is in the hydraulic brake system.
	    If brake warning light does not come on, the problem is in the vacuum pump (perform Test 2).

Test 2	Vacuum Pump Output Check
	A. Hook up vacuum gauge to hose at brake booster. At normal idle, vacuum should reach 21 inches Hg within 30 seconds (approximately 16 inches Hg at high altitudes—5,000 ft.).
	    If vacuum is okay, reconnect booster base and "TEE" vacuum gauge near pump inlet. Check vacuum at idle. There should be no more than 3 inches Hg vacuum drop. If drop is greater, look for vacuum leaks at hoses or vacuum accessories.
	    If vacuum is okay, repeat test with brake pedal held down. If vacuum drops, replace brake booster. If vacuum is within specs, check brake hydraulic system.
	    If vacuum is not okay, check gauge and connector for leaks. Make sure pulley is not slipping on shaft, and belt tension is okay. Make sure engine idle speed is correct. If vacuum output is still low, replace vacuum pump.

NOTE: When making tests, block all wheels, place transmission in Park or Neutral before starting engine.

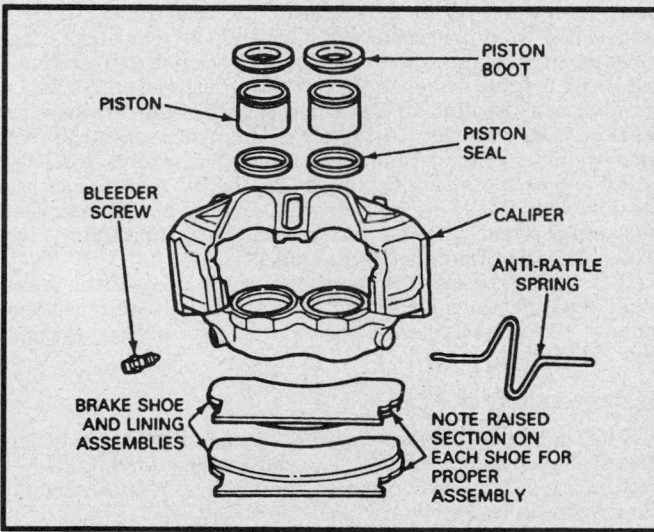

Front caliper—Ford HD rail slider

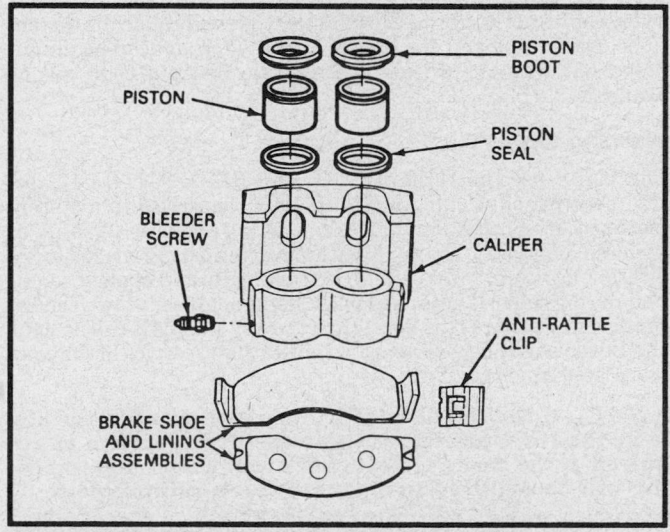

Disc caliper—Front and rear, F-Super Duty

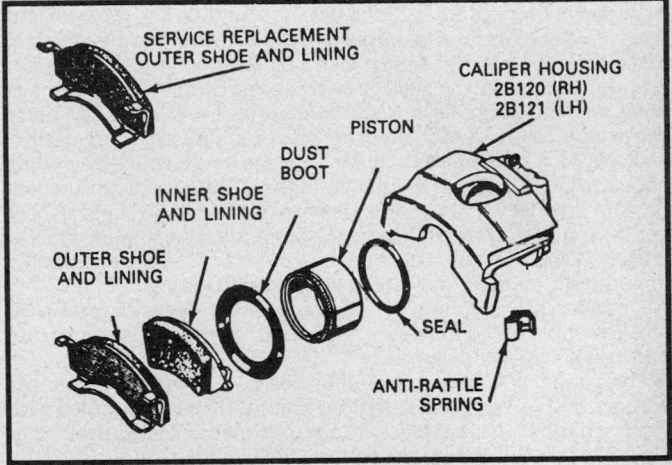

Disc caliper—Ford LD sliding caliper

3. Remove and discard seal boot, being careful not to scratch bore.

4. Remove and discard square cut seal from caliper bore groove.

5. Remove bleeder valve.

6. Clean all parts with denatured alcohol, blow dry with compressed air. Inspect all parts for scoring, corrosion or damage. If the caliper assembly is leaking, replace the piston assemblies. If the cylinder bores are scored, corroded or excessively worn, replace the caliper. Do not hone the cylinder bores. Piston assemblies are not available for oversize bores.

NOTE: Some versions of Ford calipers came with phenolic (plastic) pistons. These do not have to be replaced for small cosmetic surface irregularities or small chips between the piston boot grooves and the shoe face.

7. Lubricate the new piston seals, caliper bore and piston with clean brake fluid and install the seal in the caliper bore groove. Make sure seal is not twisted.

8. Lubricate the retaining lips of the dust boots with clean brake fluid and install them in the boot retaining grooves in the cylinder bores. Insert the pistons into the dust boots and start them into the cylinder by hand until they are beyond the piston seals. Be careful not to damage or dislodge the piston seal. Place a wood block over one piston and press the piston into the cylinder being careful not to cock the piston in the cylinder. Install

the second (of dual piston calipers) in the same manner. Make sure boots are correctly seated.

9. Install bleeder screw.

10. Install shoe and lining assemblies, using care to get the anti-rattle clips correctly positioned. New copper washers should be used when the caliper is installed and the brake hose reconnected. The machined surfaces of the caliper mount should be wire brushed smooth and clean so the caliper will be able to more freely.

NOTE:After the caliper has been installed and the system bled, before moving the vehicle, pump the brake pedal several times until the pedal is firm. Do not move the vehicle until a firm pedal is obtained. Check the fluid level in the master cylinder after pumping the brakes.

Wheel Cylinder Service

The rear brakes are drum type with internal expanding shoes. The rear brakes are of the single anchor type, mounted to the same anchor and actuated by one wheel cylinder. The wheel cylinder has 2 pistons. Brake adjustments are automatic and are made during reverse brake applications.

Wheel cylinders may need reconditioning or replacement whenever the brake shoes are replaced or when required to correct a leak condition. Leaks which coat the boot and the cylinder with fluid, or result in a dropped reservoir fluid level, or dampen and stain the brake linings are dangerous. Such leaks can cause the brakes to grab or fail and should be immediately corrected. A leakage, not immediately apparent, can be detected by pulling back the cylinder boot. A small amount of fluid seepage dampening the interior of the boot is normal. However, a dripping boot is not. Unless other conditions causing a brake to pull, grab or drag become obvious, the wheel cylinder is suspect and should and should be included in general reconditioning.

Cylinder binding may be caused by rust, deposits, grime, or swollen cups due to fluid contamination, or by a cup wedged into an excessive piston clearance.

Hydraulic system parts should not be allowed to come into contact with oil or grease, neither should those be handled with greasy hands. Even a trace of any petroleum based product is sufficient to cause damage to the rubber parts.

Disassembly and Assembly

1. Remove the brake bleeder screw.
2. Remove the dust boots, allow any brake fluid to drain out.
3. Remove the pistons, seals and inner spring.
4. Inspect the bore for scoring and corrosion. The inside of the bore may be cleaned with fine crocus cloth. If bore is scored, replace cylinder. Clean the cylinder with brake fluid.
5. Lubricate the seals with brake fluid and install. Cup lips should always face inward. Install the spring assembly and seals.
6. Carefully install the pistons and dust boots.
7. Install the bleeder screw.

Anti-Lock Braking Systems

Despite advances in brake design over the years, even the best systems in use can still lock up during certain road conditions, such as wet road surfaces. When the brakes lock up, the driver can lose control of the vehicle, because a locked wheel cannot absorb any cornering or lateral forces, and steering is lost. It is impossible to brake to a maximum and at the same time steer the vehicle when the front wheels are locked. If the back wheels are locked the vehicle will become unstable and start to slide.

While many different ways have been tried over the years to solve this problem, mechanical sensors could not provide sufficient information about wheel rotation speed and mechanical

control units could not operate the brakes fast enough to prevent brake lockup.

The growth of the electronics industry has allowed small computers (microprocessors) to be reduced in both size and cost. Coupled with fast reacting electronic sensors, anti-lock braking has become more reliable with widespread application.

REAR WHEEL ANTI-LOCK BRAKE SYSTEM

Ford Motor Company's Rear Antilock Brake System (RABS) continually monitors rear wheel speed with a sensor mounted on the rear axle. When the teeth on an exciter ring, mounted inside the rear axle on the differential gear case, pass the sensor pole piece, an AC voltage is induced in the sensor circuit with a frequency proportional to the average rear wheel speed. In the event of an impending lockup condition during braking, the RABS modulates hydraulic pressure to the rear brakes. This inhibits rear wheel lockup.

When the brake pedal is applied, the RABS module senses the drop in rear wheel speed. If the rate of deceleration is too great, indicating the wheel lockup is going to occur, the RABS module activates the electro-hydraulic valve causing isolation valve to close. With the isolation valve closed, the rear wheel cylinders are isolated from the master cylinder and the rear brake pressure cannot increase. If the rate of deceleration is still too great, the RABS module will energize the dump solenoid with a series of rapid pulses to bleed off rear wheel cylinder fluid into an accumulator built into the RABS valve. This will reduce the rear wheel cylinder pressure and allow the rear wheels to spin back up to vehicle speed. Continuing under RABS module control, the dump and isolation solenoids will be pulsed in a manner that will keep the rear wheels rotating while still maintaining high levels of deceleration during braking.

At the end of the stop, when the operator releases the brake pedal, the isolation valve de-energizes and any fluid in the accumulator is returned to the master cylinder. Normal brake operation is resumed.

System Self Test

The RABS module performs system tests and self-tests during startup and normal operation. The valve, sensor, and fluid level circuits are monitored for proper operation. If a fault is found the RABS will be deactivated and the REAR ANTILOCK light will be illuminated. Most faults will cause the light to stay illuminated until the ignition is turned **OFF**. While the light is illuminated a diagnostic flashout code may be obtained. However, there are certain faults (those associated with the fluid level switch or loss of power to the module) that will cause the system to be deactivated and the REAR ANTILOCK light to be illuminated but will not provide a diagnostic flashout code will be available.

Warning Lights

The RABS uses both the BRAKE and REAR ANTILOCK instrument panel warning lights to alert the driver to a system malfunction. Both lights must be working properly to assist in problem diagnosis. The red BRAKE warning light is used to indicate a low fluid level condition, parking brake applied condition or, for vehicles equipped with diesel engines, a low vacuum condition. To check this light, turn the key to **START**. The light should glow in this position. If it fails to glow, service of the electrical system is required.

NOTE: If the red light continues to glow after the key is in the RUN position, repair the brake system as required. If the brake system checks out OK, troubleshooting will be required to diagnose the RABS problem.

The yellow REAR ANTILOCK warning light is used to indicate an RABS malfunction and a deactivation of the RABS. To check

this light, turn the key to **ON** or **START**. The light should perform a self-check, glowing for about 2 seconds. If the light fails to glow or continues to glow after two seconds, troubleshooting of the warning lights is required.

A diode/resistor is located on the main trunk of the instrument panel wiring harness where the RABS module connector pigtail intersects the main trunk. The diode/resistor isolates the RABS module from the parking brake switch and the low vacuum switch (diesel engines). If the diode/resistor did not prevent voltage from reaching the RABS module, the yellow REAR ANTILOCK lamp would turn on and the system would be shut down whenever the parking brake was applied or the low vacuum switch was closed.

Flashout Codes

Whenever the yellow REAR ANTILOCK light comes on during normal operation, a flashout code may be obtained to aid in problem diagnosis. If the vehicle is shut off before the code is read, the code will be lost. In some cases the code may reappear when the vehicle is restarted. In other cases, the vehicle may have to be driven to reproduce the problem and, if the problem was associated with an intermittent condition, it may be difficult to reproduce. Therefore, whenever possible, it is recommended that the code be read before the vehicle is shut off.

NOTE: Place blocks behind the rear wheels and in front of the front wheels to prevent the vehicle from moving while the flashout code is being taken. If the BRAKE light is also on, due to a grounding of the fluid level circuit (perhaps low brake fluid), no flashout code will be flashed and the REAR ANTILOCK light will remain on steadily. If there is more than one system fault only the first recognized flashout code may be obtained.

Obtaining the Flashout Code

A flashout code may be obtained only when the yellow REAR ANTILOCK light is ON. No code will be flashed if the system is operating properly.

Before obtaining the flashout code, drive the vehicle to a level area, and place the shift lever in **P** for automatic transmissions and neutral for manual transmissions.

Notice whether the red BRAKE light is on or not (for future reference) and then apply the parking brake. Keep the ignition ON so that the code will not be lost.

NOTE: Place blocks behind the rear wheels and in front of the front wheels to prevent the vehicle from moving while the flashout code is being taken.

To obtain the flashout code, locate the RABS diagnostic connector (with the black/orange wire) and attach a jumper wire to it. Momentarily ground it to the chassis. When the ground is made and then broken the REAR ANTILOCK light should begin to flash.

NOTE: If the red BRAKE light was on (as noticed before the parking brake was applied) the problem may be with the low fluid level circuit and, in this case, no flashout code will be flashed and the light will remain on steadily.

The code consists of a number of short flashes and ends with a long flash. Count the short flashes and include the following long flash in the count to obtain the proper code number. For example, three short flashes followed by one long flash indicates Flashout Code Four. The code will continue to repeat itself until the key is turned off. It is recommended that the code be verified by reading it several times. In addition, the first code flashed may be too short because it may have been started in the middle. It should be ignored.

COMPONENT LOCATION

F SERIES AND BRONCO

The RABS consists of the following components:
1. RABS module located in the cab to the right of the brake pedal under the upper dash panel.
2. RABS valve (dual solenoid electro-hydraulic) is located on the left frame rail just behind the number one crossmember.
3. RABS speed sensor located on the rear axle housing and the exciter ring is located inside on the gear carrier.
4. Yellow REAR ANTILOCK warning light is in the instrument cluster.
5. RABS diagnostic connector is located in the cab and clipped on the main instrument panel wiring harness about six inches from the firewall near the parling brake pedal.
6. Diode/resistor element is located on the main trunk of the instrument panel wiring harness where the RABS module connector pigtail intersects the main harness trunk.

FORD REAR WHEEL ANTILOCK BRAKE SYSTEM DIAGNOSTIC CODES

Codes Are Yellow REAR ANTILOCK Light Flashing—Count Flashes

CODE	SYSTEM PROBLEM
CODE 1	This code is not used and should not occur
CODE 2	Open isolate circuit
CODE 3	Open dump circuit
CODE 4	Check RABS valve
CODE 5	Check RABS valve/4 × 4 indicator switch (4WD)
CODE 6	Check sensor for loose connections, chips, bad exciter ring
CODE 7	No isolate valve self test
CODE 8	No dump valve self test
CODE 9	Check sensor wiring for high resistance
CODE 10	Check sensor wiring for low resistance (shorted)
CODE 11	Check stop lamp switch
CODE 12	Check for low fluid level, bad brake light wiring
CODE 13	RABS module failure—replace
CODE 14	RABS module failure—replace
CODE 15	RABS module failure—replace
CODE 16	This code is not used and should not occur

NOTE: CODES 1 and 16 are not used. When checking resistance in the antilock brake system, always disconnect the battery. Improper resistance readings will occur with the vehicle battery connected.

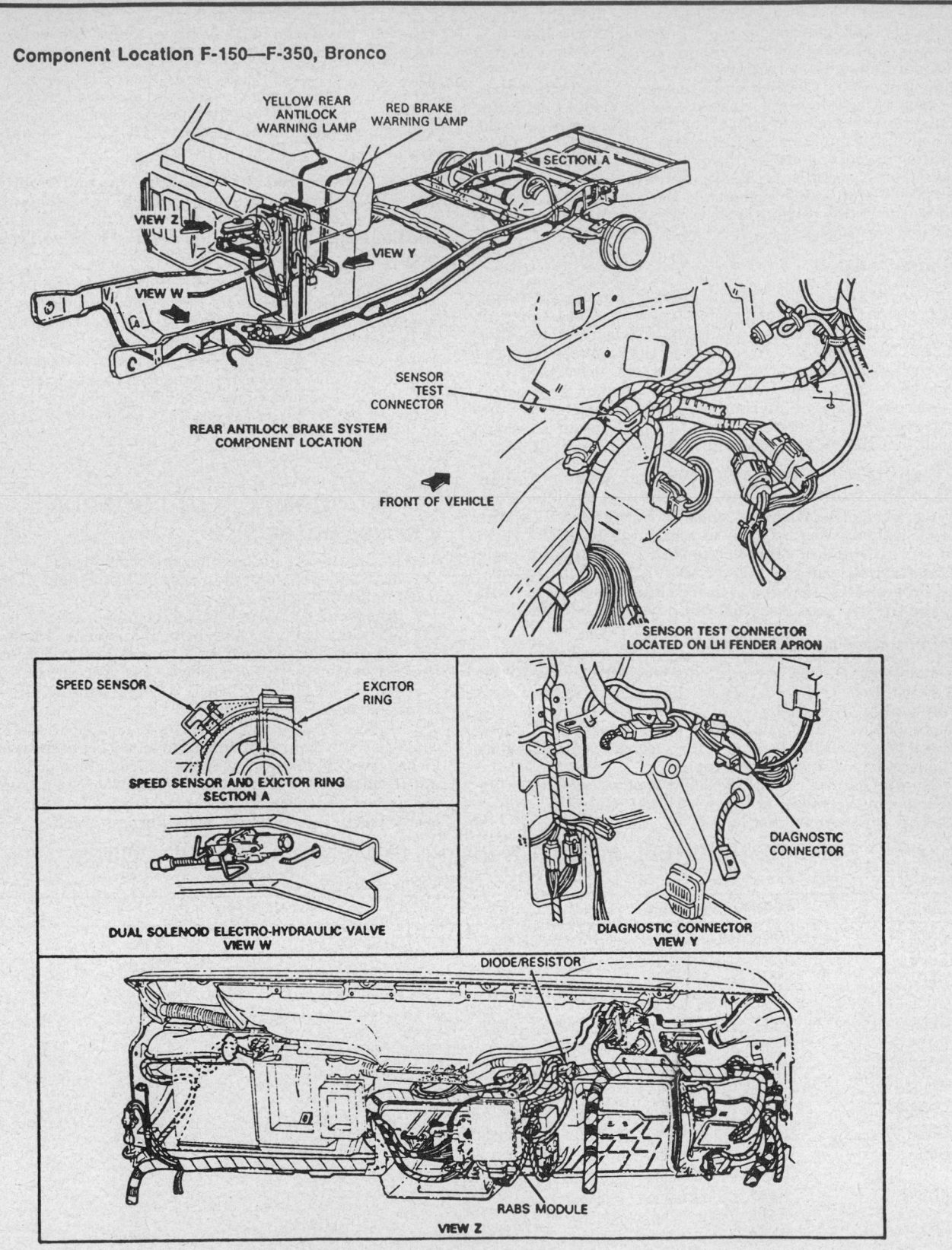

Component Location F-150—F-350, Bronco

YELLOW REAR
ANTILOCK
WARNING LAMP

RED BRAKE
WARNING LAMP

SECTION A

VIEW Z

VIEW Y

VIEW W

SENSOR
TEST
CONNECTOR

REAR ANTILOCK BRAKE SYSTEM
COMPONENT LOCATION

FRONT OF VEHICLE

SENSOR TEST CONNECTOR
LOCATED ON LH FENDER APRON

SPEED SENSOR

EXCITOR
RING

SPEED SENSOR AND EXCITOR RING
SECTION A

DIAGNOSTIC
CONNECTOR

DUAL SOLENOID ELECTRO-HYDRAULIC VALVE
VIEW W

DIAGNOSTIC CONNECTOR
VIEW Y

DIODE/RESISTOR

RABS MODULE

VIEW Z

RABS Component Location—F Series, Bronco shown—typical

7. Speed Sensor test connector (with weatherproof cap) is located under the hood on the left wheel well.

E SERIES

The RABS consists of the following components:

1. RABS module is located in the cab on the driver's inside cowl panel just outboard of the parking brake mechanism.

2. RABS valve (dual solenoid electro-hydraulic) is located on the left inside frame rail just behind the engine mount crossmember.

3. RABS speed sensor located on the rear axle housing and the exciter ring is located inside on the gear carrier.

4. Yellow REAR ANTILOCK warning light is in the instrument cluster.

5. RABS diagnostic connector is located just off the module connector harness.

6. Diode/resistor element is located on the main trunk of the instrument panel wiring harness where the RABS module connector pigtail intersects the main harness trunk.

7. Speed sensor test connector (with weatherproof cap) is located under the hood between the battery and the right side engine compartment wall.

Removal and Installation

RABS MODULE

The RABS module, valve and sensor are serviced as assemblies and are not to be disassembled. The exciter ring is pressed on the differential case and, if removed for any reason, must be discarded.

F Series and Bronco

1. Disconnect the wire harness from the RABS module by depressing the plastic tab on the connector and pulling the connector off.

2. Remove the 2 screws that retain the module to the dash panel. Remove the module.

3. Place the module in position on the dash panel. Install and tighten the 2 retaining screws.

4. Connect the wiring harness to the module. Check the system for proper operation.

E Series

1. Remove the parking brake actuator assembly. Start by loosening the adjusting nut at the equalizer. On F-Super Duty series vehicles remove the clevis pin at the parking brake. Working from the engine compartment, remove the nuts attaching the parking brake control assembly to the dash panel.

2. Working under the instrument panel, remove the bolt attaching the control assembly to the lower flange of the instrument panel. Remove the parking brake cable from the control assembly clevis by compressing the conduit end fitting prongs (using ½ inch box wrench) holding the cable assembly to the control, remove the cable from the control. Remove the parking brake control.

3. Remove the 2 screws that hold the module to the cowl panel. Remove the module.

4. Disconnect the wiring harness from the RABS module by depressing the plastic tab on the connector and pulling the connector off.

5. Connect the wiring harness to the RABS module.

6. Place module in position on the cowl panel. Install and tighten the two retaining screws.

7. Install the parking brake actuator by connecting the forward ball end of the parking brake cable to the clevis of the control assembly, and insert the cable assembly into the control assembly. Install hair pin retainer.

8. Position the control assembly on the lower flange of the instrument panel and install the attaching bolt.

9. Working from the engine compartment, install and tighten

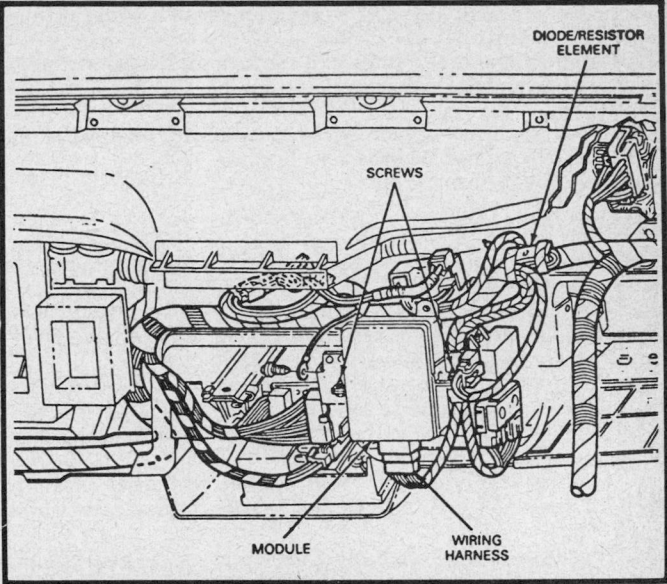

RABS Module—F Series, Bronco

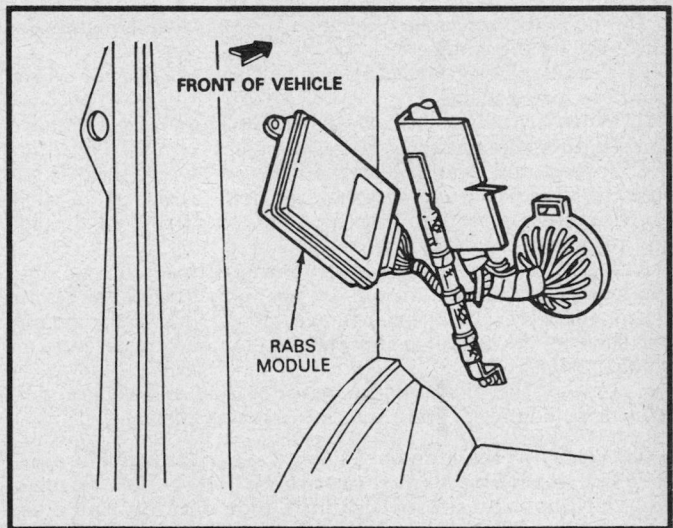

RABS Module—E Series

the nuts that attach the parking brake control assembly to the dash panel. Torque to 15 ft. lbs.

10. Adjust the parking brake equalizer lever to its original position. On Super Duty series vehicles, install the parking brake clevis pin. Check cable tension and adjust if necessary.

11. Check the RABS and parking brake systems for proper operation.

RABS DUAL SOLENOID ELECTRO-HYDRAULIC VALVE

The dual solenoid electro-hydraulic valve is located on the left frame rail slightly behind the number one crossmember. The purpose of this valve assembly is to control hydraulic fluid pressure to the rear wheels based on RABS module signals.

F Series and Bronco

1. Disconnect the inlet and outlet brake lines from the RABS valve. Cap the lines.

2. Disconnect the wiring harness to the valve.

3. Remove the nuts retaining the valve to the frame rail and remove the valve.

4. Position the RABS valve on the frame rail. Install the three nuts and torque to 12–17 ft. lbs.

5. Connect the brake lines and tighten the larger fitting to 10–17 ft. lbs. and the smaller to 10–15 ft. lbs. Do not overtighten the fittings.

6. Bleed the brake system. It is not necessary to energize the valve electrically to bleed the rear brakes.

RABS VALVE

E Series

1. Disconnect the inlet and outlet brake lines from the RABS valve. Cap the lines.

2. Disconnect the wiring harness from the valve harness.

3. Remove the three screws holding the valve to the frame rail liner and remove the valve.

4. Position the RABS valve on the frame rail liner, install the three screws and torque to 19–24 ft. lbs.

5. Connect the brake valve wiring harness to the main harness connector.

6. Connect the brake lines and tighten the larger fitting to 10–17 ft. lbs. and the smaller to 10–15 ft. lbs. Do not overtighten the fittings.

7. Bleed the brake system. It is not necessary to energize the valve electrically to bleed the rear brakes.

RABS SENSOR

1. The RABS sensor is located on the rear axle housing. Remove the wiring connector.

2. Remove the sensor hold-down bolt and remove the sensor from the axle housing.

3. When installing, clean the axle mounting surface. Use care to keep dirt from entering the axle housing.

4. Inspect and clean the magnetized sensor pole piece to ensure that it is free from loose metal particles which could cause erratic system operation. Inspect the sensor O-ring for damage and replace if necessary.

5. Lightly lubricate the sensor O-ring with motor oil, align the sensor bolt hole and install. Do not apply force to the plastic sensor connector. The sensor flange should slide to the mounting surface. This will insure the air gap setting is between 0.005–0.045 in.

6. Inspect the blue sensor connector seal and replace it if missing or damaged. Push the connector on the sensor.

NOTE: The clearance between the sensor and the exciter ring should be no greater than 0.050 inches. To measure, remove the sensor from the axle carrier, and measure the height of the pole piece from the mounting face of the flange. Sensor pole should be 1.07–1.08 in. Measure the depth from axle housing mounting surface to the top of the exciter teeth. Subtract the two measurements to get the sensor gap.

EXCITER RING

The exciter ring is pressed onto the differential case. To inspect it, remove the sensor from the axle housing.

View the exciter ring teeth through the sensor hole. Rotate the rear axle and check the exciter ring teeth for damage or breakage. Dented or broken teeth could cause the RABS system

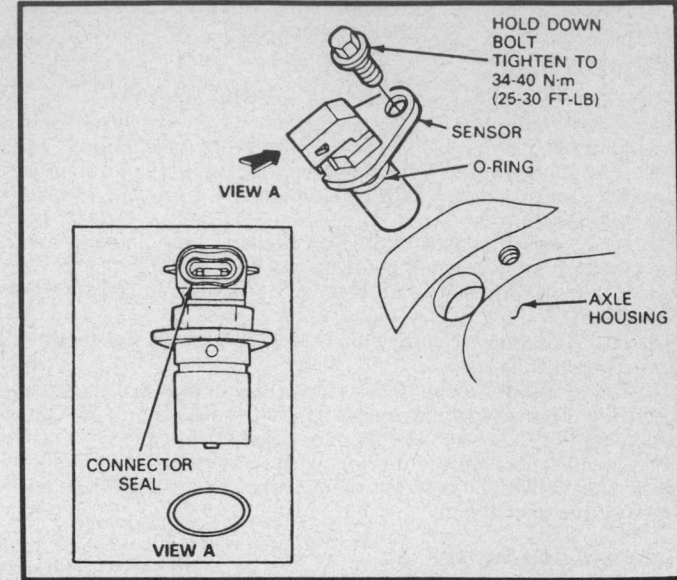

Speed sensor mounts to rear axle housing

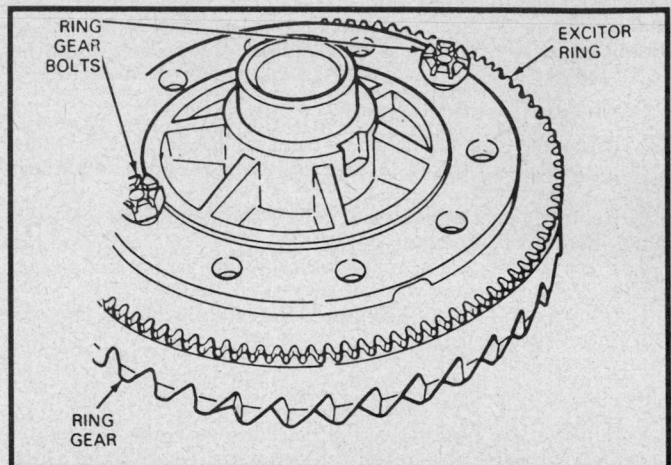

Exciter ring for speed sensor is pressed on gear carrier

to function when not required. To replace the exciter ring, the differential case must be removed from the axle housing and the exciter ring pressed off the case. Upon removal, the exciter ring must be discarded. It is not to be reused.

FUSES

Three replaceable fuses are involved with RABS. The fuses are located in the fuse box. A 20 amp fuse protects the total RABS. A 15 amp fuse protects the red BRAKE and yellow REAR ANTILOCK warning lights. Another 15 amp fuse protects the four-way stop lamp cluster.

CHRYSLER CORPORATION

Master Cylinder Service

Chrysler Corporation uses a dual master cylinder which contains a double hydraulic cylinder with two fluid reservoirs and primary and secondary hydraulic pistons. On most models, the master cylinder is assisted by a vacuum booster. The unit is mounted on a 90 degree bracket on some models, directly to the dashboard on others. Hydraulic rear drum brakes with automatic adjusters and self-adjusting front disc brakes are standard on all models.

The front outlet tube of the master cylinder is connected to the hydraulic system control valve and then to the rear brakes. This is referred the secondary system. The rear outlet tube is connected to the control valve and to the front brakes. This system is referred to as the primary system. No residual pressure valves are used in the master cylinder outlets.

During normal operation, the fluid level in the master cylinder will rise during brake operation and fall during release. It is also expected that the fluid level will decrease with brake pad wear. In addition, a trace of brake fluid on the booster shell below the master cylinder mounting flange will often be found as a result of the normal lubricating action of the master cylinder bore and seal. All of these conditions are considered normal and are not indications the master cylinder needs service.

Two types of master cylinders were used by Chrysler Corporation; 1) a cast iron master cylinder with built-in reservoir and separate proportioning valve and, 2) a master cylinder with a pressed on plastic reservoir. The body of the two-piece master cylinder is made of anodized aluminum and the reservoir is made of nylon. Both compartments of the reservoir are interconnected to permit equalization of the fluid level. However, a sufficient quantity of fluid is retained in the reservoir of the unaffected system to permit operation of that half of the master cylinder even if the other half of the reservoir is drained due to a hydraulic leak.

Use extra care when servicing aluminum master cylinders not to cross thread brake line fittings and do not overtighten any threaded connection.

In the event of a front brake system malfunction the proportioning valve with a bypass feature allows full hydraulic pressure to the rear brake system.

Disassembly and Assembly

The manufacturer does not recommend that either the cast iron or the aluminum master cylinder be overhauled, but replaced only. Do not attempt to hone the bore of the aluminum master cylinder or the hard anodized surface will be removed.

On the aluminum master cylinders, the plastic reservoir may be replaced using the following procedure:

1. Clean the outside of the master cylinder and remove the caps. Drain and discard remaining brake fluid.

2. Hold the master cylinder in a soft-jaw vise and grasp the plastic reservoir. Firmly rock reservoir from side to side to and remove it from the master cylinder housing. Don't pry the reservoir off with a tool that could damage the plastic body.

3. Remove and discard the reservoir grommets from the master cylinder body.

4. To install, lubricate the new grommets with brake fluid and install in the master cylinder body.

5. Place the reservoir in position. Make sure it is positioned properly and that the lettering can be read from the left side of the master cylinder. Install by rocking the reservoir while pressing down. Seat the reservoir until the bottom of the reservoir touches the top of the grommets.

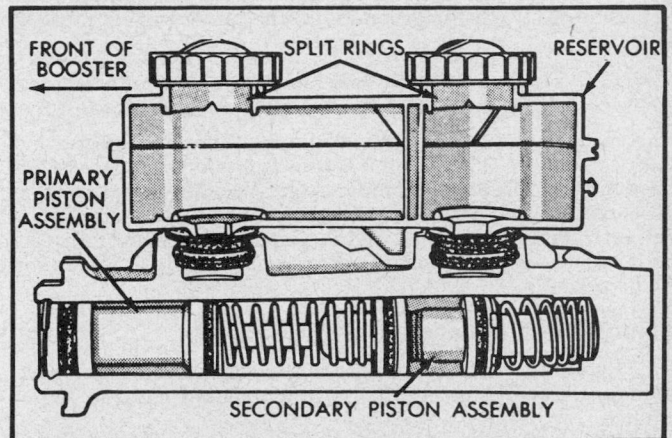

Chrysler aluminum master cylinder

Removing plastic reservoir from master cylinder housing

Brake Booster Service

Chrysler Corporation models covered here are equipped with vacuum boosters.

Under normal operating conditions, with brakes released, a vacuum suspended booster operates with vacuum on both sides of its diaphragm (or both diaphragms in a tandem diaphragm unit). When the brakes are applied, air at atmospheric pressure is admitted to one side of the diaphragm (or both diaphragms in a tandem diaphragm unit) to provide the power assist.

Brake boosters used by Chrysler Corporation are not repairable and if defective, the booster must be replaced as a unit, including the check valve. Do not remove the check valve.

Brake Booster Vacuum Pump

On gasoline engine vehicles, engine vacuum is used to power the vacuum booster brake. On diesel engines, there is not enough vacuum available for vacuum booster brake operation.

On diesel engine vehicles, vacuum is supplied from a pump. On Chrysler Corporation vehicles equipped with Cummins Turbo Diesels, the vacuum pump and power steering pump is one assembly which is driven from a common shaft from the front gear train. To service either pump, the complete assembly must be removed from the front gear housing.

In addition, these vehicles will have an engine warning light

panel on the dash which contains 5 warning indicator lights: Brake, Water In Fuel, Wait To Start, Anti-Lock and Low Fuel. The Brake light is connected to a sensor that monitors vacuum in the brake booster system. The Brake light when lit indicates low vacuum. If this light comes on, the brake system must be serviced.

NOTE: The brake light will also be activated when the parking brake is on or there is a hydraulic brake failure.

The vacuum pump provides vacuum for the brake booster and dash controllers. The vacuum sensor is mounted under the left hood hinge in the engine compartment. Vacuum is supplied by a hose Teed off the check valve in the brake booster. The sensor will activate the brake light on the warning light panel in 10 seconds or less when the vacuum drops to 8.5 in. Hg or less in the brake system.

Removal and Installation

1. Remove the vacuum pump and power steering pump assembly by removing the 2 bolts which should need an 18mm wrench.
2. Clean the gasket from the engine rear cover.
3. Install the pump assembly with a new gasket. Torque the bolts to 57 ft. lbs.

Disassembly and Assembly

1. Before starting pump disassembly, make a pin 2 in. long and 0.312 in. diameter. Use an 8mm bolt or a piece of drill rod. This pin must be hard so make it from a 10.9 grade metric bolt or at least an SAE Grade 8 capscrew.
2. Insert the pin into the pump shaft and screw a M14-2mm threaded capscrew in against the pin.
3. Tighten the capscrew against the pin to draw off the gear/eccentric/bearing assembly off of the power steering pump shaft.
4. Inspect the gear for excessive wear or damage. If the gear/eccentric is not damaged, do not separate them. If the gear is damaged, use a press to press the eccentric out of the gear. Use a flat plate over the new gear and press it onto the eccentric until it bottoms.
5. Inspect the bearing, turning it by hand. If the bearing looks good, and feels smooth to turn, do not separate them. If the bearing/eccentric is bad, press the eccentric out of the bearing, using the appropriate size socket or tool that will press only on the inner race of the bearing. Press it on until it bottoms.
6. With a 15mm wrench, remove the 4 nuts and separate the power steering pump from the vacuum pump housing. Remove the two short pushrods from the housing. Inspect the pushrods. They should move smoothly, but should not move side to side.
7. With a 10mm wrench, remove the diaphragm assemblies

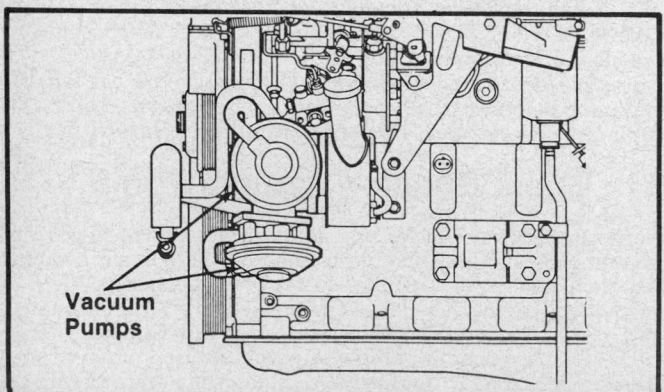

Vacuum Pumps

Power steering and vacuum pump on Cummins diesel engine

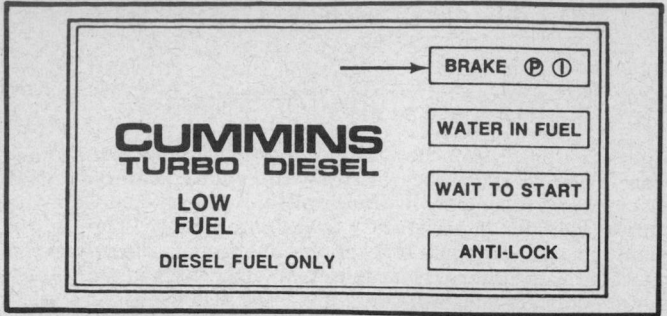

Message center includes low vacuum and antilock system warning lights

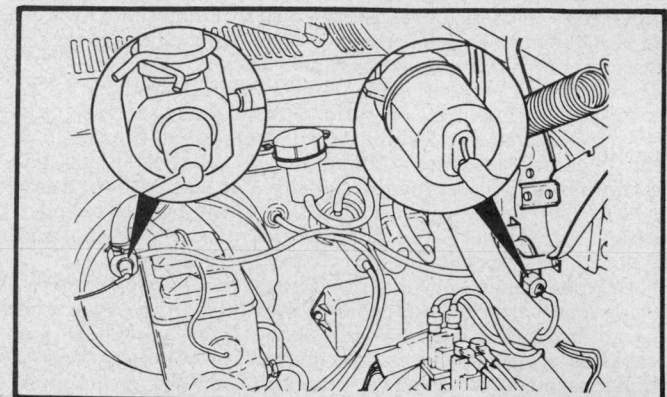

Vacuum sensor under the left hood hinge is supplied by line from booster check valve

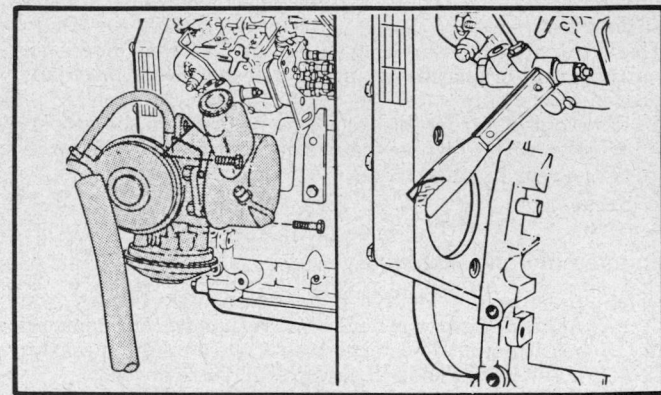

Removing power steering and vacuum pump assembly from engine's gear drive

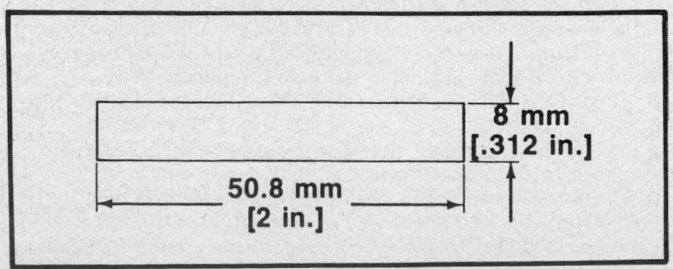

Fabricate pin for pressing off drive gear

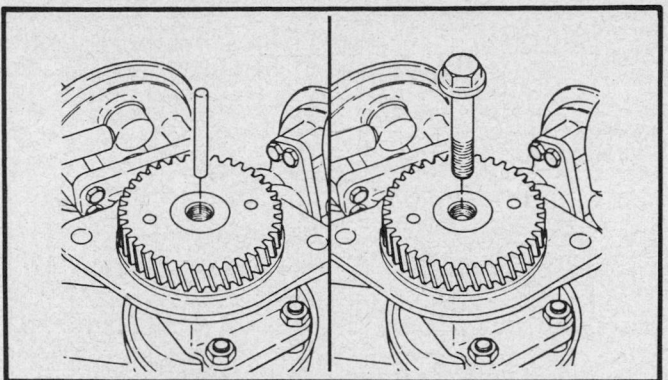

Insert pin, tighten capscrew against pin to draw gear assembly from pump shaft

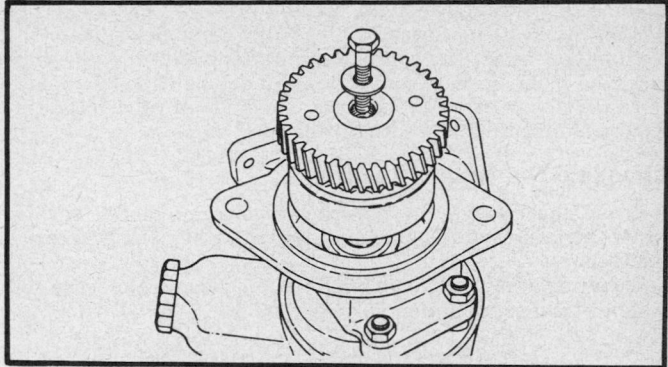

Use ⅜-18 Grade 8 capscrew to draw assembly onto pump shaft

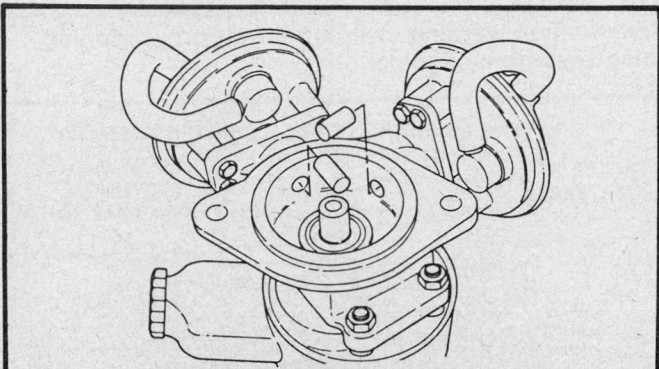

Remove the pushrods from the housing

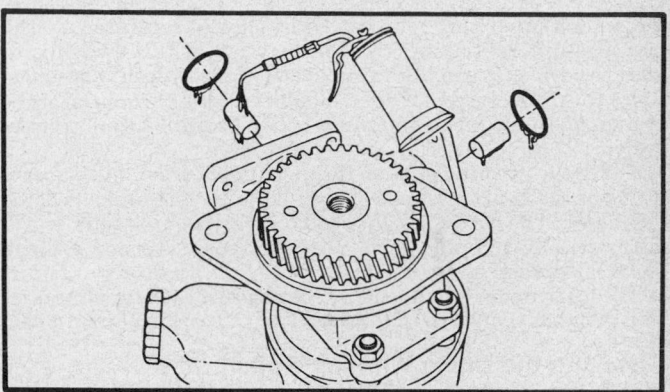

Lube pushrods and O-rings with engine oil at assembly

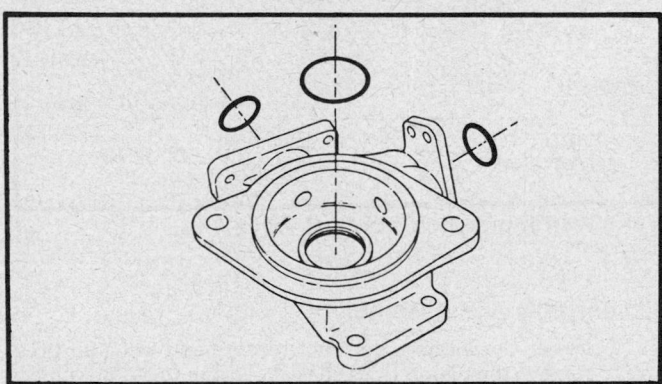

Remove vacuum diaphragm assemblies, then O-rings

from the housing. If the diaphragms are bad, they must be replaced as a unit. Remove and discard the O-rings from the center bore and push rod bores.

8. Clean all parts and dry with compressed air.

9. Install the two spacers on the studs on the back of the power steering pump.

10. Install the vacuum pump housing onto the power steering pump using a new O-ring lubricated with engine oil. Install the four retaining nuts and with a 15mm wrench, torque to 18 ft. lbs.

11. Install the gear/eccentric/bearing assembly by pulling it onto the power steering shaft with a ⅜–18 thread capscrew with a flat washer threaded into the power steering pump shaft. Pull it on until it bottoms. Remove capscrew and washer.

NOTE: This is a press fit and will require a minimum of SAE Grade 8 capscrew for thread strength.

12. Lubricate the pushrods with engine oil and install then in the housing. Install new O-rings, also lubricated with engine oil.

13. With a 10mm wrench, install the diaphragm assemblies. Torque to 7 ft. lbs.

14. Install the assembly to the engine with new gaskets. Torque bolts to 57 ft. lbs.

Combination Valve

All models have a hydraulic system control valve in the brake system. The valve is usually mounted on the frame rail below the master cylinder. The control valve assembly in B-150 and B-250 models combines a brake warning switch with a hold-off and proportioning valve assembly. A brake warning switch and hold-off valve assembly are combined and used on B-350 models. Hold-off and Proportioning valves are used because of different braking characteristics between disc and drum brakes.

A height sensing proportioning valve regulates the front to rear braking balance based upon vehicle load conditions. The valve senses vehicle loads through variations in rear suspension height. With a light load on the rear axle, the valve reduces hydraulic pressure to the rear brakes. As the load increases, more hydraulic pressure is released to the rear brakes.

HOLD-OFF VALVE

The hold-off valve section of the combination valve holds off pressure to the front disc brakes to allow the rear drum brake shoes to overcome the return springs and begin to contact the drums. This valve keeps the output pressure to the front brakes

in the 3–30 psi range until the hold-off pressure is reached (117 psi) and then blends back to give full output pressure to the front brakes under heavy brake applications. This feature helps keep the front brakes from locking under light pedal applications when driving on icy surfaces. The hold-off valve has no effect on front brake pressure during hard stops.

Checking the Hold-Off Valve

A visual check will show that the valve stem extends slightly when the brakes are applied and retracts when the brakes are released.

In case of a hold-off valve malfunction, remove the valve and install a new combination valve assembly.

BRAKE WARNING SWITCH

The hydraulic brake system is split. The front brakes are part of one system and the rear brakes are part of the other. Both systems are routed through, but hydraulically separated by the pressure differential swicth. The function of this switch is to alert the driver to a malfunction in one of the hydraulic systems. Since the brake system is split, a failure in one part of the brake system does not result in failure of the entire hydraulic brake system.

The brake warning light on the instrument panel will come on if one of the brake systems should fail after the brake pedal is depressed. The warning light switch is the latching type. It will automatically recenter itself after the repair is made and the pedal is depressed.

The instrument panel bulb can be checked each time the ignition switch is turned to **ON, START** or the parking brake is set.

Checking the Brake Warning Switch Unit

The brake warning light is lit only when the parking brake is applied with the ignition key turned **ON**. The same light will also illuminate should one of the two service brake systems fail.

To test the service brake warning system, raise the car on a hoist and open a wheel cylinder bleeder while a helper depresses the brake pedal and watches the warning light. If the light fails to light, check for a burned out bulb, disconnected socket, or a broken or disconnected wire at the switch. If the bulb is not burned out and the wire continuity is uninterupted check the service brake warning switch operation with a test lamp between the switch terminal and a voltage source.

If the light still fails to light, disconnect the brake tubes from the valve assembly and install a new valve assembly. If a new is installed, bleed the system. The warning switch is not serviced separately. Do not remove the swicth or attempt to repair.

After repairing and bleeding the brake system applying the brakes with moderate force will hydraulically recenter the valve's piston and automatically turn off the warning light. Do not disassemble to reset the piston.

Caliper Service

Chrysler Corporation calipers are one-piece castings with the inboard side containing the piston bore. A square cut rubber seal is located in a groove in the piston bore which provides the hydraulic seal between the piston and the cylinder wall.

As the brake pedal is pressed, hydraulic pressure is applied against the piston. This pressure pushes the inboard brake lining against the inboard braking surface of the rotor. As the force increases against the rotor, the caliper assembly moves inboard and provides a clamping action on the car.

When brake pressure is released, the piston seal returns to its normal position, pulling the piston back into the caliper bore. This creates a running clearance between the inner brake lining and rotor.

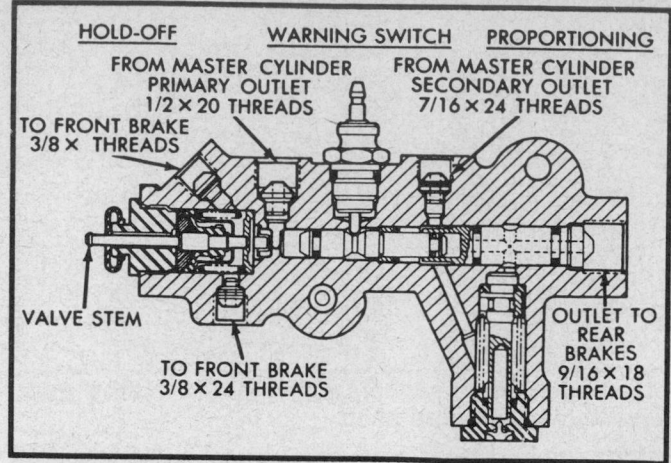

Combination warning switch/hold-off/proportioning valve assembly—Typical

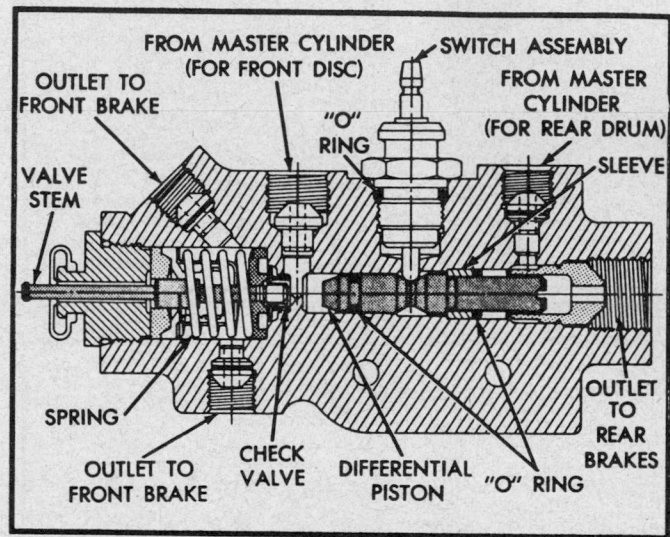

Brake warning switch/hold-off valve

Disassembly and Assembly

1. Chrysler Corporation does not recommend using air pressure to remove the piston from the caliper due to the possibility of personal injury. Their suggested procedure is to remove the caliper from its vehicle mount, remove the outboard shoe and support the caliper on top of the control arm on shop towels to absorb brake fluid. Carefully depress the brake pedal and allow hydraulic pressure to push the piston out of the bore.

NOTE: The brake pedal will fall away when the piston has passed the bore opening. Prop the brake pedal to any position below the first inch of pedal travel to prevent loss of brake fluid. If both front caliper pistons are to be removed, disconnect the flexible brake line at the frame bracket after removing the first piston. Plug the brake line to remove the piston from the opposite caliper.

2. Remove the flexible brake line from the caliper.
3. Mount the caliper in a soft-jaw vise. Do not use too much pressure or the bore will be distorted and the piston will bind.
4. Remove the dust boot and, using a small, pointed wooden stick, work the piston seal out of its groove in the caliper bore.

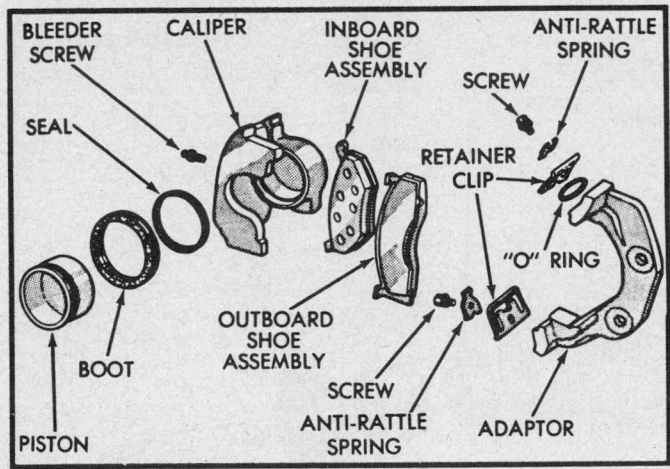

Caliper assembly—typical

Labels: BLEEDER SCREW, CALIPER, INBOARD SHOE ASSEMBLY, SCREW, ANTI-RATTLE SPRING, SEAL, RETAINER CLIP, "O" RING, BOOT, OUTBOARD SHOE ASSEMBLY, SCREW, ANTI-RATTLE SPRING, ADAPTOR, PISTON

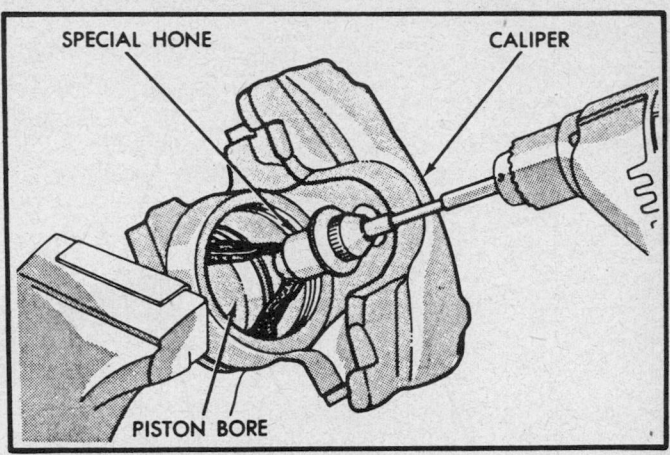

Clean up bore with light honing

Labels: SPECIAL HONE, CALIPER, PISTON BORE

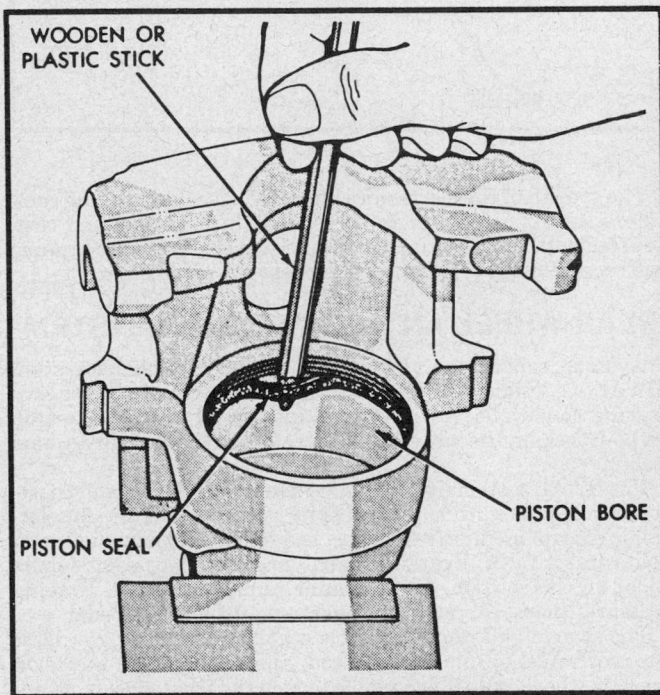

Remove piston seal without scratching bore

Labels: WOODEN OR PLASTIC STICK, PISTON BORE, PISTON SEAL

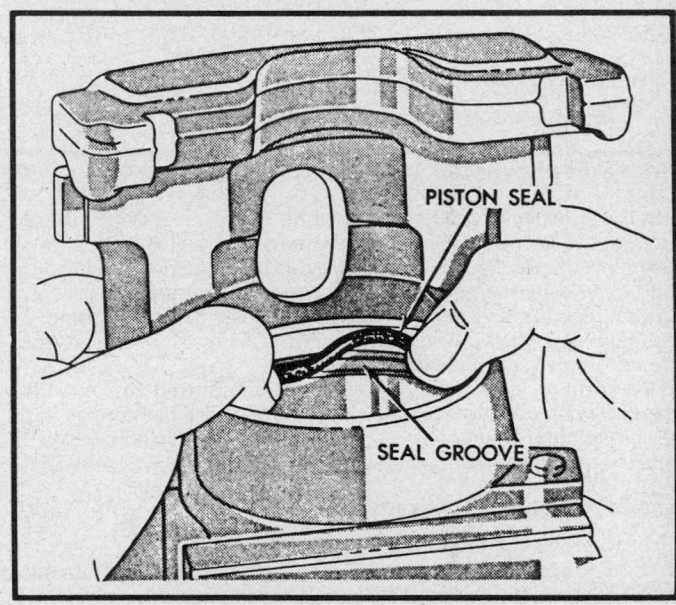

Lubricate piston seal with brake fluid and install

Labels: PISTON SEAL, SEAL GROOVE

Do not use any metal tool which might nick or scratch the bore. Discard the seal.

5. Clean all parts well using alcohol and blow dry. Inspect the piston bore for scoring or pitting. Install a new piston if it is pitted, scored or the plating is worn. Some pistons are plastic. Bores that show light scratches can be cleaned with fine crocus cloth. Deeper scratches may need to be hones.

NOTE: The bore must not be honed more than 0.002 in. oversize (only 0.001 in. oversize on Caravan, Voyager and Town & Country models). Measure the bore accurately before honing. If the bore does not clean up within this specification, a new housing must be installed. Black stains on the piston are caused by the piston seal and will do no harm.

6. Clean all parts well, dip the new piston seal in brake fluid and install in the bore. Position the seal at one area at a time and, using fingers, gently work the seal into the groove.

7. Coat the new piston boot with brake fluid leaving a generous amount inside the boot. Position the boot on the piston and install the piston into the bore, pushing it past the piston seal until it bottoms in the bore.

8. Position the dust boot and with a circular driver, seal into the caliper.

9. Install the flexible brake hose with new seals.

Wheel Cylinder Service

The rear brakes are drum type with internal expanding shoes. The rear brakes are of the single anchor type, mounted to the same anchor and actuated by 1 wheel cylinder. The wheel cylinder has 2 pistons. Brake adjustments are automatic and are made during reverse brake applications.

Wheel cylinders may need reconditioning or replacement whenever the brake shoes are replaced or when required to correct a leak condition. Leaks which coat the boot and the cylinder with fluid, or result in a dropped reservoir fluid level, or dampen and stain the brake linings are dangerous. Such leaks can cause the brakes to grab or fail and should be immediately corrected. A leakage, not immediately apparent, can be detected by pulling back the cylinder boot. A small amount of fluid seepage dampen-

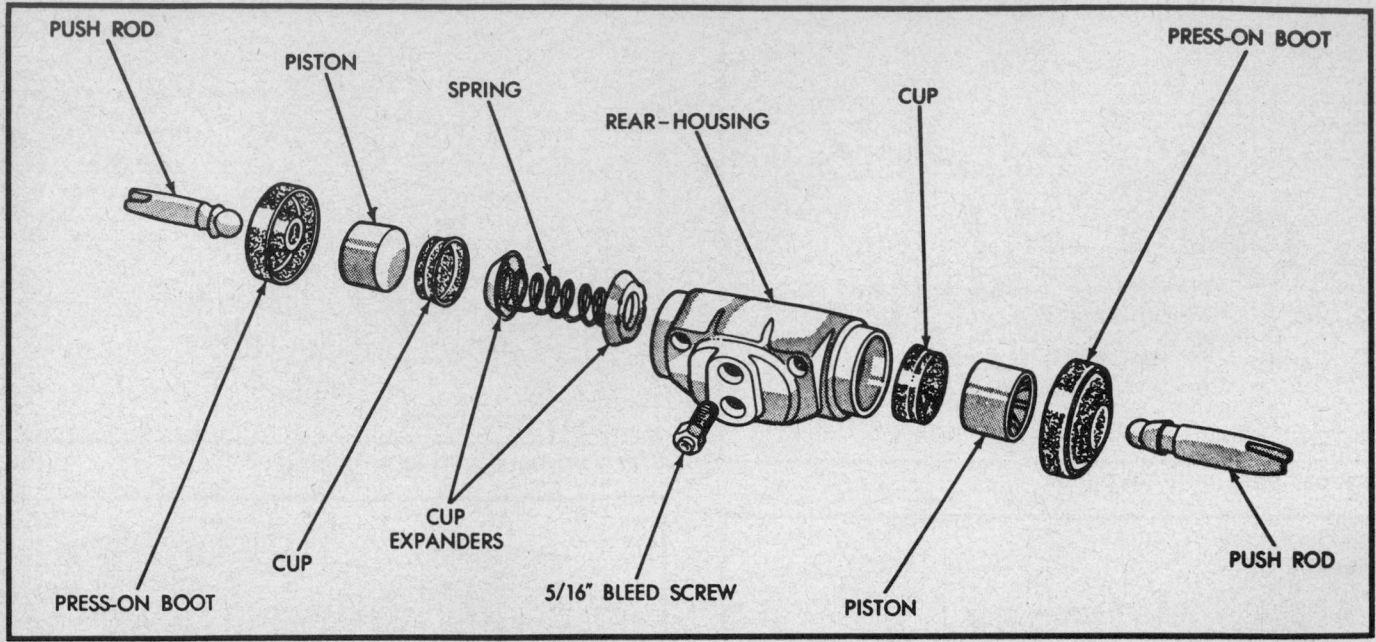

PUSH ROD — PISTON — SPRING — REAR-HOUSING — CUP — PRESS-ON BOOT — PUSH ROD — PISTON — PRESS-ON BOOT — CUP — CUP EXPANDERS — CUP — 5/16" BLEED SCREW

Rear wheel cylinder for 11 and 12 inch brakes — typical

ing the interior of the boot is normal. However, a dripping boot is not. Unless other conditions causing a brake to pull, grab or drag become obvious, the wheel cylinder is suspect and should and should be included in general reconditioning.

Cylinder binding may be caused by rust, deposits, grime, or swollen cups due to fluid contamination, or by a cup wedged into an excessive piston clearance.

Hydraulic system parts should not be allowed to come into contact with oil or grease, neither should those be handled with greasy hands. Even a trace of any petroleum based product is sufficient to cause damage to the rubber parts.

Disassembly and Assembly

1. Remove the brake bleeder screw.
2. Remove the dust boots, allow any brake fluid to drain out.
3. Remove the pistons, seals and inner spring.
4. Inspect the bore for scoring and corrosion. The inside of the bore may be cleaned with fine crocus cloth. If bore is scored, replace cylinder. Black stains on the cylinder walls are caused by the piston cups and will not impair operation of the cylinder. Clean the cylinder with alcohol or brake fluid.
5. Lubricate the seals with brake fluid and install. Cup lips should always face inward. Install the spring assembly and seals.
6. Carefully install the pistons and dust boots.
7. Install the bleeder screw.

Anti-Lock Braking Systems

Despite advances in brake design over the years, even the best systems in use can still lock up during certain road conditions, such as wet road surfaces. When the brakes lock up, the driver can lose control of the vehicle, because a locked wheel cannot absorb any cornering or lateral forces, and steering is lost. It is impossible to brake to a maximum and at the same time steer the vehicle when the front wheels are locked. If the back wheels are locked the vehicle will become unstable and start to slide.

While many different ways have been tried over the years to solve this problem, mechanical sensors could not provide sufficient information about wheel rotation speed and mechanical control units could not operate the brakes fast enough to prevent brake lockup.

The growth of the electronics industry has allowed small computers (microprocessors) to be reduced in both size and cost. Coupled with fast reacting electronic sensors, anti-lock braking has become more reliable with widespread application.

REAR WHEEL ANTI-LOCK BRAKE SYSTEM

Chrysler Corporation's Rear Wheel Antilock brake system (RWAL) is designed to prevent rear wheel lockup under heavy braking conditions. Anti-lock braking allows a vehicle to stop without locking the wheels and therefore maintains directional stability.

The RWAL system uses a standard master cylinder and booster arrangement with a vertical split hydraulic circuit. An electronic control module, rear wheel speed sensor, and a dual solenoid control valve (hydraulic valve) are the major components added to this system. No hydraulic pumps are used. Braking pressure comes directly from pushing on the brake pedal.

The system will provide vehicle stability by allowing at least one rear wheel to remain unlocked. Since the system works on the rear wheels only it is possible to lock the front wheels. In addition, the system benefit is somewhat limited when a 4WD vehicle is in the 4WD mode.

The system utilizes an amber antilock warning lamp in the instrument panel along with the standard red brake warning light. These two lights work together to notify the driver the driver that the system is working correctly. These lamps are also used to blink fault codes for system diagnosis.

Major Components

The system continually monitors rear wheel speed with a sensor mounted on the rear axle. A toothed exciter ring is press fit onto the differential case next to the differential ring gear and provides a signal for the sensor. When the teeth on the exciter ring pass the sensor pole piece, an AC voltage is induced in the sensor circuit with a frequency proportional to the average rear wheel speed. In the event of an impending lockup condition during braking, the RWAL modulates hydraulic pressure to the rear brakes. This inhibits rear wheel lockup.

The electronic brake control module is located behind the glove box on most models. The control module monitors the rear wheel speed and controls the dual solenoid valve.

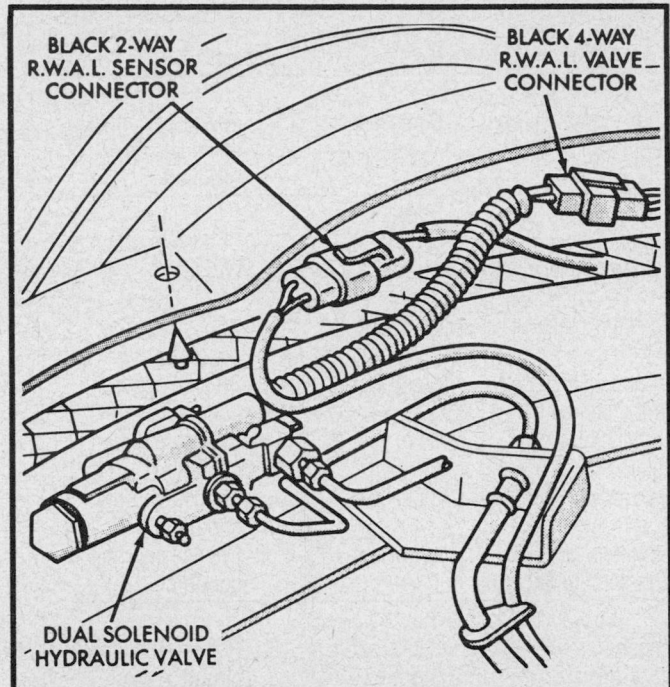

RWAL connection locations—typical

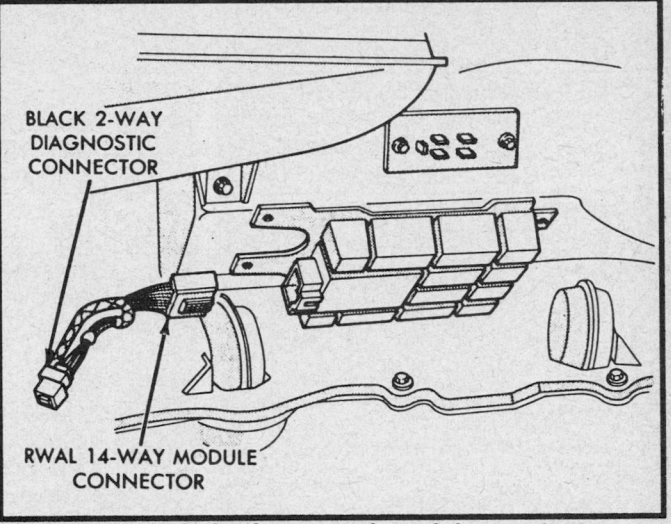

RWAL electronic brake control module—typical

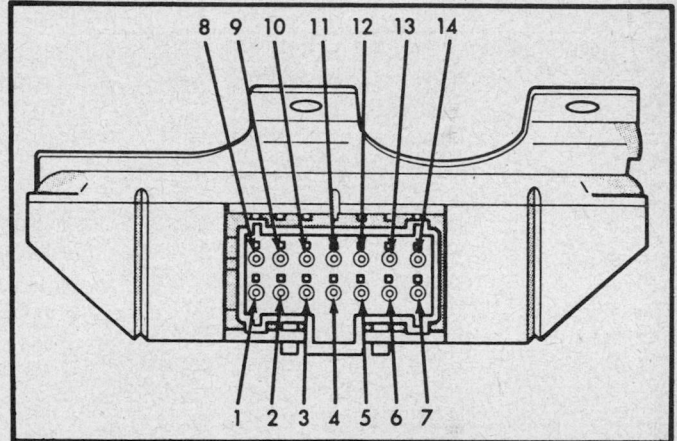

RWAL electronic brake control module pin locations

The control module determines if the rear wheels are decelerating too quickly and sends a signal to the dual solenoid hydraulic valve to prevent rear wheel lockup. The control module also performs a system self check every time the ignition key is turned **ON**.

The dual solenoid hydraulic valve is located between the rear brakes and the proportioning valve and is attached on the left frame rail near the rear axle.

Under normal conditions, the valve will allow brake fluid to flow freely between the master cylinder and the rear brakes. Once antilock braking begins the control module will trigger the valve to either isolate or reduce pressure to the rear wheels.

The electronic control module has the capability of generating and storing fault codes. Only one code can be stored and shown at any one time. Also, if a fault code is generated the electronic control module will retain the code even after a key **OFF** condition.

If a problem is detected the electronic control module will illuminate the amber antilock brake warning lamp and set a fault code. When a fault code is set the red brake warning lamp will also be lit. To determine what the fault code is, momentarily ground the RWAL diagnostic connector and count the flashes of the amber antilock warning lamp. The initial flash will be a long flash followed by a number of short flashes. The long flash indicates the beginning of the fault number sequence and the short flashes are a continuation of that sequence. Count the long flash with the short flashes to have an accurate fault code count.

To clear a fault code disconnect the control module connector from the module or disconnect the battery for at least five seconds. During system retest, wait 30 seconds to make sure the fault code does not reappear.

Removal and Installation
RWAL SPEED SENSOR

1. Raise and safely support vehicle.
2. Remove sensor hold down-bolt.
3. Remove sensor shield and sensor from differential by pulling sensor out of differential.
4. Disconnect wiring from sensor.

5. To install, connect wiring to sensor. Be sure the seal is in place between the sensor and wiring connector.
6. Install the sensor into the differential housing with a new O-ring.
7. Install sensor shield.
8. Install sensor hold down bolt. Torque to 170–230 inch lbs.
9. Lower vehicle.

ELECTRONIC BRAKE CONTROL MODULE
1. Remove the right side sill plate.
2. Remove the right side cowl cover.
3. Remove the three screws that attach electronic brake control module to side cowl.
4. Disconnect the wiring from the module.
5. When installing, connect the wiring first, then install the three mounting screws.
6. Install the right side cowl cover and sill plate.

DUAL SOLENOID HYDRAULIC VALVE
1. Raise and safely support vehicle.
2. Remove the brake lines from the valve.
3. Remove the 2 nuts that hold the valve to the frome.
4. Remove the valve from the frame and disconnect the wiring.
5. When installing, connect the wiring first, then install the valve. Torque the hold-down nuts to 16–25 ft. lbs.
6. Bleed the solenoid valve and the rear brakes.
7. Lower hoist.

Test Step	What to do	Condition	Yes	No
TEST 1 VISUAL INSPECTION				
1.1	Inspect RWAL connectors and ground for defects and good connections	Are connectors free of defects and connected properly?	Go to Test 2	Repair or connect terminals as required
TEST 2 SYSTEM SELF CHECK				
2.1	Turn ignition switch to run position	Both lamps illuminate for 2 seconds then go out as system performs self check	Go to Test 3	Choose another condition
		Antilock and brake lamp stay on	Go to Test 6	Choose another condition
		Antilock lamp off and will not self check, brake lamp checked OK	Go to Test 7	Choose another condition
		Brake lamp on, antilock lamp off and does self check	Go to Test 8	Choose another condition
		Antilock and brake lamps flashing	Go to Test 9	Choose another condition
		Brake lamp off, antilock lamp on, antilock lamp does self check	Go to Test 10	Choose another condition
TEST 3 CHECKING SENSOR OUTPUT AND PHYSICAL CONDITION				
3.1	Apply service brakes and check stop lights	Stop lamps illuminate	Go to Test 3.2	Repair stop lamp circuit
3.2	Remove sensor from differential and inspect exciter ring for damage	Exciter ring in good condition	Reinstall sensor. Go to Test 3.3	Replace exciter ring and retest system
3.3	Lift rear wheels, start engine, run wheels at 5 mph. Make sure vehicle is properly positioned on hoist or jack stands. **WARNING: STAY CLEAR OF ROTATING WHEELS.** Using a voltmeter set on 2 volt AC scale and connect between B01 PK and B02 LG/OR wires of the sensor connector	Is voltage 650 MV (RMS) or greater?	Go to Test 5	Go to Test 3.4
3.4		Has sensor been replaced?	Go to Test 3.5	Replace sensor and go to Test 3.3
3.5	Disconnect 14 way module connector. Disconnect sensor connector and connect an ohmmeter between B01 RD/VT wire in module connector and B01 PK wire in sensor connector	Is there continuity?	Go to Test 3.6	Repair open circuit
3.6	Connect an ohmmeter between B01 RD/VT wire in module connector and ground	Is there continuity?	Repair circuit for a short to ground	Go to Test 3.7
3.7	Connect an ohmmeter between B02 WT/VT wire in module connector and B02 LG/OR wire in sensor connector	Is there continuity?	Repair circuit for an open circuit	Go to Test 3.8
3.8	Connect an ohmmeter between B02 WT/VT wire in module connector and ground	Is there a short to ground?	Repair circuit for short to ground	Go to Test 4

Test Step	What to do	Condition	Yes	No
TEST 4 CHECKING SENSOR GAP				
4.1	Remove sensor from differential. Measure height of sensor pole piece from mounting face of sensor (should be 1.07″–1.08″). Measure top of exciter ring teeth from sensor mounting face on differential (should be 1.085″–1.12″). Subtract measurements as shown to obtain sensor gap. Gap must be a minimum of 0.005″ and a maximum of 0.05″	Was gap within specifications?	Go to Test 5	Go to Test 4.2
4.2	Look at sensor measurement from Test 4.1 (should be 1.07″–1.08″)	Was sensor measurement within specifications?	Repair differential and retest system	Replace sensor and retest system
TEST 5 CHECKING FOR BRAKE MECHANICAL PROBLEMS				
5.1	Check rear brakes for mechanical problems such as grabbing, locking or pulling	Are the rear brakes functioning properly?	Replace module and retest system	Repair mechanical problem and retest system
TEST 6 CHECKING THE DIAGNOSTIC CONNECTOR GROUND				
6.1	Locate the black 2-way diagnostic connector below RWAL module. Connect a jumper wire between the diagnostic connector and ground	Is there a flashout code?	Go to Test 11	Go to 6.2
6.2	Turn ignition off. Disconnect 14-way connector from module and connect an ohmmeter between the BK in the 14-way connector and the BK in the 2-way diagnostic connector	Is there continuity?	Go to Test 6.3	Repair open circuit and retest system
6.3	Check brake fluid level in master cylinder reservoir	Is brake fluid level correct?	Go to Test 6.4	Find and repair leak and retest system
6.4	Reconnect 14-way module connector. Disconnect connector from the pressure differential switch. Turn ignition to run position	Do both antilock lamp and brake lamp stay on?	Go to Test 6.5	Check brake system for air in lines or mechanical damage
6.5		Does the vehicle have a diesel engine?	Go to Test 6.6	Go to Test 6.7
6.6	Disconnect harness connector from vacuum warning switch. Turn the ignition switch to the run position	Do both lamps stay on?	Go to Test 6.7	Check complete vehicle vacuum system, repair as required and retest system
6.7	Disconnect 14-way module connector. Turn ignition switch to the run position	Are both antilock lamp and brake lamp off?	Go to Test 6.8	Choose another condition
		Antilock lamp on, brake lamp off	Repair AT1 orange wire for short to ground between module and antilock lamp	Repair short to ground in differential switch sensor wiring, B01 PK and B02 LG/OR
6.8	Remove and inspect antilock fuse	Is fuse open?	Check and repair all circuits fuse is protecting. Replace fuse	Go to Test 6.9

Test Step	What to do	Condition	Yes	No
TEST 6 CHECKING THE DIAGNOSTIC CONNECTOR GROUND				
6.9	Connect a voltmeter between pin 3 RD/YL wire of 14-way module connector and ground	Is voltage greater than 9 volts?	Go to Test 6.10	Repair the D1 RD/YL wire for an open
6.10	Remove and inspect the stop lamp fuse.	Is the fuse open?	Check and repair all circuits fuse is protecting for shorts and replace fuse	Go to Test 6.11
6.11	Connect a voltmeter between pin 9 of the 14-way module connector and ground	Is voltage greater than 9 volts?	Replace module and retest system	Repair the D3B PK/DB wire for open circuit.
TEST 7 CHECKING MODULE GROUND AND POWER				
7.1	Make sure module connector is fully-plugged into module	Is connector plugged in?	Go to Test 7.2	Plug connector in and retest system
7.2	Disconnect battery and 14-way module connector. With an ohmmeter set on 200 ohm scale, check resistance between pin 10 BK/LG wire on the 14-way harness connector and ground	Is resistance less than 1 ohm?	Go to Test 7.3	Repair H40 BK/LG for an open or damaged circuit
7.3	Remove and inspect antilock lamp fuse	Is fuse open?	Check and repair all circuits fuse is protecting for shorts and replace fuse	Go to Test 7.4
7.4	Connect battery and turn ignition to run position. With a voltmeter set on 20 volt DC scale, check voltage between Pin 2 Orange wire of the 14-way module connector and ground	Is voltage less than 9 volts?	Go to Test 7.5	Replace the module and retest system
7.5	Check antilock bulb	Is bulb open?	Replace bulb and retest system	Repair AT1 orange wire for open circuit between pin 2 and fuse
TEST 8 CHECKING PARKING SYSTEM AND MODULE				
8.1	Turn ignition to run position. Pull lever to release parking brake	Does the brake lamp go off?	Disregard failure, retest antilock and brake lamp for 2 second self check	Go to Test 8.2
8.2	Pull park brake release lever with one hand and pull pedal up with other hand	Did brake lamp go off	Repair park brake mechanism or switch	Go to Test 8.3
8.3	Disconnect black 1-way park brake switch connector	Did brake lamp go off	Adjust or replace park brake switch and retest system	Go to Test 8.4
8.4	Disconnect 14-way module connector	Did brake lamp go off?	Replace module and retest system	Repair P5 BK/GY wire for a short to ground

Test Step	What to do	Condition	Yes	No
TEST 9 CHECKING FOR INTERMITTENT PROBLEMS				
9.1	Disconnect 14-way module connector. With a voltmeter set on 20 volt DC scale, check voltage between pin 3 RD/YL wire on the 14-way module connector and ground. Turn ignition to run position and shake the instrument panel harness	Is voltage steady at 9 volts?	Go to Test 9.2	Repair D1 RD/YL for open circuit
9.2	Disconnect battery, set ohmmeter on 200 scale and connect between pin 12 BK wire of the 14-way module connector and ground, then shake the instrument panel harness	Is resistance 100K or greater and steady?	Go to Test 9.3	Repair DK/BK/ wire for a short to ground
9.3	With ohmmeter set on 200 ohm scale, connect between Pin 10 BK/LG wire of the 14-way module connector and ground, then shake instrument panel harness.	Is resistance steady at 1 ohm?	Replace module and retest system	Repair open circuit in H40 BK/LG
TEST 10 CHECKING FOR OPEN OR DISCONNECTED PARK BRAKE SWITCH CONNECTOR				
10.1	Make sure the P5 BK/GY wire at the park brake switch is connected	Is P5 wire connected to park brake switch?	Go to Test 10.2	Connect and retest system
10.2	Disconnect park brake switch connector. Disconnect message center black 6-way connector. Connect an ohmmeter between P5 BK/BY wire in both connectors	Is there continuity?	Go to Test 10.3	Repair P5 BK/GY wire for open circuit
10.3	Inspect instrument cluster printed circuit board for damage	Is printed circuit board damaged?	Replace printed circuit board	Replace brake warning lamp bulb
TEST 11 FLASHCODES				
11.1	Connect a jumper wire between the diagnostic connector and ground. Count the flashes including the long flash that starts the flash code count. Choose the proper condition	Antilock lamp and brake lamp flash 1 time	Go to Test 12	
		Antilock lamp and brake lamp flash 2 times.	G to Test 13	
		Antilock lamp and brake lamp flash 3 times.	G to Test 14	
		Antilock lamp and brake lamp flash 4 times.	G to Test 15	
		Antilock lamp and brake lamp flash 5 times.	G to Test 16	
		Antilock lamp and brake lamp flash 6 times.	G to Test 17	
		Antilock lamp and brake lamp flash 7 times.	G to Test 18	
		Antilock lamp and brake lamp flash 8 times.	G to Test 19	
		Antilock lamp and brake lamp flash 9 times.	G to Test 20	
		Antilock lamp and brake lamp flash 10 times.	G to Test 21	
		Antilock lamp and brake lamp flash 11 times.	G to Test 22	
		Antilock lamp and brake lamp flash	G to Test 23	

Test Step	What to do	Condition	Yes	No
TEST 11 FLASHCODES				
11.1		12 times. Antilock lamp and brake lamp flash 13 times.	G to Test 24	
		Antilock lamp and brake lamp flash 14 times.	G to Test 25	
		Antilock lamp and brake lamp flash 15 times.	G to Test 26	
		Antilock lamp and brake lamp flash 16 times.	G to Test 27	
TEST 12 ONE FLASH				
12.1	One flash code should not occur. Perform flashcode procedure several times	Are you still getting code 1?	Go to Test 5	Go to Test 11
TEST 13 TWO FLASHES				
13.1	Disconnect battery and 14-way module connector. Set an ohmmeter on 200 ohm scale and connect between pin 1 LG wire of the 14-way module connector and ground	Does the circuit have over 6 ohms?	Go to test 13.2	Replace the module and retest system
13.2	Disconnect valve harness connector from valve connector. Connect an ohmmeter between B09 GY/WT of harness connector and ground	Is resistance greater than 1 ohm?	Repair B09 GY/WT wire for an open circuit or high resistance. Check for contaminated or loose connector pins and retest system	Go to Test 13.3
13.3	Connect an ohmmeter between IS1 LG/ and B09 GY/WT wires in the 4-way black valve connector	Does circuit have over 6 ohms?	Replace antilock valve and retest system	Repair the IS1 LG/ for open circuit from valve to computer module and retest system
TEST 14 THREE FLASHES				
14.4	Disconnect battery. Remove 14-way module harness connector from module. Set ohmmeter on 200 ohm scale and connect to pin 8 DS1 WT/BR and ground	Does circuit have over 3 ohms?	Go to Test 14.2	Replace module and retest system
14.2	Disconnect the 4-way valve harness connector. Connect an ohmmeter between DS1 WT and B09 GY/NT wires in valve connector	Does circuit have over 3 ohms?	Replace antilock valve and retest system	Repair DS1 WT wire for open between module connector and valve connector
TEST 15 FOUR FLASHES				
15.1	Disconnect the 4-way valve harness connector from valve connector. Set ohmmeter on 20K scale and connect between VS1 LB wire in valve body and ground	Is resistance greater than 10K ohms?	Go to Test 15.2	Replace the antilock valve and retest system
15.2	Connect an ohmmeter between VS1 LB and B09 GY/WY wires in the valve connector	Is resistance greater than 10K ohms?	Go to Test 15.3	Replace the antilock valve and retest system

Test Step	What to do	Condition	Yes	No
TEST 15 FOUR FLASHES				
15.3	Disconnect battery. Disconnect the 14-way module harness connector from module. Set ohmmeter on 200K scale and connect to pin 11, VS1 LB of 14-way connector and ground	Is resistance greater than 100K ohms?	Replace module and retest system	Repair VS1 LB wire for a short to ground between valve and module. Retest system
TEST 16 FIVE FLASHES				
16.1	Did the failure occur in 2 wheel drive mode?		Go to Test 16.2	Go to Test 16.3
16.2	Disconnect 14-way module connector from module to deactivate antilock system. Drive the vehicle in 2 wheel drive mode and make normal and safe stops to determine the condition of the rear brakes	Are the brakes functioning normally?	Replace the antilock valve and retest system	Repair rear brakes and retest system
16.3	Disconnect 14-way module connector from module. Turn ignition key to run position. Shift into 4 wheel drive. Set a voltmeter to 20 vdc and connect between pin 4, X4 LG/BR wire and ground	Is voltage greater than 1 volt?	Repair X4 wire for an open or 4 wheel drive indicator switch. Retest system	Replace antilock valve and retest system
TEST 17 SIX FLASHES				
17.1	Recheck flashcode after driving vehicle	Antilock light and brake light flash 6 times	Go to Test 17.2	Go to Test 11
17.2	Disconnect battery. Disconnect 14-way module connector. Set ohmmeter on 200 ohm scale and connect between pin 13, B02 WT/VT and pin 14, B01 RD/VT of harness connector. Shake antilock wiring harness from differential to module	Is resistance constant at 1000–2000 ohms?	Go to Test 17.3	Repair circuit. Retest system
17.3	Remove sensor from the differential and inspect for build up of metal chips on sensor pole piece	Are metal chips present?	Drain and clean differential. Check exciter ring for broken or chipped teeth. Retest system	Go to Test 17.4
17.4	Look into sensor hole in differential and rotate exciter ring and check for damage (missing or bent teeth)	Is exciter ring intact?	Go to 17.5	Replace exciter ring. Retest system
17.5	Reinstall sensor. Disconnect 2-way RWAL sensor connector. With a voltmeter on 2 volt scale, connect between B01 PK and B2 LG/OR wires of sensor connector. Raise rear wheels off floor and run at 5 mph. **WARNING: STAY CLEAR OF ROTATING WHEELS**	Is voltage greater than 650 MV and steady?	Replace module. Retest system	Replace sensor. Recheck sensor output. Retest system
TEST 18 SEVEN FLASHES				
18.1	Disconnect 4-way valve harness connector from valve connector. Connect an ohmmeter between IS1 LG/ and B09 GY/WT wire in valve connector	Is resistance less than 3 ohms?	Replace antilock valve. Retest system	Go to Test 18.2

Test Step	What to do	Condition	Yes	No
TEST 18 SEVEN FLASHES				
18.2	Disconnect battery. Disconnect 4-way valve harness connector from valve connector. Disconnect 14-way module harness connector from module. Set ohmmeter on 20K ohms scale and connect between Pin 1, IS1 LG/ wire in harness connector and ground	Is resistance greater than 20K ohms?	Replace module. Retest system	Repair IS1 LG/* for a short between antilock valve and module. Retest system
TEST 19 EIGHT FLASHES				
19.1	Disconnect 4-way valve harness from valve connector. Set ohmmeter on 200 ohm scale and connect between DS1 WT and B09 GY/WT wires in valve connector	Is resistance less than 1 ohm?	Replace antilock valve. Retest system	Go to Test 19.2
19.2	Disconnect battery. Disconnect 4-way valve connector. Disconnect 14-way module connector. Set ohmmeter on 20K ohm scale and connect between pin 8, DS1 WT/BR and ground	Is resistance greater than 20K ohms?	Replace module	Repair DS1 WT/BR for a short to ground between antilock valve and module. Retest system
TEST 20 NINE FLASHES				
20.1	Disconnect 2-way sensor harness connector from sensor on differential housing. Set ohmmeter on 20K scale and connect to B01 PK and B02 LG/OR wire on sensor	Is resistance greater than 2500 ohms?	Replace sensor. Recheck resistance. **Make sure seal is in place between sensor and connector.** Retest system	Go to Test 20.2
20.2	Reconnect sensor harness **making sure seal is in place.** Disconnect battery. Disconnect 14-way module connector. Connect an ohmmeter between pin 13, B02 WT/VT and pin 14, B01 RD/VT wires in module harness connector	Is resistance greater than 2500 ohms?	Repair B02 WT/VT and B01 RD/VT for open circuits between the module and sensor. Retest system	Replace computer module. When reconnecting sensor, **make sure seal is in place.** Retest system
TEST 21 TEN FLASHES				
21.1	Set ohmmeter on 20K ohm scale. Disconnect 2-way sensor connector from sensor on differential. Connect an ohmmeter between B01 PK and B02 LG/OR wires on sensor	Is resistance less then 1000 ohms?	Replace sensor. Recheck resistance. **Make sure seal is in place between sensor and connector.** Retest system	Go to Test 21.2
21.2	Disconnect battery. Disconnect 14-way module. Connect an ohmmeter between pin 14, B01 RD/VT and ground	Is resistance greater than 20K ohms?	Go to Test 21.3	Repair B01 RD/VT circuit between the module and sensor. When reconnecting sensor, **make sure seal is in place.** Retest system

Test Step	What to do	Condition	Yes	No
TEST 21 TEN FLASHES				
21.3	Connect an ohmmeter between pin 13, B02 WT/VT and pin 14 B01 RD/VT wire in module harness connector	Is resistance greater than 20K ohms?	Replace module. Retest system	Repair B01 RD/ VT and B02 WT/ VT circuit. When reconnecting sensor, **make sure seal is in place.** Retest system
TEST 22 ELEVEN FLASHES				
22.1	Recheck flash code after driving vehicle at 35 mph or greater.	Antilock light and brake light flash 11 times	Go to Test 22.1	Go to Test 11
22.2	Apply vehicle service brakes and check vehicle stop lights	Are stop lights operating correctly?	Go to Test 22.3	Repair the stop lamp circuit. Retest system
22.3	Turn ignition switch off. Disconnect 14-way module connector from module. Connect a voltmeter between pin 7, D4 WT of harness connector and ground while stepping on brake pedal	Is voltage less than 9 volts?	Repair D4 WT for open circuit between stop light switch and module. Retest system	Check 4-way flasher, directional wiring, and feedback through stop light circuit. Also check for proper operation of cruise control. Recheck antilock and brake lights for proper 2 second bulb check
TEST 23 TWELVE FLASHES				
23.1	This code should not occur. Read flashcodes several times	Are 12 flashes still present?	Replace module. Retest system	Go to Test 11
TEST 24 THIRTEEN FLASHES				
24.1	Read flashcode	Are 13 flashes present?	Replace module. Retest system	Go to Test 11
TEST 25 FOURTEEN FLASHES				
25.1	Read flashcode	Are 14 flashes present?	Replace module. Retest system	Go to Test 11
TEST 26 FIFTEEN FLASHES				
26.1	Read flashcode	Are 15 flashes present?	Replace module. Retest system	Go to Test 11
TEST 27 SIXTEEN OR MORE FLASHES				
27.1	Read flashcode	Are 16 or more flashes present?	Replace module. Retest system	Go to Test 11

JEEP CORPORATION

Master Cylinder Service

Jeep uses a dual master cylinder which contains a double hydraulic cylinder with 2 fluid reservoirs and primary and secondary hydraulic pistons. The master cylinder is assisted by a vacuum booster. Hydraulic rear drum brakes with automatic adjusters and self-adjusting front disc brakes are standard on all models.

The front outlet tube of the master cylinder is connected to the hydraulic system control valve and then to the rear brakes. This is referred the secondary system. The rear outlet tube is connected to the control valve and to the front brakes. This system is referred to as the primary system. No residual pressure valves are used in the master cylinder outlets.

During normal operation, the fluid level in the master cylinder will rise during brake operation and fall during release. It is also expected that the fluid level will decrease with brake pad wear. In addition, a trace of brake fluid on the booster shell below the master cylinder mounting flange will often be found as a result of the normal lubricating action of the master cylinder bore and seal. All of these conditions are considered normal and are not indications the master cylinder needs service.

Two types of master cylinders were used; 1) a cast iron master cylinder with built-in reservoir and separate proportioning valve and, 2) a master cylinder with a pressed on plastic reservoir. The body of the two-piece master cylinder is made of anodized aluminum and the reservoir is made of nylon. The two compartments of the reservoir are interconnected to permit equalization of the fluid level. However, a sufficient quantity of fluid is retained in the reservoir of the unaffected system to permit operation of that half of the master cylinder even if the other half of the reservoir is drained due to a hydraulic leak. There is another type of master cylinder used on vehicles equipped with anti-lock brakes. See anti-lock section.

Use extra care when servicing aluminum master cylinders not to cross thread brake line fittings and do not overtighten any threaded connection.

In the event of a front brake system malfunction the proportioning valve with a bypass feature allows full hydraulic pressure to the rear brake system.

Disassembly and Assembly

While the manufacturer does give overhaul procedures for the master cylinder, the manufacturer does not permit that either the cast iron or aluminum master cylinder be honed in an attempt to restore the surface. Replace the cylinder if the bore is corroded or if doubt exists about cylinder bore condition.

CAST IRON MASTER CYLINDER – EXCEPT ANTI-LOCK

1. Remove the cover and drain fluid. Examine cover seal for damage.
2. Mount cylinder in vise and press in primary piston. Remove snapring.
3. Remove the primary piston and discard. It is serviced only as an assembly.
4. Apply a small amount of compressed air to secondary outlet while covering small ports at bottom of rear reservoir to ease secondary piston from bore.
1. Place shop towels under the caliper piston to protect it during removal. Apply a little compressed air to slowly ease the piston out of the bore.
2. Remove the dust boot and, using a small, pointed wooden stick, work the piston seal out of its groove in the caliper bore. Do not use a screwdriver or metal tool which might nick or scratch the bore. Discard the seal.

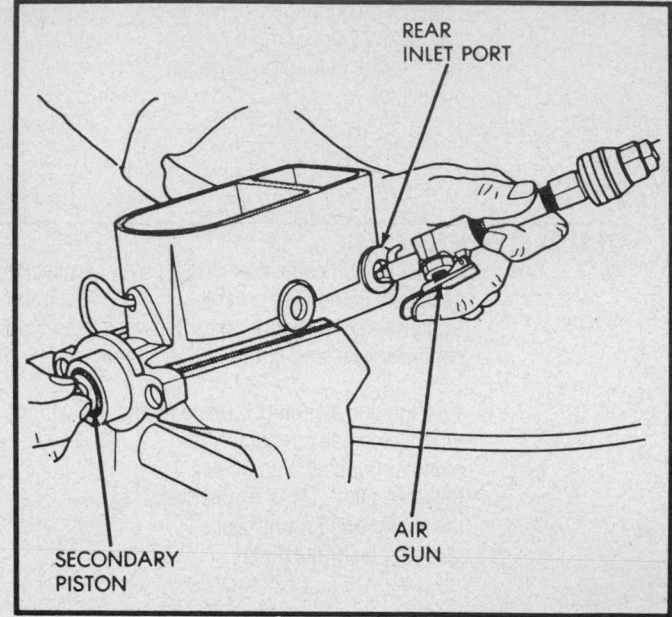

Use air pressure to remove secondary piston

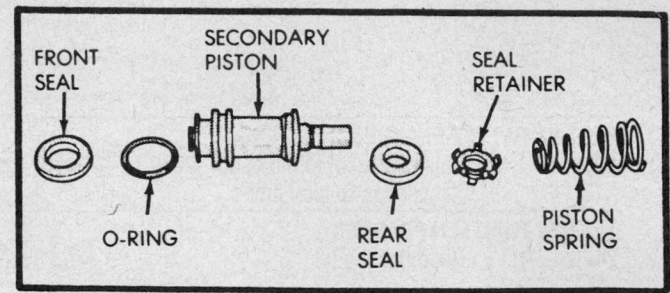

Secondary piston components

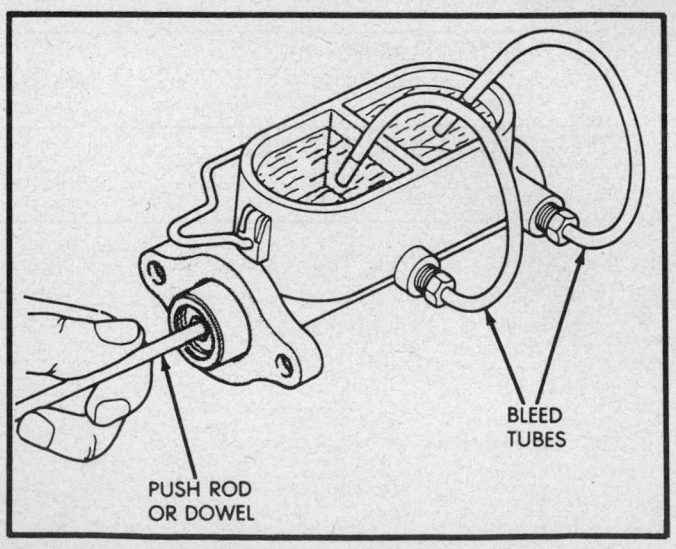

Bleeding master cylinder—typical

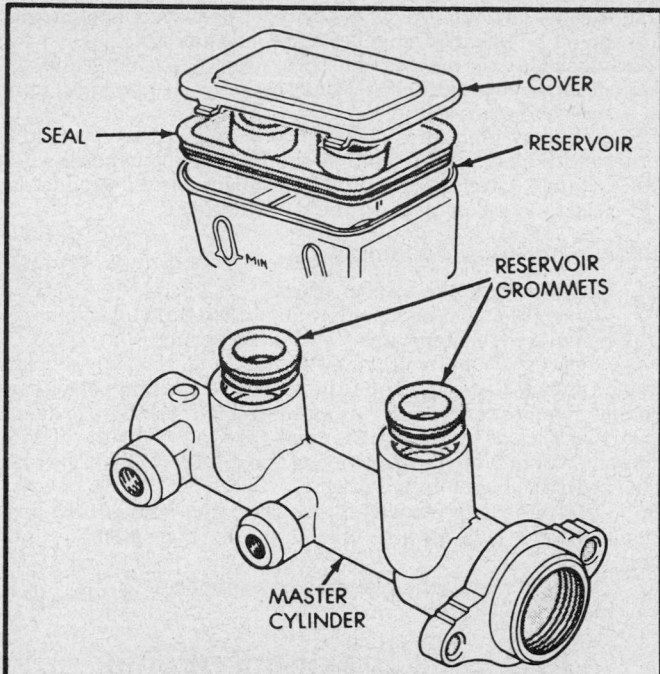

Aluminum master cylinder

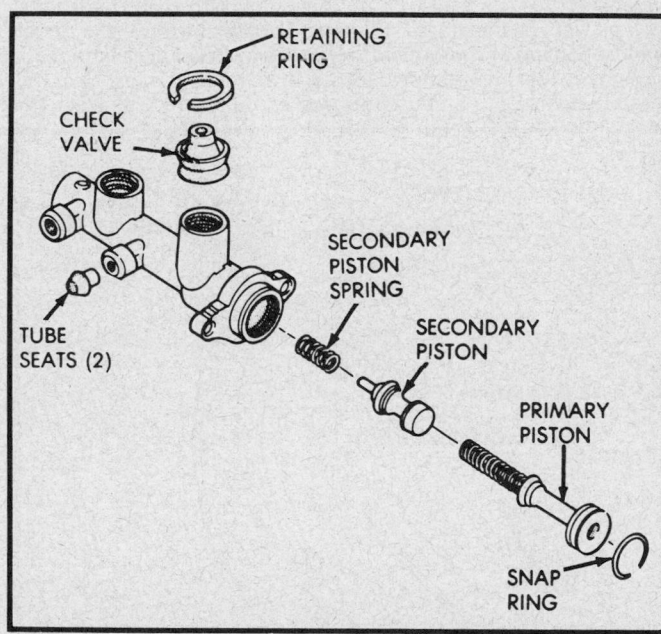

Aluminum master cylinder components

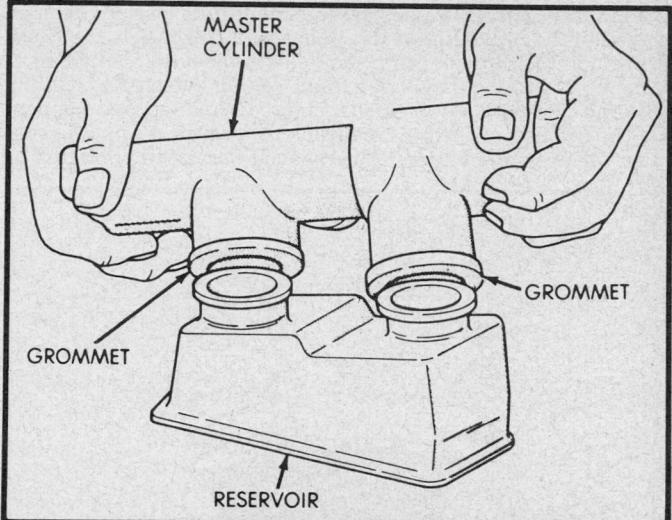

Installing the reservoir to the master cylinder body

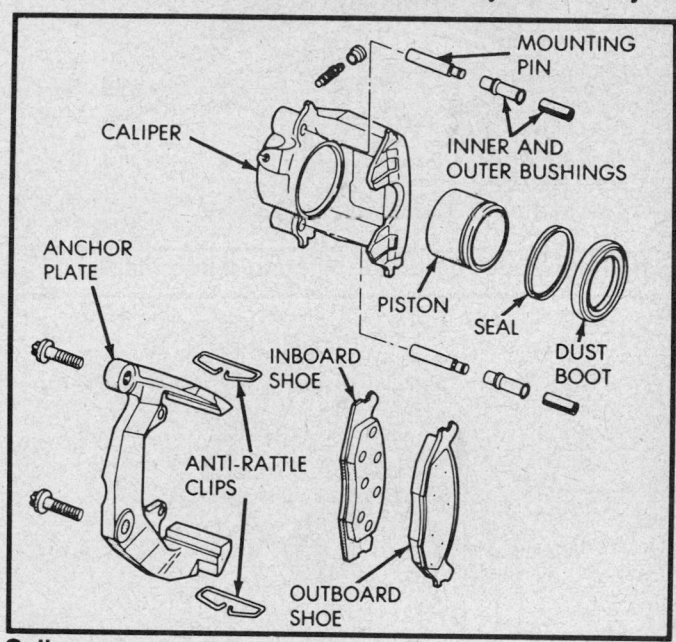

Caliper components—typical

3. Clean all parts well using alcohol and blow dry. Inspect the piston bore for scoring or pitting. Install a new piston if it is pitted, scored or the plating is worn. Jeep does not recommend honing calipers or using any type of abrasives on the basis that abrasives will ruin the piston plating and cause it to corrode and bind. Replace the piston if damaged in any way.

4. Clean all parts well, dip the new piston seal in brake fluid and install in the bore. Position the seal at one area at a time and, using fingers, gently work the seal into the groove.

5. Slide the metal retainer part of the new dust boot over the open end of the piston. Pull the retainer rearward until the boot lip seats in the groove at the end of the piston. Push the metal retainer part of the boot forward until flush with the rim at the open end of the piston. Then snap boot folds in place. Finally, install the piston in the caliper bore with a twisting motion being careful not to unseal the piston seal.

6. Seal the metal retainer part of the dust boot in the caliper with a circular driver.

7. Install new mounting bushings in the caliper as required. Install bleeder screw if removed.

8. Install the flexible brake hose with new seals.

Wheel Cylinder Service

The rear brakes are drum type with internal expanding shoes. The rear brakes are of the single anchor type, mounted to the same anchor and actuated by one wheel cylinder. The wheel cylinder has two pistons. Brake adjustments are automatic and are made during reverse brake applications.

Wheel cylinders may need reconditioning or replacement whenever the brake shoes are replaced or when required to correct a leak condition. Leaks which coat the boot and the cylinder

with fluid, or result in a dropped reservoir fluid level, or dampen and stain the brake linings are dangerous. Such leaks can cause the brakes to grab or fail and should be immediately corrected. A leakage, not immediately apparent, can be detected by pulling back the cylinder boot. A small amount of fluid seepage dampening the interior of the boot is normal. However, a dripping boot is not. Unless other conditions causing a brake to pull, grab or

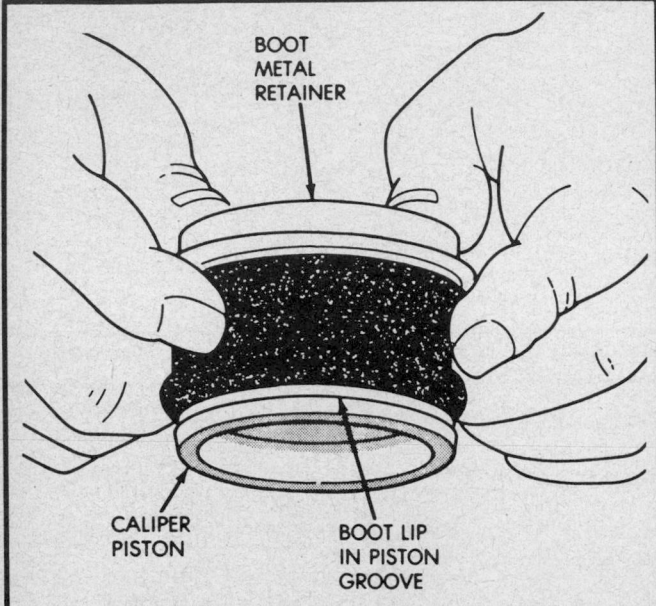

Install dust boot on piston, then fold into place

drag become obvious, the wheel cylinder is suspect and should and should be included in general reconditioning.

Cylinder binding may be caused by rust, deposits, grime, or swollen cups due to fluid contamination, or by a cup wedged into an excessive piston clearance.

Hydraulic system parts should not be allowed to come into contact with oil or grease, neither should those be handled with greasy hands. Even a trace of any petroleum based product is sufficient to cause damage to the rubber parts.

Disassembly and Assembly

1. Remove the brake bleeder screw.
2. Remove the dust boots, allow any brake fluid to drain out.
3. Remove the pistons, seals and inner spring.
4. Inspect the bore for scoring and corrosion. If bore is scored, replace cylinder. Do not hone the cylinder bores or polish the pistons. Replace the cylinder as an assembly if the bore is damaged. Black stains on the cylinder walls are caused by the piston cups and will not impair operation of the cylinder. Clean the cylinder with alcohol or brake fluid.
5. Lubricate the seals with brake fluid and install. Cup lips should always face inward. Install the spring assembly and seals.
6. Carefully install the pistons and dust boots.
7. Install the bleeder screw.

Anti-Lock Braking Systems

Despite advances in brake design over the years, even the best systems in use can still lock up during certain road conditions, such as wet road surfaces. When the brakes lock up, the driver can lose control of the vehicle, because a locked wheel cannot absorb any cornering or lateral forces, and steering is lost. It is impossible to brake to a maximum and at the same time steer the

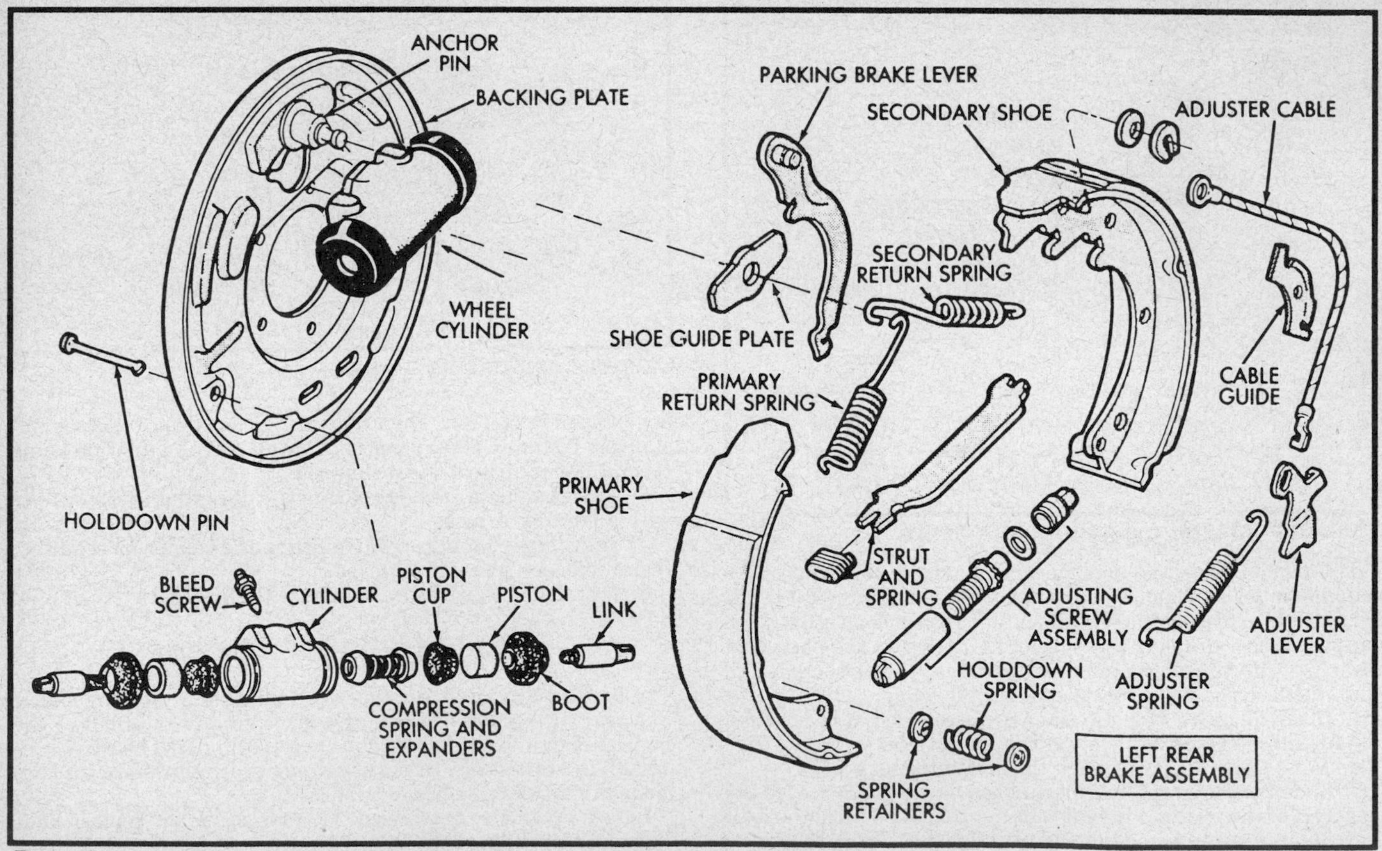

Rear drum brakes—Comanchee, Cherokee, Wrangler shown—typical

vehicle when the front wheels are locked. If the back wheels are locked the vehicle will become unstable and start to slide.

While many different ways have been tried over the years to solve this problem, mechanical sensors could not provide sufficient information about wheel rotation speed and mechanical control units could not operate the brakes fast enough to prevent brake lockup.

The growth of the electronics industry has allowed small computers (microprocessors) to be reduced in both size and cost. Coupled with fast reacting electronic sensors, anti-lock braking has become more reliable with widespread application.

Jeep's antilock brake system is available on 70 Series (Cherokee/Wagoneer Sport trucks) models with Select-Track four wheel drive. It is an electronically operated, power assisted, all wheel brake control system. The system is designed to retard wheel lockup during periods of high wheel slip when braking. Retarding wheel lockup is accomplished by modulating fluid pressures to the wheel brake units.

The 70 Series anti-lock system is a 3 channel design. The front wheel brakes are controlled individually and the rear wheel brakes in tandem.

System pressure is modulated according to wheel speed, degree of wheel slip and rate of deceleration. A sensor at each wheel converts wheel speed into electronic signals. The signals are transmitted to the brake system control unit for processing and determination of deceleration rate and wheel slip.

Basic system components include wheel sensors, fluid level and pressure switches, a pressure modulator, an accumulator, an electric booster pump, a master cylinder/power boost unit and an electronic control unit. Two instrument cluster indicator lights (one red, one yellow) are used to signal system condition and operating status.

The anti-lock electronic control system is separate from other electrical circuits in the vehicle. A specially programmed ECU is used for operational control.

The accumulator tank and the small accumulator on the booster pump both contain high pressure gas charges which assist in maintaining boost pressure. Do not puncture or attempt to disassemble either of these components at any time.

When servicing the anti-lock system, keep system components clean. Do not allow any dirt or foreign material to enter the system. Clean the reservoir cap and exterior thoroughly before removing the cap to add fluid. Dirt or foreign material in the system could result in poor brake system performance and possible component failure.

The manufacturer recommends Mopar brake fluid or equivalent meeting DOT 3 standards only. Never use reclaimed fluid or fluid from an open container that has been allowed to stand for any length of time.

CAUTION

The normal working pressure of the anti-lock boost system is 1650–2050 psi. System pressure must be pumped down before any pressure lines are loosened or disconnected. Failure to do so could result in personal injury. To reduce system pressure, turn the ignition key OFF. They apply the brakes 45–50 times (until pedal is firm) to reduce fluid pressure in the accumulator, booster, pump and lines. Wear safety goggles when disconnecting fluid lines.

MAJOR COMPONENTS

Master Cylinder/Power Booster Unit

The master cylinder and power booster pistons are located in a single, cast aluminum, cylinder body. A fluid reservoir is attached to the body with rubber seals.

The fluid reservoir is internally separated into 3 sections by bulkheads. A common fluid fill is used for the 3 sections.

The power booster is a demand type component. Power assist occurs only when the brakes are applied. Power assist is from

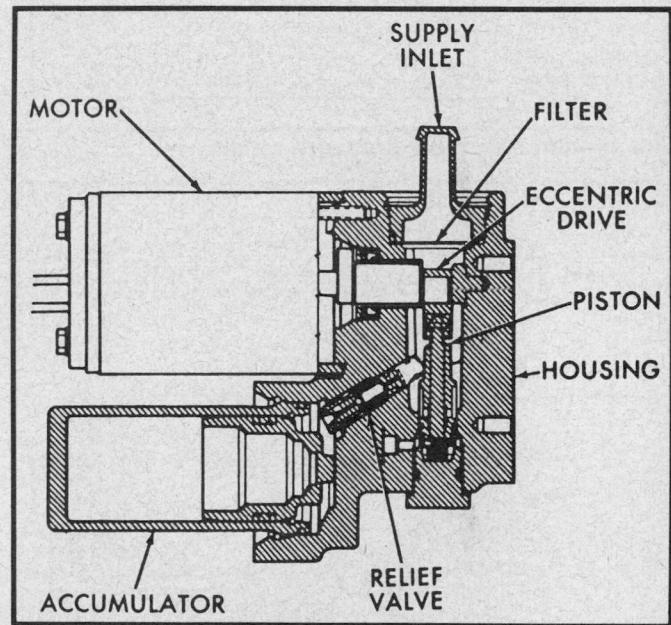

Anti-lock booster pump and motor assembly

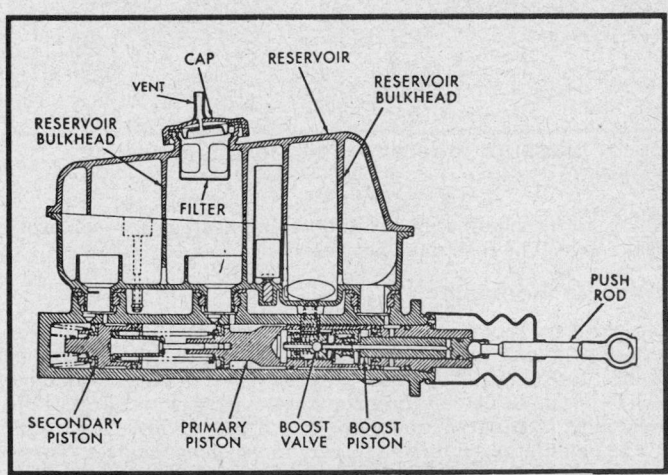

Anti-lock master cylinder/power booster unit

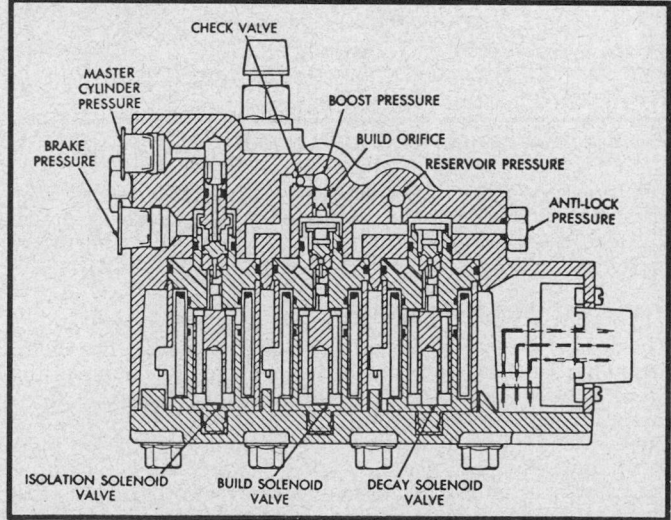

Pressure modulator channel—typical

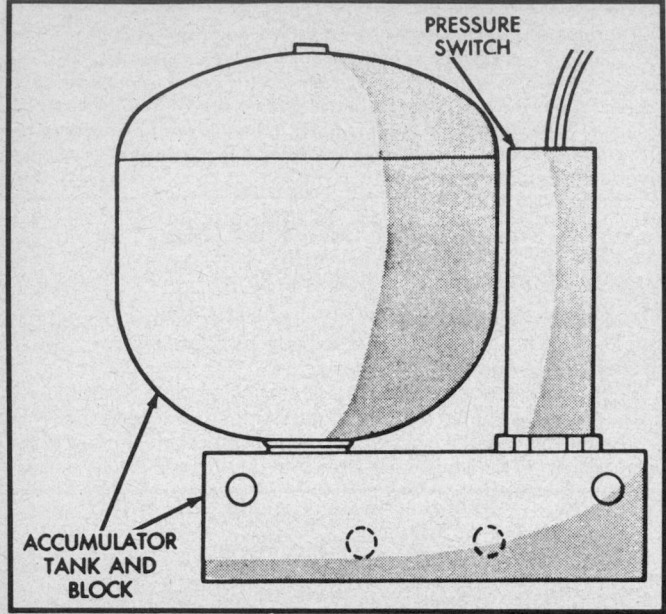

Accumulator and low pressure switch

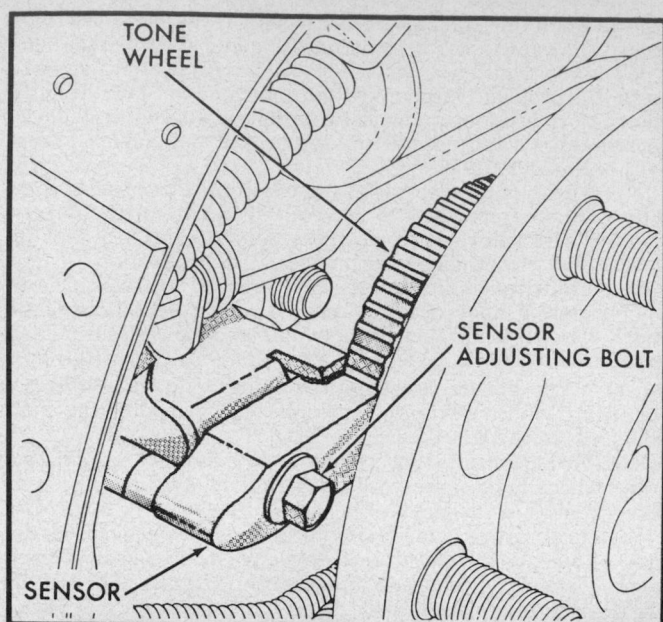

Rear wheel sensor and tone wheel

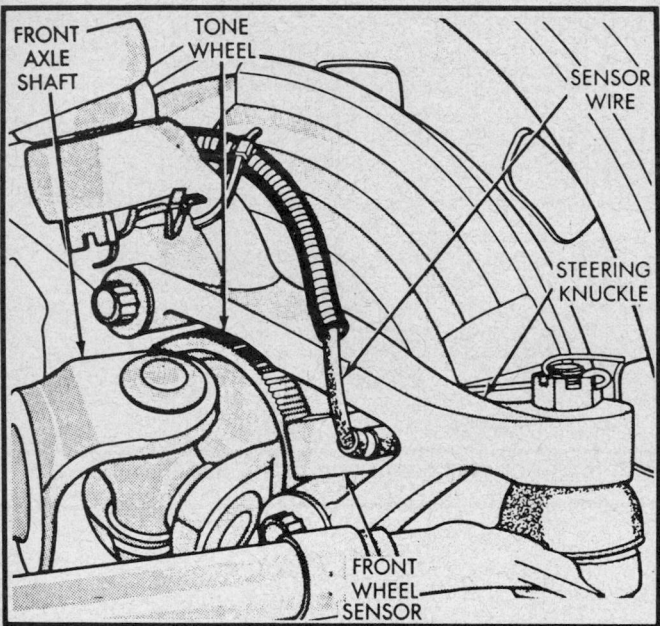

Front wheel sensor and tone wheel

high pressure brake fluid supplied by the electric motor driven booster pump. The pump is connected to the system accumulator. The accumulator is connected to the booster unit in the master cylinder.

Pump and Motor Assembly

The booster pump is powered by an electric motor. The motor and pump are combined in a common housing. The pump piston operates off an eccentric drive. An internal relief valve and a pressure switch control pump output. The housing contains a small accumulator which operates in tandem with the main accumulator.

The pump supplies fluid boost pressure for both standard and anti-lock brake operation. Pump operating pressure range is 1650–2050 psi. The pump motor is equipped with a thermal fuse

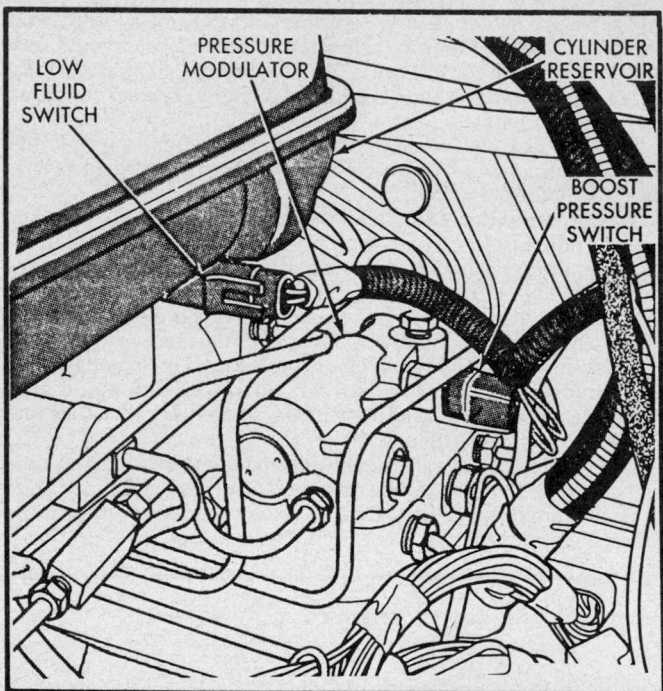

Boost pressure differential and low fluid switch locations

which stops the pump if operating temperatures approach overheat range. The fuse does not reset once it is tripped.

Pressure Modulator

The pressure modulator is a hydro-electric component. It provides three channels of pressure control to the front/rear brakes. One channel controls the rear wheel brakes in tandem. The two remaining channels control the front wheel brakes individually. Modulator inputs are both hydraulic and electronic.

The modulator contains a total of nine solenoid valves. Three valves are assigned to each control channel. The illustration shows one channel section of the modulator.

The 3 solenoid valves in each control channel have separate functions. The isolation solenoid valves isolate the master cylinder line to a caliper or wheel cylinder. The decay solenoid valves provide a controlled decrease (drop) in pressure to the wheel brakes in the anti-lock mode. The build solenoid valves provide controlled pressure build (increase) to the wheel brakes in the anti-lock mode.

Accumulator and Low Pressure Switch

The accumulator stores fluid under pressure for power brake and anti-lock operation. The low pressure switch monitors fluid pressure and is connected to the ECU.

If pressure falls below a minimum value of approximately 1050 psi, the switch triggers the ECU which stops cycling the modulator solenoids. The yellow indicator light illuminates when the solenoids cease operation in the anti-lock mode.

The pressure switch is grounded through the vehicle body during normal operation but reverts to an open circuit if pressure drop occurs. An open circuit will trigger the instrument cluster indicator lights.

The accumulator is connected to the pump and power booster unit respectively.

Wheel Sensors

A sensor is used at each wheel. The sensors convert wheel speed into an electronic signal which is transmitted to the anti-lock ECU. A toothed-type tone wheel serves as the trigger mechanism for each sensor. The tone wheels are mounted at the outboard ends of the front and rear axle shafts.

Boost Pressure Differential Switch

The boost pressure differential switch is mounted in the pressure modulator. The switch checks the pressure differential between modulated boost pressure and the master cylinder primary system pressure.

The switch is in circuit with the ECU and instrument panel indicator lights. The switch is open when pressure differential is normal. The switch will ground (through the vehicle body) if a pressure differential problem is detected. Once grounded, the switch signals the ECU to illuminate the indicator lights.

Fluid Level Switch

A fluid level switch is located in the master cylinder reservoir. The switch activates the red indicator light if the fluid level falls below the required level. The yellow light also comes on if the vehicle speed is above approximately 2.5 mph.

Electronic Control Unit

A separate electronic control unit (ECU) is used to monitor and control the entire anti-lock system. The ECU is attached to a bracket located under the rear seat. The power up voltage source for the ECU is through the ignition switch in the ON or RUN position.

The anti-lock ECU is separate from the other vehicle electronic systems. It contains a self-diagnostic program which triggers the indicator lights when a system fault is detected. Faults are stored in a diagnostic program memory. Faults remain in memory until cleared. However, if the battery is disconnected, stored faults are erased.

The ECU is also equipped with a mercury switch. The switch monitors the degree of vehicle deceleration to determine what type of surface the vehicle is on. The switch provides input to the ECU for improved operation in the 4WD mode on low traction (slippery) road surfaces.

NOTE: Proper mounting angle of the ECU is critical to correct and accurate operation of the mercury switch.

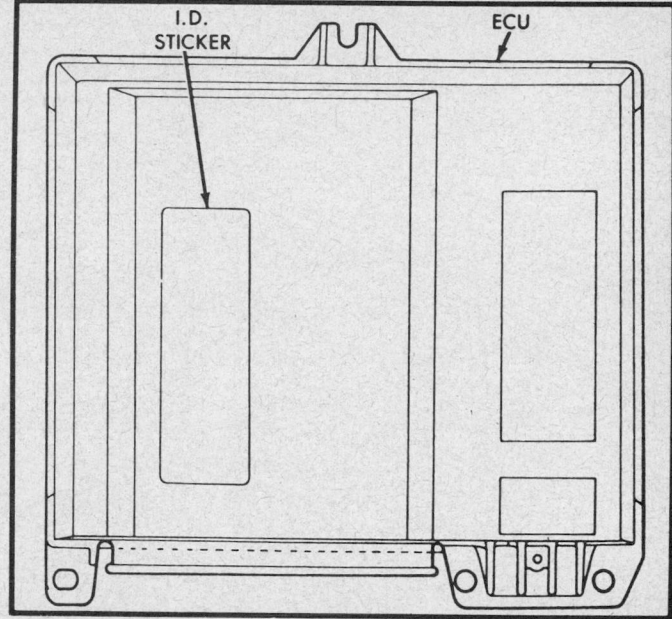

Anti-lock electronic control unit

System Relays

There are 3 system relays. The yellow indicator light and modulator power relays are located on the driver side inner fender panel. The relay wires are in the engine compartment wire harness.

The pump/motor relay is part of the pump motor harness and is located at the passenger side of the engine compartment.

The modulator power relay is connected to the pressure modulator solenoids and the ECU. When the system is powered up, the ECU supplies the operating voltage (12 volts) to the solenoids through the relay.

The indicator light relay is connected to the modulator solenoid relay and the indicator light. The relay turns the yellow light on when the modulator power relay is off. The yellow light is turned off when the modulator power relay is energized.

The pump motor relay starts/stops the pump motor when signaled by the pump switch.

Ignition Switch

The anti-lock ECU and indicator lights are in the standby mode with the ignition switch in the **OFF** or **ACCESSORY** position. No operating voltage is supplied.

In the **ON** and **RUN** positions, the switch supplies the ECU, pump motor and indicator lights with a 12 volt power supply.

In the **START** position, only the indicator lights are supplied with operating voltage. The remaining system components are in the standby mode.

System Indicator Lights

Two indicator lights are used with the anti-lock system. One light is red and the other yellow. Both are in the instrument cluster. The lights are in circuit with the self diagnostic program in the ECU and signal both normal operation and system faults.

The yellow light indicates anti-lock system condition. It is in circuit with the modulator solenoids and relay. The light illuminates at start-up and goes out when the self-diagnostic program determines system operation is normal.

If a fault occurs, the yellow light remains on until the fault is either corrected, the battery is disconnected, or the ignition switch is cycled (turned **OFF** and then **ON**). Cycling the ignition switch may not turn the light off after some faults.

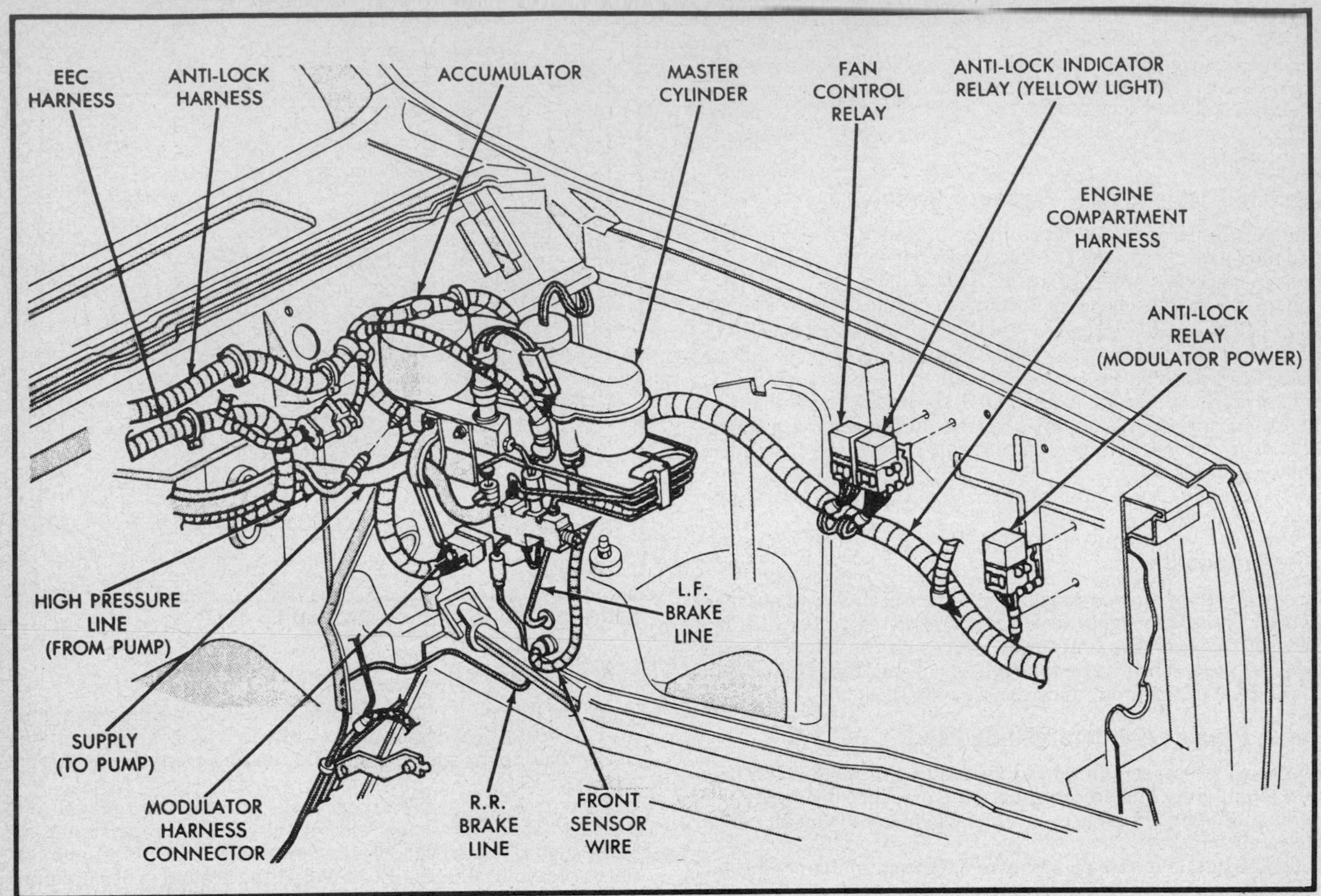

EEC
HARNESS — ANTI-LOCK
HARNESS — ACCUMULATOR — MASTER
CYLINDER — FAN
CONTROL
RELAY — ANTI-LOCK INDICATOR
RELAY (YELLOW LIGHT)

ENGINE
COMPARTMENT
HARNESS

ANTI-LOCK
RELAY
(MODULATOR POWER)

HIGH PRESSURE
LINE
(FROM PUMP)

L.F.
BRAKE
LINE

SUPPLY
(TO PUMP)

MODULATOR
HARNESS
CONNECTOR — R.R.
BRAKE
LINE — FRONT
SENSOR
WIRE

Anti-lock modulator/indicator light relays and harness location

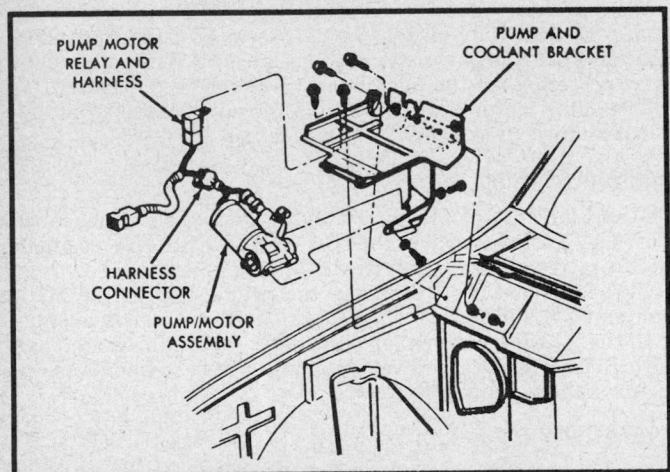

PUMP MOTOR
RELAY AND
HARNESS

PUMP AND
COOLANT BRACKET

HARNESS
CONNECTOR

PUMP/MOTOR
ASSEMBLY

Pump motor relay and harness

The yellow light illuminates in tandem with the red warning light to indicate certain types of faults. The pressure modulator solenoids are in circuit with the yellow indicator light. When the yellow light is on (system fault occurred), the solenoids are disabled.

The red light serves as the system warning light (low fluid, parking brake on, system pressure differential, etc.). The light illuminates in tandem with the yellow anti-lock light when certain system faults occur.

There are time delays built into indicator light illumination. These delays are provided as a means of identifying some system faults.

Proportioning Valve

The combination front/rear brake pressure switch and proportioning valve is connected between the master cylinder and modulator. The switch and valve operate normally in the standard braking mode. In the anti-lock mode, the proportioning valve is isolated to enable brake pressure modulation during anti-lock system operation. The pressure differential switch is only activated by a difference in pressure between the front and rear (primary and secondary) brake circuits.

Parking Brake Switch

The switch is connected to the ECU low fluid circuit. When the switch is activated, the red indicator light illuminates. If vehicle speed is above approximately 2.5 mph, the yellow light will also illuminate.

SYSTEM OPERATION

Component Connections

The booster pump and accumulator provide the fluid pressure needed for power assist. The accumulator is connected to the pump by a high pressure feed line. A second high pressure line connects the accumulator to the booster section of the master cylinder. A low pressure supply line connects the reservoir to the booster pump.

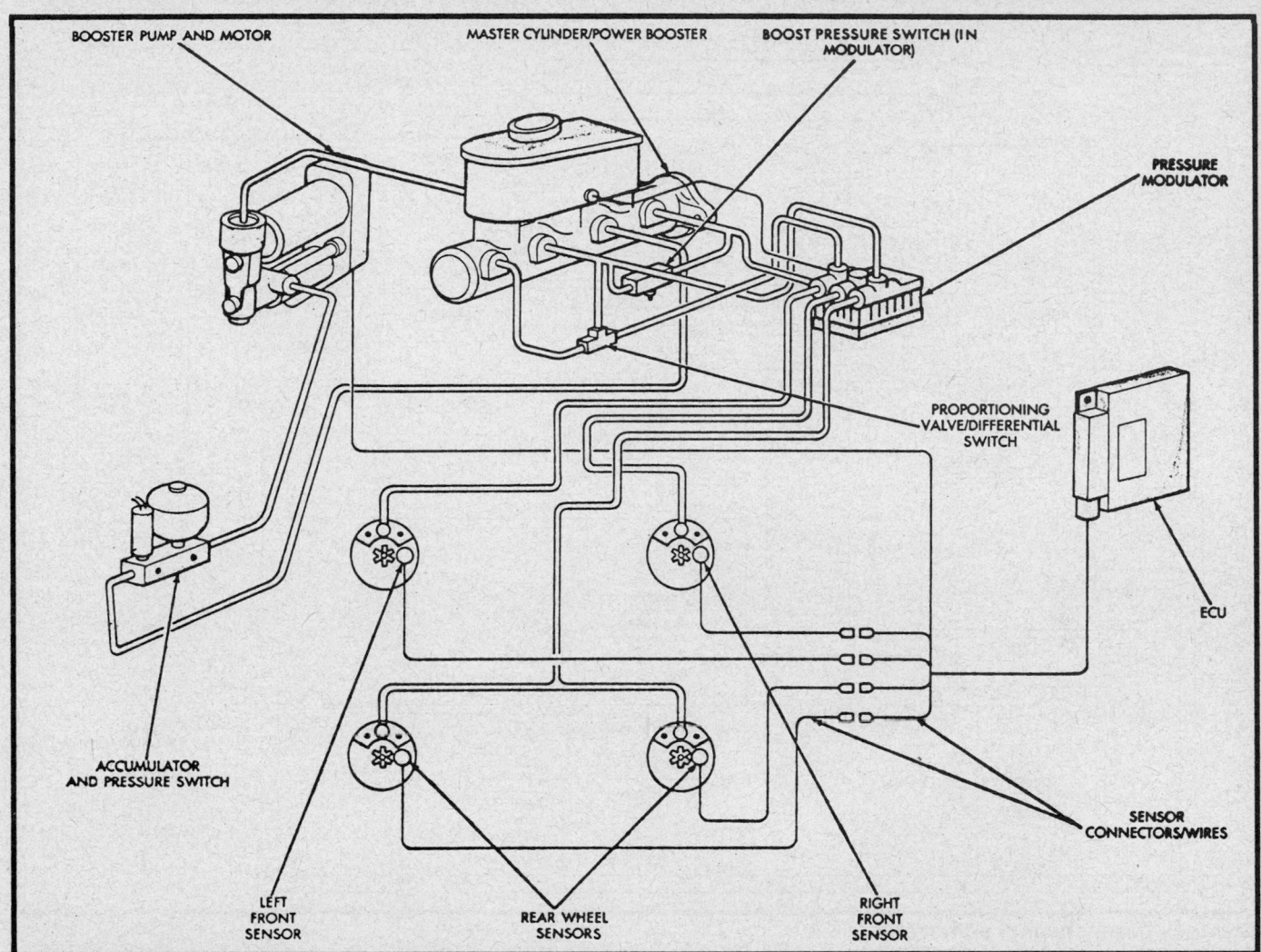

BOOSTER PUMP AND MOTOR   MASTER CYLINDER/POWER BOOSTER   BOOST PRESSURE SWITCH (IN MODULATOR)

PRESSURE MODULATOR

PROPORTIONING VALVE/DIFFERENTIAL SWITCH

ECU

ACCUMULATOR AND PRESSURE SWITCH

SENSOR CONNECTORS/WIRES

LEFT FRONT SENSOR   REAR WHEEL SENSORS   RIGHT FRONT SENSOR

Anti-lock component layout and connectors

Fluid from the master cylinder is channeled to the calipers and wheel cylinders through the pressure modulator. The 3 solenoid valves (isolation–decay–build) in each modulator control channel are contained within the modulator body.

The wheel sensors are connected directly to the ECU. The sensor triggering devices (tone wheels), are mounted on the axle shafts.

System Power Up

The anti-lock system is in standby mode with the ignition switch in **OFF** or **ACCESSORY** position. When the switch is moved to the **START** position, voltage through the switch activates the indicator lights only. The ECU and other system components are still the standby mode.

The indicator lights illuminate as part of the self test feature and remain on until the switch is in the **RUN** position.

In the **ON** and **RUN** position, 12 volts are supplied through the ignition switch to power up the ECU and system components.

When the vehicle is motionless (no wheel speed inputs) and the ignition switch is in the **ON** or **RUN** position, the modulator solenoids are activated and briefly exercised. This serves two purposes: It checks solenoid function as part of the self diagnostic feature and ensures proper solenoid operation after periods of inactivity.

Boost Pressure and Fluid Supply

The system main fluid supply is contained in the master cylinder reservoir and the accumulator. Additional fluid is also contained in the booster pump accumulator. The pump and main accumulator provide the reserve fluid pressure needed for power brake assist.

Fluid stored in the accumulator is at normal working pressure of 1650–2050 psi. The accumulator contains enough pressurized fluid for 25–30 power assisted brake applications if a pump fault should occur.

Pump motor operation is controlled by the pump relay and by a pressure switch within the pump/motor assembly. The pump operates only when the ignition switch is in the **ON** or **RUN** position.

The pump does not run continuously. It cycles on/off with the pump pressure switch. The pump is capable of running with or without connection to the ECU. Pressurized fluid from the pump is transmitted to the accumulator and power booster unit.

The booster pump motor is equipped with thermal protection. If the motor approaches an overheat condition, a thermal fuse inside the pump will blow and shut off the motor. The fuse is not a reset-type and is not serviceable.

Sensor Inputs and Pressure Modulation

The wheel sensors and tone wheels supply wheel speed inputs to

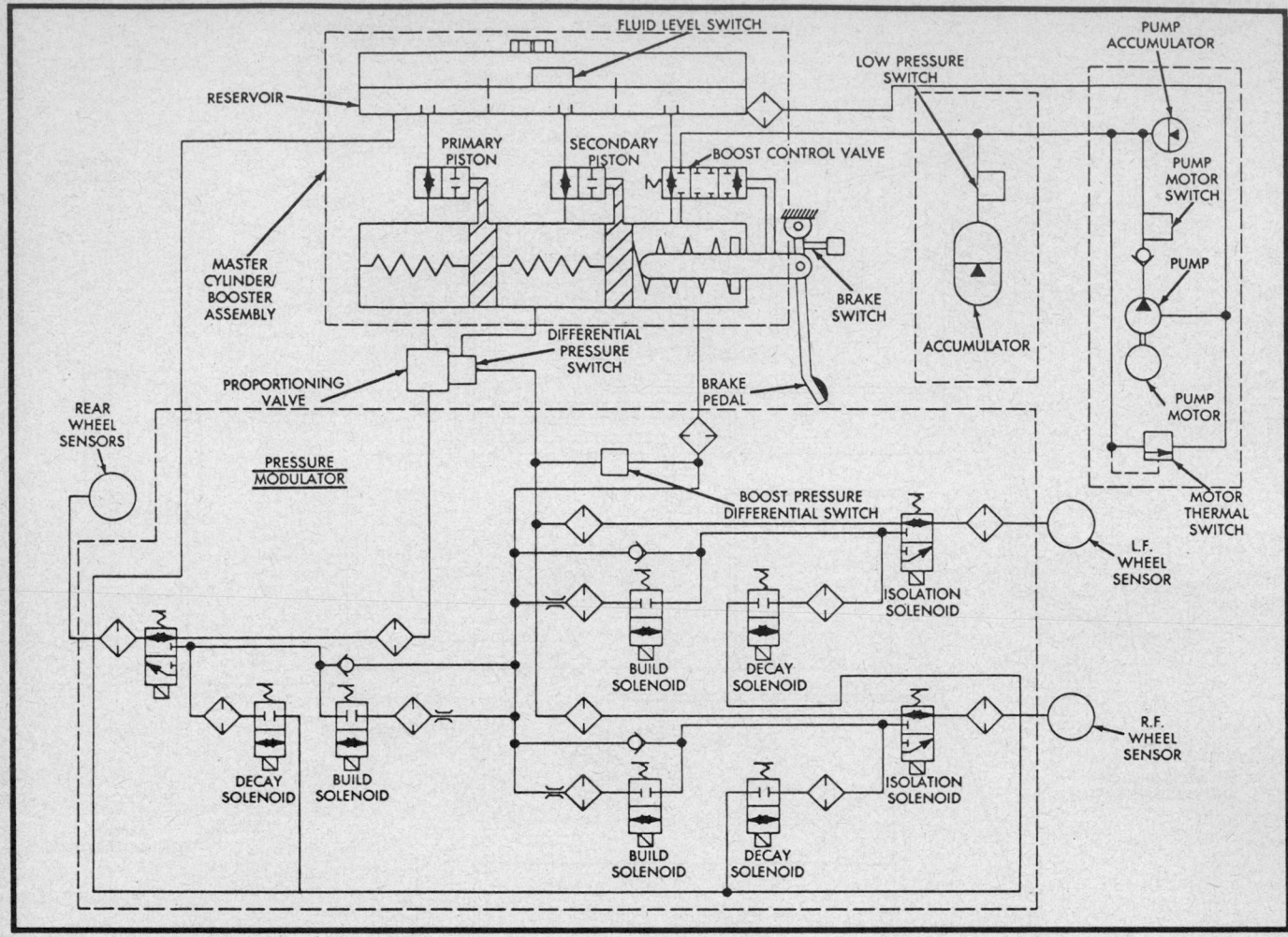

Anti-lock three channel schematic

the ECU whenever the vehicle is in motion.

The ECU determines the degree of deceleration and wheel slip and provides optimum brake pressures for each control channel based on this data. The 70 Series (Cherokee/Wagoneer) anti-lock system provides 3 channel control. The front wheels are controlled individually. The rear wheels are controlled in tandem.

The ECU activates the pressure modulator solenoids which either build (increase), decay (decrease) or hold (maintain) fluid pressure as dictated by the ECU. The isolation solenoids isolate normal fluid pressure from the master cylinder to the rear wheels or to the left or right front wheel as needed. Wheel brake isolation occurs prior to build/decay solenoid operation.

Solenoid operation is not entirely constant in the anti-lock mode. Operation occurs in brief, rapid cycles front-to-rear and side-to-side. Rapid changes in input data will produce equally rapid changes in pressure modulation. The isolation, decay, and build functions are capable of function changes and cycle times measured in milliseconds.

SERVICE DIAGNOSIS

Wheel/Tire Size and Input Signals

Anti-lock system operation is dependent on signals from the wheel sensors. The vehicle wheels and tires must all be the same size and type in order to generate accurate signals. Variations in wheel/tire size will produce inaccurate input signals resulting in incorrect pressure modulation.

Operational Sound Levels

The booster pump and/or relay may produce a clicking sound as they cycle on and off. In addition, the booster pump and motor and the pressure modulator solenoids may generate a buzzing-type sound when operating. The sound is due to normal pump motor and system operation and is not indicative of a system fault. Under most conditions, the sound should not be audible.

Vehicle Response in Anti-lock Mode

During anti-lock braking, the pressure modulator solenoids cycle rapidly in response to ECU inputs.

As the solenoids in each channel isolate, build and decay pressure as needed, the driver may experience a slight pulsing sensation within the vehicle. A firmer brake pedal and some brake pedal pulsation may also be noted during anti-lock mode braking.

The pulsing sensation occurs as the individual brake units apply/release during anti-lock mode braking. Pulsing is a result of normal front-to-rear and side-to-side pressure modulation.

Indicator Light Operation

The red warning light and the yellow anti-lock indicator light both go on at start-up and go off when the engine is running.

The one or two second illumination is part of a system self-test feature and indicates normal operation. System faults are indicated when one or both of the lights illuminate after initial start-up system check.

Driver Induced System Faults

Some driving or operational situations can induce faults in an anti-lock system that is actually operating correctly.

Induced faults are not true faults; a component malfunction as not actually occurred. Instead, they are a result of driver actions recognized by the diagnostic program as improper operation.

Improper parking brake use can induce faults in the self-diagnostic program. If a driver attempts to move the vehicle with the parking brakes applied, a system fault will register. Or, if the parking brake is applied while the vehicle is in motion, a system fault will also register. One or both indicator lights will illuminate in either situation. The red light illuminates for parking brake faults. The yellow light illuminates if a fault is sensed.

Faults can be induced in the system through excessive wheel spin. Wheel spin due to low traction surfaces or high speed acceleration can induce a fault in a system that is operating normally. In addition, if system pressure is not restored after a repair, a fault will register when the vehicle is driven.

Pumping or riding the brake pedal may also induce a fault causing the indicator light to go on.

Steering Response

A modest amount of steering input is required during extremely high deceleration braking, or when braking on differing traction surfaces. An example of differing traction surfaces would be when the left side wheels are on ice and the right side wheels are on dry pavement.

Loss of Sensor Input

Sensor malfunctions will most likely be due to loose connections, damaged sensor wires, or incorrect sensor-to-tone wheel air gap adjustment. Additional causes of sensor faults would be sensor and tone wheel misalignment or a damaged tone wheel.

System Diagnosis Procedures

Anti-lock system diagnosis involves three basic procedures. The first requires observation of indicator light display sequence. The second is a visual examination of system components for low fluid levels, leak points, or visible damage. The third involves using the manufacturer's diagnostic tester to check operation and locate a malfunctioning circuit.

The two indicator lights will illuminate separately, simultaneously, or with varying delays depending on the fault. The lights signal low fluid levels, pressure drops and other hydro-electrical faults. The service diagnosis charts for indicator light display can be used when a fault is detected.

COMPONENT SERVICEABILITY

The master cylinder/power booster unit, pressure modulator, accumulator, pump/motor and proportioning valve are not repairable components. If diagnosis indicates a malfunction has occurred, these components are to be replaced as a complete assembly.

The fluid level switch in the master cylinder and the boost pressure switch in the modulator are also not serviceable. The switches cannot be removed from their respective components.

The electrical harnesses, pump bracket, pump high pressure and supply hose, system relays and wheel sensors can be serviced individually.

The tone wheels are permanently attached to the axle shafts and are not replaceable. If a tone wheel becomes damaged, it will be necessary to replace the tone wheel and axle shaft as an assembly.

The wheel brake components such as calipers, brakeshoes, wheel cylinders, rotors and drums are all serviced the same as standard brake system components.

Wheel Sensors

The wheel sensors have a polyethylene spacer strip attached to the sensor contact face. When installing a sensor, be very sure this spacer strip actually touches the tone wheel. The strips are made in the exact thickness needed for correct sensor-to-tone wheel spacing (air gap). If the spacing (air gap) is too great, the sensors will not transmit accurate speed signals to the ECU. If the spacer strip is missing from an original, or not provided on a replacement sensor, the correct sensor-to-tone wheel air gap will have to be established with a brass feeler gauge. A brass feeler gauge must be used to avoid disrupting sensor polarity

If the spacer strip is missing from a reuseable sensor, set the sensor-to-tone wheel air gap as follows:
Set front sensor air gap to 0.013−0.019 in.
Set rear sensor air gap to 0.030−0.036 in.

Removal and Installation
FRONT WHEEL SENSOR

1. Raise and safely support vehicle and turn wheel outward for easier access to sensor.
2. Note the sensor wire routing for installation reference. Cut the tie straps holding wire to steering knuckle and brake line.
3. If sensor is covered with heavy accumulations of dirt or mud, clean the sensor and surrounding area before proceeding. This is necessary to avoid possible damage when removing the sensor.
4. Remove the sensor attaching screw and remove the sensor from the steering knuckle.
5. Unseat the grommet holding the sensor wire in the wheel house panel.
6. In the engine compartment, disconnect the sensor wire connector at the anti-lock harness plug. Remove sensor and wire.
7. Before installing a new or reinstalling an original front wheel sensor, note the condition of the spacer strip. If the strip is securely attached and in good condition, a spacing (air gap) adjustment will not be needed. However, if the strip is loose or damaged, the correct air gap will have to be established with a brass feeler gauge.
8. To install a new sensor, route the wire through the wheelhouse grommet hole and connect the sensor to the harness plug. Seat the grommet.
9. Position the sensor on the steering knuckle and install the bolt finger-tight.
10. If the sensor strip was in good condition and securely attached, lightly press the sensor against the tone wheel and tighten the bolt to 11 ft. lbs.
11. If the sensor spacer strip is missing, loose or damaged and the sensor contacts are exposed, perform the following steps:
   a. Remove the spacer strip if completely loose or torn. Wipe sensor contacts clean with a shop towel.
   b. Set sensor-to-tone wheel air gap to 0.013−0.019 in. with a brass feeler gauge.
   c. Tighten the sensor bolt to 11 ft. lbs. and recheck spacing.
12. Secure the sensor wire to the brake line and steering knuckle with new tie straps.

REAR WHEEL SENSOR REMOVAL

1. Raise and fold the rear seat forward for access to the rear sensor connectors. They are located near the ECU. Separate both sensor connections.
2. Push the sensor grommets and sensor wires through the floorpan.

SERVICE DIAGNOSIS

SYSTEM FAULT	POSSIBLE CAUSE	INDICATOR LIGHT DISPLAY
LOW FLUID	SYSTEM LEAK. ACCUMULATOR CHARGE LOW OR LOST.	RED LIGHT ON. YELLOW LIGHT ON WITHIN 1/2 SECOND WHEN VEHICLE SPEED EXCEEDS 2.5 MPH.
PARKING BRAKES APPLIED	PARKING BRAKES NOT RELEASED BEFORE DRIVING VEHICLE.	RED LIGHT ON. YELLOW LIGHT ON IF VEHICLE SPEED EXCEEDS 2.5 MPH.
PRESSURE DROP AT ACCUMULATOR	ACCUMLATOR GAS CHARGE LOST. SYSTEM LEAK. PUMP/MOTOR MALFUNCTION. PROLONGED STOP ON ICY SURFACE WITH TRANSMISSION IN GEAR.	YELLOW LIGHT ON. RED LIGHT WILL ALSO COME ON WITHIN 20 SECONDS.
DIFFERENTIAL PRESSURE SWITCH (IN PROPORTIONING VALVE) ACTUATED	SYSTEM LEAK. MASTER CYLINDER MALFUNCTION (SECONDARY PISTON). AIR IN SYSTEM.	RED LIGHT ON. YELLOW LIGHT COMES ON AT VEHICLE SPEED OF 3 MPH.
PRESSURE DROP AT BOOST PRESSURE SWITCH AND PRESSURE DIFFERENTIAL SWITCH	MASTER CYLINDER MALFUNCTION (PRIMARY PISTON). SYSTEM LEAK. AIR IN SYSTEM.	RED LIGHT ON. YELLOW LIGHT COMES ON AT VEHICLE SPEED OF 3 MPH.
WHEEL SENSOR FAULT (FRONT ONLY)	SENSOR-TO-TONE WHEEL SPACING INCORRECT (SPACE TOO LARGE). DAMAGED SENSOR WIRE, SENSOR, OR TONE WHEEL. SENSOR AND TONE WHEEL MISALIGNED. SENSOR DISCONNECTED.	YELLOW LIGHT ON. (AFTER 15 MPH)
WHEEL SENSOR FAULT (FRONT OR REAR ONE OR TWO MISSING SIGNALS)	DAMAGED SENSOR, WIRE, OR CONNECTOR. SENSOR DISCONNECTED. EXCESSIVE WHEEL SPIN. MISALIGNED OR DAMAGED TONE WHEEL. OPEN SENSOR OR WIRE.	YELLOW LIGHT ON AT 15 MPH IF FAULT OCCURRED <u>BEFORE</u> VEHICLE DRIVE-OFF. OR, ORANGE LIGHT ON AT 8 MPH IF FAULT OCCURRED <u>AFTER</u> VEHICLE DRIVE-OFF.
EXCESSIVE DECAY SOLENOID OPERATION	MODULATOR/SOLENOID FAULT. WHEEL SENSOR FAULT. EXTREMELY LOW AMBIENT TEMPERATURES. VEHICLE ON ICE COVERED SURFACE. TIRES HYDROPLANING ON WATER COVERED ROAD SURFACE.	YELLOW LIGHT ON WITHIN 1-2 SECONDS.
PRESSURE MODULATOR SOLENOID FAULT	SOLENOID SHORTED OR OPEN. DECAY AND BUILD SOLENOID ON AT SAME TIME. OPEN/SHORT IN MODULATOR HARNESS.	YELLOW LIGHT ON.
PUMP/MOTOR RUN-ON	EXCESSIVE RUN TIME. RELAY SHORTED, MOTOR SWITCH SHORTED.	RED LIGHT ON IF PUMP RUNS MORE THAN 4 MINUTES WITH NO BRAKE.
PUMP/MOTOR INOPERATIVE	PUMP RELAY FAULT. NO VOLTAGE TO MOTOR. DAMAGED PUMP OR MOTOR. PUMP GAS CHARGE LOST.	YELLOW LIGHT ON. RED LIGHT ON AFTER 20 SECONDS.
LOW VOLTAGE	SYSTEM VOLTAGE BELOW 9V. SHORT, OPEN IN FEED WIRES OR RELAY. FUSE BAD. POOR GROUND. LOOSE, DISCONNECTED WIRE IN SYSTEM. BATTERY LOW OR DISCHARGED	YELLOW LIGHT ON.
NO BRAKE SIGNAL	SYSTEM LEAK. MASTER CYLINDER MALFUNCTION. PUMP/MOTOR MALFUNCTION. ACCUMULATOR OR MODULATOR FAULT.	RED LIGHT ON DURING BRAKING.
RELAY FAULT	RELAY SHORTED OR OPEN.	YELLOW LIGHT ON.
ECU SELF DIAGNOSTIC FEATURE INOPERATIVE (SOLENOIDS NOT TEST-EXERCISED AT START-UP)	IGNITION SWITCH IN OFF POSITION. PARKING BRAKES ON (NOT RELEASED AT DRIVE-OFF). SYSTEM COMPONENT HAS MALFUNCTIONED. LOW FLUID LEVEL/LEAK IN SYSTEM.	YELLOW LIGHT ON.

Jeep Anti-lock diagnosis chart

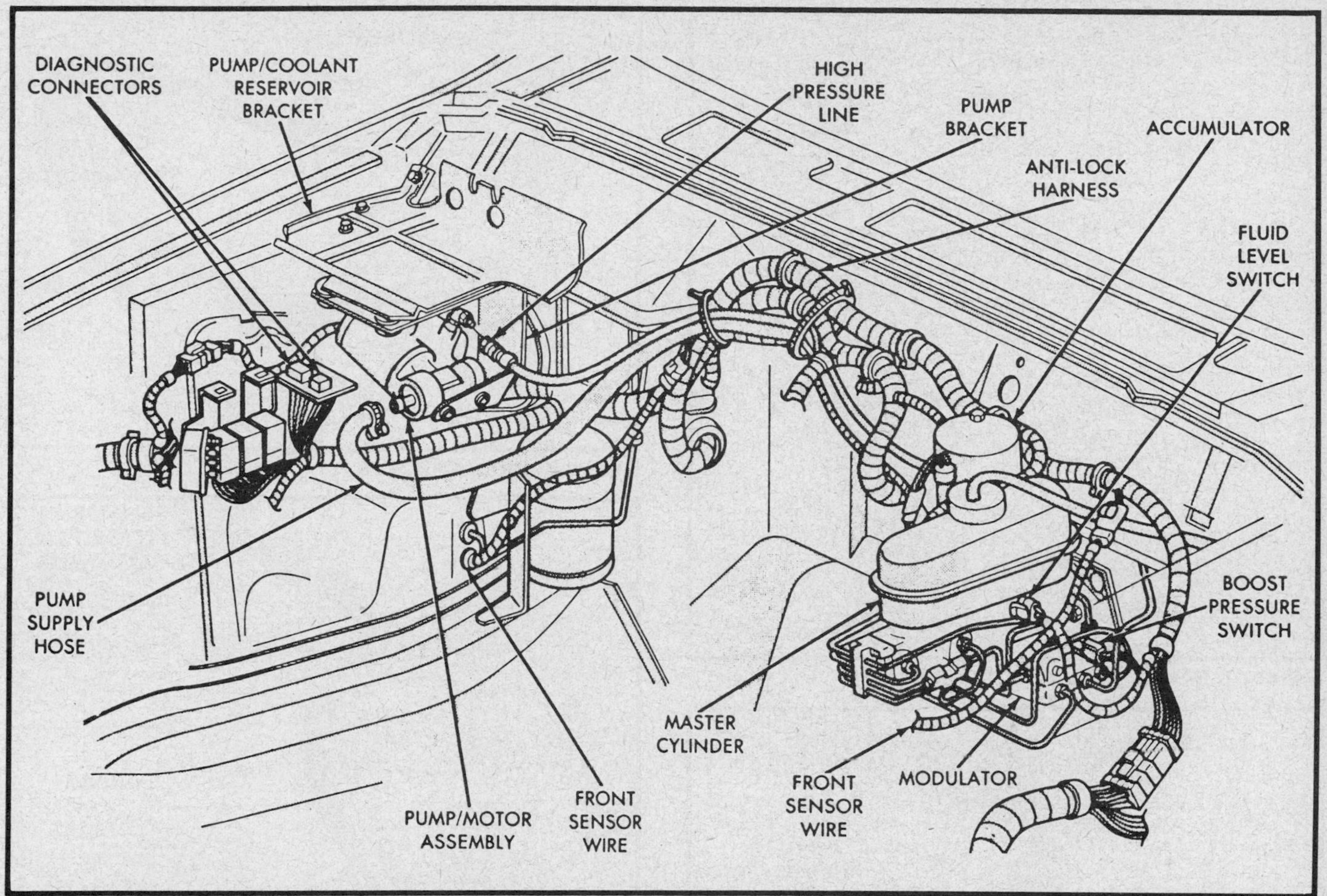

DIAGNOSTIC CONNECTORS

PUMP/COOLANT RESERVOIR BRACKET

HIGH PRESSURE LINE

PUMP BRACKET

ANTI-LOCK HARNESS

ACCUMULATOR

FLUID LEVEL SWITCH

PUMP SUPPLY HOSE

BOOST PRESSURE SWITCH

MASTER CYLINDER

FRONT SENSOR WIRE

MODULATOR

PUMP/MOTOR ASSEMBLY

FRONT SENSOR WIRE

System components and location

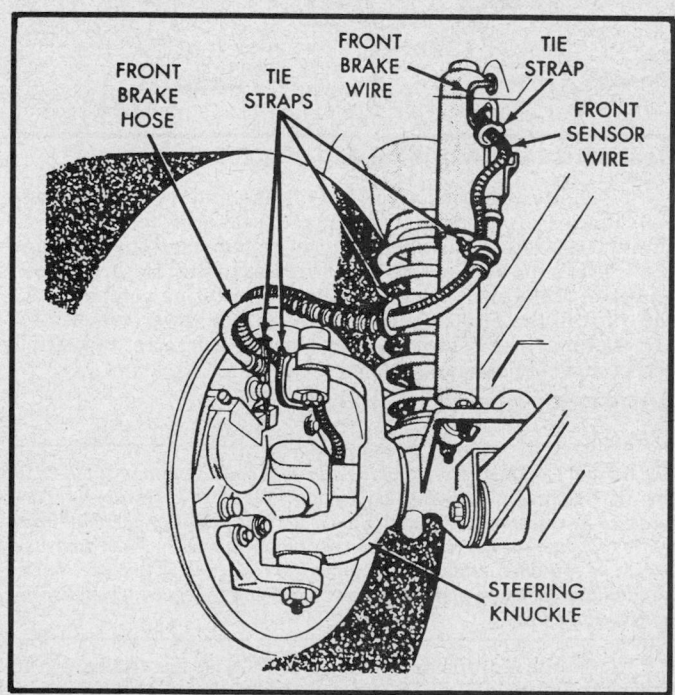

FRONT BRAKE HOSE

TIE STRAPS

FRONT BRAKE WIRE

TIE STRAP

FRONT SENSOR WIRE

STEERING KNUCKLE

Front sensor wire routing

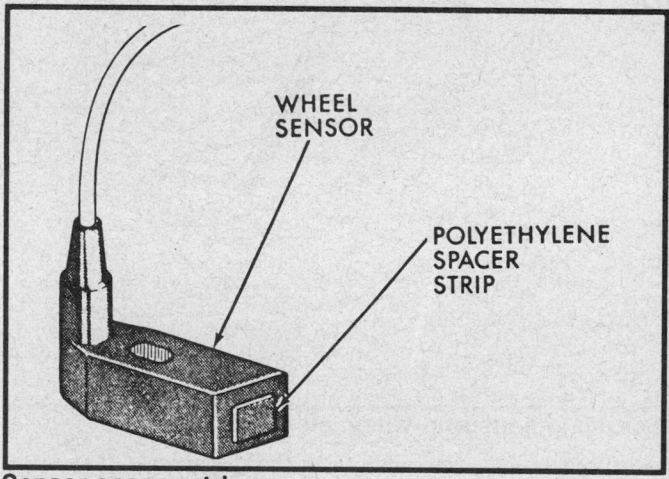

WHEEL SENSOR

POLYETHYLENE SPACER STRIP

Sensor spacer strip

3. Raise and safely support the vehicle and remove the wheel and brake drum.

4. Cut and remove the tie straps securing the sensor wires to the axle and rear brake hose.

5. Unseat the sensor backing plate grommet, remove the sensor attach bolt and remove the sensor by pulling the wire through the grommet hole in the backing plate.

6. Before installing a new or reinstalling an original rear

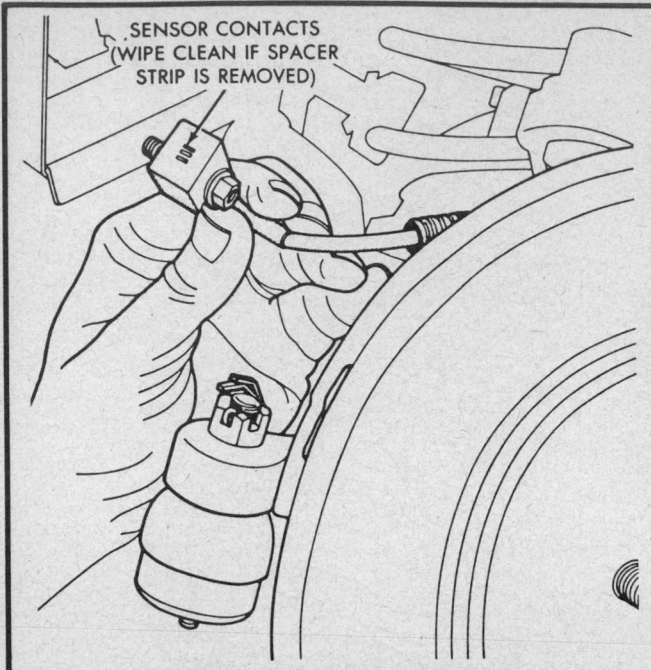

Sensor contacts (spacer strip removed)

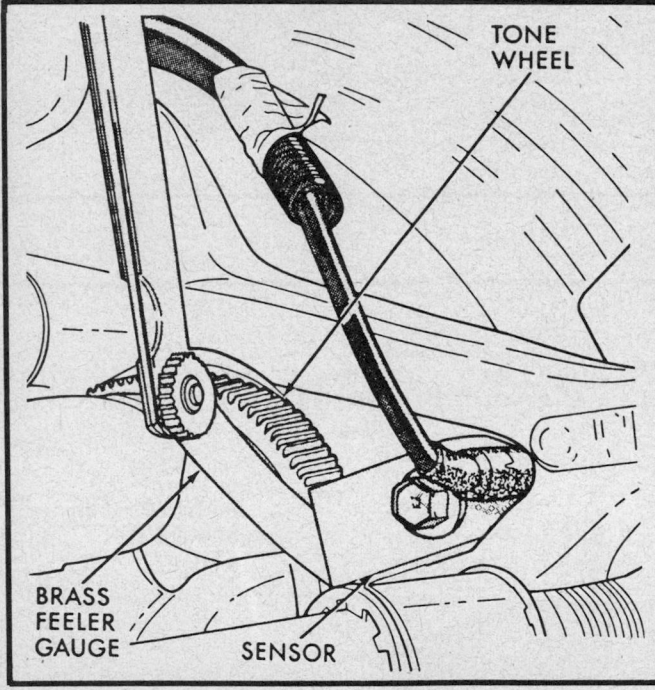

Adjusting sensor-to-wheel air gap

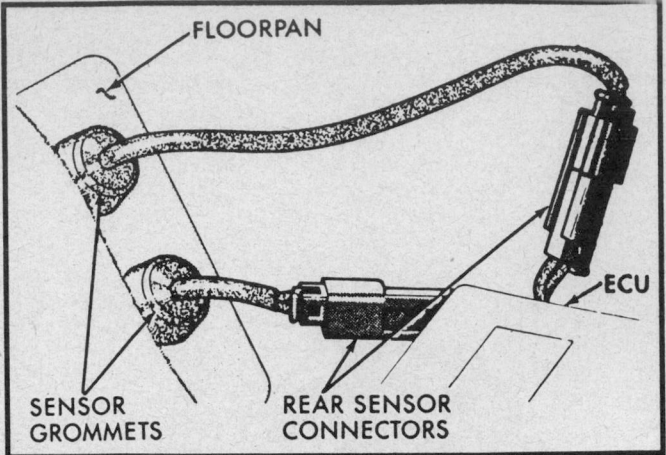

Rear sensor connectors

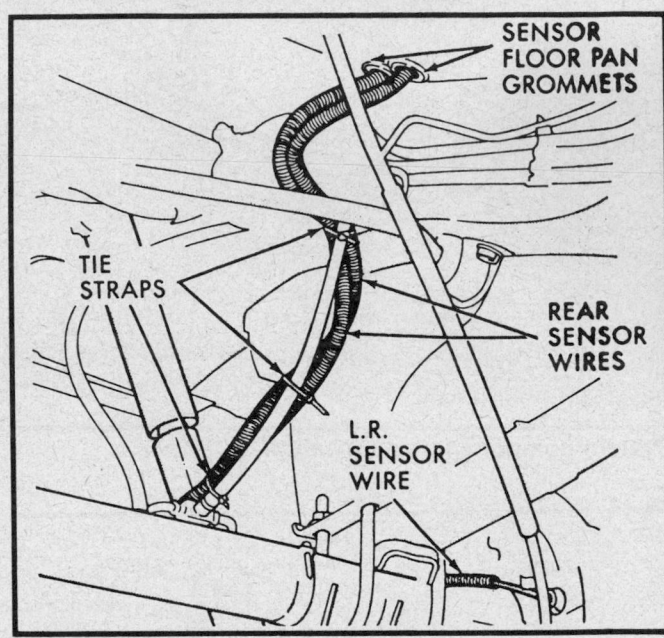

Rear sensor wire routing and attachment

wheel sensor, note the condition of the spacer strip. If the strip is securely attached and in good condition, a spacing (air gap) adjustment will not be needed. However, if the strip is loose or damaged, the correct air gap will have to be established with a brass feeler gauge.

7. If the sensor spacer strip is missing, loose or damaged and the sensor contacts are exposed, perform the following steps:

    a. Remove the spacer strip if completely loose or torn. Wipe sensor contacts clean with a shop towel.

    b. Set sensor-to-tone wheel air gap to 0.030 – 0.036 in. with a brass feeler gauge.

    c. Tighten the sensor bolt to 11 ft. lbs. and recheck spacing.

8. Route the sensor wires to the rear seat area, feed the wires through the access holes and seat the grommets in the floorpan.

9. Secure the sensor wire with wire ties to the rear brake hose and axle. Make sure the wire is clear or rotating components.

10. Install the brake drum and wheel then lower vehicle.

11. Connect the sensors to the harness connects, reposition carpet and fold down rear seat.

BOOSTER PUMP AND MOTOR

——————— CAUTION ———————

The normal working pressure of the anti-lock boost system is 1650–2050 psi. System pressure must be pumped down before any pressure lines are loosened or disconnected. Failure to do so could result in personal injury. To reduce system pressure, turn the ignition key OFF. Then apply the brakes 45–50 times (until pedal is firm) to reduce fluid pressure in the accumulator, booster, pump and lines. Wear safety goggles when disconnecting fluid lines.

1. Turn the ignition switch to the **OFF** position and apply the brakes (pump pedal) 45–50 times (until pedal is firm on initial apply) to reduce system fluid pressure.

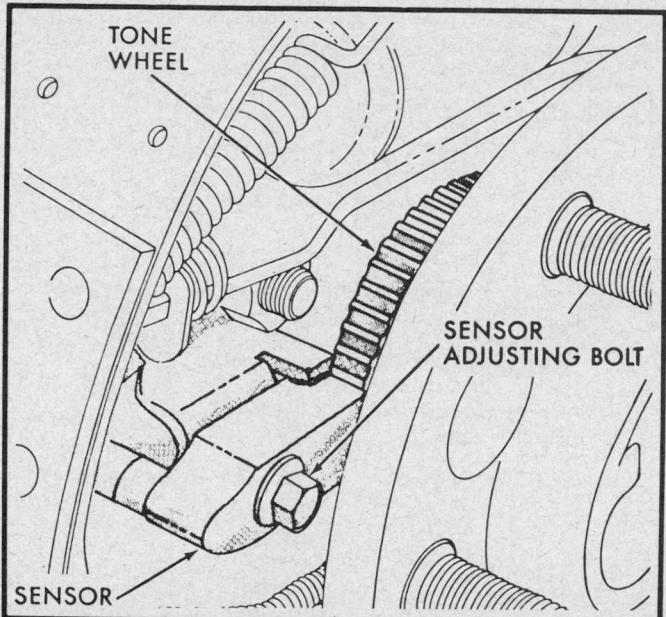

Rear sensor installation

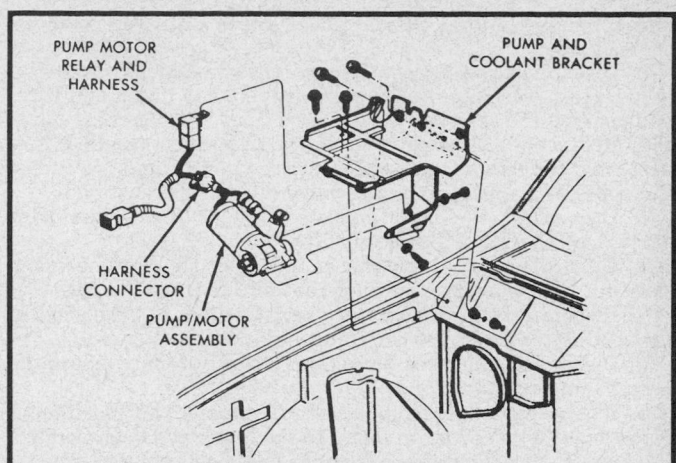

Pump motor harness and relay

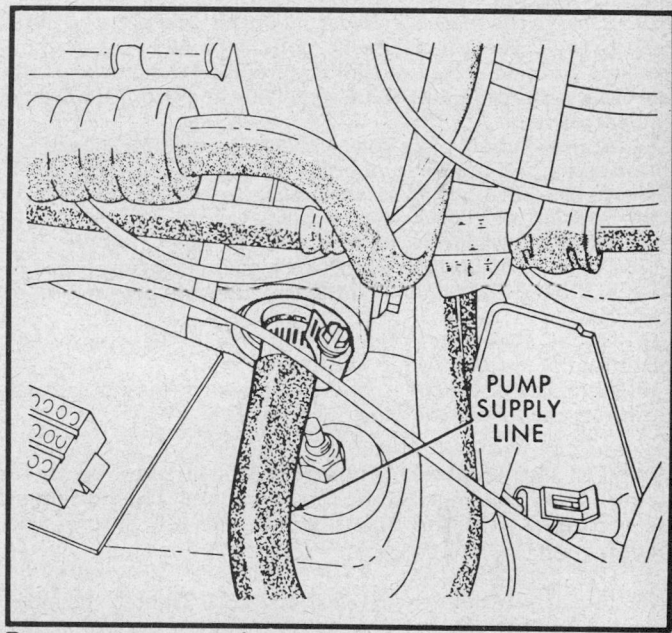

Pump pressure and supply line connections

NOTE: When the reserve pressure is depleted, the reservoir fluid level will rise above the MAX fill mark but will not overflow unless the reservoir was overfilled to begin with.

2. Disconnect the battery negative cable.

3. Remove the coolant pressure bottle retaining strap and move the reservoir aside. It is not necessary to disconnect the bottle hoses, just move the bottle aside for working clearance.

4. Remove the bolts holding the two-piece mounting bracket to the dash and inner fender panels. Rotate the bracket and pump/motor assembly to one side for access to the wires and hoses. Disconnect the pump motor harness from the engine harness.

5. Slowly loosen the pump pressure line at the pump and allow any residual fluid pressure to bleed off, then disconnect the line from the pump.

5. Put a drain container under the pump return line, loosen the return line hose clamp and remove the line from the pump. Discard any drained fluid.

6. Remove the pump/motor and bracket as an assembly.

7. Remove the relay from the bracket and separate the components.

8. When installing, position the pump/motor assembly on the bracket and install the assembly attaching screws along with the relay.

9. Connect the pressure and return lines to the pump as well as the motor harness.

10. Position the mounting bracket on the dash panel and install the attaching bolts and screws. Check the line routing, making sure the lines are not kinked or touching the engine.

11. Clean the master cylinder exterior and cap. Fill the reservior to the top of the V-shaped MAX indicator mark with DOT 3 rated brake fluid.

Note: Do not overfill the reservoir. Overfilling will cause overflow and could damage the reservoir. Add fluid to the V-shaped MAX indicator only.

12. Connect the battery and turn the ignition to **ON** to start the pump running. While the pump is running, listen for an rpm drop which indicates the pump is pressurizing. If the pump rpm does not drop after 20 seconds, immediately turn the ignition **OFF** and check the pump hydraulic connections.

NOTE: Do not allow the pump to run if it does not pressurize. If the pump rpm does not drop after 20 seconds run time, turn the ignition OFF immediately to avoid pump damage.

13. Add fluid to master cylinder reservoir if necessary.

MASTER CYLINDER

The master cylinder, modulator and accumulator are serviced as an assembly only. Do not attempt to disassemble or repair these components.

─────────── **CAUTION** ───────────

CAUTION: The normal working pressure of the anti-lock boost system is 1650–2050 psi. System pressure must be pumped down before any pressure lines are loosened or disconnected. Failure to do so could result in personal injury. To reduce system pressure, turn the ignition key OFF. Then apply the brakes 45–50 times (until pedal is firm) to reduce fluid pressure in the accumulator, booster, pump and lines. Wear safety goggles when disconnecting fluid lines.

1. Pump system pressure down by turning the ignition **OFF**

and applying the brake pedal 45–50 times until the pedal becomes firm.

2. Disconnect the battery. Remove the windshield washer fluid reservoir attaching screrws, disconnect the hoses and wires and remove the reservoir.

3. Remove the air cleaner assembly, disconnect the ECU harness wire connectors at the pressure modulator and disconnect the wires at the proportioning valve differential switch.

4. Disconnect the high pressure line at the accumulator block. Cap the line to keep out dirt.

5. Disconnect the supply line at the reservoir. Cap the line to keep out dirt. Discard any fluid that drains from the line.

6. Disconnect the low pressure switch wires, and the wires at the modulator boost pressure and fluid level switches.

7. Disconnect the front brakelines at the outboard side of the pressure modulator.

8. In the passenger compartment, remove the instrument panel lower trim cover for access to the brake pedal. Disconnect the brakelight switch wires, remove the master cylinder pushrod bolt and disconnect the pushrod from the pedal. Discard the pushrod bolt nuts as they are not reuseable.

9. Remove the master cylinder mounting bracket stud nuts.

10. In the engine compartment, pull the brake hydraulic components and mounting bracket forward until the bracket studs are clear of the dash. Lift the assembly up and out of the engine compartment.

11. At installation, place pad on the mounting bracket and position assembled bracket and brake components on dash panel. Be sure bracket studs are seated in dash panel holes.

12. Position master cylinder/modulator/accumulator assembly on dash panel. Tighten stud nuts to 27 ft. lbs.

13. Connect the harness wires to the modulator, low pressure switch, differential switch and the low fluid and boost pressure switches.

14. In the passenger compartment, install the nuts of the mounting studs and torque to 31 ft. lbs.

15. Align the brake pedal, brakelight switch, master cylinder push rod and install the pushrod bolt.

NOTE: The pushrod bolt must be installed correctly to avoid interference with the dash bracket. The bolt must be installed with the bolt head at the left side of the pedal.

16. Install new nuts on the push rod bolt. Tighten the inner lock nut to 25 ft. lbs. and the outer jam nut to only 75 in. lbs. Connect the brake light switch wires and install the lower trim panel.

17. In the engine compartment, connect the brake lines to the proportioning valve and connect the pressure and return lines to the accumulator.

18. Install the air cleaner assembly, connect the hoses and wires to the washer reservoir and install the reservoir to the fender panel.

19. Clean the master cylinder exterior and cap. Fill the reservior to the top of the V-shaped MAX indicator mark with DOT 3 rated brake fluid.

20. Connect the battery and turn the ignition to ON to start the pump running. While the pump is running, listen for an rpm drop which indicates the pump is pressurizing. If the pump rpm does not drop after 20 seconds, immediately turn the ignition OFF and check the pump hydraulic connections.

NOTE: Do not allow the pump to run if it does not pressurize. If the pump rpm does not drop after 20 seconds run time, turn the ignition OFF immediately to avoid pump damage.

21. Add fluid to master cylinder reservoir if necessary.
22. Bleed the brake system.

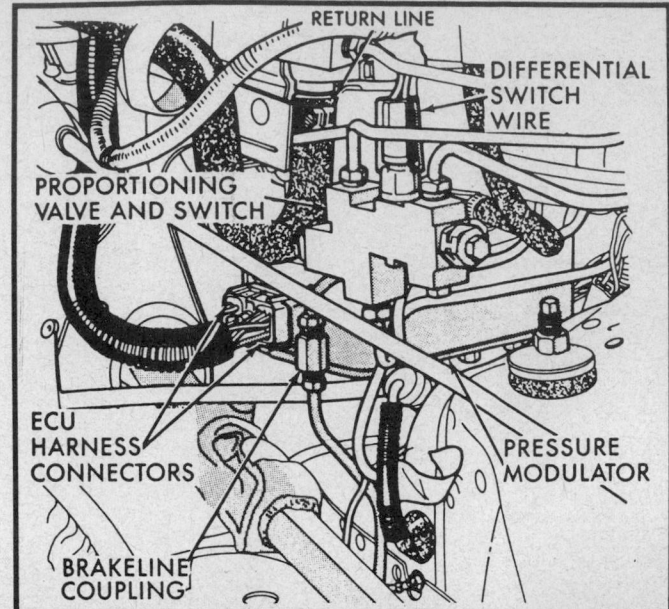

ECU harness and fluid connections

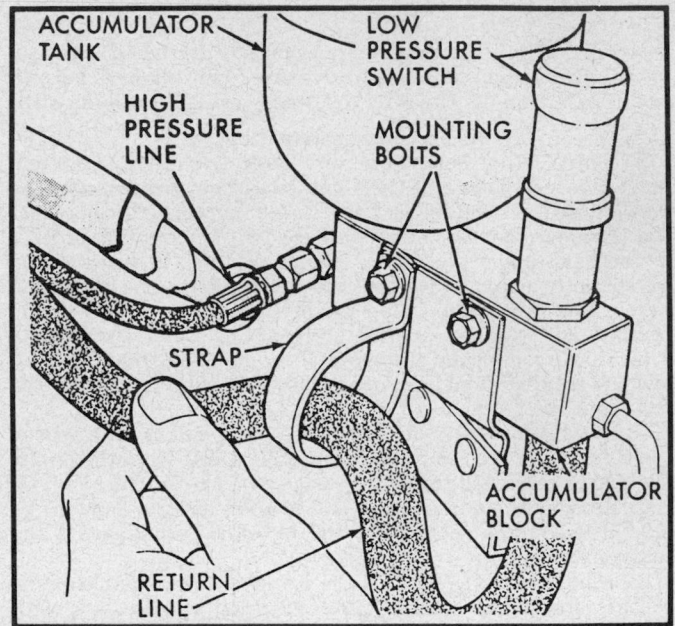

Fluid line connections

ECU

1. Make sure the ignition is **OFF**, then fold the rear seat cushion forward for access to the ECU.

2. Remove the screws attaching the ECU mounting bracket to the floorpan, remove the screws attaching the ECU to the mounting bracket, unplug the ECU and remove.

3. At installation, connect the harness of the replacement ECU.

4. Install the replacement ECU on the bracket and install the bracket to the floorpan.

5. Fold down rear seat.

SYSTEM BLEEDING

1. Fill reservoir to V-shaped maximum fill mark.

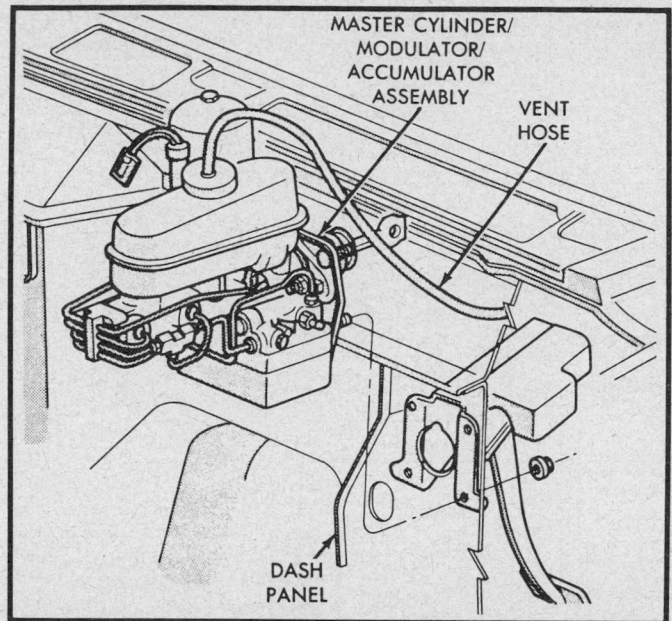

Removing/installing master cylinder, modulator and accumulator assembly

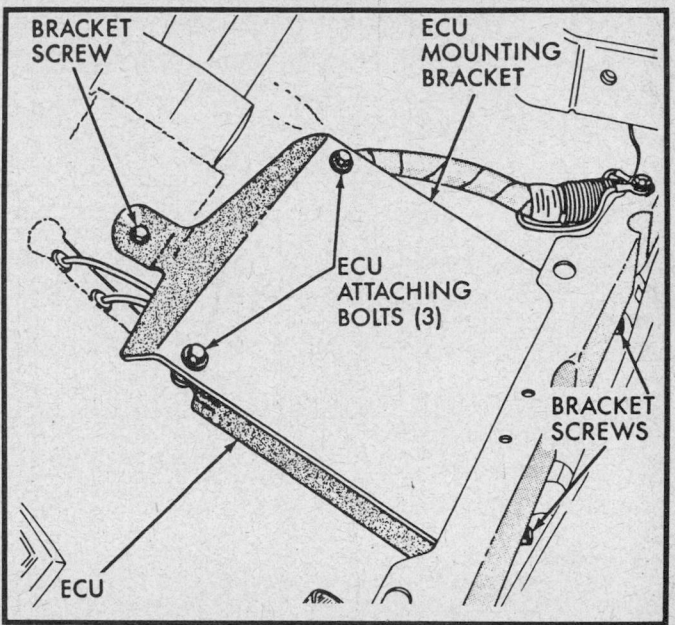

ECU mounting bracket

2. Bleed the brakes in the following sequence: right rear, left rear, right front, left front.

3. Attach a bleed hose to the caliper or wheel cylinder being bled, immerse the end of the bleed hose in a glass container partially filled with brake fluid.

4. Turn the ignition **ON** to cycle the pump.

5. Have a helper apply brake pedal to pressurize the system. Open the bleed screw ½ turn. Close the bleed screw when the fluid entering the glass container is free of bubbles.

6. Check the reservoir fluid level and add fluid to the **MAX** fill mark.

7. Repeat bleeding operations at remaining wheels.

NOTE: Do not allow the master cylinder reservoir to run dry while bleeding the brakes. Running dry will allow air to re-enter the system making a second bleeding operation necessary. More importantly, if air re-enters the system, it could damage the pump seriously enough to require replacement.

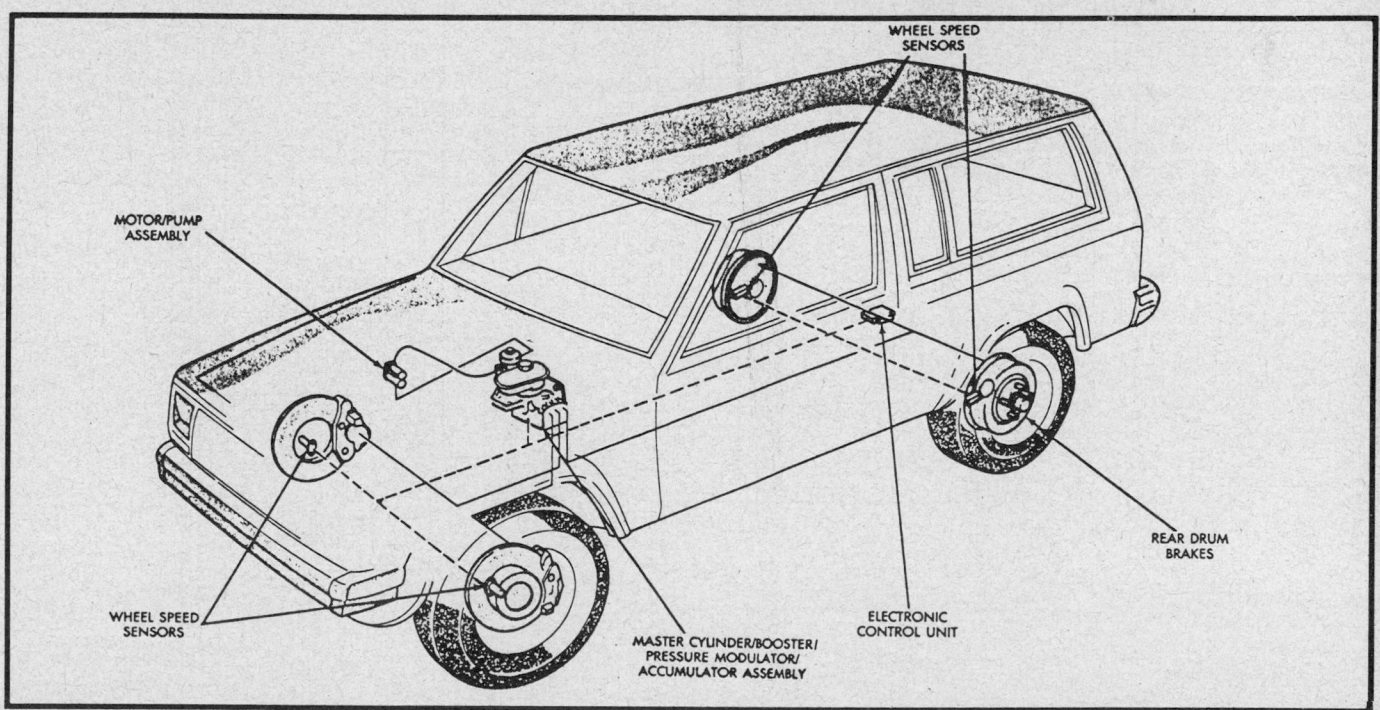

Jeep anti lock brake system

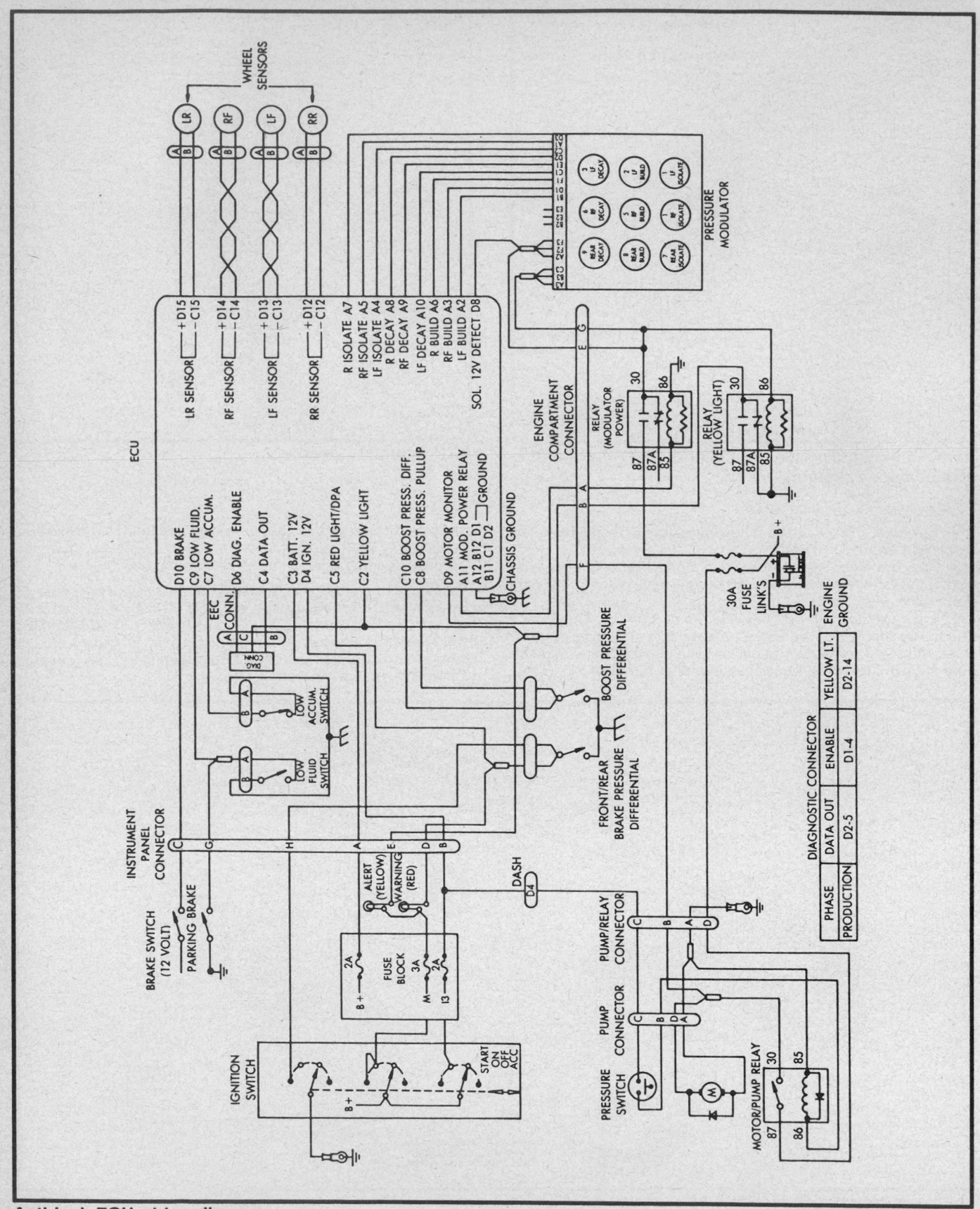

Anti-lock ECU wiring diagram

CARBURETOR IDENTIFICATION

All carburetors are identified by code numbers, either stamped on the attaching flange side, the main body or on a metal tag retained by a bowl cover screw. This identification number is important in order to obtain the correct carburetor replacement or parts and to properly adjust the carburetor when matched to a specific engine.

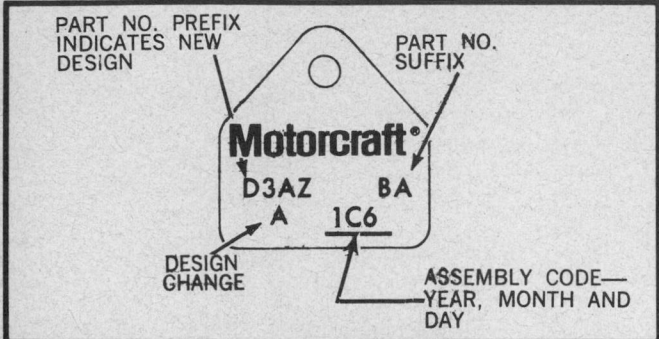

Motorcraft carburetors for Ford usage – typical

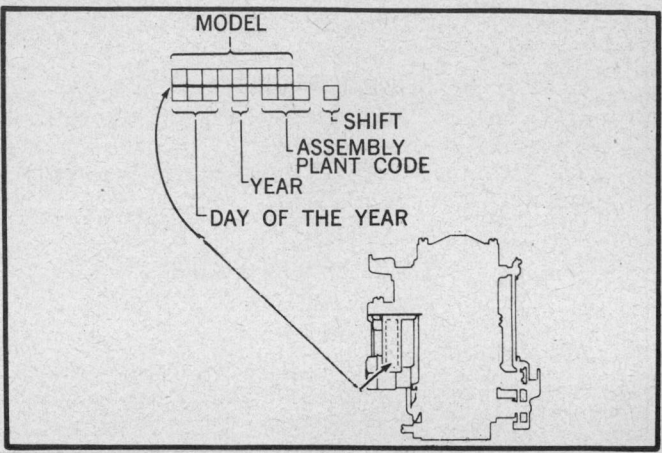

Rochester one barrel models – typical

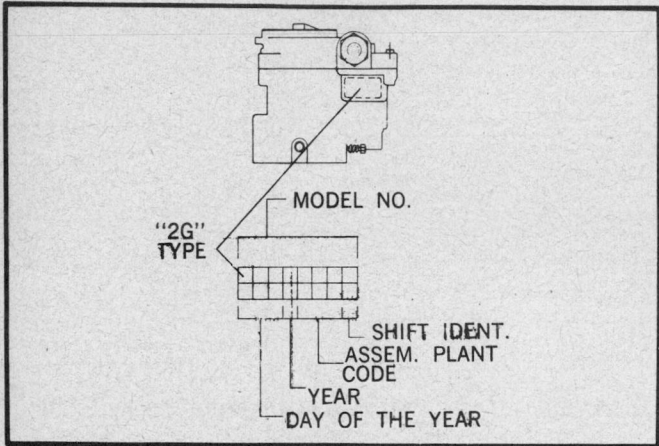

Rochester two barrel models – typical

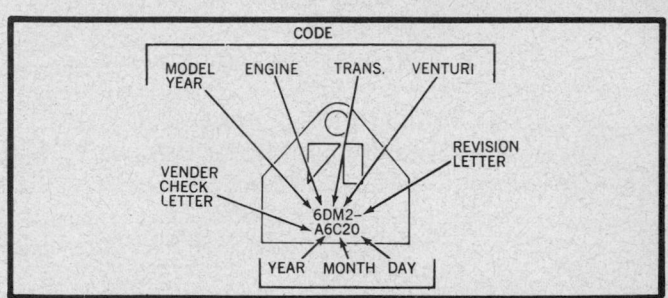

Motorcraft carburetors for Jeep usage – typical

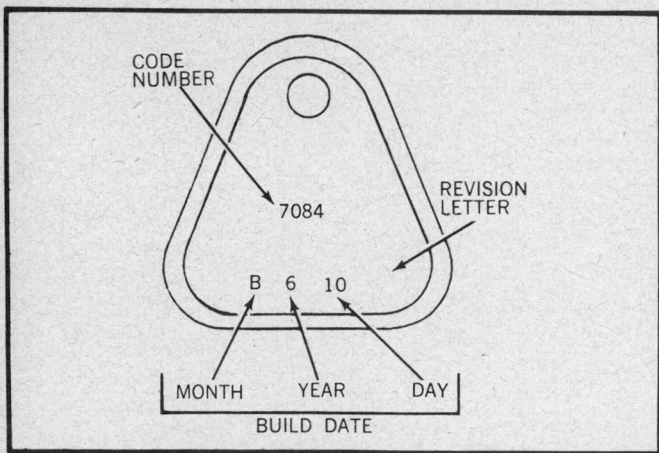

Carter carburetors for Jeep usage – typical

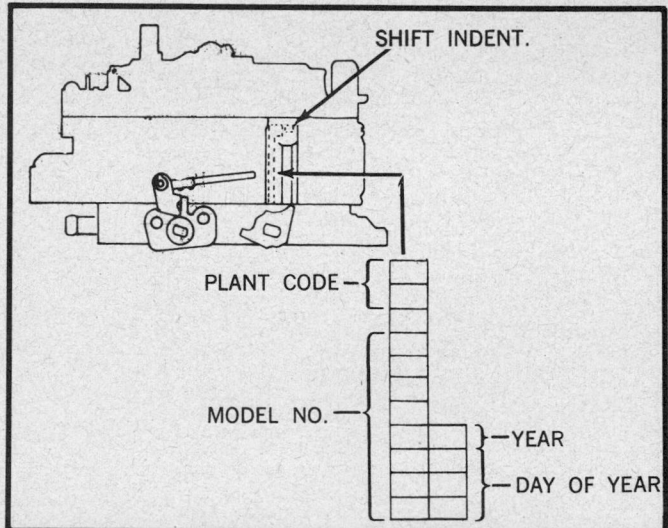

Rochester four barrel models – typical

SPECIAL TOOLS

An angle degree tool is recommended by Rochester Products Division for use to confirm adjustments to the choke valve and related linkages on late model 2 and 4 barrel carburetors in place of the plug type gauges. Decimal and degree conversion charts are provided for use with the angle degree tool. To use the angle gauge, rotate the degree scale until zero (0) is opposite the pointer. With the choke valve completely closed, place the gauge magnet squarely on top of the choke valve and rotate the bubble until it is centered. Make the necessary adjustments to have the choke valve at the specified degree angle opening as read from the degree angle tool. The carburetor may be off the engine for adjustments, but make sure the carburetor is held firmly during the use of the angle gauge.

A variety of other special adjustment tools may be necessary during the overhaul of different carburetors covered in this section. Most carburetor overhaul kits contain the float level gauges and specifications necessary for complete rebuilding, and if specifications differ from those given in the following charts, use the values listed in the overhaul instructions with a specific kit. Before beginning any overhaul procedures, read through each section to make sure all required special tools are on hand in order to complete the repair.

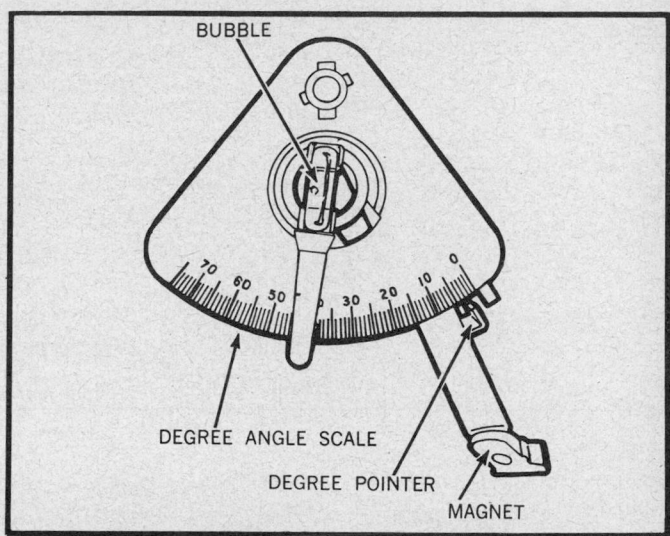

Typical degree angle tool

Carburetor Overhaul Tips

When the carburetor is disassembled, wash all parts (except diaphragms, electric choke units, pump plunger, and any other plastic, leather, fiber, or rubber parts) in clean carburetor solvent. Do not leave parts in the solvent any longer than is necessary to sufficiently loosen the deposits. Excessive cleaning may remove the special finish from the float bowl and choke valve bodies, leaving these parts unfit for service. Rinse all parts in clean solvent and blow them dry with compressed air or allow them to air dry. Wipe clean all cork, plastic, leather, and fiber parts with a clean, lint-free cloth.

Blow out all passages and jets with compressed air and be sure that there are no restrictions or blockages. Never use wire or similar tools to clean jets, fuel passages, or air bleeds. Clean all jets and valves separately to avoid accidental interchange. Check all parts for wear or damage. If wear or damage is found, replace the defective parts. Especially check the following:

1. Check the float needle and seat for wear. If wear is found, replace the complete assembly.

2. Check the float hinge pin for wear and the float(s) for dents or distortion. Replace the float if fuel has leaked into it.

3. Check the throttle and choke shaft bores for wear or an out-of-round condition. Damage or wear to the throttle arm, shaft, or shaft bore will often require replacement of the throttle body. These parts require a close tolerance of fit. Wear may allow air leakage, which could affect starting and idling.

NOTE: Throttle shafts and bushings are not included in overhaul kits. They can be purchased separately.

4. Inspect the idle mixture adjusting needles for burrs or grooves. Any such condition requires replacement of the needle, since you will not be able to obtain a satisfactory idle.

5. Test the accelerator pump check valves. They should pass air one way but not the other. Test for proper seating by blowing and sucking on the valve. Replace the valve if necessary. If the valve is satisfactory, wash the valve again to remove breath moisture.

6. Check the bowl cover for warped surfaces with a straight edge.

7. Closely inspect the valves and seats for wear and damage, replacing as necessary.

8. After the carburetor is assembled, check the choke valve for freedom of operation.

Carburetor overhaul kits are recommended for each overhaul. These kits contain all gaskets and new parts to replace those that deteriorate most rapidly. Failure to replace all parts supplied with the kit (especially gaskets) can result in poor performance later.

After cleaning and checking all components, reassemble the carburetor, using new parts and referring to the exploded view. When reassembling, make sure that all screws and jets are tight in their seats, but do not overtighten as the tips will be distorted. Tighten all screws gradually, in rotation. Do not tighten needle valves into their seats. Uneven jetting will result. Always use new gaskets. Be sure to adjust the float level, following the instructions contained in the rebuilding kit, when reassembling.

GENERAL MOTORS CARBURETORS

Rochester Carburetors

Refer to the individual truck section for idle speed and idle mixture adjustments, using the propane enrichment procedure on non-electronic controlled engine carburetors and with the use of a dwellmeter on the electronic controlled carburetor equipped engines.

ROCHESTER MODEL 1MEF
(All measurements in inches)

Year	Carburetor Number	Float Level	Choke Unloader Setting	Choke Coil Lever Setting	Fast Idle Speed (rpm)	Metering Rod Setting	Fast Idle Cam 2nd Step	Choke Vacuum Break
1986	17081009	11/32	0.520	0.120	①	0.090	0.275	0.400
	17084329	11/32	0.520	0.120	①	0.090	0.275	0.400
	17085009	11/32	0.520	0.120	①	0.090	0.275	0.400
	17085036	11/32	0.520	0.120	①	0.090	0.275	0.400
	17085044	11/32	0.520	0.120	①	0.090	0.275	0.400
	17085045	11/32	0.520	0.120	①	0.090	0.275	0.400
	17086096	11/32	0.520	0.120	①	0.090	0.275	0.400
	17086101	11/32	0.520	0.120	①	0.090	0.275	0.200
	17086102	11/32	0.520	0.120	①	0.090	0.275	0.200
1987	17081009	11/32	0.520	0.120	①	0.090	0.275	0.400
	17084329	11/32	0.520	0.120	①	0.090	0.275	0.400
	17085009	11/32	0.520	0.120	①	0.090	0.275	0.400
	17085036	11/32	0.520	0.120	①	0.090	0.275	0.400
	17085044	11/32	0.520	0.120	①	0.090	0.275	0.400
	17085045	11/32	0.520	0.120	①	0.090	0.275	0.400
	17086096	11/32	0.520	0.120	①	0.090	0.275	0.400
	17086101	11/32	0.520	0.120	①	0.090	0.275	0.200
	17086102	11/32	0.520	0.120	①	0.090	0.275	0.200
1988	17086096	11/32	0.520	0.120	①	0.090	0.275	0.200
	17086101	11/32	0.520	0.120	①	0.090	0.275	0.200
1989	17086101	11/32	0.520	0.120	①	0.090	0.275	0.200

① See emission label under hood

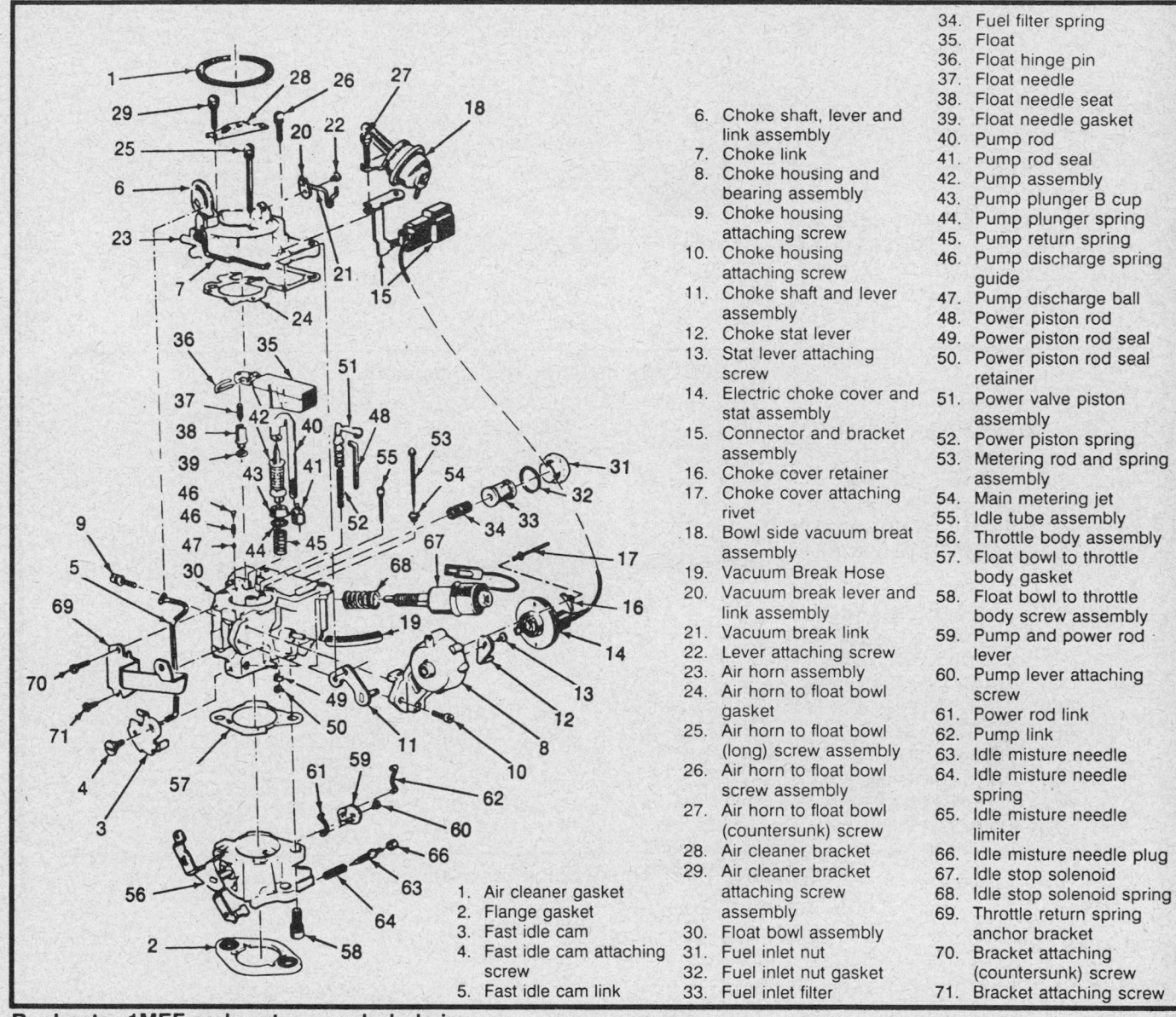

34. Fuel filter spring
35. Float
36. Float hinge pin
37. Float needle
38. Float needle seat
39. Float needle gasket
40. Pump rod
41. Pump rod seal
42. Pump assembly
43. Pump plunger B cup
44. Pump plunger spring
45. Pump return spring
46. Pump discharge spring guide
47. Pump discharge ball
48. Power piston rod
49. Power piston rod seal
50. Power piston rod seal retainer
51. Power valve piston assembly
52. Power piston spring
53. Metering rod and spring assembly
54. Main metering jet
55. Idle tube assembly
56. Throttle body assembly
57. Float bowl to throttle body gasket
58. Float bowl to throttle body screw assembly
59. Pump and power rod lever
60. Pump lever attaching screw
61. Power rod link
62. Pump link
63. Idle mixture needle
64. Idle mixture needle spring
65. Idle mixture needle limiter
66. Idle mixture needle plug
67. Idle stop solenoid
68. Idle stop solenoid spring
69. Throttle return spring anchor bracket
70. Bracket attaching (countersunk) screw
71. Bracket attaching screw

6. Choke shaft, lever and link assembly
7. Choke link
8. Choke housing and bearing assembly
9. Choke housing attaching screw
10. Choke housing attaching screw
11. Choke shaft and lever assembly
12. Choke stat lever
13. Stat lever attaching screw
14. Electric choke cover and stat assembly
15. Connector and bracket assembly
16. Choke cover retainer
17. Choke cover attaching rivet
18. Bowl side vacuum breat assembly
19. Vacuum Break Hose
20. Vacuum break lever and link assembly
21. Vacuum break link
22. Lever attaching screw
23. Air horn assembly
24. Air horn to float bowl gasket
25. Air horn to float bowl (long) screw assembly
26. Air horn to float bowl screw assembly
27. Air horn to float bowl (countersunk) screw
28. Air cleaner bracket
29. Air cleaner bracket attaching screw assembly
30. Float bowl assembly
31. Fuel inlet nut
32. Fuel inlet nut gasket
33. Fuel inlet filter

1. Air cleaner gasket
2. Flange gasket
3. Fast idle cam
4. Fast idle cam attaching screw
5. Fast idle cam link

Rochester 1MEF carburetor — exploded view

Rochester 1MEF float level adjustment

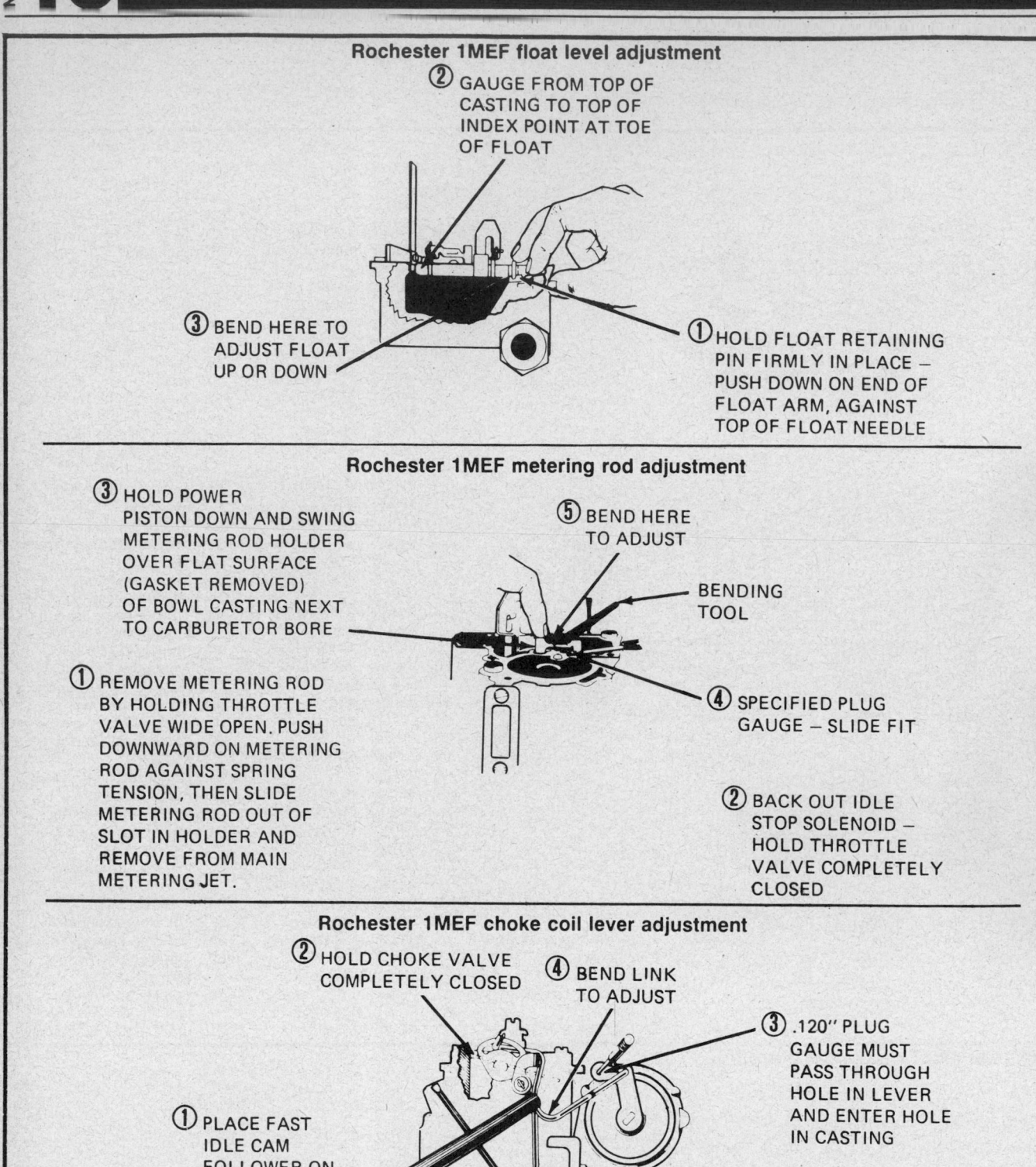

② GAUGE FROM TOP OF CASTING TO TOP OF INDEX POINT AT TOE OF FLOAT

③ BEND HERE TO ADJUST FLOAT UP OR DOWN

① HOLD FLOAT RETAINING PIN FIRMLY IN PLACE — PUSH DOWN ON END OF FLOAT ARM, AGAINST TOP OF FLOAT NEEDLE

Rochester 1MEF metering rod adjustment

③ HOLD POWER PISTON DOWN AND SWING METERING ROD HOLDER OVER FLAT SURFACE (GASKET REMOVED) OF BOWL CASTING NEXT TO CARBURETOR BORE

⑤ BEND HERE TO ADJUST

BENDING TOOL

① REMOVE METERING ROD BY HOLDING THROTTLE VALVE WIDE OPEN. PUSH DOWNWARD ON METERING ROD AGAINST SPRING TENSION, THEN SLIDE METERING ROD OUT OF SLOT IN HOLDER AND REMOVE FROM MAIN METERING JET.

④ SPECIFIED PLUG GAUGE — SLIDE FIT

② BACK OUT IDLE STOP SOLENOID — HOLD THROTTLE VALVE COMPLETELY CLOSED

Rochester 1MEF choke coil lever adjustment

② HOLD CHOKE VALVE COMPLETELY CLOSED

④ BEND LINK TO ADJUST

③ .120″ PLUG GAUGE MUST PASS THROUGH HOLE IN LEVER AND ENTER HOLE IN CASTING

① PLACE FAST IDLE CAM FOLLOWER ON HIGHEST STEP OF FAST IDLE CAM

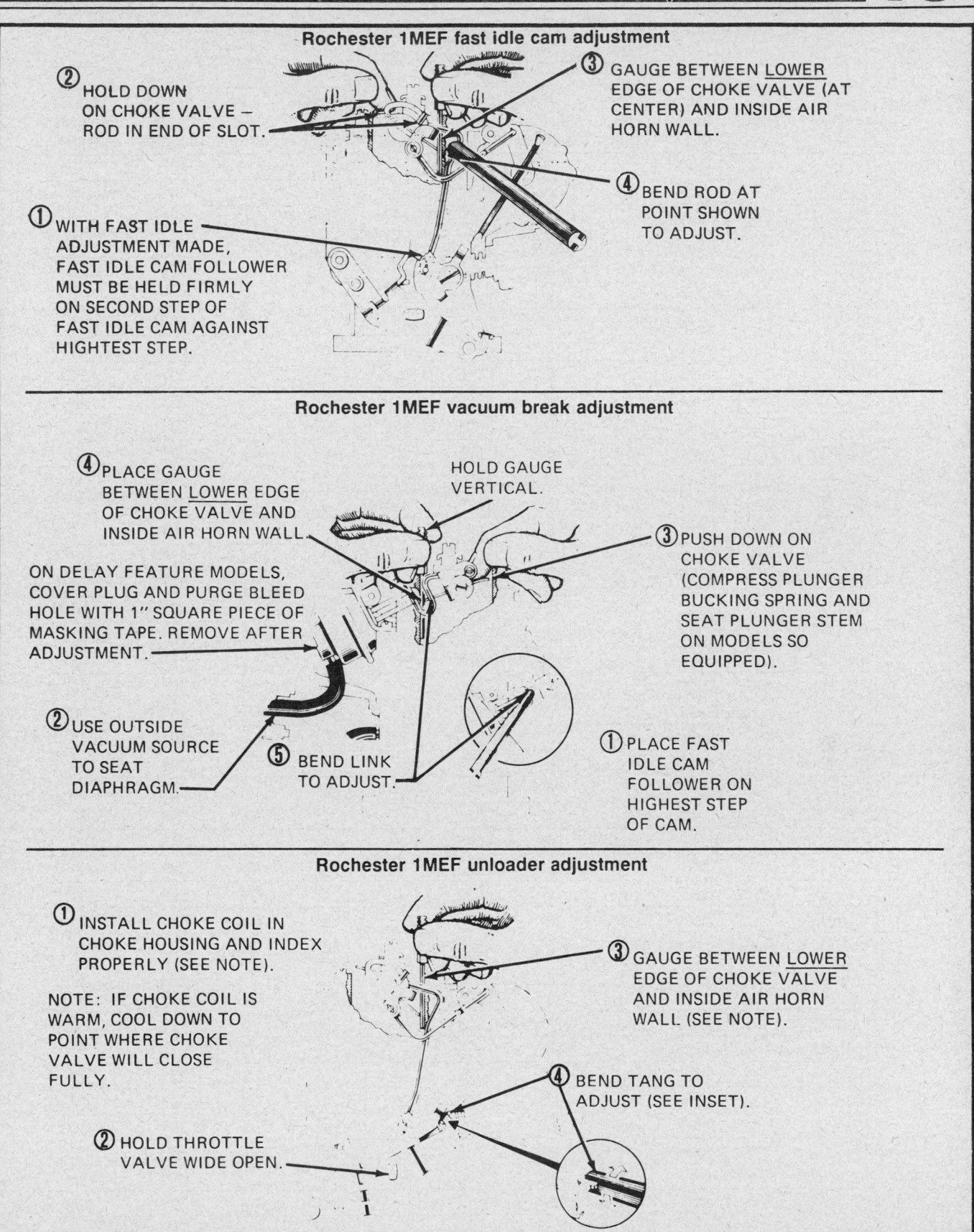

Rochester 1MEF fast idle cam adjustment

② HOLD DOWN ON CHOKE VALVE – ROD IN END OF SLOT.

③ GAUGE BETWEEN <u>LOWER</u> EDGE OF CHOKE VALVE (AT CENTER) AND INSIDE AIR HORN WALL.

④ BEND ROD AT POINT SHOWN TO ADJUST.

① WITH FAST IDLE ADJUSTMENT MADE, FAST IDLE CAM FOLLOWER MUST BE HELD FIRMLY ON SECOND STEP OF FAST IDLE CAM AGAINST HIGHTEST STEP.

Rochester 1MEF vacuum break adjustment

④ PLACE GAUGE BETWEEN <u>LOWER</u> EDGE OF CHOKE VALVE AND INSIDE AIR HORN WALL.

ON DELAY FEATURE MODELS, COVER PLUG AND PURGE BLEED HOLE WITH 1" SQUARE PIECE OF MASKING TAPE. REMOVE AFTER ADJUSTMENT.

HOLD GAUGE VERTICAL.

③ PUSH DOWN ON CHOKE VALVE (COMPRESS PLUNGER BUCKING SPRING AND SEAT PLUNGER STEM ON MODELS SO EQUIPPED).

② USE OUTSIDE VACUUM SOURCE TO SEAT DIAPHRAGM.

⑤ BEND LINK TO ADJUST.

① PLACE FAST IDLE CAM FOLLOWER ON HIGHEST STEP OF CAM.

Rochester 1MEF unloader adjustment

① INSTALL CHOKE COIL IN CHOKE HOUSING AND INDEX PROPERLY (SEE NOTE).

NOTE: IF CHOKE COIL IS WARM, COOL DOWN TO POINT WHERE CHOKE VALVE WILL CLOSE FULLY.

③ GAUGE BETWEEN <u>LOWER</u> EDGE OF CHOKE VALVE AND INSIDE AIR HORN WALL (SEE NOTE).

④ BEND TANG TO ADJUST (SEE INSET).

② HOLD THROTTLE VALVE WIDE OPEN.

ROCHESTER MODEL M4ME, M4MED, M4MEF QUADRAJET
General Motors Corporation
(All measurements in inches or degrees)

Year	Carburetor Number	Float Level	Pump Rod Hole	Pump Rod Setting	Choke Rod ① Setting	Air Valve Rod	Vacuum Break Front	Vacuum Break Rear	Air Valve Turns	Choke Unloader	Propane Enrichment (rpm)
1986	17084500	12/32	inner	9/32	37°	0.025	23°	30°	1	40°	②
	17084501	12/32	inner	9/32	37°	0.025	23°	30°	1	40°	②
	17084502	12/32	inner	9/32	46°	0.025	24°	30°	7/8	40°	②
	17085000	12/32	inner	9/32	46°	0.025	24°	30°	7/8	40°	②
	17085001	12/32	inner	9/32	46°	0.025	23°	30°	1	40°	②
	17085003	13/32	inner	9/32	46°	0.025	23°	—	7/8	35°	②
	17085004	13/32	inner	9/32	46°	0.025	23°	—	7/8	35°	②
	17085205	13/32	inner	9/32	20°	0.025	26°	38°	7/8	39°	②
	17085206	13/32	inner	9/32	46°	0.025	—	26°	7/8	39°	20
	17085208	13/32	inner	9/32	20°	0.025	26°	38°	7/8	39°	10
	17085209	13/32	outer	3/8	20°	0.025	26°	36°	7/8	39°	50
	17085210	13/32	inner	9/32	20°	0.025	26°	38°	7/8	39°	10
	17085211	13/32	outer	3/8	20°	0.025	26°	36°	7/8	39°	50
	17085212	13/32	inner	9/32	46°	0.025	23°	—	7/8	35°	②
	17085213	13/32	inner	9/32	46°	0.025	23°	—	7/8	35°	②
	17085215	13/32	inner	9/32	46°	0.025	—	26°	7/8	32°	②
	17085216	13/32	inner	9/32	20°	0.025	26°	38°	7/8	39°	②
	17085217	13/32	inner	9/32	20°	0.025	26°	36°	1/2	39°	②
	17085219	13/32	inner	9/32	20°	0.025	26°	36°	1/2	39°	②
	17085220	13/32	outer	3/8	20°	0.025	—	26°	7/8	32°	75
	17085221	13/32	outer	3/8	20°	0.025	—	26°	7/8	32°	75
	17085222	13/32	inner	9/32	20°	0.025	26°	36°	1/2	39°	20
	17085223	13/32	outer	3/8	20°	0.025	26°	36°	1/2	39°	50
	17085224	13/32	inner	9/32	20°	0.025	26°	36°	1/2	39°	20
	17085225	13/32	outer	3/8	20°	0.025	26°	36°	1/2	39°	50
	17085226	13/32	inner	9/32	20°	0.025	—	24°	7/8	32°	20
	17085227	13/32	inner	9/32	20°	0.025	—	24°	7/8	32°	20
	17085228	13/32	inner	9/32	46°	0.025	—	24°	7/8	39°	30
	17085229	13/32	inner	9/32	46°	0.025	—	24°	7/8	39°	30
	17085230	13/32	inner	9/32	20°	0.025	—	26°	7/8	32°	20
	17085231	13/32	inner	9/32	20°	0.025	—	26°	7/8	32°	40
	17085235	13/32	inner	9/32	46°	0.025	—	26°	7/8	39°	80
	17085238	13/32	outer	3/8	20°	0.025	—	26°	7/8	32°	75
	17085239	13/32	outer	3/8	20°	0.025	—	26°	7/8	32°	75
	17085283	13/32	inner	9/32	20°	0.025	—	24°	7/8	32°	20
	17085284	13/32	inner	9/32	20°	0.025	—	26°	7/8	32°	20
	17085285	13/32	inner	9/32	20°	0.025	—	24°	7/8	32°	20
	17085290	13/32	inner	9/32	46°	0.025	—	24°	7/8	39°	30
	17085291	13/32	outer	3/8	46°	0.025	—	26°	7/8	39°	100
	17085292	13/32	inner	9/32	46°	0.025	—	24°	7/8	39°	30
	17085293	13/32	outer	3/8	46°	0.025	—	26°	7/8	39°	100
	17085294	13/32	inner	9/32	46°	0.025	—	26°	7/8	39°	②
	17085298	13/32	inner	9/32	46°	0.025	—	26°	7/8	39°	②

ROCHESTER MODEL M4ME, M4MED, M4MEF QUADRAJET
General Motors Corporation
(All measurements in inches or degrees)

Year	Carburetor Number	Float Level	Pump Rod Hole	Pump Rod Setting	Choke Rod ① Setting	Air Valve Rod	Vacuum Break Front	Vacuum Break Rear	Air Valve Turns	Choke Unloader	Propane Enrichment (rpm)
1987	17084500	12/32	inner	9/32	37°	0.025	23°	30°	1	40°	②
	17084501	12/32	inner	9/32	37°	0.025	23°	30°	1	40°	②
	17084502	12/32	inner	9/32	46°	0.025	24°	30°	7/8	40°	②
	17085000	12/32	inner	9/32	46°	0.025	24°	30°	7/8	40°	②
	17085001	12/32	inner	9/32	46°	0.025	23°	30°	1	40°	②
	17085003	13/32	inner	9/32	46°	0.025	23°	—	7/8	35°	②
	17085004	13/32	inner	9/32	46°	0.025	23°	—	7/8	35°	②
	17085205	13/32	inner	9/32	20°	0.025	26°	38°	7/8	39°	②
	17085206	13/32	inner	9/32	46°	0.025	—	26°	7/8	39°	20
	17085208	13/32	inner	9/32	20°	0.025	26°	38°	7/8	39°	10
	17085209	13/32	outer	3/8	20°	0.025	26°	36°	7/8	39°	50
	17085210	13/32	inner	9/32	20°	0.025	26°	38°	7/8	39°	10
	17085211	13/32	outer	3/8	20°	0.025	26°	36°	7/8	39°	50
	17085212	13/32	inner	9/32	46°	0.025	23°	—	7/8	35°	②
	17085213	13/32	inner	9/32	46°	0.025	23°	—	7/8	35°	②
	17085215	13/32	inner	9/32	46°	0.025	—	26°	7/8	32°	②
	17085216	13/32	inner	9/32	20°	0.025	26°	38°	7/8	39°	②
	17085217	13/32	inner	9/32	20°	0.025	26°	36°	1/2	39°	②
	17085219	13/32	inner	9/32	20°	0.025	26°	36°	1/2	39°	②
	17085220	13/32	outer	3/8	20°	0.025	—	26°	7/8	32°	75
	17085221	13/32	outer	3/8	20°	0.025	—	26°	7/8	32°	75
	17085222	13/32	inner	9/32	20°	0.025	26°	36°	1/2	39°	20
	17085223	13/32	outer	3/8	20°	0.025	26°	36°	1/2	39°	50
	17085224	13/32	inner	9/32	20°	0.025	26°	36°	1/2	39°	20
	17085225	13/32	outer	3/8	20°	0.025	26°	36°	1/2	39°	50
	17085226	13/32	inner	9/32	20°	0.025	—	24°	7/8	32°	20
	17085227	13/32	inner	9/32	20°	0.025	—	24°	7/8	32°	20
	17085228	13/32	inner	9/32	46°	0.025	—	24°	7/8	39°	30
	17085229	13/32	inner	9/32	46°	0.025	—	24°	7/8	39°	30
	17085230	13/32	inner	9/32	20°	0.025	—	26°	7/8	32°	20
	17085231	13/32	inner	9/32	20°	0.025	—	26°	7/8	32°	40
	17085235	13/32	inner	9/32	46°	0.025	—	26°	7/8	39°	80
	17085238	13/32	outer	3/8	20°	0.025	—	26°	7/8	32°	75
	17085239	13/32	outer	3/8	20°	0.025	—	26°	7/8	32°	75
	17085283	13/32	inner	9/32	20°	0.025	—	24°	7/8	32°	20
	17085284	13/32	inner	9/32	20°	0.025	—	26°	7/8	32°	20
	17085285	13/32	inner	9/32	20°	0.025	—	24°	7/8	32°	20
	17085290	13/32	inner	9/32	46°	0.025	—	24°	7/8	39°	30
	17085291	13/32	outer	3/8	46°	0.025	—	26°	7/8	39°	100
	17085292	13/32	inner	9/32	46°	0.025	—	24°	7/8	39°	30
	17085293	13/32	outer	3/8	46°	0.025	—	26°	7/8	39°	100
	17085294	13/32	inner	9/32	46°	0.025	—	26°	7/8	39°	②
	17085298	13/32	inner	9/32	46°	0.025	—	26°	7/8	39°	②

ROCHESTER MODEL M4ME, M4MED, M4MEF QUADRAJET
General Motors Corporation
(All measurements in inches or degrees)

Year	Carburetor Number	Float Level	Pump Rod Hole	Pump Rod Setting	Choke Rod ① Setting	Air Valve Rod	Vacuum Break Front	Vacuum Break Rear	Air Valve Turns	Choke Unloader	Propane Enrichment (rpm)
1988	17085004	13/32	inner	9/32	46°	0.025	23°	—	7/8	35°	—
	17085212	13/32	inner	9/32	46°	0.025	23°	—	7/8	35°	—
	17088040	13/32	inner	9/32	46°	0.025	27°	—	7/8	35°	—
	17088041	13/32	inner	9/32	46°	0.025	27°	—	7/8	35°	—
1989	17085004	13/32	inner	9/32	46°	0.025	23°	—	7/8	35°	—
	17085212	13/32	inner	9/32	46°	0.025	23°	—	7/8	35°	—

NOTE: Specified angle for use with angle degree tool. Choke coil lever setting is 0.120 in. for all carburetors.
① Second step of fast idle cam
② See underhood specification sticker

MODELS M4ME, M4MED AND M4MEF

1. Air horn assembly
2. Air horn gasket
3. Pump actuating lever
4. Pump lever hinge roll pin
5. Air horn long (2) screw
6. Air horn short screw
7. Air horn countersunk (2) screw
8. Secondary (2) metering rod
9. Secondary metering rod holder and screw
10. Secondary air baffle
11. Pump plunger seal
12. Pump seal retainer
13. Front vacuum break control and bracket
14. Control attaching (2) screw
15. Vacuum hose
16. Air vavle rod
16a. Air valve rod
17. Choke rod (upper) lever
18. Choke lever screw
19. Choke rod
20. Choke rod (lower) lever
21. Intermediate choke shaft seal
22. Secondary lockout lever
23. Rear vacuum break link
24. Int. choke shaft and lever
25. Fast idle cam
26. Choke housing to bow (hot air choke) seal
27. Choke housing kit
28. Choke housing to bowl screw
29. Intermediate choke shaft (hot air choke) seal
30. Choke coil lever
31. Choke coil lever screw
32. Stat cover (hot air choke) gasket
33. Stat cover and coil assembly (hot air choke)
34. Stat cover and coil assembly (electric choke)
35. Stat cover attaching kit
36. Rear vacuum break assembly
37. Vacuum break attaching (2) screw
40. Pump discharge ball
41. Pump discharge ball retainer
42. Pump well baffle
43. Needle and seat assembly
44. Float assembly
45. Float assembly hinge pin
46. Power piston assembly
47. Power piston spring
48. Primary Metering (2) rod
49. Metering rod retainer spring
50. Float bowl insert
51. Bowl cavity insert
52. Pump return spring
53. Pump assembly
54. Pump rod
55. Secondary bores baffle
56. Idle compensator assembly
57. Idle compensator seal
58. Idle compensator cover
59. Idle compensator cover (2) screw
60. Fuel inlet filter nut
61. Filter nut gasket
62. Fuel inlet filter
63. Fuel filter spring
64. Idle stop srew
65. Idle stop screw spring
66. Idle speed solenoid and bracket assembly
67. Idle load compensator and bracket assembly
68. Throttle return spring bracket
69. Throttle lever actuator
70. Throttle lever actuator bracket
71. Actuator nut washer
72. Actuator attaching nut
73. Bracket attaching (2) screw
74. Throttle body assembly
75. Throttle body gasket
76. Throttle body (3) screw
77. Idle mixture needle and spring assembly (2)
78. Fast idle adjusting screw
79. Fast idle screw spring
80. Vacuum hose tee
81. Flange gasket

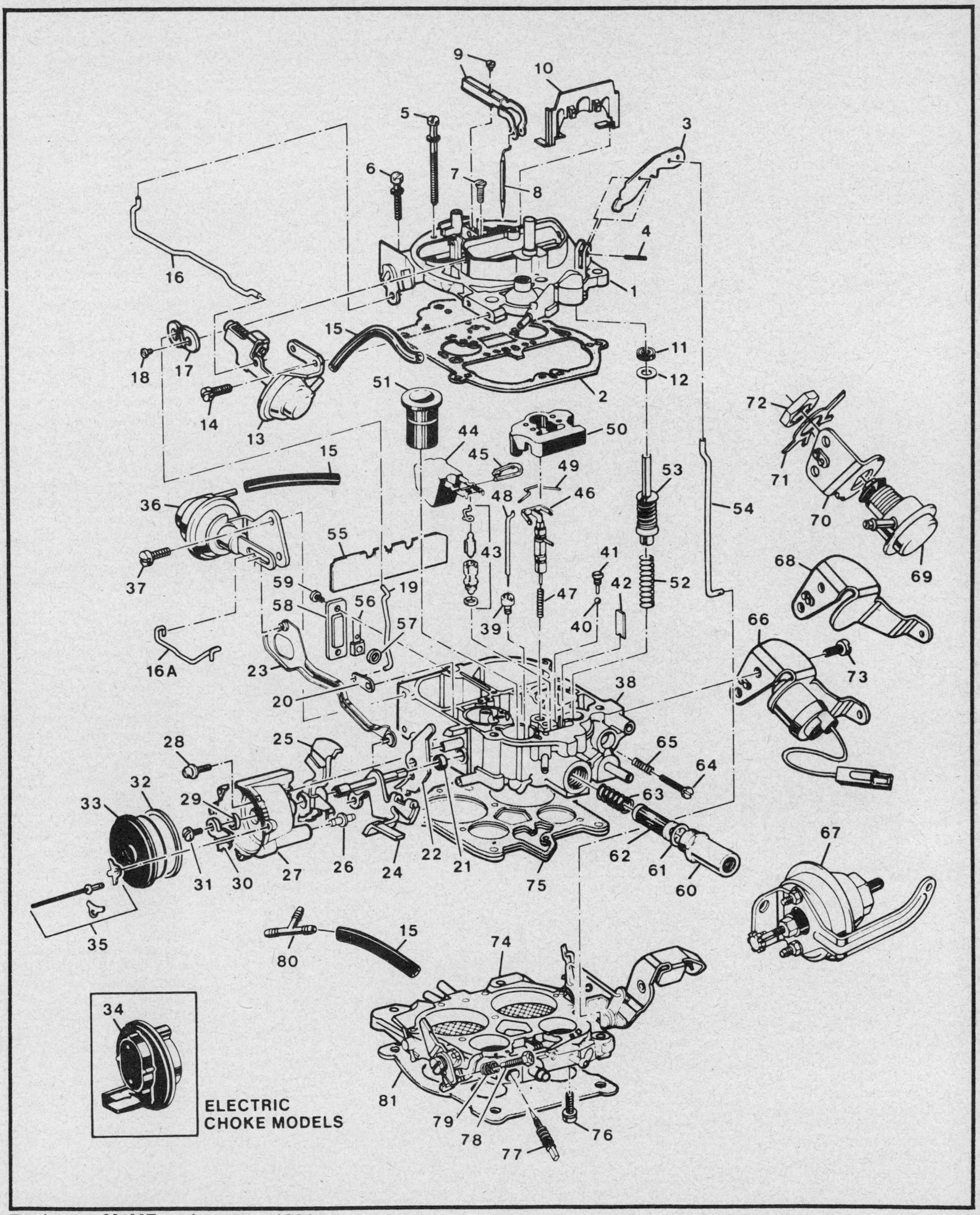

Rochester M4ME carbureter – 1986

ELECTRIC
CHOKE MODELS

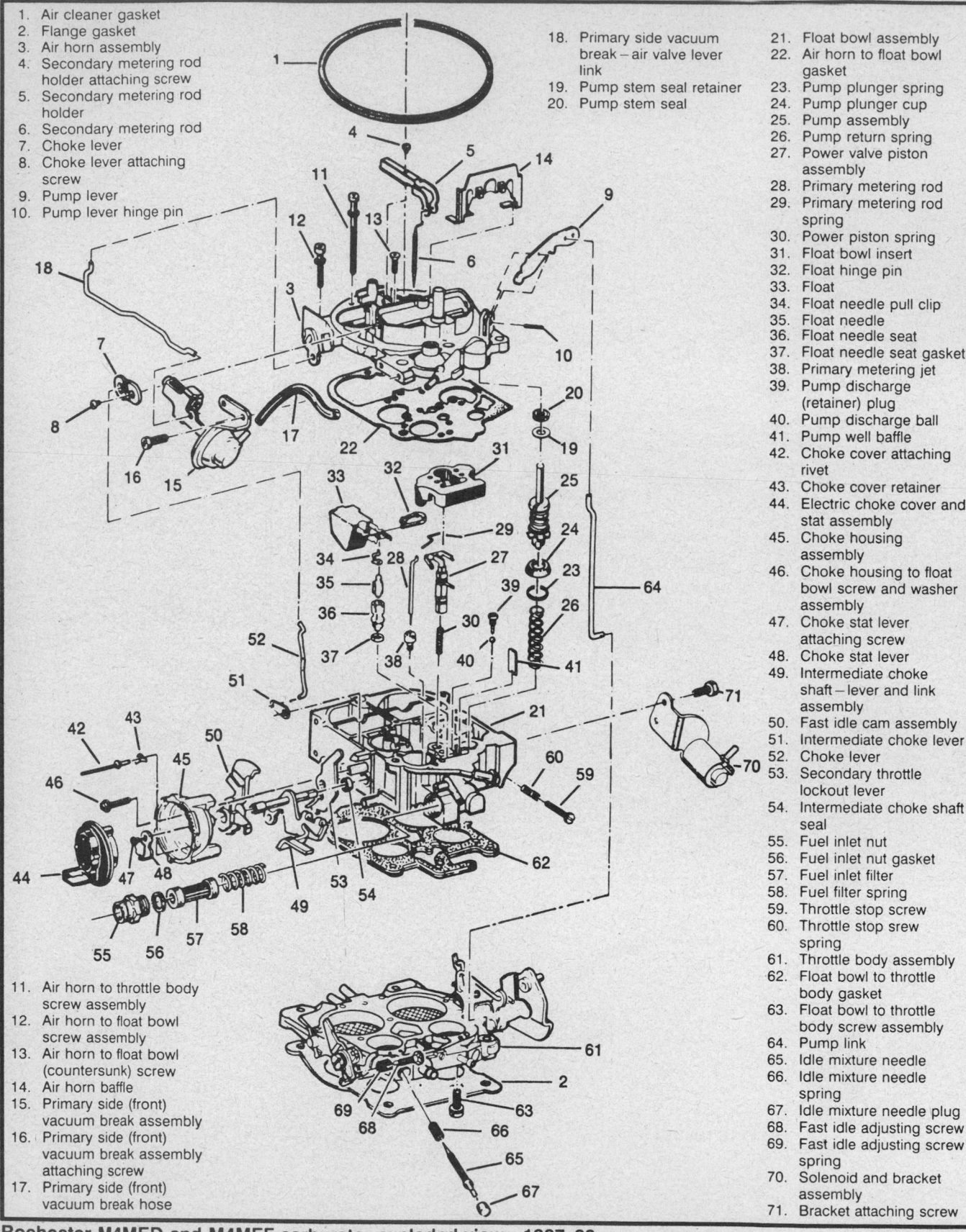

1. Air cleaner gasket
2. Flange gasket
3. Air horn assembly
4. Secondary metering rod holder attaching screw
5. Secondary metering rod holder
6. Secondary metering rod
7. Choke lever
8. Choke lever attaching screw
9. Pump lever
10. Pump lever hinge pin

11. Air horn to throttle body screw assembly
12. Air horn to float bowl screw assembly
13. Air horn to float bowl (countersunk) screw
14. Air horn baffle
15. Primary side (front) vacuum break assembly
16. Primary side (front) vacuum break assembly attaching screw
17. Primary side (front) vacuum break hose

18. Primary side vacuum break – air valve lever link
19. Pump stem seal retainer
20. Pump stem seal

21. Float bowl assembly
22. Air horn to float bowl gasket
23. Pump plunger spring
24. Pump plunger cup
25. Pump assembly
26. Pump return spring
27. Power valve piston assembly
28. Primary metering rod
29. Primary metering rod spring
30. Power piston spring
31. Float bowl insert
32. Float hinge pin
33. Float
34. Float needle pull clip
35. Float needle
36. Float needle seat
37. Float needle seat gasket
38. Primary metering jet
39. Pump discharge (retainer) plug
40. Pump discharge ball
41. Pump well baffle
42. Choke cover attaching rivet
43. Choke cover retainer
44. Electric choke cover and stat assembly
45. Choke housing assembly
46. Choke housing to float bowl screw and washer assembly
47. Choke stat lever attaching screw
48. Choke stat lever
49. Intermediate choke shaft – lever and link assembly
50. Fast idle cam assembly
51. Intermediate choke lever
52. Choke lever
53. Secondary throttle lockout lever
54. Intermediate choke shaft seal
55. Fuel inlet nut
56. Fuel inlet nut gasket
57. Fuel inlet filter
58. Fuel filter spring
59. Throttle stop screw
60. Throttle stop srew spring
61. Throttle body assembly
62. Float bowl to throttle body gasket
63. Float bowl to throttle body screw assembly
64. Pump link
65. Idle mixture needle
66. Idle mixture needle spring
67. Idle mixture needle plug
68. Fast idle adjusting screw
69. Fast idle adjusting screw spring
70. Solenoid and bracket assembly
71. Bracket attaching screw

Rochester M4MED and M4MEF carburetor exploded view – 1987–89

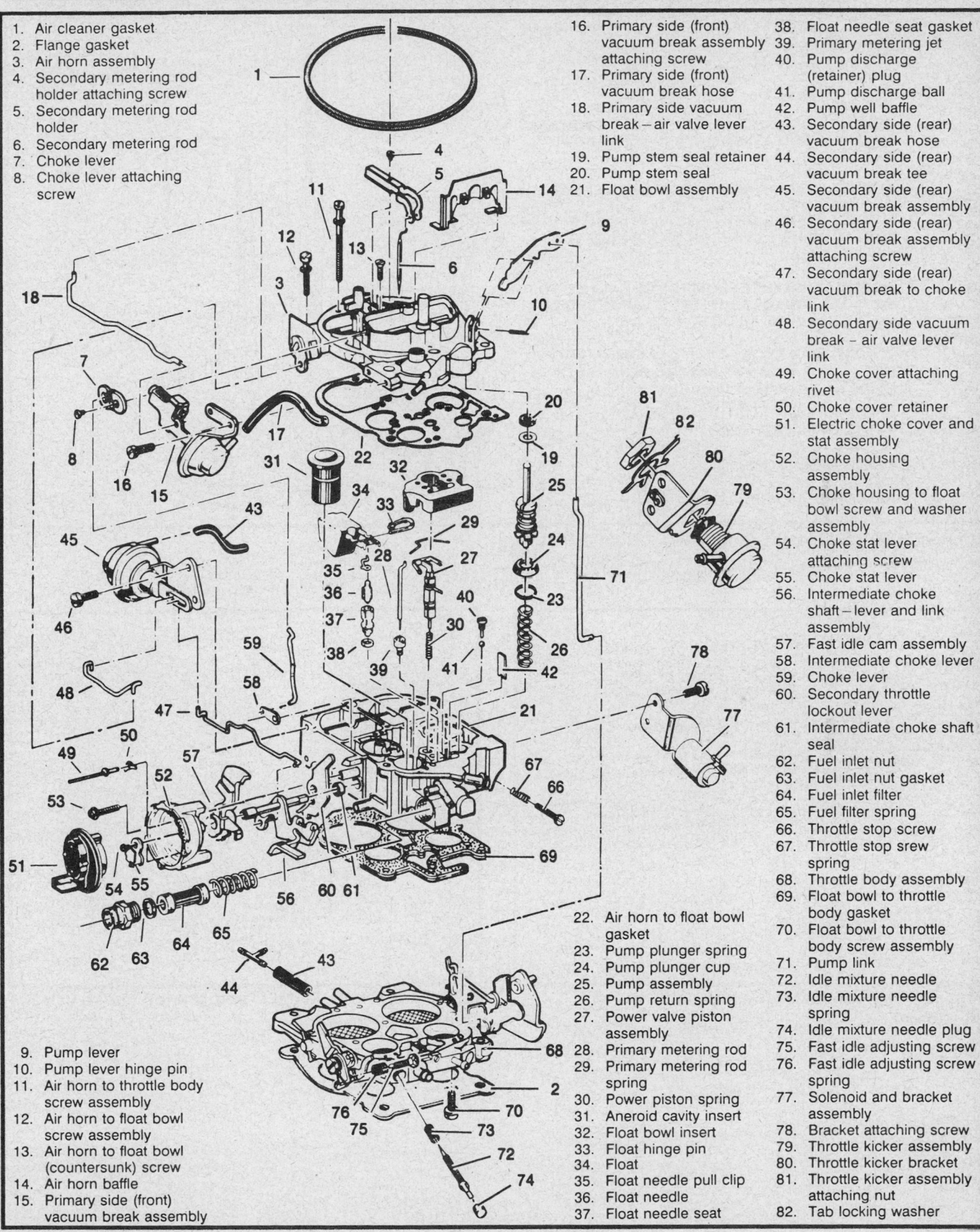

1. Air cleaner gasket
2. Flange gasket
3. Air horn assembly
4. Secondary metering rod holder attaching screw
5. Secondary metering rod holder
6. Secondary metering rod
7. Choke lever
8. Choke lever attaching screw
9. Pump lever
10. Pump lever hinge pin
11. Air horn to throttle body screw assembly
12. Air horn to float bowl screw assembly
13. Air horn to float bowl (countersunk) screw
14. Air horn baffle
15. Primary side (front) vacuum break assembly
16. Primary side (front) vacuum break assembly attaching screw
17. Primary side (front) vacuum break hose
18. Primary side vacuum break — air valve lever link
19. Pump stem seal retainer
20. Pump stem seal
21. Float bowl assembly
22. Air horn to float bowl gasket
23. Pump plunger spring
24. Pump plunger cup
25. Pump assembly
26. Pump return spring
27. Power valve piston assembly
28. Primary metering rod
29. Primary metering rod spring
30. Power piston spring
31. Aneroid cavity insert
32. Float bowl insert
33. Float hinge pin
34. Float
35. Float needle pull clip
36. Float needle
37. Float needle seat
38. Float needle seat gasket
39. Primary metering jet
40. Pump discharge (retainer) plug
41. Pump discharge ball
42. Pump well baffle
43. Secondary side (rear) vacuum break hose
44. Secondary side (rear) vacuum break tee
45. Secondary side (rear) vacuum break assembly
46. Secondary side (rear) vacuum break assembly attaching screw
47. Secondary side (rear) vacuum break to choke link
48. Secondary side vacuum break — air valve lever link
49. Choke cover attaching rivet
50. Choke cover retainer
51. Electric choke cover and stat assembly
52. Choke housing assembly
53. Choke housing to float bowl screw and washer assembly
54. Choke stat lever attaching screw
55. Choke stat lever
56. Intermediate choke shaft — lever and link assembly
57. Fast idle cam assembly
58. Intermediate choke lever
59. Choke lever
60. Secondary throttle lockout lever
61. Intermediate choke shaft seal
62. Fuel inlet nut
63. Fuel inlet nut gasket
64. Fuel inlet filter
65. Fuel filter spring
66. Throttle stop screw
67. Throttle stop srew spring
68. Throttle body assembly
69. Float bowl to throttle body gasket
70. Float bowl to throttle body screw assembly
71. Pump link
72. Idle mixture needle
73. Idle mixture needle spring
74. Idle mixture needle plug
75. Fast idle adjusting screw
76. Fast idle adjusting screw spring
77. Solenoid and bracket assembly
78. Bracket attaching screw
79. Throttle kicker assembly
80. Throttle kicker bracket
81. Throttle kicker assembly attaching nut
82. Tab locking washer

Rochester M4ME carburetor exploded view — 1987 California models

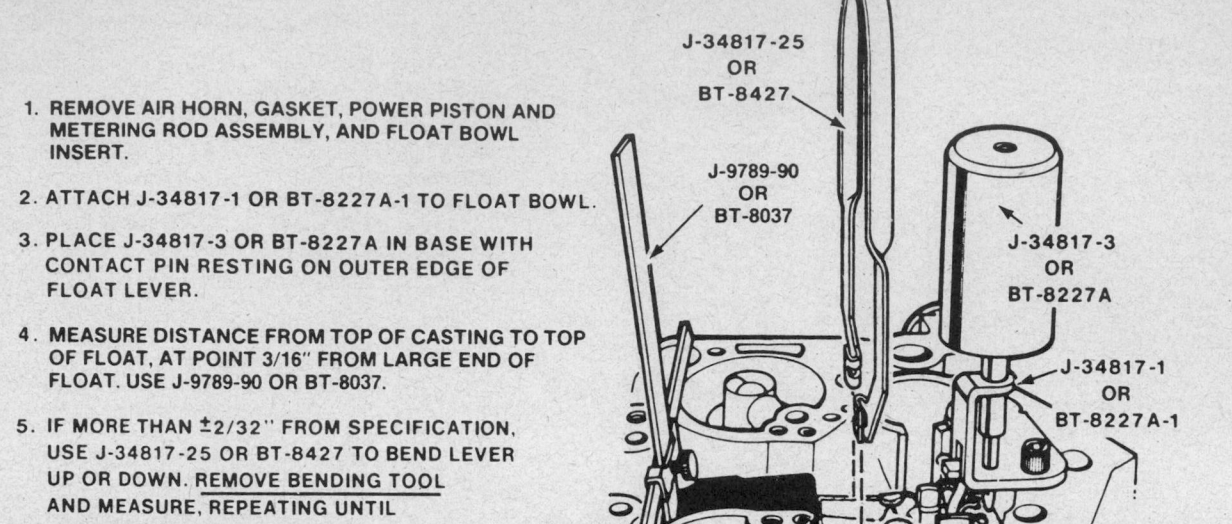

1. REMOVE AIR HORN, GASKET, POWER PISTON AND METERING ROD ASSEMBLY, AND FLOAT BOWL INSERT.

2. ATTACH J-34817-1 OR BT-8227A-1 TO FLOAT BOWL.

3. PLACE J-34817-3 OR BT-8227A IN BASE WITH CONTACT PIN RESTING ON OUTER EDGE OF FLOAT LEVER.

4. MEASURE DISTANCE FROM TOP OF CASTING TO TOP OF FLOAT, AT POINT 3/16" FROM LARGE END OF FLOAT. USE J-9789-90 OR BT-8037.

5. IF MORE THAN ±2/32" FROM SPECIFICATION, USE J-34817-25 OR BT-8427 TO BEND LEVER UP OR DOWN. REMOVE BENDING TOOL AND MEASURE, REPEATING UNTIL WITHIN SPECIFICATION.

6. CHECK FLOAT ALIGNMENT.

7. REASSEMBLE CARBURETOR.

Rochester M4ME, M4MED and M4MEF float adjustment

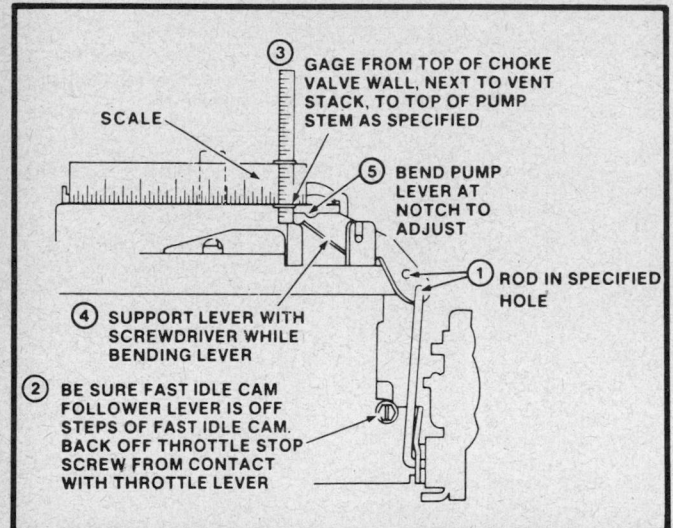

Rochester M4ME, M4MED and M4MEF pump adjustment

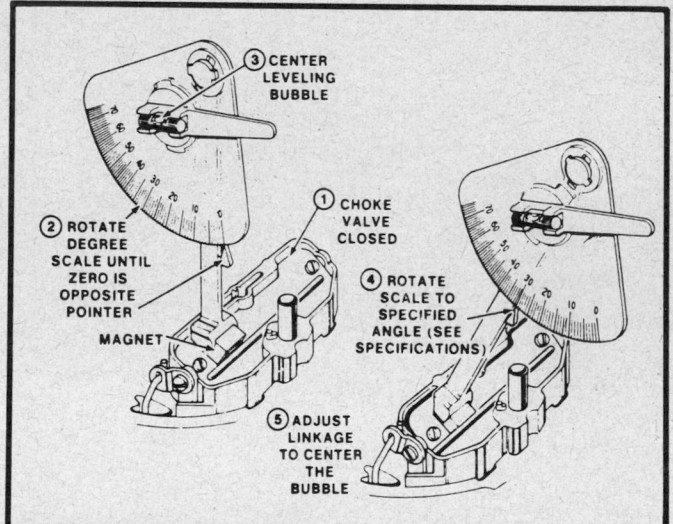

Rochester M4ME, M4MED and M4MEF choke valve angle gauge usage

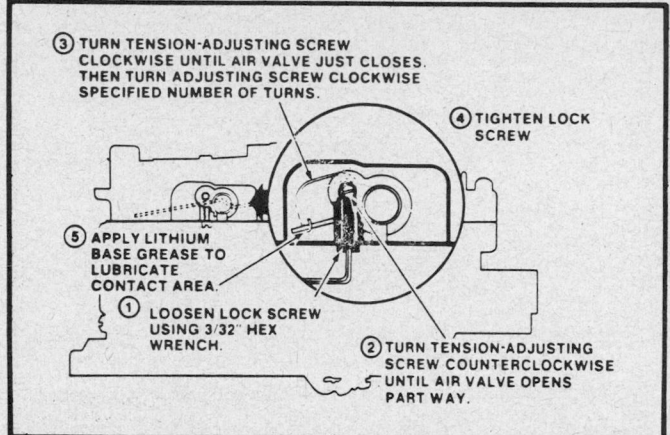

③ TURN TENSION-ADJUSTING SCREW CLOCKWISE UNTIL AIR VALVE JUST CLOSES. THEN TURN ADJUSTING SCREW CLOCKWISE SPECIFIED NUMBER OF TURNS.

④ TIGHTEN LOCK SCREW

⑤ APPLY LITHIUM BASE GREASE TO LUBRICATE CONTACT AREA.

① LOOSEN LOCK SCREW USING 3/32" HEX WRENCH.

② TURN TENSION-ADJUSTING SCREW COUNTERCLOCKWISE UNTIL AIR VALVE OPENS PART WAY.

Rochester M4ME, M4MED and M4MEF air valve spring adjustment

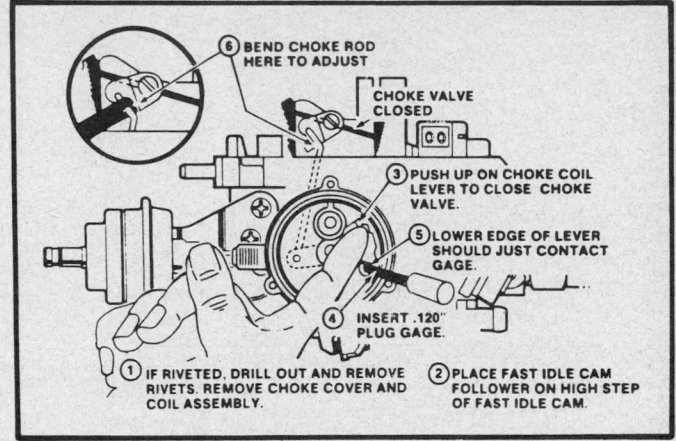

⑥ BEND CHOKE ROD HERE TO ADJUST

CHOKE VALVE CLOSED

③ PUSH UP ON CHOKE COIL LEVER TO CLOSE CHOKE VALVE.

⑤ LOWER EDGE OF LEVER SHOULD JUST CONTACT GAGE.

④ INSERT .120" PLUG GAGE.

① IF RIVETED, DRILL OUT AND REMOVE RIVETS. REMOVE CHOKE COVER AND COIL ASSEMBLY.

② PLACE FAST IDLE CAM FOLLOWER ON HIGH STEP OF FAST IDLE CAM.

Rochester M4ME, M4MED and M4MEF coil lever adjustment

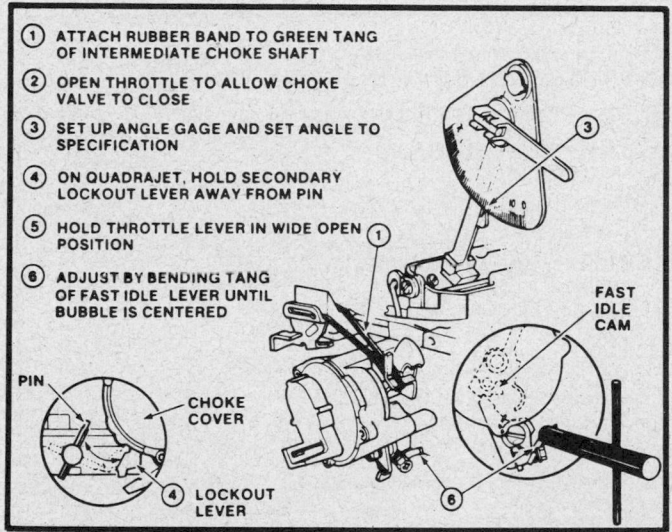

① ATTACH RUBBER BAND TO GREEN TANG OF INTERMEDIATE CHOKE SHAFT

② OPEN THROTTLE TO ALLOW CHOKE VALVE TO CLOSE

③ SET UP ANGLE GAGE AND SET ANGLE TO SPECIFICATION

④ ON QUADRAJET, HOLD SECONDARY LOCKOUT LEVER AWAY FROM PIN

⑤ HOLD THROTTLE LEVER IN WIDE OPEN POSITION

⑥ ADJUST BY BENDING TANG OF FAST IDLE LEVER UNTIL BUBBLE IS CENTERED

PIN

CHOKE COVER

FAST IDLE CAM

④ LOCKOUT LEVER

Rochester M4ME, M4MED and M4MEF unloader adjustment

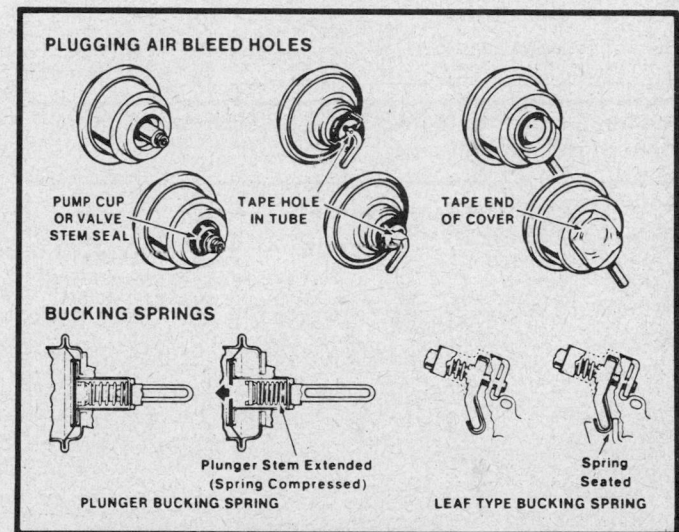

PLUGGING AIR BLEED HOLES

PUMP CUP OR VALVE STEM SEAL

TAPE HOLE IN TUBE

TAPE END OF COVER

BUCKING SPRINGS

Plunger Stem Extended (Spring Compressed)
PLUNGER BUCKING SPRING

Spring Seated
LEAF TYPE BUCKING SPRING

Rochester M4ME, M4MED and M4MEF vacuum break inspection

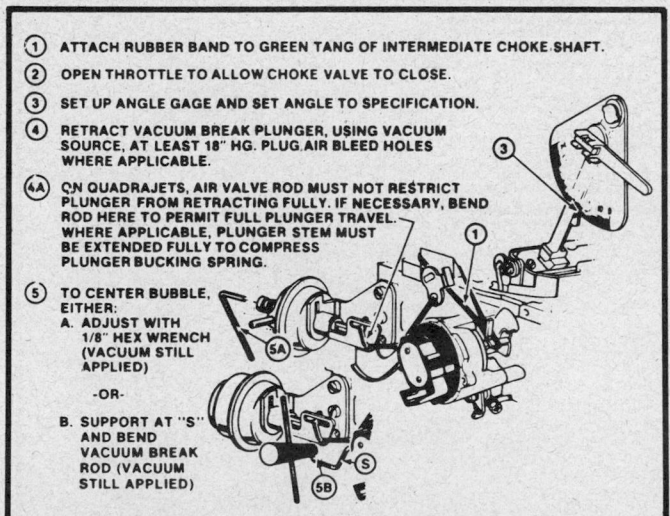

① ATTACH RUBBER BAND TO GREEN TANG OF INTERMEDIATE CHOKE SHAFT.

② OPEN THROTTLE TO ALLOW CHOKE VALVE TO CLOSE.

③ SET UP ANGLE GAGE AND SET ANGLE TO SPECIFICATION.

④ RETRACT VACUUM BREAK PLUNGER, USING VACUUM SOURCE, AT LEAST 18" HG. PLUG AIR BLEED HOLES WHERE APPLICABLE.

④A ON QUADRAJETS, AIR VALVE ROD MUST NOT RESTRICT PLUNGER FROM RETRACTING FULLY. IF NECESSARY, BEND ROD HERE TO PERMIT FULL PLUNGER TRAVEL. WHERE APPLICABLE, PLUNGER STEM MUST BE EXTENDED FULLY TO COMPRESS PLUNGER BUCKING SPRING.

⑤ TO CENTER BUBBLE, EITHER:
A. ADJUST WITH 1/8" HEX WRENCH (VACUUM STILL APPLIED)
-OR-
B. SUPPORT AT "S" AND BEND VACUUM BREAK ROD (VACUUM STILL APPLIED)

Rochester M4ME, M4MED and M4MEF rear (secondary) vacuum break adjustment

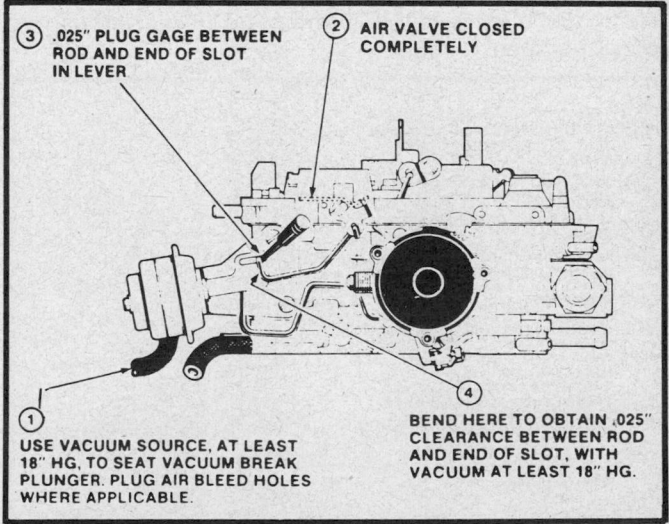

③ .025" PLUG GAGE BETWEEN ROD AND END OF SLOT IN LEVER

② AIR VALVE CLOSED COMPLETELY

① USE VACUUM SOURCE, AT LEAST 18" HG, TO SEAT VACUUM BREAK PLUNGER. PLUG AIR BLEED HOLES WHERE APPLICABLE.

④ BEND HERE TO OBTAIN .025" CLEARANCE BETWEEN ROD AND END OF SLOT, WITH VACUUM AT LEAST 18" HG.

Rochester M4ME, M4MED and M4MEF rear air valve rod adjustment – 1986

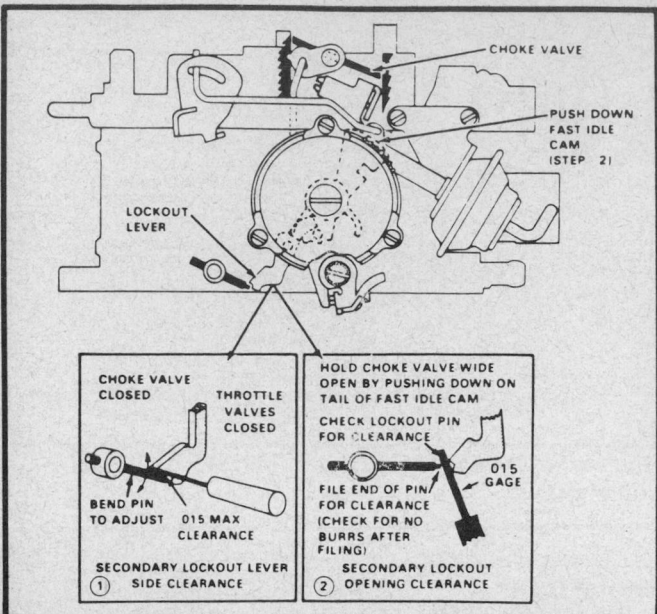

Rochester M4ME, M4MED and M4MEF secondary lockout adjustment

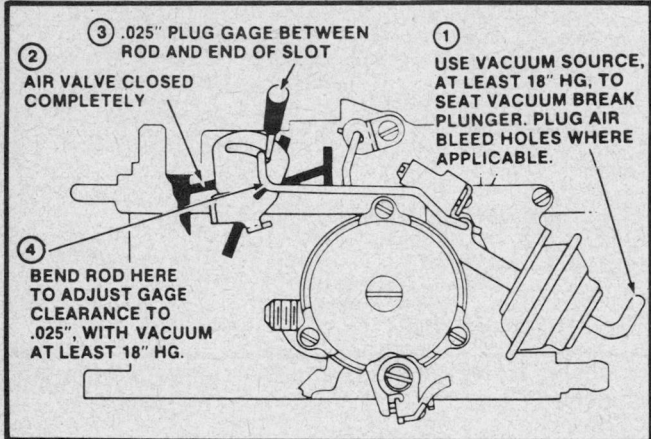

Rochester M4ME, M4MED and M4MEF rear air valve rod adjustment — 1986

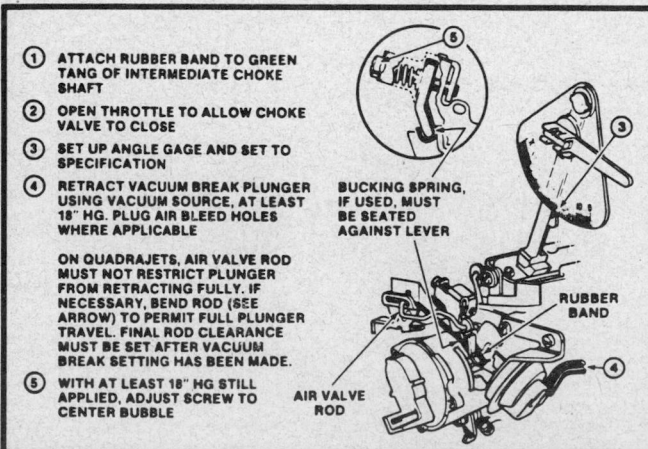

① ATTACH RUBBER BAND TO GREEN TANG OF INTERMEDIATE CHOKE SHAFT

② OPEN THROTTLE TO ALLOW CHOKE VALVE TO CLOSE

③ SET UP ANGLE GAGE AND SET TO SPECIFICATION

④ RETRACT VACUUM BREAK PLUNGER USING VACUUM SOURCE, AT LEAST 18" HG. PLUG AIR BLEED HOLES WHERE APPLICABLE

ON QUADRAJETS, AIR VALVE ROD MUST NOT RESTRICT PLUNGER FROM RETRACTING FULLY. IF NECESSARY, BEND ROD (SEE ARROW) TO PERMIT FULL PLUNGER TRAVEL. FINAL ROD CLEARANCE MUST BE SET AFTER VACUUM BREAK SETTING HAS BEEN MADE.

⑤ WITH AT LEAST 18" HG STILL APPLIED, ADJUST SCREW TO CENTER BUBBLE

Rochester M4ME, M4MED and M4MEF front (primary) vacuum break adjustment — 1986

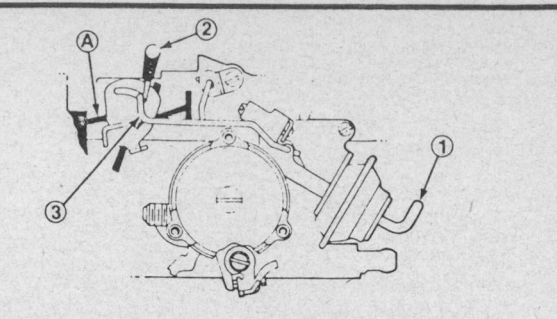

① Plug Vacuum Break bleed holes, if applicable. Air Valves Ⓐ closed. Apply 15" Hg (51 k Pa) vacuum to seat Vacuum Break Plunger.

② Gage the clearance between Air Valve Link and end of slot in lever.

③ Adjust, if necessary, by bending link.

Rochester M4ME, M4MED and M4MEF air valve rod adjustment — 1987–89

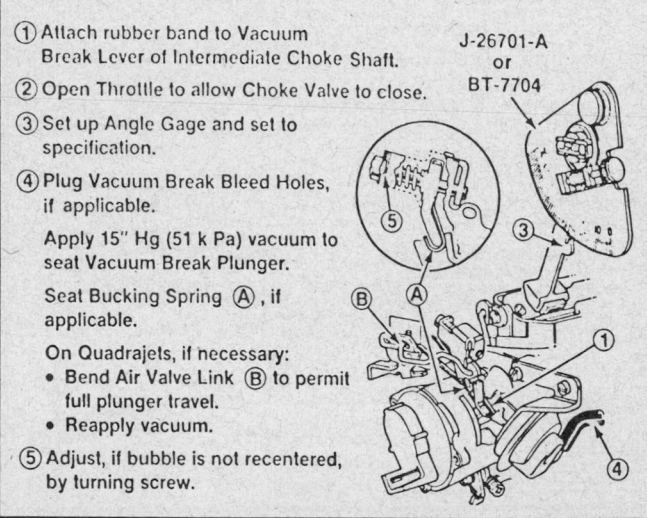

① Attach rubber band to Vacuum Break Lever of Intermediate Choke Shaft.

② Open Throttle to allow Choke Valve to close.

③ Set up Angle Gage and set to specification.

④ Plug Vacuum Break Bleed Holes, if applicable.

Apply 15" Hg (51 k Pa) vacuum to seat Vacuum Break Plunger.

Seat Bucking Spring Ⓐ, if applicable.

On Quadrajets, if necessary:
• Bend Air Valve Link Ⓑ to permit full plunger travel.
• Reapply vacuum.

⑤ Adjust, if bubble is not recentered, by turning screw.

J-26701-A or BT-7704

Rochester M4ME, M4MED and M4MEF front (primary) vacuum break adjustment — 1987–89

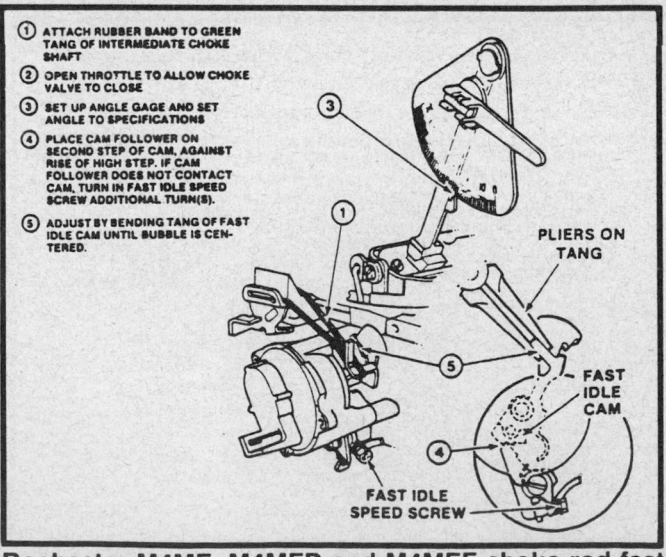

① ATTACH RUBBER BAND TO GREEN TANG OF INTERMEDIATE CHOKE SHAFT

② OPEN THROTTLE TO ALLOW CHOKE VALVE TO CLOSE

③ SET UP ANGLE GAGE AND SET ANGLE TO SPECIFICATIONS

④ PLACE CAM FOLLOWER ON SECOND STEP OF CAM, AGAINST RISE OF HIGH STEP. IF CAM FOLLOWER DOES NOT CONTACT CAM, TURN IN FAST IDLE SPEED SCREW ADDITIONAL TURN(S).

⑤ ADJUST BY BENDING TANG OF FAST IDLE CAM UNTIL BUBBLE IS CENTERED.

Rochester M4ME, M4MED and M4MEF choke rod fast idle cam adjustment

GENERAL ROCHESTER CARBURETOR SPECIFICATIONS

ANGLE DEGREE TO DECIMAL CONVERSION
Rochester Model M4MC Carburetor

Angle Degrees	Decimal Equiv. Top of Valve	Angle Degrees	Decimal Equiv. Top of Valve
5	.023	33	.203
6	.028	34	.211
7	.033	35	.220
8	.038	36	.227
9	.043	37	.234
10	.049	38	.243
11	.054	39	.251
12	.060	40	.260
13	.066	41	.269
14	.071	42	.277
15	.077	43	.287
16	.083	44	.295
17	.090	45	.304
18	.096	46	.314
19	.103	47	.322
20	.110	48	.332
21	.117	49	.341
22	.123	50	.350
23	.129	51	.360
24	.136	52	.370
25	.142	53	.379
26	.149	54	.388
27	.157	55	.400
28	.164	56	.408
29	.171	57	.418
30	.179	58	.428
31	.187	59	.439
32	.195	60	.449

ANGLE DEGREE TO DECIMAL CONVERSION
Rochester Model M4MV Carburetor

Angle Degrees	Decimal Equiv. Top of Valve	Angle Degrees	Decimal Equiv. Top of Valve
5	.019	33	.158
6	.022	34	.164
7	.026	35	.171
8	.030	36	.178
9	.034	37	.184
10	.038	38	.190
11	.042	39	.197
12	.047	40	.204
13	.051	41	.211
14	.056	42	.217

ANGLE DEGREE TO DECIMAL CONVERSION
Rochester Model M4MV Carburetor

Angle Degrees	Decimal Equiv. Top of Valve	Angle Degrees	Decimal Equiv. Top of Valve
15	.060	43	.225
16	.065	44	.231
17	.070	45	.239
18	.075	46	.246
19	.080	47	.253
20	.085	48	.260
21	.090	49	.268
22	.095	50	.275
23	.101	51	.283
24	.106	52	.291
25	.112	53	.299
26	.117	54	.306
27	.123	55	.314
28	.128	56	.322
29	.134	57	.329
30	.140	58	.337
31	.146	59	.345
32	.152	60	.353

TPS ADJUSTMENT SPECIFICATIONS
General Motors Corporation

Year	Engine Code	TPS Voltage
1986	F	0.41
	L	0.41
	N	0.25

NOTE: Measure voltage with throttle at curb idle position, ignition ON, engine and A/C OFF. All values ± 0.1 volt.

CHRYSLER CORPORATION CARBURETORS

Holley Carburetors

HOLLEY MODEL 1945
Chrysler Corporation
(All measurements in inches)

Year	Carburetor Number	Dry Float Level	Choke Unloader	Pump Stroke	Pump Rod Hole	Fast Idle Cam Position	Fast Idle Speed	Initial Choke Opening
1986	R40102A	①	0.250	1.70	1	0.080	1800	0.130
	R40244A	①	0.250	1.61	2	0.090	1600	0.130
	R40159	①	0.250	1.61	2	0.080	1600	0.130
	R40160	①	0.250	1.61	2	0.090	1600	0.130
1987	R40102A	①	0.250	1.70	1	0.080	1800	0.130
	R40244A	①	0.250	1.61	2	0.090	1600	0.130
	R40159	①	0.250	1.61	2	0.080	1600	0.130
	R40160	①	0.250	1.61	2	0.090	1600	0.130

NOTE: Choke setting is fixed and nonadjustable
① Flush with top of bowl over gasket, carb inverted

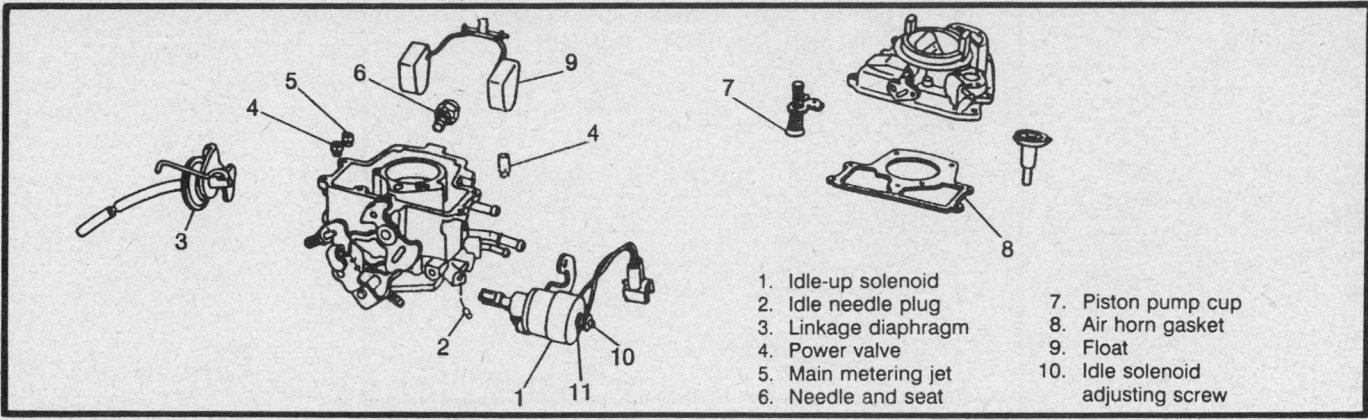

1. Idle-up solenoid
2. Idle needle plug
3. Linkage diaphragm
4. Power valve
5. Main metering jet
6. Needle and seat
7. Piston pump cup
8. Air horn gasket
9. Float
10. Idle solenoid adjusting screw

Holley 1945 carburetor—exploded view

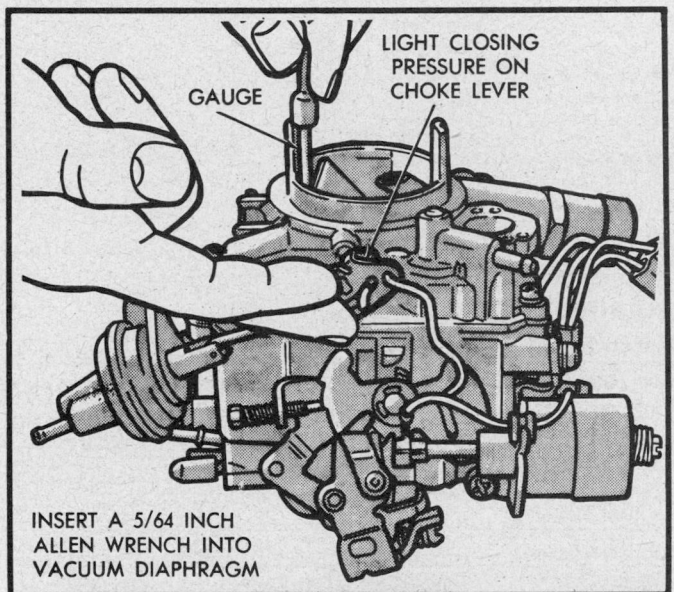

GAUGE
LIGHT CLOSING PRESSURE ON CHOKE LEVER
INSERT A 5/64 INCH ALLEN WRENCH INTO VACUUM DIAPHRAGM

Holley 1945 initial choke valve setting (vacuum kick)

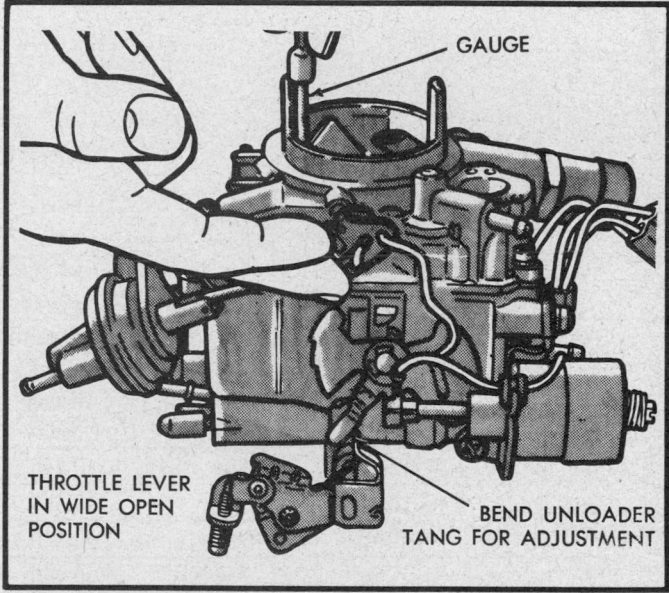

GAUGE
THROTTLE LEVER IN WIDE OPEN POSITION
BEND UNLOADER TANG FOR ADJUSTMENT

Holley 1945 choke valve unloader adjustment

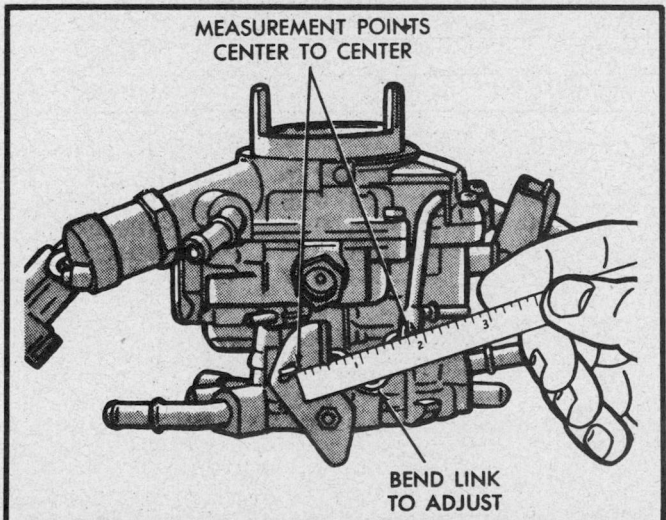

MEASUREMENT POINTS CENTER TO CENTER
BEND LINK TO ADJUST

Holley 1945 accelerator pump piston stroke adjustment

LIGHT CLOSING PRESSURE ON CHOKE LEVER
GAUGE
FAST IDLE SCREW ON SECOND HIGHEST STEP OF CAM

Holley 1945 fast idle cam adjustment

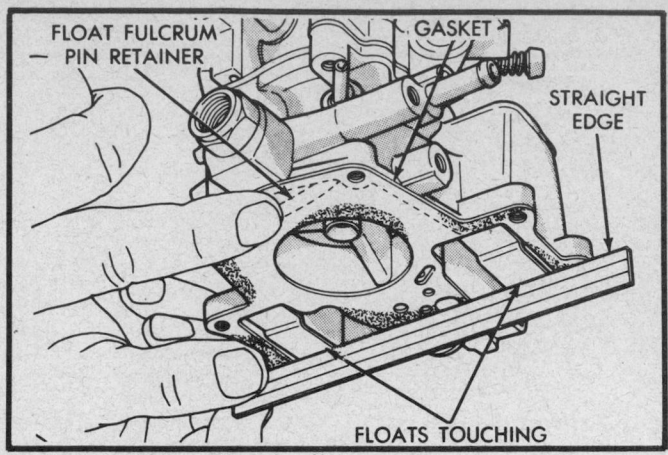

Holley 1945 float level adjustment

MODELS 2280

HOLLEY MODEL 2280
Chrysler Corporation
(All measurements in inches)

Year	Carburetor Number	Float Level ①	Choke Vacuum Kick	Fast Idle Cam	Fast Idle (rpm)	Choke Unloader	Bowl Vent Valve
1986	R40172-1A	⁹/₃₂	0.140	0.052	②	0.250	0.035
	R40216A	⁹/₃₂	0.140	0.070	②	0.250	0.035
	R40214A	⁹/₃₂	0.140	0.070	②	0.250	0.035
1987	R40172-1A	⁹/₃₂	0.140	0.052	②	0.200	0.035
	R40214A	⁹/₃₂	0.140	0.070	②	0.250	0.035
	R40216A	⁹/₃₂	0.140	0.070	②	0.250	0.035
	R40221A	⁹/₃₂	0.130	0.070	②	0.150	0.035
	R40222A	⁹/₃₂	0.130	0.070	②	0.150	0.035

① Measured from surface of fuel bowl to the toe of each float
② Refer to underhood specification sticker

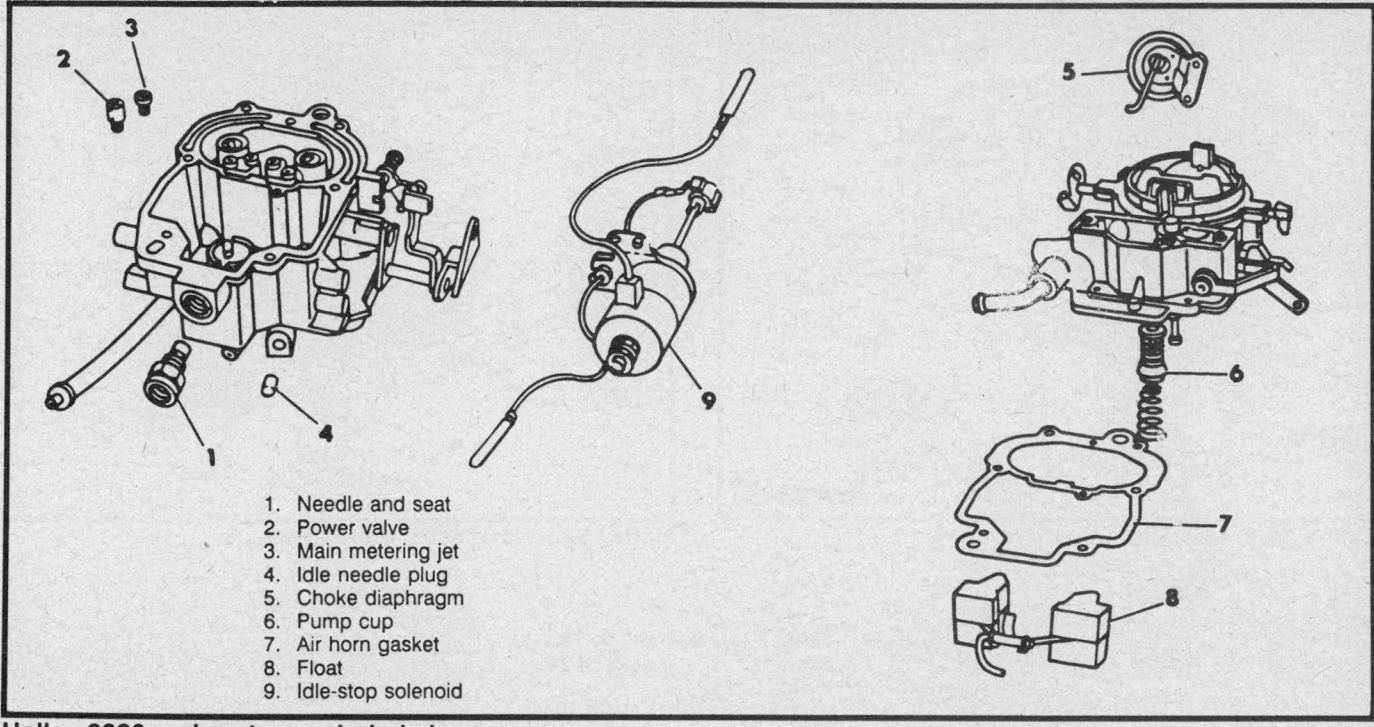

1. Needle and seat
2. Power valve
3. Main metering jet
4. Idle needle plug
5. Choke diaphragm
6. Pump cup
7. Air horn gasket
8. Float
9. Idle-stop solenoid

Holley 2280 carburetor exploded view

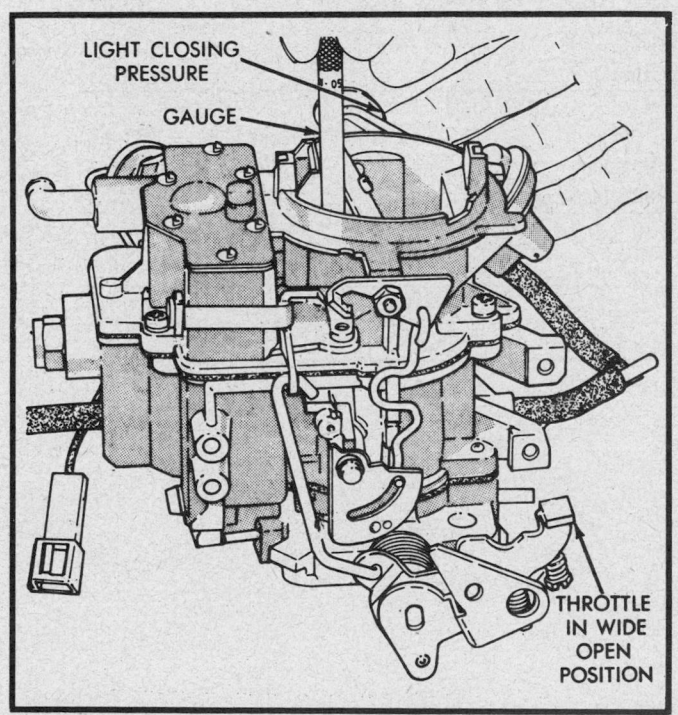

Holley 2280 choke inloader adjustment

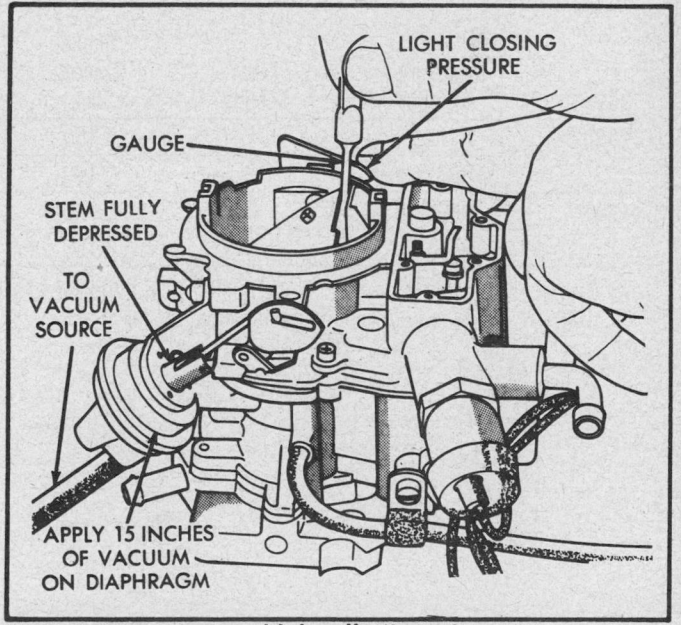

Holley 2280 vacuum kick adjustment

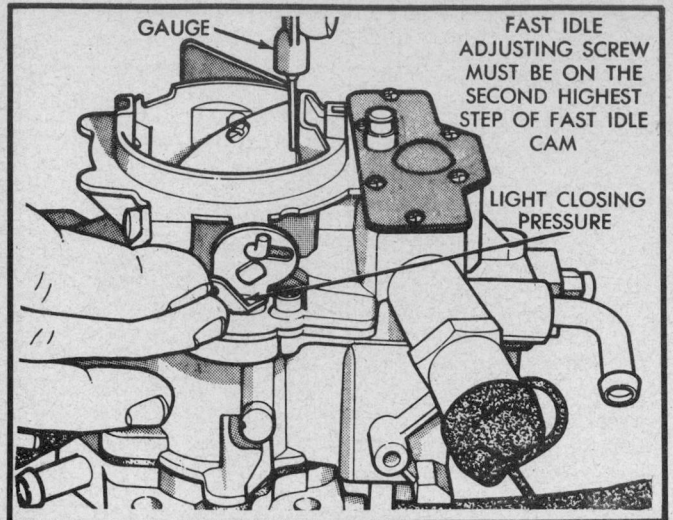

Holley 2280 fast idle adjustment

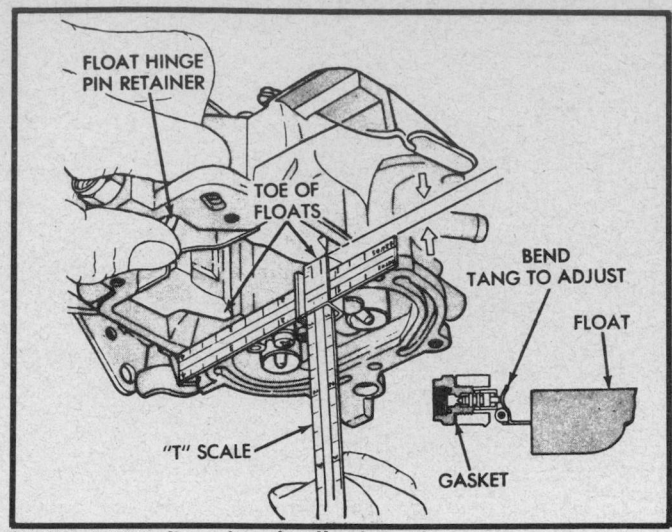

Holley 2280 float level adjustment

MODEL 6145

HOLLEY MODEL 6145
Chrysler Corporation
(All measurements in inches)

Year	Carburetor Number	Float Setting	Choke Vacuum Kick	Choke Unloader Adjustment	Fast Idle Cam Position	Fast Idle (rpm)	Pump Piston Stroke
1986	R40161	①	0.150	0.250	0.060	②	1.75
	R40162	①	0.150	0.250	0.070	②	1.75
1987	R40161	①	0.150	0.250	0.060	②	1.75
	R40162	①	0.150	0.250	0.070	②	1.75

① With bowl inverted, float lungs just touch a straightedge run along gasket surface
② 1986–87: Refer to underhood specification sticker

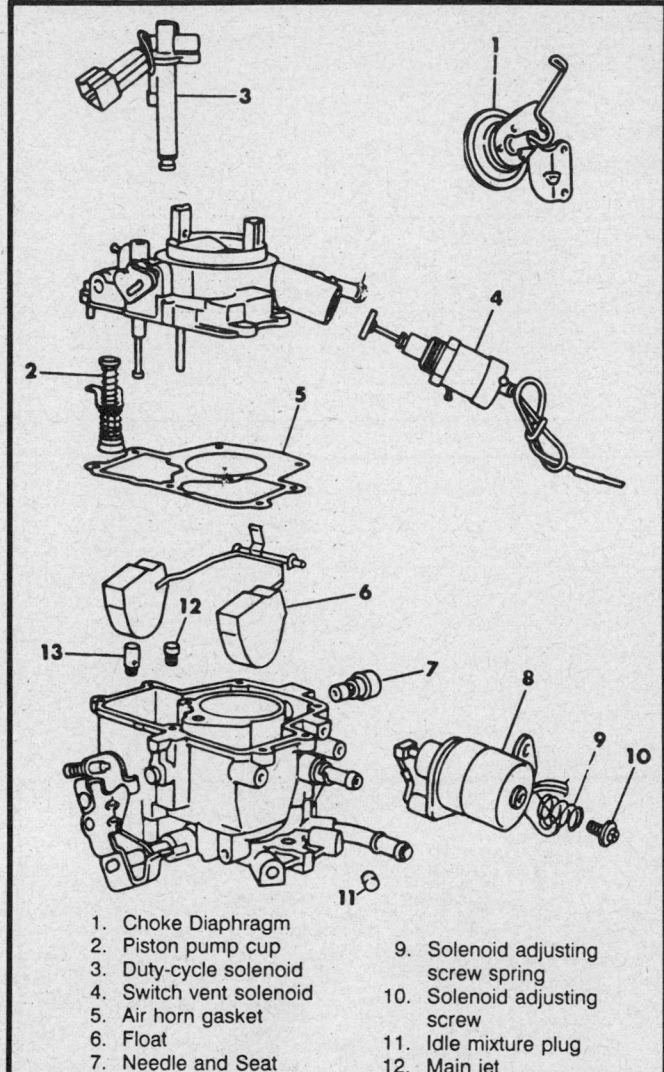

1. Choke Diaphragm
2. Piston pump cup
3. Duty-cycle solenoid
4. Switch vent solenoid
5. Air horn gasket
6. Float
7. Needle and Seat
8. Speed-up solenoid
9. Solenoid adjusting screw spring
10. Solenoid adjusting screw
11. Idle mixture plug
12. Main jet
13. Power valve

Holley 6145 carburetor—exploded view

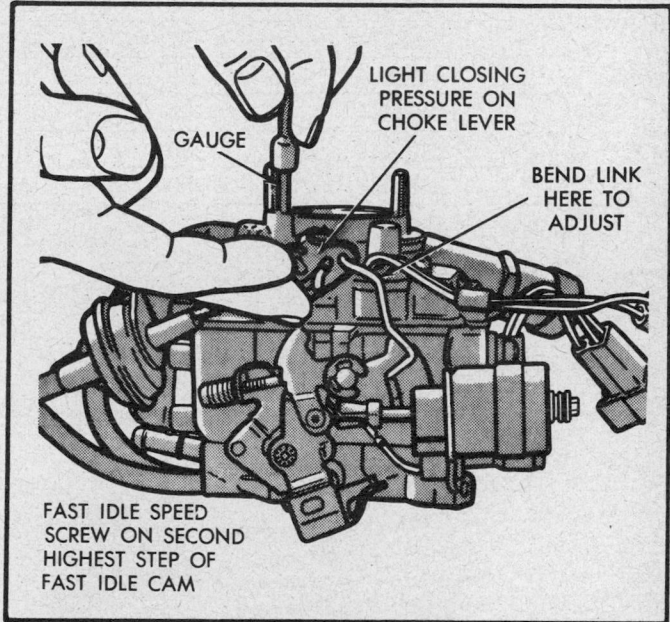

Holley 6145 float adjustment

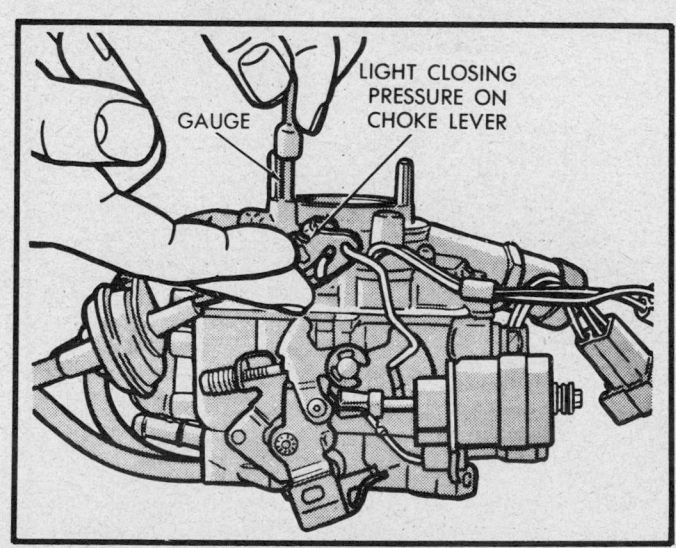

Holley 6145 vacum kick adjustment

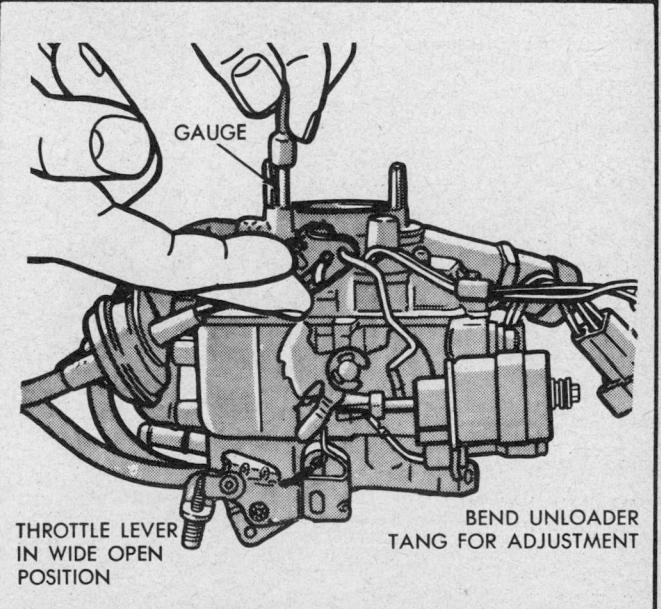

Holley 6145 fast idle cam adjustment

Holley 6145 choke unloader adjustment

MODEL 5220

HOLLEY MODEL 5220
Chrysler Corporation
(All measurements in inches)

Year	Carburetor Number	Float Level	Choke Vacuum Kick	Accelerator Pump Hole	Fast Idle Speed	Propane Idle Speed
1986	R40229A	0.480	0.130	—	①	①
	R40230A	0.480	0.130	—	①	①
	R40231A	0.480	0.130	—	①	①
	R40232A	0.480	0.130	—	①	①
1987	R40234A	0.480	0.095	—	①	①
	R40240A	0.480	0.095	—	①	①
	R40303A	0.480	0.095	—	①	①

① Refer to underhood specification sticker

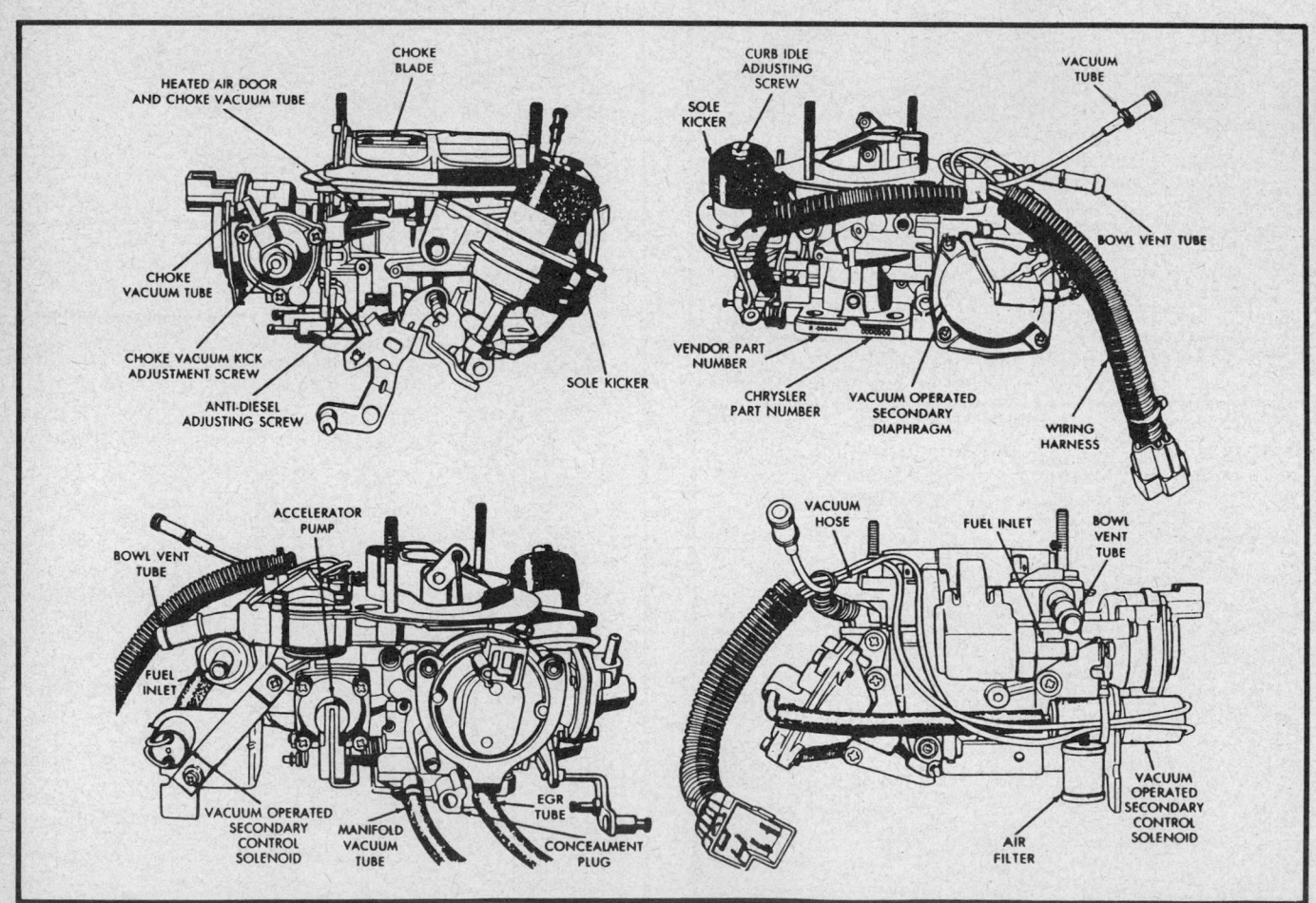

Holley 5220 carburetor side view

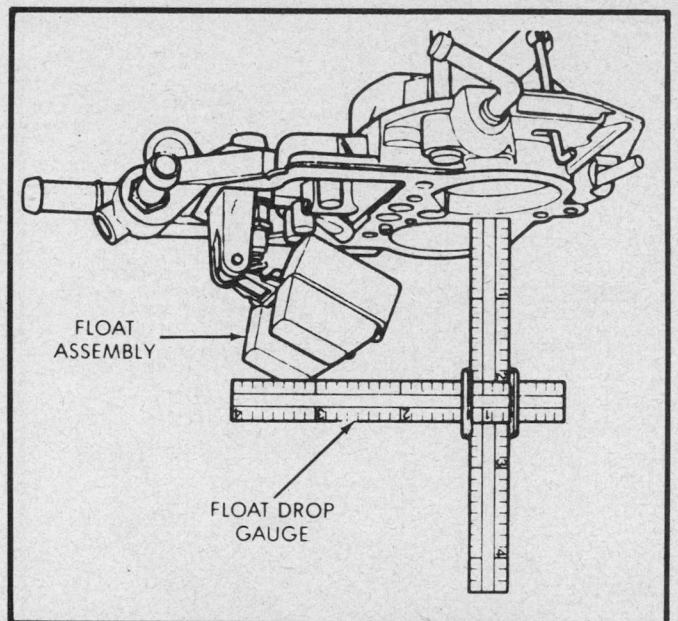

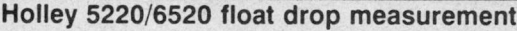

Holley 5220/6520 float drop measurement

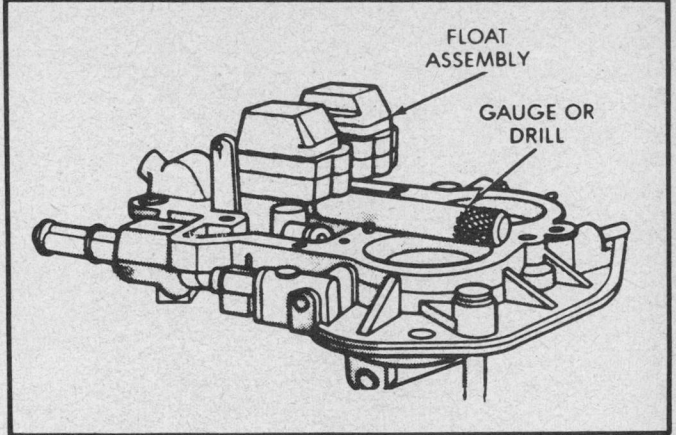

Holley 5220/6520 dry float setting

MODEL 6520

HOLLEY MODEL 6520
Chrysler Corporation
(All measurements in inches)

Year	Carburetor Number	Float Level	Choke Vacuum Kick	Accelerator Pump Hole	Fast Idle Speed	Propane Idle Speed
1986	R40233A	0.480	0.160	—	①	①
	R40234A	0.480	0.160	—	①	①
	R40240A	0.480	0.160	—	①	①
1987	R40299A	0.480	0.075	—	①	①
	R40300A	0.480	0.075	—	①	①
	R40301A	0.480	0.075	—	①	①
	R40302A	0.480	0.075	—	①	①
	R40308A	0.500	0.082	—	①	①
	R40309A	0.500	0.082	—	①	①
1988	R40308-1	0.500	0.082	—	①	①
	R40309-1	0.500	0.082	—	①	①

① Refer to underhood specification sticker

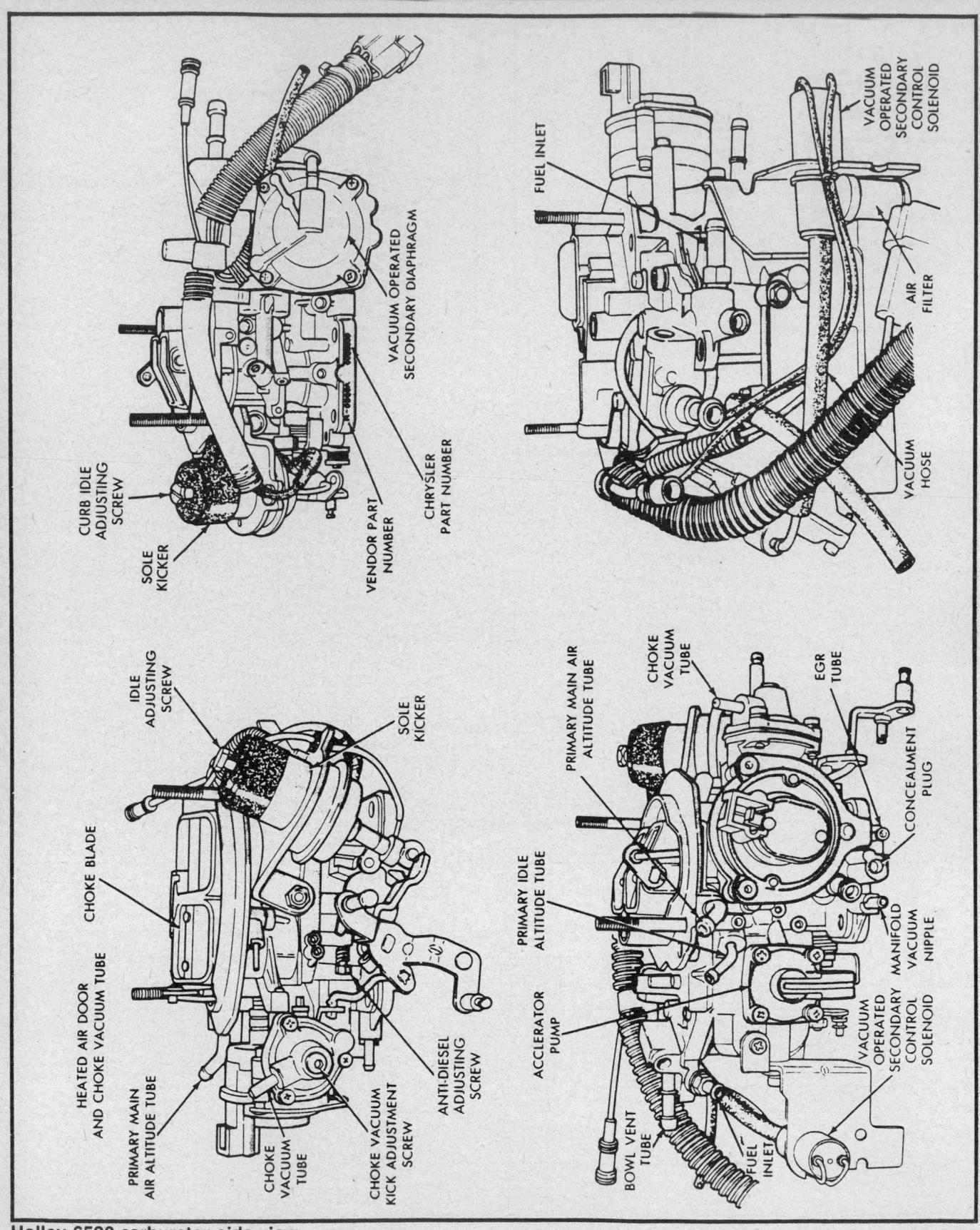

Holley 6520 carburetor side view

CURB IDLE ADJUSTING SCREW

SOLE KICKER

VENDOR PART NUMBER

CHRYSLER PART NUMBER

VACUUM OPERATED SECONDARY DIAPHRAGM

FUEL INLET

VACUUM OPERATED SECONDARY CONTROL SOLENOID

AIR FILTER

VACUUM HOSE

HEATED AIR DOOR AND CHOKE VACUUM TUBE

PRIMARY MAIN AIR ALTITUDE TUBE

CHOKE BLADE

IDLE ADJUSTING SCREW

SOLE KICKER

CHOKE VACUUM TUBE

CHOKE VACUUM KICK ADJUSTMENT SCREW

ANTI-DIESEL ADJUSTING SCREW

ACCLERATOR PUMP

PRIMARY IDLE ALTITUDE TUBE

PRIMARY MAIN AIR ALTITUDE TUBE

CHOKE VACUUM TUBE

EGR TUBE

CONCEALMENT PLUG

MANIFOLD VACUUM NIPPLE

VACUUM OPERATED SECONDARY CONTROL SOLENOID

BOWL VENT TUBE

FUEL INLET

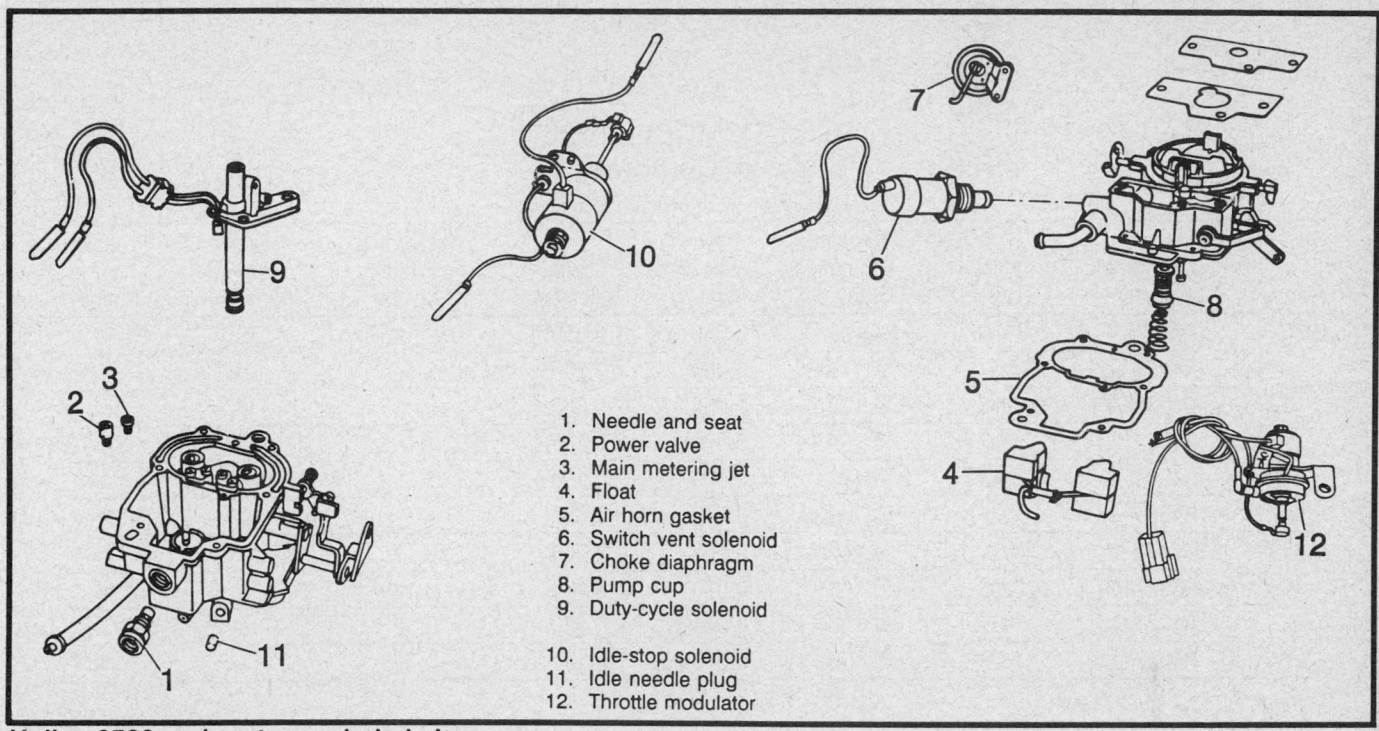

1. Needle and seat
2. Power valve
3. Main metering jet
4. Float
5. Air horn gasket
6. Switch vent solenoid
7. Choke diaphragm
8. Pump cup
9. Duty-cycle solenoid

10. Idle-stop solenoid
11. Idle needle plug
12. Throttle modulator

Holley 6520 carburetor exploded view

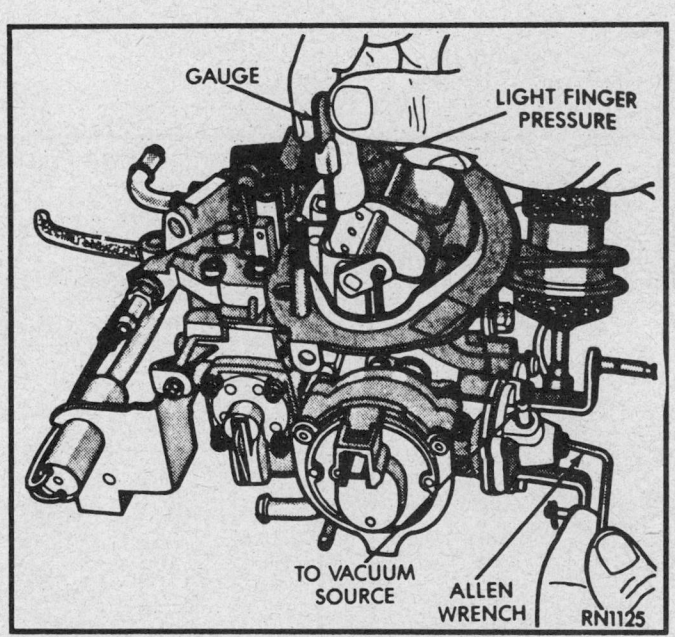

Holley 6520 choke vacuum kick adjustment

MODEL 6280

HOLLEY MODEL 6280
Chrysler Corporation
(All measurements in inches)

Year	Carburetor Number	Float Level	Choke Vacuum Kick	Fast Idle Cam	Choke Unloader	Accelerator Pump Stroke	Fast Idle Speed	Propane Idle Speed
1986	R40217A	$^9/_{32}$	0.160	0.060	0.350	0.135	②	②
	R40218A	$^9/_{32}$	0.140	0.060	0.250	0.135	②	②
	R40220A	$^9/_{32}$	0.130	0.060	0.350	0.135	②	②
	R40221A	$^9/_{32}$	0.130	0.070	0.150	①	②	②
	R40222A	$^9/_{32}$	0.130	0.070	0.150	①	②	②
	R40294A	$^9/_{32}$	0.160	0.070	0.350	—	②	②
1987	R40172-1A	$^9/_{32}$	0.140	0.052	0.200	0.135	②	②
	R40214A	$^9/_{32}$	0.140	0.070	0.250	0.135	②	②
	R40216A	$^9/_{32}$	0.140	0.070	0.250	0.135	②	②
	R40222A	$^9/_{32}$	0.130	0.070	0.150	0.135	②	②

① Flush with top of bowl vent
② Refer to underhood specification sticker

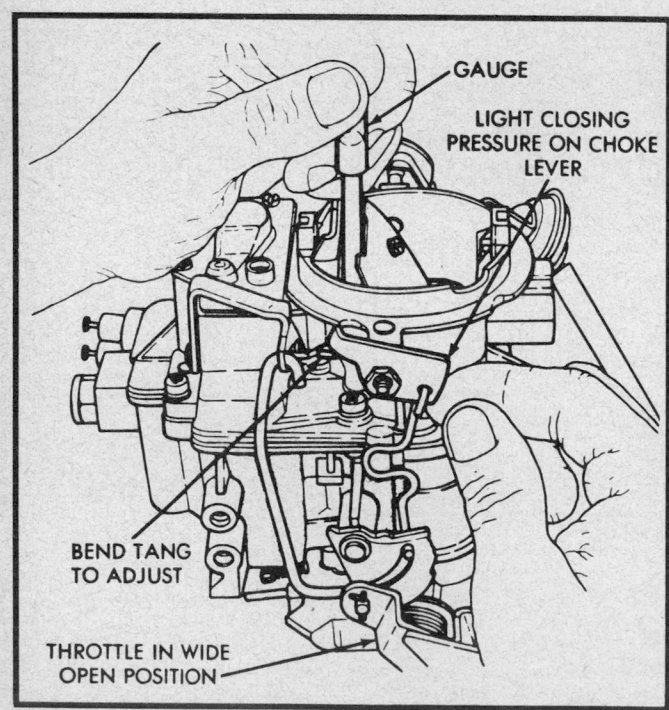

Holley 6280 choke unloader adjustment

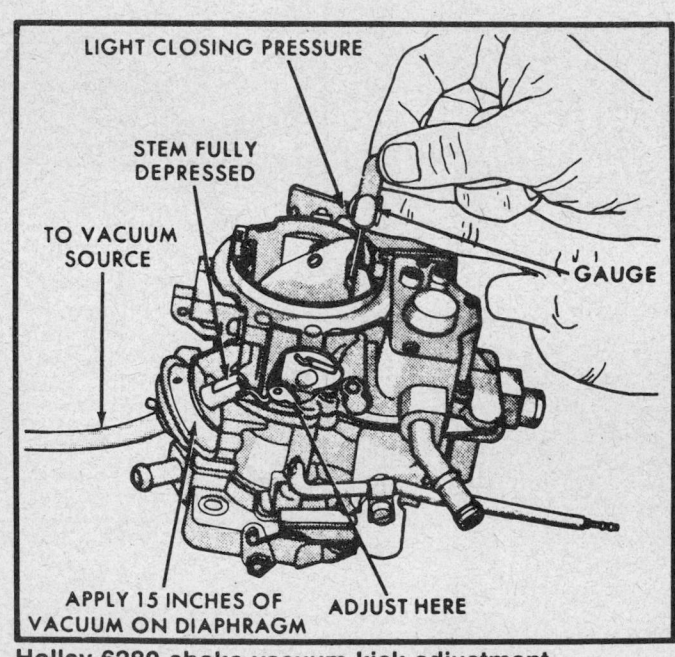

Holley 6280 choke vacuum kick adjustment

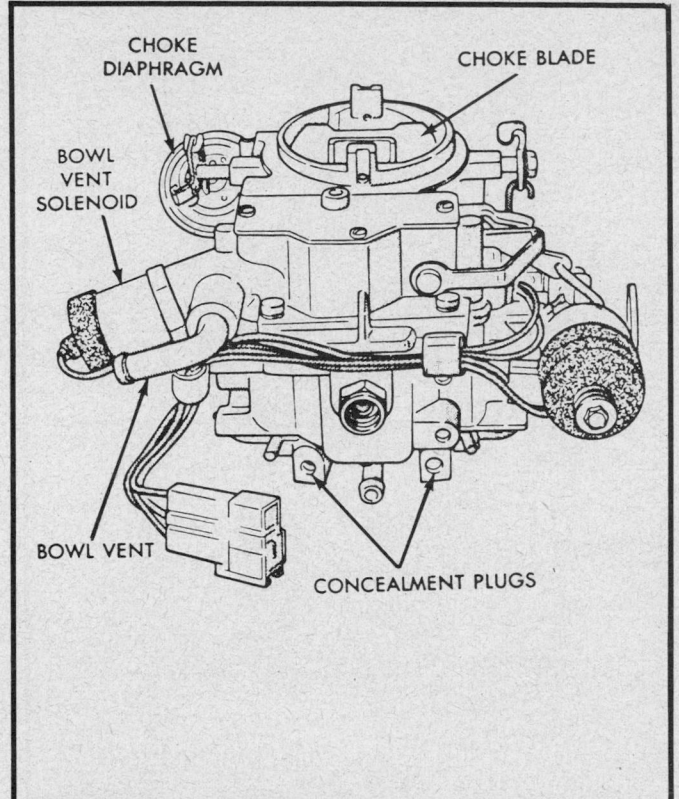

Holley 6280 carburetor

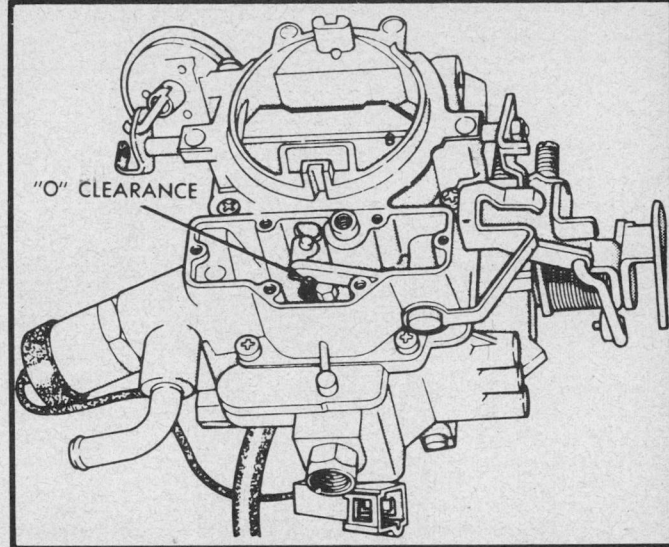

Holley 6280 accelerator pump stroke measurement

Mikuni Carburetors

MIKUNI
Chrysler Corporation
(All measurements in millimeters)

Year	Carburetor Number	Choke Breaker Opening	Choke Unloader	Fast Idle Speed	Propane Idle Speed
1986	All numbers	1.7	1.3	①	①
1987	All numbers	1.7	1.3	①	①

① Refer to the underhood specification sticker

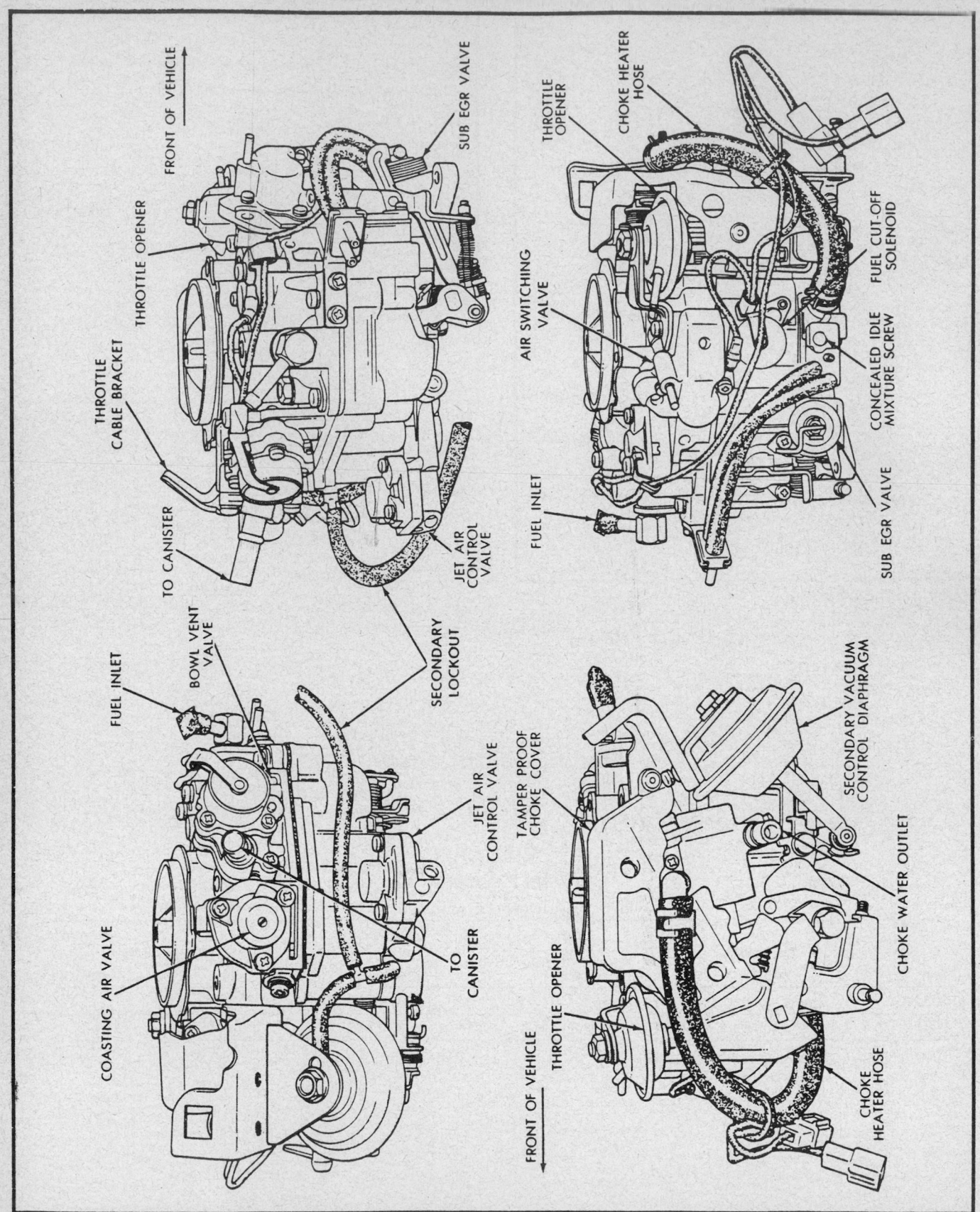

Mikuni carburetor side view—California and high altitude

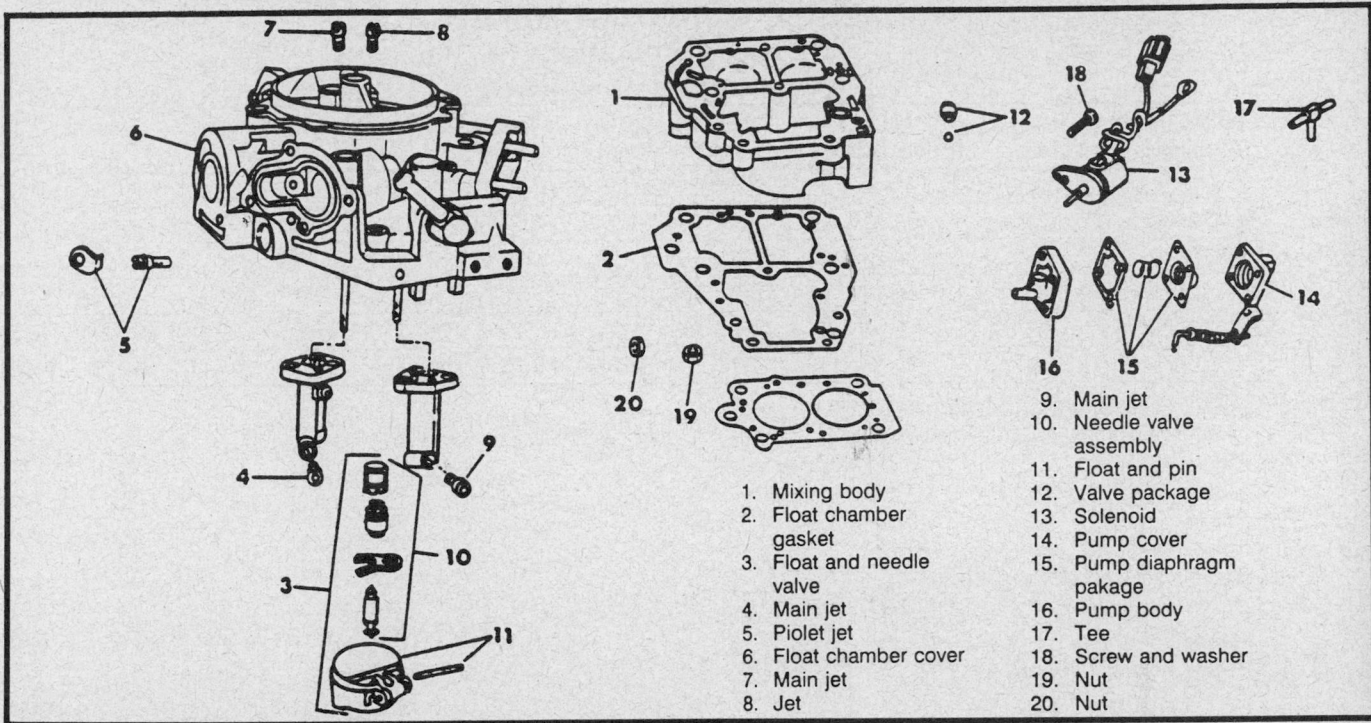

9. Main jet
10. Needle valve assembly
11. Float and pin
12. Valve package
13. Solenoid
14. Pump cover
15. Pump diaphragm pakage
16. Pump body
17. Tee
18. Screw and washer
19. Nut
20. Nut

1. Mixing body
2. Float chamber gasket
3. Float and needle valve
4. Main jet
5. Piolet jet
6. Float chamber cover
7. Main jet
8. Jet

Mikuni carburetor exploded view—federal and canadian

Rochester Carburetors

QUADRAJET

ROCHESTER QUADRAJET MODELS
Chrysler Corporation
(All measurements in inches or degrees)

Year	Carburetor Number	Float Level	Air Valve Spring Turns	Fast Idle Cam	Choke Rod	Vacuum Kick	Air Valve Rod	Choke Unloader	Propane rpm
1986	17085408	13/32	1/2	20°	0.143	27° ①	0.025	38° ②	800
	17085409	13/32	5/8	20°	0.143	27° ①	0.025	38° ②	750
	17085415	13/32	1/2	20°	0.143	27° ①	0.025	38° ②	800
	17085416	13/32	3/4	20°	0.143	27° ①	0.025	38° ②	800
	17085417	13/32	3/4	20°	0.125	27° ③	0.025	38° ④	⑤
	17085431	13/32	1/2	20°	0.125	27° ③	0.025	38° ④	⑤
1987	17085431	13/32	1/2	20°	0.125	23°	0.025	32°	⑤
	17086425	15/32	1/2	20°	0.125	23°	0.025	38°	⑤
	17087175	13/32	3/4	20°	0.125	26°	0.025	30°	⑤
	17087176	13/32	3/4	20°	0.125	26°	0.025	30°	⑤
	17087177	13/32	1	20°	0.125	27°	0.025	33°	⑤
	17087245	15/32	5/8	20°	0.125	23°	0.025	32°	⑤

ROCHESTER QUADRAJET MODELS
Chrysler Corporation
(All measurements in inches or degrees)

Year	Carburetor Number	Float Level	Air Valve Spring Turns	Fast Idle Cam	Choke Rod	Vacuum Kick	Air Valve Rod	Choke Unloader	Propane rpm
1988	17085431	$^{13}/_{32}$	$^{1}/_{2}$	20°	0.125	23°	0.025	32°	⑤
	17086425	$^{15}/_{32}$	$^{1}/_{2}$	20°	0.125	23°	0.025	32°	⑤
	17087175	$^{13}/_{32}$	$^{3}/_{4}$	20°	0.125	26°	0.025	38°	⑤
	17087176	$^{13}/_{32}$	$^{3}/_{4}$	20°	0.125	26°	0.025	30°	⑤
	17087177	$^{13}/_{32}$	1	20°	0.125	27°	0.025	33°	⑤
	17087245	$^{15}/_{32}$	$^{5}/_{8}$	20°	0.125	23°	0.025	32°	⑤

Note: specified angle for use with angle gauge tool
Choke coil lever adjustment is 0.120 in. on all models
① Plug gauge—0.214 in.
② Plug gauge—0.345 in.
③ Plug gauge—0.170 in.
④ Plug gauge—0.260 in.
⑤ Refer to underhood specification sticker

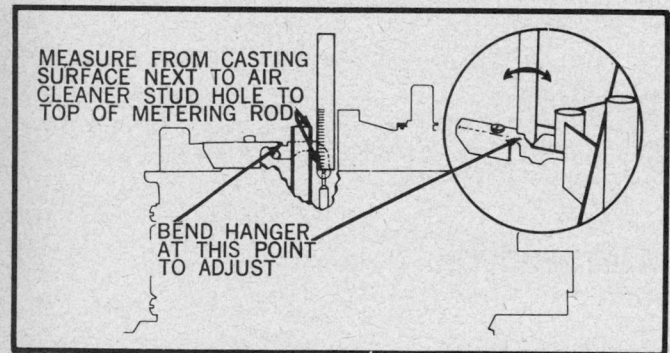

Rochester Quadrajet secondary metering adjustment

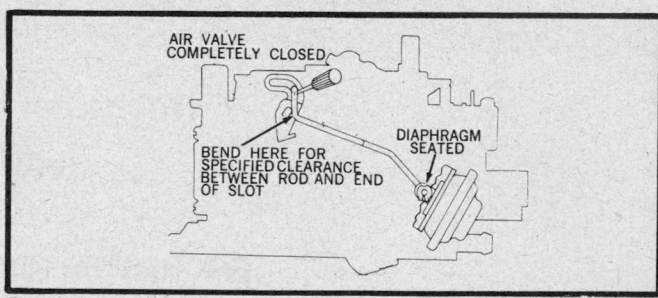

Rochester Quadrajet air valve dashpot adjustment

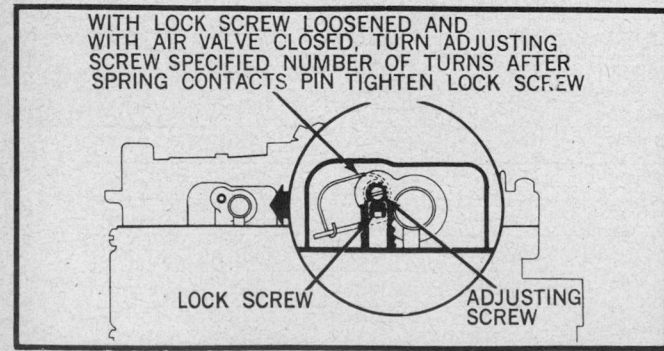

Rochester Quadrajet air valve spring adjustment

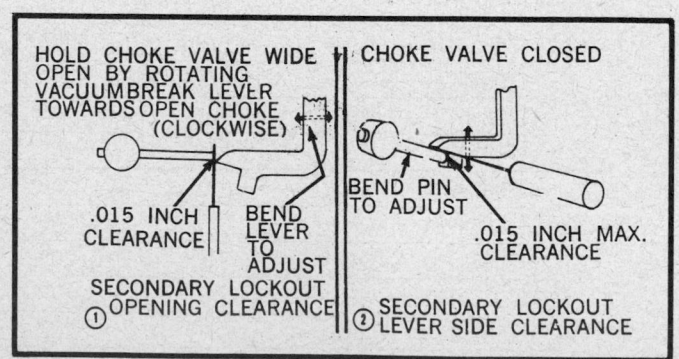

Rochester Quadrajet secondary lockout adjustment

1. Air cleaner gasket
2. Flange gasket
3. Air horn assembly
4. Secondary metering rod holder attaching screw
5. Secondary metering rod holder
6. Secondary metering rod
7. Choke lever
8. Choke lever attaching screw
9. Pump lever
10. Pump lever hinge pin
11. Air horn to throttle body screw assembly
12. Air horn to float bowl screw assembly

33. Pump discharge ball
34. Pump well baffle
35. Throttle body to "T" hose
36. Secondary side vacuum break (choke diaphragm) "T" vacuum hose
37. "T" to secondary side vacuum break (choke diaphragm) hose
38. Secondary side (rear) vacuum break assembly (choke diaphragm)
39. Secondary side (rear) vacuum break assembly (choke diaphragm) attaching screw
40. Secondary side (rear) vacuum break (choke diaphragm) to choke link
41. Secondary side vacuum break (choke diaphragm) air valve lever link
42. Choke cover attaching rivet
43. Choke cover retainer
44. Electric choke cover and stat assembly
45. Choke housing assembly
46. Choke housing to float bowl screw and washer assembly
47. Choke stat lever attaching screw
48. Choke stat lever
49. Intermediate choke shaft lever and link assembly
50. Fast idle cam assembly
51. Intermediate choke lever
52. Choke link
53. Secondary throttle lockout lever
54. Intermediate choke shaft seal
55. Fuel inlet nut
56. Fuel inlet nut gasket
57. Fule inlet filter
58. Fuel filter spring
59. Throttle stop screw
60. Throttle stop srew spring
61. Throttle body assembly
62. Float bowl to throttle body gasket
63. Float bowl to throttle body screw assembly
64. Pump link
65. Idle mixture needle
66. Idle mixture needle spring
67. Idle mixture needle plug
68. Fast idle adjusting screw
69. Fast idle adjusting screw spring
70. Hose
71. Solenoid and bracket assembly
72. Bracket attach screw

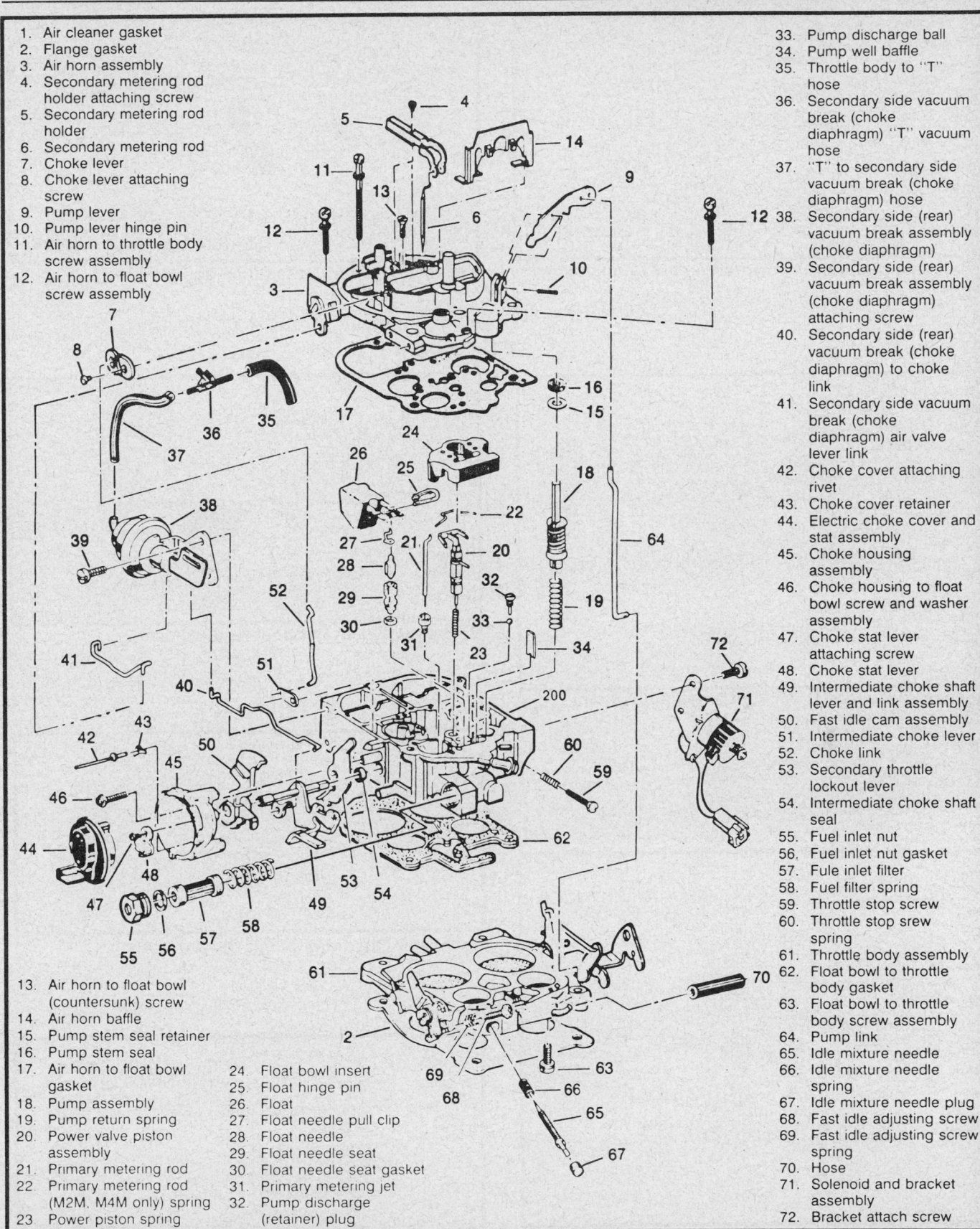

13. Air horn to float bowl (countersunk) screw
14. Air horn baffle
15. Pump stem seal retainer
16. Pump stem seal
17. Air horn to float bowl gasket
18. Pump assembly
19. Pump return spring
20. Power valve piston assembly
21. Primary metering rod
22. Primary metering rod (M2M, M4M only) spring
23. Power piston spring

24. Float bowl insert
25. Float hinge pin
26. Float
27. Float needle pull clip
28. Float needle
29. Float needle seat
30. Float needle seat gasket
31. Primary metering jet
32. Pump discharge (retainer) plug

Rochester Quadrajet carburetor exploded view

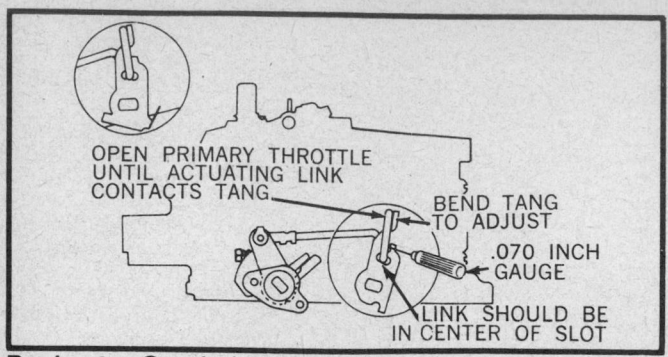

Rochester Quadrajet secondary opening adjustment

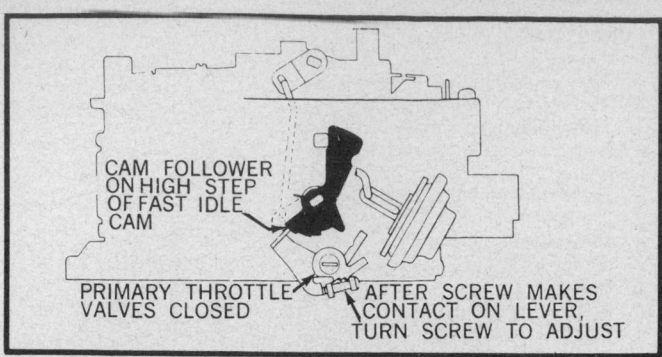

Rochester Quadrajet fast idle adjustment

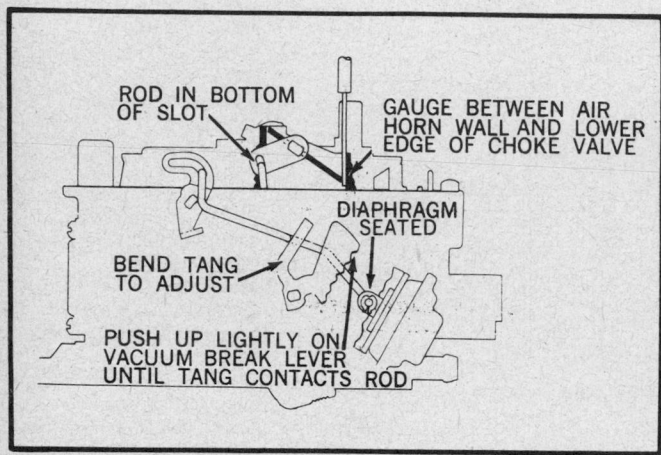

Rochester Quadrajet vacuum break adjustment

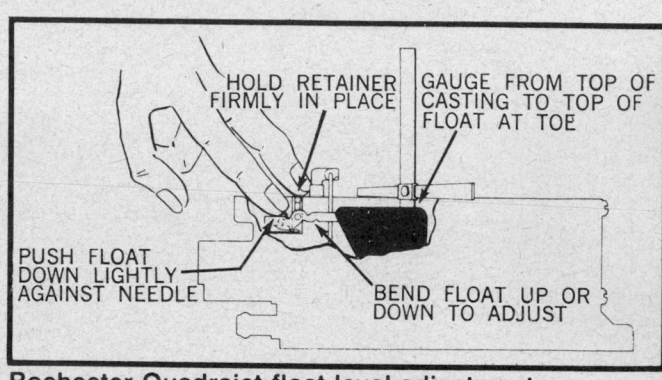

Rochester Quadrajet float level adjustment

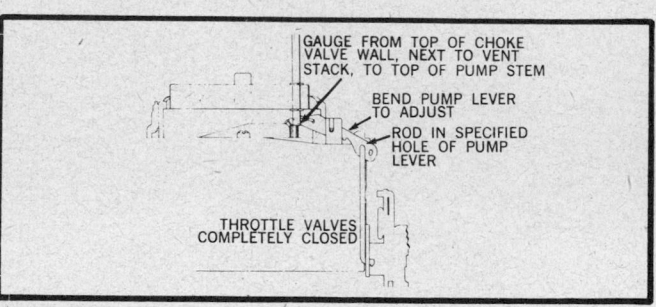

Rochester Quadrajet pump rod adjustment

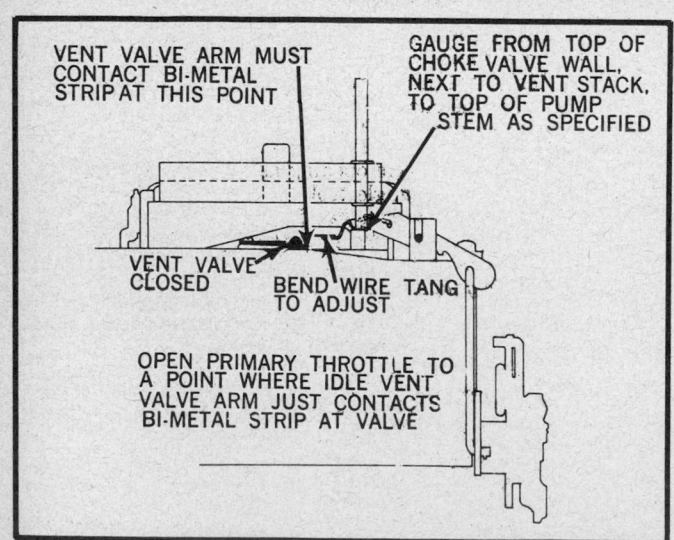

Rochester Quadrajet idle vent adjustment

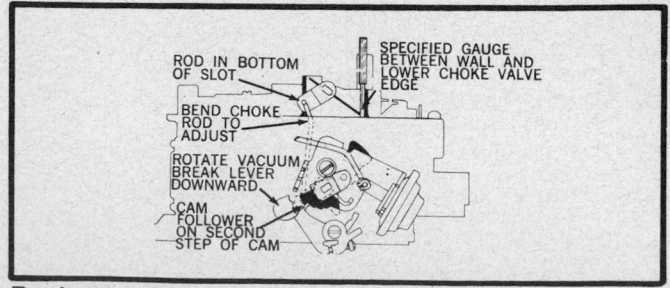

Rochester Quadrajet choke rod adjustment

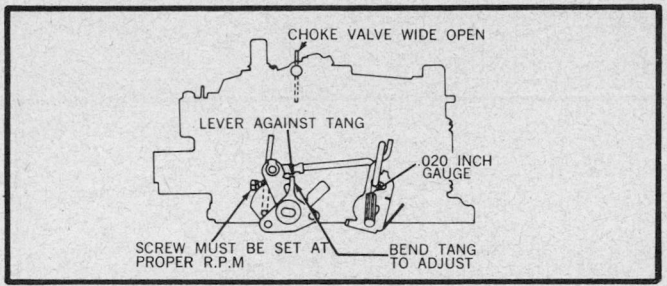

Rochester Quadrajet secondary closing adjustment

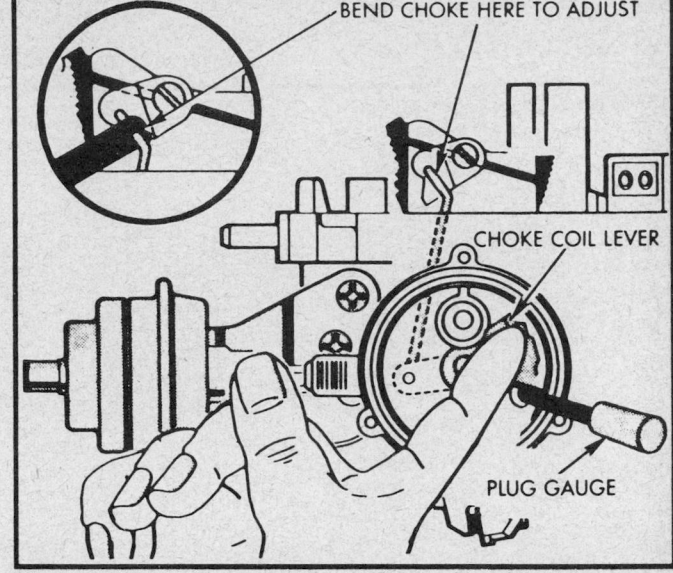

Rochester Quadrajet choke coil lever adjustment

FORD MOTOR CO. CARBURETORS

Emission Calibration Numbers

Emission calibration numbers are used by Ford Motor Company to provide the technician with the necessary specifications to adjust a specific engine to the proper emission control levels.

The calibration numbers are listed on the lower right of the Vehicle Emission Control Information label, which is attached to the engine valve cover.

The information on the decal must be used when differences exist between the decal and other specification tables, unless otherwise noted by Ford Motor Company.

CARTER MODEL YFA
Ford Motor Company
(All measurements in inches)

Year	Carburetor Number	Float Level	Float Drop	Choke Unloader Setting	Choke Setting	Dash Pot Plunger	Initial Choke Opening
1986	E57E-9510 DA,DB	0.650	—	0.270	Gray ①	—	0.320
	E5TE-9510 AA, TA, UA, VA, RA, SA, JA, BA, MA, CA, GA	0.780	—	0.330	Red ①	—	0.360
	E5TE-9510 FA	0.780	—	0.330	Red ①	—	0.340
	E5TE-9510 HA	0.780	—	0.330	Red ①	—	0.320
	D5TE-9510 AGB	0.375	—	0.280	—	—	0.230

①Choke cap index plate color

Carter Carburetors
MODEL YFA

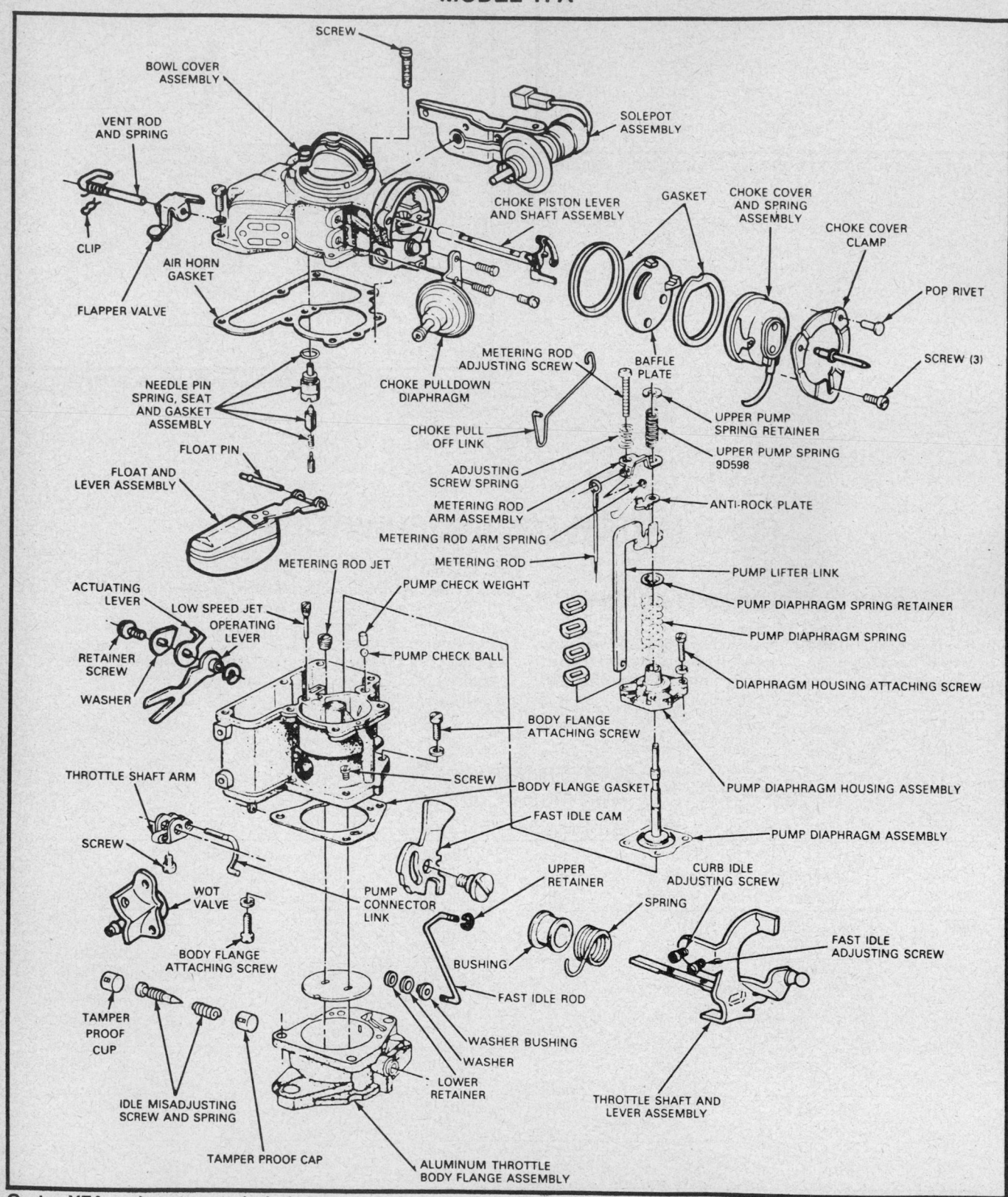

Carter YFA carburetor exploded view

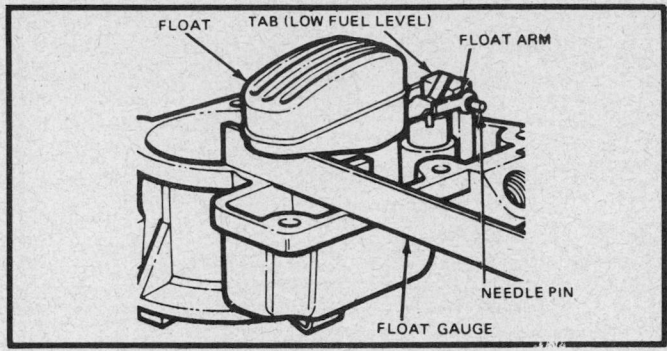

Carter YFA float drop measurement

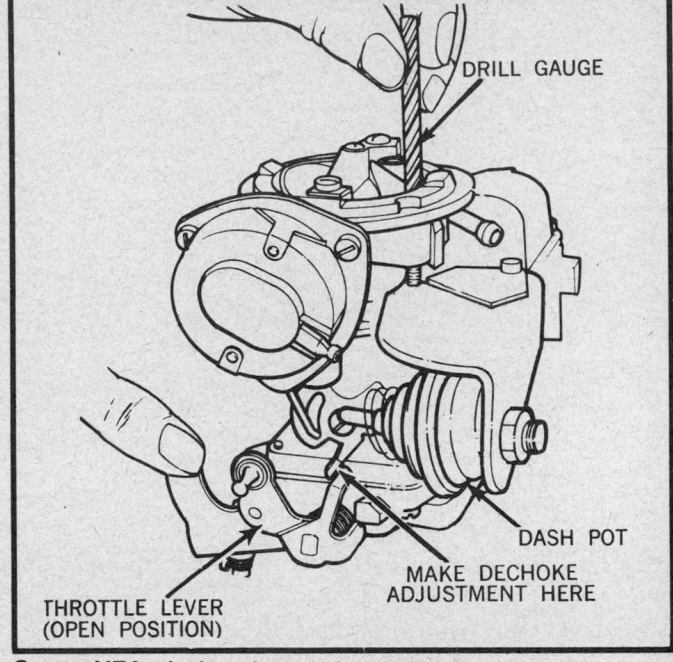

Carter YFA choke plate unloader adjustment

Holley Carburetors

MODEL 4180C

HOLLEY MODEL 4180C
Ford Motor Company
(All measurements in inches)

Year	Carburetor Number	Fuel Level (Wet)	Choke Pulldown Setting	Choke Unloader Setting	Choke Setting	Pump Lever Location	Enrichment Valve Indent.
1986	E5TE-9510 ZB	①	0.157	0.425	Orange ②	1	—
1987	E5TE-9510 ZB	①	0.144–0.170	0.425	Orange ②	1	—
	E6HE-9510 AC	①	0.144–0.170	0.425	Orange ②	1	—
	E6HE-9510 GA, GB	①	0.138–0.162	0.300	Natural ②	1	—

① At bottom of sight plug
② Choke cap color index plate

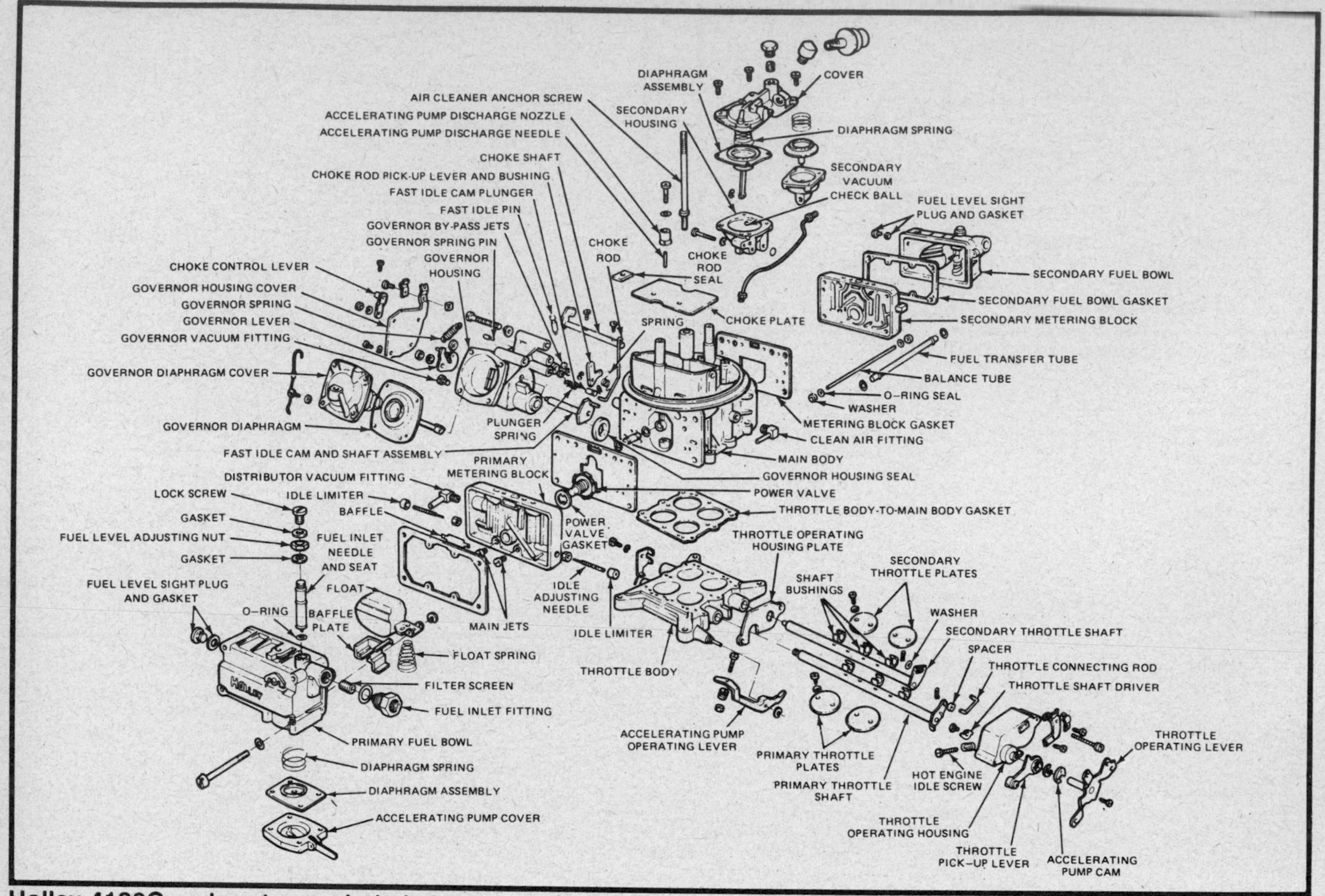

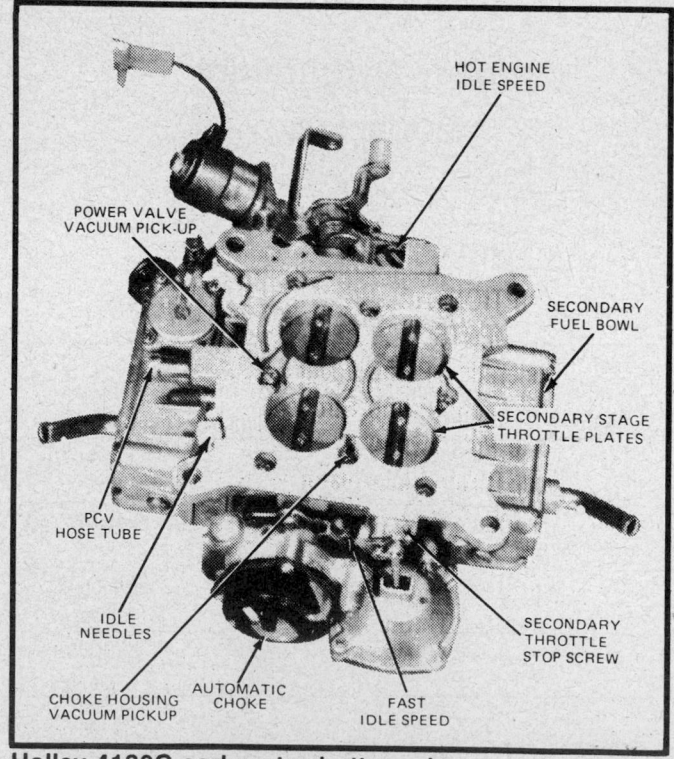

DIAPHRAGM ASSEMBLY
COVER
AIR CLEANER ANCHOR SCREW
ACCELERATING PUMP DISCHARGE NOZZLE
ACCELERATING PUMP DISCHARGE NEEDLE
SECONDARY HOUSING
DIAPHRAGM SPRING
CHOKE SHAFT
CHOKE ROD PICK-UP LEVER AND BUSHING
FAST IDLE CAM PLUNGER
FAST IDLE PIN
GOVERNOR BY-PASS JETS
GOVERNOR SPRING PIN
CHOKE ROD
CHOKE ROD SEAL
SECONDARY VACUUM CHECK BALL
FUEL LEVEL SIGHT PLUG AND GASKET
CHOKE CONTROL LEVER
GOVERNOR HOUSING COVER
GOVERNOR SPRING
GOVERNOR LEVER
GOVERNOR VACUUM FITTING
GOVERNOR HOUSING
CHOKE PLATE
SPRING
CHOKE PLATE
SECONDARY FUEL BOWL
SECONDARY FUEL BOWL GASKET
SECONDARY METERING BLOCK
GOVERNOR DIAPHRAGM COVER
FUEL TRANSFER TUBE
BALANCE TUBE
O-RING SEAL
WASHER
METERING BLOCK GASKET
CLEAN AIR FITTING
GOVERNOR DIAPHRAGM
PLUNGER SPRING
FAST IDLE CAM AND SHAFT ASSEMBLY
DISTRIBUTOR VACUUM FITTING
PRIMARY METERING BLOCK
MAIN BODY
GOVERNOR HOUSING SEAL
POWER VALVE
THROTTLE BODY-TO-MAIN BODY GASKET
LOCK SCREW
IDLE LIMITER
BAFFLE
POWER VALVE GASKET
THROTTLE OPERATING HOUSING PLATE
SHAFT BUSHINGS
SECONDARY THROTTLE PLATES
FUEL LEVEL ADJUSTING NUT
FUEL INLET NEEDLE AND SEAT
GASKET
IDLE ADJUSTING NEEDLE
WASHER
SECONDARY THROTTLE SHAFT
FUEL LEVEL SIGHT PLUG AND GASKET
FLOAT
O-RING
BAFFLE PLATE
MAIN JETS
SPACER
THROTTLE CONNECTING ROD
THROTTLE SHAFT DRIVER
IDLE LIMITER
THROTTLE BODY
FLOAT SPRING
FILTER SCREEN
FUEL INLET FITTING
PRIMARY FUEL BOWL
DIAPHRAGM SPRING
DIAPHRAGM ASSEMBLY
ACCELERATING PUMP COVER
ACCELERATING PUMP OPERATING LEVER
PRIMARY THROTTLE PLATES
PRIMARY THROTTLE SHAFT
HOT ENGINE IDLE SCREW
THROTTLE OPERATING HOUSING
THROTTLE PICK-UP LEVER
ACCELERATING PUMP CAM
THROTTLE OPERATING LEVER

Holley 4180C carburetor exploded view

HOT ENGINE IDLE SPEED
POWER VALVE VACUUM PICK-UP
SECONDARY FUEL BOWL
SECONDARY STAGE THROTTLE PLATES
PCV HOSE TUBE
IDLE NEEDLES
CHOKE HOUSING VACUUM PICKUP
AUTOMATIC CHOKE
FAST IDLE SPEED
SECONDARY THROTTLE STOP SCREW

Holley 4180C carburetor bottom view

Motorcraft Carburetors

MODEL 2150

MOTORCRAFT MODEL 2150
Ford Motor Company

(All measurements in inches)

Year	Carburetor Number	Float Level (Dry)	Choke Unloader Setting	Choke Setting	Accelerator Pump Rod Location	Fuel Level (Wet)	Choke Pulldown Setting (Min.)
1986	E69E-9510 CA, DA	1/16	0.250	V notch	4	0.810	0.126–0.146
	AA, BA	1/16	0.250	V notch	4	0.810	0.126–0.146

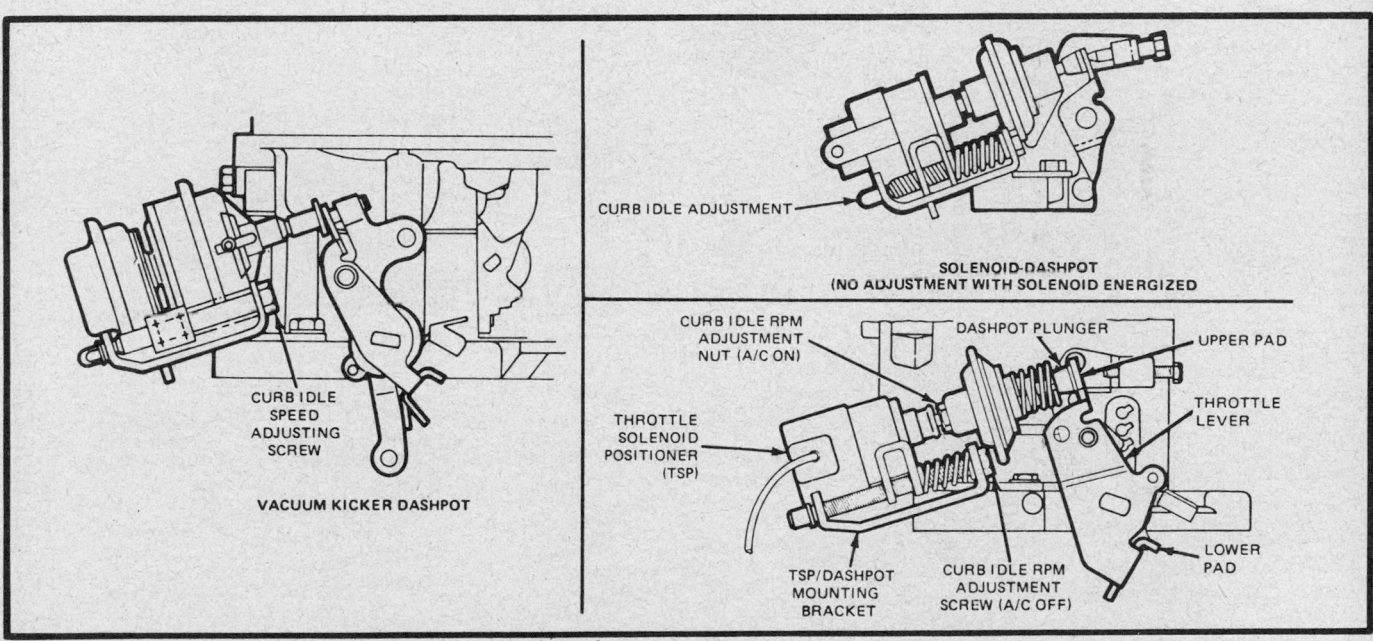

Motorcraft 2150 curb idle adjustment with throttle positioner

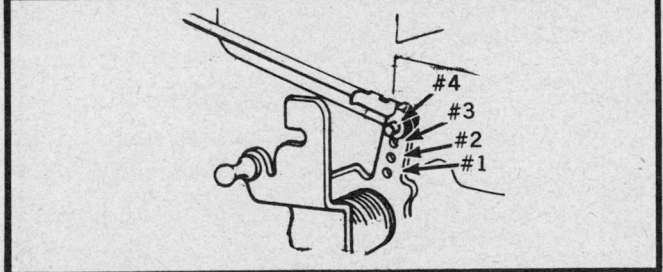

Motorcraft 2150 accelerator pump stroke hole location

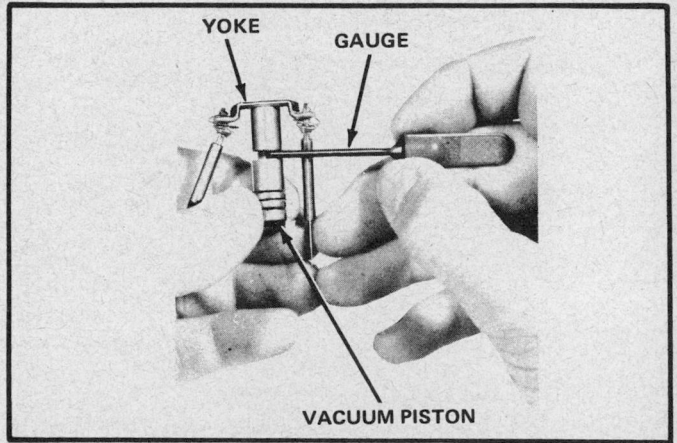

Motorcraft 2150 metering rod vacuum piston adjustment to a clearance of 0.120 in.

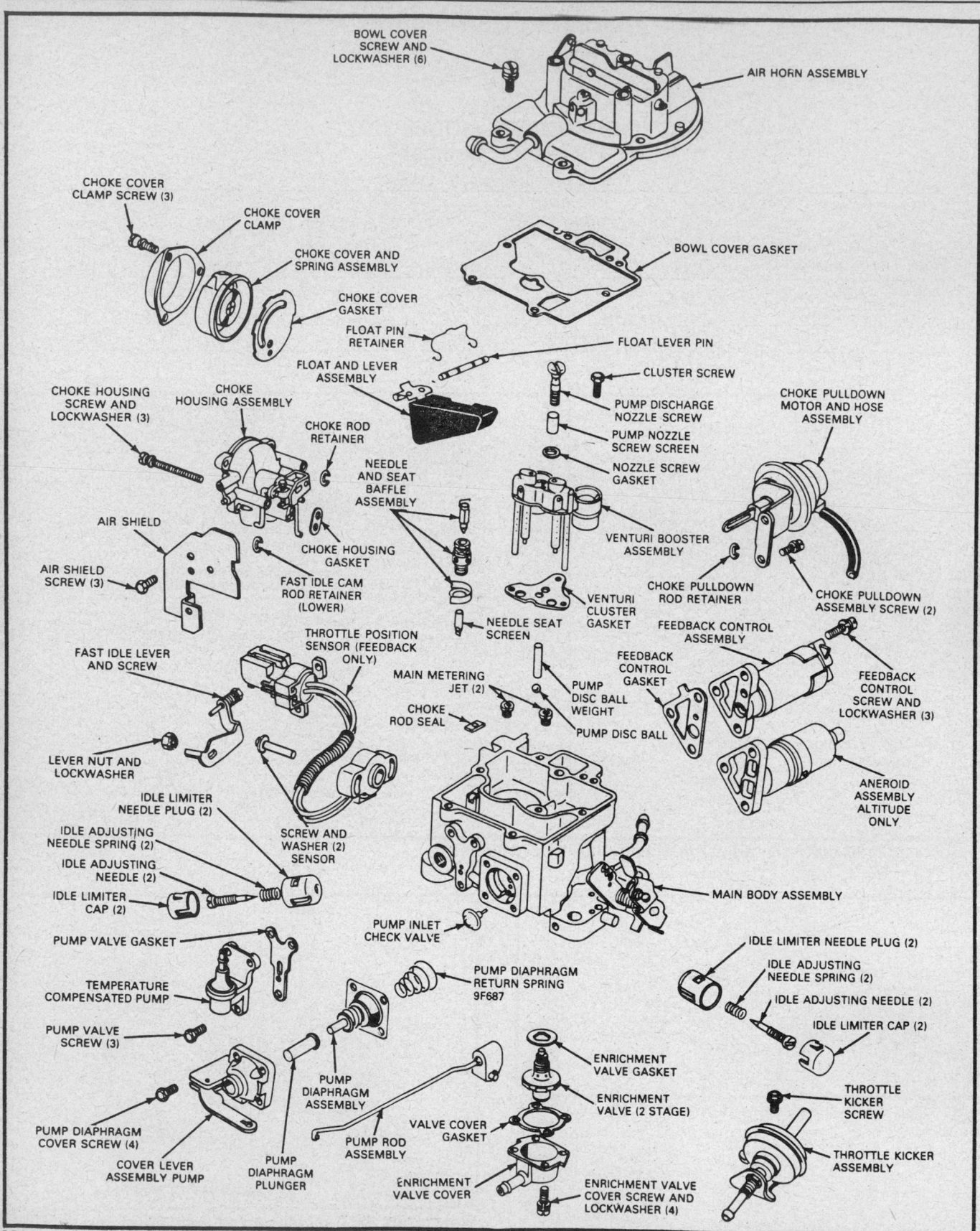

Motorcraft 2150 feedback carburetor exploded view

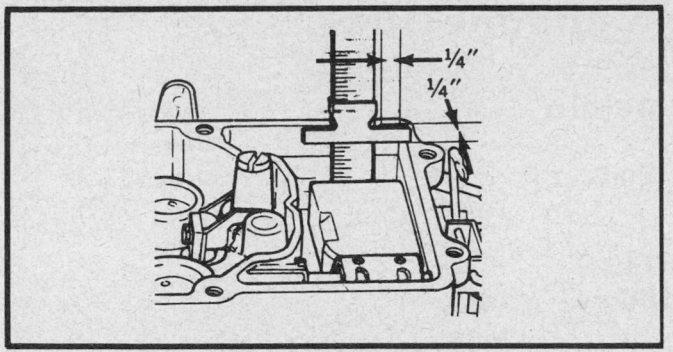

Motorcraft 2150 wet float level adjustment

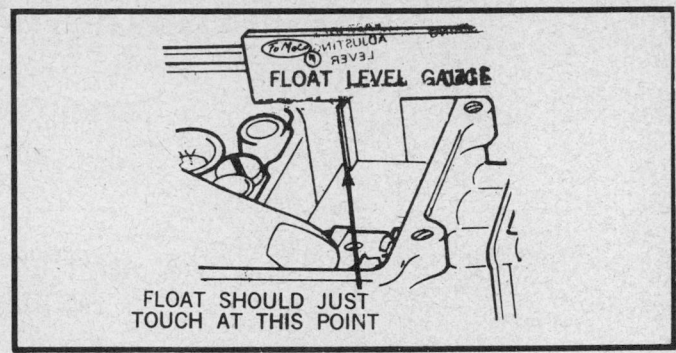

FLOAT SHOULD JUST TOUCH AT THIS POINT

Motorcraft 2150 dry float level adjustment

Asian Carburetors
ASIAN MODEL Y

Ford Motor Company
(All measurements in millimeters and degrees)

Year	Carburetor Number	Choke Pulldown Setting	Fast Idle Cam Setting	Dechoke Setting	Float Setting (Dry)	Choke Cap Setting	Fast Idle
1987	E77E-9510-AA	18°	14.5° ①	195 sec.	47.1 mm	20°C	3200 ②
1988	E87E-9510-AA	18°	14.5° ①	195 sec.	47.1 mm	20°C	3200 ②

① On step #1   ② 3100 rpm for vehicles with less than 100 miles.

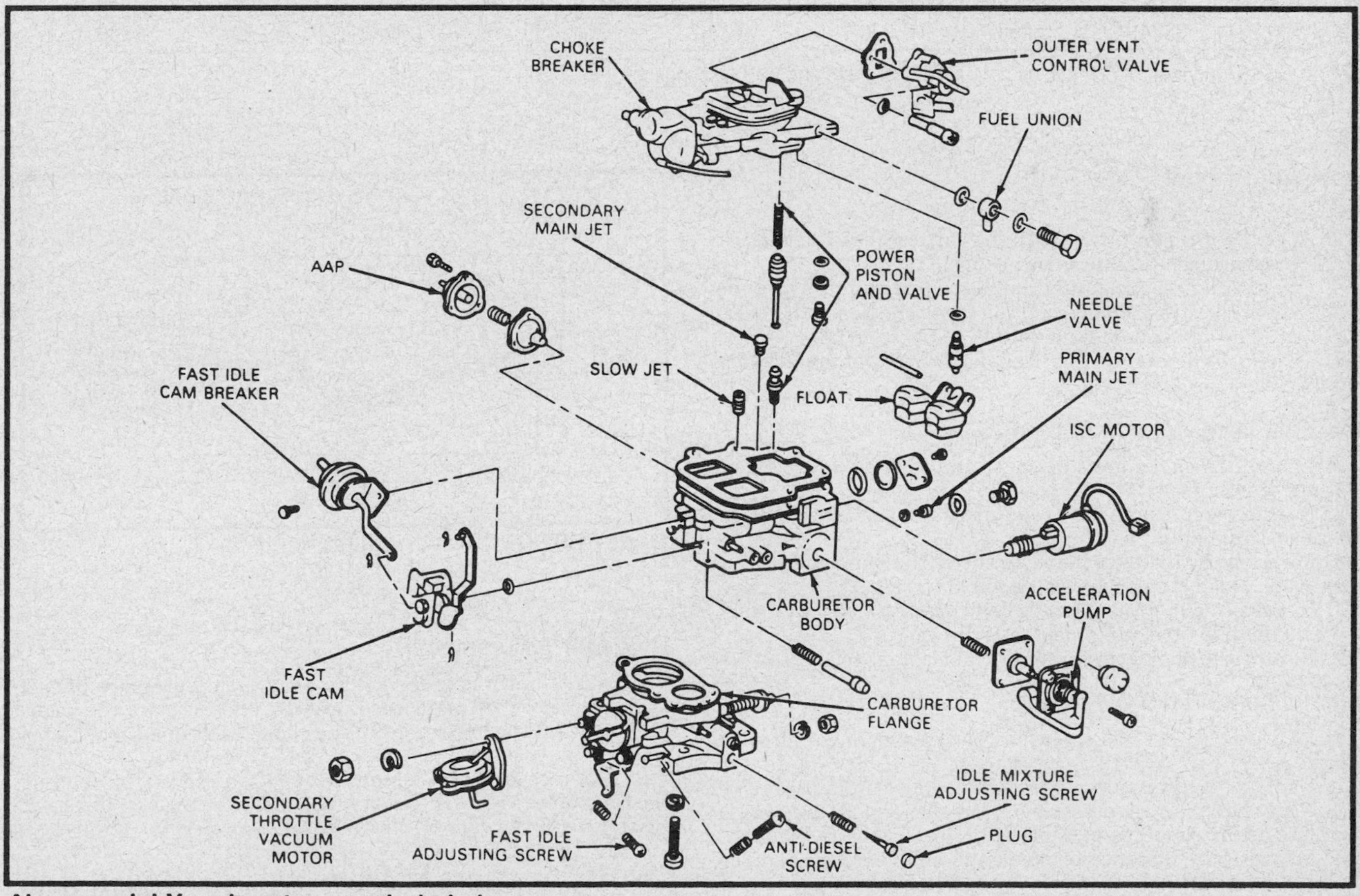

Aisan model Y carburetor — exploded view

JEEP CORPORATION CARBURETORS

Carter Carburetors

CARTER MODELS
MODEL BBD

CARTER MODEL BBD-2
Jeep
(All measurements in inches)

Year	Carburetor Number	Float Level	Step-up Piston Gap	Initial Choke Clearance	Fast Idle Cam Setting	Choke Cover Setting	Choke Unloader (Min.)	Fast Idle Speed (rpm) ①
1986	8383	0.250	0.035	0.140	0.095	1 Rich	0.280	1850
	8384	0.250	0.035	0.140	0.095	1 Rich	0.280	1700
1987	8383	0.250	0.035	0.140	0.095	1 Rich	0.280	1850
	8384	0.250	0.035	0.140	0.095	1 Rich	0.280	1700
1988	8383	0.250	0.035	0.140	0.095	1 Rich	0.280	1850
	8384	0.250	0.035	0.140	0.095	1 Rich	0.280	1700
1989	8383	0.250	0.035	0.140	0.095	1 Rich	0.280	1850
	8384	0.250	0.035	0.140	0.095	1 Rich	0.280	1700

① On second step of fast idle cam with TCS solenoid and EGR disconnected.

Float Adjustment

1. Remove the air horn.
2. Apply light finger pressure to the vertical float tab to exert gentle pressure against the inlet needle.
3. Lay a straight edge across the float bowl and measure the gap between the straight edge and the top of the float at its highest point. The gap should be 0.250 in.
4. To adjust, remove the float and bend the lower tab. Replace the float and check the gap.

Fast Idle Cam Adjustment

1. Loosen the choke housing cover and turn it ¼ turn right. Tighten one screw.
2. Slightly open the throttle and place the fast idle screw on the second cam step.
3. Measure the distance between the choke plate and the air horn wall. The distance should be 0.095 in.
4. If adjustment is necessary, bend the fast idle cam link down to increase and up to decrease the gap.
5. Return the choke cover cap to the original setting.

Initial Choke Valve Clearance

1. Position the fast idle screw on the top step of the fast idle cam.
2. Using a vacuum pump, seat the choke vacuum break.
3. Apply light closing pressure in the choke plate to position the plate as far closed as possible without forcing it.
4. Measure the distance between the air horn wall and the choke plate, it should be 0.140 in. If it is not, bend the choke vacuum break link until it is.

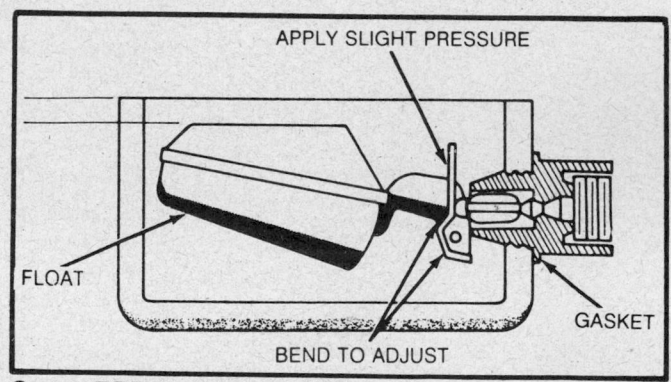

Carter BBD float level adjustment

Unloader Adjustment

1. With the throttle held fully open, apply pressure on the choke valve toward the closed position and measure the clearance between the lower edge of the choke valve and the air horn wall.
2. The measurement should be 0.280 in. Adjust by bending the tang on the throttle lever which contacts the fast idle cam. Bend toward the cam to increase the clearance.

NOTE: Do not bend the unloader down so that it binds or interferes with any other component.

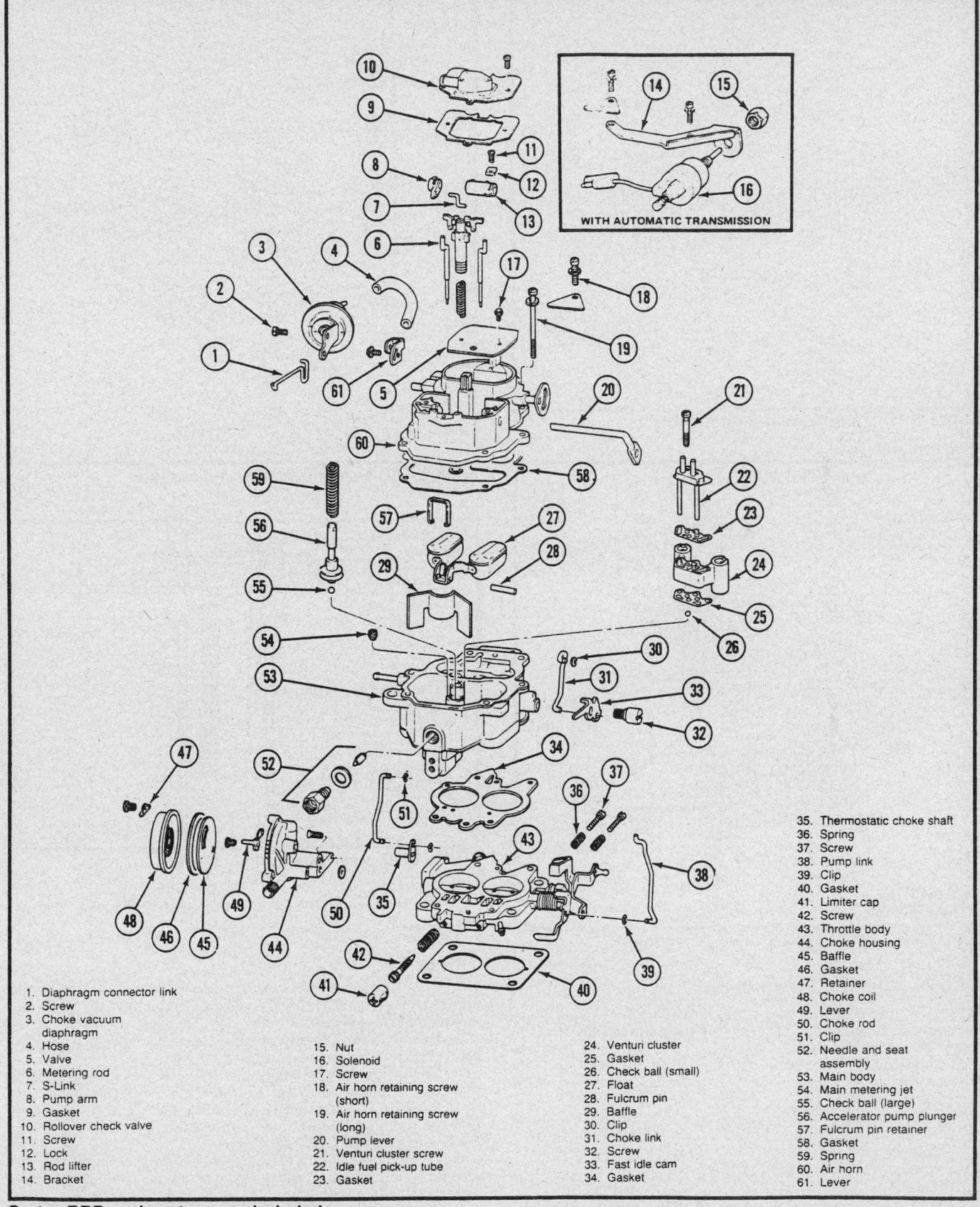

WITH AUTOMATIC TRANSMISSION

Carter BBD carburetor — exploded view

1. Diaphragm connector link
2. Screw
3. Choke vacuum diaphragm
4. Hose
5. Valve
6. Metering rod
7. S-Link
8. Pump arm
9. Gasket
10. Rollover check valve
11. Screw
12. Lock
13. Rod lifter
14. Bracket

15. Nut
16. Solenoid
17. Screw
18. Air horn retaining screw (short)
19. Air horn retaining screw (long)
20. Pump lever
21. Venturi cluster screw
22. Idle fuel pick-up tube
23. Gasket

24. Venturi cluster
25. Gasket
26. Check ball (small)
27. Float
28. Fulcrum pin
29. Baffle
30. Clip
31. Choke link
32. Screw
33. Fast idle cam
34. Gasket

35. Thermostatic choke shaft
36. Spring
37. Screw
38. Pump link
39. Clip
40. Gasket
41. Limiter cap
42. Screw
43. Throttle body
44. Choke housing
45. Baffle
46. Gasket
47. Retainer
48. Choke coil
49. Lever
50. Choke rod
51. Clip
52. Needle and seat assembly
53. Main body
54. Main metering jet
55. Check ball (large)
56. Accelerator pump plunger
57. Fulcrum pin retainer
58. Gasket
59. Spring
60. Air horn
61. Lever

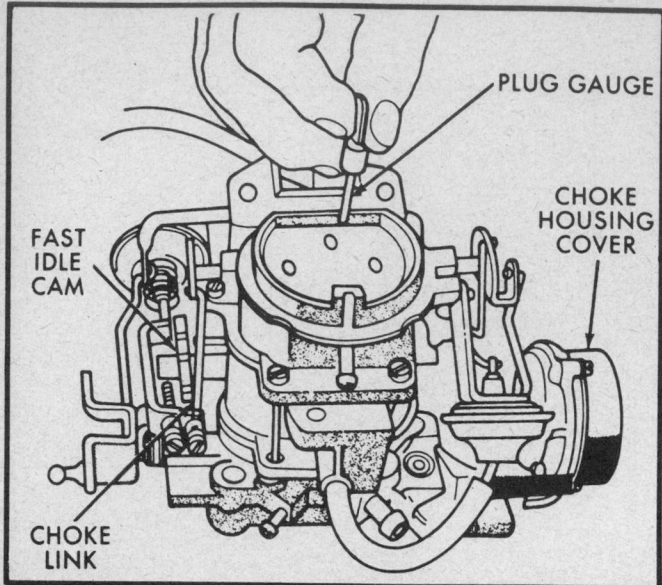

Carter BBD fast idle cam adjustment

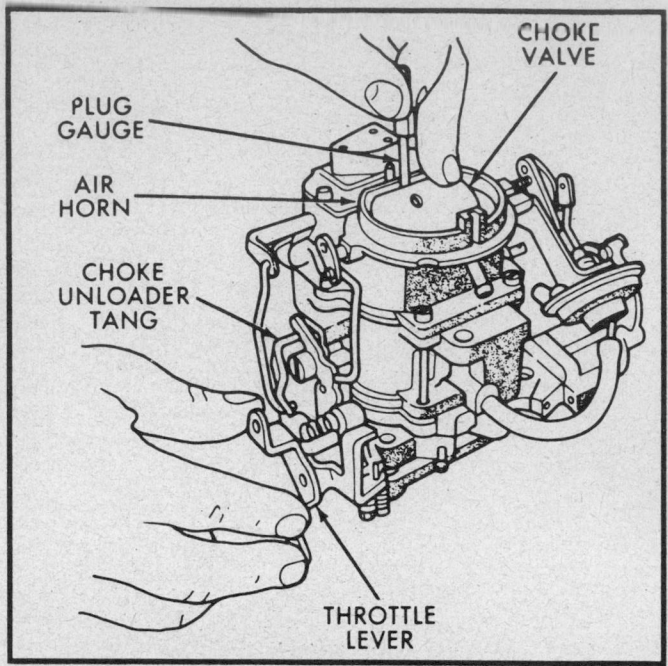

Carter BBD choke unloader adjustment

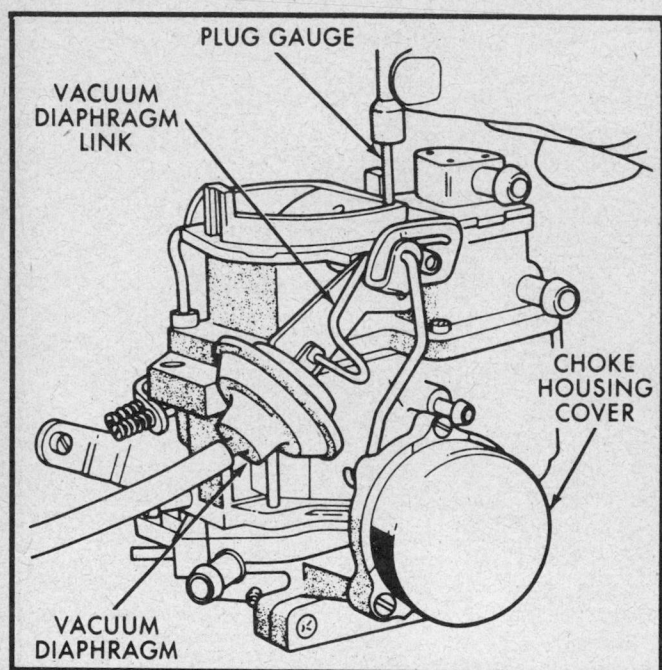

Carter BBD initial choke valve adjustment

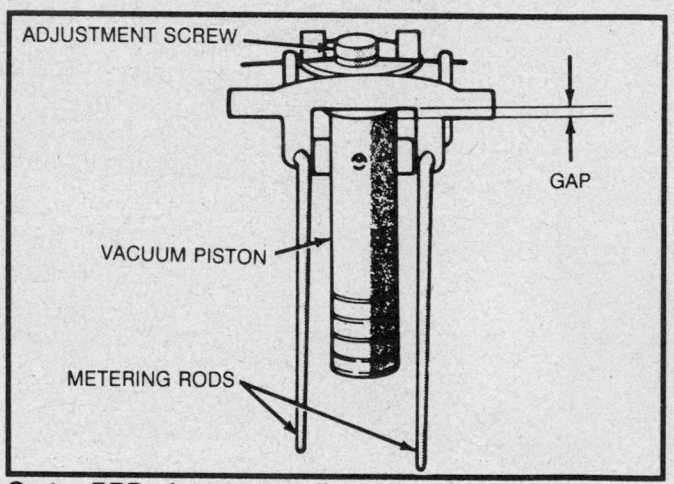

Carter BBD piston gap adjustment

5. Return the curb idle adjustment screw to its original position.

Vacuum (Step Up) Piston Gap

1. Turn the adjusting screw, mounted on top of the unit, so that the gap between the metering rod lifter lower edge, and the top of the vacuum piston, is 0.035 in.

2. Counting the number of turns involved, turn the curb idle adjustment screw counterclockwise, until the throttle valves are completely closed.

3. Fully depress the vacuum piston, while exerting moderate pressure on the metering rod lifter tab. In this position, tighten the rod lifter lock screw.

4. Release the piston and rod lifter.

NOTE: The accelerator pump should now be adjusted.

Accelerator Pump

1. Counting the number of turns involved, turn the curb idle adjustment screw counterclockwise, until the throttle valves are completely closed.

2. Open the choke valve so that the fast idle cam will allow the throttle valves to seat in their bores.

3. Turn the curb idle adjustment screw clockwise, so that it just barely touches the stop, then, turn it 2 full turns further.

4. Measure the distance between the surface of the air horn and the top of the accelerator pump shaft with a T-scale. The distance should be 0.520 in.

5. If the dimension is not correct, loosen the pump arm adjusting screw and rotate the sleeve to adjust the pump travel. Tighten the lock screw.

6. Return the curb idle screw to its original position.

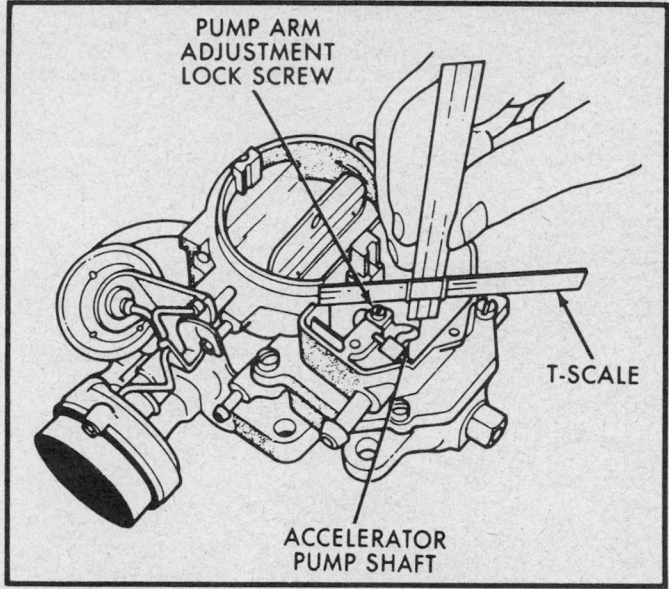

Carter BBD accelerator pump adjustment

MODEL YFA

CARTER MODEL YFA
Jeep

(All measurements in inches)

Year	Carburetor Number	Float Level	Fast Idle Cam Setting Index	Initial Choke Clearance	Choke Cover Setting	Choke Unloader (Min.)	Fast Idle Speed (rpm) ①	Bowl Vent Opens
1986	7704	0.600	0.175	0.280	Fixed	0.280	2000	—
	7705	0.600	0.175	0.280	Fixed	0.280	2300	—
	7706	0.600	0.175	0.240	Fixed	0.280	2000	—
	7707	0.600	0.175	0.280	Fixed	0.280	2300	—
1987	7704	0.600	0.175	0.280	Fixed	0.280	2000	—
	7705	0.600	0.175	0.280	Fixed	0.280	2300	—
	7706	0.600	0.175	0.280	Fixed	0.280	2000	—
	7707	0.600	0.175	0.280	Fixed	0.280	2300	—

① Engine hot, EGR valve disconnected

Float Level Adjustment

1. Remove the top of the carburetor and the gasket.
2. Invert the carburetor top and check the clearance from the top of the float to the bottom edge of the air horn with a float level gauge. Hold the carburetor top at eye level when making the check. The float arm should be resting on the inlet needle pin. To adjust, bend the float arm.

NOTE: Do Not bend the tab at the end of the arm.

Fast Idle Cam Adjustment

1. Run the engine to normal operating temperature. Connect a tachometer.
2. Disconnect and plug the EGR valve vacuum hose.

3. Position the fast idle adjustment screw on the second stop of the fast idle cam with the transmission in neutral.
4. Adjust the fast idle speed to 2300 rpm for automatic transmission and 2000 rpm for manual transmission.
5. Idle the engine and reconnect the EGR hose.

Initial Choke Valve Clearance

1. Position the fast idle screw on the top step of the fast idle cam.
2. Using a vacuum pump, seat the choke vacuum break.
3. Apply light closing pressure in the choke plate to position the plate as far closed as possible without forcing it.
4. Measure the distance between the air horn wall and the choke plate, it should be 0.280 in. If it is not, bend the choke vacuum break link until it is.

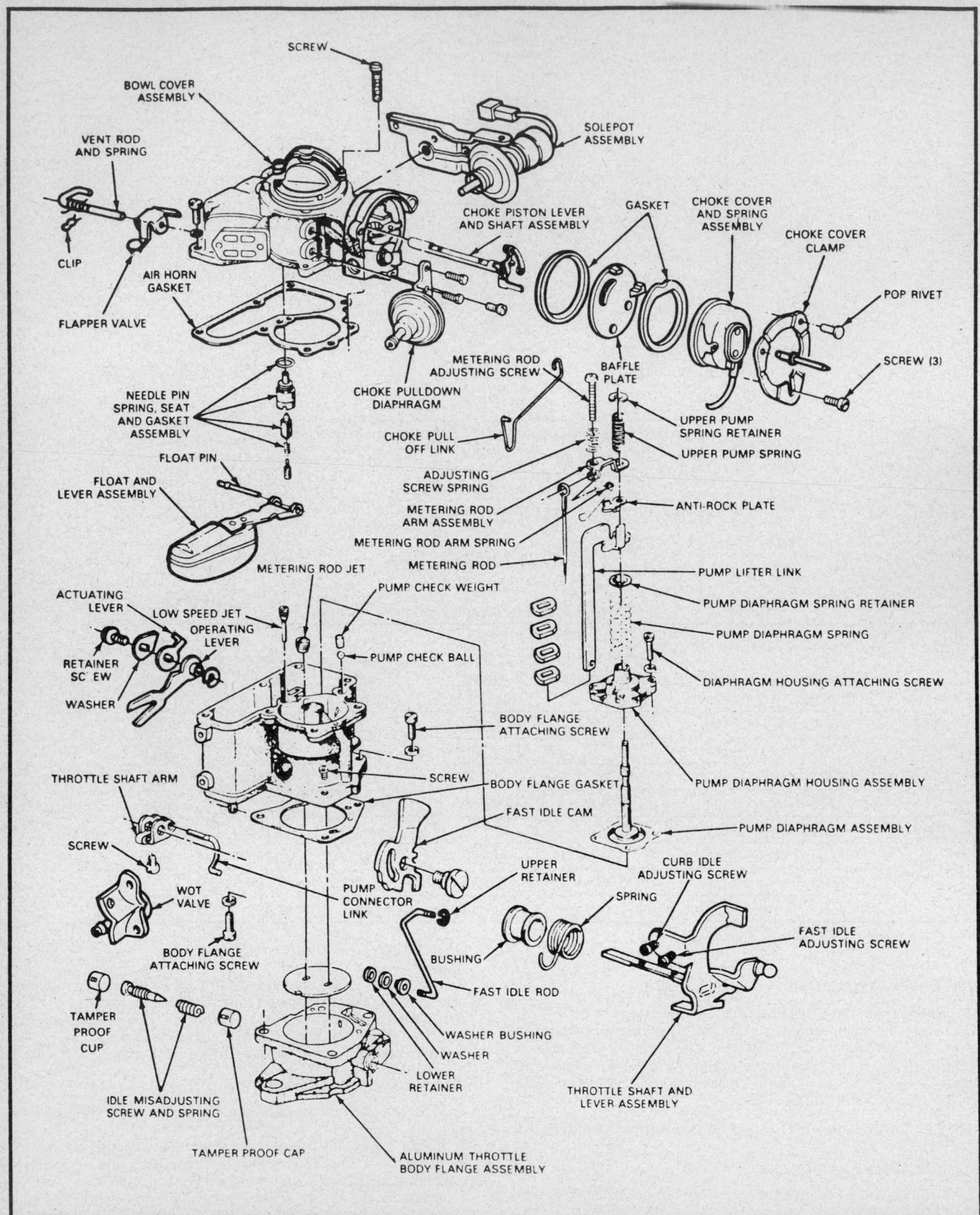

Carter YFA non-feedback carburetor — exploded view

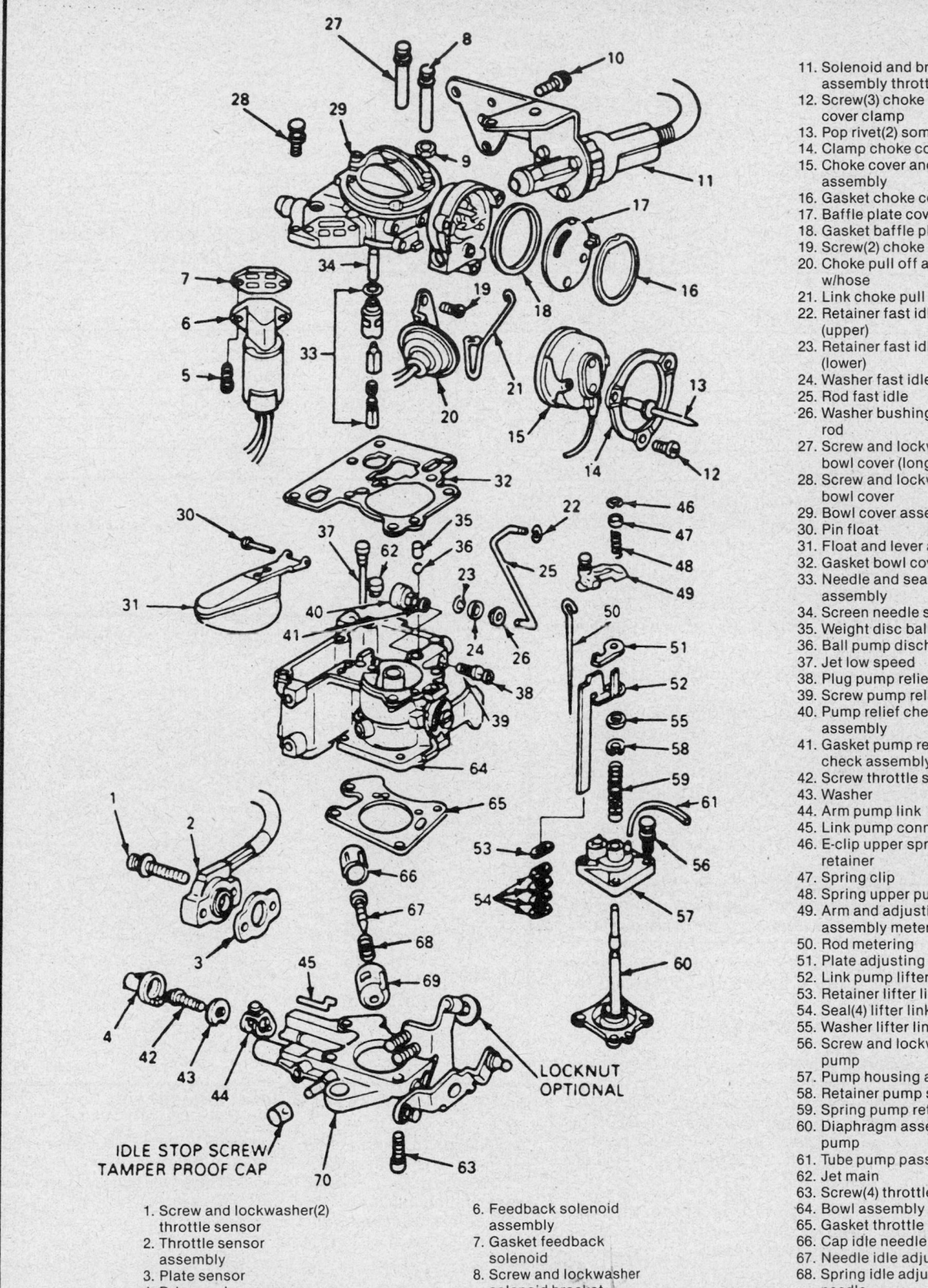

11. Solenoid and bracket assembly throttle
12. Screw(3) choke cover clamp
13. Pop rivet(2) some models
14. Clamp choke cover
15. Choke cover and spring assembly
16. Gasket choke cover
17. Baffle plate cover
18. Gasket baffle plate
19. Screw(2) choke pull off
20. Choke pull off assembly w/hose
21. Link choke pull off
22. Retainer fast idle rod (upper)
23. Retainer fast idle rod (lower)
24. Washer fast idle rod
25. Rod fast idle
26. Washer bushing fast idle rod
27. Screw and lockwasher(2) bowl cover (long)
28. Screw and lockwasher(4) bowl cover
29. Bowl cover assembly
30. Pin float
31. Float and lever assembly
32. Gasket bowl cover
33. Needle and seat assembly
34. Screen needle seat
35. Weight disc ball
36. Ball pump discharge
37. Jet low speed
38. Plug pump relief screw
39. Screw pump relief check
40. Pump relief check assembly
41. Gasket pump relief check assembly
42. Screw throttle shaft lever
43. Washer
44. Arm pump link
45. Link pump connector
46. E-clip upper spring retainer
47. Spring clip
48. Spring upper pump
49. Arm and adjusting screw assembly metering rod
50. Rod metering
51. Plate adjusting screw
52. Link pump lifter
53. Retainer lifter link seal
54. Seal(4) lifter link
55. Washer lifter link spacer
56. Screw and lockwasher(4) pump
57. Pump housing assembly
58. Retainer pump spring
59. Spring pump return
60. Diaphragm assembly pump
61. Tube pump passage
62. Jet main
63. Screw(4) throttle body
64. Bowl assembly
65. Gasket throttle body
66. Cap idle needle
67. Needle idle adjusting
68. Spring idle adjusting needle
69. Clip idle needle
70. Throttle body assembly

IDLE STOP SCREW/
TAMPER PROOF CAP

LOCKNUT
OPTIONAL

1. Screw and lockwasher(2) throttle sensor
2. Throttle sensor assembly
3. Plate sensor
4. Drive coulper sensor
5. Screw(2) feedback solenoid
6. Feedback solenoid assembly
7. Gasket feedback solenoid
8. Screw and lockwasher solenoid bracket
9. Locknut bracket screw
10. Screw(3) bracket

Carter YFA feedback carburetor — exploded view

Motorcraft Carburetors

MOTORCRAFT MODEL 2150
Jeep
(All measurements in inches)

Year	Carburetor Number	Float Level (Dry)	Fuel Level (Wet)	Initial Choke Valve Clearance	Fast Idle Cam Setting ②	Choke Cover Setting	Choke Unloader Valve Clearance	Fast Idle Speed ①	Bowl Vent Clearance	Rod Pump Location Hole
1986	4RHA2	0.575	0.930	0.136	0.086	2 Rich	0.350	1600	0.120	—
	5RHA2	0.328	0.930	0.118	0.076	Y	0.420	1600	—	—
1987	4RHA2	0.575	0.930	0.136	0.086	2 Rich	0.350	1600	0.120	—
	5RHA2	0.328	0.930	0.118	0.076	Y	0.420	1600	—	—
1988	4RHA2	0.575	0.930	0.136	0.086	2 Rich	0.350	1600	0.120	—
	5RHA2	0.328	0.930	0.118	0.076	Y	0.420	1600	—	—
1989	5RHA2	0.328	0.930	0.118	0.076	Y	0.420	1600	—	—

① TCS solenoid and EGR disconnected, fast idle screw on 2nd cam step
② Measured between choke valve and air horn fast idle screw on 2nd cam step

Dry Float Adjustment

1. With the air horn assembly and the gasket removed raise the float by pressing down on the float tab until the fuel inlet needle is lightly seated.
2. Using a T-scale, measure the distance from the fuel bowl machined surface to either corner of the float ⅛ in. (3mm) from the free end.
3. To adjust bend the float tab and hold the fuel inlet needle off its eat in order to prevent damage to the seat and the tip of the needle.

Wet Float Adjustment

— CAUTION —
Exercise extreme care when performing this adjustment as fuel vapors and liquid fuel are present and could cause personal injury if ignited.

1. Place the vehicle on a flat, level surface and run the engine to normal operating temperature. Turn off the engine and remove the air cleaner.
2. Remove the air horn attaching screws, but leave the air horn in place.
3. Start the engine and let it idle for one minute. Shut off the engine and remove the air horn and gasket.
4. Use a T-scale to measure the vertical distance between the machined surface of the carburetor body and the fuel level in the bowl. Make this measurement as near the center of the bowl as possible. The proper distance is ¼ in. To adjust, bend the float tab.

NOTE: Every time an adjustment is made, the air horn must be replaced, and the engine started and idled for one minute to stabilize the fuel level.

5. Install the air horn and gasket when adjustment is completed.

Fast Idle Cam Adjustment

1. Push down on the fast idle cam lever until the fast idle

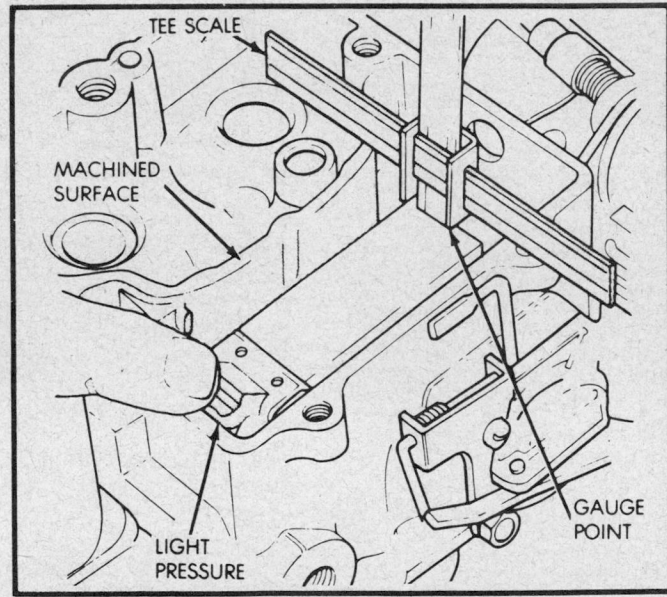

Motorcraft 2150 dry float level adjustment

speed adjusting screw is contacting the second step (index), and against the shoulder of the high step.
2. Measure the clearance between the lower edge of the choke valve and air horn wall.
3. Adjust by turning the fast idle cam lever screw to obtain the proper specification.

Initial Choke Valve Clearance

1. Remove the choke cover shield.
2. Loosen the choke cover coil retaining screws. If rivets are used grind away and replace with screws.

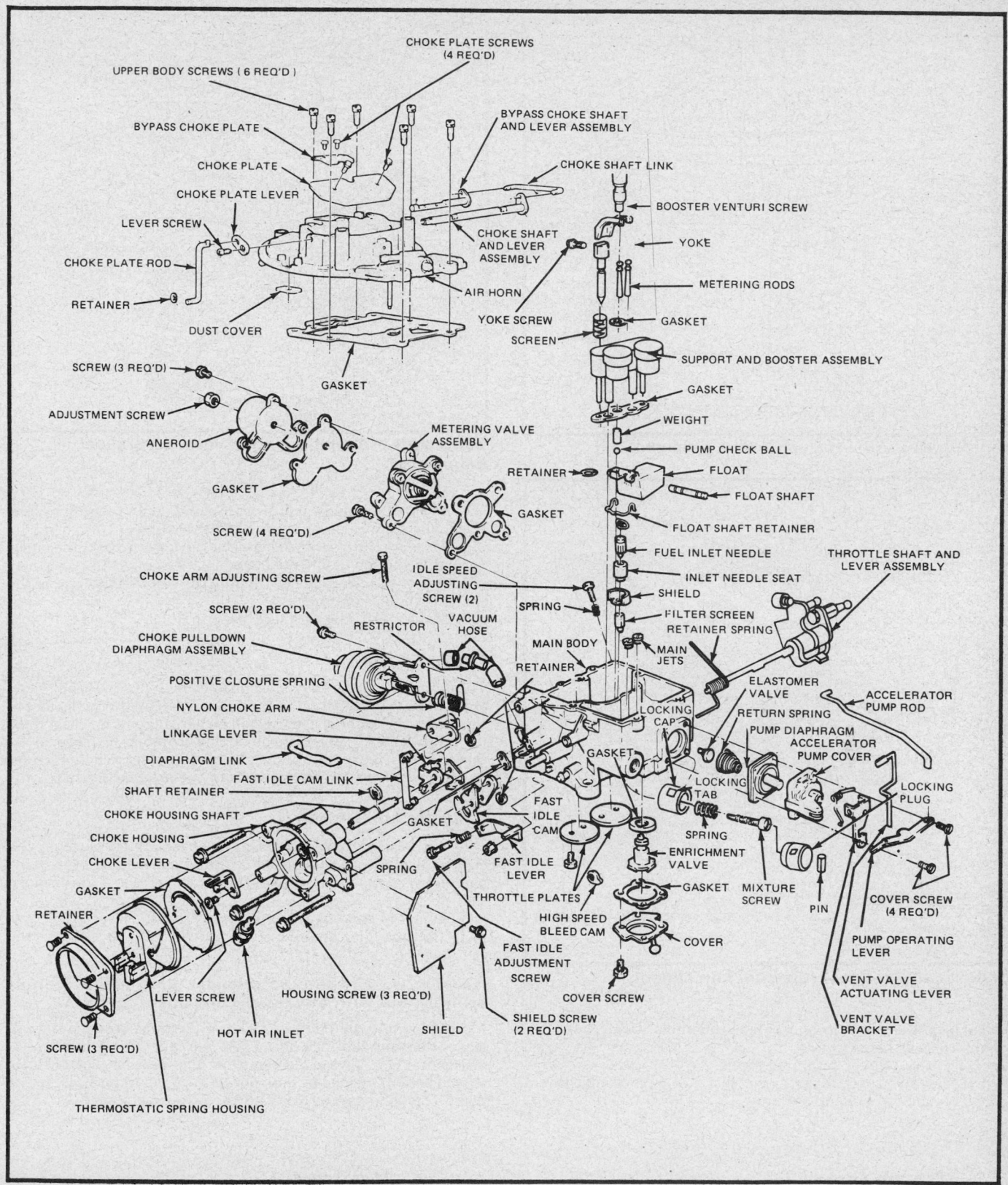

Motorcraft 2150 carburetor – exploded view

UPPER BODY SCREWS (6 REQ'D)

CHOKE PLATE SCREWS (4 REQ'D)

BYPASS CHOKE PLATE

CHOKE PLATE

CHOKE PLATE LEVER

LEVER SCREW

CHOKE PLATE ROD

RETAINER

DUST COVER

GASKET

BYPASS CHOKE SHAFT AND LEVER ASSEMBLY

CHOKE SHAFT LINK

CHOKE SHAFT AND LEVER ASSEMBLY

AIR HORN

YOKE SCREW

SCREEN

BOOSTER VENTURI SCREW

YOKE

METERING RODS

GASKET

SUPPORT AND BOOSTER ASSEMBLY

GASKET

WEIGHT

PUMP CHECK BALL

FLOAT

FLOAT SHAFT

FLOAT SHAFT RETAINER

FUEL INLET NEEDLE

INLET NEEDLE SEAT

SHIELD

FILTER SCREEN RETAINER SPRING

MAIN JETS

THROTTLE SHAFT AND LEVER ASSEMBLY

ELASTOMER VALVE

RETURN SPRING

ACCELERATOR PUMP ROD

PUMP DIAPHRAGM ACCELERATOR PUMP COVER

LOCKING PLUG

COVER SCREW (4 REQ'D)

PUMP OPERATING LEVER

VENT VALVE ACTUATING LEVER

VENT VALVE BRACKET

PIN

MIXTURE SCREW

COVER

GASKET

ENRICHMENT VALVE

SPRING

LOCKING TAB

LOCKING CAP

GASKET

MAIN BODY

RETAINER

SPRING

SHIELD

VACUUM HOSE

IDLE SPEED ADJUSTING SCREW (2)

RESTRICTOR

METERING VALVE ASSEMBLY

RETAINER

GASKET

SCREW (4 REQ'D)

ANEROID

GASKET

ADJUSTMENT SCREW

SCREW (3 REQ'D)

CHOKE ARM ADJUSTING SCREW

SCREW (2 REQ'D)

CHOKE PULLDOWN DIAPHRAGM ASSEMBLY

POSITIVE CLOSURE SPRING

NYLON CHOKE ARM

LINKAGE LEVER

DIAPHRAGM LINK

FAST IDLE CAM LINK

SHAFT RETAINER

CHOKE HOUSING SHAFT

CHOKE HOUSING

CHOKE LEVER

GASKET

RETAINER

LEVER SCREW

SCREW (3 REQ'D)

HOT AIR INLET

HOUSING SCREW (3 REQ'D)

THERMOSTATIC SPRING HOUSING

SHIELD

SHIELD SCREW (2 REQ'D)

FAST IDLE ADJUSTMENT SCREW

COVER SCREW

HIGH SPEED BLEED CAM

THROTTLE PLATES

FAST IDLE LEVER

FAST IDLE CAM

GASKET

SPRING

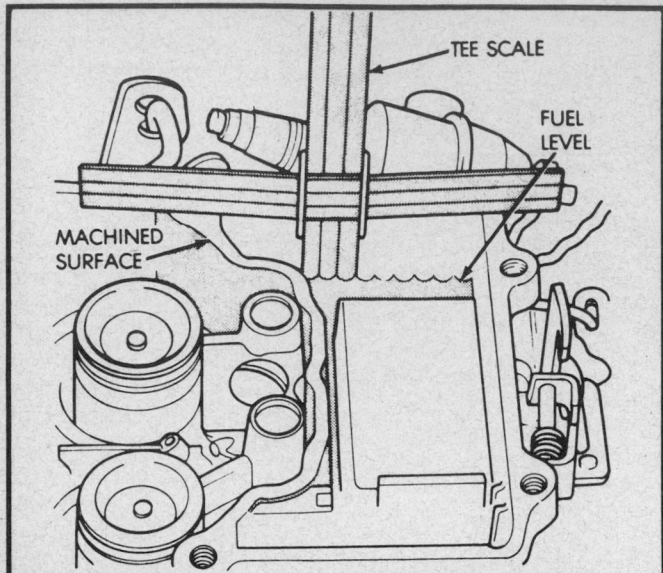

Motorcraft 2150 wet float level adjustment

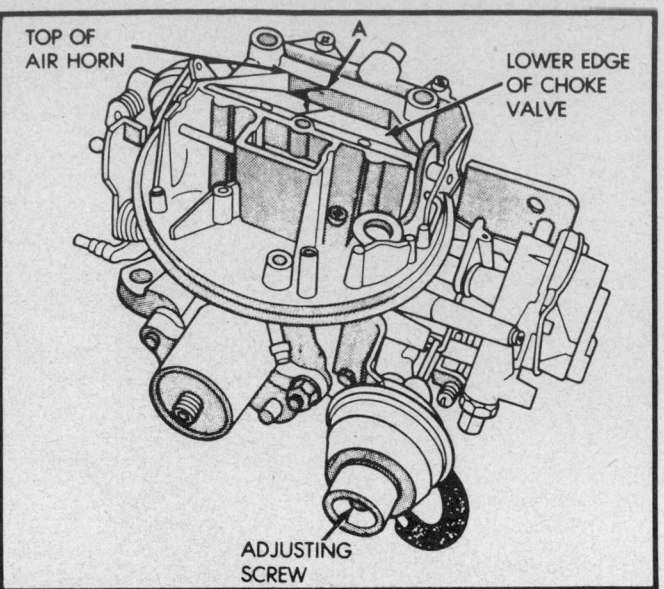

Motorcraft 2150 initial choke valve clearance adjustment

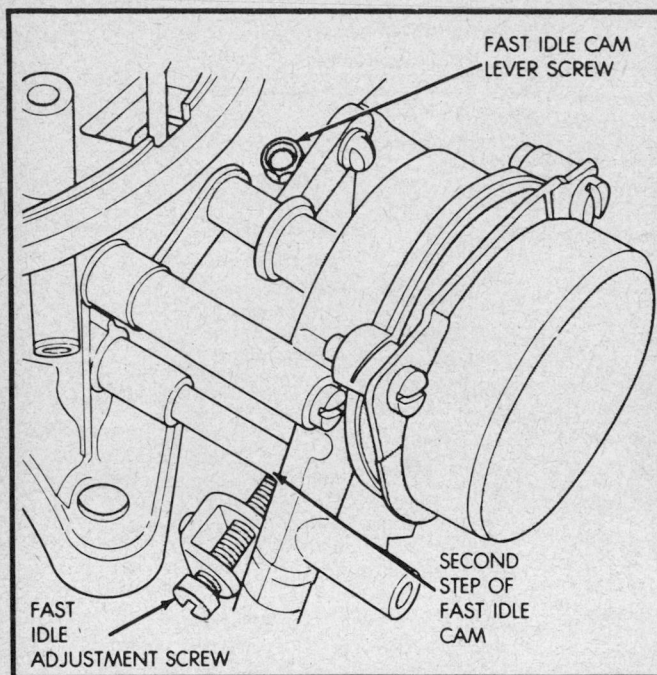

Motorcraft 2150 fast idle cam adjustment

3. Open the throttle and rotate the choke cover until the choke valve is held close.

4. Tighten 1 cover retaining screw.

5. Close the throttle with the fast idle screw adjustment screw on the top step of the cam.

6. Use a hand held vacuum pump and apply vacuum to hold the choke diaphragm aganst the setscrew.

7. Measure the clearance between the lower edge of the choke valve and the top of the air horn.

8. Adjust the clearance by turning the screw at the rear of the choke vacuum diaphragm.

9. Make a fast idle cam adjustment.

Choke Setting

The automatic choke setting is made by loosening the choke cover in the desired direction as indicated by an arrow on the face of the cover. the original setting will be satisfactory for most driving conditions. However, if the engine stumbles or stalls on acceleration during warmup, the choke may be set richer or leaner no more than two graduations from the original setting.

Unloader Adjustment

1. With the throttle held fully open, apply pressure on the choke valve toward the closed position and measure the clearance between the lower edge of the choke valve and the air horn wall.

2. Adjust by bending the tang on the throttle lever which contacts the fast idle cam. Bend toward the cam to increase the clearance.

NOTE: Do not bend the unloader down so that it binds or interferes with any other component.

3. A clearance of 0.070 in. (1.8mm) must be between the unloader tang and the edge of the fast idle cam. Final unloader adjustment must always be done on the vehicle. The throttle should be fully opened by depressing the accelerator pedal to the floor. This is to assure that full throttle is obtained.

Rochester Carburetors

ROCHESTER MODEL 2SE/E2SE
Jeep

(All measurements in inches or degrees)

Year	Carburetor Number	Float Level	Air Valve Spring	Choke Coil Level	Fast Idle Cam 2nd Step	Primary Vacuum Break	Secondary Vacuum Break	Air Valve Rod	Choke Unloader
1986	17085380	5/32	1	0.085	22°	26°	32°	1°	40°
	17085381	5/32	1	0.085	22°	26°	32°	1°	40°
	17085382	5/32	1	0.085	22°	26°	32°	1°	40°
	17085383	5/32	1	0.085	22°	26°	32°	1°	40°
	17085384	1/8	1	0.085	22°	25°	30°	1°	40°
1987	17084580	5/32	1	0.085	22°	26°	32°	1°	40°
	17084581	5/32	1	0.085	22°	26°	32°	1°	40°
	17084582	5/32	1	0.085	22°	26°	32°	1°	40°
	17084583	5/32	1	0.085	22°	26°	32°	1°	40°
	17084384	1/8	1	0.085	22°	25°	30°	1°	40°

NOTE: Specified angle for use with angle degree tool
① Maximum degree setting
② 2nd step on cam
③ Tamper resistant—riveted cover

Float and Fuel Level Adjustment

1. Start the engine and run it to normal operating temperature.
2. Remove the vent stack screws and the vent stack.
3. Remove the air horn screw adjacent to the vent stack.
4. With the engine idling and the choke fully opened, carefully insert float gauge J-9789-136 for E2SE carburetors and tool J-9789-138 for 2SE carburetors, into the air horn screw hole and vent hole. Allow the gauge to rest freely on the float.

NOTE: Do not press down on the float.

5. With the gauge at eye level, observe the mark that aligns with the top of the casting at the vent hole. The float level should be within 0.06 in. (1.5mm) of the specifications. If not, remove the air horn and adjust the float as follows:
   a. Hold the retainer pin firmly in place and push the float down, lightly, against the inlet needle.
   b. Using an adjustable T-scale, at a point 3/16 in. (5mm) from the end of the float, at the toe, measure the distance from the float bowl top surface (gasket removed) to the top of the float at the toe. If not within specification, remove the float and bend the arm.

Fast Idle Cam Adjustment

1. Make sure the choke coil adjustment is correct and that the fast idle speed is correct.
2. Obtain a choke angle gauge, tool No. J-26701-A. Rotate the degree scale to the zero degree mark opposite the pointer.
3. With the choke valve completely closed, place the magnet on the tool squarely on the choke plate. Rotate the bubble unit until it is centered.

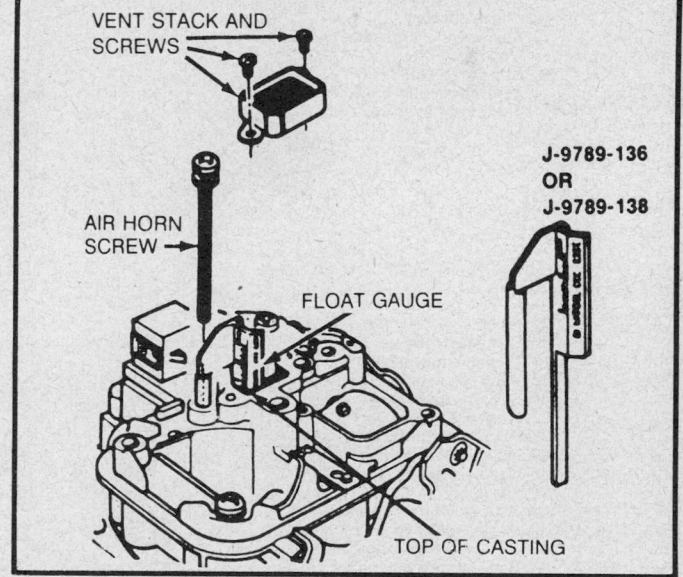

Rochester 2SE and E2SE float level measurement

4. Rotate the degree scale until the 22 degree mark is opposite the pointer.
5. Place the fast idle screw on the second step of the cam.
6. Close the choke plate by pushing on the intermediate choke lever.

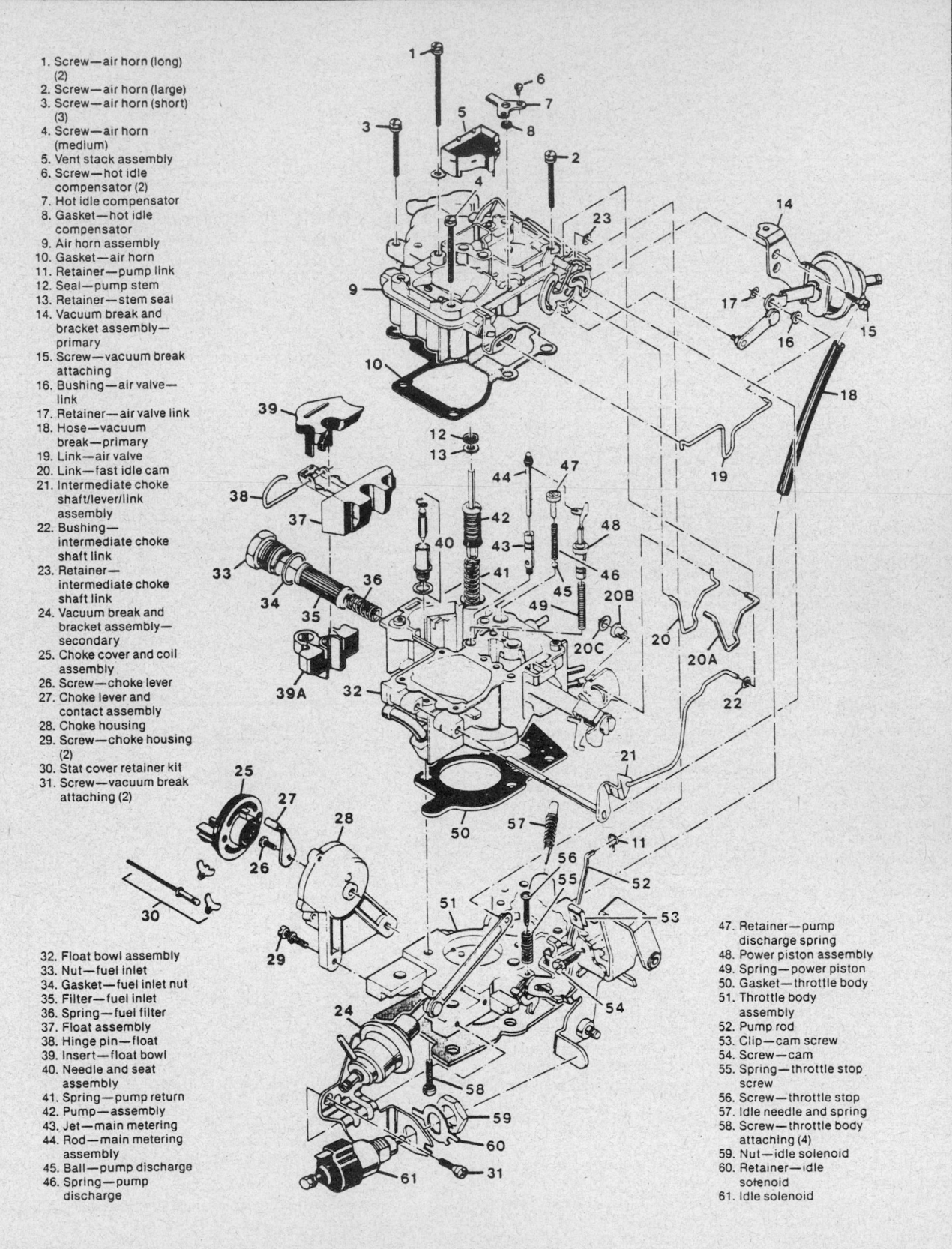

1. Screw—air horn (long) (2)
2. Screw—air horn (large)
3. Screw—air horn (short) (3)
4. Screw—air horn (medium)
5. Vent stack assembly
6. Screw—hot idle compensator (2)
7. Hot idle compensator
8. Gasket—hot idle compensator
9. Air horn assembly
10. Gasket—air horn
11. Retainer—pump link
12. Seal—pump stem
13. Retainer—stem seal
14. Vacuum break and bracket assembly— primary
15. Screw—vacuum break attaching
16. Bushing—air valve link
17. Retainer—air valve link
18. Hose—vacuum break—primary
19. Link—air valve
20. Link—fast idle cam
21. Intermediate choke shaft/lever/link assembly
22. Bushing— intermediate choke shaft link
23. Retainer— intermediate choke shaft link
24. Vacuum break and bracket assembly— secondary
25. Choke cover and coil assembly
26. Screw—choke lever
27. Choke lever and contact assembly
28. Choke housing
29. Screw—choke housing (2)
30. Stat cover retainer kit
31. Screw—vacuum break attaching (2)

32. Float bowl assembly
33. Nut—fuel inlet
34. Gasket—fuel inlet nut
35. Filter—fuel inlet
36. Spring—fuel filter
37. Float assembly
38. Hinge pin—float
39. Insert—float bowl
40. Needle and seat assembly
41. Spring—pump return
42. Pump—assembly
43. Jet—main metering
44. Rod—main metering assembly
45. Ball—pump discharge
46. Spring—pump discharge

47. Retainer—pump discharge spring
48. Power piston assembly
49. Spring—power piston
50. Gasket—throttle body
51. Throttle body assembly
52. Pump rod
53. Clip—cam screw
54. Screw—cam
55. Spring—throttle stop screw
56. Screw—throttle stop
57. Idle needle and spring
58. Screw—throttle body attaching (4)
59. Nut—idle solenoid
60. Retainer—idle solenoid
61. Idle solenoid

Rochester 2SE and E2SE carburetor—exploded view

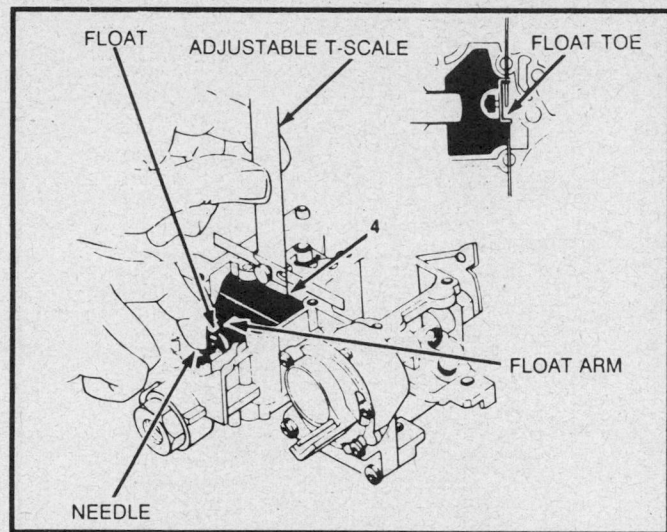

Rochester 2SE and E2SE float level adjustment

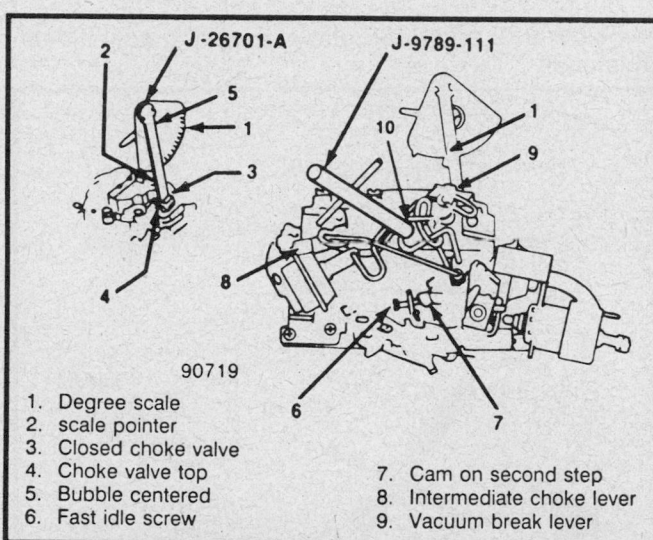

90719

1. Degree scale
2. scale pointer
3. Closed choke valve
4. Choke valve top
5. Bubble centered
6. Fast idle screw
7. Cam on second step
8. Intermediate choke lever
9. Vacuum break lever

Rochester 2SE and E2SE fast idle cam adjustment

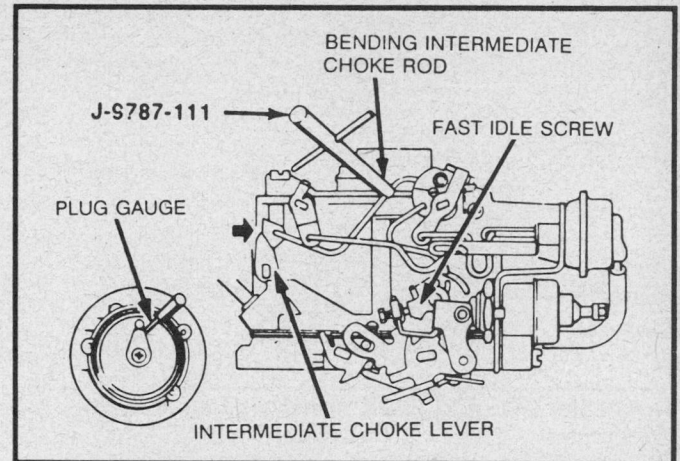

Rochester 2SE and E2SE choke coil lever adjustment

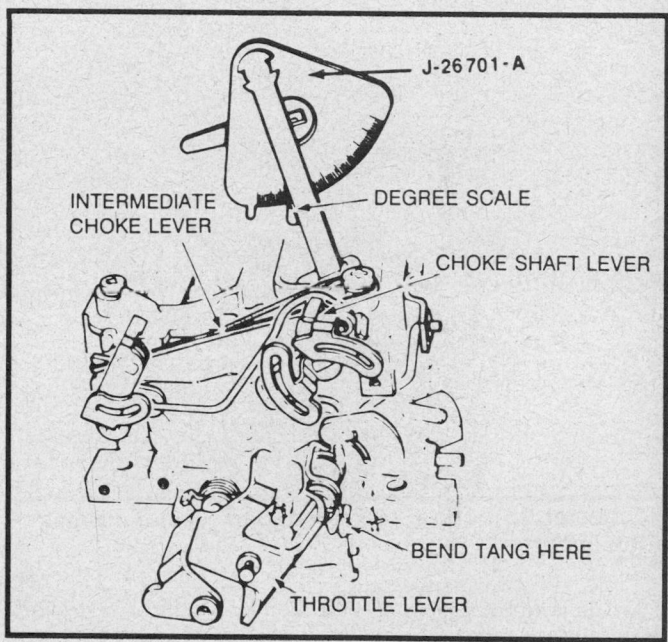

Rochester 2SE and E2SE choke unloader adjustment

7. Push the vacuum brake lever toward the open choke position until the lever is against the rear tank on the choke lever.

8. Adjust by bending the fast idle cam rod until the bubble is centered.

Choke Coil Lever Adjustment

NOTE: Once the rivets and choke cover are removed, a choke cover retainer kit is necessary for assembly.

1. Remove the rivets, retainers, choke cover and coil following the instructions found in the cover retainer kit.

2. Position the fast idle adjustment screw on the highest stop of the fast idle cam.

3. Push on the intermediate choke lever and close the choke plate.

4. Insert a 0.85 in. plug gauge, in the hole adjacent to the coil lever. The edge of the lever should barely contact the plug gauge.

5. Bend the intermediate choke rod to adjust.

Unloader Adjustment

1. Obtain a carburetor choke angle gauge, tool No. J–26701–

A. Rotate the scale on the gauge until the 0 mark is opposite the pointer.

2. Close the choke plate completely and set the magnet squarely on top of it.

3. Rotate the bubble until it is centered.

4. Rotate the degree scale until the 40° mark is opposite the pointer.

5. Hold the primary throttle valve wide open.

6. Bend the throttle lever tang until the bubble is centered.

Primary Vacuum Break Adjustment

1. Obtain a carburetor choke angle gauge, tool No. J–26701–A. Rotate the scale on the gauge until the 0 mark is opposite the pointer.

2. Rotate the degree scale until the correct specification mark is opposite the pointer.

3. Place tape over the vacuum bleed in the diaphragm.

4. Set the choke vacuum diaphragm using a hand vacuum pump.

5. Hold the choke valve at its closed position by pushing on the choke lever.

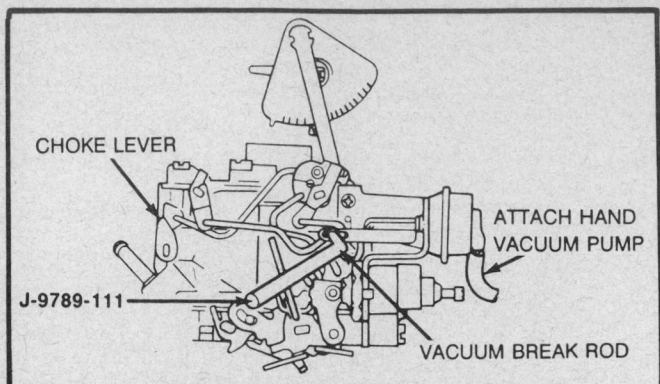

Rochester 2SE and E2SE primary vacuum break adjustment

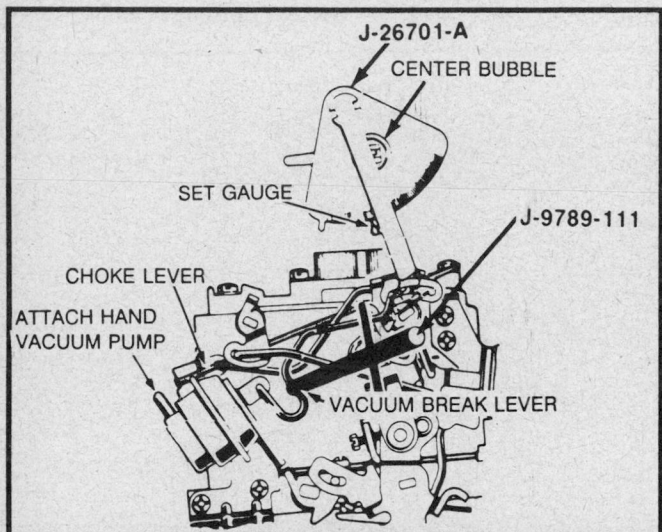

Rochester 2SE and E2SE secondary vacuum break adjustment

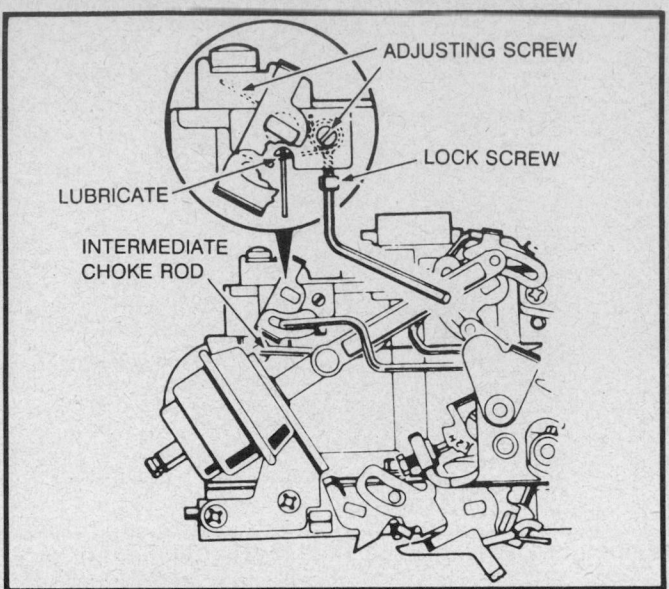

Rochester 2SE and E2SE air valve spring adjustment adjustment

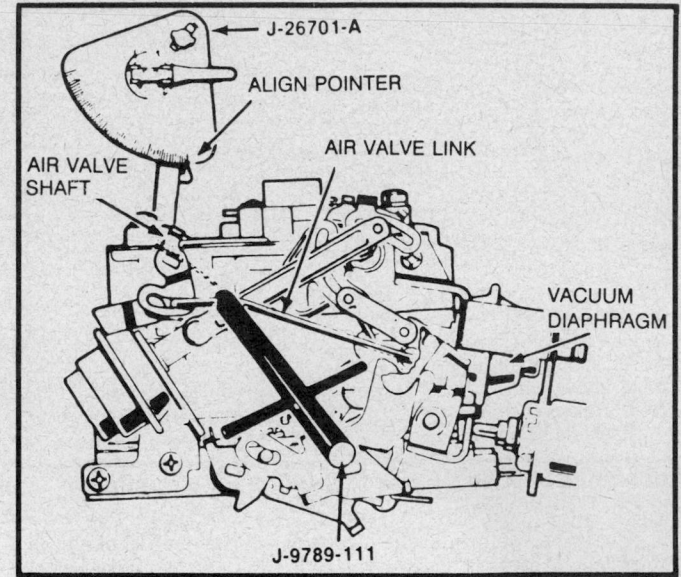

Rochester 2SE and E2SE air valve link adjustment adjustment

6. Adjust to the proper specification by bending the primary vacuum break rod.

Secondary Vacuum Break Adjustment

1. Obtain a carburetor choke angle gauge, tool No. J–26701–A. Rotate the scale on the gauge until the 0 mark is opposite the pointer.
2. Rotate the degree scale until the correct specification mark is opposite the pointer.
3. Place tape over the vacuum bleed in the diaphragm.
4. Seat the choke vacuum diaphragm using a hand vacuum pump.
5. Hold the choke valve at its closed position by pushing on the choke lever.
6. Adjust to the proper specification by bending the secondary vacuum break rod.

Air Valve Spring Adjustment

1. If necessary, remove the intermediate choke rod to gain access to the lock screw. Loosen the lock screw.
2. Turn the tension adjusting screw clockwise until the air valve opens slightly.
3. Turn the adjusting screw counterclockwise until the air valve just closes.

Continue counterclockwise to the specified number of turns.
4. Tighten the lock screw.

Air Valve Rod Adjustment

1. Obtain a carburetor choke angle gauge, tool No. J–26701–A. Rotate the scale on the gauge until the 0 mark is opposite the pointer.
2. Rotate the degree scale until the correct specification mark is opposite the pointer.
3. Seat the choke vacuum diaphragm using a hand vacuum pump.
4. Place tape over the vacuum bleed in the diaphragm.
5. Apply light pressure to the air valve shaft in the direction to open the valve to ensure all slack is removed between the air valve link and the plunger slot.
6. Bend the air valve link with tool J–97789–111 until the bubble is centered.

CHRYSLER CORPORATION

The Throttle Body Fuel Injection System is a computer regulated dual point fuel injection system that provides a precise air-fuel ratio for all driving conditions. At the center of this system is a digital pre-programmed computer known as the Single Module Engine Controller (SMEC) that regulates ignition timing, air-fuel ratio, emission control devices, charging system and idle speed. This component has the ability to update and revise its programming to meet changing operating conditions.

Various sensors provide the input necessary for the SMEC to correctly regulate the fuel flow at the injector. These include the Manifold Absolute Pressure (MAP), Throttle Position Sensor (TPS), oxygen sensor, coolant temperature sensor, throttle body temperature sensor and vehicle distance sensor. In addition to these sensors, various switches and relays also provide important information. These include the neutral-safety switch, air conditioning clutch relay and auto shut down relay.

All inputs to the SMEC are converted into signals. These signals cause changes to either the fuel flow at the injector or ignition timing or both.

The SMEC is a digital computer containing a microprocessor. The module receives input signals from various switches and sensors. It then computes the fuel injectors pulse width, spark advance, ignition coil dwell, idle speed, purge and alternator charge rate.

The SMEC tests many of its own input and output circuits. If a fault is found in a major system, this information is stored in the memory. Information on this fault can be displayed to a

technician by means of the instrument panel check engine lamp or by connecting a diagnostic read out unit and reading a numbered display code which directly relates to a general fault. When a fault code appears (either by flashes of the check engine lamp or by watching the factory diagnostic testing equipment) it indicates the SMEC has recognized an abnormal signal in the system. Fault codes indicate the results of a failure but never identify the failed component directly.

The CHECK ENGINE lamp comes on each time the ignition key is turned on and stays on for three seconds as a bulb test. If the SMEC receives an incorrect signal or no signal from certain sensors (or emission related systems on California trucks) this light is turned on. This is a warning that the SMEC has gone into a limp-in mode in an attempt to keep the system operating. It signals an immediate need for service. The lamp can also be used to display fault codes. Cycle the ignition switch **ON-OFF-ON-OFF-ON** within 5 seconds and any fault codes stored in the memory will be displayed.

The SMEC contains the circuits necessary to drive the ignition coil, fuel injector and the alternator field. These are high current devices and have been isolated to minimize and electrical noise in the passenger compartment.

The Automatic Shut Down (ASD) relay is mounted externally, but is turned on and off by the SMEC. The distributor pick-up signal goes to the SMEC. In the event of no distributor signal, the ASD relay is not activated and power is shut off from the fuel injector and ignition coil. The SMEC

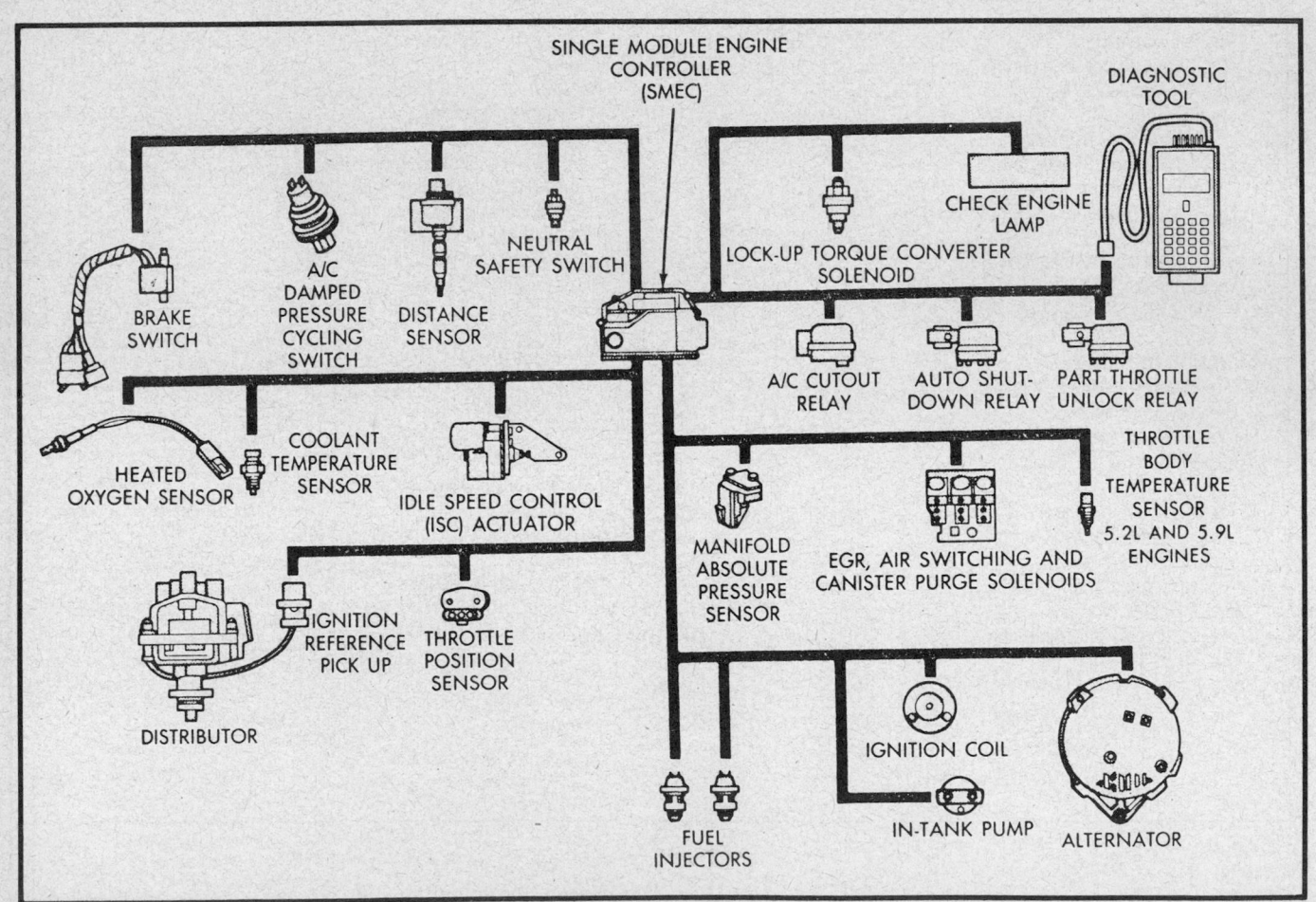

Chrysler Throttle Body Injection (TBI) components

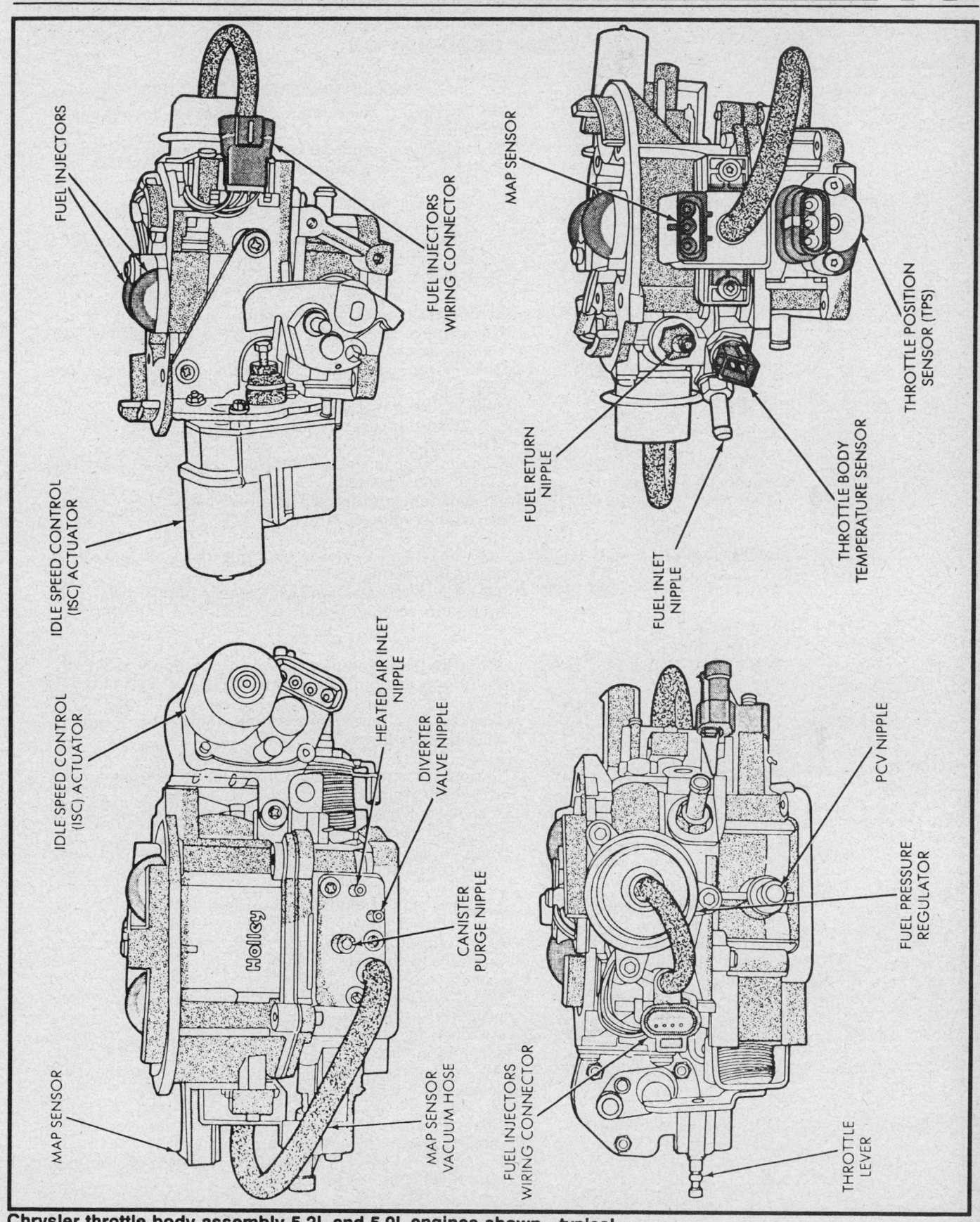

Chrysler throttle body assembly 5.2L and 5.9L engines shown—typical

FAULT CODE DESCRIPTION

CHECK ENGINE LAMP FAULT CODE	DRB II DISPLAY	DESCRIPTION OF FAULT CONDITION
11	IGN REFERENCE SIGNAL	No Distributor reference signal detected during engine cranking.
12	No. of Key-ons since last fault or since faults were erased.	Direct battery input to controller disconnected within the last 50-100 ignition key-ons.
13† **	MAP PNEUMATIC SIGNAL	No variation in MAP sensor signal is detected.
	or MAP PNEUMATIC CHANGE	No difference is recognized between the engine MAP reading and the stored barometric pressure reading.
14† **	MAP VOLTAGE TOO LOW	MAP sensor input below minimum acceptable voltage.
	or MAP VOLTAGE TOO HIGH	MAP sensor input above maximum acceptable voltage.
15 **	VEHICLE SPEED SIGNAL	No distance sensor signal detected during road load conditions.
16† **	BATTERY INPUT SENSE	Battery voltage sense input not detected during engine running.
17	LOW ENGINE TEMP	Engine coolant temperature remains below normal operating temperatures during vehicle travel (Thermostat).
21**	OXYGEN SENSOR SIGNAL	Neither rich or lean condition is detected from the oxygen sensor input.
22† **	COOLANT VOLTAGE LOW	Coolant temperature sensor input below the minimum acceptable voltage.
	or COOLANT VOLTAGE HIGH	Coolant temperature sensor input above the maximum acceptable voltage.
23	T/B TEMP VOLTAGE LOW	Throttle body temperature sensor input below the minimum acceptable voltage. (5.2L and 5.9L only)
	or T/B TEMP VOLTAGE HIGH	Throttle body temperature sensor input above the maximum acceptable voltage. (5.2L and 5.9L only)
24† **	TPS VOLTAGE LOW	Throttle position sensor input below the minimum acceptable voltage.
	or TPS VOLTAGE HIGH	Throttle position sensor input above the maximum acceptable voltage.
25**	ISC MOTOR CIRCUITS	A shorted condition detected in one or more of the ISC control circuits.
26	INJ 1 PEAK CURRENT	High resistance condition detected in the INJ 1 injector output circuit.
	or INJ 2 PEAK CURRENT	High resistance condition detected in the INJ 2 injector output circuit.
27	INJ 1 CONTROL CKT	INJ 1 injector output driver stage does not respond properly to the control signal.
	or INJ 2 CONTROL CKT	INJ 2 injector output driver stage does not respond properly to the control signal.
31**	PURGE SOLENOID CKT	An open or shorted condition detected in the purge solenoid circuit.
32**	EGR SOLENOID CIRCUIT	An open or shorted condition detected in the EGR solenoid circuit. (California emissions only)
	or EGR SYSTEM FAILURE	Required change in Fuel/Air ratio not detected during diagnostic test. (California emissions only)
33	A/C CLUTCH RELAY CKT	An open or shorted condition detected in the A/C clutch relay circuit.

FAULT CODE DESCRIPTION

CHECK ENGINE LAMP FAULT CODE	DRB II DISPLAY	DESCRIPTION OF FAULT CONDITION
36	AIR SWITCH SOLENOID	An open or shorted condition detected in the air switching solenoid circuit.
37	PTU SOLENOID CIRCUIT	An open or shorted condition detected in the torque converter part throttle unlock solenoid circuit. (Automatic transmission only)
41	CHARGING SYSTEM CKT	Output driver stage for alternator field does not respond properly to the voltage regulator control signal.
42	ASD RELAY CIRCUIT	An open or shorted condition detected in the auto shutdown relay circuit.
	or Z1 VOLTAGE SENSE	No Z1 voltage sensed when the auto shutdown relay is energized
43	IGNITION CONTROL CKT	Output driver stage for ignition coil does not respond properly to the dwell control signal.
44	FJ2 VOLTAGE SENSE	No FJ2 voltage present at the logic board during controller operation.
45	OVERDRIVE SOLENOID	An open or shorted condition detected in the overdrive solenoid circuit. (Automatic transmission only)
46**	BATTERY VOLTAGE HIGH	Battery voltage sense input above target charging voltage during engine operation.
47	BATTERY VOLTAGE LOW	Battery voltage sense input below target charging voltage during engine operation.
51**	AIR FUEL AT LIMIT	Oxygen sensor signal input indicates lean fuel/air ratio condition during engine operation.
52**	AIR FUEL AT LIMIT	Oxygen sensor signal input indicates rich fuel/air ratio condition during engine operation.
	or EXCESSIVE LEANING	Adaptive fuel value leaned excessively due to a sustained rich condition.
53	INTERNAL SELF-TEST	Internal engine controller fault condition detected,
55		Completion of fault code display on the CHECK ENGINE lamp.
62	EMR MILEAGE ACCUM	Unsuccessful attempt to update EMR mileage in the controller EEPROM.
63	EEPROM WRITE DENIED	Unsuccessful attempt to write to an EEPROM location by the controller.
	FAULT CODE ERROR	An unrecognized fault ID received by DRB II.

† Check Engine Lamp On
**Check Engine Lamp On (California Only)

contains a voltage converter which converts battery voltage to a regulated 8.0 volts output. This 8.0 volts output powers the distributor pick-up. The internal 5 volts supply powers the MAP sensor and TPS.

Throttle Body

The throttle body assembly replaces a conventional carburetor and is mounted on top of the intake manifold. The throttle body houses the fuel injectors, pressure regulator, throttle position sensor, throttle body temperature sensor, throttle body temperature sensor on 5.2L and 5.9L engines, idle speed control (ISC) actuator. Air flow through the throttle body is controlled by a cable operated throttle blade located in the base of the throttle body. The throttle body itself provides the chamber for metering, atomizing and distributing fuel throughout the air entering the engine.

─────── CAUTION ───────

The throttle body system is under a constant pressure of about 14.5 psi. Before servicing the fuel pump, fuel lines, fuel filter, throttle body or fuel injector, the fuel system pressure must be released and great care exercise to prevent personal injury. When servicing the fuel portion of the throttle body it will be necessary to bleed fuel pressure before opening any hoses. Use the following procedure:

1. Loosen the fuel filler cap to release tank pressure.
2. Disconnect injector wiring harness from engine harness.
3. Connect jumper wire to ground terminal No. 1 of injector harness to engine ground.
4. Connect jumper wire to positive terminal No. 2 of injector harness and touch to battery positive post for no longer than 5 seconds. This releases system pressure.

NOTE: Always assemble throttle body components with new O-rings and seals provided in the service packages. Never use silicone lubricants on O-rings or seals, or damage may result. Use care when removing fuel hoses to prevent damage to hose or hose nipple. Always use new hose clamps of the correct type when assembling and torque hose clamps to 10 inch lbs. Do not use Aviation style clamps on this system or hose damage may result.

Removal and Installation

1. To remove the throttle body assembly, remove the air cleaner and perform the fuel system pressure release procedure. The remove the battery negative cable.
2. Disconnect the vacuum hoses and electrical connectors.
3. Disconnect the throttle return spring, the cable and bracket. Also remove the speed control cable and transmission kickdown linkages if used.
4. Remove the fuel intake and return hoses.
5. Remove the hold-down bolts and remove the TBI assembly.
6. At installation, use new a new flange gasket. Tighten the mounting bolts to 175 inch lbs.
7. Check all electrical connections and fuel fittings for proper assembly. Use original equipment type hose clamps.
8. Install the throttle cable and bracket and kickdown cable and speed control cable if used.
9. Install air cleaner and battery negative cable.

THROTTLE BODY TEMPERATURE SENSOR

The throttle body temperature sensor is a device that monitors throttle body temperature which is the same as fuel temperature. It is mounted in the throttle body. The sensor provides information on fuel temperature which allows the SMEC to provide the correct air fuel mixture for a hot restart condition.

Disassembly and Assembly
5.2L AND 5.9L ENGINES

NOTE: It is not necessary to remove the throttle body from the intake manifold to perform component disassembly. If fuel hoses are to be replaced, only hoses marked EFI/EFM may be used. If fuel line fittings are removed, new copper sealing washers must be used.

1. Remove air cleaner.
2. Disconnect wiring connector.
3. Unscrew sensor.
4. At installation, apply heat transfer compound (provided with the new factory replacement part) to the tip portion of the sensor.
5. Install and tighten to 100 inch lbs.
6. Install wiring connector and air cleaner.

FUEL PRESSURE REGULATOR

The fuel pressure regulator is a mechanical device located in the back of the throttle body. Its function is to maintain a constant 14.5 psi across the fuel injector tip. The regulator uses a spring loaded rubber diaphragm to uncover a fuel return port. When the fuel pump becomes operational, fuel flows past the injector into the regulator and is restricted from flowing any further by the blocked return port. When fuel pressure reaches 14.5 psi, it pushes on the diaphragm, compressing the spring and uncovers the fuel return port. The diaphragm and spring will constantly move from an open to closed position to keep fuel pressure constant.

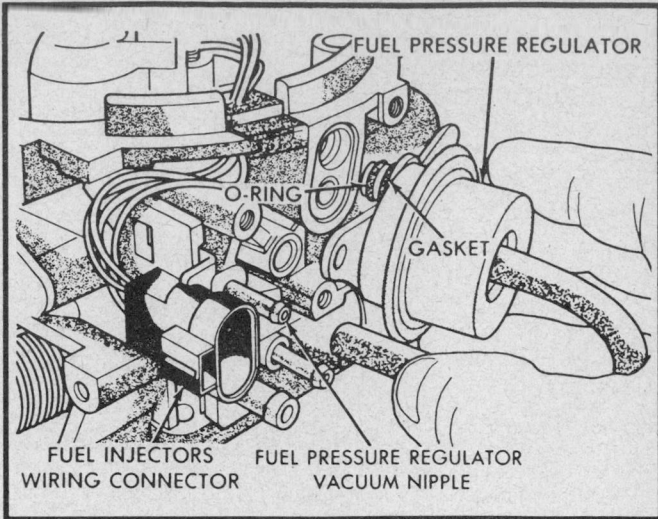

Servicing Chrysler's fuel pressure regulator

Disassembly and Assembly

1. Remove air cleaner and perform the fuel system pressure release.
2. Disconnect the negative battery cable.
3. Remove the vacuum hose from the throttle body.
4. Remove the screws attaching the pressure regulator to the throttle body.

NOTE: Place a shop towel around the fuel inlet chamber to contain any fuel remaining in the system.

5. Pull the pressure regulator from the throttle body. Discard the gasket and O-ring.
6. Place the gasket and O-ring from the service package. Do not use a substitute O-ring.
7. Position the pressure regulator on the throttle body, install the screws and tighten to 40 inch lbs.
8. Install the vacuum hose to the throttle body.
9. Reconnect the battery cable, and reinstall the air cleaner.

FUEL INJECTORS

The fuel injectors are electric solenoids driven by the SMEC.

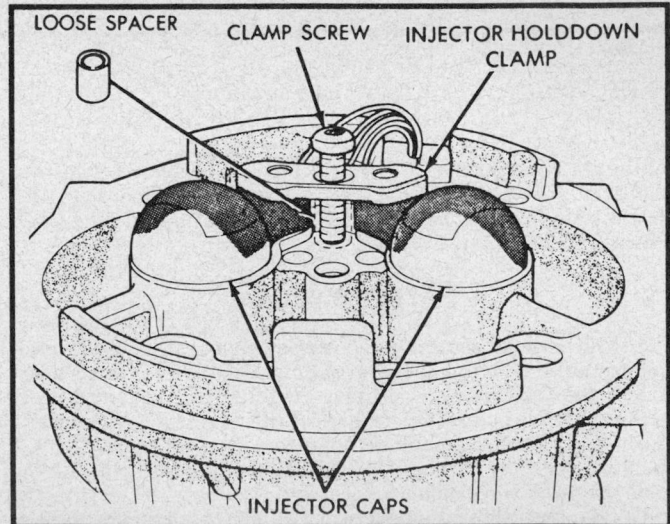

Removing the injector cap hold-down—Chrylser injection

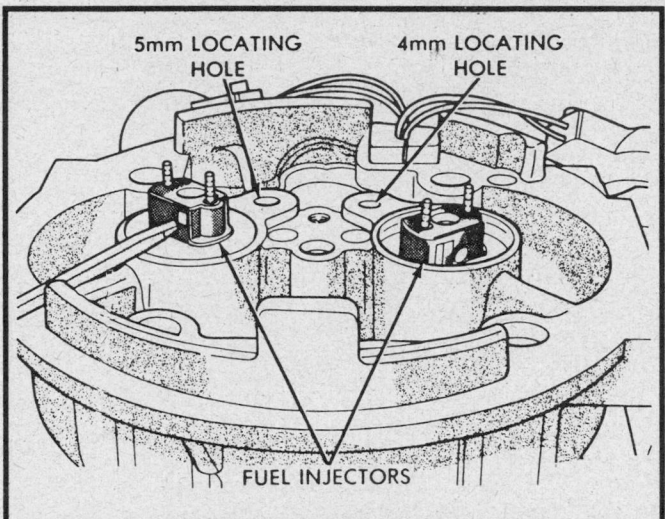

Removing the Chrylser fuel injector

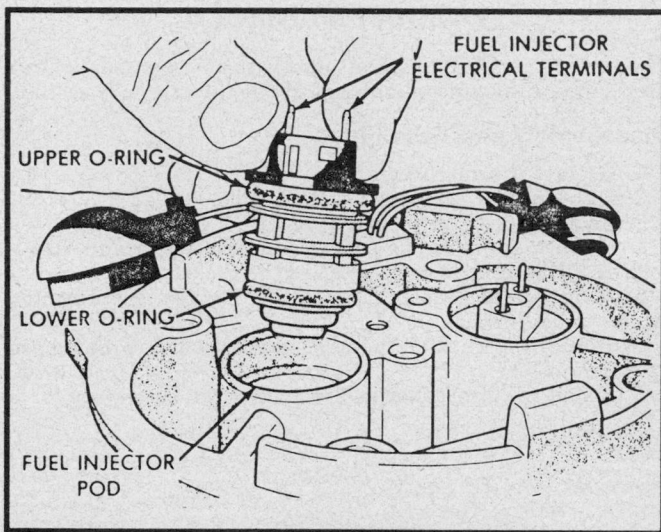

Chrylser fuel injector seals and terminals

The SMEC, based on sensor inputs determines when and how long the fuel injectors should operate. When electrical current is supplied to the injector a spring loaded ball is lifted from its seat. This allows fuel to flow through 6 spray holes and deflects off the sharp edge of the injector nozzle. This action causes the fuel to form a 45 degree cone shaped spray pattern before entering the air stream in the throttle body.

Fuel is supplied to the injectors constantly at a regulated 14.5 psi. The unused fuel is returned to the fuel tank.

Disassembly and Assembly

1. Remove air cleaner and perform the fuel system pressure release.
2. Disconnect the battery negative cable.
3. Remove the Torx screw retaining the injector hold-down clamp. Be careful of the small loose spacer under the clamp. Don't loose it or drop it down the throttle body throat.
4. Lift the top off the injector. Locate the hole in the front of the injector's electrical connector and gently pry the injector from the pod. Make sure the injector lower O-ring has been removed from the pod. Discard the O-rings.
5. Install a new lower O-ring on the injector. The O-ring should butt against the plastic filter assembly. Use only the O-ring supplied in the service package.
6. Align the injector terminal housing with the locating socket in the injector cap and press the injector into the cap so that the upper O-ring flange is flush with the lower surfaces of the cap.
7. Clean the inner surfaces of both injector pods. Brake and Carb Cleaner will work. Lightly lubricate the O-rings with petroleum jelly and place the injector and cap in the pod, aligning the cap locator pin with the locating hole in the casting.

NOTE: The passenger side cap locating pin is 5mm in diameter and will only fit in the passenger side locating hole. The driver's side locating pin is 4mm in diameter.

8. Repeat these steps with the other injector, then press firmly on the injector caps, one at a time until the cap is flush with the casting surface. Then place the injector hold-down clamp with the spacer on the rear portion of the caps, aligning the holes in the clamp with the pins on the caps. Install the clamp screw and tighten to 35 inch lbs.

NOTE: Because O-ring squeeze may cause the caps to lift up, press firmly on both caps with one hand to assure the caps are flush while installing the clamp screw.

9. Reconnect the battery cable and install the air cleaner.

MANIFOLD ABSOLUTE PRESSURE SENSOR

The Manifold Absolute Pressure (MAP) sensor is a device which monitors manifold vacuum. It is mounted on the throttle body and is connected to a vacuum nipple on the throttle body and electrically to the SMEC. The sensor transmits information on manifold vacuum conditions and barometric pressure to the SMEC. The MAP sensor data on engine load is used with data from other sensors to determine the correct air fuel mixture.

Disassembly and Assembly

1. Remove the vacuum hose and electrical connector from the MAP sensor.
2. Remove the sensor mounting screws and remove the sensor.
3. At installation, make sure the electrical connection is secure.

THROTTLE POSITION SENSOR

The Throttle Position Sensor (TPS) is mounted on the throttle body and senses the angle of the throttle blade opening. A 5 volt

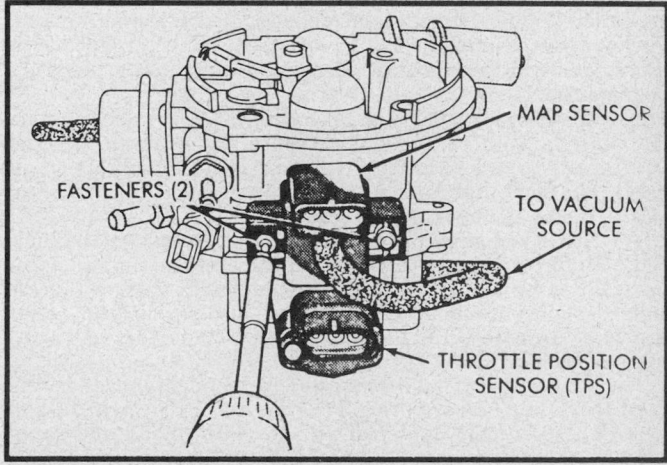

Servicing Chrylser MAP sensor

signal is supplied to the TPS and a portion of the voltage is sent back to the SMEC, based on the position of the throttle blade. The return voltage increases when the blade is opened. The signal supplied by the TPS is used to assist the SMEC in determining the correct air/fuel ratio during varying conditions like acceleration, deceleration, wide open throttle and idle.

Disassembly and Assembly

1. Disconnect the negative battery cable.
2. Remove the air cleaner.
3. Disconnect the three-way connector at the throttle position sensor.
4. Remove the screws holding the TPS to the throttle body and lift the TPS off the throttle shaft.
5. Install the TPS on the throttle body, and position it upward away from the engine. Tighten the screws to only 27 inch lbs.
6. Install the three-way electrical connector, install the air cleaner and reconnect the battery cable.

IDLE SPEED CONTROL (ISC) ACTUATOR

The Idle Speed Control (ISC) Actuator adjusts the idle speed by physically moving the throttle lever. The moving of the throttle lever will change the air flow which results in the SMEC changing the amount of fuel supplied. The ISC compensates for varying engine loads and ambient temperatures.

Disassembly and Assembly

1. Remove the air cleaner.
2. Disconnect the battery negative cable.
3. Disconnect the wiring connector at the ISC.
4. Remove the nuts which hold the ISC actuator to the bracket.
5. Install the ISC with the nuts and washers, and attach the wiring.
6. Reconnect battery negative cable and install air cleaner.
7. Check rpm at idle and if necessary, adjust to specification.

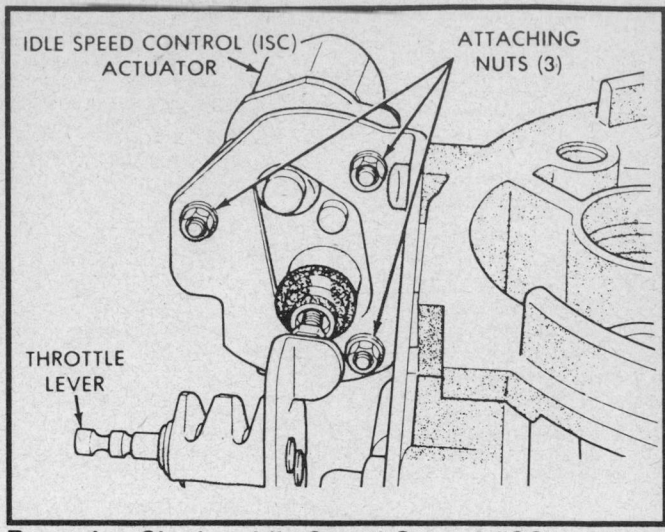

Removing Chryslser Idle Speed Control (ISC) actuator

VACUUM MANIFOLD

The vacuum manifold is a small plate with an assortment of vacuum tubes. It mounts on one side of the throttle body casting.

Disassembly and Assembly

1. Remove the air cleaner.
2. Disconnect the battery negative cable.
3. Remove the throttle body from the engine.
4. Remove the retaining screws and pull the vacuum manifold from the throttle body. Discard the gasket.
5. At installation, use a new gasket. Tighten the attaching screws to 35 inch lbs.
6. Install the throttle body assembly, using a new base gasket.
7. Install the air cleaner and reconnect the battery cable.

FORD MOTOR COMPANY

The electronic fuel injection system (EFI) is classified as a multi-point, pulse time, speed density, fuel injection system. Fuel is metered into the intake air stream in accordance with engine demand through the injectors mounted on a tuned intake manifold.

An on-board electronic engine control (EEC-IV) computer accepts inputs from various engine sensors to compute the fuel flow rate necessary to maintain a prescribed air/fuel ratio at all times. The computer then outputs a command to the fuel injectors to meter the appropriate quantity of fuel.

The EEC-IV engine control system also determines and compensates for the age of the vehicle. The system will also automatically sense and compensate for changes in altitude (for example, sea level to mountains) and will also permit push-starting the vehicle should it become necessary (manual transmission only).

The fuel delivery subsystem differs among vehicles in the Ford truck line. On E Series, F Series and Broncos (5.0L and 5.8L EFI V8), trucks equipped with the 4.9L engine, and Rangers with the 2.9L engine, the fuel delivery system consists of a low pressure in-tank mounted fuel pump, a fuel reservoir (locat-

ed to the rear of the transmission support on the left hand frame rail) and a high pressure, chassis mounted, electric fuel pump delivering fuel from the fuel tank through a chassis mounted 20 micron fuel filter to a fuel charging manifold assembly.

On Rangers equipped with 2.3L engine, the fuel delivery system consists of a high pressure, chassis-mounted electric fuel pump delivering fuel from the fuel tank to a fuel charging manifold assembly.

--- **CAUTION** ---

Fuel supply lines on 4.9L, 5.0L, 5.8L and 7.5L EFI engines will remain pressurized for some period of time after the engine is shut off. This pressure must be relieved before servicing the fuel system. Beware of the fire hazard associated with fuel under pressure which could cause personal injury.

Fuel System Pressure Relief

Before opening the fuel system on vehicles with EFI engines, relieve the fuel pressure as follows:
1. Locate and disconnect the electrical connection to either

the fuel pump relay, the inertia switch on the in-line high pressure fuel pump.

2. Crank the engine for approximately 10 seconds. The engine may start and run for a short time. If so, crank the engine an additional 5 seconds after the engine stalls.

3. Connect the electrical connector that was previously disconnected.

4. Disconnect the battery ground cable.

Push Connect Fittings

Push connect fittings are designed with two different retaining clips. The fittings used to connect to ⅜ in. and ⁵/₁₆ in. diameter tubing use a Hairpin clip. The fittings used with ¼ in. diameter tubing use a Duckbill clip. Each type of fitting requires different procedures for service. Clips should be replaced whenever a connector is removed.

The fuel lines connecting to the EFI engine fuel rails are a special, Spring-lock metal design. The fuel feed line uses a ½ in. spring lock connector. The fuel return uses a ⅜ in. spring lock connector.

Disconnect all push connect fittings from components (pump, filter, engine) prior to component removal. The push connect fittings to connect flexible fuel lines to the fuel tank sender often cannot be disconnected until the tank is partially lowered just before removing the fuel tank completely.

Removal and Installation

HAIRPIN CLIP (5/16 and 3/8 IN. FITTINGS)

1. Inspect the visible internal portion of the fitting for dirt accumulation. If more than a light coating of dust is present, clean the fitting before disassembly.

2. Some adhesion between the seals in the fitting and the tubing will occur with time. To separate, twist the fitting on the tube, then push and pull the fitting until it moves freely on the tube.

3. Remove the Hairpin type clip from the fitting by first bending the shipping tab downward so that it will clear the body. Next (using hands only) spread the two clip legs about ⅛ in. each to disengage the body and push the legs into the fitting. Complete removal is accomplished by lightly pulling from the triangular end of the clip and working it clear of the tube and fitting.

NOTE: Do not use any tool. Use hands only.

4. Grasp the fitting and hose assembly and pull to remove the fitting from the tube.

5. When the fitting is removed from the tube end, inspect the

fitting and tube for any internal parts that may have been dislodged from the fitting. Any loose internal parts should be immediately reinstalled, using the mating tube to insert the parts.

6. At installation, it is recommended that the original clip not be reused in the fitting. To install the new clip, insert the clip into any 2 adjacent openings with the triangular portion pointing away from the fitting opening. Install the clip to fully engage the body (legs of the hairpin clip locked on the outside of the body).

7. Before installing the fitting on the tube, wipe the tube end with a clean cloth. Inspect the inside of the fitting to ensure it is free of dirt.

8. To install the fitting onto the tube, align the fitting and tube and push the fitting onto the tube end. When the fitting is engaged, a definite click will be heard. Pull on the fitting to make sure it is fully engaged.

DUCKBILL CONNECTORS

This fitting consists of a body, spacers, O-rings and a Duckbill retaining clip which holds the fitting together. Since some adhesion between the seals in the fitting and the tubing will occur in time, twist the fitting on the tube until it moves freely on the tube.

To disengage this type of connector, s special tool is the preferred method. However, some fuel tubes have a secondary bead which aligns with outer surface of the clip. These beads can make tool insertion difficult. If this type of fitting is encountered, or if the special tool is unavailable, use the following method:

This method of disassembly disengages the retaining clip from the fitting body. Use with a pair of narrow pliers (6 in. channel lock type pliers are ideal). The pliers must have a jaw width of 5mm (0.2 in.) or less.

1. Align the jaws of the pliers with the openings in the side of the fitting case and compress the portion of the retaining clip

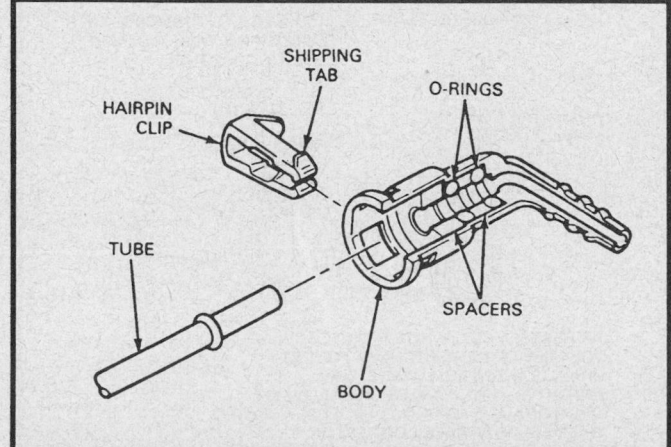

Typical Ford hairpin type push connect fitting

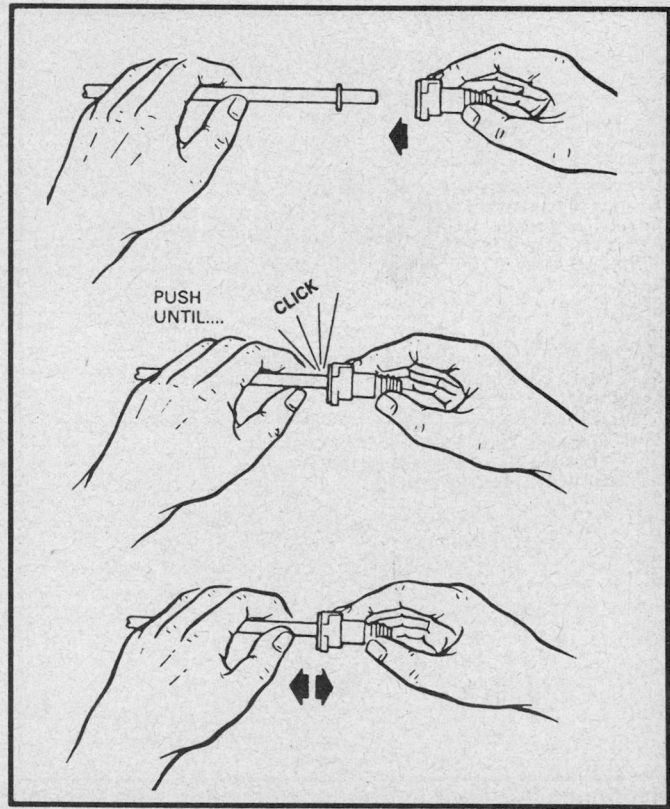

PUSH UNTIL....   CLICK

Connecting Ford duckbill type push connect fitting

that engages the fitting case. This disengages the retaining clip from the case (often one side of the clip disengage before the other. It is necessary to disengage the clip from both openings).

2. Pull the fitting off the tube. Note that only moderate effort is required if the retaining clip has been properly disengaged. Use hands only.

3. When the fitting is removed from the tube end, inspect the fitting and tube for any internal parts that may have been dislodged from the fitting. Any loose parts should be immediately installed, using the mating tube to insert the parts. The retaining clip will remain on the tube. Disengage the clip from the tube bead and remove.

4. At installation, it is recommended that the retaining clip not be reused. Install the new replacement clip into the body by inserting one of the retaining clip serrated edges on the duck bill portion into one of the window openings. Push on the other side until the clip snaps into place.

5. Before installing the fitting on the tube, wipe the tube end clean. Make sure there is no dirt on or in the tube. Align the fitting and tube and push the fitting onto the tube end. When the fitting is engaged, a definite click will be heard. Pull on the fitting to ensure it is fully engaged.

METAL SPRING-LOCK CONNECTORS

The spring lock push connect fittings work by insertion of the fitting's male end, which is surrounded by two O-rings, into a female flared end fitting. The coupling engagement is secured by a garter spring which prevents the female flared end from becoming disengaged from the male end. The barbed end of the spring lock, which is inserted into the chassis nylon tube, is made of steel and the spring lock's body is made of steel. The O-rings are made of gas-resistant viton.

These connectors require a special tool to disengage the connector. Sometimes, however, the tool will not always fit over shielded line. To fit the shielding, the hole in the tubing end of the tool must be enlarged. To do this, clamp the tool closed and drill out the existing hole with a ⅝ in. bit. Be careful to drill only the tubing hole and not the working end of the tool.

1. Always release the system pressure before disconnecting any fuel line. Clean the connection well.

2. The tool is a clam-shell like unit that goes around fuel line fitting cage. Note that there is a different tool for each size of fuel line. To disassemble this fitting, locate the white indicator ring which should be loose on the fuel line. It may have slipped down the fuel line, so look carefully. It will be required at assem-

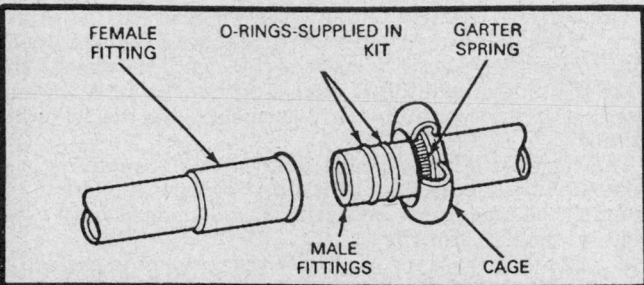

Ford spring lock coupling disconnected

FEMALE FITTING — O-RINGS-SUPPLIED IN KIT — GARTER SPRING — MALE FITTINGS — CAGE

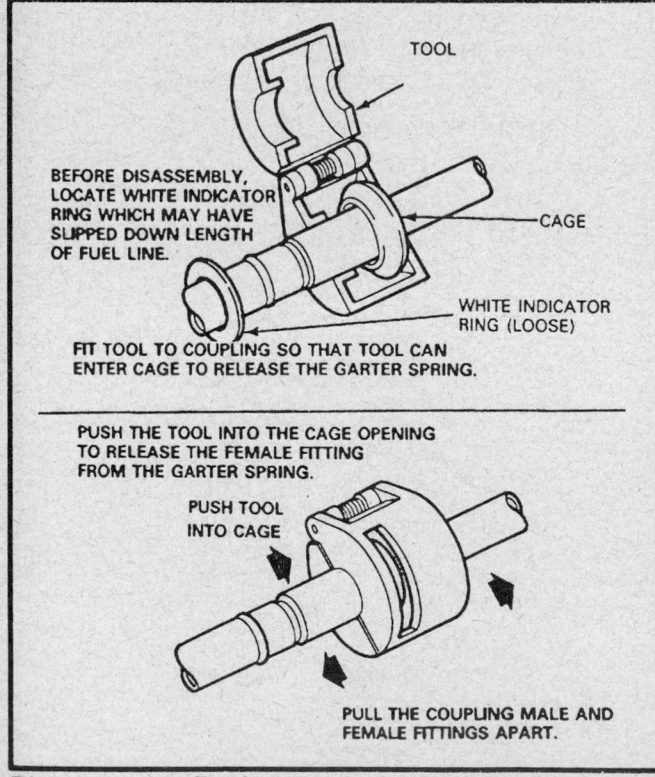

BEFORE DISASSEMBLY, LOCATE WHITE INDICATOR RING WHICH MAY HAVE SLIPPED DOWN LENGTH OF FUEL LINE.

TOOL

CAGE

WHITE INDICATOR RING (LOOSE)

FIT TOOL TO COUPLING SO THAT TOOL CAN ENTER CAGE TO RELEASE THE GARTER SPRING.

PUSH THE TOOL INTO THE CAGE OPENING TO RELEASE THE FEMALE FITTING FROM THE GARTER SPRING.

PUSH TOOL INTO CAGE

PULL THE COUPLING MALE AND FEMALE FITTINGS APART.

Disconnecting Ford spring lock coupling with special tool

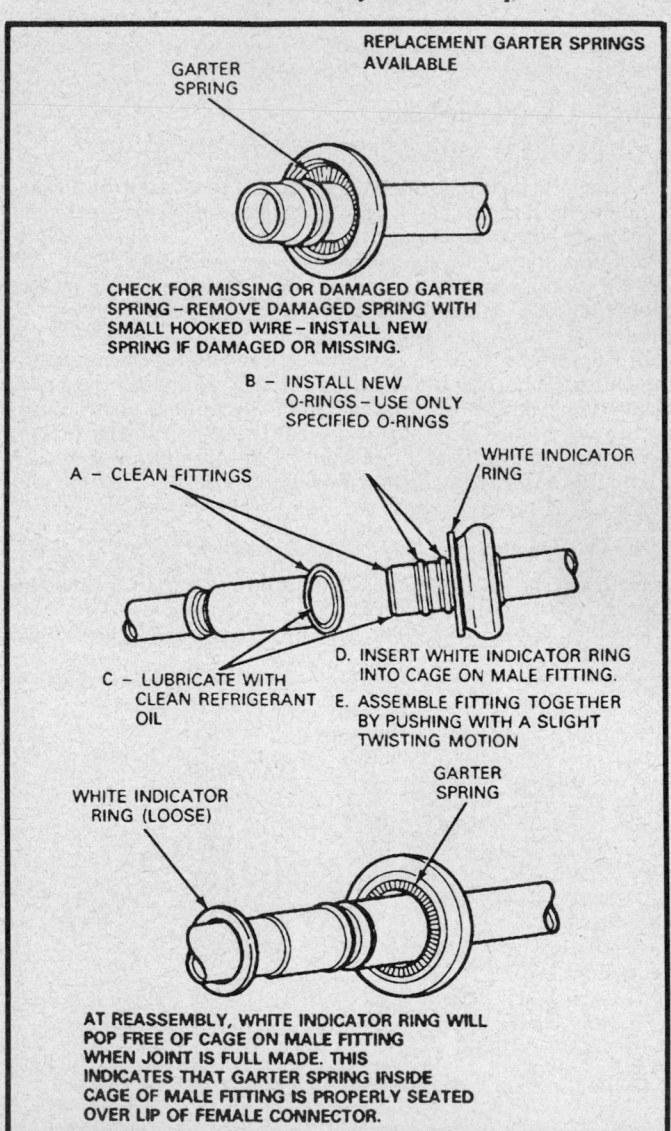

GARTER SPRING

REPLACEMENT GARTER SPRINGS AVAILABLE

CHECK FOR MISSING OR DAMAGED GARTER SPRING – REMOVE DAMAGED SPRING WITH SMALL HOOKED WIRE – INSTALL NEW SPRING IF DAMAGED OR MISSING.

B – INSTALL NEW O-RINGS – USE ONLY SPECIFIED O-RINGS

A – CLEAN FITTINGS

WHITE INDICATOR RING

C – LUBRICATE WITH CLEAN REFRIGERANT OIL

D. INSERT WHITE INDICATOR RING INTO CAGE ON MALE FITTING.

E. ASSEMBLE FITTING TOGETHER BY PUSHING WITH A SLIGHT TWISTING MOTION

WHITE INDICATOR RING (LOOSE)

GARTER SPRING

AT REASSEMBLY, WHITE INDICATOR RING WILL POP FREE OF CAGE ON MALE FITTING WHEN JOINT IS FULL MADE. THIS INDICATES THAT GARTER SPRING INSIDE CAGE OF MALE FITTING IS PROPERLY SEATED OVER LIP OF FEMALE CONNECTOR.

Connecting the Ford spring lock coupler

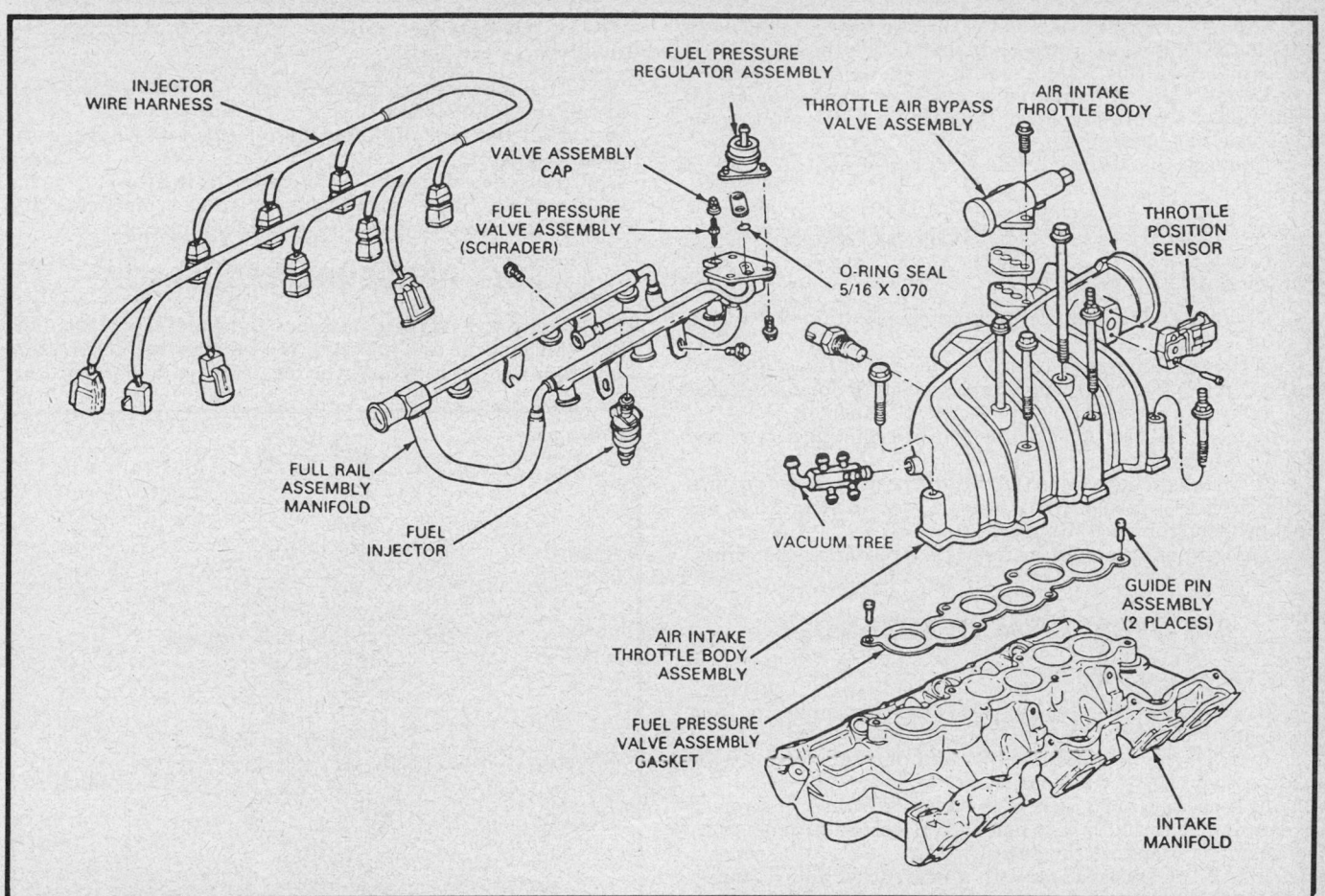

INJECTOR WIRE HARNESS

VALVE ASSEMBLY CAP

FUEL PRESSURE VALVE ASSEMBLY (SCHRADER)

FULL RAIL ASSEMBLY MANIFOLD

FUEL INJECTOR

FUEL PRESSURE REGULATOR ASSEMBLY

THROTTLE AIR BYPASS VALVE ASSEMBLY

AIR INTAKE THROTTLE BODY

THROTTLE POSITION SENSOR

O-RING SEAL 5/16 X .070

VACUUM TREE

AIR INTAKE THROTTLE BODY ASSEMBLY

FUEL PRESSURE VALVE ASSEMBLY GASKET

GUIDE PIN ASSEMBLY (2 PLACES)

INTAKE MANIFOLD

Ford throttle body fuel injection—typical

bly. Do not remove it from the fuel line after the connection is disassembled. Fit the tool to the coupling so that the tool can enter the cage to release the garter spring.

3. Push the tool into the cage opening to release the female fitting from the garter spring.

4. Pull the coupling male and female fittings apart. Remove the tool from the disconnected spring lock coupling.

5. To connect the coupling, check for missing or damaged garter spring. If the spring must be replaced, fish out the damaged spring with a small wire hook. Replacement garter springs are available from Ford. Install a new spring if required.

6. Clean the fittings and install new O-rings. Lubricate the fittings with clean refrigerant oil. Insert the white indicator ring into the cage on the male fitting. Assemble the fitting by pushing together with a slight twisting motion.

7. The white indicator ring should pop free of the cage on the male fitting when the joint is fully made. This indicates that the garter spring inside the cage is properly seated over the lip of the female connector.

THROTTLE BODY

Ford trucks and Vans, including Aerostar and Bronco II use similar fuel injection systems. Even the cast intake manifolds, with their long port runners share some similarities in appearance. Some manifolds are one piece, and others are cast in sections and held held together with bolts and gasketed joints.

Some throttle bodies use a single butterfly-type valve, the larger engines use a double butterfly. The throttle position is generally controlled by a conventional cable. An air bypass chan-

nel provides engine idle air control regulated by an air bypass valve assembly mounted on the throttle body. The valve assembly is an electromechanical device controlled by the EEC computer.

Depending on the vehicle and engine, the throttle body may also incorporate the following: An adjustment screw for idle air flow, a preset stop for Wide Open Throttle (WOT), a throttle body-mounted Throttle Position Sensor (TPS), provisions for EGR valve and sensor and individual vacuum taps.

Removal and Installation

NOTE: The throttle body removal discussed here is a general procedure. Each vehicle will be a little different. Some Aerostars, Bronco II and Ranger trucks may have extra baffles, snow shields, etc. which may need to be removed.

1. Disconnect the throttle position sensor and air bypass valve electrical connectors.

2. Mark any vacuum hoses that will be removed to make assembly easier. After removing the hose, unsnap the throttle cable (and speed control cable, if used) from the ball stud. The fittings may need to be pried off the ball stud. Use care not to kink the cable.

3. Remove the 4 throttle body screws, carefully separate the throttle body from the intake manifold and discard the gasket.

4. At assembly, make sure both the throttle body and intake manifold flanges are clean. If scraping is required, be careful not to damage the gasket surfaces or allow debris to drop into the engine.

5. It may be easiest to install the throttle body gasket on two bolts installed in the throttle body. Install the throttle body to intake manifold, then secure it with the remaining screws.

6. Connect the air bypass valve and throttle position sensor electrical connectors, reconnect the vacuum lines following the tags made at disassembly.

7. Connect the throttle cable (and speed control cable, if used).

THROTTLE POSITION SENSOR

Removal and Installation

1. Disconnect the throttle position sensor from the wiring harness.

2. Scribe a reference mark across the edge of the sensor and to the throttle body to ensure correct position during installation. Also note the relationship electrical connector.

3. Remove the throttle position sensor retaining screws and remove sensor.

4. At installation, position the throttle position sensor so that wiring harness is parallel to the venturi bores (5.0L and 5.8L engine) or facing forward (Ranger, Bronco II).

5. Tighten sensor mounting screws and reconnect the wiring.

AIR BYPASS VALVE ASSEMBLY

Removal and Installation

1. Disconnect the air bypass valve assembly connector from the wiring harness.

2. Remove the mounting screws and pull the valve off the throttle body. Discard the gasket.

3. At assembly, make sure both flanges are clean. If scraping is required, be careful not to damage the gasket surfaces or allow debris to drop into the engine.

4. Install the bypass valve with a new gasket and reconnect the wiring.

FUEL SUPPLY MANIFOLD ASSEMBLY (FUEL RAIL) AND FUEL INJECTORS

Removal and Installation

1. Perform the fuel system pressure relief procedure outlined above.

2. On E and F Series and Broncos with V8 engine, remove the upper manifold assembly. On Aerostars and some Bronco II with the V6 engine, remove the throttle body.

3. Disconnect the fuel supply and return lines.

4. Remove the bolts that hold the fuel supply manifold (fuel rail) to the lower manifold.

5. Disconnect the wiring from the injectors and the vacuum line to the fuel pressure regulator.

6. Carefully disengage the fuel rail assembly by lifting and gently rocking the rail.

NOTE: The injectors and fuel rail must be handled with care to prevent damage to sealing areas and the sensitive fuel metering orifices. Keep these parts as clean as possible. Avoid any kind of dirt or contamination.

7. The injectors are a light press-fit in the fuel rail. Grasp the injector body and pull while gently rocking the injector from side-to-side to free the O-ring. If the injector stays in the intake manifold, pull up while rocking the injector loose.

8. Inspect the fuel injectors carefully. Do not attempt to clean the injector pintle or metering orifice with tools or brushes. Install new O-rings. Lubricate the O-rings with light engine oil.

NOTE: Do not use silicone grease. It will clog the injectors.

9. Install the injectors into the intake manifold using a light, twisting, pushing motion.

10. Install the fuel rail onto the injector tops. Tighten the bracket bolts.

11. Install the electrical connectors to the injectors.

12. Install any upper manifolding or other components that may have been removed to service the fuel injectors.

FUEL PRESSURE REGULATOR

The fuel-pressure regulator attaches to the fuel supply manifold downstream of the fuel injectors. It regulates the fuel pressure supplied to the fuel injectors. The regulator is a diaphragm oper-

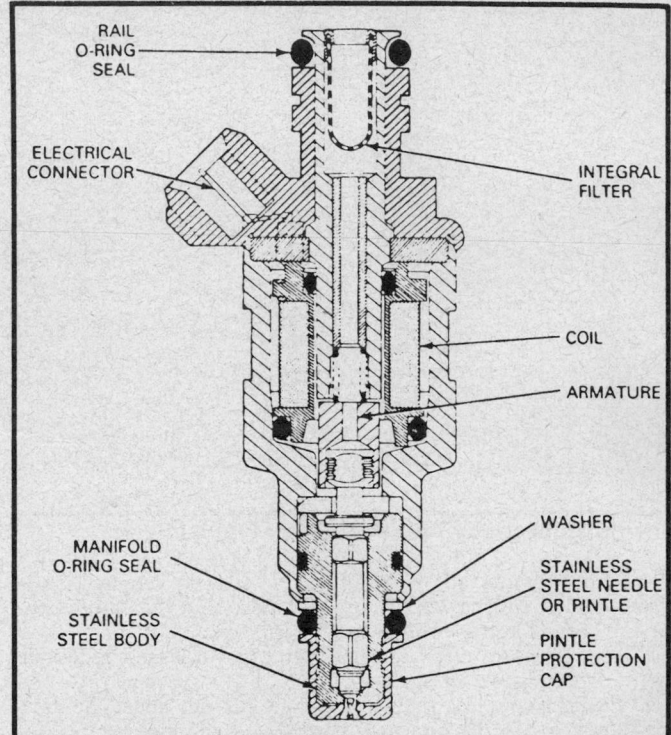

Ford fuel injector—typical

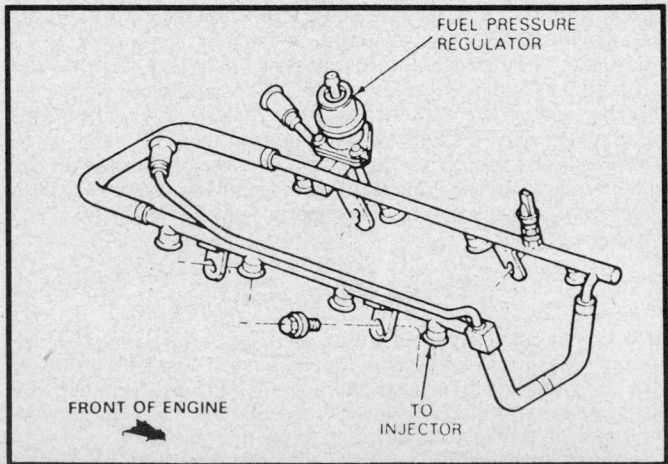

Ford fuel supply manifold assembly (fuel rail)— typical

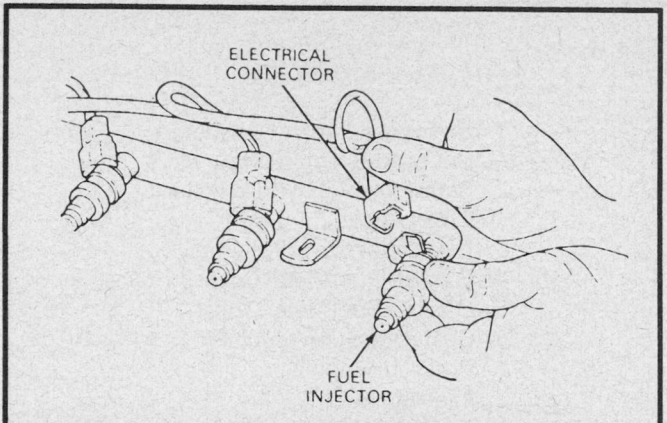

Disconnecting the injector electrical connector

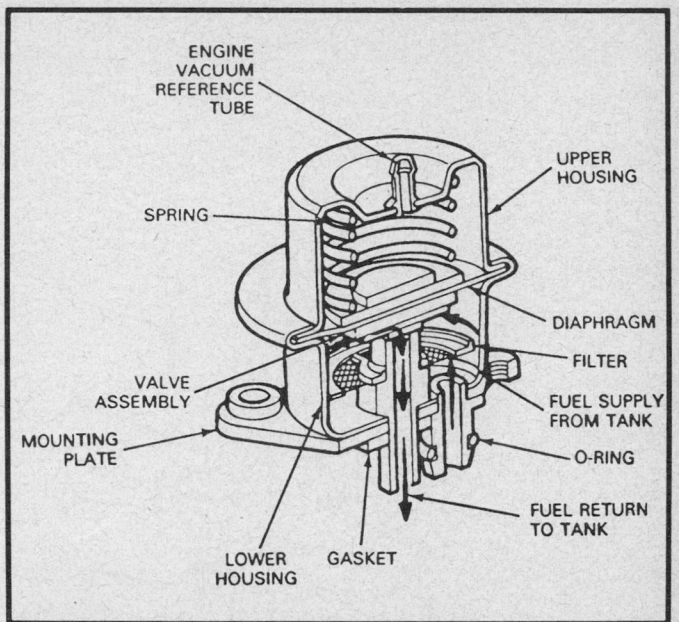

Ford fuel pressure regulator—typical

ated relief valve in which one side of the diaphragm senses fuel pressure and the other side is subject to intake manifold vacuum. The nominal fuel pressure is established by a spring preload applied to the diaphragm. Balancing one side of the diaphragm with manifold pressure maintains a constant fuel pressure drop across the injectors. Fuel in excess of that used by the engine is bypassed through the regulator and returns to the fuel tank.

Removal and Installation

1. Perform the fuel system pressure relief procedure.
2. Remove the vacuum line.
3. Remove the retaining screws, lift off the pressure regulator, discard the gasket and O-ring.
4. At installation, lubricate the new O-ring with light engine oil.

NOTE: Do not use silicone grease. It will clog the injectors.

5. Make sure the mounting surface is clean and use a new gasket. Install the pressure regulator and tighten the retaining screws.
6. Connect the vacuum hose. When the engine is restarted, check for leaks.

GENERAL MOTORS CORPORATION

Model 220 Throttle Body Injection

The fuel control system has an electric fuel pump, located in the fuel tank with the gauge sending unit, which pumps fuel to the Throttle Body Injector (TBI) through the fuel supply line, then through an in-line fuel filter. The pump is designed to provide pressurized fuel at about 18 psi. On vehicles with 2 fuel tanks, there is an electric fuel pump and gauge sending unit in each fuel tank.

A pressure regulator in the TBI keeps fuel available to the injectors at a constant pressure between 9–13 psi. Fuel in excess of injector needs is returned to the fuel tank by a separate line.

The Electronic Control Module (ECM) controls the injectors that are located in the fuel meter body assembly of the TBI. The injectors deliver fuel in one of several modes.

In order to properly control the fuel supply, the fuel pump is operated by the ECM through the fuel pump relay and oil pressure switch.

The Model 220 TBI unit, used on V6 and V8 engines consists of three major casting assemblies:
1. The fuel meter cover with pressure regulator.
2. The fuel meter body with the fuel injectors.
3. The throttle body with the Idle Air Control (IAC) valve and the Throttle Position Sensor (TPS).

Throttle Body

IDLE AIR CONTROL (IAC) VALVE

NOTE: The IAC valve is an electrical component and must not be soaked in any liquid cleaner or solvent or it will be damaged. In addition, all IAC valves on TBI Model 220 units (except those on the 7.4L engine) are thread-mounted and have a dual taper, 10mm diameter pintle. On the 7.4L engine, the IAC valve is flange-mounted and has a 12mm diameter dual taper pintle. Any replacement of an IAC valve must have the correct part number, with the appropriate pintle taper and diameter for proper seating of the valve in the throttle body.

Disassembly and Assembly

1. On thread mounted units, use a 32mm (1¼ in.) wrench and unscrew the IAC valve.
2. On flange-mounted units, remove the screws and pull out the IAC valve.
3. Discard the IAC valve O-rings. Use new ones at assembly.

NOTE: Since the IAC valve was removed during service, its operation should be tested electrically with the

Model 220 TBI

1. Screw Assembly - Fuel Meter Cover Attaching - Long
2. Screw Assembly - Fuel Meter Cover Attaching - Short
3. Fuel Meter Cover Assembly
4. Gasket - Fuel Meter Cover
5. Gasket - Fuel Meter Outlet
6. Seal - Pressure Regulator
7. Pressure Regulator
8. Injector - Fuel
9. Filter - Fuel Injector - Lower
10. O-Ring - Fuel Injector - Lower
11. O-Ring - Fuel Injector - Upper
12. Washer - Fuel Injector
13. Screw Assembly - Fuel Meter Body - Throttle Body Attaching
14. Fuel Meter Body Assembly
15. Gasket - Throttle Body to Fuel Meter Body
16. Gasket - Air Cleaner
17. O-Ring - Fuel Return Line
18. Nut - Fuel Outlet
19. O-Ring - Fuel Inlet Line
20. Nut - Fuel Inlet
21. Gasket - Fuel Outlet Nut
22. Gasket - Fuel Inlet Nut
23. Screw Assembly - TPS Attaching
24. Retainer - TPS Attaching Screw
25. Sensor - Throttle Position (TPS)
26. Plug - Idle Stop Screw
27. Screw Assembly - Idle Stop
28. Spring - Idle Stop Screw
29. Throttle Body Assembly
30. Gasket - Flange
31. Valve Assembly - Idle Air Control (IAC)
32. Gasket - Idle Air Control Valve Assembly
33. O-Ring - IACV
34. Screw Assembly - IACV Attaching

Model 220 TBI parts identification

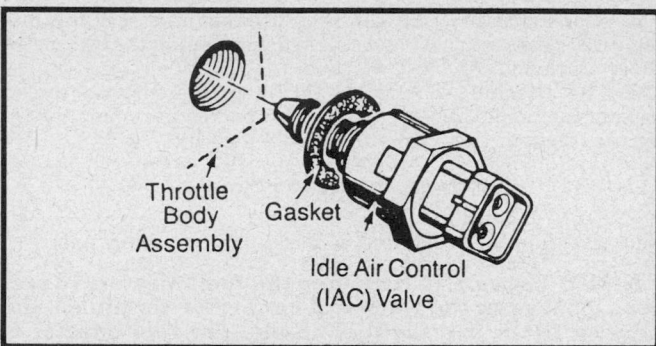

Thread-mounted type IAC valve

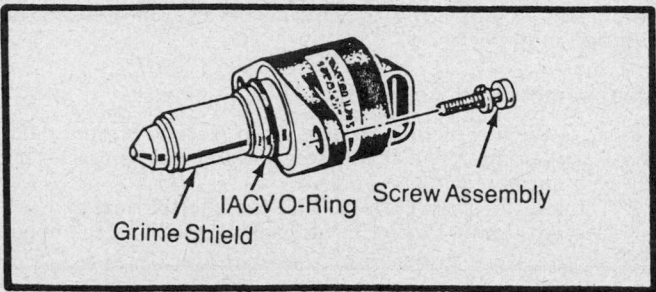

Flange-mounted type IAC valve

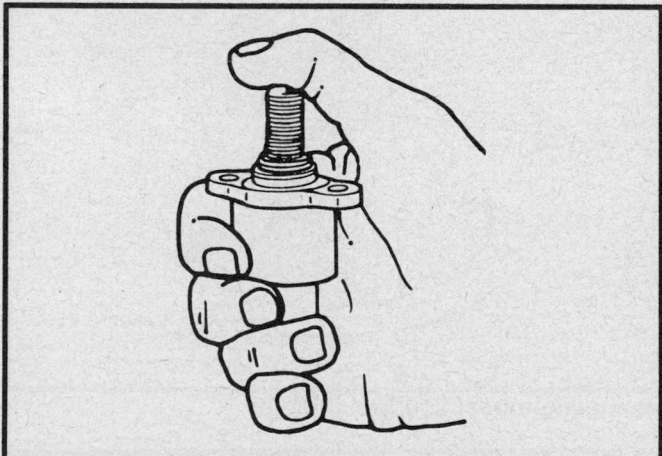

Adjusting IAC valve pintle—flange type shown—typical

factory special tool tester. However, if the valve pintle is extended electrically, it must also be retracted electrically. Before installing a IAC valve, measure the distance between the tip of the valve pintle and the mounting surface. If the dimension is greater than 28mm (1.10 in.), it must be reduced to prevent damage to the valve. This may be done electrically using the factory special tool or manually. Note that there are two different types of IAC valves: one with a collar at the electric terminal end and one without the collar. IAC valves with the collar can have the pintle pushed back in by exerting firm pressure with a slight side-to-side movement on the valve pintle to retract it. On IAC valves without the collar, compress the retaining spring and turn the pintle end clockwise. Return the spring to its original position, with the straight portion aligned in the slot under the flat surface of the valve. No physical adjustment of the IAC valve assembly is required after installation. The

IAC valve pintle is reset by turning the ignition ON for ten seconds and then OFF. The ECM then sets the pintle to the correct position. Proper idle regulation should result.

4. At installation, use a new gasket and tighten the thread-mount IAC valve to 13 ft. lbs. For the flange-mount IAC valve, lube the new O-ring and tighten the screws to 28 inch lbs.

NOTE: New IAC valves have been set at the factory and should be installed in the throttle body as is without any adjustment.

THROTTLE POSITION SENSOR (TPS)

NOTE: The TPS is an electrical component and must not be soaked in any liquid cleaner or solvent or it will be damaged. On 2.8L (V6) engines, the TPS is adjustable and is supplied with attaching screw retainers. On all other engines, it is non-adjustable, without retainers. In addition, on 2.8L (V6) and 7.4L (V8) engines, the TPS has a horizontal electrical connector; whereas on all other engines, the connector is a vertical one. Since these TPS configurations can be mounted interchangeably, be sure to order the correct one with the identical part number of the unit being replaced.

Disassembly and Assembly

1. Remove the attaching screw assemblies and retainers (if applicable).
2. Remove the TPS from the throttle body assembly.
3. Install the TPS on the throttle body assembly, while lining up the TPS lever with the TPS drive lever on the throttle body. Tighten the screws to only 18 inch lbs.
4. Reconnect the electric lead.

FUEL METER COVER

The fuel meter cover assembly contains the fuel pressure regulator assembly. The regulator has been adjusted at the factory and should only be serviced as a complete preset assembly.

─────────── CAUTION ───────────
Do not remove the 4 screws securing the pressure regulator to the fuel meter cover. The fuel pressure regulator includes a large spring under heavy compression, which, if accidentally released, could cause personal injury. Disassembly might also result in a fuel leak between the diaphragm and the regulator assembly.

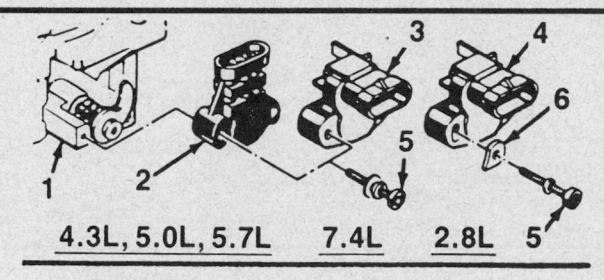

4.3L, 5.0L, 5.7L	7.4L	2.8L

1. Throttle Body Assembly
2. Throttle Position Sensor - Non-Adjustable
3. Throttle Position Sensor - Non-Adjustable
4. Throttle Position Sensor - Adjustable
5. Screw Assembly
6. Retainer

Different types of TPS used on model 220 throttle body injection

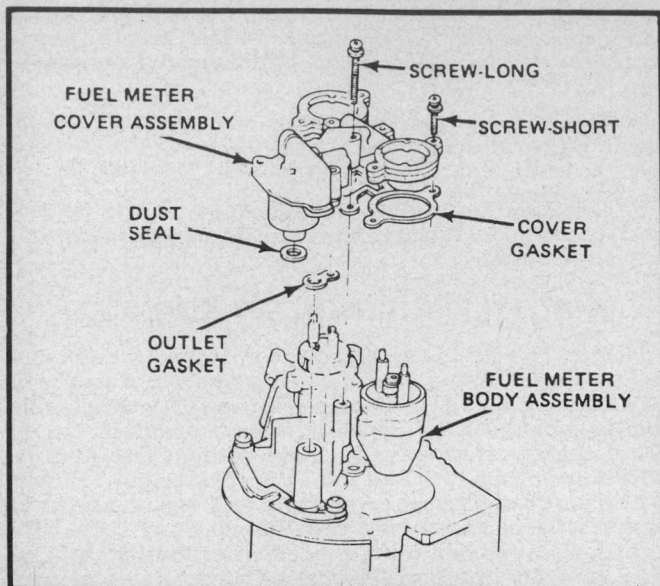

Removing model 220 fuel meter cover

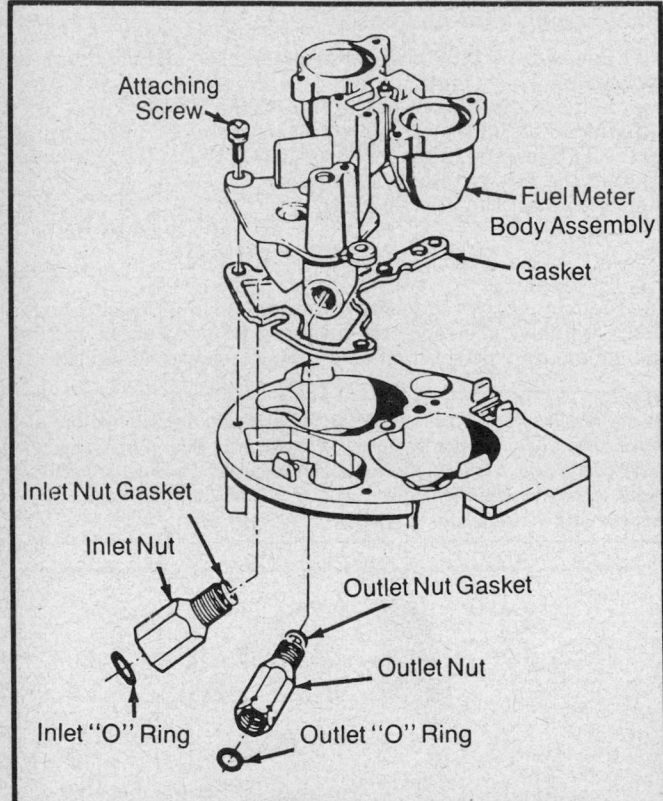

Fuel meter body assembly

Disassembly and Assembly

1. Remove the long and short fuel meter cover screws.
2. Remove the meter cover assembly.

NOTE: Do not immerse the fuel meter cover (with pressure regulator) in cleaner, as damage to the regulator diaphragm and gasket could occur.

3. Remove and discard the fuel meter outlet gasket and pressure regulator seal.

4. At installation, use a new pressure regulator seal, fuel meter outlet passage gasket and cover gasket. Install the fuel meter cover assembly.

5. The attaching screws should be precoated with thread locking compound. Make sure the short screws are next the injectors. Tighten the screws to only 28 inch lbs.

FUEL INJECTORS

Each fuel injector is serviced as a complete assembly only.

NOTE: Use care in removing the fuel injectors to prevent damage to the electrical connector terminals, the injector filter, and the fuel nozzle. The fuel injector is serviced as a complete assembly only. Also, since the injectors are electrical components, they should not be immersed in any type of liquid solvent or cleaner as damage may occur.

Disassembly and Assembly

1. With the fuel meter cover gasket in place to prevent damage to the casting, use a small lever and fulcrum to careful lift out each injector.
2. Discard the small O-rings from the injector nozzle.
3. Discard the fuel meter cover gasket as well as the upper

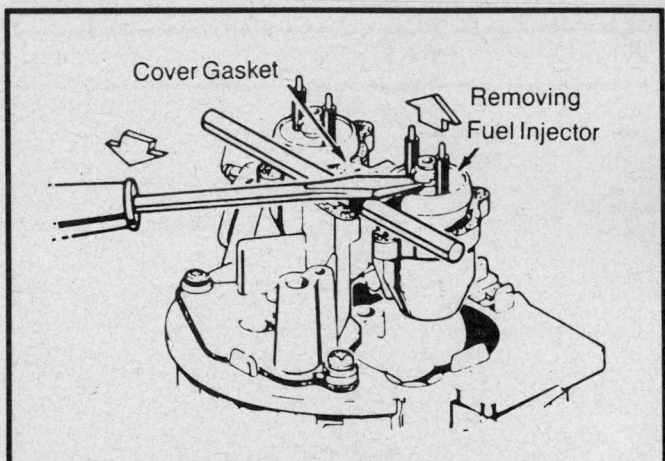

Removing model 220 fuel injector

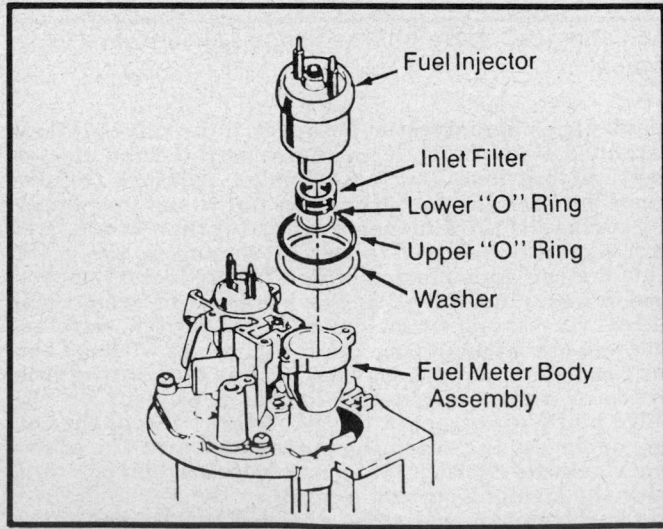

Model 220 fuel injector

(large) O-rings and steel backup washers from the top of the fuel injector cavity.

4. Inspect the fuel injector filter for dirt and contamination. If present, check for dirt in the fuel tank and lines.

5. Lube the new lower (small) O-rings with automatic transmission fluid and push the nozzle end of the injector until it presses against the injector fuel filter.

6. Install the steel injector backup washer in the counterbore of the fuel meter body. Lube the new upper (large) O-ring with automatic transmission fluid and install directly over the backup washer. Be sure the O-ring is seated properly and is flush with the top of the fuel meter body surface.

NOTE: The backup washers and O-rings must be installed before the injectors or improper seating of the large O-ring could cause fuel to leak.

7. Install the injector, aligning the raised lug on each injector base with the notch in the fuel meter body cavity. Push down on the injector until it is fully seated in the fuel meter body. The electrical terminals should be parallel with the throttle shaft.

FUEL METER BODY

Disassembly and Assembly

1. Remove the fuel inlet and outlet nuts and gaskets from the fuel meter body assembly. Discard the gaskets. Note their locations for assembly. The inlet nut has a larger passage than the outlet nut.

2. Remove the fuel meter body to throttle body attaching screw assemblies and remove the fuel meter assembly. Discard the gasket.

3. Inspect all parts for dirt or casting warpage. When cleaning, use a cold immersion type cleaner. Blow out the passages with compressed air. Do not use drill bits or pieces of wire to clean passages.

NOTE: Do not immerse the IAC valve, throttle position sensor, fuel meter cover assembly or fuel injector assemblies in cleaner or they will be damaged.

4. Install a new throttle body to fuel meter body gasket. Match the cutout portions in the gasket with the openings in the throttle body.

5. Place the fuel meter body assembly on the throttle body assembly and install the screws, precoated with thread sealer. Tighten the screws to 30 inch lbs.

6. Install the fuel inlet nut, with a new gasket and tighten to 30 ft. lbs.

7. Install the fuel outlet nut, with a new gasket and tighten to 21 ft. lbs.

Model 700 Throttle Body Injection

The fuel control system has an electric fuel pump, located in the fuel tank with the gauge sending unit, which pumps fuel to the TBI through the fuel supply line, then through an in-line fuel filter. The pump is designed to provide pressurized fuel at about 18 psi.

A pressure regulator in the TBI keeps fuel available to the injectors at a constant pressure between 9–13 psi. Fuel in excess of injector needs is returned to the fuel tank by a separate line.

The ECM controls the injectors that are located in the fuel meter body assembly of the TBI. The injectors deliver fuel in one of several modes.

In order to properly control the fuel supply, the fuel pump is operated by the ECM through the fuel pump relay and oil pressure switch.

The Model 700 TBI unit, used on the L4 engine is made up of two major casting assemblies:

1. The fuel meter assembly with pressure regulator and fuel injector.

2. The throttle body with the idle air control (IAC) valve and the throttle position sensor (TPS).

FUEL INJECTOR ASSEMBLY

The fuel injector is serviced only as a complete assembly.

NOTE: Use care in removing the injector to prevent damage to the electrical connector on top of the injector, and nozzle. Also, because the fuel injector is an elec-

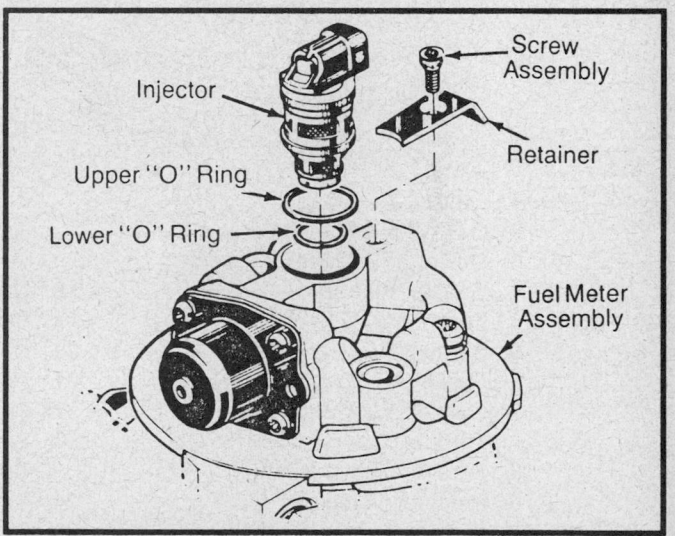

Model 700 fuel injection parts

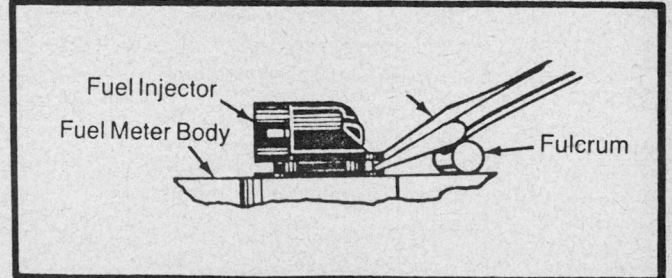

Removing TBI 700 fuel injector

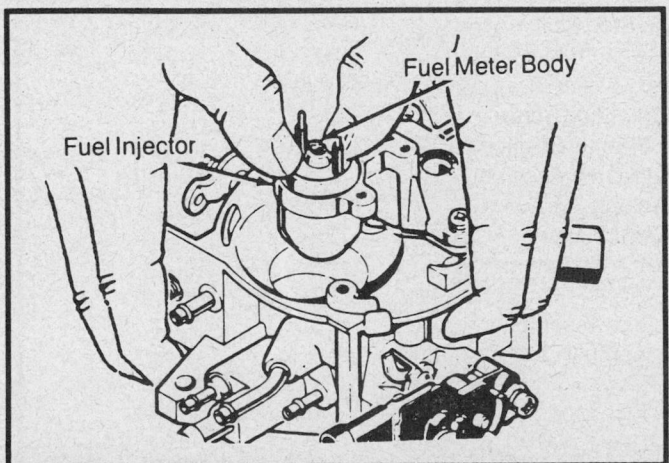

Pressing injector back into fuel meter body assembly

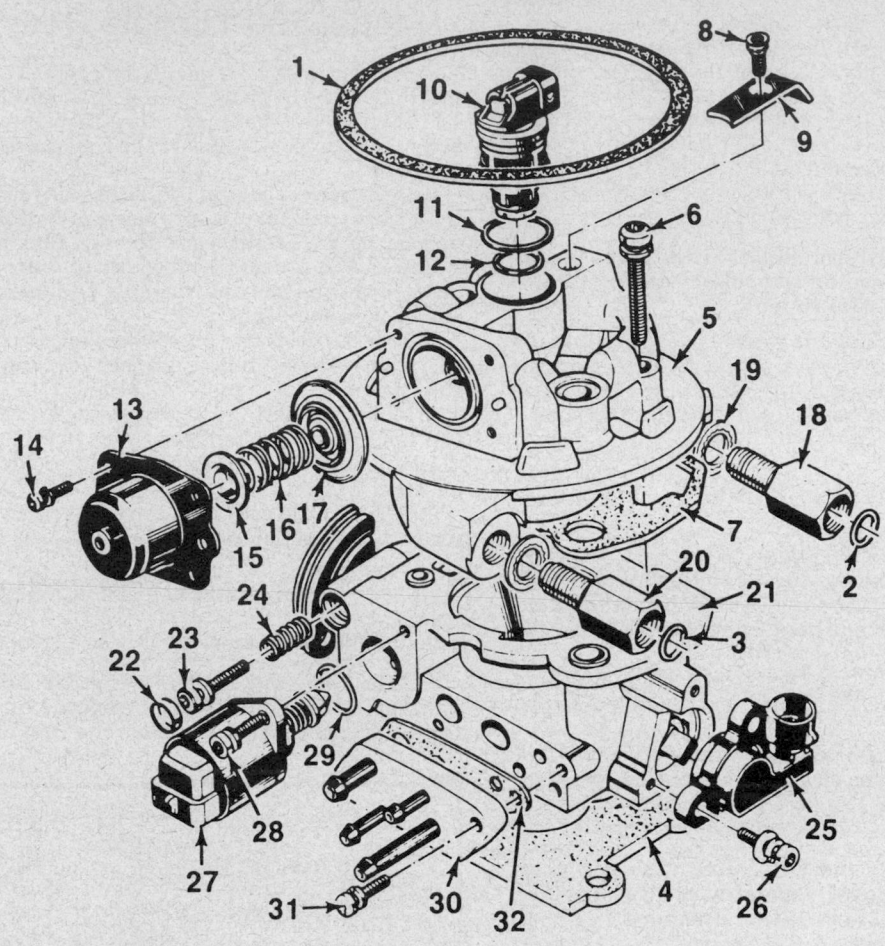

1. Gasket - Air Cleaner
2. O-Ring - Fuel Line Inlet Nut
3. O-Ring - Fuel Line Outlet Nut
4. Gasket - Flange
5. Fuel Meter Assembly
6. Screw & Washer Assembly - Fuel Meter Body Attaching
7. Gasket - Fuel Meter Body to Throttle Body
8. Screw - Injector Retainer
9. Retainer - Injector
10. Fuel Injector
11. O-Ring - Fuel Injector - Upper
12. O-Ring - Fuel Injector - Lower
13. Pressure Regulator Cover
14. Screw - Pressure Regulator Attaching
15. Seat - Spring
16. Spring - Pressure Regulator
17. Pressure Regulator Diaphragm Assembly

18. Nut - Fuel Inlet
19. Seal - Fuel Nut
20. Nut - Fuel Outlet
21. Throttle Body Assembly
22. Plug - Idle Stop Screw
23. Screw & Washer Assembly - Idle Stop
24. Spring - Idle Stop Screw
25. Sensor - Throttle Position (TPS)
26. Screw & Washer Assembly - TPS Attaching
27. Idle Air Control Valve (IACV)
28. Screw - IACV Attaching
29. O-Ring - IACV
30. Tube Module Assembly
31. Screw Assembly - Tube Module Assy.
32. Gasket - Tube Module Asembly

Model 700 TBI parts identfication

trical component, it should not be immersed in any type of liquid solvent or cleaner or it will be damage.

Disassembly and Assembly

1. Remove the electrical connector to the fuel injector.
2. Remove the injector retainer screw and flat hold-down piece.
3. Using a fulcrum, place a small lever under the ridge opposite the connector end and carefully pry the injector out. Remove and discard the upper and lower O-rings.
4. Inspect the fuel injector filter for dirt and contamination. If present, check for dirt in the fuel tank and lines.
5. Lube the new upper and lower O-rings with automatic transmission fluid, and place them on the injector. Make sure the upper O-ring is in the groove and the lower one is flush up against the filter.
6. Install the injector assembly pushing it straight into the fuel injector cavity. Be sure the electrical connector on the end of the injector is facing in the general direction of the cutout in the fuel meter body for the wire grommet. Install the injector retainer, apply thread locking compound to the screw and tighten to 27 inch lbs.

PRESSURE REGULATOR ASSEMBLY

NOTE: To prevent leaks, the pressure regulator diaphragm assembly must be replaced whenever the cover is removed.

Disassembly and Assembly

1. Remove the 4 pressure regulator attaching screws, while keeping the pressure regulator compressed.

--- CAUTION ---

The pressure regulator contains a large spring under heavy compression. Use care when removing the screws to prevent personal injury.

2. Remove the pressure regulator cover assembly.
3. Remove the regulator spring, spring seat and diaphragm assembly.
4. Check the regulator seat in the fuel meter cavity for pitting or nicks. Use a magnifying glass if necessary. If any defects are noted, the whole fuel body casting must be replaced.
5. Install a new pressure regulator diaphragm assembly, making sure it is seated in the groove in the fuel meter body.
6. Install the regulator spring seat and spring into the cover assembly and install the cover while aligning the mounting holes.

1. Pressure Regulator Cover
2. Screw Assembly
3. Spring-Seat
4. Spring
5. Diaphragm
6. Fuel Meter Assembly

Model 700 TBI pressure regulator

NOTE: Use care while installing the pressure regulator to prevent misalignment of the diaphragm and possible leaks.

7. Install the 4 cover screws using thread locking compound, while maintaining pressure on the regulator spring. Tighten the screws to 22 inch lbs.

FUEL METER ASSEMBLY

Disassembly and Assembly

1. Remove the 2 fuel meter attaching screws.
2. Remove the fuel meter assembly from the throttle body assembly and discard the gasket.
3. At installation, place new gasket in position and match the cutout portions of the gasket with the openings in the throttle body assembly.
4. Install the fuel meter assembly. Use thread locking compound on the screws and tighten to 53 inch lbs.

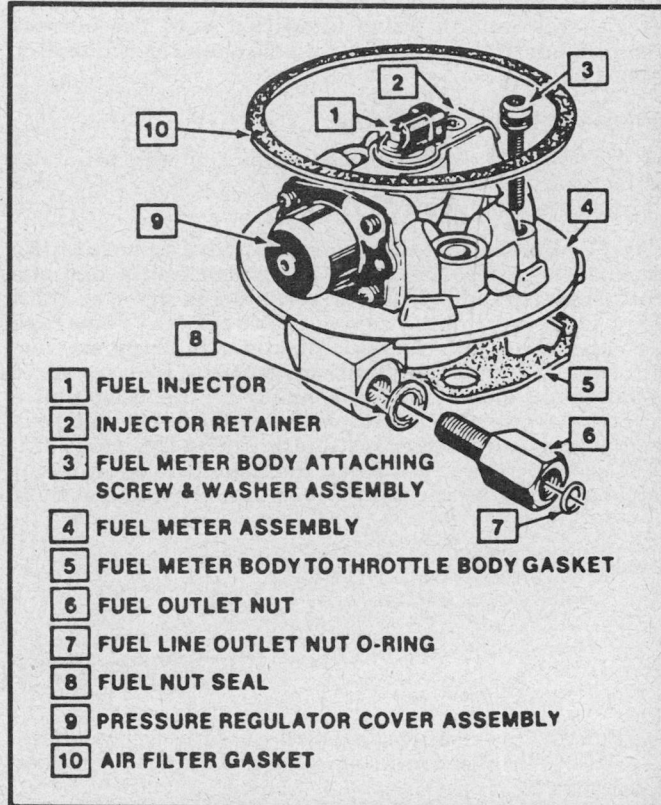

1. FUEL INJECTOR
2. INJECTOR RETAINER
3. FUEL METER BODY ATTACHING SCREW & WASHER ASSEMBLY
4. FUEL METER ASSEMBLY
5. FUEL METER BODY TO THROTTLE BODY GASKET
6. FUEL OUTLET NUT
7. FUEL LINE OUTLET NUT O-RING
8. FUEL NUT SEAL
9. PRESSURE REGULATOR COVER ASSEMBLY
10. AIR FILTER GASKET

Fuel meter assembly, Model 700 TBI

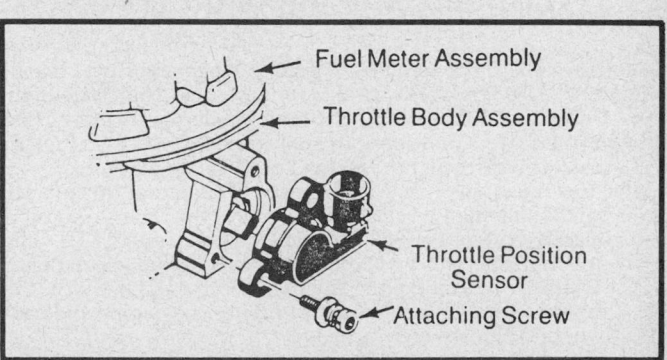

Fuel Meter Assembly
Throttle Body Assembly
Throttle Position Sensor
Attaching Screw

Throttle position sensor (TPS) Model 700 TBI

THROTTLE POSITION SENSOR

1. Remove the retainer screws.
2. Lift off throttle position sensor.

NOTE: The throttle position sensor is an electrical component, and should not be immersed in any type of liquid solvent or cleaner or it will be damaged.

3. With the throttle valve in the normally closed position, install the throttle position sensor on the throttle shaft and rotate counterclockwise to align the mounting holes. Install the screws and tighten to 18 inch lbs.

IDLE AIR CONTROL (IAC) VALVE

NOTE: The Idle Air Control (IAC) valve is an electrical component, and should not be immersed in any type of liquid solvent or cleaner or it will be damaged. On the TBI Model 700, the IAC valve is flange-mounted, with a dual taper, 10mm diameter pintle. If replacement is necessary, only an IAC valve identified with the correct part number, the appropriate pintle shape and diameter should be used.

Disassembly and Assembly

1. Remove the screw assemblies and pull the IAC valve straight out.
2. Remove and discard the O-ring.

NOTE: Before installing an IAC valve, measure the distance between the tip of the valve pintle and the mounting surface. If the dimension is greater than 28mm (1.10 in.), it must be reduced to prevent damage to the valve. This may be done electrically using the factory special tool or manually by exerting firm pressure with a slight side-to-side movement on the valve pintle to retract it. No physical adjustment of the IAC valve assembly is required after installation. The IAC valve pintle is reset by the ECM. When the vehicle is operated at normal engine temperature at about 30 mph, the ECM

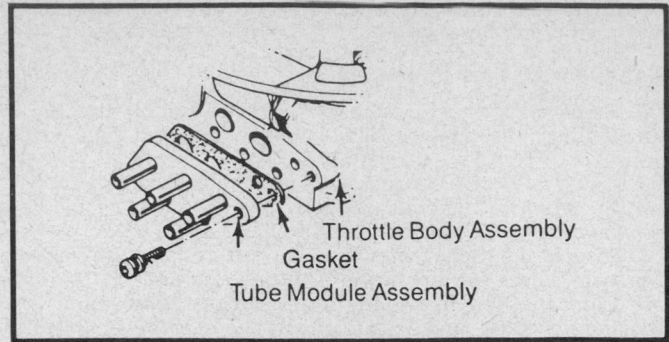

Throttle Body Assembly
Gasket
Tube Module Assembly

Tube module assembly, Model 700 TBI

causes the valve pintle to seat in the throttle body. The ECM then has a reset procedure to set the correct pintle position. Proper idle regulation should result.

3. Lubricate the new O-ring with automatic transmission fluid and install on the IAC valve. Install the valve to the throttle body. Use thread locking compound on the screws and tighten to 28 inch lbs.

NOTE: New IAC valves have been preset at the factory and should be installed in the throttle body in an as is condition, without any adjustment.

TUBE MODULE ASSEMBLY

The tube module assembly is the cluster of vacuum tube connectors located at the base of the throttle body assembly, next to the idle air control valve.

Disassembly and Assembly

1. Remove the tube module attaching screws.
2. Remove the module assembly. Discard the gasket.
3. At installation, use a new gasket and tighten the screws to 28 inch lbs.

JEEP CORPORATION

Two different fuel injection systems are used on Jeep vehicles — a Throttle Body Injection system (TBI) and a Multi-Point Injection system (MPI).

Throttle Body Injection (TBI)

Jeep series 60/70 (Comanche, Cherokee/Wagoneer Sport truck) and Model 81 (Wranger) with 2.5L engines use a Throttle Body Fuel Injection (TBI) system. TBI is a single point, pulse time system that injects fuel through an electrically operated fuel injector into the throttle body above the throttle plate.

The fuel injection pulse width (period of time that the injector is energized causing fuel to be released into the throttle body) is controlled by the engine Electronic Control Unit (ECU). The ECU accomplishes this by opening and closing the ground path to the injector. By controlling the fuel injector pulse width, the ECU is able to meter the amount of fuel to the engine and constantly adjust the air-fuel ratio.

The ECU receives inputs from sensors that react to exhaust gas oxygen content, coolant temperature, manifold absolute

pressure, engine speed (crankshaft position), throttle position, battery voltage and air fuel temperature. These inputs represent the engine's instantaneous operating conditions. Based on these inputs the ECU adjusts the air-fuel ratio and ignition timing for the current operating conditions. The sensors and switches that provide input to the ECU, the ECU and the ECU outputs (engine control devices that the ECU constantly adjusts), comprise the engine control system.

TBI fuel system pressure is bled off when the fuel pump is not operating. Fuel hoses and tubes can be removed once the vehicle is turned **OFF**. Fuel hoses and tubes can be removed once the vehicle is turned off. When removing fuel system hoses and tubes use care to avoid damaging the hoses or tube ends.

QUICK CONNECT FITTINGS

Jeep fuel injected engines use quick-connect fuel tube fittings at the ends of the nylon reinforced hoses that connect the throttle body to the fuel supply and return tubes The fittings consist of a pair of O-rings, a spacer (installed between O-rings) and an O-ring retainer.

NOTE: Whenever a fuel tube quick connect fitting is disconnected the O-rings, spacer and retainer must be replaced. A repair kit consisting of these parts is available.

Quick connect fittings are located under the vehicle along the frame rail.

The retainer has 2 tabs that are squeezed against the fuel tube and then pulled outward to disconnect the fuel tube from the quick connect fitting/hose assembly. The retainer will stay on the fuel tube when the tube is disconnected. The O-rings and spacer will remain in the connector.

The O-rings and spacer can be removed with the bent end of an **L** shaped paper clip.

O-ring Replacement

A repair kit consisting of replacement O-rings, spacer and retainer is available. The replacement parts are installed on a dis-

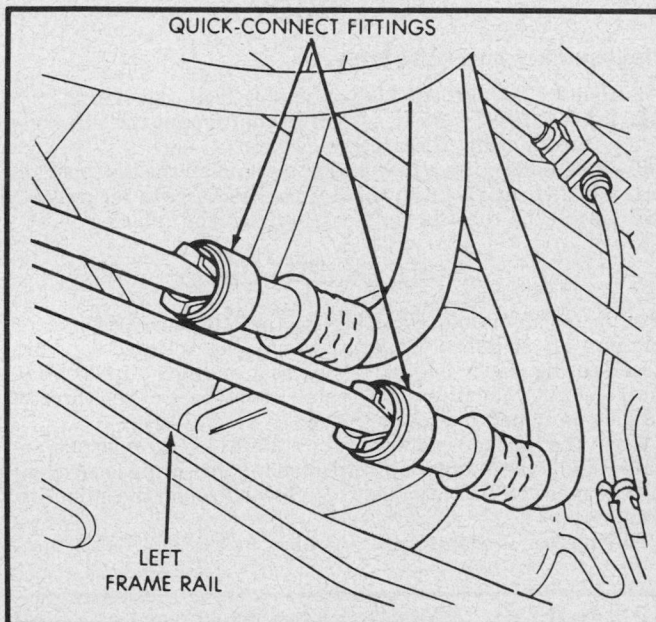

Jeep quick connect fittings—typical

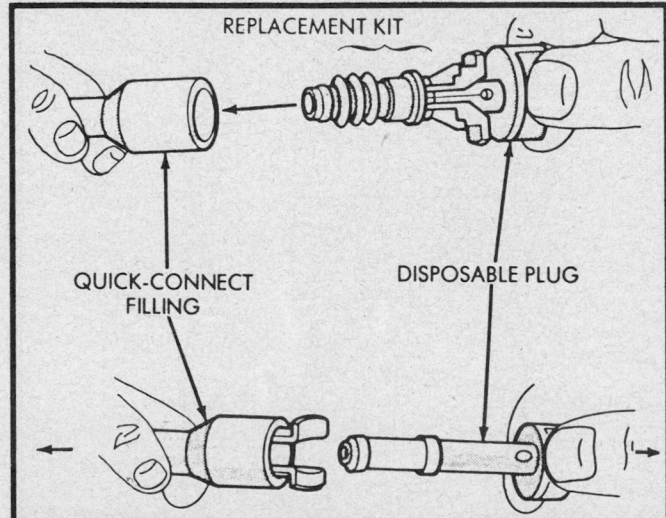

Jeep repair kit installation

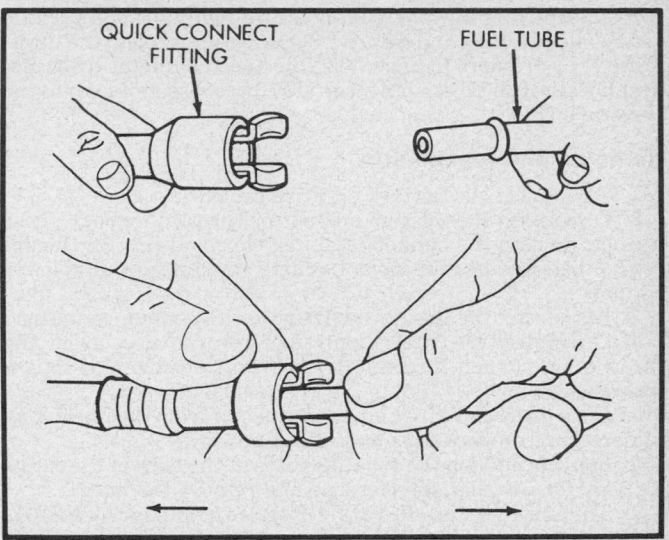

Jeep fuel tube to fitting connection

posable plastic plug. Once the connection has been separated, install the replacement kit as follows:

1. Push the kit/disposable plug assembly into the quick connect fitting until a **Click** sound is heard.

2. Grasp the end of the disposable plug and pull outward to remove it from the fitting.

3. Push the fuel tube into the quick-connect fitting until a **Click** sound is heard.

4. Verify that the connection is secure by pulling firmly back on the fuel tube. The tube should be locked in place.

THROTTLE BODY

The throttle body is mounted on top of the intake manifold and

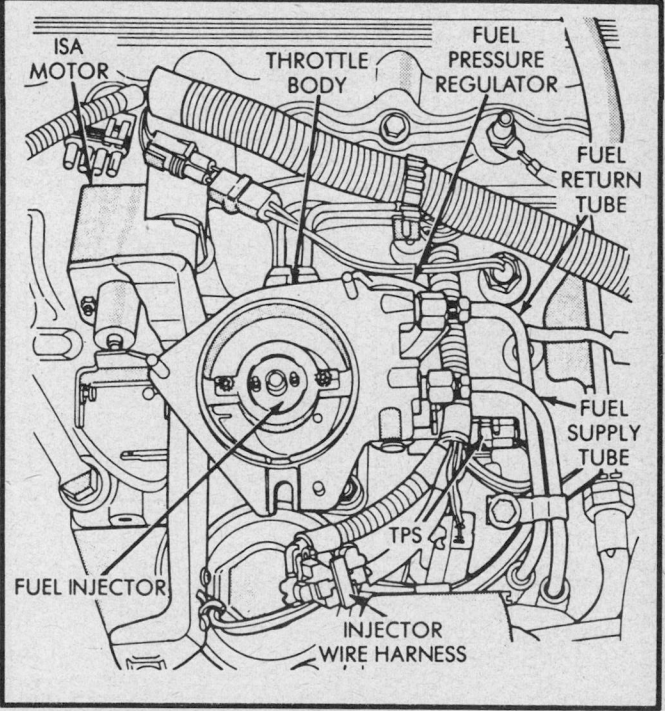

Jeep throttle body fuel injection

contains the fuel injector, fuel pressure regulator and throttle valve. The fuel inlet and return tubes are connected to the throttle body by pressure fittings. The Idle Speed Actuator (ISA) motor and Throttle Position Sensor (TPS) are also mounted to the throttle body.

Removal and Installation

1. Disconnect the battery negative cable.
2. Disconnect the vacuum hoses from the throttle body upper bonnet. Release the bonnet retaining clips and remove the upper bonnet. Remove the lower bonnet retaining bolts and lower bonnet.
3. Disconnect the Idle Speed Actuator (ISA) motor connector.
4. Disconnect the fuel supply and return tubes from the throttle body, then disconnect the throttle cable and return spring.
5. Disconnect the wire harness connector from the injector by compressing the lock tabs and lifting upward.
6. Identify and tag the vacuum hoses at the back of the throttle body for installation reference and remove the hoses.
7. Disconnect the Throttle Position Sensor (TPS). If equipped with an automatic transmission, disconnect both TPS

connectors and the Wide Open Throttle (WOT) switch (on model 81, Wrangler) connector.
8. Remove the throttle body mounting nuts and remove the throttle body. Clean the old gasket from the intake manifold.

NOTE: If the throttle body assembly is being replaced and the WOT switch, ISA motor and TPS are transferred to the replacement throttle body, they must be adjusted after installation.

9. With a new gasket, install the TPI assembly on the intake manifold and tighten the hold-down nuts to 16 ft. lbs.
10. Connect the vacuum hoses to the back of the TPI assembly and connect the fuel supply and return lines.
11. Connect the WOT switch, ISA motor and TPS connectors, as well as the fuel injector electrical connection.
12. Install the accelerator cable and return spring.
13. Install the lower then upper bonnet assembly.
14. Connect the battery negative cable.

FUEL BODY

Disassembly and Assembly

1. Remove the throttle body assembly from the vehicle.
2. Remove the 3 Torx head screws that mount the fuel body to the throttle body. Discard the gasket.
3. At assembly, use a new gasket and install the fuel body on the throttle body. Tighten the 3 Torx head screws securely.
4. Install the throttle body assembly on the vehicle.

FUEL INJECTOR

The fuel injector is located within the throttle body. The injector contains an electrically operated solenoid, plunger (or core piece), spring loaded ball valve, ball seat and fuel atomizer/discharge nozzle. The injector is seated in the bore of the throttle body by an upper and lower O-ring.

When the injector is energized by the ECU, the solenoid armature pulls the plunger upward allowing the spring loaded ball valve to move off its seat. Fuel then flows through the atomizer/spray nozzle.

The injector is exclusively controlled by the ECU. The injec-

A. INJECTOR
B. SOLENOID
C. BALL VALVE
D. VALVE SEAT
E. SPRAY NOZZLE
F. PLUNGER
G. UPPER O-RING
H. LOWER O-RING

Jeep throttle body injection parts

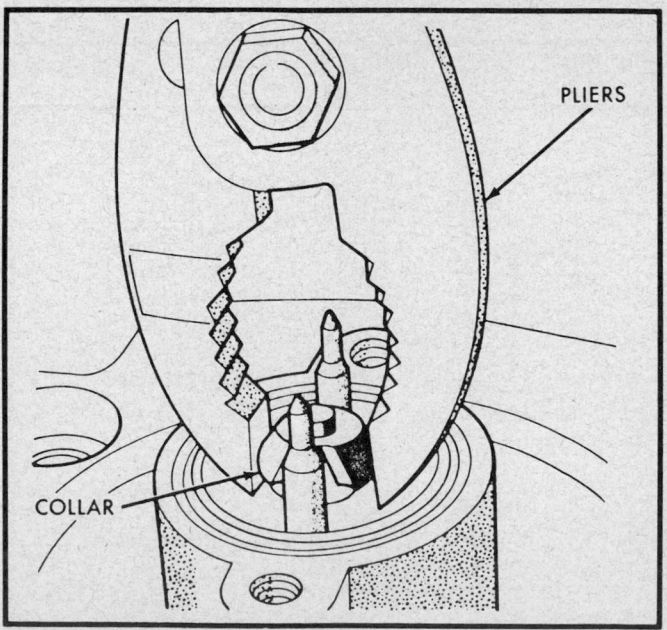

Fuel injector removal—Jeep

tion pulse width is based on the engine operating conditions, which are provided to the ECU by the input sensors.

Removal and Installation

1. Disconnect the battery negative cable.
2. Remove the throttle body upper and lower bonnet.
3. Remove the injector electrical connector by compressing the lock tabs and lifting upward.
4. Remove the injector retainer screws and remove the retainer.

NOTE: The injector has a small locating tab that fits into a slot in the bottom of the injector bore of the throttle body. Do not twist the injector during removal.

5. Using a small pair of pliers, gently grasp the center collar of the injector and carefully remove the injector by rocking it back and forth while lifting upward. Remove and discard the centering ring and the O-rings.

NOTE: Do not reuse the centering ring or the upper or lower O-rings as fuel leakage will result.

6. At assembly, lubricate the O-rings with light oil and install on the injector. Install the centering ring on top of the upper O-ring. Align the locating tab on the bottom of the injector with the slot in the bottom of the housing and install the injector.
7. Install the retainer and tighten the screws. Connect the injector electrical connection.
8. Install the lower and upper bonnet and connect the negative battery cable.

FUEL PRESSURE REGULATOR

The fuel pressure regulator used with the TBI system is an overflow type and is attached to the throttle body. The regulator is adjustable and controls the amount of pressure under which the fuel system operates.

The fuel pump delivers fuel in excess of the maximum required by the engine and the excess fuel flows back to the fuel tank from the pressure regulator via the fuel return hose.

The regulator consists of a spring chamber, calibrated spring, spring seats, diaphragm, pivot and pressure adjusting screw. A lead plug seals the adjusting screw hole.

As fuel from the fuel pump enters the top of the regulator, the relief valve and regulator spring are forced down opening a passage to the fuel return tube, allowing a certain amount of fuel to return to the fuel tank. A pivot on top of the diaphragm keeps the diaphragm from tipping to one side. The amount of pressure required to force the regulator spring down determines fuel system pressure. Fuel system pressure is controlled by the adjusting screw at the bottom of the regulator housing. Turning the screw inward increases fuel pressure, turning the screw outward decreases fuel pressure.

A small passage through the throttle body, regulator diaphragm and the regulator casing vents the spring chamber to the atmospheric pressure. The tip of the fuel injector is also vented to atmospheric pressure. Because the injector nozzle and the spring chamber are vented to the same pressure, the volume of fuel injected is dependent only on the length of time the injector is energized (injector pulse width).

Disassembly and Assembly

1. Remove the throttle body from the engine.

NOTE: To prevent release of spring pressure, keep the regulator housing forced against the throttle body while removing the regulator mounting screws.

2. Remove the pressure regulator screws.
3. Remove the housing, spring and seats, diaphragm and pivot.
4. Clean the housing well before assembly.

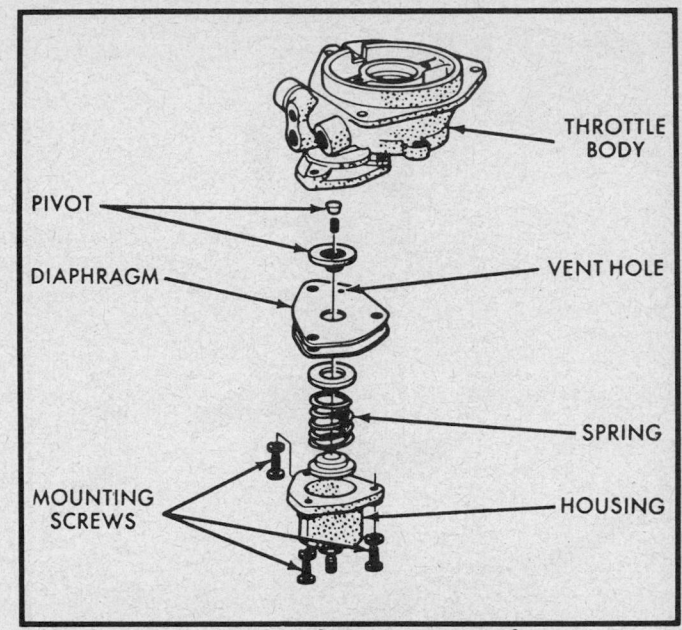

Jeep fuel pressure regulator components

NOTE: The pressure regulator diaphragm must be installed with the vent hole aligned with the vent holes in the throttle body and regulator housing.

5. Assemble the pressure regulator parts, pressing the housing and throttle body together as required to get the mounting screws installed.
6. Install throttle body on engine, start engine and check for leaks.

THROTTLE POSITION SENSOR (TPS)

The Throttle Position Sensor (TPS) is mounted on the throttle body and connected to the throttle valve shaft. The sensor is a variable resistor that provides the ECU with an input voltage that represents the throttle valve position. Input voltage to the ECU from the TPS varies in an approximate range of from 1 volt at minimum throttle opening (idle) to 5 volts at wide open throttle. The ECU uses TPS input voltage to determine current engine operating conditions.

There are two different TPS units, one used with manual transmissions and one used with automatic transmissions.

Removal and Installation

1. Remove the upper and lower air inlet bonnet.
2. If necessary, remove the throttle body assembly.
3. Remove the TPS mounting screws and remove the TPS from the throttle lever.
4. When installing the TPS, make sure that the sensor arm is underneath the arm of the throttle valve shaft.
5. Tighten the TPS. The factory recommends that the TPS be adjusted using their special diagnostic tester.
6. If removed, install the throttle body assembly on the vehicle.
7. Install the lower and upper air inlet bonnet.

IDLE SPEED ACTUATOR (ISA) MOTOR

The Idle Speed Acuator (ISA) motor is mounted to the throttle body and is controlled by the ECU. The throttle lever rests

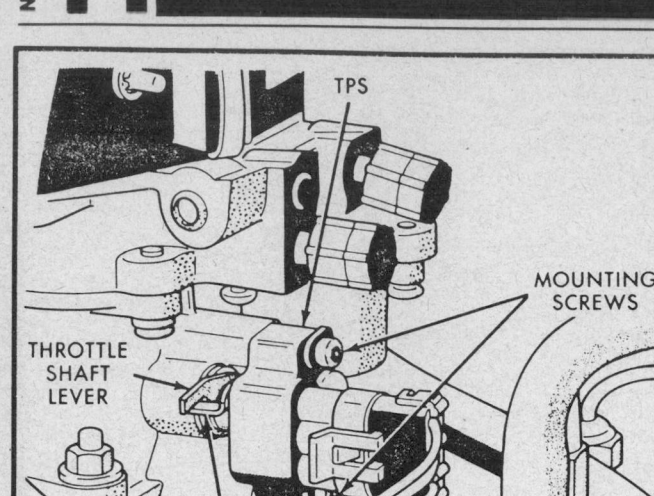

Jeep throttle position sensor

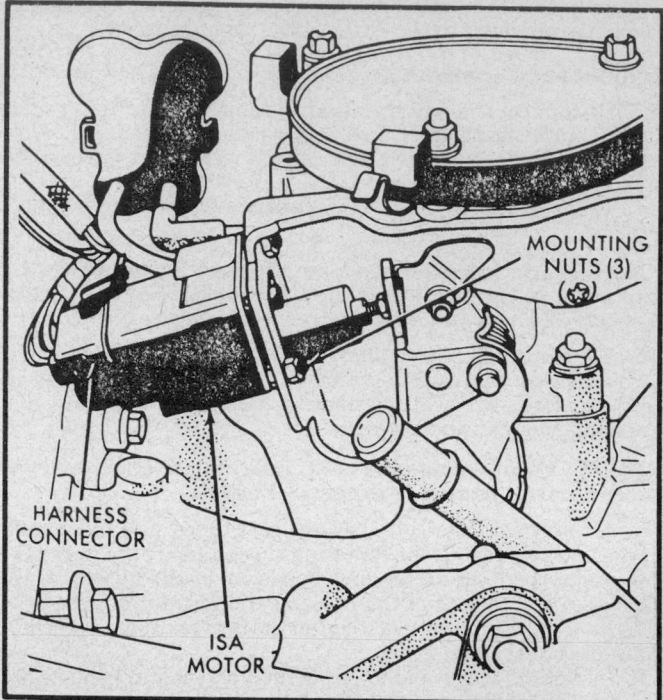

ISA motor removal—Jeep

against the initial adjustment screw of the actuator (plunger). The idle speed is not adjustable. The initial adjustment screw is only used to establish the initial positioning of the actuator when the ISA motor has been replaced.

The actuator (plunger) extends or retracts to control engine idle speed and to set the throttle stop angle during deceleration. Based on inputs from the various engine control system sensors and switches the ECU supplies current to the ISA motor to adjust the actuator (plunger) position for the particular operating conditions.

Once the engine has been shut off, current is momentarily supplied to the ISA motor through the **B+** Latch relay (located on the passenger side inner fender, between the fuel pump relay and the A/C compressor clutch relay) causing the actuator to extend to a set position for the next start-up. When the engine is next started, it operates at a fat idle until sensor inputs tell the ECU that the engine has reached normal operating temperature. The ECU then retracts the actuator until the idle is set to a programmed rpm for the current operating conditions. Idle speed varies slightly due to different operating conditions.

Removal and Installation

NOTE: The closed throttle (idle) switch is integral with the motor.

1. Disconnect the throttle return springs.
2. Disconnect the wire harness connector from the ISA motor.

NOTE: Do not attempt to remove the ISA motor-to-bracket nuts without using a backup wrench on the stud nuts. ISA internal components may be damaged if the studs disengage.

3. Remove the motor-to-bracket retaining nuts. Use a backup wrench to prevent the studs which hold the ISA motor together from turning. Remove the ISA motor from the bracket.
4. Install the ISA motor on the bracket and tighten the mounting nuts.
5. Install the wiring connector to the motor and connect the throttle return spring.

6. The factory recommends that the ISA be adjusted using their special diagnostic tester.

MANIFOLD ABSOLUTE PRESSURE (MAP) SENSOR

The Manifold Absolute Pressure (MAP) sensor reacts to absolute pressure in the intake manifold and provides an input voltage to the ECU. As engine load changes manifold pressure varies, causing the MAP sensor's resistance to change. The change in MAP sensor resistance results in a different input voltage to the ECU. The input voltage level supplies the ECU with infor-

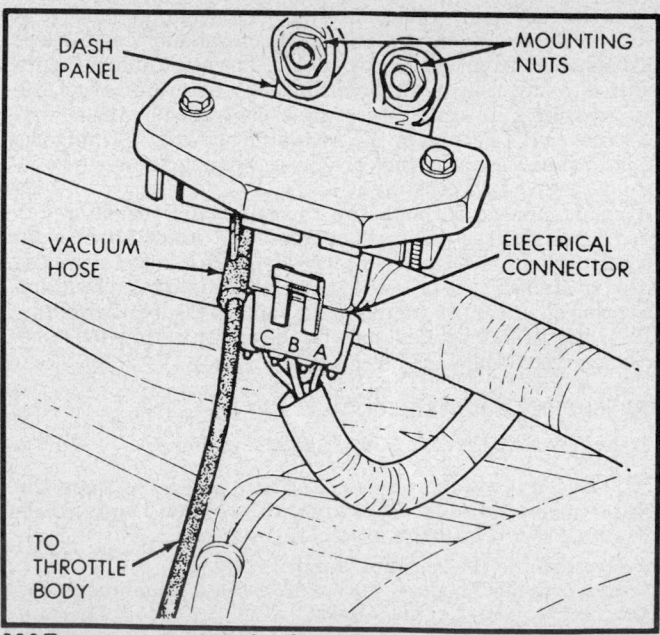

MAP sensor removal—Jeep

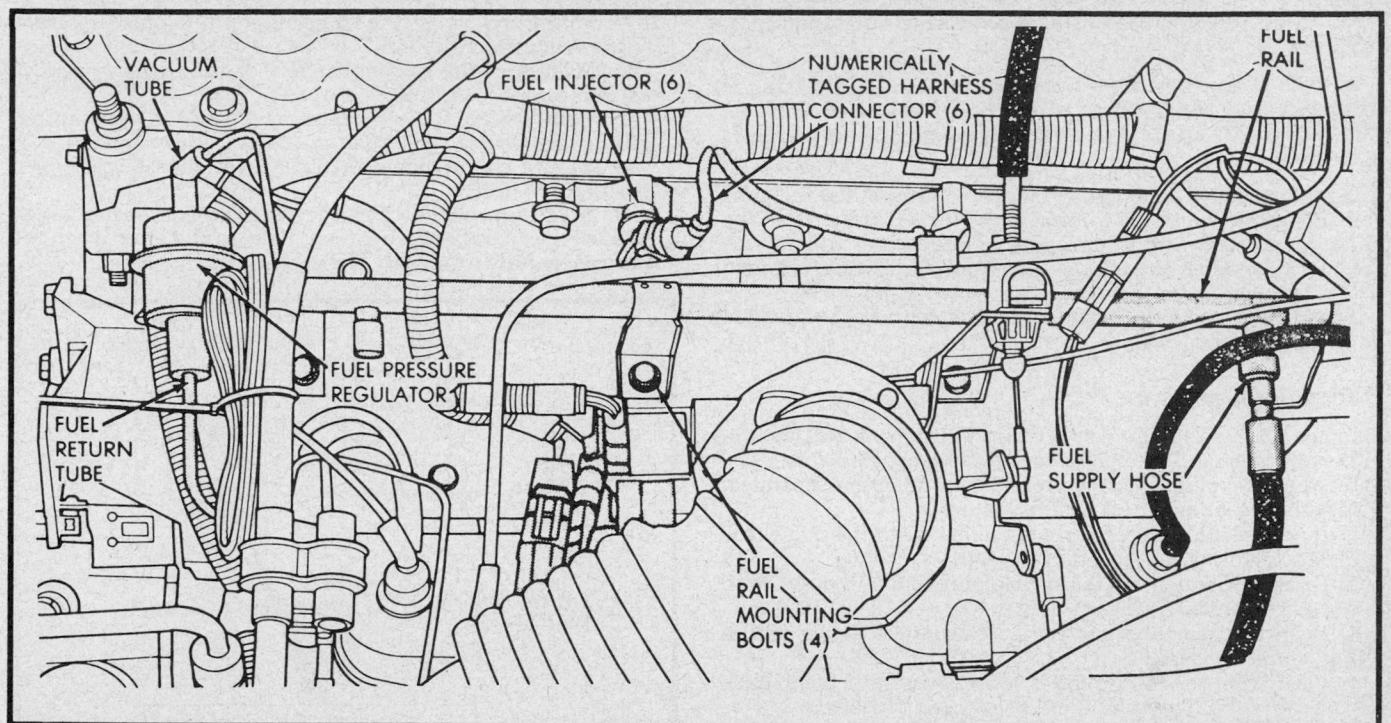

Jeep MPI injection system layout

mation relating to ambient barometric pressure during engine start-up (cranking) and to engine load while the engine is running. The ECU computes this information and adjusts the air-fuel mixture accordingly.

The MAP sensor is mounted underhood on the dash panel and is connected to the throttle body with a vacuum hose.

Removal and Installation

1. The MAP sensor gets its vacuum feed from the throttle body, but is mounted on the dash panel. Disconnect the wire harness and vacuum hose from the MAP sensor.
2. Remove the MAP sensor mounting nuts.
3. At installation, install the MAPS sensor over the studs, install the nuts and tighten to 35 inch lbs.
4. Connect the vacuum hose and wire harness.

Multi-Point Fuel Injection (MPI)

Jeep series 60/70 (Comanche, Cherokee/Wranger) vehicles with 4.0L engines use a sequential Multi-Point Fuel Injection (MPI) system. Fuel is injected into the intake manifold before the intake valve in precise metered amounts through electronically operated injectors. The injectors are fired in a specific sequence by the engine Electronic Control Unit (ECU). The ECU constantly adjusts the amount of fuel injected to meet changing operating conditions by controlling injector pulse width (the length of time the injector is energized). The ECU also adjusts ignition timing by controlling the ignition coil operation through the ignition control module. The ECU determines air-fuel mixture and ignition timing based on inputs it receives from various sensors that monitor engine operating conditions. The ECU receives inputs from sensors that react to exhaust gas oxygen content, coolant temperature, manifold absolute pressure, engine speed (crankshaft position), throttle position, battery voltage, intake manifold air temperature, engine knock and transmission gear selection. These inputs represent the engine's instantaneous operating conditions. Air-Fuel mixture and ignition timing calibrations for various driving and atmo-

spheric conditions are pre-programmed into the ECU. The ECU monitors and analyzes its various inputs, computes engine fuel and ignition timing requirements based on these inputs, and controls fuel delivery and ignition timing accordingly. The ECU, the various sensors and switches that provide input to the ECU, and the ECU outputs (engine control devices controlled by the ECU) comprise the engine control system.

The factory diagnostic tool plugs into 2 diagnostic connectors inside the engine compartment. After performing the required diagnostic test the tester will display a fault code if a malfunction is detected.

The MPI fuel system is under constant fuel pressure of 19–39 psi. Vehicles equipped with the multi-point injected 4.0L engine must have the fuel pressure released before servicing any fuel supply or return system component. Use the following procedure:

1. Disconnect the battery negative cable.
2. Remove the fuel tank filler neck cap to release fuel tank pressure.
3. Remove the cap from the pressure test port on the fuel rail.

CAUTION

Do not allow fuel to spill onto the engine intake or exhaust manifolds. Place shop towels under the pressure port to absorb fuel when the pressure is released from the fuel rail. Beware of the fire hazard that could cause personal injury.

4. Place shop towels under the fuel pressure test pot.
5. Using a small pointed tool or pin punch push the test port valve in to relieve the fuel pressure. Absorb spilled fuel with shop towels.
6. Remove the shop towels and dispose of properly.
7. Install the cap over the pressure test port.

QUICK CONNECT FITTINGS

Jeep fuel injected engines use quick-connect fuel tube fittings at the ends of the nylon reinforced hoses that connect the throttle body to the fuel supply and return tubes. The fittings consist of

a pair of O-rings, a spacer (installed between O-rings) and an O-ring retainer.

NOTE: Whenever a fuel tube quick connect fitting is disconnected the O-rings, spacer and retainer must be replaced. A repair kit consisting of these parts is available.

The retainer has 2 tabs that are squeezed against the fuel tube and then pulled outward to disconnect the fuel tube from the quick connect fitting/hose assembly. The retainer will stay on the fuel tube when the tube is disconnected. The O-rings and spacer will remain in the connector.

The O-rings and spacer can be removed with the bent end of an **L** shaped paper clip.

O-ring Replacement

A repair kit consisting of replacement O-rings, spacer and retainer is available. The replacement parts are installed on a disposable plastic plug. Once the connection has been separated, install the replacement kit as follows:

1. Push the kit/disposable plug assembly into the quick connect fitting until a **Click** sound is heard.
2. Grasp the end of the disposable plug and pull outward to remove it from the fitting.
3. Push the fuel tube into the quick-connect fitting until a **Click** sound is heard.
4. Verify that the connection is secure by pulling firmly back on the fuel tube. The tube should be locked in place.

THROTTLE BODY

Filtered air from the air cleaner enters the intake manifold through the throttle body. Fuel does not enter the intake manifold through the throttle body. Fuel is sprayed into the manifold by the fuel injectors. The throttle body, which is mounted on the intake manifold, contains an air bypass passage that is used to supply air for idle conditions and a throttle valve for above idle conditions.

The throttle position sensor and idle speed stepper motor are attached to the throttle body. The accelerator cable is connected to the throttle valve through a bellcrank and linkage mounted to the intake manifold.

There are different throttle bodies for automatic transmission and manual transmission equipped vehicles. The throttle valve is not controlled by the ECU.

Removal and Installation

1. Disconnect the battery negative cable.
2. Disconnect the air cleaner snorkel from the throttle body.
3. Disconnect the idle speed stepper motor and throttle position sensor wire connectors.
4. Disconnect the MAP sensor vacuum tube from the back of the throttle body.
5. Disconnect the throttle linkage at the throttle arm.
6. If equipped, disconnect the automatic transmission line pressure cable at the throttle arm.
7. Remove the throttle body mounting bolts, throttle body and gasket. Discard the gasket.
8. At installation, use a new gasket, install the throttle body and tighten the mounting bolts to 23 ft. lbs.
9. Connect the MAP sensor vacuum tube, the stepper motor and throttle position sensor connectors and reconnect the throttle linkage to the throttle arm.

NOTE: When the automatic transmission line pressure (Throttle Valve) cable is reconnected, it must be adjusted.

10. Connect and adjust the transmission line pressure cable. Use the following procedure:
   a. Make sure the ignition is **OFF** or the battery negative cable is still disconnected.
   b. Fully retract the cable plunger. Press the cable button all the way down. Then push the cable plunger inward.
   c. Rotate the primary throttle lever to the wide open position.
   d. Hold the primary throttle lever in the wide open position and let the cable plunger extend. Release the lever when the plunger is fully extended. The cable is now adjusted.

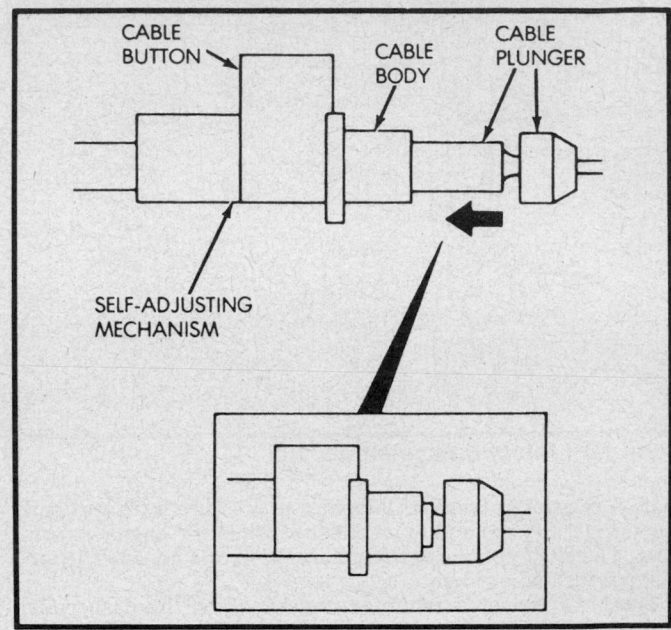

Retract the throttle valve cable end—Jeep, typical

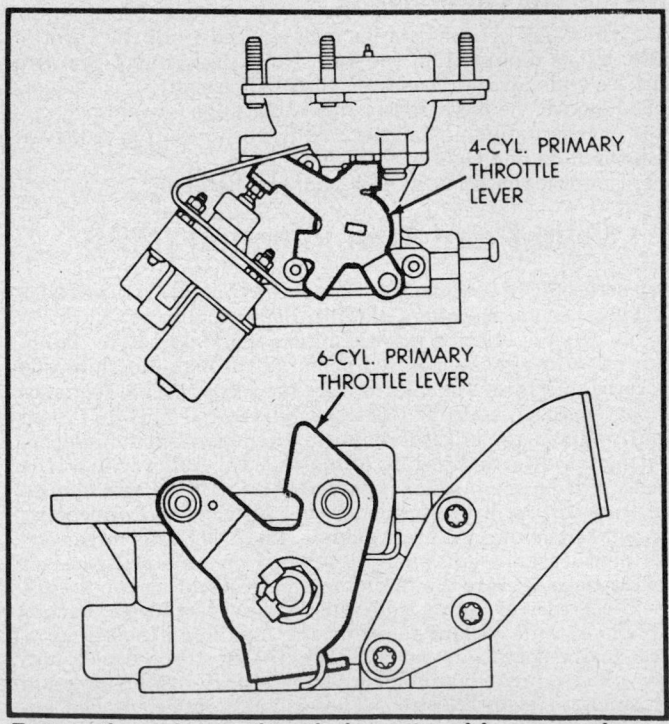

Rotate the primary throttle lever to wide open when adjusting

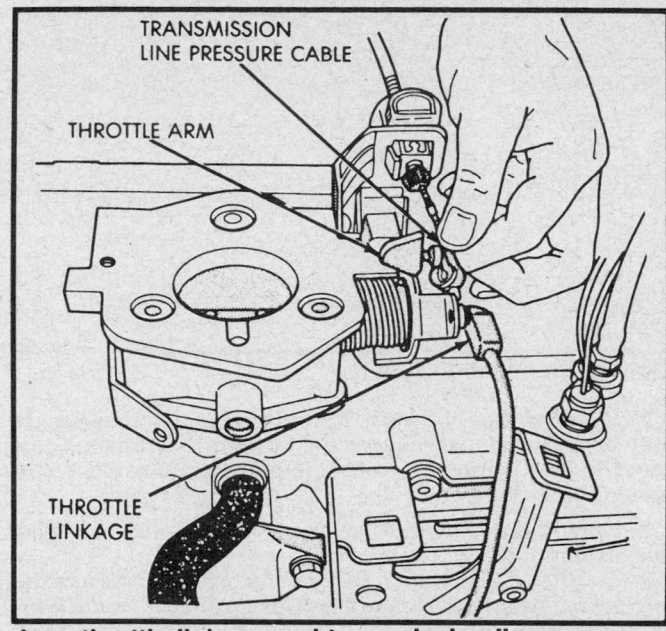

Jeep throttle linkage and transmission line pressure cable

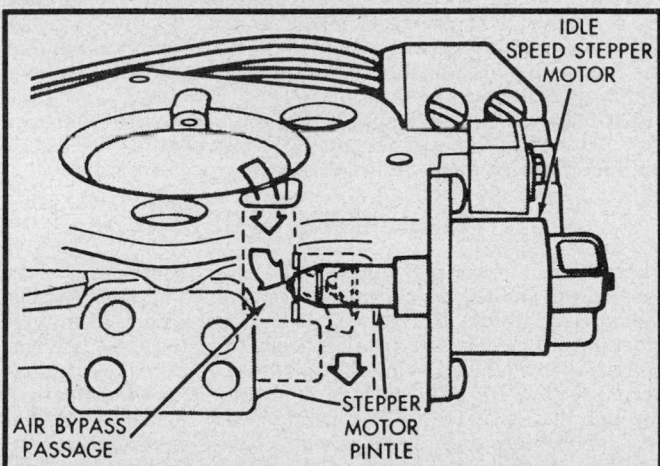

Idle speed stepper motor and bypass passage

11. Install the air cleaner snorkel and connect the battery negative cable.

IDLE SPEED STEPPER MOTOR

The idle speed stepper motor is mounted on the throttle body and is controlled by the ECU.

The throttle body has an air bypass passage that provides air for the engine at idle (the throttle plate is closed). The idle speed stepper motor pintle protrudes into the air bypass passage and regulates air flow through it. Based on various sensor inputs, the ECU adjusts the engine idle speed by moving the stepper motor pintle in and out of the bypass passage.

Removal and Installation

1. Disconnect the electrical connector from the idle speed stepper motor.
2. Remove the stepper motor retaining screws and remove the idle speed stepper motor.
3. At installation, install the stepper motor and retaining screws, and connect the electrical connection.

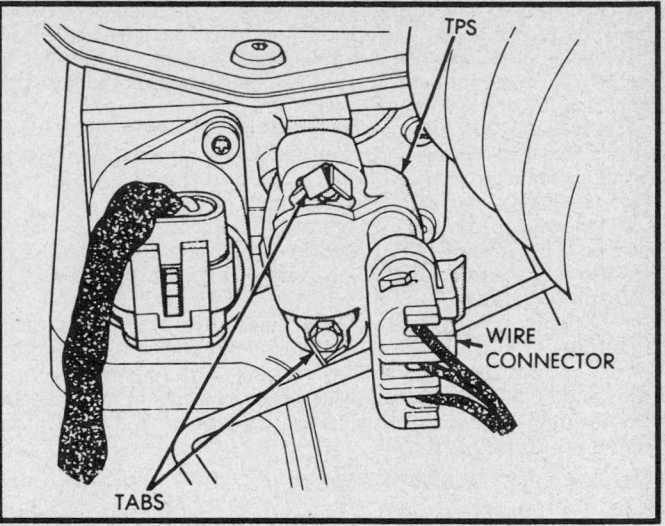

Throttle position sensor removal-typical

THROTTLE POSITION SENSOR (TPS)

The Throttle Position Sensor (TPS) is mounted on the throttle body and connected to the throttle valve shaft. The sensor is a variable resistor that provides the ECU with an input voltage that represents the throttle valve position. Input voltage to the ECU from the TPS varies in an approximate range of from 1 volt at minimum throttle opening (idle) to 5 volts at wide open throttle. The ECU uses TPS input voltage to determine current engine operating conditions.

There are 2 different throttle position sensors, 1 used with automatic transmissions and 1 used with manual transmissions. The TPS used with automatic transmissions has 2 integral wire harness connectors (one 4 pin connector and one 3 pin connector) that plug into the engine wire harness. The 4 pin connector supplies input to the ECU while the 3 pin connector supplies input to the transmission control unit. The throttle position sensor used with manual transmissions has an integral connector. The engine wire harness connects directly to the throttle position sensor.

Removal and Installation

1. Disconnect the TPS electrical connector(s).
2. Bend the lock tabs back and remove the retaining screws.
3. Remove the TPS from the throttle plate assembly.
4. At installation, position the TPS onto the throttle plate assembly and install the retaining screws. Adjust the TPS using the procedure below.
5. Bend the lock tabs over the screws and connect the TPS electrical connectors.

TPS Adjustment

Although the factory recommends their electronic diagnostic tester for this procedure, this throttle position sensor adjustment can be accomplished with a digital volt meter.

MANUAL TRANSMISSION

1. Note that the TPS terminals are marked **A, B** and **C** on the back of the harness connector. Start by turning the ignition key to **ON**.

NOTE: Do not unfasten the sensor wire harness connector. Without damaging the sensor wires, insert the voltmeter test leads through the back of the wire harness connector to make contact with the sensor terminals.

2. Check the sensor input voltage. Insert the negative lead of the voltmeter into the back of terminal **B** and the positive lead of the voltmeter into the back of terminal **A**. Make sure that the throttle plate is completely closed against the idle stop. Note the sensor input voltage.

3. Check the sensor output voltage by removing the voltmeter positive lead from sensor terminal **A** and connecting it to terminal **C**. Make sure the throttle plate is in the closed position. Note the sensor output voltage reading on the voltmeter.

4. Divide the output voltage reading by the input voltage reading. The desired ratio is 0.825 to 0.835 (0.830 desired). **Example:** if the input voltage is 5 volts and the output voltage is 4.15 volts; divide 4.15 by 5 (4.15 ÷ 5 = 0.83 or 83%).

5. If necessary, adjust the TPS sensor until the correct ratio is obtained. To adjust the input and output voltages, loosen the sensor bottom mounting screw and pivot the sensor for a fine adjustment. Adjust the TPS until the correct ratio is obtained.

6. Remove the voltmeter. Tighten the sensor mounting screws securely.

AUTOMATIC TRANSMISSION

Use the 4 terminal connector to adjust the TPS. The terminals are marked **A**, **B**, **C**, and **D**.

1. Turn the ignition key to **ON**.

NOTE: Do not unfasten the sensor wire harness connector. Without damaging the sensor wires, insert the voltmeter test leads through the back of the wire harness connector to make contact with the sensor terminals.

2. Check the TPS input voltage as follows. Locate terminal **D** and insert the negative lead of the voltmeter into the back of it. Insert the positive lead of the voltmeter into the back of terminal **A**. Note the sensor input voltage (across terminals **D** and **A**).

3. Check the TPS output voltage as follows. Disconnect the voltmeter positive lead from sensor terminal **A** and insert it into the back of terminal **B**. Note the sensor output voltage (across terminals **B** and **D**).

4. Divide the output voltage reading by the input reading. The desired ratio is 0.825 to 0.835 (0.830 desired). **Example:** if the input voltage is 5 volts and the output voltage is 4.15 volts; divide 4.15 by 5 (4.15 ÷ 5 = 0.83 or 83%).

5. If necessary, adjust the TPS sensor until the correct ratio is obtained. To adjust the input and output voltages, loosen the sensor **bottom** mounting screw and pivot the sensor for a large adjustment. Loosen the sensor **top** mounting screw and pivot the sensor for a fine adjustment. Adjust the TPS until the correct ratio is obtained.

6. Remove the voltmeter and tighten the sensor screws securely.

FUEL INJECTOR RAIL ASSEMBLY

The fuel rail supplies fuel to the injectors and is mounted to the intake manifold. The fuel pressure regulator is attached to the rail and the fuel pressure test port is integral with the rail. The fuel rail is not repairable.

Removal and Installation

1. Remove the fuel tank cap.
2. Perform the MPI fuel system pressure release procedure.
3. Disconnect the battery negative terminal.
4. Tag and remove each injector harness connector from each injector. This is important. Each injector harness connector must be returned its proper injector.
5. Disconnect the vacuum tube from the fuel pressure regulator.
6. Disconnect the fuel supply hose from the fuel rail and fuel return tube from the fuel pressure regulator.
7. Remove the fuel rail mounting bolts.

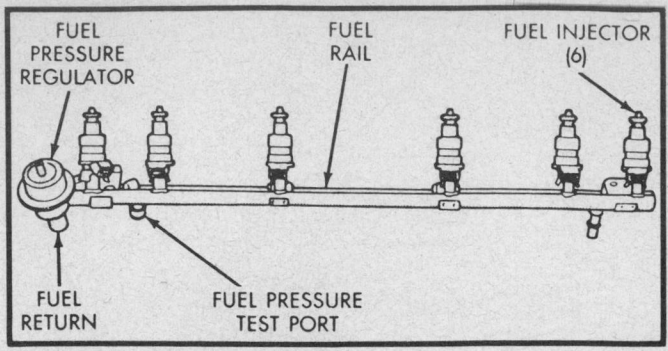

Multi-point injection fuel rail

NOTE: On models with automatic transmissions, it may be necessary to remove the automatic transmission throttle line pressure cable and bracket to remove the fuel rail assembly.

8. Remove the fuel rail by gently rocking until all the injectors are out of the intake manifold.
9. At installation, position the tips of all the injectors into the corresponding injector bore in the intake manifold. Seat the injectors into the manifold.
10. Tighten the fuel rail mounting bolts to 20 ft. lbs.
11. Connect the injector harness connectors. Make sure they are connected to the correct injector.
12. Connect the fuel return tube to the pressure regulator and the fuel supply hose to the fuel rail using a new O-ring, spacer and retainer repair kit.
13. Connect the vacuum supply tube to the pressure regulator.
14. Install the cap over the pressure test port fitting, install the fuel tank cap and connect the battery negative cable.

FUEL INJECTORS

There is one injector per cylinder. The injectors are attached to the fuel rail and the nozzle ends are positioned into openings in the intake manifold just above the intake valve ports of the cylinder head. The injectors are electrically operated and exclusively controlled by the ECU. Each injector is connected to a permanent ground. Battery voltage is supplied to the injectors through the ECU. The ECU controls injector pulse width. The ECU determines injector pulse width based on various inputs.

Removal and Installation

1. Remove the fuel tank cap.
2. Perform the MPI fuel system pressure release procedure described above.
3. Disconnect the battery negative terminal.
4. Remove the fuel rail as described above.
5. Remove the clip(s) that retain the injector(s) to the fuel rail.

NOTE: An O-ring kit is available which consists of 6 brown seals and 7 black seals. The brown seals fit on the injector tip area and seal the injector to the intake manifold when installed. The black seals fit on the rail end of the injector to seal the injector when it is installed into the fuel rail. The last black seal is for the fuel pressure regulator to seal the pressure regulator to the fuel rail. Due to the different O-ring material and useage, the brown and black O-rings cannot be interchanged.

6. Install the fuel injector(s) into the fuel rail assembly and install the retaining clips(s).
7. Install the fuel rail.
8. Install the fuel tank cap and connect the battery negative cable.

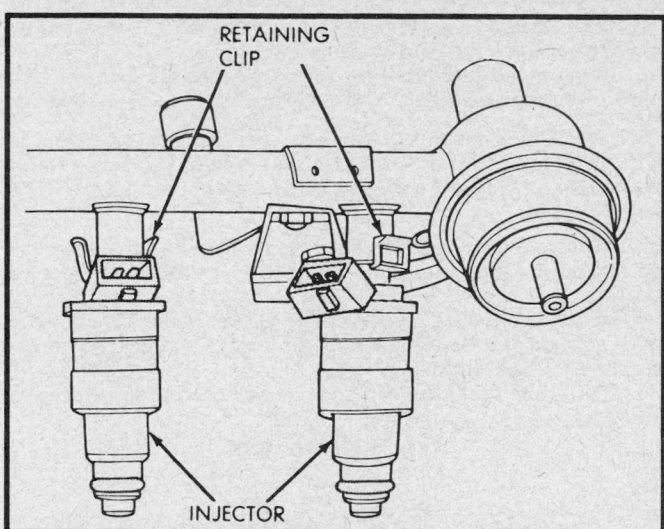

Jeep injector retaining clips

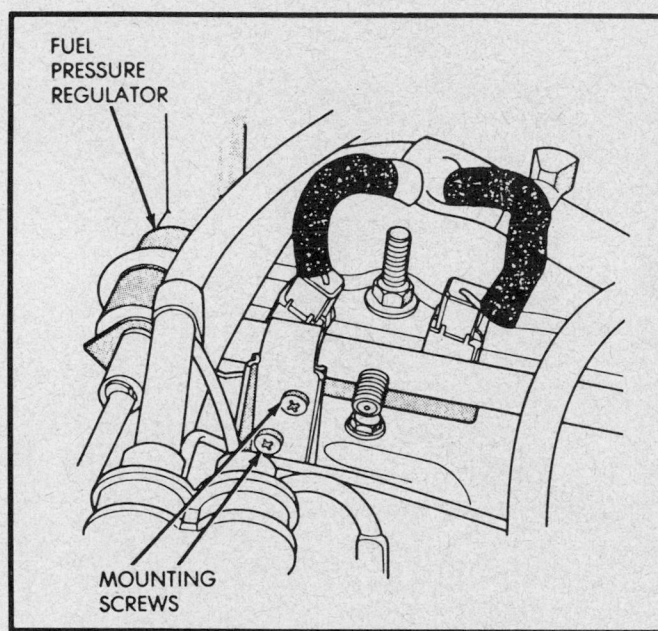

Location of fuel pressure regulator assembly

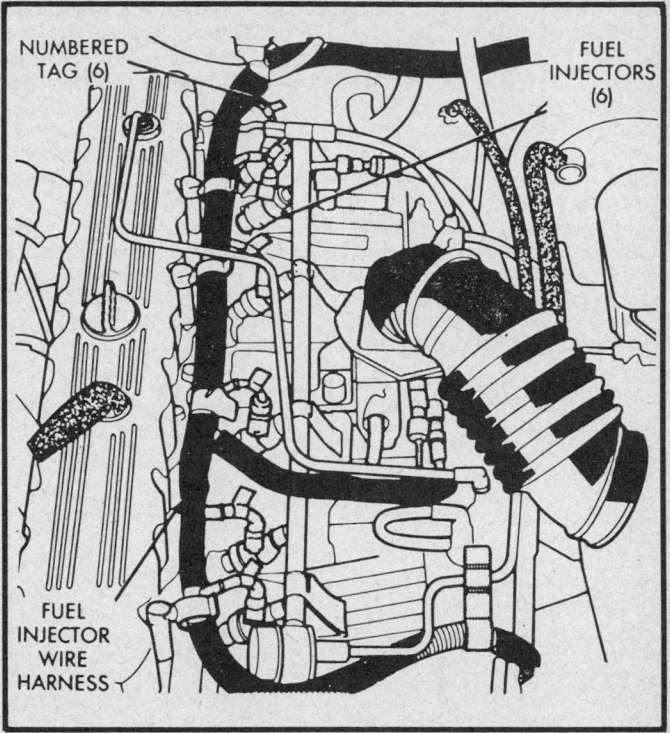

Location of fuel injector harness assembly

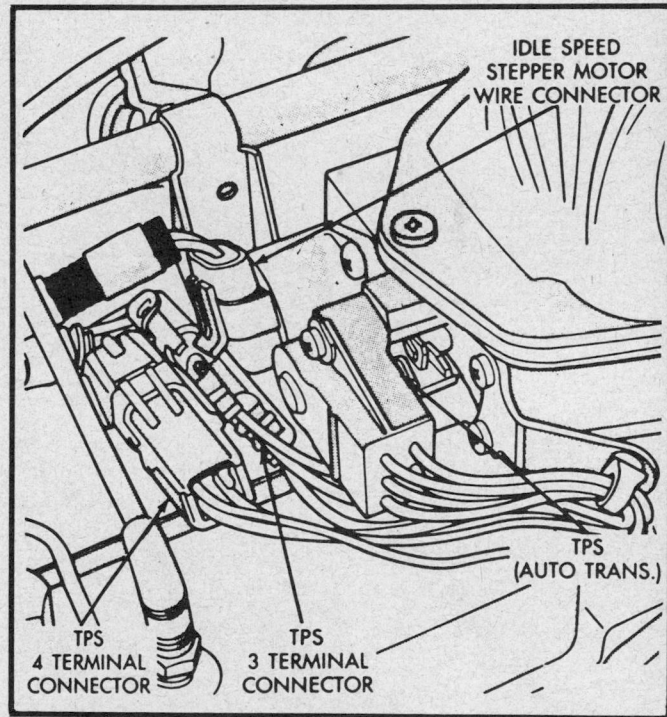

Throttle position sensor adjustment with automatic transmission

FUEL PRESSURE REGULATOR

The fuel pressure regulator used with the MPI fuel system is a vacuum assisted, nonadjustable type. The regulator is mounted on the output end of the fuel rail and is connected to intake manifold vacuum. The regulator is calibrated to maintain fuel system pressure at about 31 psi with vacuum applied while the engine is at idle. Fuel pressure will be 8–10 psi higher if vacuum is not applied to the regulator.

The pressure regulator contains a diaphragm, calibrated spring and fuel return valve. Fuel pressure operates on one side of the regulator while spring pressure and intake manifold vacuum operate on the other side. Spring pressure on the top side of the diaphragm tries to force the return valve closed. Fuel pressure on the bottom side of the diaphragm, with assistance from manifold vacuum on the spring side of the diaphragm, act against the spring pressure to open the return valve. System fuel pressure is the amount of fuel pressure required to force against spring pressure and unseat the return valve.

Without vacuum applied to the spring side of the regulator, the spring is calibrated to open the fuel return outlet when the

pressure differential between the fuel injectors and the intake manifold vacuum reaches about 39 psi. Since manifold vacuum varies with engine operating conditions, the amount of vacuum applied to the spring side of the diaphragm varies. For this reason, fuel pressure varies depending upon the intake manifold vacuum. With low vacuum, such as during wide open throttle conditions, minimal vacuum assistance is available and full spring pressure is exerted to seal the fuel outlet causing system pressure to increase. With high vacuum, such as during idle, fuel pressure on the bottom of the diaphragm is assisted by the intake manifold pressure on the spring side of the diaphragm, resulting in lower system fuel pressure. The fuel pressure regulator is not controlled by the ECU.

Removal and Installation

1. Remove the fuel tank cap.
2. Perform the MPI fuel system pressure release procedure described above.

3. Disconnect the battery negative terminal.
4. Remove the fuel rail as described above.
5. Remove the fuel pressure regulator retaining screws and remove the regulator from the fuel rail.

NOTE: An O-ring kit for the pressure regulator is available. One of the black O-ring seals in the kit is to be installed on the fuel pressure regulator before installation.

6. At installation, replace the O-ring and install the pressure regulator into the fuel rail. Tighten the mounting screws securely.
7. Install the fuel rail as described above. Make sure new O-rings, spacers and the retainer repair kit are installed when assembling the fuel lines.
8. Install the fuel tank cap and connect the battery negative cable.

MANUAL STEERING GEARS
STEERING TROUBLE DIAGNOSIS
Manual Steering

Condition	Possible Cause	Correction
Excessive play or looseness in the steering	1. Steering gear shaft adjusted too loose or shaft and/or bushing badly worn.	1. Replace worn parts and adjust according to instructions.
	2. Excessive steering gear worm end play due to bearing adjustment.	2. Adjust according to instructions.
	3. Steering linkage loose or worn.	3. Replace worn parts.
	4. Front wheel bearings improperly adjusted.	4. Adjust wheel bearings.
	5. Steering arm loose on steering gear shaft.	5. Inspect for damage to the gear shaft and steering arm, replace parts as necessary.
	6. Steering gear housing attaching bolts loose.	6. Tighten the attaching bolts to specifications.
	7. Steering arms loose at steering knuckles.	7. Tighten according to specifications.
	8. Working pins or bushings.	8. Replace king pins and bushings.
	9. Loose spring shackles.	9. Adjust or replace parts as necessary.
Hard steering	1. Low or uneven tire pressure.	1. Inflate the tires to recommended pressures.
	2. Insufficient lubricant in the steering gear housing or in steering linkage.	2. Lubricate as necessary.
	3. Steering gear shaft adjusted too tight.	3. Adjust according to instructions.
	4. Improper caster or toe-in.	4. Align the wheels.
Wheel tramp (excessive vertical motion of wheels)	1. Incorrect tire pressure.	1. Inflate the tires to recommended pressures.
	2. Improper balance of wheels, tires and brake drums.	2. Balance as necessary.
	3. Loose tie rod ends or steering connections.	3. Inspect and repair as necessary.
	4. Worn or inoperative shock absorbers.	4. Replace the shock absorbers.
Shimmy	1. Badly worn and/or unevenly worn tires.	1. Rotate tires or replace if necessary.
	2. Wheels and tires out of balance.	2. Balance wheel and tire assemblies.
	3. Worn or loose steering linkage parts.	3. Replace parts as required.
	4. Worn king pins and bushings.	4. Replace king pins and bushings.
	5. Loose steering gear adjustments.	5. Adjust steering gear as necessary.
	6. Loose wheel bearings.	6. Adjust wheel bearings.
	7. Improper caster setting.	7. Adjust caster to specifications.
	8. Weak or broken springs.	8. Replace as required.
	9. Incorrect tire pressure or tire sizes not uniform.	9. Check tire sizes and inflate tires to recommended pressure.
	10. Faulty shock absorbers.	10. Replace as necessary.
Pull to one side (tendency of the vehicle to veer in one direction only)	1. Incorrect tire pressure or tires not uniform.	1. Check tire sizes and inflate the tires to recommended pressures.
	2. Wheel bearings improperly adjusted.	2. Adjust wheel bearings.
	3. Dragging brakes.	3. Inspect for weak, or broken brake shoe spring, binding pedal.
	4. Improper caster, camber or toe-in.	4. Adjust to specifications.
	5. Grease, dirt, oil or brake fluid on brake linings.	5. Inspect, replace and adjust as necessary.
	6. Broken or sagging rear springs.	6. Replace the rear springs.
	7. Bent front axle, linkage or steering knuckle.	7. Replace the parts as necessary.
	8. Worn or tight king pin bushings.	8. Lubricate or replace as necessary.

STEERING TROUBLE DIAGNOSIS
Manual Steering

Condition	Possible Cause	Correction
Wander or weave	1. Improper caster, camber or toe-in.	1. Adjust to specifications.
	2. Worn king pin and bushings.	2. Replace parts as required.
	3. Worn or improperly adjusted front wheel bearings.	3. Adjust or replace parts as necessary.
	4. Loose spring shackles.	4. Adjust or replace parts as necessary.
	5. Incorrect tire pressure or tire sizes not uniform.	5. Check tire sizes and inflate tires to recommended pressure.
	6. Loose steering gear mounting bolts.	6. Tighten to specifications.

CHRYSLER CORPORATION

Recirculating Ball and Nut

Disassembly and Assembly

1. Position the steering gear assembly in a suitable holding and thoroughly clean the outside surface before disassembly.

2. Loosen the sector shaft adjusting screw locknut, and back out the adjusting screw about 2 turns to relieve the mesh load between the ball nut rack and the sector gear teeth.

3. Position the steering gear worm shaft in a straight ahead position.

4. Remove the attaching bolts from the sector shaft cover and slowly remove the sector shaft while sliding an arbor tool into the housing. Remove the locknut from the adjusting screw and remove the screw from the cover by turning it clockwise. Slide the adjustment screw and its shim out of the slot in the end of the sector shaft.

5. Loosen the worm shaft bearing adjuster locknut and remove the locknut. Slide the worm adjuster off the shaft.

6. Remove the wormshaft and the ball nut assembly from the housing.

NOTE: Make sure that the ball nut does not run down to either end of the wormshaft, as the ball guide ends can be damaged if the ball nut is allowed to rotate until stopped at the end of the worm.

7. Remove the remaining wormshaft bearing from the gear housing.

8. Remove the lower bearing by using a suitable tool to pry off the bearing retainer from the adjuster plug.

9. Remove the locknut from the sector shaft adjusting screw and remove the screw from the cover by turning the screw clockwise. Slide the adjuster screw and shims from the slot in the end of the sector shaft.

10. Remove the wormshaft and the sector shaft seals.

11. Support the steering gear housing in an arbor press. Press the sector shaft bearing and seal from the housing using a special tool inserted in the lower end of the housing.

12. Remove the worm shaft oil seal from the worm shaft bearing adjuster by inserting a blunt punch behind the seal and tapping alternately on each side of the seal until it is driven out of the adjuster. Remove the worm shaft in the same manner.

13. Remove the lower cup, if necessary. Pull the bearing cup out.

14. Wash all parts in clean solvent and dry thoroughly. Inspect all parts for wear, scoring, pitting, etc. Test the operation of the worm shaft and ball nut assembly. If ball nut does not travel smoothly and freely on the worm shaft or if there is binding, replace the assembly.

NOTE: The ball nut teeth are wider and deeper on one side than the other. When assembling the wormshaft and the ball nut, position the ball nut so that the wider/ deeper side of the teeth are closer to the housing cover opening after the installation.

15. Inspect the sector shaft for wear and check the fit of the shaft in the housing bearings. Inspect the fit of the shaft pilot bearing in the housing. Be sure that the worm shaft is not bent or damaged.

16. Install the sector shaft lower bearing. Press the bearing into the housing far enough to leave enough space to install the new oil seal.

17. Install the upper bearing in the same manner and press it into the inside end of the housing bore flush with the inside end of the bore surface.

18. Install the worm shaft bearing cups (upper and lower) by placing them and their spacers in the adjuster nut and press them into place.

19. Install the worm shaft oil seal by placing the seal in the worm shaft adjuster with the metal seal retainer up. Drive the seal into place with a suitable sleeve until it is just below the end of the bore in the adjuster.

NOTE: Apply a coating of steering gear lubricant to all moving parts during assembly. Also, put lubricant on and around oil seal lips.

20. Clamp the holding fixture and housing in a bench vise with the bearing adjuster opening upward.

21. With the upper bearing on the wormshaft, insert the wormshaft and ball nut assembly into the housing, positioning the wormshaft through the upper ball bearing race and seal.

22. Assemble the ball bearing and the seal into the wormshaft adjuster plug. Press the retainer into position.

23. Place the adjuster and the locknut into position guiding the wormshaft into the bearing. Tighten the adjuster until very little wormshaft endplay remains.

24. Install the sector shaft adjusting screw, with shim, in the slotted end of the sector shaft. With the adjuster screw positioned in the slot end of the sector shaft, check the end clearance of the screw.

25. Keep the clearance to 0.002 in. or less. A selection of 4 shims with various degrees is available.

26. Lubricate the the steering gear with steering gear grease. If not available, use NLGI Grade 2 E.P. or equivalent.

27. Turn the wormshaft until the ball nut is at the end of it's travel. Pack as much lubricant into the housing as possible.

28. Turn the wormshaft until the ball is at the other end of it's travel. Pack as much lubricant into the housing as possible.

29. Rotate the wormshaft to bring the ball nut to the center of it's travel.

30. Install the sector shaft assembly, including the adjuster screw and the shim, into the housing.

31. Engage the center tooth of the sector with the tooth space of the ball nut.

32. Pack more lubricant into the housing and install the side cover gasket.

33. Install the side cover.

34. Turn the the adjuster screw counterclockwise until the screw bottoms, then turn one half turn in the opposite direction. Replace the locknut, but do not tighten.

35. Install the side cover bolts and tighten to 25 ft. lbs.

36. Tighten the wormshaft adjusting locknut to 5–8 inch lbs. and the sector shaft adjusting locknut to 35 ft. lbs.

Adjustments

WORM BEARING PRELOAD

1. Remove the steering gear arm and lockwasher from the sector shaft, using a suitable gear puller.

2. Remove the horn button or horn ring.

3. Loosen the sector shaft adjusting screw locknut, and back out the adjusting screw about two turns.

4. Turn the steering wheel 2 complete turns from the straight ahead position, and place an inch lb. torque wrench on the steering shaft nut.

5. Rotate the steering shaft at least 1 turn toward the straight ahead position while measuring the torque on the torque wrench. The torque should be between 4–6 inch lbs. to move the steering wheel. If torque is not within these limits, loosen the worm shaft bearing adjuster locknut and turn the adjuster clockwise to increase the preload or counterclockwise to

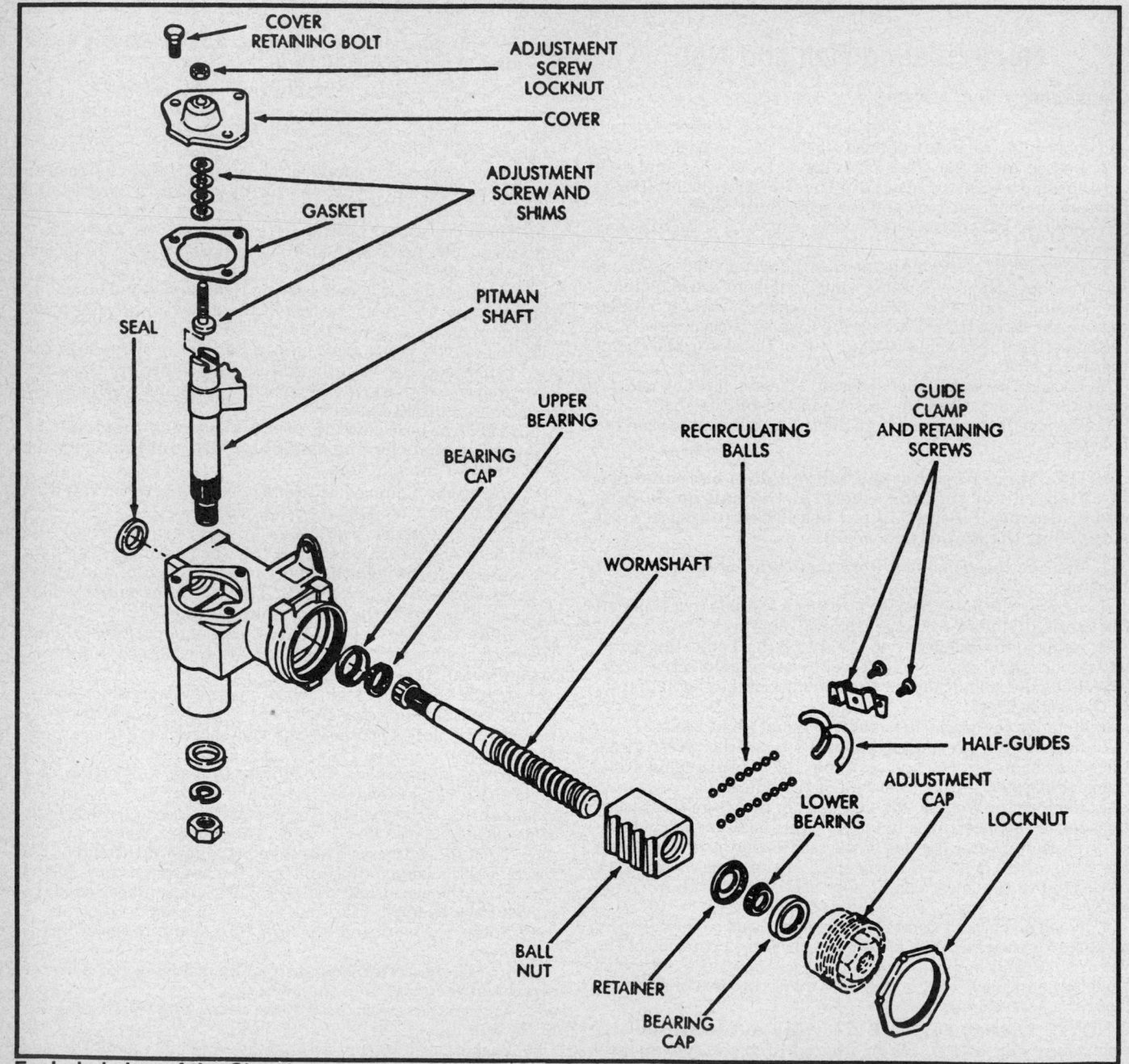

Exploded view of the Chrysler recirculating ball steering gear

decrease the preload. When the preload is correct, hold the adjuster screw steady and tighten the locknut. Recheck the preload.

BALL NUT RACK AND SECTOR MESH

NOTE: This adjustment can be accurately made only after proper preloading of worm bearing.

1. Turn the steering wheel gently stop to stop and count the number of turns. Turn the steering wheel back exactly half way, to the center position.

2. Turn the sector shaft adjusting screw clockwise to remove all lash between ball nut rack and the sector gear teeth, then tighten adjusting screw locknut to 35 ft. lbs.

3. Turn the steering wheel about ¼ turn away from the center or high spot position. With the torque wrench on the steering wheel nut measure the torque required to turn the steering

wheel through the high spot at the center position. The reading should be between 8–11 inch lbs. This is the total of the worm shaft bearing preload and the ball nut rack and sector gear mesh load. Readjust the sector shaft adjustment screw if necessary to obtain a correct torque reading.

4. After completing the adjustments, place the front wheels in a straight ahead position, and with the steering wheel and steering gear centered, install the steering arm on sector shaft. Tighten the steering arm retaining nut to 175 ft. lbs.

Manual Rack and Pinion

The manual rack and pinion gear is permanently lubricated at the factory and cannot be adjusted or serviced. If a malfunction occurs, the complete rack and pinion must be replaced.

FORD MOTOR COMPANY

Recirculating Ball and Nut (Koyo)

Disassembly and Assembly

1. Rotate the steering shaft from stop to stop, counting the total number of turns. Then turn exactly half-way back, placing the gear on center.

2. Remove the sector adjusting cover bolts, then remove the sector shaft with the cover. Remove the cover from the shaft by turning the screw clockwise. Keep the shim with the screw.

3. Using a special locknut wrench, loosen the worm bearing

adjuster locknut and remove the adjuster plug and wormshaft thrust bearing.

4. Carefully, pull the wormshaft and ball nut assembly from the housing and remove the upper thrust bearing.

NOTE: To avoid damage to the return guides, keep the ball nut from running down to either end of the worm.

5. Pry out the sector shaft and wormshaft seals and discard them.

NOTE: Do not disassemble the wormshaft assembly. If

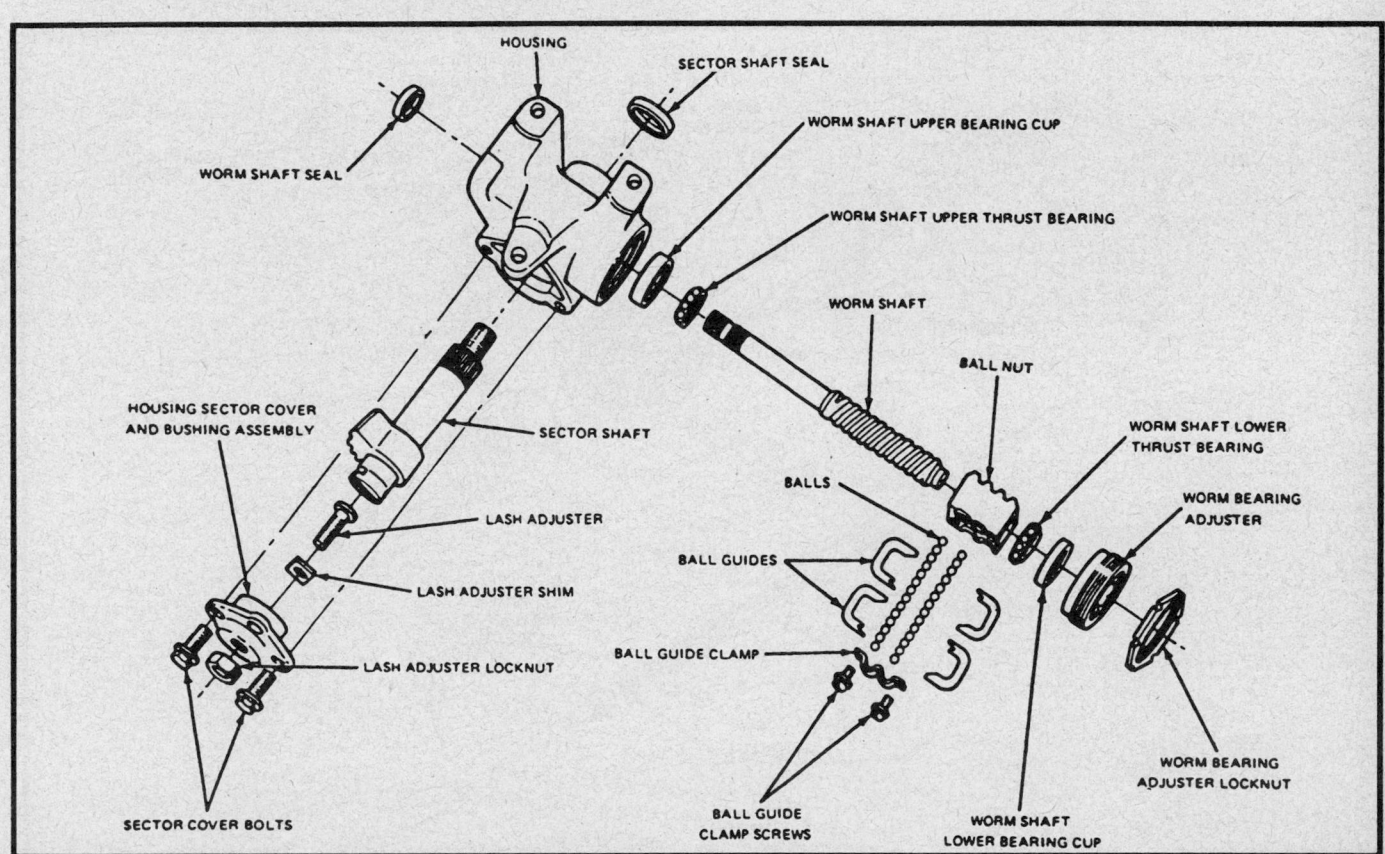

Exploded view of the Ford recirculating ball (Koyo)

the worm cannot rotate freely in the ball nut, replace the entire assembly.

6. The adjuster/plug bearing cup can be removed using a puller tool and slide hammer.

7. The housing bearing cup can be removed from the housing using a hammer and a suitable size bearing driver or socket.

8. The sector cover bushing is not serviceable. If found to be defective the entire sector cover including the bushing must be replaced.

9. The sector shaft needle bearing is serviced only as part of the housing unit and is not serviced separately. If one or more needles fall out, they may be cleaned and put back using steering gear lube to hold them in place.

10. Clean all the parts with the proper cleaning solvent and check for any cracks, chips or any excessive wear.

11. Check the clearance between the sector adjusting screw head and the bottom of the sector shaft T-slot. If the clearance is more than 0.004 in. install a new shim as required to reduce the clearance to 0.004 in. or less. A steering gear lash adjuster kit is available containing 5 different size shims. While holding the sector adjusting screw, turn the sector shaft back and forth. The sector shaft must turn freely. If the sector shaft does not turn freely, increase the T-slot clearance using an appropriate shim from the lash adjuster kit. Make sure the resulting clearance is not more than 0.004 in.

To assemble:

12. If the wormshaft bearing cup was removed from the housing, install a new cup using the proper tool for installing.

13. If the adjuster plug bearing cup was removed, install a new cup using the proper tool.

14. Install the sector shaft seal in the housing using the proper tool. Press the seal until it bottoms out.

15. Tap the wormshaft seal in the housing, using a suitable size socket and a hammer. Assemble the seal flush with the housing surface.

16. Clamp the steering gear housing in a vise with the wormshaft bore horizontal and the sector cover opening up.

17. Inspect the ball nut and wormshaft assembly for any binding. If any tightness is felt, discard and replace with a new assembly.

18. Apply steering gear grease to the wormshaft bearings, sector shaft needle bearing in the housing and the sector cover bushing.

19. Slip one of the wormshaft bearings over the wormshaft splined end. Insert the wormshaft and ball nut assembly into the housing. Feed the splined end of the wormshaft through the bearing cup and seal. Place the remaining wormshaft thrust bearing in the adjuster plug bearing cup.

20. Install the adjuster plug and locknut into the housing opening being careful to guide the wormshaft end into the bearing until nearly all endplay has been removed from the wormshaft.

21. Position the sector adjusting screw and shim into the sector shaft slot. Check the clearance between the screw head and the sector shaft T-slot. If the clearance is more than 0.004 in. install a new shim as required to reduce the clearance to 0.004 in. or less. A steering gear lash adjuster kit is available containing five different size shims. While holding the sector adjusting screw, turn the sector shaft back and forth. The sector shaft must turn freely. If the sector shaft does not turn freely, increase the T-slot clearance using an appropriate shim from the lash adjuster kit. Make sure the resulting clearance is not more than 0.004 in.

22. Lubricate the steering gear with 10.2–14.8 ounces by weight of steering gear grease. Rotate the wormshaft until the ball nut is near the end of its travel. Pack as much grease into the housing as possible without loosing it out at the sector shaft

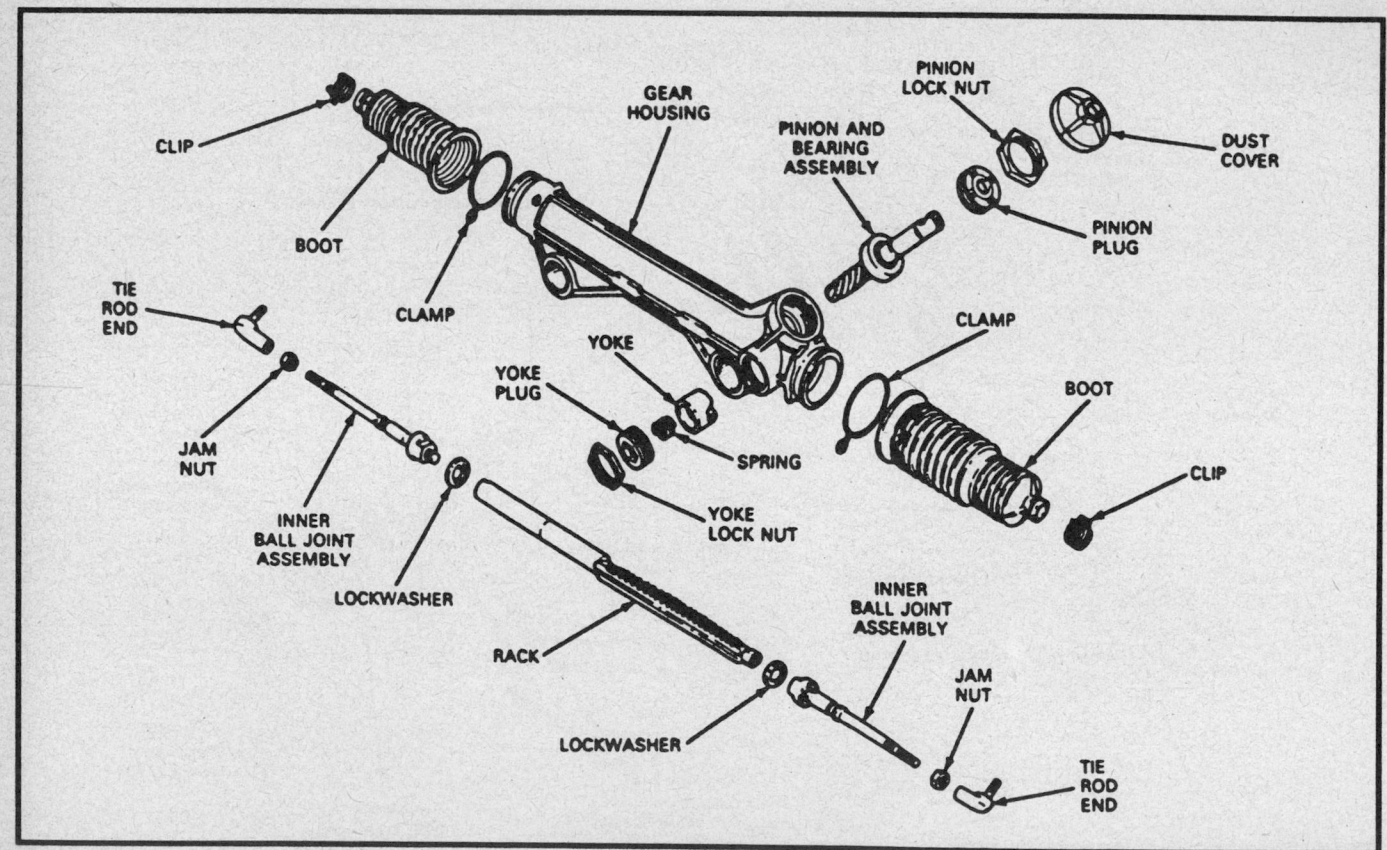

Exploded view of the Ford manual rack and pinion steering gear

opening. Rotate the wormshaft to move the ball nut near the other end of its travel and pack more grease into the housing.

23. Rotate the wormshaft until the ball nut is in the center of its travel.

24. Insert the sector shaft assembly containing the adjuster screw and shim into the housing so that the center tooth of the sector gear enters the center rack tooth space in the ball nut. Rotate the ball nut teeth slightly up to aid in alignment of the gear teeth and installation of the sector shaft.

25. Pack the remaining grease into the housing.

26. Apply an 1/8 in. wide by an 1/8 in. high bead of silicone rubber sealant to the mating surfaces of the sector cover and the housing. After waiting about 5 minutes, engage the sector adjuster screw with the tapped hole in the center of the center cover by turning the screw counterclockwise until the sector cover is flush with the housing.

27. Install the sector cover to housing attaching washer and bolts. Do not torque the bolts unless there is a lash between the sector shaft and wormshaft. The lash can be obtained by turning the screw counterclockwise.

28. Tighten the sector cover attaching bolts to 40 ft. lbs.

29. Adjust the steering gear preload and meshload.

Adjustments
PRELOAD AND MESHLOAD

1. Tighten the sector cover bolts to 40 ft. lbs.

2. Loosen the preload adjuster locknut and tighten the worm bearing adjuster nut until all end play has been removed. Lubricate the wormshaft seal with a drop of Type F automatic transmission fluid.

3. Using an 11/16 in., 12 point socket and an inch lbs. torque wrench, turn the wormshaft all the way to the right. Measure the left turn torque required to rotate the wormshaft at a constant speed for approximately 1½ turns. This torque reading is preload.

4. Tighten or loosen the adjuster nut as required until the correct preload of 7–9 inch lbs. (5–6 inch lbs. for 1988 vehicles) is obtained. Tighten the adjuster locknut to 187 ft. lbs.

5. Rotate the wormshaft from stop to stop, counting the total number of turns, then turn back halfway, placing the gear at the center.

6. Observe the highest reading while the wormshaft is turned approximately 90 degree(s) either way across center. If the highest reading (meshload) is not within 12–14 in lbs. (9–11 inch lbs. for 1988 vehicles) and at least 4 inch lbs. over the preload, turn the sector shaft adjusting screw as required.

7. Hold the sector shaft adjusting screw and tighten the locknut to 25 ft. lbs.

Manual Rack and Pinion

Disassembly and Assembly

1. Clean the exterior of the steering gear and place in a suitable holding device.

2. Place the gear in the on center position as follows:

a. Rotate the pinion shaft from one lock position to the other (entire gear travel). Record the number of pinion shaft rotations.

b. Divide the number of pinion shaft rotations by two. This provides the required number of turns to place the gear in the on-center position.

c. From one lock position, rotate the pinion the exact number of turns determined to place the gear in the on-center position. The white marks on the pinion shaft and lower bearing should be in alignment.

3. Using the proper tool, hold the yoke plug in place and remove the yoke locking nut with the proper tool

4. Remove the yoke plug.

5. Remove the spring from the yoke and remove the yoke from the housing.

NOTE: It may be necessary to use snapring pliers to remove the yoke.

6. Remove the dust cover from the pinion shaft.

7. Using the correct tool, hold the pinion plug lock plug in place and remove the pinion plug locknut.

8. Using the correct tool, remove the pinion plug.

9. Remove the pinion and bearing assembly from the housing.

To assemble:

10. Coat the pinion teeth and the upper bearing with steering grease.

11. Install the pinion and bearing assembly into the housing. Make sure the pinion is seated in the lower bearing.

12. Carefully, slide the pinion plug and seal assembly over the pinion shaft. Hand start the plug and seal into the housing. Using the proper tool, tighten the plug to 21–35 inch lbs. to set the pinion bearing preload.

13. Apply a thread lock and sealer to the pinion plug threads.

14. Hand start the pinion plug locknut onto the pinion plug. Hold the pinion plug in place using the proper tool, then tighten the locknut using tool, to 50–65 ft. lbs.

15. Pack the dust cover with steering gear grease and install it over the pinion shaft on the housing.

16. Inspect the yoke to make sure that the plastic insert is firmly seated flush with the shallow rim provided on the metal portion of the yoke assembly.

NOTE: There should be no visible gap between the plastic insert and the metal.

17. Coat the plastic yoke insert and the rack bar surface that slides against the yoke with steering gear grease.

18. Install the yoke in the housing bore against the Y-section of the rack.

19. Coat both ends of the spring with steering gear grease. Install the spring in the recess in the back of the yoke.

20. If necessary, install a new service yoke plug onto the spring. Hand tighten the plug, then tighten to 65 inch lbs.

21. Mark the housing directly across from the triangle marking on the yoke plug. Back off the yoke plug about 30 degree(s), until the bar (-) marking on the yoke plug aligns with the scribed mark on the housing. This adjusts the clearance between the yoke plug and the yoke.

22. Apply a thread lock and sealer to the yoke plug threads.

23. Hand start the locknut on the yoke plug. Hold the plug in place, then tighten the locknut using the correct tool, to 43–58 ft. lbs.

24. Verify that the bar (-) marking on the yoke plug aligns with the scribed mark on the housing.

GENERAL MOTORS CORPORATION

Saginaw 525 and 535

Disassembly and Assembly

1. Place the steering gear in a suitable holding device, clamping onto one of the mounting tabs. The wormshaft should be in a horizontal position.

2. Rotate the wormshaft from stop to stop and count the total number of turns. Turn back exactly halfway, placing the gear on center.

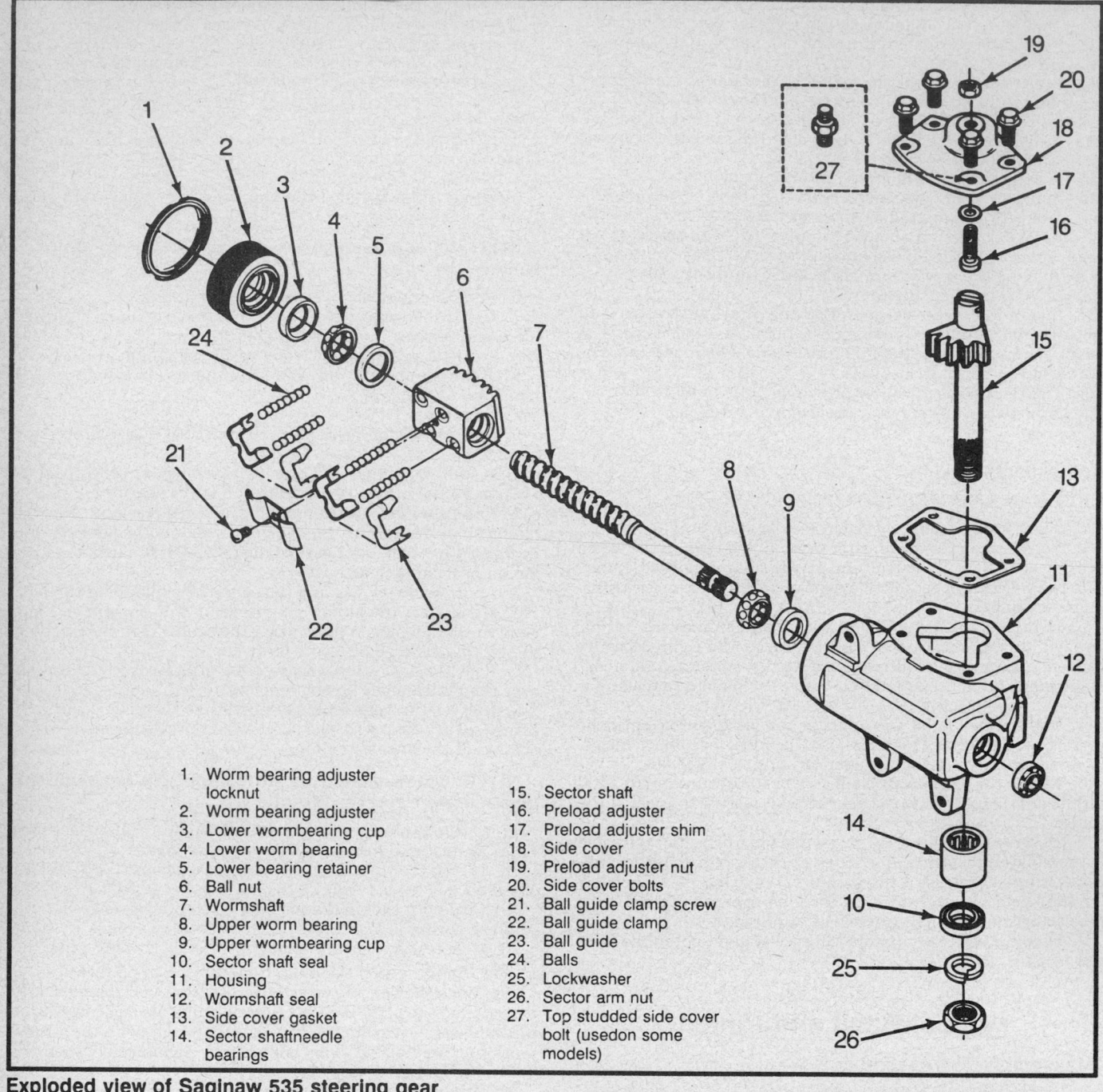

1. Worm bearing adjuster locknut
2. Worm bearing adjuster
3. Lower wormbearing cup
4. Lower worm bearing
5. Lower bearing retainer
6. Ball nut
7. Wormshaft
8. Upper worm bearing
9. Upper wormbearing cup
10. Sector shaft seal
11. Housing
12. Wormshaft seal
13. Side cover gasket
14. Sector shaftneedle bearings
15. Sector shaft
16. Preload adjuster
17. Preload adjuster shim
18. Side cover
19. Preload adjuster nut
20. Side cover bolts
21. Ball guide clamp screw
22. Ball guide clamp
23. Ball guide
24. Balls
25. Lockwasher
26. Sector arm nut
27. Top studded side cover bolt (usedon some models)

Exploded view of Saginaw 535 steering gear

3. Remove the self locking bolts which attach the sector cover to the housing.

4. Using a plastic hammer, tap lightly on the end of the sector shaft and remove the sector cover and sector shaft assembly from the gear housing.

NOTE: It may be necessary to turn the wormshaft by hand until the sector will pass through the opening in the housing.

5. Remove the locknut from the adjuster plug and remove the adjuster plug assembly.

6. Pull the wormshaft and ball nut assembly from the housing.

NOTE: Damage may result to the ends of the ball guides if the ball nut is allowed to rotate to the end of the worm.

7. Remove the worm shaft upper bearing from inside the gear housing.

8. Pry the wormshaft lower bearing retainer from the adjuster plug housing and remove the bearing.

9. Remove the locknut from the lash adjuster screw in the sector cover. Turn the lash adjuster screw clockwise and remove it from the sector cover. Slide the adjuster screw and shim out of the slot in the end of the sector shaft.

10. Pry out and discard both the sector shaft and wormshaft seals.

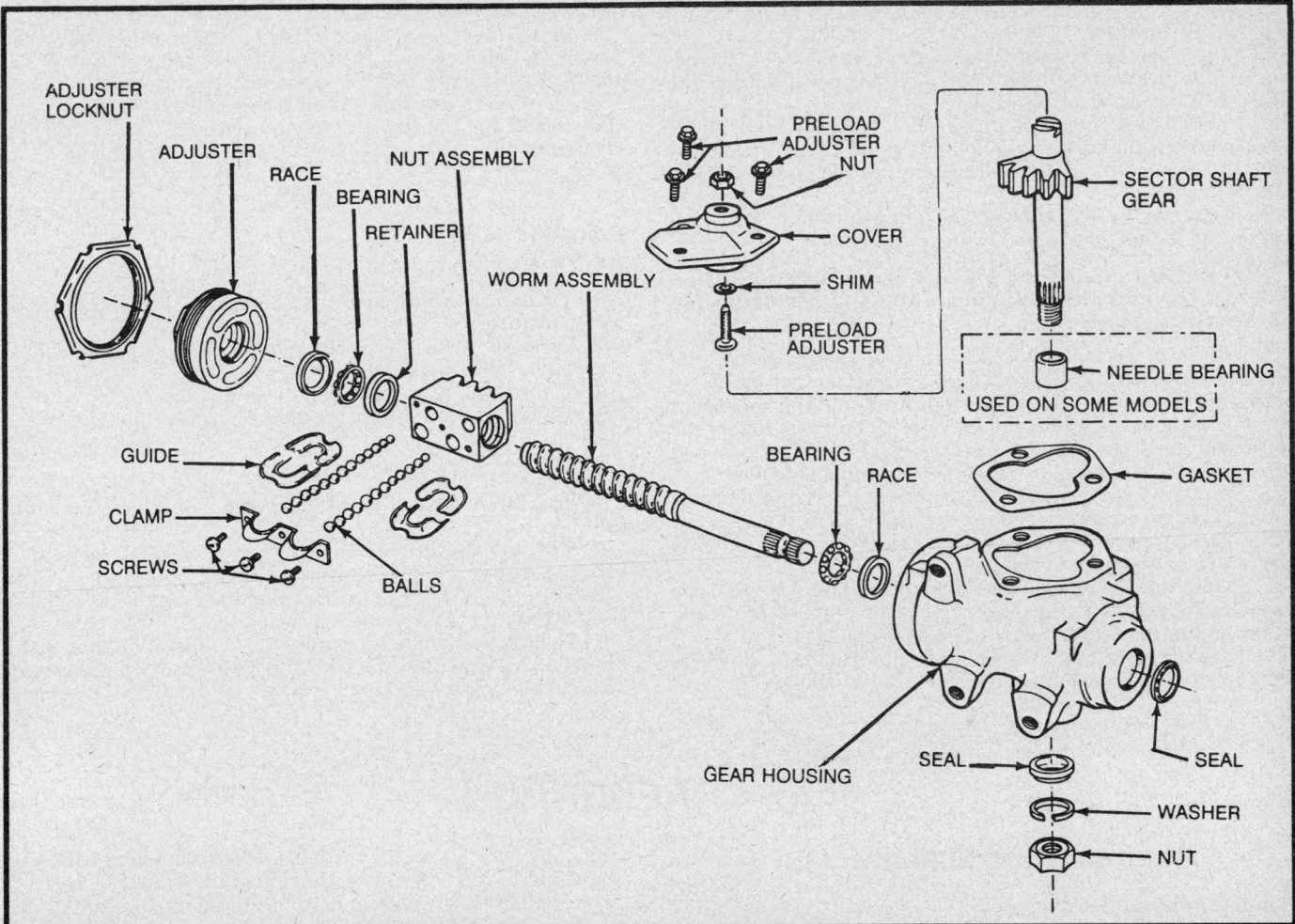

Exploded view of Saginaw 525 steering gear

11. Clean all the parts and inspect for any damage.
12. If there is any indication of binding or tightness when the ball nut is rotated on the worm, the unit should be disassembled, cleaned and inspected as follows:

    a. Remove the screws and clamp retaining the ball guides in the ball nut. Pull the guides out of the ball nut.

    b. Turn the ball nut upside down and rotate the wormshaft back and forth until all the balls have dropped out of the ball nut, count the number. The ball nut can now be pulled endwise off the worm.

    c. Clean all the parts in solvent. Inspect the worm and nut grooves and the surface of all balls for signs of indentation. Check all ball guides for damage at the ends. Replace any damaged parts.

    d. Slip the ball nut over the worm with the ball guide holes up and the narrow end of the ball nut teeth to the left from the steering wheel position. Sight through the ball guide to align the grooves in the worm.

    e. Place the 2 ball guide halves together and insert them in the upper circuit in the ball nut. Place the 2 remaining guides together and insert them in the lower circuit.

    f. Count out the correct number of balls and place them in a suitable container. This is the proper amount for one circuit.

    g. Load the correct number of balls into one of the guide holes while turning the wormshaft gradually away from that hole.

    h. Fill the remaining ball circuit in the same manner.

    i. Assemble the ball guide clamp to the ball nut and tighten the screws to 4 ft. lbs.

    j. Check the assembly by rotating the ball nut on the worm to see that it moves freely.

NOTE: Do not rotate the ball nut to the end of the worm threads as this may damage the ball guides.

To assemble:
13. Coat the threads of the adjuster plug, sector cover bolts and lash adjuster with a non-drying oil resistant sealing compound.

NOTE: Do not apply compound to the female threads. Use extreme care when applying compound to the bearing adjuster so that it does not come in contact with the wormshaft bearing.

14. Place the steering gear housing in a suitable holding device with the wormshaft bore horizontal and the sector cover opening up.
15. Make sure that all seals, bushings and bearing cups are installed in the gear housing and that the ball nut is installed on the wormshaft.
16. Slip the wormshaft upper bearing assembly over the wormshaft and insert the wormshaft and ball nut assembly into

the housing, feeding the end of the shaft through the upper ball bearing cup and seal.

17. Place the wormshaft lower bearing assembly in the adjuster plug bearing cup and press the stamped retainer into place with a suitable size socket.

18. Install the adjuster plug and locknut into the lower end of the housing while carefully guiding the end of the wormshaft into the bearing until nearly all end play has been removed from the wormshaft.

19. Position the lash adjuster including the shim in the slotted end of the sector shaft.

NOTE: End clearance should not be greater than 0.002. If the end clearance is greater than 0.002 a shim package is available.

20. Lubricate the steering gear with steering gear grease. Rotate the wormshaft until the ball nut is at the other end of its travel and then pack as much new lubricant into the housing as possible without losing out the sector shaft opening. Rotate the wormshaft until the ball nut is at the other end of its travel and pack as much lubricant into the opposite end as possible.

21. Rotate the wormshaft until the ball nut is in the center of travel. This is to make sure that the sector shaft and ball nut will engage properly with the center tooth of the sector entering the center tooth space in the ball nut.

22. Insert the sector shaft assembly including lash adjuster screw and shim into the housing so that the center tooth of the sector enters the center tooth space in the ball nut.

23. Pack the remaining portion of the lubricant into the housing and also place some in the sector cover bushing hole.

24. Place the sector cover gasket on the housing.

25. Install the sector cover onto the sector shaft, using the proper tool, and turning the lash adjuster screw counterclockwise until the screw bottoms, then back the screw off ½ turn. Loosely install a new locknut onto the adjuster screw.

26. Install and tighten the sector cover bolts. On 525 models, tighten to 30 ft. lbs; on 535 models tighten to 13 ft. lbs.

Adjustments

WORM BEARING PRELOAD

1. Tighten the worm bearing adjuster until it bottoms then loosen ¼ turn.

2. Carefully, turn the wormshaft all the way to the end of travel, then turn back ½ turn.

3. Tighten the adjuster plug to 5–8 inch lbs.

4. Tighten the locknut, using a punch against the edge of the slot.

OVER CENTER PRELOAD

1. Back off the preload adjuster until it stops, then turn it one full turn.

2. With the gear at the center of travel, check the torque to turn the stub shaft and record the reading.

3. Turn the adjuster in until the torque reads 4–10 inch lbs. greater than the above reading.

4. Tighten the adjuster locknut to 25 ft. lbs. on 525 and 22 ft. lbs on 535 gears. Prevent the adjusting screw from turning while tightening the locknut.

JEEP CORPORATION

Recirculating Ball and Nut

Disassembly and Assembly

1. Secure the gear assembly in a proper holding device.

2. Rotate the wormshaft from one stop to the other and count the total number of turns.

3. Turn the wormshaft back ½ the total numbers of turns to center the shaft and the nut.

4. Remove the sector shaft adjusting screw locknut and remove the side cover mounting bolts and the side cover.

5. Slide the adjustment screw head out of the sector shaft and remove the shim(s). Retain the shims for endplay adjustment during assembly.

6. Remove the sector shaft, wormshaft bearing adjuster locknut and the adjustment cap.

7. Remove the wormshaft and the ball nut.

NOTE: Do not allow the ball nut to rotate freely and bottom at the end of the wormshaft. This can damage the tangs at the end of the ball guides.

8. Remove the sector shaft and the wormshaft seals from the housing.

9. If there is any indication of binding or tightness when the ball nut is rotated on the worm the unit should be disassembled, cleaned and inspected as follows:

a. Remove the upper bearing from the wormshaft.

b. Remove the ball guide clamp mounting screws and remove the clamp and the ball guides.

c. Separate the guide halves and save the ball bearings that remained in the guides.

d. Remove the remaining balls from the ball nut circuits by rotating the wormshaft back and forth, until the bearings fall

out. Use a cloth to catch the balls. There are a total of 50 ball bearings in the ball nut, with 25 in each circuit.

e. Remove the wormshaft from the ball nut. Clean all the parts with the proper solvent and inspect for any damage.

f. Position the ball nut with the ball guide holes facing up and the deep side of the ball nut teeth facing down.

i. Install the wormshaft in the ball nut and thread the shaft into the nut until an equal number of shaft threads are visible at each end of the nut.

NOTE: The ball nut teeth are machined to a greater width and depth on one side. When assembling the wormshaft and the ball nut, position the ball nut so that the wider-deeper side of the teeth will face the housing side cover opening.

j. Install one bearing in each ball guide hole. Move the wormshaft up and down until the bearings roll into the ball nut threads under the wormshaft and support the wormshaft.

k. Assemble and install the ball guides in the ball nut.

l. Install 24 bearings in each ball nut circuit through the holes in the ball guides. Rotate the wormshaft back and forth to ease in the installation.

m. Position the ball guide clamp on the ball nut and install the clamp mounting screws.

n. Lubricate the wormshaft threads and upper bearing with chassis lubricant. Install the bearing on the wormshaft.

10. Clean the housing with a proper cleaning solvent and inspect the parts for any damage or excessive wear.

11. Install the wormshaft and the ball nut in the steering gear housing.

12. Install the wormshaft bearing adjustment cap in the housing and tighten it only enough to remove the wormshaft endplay.

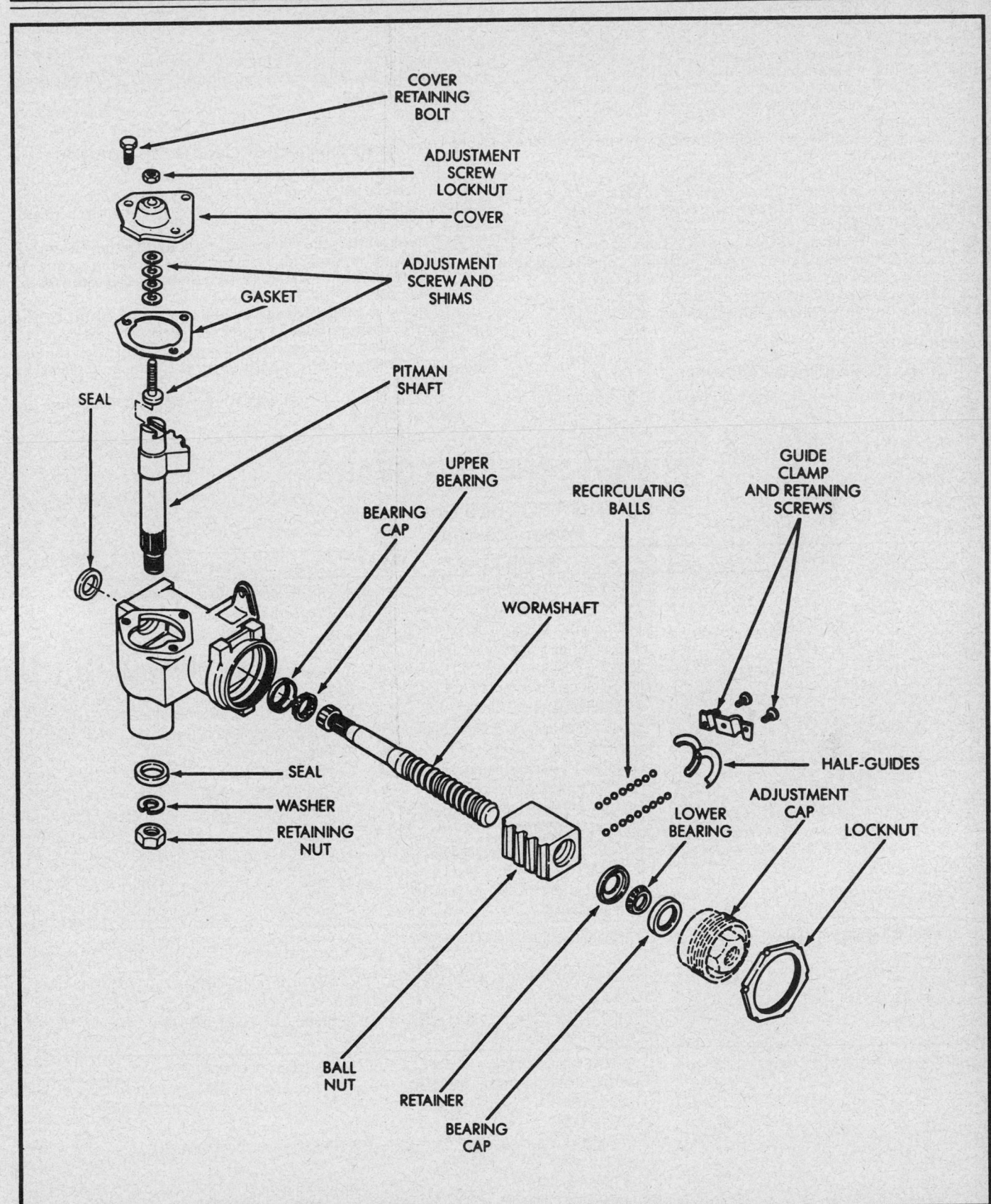

Exploded view of the Jeep manual steering gear

13. Install the locknut on the wormshaft bearing adjuster cap. Do not tighten.

14. Pack the gear housing with as much chassis grease as possible. Place the ball nut in the centered position.

15. Lubricate the sector shaft with chassis grease and insert into the gear housing. Engage the center tooth on the shaft with the center groove on the ball nut.

16. Install the shim(s) on the adjustment screw and thread the screw into the cover 2 to 3 threads.

17. Slide the head of the adjustment screw into the sector shaft and rotate the screw counterclockwise to thread it into the cover. Rotate the screw until the cover almost comes into contact with the gasket.

18. Install the cover mounting bolts. Do not tighten.

19. Tighten the adjustment screw until the cover is tight against the gasket and then loosen the screw ½ turn.

20. Tighten the cover mounting bolts to 45 ft. lbs.

21. Install the sector shaft and wormshaft seals.

Adjustments

WORMSHAFT BEARING PRELOAD

1. Tighten the worm bearing adjuster until it bottoms then loosen ¼ turn.

2. Carefully, turn the wormshaft all the way to the end of travel, then turn back ½ turn.

3. Tighten the adjuster plug to 5–8 inch lbs.

4. Tighten the adjustment cap locknut to 50 ft. lbs. Measure the preload torque.

SECTOR SHAFT OVER CENTER DRAG TORQUE

1. Rotate the wormshaft from stop-to-stop, count the number of rotations and rotate the wormshaft in the opposite direction ½ number of rotations to center the ball nut with the sector shaft.

2. While rotating the wormshaft back and forth over center, tighten the sector shaft adjustment screw until the torgue required to rotate the wormshaft over center is the same as the wormshaft bearing preload torque.

3. The over center drag torque should be equal to the wormshaft bearing preload torque plus 4–10 inch lbs.

4. While rotating the wormshaft over center, tighten the sector shaft adjustment screw until the drag torque is increased by 4–10 inch lbs.

5. Hold the sector shaft adjustment screw and tighten the locknut to 25 ft. lbs.

POWER STEERING GEARS

STEERING TROUBLE DIAGNOSIS
Power Steering

Condition	Possible Cause	Correction
Hard steering	1. Low or uneven tire pressure.	1. Inflate the tires to recommended pressure.
	2. Insufficient lubricant in the steering gear housing or in steering linkage.	2. Lubricate as necessary.
	3. Steering gear shaft adjusted too tight.	3. Adjust according to instructions.
	4. Improper caster or toe-in.	4. Align the wheels.
	5. Steering column misaligned.	5. See "Steering Gear Alignment."
	6. Loose, worn or broken pump belt.	6. Adjust or replace belt.
	7. Air in system.	7. Bleed air from system.
	8. Low fluid level in the pump reservoir.	8. Fill to correct level.
	9. Pump output pressure low.	9. See "Pressure Test."
	10. Leakage at power cylinder piston rings. (Linkage type).	10. Replace piston rings and repair as required.
	11. Binding or bent cylinder linkage. (Linkage type).	11. Replace or repair as required.
	12. Valve spool and/or sleeve sticking. (Linkage type).	12. Free-up or replace as required.
Intermittent or no power assist	1. Belt slipping and/or low fluid level.	1. Adjust or replace belt. Add fluid as necessary.
	2. Piston or rod binding in power cylinder. (Linkage type).	2. Repair or replace piston and rod.
	3. Sliding sleeve stuck in control valve. (Linkage type).	3. Free-up or replace sleeve.
Poor or no recovery from turns	1. Improper caster setting.	1. Adjust to specifications.
	2. Steering gear adjustments too tight.	2. Adjust according to instructions.
	3. Improper spool nut adjustment. (Linkage type).	3. Adjust according to instructions.
	4. Valve spool installed backwards. (Linkage type).	4. Install valve spool correctly.
	5. Low tire pressure.	5. Inflate tires to recommended pressure.
	6. Tight steering linkage.	6. Lubricate as necessary.
	7. King pins frozen.	7. Lubricate as necessary.

STEERING TROUBLE DIAGNOSIS
Power Steering

Condition	Possible Cause	Correction
Lack of effort (both turns)	1. Improper sector shaft adjustment. 2. Pressure plates on wrong side of reactions rings.	1. Adjust Sector Shaft. 2. Gear Recondition.
Lack of effort (left turn only)	1. Left turn reaction seal "O" ring worn, damaged or missing. 2. Left turn reaction oil passageway not drilled in housing or cylinder head. 3. Left turn reaction ring sticking in cylinder head.	1. Gear Recondition. 2. Replace parts as required. 3. Replace parts as required.
Lack of effort (right turn only)	1. Right turn U-shaped reaction seal worn, damaged, or missing. 2. Right turn reaction oil passageway not drilled in housing head, or ferrule pin. 3. Right turn reaction ring sticking in housing head.	1. Gear Recondition. 2. Replace parts as required. 3. Replace parts as required.
Lack of assist (left turn only)	1. Left turn reaction seal "O" ring worn, damaged, or missing.	1. Gear Recondition.
Lack of assist (right turn only)	1. Right turn U-shaped reaction seal worn, damaged, or missing. 2. Worn sealing ring (teflon) worn sleeve seal, ferrule pin "O" ring damaged or worn. 3. Excessive internal leakage thru piston end plug and/or side plugs.	1. Gear Recondition. 2. Gear Recondition. 3. Replace worn-piston assembly.
Lack of assist (both turns)	1. Low oil level in pump reservoir (usually accompanied by pump noise). 2. Loose pump belt. 3. Pump output low. 4. Engine idle too low. 5. Excessive internal leakage thru piston end plug and/or side plugs.	1. Fill to proper level. 2. Adjust belts. 3. Pressure test pump. 4. Adjust engine idle. 5. Replace worn-piston assembly.

CHRYSLER CORPORATION

Recirculating Ball Type

Disassembly and Assembly

1. Drain the gear assembly. Remove the cover retainer ring from the housing.

2. Rotate the ring until one end is near the hole in the side of the housing, then pry it out.

3. Remove the end cover from the housing by turning the stub shaft counterclockwise.

NOTE: Do not turn the stub shaft further than necessary to remove the end plug. The balls from the rack piston will fall and lay loose inside the rack piston chamber.

4. Remove the rack piston end plug.

5. Loosen the sector screw adjusting locknut. Remove the 4 side cover mounting bolts.

6. Turn the side cover until the rack piston and the sector teeth are visible, then turn the stub shaft until the sector is centered in the housing opening.

7. Remove the side cover and the sector shaft from the housing. Tap the end of the sector shaft with a soft hammer to remove.

NOTE: Do not disassemble the sector shaft, it is serviced and replaced as a unit only.

8. Insert a special tool into the rack of the piston bore with the pilot of the tool seated in the end of the worm.

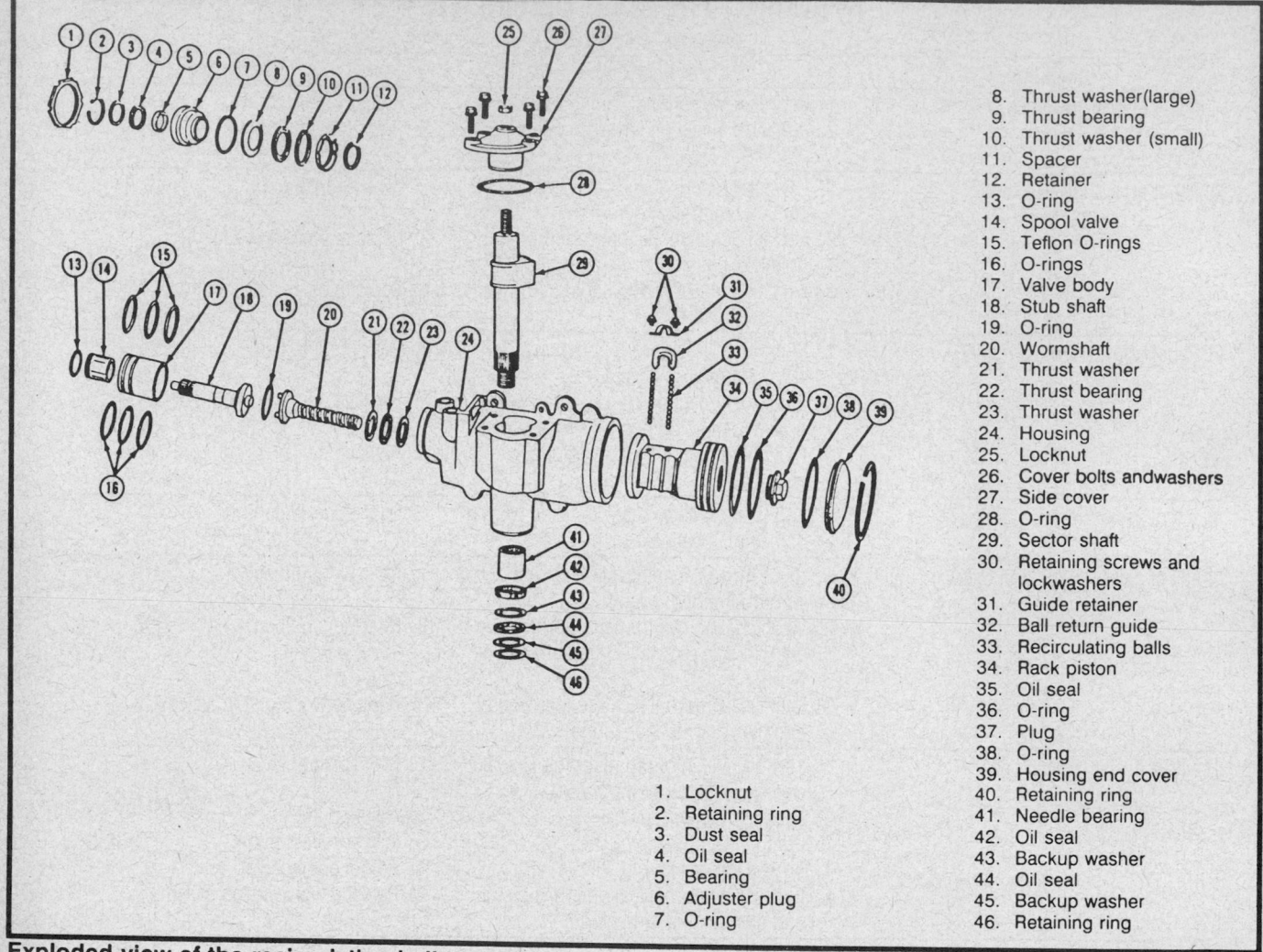

8. Thrust washer(large)
9. Thrust bearing
10. Thrust washer (small)
11. Spacer
12. Retainer
13. O-ring
14. Spool valve
15. Teflon O-rings
16. O-rings
17. Valve body
18. Stub shaft
19. O-ring
20. Wormshaft
21. Thrust washer
22. Thrust bearing
23. Thrust washer
24. Housing
25. Locknut
26. Cover bolts andwashers
27. Side cover
28. O-ring
29. Sector shaft
30. Retaining screws and lockwashers
31. Guide retainer
32. Ball return guide
33. Recirculating balls
34. Rack piston
35. Oil seal
36. O-ring
37. Plug
38. O-ring
39. Housing end cover
40. Retaining ring
41. Needle bearing
42. Oil seal
43. Backup washer
44. Oil seal
45. Backup washer
46. Retaining ring

1. Locknut
2. Retaining ring
3. Dust seal
4. Oil seal
5. Bearing
6. Adjuster plug
7. O-ring

Exploded view of the recirculating ball type steering gear

9. Turn the stub shaft counterclockwise forcing the rack piston onto the tool.

10. Remove the rack piston from the housing, keeping the ball retainer tool in place to hold the balls in position.

11. Remove the adjuster plug locknut. Remove the adjuster plug assembly, using a spanner wrench.

12. Remove the complete valve assembly from the housing by pulling outward on the splined end of the stub shaft.

13. Remove the wormshaft lower thrust bearing and the conical bearing races from the wormshaft. Note the position of each race for reinstallation.

14. Remove the dust seal from the rear of the housing and discard the seal.

15. Remove the snapring from the valve housing.

16. Turn the fixture to place the valve housing in an inverted position.

17. Insert the special tool in the valve body assembly opposite the seal end and gently tap the bearing and the seal out of the housing.

NOTE: Do not damage the housing when installing or removing the tools.

18. Remove the fluid inlet and outlet seats with the proper tool, if damaged.

19. Coat the inlet and the outlet seats with petroleum jelly or the equivalant.

20. Install the bearing with the metal side covering the rollers, facing outward.

21. Seat the bearing in the valve housing using the proper tool. Be sure that the bearing rotates freely.

22. Dip the new seal in gear lubricant (SAE 80W), then place it in the housing with the metal side of the seal facing outward.

23. Drive the seal into the housing until the outer edge of the seal does not quite clear the snapring groove.

24. Place the snapring in the housing and drive on the ring using the proper tool until the snapring seats in the groove.

25. Place the dust seal in the housing with the dished side (rubber side) facing out. Drive the dust seal into place.

26. The seal must be located behind the undercut in the input shaft when it is installed.

27. Pack the area between the 2 seals with muti-purpose grease.

28. Install the wormshaft conical bearing races and the lower thrust bearing in the same sequence that they were removed.

29. Both of the conical races must be installed so that the top of each cone faces the bottom of the gear housing.

30. Install the stub shaft seal so that it is seated against the inner edge of the stub shaft cap.

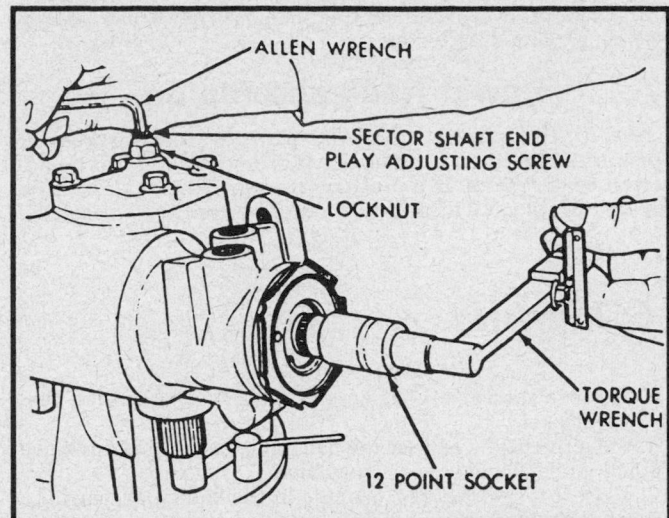

Sector shaft over center adjustment—Chrysler gear assembly

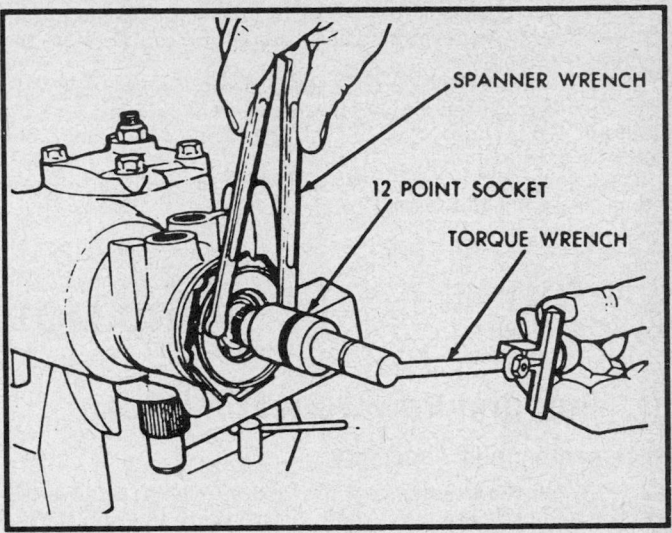

Thrust bearing preload adjustment—Chrysler gear assembly

NOTE: Do not press against the stub shaft to seat the valve body. This could cause the stub shaft and the cap to separate from the valve body and allow the spool valve dampener O-ring to slip into the valve body fluid grooves. Seat the valve body only by pushing on the outer diameter of the valve body with your fingertips. Make sure that the teflon rings do not bind inside the housing. the valve body is properly seated when all or most of the fluid return hole in the steering gear housing is visible.

31. Align the narrow slot in the valve body with the locating pin in the wormshaft and insert the valve body into the steering gear housing.
32. Install a seal protector tool over the end of the stub shaft and place the adjustment cap over the end of the stub shaft.
33. Tighten the adjustment cap, using a spanner wrench, until it seats against the valve body. Tighten to 20 ft. lbs.
34. Remove the seal protector after installing the adjustment cap.
35. Install the rack piston into the steering gear housing until the wormshaft engages with the valve body and the stub shaft.
36. Rotate the stub shaft clockwise to force the rack piston into the steering housing. Do not remove the arbor tool until the valve body piston ring has entered the housing bore.
37. Rotate the stub shaft until the rack piston center groove is aligned with the center of the sector shaft bearing bore.
38. Lubricate the sector shaft adjustment screw cover gasket and place it on the cover. Make sure that the rubber seal in the gasket is properly seated in the cover groove.
39. Place the cover over the sector shaft and thread the cover onto the adjustment screw until it makes contact with the sector shaft.
40. Install the sector shaft and with the adjustment screw cover gasket properly in place, install the cover to the steering gear housing.
41. Tighten the bolts to 45 ft. lbs.
42. Thread the adjustment screw locknut halfway on the adjustment screw and install the end plug in the rack piston. Tighten the plug to 50 ft. lbs.
43. Lubricate the steering gear housing end plug O-ring seal with power steering fluid and place it on the end plug.
44. Install and seat the end plug in the steering housing.
45. Install the end plug retaining ring with the ring end gap not aligned with the hole inside the steering gear housing. Tap the plug lightly to make sure that the ring is seated properly.

46. Adjust the wormshaft bearing preload torque and the sector shaft over center drag torque to specifications.

Adjustments

WORM THRUST BEARING

1. Remove the adjuster plug locknut and turn the adjuster plug clockwise until the thrust bearing is firmly seated, approximately 20 ft. lbs. torque.
2. Mark the housing even with one of the adjuster plugs. Measure back counterclockwise $3/16$–$1/4$ in. and mark the housing.
3. Rotate the adjuster counterclockwise until the hole in the adjuster is in line with the second mark.
4. Tighten the locknut securely and hold the adjuster plug to maintain the alignment of the hole with the mark.
5. Using a torque wrench, rotate the stub shaft clockwise to the stop then conterclockwise $1/4$ of a turn.
6. Measure the torque, the reading should be with the the torque wrench at or near the vertical position. The reading should be within 4–6 inch lbs.
7. If reading is not within specifications, loose the sector shaft preload adjustment screw locknut and turn the preload adjustment screw counterclockwise $1\frac{1}{2}$ turns.
8. Retighten the locknut, loosen (do not remove) the adjuster plug locknut.
9. Loosen the adjuster plug 1 turn counterclockwise and turn the stub shaft to the right stop and then back $1/4$ turn.
10. Measure the drag torque. Bottom the adjuster plug firmly (20 ft. lbs.) by turning it clockwise.
11. Then back it off until the total torque reading is 3–4 in lbs. in excess of the drag torgue.
12. Tighten the adjuster plug locknut securely.

NOTE: The preload torque tends to drop off when the locknut is tightened. The torque reading must be rechecked with the locknut tight. It is not possible to adjust the thrust bearing preload properly unless the adjuster plug is firmly bottomed out and the torque set while the adjuster plug is being loosened. Never attempt to adjust the thrust preload while tightening or advancing the adjuster plug into the gear assembly.

SECTOR SHAFT OVER CENTER

1. With the gear on center, loosen the locknut and tighten the sector shaft lash adjusting screw. Retighten the locknut.

2. Measure the gear over center torque, rotating the torque wrench in a 90 degree arc on each side of the center. Note the highest reading.

3. The locknut must be tight when taking this reading.

4. The over center torque of a new gear should show an increase of 4–8 inch lbs. over the thrust bearing adjustment, but not exceed 18 inch lbs.

5. The over center torque of a used gear should be a 4–5 inch lbs. increase but not exceed 14 inch lbs. total.

6. The total over center torque includes the thrust bearing, over center and drag torque.

Power Rack and Pinion

NOTE: The power rack and pinion steering gear is permanently lubricated at the factory and cannot be adjusted or serviced. If a malfunction or fluid leak occurs, the complete rack and pinion must be replaced as a unit.

FORD MOTOR COMPANY

Integral Power Steering Gear

Disassembly and Assembly

1. Position the steering gear over a drain pan in an inverted position and cycle the input shaft several times to drain the remaining fluid from the gear assembly.

2. Secure the gear in a proper holding fixture.

3. Remove the nut from the sector shaft adjusting screw.

4. Rotate the input shaft to either stop, then turn the shaft back 2 turns to the center of the gear.

NOTE: The indexing flat portion on the input shaft spline should be facing downward.

5. Remove the sector shaft cover mounting bolts.

6. Tap the lower end of the sector shaft with a soft hammer to loosen it. Remove the cover and the shaft from the housing as an assembly.

7. Remove the valve housing mounting bolts and lift the valve housing off the steering gear housing.

8. Remove the valve housing and control valve gasket. Discard the gasket.

9. Hold the piston so that the ball guide faces up and remove the ball guide clamp screws and clamp.

10. Place a finger over the opening in the ball guide, turn the piston so that the ball guide faces down. Let the guide tubes fall, using a suitable container.

11. Rotate the input shaft from stop to stop until all the balls fall from the piston.

12. Remove the valve assembly from the piston.

13. Inspect the piston bore to insure that all the balls have been removed.

14. Position the valve body in a proper holding fixture and loosen the Allen head race nut screw from the valve housing.

15. Remove the worm bearing race nut.

16. Carefully slide the input shaft, worm and valve assembly out of the valve housing.

17. Remove the dust seal from the rear of the housing and discard the seal.

18. Remove the snapring from the valve housing.

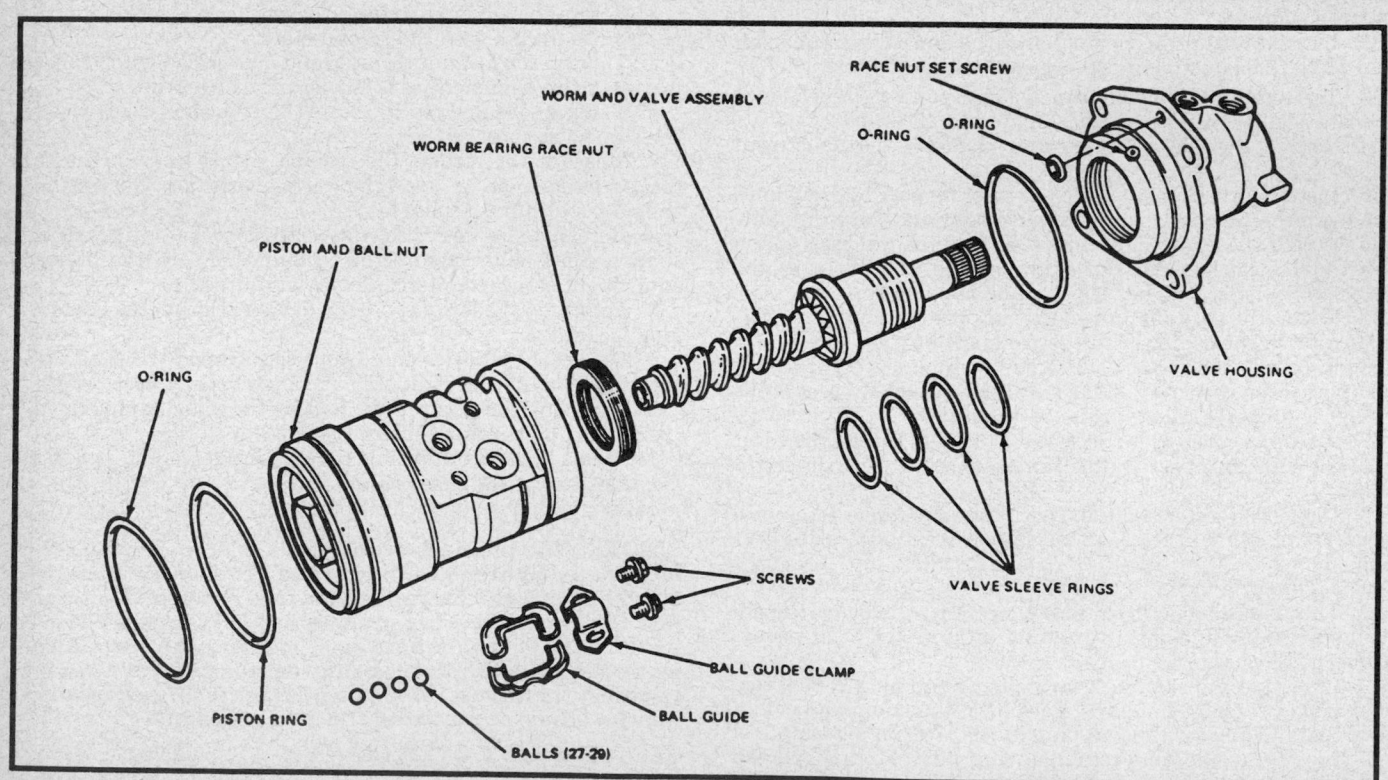

Exploded view of the Ford integral power steering gear

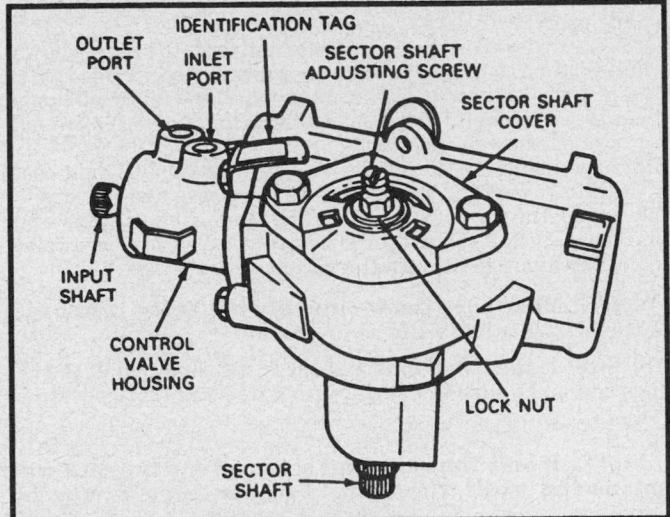

Ford integral power steering gear

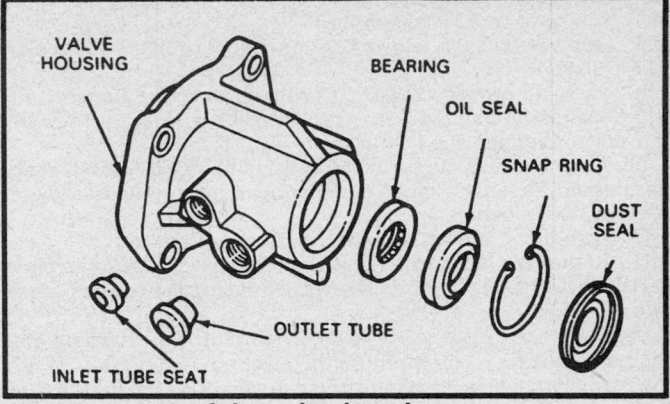

Exploded view of the valve housing

19. Turn the fixture to place the valve housing in an inverted position.

20. Insert the special tool in the valve body assembly opposite the seal end and gently tap the bearing and the seal out of the housing.

NOTE: Do not damage the housing when installing or removing the tools.

21. Remove the fluid inlet and outlet seats with the proper tool, if damaged.

22. Coat the inlet and the outlet seats with petroleum jelly or the equivalant.

23. Install the bearing with the metal side covering the rollers, facing outward.

24. Seat the bearing in the valve housing using the proper tool. Be sure that the bearing rotates freely.

25. Dip the new seal in gear lubricant (SAE 80W), then place it in the housing with the metal side of the seal facing outward.

To assemble:

26. Place the valve housing in a proper holding fixture, with the flanged end up.

27. Apply a light coat of gear lubricant (SAE 80W) or equivalent to the teflon rings on the valve sleeve.

28. Carefully, install the worm shaft and valve into the housing.

29. Install the worm bearing race nut in the housing and tighten to 55–90 ft. lbs.

30. Install the Allen head race nut set screw through the valve housing and tighten to 15–25 inch lbs.

31. Place the power cylinder piston in a proper holding fixture with the ball guide holes facing up.

32. Insert the worm shaft into position so that the first groove is in line with the hole nearest the center of the piston.

33. Install the ball guides in the piston.

34. Turn the worm shaft counterclockwise and place the same amount of balls that were removed into the ball guide. A minimum of 27 balls are required.

35. Rotate the input shaft from one stop to the other to ensure the proper input of balls into the guide.

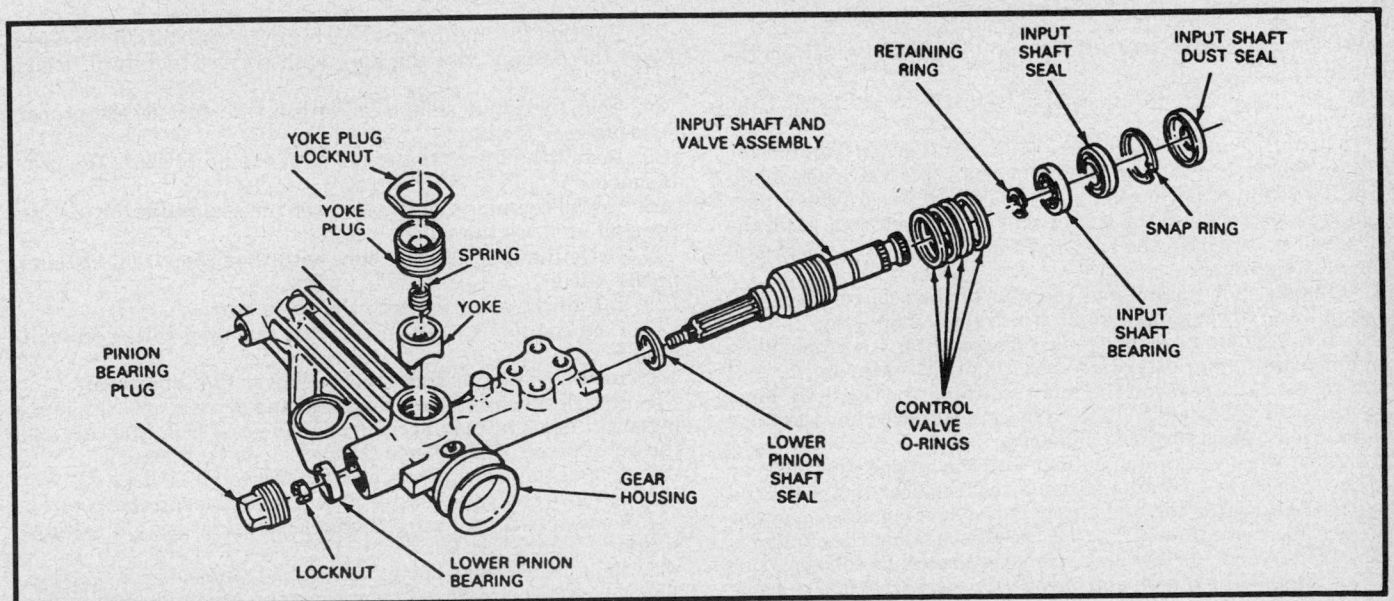

Exploded view of the input shaft and valve assembly—Aerostar

36. Secure the guides in the ball nut with the clamp and tighten the screws to 42–70 inch lbs.

37. Apply petroleum jelly or the equivalent to the teflon seal on the piston.

38. Place a new control valve O-ring on the valve housing and slide the piston and the valve into the gear housing, being careful not to damage the piston ring.

39. Align the oil passage in the valve housing with the passage in the gear housing. Place a new O-ring onto the oil passage hole of the gear housing.

40. Install the mounting bolts, do not tighten.

41. Rotate the ball nut so that the teeth are in the same plane as the sector teeth. Tighten the valve housing mounting bolts to 30–45 ft. lbs.

42. Place the sector shaft cover O-ring into the steering gear housing and turn the input shaft to center the piston.

43. Apply petroleum jelly or the equivalent to the sector shaft journal and place the sector shaft and the cover assembly in the gear housing.

44. Install the sector shaft cover mounting bolts and tighten to 55–70 ft. lbs.

45. Place a torque wrench on the input shaft and adjust the mesh load to
the proper specifications.

Integral Power Rack and Pinion

Disassembly and Assembly

1. Remove the tie rod socket assemblies from both ends of the rack. Remove the input shaft and valve assembly from the gear housing. Thoroughly clean the input shaft valve housing, yoke locknut and plug and the pinion bearing plug.

2. Position the assembly in a suitable holding fixture.

3. Do not remove the external pressure lines (right and left turn lines) unless they are leaking or damaged. If the lines are removed new teflon seals must be installed.

4. Using the proper tool, loosen the yoke plug locknut and the yoke plug to relieve pressure on the rack.

5. Remove the pinion bearing plug.

6. Install the proper tool on the input shaft. Hold the input shaft and remove the pinion bearing locknut.

NOTE: Do not allow the rack to reach full travel when loosening or tightening the locknut.

7. Using a suitable tool, pry the input shaft dust seal from the housing.

8. Remove the snapring, located beneath the dust seal, from the valve housing.

9. Install a valve body puller on the input shaft. Tighten the nut on the tool to remove the input shaft and valve assembly.

10. To remove the lower pinion shaft seal, insert the proper seal remover tool and the spacer tool until it bottoms. Hold the large nut and tighten the small nut on the tool until the expander fully tightens.

11. Install slide hammer in the rear of the seal remover tool and pull the lower pinion shaft seal from the housing.

12. If the pinion bearing needs replacement use a proper slide hammer and puller attachment to remove the bearing.

13. The 4 valve seals on the input shaft may be removed, however it is not necessary to replace these seals each time the valve is removed unless they are damaged.

14. Coat the lower pinion oil seal with the proper steering gear grease. Place the seal on a suitable seal replacer tool, with the seal facing towards the tool. Support the housing on a clean flat surface and drive the seal until it is seated against the shoulder.

15. If the valve O-rings were removed install as follows:

   a. Mount the pinion end of the valve assembly in a suitable holding device.

   b. Lubricate the proper tool with Type F automatic transmission fluid. Install the proper tool over the valve assembly. Slide one valve sleeve O-ring over the tool.

   c. Push down on the ring pusher and force the O-ring down into the fourth groove of the valve sleeve. Repeat this step 3 more times and each time add one more spacer. By adding a spacer each time, the special tool will line up with the next groove on the valve sleeve.

16. After installing the 4 valve seal O-rings, apply a light coat of the proper steering gear grease to the sleeve and O-rings.

17. Install the correct spacer over the input shaft to act as a pilot. Slowly, install the proper sizing tube over the sleeve valve end of the input shaft onto the valve sleeve O-rings.

NOTE: Make sure the O-rings are not being bent over as the sizing tube is slid over them.

18. Remove the sizing tube and check the condition of the O-rings and make sure the O-rings turn freely in the grooves.

NOTE: If only the valve was serviced and the rack was not moved while the valve was out, Step 6 may be omitted.

19. Position the rack in the housing so the right end of the rack protrudes 14mm ($^9/_{16}$ in.) from the socket to the housing.

20. Insert the propert tool into the top of the valve bore. Line up the D-flat on the input shaft 180degree(s) from the yoke plug hole center and insert the valve assembly into the bore. The D-flat must point straight to the rear when the gear is installed in the vehicle with the gear in the 'on center' (straight ahead) position. If necessary rotate the input shaft slightly from side to side to mesh the pinion to the rack teeth. Push the valve assembly in by hand until seated properly.

21. Insert the proper tool on the input shaft. Check if the pinion is centered by rotating the input shaft and counting the number of turns from center to each stop. If the number of turns is unequal, pull the valve assembly out far enough to free the pinion teeth. Rotate the input shaft 60 degree(s) (one tooth) in the direction that requires the least turns. Reinsert the valve assembly and check if the pinion is centered. Repeat if necessary.

22. Install the nut on the pinion end of the valve assembly. Hold the input shaft with the correct tool and tighten the nut to 30–40 ft. lbs. The rack must be away from the stops during this operation.

23. Position the input shaft bearing over the shaft in the bore. Drive the bearing into the bore with correct tool until firmly seated.

24. Coat the input shaft seal with a thin coat of the proper steering gear grease.

25. Install the input shaft seal with the lip towards the gear housing.

26. Install the input shaft seal over the seal protector tool, so the seal lip faces the valve.

27. Drive the seal into the bore with the proper seal installer until seated.

28. Install the snapring into the valve bore.

29. Coat the input shaft in the dust seal area with a suitable grease.

30. Install the input shaft seal tool over the input shaft.

31. Install the input shaft dust seal and drive into position using a suitable seal installer. Remove the tool from the seal and the input shaft. This allows trapped air to be released.

32. Install the bearing cap and tighten to 50 ft. lbs.

33. Remove the yoke plug locknut using the suitable tool

34 Remove the yoke plug from the housing using a suitable socket.

35. Remove the yoke spring and yoke from the gear housing. The yoke may be removed by gripping on the guide post with a pair of pliers.

36. From the right end of the gear (opposite the pinion), push

the rack into the housing far enough to gain access to the snapring.

37. Remove the snapring from the right end of the gear housing.

38. Using a hammer and a brass drift, slowly drive the rack out of the right side of the housing along with the bushing. Remove the rack from the housing.

39. To remove the high pressure rack oil seal, insert the correct tool into the housing until it bottoms.

40. Activate the expander with a wrench until the expander fully tightens against the oil seal.

41. Pull the seal from the housing, using the proper tool. Discard the seal.

NOTE: On the first attempt, the plastic insert may pull out of the seal, leaving the seal in the housing. Repeat the procedure until the seal is removed.

42. Remove the plastic O-ring and the rubber O-ring from the rack piston with a suitable tool.

43. To remove the rack bushing seal, grip the seal in a suitable holding fixture and squeeze the seal to distort it. Repeat this procedure if the bushing slips out of the holding device. With the seal distorted, it can easily removed using a suitable prying tool.

44. Mark the center tooth (the eleventh tooth) on the rack so the mark will be visible in the valve bore.

45. Slide the proper tool onto the rack until it seats on the piston. Install the rubber O-ring in the rack piston groove.

46. Slide the plastic (Teflon) O-ring over the tool into the piston groove over the rubber O-ring.

47. Remove the plastic insert from the rack seal. Save the insert for reinstallation.

48. Install the proper rack seal protector tool over the rack teeth.

49. Lubricate the rack and the protector tool with type F transmission fluid.

50. Install the seal so that the lip faces the piston. Push the seal all the way against the piston. Remove the rack seal protector tool.

51. Install the plastic insert in the rack seal.

52. Pack the rack teeth with steering gear grease and apply a light coat to the yoke contact area in back of the rack teeth.

53. Lubricate the piston seal and and rack seal outside diameter with type F transmission fluid.

54. Install the proper ring sizing tool into the end of the gear housing.

55. Carefully install the rack without scratching the housing piston bore.

56. Carefully push the piston through the sizing tool. Continue pushing on the rack until it bottoms. Remove the sizing tool.

57. Seat the rack seal with the rack by driving the end of the rack with a drift and plastic mallet.

NOTE: Do not remove the rack.

58. Install the left tie rod and ball socket on the rack and hand tighten.

59. Thread the proper sleeve protactor over the threads on the right side of the rack. Coat the protective sleeve with type F transmission fluid.

NOTE: The rack must not move too far from the center since excessive travel can cause the rack teeth to cut the left (inner) oil seal.

60. Apply steering grease to the outer rack oil seal, then install the high pressure oil seal in the rack bushing using the correct tool.

61. Lubricate the short protective sleeve on the rack end and the seal outside diameter on the rack bushing with steering grease.

62. Start the bushing on the rack with the seal facing forward. Pass the bushing and the seal over the protective sleeve and into the housing bore. Using the proper ring sizing tool, apply hand pressure to the rack bushing until the bushing seats in the gear housing. If hand pressure will not seat the bushing, use an 1⅛ in., 12 point socket or larger and a plastic mallet and tap the bushing in place.

63. Install the snapring in the right end of the gear housing.

64. Install the right tie rod assembly. Tighten both tie rod sockets at the same time to 55–65 ft. lbs. by holding one and turning the other.

65. Tap new coiled pins in the sockets until fully seated.

66. Fill the yoke plug hole with 2 ounces of steering gear grease or
the equivalent.

67. Install the yoke plug in the gear housing.

68. Install the yoke in the gear housing.

69. Install the yoke spring in the yoke.

70. Start the yoke plug and locknut in the gear housing.

71. Install the input shaft and valve assembly.

72. Adjust the rack plug preload.

73. Apply lubricant to the undercut in the tie rods where the bellows clamp to the tie rods. This is required to keep the bellows from twisting during toe-in adjustment.

74. Install the bellows and breather tube. Install new clamps retaining the bellows to the gear housing.

75. Install the clamps retaining the bellows to the tie rods.

76. Install the jam nuts to the tie rod ends on the rods.

Adjustment
RACK YOKE PLUG PRELOAD

1. Attach the gear to a proper holding device.

2. Do not remove the external pressure lines unless neccessary.

3. Drain the power steering fluid by rotating the input shaft lock-to-lock twice using the proper tool. Cover the ports with a shop towel while draining.

4. Insert an inch lb. torque wrench with a maximum capacity of 30–60 ft. lbs. into the tool, then position the adapter tool and torque wrench on the input shaft splines.

5. Loosen the yoke plug locknut, using the proper tool

6. Loosen the yoke plug with an appropriate socket.

7. Rotate the input shaft so the rack is in the center of travel by counting the number of complete revolutions of the input shaft and dividing by two.

8. Tighten the yoke plug to 45–50 inch lbs.

NOTE: Clean the threads of the yoke plug prior to tightening to prevent a false reading.

9. Back off the yoke plug approximately ⅛ turn (44 degrees minimum to 54 degrees maximum) until the torque required to initiate and sustain rotation of the input shaft is 7–18 inch lbs.

10. Install the proper tool to hold the yoke plug locknut. While holding the yoke plug, tighten the locknut 44–66 ft. lbs.

NOTE: Do not allow the yoke plug to move while tightening or the preload will be affected.

11. Recheck the input shaft torque after tightening the locknut.

GENERAL MOTORS CORPORATION

Saginaw Integral Gear

Disassembly and Assembly

1. Place the gear assembly in a proper holding fixture.
2. Pry out the retaining ring from the groove in the gear housing.
3. Turn the stub shaft counterclockwise to force the housing end plug out of the cylinder.
4. Remove the seal and the rack piston end plug.
5. Remove the adjusting nut, bolt and the side cover bolts.
6. Turn the adjuster screw clockwise to separate the side cover from the sector shaft. Remove the side cover and gasket.
7. Turn the stub shaft counterclockwise to disengage the sector shaft teeth from the rack piston. Remove the sector shaft.
8. Remove the retaining ring and the sector shaft bearing using the proper tool.
9. Remove the rack piston and balls from the bore in the gear housing.
10. Remove the adjuster plug locknut using the proper tool and remove the adjuster plug.
11. Remove the adjusting plug retaining ring and remove the seal and the bearing using the proper tool.
12. Remove the valve and the wormshaft as an assembly with both races and the bearings and separate the worm from the valve assembly.
13. Hold the valve assembly and lightly, tap the stub shaft until the shaft cap is free from the valve body.
14. Remove the shaft assembly from the spool by disengaging the shaft pin and remove the spool from the valve body by rotating it.
15. Remove the screws, clamp and ball guide from the rack piston. Remove the balls.
16. Clean and thoroughly inspect all the parts for any burrs, cracks or any other excessive wear.

To assemble:

16. Lubricate the 24 balls with power steering fluid. Install the balls, alternating by color into the ball guide.
17. Use petroleum jelly to hold the balls in the ball guide.
18. Install the ball guide to the rack piston.
19. Lubricate the stub shaft with power steering fluid and insert the stub shaft into the valve body.
20. Lubricate the valve spool and seals with power steering fluid and install into the valve body.
21. Install the O-ring in the valve body so that it is seated against the lower shaft cap and lubricate the valve body, rings and seals with power steering fluid.
22. Align the narrow notch in the valve body with the pin in the worm and install the unit into the gear housing, by exerting pressure on the valve body and not the stub shaft.
23. Install the wormshaft bearing races and bearing and insert the valve body
24. Install the seal on the adjuster plug and using the proper tool insert the needle bearing in the adjuster plug.
25. Install the seal, washer and the retaining ring in the adjuster plug.

NOTE: The retainer should not extend beyond the washer when the retainer ring is seated. The washer must be free to rotate.

26. Install the wormshaft and the valve assembly into the gear housing.
27. Install the adjuster plug into the gear housing, using the proper tool.
28. Adjust the thrust bearing preload by tightening the adjuster plug to 20 ft. lbs. to seat the thrust bearings.
29. With the ball retaining tool in position, lubricate and install the primary rack piston into the gear housing until the retaining tool bottoms against the center of the worm.

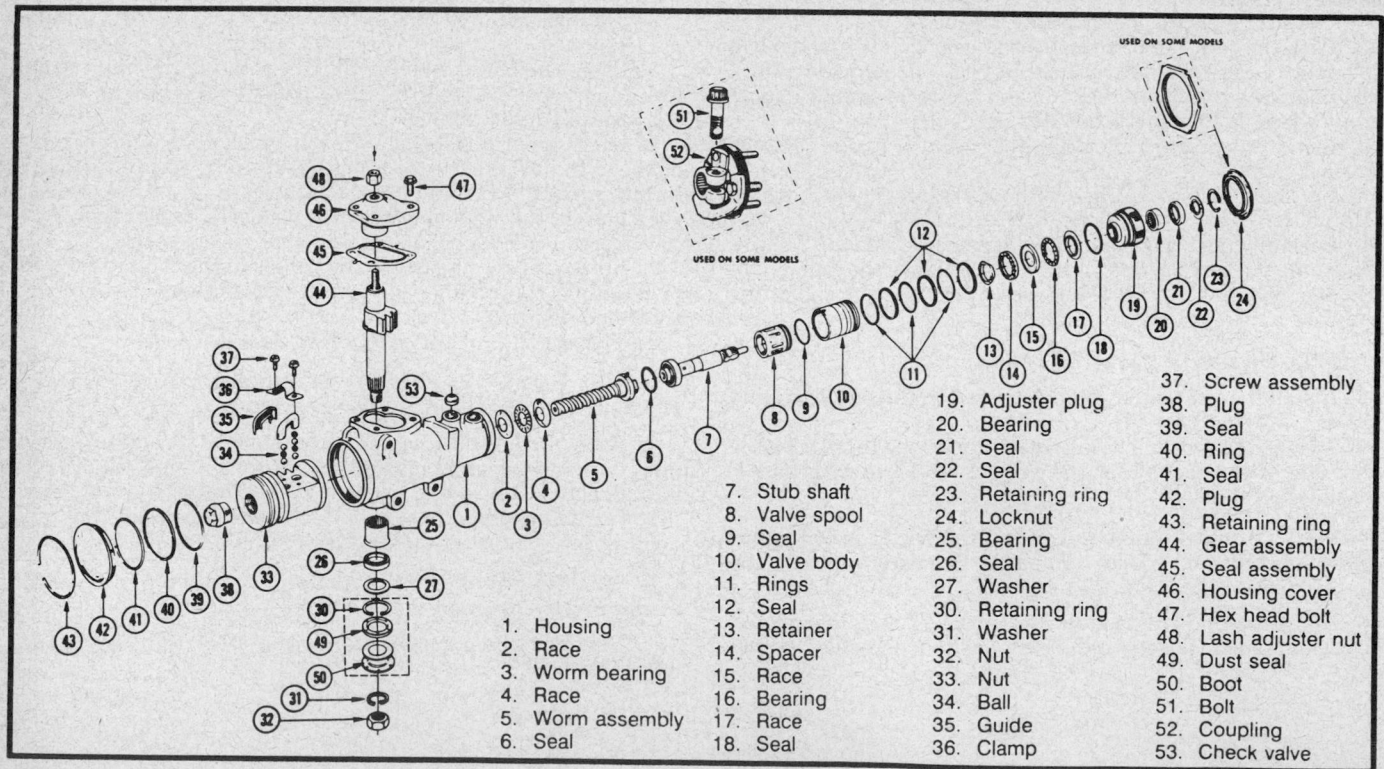

1. Housing
2. Race
3. Worm bearing
4. Race
5. Worm assembly
6. Seal
7. Stub shaft
8. Valve spool
9. Seal
10. Valve body
11. Rings
12. Seal
13. Retainer
14. Spacer
15. Race
16. Bearing
17. Race
18. Seal
19. Adjuster plug
20. Bearing
21. Seal
22. Seal
23. Retaining ring
24. Locknut
25. Bearing
26. Seal
27. Washer
30. Retaining ring
31. Washer
32. Nut
33. Nut
34. Ball
35. Guide
36. Clamp
37. Screw assembly
38. Plug
39. Seal
40. Ring
41. Seal
42. Plug
43. Retaining ring
44. Gear assembly
45. Seal assembly
46. Housing cover
47. Hex head bolt
48. Lash adjuster nut
49. Dust seal
50. Boot
51. Bolt
52. Coupling
53. Check valve

Exploded view of the Saginaw integral gear assembly — CK (GMT400)

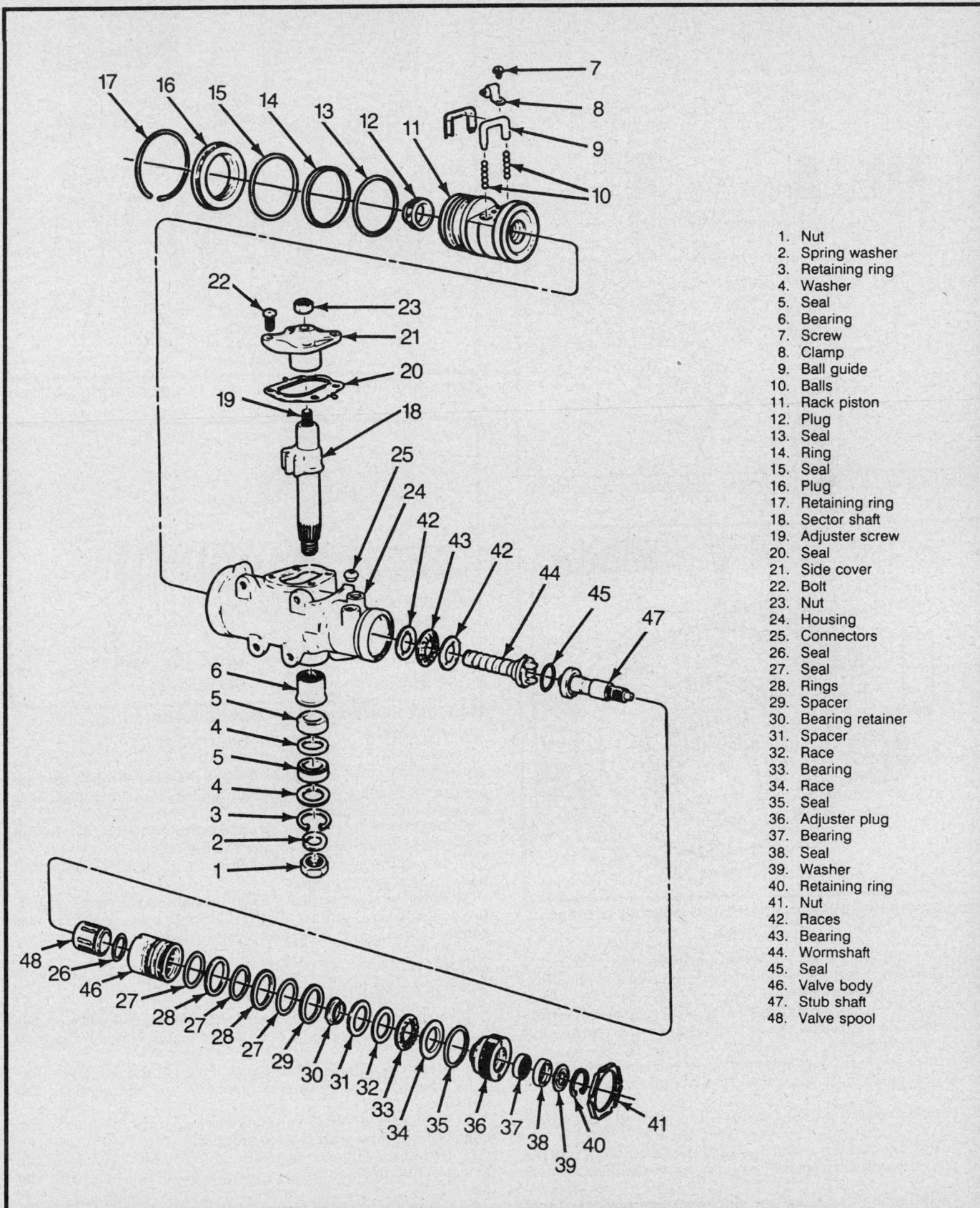

1. Nut
2. Spring washer
3. Retaining ring
4. Washer
5. Seal
6. Bearing
7. Screw
8. Clamp
9. Ball guide
10. Balls
11. Rack piston
12. Plug
13. Seal
14. Ring
15. Seal
16. Plug
17. Retaining ring
18. Sector shaft
19. Adjuster screw
20. Seal
21. Side cover
22. Bolt
23. Nut
24. Housing
25. Connectors
26. Seal
27. Seal
28. Rings
29. Spacer
30. Bearing retainer
31. Spacer
32. Race
33. Bearing
34. Race
35. Seal
36. Adjuster plug
37. Bearing
38. Seal
39. Washer
40. Retaining ring
41. Nut
42. Races
43. Bearing
44. Wormshaft
45. Seal
46. Valve body
47. Stub shaft
48. Valve spool

Exploded view of the Saginaw integral gear assembly – except CK (GMT400)

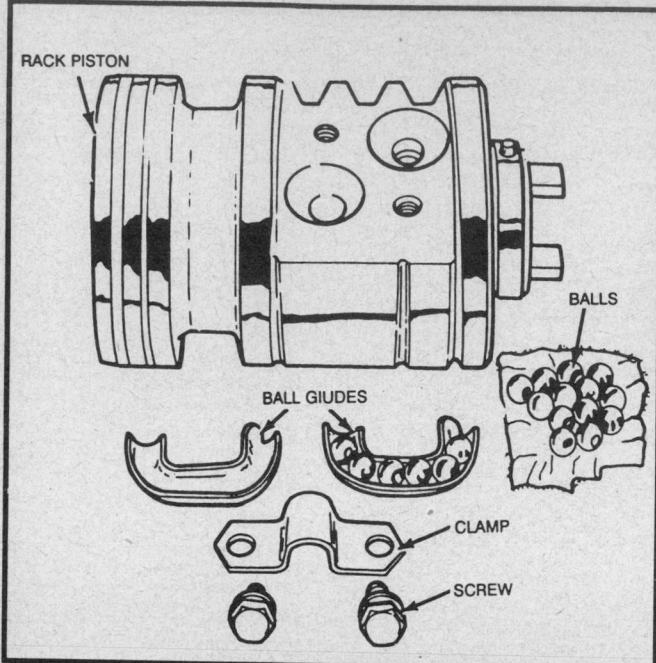

Exploded view of the Saginaw rack piston assembly

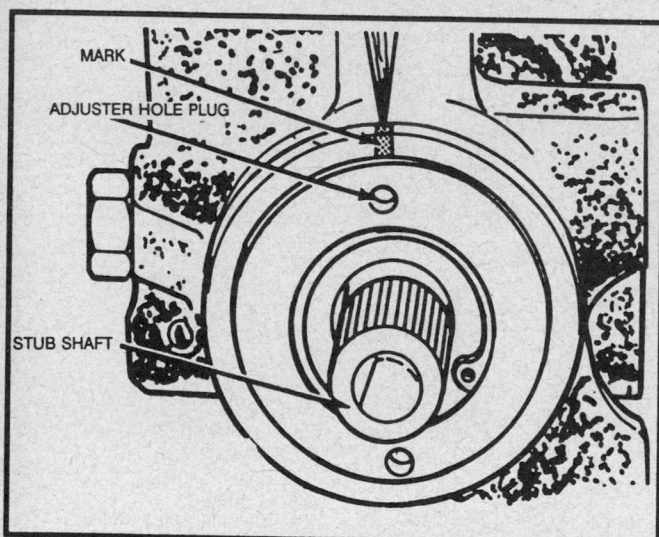

Marking the housing for the thrust bearing preload

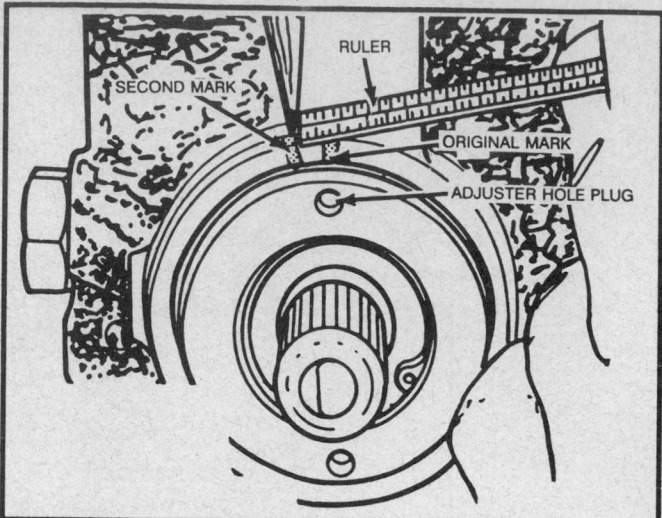

Remarking the housing for the thrust bearing preload

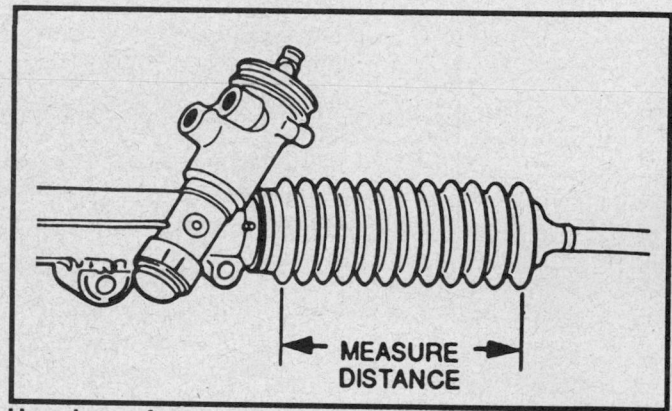

Housing reference mark and rack centering measurement

30. Turn the stub shaft clockwise to thread the rack piston onto the worm. Keep the retaining tool tight against the worm while turning the stub shaft.

31. Remove the ball retainer tool when the rack piston is completely threaded onto the worm. Center the rack teeth in the sector shaft opening.

32. Install the secondary rack piston in the gear housing and line up the center tooth space with the teeth of the primary rack piston.

33. Install the sector shaft bearing and seal, using the proper tool.

34. Install the retaining ring and slide the sector shaft into the gear housing with the tapered teeth engaging the primary rack piston.

35. Install a new O-ring on the side cover and push the cover into the housing until contact is made with the preload adjuster screw. With the aid of an Allen wrench inserted through the cover, turn the adjusting screw counterclockwise until the cover bottoms on the housing.

36. Install the side cover bolts and tighten to 40 ft. lbs. Install the rack piston plug and torque to 75 ft. lbs.

37. Install the primary and secondary end covers, O-rings, and install the retainer rings.

38. With the steering gear on center, tighten the sector adjusting screw. Install and tighten the locknut and check the over center torque.

Adjustments

THRUST BEARING PRELOAD

1 Turn the adjuster plug counterclockwise, using the proper tool, until the plug and the bearing are firmly seated—about 20 ft. lbs.

2. Mark the adjuster in line with a hole in the adjuster plug.

3. Measure back counterclockwise ½ in. and re-mark the housing.

4. Rotate the adjuster counterclockwise until the hole in the adjuster is in line with the second mark.

5. Install the adjuster nut and tighten to 80 ft. lbs. Hold the adjuster nut to maintain the alignment of the hole with the mark.

6. Check the turning torque of the stub shaft, using a suitable torque wrench. The reading should be taken with the beam

of the wrench near vertical while turning the wrench counterclockwise.

7. The reading should be 4–10 inch lbs. Lubricate the stub shaft area outside the dust seal with a suitable chassis lubricant.

SECTOR SHAFT OVER-CENTER PRELOAD

1. Center the steering gear by turning the stub shaft to the left then to the right counting the number of turns, using the proper tool.

2. Turn the shaft back ½ way to the center position.

3. Check the ball and bearing preload by turning the torque wrench through the center of travel. Note the highest reading.

4. Tighten the adjusting screw until the reading is 6–10 inch lbs. higher than the previous reading.

5. The total reading should not exceed 20 inch lbs. Tighten the adjusting nut to 20 ft. lbs.

Power Rack and Pinion

Disassembly and Assembly

1. Place the rack and pinion assembly in a suitable holding device.

2. Remove the adjuster plug locknut from the adjuster plug.

3. Remove the adjuster plug, spring and the rack bearing from the housing.

4. Remove the retaining ring from the valve bore of the housing.

5. Remove the dust cover from the bottom of the housing.

NOTE: The stub shaft must be held to prevent damage to the pinion teeth.

6. While holding the stub shaft, remove the hex locknut from the pinion and valve assembly.

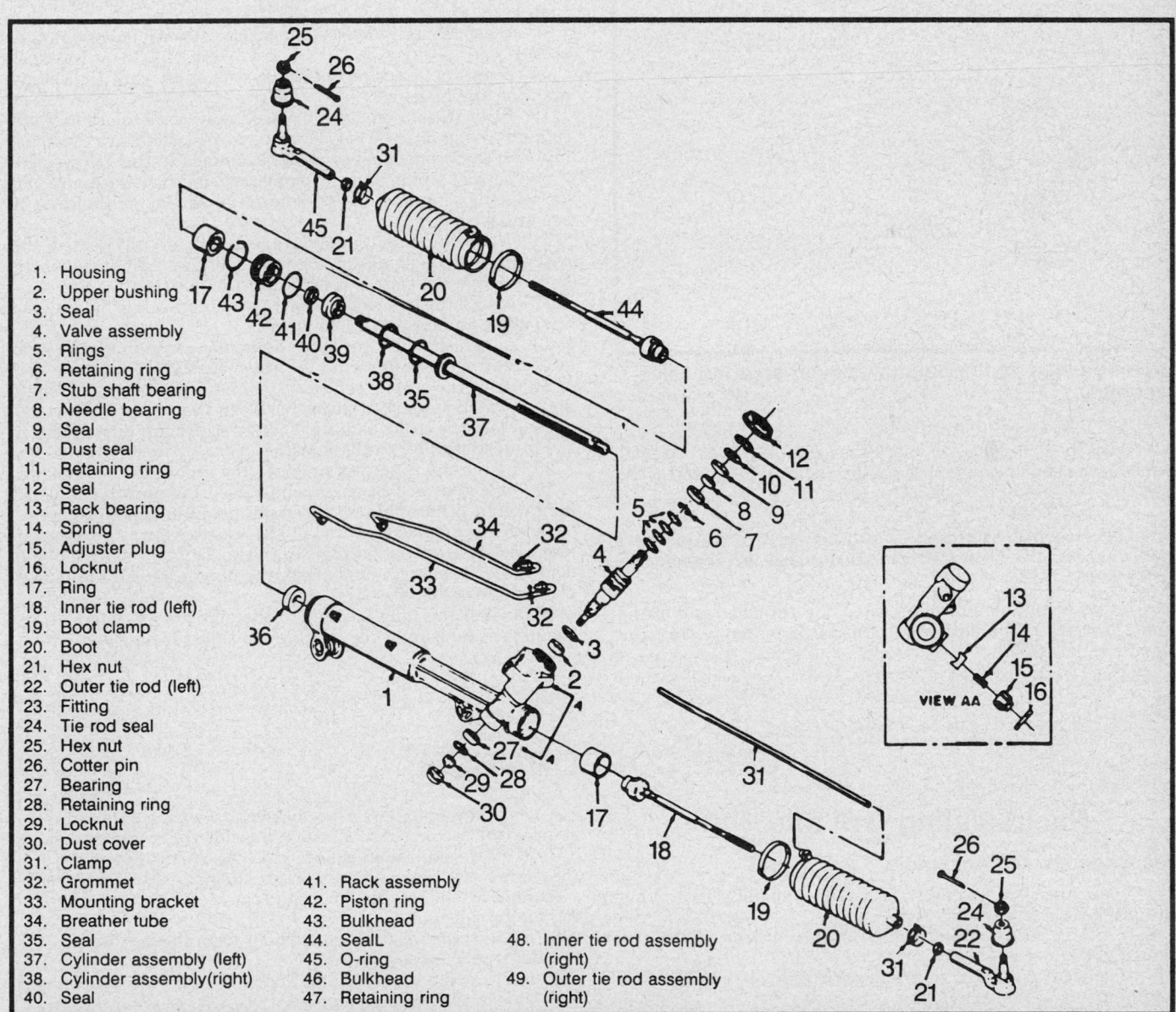

1. Housing
2. Upper bushing
3. Seal
4. Valve assembly
5. Rings
6. Retaining ring
7. Stub shaft bearing
8. Needle bearing
9. Seal
10. Dust seal
11. Retaining ring
12. Seal
13. Rack bearing
14. Spring
15. Adjuster plug
16. Locknut
17. Ring
18. Inner tie rod (left)
19. Boot clamp
20. Boot
21. Hex nut
22. Outer tie rod (left)
23. Fitting
24. Tie rod seal
25. Hex nut
26. Cotter pin
27. Bearing
28. Retaining ring
29. Locknut
30. Dust cover
31. Clamp
32. Grommet
33. Mounting bracket
34. Breather tube
35. Seal
37. Cylinder assembly (left)
38. Cylinder assembly (right)
40. Seal
41. Rack assembly
42. Piston ring
43. Bulkhead
44. SeaL
45. O-ring
46. Bulkhead
47. Retaining ring
48. Inner tie rod assembly (right)
49. Outer tie rod assembly (right)

VIEW AA

Exploded view of General Motors power rack and pinion assembly

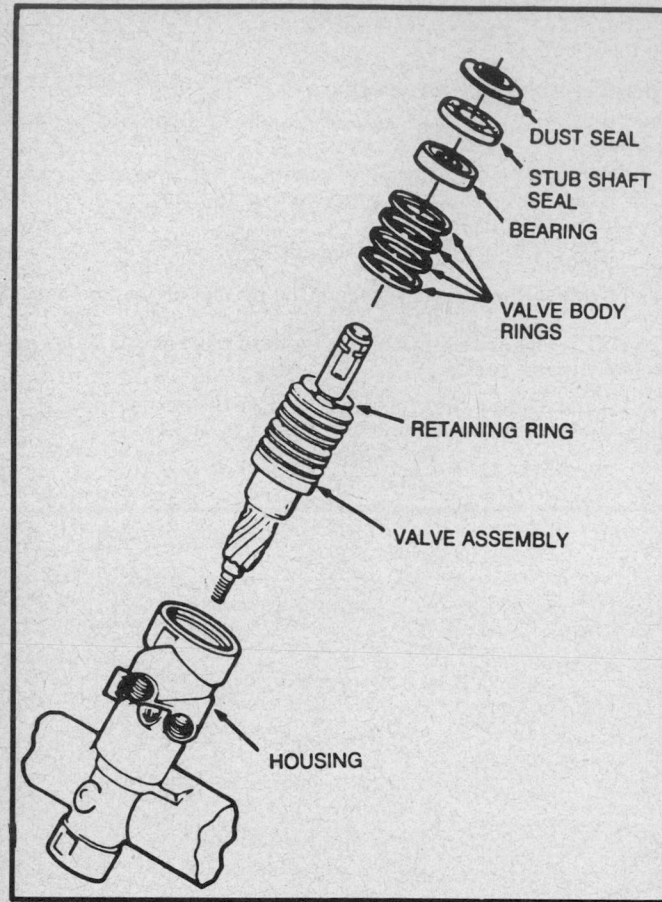

Exploded view of the Saginaw power steering valve assembly

housing. Just before the removal of the pinion and valve assembly, mark the second location of the stub shaft notch on the housing.

9. Remove the stub shaft dust seal, stub shaft seal, stub shaft bearing assembly and the pinion and valve assembly, with the retaining ring and the valve body rings attached.

10. Remove the valve body rings from the pinion and valve assembly.

11. Clean the valve assembly ring grooves. Inspect the pinion and valve assembly for a broken drive pin. If a broken pin is found, replace the gear assembly.

12. Apply grease to each ring groove and to the new valve body rings when installed to hold the rings in position.

13. Connect the new valve body rings to the pinion and the valve assembly.

14. Place the pinion and valve assembly into a clear protective device. This allows the valve rings to be properly sized.

15. Place the valve assembly in the protector so that the valve body is flush with the bottom of the protector.

16. Center the rack in the housing according to the marks that were taken.

17. Lubricate the valve housing bore with a liberal amount of grease.

18. Align the mark on the valve stub shaft with the second mark on the housing.

19. Place the pinion and valve assembly, with the spool shaft retaining rings and the valve body rings installed, into the housing. Use the proper tool to prevent damage to the valve ring.

20. Set the pinion and valve assembly onto the rack and pinion housing assembly using the proper tool. Do not hammer or use excessive force.

21. When the pinion and valve assembly is fully seated, the notch in the stub shaft and the first mark on the housing must line up while the rack is centered in the housing.

22. Install the hex locknut onto the pinion, while holding the stub shaft and tighten to 26 ft. lbs.

23. Install the dust cover to the housing and place the stub shaft bearing assembly onto the valve stub shaft.

24. Place the special protector tool onto the valve stub shaft apply a small amount of grease between the seals and the tool.

25. Place the stub shaft seal and the stub shaft dust seal over the protector and into the housing.

26. Install the retaining ring into the groove in the housing.

27. Coat the rack bearing, adjuster spring and the adjuster plug with a lithium base grease and install in the housing.

28. With the rack centered in the housing, turn the adjuster plug clockwise until it bottoms in the housing. Then back off 50 degree(s)–70 degree(s) and check the pinion. Maximum pinion preload is 18 inch lbs.

29. Install the plug locknut to the adjuster. Tighten firmly against the housing while holding the adjuster plug stationary.

7. With the rack centered, mark the location of the stub shaft notch on the housing and measure the distance to the end of the boot.

NOTE: Do not hammer or pound on the pinion and valve assembly. This will cause damage or loosen the drive pin.

8. Using a suitable press, press on the threaded end of the pinion to remove the pinion and the valve assembly from the

JEEP CORPORATION

Recirculating Ball and Nut

Disassembly and Assembly

1. Place the gear assembly in a proper holding fixture and drain the fluid from the gear.

2. Pry out the retaining ring from the groove in the gear housing.

3. Turn the stub shaft counterclockwise to force the housing end plug out of the cylinder.

4. Remove the seal and the rack piston end plug.

5. Remove the adjusting nut, bolt and the side cover bolts.

6. Turn the adjuster screw clockwise to separate the side cover from the sector shaft. Remove the side cover and gasket.

7. Turn the stub shaft counterclockwise to disengage the sector shaft teeth from the rack piston. Remove the sector shaft.

8. Remove the retaining ring and the sector shaft bearing using the proper tool.

9. Remove the rack piston and balls from the bore in the gear housing.

10. Remove the adjuster plug locknut using the proper tool and remove the adjuster plug.

11. Remove the adjusting plug retaining ring and remove the seal and the bearing using the proper tool.

12. Remove the valve and the wormshaft as an assembly with both races and the bearings attached and separate the worm from the valve assembly.

13. Hold the valve assembly and lightly, tap the stub shaft until the shaft cap is free from the valve body.

14. Remove the shaft assembly from the spool by disengaging the shaft pin and remove the spool from the valve body by rotating it.

15. Remove the screws, clamp and ball guide from the rack piston. Remove the balls.

16. Clean and thoroughly inspect all the parts for any burrs, cracks or any other excessive wear.

17. Lubricate the 24 balls with power steering fluid. Install the balls, alternating by color into the ball guide.

18. Use petroleum jelly to hold the balls in the ball guide.

19. Install the ball guide to the rack piston.

20. Lubricate the stub shaft with power steering fluid and insert the stub shaft into the valve body.

21. Lubricate the valve spool and seals with power steering fluid and install into the valve body.

22. Install the O-ring in the valve body so that it is seated against the lower shaft cap and lubricate the valve body, rings and seals with power steering fluid.

23. Align the narrow notch in the valve body with the pin in the worm and install the unit into the gear housing, by exerting pressure on the valve body and not the stub shaft.

24. Install the wormshaft bearing races and bearing and insert the valve body.

25. Install the seal on the adjuster plug and using the proper tool insert the needle bearing in the adjuster plug.

26. Install the seal, washer and the retaining ring in the adjuster plug.

NOTE: The retainer should not extend beyond the washer when the retainer ring is seated. The washer must be free to rotate.

27. Install the wormshaft and the valve assembly into the gear housing.

28. Install the adjuster plug into the gear housing, using the proper tool.

29. Adjust the thrust bearing preload by torquing the adjuster plug to 20 ft. lbs. to seat the thrust bearings.

30. With the ball retaining tool in position, lubricate and install the primary rack piston into the gear housing until the retaining tool bottoms against the center of the worm.

31. Turn the stub shaft clockwise to thread the rack piston onto the worm. Keep the retaining tool tight against the worm while turning the stub shaft.

32. Remove the ball retainer tool when the rack piston is completely threaded onto the worm. Center the rack teeth in the sector shaft opening.

33. Install the secondary rack piston in the gear housing and line up the center tooth space with the teeth of the primary rack piston.

34. Install the sector shaft bearing and seal, using the proper tool.

35. Install the retaining ring and slide the sector shaft into the gear housing with the tapered teeth engaging the primary rack piston.

36. Install a new O-ring on the side cover and push the cover into the housing until contact is made with the preload adjuster screw. With the aid of an Allen wrench inserted through the cover, turn the adjusting screw counterclockwise until the cover bottoms on the housing.

37. Install the side cover bolts and tighten to 45 ft. lbs. Install the rack piston plug and torque to 50 ft. lbs.

38. Install the primary and secondary end covers, O-rings and install the retainer rings.

39. With the steering gear on center, tighten the sector adjusting screw. Install and tighten the locknut and check the over center torque.

Adjustments
WORMSHAFT BEARING PRELOAD

1. Tighten the wormshaft bearing adjustment cap until it is seated in the gear housing.

2. Place an index mark on the gear housing opposite one of the holes in the adjuster plug. Measure back countrerclockwise from the index mark and remark the housing.

3. Turn the adjuster plug counterclockwise until hole in the adjuster plug is aligned with the second mark on the housing.

4. Install the adjuster plug locknut and tighten to 85 ft. lbs.

5. Turn the stub shaft clockwise to the stop, then turn it back ¼ turn. Record the torque reading.

6. The torque required to turn the stub shaft should be 4–10 inch lbs.

SECTOR SHAFT OVER CENTER DRAG TORQUE

1. Turn the sector shaft adjuster screw counterclockwise until fully extended, then turn back clockwise ½ turn.

2. Rotate the stub shaft from stop-to-stop and count the number of turns. Turn the stub shaft back ½ turn from either stop. This is the gear center.

NOTE: When the gear is centered, the flat potion of the stub shaft should face up and be parallel to the side cover.

3. Rotate the torque wrench 45 degree(s) on each side of center and measure the highest drag torque on or near the center.

4. Adjust the over center drag torque by turning the sector shaft adjusting screw clockwise until the desired reading is obtained.

   a. On new steering gears, add 4–8 lbs. to the previously measured worm bearing preload torque.

   b. On used gears, add 4–5 lbs. to the previously measured worm bearing preload torque.

5 Tighten the sector shaft adjusting screw locknut to 20 ft. lbs.

POWER STEERING PUMPS
STEERING TROUBLE DIAGNOSIS
Power Steering Pump

Condition	Possible Cause	Correction
Intermittent assist	1. Flow control valve sticking.	1. Pressure test pump and service as necessary.
	2. Slipping belt.	2. Adjust belt.
	3. Low fluid level.	3. Inspect and correct fluid level.
	4. Low pump efficiency.	4. Pressure test pump and service as necessary.

STEERING TROUBLE DIAGNOSIS
Power Steering Pump

Condition	Possible Cause	Correction
No assist	1. Pump seizure. 2. Broker slipper spring(s). 3. Flow control bore plug ring not in place. 4. Flow control valve sticking.	1. Replace pump. 2. Recondition pump or replace as necessary. 3. Replace snapring. Inspect groove for depth. 4. Pressure test pump and service as necessary.
No assist when parking only	1. Wrong pressure relief valve. 2. Broken "O" ring on flow control bore plug. 3. Loose pressure relief valve. 4. Low pump efficiency.	1. Install proper relief valve. 2. Replace "O" ring. 3. Tighten valve. 4. Pressure test pump and service as necessary.
Noisy pump	1. Low fluid level. 2. Belt noise. 3. Foreign material blocking pump housing oil inlet hole.	1. Inspect and correct fluid level. 2. Inspect for pulley alignment, paint or grease on pulley and correct. Adjust belt. 3. Remove reservoir, visually check inlet oil hole and service as necessary.
Pump vibration	1. Pump hose interference with sheet metal or brake lines. 2. Belt loose. 3. Pulley loose or out of round. 4. Crankshaft pulley loose or damaged. 5. Bracket pivot bolts loose.	1. Reroute hoses. 2. Adjust belt. 3. Replace pulley. 4. Replace crankshaft pulley. 5. If unable to tighten, replace bracket.
Pump leaks	1. Cap or filler neck leaks. 2. Reservoir solder joints leak. 3. Reservoir "O" ring leaking. 4. Shaft seal leaking. 5. Loose rear bracket bolts. 6. Loose or faulty high pressure ferrule. 7. Rear bolt holes stripped or casting cracked.	1. Correct fluid level. 2. Resolder or replace reservoir as necessary. 3. Inspect sealing area of reservoir. Replace "O" ring or reservoir as necessary. 4. Replace seal. 5. Tighten bolts. 6. Tighten fitting. 7. Repair, if possible, or replace pump.
Objectionable hiss	1. Noisy valve	1. Do not replace valve unless "hiss" is extremely objectionable. A replacement valve will also exhibit slight noise and is not always a cure for the objection.
Rattle or chuckle noise in steering gear	1. Gear loose on frame. 2. Steering linkages looseness. 3. Pressure hose touching other parts of truck. 4. Loose Pitman shaft over center adjustment. **NOTE:** A slight rattle may occur on turns because of increased clearance off the "high point". This is normal and clearance must not be reduced below specified limits to eliminate this slight rattle. 5. Loose Pitman arm.	1. Check gear mounting bolts. Torque bolts to specifications. 2. Check linkage pivot points for wear. Replace if necessary. 3. Adjust hose position. Do not bend tubing by hand. 4. Adjust. 5. Torque Pitman arm pinch bolt.

CHRYSLER CORPORATION

Vane Type Pump

Disassembly and Assembly

1. Secure pump securely in a suitable holding device.
2. Remove the pump pulley, using a proper puller.
3. Remove the mounting brackets from the pump.
4. Remove the 2 mounting studs and the pressure hose fittings. Gently tap the resevoir tube back and forth and remove the reservoir from the pump body.
5. Using a punch, tap the end cover retaining ring until one end of the ring is near the hole in the pump body. Insert the punch in the hole far enough to disengage the ring from the groove in the pump bore and remove the ring.
6. Tap the end cover with a plastic hammer to jar it loose and remove the cover.
7. Remove the pump body and place in a inverted position on a flat surface and tap the end of the driveshaft (with a plastic hammer) to loosen the pressure plate, rotor and thrust plate assembly from the pump body.
8. Lift the pump body from the rotor assembly. The flow control valve and spring should slide out of the bore.
   a. Remove the valve from the holding fixture and remove the pressure relief ball, guide and spring.
   b. Install the spring, guide and pressure relief ball in the end of the flow control valve.
   c. Install the flow valve spring and the valve in the bore.
9. Pry out the driveshaft oil seal. Clean and inspect the seal bore in the housing.
10. Disconnect the pressure plate and the cam ring from the rotor and remove the 10 vanes from the slots in the rotor.
11. Secure the driveshaft in a suitable holding fixture.
12. Remove the rotor lock ring and pry off the driveshaft.

13. Remove the rotor and the thrust plate from the shaft. Discard the lock ring, the reservoir O-rings, the 2 mounting stud and the pressure fitting O-rings.
14. Clean and inspect all the parts.
15. Install the new driveshaft seal into the bore until the seal bottoms on the shoulder, using the proper tool.
16. Lubricate the seal with power steering fluid and secure the pump body in a suitable fixture.
17. Install the end cover and pressure plate O-rings in the grooves of the pump cavity. Lubricate with power steering fluid.
18. Lubricate the large pump body to reservoir O-ring and install on the pump body.
19. With the driveshaft secure, install the thrust plate on the driveshaft with the ported side up.
20. Slide the rotor over the splines with the counterbore of the rotor facing down. Install the rotor lock ring making sure that the ring is seated in the groove.

NOTE: Regardless of which locking ring was originally used, always replace with a new ring.

21. Install 2 dowel pins in the holes in the pump cavity. Insert the driveshaft, rotor and thrust plate assembly into the pump cavity.
22. Slide the cam ring over the rotor on the dowel pins with the arrow on the ring facing UP.
23. Install the 10 vanes in the rotor slots and lubricate with power steering fluid.
24. Place the pressure plate on the dowel pins. Install the pressure plate assembly on the O-ring in the pump cavity with the proper tool.
25. Place the spring in the groove in the pressure plate and position the end cover lip edge up over the spring.

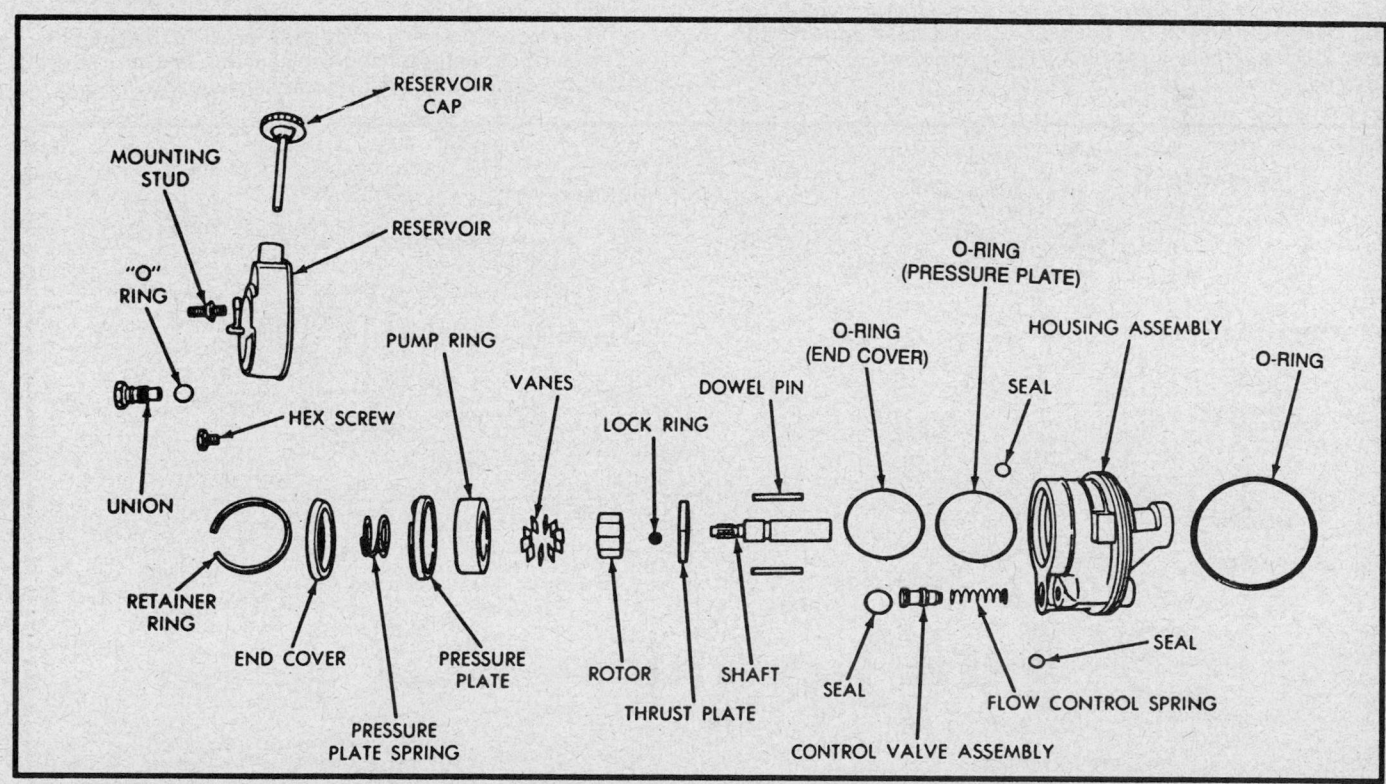

Exploded view of the vane type pump—Chrysler

26. Press the end cover down below the retaining ring groove and install the retaining ring. Make sure that it is seated in the groove.

27. Tap the retainer ring ends around in the groove until the gap is in line with the flow control valve bore.

28. Install the reservoir, the 2 mounting stud and the flow control valve O-ring on the pump body.

29. Lubricate with power steering fluid and position the reservoir on the pump body.

30 Tap the reservoir down on the pump and insert the flow control valve spring and the valve with the slotted end up.

31. Replace the O-ring on the pressure hose fitting and install the pressure hose fitting and tighten to 35 ft. lbs. Tighten the mounting studs to 35 ft. lbs.

NOTE: Be sure that the O-ring is installed on the upper groove of the pressure hose fitting.

32. Install the pulley on the shaft using the proper tool.

FORD MOTOR COMPANY

Saginaw Pump

Disassembly and Assembly

1. Drain as much fluid as possible and clean the outside of the pump.

2. Remove the bracket and the pulley from the pump using a suitable pulley remover tool.

3. Clamp the front hub of the pump in a suitable holding device so that the extending portion of the shaft points down.

NOTE: Do not clamp the pump too tightly or bearing damage might occur.

4. Remove the pressure union, O-ring assembly and both mounting bolts from the back of the reservoir. Discard the seals and the O-rings.

5. Rock the reservoir slightly back and forth to unseat the O-ring seal. Remove the O-ring and discard.

6. Remove the reservoir.

7. Remove the mounting bolt and the pressure union seals from the counterbored spaces in the pump housing. Discard the seals.

8. Rotate the end plate retaining ring so that one end of the ring is over the hole in the housing. Insert a small punch in the ⅛ in. diameter hole in the housing opposite the flow control valve hole.

9. Compress the retaining ring with the punch and pry out the retaining ring.

10. Remove the end plate. The end plate is spring loaded and will generally sit above the housing level for easy removal. If the plate sticks, rock it back and forth to free remove it.

11. Remove the pressure plate spring.

12. Remove the pump from the holding device and turn it over to allow the flow control valve and spring to fall out.

NOTE: Do not disassemble the flow control valve. Service it as a unit.

13. Tap the end of the shaft lightly until the pressure plate falls free.

14. Remove the cam ring and the vanes from the rotor.

15. Remove the retaining ring by clamping the shaft in a proper holding device and pry the ring off the shaft. Do not damage the shaft. Discard the retaining ring.

16. Remove the thrust plate from the shaft and both dowel pins from the housing.

17. Remove the pressure plate and end plate O-ring seals from the housing bore and discard them.

18. Remove the shaft seal only if it is worn and damaged. Removal will destroy the seal.

   a. To remove the rotor shaft seal insert a sharp tool between the rotor shaft seal and the housing. Pry out the seal. Do not pry against the shaft or the housing bore.

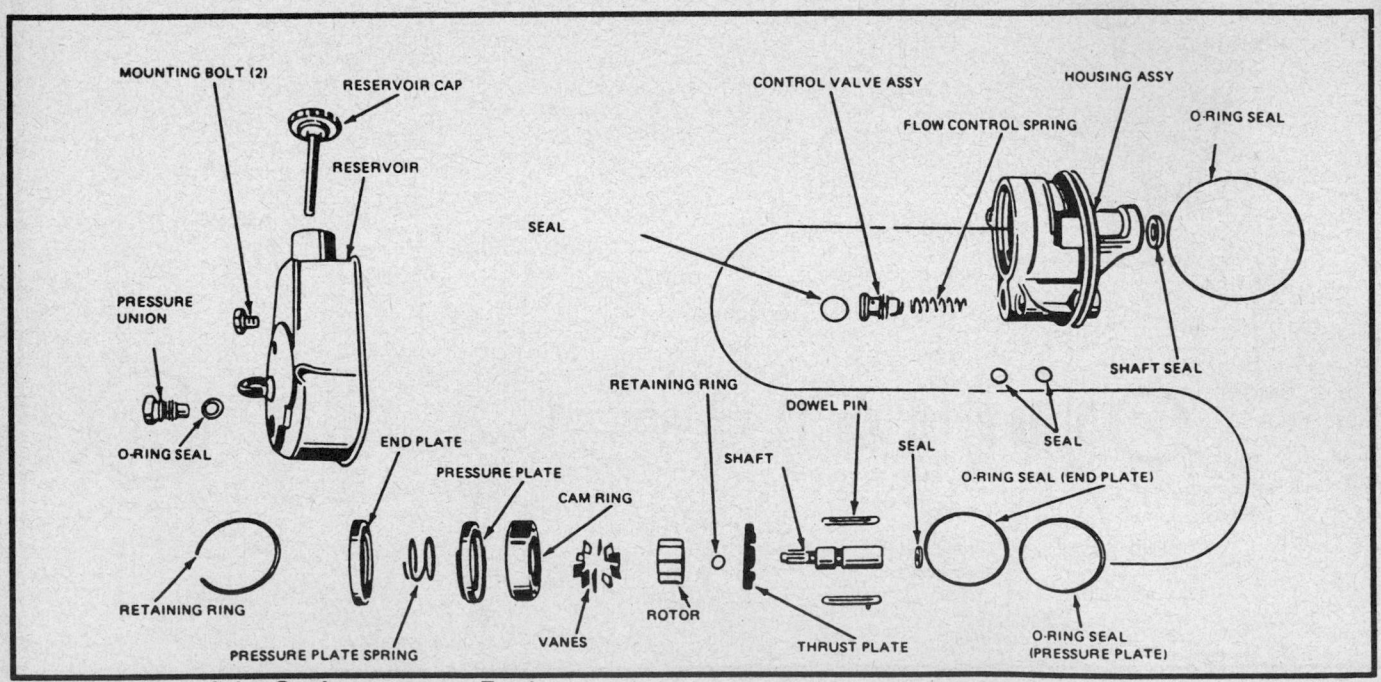

Exploded view of the Saginaw pump—Ford

b. Place the new seal on the shaft with the metal backing facing the pulley end of the shaft.

c. Install the seal using a suitable seal installer tool.

To assemble:

19. Clean all the metal parts with the proper solvent.

20. Lubricate a new pressure plate O-ring seal with a premium power steering fluid or equivalent and install it in the third groove from the rear of the housing.

21. Clamp the end hub of the housing in a suitable holding device with the extending portion of the shaft pointing down. Do not clamp too tightly.

22. Insert both dowel pins and install the thrust plate on the shaft with the ports facing the splined end of the shaft.

23. Install the rotor on the shaft with the counterbored end toward the thrust plate.

24. Clamp the shaft in a proper holding device.

25. Install a new retaining ring on the splined end of the shaft by prying the ring open and sliding it down over the shaft until it seats in the ring groove. Do not damage the shaft.

26. Insert the shaft in the housing and lubricate with a suitable power steering fluid. Make sure that the thrust plate slides properly on the dowel pins.

27. Install the cam ring on the dowel pins with the rotation arrow toward the rear of the housing.

28. Install the vanes in the rotor slots with the rounded edge of the vanes facing out. Make sure that the vanes slide freely.

29. Lubricate the pressure plate with premium power steering fluid.

30. Install the pressure plate on the dowel pins with the circular spring depression toward the rear of the housing. The narrow slots in the plate should engage the dowel pins.

31. Press the pressure plate over the O-ring about $1/16$ of an in. to seat properly.

32. Lubricate a new end plate O-ring and install it in the second groove from the rear of the housing.

33. Install the pressure plate spring in the groove in the pressure plate.

34. Lubricate the end plate with a suitable power steering fluid and press it in the housing, using a suitable arbor press. Depress the end plate just enough to install the retaining ring in it's groove.

35. Install the end plate retaining ring and release the press.

36. Place the control valve spring in it's hole and insert the control valve, with the screened end facing the front of the housing.

37. Install new mounting bolt and pressure union seals in the countersunk holes.

38. Lubricate a new O-ring seal and install it on the housing.

39. Lubricate the inside edge of the reservoir with power steering fluid and install it on the housing. Align the holes in the reservoir with the housing.

40. Install the mounting bolts and tighten to 35 ft. lbs.

41. Lubricate a new O-ring and install it on the pressure union in the groove next to the head hex. Insert the pressure union in the flow control valve hole in the back of the reservoir and tighten to 25–30 ft. lbs.

C-II Pump

Disassembly and Assembly

1. Drain as much fluid as possible and clean the outside of the pump.

2. Remove the bracket and the pulley from the pump using a suitable pulley remover tool

3. Remove the outlet fitting, flow control valve and the spring from the pump.

4. Remove the pump reservoir.

5. Place a C-clamp or equivalent in a suitable holding device.

6. Place the lower support plate tool or equivalent over the

pump rotor shaft and install the upper compressor plate tool or equivalent over the pump rotor shaft.

7. Holding the upper compressor tool, place the pump assembly in the C-clamp with the rotor shaft facing down.

NOTE: Position the contour of the upper compressor tool with the contour of the pump valve cover.

8. Tighten the C-clamp until a slight bottoming of the valve cover is felt.

9. Insert a suitable tool in the small hole in the side of the pump housing plate and push in on the valve cover retaining ring. Remove the ring.

10. Loosen the C-clamp. Remove the upper compressor plate and remove the pump assembly.

11. Remove the pump valve cover. Discard the O-ring seal.

12. Push on the rotor shaft. Remove the rotor shaft, upper plate, rotor and slippers, cam insert and the 2 dowel pins.

13. The lower plate and the disc spring will remain in the pump housing plate. To remove;

a. Place the pump housing on a flat surface. Raise slightly

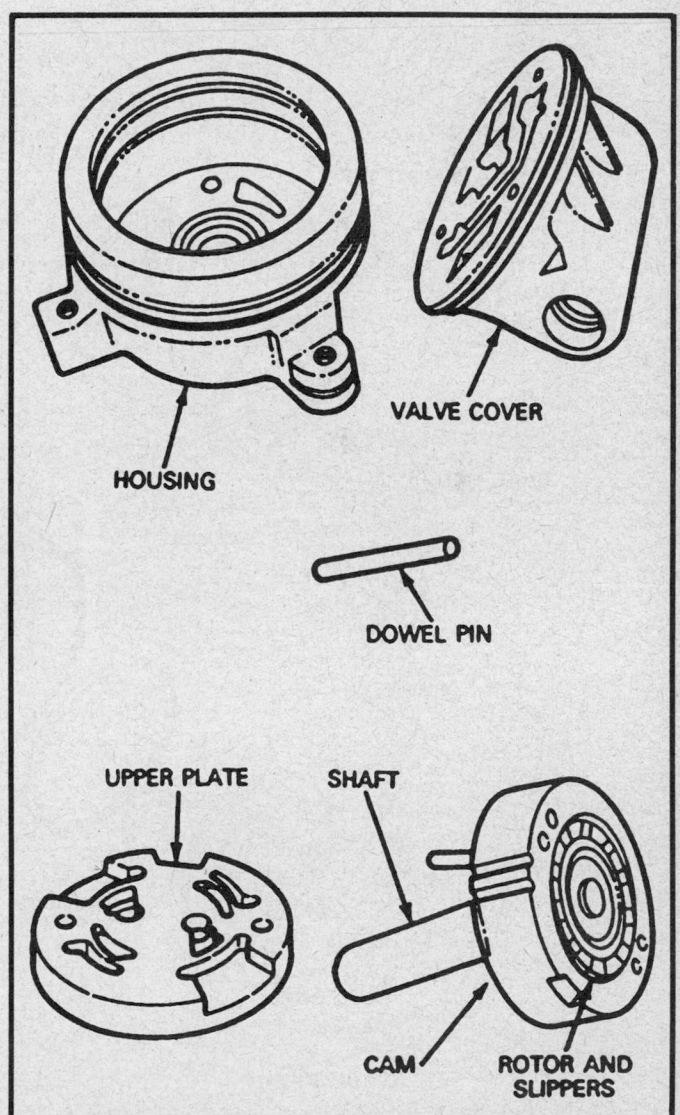

HOUSING

VALVE COVER

DOWEL PIN

UPPER PLATE   **SHAFT**

CAM   **ROTOR AND SLIPPERS**

Pump housing components—Ford power steering gear

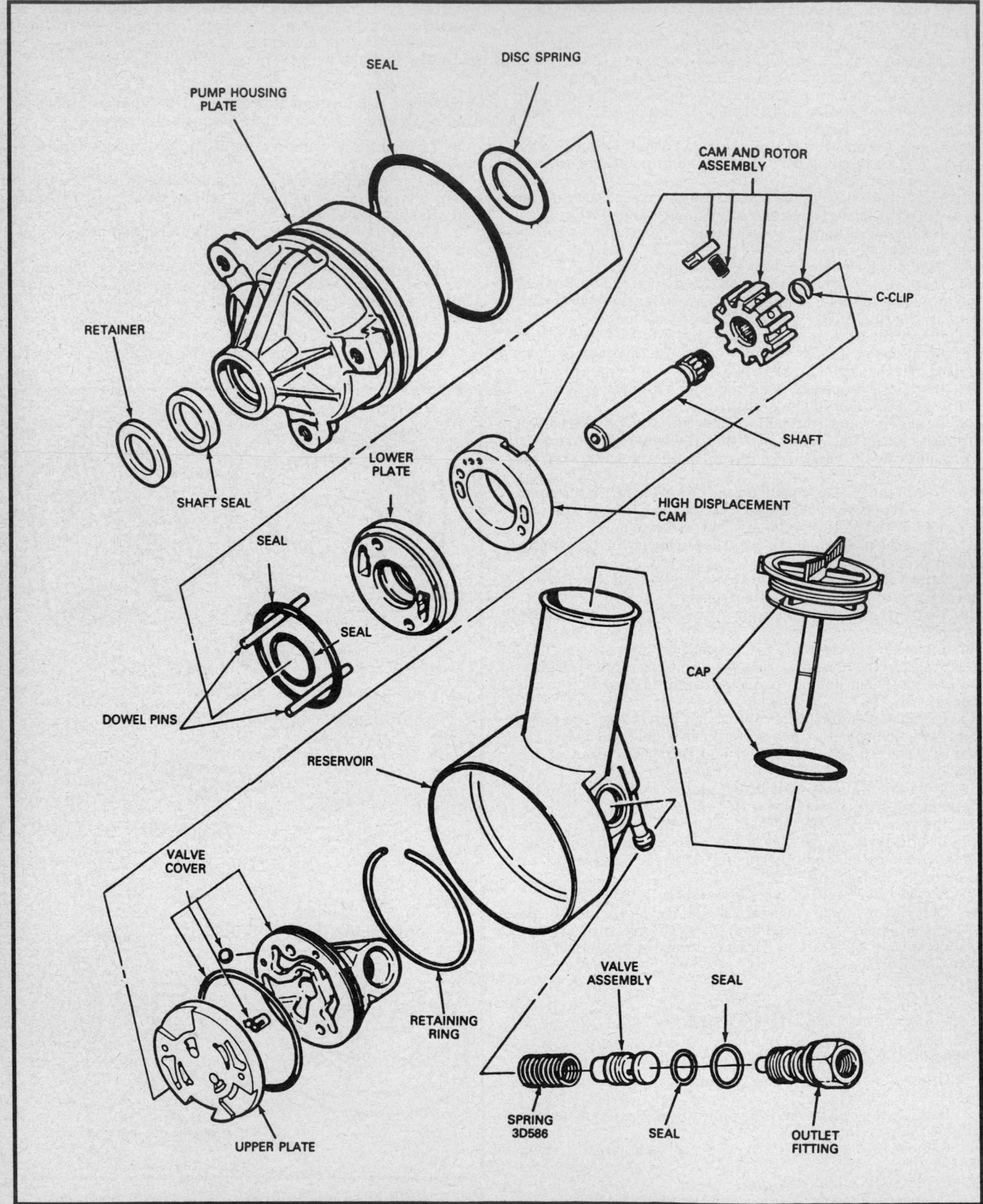

Exploded view of the C-11 power steering pump

and slam the housing plate down flatly until the lower plate and the disc spring fall out. Discard the O-rings.

14. Remove the rotor shaft seal and the retainer at the same time by prying out with a proper tool.

NOTE: This method is only used when the pump is disassembled.

To assemble:

15. Place the rotor on the rotor shaft splines and install the retaining ring in the groove at the end of the rotor shaft.

16. Position the insert cam over the rotor. Be sure the recessed flat on the insert cam is facing the reservoir.

17. With the rotor extended about ½ way out of the cam, insert a spring in a rotor spring pocket.

18. Use one of the slippers to compress the spring and install the slipper with the narrow groove facing up.

19. Hold the cam stationary, turn the rotor to the left or the right , one space at a time and install another spring and slipper until all 10 rotor cavities have been filled.

NOTE: Be careful when turning the rotor, that the springs and the slippers already installed do not fall out.

20. Install a new rotor shaft seal using a suitable seal driver tool. Using a plastic mallet, drive the seal into the bore until it bottoms out.

21. Install the seal retainer.

22. Place the pump housing plate on a flat surface, with the pulley side facing down.

23. Insert the lower pressure plate with the O-ring seals toward the front of the pump, into the pump housing plate and over the dowel pins.

24. Position the assembly on the C-clamp. Place the proper driver tool into the rotor shaft hole and press on the lower plate until it bottoms in the pump plate housing.

25. This will seat the outer O-ring.

26. Install the cam, rotor, slippers and the rotor shaft assembly into the pump housing plate over the dowel pins.

NOTE: When installing this assembly into the pump housing plate, the stepped holes must be used for dowel pins. The recessed notch in the cam insert must face toward the reservoir and be approximately 180 degrees opposite the square pump mounting boss.

27. Position the upper pressure plate over the dowel pins.

28. The square recess on the outside of the upper plate must be facing toward the reservoir and be 180 degrees opposite the pump square mounting boss.

29. Place a new O-ring seal on the valve cover and lubricate with power steering fluid.

NOTE: Be sure that the plastic baffle is securely in place in the valve cover.

30. Insert the valve cover over the dowel pins. Make sure that the outlet fitting hole in the valve cover is in line with the square mounting boss of the pump housing plate.

31. Place the assembly in the C-clamp tool and compress the valve cover into the pump housing plate, until the retaining ring groove is exposed in the pump housing plate.

32. Install the valve cover retaining ring with the ends near the hole in the pump housing plate.

33. Remove the pump assembly from the C-clamp tool.

34. Place a new O-ring on the pump housing plate and lubricate with power steering fluid.

35. Install the power steering reservoir.

36. Install the flow control spring and the flow control valve into the valve cover.

37. Place new O-ring seals on the outlet fitting and lubricate.

38. Install the outlet fitting into the valve cover and tighten to 24–34 ft. lbs.

GENERAL MOTORS CORPORATION

Saginaw Type P

Disassembly and Assembly

1. Drain the pump of any fluid. Clean the exterior of the pump.

2. Remove the reservoir mounting bolt and the line fitting. Remove the reservoir.

3. Pry off the retaining ring, using the proper tool. Remove the end plate and the pressure plate spring.

4. Remove the control valve, control valve spring and the O-ring.

5. Tap lightly on the driveshaft and remove the pressure plate.

6. Remove the pump ring and the vanes.

7. Remove the shaft retaining ring, pump rotor and the thrust plate.

8. Remove the driveshaft and pry the seal from the housing.

9. Remove the dowel pins, O-rings and the seal from the housing.

10. Clean all the parts with a suitable cleaning solvent. Lubricate the O-rings, pump ring, rotor and the vanes with power steering fluid.

11. Install the dowel pins and the O-rings.

12. Insert the driveshaft seal using the proper tool. Install the O-ring, driveshaft and the thrust plate.

13. Install the rotor, making sure that the counterbore portion of the rotor faces the driveshaft end of the housing.

14. Install the vanes with the rounded edge of the vane facing away from the rotor.

15. Install the driveshaft retaining ring, pump ring and the pressure plate in the housing.

16. Install the seal and the reservoir. Replace the mounting bolt and the fitting. Tighten the fitting to 75 ft. lbs.

Saginaw Type TC

Disassembly and Assembly

1. Clamp the pump in a suitable holding device. Remove the retaining clips, if equipped.

2. Remove the reservoir and the O-ring, or the return tube, if equipped.

3. Remove the fitting, flow control valve, flow control valve spring and the O-ring seal.

4. Remove the retaining ring, using suitable snapring pliers.

5. Remove the driveshaft and bearing. Pry out the driveshaft seal.

6. Insert a punch into the access hole and pry out the retaining ring.

7. Press out the thrust plate, using the proper tool and remove the O-ring seal.

8. Remove the pump ring, rotor, vanes and the dowel pins from the pump assembly.

9. Disconnect the pressure plate, O-ring, pressure plate ring and O-ring seal and remove the dowel pin.

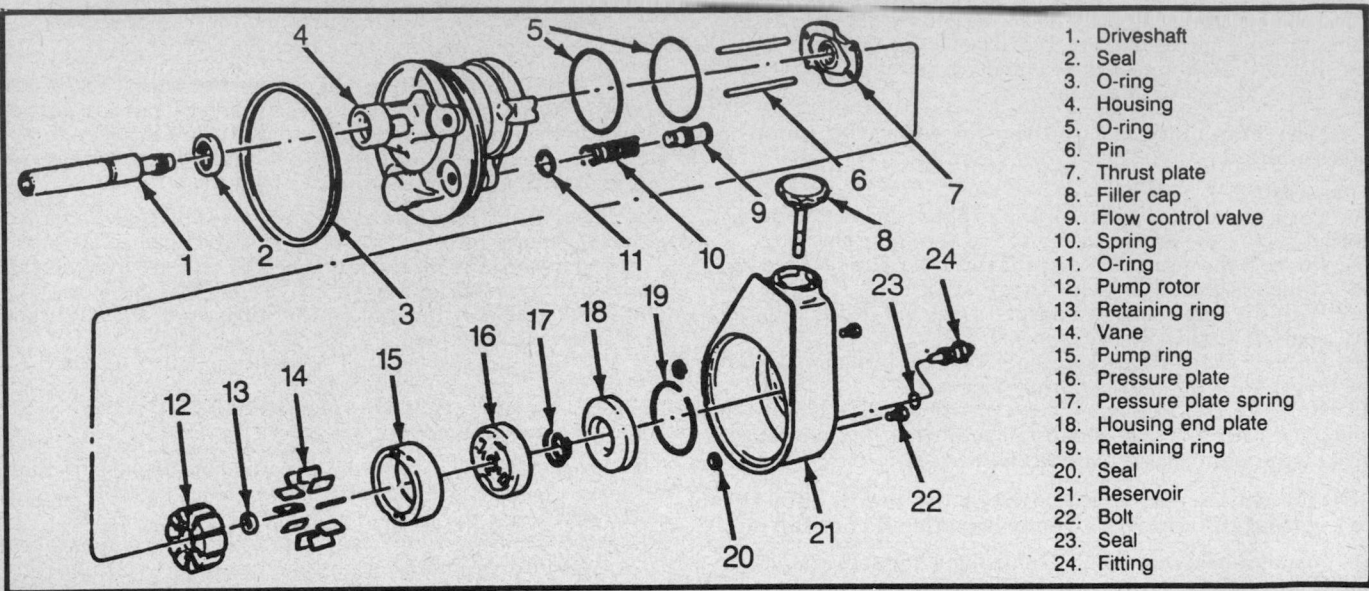

1. Driveshaft
2. Seal
3. O-ring
4. Housing
5. O-ring
6. Pin
7. Thrust plate
8. Filler cap
9. Flow control valve
10. Spring
11. O-ring
12. Pump rotor
13. Retaining ring
14. Vane
15. Pump ring
16. Pressure plate
17. Pressure plate spring
18. Housing end plate
19. Retaining ring
20. Seal
21. Reservoir
22. Bolt
23. Seal
24. Fitting

Exploded view of Saginaw type P power steering pump

A. Used on some models
1. Housing
2. Sleeve
3. Dowel pin
4. O-ring seal
5. Pressure plate spring
6. O-ring seal
7. Pressure plate
8. Dowel pin
9. Vane
10. Rotor
11. Pump ring
12. O-ring
13. Thrust plate
14. Retaining ring
15. Return tube
16. Driveshaft seal
17. Driveshaft
18. Bearing
19. Retaining ring
20. Flow control spring
21. Control valve
22. O-ring
23. Fitting
24. Reservoir
25. O-ring
26. Clips
27. Capstick

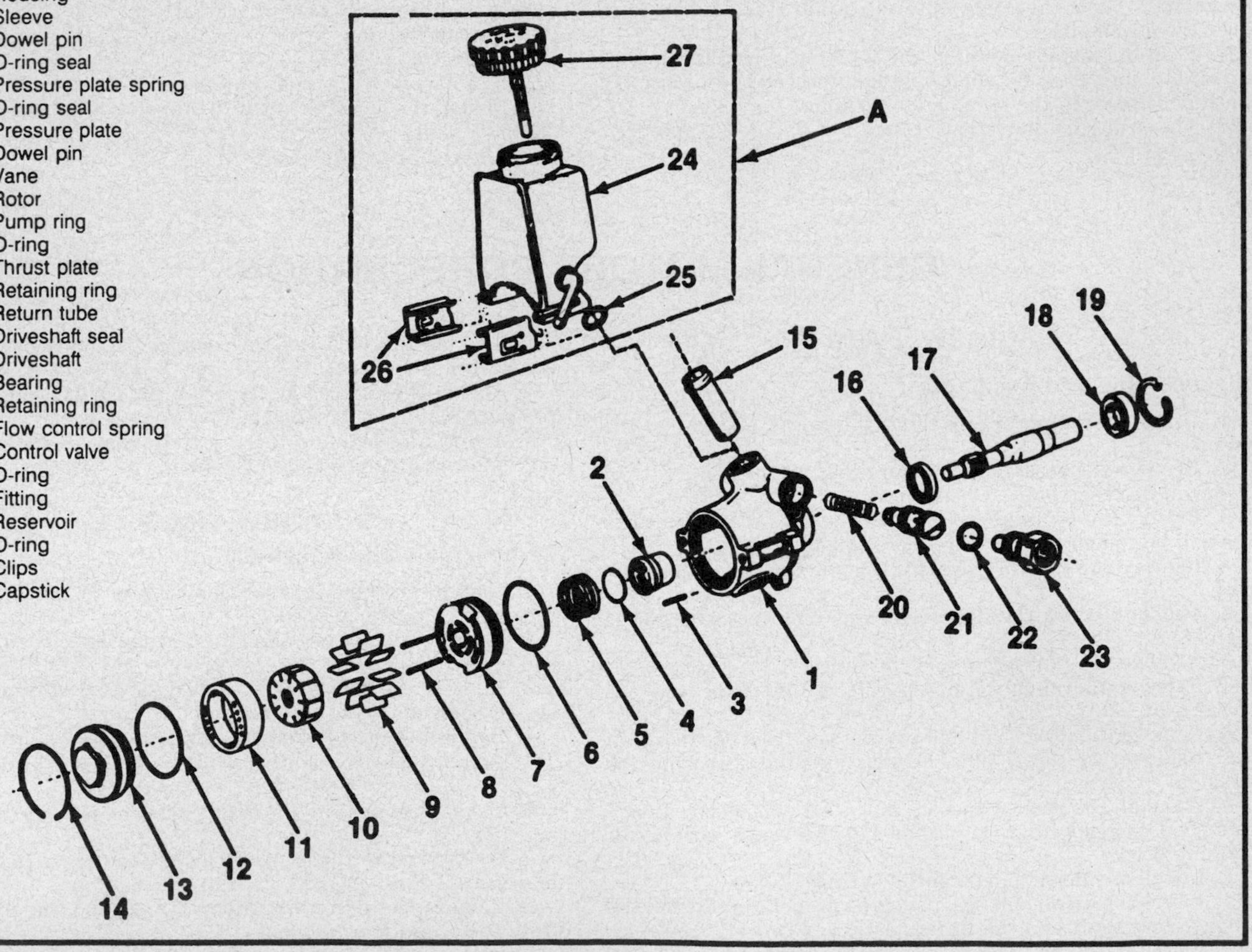

Exploded view of Saginaw type TC power steering pump

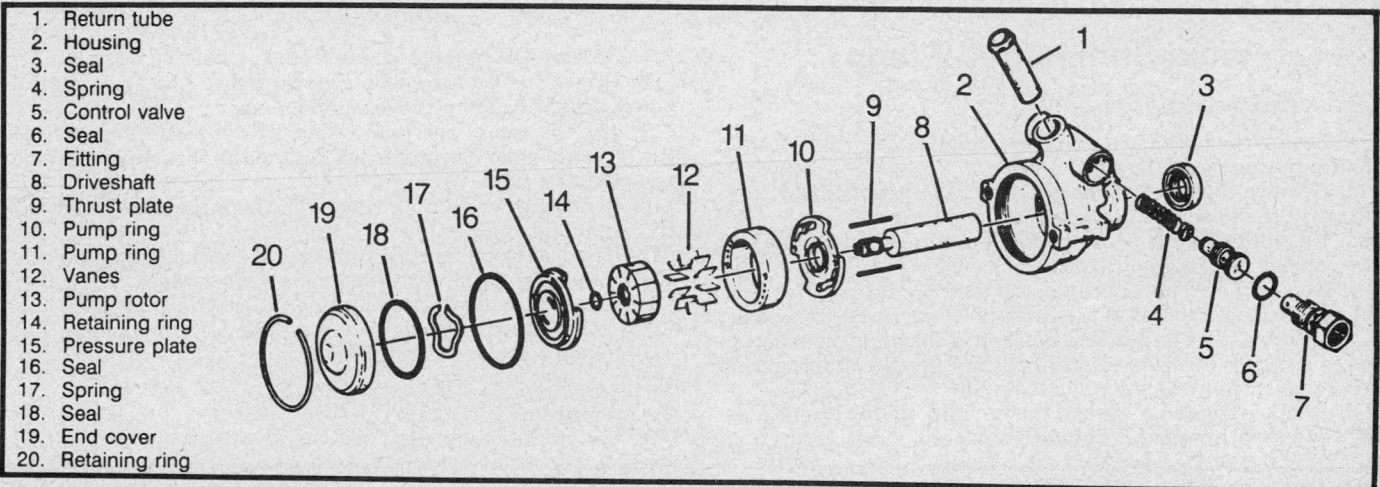

1. Housing
2. Sleeve
3. Dowel pin
4. O-ring
5. Pressure plate spring
6. O-ring
7. Pressure plate
8. Dowel pin
9. Vane
10. Rotor
11. Pump ring
12. O-ring
13. Thrust plate
14. Retaining ring
15. Return tube

Saginaw pump housing components

1. Return tube
2. Housing
3. Seal
4. Spring
5. Control valve
6. Seal
7. Fitting
8. Driveshaft
9. Thrust plate
10. Pump ring
11. Pump ring
12. Vanes
13. Pump rotor
14. Retaining ring
15. Pressure plate
16. Seal
17. Spring
18. Seal
19. End cover
20. Retaining ring

Exploded view of Saginaw type CB power steering pump

10. Remove the sleeve from the pump housing. Clean all the parts with the proper cleaning solvent.

11. Inspect all the parts for any burrs, chips or excessive wear. If heavy wear is present, or parts are faulty, relpace the entire rotating unit.

12. Install the return tube, if equipped.

13. Replace the dowel pin, O-ring seal and the pressure plate spring.

14. Install the pressure plat and mark the top of the pressure plate directly over the pin hole in the plate. Replace the dowel pin.

15. Lubricate the O-ring, pump ring, rotor and vanes with power steering fluid.

16. Install the vanes with the rounded edge of the vanes, facing away from the rotor.

17. Install the pump ring, making sure that the identification marks are facing up. Replace the O-ring seal.

18. Install the thrust plate with the dimples in the thrust plate lining up with the bolt holes on the housing. Make sure that the thrust plate engages the pump ring dowel pins.

19. Compress the thrust plate and install the retaining ring. Align the opening of the ring with the bolt hole nearest the hole.

20. Install the driveshaft seal, using the proper tool, until the seal bottoms in the housing.

21. Press the bearing onto the driveshaft and slide the assembly into the housing while rotating the driveshaft so that the shaft serrations engage with the rotor.

22. Replace the retaining ring with the proper snapring pliers.

23. Install the flow control spring and the flow control valve.

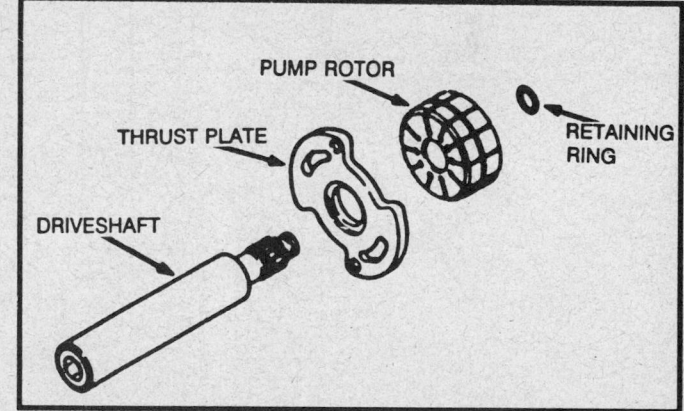

Exploded view of the driveshaft sub-assembly

24. Replace the O-ring seal and the O-ring, using a suitable seal installer tool.

25. Install the pump reservoir to the housing and connect the clips, if equipped.

Saginaw Type CB

Disassembly and Assembly

1. Remove the retaining ring, using a proper tool inserted into the access hole.

2. Push on the driveshaft and remove the U-ring, pressure plate spring, pump ring and the pump vanes and the driveshaft sub assembly.

3. Pry out the O-ring fom the pump housing. Remove the dowel pins and the driveshaft seal.

4. Remove the pressure plate, pressure plate spring and the O-ring from the end cover.

5. Remove the shaft retaining ring, pump rotor and the thrust plate from the driveshaft.

6. Clean and inspect the parts for any burrs, chips or excessive wear.

7. Lubricate the new driveshaft seal with the proper power steering fluid and install in the pump housing, using the proper tool.

8. Place the dowel pins into the housing

9. Install the thrust plate, pump rotor and the retaining ring onto the driveshaft.

10. Install the driveshaft assembly into the pump housing and place the vanes into rotor.

11. Install the pump ring with the holes aligned with the dowel pins in the housing.

12. Lubricate the new O-ring with the proper power steering fluid and install into the groove in the housing.

13. Install the pressure plate and the pressure plate spring.

14. Lubricate the new O-ring with the proper power steering fluid and install in the end cover. Lubricate the outer edge of the end cover.

15. Press the end cover into the housing and replace the retaining ring into the groove in the housing

JEEP CORPORATION

Vane-Submerged Pump

Disassembly and Assembly

1. Secure the pump in a proper holding device with the pump shaft pointing down. Drain the fluid.

2. Remove the pressure hose fitting and the mounting stud. Discard the seals and the O-ring.

3. Tilt the reservoir back and forth to unseat the O-ring seal and remove the reservoir. Discard the O-ring.

4. Remove the mounting stud and the hose fitting seals from the counterbored spaces in the pump housing. Discard the seals.

5. Insert a small punch into the hole in the pump housing opposite the flow control valve orifice. Pry up the retaining ring and remove from the pump housing.

6. Remove the end plate and the spring from the pump housing. Tap it with a plastic hammer to loosen, if neccessary.

7. Remove the pump housing from the holding device.

8. Invert the pump housing and remove the flow control valve and spring from the pump housing.

9. Tap the end of the pump shaft with a plastic hammer so the pressure plate, pump ring, rotor and the thrust plate can be removed as a unit.

10. Remove the retaining ring from the pump shaft. Discard the retaining ring.

11. Remove the pump ring, rotor and the thrust plate from the shaft. Use care to prevent dropping the rotor vanes.

12. Remove the end plate O-ring seal and the shaft seal.

13. Clean all the components and inspect for any damage. Lubricate with power steering fluid.

To assemble:

14. Install the pump shaft seal, using the proper tool.

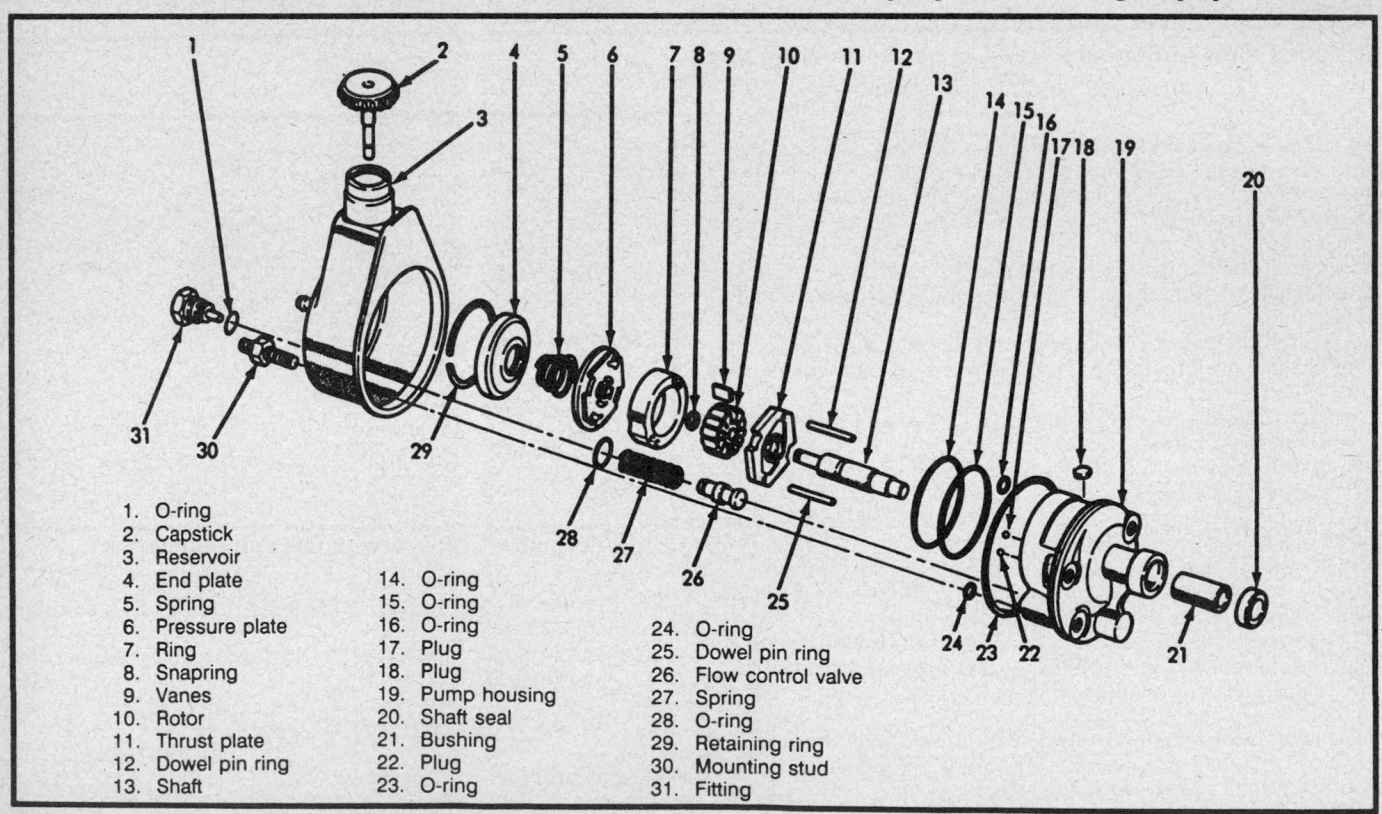

1. O-ring
2. Capstick
3. Reservoir
4. End plate
5. Spring
6. Pressure plate
7. Ring
8. Snapring
9. Vanes
10. Rotor
11. Thrust plate
12. Dowel pin ring
13. Shaft
14. O-ring
15. O-ring
16. O-ring
17. Plug
18. Plug
19. Pump housing
20. Shaft seal
21. Bushing
22. Plug
23. O-ring
24. O-ring
25. Dowel pin ring
26. Flow control valve
27. Spring
28. O-ring
29. Retaining ring
30. Mounting stud
31. Fitting

Exploded view of vane-submerged type pump

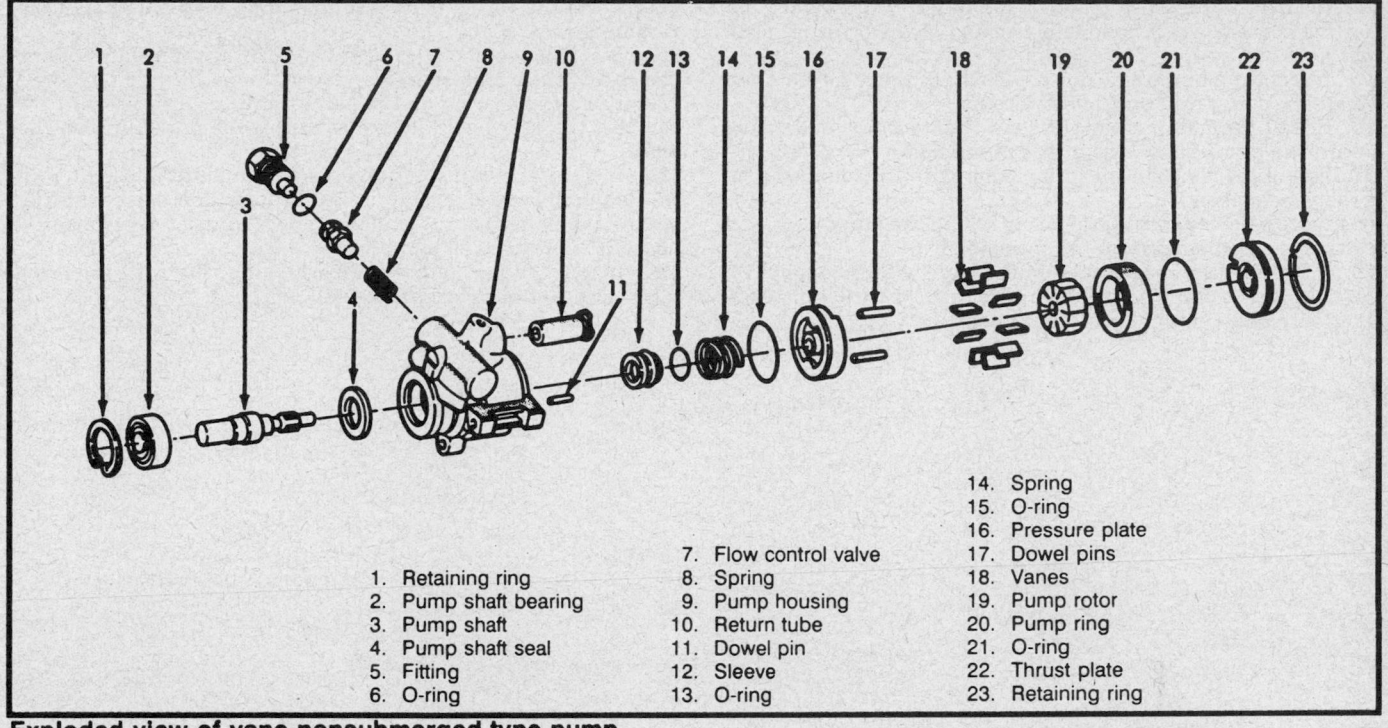

14. Spring
15. O-ring
16. Pressure plate
17. Dowel pins
18. Vanes
19. Pump rotor
20. Pump ring
21. O-ring
22. Thrust plate
23. Retaining ring

1. Retaining ring
2. Pump shaft bearing
3. Pump shaft
4. Pump shaft seal
5. Fitting
6. O-ring
7. Flow control valve
8. Spring
9. Pump housing
10. Return tube
11. Dowel pin
12. Sleeve
13. O-ring

Exploded view of vane-nonsubmerged type pump

15. Lubricate with petroleum jelly and install the replacement seal in the third groove in the housing.

16. Clamp the pump housing in a suitable holding device with the large bore facing down.

17. Insert both dowel pins in the thrust plate.

18. Insert the splined end of the pump shaft through the thrust plate and the rotor and install the retaining ring on the end of the shaft.

19. Open the retaining ring only wide enough to slide it over the end of the shaft. The rotor must slide freely on the splines.

20. Insert the pump shaft in the pump housing. Make sure that the dowel pins are properly engaged in the thrust plate.

21. Install the pump ring on the dowel pins with the pump rotation arrow facing up.

22. Install all 10 rotor vanes in the rotor slots with the rounded edges of the vanes facing outward.

23. Install the pressure plate on the dowel pins with the plate spring groove facing upward.

24. Using the proper tool, force the pressure plate down approximately $1/16$ in. to seat it.

25. Lubricate the end plate seal with petroleum jelly and install it in the second groove in the housing.

26 Install the spring in the center groove in the pressure plate.

27. Lubricate the end plate outside diameter with petroleum jelly and install the plate in the pump housing.

28. Press the end plate down and install the end plate retaining ring.

29. Install the spring over the hexnut end of the flow control valve.

30. Install the flow control valve and the spring in the pump housing bore with the hexnut end of the valve facing the inside of the housing bore.

31. Install the mounting stud seals and the pump fitting seal in the counterbored holes in the pump housing.

32. Place the reservoir O-ring on the pump housing.

33. Lubricate the inner edge of the reservoir with petroleum jelly and place the reservoir on the pump housing. Press the reservoir down to seat it on the pump housing.

34. Install the mounting studs and tighten to 35 ft. lbs.

35. Install the seal on the flow control valve fitting and install the fitting in the flow control valve bore. Tighten the fitting to 35 ft. lbs.

Vane-Nonsubmerged Pump

Disassembly and Assembly

1. Secure the pump assembly in a suitable holding device. Drain the fluid from the pump.

2. Remove the flow control valve and the valve spring from the pump housing.

3. Remove and discard the pump shaft retaining ring.

4. Support the pump shaft bearing on it's inner race and force the pump shaft from the bearing.

5. Pry the pump shaft seal from the pump body, using a suitable tool. Remove the thrust plate retaining ring.

6. Force the thrust plate from the pump body and remove and discard the thrust plate O-ring seal.

7. Remove the pressure plate spring, the dowel pin and the pump shaft sleeve O-ring seal.

8. Remove the pump shaft sleeve, using the proper tool.

9. Clean all the components with the proper cleaning solvent and inspect for any damage.

NOTE: The flow control valve is serviced as a unit only and it must not be disassembled.

To assemble:

10. Install the pump shaft sleeve into the pump body bore, using the proper tool. Make sure that the sleeve is completely seated in the bore.

11. Place a new O-ring seal in the sleeve seat and install the short dowel pin in the pump body.

12. Install the pressure plate spring over the pump shaft sleeve and place a new O-ring seal on the pressure plate.

13. Make a reference mark on the top of the pressure plate directly over the dowel pin hole.

14. Install the pressure plate in the pump body. Make sure that the short dowel is completely seated in the pressure plate hole.

15. Insert the 2 pump ring dowel pins in the pressure plate and install the pump ring on the dowel pins.

16. Install the pump rotor with it's counterbored end facing toward the pump shaft side of the pump body.

17. Install the vanes in the pump rotor with the rounded edge of the vanes facing out.

18. Place a new thrust plate O-ring seal in the pump body and position the thrust plate in the pump body.

19. Align the reference marks on the plate with the mounting bolt holes in the pump body. Make sure that the thrust plate engages with the 2 pump ring dowel pins.

20. Force the thrust plate into the pump body and install the retaining ring.

21. Install a new shaft seal into the shaft bore until it contacts the end of the counterbore.

22. Press the bearing on the pump shaft, using a proper tool. Support the bearing on it's inner race while pressing it on the shaft.

23. Insert the pump shaft and the bearing into the shaft bore in the pump body and rotate it until the splines mesh with the rotor. Make sure that the shaft bearing is completely against the end of the bore in the pump body.

24. Install the new pump shaft retaining ring with the large lug placed to the right of the small lug.

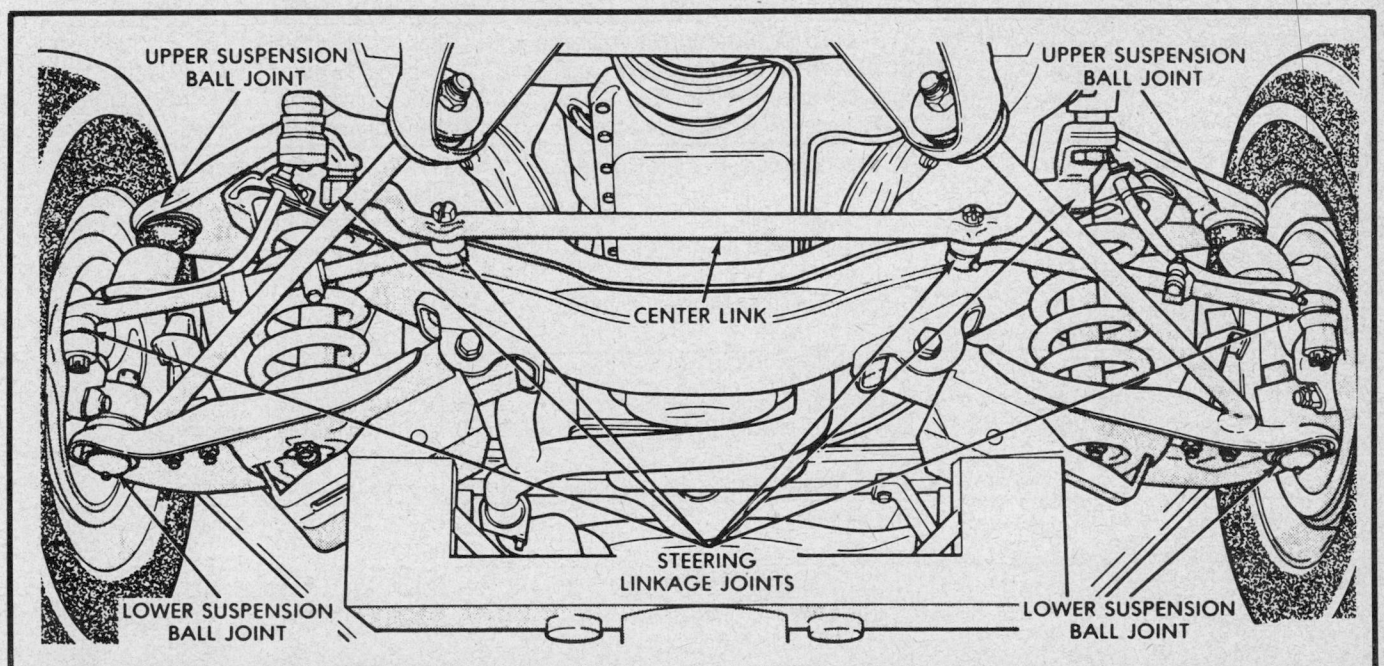

Typical front end major components

FRONT END TROUBLE DIAGNOSIS

Condition	Cause	Correction
Hard steering	1) Steering linkage needs lubrication 2) Low or uneven front tire pressure 3) Incorrect front wheel alignment (manual steering)	1) Lubricate the linkage 2) Inflate tires to the recommended pressure 3) Check and align the front suspension
Poor directional stability	1) Steering linkage need lubrication 2) Low or uneven tire pressure 3) Loose wheel bearings 4) Incorrect front wheel alignment (caster) 5) Broken springs 6) Malfunctioning shock absorber 7) Broken stabilizer bar or a missing link	1) Lubricate the linkage 2) Inflate tires to the recommended pressure 3) Adjust or replace the wheel bearings 4) Check and align the front suspension 5) Replace the springs 6) Check and replace the shock absorber 7) Replace the stabilizer bar or link
Front wheel shimmy (smooth road shake)	1) Tire and wheel are out of balance or out of round 2) Worn or loose wheel bearings 3) Worn ball joints 4) Malfunctioning shock absorber	1) Balance the tires, check run-out 2) Adjust the wheel bearings 3) Replace the ball joints 4) Check and replace the shock absorber
Vehicle pulls to one side (no braking action)	1) Low or uneven tire pressure 2) Front or rear brakes dragging 3) Broken or sagging front spring 4) Incorrect front wheel alignment (camber)	1) Inflate the tires to the recommended pressure 2) Adjust the brakes 3) Replace the spring 4) Check and align the front suspension
Noise in the front end	1) Steering linkage needs lubrication 2) Loose shock absorber or worn bushings 3) Worn control arm bushings 4) Worn or loose wheel bearings 5) Loose stabilizer bar 6) Loose wheel nuts 7) Spring is improperly positioned 8) Loose suspension bolts	1) Lubricate at the recommended intervals 2) Tighten the bolts or replace the shock absorber 3) Replace the bushings or control arm 4) Adjust or replace the wheel bearings 5) Tighten all the stabilizer bar attachments 6) Tighten the wheel nuts 7) Reposition the spring 8) Tighten to specifications or replace
Wheel tramp	1) Tire and the wheel are out of balance 2) Tire and the wheel are out of round 3) Blister or bumb on the tire 4) Improper shock absorber action	1) Balance the wheels 2) Replace the tire 3) Replace the tire 4) Replace the shock absorber
Excessive or uneven tire wear	1) Underinflated or overinflated tires 2) Improper toe-in 3) Wheels are out of balance 4) Hard driving 5) Overloading the vehicle	1) Inflate the tire to the recommended pressure 2) Adjust toe-in setting 3) Balance the wheels 4) Follow proper driving techniques 5) Do not exceed the maximum recommended payload rating
Scuffed tires	1) Toe-in is incorrect 2) Excessive speed on turns 3) Tires are improperly inflated 4) Suspension arm is bent or twisted	1) Adjust toe-in setting 2) Follow proper driving techniques 3) Inflate the tires to the recommended pressure 4) Replace the suspension arm
Noisy shocks	1) Loose mounting	1) Check all mounting torques (bolt and/or nut)
Excessive road shock	1) Tire air pressure is too high 2) Loose wheel bearings	1) Deflate to correct pressure 2) Adjust bearings

FRONT END TROUBLE DIAGNOSIS

Condition	Cause	Correction
Excessive road shock	3) Camber adjustment is incorrect (negative camber contributes to road shock)	3) Adjust camber
	4) Weak or broken front spring	4) Replace the spring
	5) Loose suspension components	5) Inspect, repair, and adjust as necessary
Leaky shocks	1) Seals are worn out	1) Replace shocks
Weak shocks	1) Shocks are worn out	1) Replace shocks
	2) Loss of shock fluid	2) Replace shocks
Vibration and shimmy	1) Seal damage resulting in loss of lubricant, corrosion, excessive wear	1) Replace damaged parts as necessary
	2) Tires and wheels, or brake drums, are out of balance	2) Balance the tires and wheels, turn the brake drums
	3) Bent wheel or tire is out of round	3) Replace the wheel and remount, or replace the tire
	4) Wheel stud nuts torqued unevenly	4) Retorque the wheel stud nuts
	5) Loose steering linkage	5) Adjust, torque or repair as necessary
	6) Wheel is loose on the hub	6) Inspect the wheel bolt for damage Replace the wheel if needed. Replace all wheel studs
	7) Driveline universal joints are rough or defective (may be confused with steering vibration)	7) Repair driveline
	8) Malfunctioning shock absorbers	8) Replace the shock absorbers
Cupped tires	1) Front shock absorbers are defective	1) Replace the shock absorbers
	2) Worn ball joints	2) Replace the ball joints
	3) Wheel bearings are incorrectly adjusted or worn	3) Adjust or replace the wheel bearings (also replace the races)
	4) Wheel and tire is out of balance	4) Balance the wheel and tire
	5) Excessive tire or wheel runout	5) Check and compensate for runout

Wheel Alignment

For a vehicle to have safe steering control with a minimum of tire wear, certain established rules must be followed. These rules fix the values of planes, angles and radii relative to each other and to vehicle and tire dimensions. Some factors are built in, with no provision for adjustment; others are adjustable within limits. The entire system depends upon all value factors, separately and combined. It is therefore difficult to change some of the established settings without influencing others.

This system is called steering geometry or wheel alignment and requires a complete check of all the factors involved. Definitions of these factors and the effect each has on the vehicle are as follows.

STEERING WHEEL POSITION

Always check steering wheel alignment in conjunction with and at the same time as toe-in. In fact, the steering wheel spoke position, with the vehicle on a straight section of highway, may be the first indication of front end misalignment.

If the vehicle has been wrecked, or indicates any evidence of steering gear or linkage disturbance, the pitman arm should be disconnected from the sector shaft. The steering wheel (or gear) should be turned from extreme right to extreme left to determine the halfway point in its turning scope. This will be the spot on the gear that is in action during straight ahead driving and in which position the steering gear should be adjusted. With the steering wheel in the straight ahead position and the steering gear adjusted to zero lash status, reconnect the pitman arm.

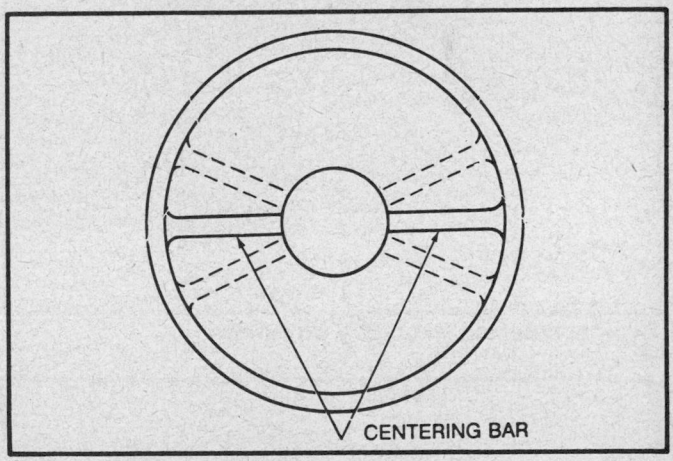

Steering wheel positioning

CAMBER ANGLE

Camber is the amount that the front wheels are inclined outward or inward at the top. Camber is spoken of, and measured, in degrees from the perpendicular. The purpose of the camber angle is to take some of the load off the spindle outboard bearing.

CASTER ANGLE

Caster is the amount that the kingpin (or in the case of vehicles

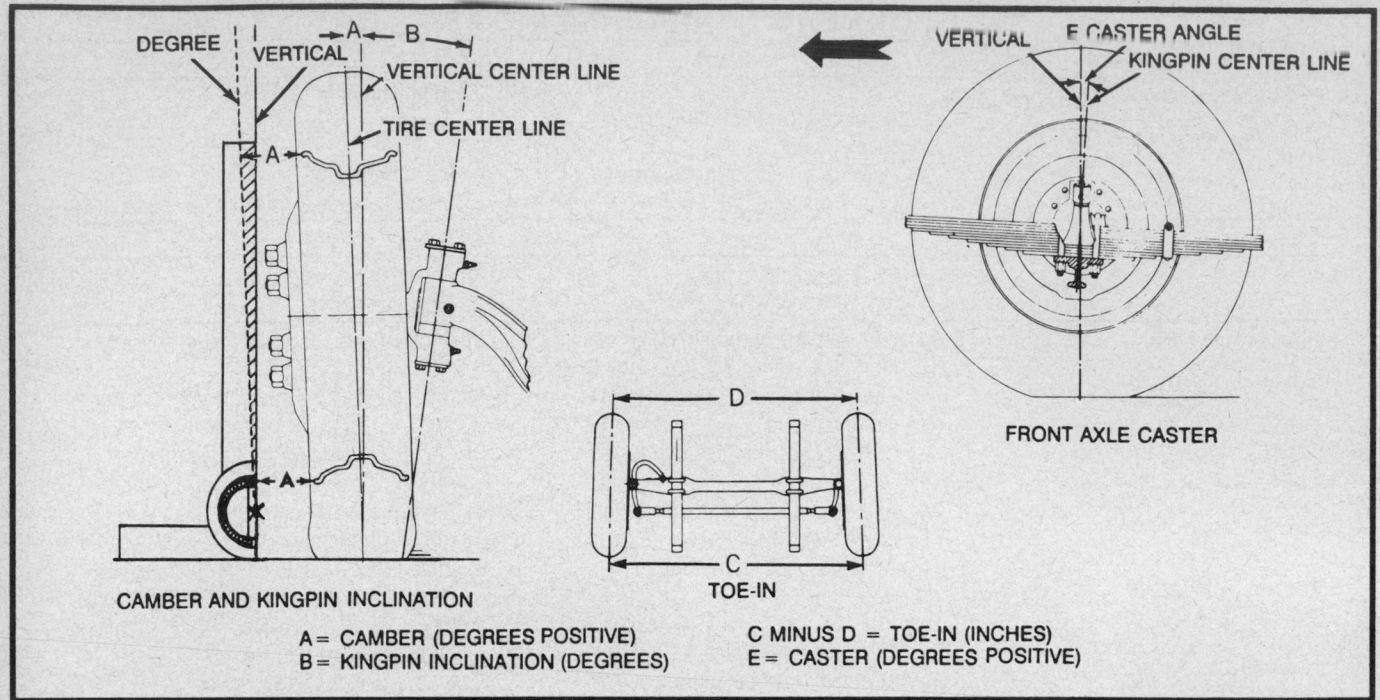

A = CAMBER (DEGREES POSITIVE)
B = KINGPIN INCLINATION (DEGREES)

C MINUS D = TOE-IN (INCHES)
E = CASTER (DEGREES POSITIVE)

Typical steering geometry

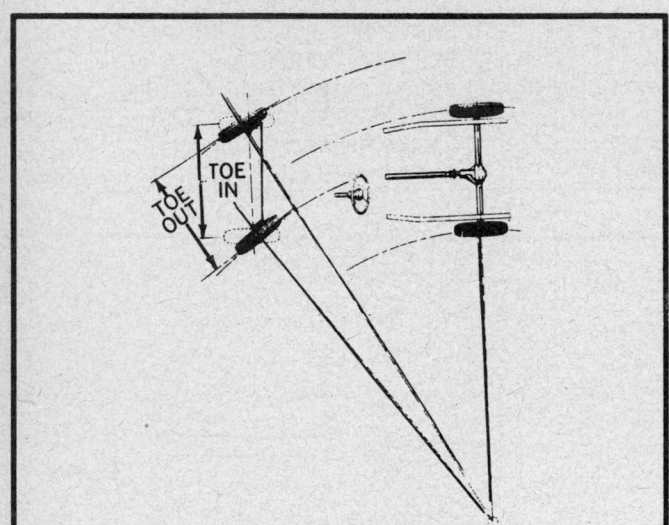

Typical steering geometry on turns

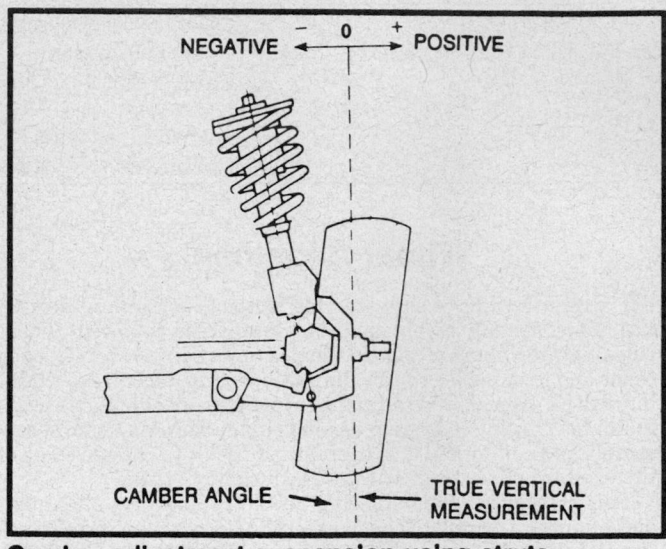

Camber adjustment suspension using struts

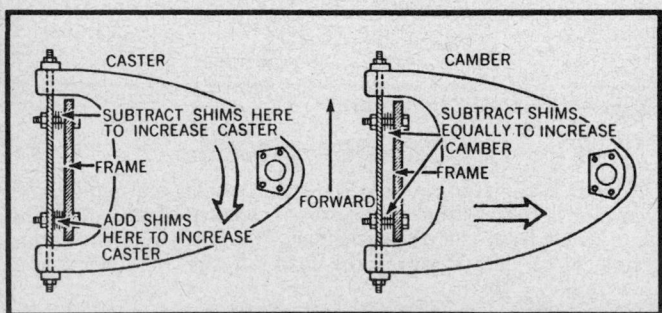

Caster/camber adjustment suspension using upper control arms

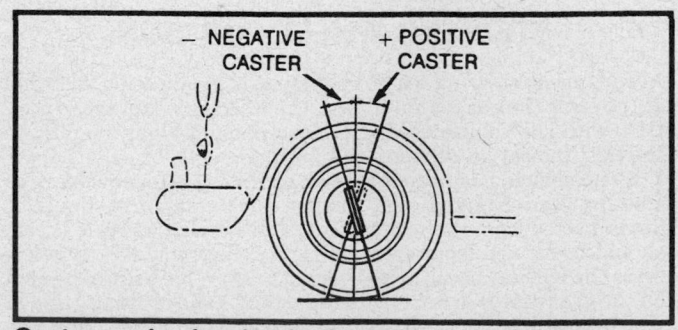

Caster angle showing both positive and negative caster

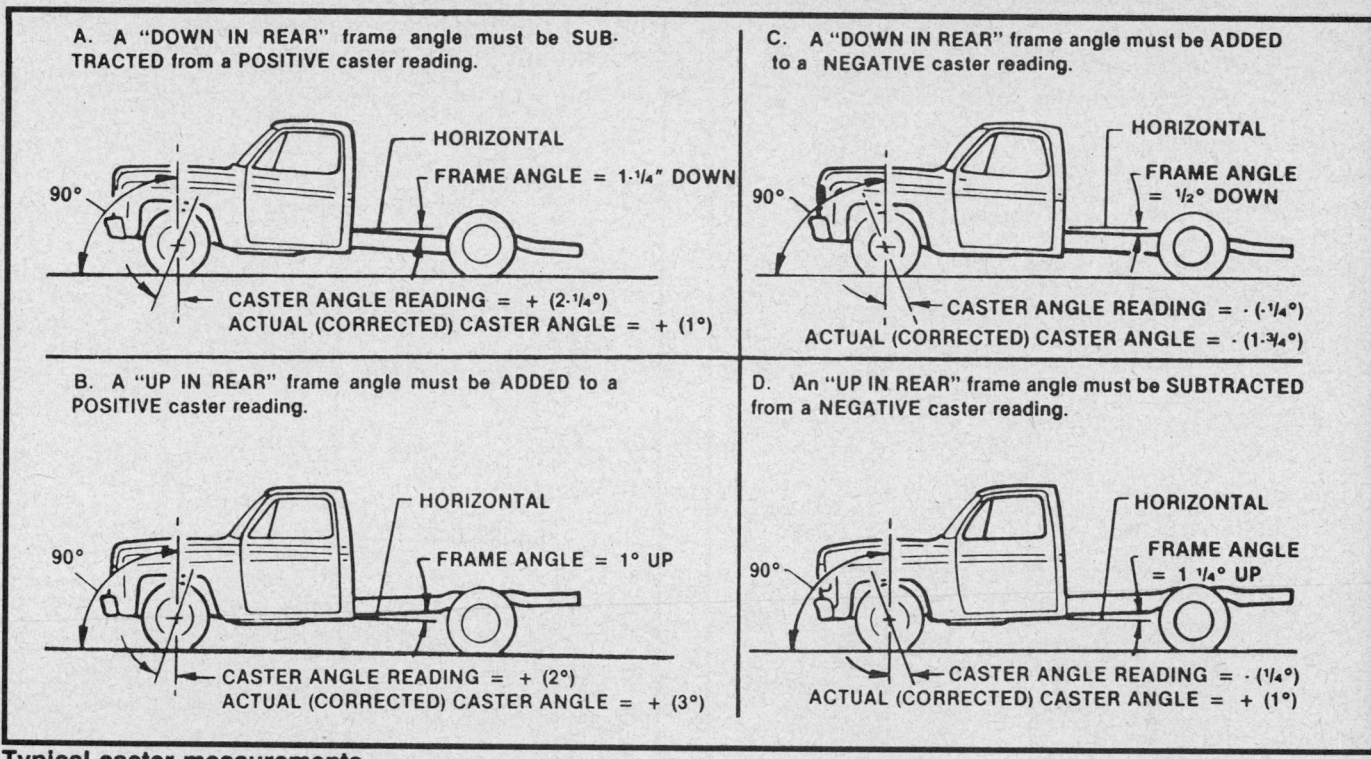

A. A "DOWN IN REAR" frame angle must be SUB-TRACTED from a POSITIVE caster reading.

90°

HORIZONTAL

FRAME ANGLE = 1-1/4" DOWN

CASTER ANGLE READING = + (2-1/4°)
ACTUAL (CORRECTED) CASTER ANGLE = + (1°)

C. A "DOWN IN REAR" frame angle must be ADDED to a NEGATIVE caster reading.

90°

HORIZONTAL

FRAME ANGLE = 1/2° DOWN

CASTER ANGLE READING = · (-1/4°)
ACTUAL (CORRECTED) CASTER ANGLE = · (1-3/4°)

B. A "UP IN REAR" frame angle must be ADDED to a POSITIVE caster reading.

90°

HORIZONTAL

FRAME ANGLE = 1° UP

CASTER ANGLE READING = + (2°)
ACTUAL (CORRECTED) CASTER ANGLE = + (3°)

D. An "UP IN REAR" frame angle must be SUBTRACTED from a NEGATIVE caster reading.

90°

HORIZONTAL

FRAME ANGLE = 1 1/4° UP

CASTER ANGLE READING = · (1/4°)
ACTUAL (CORRECTED) CASTER ANGLE = + (1°)

Typical caster measurements

without kingpins, the knuckle support pivots) is tilted towards the back or front of the vehicle. Caster is usually spoken of, and measured, in degrees. Positive caster means that the top of the kingpin is tilted toward the back of the vehicle. Positive caster is indicated by the sign +.

Negative caster is exactly the opposite; the top of the kingpin is tilted toward the front of the vehicle. This is generally indicated by the sign –. Negative caster is sometimes referred to as reverse caster.

The effect of positive caster is to cause the vehicle to steer in the direction in which it tends to go. Positive caster in the front wheels may cause the vehicle to steer down off a crowned road or steer in the direction of a cross wind. For this reason, a number of our modern vehicles are arranged with negative caster so that the opposite is true, which is that the vehicle tends to steer up a crowned road and into a cross wind.

Caster angle specifications are based on the vehicle load limits, which will usually result in a level frame. Since load requirements may vary, the frame does not always remain level and must be considered when determining the correct caster angle.

Because of their naturally straight running characteristics, front wheel drive vehicles are not overly sensitive to caster, therefore caster is not adjustable.

To measure the caster angle, the vehicle should be on a smooth and level surface. Place a bubble protractor on the frame rail and measure the degree of frame tilt and in what direction, either front or rear.

Two methods of determining caster angles are used. The first method is to determine the caster angle from the wheel with alignment equipment, and the second method is to obtain the desired caster angle from the specification charts. The frame angle is then added to or subtracted from the caster angles as necessary.

METHOD ONE

1. Determine the frame angle.
   a. If the frame is high at rear, than the frame angle is negative.

b. If the frame is low at rear, than the frame angle is positive.
2. Determine the caster angle at the wheel with the alignment checking equipment.
3. Add or subtract frame angle to determine caster angle.
   a. Negative frame angle is added to positive caster angle.
   b. Positive frame angle is subtracted from positive caster angle.
   c. Negative frame angle is subtracted from negative caster angle.
   d. Positive frame angle is added to negative caster angle.
4. Determine the correct caster angle and the specified caster angle. Correct the vehicle caster, as required.

METHOD TWO

1. Measure the frame angle.
   a. If the front of the frame is down than the frame angle is positive.
   b. If the front of the frame is up than the frame angle is negative.
2. From the specifications, determine the specified or desired caster setting.
3. Add or subtract the frame angle from the specified caster setting.
   a. Positive frame angle is subtracted from the specified setting.
   b. Negative frame angle is added to the specified caster setting.
4. Using wheel alignment equipment, obtain the measured caster angle from the wheel and determine the corrected specified setting.

KINGPIN INCLINATION ANGLE

In addition to the caster angle, the kingpins, if equipped, (or knuckle support pivots) are also inclined toward each other at the top. This angle is known as kingpin inclination and is usually spoken of, and measured, in degrees.

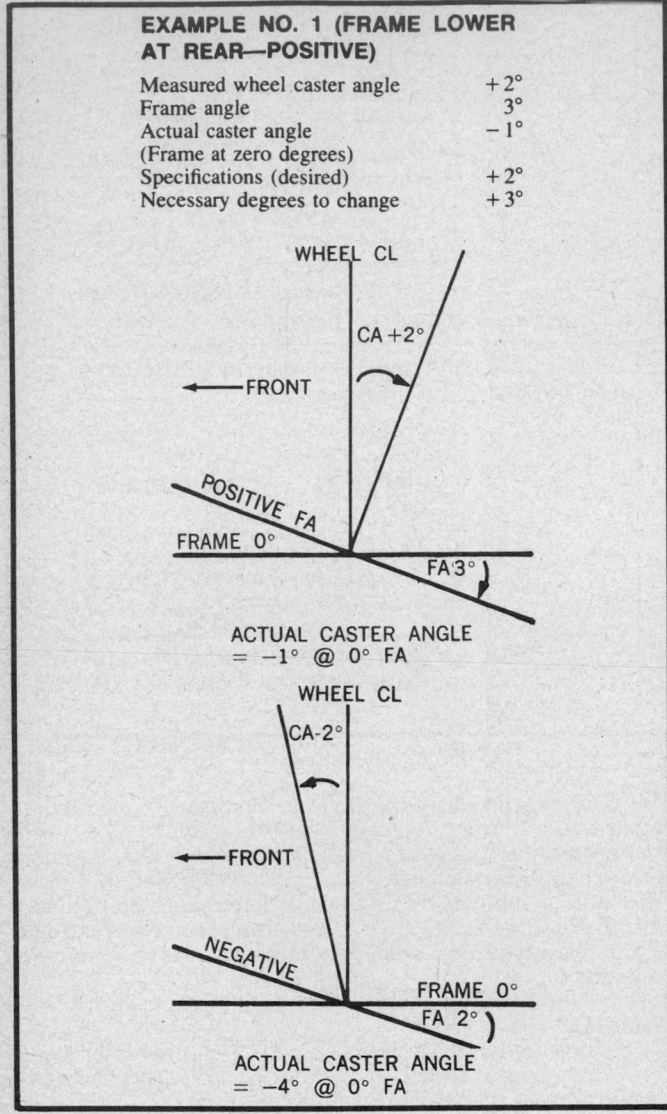

EXAMPLE NO. 1 (FRAME LOWER AT REAR—POSITIVE)

Measured wheel caster angle	+2°
Frame angle	3°
Actual caster angle	−1°
(Frame at zero degrees)	
Specifications (desired)	+2°
Necessary degrees to change	+3°

WHEEL CL
CA +2°
FRONT
POSITIVE FA
FRAME 0°
FA 3°
ACTUAL CASTER ANGLE = −1° @ 0° FA

WHEEL CL
CA-2°
FRONT
NEGATIVE
FRAME 0°
FA 2°
ACTUAL CASTER ANGLE = −4° @ 0° FA

Alignment measurement—example one

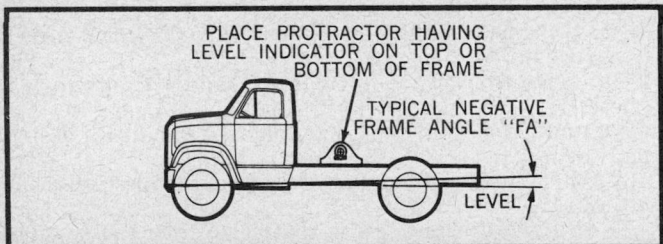

PLACE PROTRACTOR HAVING LEVEL INDICATOR ON TOP OR BOTTOM OF FRAME

TYPICAL NEGATIVE FRAME ANGLE "FA"

LEVEL

Frame angle determination—method one

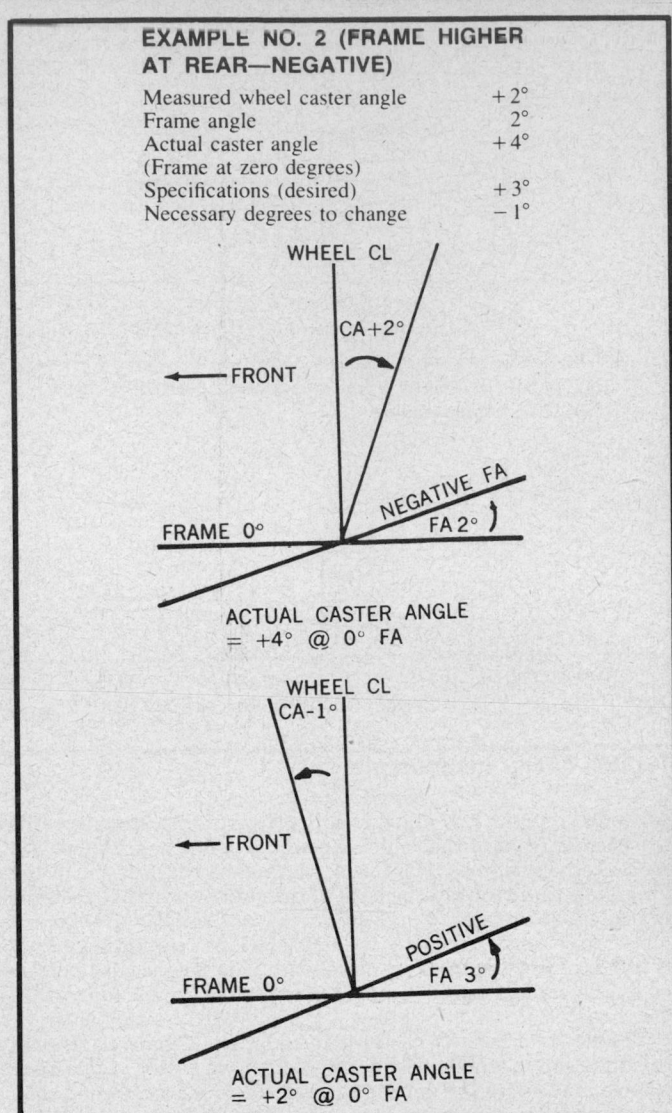

EXAMPLE NO. 2 (FRAME HIGHER AT REAR—NEGATIVE)

Measured wheel caster angle	+2°
Frame angle	2°
Actual caster angle	+4°
(Frame at zero degrees)	
Specifications (desired)	+3°
Necessary degrees to change	−1°

WHEEL CL
CA+2°
FRONT
NEGATIVE FA
FRAME 0°
FA 2°
ACTUAL CASTER ANGLE = +4° @ 0° FA

WHEEL CL
CA-1°
FRONT
POSITIVE
FRAME 0°
FA 3°
ACTUAL CASTER ANGLE = +2° @ 0° FA

Alignment measurement—example two

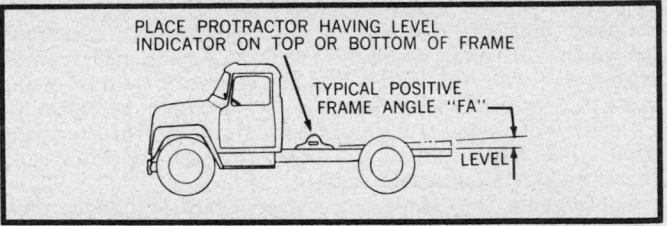

PLACE PROTRACTOR HAVING LEVEL INDICATOR ON TOP OR BOTTOM OF FRAME

TYPICAL POSITIVE FRAME ANGLE "FA"

LEVEL

Frame angle determination—method two

The effect of kingpin inclination is to cause the wheels to steer in a straight line, regardless of outside forces such as crowned roads, cross winds, etc., which may tend to make the vehicle steer at a tangent. As the spindle is moved from extreme right to extreme left it apparently rises and falls. The spindle reaches its highest position when the wheels are in the straight ahead position. In actual operation, the spindle cannot rise and fall because the wheel is in constant contact with the ground.

Therefore, the vehicle itself will rise at the extreme right turn and come to its lowest point at the straight ahead position, and again rise for an extreme left turn. The weight of the vehicle will tend to cause the wheels to come to the straight ahead position, which is the lowest position of the vehicle itself.

KINGPIN INCLUDED ANGLE

Included angle is the name given to that angle which includes kingpin inclination and camber. It is the relationship between the centerline of the wheel and the centerline of the kingpin (or the knuckle support pivots). This angle is built into the knuckle (spindle) forging and will remain constant throughout the life of the vehicle, unless the spindle itself is damaged.

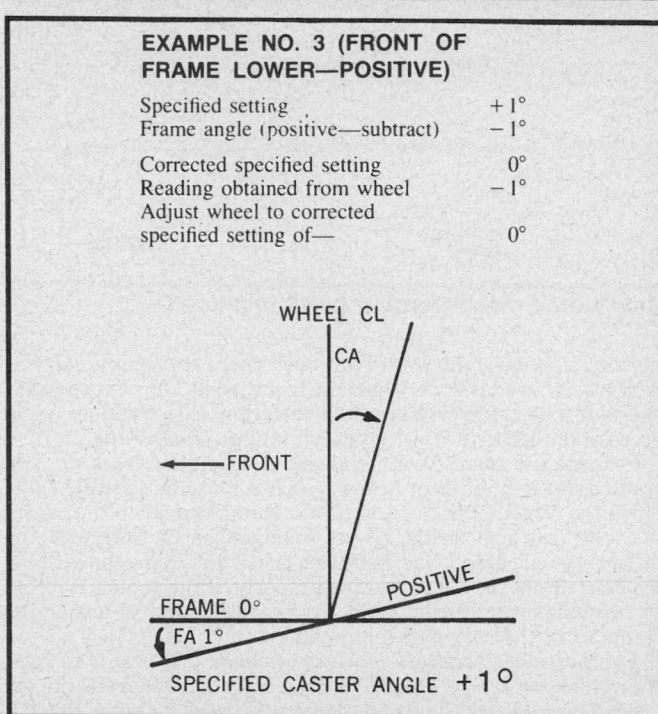

EXAMPLE NO. 3 (FRONT OF FRAME LOWER—POSITIVE)

Specified setting	+ 1°
Frame angle (positive—subtract)	– 1°
Corrected specified setting	0°
Reading obtained from wheel	– 1°
Adjust wheel to corrected specified setting of—	0°

SPECIFIED CASTER ANGLE + 1°

Alignment measurement — example three

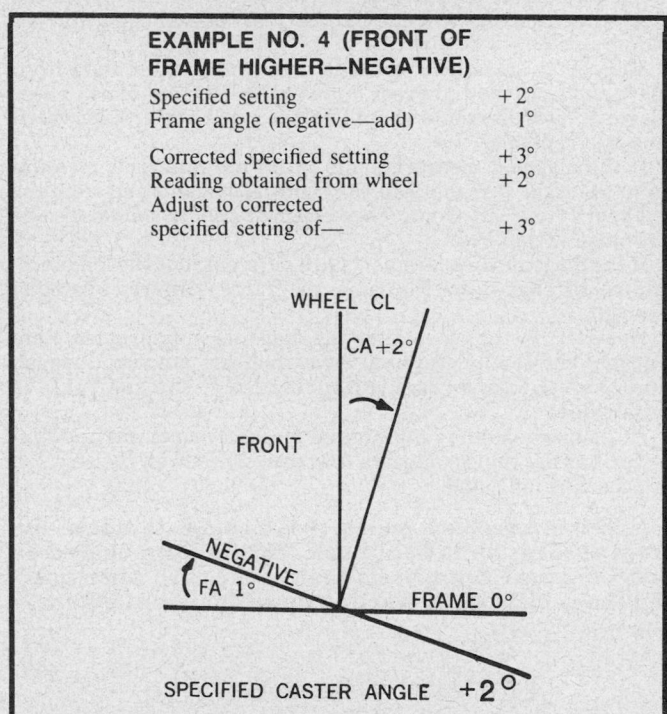

EXAMPLE NO. 4 (FRONT OF FRAME HIGHER—NEGATIVE)

Specified setting	+ 2°
Frame angle (negative—add)	1°
Corrected specified setting	+ 3°
Reading obtained from wheel	+ 2°
Adjust to corrected specified setting of—	+ 3°

SPECIFIED CASTER ANGLE + 2°

Alignment measurement — example four

When checking a vehicle on the front end alignment machine, always measure kingpin inclination as well as camber unless some provision is made on the stand for checking condition of the spindle. Where no such provision is made, add the kingpin inclination inclination to the camber for each side of the vehicle. These totals should be exactly the same, regardless of how far from the norm the readings may be.

For example, the left side of the vehicle checks 5½ degrees

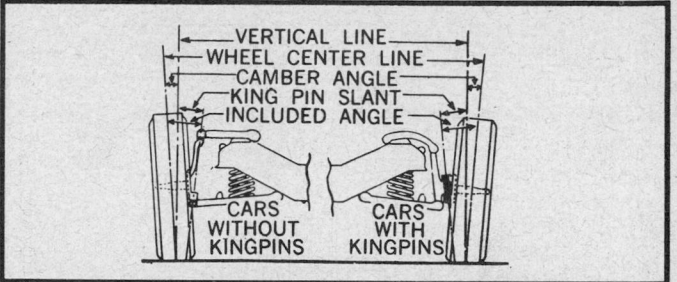

Included angle, kingpin and camber measurement locations

kingpin inclination and 1 degree positive camber the total is 6½ degrees. Since both sides check exactly the same for the included angle, it is unlikely that both spindles, in this instance, are bent. Adjusting to correct for camber will automatically set correct kingpin inclination.

A bent spindle would show up as follows. The left side of the vehicle has ¾ degree positive camber with 5¼ degree kingpin inclination, the total being 6 degrees included angle. The right side of vehicle has 1¼ degree positive camber with 6 degree kingpin inclination, the total being 7¼ degrees included angle. One of these spindles is bent and if adjustments are made to correct camber, the kingpin inclination will be incorrect due to the bent spindle.

Since the most common cause of a bent spindle is striking the curb when parking, which causes the spindle to bend upward, the side having the greater included angle usually has the bent spindle. It will be found impossible to achieve good alignment and minimum tire wear unless the bent spindle is replaced.

TOE-IN

Toe-in is the amount that the front wheels are closer together at the front than they are at the back. This dimension is usually measured, in inches or fractions of an inch.

Generally speaking, the wheels are toed-in because they are cambered. When a vehicle operates with zero degrees camber it will be found to operate with zero toe-in. As the required camber increases, so does the toe-in. The reason for this is that the cambered wheel tends to steer in the direction in which it is cambered. Therefore it is necessary to overcome this tendency by compensating very slightly in the direction opposite to that in which it tends to roll. Caster and camber both have an effect on toe-in. Therefore toe-in is the last component on the front end which should be corrected.

TOE-OUT

When a vehicle is steered into a turn, the outside wheel of the vehicle scribes a much larger circle than the inside wheel. Therefore, the outside wheel must be steered to a somewhat less angle than the inside wheel. This difference in the angle is often called toe-out.

The change in angle from toe-in in the straight ahead position to toe-out in the turn is caused by the relative position of the steering arms to the kingpin and to each other.

If a line were drawn from the center of the kingpin through the center of the steering arm tie rod attaching hole at each wheel the lines would be found to cross almost exactly in the center of the rear axle.

If the front end angles, including toe-in, are set correctly, and the toe-out is found to be incorrect, one or both of the steering arms are bent.

TRACKING

While tracking is more a function of the rear axle and frame, it is

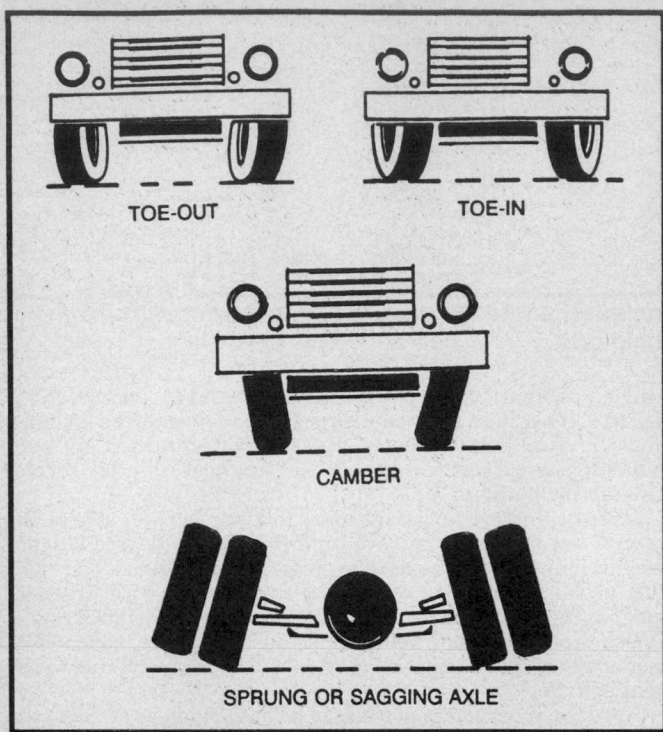

Exaggerated examples of alignment problems

TOE-OUT TOE-IN

CAMBER

SPRUNG OR SAGGING AXLE

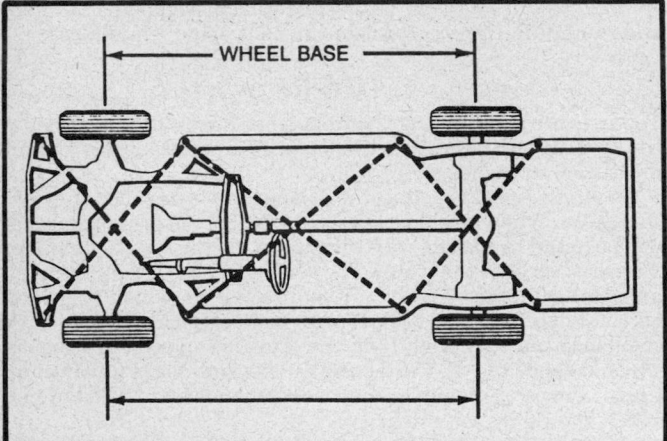

WHEEL BASE

Frame measurement point locations

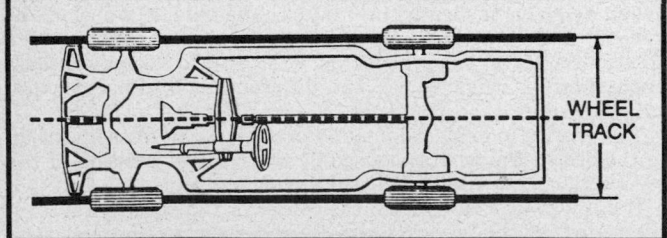

WHEEL TRACK

Parallel wheel track measurement

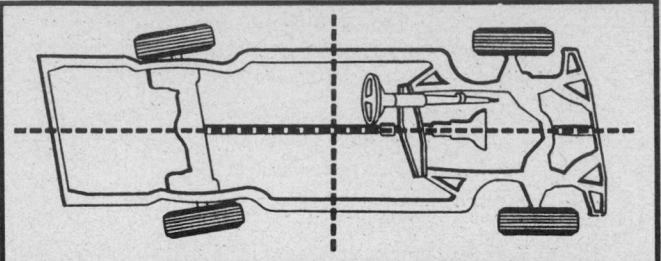

Bent frame measurement point locations

moving in a straight line. However, there are many vehicles whose rear tread is wider than the front tread. On such vehicles, the rear axle tread will straddle the front axle tread an equal amount on both sides, when moving in a straight line.

Perhaps the easiest way to check a vehicle for tracking is to stand directly in back of it and watch it more in a straight line down the street. If the observer will stand as near to the center of the vehicle as possible, he can readily observe, even with the difference in perspective between the front and rear wheels, whether or not they are tracking properly. If the vehicle is found to track incorrectly, the difficulty will be found in either the frame or in the rear axle alignment.

Another more accurate method to check tracking is to park the vehicle on a level floor and drop a plumb line from the extreme outer edge of the front suspension lower A-frame. Use the same drop point on each side of the vehicle. Make a chalk lie where the plumb line strikes the floor. Do the same with the rear axle, selecting a point on the rear axle housing for the plumb line.

Measure diagonally from the left rear mark to the right front mark and from the right rear mark to the left front mark. These diagonal measurements should be the same but a ¼ in. variation is acceptable.

If the diagonal measurements taken are different, measure from the right rear mark to the right front mark and from the left rear to the left front. These measurements should also be the same within ¼ in.

If the diagonal measurements are different, but the longitudinal measurements are the same, the frame is swayed (diamond shaped).

However, in the event that the diagonal measurements are unequal and the longitudinal measurements are also unequal, and the vehicle is tracking incorrectly, the rear axle is misaligned.

If the diagonal and longitudinal measurements are both unequal, but the vehicle appears to track correctly on the street, a kneeback is indicated.

NOTE: A kneeback means that a complete side of the front suspension is bent back. This is often caused by crimping the front wheels against the curb when parking the vehicle, then starting up without straightening the wheels out.

Tire and Wheel Service

TIRE AND WHEEL BALANCE

There are 2 types of tire and wheel balancing procedures. They are the dynamic balance and the static balance.

The dynamic balance is the equal distribution of weight on each side of the centerline, so that when the tire and wheel assembly spins there is no tendency for the assembly to move from side to side. Tire and wheel assemblies that are dynamically unbalanced may cause wheel shimmy.

The static balance is the equal distribution of weight around

difficult to align the front suspension when the vehicle does not track straight. Tracking means that the centerline of the rear axle follows exactly the path of the centerline of the front axle when the vehicle is moving in a straight line.

On vehicles that have equal tread, front and rear, the rear tires will follow in exactly the thread of the front tires, when

TIRE AND WHEEL DIAGNOSIS

Condition	Cause	Correction
Tires show excess wear on edge of tread	1) Under inflated tires 2) Vehicle overloaded 3) High-speed cornering 4) Incorrect toe setting	1) Adjust air pressure in tires 2) Correct as required 3) Correct as required 4) Set to to specification
Tires show excess wear in center of tread	1) Tires over inflated	1) Adjust air pressure in tires
Other excessive tire wear problems	1) Improper tire pressure 2) Incorrect tire/wheel usage 3) Loose or leaking shock absorbers 4) Front end out of alignment 5) Front wheel bearings out of adjustment 6) Loose, worn or damaged suspension components, bushings and ball joints 7) Wheels and tires out of balance 8) Excessive lateral and/or radial runout of wheel or tire 9) Tires need rotating	1) Adjust air pressure in tires 2) Install correct tire and wheel combination 3) Tighten or replace as necessary 4) Align front end 5) Adjust front wheel bearings 6) Inspect, repair or replace as required 7) Balance wheels and tires 8) Check, repair or replace as required. Use dial indicator to accurately determine runout 9) Rotate tires
Excessive vehicle vibration, rough steering, or severe tire wear	1) Loose or improper attaching parts 2) Overloading or unbalanced loads	1) Tighten or replace 2) Check wheel and tire specs against work load requirements. Recommend correct tire and rim. Check on loading procedure
Vehicle vibrations	1) Loose or worn driveline or suspension parts 2) Improper front end alignment 3) Excessive lateral runout (wheel or tire). Use a dial indicator to accurately verify runout reading 4) Bent or distorted wheel disc from overloading, road impact hazards or improper handling 5) Loose mountings—damaged studs, cap nuts, enlarged stud holes, worn or broken hub face or foreign material on mounting surfaces 6) Out-of-balance wheel and/or tire or hub and drum assembly 7) Out-of-round wheel or tire (excessive radial runout). Use a dial indicator to accurately verify runout reading 8) Wheel stud runout 9) Water in tires	1) Identify location of vibration carefully as it may be transmitted through frame making a rear end vibration appear to come from the front. Repair or replace loose and worn parts 2) Align front end 3) Replace wheel or tire 4) Replace wheel. Attempts to straighten wheel can result in fractures in the steel and weakening of the disc or the weld between disc and rim. Check loading and operating conditions and shop practices 5) Tighten and/or replace worn or damaged parts. Clean mounting surfaces 6) Determine the out-of-balance component and balance or replace 7) Replace the wheel or tire and check for overloading and unbalanced loads, rugged operating conditions, proper wheel and tire specifications 8) Replace hub or axle shaft 9) Remove water
Wheel mounting is difficult	1) Improper application or mismatched parts, including studs and nuts 2) Corroded or worn parts	1) Follow manufacturers' specifications 2) Clean or replace
Wheel-rust or corrosion	1) Poor maintenance	1) Keep clean and protect with paint

TIRE AND WHEEL DIAGNOSIS

Condition	Cause	Correction
Cracked or broken wheel discs. Cracks develop in the wheel disc from hand hole to hand hole, from hand hole to rim, or from hand hole to stud. Stud holes become worn, elongated or deformed. Metal builds up around stud hole edges, cracks develop from stud hole to stud hole. Related driver complaints: unusual operating noise or vibration and on the road failures	1) Metal fatigue resulting from abusive handling 2) Vehicle operated with loose wheel mounting	1) Replace wheel. Check position of wheel on vehicle for working load specifications 2) Replace wheel and check for: — Installation or correct studs and nuts, and recommend exact specifications — Cracked or broken studs, and replace — Worn hub face. Machine if not excessive, or replace if severe — Broken or cracked hub barrel, replace — Worn stud grooves, replace or install recommended serrated bolts — Clean mounting surfaces and re-torque cap nut periodically NOTE: Rust streaks fanning out from stud holes are a sure indication that the cap nuts are or have been loose
Cracks develop in rim base back flange (rim bead seat) or the gutter area (drop well radii)	1) Overloading or abuse 2) Improper use of tools	1) Replace rim or wheel. Check loading and operating conditions. Avoid over inflation of tires. Check specs for rim load capacity, working loads, tire size, ply rating and tire construction 2) Check mounting, demounting, and maintenance procedures
Damaged stud threads	1) Sliding wheel across studs during assembly	1) Replace studs. Follow proper wheel installation procedure
Loose drum	1) Stud too long	1) Replace stud with proper length stud
Broken studs	1) Loose lug nuts 2) Overloading	1) Replace studs. Follow proper torque procedure 2) Replace studs. Compare actual load against vehicle load ratings
Stripping threads	1) Excessive torque	1) Replace studs. Follow proper torque procedure
Rust streaks from stud holes	1) Loose lug nuts	1) Check complete assembly. Replace damaged parts. Follow proper torque procedure
Damaged lug nuts	1) Loose wheel assembly	1) Replace lug nuts. Check for proper stud standout. Follow proper torque procedure
Frozen lug nuts	1) Corrosion or galling	1) If corrosion is slight, wire brush away corrosion If corrosion is excessive, replace studs and nuts If condition persists, lubricate first three threads of each stud with a graphite-based lubricant NOTE: Do not permit lubricant to get on cone seats of stud holes or on cone face of lug nuts

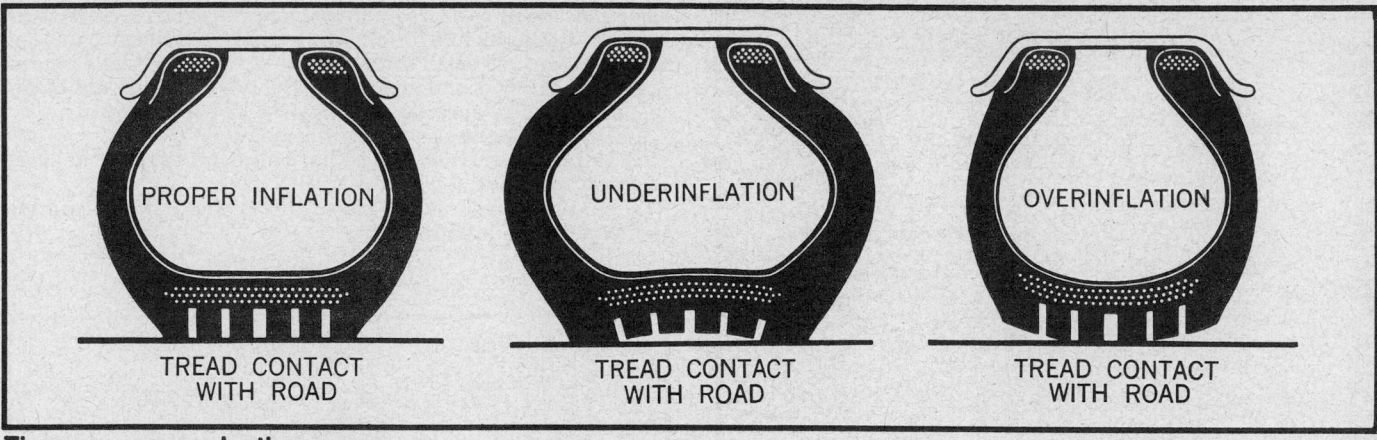

PROPER INFLATION

UNDERINFLATION

OVERINFLATION

TREAD CONTACT WITH ROAD

TREAD CONTACT WITH ROAD

TREAD CONTACT WITH ROAD

Tire pressure evaluation

the wheel. Tire and wheel assemblies that are statically unbalanced cause a bouncing action called wheel tramp. This condition will eventually cause uneven tire wear.

Before the tire and wheel assembly can be properly balanced all deposits of mud, etc must be removed from the inside of the rim area. Stones and other foreign matter should be removed from the tire tread area. The tire and wheel assembly should be inspected for any signs of external damage. Once these conditions have been met the tire and wheel assembly is ready to be balanced according to manufacturers instructions.

TIRE ROTATION

To ensure that all tires wear evenly tire rotation should be done every 8000 miles. If a tire shows excessive wear the wear problem should be corrected before rotating the tires. If the vehicle is equipped with a temporary spare tire, do not include it in the tire rotation procedure.

LUG NUT TORQUE

When reinstalling tire and wheel lug nuts, be sure that they are torqued properly and to the correct specification. Tighten the lug nuts in a criss-cross manner until all the lug nuts are snug against the wheel assembly. Torque the lug nuts to specification and in the proper sequence.

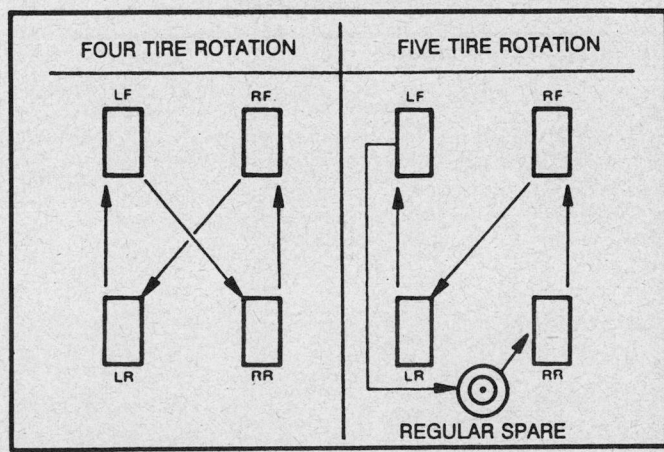

FOUR TIRE ROTATION

FIVE TIRE ROTATION

LF   RF

LF   RF

LR   RR

LR   RR

REGULAR SPARE

Tire rotation pattern

TIRE REPLACEMENT

Specialized tools and equipment have been designed for use in

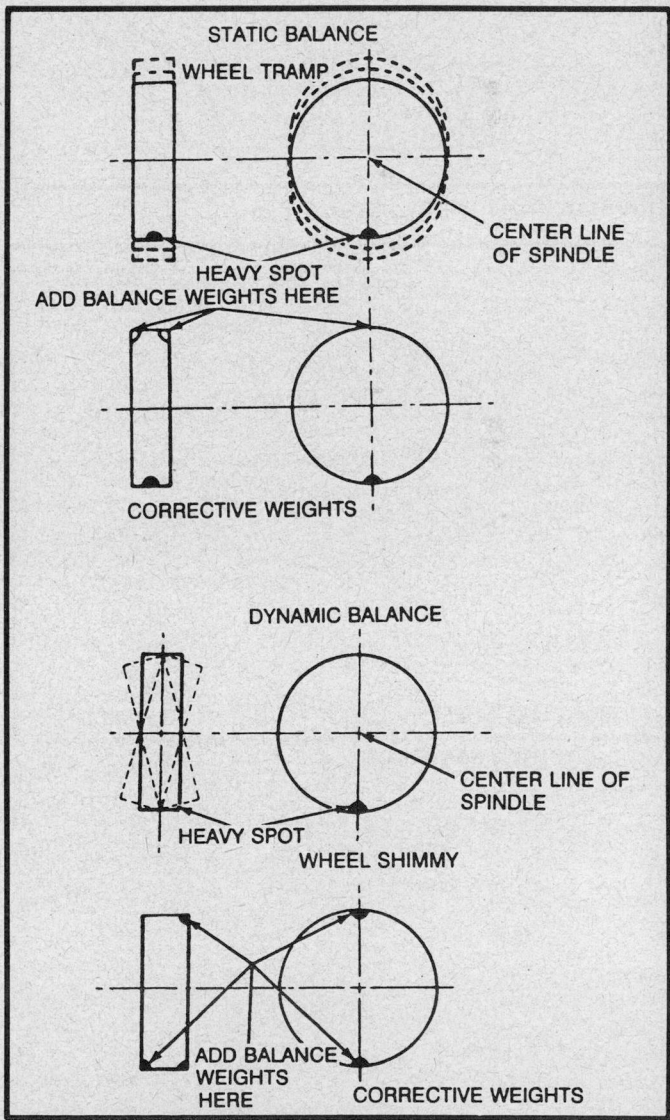

STATIC BALANCE

WHEEL TRAMP

CENTER LINE OF SPINDLE

HEAVY SPOT
ADD BALANCE WEIGHTS HERE

CORRECTIVE WEIGHTS

DYNAMIC BALANCE

CENTER LINE OF SPINDLE

HEAVY SPOT

WHEEL SHIMMY

ADD BALANCE WEIGHTS HERE

CORRECTIVE WEIGHTS

Tire and wheel balancing points

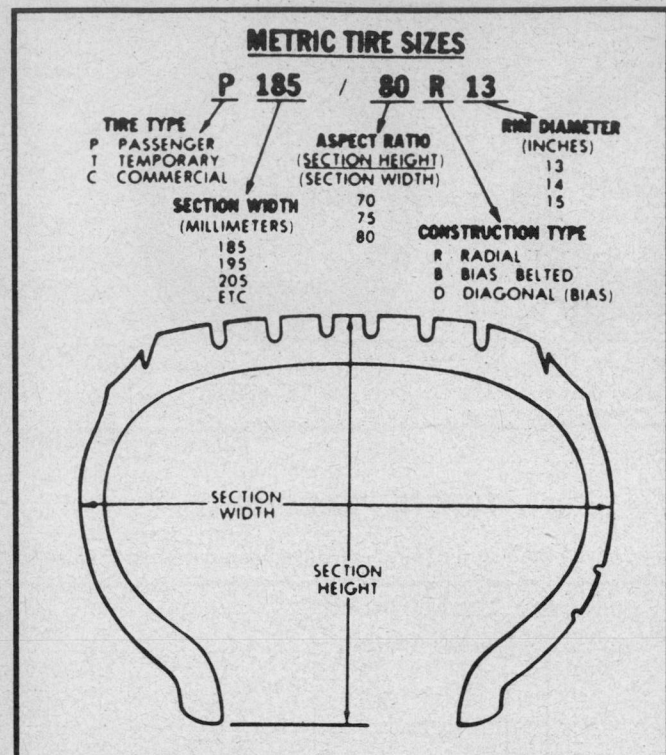

Tire data explanation

the replacement of a tire on multipiece rims. The manufacturers instructions should be followed in the use of the machines in the mounting and dismounting of tires to avoid personal injury.

For the safety of the repairman, the word **DIP** should be remembered when working with tires and wheels.

1. **D**—deflate the tire before working on it.
2. **I**—inspect the rim, rings, lug holes and tires for damage and proper sealing.
3. **P**—protect yourself by placing the tire and wheel assembly in a cage before inflating it.

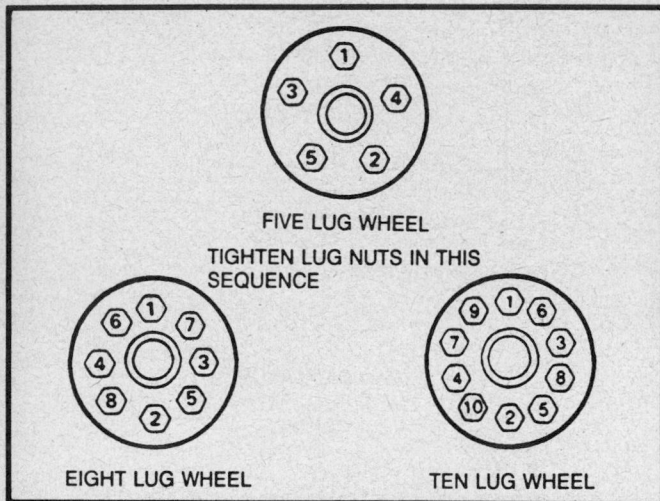

Lug nut torque sequence

Tire servicing procedure

GENERAL INFORMATION

Drive Axle Types

FULL FLOATING AXLES

Support of the vehicle and the payload weight is by the axle housing. The wheels are driven by splined shafts which float within the axle housing.

SEMI-FLOATING AXLE

This axle design provides for the support of the payload and vehicle weight to be carried by the axle shaft through the wheel bearings to the axle housing.

SINGLE REDUCTION AXLE

Final drive ratio is obtained by the use of a single ring gear and pinion set.

LOCK-UP TYPE DIFFERENTIALS

Unlike the standard differential, the locking differential equally divides the torque load between the driving wheels. The vehicle equipped with a locking differential can be operated on any surface (sand, snow, etc.) with a minimum of slippage through one wheel and provides the greatest power to the wheel getting traction. The vehicle with the standard differential provides power to the wheel that's easiest to turn; that is, the one experiencing the poorest traction while the other wheel may be gripping well.

When negotiating a turn, the locking differential allows the outer wheel to turn faster than the inner. When traveling in a straight direction, and the vehicle loses traction over a rough or slippery road, the clutches will lock-up and neither wheel will spin. A specified lubricant must be used for locking differentials.

The overhaul procedures are basically the same as for the conventional rear axle assemblies. The noted differences are within the differential carrier case where the lock-up mechanism is located. In some instances where wear is noted within the lock-up mechanism, the lock-up assembly should be replaced as a unit.

Drive Axle Service

COMPONENT INSPECTION AND REPLACING

Cleaning Bearings

Proper bearing cleaning is important. Bearings should always be cleaned separately from other rear axle parts.
 1. Soak all bearings in clean kerosene or diesel fuel oil.

NOTE: Ordinary gasoline should not be used nor should bearings should not be cleaned in hot solution tank.

 2. Slush bearings in cleaning solution until all oil lubricant is loosened. Brush bearings with soft bristled brush until all dirt has been removed. Remove loose particles of dirt by striking flat against a wood block.
 3. Rinse bearings in clean fluid. While holding races to prevent rotation, blow dry with compressed air.

NOTE: Do not spin bearings while drying.

 4. After bearings have been inspected, lubricate thoroughly with regular axle lubricant; then wrap each bearing in clean cloth until ready to use.

Checking the drive gear run-out

Cleaning Parts

Immerse all parts in cleaning fluid and clean thoroughly. Use a stiff bristle brush as required to remove foreign deposits. Clean all lubricant passages or channels in pinion cage, carrier, caps and retainers. Make certain the interior of housing is thoroughly cleaned. Clean vent plugs and breathers.

Small parts such as cap screws, bolts, studs, nuts and etc., should be cleaned thoroughly.

Inspection

Magna flux all steel parts, except ball and roller bearings, to detect presence of wear and cracks.

Bearings

Rotate each bearing and check to see if the rollers are worn, chipped, rough or in any other way damaged. Check the cage to see if it is in any way damaged. If either the bearing rollers or the cage are damaged the bearing must be replaced.

Gears

Examine drive gear and drive pinion, differential pinions and differential side gears carefully, for damaged teeth, worn spots in surface hardening, distortion and where drive gear is attached to differential case with rivets, inspect rivets for looseness, replace loose rivets. Check radial clearances between differential side gears and differential case. Check fit of differential pinions on spider.

Differential Case

Inspect case for cracks, distortion or damage, if in good condition, thoroughly clean case and cover; then assemble case with bolts and mount in lathe centers of V-block stand. If lathe is not available, install differential side bearings and mount case in differential carrier. Install dial indicator and check differential case run out.

Differential case with drive gear installed is checked in the same manner, except the dial indicator reading must be taken at the gear instead of the case flange.

Axle Shafts

Examine splined end of axle shaft for twisted or cracked splines, twisted shaft and worn dowel holes in flange; install new shafts, if necessary.

Install axle shaft assembly in lathe centers and check shaft run-out with dial indicator so the indicator shaft end contacts inner surface of flange near outer edge of flange and check flange run-out.

Shims

Carefully inspect shims for uniform thickness. Where various thickness of shims are used in a pack, it is recommended the thickest shims be used between the thin shims.

Thrust Washers

Replace all thrust washers.

Spider Arms

Carefully inspect spider arms for wear or defects.

Differential Pinion Bushings

Examine bushings (when used) for excessive wear, looseness or damage. Check fit or gears on spider for excessive clearance.

Axle Housing Sleeves

Sleeves showing damaged threads, wear or other damage should be replaced, if a hydraulic press is available, otherwise replace housing.

Housing Check
BEFORE REMOVAL

A check for bent axle housing can be made with unit in vehicle; however, conventional alignment instruments can be used, if available.

1. Raise and safely support rear axle. Block the axle under each spring seat.
2. Check wheel bearing adjustment and adjust, if necessary; then, check wheels for looseness and tighten wheel nuts, if necessary.
3. Place a chalk mark on outer side wall of tires at bottom. Measure across tires at chalk marks with a toe-in gauge.
4. Turn wheels half-way around so the chalk marks are positioned at top of wheel. Measure across tires again. If measurement at top is ⅓ in. or more, smaller than measurement at bottom of wheels, axle housing has sagged and is bent. If measurement at top exceeds bottom dimension by ⅓ in. or more, axle housing is bent at ends.
5. Turn chalk marks on both wheels so the marks are level with axle and at rear of vehicle. Take measurement with toe-in gauge at chalk marks; then, turn both chalk marks to front and level with axle and take another measurement. If measurement at front exceeds rear dimension by ⅓ in. or more, axle is bent to the rear. If the measurement condition is the reverse, the axle is bent forward.

AFTER REMOVAL

Place two straightedges across the housing flanges and measure the distance between the ends of the straightedges at a point 11 inches from the tube center. Relocate the straightedge 180 degrees and remeasure. If the straightedges are parallel in both measurements within ³⁄₃₂ in., the housing is serviceable.

Oil Seal

Surface of parts, contacted by oil seals must be free of corrosion, pits and grooves. When abrasive cleaning fails to clean up the seal contact surface and restore smooth finish, a new part must be installed.

Oil seals can be removed with a drift pin. When removing a seal, be careful it does not become cocked and result in damage to the retainer. Clean surface of retainer carefully, so the seal will seat properly in retainer. Coat outer surface of seal retainer with a light coat of sealer, to prevent lubricant leaks. Carefully start seal in retainer. Cutting, scratching or curling of lip of seal seriously impairs its efficiency and usually results in premature replacement. Lip of seal should be coated with a high temperature grease containing zinc oxide to help prevent scoring and

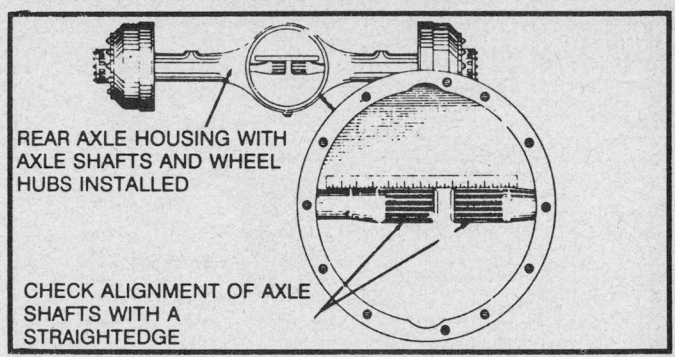

Method of checking the axle housing alignment with full floating axles

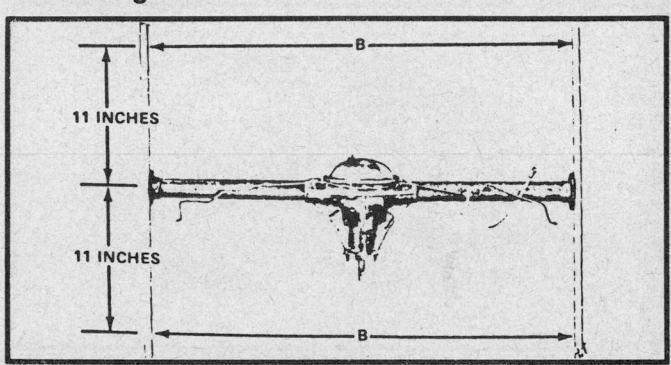

Checking the housing alignment with straight edge bars

damage to parts during installation. Seals must always be installed so the seal lip is toward the lubricant.

Pinion Bearing
Adjustments (Preload)

Pinion bearing must be adjusted for preload before assembly is installed in carrier.

Do not install oil seal until after adjustment is made. Installation of seal would produce false rotating torque.

1. With pinion bearings and adjusting spacers (or shims) installed in cage, check bearing contact by rotating cage.
2. Using a press, apply pressure (approx. 20,000 lbs.) to outer bearing.
3. Wrap soft wire around cage and pull on horizontal line with spring scale. Rotating (not starting) torque should be within limits recommended by manufacturer.

Adjustments (Preload)

Pinion bearing must be adjusted for preload before assembly is installed in carrier.

Do not install oil seal until after adjustment is made. Installation of seal would produce false rotating torque.

1. With pinion bearings and adjusting spacers (or shims) installed in cage, check bearing contact by rotating cage.
2. Using a press, apply pressure (approx. 20,000 lbs.) to outer bearing.
3. Wrap soft wire around cage and pull on horizontal line with spring scale. Rotating (not starting) torque should be within limits recommended by manufacturer.

NOTE: Method of determining inch-pounds torque with scale is to determine radius of cage. Multiply radius in inches by pounds pull required to rotate cage to determine inch-pounds torque. Example: An 8 in. diameter divided by 2 equals 4 in. radius. Multiply 4 in. (radius) by 5 pounds (pull) equals 20 in. pounds torque.

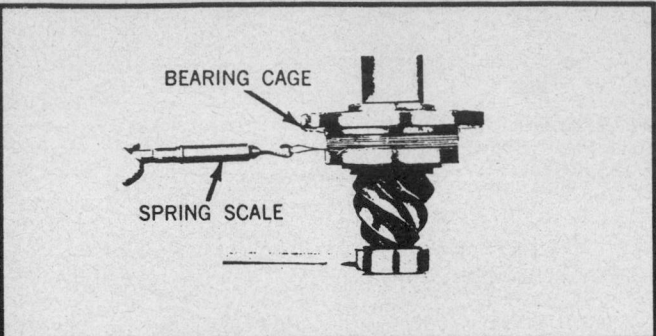

Checking the pinion pre-load

Checking the pre-load on bevel gear cross shaft

4. If press is not available, check preload torque by installing propeller shaft yoke, washer, and nut and torque to specifications; then check as previously explained. Remove yoke after correct adjustment is obtained.

Bevel Gear Shaft Bearing Adjustment

Bevel gear shaft bearings must be adjusted for preload before pinion and cage assembly and differential assembly are installed in carrier.

1. Wrap several turns of soft wire around gear teeth on cross shaft and pull on a horizontal line with spring scale. Rotating (not starting) torque should be used.

NOTE: Method of determining inch lbs. torque with scale is to determine radius. Multiply radius in inches by pounds pull required to rotate shaft to determine inch-pounds torque. Example: An 8 in. diameter divided by 2 equals 4 in. radius times 5 pounds (pull) equals 20 inch lbs. torque.

2. Remove or add shims from under cage or cap opposite bevel gear to obtain specified bearing preload.

3. When making bevel gear and pinion tooth contact or backlash adjustments it is sometimes necessary to remove or add shims from one side.

NOTE: Always remove or add an equal thickness to the opposite side so to maintain correct preload.

Gear Tooth Contact and Backlash

PINION DEPTH MEASUREMENT METHOD

Methods of adjusting pinions to obtain the proper depths will vary with the axle type and the manufacturers recommendations. Pinion depth settings and gear teeth contact may be determined by the use of pinion setting gauges or by the use of marking dye on the gear teeth.

When using the gauge method, backlash is established after the pinion has been properly set. With the dye method, backlash is obtained first, then, the proper pinion tooth contact is established.

The pinion gauge method can be a direct reading micrometer, mounted on or through an arbor bar, set in adapter discs and located in the side carrier bearing cup locations on the differential housing and held in place by the bearing cup caps. The arbor bar coincides and represents the center line of the axle shafts. A reading is taken by the mounted micrometer, from the arbor bar to the head of the pinion to determine the need to add to or remove shims from the shim pack total, to adjust the pinion to the proper nominal assembly dimension or standard pinion depth.

Another method using the arbor bar and discs, is the use of a gauge block with a spring loaded plunger and a thumb screw to lock the plunger upon expansion. A micrometer is used to measure the gauge block after the plunger has been allowed to expand between the arbor bar and the pinion head. As in the mounted micrometer procedure, the shim pack thickness is determined by the reading obtained.

A third method is the use of a gauge block tool, installed in the housing in place of the pinion gear, and a large arbor bar placed in the axle housing differential bearing seats and tightened securely. A measurement is taken between the arbor bar and the pinion tool by either a feeler gauge or the use of individual shims from the shim pack. This measurement represents the shim pack needed for a zero marked pinion.

SETTING NEW PINION (WITHOUT GAUGE)

Whenever a pinion setting gauge is not available, the approximate thickness of the pinion shim pack at the rear pinion bearing cup, change the sign of the marking (individual variation distance) on the new pinion (plus to minus or minus to plus), then add the variation of the old pinion (sign unchanged) which will determine the amount the original shim pack must be changed when installing a new pinion.

On those types of axles where the shims are located between

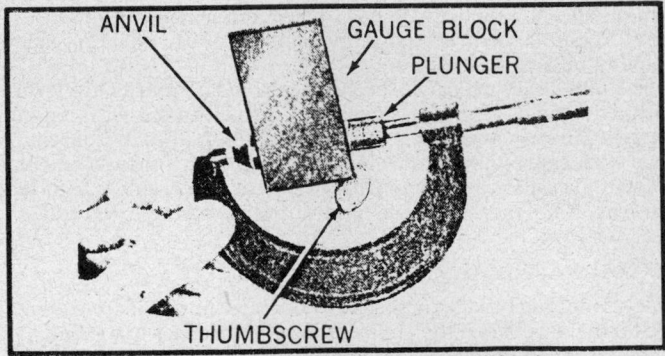

Method of measurement of the gauge block

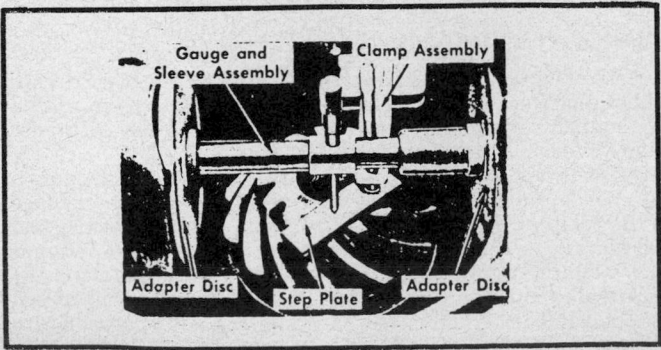

Installment of the pinion gauge

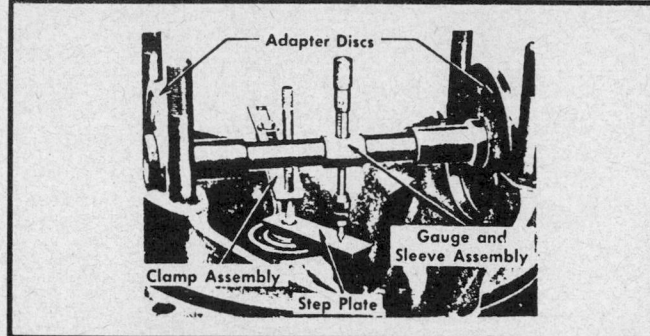

Position of pinion setting gauge

Checking the gear backlash-bevel gear

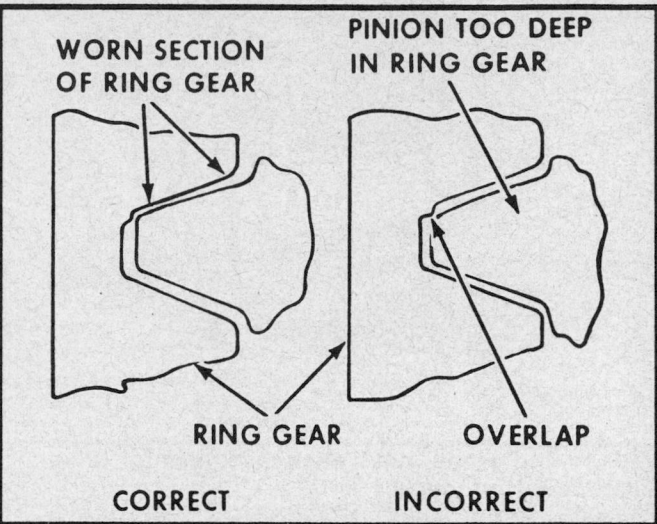

Avoid overlap of worn section of gear teeth during backlash adjustments when using original gears

the pinion cage and differential carrier, change the sign of the marking (individual variation distance) on the old pinion (plus to minus or minus to plus), then, add variation of the new pinion (sign unchanged) which will determine how much the original shim pack must be altered when installing a new pinion.

When the approximate thickness of shim pack has been determined, final check of gear tooth contact must be made using dye method.

GEAR TOOTH CONTACT (DYE)

Gear tooth contact cannot be successfully accomplished until pinion and bevel gear bearings are in proper adjustment and gear backlash is within specified limits.

Check for proper tooth contact by painting a few teeth of bevel gear with marking dye. Turn pinion in direction of normal rotation, then check tooth impression on bevel gear.

GEAR BACKLASH

Gears used in extended service, form running contacts due to wear of teeth; therefore, the original shim pack (between pinion cage and carrier) should be maintained when checking backlash. If backlash exceeds maximum tolerance, reduce backlash only in the amount that will avoid overlap of worn tooth section. Smoothness and roughness can be noted by rotating bevel gear.

If a slight overlap is present at worn tooth section, rotation will be rough.

If new gears are installed, check backlash with dial indicator.

Backlash is increased by moving bevel gear away from pinion and may be decreased by moving bevel gear toward pinion.

When the drive gear is attached to the differential, backlash is accomplished is differential bearing adjusting rings. It should be remembered, when one ring is tightened, the opposite ring must be loosened an equal amount to maintain previously established bearing adjustment.

On axles where the bevel gear is supported by cross shaft, backlash is accomplished by adding or removing shims under bearing cages.

TERMS USED

Certain dimensions must be determined when using the pinion setting gauge:

1. **Nominal Assembly Dimension:** (standard pinion depth) This dimension (varying with axle model) is the distance between the center line of the drive gear (or differential carrier bore) and the end of the drive pinion. This dimension may be marked on the pinion or listed on the Nominal Assembly Dimension and Adapter Disc chart.

2. **Individual Variation Distance:** (pinion depth variance) This dimension is a plus or minus variation of the **Nominal Assembly Dimension** on each individual pinion which may be caused by manufacturing variations.

3. **Corrected Nominal Dimension:** (desired pinion depth) This dimension is the **Nominal Assembly Dimension** plus or minus the **Individual Variation Distance.**

4. **Corrected Micrometer Distance** is the **Corrected Nominal Dimension** less the thickness of the gauge set step plate (0.400 in.) mounted on end of pinion.

5. **Initial Micrometer Reading** is the dimension taken by micrometer to the gauge step plate.

6. **Shim Pack Correction** is determined by the difference between the **Corrected Micrometer Distance** and the **Initial Micrometer Reading** and represents the amount of shim pack to be added or removed as later explained.

7. **Measured Pinion Depth.** This measurement is the distance between the axle center line and the top of the pinion gear. If a step plate or other type gauge tool is used, this measurement is included in the total.

Pinion and Drive Gear Identification

Drive gears and pinions are tested at the time of manufacture to detect machining variances and to obtain desirable tooth contact and quietness. When the correct setting is achieved, the gears are considered matched and a set of numbers, along with other identifying marks are etched on the gear set.

A plus (+) or minus (−) sign is used, followed by a digit to represent the factory setting where the tooth contact and quietness were the best. This is called the pinion depth variance or individual variation distance.

If the pinion is marked + 5 for example, this means the distance from the pinion gear rear face to the axle shaft center line is 0.005 in. more than the standard setting and if the pinion gear is marked − 5, this means the distance is 0.005 in. less than the

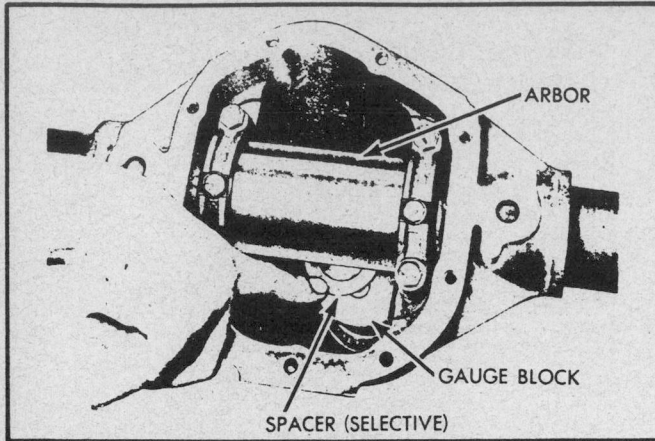

Determining proper shim pack thickness for drive pinion depth of mesh

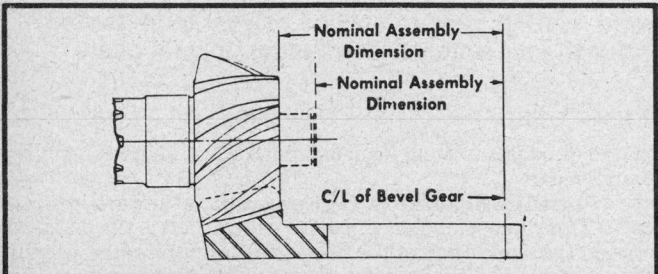

Nominal assembly dimension

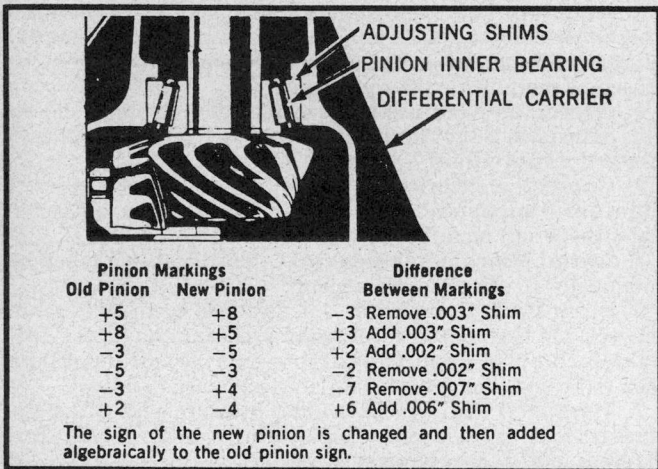

| Pinion Markings | | Difference |
Old Pinion	New Pinion	Between Markings
+5	+8	−3 Remove .003" Shim
+8	+5	+3 Add .003" Shim
−3	−5	+2 Add .002" Shim
−5	−3	−2 Remove .002" Shim
−3	+4	−7 Remove .007" Shim
+2	−4	+6 Add .006" Shim

The sign of the new pinion is changed and then added algebraically to the old pinion sign.

Determining pinion shim pack thickness, if the shim pack is located at the rear pinion bearing cup

standard setting. To move the pinion to the standard setting, compensating for the variation, shims must be either added to subtracted from the total shim pack, located under the rear pinion bearing cup, between the pinion cage and the differential carrier or under the rear pinion bearing, depending upon the differential model being serviced.

The procedures to follow in the adjustment of the pinion and drive gears are outlined in the respective differential model disassembly and assembly chapters.

As a rule of thumb on the addition or removal of shims for the pinion depth adjustment, draw a diagram as shown and determine which way the pinion must be moved to obtain the desired pinion depth.

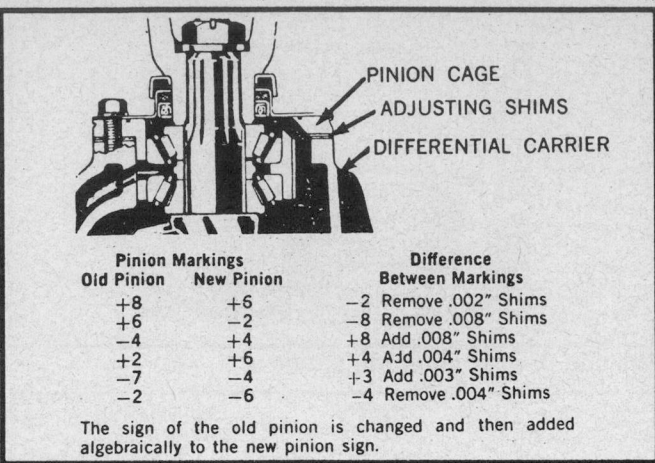

| Pinion Markings | | Difference |
Old Pinion	New Pinion	Between Markings
+8	+6	−2 Remove .002" Shims
+6	−2	−8 Remove .008" Shims
−4	+4	+8 Add .008" Shims
+2	+6	+4 Add .004" Shims
−7	−4	+3 Add .003" Shims
−2	−6	−4 Remove .004" Shims

The sign of the old pinion is changed and then added algebraically to the new pinion sign.

Determining pinion shim pack thickness, if the shim pack is located between the pinion cage and differential

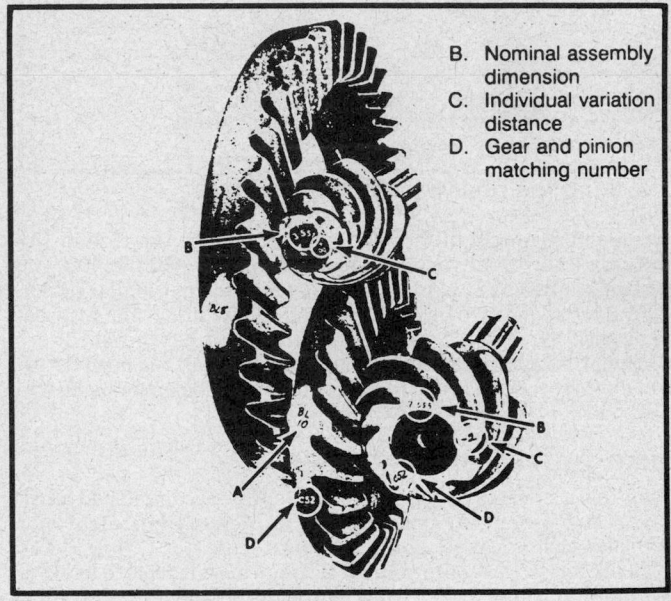

B. Nominal assembly dimension
C. Individual variation distance
D. Gear and pinion matching number

Typical gear set marking code

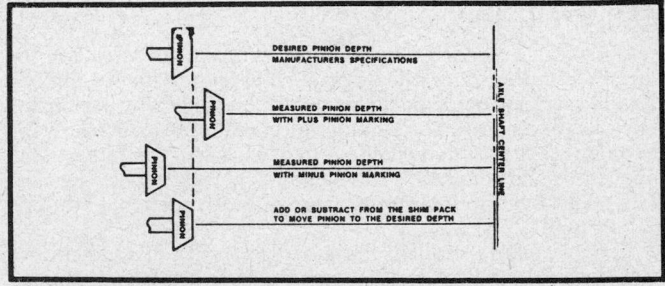

Movement of pinion to obtain desired pinion depth

Standard Torque Specifications and Capscrew Markings

Because of the varied bolt sizes used in the many models of differentials, the torque specifications are not always available for a specific bolt. By determining the grade of bolt, size and thread, the proper torque limit can be determined.

CHRYSLER CORPORATION

Front Axle Assembly

7¼ INCH RING GEAR AXLE

Disassembly

DIFFERENTIAL

1. Remove the axle housing cover.
2. Clean the inside of the differential case with solvent and blow dry with compressed air.
3. Turn the differential case to make the differential pinion shaft lock screw accessible and remove the lock screw and pinion shaft.
4. Remove the left axle shaft by performing the following procedures:
    a. Remove the C-lock from the recessed groove of the axle shaft.
    b. Remove the axle shaft from the housing.
5. Remove the right axle shaft and inner axle shaft by performing the following procedures:
    a. Remove the disconnect housing cover assembly-to-axle housing screws and the assembly and the gasket.
    b. Remove the axle bearing seal retainer-to-axle housing

screws and the axle/bearing retainer assembly from the axle housing.
    c. Remove the shift collar from the disconnect housing.
    d. Remove the C-lock from the recessed groove of the axle shaft.
    e. Remove the needle bearing from the inner axle shaft.
    f. Using an axle puller tool, pull the inner axle shaft from the axle housing.
6. Check for differential side-play by inserting a pry-bar between the left side of the axle housing and the differential case flange. Using a prying motion, determine whether side-play exists; there should be no side-play.
7. Paint the ring gear teeth and make a gear tooth contact pattern. Determine if proper depth of mesh can be obtained.
8. If side-play was found in step 6, proceed to step 9. If no side-play was found in step 6, check the drive gear run-out by performing the following procedures:
    a. Mount a dial indicator and index the indicator stem at right angles in the rear face of the ring gear.
    b. Rotate the ring gear and mark the ring gear and case at the point of greatest run-out.
    c. Total indicator reading should not exceed 0.005 in.; if it does, the possibility exists that the case must be replaced.

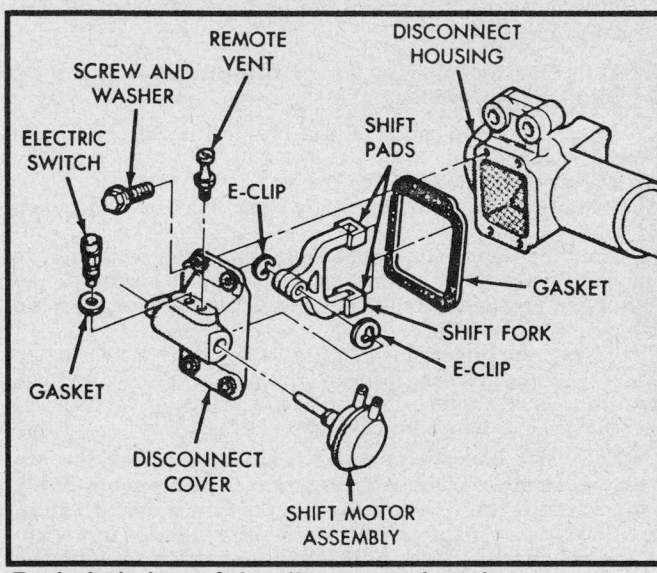

Exploded view of the disconnect housing cover assembly—front axle assembly

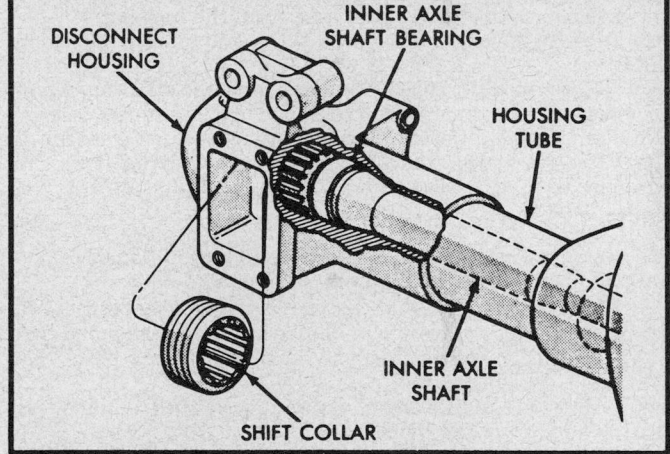

View of the inner axle shaft, bearing and shift collar—front axle assembly

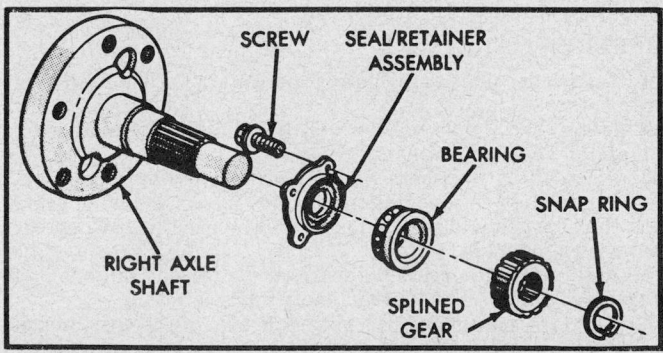

Exploded view of the right axle shaft—front axle assembly

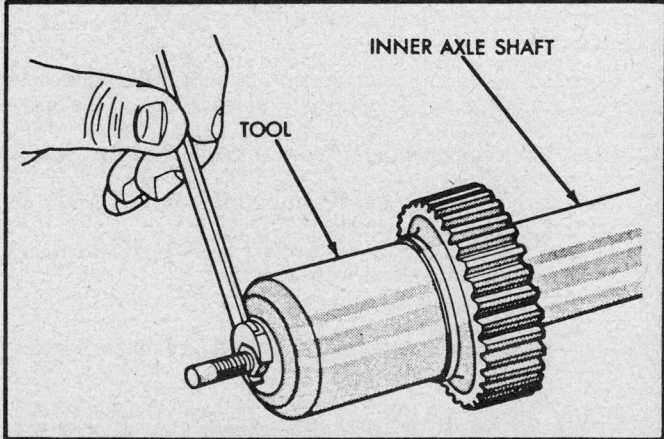

Removing the needle bearing from the inner axle shaft—front axle assembly

9. Using an inch lb. torque wrench, measure and record the pinion bearing preload.

10. Matchmark the axle housing and the differential bearing caps.

11. Remove the threaded adjusters and the differential bearing caps; there is a special wrench to do this through the axle tube.

12. Remove the differential case from the housing.

NOTE: The differential bearing cups and threaded adjuster must be kept together so they can be installed in their original position.

13. Clamp the differential case and ring gear in a vise with soft jaws.

14. Remove the ring gear bolts (left-hand thread). Tap the ring gear loose with a soft-faced mallet.

15. If the ring gear run-out exceeded 0.005 in., recheck the case as follows:

    a. Install the differential case, cups, caps and adjusters into the housing.

    b. Turn the adjusters to eliminate all side-play and tighten the differential cap bolts snugly.

    c. Measure the run-out at the ring gear flange face; total indicator reading should not exceed 0.003 in.

NOTE: It is often possible to reduce run-out by removing the ring gear and reinstalling it 180 degrees from its original position.

    d. Remove the differential case from the housing.

16. Remove the pinion shaft lock-screw and remove the pinion shaft.

17. Rotate the differential side gears until the differential pinion shafts can be removed through the opening in the case.

18. Remove the differential side gears and thrust washers.

19. Using a bearing puller, press side bearing from the differential.

PINION GEAR

1. Remove the pinion nut, washer and pinion flange.

2. Remove and discard the pinion oil seal.

3. Using a brass hammer, drive the pinion rearward out of the bearing. This will result in damage to the bearing and cup. The bearing cone and cup must be replaced with new parts. Discard the collapsible spacer.

4. Using a brass drift and a hammer, drive the front and rear bearing cups from the housing.

5. Remove the shim from behind the rear bearing cup and record the thickness.

6. Using a bearing puller, press the rear bearing cone from the pinion stem.

Inspection

1. Clean the differential components in solvent and use compressed air to dry them; do not use compressed air on the bearings, only shop towels.

2. Check the components for wear or damage; replace them, if necessary.

3. Inspect the bearings and bearing cups for wear, cracks or scoring; replace them, if necessary.

4. Inspect the differential side and pinion gears for wear, cracks or chips; replace them, if necessary.

5. Inspect the ring and pinion gears for wear and/or damage; replace them, if necessary.

6. Inspect the differential case for cracks or damage; replace it, if necessary.

Assembly
PINION GEAR

1. The proper pinion setting (relative to the ring gear) is de-termined by a shim which has been selected before the pinion is to be installed in the carrier. Pinion bearing shims are available in 0.001 in. increments.

2. The head of the pinion is marked with a plus (+) or a minus (−) mark that is followed by a number ranging from 0–4. If the old and new pinions have the same marking and the old bearing is being installed, use a shim of the original thickness. If the old pinion is marked zero (0), however and the new pinion is marked +2, try a shim that is 0.002 in. thinner. If the new pinion is marked axle housing cup bore and install −2, try a shim that is 0.002 in. thicker.

3. Position the selected shim in the bore of the rear bearing cup. Install the cup.

NOTE: Special pinion depth measuring tools are available. When using the special tools, follow the manufacturer's recommended procedures. Without the special tools, complete the following procedure and check the pinion depth by examining the pinion to ring gear tooth contact pattern. Correct as required by adding or subtracting shims controlling the pinion depth.

4. Place the rear pinion bearing cone on the pinion stem (small side away from pinion head).

5. Lubricate the front and rear bearing cones and install the rear pinion bearing cone onto the pinion stem with an arbor press.

6. Insert the pinion bearing and collapsible spacer assembly through the carrier and install the front bearing cone. Install the companion flange.

NOTE: During installation of the pinion bearing do not collapse the spacer.

7. Install the drive pinion oil seal into the carrier; be sure to properly seat the seal.

8. Support the pinion in the carrier.

9. Install the belleville washer (convex side up) and pinion nut.

10. Hold the companion flange and tighten the pinion nut to remove all endplay, while rotating the pinion to ensure proper bearing seating. Remove the tools and rotate the pinion several revolutions.

11. Torque the pinion nut to 210 ft. lbs. (285 Nm). Using an inch lbs. torque wrench, measure the pinion bearing preload; the torque is 20–35 inch lbs. for new bearings or 10 inch lbs. over the original figure for the old pinion bearing.

NOTE: The correct preload reading can only be obtained with the carrier nose upright. The final assembly is incorrect if the final pinion nut torque is below 210 ft. lbs. (285 Nm) or if the pinion bearing preload is not within specifications. Under no circumstances should the pinion nut be backed off to reduce the pinion bearing preload; if this is done, a new collapsible spacer will have to be installed and the unit adjusted again until proper preload is obtained.

DIFFERENTIAL

1. Lubricate all parts, before assembly, with rear axle lubricant.

2. Install the thrust washers on the differential side gears and install the side gears into the case.

3. Place thrust washers on both differential pinions and, working through the opening in the case, mesh the pinion gears with the side gears. The pinions should be exactly 180 degrees apart.

4. Rotate the side gears 90 degrees to align the pinions and thrust washers with the pinion shaft holes.

5. From the pinion shaft lockpin hole side of the case, insert the slotted end of the pinion shaft through the case and conical thrust washer; install the pinion shaft through one of the pinion gears.

6. Install a thrust block through the side gear hub, so the slot is centered between the side gears.

7. Hold all of the parts in alignment and align the lockpin holes in the pinion shaft and case. Install the lockpin from the pinion shaft side of the ring gear flange, temporarily.

8. With a stone, relieve the edge of the chamfer on the inside diameter of the ring gear.

9. Heat the ring gear (fluid bath or heat lamp) to a temperature not exceeding 300°F; do not heat ring gear with a torch.

10. Align the ring gear with the case. Insert the ring gear screws through the case flange and into the ring gear.

11. Alternately, tighten each cap screw to 80 ft. lbs. (108 Nm).

12. Position each differential bearing cone on the hub of the differential case (taper away from ring gear) and install the bearing cones; a shop press may be helpful.

13. Install the differential into the axle housing.

14. Install the right and inner axle shaft by performing the following procedures:

a. Using the axle shaft removal/installation tool, install the inner axle shaft into the housing.

b. Install the C-clip on the other end of the shaft to retain it.

c. Install the needle bearing into the end of the inner axle shaft.

d. Install the shift collar onto the splined end of the inner axle shaft.

e. Install the axle shaft/bearing retainer assembly into the disconnect housing and torque the bearing retainer-to-disconnect housing screws to 200 inch lbs. (23 Nm).

f. Using a new gasket, install the disconnect housing cover assembly onto the disconnect housing and torque the bolts to 10 ft. lbs. (14 Nm).

15. Install the left axle shaft into the axle housing and secure it with the C-clip.

16. To complete the installation, reverse the removal procedures.

Adjustment

DIFFERENTIAL BEARING PRELOAD AND RING GEAR-TO-PINION BACKLASH

The threaded adjuster uses a hex drive hole and requires a special tool C–4164 to adjust the side bearing preload through the axle tube. An adjuster lock with 2 pointed teeth which engage in the exposed adjuster thread when the lock is tightened is provided. The shims will range from 0.020–0.038 in. and will be equipped with internal centering tabs. The shims, marked with a number which represents its thickness in thousandths of an in., can be installed with either side against the pinion head.

1. Index the gears so the same gear teeth are in contact throughout the adjustment.

2. The differential bearing cups will not always move with the adjusters. It is important to seat the bearings by rotating them 5–10 times in each direction, each time the adjusters are moved.

3. With the pinion bearings installed and the preload set, install the differential with adjusters, caps and bearings. Lubricate the bearings and adjuster threads. Tighten the top cap screws on the right and left to 10 ft. lbs. Tighten the bottom cap screws finger tight until the head is just seated on the bearing cap.

4. Using the tool, make sure the adjuster rotates freely. Turn both adjusters in until bearing play is eliminated with some drive gear backlash (0.010 in.). Seat the bearing rollers.

5. Install and register a dial indicator against the drive side of a gear tooth. Check the backlash at 4 positions to find the point of minimum backlash. Rotate the gear to the position of least backlash and mark the tooth so the readings will be taken at the same point.

6. Loosen the right adjuster and turn it until the backlash is 0.003–0.004 in. with each adjuster tightened to 10 ft. lbs. Seat the bearings rollers.

7. Tighten the differential bearing cap screws to 45 ft. lbs. (61 Nm).

8. Tighten the right adjuster to 70 ft. lbs. and seat the rollers, until the torque remains constant at 70 ft. lbs. Measure the backlash, if the backlash is not 0.006–0.008 in. increase the torque on the right adjusters and seat the rollers until the correct backlash is obtained.

9. Tighten the left adjuster to 70 ft. lbs. and seat the bearings until the torque remains constant.

10. If the assembly is properly done, the initial reading on the left adjuster will be approximately 70 ft. lbs. If it is substantially less, the entire procedure should be repeated.

11. After the adjustments are complete, install the adjuster locks; be sure the teeth are engaged in the adjuster threads. Torque the lockscrews to 90 inch lbs.

SPICER MODEL 44 AXLE

Disassembly

DIFFERENTIAL

1. Remove the housing cover and drain the lubricant.

2. Remove the left axle shaft and the inner axle shaft by performing the following procedures:

a. Using an axle puller, press the left axle shaft from the axle housing.

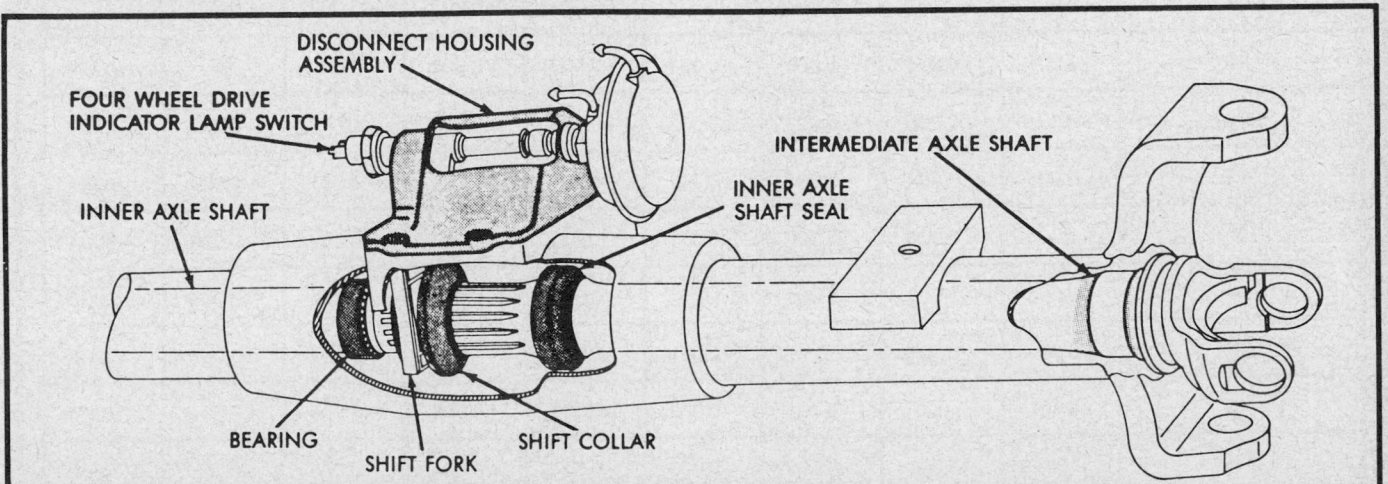

Sectional view of the of the left disconnect axle assembly—model 44 front axle assembly

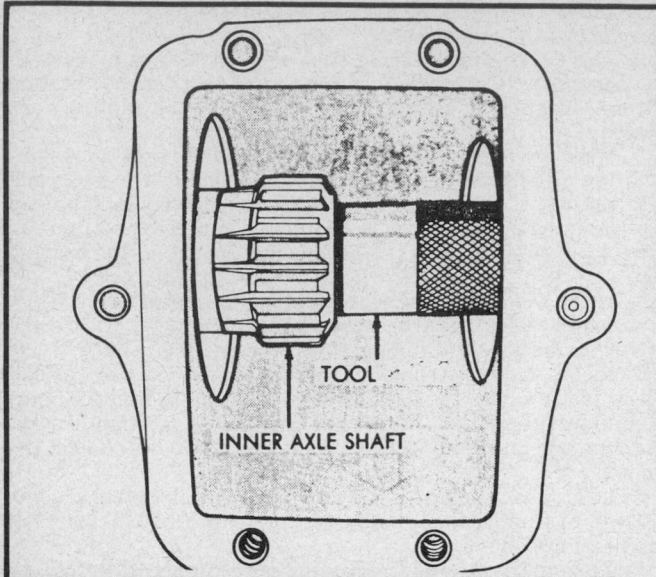

Removing the inner axle shaft—model 44 front axle assembly

b. Remove the disconnect housing assembly-to-axle housing screws, the housing and the gasket.

c. Remove the shift collar from the inner axle shaft.

d. Using an inner axle shaft removal/installation tool, attach it to the inner axle shaft and carefully, slide the inner axle shaft from the axle housing.

3. Using an axle spreader tool, mount it onto the axle housing and spread the housing enough to remove the differential.

4. Using a dial indicator, measure the amount the opening is being spread; do not spread the housing more than 0.015 in. (0.38mm), for damage to the housing may occur.

5. Mark the differential bearing caps for reassembly purposes.

6. Loosen the bearing caps until 2–3 threads are engaged.

7. Using a prybar, pry the differential loose.

8. Remove the bearing caps and the differential.

9. Mount the differential into a vise.

10. Remove and discard the ring gear bolts; they are not reusable.

11. Using a brass drift and a hammer, tap the ring gear from the differential.

12. Using a differential bearing puller, press the differential bearings from the differential.

13. Remove the differential bearing shims.

14. Remove the pinion shaft lockpin and pinion shaft.

15. Rotate the pinions to remove them through the case opening.

16. Remove the side gears and thrust washers.

PINION GEAR

1. Remove the differential case from the axle housing.

2. Using a pinion yoke holding tool, remove the pinion gear nut.

3. Remove the pinion washer. Using a pinion yoke holder tool and a pinion puller tool, press the yoke from the pinion gear.

4. Using an oil seal remover tool, remove the pinion gear oil seal and discard it. Remove the slinger, the gasket, the upper pinion bearing cone and preload shim pack; measure and record the shim thicknesses.

5. Press drive the pinion gear and inner bearing cone assembly from the axle housing.

6. Using a shop press, press the inner bearing cone from the pinion gear.

7. Remove and record the shim thicknesses from behind the inner pinion bearing cup.

Inspection

1. Clean the differential components in solvent and use compressed air to dry them; do not use compressed air on the bearings, only shop towels.

2. Check the components for wear or damage; replace them, if necessary.

3. Inspect the bearings and bearing cups for wear, cracks or scoring; replace them, if necessary.

Original Pinion Gear Depth Variance	Replacement Pinion Gear Depth Variance								
	−4	−3	−2	−1	0	+1	+2	+3	+4
+4	+0.008	+0.007	+0.006	+0.005	+0.004	+0.003	+0.002	+0.001	0
+3	+0.007	+0.006	+0.005	+0.004	+0.003	+0.002	+0.001	0	−0.001
+2	+0.006	+0.005	+0.004	+0.003	+0.002	+0.001	0	−0.001	−0.002
+1	+0.005	+0.004	+0.003	+0.002	+0.001	0	−0.001	−0.002	−0.003
0	+0.004	+0.003	+0.002	+0.001	0	−0.001	−0.002	−0.003	−0.004
−1	+0.003	+0.002	+0.001	0	−0.001	−0.002	−0.003	−0.004	−0.005
−2	+0.002	+0.001	0	−0.001	−0.002	−0.003	−0.004	−0.005	−0.006
−3	+0.001	0	−0.001	−0.002	−0.003	−0.004	−0.005	−0.006	−0.007
−4	0	−0.001	−0.002	−0.003	−0.004	−0.005	−0.006	−0.007	−0.008

4. Inspect the differential side and pinion gears for wear, cracks or chips; replace them, if necessary.

5. Inspect the ring and pinion gears for wear and/or damage; replace them, if necessary.

6. Inspect the differential case for cracks or damage; replace it, if necessary.

Assembly

PINION GEAR

1. Make sure the ring and pinion are a matched set.

2. Measure the thickness of the original pinion shim and note the variance on the pinion gear.

3. Perform the following procedure to determine the pinion starter shim thickness:

    a. If the original ring and pinion are being installed, use the original shim.

    b. If a replacement gear set is being installed, determine the best starter shim thickness.

    c. Refer to the pinion variance chart and observe where the old and new pinion marking column intersect.

    d. If the old pinion is + 2 and the new pinion is − 2, the intersecting figure is + 0.004 in. (0.10mm); add this amount to the original shim. Or, if the old pinion is − 3 and the new pinion is − 2, the intersecting figure is − 0.001 in. (− 0.025mm); subtract this amount from the original shim.

4. Install the starter shim in the pinion rear bearing cup bore; if the shim is chamfer on one side, position the chamfered side so it faces the bottom of the bore.

5. Using a driver tool, install the pinion rear bearing cup into the axle housing.

6. Install the front bearing cup.

7. Using a shop press, press the rear bearing onto the pinion gear.

8. Install the pinion gear into the axle housing and the front bearing onto the pinion; do not install the slinger or the seal.

9. Install the yoke, the pinion nut washer and the old pinion nut; tighten the nut enough to remove the endplay.

10. Adjust the backlash and gear tooth contact.

DIFFERENTIAL

1. Install the side gears, the thrust washers and the pinion gears into the differential case.

NOTE: If new gears and washers are used, it will not be necessary to check the gear backlash. Correct fit is provided due to the close manufacturing tolerances.

2. Install the pinion shaft and lockpin into the case.

3. Assemble the original differential bearing shim packs, then, remove approximately 0.20 in. (0.50mm) shim thickness from each pack; the remaining shims will serve as a starter shim pack.

4. Install the starter shim packs and bearing onto the case.

5. Align and install the ring gear. Using new bolts, torque the ring gear-to-differential case bolts to 45–60 ft. lbs. (61–81 Nm).

6. Install the spreader tool onto the axle housing. Using a dial indicator, spread the axle housing no more than 0.015 in. (0.38mm).

NOTE: Do not spread the housing more than 0.015 in. (0.038mm), for damage may occur to the case.

7. Install the differential; it may be necessary to tap the differential bearing cups, with a soft hammer, to seat them.

8. Install the differential bearing caps and torque the bolts to 70–90 ft. lbs. (95–122 Nm).

9. Remove the spreader tool and dial indicator.

10. Adjust the ring and pinion gear.

11. Using silicone sealant, apply a bead of it to the axle housing. Install the cover and torque the bolts to 35 ft. lbs. (47 Nm).

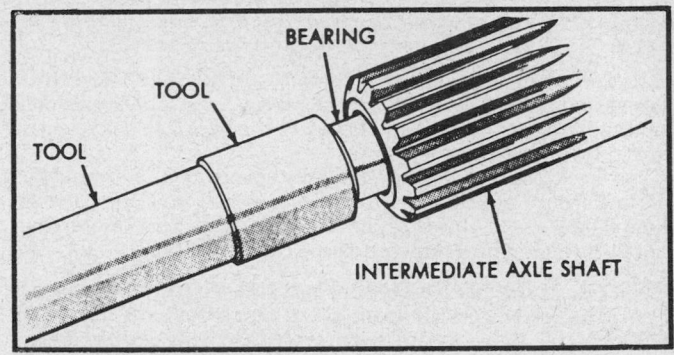

Installing the inner axle shaft bearing—model 44 front axle assembly

Adjustment

PINION BEARING PRELOAD

1. Using a yoke holding tool, torque the pinion nut to 200–220 ft. lbs. (271–298 Nm). Rotate the drive pinion several complete revolutions to seat the bearing rollers.

2. Using an inch lb. torque wrench, measure the torque necessary to rotate the pinion; the torque should be 20–40 inch lbs. (2–5 Nm).

NOTE: If the torque is not correct, add a shim to decrease the preload or subtract a shim to increase the preload.

3. Remove the pinion nut, the washer and the yoke after setting the preload; be sure to discard the old nut.

4. Lubricate the new pinion oil seal lip and install the seal into the axle housing.

5. Install the yoke, the washer and a new pinion nut; torque the nut to 200–220 ft. lbs. (271–298 Nm).

DIFFERENTIAL BEARING PRELOAD AND DRIVE GEAR AND PINION BACKLASH

1. Install the differential and tighten the bearing caps.

2. Using a dial indicator, mount it onto the housing, position the stylus against the drive side of one ring gear tooth; be sure the stylus is at a right angle to the tooth.

3. Move the ring gear toward the dial indicator and zero it.

4. Move the ring gear away from the pinion until the backlash and note the reading on the dial indicator.

NOTE: The reading represents the thickness of the shim pack necessary to take up the clearance between the bearing cup and the case on the ring gear side of the differential assembly.

5. Subtract this reading from the previously recorded total reading to obtain the amount of shims necessary to take up the clearance between the bearing cup and the case at the pinion side of the differential.

6. Remove the differential and ring gear assembly from the carrier.

7. Remove the differential bearing covers. Install the correct thickness shim pack between the bearing cone and differential case hub shoulder. Add an additional 0.015 in. (0.38mm) shim to the drive gear side of the differential and install the differential bearing cones.

8. Install the spreader tool to the axle housing. Using a dial indicator, spread the housing to 0.015–0.020 (0.38–0.51mm). Install the differential assembly into the axle housing.

9. Install the bearing caps, remove the spreader tool and torque the bearing caps snugly.

10. Using a soft hammer, tap the drive gear to seat the differential bearing and cups.

NOTE: **When seating the bearing and cups, be careful not to nick the ring gear or drive pinion teeth.**

11. Torque the bearing cap bolts to 70–90 ft. lbs. (95–122 Nm).

12. Attach a dial indicator to the carrier, with the stylus contacting a ring gear tooth, and measure the backlash between the ring gear and the drive pinion.

13. Check the backlash at 4 equally spaced points around the circumference of the ring gear; the backlash must be between 0.04–0.009 in. (0.102–0.229mm) and cannot vary more than 0.002 in. (0.508mm) between the 4 check positions.

NOTE: **If the backlash does not fall within these specifications, change the shim pack thickness on both the differential bearing hubs to maintain the proper bearing preload and backlash.**

SPICER – MODEL 60 AXLE

For overhaul information, refer to the Spicer 60 axle, in the rear axle assembly section.

Rear Axle Assembly

While some Dodge/Plymouth trucks use a 7¼, 8¼, 8⅜ or 9¼ in. semi-floating axle others use a Spicer 60, 60 HD (heavy duty) or 70 full-floating axle.

7¼, 8¼, 8⅜ AND 9¼ INCH RING GEAR AXLE

Disassembly
DIFFERENTIAL

1. Remove the axle housing cover.

2. Clean the inside of the differential case with solvent and blow dry with compressed air.

3. Check for differential side-play by inserting a pry-bar between the left side of the axle housing and the differential case flange. Using a prying motion, determine whether side-play exists; there should be no side-play.

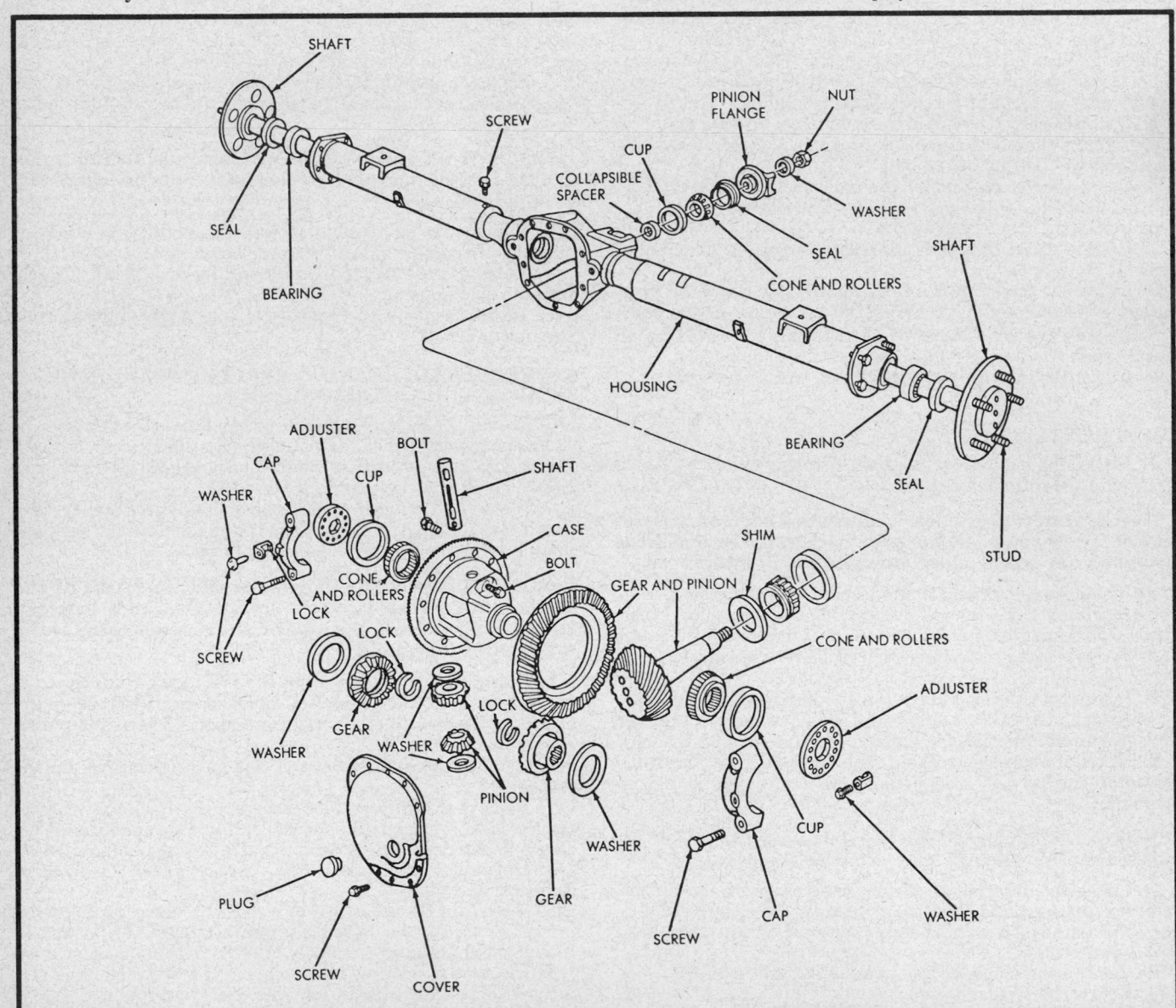

Exploded view of the 7¼ inch rear axle assembly

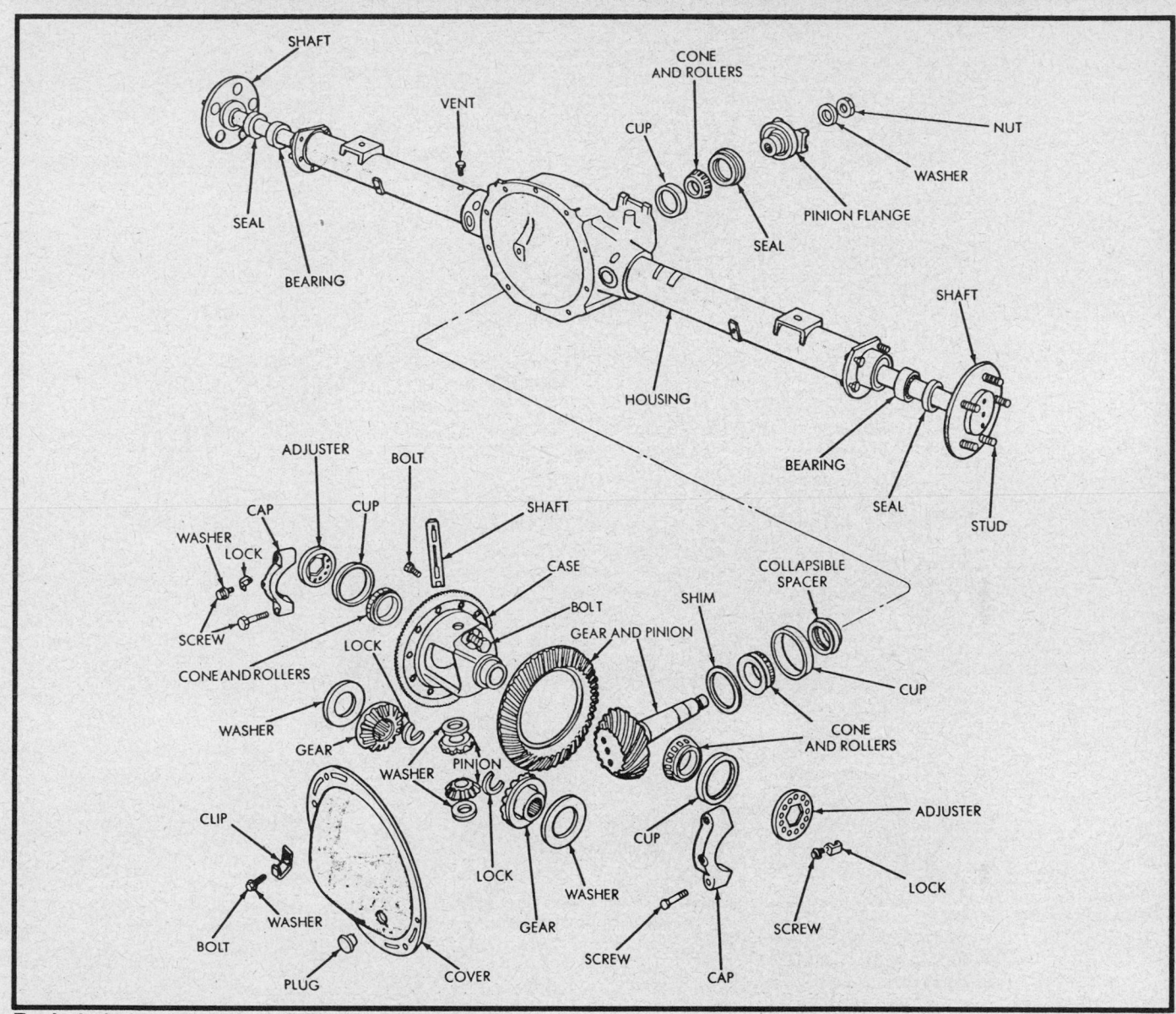

Exploded view of the 8¼ inch rear axle assembly

4. Paint the ring gear teeth and make a gear tooth contact pattern. Determine if proper depth of mesh can be obtained.

5. If side-play was found in step 3, proceed to step 6. If no side-play was found in step 3, check the drive gear run-out by performing the following procedures:

    a. Mount a dial indicator and index the indicator stem at right angles in the rear face of the ring gear.

    b. Rotate the ring gear and mark the ring gear and case at the point of greatest run-out.

    c. Total indicator reading should not exceed 0.005 in.; if it does, the possibility exists that the case must be replaced.

6. Using an inch lb. torque wrench, measure and record the pinion bearing preload.

7. Matchmark the axle housing and the differential bearing caps.

8. Remove the threaded adjusters and differential bearing caps; there is a special wrench to do this through the axle tube.

9. Remove the differential case from the housing.

NOTE: The differential bearing cups and threaded adjuster must be kept together so they can be installed in their original position.

10. Clamp the differential case and ring gear in a vise with soft jaws.

11. Remove the ring gear bolts (left-hand thread). Tap the ring gear loose with a soft-faced mallet.

12. If the ring gear run-out exceeded 0.005 in., recheck the case as follows:

    a. Install the differential case, cups, caps and adjusters into the housing.

    b. Turn the adjusters to eliminate all side-play and tighten the differential cap bolts snugly.

    c. Measure the run-out at the ring gear flange face; total indicator reading should not exceed 0.003 in.

NOTE: It is often possible to reduce run-out by removing the ring gear and reinstalling it 180 degrees from its original position.

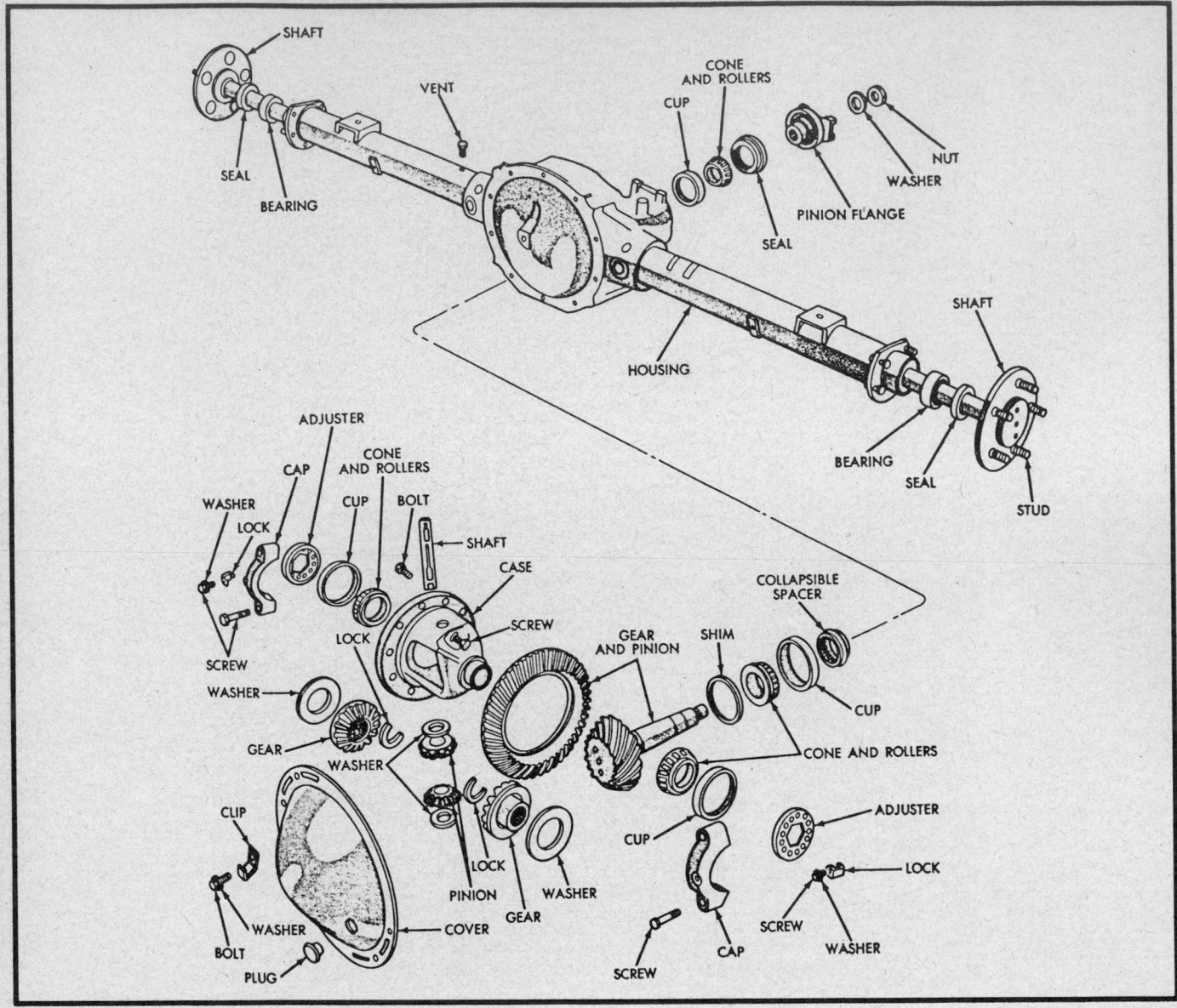

Exploded view of the 8⅜ inch rear axle assembly

d. Remove the differential case from the housing.

13. Remove the pinion shaft lock-screw and remove the pinion shaft.

14. Rotate the differential side gears until the differential pinion shafts can be removed through the opening in the case.

15. Remove the differential side gears and thrust washers.

16. Using a bearing puller, press side bearing from the differential.

PINION GEAR

1. Remove the pinion nut, washer and pinion flange.

2. Remove and discard the pinion oil seal.

3. Using a brass hammer, drive the pinion rearward out of the bearing. This will result in damage to the bearing and cup. The bearing cone and cup must be replaced with new parts. Discard the collapsible spacer.

4. Using a brass drift and a hammer, drive the front and rear bearing cups from the housing.

5. Remove the shim from behind the rear bearing cup and record the thickness.

6. Using a bearing puller, press the rear bearing cone from the pinion stem.

Inspection

1. Clean the differential components in solvent and use compressed air to dry them; do not use compressed air on the bearings, only shop towels.

2. Check the components for wear or damage; replace them, if necessary.

3. Inspect the bearings and bearing cups for wear, cracks or scoring; replace them, if necessary.

4. Inspect the differential side and pinion gears for wear, cracks or chips; replace them, if necessary.

5. Inspect the ring and pinion gears for wear and/or damage; replace them, if necessary.

6. Inspect the differential case for cracks or damage; replace it, if necessary.

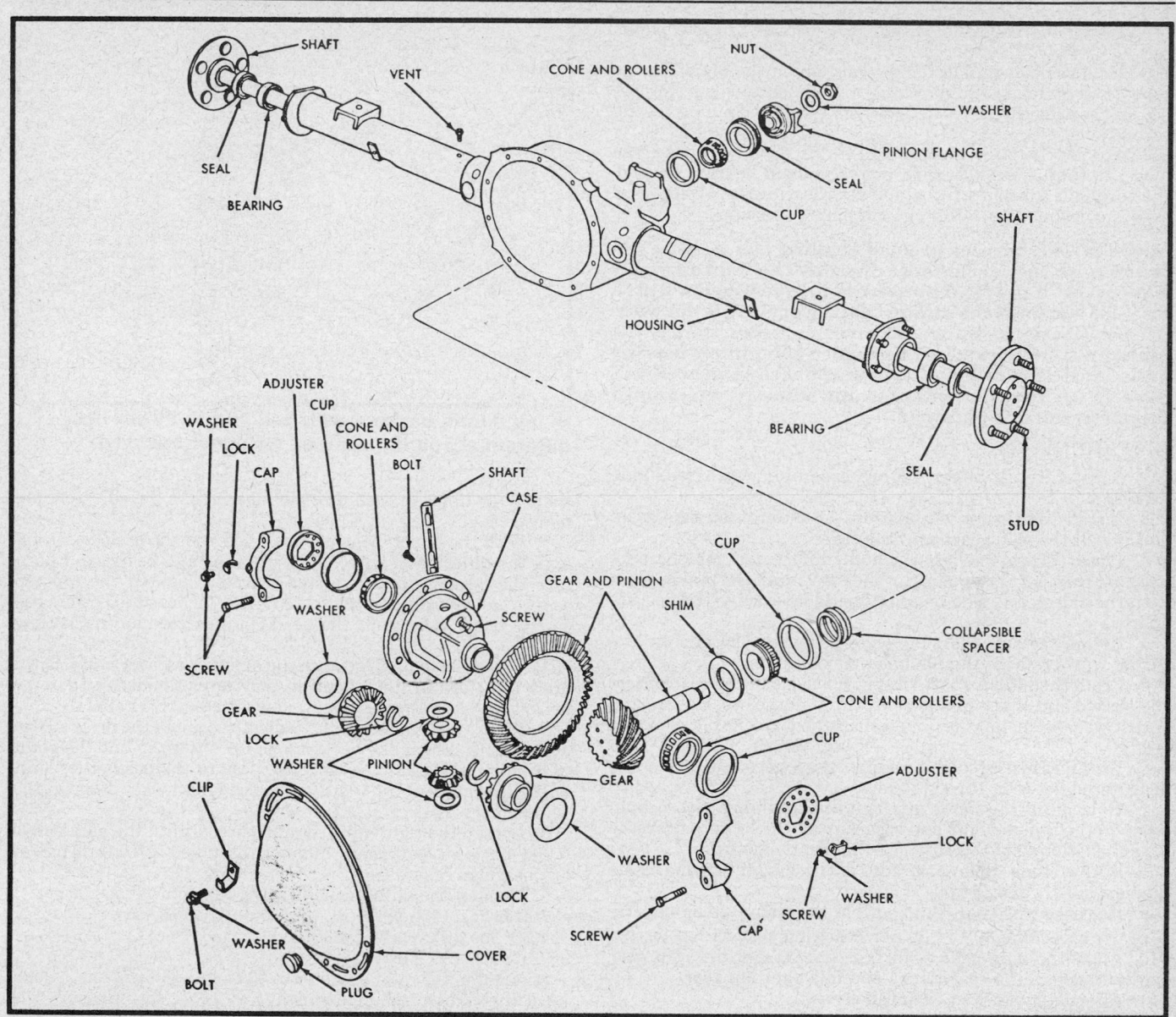

Exploded view of the 9¼ inch rear axle assembly

Assembly

PINION GEAR

1. The proper pinion setting (relative to the ring gear) is determined by a shim which has been selected before the pinion is to be installed in the carrier. Pinion bearing shims are available in 0.001 in. increments.

2. The head of the pinion is marked with a plus (+) or a minus (−) mark that is followed by a number ranging from 0–4. If the old and new pinions have the same marking and the old bearing is being installed, use a shim of the original thickness. If the old pinion is marked zero (0), however and the new pinion is marked +2, try a shim that is 0.002 in. thinner. If the new pinion is marked axle housing cup bore and install −2, try a shim that is 0.002 in. thicker.

3. Position the selected shim in the bore of the rear bearing cup. Install the cup.

NOTE: Special pinion depth measuring tools are available. When using the special tools, follow the manu-facturer's recommended procedures. Without the special tools, complete the following procedure and check the pinion depth by examining the pinion to ring gear tooth contact pattern. Correct as required by adding or subtracting shims controlling the pinion depth.

4. Place the rear pinion bearing cone on the pinion stem (small side away from pinion head).

5. Lubricate the front and rear bearing cones and install the rear pinion bearing cone onto the pinion stem with an arbor press.

6. Insert the pinion bearing and collapsible spacer assembly through the carrier and install the front bearing cone. Install the companion flange.

NOTE: During installation of the pinion bearing do not collapse the spacer.

7. Install the drive pinion oil seal into the carrier; be sure to properly seat the seal.

8. Support the pinion in the carrier.

9. Install the belleville washer (convex side up) and pinion nut.

10. Hold the companion flange and tighten the pinion nut to remove all endplay, while rotating the pinion to ensure proper bearing seating. Remove the tools and rotate the pinion several revolutions.

11. Torque the pinion nut to 210 ft. lbs. (285 Nm). Using an inch lbs. torque wrench, measure the pinion bearing preload; the torque is 20–35 inch lbs. for new bearings or 10 inch lbs. over the original figure for the old pinion bearing.

NOTE: The correct preload reading can only be obtained with the carrier nose upright. The final assembly is incorrect if the final pinion nut torque is below 210 ft. lbs. (285 Nm) or if the pinion bearing preload is not within specifications. Under no circumstances should the pinion nut be backed off to reduce the pinion bearing preload; if this is done, a new collapsible spacer will have to be installed and the unit adjusted again until proper preload is obtained.

DIFFERENTIAL

1. Lubricate all parts, before assembly, with rear axle lubricant.

2. Install the thrust washers on the differential side gears and install the side gears into the case.

3. Place thrust washers on both differential pinions and, working through the opening in the case, mesh the pinion gears with the side gears. The pinions should be exactly 180 degrees apart.

4. Rotate the side gears 90 degrees to align the pinions and thrust washers with the pinion shaft holes.

5. From the pinion shaft lockpin hole side of the case, insert the slotted end of the pinion shaft through the case and conical thrust washer; install the pinion shaft through one of the pinion gears.

6. Install a thrust block through the side gear hub, so the slot is centered between the side gears.

7. Hold all of the parts in alignment and align the lockpin holes in the pinion shaft and case. Install the lockpin from the pinion shaft side of the ring gear flange, temporarily.

8. With a stone, relieve the edge of the chamfer on the inside diameter of the ring gear.

9. Heat the ring gear (fluid bath or heat lamp) to a temperature not exceeding 300°F; do not heat ring gear with a torch.

10. Align the ring gear with the case. Insert the ring gear screws through the case flange and into the ring gear.

11. Alternately tighten each cap screw to:
80 ft. lbs. (108 Nm) — 7¼ in axle
70 ft. lbs. (95 Nm) — 8¼ in., 8⅜ in. and 9¼ in. axles

12. Position each differential bearing cone on the hub of the differential case (taper away from ring gear) and install the bearing cones; a shop press may be helpful.

Adjustment

DIFFERENTIAL BEARING PRELOAD AND RING GEAR-TO-PINION BACKLASH

The threaded adjuster uses a hex drive hole and requires a special tool C–4164 to adjust the side bearing preload through the axle tube. An adjuster lock with 2 pointed teeth which engage in the exposed adjuster thread when the lock is tightened is provided. The shims will range from 0.020–0.038 in. and will be equipped with internal centering tabs. The shims, marked with a number which represents its thickness in thousandths of an in., can be installed with either side against the pinion head.

1. Index the gears so the same gear teeth are in contact throughout the adjustment.

2. The differential bearing cups will not always move with the adjusters. It is important to seat the bearings by rotating

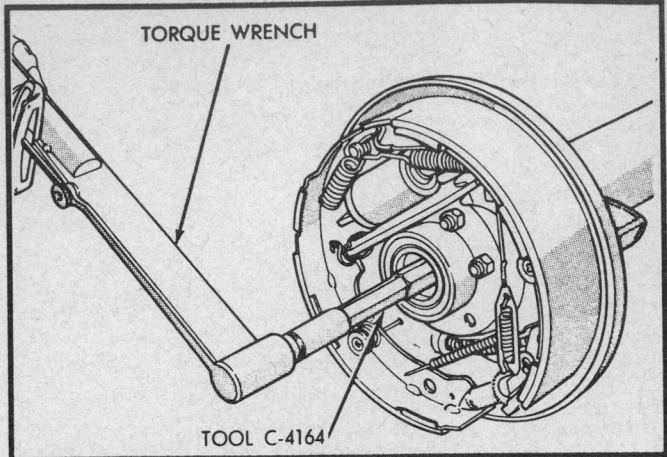

Using a long bar tool with hex end to adjust the differential bearing preload and gear backlash

them 5–10 times in each direction, each time the adjusters are moved.

3. With the pinion bearings installed and the preload set, install the differential with adjusters, caps and bearings. Lubricate the bearings and adjuster threads. Tighten the top cap screws on the right and left to 10 ft. lbs. Tighten the bottom cap screws finger tight until the head is just seated on the bearing cap.

4. Using the tool, make sure the adjuster rotates freely. Turn both adjusters in until bearing play is eliminated with some drive gear backlash (0.010 in.). Seat the bearing rollers.

5. Install and register a dial indicator against the drive side of a gear tooth. Check the backlash at 4 positions to find the point of minimum backlash. Rotate the gear to the position of least backlash and mark the tooth so the readings will be taken at the same point.

6. Loosen the right adjuster and turn it until the backlash is 0.003–0.004 in. with each adjuster tightened to 10 ft. lbs. Seat the bearings rollers.

7. Tighten the differential bearing cap screws to:
100 ft. lbs. (136 Nm) — 8¼ in. and 9¼ in axles
45 ft. lbs. (61 Nm) — 7¼ in. axle
70 ft. lbs. (95 Nm) — 8⅜ in axle

8. Tighten the right adjuster to 70 ft. lbs. and seat the rollers, until the torque remains constant at 70 ft. lbs. Measure the backlash, if the backlash is not 0.006–0.008 in. increase the torque on the right adjusters and seat the rollers until the correct backlash is obtained.

9. Tighten the left adjuster to 70 ft. lbs. and seat the bearings until the torque remains constant.

10. If the assembly is properly done, the initial reading on the left adjuster will be approximately 70 ft. lbs. If it is substantially less, the entire procedure should be repeated.

11. After the adjustments are complete, install the adjuster locks; be sure the teeth are engaged in the adjuster threads. Torque the lockscrews to 90 inch lbs.

SPICER—MODELS 60, 60 HD AND 70 AXLES

Disassembly

DIFFERENTIAL

1. Remove the housing cover and drain the lubricant.

2. Using an axle spreader tool, mount it onto the axle housing and spread the housing enough to remove the differential.

3. Using a dial indicator, measure the amount the opening is

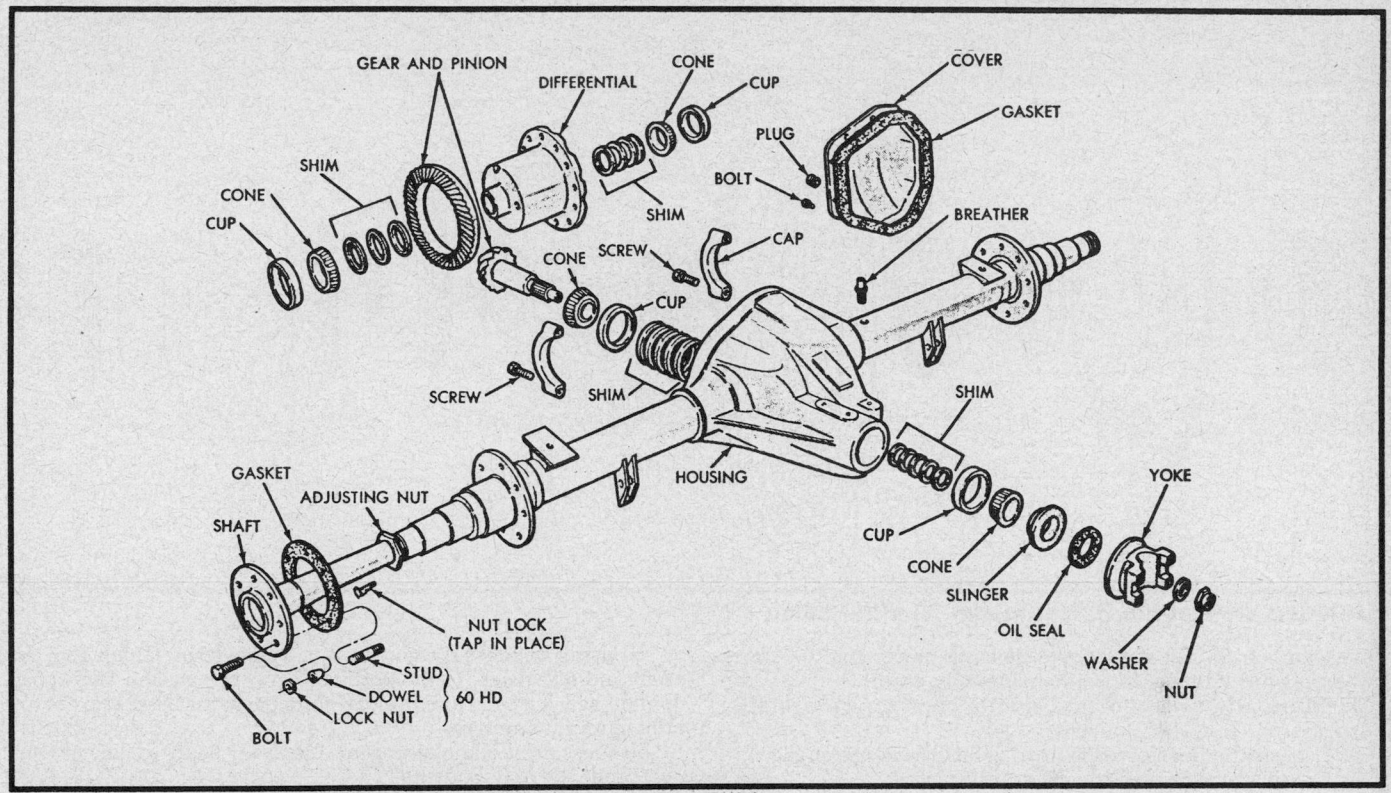

Exploded view of the Spicer 60 and 60 HD rear axle assembly

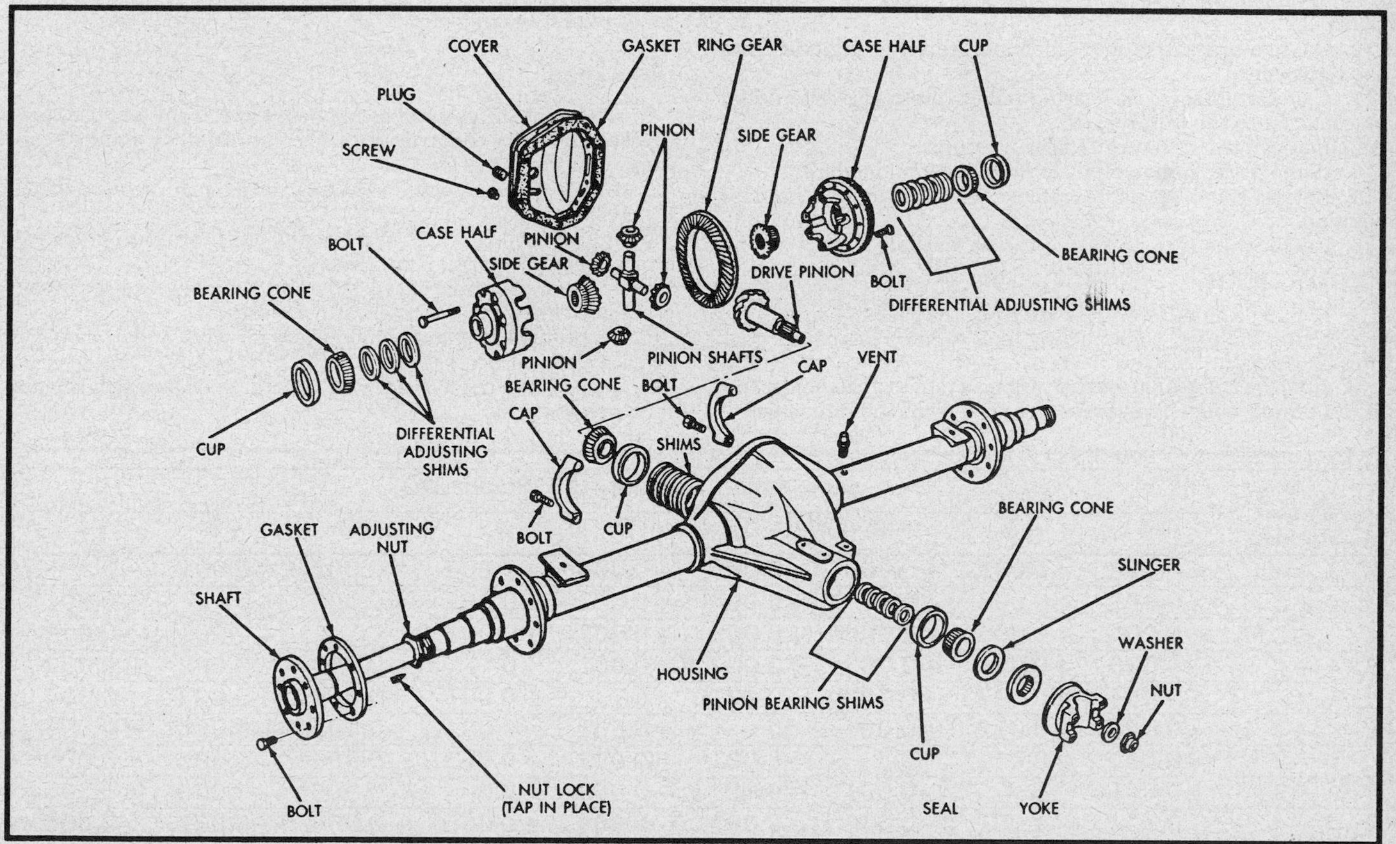

Exploded view of the Spicer model 70 rear axle assembly

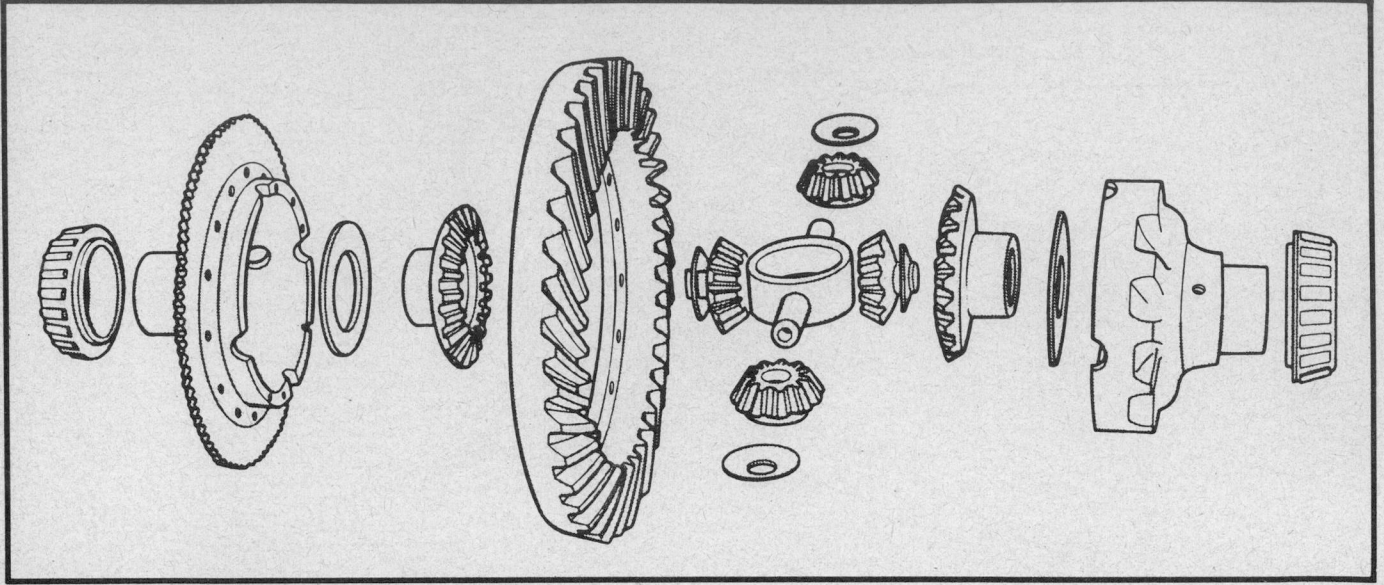

Exploded view of the Spicer model 70 differential

being spread; do not spread the housing more than 0.015 in. (0.38mm), for damage to the housing may occur.

4. Mark the differential bearing caps for reassembly purposes.

5. Loosen the bearing caps until 2–3 threads are engaged.

6. Using a prybar, pry the differential loose.

7. Remove the bearing caps and the differential.

8. Mount the differential into a vise.

9. Remove and discard the ring gear bolts; they are not reusable.

10. Using a brass drift and a hammer, tap the ring gear from the differential.

11. Using a differential bearing puller, press the differential bearings from the differential.

12. Remove the differential bearing shims.

13. Remove the pinion shaft lockpin and pinion shaft.

14. Rotate the pinions to remove them through the case opening.

15. Remove the side gears and thrust washers.

PINION GEAR

1. Remove the differential case from the axle housing.

2. Using a pinion yoke holding tool, remove the pinion gear nut.

3. Remove the pinion washer. Using a pinion yoke holder tool and a pinion puller tool, press the yoke from the pinion gear.

4. Using an oil seal remover tool, remove the pinion gear oil seal and discard it. Remove the slinger, the gasket, the upper pinion bearing cone and preload shim pack; measure and record the shim thicknesses.

5. Press drive the pinion gear and inner bearing cone assembly from the axle housing.

6. Using a shop press, press the inner bearing cone from the pinion gear.

7. Remove and record the shim thicknesses from behind the inner pinion bearing cup.

Inspection

1. Clean the differential components in solvent and use compressed air to dry them; do not use compressed air on the bearings, only shop towels.

2. Check the components for wear or damage; replace them, if necessary.

3. Inspect the bearings and bearing cups for wear, cracks or scoring; replace them, if necessary.

4. Inspect the differential side and pinion gears for wear, cracks or chips; replace them, if necessary.

5. Inspect the ring and pinion gears for wear and/or damage; replace them, if necessary.

6. Inspect the differential case for cracks or damage; replace it, if necessary.

Old Pinion Marking	New Pinion Marking (U.S. Standards)								
	—4	—3	—2	—1	0	+1	+2	+3	+4
+4	+0.008	+0.007	+0.006	+0.005	+0.004	+0.003	+0.002	+0.001	0
+3	+0.007	+0.006	+0.005	+0.004	+0.003	+0.002	+0.001	0	—0.001
+2	+0.006	+0.005	+0.004	+0.003	+0.002	+0.001	0	—0.001	—0.002
+1	+0.005	+0.004	+0.003	+0.002	+0.001	0	—0.001	—0.002	—0.003
0	+0.004	+0.003	+0.002	+0.001	0	—0.001	—0.002	—0.003	—0.004
—1	+0.003	+0.002	+0.001	0	—0.001	—0.002	—0.003	—0.004	—0.005
—2	+0.002	+0.001	0	—0.001	—0.002	—0.003	—0.004	—0.005	—0.006
—3	+0.001	0	—0.001	—0.002	—0.003	—0.004	—0.005	—0.006	—0.007
—4	0	—0.001	—0.002	—0.003	—0.004	—0.005	—0.006	—0.007	—0.008

Assembly

PINION GEAR

1. Make sure the ring and pinion are a matched set.
2. Measure the thickness of the original pinion shim and note the variance on the pinion gear.
3. Perform the following procedure to determine the pinion starter shim thickness:

    a. If the original ring and pinion are being installed, use the original shim.

    b. If a replacement gear set is being installed, determine the best starter shim thickness.

    c. Refer to the pinion variance chart and observe where the old and new pinion marking column intersect.

    d. If the old pinion is +2 and the new pinion is −2, the intersecting figure is +0.004 in. (0.10mm); add this amount to the original shim. Or, if the old pinion is −3 and the new pinion is −2, the intersecting figure is −0.001 in. (−0.025mm); subtract this amount from the original shim.

4. Install the starter shim in the pinion rear bearing cup bore; if the shim is chamfer on one side, position the chamfered side so it faces the bottom of the bore.
5. Using a driver tool, install the pinion rear bearing cup into the axle housing.
6. Install the front bearing cup.
7. Using a shop press, press the rear bearing onto the pinion gear.
8. Install the pinion gear into the axle housing and the front bearing onto the pinion; do not install the slinger or the seal.
9. Install the yoke, the pinion nut washer and the old pinion nut; tighten the nut enough to remove the endplay.
10. Adjust the backlash and gear tooth contact.

DIFFERENTIAL

1. Install the side gears, the thrust washers and the pinion gears into the differential case.

NOTE: If new gears and washers are used, it will not be necessary to check the gear backlash. Correct fit is provided due to the close manufacturing tolerances.

2. Install the pinion shaft and lockpin into the case.
3. Assemble the original differential bearing shim packs, then, remove approximately 0.20 in. (0.50mm) shim thickness from each pack; the remaining shims will serve as a starter shim pack.
4. Install the starter shim packs and bearing onto the case.
5. Align and install the ring gear. Using new bolts, torque the ring gear-to-differential case bolts to 100–120 ft. lbs. (136–163 Nm).
6. Install the spreader tool onto the axle housing. Using a dial indicator, spread the axle housing no more than 0.015 in. (0.38mm).

NOTE: Do not spread the housing more than 0.015 in. (0.038mm), for damage may occur to the case.

7. Install the differential; it may be necessary to tap the differential bearing cups, with a soft hammer, to seat them.
8. Install the differential bearing caps and torque the bolts to 70–90 ft. lbs. (95–122 Nm).
9. Remove the spreader tool and dial indicator.
10. Adjust the ring and pinion gear.
11. Using silicone sealant, apply a bead of it to the axle housing. Install the cover and torque the bolts to 35 ft. lbs. (47 Nm).

Adjustment

PINION BEARING PRELOAD

1. Using a yoke holding tool, torque the pinion nut to 250–270 ft. lbs. (339–366 Nm). Rotate the drive pinion several complete revolutions to seat the bearing rollers.

2. Using an inch lb. torque wrench, measure the torque necessary to rotate the pinion; the torque should be 10–20 inch lbs. (1–3 Nm).

NOTE: If the torque is not correct, add a shim to decrease the preload or subtract a shim to increase the preload.

3. Remove the pinion nut, the washer and the yoke after setting the preload; be sure to discard the old nut.
4. Lubricate the new pinion oil seal lip and install the seal into the axle housing.
5. Install the yoke, the washer and a new pinion nut; torque the nut to 250–270 ft. lbs. (339–366 Nm).

DIFFERENTIAL BEARING PRELOAD AND DRIVE GEAR AND PINION BACKLASH

1. Install the differential and tighten the bearing caps.
2. Using a dial indicator, mount it onto the housing, position the stylus against the drive side of one ring gear tooth; be sure the stylus is at a right angle to the tooth.
3. Move the ring gear toward the dial indicator and zero it.
4. Move the ring gear away from the pinion until the backlash and note the reading on the dial indicator.

NOTE: The reading represents the thickness of the shim pack necessary to take up the clearance between the bearing cup and the case on the ring gear side of the differential assembly.

5. Subtract this reading from the previously recorded total reading to obtain the amount of shims necessary to take up the clearance between the bearing cup and the case at the pinion side of the differential.
6. Remove the differential and ring gear assembly from the carrier.
7. Remove the differential bearing covers. Install the correct thickness shim pack between the bearing cone and differential case hub shoulder. Add an additional 0.015 in. (0.38mm) shim to the drive gear side of the differential and install the differential bearing cones.
8. Install the spreader tool to the axle housing. Using a dial indicator, spread the housing to 0.015–0.020 (0.38–0.51mm). Install the differential assembly into the axle housing.
9. Install the bearing caps, remove the spreader tool and torque the bearing caps snugly.
10. Using a soft hammer, tap the drive gear to seat the differential bearing and cups.

NOTE: When seating the bearing and cups, be careful not to nick the ring gear or drive pinion teeth.

11. Torque the bearing cap bolts to 70–90 ft. lbs. (95–122 Nm).
12. Attach a dial indicator to the carrier, with the stylus contacting a ring gear tooth, and measure the backlash between the ring gear and the drive pinion.
13. Check the backlash at 4 equally spaced points around the circumference of the ring gear; the backlash must be between 0.04–0.009 in. (0.102–0.229mm) and cannot vary more than 0.002 in. (0.508mm) between the 4 check positions.

NOTE: If the backlash does not fall within these specifications, change the shim pack thickness on both the differential bearing hubs to maintain the proper bearing preload and backlash.

TRAC-LOK DIFFERENTIAL

Operational Test

If a noisy or rough operation such as a chatter occurs when turning corners, the most probable cause of this chatter or noise is incorrect or contaminated lubricant. Before removing the Trac-Lok unit for repair, drain, flush and refill the axle with the

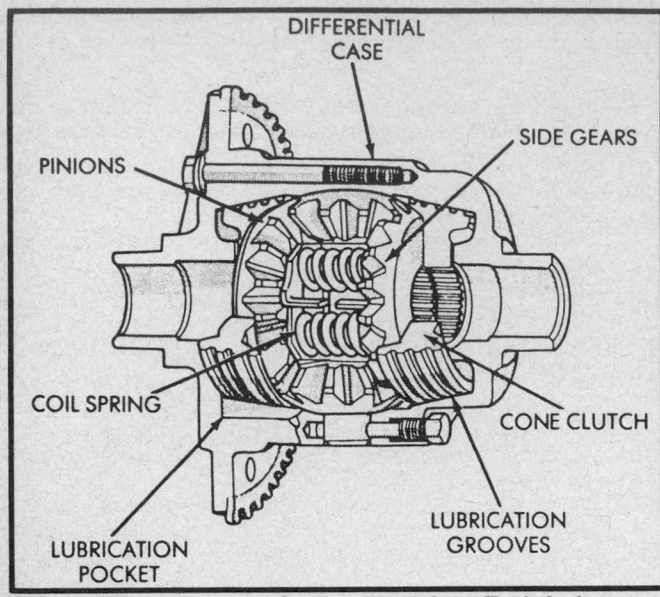

Sectional view of the Spicer model 70 Trak-Lok differential

specified lubricant. A complete lubricant drain and refill with the specified fluid will usually correct the chatter problem. A quick operational test of the Trac-Lok differential can be done easily by performing the following steps.

1. Position one wheel on solid dry pavement and the opposite wheel on ice, mud grease or a similar low traction surface.

2. Gradually, increase the engine rpm to obtain the maximum traction prior to a breakaway. The ability to move the vehicle effectively will demonstrate the proper performance.

NOTE: If the test is performed on extremely slick surfaces such as ice or grease coated surfaces, some question may exist as to proper performance. In these extreme cases, a properly performing Trac-Lok will provide greater pulling power by lightly applying the parking brake.

Disassembly

DIFFERENTIAL

1. Remove the housing cover and drain the lubricant.

2. Using an axle spreader tool, mount it onto the axle housing and spread the housing enough to remove the differential.

3. Using a dial indicator, measure the amount the opening is being spread; do not spread the housing more than 0.015 in. (0.38mm), for damage to the housing may occur.

4. Mark the differential bearing caps for reassembly purposes.

5. Loosen the bearing caps until 2–3 threads are engaged.

6. Using a prybar, pry the differential loose.

7. Remove the bearing caps and the differential.

8. Mount the differential into a vise.

9. Remove and discard the ring gear bolts; they are not reusable.

10. Using a brass drift and a hammer, tap the ring gear from the differential.

11. Using a differential bearing puller, press the differential bearings from the differential.

12. Remove the differential bearing shims.

13. Remove the pinion shaft lockpin and pinion shaft.

14. Rotate the pinions to remove them through the case opening.

15. Remove the side gears and thrust washers.

Inspection

If any member of either clutch pack shows evidence of excessive wear or scoring, the complete clutch pack must be replaced on both sides.

1. Thoroughly, clean each part in solvent.

2. Towel dry bearings or allow them to air dry, do not use compressed air to dry bearings as damage might result. Dry all other parts with compressed air or shop towels. If the parts are not to be assembled immediately, cover them to prevent dust or dirt contamination.

3. Inspect the housing for cracks and sand holes. Replace the housing if it is cracked or porous. Check for burrs and deep scratches or nicks on the gasket and oil seal surfaces. An oil stone or fine tooth file may be used to remove nicks or burrs.

4. Inspect the bearing cup bores for nicks or burrs that may have been created during bearing cup removal.

5. Inspect and clean the axle tubes. Inspect the vent to be sure it is not obstructed.

6. Check housing for bent or loose tubes or other physical damage.

7. Inspect the side gears for worn, cracked or chipped teeth. The gears should fit snugly on the axle shaft splines. Also, inspect the fit of the gears in the differential case bore.

Assembly

DIFFERENTIAL

1. Install the side gears, the thrust washers and the pinion gears into the differential case.

NOTE: If new gears and washers are used, it will not be necessary to check the gear backlash. Correct fit is provided due to the close manufacturing tolerances.

2. Install the pinion shaft and lockpin into the case.

3. Assemble the original differential bearing shim packs, then, remove approximately 0.20 in. (0.50mm) shim thickness from each pack; the remaining shims will serve as a starter shim pack.

4. Install the starter shim packs and bearing onto the case.

5. Align and install the ring gear. Using new bolts, torque the ring gear-to-differential case bolts to 100–120 ft. lbs. (136–163 Nm).

6. Install the spreader tool onto the axle housing. Using a dial indicator, spread the axle housing no more than 0.015 in. (0.38mm).

NOTE: Do not spread the housing more than 0.015 in. (0.038mm), for damage may occur to the case.

7. Install the differential; it may be necessary to tap the differential bearing cups, with a soft hammer, to seat them.

8. Install the differential bearing caps and torque the bolts to 70–90 ft. lbs. (95–122 Nm).

9. Remove the spreader tool and dial indicator.

10. Adjust the ring and pinion gear.

11. Using silicone sealant, apply a bead of it to the axle housing. Install the cover and torque the bolts to 35 ft. lbs. (47 Nm).

FORD MOTOR COMPANY

Front Axle Assembly

DANA—MODEL 28, 44 AND 50 AXLES

Disassembly

DIFFERENTIAL

1. Remove the left axle arm-to carrier case bolts, the left arm and drain the lubricant.
2. Remove the right axle stub shaft by performing the following procedures:
    a. Rotate the stub shaft so the open end of the snapring is exposed.
    b. Using 2 prybars, force the snapring from the stub shaft.
    c. Remove the stub shaft from the carrier.
3. Using an axle spreader tool, mount it onto the axle housing and spread the housing enough to remove the differential.
4. Using a dial indicator, measure the amount the opening is being spread; do not spread the housing more than 0.010 in. (0.25mm), for damage to the housing may occur.
5. Mark the differential bearing caps for reassembly purposes.
6. Loosen the bearing caps until 2–3 threads are engaged.
7. Using a prybar, pry the differential loose.
8. Remove the bearing caps and the differential.
9. Mount the differential into a vise.
10. Remove and discard the ring gear bolts; they are not reusable.
11. Using a brass drift and a hammer, tap the ring gear from the differential.
12. Using a differential bearing puller, press the differential bearings from the differential.
13. Remove the differential bearing shims.
14. Remove the pinion shaft lockpin and pinion shaft.
15. Rotate the pinions to remove them through the case opening.
16. Remove the side gears and thrust washers.

PINION GEAR

1. Remove the differential case from the axle carrier housing.
2. Using a pinion yoke holding tool, remove the pinion gear nut.
3. Remove the pinion washer. Using a pinion yoke holder tool and a pinion puller tool, press the yoke from the pinion gear.
4. Using a soft hammer, drive the pinion gear assembly from the axle carrier housing.
5. Using a bearing cup puller tool and a slide hammer, remove the pinion gear oil seal and discard it. Remove the outer pinion bearing and the oil slinger from the carrier input bore.
6. Remove the pinion bearing preload shims.
7. Using a shop press, press the inner pinion bearing cup and baffle from the bore.
8. Rotate the carrier housing. Using a shop press, press the outer pinion bearing cup from the bore.
9. Using a universal bearing remover tool, press the bearing and the oil slinger from the pinion gear.

Inspection

1. Clean the differential components in solvent and use compressed air to dry them; do not use compressed air on the bearings, only shop towels.
2. Check the components for wear or damage; replace them, if necessary.
3. Inspect the bearings and bearing cups for wear, cracks or scoring; replace them, if necessary.
4. Inspect the differential side and pinion gears for wear, cracks or chips; replace them, if necessary.
5. Inspect the ring and pinion gears for wear and/or damage; replace them, if necessary.
6. Inspect the differential case for cracks or damage; replace it, if necessary.

Assembly

PINION GEAR

1. Make sure the ring and pinion are a matched set.
2. Perform the depth gauge check, performing the following procedures:
    a. Using pinion bearing cup replacer tools and the forcing screw from the depth gauge tool set, install the inner and outer pinion cups.
    b. Place a new rear pinion bearing over the aligning adapter and insert it into the pinion bearing retainer assembly. Place the front pinion bearing into the bearing cup in the carrier and assemble the handle onto the screw and hand tighten.

NOTE: The ⅜ in. drive in the handle is to be used for obtaining the proper pinion bearing preload.

    c. Center the gauge tube into the differential bearing bore. Install the bearing caps and tighten the handle until the bearing preload is 20–40 inch lbs. (2.3–4.5 Nm).
    d. Using a feeler gauge or shims, select the thickest feeler shim that will fit between the gauge tube and the gauge block. Insert the feeler gauge or shims directly along the gauge block to insure a correct reading. The feeler gauge, installed between the gauge tube and the gauge block, should have a slight drag feeling.
    e. After the correct shims or feeler gauge thickness is obtained, check the reading, this is the thickness of shim(s) required, provided that upon inspection of the service pinion gear, the button is etched 0.

NOTE: If the service pinion gear is marked with a (+) plus reading, this amount must be subtracted from the thickness dimension obtained in step d; example: +2 (−0.002 in.). If the service pinion gear is marked with a (−) minus reading, this amount must be added to the thickness dimension obtained in step d; example: −2 (+0.002 in.). Be sure to use the exact same new rear pinion bearing that was used in the previous steps.

    f. Using a micrometer, measure the shims to verify the sizes.
3. Place the oil slinger (if used) onto the pinion. Using a pin-

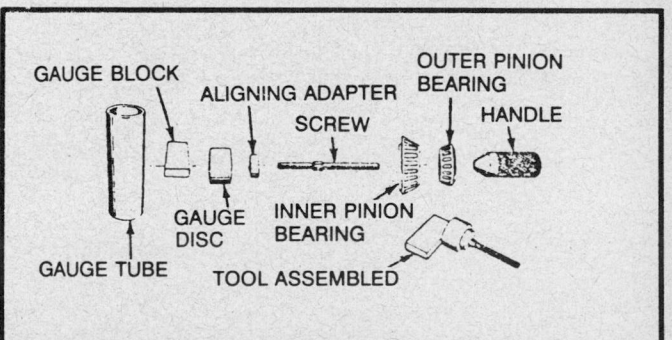

View of the depth gauge tool set

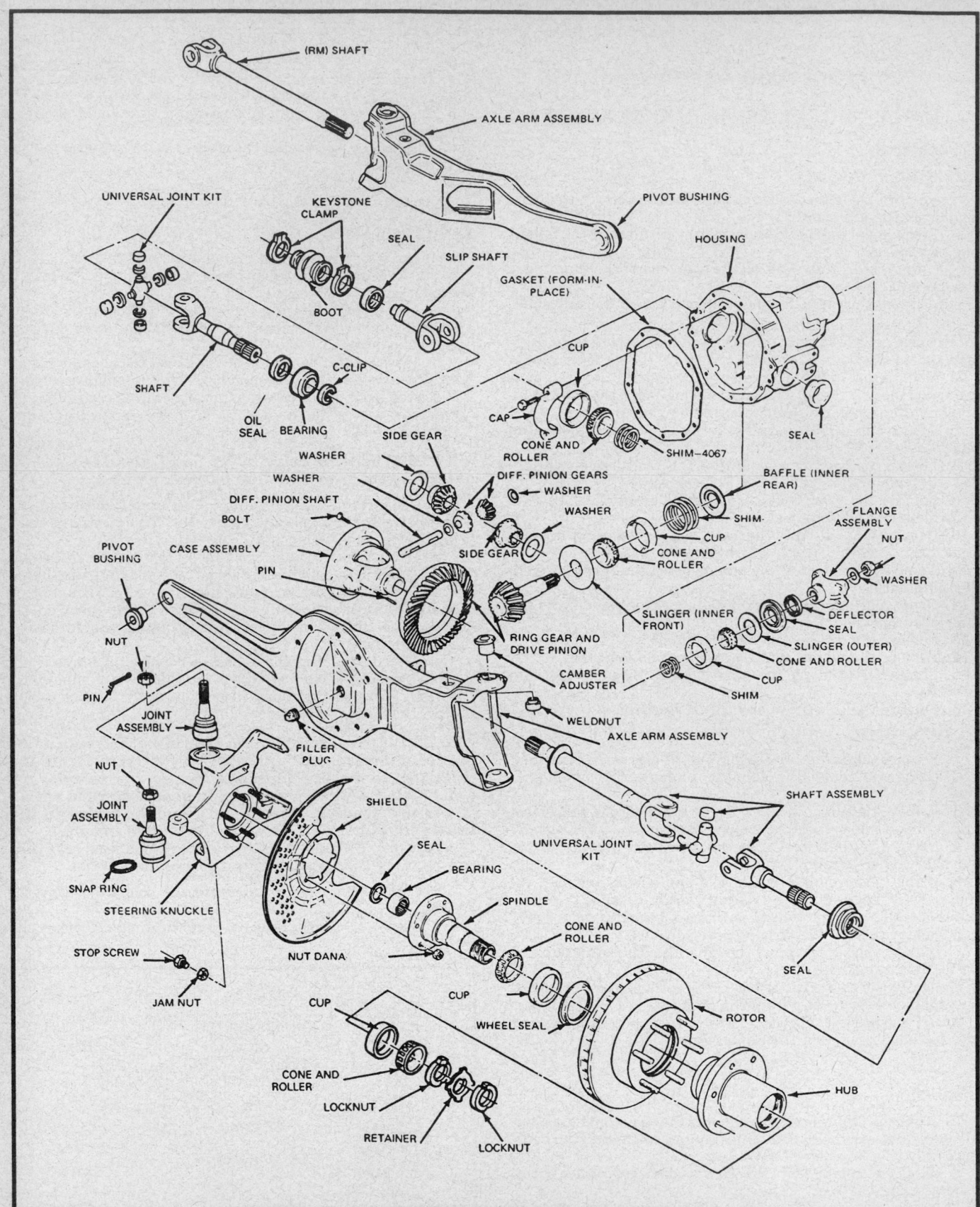

Exploded view of the Dana model 44 front axle assembly—model 50 is similar

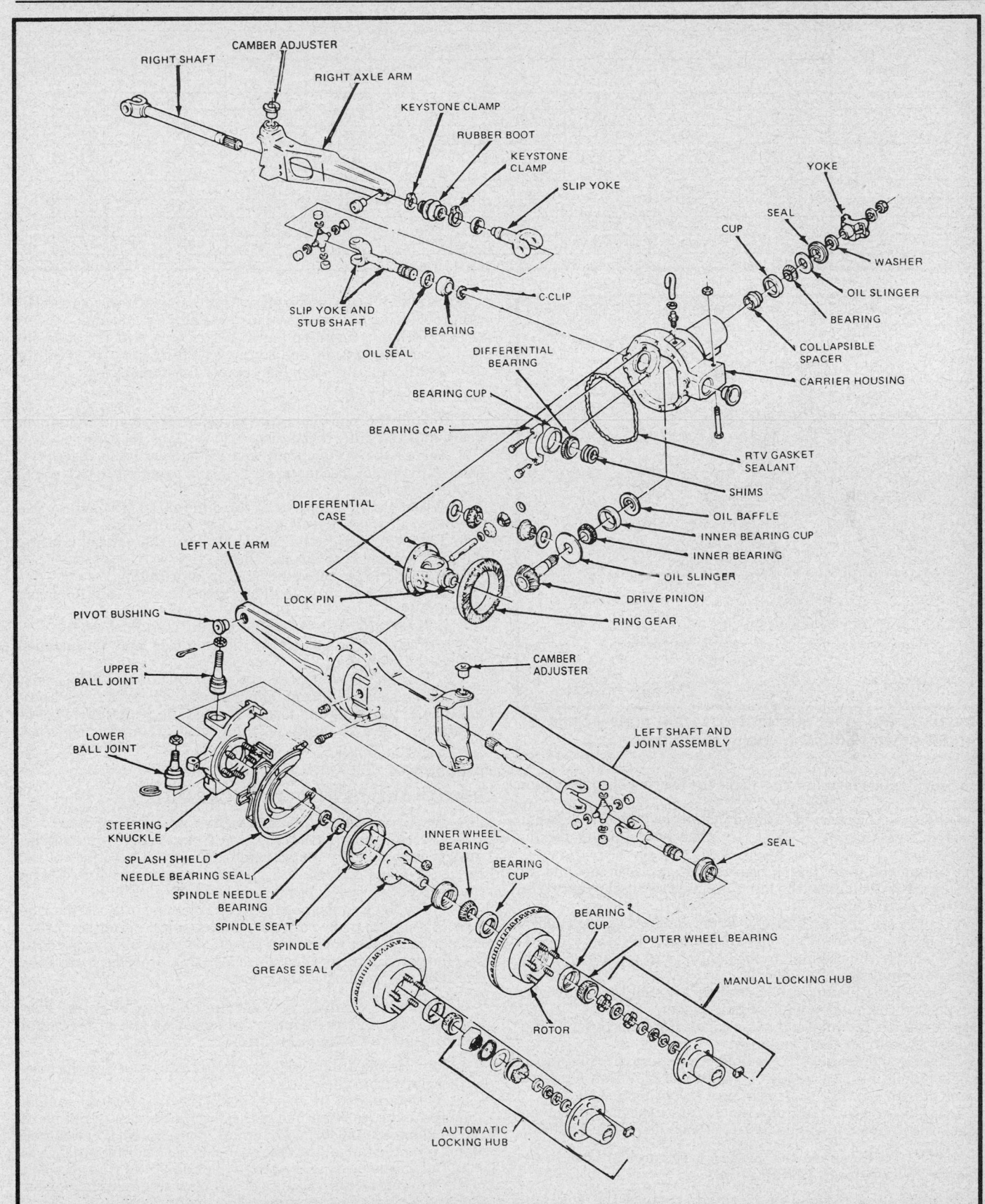

RIGHT SHAFT

CAMBER ADJUSTER

RIGHT AXLE ARM

KEYSTONE CLAMP

RUBBER BOOT

KEYSTONE CLAMP

SLIP YOKE

YOKE

CUP

SEAL

WASHER

OIL SLINGER

BEARING

COLLAPSIBLE SPACER

CARRIER HOUSING

SLIP YOKE AND STUB SHAFT

OIL SEAL

BEARING

C-CLIP

DIFFERENTIAL BEARING

BEARING CUP

BEARING CAP

RTV GASKET SEALANT

SHIMS

OIL BAFFLE

INNER BEARING CUP

INNER BEARING

OIL SLINGER

DRIVE PINION

RING GEAR

DIFFERENTIAL CASE

LEFT AXLE ARM

LOCK PIN

PIVOT BUSHING

UPPER BALL JOINT

LOWER BALL JOINT

CAMBER ADJUSTER

LEFT SHAFT AND JOINT ASSEMBLY

SEAL

STEERING KNUCKLE

SPLASH SHIELD

NEEDLE BEARING SEAL

SPINDLE NEEDLE BEARING

SPINDLE SEAT

SPINDLE

GREASE SEAL

INNER WHEEL BEARING

BEARING CUP

BEARING CUP

OUTER WHEEL BEARING

MANUAL LOCKING HUB

ROTOR

AUTOMATIC LOCKING HUB

Exploded view of the Dana model 28 front axle assembly

Old Pinion Marking	New Pinion Marking								
	−4	−3	−2	−1	0	+1	+2	+3	+4
+4	+0.008	+0.007	+0.006	+0.005	+0.004	+0.003	+0.002	+0.001	0
+3	+0.007	+0.006	+0.005	+0.004	+0.003	+0.002	+0.001	0	−0.001
+2	+0.006	+0.005	+0.004	+0.003	+0.002	+0.001	0	−0.001	−0.002
+1	+0.005	+0.004	+0.003	+0.002	+0.001	0	−0.001	−0.002	−0.003
0	+0.004	+0.003	+0.002	+0.001	0	−0.001	−0.002	−0.003	−0.004
−1	+0.003	+0.002	+0.001	0	−0.001	−0.002	−0.003	−0.004	−0.005
−2	+0.002	+0.001	0	−0.001	−0.002	−0.003	−0.004	−0.005	−0.006
−3	+0.001	0	−0.001	−0.002	−0.003	−0.004	−0.005	−0.006	−0.007
−4	0	−0.001	−0.002	−0.003	−0.004	−0.005	−0.006	−0.007	−0.008

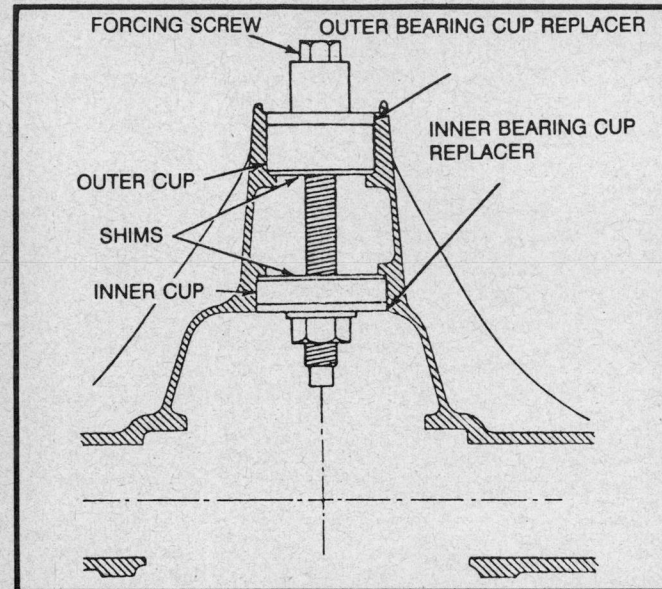

Installing the inner and outer bearing cups — Dana model 44 and 50 front axle assemblies

ion bearing cone installer tool, press the bearing onto the pinion gear.

4. Remove the bearing cup and install the oil baffle (1st) and the required amount of shims into the inner pinion bearing bore.

5. Using the inner pinion bearing cup replacer tool and the forcing screw tool, press the inner pinion bearing cup; be careful not to cock the cup.

6. Lubricate the ends of the outer pinion bearings rollers with long life lubricant and install the outer bearing cone.

7. Measure the original preload shims and replace with new shims of equal size.

8. Install the pinion into the carrier. Install the shims over the pinion, the outer pinion and oil slinger.

9. Assemble the yoke end, the washer, the deflector and slinger onto the pinion shaft and align.

10. Using a companion flange holder tool, seat the yoke, install a new pinion nut and torque to 175 ft. lbs. (237 Nm) for model 28 or 200–220 ft. lbs. (271–298 Nm) except for model 28.

11. Using an inch lb. torque wrench, rotate the pinion gear and check the preload; it should be 20–40 inch lbs. (2.25–4.52 Nm).

NOTE: To increase the preload, remove shims; to decrease the preload, install shims.

12. After the preload is adjusted, remove the yoke and washer.

13. Lubricate the pinion oil seal lip. Using an oil seal installation tool, drive a new oil seal into the carrier housing.

14. Using a companion flange holder tool, seat the yoke, install a new pinion nut and torque to 175 ft. lbs. (237 Nm) or 200–220 ft. lbs. (271–298 Nm) except for model 28.

DIFFERENTIAL

1. Install the side gears, the thrust washers and the pinion gears into the differential case.

2. Install the pinion shaft and lockpin into the case; peen some differential case metal over the pin to lock it in two places 180 degress apart.

3. Assemble the ring gear to the differential case and torque the bolts, alternately, to 45–60 ft. lbs. (61–81 Nm).

4. Place the differential assembly into the carrier housing with the master bearings installed.

5. Adjust the pinion and ring gear backlash.

6. Install the right stub shaft by performing the following procedures:

    a. Insert the stub shaft into the differential carrier.

    b. Position the carrier so the snapring may be installed onto the stub shaft.

    c. Using 2 prybars, press the snapring onto the stub shaft.

7. Using silicone sealant, apply a bead of it to the axle housing. Install the cover and torque the bolts to 35 ft. lbs. (47 Nm) except for model 28 or 40–50 ft. lbs. (54–68 Nm) for model 28.

Adjustment

PINION AND RING GEAR BACKLASH

1. Install the differential and tighten the bearing caps.

2. Force the differential case away from the drive pinion gear, until it is completely seated against the cross bore face of the carrier. Using a dial indicator, position it so the stylus rests on the differential case bolt and zero the indicator.

3. Force the ring gear against the pinion gear. Rock the ring gear, slightly, to make sure the gear teeth are in contact. Then, force the ring gear away from the pinion gear, making sure the dial indicator returns to zero; repeat this procedure until the dial indicator reading is the same.

NOTE: The reading reveals the amount of shims necessary between the differential case and the differential bearing on the ring gear side.

4. Remove the differential case from the carrier and the master bearings from the case.

5. As determined in step 3, place the required amount of shims onto the ring gear hub of the differential case. Example: if the reading was 0.045 in. (1.14mm), place 0.045 in. (1.14mm) shims onto the hub of the ring gear side of the differential case.

6. Install the bearing cone onto the hub of the ring gear side of the differential case. Using a differential side bearing replacer tool and a shop press, press the bearing onto the hub.

7. To determine the correct amount of shims to be installed

on the hub of the drive pinion side, subtract the reading obtained in step 3 from the differential total case endplay. When this amount is determined, add 0.010 in. (0.26mm) to the amount; this is the required amount of shims to be placed on the hub of the drive pinion side of the differential.

Example: Total case endplay was 0.091 in. (2.30mm) and the reading in step 3 was 0.045 in. (1.14mm). Subtract the reading from the endplay; the result is 0.046 in. (1.16mm). Then, add 0.010 in. (0.26mm) to the result; 0.056 in. (1.42mm) is the amount of shims to be added on the hub of the drive pinion side of the differential case.

8. Place the required amount of shims onto the hub of the drive pinion side of the differential case.

9. Install the bearing cone onto the hub of the drive pinion side of the differential case. Using a step plate tool, placed on the ring gear side bearing, and a differential side bearing replacer tool, drive the bearing onto the hub of the drive pinion side of the differential case.

10. Using a differential bearing replacer tool, install the bearing cone onto the pinion side of the differential case; be sure to position a pinion bearing cone replacer tool on the ring gear bearing to prevent damage to it.

11. Install the differential bearing cups onto the bearing cones.

12. Using a case spreader tool and a dial indicator, spread the carrier housing to 0.015 in. (0.25mm) max.

13. Install the differential case into the carrier; it may be necessary to use a soft hammer to seat the differential case into the carrier case cross bore.

14. Install the bearing caps; make sure the letters or numbers stamped on the caps correspond in both direction and position with the numbers stamped in the carrier. Torque the bolts to 35–40 ft. lbs. (48–54 Nm) for model 28 or 80–90 ft. lbs. (108–122 Nm) except for model 28.

15. Install a dial indicator to the case and check the ring gear backlash at 3 equally spaced points; the backlash should be 0.005–0.009 in. (0.13–0.23mm) and should not vary more than 0.003 in. (0.08mm) between the points.

NOTE: If the backlash is high, the ring gear must be moved closer to the pinion, by moving the shims to the ring gear side from the opposite side. If the backlash is low, the ring gear must be moved away from the pinion by moving the shims from the ring gear side to the opposite side.

16. Check and/or adjust the gear tooth pattern.
17. Install the right stub shaft by performing the following procedures:
   a. Insert the stub shaft into the differential carrier.
   b. Position the carrier so the snapring may be installed onto the stub shaft.
   c. Using 2 prybars, press the snapring onto the stub shaft.
18. Using silicone sealant, apply it to the mating surface of the carrier support arm.

NOTE: Allow silicone sealant 1 hour to cure.

19. Using 2 guide pins, assemble the carrier housing to the carrier support arm and torque the new bolts to 30–40 ft. lbs. (41–54 Nm) except for model 28 or 40–50 ft. lbs. (54–68 Nm) for model 28.
20. Except for model 28, install the support arm tab bolt to the side of the carrier and torque the bolts to 85 ft. lbs. (115–136 Nm).
21. For model 28, assemble the carrier shear bolt and nut, then, torque to 75–95 ft. lbs. (102–129 Nm).

DANA 60 MONOBEAM AXLE

The differential side bearing shims are located between the side bearing cup assembly and the differential case. The axle use inner and outer shims on the pinion gear. The inner shims are

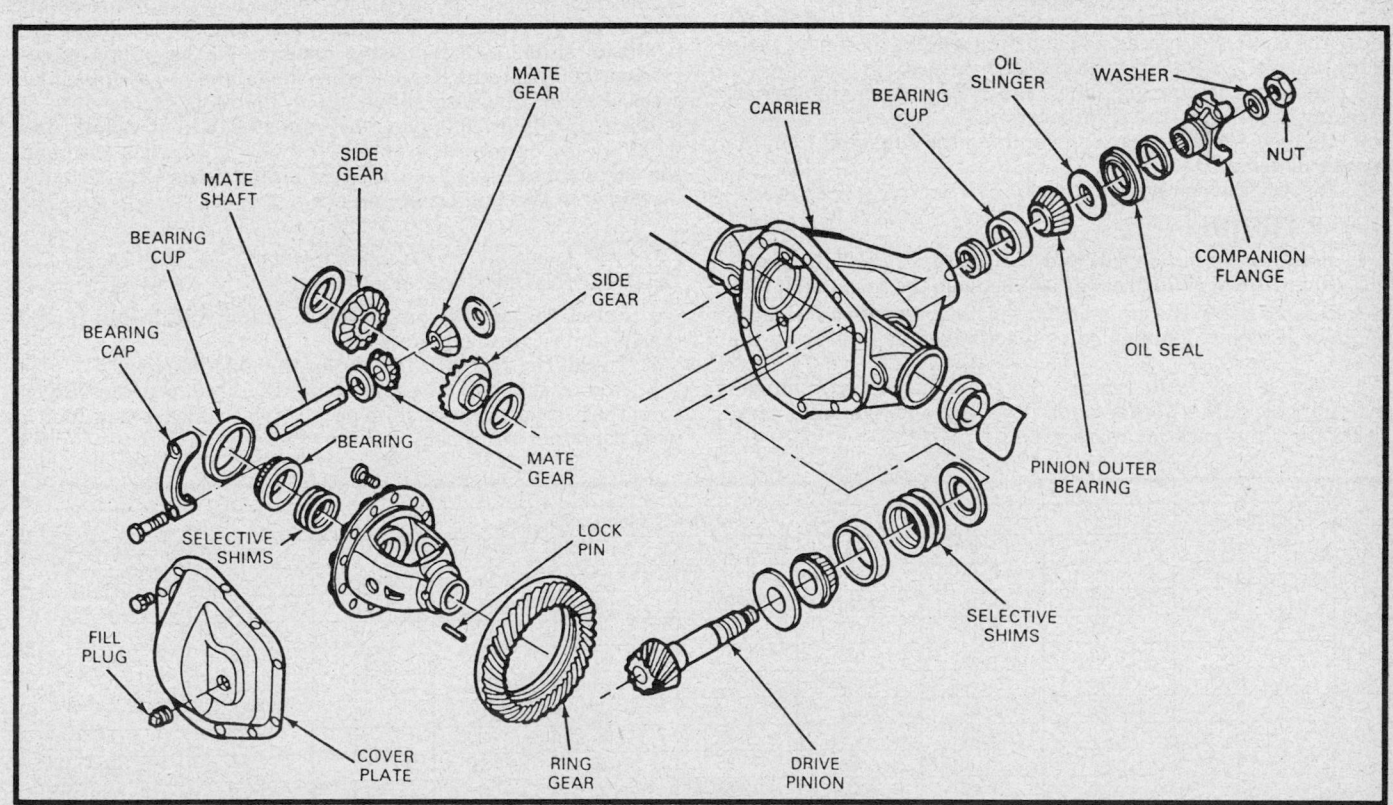

Exploded view of the Dana 60 Monobeam front axle differential assembly

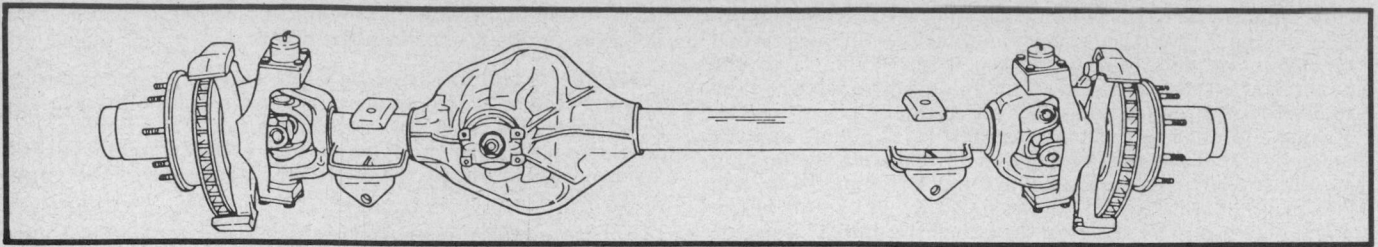

Assembled view of the Dana 60 Monobeam front axle assembly

used to control the pinion depth in the housing, while the outer shims are used to preload the pinion bearings. The axle uses a solid differential carrier with a removable side and pinion gear shaft.

Disassembly

DIFFERENTIAL CARRIER

1. The axle assembly can be overhauled either in or out of the vehicle. Either way, the free-floating axles must be removed.
2. Drain the lubricant and remove the rear cover and gasket.
3. Matchmark the bearing caps and the housing for reassembly in the same position. Remove the bearing caps and bolts.
4. Using a spreader tool mounted to the carrier housing, spread the housing a maximum of 0.015 in.

NOTE: Do not exceed this measurement. The housing could be permanently damaged. The use of a dial indicator is recommended to prevent over-stretching the housing.

5. Using a pry bar, remove the differential case from the housing. Remove the spreader tool from the housing.
6. Remove the differential side bearing cups and tag to identify the side, if they are to be used again.
7. Remove the differential gear pinion shaft lock pin and remove the shaft. Rotate the side and pinion gears to remove them from the carrier. Remove the thrust bearings.
8. Remove the bearing cones and rollers from the carrier, marking and noting the shim locations.
9. Remove the ring gear bolts and tap the ring gear from the carrier housing.
10. Inspect the components.

DRIVE PINION

1. Remove the pinion nut and flange from the pinion gear.
2. Remove the pinion gear assembly from the housing. It may be necessary to tap the pinion from the housing with a soft faced hammer. Catch the pinion so as not to allow it to drop on the floor.
3. With a long drift, remove the inner bearing cup, pinion seal, slinger, gasket, outer pinion bearing and the shim pack. Label the shim pack for reassembly.

4. Remove the rear pinion bearing cup and shim pack from the housing. Label the shims for reassembly.
5. Remove the rear pinion bearing from the pinion gear with an arbor press and special plates.

Inspection

1. Clean the gears, bearings and component parts with solvent and inspect for scoring, chipping or excessive wear.
2. Inspect the flanges and splines for excessive wear.
3. Replace the necessary parts as required.

PINION SHIM SELECTION

Ring gears and pinions are supplied in matched sets only. The matched numbers are etched on both gears for verification. On the rear face of the pinion, a plus (+) or a minus (−) number will be etched, indicating the best running position for each particular gear set. This dimension is controlled by the shimming behind the inner bearing cup. Whenever baffles or oil slingers are used, they become part of the adjusting shim pack. An example: If a pinion is etched +3, this pinion would require 0.003 in. less shims than a pinion etched 0. This means by removing shims, the mounting distance of the pinion is increased by 0.003 in., which is just what a plus (+) etching indicates. If a pinion is etched −3, it would be necessary to add 0.003 in. more shims than would be required if the pinion was etched 0. By adding the 0.003 in. shims, the mounting distance of the pinion is decreased 0.003 in., which is just what the minus (−) etching indicates. Pinion adjusting shims are available in thicknesses of 0.003 in. (0.08mm), 0.005 in. (0.13mm), 0.010 in. (0.25mm) and 0.030 in. (0.76mm). An example: If a new gear set is used and the old pinion reads +2 and the new pinion reads −2, add 0.004 in. shims to the original shim pack.

Assembly

DRIVE PINION

1. Select the correct pinion depth shims and install in the rear pinion bearing cup bore.
2. Install the rear bearing cup in the axle housing.
3. Add or subtract an equal amount of shim thickness to or from the preload or outer shim pack, as was added or subtracted from the inner shim pack.

Old Pinion Marking	New Pinion Marking								
	−10	−8	−5	−3	0	+3	+5	+8	+10
+10	+.20	+.18	+.15	+.13	+.10	+.08	+.05	+.03	0
+8	+.18	+.15	+.13	+.10	+.08	+.05	+.03	0	−.03
+5	+.15	+.13	+.10	+.08	+.05	+.03	0	−.03	−.05
+3	+.13	+.10	+.08	+.05	+.03	0	−.03	−.05	−.08
0	+.10	+.08	+.05	+.03	0	−.03	−.05	−.08	−.10
−3	+.08	+.05	+.03	0	−.03	−.05	−.08	−.10	−.13
−5	+.05	+.03	0	−.03	−.05	−.08	−.10	−.13	−.15
−8	+.03	0	−.03	−.05	−.08	−.10	−.13	−.15	−.18
−10	0	−.03	−.05	−.08	−.10	−.13	−.15	−.18	−.20

4. Install the front pinion bearing cup into its bore in the axle housing.

5. Press the rear pinion bearing onto the pinion gear shaft and install the pinion gear with bearing into the axle housing.

6. Install the preload shims and the front pinion bearing; do not install the oil seal at this time.

7. Install the flange with the holding bar tool attached, the washer and the nut on the pinion shaft end. Torque the nut to 240–300 ft. lbs. (326–406 Nm).

8. Remove the holding bar from the flange and with an inch lb. torque wrench, measure the rotating torque of the pinion gear. The rotating torque should be 10–20 inch lbs. with the original bearings or 20–40 inch lbs. with new bearings. Disregard the torque reading necessary to start the shaft to turn.

9. If the preload torque is not in specifications, adjust the shim pack as required.

a. To increase preload, decrease the thickness of the preload shim pack.

b. To decrease preload, increase the thickness of the preload shim pack.

10. When the proper preload is obtained, remove the nut, washer and flange from the pinion shaft.

11. Install a new pinion seal into the housing and reinstall the flange, washer and nut. Using the holder tool, torque the nut to 240–300 ft. lbs. (326–406 Nm).

DIFFERENTIAL CARRIER

1. Install the differential side gears, the differential pinion gears and new thrust washers into the differential carrier.

2. Align the pinion gear shaft holes and install the pinion shaft into the carrier. Align the lock pin hole in the shaft and carrier. Install the lock pin and peen the hole to avoid having the pin drop from the carrier.

3. Install the differential case side bearings with the proper installation tools. Do not install the shims at this time.

4. Place the carrier assembly into the axle housing with the bearing cups on the bearing cones. Install the bearing caps in their original position and tighten the bearing cap bolts enough to keep the bearing caps in place.

5. Install a dial indicator on the housing so the indicator button contacts the carrier flange. Press the differential carrier to prevent sideplay and center the dial indicator. Rotate the carrier and check the flange for run-out. If the run-out is greater than 0.002 in., the defect is probably due to the bearings or to the carrier and should be corrected.

6. Remove the assembly and install the ring gear. Torque the retaining bolts and reinstall the assembly into the housing. Install the bearing caps in their original position and tighten the cap bolts to keep the bearings caps in place.

7. Install the dial indicator and position the indicator button to contact the ring gear back surface. Rotate the assembly and the run-out should be less than 0.002 in. If over 0.002 in., remove the assembly and relocate the ring gear 180 degrees. Reinstall the assembly and recheck. If the run-out remains over the 0.002 in. tolerance, the ring gear is defective. If the measurement is within tolerances, continue on with the assembly.

8. Position 2 pry bars between the bearing cap and the housing on the side opposite the ring gear. Pull on the pry bars and force the differential carrier as far as possible towards the dial indicator. Rock the assembly to seat the bearings and reset the dial indicator to zero.

9. Reposition the prybars to the opposite side of the carrier and force the carrier assembly as far towards the center of the housing. Read the dial indicator scale. This will be the total amount of shims required for setting the backlash during the reassembly, less the bearing preload. Record the measurement.

10. With the pinion gear installed and properly set, position the differential carrier assembly into the axle housing and install the bearing caps in their proper positions. Tighten the cap bolts just to hold the bearing cups in place.

11. Install a dial indicator on the axle housing with the indicator button contacting the back of the ring gear.

12. Position 2 prybars between the bearing cup and the axle housing on the ring gear side of the case and pry the ring gear into mesh with the pinion gear teeth, as far as possible. Rock the ring gear to allow the teeth to mesh and the bearings to seat. With the pressure still applied by the prybars, set the dial indicator to zero.

13. Reposition the prybars on the opposite side of ring gear and pry the gear as far as it will go. Take the dial indicator reading. Repeat this procedure until the same reading is obtained each time. This reading represents the necessary amount of shims between the differential carrier and the bearing on the ring gear side.

14. Remove the bearing from the differential carrier on the ring gear side and install the proper amount of shims. Reinstall the bearing.

15. Remove the differential carrier bearing from the opposite side of the ring gear. To determine the amount of shims needed, use the following method.

a. Subtract the size of the shim pack just installed on the ring gear side of the carrier from the reading obtained and recorded when measurement was taken without the pinion gear in place.

b. To this figure, add an additional 0.015 in. to compensate for preload and backlash. An example: If the first reading was 0.085 in. and the shims installed on the ring gear side of the carrier were 0.055 in., the correct amount of shims would be 0.085 − 0.055 + 0.015 = 0.045 in.

16. Install the required shims as determined under step 15 and install the differential side bearing. The installation of the shims should give the proper preload to the bearings and the proper backlash to the ring and pinion gears.

17. Spread the axle housing with the spreader tool no more than 0.015 in. Install the differential bearing outer cups in their correct locations and install the cups in their respective locations.

18. Install the bolts and tighten finger-tight. Rotate the differential carrier and ring gear and tap with a soft-faced hammer to insure proper seating of the assembly in the axle housing.

19. Remove the spreader tool and torque the cap bolts to 80–90 ft. lbs. (108–122 Nm).

20. Install a dial indicator and check the ring gear backlash at 4 equally spaced points of the ring gear circle. The backlash must be within a range of 0.004–0.009 in. and must not vary more than 0.003 in. between the points checked.

21. If the backlash is not within specifications, the shim packs must be corrected to bring the backlash within limits.

22. Check the tooth contact pattern and verify.

23. Install the cover and torque the bolts to 30–40 ft. lbs. (41–54 Nm). Refill to proper level with lubricant and operate to verify proper assembly.

Rear Axle Assembly

FORD—10¼ AND 8.8 INCH RING GEAR AXLES

Disassembly

DIFFERENTIAL CARRIER

1. Remove the cover and clean the lubricant from the internal parts.

2. Using a dial indicator, measure and record the ring gear backlash and the runout; the backlash should be 0.008–0.015 in. and the runout should be less than 0.004 in.

3. Mark 1 differential bearing cap to ensure it is installed its original position.

4. Loosen the differential bearing cap bolts.

5. Using a prybar, pry the differential carrier until the bearing cups and shims are loose in the bearing caps.

6. Remove the bearing caps and the differential assembly.

7. If necessary, remove ring gear-to-differential case bolts. Using a hammer and a punch, strike the alternate bolt holes around the ring gear to dislodge it from the differential.

8. If necessary, remove the excitor ring by striking it with a soft hammer.

9. Remove the pinion shaft lock bolt from the differential case. Remove the differential pinion shaft, the pinion gears and the thrust washers.

10. Remove the side gears and thrust washers.

11. Using a bearing puller tool, press the bearings from the differential carrier.

PINION GEAR

1. Remove the differential carrier assembly.

2. Using a companion flange holding tool, remove the companion flange nut.

3. Using a puller tool, press the companion flange from the pinion gear.

4. Using a soft hammer, drive the pinion gear from the housing.

5. Using a prybar, remove the pinion gear oil seal from the housing.

6. Remove the oil slinger and the front pinion bearing.

7. Using a shop press, press the bearing cone from from the pinion gear.

8. Remove and record the shim from the pinion gear.

Inspection

1. Clean the differential components in solvent and use compressed air to dry them; do not use compressed air on the bearings, only shop towels.

2. Check the components for wear or damage; replace them, if necessary.

3. Inspect the bearings and bearing cups for wear, cracks or scoring; replace them, if necessary.

4. Inspect the differential side and pinion gears for wear, cracks or chips; replace them, if necessary.

5. Inspect the ring and pinion gears for wear and/or damage; replace them, if necessary.

6. Inspect the differential case for cracks or damage; replace it, if necessary.

Assembly

PINION GEAR

NOTE: When replacing the ring and pinion gear, the correct shim thickness for the new gear set to be installed is determined by following procedure using a pinion depth gauge tool set.

1. Assemble the appropriate aligning adapter, the gauge disc and gauge block to the screw.

2. Place the rear pinion bearing over the aligning tool and insert it into the rear portion of the bearing cup of the carrier. Place the front bearing into the front bearing cup and assemble the tool handle into the screw. Roll the assembly back and forth a few times to seat the bearings while tightening the tool handle, by hand, to 20 ft. lbs. (27 Nm).

NOTE: The gauge block must be offset 45 degrees to obtain an accurate reading.

3. Center the gauge tube into the differential bearing bore. Install the bearing caps and tighten the bolts to 70–85 ft. lbs. (96–115 Nm); be sure to install the caps with the triangles pointing outward.

4. Place the selected shim(s) on the pinion and press the pinion bearing cone and roller assembly until it is firmly seated on the shaft, using the pinion bearing cone replacer and the axle bearing/seal plate.

5. Place the collapsible spacer on the pinion stem against the pinion stem shoulder.

6. Install the front pinion bearing and oil slinger in the housing bore and install the pinion seal on the pinion seal replacer. Using a hammer, install the seal until it seats.

7. From the rear of the axle housing, install the drive pinion assembly into the housing pinion shaft bore.

8. Lubricate the pinion shaft splines and install the companion flange.

9. Using a companion flange holder tool, torque the pinion nut to 160 ft. lbs. (217 Nm); rotate the pinion gear, occasionally, to ensure proper bearing seating.

10. Using an inch pound torque wrench, frequently, measure the pinion bearing preload; it should be 9–14 inch lbs. for used bearings or 16–29 inch lbs. for new bearings.

NOTE: If the preload is higher than the specification, tighten to the original reading as recorded; never back off the pinion nut.

DIFFERENTIAL CARRIER

1. If the bearings were removed, use a shop press to press them onto the differential case.

2. Install the side gears and thrust washers. Install the pinion gears, the thrust washer, the pinion shaft and the pinion shaft lock bolt.

3. Using a shop press, align the excitor ring tab with the differential case slot and press the ring gear and excitor ring onto the differential case. Install the ring gear-to-differential case bolts and torque them to 100–120 ft. lbs. (135–162 Nm).

4. Place the differential case with the bearing cups into the housing.

5. On the left side, install a 0.265 in shim. Install the bearing cap and tighten the bolts finger tight.

6. On the right side, install progressively larger shims until the largest can be installed by hand. Install the bearing cap.

7. Torque the bearing cap-to-housing bolts to 70–85 ft. lbs. (95–115 Nm).

8. Rotate the assembly to ensure free rotation.

9. Adjust the ring gear backlash.

Adjustment

RING GEAR AND PINION BACKLASH

1. Using a dial indicator, measure the ring gear and pinion backlash; it should be 0.008–0.015 in. If the backlash is 0.001–0.007 in. or greater than 0.015 in. proceed to step 3. If the backlash is zero, proceed to step 2.

2. If the backlash is zero, add 0.020 in. shim(s) to the right side and subtract a 0.020 in. shim(s) from the left side.

Backlash Change Required	Thickness Change Required	Backlash Change Required	Thickness Change Required
.001	.002	.009	.012
.002	.002	.010	.014
.003	.004	.011	.014
.004	.006	.012	.016
.005	.006	.013	.018
.006	.008	.014	.018
.007	.010	.015	.020
.008	.010		

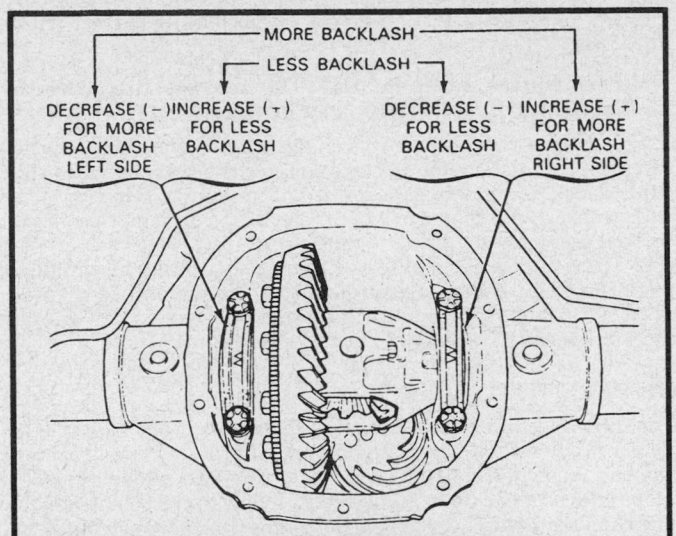

backlash adjustment by changing shims

3. If the backlash is within specification, go to step 7. If the backlash is 0.001–0.007 in. or greater than 0.015 in., increase the thickness of a shim on 1 side and decrease the same thickness of another shim on the other side, until the backlash comes within range.

4. Install and torque the bearing cap bolts to 80–95 ft. lbs. (109–128 Nm).

5. Rotate the assembly several times to ensure proper seating.

6. Recheck the backlash, if it is not within specification, go to step 7.

7. Remove the bearing caps. Increase the shim sizes, on both sides by 0.006 in.; make sure the shims are fully seated and the assembly turns freely. Use a shim driver to install the shims.

8. Install the bearing caps and torque the bearing caps to 80–95 ft. lbs. (109–128 Nm). Recheck the backlash; if not to specification, repeat this entire procedure.

FORD — 7½ INCH RING GEAR AXLE

Disassembly

DIFFERENTIAL CASE

1. Check and record the ring gear runout and backlash.

2. Mark on differential bearing cap to help position the caps properly during assembly.

3. Loosen the differential bearing cap bolts and bearing caps.

NOTE: The direction of arrows on bearing caps must be noted. When reassembled, the arrows must be pointing in the same direction as before removal.

4. Pry the differential case, bearing cups and shims out until they are loose in the bearing caps. Remove the bearing caps and the differential assembly from the carrier.

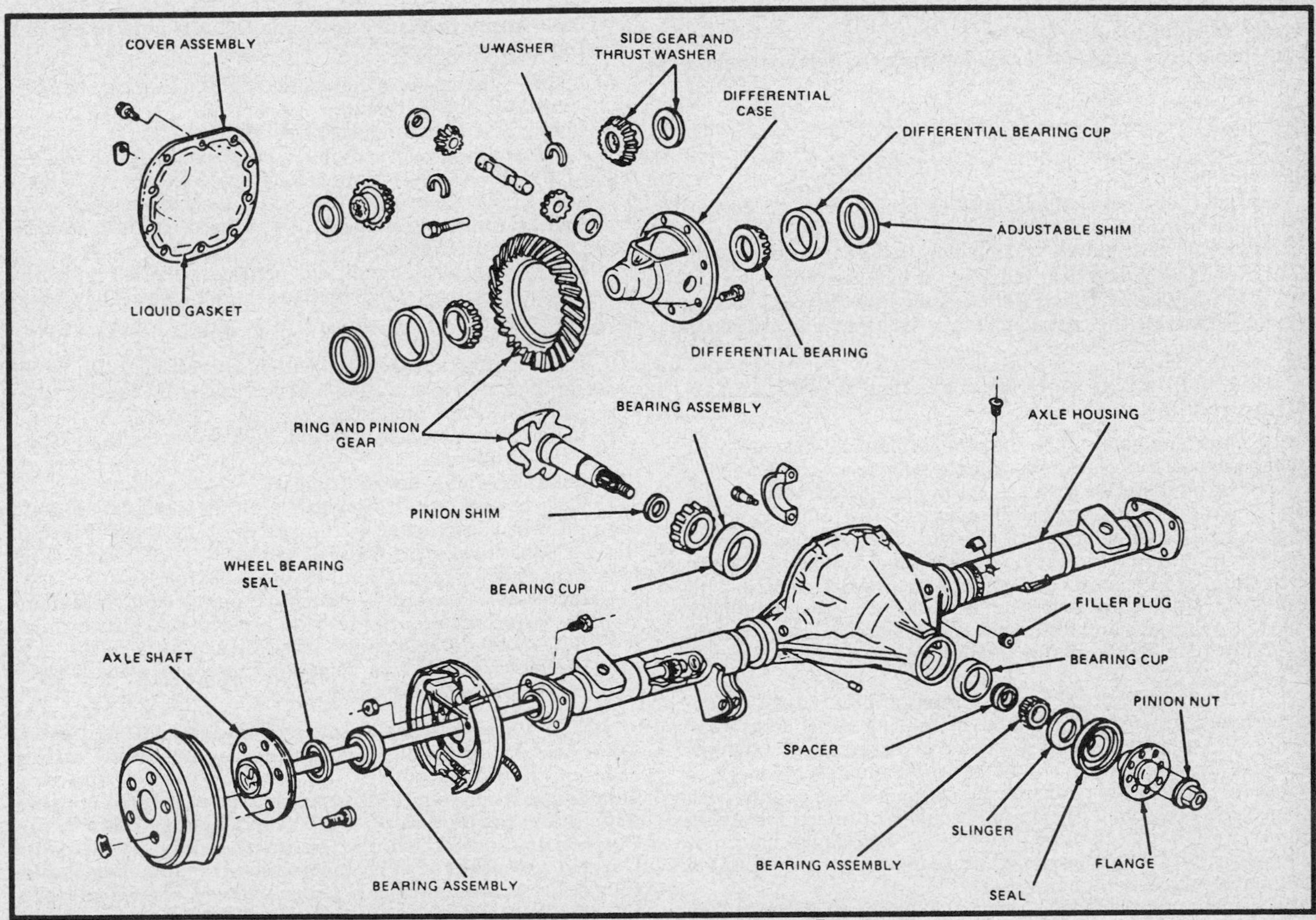

Exploded view of the 7½ inch ring gear axle assembly — Ford Motor Company

If the ring is removed, discard the bolts. Install new bolts, coated with Loctite® or equivalent. Tighten to 70–85 ft. lbs. (95–115 Nm).

DRIVE PINION

1. Hold the rear axle companion flange with the proper tool and remove the pinion nut.
2. Remove the companion flange. With a soft-faced hammer, drive the pinion out of the front bearing cone and remove it through the rear of the carrier casting.
3. Remove the drive pinion oil seal with tool 1125–AC and T50T–100–A or their equivalent. Remove the front pinion bearing cone, the roller and slinger from the housing.
4. To remove the pinion rear bearing cone, use tool T71P–4621–B or equivalent. Measure the shim found under the bearing cone with a micrometer. Record the thickness of the shim.

NOTE: Before assembling the rear bearing cone to the pinion, it will be necessary to adjust pinion depth.

Inspection

1. Clean the differential components in solvent and use compressed air to dry them; do not use compressed air on the bearings, only shop towels.
2. Check the components for wear or damage; replace them, if necessary.
3. Inspect the bearings and bearing cups for wear, cracks or scoring; replace them, if necessary.
4. Inspect the differential side and pinion gears for wear, cracks or chips; replace them, if necessary.
5. Inspect the ring and pinion gears for wear and/or damage; replace them, if necessary.
6. Inspect the differential case for cracks or damage; replace it, if necessary.

Assembly

DRIVE PINION

1. Place the selected shim(s) on the pinion shaft an depress the pinion bearing until firmly seated on the shaft.
2. Place the rear pinion bearing (new or used if in good condition) over the aligning disc and insert it into the pinion bearing cup of the carrier. Place the front bearing into the front bearing cup and assemble the tool handle into the screw and tighten to 20 ft. lbs. (27 Nm).

NOTE: The gauge block must be offset to obtain an accurate reading.

3. Center the gauge tube into the differential bearing bore. Install the bearing caps and torque the bolts to specification; the caps must be installed with the arrows point outboard.
4. Make sure the gauge handle adapter screw, aligning adapter, gauge disc and gauge block assembly are securely mounted between front and rear bearing. Recheck tool handle torque prior to gauging to ensure the bearings are properly seated. This can affect final shim selection when improperly assembled. Clean bearing cups and differential pedestal surfaces thoroughly. Apply only light oil film on bearing assemblies prior to gauging.
5. Gauge block should then be rotated several ½ turns to ensure rollers are properly seated in bearing cups. Rotational torque on the gauge assembly should be 20 inch lbs. with new bearings. Final position should be approximately 45 degrees across the gauge tube to ensure the gauge block is aligned with gauge tube high point. This area should be utilized for pinion shim selection. Selection of pinion shim with gauge block not aligned with tube high point will cause improper shim selection and may result in axle noise.
6. Utilize pinion shims as the gauge for shim selection. This will minimize errors in attempting to stack feeler gauge stock together or simple addition errors in calculating correct shim thickness.

NOTE: Shims must be flat. Do not use dirty, bent, nicked or mutilated shims as a gauge.

7. It is important to utilize a light drag on the shim for the correct selection. Do not attempt to force the shim between the gauge block and gauge tube. This will minimize selection of a shim thicker than required which results in a deep tooth contact in final assembly for integral axles.
8. If the pinion has a plug (+) marking, subtract his amount from the feeler gauge measurement. If the pinion has a minimum (−) marking, add this amount to the feeler gauge measurement.

DIFFERENTIAL CASE

For shim selection after a complete replacement of the rear axle housing, the differential assembly or differential side bearings use the following instructions. For a ring and pinion replacement only or a backlash adjustment, follow Steps 9 through 13 and Step 15, using the side bearing shims that were originally in the axle.

1. With pinion depth set and pinion installed, place differential case gear assembly with bearings and cups into the carrier.
2. Install a 0.265 in. (6.73mm) shim on left side.
3. Install left bearing cap and tighten bolts finger tight.
4. Install progressively larger shims on the right side until the largest shim selected can be assembled with a slight drag feel.

NOTE: Apply pressure towards the left side to ensure bearing cup is seated.

5. Install right side bearing cap and tighten bearing cup bolts to 70–85 ft. lbs. (95–115 Nm).
6. Rotate assembly to ensure free rotation.
7. Check the ring gear and pinion backlash. If the backlash is 0.008–0.015 in. (0.20–0.38mm) with 0.012–0.015 in. (0.304–0.381mm) preferred, proceed to Step 14. If backlash is not within specifications, go to Step 10, unless zero backlash is measured, then, go to Step 8.
8. If a zero backlash conditions occurs, add 0.020 in. to the right side and subtract 0.020 in. from the left side to allow backlash indication.
9. Recheck backlash.
10. If backlash is not to specification, correct backlash by increasing thickness of one shim and decreasing thickness on the other shim the same amount.
11. Install shim and bearing caps. Tighten cap bolts to 70–85 ft. lbs. (95–115 Nm).
12. Rotate assembly several times.
13. Recheck backlash. If backlash is within specification, go to Step 14. If backlash is not within specification, repeat Step 10. Backlash specification is 0.008–0.015 in. (0.20–0.38mm). Preferred range is 0.012–0.015 in. (0.304–0.381mm).
14. Increase both left and right shim sizes by 0.006 in. and install for correct differential bearing preload; make sure shims are fully seated and assembly turns freely.
15. Utilize white marking compound to obtain a tooth mesh contact pattern in the assembly.

NOTE: Pattern inspection is intended to detect gross errors in set up prior to complete reassembly. Pattern contact should be within the primary area of the ring gear tooth surface avoiding any narrow or hard contact with outer perimeter of tooth (top to root, toe to heel). Pattern inspection should be on the drive (pull) side. Correct assembly of drive pattern will result in satisfactory coast performance. If gross pattern error is detected, the preferred backlash of 0.012–0.015 in. (0.30–0.38mm), recheck pinion shim selection.

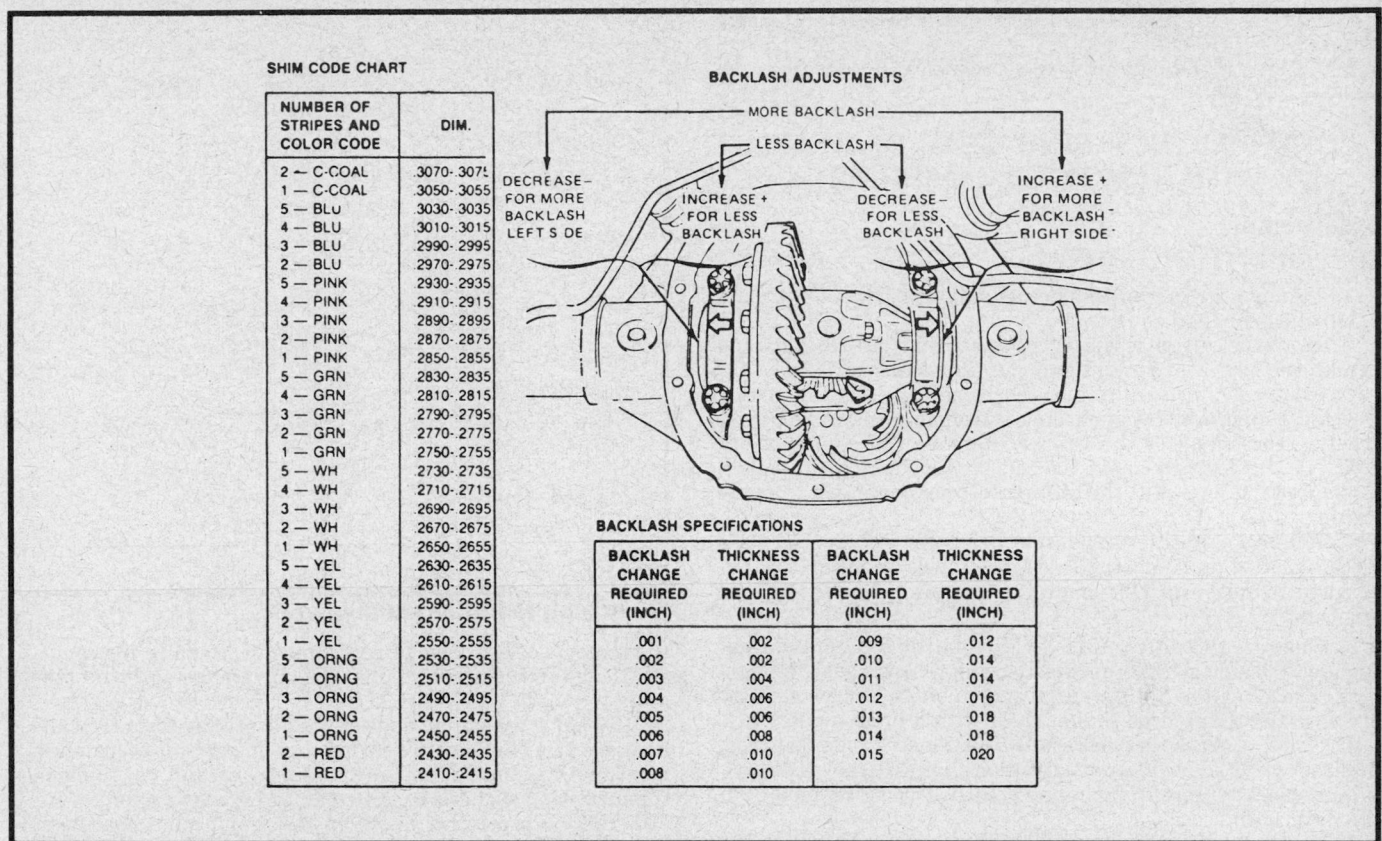

SHIM CODE CHART

NUMBER OF STRIPES AND COLOR CODE	DIM.
2 — C-COAL	.3070-.3075
1 — C-COAL	.3050-.3055
5 — BLU	.3030-.3035
4 — BLU	.3010-.3015
3 — BLU	.2990-.2995
2 — BLU	.2970-.2975
5 — PINK	.2930-.2935
4 — PINK	.2910-.2915
3 — PINK	.2890-.2895
2 — PINK	.2870-.2875
1 — PINK	.2850-.2855
5 — GRN	.2830-.2835
4 — GRN	.2810-.2815
3 — GRN	.2790-.2795
2 — GRN	.2770-.2775
1 — GRN	.2750-.2755
5 — WH	.2730-.2735
4 — WH	.2710-.2715
3 — WH	.2690-.2695
2 — WH	.2670-.2675
1 — WH	.2650-.2655
5 — YEL	.2630-.2635
4 — YEL	.2610-.2615
3 — YEL	.2590-.2595
2 — YEL	.2570-.2575
1 — YEL	.2550-.2555
5 — ORNG	.2530-.2535
4 — ORNG	.2510-.2515
3 — ORNG	.2490-.2495
2 — ORNG	.2470-.2475
1 — ORNG	.2450-.2455
2 — RED	.2430-.2435
1 — RED	.2410-.2415

BACKLASH SPECIFICATIONS

BACKLASH CHANGE REQUIRED (INCH)	THICKNESS CHANGE REQUIRED (INCH)	BACKLASH CHANGE REQUIRED (INCH)	THICKNESS CHANGE REQUIRED (INCH)
.001	.002	.009	.012
.002	.002	.010	.014
.003	.004	.011	.014
.004	.006	.012	.016
.005	.006	.013	.018
.006	.008	.014	.018
.007	.010	.015	.020
.008	.010		

Shim changes for ring gear and pinion backlash

16. Install bearing caps and tighten cap bolts to 70–85 ft. lbs. (95–115 Nm).

17. Install the axle shafts.

18. Remove the oil seal replacer from the transmission extension housing. Install the driveshaft in the extension housing. align the scribe marks on the flange and driveshaft and connect the driveshaft at the drive pinion flange. Apply Loctite® to the threads of the attaching bolts and torque to 70–95 ft. lbs. (90–128 Nm).

19. Install the brake drum and attaching shakeproof retainers. Install the wheel and tire on the brake drum. Install the wheel covers.

20. Clean the gasket mating surface of the rear axle housing and cover.

Apply a new continuous bead of silicone rubber sealant to the carrier casting face.

NOTE: Make sure the machined surfaces on both cover and carrier are clean before installing the new silicone sealant. Inside of axle must be covered when cleaning the machined surface to prevent axle contamination.

21. Install the cover and torque the bolts to 25–35 ft. lbs. (34–47 Nm), except the ratio tag bolt, which is tightened to 15–25 ft. lbs. (20–34 Nm).

NOTE: Cover assembly must be installed within 15 minutes of application of the silicone or new sealant must be reapplied.

22. Add EOAZ–19580–A (ESP–MC2154–A) or equivalent, through the filler hole until the lubricant level is ⅜ in. (9.5mm) below the filler hole with the axle in the running position.

23. Lower vehicle and road test.

Adjustment

DRIVE PINION AND DRIVE PINION BEARING PRELOAD

1. Install the pinion front bearing and slinger.

2. Apply grease, C1AZ–19590–B or equivalent, between the lips of the pinion seal and install the pinion seal.

3. Insert the companion flange into the seal and hold it firmly against the pinion front bearing cone. From the rear of the carrier casting, insert the pinion shaft, with a new spacer, into the flange.

4. Start new pinion nut. Hold the flange with special tool T78P–4851–A or equivalent, and tighten the pinion nut. As the nut is tightened, the pinion shaft is pulled into the front bearing cone and into the flange.

5. As the pinion shaft is pulled into the front bearing cone, pinion shaft endplay is reduced. While there is still endplay in the pinion shaft, the flange and bearing cone will be felt to bottom on the collapsible spacer.

6. From this point, a much greater torque must be applied to turn the pinion nut, since the spacer must be collapsed. Very slowly, tighten the nut but check the pinion shaft endplay often to see the pinion bearing preload does not exceed the limits.

7. If the pinion nut is tightened to the point that pinion bearing preload exceeds the limits, the pinion shaft must be removed and a new collapsible spacer installed.

NOTE: Do not decrease the preload by loosening the pinion nut. This will remove the compression between the pinion front and rear bearing cones and the collapsible spacer and may permit the front bearing cone to turn on the pinion shaft.

8. As soon as there is a preload on the bearings, turn the pin-

ion shaft in both directions several times to set the bearing rollers.

9. Adjust the bearing preload to specification. Measure the preload.

FORD—9.0 INCH RING GEAR REAR AXLE WITH REMOVABLE CARRIER

Disassembly

DIFFERENTIAL CARRIER

1. Remove the carrier-to-axle housing bolts, the carrier and drain the gear lube.

2. Place the carrier assembly into a holding fixture, check and record the ring gear runout and the ring gear backlash.

3. Mark one of the differential bearing caps and the mating bearing support with punch marks to help position the parts during reassembly of the carrier. Remove the adjusting nut locks, bearing caps, (remove the bearing caps with a soft mallet) and adjusting nuts. Lift the differential case assembly from the carrier.

4. Remove the differential side bearings with special tools T57L–4220–A or T66P–4220–A. Mark the differential case, differential cover and ring gear for assembly in the original position.

5. Separate the differential cover from the differential case. Remove the side gear thrust washer and the side gear. Using a drift, drive out the 3 differential pinion shaft lock pins. Drive out the long differential pinion shaft with a brass drift.

6. Using a brass drift carefully positioned inside the case, drive out the 2 short differential pinion shafts. Remove the positioning block, differential pinions and the thrust washers from the differential case.

7. Remove the side gear and side gear thrust washer from the case.

8. Position the carrier assembly in a manner that will permit

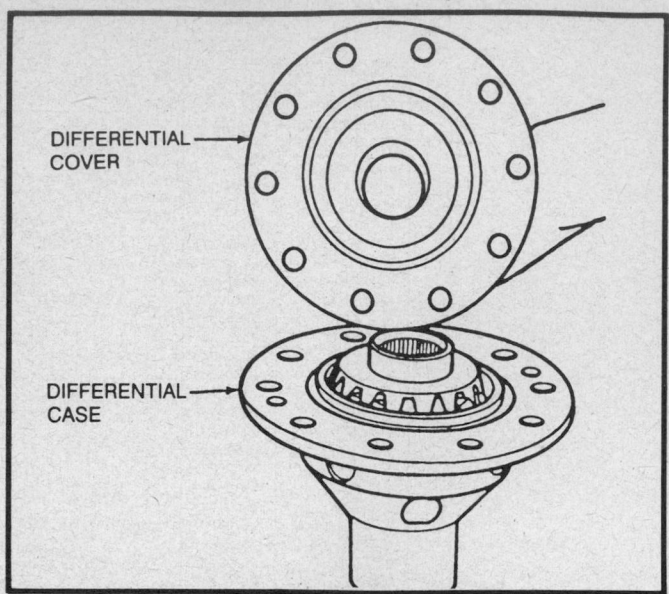

Removing the differential cover

the removal of the drive pinion shaft nut. Remove the companion flange from the drive pinion shaft and remove the pinion seal.

9. Remove the pinion and retainer assembly from the carrier housing. If a new pinion bearing and or gear set is installed, a new shim will have to installed. Be very careful not to damage the mounting surfaces of the retainer and the carrier.

10. Place a protective sleeve on the pinion pilot bearing surface. Press the pinion shaft out of the pinion retainer. Press the pinion shaft out of the pinion rear bearing cone, using tool T71P–4621–B.

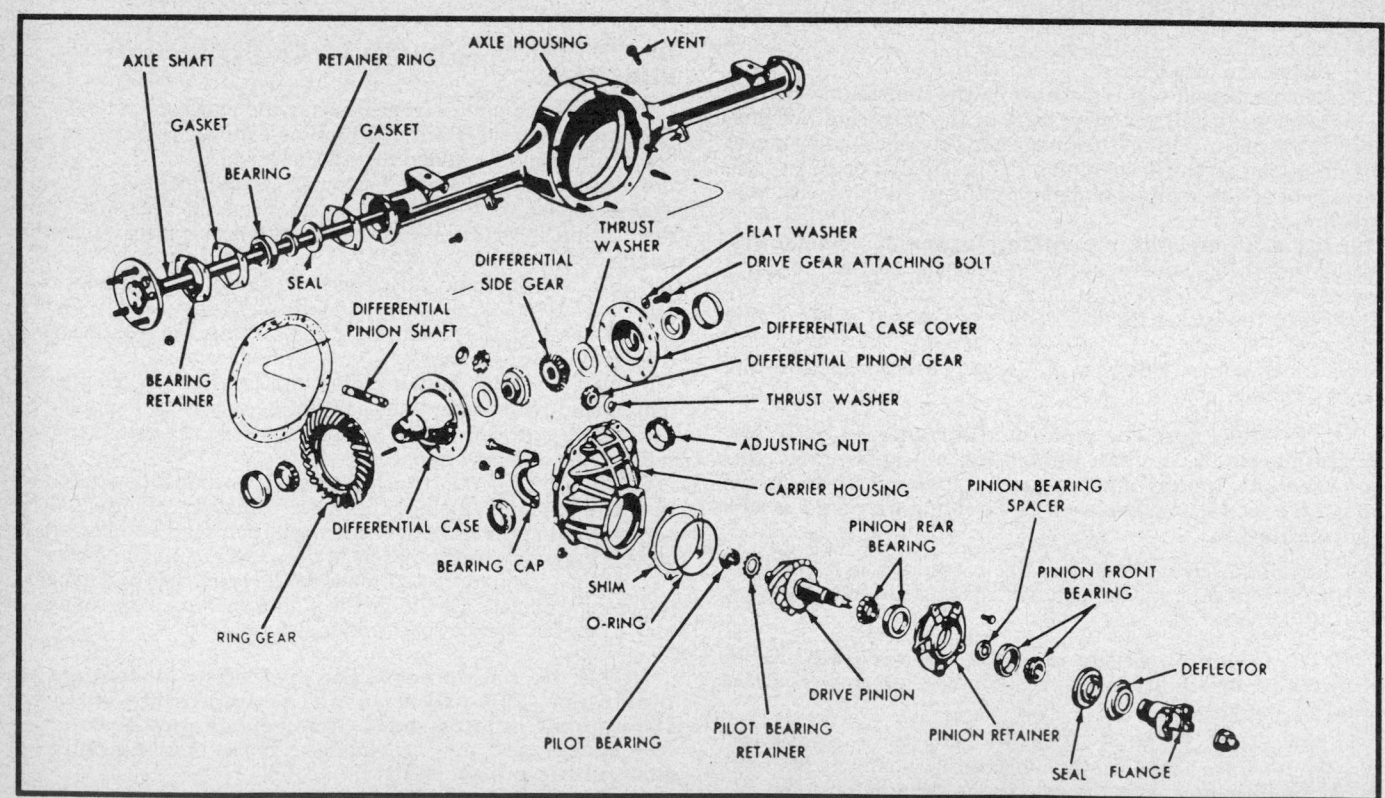

Exploded view of the 9 in. ring gear axle with a removable carrier—Ford Motor Company

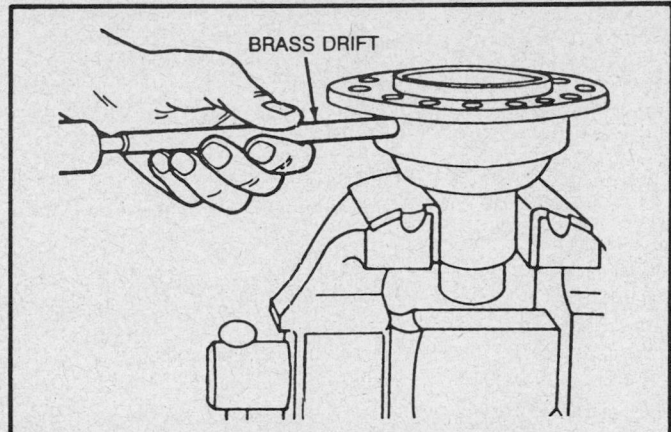

Removing the long differential pinion shaft

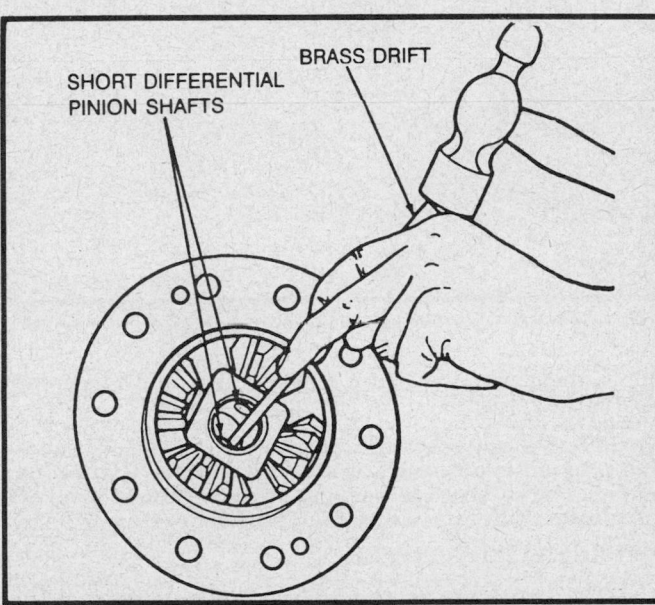

Removing the side gear and thrust washer

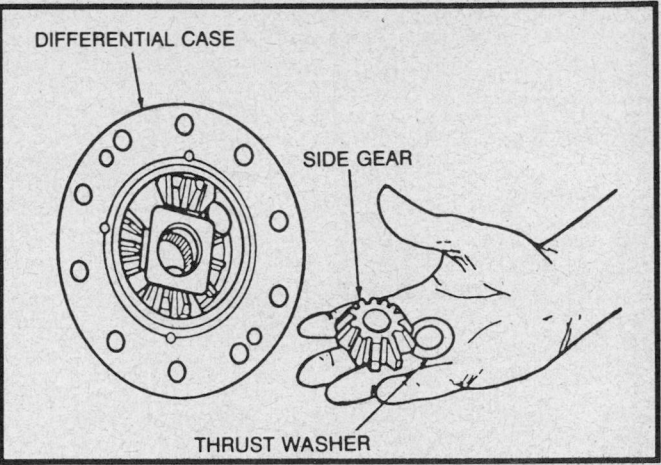

Removing the short differential pinion shaft

2. Using a seal puller, remove the pinion seal from the retainer assembly.

3. Remove the retainer assembly-to-carrier bolts and the carrier. Measure and record the thickness of the shim that was between the retainer and the carrier assembly.

4. Install a piece of hose on the pinion pilot bearing surface in front of the pinion gear. Mount the retainer assembly in a press and press the pinion gear out of the retainer.

5. Mount the pinion shaft in a press and press the rear bearing from the pinion shaft.

6. Mount the retainer assembly into a shop press and press the front and rear bearing cups from the assembly.

7. Using a bearing driver, drive the pilot bearing and retainer out of the carrier assembly.

Inspection

1. Clean the differential components in solvent and use compressed air to dry them; do not use compressed air on the bearings, only shop towels.

2. Check the components for wear or damage; replace them, if necessary.

3. Inspect the bearings and bearing cups for wear, cracks or scoring; replace them, if necessary.

4. Inspect the differential side and pinion gears for wear, cracks or chips; replace them, if necessary.

5. Inspect the ring and pinion gears for wear and/or damage; replace them, if necessary.

6. Inspect the differential case for cracks or damage; replace it, if necessary.

Assembly
DRIVE PINION AND RING GEAR SET

NOTE: When replacing a ring gear and a drive pinion or pinion bearings, select the proper pinion shim thickness by using the following procedure and tool T79P-4020-A or equivalent.

1. Select the proper rear pinion bearing aligning adapter and gauge disc to correspond to the axle size. Slide these adapters over the screw or threaded shaft and install the gauge block on the threaded shaft and tighten it securely.

2. Place this assembly, along with the rear drive pinion bearing, into the pinion bearing retainer assembly. Install the front pinion bearing (new or used, if in good condition) and screw the handle onto the threaded shaft, with the tapered end into the front pinion bearing.

3. The flat end of the handle has a ⅜ in. square hole broached

11. Remove and install a new pinion shaft pilot bearing. Remove the old pinion shaft pilot bearing by pressing it off and install the new one by pressing it on. Install a new pinion shaft pilot bearing retainer, concave side up, on the same press.

NOTE: Do not remove the drive pinion bearing cups from the retainer unless the cups are worn or damaged or if the cone and roller assemblies are damaged.

12. If the cups are worn or damaged, remove them with the use of bearing cup puller T77F-1102-A or T78P-1225-B or equivalent. Install the new bearing cups by pressing them into the retainer with pinion bearing cup replacer T71P-4616-A or equivalent.

13. After the new cups have been installed, make sure they are seated in the retainer by trying to insert a 0.0015 in. feeler gauge between the cup and the bottom of the bore. Whenever the cups are replaced, the cone and roller assemblies should also be replaced.

DRIVE PINION AND BEARING RETAINER

1. Install a holding fixture onto the flange, then, remove the pinion nut and washer. Leave the holding fixture on the flange and using a puller, remove the flange from the pinion shaft.

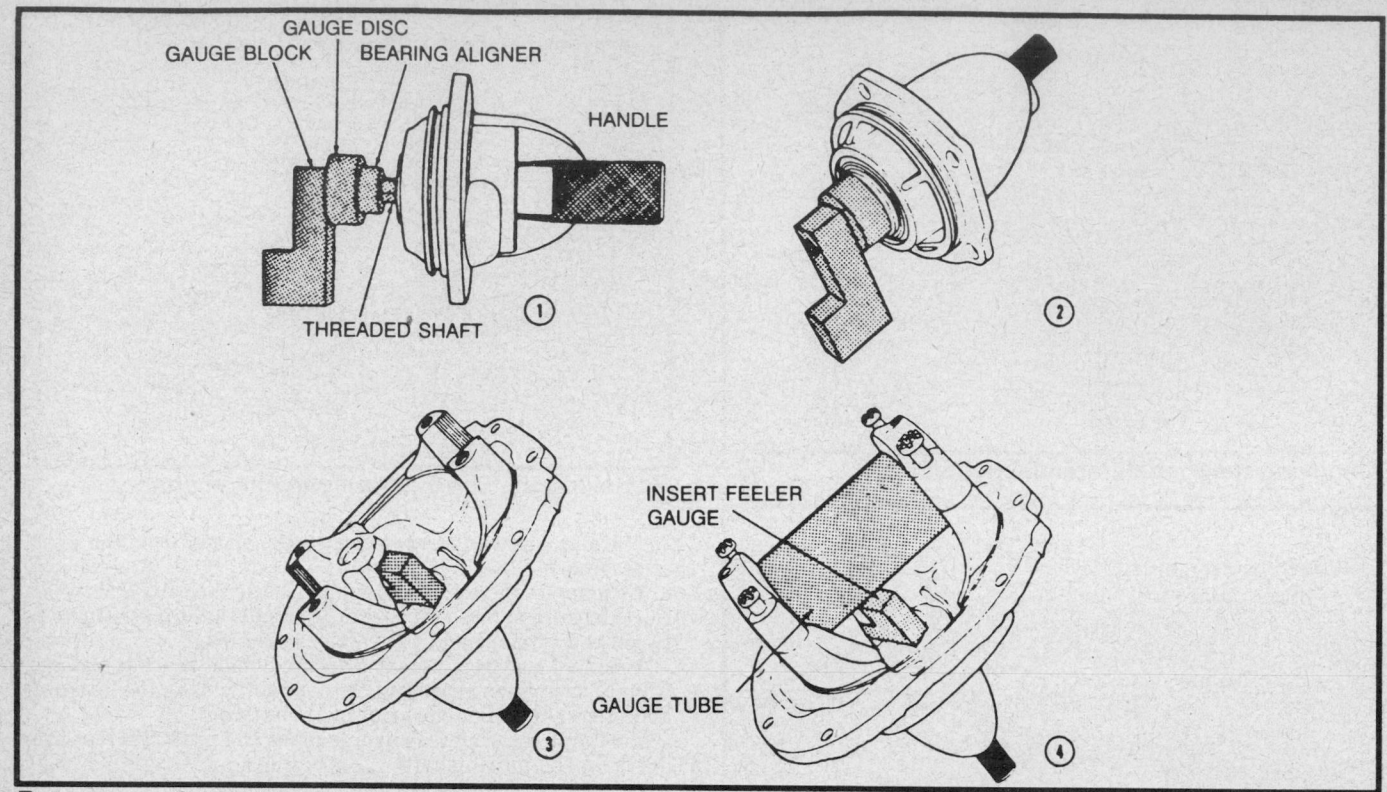

Proper use of the pinion depth gauge tool

in it. This is designed so an inch pound torque wrench may be used to obtain the proper pinion bearing preload.

4. Install the pinion bearing retainer assembly into the carrier (without a pinion shim) and tighten the attaching bolts to 30–45 ft. lbs. Rotate the gauge block so it rests against the pilot boss.

5. Place the differential gauge tube into the differential bearing bore and tighten the bearing caps to the specified torque. Using a feeler gauge, gauge the space between the differential bearing gauge block and gauge tube. Insert a feeler blade directly along the gauge block top to ensure a correct reading. The fit should be a slight drag-type feeling.

6. After a correct feeler gauge is obtained, use the conversion chart provided to find the correct shim thickness needed according to the feeler gauge reading.

7. After determining the correct shim thickness as just outlined in this procedure, assemble the pinion bearing retainer as follows.

NOTE: A new ring gear and drive pinion should always be installed in an axle as a matched set, never separately. Be sure the same matching number appears on the ring gear and on the head of the drive pinion.

8. Install the pinion retainer attaching bolts and torque them to 30–45 ft. lbs. Install the oil slinger, if equipped.

9. Install a new pinion oil seal in the bearing retainer, install the companion flange. Start a new pinion nut on the drive pinion shaft and apply a small amount of thread lubricant to the flange side of the nut.

10. Hold the flange with tool T57T–4851–B and tighten the pinion nut: do not use impact tools. Check the pinion bearing preload, the correct preload will be obtained when the torque required to rotate the pinion in the retainer is as specified in the specifications.

11. If torque required to rotate pinion is less than specified,

tighten the pinion shaft nut a little at a time until the proper preload is established.

NOTE: Do not over-tighten the pinion nut. If excessive preload is obtained as a result of over tightening, replace the collapsible bearing spacer. Do not back off the pinion shaft nut to establish pinion bearing preload.

DIFFERENTIAL CARRIER

NOTE: Lubricate all the differential components liberally with hypoid gear lubricant, EOAZ–19580–A or equivalent, during assembly.

1. Place a side gear thrust washer and side gear in the differential case bore. With a soft faced hammer, drive a short differ-

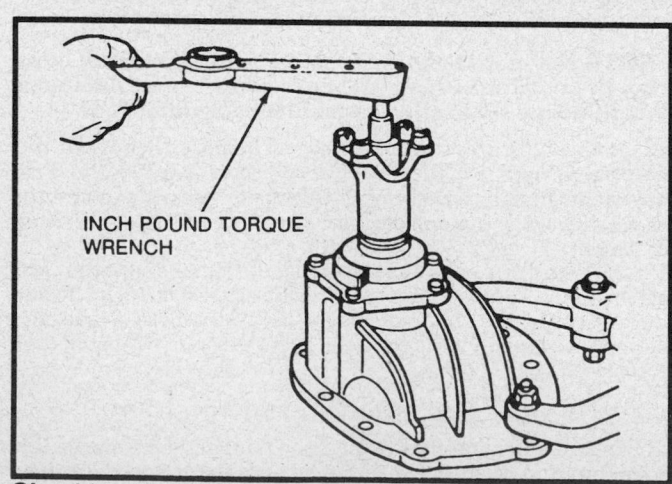

Checking the pinion bearing preload

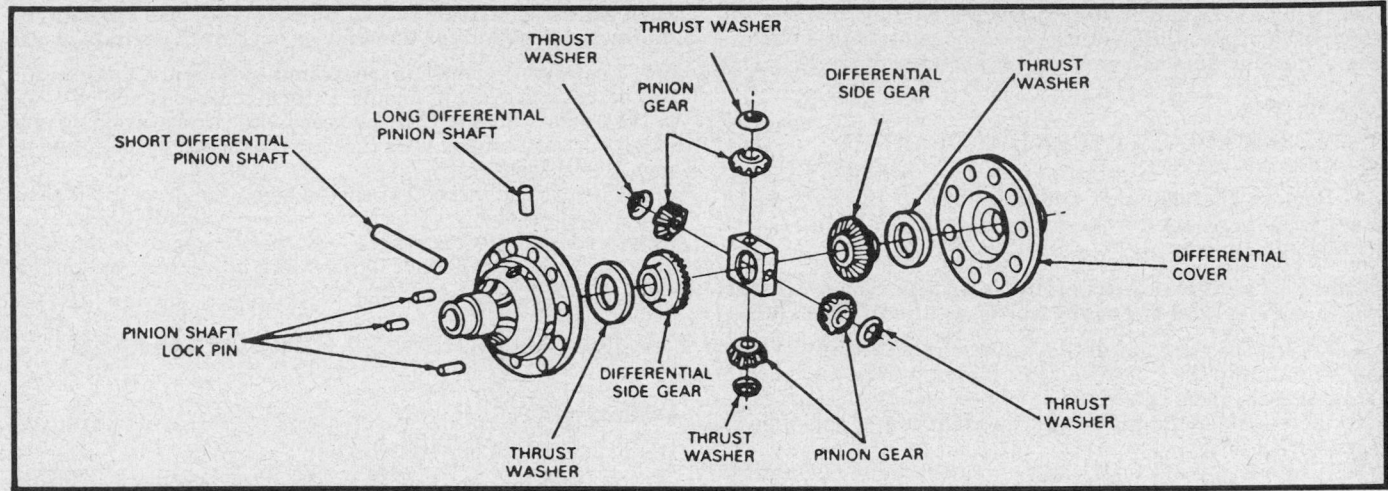

Exploded view of the differential case

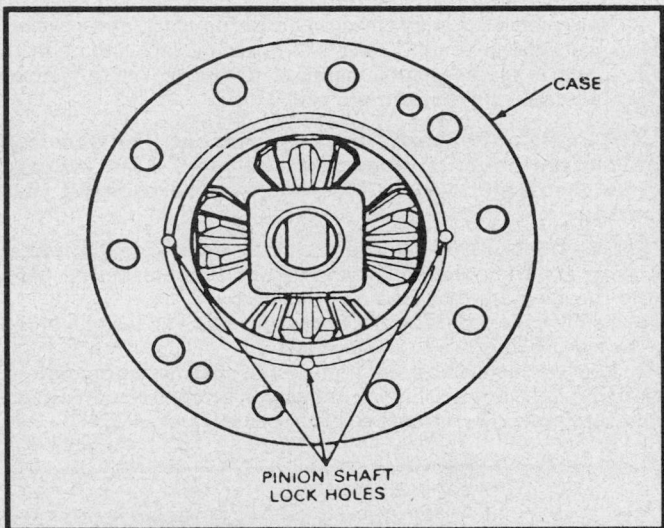

Location of the pinion shaft lock holes

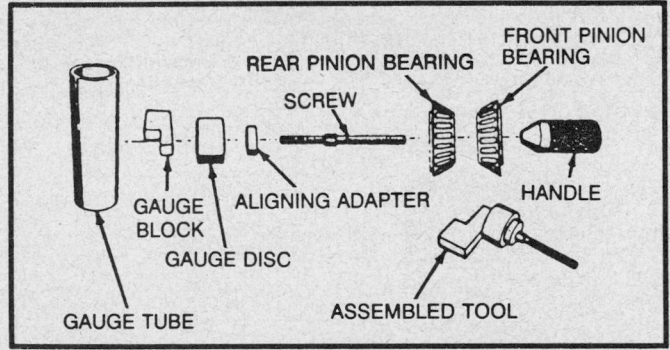

Typical rear axle pinion depth gauge tool

ential pinion shaft into the case far enough to retain a pinion thrust washer and pinion gear.

2. Carefully, align the pinion shaft lock pin holes with the holes provided in the case. Drive a short differential pinion shaft only far enough into the case to retain the pinion thrust washer pinion gear.

3. Install the remaining 2 pinion thrust washers along with the pinion gears into the case. Install the positioning block into

the case. Use a soft face hammer, to drive the short differential pinion shafts into the case until the shafts are flush with the side of the case.

4. Insert the long differential pinion shaft and drive it into the case. Be sure the pinion shaft lock holes align with the holes in the case. Place a 2nd side gear and thrust washer into position. Install the 3 pinion shaft lock pins. Press the differential cover on the case.

5. Clean the tapped holes in the ring gear with a suitable solvent. Insert $2 - \frac{7}{16}$ (N.F.) $\times$ 2 bolts through the differential case flange and turn them 3–4 turns into the ring gear as a guide in aligning the ring gear bolt holes. Press or tap the ring gear into position.

6. If the new bolts are coated with a green or yellow coating of approximately ½ in. or over the threaded area, use as is. If it is not coated, apply a suitable thread sealer and torque the bolts to 70–85 ft. lbs; do not reuse the old bolts.

7. If the differential bearings have been removed, press them in using tool T57L-4221-A2 or equivalent. Wipe a thin coating of axle lubricant on the differential bearing bores so the differential bearing cups will move easily.

8. Place the cups on the bearings and set the differential case assembly in the carrier. Assemble the differential case and ring gear assembly in the carrier so the marked tooth on the drive pinion indexes between the marked teeth on the ring gear; be sure to match the marked gears as indicated. When assembled out of time, the result is noise and improper mating.

9. Slide the assembly along the bores until a slight backlash is felt between the gear teeth. Set the adjusting nuts in the bores using differential bearing nut wrench T70P-4067-A so they just contact the bearing cups.

10. The nuts should be engaged about the same number of threads (turns) on each side. Carefully position the differential bearing caps on the carrier. Match the marks made when the caps were removed. Before tightening the bearing cap bolts, be sure the adjuster nuts are properly threaded in the cap and carrier and turn freely.

11. Install the bearing cap bolts and alternately torque them to 70–85 ft. lbs. If the adjusting nuts do not turn freely as the cap bolts are tightened, remove the differential bearing caps and again inspect for damaged threads or incorrectly positioned caps.

12. Tightening the bolts to the specified torque is done to be sure the cups and adjusting nuts are seated. Loosen the cap bolts and tighten them to only 25 ft. lbs. before making adjustments.

13. Adjust the backlash between the ring gear and pinion and the differential bearing preload as described in the following section.

14. Using a new gasket and silicone sealant, position the differential carrier on the studs in the axle housing. Install the carrier-to-housing nuts and washers; torque them to 25–40 ft. lbs.

Adjustment

BACKLASH AND DIFFERENTIAL BEARING PRELOAD

1. Remove the adjusting nut locks, loosen the differential bearing cap bolts and torque the bolts to 15–20 ft. lbs. before making adjustments.

NOTE: The left adjusting nut is on the ring gear side of the carrier and the right nut is on the pinion side.

2. Loosen the right nut until it is away from the cup. Tighten the left nut until the ring gear is just forced into the pinion with zero backlash, then, rotate the pinion several revolutions to be sure there is no binding. Recheck the right nut at this time to make sure it is still loose.

3. Install a dial indicator and tighten the right nut until it first contacts the bearing cups. Set the dial indicator to zero and apply pressure to the bearing by tightening the right nut until the indicator reading shows 0.008–0.012 in. case spread.

4. Turn the pinion gear several times in each direction to seat the bearings in the cups and be sure no bind is evident (this step is important). Tighten the bearing cap bolts to 70–85 ft. lbs.

5. Measure the backlash on several teeth around the ring gear. If the backlash is out of specification, loosen 1 adjusting nut and tighten the opposite nut an equal amount, to move the ring gear away from or toward the pinion.

6. Tightening the left nut moves the ring gear into the pinion to decrease the backlash and tightening the right nut moves the ring gear away.

NOTE: When moving the adjusting nuts, the final movement should always be made in a tightening direction. An example of this is, if the left nut had to be loosened 1 notch, loosen the nut 2 turns and tighten it 1; this ensures the nut is contacting the bearing cup and the cup can not shift after being put in service. After all such adjustments, check to be sure the case spread remains as specified for the new or original bearings used.

7. Use a white marking compound to obtain a tooth mesh contact pattern in the assembly. Pattern contact should be within the primary area of the ring gear tooth surface avoiding any narrow or hard contact with the outer perimeter of tooth (top to root, toe to heel).

8. The pattern inspection should be on the drive (pull) side. The correct assembly of the drive pattern will result in a satisfactory coast performance. If gross pattern error is detected with preferred backlash of 0.012–0.015 in. recheck the pinion shim selection.

DANA—MODEL 30 RING GEAR AXLE

Disassembly

DIFFERENTIAL CARRIER

1. The axle assembly can be overhauled either in or out of the vehicle. Either way, the free-floating axles must be removed.

2. Drain the lubricant and remove the rear cover and gasket.

3. Matchmark the bearing caps and the housing for reassembly in the same position. Remove the bearing caps and bolts.

4. Using a spreader tool mounted to the carrier housing, spread the housing a maximum of 0.015 in.

NOTE: Do not exceed this measurement. The housing could be permanently damaged. The use of a dial indicator is recommended to prevent over-stretching the housing.

5. Using a pry bar, remove the differential case from the housing. Separate the shims and record the dimensions. Remove the spreader tool from the housing.

6. Remove the differential side bearing cups and tag to identify the side, if they are to be used again.

7. Remove the differential gear pinion shaft lock pin and remove the shaft. Rotate the side and pinion gears to remove them from the carrier. Remove the thrust bearings.

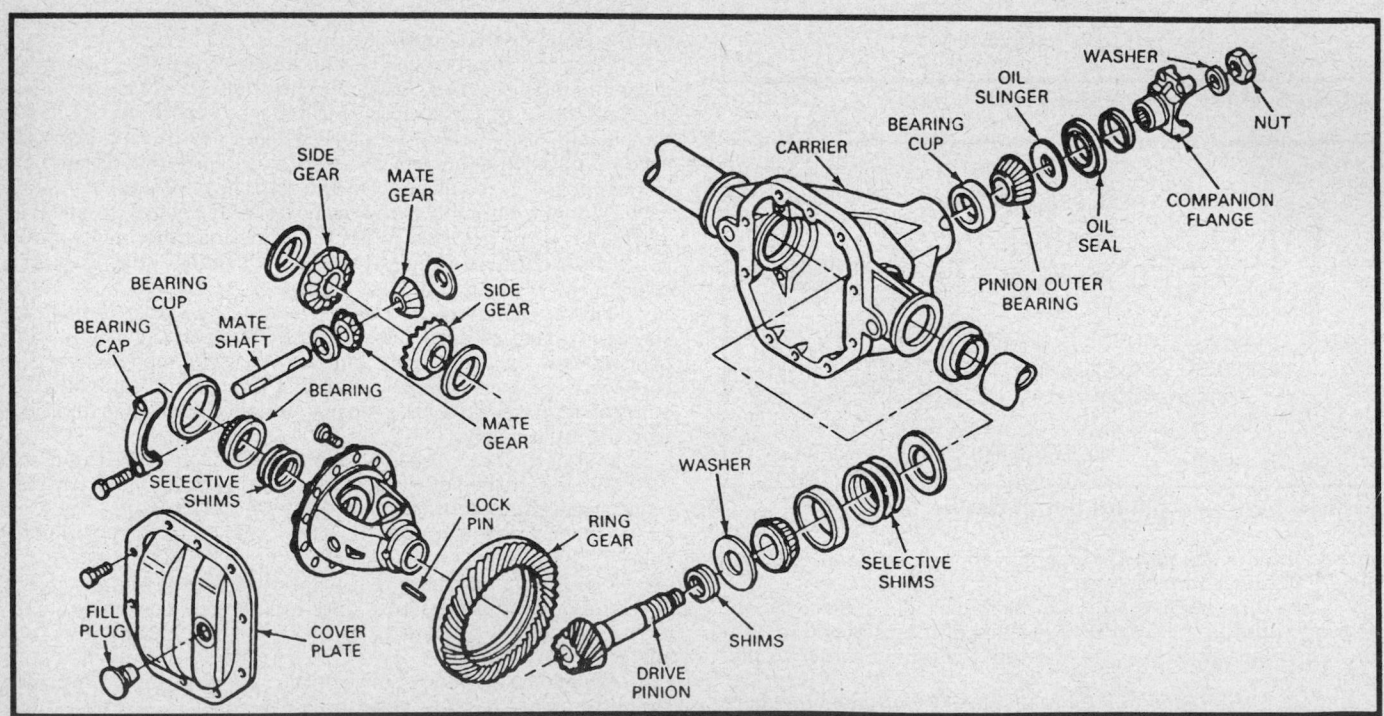

Exploded view of the Dana model 30 rear axle assembly

8. Remove the bearing cones and rollers from the carrier, marking and noting the shim locations.

9. Remove the ring gear bolts and tap the ring gear from the carrier housing.

10. Inspect the components.

DRIVE PINION

1. Remove the pinion nut and flange from the pinion gear.

2. Remove the pinion gear assembly from the housing. It may be necessary to tap the pinion from the housing with a soft faced hammer. Catch the pinion so as not to allow it to drop on the floor.

3. With a long drift, remove the inner bearing cup, pinion seal, slinger, gasket, outer pinion bearing and the shim pack. Label the shim pack for reassembly.

4. Remove the rear pinion bearing cup and shim pack from the housing. Label the shims for reassembly.

5. Remove the rear pinion bearing from the pinion gear with an arbor press and special plates.

Inspection

1. Clean the gears, bearings and component parts with solvent and inspect for scoring, chipping or excessive wear.

2. Inspect the flanges and splines for excessive wear.

3. Replace the necessary parts as required.

PINION SHIM SELECTION

Ring gears and pinions are supplied in matched sets only. The matched numbers are etched on both gears for verification. On the rear face of the pinion, a plus (+) or a minus (−) number will be etched, indicating the best running position for each particular gear set. This dimension is controlled by the shimming behind the inner bearing cup. Whenever baffles or oil slingers are used, they become part of the adjusting shim pack. An example: If a pinion is etched +3, this pinion would require 0.003 in. less shims than a pinion etched 0. This means by removing shims, the mounting distance of the pinion is increased by 0.003 in., which is just what a plus (+) etching indicates. If a pinion is etched −3, it would be necessary to add 0.003 in. more shims than would be required if the pinion was etched 0. By adding the 0.003 in. shims, the mounting distance of the pinion is decreased 0.003 in., which is just what the minus (−) etching indicates. Pinion adjusting shims are available in thicknesses of 0.003, 0.005 and 0.010 in. An example: If a new gear set is used and the old pinion reads +2 and the new pinion reads −2, add 0.004 in. shims to the original shim pack.

Assembly

DRIVE PINION

1. Select the correct pinion depth shims and install in the rear pinion bearing cup bore.

2. Install the rear bearing cup in the axle housing.

3. Add or subtract an equal amount of shim thickness to or from the preload or outer shim pack, as was added or subtracted from the inner shim pack.

4. Install the front pinion bearing cup into its bore in the axle housing.

5. Press the rear pinion bearing onto the pinion gear shaft and install the pinion gear with bearing into the axle housing.

6. Install the preload shims and the front pinion bearing; do not install the oil seal at this time.

7. Install the flange with the holding bar tool attached, the washer and the nut on the pinion shaft end. Torque the nut to 200–220 ft. lbs. (271–298 Nm).

8. Remove the holding bar from the flange and with an inch lb. torque wrench, measure the rotating torque of the pinion gear. The rotating torque should be 10–20 inch lbs. with the original bearings or 20–40 inch lbs. with new bearings. Disregard the torque reading necessary to start the shaft to turn.

9. If the preload torque is not in specifications, adjust the shim pack as required.

   a. To increase preload, decrease the thickness of the preload shim pack.

   b. To decrease preload, increase the thickness of the preload shim pack.

10. When the proper preload is obtained, remove the nut, washer and flange from the pinion shaft.

11. Install a new pinion seal into the housing and reinstall the flange, washer and nut. Using the holder tool, torque the nut to 200–220 ft. lbs. (271–298 Nm).

DIFFERENTIAL CARRIER

1. Install the differential side gears, the differential pinion gears and new thrust washers into the differential carrier.

2. Align the pinion gear shaft holes and install the pinion shaft into the carrier. Align the lock pin hole in the shaft and carrier. Install the lock pin and peen the hole to avoid having the pin drop from the carrier.

3. Install the differential case side bearings with the proper installation tools. Do not install the shims at this time.

4. Place the carrier assembly into the axle housing with the bearing cups on the bearing cones. Install the bearing caps in their original position and tighten the bearing cap bolts enough to keep the bearing caps in place.

5. Install a dial indicator on the housing so the indicator button contacts the carrier flange. Press the differential carrier to prevent sideplay and center the dial indicator. Rotate the carrier and check the flange for run-out. If the run-out is greater than 0.002 in., the defect is probably due to the bearings or to the carrier and should be corrected.

6. Remove the assembly and install the ring gear. Torque the retaining bolts and reinstall the assembly into the housing. Install the bearing caps in their original position and tighten the cap bolts to keep the bearings caps in place.

7. Install the dial indicator and position the indicator button to contact the ring gear back surface. Rotate the assembly and the run-out should be less than 0.002 in. If over 0.002 in., remove the assembly and relocate the ring gear 180 degrees. Reinstall the assembly and recheck. If the run-out remains over the 0.002 in. tolerance, the ring gear is defective. If the measurement is within tolerances, continue on with the assembly.

8. Position 2 pry bars between the bearing cap and the housing on the side opposite the ring gear. Pull on the pry bars and force the differential carrier as far as possible towards the dial indicator. Rock the assembly to seat the bearings and reset the dial indicator to zero.

9. Reposition the prybars to the opposite side of the carrier and force the carrier assembly as far towards the center of the housing. Read the dial indicator scale. This will be the total amount of shims required for setting the backlash during the reassembly, less the bearing preload. Record the measurement.

10. With the pinion gear installed and properly set, position the differential carrier assembly into the axle housing and install the bearing caps in their proper positions. Tighten the cap bolts just to hold the bearing cups in place.

11. Install a dial indicator on the axle housing with the indicator button contacting the back of the ring gear.

12. Position 2 prybars between the bearing cup and the axle housing on the ring gear side of the case and pry the ring gear into mesh with the pinion gear teeth, as far as possible. Rock the ring gear to allow the teeth to mesh and the bearings to seat. With the pressure still applied by the prybars, set the dial indicator to zero.

13. Reposition the prybars on the opposite side of ring gear and pry the gear as far as it will go. Take the dial indicator reading. Repeat this procedure until the same reading is obtained each time. This reading represents the necessary amount of shims between the differential carrier and the bearing on the ring gear side.

14. Remove the bearing from the differential carrier on the ring gear side and install the proper amount of shims. Reinstall the bearing.

15. Remove the differential carrier bearing from the opposite side of the ring gear. To determine the amount of shims needed, use the following method.

    a. Subtract the size of the shim pack just installed on the ring gear side of the carrier from the reading obtained and recorded when measurement was taken without the pinion gear in place.

    b. To this figure, add an additional 0.015 in. to compensate for preload and backlash. An example: If the first reading was 0.085 in. and the shims installed on the ring gear side of the carrier were 0.055 in., the correct amount of shims would be $0.085 - 0.055 + 0.015 = 0.045$ in.

16. Install the required shims as determined under step 15 and install the differential side bearing. The installation of the shims should give the proper preload to the bearings and the proper backlash to the ring and pinion gears.

17. Spread the axle housing with the spreader tool no more than 0.015 in. Install the differential bearing outer cups in their correct locations and install the cups in their respective locations.

18. Install the bolts and tighten finger-tight. Rotate the differential carrier and ring gear and tap with a soft-faced hammer to insure proper seating of the assembly in the axle housing.

19. Remove the spreader tool and torque the cap bolts to specifications.

20. Install a dial indicator and check the ring gear backlash at 4 equally spaced points of the ring gear circle. The backlash must be within a range of 0.004–0.009 in. and must not vary more than 0.002 in. between the points checked.

21. If the backlash is not within specifications, the shim packs must be corrected to bring the backlash within limits.

22. Check the tooth contact pattern and verify.

23. Complete the assembly, refill to proper level with lubricant and operate to verify proper assembly.

GENERAL MOTORS CORPORATION

Front Axle Assembly

GMC — 8½ INCH RING GEAR AXLE

For overhaul information, refer to the General Motors Corporation 8½ in. ring gear axle, in the rear axle assembly section.

DANA — 9¾ INCH RING GEAR AXLE

For overhaul information, refer to the Dana 9¾ in. ring gear axle, in the rear axle assembly section.

GMC — 8¼ AND 9¼ INCH RING GEAR AXLE

Disassembly

1. Remove the drain plug and drain the fluid from the axle.
2. Measure and record the backlash for it may help to determine the cause of an axle problem.
3. Using a holding tool, remove the pinion flange nut and washer.
4. Using a pinion flange removal tool, press the pinion flange from the differential.
5. Using an oil seal puller, pull the pinion oil seal from the differential.
6. Remove the solenoid and the indicator switch.
7. Remove the right axle tube-to-carrier case bolts and the tube with the shaft.
8. Remove the sleeve, the shift fork, the shaft, the spring and the shim.
9. Clamp the axle shaft tube in a vise, using the mounting flange. Strike the inside of the shaft flange to dislodge the carrier connector. Remove the carrier connector and the retaining ring.
10. Remove the snapring, the washer and the thrust washer.
11. Remove the axle shaft with the deflector.
12. Remove the sleeve, the bearing and the output shaft.
13. Using a removal tool, press the differential pilot bearing.
14. Using a prybar and a soft faced hammer, remove the shaft and the deflector.
15. Using a prybar, remove the seal from the axle tube.
16. Remove the bearing from the carrier case.

17. Remove the carrier case bolts, tap on the carrier case lugs to separate the right side carrier case half.
18. Pry up the locks and remove the differential assembly.
19. Remove the bolt, the lock, the sleeves and the side bearing cups; turn the sleeves to push the cups from the bores.
20. Remove the adjuster plug with the side bearing cup and the O-ring, if equipped.
21. Remove the pinion with the shim, the bearing cone and the spacer.
22. Using a bearing removal tool, press the bearing from the pinion.
23. Remove the shim, the seal, the bearing cup and the cone.
24. Using the puller tool, press the bearing cup from the pinion.
25. Remove the side bearings.

NOTE: The ring gear bolts are equipped with left handed threads.

26. Remove the ring gear bolts. Using a brass drift, drive the ring gear from the differential case.
27. Using a drift and a hammer, drive the roll pin from the differential case.

Inspection

1. Clean the gears, bearings and component parts with solvent and inspect for scoring, chipping or excessive wear.
2. Inspect the flanges and splines for excessive wear.
3. Replace the parts, if necessary.

Assembly

1. Install the roll pin into the differential case.
2. Install the ring gear to the differential case and torque the bolts to 52–66 ft. lbs. (70–90 Nm).
3. Install the side bearings.
4. Using a shop press, press the bearing cup onto the pinion.
5. Install the cone, the bearing cup, the seal and the shim onto the pinion.
6. Using a shop press, press the bearing onto the pinion.
7. Install the spacer, the bearing cone and the shim onto the pinion.

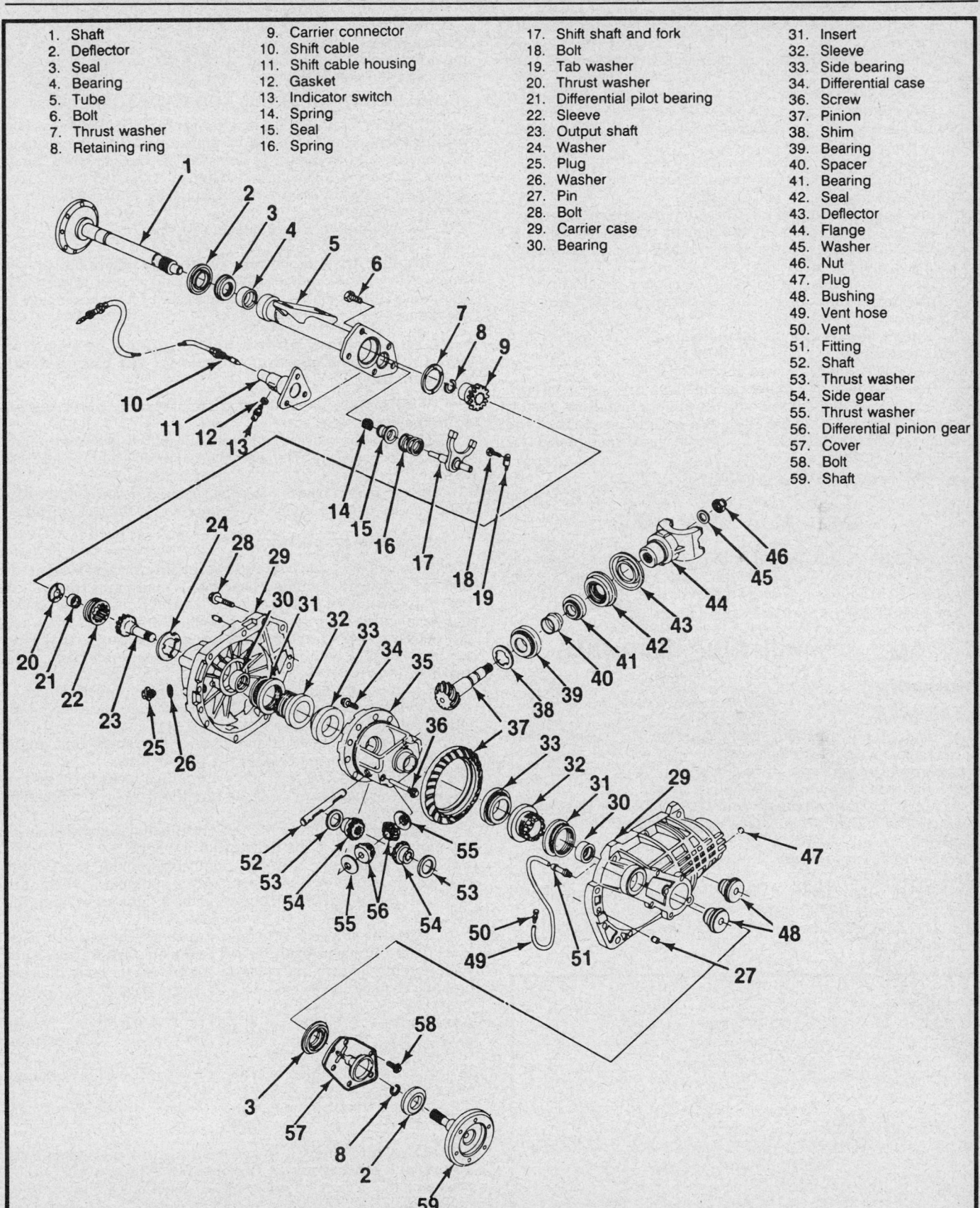

1. Shaft
2. Deflector
3. Seal
4. Bearing
5. Tube
6. Bolt
7. Thrust washer
8. Retaining ring
9. Carrier connector
10. Shift cable
11. Shift cable housing
12. Gasket
13. Indicator switch
14. Spring
15. Seal
16. Spring
17. Shift shaft and fork
18. Bolt
19. Tab washer
20. Thrust washer
21. Differential pilot bearing
22. Sleeve
23. Output shaft
24. Washer
25. Plug
26. Washer
27. Pin
28. Bolt
29. Carrier case
30. Bearing
31. Insert
32. Sleeve
33. Side bearing
34. Differential case
36. Screw
37. Pinion
38. Shim
39. Bearing
40. Spacer
41. Bearing
42. Seal
43. Deflector
44. Flange
45. Washer
46. Nut
47. Plug
48. Bushing
49. Vent hose
50. Vent
51. Fitting
52. Shaft
53. Thrust washer
54. Side gear
55. Thrust washer
56. Differential pinion gear
57. Cover
58. Bolt
59. Shaft

Exploded view of the 8¼ and 9¼ inch front differential assembly—General Motors

8. Install the O-ring, if equipped, and the adjuster plug with the side bearing cup.

9. While turning the sleeves to install the cups, install the side bearing cups, the sleeves, the lock and the bolt.

10. Install the differential assembly and secure with the locks.

11. Using a new gasket, assemble the carrier case halves and install the bolts; torque the carrier bolts to 30–40 ft. lbs. (40–55 Nm).

12. Press the bearing into the carrier case.

13. Install the new seal into the axle tube.

14. Install the deflector and the shaft.

15. Press the differential pilot bearing into the carrier case.

16. Install the output shaft, the bearing and the sleeve.

17. Install the deflector with the axle shaft, the thrust washer, the washer and the snapring.

18. Install the retaining ring and the carrier connector.

19. Install the shim, the spring, the shaft, the shift fork and the sleeve.

20. Using a new gasket, install the axle shaft tube to the carrier case and torque the bolts to 15–20 ft. lbs. (20–27 Nm).

21. Install the indicator switch and the solenoid.

22. Using an oil seal installer tool, install a new pinion oil seal.

23. Install the pinion flange onto the pinion. Install the washer and the flange nut. Tighten the nut a little at a time until the preload is 3–5 inch lbs. (0.3–0.6 Nm). The maximum pinion nut torque is 15 ft. lbs. (20 Nm).

24. Refill the axle with lubricant.

Rear Axle Assembly

The rear axles are categorized by the ring gear diameter and are identified as follows: 7½, 8½, 9½ in. (GMC) semi-floating axles; 9¾, 10½ in. (Dana) full floating axles; 10½ in. (GMC) full floating axles and 12 in. (Rockwell) full floating axles.

GMC — 7½ INCH RING GEAR AXLE

Disassembly
REAR AXLE CASE

1. Before removing the rear axle case from the housing, check the ring gear-to-drive pinion backlash. This will indicate gear or bearing wear or an error in backlash or preload setting which will help in determining cause of axle noise.

2. Mark the bearing caps **R** and **L** to make sure they will be reassembled in their original location. Remove rear axle bearing cap bolts.

3. Remove rear axle case. Exercise caution in prying on carrier so the gasket sealing surface is not damaged. Place right and left bearing outer races and shims in sets with marked bearing caps so they can be reinstalled in their original positions.

4. If rear axle side bearings are to be replaced, use a puller to remove them.

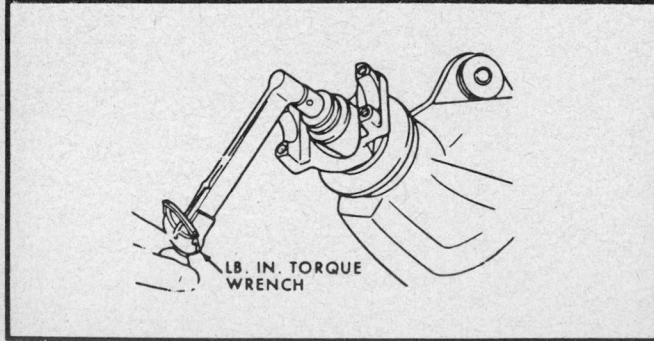

Checking the pinion pre-load

5. Remove rear axle pinions, side gears and thrust washers from case. Mark the side gear and case after removing bolts. Using a brass drift and hammer, drive it off; do not pry between ring gear and case.

DRIVE PINION, BEARING AND RACES

1. Check drive pinion bearing preload. If there is no preload reading, check for looseness of pinion assembly by shaking. Looseness could be caused by defective bearings or worn pinion flange. If rear axle was operated for an extended period with very loose bearings, the ring gear and drive pinion will also require replacement.

2. Remove pinion flange nut and washer.

3. Remove pinion flange.

4. Install a drive pinion remover tool and drive out pinion. Apply heavy hand pressure on the pinion remover toward rear axle housing to keep front bearing seated to avoid damage to outer race.

NOTE: The rear pinion bearing must be removed when it becomes necessary to change the pinion depth adjustment.

5. With drive pinion removed from carrier, press bearing from the pinion gear.

6. Drive pinion oil seal from carrier and remove front pinion bearing. If this bearing is to be replaced, remove outer race from carrier.

7. If rear pinion bearing is to be replaced, remove outer race from carrier using a punch in slots provided for this purpose.

Cleaning and Inspection

1. Clean all rear axle bearings thoroughly in clean solvent (do not use a brush). Examine bearings visually and by feel. All bearings should feel smooth when oiled and rotated while applying as much hand pressure as possible. Minute scratches and pits appear on rollers and races at low mileage are due to the initial preload and bearings having these marks should not be rejected.

2. Examine sealing surface of pinion flange for nicks, burrs or rough tool marks which would cause damage to the seal and result in an oil leak. Replace if damaged.

3. Examine carrier bore and remove any burrs that might cause leaks around the O.D. of the pinion seal.

4. Examine the ring gear and drive pinion teeth for excessive wear and scoring. If any of these conditions exist, replacement of the gear set will be required.

5. Inspect the pinion gear shaft for unusual wear; also check the pinion and side gears and thrust washers.

6. Check the press fit of the side bearing inner race on the rear axle case hub by prying against the shoulder at the puller recess in the case. Side bearings must be a tight press fit on the hub.

7. Diagnosis of a rear axle failure such as: chipped bearings, loose (lapped-in) bearings, chipped gears, etc., is a warning that some foreign material is present; therefore, the axle housing must be cleaned.

Assembly
DRIVE PINION

1. If a new rear pinion bearing is to be installed, install new outer races.

2. If a new front pinion bearing is to be installed, install new outer race.

NOTE: Pinion depth is set with pinion setting gauge. The pinion setting gauge provides in effect, a normal or zero pinion as a gauging reference. Instructions are included in gauge set.

3. Make certain all of the gauge parts are clean.

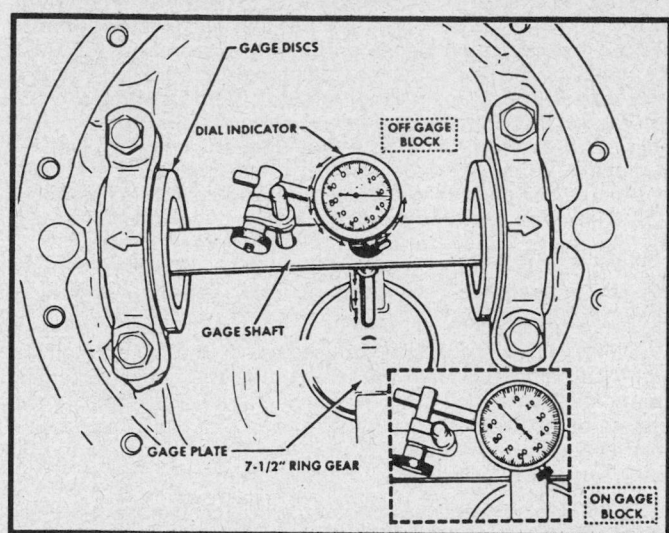

Checking the pinion depth

4. Lubricate front and rear pinion bearings liberally with rear axle lubricant.

5. While holding bearings in position, install depth setting gauge assembly.

6. Hold stud stationary with a wrench positioned over the flats on the ends of stud and tighten nut to 20 inch lbs. (2.2 Nm) torque. Rotate gauge plate assembly several complete revolutions to seat the bearings. Tighten nut until a torque between 15–25 inch lbs. (1.6–2.2 Nm) is obtained to keep the gauge plate in rotation.

7. Rotate the gauge plate tool until the gauging areas are parallel with the discs.

8. Make certain rear axle side bearing support bores are clean and free of burrs.

9. Install the correct discs on the gauge shaft.

10. Position the gauge shaft assembly in the carrier so the dial indicator rod is centered on the gauging area of the gauge block and the discs seated fully in the side bearing bores. Install side bearing caps and torque bolts to 55 ft. lbs. (75 Nm). Use a dial indicator reading from 0.00–100.0 inch (0.0–2.5mm).

11. Set dial indictor at zero. Then position on mounting post of the gauge shaft with the contact button touching the indicator pad. Push dial indicator downward until the needle rotates approximately ¾ turn clockwise. Tighten the dial indicator in this position and recheck.

12. Rotate gauge shaft slowly back and forth until the dial indicator reads the greatest deflection. At the point of greatest deflection, set the dial indicator to zero. Repeat rocking action of gauge shaft to verify the zero setting.

13. After the zero setting is obtained, rotate gauge shaft until the dial indicator rod does not touch the gauge block.

14. Record dial reading at pointer position. Example: If pointer moved counterclockwise 0.067 in. (1.70mm) to a dial reading of 0.033 in. (0.84mm) except as follows: dial indicator reading should be within the range of 0.50–0.020–0.050 in. (1.27mm).

15. Loosen the stud tool and remove gauge plate, washer and both bearings from carrier.

16. Position correct shim on drive pinion and install the drive pinion rear bearings.

REAR AXLE CASE

Before assembling the rear axle case, lubricate all parts with rear axle lubricant.

1. Place side gear thrust washer over side gear hubs and install side gears in case. If same parts are reused, install in original sides.

2. Position one pinion, without washer, between the side gears and rotate gears until pinion is directly opposite from loading opening in case. Place other pinion between side gears so the pinion shaft holes are in line; then, rotate gears to make sure holes in pinions align with the holes in case.

3. If the holes align, rotate pinions back toward loading opening just enough to permit sliding in pinion thrust washers.

4. After making certain the mating surfaces of case and ring gear are clean and free of burrs, thread 2 bolts into opposite sides of ring gear; then, install ring gear on case. Install new ring gear attaching bolts snug; never reuse old bolts. Torque bolts alternately in progressive stages to 90 ft. lbs. (120 Nm).

5. If case side bearings were removed, reinstall bearings.

NOTE: The side bearing preload adjustment is to be made before installing the pinion.

6. If the pinion is installed, remove ring gear. Case side bearing preload is adjusted by changing the thickness of both the right and left shims by an equal amount. By changing the thickness of both shims equally, the original backlash will be maintained. Production shims are cast iron and vary in thickness from 0.210–0.272 in. (5.33–6.91mm) in increments of 0.002 in. (0.05mm). Standard service spacers are 0.170 in. (4.32mm) thick and steel service shims are available from 0.040–0.082 in. (1.02–2.08mm) in increments of 0.002 in. (0.05mm).

NOTE: Do not attempt to reinstall the production shims as they may break when tapped into place. If service shims were previously installed, they can be reused but, whether using new or old bearings, adhere to the following procedure in all cases.

7. Before installing of the case assembly, make sure the side bearing surfaces in the carrier are clean and free of burrs. If the same bearings are being reused, they must have the original outer races in place.

8. Determine the approximate thickness of shims needed by measuring each production shim or each service spacer and shim pack.

9. In addition to the service spacer, a service shim will be needed. To select a starting point in service shim thickness, use the following chart.

10. Place case with bearing outer races in position in carrier. Slip the service spacer between each bearing race and carrier housing with chamfered edge against housing.

4.32mm (.170″) SERVICE SPACER	
Total Thickness of Both Prod. Shims Removed	Total Thickness of Service Shims to be Used as a Starting Point
10.57mm .420″	1.52mm .060″
10.92mm .430″	1.78mm .070″
11.18mm .440″	2.03mm .080″
11.43mm .450″	2.29mm .090″
11.68mm .460″	2.54mm .100″
11.94mm .470″	2.79mm .110″
12.19mm .480″	3.05mm .120″
12.45mm .490″	3.30mm .130″
12.70mm .500″	3.56mm .140″
12.95mm .510″	3.81mm .150″
13.21mm .520″	4.06mm .160″
13.46mm .530″	4.32mm .170″
13.97mm .550″	4.83mm .190″

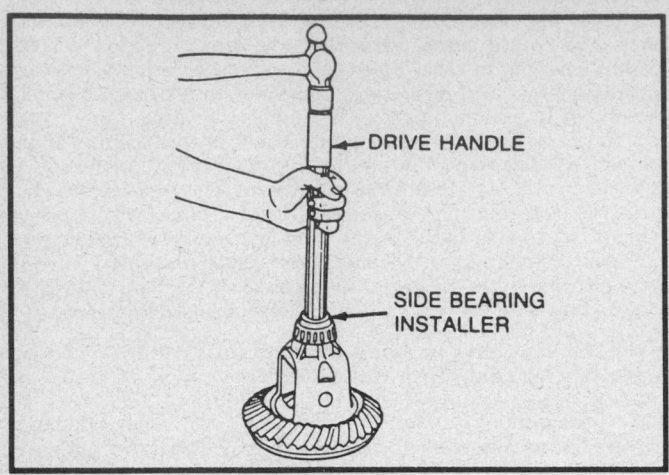

DRIVE HANDLE

SIDE BEARING INSTALLER

Installing the case side bearings

NOTE: **Install the left bearing cap loose so the case may be moved while checking adjustments. Another bearing cap bolt can be added in the lower right bearing cap hole. This will prevent case from dropping while making shim adjustments.**

11. Select 1 or 2 shims totaling the amount shown in the right-hand column and position between the right bearing race and the service spacer. Be sure left bearing race and spacer are against left side of housing.

12. Insert progressively larger feeler gauge sizes 0.010 in. (0.25mm), 0.012 in. (0.30mm), 0.014 in. (0.36mm) or etc. between the right shim and service spacer until there is noticeable increased drag. Push the feeler gauge downward until the end of the gauge makes contact with the carrier bore so as to obtain a correct reading. The point just before additional drag begins is correct feeler gauge thickness. Rotate case while using feeler gauge to assure an even reading.

NOTE: **The original light drag is caused by weight of the case against the carrier while additional drag is caused by side bearing preload. By starting with a thin feeler gauge, a sense of feel is obtained so the beginning of preload can be recognized to obtain zero clearance. It will be necessary to work case in and out and to the left in order to insert the feeler gauge.**

13. Remove left bearing cap and shim from carrier. The total shim pack needed (with no preload on side bearings) is the feeler gauge reading in step 12 plus thickness of shims installed in step 10.

14. Select 2 shims of approximately equal size whose total thickness is equal to the valuelo obtained in Step 12. These shims will be installed between each side bearing race and service spacer when the case is installed in the carrier.

NOTE: **The objective is to obtain the equivalent of a slip fit of the case in the carrier. For convenience in setting backlash, the preload will not be added until the final step.**

15. If the pinion is in position, install the ring gear and adjust the rear axle backlash.

DRIVE PINION, BEARING AND RACES

1. Install a new collapsible spacer on pinion and position assembly in carrier. Lubricate the pinion bearings with rear axle lubricant before installing pinion.

2. Hold the pinion forward in the case assembly.

3. Install the front bearing onto pinion and the drive bearing onto pinion shaft until sealed in the race.

4. Position and install the pinion oil seal in the carrier.

5. Lubricate the pinion oil seal lips and seal surface of pinion flange. Install pinion flange on pinion by tapping with a soft hammer until a few pinion threads project through the flange.

6. Install the pinion washer and nut. While holding the pinion flange, intermittently, rotate the pinion to seat pinion bearings. Tighten the pinion flange nut until the endplay begins to disappear. When no further endplay is detectable and the holder will no longer pivot freely as the pinion is rotated, the preload specifications are being approached; no further tightening should be attempted until the preload has been checked.

7. Check the preload by using an inch lb. torque wrench. After the preload has been checked, final tightening should be done very carefully.

NOTE: If when checking, preload was found to be 5 inch lbs. (0.6 Nm), any additional tightening of the pinion nut can add many additional inch lbs. of torque. Therefore, the pinion nut should be further tightened only a little at a time, for the preload specifications will compress the collapsible spacer too far and require the installation of a new collapsible spacer.

8. While observing the preceding note, carefully set preload at 24–32 inch lbs. (2.7–3.6 Nm) on new bearings or 8–12 inch lbs. (1.0–1.4 Nm) for used bearings.

9. Rotate pinion several times to assure the bearings have been seated. Check the preload again, if preload has been reduced by rotating pinion, reset preload to specifications.

Adjustment

REAR AXLE BACKLASH

1. Install rear axle case into carrier, using shims as determined by the side bearing preload adjustment.

2. Rotate the rear axle case several times to seat bearings, then, mount a dial indicator. Use a small button on the indicator stem so contact can be made near heel end of tooth. Set the dial indicator so the stem is aligned as nearly as possible with gear rotation and perpendicular to tooth angle for accurate backlash reading.

3. Check the backlash at 3 or 4 points around ring gear. Lash must not vary more than 0.002 in. (0.05mm) around ring gear. The pinion must be held stationary when checking backlash; if variation is greater than 0.002 in. (0.05mm) check for burrs, uneven bolting conditions or distorted case flange and make corrections, as necessary.

4. Backlash at the point of minimum lash should be between 0.005–0.009 in. (0.13–0.23mm) for all new gears.

5. If backlash is not within specifications, correct by increasing thickness of one shim and decreasing thickness of other shim the same amount. This will maintain correct rear axle side bearing preload.

   a. For each 0.001 in. (0.03mm) change in backlash desired, transfer 0.002 in. (0.05mm) in shim thickness.

   b. To decrease backlash 0.001 in. (0.03mm), decrease thickness of right shim 0.002 in. (0.05mm) and increase thickness of left shim 0.002 in. (0.05mm).

   c. To increase backlash 0.002 in. (0.05mm), increase thickness of right shim 0.004 in. (0.10mm) and decrease thickness of left shim 0.004 in. (0.10mm).

6. When the backlash is correctly adjusted, remove both bearing caps and both shim packs. Keep the packs in their respective position, right or left side. Select a shim 0.004 in. (0.10mm) thicker than the one removed from left side, then, insert left side shim pack between the spacer and the left bearing race. Loosely install bearing cap.

7. Select a shim 0.004 in. (0.10mm) thicker than the one removed from right side and insert between the spacer and the right bearing race; it will be necessary to drive the right shim into position.

8. Torque to 55 ft. lbs. (75 Nm).

9. Recheck backlash and correct if necessary.

10. Install the axles.

11. Install a new cover gasket, the cover and torque the bolts to 20 ft. lbs. (27 Nm).

12. Refill the rear axle to the proper level.

GMC—8½ AND 9½ INCH RING GEAR AXLE

This axle assembly is the semi-floating type with a hypoid type drive pinion and ring gears. The drive pinion gear is supported by 2 bearings. The differential case contains 2 pinion gears. The carrier assembly is not removable since it is part of the axle assembly but the design allows for the differential assembly to be serviced while the axle is still in the vehicle. The ring gear bolted to a one piece differential case is supported by 2 preloaded roller bearings.

Disassembly

DIFFERENTIAL CASE

1. Remove the inspection cover from the axle housing and drain the gear lubricant into a pan.

2. Remove the screw or pin that holds the pinion shaft in place and remove the shaft.

3. Push the axle shaft(s) in a little and remove the C-locks from the ends of the shafts. Remove the axle shafts from the housing.

4. Measure and record the backlash; this will allow the old gears to be reassembled at the same amount of lash to avoid changing the gear tooth pattern. It also helps to indicate if there is gear or bearing wear and if there is any error in the original backlash setting.

5. Remove the differential pinions, the side gears and thrust washers from the case; be sure to mark the pinions and side gears so they may be reassembled in their original position.

6. Mark the bearing caps and housing and loosen the retaining bolts. Tap the caps lightly to loosen them. When the caps are loose, remove the bolts and reinstall them, just a few turns; this will keep the case from falling out of the housing when it is pried loose.

7. Using a pry bar, carefully, pry the case assembly loose; be careful not to damage the gasket surface on the housing when prying. The case assembly may suddenly come free if the bearings were preloaded, so pry very slowly.

8. When the case assembly is loose, remove the bearing cap bolts and the caps. Place the caps so they may be reinstalled in the same position. Place any shims that were removed with the cap.

9. Using a bearing puller, pull the differential bearing from the case.

10. To remove the drive pinion bearing, perform the following procedures:

    a. Depending on the bearing that is being replaced, remove the front or rear bearing cup from the carrier assembly.

    b. With the pinion gear mounted in a press, press the rear bearing from the pinion shaft. Be sure to record the thicknesses of the shims that were removed from between the bearing and the gear.

DRIVE PINION

1. With the differential removed, check the pinion preload. Do this by checking the amount of torque needed to turn the pinion gear. For a new bearing, it should be 20–25 inch lbs. and for a used bearing it should be 10–15 inch lbs. If there is no preload reading check the pinion for looseness. If there is any looseness, replace the bearing.

2. Using a holder assembly to secure the flange, remove the flange nut and washer.

3. Using a puller, press the flange from the pinion splines.

4. Thread the pinion nut, a few turns, onto the pinion shaft. Using a brass drift and hammer, lightly tap the end of the pinion shaft to remove the pinion from the carrier; be careful not to allow the pinion to fall out of the carrier.

5. With the pinion removed from the carrier, discard the old seal pinion nut and collapsible spacer; install new ones when reassembling.

RING GEAR

1. Remove the ring gear-to-differential case bolts and tap the ring gear from the case with a soft hammer.

NOTE: Do not try to pry the ring gear off the case. This will damage the machined surfaces.

2. Clean all dirt from the case assembly and lubricate the case with gear lube.

Cleaning and Inspection

1. Clean all parts in solvent and blow dry.

2. Check all of the parts for any signs of wear, chips, cracks or distortion; replace any parts that are defective.

3. Check the fit of the differential side gears in the case and the fit of the side gear and axle shaft splines.

Assembly

DRIVE PINION BEARING

1. Using a bearing driver, install a new bearing cup for each one that was removed; make sure the cups are seated fully against the shoulder in the housing.

2. The pinion depth must be checked to determine the nominal setting. This allows for machining variations in the housing and enables selection of the proper shim so the pinion depth can be set for the best bear tooth contact.

3. Clean the housing and carrier assemblies to insure accurate measurement of the pinion depth.

4. Lubricate the front and rear pinion bearings with gear lubricant and install them in their races in the carrier assembly.

1. Companion Flange
2. Deflector
3. Pinion oil seal
4. Pinion front bearing
5. Pinion bearing spacer
6. Differential carrier
7. Differential case
8. Shim (A) with service shim
9. Gasket
10. Differential bearing
11. C-lock
12. Pinion shaft lock bolt
13. Cover
14. Pinion shaft
15. Ring gear
16. Side gear
17. Bearing cap
18. Axle shaft
19. Thrust washer
20. Differential pinion
21. Shim
22. Pinion rear bearing
23. Drive pinion

Cross-sectional view of the General Motors 8½ and 9½ inch rear axle assembly

5. Using a pinion setting gauge, select the proper clover leaf plate and install it on the preload stud.

6. Using the proper pilot, insert the stud through the rear bearing, with the proper size pilot on the stud and through the front bearing. Install the hex nut and tighten it until it is snug.

7. Using a wrench to hold the preload stud, torque the hex nut until 20 inch lbs. of torque are required to rotate the bearings.

8. Install the side bearing discs on the ends of the arbor assembly, using the step of the disc that fits the bore of the carrier.

9. Install the arbor and plunger assembly into the carrier; make sure the side bearing discs fit properly.

10. Install the bearing caps in the carrier assembly finger tight; make sure the discs do not move.

11. Mount a dial indicator on the mounting post of the arbor with the contact button resting on the top surface of the plunger.

13. Preload the dial indicator by turning it ½ revolution and tightening it in this position.

14. Use the button on the gauge plate that corresponds to the ring gear size and turn the plate so the plunger rests on top of it.

15. Rock the plunger rod back and forth across the top of the button until the dial indicator reads the greatest amount of variation. Set the dial indicator to zero at the point of most variation. Repeat the rocking of the plunger several times to check the setting.

16. Turn the plunger until it is removed from the gauge plate button. The dial indicator will now read the pinion shim thickness required to set the nominal pinion depth; record the reading.

17. Check for the pinion code number, located on the rear face of the pinion gear; the number will indicate the necessary change to the pinion shim thickness.

NOTE: If the pinion is marked with a plus (+) and a number, add that much to the reading of the dial indicator. If the pinion has no mark, use the reading from the dial indicator as the correct shim thickness. If the pinion is marked with a minus (−) and a number, subtract that amount from the reading on the dial indicator.

18. Remove the depth gauge tools from the carrier assembly and install the proper size shim on the pinion gear.

19. Lubricate the bearing with gear lubricant and use a shop press to press the bearing onto the pinion shaft.

DRIVE PINION

1. Lubricate the front bearing and install it into the front cup.

2. Using a seal driver and a gauge plate, drive the pinion seal into the bore until the gauge plate is flush with the shoulder of the carrier.

3. Lubricate the seal lips and install a new bearing spacer on the pinion gear.

4. Install the pinion gear into the carrier assembly. Using a large washer and nut, draw the pinion gear through the front bearing, far enough to install the companion flange.

5. With the companion flange installed on the pinion shaft, use a holder assembly and tighten the pinion nut until all of the endplay is removed from the drive pinion.

6. When no more endplay exists, check the preload; the preload should be 20–25 inch lbs. on new bearings or 10–15 inch lbs. on used bearings. Tighten the pinion nut until these figures are reached; do not over tighten the pinion, for this will collapse the spacer too much and make it necessary to replace it.

7. Turn the pinion gear several times to make sure the bearings are seated and recheck the preload.

RING GEAR

1. Align the ring gear bolt holes with the carrier holes and lightly press the ring gear onto the case assembly.

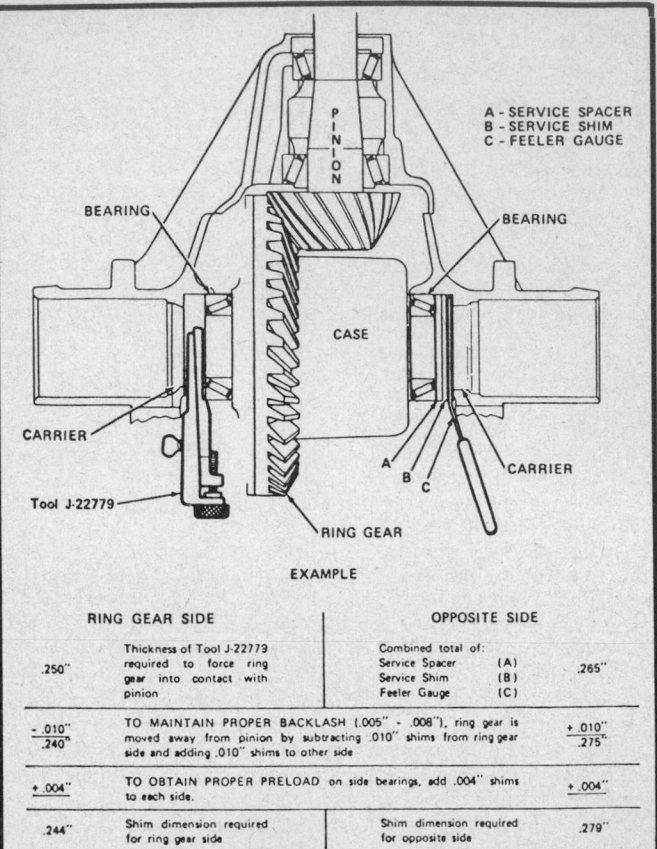

A - SERVICE SPACER
B - SERVICE SHIM
C - FEELER GAUGE

EXAMPLE

RING GEAR SIDE		OPPOSITE SIDE	
.250"	Thickness of Tool J-22779 required to force ring gear into contact with pinion	Combined total of: Service Spacer (A) Service Shim (B) Feeler Gauge (C)	.265"
− .010" .240"	TO MAINTAIN PROPER BACKLASH (.005" − .008"), ring gear is moved away from pinion by subtracting .010" shims from ring gear side and adding .010" shims to other side	+ .010" .275"
+ .004"	TO OBTAIN PROPER PRELOAD on side bearings, add .004" shims to each side.	+ .004"
.244"	Shim dimension required for ring gear side	Shim dimension required for opposite side	.279"

Shim pack selection chart

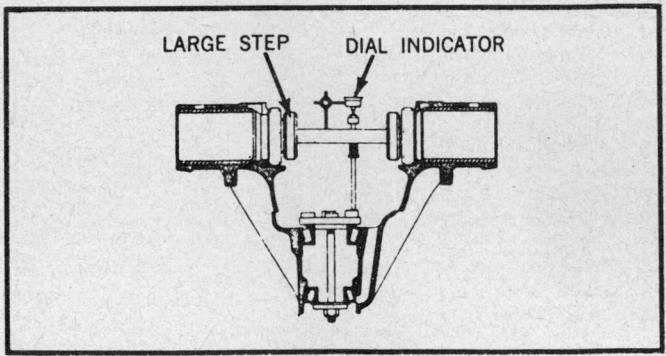

LARGE STEP   DIAL INDICATOR

Gauge tools installed in the carrier

2. Install the bolts and tighten them all evenly, using a crisscross pattern to avoid cocking the ring gear.

3. When the ring gear is firmly seated against the case, torque the bolts to 60 ft. lbs.

DIFFERENTIAL CASE ASSEMBLY

1. Place the new differential bearing onto the case hub with the thick side of the inner race toward the case. Using a bearing driver, drive the bearing onto the case until it seats against the shoulder on the case.

2. Install the thrust washers and side gears into the case assembly. If the original parts are being used, be sure to place them in their original position.

3. Place the pinions in the case so they are 180 degrees apart as they engage the side gears.

4. Turn the pinion gears so the case holes align with the gear holes. When the holes are aligned, install the pinion shaft and

lock screw; do not tighten the lock screw too tightly at this time.

5. Check the bearings, bearing cups, cup seat and carrier caps to make sure they are in good condition.

6. Lubricate the bearings with gear lube. Install the cups on the bearings and the differential assembly into the carrier. Support the carrier assembly to keep it from falling.

7. Install a support strap on the left side bearing and tighten the bearing bolts to an even, snug fit.

8. With the ring gear tight against the pinion gear, insert a gauge tool between the left side bearing cup and the carrier housing.

9. While lightly shaking the tool back and forth, turn the adjusting wheel until a slight drag is felt and tighten the locknut.

10. Between the right side bearing and carrier, install a 0.170 in. thick service spacer, a service shim and a feeler gauge. The feeler gauge must be thick enough so a light drag is felt when it is moved between the carrier and the shim.

11. Add the total of the service spacer, service shim and the feeler gauge. Remove the gauge tool from the left side of the carrier, then, using a micrometer, measure the thickness in at least 3 places. Average the readings and record the result.

12. Refer to the chart to determine the proper thickness of the shim packs.

13. Install the left side shim first, then, the right side shim between the bearing cup and spacer. Position the shim so the chamfered side is facing outward or next to the spacer.

NOTE: If there is not enough chamfer around the outside of the shim, file or grind the chamfer a little to allow for easy installation.

14. If there is difficulty in installing the shim, partially remove the case from the carrier and slide both the shim and case back into place.

15. Install the bearing caps and torque them to 60 ft. lbs. Tighten the pinion shaft lock screw.

NOTE: The differential side bearings are now preloaded. If any adjustments are made in later procedures, make sure not to change the preload. Do not change the total thickness of the shim packs.

16. Mount a dial indicator on the carrier assembly with the indicator button perpendicular to the tooth angle and aligned with the gear rotation.

17. Measure the amount of backlash between the ring and pinion gears; it should be between 0.005–0.008 in. Take readings at 4 different spots on the gear; there should not be variations greater than 0.002 in.

18. If there are variations greater than 0.002 in. between the readings, check the runout between the case and ring gear; the gear runout should not be greater than 0.003 in. If the runout exceeds 0.003 in., check the case and ring gear for the deformation or dirt between the case and gear.

19. If the gear backlash exceeds 0.008 in., increase the thickness of the shims on the ring gear side and decrease the thickness of the shims on the opposite side, an equal amount.

20. If the backlash is less than 0.005 in., decrease the shim thickness on the ring gear side and increase the shim thickness on the opposite side an equal amount.

GEAR PATTERN CHECK

Before final assembly of the differential, a pattern check of the gear teeth must be made. This determines if the teeth of the ring and pinion gears are meshing properly, for low noise level and long life of the gear teeth. The most important thing to note is if the pattern is located centrally up and down on the face of the ring gear.

1. Wipe any oil from the carrier and all dirt and oil from the teeth of the ring gear.

2. Coat the teeth of the ring gear with a gear marking compound.

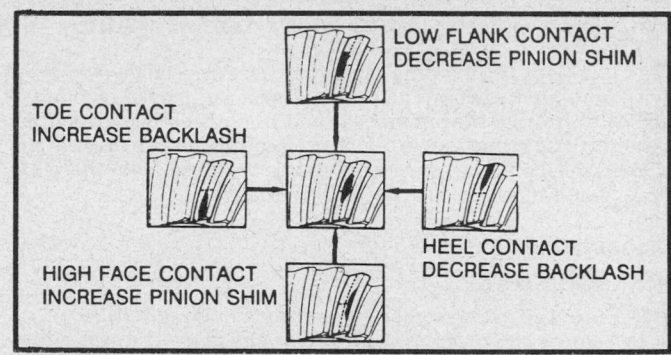

Checking the gear tooth contact

3. With the bearing caps torqued to 55 ft. lbs., expand the brake shoes until it takes 20–30 ft. lbs. of torque to turn the pinion gear.

4. Turn the companion flange so the ring gear makes a full rotation in 1 direction, then, turn it a full rotation in the opposite direction.

5. Check the pattern on the teeth and refer to the chart for any adjustments necessary.

6. With the gear tooth pattern checked and properly adjusted, install the axle housing cover gasket and cover and tighten securely. Refill the axle with gear lube to the correct level.

7. Road test the vehicle to check for any noise and proper operation of the rear.

1. Companion flange	17. Side bearing adjusting nut
2. Oil deflector	
3. Oil seal	18. Adjusting nut retainer
4. Bearing retainer	19. Retainer screw
5. Shim	20. Bearing cap
6. Pinion front bearing	21. Case-to-ring gear bolt
7. Collapsible spacer	22. Differential cover
8. Pinion rear bearing	23. Bearing cap bolt
9. Drive pinion	24. Cover screw
10. Straddle bearing	25. Axle shaft
11. Ring gear	
12. Differential spider	
13. Differential case	
14. Differential pinion	
15. Differential side gear	
16. Side bearing	

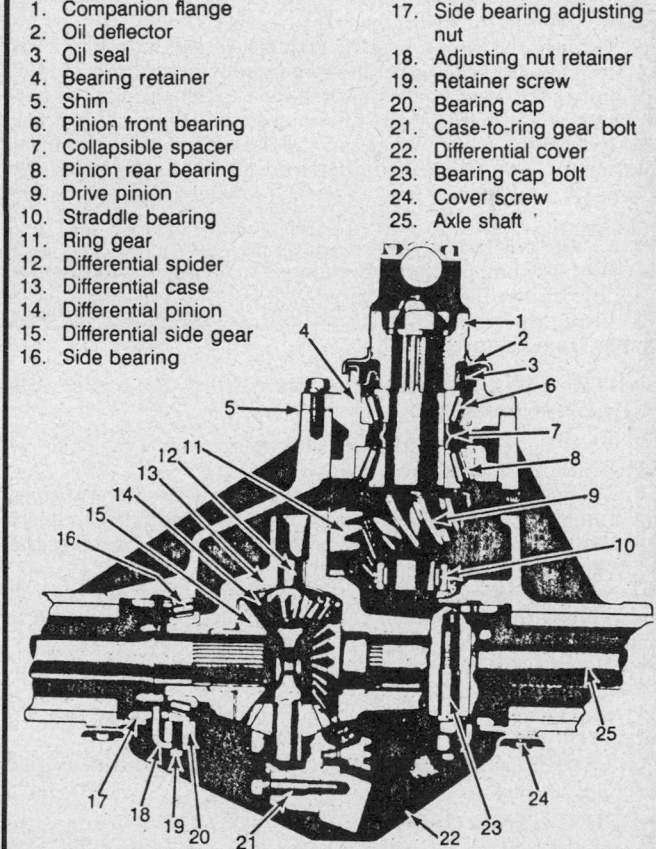

Cross-sectional view of the General Motors 10½ inch rear axle

GMC — 10½ INCH RING GEAR AXLE

This axle is a full floating type that uses special hypoid type drive and pinion gears. The pinion gear is supported by 3 bearings, 2 in front of the pinion gear and 1 behind. The differential assembly has either 2 or 4 pinions depending on the application of the axle. This axle assembly must be removed from the vehicle to remove and service the differential.

Disassembly
DIFFERENTIAL

1. Place the axle assembly in a vise or holding fixture.
2. Remove the cover bolts, the cover and allow the gear lubricant to drain into a pan.
3. Remove the axle shafts from the axle assembly.

NOTE: Measure and record the pinion backlash so if the same gears are reused they may be installed at the same backlash to avoid changing the gear tooth pattern.

4. From the bearing caps, remove the adjusting nut lock retainers.
5. Mark the bearing caps so they may be reinstalled in the same position and remove the bearing caps.
6. Loosen the side bearing adjusting nut and remove the differential carrier from the axle housing.

PINION

1. Remove the differential assembly from the axle.
2. Check the pinion bearing for the proper preload. The force required to turn the pinion should be 25–35 inch lbs. for used bearings. If there is no reading, shake the companion flange to check for any looseness in the bearing. If there is any looseness present, replace the bearing.
3. Remove the pinion bearing retainer-to-axle housing bolts.
4. Remove the bearing retainer and pinion assembly from the axle housing. It may be necessary to tap the pilot end of the pinion shaft to help remove the pinion assembly from the carrier.
5. Record the thickness of the shims that are removed from between the carrier assembly and the bearing retainer assembly.

DRIVE PINION

1. With the pinion assembly clamped in a vise, install a holder assembly on the flange.
2. Using the proper size socket, remove the pinion nut and washer from the pinion.

NOTE: When reassembling the pinion use a new nut and washer assembly.

3. With the holder assembly still in place, use a puller to remove the flange from the pinion.
4. With the bearing retainer supported in a shop press, press the pinion out of the retainer assembly; be careful not to allow the pinion gear to fall onto the floor because this can damage the gear.
5. Separate the pinion flange, the oil seal, the front bearing and the bearing retainer; if the oil seal needs to be replaced it may have to be driven from the retainer.
6. Using a drift, drive the front and rear bearing cups from the bearing retainer.
7. Support the pinion assembly in a press, with the bearing supported. Press the bearing from the pinion gear.
8. Using a drift, drive the straddle bearing from the carrier assembly.

DIFFERENTIAL CASE

1. Scribe a line across both halves of the differential case so they may be reassembled in the same position and with the ring gear removed, separate the halves.

2. Remove the ring gear bolts and washers; using a soft hammer tap the ring gear from the case.
3. Remove the internal parts from the case and set them aside in order so they may be reassembled in the same position.
4. If removing the side bearing, perform the following procedures:
   a. Install a bearing puller on the bearing and press the bearing assembly from the differential case.
   b. Check the bearings for any signs of wear on distortion.

Cleaning and Inspection

1. Clean all of the parts in solvent and blow dry.
2. Check the differential gears, pinions, thrust washers and spider for any signs of unusual wear, chips, cracks or pitting.
3. Check the pinion gear for signs of wear, chips, cracks or any other imperfections. Check the splines for signs of wear or distortion.
4. Check all mating surfaces for signs of wear.
5. Check the bearings for signs of wear or pitting on the rollers and races and check the bearing cage for dents and bends. Check the bearing retainer for any cracks, pits, grooves or corrosion.
6. Check the pinion flange splines for any signs of wear or distortion.
7. Replace parts that show any of the signs mentioned above.

Assembly
DIFFERENTIAL CASE

1. If the side bearing was removed, perform the following procedures:
   a. Install a new bearing on the differential case.
   b. Using a bearing driver, drive the bearing onto the case assembly until it seats against the shoulder on the case.
2. Using a good quality gear lubricant coat all of the parts.
3. Assemble the differential pinions and thrust washers onto the spider and install the assembly into the differential case.
4. Align the scribe marks on both halves of the differential case and install the ring gear.
5. Install the ring gear washers and bolts and torque the bolts to approx. 10 ft. lbs.

DRIVE PINION

1. Coat all of the parts with a good quality gear lubricant.
2. Position the pinion gear into a shop press and press the rear bearings onto the pinion assembly.
3. Using a bearing driver, install the front and rear bearing cups into the bearing retainer.
4. Using a bearing driver, install the straddle bearing assembly in the axle housing.
5. Install the bearing retainer, with the bearing cups, onto the pinion gear and install a new collapsible spacer.
6. Using a shop press, press the front bearing onto the pinion gear.
7. Lubricate the oil seal with a good quality high pressure grease and install the seal into the retainer bore; be sure to press the seal until it rests against the internal shoulder.
8. Install the pinion flange and oil deflector onto the pinion gear splines, then, install a new lock washer and pinion nut.
9. With the pinion flange clamped in a vise and a holder assembly installed on the flange, tighten the nut to obtain the proper preload; 25–35 inch lbs. for a new bearing or 5–15 inch lbs. for a used bearing. To preload the bearing, tighten the pinion nut to approx. 350 ft. lbs. and take a reading of the torque required to turn the pinion. Continue tightening the nut until the proper preload is obtained.

NOTE: Do not tighten the nut too tightly because it will collapse the spacer too much. This will make replacement necessary.

		CODE NUMBER ON ORIGINAL PINION				
		+2	+1	0	-1	-2
CODE NUMBER ON SERVICE PINION	+2	-	ADD .001	ADD .002	ADD .003	ADD .004
	+1	SUBT .001	-	ADD .001	ADD .002	ADD .003
	0	SUBT .002	SUBT .001	-	ADD .001	ADD .002
	-1	SUBT .003	SUBT .002	SUBT .001	-	ADD .001
	-2	SUBT .004	SUBT .003	SUBT .002	SUBT .001	-

Pinion depth codes and corresponding shim thicknesses

DRIVE PINION

1. If installing a new pinion gear, check the top of the new gear for the depth code number.
2. Compare the new number with the old number on top of the old pinion and check the pinion depth chart for preliminary setting of the pinion depth.
3. Check the thickness of the original shims removed from the pinion and either add or subtract from the shims according to the chart.
4. Place the shim on the carrier assembly and align the holes with those in the axle housing; make sure the surfaces are clean of all dirt and grease.
5. Install the retainer and pinion assembly in the housing making sure the holes align. Install the retaining bolts and torque to approx. 45 ft. lbs.

DIFFERENTIAL CASE

1. Place the bearing cups over the side bearings on the differential assembly and place the unit into the carrier in the axle housing.
2. Align the marks and install the bearing caps and the bolts. Tighten the bearing retaining bolts.
3. Loosen the right side nut and tighten the left side nut until the ring gear comes in contact with the pinion gear; do not force the gears together. This brings the gears to zero lash.
4. Back off the left side adjusting nut about 2 slots and install the lock fingers into the nut.
5. In this order, tighten the right side adjusting nut firmly to force the case assembly into tight contact with the left side adjusting nut, then, loosen the right side nut until it is free from the bearing.
6. Again, retighten the right side adjusting nut until it comes in contact with the bearing. Tighten the right adjusting nut about 2 slots for an old bearing or 3 slots for a new bearing.
7. Install the lock retainers into the slots and torque the bearing cap bolts to 100 ft. lbs.; this procedure now insures the bearings are preloaded properly. If more adjustments are made, make sure the preload stays the same. To do this, 1 adjusting nut must be loosened the same amount the other nuts is tightened.
8. Install a dial indicator on the housing and measure the amount of backlash between the ring and pinion gear. The backlash should measure between 0.003–0.012 in. with the best figure being between 0.005–0.008 in.
9. If the backlash is more than 0.012 in., loosen the right side adjusting nut 1 slot and tighten the left side 1 slot. If the backlash is less than 0.003 in., loosen the left side nut 1 slot and tighten the right side 1 slot. These adjustments should bring the backlash measurement into an acceptable range.

PATTERN CHECK

1. Clean all the oil from the ring gear. Using a gear marking compound, coat the teeth of the ring gear.

2. Make sure the bearing caps are torqued to 110 ft. lbs. and apply load to the gears while rotating the pinion. Rotate the ring gear a full turn in both directions.

NOTE: Load must be applied to the assembly while rotating or the pattern will not show completely.

3. Check the pattern on the ring gear, adjust the assembly to get the contact pattern located centrally on the face of the ring gear teeth.

DANA — 9¾ AND 10½ INCH RING GEAR AXLES

The Dana Corporation's 9¾ and 10½ in. ring gear axle assemblies are basically the same but with certain exceptions. The differential side bearing shims are located between the side bearing cup assembly and the differential case on the 9¾ in. ring gear axle assembly, while on the 10½ in. ring gear axle assembly, the side bearing shims are located between the side bearing cup and the axle housing. Both axles use inner and outer shims on the pinion gear. The inner shims are used to control the pinion depth in the housing, while the outer shims are used to preload the pinion bearings. The 9¾ in. ring gear axle uses a solid differential carrier with a removable side and pinion gear shaft. The 10½ in. ring gear axle uses a split differential carrier with the side and pinion gears mounted on a cross shaft.

Disassembly

DIFFERENTIAL CARRIER

9¾ Inch

1. The axle assembly can be overhauled either in or out of the vehicle. Either way, the free-floating axles must be removed.
2. Drain the lubricant and remove the rear cover and gasket.
3. Matchmark the bearing caps and the housing for reassembly in the same position. Remove the bearing caps and bolts.
4. Using a spreader tool mounted to the carrier housing, spread the housing a maximum of 0.015 in.

NOTE: Do not exceed this measurement. The housing could be permanently damaged. The use of a dial indicator is recommended to prevent over-stretching the housing.

5. Using a pry bar, remove the differential case from the housing. Separate the shims and record the dimensions and location on the 10½ in. ring gear axle. Remove the spreader tool from the housing.
6. Remove the differential side bearing cups and tag to identify the side, if they are to be used again.
7. Remove the differential gear pinion shaft lock pin and remove the shaft. Rotate the side and pinion gears to remove them from the carrier. Remove the thrust bearings.
8. Remove the bearing cones and rollers from the carrier, marking and noting the shim locations.
9. Remove the ring gear bolts and tap the ring gear from the carrier housing.
10. Inspect the components.

10½ Inch

1. The axle assembly can be overhauled either in or out of the vehicle. Either way, the free-floating axles must be removed.
2. Drain the lubricant and remove the rear cover and gasket.
3. Matchmark the bearing caps and the housing for reassembly in the same position. Remove the bearing caps and bolts.
4. Using a spreader tool mounted to the carrier housing, spread the housing a maximum of 0.015 in.

NOTE: Do not exceed this measurement. The housing could be permanently damaged. The use of a dial indicator is recommended to prevent over-stretching the housing.

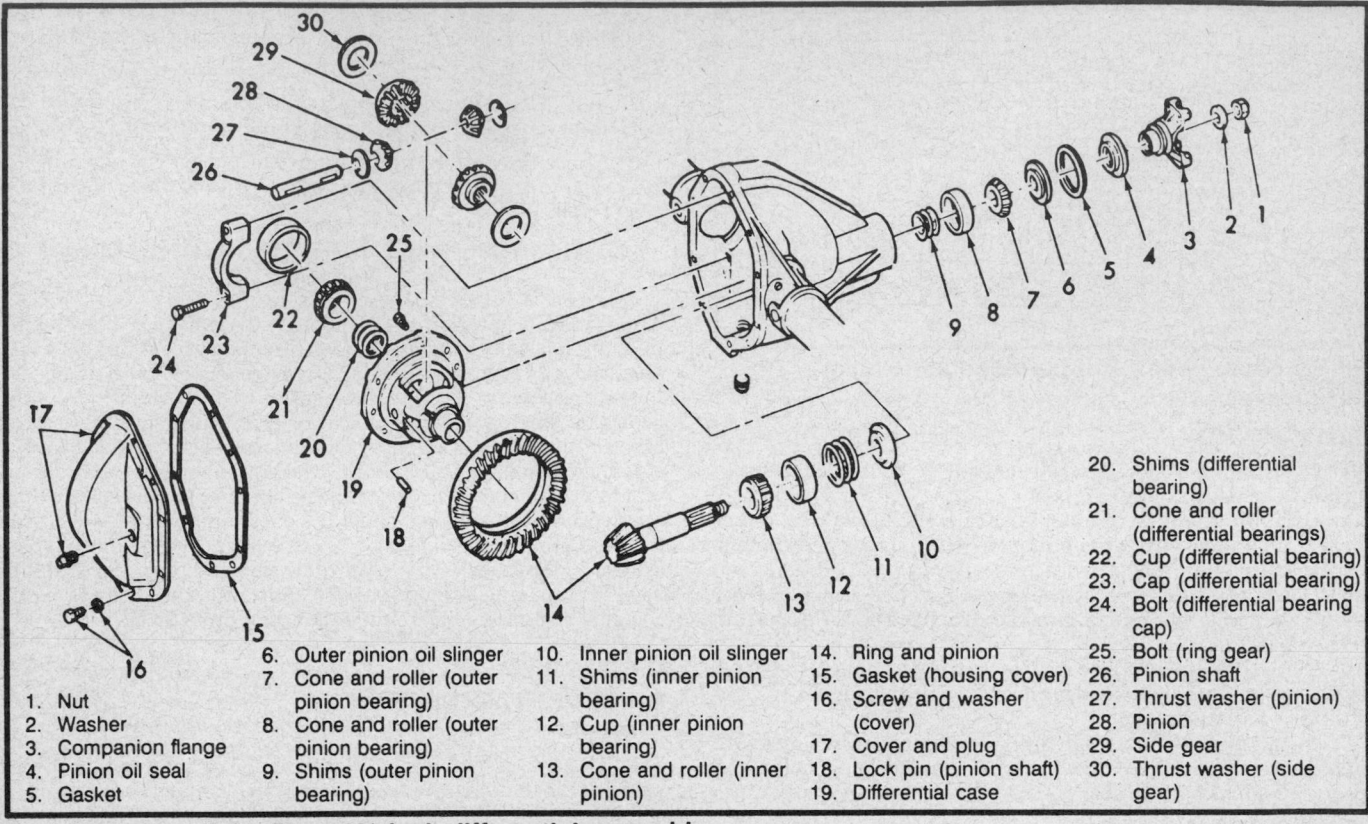

6. Outer pinion oil slinger
7. Cone and roller (outer pinion bearing)
8. Cone and roller (outer pinion bearing)
9. Shims (outer pinion bearing)
10. Inner pinion oil slinger
11. Shims (inner pinion bearing)
12. Cup (inner pinion bearing)
13. Cone and roller (inner pinion)
14. Ring and pinion
15. Gasket (housing cover)
16. Screw and washer (cover)
17. Cover and plug
18. Lock pin (pinion shaft)
19. Differential case

1. Nut
2. Washer
3. Companion flange
4. Pinion oil seal
5. Gasket

20. Shims (differential bearing)
21. Cone and roller (differential bearings)
22. Cup (differential bearing)
23. Cap (differential bearing)
24. Bolt (differential bearing cap)
25. Bolt (ring gear)
26. Pinion shaft
27. Thrust washer (pinion)
28. Pinion
29. Side gear
30. Thrust washer (side gear)

Exploded view of the Dana 9¾ inch differential assembly

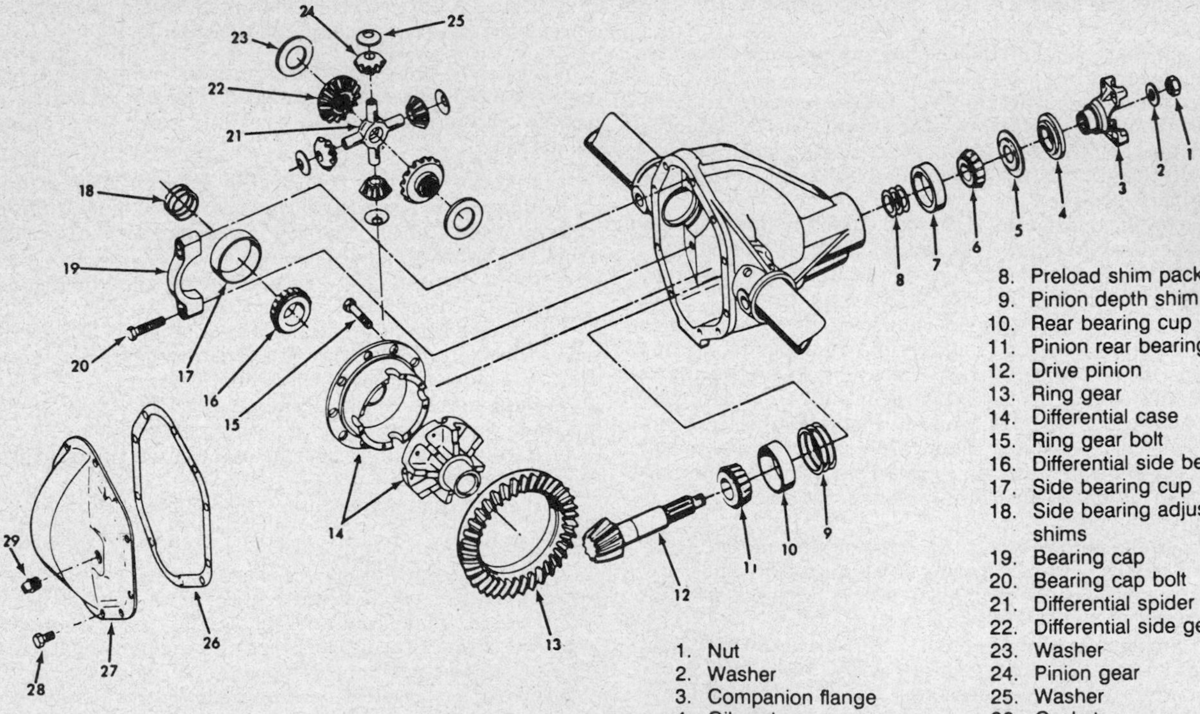

1. Nut
2. Washer
3. Companion flange
4. Oil seal
5. Oil slinger
6. Pinion front bearing
7. Front bearing cup

8. Preload shim pack
9. Pinion depth shim pack
10. Rear bearing cup
11. Pinion rear bearing
12. Drive pinion
13. Ring gear
14. Differential case
15. Ring gear bolt
16. Differential side bearing
17. Side bearing cup
18. Side bearing adjusting shims
19. Bearing cap
20. Bearing cap bolt
21. Differential spider
22. Differential side gear
23. Washer
24. Pinion gear
25. Washer
26. Gasket
27. Cover
28. Cover screw
29. Drain plug

Exploded view of the Dana 10½ inch differential assembly

5. Using a pry bar, remove the differential case from the housing. Separate the shims and record the dimensions and location on the 10½ in. ring gear axle. Remove the spreader tool from the housing.

6. Using puller tools, press the differential side bearings from the case.

7. Remove the ring gear bolts and tap the ring gear from the case with a soft-faced hammer.

8. Matchmark the case halves for reassembly and remove the retaining bolts.

9. Tap the upper case ½ to separate it from the bottom ½. Remove the internal gears, washers and cross.

DRIVE PINION

1. Remove the pinion nut and flange from the pinion gear.

2. Remove the pinion gear assembly from the housing. It may be necessary to tap the pinion from the housing with a soft faced hammer. Catch the pinion so as not to allow it to drop on the floor.

3. With a long drift, remove the inner bearing cup, pinion seal, slinger, gasket, outer pinion bearing and the shim pack. Label the shim pack for reassembly.

4. Remove the rear pinion bearing cup and shim pack from the housing. Label the shims for reassembly.

5. Remove the rear pinion bearing from the pinion gear with an arbor press and special plates.

Inspection

1. Clean the gears, bearings and component parts with solvent and inspect for scoring, chipping or excessive wear.

2. Inspect the flanges and splines for excessive wear.

3. Replace the necessary parts as required.

SIDE BEARING SHIM SELECTION

10½ Inch

1. With the pinion gear not in the axle housing, place the bearing cups over the side bearings and install the differential carrier into the axle housing.

2. Place the shim that was originally installed on the ring gear side into its original position.

3. Install the bearing caps in their proper positions and tighten the bolts to keep the bearings in place.

4. Mount a dial indicator on the axle housing with the indicator button contacting the back of the ring gear.

5. Position 2 prybars between the bearing shim and the housing on the ring gear side of the differential carrier. Force the differential carrier away from the dial indicator and set the indicator to zero.

6. Reposition the prybars to the opposite side of the differential carrier and force the carrier back towards the dial indicator. Repeat several times until the same reading is obtained each time.

7. To the dial indicator reading, add the thickness of the shim and record the results to be used later in the assembly.

PINION SHIM SELECTION

Ring gears and pinions are supplied in matched sets only. The matched numbers are etched on both gears for verification. On the rear face of the pinion, a plus (+) or a minus (−) number will be etched, indicating the best running position for each particular gear set. This dimension is controlled by the shimming behind the inner bearing cup. Whenever baffles or oil slingers are used, they become part of the adjusting shim pack. An example: If a pinion is etched + 3, this pinion would require 0.003 in. less shims than a pinion etched 0. This means by removing shims, the mounting distance of the pinion is increased by 0.003 in., which is just what a plus (+) etching indicates. If a pinion is etched − 3, it would be necessary to add 0.003 in. more shims than would be required if the pinion was etched 0. By adding the 0.003 in. shims, the mounting distance of the pinion is decreased 0.003 in., which is just what the minus (−) etching indicates. Pinion adjusting shims are available in thicknesses of 0.003, 0.005 and 0.010 in. An example: If a new gear set is used and the old pinion reads + 2 and the new pinion reads − 2, add 0.004 in. shims to the original shim pack.

Assembly

DRIVE PINION

1. Select the correct pinion depth shims and install in the rear pinion bearing cup bore.

2. Install the rear bearing cup in the axle housing.

3. Add or subtract an equal amount of shim thickness to or from the preload or outer shim pack, as was added or subtracted from the inner shim pack.

4. Install the front pinion bearing cup into its bore in the axle housing.

5. Press the rear pinion bearing onto the pinion gear shaft and install the pinion gear with bearing into the axle housing.

6. Install the preload shims and the front pinion bearing; do not install the oil seal at this time.

Old Pinion Marking	New Pinion Marking								
	− 4	− 3	− 2	− 1	0	+ 1	+ 2	+ 3	+ 4
+ 4	+ 0.008	+ 0.007	+ 0.006	+ 0.005	+ 0.004	+ 0.003	+ 0.002	+ 0.001	0
+ 3	+ 0.007	+ 0.006	+ 0.005	+ 0.004	+ 0.003	+ 0.002	+ 0.001	0	− 0.001
+ 2	+ 0.006	+ 0.005	+ 0.004	+ 0.003	+ 0.002	+ 0.001	0	− 0.001	− 0.002
+ 1	+ 0.005	+ 0.004	+ 0.003	+ 0.002	+ 0.001	0	− 0.001	− 0.002	− 0.003
0	+ 0.004	+ 0.003	+ 0.002	+ 0.001	0	− 0.001	− 0.002	− 0.003	− 0.004
− 1	+ 0.003	+ 0.002	+ 0.001	0	− 0.001	− 0.002	− 0.003	− 0.004	− 0.005
− 2	+ 0.002	+ 0.001	0	− 0.001	− 0.002	− 0.003	− 0.004	− 0.005	− 0.006
− 3	+ 0.001	0	− 0.001	− 0.002	− 0.003	− 0.004	− 0.005	− 0.006	− 0.007
− 4	0	− 0.001	− 0.002	0.003	− 0.004	− 0.005	− 0.006	− 0.007	− 0.008

7. Install the flange with the holding bar tool attached, the washer and the nut on the pinion shaft end. Torque the nut to 250 ft. lbs. for the 10½ in. and 255 ft. lbs. for the 9¾ in.

8. Remove the holding bar from the flange and with an inch lb. torque wrench, measure the rotating torque of the pinion gear. The rotating torque should be 10–20 inch lbs. with the original bearings or 20–40 inch lbs. with new bearings. Disregard the torque reading necessary to start the shaft to turn.

9. If the preload torque is not in specifications, adjust the shim pack as required.

    a. To increase preload, decrease the thickness of the preload shim pack.

    b. To decrease preload, increase the thickness of the preload shim pack.

10. When the proper preload is obtained, remove the nut, washer and flange from the pinion shaft.

11. Install a new pinion seal into the housing and reinstall the flange, washer and nut. Using the holder tool, torque the nut to 250 ft. lbs. for the 10½ in. and 255 ft. lbs. for the 9¾ in.

DIFFERENTIAL CARRIER

9¾ Inch

1. Install the differential side gears, the differential pinion gears and new thrust washers into the differential carrier.

2. Align the pinion gear shaft holes and install the pinion shaft into the carrier. Align the lock pin hole in the shaft and carrier. Install the lock pin and peen the hole to avoid having the pin drop from the carrier.

3. Install the differential case side bearings with the proper installation tools. Do not install the shims at this time.

4. Place the carrier assembly into the axle housing with the bearing cups on the bearing cones. Install the bearing caps in their original position and tighten the bearing cap bolts enough to keep the bearing caps in place.

5. Install a dial indicator on the housing so the indicator button contacts the carrier flange. Press the differential carrier to prevent sideplay and center the dial indicator. Rotate the carrier and check the flange for run-out. If the run-out is greater than 0.002 in., the defect is probably due to the bearings or to the carrier and should be corrected.

6. Remove the assembly and install the ring gear. Torque the retaining bolts and reinstall the assembly into the housing. Install the bearing caps in their original position and tighten the cap bolts to keep the bearings caps in place.

7. Install the dial indicator and position the indicator button to contact the ring gear back surface. Rotate the assembly and the run-out should be less than 0.002 in. If over 0.002 in., remove the assembly and relocate the ring gear 180 degrees. Reinstall the assembly and recheck. If the run-out remains over the 0.002 in. tolerance, the ring gear is defective. If the measurement is within tolerances, continue on with the assembly.

8. Position 2 pry bars between the bearing cap and the housing on the side opposite the ring gear. Pull on the pry bars and force the differential carrier as far as possible towards the dial indicator. Rock the assembly to seat the bearings and reset the dial indicator to zero.

9. Reposition the prybars to the opposite side of the carrier and force the carrier assembly as far towards the center of the housing. Read the dial indicator scale. This will be the total amount of shims required for setting the backlash during the reassembly, less the bearing preload. Record the measurement.

10. With the pinion gear installed and properly set, position the differential carrier assembly into the axle housing and install the bearing caps in their proper positions. Tighten the cap bolts just to hold the bearing cups in place.

11. Install a dial indicator on the axle housing with the indicator button contacting the back of the ring gear.

12. Position 2 prybars between the bearing cup and the axle housing on the ring gear side of the case and pry the ring gear into mesh with the pinion gear teeth, as far as possible. Rock the ring gear to allow the teeth to mesh and the bearings to seat. With the pressure still applied by the prybars, set the dial indicator to zero.

13. Reposition the prybars on the opposite side of ring gear and pry the gear as far as it will go. Take the dial indicator reading. Repeat this procedure until the same reading is obtained each time. This reading represents the necessary amount of shims between the differential carrier and the bearing on the ring gear side.

14. Remove the bearing from the differential carrier on the ring gear side and install the proper amount of shims. Reinstall the bearing.

15. Remove the differential carrier bearing from the opposite side of the ring gear. To determine the amount of shims needed, use the following method.

    a. Subtract the size of the shim pack just installed on the ring gear side of the carrier from the reading obtained and recorded when measurement was taken without the pinion gear in place.

    b. To this figure, add an additional 0.015 in. to compensate for preload and backlash. An example: If the first reading was 0.085 in. and the shims installed on the ring gear side of the carrier were 0.055 in., the correct amount of shims would be $0.085 - 0.055 + 0.015 = 0.045$ in.

16. Install the required shims as determined under step 15 and install the differential side bearing. The installation of the shims should give the proper preload to the bearings and the proper backlash to the ring and pinion gears.

17. Spread the axle housing with the spreader tool no more than 0.015 in. Install the differential bearing outer cups in their correct locations and install the cups in their respective locations.

18. Install the bolts and tighten finger-tight. Rotate the differential carrier and ring gear and tap with a soft-faced hammer to insure proper seating of the assembly in the axle housing.

19. Remove the spreader tool and torque the cap bolts to specifications.

20. Install a dial indicator and check the ring gear backlash at 4 equally spaced points of the ring gear circle. The backlash must be within a range of 0.004–0.009 in. and must not vary more than 0.002 in. between the points checked.

21. If the backlash is not within specifications, the shim packs must be corrected to bring the backlash within limits.

22. Check the tooth contact pattern and verify.

23. Complete the assembly, refill to proper level with lubricant and operate to verify proper assembly.

10½ Inch

1. Install new thrust washers to the side gears and lubricate the contact surfaces.

2. Assemble the side gears, pinion bears, washers and cross shaft into the flanged case ½.

3. Install the upper case ½ to the bottom ½, making sure the scribe marks are aligned.

4. Install the retaining bolts finger tight, then, torque the bolts alternately.

5. If a new ring gear is to be installed or the old one used, install it to the differential case and align the bolt holes and torque the bolts alternately.

6. Install the side carrier bearings.

7. Install the differential carrier, with the side bearings and cups installed, in place in the axle housing.

8. Select the smallest of the original shims as a gauge shim and place it between the bearing cup and the housing on the ring gear side.

9. Install the bearing caps and tighten the bolts to hold the cups in place.

10. Mount a dial indicator on the ring gear side of the axle housing and position the indicator button on the rear side of the ring gear.

11. Position 2 prybars between the bearing cup and the housing on the side opposite the ring gear. With the prybars, force the differential carrier towards the dial indicator and set the indicator dial to zero.

12. Reposition the prybars on the ring gear side of the carrier and force the ring gear into mesh with the pinion gear while observing the dial indicator reading. Repeat this operation until the same reading is obtained each time.

13. Add this indicator reading to the gauging shim thickness to determine the correct shim dimension for installation on the ring gear side of the differential carrier.

14. An example: If the gauging shim was 0.115 in. and the indicator reading was 0.017 in., the correct shim would be 0.115 + 0.017 = 0.172 in.

15. Remove the gauge shim and install the correct shim into position between the bearing cup and the axle housing on the ring gear side of the housing.

16. To determine the correct dimension for the remaining shim, refer to the side bearing shim selection for the 10½ in. and obtain the recorded shim size. From that figure, subtract the size of the shim installed in step 14 and add 0.006 in. for the bearing preload and backlash.

17. An example: If the reading of the shim just installed on the ring gear side of the carrier was 0.172 in. and the reading obtained during the checking of clearance without the pinion installed was 0.329, the correct shim dimension would be as follows: 0.329 − 0.172 = 0.157 + 0.006 = 0.163 in.

18. Spread the axle housing with a spreader tool, no more than 0.015 in. The carrier assembly is in place in the housing.

19. Assemble the shim, as determined previously, into place between the bearing cup and the housing. Remove the spreader tool.

20. Install the bearing caps in their marked positions and torque the bolts to specifications.

21. Install a dial indicator and check the ring gear backlash at 4 equally spaced points around the ring gear.

22. The backlash must be within 0.004–0.009 in. and must not vary more than 0.002 in. between the positions checked.

23. Whenever the backlash is not within the allowable limits, it must be corrected. Changing of the shim packs is required.

    a. Low backlash is corrected by decreasing the shim on the ring gear side and increasing the opposite side shim an equal amount.

    b. High backlash is corrected by increasing the shim on the ring gear side and decreasing the opposite side shim an equal amount.

24. Check the tooth contact pattern and correct as required.

25. Complete the assembly, refill to the correct level and operate to verify correct repairs.

ROCKWELL – 12 INCH RING GEAR AXLE

Disassembly

DIFFERENTIAL

1. Remove locknut, adjusting screw and thrust block.
2. Remove 2 adjuster lock cap screws and locks.
3. Punch-mark bearing caps and carrier to help in locating caps for assembly. Remove bearing adjusters and bearing caps.

NOTE: Do not pry caps free with a prybar or distort locating dowels.

4. Carefully remove differential assembly from carrier.
5. Use a differential side bearing remover to pull bearing cones off each side of case.
6. Make sure the differential case halves are punch-marked so they can be reassembled in same position.
7. Remove drive gear and separate case halves.

8. Remove 2 side gears, the differential spider and the 4 differential pinions.
9. Remove pinion and side gear thrust washers.

DRIVE PINION

1. Remove seal retainer and gasket from carrier.
2. Using brass drift against inner end of pinion, drive out the pinion and bearing assembly.
3. Remove shim pack from carrier from those models having tapered roller outer bearings.
4. It may be necessary to use a drift to remove the pinion rear bearing.
5. Clamp yoke in soft-jawed vise. Remove yoke nut and washer and separate drive pinion from yoke.
6. Separate yoke from oil seal retainer.
7. Place retainer in a soft-jawed vise and, using a hammer and chisel, remove oil seal and then the felt oil seal.
8. If equipped with a tapered roller outer bearing, remove bearing cup, outer tapered bearing cone and bearing spacer from drive pinion.
9. Using a bearing remover press plate with shop press, press the bearing cone or roller bearing from the drive pinion.
10. If equipped, remove the bearing lock ring and use press plates with shop press to press the roller bearing from inner end of drive pinion.

Inspection

1. Clean the gears, bearings and component parts with solvent and inspect for scoring, chipping or excessive wear.
2. Inspect the flanges and splines for excessive wear.
3. Replace the necessary parts as required.

Assembly

NOTE: Thoroughly, clean and lubricate all components with axle lubricant before reassembling.

DRIVE PINION

1. Clean counterbore of oil seal retainer. Saturate the felt seal in oil and install evenly in retainer. Soak oil seal in light engine oil for about 1 hour before installing. Coat outer surface of seal lightly with sealing compound to prevent oil leaks between seal and retainer.
2. Install oil seal into retainer with lip of seal toward inner side of retainer. Using a seal installer, press oil seal into retainer with face of seal flush with retainer face.
3. Retainer surface must be clean and smooth to prevent oil leaks between retainer and carrier.
4. Using a shop press, press bearing into place into carrier bore or the roller bearing into position on drive pinion with chamfered side of inner race facing toward pinion shoulder. Position bearing lock ring to secure bearing on drive pinion.

NOTE: Opposed tapered roller bearing cones, 2 bearing cups and spacer are serviced and replaced as a unit. The spacer is a preselected one to provide proper bearing adjustment.

5. Models with tapered roller bearings:

    a. Press inner bearing cone into place with largest side of cone facing the pinion gear end.

    b. Install original shim pack in carrier. If original ring gear and pinion are reinstalled, use shims that were removed. Shims are available in 5 thicknesses: 0.012, 0.015, 0.018, 0.021 and 0.024 in. When using new gears, start with a 0.021 in. shim and check the pinion depth.

    c. Insert the pinion assembly into carrier, align roller bearing with carrier boss. Install bearing spacer, bearing cup and bearing cone with the wide side facing pinion splines.

6. If equipped with double-row ball bearing: Using a 2 in. pipe or tubing, drive bearing unit into proper seating position.

7. With pinion assembly properly positioned in carrier, install new gasket. Install seal retainer onto yoke and assemble yoke and retainer assembly onto splined end of drive pinion.

8. Secure the retainer to carrier with lock washers and cap screws and torque.

9. Secure the pinion assembly with yoke washer and nut and torque to 220 ft. lbs.

DIFFERENTIAL

1. To facilitate installation of drive gear, install 2 guide pins ($\frac{1}{2} \times 20 \times 2$ in. bolts) in gear. Start the guide pins through the case flange holes and tap drive gear onto case. If a differential gear is bad, the complete set should be replaced.

2. Lubricate the differential case inner walls and all component parts with axle lubricant. Place the differential pinions and thrust washers onto the spider.

3. Assemble the side gears, pinions, side gear and pinion thrust washers onto the left half of differential.

4. Assemble the drive gear half, right half of differential, being sure to align marks on both halves.

5. Install differential-to-drive gear cap screw and lock washers and tighten evenly until drive gear is flush with case flange. Remove guide pins and install cap screws and torque.

6. Using an installer tool, install the differential side bearing cones.

7. Install the bearing cap locating dowels into the caps. Lubricate the side bearings and place the bearing cups on bearings.

8. Install the differential assembly into the carrier. Carefully install the bearing adjusters into the carrier.

9. Install the bearing caps by aligning the punch marks previously made. Be sure the bearing adjuster threads are engaged with carrier and caps. Tighten the adjusters alternately and evenly. Tighten the bearing cap screws until the lock washers are flat.

Adjustment

DRIVE GEAR AND PINION

1. Loosen the bearing cap screws, enough, to loosen the right-hand bearing adjuster (pinion side) and tighten the left-hand bearing adjuster (opposite pinion side.) Using the adjuster, remove all backlash between the drive gear and pinion.

2. Back off the left-hand bearing adjuster about 2 notches to point where notch in adjuster is aligned with lock. Tighten the right-hand bearing adjuster solidly to seat the bearing. Loosen right-hand adjuster, enough, to free the bearing; then, retighten against the bearing. Draw up right-hand adjuster 1-2 more notches until adjuster notch aligns with the lock.

3. Using a dial indicator on carrier adjuster, slowly oscillate the drive gear and measure the backlash; it should be 0.005-0.008 in.

4. If backlash exceeds 0.008 in., loosen the right-hand adjuster 1 notch; then, tighten the left-hand adjuster 1 notch. If less than 0.005 in., loosen the left-hand adjuster 1 notch and tighten the right-hand adjuster 1 notch.

5. After the backlash has been adjusted, tighten the bearing cap screws until their respective lock washers flatten out.

6. Check the drive gear run-out.

7. Install the side bearing adjusting locknut and secure with cap screws and lock washers.

CHECKING PINION DEPTH

NOTE: This procedure is performed if the pinion is equipped with tapered roller bearings.

1. Coat the drive gear with red lead.

2. Turn the pinion shaft several revolutions in both directions while applying considerable drag on drive gear.

3. Pinion depth is determined by shim pack selection. Shim packs are available in thicknesses of: 0.012, 0.015, 0.018, 0.021 and 0.024 in.

4. Changing the pinion depth will again require adjusting backlash. After pinion depth and backlash have been adjusted, torque bearing caps.

THRUST BLOCK

1. Install the thrust block and locknut to the adjusting screw.

2. Thread the screw and block into the carrier until the block contacts the drive gear.

3. Rotate the gear and note the drag change.

4. Adjust these parts until point of greatest drag is reached. Back off the screw about a 30 degrees to provide 0.005-0.007 in. clearance between the block and gear. Make certain screw does not turn at all when torquing the locknut to 135 ft. lbs.

JEEP CORPORATION

Jeep models are using Dana $7\frac{9}{16}$ in. and $8\frac{7}{8}$ in. semi-floating and $8\frac{1}{2}$ in. full-floating type rear axles. The axle housings are made of a modular cast iron center section and 2 steel tubes which are pressed into the center section. The rear drum brake support plates are attached to the mounting flanges at the axle tube outboard ends.

The differential assembly consists of a cast iron case containing 2 differential side gears, 2 differential pinion gears and a pinion shaft on which the pinion gears are mounted. The differential side and pinion gears are in constant mesh.

The axle ratio and the ring and pinion gear tooth combinations are stamped on a tag attached to the differential housing cover. On the Jeep rear axles, the axle code letters are stamped on the right side axle housing tube boss.

NOTE: The Trac-Lok limited slip differentials are available as an option. The Trac-Lok is used only in rear axles and there are 2 Trac-Lok units used.

Front Axle Assembly

DANA — $7\frac{9}{16}$ INCH AND $8\frac{7}{8}$ INCH RING GEAR AXLE

For overhaul information, refer to the Dana $7\frac{9}{16}$ in. and $8\frac{7}{8}$ in. ring gear axle, in the rear axle assembly section.

DANA — $8\frac{1}{2}$ INCH RING GEAR AXLE

For overhaul information, refer to the Dana $8\frac{1}{2}$ in. ring gear axle, in the rear axle assembly section.

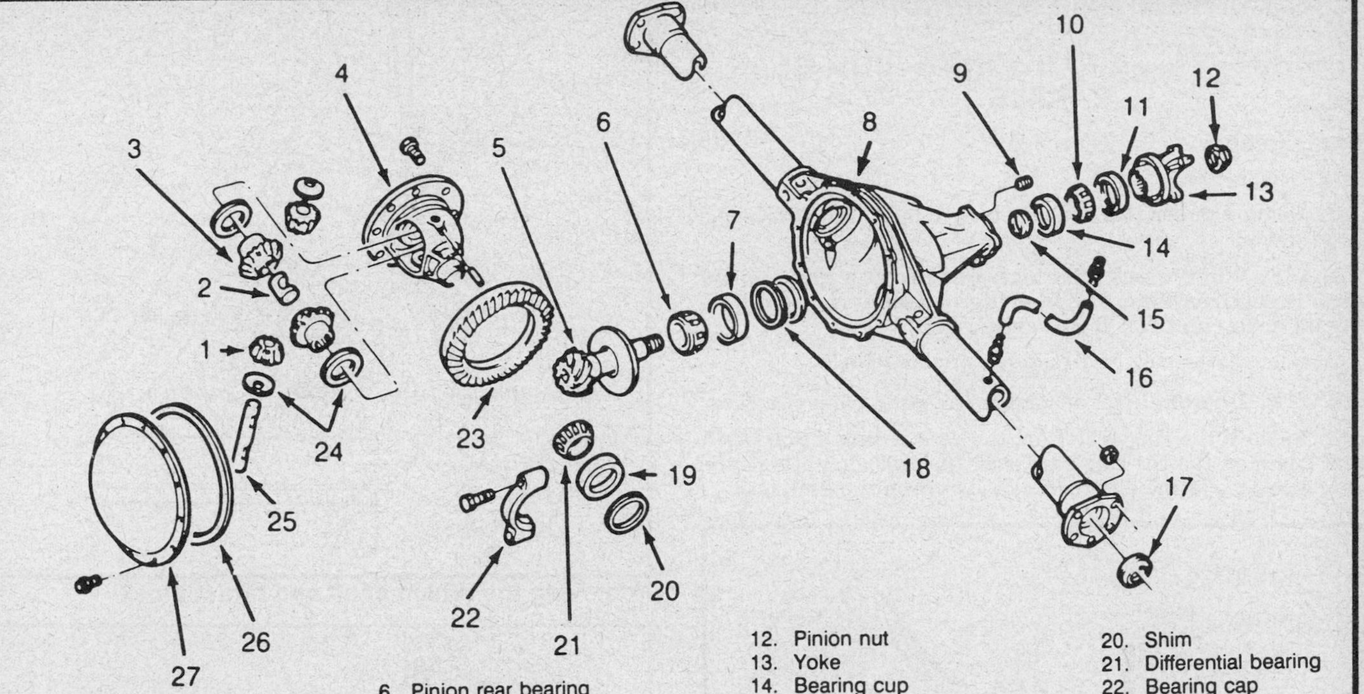

12. Pinion nut	20. Shim
13. Yoke	21. Differential bearing
14. Bearing cup	22. Bearing cap
15. Collapsible spacer	23. Ring gear
16. Vent assembly	24. Thrust washer
17. Oil seal	25. Pinion mate shaft
18. Pinion depth shim	26. Gasket
19. Bearing cup	27. Cover

1. Differential pinion gear	6. Pinion rear bearing
2. Thrust block	7. Bearing cup
3. Differential side gear	8. Housing
4. Differential case	9. Fill plug
5. Pinion gear	10. Pinion front bearing
	11. Oil seal

Exploded view of the Dana 8⁷⁄₈ inch rear differential assembly

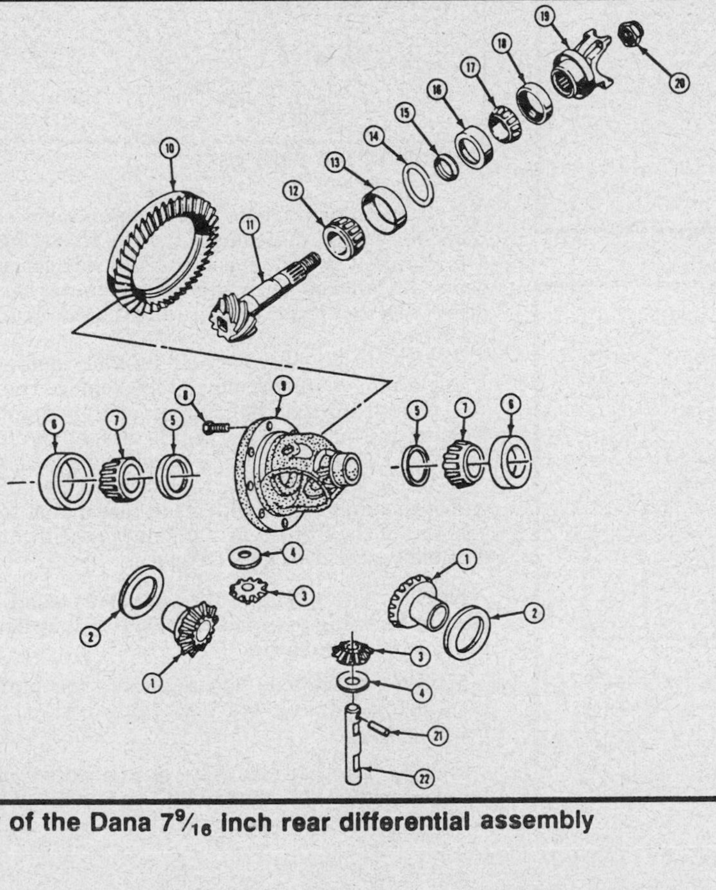

1. Differential side gear
2. Side gear thrust washer
3. Differential pinion
4. Pinion thrust washer
5. Differential bearing shim
6. Differential bearing cup
7. Differential bearing
8. Rear gear bolt
9. Differential case
10. Ring gear
11. Pinion gear
12. Pinion gear rear bearing
13. Rear bearing cup
14. Pinion depth shim
15. Pinion bearing preload spacer
16. Front bearing cup
17. Pinion gear front bearing
18. Pinion seal
19. Pinion yoke
20. Pinion nut
21. Pinion shaft lock pin
22. Differential pinion shaft

Exploded view of the Dana 7⁹⁄₁₆ inch rear differential assembly

Rear Axle Assemblies

DANA — 7⁹/₁₆ AND 8⁷/₈ INCH RING GEAR AXLE

Disassembly

DIFFERENTIAL

1. Using a puller tool and adapters, remove the differential bearings.

NOTE: When using this tool, be sure the differential case is secure. When the bearing is removed the differential case can drop if not supported.

2. Remove the ring gear-to-differential case bolts.

NOTE: Do not chisel or wedge the gear from the case.

3. Remove the ring gear from the case. Using a brass drift and hammer, tap the ring gear from the case; do not nick the ring gear face of the differential case or drop the gear.

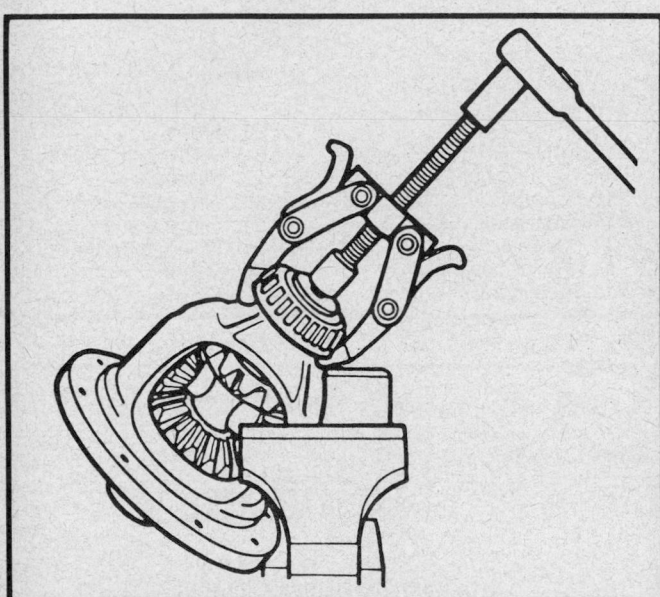

Removing the differential bearing

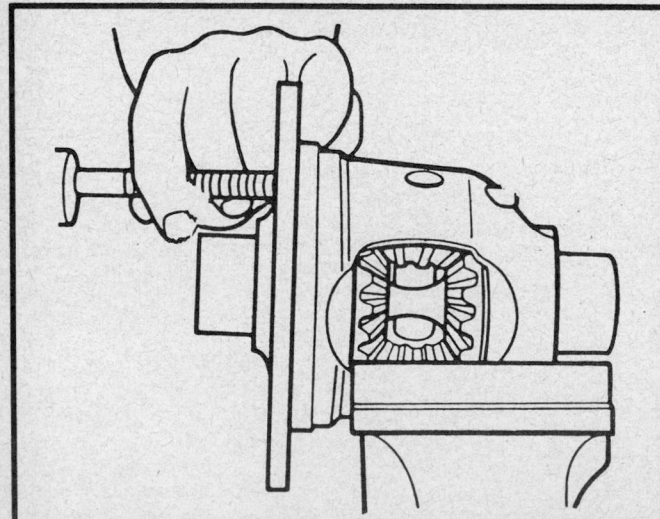

Removing the pinion lock pin

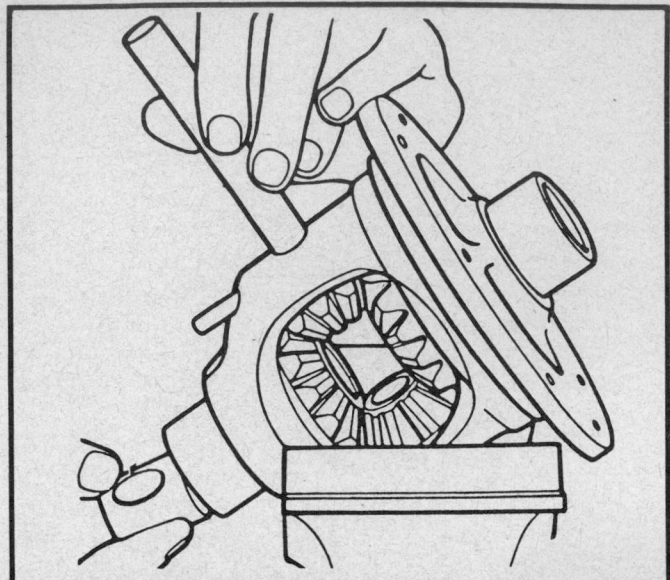

Removing the pinion shaft and thrust block

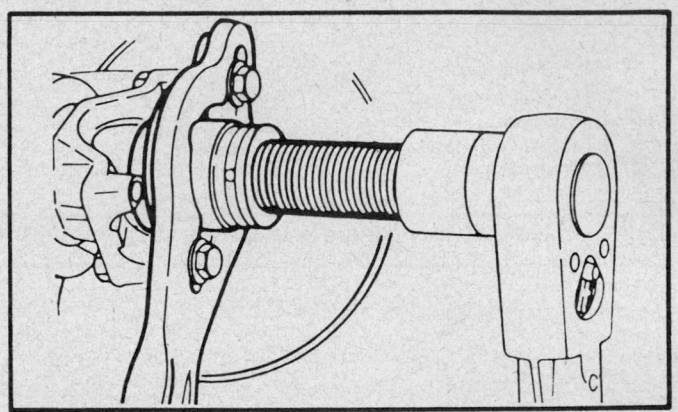

Removing the axle yoke

4. Using a drift, remove the pinion mate shaft lockpin. Remove the pinion mate shaft and the thrust block.

5. Rotate the pinion gears on the side gears until the pinion gears are aligned with the case opening. Remove the pinion gears with the thrust washers and the side gears with the thrust washers.

6. Using a pinion yoke holding tool, remove the pinion nut. Using a pinion yoke removal tool, remove the axle yoke.

7. Install the axle housing cover to prevent the pinion gear from falling out when the gear is driven out of the bearings and housing. Loosely attach the cover using 2 bolts.

8. Using a seal removal tool, remove the pinion seal. Tap the end of the pinion gear with a soft face mallet to drive the pinion gear out of the front bearing. Remove the front bearing and collapsible spacer. Discard the spacer.

NOTE: The collapsible spacer is used to control the pinion bearing preload. Discard this spacer after removal, it is not reusable.

9. Remove the axle housing cover, the pinion gear and the rear bearing. Using bearing removal tools, remove the rear bearing cup.

NOTE: The pinion gear depth adjustment shims are located under the rear bearing cup; label these shims for assembly reference.

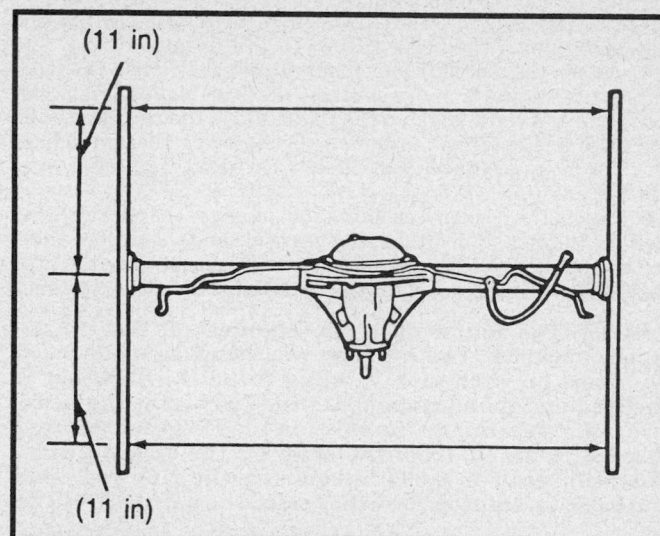

Checking the axle housing alignment

10. Using bearing removal tool, remove the front bearing cup.

NOTE: Keep the bearing cup remover tool seated squarely on the cup to prevent damaging the cup bores during removal.

Inspection
AXLE HOUSING

1. Place 2 straight-edges across the tube flanges and measure the distance between the flange ends. If the straightedges are parallel within ³/₃₂ in. at a distance of 11 inches from the tube centerline, the axle housing is serviceable.
2. Perform this inspection with the straightedges placed in horizontal and vertical positions.

DIFFERENTIAL

1. Clean each part thoroughly in solvent.
2. Towel dry the bearings or allow them to air dry, do not use compressed air to dry bearings as damage might result. Dry all other parts with compressed air or shop towels. If the parts are not to be assembled immediately, cover them to prevent dust or dirt contamination.
3. Inspect the housing for cracks and sand holes. Replace the housing if it is cracked or porous. Check for burrs and deep scratches or nicks on the gasket and oil seal surfaces. An oil stone or fine tooth file may be used to remove nicks or burrs.
4. The bearing cup bores should be carefully inspected for nicks or burrs that may have been created during bearing cup removal.
5. Inspect and clean the axle tubes. Inspect the vent to be sure it is not obstructed.
6. Check housing for bent or loose tubes or other physical damage.
7. Inspect the shaft for scoring and wear. The shaft should be a press fit of 0.000–0.010 in. in the case. Replace the shaft if worn or scored.
8. Inspect the side gears for worn, cracked or chipped teeth. The gears should fit snugly on the axle shaft splines. Also inspect the fit of the gears in the differential case bore.
9. With the gears installed, side clearance must not exceed 0.007 in. Excessive side clearance must be corrected to avoid driveline backlash resulting in a clunk noise when the transmission is initially engaged in **D** or **R** with automatic transmission.

Assembly
PINION GEAR

Ring and pinion gear sets are factory tested to detect machining variances. Tests are started at a standard setting which is then varied to obtain the most desirable tooth contact pattern and quiet operation. When this setting is determined, the ring and pinion gear are etched with identifying numbers.

The ring gear receives one number. The pinion gear receives 2 numbers which are separated by a plus (+) or a minus (−) sign.

The 2nd number on the pinion gear indicates pinion position, in relation to the centerline of the axle shafts, where tooth contact was best and gear operation was most quiet. This number represents pinion depth variance and indicates the amount in thousands of an inch the gear set varied from the standard setting.

The number on the ring gear and 1st number on the pinion gear identify the gears as a matched set; do not attempt to use a ring and pinion set having different numbers. The standard setting for Jeep axles is 2.547 in. If the pinion is marked +2, the gear set varied from standard by +0.002 in. and will require 0.002 in. less shims than a gear set marked zero (0).

When a gear set is marked plus (+), the distance from the pinion end face to the axle shaft centerline must be more than the standard setting. If the pinion gear is marked −3, the gear set varied from standard by 0.003 in. more shims than a set marked zero (0). When a set is marked minus (−), the distance from the pinion end face to the axle shaft centerline must be less than the standard setting.

NOTE: On some factory installed gear sets, an additional 0.010 or 0.020 in. may have been machined off the pinion gear bottom face. This does not affect the gear operation but does affect the pinion gear marking and depth measurement.

Pinion gears machined in this fashion have different identifying numbers. For example, if the pinion is marked +23, the number 2 indicates 0.020 in. was removed from the pinion bottom face and the number 3 indicates variance from the standard setting is +0.003 in. If the pinion is marked +16, the number 1 indicates 0.010 in. was removed from the pinion bottom face and the number 6 indicates variance from the standard setting is +0.006 in.

Gear sets with additional amounts machined off the pinion bottom face are factory installed items exclusively. All service replacement gear sets will be machined to standard settings only. In addition, replacement gear sets marked ±0.009 in. or

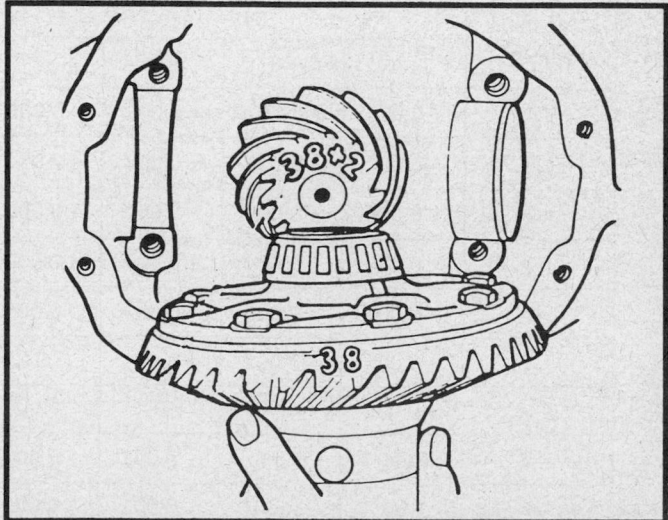

Pinion and ring gear identifying numbers

more or sets with mismatched identifying numbers must be returned to the parts distributor center; do not attempt to install these gear sets.

The chart provided in this section will help to determine the approximate starter shim thickness needed for the initial pinion depth measurement. However, the chart will not provide the exact shim thickness required for final adjustment and must not be used as a substitute for an actual pinion depth measurement. The chart should be used as follows.

1. Measure the thickness of the original pinion depth shim. Note the pinion depth variance numbers marked on the old and new pinion gears.

2. Now use the chart to determine the starter shim thickness. An example of this is as follows:

If the old pinion is marked − 3 and the new pinion is marked + 2, the chart procedure would be as follows. Go to the old pinion column and locate the − 3, then go across the chart until the + 2 figure is reached in the new pinion column. The box where the 2 columns intersect will indicate the amount of starter shim thickness required.

DIFFERENTIAL

1. Install the differential bearings on the case using tools J– 21784 and J–8092 or equivalent.

2. Install the thrust washers on the differential side gears and install the gears in the differential case. Install the differential pinion gears in the case. Install the thrust washers behind the pinion gears and align the pinion gear bores.

3. Rotate the differential side and pinion gears until the pinion mate shaft bores in the pinion gears are aligned with the shaft bores in the case.

4. Install thrust block in the case. Insert the block through the side gear bore. Align the bore in the block with the pinion mate shaft bores in the pinion gears and case.

5. Install the pinion mate shaft. Align the lockpin bore in the shaft with the bore in the case and install shaft lockpin.

RING GEAR

1. Position the ring gear on the differential case. Install the 2 ring gear bolts in the opposite holes and tighten the bolts to pull the gear into position.

2. Install the remaining ring gear bolts and tighten to within 105 ft. lbs. torque.

3. Position the shims previously selected to remove the differential bearing sideplay on the bearing cups and install the differential assembly in the axle housing. Install the bearing cap bolts and tighten the bolts with 85 ft. lbs. torque.

4. Attach the dial indicator to the housing. Position the indicator so the indicator stylus contacts the drive side of a ring gear tooth and at a right angle to the tooth. Move the ring gear back and forth and note the movement registered on the dial indicator. The ring gear backlash should be 0.005–0.009 in., with 0.008 in. desired.

5. Adjust the backlash as follows: to increase the backlash, install the thinner shim on the ring gear side and the thicker shim on the opposite side. To decrease the backlash, reverse the procedure; however, do not change the total thickness of the shims.

NOTE: The following is an example on how to decrease backlash. The sideplay was removed using 0.090 in. shims on each side totaling 0.180 in. Backlash is checked and found to be 0.011 in. To correct the backlash, add 0.004 in. the shim on the ring gear side and subtract 0.004 in. from the shim on the opposite side. This will result in 0.094 in. shim on the ring gear side and 0.086 in. shim on the other side. The backlash will be

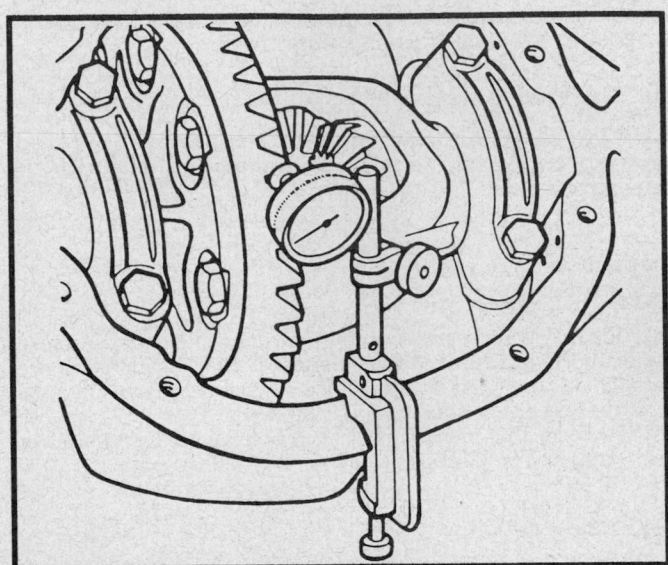

Measuring the ring gear backlash

Old Pinion Marking	New Pinion Marking								
	− 4	− 3	− 2	− 1	0	+ 1	+ 2	+ 3	+ 4
+ 4	+ 0.008	+ 0.007	+ 0.006	+ 0.005	+ 0.004	+ 0.003	+ 0.002	+ 0.001	0
+ 3	+ 0.007	+ 0.006	+ 0.005	+ 0.004	+ 0.003	+ 0.002	+ 0.001	0	− 0.001
+ 2	+ 0.006	+ 0.005	+ 0.004	+ 0.003	+ 0.002	+ 0.001	0	− 0.001	− 0.002
+ 1	+ 0.005	+ 0.004	+ 0.003	+ 0.002	+ 0.001	0	− 0.001	− 0.002	− 0.003
0	+ 0.004	+ 0.003	+ 0.002	+ 0.001	0	− 0.001	− 0.002	− 0.003	− 0.004
− 1	+ 0.003	+ 0.002	+ 0.001	0	− 0.001	− 0.002	− 0.003	− 0.004	− 0.005
− 2	+ 0.002	+ 0.001	0	− 0.001	− 0.002	− 0.003	− 0.004	− 0.005	− 0.006
− 3	+ 0.001	0	− 0.001	− 0.002	− 0.003	− 0.004	− 0.005	− 0.006	− 0.007
− 4	0	− 0.001	− 0.002	0.003	− 0.004	− 0.005	− 0.006	− 0.007	− 0.008

approximately 0.007–0.008 in. The total shim thickness remains 0.180 in.

Adjustment

PINION DEPTH MEASUREMENT

1. Measure the thickness of the original pinion depth shim. Note the pinion depth variance numbers marked on the old and new pinion gears.

2. Determine the starter shim thickness. Using the chart, determine the amount to be added or subtracted from the original shim thickness for starter shim thickness.

NOTE: The starter shim thickness must not be used as a final shim setting. An actual pinion depth measurement must be performed and the final shim thickness adjusted, as necessary.

3. Install the ring bearing on the pinion gear with the large diameter of the bearing cage facing the gear end of the pinion. Press the bearing against the rear face of the gear.

4. Clean the pinion bearing bores in the axle housing thoroughly. This is important in obtaining the correct pinion gear depth adjustment. Install the starter pinion depth shim in the housing rear bearing cup bore. Be sure the shim is centered in the bearing cup bore.

NOTE: If the shim is chamfered, be sure the chamfered side faces the bottom of the bearing cup bore.

5. Install the ring bearing cup using tools J–8092 and J–8608 or equivalent. Install the front bearing cup using tools J–8092 and J–8611–01 or equivalent. Install the pinion gear in the rear bearing cup.

6. Install the front bearing, rear universal joint yoke and original pinion nut on the pinion gear. Tighten the pinion nut only enough to remove the bearing endplay.

NOTE: Do not install a replacement pinion nut and collapsible spacer at this time as the pinion gear will be removed after depth measurement.

7. Note the pinion depth variance marked on the pinion gear. If the number is preceded by a plus (+) sign, add that amount (in thousandths) to the standard setting for the axle model being overhauled. If the number is preceded by a minus (−) sign, subtract that amount (in thousandths) from the standard setting. The result of this addition or subtraction is the desired pinion depth. Record this figure for future reference.

8. Assemble an arbor tool J–5223–4 and discs J–5223–23 or equivalent, install the assembled tools in the differential bearing cup bores; be sure the discs are completely seated in bearing cup bores.

9. Install the bearing caps over the discs and install the bearing cap bolts. Tighten the bearing cap bolts securely but not with the specified torque.

10. Position a gauge block tool J–5223–20 or equivalent, on the end face of the pinion gear with the anvil end of the gauge block seated on the gear and the gauge plunger under the arbor tool J–5223–4 or equivalent.

11. Assemble and mount the clamp tool J–5223–24 and bolt J–5223–29 or equivalent, on the axle housing. Use the axle housing cover bolt to attach the clamp to the housing.

12. Extend the clamp bolt until it presses against the gauge block with enough force to prevent the gauge block from moving. Loosen the gauge block thumb screw to release the gauge block plunger. When the plunger contacts the arbor tool, tighten the thumbscrew to lock the plunger in position; do not disturb the plunger position.

13. Remove the clamp and bolt assembly from the axle housing. Remove the gauge block and measure the distance from the end of the anvil to the end of the plunger using a 2 3 in. microm-

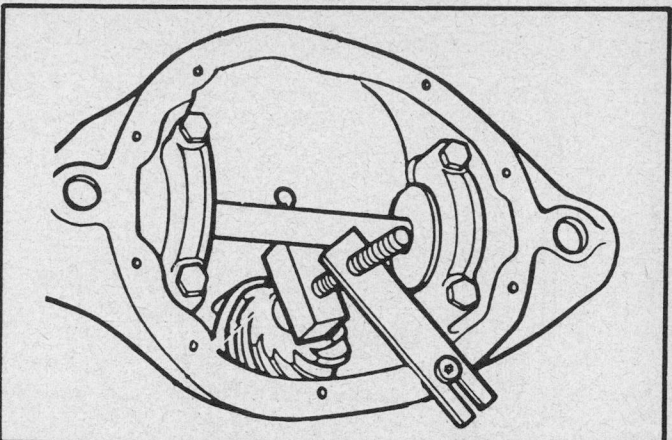

Installing the gauge arbor tool, discs and the gauge block tool

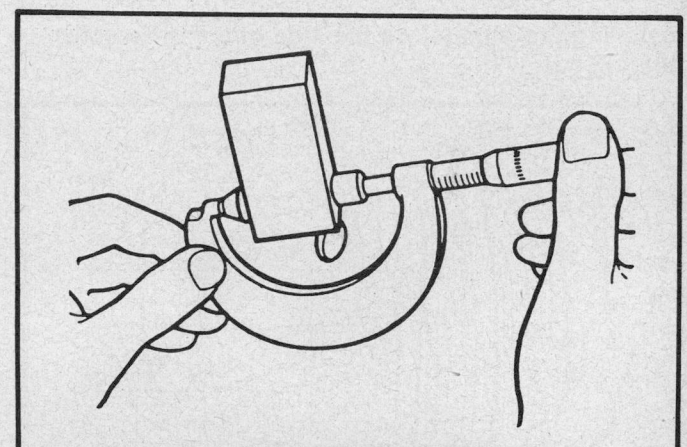

Measuring the anvil with a micrometer

eter. This dimension represents the measured pinion depth. Record this dimension for assembly reference.

14. Remove the bearing caps, the arbor tool and discs from the axle housing. Remove the pinion gear, the rear bearing cup and pinion depth shim from the axle housing.

15. Measure the thickness or the depth shim. Add this dimension to the measured pinion depth. From this total, subtract the desired pinion depth. The result represents the correct shim thickness required.

NOTE: The desired pinion depth is the standard setting plus or minus the pinion depth variance.

PINION GEAR BEARING PRELOAD

1. Install the correct thickness pinion depth shim(s) in the axle housing bearing cup bore. Install the rear bearing cup and pinion gear.

NOTE: The collapsible spacer controls the pinion bearing preload; do not reuse the old spacer, use a replacement spacer only.

2. Install the replacement collapsible spacer and front bearing on the pinion gear. Install the pinion oil seal using tool J–22661 or equivalent.

3. Install the pinion yoke, replace the pinion nut and tighten the pinion nut finger-tight. Tighten the pinion nut enough to remove endplay and seat the pinion bearings. Using tool J–22575 or equivalent, tighten the nut and use tool J–86141–01 or equivalent, to hold the yoke while tightening the nut.

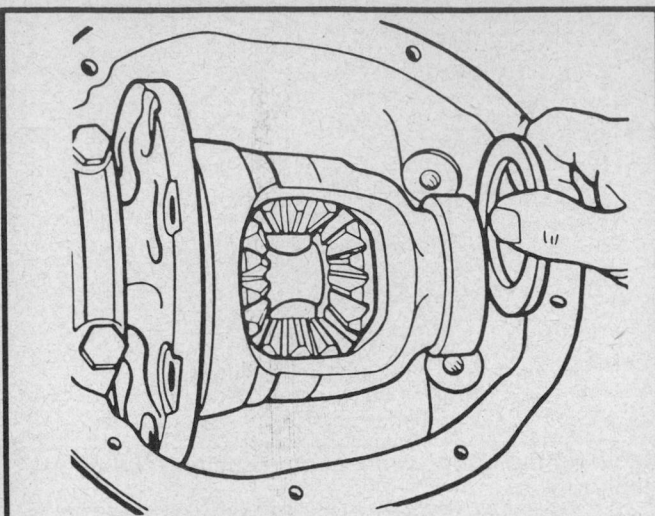

Installing the shim(s) on the side of the differential bearing cup

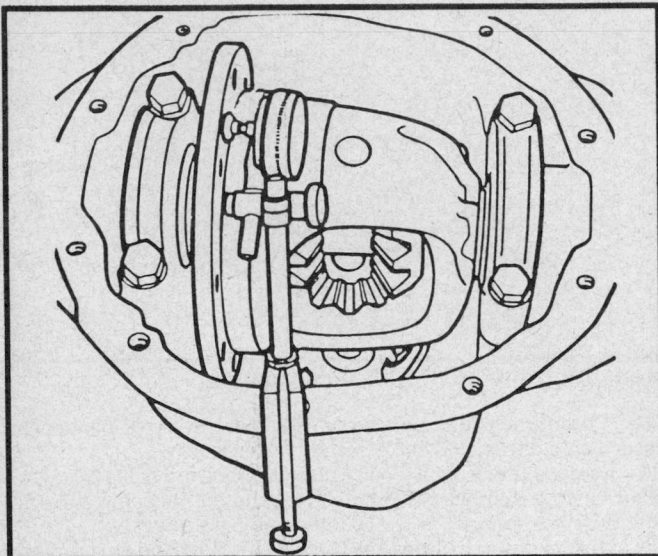

Installation of the dial indicator

4. Rotate the pinion, while tightening the nut, to seat the bearings evenly. Remove the tools.

NOTE: Do not exceed the specified preload torque or loosen the nut to reduce the preload torque, if the specified torque is exceeded.

5. Using an inch lb. torque wrench and adapter tool J–22575 or equivalent, measure the torque required to turn the pinion gear; the correct pinion bearing preload torque is 17–25 inch lbs. Continue tightening the pinion nut until the required preload torque is obtained.

6. If the pinion bearing preload torque is exceeded, remove the pinion gear, replace the collapsible spacer and pinion nut and adjust the preload again.

DIFFERENTIAL BEARING

1. Place the bearing cup over each differential bearing and install the differential case assembly in the axle housing.

2. Install the shim on each side between the bearing cup and the housing; use 0.080 in. shims as the starting point.

3. Install the bearing caps and tighten the bolts finger-tight. Mount the dial indicator on the housing. Using a prybar, pry between the shims and housing. Pry the assembly to one side and zero the indicator, then, pry the assembly to the opposite side and read the indicator.

NOTE: Do not zero or read the indicator while prying.

4. The amount read on the indicator is the shim thickness that should be added to arrive at the zero preload and zero endplay. Repeat the procedure to ensure accuracy and adjust if necessary; shims are available in thicknesses from 0.080–0.110 in. in increments of 0.002 in.

5. When the sideplay is eliminated, a slight bearing drag will be noticed. Install the bearing caps and tighten the bearing cap bolts to with 85 ft. lbs. torque.

6. Attach the dial indicator to the axle housing and check the ring gear mounting face of the differential case for runout; runout should not exceed 0.002 in.

7. Remove the case from the housing. Retain the shims used to adjust the sideplay.

DIFFERENTIAL AND BEARING PRELOAD

NOTE: The differential bearings must be preloaded to compensate for heat and loads during operation. The differential bearings are preloaded by increasing the shim pack thickness at each side of the differential by 0.004 in. for a total of 0.008 in.

1. Remove the differential assembly from the housing. Be sure to keep the differential bearing shim packs together for the proper assembly. Do not distort the shims in the axle housing bearing bores.

2. Install the differential bearing cups on the differential bearings. The cups should cover the differential bearing rollers completely. Position the differential assembly in the housing so the bearings just start into the housing bearing bores.

NOTE: Slightly tipping the bearing cups will ease starting them into the bores. Also keep the differential assembly square in the housing during installation and push it in as far as possible.

3. Tap the outer edge of the bearing cups until the differential is seated in the housing.

4. Install the differential bearing caps. Position the caps accordingly to the alignment punch marks made at disassembly. Tighten the bearing cap bolts with 85 ft. lbs. torque. Preloading the differential bearings may change the backlash setting. Check and correct the backlash, if necessary.

5. Install the propeller shaft, aligning the index marks made at disassembly. Install the axle shafts, bearings, seals and brake support plates. Fill the rear axle with the specified axle lubricant.

6. Check and adjust the axle shaft endplay, if necessary. Adjust the endplay at the left side of the axle shaft only. Install the hubs, drums and wheels.

Lower the vehicle and road test the vehicle to check the rear axle assembly for proper operation.

DANA–8½ INCH RING GEAR AXLE

Disassembly

DIFFERENTIAL

1. Remove the housing cover and drain the lubricant.

2. Using an axle spreader tool, mount it onto the axle housing and spread the housing enough to remove the differential.

3. Using a dial indicator, measure the amount the opening is being spread; do not spread the housing more than 0.015 in. (0.38mm), for damage to the housing may occur.

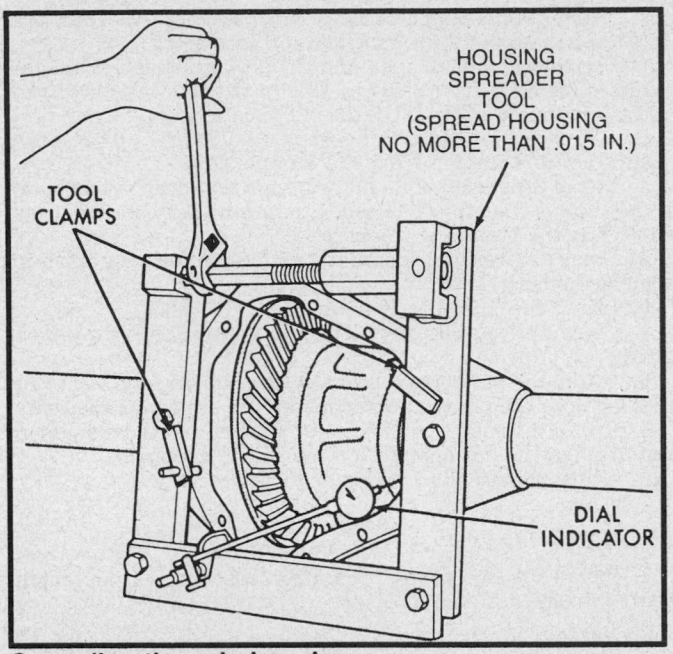

Spreading the axle housing

4. Mark the differential bearing caps for reassembly purposes.
5. Loosen the bearing caps until 2–3 threads are engaged.
6. Using a prybar, pry the differential loose.
7. Remove the bearing caps and the differential.
8. Mount the differential into a vise.
9. Remove and discard the ring gear bolts; they are not reusable.
10. Using a brass drift and a hammer, tap the ring gear from the differential.

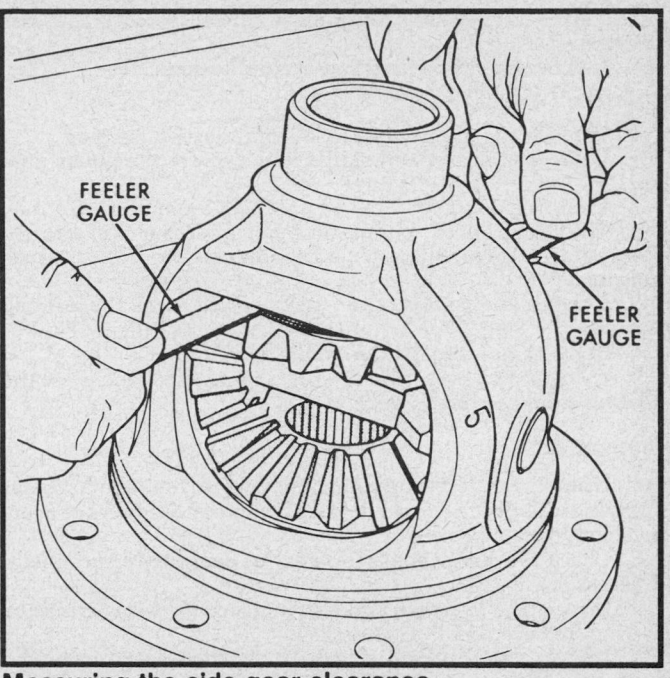

Measuring the side gear clearance

11. Using a differential bearing puller, press the differential bearings from the differential.
12. Remove the differential bearing shims.
13. Using 2 sets of feeler gauges, insert them between each side of the side gear thrust washer and differential case and measure the side gear clearance; the clearance should not exceed 0.007 in. (0.18mm). Replace both thrust washers, if the clearance exceeds the tolerance.
14. Remove the pinion shaft lockpin and pinion shaft.

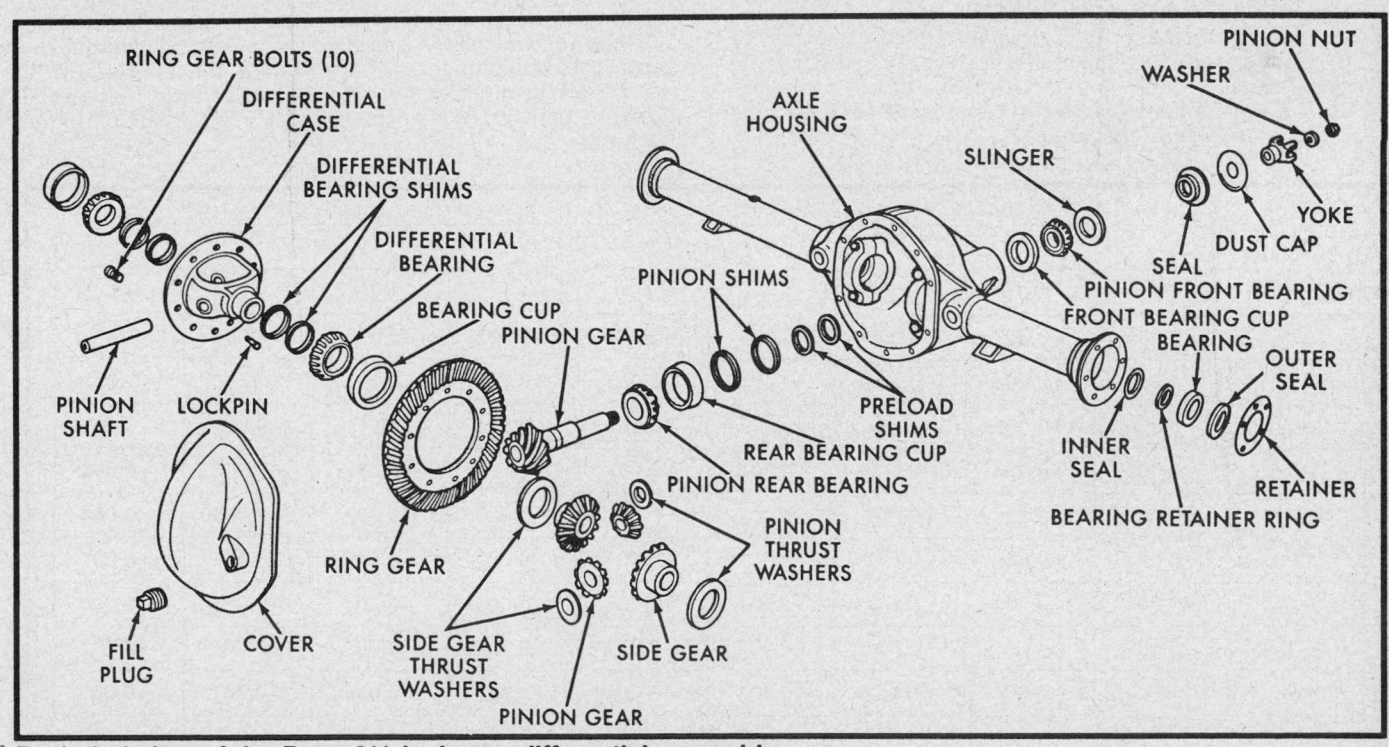

Exploded view of the Dana 8½ inch rear differential assembly

15. Rotate the pinions to remove them through the case opening.

16. Remove the side gears and thrust washers.

PINION GEAR

1. Remove the differential case from the axle housing.

2. Using a pinion yoke holding tool, remove the pinion gear nut.

3. Using a pinion yoke holder tool and a pinion puller tool, press the yoke from the pinion gear. Remove the pinion washer.

4. Using a soft mallet, drive the pinion gear from the axle housing.

5. Remove the pinion gear, the bearings and the preload spacers.

6. Remove and discard the pinion seal.

7. Using a shop press and the bearing removal tool, press the bearing from the pinion gear.

Inspection

1. Clean the differential components in solvent and use compressed air to dry them; do not use compressed air on the bearings, only shop towels.

2. Check the components for wear or damage; replace them, if necessary.

3. Inspect the bearings and bearing cups for wear, cracks or scoring; replace them, if necessary.

4. Inspect the differential side and pinion gears for wear, cracks or chips; replace them, if necessary.

5. Inspect the ring and pinion gears for wear and/or damage; replace them, if necessary.

6. Inspect the differential case for cracks or damage; replace it, if necessary.

Assembly

PINION GEAR

1. Make sure the ring and pinion are a matched set.

2. Measure the thickness of the original pinion shim and note the variance on the pinion gear.

3. Perform the following procedure to determine the pinion starter shim thickness:

   a. If the original ring and pinion are being installed, use the original shim.

   b. If a replacement gear set is being installed, determine the best starter shim thickness.

c. Refer to the pinion variance chart and observe where the old and new pinion marking column intersect.

d. If the old pinion is +1 and the new pinion is −3, the intersecting figure is +0.004 in. (0.10mm); add this amount to the original shim. Or, if the old pinion is −3 and the new pinion is −2, the intersecting figure is −0.001 in. (−0.025mm); subtract this amount from the original shim.

4. Install the starter shim in the pinion rear bearing cup bore; if the shim is chamfer on one side, position the chamfered side so it faces the bottom of the bore.

5. Using a driver tool, install the pinion rear bearing cup into the axle housing.

6. Install the front bearing cup.

7. Using a shop press, press the rear bearing onto the pinion gear.

8. Install the pinion gear into the axle housing and the front bearing onto the pinion; do not install the slinger or the seal.

9. Install the yoke, the pinion nut washer and the old pinion nut; tighten the nut enough to remove the endplay.

10. Adjust the backlash and gear tooth contact.

DIFFERENTIAL

1. Install the side gears, the thrust washers and the pinion gears into the differential case.

NOTE: Be sure to install new side gear thrust washers, if the clearance measured at disassembly exceeded 0.007 in. (0.18mm).

2. Using 2 sets of feeler gauges, insert them between each side of the side gear thrust washer and differential case and measure the side gear clearance; the clearance should not exceed 0.007 in. (0.18mm). Replace both thrust washers, if the clearance exceeds the tolerance.

3. Install the pinion shaft and lockpin into the case.

4. Assemble the original differential bearing shim packs, then, remove approximately 0.20 in. (0.50mm) shim thickness from each pack; the remaining shims will serve as a starter shim pack.

5. Install the starter shim packs and bearing onto the case.

6. Align and install the ring gear. Using new bolts, torque the ring gear-to-differential case bolts to 55 ft. lbs. (75 Nm).

7. Install the spreader tool onto the axle housing. Using a dial indicator, spread the axle housing no more than 0.015 in. (0.38mm).

OLD PINION MARKING	NEW PINION MARKING								
	−4	−3	−2	−1	+0	+1	+2	+3	+4
+4	+0.008	+0.007	+0.006	+0.005	+0.004	+0.003	+0.002	+0.001	0
+3	+0.007	+0.006	+0.005	+0.004	+0.003	+0.002	+0.001	0	−0.001
+2	+0.006	+0.005	+0.004	+0.003	+0.002	+0.001	0	−0.001	−0.002
+1	+0.005	+0.004	+0.003	+0.002	+0.001	0	−0.001	−0.002	−0.003
0	+0.004	+0.003	+0.002	+0.001	0	−0.001	−0.002	−0.003	−0.004
−1	+0.003	+0.002	+0.001	0	−0.001	−0.002	−0.003	−0.004	−0.005
−2	+0.002	+0.001	0	−0.001	−0.002	−0.003	−0.004	−0.005	−0.006
−3	+0.001	0	−0.001	−0.002	−0.003	−0.004	−0.005	−0.006	−0.007
−4	0	−0.001	−0.002	−0.003	−0.004	−0.005	−0.006	−0.007	−0.008

NOTE: **Do not spread the housing more than 0.015 in. (0.038mm), for damage may occur to the case.**

8. Install the differential; it may be necessary to tap the differential bearing cups, with a soft hammer, to seat them.

9. Install the differential bearing caps and torque the bolts to 57 ft. lbs. (77 Nm).

10. Remove the spreader tool and dial indicator.

11. Adjust the ring and pinion gear.

12. Using silicone sealant, apply a bead of it to the axle housing. Install the cover and torque the bolts to 35 ft. lbs. (47 Nm).

Adjustment

RING AND PINION

1. Using yellow ferrous oxide compound, coat the drive and coast sides of the ring gear teeth.

2. Install the differential and tighten the bearing caps.

3. Using a dial indicator, mount it onto the housing, position the stylus against the drive side of one ring gear tooth; be sure the stylus is at a right angle to the tooth.

4. Move the ring gear toward the dial indicator and zero it.

5. Move the ring gear away from the pinion until the backlash is 0.005–0.009 in. (0.1 3–0.23mm). Insert shims or feeler gauges between the differential bearings and housing to maintain the backlash during the remainder of the adjustment.

NOTE: **To increase the backlash, subtract shims from the ring gear side of the case. To decrease the backlash, add shims to the ring gear side of the case.**

6. Move the dial indicator aside and recoat any necessary ring gear teeth with the ferrous oxide compound.

7. Rotate the ring gear a complete revolution in both directions and note the tooth contact pattern imprinted in the compound.

8. Adjustments can be made as follows:

   a. Decreasing the backlash moves the drive and coast side pattern slightly lower and toward the toe.

   b. Increasing the backlash move the drive and coast side pattern slightly higher and toward the heel.

   c. A thicker pinion shim moves the pinion closer to the ring gear. The drive pattern moves deeper on the tooth and slightly towards the heel.

   d. A thinner pinion shim moves the pinion away from the ring gear. Drive pattern moves toward the top of the tooth and toward the heel. Coast pattern moves toward the top of the tooth and slightly toward the toe.

9. Remove the differential and pinion gear.

10. Change the pinion and differential shims, as necessary.

11. Install the pinion and differential.

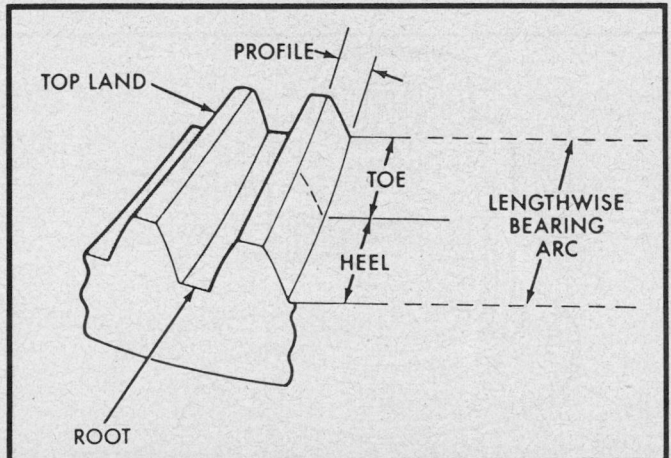

View of the gear tooth nomenclature

12. Recheck the tooth contact pattern and backlash; adjust, as necessary.

PINION BEARING PRELOAD

1. Using a yoke holding tool, torque the pinion nut to a minimum of 210 ft. lbs. (285 Nm).

2. Using an inch lb. torque wrench, measure the torque necessary to rotate the pinion; the torque should be 20–40 inch lbs. (2–5 Nm).

NOTE: **If the torque is not correct, add shims to increase the preload or subtract shims to decrease the preload.**

3. Remove the pinion nut, the washer and the yoke after setting the preload; be sure to discard the old nut.

4. Lubricate the new pinion oil seal lip and install the seal into the axle housing.

5. Install the yoke, the washer and a new pinion nut; torque the nut to a minimum of 210 ft. lbs. (285 Nm).

DIFFERENTIAL BEARING PRELOAD

1. Remove the differential bearing from the side of the case opposite the ring gear.

2. Add a 0.015 in (0.38mm) shim the shim pack on the side of the case.

3. Reistall the bearing onto the case.

4. Clean the ferrous oxide compound from the ring and pinion gears, then, lubricate the differential gears and bearings with axle lubricant.

5. Install the spreader tool onto the axle housing. Using a dial indicator, spread the axle housing no more than 0.015 in. (0.38mm).

NOTE: **Do not spread the housing more than 0.15 in. (0.38mm), for damage may occur to the case.**

6. Install the differential; it may be necessary to tap the differential bearing cups, with a soft hammer, to seat them.

7. Install the differential bearing caps and torque the bolts to 57 ft. lbs. (77 Nm).

8. Recheck the backlash; it should be 0.005–0.009 in. (0.13–0.23mm). If necessary, reset the backlash.

TRAC-LOK DIFFERENTIAL

Operational Test

If a noisy or rough operation such as a chatter occurs when turning corners, the most probable cause of this chatter or noise is incorrect or contaminated lubricant. Before removing the Trac-Lok unit for repair, drain, flush and refill the axle with the specified lubricant. A complete lubricant drain and refill with the specified fluid will usually correct the chatter problem. A quick operational test of the Trac-Lok differential can be done easily by performing the following steps.

1. Position one wheel on solid dry pavement and the opposite wheel on ice, mud grease or a similar low traction surface.

2. Gradually, increase the engine rpm to obtain the maximum traction prior to a breakaway. The ability to move the vehicle effectively will demonstrate the proper performance.

NOTE: **If the test is performed on extremely slick surfaces such as ice or grease coated surfaces, some question may exist as to proper performance. In these extreme cases, a properly performing Trac-Lok will provide greater pulling power by lightly applying the parking brake.**

Disassembly

DIFFERENTIAL

1. Remove the differential from the axle housing as previous-

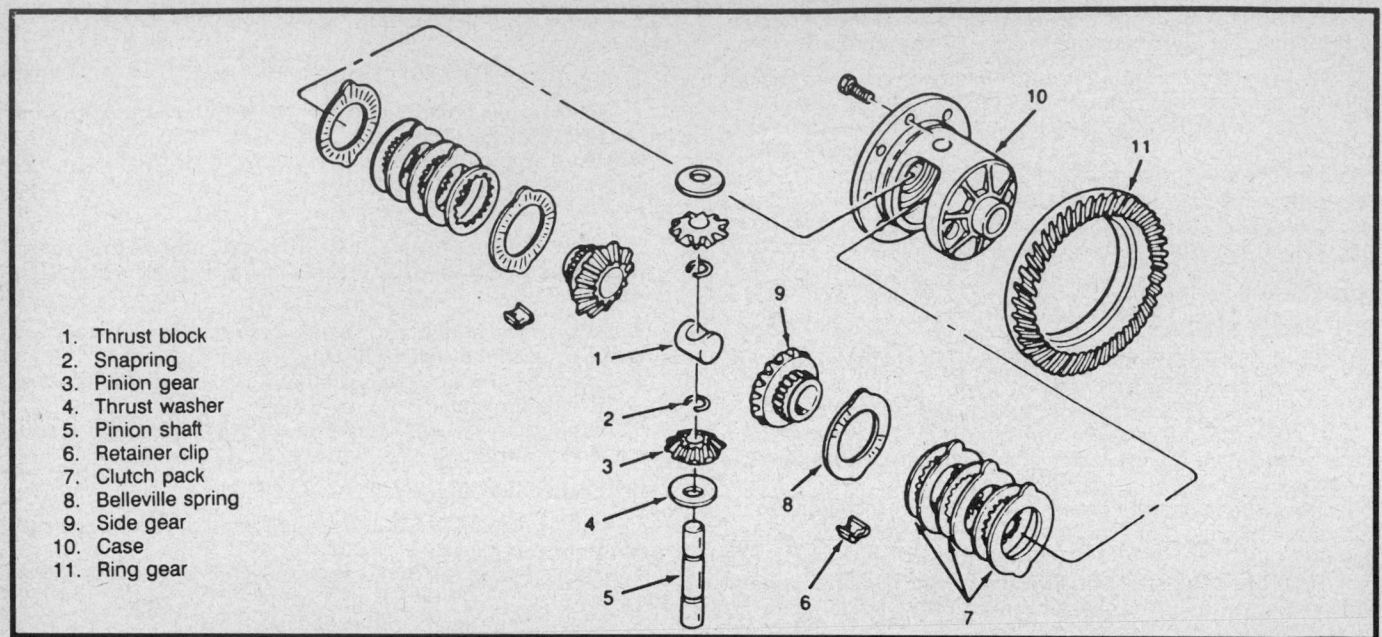

1. Thrust block
2. Snapring
3. Pinion gear
4. Thrust washer
5. Pinion shaft
6. Retainer clip
7. Clutch pack
8. Belleville spring
9. Side gear
10. Case
11. Ring gear

Exploded view of the Trac-Loc differential

ly outlined in this section. Install one axle shaft in the vise with the spline end facing upward and tighten the vise.

2. Do not allow more than 2¾ in. of the shaft to extend above the top of the vise. This prevents the shaft from fully entering the side gear, causing interference with the step plate tool used to remove the differential gears.

3. Mount the differential case on the axle shaft with the ring gear bolt heads facing upward. Place some shop towels under the ring gear to protect the gear when it is removed from the case.

4. Remove and discard the ring gear bolts. Remove the ring gear from the case, using a rawhide hammer. Remove the differential case from the axle shaft and remove the ring gear and remount the differential case on the axle shaft.

5. Use suitable tools to disengage the snaprings from the pinion mate shaft. Place a shop towel on the opposite opening of the case to prevent the snaprings from flying out of the case. Remove the pinion mate shaft using a hammer and brass drift.

NOTE: A special gear rotating tool J–23781–3 or equivalent, is required to perform the following steps. The tool consists of 3 parts; the gear rotating tool, forcing screw and step plate.

6. Install step plate tool into the lower differential side gear. Position the pawl end of the gear rotating tool onto the step plate.

7. Insert the forcing screw tool through the top of the case and thread it into the gear rotating tool. Before using the forcing screw tool, apply a small amount of grease to the centering hole in the step plate and oil the threads of the forcing screw.

8. Center the forcing screw in the step plate and tighten the screw to move the differential side gears away from the differential pinion gears. Remove the differential pinion gear thrust washers using a feeler gauge or a shim stock of 0.030 in. thickness. Insert the feeler gauge or shim stock between the washer and the case and withdraw the shim stock with the thrust washer.

9. Tighten the forcing screw until a slight movement of the differential pinion gear is observed. Insert the pawl end of the gear rotating tool between the teeth of one differential side gear.

10. Pull the handle of the tool to rotate the side gears and pin-

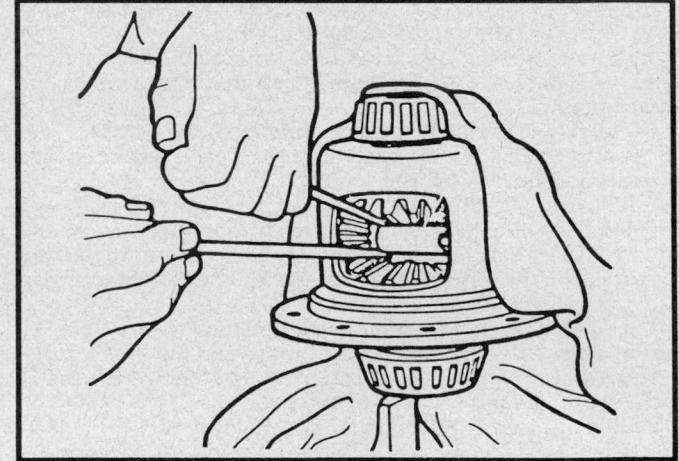

Removing the snapring from the pinion mate shaft

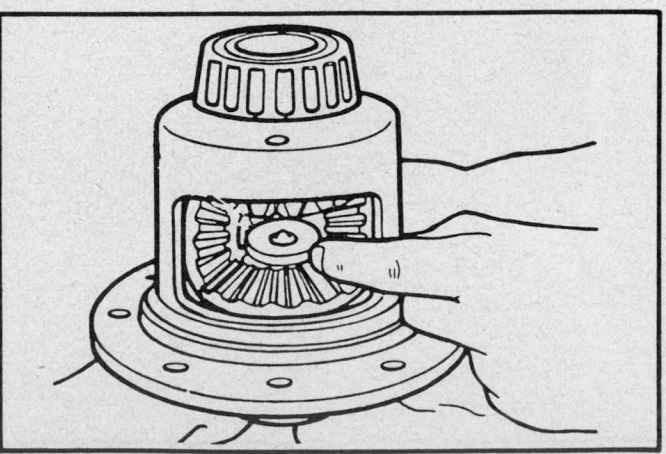

Install the step plate tool

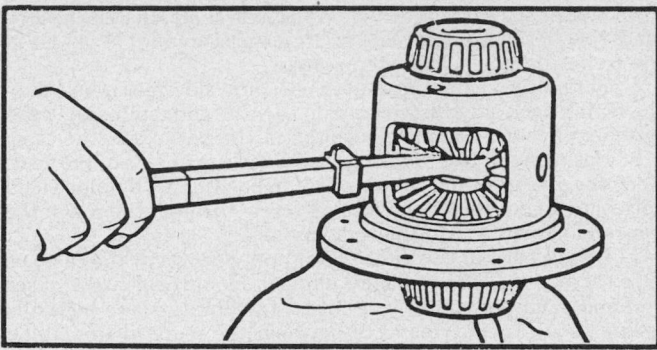

Install the gear rotating tool

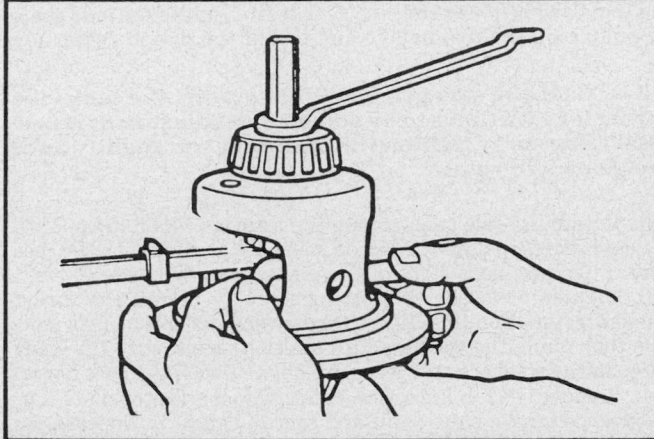

Removing the pinion gear thrust washers

ion gears. Remove the pinion gears as they appear in the case opening. It could be necessary to adjust the tension applied on the belleville springs by the forcing screw before the gears can be rotated in the case.

11. Retain the upper side gear and clutch pack in the case by placing a hand on the bottom of the rotating tool while removing the forcing screw. Remove the rotating tool, upper side gear and clutch pack.

12. Remove the differential case from the axle shaft. Invert the case with the flange or ring gear side up and remove the step plate tool, lower the side gear and clutch pack from the case. Remove the retainer clips from both the clutch packs to allow separation of the plates and discs.

Inspection

If any member of either clutch pack shows evidence of excessive wear or scoring, the complete clutch pack must be replaced on both sides.

1. Thoroughly, clean each part in solvent.

2. Towel dry bearings or allow them to air dry, do not use compressed air to dry bearings as damage might result. Dry all other parts with compressed air or shop towels. If the parts are not to be assembled immediately, cover them to prevent dust or dirt contamination.

3. Inspect the housing for cracks and sand holes. Replace the housing if it is cracked or porous. Check for burrs and deep scratches or nicks on the gasket and oil seal surfaces. An oil stone or fine tooth file may be used to remove nicks or burrs.

4. Inspect the bearing cup bores for nicks or burrs that may have been created during bearing cup removal.

5. Inspect and clean the axle tubes. Inspect the vent to be sure it is not obstructed.

6. Check housing for bent or loose tubes or other physical damage.

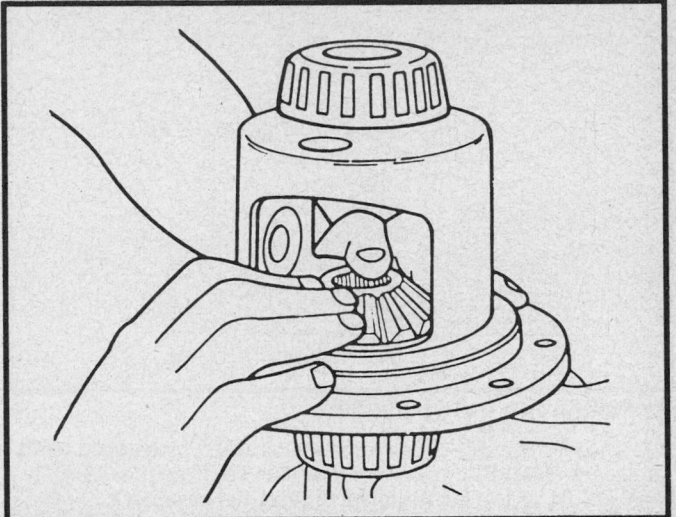

Installing the clutch packs

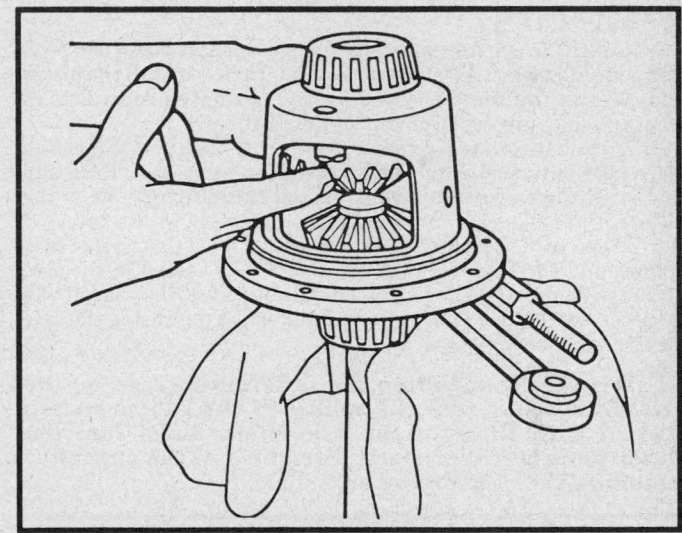

Keeping the side gear rotating tool in position

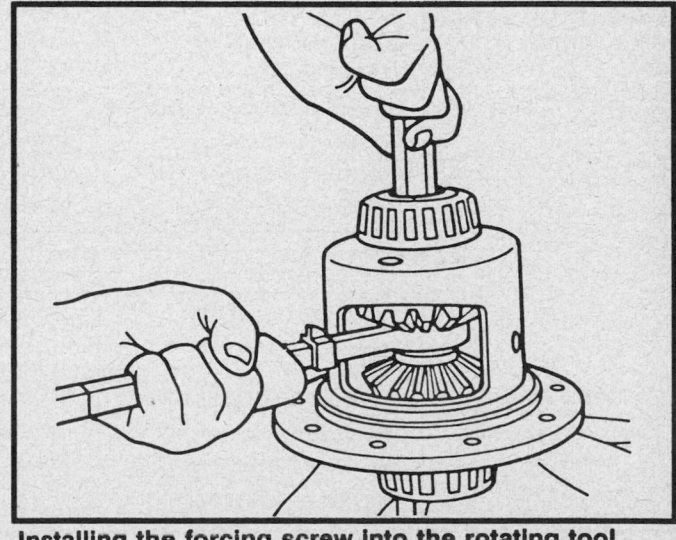

Installing the forcing screw into the rotating tool

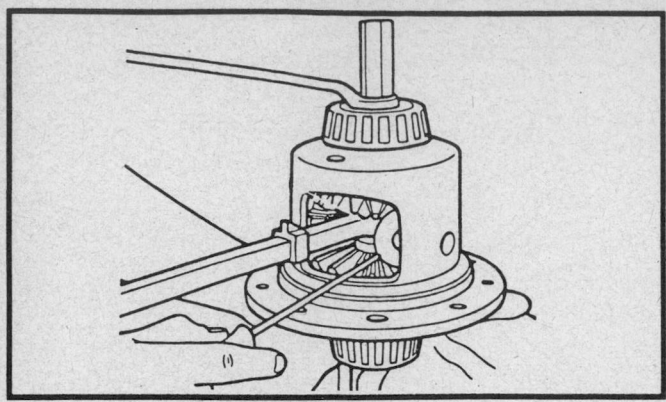

Installing the thrust washers

7. Inspect the side gears for worn, cracked or chipped teeth. The gears should fit snugly on the axle shaft splines. Also, inspect the fit of the gears in the differential case bore.

Assembly

DIFFERENTIAL

1. Lubricate all the differential components with the specified gear lubricant. Assemble the clutch packs. Install the plates and discs in the same position as when removed regardless of whether they are replacement or original parts.

2. Install the clutch retainer clips on the ears of the clutch plates. Be sure the clutch packs are completely assembled and seated on the ears of the plates. Install the clutch packs on the differential side gears and install the assembly in the case.

3. Make sure the clutch pack stays assembled on the side gear splines and the retainer clips are completely seated in the case pockets. To prevent the pack from falling out of the case, it will be necessary to hold it in place by hand while mounting the case on the axle shaft.

NOTE: When installing the differential case on the axle shaft, make sure the splines of the side gears are aligned with those of the axle shaft. Make sure the clutch pack is still properly assembled in the case after installing the case on the axle shaft.

4. Mount the case assembly on the axle shaft. Install the step plate tool in the side gear and apply a small amount of grease in the centering hole of the step plate.

5. Install the remaining clutch pack and side gear. Make sure the clutch pack stays assembled on the side gear splines and the retainer clips are completely seated in the pockets of the case.

6. Position the gear rotating tool in the upper side of the gear. Keep the side gear and rotating tool in position by holding them with your hand. Insert the forcing screw through the top of the case and thread it into the rotating tool.

7. Install both of the differential pinion gears in the case; be sure the bores of the gears are aligned. Hold the gears in place by hand. Tighten the forcing screw to compress the belleville springs and provide clearance between the teeth of the pinion gears and the side gears.

8. Position the pinion gears in the case and insert the rotating tool pawl between the side gear teeth. Rotate the side gears by pulling on the tool handle and install the pinion gears.

NOTE: If the side gears will not rotate, the belleville spring load will have to be adjusted. If adjustment is necessary, loosen or tighten the forcing screw slightly until the gears will rotate.

9. Rotate the side gears, using the rotating tool handle, until the shaft bores in both the pinion gears are aligned with the case bore. Lubricate both sides of the pinion gear thrust washers.

10. Tighten or loosen the forcing screw to permit the thrust washer installation. Install the thrust washers and using a suitable tool, guide the washers into position. Make sure the shaft bores in the washers and gears are aligned with the case bores.

11. Remove the forcing screw, rotating tool and step plate. Lubricate the pinion mate shaft and seat the shaft in the case. Be sure the snapring grooves in the shaft are exposed to allow the snapring installation.

12. Install the pinion mate shaft snaprings, remove the case from the axle shaft and install the ring gear on the case. Be sure to use replacement ring bolts only; do not reuse the original bolts.

13. Align the ring gear and case bolt holes and install the ring gear bolts finger tight only. Remove the case on the axle shaft and tighten the bolts evenly to the proper torque specifications.

14. Install the differential assembly into the axle housing.

Component	Service Set-To Torque	Service Recheck Torque
Wheel Lug Nuts	102 N·m (75 ft-lbs)	81-122 N·m (60-90 ft-lbs)
Brake Support Plate Nuts	43 N·m (32 ft-lbs)	34-54 N·m (25-40 ft-lbs)
U-Joint Strap Bolts	19 N·m (170 in-lbs)	15-23 N·m (140-200 in-lbs)
Differential Bearing Cap Bolts	77 N·m (57 ft-lbs)	64-91 N·m (47-67 ft-lbs)
Ring Gear-to-Case Bolts	70 N·m (52 ft-lbs)	57-88 N·m (42-65 ft-lbs)
Rear Axle Cover Screws	19 N·m (170 in-lbs)	17-21 N·m (150-190 in-lbs)
Rear Axle Filler Plug	34 N·m (25 ft-lbs)	27-41 N·m (20-30 ft-lbs)

Component	Service Set-To Torque	Service Recheck Torque
Axle Housing Cover Bolts	19 N·m (170 in-lbs)	17-21 N·m (150-190 in-lbs)
Brake Tube-to-Rear Wheel Cylinder	11 N·m (97 in-lbs)	10-12 N·m (90-105 in-lbs)
Differential Bearing Cap Bolts	115 N·m (85 ft-lbs)	102-129 N·m (75-95 ft-lbs)
Ring Gear-to-Case Bolt	142 N·m (105 ft-lbs)	135-149 N·m (95-115 ft-lbs)
Rear Brake Support Plate Bolts	43 N·m (32 ft-lbs)	34-54 N·m (25-40 ft-lbs)
Universal Joint Strap Bolts	19 N·m (170 in-lbs)	16-22 N·m (140-200 in-lbs)

Torque specifications for the Trac-Lock differential

GROUP INDEX

ALPHABETICAL INDEX

LABOR — 1 TUNE UP 1 — LABOR

	(Factory Time)	Chilton Time
Compression Test		
Four		
S-series		.6
Astro		.9
Six		.9
V-6		
Vans-Astro		.9
All other models		.7
V-8		1.4
Diesel		1.3

Engine Tune Up, (Electronic Ignition)
Includes: Test battery and clean connections. Tighten manifold and carburetor mounting bolts. Check engine compression, clean and adjust or renew spark plugs. Test resistance of spark plug cables. Inspect distributor cap and rotor. Adjust distributor air gap. Check vacuum advance operation. Reset ignition timing. Adjust idle mixture and idle speed. Service air cleaner. Inspect and adjust drive belts. Inspect choke operation and adjust or free up. Check operation of EGR valve.

	(Factory Time)	Chilton Time
Four–1986-90		
S-series		1.5
Astro		1.8
Six–1986-90		
Vans		2.5
All other models		2.3
V-6–1986-90		
Vans-Astro		2.3
All other models		2.0
V-8–1986-90		
Vans		3.4
All other models		3.0
w/A.C. add		.5

LABOR — 2 IGNITION SYSTEM 2 — LABOR

GASOLINE ENGINES

Spark Plugs, Clean and Reset or Renew

Vans-Astro-Safari
	(Factory Time)	Chilton Time
Four (.6)		.8
Six (.4)		*.8
V-6 (.6)		.8
V-8 (.9)		1.3

All Other Models
Four (.3)		.5
Six (.3)		.6
V-6 (.4)		.6
V-8 (.6)		.9
*w/A.C. add (.5)		.5

Ignition Timing, Reset
All models (.3)		.5

Distributor, Renew
Includes: Reset ignition timing.

Vans-Astro-Safari
Four (.6)		.9
Six (.3)		*.9
V-6 (.8)		1.1
V-8 (.6)		1.1

All Other Models
Four		
eng code A (.3)		.5
eng code Y (.6)		.9
eng code E (.6)		.9
Six (.6)		.8
V-6 (.6)		1.0
V-8 (.4)		.6
*w/A.C. add (.5)		.5

Distributor, R&R and Recondition
Includes: Reset ignition timing.

Vans-Astro-Safari
Four (.9)		1.5
Six (.5)		*1.4
V-6 (1.1)		1.8
V-8 (.8)		1.6

All Other Models
Four		
eng code A (.6)		1.0
eng code Y (.9)		1.5
eng code E (.9)		1.5
Six (.8)		1.5
V-6 (.9)		1.5
V-8 (.9)		1.1
*w/A.C. add (.5)		.5

Distributor Cap and/or Rotor, Renew

Vans-Astro-Safari
Four (.3)		.5
Six (.4)		*.6
V-6 (.5)		.7

V-8 (.5)		.7
All Other Models		
All engs (.3)		.5
*w/A.C. add (.5)		.5

Ignition Coil, Renew
Includes: Test coil.

Four
eng code Y (2.0)		2.8
eng code E (.6)		.9
eng code A (.3)		.5
Six (.6)		*.8
V-6		
S-series (.7)		1.0
Vans-Astro-Safari (.5)		.8
All other models (.4)		.7
V-8 (.5)		.8
*w/A.C. add (.5)		.5

Vacuum Advance Assembly, Renew
Includes: Adjust dwell and timing.

Vans
Six (.7)		*1.1
V-6 (.3)		.6
V-8 (1.0)		1.4

All Other Models
Four		
eng code A (.4)		.7
eng code Y (.6)		.9
eng code E (.6)		.9
Six (.5)		.6
V-6 (.6)		.9
V-8 (.4)		.8
*w/A.C. add (.5)		.5

Vacuum Advance Solenoid, Renew
All models (.2)		.3

Spark Plug Wires, Renew

Vans
Six (.3)		*.7
V-6 (.3)		.6
V-8 (.7)		1.2

All Other Models
Four		
S-series (.3)		.5
Astro-Safari (.5)		.7
Six (.5)		.6
V-6 (.5)		.8
V-8 (.5)		.8
*w/A.C. add (.5)		.5

Ignition Switch, Renew
All models (.6)		1.0

Ignition Switch Lock Cylinder, Renew
All models (.4)		.7
w/Tilt whl add (.1)		.1

Recode cyl add (.3)		.3
Vans, add		.2

ELECTRONIC IGNITION

Distributor Module, Renew

Vans
Six (.3)		*.7
V-6 (.5)		.8
V-8 (.5)		.8

All Other Models
Four (.3)		.6
Six (.3)		.6
V-6 (.6)		.9
V-8 (.3)		.6
*w/A.C. add (.5)		.5

Distributor Hall Effect Switch, Renew
S-series (.5)		.8
Astro (.7)		1.0

ESC Detonation Sensor, Renew (Knock Sensor)
10-30 Series (.7)		1.0
All other models (.6)		.9

ESC Module, Renew
S-series (.9)		1.2
All other models (.5)		.7

Distributor Capacitor and/or Module Wiring Harness, Renew

Vans
Six (.4)		*.8
V-6 (.5)		.8
V-8 (.5)		.9

All Other Models
Four (.4)		.7
Six (.4)		.7
V-6 (.6)		.8
V-8 (.5)		.7
*w/A.C. add (.5)		.5

Distributor Pick-Up Coil and/or Pole Piece, Renew
Includes: R&R distributor and reset ignition timing.

Vans
Six (.5)		*1.1
V-6 (.8)		1.3
V-8 (.8)		1.3

All Other Models
Four		
eng code A (.3)		.6
eng code Y (1.0)		1.5
Six (.5)		.7
V-6		
S-series (.7)		1.1
Astro-Safari (.9)		1.3

LABOR   2   IGNITION SYSTEM   2   LABOR

(Factory Time)	Chilton Time	(Factory Time)	Chilton Time	(Factory Time)	Chilton Time
V-8 (.6)	.8	**Fast Idle Solenoid, Renew**		**Glow Plug Module, Renew**	
*w/A.C. add (.5)	.5	Vans (.5)	.7	All models (.3)	.5
		All other models (.3)	.4	**Glow Plug Control Switch, Renew**	
DIESEL IGNITION COMPONENTS				Vans (.5)	.7
Coolant Fast Idle Temperature Switch, Renew		**Glow Plugs, Renew**		All other models (.3)	.4
		All models			
All models (.3)	.4	Four (.5)	.7	**Fast Idle Relay, Renew**	
		V-8		All models (.3)	.4
Glow Plug Relay, Renew		one	.4	**Starter Lockout Relay, Renew**	
Vans (.4)	.6	one-each bank	.7	All models (.2)	.3
All other models (.2)	.3	all-both banks	1.3		

LABOR   3   FUEL SYSTEM   3   LABOR

(Factory Time)	Chilton Time	(Factory Time)	Chilton Time	(Factory Time)	Chilton Time
GASOLINE ENGINES		2 bbl (.7)	1.0	**Fuel Gauge (Dash), Renew**	
Fuel Pump, Test		4 bbl (.8)	1.1	1986	
Includes: Disconnect line at carburetor, attach pressure gauge.		To perform C.C.C. system test add (.5)	1.0	S-series (.3)	.5
All models	.3	**Fuel Filter, Renew**		Astro-Safari (.9)	1.4
		Vans (.5)	.6	All other models (.5)	.9
Carburetor, Adjust (On Truck)		All other models (.3)	.4	1987-90	
Vans				S-series-Astro-Safari (.9)	1.4
Curb & Fast Idle (.5)	.6	**Anti-Dieseling or Idle Stop Solenoid, Renew**		Vans (.8)	1.3
Vacuum Break (.4)	.5	S-series (.5)	.7	C-K series (.5)	.8
Complete (1.3)	1.8	Vans (.4)	.5	R-V series (.7)	1.2
Accelerator Pump Dual Capacity Solenoid, Renew		All other models (.2)	.3		
Vans (.8)	1.1	**Automatic Choke Vacuum Diaphragm, Renew (One)**		**Intake Manifold, Renew**	
Choke Coil, Cover and/or Gasket, Renew		S-series-Astro-Safari		Six	
Vans (1.1)	1.5	Rochester (.6)	.8	Vans (2.7)	3.9
Fast Idle Solenoid, Renew		Isuzu (.9)	1.2	All other models (1.2)	1.8
Vans (.6)	.8	Vans (.9)	1.2	w/P.S. add (.5)	.5
Fast Idle Actuator Vacuum Switching Valve, Renew		All other models (.4)	.6		
Vans (.3)	.5	**Carburetor Base Gasket EFE Heater, Renew**		**Intake and Exhaust Manifold Gaskets, Renew**	
Fast Idle Actuator, Renew		S-series (.6)	1.0	Six	
Vans (.3)	.5	**Fuel Pump, Renew**		Vans (2.5)	3.6
Throttle Return Control Actuator, Renew		Four (.6)	*.9	All other models (1.4)	2.0
Vans (.5)	.7	Six (.5)	.7	w/P.S. add (.5)	.5
Carburetor, Renew		V-6 (.6)	*.9		
Includes: Necessary adjustments.		V-8 (1.0)	1.4	**Intake Manifold or Gasket, Renew**	
S-series		w/A.I.R. add (.3)	.3	Four	
Rochester (.6)	1.0	*Astro-Safari, add	.4	eng code A (1.7)	2.5
Isuzu (.8)	1.2			eng code Y (1.9)	2.7
Astro-Safari (1.2)	1.7	**Fuel Tank, Renew**		eng code E	
Vans (1.0)	1.4	Includes: Drain and refill tank.		S-series	
All other models (.6)	1.0	**Cab Mount**		4X2 (1.8)	2.5
To perform C.C.C. system test add (.5)	1.0	All models (.5)	1.0	4X4 (2.3)	3.2
		Frame Mount		Astro-Safari (2.2)	3.1
Carburetor, R&R and Clean or Recondition		side tank-each (1.2)	1.7	w/Cruise control add	.2
Includes: Necessary adjustments.		Pick-Ups (1.0)	1.6	Six-All models (2.7)	3.9
Vans		Vans (1.0)	1.6	V-6	
1 bbl (2.5)	3.2	Suburban & Blazer (.9)	1.4	1986	
2 bbl (2.5)	3.2	Jimmy (.9)	1.4	S-series (3.9)	5.5
4 bbl (2.7)	3.5	S-series		Astro-Safari (2.2)	3.1
All Other Models		rear (1.1)	1.7	exc Vans (2.1)	3.0
1 bbl (2.3)	3.0	left (1.3)	1.9	Vans (2.3)	3.3
2 bbl (2.3)	3.0	Astro-Safari (1.3)	1.9	w/A.C. add (.2)	.2
4 bbl (2.5)	3.2	w/Fuel tank shield add (.3)	.4	w/C.C.C. add (.2)	.2
To perform C.C.C. system test add (.5)	1.0			1987-90	
		Fuel Gauge (Tank), Renew		eng code R (3.0)	4.2
Needle Valve and Seat, Renew		Includes: Drain and refill tank.		eng code Z	
Includes: R&R carb air horn and floats. Adjust idle speed.		**Cab Mounted Tank**		S-series (2.3)	3.3
Vans		All models (.5)	.9	Astro-Safari (2.8)	3.9
1 bbl (1.1)	1.5	**Frame Mounted Tank**		Vans (2.0)	2.9
2 bbl (.8)	1.2	side tank-each (1.0)	1.5	C-K series (2.1)	3.0
4 bbl (.9)	1.3	Pick-Ups (1.3)	1.9	w/A.C. add (.2)	.2
S-series		Vans (1.1)	1.7	w/AIR add (.1)	.1
Rochester (.9)	1.3	Suburban & Blazer (.9)	1.3	w/Cruise control add (.2)	.2
Isuzu (.8)	1.2	Jimmy (.9)	1.3	w/A.T. add (.1)	.1
All Other Models		S-series		V-8-454 eng	
1 bbl (.5)	.9	rear (1.3)	1.8	All models (2.0)	2.7
		left (1.5)	2.0	V-8-All other engs	
		Astro-Safari (1.5)	2.0	exc Vans (1.7)	2.5
		w/Fuel tank shield add (.3)	.4	Vans (2.7)	3.9
				w/A.C. add (.2)	.2
				Renew manif add (.3)	.5

LABOR 3 FUEL SYSTEM 3 LABOR

	(Factory Time)	Chilton Time
FUEL INJECTION		
Fuel Filter Element, Renew		
C-K series (.3)		.5
R-V series (.3)		.5
Vans-Astro-Safari (.4)		.6
S-series		
4X2 (.4)		.6
4X4 (.5)		.7
Fuel Injectors, Clean (On Truck) (w/TBI or MFI)		
Includes: Hook up pressurized fuel injection cleaning equipment.		
All models		.5
Vans-Astro-Safari add		.2
Throttle Body, R&R or Renew		
1986		
Astro (.9)		1.3
S-series (.6)		1.1
All other models (.3)		.5
Renew throttle body kit		
add (.3)		.3
Renew fuel meter body add (.3)		.3
1987-90		
Astro-Safari (.6)		.9
S-series (.8)		1.1
All other models (.5)		.8
Renew throttle body add (.5)		.5
Throttle Body Fuel Meter Assy., and/or Gasket, Renew		
1986		
Vans-Astro-Safari (.6)		.8
S-series (.4)		.6
All other models (.6)		.8
1987-90		
Astro-Safari (.9)		1.1
S-series (.9)		1.1
Vans (.8)		1.0
All other models (.6)		.8
Throttle Position Switch, Renew		
Vans (1.0)		1.4
All other models (.5)		.8
Idle Air Control Valve, Renew		
1986		
Astro-Safari (.7)		1.0
S-series (.5)		.8
All other models (.5)		.8
1987-90		
Vans-Astro-Safari (.7)		1.0
S-series (.6)		.9
All other models (.5)		.8
Throttle Body Injector and/or Gasket, Renew		
1986		
Astro-Safari-one (.6)		.8
both (.6)		.9
S-series-one (.8)		1.2
both (.9)		1.3
All other models		
one (.4)		.6
both (.4)		.7
1987-90		
Vans-Astro-Safari		
one (.6)		.8
both (.6)		.9

	(Factory Time)	Chilton Time
S-series		
one (.7)		.9
both (.7)		1.0
All other models		
one (.4)		.6
both (.4)		.7
Minimum Idle Speed, Adjust		
1986		
Astro-Safari (.9)		1.2
S-series (.5)		.8
Vans (.7)		1.0
All other models (.3)		.4
1987-90		
Vans-Astro-Safari (.5)		.8
S-series (.6)		.9
All other models (.3)		.4
Fuel Pressure Regulator and/or Gaskets, Renew		
1986		
Vans-Astro-Safari (.7)		1.3
S-series (.7)		1.1
All other models (.5)		.7
1987-90		
Vans (.8)		1.2
Astro-Safari (.7)		1.1
S-series (.7)		1.1
All other models (.5)		.7
Fuel Pump, Renew (In Tank)		
Left Tank		
S-series (1.6)		2.3
All other models (1.3)		1.8
Rear Tank		
S-series (1.5)		2.0
All other models (1.2)		1.7
Right Tank		
All models (1.4)		1.9
Fuel Pump Relay, Renew		
Astro-Safari (.7)		.9
S-series (.5)		.7
All other models (.5)		.7
DIESEL ENGINE		
Air Cleaner, Service		
All models (.2)		.4
Air Intake Crossover, Renew		
All models (.3)		.5
Fuel Filter, Renew		
All models (.2)		.4
Idle Speed, Adjust		
All models (.2)		.4
Injection Timing, Check and Adjust		
All models (.9)		.9
Throttle Position Sensor, Renew		
All models (.5)		.7
Fuel Solenoid, Renew		
Vans (2.0)		*2.7
All other models (.5)		.7
*w/A.C. add (.2)		.2
Cold Advance Solenoid, Renew		
Vans (2.1)		*2.8
All other models (.6)		.8
*w/A.C. add (.2)		.2

	(Factory Time)	Chilton Time
Fuel Injection Head Seal, Renew		
Includes: Renew head and drive shaft seals. Renew governor weight retaining ring.		
All models		
5.7L eng (3.3)		4.7
6.2L eng		
Vans (4.0)		5.3
All other models (3.2)		4.1
Fuel Injection Pump, Renew		
Includes: Pressure and electrical tests. Adjust timing.		
All models		
2.2L eng (1.9)		2.7
5.7L eng (2.6)		3.5
6.2L eng		
Vans (3.8)		*4.9
All other models (3.3)		4.4
*w/A.C. add (.2)		.2
Fuel Return Lines (At Nozzles), Renew		
All models-one side (.3)		.5
both sides (.4)		.7
return hose (.2)		.3
w/A.C. add (.2)		.2
High Pressure Fuel Lines, Renew		
Includes: Flush lines.		
Four-one (.4)		.7
all (.5)		.8
V-8-one (1.7)		2.0
one-each bank (1.9)		2.2
all-both banks (2.2)		2.8
w/A.C. add (.2)		.2
Injector Nozzle and/or Seal, Renew		
Four		
one or all (.6)		1.0
V-8-one (.8)		1.2
one-each bank (1.0)		1.4
all-both banks (1.5)		3.0
w/A.C. add (.2)		.2
Clean nozzles add-each		.2
Fuel Supply Pump, Renew		
All models (.5)		.7
w/A.C. add (.2)		.2
Fuel Injection Pump Throttle Shaft Seal, Renew		
All models		
5.7L eng (.9)		1.3
6.2L eng		
Vans (2.0)		*2.5
All other models (1.7)		2.3
*w/A.C. add (.2)		.2
Injection Pump Adapter and/or Seal, Renew		
All models		
5.7L eng (1.9)		2.4
Locate new timing mark add (.1)		.1
Vacuum Pump, Renew		
Vans (.9)		1.6
All other models (.5)		.8
w/A.C. add (.2)		.2
Intake Manifold or Gasket, Renew		
All models		
2.2L eng (.7)		1.2
5.7L eng (2.7)		3.5
6.2L eng (1.6)		2.3
w/A.C. add (.2)		.2
Renew manif add (.2)		.5

LABOR 3A EMISSION CONTROLS 3A LABOR

	(Factory Time)	Chilton Time
GASOLINE ENGINES		
Emission Control Check		
Includes: Check and adjust engine idle speed, mixture and ignition timing.		
All models		.6

	(Factory Time)	Chilton Time
CRANKCASE EMISSION		
Positive Crankcase Ventilation Valve, Renew		
All models (.2)		.3
Crankcase Vent Filter, Renew		
All models (.2)		.3

	(Factory Time)	Chilton Time
AIR INJECTION REACTOR TYPE		
A.I.R. Air Pump Cleaner, Renew		
All models (.2)		.4
Air Pump, Renew		
Four (.4)		*.6

LABOR   3A   EMISSION CONTROLS 3A   LABOR

	(Factory) Time	Chilton Time
Six (.6)		.8
V-6 (.4)		*.7
V-8 (.8)		1.0
*Astro add		.2

Air Pump Relief Valve, Renew

Six (.8)		1.0
V-8 (1.0)		1.2

Diverter or Gulp Valve, Renew

Vans-Astro-Safari (.4)		.6
All other models (.2)		.4

Check Valve, Renew (One)

Vans (.4)		.6
All other models (.2)		.4
each adtnl		.1

Combustion Pipes and/or Extensions, Renew
Vans

Six (.6)		.9
V-8-one (.6)		.9
both (.8)		1.2

All Other Models

Four (.6)		1.0
Six (.5)		.8
V-6-each (.3)		.6
V-8-one (.3)		.6
both (.5)		.9

Vacuum Delay Valve, Renew

All models (.3)		.4

Deceleration Valve, Renew

All models (.3)		.4

CONTROLLED COMBUSTION TYPE

Air Cleaner Vacuum Motor, Renew

Vans-Astro-Safari (.6)		.8
All other models (.3)		.6

Air Cleaner Temperature Sensor, Renew

Vans-Astro-Safari (.4)		.5
All other models (.3)		.4

EGR/EFE Thermal Vacuum Switch, Renew

Vans-Astro (.4)		.6
All other models (.3)		.5

EVAPORATIVE EMISSION TYPE

Charcoal Canister, Renew

Vans (.7)		1.0
All other models (.2)		.4

Canister Purge Thermal Vacuum Switch, Renew

exc Vans (.3)		.4
Vans-Astro (.5)		.6

TRANSMISSION CONTROLLED SPARK

Transmission Controlled Spark Solenoid, Renew

Vans (.4)		.5
All other models (.2)		.3

Thermostatic Vacuum Switch or Temperature Switch, Renew

Vans (.5)		.6
All other models (.3)		.4

Controlled Spark Relay, Renew (On Firewall)

All models (.2)		.3

Thermal Vacuum Switch, Renew

All models (.3)		.4

EXHAUST GAS RECIRCULATION SYSTEM

E.G.R. Valve, Renew
Four

eng code A (.8)		1.1
eng code Y (.3)		.5

eng code E

Astro (.9)		1.2
S-series (.5)		.8
Vans (.5)		.8

Diesel

5.7L eng (.6)		1.0
6.2L eng (.2)		.4
All other models (.3)		.5

E.G.R. Vacuum Delay Valve, Renew

S-series (.2)		.3

EARLY FUEL EVAPORATION SYSTEM

E.F.E. Valve, Renew

Six (.3)		.6
V-6 & V-8 (.6)		1.0
dual exhaust (.5)		.9

E.F.E. Actuator and Rod Assy., Renew

All models (.3)		.6

E.F.E. Vacuum Check Valve, Renew

All models (.2)		.3

COMPUTER COMMAND CONTROL SYSTEM (C.C.C.)

Computer Command Control System Performance Check

All models (.5)		1.0

Throttle Position Sensor, Adjust
Does not include system performance check.

All models (.4)		.9

Manifold Absolute Pressure Sensor, Renew
Does not include system performance check.

S-series (.4)		.6
All other models (.5)		.7

Engine Speed Sensor, Renew
Does not include system performance check.

Vans (.7)		.9
All other models (.5)		.7

Calpak, Renew
Does not include system performance check.

All models (.5)		.7

Electronic Control Module, Renew
Does not include system performance check.

All models (.5)		.6

Mixture Control Solenoid, Renew
Does not include system performance check.

Vans-Astro-Safari (1.4)		1.8
All other models-2 bbl (1.1)		1.4
4 bbl (1.2)		1.5

Prom, Renew
Does not include system performance check.

All models (.5)		.8

Coolant Temperature Sensor, Renew
Does not include system performance check.

Vans-Astro-Safari (.7)		.9
All other models (.5)		.6

Oxygen Sensor, Renew
Does not include system performance check.

All models (.5)		.7

Barometric Sensor, Renew
Does not include system performance check.

All models (.5)		.7

Manifold Differential Pressure Sensor, Renew
Does not include system performance check.

All models (.5)		.7

Throttle Position Sensor, Renew
Does not include system performance check.

Vans-Astro-Safari (1.3)		1.7
All other models-2 bbl (1.1)		1.4
4 bbl (1.2)		1.5

Idle Speed Control Motor, Renew
Does not include system performance check.

All models (.5)		.8

Air Control/Air Switching Valve, Renew
Does not include system performance check.

All models (.6)		.8

E.G.R. Vacuum Control Solenoid, Renew
Does not include system performance check.

All models (.6)		.8

Vehicle Speed Sensor, Renew
Does not include system performance check.

All models (1.0)		1.5

E.G.R. Bleed Control Solenoid, Renew
Does not include system performance check.

Vans-Astro-Safari (.5)		.7
All other models (.4)		.6

EFE/EGR Relay, Renew
Does not include system performance check.

All models (.3)		.4

Tachometer Filter, Renew
Does not include system performance check.

All models (.3)		.3

COASTING RICHER SYSTEM (C.R.S.)

Engine Speed Sensor, Renew

S-series (.3)		.4

Accelerator Switch, Renew

S-series (.3)		.4

Clutch Switch, Renew

S-series (.3)		.4

Transmission Switch, Renew

S-series (.4)		.7

Coasting Valve Solenoid, Renew

S-series (.3)		.4

DIESEL ENGINE

Crankcase Depression Regulator Valve, Renew

Vans (.5)		.7
All other models (.3)		.4

Crankcase Ventilation Filter, Renew

All models (.3)		.4

E.G.R. Valve and/or Gasket, Renew
All models

5.7L eng (.6)		1.0
6.2L eng (.2)		.4

E.G.R. Control Valve Solenoid, Renew

Vans (.5)		.7
All other models (.2)		.3

E.P.R. Valve, Renew

Vans (.3)		.4
All other models (.6)		.8

E.P.R. Control Valve Switch, Renew

All models (.5)		.7

E.P.R. Control Valve Solenoid, Renew

Vans (.7)		1.0
All other models (.5)		.7

Vacuum Regulator Valve, Renew

Vans (.8)		1.1
All other models (.5)		.7

LABOR 4 ALTERNATOR AND REGULATOR 4 LABOR

	(Factory Time)	Chilton Time
Delcotron Circuits, Test		
Includes: Test battery, regulator and Delcotron output.		
All models		.6
Alternator Drive Belt, Renew		
Four		
eng code A (.2)		.2
w/P.S. add (.2)		.2
eng code E (.2)		.3
eng code Y (.2)		.3
w/A.C. add (.1)		.1
Six—exc Vans (.2)		.3
Vans (.4)		.5
w/AIR add (.2)		.2
V-6 (.2)		.3
w/AIR add (.1)		.1
V-8—exc Vans (.2)		.3
Vans (.3)		.4
w/AIR add (.2)		.2
Diesel (.2)		.3
Delcotron, Renew		
Includes: Transfer fan and pulley.		
Four—		
eng code A (.6)		.8
eng code Y (.3)		.5
eng code E (.3)		.5
Six—exc Vans (.4)		.6
Vans (.6)		.8
V-6		
Astro-Safari (.7)		.9
All other models (.5)		.7
V8—exc Vans (.6)		.8
Vans (.8)		1.0
Diesel—exc Vans (.4)		.6
Vans (.7)		1.0
Add circuit test if performed.		
Delcotron, R&R and Recondition		
Includes: Complete disassembly, replace parts as required, reassemble.		
Four—		
eng code A (1.5)		2.2
eng code Y (1.3)		2.0
eng code E (1.1)		2.0
Six—exc Vans (1.2)		1.8
Vans (1.3)		1.9
V-6		
Astro-Safari (1.3)		2.2
All other models (1.1)		1.8
V-8—exc Vans (1.2)		2.0
Vans (1.4)		2.2
Diesel—exc Vans (1.3)		2.0
Vans (1.8)		2.7
Add circuit test if performed.		
Delcotron Bearings, Renew (Both)		
Includes: R&R Delcotron, separate end frames.		
Four—		
eng code A (.8)		1.1
eng code Y (.6)		1.0
eng code E (.6)		1.0
Six—exc Vans (.6)		.9
Vans (.7)		1.0
V-6		
Astro-Safari (.8)		1.1
All other models (.6)		1.0
V-8—exc Vans (.6)		.9
Vans (.8)		1.1
Diesel—exc Vans (.6)		.9
Vans (1.0)		1.4
Voltage Regulator, Test and Renew		
Includes: Disassemble and reassemble Delcotron.		
Four—		
eng code A (.7)		1.0
eng code Y (.6)		1.1
eng code E (.6)		1.1
Six—exc Vans (.9)		1.2
Vans (.6)		.9
V-6		
Astro-Safari (.8)		1.2
All other models (.6)		1.1
V-8—exc Vans (.8)		1.1
Vans (.8)		1.1
Diesel—exc Vans (.6)		1.0
Vans (1.3)		1.6
Voltmeter, Renew		
1986		
S-series (.3)		.6
Astro-Safari (.9)		1.4
All other models (.6)		1.0
1987-90		
S-series-Astro-Safari (.9)		1.4
Vans (.8)		1.3
All other models (.6)		1.2

LABOR 5 STARTING SYSTEM 5 LABOR

	(Factory Time)	Chilton Time
Starter Draw Test (On Truck)		
All models		.3
Starter, Renew		
Four		
eng code A (.6)		1.0
eng code Y (.8)		1.2
eng code E		
4X2 (1.0)		1.5
4X4 (1.5)		2.1
Six (.4)		.7
V-6		
4X2 (.6)		1.0
4X4 (.9)		1.5
V-8 (.5)		.8
Diesel (.6)		1.1
Add draw test if performed.		
Starter, R&R and Recondition		
Includes: Turn down armature.		
Four		
eng code A (1.5)		2.3
eng code Y (2.0)		2.8
eng code E		
4X2 (1.6)		2.4
4X4 (2.1)		3.4
Six (1.2)		2.0
V-6		
4X2 (1.5)		2.3
4X4 (2.0)		2.8
V-8 (1.5)		2.1
Diesel (1.6)		2.2
Renew field coils add (.2)		.5
Add draw test if performed.		
Starter Solenoid, Renew		
Includes: R&R starter.		
Four		
eng code A (.6)		1.0
eng code Y (.9)		1.3
eng code E		
4X2 (1.1)		1.6
4X4 (1.5)		2.2
Six (.5)		.8
V-6		
4X2 (.6)		1.0
4X4 (1.1)		1.5
V-8 (.7)		.9
Diesel (.8)		1.1
Starter Drive, Renew		
Includes: R&R starter.		
Four		
eng code A (.8)		1.2
eng code Y (1.0)		1.4
eng code E		
4X2 (.9)		1.2
4X4 (1.8)		2.4
Six (.7)		1.0
V-6		
4X2 (.8)		1.2
4X4 (1.4)		1.8
V-8 (.8)		1.1
Diesel (1.0)		1.3
Battery Cables, Renew		
Positive-exc Vans (.3)		.4
Vans (.5)		.6
Negative		
S-series (.4)		.5
All other models (.2)		.3
batt to batt		
Vans (.7)		1.0
All other models (.3)		.4

LABOR 6 BRAKE SYSTEM 6 LABOR

	(Factory Time)	Chilton Time
Brakes, Adjust (Minor)		
Includes: Adjust brake shoes, fill master cylinder.		
two wheels		.4
Bleed Brakes (Four Wheels)		
Includes: Fill master cylinder.		
All models (.4)		.6
Brake Pedal Free Play, Adjust		
All models		.3
Brake Shoes and/or Pads, Renew		
Includes: Install new or exchange shoes or pads, adjust service and hand brake. Bleed system.		
With Single Rear Wheels		
front-disc (.9)		1.2
rear-drum (1.0)		1.7
All four wheels		2.8
With Dual Rear Wheels		
front-disc (.9)		1.2
rear-drum (2.1)		3.0

LABOR — 6 BRAKE SYSTEM 6 — LABOR

	(Factory Time)	Chilton Time
All four wheels		4.0
Resurface brake rotor add, each		.9
Resurface brake drum add, each		.5
Brake Drum, Renew (One)		
w/Single rear wheels (.3)		.6
w/Dual rear wheels (1.0)		1.4
Free-Up or Renew Brake Self Adjusting Units (One)		
w/Single rear wheels (.4)		.7
w/Dual rear wheels (.7)		1.0
Brake Combination Valve and/or Switch, Renew		
Includes: Bleed system.		
Vans (.8)		1.1
All other models		
w/2 wheel drive (.7)		1.0
w/4 wheel drive (.7)		1.0

BRAKE HYDRAULIC SYSTEM

Wheel Cylinder, Renew		
Includes: Bleed system.		
With Single Rear Wheels		
one (.8)		1.3
both (1.1)		1.8
With Dual Rear Wheels		
one (1.0)		1.7
both (1.8)		2.6
Wheel Cylinder, R&R and Recondition		
Includes: Home cylinder and bleed system.		
With Single Rear Wheels		
one (1.0)		1.6
both (1.5)		2.4
With Dual Rear Wheels		
one (1.2)		2.0
both (2.2)		3.2
Brake Hose, Renew		
Includes: Bleed system.		
All models-front-one (.5)		.8
rear-one (.5)		.8
Master Cylinder, Renew		
Includes: Bleed system.		
All models (.6)		1.0
Master Cylinder, R&R and Recondition		
All models (1.4)		1.8

POWER BRAKES

Vacuum Power Brake Booster, Renew		
S-series (1.2)		1.8
All other models (.6)		1.0
Vacuum Power Brake Booster, R&R and Recondition		
S-series		
single (1.7)		2.5
tandem (1.8)		2.6
All other models		
single (1.1)		1.8
tandem (1.3)		2.0
Brake Booster Check Valve, Renew		
All models (.3)		.3

COMBINATIONS
Add to Brakes, Renew

See Machine Shop Operations

	(Factory Time)	Chilton Time
RENEW WHEEL CYLINDER		
Each (.3)		.4
REBUILD WHEEL CYLINDER		
Each (.3)		.6
REBUILD CALIPER ASSEMBLY		
Each (.5)		.5
RENEW BRAKE HOSE		
Each		.3
RENEW REAR WHEEL GREASE SEALS		
Semi-floating axle		
one (.2)		.3
Full-floating axle		
one (.3)		.4
RENEW BRAKE DRUM (ONE)		
With single rear whls (.4)		.5
With dual rear whls (.5)		.6
REPACK FRONT WHEEL BEARINGS (BOTH WHEELS)		
All models (.6)		.6
RENEW DISC BRAKE ROTOR		
Each-w/2 whl drive (.3)		.5
Each-w/4 whl drive (.6)		.8

	(Factory Time)	Chilton Time
Hydraulic Brake Booster, Renew		
Vans (1.2)		1.7
All other models (1.1)		1.6
Hydraulic Brake Booster, R&R and Recondition		
Vans (1.8)		2.7
All other models (1.5)		2.4
Hydra-Boost Pump, Renew		
All models (.9)		1.3
w/A.C. add (.2)		.2
Hydra-Boost Pump, R&R and Recondition		
All models (1.3)		1.9
w/A.C. add (.2)		.2
Hydra-Boost Pump Line, Renew		
All models-one (.5)		.7
Hydra-Boost Pump Drive Belt, Renew		
All models (.2)		.3
Accumulator (Hydra-Boost), R&R or Renew		
All models (.3)		.7

DISC BRAKES

Brake Shoes and/or Pads, Renew		
Includes: Install new or exchange shoes or pads, adjust service and hand brake. Bleed system.		
With Single Rear Wheels		
front-disc (.9)		1.2

	(Factory Time)	Chilton Time
rear-drum (1.0)		1.7
All four wheels		2.8
With Dual Rear Wheels		
front-disc (.9)		1.2
rear-drum (2.1)		3.0
All four wheels		4.0
Resurface brake rotor add, each		.9
Resurface brake drum add, each		.6
Disc Brake Pads, Renew		
Includes: Install new disc brake pads only.		
All models (.9)		1.2
Disc Brake Rotor, Renew		
With Two Wheel Drive		
All models-one (.7)		1.0
both (1.2)		1.8
With Four Wheel Drive		
S-series-one (.5)		.8
both (.8)		1.4
All other models-one (1.0)		1.2
both (1.8)		2.1
Caliper Assembly, Renew		
Includes: Bleed system.		
All models-one (.7)		1.1
both (1.1)		1.7
Caliper Assembly, R&R and Recondition		
Includes: Bleed system.		
All models-one (1.2)		1.6
both (2.1)		2.5

PARKING BRAKE

Parking Brake, Adjust		
10-30 series (.8)		1.0
All other models (.3)		.4
Parking Brake Equalizer, Renew		
10-30 series (.9)		1.2
All other models (.3)		.6
Parking Brake Control Assembly, Renew		
S-series (1.0)		1.7
Vans (.9)		1.5
Astro-Safari (1.6)		2.3
All other models (.6)		.9
w/Diesel eng add		.4
Parking Brake Cables, Renew		
Front		
All models (.6)		1.0
Intermediate		
All models (.3)		.5
Rear-one		
with single rear whls (.7)		1.0
with dual rear whls (.9)		1.2

ANTI-SKID BRAKE SYSTEM (ABS)

Electronic Brake Control Module, Renew		
All models (.3)		.4
Brake Pressure Modulator Valve, Renew		
Includes: Bleed brakes.		
All models (.4)		.7

LABOR — 7 COOLING SYSTEM 7 — LABOR

	(Factory Time)	Chilton Time
Winterize Cooling System		
Includes: Run engine to check for leaks, tighten all hose connections. Test radiator and pressure cap, drain radiator and engine block. Add antifreeze and refill coolant.		
All models		.8

	(Factory Time)	Chilton Time
Thermostat, Renew		
C-K series		
Gas (.5)		.7
Diesel (.4)		.6
Vans		
Six (.4)		.6
V-6 (.5)		.7

	(Factory Time)	Chilton Time
V-8 (.8)		*1.0
Diesel (.8)		1.0
*w/A.C. add (.5)		.5
Astro-Safari		
Four (.5)		.7
V-6 (.7)		.9

LABOR   7 COOLING SYSTEM 7   LABOR

(Factory Time)	Chilton Time
S-series	
Four (.5)	.7
V-6 (.4)	.6
R-V series	
Six (.4)	.6
V-8 (.4)	.6
Diesel (.4)	.6

Radiator Assembly, R&R or Renew

C-K series	
Gas (.5)	.9
Diesel (.8)	1.2
Vans	
Gas (.7)	1.1
Diesel (1.0)	1.5
w/A.C. add (.3)	.3
Astro-Safari	
All models (.7)	1.1
S-series	
All models (.5)	.9
R-V series	
Gas	
4X2 (.5)	.9
4X4 (.7)	1.1
Diesel (1.0)	1.5
Renew side tank add	
one side (.7)	.7
both sides (1.2)	1.2

ADD THESE OPERATIONS TO RADIATOR R&R

Boil & Repair	1.5
Rod Clean	1.9
Repair Core	1.3
Renew Tank	1.6
Renew Trans. Oil Cooler	1.9
Recore Radiator	1.7

Radiator Hoses, Renew

All models	
upper (.4)	.5
lower (.5)	.6
both (.6)	.9

Thermostat By-Pass Hose or Pipe, Renew

Vans (.6)	.9
All other models (.3)	.5

Fan Blade or Clutch Assy., Renew

C-K series	
Gas (.3)	.5
Diesel (.6)	.8
Vans	
Gas (.6)	.8
Diesel (.7)	.9
w/P.S. add (.1)	.1
w/one piece shroud add (.3)	.3
Astro-Safari	
All models (.6)	.8
w/A.C. add (.1)	.1
S-series	
All models (.4)	.6
R-V series	
Gas (.7)	.9
Diesel (.4)	.6

Drive Belt, Renew

Four	
Serpentine	
Astro-Safari (.3)	.4
All other models (.2)	.3
Renew tensioner add (.1)	.1
Six	
A.C. (.4)	.5
A.I.R. (.3)	.4
Fan (.4)	.5
w/A.C. add (.2)	.2
V-6	
Serpentine (.2)	.3
Renew tensioner add (.1)	.1
V-8–exc 454 eng	
A.C.	
Vans (.5)	.6
R-V series (.2)	.3

(Factory Time)	Chilton Time
w/AIR add (.2)	.2
AIR	
Vans (.3)	.4
R-V series (.2)	.3
Fan	
Vans (.3)	.4
R-V series (.2)	.3
P.S.	
Vans (.5)	.6
R-V series (.3)	.4
w/AIR add (.2)	.2
w/A.C. add (.3)	.3
Serpentine	
All models (.2)	.4
V-8–454 eng	
A.C. (.3)	.4
A.I.R. (.2)	.3
Fan (.2)	.3
P.S. (.5)	.6
Serpentine (.2)	.4
Diesel	
A.C.	
Vans (.9)	1.2
R-V series (.3)	.4
Fan	
Vans (.5)	.6
R-V series (.2)	.3
P.S.	
Vans (.8)	1.1
R-V series (.3)	.4
w/A.C. add	
Vans (.4)	.4
R-V series (.1)	.1
Serpentine (.2)	.4

Drive Belt, Adjust

Six-V-8	
one (.2)	.3
each adtnl (.1)	.1

Water Pump, Renew

C-K Series	
Gas (.8)	1.5
Diesel (1.6)	2.4
w/A.C. add (.1)	.1
w/P.S. add (.3)	.3
Vans	
Six (1.2)	1.8
V-6 (.9)	1.6
V-8 (1.2)	1.8
Diesel (2.0)	3.0
w/A.C. add (.5)	.5
w/P.S. add (.4)	.4
w/AIR add (.2)	.2
Astro-Safari	
Four (.9)	1.3
V-6 (1.1)	1.9
S-series	
Four (.9)	1.3
V-6 (.9)	2.0
w/A.C. add (.2)	.2
w/P.S. add (.2)	.2
R-V series	
Six (1.2)	1.8
V-8 (.8)	1.5
Diesel (1.9)	2.9
w/A.C. add (.2)	.2
w/P.S. add (.6)	.6

Water Jacket Expansion Plugs, Renew (Engine Block)

All models–each (.3)	.5

Note: If necessary to R&R any component to gain access to plug, add appropriate time.

Electric Cooling Fan Blade and/or Motor, Renew (Right or Single)

Vans (.6)	.9
C-K-R-V series (.5)	.8

Engine Cooling Fan Relay, Renew

All models (.2)	.3

(Factory Time)	Chilton Time
Temperature Gauge (Engine Unit), Renew	
Astro-Safari (.6)	.9
All other models (.4)	.5

Temperature Gauge (Dash Unit), Renew

1986	
exc Vans (.6)	1.0
Vans (.5)	1.0
S-series (.3)	.6
Astro-Safari (.9)	1.4
1987-90	
S-series-Astro-Safari (.9)	1.4
Vans (.8)	1.3
All other models (.6)	1.2

Heater Hoses, Renew

Includes: Drain coolant at hose.

C-K series	
one (.4)	.5
both (.5)	.7
Vans	
one (.2)	.3
both (.4)	.5
Astro-Safari	
one (.9)	1.2
both (1.0)	1.4
S-series	
one (.4)	.5
both (.4)	.6
R-V series	
one (.2)	.3
both (.3)	.4

Auxiliary Heater Hoses, Renew (One or All)

Includes: Drain coolant at hose.

All models (1.8)	2.4

Hot Water Shut Off Valve, Renew (Auxiliary Heater)

Astro-Safari (.9)	1.3
All other models (.7)	1.1

Heater Core, R&R or Renew (w/o A.C.)

C-K series	
Gas (.7)	1.5
Diesel (1.1)	2.0
Vans (2.1)	4.0
Astro-Safari (1.3)	2.5
S-series (.9)	1.7
R-V series	
Gas (.8)	1.5
Diesel (1.7)	3.3

(w/A.C.)

C-K series	
Gas (.7)	1.5
Diesel (.4)	.8
Vans	
Gas (3.3)	6.5
Diesel (2.7)	5.3
Astro-Safari (.9)	1.7
S-series (1.4)	2.7
R-V series	
Gas (1.4)	2.5
Diesel (2.1)	4.0

Add time to evacuate and charge A.C. system if required.

ADD THESE OPERATIONS TO HEATER CORE R&R

Boil & Repair	1.2
Repair Core	.9
Recore	1.2

Auxiliary Heater Core, R&R or Renew

Vans (.5)	.9
Astro-Safari (.7)	1.3
R-V series (.6)	1.1

Heater Water Control Valve, Renew

All models (.6)	.8

Heater Blower Motor, Renew

C-K series	
wo/A.C. (.3)	.5

LABOR — 7 COOLING SYSTEM 7 — LABOR

(Factory Time)	Chilton Time
w/A.C.	
Gas (.5)	.7
Diesel (1.9)	2.6
Astro-Safari	
wo/A.C. (.6)	.8
w/A.C. (.5)	.7
Vans	
w/ or wo/A.C.	
Gas (.3)	.5
Diesel (.5)	.7
S-series	
wo/A.C. (.3)	.5
w/A.C. (.3)	.5

(Factory Time)	Chilton Time
R-V series	
Gas	
wo/A.C. (.3)	.5
w/A.C. (.3)	.5
Diesel	
wo/A.C. (1.0)	1.5
w/A.C. (2.0)	3.0
Add time to recharge A.C. system if required.	
Heater Blower Motor Switch, Renew	
All models (.4)	.7
Heater Blower Motor Resistor, Renew	
All models (.2)	.4

(Factory Time)	Chilton Time
Heater Control Assembly, Renew	
R-V series (.6)	.9
Vans-Astro-Safari (.4)	.7
All other models (.3)	.5
Auxiliary Heater Blower Motor, Renew	
Vans-Astro-Safari (.3)	.5
R-V series (.5)	.8
Rear A.C. Blower Motor, Renew	
Vans (.6)	.9
Astro-Safari (.4)	.7
R-V series (.9)	1.2
Blower Motor Relay, Renew	
All models (.3)	.4

LABOR — 8 EXHAUST SYSTEM 8 — LABOR

(Factory Time)	Chilton Time
Muffler, Renew	
All models	
single exh–each (.6)	.9
dual exh	
right (.7)	1.0
left (.8)	1.1
Tail Pipe, Renew	
All models–each (.5)	.7
Front Catalytic Converter, Renew	
C-K series (.9)	1.3
Vans (.5)	.8
Astro-Safari (.5)	.8
S-series (.6)	.9
R-V series (.7)	1.0
Front Exhaust Pipe, Renew	
All models	
right side (.7)	.9
left side (.6)	.9
Crossover Exhaust Pipe, Renew	
C-K series (.7)	1.1
Vans (.4)	.7
Astro-Safari (.5)	.8
S-series	
Four (1.2)	1.6
V-6 (.9)	1.3
R-V series (.5)	.8
Rear Exhaust Catalytic Converter, Renew	
All models (.5)	.8
Front Exhaust Pipe, Renew (To Converter)	
S-series (.6)	1.0
All other models (.4)	.7
Rear Exhaust Pipe, Renew	
All models	
right side (.4)	.9
left side (1.0)	1.3
crossover (.7)	1.3
Intermediate Exhaust Pipe, Renew	
C-K series (.9)	1.3
All other models (.4)	.7
Resonator and Pipe Assy., Renew	
All models (.4)	.6

(Factory Time)	Chilton Time
E.F.E. Valve (Heat Riser), Renew	
Six (.3)	.6
V-6 & V-8–single exh (.6)	1.0
dual exh (.5)	.9
E.F.E. Actuator and Rod Assy., Renew	
All models (.3)	.6
Exhaust Manifold, Renew	
Four–	
eng codes A-Y (1.0)	1.5
w/A.C. add (.8)	.8
w/P.S. add (.4)	.4
eng code E	
S-series (.8)	1.1
Astro-Safari (.9)	1.3
w/A.C. add (.2)	.4
Six	
1986	
exc Vans (1.6)	2.3
Vans (1.8)	2.5
1987-90	
exc Vans (2.4)	3.4
Vans (2.6)	3.6
V-6	
S-series	
eng Code R	
right side (.9)	1.5
left side (.8)	1.4
w/P.S. add (.1)	.1
eng Code Z	
4X2	
right side (.9)	1.5
left side (1.1)	1.7
4X4	
right side (.9)	1.5
left side (2.4)	3.4
Astro-Safari	
right side (1.1)	1.7
left side (.7)	1.5
exc Vans	
right side (.6)	1.0
left side (.7)	1.1
Vans	
right side (.9)	1.5
left side (.7)	1.1

(Factory Time)	Chilton Time
w/P.S. add (.3)	.3
w/A.I.R. add (.3)	.3
V-8–454 eng	
right side (1.6)	2.3
left side (1.3)	2.0
w/A.C. add (.5)	.5
V-8–All other engs	
exc Vans–right side (.6)	1.0
left side (.8)	1.5
Vans–right side (.9)	1.5
left side (.9)	1.5
w/P.S. add (.2)	.2
w/A.C. add (.3)	.3
w/A.I.R. add (.1)	.1
Diesel	
2.2L eng (.7)	1.2
5.7L eng	
right side (.9)	1.3
left side (.7)	1.1
6.2L eng	
C-K series	
right side (.8)	1.2
left side (1.1)	1.5
Vans	
right side (.9)	1.3
left side (.8)	1.2
w/A.C. add (.6)	.6
R-V series	
right side (1.5)	1.9
left side (1.4)	1.8
w/A.C. add (.3)	.3
Intake and Exhaust Manifold Gasket, Renew	
Six	
exc Vans (2.1)	3.1
Vans (2.5)	3.5
COMBINATIONS	
Muffler, Exhaust and Tail Pipe, Renew	
Four (1.2)	1.7
Six (1.3)	1.9
V-6 (.7)	1.2
V-8–one side (1.1)	1.6

LABOR — 9A FRONT SUSPENSION (RWD) 9A — LABOR

(Factory Time)	Chilton Time
Note: On all front suspension operations alignment charges must be added if performed. Time given does not include alignment.	
Check Alignment of Front End	
All models	.5
Note: Deduct if alignment is performed.	

(Factory Time)	Chilton Time
Toe-In, Adjust	
All models (.4)	.6
Align Front End	
Includes: Adjust front wheel bearings.	
S-series	
4X2 (.7)	1.4
4X4 (1.1)	2.0

(Factory Time)	Chilton Time
C-K Series	
1987-90	
wo/Cam Kit	
4X2 (1.7)	3.0
4X4 (1.2)	2.0
w/Cam Kit (.6)	1.0
All other models (1.1)	2.0

LABOR　9A　FRONT SUSPENSION (RWD)　9A　LABOR

	(Factory Time)	Chilton Time
Front Wheel Bearings, Clean and Repack		
Two Wheel Drive		
one wheel (.7)		.8
both wheels (1.2)		1.4
Four Wheel Drive		
one wheel (1.2)		1.4
both wheels (2.2)		2.5
Front Wheel Grease Seal, Renew		
Two Wheel Drive		
one wheel (.7)		.7
both wheels (1.2)		1.2
Four Wheel Drive		
one wheel (1.2)		1.3
both wheels (2.2)		2.4
Front Wheel Bearings and Cups, Renew		
Two Wheel Drive		
one wheel (.7)		.9
both wheels (1.1)		1.5
Four Wheel Drive		
one wheel (1.2)		1.5
both wheels (2.2)		2.6
Front Wheel Bearing and Hub Assy., Renew		
S-series-4X4		
one side (.9)		1.1
both sides (1.6)		2.0
Renew inner seal add		
one (.4)		.4
both (.6)		.6
K-Series-4X4		
one (.7)		1.0
both (1.0)		1.6
Renew inner seal add		
one (.1)		.1
both (.2)		.2
Front Shock Absorbers, Renew		
S-series		
one (.5)		.7
both (.9)		1.1
w/Dual Shocks		
right (.6)		.8
left (.4)		.6
both (.8)		1.2
All other models-one (.3)		.5
both (.4)		.8
Steering Arm and Knuckle (Integral), Renew		
Add alignment charges.		
Two Wheel Drive		
S-series-one (1.3)		1.6
both (2.4)		3.0
All other models-one (1.0)		1.3
both (1.7)		2.5
Steering Knuckle, Renew		
Add alignment charges.		
Four Wheel Drive		
S-series		
one (1.3)		1.6
both (2.4)		3.0
All other models-one (1.4)		1.6
both (2.5)		2.9
Lower Control Arm Assy., Renew		
Add alignment charges.		
S-series-4X2-one (1.2)		1.6
both (2.2)		3.1
4X4-one (1.6)		2.0
both (3.0)		3.8
All other models		
4X2		
one (.9)		1.3
both (1.7)		2.5
4X4		
one (1.6)		2.0
both (3.0)		3.8

	(Factory Time)	Chilton Time
Lower Control Arm Bushings and Shaft, Renew		
Add alignment charges.		
S-series-4X2		
1986-87-one side (1.2)		1.9
both sides (2.3)		3.5
1988-90-one side (.9)		1.4
both sides (1.6)		2.6
4X4-one side (1.4)		2.1
both sides (2.5)		4.0
Astro-one side (1.2)		1.9
both sides (2.3)		3.5
All other models		
4X2		
one side (.9)		1.5
both sides (1.7)		2.9
4X4		
one side (1.8)		2.3
both sides (3.4)		4.4
Upper Control Arm Assy., Renew		
Add alignment charges.		
S-series-4X2-one (.9)		1.3
both (1.5)		2.2
4X4-one (1.0)		1.4
both (1.8)		2.7
All other models		
exc Vans		
one side (.6)		1.1
both sides (1.1)		2.1
Vans		
one side (.8)		1.2
both sides (1.4)		2.3
Upper Control Arm Bushings and Shaft, Renew		
Add alignment charges.		
S-series-one side (1.1)		1.7
both sides (2.0)		3.0
Astro-Safari-one side (1.0)		1.6
both sides (1.8)		2.8
C-K Series		
1987-90		
4X2-one side (1.1)		1.5
both sides (2.1)		2.9
4X4-one side (.9)		1.2
both sides (1.4)		2.0
All other models-one side (.9)		1.4
both sides (1.6)		2.7
Upper Ball Joint, Renew		
Add alignment charges.		
S-series-4X4		
one (.8)		1.3
both (1.4)		2.4
C-K Series		
1987-90		
4X2-one (.9)		1.3
both (1.6)		2.4
4X4-one (1.0)		1.4
both (1.8)		2.6
All other models-one (.7)		1.1
both (1.2)		2.1
Lower Ball Joint, Renew		
Add alignment charges.		
S-series-4X4		
one (1.1)		1.5
both (2.0)		2.8
K-Series		
1987-90		
4X4-one (1.8)		2.4
both (3.4)		4.5
All other models-one (.7)		1.2
both (1.2)		2.3
Ball Joints or King Pins (Upper and Lower), Renew		
Four Wheel Drive		
Add alignment charges.		
All models-one side (1.8)		2.4
both sides (3.5)		4.7

	(Factory Time)	Chilton Time
Front Spring, Renew		
Coil		
All models-one (.8)		1.2
both (1.4)		2.3
Leaf		
All models-one (.8)		1.4
both (1.5)		2.7
Front Spring Shackle or Pin, Renew		
All models-one (.3)		.5
both (.5)		.9
Front Stabilizer Shaft, Renew		
K Series-1987-90 (.8)		1.1
All models (.6)		.9
Front Stabilizer Shaft Bushings, Renew		
K-series-1987-90		
one (.5)		.7
both (.9)		1.2
All other models-one (.4)		.7
both (.5)		.8
FOUR WHEEL DRIVE		
K-V-10-20-30 SERIES		
Steering Knuckle Spindle Bearings, Renew		
All models-one (1.1)		1.4
both (2.1)		2.7
Renew spindle add,		
each (.1)		.2
Renew knuckle add,		
each (.5)		.6
Front Wheel Hub, Renew		
All models-one (.6)		.9
both (1.1)		1.7
Free Wheeling Hub Control Mechanism, Recondition		
All models-one (.4)		.5
both (.6)		.8
Recond add each (.5)		.6
Front Axle Shaft Oil Seals, Renew		
All models-one (3.0)		4.0
both (3.1)		4.3
Front Differential Housing Assy., Renew		
Includes: R&R drive shaft, transfer all parts as required. Bleed brakes and make all necessary adjustments.		
All models (7.4)		10.0
Front Drive Axle Differential Case, R&R or Renew		
All models		
Corp axle (3.4)		4.2
Dana axle (4.4)		5.4
Ring Gear and Pinion Set, Renew		
Includes: R&R differential case.		
All models		
Corp axle (4.3)		5.4
Dana axle (5.5)		6.9
Pinion Bearings, Renew		
Includes: R&R differential case.		
All models		
Corp axle (4.0)		5.5
Dana axle (5.2)		6.6
Differential Side Bearings, Renew		
Includes: R&R differential case.		
All models		
Corp axle (3.3)		4.4
Dana axle (4.1)		5.6
Front Axle Housing Cover and/or Gasket, Renew		
All models (.4)		.7
Pinion Shaft Oil Seal, Renew		
All models (.5)		.9

LABOR 9A FRONT SUSPENSION (RWD) 9A LABOR

(Factory Time)	Chilton Time
Front Drive Shaft, R&R or Renew	
All models (.4)	.6
w/Transfer case shield add (.1)	.1
Front Propeller Shaft U-Joints, Renew	
All models	
front (.6)	.9
rear (1.1)	1.5
both (1.3)	2.0
w/Transfer case shield add (.1)	.1
Front Axle Shaft and/or Universal Joint, Renew (One Side)	
All models (1.2)	1.7
Renew inner shaft add	.4
Renew outer shaft add	.4
Renew U-Joint add	.4
Renew spindle brg add	.1
Front Drive Axle, R&R or Renew	
All models-one (1.1)	1.5
both (2.0)	2.8
Renew or recond outer	
C.V. Joint add-each (.6)	.6
Renew or recond inner	
C.V. Joint add-each (.4)	.4
Renew shaft add-each (.3)	.3
S-SERIES	
Front Torsion Bar, Adjust	
S-Series (.4)	.5
Front Torsion Bar, Renew	
S-Series-one side (.9)	1.2
both sides (1.1)	1.6
w/Skid plate add (.3)	.3
w/V-6 add	.2
Torsion Bar Pivot Arm, Renew	
S-Series-one side (.5)	.7
both sides (.7)	1.1
w/Skid plate add (.2)	.2
Torsion Bar Support Crossmember, Renew	
S-Series (1.0)	1.5
w/Skid plate add (.2)	.2
Front Differential Vacuum Locking Actuator, Renew	
S-series (.2)	.5
w/V-6 add	.3
Front Differential Locking Cable, Renew	
S-series (.4)	.6
w/Skid plate add (.1)	.1
w/V-6 add	.4
Front Propeller Shaft U-Joints, Renew	
S-series	
front (.6)	.9
rear (1.1)	1.5
both (1.3)	2.0
Front Propeller Shaft Assy., Renew	
S-series (.6)	.9
w/Transfer case shield add	.3
Output Shaft, Renew	
S-Series	
right side (1.5)	2.1
left side (1.3)	1.8
both sides (2.7)	3.8
Renew shaft seal add	
each (.2)	.2

(Factory Time)	Chilton Time
Drive Axle Assy., R&R or Renew	
S-Series	
one (1.1)	1.5
both (1.9)	2.6
Renew axle shaft, add	
each (.6)	.6
Renew C/V joint boot or seal, add	
each side (.3)	.3
Renew outer C/V joint, add	
each (.4)	.4
Renew D.O. joint, add	
each (.3)	.3
Repack or Recond joints, add	
inner (.4)	.4
outer (.6)	.6
Front Differential Cover or Gasket, Renew	
All models (.4)	.6
Differential Pinion Shaft Oil Seal and/or Flange, Renew	
1986-87 (3.7)	5.2
1988-90	
exc. 4.3L-V-6 (1.1)	1.5
4.3L-V-6 (.7)	1.0
Differential Output Shaft Tube Assy., R&R or Renew	
All models (1.4)	1.9
Renew output shaft seal	
add (.1)	.1
Renew pilot brg add (.2)	.2
Renew shaft assy add (.1)	.1
Recond tube assy add (.3)	.3
Differential Carrier Assy., Remove & Install	
All models (2.8)	4.3
Renew pinion shaft and/or side pinion gears add (.4)	.4
Renew side brgs add (1.0)	1.0
Renew pinion brgs add (1.7)	1.7
Renew ring and pinion assy, add (1.6)	1.6
Renew case add (1.2)	1.2
Renew carrier add (1.8)	1.8
Renew output shaft brgs add (.9)	.9
Renew mount bushs add (.2)	.2
Recond complete add (2.2)	3.0
Recond tube add (.3)	.3
K-SERIES 1987-89	
Steering Knuckle Inner Dust Seal, Renew	
K-Series-one (.8)	1.1
both (1.4)	1.9
Steering Knuckle Assy., Renew	
Add alignment charges.	
K-Series-one (1.4)	1.9
both (2.5)	3.3
Front Axle Engagement Switch, Renew	
K-Series (.4)	.6
w/Skid plate add (1.)	.3
Front Differential Locking Actuator, Renew	
K-Series (.3)	.5
Front Torsion Bar, Adjust	
K-Series (.4)	.5
Front Torsion Bar, Renew	
K-Series-one (1.0)	1.4
both (1.0)	1.5

(Factory Time)	Chilton Time
Torsion Bar Pivot Arm, Renew	
K-Series-one (.4)	.6
both (.6)	.8
Torsion Bar Support Crossmember, Renew	
K-Series (1.0)	1.5
Front Propeller Shaft U-Joints, Renew	
K-Series	
front (.6)	.9
rear (1.1)	1.5
both (1.3)	2.0
Front Propeller Shaft Assy., Renew	
K-Series (.4)	.6
Output Shaft, R&R or Renew	
K-series	
right (1.0)	1.4
left (.6)	.8
both (1.5)	2.1
Renew shaft seal add-each	.1
w/Stabilizer bar add	.3
Drive Axle Assy., R&R or Renew	
K-Series-one (.5)	.8
both (.9)	1.5
Renew axle shaft, add	
each (.6)	.6
Renew C/V joint boot or seal, add	
each side (.3)	.3
Renew outer C/V joint, add	
each (.4)	.4
Renew inner C/V joint, add	
each (.4)	.4
Renew outer seal protector, add-each (.1)	.1
w/Skid plate add	.1
w/Stabilizer Bar add	.3
Front Differential Cover or Gasket, Renew	
K-Series (.5)	.6
Differential Pinion Shaft Oil Seal and/or Flange, Renew	
K-Series (.6)	.9
Differential Output Shaft Tube Assy., R&R or Renew	
K-Series (1.0)	1.4
Renew output shaft seal add (.1)	.1
Renew pilot brg add (.1)	.1
Renew shift assy add (.1)	.1
Recond tube assy add (.3)	.3
w/Skid plate add	.1
w/Stabilizer bar add	.3
Differential Carrier Assy., Remove & Install	
K-Series (2.1)	3.0
Renew pinion shaft and/or side pinion gears add (.8)	.8
Renew side brgs add (1.5)	1.5
Renew pinion brgs add (2.0)	2.0
Renew ring and pinion assy, add (2.6)	2.6
Renew case add (1.9)	1.9
Renew carrier add (2.6)	2.6
Renew output shaft brgs add (1.6)	1.6
Recond complete add (3.0)	4.0
Recond tube add (.3)	.3

LABOR 10 STEERING LINKAGE 10 LABOR

(Factory Time)	Chilton Time
Tie Rods or Tie Rod Ends, Renew	
Includes: Reset toe-in.	
Two Wheel Drive	
one (.7)	.9
both (.9)	1.4

(Factory Time)	Chilton Time
Four Wheel Drive	
one (.8)	1.1
both (1.0)	1.6

(Factory Time)	Chilton Time
Idler Arm, Renew	
All models (.7)	1.0
4X4 add	.2
Astro-both, add	.3

LABOR 10 STEERING LINKAGE 10 LABOR

(Factory Time)	Chilton Time
Drag Link, Renew	
All models (.4)	.9
Intermediate Rod, Renew	
Includes: Reset toe-in.	
Vans-S-series 4X4 (1.0)	1.4
All other models (.9)	1.3
Pitman Arm, Renew	
1986	
All models (.5)	.8

(Factory Time)	Chilton Time
S-series 4X4 add	.7
1987-90	
S-series	
4X2 (.4)	.6
4X4 (1.0)	1.5
C-K series	
4X2 (.4)	.6
4X4 (.9)	1.3
Van (.7)	1.1
w/P.S. add (.3)	.3
All other models (.5)	.8

(Factory Time)	Chilton Time
Steering Knuckle Arm, Renew	
Includes: Reset toe-in.	
All models-one (.9)	1.3
both (1.1)	1.7
Steering Damper, Renew	
All models (.3)	.6
S-series 4X4 add	.3
Idler Arm Bracket and Bushing, Renew	
All models (.4)	.8

LABOR 11 STEERING GEAR 11 LABOR

MANUAL STEERING

(Factory Time)	Chilton Time
Steering Wheel, Renew	
All models (.3)	.4
Upper Mast Jacket Bearing, Renew	
All models-std column (.8)	1.4
tilt column (.9)	1.6
w/Cruise control add (.2)	.2
Steering Column Shift Bowl, Renew	
All models	
std colm (1.4)	2.0
tilt colm (1.7)	2.3
Steering Shaft Lower Coupling (Pot Joint), Renew	
Includes: R&R intermediate shaft.	
S-series (.4)	*.7
w/P.S. add (.3)	.3
All other models (.7)	1.0
*LLV model	
one (.6)	.9
both (.8)	1.2
Flexible Coupling (Rag Joint), Renew	
All models (.6)	1.0
Steering Column, Remove & Install	
All models (.8)	1.2
Renew colm assy add	.4
Recond std colm add (.7)	.9
Recond tilt colm add (1.0)	1.6
Steering Column Lock Actuator Parts, Renew	
All models	
std colm (.8)	1.4
tilt colm (.9)	1.6
w/Cruise control add (.2)	.2
Steering Gear, Adjust (On Truck)	
All models (.4)	.6
S-series 4X4 add	.2
Steering Gear, R&R or Renew	
All models (.6)	1.0
S-series 4X4 add	.2
Steering Gear, R&R and Recondition	
Includes: Disassemble, renew necessary parts, reassemble and adjust.	
All models (1.6)	2.4
S-series 4X4 add	.2
Pitman Shaft Seal, Renew	
Does not require gear R&R.	
All models (.9)	1.4
S-series 4X4 add	.2

POWER STEERING

(Factory Time)	Chilton Time
Trouble Shoot Power Steering	
Includes: Test pump and system pressure. Check pounds pull on steering wheel and check for leaks.	
All models	.5
Power Steering Gear, Adjust (On Truck)	
All models (.7)	1.0
S-series 4X4 add	.2
Power Steering Belt, Renew	
All models (.2)	.4
Power Steering Gear, R&R or Renew	
S-series (.9)	1.4
Astro-Safari (1.0)	1.5
All other models (.8)	1.3
w/Stabilizer bar add (.2)	.2
w/Hydraulic brake booster add	.1
Power Steering Gear, R&R and Recondition	
S-series (1.8)	3.0
Astro-Safari (2.0)	3.2
All other models (1.8)	3.0
w/Stabilizer bar add (.2)	.2
w/Hydraulic brake booster add	.1
Valve Body, Recondition	
Includes: R&R gear assy.	
S-series (1.2)	1.7
Astro-Safari (1.3)	1.8
All other models (1.2)	1.8
w/Stabilizer bar add (.2)	.2
w/Hydraulic brake booster add	.1
Adjuster Plug, Recondition	
Includes: R&R gear assy.	
S-series (1.1)	1.6
Astro-Safari (1.2)	1.7
All other models (1.0)	1.5
w/Stabilizer bar add (.2)	.2
w/Hydraulic brake booster add	.1
Rack Piston Assy., Recondition	
Includes: R&R gear assy.	
S-series (1.3)	1.8
Astro-Safari (1.4)	1.9
All other models (1.2)	1.8
w/Stabilizer bar add (.2)	.2
w/Hydraulic brake booster add	.1
Power Steering Pump, R&R or Renew	
1986	
All models (.8)	1.2
1987-90	
C-K series (1.0)	1.4
Vans (1.0)	1.4
Astro-Safari	
Four (.7)	.9
V-6 (1.1)	1.5

(Factory Time)	Chilton Time
S-series	
Four (.5)	.8
V-6 (.8)	1.2
R-V series	
Gas (.8)	1.2
Diesel (.4)	.7
w/A.C. add (.2)	.2
Vans-w/Diesel eng add	.2
w/Hyd. Brake Booster add	.1
Power Steering Pump, R&R and Recondition	
1986	
All models (1.2)	1.8
1987-90	
C-K series (1.5)	2.0
Vans (1.5)	2.0
Astro-Safari	
Four (1.2)	1.5
V-6 (1.6)	2.1
S-series	
Four (1.0)	1.4
V-6 (1.3)	1.8
R-V series	
Gas (1.3)	1.8
Diesel (.9)	1.3
w/A.C. add (.2)	.2
Vans-w/Diesel eng add	.2
w/Hyd. Brake Booster add	.1
Power Steering Reservoir and/or 'O' Ring Seal, Renew	
1986	
All models (1.0)	1.4
1987-90	
C-K series (1.2)	1.7
Vans (1.1)	1.6
Astro-Safari	
Four (.8)	1.1
V-6 (1.2)	1.7
S-series	
Four (.6)	1.0
V-6 (.9)	1.4
R-V series	
Gas (.9)	1.4
Diesel (.5)	.9
w/A.C. add (.2)	.2
Vans-w/Diesel eng add	.2
w/Hyd. Brake Booster add	.1
Pump Flow Control Valve, Renew	
S-series (.3)	.7
All other models (.6)	1.0
w/A.C. add (.2)	.2
Power Steering Hoses, Renew	
All models	
pressure (.4)	.6
return (.5)	.8
w/A.C. add (.2)	.2
w/Hyd. Brake Booster add	.1

LABOR   12   CYLINDER HEAD & VALVE SYSTEM   12   LABOR

GASOLINE ENGINES

	(Factory) Time	Chilton Time
Compression Test		
Four		.6
Six		.9
V-6		.9
V-8		1.4

Cylinder Head Gasket, Renew
Includes: Clean carbon and make all necessary adjustments.

		Chilton Time
Four		
eng code A (3.4)		4.7
eng code Y (3.7)		5.1
eng code E		
S-series (4.0)		5.6
Astro-Safari (4.4)		6.2
w/Cruise control add		.2
w/A.C. add (.8)		.8
w/P.S. add (.4)		.4
Six-exc Vans (4.6)		6.4
Vans (4.7)		6.5
w/A.C. add (.3)		.3
V-6-		
1986		
S-series-Astro-Safari		
one (5.7)		8.1
both (7.6)		10.8
All other models		
one (4.2)		6.0
both (6.5)		9.2
w/A.C. add (.5)		.5
w/P.S. add (.5)		.5
w/C.C.C. add (.3)		.3
1987-90		
eng code R		
one side (4.9)		6.8
both sides (6.4)		8.9
w/A.C. add (.2)		.2
w/P.S. add (.2)		.2
eng code Z		
S-series		
right (4.8)		6.7
left (6.4)		8.9
both (8.8)		12.3
Astro-Safari		
one side (5.4)		7.5
both sides (7.7)		10.7
w/A.C. add		.3
w/P.S. add		.5
w/AIR add		.3
w/Cruise control add		.2
C-K series		
one side (4.4)		6.1
both sides (6.6)		9.2
w/A.C. add (.2)		.2
w/AIR add (.4)		.4
Vans		
one side (4.7)		6.5
both sides (6.9)		9.7
w/A.C. add (.3)		.3
w/P.S. add (.1)		.1
w/Cruise control add (.1)		.1
w/A.T. add (.1)		.1
V-8-454 eng		
one (5.2)		7.5
both (7.1)		10.2
V-8-all other engs		
exc Vans-one (4.5)		6.2
both (6.4)		8.8
Vans-left (4.8)		6.9
right (5.6)		8.1
both (7.0)		10.4
w/P.S. add (.2)		.2
w/A.C. add (.7)		.7
w/A.I.R. add (.2)		.2

Cylinder Head, Renew
Includes: Transfer all components, reface valves, clean carbon.

		Chilton Time
Four		
eng code A (5.7)		7.9

COMBINATIONS

Add to Valve Job

See Machine Shop Operations

	(Factory) Time	Chilton Time
GASOLINE ENGINES		
DRAIN, EVACUATE & RECHARGE AIR CONDITIONING SYSTEM		
All models (.5)		1.0
ROCKER ARM STUD, RENEW		
Each (.3)		.3
HYDRAULIC VALVE LIFTERS, DISASSEMBLE AND CLEAN		
Each		.2
DISTRIBUTOR, RECONDITION		
All models (.5)		.9
CARBURETOR, RECONDITION		
1 BBL (1.0)		1.0
2 BBL (1.0)		1.2
4 BBL (.8)		1.5
VALVE GUIDES, REAM OVERSIZE		
Each (.1)		.1

	(Factory) Time	Chilton Time
eng code Y (6.2)		8.7
eng code E		
S-series (5.5)		7.7
Astro-Safari (5.7)		8.0
w/Cruise control add		.2
w/A.C. add (.8)		.8
w/P.S. add (.4)		.4
Six-exc Vans (6.0)		8.4
Vans (6.2)		8.6
w/A.C. add (.3)		.3
V-6-		
1986		
S-series-Astro-Safari		
one (6.5)		9.2
both (9.0)		12.8
All other models		
one (5.0)		7.1
both (7.6)		10.8
w/A.C. add (.5)		.5
w/P.S. add (.5)		.5
w/C.C.C. add (.3)		.3
1987-90		
eng code R		
one side (5.9)		8.2
both sides (8.3)		11.6
w/A.C. add (.2)		.2
w/P.S. add (.2)		.2
eng code Z		
S-series		
right (5.7)		7.9
left (7.2)		10.0
both (10.3)		14.4
Astro-Safari		
one side (6.3)		8.8
both sides (9.3)		13.0
w/A.C. add		.3
w/P.S. add		.5
w/AIR add		.3
w/Cruise control add		.2
C-K series		
one side (5.2)		7.2
both sides (8.0)		11.2
w/A.C. add (.2)		.2
w/AIR add (.4)		.4
Vans		
one side (5.5)		7.7
both sides (8.4)		11.8

	(Factory) Time	Chilton Time
w/A.C. add (.3)		.3
w/P.S. add (.1)		.1
w/Cruise Control add (.1)		.1
w/A.T. add (.1)		.1
V-8-454 eng		
one (6.2)		8.9
both (9.2)		13.3
V-8-all other engs		
exc Vans-one (5.4)		7.4
both (8.1)		11.1
Vans-left (5.6)		8.1
right (6.5)		9.4
both (8.8)		12.7
w/P.S. add (.2)		.2
w/A.C. add (.7)		.7
w/A.I.R. add (.2)		.2

Clean Carbon and Grind Valves
Includes: R&R cylinder heads, grind valves and seats. Minor tune up.

		Chilton Time
Four		
eng code A (5.2)		7.3
eng code Y (5.3)		7.4
eng code E		
S-series (5.6)		8.0
Astro-Safari (6.0)		8.5
w/Cruise control add		.2
w/A.C. add (.8)		.8
w/P.S. add (.4)		.4
Six-exc Vans (6.4)		8.9
Vans (6.6)		9.2
w/A.C. add (.3)		.3
V-6-		
1986		
S-series-Astro-Safari		
one side (7.0)		9.9
both sides (9.4)		13.3
All other models		
one side (5.3)		7.5
both sides (7.8)		11.1
w/A.C. add (.5)		.5
w/P.S. add (.5)		.5
w/C.C.C add (.3)		.3
1987-90		
eng code R		
one side (6.0)		8.4
both sides (8.6)		12.0
w/A.C. add (.2)		.2
w/P.S. add (.2)		.2
eng code Z		
S-series		
right side (5.8)		8.1
left side (7.5)		10.5
both sides (10.8)		15.1
Astro-Safari		
one side (6.5)		9.1
both sides (9.7)		13.5
w/A.C. add		.3
w/P.S. add		.5
w/AIR add		.3
w/Cruise control add		.2
C-K series		
one side (5.5)		7.7
both sides (8.6)		12.0
w/A.C. add (.2)		.2
w/AIR add (.4)		.4
Vans		
one side (5.8)		8.1
both sides (8.1)		11.3
w/A.C. add (.3)		.3
w/P.S. add (.1)		.1
w/Cruise Control add (.1)		.1
w/A.T. add (.1)		.1
V-8-454 eng		
one bank (6.5)		9.4
both banks (9.5)		13.7
V-8-all other engs		
exc Vans-one bank (5.8)		8.0
both banks (8.8)		12.1
Vans-left bank (6.1)		8.8
right bank (6.9)		10.0

LABOR   12   CYLINDER HEAD & VALVE SYSTEM   12   LABOR

	(Factory) Time	Chilton Time
both banks (9.6)		13.9
w/P.S. add (.2)		.2
w/A.C. add (.7)		.7
w/A.I.R. add (.2)		.2
Valves, Adjust		
Six (.5)		1.4
V-8 (.8)		1.9
w/A.C. add		.7
w/P.A.I.R. add		.6
Valve Cover Gasket, Renew		
Four		
eng code A (.4)		.7
eng code Y (.6)		.9
eng code E		
S-series (.9)		1.3
Astro-Safari (1.4)		2.0
Six–exc Vans (.8)		1.1
Vans (1.1)		1.6
V-6–		
1986		
S-series–Astro-Safari		
one side (.9)		1.3
both sides (1.8)		2.6
exc Vans		
right side (.7)		1.0
left side (.3)		.5
both sides (.9)		1.4
Vans		
right side (.9)		1.3
left side (.5)		.8
both sides (1.1)		1.7
w/A.C. add (.3)		.3
w/C.C.C. add (.3)		.3
1987-90		
eng code R		
right side (1.0)		1.4
left side (.6)		.8
both sides (1.4)		2.0
eng code Z		
S-series		
right side (.6)		.8
left side (.5)		.7
both sides (.9)		1.3
Astro-Safari		
right side (.7)		1.0
left side (.5)		.8
both sides (.8)		1.4
w/A.C. add (.1)		.1
w/AIR add (.2)		.2
w/Cruise control add (.2)		2
C-K series		
one (.3)		.5
both (.5)		.8
Vans		
one (.5)		.8
both (.6)		1.0
w/A.C. add (.1)		.1
w/Cruise control add (.2)		.2
w/A.I.R. add (.2)		.2
V-8–454 eng		
one (.6)		.8
both (1.1)		1.5
V-8–all other engs		
exc Vans–one (.6)		.8
both (1.0)		1.3
Vans–right (1.5)		2.1
left (.8)		1.1
both (1.9)		2.7
w/A.C. add (.7)		.7
w/A.I.R. add (.2)		.2
Push Rod Side Cover Gasket, Renew		
Four		
eng code E		
S-series		
4X2 (2.1)		2.7
4X4 (1.6)		2.2
LLV model (.8)		1.2
Astro-Safari (1.8)		2.5
Six–exc Vans		
front (.5)		.7
rear (.3)		.4
both (.9)		1.2
Vans		
front (.7)		1.0
rear (.3)		.4
both (1.0)		1.4
Valve Push Rods and/or Rocker Arms, Renew		
Four		
eng code A-all (.9)		1.2
eng code Y-all (1.0)		1.4
eng code E		
S-series-all (1.2)		2.0
Astro-Safari-all (1.7)		2.7
Six–exc Vans		
one cyl (1.0)		1.4
all cyls (1.4)		2.0
Vans		
one cyl (1.3)		1.9
all cyls (1.7)		2.4
V-6–		
1986		
S-series–Astro-Safari		
one cyl (1.0)		1.5
one cyl–each side (1.8)		2.7
exc Vans		
one cyl–right side (.9)		1.4
one cyl–left side (.5)		1.0
one cyl–both sides (1.2)		1.9
Vans		
one cyl–right side (1.1)		1.7
one cyl–left side (.7)		1.2
one cyl–each side (1.4)		2.2
each adtnl cyl		.1
w/A.C. add (.3)		.3
w/C.C.C. add (.3)		.3
1987-90		
eng code R		
one cyl–right side (1.2)		1.6
one cyl–left side (.8)		1.1
one cyl–each side (1.7)		2.3
all cyls–both sides (2.0)		2.8
eng code Z		
S-series		
one cyl (.7)		.9
one cyl–each side (1.2)		1.6
all cyls–both sides (1.5)		2.1
Astro-Safari		
one cyl (.7)		.9
one cyl–each side (.9)		1.2
all cyls–both sides (1.2)		1.6
w/A.C. add (.1)		.1
w/AIR add (.2)		.2
w/Cruise control add (.2)		.2
C-K series		
one cyl (.5)		.7
one cyl–each side (.8)		1.1
all cyls–both sides (1.1)		1.5
Vans		
one cyl (.7)		1.0
one cyl–each side (.9)		1.2
all cyls–both sides (1.2)		1.8
w/A.C. add (.1)		.1
w/Cruise control add (.2)		.2
w/A.I.R. add (.2)		.2
V-8–454 eng		
one cyl (.8)		1.1
one cyl–each bank (1.4)		2.0
all–both banks (1.9)		2.7
V-8–all other engs		
exc Vans		
one cyl (.8)		1.1
one cyl–each bank (1.4)		1.9
all cyls–both banks (1.9)		2.6
Vans		
one cyl–right bank (1.7)		2.5
one cyl–left bank (1.1)		1.6
one cyl–both banks (2.3)		3.3
all cyls–both banks (2.8)		4.0
w/A.C. add (.7)		.7
w/A.I.R. add (.2)		.2
Valve Lifters, Renew (Tappets)		
Includes: R&R intake manifold on V-6 & V-8 engs. Make all necessary adjustments.		
Four		
eng code E		
S-series-all (3.2)		4.3
LLV model-all (1.8)		2.5
Astro-Safari-all (3.3)		4.6
Six–exc Vans–one cyl (1.5)		2.1
all cyls (2.1)		2.9
Vans–one cyl (1.9)		2.7
all cyls (2.7)		3.9
V-6–		
1986		
S-series		
one cyl (4.1)		6.0
one cyl–each side (4.2)		6.2
all cyls–both sides (4.7)		6.9
Astro-Safari		
one cyl (3.0)		4.4
one cyl–each side (3.3)		4.8
all cyls–both sides (3.8)		5.5
All other models		
one cyl (2.6)		3.8
one cyl–each side (2.8)		4.1
all cyls–both sides (3.3)		4.8
w/A.C. add (.3)		.3
w/C.C.C. add (.3)		.3
1987-90		
eng code R		
one cyl (3.2)		4.4
all cyls (3.7)		5.1
eng code Z		
S-series		
one cyl (2.6)		3.6
all cyls (3.3)		4.6
Astro-Safari		
one cyl (3.4)		4.7
all cyls (4.0)		5.6
w/A.C. add (.1)		.1
w/Cruise control (.1)		.1
w/A.T. add (.1)		.1
C-K series		
one cyl (2.5)		3.5
one cyl–each side (2.7)		3.7
all cyls–both sides (3.1)		4.3
w./A.C. add (.2)		.2
Vans		
one cyl (2.4)		3.3
one cyl–each side (2.7)		3.7
all cyls–both sides (3.1)		4.3
w/A.C. add (.1)		.1
w/Cruise control add (.2)		.2
w/A.I.R. add (.2)		.2
V-8–454 eng		
one cyl (2.5)		3.6
all cycls (3.5)		5.0
V-8–all other engs		
exc Vans–one cyl (2.8)		3.8
all cyls (3.4)		4.6
Vans–one cyl (3.2)		4.6
one cyl–each bank (3.6)		5.2
all cyls–both banks (4.2)		6.0
w/A.C. add (.7)		.7
w/A.I.R. add (.2)		.2
Valve Springs or Valve Stem Oil Seals, Renew (Head on Truck)		
Four		
eng code A		
one cyl (.8)		1.3
all cyls (1.4)		2.2
eng code Y		
one cyl (1.1)		1.6
all cyls (2.0)		3.0

LABOR 12 CYLINDER HEAD & VALVE SYSTEM 12 LABOR

	(Factory) Time	Chilton Time
eng code E		
S-series		
one cyl (1.2)		1.9
all cyls (2.2)		3.1
Astro-Safari		
one cyl (1.8)		2.6
all cyls (2.8)		3.8
Six—exc Vans		
one cyl (1.3)		1.8
all cyls (2.7)		3.7
Vans		
one cyl (1.5)		2.1
all cyls (2.9)		4.0
V-6		
1986		
S-series-Astro-Safari		
one cyl (1.3)		1.9
one cyl-each side (2.3)		3.4
all cyls-both sides (3.6)		5.3
All other models		
one cyl-right side (1.4)		2.0
one cyl-left side (1.0)		1.5
one cyl-each side (2.0)		2.9
all cyls-both sides (3.2)		4.7
1987-90		
eng code R		
one cyl-right side (1.5)		2.1
one cyl-left side (1.1)		1.5
one cyl-each side (2.3)		3.2
all cyls-both sides (3.7)		5.1
eng code Z		
S-series		
one cyl (1.2)		1.6
one cyl-each side (1.9)		2.6
all cyls-both sides (3.6)		5.0
Astro-Safari		
one cyl (1.2)		1.6
one cyl-each side (1.7)		2.3
all cyls-both sides (3.1)		4.3
C-K series		
one cyl (.9)		1.2
one cyl-each side (1.4)		1.9
all cyls-both sides (2.8)		3.9
Vans		
one cyl (1.0)		1.4
one cyl-each side (1.5)		2.1
all cyls-both sides (2.9)		4.0
w/A.C. add (.1)		.1
w/Cruise control add (.2)		.2
w/A.I.R. add (.2)		.2
V-8-454 eng		
one cyl (1.1)		1.6
all cyls (3.7)		5.3
V-8-all other engs		
exc Vans		
one cyl (1.1)		1.5
all cyls (3.6)		5.0
Vans		
one cyl-right bank (2.1)		3.0
one cyl-left bank (1.4)		2.0
one cyl-each bank (3.0)		4.3
all cyls-both banks (4.7)		6.8
w/A.C. add (.7)		.7
w/A.I.R. add (.2)		.2

Valve Rocker Arm Stud, Renew (One)
Includes: Drain and refill cooling system.

Four		
eng code E		
S-series (1.0)		1.5
Astro-Safari (1.5)		2.2
Six—exc Vans (1.1)		1.5
Vans (1.5)		2.1

	(Factory) Time	Chilton Time
V-6		
1986		
S-series-Astro-Safari (1.3)		1.8
All other models		
right side (1.3)		1.8
left side (.9)		1.4
w/A.C. add (.3)		.3
w/C.C.C. add (.3)		.3
1987-90		
eng code R		
right side (1.1)		1.5
left side (.8)		1.1
eng code Z		
S-series		
Astro-Safari		
right side (1.1)		1.5
left side (.9)		1.2
C-K series		
one (.7)		.9
Vans		
one (.9)		1.2
w/A.C. add (.1)		.1
w/Cruise control add (.2)		.2
w/A.I.R. add (.2)		.2
V-8-454 eng (.8)		1.1
V-8-all other engs		
exc Vans (1.1)		1.5
Vans (.8)		1.1
each adtnl-all engs (.3)		.3
w/A.C. add (.2)		.2
w/A.I.R. add (.3)		.3

DIESEL ENGINE

Compression Test

All models		1.3

Cylinder Head Gasket, Renew

Includes: R&R injector pump and lines. R&R intake manifold and disconnect exhaust manifolds. Clean gasket surfaces, bleed litters and adjust timing. Drain and refill cooling system.

All models-5.7L eng		
right side (5.0)		6.1
left side (4.9)		6.0
both sides (7.2)		9.1
6.2L eng		
one side (5.8)		8.0
both sides (8.1)		11.2
2.2L eng (2.6)		3.8
w/A.C. add (.3)		.3
Vans-w/A.C. add (2.0)		2.0

Cylinder Head, Renew

Includes: R&R injector pump and lines. R&R intake manifold and disconnect exhaust manifolds. Clean gasket surfaces. Transfer parts, reface valves. Bleed lifters and adjust timing. Drain and refill cooling system.

All models-5.7L eng		
right side (5.5)		6.9
left side (5.4)		6.8
both sides (8.1)		10.7
6.2L eng		
one side (6.8)		9.5
both sides (9.6)		13.3
2.2L eng (3.9)		5.7
w/A.C. add (.3)		.3
Vans-w/A.C. add (2.0)		2.0

Clean Carbon and Grind Valves

Includes: R&R injector pump and lines. R&R cylinder heads, clean carbon. Recondition valves and valve seats. Check and adjust valve stem length. Bleed lifters, drain and refill cooling system.

All models-5.7L eng		
right side (5.4)		7.2

	(Factory) Time	Chilton Time
left side (5.3)		7.1
both sides (9.1)		12.6
6.2L eng		
one side (7.1)		9.8
both sides (10.4)		14.4
2.2L eng (3.9)		5.7
w/A.C. add (.3)		.3
Vans-w/A.C. add (2.0)		2.0

Rocker Arm Cover or Gasket, Renew
Includes: R&R injector pump and lines.

All models-5.7L eng		
one side (2.0)		2.6
both sides (2.2)		2.9
6.2L eng		
one side (2.6)		3.6
both sides (3.1)		4.3
2.2L eng (.4)		.6
Vans-w/A.C. add (2.0)		2.0

Valve Spring or Valve Stem Oil Seals, Renew (Head on Truck)
Includes: R&R injector pump and lines.

All models-5.7L eng		
one (2.2)		3.1
one-each bank (2.6)		3.7
each adtnl(.3)		.3
6.2L eng		
one cyl (3.0)		4.2
one cyl-each side (3.9)		5.4
each adtnl cyl (.4)		.4
2.2L eng		
one cyl (.8)		1.2
all cyls (1.3)		2.0
Vans-w/A.C. add (2.0)		2.0

Rocker Arm and/or Push Rod, Renew
Includes: R&R injector pump and lines.

All models-5.7L eng		
one cyl (2.1)		3.0
one cyl-each side (2.5)		3.5
each adtnl cyl (.1)		.1
6.2L eng		
one cyl (2.7)		3.7
one cyl-each side (3.3)		4.6
each adtnl cyl (.1)		.1
2.2L eng		
one or all (.7)		1.2
Vans-w/A.C. add (2.0)		2.0

Valve Lifters, Renew
Includes: R&R fuel injection pump and lines.

All models-5.7L eng		
one cyl (3.2)		4.2
one cyl-each side (3.5)		4.5
each adtnl cyl (.1)		.2
6.2L eng-exc Vans		
one cyl (3.4)		4.7
one cyl-each side (4.6)		6.4
each adtnl cyl (.1)		.2
Vans		
one cyl (6.7)		9.3
one cyl-each side (8.8)		12.2
each adtnl cyl (.1)		.1
2.2L eng-all (6.9)		10.0
w/A.C. add (.8)		.8
w/P.S. add (.3)		.3
Vans-w/A.C. add (2.0)		2.0

Push Rod Side Cover Gasket, Renew

All models		
2.2L eng (1.1)		1.5

Valve Clearance, Adjust

All models		
2.2L eng (.6)		1.0

LABOR   13   ENGINE ASSEMBLY & MOUNTS   13   LABOR

	(Factory Time)	Chilton Time

Note: All engine operations listed in this group are for assemblies as supplied by the original equipment manufacturer. Time to replace assemblies from independent rebuilders may vary.

GASOLINE ENGINES

Engine Assembly, R&R

Does not include transfer of any parts or equipment.

	Factory	Chilton
Four		5.0
w/A.C. add		.9
w/P.S. add		.4
w/A.T. add		.3
w/Cruise control add		.2
w/Skid plate add		.3
Six—exc Vans		5.1
Vans		7.7
w/P.S. add		.3
w/A.C. add		1.3
w/M.T. add		.5
V-6		
S-series		
4X2		5.5
4X4		*6.7
*w/M.T. add	(2.0)	2.0
Astro-Safari		6.9
exc Vans		4.9
Vans		5.9
w/P.S. add		.3
w/C.C.C. add		.6
w/A.T. add		.4
w/A.C. add		
Vans		1.1
Astro-Safari		.9
All other models		.4
V-8—454 eng		6.2
V-8—all other engs		
exc Vans		6.2
Vans		8.6
w/A.C. add		.4
w/P.S. add		.3
w/A.I.R. add		.4
w/M.T. add		.5
w/A.T. add		.3
Vans with A.C. add		1.7

Engine Assembly, Renew

Includes: R&R engine and transmission assy. Transfer all component parts not supplied with replacement engine. Minor tune up.

	Factory	Chilton
Four		
eng code Y		
4X2 (5.4)		8.0
4X4 (8.4)		12.0
w/A.C. add		.4
w/P.S. add		.4
eng code E		
S-series		
4X2 (4.8)		7.0
4X4 (5.6)		8.1
Astro-Safari (6.6)		9.6
w/A.C. add		.9
w/P.S. add		.3
w/A.T. add		.3
w/Cruise control add		.2
w/Skid plate add		.3
Six—exc Vans (4.9)		8.2
Vans (5.5)		9.6
w/P.S. add (.3)		.3
w/A.C. add (1.3)		1.3
w/M.T. add		.5
V-6		
S-series		
eng Code R		
4X2 (5.7)		8.0
4X4 (6.2)		*8.6
w/A.C. add (.2)		.2
w/P.S. add (.2)		.2
w/M.T. add (.2)		.2

	Factory	Chilton
w/Skid plate add (.2)		.2
*1986—w/M.T. add		2.0
eng Code Z		
4X2 (6.1)		9.0
4X4 (7.1)		10.2
w/A.C. add (.2)		.2
w/P.S. add (.2)		.2
w/A.T. add (.1)		.1
Astro-Safari (7.2)		10.4
exc Vans (5.8)		8.4
Vans (6.5)		9.4
w/P.S. add (.3)		.3
w/C.C.C. add (.6)		.6
w/A.T. add (.4)		.4
w/A.C. add		
Vans (1.1)		1.1
Astro-Safari (.9)		.9
All other models (.4)		.4
V-8—454 eng (6.9)		9.3
V-8—all other engs		
exc Vans (6.0)		8.2
Vans (7.8)		11.3
w/A.C. add (.4)		.4
w/P.S. add (.3)		.3
w/A.I.R. add (.4)		.4
w/M.T. add (.5)		.5
w/A.T. add (.3)		.3
Vans with A.C. add (1.7)		1.7

**Cylinder Block, Renew (Partial-Basic)
(w/All Internal Parts Less Head(s) and Oil Pan)**

Includes: R&R engine and transmission assy. Transfer all components parts not supplied with replacement engine. Minor tune up.

	Factory	Chilton
Four		
eng code A		
4X2 (8.0)		12.0
4X4 (8.9)		13.0
eng code Y		
4X2 (9.9)		14.5
4X4 (13.1)		19.0
w/A.C. add (.4)		.4
w/P.S. add (.4)		.4
eng code E		
S-series		
4X2 (7.5)		11.2
4X4 (8.5)		12.6
Astro-Safari (9.5)		14.0
w/A.C. add		.9
w/P.S. add		.3
w/A.T. add		.3
w/Cruise control add		.2
w/Skid plate add		.3
Recond valves add (1.3)		1.8
Six—exc Vans (8.3)		11.6
Vans (9.5)		13.3
w/P.S. add (.3)		.3
w/A.C. add (1.3)		1.3
w/M.T. add		.5
Recond valves add (1.9)		2.5
V-6		
1986		
S-series		
4X2 (9.7)		13.5
4X4 (10.5)		*14.7
*w/M.T. add		2.0
Astro-Safari (11.1)		15.5
exc Vans (9.6)		13.4
Vans (10.4)		14.5
Recond valves add (1.9)		2.5
w/P.S. add (.3)		.3
w/C.C.C. add (.6)		.6
w/A.C. add		
Vans (1.1)		1.1
Astro (.9)		.9
All other models (.4)		.4

	Factory	Chilton
1987-90		
S-series		
eng code R		
4X2 (9.5)		13.3
4X4 (10.0)		14.0
w/A.C. add (.2)		.2
w/P.S. add (.2)		.2
w/M.T. add (.2)		.2
w/Skid plate add (.3)		.3
Recond valves add (1.9)		2.5
eng code Z		
S-series		
4X2 (9.2)		13.3
4X4 (10.2)		14.7
w/A.C. add (.2)		.2
w/P.S. add (.2)		.2
w/A.T. add (.2)		.2
Recond valves add (1.9)		2.5
Vans-Astro-Safari (10.5)		14.7
w/A.C. add (1.1)		1.1
w/P.S. add (.3)		3
w/AIR add (.4)		.4
w/Cruise control add (.2)		.2
w/A.T. add (.4)		.4
Recond valves add (1.9)		2.5
C-K series (8.8)		12.3
w/A.C. add (.2)		.2
w/AIR add (.2)		.2
w/A.T. add (.1)		1
Recond valves add (1.9)		2.5
V-8—454 eng (11.4)		15.9
V-8—all other engs		
exc Vans (8.8)		12.3
Vans (12.3)		17.2
w/A.C. add (.4)		.4
w/P.S. add (.3)		.3
w/A.I.R. add (.4)		.4
w/M.T. add (.5)		.5
w/A.T. add (.3)		.3
Vans with A.C. add (1.7)		1.7
Recond valves add (2.7)		3.5

**Cylinder Block, Renew (Fitted)
(w/Pistons, Rings and Bearings)**

Includes: R&R engine and transmission assy. Transfer all component parts not supplied with replacement engine. Clean carbon, grind valves. Minor tune up.

	Factory	Chilton
Four		
eng code E		
S-series		
4X2 (11.3)		16.4
4X4 (12.1)		17.5
Astro-Safari (13.1)		19.0
w/A.C. add		.9
w/P.S. add		.3
w/A.T. add		.3
w/Cruise control add		.2
w/Skid plate add		.3
Six—exc Vans (13.2)		18.4
Vans (13.7)		19.1
w/P.S. add (.3)		.3
w/A.C. add (1.3)		1.3
w/M.T. add		.5
V-6		
S-series		
eng Code R		
4X2 (14.6)		21.1
4X4 (15.0)		*21.7
w/A.C. add (.2)		.2
w/P.S. add (.2)		.2
w/M.T. add (.2)		.2
w/Skid plate add (.2)		.2
*1986—w/M.T. add (2.0)		2.0
eng Code Z		
4X2 (14.7)		21.3
4X4 (15.4)		22.3
w/A.C. add (.2)		.2
w/P.S. add (.2)		.2

LABOR 13 ENGINE ASSEMBLY & MOUNTS 13 LABOR

(Factory Time)	Chilton Time
w/A.T. add (.1)............................	.1
Astro-Safari (16.0)	23.2
exc Vans (14.5)...........................	21.0
Vans (15.3)................................	22.2
w/P.S. add (.3)............................	.3
w/C.C.C. add (.6).........................	.6
w/A.T. add (.4)............................	.4
w/A.C. add	
Vans (1.1)................................	1.1
Astro-Safari (.9).........................	.9
All other models (.4)	.4
V-8–454 eng (17.7).......................	23.8
V-8–all other engs	
exc Vans (17.0)..........................	23.4
Vans (17.8)...............................	25.8
w/A.C. add (.4)...........................	.4
w/P.S. add (.3)...........................	.3
w/A.I.R. add (.4).........................	.4
w/M.T. add (.5)...........................	.5
w/A.T. add (.3)...........................	.3
Vans with A.C. add (1.7)...............	1.7

Engine Assy., R&R and Recondition
Includes: Rebore block, install new pistons, rings, rod and main bearings. Clean carbon, grind valves. Tune engine.

Four

eng code A	
4X2 (13.2)............................	19.7
4X4 (14.1)............................	21.0
eng code Y	
4X2 (16.0)............................	23.8
4X4 (18.6)............................	27.7
w/A.C. add (.4)	.4
w/P.S. add (.4)	.4
eng code E	
S-series	
4X2 (13.5).........................	19.5
4X4 (14.4).........................	20.8
Astro-Safari (15.4)...............	22.3
w/A.C. add.............................	.9
w/P.S. add.............................	.3
w/A.T. add.............................	.3
w/Cruise control add	.2
w/Skid plate add	.3
Six–exc Vans (25.0)................	32.0
Vans (27.6).............................	34.6
w/P.S. add (.3)	.3
w/A.C. add (1.3)	1.3
w/M.T. add	.5

V-6

S-series	
eng Code R	
4X2 (20.3).........................	28.4
4X4 (20.7).........................	*28.9
w/A.C. add (.2)	.2
w/P.S. add (.2)	.2
w/M.T. add (.2)	.2
w/Skid plate add (.2)	.2
*1986–w/M.T. add (2.0)	2.0
eng Code Z	
4X2 (20.3).........................	28.4
4X4 (21.3).........................	29.8

(Factory Time)	Chilton Time
w/A.C. add (.2)...........................	.2
w/P.S. add (.2)...........................	.2
w/A.T. add (.1)...........................	.1
Astro-Safari (23.4)......................	31.5
exc Vans (20.9).........................	28.8
Vans (21.7)...............................	29.2
w/P.S. add (.3)...........................	.3
w/C.C.C. add (.6).......................	.6
w/A.T. add (.4)...........................	.4
w/A.C. add	
Vans (1.1)................................	1.1
Astro-Safari (.9).........................	.9
All other models (.4)	.4
V-8–454 eng (32.5)......................	41.9
V-8–all other engs	
exc Vans (30.7)..........................	43.5
Vans (32.2)...............................	45.0
w/A.C. add (.4)...........................	.4
w/P.S. add (.3)...........................	.3
w/A.I.R. add (.4).........................	.4
w/M.T. add (.5)...........................	.5
w/A.T. add (.3)...........................	.3
Vans with A.C. add (1.7)...............	1.7

Engine Mounts, Renew
Front

Four–one (.5)..........................	.7
both (.7)..............................	1.0
4X2 add–each...........................	.2
w/P.S. add (.2)..........................	.2
Six–exc Vans–one (.7)...............	1.1
both (.9)..............................	1.4
Vans–one (.9).........................	1.3
both (1.2)............................	1.6

V-6

1986-87	
S-series	
one (1.0).........................	1.4
both (1.4)........................	1.9
1988-90	
eng Code R	
4X2	
right (1.8)	2.4
left (2.0)	2.6
both (3.2)	4.5
4X4	
right (1.5)	2.0
left (1.6)	2.1
both (1.7)	2.3
w/Skid plate add (.1)...............	.1
eng Code Z	
one (1.7)........................	2.3
both (2.2).......................	3.0
All other models	
one (.7).........................	1.1
both (1.2).......................	1.7

V-8–all engines

one (.8)...............................	1.3
both (1.2).............................	1.9
Rear	
All models (.4).........................	.7

(Factory Time)	Chilton Time
DIESEL ENGINE	

Engine Assembly, Remove & Install
Does not include transfer of any parts or equipment.

All models................................	5.0
w/A.C. add	1.2
w/A.T. add	.8

Engine Assembly, Renew (Universal)
Includes: R&R engine assembly. Transfer all component parts not supplied with replacement engine. Make all necessary adjustments.

All models	
5.7L eng	20.0
6.2L eng	22.0
w/A.C. add	1.2
w/A.T. add	.8

Cylinder Block, Renew (Partial)
Includes: Transfer all component parts not supplied with replacement block. Clean carbon, grind valves. Make all necessary adjustments.

All models	
2.2L eng (11.1).....................	18.0
5.7L eng	21.3
6.2L eng	
Vans (17.4).......................	29.5
All other models (15.5)...........	27.6
w/A.C. add	1.2
w/A.T. add	.8

Engine Assembly, R&R and Recondition
Includes: Rebore block, install new pistons, rings, rod and main bearings. Clean carbon, grind valves. Make all necessary adjustments.

All models	
2.2L eng	27.3
5.7L eng	37.2
6.2L eng	40.0
w/A.C. add	1.2
w/A.T. add	.8

Engine Assembly, Recondition (In Truck)
Includes: Expand or renew pistons, install new rings, pins, rod and main bearings. Clean carbon, grind valves. Make all necessary adjustments.

All models	
2.2L eng..............................	20.1
5.7L eng	28.5
6.2L eng	32.9
w/A.C. add (.3).........................	.3

Engine Mounts, Renew
Front

All models–5.7L eng	
one (.5).............................	.8
both (.6)............................	1.0
6.2L eng	
one (.7).............................	1.0
both (1.1)...........................	1.5
2.2L eng	
one (1.0)............................	1.4
both (1.8)...........................	2.6
Rear	
All models (.4).........................	.6

LABOR 14 PISTONS, RINGS & BEARINGS 14 LABOR

(Factory Time)	Chilton Time
GASOLINE ENGINES	

Rings, Renew (See Engine Combinations)
Includes: Remove cylinder top ridge, deglaze cylinder walls, replace rod bearings, clean carbon from cylinder heads. Clean piston and ring grooves. Minor tune up.

Four

eng code A	
one cyl (5.9)........................	8.5

(Factory Time)	Chilton Time
each adtnl cyl......................	.7
4X4 add (.9)	.9
eng code Y	
one cyl (6.9)........................	10.0
each adtnl cyl......................	.7
4X4 add (.4)	.4
w/A.C. add (.4)	.4
w/P.S. add (.4)	.4
eng code E S-series	
4X2–one cyl (6.5)...................	10.5

(Factory Time)	Chilton Time
4X4–one cyl (8.5)...................	13.0
Astro-Safari–one cyl (6.4)	10.0
each adtnl cyl......................	.7
w/A.C. add	.6
w/P.S. add	.1
w/Cruise control add	.2
w/A.T. add	.2
w/Skid plate add	.3
Six–exc Vans–one cyl (7.0)........	9.8
all cyls (8.6)........................	12.0

LABOR   14   PISTONS, RINGS & BEARINGS   14   LABOR

	Factory Time	Chilton Time
Vans–one cyl (7.0)		10.0
all cyls (8.6)		12.2
w/A.C. add (.3)		.3
V-6		
S-series–Astro-Safari		
eng Code R		
one cyl (8.4)		11.7
one cyl–each side (10.4)		14.5
all cyls–both sides (11.2)		15.6
eng Code Z		
4X2		
one cyl (8.0)		11.2
one cyl–each side (9.0)		12.6
all cyls–both sides (9.8)		13.7
4X4		
one cyl–right side (8.4)		11.7
one cyl–left side (10.1)		14.1
one cyl–each side (13.5)		18.9
all cyls–both sides (14.3)		20.0
w/A.C. add (.2)		.2
w/P.S. add (.2)		.2
w/A.T. add (.1)		.1
w/Skid plate add (.1)		.1
All other models		
one cyl (6.6)		9.5
one cyl–each side (8.8)		12.8
all cyls–both sides (10.7)		15.5
w/A.C. add (.5)		.5
w/P.S. add (.5)		.5
w/C.C.C. add (.3)		.3
V-8–454 eng–one (6.6)		9.1
all (10.9)		14.8
V-8–all other engs		
exc Vans–one (6.1)		8.4
all (10.8)		14.9
Vans–one cyl (7.7)		11.1
all cyls (12.7)		18.4
w/A.C. add (.7)		.7
w/P.S. add (.2)		.2
w/A.I.R. add (.2)		.2

Piston or Connecting Rod, Renew

Includes: Remove cylinder top ridge, deglaze cylinder walls, replace rod bearings, clean carbon from cylinder heads. Minor tune up.

Four		
eng code A		
one cyl (6.3)		9.1
each adtnl cyl		.7
4X4 add (.9)		.9
eng code Y		
one cyl (7.3)		10.5
each adtnl cyl		.7
4X4 add (.4)		.4
w/A.C. add (.4)		.4
w/P.S. add (.4)		.4
eng code E		
S-series		
4X2–one cyl (7.0)		10.8
4X4–one cyl (9.0)		13.3
Astro-Safari–one cyl (6.9)		10.3
each adtnl cyl		.7
w/A.C. add		.6
w/P.S. add		.1
w/Cruise control add		.2
w/A.T. add		.2
w/Skid plate add		.3
Six–exc Vans–one cyl (7.5)		10.5
all cyls (9.4)		13.1
Vans–one cyl (7.5)		10.7
all cyls (9.4)		13.3
w/A.C. add (.3)		.3
V-6		
S-series–Astro-Safari		
eng Code R		
one cyl (8.5)		12.0
one cyl–each side (10.6)		15.1
all cyls–both sides (12.5)		17.4
eng Code Z		
4X2		
one cyl (8.1)		11.5
one cyl–each side (9.2)		13.2

COMBINATIONS
Add to Engine Work
See Machine Shop Operations
GASOLINE ENGINES

	Factory Time	Chilton Time		Factory Time	Chilton Time
DRAIN, EVACUATE AND RECHARGE AIR CONDITIONING SYSTEM			**REMOVE CYLINDER TOP RIDGE**		
All models (.5)		1.0	Each (.3)		.3
ROCKER ARM STUD, RENEW			**VALVES, RECONDITION**		
Each (.3)		.3	Four (1.8)		2.5
HYDRAULIC VALVE LIFTERS, DISASSEMBLE AND CLEAN			Six (2.1)		3.0
			V-6 (2.0)		3.0
Each		.2	V-8 (2.7)		3.5
DISTRIBUTOR, RECONDITION			**PLASTIGAUGE BEARINGS**		
All models (.5)		.9	Each (.1)		.1
CARBURETOR, RECONDITION			**OIL PUMP, RECONDITION**		
1 BBL (1.0)		1.0	All models		.6
2 BBL (1.0)		1.2	w/P.S. add (.2)		.2
4 BBL (.8)		1.5	w/C.C.C. add (.2)		.2
VALVE GUIDES, REAM OVERSIZE			**OIL FILTER, RENEW**		
Each (.1)		.1	Four (.3)		.4
DEGLAZE CYLINDER WALLS			Six (.2)		.3
Each (.1)		.1	V-6 (.3)		.4
			V-8 (.3)		.4

	Factory Time	Chilton Time
all cyls–both sides (11.1)		15.5
4X4		
one cyl–right side (8.5)		12.0
one cyl–left side (10.2)		14.7
one cyl–each side (13.7)		19.5
all cyls–both sides (14.6)		21.8
w/A.C. add (.2)		.2
w/P.S. add (.2)		.2
w/A.T. add (.1)		.1
w/Skid plate add (.1)		.1
All other models		
one cyl (6.6)		9.8
one cyl–each side (8.8)		13.4
all cyls–both sides (13.3)		17.3
w/A.C. add (.5)		.5
w/P.S. add (.5)		.5
w/C.C.C. add (.3)		.3
V-8–454 eng–one (6.6)		9.4
all (10.9)		17.2
V-8–all other engs		
exc Vans–one (6.1)		8.7
all (10.8)		17.3
Vans–one cyl (7.9)		11.4
all cyls (13.8)		20.8
w/A.C. add (.7)		.7
w/P.S. add (.2)		.2
w/A.I.R. add (.2)		.2

Connecting Rod Bearings, Renew

Four		
eng code A (4.8)		6.7
eng code Y		
4X2 (5.7)		8.0
4X4 (4.7)		6.5
w/A.C. add (.4)		.4
w/P.S. add (.4)		.4
eng code E		
S-series		
4X2 (3.7)		5.5
4X4 (5.5)		7.8
Astro-Safari–(3.0)		4.2
w/P.S. add		.1
w/A.T. add		.2
w/Skid plate add		.2
Six–one (2.2)		2.8
all (3.3)		4.9
V-6		
S-series		
4X2 (6.4)		9.4

	Factory Time	Chilton Time
4X4 (4.9)		7.3
All other models (3.4)		4.9
w/A.C. add (.2)		.2
w/P.S. add (.2)		.2
w/C.C.C. add (.2)		.2
w/A.T. add (.3)		.3
V-8–454 eng–one (1.8)		2.8
all (3.9)		5.4
V-8–all other engs		
All models–one (1.4)		2.0
all (3.4)		4.9
w/M.T. add (.2)		.2

DIESEL ENGINE

Rings, Renew (See Engine Combinations)

Includes: Remove cylinder to ridge, deglaze cylinder walls. Clean piston and ring grooves. Make all necessary adjustments.

All models		
2.2L eng (10.0)		14.5
w/A.C. add (.8)		.8
w/P.S. add (.3)		.3
5.7L eng (10.6)		14.0
6.2L eng (15.4)		21.5
w/A.C. add (.3)		.3

Piston or Connecting Rod, Renew

Includes: Remove cylinder top ridge, deglaze cylinder walls. Make all necessary adjustments.

All models		
2.2L eng (10.0)		16.3
w/A.C. add (.8)		.8
w/P.S. add (.3)		.3
5.7L eng (10.7)		16.8
6.2L eng (16.5)		23.9
w/A.C. add (.3)		.3

Connecting Rod Bearings, Renew

Includes: Raise engine and clean oil pump screen.

All models		
2.2L eng (7.5)		10.8
w/A.C. add (.8)		.8
w/P.S. add (.3)		.3
5.7L eng (4.0)		5.6
6.2L eng		
Vans (5.6)		7.8
All other models (4.0)		5.8

LABOR   15   CRANKSHAFT & DAMPER   15   LABOR

(Factory Time)	Chilton Time
GASOLINE ENGINES	
Crankshaft and Main Bearings, Renew	
Includes: R&R engine, plastigauge bearings.	
Four	
eng code A	
4X2 (7.8)	11.3
4X4 (8.9)	12.9
eng code Y	
4X2 (7.8)	11.5
4X4 (10.4)	15.0
w/A.C. add (.4)	.4
w/P.S. add (.4)	.4
eng code E	
S-series	
4X2 (6.3)	9.3
4X4 (7.3)	10.6
Astro-Safari (8.3)	12.0
w/A.C. add	.9
w/P.S. add	.3
w/A.T. add	.3
w/Cruise control add	.2
w/Skid plate add	.3
Six—exc Vans (7.3)	10.2
Vans (9.3)	13.4
w/P.S. add (.3)	.3
w/A.C. add (1.2)	1.2
w/M.T. add	.5
V-6	
S-series	
4X2 (8.5)	12.3
4X4 (9.0)	•13.0
*w/M.T. add	2.0
Astro-Safari (10.2)	14.8
exc Vans (9.1)	13.2
Vans (9.7)	14.0
w/P.S. add (.3)	.3
w/C.C.C. add (.6)	.6
w/A.T. add (.4)	.4
w/A.C. add	
Vans (1.1)	1.1
Astro-Safari (.9)	.9
All other models (.4)	.4
V-8-454 eng (9.2)	12.4
V-8—all other engs	
exc Vans (8.8)	12.3
Vans (10.3)	14.8
w/A.C. add (.4)	.4
w/P.S. add (.3)	.3
w/A.I.R. add (.4)	.4
w/M.T. add (.5)	.5
w/A.T. add (.3)	.3
Vans with A.C. add (1.7)	1.7
Main Bearings, Renew	
Includes: Plastigauge bearings.	
Four	
eng code A (5.2)	7.5
eng code Y	
4X2 (5.8)	8.4
4X4 (4.7)	6.8
w/A.C. add (.4)	.4
w/P.S. add (.4)	.4
eng code E	
S-series	
4X2 (3.7)	5.8
4X4 (5.5)	8.1
Astro-Safari (3.0)	4.5
w/P.S. add	.1
w/A.T. add	.2
w/Skid plate	.2
Six—exc Vans (3.1)	4.9
Vans (3.3)	5.2
V-6	
S-series	
4X2 (6.1)	9.5
4X4 (4.9)	7.8
All other models (3.1)	4.5

(Factory Time)	Chilton Time
w/A.C. add (.2)	.2
w/P.S. add (.2)	.2
w/C.C.C. add (.2)	.2
w/A.T. add (.3)	.3
w/Skid plate add (.3)	.3
V-8-454 eng (3.2)	5.0
V-8—all other engs	
All models (3.9)	5.6
w/M.T. add (.2)	.2
Rear Main Bearing Oil Seal, Renew	
Four	
eng code A (4.1)	•6.3
eng code Y	
4X2 (6.7)	•9.7
4X4 (9.2)	•13.3
w/A.C. add (.4)	.4
w/P.S. add (.4)	.4
eng code E	
S-series	
4X2 (2.9)	4.2
4X4 (3.4)	5.0
Astro-Safari (2.1)	3.2
w/Skid plate add	.3
w/A.T. add (.4)	.4
w/M.T. add (.4)	.4
Six—exc Vans (1.9)	2.7
Vans (2.2)	3.2
V-6	
S-series	
1986-87	
4X2	
w/M.T. (2.8)	4.0
w/A.T. (3.8)	5.5
4X4	
w/M.T. (3.7)	5.3
w/A.T. (3.9)	5.6
w/Skid plate add (.3)	.3
1988-90	
eng Code R	
4X2	
w/M.T. (2.6)	4.0
w/A.T. (4.0)	5.8
4X4	
w/M.T. (4.0)	5.8
w/A.T. (3.3)	4.7
w/Skid plate add(.3)	.3
eng Code Z	
4X2 (2.4)	3.5
4X4 (4.1)	5.9
Vans-Astro-Safari	
w/M.T. (2.2)	3.2
w/A.T. (2.9)	4.2
All other models	
4X2	
w/M.T. (2.5)	3.6
w/A.T. (2.3)	3.3
4X4	
w/M.T. (3.1)	4.5
w/A.T. (3.2)	4.7
V-8-454 eng (2.0)	3.3
V-8—all other engs	
4X2	
w/M.T. (2.1)	3.0
w/A.T. (2.2)	3.1
4X4	
w/M.T. (2.9)	4.2
w/A.T. (2.6)	3.7
Harmonic Balancer (Vibration Damper), Renew	
Includes: Renew timing cover oil seal.	
Four	
eng code A (.9)	1.5
eng code Y (.7)	1.4
eng code E (.5)	1.1

(Factory Time)	Chilton Time
w/A.C. add (.2)	.2
w/P.S. add (.2)	.2
Six—exc Vans (1.5)	2.1
Vans (1.1)	1.5
w/A.C. add (.2)	.2
V-6	
All models (.8)	1.3
w/A.C. add (.2)	.2
w/P.S. add (.2)	.2
V-8-454 eng (1.2)	1.6
V-8—all other engs	
All models (1.0)	1.5
w/A.C. add (.2)	.2
w/P.S. add (.2)	.2
w/A.I.R. add (.2)	.2
DIESEL ENGINE	
Crankshaft and Main Bearings, Renew	
Includes: R&R engine, plastigauge bearings.	
All models	
2.2L eng (8.9)	13.0
w/A.C. add (.8)	.8
w/P.S. add (.3)	.3
5.7L eng (7.5)	10.9
6.2L eng	
Vans (13.4)	19.5
All other models (8.5)	12.3
w/A.C. add (.3)	.3
w/A.T. add	.8
Main Bearings, Renew	
Includes: Plastigauge bearings.	
All models	
2.2L eng (7.9)	11.4
w/A.C. add (.8)	.8
w/P.S. add (.3)	.3
5.7L eng (3.5)	5.4
6.2L eng	
Vans (4.9)	7.0
All other models (3.5)	5.0
Main and Rod Bearings, Renew	
Includes: Check all bearing clearance.	
All models	
2.2L eng (9.1)	12.6
w/A.C. add (.8)	.8
w/P.S. add (.3)	.3
5.7L eng (5.1)	7.8
6.2L eng	
Vans (7.3)	9.4
All other models (5.3)	7.4
Rear Main Bearing Oil Seals, Renew or Repack (Upper and Lower)	
Includes: R&R oil pan and rear main bearing cap.	
All models	
2.2L eng (1.9)	2.8
5.7L eng (2.8)	4.0
6.2L eng	
Vans (3.7)	5.4
All other models (2.5)	3.6
Harmonic Balancer (Vibration Damper), Renew	
All models	
5.7L eng (.9)	1.3
6.2L eng	
Vans (1.2)	1.6
All other models (.8)	1.2
w/A.C. add (.4)	.4
Crankshaft Front Oil Seal, Renew	
All models	
5.7L eng (1.0)	1.5
6.2L eng	
Vans (1.2)	1.8
All other models (.8)	1.4
w/A.C. add (.4)	.4

LABOR 16 CAMSHAFT & TIMING GEARS 16 LABOR

GASOLINE ENGINES

Timing Cover Oil Seal, Renew

	(Factory Time)	Chilton Time
Four		
eng code A (.9)		1.7
eng code Y (.7)		1.6
eng code E (.5)		1.2
w/A.C. add (.2)		.2
w/P.S. add (.2)		.2
Six–exc Vans (1.5)		2.2
Vans (1.1)		1.6
w/A.C. add (.2)		.2
V-6		
All models (.8)		1.4
w/A.C. add (.2)		.2
w/P.S. add (.2)		.2
V-8–454 eng (1.2)		1.6
V-8–all other engs		
All models (1.0)		1.6
w/A.C. add (.2)		.2
w/P.S. add (.2)		.2
w/A.I.R. add (.2)		.2

Timing Cover Gasket, Renew
Includes: Renew oil seal.

	(Factory Time)	Chilton Time
Four		
eng code A (5.6)		8.0
eng code Y (1.7)		2.5
eng code E		
S-series (1.8)		2.5
Astro-Safari (1.3)		2.0
w/A.C. add (.2)		.2
w/P.S. add (.2)		.2
Six–exc Vans (1.8)		2.5
Vans (1.5)		2.1
w/A.C. add (.2)		.2
V-6		
1986		
S-series (2.0)		3.0
Astro-Safari (2.9)		4.2
exc Vans (2.4)		3.4
Vans (3.4)		4.9
w/A.C. add (.2)		.2
w/P.S. add (.3)		.3
1987-90		
eng code R (1.7)		2.4
eng code Z		
S-series		
4X2 (5.3)		7.4
4X4 (3.9)		5.4
Astro-Safari (2.4)		3.3
w/A.C. add (.2)		.2
C-K series–Vans (2.5)		3.5
V-8–454 eng (2.2)		2.8
V-8–all other engs		
exc Vans (2.0)		3.0
Vans (2.7)		3.9
w/A.C. add (.5)		.5
w/P.S. add (.2)		.2
w/A.I.R. add (.3)		.3
Vans w/A.C. add (1.2)		1.2

Timing Chain, Renew
Includes: R&R engine front cover.

	(Factory Time)	Chilton Time
Four		
eng code A (5.7)		8.5
eng code Y (2.0)		3.0
w/A.C. add (.4)		.4
w/P.S. add (.4)		.4
V-6		
1986		
S-series (2.3)		3.5
Astro-Safari (3.0)		4.7
exc Vans (2.5)		3.9
Vans (3.5)		5.4
w/A.C. add (.2)		.2
w/P.S. add (.3)		.3
1987-90		
eng code R (1.8)		2.7

	(Factory Time)	Chilton Time
eng code Z		
S-series		
4X2 (5.4)		7.7
4X4 (4.0)		5.7
Astro-Safari (2.5)		3.6
w/A.C. add (.2)		.2
C-K series–Vans (2.6)		3.8
V-8–454 eng (2.6)		3.3
V-8–all other engs		
exc Vans (2.2)		3.5
Vans (3.0)		4.4
w/A.C. add (.5)		.5
w/P.S. add (.2)		.2
w/A.I.R. add (.3)		.3
Vans w/A.C. add (1.2)		1.2

Camshaft, Renew
Includes: R&R engine and front cover, where required.

	(Factory Time)	Chilton Time
Four		
eng code A (1.0)		1.5
eng code Y (4.0)		6.0
eng code E		
S-series (5.0)		7.2
Astro-Safari (6.0)		8.7
w/A.C. add		.5
w/P.S. add		.3
w/A.T. add		.1
Six–exc Vans (4.8)		7.1
Vans (4.7)		7.0
w/A.C. add (.8)		.8
V-6		
1986		
S-series (5.1)		8.5
Astro-Safari (5.7)		8.8
exc Vans (5.0)		7.2
Vans (7.5)		10.8
w/C.C.C. add (.3)		.3
w/A.C. add (.3)		.3
w/P.S. add (.3)		.3
1987-90		
eng code R (5.2)		7.2
w/A.C. add (.4)		.4
w/P.S. add (.2)		.2
w/A.T. add (.1)		.1
eng code Z		
S-series		
4X2 (6.5)		9.8
4X4 (7.9)		11.0
w/A.C. add (.5)		.5
w/A.T. add (.1)		.1
Astro-Safari (6.3)		8.8
w/A.C. add (.3)		.3
w/A.T. add (.3)		.3
C-K series–Vans (5.3)		7.4
w/A.C. add (.3)		.3
w/A.T. add (.1)		.1
V-8–454 eng (6.2)		9.3
V-8–all other engs		
exc Vans (4.9)		8.0
Vans (6.7)		9.5
w/A.C. add (.6)		.6
w/P.S. add (.4)		.4
w/A.I.R. add (.4)		.4

Camshaft Timing Gear, Renew

	(Factory Time)	Chilton Time
Four		
eng code A (.5)		.9
eng code Y (2.0)		3.0
eng code E		
S-series (5.0)		7.2
Astro-Safari (6.0)		8.7
w/A.C. add		.5
w/P.S. add		.3
w/A.T. add		.1
Renew crank gear add		.2
Six		
Use Camshaft R&R.		

	(Factory Time)	Chilton Time
V-6		
1986		
S-series (2.3)		3.5
Astro-Safari (3.0)		4.7
exc Vans (2.5)		3.9
Vans (3.5)		5.4
w/A.C. add (.2)		.2
w/P.S. add (.3)		.3
1987-90		
eng code R (1.8)		2.5
w/A.C. add (.2)		.2
w/P.S. add (.2)		.2
eng code Z		
S-series		
4X2 (5.4)		7.7
4X4 (4.0)		5.7
Astro-Safari-Vans (2.5)		3.5
C-K series (2.6)		3.6
w/A.C. add (.2)		.2
w/P.S. add (.2)		.2
Renew crank gear add (.2)		.2

DIESEL ENGINE

Timing Cover or Gasket, Renew
Includes: R&R fan blade, crankshaft pulley and balancer. Drain and refill oil and coolant.

	(Factory Time)	Chilton Time
All models		
2.2L eng (2.5)		3.6
5.7L eng (2.3)		3.3
6.2L eng (4.3)		6.2
w/A.C. add (.4)		.4

Timing Cover Oil Seal, Renew
Includes: R&R fan blade, crankshaft pulley and balancer. Drain and refill oil and coolant.

	(Factory Time)	Chilton Time
All models		
2.2L eng (1.1)		2.0
5.7L eng (1.0)		1.6
6.2L eng		
Vans (1.2)		2.0
All other models (.8)		1.5
w/A.C. add (.4)		.4

Camshaft Gear and/or Timing Chain, Renew
Includes: R&R fan blades, crankshaft pulley and balancer. Drain and refill oil and coolant.

	(Factory Time)	Chilton Time
All models		
5.7L eng (3.6)		4.8
6.2L eng (4.5)		6.7
w/A.C. add (.4)		.4

Injector Pump Drive Gear, Renew
Includes: R&R timing gear and chain. R&R intake manifold and lifters. Drain and refill oil and coolant, where required.

	(Factory Time)	Chilton Time
All models		
2.2L eng (.9)		1.5
5.7L eng (5.2)		7.2
6.2L eng (4.4)		6.6
w/A.C. add (.4)		.4

Camshaft, Renew
Includes: R&R radiator, front cover, fuel pump, timing gear and chain. R&R injector pump, intake manifold and lifters. Disconnect exhaust system. Drain and refill oil and coolant. Make all necessary adjustments.

	(Factory Time)	Chilton Time
All models		
2.2L eng (6.9)		10.0
w/A.C. add (.6)		.6
w/P.S. add (.3)		.3
5.7L eng (6.5)		10.8
6.2L eng (12.0)		17.4
w/A.C. add (2.0)		2.0
w/A.T. add (.3)		.3

LABOR 16 CAMSHAFT & TIMING GEARS 16 LABOR

	(Factory) Time	Chilton Time
Camshaft Bearings, Renew		
Includes: R&R radiator, front cover, fuel pump, timing gear and chain. R&R injector pump, intake manifold and lifters. Disconnect exhaust system. Drain and refill oil and coolant. Make all necessary adjustments.		
All models		
5.7L eng (9.5)		14.6
w/A.C. add (.2)		.2
Camshaft Rear Bearing Plug, Renew		
Note: Use appropriate labor operation for removal of necessary components to gain access to plug.		
All models (.3)		.6

	(Factory) Time	Chilton Time
Camshaft Timing Gear, Renew		
All models		
2.2L eng (.9)		1.6
w/A.C. add (.1)		.1
Crankshaft Timing Gear, Renew		
All models		
2.2L eng (.9)		1.6
w/A.C. add (.1)		.1
Camshaft Idler Pulley, Renew		
All models		
2.2L eng (.4)		.6
w/A.C. add (.1)		.1

	(Factory) Time	Chilton Time
Camshaft Drive Belt, Renew		
All models		
2.2L eng (.8)		1.5
w/A.C. add (.1)		.1
Camshaft Drive Belt Covers and/or Gaskets, Renew		
All models		
2.2L eng		
upper (.3)		.5
lower or both (.6)		1.0
w/A.C. add (.1)		.1

LABOR 17 ENGINE OILING SYSTEM 17 LABOR

	(Factory) Time	Chilton Time
GASOLINE ENGINE		
Oil Pan and/or Gasket, Renew		
Four		
eng code A (3.7)		5.5
eng code Y		
4X2 (4.3)		6.2
4X4 (3.2)		4.6
w/A.C. add (.4)		.4
w/P.S. add (.4)		.4
eng code E		
S-series		
4X2 (2.5)		3.6
4X4 (4.1)		6.0
LLV model (1.7)		2.4
Astro-Safari (1.6)		2.3
w/A.T. add (.2)		.2
w/P.S. add (.1)		.1
w/Skid plate add (.3)		.3
Six—exc Vans (1.7)		2.5
Vans (1.8)		2.6
V-6		
S-series		
1986-87		
4X2 (4.9)		7.3
4X4 (3.4)		5.1
1988-90		
eng Code R		
4X2 (4.8)		7.2
4X4 (2.4)		3.6
w/A.C. add (.2)		.2
w/P.S. add (.2)		.2
w/A.T. add (.4)		.4
w/Skid plate add (.3)		.3
eng Code Z		
4X2 (4.8)		7.2
4X4 (2.5)		3.7
w/A.C. add (.2)		.2
w/P.S. add (.1)		.1
w/A.T. add (.1)		.1
Astro-Safari-Vans (.9)		1.4
w/A.C. add (.2)		.2
w/P.S. add (.2)		.2
w/C.C.C. add (.2)		.2
w/A.T. add (.3)		.3
C-K series (1.3)		1.8
w/Skid plate add (.2)		.3
All other models (1.7)		2.5
V-8—454 eng (1.4)		2.5
V-8—all other engs (1.1)		1.6
w/M.T. add (.2)		.2
Pressure Test Engine Bearings (Pan Off)		
All models		1.0
Oil Pump, Renew		
Four		
eng code A (3.8)		5.7
eng code Y		
4X2 (4.4)		6.4

	(Factory) Time	Chilton Time
4X4 (3.4)		4.8
w/A.C. add (.4)		.4
w/P.S. add (.4)		.4
eng code E		
S-series		
4X2 (2.7)		3.9
4X4 (4.2)		6.2
LLV model (1.8)		2.6
Astro-Safari (1.7)		2.5
w/A.T. add		.2
w/P.S. add		.1
w/Skid plate add		.3
Six—exc Vans (1.9)		2.7
Vans (1.9)		2.8
V-6		
S-series		
1986-87		
4X2 (4.9)		7.5
4X4 (3.4)		5.3
1988-90		
eng Code R		
4X2 (4.9)		7.4
4X4 (2.5)		3.8
w/A.C. add (.2)		.2
w/P.S. add (.2)		.2
w/A.T. add (.4)		.4
w/Skid plate add (.3)		.3
eng Code Z		
4X2 (4.9)		7.4
4X4 (2.6)		3.9
w/A.C. add (.2)		.2
w/P.S. add (.1)		.1
w/A.T. add (.1)		.1
Astro-Safari-Vans (1.0)		1.6
w/A.C. add (.2)		.2
w/P.S. add (.2)		.2
w/C.C.C. add (.2)		.2
w/A.T. add (.3)		.3
C-K series (1.4)		2.0
w/Skid plate add (.2)		.3
All other models (1.8)		2.7
V-8—454 eng (1.5)		2.7
V-8—all other engs (1.2)		1.8
w/M.T. add (.2)		.2
Oil Pressure Gauge (Dash), Renew		
1986		
S-series (.3)		.5
Astro-Safari (.9)		1.4
All other models (.6)		1.0
1987-90		
S-series (.9)		1.4
Astro-Safari (.9)		1.4
C-K series (.5)		.8
All other models (.7)		1.2
Oil Pressure Gauge (Engine Unit), Renew		
All models (.2)		.5
w/A.C. add (.2)		.2

	(Factory) Time	Chilton Time
w/Cruise control add (.4)		.4
Oil Filter By-Pass Valve, Renew		
Four—eng code Y (.3)		.4
Six (.2)		.3
V-6 (.3)		.4
V-8 (.3)		.4
Oil Filter Element, Renew		
Four (.3)		.4
Six (.2)		.3
V-6 (.3)		.4
V-8 (.3)		.4
DIESEL ENGINE		
Oil Pan and/or Gasket, Renew		
Includes: Raise engine, R&R and clean oil pump screen.		
All models		
2.2L eng (.7)		1.2
5.7L eng (2.1)		3.0
6.2L eng		
Vans (3.2)		4.6
All other models (2.0)		2.9
w/M.T. add (.3)		.3
Pressure Test Engine Bearings (Pan Off)		
All models		1.0
Oil Pump, Renew		
Includes: Raise engine, R&R and clean oil pump screen.		
All models		
2.2L eng (5.9)		8.5
w/A.C. add (.6)		.6
w/P.S. add (.3)		.3
5.7L eng (2.2)		3.2
6.2L eng		
Vans (3.2)		4.8
All other models (2.1)		3.1
w/M.T. add (.3)		.3
Oil Pump, R&R and Recondition		
Includes: Raise engine, R&R and clean oil pump screen.		
All models		
5.7L eng (2.4)		3.4
Oil Pressure Sending Unit, Renew		
All models		
5.7L eng (.3)		.5
6.2L eng (1.4)		1.8
Oil Filter Element, Renew		
All models (.3)		.4
Crankcase and/or Gasket, Renew		
All models		
2.2L eng (5.8)		8.4
w/A.C. add (.6)		.6
w/P.S. add (.3)		.3

LABOR 18 CLUTCH & FLYWHEEL 18 LABOR

	(Factory) Time	Chilton Time
Clutch Pedal Free Play, Adjust		
All models (.3)		.4
Bleed Clutch Hydraulic System		
All models (.5)		.6
Clutch Master Cylinder, Renew		
Includes: Bleed system.		
10-30 Series (.5)		.8
All other models (.8)		1.2
Recond cyl add (.2)		.4
Clutch Slave (Actuator) Cylinder, Renew		
Includes: Bleed system.		
All models (.6)		1.0
Recond cyl add (.2)		.4
Clutch Assembly, Renew		
Includes: R&R trans and adjust clutch free play.		
3 Speed		
2 WD (1.5)		2.0
4 WD (1.7)		2.2
4 Speed		
C-K series–1986		
Muncie-New Process		
2 WD (2.4)		3.2
4 WD (2.8)		3.8
Muncie Getrag		
2 WD (2.6)		3.5
4 WD (2.8)		3.8
R-V series		
Muncie-Isuzu		
4X2 (2.7)		3.6
4X4 (3.7)		5.0
New Process		
4X2 (1.8)		2.4
4X4 (2.7)		3.6
C-K series–1987-90		
4X2		
Muncie-Isuzu (1.5)		2.0
HM290 (2.3)		3.1
4X4		
Muncie (2.2)		2.9
HM290 (4.0)		5.4
Vans		
Muncie-Warner-New Process (2.0).		2.6
Astro-Safari		
Muncie (1.8)		2.3
S-series		
Isuzu-Muncie		
Four		
4X2 (2.6)		3.5
4X4 (3.1)		4.2
V-6		
4X2 (2.2)		2.9
4X4 (3.2)		4.3
New Process-Warner		
4X2 (1.7)		2.2
4X4 (3.2)		4.3
5 Speed		
C-K series–1986		
4X2 (2.6)		3.5
4X4 (2.8)		3.8
C-K series–1987-90		
4X2 (2.3)		3.1
4X4 (4.0)		5.4
Astro-Safari		
All models (1.6)		2.1
S-series		
Four		
4X2 (1.7)		2.2
4X4 (2.6)		3.5

	(Factory) Time	Chilton Time
V-6		
4X2 (1.7)		2.2
4X4 (3.1)		4.2
w/Skid plate add (.3)		.3
w/Catalytic converter add (.4)		.4
w/Power take off add (.3)		.3
Renew pilot brg add (.2)		.2
Clutch Release Bearing, Fork and/or Ball Stud, Renew		
Includes: R&R trans, and adjust clutch free play.		
3 Speed		
2 WD (1.2)		1.7
4 WD (1.4)		1.9
4 Speed		
C-K series–1986		
Muncie-New Process		
2 WD (2.1)		2.9
4 WD (2.5)		3.5
Muncie Getrag		
2 WD (2.3)		3.2
4 WD (2.5)		3.5
R-V series		
Muncie-Isuzu		
4X2 (2.4)		3.3
4X4 (3.4)		4.7
New Process		
4X2 (1.5)		2.1
4X4 (2.4)		3.3
C-K series–1987-90		
4X2		
Muncie-Isuzu (1.2)		1.7
HM290 (2.0)		2.8
4X4		
Muncie (1.9)		2.6
HM290 (3.7)		5.1
Vans		
Muncie-Warner-New Process (1.7).		2.3
Astro-Safari		
Muncie (1.5)		2.0
S-series		
Isuzu-Muncie		
Four		
4X2 (2.3)		3.2
4X4 (2.8)		3.9
V-6		
4X2 (1.9)		2.6
4X4 (2.9)		4.0
New Process-Warner		
4X2 (1.4)		1.9
4X4 (2.9)		4.0
5 Speed		
C-K series–1986		
4X2 (2.3)		3.2
4X4 (2.5)		3.5
C-K series–1987-90		
4X2 (2.0)		2.8
4X4 (3.7)		5.1
Astro-Safari		
All models (1.3)		1.8
S-series		
Four		
4X2 (1.4)		1.9
4X4 (2.3)		3.2
V-6		
4X2 (1.4)		1.9
4X4 (2.8)		3.9
Renew fork assy add (.3)		.3
w/Skid plate add (.3)		.3

	(Factory) Time	Chilton Time
w/Catalytic converter add (.4)		.4
w/Power take off add (.3)		.3
Clutch Cross Shaft Assy., Renew		
Includes: Raise vehicle and adjust linkage.		
All models (.4)		.9
Flywheel, Renew		
Includes: R&R transmission.		
3 Speed		
2 WD (1.8)		2.3
4 WD (2.0)		2.5
4 Speed		
C-K series–1986		
Muncie-New Process		
2 WD (2.7)		3.5
4 WD (3.1)		4.1
Muncie Getrag		
2 WD (2.9)		3.8
4 WD (3.1)		4.1
R-V series		
Muncie-Isuzu		
4X2 (3.0)		3.9
4X4 (4.0)		5.3
New Process		
4X2 (2.1)		2.7
4X4 (3.0)		3.9
C-K series–1987-90		
4X2		
Muncie-Isuzu (1.8)		2.3
HM290 (2.3)		3.4
4X4		
Muncie (2.5)		3.2
HM290 (4.3)		5.7
Vans		
Muncie-Warner-New Process (2.3).		2.9
Astro-Safari		
Muncie (2.1)		2.6
S-series		
Isuzu-Muncie		
Four		
4X2 (2.9)		3.8
4X4 (3.4)		4.5
V-6		
4X2 (2.5)		3.2
4X4 (3.5)		4.6
New Process-Warner		
4X2 (2.0)		2.5
4X4 (3.5)		4.6
5 Speed		
C-K series–1986		
4X2 (2.9)		3.8
4X4 (3.1)		4.1
C-K series–1987-90		
4X2 (2.6)		3.4
4X4 (4.3)		5.7
Astro-Safari		
All models (1.9)		2.4
S-series		
Four		
4X2 (2.0)		2.5
4X4 (2.9)		3.8
V-6		
4X2 (2.0)		2.5
4X4 (3.4)		4.5
Renew pilot brg add (.2)		.2
w/Skid plate add (.3)		.3
w/Catalytic converter add (.3)		.4
w/Power take off add (.3)		.3
Renew ring gear add		.5

LABOR · 19A · MANUAL TRANSMISSION (RWD) · 19A · LABOR

(Factory Time)	Chilton Time
Transmission Assy., R&R or Renew	
Includes: Raise vehicle and perform necessary adjustments. Transfer all attaching parts.	
3 Speed	
4X2 (1.2)	1.7
4X4 (1.4)	1.9
4 Speed	
10-30 Series–1986	
Muncie–New Process	
4X2 (2.1)	2.9
4X4 (2.5)	3.5
Muncie Getrag	
4X2 (2.3)	3.2
4X4 (2.5)	3.5
R-V series	
Muncie-Isuzu	
4X2 (2.4)	3.3
4X4 (3.4)	4.7
New Process	
4X2 (1.5)	2.1
4X4 (2.4)	3.3
C-K series	
1987-90	
4X2	
Muncie-Isuzu (1.2)	1.7
HM290 (2.0)	2.8
4X4	
Muncie (1.9)	2.6
HM290 (3.7)	5.1
Vans	
Muncie-Warner–New Process (1.7)	2.3
Astro-Safari	
Muncie (1.5)	2.0
S-series	
Isuzu-Muncie	
Four	
4X2 (2.3)	3.2
4X4 (2.8)	3.9
V-6	
4X2 (1.9)	2.6
4X4 (2.9)	4.0
New Process-Warner	
4X2 (1.4)	1.9
4X4 (2.9)	4.0
5 Speed	
10-30 Series	
4X2 (2.3)	3.2
4X4 (2.5)	3.5
C-K series	
1987-90	
4X2 (2.0)	2.8
4X4 (3.7)	5.1
Astro-Safari	
All models (1.3)	1.8

(Factory Time)	Chilton Time
S-series	
Four	
4X2 (1.4)	1.9
4X4 (2.3)	3.2
V-6	
4X2 (1.4)	1.9
4X4 (2.8)	3.9
w/Skid plate add (.3)	.3
w/Catalytic converter add (.4)	.4
w/Power take off add (.3)	.3
Transmission Assy., R&R and Recondition	
Includes: Raise vehicle and perform all necessary adjustments.	
3 Speed	
4X2 (3.2)	4.5
4X4 (3.4)	4.7
4 Speed	
10-30 Series–1986	
Muncie	
4X2 (4.7)	6.5
4X4 (5.2)	7.2
Muncie Getrag	
4X2 (5.0)	7.0
4X4 (5.2)	7.2
R-V series	
Muncie-Isuzu	
4X2 (5.1)	7.1
4X4 (6.1)	8.5
New Process	
4X2 (3.6)	5.0
4X4 (4.5)	6.3
C-K series	
1987-90	
4X2	
Muncie-Isuzu (3.9)	5.4
HM290 (6.9)	9.6
4X4	
Muncie (4.6)	6.4
HM290 (8.5)	11.9
Vans	
Muncie-Warner-New Process (3.6)	5.0
Astro-Safari	
Muncie (3.3)	4.6
S-series	
Isuzu-Muncie	
Four	
4X2 (4.2)	6.7
4X4 (5.5)	7.7
V-6	
4X2 (3.8)	5.3
4X4 (4.6)	6.4
New Process-Warner	
4X2 (3.2)	4.4
4X4 (4.6)	6.4

(Factory Time)	Chilton Time
5 Speed	
C-K series	
1987-90	
4X2 (6.9)	9.6
4X4 (8.5)	11.9
Astro-Safari	
All models (3.3)	4.6
S-series	
4X2 (3.4)	4.7
4X4 (4.8)	6.7
w/Skid plate add (.3)	.3
w/Catalytic converter add (.4)	.4
w/Power take off add (.3)	.3
Transmission Shift Cover, Renew or Recondition	
Includes: Raise vehicle and adjust linkage.	
3 Speed	
exc Vans (.7)	1.3
Vans (.6)	1.0
Recond cover add (.3)	.5
4 Speed	
Saginaw (1.9)	2.6
New Process (.6)	1.0
Isuzu (.5)	.9
Warner (.8)	*1.4
Muncie	
10-30-C-K Series	
4X2 (1.4)	2.0
4X4 (2.1)	2.8
R-V series	
4X2 (2.6)	3.5
4X4 (3.6)	4.8
Astro-Safari (.6)	.8
S-series (.8)	1.2
*Recond add (.6)	.8
5 Speed	
S-series (.8)	*1.4
Astro-Safari (1.8)	2.5
*Recond add (.6)	.8
Transmission Rear Oil Seal, Renew	
Includes: Raise vehicle, R&R drive shaft.	
All models (.5)	.9
Renew bush add (.1)	.1
Speedometer Driven Gear, Renew	
All models (.3)	.6
Speedometer Drive Gear, Renew	
4 Speed	
All models (.9)	1.4
5 Speed	
Astro (1.8)	2.5
Transmission Speed Sensor, Renew	
All models	
1987-90 (.4)	.6

LABOR · 20 · TRANSFER CASE · 20 · LABOR

(Factory Time)	Chilton Time
Transfer Case Assy., R&R or Renew	
Dana (3.1)	4.5
New Process Model 241 (1.3)	2.0
New Process Model 231 (2.2)	3.1
New Process Model 208 (1.6)	2.3
New Process Model 207 (1.4)	2.1
New Process Model 205 (1.4)	2.1
New Process Model 203 (2.5)	3.8
Borg Warner Model 1370 (1.3)	2.0
w/Power take off add (.3)	.3
w/Skid plate add (.3)	.3
Transfer Case Assy., R&R and Recondition	
Dana (5.2)	7.1
New Process Model 241 (3.5)	5.6
New Process Model 231 (4.6)	6.6
New Process Model 208 (4.1)	5.9
New Process Model 207 (3.4)	5.5
New Process Model 206 (3.9)	6.0
New Process Model 203 (6.8)	8.7

(Factory Time)	Chilton Time
Borg Warner Model 1370 (4.4)	6.3
w/Power take off add (.3)	.3
w/Skid plate add (.3)	.3
Transfer Case Oil Seals, Renew	
Dana	
front (1.1)	1.7
rear (.6)	1.0
New Process Model 241	
front (.5)	.9
rear (.3)	.6
New Process Model 231	
front (.6)	1.0
rear (.4)	.7
New Process Model 208	
front (.5)	.9
rear (.3)	.6
New Process Model 207	
front (.5)	.9
rear (.4)	.7

(Factory Time)	Chilton Time
New Process Model 205	
front (1.1)	1.7
rear (.6)	1.0
New Process Model 203	
front (.8)	1.4
rear (.7)	1.3
Borg Warner Model 1370	
front (.5)	.9
rear (.4)	.7
Transfer Case Power Take Off Cover Gasket, Renew	
All models (.4)	.7
Transfer Case Rear Output Shaft Housing Gasket, Renew	
All models	
New Process	
Model 241 (.5)	.8
Model 231 (.6)	1.0

LABOR 20 TRANSFER CASE 20 LABOR

(Factory Time)	Chilton Time	(Factory Time)	Chilton Time	(Factory Time)	Chilton Time
Model 208 (.5)	.8	New Process Model 208 (1.0)	1.4	Model 231 (.6)	1.1
Model 207 (.6)	1.0	New Process Model 207 (.6)	1.0	Model 208 (1.0)	1.5
Model 205 (.8)	1.2	New Process Model 205 (.6)	1.0	Model 207 (.6)	1.0
Borg Warner		New Process Model 203 (.9)	1.2	Model 205 (.6)	1.0
Model 1370 (.5)	.8	Borg Warner Model 1370 (.5)	.8	Borg Warner	
Transfer Case Speedometer Drive Gear, Renew		**Rear Output Shaft Housing, Renew**		Model 1370 (.5)	.9
New Process Model 241 (.5)	.7	All models		**Vacuum Control Switch, Renew**	
New Process Model 231 (.6)	1.0	New Process Model 241 (.5)	.9	S-series (.3)	.5

LABOR 21 SHIFT LINKAGE 21 LABOR

(Factory Time)	Chilton Time	(Factory Time)	Chilton Time	(Factory Time)	Chilton Time
MANUAL		**Gear Shift Tube and/or Levers, Renew**		Trans vacuum valve (.5)	.6
Shift Linkage, Adjust		Tilt column (1.7)	2.5	Complete (.6)	1.0
All models (.3)	.4	Std column (1.4)	2.2	Note: Does not apply to Vans with THM 400 trans.	
Gearshift Control Lever, Renew		**AUTOMATIC**			
All models–column mount (.2)	.4	**Linkage, Adjust**		**Column Shift Selector Lever, Renew**	
floor mount (.3)	.6	All models		All models (.2)	.3
Transfer Case Gearshift Lever, Renew		Neutral Safety Switch (.2)	.3	**Shift Control Rods, Renew**	
S-series (.4)	.6	Shift Indicator Needle (.2)	.3	Includes: Necessary adjustments.	
All other models (.3)	.5	Shift Linkage (.3)	.4	All models–one (.4)	.5
		T.V. Cable (.4)	.5		
Transfer Case Shifter Assy., Renew		**Shift Linkage, Adjust (w/Diesel Eng)**		**Cross Shaft Assembly, Renew**	
New Process Model 203 (1.4)	2.1	All models		Includes: Necessary adjustments.	
Gearshift Control Rods, Renew		Fast idle speed (.2)	.3	All models (.3)	.6
All models–one (.4)	.6	Throttle rod/T.V.		**Shift Indicator Needle, Renew**	
two (.5)	.9	cable (.5)	.6	All models (.6)	1.0

LABOR 23A AUTOMATIC TRANSMISSION (RWD) 23A LABOR

(Factory Time)	Chilton Time	(Factory Time)	Chilton Time	(Factory Time)	Chilton Time
TURBO HYDRA-MATIC - 180		**Detent Valve, Renew**		**Valve Body Assy., R&R and Recondition**	
ON CAR SERVICES		Includes: R&R oil pan and valve body, servo cover and reinforcement plate.		Includes: R&R oil pan, reinforcement plate, screen and servo cover. Replace parts as required.	
Drain & Refill Unit		All models (1.6)	2.2	All models (1.6)	2.2
All models	1.0	**Extension Housing or Gasket, Renew**		**Parking Pawl, Renew**	
Oil Pressure Check		All models (1.1)	1.6	Includes: R&R oil pan and extension housing.	
All models	.5	Renew bushing add (.2)	.2	All models (1.1)	1.9
Check Unit for Oil Leaks		**Extension Housing Rear Oil Seal, Renew**		**Transmission Mount, Renew**	
Includes: Clean and dry outside of case and run unit to determine point of leak.		All models (.5)	.7	All models	
All models	.9	**Governor Assembly, Renew**		rear (.4)	.6
		Includes: R&R drive shaft and extension housing.		**SERVICES REQUIRING R&R**	
Neutral Safety Switch, Renew		All models (1.0)	1.6	**Transmission Assy., Renew**	
All models (.3)	.5	Recond governor hub add (.1)	.3	Includes: R&R converter and front pump seal. Renew assy with new or exchange unit.	
Shift Linkage, Adjust		**Oil Pan Gasket, Renew**		S-series (3.2)	4.6
All models		All models (.6)	1.0	**Transmission and Converter Assy., R&R and Recondition**	
Neutral Safety Switch (.2)	.3	**Governor Pressure Switch and/or Electrical Connector, Renew**		Includes: Disassemble trans, inspect and replace parts as required. Make all necessary adjustments. Road test.	
Shift Indicator Needle (.3)	.4	Includes: R&R oil pan.		S-series (6.6)	10.0
Shift Linkage (.3)	.4	All models (.6)	1.1	**Transmission Assembly, Reseal**	
T.V. Cable (.4)	.5	**Converter Clutch Solenoid Assy., Renew**		Includes: R&R transmission and install all new gaskets and seals.	
Vacuum Modulator, Renew		Includes: R&R oil pan.		S-series	7.1
All models (.4)	.5	All models (.7)	1.2	**Transmission Assembly, Recondition (Off Truck)**	
Speedometer Driven Gear, Renew		**Low Band Servo, Renew**		All models (3.4)	5.4
All models (.3)	.5	Includes: R&R oil pan, reinforcement plate, servo cover and valve body. Adjust servo.		**Front Pump Oil Seal, Renew**	
Torque Converter Clutch Switches, Renew		All models (1.1)	1.6	Includes: R&R converter and seal.	
All models		Recond servo add (.1)	.2	S-series (2.6)	3.8
Third Clutch (.6)	.8	**Valve Body Assembly, Renew**			
Detent Cable, Adjust		Includes: R&R oil pan, reinforcement plate, screen and servo cover.			
All models (.2)	.4	All models (1.0)	1.5		
Detent Cable, Renew					
All models (.5)	.9				

LABOR 23A AUTOMATIC TRANSMISSION (RWD) 23A LABOR

Torque Converter, Renew
S-series (3.2) 4.6

Flywheel (Flexplate), Renew
S-series (3.4) 4.9

Front Oil Pump, Renew
S-series (3.6) 5.2
Renew pump bushing add (.3) 3
Renew conver housing bushing
add (.2) 2

Front Oil Pump, R&R and Recondition
S-series (4.2) 6.1
Renew pump bushing add (.3) 3
Renew cover housing bushing
add (.2) 2

Apply and Actuator Valve and/or Bushing, Renew
Includes: R&R trans, converter and oil pump.
S-series (3.1) 4.5

Second and Third Clutch Assemblies, Renew
Includes: R&R trans and converter.
S-series (3.5) 5.1
Overhaul second clutch add (.5) 5
Overhaul third clutch add (.4) 4
R&R planetary carrier and reaction
sun gear add (.6) 6
Renew sun gear drum bushing
add (.3) 3

Low Band, Renew
Includes: R&R trans and converter, housing, pump valve body and servo. Remove second and third clutch assys., extension housing and speedometer drive and driven gears. Remove governor body and hub sun gear, planetary carrier and modulator.
S-series (4.4) 6.4
Recond valve body add (.6) 7
Recond oil pump add (.6) 8
Recond low servo add (.1) 2
Renew parking pawl rod add (.1) 1
Renew selector shaft seal add (.1) 1
Recond second clutch add (.5) 6
Recond third clutch add (.4) 5
Renew reaction sun gear and
drum bushing add (.3) 4
Recond gov and hub add (.1) 2
Renew bushings add—each 1

TURBO HYDRA-MATIC 200C
ON TRUCK SERVICES

Drain & Refill Unit
All models 9

Oil Pressure Check
All models (.5) 7

Check Unit For Oil Leaks
Includes: Clean and dry outside of case and run unit to determine point of leak.
All models 9

Neutral Safety Switch, Renew
All models (.3) 4

Throttle Valve Control Cable and/or 'O' Ring, Renew
Includes: Adjust cable.
All models (.5) 8

Speedometer Driven Gear and/or Seal, Renew
All models (.3) 5

Transmission Rear Oil Seal, Renew
Includes: R&R driveshaft.
All models (.4) 8

Torque Converter Clutch Switches, Renew
All models
Brake (.2) 4
Thermal Vacuum (.3) 5
Temp Indicator (.3) 5

Governor Assy., R&R or Renew
Includes: Renew governor seal.
All models (1.1) 1.7

Governor Assy., R&R and Recondition
Includes: Clean and inspect governor, renew seal and gear.
All models (1.3) 2.0

Oil Pan and/or Gasket, Renew
Includes: Clean pan and service screen.
All models (.6) 9

Manual Shaft Seal and/or Detent Lever, Renew
Includes: R&R oil pan.
All models (.7) 1.1

Valve Body Assembly, Renew
Includes: R&R oil pan and renew filter.
All models (.9) 1.5

Valve Body Assy., R&R and Recondition
Includes: R&R oil pan and renew filter. Disassemble, clean, inspect and free all valves. Replace parts as required.
All models (1.6) 2.8

Intermediate Servo Assy., R&R or Renew
All models (1.1) 1.7
Recond servo add (.2) 2

Parking Pawl, Shaft, Rod or Spring, Renew
Includes: R&R oil pan.
All models (1.3) 2.0

1-2 Accumulator Piston and/or Spring, R&R or Renew
Includes: R&R oil pan.
All models (.9) 1.4
Recond accumulator add (.2) 2

SERVICES REQUIRING R&R

Transmission Assembly, R&R or Renew
All models
4X2 (2.6) 3.7
4X4 (3.2) 4.6

Transmission and Converter, R&R and Recondition
Includes: Disassemble transmission completely, including valve body. Clean and inspect all parts. Renew all parts as required. Make all necessary adjustments. Road test.
All models
4X2 (6.2) 11.2
4X4 (6.8) 11.8

Transmission Assy., R&R and Reseal
Includes: Install all new gaskets and seals.
All models 6.5
4X2 .... 6.5
4X4 .... 7.0

Flywheel (Flexplate), Renew
Includes: R&R transmission.
All models
4X2 (2.8) 3.9
4X4 (3.4) 4.8

Torque Converter, Renew
Includes: R&R transmission.
All models
4X2 (2.6) 3.8
4X4 (3.2) 4.7

Front Pump Oil Seal, Renew
Includes: R&R transmission.
All models
4X2 (2.6) 3.8
4X4 (3.2) 4.7

Front Pump Assy., Renew or Recondition
Includes: R&R transmission.
All models
4X2 (3.0) 4.3
4X4 (3.6) 5.2
Recond front pump add (.5) 8
Renew bushing add (.1) 1

Converter Clutch Solenoid Assy., Renew
Includes: R&R transmission, converter and oil pump.
All models
4X2 (2.6) 4.0
4X4 (3.2) 4.9

Apply and Actuator Valves and/or Bushing, Renew
Includes: R&R transmission, converter and oil pump.
All models
4X2 (2.6) 4.0
4X4 (3.2) 4.9

Direct, Forward Clutches and Intermediate Band, Renew
Includes: R&R transmission, converter, pump and seal, oil pan, valve body and servo.
All models
4X2 (3.4) 4.9
4X4 (4.0) 5.8
Recond valve body add (.7) 1.0
Recond oil pump add (.5) 8
Recond servo add (.2) 2
Recond direct clutch add (.3) 4
Recond forward clutch add (.4) 5
Renew bushings add—each (.1) 1

Output Carrier, Sun Gear and Drive Shell, R&R or Renew
Includes: R&R transmission, converter, pump and seal, oil pan, valve body, direct and forward clutches, intermediate band and servo.
All models
4X2 (3.5) 5.5
4X4 (4.1) 5.9
Recond valve body add (.7) 1.0
Recond oil pump add (.5) 8
Recond servo add (.2) 2
Recond direct clutch add (.3) 4
Recond forward clutch add (.4) 5
Recond sun gear and drum,
add (.3) 4
Renew output shaft add (.7) 1.0
Renew bushings add—each (.1) 1

TURBO HYDRA-MATIC '350'
ON TRUCK SERVICE

Drain and Refill Unit
All models (.5) 1.0

Oil Pressure Check
All models (.5) 7

Check Unit for Leaks
Includes: Clean and dry outside of case and run unit to determine point of leak.
All models 9

Vacuum Modulator, Renew
w/2 whl drive (.3) 4
w/4 whl drive (.5) 6

Detent Valve Control Cable or Seal, Renew
All models 9

Speedometer Drive Gear, Renew
Includes: R&R extension housing.
w/2 whl drive (.7) 1.2
w/4 whl drive (.6) 1.1

LABOR 23A AUTOMATIC TRANSMISSION (RWD) 23A LABOR

	(Factory Time)	Chilton Time

Speedometer Driven Gear, Renew
All models (.3) 5

Governor Assy., R&R or Renew
Includes: R&R cover and gasket.
All models (.4) 6

Governor Assy., R&R and Recondition
Includes: R&R cover and gasket.
All models (.6) 1.1

Extension Housing Rear Oil Seal, Renew
Includes: R&R drive shaft.
exc Vans (.5) 8
Vans (.4) 7

Torque Converter Clutch Brake Switch, Renew
All models (.2) 4

Torque Converter Clutch Thermal Vacuum Switch, Renew
All models (.3) 5

Torque Converter Clutch Vacuum Delay Valve, Renew
All models (.2) 3

Engine Low Vacuum Switch, Renew
All models (.2) 4

High Vacuum Switch, Renew
All models (.3) 5

Oil Pan and/or Gasket, Renew
Includes: Clean oil pan and service screen.
All models (.6) 1.0

Parking Pawl, Renew
Includes: R&R oil pan.
All models (1.4) 1.9

Intermediate Servo, Renew
Includes: R&R oil pan, valve body and adjust servo.
All models (.8) 1.4
Recond servo add (.2) 2

Governor Pressure Switch and/or Electrical Connector, Renew
Includes: R&R oil pan.
All models (.6) 1.1

Auxiliary Valve Body and/or Apply Valve, Renew
Includes: R&R oil pan.
All models (.9) 1.4
Renew body gskt add (.2) 2

Converter Clutch Solenoid, Renew
Includes: R&R oil pan.
All models (.6) 1.1

Intermediate Clutch Accumulator, Renew
All models (.7) 1.2

Valve Body Assy., R&R or Renew
Includes: R&R oil pan and vacuum modulator, clean pan and strainer.
All models (.8) 1.6

Valve Body, R&R and Recondition
Includes: R&R oil pan and vacuum modulator, clean pan and strainer. Disassemble, clean, inspect, free all valves. Replace parts as required.
All models (1.4) 2.4

SERVICES REQUIRING R&R

Transmission, R&R or Renew
2 whl drive (2.0) 3.6
4 whl drive (4.3) 6.1
w/Skid plate add (.3) 3
Pressure check converter add (.2) 2

Transmission and Converter, R&R and Recondition
Includes: Disassemble trans including valve body, clean, inspect and replace parts as required.
2 whl drive (6.3) 10.0
4 whl drive (8.3) 12.3
w/Skid plate add (.3) 3
Pressure check converter add (.2) 2

Transmission Assembly, Reseal
Includes: R&R transmission and renew all seals and gaskets.
2 whl drive (3.5) 5.5
4 whl drive (5.3) 8.1
w/Skid plate add (.3) 3

Front Pump Seal, Renew
Includes: R&R transmission.
2 whl drive (2.1) 3.7
4 whl drive (4.0) 6.4
w/Skid plate add (.3) 3

Flywheel (Flexplate), Renew
Includes: R&R transmission.
2 whl drive (2.2) 3.8
4 whl drive (4.0) 6.4
w/Skid plate add (.3) 3

Torque Converter, Renew
Includes: R&R transmission and check end play of converter.
2 whl drive (2.0) 3.6
4 whl drive (4.4) 6.7
w/Skid plate add (.3) 3

Forward, Direct or Intermediate Clutch, R&R or Renew
Includes: R&R transmission, converter and pump seal, intermediate, direct and forward clutches, oil pan, valve body and intermediate servo piston.
2 whl drive (3.2) 5.7
4 whl drive (5.2) 7.4
w/Skid plate add (.3) 3

Forward, Direct or Intermediate Clutch, R&R and Recondition
Includes: R&R transmission, converter and pump seal, intermediate, direct and forward clutches, oil pan, valve body and intermediate servo piston.
2 whl drive (3.6) 6.4
4 whl drive (6.1) 8.8
w/Skid plate add (.3) 3

Front Oil Pump, Renew
Includes: R&R transmission, converter and pump seal.
2 whl drive (2.2) 3.9
4 whl drive (4.5) 6.6
w/Skid plate add (.3) 3

Front Oil Pump, R&R and Recondition
Includes: R&R transmission, converter and pump seal.
2 whl drive (2.7) 4.8
4 whl drive (5.0) 7.3
w/Skid plate add (.3) 3

Low and Reverse Clutch Piston Assembly, R&R or Renew
Includes: R&R trans, converter, pump and seal, intermediate clutch, oil pan, valve body, intermediate servo piston, direct and forward clutches, intermediate band, output carrier, sungear and drive shell, extension housing, speedometer drive gears, governor, output ring gear, low and reverse roller clutch support, reaction carrier and output shell.
2 whl drive (3.6) 6.4
4 whl drive (5.7) 8.1
w/Skid plate add (.3) 3

Low and Reverse Clutch Piston Assembly, R&R and Recondition
Includes: R&R trans, converter, pump and seal, intermediate clutch, oil pan, valve body, intermediate servo piston, direct and forward clutches, intermediate band, output carrier, sungear and drive shell, extension housing, speedometer drive gears, governor, output ring gear, low and reverse roller clutch support, reaction carrier and output shell.
2 whl drive (3.8) 6.8
4 whl drive (6.2) 8.9
w/Skid plate add (.3) 3

Intermediate Band, Renew
Includes: R&R transmission, converter and pump seal, intermediate clutch, oil pan, valve body and intermediate servo piston.
2 whl drive (3.4) 6.1
4 whl drive (5.2) 7.6
w/Skid plate add (.3) 3

TURBO HYDRA-MATIC '400'

ON TRUCK SERVICES

Drain and Refill Unit
All models (.5) 1.0

Oil Pressure Check
All models (.5) 7

Check Unit for Leaks
Includes: Clean and dry outside of case and run unit to determine point of leak.
All models 9

Vacuum Modulator, Renew
w/2 whl drive (.3) 4
w/4 whl drive (.4) 6

Detent Solenoid, Renew or Adjust
Includes: R&R oil pan.
All models (.7) 1.1

Down Shift Control Switch, Renew
All models (.2) 4

Detent Solenoid Connector, Renew
Includes: R&R oil pan.
All models (.7) 1.1

Transmission speed sensor, renew
All models (.4) 6

Speedometer Drive Gear, Renew
Includes: R&R extension housing.
All models (.8) 1.5

Speedometer Driven Gear, Renew
All models (.3) 5

Governor Assy., R&R or Renew
Includes: R&R cover and gasket.
All models (.5) 8

Governor Assy., R&R and Recondition
Includes: R&R cover and gasket.
All models (.8) 1.1

Extension Housing Rear Oil Seal, Renew
Includes: R&R drive shaft.
All models (.5) 1.0
Renew bushing add (.1) 1

Oil Pan and/or Gasket, Renew
Includes: Clean oil pan and service screen.
All models (.6) 1.0

Parking Pawl, Renew
Includes: R&R oil pan.
All models (.9) 1.5

Servos, Renew or Recondition
Includes: R&R oil pan, detent solenoid, servo cover and valve body. Adjust servo.
All models-front (1.2) 1.8

LABOR 23A AUTOMATIC TRANSMISSION (RWD) 23A LABOR

	(Factory) Time	Chilton Time
rear (1.5)		2.1

Pressure Regulator Valve, Renew
Includes: R&R oil pan.

| All models (.8) .... | | 1.4 |

Valve Body Assy., R&R or Renew
Includes: R&R oil pan and vacuum modulator, clean pan and strainer.

| All models (.8) .... | | 1.6 |

Valve Body, R&R and Recondition
Includes: R&R oil pan and vacuum modulator, clean pan and strainer. Disassemble, clean, inspect, free all valves. Replace parts as required.

| All models (1.3) .... | | 2.6 |

SERVICES REQUIRING R&R

Transmission Assembly, Renew
Includes: Renew assy with new or exchange unit.

2 whl drive (2.8)		3.7
4 whl drive (3.6)		4.7
w/Skid plate add (.3)		.3

Transmission and Converter, R&R and Recondition
Includes: Disassemble trans including valve body, clean, inspect and replace parts as required.

2 whl drive (6.8)		9.5
4 whl drive (7.8)		10.9
w/Skid plate add (.3)		.3
Pressure check converter add (.2)		.2

Transmission Assembly, Reseal
Includes: R&R transmission and renew all seals and gaskets.

2 whl drive (3.6)		6.9
4 whl drive (5.6)		8.2
w/Skid plate add (.3)		.3

Front Pump Seal, Renew
Includes: R&R transmission.

2 whl drive (2.0)		2.8
4 whl drive (3.0)		4.2
w/Skid plate add (.3)		.3

Flywheel (Flexplate), Renew
Includes: R&R transmission.

2 whl drive (2.7)		3.7
4 whl drive (3.7)		5.1
w/Skid plate add (.3)		.3

Torque Converter, Renew
Includes: R&R transmission and check end play of converter.

2 whl drive (2.5)		3.5
4 whl drive (3.5)		4.9
w/Skid plate add (.3)		.3

Front Oil Pump, Renew
Includes: R&R transmission and converter.

2 whl drive (3.5)		4.9
4 whl drive (4.5)		6.3
w/Skid plate add (.3)		.3

Front Oil Pump, R&R and Recondition
Includes: R&R transmission and converter.

2 whl drive (3.8)		5.4
4 whl drive (4.8)		6.8
w/Skid plate add (.3)		.3

Forward, Direct or Intermediate Clutch, R&R or Renew
Includes: R&R transmission, converter, oil pan, oil pump and seal.

2 whl drive (4.2)		5.8
4 whl drive (5.2)		7.2
w/Skid plate add (.3)		.3

Forward, Direct or Intermediate Clutch, R&R and Recondition
Includes: R&R transmission, converter, oil pan, oil pump and seal, forward clutch, sun gear shaft, front brake band and adjust end play.

2 whl drive (4.8)		6.7
4 whl drive (5.8)		8.1
w/Skid plate add (.3)		.3

Center Support and Gear Unit Assy., Renew
Includes: R&R transmission, converter, pump and seal, forward clutch, front brake band, valve body, case extension, speedometer driven gear. Check end play.

2 whl drive (5.0)		7.0
4 whl drive (6.0)		8.4
w/Skid plate add (.3)		.3

TURBO HYDRA-MATIC 700-R4
ON TRUCK SERVICES

Drain & Refill Unit

| All models .... | | .9 |

Oil Pressure Check

| All models (.5) .... | | .7 |

Check Unit For Oil Leaks
Includes: Clean and dry outside of case and run unit to determine point of leak.

| All models .... | | .9 |

Neutral Safety Switch, Renew

| All models (.3) .... | | .4 |

Shift Linkage, Adjust

| All models (.4) .... | | .6 |

Torque Converter Clutch Switches, Renew
All models

Brake (.2)		.4
Thermal Vacuum (.3)		.5
Temp Indicator (.3)		.5

Detent Valve Control Cable and/or 'O' Ring, Renew
Includes: Adjust cable.

| All models (.7) .... | | .9 |

Transmission Speed Sensor, Renew

| All models (.5) .... | | .7 |

Speedometer Driven Gear and/or Seal, Renew

| All models (.3) .... | | .5 |

Extension Housing Rear Oil Seal, Renew
Includes: R&R driveshaft.

| S-series 4X4 (1.4) .... | | 1.9 |
| All models (.4) .... | | .8 |

Governor Cover and/or Seal, Renew
S-series

4 WD (1.0)		*1.4
All other models (.4)		.6
*w/V-6 add		.2
w/Skid plate add		.2

Governor Assembly, R&R or Renew
S-series

4 WD (1.0)		*1.4
All other models (.5)		.7
*w/V-6 add		.2
w/Skid Plate add		.2

Governor Assy., R&R and Recondition
S-series

4 WD (1.2)		*1.7
All other models (.7)		1.0
*w/V-6 add		.2
w/Skid plate add		.2

Oil Pan and/or Gasket, Renew

| Vans (.8) .... | | 1.1 |
| S-series 4X4-V-6 (1.1) .... | | 1.5 |

| All other models (.6) .... | | .9 |
| w/Skid plate add (.3) .... | | .3 |

Governor Pressure Switch, Renew
Includes: R&R oil pan.

Vans (.8)		1.3
S-series 4X4-V-6 (1.5)		2.0
All other models (.6)		1.1
w/Skid plate add (.3)		.3

Converter Clutch Solenoid, Renew
Includes: R&R oil pan.

Vans (.8)		1.3
S-series 4X4-V-6 (1.5)		2.0
All other models (.6)		1.1
w/Skid plate add (.3)		.3

Valve Body Assembly, Renew
Includes: R&R oil pan and renew filter.

Vans (1.1)		1.7
S-series 4X4-V-6 (1.4)		1.9
All other models (1.0)		1.6
w/Skid plate add (.3)		.3

Valve Body Assy., R&R and Recondition
Includes: R&R oil pan and renew filter. Disassemble, clean, inspect and free all valves. Replace parts as required.

Vans (2.0)		2.8
S-series 4X4 (2.3)		3.1
All other models (2.0)		2.8
w/Skid plate add (.3)		.3

2-4 Servo Assy., R&R or Renew

S-series (1.3)		1.9
S-series 4X4-V-6 (3.2)		4.4
All other models (.6)		1.0
w/Skid plate add (.3)		.3
Recond servo add (.2)		.3

Parking Pawl, Shaft, Rod or Spring, Renew
Includes: R&R oil pan.

Vans (.9)		1.4
S-series 4X4-V-6 (1.4)		1.9
All other models (.9)		1.4
Renew pawl add (.5)		.5
w/Skid plate add (.3)		.3

1-2 Accumulator Piston and/or Spring, Renew
Includes: R&R oil pan.

Vans (1.0)		1.6
S-series 4X4-V-6 (1.2)		1.8
All other models (.8)		1.5
w/Skid plate add (.3)		.3
Recond add (.1)		.2

SERVICES REQUIRING R&R

Transmission Assy., Renew
Includes: Renew assy with new or exchange unit.

1986		
2 whl drive (2.2)		3.1
4 whl drive (4.0)		5.8
1987-90		
Vans (2.6)		3.5
Astro-Safari (3.0)		4.0
S-series		
4X2 (4.0)		5.4
4X4 (4.8)		6.4
C-K series		
4X2 (2.8)		3.7
4X4 (4.2)		5.6
R-V series		
4X2 (2.6)		3.5
4X4 (3.5)		4.7
w/Skid plate add (.3)		.3

LABOR 23A AUTOMATIC TRANSMISSION (RWD) 23A LABOR

	(Factory Time)	Chilton Time
Transmission and Converter, R&R and Recondition		
Includes: Disassemble transmission completely, including valve body and overhaul unit. Clean and inspect all parts. Renew all parts as required. Make all necessary adjustments. Road test.		
1986		
2 whl drive (6.3)		12.0
4 whl drive (7.1)		15.0
1987-90		
Vans (8.1)		10.9
Astro-Safari (8.5)		11.4
S-series		
4X2 (9.5)		12.8
4X4 (10.3)		13.9
C-K series		
4X2 (8.3)		11.2
4X4 (9.7)		13.0
R-V series		
4X2 (8.1)		10.9
4X4 (9.0)		12.1
w/Skid plate add (.3)		.3
Clean and leak check converter add (.2)		.4
Check end play add (.2)		.3
Transmission Assy., R&R and Reseal		
Includes: Install all new gaskets and seals.		
1986		
2 whl drive		4.7
4 whl drive		7.4
1987-90		
Vans		6.4
Astro-Safari		6.9
S-series		
4X2		8.3
4X4		9.3
C-K series		
4X2		6.6
4X4		8.5
R-V series		
4X2		6.4
4X4		7.6
w/Skid plate add		.3
Flywheel (Flexplate), Renew		
Includes: R&R transmission.		
1986		
2 whl drive (2.4)		3.3
4 whl drive (4.2)		6.0
1987-90		
Vans (2.8)		3.8
Astro-Safari (3.3)		4.3
S-series		
4X2 (4.2)		5.4
4X4 (5.0)		6.7
C-K series		
4X2 (3.0)		4.0
4X4 (4.4)		5.9
R-V series		
4X2 (2.8)		3.8
4X4 (3.7)		5.0
w/Skid plate add (.3)		.3
Torque Converter, Renew		
Includes: R&R transmission.		
1986		
2 whl drive (2.1)		2.9
4 whl drive (3.9)		5.6

	(Factory Time)	Chilton Time
1987-90		
Vans (2.5)		3.7
Astro-Safari (2.9)		4.2
S-series		
4X2 (3.9)		5.6
4X4 (4.7)		6.6
C-K series		
4X2 (2.7)		3.9
4X4 (4.0)		5.8
R-V series		
4X2 (2.5)		3.7
4X4 (3.4)		4.9
w/Skid plate add (.3)		.3
Front Pump Oil Seal, Renew		
Includes: R&R transmission.		
1986		
2 whl drive (2.1)		3.0
4 whl drive (3.9)		5.6
1987-90		
Vans (1.9)		3.6
Astro-Safari (2.2)		4.1
S-series		
4X2 (3.3)		5.5
4X4 (4.1)		6.5
C-K series		
4X2 (2.0)		3.8
4X4 (3.4)		5.7
R-V-series		
4X2 (1.9)		3.6
4X4 (2.8)		4.8
w/Skid plate add (.3)		.3
Front Pump Assy., Renew or Recondition		
Includes: R&R transmission.		
1986		
2 whl drive (2.7)		4.0
4 whl drive (4.5)		6.5
1987-90		
Vans (3.2)		4.3
Astro-Safari (3.6)		4.8
S-series		
4X2 (4.6)		6.2
4X4 (5.4)		7.2
C-K series		
4X2 (3.4)		4.5
4X4 (4.7)		6.3
R-V series		
4X2 (3.2)		4.3
4X4 (4.1)		5.5
w/Skid plate add (.3)		.3
Recond front pump add (.5)		.6
Renew bushing add (.1)		.1
Input Drum, Reverse and Input Clutch, Renew		
Includes: R&R transmission.		
1986		
2 whl drive (3.2)		4.6
4 whl drive (5.0)		7.2
1987-90		
Vans (5.0)		6.7
Astro-Safari (5.4)		7.2
S-series		
4X2 (6.4)		8.6
4X4 (7.2)		9.7

	(Factory Time)	Chilton Time
C-K series		
4X2 (5.2)		7.0
4X4 (6.5)		8.7
R-V series		
4X2 (5.0)		6.7
4X4 (5.9)		7.9
w/Skid plate add (.3)		.3
Recond valve body add (.4)		.5
Recond front pump add (.5)		.6
Renew bushings add–each (.1)		.1
Reaction Gear Set, Renew		
Includes: R&R transmission.		
1986		
2 whl drive (3.5)		5.2
4 whl drive (5.3)		7.6
1987-90		
Vans (5.0)		6.7
Astro-Safari (5.4)		7.2
S-series		
4X2 (6.4)		8.6
4X4 (7.2)		9.7
C-K series		
4X2 (5.2)		7.0
4X4 (6.5)		8.7
R-V series		
4X2 (5.0)		6.7
4X4 (5.9)		7.9
w/Skid plate add (.3)		.3
Recond valve body add (.4)		.5
Recond front pump add (.5)		.6
Renew input clutch drum add (.2)		.3
Recond reaction gear set add (.2)		.2
Renew bushings add–each (.1)		.1
Low and Reverse Clutch Piston Assy., Renew		
Includes: R&R transmission.		
1986		
2 whl drive (3.7)		5.7
4 whl drive (5.5)		7.9
1987-90		
Vans (5.2)		7.0
Astro-Safari (5.6)		7.5
S-series		
4X2 (6.6)		8.9
4X4 (7.4)		9.9
C-K series		
4X2 (5.4)		7.2
4X4 (6.7)		9.0
R-V series		
4X2 (5.2)		7.0
4X4 (6.1)		8.2
w/Skid plate add (.3)		.3
Recond valve body add (.4)		.5
Recond front pump add (.5)		.6
Recond reverse clutch add (.4)		.5
Recond input clutch add (.4)		.5
Renew input clutch drum add (.2)		.2
Recond reaction gear set add (.2)		.3
Recond low and reverse clutch add (.1)		.2
Recond reverse piston add (.3)		.4
Recond gov or renew gear add (.2)		.3
Renew gov bushing add (.4)		.5
Renew bushings add–each (.1)		.1

LABOR 25 U-JOINTS & DRIVESHAFT 25 LABOR

	(Factory Time)	Chilton Time
Universal Joints, Renew		
All models–one (.6)		1.0
each adtnl (.3)		.4
Drive Shaft, R&R or Renew		
One Piece Shaft		
All models (.3)		.5

	(Factory Time)	Chilton Time
Two Piece Shaft		
front shaft (.4)		.7
rear shaft (.3)		.5

	(Factory Time)	Chilton Time
Center Support Bearing, Renew		
All models (.5)		1.0
Driveshaft Slip Joint, Renew		
All models (.6)		.9

LABOR — 26 DRIVE AXLE 26 — LABOR

	Factory Time	Chilton Time
Rear Axle, Drain and Refill		
All models		.6
Rear Axle Housing Cover Gasket, Renew		
All models (.4)		.6
Rear Wheel Hub Assembly, Renew		
All models-one side (1.0)		1.3
both sides (1.8)		2.4
w/Dual whls add-each side		.1
Rear Wheel Hub Oil Seal, Renew		
All models-one side (.6)		.9
both sides (1.0)		1.6
w/Dual whls add-each side		.1
Axle Shaft, Renew		
Semi-Floating Axle		
one (.7)		.9
both (.8)		1.2
Full Floating Axle		
one (.3)		.6
both (.5)		.8
Axle Shaft Oil Seal, Renew		
Semi-Floating Axle		
one (.7)		1.1
both (.8)		1.4
Full Floating Axle		
one (.7)		1.1
both (1.2)		1.6
w/Dual whls add, each side (.1)		.1

	Factory Time	Chilton Time
Axle Shaft Bearing, Renew		
Semi-Floating Axle		
one (.8)		1.1
both (.9)		1.4
Full Floating Axle		
one (1.0)		1.4
both (1.6)		2.7
w/Dual whls add-each side		.1
Pinion Shaft Oil Seal, Renew		
Includes: Renew pinion flange if necessary.		
All models		
Semi-Floating (.6)		.8
Full Floating (.7)		1.1
Differential Case, Renew		
Standard		
Semi-Floating (2.0)		3.1
Full Floating (2.2)		3.3
Limited Slip (Semi-Floating)		
Eaton Case (2.4)		3.5
exc Eaton Case (2.6)		3.7
Limited Slip (Full Floating)		
Eaton Case (2.4)		3.5
exc Eaton Case (2.1)		3.2
Ring and Pinion Gears, Renew		
Semi-Floating Axle (2.4)		4.1
Full Floating Axle (2.8)		4.6

	Factory Time	Chilton Time
Recond diff case add		
std (.3)		.5
limited slip (.7)		1.0
Pinion Bearings, Renew		
Note: Does not require case removal on semi-floating axles.		
Semi-Floating Axle (2.2)		3.1
Full Floating Axle (1.9)		2.8
Renew side brgs add (.3)		.5
Limited Slip Clutch Plates, Renew		
Semi-Floating Axle		
Eaton Case (2.4)		3.5
exc Eaton Case (1.1)		2.0
S-series (1.2)		2.1
Full Floating Axle		
Eaton Case (2.4)		3.5
exc Eaton Case (2.3)		3.4
Side Bearings, Renew		
Semi-Floating Axle (1.9)		2.6
Full Floating Axle (1.8)		2.5
Rear Axle Housing, Renew		
Semi-Floating Axle (4.5)		6.1
Full Floating Axle (5.1)		6.7
w/Dual whls add (.2)		.4
Differential Assy., Renew (Complete)		
Includes: Transfer parts as required. Bleed brake system.		
All models (2.1)		3.5

LABOR — 27 REAR SUSPENSION 27 — LABOR

	Factory Time	Chilton Time
Rear Spring, Renew		
S-series-one (.7)		1.1
both (1.2)		2.0
Vans-Astro-one (1.0)		1.3
both (1.9)		2.5
All other models-one (.7)		1.1
both (.9)		1.5
w/Aux fuel tank add (.6)		.6
w/Dual whls add-each side		.1
w/Skid plate add (.3)		.3
Recond add-each side		.5
Rear Spring Shackle and/or Bushing, Renew		
S-series-one (.4)		.6

	Factory Time	Chilton Time
both (.6)		1.0
Vans-Astro-one (1.1)		1.4
both (1.9)		2.6
All other models-one (.5)		.7
both (.7)		1.1
Rear Spring Eye Bushing, Renew		
Vans-one side (1.2)		1.6
both sides (1.4)		2.0
All other models-one side (.9)		1.3
both sides (1.2)		1.8
w/Dual whls add-each side		.1

	Factory Time	Chilton Time
w/Skid plate add (.3)		.3
Rear Spring Rear Eye Bushings, Renew		
Astro-Safari-one side (1.1)		1.5
both sides (2.1)		3.0
Rear Shock Absorber, Renew		
All models-one (.3)		.5
both (.4)		.8
Rear Stabilizer Bar, Renew		
C-R models (.4)		.5
S-series (.6)		.8

LABOR — 28 AIR CONDITIONING 28 — LABOR

	Factory Time	Chilton Time
Note: If more than one item requires replacement where evacuation and discharging the system is already included in the operation, deduct 1.0 hour for each additional item to the times listed.		
Drain, Evacuate and Recharge System		
All models (.5)		1.0
Flush Refrigerant System, Complete		
To be used in conjunction with component replacement which could contaminate system.		
All models		1.3
Leak Test		
Includes: Check all lines and connections.		
All models		.6
Refrigerant, Add Partial Charge		
All models		.6
Compressor Bolt, Renew		
All models (.2)		.5

	Factory Time	Chilton Time
If necessary to R&R fan pulley,		
add (.3)		.3
w/P.S. add (.2)		.2
w/AIR add (.2)		.2
COMPRESSOR - 6 CYLINDER AXIAL		
Compressor Assembly, Renew		
Includes: Transfer all necessary attaching parts. Evacuate and charge system.		
exc Vans (1.1)		2.0
Vans		
Gas (1.3)		2.2
Diesel (1.7)		2.6
Compressor Clutch Plate and Hub Assy., Renew		
Includes: Check air gap. Does not include R&R compressor.		
exc Vans (.3)		.6
Vans (.8)		1.1

	Factory Time	Chilton Time
Compressor Pulley and/or Bearing, Renew		
Includes: R&R hub and drive plate.		
exc Vans (.5)		.9
Vans (.9)		1.2
Compressor Clutch Holding Coil, Renew		
Includes: R&R hub and drive plate, pulley and bearing.		
exc Vans (.6)		1.1
Vans (1.0)		1.4
Compressor Shaft Seal Kit, Renew		
Includes: R&R clutch hub and drive plate. Evacuate and charge system.		
exc Vans (1.1)		2.0
Vans		
Gas (1.6)		2.5
Diesel (1.9)		2.8

LABOR 28 AIR CONDITIONING 28 LABOR

	(Factory) Time	Chilton Time
Compressor Rear Head, Oil Pump Gears and/or Rear Reed Assembly, Renew		
Includes: R&R compressor. R&R rear head and rear reed plate assy. Clean and test parts. Add oil. Evacuate and charge system.		
exc Vans (1.9)		2.8
Vans		
Gas (2.1)		3.0
Diesel (2.5)		3.4
Compressor Front Head and/or Front Reed Assembly, Renew		
Includes: R&R compressor. R&R rear head and reed plate assy. Disassemble shell to internal mechanism and front head assy. R&R front valve and reed plate and shaft seal assy. Clean and inspect parts. Add oil. Evacuate and charge system.		
exc Vans (2.2)		3.1
Vans		
Gas (2.4)		3.3
Diesel (2.8)		3.7

COMPRESSOR - 4 CYLINDER RADIAL

Compressor Assembly, Renew
Includes: Transfer all necessary attaching parts. Evacuate and charge system.

Astro-Safari–Vans (1.5)		2.5
All other models (1.0)		2.0
Astro-Safari-w/AIR add		.5

Compressor Clutch Hub and Drive Plate, Renew
Includes: Check air gap. Does not include R&R compressor.

All models (.5)		.8

Compressor Rotor and/or Bearing, Renew

Astro-Safari–Vans (1.4)		2.3
All other models (.6)		1.0

Add time to evacuate and charge system if required.

Compressor Clutch Coil and/or Pulley Rim, Renew

Astro-Safari–Vans (1.4)		2.3
All other models (.6)		.8

Add time to evacuate and charge system if required.

Compressor Shaft Seal Kit, Renew
Includes: R&R clutch hub and drive plate. Evacuate and charge system.

All models (1.3)		2.5

Compressor Front Bearing, Front Head and/or Seal, Renew
Includes: R&R clutch hub and drive plate, rotor, pulley and coil. Evacuate and charge system.

Astro-Safari–Vans (2.0)		3.0
All other models (1.5)		2.8

Compressor Outer Shell and/or 'O' Rings, Renew
Includes: R&R compressor. R&R clutch hub and drive plate, rotor, pulley and coil. Evacuate and charge system.

Astro-Safari–Vans (2.1)		3.2
All other models (1.7)		2.9

Compressor Discharge Valve Plate Assy., Renew
Includes: R&R compressor. R&R clutch hub and drive plate, rotor, pulley and coil. Evacuate and charge system.

Astro-Safari–Vans (2.2)		3.4
All other models (1.8)		2.9
Renew two or more valves add (.1)		.2

Compressor Cylinder and Shaft Assy., Renew
Includes: R&R compressor. Transfer clutch hub, drive plate, rotor, pulley, and coil. Inspect front head. Add oil. Evacuate and charge system.

Astro-Safari–Vans (2.3)		3.5
All other models (1.9)		3.0

COMPRESSOR ASSEMBLY DA-6–HR-6

Compressor Assembly, Renew
Includes: Transfer parts as required. Evacuate and charge system.

Vans-Safari-Astro (1.3)		2.4
All other models (1.0)		2.0
Astro-Safari-w/AIR add		.5

Compressor Clutch Plate and Hub Assy., Renew
Includes: R&R hub and drive plate assy. Check air gap.

Vans-Safari-Astro (.4)		.7
All other models (.3)		.6

Compressor Clutch Coil and/or Pulley Rim, Renew
Includes: R&R hub and drive plate assy.

Vans-Safari-Astro (1.0)		1.5
All other models (.8)		1.3

Add time to evacuate and charge system if required.

Compressor Rotor and/or Bearing, Renew
Includes: R&R hub and drive plate assy.

Vans-Safari-Astro (.9)		1.4
All other models (.7)		1.2

Add time to evacuate and charge system if required.

Compressor Shaft Seal Kit, Renew
Includes: Evacuate and charge system.

Vans-Safari-Astro (1.2)		2.6
All other models (1.1)		2.5

Compressor Front Head and/or Seal, Renew
Includes: R&R compressor. R&R clutch and pulley assy. R&R shaft seal assy. Clean and inspect parts. Evacuate and charge system.

Vans-Safari-Astro (1.6)		3.0
All other models (1.4)		2.8

Compressor Cylinder and Shaft Assy., Renew
Includes: R&R compressor. R&R clutch and pulley assy. R&R shaft seal assy., remove and transfer front head assy. R&R compressor shell and 'O' rings. R&R compressor valve plates. Clean and inspect parts. Evacuate and charge system.

Vans-Safari-Astro (2.3)		3.7
All other models (1.9)		3.3

Compressor Relief Valve, Renew
Includes: Evacuate and charge system.

exc Vans (.9)		1.5
Vans-Safari-Astro (1.4)		2.0

Condenser, Renew
Includes: Evacuate and charge system.

S-series		
Four (1.3)		2.8
V-6 (1.9)		3.4
exc Vans (1.3)		2.8
Vans-Astro-Safari (1.3)		2.8
w/Aux oil cooler add (.3)		.3

Evaporator Core, Renew
Includes: Evacuate and charge system.
Front Unit

S-series (1.4)		2.8

Vans		
Gas (1.8)		3.5
Diesel (2.0)		3.9
Astro-Safari (1.6)		3.0
C-K series		
Gas (2.5)		4.9
Diesel (1.1)		2.0
R-V series		
Gas (1.1)		2.0
Diesel (2.8)		5.5

Rear Unit

exc Vans (1.6)		3.6
Vans (1.9)		4.3

Accumulator, Renew
Includes: Evacuate and charge system.

All models (.9)		1.5

Expansion Tube (Orifice), Renew
Includes: Evacuate and charge system.

All models (.7)		1.4

Pressure Cycling Switch, Renew

All models (.2)		.3

Rear Expansion Valve, Renew
Includes: Evacuate and charge system.

Vans (1.2)		1.7
Astro-Safari (1.6)		2.1
R-V series (1.3)		1.8

Expansion Tube and Screen, Clean and Inspect or Renew
Includes: Evacuate and charge system.

All models (.9)		1.5

A.C. or Heater Blower Motor, Renew

C-K series		
wo/A.C. (.3)		.5
w/A.C.		
Gas (.5)		.7
Diesel (1.9)		2.6
Astro-Safari		
wo/A.C. (.6)		.8
w/A.C. (.5)		.7
Vans		
w/ or wo/A.C.		
Gas (.3)		.5
Diesel (.5)		.7
S-series		
wo/A.C. (.3)		.5
w/A.C. (.3)		.5
R-V series		
Gas		
wo/A.C. (.3)		.5
w/A.C. (.3)		.5
Diesel		
wo/A.C. (1.0)		1.5
w/A.C. (2.0)		3.0

Add time to recharge A.C. system if required.
Rear Unit

All models (.6)		1.1

Blower Motor Switch, Renew

Front unit (.5)		.9
Rear unit (.3)		.6

Temperature Control Assy., Renew

All models (.7)		1.1

Blower Motor Resistor, Renew

Front unit (.2)		†.4
Rear unit (.3)		*.5
*R&R seat add		.2
†1987-90 C & K models add		.4

Blower Motor Relay, Renew

All models (.3)		.5

Air Conditioning Hoses, Renew
Includes: Evacuate and charge system.
Condenser Outlet

Astro (1.1)		2.2

LABOR 28 AIR CONDITIONING 28 LABOR

	(Factory Time)	Chilton Time
Liquid Line		
Vans-Astro-Safari (1.1)		1.8
S-series (1.0)		1.7
All other models (.9)		1.6
Suction & Discharge Hose Assy		
w/Front A.C.		
Vans (1.3)		2.0

	(Factory Time)	Chilton Time
Astro-Safari (1.1)		1.8
All other models (1.0)		1.7
w/Rear A.C.		
Vans (2.0)		3.0
V-series (1.4)		2.1

	(Factory Time)	Chilton Time
Front to Rear Unit		
All models (1.3)		2.0
Hose & Plate Assy		
All models (1.4)		2.1
R&R seat for rear A.C. add		.2
R&R trim panel for rear A.C. add		.5

LABOR 30 HEAD AND PARKING LAMPS 30 LABOR

	(Factory Time)	Chilton Time
Aim Headlamps		
two		.4
four		.6
Headlamp Sealed Beam Bulb, Renew		
All models-each (.2)		.3
Turn Signal or Parking Lamp Assy., Renew		
R-V series-each (.4)		.5

	(Factory Time)	Chilton Time
All other models-each (.2)		.4
Side Marker Lamp Assy., Renew		
All models-each (.2)		.3
Tail and Stop Lamp Assy., Renew		
Includes: Back-up and/or marker lamp assy. on combination units.		
All models-each (.3)		.4

	(Factory Time)	Chilton Time
License Lamp Assy., Renew		
All models-each (.2)		.3
Roof Marker Lamp Assy., Renew		
All models-each (.2)		.3
Reflectors, Renew		
All models-each		.2

LABOR 31 WINDSHIELD WIPER & SPEEDOMETER 31 LABOR

	(Factory Time)	Chilton Time
Wiper Motor, Renew		
C-K series (.7)		1.0
Vans (.9)		1.2
Astro-Safari (.3)		.5
S-series		
Front (.6)		.8
Rear (.4)		.6
R-V series (.3)		.5
Recond motor add (.3)		.5
Wiper Transmission, Renew (One Side)		
All models (.6)		.8
Wiper Switch, Renew		
std whl (1.2)		1.7
tilt whl (1.0)		1.5
Washer Pump Assy., Renew		
C-K series (.4)		.5
Vans (.2)		.3
Astro-Safari (.3)		.4
S-series		
Front (.2)		.3
Rear (.2)		.3

	(Factory Time)	Chilton Time
R-V series (.3)		.4
Intermittent Wiper Controller Assy., Renew		
S-series (.3)		.5
All other models (.5)		.8
Pulse Wiper Control Module, Renew		
All models (.3)		.5
Windshield Washer Pump Valve, Renew		
All models (.2)		.4
Speedometer Head, R&R or Renew		
1986		
S-series (.4)		.8
exc Vans (.6)		1.0
Vans (.5)		.9
Astro-Safari (.7)		1.2
1987-90		
S-series-Astro-Safari (.7)		1.2
exc Vans (.5)		.9
Vans (.6)		1.0
Reset odometer add		.2

	(Factory Time)	Chilton Time
Speedometer Cable and Casing, Renew		
1986		
upper cable (.4)		.6
lower cable (.3)		.5
one piece cable		
conv cab (.4)		.6
All other models (.7)		1.1
1987-90		
One Piece Cable		
Astro-Safari (.7)		1.1
All other models (.8)		1.2
Two Piece Cable		
upper (.4)		.6
lower (.3)		.5
Instrument Panel Cluster Assy., R&R or Renew		
C-K series (.4)		.7
Odometer and/or Motor, Renew		
C-K series (.5)		.8

LABOR 32 LIGHT SWITCHES & WIRING 32 LABOR

	(Factory Time)	Chilton Time
Headlamp Switch, Renew		
S-series (.4)		.7
exc Vans (.5)		.8
Vans-Astro-Safari (.3)		.6
Headlamp Dimmer Switch, Renew		
S-series (.6)		.9
Vans-Astro (.4)		.7
All other models (.5)		.8
Turn Signal and Hazard Warning Switch, Renew		
All models-std colm (.6)		1.1
tilt colm (1.0)		1.5

	(Factory Time)	Chilton Time
Back-Up Lamp and Park/Neutral Switch, Renew		
S-series (.4)		.6
All other models (.3)		.5
Starter Safety Switch, Renew		
w/A.T.-column mount (.3)		.5
w/M.T.-clutch mount (.2)		.4
Back-Up Lamp Switch, Renew		
w/A.T. (.3)		.5
w/M.T.-floor shift (.2)		.4
w/M.T.-column shift (.3)		.5
Stop Light Switch, Renew		
All models (.2)		.3

	(Factory Time)	Chilton Time
Parking Brake Warning Lamp Switch, Renew		
S-series (.4)		.6
All other models (.2)		.4
Turn Signal or Hazard Warning Flasher, Renew		
S-series (.4)		.5
All other models (.2)		.3
Horn, Renew		
Astro-Safari-R-V series (.4)		.5
All other models (.2)		.4

LABOR   34 CRUISE CONTROL 34   LABOR

	(Factory Time)	Chilton Time
Engagement Switch, Renew		
All models (.5)		.9
Cruise Control Release Switch, Renew		
All models		
Brake (.4)		.5
Clutch (.4)		.5
Cruise Control Servo, Renew		
exc Vans (.6)		.8
Vans-Astro-Safari (.7)		.9

	(Factory Time)	Chilton Time
Renew bracket add (.1)		.2
Vacuum Hoses, Renew		
exc Vans (.2)		.3
Vans-Astro-Safari (.4)		.6
Cruise Control Cable or Chain, Renew		
Vans-Astro-Safari (.5)		.7
All other models (.3)		.5
Cruise Control Resume Solenoid, Renew		
All models (.2)		.3

	(Factory Time)	Chilton Time
Cruise Control Module, Renew		
Astro-Safari (.5)		.7
All other models (.3)		.5
Cruise Control Speed Sensor, Renew		
S-series–Vans-Astro-Safari (.6)		.9
All other models (.7)		1.0
Cruise Control Check Valve, Renew		
All models (.2)		.4

GROUP INDEX

ALPHABETICAL INDEX

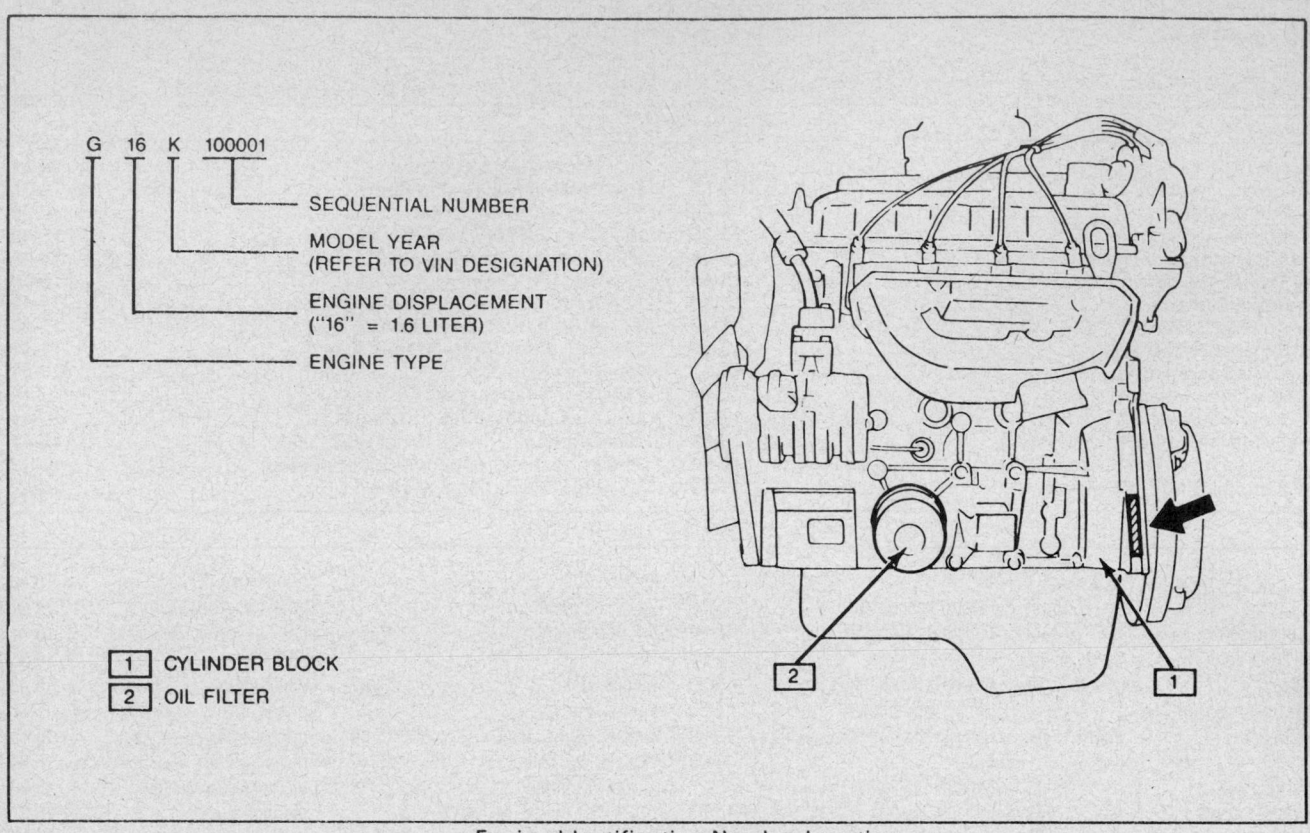

G 16 K 100001

—— SEQUENTIAL NUMBER

—— MODEL YEAR
(REFER TO VIN DESIGNATION)

—— ENGINE DISPLACEMENT
("16" = 1.6 LITER)

—— ENGINE TYPE

1 CYLINDER BLOCK
2 OIL FILTER

Engine Identification Number Location

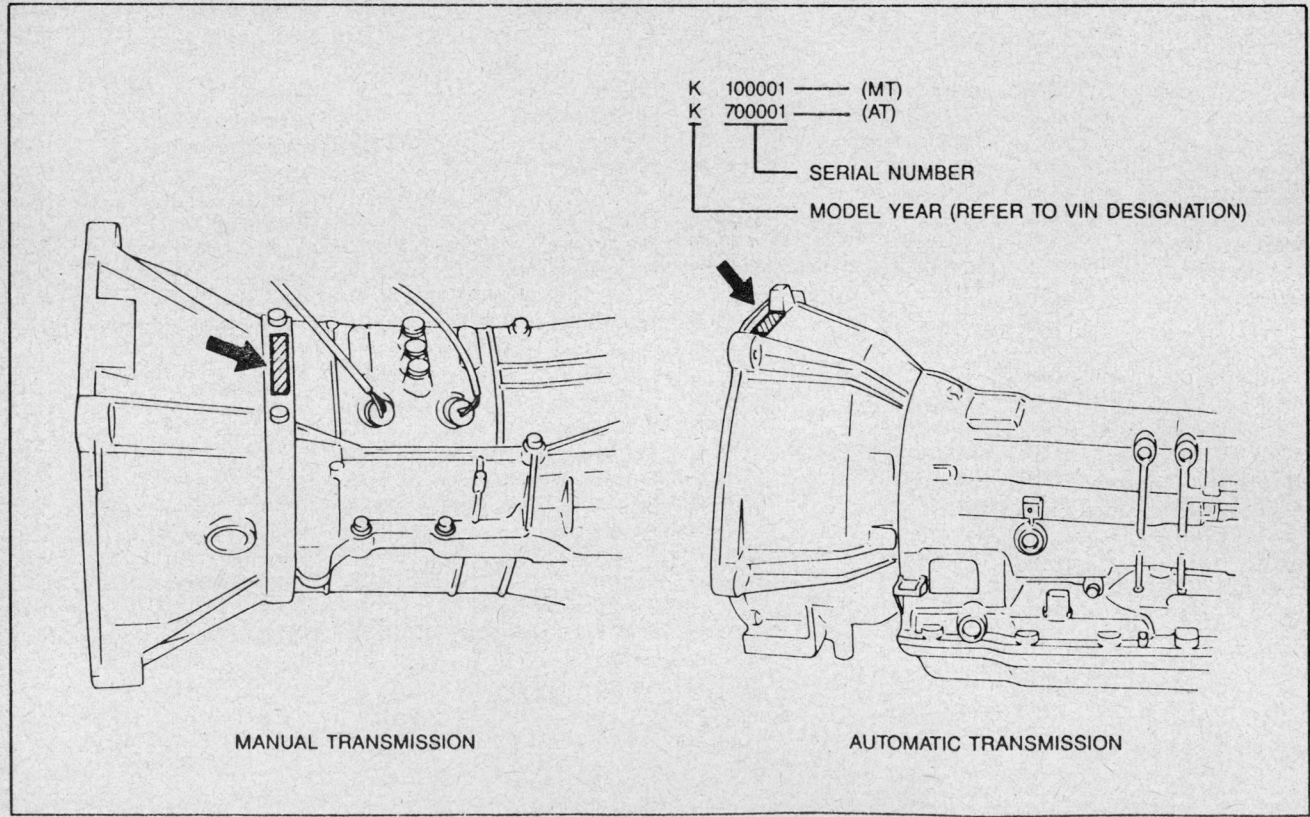

K 100001 ——— (MT)
K 700001 ——— (AT)

—— SERIAL NUMBER

—— MODEL YEAR (REFER TO VIN DESIGNATION)

MANUAL TRANSMISSION

AUTOMATIC TRANSMISSION

Transmission Identification Number Location

LABOR 1 TUNE UP 1 LABOR

	(Factory Time)	Chilton Time
Compression Test		
Four—1989-90		.6
Engine Tune Up, (Electronic Ignition)		

Includes: Test battery and clean connections. Check engine compression, clean and adjust or renew spark plugs. Test resistance of spark plug cables. Inspect distributor cap and rotor. Check vacuum advance operation. Reset ignition timing. Adjust minimum idle speed. Service air cleaner. Inspect and adjust drive belts. Check operation of EGR valve.

	(Factory Time)	Chilton Time
Four—1989-90		1.5

LABOR 2 IGNITION SYSTEM 2 LABOR

	(Factory Time)	Chilton Time
Spark Plugs, Clean and Reset or Renew		
1989-90 (.3)		.4
Ignition Timing, Reset		
All models (.3)		.4
Distributor, Renew		
Includes: Reset ignition timing.		
1989-90 (.4)		.7
Distributor, R&R and Recondition		
Includes: Reset ignition timing.		
1989-90 (.7)		1.4

	(Factory Time)	Chilton Time
Vacuum Advance Unit, Renew		
Includes: Reset ignition timing.		
1989-90 (.3)		.5
Distributor Cap and/or Rotor, Renew		
1989-90 (.3)		.4
Ignition Coil, Renew		
1989-90 (.3)		.4
Ignition Cables, Renew		
1989-90 (.3)		.4

	(Factory Time)	Chilton Time
Distributor Capacitor and/or Module Wiring Harness, Renew		
1989-90 (.3)		.5
Distributor Pick-Up Coil and/or Pole Piece, Renew		
1989-90 (.4)		.6
Ignition Switch, Renew		
1989-90 (.7)		1.0

LABOR 3 FUEL SYSTEM 3 LABOR

	(Factory Time)	Chilton Time
FUEL INJECTION		
Fuel Injectors, Clean (On Car) (w/TBI or MFI)		
Includes: Hook up pressurized fuel injection cleaning equipment.		
All models		.5
Fuel Filter Element, Renew		
All models (.3)		.4
Throttle Body, R&R or Renew		
1989-90 (.9)		1.2
Renew throttle body add (.3)		.3
Minimum Idle Speed, Adjust		
All models (.5)		.6

	(Factory Time)	Chilton Time
Fuel Pressure Regulator, Renew		
1989-90 (.4)		.6
Throttle Body Injector and/or Gasket, Renew		
1989-90 (.3)		.5
Fuel Pump, Renew (In Tank)		
1989-90 (1.3)		1.8
w/Trailer hitch add (.2)		.2
Fuel Pump Relay, Renew		
1989-90 (.3)		.4
Fast Idle Actuator Vacuum Switching Valve, Renew		
1989-90 (.3)		.4

	(Factory Time)	Chilton Time
TBI Heater and/or Gasket, Renew		
1989-90 (.7)		1.0
Fuel Tank, Renew		
1989-90 (1.3)		1.8
w/Trailer hitch add (.2)		.2
Fuel Gauge (Tank Unit), Renew		
1989-90 (1.0)		1.5
w/Trailer hitch add (.2)		.2
Fuel Gauge (Dash Unit), Renew		
1989-90 (.5)		.8
Intake Manifold and/or Gasket, Renew		
1989-90 (1.2)		1.7
w/A.T. add (.1)		.1
Renew manif add (.4)		.5

LABOR 3A EMISSION CONTROLS 3A LABOR

	(Factory Time)	Chilton Time
Emission Control Check		
Includes: Check and adjust minimum idle speed and ignition timing. Check operation of EGR valve.		
All models		.6
EVAPORATIVE EMISSION TYPE		
Positive Crankcase Vent Valve, Renew		
All models (.2)		.2
Charcoal Canister, Renew		
All models (.3)		.3
EXHAUST GAS RECIRCULATION SYSTEM		
E.G.R. Valve, Renew		
1989-90 (.4)		.5

	(Factory Time)	Chilton Time
Thermostatic Vacuum Control Switch, Renew		
1989-90 (.2)		.3
E.G.R. Modulator, Renew		
1989-90 (.2)		.3
ELECTRONIC EMISSION CONTROLS		
Throttle Position Sensor, Adjust		
1989-90 (.2)		.4
Electronic Control Module, Renew		
1989-90 (.5)		.7
Coolant Temperature Sensor, Renew		
1989-90 (.4)		.6

	(Factory Time)	Chilton Time
Manifold Absolute Pressure Sensor, Renew		
1989-90 (.4)		.6
Manifold Air Temperature Sensor, Renew		
1989-90 (.4)		.6
Oxygem Sensor, Renew		
1989-90 (.4)		.6
E.C.M. Relay, Renew		
1989-90 (.3)		.5
Throttle Position Sensor, Renew		
1989-90 (.6)		.8
Cancel Switch, Renew		
1989-90 (.3)		.5

LABOR 4 ALTERNATOR AND REGULATOR 4 LABOR

	(Factory Time)	Chilton Time
Generator Circuits, Test		
Includes: Test battery, regulator and generator output.		
All models		.6

	(Factory Time)	Chilton Time
Generator Drive Belt, Renew		
1989-90 (.3)		.4

	(Factory Time)	Chilton Time
Generator Assembly or Fan Pulley, Renew		
1989-90 (.6)		.9

LABOR   4 ALTERNATOR AND REGULATOR 4   LABOR

(Factory Time)	Chilton Time	(Factory Time)	Chilton Time	(Factory Time)	Chilton Time
Generator, R&R and Recondition		**Generator Front Bearing, Renew**		**Generator Voltage Regulator, Test and Renew**	
Includes: Test, disassemble, replacement of parts as required, reassemble.		Includes: R&R generator, separate end frames.		Includes: R&R generator, disassemble and reassemble.	
1989-90 (1.4)	2.0	1989-90 (.8)	1.1	1989-90 (1.0)	1.4
		Renew rear brg add	.1		

LABOR   5 STARTING SYSTEM 5   LABOR

(Factory Time)	Chilton Time	(Factory Time)	Chilton Time	(Factory Time)	Chilton Time
Starter Draw Test (On Car)		**Starter Drive, Renew**		**Ignition Switch, Renew**	
All models	.3	Includes: R&R starter.		1989-90 (.7)	1.0
Starter Assembly, Renew		1989-90 (.6)	.9	**Battery Cables, Renew**	
1989-90 (.4)	.6	**Starter Motor Solenoid, Renew**		All models	
Starter Assy., R&R and Recondition		Includes: R&R starter.		positive (.4)	.5
Includes: Turn down armature.		1989-90 (.5)	.8	negative (.3)	.4
1989-90 (1.1)	2.0	**Clutch Start Switch, Renew**		**Battery Terminals, Clean**	
Renew field coils add (.2)	.5	1989-90 (.4)	.5	All models	.3

LABOR   6 BRAKE SYSTEM 6   LABOR

(Factory Time)	Chilton Time
Brake Pedal Free Play, Adjust	
All models	.3
Brakes, Adjust (Minor)	
Includes: R&R wheels and adjust brakes thru access holes in drums. Fill master cylinder.	
two wheels	.4
Remove knock out plugs add, each	.1
Bleed Brakes (Four Wheels)	
Includes: Fill master cylinder.	
All models (.4)	.5
Brake Shoes and/or Pads, Renew	
Includes: Install new or exchange brake shoes or pads, adjust service and hand brake. Bleed system.	
1989-90	
front-disc (.6)	.9
rear drum (1.1)	1.5
all four wheels	2.3
Resurface disc rotor add-each	.5
Resurface brake drum add-each	.5
Brake Drums, Renew	
1989-90-one (.4)	.6
both (.7)	1.1
Brake System Failure Warning Switch, Renew	
1989-90 (.3)	.4

BRAKE HYDRAULIC SYSTEM

(Factory Time)	Chilton Time
Wheel Cylinders, Renew	
Includes: Bleed system.	
1989-90-one (.9)	1.0
both (1.2)	1.9
Wheel Cylinders, R&R and Recondition	
Includes: Bleed system.	
1989-90-one (1.1)	1.1
both (1.6)	2.1
Brake Hose, Renew (Flex)	
Includes: Bleed system.	
1989-90-front-one (.6)	.8
rear-one (.6)	.8
each adtnl	.3

COMBINATIONS

Add to Brakes, Renew

See Machine Shop Operations

(Factory Time)	Chilton Time
RENEW WHEEL CYLINDER	
Each	.2
REBUILD WHEEL CYLINDER	
Each	.3
REBUILD CALIPER ASSEMBLY	
Each	.4
RENEW MASTER CYLINDER	
All models	.4
REBUILD MASTER CYLINDER	
All models	.9
RENEW BRAKE HOSE	
Each	.3
RENEW BRAKE DRUM	
Each	.2
RENEW DISC BRAKE ROTOR	
Each	.3
RENEW DISC BRAKE ROTOR STUDS	
Each	.1

(Factory Time)	Chilton Time
Master Cylinder, Renew	
Includes: Bleed complete system.	
1989-90 (.6)	.9
Master Cylinder, R&R and Rebuild	
Includes: Bleed complete system.	
1989-90 (.9)	1.4
Brake System, Flush and Refill	
All models	1.2

POWER BRAKES

(Factory Time)	Chilton Time
Power Brake Booster, Renew	
1989-90 (.4)	.7
Recond m/Cyl and bleed brakes add	.6
Power Brake Booster, R&R and Recondition	
1989-90 (.8)	1.4
Vacuum Check Valve, Renew	
1989-90 (.3)	.3

DISC BRAKES

(Factory Time)	Chilton Time
Disc Brake Pads, Renew	
Includes: Install new disc brake pads only.	
1989-90 (.6)	.9
Disc Brake Rotor, Renew	
1989-90-one (.5)	.7
both (.7)	1.1
Caliper Assembly, Renew	
Includes: Bleed complete system.	
1989-90-one (.8)	.8
both (1.1)	1.4
Caliper Assy., R&R and Recondition	
Includes: Bleed complete system.	
1989-90-one (1.1)	1.2
both (1.7)	2.2
Brake Combination Valve, Renew	
1989-90 (.7)	1.0
Height Sensing Brake Proportioner Valve, Renew	
1989-90 (.7)	1.0

PARKING BRAKE

(Factory Time)	Chilton Time
Parking Brake, Adjust	
All models (.3)	.4
Parking Brake Warning Lamp Switch, Renew	
1989-90 (.3)	.4
Parking Brake Control, Renew	
1989-90 (.5)	.8
Parking Brake Cables, Renew	
1989-90-rear-one (1.1)	1.4
both (1.7)	2.3

LABOR 7 COOLING SYSTEM 7 LABOR

	Factory Time	Chilton Time
Winterize Cooling System		
Includes: Run engine to check for leaks, tighten all hose connections. Test radiator and pressure cap, drain radiator and engine block. Add antifreeze and refill system.		
All models		.5
Thermostat, Renew		
1989-90 (.3)		.4
Radiator Assembly, R&R or Renew		
Includes: Drain and refill cooling system.		
1989-90 (.5)		.8
ADD THESE OPERATIONS TO RADIATOR R&R		
Boil & Repair		1.5
Rod Clean		1.9
Repair Core		1.3
Renew Tank		1.6
Renew Trans. Oil Cooler		1.9
Recore Radiator		1.7
Radiator Hoses, Renew		
1989-90		
upper (.3)		.4
rad to outlet pipe (.4)		.5

	Factory Time	Chilton Time
outlet to inlet pipe (.4)		.5
both (.5)		.7
Thermostat By-Pass Hose or Pipe, Renew		
1989-90 (.3)		.5
Water Pump, Renew		
Includes: Drain and refill cooling system.		
1989-90 (1.2)		1.7
w/A.C. add (.5)		.5
Drive Belt, Adjust		
All models-one		.3
all		.4
Drive Belt, Renew		
All models		
A.C. (.4)		.5
Fan/Gen (.3)		.4
Temperature Gauge (Dash Unit), Renew		
1989-90 (.5)		.8
Water Jacket Expansion Plugs, Renew		
Each		.5
Add time to gain access.		
Heater Blower Motor Switch, Renew		
1989-90 (.3)		.4

	Factory Time	Chilton Time
Master Electrical Switch, Renew (A.C. On-Off)		
1989-90 (.3)		.4
Temperature Control Assy., Renew		
1989-90 (1.2)		1.6
Heater Blower Motor Resistor, Renew		
1989-90 (.2)		.3
Heater Blower Motor, Renew		
1989-90 (.4)		.6
Heater Core, R&R or Renew		
1989-90-wo/A.C. (1.5)		2.9
w/A.C. (1.5)		2.9
Add time to evacuate and charge A.C. system if reqd.		
ADD THESE OPERATIONS TO HEATER CORE R&R		
Boil & Repair		1.2
Repair Core		.9
Recore		1.2
Heater Hoses, Renew		
1989-90-one (.3)		.4
all (.4)		.5

LABOR 8 EXHAUST SYSTEM 8 LABOR

	Factory Time	Chilton Time
Muffler, Renew		
1989-90 (.4)		.6
Tail Pipe, Renew		
1989-90 (.3)		.4

	Factory Time	Chilton Time
Catalytic Converter, Renew		
1989-90 (.5)		.7
Exhaust Manifold, Renew		
1989-90 (.6)		1.0

	Factory Time	Chilton Time
COMBINATIONS		
Exhaust System, Renew (Complete)		
1989-90		1.1
Muffler and Tail Pipe, Renew		
1989-90		.7

LABOR 9A FRONT SUSPENSION (RWD) 9A LABOR

	Factory Time	Chilton Time
Note: On all front suspension operations alignment charges must be added if performed. Time given does not include alignment.		
Wheel, Renew		
one		.5
Wheels, Rotate (All)		
All models		.5
Wheels, Balance		
one		.3
each adtnl		.2
Check Alignment of Front End		
All models		.5
Note: Deduct if alignment is performed.		
Toe-In, Adjust		
All models (.6)		.6
Front Wheel Bearings, Renew		
Add alignment charges.		
1989-90-one side (1.0)		1.4
both sides (1.7)		2.3
Front Wheel Bearing Seal or Hub Assy., Renew		
1989-90-one side (1.1)		1.5
both sides (2.0)		2.7
Front Spindle, Renew		
Add alignment charges if required.		
1989-90-one side (.7)		1.0
both sides (1.4)		2.0

	Factory Time	Chilton Time
Steering Knuckle, Renew		
Add alignment charges.		
1989-90-one side (1.1)		1.5
both sides (1.9)		2.6
Steering Knuckle Inner Dust Seal, Renew		
Add alignment charges.		
1989-90-one side (1.0)		1.5
both sides (1.9)		2.6
Lower Ball Joints, Renew		
Add alignment charges.		
1989-90-one (.5)		.8
both (.7)		1.3
Front Coil Springs, Renew		
Add alignment charges.		
1989-90-one (.5)		.8
both (.7)		1.3
Lower Control Arm Assy., Renew		
Add alignment charges.		
1989-90-one (.7)		1.0
both (1.3)		1.7
w/Skid plate add (.1)		.1
Front Strut Shock Absorbers, Renew		
Add alignment charges.		
1989-90-one (.6)		.9
both (1.0)		1.5
Front Spring Seats and/or Insulators, Renew		
Add alignment charges.		
1989-90-one side (.5)		.8
both (.7)		1.3

	Factory Time	Chilton Time
Front Strut Bearing Mount, Renew		
Add alignment charges.		
1989-90-one side (.6)		.9
both sides (.9)		1.5
Front Stabilizer Shaft Bushings, Renew		
1989-90-one (.3)		.4
both (.3)		.5
Front Stabilizer Shaft, Renew		
1989-90 (.6)		.9
4 WHEEL DRIVE FRONT AXLE		
Front Propeller Shaft, Renew		
1989-90 (.3)		.5
Front Universal Joints, Renew or Recondition		
1989-90		
front (.6)		.8
rear (.6)		.8
both (1.0)		1.4
Halfshaft Assy., R&R or Renew		
1989-90-one (1.0)		1.3
both (1.8)		2.4
Renew Outer C.V. Joint add each (.3)		.4
Renew Tri-Pot Joint add- each (.3)		.4
Renew C.V. Joint Seal (Boot), add-each (.4)		.5
w/Skid plate add (.1)		.1
Axle Shaft, Renew		
1989-90-left side (.6)		.9
w/Skid plate add (.1)		.1

LABOR 9A FRONT SUSPENSION (RWD) 9A LABOR

(Factory Time)	Chilton Time	(Factory Time)	Chilton Time	(Factory Time)	Chilton Time
Axle Shaft Oil Seal, Renew		**Differential Carrier Assy., Remove & Install**		Recond complete add (1.4)...............	1.9
1989-90–right (.5)............	.8	1989-90 (1.3)........................	1.9	**Front Differential Housing, Renew**	
left (.6)............	.9	Renew pinion shaft and/or		1989-90 (1.5)........................	2.4
both (.9)............	1.5	side & pinion gears add (1.0)	1.4	**Front Differential Mount and/or Bracket,**	
w/Skid plate add (.1)............	.1	Renew side brgs add (.7)................	1.0	**Renew**	
Axle Shaft Bearing, Renew		Renew pinion brgs add (1.1)........	1.5	1989-90–right (.4)........................	.6
1989-90–left side (.7)............	1.0	Renew ring gear and		left (.4)........................	.6
w/Skid plate add (.1)............	.1	pinion add (1.3)........	1.8	rear (.3)........................	.5
Front Pinion Shaft Oil Seal, Renew		Renew diff case add (1.0)........	1.4	w/Skid plate add (.1)........................	.1
1989-90 (.5)............	.7	Renew carrier add (1.0)........	1.4		

LABOR 10 STEERING LINKAGE 10 LABOR

(Factory Time)	Chilton Time	(Factory Time)	Chilton Time	(Factory Time)	Chilton Time
Inner Tie Rod, Renew		**Tie Rod Ends and/or Adjusting Sleeve,**		**Idler Arm, Renew**	
Includes: Reset toe-in.		**Renew**		Includes: Reset toe-in.	
1989-90–one (.8)............	.9	Includes: Reset toe-in.		1989-90 (1.0)........................	1.3
both (.9)............	1.2	1989-90–one (.9)........	1.0	w/Skid plate add (.1)........................	.1
w/Skid plate add (.1)............	.1	both (1.1)........	1.4	**Steering Relay Rod, Renew**	
Pitman Arm, Renew		w/Skid plate add (.1)........	.1	Includes: Reset toe-in.	
1989-90 (.5)............	.7			1989-90 (1.1)........................	1.4
w/Skid plate add (.1)............	.1			w/Skid plate add (.1)........................	.1

LABOR 11 STEERING GEAR 11 LABOR

(Factory Time)	Chilton Time	(Factory Time)	Chilton Time	(Factory Time)	Chilton Time
MANUAL STEERING		**Steering Column, Renew**		**Manual Steering Gear, Renew**	
Steering Wheel, Renew		1989-90 (.8)........................	1.3	Includes: Reset toe-in.	
1989-90 (.3)............	.4	**Steering Intermediate Shaft, Renew**		1989-90 (1.1)........................	1.9
Horn Contact or Cancelling Cam, Renew		1989-90 (.6)........................	.9	w/Skid plate add (.1)........................	.1
1989-90 (.3)............	.5				

LABOR 12 CYLINDER HEAD & VALVE SYSTEM 12 LABOR

(Factory Time)	Chilton Time	(Factory Time)	Chilton Time	(Factory Time)	Chilton Time
Compression Test		**Clean Carbon and Grind Valves**		w/A.C. add (.6)........................	.6
1989-90	.6	Includes: R&R cylinder head, grind valves and		w/A.T. add (.1)........................	.1
		seats. Minor tune up.		**Valve Springs and/or Valve Stem Oil**	
Cylinder Head Gasket, Renew		1989-90 (5.5)........................	7.7	**Seals, Renew**	
Includes: Clean carbon and make all necessary		w/A.C. add (.6)........................	.6	Includes: R&R cylinder head.	
adjustments.		w/A.T. add (.1)........................	.1	1989-90–one cyl (3.3)........................	4.6
1989-90 (2.9)............	4.0	**Rocker Arm Cover Gasket, Renew**		all cyls (4.0)........................	5.6
w/A.C. add (.6)............	.6	1989-90 (.5)........................	.8	w/A.C. add (.6)........................	.6
w/A.T. add (.1)............	.1	**Valve Rocker Arms, Renew**		w/A.T. add (.1)........................	.1
		Includes: R&R cylinder head.		**Valve Adjusters, Renew**	
Cylinder Head, Renew		1989-90 (3.0)........................	4.4	1989-90–one cyl (.8)........................	1.3
Includes: Transfer all components, clean car-		w/A.C. add (.6)........................	.6	all cyls (1.0)........................	1.7
bon. Make all necessary adjustments.		w/A.T. add (.1)........................	.1	w/A.C. add (.5)........................	.5
1989-90 (3.8)............	5.3	**Valve Rocker Arm Shaft, Renew**		**Valve Lash, Adjust**	
w/A.C. add (.6)............	.6	Includes: R&R cylinder head.		1989-90 (.8)........................	1.2
w/A.T. add (.1)............	.1	1989-90–one or both (3.0)............	4.3	w/A.C. add (.5)........................	.5

LABOR 13 ENGINE ASSEMBLY & MOUNTS 13 LABOR

(Factory Time)	Chilton Time	(Factory Time)	Chilton Time	(Factory Time)	Chilton Time
Note: All engine operations listed in this		w/A.C. add	.7	w/Skid plate add (.1)........................	.1
group are for assemblies as supplied by the		w/Skid plate add	.1	Recond valves add	2.5
original equipment manufacturer. Time to					
replace assemblies from independent re-		**Cylinder Block, Renew (Partial)**		**Cylinder Assembly, Renew (Fitted)**	
builders may vary.		Includes: R&R engine assembly, transfer all		**(w/Pistons, Rings & Bearings)**	
		component parts not supplied with replace-		Includes: R&R engine assembly, transfer all	
Engine Assembly, Remove & Install		ment engine. Minor tune up.		component parts not supplied with replace-	
Does not include transfer of any parts or equip-		1989-90 (5.5)........................	7.7	ment engine. Minor tune up.	
ment.		w/A.C. add (.7)........................	.7	1989-90 (7.7)........................	10.8
1989-90	4.2				

LABOR 13 ENGINE ASSEMBLY & MOUNTS 13 LABOR

(Factory Time)	Chilton Time	(Factory Time)	Chilton Time	(Factory Time)	Chilton Time
w/A.C. add (.7)	.7	w/A.C. add (.7)	.7	w/A.C. add (.6)	.6
w/Skid plate add (.1)	.1	w/Skid plate add (.1)	.1	w/Skid plate add (.1)	.1

Engine Assembly, R&R and Recondition
Includes: Rebore block, install new pistons, rings, rod and main bearings. Clean carbon, grind valves. Tune engine.
1989-90 (13.6) **19.0**

Engine Assembly, Recondition (In Car)
Includes: Expand or renew pistons, install new rings, pins, rod and main bearings. Clean carbon, grind valves. Tune engine.
1989-90 (10.6) **14.8**

Engine Mounts, Renew
1989-90
right side (.8) **1.1**
left side (.6) .... **.9**

LABOR 14 PISTONS, RINGS & BEARINGS 14 LABOR

Rings, Renew (See Engine Combinations)
Includes: Remove cylinder top ridge, deglaze cylinder walls. Clean ring grooves. Minor tune up.

	Chilton Time
1989-90-one cyl (5.2)	7.2
all cyls (6.6)	9.4
w/A.C. add (.6)	.6
w/A.T. add (.1)	.1
w/Skid plate add (.1)	.1

Pistons or Connecting Rods, Renew
Includes: Remove cylinder top ridge, deglaze cylinder walls. Minor tune up.

	Chilton Time
1989-90-one cyl (5.9)	7.5
all cyls (7.2)	10.6
w/A.C. add (.6)	.6
w/A.T. add (.1)	.1
w/Skid plate add (.1)	.1

Connecting Rod Bearings, Renew

	Chilton Time
1989-90 (2.9)	4.0
w/Skid plate add (.1)	.1

COMBINATIONS
Add to Engine Work
See Machine Shop Operations

(Factory Time)	Chilton Time	(Factory Time)	Chilton Time
DRAIN, EVACUATE & RECHARGE AIR CONDITIONING SYSTEM		**CONNECTING ROD, RENEW (ENGINE DISASSEMBLED)**	
All models............	1.0	Each	.4
DISTRIBUTOR, RECONDITION		**DEGLAZE CYLINDER WALLS**	
All models............	.8	Each	.1
VALVE GUIDES, REAM OVERSIZE		**REMOVE CYLINDER TOP RIDGE**	
Each	.2	Each	.3
		PLASTIGAUGE BEARINGS	
CYLINDER HEAD, R&R (ENGINE REMOVED)		Each	.1
		OIL FILTER ELEMENT, RENEW	
All models............	1.0	All models............	.3

LABOR 15 CRANKSHAFT & DAMPER 15 LABOR

(Factory Time)	Chilton Time	(Factory Time)	Chilton Time	(Factory Time)	Chilton Time

Crankshaft and Main Bearings, Renew
Includes: R&R engine, check all bearing clearances.

	Chilton Time
1989-90 (5.7)	8.0
w/A.C. add (.6)	.6
w/A.T. add (.1)	.1
w/Skid plate add (.1)	.1

Main Bearings, Renew
Includes: Check all bearing clearances.
1989-90 (3.2) **4.5**

w/Skid plate add (.1) .... **.1**

Main and Rod Bearings, Renew
Includes: Check all bearing clearances.
1989-90 (4.2) **5.7**
w/Skid plate add (.1) .... **.1**

Crankshaft Rear Main Seals, Renew
1989-90
w/M.T. (2.3) **3.3**
w/A.T. (2.4) **3.5**

Rear Main Seal Housing and/or Gasket, Renew
1989-90
w/M.T. (2.3) **3.4**
w/A.T. (2.5) **3.6**

Crankshaft Pulley, Renew
1989-90 (.8) **1.3**
w/A.C. add (.6) .... **.6**

Crankshaft Timing Sprocket, Renew
1989-90 (1.3) **1.8**
w/A.C. add (.6) .... **.6**

LABOR 16 CAMSHAFT & TIMING GEARS 16 LABOR

(Factory Time)	Chilton Time	(Factory Time)	Chilton Time	(Factory Time)	Chilton Time

Camshaft Drive Belt Cover, R&R or Renew
1989-90 (1.0) **1.4**
w/A.C. add (.6) .... **.6**

Camshaft Drive Belt, Renew (Timing Belt)
1989-90 (1.1) **1.5**
w/A.C. add (.6) .... **.6**

Camshaft Idler Pulley, Renew
1989-90 (1.1) **1.6**
w/A.C. add (.6) .... **.6**

Camshaft Timing Sprocket, Renew
1989-90 (1.3) **1.8**

w/A.C. add (.6) .... **.6**

Camshaft and/or Bearings, Renew
1989-90 (3.1) **4.3**
w/A.C. add (.6) .... **.6**
w/A.T. add (.1) .... **.1**

LABOR 17 ENGINE OILING SYSTEM 17 LABOR

(Factory Time)	Chilton Time	(Factory Time)	Chilton Time	(Factory Time)	Chilton Time

Oil Pan and/or Gasket, Renew
1989-90 (1.9) **2.6**
w/Skid plate add (.1) .... **.1**

Pressure Test Engine Bearings (Pan Off)
All models............ **1.0**

Oil Pump, Renew
1989-90 (2.9) **4.0**
w/A.C. add (.6) .... **.6**
w/Skid plate add (.1) .... **.1**
Recond pump add (.3) .... **.3**

Oil Pressure Sending Unit, Renew
1989-90 (.2) .... **.4**

Oil Filter Element, Renew
1989-90 (.3) .... **.3**

LABOR 18 CLUTCH & FLYWHEEL 18 LABOR

	(Factory Time)	Chilton Time

Clutch Pedal Free Play, Adjust
All models................................ .3

Clutch Release Bearing, Renew
Includes: R&R trans and adjust linkage.
1989-90 (2.1)............................... 3.0

Clutch Assembly, Renew
Includes: R&R trans. Renew clutch disc, pressure plate and release bearing. Adjust linkage.
1989-90 (2.2) 3.3
Renew clutch fork and/or bushings
add (.2) 2

Clutch Control Cable, Renew
1989-90 (.5)............................ .8
Flywheel, Renew
Includes: R&R trans and adjust linkage.
1989-90 (2.3)............................... 3.6
Renew pilot brg add (.2) 2

LABOR 19A MANUAL TRANSMISSION (RWD) 19A LABOR

Transmission Assembly, R&R or Renew
1989-90 (2.2)............................ 3.0
Renew front retainer or
gasket add 3
Renew assy add (.2) 3

Transmission Assy., R&R and Recondition
Includes: Complete disassembly, clean and in-
spect or renew all parts. Install new gaskets and seals.
1989-90 (5.2)............................... 7.2
Transmission, Recondition (Off Car)
All models (3.0) 4.2
Rear Transmission Mount, Renew
1989-90 (.5)................................... .7

Transmission Shift Cover and/or Gasket, Renew
1989-90 (1.9)................................ 2.7
Recond cover add (.2) 3
Speedometer Driven Gear and/or Seal, Renew
1989-90 (.3)................................... .4

LABOR 20 TRANSFER CASE 20 LABOR

Transfer Case Oil Seals, Renew
1989-90
front (.4) 6
rear (.4) 6
Speedometer Driven Gear and/or Seal, Renew
1989-90 (.3) 4

Transfer Case Speedometer Drive Gear, Renew
1989-90 (1.5) 2.0
Transfer Case to Adapter Gasket, Renew
1989-90 (2.4) 3.2
Rear Output Shaft Housing, Renew
1989-90 (1.5) 2.0

Transfer Case Assy., R&R or Renew
1989-90 (2.4) 3.3
Renew assy add (.1) 2

Transfer Case Assy., R&R and Recondition
1989-90 (4.2)................................. 5.9

LABOR 21 SHIFT LINKAGE 21 LABOR

MANUAL
Gearshift Control Lever, Renew
1989-90 (.3)........................... .5
AUTOMATIC
Shift Linkage, Adjust
All models
Neutral Start Switch (.3) 4

Shift Linkage (.3)........................ .4
T.V. Cable (.4)........................... .5
Park Lock Cable, Adjust
1989-90 (.2)............................... .3
Park Lock Cable, Renew
1989-90 (.6)............................... .9

Shift Control Cable, Renew
1989-90 (.5).................................. .8

Floor Shift Control Assy., Renew
1989-90 (.6)................................ 1.0

LABOR 23A AUTOMATIC TRANSMISSION (RWD) 23A LABOR

TURBO HYDRA-MATIC 180
ON CAR SERVICES
Drain & Refill Unit
All models..................................... 1.0
Oil Pressure Check
All models..................................... .5
Check Unit for Oil Leaks
Includes: Clean and dry outside of case and run unit to determine point of leak.
All models..................................... .9
Neutral Start Switch, Renew
All models (.3) 5
Shift Linkage, Adjust
All models
Neutral Start Switch (.3) 4
Shift Linkage (.3)....................... .4
T.V. Cable (.4)............................ .5
Vacuum Modulator, Renew
All models (.3) 5

Detent Cable, Renew
All models (.4) 6
Detent Valve, Renew
Includes: R&R oil pan and valve body, servo cover and reinforcement plate.
All models (.9) 1.3
Oil Pan and/or Gasket, Renew
All models (.6) 1.0
Manual Shaft Seal, Renew
Includes: R&R oil pan.
All models (1.0) 1.4
Governor Pressure Switch and/or Electrical Connector, Renew
Includes: R&R oil pan.
All models (.7) 1.2
Converter Clutch Solenoid, Renew
Includes: R&R oil pan.
All models (.6) 1.1

Low Band Servo, Renew
Includes: R&R oil pan, reinforcement plate, servo cover and valve body. Adjust servo.
All models (1.0) 1.5
Valve Body Assembly, Renew
Includes: R&R oil pan, reinforcement plate, screen and servo cover.
All models (.8) 1.3
Valve Body Assy., R&R and Recondition
Includes: R&R oil pan, reinforcement plate, screen and servo cover. Disassemble, clean, inspect all valves. Replace parts as required.
All models (1.6) 2.5
Transmission Mount, Renew
All models
rear (.5) 8
SERVICES REQUIRING R&R
Transmission Assembly, Renew
Includes: Renew assy with new or exchange unit.
1989-90 (3.5).................................. 4.9

LABOR 23A AUTOMATIC TRANSMISSION (RWD) 23A LABOR

(Factory Time)	Chilton Time
Transmission and Converter Assy., R&R and Recondition	
Includes: Disassemble trans, inspect and replace parts as required. Make all necessary adjustment. Road test.	
1989-90 (6.7)	9.7
Transmission Assembly, Reseal	
Includes: R&R transmission and install all new gaskets and seals.	
1989-90	6.9
Transmission, Recondition (Off Truck)	
All models (3.4)	4.8
Front Pump Oil Seal, Renew	
Includes: R&R converter and seal.	
1989-90 (3.1)	4.3

(Factory Time)	Chilton Time
Torque Converter, Renew	
Includes: R&R trans.	
1989-90 (3.3)	4.5
Flywheel (Flexplate), Renew	
Includes: R&R trans.	
1989-90 (2.4)	3.4
Front Oil Pump, Renew	
Includes: R&R trans.	
1989-90 (3.7)	5.1
Front Oil Pump, R&R and Recondition	
Includes: R&R trans.	
1989-90 (4.0)	5.6

(Factory Time)	Chilton Time
Apply and Actuator Valve and/or Bushing, Renew	
Includes: R&R trans, converter and oil pump.	
1989-90 (2.8)	3.9
Second and Third Clutch Assemblies, Renew	
Includes: R&R trans and converter, housing and pump reverse clutch assy., second clutch bushing.	
1989-90 (3.6)	5.0
Governor Assembly, Renew	
Includes: R&R trans.	
1989-90 (2.7)	3.8
Recond gover add (.1)	.2
Parking Pawl, Renew	
Includes: R&R trans.	
1989-90 (3.0)	4.2

LABOR 25 U-JOINTS & DRIVESHAFT 25 LABOR

(Factory Time)	Chilton Time
Rear Propeller Shaft, R&R or Renew	
1989-90 (.3)	.5
Pinion Shaft Flange, Renew	
1989-90 (.7)	1.0

(Factory Time)	Chilton Time
Universal Joints, Renew or Recondition	
1989-90	
front (.6)	.8
rear (.6)	.8
both (.9)	1.3

LABOR 26 DRIVE AXLE 26 LABOR

(Factory Time)	Chilton Time
Rear Axle Shaft, Renew	
1989-90–one (.6)	.8
both (.9)	1.3
Axle Shaft Inner Oil Seal, Renew	
1989-90–one (.6)	.8
both (.8)	1.2
Axle Shaft Oil Seal and/or Bearing, Renew	
1989-90–one (.7)	.9
both (1.2)	1.6
Pinion Shaft Oil Seal, Renew	
1989-90 (.8)	1.1

(Factory Time)	Chilton Time
Differential Carrier, Renew (Complete)	
1989-90 (1.1)	1.8
Pinion Shaft, Pinion Gears and/or Side Gears, Renew	
1989-90 (2.7)	3.6
Differential Case, Renew	
1989-90 (2.3)	3.1
Differential Side Bearings, Renew	
1989-90 (2.1)	2.8

(Factory Time)	Chilton Time
Ring and Pinion Bearings, Renew (Front and Rear)	
1989-90 (2.4)	3.2
Ring Gear and Pinion Assy., Renew	
1989-90 (2.6)	3.5
Rear Axle Housing, Renew	
Includes: Transfer parts as required, bleed brakes.	
1989-90 (2.2)	2.9
Rear Differential Assy., Renew (Complete)	
1989-90 (2.0)	2.7

LABOR 27 REAR SUSPENSION 27 LABOR

(Factory Time)	Chilton Time
Rear Wheel Spindle Rod, Renew	
1989-90–one (.4)	.6
both (.7)	1.0
Rear Coil Springs, Renew	
1989-90–one (.4)	.5
both (.6)	.7

(Factory Time)	Chilton Time
Rear Control Arm Assy., Renew	
1989-90	
upper center (.5)	.8
Renew ball joint seal add (.1)	.1

(Factory Time)	Chilton Time
Rear Control Arm Ball Joint Boss, Renew	
1989-90 (.5)	.8
Renew ball joint seal add (.1)	.1
Rear Shock Absorbers, Renew	
1989-90–one (.5)	.6
both (.7)	1.0

LABOR 28 AIR CONDITIONING 28 LABOR

(Factory Time)	Chilton Time
Note: If more than one item requires replacement where evacuation and discharging the system is already included in the operation, deduct 1.0 hour for each additional item to the time listed.	
Drain, Evacuate and Recharge System	
All models	1.0
Flush Refrigerant System, Complete	
To be used in conjunction with component replacement which could contaminate system.	
All models	1.3

(Factory Time)	Chilton Time
Leak Test	
Includes: Check all lines and connections.	
All models	.5
Refrigerant, Add (Partial Charge)	
All models	.6
Compressor Drive Belt, Renew	
All models (.4)	.5

(Factory Time)	Chilton Time
Compressor Assembly, Renew	
Includes: Transfer all necessary attaching parts. Evacuate and charge system.	
All models (.8)	1.5
Install liquid line filter add (.9)	1.2
Compressor Clutch Plate and Hub Assy., Renew	
Includes: R&R compressor. Evacuate and charge system.	
1989-90 (1.2)	1.9

LABOR 28 AIR CONDITIONING 28 LABOR

Compressor Clutch Rotor and/or Bearing, Renew
Includes: R&R compressor. Evacuate and charge system.
1989-90 (1.2) 1.9

Compressor Clutch Coil and/or Pulley Rim Assy., Renew
Includes: R&R compressor. Evacuate and charge system.
1989-90 (1.3) 2.0

Compressor Front Seal, Seat and 'O' Ring, Renew
Includes: R&R compressor. Evacuate and charge system.
1989-90 (1.2) 2.0

Compressor Front or Rear Head, Reed Assy., and/or Gaskets and Seals, Renew
Includes: R&R compressor. R&R clutch and hub assy. Evacuate and charge system.
1989-90 (1.5) 2.5

Compressor Shaft and Cylinder Assy., Renew
Includes: R&R compressor. R&R clutch hub and drive plate assy. Clean and inspect all parts. Evacuate and charge system.
1989-90 (1.8) 2.8

Condenser, Renew
Includes: Evacuate and charge system.
1989-90 (1.2) 2.0

Evaporator Core, Renew
Includes: Evacuate and charge system.
1989-90 (1.6) 3.0

Expansion Valve, Renew
Includes: Evacuate and charge system.
1989-90 (1.6) 3.0

In-Line Filter Dryer, Renew
Includes: Evacuate and charge system.
1989-90 (.8) 1.4
Install liquid line filter add (.9) 1.2

Blower Motor and/or Fan, Renew
1989-90 (.4) 6

Blower Motor Resistor, Renew
1989-90 (.2) 3

Blower Motor Switch, Renew
1989-90 (.3) 4

Master Electrical Switch, Renew
1989-90 (.3) 4

Temperature Control Assy., Renew
1989-90 (1.2) 1.6

Compressor Cut-Off Switches, Renew
1989-90
Low Pressure (.2) 3
Coolant High Temp (.2) 3
High Pressure (.2) 3
Add time to recharge A.C. system if required.

Air Conditioning Hoses, Renew
Includes: Evacuate and charge system.
1989-90-one (.8) 1.5
each adtnl 5

LABOR 29 LOCKS, HINGES & WIND. REGULATORS 29 LABOR

Hood Latch, Renew
1989-90 (.2) 3

Hood Hinge, Renew
1989-90-one (.3) 4
both (.5) 7

Hood Release Cable, Renew
1989-90 (.5) 8

Door Handle (Outside), Renew
1989-90 (.4) 6

Front Door Lock Cylinder, Renew
1989-90 (.5) 7

Lock Striker Plate, Renew
1989-90 (.2) 3

Front Door Lock, Renew
1989-90 (.5) 7

Front Door Lock Remote Control, Renew
1989-90 (.2) 5

Tailgate Lock Cylinder, Renew
1989-90 (.3) 4

Front Door Window Regulator, Renew
1989-90-manual (.6) 9

LABOR 30 HEAD AND PARKING LAMPS 30 LABOR

Aim Headlamps
two 4
four 6

Composite Headlamp Bulb, Renew
All models-one (.2) 3

Back-Up Lamp Bulb, Renew
All models-one 2
all 3

Park and Turn Signal Lamp Bulb, Renew
All models-one 2
all 3

License Lamp Bulb, Renew
All models-one or all 2

Side Marker Lamp Bulb, Renew
All models-one 2
each adtnl 1

Stop, Tail and Turn Signal Lamp Bulb, Renew
All models-one 2
each adtnl 1

Park and Turn Signal Lamp Assy., Renew
All models-each (.4) 5

Rear Combination Lamp Assy., Renew
All models-each (.3) 5

LABOR 31 WINDSHIELD WIPER & SPEEDOMETER 31 LABOR

Windshield Wiper Motor, Renew
1989-90 (.4) 6

Back Window Wiper Motor, Renew
1989-90 (.5) 7

Windshield Wiper Switch, Renew
1989-90 (.3) 4

Back Window Wiper Switch, Renew
1989-90 (.3) 4

Washer Pump, Renew
1989-90-front (.3) 4
rear (.3) 4

Wiper Transmission, Renew
1989-90-both (1.5) 2.0

Pulse Wiper Control Module or Relay, Renew
1989-90 (.3) 4

Speedometer Head, R&R or Renew
1989-90 (.5) 9
Reset odometer add 2

Tachometer, R&R or Renew
1989-90 (.5) 9

Radio, R&R
1989-90 (.3) 5

LABOR 32 LIGHT SWITCHES 32 LABOR

Headlamp Switch, Renew
1989-90 (.3) 5

Headlamp Dimmer Switch, Renew
1989-90 (.3) 5

Clutch Start Switch, Renew
1989-90 (.4) 6

Back-Up Lamp Switch, Renew
1989-90 (.3) 4

Parking Brake Warning Lamp Switch, Renew
1989-90 (.3) 4

Turn Signal or Hazard Warning Switch, Renew
1989-90 (.3) 5

Turn Signal or Hazard Warning Flasher, Renew
1989-90
turn signal (.2) 3

Horn Relay, Renew
1989-90 (.2) 3

Horn, Renew
1989-90 (.2) 3

GROUP INDEX

ALPHABETICAL INDEX

FRONT SUSPENSION AND STEERING LINKAGE DIAGNOSIS

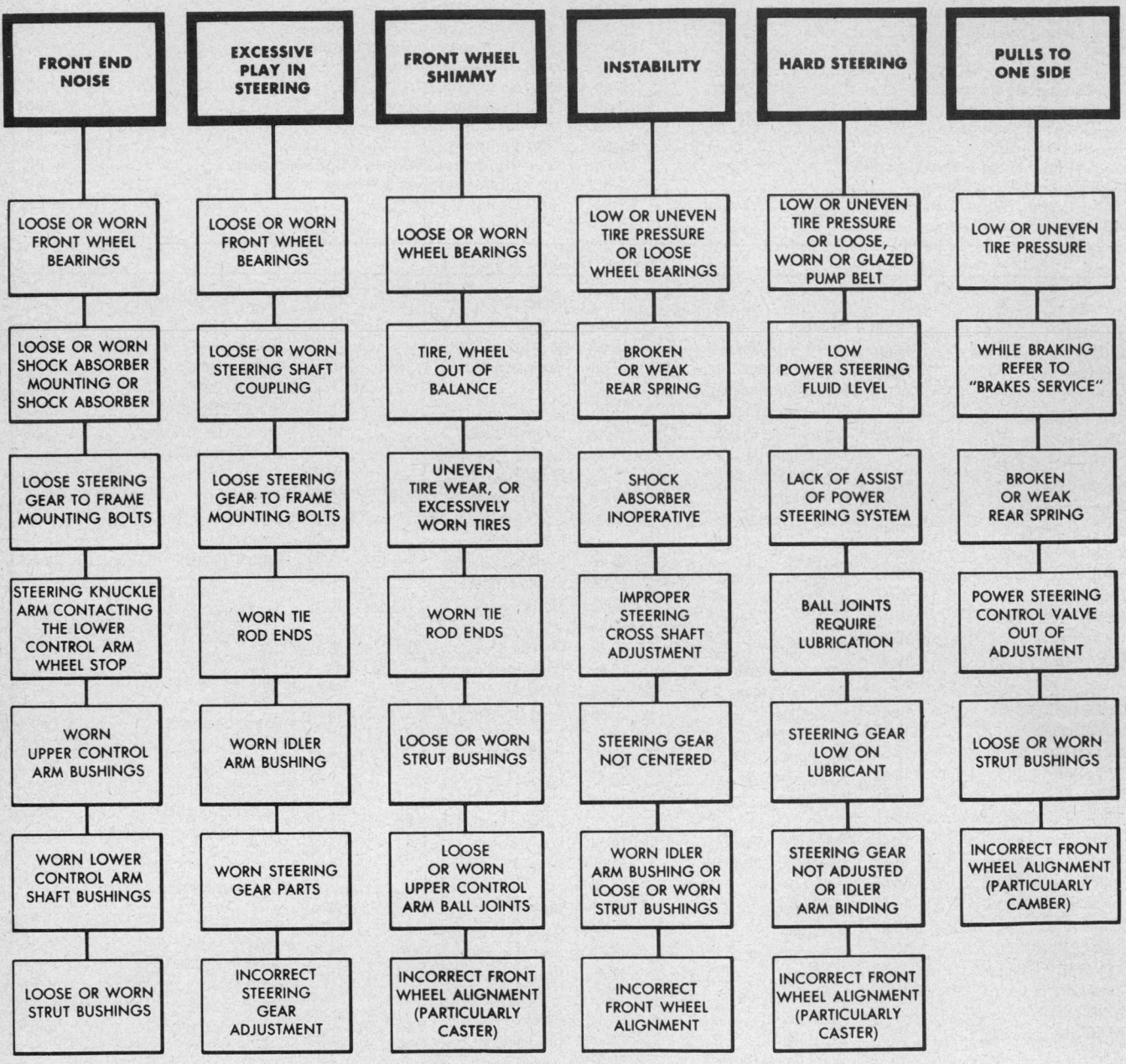

FRONT END NOISE	EXCESSIVE PLAY IN STEERING	FRONT WHEEL SHIMMY	INSTABILITY	HARD STEERING	PULLS TO ONE SIDE
LOOSE OR WORN FRONT WHEEL BEARINGS	LOOSE OR WORN FRONT WHEEL BEARINGS	LOOSE OR WORN WHEEL BEARINGS	LOW OR UNEVEN TIRE PRESSURE OR LOOSE WHEEL BEARINGS	LOW OR UNEVEN TIRE PRESSURE OR LOOSE, WORN OR GLAZED PUMP BELT	LOW OR UNEVEN TIRE PRESSURE
LOOSE OR WORN SHOCK ABSORBER MOUNTING OR SHOCK ABSORBER	LOOSE OR WORN STEERING SHAFT COUPLING	TIRE, WHEEL OUT OF BALANCE	BROKEN OR WEAK REAR SPRING	LOW POWER STEERING FLUID LEVEL	WHILE BRAKING REFER TO "BRAKES SERVICE"
LOOSE STEERING GEAR TO FRAME MOUNTING BOLTS	LOOSE STEERING GEAR TO FRAME MOUNTING BOLTS	UNEVEN TIRE WEAR, OR EXCESSIVELY WORN TIRES	SHOCK ABSORBER INOPERATIVE	LACK OF ASSIST OF POWER STEERING SYSTEM	BROKEN OR WEAK REAR SPRING
STEERING KNUCKLE ARM CONTACTING THE LOWER CONTROL ARM WHEEL STOP	WORN TIE ROD ENDS	WORN TIE ROD ENDS	IMPROPER STEERING CROSS SHAFT ADJUSTMENT	BALL JOINTS REQUIRE LUBRICATION	POWER STEERING CONTROL VALVE OUT OF ADJUSTMENT
WORN UPPER CONTROL ARM BUSHINGS	WORN IDLER ARM BUSHING	LOOSE OR WORN STRUT BUSHINGS	STEERING GEAR NOT CENTERED	STEERING GEAR LOW ON LUBRICANT	LOOSE OR WORN STRUT BUSHINGS
WORN LOWER CONTROL ARM SHAFT BUSHINGS	WORN STEERING GEAR PARTS	LOOSE OR WORN UPPER CONTROL ARM BALL JOINTS	WORN IDLER ARM BUSHING OR LOOSE OR WORN STRUT BUSHINGS	STEERING GEAR NOT ADJUSTED OR IDLER ARM BINDING	INCORRECT FRONT WHEEL ALIGNMENT (PARTICULARLY CAMBER)
LOOSE OR WORN STRUT BUSHINGS	INCORRECT STEERING GEAR ADJUSTMENT	INCORRECT FRONT WHEEL ALIGNMENT (PARTICULARLY CASTER)	INCORRECT FRONT WHEEL ALIGNMENT	INCORRECT FRONT WHEEL ALIGNMENT (PARTICULARLY CASTER)	

MODEL IDENTIFICATION CHART

B 100 - DODGE TRADESMAN VAN	CB 400 - FRONT SECTION - KARY VAN	D 200 - DODGE PICK-UP - 2 WHEEL DRIVE
B 100 - DODGE SPORTSMAN WAGON	AW 100 - RAMCHARGER - 4 WHEEL DRIVE	RD 200 - DODGE RAIL-TRACK - 2 WHEEL DRIVE
B 200 - DODGE TRADESMAN VAN	PW 100 - TRAILDUSTER - 4 WHEEL DRIVE	D 300 - DODGE PICK-UP - 2 WHEEL DRIVE
B 200 - DODGE SPORTSMAN WAGON	AD 100 - RAMCHARGER - 2 WHEEL DRIVE	W 100 - DODGE PICK-UP - 4 WHEEL DRIVE
B 300 - DODGE TRADESMAN VAN	AD 150 - SPORT UTILITY - 2 WHEEL DRIVE	AW 150 - SPORT UTILITY - 4 WHEEL DRIVE
B 300 - DODGE SPORTSMAN WAGON	PD 100 - TRAILDUSTER - 2 WHEEL DRIVE	W 200 - DODGE PICK-UP - 4 WHEEL DRIVE
PB 100 - PLYMOUTH VOYAGER WAGON	D 100 - DODGE PICK-UP - 2 WHEEL DRIVE	W 300 - DODGE PICK-UP - 4 WHEEL DRIVE
PB 200 - PLYMOUTH VOYAGER WAGON	D 150 - DODGE PICK-UP - 2 WHEEL DRIVE	W 400 - DODGE PICK-UP - 4 WHEEL DRIVE
PB 300 - PLYMOUTH VOYAGER WAGON		
CB 300 - FRONT SECTION - KARY VAN		

LABOR   1   TUNE UP   1   LABOR

	(Factory) Time	Chilton Time
Compression Test		
Six(.6)		.9
V-8-318-360 engs (.7)		1.0

Engine Tune Up, (Electronic Ignition)
Includes: Test battery and clean connections. Tighten manifold and carburetor mounting bolts. Check engine compression, clean and adjust or renew spark plugs. Test resistance of spark plug wires. Inspect distributor cap and rotor. Adjust distributor air gap. Check vacuum advance operation. Reset ignition timing. Adjust idle mixture and idle speed. Service carburetor air cleaner. Inspect crankcase ventilation system. Inspect and adjust drive belts. Inspect and adjust drive belts. Inspect choke operation, adjust or free up as necessary. Check operation of E.G.R. valve.

	(Factory) Time	Chilton Time
Six		2.8
V-8-318-360 engs		3.2
w/A.C. add		.6

LABOR   2   IGNITION SYSTEM   2   LABOR

	(Factory) Time	Chilton Time
Spark Plugs, Clean and Reset or Renew		
Six(.4)		.7
V-8-318-360 eng (.5)		.8
Ignition Timing, Reset		
B-PB-CB Models (.3)		.5
All other models (.2)		.4
Distributor, Renew		
Includes: Adjust ignition timing and renew oil seal if required.		
Six-B-PB-CB Models (.7)		1.0
All other models (.6)		.9
V-8-318-360 engs		
B-PB-CB Models (.6)		1.0
All other models (.5)		.9
Distributor, R&R and Recondition		
Includes: Adjust ignition timing and renew oil seal if required.		
Six-B-PB-CB Models (1.4)		2.0
All other models (1.3)		1.9
V-8-318-360 engs		
B-PB-CB Models (1.4)		2.0
All other models (1.3)		1.9

	(Factory) Time	Chilton Time
Distributor Pick-Up Plate and Coil Assembly, Renew		
Includes: R&R distributor, reset ignition timing.		
Six-B-PB-CB Models (.9)		1.3
All other models (.8)		1.2
V-8-318-360 engs		
B-PB-CB Models (.7)		1.3
All other models (.6)		1.2
Electronic Distributor Reluctor, Renew		
Includes: R&R distributor and reset ignition timing.		
Six-B-PB-CB Models (.8)		1.2
All other models (.7)		1.1
V-8-318-360 engs		
B-PB-CB Models (.7)		1.2
All other models (.6)		1.1
Vacuum Control Unit, Renew		
Includes: R&R distributor and reset ignition timing.		
Six-B-PB-CB Models (.8)		1.2
All other models (.7)		1.1
V-8-318-360 engs		
B-PB-CB Models (.7)		1.2
All other models (.6)		1.1

	(Factory) Time	Chilton Time
Distributor Cap and/or Rotor, Renew		
B-PB-CB Models (.4)		.5
All other models (.3)		.4
Single Module Engine Controller, Renew		
All models (.3)		.5
Electronic Ignition Control Unit, Renew		
B-PB-CB Models (.3)		.5
All other models (.2)		.4
Spark Control Computer, Renew		
B-PB-CB models (.7)		1.1
All other models (.6)		1.0
Ignition Cables, Renew		
Six(.5)		.8
V-8-318-360 engs (.6)		.9
Ignition Coil, Renew		
B-PB-CB Models (.4)		.6
All other models (.3)		.5
Electronic Ignition Ballast Resistor, Renew		
B-PB-CB Models (.3)		.5
All other models (.2)		.4
Ignition Switch, Renew		
Includes: Renew lock cylinder if required.		
1986-90		
std colm (.7)		1.2
tilt colm (.4)		.7

CHRYSLER CORPORATION
PICK-UP • RAMCHARGER • VAN

LABOR — 3 FUEL SYSTEM 3 — LABOR

(Factory Time)	Chilton Time
GASOLINE ENGINES	
Fuel Pump, Test	
Includes: Disconnect line at carburetor, attach pressure gauge.	
All models	.3
Carburetor, Adjust (On Truck)	
All models (.6)	.8
Air Cleaner Vacuum Diaphragm, Renew	
All models (.3)	.5
Air Cleaner Vacuum Sensor, Renew	
All models (.3)	.5
Coolant Temperature Sensor/Switch, Renew	
B-PB-CB models (.4)	.6
All other models (.3)	.5
Fuel Filter Element, Renew	
All models (.2)	.3
Accelerator Pump, Renew	
Holly-1 bbl (.5)	.8
Carter-Holly-2 bbl (.5)	.8
Carter-Rochester-4 bbl (.6)	.9
Float and/or Needle Valve and Seat, Renew	
Holly-1 bbl (.8)	1.1
Carter-Holly-2 bbl (.5)	.8
Carter-Rochester-4 bbl (1.0)	1.4
Carburetor, Renew	
Includes: All necessary adjustments.	
1 bbl (.7)	1.1
2 bbl (.7)	1.1
4 bbl (.8)	1.2
Carburetor, R&R and Clean or Recondition	
Includes: All necessary adjustments.	
Holly-1 bbl (1.9)	2.5
Carter-2 bbl (2.3)	3.1
Holly-2 bbl (1.9)	2.5
Carter-4 bbl (2.6)	3.5
Rochester-4 bbl	3.5
Fuel Pump, Renew	
Six-B-PB-CB Models (.6)	.9
All other models (.5)	.8
V-8-318-360 engs (.5)	.8
Add pump test if performed.	
Fuel Tank, Renew	
Includes: Drain and refill, test and renew tank gauge if necessary.	
Main Tank	
frame mount (1.0)	1.5

(Factory Time)	Chilton Time
cab mount (.7)	1.2
plastic tank (1.0)	1.5
Auxiliary Tank	
cab mount (1.2)	1.7
frame mount (1.0)	1.5
w/Skid plate add (.3)	.3
w/Towing pkg add	.5
Fuel Gauge (Tank), Renew Main Tank	
frame mount (.7)	1.2
cab mount (.5)	.9
plastic tank (1.0)	1.4
Auxiliary Tank	
cab mount (.5)	.9
frame mount (.6)	1.0
w/Skid plate add (.3)	.3
w/Towing pkg add	.5
Fuel Gauge (Dash), Renew	
1986-90 (.6)	1.1
Intake and Exhaust Manifold Gaskets, Renew Six	
B-PB-CB Models (2.0)	3.0
All other models (1.8)	2.8
w/A.C. add (.4)	.4
Renew manif add	.5
Intake Manifold Gasket, Renew V-8	
B Models (3.0)	4.0
w/A.C. add (.8)	.8
All other models (2.5)	3.5
w/A.C. add (.4)	.4
w/Air inj add	.6
Renew manif add	.5
ELECTRONIC FUEL INJECTION	
Fuel Pump, Test	
All models	
electric	.4
Air Cleaner, Service	
All models	.2
Fuel Filter, Renew	
All models	
in line	.3
in tank	1.3
Fuel Injectors, Clean (On Truck) (w/TBI or MFI)	
Includes: Hook up pressurized fuel injection cleaning equipment.	
All models	.5
Throttle Body, Renew	
All models (.6)	1.0

(Factory Time)	Chilton Time
Fuel Pressure Regulator, Renew	
All models (.3)	.5
Fuel Pump, Renew (In Tank)	
All models (.9)	1.3
Automatic Idle Speed Motor, Renew	
All models (.3)	.5
Fuel Injector, Renew	
All models (.3)	.5
Throttle Body Temperature Sensor, Renew	
All models (.2)	.4
Throttle Position Sensor (Potentiometer), Renew	
All models (.3)	.4
M.A.P. Sensor, Renew	
All models (.2)	.4
Automatic Shutdown Relay, Renew	
All models (.2)	.3
DIESEL ENGINE	
Intake Air Heater Thermister, Renew	
All models (.5)	.7
Intake Air Heater Controller, Renew	
All models (.2)	.4
Coolant Temperature Sensor/Switch, Renew	
All models (.3)	.4
Fuel Injectors, Renew	
All models-one (.3)	.5
all (.9)	1.5
Fuel Cut-Off Solenoid, Renew	
All models (.3)	.4
Fuel Filter, Renew	
All models (.2)	.3
Fuel Injection Pump, Renew	
All models (1.1)	1.5
Injection Pump Drive Gear, Renew	
All models (1.2)	1.7
Accessory Drive Adapter, Renew	
All models (1.0)	1.4
Turbocharger Assy., Remove & Install	
All models (.5)	.8
Renew assy add (.1)	.2
Renew mounting gskts add (.5)	.5
Renew compressor cover add (.5)	.5
Intake Manifold Cover Gasket, Renew	
All models (.5)	.8

LABOR — 3A EMISSION CONTROLS 3A — LABOR

(Factory Time)	Chilton Time
CRANKCASE EMISSION	
Positive Crankcase Ventilation Valve, Renew	
All models (.2)	.3
EVAPORATIVE EMISSION	
Vapor Canister, Renew	
All models (.3)	.5
Vapor Canister Hoses, Renew	
All models-one (.2)	.3
Vapor Canister Filter, Renew	
All models (.2)	.3
Vapor Separator, Renew	
All models (.9)	1.2

(Factory Time)	Chilton Time
AIR INJECTION SYSTEM	
Air Pump, Renew	
Six (.9)	1.2
V-8	
SINGLE PUMP	
B-PB models (.8)	1.1
All other models (.5)	.8
DUAL PUMP	
Upper	
B-PB models (1.3)	1.7
All other models (1.0)	1.4
Lower	
B-PB models (2.2)	2.8
All other models (1.9)	2.5
Aspirator, Renew	
All models (.3)	.4

(Factory Time)	Chilton Time
Diverter/Control Valve, Renew	
Six (.3)	.6
V-8 (.4)	.7
Injection Tube and Check Valve Assy., Renew	
Six (.4)	.7
V-8 (.5)	.8
Orifice Spark Advance Control Valve, Renew	
All models (.2)	.4
HEATED AIR SYSTEM	
Air Cleaner Vacuum Diaphragm, Renew	
1986-90 (.3)	.5

LABOR 3A EMISSION CONTROLS 3A LABOR

Factory Time	Chilton Time
Air Cleaner Vacuum Sensor, Renew 1986-90 (.3)	.5
EXHAUST GAS RECIRCULATION SYSTEM	
E.G.R. Valve, Renew Six (.4)	.6
V-8 (.5)	.7
E.G.R. Coolant Control Valve, Renew All models (.3)	.5
E.G.R. Vacuum Amplifier, Renew All models (.3)	.5
E.G.R. Time Delay Timer, Renew All models (.2)	.4
E.G.R. Time Delay Solenoid, Renew All models (.2)	.4
Charge Temperature Switch, Renew All models (.2)	.3
Coolant Vacuum Switch Valve, Renew All models (.3)	.4
Spark Advance Delay Valve, Renew All models (.2)	.3
E.G.R. Purge Control Solenoid Bank, Renew All models (.3)	.4
E.F.C. SYSTEM	
Oxygen Sensor, Renew All models (.3)	.5
Emission Maintenance Reminder Module, Renew All models (.2)	.4
Electronic Speed Switch, Renew All models (.3)	.4

LABOR 4 ALTERNATOR AND REGULATOR 4 LABOR

Factory Time	Chilton Time
Alternator Circuits, Test Includes: Test battery, regulator and alternator output. All models	.6
Alternator, Renew Six (.7)	1.2
V-8–318-360 engs B-PB-CB Models (.9)	1.4
All other models (.7)	1.2
Add circuit test if performed.	
Alternator, R&R and Recondition Six (2.0)	3.1
V-8–318-360 engs B-PB-CB Models (2.2)	3.3
All other models (2.0)	3.1
Add circuit test if performed.	
Alternator Drive End Frame Bearing, Renew Six (1.0)	1.5
V-8–318-360 engs B-PB-CB Models (1.2)	1.7
All other models (1.0)	1.5
Renew rear brg add	.2
Voltage Regulator, Test and Renew All models (.3)	.6
Alternator Gauge, Renew 1986-90 (.6)	1.1

LABOR 5 STARTING SYSTEM 5 LABOR

Factory Time	Chilton Time
Starter Draw Test (On Truck) All models	.3
Starter, Renew Six (.6)	1.0
V-8–318-360 engs (.6)	1.0
Diesel (.5)	.8
Add draw test if performed.	
Starter, R&R and Recondition Six (1.8)	2.7
V-8–318-360 engs (1.9)	2.8
Diesel	2.5
Renew field coils add	.5
Add draw test if performed.	
Starter Drive, Renew Includes: R&R starter. Six (1.1)	1.5
V-8–318-360 engs (.9)	1.3
Diesel (.8)	1.2
Starter Solenoid, Renew Includes: R&R starter. Six (1.1)	1.5
V-8–318-360 engs (.9)	1.3
Diesel (.8)	1.2
Starter Relay, Renew All models (.3)	.5
Battery Cables, Renew All models-positive (.4)	.6
ground (.2)	.3
starter to relay (.3)	.5

LABOR 6 BRAKE SYSTEM 6 LABOR

Factory Time	Chilton Time
Brakes, Adjust (Minor) Includes: Adjust brakes, fill master cylinder. two wheels	.5
four wheels	.8
Brake Pedal Free Play, Adjust All models	.4
Bleed Brakes (Four Wheels) Includes: Fill master cylinder. All models (.4)	.6
Brake Drum and Hub Assy., Renew Includes: Repack and/or renew wheel bearings. front-one (1.0)	1.6
rear-one (.8)	1.4
w/Dual rear whls add	.3
Rear Brake Drum, Renew (One) All models semi-floating axle (.3)	.6
full floating axle (1.8)	2.3
w/Dual rear whls add (.2)	.3
Brake System Indicator Switch, Renew All models (.3)	.5

COMBINATIONS
Add to Brakes, Renew
See Machine Shop Operations

Factory Time	Chilton Time
RENEW WHEEL CYLINDER Each	.2
REBUILD WHEEL CYLINDER Each	.3
RENEW BRAKE HOSE Each	.3
REBUILD CALIPER ASSEMBLY Each (.4)	.6
RENEW BRAKE DRUM Front Each	.3
Rear Full Floating Axle-each	.3
Semi-Floating Axle-each	1.0
RENEW DISC BRAKE ROTOR Each (.3)	.4
RENEW REAR WHEEL GREASE SEALS OR BEARINGS Full Floating Axle-each	.2
Semi-Floating Axle-each	.8
RENEW FRONT WHEEL BEARINGS (One Wheel) one or both Drum Brakes	.2
Disc Brakes	.4
FRONT WHEEL BEARINGS, REPACK OR RENEW SEALS (Both Wheels) Drum Brakes	.4
Disc Brakes	.8

LABOR 6 BRAKE SYSTEM 6 LABOR

	(Factory Time)	Chilton Time
Brake Shoes and/or Pads, Renew		
Includes: Install new or exchange shoes or pads. Service adjusters. Adjust service and hand brake. Bleed system.		
front-disc (.6)		1.2
rear-drum		
semi-floating axle (.7)		1.4
full floating axle (1.5)		2.5
All four wheels		
semi-floating axle		2.5
full floating axle		4.4
Resurface brake rotor add, each		1.0
Resurface brake drum add, each		.6

BRAKE HYDRAULIC SYSTEM

	(Factory Time)	Chilton Time
Rear Wheel Cylinder, Renew		
Includes: Bleed brake system.		
Semi-floating axle		
one (.8)		1.0
both (1.4)		1.8
Full floating axle		
one (1.1)		1.5
both (2.0)		2.9
w/Dual rear whls add		.3
Rear Wheel Cylinder, R&R and Recondition		
Includes: Hone cylinder, bleed brake system.		
Semi-floating axle		
one (1.1)		1.3
both (2.0)		2.4
Full floating axle		
one (1.4)		1.8
both (2.6)		3.5
w/Dual rear whls add		.3
Brake Hose, Renew (Flex)		
Includes: Bleed brake system.		
front-one (.4)		.6
rear (.5)		.7
each adtnl		.3
Master Cylinder, Renew		
Includes: Bleed brake system.		
Cast Iron (.4)		.8
Aluminum		
w/Manual brks (.6)		1.0
w/Power brks (.4)		.8

	(Factory Time)	Chilton Time
Master Cylinder, R&R and Recondition		
Includes: Bleed brake system.		
Cast Iron		1.5
Aluminum		
w/Manual brks		1.7
w/Power brks		1.5
Brake System Combination Valve, Renew		
Includes: Bleed brake system.		
B-PB-CB models (.9)		1.3
All other models (.8)		1.2

POWER BRAKES

	(Factory Time)	Chilton Time
Power Brake Unit, Renew		
All models (.5)		1.1
w/A.C. add (.1)		.3
Power Brake Check Valve, Renew		
All models (.2)		.4
Power Brake Vacuum Hose, Renew		
All models (.3)		.4

DISC BRAKES

	(Factory Time)	Chilton Time
Brake Shoes and/or Pads, Renew		
Includes: Install new or exchange shoes or pads. Service adjusters. Adjust service and hand brake. Bleed system.		
front-disc (.6)		1.2
rear-drum		
semi-floating axle (.7)		1.4
full floating axle (1.5)		2.5
All four wheels		
semi-floating axle		2.5
full floating axle		4.4
Resurface brake rotor add, each		1.0
Resurface brake drum add, each		.6
Disc Brake Pads, Renew		
Includes: Install new disc brake pads only.		
All models (.6)		1.2
Disc Brake Rotor (w/Hub), Renew (One)		
Includes: Repack and/or renew bearings.		
2 WD		
All models (.8)		1.4

	(Factory Time)	Chilton Time
4 WD		
44 FBJ front axle (1.1)		2.0
60 F front axle (.9)		1.7
Disc Brake Rotor, Renew (8 Hole)		
All models-one (.9)		1.2
both (1.4)		2.0
Disc Brake Caliper, Renew (One)		
Includes: Bleed front brake lines only.		
All models (.6)		1.0
Disc Brake Caliper, R&R and Recondition (One)		
Includes: Renew parts as required, bleed front brake lines only.		
All models (.8)		1.6

PARKING BRAKE

	(Factory Time)	Chilton Time
Parking Brake, Adjust		
All models (.3)		.5
Parking Brake Lever Assembly, Renew		
All models (.6)		.9
Parking Brake Warning Lamp Switch, Renew		
All models (.3)		5
Parking Brake Cables, Renew		
Front		
All models (.6)		.8
Intermediate		
All models (.3)		.5
Rear		
2 wd-each (.6)		.8
4 wd-each (1.0)		1.4
w/Dual rear whls add		.3

ANTI-SKID BRAKE SYSTEM (ABS)

	(Factory Time)	Chilton Time
Anti-Lock Brake Solenoid Valve, Renew		
All models (.7)		1.0
Anti-Lock Brake Control Module, Renew		
All models (.7)		1.0
Anti-Lock Speed Sensor, Renew		
All models-one (.3)		.5

LABOR 7 COOLING SYSTEM 7 LABOR

	(Factory Time)	Chilton Time
Winterize Cooling System		
Includes: Run engine to check for leaks, tighten all hose connections. Test radiator and pressure cap, drain radiator and engine block. Add anti-freeze and refill coolant.		
All models		.5
Thermostat, Renew		
All models (.5)		.8
w/A.C. add (.1)		.1
w/Diesel eng add		.2
Radiator Assembly, R&R or Renew		
B-PB-CB Models (1.0)		1.5
All other models (.7)		1.3
w/A.C. add (.1)		.1
w/A.T. add (.1)		.1
w/Aux oil cooler add		.1

ADD THESE OPERATIONS TO RADIATOR R&R

Boil & Repair		1.5
Rod Clean		1.9
Repair Core		1.3
Renew Tank		1.6
Renew Trans. Oil Cooler		1.9
Recore Radiator		1.7

	(Factory Time)	Chilton Time
Radiator Hoses, Renew		
All models-upper (.3)		.5
lower (.4)		.6
by-pass (.5)		*.7
w/A.C. add (.1)		.1
*w/Air inj add (.1)		.1
Fan Belt, Renew		
All models (.3)		.5
w/Air inj add (.1)		.1
w/A.C. add (.1)		.1
w/P.S. add (.2)		.2
Fluid Fan Drive Unit, Renew		
B-PB-CB Models (.8)		1.1
All other models (.5)		.7
w/A.C. add (.1)		.1
w/Air inj add (.1)		.1
Idler Pulley, Renew		
All models (.3)		.5
Fan Pulley, Renew		
All models (.3)		.5
w/A.C. add (.3)		.3
Coolant Reserve Tank, Renew		
All models (.2)		.3

	(Factory Time)	Chilton Time
Water Pump, Renew		
Six-1986-87		
B-PB-CB Models (.9)		1.4
D-AD-PD Models (.7)		1.3
AW-PW-W Models (1.0)		1.6
w/A.C. add (.3)		.3
V-8-318-360 engs		
B-PB-CB Models		
1986-90		
wo/A.C. (1.3)		1.8
w/A.C. (1.8)		2.6
w/P.S. add (.2)		.2
w/100 Amp alt add (.6)		.6
All other models		
1986-90 (1.0)		1.5
w/A.C. add (.2)		.2
w/P.S. add (.2)		.2
w/Air inj add (.2)		.2
Diesel		
All models (.6)		1.0
Water Jacket Expansion Plugs, Renew (Engine Block)		
Six-All models		
left side-one (1.9)		2.3

LABOR 7 COOLING SYSTEM 7 LABOR

	(Factory Time)	Chilton Time
V-8–318-360 engs		
All models		
front-right or left-one (.6)		1.1
center-right or left-one (.6)		1.1
rear-right side (.5)		1.0
rear-left side (.8)		1.2
Water Jacket Expansion Plugs, Renew (Cylinder Head)		
V-8–318-360 engs		
front-one-all models (.3)		.6
Rear-one		
B-PB-CB Models (.3)		.6
All other models (3.1)		4.2
Temperature Gauge (Engine Unit), Renew		
All models (.3)		.5
Temperature Gauge (Dash Unit), Renew		
1986-90 (.6)		1.1
Heater Core, R&R or Renew		
Without Air Conditioning		
Front		
B-PB-CB Models		
1986-90 (.7)		1.6

	(Factory Time)	Chilton Time
All other models		
1986-90 (1.3)		2.2
Rear		
1986-90-All models (.8)		1.5
With Air Conditioning		
Front		
B-PB-CB Models		
1986-90 (2.7)		*5.0
All other models		
1986-90 (2.1)		*4.0
Rear		
1986-90-All models (1.5)		*3.0
Front Unit		
w/Front & Rear A.C.		
All models (3.0)		*5.5
°Includes Recharge A.C. System.		
ADD THESE OPERATIONS TO HEATER CORE R&R		
Boil & Repair		1.2
Repair Core		.9
Recore		1.2

	(Factory Time)	Chilton Time
Heater Water Valve, Renew		
All models		
w/Heater (.4)		.7
w/A.C. (.5)		.8
Heater Hoses, Renew		
All models-one or both (.4)		.6
Heater Blower Motor, Renew		
Front		
1986-90-All models (.4)		.9
Rear		
1986-90-All models (.4)		.9
Heater Blower Motor Resistor, Renew		
All models (.2)		.5
Heater Blower Motor Switch, Renew		
B-PB-CB Models		
1986-90 (.4)		.6
All other models		
1986-90 (.3)		.6
Heater Temperature Control Assembly, Renew		
All models (.4)		.7

LABOR 8 EXHAUST SYSTEM 8 LABOR

	(Factory Time)	Chilton Time
Muffler, Renew		
All models		
4X2 (.5)		.8
4X4 (.7)		1.1
Renew ex pipe add		.3
Tail Pipe, Renew		
All models (.4)		.7
Exhaust Pipe, Renew		
Six(.6)		1.0
V-8–318-360 engs (.8)		1.2
Renew ext add		.2
Exhaust Pipe Extension, Renew		
All models (.7)		1.1
Catalytic Converter, Renew		
All models (.9)		1.3
dual exh-both (1.0)		1.5
Catalytic Converter Heat Shield, Renew		
upper (.6)		.9

	(Factory Time)	Chilton Time
lower (.2)		.4
intermediate (.2)		.5
frame rail mount-each (.2)		.4
Exhaust Manifold Heat Control Valve, Recondition		
Six(2.7)		3.4
w/A.C. add (.3)		.3
V-8–318-360 engs (1.2)		1.9
Intake and Exhaust Manifold Gaskets, Renew		
Six		
B-PB-CB Models (2.0)		3.0
All other models (1.8)		2.8
w/A.C. add (.4)		.4
Renew manif add		.5
Exhaust Manifold or Gaskets, Renew		
Six		
B-PB-CB Models		
1986-87 (2.1)		2.7

	(Factory Time)	Chilton Time
D-AD-PD Models		
1986-90 (1.9)		2.5
W-AW-PW Models		
1986-90 (1.9)		2.5
V-8–1986-90-318-360 engs		
right side (.5)		1.1
left side (.7)		1.3
w/Air inj add (.2)		.2
Diesel		
All models (.7)		1.2
COMBINATIONS		
Muffler, Exhaust and Tail Pipe, Renew		
Six		1.6
V-8		1.8
Muffler and Tail Pipe, Renew		
All models		1.2

LABOR 9A FRONT SUSPENSION (RWD) 9A LABOR

	(Factory Time)	Chilton Time
Note: On all front suspension operations alignment charges must be added if performed. Time given does not include alignment.		
Check Alignment of Front End		
All models		.8
Note: Deduct if alignment is performed.		
Toe-In, Adjust		
All models		.7
Align Front End		
Includes: Adjust front wheel bearings.		
All models (1.0)		1.5
Wheels, Balance		
one		.5
each adtnl		.3
Front Wheel Bearings, Clean and Repack (Both Wheels)		
All models		
w/Drum Brakes		1.0
w/Disc Brakes		1.5

	(Factory Time)	Chilton Time
w/4 wd		2.0
Front Wheel Bearings and Cups, Renew (One Wheel)		
Drum Brakes (.6)		.9
Disc Brakes		
w/2 wd (.7)		1.1
w/4 wd (1.2)		1.7
Front Wheel Grease Seals, Renew (One Wheel)		
All models		
w/2 wd (.6)		.8
w/4 wd (1.1)		1.5
Front Shock Absorbers, Renew		
1986-90-one (.3)		.6
both (.5)		.9
Steering Knuckle, Renew (One)		
w/2 WD		
1986-90 (1.1)		1.7
w/4 WD		
1986-90		
w/44 FBJ Axle (1.5)		2.1

	(Factory Time)	Chilton Time
w/60 F Axle (1.2)		1.8
Lower Control Arm, Renew (One)		
Add alignment charges.		
1986-90 (1.3)		1.9
Lower Ball Joint, Renew (One)		
Add alignment charges.		
1986-90		
w/2 wd (1.4)		2.0
w/4 wd (1.9)		2.7
Lower Control Arm Strut Bushings, Renew (One Side)		
Add alignment charges.		
1986-90 (.3)		.6
Lower Control Arm Bushings, Renew (One Side)		
Add alignment charges.		
1986-90 (1.5)		2.3
Upper Control Arm, Renew (One)		
Includes: Align front end.		
1986-90 (1.9)		2.7

CHRYSLER CORPORATION
PICK-UP • RAMCHARGER • VAN

LABOR   9A FRONT SUSPENSION (RWD) 9A   LABOR

	Factory Time	Chilton Time
Upper Ball Joint, Renew (One)		
Add alignment charges.		
1986-90		
w/2 wd (.9)		1.4
w/44 FBJ Axle (2.0)		3.2
w/60 F Axle (1.8)		3.0
Upper Control Arm Bushings, Renew (One Side)		
Includes: Align front end.		
1986-90 (1.8)		2.6
Front Sway Bar Bushings, Renew (One or All)		
D-AD-PD 150		
D-RD 250		
D350-450 models (.6)		.8
All other models (.4)		.6
Front Sway Bar, Renew		
All models (.4)		.6
Front Spring, Renew (One)		
Coil		
1986-90 (1.0)		1.4
Leaf		
1986-90 (.7)		1.1
Front Spring Shackle, Renew (One)		
Includes: Renew bushings.		
1986-90		
right side (.7)		1.0
left side (.5)		.8

FOUR WHEEL DRIVE

	Factory Time	Chilton Time
Front Axle Shaft, R&R or Renew (One or Both—One Side)		
1986-90		
44 FBJ Axle (1.2)		1.8
60 F Axle (1.3)		1.9
Recond U-Joint add-each		.2

	Factory Time	Chilton Time
Front Axle Inner Oil Seals, Renew (Both Sides)		
1986-90		
44 FBJ Axle (4.1)		6.0
60 F Axle (3.5)		5.0
Front Axle Shaft Spindle, Renew		
All models		
44 FBJ Axle (.6)		1.0
60F Axle (.8)		1.2
Locking Hub Assy., Renew or Recondition		
All models		
44 FBJ Axle		
Spicer (.5)		.9
Auto (.4)		.8
60F Axle		
Dualmatic (.2)		.5
Vacuum Shift Motor, Renew		
All models (.2)		.3
Inner Axle Shaft or Bearing, Renew		
Includes: Renew shift collar.		
All models (.9)		1.2
Intermediate Axle Shaft, Renew		
Includes: Renew inner and outer bearings and seal.		
All models (.7)		1.0
Drive Pinion Oil Seal, Renew		
1986-90 (.5)		.9
Front Axle Housing Cover and/or Gasket, Renew or Reseal		
All models (.4)		.6
Front Drive Shaft, Renew (Transfer Case To Front Axle)		
1986-90 (.4)		.7
w/Skid plate add (.3)		.3
Front Drive Shaft Universal Joint, Renew At Transfer Case		
Dana-CV Type (.8)		1.3
Saginaw-CV Type (1.3)		2.0

	Factory Time	Chilton Time
At Front Axle(.6)		1.0
Front Axle Shaft Outer Oil Seal, Renew		
44 FBJ Axle		
right (.7)		1.0
left (1.0)		1.3
60 F Axle-one (.9)		1.2
Front Axle Assy., R&R or Renew		
Includes: Renew oil seals, transfer axle shafts and brake assemblies.		
All models		
44 FBJ Axle (3.8)		5.6
60 F Axle (3.7)		5.5
Renew axle shafts add-each		.5
Differential Side Bearings, Renew		
Includes: R&R ring and pinion, if necessary. Renew axle inner oil seals and adjust side bearing preload and backlash.		
All models		
44 FBJ Axle (5.5)		8.1
60 F Axle (4.9)		7.2
Differential Case, Renew		
Includes: R&R ring and pinion, if necessary. Renew bearings and gears. Renew pinion seal and axle inner oil seals. Adjust backlash.		
All models		
44 FBJ Axle (5.8)		8.5
60 F Axle (5.4)		7.9
Differential Side Gears, Renew		
Includes: Renew axle inner oil seals if required.		
All models		
44 FBJ Axle (4.4)		6.6
60 F Axle (3.8)		5.5
Ring Gear and Pinion Set, Renew		
Includes: Renew pinion bearing, side bearings and all seals. Make all necessary adjustments.		
All models		
44 FBJ Axle (6.5)		9.6
60 F Axle (5.8)		8.5
Renew diff case add (.3)		.5

LABOR   10 STEERING LINKAGE 10   LABOR

	Factory Time	Chilton Time
Tie Rods or Tie Rod Ends, Renew		
Includes: Reset toe-in.		
1986-90		
inner & outer-one side (.7)		1.0
Steering Knuckle Arm, Renew (One)		
w/2 wd		
1986-90 (1.1)		1.5
w/4 wd		
1986-90 (.6)		.9

	Factory Time	Chilton Time
Center Link, Renew		
B-PB-CB Models		
1986-90 (.6)		.8
All other models		
1986-90 (.4)		.6
Idler Arm, Renew		
1986-90-one (.3)		.5
both (.5)		.7

	Factory Time	Chilton Time
Pitman Arm, Renew		
B-PB-CB Models		
1986-90 (.5)		.8
All other models		
1986-90 (.4)		.7
Drag Link, Renew		
B-PB-CB-AD-D models (.3)		.6
All other models (.6)		.9

LABOR   11 STEERING GEAR 11   LABOR

	Factory Time	Chilton Time
STANDARD STEERING		
Steering Gear, Adjust (On Truck)		
All models (.9)		1.1
Steering Gear Assembly, Renew		
B-PB-CB Models		
1986-90 (1.3)		1.9
D-AD-PD-RD Models		
1986-90 (.6)		1.2
Steering Gear Assy., R&R and Recondition		
Includes: Disassemble, renew necessary parts, reassemble and adjust.		
B-PB-CB Models		
1986-90 (1.9)		2.9

	Factory Time	Chilton Time
D-AD-PD-RD Models		
1986-90 (1.3)		2.2
Steering Column Mast Jacket, Renew		
Does not include painting.		
B-PB-CB Models		
1986-90		
column shift (1.3)		2.0
floor shift (1.1)		1.6
All other models		
1986-90		
column shift (1.6)		2.4
floor shift (1.1)		1.6
Tilt Column		
All models (2.3)		3.3

	Factory Time	Chilton Time
Upper Mast Jacket Bearing, Renew		
All models		
w/Std column (.5)		1.0
w/Tilt column (1.1)		1.5
Steering Column Shift Housing, Renew		
All models		
w/Std column (.9)		1.5
w/Tilt column (2.2)		3.3
Steering Gear Cross Shaft Oil Seal, Renew		
All models (.8)		1.4
Steering Wheel, R&R or Renew		
All models (.3)		.5

LABOR   11   STEERING GEAR   11   LABOR

(Factory Time)	Chilton Time	(Factory Time)	Chilton Time	(Factory Time)	Chilton Time
POWER STEERING		**Steering Gear Cross Shaft Oil Seals, Renew (Inner and Outer)**		**Power Steering Pump, R&R and Recondition**	
Trouble Shoot Power Steering		B-PB-CB Models		B-PB-CB Models	
Includes: Test pump and system pressure. Check pounds pull on steering wheel and check for leaks.		1986-90 (.9)	1.6	1986-90 (1.6)	2.5
All models	.5	All other models		All other models	
		1986-90 (1.2)	1.9	1986-90 (1.1)	2.3
Power Steering Belt, Renew				w/Air inj add (.2)	.2
All models (.3)	.5	**Gear Control Valve Assy., Renew**		**Pump Flow Control Valve, Test and Clean or Renew**	
w/Air inj add (.1)	.1	B-PB-CB Models		B-PB-CB models (1.1)	1.6
w/A.C. add (.1)	.1	1986-90 (.5)	.9	All other models (.9)	1.3
Power Steering Gear Assy., Renew		All other models		w/Air inj add (.2)	.2
B-PB-CB Models		1986-90 (1.5)	2.2	**Power Steering Pump Reservoir and/or Seals, Renew**	
1986-90 (1.3)	1.7			B-PB-CB models (.8)	1.1
All other models		**Pressure Control Valve, Renew**		All other models (.7)	1.0
1986-90 (1.1)	1.6	B-PB-CB Models		w/Air inj add (.2)	.2
Power Steering Gear, R&R and Recondition		1986-90 (.4)	.8	**Pump Drive Shaft Oil Seal, Renew**	
B-PB-CB Models				All models (.9)	1.3
1986-90 (2.7)	3.9	**Power Steering Pump, Test and Renew**		w/Air inj add (.2)	.2
All other models		Includes: Transfer or renew pulley.			
1986-90 (2.2)	3.2	B-PB-CB Models		**Power Steering Hoses, Renew**	
Power Steering Gear Assy., Renew (w/ Remanufactured Unit)		1986-90 (1.1)	1.5	All models	
B-PB-CB Models		All other models		pressure–each (.4)	.7
1986-90 (1.2)	1.7	1986-90 (.9)	1.4	return–each (.3)	.6
		w/Air inj add (.2)	.2		

LABOR   12   CYLINDER HEAD & VALVE SYSTEM   12   LABOR

(Factory Time)	Chilton Time		(Factory Time)	Chilton Time
GASOLINE ENGINES			All other models	
Compression Test			1986-87 (4.9)	7.8
Six (.6)	.9		**V-8–318-360 engs**	
V-8			B-PB-CB Models	
318-360 engs (.7)	1.0		1986-90 (7.0)	10.6
Cylinder Head Gasket, Renew			All other models	
Includes: Clean gasket surfaces, clean carbon, make all necessary adjustments.			1986-90 (6.0)	9.9
Six			w/100 Amp alt add (.6)	.6
B-PB-CB Models			w/Air inj add (.6)	.6
1986-87 (3.6)	5.0		w/A.C. add (.4)	.4
All other models			w/P.S. add (.2)	.2
1986-87 (2.5)	4.0		**Valves, Adjust**	
V-8–318-360 engs			**Six**	
B-PB-CB Models			B-PB-CB Models (.8)	1.2
1986-90–one (3.7)	4.5		All other models (.7)	1.1
both (4.9)	6.6		**Valve Cover Gasket, Renew**	
All other models			**Six**	
1986-90–one (3.2)	4.3		B-PB-CB Models	
both (4.0)	5.9		1986-87 (.9)	1.2
w/100 Amp alt add (.6)	.6		All other models	
w/Air inj add (.6)	.6		1986-87 (.8)	1.1
w/A.C. add (.4)	.4		**V-8–318-360 engs**	
w/P.S. add (.2)	.2		B-PB-CB Models	
			1986-90–one (.5)	.8
Cylinder Head, Renew			both (.8)	1.2
Includes: Transfer all parts, reface valves, make all necessary adjustments.			All other models	
Six			1986-90–one (.5)	.8
B-PB-CB Models			both (.8)	1.2
1986-87 (5.9)	8.2		w/Air inj add (.2)	.2
All other models			**Valve Push Rod and/or Rocker Arm, Renew**	
1986-87 (5.0)	7.0		**Six**	
V-8–318-360 engs			B-PB-CB Models	
B-PB-CB Models			1986-87–one or all (1.1)	1.7
1986-90–one (5.0)	6.5		All other models	
both (7.6)	9.6		1986-87–one or all (.9)	1.5
All other models			**V-8–318-360 engs**	
one (4.2)	6.3		B-PB-CB Models	
both (6.9)	8.9		1986-90–one side (.7)	1.1
w/100 Amp alt add (.6)	.6		both sides (1.0)	2.1
w/Air inj add (.6)	.6		All other models	
w/A.C. add (.4)	.4		1986-90–one side (.6)	.9
w/P.S. add (.2)	.2		both sides (.9)	1.6
			w/Air inj add (.5)	.5

COMBINATIONS

Add to Valve Job
See Machine Shop Operations

GASOLINE ENGINES

(Factory Time)	Chilton Time
DRAIN, EVACUATE AND RECHARGE AIR CONDITIONING SYSTEM	
All Models	1.4
ROCKER ARMS & SHAFT ASSY., DISASSEMBLE AND CLEAN OR RECONDITION	
Six (.5)	.6
V-8–one side (.5)	.6
both sides (.9)	1.1
HYDRAULIC VALVE LIFTERS, DISASSEMBLE AND CLEAN	
Each	.2
DISTRIBUTOR, RECONDITION	
All Models (.7)	1.0
CARBURETOR, RECONDITION	
1 BBL (.9)	1.4
2 BBL (1.1)	1.6
4 BBL (1.6)	2.1
VALVE GUIDES, REAM OVERSIZE	
Each (.2)	.3
VALVES, RECONDITION (ALL)	
Cylinder Head Removed	
Six (2.2)	3.0
V-8 (2.7)	4.0

(Factory Time)	Chilton Time
Clean Carbon and Grind Valves	
Includes: R&R cylinder heads, clean gasket surfaces, clean carbon, reface valves and seats. Minor tune up.	
Six	
B-PB-CB Models	
1986-87 (5.4)	7.8

LABOR 12 CYLINDER HEAD & VALVE SYSTEM 12 LABOR

	(Factory Time)	Chilton Time
Valve Tappets, Renew (SEE NOTE)		
Includes: R&R cylinder head on 6 cyl engine, where required.		
Six		
B-PB-CB Models		
1986-87–one (1.6)		2.1
each adtnl (.1)		.1
All other models		
1986-87–one (1.5)		2.0
each adtnl (.1)		.1
V-8–318-360 engs–all models		
1986-90–one (1.0)		3.1
one–each bank (1.5)		3.6
all–both banks (2.4)		4.4
w/A.C. add (.2)		.2
w/Air inj add (.2)		.2

NOTE: Factory time for V-8 engines is based on using magnetic tool through push rod opening to remove lifters. Chilton experience finds it better and safer to R&R intake manifold, since the lifters have a tendency to stick in the block and sometimes come apart.

	(Factory Time)	Chilton Time
Valve Spring and/or Valve Stem Oil Seals, Renew (Head on Truck)		
Six–1986-87		
All models–one (1.0)		1.4
all (2.6)		3.6
V-8–318-360 engs–all models		
1986-90–one (1.1)		1.5
one–each bank (1.7)		2.4
all–both banks (4.4)		5.2
w/Air inj add (.2)		.2

DIESEL ENGINE

	(Factory Time)	Chilton Time
Cylinder Head Gasket, Renew		
Includes: Clean gasket surfaces, clean carbon, make all necessary adjustments.		
All models (2.6)		3.6
Cylinder Head, Renew		
Includes: Transfer all parts, reface valves, make all necessary adjustments.		
All models (3.7)		5.1

	(Factory Time)	Chilton Time
Compression Test		
All models		1.7
Clean Carbon and Grind Valves		
Includes: R&R cylinder head, clean gasket surfaces, clean carbon, reface valves and seats. Make all necessary adjustments.		
All models (4.5)		6.3
Valve Cover Gaskets, Renew (All)		
All models (.5)		.7
Valve Rocker Arms and/or Supports, Renew		
All models–one (.3)		.5
all (1.5)		2.1
Valve Tappet Cover, Renew		
All models (1.5)		2.1
Valve Stem Oil Seals, Renew (Head on Truck)		
All models–all (2.2)		3.0

LABOR 13 ENGINE ASSEMBLY & MOUNTS 13 LABOR

	(Factory Time)	Chilton Time
GASOLINE ENGINES		
Note: All engine operations listed in this group are for assemblies as supplied by the original equipment manufacturer. Time to replace assemblies from independent rebuilders may vary.		
Engine Assembly, Remove & Install		
Does not include transfer of any parts or equipment.		
Six		
B-PB-CB Models		
1986-87–w/M.T.		8.7
w/A.T.		7.8
All other models		
1986-87–w/M.T.		7.8
w/A.T.		6.6
V-8–318-360 engs		
B-PB-CB Models		
1986-90–w/M.T.		9.6
w/A.T.		9.2
All other models		
1986-90–w/M.T.		7.7
w/A.T.		6.5
w/P.S. add (.2)		.2
w/Skid plate add (.3)		.3
w/Air inj add (.3)		.3
Six–w/A.C. add (1.0)		1.0
V-8–w/A.C. add (1.7)		*1.7
*Includes recharge A.C. system.		
(G) Rebuilt Engine Assembly, Renew (w/Cyl. Head(s) and Oil Pan)		
Includes: R&R engine assy. Transfer all component parts not supplied with replacement engine.		
Six		
B-PB-CB models		
1986-87–w/M.T.		11.7
w/A.T.		10.8
All other models		
1986-87–w/M.T.		10.8
w/A.T.		9.6
V-8		
318-360 engs		
B-PB-CB models		
1986-90–w/M.T.		12.6
w/A.T.		12.2
All other models		
1986-90–w/M.T.		10.7
w/A.T.		9.5

	(Factory Time)	Chilton Time
w/A.C. add		1.0
w/P.S. add		.2
w/Air inj add		.3
w/Skid plate add		.3
w/Air inj add (.3)		.3
Six–w/A.C. add (1.0)		1.0
V-8–w/A.C. add		*1.7
*Includes: Recharge A.C. system.		
Short Engine Assy., Renew (w/All Internal Parts Less Cylinder Head(s) and Oil Pan)		
Includes: R&R engine, transfer all component parts not supplied with replacement engine. Tune engine.		
Six		
B-PB-CB Models		
1986-87–w/M.T. (10.9)		16.0
w/A.T. (10.0)		15.1
All other models		
1986-87–w/M.T. (8.5)		14.1
w/A.T. (7.3)		13.2
V-8–318-360 engs		
B-PB-CB Models		
1986-90–w/M.T. (11.0)		17.5
w/A.T. (10.1)		16.6
All other models		
1986-90–w/M.T. (9.6)		15.7
w/A.T. (8.7)		14.8
w/P.S. add (.2)		.2
w/Skid plate add (.3)		.3
w/Air inj add (.3)		.3
Six–w/A.C. add (1.0)		1.0
V-8–w/A.C. add (1.7)		*1.7
*Includes recharge A.C. system, Recond valves add		
Six (1.8)		2.5
V-8 (2.7)		3.5
Cylinder Block, Renew (w/Pistons and Rings)		
Includes: R&R engine, transfer all component parts not supplied with replacement engine, clean carbon, grind valves. Tune engine.		
Six		
B-PB-CB Models		
1986-87–w/M.T. (15.5)		22.7
w/A.T. (14.7)		21.8
All other models		
1986-87–w/M.T. (14.6)		21.6
w/A.T. (13.7)		20.7

	(Factory Time)	Chilton Time
w/P.S. add (.2)		.2
w/Skid plate add (.3)		.3
w/Air inj add (.3)		.3
Six–w/A.C. add (1.0)		1.0
V-8–w/A.C. add (1.7)		*1.7
*Includes recharge A.C. system.		
Engine Assembly, R&R and Recondition		
Includes: Rebore block, install new pistons, rings, rod and main bearings. Clean carbon, grind valves. Tune engine.		
Six		
B-PB-CB Models		
1986-87–w/M.T. (30.0)		35.2
w/A.T. (29.1)		34.3
All other models		
1986-87–w/M.T. (28.6)		33.0
w/A.T. (27.4)		32.6
V-8–318-360 engs		
B-PB-CB Models		
1986-90–w/M.T. (36.3)		41.5
w/A.T. (35.9)		40.1
All other models		
1986-90–w/M.T. (33.7)		38.9
w/A.T. (32.5)		37.7
w/P.S. add (.2)		.2
w/Skid plate add (.3)		.3
w/Air inj add (.3)		.3
Six–w/A.C. add (1.0)		1.0
V-8–w/A.C. add (1.7)		*1.7
*Includes recharge A.C. system.		
Engine Mounts, Renew		
Front		
Six–all models		
1986-87–one (.4)		1.0
V-8–318-360 engs		
B-PB-CB Models		
1986-90–one (.9)		1.2
All other models		
1986-90–one (.3)		.5
Rear		
Six–1986-87 (.5)		1.0
V-8		
B-PB-CB Models		
1986-90 (.6)		1.0
All other models		
1986-90 (1.0)		1.4

LABOR 13 ENGINE ASSEMBLY & MOUNTS 13 LABOR

(Factory Time)	Chilton Time
DIESEL ENGINE	
Engine Assembly, Remove & Install	
Does not include transfer of any parts or equipment.	
All models	7.0
w/P.S. add	.2

(Factory Time)	Chilton Time
Short Engine Assy., Renew (w/All Internal Parts Less Cylinder Head and Oil Pan)	
Includes: R&R engine, transfer all component parts not supplied with replacement engine. Make all necessary adjustments.	
All models (9.8)	13.7
w/P.S. add (.2)	.2
Recond valves add (1.8)	2.5

(Factory Time)	Chilton Time
Engine Assembly, R&R and Recondition	
Includes: Rebore block, install new pistons, rings, rod and main bearings. Clean carbon, grind valves. Make all necessary adjustments.	
All models (19.1)	26.7
w/P.S. add (.2)	.2
Engine Mounts, Renew	
All models—right or left (.5)	.8

LABOR 14 PISTONS, RINGS & BEARINGS 14 LABOR

(Factory Time)	Chilton Time
GASOLINE ENGINES	
Rings, Renew (See Engine Combinations)	
Includes: R&R pistons, remove cylinder top ridge, hone cylinder walls.	
Six	
B-PB-CB Models	
1986-87 (6.8)	9.5
All other models	
1986-87 (6.9)	10.1
V-8—318-360 engs	
B-PB-CB Models	
1986-90 (9.6)	13.4
All other models	
1986-90 (9.1)	13.0
w/100 Amp alt add (.6)	.6
w/Air inj add (.6)	.6
w/A.C. add (.2)	.2
Pistons (w/Pin), Renew	
Includes: Remove cylinder top ridge, hone cylinder walls, renew connecting rod bearings if required.	
Six	
B-PB-CB Models	
1986-87 (8.5)	11.3
All other models	
1986-87 (9.2)	12.0
V-8—318-360 engs	
B-PB-CB Models	
1986-90 (12.1)	15.8
All other models	
1986-90 (10.5)	12.9
w/100 Amp alt add (.6)	.6
w/Air inj add (.6)	.6
w/A.C. add (.2)	.2
Connecting Rod Bearings, Renew	
Six	
B-PB-CB Models	
1986-87—one (1.6)	2.3
all (2.6)	4.5
All other models	
1986-87—one (2.3)	3.3
all (3.3)	5.9

COMBINATIONS
Add to Engine Work
See Machine Shop Operations

(Factory Time)	Chilton Time	(Factory Time)	Chilton Time
DRAIN, EVACUATE AND RECHARGE AIR CONDITIONING SYSTEM		**VALVE GUIDES, REAM OVERSIZE**	
All models	1.4	Each (.2)	.3
ROCKER ARMS & SHAFT ASSY., DISASSEMBLE AND CLEAN OR RECONDITION		**VALVE, RECONDITION (ALL)**	
		Cylinder Head Removed	
Six (.5)	.6	Six (2.2)	3.0
V-8—one side (.5)	.6	V-8 (2.7)	4.0
both sides (.9)	1.1	Diesel (1.8)	2.5
HYDRAULIC VALVE LIFTERS, DISASSEMBLE AND CLEAN		**DEGLAZE CYLINDER WALLS**	
Each	.2	Each (.1)	.2
		REMOVE CYLINDER TOP RIDGE	
		Each (.3)	.3
DISTRIBUTOR, RECONDITION		**PLASTIGAUGE BEARINGS**	
All Models (.7)	1.0	Each (.1)	.1
CARBURETOR, RECONDITION		**OIL PUMP, RECONDITION**	
1 BBL (.9)	1.4	Six (.2)	.4
2 BBL (1.1)	1.6	V-8 (.2)	.4
4 BBL (1.6)	2.1	**OIL FILTER ELEMENT, RENEW**	
		All Models (.2)	.3

(Factory Time)	Chilton Time
V-8—318-360 engs	
B-PB-CB Models	
1986-90—one (2.4)	3.6
all (3.8)	6.6
All other models	
1986-90—one (1.3)	2.4
all (2.7)	5.1
DIESEL ENGINE	
Rings, Renew (See Engine Combinations)	
Includes: R&R pistons, remove cylinder top ridge, hone cylinder walls.	
All models—one cyl (7.6)	10.6

(Factory Time)	Chilton Time
all cyls (11.0)	15.4
Pistons or Connecting Rods, Renew	
Includes: R&R pistons, remove cylinder top ridge, hone cylinder walls.	
All models—one cyl (7.6)	10.9
all cyls (11.1)	17.2
Piston Cooling Nozzles, Renew	
All models—all (9.4)	13.2
Connecting Rod Bearings, Renew	
Includes: R&R engine assy.	
All models (6.8)	9.5

LABOR 15 CRANKSHAFT & DAMPER 15 LABOR

(Factory Time)	Chilton Time
GASOLINE ENGINES	
Crankshaft and Main Bearings, Renew	
Includes: R&R engine assembly, plastigauge all bearings.	
Six	
B-PB-CB Models	
1986-87—w/M.T. (10.1)	13.6
w/A.T. (9.2)	12.7
All other models	
1986-87—w/M.T. (6.6)	10.4
w/A.T. (6.1)	9.6
V-8—318-360 engs	
B-PB-CB Models	
1986-90 w/M.T. (9.6)	14.7
w/A.T. (8.7)	14.2

(Factory Time)	Chilton Time
All other models	
1986-90—w/M.T. (8.4)	12.2
w/A.T. (7.9)	11.0
w/P.S. add (.2)	.2
w/Skid plate add (.3)	.3
V-8—w/A.C. add (1.7)	•1.7
*Includes recharge A.C. system.	
Main Bearings, Renew	
Includes: Plastigauge bearings.	
Six	
B-PB-CB Models	
1986-87—one (2.7)	3.9
all (4.2)	6.0

(Factory Time)	Chilton Time
All other models	
1986-87—one (1.6)	4.0
all (3.2)	5.4
V-8—318-360 engs	
B-PB-CB Models	
1986-90—one (2.6)	3.7
all (3.2)	5.7
All other models	
1986-90—one (1.8)	3.2
all (3.2)	4.5
Rod and Main Bearings, Renew	
Includes: Plastigauge bearings.	
Six	
B-PB-CB Models	
1986-87 (6.0)	7.8

LABOR 15 CRANKSHAFT & DAMPER 15 LABOR

(Factory Time)	Chilton Time	(Factory Time)	Chilton Time	(Factory Time)	Chilton Time
All other models		**Vibration Damper, Renew**		**DIESEL ENGINE**	
1986-87 (4.2)	7.2	**Six**		**Crankshaft and Main Bearings, Renew**	
V-8–318-360 engs		B-PB-CB Models		Includes: R&R engine assembly, plastigauge all	
B-PB-CB Models		1986-87 (.9)	1.4	bearings.	
1986-90 (5.6)	8.1	D-AD-PD Models		All models (9.2)	12.9
All other models		1986-87 (.8)	1.2	w/P.S. add (.2)	.2
1986-90 (4.5)	6.9	W-AW-PW Models		**Main Bearings, Renew**	
		1986-87 (.8)	1.4	Includes: R&R engine assembly.	
Rear Main Bearing Oil Seals, Renew				All models (7.0)	9.8
(Upper & Lower)		**V-8–318-360 engs**		**Main and Rod Bearings, Renew**	
Six		B-PB-CB Models		Includes: R&R engine assembly.	
B-PB-CB Models		1986-90 (.7)	1.3	All models (8.8)	11.6
1986-87 (1.4)	2.0	All other models		**Rear Main Bearing Oil Seals, Renew**	
All other models		1986-90 (.6)	1.2	**(Complete)**	
1986-87 (1.6)	2.5	w/A.C. add (.2)	.2	All models (2.4)	3.5
V-8–318-360 engs		w/P.S. add (.1)	.1	**Vibration Damper, Renew**	
B-PB-CB Models				All models (.4)	.6
1986-90 (1.9)	2.7	**Crankshaft Pulley, Renew**		**Crankshaft Front Oil Seal, Renew**	
All other models		All models		All models (1.0)	1.4
1986-90 (1.4)	2.0	1986-90 (.5)	.9		

NOTE: Upper seal removed with special tool. If necessary to R&R crankshaft, use Crankshaft and Main Bearings, Renew.

w/A.C. add (.2) .2
w/P.S. add (.1) .1

LABOR 16 CAMSHAFT & TIMING GEARS 16 LABOR

(Factory Time)	Chilton Time	(Factory Time)	Chilton Time	(Factory Time)	Chilton Time
GASOLINE ENGINES		w/P.S. add (.2)	.2	**V-8–318-360 engs**	
Timing Chain Case Cover Gasket, Renew		w/A.C. add (.4)	.4	B-PB-CB Models	
Six				1986-90 (5.3)	7.6
All models		**Timing Chain or Gear, Renew**		All other models	
1986-87 (1.4)	2.5	Includes: Renew cover oil seal and crankshaft		1986-90 (4.7)	7.1
V-8–318-360 engs		gear if necessary.		w/A.C. add (.8)	.8
B-PB-CB Models		**Six**		w/P.S. add (.2)	.2
1986-90 (2.0)	2.9	1986-87 (2.2)	2.9	w/100 Amp alt add (.5)	.5
All other models		**V-8–318-360 engs**		w/Air inj add (.8)	.8
1986-90 (1.8)	2.6	B-PB-CB Models			
w/P.S. add (.2)	.2	1986-90 (2.4)	3.5	**Camshaft Bearings, Renew**	
w/A.C. add (.2)	.2	All other models		**(Engine Removed and Disassembled)**	
w/100 Amp alt add (.5)	.5	1986-90 (2.3)	3.0	All models (2.0)	2.6
w/Air inj add (.2)	.2	w/P.S. add (.2)	.2		
		w/A.C. add (.4)	.4	**DIESEL ENGINE**	
Timing Chain Case Cover Oil Seal, Renew		w/100 Amp alt add (.5)	.5	**Timing Chain Case Cover Gasket, Renew**	
Six		w/Air inj add (.2)	.2	All models (1.1)	1.5
B-PB-CB Models				**Timing Chain Case Cover Oil Seal, Renew**	
1986-87 (1.1)	1.7	**Camshaft, Renew**		All models (1.0)	1.4
D-AD-PD Models		Includes: Renew valve tappets and adjust valve		**Timing Pin Assy., Renew**	
1986-87 (.9)	1.2	clearance when required.		All models (1.2)	1.7
W-AW-PW Models		**Six**			
1986-87 (.9)	1.2	All models		**Camshaft, Renew**	
V-8–318-360 engs		1986-87 (4.4)	6.4	Includes: R&R engine assy.	
All models		w/A.C. add (.8)	.8	All models (6.4)	9.1
1986-90 (.9)	1.3				

LABOR 17 ENGINE OILING SYSTEM 17 LABOR

(Factory Time)	Chilton Time	(Factory Time)	Chilton Time	(Factory Time)	Chilton Time
GASOLINE ENGINES		**V-8–318-360 engs**		**Oil Pressure Gauge (Dash), Renew**	
Oil Pan or Gasket, Renew		B-PB-CB Models		1986-90 (.6)	1.1
Six		1986-90 (1.7)	2.3	**Oil Pressure Gauge (Engine), Renew**	
B-PB-CB Models		All other models		All models (.4)	.6
1986-87 (1.1)	1.7	1986-90 (1.1)	1.8	**Oil Filter Element, Renew**	
All other models				All models (.2)	.3
1986-87 (1.4)	2.0	**Oil Pump, R&R and Recondition**			
V-8–318-360 engs		**Six**			
B-PB-CB Models		B-PB-CB Models		**DIESEL ENGINE**	
1986-90 (1.4)	2.0	1986-90 (.8)	1.5		
All other models		All other models		**Oil Pan and/or Gasket, Renew**	
1986-90 (1.0)	1.6	1986-87 (1.4)	1.8	Includes: R&R engine assy.	
		V-8–318-360 engs		All models (5.6)	7.8
Oil Pump, Renew		B-PB-CB Models		**Oil Pump or Gasket, Renew**	
Six		1986-90 (2.1)	2.7	All models (1.2)	1.7
B-PB-CB models		All other models		**Oil Filter Element, Renew**	
1986-87 (.6)	1.2	1986-90 (1.6)	2.2	All models (.2)	.3
All other models		**Pressure Test Engine Bearings (Pan Off)**			
1986-87 (.8)	1.3	All models	1.2		

LABOR 18 CLUTCH & FLYWHEEL 18 LABOR

(Factory Time)	Chilton Time
Clutch Pedal Free Play, Adjust	
All models (.3)	.5
Bleed Clutch Hydraulic System	
All models	.4
Clutch Master Cylinder, Renew	
Includes: Bleed system.	
All models (.5)	.8
Recond cyl add	.4
Clutch Slave Cylinder, Renew	
Includes: Bleed system.	
All models (.4)	.6
Recond cyl add	.4
Hydraulic Clutch Assy., Renew	
4X2 models (.9)	1.3
4X4 models (1.4)	1.8
Clutch Assembly, Renew	
4 Speed	
B-PB models (3.2)	4.4
All other models	
w/2 wheel drive (2.9)	4.0
w/4 wheel drive (3.9)	5.4

(Factory Time)	Chilton Time
5 Speed	
All models (2.0)	2.9
w/Skid plate add (.3)	.3
w/P.T.O. add (.3)	.5
w/2 piece drive shaft add	.2
w/Dual exh add (.3)	.3
Clutch Release Bearing, Renew	
4 Speed	
B-PB models (2.5)	3.5
All other models	
w/2 wheel drive (2.3)	3.2
w/4 wheel drive (3.5)	4.9
5 Speed	
All models (1.9)	2.6
w/Skid plate add (.3)	.3
w/P.T.O. add (.3)	.5
w/2 piece drive shaft add	.2
w/Dual exh add (.3)	.3
Clutch Release Fork, Renew	
4 Speed	
B-PB-CB Models (.3)	.6
D-AD Models (.4)	.7
W-AW-PW Models (.4)	.7

(Factory Time)	Chilton Time
5 Speed	
All models (2.1)	2.7
Clutch Torque Shaft, Renew	
Includes: Renew bearings.	
B-PB-CB Models (.3)	.6
All other models (.5)	.9
Flywheel Assembly, Renew	
4 Speed	
1986-90	
w/Overdrive (2.8)	3.9
w/NP-435-445	
and 2/wd (3.0)	4.2
w/NP-435-445	
and 4/wd (4.3)	6.0
5 Speed	
Diesel (2.5)	3.5
Gas (2.3)	3.2
Renew ring gear add (.6)	.6
w/Skid plate add (.3)	.3
w/Dual exh add (.3)	.3
w/2 piece drive shaft add	.2

LABOR 19A MANUAL TRANSMISSION (RWD) 19A LABOR

(Factory Time)	Chilton Time
Transmission Assy., R&R or Renew	
4 Speed	
O/Drive 4	
B-models (1.4)	2.0
AD-D models (1.6)	2.2
NP-435-445	
w/2 wheel drive (2.2)	3.0
w/4 wheel drive (3.5)	4.9
5 Speed	
All models (1.2)	2.0
w/Skid plate add (.3)	.3
w/P.T.O. add (.3)	.5
w/2 piece drive shaft add	.2
w/Dual exh add (.3)	.3
Renew assy add (.4)	.6
Transmission Assy., R&R and Recondition	
4 Speed	
O/Drive 4	
B-models (4.3)	6.0

(Factory Time)	Chilton Time
AD-D models (4.5)	6.3
NP-435-445	
w/2 wheel drive (5.4)	7.5
w/4 wheel drive (6.4)	8.5
5 Speed	
All models (4.4)	6.4
w/Skid plate add (.3)	.3
w/P.T.O. add (.3)	.5
w/2 piece drive shaft add	.2
w/Dual exh add (.3)	.3
Transmission, Recondition (Off Truck)	
Overdrive 4 (2.9)	3.9
NP-435-445 (2.7)	3.6
NP2500 (3.2)	4.4
Transmission Front Oil Seal, Renew	
Includes: R&R transmission.	
4 Speed	
O/Drive 4	
B-models (1.6)	2.2

(Factory Time)	Chilton Time
AD-D models (1.8)	2.4
NP-435-445	
w/2 wheel drive (2.8)	4.2
w/4 wheel drive (3.8)	5.2
5 Speed	
All models (1.5)	2.3
w/Skid plate add (.3)	.3
w/P.T.O. add (.3)	.5
w/2 piece drive shaft add	.2
w/Dual exh add (.3)	.3
Extension Housing Oil Seal, Renew	
All models (.5)	.7
Speedometer Drive Pinion, Renew	
All models (.3)	.6

LABOR 20 TRANSFER CASE 20 LABOR

(Factory Time)	Chilton Time
Transfer Case Assy., R&R or Renew	
All models (1.5)	2.0
w/Skid plate add (.3)	.3
Renew assy add (.3)	.5
Transfer Case Assy., R&R and Recondition	
All models	
NP 208 (4.5)	6.6
NP 205 (4.6)	6.7
NP 231-241 (4.6)	6.7
w/Skid plate add (.3)	.3
Transfer Case Adapter, Renew	
All models (1.5)	2.1
w/Skid plate add (.3)	.3
Transfer Case Adapter Gasket, Renew	
All models (1.2)	1.7
w/Skid plate add (.3)	.3

(Factory Time)	Chilton Time
Transfer Case Shift Lever, Renew	
All models (.2)	.4
Rear Output Shaft Seal, Renew	
All models (1.2)	1.6
Transfer Case Shift Rod, Renew	
All models–one (.3)	.5
both (.4)	.7
Transfer Case Front Yoke, Renew	
All models (.4)	.7
Front Output Shaft Bearing and/or Gasket, Renew	
All models (1.2)	1.6
w/Skid plate add (.3)	.3

(Factory Time)	Chilton Time
Speedometer Drive Pinion, Renew	
All models (.8)	1.1
Power Take Off Assy., R&R or Renew	
1986-87 (1.4)	2.5
Power Take Off Assy., R&R and Recondition	
1986-87 (3.1)	4.9
Power Take Off Mounting Gasket, Renew	
1986-87 (1.3)	2.4
Power Take Off Cover Gasket, Renew	
1986-87 (.4)	.7
Power Take Off Control Cable, Renew	
1986-87 (.6)	1.0

LABOR 21 SHIFT LINKAGE 21 LABOR

(Factory Time)	Chilton Time	(Factory Time)	Chilton Time	(Factory Time)	Chilton Time
STANDARD		**Gearshift Control Rod and/or Swivels, Renew**		**Gearshift Control Rod, Renew**	
Shift Linkage, Adjust		All models–one (.3)	.4	All models (.4)	.6
All models (.3)	.5	**Gearshift Mechanism, Renew (4 Speed)**		**Gear Selector Indicator, Renew**	
		All models–w/Overdrive (.6)	1.1	All models	
Gearshift Lever, Renew		**AUTOMATIC**		inst panel mount (.7)	1.0
All models		**Throttle Linkage, Adjust**		column mount (.2)	.4
Overdrive (.2)	.4	All models (.3)	.5	**Steering Column Shift Housing, Renew**	
NP435-445 (.5)	.7	**Gearshift Lever, Renew**		1986-90	
5 Speed (.4)	.6	All models (.4)	.6	w/Std column (.9)	1.5
				w/Tilt column (2.2)	3.3

LABOR 23A AUTOMATIC TRANSMISSION (RWD) 23A LABOR

(Factory Time)	Chilton Time	(Factory Time)	Chilton Time	(Factory Time)	Chilton Time
A904–A727		**Oil Pan Gasket, Renew**		**Transmission Assembly, Reseal**	
ON TRUCK SERVICES		All models (.5)	1.0	Includes: R&R trans and renew all seals and gaskets.	
Drain and Refill Unit		**Oil Filter, Renew**		B-PB-CB Models	
All models	1.0	All models (.6)	1.1	1986-90 (4.2)	6.8
Oil Pressure Test		**Parking Lock Sprag Control Rod, Renew**		D-AD-PD-RD Models	
Note: Using 3 pressure test points.		Includes: R&R oil pan and remove valve body.		1986-90 (4.5)	7.1
All models	1.5	All models (.9)	1.5	W-AW-PW Models	
Check Unit For Oil Leaks		**Accumulator Piston, Renew or Recondition**		1986-90 (6.3)	8.9
Includes: Clean and dry outside of case and run unit to determine point of leak.		Includes: R&R oil pan and adjust band.		w/Skid plate add (.3)	.3
All models	1.0	All models (1.1)	1.7	w/Dual exh add (.3)	.3
Neutral Safety Switch, Renew		**Kickdown Servo, Renew or Recondition**		**Transmission and Converter, R&R and Recondition**	
All models (.3)	.4	Includes: R&R oil pan and adjust band.		Includes: Disassemble trans including valve body, clean, inspect and replace parts as required.	
Oil Cooler Lines, Renew		All models (.9)	1.5	B-PB-CB Models	
Includes: Cut and form to size.		**Reverse Servo, Renew or Recondition**		1986-90 (6.5)	11.8
All models–one (.6)	1.0	Includes: R&R oil pan and adjust band.		D-AD-PD-RD Models	
Transmission Auxiliary Oil Cooler, Renew		All models (.8)	1.4	1986-90 (6.8)	12.1
All models (.7)	1.2	**Valve Body Assembly, Renew**		W-AW-PW Models	
Throttle Linkage, Adjust		Includes: R&R oil pan and replace filter.		1986-90 (8.6)	13.9
All models (.3)	.5	All models (.9)	1.5	w/Skid plate add (.3)	.3
Kickdown Band, Adjust		**Valve Body Assy., R&R and Recondition**		w/Dual exh add (.3)	.3
All models (.3)	.5	Includes: R&R oil pan and replace filter. Disassemble, clean, inspect, free all valves. Replace parts as required.		Flush converter and lines add (.5)	.7
Throttle Valve Lever Shaft Seal, Renew		All models (1.7)	2.4	**Torque Converter, Renew**	
All models (.3)	.7	**Bands, Adjust**		Includes: R&R transmission.	
Valve Body Manual Lever Shaft Seal, Renew		Includes: R&R oil pan.		B-PB-CB Models	
All models (.4)	.8	All models		1986-90 (2.2)	5.1
Extension Housing Oil Seal, Renew		reverse & kickdown (.6)	1.2	D-AD-PD-RD Models	
All models (.5)	1.1	**SERVICES REQUIRING R&R**		1986-90 (2.5)	5.4
Extension Housing or Adapter Gasket, Renew		**Transmission Assembly, Remove and Reinstall**		W-AW-PW Models	
All models		B-PB-CB Models		1986-90 (4.3)	7.3
w/2 wheel drive (1.4)	2.0	1986-90 (2.0)	4.7	w/Skid plate add (.3)	.3
w/4 wheel drive (1.9)	2.5	D-AD-PD-RD Models		w/Dual exh add (.3)	.3
w/Skid plate add (.3)	.3	1986-90 (2.3)	5.0	**Kickdown Band, Renew**	
Governor Assy., R&R or Recondition		W-AW-PW Models		Includes: R&R transmission.	
Includes: R&R extension housing.		1986-90 (4.1)	6.9	B-PB-CB Models	
All models		Renew trans add (.4)	.5	1986-90 (2.7)	6.1
w/2 wheel drive (1.8)	2.5	Flush converter and lines add (.5)	.7	D-AD-PD-RD Models	
w/4 wheel drive (2.3)	3.0	w/Skid plate add (.3)	.3	1986-90 (3.0)	6.4
w/Skid plate add (.3)	.3	w/Dual exh add (.3)	.3	W-AW-PW Models	
Parking Lock Sprag, Renew		**Transmission Assembly, Renew (w/Remanufactured Unit)**		1986-90 (4.8)	8.3
Includes: R&R extension housing.		Includes: Remove and install all necessary interfering parts. Transfer all parts not supplied with replacement unit. Road test.		w/Skid plate add (.3)	.3
All models		B-PB-CB Models		w/Dual exh add (.3)	.3
w/2 wheel drive (1.3)	2.2	1986-90 (2.3)	5.2	**Reverse Band, Renew**	
w/4 wheel drive (1.8)	2.4	D-AD-PD-RD Models		Includes: R&R transmission.	
w/Skid plate add (.3)	.3	1986-90 (2.6)	5.5	B-PB-CB Models	
Output Shaft Bearing and Oil Seal, Renew		W-AW-PW Models		1986-90 (3.1)	6.7
Includes: R&R extension housing.		1986-90 (4.5)	7.4	D-AD-PD-RD Models	
All models		Pressure test governor add (.7)	1.1	1986-90 (3.4)	7.0
w/2 wheel drive (1.4)	2.3	w/Skid plate add (.3)	.3	W-AW-PW Models	
w/4 wheel drive (1.9)	2.5	w/Dual exh add (.3)	.3	1986-90 (5.2)	8.9
w/Skid plate add (.3)	.3			w/Skid plate add (.3)	.3
				w/Dual exh add (.3)	.3
				Transmission Case, Renew	
				Includes: R&R transmission.	
				B-PB-CB Models	
				1986-90 (3.9)	7.7

LABOR 23A AUTOMATIC TRANSMISSION (RWD) 23A LABOR

(Factory Time)	Chilton Time
D-AD-PD-RD Models	
1986-90 (4.2)	8.0
W-AW-PW Models	
1986-90 (6.0)	9.9
w/Skid plate add (.3)	.3
w/Dual exh add (.3)	.3
Front Pump Assembly, Renew or Recondition	
Includes: R&R trans, replace reaction shaft if necessary.	
B-PB-CB Models	
1986-90 (2.6)	5.9
D-AD-PD-RD Models	
1986-90 (2.9)	6.2
W-AW-PW Models	
1986-90 (4.7)	8.1
w/Skid plate add (.3)	.3
w/Dual exh add (.3)	.3
Front Pump Oil Seal, Renew	
Includes: R&R transmission.	
B-PB-CB Models	
1986-90 (2.2)	5.1
D-AD-PD-RD Models	
1986-90 (2.5)	5.4
W-AW-PW Models	
1986-90 (4.3)	7.3
w/Skid plate add (.3)	.3
w/Dual exh add (.3)	.3

A500 ON TRUCK SERVICES

Drain and Refill Unit	
All models	1.0
Oil Pressure Test	
Note: Using 3 pressure test points.	
All models	1.5
Check Unit for Oil Leaks	
Includes: Clean and dry outside of case and run unit to determine point of leak.	
All models	1.0
Neutral Safety Switch, Renew	
All models (.3)	.4
Overdrive Cancel Switch, Renew	
All models (.4)	.6
Oil Cooler Lines, Renew	
Includes: Cut and form to size.	
All models-one (.6)	1.0
Transmission Auxiliary Oil Cooler, Renew	
All models (.7)	1.2
Throttle Linkage, Adjust	
All models (.3)	.5
Throttle Valve Lever Shaft Seal, Renew	
All models (.3)	.7

(Factory Time)	Chilton Time
Valve Body Manual Lever Shaft Seal, Renew	
All models (.4)	.8
Extension Housing Oil Seal, Renew	
All models (.5)	1.1
Extension Housing/Overdrive Unit, Remove and Install	
All models (1.2)	1.7
Renew assy add (.7)	.7
Governor Assy: Renew or Recondition	
Includes: R&R extension housing.	
All models (1.7)	2.4
Parking Lock Sprag, Renew	
Includes: R&R extension housing.	
All models (2.2)	3.1
Output Shaft Bearings, Renew (Front or Rear)	
Includes: R&R extension housing.	
All models (1.8)	2.5
Extension Housing Bushing, Renew	
Includes: R&R extension housing.	
All models (1.8)	2.5
Overdrive Sliding Hub, Renew	
Includes: R&R extension housing.	
All models (2.2)	3.1
Overdrive Direct Clutch Drum, Renew	
Includes: R&R extension housing.	
All models (2.2)	3.1
Overdrive Clutches and Seals, Renew	
Includes: R&R extension housing.	
All models (2.2)	3.1
Overdrive Sungear, Renew	
Includes: R&R extension housing.	
All models (2.1)	3.0
Planetary Pinion Assy., Renew	
Includes: R&R extension housing.	
All models (2.0)	2.9
Annulus/Parking Gear, Renew	
Includes: R&R extension housing.	
All models (2.2)	3.1
Overrunning Clutch Assy., Renew	
Includes: R&R extension housing.	
All models (2.2)	3.1
Overdrive Output Shaft, Renew	
Includes: R&R extension housing.	
All models (2.4)	3.4
Oil Pan and/or Gasket, Renew	
All models (.5)	1.0

(Factory Time)	Chilton Time
Parking Lock Sprag Control Rod, Renew	
Includes: R&R oil pan and remove valve body.	
All models (.9)	1.5
Accumulator Piston, Renew or Recondition	
Includes: R&R oil pan and adjust band.	
All models (1.1)	1.7
Kickdown Servo, Renew or Recondition	
Includes: R&R oil pan and adjust band.	
All models (.9)	1.5
Reverse Servo, Renew or Recondition	
Includes: R&R oil pan and adjust band.	
All models (.8)	1.4
Valve Body Assembly, Renew	
Includes: R&R oil pan and renew filter.	
All models (.9)	1.5
Valve Body Assy; R&R and Recondition	
Includes: R&R oil pan and replace filter. Disassemble, clean, inspect, free all valves. Replace parts as required.	
All models (1.7)	2.4
Bands, Adjust	
Includes: R&R oil pan.	
All models	
reverse (.6)	1.2
kickdown (.6)	1.2
Torque Converter Lock Up Solenoid, Renew	
Includes: R&R oil pan.	
All models (1.2)	1.8

SERVICES REQUIRING R&R
Transmission Assembly, Remove and Install	
All models (3.6)	5.0
Renew trans add (.4)	.5
Flush conver and lines add (.5)	.5
Transmission Assembly, Reseal	
Includes: R&R trans and renew all seals and gaskets.	
All models	6.5
Transmission and Converter, R&R and Recondition	
Includes: Disassemble trans including valve body, clean, inspect and replace parts as required.	
All models (8.3)	11.6
Torque Converter, Renew	
Includes: R&R transmission.	
All models (3.8)	5.2
Flywheel (Flexplate), Renew	
Includes: R&R transmission.	
All models (3.7)	5.1

LABOR 25 U-JOINTS & DRIVESHAFT 25 LABOR

(Factory Time)	Chilton Time
Drive Shaft, R&R or Renew	
All Models	
trans to rear axle (.4)	.7
center bearing	
to rear axle (.4)	.7
transfer case to front axle (.5)	.8
transfer case to rear axle (.4)	.7
trans to center brg (1.2)	1.7
w/Skid plate add (.3)	.3
Universal Joints, Renew or Recondition	
Includes: R&R drive shaft.	
Single Piece Shaft	
(without center bearing)	
trans to rear axle (.6)	.9

(Factory Time)	Chilton Time
at rear axle (.5)	.8
transfer case to rear axle (.5)	.8
transfer case to	
rear axle (.9)	1.2
(transfer case to front axle)	
Dana CV Type (.8)	1.3
Saginaw CV Type (1.5)	2.0
at front axle (.6)	.9
Two Piece Shaft	
trans to center brg (.9)	1.2
center brg to rear	
axle (.6)	.9
at rear axle (.6)	.8
w/Skid plate add (.3)	.3

(Factory Time)	Chilton Time
Drive Shaft Center Bearing, Renew	
Includes: Renew insulator if necessary.	
All models (1.1)	1.5
Universal Joint Ball and Socket Assy., Renew	
Front shaft-Saginaw	
C/V type (1.3)	1.7
w/Skid plate add (.2)	.3
Universal Joint Center Yoke or Flange, Renew	
Front shaft-Saginaw	
C/V type (1.3)	1.7
w/Skid plate add (.2)	.3

LABOR — 26 DRIVE AXLE 26 — LABOR

	Factory Time	Chilton Time
Differential, Drain & Refill		
All models		.6
Rear Axle Housing Cover, Renew or Reseal		
All models (.4)		.6
Axle Shaft, Renew		
Includes: Renew outer oil seal, bearing and gasket on 8⅝ - 9¼ axles.		
8¼ - 8⅜ - 9¼ Axles		
1986-90-one (.7)		1.0
Spicer 60 - 70 Axle		
1986-90-one (.5)		.8
Axle Shaft Bearing, Renew		
Includes: Renew oil seal.		
8¼ - 8⅜ - 9¼ Axles		
1986-90-one (.6)		.9
Axle Shaft Oil Seal, Renew		
8¼ - 8⅜ - 9¼ Axles		
1986-90-one (.6)		.9
Pinion Shaft Oil Seal, Renew		
All models (.6)		1.0

	Factory Time	Chilton Time
Rear Axle Housing, Renew		
Includes: Renew pinion oil seal, inner and outer axle shaft or wheel bearing oil seals and gaskets.		
8¼ - 8⅜ - 9¼ Axles		
All models (4.2)		6.3
Spicer 60 - 70 Axles		
All models (5.7)		8.5
Differential Carrier Assembly, Renew		
Note: Assembly includes axle housing.		
8¼ - 8⅜ - 9¼ Axles		
All models (2.0)		3.1
Spicer 60 - 70 Axles		
All models (3.0)		4.6
Differential Side Bearings, Renew		
Includes: Renew pinion oil seal and adjust backlash.		
8¼ - 8⅜ - 9¼ Axles		
All models (1.5)		2.5
Spicer 60 - 70 Axles		
All models (3.1)		4.6
Renew pinion bearings, add (.9)		1.4

	Factory Time	Chilton Time
Differential Case, Renew		
Includes: Renew ring gear and pinion, bearings and side gears if necessary.		
8¼ - 8⅜ - 9¼ Axles		
Std & Sure Grip		
All models (3.0)		4.5
Spicer 60 - 70 Axles		
All models (3.6)		5.4
Differential Side Gears, Renew		
Includes: Renew axle shaft oil seals.		
8¼ - 8⅜ - 9¼ Axles		
All models (1.1)		2.0
Spicer 60 - 70 Axles		
All models (1.4)		3.0
Ring Gear and Pinion Set, Renew		
Includes: Renew wheel bearing or inner axle shaft oil seals, pinion oil seal and gaskets.		
8¼ - 8⅜ - 9¼ Axles		
All models (3.7)		7.0
Spicer 60 - 70 Axles		
All models (3.7)		7.0
Renew side bearings add (.3)		.7

LABOR — 27 REAR SUSPENSION 27 — LABOR

	Factory Time	Chilton Time
Rear Spring, Renew		
All models-one (.5)		.9
both (1.0)		1.7
w/Aux. rear spring add,		
each (.5)		.5
w/Skid plate add (.3)		.3

	Factory Time	Chilton Time
Auxiliary Rear Spring, Renew		
All models-one (.7)		1.5
Rear Spring Shackle, Renew		
Includes: Renew bushings.		
B-PB-CB Models		
one (.3)		.7

	Factory Time	Chilton Time
All other models		
one (.6)		1.0
w/Skid plate add (.3)		.3
Rear Shock Absorbers, Renew		
All models-one (.2)		.4
both (.4)		.6

LABOR — 28 AIR CONDITIONING 28 — LABOR

	Factory Time	Chilton Time
Note: If more than one item requires replacement where evacuation and discharging the system is already included in the operation, deduct 1.0 hour for each additional item to the times listed.		
Drain, Evacuate, Leak Test and Charge System		
All models		1.7
Flush Refrigerant System, Complete		
To be used in conjunction with component replacement which could contaminate system.		
All models		1.3
Partial Charge		
Includes: Leak test.		
All models		
w/Front unit (.5)		1.1
w/Front and rear unit (.9)		1.4
Performance Test		
All models		.8
Vacuum Leak Test		
All models		.9
ON TRUCK SERVICES		
Compressor Belt, Renew		
B-PB-CB Models (.4)		.6
All other models (.3)		.5
w/Air inj add (.1)		.1
w/P.S. add (.1)		.1
Compressor Clutch Field Coil, Renew		
Includes: Renew pulley w/Hub, if necessary.		
B-PB-CB Models		
w/C-171 comp (.5)		.9

	Factory Time	Chilton Time
All other models (.5)		.9
Compressor Clutch Assembly, Renew		
B-PB-CB Models		
w/C-171 comp (.5)		.8
All other models (.5)		.8
C-171 COMP		
Compressor Assembly, Renew		
Includes: Transfer parts as required. Pressure test and charge system.		
Six		
All models (1.8)		3.2
V-8		
B-PB-CB models (2.1)		3.5
All other models (1.7)		3.1
Diesel		
All models (2.0)		3.4
w/Rear A.C. add (.3)		.3
w/114 Amp alter add (.6)		.6
Compressor Front Cover and/or Seal, Renew		
Includes: Pressure test and charge system.		
Six		
All models (2.2)		3.5
V-8		
B-PB-CB models (2.5)		3.8
All other models (2.1)		3.4
Diesel		
All models (2.4)		3.7
w/114 Amp alter add (.6)		.6

	Factory Time	Chilton Time
Compressor Rear Cover and/or Seal, Renew		
Includes: Pressure test and charge system.		
Six		
All models (2.1)		3.4
V-8		
B-PB-CB models (2.4)		3.7
All other models (2.0)		3.3
Diesel		
All models (2.3)		3.6
w/114 Amp alter add (.6)		.6
Compressor Center Seal, Renew		
Includes: Pressure test and charge system.		
Six		
All models (2.3)		3.6
V-8		
B-PB-CB models (2.6)		3.9
All other models (2.2)		3.5
Diesel		
All models (2.5)		3.8
w/114 Amp alter add (.6)		.6
Compressor Shaft Gas Seal, Renew		
Includes: Pressure test and charge system.		
Six		
All models (2.2)		3.5
V-8		
B-PB-CB models (2.5)		3.8
All other models (2.1)		3.4
Diesel		
All models (2.4)		3.7
w/114 Amp alter add (.6)		.6

LABOR 28 AIR CONDITIONING 28 LABOR

(Factory Time)	Chilton Time	(Factory Time)	Chilton Time	(Factory Time)	Chilton Time
Expansion Valve, Renew		w/Front and rear unit (1.9)	3.0	**Temperature Control Assembly, Renew**	
Includes: Pressure test and charge system.		All other models (1.2)	2.2	B-PB-CB Models	
B-PB-CB Models		Renew receiver drier add	.2	1986-90 (.6)	1.0
front unit (1.1)	2.0	**Evaporator Coil, Renew**		All other models	
rear unit (1.9)	2.8	Includes: Add partial charge, leak test and		1986-90 (.5)	.9
All other models (1.0)	1.9	charge system.			
Renew receiver drier add	.2	B-PB-CB Models		**A.C. Push Button Vacuum Switch, Renew**	
Receiver Drier, Renew		Front Unit (2.9)	5.4	All models (.6)	1.0
Includes: Add partial charge, leak test and		Front Unit–Front and Rear			
charge system.		Unit Equipped (3.2)	6.0	**Air Conditioning Hoses, Renew**	
B-PB-CB Models		Rear Unit (1.6)	2.8	Includes: Evacuate and charge system.	
w/Front unit (1.1)	1.9	All other models (2.3)	4.7	SUCTION ASSY	
w/Front and rear unit (1.5)	2.3			B-PB Models (1.2)	*2.0
All other models (1.1)	1.9	**Blower Motor, Renew**		All other models (1.1)	1.9
Low Pressure Cut Off Switch, Renew		B-PB-CB Models		DISCHARGE ASSY	
Includes: Evacuate and charge system.		1986-90		All models (1.1)	*1.9
B-PB-CB Models		Front (.9)	1.5	REAR UNIT TUBE ASSY	
w/Front unit (1.0)	1.8	Rear (.4)	.9	B-PB Models (3.7)	5.0
w/Front and rear unit (1.3)	2.1	All other models		SUCTION HOSE	
All other models (1.0)	1.8	1986-90 (.4)	.9	Rear unit to rear evap. (1.3)	2.1
Clutch Cycling (Thermostatic Control)				DISCHARGE HOSE	
Switch, Renew		**Blower Motor Resistor, Renew**		Rear unit to rear evap. (1.3)	2.1
All models (.3)	.5	All models (.3)	.4	SUCTION HOSE	
Condenser Assembly, Renew				Rear unit to front tube (1.3)	2.1
Includes: Add partial charge, leak test and		**Blower Motor Switch, Renew**		DISCHARGE HOSE	
charge system.		All models		Rear unit to front tube (1.3)	2.1
B-PB-CB Models		Front unit (.5)	.9	*w/Rear A.C. add (.3)	.3
w/Front unit (1.6)	2.5	Rear unit (.3)	.6	Renew receiver drier add	.2

LABOR 30 HEAD AND PARKING LAMPS 30 LABOR

(Factory Time)	Chilton Time	(Factory Time)	Chilton Time	(Factory Time)	Chilton Time
Aim Headlamps		**Parking Lamp or Turn Signal Lamp Lens or**		**Cargo Lamp Assembly, Renew**	
two	.4	**Bulb, Renew**		All models-one (.2)	.3
four	.6	All models-one (.2)	.3	**License Lamp Lens Or Bulb, Renew**	
		Tail and Stop Lamp Lens or Bulb, Renew		All models (.2)	.2
Headlamp Sealed Beam Bulb, Renew		All models-one (.2)	.3	**Clearance Lamp Assembly, Renew**	
Does not include aim headlamps.		**Reflectors, Renew**		All models-one (.2)	.3
All models-one (.3)	.3	All models-one (.2)	.2	**Side Marker Lamp, Renew**	
				All models-one (.2)	.3

LABOR 31 WINDSHIELD WIPER & SPEEDOMETER 31 LABOR

(Factory Time)	Chilton Time	(Factory Time)	Chilton Time	(Factory Time)	Chilton Time
Windshield Wiper Motor, Renew		1987-90		**Speedometer Head, R&R or Renew**	
B-PB-CB Models		std colm (.8)	1.2	B-PB-CB Models	
1986-90 (.6)	.9	tilt colm (1.2)	1.6	1986-90 (.3)	.6
All other models		All other models		All other models	
1986-87 (.4)	.6	1986-88 (.4)	.6	1986-90 (.4)	.7
1987-90 (.7)	1.0	1989-90		Reset odometer add	.2
Windshield Wiper Pivot, Renew		std colm (.8)	1.2		
All models-one (.5)	.7	tilt colm (1.2)	1.6	**Speedometer Cable and Casing, Renew**	
Wiper Link, Renew		**Wiper Delay Control Module, Renew**		All models-each (.5)	.7
All models-one (.5)	.8	All models (.3)	.5		
Wiper Switch, Renew		**Windshield Washer Pump, Renew**		**Radio, R&R**	
B-PB-CB Models		All models (.3)	.5	All models (.3)	.5
1986 (.3)	.7				

LABOR 32 LIGHT SWITCHES & WIRING 32 LABOR

(Factory Time)	Chilton Time	(Factory Time)	Chilton Time	(Factory Time)	Chilton Time
Headlamp Switch, Renew		**Neutral Safety Switch, Renew**		w/Tilt column (.9)	1.4
1986-90 (.4)	.7	All models (.3)	.4	**Turn Signal or Hazard Warning Flasher,**	
Headlamp Dimmer Switch, Renew		**Stop Light Switch, Renew**		**Renew**	
All models (.3)	.5	All models (.3)	.4	All models (.2)	.3
		w/Cruise control add (.1)	.1	**Horn, Renew**	
Back-Up Lamp Switch, Renew		**Turn Signal Switch, Renew**		B-PB models (.3)	.4
(w/Manual Trans)		1986-90		All other models (.2)	.3
All models (.3)	.4	w/Std column (.5)	.9	w/A.C. or Aux. Oil Cooler add (.3)	.3

LABOR   34   CRUISE CONTROL   34   LABOR

	(Factory Time)	Chilton Time
Cruise Control Servo, Renew		
All models (.2)		.6
Cruise Control Cable, Renew		
All models (.3)		.5
Cruise Control Vacuum Hoses, Renew		
All models (.2)		.3

	(Factory Time)	Chilton Time
Cruise Control Switch (Turn Signal Lever), Renew		
1986-90		
w/Std column (.5)		.9
w/Tilt column (.9)		1.4
Cruise Control Cut-Off Safety Switch, Renew		
All models (.3)		.4

GROUP INDEX

ALPHABETICAL INDEX

LABOR — SERVICE BAY OPERATIONS — LABOR

	(Factory Time)	Chilton Time
COOLING		
Winterize Cooling System		
Includes: Run engine to check for leaks, tighten all hose connections. Test radiator and pressure cap, drain radiator and engine block. Add antifreeze and refill system.		
All models		.5
Thermostat, Renew		
1986-90 (.4)		.5
Drive Belts, Adjust		
All models-one		.2
each adtnl		.1
Drive Belts, Renew		
1986-90		
Water Pump		
2.6L eng (.3)		.3
Fan & alter (.2)		*.3
Air pump (.3)		.4
Pow str (.4)		*.6
P.S. & alter (.2)		*.3
A.C. (.2)		.3
*w/A.C. add (.1)		.1
Radiator Hoses, Renew		
1986-90-upper (.3)		.4
lower (.4)		.6
FUEL		
Carburetor Air Cleaner, Service		
All models		.3
Carburetor, Adjust (On Car)		
Includes: Adjust idle mixture and idle speed. Check and reset ignition timing.		
All models		
Holly 2 bbl		.6
All others		.5
Automatic Choke, Renew		
1986-87 (.7)		1.0

	(Factory Time)	Chilton Time
Carburetor Choke Vacuum Kick, Adjust		
1986-87		
Holly (.2)		.4
BRAKES		
Brake Pedal Free Play, Adjust		
All models		.3
Brakes, Adjust (Minor)		
Includes: Adjust brake shoes, fill master cylinder.		
two wheels		.4
Bleed Brakes (Four Wheels)		
Includes: Add fluid.		
All models (.4)		.6
Parking Brake, Adjust		
All models		.4
LUBRICATION SERVICE		
Lubricate Chassis, Change Oil & Filter		
Includes: Inspect and correct all fluid levels.		
All models		.6
Install grease fittings add		.1
Engine Oil & Filter, Change		
Includes: Inspect and correct all fluid levels.		
All models		.4
Lubricate Chassis		
Includes: Inspect and correct all fluid levels.		
All models		.4
Install grease fittings add		.1
WHEELS		
Wheels, Balance		
one		.3
each adtnl		.2
Wheel, Renew		
one		.5

	(Factory Time)	Chilton Time
Wheels, Rotate (All)		
All models		.5
ELECTRICAL		
Aim Headlamps		
two		.4
four		.6
Headlamp Sealed Beam Bulb, Renew		
Does not include aim headlamps.		
All models-each (.2)		.3
Halogen Headlamp Bulb, Renew		
All models-each (.2)		.3
License Lamp Lens, Renew		
All models (.2)		.2
License Lamp Assembly, Renew		
All models (.2)		.3
Turn Signal and Parking Lamp Assy., Renew		
All models (.2)		.4
Tail Lamp Assembly, Renew		
1986 (.5)		.8
1987-90 (.2)		.4
w/Dual rear doors add (.2)		.2
Side Marker Lamp Assy., Renew		
All models-each (.2)		.3
Turn Signal or Hazard Warning Flasher, Renew		
All models (.2)		.3
Horn Relay, Renew		
All models (.2)		.3
Horn, Renew		
1986-88-one (.2)		.4
1989-90 (.5)		.7
Battery Cables, Renew		
All models		
positive (.5)		.6
negative (.2)		.2

LABOR — 1 TUNE UP 1 — LABOR

	(Factory Time)	Chilton Time
Compression Test		
Four-1986-90		.6
V-6-1978-90		.8
Engine Tune Up, (Electronic Ignition)		
Includes: Test battery and clean connections. Tighten manifold and carburetor mounting bolts. Check engine compression, clean and adjust or renew spark plugs. Test resistance of spark plug cables. Inspect distributor cap and		

rotor, reluctor and pick up plate. Check vacuum advance operation. Reset ignition timing. Adjust idle mixture and idle speed. Service air cleaner. Inspect crankcase ventilation system. Inspect and adjust drive belts. Inspect choke operation and adjust or free up. Check operation of EGR valve.

	(Factory Time)	Chilton Time
Four-1986-90		1.5
V-6-1987-90		1.8
w/Turbo add		.5

LABOR — 2 IGNITION SYSTEM 2 — LABOR

	(Factory Time)	Chilton Time
Spark Plugs, Clean and Reset or Renew		
1986-90-Four (.3)		.6
V-6(.5)		.8
Ignition Timing, Reset		
1986-90 (.3)		.4
Spark Control Computer, Renew (SCC)		
1986-87 (.3)		1.0
Single Module Engine Controller, Renew		
1987-90 (.3)		.5

	(Factory Time)	Chilton Time
Electronic Control Unit, Renew		
1986-87		
2.6L eng (.3)		.5
Distributor Assembly, Renew		
Includes: Reset ignition timing.		
1986-90-Four (.5)		.8
V-6 (.5)		.8
w/Turbo add (.1)		.1
Distributor, R&R and Recondition		
Includes: Reset ignition timing.		
1986-90-Four (.9)		1.6
V-6 (1.0)		1.6

	(Factory Time)	Chilton Time
Distributor Pick-Up Plate and Coil Assy., Renew (Hall Effect)		
Does not require R&R of distributor.		
1986-90		
2.2L & 2.5L engs (.3)		.6
Distributor Control Unit or Disc, Renew		
1987-90		
V-6 (.6)		.9
Distributor Pick-Up Set, Renew		
Does not require R&R of distributor.		
1986-90		
2.6L & 3.0L engs (.5)		.7

LABOR · 2 IGNITION SYSTEM 2 · LABOR

(Factory Time)	Chilton Time
Distributor Ignitor Set, Renew	
Does not require R&R of distributor.	
1986-87	
2.6L eng (.4)	.6
Distributor Breaker Assy., Renew	
Does not require R&R of distributor.	
1986-87	
2.6L eng (.4)	.6
Distributor Reluctor and Governor Assy., Renew	
Does not require R&R of distributor.	
1986-87	
2.6L eng (.3)	.5

(Factory Time)	Chilton Time
Distributor Vacuum Advance Control Unit, Renew	
Does not require R&R of distributor.	
1986-87	
2.6L eng (.6)	.9
Distributor Cap and/or Rotor, Renew	
1986-90 (.2)	.4
Ignition Coil, Renew	
1986-90 (.2)	.4
Ignition Cables, Renew	
1986-90–Four (.2)	.4
V-6 (.3)	.5
Ignition Switch, Renew	
1986-90	
std column (.4)	.8

(Factory Time)	Chilton Time
tilt column (.4)	.9
Ignition Key Warning Buzzer or Chime, Renew	
1986-90 (.2)	.3
Ignition Switch Time Delay Relay, Renew	
1986-90 (.2)	.3
Ignition Key Buzzer/Chime Switch, Renew	
1986-90	
std column (.6)	1.2
tilt column (.5)	1.0
Ignition Lock Housing, Renew	
1986-90–std colm (.8)	1.3
Tilt Column	
console shift (1.1)	1.7
column shift (.8)	1.3

LABOR · 3 FUEL SYSTEM 3 · LABOR

(Factory Time)	Chilton Time
Fuel Pump, Test	
All models	.3
Carburetor Air Cleaner, Service	
All models	.3
Carburetor Idle Speed and Mixture, Adjust	
Includes: Check and reset ignition timing.	
All models	
Holly-2 bbl	.6
All others	.5
Idle Solenoid, Renew	
1986-87 (.4)	.6
Coolant Temperature Sensor/Switch, Renew	
1986-90 (.2)	.4
Choke Vacuum Kick, Adjust	
1986-87 (.2)	.3
Choke Vacuum Kick Diaphragm, Renew	
1986-87 (.2)	.4
Accelerator Pump, Renew	
1986-87	
Holly (.4)	.8
All others (.8)	1.1
Heated Air Door Sensor, Renew	
1986-90 (.2)	.3
Carburetor Assembly, Renew	
Includes: All necessary adjustments.	
1986-87	
Holly (.8)	1.3
All others (.7)	1.2
Carburetor, R&R and Clean or Recondition	
Includes: All necessary adjustments.	
1986-87	
Holly (1.2)	2.4
All others (2.5)	3.5
Carburetor Needle and Seat, Renew	
Includes: Adjust float level, idle speed and mixture.	
1986-87	
Holly (.7)	1.1
All others (1.1)	1.5
Fuel Filter, Renew	
1986-87	
in line (.2)	.3
in tank (.5)	.8
Fuel Pump, Renew	
1986-87 (.4)	.7
Add pump test if performed.	

(Factory Time)	Chilton Time
Fuel Tank, Renew	
1986-87 (.9)	1.4
1988-90 (1.1)	1.5
Fuel Gauge (Tank Unit), Renew	
1986-87 (.6)	1.0
1988-90 (1.1)	1.5
Fuel Gauge (Dash Unit), Renew	
1986-90 (.5)	.9
Intake Manifold or Gasket, Renew	
1986-90	
2.2L & 2.5L engs (2.2)	3.7
2.6L eng (1.9)	3.0
w/P.S. add (.4)	.4
Renew manif add (.2)	.5
Intake and Exhaust Manifold Gaskets, Renew	
1986-90	
2.2L & 2.5L engs (1.9)	3.5
w/P.S. add (.4)	.4
Two Piece Intake Manifold Gaskets, Renew	
1987-90	
3.0L eng-upper (.6)	.9
lower (1.3)	1.7
Renew manif add-each (.2)	.3
ELECTRONIC FUEL INJECTION	
Fuel Injectors, Clean (On Car) (w/TBI or MFI)	
Includes: Hook up pressurized fuel injection cleaning equipment.	
All models	.5
Fuel Filter, Renew	
in line (.3)	.4
in tank (.5)	.8
Throttle Body, Renew	
1987-90–Four (.7)	1.2
V-6 (.4)	.7
Fuel Pressure Regulator, Renew	
1987-90–Four (.2)	.4
V-6 (.7)	1.0
Fuel Pump, Renew (In Tank)	
1987–Four (.7)	1.0
V-6 (.7)	1.0
1988-90–Four (1.0)	1.4
V-6 (1.0)	1.4
Fuel Pump Relay, Renew	
1987-90 (.3)	.4

(Factory Time)	Chilton Time
Automatic Idle Speed Assy., Renew	
1987-90–Four (.3)	.5
V-6 (.5)	.7
Fuel Injector, Renew	
1987-90	
Four-one (.3)	.5
V-6-one (.8)	1.2
each adtnl (.1)	.2
Throttle Body Temperature Sensor, Renew	
1987-90 (.2)	.4
Fuel Injector Rail, Renew	
1987-90 (.8)	1.1
Throttle Position Sensor (Potentiometer), Renew	
1987-90–Four (.2)	.3
V-6 (.3)	.4
M.A.P. Sensor, Renew	
1987 (.4)	.6
1988-90	
under hood (.2)	.4
Automatic Shutdown Relay, Renew	
1988-90 (.2)	.3
TURBOCHARGER	
(G) Throttle Body, Renew	
1989-90 (.5)	.9
(G) Turbocharger Assy., R&R or Renew	
Includes: Renew gaskets.	
1989-90 (3.5)	4.9
(G) Fuel Pressure Regulator, Renew	
1989-90 (.3)	.5
(G) M.A.P. Sensor, Renew	
1989-90	
under hood (.2)	.4
(G) Throttle Position Sensor (Potentiometer), Renew	
1989-90 (.2)	.3
(G) Detonation Sensor, Renew	
1989-90 (.2)	.4
(G) Charge Temperature Sensor, Renew	
1989-90 (.2)	.4
(G) Fuel Pump, Renew (In Tank)	
1989-90 (1.0)	1.6
(G) Fuel Injector Rail, Renew	
1989-90 (.6)	1.0
(G) Fuel Injector, Renew	
1989-90-one (.3)	.5
each adtnl (.1)	.2

LABOR 3A EMISSION CONTROLS 3A LABOR

	(Factory) Time	Chilton Time
CRANKCASE EMISSION		
Crankcase Vent Valve, Renew		
1986-90 (.2)		.3
AIR INJECTION SYSTEM		
Air Pump, Renew		
1986-87		
2.2L & 2.5L engs (.4)		.7
Injection Tube and Check Valve Assy., Renew		
1986-87–2.2L & 2.5L engs		
ex manif mount (.5)		.8
to conv		
one or both (.4)		.6
EFI engs		
to conv (.5)		.8
Aspirator Valve, Renew		
1986-90 (.2)		.4
w/EFI add (.1)		.1
Air Pump Diverter/Switching Valve, Renew		
1986-87		
2.2L & 2.5L engs (.3)		.5
Aspirator Silencer, Renew		
1986-90 (.2)		.3
Enrichment Solenoid Valve, Renew		
1986-87		
2.6L eng (.3)		.4
Jet Air Control Valve, Renew		
1986-87 (.5)		.7
Jet Mixture Solenoid Valve, Renew		
1986-87		
2.6L eng (.4)		.6
Deceleration Solenoid Valve, Renew		
1986-87		
2.6L eng (.3)		.6

	(Factory) Time	Chilton Time
Thermal Check Valve, Renew		
1986-87		
2.6L eng (.2)		.3
Air Switching Valve, Renew		
1986-87		
2.6L eng (.4)		.5
Distributor/Air Switching Valve Solenoid Assy., Renew		
1986-87 (.2)		.3
Intake Air Temperature Sensor, Renew		
1986-87 (.2)		.3
EVAPORATIVE EMISSION		
Vapor Canister, Renew		
1986-90 (.3)		.4
Vapor Canister Filter, Renew		
1986-90 (.2)		.3
Vapor Canister Valve, Renew		
1986-90 (.2)		.3
E.G.R. SYSTEM		
Coolant Vacuum Switch, Renew (CCEVS)		
1986-87 (.3)		.4
Exhaust Gas Recirculation Control Valve, Renew		
1986-90		
2.2L & 2.5L engs (.6)		.7
2.6L eng (.4)		.5
3.0L eng (.4)		.5
E.G.R. and Purge Control Solenoid Bank, Renew		
1986-90 (.2)		.3

	(Factory) Time	Chilton Time
Coolant Vacuum Switch/Valve, Renew (CCEGR)		
1986-87–one (.3)		.5
both (.4)		.6
(G) Coolant Temperature Sensor/Switch, Renew		
1986-90 (.2)		.4
Emissions Maintenance Reminder Switch, Renew		
1988-90 (.3)		.5
EFE SYSTEM		
Oxygen Sensor, Renew		
1986-90		
2.2L & 2.5L engs (.2)		.4
2.6L eng (.5)		.7
3.0L eng (.4)		.6
Charge Temperature Sensor, Renew		
1988-90 (.2)		.4
High Altitude Compensator, Renew		
1986-87 (.3)		.5
HEATED INLET AIR SYSTEM		
Carburetor Air Cleaner, Service		
1986-90		.3
Air Cleaner Vacuum Sensor, Renew		
1986-90–one (.2)		.3
Heated Air Door Sensor, Renew		
1986-90 (.2)		.3
PULSE AIR SYSTEM		
Pulse Air Feeder, Renew		
1986-87 (.6)		.9
Pulse Air Feeder Tube, Renew		
1986-87 (.7)		1.1
EFI eng (.4)		.6

LABOR 4 ALTERNATOR AND REGULATOR 4 LABOR

	(Factory) Time	Chilton Time
Alternator Circuits, Test		
Includes: Test battery, regulator and alternator output.		
All models		.6
Alternator Drive Belt, Renew		
1986-90 (.2)		.3
w/A.C. add (.1)		.1
Alternator Assembly, Renew		
Includes: Transfer pulley if required.		
1986-90		
Four (.8)		1.2
V-6 (.7)		1.1

	(Factory) Time	Chilton Time
w/A.C. add (.3)		.3
Add circuit test if performed.		
Alternator, R&R and Recondition		
Includes: Test and disassemble.		
1986-90		
Four (1.5)		2.1
V-6 (1.4)		2.0
w/A.C. add (.3)		.3
Alternator Front Bearing or Retainer, Renew		
1986-90 (.9)		1.3
w/A.C. add (.3)		.3

	(Factory) Time	Chilton Time
Renew rear brg add		.2
Voltage Regulator, Test and Renew		
1986-90		
external type (.3)		.5
internal type		
Four (.9)		*1.6
V-6 (.8)		*1.5
*w/A.C. add (.3)		.3
Alternator Gauge, Renew		
1986-90 (.3)		.6
Gauge Alert Module, Renew		
1986-90 (.7)		1.1

LABOR 5 STARTING SYSTEM 5 LABOR

	(Factory) Time	Chilton Time
Starter Draw Test (On Truck)		
All models		.3
Starter Assy., Renew		
Includes: Test starter relay, starter solenoid and amperage draw.		
1986-90		
2.2L & 2.5L engs (1.0)		1.3
2.6L & 3.0L engs (.6)		1.0
w/Turbo add (.5)		.5

	(Factory) Time	Chilton Time
Starter, R&R and Recondition		
Includes: Turn down armature.		
1986-90		
2.2L & 2.5L engs		2.8
2.6L & 3.0L engs		2.5
w/Turbo add (.5)		.5
Renew field coils add (.5)		.5
Starter Drive, Renew		
Includes: R&R starter.		
1986-90		
2.2L & 2.5L engs (1.4)		1.8

	(Factory) Time	Chilton Time
2.6L & 3.0L engs (.8)		1.1
w/Turbo add (.5)		.5
Starter Solenoid or Switch, Renew		
Includes: R&R starter.		
1986-90		
2.2L & 2.5L engs (1.0)		1.4
2.6L & 3.0L engs (1.0)		1.4
w/Turbo add (.5)		.5
Starter Relay, Renew		
1986-90 (.2)		.3

LABOR — 5 STARTING SYSTEM 5 — LABOR

	(Factory Time)	Chilton Time
Neutral Start and Back-Up Lamp Switch, Renew		
1986-90 (.3)		.4
Battery Terminals, Clean		
All models		.3

	(Factory Time)	Chilton Time
Ignition Switch, Renew		
1986-90		
std column (.4)		.8
tilt column (.4)		.9

	(Factory Time)	Chilton Time
Battery Cables, Renew		
1986-90		
positive (.5)		.6
negative (.2)		.2

LABOR — 6 BRAKE SYSTEM 6 — LABOR

	(Factory Time)	Chilton Time
Brake Pedal Free Play, Adjust		
All models		.3
Brakes, Adjust (Minor)		
Includes: Adjust brake shoes, fill master cylinder.		
two wheels		.4
Bleed Brakes (Four Wheels)		
Includes: Add fluid.		
All models (.4)		.6
Free-Up or Renew Brake Self Adjusting Units		
one		.6
each adtnl		.4
Brake Shoes and/or Pads, Renew		
Includes: Install new or exchange brake shoes or pads. Adjust service and hand brake. Bleed system.		
1986-90-front-disc (.5)		.8
rear-drum (.8)		1.5
all four wheels (1.3)		2.2
Resurface disc rotor, add-each		.9
Resurface brake drum, add-each		.5
Rear Brake Drum, Renew (One)		
1986-90 (.5)		.6

BRAKE HYDRAULIC SYSTEM

	(Factory Time)	Chilton Time
Wheel Cylinder, Renew		
Includes: Bleed system.		
1986-90 (.7)		1.1
both (1.3)		2.1
Wheel Cylinder, R&R and Rebuild		
Includes: Hone cylinder and bleed system.		
1986-90-one		1.2
both		2.3
Brake Hose, Renew (Flex)		
Includes: Bleed system.		
1986-90-front-one (.4)		.8
rear-one (.4)		.8
each adtnl		.3
Master Cylinder, Renew		
Includes: Bleed complete system.		
1986-90 (.5)		.9
Master Cylinder, R&R and Rebuild		
Includes: Bleed complete system.		
1986-90		1.6

COMBINATIONS
Add to Brakes, Renew

See Machine Shop Operations

	(Factory Time)	Chilton Time
RENEW WHEEL CYLINDER		
Each		.3
REBUILD WHEEL CYLINDER		
Each		.4
REBUILD CALIPER ASSEMBLY		
Each		.4
RENEW MASTER CYLINDER		
All models		.6
REBUILD MASTER CYLINDER		
All models		.8

	(Factory Time)	Chilton Time
RENEW BRAKE HOSE		
Each		.3
RENEW REAR WHEEL GREASE SEALS		
One side		.3
RENEW DISC BRAKE ROTOR		
Each		.2
RENEW BRAKE DRUM		
Each		.3
DISC BRAKE ROTOR STUDS, RENEW		
Each		.1

	(Factory Time)	Chilton Time
Master Cylinder Reservoir, Renew		
Includes: Bleed complete system.		
1986-90 (.6)		1.0
Brake System, Flush and Refill		
All models		1.2

POWER BRAKES

	(Factory Time)	Chilton Time
Brake Booster Assembly, Renew		
1986-90 (.8)		1.2
Brake Booster Check Valve, Renew		
1986-90 (.2)		.2

DISC BRAKES

	(Factory Time)	Chilton Time
Disc Brake Pads, Renew		
Includes: Install new disc brake pads only.		
1986-90 (.5)		.8
Disc Brake Rotor, Renew		
1986-90-one (.3)		.6
Disc Brake Rotor and Hub, Renew		
1986-90-one (1.1)		1.4
Caliper Assembly, Renew		
Includes: Bleed system.		
1986-90-one (.5)		.7
both		1.2

	(Factory Time)	Chilton Time
Caliper Assy., R&R and Recondition		
Includes: Bleed system.		
1986-90-one (.8)		1.1
both		2.0
Brake System Combination Valve, Renew		
Includes: Bleed complete system.		
1986-90 (1.2)		1.5
Load Sensing Valve Actuator, Renew		
1986-90 (.3)		.5
Load Sensing Proportioning Valve, Renew		
Includes: Adjust valve and bleed brakes.		
1986-90 (.7)		1.0

PARKING BRAKE

	(Factory Time)	Chilton Time
Parking Brake, Adjust		
1986-90 (.3)		.4
Parking Brake Warning Lamp Switch, Renew		
1986-90 (.8)		1.1
Parking Brake Control, Renew		
1986-90 (.9)		1.4
Parking Brake Cables, Renew		
Includes: Adjust parking brake.		
1986-90-front (.5)		.7
intermediate (.3)		.5
rear-each (.6)		.8
assembly (1.0)		1.5

LABOR — 7 COOLING SYSTEM 7 — LABOR

	(Factory Time)	Chilton Time
Winterize Cooling System		
Includes: Run engine to check for leaks, tighten all hose connections. Test radiator and pressure cap. Drain radiator and engine block. Add antifreeze and refill system.		
All models		.5

	(Factory Time)	Chilton Time
Thermostat, Renew		
1986-90 (.4)		.6
Radiator Assembly, R&R or Renew		
1986-90 (.5)		.9
w/A.T. add (.1)		.1

	Chilton Time
ADD THESE OPERATIONS TO RADIATOR R&R	
Boil & Repair	1.5
Rod Clean	1.9
Repair Core	1.3
Renew Tank	1.6

LABOR — 7 COOLING SYSTEM 7 — LABOR

	(Factory Time)	Chilton Time
Renew Trans. Oil Cooler		1.9
Recore Radiator		1.7
Fan Blades, Renew		
1986-90 (.2)		.5
Drive Belts, Renew		
1986-90		
Water Pump		
2.6L eng (.3)		.4
Fan & alter (.2)		*.3
Pow str (.4)		*.6
A.C. (.2)		.3
Air pump (.3)		.4
P.S. & alter (.2)		*.3
*w/A.C. add (.1)		.1
Drive Belts, Adjust		
All models-one		.2
each adtnl		.1
Radiator Hoses, Renew		
1986-90-upper (.3)		.4
lower (.4)		.6
Water Pump, Renew		
1986-90		
2.2L & 2.5L engs (1.0)		1.6
2.6L eng (.7)		1.2
3.0L eng (2.2)		3.0
w/A.C. add		.3
Coolant Temperature Sensor/Switch, Renew		
1986-90 (.2)		.4
Radiator Fan Coolant Sensor, Renew		
1986-87 (.2)		.3
Radiator Fan Motor, Renew		
1986-90-wo/A.C. (.4)		.5
w/A.C. (.4)		.5
Condenser Fan Switch, Renew		
1986-87 (.3)		.6
Radiator Fan Motor Relay, Renew		
1986-90 (.2)		.3
Transaxle Auxiliary Oil Cooler, Renew		
1986-90 (.5)		.9
Water Jacket Expansion Plugs, Renew (Cylinder Block)		
1986-90		
2.6L & 3.0L engs		
right side		
front (.7)		1.0
center or rear (1.1)		1.5

	(Factory Time)	Chilton Time
left side		
upper front or center (2.1)		3.0
lower front or center (.3)		.5
rear (1.0)		1.4
rear of engine (3.7)		5.0
2.2L & 2.5L engs		
left side		
front (.7)		1.0
rear (.4)		.6
right side		
front or center (.6)		.9
rear (1.0)		1.4
w/P.S. add (.3)		.3
w/Pulse air add (.6)		.6
Water Jacket Expansion Plugs, Renew (Cylinder Head)		
1986-90		
2.2L & 2.5L engs		
front (.6)		.9
rear (.8)		1.1
2.6L eng		
rear (.5)		.7
Temperature Gauge (Dash Unit), Renew		
1986-90 (.3)		.6
Temperature Gauge (Engine Unit), Renew		
1986-90		
sending unit (.3)		.4
light switch (.3)		.4
Heater Hoses, Renew		
1986-90-one (.4)		.4
each adtnl (.1)		.2
Heater Water Valve, Renew (Front Heater)		
1986-90-w/A.C. (.3)		.5
Heater Control Assembly, Renew (Front Heater)		
1986-90-wo/A.C. (.4)		.7
w/A.C. (.3)		.6
w/Console add (.2)		.2
Vacuum Switch (Push Button), Renew		
1986-90-w/A.C. (.4)		.7
w/Console add (.2)		.2
Blower Motor Switch, Renew (Front Heater)		
1986-90-wo/A.C. (.4)		.7
w/A.C. (.5)		.8
w/Console add (.2)		.2
Heater Core, R&R or Renew (Front Heater)		
1986-90-wo/A.C. (1.8)		3.5
w/A.C. (2.4)		*5.5

	(Factory Time)	Chilton Time
1989-90-wo/A.C. (2.0)		3.7
w/A.C. (2.6)		*5.5
w/Console add (.2)		.2
*Includes: Recharge A.C. system.		
ADD THESE OPERATIONS TO HEATER CORE R&R		
Boil & Repair		1.2
Repair Core		.9
Recore		1.2
Heater Blower Motor, Renew (Front Heater)		
1986-90-wo/A.C. (.4)		.6
w/A.C. (.6)		1.2
Blower Motor Resistor, Renew (Front Heater)		
1986-90-wo/A.C. (.2)		.3
w/A.C. (.2)		.4
Rear Heater Coolant Line, Renew		
1987-90-w/A.C. (.4)		.5
wo/A.C. (.7)		1.0
Rear Heater Water Valve, Renew		
1987 (.9)		1.2
1988-90 (1.3)		1.7
Rear Heater Control Assembly, Renew		
1987-90		
wo/A.C. (.8)		1.2
w/A.C. (.3)		.5
Rear Heater Blower Motor Switch, Renew		
1987-90 (.4)		.6
Rear Heater Blower Motor, Renew		
1987-90		
wo/A.C. (.9)		1.3
w/A.C. (.7)		1.1
Rear Heater Blower Motor Resistor, Renew		
1987-90		
wo/A.C. (.8)		1.2
w/A.C. (.5)		.7
Rear Heater Blower Fan, Renew		
1987-90		
wo/A.C. (1.4)		2.0
w/A.C. (.9)		1.3
Rear Heater Core, R&R or Renew		
1987-90		
wo/A.C. (1.5)		2.2
w/A.C. (.7)		1.3
Rear Heater/A.C. Mode Motor, Renew		
1987-90 (.9)		1.3

LABOR — 8 EXHAUST SYSTEM 8 — LABOR

	(Factory Time)	Chilton Time
Muffler, Renew		
1986-90 (.4)		.7
Cut exhaust pipe add (.2)		.2
Exhaust Pipe, Renew		
1986-90 (.7)		1.1
Cut at muffler add (.2)		.2
Exhaust Pipe Extension, Renew		
1986-90 (.6)		1.0

	(Factory Time)	Chilton Time
Tail Pipe, Renew		
1986-90 (.4)		.6
Cut at muffler add (.2)		.2
Catalytic Converter, Renew		
1986-90		
exh pipe mount (.7)		.9
manif mount (.9)		1.3
Exhaust Manifold or Gasket, Renew		
1986-90		
2.2L eng (2.7)		3.7

	(Factory Time)	Chilton Time
2.5L eng (2.1)		3.3
2.6L eng (.7)		1.2
3.0L eng		
Front (.6)		1.0
Rear (.8)		1.2
w/P.S. add (.4)		.4
COMBINATIONS		
Exhaust System, Renew (Complete)		
1986-90		1.5

LABOR 9 FRONT SUSPENSION & HALFSHAFTS (FWD) 9 LABOR

Note: On all front suspension operations alignment charges must be added if performed. Time given does not include alignment.

	(Factory Time)	Chilton Time		(Factory Time)	Chilton Time
Wheel, Renew			**Wheels, Rotate (All)**		
one		.5	All models		.5

LABOR 9 FRONT SUSPENSION & HALFSHAFTS (FWD) 9 LABOR

(Factory Time)	Chilton Time
Wheels, Balance	
one	.3
each adtnl	.2
Check Alignment of Front End	
All models	.5
Note: Deduct if alignment is performed.	
Toe-Out, Adjust	
All models	.6
Align Front End	
Includes: Adjust camber, toe, car height and center steering wheel.	
All models (.8)	1.4
(G) Rear Suspension, Align	
All models	1.5
Steering Knuckle Bearing, Renew (Wheel Bearing)	
Add alignment charges.	
1986-90-one (1.1)	1.6
both (2.1)	3.0
Steering Knuckle, Renew (One)	
Add alignment charges.	
1986-88 (1.0)	1.6
1989-90 (1.2)	1.7
Front Wheel Bearing & Hub Assy., Renew	
1986-90-one (.5)	.7
both (.9)	1.3
Front Strut Assy., R&R or Renew	
Add alignment charges.	
1986-90-one (1.1)	1.4

(Factory Time)	Chilton Time
both (2.0)	2.7
Lower Control Arm Assy., Renew	
Includes: Reset toe-in.	
1986-90-one (1.1)	1.6
Lower Ball Joint, Renew (One)	
Add alignment charges.	
1986-90 (.8)	1.2
Lower Control Arm Strut Bushings, Renew	
Add alignment charges.	
1986-90-one side (.6)	.9
Front Coil Spring, Renew	
Includes: R&R front strut.	
Add alignment charges.	
1986-90-one (.8)	1.5
both (1.5)	2.8
Front Sway Bar, Renew	
1986-87 (.4)	.7
1988-90 (.3)	.5
Sway Bar Bracket and Bushings, Renew	
1986-87-both (.5)	.9
1988-90 (.3)	.5
Front Suspension Strut Mount Assy., Renew	
Includes: Renew bearing.	
1986-90 (.8)	1.5
K-Frame Assembly, Renew	
Add alignment charges.	
All models (2.5)	4.0

(Factory Time)	Chilton Time
Half Shaft Boot, Renew	
Includes: Clean and lubricate C/V joint.	
All models	
1986-90	
one-inner or outer (.7)	1.0
both-one side (1.0)	1.4
Renew shaft seal, add	
right side (.1)	.1
left side (.3)	.3
Half Shaft C/V Joint, Renew	
All models	
1986-90	
one-inner or outer (.7)	1.0
both-one side (1.0)	1.4
inter shaft U-joint (.6)	1.0
Renew shaft seal, add	
right side (.1)	.1
left side (.3)	.3
Front Wheel Half Shaft Assy., Renew	
All models	
1986-90	
inter spline yoke (.6)	1.0
inter stub shaft (.6)	1.0
all others-each (1.0)	1.4
Renew shaft seal, add	
right side (.1)	.1
left side (.3)	.3
Intermediate Shaft Support Bearing, Renew	
1986-90-each (.6)	1.0
Half Shaft Oil Seal, Renew	
All models	
1986-90	
right side (.5)	.8
left side (.7)	1.1

LABOR 11 STEERING GEAR 11 LABOR

(Factory Time)	Chilton Time
Tie Rods or Tie Rod Ends, Renew	
Includes: Reset toe-out.	
1986-88	
outer-one (.9)	1.2
inner & outer-w/P.S.	
one side (1.9)	2.5
1989-90	
outer-one (.9)	1.2
inner & outer-w/P.S.	
one side (2.2)	2.8
STANDARD STEERING	
Horn Contact Cable and Ring, Renew	
1986-90 (.2)	.4
Horn Switch, Renew	
1986-90 (.2)	.3
Steering Wheel, Renew	
1986-90 (.2)	.3
Steering Column Jacket, Renew	
Does not include painting.	
1986-90	
Std Column	
console shift (1.1)	1.8
column shift (1.5)	2.3
Tilt Column	
console shift (1.5)	2.6
column shift (1.6)	2.8
Upper Mast Jacket Bearing, Renew	
Includes: Replace insulators if necessary.	
1986-90	
std column (.4)	.9
tilt column (1.2)	2.0
Steering Column Gear Shift Tube, Renew	
1986-90	
std column (1.3)	2.1
tilt column (1.8)	2.6

(Factory Time)	Chilton Time
Steering Column Lower Shaft Bearing, Renew	
Includes: Replace support if necessary.	
1986-90	
Std Column	
console shift (.8)	1.6
column shift (.9)	1.7
Tilt Column	
console shift (.6)	1.0
column shift (.6)	1.0
Steering Gear Assy., R&R or Renew	
Add alignment charges.	
1986-90 (1.6)	3.0
POWER STEERING	
Power Steering Pump Pressure Check	
All models	.5
Power Steering Pump Belt, Renew	
1986-90 (.4)	.6
P.S. & alter belt (.2)	.3
w/A.C. add (.1)	.1
w/Air inj add (.1)	.1
Power Steering Gear Assy., R&R or Renew	
Includes: Reset toe-in.	
1986-90 (1.9)	3.1
Steering Gear Oil Seals, Renew (All)	
Includes: R&R gear assy. and reset toe-in.	
1986-88 (3.1)	5.1
Upper and Lower Valve Pinion Seals, Renew	
1986-87 (1.4)	2.0
Renew brgs add (.3)	.5

(Factory Time)	Chilton Time
Power Steering Pump, Renew	
Includes: Test pump and transfer pulley.	
1986	
2.2L & 2.5L engs (1.0)	1.4
2.6L eng (.8)	1.2
1987-90	
2.2L & 2.5L engs (1.2)	1.6
2.6L eng (.8)	1.2
3.0L eng (1.2)	1.6
Power Steering Pump, R&R and Recondition	
1986-90	
2.2L & 2.5L engs (1.6)	2.3
2.6L eng (1.3)	2.0
3.0L eng (1.6)	2.3
Pump Flow Control Valve, Test and Clean or Renew	
1986-90	
2.2L & 2.5L engs (.6)	1.0
2.6L eng (.7)	1.1
3.0L eng (.6)	1.0
Power Steering Reservoir or Seals, Renew	
1986 (.7)	1.1
1987-90	
2.2L & 2.5L engs (1.3)	1.8
2.6L eng (.7)	1.1
3.0L eng (1.3)	1.8
Pump Drive Shaft Oil Seal, Renew	
1986	
2.2L & 2.5L engs (.9)	1.4
2.6L eng (.7)	1.1
1987-90	
2.2L & 2.5L engs (1.3)	1.8
2.6L eng (.7)	1.1
3.0L eng (1.3)	1.8
Power Steering Hoses, Renew	
1986-90-each (.4)	.5

LABOR 12 CYLINDER HEAD & VALVE SYSTEM 12 LABOR

	(Factory Time)	Chilton Time
Compression Test		
Four–1986-90		.6
V-6–1987-90		.8
Cylinder Head Gasket, Renew		
Includes: Clean carbon.		
1986-90		
2.2L & 2.5L engs (3.2)		4.8
w/Turbo add (.5)		.5
2.6L eng (2.8)		4.5
3.0L eng		
front (4.2)		5.6
rear (4.6)		6.4
both (4.9)		6.9
w/A.C. add (.2)		.2
w/P.S. add (.2)		.2
w/Air inj add (.2)		.2
Renew timing belt add (.5)		.5
Cylinder Head, Renew		
Includes: Transfer parts as required. Clean carbon, make all necessary adjustments.		
1986-90		
2.2L & 2.5L engs (4.7)		6.5
w/Turbo add (.5)		.5
2.6L eng (4.7)		7.4
3.0L eng		
front (4.7)		6.1
rear (5.2)		7.2
both (6.1)		8.5
w/A.C. add (.2)		.2
w/P.S. add (.2)		.2
w/Air inj add (.2)		.2
Clean Carbon and Grind Valves		
Includes: R&R cylinder head. Reface valves and seats. Minor tune up.		
1986-90		
2.2L & 2.5L engs (4.8)		6.8
w/Turbo add (.5)		.5
2.6L eng (5.4)		8.0
3.0L eng		
front (5.2)		7.3
rear (5.6)		7.8
both (7.0)		9.8
w/A.C. add (.2)		.2
w/P.S. add (.2)		.2
w/Air inj add (.2)		.2

COMBINATIONS

Add To Valve Job

See Machine Shop Operations

	(Factory Time)	Chilton Time
DRAIN, EVACUATE & RECHARGE AIR CONDITIONING SYSTEM		
All models		1.0
CARBURETOR, RECONDITION		
Holly (.5)		.9
DISTRIBUTOR, RECONDITION		
All models (.7)		.7
RECONDITION CYL. HEAD (HEAD REMOVED)		
2.2L eng (1.4)		2.0
2.5L eng (1.4)		2.0
3.0L eng (3.6)		4.8
CAMSHAFT, RENEW (HEAD DISASSEMBLED)		
OHC engs (.1)		.2
VALVE GUIDES, REAM OVERSIZE		
Each		.2
REMOVE CYLINDER TOP RIDGE		
Each (.3)		.3
RENEW OIL PUMP		
All engs (.2)		.3
ROD BEARINGS, RENEW (PAN REMOVED)		
Four (.7)		1.2
V-6		1.8
DEGLAZE CYLINDER WALLS		
Each (.1)		.1
PLASTIGAUGE BEARINGS		
Each (.1)		.1
OIL FILTER ELEMENT, RENEW		
All models (.3)		.3

	(Factory Time)	Chilton Time
Cylinder Head Cover Gasket, Renew or Reseal		
1986-90		
2.2L & 2.5L engs (.7)		1.1
2.6L eng (.4)		.6
3.0L eng		
front (.3)		.5
rear (.5)		.7
Valve Rocker Arms or Shafts, Renew		
1986-90		
2.2L & 2.5L engs		
all arms (1.3)		1.8
2.6L eng-one shaft (1.0)		1.4
both shafts (1.1)		1.7
3.0L eng		
one head (.9)		1.3
both heads (1.8)		2.5
Valve Tappets, Renew		
1986-90		
2.2L & 2.5L engs		
one (1.3)		1.8
each adtnl (.1)		.1
3.0L eng		
one bank (.8)		1.2
both banks (1.6)		2.4
Valve Tappets, Adjust		
1986-87		
2.6L eng (.9)		1.5
Jet Valves, Renew		
1986-87		
2.6L eng-one or all (.9)		1.1
Valve Springs and/or Valve Stem Oil Seals, Renew		
1986-90		
2.2L & 2.5L engs		
one (1.5)		2.1
all (2.0)		3.0
2.6L eng (4.7)		6.0
*w/Head on car		3.5
3.0L eng		
one cyl (2.0)		2.8
all cyls (3.2)		4.5

LABOR 13 ENGINE ASSEMBLY & MOUNTS 13 LABOR

Note: All engine operations listed in this group are for assemblies as supplied by the original equipment manufacturer. Time to replace assemblies from independent rebuilders may vary.

Engine Assembly, Remove & Install
Includes: R&R engine and transmission as a unit. Does not include transfer of any parts or equipment.
1986-90
2.2L & 2.5L engs ... 6.0
w/M.T. add (1.0) ... 1.0
2.6L eng ... 5.2
3.0L eng ... 6.5
w/A.C. add 3
w/P.S. add 3
w/Turbo add 5

Short Engine Assembly, Renew (w/All Internal Parts Less Cyl. Head and Oil Pan)
Includes: R&R engine and transmission as a unit. Transfer all necessary parts not supplied with replacement engine. Minor tune up.
1986-90
2.2L & 2.5L engs (7.6) ... 13.0

w/M.T. add (1.0) ... 1.0
Recond valves add (1.4) ... 2.0
2.6L eng (7.2) ... 12.0
Recond valves add (2.6) ... 3.5
3.0L eng (7.2) ... 10.5
Recond valves add (3.6) ... 4.8
w/A.C. add (.3) 3
w/P.S. add (.3) 3
w/Turbo add 5

(G) Complete Engine Assembly, Renew
Includes: Transfer necessary parts as required.
2.6L eng ... 12.0
w/P.S. add 2
w/A.C. add 4

(P) Engine Assy., R&R and Recondition (Complete)
Includes: Rebore block, install new pistons, rings, rod and main bearings. Clean carbon, grind valves. Replace valve stem oil seals. Tune engine.
1986-90
2.2L & 2.5L engs (17.8) ... 25.2

w/M.T. add (1.0) ... 1.0
2.6L eng (17.0) ... 23.4
3.0L eng (19.5) ... 28.2
w/A.C. add (.3) 3
w/P.S. add (.3) 3
w/Turbo add 5

Engine Assembly, Recondition (In Car)
Includes: Expand or renew pistons, install rings, pins, rod and main bearings. Clean carbon, grind valves. Tune engine.
1986-90
2.2L & 2.5L engs (15.2) ... 20.8
2.6L eng (14.4) ... 19.0
3.0L eng (15.8) ... 22.3
w/A.C. add (.4) 4
w/Turbo add 5

Engine Support, Renew
1986-90-right side (.3) 5
left side (.3) 5
center (.4) 6
Trans/Axle
Roll rod (.2) 5

LABOR 14 PISTONS, RINGS & BEARINGS 14 LABOR

	(Factory Time)	Chilton Time
Rings, Renew (See Engine Combinations)		
Includes: Replace connecting rod bearings, deglaze cylinder walls, clean carbon. Minor tune up.		
1986-90		
2.2L eng		
one cyl (4.6)		6.9
all cyls (5.9)		8.1
2.5L eng		
one cyl (4.9)		7.1
all cyls (6.4)		9.2
2.6L eng-one cyl (4.1)		6.3
all cyls (5.7)		8.0
3.0L eng		
one cyl (4.4)		6.1
one cyl-each bank (5.4)		7.5
all cyls-both banks (7.7)		10.7
w/A.C. add (.2)		.2
w/P.S. add (.2)		.2
w/Air inj add (.2)		.2
w/Turbo add (.5)		.5

Pistons or Connecting Rods, Renew

Includes: Replace connecting rod bearings and piston rings, deglaze cylinder walls. Clean carbon from cylinder head.

	(Factory Time)	Chilton Time
1986-90		
2.2L eng		
one cyl (4.9)		7.2
all cyls (6.1)		9.3
2.5L eng		
one cyl (5.2)		7.5
all cyls (7.3)		10.5
2.6L eng-one cyl (4.7)		6.6
all cyls (7.2)		9.2
3.0L eng		
one cyl (4.4)		6.4
one cyl-each bank (5.4)		8.1
all cyls-both banks (7.8)		12.5
w/A.C. add (.2)		.2
w/P.S. add (.2)		.2
w/Air inj add (.2)		.2
w/Turbo add (.5)		.5

COMBINATIONS
Add To Engine Work

See Machine Shop Operations

	Chilton Time
DRAIN, EVACUATE & RECHARGE AIR CONDITIONING SYSTEM	
All models	1.0
CARBURETOR, RECONDITION	
Holly (.5)	.9
DISTRIBUTOR, RECONDITION	
All models (.7)	.7
R&R CYLINDER HEAD (ENGINE REMOVED)	
Four	1.5
CONNECTING ROD, RENEW (ENGINE DISASSEMBLED)	
Each	.4
RECONDITION CYL. HEAD (HEAD REMOVED)	
2.2L eng (1.4)	2.0
2.5L engs (1.4)	2.0
3.0L eng (3.6)	4.8
CAMSHAFT, RENEW (HEAD DISASSEMBLED)	
OHC engs (.1)	.2
REMOVE CYLINDER TOP RIDGE	
Each (.3)	.3
RENEW OIL PUMP	
All engs (.2)	.3
ROD BEARINGS, RENEW (PAN REMOVED)	
Four (.7)	1.2
V-6	1.8
DEGLAZE CYLINDER WALLS	
Each (.1)	.1
PLASTIGAUGE BEARINGS	
Each (.1)	.1
OIL FILTER ELEMENT, RENEW	
All models (.3)	.3

	(Factory Time)	Chilton Time
Connecting Rod Bearings, Renew (All)		
1986-90		
2.2L eng (2.1)		3.0
2.5L eng (2.6)		3.6
2.6L eng (1.2)		2.2
3.0L eng (2.4)		3.4
Renew oil pump add (.2)		.3

LABOR 15 CRANKSHAFT & DAMPER 15 LABOR

	(Factory Time)	Chilton Time
Crankshaft and Main Bearings, Renew		
Includes: R&R engine assembly.		
1986-90		
2.2L & 2.5L engs (7.3)		11.2
w/M.T. add (1.0)		1.0
w/Turbo add (.5)		.5
2.6L eng (7.6)		12.1
3.0L eng (6.5)		10.0
w/A.C. add (.3)		.3
w/P.S. add (.3)		.3
Main Bearings, Renew		
1986-90		
2.2L eng		
No 2-3 or 4 (1.8)		2.8
No 1 (3.0)		4.0
No 5 (5.6)		8.8
all (7.0)		11.0
2.5L eng		
No 2-3 or 4 (2.3)		3.2
No 1 (3.5)		4.9

	(Factory Time)	Chilton Time
No 5 (5.6)		8.8
all (7.3)		11.2
w/A.C. add (.3)		.3
w/P.S. add (.3)		.3
w/Turbo add (.5)		.5
No. 5 brg. w/A520-A555		
Trans/axle add (.3)		.3
2.6L eng (2.2)		3.0
3.0L eng (2.0)		2.8
Main and Rod Bearings, Renew		
1986-90		
2.5L eng (8.0)		12.4
2.6L eng (2.9)		4.2
3.0L eng (3.1)		4.6
Rear Main Bearing Oil Seals, Renew (Complete)		
1986-90		
2.2L & 2.5L engs (3.0)		5.4
2.6L eng-w/A.T. (3.2)		5.5

	(Factory Time)	Chilton Time
3.0L eng (3.0)		5.4
w/A520-A555		
Trans/axle add (.3)		.3
Crankshaft Pulley, Renew		
1986-90		
2.2L eng (.5)		.7
2.5L eng (.4)		.6
2.6L eng (.4)		.6
3.0L eng (.4)		.6
w/A.C. add (.2)		.2
w/P.S. add (.2)		.2
Crankshaft Front Oil Seal, Renew		
1986-90		
2.2L eng (1.3)		2.0
2.5L eng (1.1)		1.6
3.0L eng (1.4)		2.1
w/A.C. add (.2)		.2
w/P.S. add (.2)		.2

LABOR 16 CAMSHAFT & TIMING GEARS 16 LABOR

	(Factory Time)	Chilton Time
Timing Chain or Belt Case/Cover, Renew		
Includes: Renew gasket.		
1986-90		
2.2L & 2.5L engs		
upper cover (.2)		.4
lower cover (.6)		1.0
2.6L eng (3.2)		4.5
3.0L eng		
lower cover (1.0)		1.3

	(Factory Time)	Chilton Time
upper cover-one (.2)		.4
w/A.C. add (.2)		.2
w/P.S. add (.2)		.2
Timing Belt, Renew		
1986-90		
2.2L & 2.5L engs (1.6)		2.3
3.0L eng (1.3)		2.0
w/A.C. add (.2)		.2

	(Factory Time)	Chilton Time
w/P.S. add (.2)		.2
Balance Shafts Chain and/or Sprockets, Renew		
1986-90		
2.5L eng (2.4)		3.4
w/A.C. add (.6)		.6
w/P.S. add (.1)		.1
Renew carrier add (.6)		.6

LABOR 16 CAMSHAFT & TIMING GEARS 16 LABOR

(Factory Time)	Chilton Time
(G) Balance Shaft Chain Tensioner and/or Guide, Renew	
1986-90	
2.5L eng (1.2)	1.9
Balance Shaft Gears Cover, R&R or Renew	
1986-90	
2.5L eng (1.3)	1.8
Balance Shaft Gears, Renew	
1986-90	
2.5L eng (1.5)	2.1
Balance Shafts, Renew	
1986-90	
2.5L eng-one or both (1.8)	2.5
Balance Shaft Carrier, Renew	
Includes: Renew balance shafts if required.	
1986-90	
2.5L eng (1.8)	2.6
Timing Chain, Renew	
Includes: Renew cover seal.	
1986-87	
2.6L eng	
cam drive (3.6)	5.0
shaft drive (3.4)	4.8
w/A.C. add (.2)	.2
w/P.S. add (.1)	.1
Timing Chain, Adjust	
1986-87	
2.6L eng (.4)	.8
Timing Chain Guide, Renew	
1986-87	
2.6L eng-cam drive	
right or left (3.2)	4.6
silent shaft-upper (3.2)	4.6
lower (3.2)	4.6
w/A.C. add (.2)	.2
w/P.S. add (.1)	.1
Timing Chain Tensioner, Renew	
1986-87	
2.6L eng (3.5)	4.9

(Factory Time)	Chilton Time
w/A.C. add (.2)	.2
w/P.S. add (.1)	.1
Timing Belt Tensioner, Renew	
1986-90	
2.2L & 2.5L engs (.9)	1.5
3.0L eng (1.2)	1.8
w/A.C. add (.2)	.2
w/P.S. add (.2)	.2
Timing Chain Cover Oil Seal, Renew	
1986-87	
2.6L eng (.5)	.9
w/P.S. add (.1)	.1
Camshaft Sprocket, Renew	
Includes: Renew cover oil seal, timing chain and crankshaft sprocket, where required.	
1986-90	
2.2L & 2.5L engs (1.7)	2.4
2.6L eng (3.6)	5.0
3.0L eng	
front head (1.7)	2.4
rear head (1.7)	2.4
w/A.C. add (.2)	.2
w/P.S. add (.2)	.2
Camshaft Oil Seal, Renew	
1986-90	
2.2L & 2.5L engs-front (.7)	1.1
2.2-2.5-2.6L engs-rear (.4)	.8
3.0L eng	
front of engine	
one (2.1)	2.9
rear of engine	
front head (.5)	.8
rear head (.6)	.9
w/A.C. add (.2)	.2
Camshaft, Renew	
1986-90	
2.2L eng (1.7)	2.8
2.5L eng (1.4)	2.0
2.6L eng (1.6)	2.2

(Factory Time)	Chilton Time
3.0L eng	
front head (2.1)	2.9
rear head (2.1)	2.9
w/A.C. add (.2)	.2
Renew valve springs add	
Four (1.1)	1.1
V-6 (1.5)	1.5
Camshaft Distributor Drive Gear, Renew	
1986-87	
2.6L eng (.7)	1.1
Intermediate Shaft, Renew	
1986-90	
2.2L eng (1.3)	2.5
2.5L eng (1.4)	2.0
w/A.C. add (.2)	.2
w/P.S. add (.2)	.2
Silent Shaft Sprocket, Renew	
1986-87	
2.6L eng-one or both (3.4)	4.7
w/A.C. add (.2)	.2
w/P.S. add (.1)	.1
Intermediate Shaft Sprocket, Renew	
1986-90	
2.2L & 2.5L engs (1.7)	2.7
w/A.C. add (.2)	.2
w/P.S. add (.2)	.2
Silent Shaft, Renew	
1986-87	
2.6L eng-right (4.0)	5.6
left (5.0)	7.0
both (5.3)	7.5
w/A.C. add (.4)	.4
w/P.S. add (.1)	.1
Intermediate Shaft Oil Seal, Renew	
1986-90	
2.2L & 2.5L engs (1.1)	1.8
w/A.C. add (.2)	.2
w/P.S. add (.2)	.2

LABOR 17 ENGINE OILING SYSTEM 17 LABOR

(Factory Time)	Chilton Time
Oil Pan or Gasket, Renew or Reseal	
1986-90	
2.2L & 2.5L engs (1.0)	1.4
2.6L eng (.6)	1.0
3.0L eng (1.0)	1.4
Pressure Test Engine Bearings (Pan Off)	
All models	1.0
Oil Pump, Renew	
1986-90	
2.2L & 2.5L engs (1.3)	1.7

(Factory Time)	Chilton Time
2.6L eng (3.8)	5.2
3.0L eng (2.0)	2.8
w/A.C. add (.2)	.2
w/P.S. add (.1)	.1
Oil Pump, R&R and Recondition	
1986-90	
2.2L & 2.5L engs (1.7)	2.2
Oil Pressure Relief Valve Spring, Renew	
1986-90	
2.2L eng (1.6)	2.2

(Factory Time)	Chilton Time
2.5L eng (1.4)	2.0
2.6L eng (3.4)	4.7
3.0L eng (1.1)	1.5
Oil Pressure Gauge (Engine Unit), Renew	
1986-90 (.3)	.4
Oil Pressure Gauge (Dash), Renew	
1986-90 (.3)	.6
Oil Filter Element, Renew	
1986-90 (.2)	.3

LABOR 18 CLUTCH & FLYWHEEL 18 LABOR

(Factory Time)	Chilton Time
Clutch Self-Adjusting Mechanism, Renew	
1986-90 (.3)	.6
Clutch Release Cable, Renew	
1986-90 (.4)	.5
Clutch Release Lever and/or Seal, Renew	
1986-90 (.5)	.8

(Factory Time)	Chilton Time
Clutch Release Bearing or Fork, Renew	
1986-90 (2.8)	3.8
w/A520-A555	
Trans/axle add (.3)	.3
w/Turbo add (.3)	.3
Clutch Assembly, Renew	
1986-90 (2.9)	4.0

(Factory Time)	Chilton Time
w/A520-A555	
Trans/axle add (.3)	.3
w/Turbo add (.3)	.3
Renew input seal add (.2)	.2
Flywheel, Renew	
1986-90 (3.0)	4.2
w/A520-A555	
Trans/axle add (.3)	.3
w/Turbo add (.3)	.3

LABOR   19   MANUAL TRANSAXLE (FWD)   19   LABOR

(Factory Time)	Chilton Time	(Factory Time)	Chilton Time	(Factory Time)	Chilton Time
Half Shaft Boot, Renew		Renew shaft seal, add		w/A520-A555	
Includes: Clean and lubricate C/V joint.		right side (.1)	.1	Trans/axle add (.3)	.3
1986-90		left side (.3)	.3	w/Turbo add (.3)	.3
one-inner or outer (.7)	1.0	**Half Shaft Oil Seal, Renew**		Renew assy add (.4)	.6
both-one side (1.0)	1.4	1986-90–right (.5)	.8	Renew input shaft seal add	.2
Renew shaft seal, add		left (.7)	1.1	**Manual Trans/Axle Assy., R&R and**	
right side (.1)	.1	**Differential Gear Cover, Renew or Reseal**		**Recondition (Complete)**	
left side (.3)	.3	1986-90 (1.0)	1.3	1986-90 (5.5)	8.0
				w/A520-A555	
Half Shaft C/V Joint, Renew		**Selector Shaft Seal, Renew**		Trans/axle add (.3)	.3
1986-90		1986-90 (.8)	1.1	w/Turbo add (.3)	.3
one-inner or outer (.7)	1.0	**Selector Shaft Housing, Renew**		Renew ring gear and pinion add (.7)..	1.5
both-one side (1.0)	1.4	1988-90 (1.3)	1.7	Renew clutch assy add (.2)	.2
Renew shaft seal, add				**Manual Trans/Axle Assy., Recondition (Off**	
right side (.1)	.1	**Manual Trans/Axle Assembly, Remove &**		**Car)**	
left side (.3)	.3	**Install**		1986-90	
		Does not include transfer of any parts.		A460 (2.5)	3.9
Front Wheel Half Shaft Assy., Renew		1986-90 (2.7)	3.7	A465-A525 (2.8)	4.2
1986-90–each (1.0)	1.4			A520-A555 (3.2)	4.5

LABOR   21   SHIFT LINKAGE   21   LABOR

(Factory Time)	Chilton Time	(Factory Time)	Chilton Time	(Factory Time)	Chilton Time
MANUAL		**Selector Shaft Seal, Renew**		**Selector Lever, Renew**	
Gearshift Linkage, Adjust		1986-90 (.8)	1.1	1986-90 (.3)	.4
1986-90 (.2)	.4	**Trans/Axle Selector Shaft, Renew**		**Gearshift Mechanism, Renew**	
Gearshift Lever, Renew		1986-90 (1.3)	1.7	1986-87 (.4)	.8
1986-87 (.4)	.6	**Gearshift Selector Cable, Renew**			
Gearshift Control Rod and/or Swivel,		1986-90 (.9)	1.4	**Gearshift Control Cable, Renew**	
Renew		**Gearshift Crossover Cable, Renew**		1986-90 (.5)	.8
1986-90 (.3)	.4	1986-90 (.8)	1.3	**Throttle Lever Control Cable, Renew**	
Gearshift Mechanism, Renew		**AUTOMATIC**		1986-90 (.3)	.6
1986-90		**Throttle Linkage, Adjust**		**Gear Selector Dial, Renew**	
cable shift (.7)	1.1	1986-90 (.2)	.4	1986-90 (.7)	1.1

LABOR   23   AUTOMATIC TRANSAXLE (FWD)   23   LABOR

(Factory Time)	Chilton Time	(Factory Time)	Chilton Time	(Factory Time)	Chilton Time
A404 - A413 - A470		**Extension Housing, Reseal**		**Drive Shaft Seal, Renew**	
ON CAR SERVICES		1986-90 (.5)	.7	1986-90–right side (.5)	.8
Drain & Refill Unit		**Differential Gear Cover, Renew or Reseal**		left side (.7)	1.1
All models	1.2	1986-90 (.8)	1.2	**Transfer Gear Cover, Renew or Reseal**	
Oil Pressure Check		**Drive Shaft Boot, Renew**		1986-90 (.5)	.7
All models	.8	Includes: Clean and lubricate C/V joint.		**Transfer Gear Set, Renew**	
Check Unit For Oil Leaks		All models		Includes: R&R cover, renew bearing.	
Includes: Clean and dry outside of case and run		1986-90		1986-90 (1.0)	1.3
unit to determine point of leak.		one-inner or outer (.7)	1.0	**Governor Assy., Renew or Recondition**	
All models	.9	both-one side (1.0)	1.4	Includes: R&R oil pan.	
Neutral Safety Switch, Renew		Renew shaft seal, add		1986-90 (1.4)	2.4
All models (.3)	.4	right side (.1)	.1	**Governor Support and Parking Gear,**	
Transmission Auxiliary Oil Cooler, Renew		left side (.3)	.3	**Renew**	
1986-90 (.5)	.9	**Drive Shaft C/V Joint, Renew**		Includes: R&R oil pan.	
Oil Cooler Lines, Renew		All models		1986-90 (2.0)	2.9
Includes: Cut and form to size.		1986-90			
1986-90 (.4)	.6	one-inner or outer (.7)	1.0	**Oil Pan and/or Gasket, Renew**	
Throttle Linkage, Adjust		both-one side (1.0)	1.4	1986-90 (.7)	1.2
1986-90 (.2)	.4	inter shaft U-joint (.6)	1.0	**Oil Filter Element, Renew**	
Kickdown Band, Adjust		Renew shaft seal, add		Includes: R&R oil pan.	
1986-90 (.2)	.4	right side (.1)	.1	1986-90 (.8)	1.4
Throttle Valve Lever Shaft Seal, Renew		left side (.3)	.3	**Parking Lock Sprag, Renew**	
1986-90 (.5)	.8	**Front Wheel Drive Shaft Assy., Renew**		Includes: R&R oil pan.	
Valve Body Manual Lever Shaft Seal,		All models		1986-90 (1.6)	2.6
Renew		1986-90		**Accumulator Piston, Renew or Recondition**	
1986-90 (.3)	.6	inter spline yoke (.6)	1.0	Includes: R&R oil pan.	
		inter stub shaft (.6)	1.0	1986-90 (1.2)	2.2
		all others–each (1.0)	1.4		
		Renew shaft seal, add			
		right side (.1)	.1		
		left side (.3)	.3		

LABOR   23   AUTOMATIC TRANSAXLE (FWD)   23   LABOR

	Factory Time	Chilton Time
Kickdown Servo, Renew		
Includes: R&R oil pan.		
1986-90 (1.5)		2.5
Reverse Servo, Renew		
Includes: R&R oil pan.		
1986-90 (1.3)		2.2
Lock-Up Torque Converter Solenoid, Renew		
Includes: R&R oil pan.		
1986-90 (1.3)		2.2
Valve Body, Renew		
Includes: R&R oil pan.		
1986-90 (1.1)		2.1
Valve Body, R&R and Recondition		
Includes: R&R oil pan and renew filter.		
1986-90 (1.8)		3.2
SERVICES REQUIRING R&R		
Trans/Axle Assy., Remove & Install		
1986-90		
2.2L & 2.5L engs (2.7)		3.7
2.6L eng (3.0)		4.1
3.0L eng (3.0)		4.2
w/Turbo add (.3)		.3
Renew assy add (.4)		.6
Trans/Axle Assembly, Reseal		
Includes: R&R trans/axle and renew all seals and gaskets.		
1986-90		
2.2L & 2.5L engs (5.4)		7.0
2.6L eng (5.6)		7.4
3.0L eng (5.7)		7.5
w/Turbo add (.3)		.3
Trans/Axle Assy., R&R and Recondition		
Includes: Disassemble complete, clean, inspect and replace all parts as required.		
1986-90		
2.2L & 2.5L engs		12.5
2.6L eng		12.9
3.0L eng		12.5
w/Turbo add (.3)		.3
Flush conv and cooler lines add		.5
Kickdown Band, Renew		
1986-90		
2.2L & 2.5L engs (4.0)		4.9
2.6L eng (4.3)		5.3
3.0L eng (4.3)		5.3
w/Turbo add (.3)		.3
Reverse Band, Renew		
1986-90		
2.2L & 2.5L engs (4.2)		5.2
2.6L eng (4.5)		5.6
3.0L eng (4.5)		5.6
w/Turbo add (.3)		.3
Trans/Axle Case, Renew		
1986-90		
2.2L & 2.5L engs (7.7)		10.0
2.6L eng (8.0)		10.4
3.0L eng (8.0)		10.4
w/Turbo add (.3)		.3
Front and Rear Clutch Seals, Renew		
1986-90		
2.2L & 2.5L engs (4.2)		5.2
2.6L eng (4.5)		5.6
3.0L eng (4.5)		5.6
w/Turbo add (.3)		.3
Torque Converter, Renew		
1986-90		
2.2L & 2.5L engs (3.3)		4.0
2.6L eng (3.6)		4.4
3.0L eng (3.6)		4.4
w/Turbo add (.3)		.3

	Factory Time	Chilton Time
Torque Converter Drive Plate, Renew (w/ Ring Gear)		
1986-90		
2.2L & 2.5L engs (3.3)		4.0
2.6L eng (3.6)		4.4
3.0L eng (3.6)		4.4
w/Turbo add (.3)		.3
Front Oil Pump, Renew		
1986-90		
2.2L & 2.5L engs (3.7)		4.5
2.6L eng (4.0)		4.9
3.0L eng (4.0)		4.9
w/Turbo add (.3)		.3
Front Pump Oil Seal, Renew		
1986-90		
2.2L & 2.5L engs (3.3)		4.0
2.6L eng (3.6)		4.4
3.0L eng (3.6)		4.4
w/Turbo add (.3)		.3
Reaction Shaft and/or Bushing, Renew		
Includes: Renew front pump if necessary.		
1986-90		
2.2L & 2.5L eng (3.7)		4.5
2.6L eng (4.0)		4.9
3.0L eng (4.0)		4.9
w/Turbo add (.3)		.3
Trans/Axle Differential Assy., Recondition		
Includes: R&R trans/axle, completely recondition differential assembly only.		
1986-90		
2.2L & 2.5L engs (6.6)		9.0
2.6L eng (6.9)		9.4
3.0L eng (6.9)		9.4
w/Turbo add (.3)		.3

CHRYSLER TORQUEFLITE - A604

ON CAR SERVICES

	Factory Time	Chilton Time
(G) Drain & Refill Unit		
All models		1.0
(G) Oil Pressure Check		
All models		.8
(M) Check Unit For Oil Leaks		
Includes: Clean and dry outside of case and run unit to determine point of leak.		
All models		.9
(G) Neutral Safety Switch, Renew		
All models (.3)		.4
(G) Transmission Auxiliary Oil Cooler, Renew		
1989-90		
Ramvan-Caravan-Voyager (.5)		.9
All other models (.3)		.6
(G) Oil Cooler Lines, Renew		
Includes: Cut and form to size.		
All models (.4)		.6
(G) Extension Housing, Reseal		
1989-90 (.5)		.7
(G) Throttle Valve Lever Shaft Seal, Renew		
1989-90 (.5)		.8
(G) Valve Body Manual Lever Shaft Seal, Renew		
1989-90 (.3)		.6
(G) Differential Gear Cover, Renew or Reseal		
1989-90 (.8)		1.2
(G) Trans/Axle Solenoid Assy., and/or Gasket, Renew		
1989-90 (.3)		.5

	Factory Time	Chilton Time
(G) Half Shaft Boot, Renew		
Includes: Clean and lubricate C/V joint.		
All models		
1989-90		
one-inner or outer (.7)		1.0
both-one side (1.0)		1.4
Renew shaft seal, add		
right side (.1)		.1
left side (.3)		.3
(G) Half Shaft C/V Joint, Renew		
All models		
1989-90		
one-inner or outer (.7)		1.0
both-one side (1.0)		1.4
Renew shaft seal, add		
right side (.1)		.1
left side (.3)		.3
(G) Front Wheel Half Shaft Assy., Renew		
All models		
1989-90-each (1.0)		1.4
Renew shaft seal, add		
right side (.1)		.1
left side (.3)		.3
(G) Half Shaft Seal, Renew		
1989-90		
right side (.5)		.8
left side (.7)		1.1
(G) Transfer Gear Cover, Renew or Reseal		
1989-90 (.5)		.7
(G) Transfer Gear Set, Renew		
Includes: R&R cover, renew bearing.		
1989-90 (1.0)		1.3
(G) Oil Pan and/or Gasket, Renew		
1989-90 (.7)		1.0
(G) Parking Lock Sprag, Renew		
Includes: R&R oil pan.		
1989-90 (1.6)		2.2
(G) Accumulator Piston, Renew or Recondition		
Includes: R&R oil pan.		
1989-90 (1.2)		1.7
(G) Valve Body, Renew		
Includes: R&R oil pan and renew filter.		
1989-90 (1.1)		1.5
(P) Valve Body, R&R and Recondition		
Includes: R&R oil pan and renew filter.		
1989-90 (1.8)		2.5
SERVICES REQUIRING R&R		
(G) Trans/Axle Assy., Remove & Install		
All models		
1989-90 (3.0)		4.1
(P) Trans/Axle Assy., R&R and Recondition		
Includes: Disassemble complete, clean, inspect and replace all parts as required.		
All models		
1989-90 (7.4)		10.3
(G) Trans/Axle Assembly, Reseal		
Includes: R&R trans/axle and renew all seals and gaskets.		
All models		
1989-90		7.4
(P) Trans/Axle Differential Assy., Recondition		
Includes: R&R trans/axle, completely recondition differential assembly only.		
All models		
1989-90 (6.3)		8.8

LABOR 27 REAR SUSPENSION 27 LABOR

(Factory Time)	Chilton Time		(Factory Time)	Chilton Time		(Factory Time)	Chilton Time
Rear Wheel Bearings, Renew or Repack			both (1.6)	2.2		**Rear Spring Shackle, Renew**	
1986-90–one side (.6)	.9		**Lower Control Arm Bushings, Renew**			1986-90–one (.4)	.6
both sides (1.1)	1.7		1986-87–one side (.6)	1.0		**Rear Spring Bushing, Renew**	
Rear Wheel Grease Seal, Renew			**Stub Axle Spindle, Renew**			1986-90–each (.4)	.6
1986-90–one side (.4)	.7		1986-90–each (.5)	.7		**Rear Spring Front Hanger, Renew**	
Rear Shock Absorbers, Renew						1986-90–one (.7)	1.1
1986-90–one (.3)	.5		**Rear Wheel Mounting Studs, Renew**			**Rear Trailing Arm, Renew**	
both (.4)	.7		1986-90–one (.5)	.8		1986-90 (1.6)	2.3
Rear Springs, Renew			each adtnl	.1			
1986-90–one (.9)	1.2						

LABOR 28 AIR CONDITIONING 28 LABOR

(Factory Time)	Chilton Time
Note: If more than one item requires replacement where evacuation and discharging the system is already included in the operation, deduct 1.0 hour for each additional item to the times listed.	
Drain, Evacuate, Leak Test and Charge System	
All models	1.0
Flush Refrigerant System, Complete	
To be used in conjunction with component replacement which could contaminate system.	
All models	1.3
Partial Charge	
Includes: Leak test.	
All models (.4)	.6
Performance Test	
All models	.8
Vacuum Leak Test	
All models	.8
Compressor Drive Belt, Renew	
1986-90 (.2)	.3
C-171 COMPRESSOR	
Compressor Assembly, Renew	
Includes: Transfer parts as required. Pressure test and charge system.	
1986-88	
2.2L & 2.5L engs (1.4)	2.5
2.6L eng (1.9)	3.0
3.0L eng (1.4)	2.5
Compressor Clutch Field Coil, Renew	
1986-88	
2.2L & 2.5L engs (.6)	.9
2.6L eng (.9)	1.4
3.0L eng (.6)	.9
Compressor Clutch Pulley (w/Hub), Renew	
1986-88	
2.2L & 2.5L engs (.4)	.5
2.6L eng (.7)	1.0
3.0L eng (.4)	.5
Compressor Clutch Assembly, Renew	
1986-88	
2.2L & 2.5L engs (.6)	.8
2.6L eng (.9)	1.3
3.0L eng (.6)	.8
Compressor Front Cover Seal, Renew	
Includes: R&R compressor. Pressure test and charge system.	
1986-88	
2.2L & 2.5L engs (1.8)	3.1
2.6L eng (2.3)	3.6
3.0L eng (1.8)	3.1

(Factory Time)	Chilton Time
Compressor Rear Cover Seal, Renew	
Includes: R&R compressor. Pressure test and charge system.	
1986-88	
2.2L & 2.5L engs (1.7)	3.0
2.6L eng (2.2)	3.5
3.0L eng (1.7)	3.0
Compressor Center Seal, Renew	
Includes: R&R compressor. Pressure test and charge system.	
1986-88	
2.2L & 2.5L engs (1.9)	3.2
2.6L eng (2.4)	3.7
3.0L eng (1.9)	3.2
Compressor Shaft Gas Seal, Renew	
Includes: R&R compressor. Pressure test and charge system.	
1986-88	
2.2L & 2.5L engs (1.8)	3.1
2.6L eng (2.3)	3.6
3.0L eng (1.8)	3.1
A-590 COMPRESSOR	
VARIABLE DISPLACEMENT COMP.	
(G) Compressor Clutch Field Coil, Renew	
Includes: Replace pulley w/hub if necessary.	
1989-90 (.6)	.9
(G) Compressor Clutch Pulley (W/Hub), Renew	
1989-90 (.4)	.7
(G) Compressor Clutch Assembly, Renew	
1989-90 (.6)	.9
(G) Compressor Assembly, Renew	
Includes: Transfer parts as required. Pressure test and charge system.	
1989-90 (1.4)	2.0
(G) Compressor Front Cover or Seal, Renew	
Includes: R&R compressor. Pressure test and charge system.	
1989-90 (1.8)	2.5
(G) Compressor Rear Cover or Seal, Renew	
Includes: R&R compressor. Pressure test and charge system.	
1989-90 (1.7)	2.4
(G) Compressor Center Seal, Renew	
Includes: R&R compressor. Pressure test and charge system.	
1989-90 (1.9)	2.7
(G) Compressor Shaft Gas Seal, Renew	
Includes: R&R compressor. Pressure test and charge system.	
1989-90 (1.8)	2.5

(Factory Time)	Chilton Time
Expansion Valve, Renew	
Includes: Pressure test and charge system.	
1986-90	
Front (1.0)	1.7
Rear (1.5)	2.2
Renew receiver drier add	.2
Receiver Drier, Renew	
Includes: Add partial charge, leak test and charge system.	
1986-90 (.9)	1.6
Low Pressure Cut Off Switch, Renew	
Includes: Charge system.	
1986-87 (.9)	1.4
Low Pressure/Clutch Cycling Switch, Renew	
1986-90	
electric (.2)	.4
pressure activated (.2)	.4
Condenser Assembly, Renew	
Includes: Add partial charge, leak test and charge system.	
1986-90 (1.1)	2.0
Renew receiver drier add	.2
Evaporator Coil, Renew	
Includes: Add partial charge, leak test and charge system.	
1986-90	
Front (2.9)	4.5
Rear (1.7)	3.5
w/Console add (.2)	.2
Temperature Control Assembly, Renew	
1986-90 (.4)	.7
w/Console add (.2)	.2
Push Button Vacuum Switch, Renew	
1986-90 (.4)	.7
w/Console add (.2)	.2
Blower Motor Switch, Renew	
1986-90 (.5)	.8
w/Console add (.2)	.2
Temperature Control Cable, Renew	
1986-90 (1.2)	1.8
w/Console add (.2)	.2
Blower Motor, Renew	
1986-90 (.6)	1.2
Blower Motor Resistor, Renew	
1986-90 (.2)	.4
Vacuum Actuators, Renew	
1986-88	
outside air door (.2)	.4
heater/defroster door (.3)	.6
A/C mode door (.8)	1.5
1989-90	
outside air door (.2)	.4
heater/defroster door (.3)	.6
A/C mode door (.3)	.6

LABOR 28 AIR CONDITIONING 28 LABOR

(Factory Time)	Chilton Time
Air Conditioning Hoses, Renew	
Includes: Add partial charge, leak test and charge system.	
1986-90	
Suction Hose	
2.2L & 2.5L engs (1.1)	1.5

(Factory Time)	Chilton Time
2.6L eng (1.3)	1.7
3.0L eng (1.1)	1.5
Discharge Hose	
2.2L eng (1.1)	1.5

(Factory Time)	Chilton Time
2.6L eng (1.3)	1.7
3.0L eng (1.1)	1.5
Discharge/Liquid line	
rear (1.3)	1.7
Renew receiver drier add	.2

LABOR 30 HEAD AND PARKING LAMPS 30 LABOR

(Factory Time)	Chilton Time
Aim Headlamps	
two	.4
four	.6
Headlamp Sealed Beam Bulb, Renew	
Does not include aim headlamp.	
All models-each (.2)	.3
Halogen Headlamp Bulb, Renew	
All models-each (.2)	.3

(Factory Time)	Chilton Time
License Lamp Lens, Renew	
All models (.2)	.2
License Lamp Assembly, Renew	
1986-90 (.2)	.3
Turn Signal and Parking Lamp Assy., Renew	
All models (.2)	.3

(Factory Time)	Chilton Time
Tail Lamp Assembly, Renew	
1986 (.5)	.8
1987-90 (.2)	.4
w/Dual rear doors add (.2)	.2
Side Marker Lamp Assy., Renew	
All models-each (.2)	.3

LABOR 31 WINDSHIELD WIPER & SPEEDOMETER 31 LABOR

(Factory Time)	Chilton Time
Windshield Wiper Motor, Renew	
1986-90 (.4)	.6
Wiper/Washer Switch Assy., Renew	
1986-90	
std column (.8)	1.2
tilt column (1.1)	1.5
Rear Window Wiper/Washer Switch, Renew	
1986-90 (.5)	.7
Rear Window Wiper Motor, Renew	
1986-88 (.3)	.5
1989-90 (.5)	.7
Washer Pump, Renew	
1986-90	
front (.3)	.4

(Factory Time)	Chilton Time
rear (.7)	1.0
Wiper Link Assembly, Renew	
1986-90 (.5)	.7
Windshield Wiper Pivot, Renew	
1986-90-one (.4)	.6
Intermittent Wiper Control Module, Renew	
1986-90 (.2)	.4
Speedometer Head, R&R or Renew	
Does not include reset odometer.	
1986-90 (.6)	1.1
Reset odometer add	.2
Speedometer Cable and Casing, Renew	
1986-90	
upper (.5)	.9

(Factory Time)	Chilton Time
lower (.3)	.6
one piece (.6)	1.0
Speedometer Cable (Inner), Renew or Lubricate	
1986-90	
upper (.3)	.5
lower (.4)	.8
one piece (.4)	.8
trans to speedo (.3)	.5
Speedometer Drive Pinion, Renew	
Includes: Renew oil seal.	
1986-90 (.3)	.4
Radio, R&R	
1986-90 (.3)	.5
w/Console add (.2)	.2

LABOR 32 LIGHT SWITCHES & WIRING 32 LABOR

(Factory Time)	Chilton Time
Headlamp Switch, Renew	
1986-90 (.5)	.7
Headlamp Dimmer Switch, Renew	
1986-90 (.3)	.6
Back-Up Lamp Switch, Renew	
(w/Manual Trans)	
1986-90 (.2)	.4
Neutral Safety Switch, Renew	
1986-90 (.3)	.4
Stop Light Switch, Renew	
1986-90 (.3)	.4
w/Cruise control add (.1)	.1

(Factory Time)	Chilton Time
Parking Brake Warning Lamp Switch, Renew	
1986-90 (.8)	1.1
Turn Signal Switch, Renew	
1986-90	
std column (.6)	1.0
tilt column (.8)	1.5
Turn Signal or Hazard Warning Flasher, Renew	
1986-90 (.2)	.3

(Factory Time)	Chilton Time
Horn, Renew	
1986-88-one (.2)	.4
1989-90-one (.5)	.7
Horn Relay, Renew	
1986-90 (.2)	.3
Horn Switch, Renew	
1986-90 (.2)	.3
Wiring Harness, Renew	
1986-90	
Main harness to dash (2.7)	4.5
Body harness (1.3)	2.5
Intermediate harness (.9)	1.7

LABOR 34 CRUISE CONTROL 34 LABOR

(Factory Time)	Chilton Time
Speed Control Servo Assy., Renew	
1986-87 (.3)	.5
1988-90 (.5)	.7
w/Turbo add (.1)	.1
Speed Control Cable, Renew	
1986-90 (.4)	.6

(Factory Time)	Chilton Time
Speed Control Turn Signal Lever Switch, Renew	
1986-90	
std column (.5)	.9
tilt column (1.0)	1.5
Speed Control Wiring Harness, Renew	
1986-90 (.3)	.6

(Factory Time)	Chilton Time
Speed Control Safety (Cut-Out) Switch, Renew	
1986-87 (.3)	.4
Electronic Speed Control Module, Renew	
1986-90 (.3)	.4
Speed Control Vacuum Hoses, Renew	
1986-90 (.2)	.4

GROUP INDEX

ALPHABETICAL INDEX

LABOR   1   TUNE UP   1   LABOR

	(Factory Time)	Chilton Time
Compression Test		
Four		.5
V-6		.7

Engine Tune Up, (Electronic Ignition)
Includes: Test battery and clean connections. Tighten manifold and carburetor mounting bolts. Check engine compression, clean and adjust or renew spark plugs. Test resistance of

spark plug cables. Inspect distributor cap and rotor. Check vacuum advance operation. Reset ignition timing. Adjust idle mixture and idle speed. Service carburetor air cleaner. Inspect crankcase ventilation system. Inspect and adjust drive belts. Inspect choke operation and adjust or free up. Check operation of EGR valve.

	(Factory Time)	Chilton Time
Four		1.5
V-6		1.8

LABOR   2   IGNITION SYSTEM   2   LABOR

	(Factory Time)	Chilton Time
Spark Plugs, Clean and Reset or Renew		
Four (.3)		.4
V-6 (.5)		.6
Ignition Timing, Reset		
All models (.3)		.5
Distributor, Renew		
Includes: Reset ignition timing and renew oil seal if required.		
Four (.5)		.8
V-6 (.5)		.8
Distributor, R&R and Recondition		
Includes: Reset ignition timing.		
Four (1.0)		1.5
V-6 (1.0)		1.5
Distributor Pick-Up Plate and Coil Assembly, Renew		
Includes: R&R distributor, reset ignition timing.		
Four (.5)		1.0

	(Factory Time)	Chilton Time
V-6 (.5)		1.0
w/Dual coil add (.1)		.1
Electronic Distributor Reluctor, Renew		
Includes: R&R distributor and reset ignition timing.		
Four (.5)		1.0
V-6 (.5)		1.0
Vacuum Control Unit, Renew		
Includes: R&R distributor and reset ignition timing.		
Four (.5)		.9
V-6 (.5)		.9
Distributor Cap and/or Rotor, Renew		
All models (.3)		.5
Electronic Ignition Control Unit, Renew		
All models (.2)		.4

	(Factory Time)	Chilton Time
Single Module Engine Controller, Renew		
All models (.3)		.5
Ignition Cables, Renew		
Four (.3)		.4
V-6 (.2)		.6
Spark Control Computer, Renew		
All models (.2)		.4
Ignition Coil, Renew		
All models (.3)		.5
Electronic Ignition Ballast Resistor, Renew		
All models (.2)		.4
Ignition Switch, Renew		
All models		
std colm (.7)		1.2
tilt colm (.4)		.7

LABOR   3   FUEL SYSTEM   3   LABOR

	(Factory Time)	Chilton Time
Fuel Pump, Test		
Includes: Disconnect line at carburetor, attach pressure gauge.		
All models		.3
Fuel Filter, Renew		
All models		
in line (.2)		.3
in tank (.9)		1.3
Carburetor, Adjust (On Truck)		
All models (.6)		.8
Air Cleaner Vacuum Diaphragm, Renew		
All models (.2)		.3
Air Cleaner Vacuum Sensor, Renew		
All models (.2)		.3
Coolant Temperature Sensor/Switch, Renew		
All models (.3)		.4
Choke Vacuum Kick, Adjust		
All models (.2)		.3
Choke Vacuum Kick, Renew		
All models (.2)		.4
Accelerator Pump, Renew		
All models (.4)		.8
Needle Valve and Seat, Renew		
Includes: Reset float level.		
All models (.4)		.7
Choke Control Switch, Renew		
All models (.2)		.4
Carburetor, Renew		
Includes: All necessary adjustments.		
All models		
Holly 2 bbl (.6)		1.0

	(Factory Time)	Chilton Time
Carburetor, R&R and Clean or Recondition		
Includes: All necessary adjustments.		
All models		
Holly 2 bbl (1.5)		2.4
Fuel Pump, Renew (Mechanical)		
Four (.5)		.7
V-6 (.5)		.7
Add pump test if performed.		
Fuel Tank, Renew		
Includes: Drain and refill tank, transfer or renew tank gauge.		
All models (1.0)		1.4
Fuel Gauge (Tank Unit), Renew		
All models (1.0)		1.4
Fuel Gauge (Dash Unit), Renew		
All models (.6)		1.1
Intake and Exhaust Manifold Gaskets, Renew		
Four (1.8)		2.5
w/A.C. add (.2)		.2
Renew intake manif add		.4
Intake Manifold Gaskets, Renew		
V-6 (1.9)		2.7
w/A.C. add (.4)		.4
w/AIR inj add (.3)		.3
Renew manif add		.5

ELECTRONIC FUEL INJECTION

	(Factory Time)	Chilton Time
Fuel Pump, Test		
All models		
electric		.4

	(Factory Time)	Chilton Time
Air Cleaner, Service		
All models		.2
Fuel Filter, Renew		
All models		
in line (.2)		.3
in tank (.9)		1.3
Fuel Injectors, Clean (On Truck) (w/TBI or MFI)		
Includes: Hook up pressurized fuel injection cleaning equipment.		
All models		.5
Throttle Body, Renew		
V-6 (.6)		1.0
Fuel Pressure Regulator, Renew		
V-6 (.3)		.5
Fuel Pump, Renew (In Tank)		
V-6 (.9)		1.3
Automatic Idle Speed Motor, Renew		
V-6 (.3)		.5
Fuel Injector, Renew		
V-6 (.3)		.5
Throttle Body Temperature Sensor, Renew		
V-6 (.2)		.4
Throttle Position Sensor (Potentiometer), Renew		
V-6 (.3)		.4
M.A.P. Sensor, Renew		
V-6 (.2)		.4
Automatic Shutdown Relay, Renew		
V-6 (.2)		.3

CHRYSLER CORPORATION
DAKOTA

SECTION 15

LABOR — 3A EMISSION CONTROLS 3A — LABOR

(Factory Time)	Chilton Time
CRANKCASE EMISSION	
Positive Crankcase Ventilation Valve, Renew	
All models (.2)	.3
EVAPORATIVE EMISSION	
Vapor Canister or Filter, Renew	
All models (.2)	.3
AIR INJECTION SYSTEM	
Air Pump, Renew	
Four (.4)	.7
V-6 (.5)	.8
Aspirator, Renew	
All models (.2)	.4
Diverter/Control Valve, Renew	
Four (.2)	.3
V-6 (.3)	.4
Injection Tube and Check Valve Assy., Renew	
Four (.7)	1.0
V-6 (.6)	.9

(Factory Time)	Chilton Time
Orifice Spark Advance Control Valve, Renew	
All models (.2)	.4
HEATED AIR SYSTEM	
Air Cleaner Vacuum Diaphragm, Renew	
All models (.2)	.3
Air Cleaner Vacuum Sensor, Renew	
All models (.2)	.3
EXHAUST GAS RECIRCULATION SYSTEM	
E.G.R. Valve, Renew	
1986-88	
Four (.7)	1.0
V-6 (.3)	.5
1988-90	
Four (.2)	.4
V-6 (.3)	.5
Coolant Vacuum Switch Valve, Renew	
All models (.2)	.3
Idle/EGR Speed Switch Timer, Renew	
All models (.2)	.4

(Factory Time)	Chilton Time
E.G.R. Vacuum Amplifier, Renew	
All models (.2)	.4
Charge Temperature Switch, Renew	
All models (.2)	.3
EGR/Purge Control Solenoid Bank, Renew	
All models (.2)	.3
Coolant Temperature Sensor/Switch, Renew	
All models (.3)	.5
E.F.C. SYSTEM	
Oxygen Sensor, Renew	
All models (.2)	.4
Carburetor Solenoid, Renew	
All models (.6)	1.0
Electronic Speed Switch, Renew	
All models (.2)	.4
Emission Maintenance Reminder Module, Renew	
All models (.4)	.6
High Altitude Compensator, Renew	
All models (.3)	.5

LABOR — 4 ALTERNATOR AND REGULATOR 4 — LABOR

(Factory Time)	Chilton Time
Alternator Circuits, Test	
Includes: Test battery, regulator and alternator output.	
All models	.6
Alternator, Renew	
Four (1.0)	1.3
V-6 (.7)	1.0
Add circuit test if performed.	

(Factory Time)	Chilton Time
Alternator, R&R and Recondition	
Four	2.3
V-6	2.0
Add circuit test if performed.	
Alternator Drive End Frame Bearing, Renew	
Four (.8)	1.1

(Factory Time)	Chilton Time
V-6 (.6)	.9
Renew rear brg add	.2
Voltage Regulator, Test and Renew	
All models (.3)	.6
Alternator Gauge, Renew	
All models (.6)	1.1

LABOR — 5 STARTING SYSTEM 5 — LABOR

(Factory Time)	Chilton Time
Starter Draw Test (On Truck)	
All models	.3
Starter, Renew	
Four (.9)	1.2
V-6 (.8)	1.1
Starter, R&R and Recondition	
Four (1.9)	2.6
V-6 (1.8)	2.5

(Factory Time)	Chilton Time
Renew field coils add	.5
Add draw test if performed.	
Starter Drive, Renew	
Includes: R&R starter.	
Four (1.2)	1.5
V-6 (1.1)	1.4
Starter Solenoid, Renew	
Includes: R&R starter.	
Four (1.2)	1.5

(Factory Time)	Chilton Time
V-6 (1.1)	1.4
Starter Relay, Renew	
All models (.2)	.3
Battery Cables, Renew	
All models-positive (.3)	.4
negative (.2)	.3
Battery Terminals, Clean	
All models	.3

LABOR — 6 BRAKE SYSTEM 6 — LABOR

(Factory Time)	Chilton Time
Brakes, Adjust (Minor)	
Includes: Adjust brakes, fill master cylinder.	
two wheels	.5
Brake Pedal Free Play, Adjust	
All models	.4
Bleed Brakes (Four Wheels)	
Includes: Fill master cylinder.	
All models (.4)	.6
Rear Brake Drum, Renew	
All models-one (.3)	.6

(Factory Time)	Chilton Time
Brake Shoes and/or Pads, Renew	
Includes: Install new or exchange brake shoes or pads. Service adjusters. Adjust service and hand brake. Bleed system.	
All models	
front-disc (.6)	1.1
rear-drum (.7)	1.4
all four wheels	2.3
Resurface brake rotor add, each	.9
Resurface brake drum add, each	.5
BRAKE HYDRAULIC SYSTEM	
Wheel Cylinders, Renew	
Includes: Bleed brake system.	
All models-one (.8)	1.3

(Factory Time)	Chilton Time
both (1.5)	2.4
Wheel Cylinders, R&R and Recondition	
Includes: Bleed brake system.	
All models-one	1.5
both	2.8
Brake Hose, Renew (Flex)	
Includes: Bleed system.	
All models	
front-one (.4)	.6
rear-one (.5)	.7
each adtnl	.3

15-77

LABOR 6 BRAKE SYSTEM 6 LABOR

(Factory Time)	Chilton Time
Master Cylinder, Renew	
Includes: Bleed brake system.	
All models	
w/Manual brks (.6)	1.0
w/Power brks (.4)	.8
Master Cylinder, R&R and Recondition	
Includes: Bleed brake system.	
All models	
w/Manual brks	1.7
w/Power brks	1.5
Master Cylinder Reservoir, Renew	
Includes: Bleed system.	
All models (.6)	1.0
Brake System Combination Valve, Renew	
Includes: Bleed brake system.	
All models (.8)	1.2

POWER BRAKES

Power Brake Unit, Renew	
All models (1.0)	1.4
w/A.C. add (.1)	.1
Power Brake Check Valve, Renew	
All models (.2)	.3

DISC BRAKES

Brake Shoes and/or Pads, Renew	
Includes: Install new or exchange brake shoes or pads. Service adjusters. Adjust service and hand brake. Bleed system.	
All models	
front-disc (.6)	1.1
rear-drum (.7)	1.4
all four wheels	2.3
Resurface brake rotor add, each	.9
Resurface brake drum add, each	.5

COMBINATIONS

Add to Brakes, Renew

See Machine Shop Operations

(Factory Time)	Chilton Time
RENEW WHEEL CYLINDER	
Each	.2
REBUILD WHEEL CYLINDER	
Each	.3
RENEW BRAKE HOSE	
Each	.3
REBUILD CALIPER ASSEMBLY	
Each	.4
RENEW BRAKE DRUM	
Each	.3
RENEW DISC BRAKE ROTOR	
Each	.4
RENEW REAR WHEEL GREASE SEALS OR BEARINGS	
Each side	.2
FRONT WHEEL BEARINGS, CLEAN AND REPACK (BOTH WHEELS)	
All models	.6
DISC BRAKE ROTOR STUD, RENEW	
Each	.1

(Factory Time)	Chilton Time
Disc Brake Pads, Renew	
Includes: Install new disc brake pads only.	
All models (.6)	1.1
Disc Brake Rotor (w/Hub), Renew (One)	
All models	
7¼ axle (.5)	.7

(Factory Time)	Chilton Time
8¼ axle (.5)	.7
Disc Brake Caliper Assy., Renew	
Includes: Bleed front brake lines only.	
All models-one (.6)	.8
both	1.3
Caliper Assy., R&R and Recondition	
Includes: Bleed front brake lines only.	
All models-one (.8)	1.2
both	2.1
Load Sensing Proportioning Valve, Renew	
Includes: Adjust brakes and bleed system.	
All models (.7)	1.0
Load Sensing Proportioning Valve Lever or Actuator, Renew	
All models (.3)	.5

PARKING BRAKE

Parking Brake, Adjust	
All models (.3)	.5
Parking Brake Lever Assembly, Renew	
1986-88 (.4)	.7
1989-90 (.6)	.9
Parking Brake Cables, Renew	
All models	
front (.6)	.8
intermediate (.3)	.5
rear (.6)	.8

ANTI-SKID BRAKE SYSTEM (ABS)

Anti-Lock Brake Solenoid Valve, Renew	
All models (.7)	1.0
Anti-Lock Brake Control Module, Renew	
All models (.7)	1.0
Anti-Lock Speed Sensor, Renew	
All models-one (.3)	.5

LABOR 7 COOLING SYSTEM 7 LABOR

(Factory Time)	Chilton Time
Winterize Cooling System	
Includes: Run engine to check for leaks, tighten all hose connections. Test radiator and pressure cap, drain radiator and engine block. Add anti-freeze and refill system.	
All models	.5
Thermostat, Renew	
All models (.4)	.6
w/A.C. add (.1)	.1
Radiator Assembly, R&R or Renew	
All models (.7)	1.3
w/A.T. add (.1)	.1
w/Aux trans cooler add (.1)	.1

ADD THESE OPERATIONS TO RADIATOR R&R

Boil & Repair	1.5
Rod Clean	1.9
Repair Core	1.3
Renew Tank	1.6
Renew Trans. Oil Cooler	1.9
Recore Radiator	1.7
Drive Belts, Renew	
Alter. (.2)	.3
P.S. (.2)	.3
A.C. (.2)	.3
Air inj (.2)	.3
*w/P.S. add (.2)	.2
*w/A.C. add (.1)	.1
*w/Air inj add (.1)	.1

(Factory Time)	Chilton Time
Drive Belts, Adjust	
All models-one (.2)	.3
each adtnl	.1
Radiator Hoses, Renew	
All models	
upper (.4)	.6
lower (.4)	.6
by-pass (.3)	.5
w/A.C. add (.1)	.1
*w/Air inj add (.1)	.1
Fluid Fan Drive, Renew	
All models (.5)	.7
w/A.C. add (.1)	.1
w/Air inj add (.1)	.1
Water Pump, Renew	
Four (1.1)	1.6
V-6 (1.0)	1.5
w/A.C. add (.3)	.3
w/P.S. add (.2)	.2
w/Air inj add (.2)	.2
Water Jacket Expansion Plugs, Renew Engine Block	
Four	
Front	
right side-one (.6)	.9
all (1.0)	1.7
Left side	
upper (.9)	1.3
lower (.5)	.8

(Factory Time)	Chilton Time
V-6	
Side	
front or center (.6)	1.1
right rear (.8)	1.0
left rear (.8)	1.2
Front	
right or left (.4)	.7
Engine Rear	
w/A.T. (2.9)	4.0
Water Jacket Expansion Plugs, Renew Cylinder Head	
V-6	
front-one (.3)	.6
rear (3.1)	4.2
Temperature Gauge (Engine Unit), Renew	
All models (.3)	.5
Temperature Gauge (Dash Unit), Renew	
All models (.6)	1.1
Coolant Temperature Sensor/Switch, Renew	
All models (.3)	.5
Heater Core, R&R or Renew	
All models	
wo/A.C. (1.9)	3.0
w/A.C. (2.6)	*5.0
*Includes: Recharge A.C. system.	

ADD THESE OPERATIONS TO HEATER CORE R&R

Boil & Repair	1.2
Repair Core	.9

LABOR — 7 COOLING SYSTEM 7 — LABOR

(Factory Time)	Chilton Time
Recore	1.2
Heater Hose, Renew	
All models-one (.4)	.5
each adtnl	.2
Heater Water Valve, Renew	
All models (.4)	.6

(Factory Time)	Chilton Time
Heater Blower Motor, Renew	
All models (1.1)	1.6
Heater Blower Motor Resistor, Renew	
All models (.2)	.4

(Factory Time)	Chilton Time
Heater Blower Motor Switch, Renew	
All models (.4)	.7
Temperature Control Assembly, Renew	
All models	
wo/A.C. (.3)	.5
w/A.C. (.5)	.8

LABOR — 8 EXHAUST SYSTEM 8 — LABOR

(Factory Time)	Chilton Time
Muffler, Renew	
All models (.5)	.8
Renew exh pipe add	.3
Tail Pipe, Renew	
All models (.4)	.7
Exhaust Pipe, Renew	
Four (.6)	1.0
V-6 (.8)	1.2
4X4 add (1.7)	2.0
Renew exten. add	.2
Exhaust Pipe Extension, Renew	
All models (.7)	1.1
Catalytic Converter, Renew	
All models (.9)	1.1

(Factory Time)	Chilton Time
Catalytic Converter Heat Shield, Renew	
All models	
upper (.6)	.9
lower (.2)	.4
Power Heat Control Valve, Renew	
V-6 (.4)	7
Exhaust Manifold Heat Control Valve, Recondition	
V-6 (1.0)	1.7
Intake and Exhaust Manifold Gaskets, Renew	
Four (1.8)	2.5
w/A.C. add (.2)	.2

(Factory Time)	Chilton Time
Renew manif add	.5
Exhaust Manifold and/or Gaskets, Renew	
Four (2.6)	3.6
V-6	
right side (.4)	1.1
left side (.7)	1.3
w/Air inj add (.2)	.2
COMBINATIONS	
Muffler, Exhaust and Tail Pipe, Renew	
Four	2.0
V-6	2.1
4X4 add	2.0
Muffler and Tail Pipe, Renew	
All models	1.2

LABOR — 9A FRONT SUSPENSION (RWD) 9A — LABOR

(Factory Time)	Chilton Time
Note: On all front suspension operations alignment charges must be added if performed. Time given goes not include alignment.	
Check Alignment of Front End	
All models	.5
Note: Deduct if alignment is performed.	
Vehicle Height, Adjust	
All models (.2)	.4
Adjust headlamps add	.3
Toe-In, Adjust	
All models (.4)	.6
Align Front End	
Includes: Adjust front wheel bearings.	
All models (.8)	1.5
Wheels, Balance	
one	.5
each adtnl	.3
Front Wheel Bearings, Clean and Repack (Both Wheels)	
2 WD models	1.5
4 WD models	2.0
Front Wheel Bearings and Cups, Renew	
All models	
one side (.6)	.8
both sides (1.1)	1.5
Front Wheel Grease Seal, Renew	
All models-one (.5)	.7
both (.9)	1.3
Steering Knuckle, Renew	
7¼ axle (.8)	1.1
8¼ axle (1.1)	1.5
Lower Control Arm, Renew	
Add alignment charges.	
4X2 models (1.5)	2.0
4X4 models (.7)	1.0

(Factory Time)	Chilton Time
Lower Control Arm Bushings, Renew	
Add alignment charges.	
4X2 models (1.5)	2.2
Lower Ball Joint, Renew	
Add alignment charges.	
4X2 models (1.4)	1.9
Upper Control Arm, Renew	
Add alignment charges.	
4X2 models (1.9)	2.6
4X4 models (1.7)	2.3
Upper Ball Joint, Renew	
Add alignment charges.	
4X2 models (.9)	1.2
Upper Control Arm Bushings, Renew	
Add alignment charges.	
4X2 models (1.8)	2.5
Front Shock Absorbers, Renew	
All models-one (.3)	.4
both (.5)	.7
Front Sway Bar, Renew	
All models (.4)	.6
Front Sway Bar Links, Renew	
All models-one (.3)	.4
both (.4)	.6
Front Sway Bar Bushings, Renew	
All models	
one or all (.4)	.6
Torsion Bar, Renew	
All models-one (.3)	.4
both (.5)	.7
Torsion Bar Anchor or Adjusting Bolt, Renew	
All models-each (.4)	.6
Front Coil Spring, Renew	
Add alignment charges.	
All models (1.4)	1.9

(Factory Time)	Chilton Time
FOUR WHEEL DRIVE	
Front Axle Housing Cover, Renew or Reseal	
All models (.4)	.6
Front Axle Shaft, Renew	
All models	
one or both-one side (.4)	.6
Drive Shaft Boot, Renew	
All models	
one or both-one side (.6)	.9
Axle Shaft Outer Grease Seals, Renew	
7¼ axle	
right side (1.0)	1.4
left side (1.2)	1.6
Drive Pinion Oil Seal, Renew	
All models (.5)	.9
Inner Drive Shaft C/V Joint, Renew	
All models (.6)	.9
Vacuum Shift Motor, Renew	
All models (.2)	.4
Front Axle Housing, Renew	
All models (4.0)	5.4
Differential Side Bearings, Renew	
Includes: R&R ring and pinion, renew inner oil seals and adjust side bearing preload and backlash.	
All models (4.0)	5.5
Differential Case, Renew	
Includes: R&R ring and pinion, renew bearings and gears, renew pinion seal and inner oil seals. Adjust backlash.	
All models (4.8)	6.6
Differential Side Gears, Renew	
Includes: Renew axle shaft oil seals and side gear thrust washers.	
All models (2.9)	4.0

LABOR — 9A FRONT SUSPENSION (RWD) 9A — LABOR

	(Factory Time)	Chilton Time
Ring Gear and Pinion Set, Renew		
Includes: Renew inner axle shaft oil seals, pinion seal and gaskets. Renew pinion bearings.		
All models (4.9)		6.8
Renew diff case add		.3

	(Factory Time)	Chilton Time
Output Shaft or Bearing, Renew		
All models (1.1)		1.5
Renew pilot brg add (.3)		.3

	(Factory Time)	Chilton Time
Intermediate Axle Shaft, Renew		
Includes: Renew outer seals and bearings.		
All models (1.4)		1.8

LABOR — 11 STEERING GEAR 11 — LABOR

	(Factory Time)	Chilton Time
STANDARD STEERING		
Steering Wheel, Renew		
All models (.2)		.4
Upper Mast Jacket Bearing, Renew		
All models		
Standard Column (.5)		1.0
Tilt Column (1.1)		1.5
Steering Column Shift Housing, Renew		
All models		
Standard Column (.9)		1.5
Tilt Column (2.2)		3.3
Steering Column Mast Jacket, Renew		
Does not include painting.		
All models		
Standard Column		
column shift (1.6)		2.4
floor shift (1.1)		1.6
Tilt Column		
All models (2.3)		3.3
Tie Rods or Tie Rod Ends, Renew		
Includes: Reset toe-in.		
All models		
outer-each (.7)		1.0
inner and outer-		
one side (2.3)		3.0
Steering Gear Rack End Boot, Renew		
Includes: Reset toe-in.		
All models		
one side		1.3

	(Factory Time)	Chilton Time
Steering Gear Assembly, Renew		
All models (.6)		1.2
POWER STEERING		
Trouble Shoot Power Steering		
Includes: Test pump and system pressure. Check pounds pull on steering wheel and check for leaks.		
All models		.5
Power Steering Belt, Renew		
All models (.2)		.3
w/A.C. add (.1)		.1
w/Air inj add (.1)		.1
Tie Rods or Tie Rod Ends, Renew		
Includes: Reset toe-in.		
All models		
outer-each (.7)		1.0
inner and outer-		
one side (2.3)		3.0
Steering Gear Rack End Boot, Renew		
Includes: Reset toe-in.		
All models		
one side		1.3
Power Steering Gear Assy., Renew		
Includes: Reset toe-in.		
4X2 models (1.3)		2.0
4X4 models (.9)		1.5

	(Factory Time)	Chilton Time
Steering Gear Oil Seals, Renew (All)		
Includes: R&R gear assy. Reset toe-in.		
All models (2.4)		4.0
Renew housing add (.1)		.1
Upper and Lower Valve Pinion Seals, Renew		
All models (1.4)		2.0
Renew pinion brgs add (.3)		.5
Power Steering Pump, Test and Renew		
All models (.9)		1.4
w/Air inj add (.2)		.2
Power Steering Pump, R&R and Recondition		
All models (1.4)		1.9
w/Air inj add (.2)		.2
Pump Flow Control Valve, Test and Clean or Renew		
All models (.9)		1.3
w/Air inj add (.2)		.2
Power Steering Reservoir and/or Seals, Renew		
All models (.7)		1.0
w/Air inj add (.2)		.2
Pump Drive Shaft Oil Seal, Renew		
All models (.9)		1.3
w/Air inj add (.2)		.2
Power Steering Hoses, Renew		
All models		
pressure (.4)		.7
return (.3)		.6

LABOR — 12 CYLINDER HEAD & VALVE SYSTEM 12 — LABOR

	(Factory Time)	Chilton Time
Compression Test		
Four		.5
V-6		.7
Cylinder Head Gasket, Renew		
Includes: Clean gasket surfaces, clean carbon, make all necessary adjustments.		
Four (3.4)		4.8
V-6-one side (2.8)		4.0
both sides (3.8)		5.5
w/A.C. add (.2)		.2
w/Air inj add (.4)		.4
w/100 amp alter add (.6)		.6
w/P.S. add (.2)		.2
Cylinder Head, Renew		
Includes: Transfer all parts, reface valves, make all necessary adjustments.		
Four (4.7)		8.0
V-6-one side (3.8)		5.5
both sides (6.1)		8.8
w/A.C. add (.2)		.2
w/Air inj add (.4)		.4
w/100 amp alter add (.6)		.6
w/P.S. add (.2)		.2

COMBINATIONS
Add to Valve Job
See Machine Shop Operations

	(Factory Time)	Chilton Time
DRAIN, EVACUATE AND RECHARGE AIR CONDITIONING SYSTEM		
All models		1.0
ROCKER ARM SHAFT ASSY., DISASSEMBLE AND CLEAN OR RECONDITION		
V-6-one side		.5
both sides		.9
HYDRAULIC VALVE LIFTERS, DISASSEMBLE AND CLEAN		
Each		.2
DISTRIBUTOR, RECONDITION		
All models		1.0
VALVE GUIDES, REAM OVERSIZE		
Each		.3
VALVES, RECONDITION (HEAD REMOVED)		
Four		2.0
V-6		3.0
CARBURETOR, RECONDITION		
All models		1.5

	(Factory Time)	Chilton Time
Clean Carbon and Grind Valves		
Includes: R&R cylinder head(s), clean gasket surfaces, clean carbon, reface valves and seats. Minor tune up.		
Four (4.2)		6.8
V-6-one side (3.1)		4.5
both sides (6.2)		8.9
w/A.C. add (.2)		.2
w/Air inj add (.4)		.4
w/100 amp alter add (.6)		.6
w/P.S. add (.2)		.2
Valve Cover Gasket, Renew		
Four (.6)		1.0
V-6-one (.4)		.6
both (.7)		1.0
w/Air inj add (.2)		.2
Valve Push Rods and/or Rocker Arms, Renew		
V-6-one cyl (.6)		.8
one cyl-each side (1.1)		1.4
all cyls-both sides (1.3)		1.7
w/Air inj add (.5)		.5
Valve Tappets (Lifters), Renew		
Four-all (1.7)		2.5

LABOR 12 CYLINDER HEAD & VALVE SYSTEM 12 LABOR

(Factory Time)	Chilton Time	(Factory Time)	Chilton Time	(Factory Time)	Chilton Time
V-6-one cyl (1.0).....................	1.5	Roller Type Valve Tappets (Lifters), Renew		Valve Springs and/or Valve Stem Oil Seals, Renew (Head on Truck)	
one cyl-each side (1.4)........	2.0	V-6		Four-all (1.8)........................	2.9
all cyls-both sides (2.3)........	3.3	one cyl (2.2).....................	3.0	V-6-one cyl (1.1)...................	1.6
w/A.C. add (.2)......................	.2	all cyls (3.0).....................	4.2	one cyl-each side (1.6)........	2.3
w/Air inj add (.2)....................	.2	w/A.C. add (.2).....................	.2	all cyls-both sides (4.0)...........	5.8
				w/Air inj add (.2)....................	.2

LABOR 13 ENGINE ASSEMBLY & MOUNTS 13 LABOR

(Factory Time)	Chilton Time	(Factory Time)	Chilton Time	(Factory Time)	Chilton Time
Note: All engine operations listed in this group are for assemblies as supplied by the original equipment manufacturer. Time to replace assemblies from independent rebuilders may vary.		Short Engine Assy., Renew (w/All Internal Parts Less Cylinder Head(s) and Oil Pan)		Engine Assembly, R&R and Recondition	
		Includes: R&R engine assy. Transfer all component parts not supplied with replacement engine. Tune up.		Includes: Rebore block, install new pistons, rings, pins, rod and main bearings. Clean carbon, grind valves. Tune engine.	
Engine Assembly, Remove & Install		Four (7.3)...........................	13.0	Four (14.2).........................	21.3
Does not include transfer of any parts or equipment.		V-6 (8.6)............................	14.5	V-6 (19.9)..........................	28.6
		w/P.S. add (.3)....................	.3	w/P.S. add (.3)....................	.3
Four..................................	4.6	w/M.T. add (1.9)..................	1.9	w/M.T. add (1.9)..................	1.9
V-6...................................	6.0	w/A.C. add (1.0)..................	1.0	w/A.C. add (1.0)..................	1.0
w/P.S. add...........................	.3	w/Air inj add (.2).................	.2	w/Air inj add (.2).................	.2
w/M.T. add...........................	1.9	4X4 add (1.5)......................	2.0	4X4 add (1.5)......................	2.0
w/A.C. add...........................	1.0	w/A500 trans add (.4).............	.4	w/A500 trans add (.4).............	.4
w/Air inj add........................	.2	Recond valves add		**Engine Mounts, Renew (Front)**	
4X4 add (1.5)........................	2.0	Four.............................	2.0	Four	
w/A500 trans add (.4)................	.4	V-6..............................	3.0	right (.8).......................	1.1
				left (.3)........................	.5
				4X4 add (.3)......................	.3
				V-6-each (.6).....................	.9

LABOR 14 PISTONS, RINGS & BEARINGS 14 LABOR

(Factory Time)	Chilton Time
Rings, Renew	
Includes: Remove cylinder top ridge, deglaze cylinder walls.	
Four-one cyl (4.6)..................	6.4
all cyls (5.6).....................	7.8
V-6-one cyl (4.5)...................	6.3
one cyl-each side (6.2)...........	8.6
all cyls (8.3).....................	11.6
w/A.C. add (.2).....................	.2
w/Air inj add (.1).................	.1
w/100 amp alter add (.6)...........	.6
4X4 add (1.5)......................	2.0
w/A500 trans add (.4).............	.4
Pistons or Connecting Rods, Renew	
Includes: Remove cylinder top ridge, deglaze cylinder walls.	
Four-one cyl (4.9)..................	6.7
all cyls (7.0).....................	9.0
V-6-one cyl (4.6)...................	6.6
one cyl-each side (6.3)...........	9.2
all cyls (9.1).....................	13.4
w/A.C. add (.2).....................	.2
w/Air inj add (.1).................	.1
w/100 amp alter add (.6)...........	.6
4X4 add (1.5)......................	2.0
w/A500 trans add (.4).............	.4
Connecting Rod Bearings, Renew	
Four (2.1)..........................	3.0
V-6 (2.3)...........................	3.5
4X4 add (1.5)......................	2.0
w/A500 trans add (.4).............	.4

COMBINATIONS

Add to Engine Work

See Machine Shop Operations

(Factory Time)	Chilton Time	(Factory Time)	Chilton Time
DRAIN, EVACUATE AND RECHARGE AIR CONDITIONING SYSTEM		**VALVES, RECONDITION (ALL)**	
All models........................	1.0	Cylinder Head Removed	
ROCKER ARMS & SHAFT ASSY., DISASSEMBLE AND CLEAN OR RECONDITION		Four.............................	2.0
		V-6..............................	3.0
V-6-one side.....................	.5	**DEGLAZE CYLINDER WALLS**	
both sides.......................	.9	Each.............................	.2
HYDRAULIC VALVE LIFTERS, DISASSEMBLE AND CLEAN		**REMOVE CYLINDER TOP RIDGE**	
Each.............................	.2	Each.............................	.3
DISTRIBUTOR, RECONDITION		**PLASTIGAUGE BEARINGS**	
All models.......................	1.0	Each.............................	.1
CARBURETOR, RECONDITION		**OIL PUMP, RECONDITION**	
All models.......................	1.2	V-6..............................	.4
VALVE GUIDES, REAM OVERSIZE		**OIL FILTER ELEMENT, RENEW**	
Each.............................	.3	All models.......................	.3

LABOR 15 CRANKSHAFT & DAMPER 15 LABOR

(Factory Time)	Chilton Time	(Factory Time)	Chilton Time	(Factory Time)	Chilton Time
Crankshaft and Main Bearings, Renew		V-6 (7.9)...........................	12.0	w/100 amp alter add (.2)..........	.2
Includes: R&R engine assy, plastigauge all bearings.		w/P.S. add (.3)....................	.3	w/A.C. add (1.0)...................	1.0
Four (6.7)..........................	11.2	w/M.T. add (.5)....................	.5	4X4 add (1.5)......................	2.0
		w/Air inj add (.2).................	.2	w/A500 trans add (.4).............	.4

LABOR 15 CRANKSHAFT & DAMPER 15 LABOR

(Factory Time)	Chilton Time	(Factory Time)	Chilton Time	(Factory Time)	Chilton Time
Main Bearings, Renew		**Rod and Main Bearings, Renew**		4X4 add (1.5)	2.0
Includes: Plastigauge bearings.		V-6 (3.6)	5.8	w/A500 trans add (.4)	.4
Four		4X4 add (1.5)	2.0	**Vibration Damper or Pulley, Renew**	
No. 2-3-4 (1.8)	2.8	w/A500 trans add (.4)	.4	V-6 (.6)	1.0
No. 1 (3.0)	4.0	**Rear Main Bearing Oil Seals, Renew**		w/P.S. add (.1)	.1
No. 5 (5.6)	8.8	**(Upper and Lower)**		w/A.C. add (.2)	.2
V-6 (2.6)	4.0	Four		**Crankshaft Front Oil Seal, Renew**	
4X4 add (1.5)	2.0	w/A.T. (2.7)	5.1	Four (1.3)	1.8
w/A500 trans add (.4)	.4	w/M.T. (3.0)	5.4	w/P.S. add (.2)	2
		V-6 (2.1)	4.0		

LABOR 16 CAMSHAFT & TIMING GEARS 16 LABOR

(Factory Time)	Chilton Time	(Factory Time)	Chilton Time	(Factory Time)	Chilton Time
Timing Belt Cover, Renew		w/P.S. add (.2)	.2	**Balance Shafts, Renew**	
Four		w/A.C. add (.4)	.4	Four	
upper (.2)	.4	w/Air inj add (.2)	.2	2.5L eng-one or both (1.8)	2.5
lower (.6)	1.0	w/100 amp alter add (.5)	.5	**Balance Shaft Carrier, Renew**	
w/A.C. add (.2)	.2	**Timing Cover Oil Seal, Renew**		Includes: Renew balance shafts if required.	
w/100 amp alter add (.5)	.5	Four (1.3)	2.0	Four	
Timing Belt, Renew		V-6 (.9)	1.3	2.5L eng (1.8)	2.6
Four (.9)	1.5	w/P.S. add (.2)	.2	**Intermediate Shaft, Renew**	
w/P.S. add (.1)	.1	w/A.C. add (.4)	.4	Four (1.5)	2.1
w/A.C. add (.5)	.5	**Balance Shaft Chain Tensioner and/or**		w/A.C. add (.5)	5
Timing Belt Tensioner, Renew		**Guide, Renew**		w/P.S. add (.1)	.1
Four (.9)	1.5	Four		**Intermediate Shaft Oil Seal, Renew**	
w/P.S. add (.2)	.2	2.5L eng (1.2)	1.9	Four (1.0)	1.6
w/A.C. add (.2)	.2			w/A.C. add (.5)	.5
Camshaft Seals, Renew		**Balance Shafts Chain and/or Sprockets,**		w/P.S. add (.1)	.1
Four		**Renew**			
front (.7)	1.1	Four		**Intermediate Shaft Sprocket, Renew**	
rear (.9)	1.3	2.5L eng (2.4)	3.4	Four (1.0)	1.6
w/P.S. add (.1)	.1	w/A.C. add (.6)	.6	w/A.C. add (.5)	.5
Timing Chain Case Cover Gasket, Renew		w/P.S. add (.1)	.1	w/P.S. add (.1)	1
Includes: Renew oil seal.		Renew carrier add (.6)	.6	**Camshaft, Renew**	
V-6 (1.8)	2.6			Four (1.7)	2.8
w/P.S. add (.2)	.2	**Balance Shaft Gears Cover, R&R or Renew**		V-6 (3.9)	7.0
w/A.C. add (.4)	.4	Four		w/P.S. add (.2)	.2
w/Air inj add (.2)	.2	2.5L eng (1.3)	1.8	w/Aux trans cooler add (.3)	.3
w/100 amp alter add (.5)	.5	**Balance Shaft Gears, Renew**		w/A.C. add (.8)	.8
Timing Chain, Renew		Four		w/Air inj add (.2)	.2
V-6 (2.3)	3.0	2.5L eng (1.5)	2.1	w/100 amp alter add (.5)	.5

LABOR 17 ENGINE OILING SYSTEM 17 LABOR

(Factory Time)	Chilton Time	(Factory Time)	Chilton Time	(Factory Time)	Chilton Time
Oil Pan and/or Gasket, Renew		**Oil Pump, Renew**		**Oil Pressure Gauge (Dash Unit), Renew**	
Four (.9)	1.4	Four (1.2)	1.7	All models (.6)	1.1
V-6 (1.1)	1.6	V-6 (1.1)	1.7	**Oil Pressure Gauge (Engine Unit), Renew**	
4X4 add (1.5)	2.0	4X4 add (1.5)	2.0	All models	
w/A500 trans add (.4)	.4	w/A500 trans add (.4)	.4	w/Gauge (.4)	.6
		Oil Pump, R&R and Recondition		w/Light (.2)	.3
Pressure Test Engine Bearings (Pan Off)		Four (1.7)	2.2	**Oil Filter Element, Renew**	
All models	1.0	V-6 (1.5)	2.0	All models (.2)	.3
		4X4 add (1.5)	2.0		

LABOR 18 CLUTCH & FLYWHEEL 18 LABOR

(Factory Time)	Chilton Time	(Factory Time)	Chilton Time	(Factory Time)	Chilton Time
Clutch Pedal Free Play, Adjust		**Clutch Slave Cylinder, Renew**		w/Two piece shaft add (.2)	.2
All models (.3)	.5	Includes: Bleed system.		w/Skid plate add	.3
Bleed Clutch Hydraulic System		All models (.4)	.6	4X4 add (.7)	.7
All models	.4	Recond cyl add	.4	**Clutch Release Bearing, Renew**	
Clutch Master Cylinder, Renew		**Hydraulic Clutch Assy., Renew**		5 Speed	
Includes: Bleed system.		All models (.9)	1.3	All models (1.9)	2.7
All models (.4)	.6	**Clutch Assembly, Renew**		w/Two piece shaft add (.2)	.2
Recond cyl add	.4	5 Speed		w/Skid plate add	.3
		All models (2.1)	3.0	4X4 add (.7)	.7

LABOR 18 CLUTCH & FLYWHEEL 18 LABOR

	(Factory Time)	Chilton Time
Clutch Release Fork, Renew		
5 Speed		
All models (2.1)		2.9
w/Two piece shaft add (.2)		.2
w/Skid plate add		.3
4X4 add (.7)		.7

	(Factory Time)	Chilton Time
Flywheel, Renew		
5 Speed		
All models (2.0)		3.3
Renew pilot brg add (.2)		.2
Renew ring gear add (.3)		.5
w/Two piece shaft add (.2)		.2
w/Skid plate add		.3
4X4 add (.7)		.7

LABOR 19A MANUAL TRANSMISSION (RWD) 19A LABOR

	(Factory Time)	Chilton Time
Transmission Assy., R&R or Renew		
5 Speed		
NP2500		
4X2 (1.2)		1.7
4X4 (1.9)		2.7
Renew assy add (.2)		.4
w/Skid plate add (.1)		.3
Transmission Assy., R&R and Recondition		
5 Speed		
NP2500		
4X2 (4.4)		6.1

	(Factory Time)	Chilton Time
4X4 (5.1)		7.1
w/Skid plate add (.1)		.3
Transmission Assembly, Recondition (Off Truck) 5 Speed		
NP2500 (3.2)		4.5
Transmission Front Oil Seal, Renew		
Includes: R&R transmission.		
5 Speed		
NP2500		
4X2 (1.5)		2.0

	(Factory Time)	Chilton Time
4X4 (2.2)		3.0
w/Skid plate add (.1)		.3
Speedometer Drive Pinion, Renew		
All models (.3)		.6
Extension Housing Oil Seal, Renew		
All models (.5)		.8

LABOR 20 TRANSFER CASE 20 LABOR

	(Factory Time)	Chilton Time
Transfer Case Adapter, Renew		
All models (1.7)		2.2
Transfer Case Adapter Gasket, Renew		
All models (1.4)		1.8
Transfer Case Shift Lever, Renew		
All models (.4)		.6
Transfer Case Yoke, Renew		
All models		
front (.5)		.7
rear (.4)		.6
Rear Output Shaft Seal, Renew		
All models (.4)		.7

	(Factory Time)	Chilton Time
Rear Output Shaft Housing, Renew		
Includes: Renew bearing.		
All models (1.0)		1.4
Speedometer Drive Pinion, Renew		
All models (.3)		.4
Vacuum Engagement Switch, Renew		
All models (.4)		.6
Transfer Case Assy., R&R or Renew		
All models (1.5)		1.9
Renew assy. add (.3)		.3

	(Factory Time)	Chilton Time
Transfer Case Assy., R&R and Recondition (Complete)		
All models (4.1)		5.4
Transfer Case Rear Housing, Renew		
Includes: R&R transfer case.		
All models (2.4)		3.1
Transfer Case Front Housing, Renew		
Includes: R&R transfer case.		
All models (3.4)		4.5
Transfer Case Drive Chain, Renew		
Includes: R&R transfer case.		
All models (2.5)		3.3

LABOR 21 SHIFT LINKAGE 21 LABOR

	(Factory Time)	Chilton Time
STANDARD		
Shift Linkage, Adjust		
All models (.3)		.5
Gearshift Lever, Renew		
All models (.4)		.6

	(Factory Time)	Chilton Time
AUTOMATIC		
Throttle Linkage, Adjust		
All models (.3)		.5
Gearshift Lever, Renew		
All models (.3)		.5
Gearshift Control Rod, Renew		
All models (.4)		.6

	(Factory Time)	Chilton Time
Gear Selector Indicator, Renew		
All models (.5)		.8
Steering Column Shift Housing, Renew		
All models		
w/Std column (.9)		1.5
w/Tilt column (2.2)		3.3

LABOR 23A AUTOMATIC TRANSMISSION (RWD) 23A LABOR

	(Factory Time)	Chilton Time
A998		
ON TRUCK SERVICES		
Drain and Refill Unit		
All models		1.0
Oil Pressure Test		
Note: Using 3 pressure test points.		
All models		1.5

	(Factory Time)	Chilton Time
Check Unit for Oil Leaks		
Includes: Clean and dry outside of case and run unit to determine point of leak.		
All models		1.0
Neutral Safety Switch, Renew		
All models (.3)		.4
Oil Cooler Lines, Renew		
Includes: Cut and form to size.		
All models-one (.6)		1.0

	(Factory Time)	Chilton Time
Transmission Auxiliary Oil Cooler, Renew		
All models (.7)		1.2
Throttle Linkage, Adjust		
All models (.3)		.5
Kickdown Band, Adjust		
All models (.3)		.5
Throttle Valve Lever Shaft Seal, Renew		
All models (.3)		.7

LABOR 23A AUTOMATIC TRANSMISSION (RWD) 23A LABOR

	(Factory) Time	Chilton Time
Valve Body Manual Lever Shaft Seal, Renew		
All models (.4)		.8
Extension Housing Oil Seal, Renew		
All models (.5)		1.1
Extension Housing or Adapter Gasket, Renew		
All models (1.4)		2.0
Governor Assy., Renew or Recondition		
Includes: R&R extension housing.		
All models (1.6)		2.5
Parking Lock Sprag, Renew		
Includes: R&R extension housing.		
All models (1.3)		2.2
Output Shaft Bearing and/or Oil Seal, Renew		
Includes: R&R extension housing.		
All models (1.4)		2.3
Oil Pan and/or Gasket, Renew		
All models (.5)		1.0
Parking Lock Sprag Control Rod, Renew		
Includes: R&R oil pan and remove valve body.		
All models (.9)		1.5
Accumulator Piston, Renew or Recondition		
Includes: R&R oil pan and adjust band.		
All models (1.1)		1.7
Kickdown Servo, Renew or Recondition		
Includes: R&R oil pan and adjust band.		
All models (.9)		1.5
Reverse Servo, Renew or Recondition		
Includes: R&R oil pan and adjust band.		
All models (.8)		1.4
Valve Body Assembly, Renew		
Includes: R&R oil pan and renew filter.		
All models (.9)		1.5
Valve Body Assy., R&R and Recondition		
Includes: R&R oil pan and replace filter. Disassemble, clean, inspect, free all valves. Replace parts as required.		
All models (1.7)		2.4
Bands, Adjust		
Includes: R&R oil pan.		
All models		
reverse (.6)		1.2
kickdown (.6)		1.2
Torque Converter Lock Up Solenoid, Renew		
Includes: R&R oil pan.		
All models (1.2)		1.8

SERVICES REQUIRING R&R

	(Factory) Time	Chilton Time
Transmission Assembly, Remove and Reinstall		
4X2 models (2.3)		3.2
4X4 models (3.9)		5.4
Renew trans add (.4)		.5
Flush conver and lines add (.5)		.5
w/Skid plate add (.2)		.3
Transmission Assembly, Renew (w/Remanufactured Unit)		
Includes: Remove and install all necessary interfering parts. Transfer all parts not supplied with replacement unit. Road test.		
4X2 models (2.6)		3.7
4X4 models (4.2)		5.9
w/Skid plate add (.2)		.3
Transmission Assembly, Reseal		
Includes: R&R trans and renew all seals and gaskets.		
4X2 models (4.5)		6.0

	(Factory) Time	Chilton Time
4X4 models (6.1)		8.5
w/Skid plate add (.2)		.3
Transmission and Converter, R&R and Recondition		
Includes: Disassemble trans including valve body, clean, inspect and replace parts as required.		
4X2 models (6.8)		9.5
4X4 models (8.4)		11.7
w/Skid plate add (.2)		3
Flywheel (Flexplate), Renew		
Includes: R&R transmission.		
4X2 models (2.4)		3.3
4X4 models (4.0)		5.5
Torque Converter, Renew		
Includes: R&R transmission.		
4X2 models (2.5)		3.5
4X4 models (4.1)		5.7
w/Skid Plate add (.2)		.3
Kickdown Band, Renew		
Includes: R&R transmission.		
4X2 models (3.0)		4.2
4X4 models (4.6)		6.4
w/Skid plate add (.2)		3
4X4 models (4.0)		5.5
Reverse Band, Renew		
Includes: R&R transmission.		
4X2 models (3.4)		4.7
4X4 models (5.0)		7.0
w/Skid plate add (.2)		.3
Transmission Case, Renew		
Includes: R&R transmission.		
4X2 models (4.2)		5.8
4X4 models (5.8)		8.1
w/Skid plate add (.2)		.3
Front Pump Assembly, Renew or Recondition		
Includes: R&R transmission. Renew reaction shaft if necessary.		
4X2 models (2.9)		4.0
4X4 models (4.5)		6.3
w/Skid plate add (.2)		.3
Front Pump Oil Seal, Renew		
Includes: R&R transmission.		
4X2 models (2.5)		3.5
4X4 models (4.1)		5.7
w/Skid plate add (.2)		.3

A500
ON TRUCK SERVICES

	(Factory) Time	Chilton Time
Drain and Refill Unit		
All models		1.0
Oil Pressure Test		
Note: Using 3 pressure test points.		
All models		1.5
Check Unit for Oil Leaks		
Includes: Clean and dry outside of case and run unit to determine point of leak.		
All models		1.0
Neutral Safety Switch, Renew		
All models (.3)		.4
Overdrive Cancel Switch, Renew		
All models (.4)		.6
Oil Cooler Lines, Renew		
Includes: Cut and form to size.		
All models-one (.6)		1.0
Transmission Auxiliary Oil Cooler, Renew		
All models (.7)		1.2
Throttle Linkage, Adjust		
All models (.3)		.5

	(Factory) Time	Chilton Time
Throttle Valve Lever Shaft Seal, Renew		
All models (.3)		.7
Valve Body Manual Lever Shaft Seal, Renew		
All models (.4)		.8
Extension Housing Oil Seal, Renew		
All models (.5)		1.1
Extension Housing/Overdrive Unit, Remove and Install		
All models (1.2)		1.7
Renew assy add (.7)		.7
Governor Assy: Renew or Recondition		
Includes: R&R extension housing.		
All models (1.7)		2.4
Parking Lock Sprag, Renew		
Includes: R&R extension housing.		
All models (2.2)		3.1
Output Shaft Bearings, Renew (Front or Rear)		
Includes: R&R extension housing.		
All models (1.8)		2.5
Extension Housing Bushing, Renew		
Includes: R&R extension housing.		
All models (1.8)		2.5
Overdrive Sliding Hub, Renew		
Includes: R&R extension housing.		
All models (2.2)		3.1
Overdrive Direct Clutch Drum, Renew		
Includes: R&R extension housing.		
All models (2.2)		3.1
Overdrive Clutches and Seals, Renew		
Includes: R&R extension housing.		
All models (2.2)		3.1
Overdrive Sungear, Renew		
Includes: R&R extension housing.		
All models (2.1)		3.0
Planetary Pinion Assy., Renew		
Includes: R&R extension housing.		
All models (2.0)		2.9
Annulus/Parking Gear, Renew		
Includes: R&R extension housing.		
All models (2.2)		3.1
Overrunning Clutch Assy., Renew		
Includes: R&R extension housing.		
All models (2.2)		3.1
Overdrive Output Shaft, Renew		
Includes: R&R extension housing.		
All models (2.4)		3.4
Oil Pan and/or Gasket, Renew		
All models (.5)		1.0
Parking Lock Sprag Control Rod, Renew		
Includes: R&R oil pan and remove valve body.		
All models (.9)		1.5
Accumulator Piston, Renew or Recondition		
Includes: R&R oil pan and adjust band.		
All models (1.1)		1.7
Kickdown Servo, Renew or Recondition		
Includes: R&R oil pan and adjust band.		
All models (.9)		1.5
Reverse Servo, Renew or Recondition		
Includes: R&R oil pan and adjust band.		
All models (.8)		1.4

LABOR 23A AUTOMATIC TRANSMISSION (RWD) 23A LABOR

(Factory Time)	Chilton Time

Valve Body Assembly, Renew
Includes: R&R oil pan and renew filter.
All models (.9) ... 1.5

Valve Body Assy: R&R and Recondition
Includes: R&R oil pan and replace filter. Disassemble, clean, inspect, free all valves. Replace parts as required.
All models (1.7) ... 2.4

Bands, Adjust
Includes: R&R oil pan.
All models
reverse (.6) ... 1.2
kickdown (.6) ... 1.2

Torque Converter Lock Up Solenoid, Renew
Includes: R&R oil pan.
All models (1.2) ... 1.8

SERVICES REQUIRING R&R

Transmission Assembly, Remove and Install
All models (3.6) ... 5.0
Renew trans add (.4) 5
Flush conver and lines add (.5) 5

Transmission Assembly, Reseal
Includes: R&R trans and renew all seals and gaskets.
All models ... 6.5

Transmission and Converter, R&R and Recondition
Includes: Disassemble trans including valve body, clean, inspect and replace parts as required.
All models (8.3) ... 11.6

Torque Converter, Renew
Includes: R&R transmission.
All models (3.8) ... 5.2

Flywheel (Flexplate), Renew
Includes: R&R transmission.
All models (3.7) ... 5.1

LABOR 25 U-JOINTS & DRIVESHAFT 25 LABOR

Drive Shaft, R&R or Renew
All models
trans to rear axle (.4) 6
center brg to rear axle (.4) 6
transfer case to front axle (.5) 8
trans to center brg (1.2) ... 1.5

Universal Joints, Renew or Recondition
SINGLE PIECE SHAFT
at rear axle (.5) 7

trans rear-to rear axle (.6) 9
both (1.2) ... 1.5
transfer case to
rear axle (.9) ... 1.2
transfer case rear,
to rear axle (.5) 7
at front axle (.6) 9
transfer case to front axle
Saginaw C/V Type (1.3) ... 1.8

TWO PIECE SHAFT
trans to center brg (.7) ... 1.0
center brg to rear axle (.7) ... 1.0
at rear axle (.5) 7
center brg to rear
axle-all (1.2) ... 1.6
both shafts-all three (1.4) ... 2.0

Center Bearing, Renew
All models (.8) ... 1.1

LABOR 26 DRIVE AXLE 26 LABOR

Differential, Drain & Refill
All models 6

Rear Axle Housing Cover, Renew or Reseal
All models (.4) 6

Rear Axle Shaft, Renew
All models (.7) ... 1.0

Axle Shaft Bearing, Renew
All models (.6) 9

Axle Shaft Oil Seal, Renew
All models (.6) 9

Pinion Shaft Oil Seal, Renew
All models (.4) 6

Differential Backlash, Adjust
All models
7¼ axle (1.1) ... 1.5
8¼ axle (1.3) ... 1.8

Rear Axle Housing, Renew
Includes: Renew pinion oil seal, inner and outer axle shaft or wheel bearing oil seals and gaskets.
All models (4.2) ... 6.3

Rear Axle Assembly, Renew
Includes: Renew oil seals and gaskets. Transfer axle shafts and brake assemblies.
All models (2.0) ... 3.1

Differential Side Bearings, Renew
Includes: Adjust backlash and renew axle shaft oil seals.
All models (1.5) ... 2.5

Differential Case, Renew
Includes: Renew side bearings and thrust washers, side gears if necessary.
All models (3.0) ... 4.5

Differential Side Gears, Renew
Includes: Renew axle shaft oil seals.
All models (1.1) ... 2.0

Ring Gear and Pinion Set, Renew
Includes: Renew wheel bearing or inner axle shaft oil seals, pinion oil seal and gaskets.
All models (2.7) ... 4.0
Renew side bearings add (.2) 5

LABOR 27 REAR SUSPENSION 27 LABOR

Rear Spring, Renew
All models-right (.5) 7
left (.6) 8
both (1.1) ... 1.5

Auxiliary Rear Spring, Renew
All models-one (.7) ... 1.0

Rear Spring Shackle, Renew
Includes: Renew bushings.
All models-one side (.6) ... 1.0

Rear Shock Absorbers, Renew
All models-one (.2) 4
both (.4) 6

LABOR 28 AIR CONDITIONING 28 LABOR

Note: If more than one item requires replacement where evacuation and discharging the system is already included in the operation, deduct 1.0 hour for each additional item to the times listed.

Drain, Evacuate, Leak Test and Charge System
All models ... 1.0

Flush Refrigerant System, Complete
To be used in conjunction with component replacement which could contaminate system.
All models ... 1.3

LABOR 28 AIR CONDITIONING 28 LABOR

	(Factory Time)	Chilton Time
Partial Charge		
Includes: Leak test.		
All models		.6
Compressor Belt, Renew		
All models (.2)		.3
w/Air inj add (.1)		.1
w/P.S. add (.1)		.1
Compressor Clutch Field Coil, Renew		
Includes: Renew pulley w/Hub if necessary.		
All models (.5)		.9
Compressor Clutch Assembly, Renew		
All models (.5)		.8
Compressor Assembly, Renew		
Includes: Transfer parts as required. Pressure test and charge system.		
Four (1.3)		2.7
V-6 (1.7)		3.1
w/114 amp alt add (.6)		.6
Compressor Front Cover and/or Seal, Renew		
Includes: Pressure test and charge system.		
Four (1.7)		3.0
V-6 (2.1)		3.4
w/114 amp alt add (.6)		.6
Compressor Rear Cover and/or Seal, Renew		
Includes: Pressure test and charge system.		
Four (1.6)		2.9

	(Factory Time)	Chilton Time
V-6 (2.0)		3.3
w/114 amp alt add (.6)		.6
Compressor Center Seal, Renew		
Includes: Pressure test and charge system.		
Four (1.8)		3.1
V-6 (2.2)		3.5
w/114 amp alt add (.6)		.6
Compressor Shaft Gas Seal, Renew		
Includes: Pressure test and charge system.		
Four (1.7)		3.0
V-6 (2.1)		3.4
w/114 amp alt add (.6)		.6
Expansion Valve, Renew		
Includes: Pressure test and charge system.		
All models (1.1)		1.6
Renew receiver drier add (.2)		.2
Receiver Drier, Renew		
Includes: Add partial charge, leak test and charge system.		
All models (1.1)		1.6
Low Pressure Cut Off Switch, Renew		
Includes: Pressure test and charge system.		
All models (1.0)		1.5
Clutch Cycling (Thermostatic Control) Switch, Renew		
All models (.3)		.5

	(Factory Time)	Chilton Time
Condenser Assembly, Renew		
Includes: Add partial charge, leak test and charge system.		
All models (1.4)		2.0
Renew receiver drier add (.2)		.2
Evaporator Coil, Renew		
Includes: Add partial charge, leak test and charge system.		
All models (2.7)		4.2
Blower Motor, Renew		
All models (1.1)		1.6
Blower Motor Resistor, Renew		
All models (.3)		.4
Blower Motor Switch, Renew		
All models (.5)		.9
Temperature Control Assembly, Renew		
All models (.5)		.9
A.C. Push Button Switch, Renew		
All models (.6)		1.0
Air Conditioning Hoses, Renew		
Includes: Pressure test and charge system.		
All models		
suction/liquid line (1.1)		1.9
discharge/liquid line (1.1)		1.9
Renew receiver drier add (.2)		.2

LABOR 30 HEAD AND PARKING LAMPS 30 LABOR

	(Factory Time)	Chilton Time
Aim Headlamps		
two		.4
four		.6
Headlamp Sealed Beam Bulb, Renew		
Does not include aim headlamp.		
All models-one (.3)		.3

	(Factory Time)	Chilton Time
Parking Lamp Lens or Bulb, Renew		
All models-one (.2)		.3
Turn Signal Lamp Lens or Bulb, Renew		
All models-one (.2)		.3
Tail and Stop Lamp Lens or Bulb, Renew		
All models-one (.2)		.3

	(Factory Time)	Chilton Time
Back-Up Lamp Lens or Bulb, Renew		
All models-one (.2)		.3
License Lamp Lens or Bulb, Renew		
All models-one (.2)		.3
Reflectors, Renew		
All models-one (.2)		.2

LABOR 31 WINDSHIELD WIPER & SPEEDOMETER 31 LABOR

	(Factory Time)	Chilton Time
Windshield Wiper Motor, Renew		
All models (.7)		1.0
Windshield Wiper Pivot, Renew		
All models-one (.5)		.8
Wiper Links, Renew		
All models-one or both (.5)		.8
Windshield Wiper and Washer Switch, Renew		
All models		
Std column (.8)		1.2

	(Factory Time)	Chilton Time
Tilt column (1.2)		1.7
Wiper Delay Control Module, Renew		
All models (.3)		.5
Windshield Washer Pump, Renew		
All models (.3)		.5
Speedometer Head, R&R or Renew		
All models (.4)		.7
Reset odometer add		.2

	(Factory Time)	Chilton Time
Speedometer Cable and Casing, Renew		
All models		
lower (.3)		.6
upper (.5)		.8
one piece (.4)		.7
Speedometer Driven Pinion, Renew		
Includes: Renew oil seal.		
All models (.3)		.4

LABOR 32 LIGHT SWITCHES & WIRING 32 LABOR

	(Factory Time)	Chilton Time
Headlamp Switch, Renew		
All models (.4)		.6
Headlamp Dimmer Switch, Renew		
All models (.3)		.5
Back-Up Lamp Switch, Renew		
(w/Manual Trans)		
All models (.3)		.4

	(Factory Time)	Chilton Time
Neutral Safety Switch, Renew		
All models (.3)		.4
Parking Brake Warning Lamp Switch, Renew		
All models (.3)		.4
Stop Light Switch, Renew		
All models (.3)		.4

	(Factory Time)	Chilton Time
w/Cruise control add (.1)		.1
Turn Signal Switch, Renew		
All models		
Std column (.5)		.9
Tilt column (.9)		1.4
Turn Signal or Hazard Warning Flasher, Renew		
All models (.2)		.3

GROUP INDEX

ALPHABETICAL INDEX

LABOR — 1 TUNE UP 1 — LABOR

	Factory Time	Chilton Time
Compression Test		
Four		.5
Two plug engine add		.2
Six		.6
V-6		.7
V-8		.9

Engine Tune Up, (Electronic Ignition)
Includes: Test battery and clean connections. Tighten manifold and carburetor mounting bolts. Check engine compression, clean and adjust or renew spark plugs. Test resistance of spark plug cables. Inspect distributor cap and rotor. Adjust air gap. Reset ignition timing. Adjust idle mixture and idle speed. Service air cleaner. Inspect and adjust drive belts. Inspect choke operation and adjust or free up. Check operation of EGR valve.

	Factory Time	Chilton Time
Four		1.5
Two plug engine add		.2
Six		2.1
V-6		2.0
V-8		2.7
w/A.C. add		.6

LABOR — 2 IGNITION SYSTEM 2 — LABOR

	Factory Time	Chilton Time
Diagnosis Ignition System		
Includes: Scope engine.		
All models (.5)		1.0
Spark Plugs, Clean and Reset or Renew		
RANGER-BRONCO		
Four		
Single plug (.4)		.6
Dual plug (.7)		.9
Six (.4)		.6
V-6 (.6)		.8
V-8 (.6)		.8
AEROSTAR		
Four (.5)		.7
V-6		
2.8L eng (1.0)		1.4
3.0L eng (1.6)		2.5
ECONOLINE-Six (.5)		.7
V-8		
5.0L-5.8L engs (.7)		1.0
7.5L eng (1.0)		1.4
F100-350-Six (.4)		.8
V-6 (.4)		.6
V-8 (.6)		.8
Ignition Timing, Reset		
Econoline-Aerostar (.6)		.8
All other models (.3)		.4
Distributor, R&R or Renew		
Includes: Reset ignition timing.		
RANGER (.7)		1.1
AEROSTAR		
Four (.6)		1.0
V-6 (.7)		1.3
BRONCO (.6)		.9
BRONCO II (.7)		1.1
ECONOLINE (.8)		1.2
F100-350-Six (.6)		.9
V-6 (.5)		.9
V-8 (.6)		1.0
Renew vac. diaph add		.2
Distributor, R&R and Recondition		
Includes: Reset ignition timing.		
BRONCO-Six (1.2)		1.7
V-8 (1.5)		2.0
ECONOLINE-Six (1.4)		1.9
V-8 (1.6)		2.1
F100-350-Six (1.2)		1.7
V-6 (1.5)		2.0
V-8 (1.7)		2.2
Distributor Cap and/or Rotor, Renew		
RANGER-BRONCO II (.5)		.6

	Factory Time	Chilton Time
BRONCO (.3)		.5
ECONOLINE (.4)		.6
F100-350 (.3)		.5
AEROSTAR (.5)		.6
Distributor Vacuum Control Valve, Renew		
All models (.3)		.5
Ignition Coil, Renew		
Includes: Test.		
AEROSTAR (.3)		.5
RANGER (.4)		.6
BRONCO (.5)		.7
BRONCO II (.3)		.5
ECONOLINE (.6)		.8
F100-350 (.5)		.7
Profile Ignition Pick-Up Sensor, Renew		
All models		
Dura-Spark (.5)		.8
Test system add		.3
Ignition Maintenance Warning Module, Renew or Reset		
All models (.4)		.6
Ignition Module Assembly, Renew		
All models		
Dura-Spark II (.2)		.4
Perform system test add (.3)		.3
Distributor Armature, Renew		
All models (.3)		.6
Distributor Stator, Renew		
Does not include system test.		
Econoline-Aerostar (.7)		.9
All other models (.6)		.8
Renew TFI module add (.2)		.2
Thick Film Ignition Module, Renew		
Does not include system test.		
Econoline-Aerostar (.6)		.8
All other models (.5)		.7
Ignition Cables, Renew		
Includes: Test wiring.		
AEROSTAR		
Four (.5)		.7
V-6		
2.8L eng (.7)		1.0
3.0L eng (1.6)		2.1
RANGER-BRONCO II (.6)		.8
BRONCO (.5)		.7
ECONOLINE		
Six (.5)		.6

	Factory Time	Chilton Time
V-8		
5.0L-5.8L eng (.6)		.8
7.5L eng (.7)		1.0
F100-350 (.4)		.7
Ignition Switch, Renew		
Aerostar (.9)		1.2
All other models (.5)		.8
DISTRIBUTORLESS IGNITION SYSTEM		
Diagnosis Ignition System		
All models (.5)		1.3
DIS Ignition Module, Renew		
Does not include system test.		
Ranger (.2)		.4
Camshaft Position Sensor, Renew		
Does not include system test.		
Ranger (.7)		1.1
Crankshaft Position Sensor, Renew		
Does not include system test.		
Ranger (.5)		.8
DIESEL IGNITION SYSTEM		
Diagnosis Glow Plug System		
Four (.3)		.5
V-8 (.7)		1.0
Glow Plug Relay, Renew		
Does not include system test.		
All models (.3)		.4
Glow Plug Wiring (Buss Bar), Renew		
Does not include system test.		
Four (.5)		.7
V-8 (.9)		1.1
Glow Plug Control Module, Renew		
Does not include system test.		
All models (.4)		.5
Glow Plugs, Renew		
Does not include system test.		
Four		
one or all (.3)		.5
V-8		
one (.4)		.5
each adtnl (.1)		.1
all (.8)		1.0
Idle Speed Control Modulator Solenoid, Renew		
All models (.4)		.6

LABOR 3 FUEL SYSTEM 3 LABOR

	(Factory) Time	Chilton Time
GASOLINE ENGINES		
Fuel Pump, Test		
Includes: Disconnect line at carburetor, attach pressure gauge.		
All models		
mechanical		.4
electric		.5
Fuel Filter, Renew		
RANGER-BRONCO (.3)		.4
AEROSTAR		
Four (.7)		.9
V-6		
2.8L (.3)		.4
3.0L (.6)		.8
ECONOLINE-Six (.4)		.5
V-8 (.3)		.4
F100-350		
Six (.4)		.5
V-8 (.3)		.4
Carburetor, Adjust (On Truck)		
All models (.3)		.4
Carburetor, R&R or Renew		
Includes: Necessary adjustments.		
RANGER-BRONCO I & II		
Four (.4)		.7
Six (.5)		.9
V-6 (.6)		1.0
V-8 (.6)		1.0
AEROSTAR		
V-6 (.7)		1.1
ECONOLINE-Six (.7)		1.2
V-8 (1.0)		1.5
F100-350-Six (.5)		.9
V-6 (.5)		.9
V-8 (.8)		1.2
Carburetor, R&R and Clean or Recondition		
Includes: Necessary adjustments.		
RANGER-BRONCO I & II		
Four (1.2)		1.8
Six (1.3)		2.0
V-6 (2.2)		3.0
V-8		
2150-2V (1.6)		2.4
2150-2V FB (2.6)		3.9
AEROSTAR		
V-6 (2.3)		3.4
ECONOLINE-Six (1.5)		2.0
V-8		
2150-2V (1.6)		2.4
2150-2V FB (2.2)		3.3
4160 4V (2.8)		4.2
F100-350-Six (1.1)		1.7
V-6 (1.3)		2.2
V-8-2 bbl		
w/Auto choke (1.8)		2.5
w/Manual choke (1.3)		1.9
4 bbl		
Motorcraft (1.8)		2.5
Holly (2.6)		3.9
Mechanical Fuel Pump, R&R or Renew		
RANGER-Four (.3)		.5
V-6 (.5)		.8
AEROSTAR		
V-6 (.8)		1.1
BRONCO		
Six (.5)		.8
V-8 (.7)		1.0
ECONOLINE		
Six (.4)		.7
V-8		
Gas (.7)		1.0
Diesel (.5)		.8
F100-350		
Six (.4)		.7
V-8 (.7)		1.0
Add pump test if performed.		

	(Factory) Time	Chilton Time
Fuel Tank Switch Assy., Renew		
All models (.3)		.5
Fuel Tank Selector Valve, Renew		
RANGER-BRONCO II (.8)		1.1
F-SERIES-ECONOLINE (.6)		.9
Fuel Tank, Renew		
RANGER		
aft tank		
4X2 (1.0)		1.4
4X4 (1.3)		1.9
mid tank (1.2)		1.8
AEROSTAR (1.2)		1.8
BRONCO (1.4)		2.0
BRONCO II		
4X2 (1.0)		1.4
4X4 (1.3)		1.9
ECONOLINE		
aft tank (1.0)		1.5
mid tank (1.2)		2.0
F100-350		
aft tank (1.4)		2.0
mid tank (1.1)		1.5
Auxiliary Fuel Tank, R&R or Renew		
BRONCO (.7)		1.3
ECONOLINE (.9)		1.5
F100-350 (.9)		1.5
Fuel Tank Sending Unit (w/Pump), Renew		
RANGER		
aft tank (.9)		1.3
mid tank (1.2)		1.8
AEROSTAR (1.2)		1.8
BRONCO (1.4)		2.0
BRONCO II (1.2)		1.8
ECONOLINE		
rear mounted (.3)		.6
side mounted (1.1)		1.9
aft tank (1.0)		1.5
mid tank (1.2)		2.0
F100-350		
aft tank (1.4)		2.0
mid tank (1.1)		1.5
Fuel Gauge (Dash), Renew		
RANGER (.6)		1.0
AEROSTAR (.6)		1.0
BRONCO (.6)		1.0
BRONCO II (.6)		1.0
ECONOLINE (.7)		1.1
F100-350 (.7)		1.1
Intake Manifold or Gaskets, Renew		
RANGER-BRONCO II		
Four		
2.0L eng (1.2)		2.0
w/P.S. add		.2
V-6 (2.8)		3.8
F-SERIES-BRONCO		
Six		4.4
V-8		
5.0L eng (1.9)		2.7
5.8L eng (2.3)		3.2
5.8L eng-w/Dual Ther (3.7)		5.1
7.5L eng (3.7)		5.1
ECONOLINE		
Six		4.4
V-8		
5.0L eng (1.9)		2.7
5.8L eng (3.2)		4.4
5.8L eng-w/Dual Ther (4.6)		6.4
7.5L eng (4.6)		6.4
Renew manif add (.4)		.5
ELECTRONIC FUEL INJECTION (EFI)		
(G) Fuel Injectors, Clean (On Car) (w/CFI or EFI)		
Includes: Hook up pressurized fuel injection cleaning equipment.		
Aerostar		1.0
All other models		.5

	(Factory) Time	Chilton Time
Fuel Filter Assembly, Renew		
RANGER-BRONCO II		
All models (.3)		.4
AEROSTAR		
Four (.7)		1.0
V-6 (.6)		.9
F-Series-BRONCO-ECONOLINE		
Six (.4)		.5
V-8 (.4)		.5
Diesel (.4)		.5
Fuel Injection Manifold Assy., Renew (Fuel Rail)		
Four		
Ranger (.8)		1.2
Aerostar (.9)		1.3
Six		
F-Series-Bronco (1.9)		2.6
Econoline (2.1)		2.9
V-6		
2.9L eng (1.2)		1.7
3.0L eng (1.1)		1.6
V-8		
5.0L-5.8L engs		
two piece		
right (1.3)		1.8
left (.8)		1.3
both (1.7)		2.8
one piece		
F-Series (1.9)		2.6
Econoline (2.1)		3.0
7.5L eng		
F-Series (1.7)		2.4
Econoline (1.9)		2.6
Air Intake Charge Throttle Body, Renew		
Four (.6)		1.0
Six		
F-series-Bronco (.7)		1.1
Econoline (1.0)		1.4
V-6		
2.9L eng (.6)		1.0
3.0L eng (1.1)		1.5
V-8		
5.0L-5.8L engs		
F-Series-Bronco (1.0)		1.4
Econoline (1.1)		1.5
7.5L eng		
F-Series (.7)		1.1
Econoline (1.0)		1.4
Fuel Charging Wiring Assy., Renew		
Four (.3)		.6
Six		
F-Series-Bronco (1.6)		2.2
Econoline (2.0)		2.6
V-6 (1.2)		1.7
V-8		
5.0L-5.8L engs		
F-Series-Bronco (1.2)		1.7
Econoline (1.7)		2.3
7.5L eng		
F-Series-Bronco (1.4)		1.9
Econoline (1.5)		2.0
Fuel Pressure Regulator, Renew		
Four (1.0)		1.5
Six		
F-Series-Bronco (1.8)		2.5
Econoline (2.2)		2.9
V-6		
2.9L eng (.3)		.6
3.0L eng (.5)		.8
V-8		
5.0L-5.8L engs (.8)		1.3
7.5L eng (.5)		.8
Electric Fuel Pump, Renew		
Ranger-Bronco II (.6)		.8
All other models (.5)		.7
Test pump add (.4)		.4

LABOR   3 FUEL SYSTEM 3   LABOR

	(Factory) Time	Chilton Time
Fuel Injectors, Renew		
Does not include system test.		
Ranger-Bronco II		
Four-one (.8)		1.2
all (.9)		1.4
V-6-one (1.0)		1.3
all (1.2)		1.8
F-Series-Bronco		
Six-one (1.6)		2.2
all (1.8)		2.5
V-8-one (1.5)		2.1
all (1.7)		2.4
Econoline		
Six-one (1.9)		2.5
all (2.1)		2.8
V-8-one (1.8)		2.4
all (2.0)		2.7
Aerostar		
Four-one (1.0)		1.3
all (1.1)		1.7
V-6-one (.9)		1.2
all (1.1)		1.5
Clean injectors add		.5
Intake Manifold and/or Gasket, Renew		
Four		
2.3L EFI		
upper (1.1)		1.5
lower (2.2)		3.1
V-6		
2.9L eng		
upper (1.0)		1.4
lower (2.2)		3.1
3.0L eng (3.4)		4.7
Six		
F-Series-Bronco		
upper (1.2)		1.7
upper & lower (2.6)		3.6
Econoline		
upper (1.2)		1.7
upper & lower (2.7)		3.7
V-8		
5.0L-5.8L engs		
F-Series-Bronco		
upper (1.1)		1.5
upper & lower (3.0)		4.2

	(Factory) Time	Chilton Time
Econoline		
upper (1.6)		2.2
upper & lower (3.5)		4.9
7.5L eng		
F-Series-Bronco		
upper (1.2)		1.7
upper & lower (3.2)		4.5
Econoline		
upper (1.3)		1.8
upper & lower (3.4)		4.7
w/A.C. add (.2)		.2
w/Cruise control add (.1)		.1
w/P.S. add (.2)		.2
DIESEL ENGINE		
Diagnosis Glow Plug System		
Four (.3)		.5
V-8 (.7)		1.0
Glow Plug Relay, Renew		
Does not include system test.		
All models (.3)		.4
Glow Plug Wiring (Buss Bar), Renew		
Does not include system test.		
Four (.5)		.7
V-8 (.9)		1.1
Glow Plug Control Module, Renew		
Does not include system test.		
All models (.4)		.5
Glow Plugs, Renew		
Does not include system test.		
Four		
one or all (.3)		.5
V-8		
one (.4)		.5
each adtnl (.1)		.1
all (.8)		1.0
Idle Speed Control Modulator Solenoid, Renew		
All models (.4)		.6
Fuel/Water Separator, Renew		
V-8		
F series (.6)		.8

	(Factory) Time	Chilton Time
Econoline (.8)		1.0
Fuel Pump, Renew		
V-8		
All models (.5)		.7
Fuel Filter Element, Renew		
All models		
Four & V-8 (.3)		.4
Intake Manifold and or Gaskets, Renew		
Four		
2.2L eng (1.4)		2.2
2.3L eng (2.4)		3.3
V-8		
F series (2.9)		4.0
Econoline (4.5)		6.3
Renew manif add (.2)		.5
Fuel Injection Pump Nozzles, Renew		
Four-2.3L eng		
one (.8)		1.1
each adtnl (.2)		.2
all (1.2)		1.7
V-8		
one (.7)		1.0
each adtnl (.5)		.6
all (1.7)		2.4
Fuel Injection Pump, Renew		
Four		
2.2L eng (1.6)		2.4
2.3L eng (1.4)		1.9
V-8		
F series (2.0)		2.7
Econoline (3.7)		5.0
Transfer vac regul add		.2
Injection Pump Drive Gear, Renew		
Four		
2.2L eng (1.9)		2.9
2.3L eng (1.2)		2.0
V-8		
F series (1.8)		2.5
Econoline (3.4)		4.7
Turbocharger Assy., R&R or Renew		
Four		
2.3L eng (1.7)		2.5
Renew wastegate actuator add (.2)		.2

LABOR   3A EMISSION CONTROLS 3A   LABOR

	(Factory) Time	Chilton Time
Emission Control Check		
Includes: Check and adjust engine idle speed and mixture, reset ignition timing. Check PCV valve.		
All models (.4)		.6
CRANKCASE EMISSION		
Positive Crankcase Ventilation Valve, Clean or Renew		
All models-clean (.4)		.5
renew (.2)		.3
EVAPORATIVE EMISSION TYPE		
Fuel Vapor Canister, Renew		
Bronco (.3)		.4
Econoline (.3)		.4
F100-350 (.4)		.6
Vapor Separator, Renew		
Bronco (.2)		.4
Econoline (.2)		.4
F100-350		
cab mounted (.2)		.4
frame mounted (.3)		.5

	(Factory) Time	Chilton Time
CONTROLLED COMBUSTION TYPE		
Air Cleaner Motor, Renew		
All models (.2)		.3
Air Cleaner Sensor, Renew		
All models (.2)		.3
THERMACTOR TYPE		
Thermactor Air Pump, Renew		
Four (.3)		.5
V-6 (.5)		.7
Six (.3)		.5
V-8-302-351 W engs (.4)		.7
351M, 400 engs (.7)		1.0
460 eng (.5)		.8
*Aerostar add		.2
Thermactor Drive Belt, Renew		
All models (.3)		.5
Anti-Backfire Valve, Renew		
All models (.3)		.4
Relief Valve, Renew		
All models (.3)		.4
Thermactor Air By-Pass Valve, Renew		
All models (.4)		.7

	(Factory) Time	Chilton Time
E.G.R. TYPE		
E.G.R. Valve, Renew		
1986		
Four (.3)		.5
V-6 (.7)		1.0
Six (.3)		.5
V-8 (.7)		.7
w/Dual Pumps		
one (.5)		.8
both (.8)		1.2
1987-90		
Four (.3)		.5
Six		
F-Series-Bronco (.7)		1.0
Econoline (1.0)		1.4
V-8		
5.0L eng		
F-Series (.5)		.8
Econoline (1.1)		1.5
5.8L eng (.4)		.6
5.8L-7.5L engs		
w/Dual Pumps		
one (.5)		.8
both (.8)		1.2
7.5L eng		
F-Series (.7)		1.0
Econoline (.4)		.6

LABOR   3A   EMISSION CONTROLS   3A   LABOR

	(Factory Time)	Chilton Time
E.G.R. Switch, Renew		
All models (.3)		.4
Vacuum Switch, Renew		
All models (.3)		.4
Air Supply Pump, Renew		
All models (.3)		.4
Thermostatic Exhaust Control Valve, Renew		
Econoline-Six (1.7)		2.4
F100-350-Six (1.5)		2.2

ELECTRONIC EMISSION CONTROL

	(Factory Time)	Chilton Time
EEC System, Test		
BRONCO (.7)		1.0
EGR Cooler, Renew		
Does not include system test.		
BRONCO (.6)		1.0
Power Relay, Renew		
Does not include system test.		
BRONCO (.3)		.4
Calibrator Assembly, Renew		
Does not include system test.		
BRONCO (.2)		.4
Processor Assembly, Renew		
Does not include system test.		
BRONCO (.3)		.6
Feedback Carburetor Actuator, Renew		
Does not include system test.		
BRONCO (.3)		.4
Exhaust Gas Oxygen Sensor, Renew		
Does not include system test.		
BRONCO (.4)		.7
Barometric Manifold Absolute Pressure Sensor, Renew		
Does not include system test.		
BRONCO (.3)		.5
Thermactor Air Bypass and Air Diverter Solenoid, Renew		
Does not include system test.		
BRONCO (.3)		.5

MCU SYSTEM

	(Factory Time)	Chilton Time
MCU System, Test		
All models (.4)		.6
Oxygen Sensor, Renew		
Does not include system test.		
All models (.3)		.7
Thermactor Air Valve, Renew		
Does not include system test.		
All models (.5)		.7
Ported Vacuum Switch, Renew		
Does not include system test.		
All models (.1)		.2
Fuel Control Solenoid, Renew		
Does not include system test.		
All models (.1)		.2
E.G.R. Valve, Renew		
Does not include system test.		
All models (.3)		.4
TAB/TAD Solenoid, Renew		
Does not include system test.		
All models (.1)		.2
Canister Purge Solenoid, Renew		
Does not include system test.		
All models (.1)		.2

	(Factory Time)	Chilton Time
Vacuum Switch, Renew		
Does not include system test.		
All models (.3)		.4
MCU/ECU Module, Renew		
Does not include system test.		
All models (.3)		.5
Low Temperature Switch, Renew (Electric or Vacuum)		
Does not include system test.		
All models		
2 port (.4)		.5
3 port (.3)		.4
Feedback Carburetor Actuator, Renew		
Does not include system test.		
All models (.4)		.6
Solenoid, Renew		
Does not include system test.		
All models-one (.3)		.4
Mid Temperature Switch, Renew (Electric or Vacuum)		
Does not include system test.		
All models (.3)		.4
Throttle Positioner Assembly, Renew		
Does not include system test.		
All models (.3)		.4

ELECTRONIC ENGINE CONTROL IV

	(Factory Time)	Chilton Time
E.E.C. System, Test		
All models (.5)		1.0
Throttle Position Sensor, Renew		
Does not include system test.		
Ranger-Bronco II		
Four (.6)		.8
V-6		
2.8L eng (.3)		.5
2.9L eng (.1)		.3
F-Series-Bronco		
wo/EFI		
Six & V-8 (.3)		.5
w/EFI		
Six (.3)		.5
V-8 (.6)		.8
Econoline		
wo/EFI		
Six & V-8 (.5)		.7
w/EFI		
Six (.5)		.7
V-8 (.7)		1.0
Aerostar		
Four (.7)		1.0
V-6 (.2)		.4
Air Change Temperature Sensor, Renew		
Does not include system test.		
All models (.1)		.3
Throttle Air By-Pass Valve, Renew		
Does not include system test.		
Ranger-Bronco II		
Four (.3)		.5
V-6 (.2)		.4
F-Series-Bronco		
Six (.2)		.4
V-8 (.3)		.5
Econoline		
Six & V-8 (.3)		.5
Aerostar		
Four (.3)		.5
V-6 (.2)		.4
Exhaust Gas Oxygen Sensor, Renew		
Does not include system test.		
Ranger-Bronco II		
Four (.2)		.4
V-6 (.1)		.3

	(Factory Time)	Chilton Time
F-Series-Bronco		
Six (.1)		.3
V-8 (.2)		.4
Econoline		
Six & V-8 (.2)		.4
Aerostar		
Four & V-6 (.3)		.5
Processor Assembly, Renew		
Does not include system test.		
All models (.2)		.3
Electronic Control Power Relay, Renew		
Does not include system test.		
Four		
All models (.2)		.4
V-6		
All models (.2)		.4
Six & V-8		
All models (.2)		.4
Electronic Vacuum Regulator, Renew		
Does not include system test.		
Six (.2)		.4
V-6 (.1)		.3
V-8 (.2)		.4
E.G.R. Pressure Feedback Sensor, Renew		
Does not include system test.		
V-6 (.2)		.4
Choke Cap, Renew		
Does not include system test.		
V-6		
All models (.3)		.5
E.G.R. Shut-Off Solenoid, Renew		
Does not include system test.		
Econoline (.2)		.3
All other models (.1)		.2
Fuel Pump Relay, Renew		
Does not include system test.		
Four		
All models (.1)		.2
Fuel Pump Inertia Switch Assy., Renew		
Does not include system test.		
Four		
All models (.2)		.3
Throttle Positioner Assembly, Renew		
Does not include system test.		
All models		
Six (.5)		.7
V-6 (.4)		.6
Fuel Injector Assembly, Renew		
Does not include system test.		
Ranger-Bronco II		
Four-one (.8)		1.2
all (.9)		1.4
V-6-one (1.0)		1.3
all (1.2)		1.8
F-Series-Bronco		
Six-one (1.6)		2.2
all (1.8)		2.5
V-8-one (1.5)		2.1
all (1.7)		2.4
Econoline		
Six-one (1.9)		2.5
all (2.1)		2.8
V-8-one (1.8)		2.4
all (2.0)		2.7
Aerostar		
Four-one (1.0)		1.3
all (1.1)		1.7
V-6-one (.9)		1.2
all (1.1)		1.5
Clean injectors add		.5

LABOR 3A EMISSION CONTROLS 3A LABOR

	(Factory Time)	Chilton Time
Knock Sensor, Renew		
Does not include system test.		
All models		
Four (.2)		.4
V-6 (.2)		.4
Six (.3)		.5
V-8 (.4)		.6
Air Change Temperature Sensor, Renew		
Does not include system test.		
Econoline (.3)		.5
All other models (.1)		.3
Canister Purge Solenoid, Renew		
Does not include system test.		
Econoline (.2)		.4
All other models (.1)		.3
Engine Coolant Temperature Sensor, Renew		
Does not include system test.		
All models (.2)		.4
Feedback Control Solenoid, Renew		
Does not include system test.		
V-6		
All models (.3)		.4
Six		
All models (.2)		.4
V-8		
All models (.6)		.8

	(Factory Time)	Chilton Time
Manifold Absolute Pressure Sensor, Renew		
Does not include system test.		
All models (.1)		.3
E.G.R. Valve Position Sensor, Renew		
Does not include system test.		
Econoline–Aerostar (.3)		.5
All other models (.2)		.4
Renew E.G.R. valve add (.1)		.1
Thick Film Ignition Module, Renew		
Does not include system test.		
Four		
All models (.5)		.7
V-6		
All models (.6)		.8
Six		
All models (.5)		.7
V-8		
All models (.6)		.8
Profile Ignition Pick-Up Sensor, Renew		
Does not include system test.		
Four (.6)		.8
Six (.6)		.8
V-6 (.7)		1.0
V-8 (.7)		1.0
Renew TFI module add (.2)		.2

	(Factory Time)	Chilton Time
E.G.R. Valve, Renew		
Does not include system test.		
Four		
Ranger (.2)		.4
Aerostar (.4)		.7
Six		
All models (.1)		.3
V-6		
All models (.1)		.3
V-8		
Econoline (.2)		.4
All other models (.1)		.3
Throttle Kicker Actuator, Renew		
Does not include system test.		
All models (.5)		.7
Tab/Tad Solenoids, Renew		
Does not include system test.		
All models (.2)		.3
E.G.R. Control Solenoids, Renew		
Does not include system test.		
All models (.2)		.3
Throttle Kicker Solenoid, Renew		
Does not include system test.		
All models (.2)		.3

LABOR 4 ALTERNATOR AND REGULATOR 4 LABOR

	(Factory Time)	Chilton Time
Alternator Circuits, Test		
Includes: Test battery, regulator and alternator output.		
All models (.4)		.6
Alternator Drive Belt, Renew		
Gas (.3)		.4
Diesel (.4)		.5
Alternator, R&R or Renew		
Four (.4)		.7
Six		
Econoline (1.1)		1.5
All other models (.4)		.7

	(Factory Time)	Chilton Time
V-6		
2.8L-2.9L engs (.5)		.9
3.0L eng (1.0)		1.5
V-8		
Econoline		
5.0L-5.8L engs (.9)		1.4
6.9L-7.3L engs (.9)		1.4
7.5L eng (1.2)		*1.6
All other models (.5)		.9
*w/Dual Therm. pumps add		.5
Renew regulator add		.4
Renew brushes add		.3
Renew drive brg add		.3

	(Factory Time)	Chilton Time
Renew end brg add		.3
Renew rectifier assy add		.4
Renew stator assy add		.4
Alternator Regulator, Renew (External)		
All models (.3)		.5
Add circuit test if performed.		
Ammeter, Renew		
All models (.5)		.9
Instrument Cluster Voltage Regulator, Renew		
All models (.5)		.8

LABOR 5 STARTING SYSTEM 5 LABOR

	(Factory Time)	Chilton Time
Starter Draw Test (On Truck)		
All models (.3)		.3
Starter, R&R or Renew		
Gas Engines		
All models (.4)		.7
Diesel Engines		
Four (.8)		1.1
V-8 (.6)		.9

	(Factory Time)	Chilton Time
Renew brushes add		
TK		.5
Motorcraft		.6
Delco		.2
Renew starter drive add		
TK		.6
Motorcraft		.2
Delco		.4
Recond complete add		
TK		1.5

	(Factory Time)	Chilton Time
Motorcraft & Delco		1.0
Renew field coils add		.5
Add draw test if performed.		
Starter Solenoid Relay, Renew		
All models (.3)		.5
Battery Cables, Renew		
All models–each (.3)		.4

LABOR 6 BRAKE SYSTEM 6 LABOR

	(Factory Time)	Chilton Time
Brake Pedal Free Play, Adjust		
All models (.3)		.4

	(Factory Time)	Chilton Time
Brakes, Adjust (Minor)		
Includes: Adjust brakes, fill master cylinder.		
two wheels		.4
four wheels		.7

	(Factory Time)	Chilton Time
Bleed Brakes (Four Wheels)		
Includes: Fill master cylinder.		
All models (.3)		.6

LABOR 6 BRAKE SYSTEM 6 LABOR

Brake Shoes, Renew

Includes: Install new or exchange shoes, service self adjustors. Adjust service and hand brake. Bleed system.

	Factory Time	Chilton Time
BRONCO—front (1.5)		2.0
rear (1.3)		1.8
All four wheels (2.2)		3.7
ECONOLINE—F100-350		
front (1.1)		1.5
rear (1.7)		2.2
All four wheels (2.3)		3.5
F100-350 4X4		
front (1.3)		1.8
rear (1.7)		2.2
All four wheels (2.5)		3.7
Resurface brake drum add, each		.5

Brake Shoes and/or Pads, Renew

Includes: Install new or exchange brake shoes or pads. Adjust service and hand brake. Bleed system.

	Factory Time	Chilton Time
5 lug wheel		
front-disc (.7)		1.1
rear-drum (.9)		*1.8
all four wheels (1.3)		2.8
8 lug wheel		
front (.8)		1.1
rear (1.0)		1.3
all four wheels (1.5)		2.2
10 lug wheel		
front (1.2)		1.5
rear (1.2)		1.5
all four wheels (2.1)		2.8
*w/Full floating axle add		.6
Resurface brake rotor add, each		.9
Resurface brake drum add, each		.5

Front Brake Drum and Hub Assy., Renew

	Factory Time	Chilton Time
BRONCO—one (.7)		.9
both (1.2)		1.6
ECONOLINE—one (.5)		.8
both (.7)		1.1
F100-350—one (.5)		.8
both (.8)		1.2

Rear Brake Drum, Renew

All models

	Factory Time	Chilton Time
Semi-Floating Axle		
one (.4)		.6
both (.6)		.9
Ford Axle (Full Floating)		
one (.4)		.6
both (.6)		.9
Dana Axle (Full Floating)		
one (.7)		1.1
both (1.1)		1.9

Brake Pressure Warning Light Switch, Renew

	Factory Time	Chilton Time
All models (.3)		.5

BRAKE HYDRAULIC SYSTEM

Wheel Cylinder, Renew

Includes: Bleed system.

Front

	Factory Time	Chilton Time
BRONCO—one (1.1)		1.5
both (2.1)		2.9
ECONOLINE, F100-350		
one (.9)		1.3
both (1.7)		2.5
F100-350 4X4		
one (1.0)		1.4
both (1.9)		2.7

Rear

	Factory Time	Chilton Time
RANGER-AEROSTAR—one (.8)		1.4
both (1.5)		2.6
BRONCO—one (1.0)		1.5
both (1.9)		2.9
ECONOLINE, F-SERIES 4X2		
one (1.2)		1.6
both (2.3)		3.0

COMBINATIONS

Add to Brakes, Renew

See Machine Shop Operations

	Factory Time	Chilton Time
RENEW WHEEL CYLINDER		
Each (.3)		.4
REBUILD WHEEL CYLINDER		
Each (.3)		.6
REBUILD CALIPER ASSEMBLY		
Single piston		.3
Dual piston		.5
RENEW MASTER CYLINDER		
All models (.4)		.7
REBUILD MASTER CYLINDER		
All models		1.3
RENEW BRAKE HOSE		
Each (.3)		.3
RENEW REAR WHEEL GREASE SEALS		
One side (.2)		.4
FRONT WHEEL BEARINGS, REPACK OR RENEW SEALS (BOTH WHEELS)		
Drum brakes (.3)		.6
Disc brakes (.4)		.7
4X4 (.6)		.8
RENEW BRAKE DRUM		
Each (.2)		.3
RENEW DISC BRAKE ROTOR		
4X2 (.2)		.3
4X4 (.3)		.5

	Factory Time	Chilton Time
F-SERIES 4X4		
one (1.2)		1.9
both (2.3)		3.3

Wheel Cylinder, R&R and Recondition

Includes: Hone cylinder and bleed system.

Front

	Factory Time	Chilton Time
BRONCO—one (1.1)		1.8
both (2.1)		3.5
ECONOLINE, F100-350 F-SERIES 4X2		
one (.9)		1.6
both (1.7)		3.1
F-SERIES F100-350 4X4		
one (1.0)		1.7
both (1.9)		3.3

Rear

	Factory Time	Chilton Time
RANGER-AEROSTAR—one (.8)		1.6
both (1.5)		3.0
BRONCO—one (1.0)		1.8
both (1.9)		3.5
ECONOLINE, F-SERIES 4X2		
one (1.2)		1.9
both (2.3)		3.7
F-SERIES 4X4		
one (1.2)		2.2
both (2.3)		3.6

Brake Hose, Renew (Flex)

Includes: Bleed system.

Front

	Factory Time	Chilton Time
RANGER-AEROSTAR—one (.5)		.8
both (.6)		1.0
BRONCO, F100-350, F100-350 4X4		
one (.5)		.8
both (.6)		1.0
ECONOLINE 100-350		
one (.6)		.9
both (.8)		1.1

Rear

	Factory Time	Chilton Time
RANGER-AEROSTAR—one (.5)		.8
BRONCO, F100-350 4X4		
one (.5)		.8

	Factory Time	Chilton Time
ECONOLINE 100-350, F100-350		
one (.6)		.9
each adtnl		.3

Master Cylinder, Renew

Includes: Bleed complete system.

	Factory Time	Chilton Time
Aerostar (.7)		1.1
All other models		
wo/Booster (.6)		1.0
w/Booster (.5)		.9

Master Cylinder, R&R and Recondition

Includes: Hone cylinder and bleed complete system.

	Factory Time	Chilton Time
Aerostar (1.0)		1.6
All other models		
wo/Booster (.8)		1.5
w/Booster (.7)		1.4

Vacuum Pump, Renew (w/Diesel Eng)

	Factory Time	Chilton Time
ECONOLINE-F-series (.6)		.9
All other models (.4)		.6

Brake Differential Valve, R&R or Renew

Includes: Bleed complete system and transfer switch.

	Factory Time	Chilton Time
All models (.7)		1.2

POWER BRAKES

Power Brake Booster, R&R or Renew

	Factory Time	Chilton Time
Aerostar (1.0)		1.5
All other models (.6)		1.1
w/Cruise control add (.2)		.2

Brake Booster Check Valve, Renew

	Factory Time	Chilton Time
All models (.3)		.4

Hydra-Boost Brake Booster, Renew

	Factory Time	Chilton Time
Diesel models (.8)		1.2

DISC BRAKES

Brake Shoes and/or Pads, Renew

Includes: Install new or exchange brake shoes or pads. Adjust service and hand brake. Bleed system.

	Factory Time	Chilton Time
5 lug wheel		
front-disc (.7)		1.1
rear-drum (.9)		*1.8
all four wheels (1.3)		2.8
8 lug wheel		
front (.8)		1.1
rear (1.0)		1.3
all four wheels (1.5)		2.2
10 lug wheel		
front (1.2)		1.5
rear (1.2)		1.5
all four wheels (2.1)		2.8
*w/Full floating axle add		.6
Resurface brake rotor add, each		.9
Resurface brake drum add, each		.5

Disc Brake Rotor, Renew

Includes: Renew front wheel bearings and grease retainer and repack bearings.

	Factory Time	Chilton Time
4X2 models		
one (.5)		.8
both (.8)		1.4
4X4 models		
Ranger-Bronco II		
one (.5)		.8
both (.8)		1.4
F-Series-Bronco		
one (.7)		1.0
both (1.1)		1.8
8 lug wheel		
one (.7)		1.1
both (1.2)		1.9
10 lug wheel		
one (1.5)		1.9
both (2.6)		3.2

LABOR   6 BRAKE SYSTEM 6   LABOR

(Factory Time)	Chilton Time
Caliper Assembly, Renew	
Includes: Bleed complete system.	
5 lug wheel	
one (.6)	1.0
both (.8)	1.4
8 lug wheel	
one (.7)	1.0
both (.9)	1.4
10 lug wheel	
one–front or rear (.8)	1.1
two–same axle (1.2)	1.8
all four wheels (2.1)	3.0
Recond caliper add	
Single Piston–each (.2)	.3
Dual Piston–each (.3)	.5
PARKING BRAKE	
Parking Brake, Adjust	
All models (.3)	.5
Parking Brake Control, Renew	
AEROSTAR (.6)	.9

(Factory Time)	Chilton Time
RANGER–BRONCO II (.5)	.8
ECONOLINE (.6)	.9
F-SERIES–BRONCO (.6)	.9
Super Duty (.8)	1.1
Parking Brake Cable, Renew	
Front–All models (.7)	1.0
Rear	
Semi-Floating Axle	
one (.5)	.8
both (.7)	1.1
Dana Full Floating Axle	
one (.8)	1.1
both (1.4)	2.0
Ford Full Floating Axle	
one (.6)	.9
both (.9)	1.4
Parking Brake Assy., (Trans Mount), Remove & Install	
F-Series (1.2)	1.5
Renew assy add (1.4)	1.4

(Factory Time)	Chilton Time
ANTI-SKID BRAKE SYSTEM (ABS)	
Anti-Skid Brake System Diagnosis	
All models (.3)	.6
Brake Computer Module, Renew	
Does not include system test.	
All models (.3)	.4
Electro Hydraulic Proportioning Valve, Renew	
Does not include system test.	
All models (.6)	.9
Excitor Ring, Renew	
Does not include system test.	
All models (1.1)	1.5
Sensor Assembly, Renew	
Does not include system test.	
All models (.3)	.5

LABOR   7 COOLING SYSTEM 7   LABOR

(Factory Time)	Chilton Time
Winterize Cooling System	
Includes: Run engine to check for leaks, tighten all hose connections. Test radiator and pressure cap, drain radiator and engine block. Add antifreeze and refill system.	
All models	.5
Thermostat, Renew	
Gas Engines	
Four (.5)	.6
Six (.4)	*.6
V-6 (.6)	.9
V-8 (.9)	†1.0
Diesel Engines	
Four (.7)	.9
V-8 (1.1)	1.4
*ECONOLINE add	.3
†ECONOLINE add	.5
Radiator Assembly, R&R or Renew	
Includes: Drain and refill cooling system.	
RANGER–AEROSTAR	
Gas (.6)	1.0
Diesel (.7)	1.1
BRONCO I & II	
Six (.9)	1.5
V-6 (.6)	1.0
V-8 (.6)	1.0
ECONOLINE–Six (1.1)	1.7
V-8 (1.0)	1.6
Diesel (.9)	1.5
F100-350	
Six (.9)	1.5
V-8 (.6)	1.0
Diesel (1.4)	2.0
ADD THESE OPERATIONS TO RADIATOR R&R	
Boil & Repair	1.5
Rod Clean	1.9
Repair Core	1.3
Renew Tank	1.6
Renew Trans. Oil Cooler	1.9
Renew Side Tank	.7
Recore Radiator	1.7
Radiator Hoses, Renew	
RANGER–BRONCO II–upper (.3)	.4
lower (.4)	.5
both (.5)	.6
ALL OTHER MODELS	
upper (.4)	.5

(Factory Time)	Chilton Time
lower (.4)	.5
both (.5)	.7
Water Pump, Renew	
RANGER–BRONCO II	
Four (1.1)	1.7
w/A.C. add (.5)	.5
w/P.S. add (.2)	.2
V-6 (1.4)	2.0
w/A.C. add (.1)	.1
Diesel	
2.2L eng (1.1)	1.7
2.3L eng (1.6)	2.3
AEROSTAR	
Four (1.1)	1.7
V-6 (1.3)	2.0
w/A.C. add (.3)	.3
w/P.S. add (.2)	.2
BRONCO–Six (.9)	1.5
V-6 (1.4)	2.0
w/A.C. add (.4)	.4
V-8 (1.3)	1.9
w/A.C. add (.2)	.2
ECONOLINE	
1986-90	
Six (1.3)	2.0
w/A.C. add (.2)	.2
V-8	
302-351 engs (1.7)	2.7
w/Dual Therm add (1.0)	1.4
460 eng (1.9)	3.4
Diesel (2.5)	3.7
w/A.C. add (.3)	.3
F100-350–Six (.9)	1.6
V-6 (1.1)	1.7
V-8	
302-351W engs (1.3)	2.0
351M-400 engs (1.3)	2.0
w/Dual Therm add (.5)	.7
460 eng (1.7)	2.7
Diesel (1.9)	2.9
w/P.S. add	.3
w/A.C. add	.3
Fan Blade, Renew	
V-8–Diesel (.7)	1.0
All other engs	
wo/Viscous drive (.4)	.6
w/Viscous drive (.5)	.7
Drive Belt, Adjust	
All models–one (.3)	.4
each adtnl (.2)	.3

(Factory Time)	Chilton Time
Vacuum Pump Drive Belt, Renew	
All models (.3)	.4
Serpentine Drive Belt, Renew	
Econoline (.4)	.6
All other models (.3)	.5
Thermactor Drive Belt, Renew	
All models (.3)	.4
Temperature Gauge (Engine), Renew	
All models (.3)	.5
Temperature Gauge (Dash), Renew	
All models (.6)	1.0
Water Jacket Expansion Plugs, Renew (Side of Block)	
All models–each	.5
Add time to gain accessibility.	
Heater Core, R&R or Renew	
Without Air Conditioning	
AEROSTAR–Main (.8)	1.4
Auxiliary (.8)	1.4
RANGER (.5)	.9
BRONCO (.8)	1.6
BRONCO II (.5)	.9
ECONOLINE–Main (1.1)	1.0
Auxiliary (.8)	1.4
F100-350 (.8)	1.6
WITH AIR CONDITIONING	
Aerostar (.8)	1.4
Econoline (1.1)	2.0
All other models (.5)	1.1
ADD THESE OPERATIONS TO HEATER CORE R&R	
Boil & Repair	1.2
Repair Core	.9
Recore	1.2
Heater Water Control Valve, Renew	
All models (.3)	.6
Heater Blower Motor, Renew	
AEROSTAR–Main (.5)	.9
Auxiliary (.4)	.7
RANGER (.5)	.7
BRONCO (.5)	.7
ECONOLINE–Main (.5)	.9
Auxiliary (.6)	.9
F100-350 (.3)	.6
Heater Control Assembly, Renew	
All models (.6)	1.1

LABOR 7 COOLING SYSTEM 7 LABOR

(Factory Time)	Chilton Time	(Factory Time)	Chilton Time	(Factory Time)	Chilton Time
Heater Blower Motor Switch, Renew		BRONCO (.4)	.7	ECONOLINE—Main (.4)	.7
AEROSTAR		BRONCO II (.5)	.9	Auxiliary (.5)	.8
main (.6)	.9	ECONOLINE (.5)	.9	F100-350 (.4)	.7
front (.6)	.9	F100-350 (.4)	.7	AEROSTAR—Main (.3)	.6
rear (.4)	.6	**Heater Blower Motor Resistor, Renew**		Auxiliary (.5)	.8
RANGER (.5)	.9	RANGER, BRONCO (.3)	.6		

LABOR 8 EXHAUST SYSTEM 8 LABOR

(Factory Time)	Chilton Time	(Factory Time)	Chilton Time	(Factory Time)	Chilton Time
Catalytic Converter, Renew		Diesel (.6)	.9	both (2.9)	4.0
1986-90		Aerostar		3.0L eng	
Ranger-Bronco II-		Four (.8)	1.1	right (1.6)	2.2
Aerostar		V-6		left (1.9)	2.6
Four (.5)	.8	2.8L eng (.7)	1.0	both (2.5)	3.5
V-6 (.9)	1.4	3.0L eng (.8)	1.1	**V-8**	
All other models		**Tail Pipe, Renew**		302-351W engs	
Six (1.9)	2.6	BRONCO (.5)	.7	one side (.7)	1.1
V-8 (1.8)	2.5	ECONOLINE (.5)	.7	both sides (1.1)	1.9
Muffler, Renew		F100-350 (.4)	.6	w/Dual Therm Pumps	
1986-90		**Exhaust Manifold, Renew**		right (1.4)	1.9
Ranger-Bronco II		**Four**		left (1.7)	2.4
Four		Gas		both (2.7)	3.8
Gas (.4)	.7	2.0L eng (.9)	1.5	351M-400 engs	
Diesel (.5)	.8	2.3L eng (1.4)	2.0	one side (.8)	1.3
V-6 (.8)	1.2	Diesel		both sides (1.2)	2.3
F-Series-Bronco-Econoline		2.2L eng (.9)	1.6	460 eng-F-series	
Six (.8)	1.2	2.3L eng (2.4)	3.4	one side (1.3)	1.8
V-8		**Six—wo/EFI**	4.5	both sides (2.2)	3.0
302-351 engs (.8)	1.2	w/EFI		460 eng-Econoline	
460 eng (.6)	.9	front (3.7)	5.1	right side (2.7)	3.8
Diesel (.5)	.8	rear (3.1)	4.3	left side (1.5)	2.1
Aerostar		both (3.9)	5.4	both sides (3.8)	5.3
Four (.5)	.8	**V-6**		**Diesel**	
V-6		2.8L eng		right side (1.7)	2.3
2.8L eng (.6)	.9	Ranger-Bronco II		left side (1.6)	2.2
3.0L eng (.4)	.7	right (1.5)	2.1	both sides (2.6)	3.8
Intermediate Exhaust Pipe, Renew		left (1.4)	2.0	* w/A.C. add (.3)	.3
1986-90		both (2.4)	3.6		
Ranger		Aerostar		**COMBINATIONS**	
Four		right (1.1)	1.5	**Muffler, Exhaust and Tail Pipe, Renew**	
Gas (.7)	1.0	left (.8)	1.1	RANGER	1.1
Diesel (.6)	.9	both (1.5)	2.1	BRONCO	1.9
F-Series-Bronco-Econoline		2.9L eng		ECONOLINE	1.9
Six (.6)	.9	right (1.4)	2.0	F100-350-one side	1.8
V-8 (.7)	1.0	left (1.8)	2.5	both sides	2.7

LABOR 9A FRONT SUSPENSION (RWD) 9A LABOR

(Factory Time)	Chilton Time	(Factory Time)	Chilton Time	(Factory Time)	Chilton Time
Note: On all front suspension operations alignment charges must be added if performed. Time given does not include alignment.		**Front Wheel Bearings and Cups, Renew (One Wheel)**		10 Lug	
		4X2		Super Duty (.8)	1.1
		All models (.7)	1.1	**Front Hub Assembly, Renew**	
		4X4		F-Series-Super Duty	
Check Alignment of Front End		Ranger-Bronco II (.7)	1.1	one (1.5)	1.9
All models (.5)	.6	F-Series-Bronco (.8)	1.2	both (2.6)	3.2
Note: Deduct if alignment is performed.		Super Duty (.9)	1.3		
Toe-In, Adjust		**Front Wheel Grease Seal, Renew (One Wheel)**		**Front Shock Absorber or Bushings, Renew**	
All models (.4)	.7	5 lug-4X2		All models-one (.4)	.6
		Ranger-Aerostar (.5)	.8	both (.5)	.8
Align Front End		F-Series-Bronco (.6)	.9		
Includes: Adjust front wheel bearings.		Econoline (.6)	.9	**Upper Control Arms, Renew**	
Aerostar (1.2)	1.5	5 lug-4X4		Add alignment charges.	
All other models (1.9)	2.5	Ranger-Bronco II (.5)	.8	Aerostar-one (1.0)	1.3
		F-Series-Bronco (.7)	1.0	both (1.5)	2.0
Front Wheel Bearings, Clean and Repack (Both Wheels)		8 Lug-4X2			
drum brakes	1.0	F-Series-Econoline (.7)	1.0	**Upper Control Arm Bushings, Renew**	
disc brakes	1.4	8 Lug-4X4		Add alignment charges.	
4 wheel drive	2.5	F-Series-Econoline (.8)	1.1	Aerostar-one side (1.6)	2.2
				both sides (2.5)	3.4

LABOR 9A FRONT SUSPENSION (RWD) 9A LABOR

	(Factory Time)	Chilton Time

Lower Control Arms, Renew
Add alignment charges.
Aerostar-one side (1.5)	2.0
both sides (2.4)	3.2

Front Axle 'I' Beam, Renew
Includes: R&R wheels and brake backing plates.
Add alignment charges.
STAMPED AXLE 4X2
one side (2.3)	3.1
both sides (3.9)	5.3

FORGED AXLE 4X2
one side (1.8)	2.4
both sides (2.7)	3.6
Super Duty (4.5)	6.4

Renew ball joints
add-each (.2)	.3

Renew pivot bushings
add-each (.2)	.3

Front Spindle Assembly, Renew
CONTROL ARM AXLE
one side (1.4)	1.9
both sides (1.9)	2.9

STAMPED AXLE 4X2
one side (1.6)	2.1
both sides (2.3)	3.1

FORGED AXLE 4X2
one side (1.4)	1.9
both sides (1.9)	2.5

STAMPED AXLE 4X4
one side (.6)	.9
both sides (.9)	1.3

FORGED AXLE 4X4
one side (1.5)	1.9
both sides (2.0)	2.5

MONOBEAM
one (.7)	1.0
both (1.1)	1.5

8 LUG WHEEL
one (.8)	1.1
both (1.2)	1.6

10 LUG WHEEL
one (1.8)	2.5
both (2.9)	4.0

Rebush spindle, add
each side (.4)	.5

Renew needle brgs, add
each (.1)	.2

Steering Shock Absorber, Renew
BRONCO, F100-250 4X4 (.3)	.6

Track Bar Assembly, Renew
BRONCO, F100-250 4X4 (.6)	1.0

Radius Arm, Renew
All models-one (1.5)	1.9
both (2.2)	2.8

Radius Arm Bushings, Renew
Add alignment charges if required.
All models-each side	1.0

Front Spring, Renew
AEROSTAR
one (.9)	1.2
both (1.6)	2.1

4X2
All models
one (.4)	.7
both (.7)	1.3

4X4
Ranger-Bronco II
one (.4)	.7
both (.7)	1.3

F-Series-Bronco
one (.7)	1.1
both (1.1)	2.0

Super Duty
right (1.1)	1.5
left (.6)	.9
both (1.5)	2.2

Renew tie bolt
add-each (.5)	.5

Front Stabilizer Bushings, Renew
All models (.5)	.8

Front Stabilizer Bar, Renew
All models (.6)	.9

Front Stabilizer End Kit, Renew
All models (.4)	.5

Ball Joints, Renew
Add alignment charges if required.
4X4 models-each side	2.0

Ball Joints, Renew (4X2 models)
Includes: Alignment charges.
All models
one (1.7)	2.5
one side (2.6)	3.5

FRONT WHEEL DRIVE

Front Axle Housing and Differential Assy., R&R (Complete)
Includes: Drain and refill axle, R&R wheels, hubs and axle shafts. Road test.
BRONCO (3.9)	5.4
F100 (3.7)	5.2
F250 (2.8)	4.2

Front Axle Housing, Renew (One Piece Assy)
Includes: R&R housing and differential assy. Transfer all parts. Adjust ring gear and pinion. Does not include disassembly of differential case.
BRONCO (8.0)	9.6
F100 (7.4)	9.0
F250 (7.2)	9.0

Axle Housing Cover or Gasket, Renew
All models (.5)	.7

Front Axle Arm (Beam), Renew (Independent Front Suspension)
w/coil springs
left side (3.8)	5.1
right side (2.9)	3.9
both sides (5.9)	7.9

w/leaf springs
left side (3.8)	5.1
right side (3.0)	4.0
both sides (6.1)	8.2
monobeam (4.6)	6.5

Renew ball joints
add-each (.2)	.3

Renew pivot bushings
add-each (.2)	.3

Front Axle Shaft, Renew
Stamped Axle
Ranger-Bronco II
one (.7)	.9
both (1.2)	1.8

F-Series-Bronco
left (.8)	1.0
right (.9)	1.2
both (1.4)	1.9

MonoBeam
one (.8)	1.0
both (1.3)	1.8

8 Lug Wheel
one (.8)	1.1
both (1.4)	1.9

O/haul or renew U-Joints,
add-each (.3)	.3

Front Axle Stub Shaft and Slip Joint, Renew
Includes: Renew U-Joint.
Ranger-Bronco II (2.3)	3.2
F-Series-Bronco (2.6)	3.6

Front Axle Housing Oil Seals, Renew
Stamped Axle
Ranger-Bronco II
left (.7)	1.0
right (2.1)	2.8
both (2.1)	2.9

F-series-Bronco
left (.8)	1.1
right (2.2)	2.9
both (2.3)	3.0

Monobeam
one (3.4)	4.5
both (3.4)	4.5

8 Lug Wheel
one (2.4)	3.1
both (2.5)	3.3

Steering Knuckle, Renew
Add alignment charges.
Stamped Axle 4X4
one side (2.4)	3.1
both sides (4.3)	5.5

Monobeam 4X4
one side (1.7)	2.2
both sides (2.9)	3.8

Renew king pin add,
each (.1)	.2

Renew brg and cup add,
each (.1)	.1

Front Axle Pinion Oil Seal, Renew
All models (.6)	1.0

Front Axle Pivot Bushings, Renew
All models-one side (.5)	.8
both sides (.7)	1.3

Front Drive Shaft, R&R
All models (.5)	.7

Recond U-Joint, Add
one (.3)	.4
all (.5)	.6

Differential Carrier, R&R or Reseal
All models
w/coil springs (2.3)	3.2
w/leaf springs (2.4)	3.3
w/monobeam (3.6)	5.0

Ring Gear Backlash, Adjust
All models
w/coil springs (3.1)	4.3
w/leaf springs (3.2)	4.4
w/monobeam (4.4)	6.1

Ring Gear and Pinion Set, Renew
All models
w/coil springs (3.9)	5.4
w/leaf springs (4.0)	5.6
w/monobeam (5.2)	7.2

Renew pinion brgs add (.2)
	.4
Recond diff assy add (.2)
	.5

Differential Case, Renew
All models
w/coil springs
std (3.2)	4.5
locker (3.5)	4.9

w/leaf springs
std (3.3)	4.6
locker (3.6)	5.0

w/monobeam
std (4.5)	6.3
locker (4.8)	6.7

Renew diff brgs add (.2)
	.4

LABOR   10   STEERING LINKAGE   10   LABOR

	(Factory Time)	Chilton Time
Tie Rod Ends, Renew (One Side)		
Includes: Reset toe-in.		
All models (.8)		1.1
Tie Rod, Renew (One)		
Includes: Reset toe-in.		
All models (.8)		1.2
Drag Link, Renew		
Does not include toe-in adjustment.		
All models (.5)		.7

	(Factory Time)	Chilton Time
Pitman Arm, Renew		
All models (.5)		.7
Front Spindle Arm, Renew		
Includes: R&R wheel hub and brake drum/ rotor where required. Reset toe-in.		
BRONCO-Part Time Hub		
one (1.0)		1.4
both (1.9)		2.7
Full Time Hub		
one (.9)		1.3

	(Factory Time)	Chilton Time
both (1.6)		2.4
ECONOLINE-one (.6)		1.0
both (1.0)		1.8
F100-350-one (1.1)		1.5
both (1.6)		2.2
F100-350 4X4		
Part Time Hub-one (1.0)		1.4
both (1.9)		2.7
Full Time Hub-one (.9)		1.3
both (1.6)		2.4

LABOR   11   STEERING GEAR   11   LABOR

	(Factory Time)	Chilton Time
MANUAL		
Steering Wheel, Renew		
All models (.3)		.5
Upper Mast Jacket Bearing, Renew		
All models		
std colm (.5)		.9
tilt colm (.6)		1.0
Steering Column Lock Actuator, Renew		
All models		
std colm (1.0)		1.5
tilt colm (1.4)		2.0
Steering Gear, Adjust (On Truck)		
Includes: Bearing preload and gear mesh adjustments.		
All models (.6)		1.0
Steering Gear, R&R or Renew		
All models (.7)		1.2
Steering Gear, R&R and Recondition		
Includes: Disassemble, renew necessary parts, reassemble and adjust.		
All models (1.4)		2.2
POWER STEERING		
Trouble Shoot Power Steering		
Includes: Test pump and system pressure. Check pounds pull on steering wheel and check for leaks.		
All models (.7)		1.0
Power Steering Belt, Renew		
Four		
Gas (.3)		.5
Diesel (.3)		.5
Six (.5)		.7
V-6 (.3)		.5
V-8		
302-351 engs (.4)		.6
460 eng		
1986-87 (.8)		1.0
1988-90 (.4)		.6
Diesel (.4)		.6
Power Steering Gear, R&R or Renew		
All models (.8)		1.4
w/V-8 Diesel add		.4
Power Steering Gear, R&R and Recondition		
Includes: Disassemble, renew necessary parts, reassemble and adjust.		
All models (2.2)		3.8

	(Factory Time)	Chilton Time
Power Steering Pump, R&R or Renew		
Includes: Transfer pulley where required.		
Aerostar-Four (1.1)		1.5
V-6		
2.8L (1.0)		1.4
3.0L (.9)		1.3
All other models		
Four		
Gas (.7)		1.0
Diesel		
2.2L eng (.8)		1.2
2.3L eng (1.2)		1.6
Six		
1986-87 (.6)		1.0
1988-90 (.9)		1.3
V-6 (.8)		1.2
V-8		
302-351W engs (.6)		1.0
460 eng (.8)		1.2
w/A.C. add (.4)		.4
Diesel (1.0)		1.4
Power Steering Pump, R&R and Recondition		
Aerostar-Four (1.5)		2.3
V-6		
2.8L (1.4)		2.2
3.0L (1.3)		2.1
All other models		
Four		
Gas (1.1)		1.8
Diesel		
2.2L eng (1.2)		2.0
2.3L eng (1.6)		2.4
Six		
1986-87 (1.0)		1.5
1988-90 (1.3)		1.8
V-6 (1.3)		2.2
V-8		
302-351W engs (1.1)		1.8
460 eng (1.2)		1.7
w/A.C. add (.4)		.4
Diesel (1.6)		2.2
Power Steering Pump Shaft Seal, Renew		
Includes: R&R pump.		
Aerostar-Four (1.2)		1.7
V-6		
2.8L (1.1)		1.6
3.0L (1.0)		1.5
All other models		
Four		
Gas (.7)		1.2
Diesel		
2.2L eng (.9)		1.4
2.3L eng (1.3)		1.8

	(Factory Time)	Chilton Time
Six		
1986-87 (.7)		1.2
1988-90 (1.0)		1.5
V-6 (.9)		1.4
V-8		
302-351W engs (.6)		1.2
460 eng (.9)		1.4
w/A.C. add (.4)		.4
Diesel (1.1)		1.6
Power Steering Hoses, Renew		
AEROSTAR		
pressure (.6)		.8
return (.5)		.7
BRONCO, F-Series		
pressure (.6)		.8
return (.5)		.7
ECONOLINE-pressure (.5)		.7
return (.6)		.8
RANGER		
pressure (.5)		.7
return (.5)		.7
cooling (.3)		.5
V-8-Diesel		
cooling (.5)		.7
return (.8)		1.0
pressure (.7)		.9
RACK AND PINION STEERING		
Steering Gear, R&R or Renew		
All models		
manual (.8)		1.3
power (1.0)		1.6
Purge system add (.3)		.3
Steering Gear, R&R and Recondition		
All models		
manual (2.4)		3.8
power (3.0)		4.8
Purge system add (.3)		.3
Steering Gear, Adjust (On Truck)		
All models (.3)		.5
Tie Rod Ball Joint Sockets and Bellows, Renew		
All models		
manual (1.2)		1.9
power (2.0)		3.0
Purge system add (.3)		.3
Input Shaft and Valve Assy., Recondition		
All models		
manual (1.4)		2.2
power (1.6)		2.5
Purge system add (.3)		.3

LABOR   12   CYLINDER HEAD & VALVE SYSTEM   12   LABOR

GASOLINE ENGINES

	Factory Time	Chilton Time
Compression Test		
Four		.5
Two plug engine add		.2
Six		.6
V-6		.7
V-8		.9

Cylinder Head Gasket, Renew
Includes: Check cylinder head and block flatness. Clean carbon and make all necessary adjustments.

RANGER-BRONCO II		
Four		
2.0L eng (3.7)		5.1
2.3L eng (4.3)		6.0
V-6		
2.8L eng		
one side (4.3)		6.0
both sides (5.3)		7.4
2.9L eng		
one side (3.6)		5.0
both sides (4.8)		6.7
AEROSTAR		
Four (4.4)		6.1
V-6		
2.8L eng		
one side (4.4)		6.1
both sides (5.7)		7.9
3.0L eng		
one side (5.0)		7.0
both sides (7.3)		10.2
ECONOLINE		
Six		
wo/EFI (3.4)		4.7
w/EFI (5.2)		7.2
V-8		
5.0L eng		
wo/EFI		
one side (3.1)		4.3
both sides (4.4)		6.1
w/EFI		
one side (6.3)		8.8
both sides (8.6)		12.0
5.8L eng-wo/EFI		
one side (5.2)		7.2
both sides (7.5)		10.5
5.8L-7.5L engs		
w/Dual Thermactor		
one side (7.3)		10.2
both sides (9.7)		13.5
F-Series-BRONCO		
Six		
wo/EFI (2.8)		3.9
w/EFI (4.6)		6.4
V-8		
5.0L eng		
wo/EFI		
one side (3.1)		4.3
both sides (4.4)		6.1
w/EFI		
one side (4.7)		7.0
both sides (6.7)		9.5
5.8L eng-wo/EFI		
one side (4.7)		6.5
both sides (6.5)		9.1
5.8L-7.5L engs		
w/Dual Thermactor		
one side (5.5)		7.7
both sides (7.1)		9.9

Cylinder Head, Renew
Includes: Transfer all components, clean carbon. Reface valves, check valve spring tension, assembled height and valve head runout.

RANGER-BRONCO II		
Four		
2.0L eng (5.6)		7.8
2.3L eng (6.2)		8.6

COMBINATIONS
Add to Valve Job

	Factory Time	Chilton Time
DRAIN, EVACUATE & RECHARGE AIR CONDITIONING SYSTEM		
All models (.7)		1.5
ROCKER ARMS OR SHAFT ASSY. DISASSEMBLE AND CLEAN OR RECONDITION		
Six (.6)		1.0
V-8–One side (.5)		.7
Both sides (1.0)		1.3
HYDRAULIC VALVE LIFTERS, DISASSEMBLE AND CLEAN		
Each (.2)		.2
ROCKER ARM STUD, RENEW		
Each (.3)		.3
DISTRIBUTOR, RECONDITION		
All models (.7)		1.0
CARBURETOR, RECONDITION		
1 BBL (.9)		1.2
2 BBL (1.0)		1.3
4 BBL		
Ford (1.0)		1.5
Holly (1.3)		2.0
VALVE GUIDES, REAM OVERSIZE		
Each (.1)		.2
VALVE SEAT INSERT, RENEW		
DIESEL		
V-8–one (.2)		.3
each adtnl (.2)		.2
VALVE GUIDES, RENEW		
DIESEL		
V-8–one (.5)		.6
each adtnl (.5)		.5

	Factory Time	Chilton Time
V-6		
2.8L eng		
one side (5.3)		7.4
both sides (8.1)		11.3
2.9L eng		
one side (4.6)		6.4
both sides (6.9)		9.6
AEROSTAR		
Four (6.3)		8.8
V-6		
2.8L eng		
one side (5.4)		7.5
both sides (7.8)		10.9
3.0L eng		
one side (6.0)		8.4
both sides (9.4)		13.1
ECONOLINE		
Six		
wo/EFI (6.3)		8.8
w/EFI (8.1)		11.3
V-8		
5.0L eng		
wo/EFI		
one side (4.5)		6.3
both sides (7.2)		10.0
w/EFI		
one side (7.7)		10.7
both sides (11.4)		15.9
5.8L eng-wo/EFI		
one side (6.6)		9.2
both sides (10.3)		14.4
5.8L-7.5L engs		
w/Dual Thermactor		
one side (8.7)		12.1
both sides (12.5)		17.5

F-Series-BRONCO	Factory	Chilton
Six		
wo/EFI (5.7)		7.9
w/EFI (7.5)		10.5
V-8		
5.0L eng		
wo/EFI		
one side (4.5)		6.3
both sides (7.2)		10.0
w/EFI		
one side (6.1)		8.9
both sides (9.5)		13.4
5.8L eng-wo/EFI		
one side (6.1)		8.5
both sides (9.3)		13.0
5.8L-7.5L engs		
w/Dual Thermactor		
one side (6.9)		9.6
both sides (9.9)		13.8

Clean Carbon and Grind Valves
Includes: R&R cylinder heads, check valve spring tension, valve seat and head runout, stem to guide clearance and spring assembled height. Minor tune up.

RANGER-BRONCO II		
Four		
2.0L eng (6.3)		8.8
2.3L eng (6.9)		9.6
V-6		
2.8L eng		
one side (5.8)		8.1
both sides (8.4)		11.7
2.9L eng		
one side (5.1)		7.1
one side (7.9)		11.0
AEROSTAR		
Four (7.0)		9.8
V-6		
2.8L eng		
one side (5.9)		8.2
both sides (8.8)		12.3
3.0L eng		
one side (6.4)		8.9
both sides (10.1)		14.1
ECONOLINE		
Six		
wo/EFI (6.1)		8.5
w/EFI (7.9)		11.0
V-8		
5.0L eng		
wo/EFI		
one side (4.8)		6.7
both sides (7.8)		10.9
w/EFI		
one side (6.4)		11.2
both sides (10.1)		16.8
5.8L eng-wo/EFI		
one side (6.9)		9.6
both sides (10.9)		15.2
5.8L-7.5L engs		
w/Dual Thermactor		
one side (9.0)		12.6
both sides (13.1)		18.3
F-Series-BRONCO		
Six		
wo/EFI (5.5)		7.7
w/EFI (7.3)		10.2
V-8		
5.0L eng		
wo/EFI		
one side (4.8)		6.7
both sides (7.8)		10.9
w/EFI		
one side (6.7)		9.3
both sides (10.2)		14.2
5.8L eng-wo/EFI		
one side (6.4)		8.9
both sides (9.9)		13.8

LABOR 12 CYLINDER HEAD & VALVE SYSTEM 12 LABOR

	(Factory Time)	Chilton Time
5.8L-7.5L engs		
w/Dual Thermactor		
one side (7.2)		10.0
both sides (10.5)		14.7
Rocker Arm Cover or Gasket, Renew		
RANGER-BRONCO II		
Four		
2.0L eng (.7)		1.0
2.3L eng (1.3)		1.8
V-6		
2.8L eng		
one side (.8)		1.1
both sides (1.2)		1.7
2.9L eng		
one side (.9)		1.3
both sides (1.6)		2.3
AEROSTAR		
Four (1.2)		1.7
V-6		
2.8L eng		
one side (1.3)		1.9
both sides (2.5)		3.6
3.0L eng		
one side (1.5)		2.2
both sides (2.8)		4.0
ECONOLINE		
Six		
wo/EFI (1.0)		1.5
w/EFI (2.1)		3.0
V-8		
5.0L eng		
wo/EFI		
right side (.8)		1.2
left side (.6)		.9
both sides (1.0)		1.5
w/EFI		
right side (2.2)		3.1
left side (1.2)		1.7
both sides (2.9)		4.1
5.8L eng-wo/EFI		
right side (.8)		1.2
left side (.6)		.9
both sides (1.0)		1.5
5.8L-7.5L engs		
w/Dual Thermactor		
right side (2.5)		3.6
left side (1.5)		2.2
both sides (3.5)		5.0
F-Series-BRONCO		
Six		
wo/EFI (.9)		1.3
w/EFI (1.7)		2.4
V-8		
5.0L eng		
wo/EFI		
right side (.7)		1.0
left side (.5)		.8
both sides (.9)		1.3
w/EFI		
right side (1.5)		2.2
left side (.8)		1.2
both sides (1.9)		2.7
5.8L eng-wo/EFI		
right side (.7)		1.0
left side (.5)		.8
both sides (.9)		1.3
5.8L-7.5L engs		
w/Dual Thermactor		
right side (1.7)		2.4
left side (1.0)		1.5
both sides (2.4)		3.4
Rocker Arm Shaft Assy., Recondition		
Includes: R&R rocker arm cover.		
BRONCO-Six (1.1)		1.6

	(Factory Time)	Chilton Time
Valve Push Rod and/or Rocker Arm, Renew		
Includes: R&R rocker arm cover.		
RANGER-BRONCO II		
Four		
2.0L eng-one (.8)		1.2
all (1.1)		1.6
2.3L eng-one (1.8)		2.6
all (2.3)		3.3
V-6		
2.8L eng		
one side (1.3)		1.9
both sides (2.2)		3.1
2.9L eng		
one side (1.2)		1.7
both sides (2.2)		3.1
AEROSTAR		
Four-one (1.3)		1.9
all (1.6)		2.3
V-6		
2.8L eng		
one side (1.8)		2.6
both sides (3.5)		5.0
3.0L eng		
one side (1.8)		2.6
both sides (3.4)		4.8
ECONOLINE		
Six		
wo/EFI-one (1.1)		1.6
all (1.4)		2.0
w/EFI-one (2.2)		3.1
all (2.5)		3.6
V-8		
5.0L eng		
wo/EFI		
one side (1.0)		1.5
both sides (1.4)		2.0
w/EFI		
right side (2.4)		3.4
left side (1.4)		2.0
both sides (3.3)		4.7
5.8L eng-wo/EFI		
one side (1.0)		1.5
both sides (1.4)		2.0
5.8L-7.5L engs		
w/Dual Thermactor		
right side (2.7)		3.8
left side (1.7)		2.4
both sides (3.9)		5.5
F-Series-BRONCO		
Six		
wo/EFI-one (1.0)		1.5
all (1.8)		2.6
w/EFI-one (1.8)		2.6
all (2.1)		3.0
V-8		
5.0L eng		
wo/EFI		
one side (.9)		1.3
both sides (1.3)		1.9
w/EFI		
right side (1.7)		2.4
left side (1.0)		1.5
both sides (2.3)		3.3
5.8L eng-wo/EFI		
one side (.9)		1.3
both sides (1.3)		1.9
5.8L-7.5L engs		
w/Dual Thermactor		
right side (1.9)		2.7
left side (1.2)		1.7
both sides (2.8)		4.0
Valve Tappets, Renew (All)		
Includes: R&R intake manifold where required. Adjust carburetor and ignition timing.		
RANGER-BRONCO II		
Four		
2.0L eng (1.2)		1.7
2.3L eng (1.6)		2.3

	(Factory Time)	Chilton Time
V-6		
2.8L eng (5.6)		7.9
2.9L eng (5.0)		7.1
AEROSTAR		
Four (5.0)		7.1
V-6		
2.8L eng (6.4)		9.0
3.0L eng (5.2)		7.3
ECONOLINE		
Six		
wo/EFI (2.1)		3.0
w/EFI (3.0)		4.3
V-8		
5.0L eng		
wo/EFI (4.3)		6.1
w/EFI (4.8)		6.8
5.8L eng-wo/EFI (4.3)		6.1
5.8L-7.5L engs		
w/Dual Thermactor (6.5)		9.2
F-Series-BRONCO		
Six		
wo/EFI (1.7)		2.4
w/EFI (2.6)		3.7
V-8		
5.0L eng		
wo/EFI (2.8)		4.0
w/EFI (4.3)		6.1
5.8L eng-wo/EFI (3.8)		5.4
5.8L-7.5L engs		
w/Dual Thermactor (4.9)		6.9
Valve Spring or Valve Stem Oil Seals, Renew (Head on Truck)		
Includes: R&R rocker arms or assy. and adjust valves, if adjustable.		
RANGER-BRONCO II		
Four		
2.0L eng-one (.9)		1.3
all (1.9)		2.7
2.3L eng-one (1.5)		2.2
all (2.7)		3.8
V-6		
2.8L eng		
one side (1.7)		2.4
both sides (3.0)		4.2
2.9L eng		
one side (2.0)		2.9
both sides (3.8)		5.4
AEROSTAR		
Four-one (1.4)		2.0
all (2.6)		3.7
V-6		
2.8L eng		
one side (2.2)		3.1
both sides (4.3)		6.1
3.0L eng		
one side (2.6)		3.7
both sides (5.0)		7.1
ECONOLINE		
Six		
wo/EFI-one (1.2)		1.7
all (2.8)		4.0
w/EFI-one (2.3)		3.3
all (3.9)		5.5
V-8		
5.0L eng		
wo/EFI		
one side (2.0)		2.9
both sides (3.4)		4.8
w/EFI		
right side (3.4)		4.8
left side (2.4)		3.4
both sides (5.3)		7.5
5.8L eng-wo/EFI		
one side (2.0)		2.9
both sides (3.4)		4.8
5.8L-7.5L engs		
w/Dual Thermactor		
right side (3.7)		5.2
left side (2.7)		3.8

LABOR 12 CYLINDER HEAD & VALVE SYSTEM 12 LABOR

	(Factory Time)	Chilton Time
both sides (5.9)		8.3
F-Series-BRONCO		
Six		
wo/EFI-one (1.1)		1.6
all (2.7)		3.8
w/EFI-one (1.9)		2.7
all (3.5)		5.0
5.0L eng		
wo/EFI		
one side (1.9)		2.7
both sides (3.3)		4.7
w/EFI		
right side (2.7)		3.8
left side (2.0)		2.9
both sides (4.3)		6.1
5.8L eng-wo/EFI		
one side (1.9)		2.7
both sides (3.3)		4.7
5.8L-7.5L engs		
w/Dual Thermactor		
right side (2.9)		4.1
left side (2.2)		3.1
both sides (4.8)		6.8
one-each side (1.1)		1.5
all-both sides (2.8)		3.5

Valve Clearance, Adjust		
Four		1.8
V-6		2.7

DIESEL ENGINE

Compression Test		
FOUR		1.0
V-8		1.8

Cylinder Head Gasket, Renew		
Four		
2.2L eng (2.8)		3.9
2.3L eng (4.2)		5.8
V-8–6.9L-7.3L		
F Series		
right side (6.9)		9.6
left side (6.3)		8.8
both sides (9.6)		13.4
Econoline		
right side (9.2)		12.8
left side (9.4)		11.7
both sides (12.0)		16.8
w/A.C. add (.4)		.4
w/P.S. add (.5)		.5

Cylinder Head, Renew

Includes: Transfer all components. Clean, replace and lap valves. Make all necessary adjustments.

Four		
2.2L eng (4.4)		6.1
2.3L eng (6.4)		8.9
V-8–6.9L-7.3L		
F Series		
right side (8.4)		11.7
left side (7.8)		10.9
both sides (12.5)		17.5
Econoline		
right side (10.7)		14.9
left side (9.9)		13.8
both sides (14.9)		20.8
w/A.C. add (.4)		.4
w/P.S. add (.5)		.5

Clean Carbon and Grind Valves

Includes: R&R cylinder head. Reface valves and seats. Make all necessary adjustments.

Four		
2.2L eng (5.9)		8.0
2.3L eng (6.7)		9.4
V-8–6.9L-7.3L		
F Series		
right side (8.8)		12.3
left side (8.2)		11.4
both sides (13.3)		18.6
Econoline		
right side (11.1)		15.5
left side (10.3)		14.4
both sides (15.7)		21.9
w/A.C. add (.4)		.4
w/P.S. add (.5)		.5

Rocker Arm Cover and/or Gasket, Renew

Four		
2.2L eng (.4)		.7
2.3L eng (.5)		.8
V-8–6.9L-7.3L		
F Series		
right side (.8)		1.1
left side (.6)		.9
both sides (1.1)		1.7
Econoline		
right side (1.7)		2.3
left side (.9)		1.2
both sides (2.1)		2.9

Valve Push Rods and/or Rocker Arms, Renew		
Four		
2.2L eng-one (.7)		1.2
all (.9)		1.6
2.3L eng-one (.7)		1.0
all (1.2)		1.7
V-8–6.9L-7.3L		
F Series		
right side (1.1)		1.5
left side (.9)		1.3
both sides (1.6)		2.4
Econoline		
right side (2.0)		2.8
left side (1.2)		1.6
both sides (2.6)		3.6

Note: If necc to tilt eng to renew rods for # 3 & 5 cyls add **2.0**

Valve Springs and/or Valve Stem Oil Seals, Renew (Head on Truck)		
Four		
2.2L eng-one (.9)		1.6
all (1.4)		2.4
2.3L eng-one (.7)		1.1
all (1.7)		2.4
V-8–6.9L-7.3L		
F Series		
one cyl (1.1)		1.5
one cyl-each side (1.7)		2.3
all cyls-both sides (4.0)		5.6
Econoline		
right side (3.2)		4.4
left side (2.4)		3.3
both sides (5.0)		7.0

Valve Tappets, Renew		
Four		
2.2L eng		
all (6.1)		8.8
V-8–6.9L-7.3L		
F Series		
one cyl (2.9)		4.2
all cyls-one side (3.2)		4.6
all cyls-both sides (4.0)		5.8
Econoline		
one cyl (4.5)		6.3
all cyls-both sides (5.5)		7.7
w/A.C. add (.4)		.4
w/P.S. add (.5)		.5

LABOR 13 ENGINE ASSEMBLY & MOUNTS 13 LABOR

Note: All engine operations listed in this group are for assemblies as supplied by the original equipment manufacturer. Time to replace assemblies from independent rebuilders may vary.

GASOLINE ENGINES

Engine Assembly, Remove & Install

Includes: R&R hood and radiator, adjust carburetor and linkage.

Does not include transfer of any parts or equipment.

RANGER–BRONCO II		
Four		
2.0L eng (3.1)		4.3
2.3L eng		
4X2		
w/M.T. (4.5)		6.3
w/A.T. (3.4)		4.7
4X4 (4.8)		6.7

V-6		
2.8L eng		
4X2		
w/M.T. (4.8)		6.7
w/A.T. (5.2)		7.2
4X4		
w/M.T. (5.1)		7.0
w/A.T. (5.3)		7.4
2.9L eng		
4X2 or 4X4		
w/M.T. (4.3)		6.0
w/A.T. (4.3)		6.0
AEROSTAR		
Four		
w/M.T. (5.8)		8.1
w/A.T. (5.9)		8.3
V-6		
2.8L eng (5.9)		8.3
3.0L eng (6.1)		8.5
ECONOLINE		
Six		
wo/EFI (6.8)		9.5
w/EFI (7.2)		10.0

V-8		
5.0L-5.8L engs		
wo/EFI (5.3)		7.4
w/EFI (6.3)		8.8
7.5L eng (6.2)		8.6
F-Series-BRONCO		
4X2		
Six		
wo/EFI (4.5)		6.3
w/EFI (6.6)		9.2
V-8		
5.0L-5.8L engs		
w/M.T. (3.5)		4.9
w/A.T. (4.6)		6.4
7.5L eng (4.6)		6.4
4X4		
Six		
wo/EFI		
w/M.T. (3.9)		5.4
w/A.T. (4.2)		5.8
w/EFI		
w/M.T. (6.5)		9.1
w/A.T. (6.6)		9.2

LABOR 13 ENGINE ASSEMBLY & MOUNTS 13 LABOR

(Factory Time)	Chilton Time
V-8	
5.0L-5.8L engs	
w/M.T. (3.6)	5.0
w/A.T. (4.7)	6.5
7.5L eng (4.7)	6.5
w/P.S. add (.4)	.4
w/A.C. add (.6)	.6

Engine Assembly, Replace With New or Rebuilt Unit (With Cyl. Heads and Oil Pan)

Includes: R&R hood and radiator. R&R engine assembly, transfer all necessary parts, fuel and electrical units. Tune engine. Road test.

(Factory Time)	Chilton Time
RANGER-BRONCO II	
Four	
2.0L eng (5.2)	7.2
2.3L eng	
4X2	
w/M.T. (7.0)	9.8
w/A.T. (5.9)	8.2
4X4 (6.9)	9.7
V-6	
2.8L eng	
4X2	
w/M.T. (7.1)	9.9
w/A.T. (7.5)	10.5
4X4	
w/M.T. (7.4)	10.3
w/A.T. (7.6)	10.6
2.9L eng	
4X2 or 4X4	
w/M.T. (6.8)	9.5
w/A.T. (6.8)	9.5
AEROSTAR	
Four	
w/M.T. (8.3)	11.6
w/A.T. (8.4)	11.8
V-6	
2.8L eng (8.4)	11.8
3.0L eng (8.6)	12.0
ECONOLINE	
Six	
wo/EFI (10.2)	14.2
w/EFI (10.6)	14.8
V-8	
5.0L-5.8L engs	
wo/EFI (7.6)	10.6
w/EFI (8.6)	12.0
7.5L eng (8.5)	11.8
F-Series-BRONCO	
4X2	
Six	
wo/EFI (6.8)	9.5
w/EFI (8.9)	12.4
V-8	
5.0L-5.8L engs	
w/M.T. (5.8)	8.1
w/A.T. (6.9)	9.6
7.5L eng (6.9)	9.6
4X4	
Six	
wo/EFI	
w/M.T. (6.2)	8.6
w/A.T. (6.5)	9.1
w/EFI	
w/M.T. (8.8)	12.3
w/A.T. (8.9)	12.5
V-8	
5.0L-5.8L engs	
w/M.T. (5.9)	8.2
w/A.T. (7.0)	9.8
7.5L eng (7.0)	9.8
w/P.S. add (.4)	.4
w/A.C. add (.6)	.6

Cylinder Assembly, Renew (w/All Internal Parts Less Head(s) and Oil Pan)

Includes: R&R hood and radiator. R&R engine, transfer all component parts not supplied with replacement engine, clean carbon, grind valves, Minor tune up. Road test.

(Factory Time)	Chilton Time
RANGER-BRONCO II	
Four	
2.0L eng (9.7)	13.5
2.3L eng	
4X2	
w/M.T. (11.3)	15.8
w/A.T. (10.2)	14.2
4X4 (10.9)	15.2
V-6	
2.8L eng	
4X2	
w/M.T. (12.4)	17.3
w/A.T. (12.8)	17.9
4X4	
w/M.T. (12.7)	17.7
w/A.T. (12.9)	18.0
2.9L eng	
4X2 or 4X4	
w/M.T. (12.2)	17.0
w/A.T. (12.2)	17.0
AEROSTAR	
Four	
w/M.T. (12.6)	17.6
w/A.T. (12.7)	17.8
V-6	
2.8L eng (13.3)	18.6
3.0L eng (14.0)	19.6
ECONOLINE	
Six	
wo/EFI (13.2)	18.4
w/EFI (13.6)	19.0
V-8	
5.0L-5.8L engs	
wo/EFI (14.9)	20.8
w/EFI (15.9)	22.2
7.5L eng (14.9)	20.8
F-Series-BRONCO	
4X2	
Six	
wo/EFI (10.9)	15.2
w/EFI (13.0)	18.2
V-8	
5.0L-5.8L engs	
w/M.T. (13.1)	18.3
w/A.T. (14.2)	19.8
7.5L eng (14.2)	19.8
4X4	
Six	
wo/EFI	
w/M.T. (10.3)	14.4
w/A.T. (10.6)	14.8
w/EFI	
w/M.T. (12.9)	18.0
w/A.T. (13.0)	18.2
V-8	
5.0L-5.8L engs	
w/M.T. (13.2)	18.4
w/A.T. (14.3)	20.0
7.5L eng (13.4)	18.7
w/P.S. add (.4)	.4
w/A.C. add (.6)	.6

Engine Assembly, R&R and Recondition (Complete)

Includes: R&R hood and radiator. Rebore block, install new pistons, rings, rod and main bearings. Clean carbon, grind valves. Tune engine. Road test.

(Factory Time)	Chilton Time
RANGER-BRONCO II	
Four	
2.0L eng (15.6)	22.4
2.3L eng	
4X2	
w/M.T. (16.6)	23.9
w/A.T. (15.5)	22.3
4X4 (16.2)	22.7
V-6	
2.8L eng	
4X2	
w/M.T. (19.0)	27.3
w/A.T. (19.4)	27.9
4X4	
w/M.T. (19.3)	27.7
w/A.T. (19.5)	28.0
2.9L eng	
4X2 or 4X4	
w/M.T. (18.7)	26.9
w/A.T. (18.7)	26.9
AEROSTAR	
Four	
w/M.T. (17.9)	25.7
w/A.T. (18.0)	25.9
V-6	
2.8L eng (20.1)	28.9
3.0L eng (20.3)	29.2
ECONOLINE	
Six	
wo/EFI (21.4)	30.8
w/EFI (21.8)	31.3
V-8	
5.0L-5.8L engs	
wo/EFI (22.6)	32.5
w/EFI (23.6)	33.9
7.5L eng (24.0)	34.5
F-Series-BRONCO	
4X2	
Six	
wo/EFI (19.1)	27.5
w/EFI (21.2)	30.5
V-8	
5.0L-5.8L engs	
w/M.T. (20.8)	29.9
w/A.T. (21.9)	31.5
7.5L eng (22.4)	32.2
4X4	
Six	
wo/EFI	
w/M.T. (18.5)	26.6
w/A.T. (18.8)	27.0
w/EFI	
w/M.T. (21.1)	30.3
w/A.T. (21.2)	30.5
V-8	
5.0L-5.8L engs	
w/M.T. (20.9)	30.0
w/A.T. (22.0)	31.6
7.5L eng (22.5)	32.4
w/P.S. add (.4)	.4
w/A.C. add (.6)	.6

Engine Mounts, Renew

(Factory Time)	Chilton Time
RANGER-BRONCO II	
FRONT	
Four	
2.0L eng	
one (.4)	.6
both (.5)	.9
2.3L eng	
one (1.4)	1.9
both (1.5)	2.0
V-6	
2.8L eng	
one (.4)	.6
both (.5)	.9
2.9L eng	
one (.6)	.9
both (.8)	1.2
AEROSTAR	
Four	
one (1.4)	1.9
both (1.5)	2.0
V-6	
2.8L eng	
one (.7)	1.0
both (.9)	1.3

LABOR 13 ENGINE ASSEMBLY & MOUNTS 13 LABOR

	(Factory Time)	Chilton Time
3.0L eng		
right (.5)		.7
left (.8)		1.2
both (.9)		1.4
ECONOLINE		
Six		
one (.4)		.6
both (.5)		.9
V-8		
5.0L eng		
one (1.0)		1.5
both (1.1)		1.7
5.8L eng		
one (.8)		1.2
both (1.0)		1.5
7.5L eng		
right (.7)		1.0
left (.5)		.7
both (.8)		1.4
F-Series-BRONCO		
Six		
one (.4)		.6
both (.5)		.9
V-8		
5.0L-5.8L engs		
one (.4)		.6
both (.6)		1.0
7.5L eng		
one (.4)		.6
both (.6)		.9
Rear		
Ranger (.4)		.6
Bronco (.6)		.8
Aerostar (.4)		.7
Econoline (.4)		.7
F100-350 (.6)		.8

DIESEL ENGINE

Engine Assembly, Remove & Install

Includes: R&R hood and radiator. Does not include transfer of any parts or equipment.

	(Factory Time)	Chilton Time
Four		
2.2L eng (3.7)		5.1
2.3L eng (4.6)		6.5
w/A.C. add (.4)		.4
w/P.S. add (.5)		.5
V-8—6.9L-7.3L		
F Series (6.2)		8.6
w/A.T. add (.6)		.6
4X4 add (.2)		.2
Econoline (7.1)		9.9
w/A.C. add		
F Series (.3)		.3
Econoline (1.0)		1.0

Cylinder Assembly, Renew
(w/All Internal Parts Less Head(s) and Oil Pan)

Includes: R&R hood and radiator. R&R engine, transfer all component parts not supplied with replacement engine. Clean carbon, grind valves. Make all necessary adjustments.

	(Factory Time)	Chilton Time
Four		
2.2L eng (12.6)		17.3
2.3L eng (11.6)		16.5
w/A.C. add (.4)		.4
w/P.S. add (.5)		.5
V-8—6.9L-7.3L		
F Series (19.6)		27.4
w/A.T. add (.6)		.6
4X4 add (.2)		.2
Econoline (20.5)		28.7
w/A.C. add		
F Series (.3)		.3

	(Factory Time)	Chilton Time
Econoline (1.0)		1.0

Engine Assembly, R&R and Recondition (Complete)

Includes: R&R hood and radiator. Install new cylinder sleeves, pistons, rings, rod and main bearings. Clean carbon, grind valves. Make all necessary adjustments.

	(Factory Time)	Chilton Time
Four		
2.2L eng (17.7)		24.7
2.3L eng (16.6)		23.5
w/A.C. add (.4)		.4
w/P.S. add (.5)		.5
V-8—6.9L-7.3L		
F Series (27.2)		38.0
w/A.T. add (.6)		.6
4X4 add (.2)		.2
Econoline (28.0)		39.2
w/A.C. add		
F Series (.3)		.3
Econoline (1.0)		1.0
Engine Mounts, Renew		
Front		
Four—one (.6)		.8
both (.9)		1.2
V-8—6.9L-7.3L		
F Series		
right (1.8)		2.4
left (1.6)		2.1
both (1.9)		2.6
Econoline		
right (1.9)		2.5
left (1.8)		2.3
both (2.1)		2.8
Rear		
Four (.4)		.6
V-8 (.4)		.6

LABOR 14 PISTONS, RINGS & BEARINGS 14 LABOR

GASOLINE ENGINES

Rings, Renew (All)

Includes: Remove cylinder top ridge, deglaze cylinder walls, replace rod bearings, clean carbon. Minor tune up.

	(Factory Time)	Chilton Time
RANGER-BRONCO II		
Four		
2.0L eng (8.2)		11.4
2.3L eng (7.9)		11.0
V-6		
2.8L eng (10.8)		15.1
2.9L eng		
4X2 (10.8)		15.1
4X4 (11.7)		16.3
AEROSTAR		
Four (8.0)		11.2
V-6		
2.8L eng (10.7)		14.9
3.0L eng (11.0)		15.4
ECONOLINE		
Six		
wo/EFI (8.3)		11.6
w/EFI (12.7)		17.7
V-8		
5.0L eng		
wo/EFI (11.8)		16.5
w/EFI (14.2)		19.8
5.8L eng (11.8)		16.5
5.8L-7.5L engs		
w/Dual Thermactor (13.7)		19.1
F-Series-BRONCO		
Six		
wo/EFI (7.5)		10.5
w/EFI (9.2)		12.8

COMBINATIONS
Add to Engine Work

	(Factory Time)	Chilton Time		(Factory Time)	Chilton Time
DRAIN, EVACUATE & RECHARGE AIR CONDITIONING SYSTEM			**TIMING CHAIN, RENEW (COVER REMOVED)**		
All models (.7)		1.5	All models (.3)		.5
ROCKER ARMS OR SHAFT ASSY. DISASSEMBLE AND CLEAN OR RECONDITION			**VALVE GUIDES, REAM OVERSIZE**		
Six (.6)		1.0	Each (.1)		.2
V-8—One side (.5)		.7	**DEGLAZE CYLINDER WALLS**		
Both sides (1.0)		1.3	Each (.1)		.2
HYDRAULIC VALVE LIFTERS, DISASSEMBLE AND CLEAN			**REMOVE CYLINDER TOP RIDGE**		
Each (.2)		.2	Each (.3)		.3
ROCKER ARM STUD, RENEW			**MAIN BEARINGS, RENEW (PAN REMOVED)**		
Each (.3)		.3	Four (1.9)		2.9
DISTRIBUTOR, RECONDITION			Six (1.6)		2.5
All models (.7)		1.0	V-6 (1.5)		2.0
CARBURETOR, RECONDITION			V-8 (1.9)		2.9
1 BBL (.9)		1.2	**PLASTIGAUGE BEARINGS**		
2 BBL (1.0)		1.3	Each (.1)		.1
4 BBL			**OIL PUMP, RECONDITION**		
Ford (1.0)		1.5	All models (.4)		.6
Holly (1.3)		2.0	**OIL FILTER ELEMENT, RENEW**		
			All models (.3)		.4

	(Factory Time)	Chilton Time		(Factory Time)	Chilton Time
V-8			**w/EFI**		
5.0L eng			4X2 (13.2)		18.4
wo/EFI			4X4 (13.4)		18.7
4X2 (10.2)		14.2			
4X4 (13.4)		18.7			

LABOR 14 PISTONS, RINGS & BEARINGS 14 LABOR

	(Factory Time)	Chilton Time
5.8L-7.5L engs		
w/Dual Thermactor		
4X2 (11.8)		16.5
4X4 (11.8)		16.5
Piston or Connecting Rod, Renew (One)		
Includes: Remove cylinder top ridge, deglaze cylinder walls, replace rod bearings, clean carbon. Minor tune up.		
RANGER-BRONCO II		
Four		
2.0L eng (7.2)		10.0
2.3L eng (7.3)		10.2
V-6		
2.8L eng (7.9)		11.0
2.9L eng		
4X2 (7.1)		9.9
4X4 (8.0)		11.2
AEROSTAR		
Four (7.3)		10.2
V-6		
2.8L eng (7.3)		10.2
3.0L eng (7.1)		9.9
ECONOLINE		
Six		
wo/EFI (6.3)		8.8
w/EFI (10.5)		14.7
V-8		
5.0L eng		
wo/EFI (8.1)		11.3
w/EFI (11.1)		15.5
5.8L eng (8.1)		11.3
5.8L-7.5L engs		
w/Dual Thermactor (9.9)		13.8
F-Series-BRONCO		
Six		
wo/EFI (5.4)		7.5
w/EFI (7.2)		10.0
V-8		
5.0L eng		
wo/EFI		
4X2 (5.6)		7.8
4X4 (8.4)		11.7
w/EFI		
4X2 (8.1)		11.3
4X4 (8.4)		11.7
5.8L-7.5L engs		
w/Dual Thermactor		
4X2 (7.6)		10.6
4X4 (7.6)		10.6

	(Factory Time)	Chilton Time
Connecting Rod Bearings, Renew		
Includes: R&R oil pan, plastigauge and install new bearings. Clean oil pump pick up tube and screen. Renew oil filter.		
RANGER-BRONCO II		
Four		
2.0L eng (3.2)		4.4
2.3L eng		
4X2 (3.3)		4.6
4X4 (3.9)		5.4
V-6		
2.8L eng		
w/M.T. (4.4)		6.1
w/A.T. (4.6)		6.4
2.9L eng		
1986-87		
Ranger		
4X2 (3.6)		5.2
4X4 (4.9)		7.1
Bronco II (4.9)		7.1
1988-90		
Ranger		
4X2 (3.6)		5.2
4X4 (5.1)		7.3
Bronco II		
4X2 (4.9)		7.1
4X4 (5.1)		7.3
AEROSTAR		
Four (2.6)		3.6
V-6		
2.8L eng (3.2)		4.4
3.0L eng (2.9)		4.0
ECONOLINE		
Six		
wo/EFI (3.9)		5.4
w/EFI (5.1)		7.1
V-8		
5.0L-5.8L engs (6.3)		8.8
7.5L eng (4.3)		6.0
F-Series-BRONCO		
Six		
wo/EFI (3.7)		5.1
w/EFI (4.6)		6.4
V-8		
5.0L-5.8L engs		
4X2		
w/M.T. (5.1)		7.1
w/A.T. (5.3)		7.4

	(Factory Time)	Chilton Time
4X4		
w/M.T. (5.7)		7.9
w/A.T. (5.9)		8.2
7.5L eng		
4X2		
w/M.T. (3.9)		5.4
w/A.T. (4.1)		5.7
4X4		
w/M.T. (4.5)		6.3
w/A.T. (4.7)		6.5
DIESEL ENGINE		
Rings, Renew (All)		
Includes: Remove cylinder top ridge, deglaze cylinder walls, replace rod bearings, clean carbon. Make all necessary adjustments.		
Four		
2.2L eng (8.8)		12.3
2.3L eng (8.8)		12.3
V-8–6.9L-7.3L		
F Series (15.6)		22.6
Econoline (16.2)		23.4
w/A.C. add		
F Series (.3)		.3
Econoline (1.0)		1.0
Piston or Connecting Rod, Renew (One)		
Includes: Remove cylinder top ridge, deglaze cylinder wall, replace rod bearing, clean carbon. Make all necessary adjustments.		
Four		
2.2L eng (7.9)		11.0
2.3L eng (7.7)		11.0
V-8–6.9L-7.3L		
F Series (12.4)		17.9
Econoline (13.0)		18.8
w/A.C. add		
F Series (.3)		.3
Econoline (1.0)		1.0
Connecting Rod Bearings, Renew		
Four		
2.2L eng (4.2)		6.0
2.3L eng (3.7)		5.2
V-8–6.9L-7.3L		
F Series		
4X2 (4.9)		7.1
4X4 (5.2)		7.5
Econoline (5.4)		7.8

LABOR 15 CRANKSHAFT & DAMPER 15 LABOR

	(Factory Time)	Chilton Time
GASOLINE ENGINES		
Crankshaft and Main Bearings, Renew		
Includes: R&R hood and radiator. R&R engine, check all bearing clearances.		
RANGER-BRONCO II		
Four		
2.0L eng (6.9)		9.7
2.3L eng		
4X2		
w/M.T. (7.9)		11.0
w/A.T. (6.8)		9.5
4X4 (8.3)		11.6
V-6		
2.8L eng		
4X2		
w/M.T. (8.2)		11.4
w/A.T. (8.6)		12.0
4X4		
w/M.T. (8.5)		11.9
w/A.T. (8.7)		12.1
2.9L eng		
4X2 or 4X4		
w/M.T. (7.9)		11.0
w/A.T. (7.9)		11.0

	(Factory Time)	Chilton Time
AEROSTAR		
Four		
w/M.T. (9.2)		12.9
w/A.T. (9.3)		13.0
V-6		
2.8L eng (9.3)		13.0
3.0L eng (9.6)		13.4
ECONOLINE		
Six		
wo/EFI (10.9)		15.2
w/EFI (11.3)		15.8
V-8		
5.0L-5.8L engs		
wo/EFI (9.1)		12.7
w/EFI (10.1)		14.1
7.5L eng (10.2)		14.3
F-Series-BRONCO		
4X2		
Six		
wo/EFI (8.6)		12.0
w/EFI (10.7)		15.0
V-8		
5.0L-5.8L engs		
w/M.T. (7.3)		10.2

	(Factory Time)	Chilton Time
w/A.T. (8.4)		11.7
7.5L eng (8.6)		12.0
4X4		
Six		
wo/EFI		
w/M.T. (8.0)		11.2
w/A.T. (8.3)		11.6
w/EFI		
w/M.T. (10.6)		14.8
w/A.T. (10.7)		15.0
V-8		
5.0L-5.8L engs		
w/M.T. (7.4)		10.3
w/A.T. (8.5)		11.9
7.5L eng (8.7)		12.1
Main Bearings, Renew		
Includes: R&R oil pan or engine as required. Plastigauge and install new main bearings. Recondition oil pump and renew oil filter.		
RANGER-BRONCO II		
Four		
2.0L eng (4.1)		5.7
2.3L eng		
4X2 (4.2)		5.9

LABOR 15 CRANKSHAFT & DAMPER 15 LABOR

(Factory Time)	Chilton Time
4X4 (4.8)	6.7
V-6	
2.8L eng	
w/M.T. (8.0)	11.2
w/A.T. (8.4)	11.7
2.9L eng	
w/M.T. (6.8)	.9.8
w/A.T. (6.9)	10.0
AEROSTAR	
Four (3.5)	4.9
V-6	
2.8L eng	
w/M.T. (9.4)	13.1
w/A.T. (9.8)	13.7
3.0L eng	
w/M.T. (8.7)	12.1
w/A.T. (9.0)	12.6
ECONOLINE	
Six	
wo/EFI (4.1)	5.7
w/EFI (5.3)	7.4
V-8	
5.0L-5.8L engs (4.7)	6.5
7.5L eng	
1986-87 (4.4)	6.1
1988-90 (6.9)	9.6
F-Series-BRONCO	
Six (3.9)	5.4
V-8	
4X2	
5.0L-5.8L engs	
w/M.T. (5.7)	7.9
w/A.T. (5.8)	8.1
4X4	
w/M.T. (6.5)	9.1
w/A.T. (6.6)	9.2
7.5L eng	
4X2	
1986-87	
w/M.T. (4.0)	5.6
w/A.T. (4.2)	5.8
1988-90	
w/M.T. (8.5)	11.9
w/A.T. (8.2)	11.4
4X4	
1986-87	
w/M.T. (4.6)	6.4
w/A.T. (4.8)	6.7
1988-90	
w/M.T. (8.8)	12.3
w/A.T. (8.4)	11.7

Main and Rod Bearings, Renew

Includes: R&R oil pan or engine as required. Plastigauge and install new rod and main bearings. Recondition oil pump and renew oil filter.

(Factory Time)	Chilton Time
RANGER-BRONCO II	
Four	
2.0L eng (5.1)	7.1
2.3L eng	
4X2 (5.2)	7.3
4X4 (5.8)	8.1
V-6	
2.8L eng	
w/M.T. (9.0)	12.6
w/A.T. (9.4)	13.1
2.9L eng	
w/M.T. (8.3)	12.0
w/A.T. (8.4)	12.2
AEROSTAR	
Four (4.5)	6.3
V-6	
2.8L eng	
w/M.T. (10.4)	14.5
w/A.T. (10.8)	15.1
3.0L eng	
w/M.T. (10.2)	14.2
w/A.T. (10.5)	14.7
ECONOLINE	
Six	
wo/EFI (5.5)	7.7
w/EFI (6.7)	9.3
V-8	
5.0L-5.8L engs (6.5)	9.1
7.5L eng	
1986-87 (6.2)	8.6
1988-90 (8.7)	12.1
F-Series-BRONCO	
Six (5.3)	7.4
V-8	
4X2	
5.0L-5.8L engs	
w/M.T. (7.5)	10.5
w/A.T. (7.6)	10.6
4X4	
w/M.T. (8.3)	11.6
w/A.T. (8.4)	11.7
7.5L eng	
4X2	
1986-87	
w/M.T. (5.8)	8.1
w/A.T. (6.0)	8.4
1988-90	
w/M.T. (10.3)	14.4
w/A.T. (10.0)	14.0
4X4	
1986-87	
w/M.T. (6.4)	8.9
w/A.T. (6.6)	9.2
1988-90	
w/M.T. (10.6)	14.8
w/A.T. (10.2)	14.2

Rear Main Bearing Oil Seal, Renew (Upper & Lower)
Split Lip or Full Circle Type

Includes: R&R transmission on all 6 cyl models. Includes R&R oil pan or trans on V-8 models.

(Factory Time)	Chilton Time
RANGER-BRONCO II	
4X2	
Four	
2.0L eng (2.1)	2.9
2.3L eng	
w/M.T. (2.0)	2.8
w/A.T. (2.6)	3.6
V-6	
2.8L eng	
w/M.T. (3.3)	4.6
w/A.T. (3.5)	4.9
2.9L eng	
Ranger (3.0)	4.3
Bronco II (3.9)	5.6
4X4	
Four	
TK-MRI (3.3)	4.6
MMC5 (3.5)	4.9
V-6 (3.5)	4.9
AEROSTAR	
Four	
w/M.T. (2.0)	2.8
w/A.T. (2.6)	3.6
V-6	
w/M.T. (3.0)	4.3
w/A.T. (3.0)	4.3
ECONOLINE	
1986-87	
Six	
NP 435 (2.5)	3.7
Tremec (2.0)	3.0
C-6 (2.7)	4.0
AOD (2.6)	3.9
V-8	
5.0L-5.8L engs (2.7)	4.0
7.5L eng	
split lip (5.3)	7.9
1988-90	
Six	
MR-2 (2.7)	4.0
ZF-5 (3.3)	4.9
C-6 (2.7)	4.0
AOD (2.6)	3.9
V-8	
5.0L-5.8L engs (2.7)	4.0
7.5L eng	
split lip (5.3)	7.9
F-Series-BRONCO	
4X2	
1986-87	
Six	
Tremec (1.8)	2.7
T-18 (2.5)	3.7
NP 435 (2.5)	3.7
TOD (2.3)	3.4
C-5 (2.3)	3.4
C-6 (2.3)	3.4
AOD (2.9)	4.3
V-8	
5.0L-5.8L engs	
T-18 (2.6)	3.9
T-19 (2.6)	3.9
NP 435 (2.6)	3.9
TOD (2.4)	3.6
C-6 (2.7)	4.0
AOD (2.9)	4.3
7.5L eng	
split lip (3.2)	4.8
4X4	
Six	
T-18 (4.2)	6.3
TOD (4.2)	6.3
C-6 (4.0)	6.0
V-8	
5.0L-5.8L engs	
T-18 (4.3)	6.4
NP 435 (4.3)	6.4
C-6 (4.3)	6.4
AOD (4.2)	6.3
7.5L eng	
split lip (3.4)	5.1
4X2	
1988-90	
Six	
MR-2 (2.6)	3.9
T-18 (2.5)	3.8
ZF-5 (3.6)	5.4
C-6 (2.3)	3.4
AOD (2.9)	4.3
V-8	
5.0L eng	
MR-2 (2.8)	4.2
T-18 (2.5)	3.8
AOD (2.9)	4.3
5.8L eng	
ZF-5 (3.7)	5.5
E4OD-C-6 (2.7)	4.0
AOD (2.9)	4.3
7.3L Super Duty	
ZF-5 (4.0)	6.0
E4OD (3.2)	4.8
7.5L-7.5L Super Duty	
split lip (7.4)	11.1
4X4	
Six	
MR-2 (3.6)	5.4
T-18 (4.4)	6.6
ZF-5 (4.6)	6.9
C-6 (4.0)	6.0
V-8	
5.0L eng	
MR-2 (3.8)	5.7
T-18 (4.3)	6.4
C-6 (4.3)	6.4
AOD (4.2)	6.3
5.8L eng	
ZF-5 (4.8)	7.2
E4OD-C-6 (4.3)	6.4
AOD (4.2)	6.3
7.5L eng	
split lip (7.8)	11.7

LABOR 15 CRANKSHAFT & DAMPER 15 LABOR

(Factory Time)	Chilton Time
Crankshaft Front Oil Seal, Renew	
Does not require R&R of front cover on V-6 & V-8 engines.	
RANGER-BRONCO II	
Four	
2.0L eng	
Crank (1.7)	2.4
Cam (1.7)	2.4
Aux (1.8)	2.5
All (2.0)	2.8
2.3L eng	
Crank (1.6)	2.2
Cam (1.5)	2.1
Aux (1.5)	2.1
All (1.9)	2.6
V-6	
2.8L eng	
w/M.T. (1.0)	1.4
w/A.T. (1.1)	1.5
2.9L eng (1.4)	1.9
AEROSTAR	
Four	
Crank (1.6)	2.2
Cam (1.5)	2.1
All (1.9)	2.6
V-6	
2.8L eng	
w/M.T. (1.0)	1.4
w/A.T. (1.1)	1.5
3.0L eng (.9)	1.3
ECONOLINE	
Six (1.1)	1.5
V-8	
5.0L eng (1.7)	2.3
5.8L eng (1.8)	2.4
7.5L eng (4.4)	6.1
F-Series-BRONCO	
Six (1.1)	1.5
V-8	
5.0L-5.8L engs (1.2)	1.6
7.5L engs (3.0)	4.2

(Factory Time)	Chilton Time
DIESEL ENGINE	
Crankshaft and Main Bearings, Renew	
Includes: R&R engine assy., check all bearing clearances.	
Four	
2.2L eng (7.4)	10.7
2.3L eng (8.0)	11.6
V-8–6.9L-7.3L	
F Series (12.7)	18.4
w/A.T. add (.6)	.6
4X4 add (.2)	.2
Econoline (13.6)	19.7
w/A.C. add	
F Series (.3)	.3
Econoline (1.0)	1.0
Main Bearings, Renew	
Includes: Check all bearing clearances.	
Four	
2.2L eng (5.0)	7.0
2.3L eng (4.6)	6.6
V-8–6.9L-7.3L	
F Series	
4X2 (5.6)	8.1
4X4 (6.0)	8.7
Econoline (6.1)	8.8
Main and Rod Bearings, Renew	
Includes: Check all bearing clearances.	
Four	
2.2L eng (6.0)	8.2
2.3L eng (5.6)	7.8
V-8–6.9L-7.3L	
F Series	
4X2 (7.7)	11.1
4X4 (8.1)	11.7
Econoline (8.2)	11.2
Crankshaft Front Oil Seal, Renew	
Four	
both sides (7.9)	11.0

(Factory Time)	Chilton Time
2.3L eng (1.7)	2.5
V-8-6.9L-7.3L	
F Series (1.6)	2.5
Econoline (1.2)	1.8
w/A.C. add (.4)	.4
w/P.S. add (.5)	.5
Crankshaft Rear Oil Seal, Renew	
Four	
2.2L eng (1.9)	2.7
2.3L eng	
4X2 (1.7)	2.7
4X4 (3.5)	5.0
V-8-6.9L-7.3L	
F Series	
4X2-w/M.T. (3.3)	4.8
w/A.T. (3.0)	4.3
4X4-w/M.T. (4.3)	6.2
w/A.T. (4.0)	6.0
Econoline (3.1)	4.5
Crankshaft and/or Camshaft Sprockets, Renew	
Four	
2.2L eng (1.9)	2.7
2.3L eng (1.1)	1.6
V-8-6.9L-7.3L	
F Series (4.1)	5.9
Econoline (4.7)	6.8
w/A.C. add (.4)	.4
w/P.S. add (.5)	.5
Vibration Damper or Pulley, Renew	
Four	
2.2L eng (.8)	1.2
2.3L eng (.4)	.7
V-8-6.9L-7.3L	
F Series (1.5)	2.1
Econoline (1.1)	1.5
w/A.C. add (.1)	.1

LABOR 16 CAMSHAFT & TIMING GEARS 16 LABOR

(Factory Time)	Chilton Time
GASOLINE ENGINES	
Timing Case Cover, Gasket or Oil Seal, Renew	
Includes: R&R radiator if required.	
RANGER-BRONCO II	
Four	
2.0L eng (2.0)	2.8
2.3L eng (1.9)	2.6
V-6	
2.8L eng (4.6)	6.4
2.9L eng	
1986-87 (4.6)	6.4
1988-89 (2.4)	3.5
AEROSTAR	
Four (1.9)	2.6
V-6	
1986-87 (4.8)	6.7
1988-90 (2.4)	3.5
ECONOLINE	
Six (2.7)	3.7
V-8	
5.0L eng (3.1)	4.3
5.8L engs (3.4)	4.7
5.8-7.5L engs	
w/Dual Thermactor (4.4)	6.1
F-Series-BRONCO	
Six (2.6)	3.6
V-8	
5.0L-5.8L engs (2.5)	3.5
5.8L-7.5L engs	
w/Dual Thermactor (3.0)	4.2

(Factory Time)	Chilton Time
Timing Belt, Renew	
RANGER-AEROSTAR	
Four	
2.0L eng (1.6)	2.5
2.3L eng (1.3)	2.2
w/P.S. add (.2)	.2
w/A.C. add (.3)	.3
Timing Chain or Gears, Renew (SIX)	
Includes: R&R timing case cover and radiator, renew gears or chain. Reset ignition timing.	
BRONCO-Six (2.7)	3.9
ECONOLINE-Six (3.5)	5.4
F100-350	
Six (2.7)	4.0
CRANKSHAFT GEAR ONLY. FOR CAMSHAFT FIBER GEAR USE CAMSHAFT, RENEW	
Timing Chain or Gears, Renew (V-6 & V-8)	
Includes: R&R timing case cover and radiator. Renew gears or chain. Reset ignition timing.	
RANGER-BRONCO	
V-6	
2.9L eng	
1986-87 (4.4)	6.7
1988-90 (2.5)	3.8
AEROSTAR	
V-6	
3.0L eng	
1986-87 (4.2)	7.0
1988-90 (2.5)	3.8

(Factory Time)	Chilton Time
F-Series-BRONCO	
V-8	
5.0L-5.8L engs (2.7)	4.0
5.8L-7.5L engs	
w/Dual Thermactor (3.1)	4.7
ECONOLINE	
V-8	
5.0L eng (3.5)	4.8
5.8L eng (3.7)	5.2
5.8L-7.5L engs	
w/Dual Thermactor (4.5)	6.6
Camshaft or Camshaft Gear, Renew	
Includes: R&R radiator, timing case cover.	
RANGER-BRONCO	
Four	
2.0L eng (2.2)	3.0
2.3L eng (4.2)	5.9
*Renew cam brgs add	.5
V-6	
2.8L eng	
w/M.T. (8.9)	12.5
w/A.T. (9.1)	12.7
2.9L eng (8.0)	11.2
AEROSTAR	
Four (5.4)	7.5
V-6	
2.8L eng (9.4)	13.1
3.0L eng (6.9)	9.7
ECONOLINE	
Six	
wo/EFI (6.6)	9.2

LABOR 16 CAMSHAFT & TIMING GEARS 16 LABOR

(Factory Time)	Chilton Time
w/EFI (6.3)	8.8
V-8	
5.0L eng	
wo/EFI (5.6)	7.8
w/EFI (8.1)	11.3
5.8L eng (6.1)	8.5
5.8L-7.5L engs	
w/Dual Thermactor (9.7)	13.5
F-Series-BRONCO	
Six	
wo/EFI (5.9)	8.2
w/EFI (6.1)	8.5
V-8	
5.0L eng	
wo/EFI (5.2)	7.3
w/EFI (6.7)	9.4
5.8L-7.5L engs (7.5)	10.5
5.8L eng	
w/Dual Thermactor (10.9)	15.2

Camshaft Bearings, Renew
Includes: R&R hood, radiator and engine assembly where required. R&R camshaft and renew bearings. Adjust carburetor and ignition timing.

(Factory Time)	Chilton Time
RANGER-BRONCO II	
Four	
2.0L eng (2.7)	4.1
w/P.S. add (.2)	.2
w/A.C. add (.3)	.3

DIESEL ENGINE

(Factory Time)	Chilton Time
Timing Cover Gasket, Renew	
Four	
2.2L eng (5.5)	7.9
2.3L eng (2.0)	3.0
V-8-6.9L-7.3L	
F Series (3.1)	4.5
Econoline (3.1)	4.5
w/A.C. add (.4)	.4
w/P.S. add (.5)	.5
Camshaft, Renew	
Four	
2.2L eng (6.1)	8.8
2.3L eng (1.5)	2.2
V-8-6.9L-7.3L	
F Series (11.6)	16.8

(Factory Time)	Chilton Time
Econoline (11.7)	17.0
w/A.C. add	
F Series (.3)	.3
Econoline (1.0)	1.0
Camshaft and/or Crankshaft Sprockets, Renew	
Four	
2.2L eng (1.9)	2.7
2.3L eng (1.1)	1.6
V-8-6.9L-7.3L	
F Series (3.3)	4.7
Econoline (3.3)	4.7
w/A.C. add (.4)	.4
w/P.S. add (.5)	.5
Camshaft Idler Gear, Renew	
Four	
2.2L eng (2.0)	2.7
2.3L eng (1.0)	1.5
w/A.C. add (.4)	.4
w/P.S. add (.5)	.5
Timing Belt, Renew	
Four	
2.3L eng (1.0)	1.5

LABOR 17 ENGINE OILING SYSTEM 17 LABOR

GASOLINE ENGINES

Oil Pan or Gasket, Renew
Includes: Clean oil pick up tube and screen. Renew oil filter.

(Factory Time)	Chilton Time
RANGER-BRONCO II	
Four	
2.0L eng (2.2)	3.0
2.3L eng	
4X2 (2.9)	4.0
4X4 (2.9)	4.0
V-6	
2.8L eng	
w/M.T. (3.4)	4.7
w/A.T. (3.6)	5.0
2.9L eng	
1986-87	
Ranger	
4X2 (2.0)	2.9
4X4 (3.3)	4.7
Bronco II (3.3)	4.7
1988-90	
Ranger	
4X2 (2.0)	2.9
4X4 (3.5)	5.0
Bronco II	
4X2 (3.3)	4.7
4X4 (3.5)	5.0
AEROSTAR	
Four (1.6)	2.2
V-6	
2.8L eng (2.2)	3.0
3.0L eng (1.4)	1.9
ECONOLINE	
Six	
wo/EFI (2.5)	3.5
w/EFI (3.7)	5.1
V-8	
5.0L-5.8L engs (2.8)	3.9
7.5L eng	
1986-87 (2.5)	3.5
1988-90 (5.0)	7.0
F-Series-BRONCO	
Six	
wo/EFI (2.3)	3.2
w/EFI (3.2)	4.4

(Factory Time)	Chilton Time
V-8	
5.0L-5.8L engs	
4X2	
w/M.T. (3.8)	5.3
w/A.T. (3.9)	5.4
4X4	
w/M.T. (4.6)	6.4
w/A.T. (4.7)	6.5
7.5L eng	
4X2	
1986-87	
w/M.T. (2.1)	2.9
w/A.T. (2.3)	3.2
1988-90	
w/M.T. (6.6)	9.2
w/A.T. (6.3)	8.8
4X4	
1986-87	
w/M.T. (2.7)	3.7
w/A.T. (2.9)	4.0
1988-90	
w/M.T. (6.9)	9.6
w/A.T. (6.5)	9.1

Oil Pump, R&R or Renew
Includes: R&R oil pan, clean oil pump pick up tube and screen. Renew oil filter.

(Factory Time)	Chilton Time
RANGER-BRONCO II	
Four	
2.0L eng (2.4)	3.3
2.3L eng	
4X2 (3.0)	4.2
4X4 (3.0)	4.2
V-6	
2.8L eng	
w/M.T. (3.5)	4.9
w/A.T. (3.7)	5.1
2.9L eng	
1986-87	
Ranger	
4X2 (2.1)	3.1
4X4 (3.4)	4.9
Bronco II (3.4)	4.9
1988-90	
Ranger	
4X2 (2.1)	3.1
4X4 (3.6)	5.2
Bronco II	
4X2 (3.4)	4.9

(Factory Time)	Chilton Time
4X4 (3.6)	5.2
AEROSTAR	
Four (1.7)	2.3
V-6	
2.8L eng (2.3)	3.2
3.0L eng (1.5)	2.1
ECONOLINE	
Six	
wo/EFI (2.6)	3.6
w/EFI (3.8)	5.3
V-8	
5.0L-5.8L engs (2.9)	4.0
7.5L eng	
1986-87 (2.6)	3.6
1988-90 (5.1)	7.1
F-Series-BRONCO	
Six	
wo/EFI (2.4)	3.3
w/EFI (3.3)	4.6
V-8	
5.0L-5.8L engs	
4X2	
w/M.T. (3.9)	5.4
w/A.T. (4.0)	5.5
4X4	
w/M.T. (4.7)	6.5
w/A.T. (4.8)	6.6
7.5L eng	
4X2	
1986-87	
w/M.T. (2.2)	3.0
w/A.T. (2.4)	3.3
1988-90	
w/M.T. (6.7)	9.3
w/A.T. (6.4)	8.9
4X4	
1986-87	
w/M.T. (2.8)	3.9
w/A.T. (3.0)	4.2
1988-90	
w/M.T. (7.0)	9.8
w/A.T. (6.6)	9.2
Recond pump add (.4)	.5
Pressure Test Engine Bearings (Pan Off)	
All models	1.0
Oil Pressure Gauge (Engine), Renew	
All models (.3)	.5

LABOR 17 ENGINE OILING SYSTEM 17 LABOR

(Factory Time)	Chilton Time	(Factory Time)	Chilton Time	(Factory Time)	Chilton Time
Oil Pressure Gauge (Dash), Renew		2.3L eng		2.3L eng (1.4)............	1.9
RANGER (.6)........................	1.0	4X2 (1.6)..............	2.2	V-8-6.9L-7.3L	
BRONCO (.7)........................	1.1	4X4 (2.7)..............	3.7	F Series	
BRONCO II (.6).....................	1.0	V-8-6.9L-7.3L		4X2 (2.8)................	3.9
AEROSTAR (.6)......................	1.0	F Series............	3.6	4X4 (3.3)................	4.6
ECONOLINE (.5).....................	.8	4X2 (2.6).............	3.6	Econoline (3.5)...........	5.0
F100-350 (.7)......................	1.1	4X4 (3.1).............	4.3	Recond pump add............	.5
Oil Filter Element, Renew		Econoline (3.3)......	4.7	**Oil Cooler Assembly, Renew**	
All models (.3)	.4	**Pressure Test Engine Bearings (Pan Off)**		V-8-6.9L-7.3L	
DIESEL ENGINE		All models............	1.0	F-Series (2.5)..........	3.4
		Oil Pump, Renew		Econoline (1.9).........	2.5
Oil Pan and/or Gasket, Renew		Four		**Oil Filter Element, Renew**	
Four		2.2L eng (3.4)......	4.8	All models (.3)..........	.4
2.2L eng (3.2).................	4.5				

LABOR 18 CLUTCH & FLYWHEEL 18 LABOR

(Factory Time)	Chilton Time	(Factory Time)	Chilton Time	(Factory Time)	Chilton Time
Clutch Pedal Free Play, Adjust		4X4		Diesel............	6.1
All models (.3)	.4	Warner T-18	5.7	w/Skid plate add (.2)........	.3
Bleed Hydraulic Clutch System		New Process 435	5.2	w/Full carpet add (.7).......	1.0
All models (.3)	.4	TOD	4.7	w/P.T.O. add (.6)............	.8
Clutch Master Cylinder, Renew		Warner T-19-MR-2	4.9	w/Coupling shaft add (.2)....	.3
Does not include bleed system.		ZF-5			
Econoline (.7).................	1.1	Gas	6.3	**Flywheel, Renew**	
Aerostar (.7).................	1.1	Diesel.....................	6.4	Includes: R&R trans and transfer case as a unit.	
All other models (.5).........	.8	w/Skid plate add (.2).........	.3	R&R clutch and adjust free play.	
Hydraulic Clutch Slave Cylinder, Renew		w/Full carpet add (.7)........	1.0	Ranger	
(External)		w/P.T.O. add (.6).............	.8	4X2	
For Internal Slave Cyl See Trans R&R–Group		w/Coupling shaft add (.2).....	.3	Four	
19.		**Clutch Release Bearing, Renew**		Gas	2.6
F-Series-Bronco		Includes: R&R trans and transfer case as a unit.		Diesel	3.4
4X2 (.5)....................	1.0	Adjust clutch pedal free play.		V-6	
4X4 (.5)	1.0	Ranger		4X4	
Econoline		4X2		Four	5.2
All models (.7)	1.1	Four		V-6	5.5
		Gas	2.5	Bronco II	
Clutch Assembly, Renew		Diesel	2.0	TK-5	5.0
Includes: R&R trans and transfer case as a unit.		V-6	2.8	MMC5.....................	5.5
Adjust clutch pedal free play.		4X4		Aerostar	
Ranger		Four	4.6	Four-TK-5	3.1
4X2		V-6	4.9	V-6-TK-5	3.4
Four		Bronco II		Bronco	
Gas	2.8	TK-5	4.4	T-18.....................	6.3
Diesel	2.3	MMC5.........................	4.9	N.P. 435-MR-2.............	5.2
V-6	3.1	Aerostar		TOD......................	5.0
4X4		Four-TK-5	2.5	ZF-5.....................	6.3
Four	4.9	V-6-TK-5	2.8	Econoline	
V-6	5.2	Bronco		3 Speed	2.1
Bronco II		T-18.........................	5.7	4 Speed O.D.	2.4
TK-5	4.7	N.P. 435-MR-2................	4.6	MR-2	3.6
MMC5.........................	5.2	TOD.........................	4.4	ZF-5	4.5
Aerostar		ZF-5.........................	6.0	New Process 435	3.2
Four-TK-5	2.8	Econoline			
V-6-TK-5	3.1	3 Speed	1.5	F-Series	
Bronco		4 Speed O.D.	1.8	4X2	
T-18.........................	6.0	MR-2	3.0	3 Speed	2.1
N.P. 435-MR-2................	4.9	ZF-5	3.9	4 Speed	
TOD.........................	4.7	New Process 435	2.6	TOD...................	3.2
ZF-5.........................	6.3	F-Series		Warner T-18	3.8
Econoline		4X2		New Process 435	3.2
3 Speed	1.8	3 Speed	1.5	Warner T-19	3.6
4 Speed O.D.	2.1	4 Speed		MR-2	3.8
MR-2	3.3	TOD.......................	2.6	ZF-5	
ZF-5	4.2	Warner T-18	3.2	Gas	5.0
New Process 435	2.9	New Process 435	2.6	Diesel................	5.3
F-Series		Warner T-19	3.0	4X4	
4X2		MR-2	3.2	Warner T-18	6.0
3 Speed	1.8	ZF-5		New Process 435	5.5
4 Speed		Gas	4.4	TOD..................	5.0
TOD.......................	2.9	Diesel................	4.7	Warner T-19-MR-2	5.2
Warner T-18	3.5	4X4		ZF-5	
New Process 435	2.9	Warner T-18	5.4	Gas	6.6
Warner T-19	3.3	New Process 435	4.9	Diesel................	6.7
MR-2	3.5	TOD......................	4.4	w/Skid plate add (.2)........	.3
ZF-5		Warner T-19-MR-2	4.6	w/Full carpet add (.7).......	1.0
Gas	4.7	ZF-5		Renew ring gear add (.2).....	.4
Diesel	5.0	Gas	6.0	w/P.T.O. add (.6)............	.8
				w/Coupling shaft add (.2)....	.3

LABOR   19A   MANUAL TRANSMISSION (RWD)   19A   LABOR

	Factory Time / Chilton Time		Factory Time / Chilton Time		Factory Time / Chilton Time

Transmission Assy., Remove and Reinstall
Includes: R&R transmission and transfer case as a unit.

Ranger
4X2
Four
Gas (1.8)............ 2.5
Diesel (1.4)............ 2.0
V-6 (2.0)............ 2.8
4X4
Four (3.3)............ 4.6
V-6 (3.5)............ 4.9

Bronco II
TK-5 (3.2)............ 4.4
MMC5 (3.5)............ 4.9

Aerostar
Four–TK-5 (1.7)............ 2.5
V-6–TK-5 (2.0)............ 2.8

Bronco
T-18 (4.1)............ 5.7
N.P. 435–MR-2 (3.5)............ 4.6
TOD (3.2)............ 4.4
ZF-5 (4.3)............ 6.0

Econoline
3 Speed (.8)............ 1.5
4 Speed O.D. (.9)............ 1.8
MR-2 (2.2)............ 3.0
ZF-5 (2.8)............ 3.9
New Process 435 (1.7)............ 2.6

F-Series
4X2
3 Speed (.8)............ 1.5
4 Speed
TOD (1.9)............ 2.6
Warner T-18 (2.3)............ 3.2
New Process 435 (1.7)............ 2.6
Warner T-19 (2.2)............ 3.0
MR-2 (2.3)............ 3.2
ZF-5
Gas (3.2)............ 4.4
Diesel (3.4)............ 4.7
4X4
Warner T-18 (3.9)............ 5.4
New Process 435 (3.5)............ 4.9
TOD (3.2)............ 4.4
Warner T-19–MR-2 (3.3)............ 4.6
ZF-5
Gas (4.3)............ 6.0
Diesel (4.4)............ 6.1
Renew slave cyl add............ .4
w/Skid plate add (.2)............ .3

w/Full carpet add (.7)............ 1.0
w/P.T.O. add (.6)............ .8
w/Coupling shaft add (.2)............ .3

Transmission Assy., R&R and Recondition
Includes: R&R trans and transfer case as a unit. Separate and overhaul transmission only.

RANGER
4X2
Four
Gas (5.3)............ 7.4
Diesel (4.9)............ 6.8
V-6 (5.5)............ 7.7
4X4
Four (6.8)............ 9.5
V-6 (7.0)............ 9.8

Bronco II
TK-5 (7.5)............ 10.5
MMC5 (7.0)............ 9.8

Aerostar
Four–TK-5 (6.0)............ 8.4
V-6–TK-5 (5.5)............ 7.7

Bronco
T-18 (6.0)............ 8.4
N.P. 435–MR-2 (7.0)............ 9.8
TOD (5.0)............ 7.0
ZF-5 (9.6)............ 13.4

Econoline
3 Speed (2.9)............ 4.0
4 Speed O.D. (2.7)............ 3.7
MR-2 (5.7)............ 7.9
ZF-5 (8.1)............ 11.3
New Process 435 (3.9)............ 5.4

F-Series
4X2
3 Speed (2.9)............ 4.0
4 Speed
TOD (3.7)............ 5.1
Warner T-18 (4.2)............ 5.8
New Process 435 (3.9)............ 5.4
Warner T-19 (4.1)............ 5.7
MR-2 (5.8)............ 8.1
ZF-5
Gas (8.5)............ 11.9
Diesel (8.7)............ 12.1
4X4
Warner T-18 (5.8)............ 8.1
New Process 435 (5.7)............ 7.9
TOD (5.0)............ 7.0
Warner T-19–MR-2 (6.8)............ 9.5

ZF-5
Gas (9.6)............ 13.4
Diesel (9.7)............ 13.6
w/Skid plate add (.2)............ .3
w/Full carpet add (.7)............ 1.0
w/P.T.O. add (.6)............ .8
w/Coupling shaft add (.2)............ .3

Transmission, Recondition (Off Truck)
3 Speed (2.1)............ 3.2
4 Speed
TOD (1.8)............ 2.5
New Process (2.2)............ 3.4
Warner (1.9)............ 3.0
Overdrive (2.3)............ 3.4
SROD (1.9)............ 3.0
TK (2.2)............ 3.0
5 Speed
TK-5 (4.3)............ 6.0
MMC5-MR-1 (3.5)............ 4.9
MR-2 (3.5)............ 4.9
ZF-5 (5.3)............ 7.4

Extension Housing, Bearing Retainer or Gasket, Renew
Includes: Renew oil seal.
All models 4X2
3 Speed (1.2)............ 1.7
4 Speed-O/D (1.3)............ 1.8
4 Speed-TOD (1.3)............ 1.8
4 Speed-SROD (1.4)............ 1.9
4 Speed-TK (1.2)............ 1.7
4 Speed-Warner T-19 (1.1)............ 1.7
4 Speed-Warner T-18 (1.3)............ 1.8
New Process 435 (1.2)............ 1.8
5 Speed-TK (1.2)............ 1.7
4X4
TK (2.2)............ 2.8
TOD (2.2)............ 2.8
MMC5-MR-1 (2.2)............ 2.8
Warner T-18 (2.3)............ 3.0
New Process 435 (2.3)............ 3.0
Warner T-19 (2.0)............ 2.8
w/Coupling shaft add (.2)............ .3

Transmission Rear Oil Seal and/or Bushing, Renew
F-Series–Super Duty (1.3)............ 2.0
BRONCO (.7)............ 1.0
All other models (.5)............ .8
w/Coupling shaft add (.2)............ .3

LABOR   20   TRANSFER CASE   20   LABOR

	Factory Time / Chilton Time		Factory Time / Chilton Time		Factory Time / Chilton Time

Transfer Case Assembly, R&R or Renew
Ranger-Bronco II
4X2 (1.5)............ 2.0
4X4 (1.2)............ 1.7
F-Series (1.8)............ 2.5
Bronco (2.0)............ 2.7
Renew assy add............ .5
w/P.T.O. add (.6)............ .8
w/Coupling shaft add (.2)............ .3

Transfer Case, R&R and Recondition
Includes: R&R trans and/or transfer case. Separate units and overhaul transfer case only.
All models
New Process 208
Part Time (4.7)............ 6.4

Borg Warner 1345-1356
Part Time (3.8)............ 5.3
Borg Warner 1350
4X2 (2.1)............ 3.0
4X4 (4.8)............ 6.7
w/P.T.O. add (.6)............ .8
w/Coupling shaft add (.2)............ .3

ELECTRONIC SHIFT CONTROL

Electronic Shift Control Circuit Test
All models (.4)............ .6

Electronic Shift Control Module, Renew
Does not include system test.
All models (.2)............ .3

Electronic Shift Control Switch, Renew
Does not include system test.
All models (.3)............ .5

Electronic Shift Control Motor, Renew
Does not include system test.
All models (.4)............ .6

Electronic Shift Control Speed Sensor, Renew
Does not include system test.
Ranger-Bronco II (.3)............ .5
Bronco (.7)............ 1.0

Electronic Shift Transfer Case Coil, Renew
Does not include system test.
Ranger-Bronco II (2.9)............ 3.6
F-Series–Bronco (1.8)............ 2.4

LABOR 21 SHIFT LINKAGE 21 LABOR

(Factory Time)	Chilton Time
MANUAL	
Shift Linkage, Adjust	
All models (.3)	.4
Gear Shift Tube Assy., Renew (3 SPEED)	
Bronco (.5)	1.1
ECONOLINE (.6)	1.1
F100-250 (1.1)	1.7
Gear Shift Rods, Renew	
Includes: Adjust shift linkage.	
BRONCO (.4)	.7

(Factory Time)	Chilton Time
ECONOLINE-3 spd (.5)	.7
F100-250-3 spd (.5)	.7
Transfer Case Control Lever, Renew	
All models (.5)	.7
AUTOMATIC	
Gear Shift Tube Assembly, Renew	
F100-350 (.7)	1.5

(Factory Time)	Chilton Time
Shift Linkage, Adjust	
Includes: Adjust neutral safety switch.	
All models	
manual (.3)	.5
manual & kickdown (.4)	.6
Gear Selector Lever, Renew	
All models	
column shift (.2)	.5
floor shift (.4)	.6

LABOR 23A AUTOMATIC TRANSMISSION (RWD) 23A LABOR

(Factory Time)	Chilton Time
ON TRUCK SERVICES	
Drain and Refill Unit	
A4LD	1.2
E4OD	1.1
All other models	1.0
Oil Pressure Check	
All models (.3)	.5
Check Unit for Oil Leaks	
Includes: Clean and dry outside of case, run unit to determine point of leak.	
All models (.7)	.9
Neutral Safety Switch, Renew	
All models (.3)	.4
Vacuum Modulator, Renew	
A4LD (.4)	.6
C-5 (.4)	.6
C-6 (.3)	.5
Vacuum Modulator, Adjust	
Includes: Pressure check.	
All models (.5)	.9
Linkage, Adjust	
manual (.3)	.5
manual & kickdown (.4)	.6
Kickdown Linkage Rod or Cable, Adjust	
All models (.4)	.6
Manual Lever Position Sensor, Renew	
E4OD (.3)	.5
Front Band, Adjust	
A4LD (.3)	.5
C-5 (.3)	.5
C-6 (.2)	.4
Rear Band, Adjust	
A4LD (.2)	.4
C-5 (.2)	.4
Front and Rear Bands, Adjust	
A4LD (.5)	.8
C-5 (.5)	.8
Servo Assembly, Recondition (External)	
A4LD	
Inter or Overdrive (.4)	.7
C-6	
Intermediate (1.0)	1.5
Extension Housing and/or Gasket, Renew	
4X2	
A4LD (1.0)	1.6
C-5 (.9)	1.5
C-6	
F-Series (1.0)	1.6
Econoline (1.1)	1.7
AOD (1.5)	2.1
E4OD	
F-Series-Econoline (1.1)	1.7
Super Duty (1.6)	2.2

(Factory Time)	Chilton Time
4X4	
A4LD (1.5)	2.1
AOD-C-6 (2.2)	2.8
E4OD (1.8)	2.4
w/Coupling shaft add (.2)	.2
Governor Assembly, Renew	
4X2	
A4LD (1.0)	1.7
C-5 (1.2)	1.8
C-6 (1.2)	1.8
AOD (1.2)	2.2
4X4	
A4LD (1.8)	2.4
AOD-C-6 (2.2)	2.9
w/Coupling shaft add (.2)	.2
Extension Housing Rear Oil Seal and/or Bushing, Renew	
All models (.5)	.8
w/Coupling shaft add (.2)	.2
Front Servo, Recondition	
Includes: R&R oil pan.	
AOD (1.0)	1.5
Rear Servo, Recondition	
Includes: R&R oil pan.	
AOD (1.0)	1.5
Oil Pan or Gasket, Renew	
RANGER-BRONCO II	
A4LD (.9)	1.2
AEROSTAR	
A4LD (.9)	1.2
F-Series-BRONCO	
C-5 (.7)	1.0
C-6 (.7)	1.0
AOD (.7)	1.0
E4OD (.8)	1.1
ECONOLINE	
C-6 (.7)	1.0
AOD (.7)	1.0
E4OD (.8)	1.1
Adj linkage add (.2)	.2
Adj band add (.1)	.1
Valve Body Assembly, Renew	
Includes: R&R oil pan.	
RANGER-BRONCO II	
A4LD (1.2)	1.7
AEROSTAR	
A4LD (1.2)	1.7
F-Series-BRONCO	
C-5 (.9)	1.4
C-6 (.9)	1.4
AOD (1.0)	1.5
E4OD (1.0)	1.4
ECONOLINE	
C-6 (.9)	1.4
AOD (1.0)	1.5
E4OD (1.0)	1.4

(Factory Time)	Chilton Time
Adj linkage add (.2)	.2
Adj band add (.1)	.1
Valve Body Assy., R&R and Recondition	
Includes: R&R oil pan and replace filter. Disassemble, clean, inspect, free all valves. Replace parts as required.	
RANGER-BRONCO II	
A4LD (1.7)	2.5
AEROSTAR	
A4LD (1.7)	2.5
F-Series-BRONCO	
C-5 (1.6)	2.4
C-6 (1.5)	2.3
AOD (1.9)	2.7
E4OD (1.5)	2.3
ECONOLINE	
C-6 (1.5)	2.3
AOD (1.9)	2.7
E4OD (1.5)	2.3
Adj linkage add (.2)	.2
Adj band add (.1)	.1
Accumulator Body, Renew	
Includes: R&R oil pan.	
F-Series-ECONOLINE	
E4OD (1.0)	1.4
Clean accumulator add (.4)	.4
Solenoid Body, Renew	
Includes: R&R oil pan.	
F-Series-ECONOLINE	
E4OD (1.0)	1.4
Throttle and Manual Seals and/or Levers, Renew	
Includes: R&R oil pan and valve body.	
RANGER-BRONCO	
A4LD (1.2)	1.8
AEROSTAR	
A4LD (1.2)	1.8
F-Series-BRONCO	
C-5 (1.0)	1.6
C-6 (1.1)	1.7
AOD (1.0)	1.6
ECONOLINE	
C-6 (1.1)	1.7
AOD (1.0)	1.6
Adj linkage add (.2)	.2
Adj band add (.1)	.1
SERVICES REQUIRING R&R	
Transmission Assembly, R&R	
Includes: R&R transmission and converter assembly. Drain and refill unit. Adjust linkage.	
RANGER	
A4LD	
4X2 (2.4)	3.4
4X4 (3.9)	5.5

LABOR 23A AUTOMATIC TRANSMISSION (RWD) 23A LABOR

(Factory) Time	Chilton Time
BRONCO II	
A4LD	
4X2 (3.9)	5.5
4X4 (3.9)	5.5
AEROSTAR	
A4LD	
Four (2.5)	3.5
V-6 (2.1)	2.9
F-Series-BRONCO	
4X2	
C-5 (2.4)	3.4
C-6	
Six (2.6)	3.6
V-8 (2.9)	4.0
AOD (2.8)	3.9
E4OD (2.9)	4.0
4X4	
C-6	
Six (4.2)	5.9
V-8	
5.0L eng (4.3)	6.0
5.8L eng (4.3)	6.0
6.9L-7.3L engs (3.8)	5.3
7.5L eng (3.8)	5.3
AOD (4.2)	5.9
E4OD (3.9)	5.4
ECONOLINE	
C-6	
Six (2.7)	3.8
V-8	
5.8L eng (2.7)	3.8
6.9L-7.3L engs (2.8)	3.9
7.5L eng (3.0)	4.2
AOD	
Six (2.5)	3.5
V-8 (2.6)	3.6
E4OD (2.8)	3.9
w/Skid plate add (.2)	.3
w/P.T.O. add (.6)	.8
w/Coupling shaft add (.2)	.3

Transmission and Converter Assy., R&R and Recondition

Includes: Drain and refill unit. Disassemble trans including valve body, clean, inspect and replace parts as required. Adjust linkage. Road test.

(Factory) Time	Chilton Time
RANGER	
A4LD	
4X2 (9.3)	13.0
4X4 (10.8)	15.1
BRONCO II	
A4LD	
4X2 (10.8)	15.1
4X4 (10.8)	15.1
AEROSTAR	
A4LD	
Four (9.4)	13.1
V-6 (9.0)	12.6
F-Series-BRONCO	
4X2	
C-5 (6.0)	8.4
C-6	
Six (6.4)	9.0
V-8 (6.7)	9.4
AOD (7.7)	9.4
E4OD (8.6)	12.0
4X4	
C-6	
Six (8.0)	11.2
V-8	
5.0L eng (8.1)	11.3
5.8L eng (8.1)	11.3
6.9L-7.3L engs (7.6)	10.6
7.5L eng (7.6)	10.6
AOD (9.1)	12.7
E4OD (9.6)	13.4
ECONOLINE	
C-6	
Six (6.5)	9.1

(Factory) Time	Chilton Time
V-8	
5.8L eng (6.5)	9.1
6.9L-7.3L engs (6.6)	9.2
7.5L eng (6.8)	9.5
AOD	
Six (7.4)	10.4
V-8 (7.5)	10.5
E4OD (8.5)	11.9
Clean and check converter add (.5)	.5
Flush oil cooler and lines add (.2)	.2
w/Skid plate add (.2)	.3
w/P.T.O. add (.6)	.8
w/Coupling shaft add (.2)	.3

Transmission Assembly, Reseal

Includes: R&R transmission, drain and refill unit. Renew all seals and gaskets. Adjust linkage. Road test.

(Factory) Time	Chilton Time
RANGER	
A4LD	
4X2	6.4
4X4	8.5
BRONCO II	
A4LD	
4X2	8.5
4X4	8.5
AEROSTAR	
A4LD	
Four	6.5
V-6	5.9
F-Series-BRONCO	
4X2	
C-5	6.4
C-6	
Six	6.6
V-8	7.0
AOD	6.9
E4OD	7.0
4X4	
C-6	
Six	8.9
V-8	
5.0L eng	9.0
5.8L eng	9.0
6.9L-7.3L engs	8.3
7.5L eng	8.3
AOD	8.9
E4OD	8.4
ECONOLINE	
C-6	
Six	6.8
V-8	
5.8L eng	6.8
6.9L-7.3L engs	6.9
7.5L eng	7.2
AOD	
Six	6.5
V-8	6.6
E4OD	6.9
w/Skid plate add (.2)	.3
w/P.T.O. add (.6)	.8
w/Coupling shaft add (.2)	.3

Torque Converter, Renew

Includes: R&R transmission. Drain and refill unit. Adjust linkage. Road test.

(Factory) Time	Chilton Time
RANGER	
A4LD	
4X2 (2.5)	3.5
4X4 (4.0)	5.6
BRONCO II	
A4LD	
4X2 (4.0)	5.6
4X4 (4.0)	5.6
AEROSTAR	
A4LD	
Four (2.6)	3.6
V-6 (2.1)	2.9
F-Series-BRONCO	
4X2	
C-5 (2.5)	3.5

(Factory) Time	Chilton Time
C-6	
Six (2.7)	3.7
V-8 (3.0)	4.2
AOD (2.9)	4.0
E4OD	4.1
4X4	
C-6	
Six (4.3)	6.0
V-8	
5.0L eng (4.4)	6.1
5.8L eng (4.4)	6.1
6.9L-7.3L engs (3.9)	5.4
7.5L eng (3.9)	5.4
AOD (4.3)	6.0
E4OD	5.5
ECONOLINE	
C-6	
Six (2.8)	3.9
V-8	
5.8L eng (2.8)	3.9
6.9L-7.3L engs (2.9)	4.0
7.5L eng (3.1)	4.3
AOD	
Six (2.6)	3.6
V-8 (2.7)	3.7
E4OD	4.0
w/Skid plate add (.2)	.3
w/P.T.O. add (.6)	.8
w/Coupliong shaft add (.2)	.3

Bands, Renew (One or Both)

Includes: R&R transmission. Drain and refill unit. Renew gaskets and seals as necessary. Adjust linkage. Road test.

(Factory) Time	Chilton Time
RANGER	
A4LD	
4X2 (4.3)	6.0
4X4 (5.8)	8.1
BRONCO II	
A4LD	
4X2 (5.8)	8.1
4X4 (5.8)	8.1
AEROSTAR	
A4LD	
Four (4.4)	6.1
V-6 (4.0)	5.6
F-Series-BRONCO	
4X2	
C-5 (3.6)	5.0
C-6	
Six (3.7)	5.1
V-8 (4.0)	5.6
AOD (4.3)	6.0
E4OD (4.6)	6.4
4X4	
C-6	
Six (5.3)	7.4
V-8	
5.0L eng (5.4)	7.5
5.8L eng (5.4)	7.5
6.9L-7.3L engs (4.9)	6.8
7.5L eng (4.9)	6.8
AOD (5.7)	7.9
E4OD (5.6)	7.8
ECONOLINE	
C-6	
Six (3.8)	5.3
V-8	
5.8L eng (3.8)	5.3
6.9L-7.3L engs (3.9)	5.4
7.5L eng (4.1)	5.7
AOD	
Six (4.0)	5.6
V-8 (4.1)	5.7
E4OD (4.5)	6.3
w/Skid plate add (.2)	.3
w/P.T.O. add (.6)	.8
w/Coupling shaft add (.2)	3

LABOR 23A AUTOMATIC TRANSMISSION (RWD) 23A LABOR

(Factory Time)	Chilton Time
Front Oil Pump Seal, Renew	
Includes: R&R transmission. Drain and refill unit. Adjust linkage. Road test.	
RANGER	
A4LD	
4X2 (2.5)	3.5
4X4 (4.0)	5.6
BRONCO II	
A4LD	
4X2 (4.0)	5.6
4X4 (4.0)	5.6
AEROSTAR	
A4LD	
Four (2.6)	3.6
V-6 (2.2)	3.0
F-Series-BRONCO	
4X2	
C-5 (2.5)	3.5
C-6	
Six (2.7)	3.7
V-8 (3.0)	4.2
AOD (2.9)	4.0
E4OD (3.0)	4.2
4X4	
C-6	
Six (4.3)	6.0
V-8	
5.0L eng (4.4)	6.1
5.8L eng (4.4)	6.1
6.9L-7.3L engs (3.9)	5.4
7.5L eng (3.9)	5.4
AOD (4.3)	6.0
E4OD (4.0)	5.6
ECONOLINE	
C-6	
Six (2.8)	3.9
V-8	
5.8L eng (2.8)	3.9
6.9L-7.3L engs (2.9)	4.0
7.5L eng (3.1)	4.3
AOD	
Six (2.6)	3.6
V-8 (2.7)	3.7
E4OD (2.9)	4.0
w/Skid plate add (.2)	.3
w/P.T.O. add (.6)	.8
w/Coupling shaft add (.2)	.3
Front Oil Pump, R&R and Recondition	
Includes: R&R transmission. Drain and refill unit. Renew gaskets and seals as necessary. Adjust linkage. Road test.	
RANGER	
A4LD	
4X2 (2.8)	3.9
4X4 (4.3)	6.0
BRONCO II	
A4LD	
4X2 (4.3)	6.0
4X4 (4.3)	6.0
AEROSTAR	
A4LD	
Four (2.9)	4.0
V-6 (2.5)	3.5

(Factory Time)	Chilton Time
F-Series-BRONCO	
4X2	
C-5 (2.9)	4.0
C-6	
Six (3.2)	4.4
V-8 (3.5)	4.9
AOD (3.4)	4.7
E4OD (3.8)	5.3
4X4	
C-6	
Six (4.8)	6.7
V-8	
5.0L eng (4.9)	6.8
5.8L eng (4.9)	6.8
6.9L-7.3L engs (4.4)	6.1
7.5L eng (4.4)	6.1
AOD (4.7)	6.5
E4OD (4.8)	6.7
ECONOLINE	
C-6	
Six (3.3)	4.6
V-8	
5.8L eng (3.3)	4.6
6.9L-7.3L engs (3.4)	4.7
7.5L eng (3.6)	5.0
AOD	
Six (3.1)	4.3
V-8 (3.2)	4.4
E4OD (3.7)	5.1
w/Skid plate add (.2)	.3
w/P.T.O. add (.6)	.6
w/Coupling shaft add (.2)	.3
Flywheel and Ring Gear Assy., Renew	
Includes: R&R transmission. Drain and refill unit. Adjust linkage. Road test.	
RANGER	
A4LD	
4X2 (2.7)	3.7
4X4 (4.2)	5.8
BRONCO II	
A4LD	
4X2 (4.2)	5.8
4X4 (4.2)	5.8
AEROSTAR	
A4LD	
Four (2.8)	3.9
V-6 (2.4)	3.3
F-Series-BRONCO	
4X2	
C-5 (2.7)	3.7
C-6	
Six (2.9)	4.0
V-8 (3.2)	4.4
AOD (3.1)	4.3
E4OD (3.2)	4.4
4X4	
C-6	
Six (4.5)	6.3
V-8	
5.0L eng (4.6)	6.4
5.8L eng (4.6)	6.4
6.9L-7.3L engs (4.1)	5.7
7.5L eng (4.1)	5.7
AOD (4.5)	6.3

(Factory Time)	Chilton Time
E4OD (4.2)	5.8
ECONOLINE	
C-6	
Six (3.0)	4.2
V-8	
5.8L eng (3.0)	4.2
6.9L-7.3L engs (3.1)	4.3
7.5L eng (3.3)	4.6
AOD	
Six (2.8)	3.9
V-8 (2.6)	3.6
E4OD (3.1)	4.3
w/Skid plate add (.2)	.3
w/P.T.O. add (.6)	.8
w/Coupling shaft add (.2)	.3
Parking Pawl, Renew	
Includes: Disassemble as required. Drain and refill unit. Renew gaskets and seals as necessary. Adjust linkage. Road test.	
RANGER	
A4LD	
4X2 (1.0)	1.5
4X4 (2.6)	3.6
BRONCO II	
A4LD	
4X2 (2.6)	3.6
4X4 (2.6)	3.6
AEROSTAR	
A4LD	
Four (1.0)	1.5
V-6 (1.0)	1.5
F-Series-BRONCO	
4X2	
C-5 (3.4)	4.7
C-6	
Six (3.6)	5.0
V-8 (3.9)	5.4
AOD (1.5)	2.1
E4OD	
F-Series (1.0)	1.5
Super Duty (1.2)	1.7
4X4	
C-6	
Six (5.0)	7.0
V-8	
5.0L eng (5.3)	7.4
5.8L eng (5.3)	7.4
6.9L-7.3L eng (5.5)	7.7
7.5L eng (5.5)	7.7
AOD (2.8)	3.9
ECONOLINE	
C-6	
Six (3.7)	5.1
V-8	
5.8L eng (3.7)	5.1
6.9L-7.3L eng (3.9)	5.4
7.5L eng (3.7)	5.1
AOD	
Six (1.5)	2.1
V-8 (1.5)	2.1
E4OD (1.0)	1.5
w/Skid plate add (.2)	.3
w/P.T.O. add (.6)	.8
w/Coupling shaft add (.2)	.3

LABOR 25 U-JOINTS & DRIVESHAFT 25 LABOR

(Factory Time)	Chilton Time
Drive Shaft, Renew	
RANGER-BRONCO (.4)	.6
AEROSTAR (.4)	.6
F-series-ECONOLINE	
wo/Coupling shaft (.3)	.5
w/Coupling shaft (.6)	.8
Recond U-Joints add,	
4X2	
RANGER-each (.4)	.5

(Factory Time)	Chilton Time
AEROSTAR-each (.3)	.4
F-series-ECONOLINE	
wo/Coupling shaft	
each (.4)	.5
w/Coupling shaft	
each (.4)	.5
4X4	
Single Cardan	
each (.4)	.5

(Factory Time)	Chilton Time
Double Cardan	
each (.6)	.8
Install yoke seal kit	
add-each (.1)	.1
Drive Shaft Center Support Bearing, Renew	
All models (.8)	1.2

LABOR — 26 DRIVE AXLE 26 — LABOR

(Factory Time)	Chilton Time
Rear Axle, Drain and Refill	
All models (.5)	.6
Axle Housing Cover or Gasket, Renew (Integral Type)	
All models (.5)	.6
Axle Shaft, Renew	
All models	
Removable Carrier	
one (.5)	.8
both (.8)	1.3
Integral Carrier	
one (.7)	1.0
both (.9)	1.4
Rear Wheel Bearing or Oil Seal, Renew (One Wheel)	
All models	
6.75 axle (.6)	.9
7.5 axle (.6)	.9
ball bearing (.6)	.9
roller brg	
Ford-Dana (.7)	1.0
Dana 250 (.9)	1.3
Semi-Floating (.9)	1.3
tapered roller brg (.7)	1.0
full floating axle (.7)	1.0
Rear Axle Shaft Gasket or Outer Oil Seal, Renew	
All models	
Semi-Floating Axle	
one side (.5)	.7
both sides (.6)	.9
Dana Full Floating Axle	
one side (.4)	.6
both sides (.7)	1.0

(Factory Time)	Chilton Time
Ford Full Floating Axle	
one side (.3)	.5
both sides (.5)	.8
Integral Carrier	
one side (.8)	1.1
both sides (1.2)	1.6
Removable Carrier	
one side (.6)	.9
both sides (.9)	1.3
Pinion Shaft Oil Seal, Renew	
All models (1.0)	1.4

INTEGRAL CARRIER

Rear Axle Housing, Renew
Includes: Drain and refill axle. R&R wheels, hubs and axle shafts. Renew inner oil seals, remove brake backing plates without disconnecting brake lines. Transfer all parts and adjust ring gear and pinion. Does not include disassembly of differential assembly.

All models	
Ford 7.5 (3.5)	5.0
Ford 10.25 (4.8)	6.7
Dana 60 Semi-Float (6.6)	9.5
Dana 60-61 Full Float (6.9)	10.0
Dana 70 (6.3)	9.1
Dana 80 (6.6)	9.5
w/Dual whls add (.3)	.5
Recond diff add	1.0

Ring Gear and Pinion, Adjust
Includes: Drain and refill axle. Adjust ring and pinion backlash. Road test.

All models	
std axle (1.5)	2.2

(Factory Time)	Chilton Time
limited slip/Trac-Lok (1.8)	2.6
Ring and Pinion Gear, Renew	
Includes: Drain and refill axle. Adjust backlash. Road test.	
All models	
Ford axle (2.4)	4.0
Dana axle (2.1)	3.5
w/Limited slip add (.1)	.2
Renew pinion brgs and cups add (.6)	.8
Recond diff assy add	
Ford 7.5 (.4)	.6
Dana-std (.5)	.7
Trac-Lok 2 pinion (.6)	.8
Trac-Lok 4 pinion (.7)	1.0

REMOVABLE CARRIER

Differential Carrier, Remove & Install
Includes: Remove or renew axle shafts. Drain and refill axle. Renew oil seal and housing gasket.

All models	
one piece shaft (1.7)	2.5
two piece shaft (1.8)	2.7
Adjust ring gear add (.2)	.3
Check case run out add (.3)	.4
Renew ring gear & pinion add	
std (1.1)	1.5
limited slip/Trac-Lok (2.0)	2.9
Renew pinion brg cups add (.2)	.3
Renew case add (1.0)	1.4
Renew diff brg add (.2)	.3

LABOR — 27 REAR SUSPENSION 27 — LABOR

(Factory Time)	Chilton Time
Rear Spring, Renew	
4 lug wheel	
Aerostar	
one (.5)	.8
both (.8)	1.4
All other models	
one (.9)	1.3
both (1.6)	2.4
5 lug wheel	
one (1.0)	1.5
both (1.8)	2.8
8 lug wheel	
one (1.1)	1.6

(Factory Time)	Chilton Time
both (1.9)	3.0
10 lug wheel	
one (1.2)	1.6
both (2.1)	3.0
Renew spring bushings add—each (.3)	.3
Rear Spring Shackle Bushings, Renew	
All models	
one (.8)	1.2
both (1.2)	2.1
Rear Spring Shackles, Renew	
All models—one side (.4)	.7

(Factory Time)	Chilton Time
both sides (.6)	1.3
Rear Shock Absorbers, Renew	
All models-one (.3)	.6
both (.4)	.8
Rear Stabilizer Bar, Renew	
All models (.5)	.9
Upper Control Arm Bushings, Renew	
Aerostar	
one side (.7)	1.0
both sides (1.1)	1.7

LABOR — 28 AIR CONDITIONING 28 — LABOR

(Factory Time)	Chilton Time
Note: If more than one item requires replacement where evacuation and discharging the system is already included in the operation, deduct 1.0 hour for each additional item to the times listed.	
Drain, Evacuate and Recharge System	
Includes: Check for leaks.	
All models (.7)	1.2
Flush Refrigerant System, Complete	
To be used in conjection with component replacement which could contaminate system.	
All models	1.3
Refrigerant, Add (Partial Charge)	
All models	.6
Compressor Belt, Renew	
Four (.5)	.7

(Factory Time)	Chilton Time
All other engs (.3)	.6
Compressor Assembly, Renew	
Includes: Evacuate and charge system.	
Four	
Gas	
2.0L eng (2.0)	3.0
2.3L eng	
Ranger (2.1)	3.1
Aerostar (2.6)	3.7
Diesel	
2.3L eng (1.5)	2.3
Six (1.8)	2.5
V-6	
Ranger-Bronco II (1.5)	2.3
Aerostar (1.9)	2.7
V-8	
Gas (1.6)	2.3

(Factory Time)	Chilton Time
Diesel (1.8)	2.5
Recond comp add (1.2)	1.5
Compressor Shaft Seal Kit, Renew	
Includes: Evacuate and charge system.	
Four	
Gas	
2.0L eng (2.5)	3.5
2.3L eng	
Ranger (2.6)	3.4
Aerostar (3.1)	4.2
Diesel (2.2)	3.0
Six (1.9)	2.6
V-6	
2.8L-2.9L eng (2.0)	2.8
3.0L eng (2.3)	3.0
V-8	
Gas (1.9)	2.6

LABOR 28 AIR CONDITIONING 28 LABOR

(Factory Time)	Chilton Time	(Factory Time)	Chilton Time	(Factory Time)	Chilton Time
Diesel (2.1)	2.9	F100-350 (1.3)	2.5	**AEROSTAR**	
Condenser Assembly, Renew		**Dehydrator Receiver Tank, Renew**		main (.4)	.7
Includes: Evacuate and charge system.		Includes: Evacuate and charge system.		auxiliary (.4)	.7
RANGER (1.0)	2.0	ECONOLINE (1.2)	1.9	BRONCO II (.5)	.9
AEROSTAR (1.1)	2.3	**Accumulator Assembly, Renew**		ECONOLINE	
BRONCO (1.1)	2.3	Includes: Evacuate and charge system.		std (.6)	1.0
BRONCO II (1.0)	2.0	RANGER-BRONCO II (.9)	1.5	aux (.6)	1.0
ECONOLINE (1.4)	2.7	AEROSTAR (1.2)	1.8	F-Series-BRONCO (.3)	.5
F100-350 (1.1)	2.4	BRONCO-F100-350 (.9)	1.6	**Blower Motor Switch, Renew**	
Expansion Valve, Renew		**Suction or Discharge Manifold Assy., Renew**		RANGER (.5)	.7
Includes: Evacuate and charge system.				AEROSTAR (.6)	.9
All models		Includes: Evacuate and charge system.		BRONCO (.5)	.7
std (1.0)	1.7	All models (.8)	1.5	ECONOLINE (.5)	.7
aux (1.2)	2.0	**Orifice Valve, Renew**		F100-350 (.4)	.7
Evaporator Core, Renew		Includes: Evacuate and charge system.		**Evaporator Thermostatic Switch, Renew**	
Includes: Evacuate and charge system.		RANGER-BRONCO II (1.0)	1.7	BRONCO (.6)	1.0
RANGER (1.5)	2.9	AEROSTAR		ECONOLINE (.3)	.6
AEROSTAR		main (1.0)	1.5	F100-350 (.7)	1.2
main (1.6)	3.0	auxiliary (1.2)	1.8	**A/C Clutch Cycling Pressure Switch Assy., Renew**	
aux (1.3)	2.5	BRONCO-F100-350 (.9)	1.4		
BRONCO (1.3)	2.5	ECONOLINE (.9)	1.4	All models (.2)	.4
BRONCO II (1.5)	2.9	**Blower Motor, Renew**		**Air Conditioning Hoses, Renew**	
ECONOLINE		RANGER (.5)	.9	Includes: Evacuate and charge system.	
std (2.4)	4.6			Ail models-one (.9)	1.7
aux (1.8)	3.5			each adtnl (.3)	.5

LABOR 30 HEAD AND PARKING LAMPS 30 LABOR

(Factory Time)	Chilton Time	(Factory Time)	Chilton Time	(Factory Time)	Chilton Time
Aim Headlamps		**Parking Lamp Assembly, Renew**		**License Lamp Assembly, Renew**	
two	.4	RANGER-BRONCO II (.2)	.3	Aerostar (.4)	.5
four	.6	AEROSTAR (.3)	.4	All other models (.3)	.4
		ECONOLINE (.2)	.3		
Headlamp Sealed Beam Bulb, Renew		F-Series-BRONCO		**Reflector, Renew**	
All models-each (.2)	.3	1986 (.3)	.5	All models-each	.2
		1987-90 (.6)	.9		
Halogen Headlamp Bulb, Renew		**Rear Lamp Assembly, Renew**		**Side Marker Lamp Assy., Renew**	
All models-one (.3)	.3	All models (.2)	.3	All models-one (.2)	.3

LABOR 31 WINDSHIELD WIPER & SPEEDOMETER 31 LABOR

(Factory Time)	Chilton Time	(Factory Time)	Chilton Time	(Factory Time)	Chilton Time
Wiper Motor, Renew		**Windshield Wiper Governor Assy., Renew**		lower (.4)	.7
RANGER-BRONCO II (.4)	.6	Aerostar-F-Series-Bronco (.5)	.7	w/V-8 Diesel	
AEROSTAR		All other models (.4)	.6	upper (.9)	1.4
front (.9)	1.4	**Speedometer Head, R&R or Renew**		lower (.7)	1.2
rear (.7)	1.1	All models			
BRONCO (.9)	1.4	Standard (.6)	1.2	**ELECTRONIC INSTRUMENTATION**	
ECONOLINE (.9)	*1.4	Reset odometer add	.2		
F100-350 (.9)	1.4	**Speedometer Cable and Casing, Renew**		**Electronic Instrument Cluster and Message Center Diagnosis**	
*w/Cruise control add (.3)	.3	RANGER-BRONCO II (.4)	.7	Includes: Test system with approved test equipment and following recommended service procedures.	
Wiper Switch, Renew		AEROSTAR (.4)	.7		
Aerostar		F-Series-BRONCO		Aerostar (.5)	1.0
front (.5)	.8	one piece (.6)	1.1	**Multigauge and Message Center, Renew**	
rear (.5)	.8	upper (.3)	.5	Does not include system test.	
All other models		lower (.3)	.5	Aerostar (.6)	.9
front (.3)	.6	ECONOLINE		**Electronic Speedometer, Renew**	
rear (.2)	.4	one piece (.7)	1.3	Does not include system test.	
Wiper Pivot, Renew		upper or lower (.5)	.9	Aerostar (.6)	.9
RANGER-BRONCO II-one (.4)	.7	w/V-8 Diesel (.8)	1.3	**Tripmeter and Fuel Computer, Renew**	
both (.5)	.9	**Speedometer Cable (Inner), Renew or Lubricate**		Does not include system test.	
BRONCO-each (.8)	1.1			Aerostar (.6)	.9
AEROSTAR-both (.4)	.7	RANGER-BRONCO II (.4)	.7	**Keyboard Message Center, Renew**	
ECONOLINE (.6)	.9	AEROSTAR (.4)	.7	Does not include system test.	
F100-350-each (.8)	1.1	F-Series-BRONCO		Aerostar (.6)	.9
Washer Pump, Renew		one piece (.4)	.8	**Instrument Cluster Printed Circuit, Renew**	
Aerostar		upper (.4)	.6	Does not include system test.	
front (.6)	.9	lower (.4)	.6	Aerostar (.5)	.8
rear (.3)	.5	ECONOLINE			
All other models-front (.3)	.4	one piece (.6)	1.1		
rear (.8)	1.1	upper (.6)	1.1		

LABOR 32 LIGHT SWITCHES & WIRING 32 LABOR

(Factory Time)	Chilton Time	(Factory Time)	Chilton Time	(Factory Time)	Chilton Time
Headlamp Switch, Renew		ECONOLINE–std whl (.6)	1.2	**Parking Brake Warning Lamp Switch, Renew**	
All models (.4)	.6	tilt whl (.7)	1.3	All models (.3)	.4
Headlamp Dimmer Switch, Renew		F100-350–std whl (.6)	1.1	**Back-Up Lamp Switch, Renew (w/Manual Trans)**	
All models		tilt whl (.7)	1.2	All models (.3)	.4
floor mount (.3)	.5	**Turn Signal or Hazard Warning Flasher, Renew**		**Neutral Safety Switch, Renew**	
column mount (.5)	.9	ECONOLINE (.3)	.4	All models (.3)	.4
Turn Signal Switch Assy., Renew		All other models (.2)	.3	**Horns, Renew**	
RANGER (.5)	1.0	**Stop Light Switch, Renew**		All models–each (.2)	.3
AEROSTAR (.7)	1.0	All models (.3)	.5	**Horn Relay, Renew**	
BRONCO–std whl (.6)	1.1	**Emergency Flasher Switch Assy., Renew**		All models (.3)	.4
tilt whl (.7)	1.2	BRONCO (.3)	.6		
BRONCO II–std whl (.5)	1.1				
tilt whl (.6)	1.2				

LABOR 34 CRUISE CONTROL 34 LABOR

(Factory Time)	Chilton Time	(Factory Time)	Chilton Time	(Factory Time)	Chilton Time
Cruise Control System Diagnosis		Road test add (.3)	.3	**Speed Control Actuator Switch Assy., Renew**	
All models (.4)	.6	**Speed Control Sensor Assy., Renew**		All models (.2)	.4
Cruise Control Chain/Cable, Renew		All models (.2)	*.4	Road test add (.3)	.3
All models (.2)	.4	Road test add (.3)	.3	**Speed Control Metering (Dump) Valve, Renew**	
Speed Control Servo Assy., Renew		*Econoline		All models (.1)	.3
All models (.3)	.5	w/V-8 Diesel add	.3	**Speed Control Clutch Switch, Renew**	
Road test add (.3)	.3	**Speed Control Amplifier Assy., Renew**		All models (.3)	.4
Speed Control Relay, Renew		All models (.2)	.3	Road test add (.3)	.3
All models (.1)	.3	Road test add (.3)	.3		

SPECIFICATIONS

ENGINE IDENTIFICATION

Year	Model	Engine Displacement cu. in. (cc/liter)	Engine Series Identification	No. of Cylinders	Engine Type
1986	Montero	156 (2555/2.6)	G54B	4	SOHC
	Pick-Up	122 (1997/2.0)	G63B	4	SOHC
	Pick-Up	156 (2555/2.6)	G54B	4	SOHC
	Ram 50	122 (1997/2.0)	G63B	4	SOHC
	Ram 50	156 (2555/2.6)	G54B	4	SOHC
	Ram Raider	156 (2555/2.6)	G54B	4	SOHC
1987	Montero	156 (2555/2.6)	G54B	4	SOHC
	Pick-Up	122 (1997/2.0)	G63B	4	SOHC
	Pick-Up	156 (2555/2.6)	G54B	4	SOHC
	Ram 50	122 (1997/2.0)	G63B	4	SOHC
	Ram 50	156 (2555/2.6)	G54B	4	SOHC
	Ram Raider	156 (2555/2.6)	G54B	4	SOHC
	Van	143 (2350/2.4)	G64B	4	SOHC
1988	Montero	156 (2555/2.6)	G54B	4	SOHC
	Pick-Up	122 (1997/2.0)	G63B	4	SOHC
	Pick-Up	156 (2555/2.6)	G54B	4	SOHC
	Ram 50	122 (1997/2.0)	G63B	4	SOHC
	Ram 50	156 (2555/2.6)	G54B	4	SOHC
	Ram Raider	156 (2555/2.6)	G54B	4	SOHC
	Van	143 (2350/2.4)	G64B	4	SOHC
1989	Montero	156 (2555/2.6)	G54B	4	SOHC
	Montero	181 (2972/3.0)	6G72	6	DOHC
	Pick-Up	122 (1997/2.0)	G63B	4	SOHC
	Pick-Up	156 (2555/2.6)	G54B	4	SOHC
	Ram 50	122 (1997/2.0)	G63B	4	SOHC
	Ram 50	156 (2555/2.6)	G54B	4	SOHC
	Ram Raider	156 (2555/2.6)	G54B	4	SOHC
	Ram Raider	181 (2972/3.0)	6G72	6	DOHC
	Van	143 (2350/2.4)	4G64	4	SOHC
1990	Montero	181 (2972/3.0)	6G72	6	DOHC
	Pick-Up	143 (2350/2.4)	4G64	4	SOHC
	Pick-Up	181 (2972/3.0)	6G72	6	DOHC
	Ram 50	143 (2350/2.4)	4G64	4	SOHC
	Ram 50	181 (2972/3.0)	6G72	6	DOHC
	Van	143 (2350/2.4)	4G64	4	SOHC

GENERAL ENGINE SPECIFICATIONS

Year	Model	Engine Displacement cu. in. (cc)	Fuel System Type	Net Horsepower @ rpm	Net Torque @ rpm (ft. lbs.)	Bore × Stroke (in.)	Compression Ratio	Oil Pressure @ rpm
1986	Montero	156 (2555)	2bbl	109 @ 5000	142 @ 3000	3.59 × 3.86	8.7:1	45–90 @ 3000
	Pick-Up	122 (1997)	2bbl	88 @ 5000	108 @ 3500	3.31 × 3.54	8.5:1	45–90 @ 3000
	Pick-Up	156 (2555)	2bbl	109 @ 5000	142 @ 3500	3.59 × 3.86	8.7:1	45–90 @ 3000
	Ram 50	122 (1997)	2bbl	88 @ 5000	108 @ 3500	3.31 × 3.54	8.5:1	45–90 @ 3000
	Ram 50	156 (2555)	2bbl	109 @ 5000	142 @ 3500	3.59 × 3.86	8.7:1	45–90 @ 3000
	Ram Raider	156 (2555)	2bbl	109 @ 5000	142 @ 3500	3.59 × 3.86	8.7:1	45–90 @ 3000
1987	Montero	156 (2555)	2bbl	109 @ 5000	142 @ 3500	3.59 × 3.86	8.7:1	45–90 @ 3000
	Pick-Up	122 (1997)	2bbl	88 @ 5000	108 @ 3500	3.31 × 3.54	8.5:1	45–90 @ 3000
	Pick-Up	156 (2555)	2bbl	109 @ 5000	142 @ 3500	3.59 × 3.86	8.7:1	45–90 @ 3000
	Ram 50	122 (1997)	2bbl	88 @ 5000	108 @ 3500	3.31 × 3.54	8.5:1	45–90 @ 3000
	Ram 50	156 (2555)	2bbl	109 @ 5000	142 @ 3500	3.59 × 3.86	8.7:1	45–90 @ 3000
	Ram Raider	156 (2555)	2bbl	88 @ 5000	108 @ 3500	3.31 × 3.54	8.7:1	45–90 @ 3000
	Van	143 (2350)	MPI	107 @ 5000	132 @ 3500	3.41 × 3.94	8.5:1	40–85 @ 3000
1988	Montero	156 (2555)	2bbl	109 @ 5000	142 @ 3500	3.59 × 3.86	8.7:1	45–90 @ 3000
	Pick-Up	122 (1997)	2bbl	88 @ 5000	108 @ 3500	3.31 × 3.54	8.5:1	45–90 @ 3000
	Pick-Up	156 (2555)	2bbl	109 @ 5000	142 @ 3500	3.59 × 3.86	8.7:1	45–90 @ 3000
	Ram 50	122 (1997)	2bbl	88 @ 5000	108 @ 3500	3.31 × 3.54	8.5:1	45–90 @ 3000
	Ram 50	156 (2555)	2bbl	109 @ 5000	142 @ 3500	3.59 × 3.86	8.7:1	45–90 @ 3000
	Ram Raider	156 (2555)	2bbl	109 @ 5000	142 @ 3500	3.59 × 3.86	8.7:1	45–90 @ 3000
	Van	143 (2350)	MPI	107 @ 5000	132 @ 3500	3.41 × 3.94	8.5:1	40–85 @ 3000
1989	Montero	156 (2555)	2bbl	109 @ 5000	142 @ 3500	3.59 × 3.86	8.7:1	45–90 @ 3000
	Montero	181 (2972)	MPI	143 @ 5000	168 @ 2500	3.59 × 2.99	8.9:1	30–80 @ 3000
	Pick-Up	122 (1997)	2bbl	88 @ 5000	108 @ 3500	3.31 × 3.54	8.5:1	45–90 @ 3000
	Pick-Up	156 (2555)	2bbl	109 @ 5000	142 @ 3500	3.59 × 3.86	8.7:1	45–90 @ 3000
	Ram 50	122 (1997)	2bbl	88 @ 5000	108 @ 3500	3.31 × 3.54	8.5:1	45–90 @ 3000
	Ram 50	156 (2555)	2bbl	109 @ 5000	142 @ 3500	3.59 × 3.86	8.7:1	45–90 @ 3000
	Ram Raider	156 (2555)	2bbl	109 @ 5000	142 @ 3500	3.59 × 3.86	8.7:1	45–90 @ 3000
	Ram Raider	181 (2972)	MPI	143 @ 5000	168 @ 2500	3.59 × 2.99	8.9:1	30–80 @ 3000
	Van	143 (2350)	MPI	107 @ 5000	132 @ 3500	3.41 × 3.94	8.5:1	40–85 @ 3000
1990	Montero	181 (2972)	MPI	143 @ 5000	168 @ 2500	3.59 × 2.99	8.9:1	30–80 @ 3000
	Pick-Up	143 (2350)	MPI	116 @ 5000	132 @ 3500	3.41 × 3.94	8.5:1	40–85 @ 3000
	Pick-Up	181 (2972)	MPI	143 @ 5000	168 @ 2500	3.59 × 2.99	8.9:1	30–80 @ 3000
	Ram 50	143 (2350)	MPI	116 @ 5000	132 @ 3500	3.41 × 3.94	8.5:1	40–85 @ 3000
	Ram 50	181 (2972)	MPI	143 @ 5000	168 @ 2500	3.59 × 2.99	8.9:1	30–80 @ 3000
	Van	143 (2350)	MPI	107 @ 5000	132 @ 3500	3.41 × 3.94	8.5:1	40–85 @ 3000

GASOLINE ENGINE TUNE-UP SPECIFICATIONS

Year	Model	Engine Displacement cu. in. (cc)	Spark Plugs Type	Gap (in.)	Ignition Timing (deg.) MT	AT	Compression Pressure (psi)	Fuel Pump (psi)	Idle Speed (rpm) MT	AT	Valve Clearance ③ In.	Ex.
1986	Montero	156 (2555)	RN9YC	0.039–0.043	7B	7B	170	3–4	800	800	Hyd.	Hyd.
	Pick-Up	122 (1997)	RN9YC	0.039–0.043	5B	5B	170	3–4	750	750	Hyd.	Hyd.
		156 (2555)	RN9YC	0.039–0.043	7B	7B	170	3–4	800	800	Hyd.	Hyd.
	Ram 50	122 (1997)	RN9YC	0.039–0.043	5B	5B	170	3–4	750	750	Hyd.	Hyd.
		156 (2555)	RN9YC	0.039–0.043	7B	7B	170	3–4	800	800	Hyd.	Hyd.
	Ram Raider	156 (2555)	RN9YC	0.039–0.043	7B	7B	170	3–4	800	800	Hyd.	Hyd.
1987	Montero	156 (2555)	RN9YC	0.039–0.043	7B	7B	170	3–4	800	800	Hyd.	Hyd.
	Pick-Up	122 (1997)	RN9YC	0.039–0.043	8B	8B	170	3–4	750	750	Hyd.	Hyd.
		156 (2555)	RN9YC	0.039–0.043	7B	7B	170	3–4	800	800	Hyd.	Hyd.
	Ram 50	122 (1997)	RN9YC	0.039–0.043	8B	8B	170	3–4	750	750	Hyd.	Hyd.
		156 (2555)	RN9YC	0.039–0.043	7B	7B	170	3–4	800	800	Hyd.	Hyd.
	Ram Raider	156 (2555)	RN9YC	0.039–0.043	7B	7B	170	3–4	800	800	Hyd.	Hyd.
	Van	143 (2350)	RN9YC	0.039–0.043	—	①	120	28	—	750	Hyd.	Hyd.
1988	Montero	156 (2555)	RN9YC	0.039–0.043	7B	7B	170	3–4	800	800	Hyd.	Hyd.
	Pick-Up	122 (1997)	RN9YC	0.039–0.043	8B	8B	170	3–4	750	750	Hyd.	Hyd.
		156 (2555)	RN9YC	0.039–0.043	7B	7B	170	3–4	800	800	Hyd.	Hyd.
	Ram 50	122 (1997)	RN9YC	0.039–0.043	8B	8B	170	3–4	750	750	Hyd.	Hyd.
		156 (2555)	RN9YC	0.039–0.043	7B	7B	170	3–4	800	800	Hyd.	Hyd.
	Ram Raider	156 (2555)	RN9YC	0.039–0.043	7B	7B	170	3–4	800	800	Hyd.	Hyd.
	Van	143 (2350)	RN9YC	0.039–0.043	—	①	120	28	—	750	Hyd.	Hyd.
1989	Montero	156 (2555)	RN9YC	0.039–0.043	7B	7B	170	3–4	800	800	Hyd.	Hyd.
		181 (2972)	RN114C4	0.039–0.043	②	②	120	38	700	700	Hyd.	Hyd.
	Pick-Up	122 (1997)	RN9YC	0.039–0.043	8B	8B	170	3–4	750	750	Hyd.	Hyd.
		156 (2555)	RN9YC	0.039–0.043	7B	7B	170	3–4	800	800	Hyd.	Hyd.

GASOLINE ENGINE TUNE-UP SPECIFICATIONS

Year	Model	Engine Displacement cu. in. (cc)	Spark Plugs Type	Gap (in.)	Ignition Timing (deg.) MT	AT	Compression Pressure (psi)	Fuel Pump (psi)	Idle Speed (rpm) MT	AT	Valve Clearance ③ In.	Ex.
1989	Ram 50	122 (1997)	RN9YC	0.039–0.043	8B	8B	170	3–4	750	750	Hyd.	Hyd.
		156 (2555)	RN9YC	0.039–0.043	7B	7B	170	3–4	800	800	Hyd.	Hyd.
	Ram Raider	156 (2555)	RN9YC	0.039–0.043	7B	7B	170	3–4	800	800	Hyd.	Hyd.
		181 (2972)	RN114C4	0.039–0.043	②	②	120	38	700	700	Hyd.	Hyd.
	Van	143 (2350)	RN9YC	0.039–0.043	—	①	120	38	—	750	Hyd.	Hyd.
1990	Montero	181 (2972)	RN114C4	0.039–0.043	②	②	120	38	700	700	Hyd.	Hyd.
	Pick-Up	143 (2350)	RN9YC	0.039–0.043	①	①	120	38	750	750	Hyd.	Hyd.
		181 (2972)	RN114C4	0.039–0.043	②	②	120	38	700	700	Hyd.	Hyd.
	Ram 50	143 (2350)	RN9YC	0.039–0.043	①	①	120	38	750	750	Hyd.	Hyd.
		181 (2972)	RN114C4	0.039–0.043	②	②	120	38	700	700	Hyd.	Hyd.
	Van	143 (2350)	RN9YC	0.039–0.043	—	①	120	38	—	750	Hyd.	Hyd.

① Basic timing: 5B
  Actual timing: 8B
② Basic timing: 5B
  Actual timing: 15B
③ Jet valve clearance (all engines): 0.010 in. (0.25 mm)

FIRING ORDERS

NOTE: To avoid confusion, always replace spark plug wires one at a time.

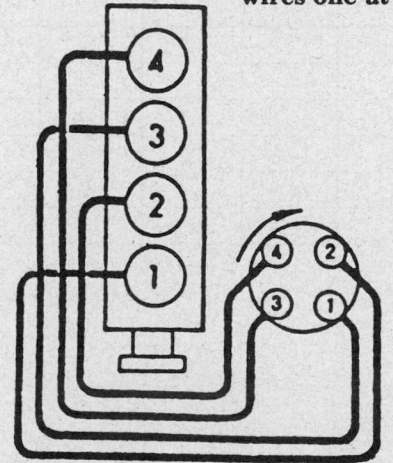

Mitsubishi 2.0L, 2.4L and 2.6L
Firing order: 1–3–4–2
Distributor rotation: clockwise

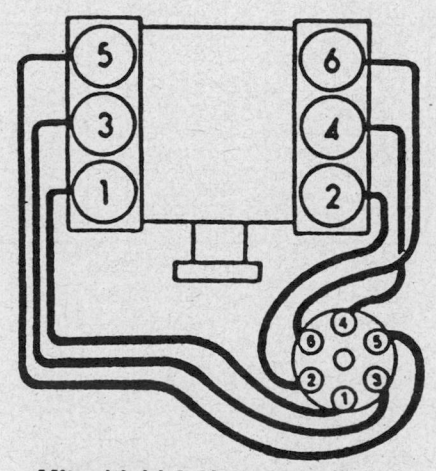

Mitsubishi 3.0L
Firing order: 1–2–3–4–5–6
Distributor rotation: clockwise

CAPACITIES

Year	Model	Engine Displacement cu. in. (cc)	Engine Crankcase with Filter	Engine Crankcase without Filter	Transmission (pts.) 4-Spd	Transmission (pts.) 5-Spd	Transmission (pts.) Auto.	Drive Axle (pts.)	Fuel Tank (gal.)	Cooling System (qts.)
1986	Montero	156 (2555)	6	5.5	—	4.6	14.4	⑦	16	8.5
	Pick-Up	122 (1997)	4	3.5	—	5	14.4	3.2	⑨	9.5
		156 (2555)	①	②	—	5	14.4	⑧	⑨	9.5
	Ram 50	122 (1997)	4	3.5	—	5	14.4	3.2	⑨	9.5
		156 (2555)	①	②	—	5	14.4	⑧	⑨	9.5
	Ram Raider	156 (2555)	6	5.5	—	4.6	14.4	⑦	16	8.5
1987	Montero	156 (2555)	6	5.5	—	4.7	15.2	⑩	16	8.5
	Pick-Up	122 (1997)	4	3.5	—	5	12.7	2.7	⑬	7.4
		156 (2555)	①	②	—	5	⑪	⑫	⑬	8.3
	Ram 50	122 (1997)	4	3.5	—	5	12.7	2.7	⑬	7.4
		156 (2555)	①	②	—	5	⑪	⑫	⑬	8.3
	Ram Raider	156 (2555)	6	5.5	—	4.7	15.2	⑩	16	8.5
	Van	143 (2350)	4	3.5	—	—	14.4	2.7	14	8.5 ⑭
1988	Montero	156 (2555)	5	4.5	—	4.7	15.2	⑩	16	8.5
	Pick-Up	122 (1997)	4	3.5	—	5	14.4	3.2	⑬	8.3
		156 (2555)	③	④	—	5	⑮	⑫	⑬	8.3
	Ram 50	122 (1997)	4	3.5	—	5	14.4	3.2	⑬	8.3
		156 (2555)	③	④	—	5	⑮	⑫	⑬	8.3
	Ram Raider	156 (2555)	5	4.5	—	4.7	15.2	⑩	16	8.5
	Van	143 (2350)	4	3.5	—	—	14.4	3.2	14	8.5 ⑭
1989	Montero	156 (2555)	5	4.5	—	5	—	⑦	16	8.5
		181 (2972)	5	4.5	—	5	15.2	⑯	⑰	9.5
	Pick-Up	122 (1997)	4	3.5	—	5	14.4	3.2	⑬	8.3
		156 (2555)	③	④	—	5	⑮	⑧	⑬	8.3
	Ram 50	122 (1997)	4	3.5	—	5	14.4	3.2	⑬	8.3
		156 (2555)	③	④	—	5	⑮	⑧	⑬	8.3
	Ram Raider	156 (2555)	5	4.5	—	5	—	⑦	16	8.5
		181 (2972)	5	4.5	—	5	15.2	⑯	16	9.5
	Van	143 (2350)	4	3.5	—	—	14.4	3.2	14	8.5 ⑭
1990	Montero	181 (2972)	5.5	5	—	5	15.2	⑯	⑰	9.5
	Pick-Up	143 (2350)	⑤	⑥	—	5	14.8	3.2	⑬	6.5
		181 (2972)	5.5	5	—	5	14.8	5.4	⑬	9
	Ram 50	143 (2350)	⑤	⑥	—	5	14.8	3.2	⑬	6.5
		181 (2972)	5.5	5	—	5	14.8	5.4	⑬	9
	Van	143 (2350)	4	3.5	—	—	14.4	3.2	14	8.5 ⑭

① 2WD: 5.3 qts.
  4WD: 6 qts.
② 2WD: 4.8 qts.
  4WD: 5.5 qts.
③ 2WD: 4.5 qts.
  4WD: 5 qts.
④ 2WD: 4 qts.
  4WD: 4.5 qts.
⑤ 2WD: 4.5 qts.
  4WD: 5.5 qts.

⑥ 2WD: 4 qts.
  4WD: 5 qts.
⑦ Front axle: 2.3 pts.
  Rear axle: 3.8 pts.
⑧ Front axle: 2.3 pts.
  Rear axle: 3.2 pts.
⑨ 2WD: 15 gals.
  4WD: 18 gals.

⑩ Front axle: 2.3 pts.
  Conventional rear axle: 2.3 pts.
  Limited-slip rear axle: 3.8 pts.
⑪ 2WD: 12.7 pts.
  4WD: 15.2 pts.
⑫ Front axle
  Conventional rear axle: 2.7 pts.
  Limited-slip rear axle: 3.2 pts.

⑬ 2WD standard body: 14 gals.
  2WD long body: 18 gals.
  4WD standard body: 16 gals.
  4WD long body: 20 gals.
⑭ Add ½ qt. with rear heater
⑮ 2WD: 14.4 pts.
  4WD: 15.2 pts.
⑯ Front axle:
  Rear axle:
⑰ 2 door: 20 gal.
  4 door: 24 gal.

CAMSHAFT SPECIFICATIONS

All measurements given in inches.

Year	Engine Displacement cu. in. (cc)	Journal Diameter					Lobe Lift ①		Bearing Clearance	Camshaft End Play
		1	2	3	4	5	In.	Ex.		
1986	122 (1997)	1.34	1.34	1.34	1.34	1.34	1.66–1.68	1.66–1.68	0.002–0.004	0.004–0.016
	156 (2555)	1.34	1.34	1.34	1.34	1.34	1.65–1.67	1.65–1.67	0.001–0.002	0.004–0.016
1987	122 (1997)	1.34	1.34	1.34	1.34	1.34	1.66–1.68	1.66–1.68	0.002–0.004	0.004–0.016
	143 (2350)	1.34	1.34	1.34	1.34	1.34	1.65–1.67	1.65–1.67	0.002–0.004	0.004–0.016
	156 (2555)	1.34	1.34	1.34	1.34	1.34	1.65–1.67	1.65–1.67	0.001–0.002	0.004–0.016
1988	122 (1997)	1.34	1.34	1.34	1.34	1.34	1.66–1.68	1.66–1.68	0.002–0.004	0.004–0.016
	143 (2350)	1.34	1.34	1.34	1.34	1.34	1.65–1.67	1.65–1.67	0.002–0.004	0.004–0.016
	156 (2555)	1.34	1.34	1.34	1.34	1.34	1.65–1.67	1.65–1.67	0.001–0.002	0.004–0.016
1989	122 (1997)	1.34	1.34	1.34	1.34	1.34	1.66–1.68	1.66–1.68	0.002–0.004	0.004–0.016
	143 (2350)	1.34	1.34	1.34	1.34	1.34	1.65–1.67	1.65–1.67	0.002–0.004	0.004–0.016
	156 (2555)	1.34	1.34	1.34	1.34	1.34	1.65–1.67	1.65–1.67	0.001–0.002	0.004–0.016
	181 (2972)	1.34	1.34	1.34	1.34	—	1.60–1.62	1.60–1.62	0.002–0.004	NA
1990	143 (2350)	1.34	1.34	1.34	1.34	1.34	1.65–1.67	1.65–1.67	0.002–0.004	0.004–0.016
	181 (2972)	1.34	1.34	1.34	1.34	—	1.60–1.62	1.60–1.62	0.002–0.004	NA

① Diameter of cam lobe

CRANKSHAFT AND CONNECTING ROD SPECIFICATIONS

All measurements are given in inches.

Year	Engine Displacement cu. in. (cc)	Crankshaft				Connecting Rod		
		Main Brg. Journal Dia.	Main Brg. Oil Clearance	Shaft End-play	Thrust on No.	Journal Diameter	Oil Clearance	Side Clearance
1986	122 (1997)	2.24	0.001–0.004	0.002–0.016	3	NA	0.001–0.002	0.004–0.016
	156 (2555)	2.36	0.001–0.004	0.002–0.016	3	2.87	0.001–0.002	0.004–0.016
1987	122 (1997)	2.24	0.001–0.004	0.002–0.016	3	NA	0.001–0.002	0.004–0.016
	143 (2350)		0.001–0.004	0.002–0.016	3	NA	0.001–0.004	0.004–0.016
	156 (2555)	2.36	0.001–0.004	0.002–0.016	3	2.87	0.001–0.002	0.004–0.016

CRANKSHAFT AND CONNECTING ROD SPECIFICATIONS
All measurements are given in inches.

Year	Engine Displacement cu. in. (cc)	Crankshaft Main Brg. Journal Dia.	Main Brg. Oil Clearance	Shaft End-play	Thrust on No.	Connecting Rod Journal Diameter	Oil Clearance	Side Clearance
1988	122 (1997)	2.24	0.001–0.004	0.002–0.016	3	NA	0.001–0.002	0.004–0.016
	143 (2350)	2.24	0.001–0.004	0.002–0.016	3	NA	0.001–0.004	0.004–0.016
	156 (2555)	2.36	0.001–0.004	0.002–0.016	3	2.87	0.001–0.002	0.004–0.016
1989	122 (1997)	2.24	0.001–0.004	0.002–0.016	3	NA	0.001–0.002	0.004–0.016
	143 (2350)	2.24	0.001–0.004	0.002–0.016	3	NA	0.001–0.004	0.004–0.016
	156 (2555)	2.36	0.001–0.004	0.002–0.016	3		0.001–0.002	0.004–0.016
	181 (2972)	2.36	0.001–0.004	0.002–0.012	3	1.97	0.001–0.004	0.004–0.016
1990	143 (2350)	2.24	0.001–0.004	0.002–0.016	3	NA	0.001–0.004	0.004–0.016
	181 (2972)	2.36	0.001–0.004	0.002–0.012	3	1.97	0.001–0.004	0.004–0.016

VALVE SPECIFICATIONS

Year	Engine Displacement cu. in (cc)	Seat Angle (deg.)	Face Angle (deg.)	Spring Test Pressure (lbs.)	Spring Installed Height (in.)	Stem-to-Guide Clearance (in.) Intake	Exhaust	Stem Diameter (in.) Intake	Exhaust
1986	122 (1997)	45	45–45.5	72	1.60	0.001–0.004	0.002–0.006	0.315	0.315
	156 (2555)	45	45–45.5	72	1.60	0.001–0.004	0.002–0.006	0.315	0.315
1987	122 (1997)	45	45–45.5	72	1.60	0.001–0.004	0.002–0.006	0.315	0.315
	143 (2350)	44–44.5	45–45.5	73	1.60	0.001–0.004	0.002–0.006	0.310	0.310
	156 (2555)	45	45–45.5	72	1.60	0.001–0.004	0.002–0.006	0.315	0.315
1988	122 (1997)	45	45–45.5	72	1.60	0.001–0.004	0.002–0.006	0.315	0.315
	143 (2350)	44–44.5	45–45.5	73	1.60	0.001–0.004	0.002–0.006	0.310	0.310
	156 (2555)	45	45–45.5	72	1.60	0.001–0.004	0.002–0.006	0.315	0.315

VALVE SPECIFICATIONS

Year	Engine Displacement cu. in (cc)	Seat Angle (deg.)	Face Angle (deg.)	Spring Test Pressure (lbs.)	Spring Installed Height (in.)	Stem-to-Guide Clearance (in.) Intake	Stem-to-Guide Clearance (in.) Exhaust	Stem Diameter (in.) Intake	Stem Diameter (in.) Exhaust
1989	122 (1997)	45	45–45.5	72	1.60	0.001–0.004	0.002–0.006	0.315	0.315
	143 (2350)	44–44.5	45–45.5	73	1.60	0.001–0.004	0.002–0.006	0.310	0.310
	156 (2555)	45	45–45.5	72	1.60	0.001–0.004	0.002–0.006	0.315	0.315
	181 (2972)	44–44.5	45–45.5	74	1.60	0.001–0.004	0.002–0.006	0.313	0.312
1990	143 (2350)	44–44.5	45–45.5	73	1.60	0.001–0.004	0.002–0.006	0.310	0.310
	181 (2972)	44–44.5	45–45.5	74	1.60	0.001–0.004	0.002–0.006	0.313	0.312

PISTON AND RING SPECIFICATIONS
All measurements are given in inches.

Year	Engine Displacement cu. in. (cc)	Piston Clearance	Ring Gap Top Compression	Ring Gap Bottom Compression	Ring Gap Oil Control	Ring Side Clearance Top Compression	Ring Side Clearance Bottom Compression	Ring Side Clearance Oil Control
1986	122 (1997)	0.0004–0.0012	0.010–0.031	0.008–0.031	0.008–0.039	0.001–0.004	0.001–0.004	NA
	156 (2555)	0.0008–0.0016	0.012–0.031	0.010–0.031	0.008–0.039	0.002–0.005	0.001–0.004	NA
1987	122 (1997)	0.0004–0.0012	0.010–0.031	0.008–0.031	0.008–0.039	0.001–0.004	0.001–0.004	NA
	143 (2350)	0.0008–0.0016	0.010–0.031	0.008–0.031	0.008–0.039	0.001–0.004	0.001–0.004	NA
	156 (2555)	0.0008–0.0016	0.012–0.031	0.010–0.031	0.008–0.039	0.002–0.005	0.001–0.004	NA
1988	122 (1997)	0.0004–0.0012	0.010–0.031	0.008–0.031	0.008–0.039	0.001–0.004	0.001–0.004	NA
	143 (2350)	0.0008–0.0016	0.010–0.031	0.008–0.031	0.008–0.039	0.001–0.004	0.001–0.004	NA
	156 (2555)	0.0008–0.0016	0.012–0.031	0.010–0.031	0.008–0.039	0.002–0.005	0.001–0.004	NA
1989	122 (1997)	0.0004–0.0012	0.010–0.031	0.008–0.031	0.008–0.039	0.001–0.004	0.001–0.004	NA
	143 (2350)	0.0008–0.0016	0.010–0.031	0.008–0.031	0.008–0.039	0.001–0.004	0.001–0.004	NA
	156 (2555)	0.0008–0.0016	0.012–0.031	0.010–0.031	0.008–0.039	0.002–0.005	0.001–0.004	NA
	181 (2972)	0.0008–0.0016	0.012–0.031	0.010–0.031	0.008–0.039	0.001–0.004	0.001–0.004	NA
1990	143 (2350)	0.0008–0.0016	0.010–0.031	0.008–0.031	0.008–0.039	0.001–0.004	0.001–0.004	NA
	181 (2972)	0.0008–0.0016	0.012–0.031	0.010–0.031	0.008–0.039	0.001–0.004	0.001–0.004	NA

TORQUE SPECIFICATIONS
All readings in ft. lbs.

Year	Engine Displacement cu. in. (cc)	Cylinder Head Bolts	Main Bearing Bolts	Rod Bearing Bolts	Crankshaft Pulley Bolts	Flywheel Bolts	Manifold Intake	Manifold Exhaust	Spark Plugs
1986	122 (1997)	70	38	38	20	95	13	13	18–20
	156 (2555)	70	58	34	87	95	13	13	18–20
1987	122 (1997)	70	38	38	20	95	13	13	18–20
	143 (2350)	70	38	38	20	95	13	13	18–20
	156 (2555)	70	58	34	87	95	13	13	18–20
1988	122 (1997)	70	38	38	20	95	13	13	18–20
	143 (2350)	70	38	38	20	95	13	13	18–20
	156 (2555)	70	58	34	87	95	13	13	18–20
1989	122 (1997)	70	38	38	20	95	13	13	18–20
	143 (2350)	70	38	38	20	95	13	13	18–20
	156 (2555)	70	58	34	87	95	13	13	18–20
	181 (2972)	70	60	38	110	55	13	13	18–20
1990	143 (2350)	70	38	34	20	95	13	13	18–20
	181 (2972)	70	60	38	110	55	13	13	18–20

BRAKE SPECIFICATIONS
All measurements in inches unless noted

Year	Model	Lug Nut Torque (ft. lbs.)	Master Cylinder Bore	Brake Disc Minimum Thickness	Brake Disc Maximum Runout	Standard Brake Drum Diameter	Minimum Lining Thickness Front	Minimum Lining Thickness Rear
1986	Montero	72–87	0.87	0.72	0.006	10	0.06	0.06
	Pick-Up	51–57	0.87	0.72	0.006	②	0.06	0.06
	Ram 50	51–57	0.87	0.72	0.006	②	0.06	0.06
	Ram Raider	72–87	0.87	0.72	0.006	10	0.06	0.06
1987	Montero	72–87	0.87	0.72	0.006	10	0.06	0.06
	Pick-Up	87–101	0.87	0.80	0.006	10	0.06	0.06
	Ram 50	87–101	0.87	0.80	0.006	10	0.06	0.06
	Ram Raider	72–87	0.87	0.72	0.006	10	0.06	0.06
	Van	87–101	0.94	0.80	0.006	10	0.06	0.06
1988	Montero	72–87	0.94	0.80	0.006	10	0.06	0.06
	Pick-Up	87–101	①	0.80	0.006	10	0.06	0.06
	Ram 50	87–101	①	0.80	0.006	10	0.06	0.06
	Ram Raider	72–87	0.94	0.80	0.006	10	0.06	0.06
	Van	87–101	0.94	0.80	0.006	10	0.06	0.06
1989	Montero	72–87	0.94	0.80	0.006	10	0.06	0.06
	Pick-Up	87–101	0.94	0.80	0.006	10	0.06	0.06
	Ram 50	87–101	0.94	0.80	0.006	10	0.06	0.06
	Ram Raider	72–87	0.94	0.80	0.006	10	0.06	0.06
	Van	87–101	0.94	0.80	0.006	10	0.06	0.06

BRAKE SPECIFICATIONS

All measurements in inches unless noted

Year	Model	Lug Nut Torque (ft. lbs.)	Master Cylinder Bore	Brake Disc Minimum Thickness	Brake Disc Maximum Runout	Standard Brake Drum Diameter	Minimum Lining Thickness Front	Minimum Lining Thickness Rear
1990	Montero	72–87	0.94	0.80	0.006	10	0.06	0.06
	Pick-Up	87–101	0.94	0.80	0.006	10	0.06	0.06
	Ram 50	87–101	0.94	0.80	0.006	10	0.06	0.06
	Van	87–101	0.94	0.80	0.006	10	0.06	0.06

① 2WD: 0.87 in.
   4WD: 0.94 in.
② 2WD: 9.5 in.
   4WD: 10 in.

WHEEL ALIGNMENT

Year	Model	Caster Range (deg.)	Caster Preferred Setting (deg.)	Camber Range (deg.)	Camber Preferred Setting (deg.)	Toe-in (in.)	Steering Axis Inclination (deg.)
1986	Montero	$2\frac{1}{2}$P–$3\frac{1}{2}$P	3P	$\frac{1}{2}$P–$1\frac{1}{2}$P	1P	0.20	8
	2WD Pick-Up	$1\frac{1}{2}$P–$3\frac{1}{2}$P	$2\frac{1}{2}$P	$\frac{1}{2}$P–$1\frac{1}{2}$P	1P	0.20	8
	4WD Pick-Up	$1\frac{1}{2}$P–$2\frac{1}{2}$P	2P	$\frac{1}{2}$P–$1\frac{1}{2}$P	1P	0.20	8
	2WD Ram 50	$1\frac{1}{2}$P–$3\frac{1}{2}$P	$2\frac{1}{2}$P	$\frac{1}{2}$P–$1\frac{1}{2}$P	1P	0.20	8
	4WD Ram 50	$1\frac{1}{2}$P–$2\frac{1}{2}$P	2P	$\frac{1}{2}$P–$1\frac{1}{2}$P	1P	0.20	8
	Ram Raider	$2\frac{1}{2}$P–$3\frac{1}{2}$P	3P	$\frac{1}{2}$P–$1\frac{1}{2}$P	1P	0.20	8
1987	Montero	$2\frac{1}{2}$P–$3\frac{1}{2}$P	3P	$\frac{1}{2}$P–$1\frac{1}{2}$P	1P	0.20	8
	2WD Pick-Up	2P–4P	3P	$\frac{1}{4}$P–$1\frac{1}{4}$P	$\frac{2}{3}$P	0.10	NA
	4WD Pick-Up	1P–3P	2P	$\frac{1}{2}$P–$1\frac{1}{2}$P	1P	0.10	NA
	2WD Ram 50	2P–4P	3P	$\frac{1}{4}$P–$1\frac{1}{4}$P	$\frac{2}{3}$P	0.10	NA
	4WD Ram 50	1P–3P	2P	$\frac{1}{2}$P–$1\frac{1}{2}$P	1P	0.10	NA
	Ram Raider	$2\frac{1}{2}$P–$3\frac{1}{2}$P	3P	$\frac{1}{2}$P–$1\frac{1}{2}$P	1P	0.20	8
	Van	$2\frac{1}{2}$P–$3\frac{1}{2}$P	3P	0–1P	$\frac{1}{2}$P	0.12	NA
1988	Montero	$2\frac{1}{2}$P–$3\frac{1}{2}$P	3P	$\frac{1}{2}$P–$1\frac{1}{2}$P	1P	0.20	8
	2WD Pick-Up	2P–4P	3P	$\frac{1}{4}$P–$1\frac{1}{4}$P	$\frac{2}{3}$P	0.10	NA
	4WD Pick-Up	1P–3P	2P	$\frac{1}{2}$P–$1\frac{1}{2}$P	1P	0.10	NA
	2WD Ram 50	2P–4P	3P	$\frac{1}{4}$P–$1\frac{1}{4}$P	$\frac{2}{3}$P	0.10	NA
	4WD Ram 50	1P–3P	2P	$\frac{1}{2}$P–$1\frac{1}{2}$P	1P	0.10	NA
	Ram Raider	$2\frac{1}{2}$P–$3\frac{1}{2}$P	3P	$\frac{1}{2}$P–$1\frac{1}{2}$P	1P	0.20	8
	Van	$2\frac{1}{2}$P–$3\frac{1}{2}$P	3P	0–1P	$\frac{1}{2}$P	0.12	NA
1989	Montero	2P–4P	3P	$\frac{1}{2}$P–$1\frac{1}{2}$P	1P	0.20	8
	2WD Pick-Up	$1\frac{1}{2}$P–$3\frac{1}{2}$P	$2\frac{1}{2}$P	$\frac{1}{4}$P–$1\frac{1}{4}$P	$\frac{2}{3}$P	0.20	NA
	4WD Pick-Up	1P–3P	2P	$\frac{1}{2}$P–$1\frac{1}{2}$P	1P	0.20	NA
	2WD Ram 50	$1\frac{1}{2}$P–$3\frac{1}{2}$P	$2\frac{1}{2}$P	$\frac{1}{4}$P–$1\frac{1}{4}$P	$\frac{2}{3}$P	0.20	NA
	4WD Ram 50	1P–3P	2P	$\frac{1}{2}$P–$1\frac{1}{2}$P	1P	0.20	NA
	Ram Raider	2P–4P	3P	$\frac{1}{2}$P–$1\frac{1}{2}$P	1P	0.20	8
	Van	$2\frac{1}{2}$P–$3\frac{1}{2}$P	3P	0–1P	$\frac{1}{2}$P	0.08	NA

WHEEL ALIGNMENT

Year	Model	Caster Range (deg.)	Caster Preferred Setting (deg.)	Camber Range (deg.)	Camber Preferred Setting (deg.)	Toe-in (in.)	Steering Axis Inclination (deg.)
1990	Montero	2P–4P	3P	$1/2$P–$1\frac{1}{2}$P	1P	0.20	8
	2WD Pick-Up	$1\frac{1}{2}$P–$3\frac{1}{2}$P	$2\frac{1}{2}$P	$1/4$P–$1\frac{1}{4}$P	$2/3$P	0.20	NA
	4WD Pick-Up	1P–3P	2P	$1/2$P–$1\frac{1}{2}$P	1P	0.20	NA
	2WD Ram 50	$1\frac{1}{2}$P–$3\frac{1}{2}$P	$2\frac{1}{2}$P	$1/4$P–$1\frac{1}{4}$P	$2/3$P	0.20	NA
	4WD Ram 50	1P–3P	2P	$1/2$P–$1\frac{1}{2}$P	1P	0.20	NA
	Van	2P–4P	3P	$1/4$N–$1\frac{1}{4}$P	$1/2$P	0.08	NA

ENGINE ELECTRICAL

NOTE: Disconnecting the negative battery cable on some vehicles may interfere with the functions of the on board computer systems and may require the computer to undergo a relearning process, once the negative battery cable is reconnected.

Distributor

Removal and Installation

1. Disconnect the negative battery cable.
2. To gain access to the distributor on the Van:
   a. Remove the battery cover.
   b. Disconnect the negative battery cable.
   c. Release the 2 catches and flip the passenger seat up.
   d. Remove the driver's seat.
   e. Remove the parking brake lever cover.
   f. Remove the parking brake lever and fuel filler fuel release lever retaining screws and remove the levers from the seat under frame.
   g. Remove the seat under frame retaining screws and remove the seat under frame from the vehicle.
3. Disconnect the distributor pickup lead wires and vacuum hose(s), if equipped.
4. Unfasten the distributor cap retaining clips or screws and lift off the distributor cap with all ignition wires still connected. Remove the coil wire if necessary.
5. Matchmark the rotor to the distributor housing and the distributor housing to the engine.

NOTE: Do not crank the engine during this procedure. If the engine is cranked, the matchmark must be disregarded.

6. Remove the retaining nut and remove the distributor from the engine.
To install:
7. Install a new distributor housing O-ring.
8. Install the distributor in the engine so the rotor is lined up with the matchmark on the housing and the housing is lined up with the matchmark on the engine. Make sure the distributor is fully seated and that the distributor shaft is fully engaged.
9. If the engine has been cranked, position the engine so that the No. 1 piston is at TDC of the compression stroke and the mark on the vibration damper is lined up with **0** on the timing indicator. Then install the distributor so the rotor is aligned with the position of the No. 1 ignition wire on the distributor cap.

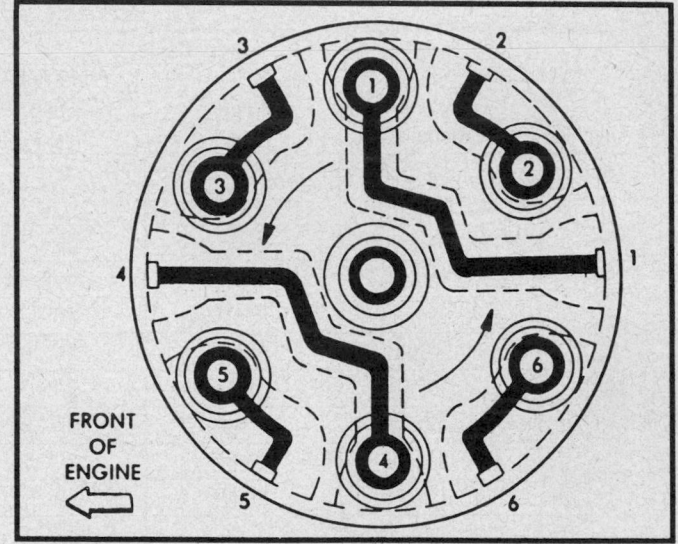

Distributor cap terminal routing viewed from the top of the cap—3.0L engine

NOTE: There are distributor cap runners inside the cap on vehicles with a 3.0L engine. Make sure the rotor is pointing to where the No. 1 runner originates inside the cap and not where the No. 1 ignition wire plugs into the cap.

10. Install the retaining nut and snug it. Connect the vacuum hose(s), if equipped.
11. Connect the distributor pickup lead wires.
12. Install the distributor cap and snap the retaining clips into place or tighten the screws.
13. Connect the negative battery cable.
14. Adjust the ignition timing and tighten the retaining nut.

Ignition Timing

Adjustment

CARBURETED ENGINE

1. Start the engine, set the parking brake and run the engine until at normal operating temperature. Keep all lights and accessories **OFF** and place the transmission in neutral.

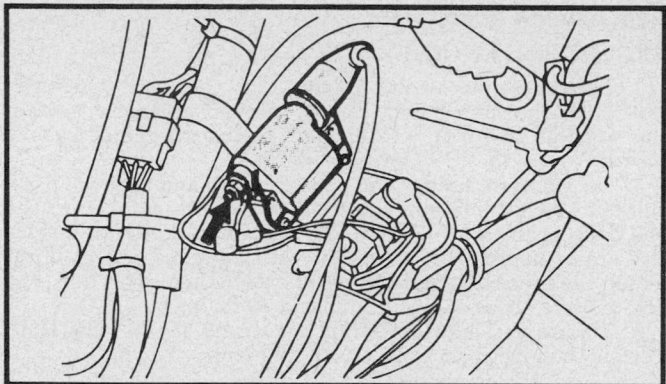

Tachometer terminal—1987–89 Pick-Up and Ram 50

2. Connect a conventional power timing light to the No. 1 cylinder spark plug wire.

3. Connect the red lead of a tachometer to the negative primary terminal of the coil and connect the black lead to a good ground. Set the idle speed to specifications.

4. On 1986–87 vehicles, if working at an altitude of 3900 ft. (1200 meters) or higher, disconnect and plug the vacuum hose to the distributor diaphragm, turn the engine off and then restart the engine. On 1988–89 vehicles at the same altitude, disconnect and plug the white-striped hose running to the sub-vacuum chamber on the bottom of the distributor. (This step also applies to California engines equipped with dual-diaphragm distributor).

5. Aim the timing light at the timing scale.

6. Loosen the distributor nut just enough so the disributor can be rotated.

7. Turn the distributor in the proper direction until the speci-

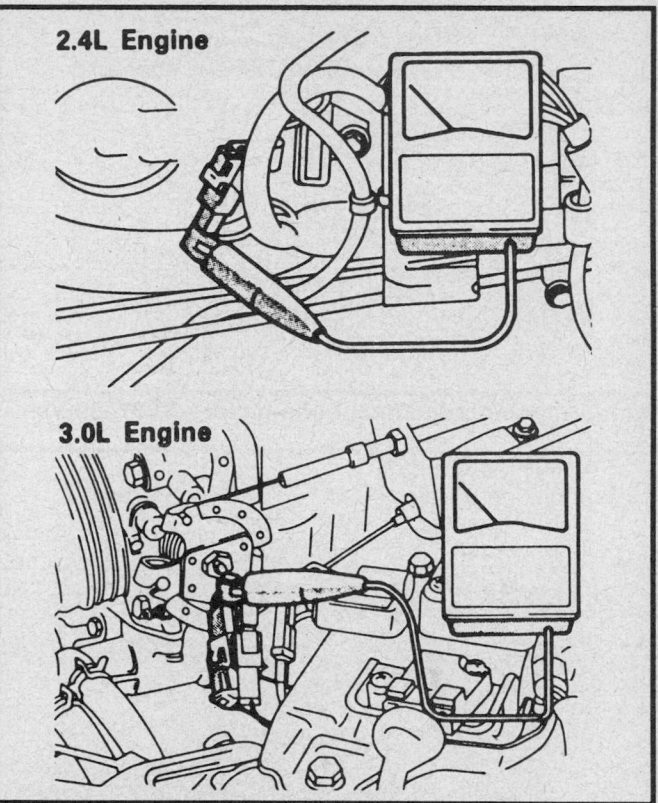

Tachometer connector—1990 Pick-Up and Ram 50

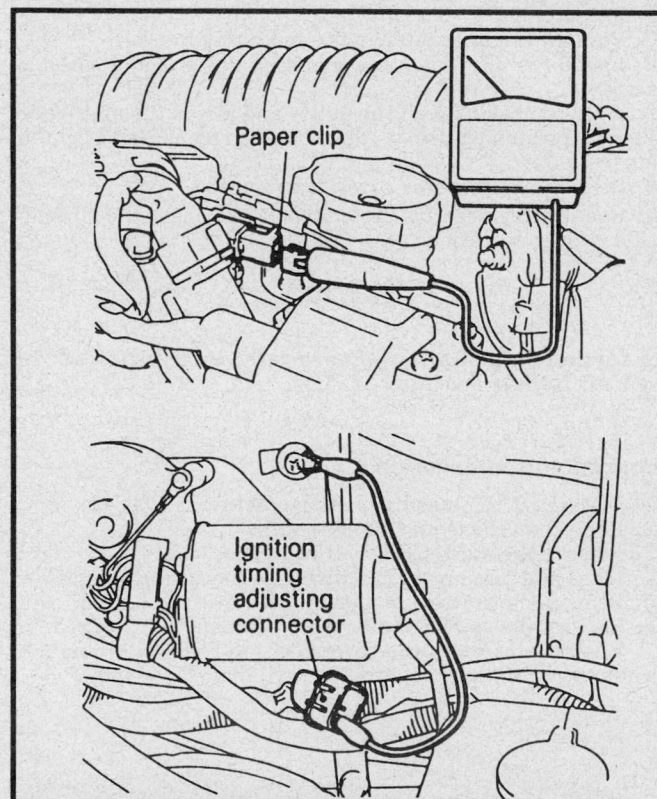

Tachometer terminal and ignition timing adjusting connector—Montero and Raider with 3.0L engine

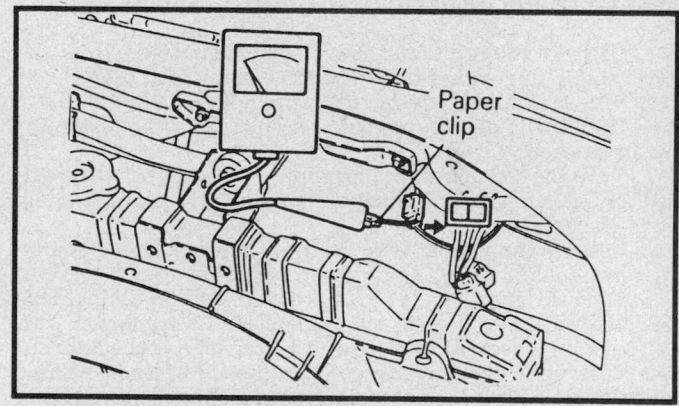

Tachometer connector—Van

fied timing is reached. Tighten the nut and recheck the timing.

8. Turn the engine off and connect the vacuum hose. Start the engine and check the timing with the vacuum hose plugged in. This reading should be basic timing plus 5 degrees.

9. Turn the engine off and remove all test equipment.

FUEL INJECTED ENGINE

1. Start the engine, set the parking brake and run the engine until at normal operating temperature. Keep all lights and accessories **OFF** and place the transmission in neutral.

2. Without unplugging the connector, insert a paper clip into the tachometer terminal. Connect the red lead of a tachometer to the paper clip and connect the black lead to a good ground. Set the idle speed to specifications.

3. Turn the engine off. Remove the water-proof cover from the ignition timing adjusting connector. Connect a jumper wire from the ignition timing adjusting terminal to a good ground.

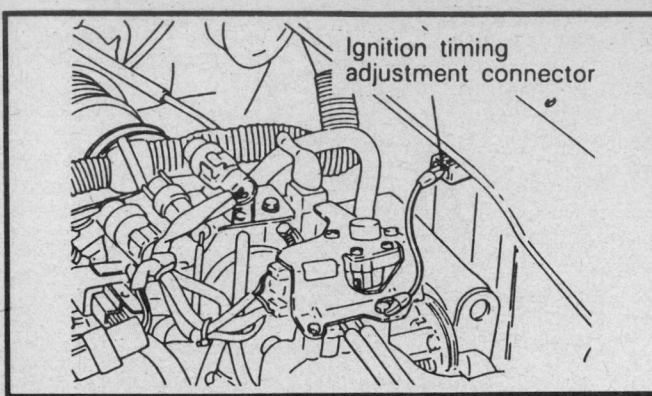

Ignition timing adjustment connector—1987–89 Van

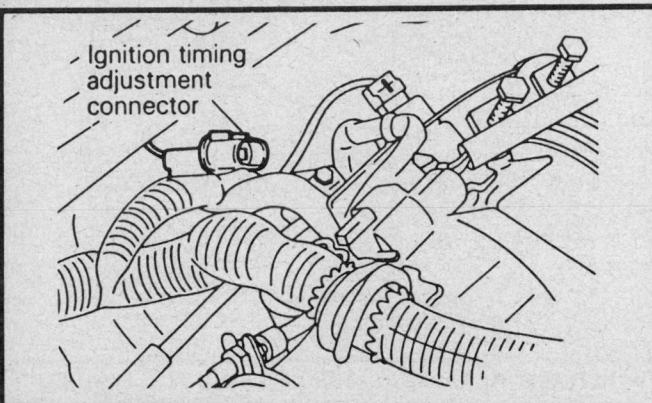

Ignition timing adjustment connector—1990 Van

4. Connect a conventional power timing light to the No. 1 cylinder spark plug wire. Start the engine and run at idle.

5. Aim the timing light at the timing scale.

6. Loosen the distributor nut just enough so the disributor can be rotated.

7. Turn the distributor in the proper direction until the specified timing is reached. Tighten the nut and recheck the timing. Turn the engine off.

8. Remove the jumper wire from the ignition timing adjusting terminal and install the water-proof cover.

9. Start the engine and check the actual ignition timing. This reading should be 3 degrees more than basic timing for the 2.4L engine and 10 degrees more than basic timing for the 3.0L engine. This value may increase according to the altitude. As long as the basic timing is correct, the vehicle is timed correctly.

NOTE: The actual timing may fluctuate according to the control mode of the engine control unit; this is normal. As long as the timing did not fluctuate when basic timing was checked, there is no problem.

10. Turn the engine off and remove all test equipment.

Alternator

For further information, please refer to "Electrical" in the Unit Repair section.

Belt Tension Adjustment
EXCEPT 3.0L ENGINE

1. Loosen the pivot bolt slightly.

2. Raise the vehicle and support safely if necessary. Loosen the adjuster slot bolt just enough so the alternator can be moved.

3. On Montero, Raider and 1986 Pick-Up and Ram 50, use a suitable pry bar and apply tension to the alternator until the belt deflects about ¼–½ in. under a 10 lb. load. All other vehicles are equipped with a bracket with an adjuster bolt. First loosen the brace bolt and tighten the adjustment bolt until the belt deflects about ¼–½ in. under a 10 lb. load.

4. Torque the adjuster strap bolt to 10 ft. lbs. (15 Nm). Torque the pivot bolt to 16 ft. lbs. (23 Nm).

3.0L ENGINE

1. Loosen the tensioner pulley locknut.

2. Turn the adjusting bolt until the belt deflects about ¼–½ in. under a 10 lb. load.

3. Tighten the locknut.

Removal and Installation

1. Disconnect the negative battery cable.

2. Remove the alternator cover, if equipped.

3. Remove the alternator adjustment bolt or loosen the tensioner and remove the belt.

4. Remove the alternator brace bolt(s), nut(s) and applicable spacers.

5. Remove the alternator from the mounting bracket, label and disconnect all wires from the rear of the unit.

To install:

6. Connect all wiring to their proper terminals on the rear of the alternator.

7. Position the alternator in the mounting bracket.

8. Install the alternator brace bolt(s), nut(s) and applicable spacers.

9. Wrap the belt around the pulley and install the alternator adjustment bolt, if equipped. Adjust the belt tension and tighten the bolts.

10. Install the alternator cover, if equipped.

11. Connect the negative battery cable and check the alternator for proper operation.

Starter

For further information, please refer to "Electrical" in the Unit Repair section.

Removal and Installation

1. Disconnect the negative battery cable.

2. Raise the vehicle and support safely.

3. Remove the starter cover, if equipped.

4. Label and disconnect the wiring to the starter motor.

5. Remove the starter mounting bolts.

6. Remove the starter motor from the vehicle.

7. The installation is the reverse of the removal procedure. Torque the mounting bolts to 20–25 ft. lbs. (27–34 Nm).

CHASSIS ELECTRICAL

Heater Blower Motor

Removal and Installation

MONTERO AND RAIDER

1. Disconnect the negative battery cable.
2. On some vehicles, the blower motor is not accessible without removing the blower motor housing.
   a. Remove the lap heater duct.
   b. Open the glove box lid and release the glove box stoppers. Remove the glove box from its hinge.
   c. Use a small suitable prying device to remove the clip that holds the air selection control cable.
   d. Disconnect the air selection control cable from the end of the air selection damper lever.
   e. Remove the air distribution duct from the left side of the blower assembly.
   f. Disconnect the connector to the resistor block and remove the grounding bolt.
   g. Remove the blower housing mounting bolts and remove the housing from the vehicle.
   h. Remove the resistor block and vent hose from the housing.
3. Remove the blower motor retaining screws and remove the assembly from the housing. Remove the fan from the motor.

To install:

4. Inspect the gasket for cracking or breaks and replace or repair it as required. Install to the blower motor.
5. Install the fan to the blower motor shaft. Install the blower assembly to the housing and install the retaining screws.
6. If the heater box was removed:
   a. Install the vent hose and resistor block.
   b. Install the assembled blower housing to the vehicle.

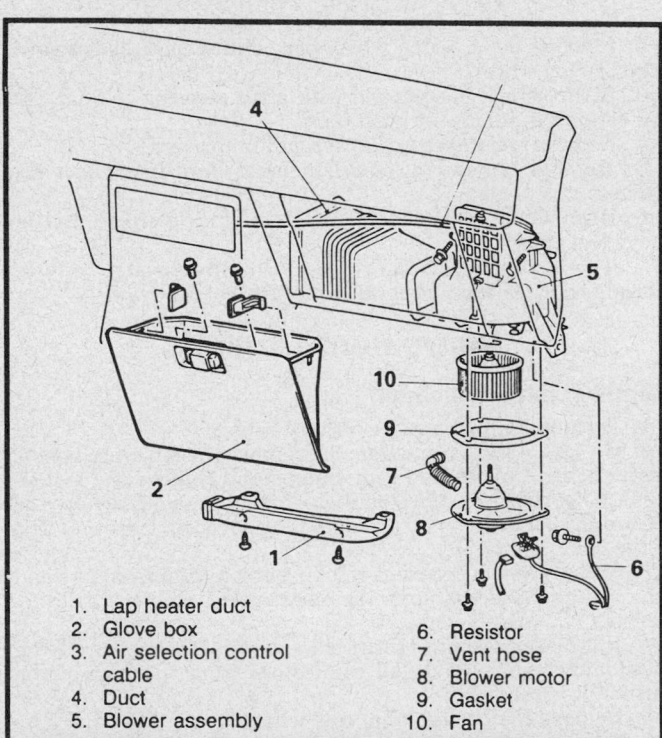

1. Lap heater duct
2. Glove box
3. Air selection control cable
4. Duct
5. Blower assembly
6. Resistor
7. Vent hose
8. Blower motor
9. Gasket
10. Fan

Typical blower motor removal and installation— except Van

c. Position the ground wire and install the grounding bolt.
d. Connect the resistor block connector.
e. Install the air distribution duct to the blower housing.
f. Move the air selection control lever to the recirculation position. Pull the air selection control damper lever up and connect the air selection control cable to the end of the air selection damper lever. Secure the cable with the clip.
g. Install the lap heater duct, glove box and stopper.
7. Connect the negative battery cable and check the blower motor for proper operation.

PICK-UP AND RAM 50

1. Disconnect the negative battery cable. On 1986 vehicles, remove the fan switch knob, heater control knobs and radio knobs and remove the instrument panel bezel.
2. Disconnect the blower motor connector.
3. Remove the blower motor retaining screws and remove the assembly from the housing.
4. Remove the fan from the motor.
5. The installation is the reverse of the removal procedure.

VAN

Front Heater Unit

1. Disconnect the negative battery cable.
2. Remove the lap heater duct.
3. Remove the left side defroster duct.
4. Disconnect the resistor block connector.
5. Remove the resistor block.
6. Remove the blower motor retaining screws and remove the assembly from the housing.
7. Remove the fan from the motor.
8. The installation is the reverse of the removal procedure.

Rear Heater Unit

1. Disconnect the negative battery cable.
2. Disconnect the blower motor connector.
3. Remove the blower motor cover.
4. Remove the vent hose.
5. Remove the blower motor retaining screws and remove the assembly from the housing. Remove the fan from the motor.
6. The installation is the reverse of the removal procedure.

Front Windshield Wiper Motor

Removal and Installation

EXCEPT VAN

1. Disconnect the negative battery cable.
2. Disconnect the wiper motor connector.
3. Remove the wiper motor retaining bolts and pull the motor out far enough to gain access to the wiper linkage.
4. Matchmark and pry the wiper linkage from the motor output shaft.
5. Remove the wiper motor from the vehicle.
6. The installation is the reverse of the removal procedure.

VAN

1. Disconnect the negative battery cable.
2. Remove the steering wheel and column covers.
3. If the vehicle is equipped with a tilt column, lower it to its lowest position. If the vehicle is not equipped with a tilt column, remove the combination switch.
4. Remove the brake fluid level inspection cover on the left side of the instrument panel.
5. Remove the lap heater ducts. Remove the switch panel and remove the instrument cluster assembly.
6. Remove the brake fluid reservoir mounting screws. Do not

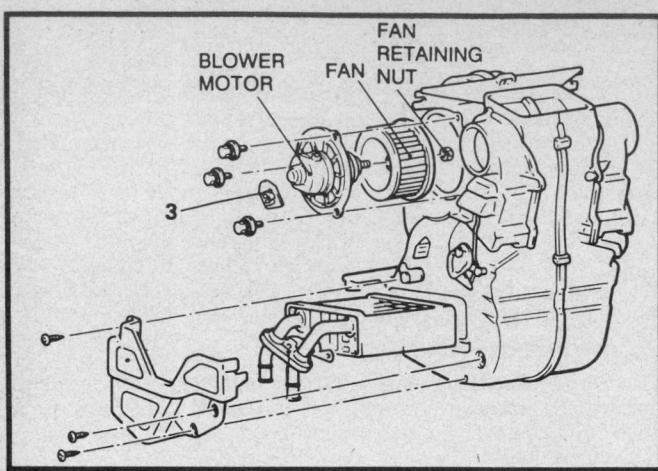

Front heater blower motor removal and installation—Van

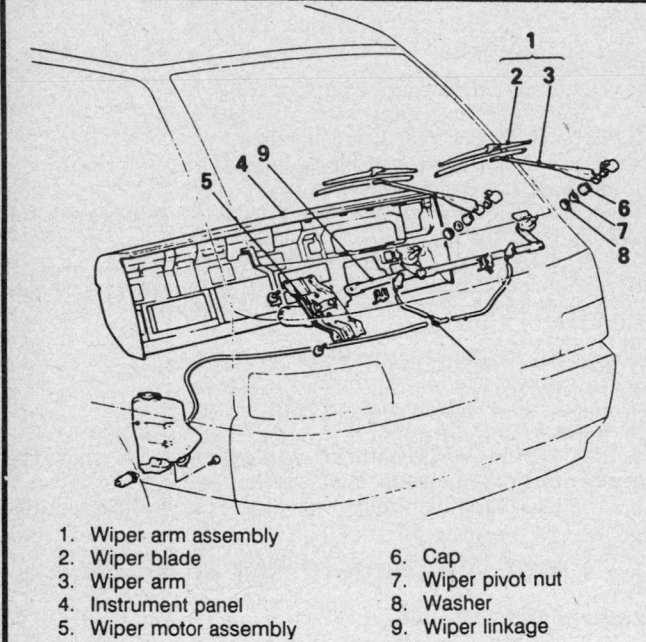

1. Wiper arm assembly
2. Wiper blade
3. Wiper arm
4. Instrument panel
5. Wiper motor assembly
6. Cap
7. Wiper pivot nut
8. Washer
9. Wiper linkage

Front wiper system—Van

allow fluid to spill out onto any painted surface; brake fluid will ruin the paint.

7. Remove the heater control knobs and remove the center panel.

8. Remove the heater control mounting screws and push the control panel into the instrument panel.

9. Disconnect the harnesses below the center of the instrument panel.

10. Remove the radio.

11. Remove the mounting screws across the bottom of the instrument panel.

12. Remove the bolt covers across the top of the instrument panel and remove the bolts.

13. Remove the defroster ductwork from the heater unit.

14. Carefully remove the instrument panel from the vehicle.

15. Disconnect the wiper motor connector.

16. Remove the wiper motor retaining bolts and pull the motor out far enough to gain access to the wiper linkage.

17. Matchmark and pry the wiper linkage from the motor output shaft.

18. Remove the wiper motor from the vehicle.

To install:

19. Position the wiper motor and connect the linkage.

20. Install the motor retaining bolts and connect the connector. Make sure the motor works properly in all modes before installing the remaining parts. Disconnect the battery before proceding.

21. Install the instrument panel and all related parts. Adjust control cables if necessary.

22. Install the combination switch, if it was removed. Install the steering wheel and column covers.

23. Connect the negative battery cable.

24. Check the entire climate control system and all gauges for proper operation.

Rear Wiper Motor

Removal and Installation

1. Disconnect the negative battery cable.

2. Tilt the wiper mount nut cover up and remove the nut. Remove the wiper arm from the shaft. Remove the wiper pivot nut and washer, if equipped.

3. Remove the tailgate or back door trim and waterproof film.

4. Disconnect the wiper motor connector.

5. Remove the wiper motor retaining bolts and remove the motor from the vehicle.

6. The installation is the reverse of the removal procedure.

Combination Switch

Removal and Installation

NOTE: The combination switch incorporates the windshield, headlight, dimmer, and turn signal switches into a single switch assembly.

1. Disconnect the negative battery cable.

2. Remove the steering wheel pad. Matchmark and remove the steering wheel.

3. If the vehicle is equipped with a tilt steering column, put the column in its lowest position.

4. Remove the upper and lower column covers.

5. Remove the wiring harness band and disconnect the harness.

6. Remove the combination switch mounting screws and remove the switch.

7. The installation is the reverse of the removal procedure. Torque the steering wheel nut to 30 ft. lbs. (41 Nm).

Instrument Cluster

Removal and Installation

1. Disconnect the negative battery cable.

2. On 1986 Pick-Up and Ram 50, remove the fan switch knob, heater control knobs and radio knobs and remove the instrument panel bezel. On 1987–90 Pick-Up and Ram 50, remove the hazard flasher switch and the matching cover on the other side of the column.

3. Remove the instrument cluster hood retaining screws and remove the hood. Remove the instrument cluster retaining screws.

4. Pull the cluster out, unclip the speedometer cable from the speedometer and unplug all connectors from the rear of the cluster.

5. Remove the cluster from the vehicle.

6. Remove the cover and glass. Remove the retaining screws and remove the speedometer, gauges, etc. as required.

7. The installation is the reverse of the removal procedure.

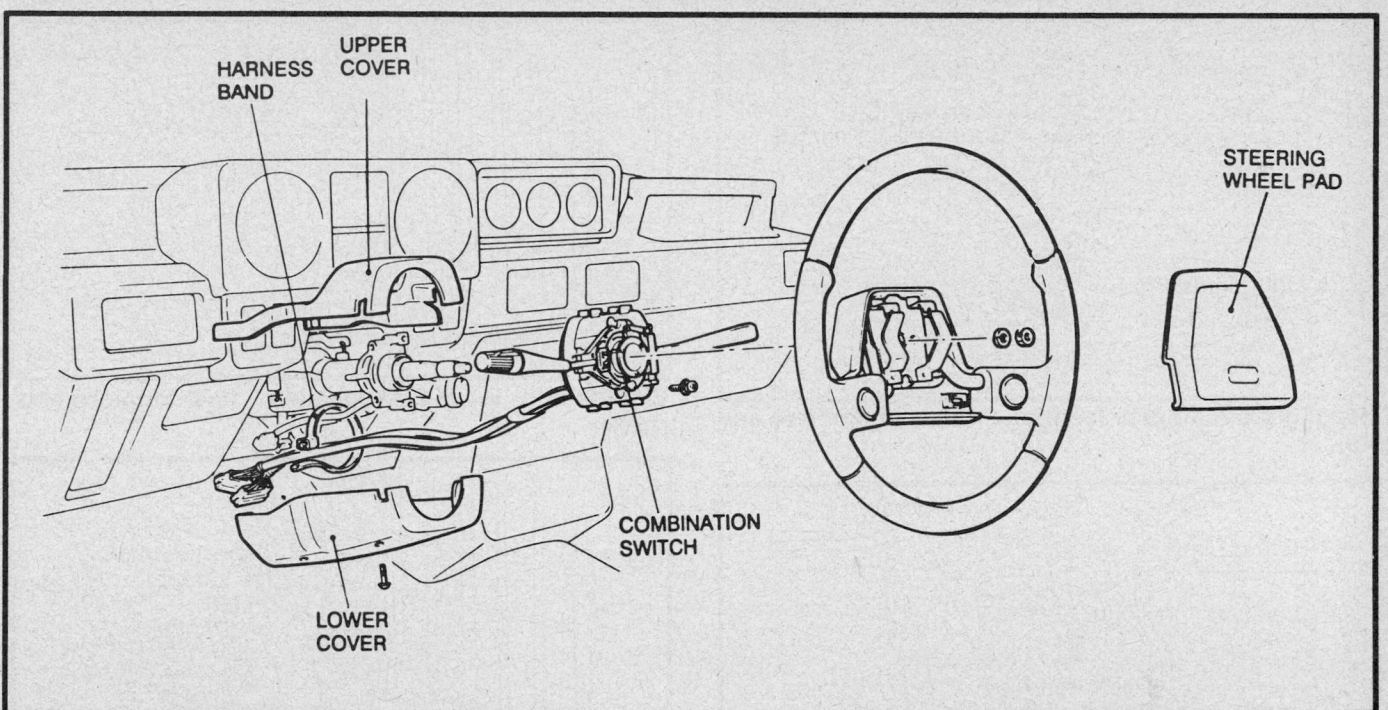

Typical combination switch mounting

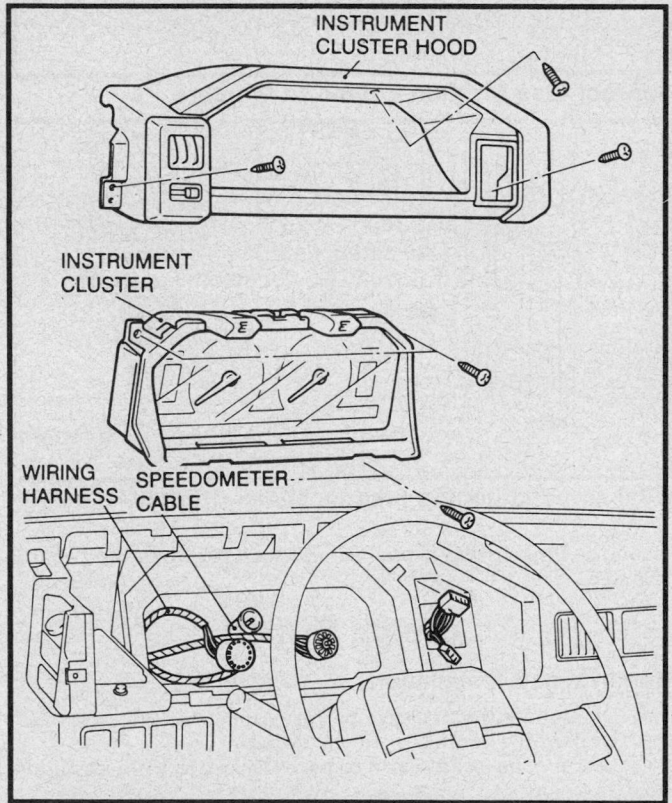

Typical instrument cluster mounting

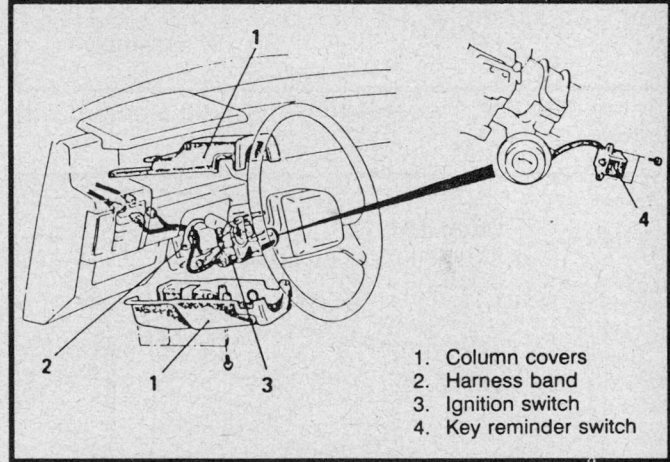

1. Column covers
2. Harness band
3. Ignition switch
4. Key reminder switch

Typical ignition switch and lock assembly

Ignition Switch and Lock

Removal and Installation

1. Disconnect the negative battery cable.

2. If the vehicle is equipped with a tilt steering column, put the column in its lowest position.

3. Remove the upper and lower column covers.

4. Remove the wiring harness band and disconnect the ignition switch harness.

5. Remove the ignition switch to lock attaching screws, if equipped and remove the switch from the lock.

6. Using a hacksaw blade, cut a groove into the head of the special ignition switch and lock assembly mounting screws and remove the screws.

7. Remove the assembly from the steering column.

To install:

8. With the key inserted in the switch, install the switch and lock assembly to the steering column. Tighten the screws gradually making sure the key does not bind at any time.

9. If using the special break-off bolts, tighten them until the heads break off.

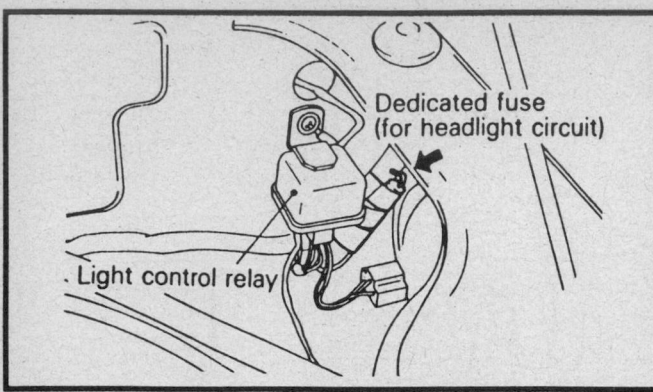

Headlight circuit fuse location – 1986–90 Montero and Raider

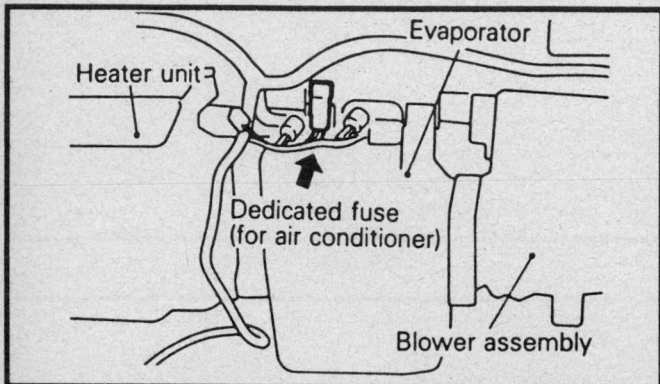

Air conditioning fuse location – 1987–90 Montero and Raider

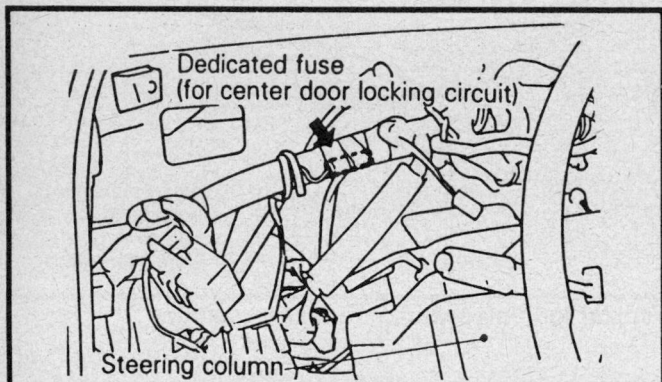

Electric door locks fuse location – 1989 Montero and Raider

Electric door locks fuse location – 1990 Montero and Raider

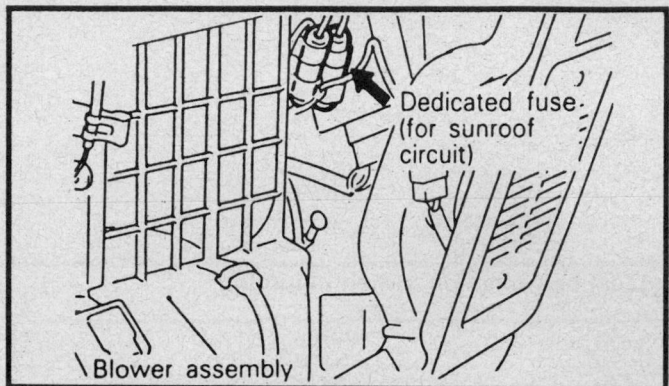

Sunroof fuse location – 1989–90 Montero

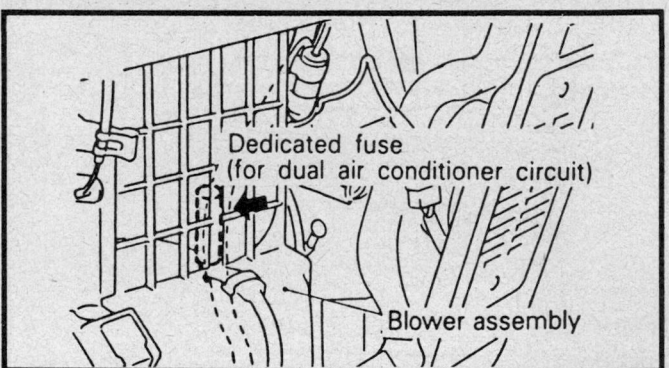

Dual air conditioning fuse location – 1989–90 Montero

10. Connect the switch harness and check the assembly for proper operation.
11. Install the upper and lower column covers.

Stoplight Switch

Removal and Installation

1. Disconnect the negative battery cable.
2. Unplug the connector to the switch.
3. Remove the locknut and remove the switch from its mount bracket.
4. The installation is the reverse of the removal procedure.
5. Adjust the switch so that the brake lights come on only when the brake pedal is pushed and turn off when the pedal is released.

Clutch Switch

Removal and Installation

1. Disconnect the negative battery cable.
2. Unplug the connector to the switch.
3. Remove the locknut and remove the switch from its mount bracket.
4. The installation is the reverse of the removal procedure.
5. Adjust the switch so that the distance from the floorboard to the face of the pedal pad is 7½ in. for Montero and Raider or 6½ in. for Pick-Up and Ram 50.
6. Make sure the cruise control system is not operational when the pedal is pushed in and does operate properly with the pedal released.

Fuses and Circuit Breakers

Location

MONTERO AND RAIDER

The main fuse block is located on the left side of the instrument panel, covered by a removeable access panel. There are also several dedicated fuses located throughout the vehicle.

PICK-UP, RAM 50 AND VAN

The fuse block is located to the left of the steering column, covered by a removeable access panel or mounted to the left kick-panel.

ENGINE COOLING

Radiator

Removal and Installation

EXCEPT VAN

1. Disconnect the negative battery cable.
2. Drain the radiator.
3. Remove the upper hose and coolant reserve tank hose from the radiator.
4. Remove the shroud assembly from the radiator.
5. Raise the vehicle and support safely.
6. Remove the lower hose from the radiator.
7. Disconnect and plug the automatic transmission cooler hoses, if equipped. Lower the vehicle.
8. Remove the mounting screws and carefully lift the radiator out of the engine compartment.

To install:

9. Lower the radiator into position and install the mounting screws.
10. Raise the vehicle and support safely. Connect the automatic transmission cooler hoses, if they were removed.
11. Connect the lower hose. Lower the vehicle.
12. Install the shroud assembly.
13. Connect the upper hose and coolant reserve tank hose.
14. Fill the system with coolant.
15. Connect the negative battery cable, run the vehicle until the thermostat opens, fill the radiator completely and check the automatic transmission fluid level, if equipped.
16. Check for leaks. Once the vehicle has cooled, recheck the coolant level.

VAN

1. Disconnect the negative battery cable.
2. Release the 2 catches and flip the passenger seat up.
3. Remove the driver's seat.
4. Remove the parking brake lever cover.
5. Remove the parking brake lever and fuel filler fuel release lever retaining screws and remove the levers from the seat under frame.
6. Remove the battery cover, if necessary.
7. Remove the seat underframe retaining screws and remove the seat underframe from the vehicle.
8. Raise the vehicle and support safely. Drain the radiator.
9. Disconnect and plug the automatic transmission cooler hoses.
10. Remove the lower radiator mounting screws. Lower the vehicle.
11. Remove the upper hose and coolant reserve tank hose from the radiator.
12. Remove the shroud assembly from the radiator.
13. Remove the lower hose from the radiator.
14. Remove the upper mounting screws and carefully lift the radiator out of the engine compartment.

To install:

15. Lower the radiator into position and install the mounting screws.
16. Raise the vehicle and support safely. Connect the automatic transmission cooler hoses. Lower the vehicle.
17. Connect the lower hose.
18. Install the shroud assembly.
19. Connect the upper hose and coolant reserve tank hose.
20. Fill the system with coolant.
21. Connect the negative battery cable, run the vehicle until the thermostat opens, fill the radiator completely and check the automatic transmission fluid level.
22. Check for leaks. Once the vehicle has cooled, recheck the coolant level.
23. Install the seat underframe and all related parts.

Heater Core

Removal and Installation

MONTERO AND RAIDER

1. Disconnect the negative battery cable.
2. Drain the coolant.
3. Remove the lap heater ducts and lower the hood release calble bracket.
4. Remove the side demister grills by carefully prying them from the instrument panel.
5. Remove the glove box and center console assembly. Remove the center reinforcement.
6. Remove the steering wheel.
7. Remove the instrument cluster.
8. Remove the oil pressure gauge, inclinometer and voltmeter pod cover and remove the gauge assembly.
9. Label and disconnect the recirculation/fresh air door control cable.
10. Label and disconnect the mode selection control cable.
11. Label and disconnect the water valve control cable.
12. Remove the fuse box retaining screw and position the fuse box out of the way as far as it will go.
13. Remove the instrument panel retaining nuts and bolts and carefully remove the instrument panel from the vehicle.
14. Remove the air cleaner or air intake plenum, as required.
15. Disconnect the heater hoses from the heater core tubes.
16. Remove the duct from the top of the heater case.
17. Remove the retaining nuts and bolts and remove the heater case from the vehicle.
18. Remove the water valve cover and carefully remove the water valve from the case.
19. Remove the foot/defroster selection link from the mode selection lever.
20. Move the lever up to a position which will not interfere with the removal of the heater core.

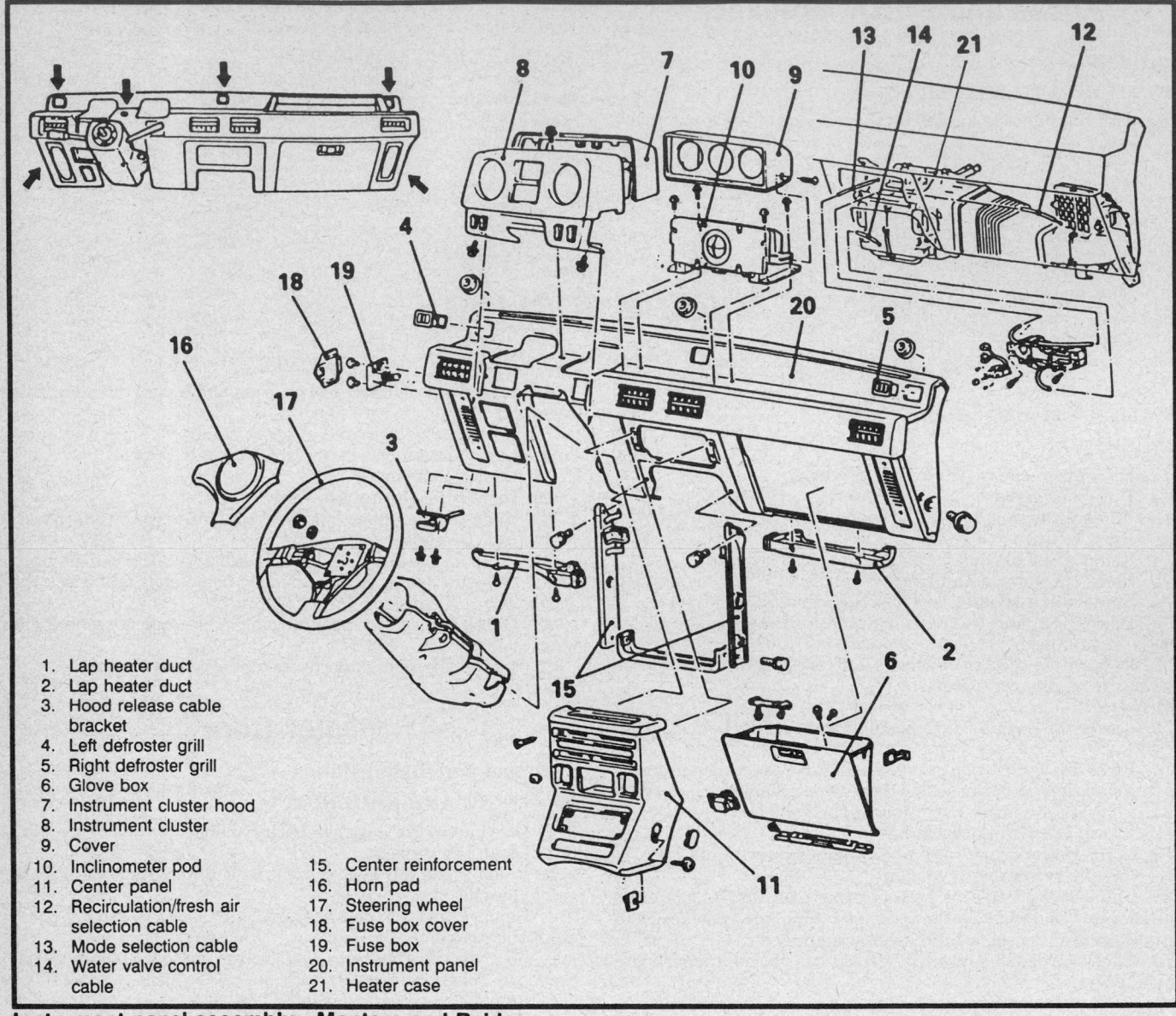

1. Lap heater duct
2. Lap heater duct
3. Hood release cable bracket
4. Left defroster grill
5. Right defroster grill
6. Glove box
7. Instrument cluster hood
8. Instrument cluster
9. Cover
10. Inclinometer pod
11. Center panel
12. Recirculation/fresh air selection cable
13. Mode selection cable
14. Water valve control cable
15. Center reinforcement
16. Horn pad
17. Steering wheel
18. Fuse box cover
19. Fuse box
20. Instrument panel
21. Heater case

Instrument panel assembly—Montero and Raider

21. Remove the heater core from the heater case. If the mode lever is in the way, remove it.
To install:
22. Install the heater core to the heater case. Install the mode lever, if it was removed.
23. Install the foot/defroster selection link to the mode selection lever.
24. Install the water valve assembly and its cover to the case.
25. Install the assembled heater case to the vehicle and install the retaining nuts and bolts.
26. Install the duct to the top of the case.
27. Connect the heater hoses to the core tubes and install the air cleaner or intake plenum.
28. Install the instrument panel and all related parts. Adjust the control cables if necessary.
29. Fill the system with coolant.
30. Connect the negative battery cable, run the vehicle until the thermostat opens and fill the radiator completely.
31. Check for leaks. Once the vehicle has cooled, recheck the coolant level.

32. Check the entire climate control system and all gauges for proper operation.

1986 PICK-UP AND RAM 50
1. Disconnect the negative battery cable.
2. Drain the coolant.
3. Place the water control valve (inside the cab) in the **OFF** position.
4. Remove the parcel tray, center ventilator grille and duct and the defroster duct.
5. Label and disconnect all cables from the heater case.
6. Disconnect the heater hoses from the heater core tubes.
7. Disconnect the blower motor connector.
8. Remove the top mounting bolts and center mounting nuts and remove the heater case from the vehicle.
9. Remove the heater core from the heater case.
10. The installation is the reverse of the removal procedure. If the heater hose grommets were disturbed, reseal them completely with suitable sealer.
11. Fill the system with coolant.

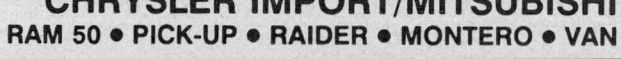

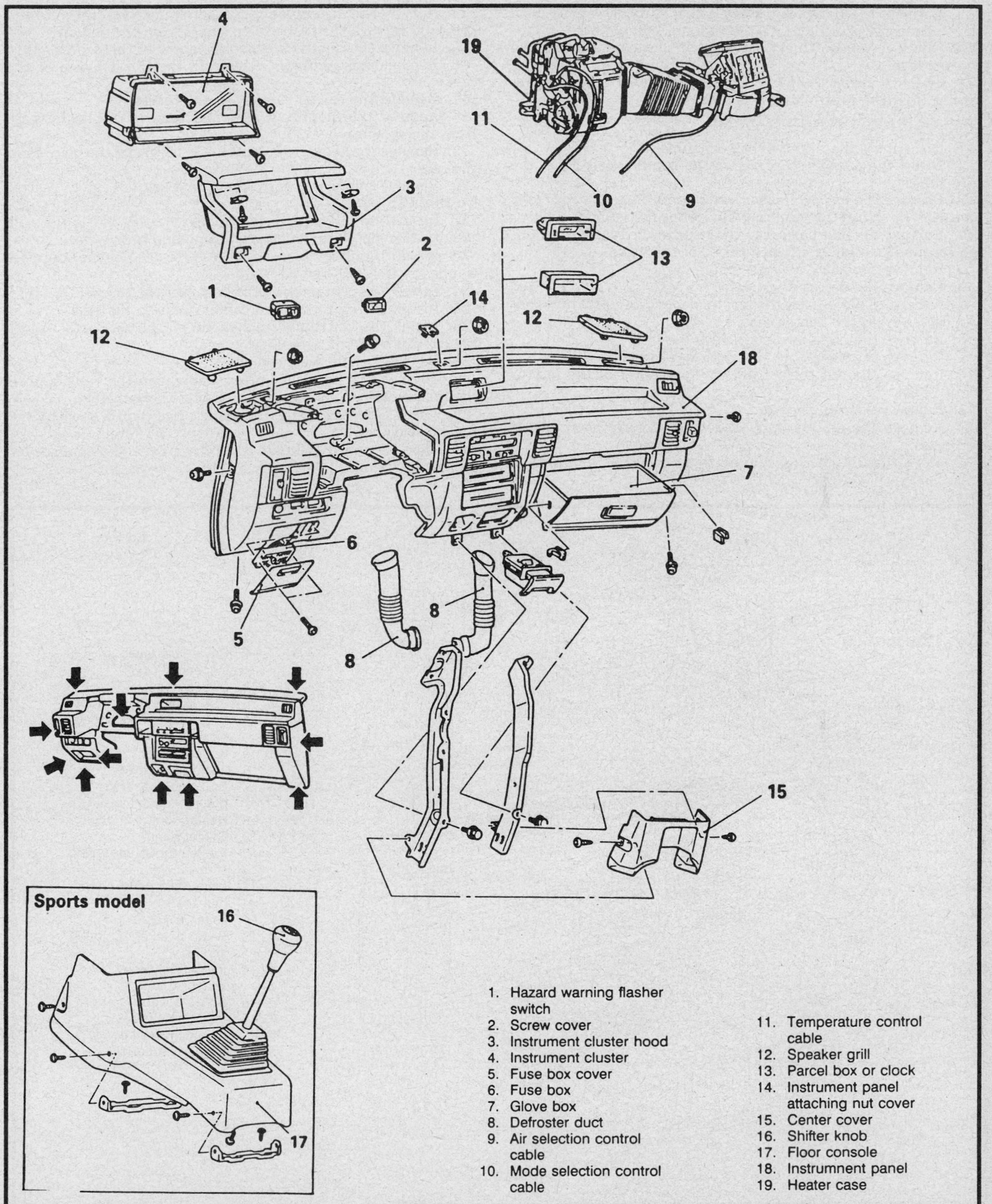

Sports model

1. Hazard warning flasher switch
2. Screw cover
3. Instrument cluster hood
4. Instrument cluster
5. Fuse box cover
6. Fuse box
7. Glove box
8. Defroster duct
9. Air selection control cable
10. Mode selection control cable
11. Temperature control cable
12. Speaker grill
13. Parcel box or clock
14. Instrument panel attaching nut cover
15. Center cover
16. Shifter knob
17. Floor console
18. Instrunment panel
19. Heater case

Instrument panel assembly — 1987–90 Pick-Up and Ram 50

12. Connect the negative battery cable, run the vehicle until the thermostat opens and fill the radiator completely.

13. Check for leaks. Once the vehicle has cooled, recheck the coolant level.

14. Check the entire climate control system for proper operation. Adjust the control cables if necessary.

1987–90 PICK-UP AND RAM 50

1. Disconnect the negative battery cable.

2. Drain the coolant. Disconnect the heater hoses from the core tubes.

3. Remove the hazard flasher switch and the matching cover on the other side of the column. Remove the instrument cluster.

4. Remove the fuse box cover and remove the fuse box retaining screws. Position the fuse box out of the way.

5. Remove the glove box assembly.

6. Remove the defroster ducts.

7. Label and disconnect the air, mode, and temperature control cables from the heater case.

8. Remove the front speaker grilles.

9. Remove the parcel box or clock, as equipped.

10. Remove the nut cover from the top center of the instrument panel.

11. Remove the center cover.

12. Remove the shifter knob and floor console assembly, if equipped.

13. Move the tilt steering column down as far as it will go.

14. Remove the instrument panel retaining nuts and bolts and carefully remove the instrument panel from the vehicle.

15. Remove the duct from the top center of the heater case.

16. Remove the defroster duct from the the left side of the case.

17. Remove the center reinforcement braces.

18. Remove the mounting nuts and remove the heater case from the vehicle.

19. Remove the hose cover, joint hose clamp and the plate from the case.

20. Remove the heater core from the case.

To install:

21. Install the heater core to the heater case.

22. Install the plate, joint hose clamp and hose cover.

23. Install the assembled heater case to the vehicle. Connect the heater hoses to the core tubes.

24. Install the center reinforcement braces.

25. Install the defroster and center ducts to the case.

26. Install the instrument panel and all related parts. Adjust the control cables if necessary.

27. Fill the system with coolant.

28. Connect the negative battery cable, run the vehicle until the thermostat opens and fill the radiator completely.

29. Check for leaks. Once the vehicle has cooled, recheck the coolant level.

30. Check the entire climate control system and all gauges for proper operation.

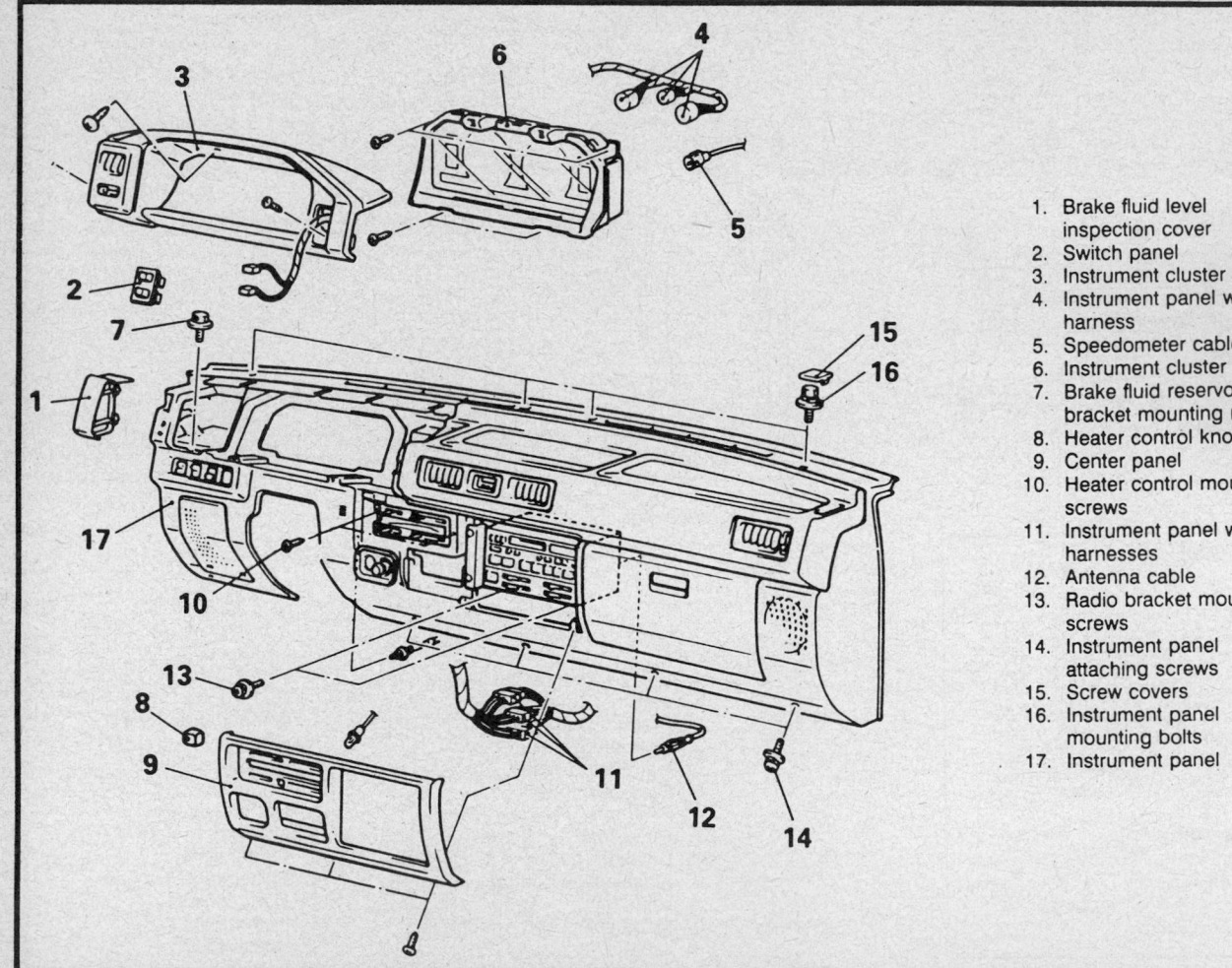

1. Brake fluid level inspection cover
2. Switch panel
3. Instrument cluster hood
4. Instrument panel wiring harness
5. Speedometer cable
6. Instrument cluster
7. Brake fluid reservoir bracket mounting nut
8. Heater control knob
9. Center panel
10. Heater control mounting screws
11. Instrument panel wiring harnesses
12. Antenna cable
13. Radio bracket mounting screws
14. Instrument panel attaching screws
15. Screw covers
16. Instrument panel mounting bolts
17. Instrument panel

Instrument panel assembly–Van

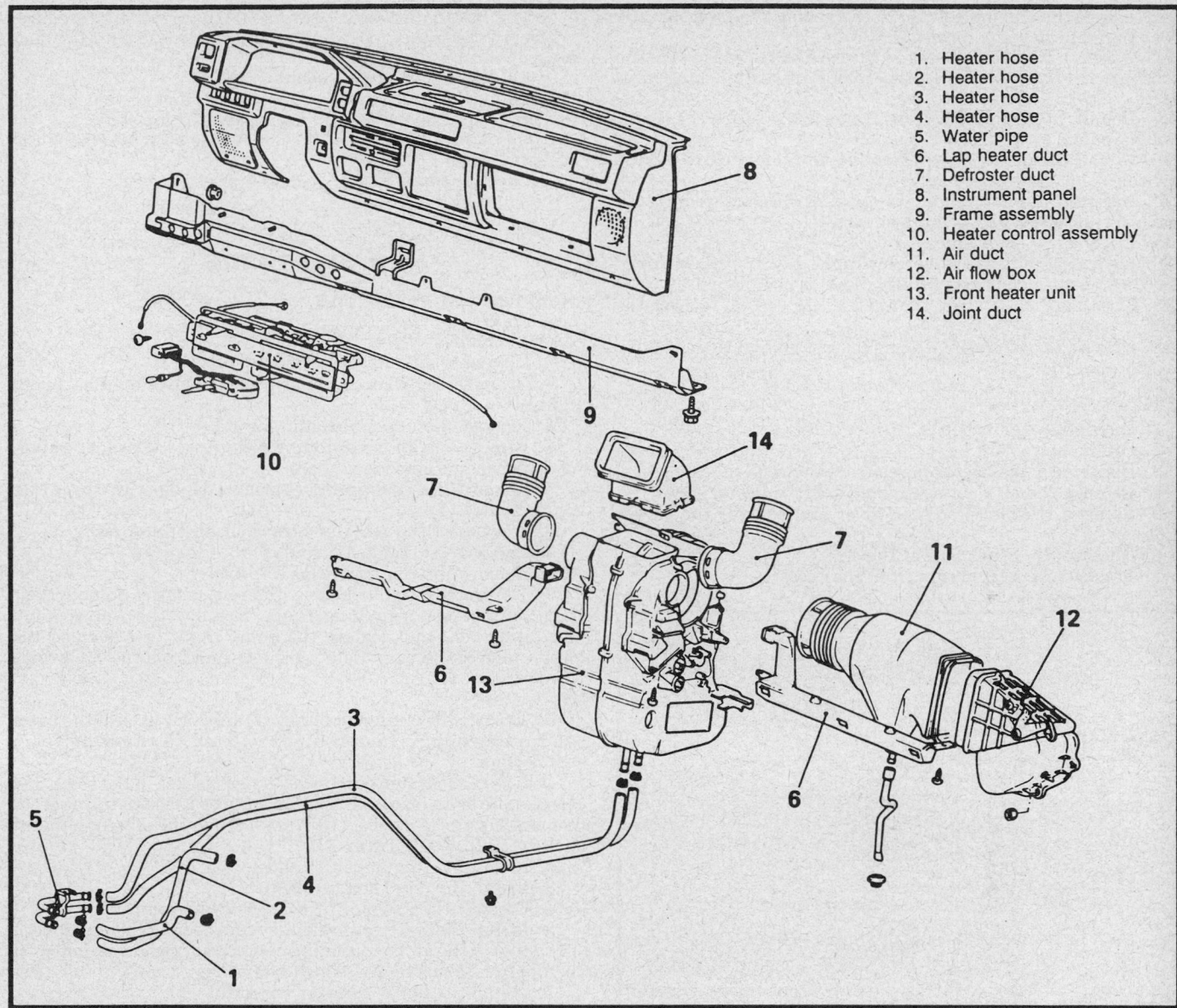

1. Heater hose
2. Heater hose
3. Heater hose
4. Heater hose
5. Water pipe
6. Lap heater duct
7. Defroster duct
8. Instrument panel
9. Frame assembly
10. Heater control assembly
11. Air duct
12. Air flow box
13. Front heater unit
14. Joint duct

Front heater case and related parts — Van

VAN

Front Heater Core

1. Disconnect the negative battery cable.
2. Drain the coolant.
3. Remove the steering wheel and column covers. If the vehicle is equipped with a tilt column, lower it to its lowest position. If the vehicle is not equipped with a tilt column, remove the combination switch.
4. Remove the brake fluid level inspection cover on the left side of the instrument panel.
5. Remove the lap heater ducts. Remove the switch panel and remove the instrument cluster assembly.
6. Remove the brake fluid reservoir mounting screws. Do not allow fluid to spill out onto any painted surface; brake fluid will ruin the paint.
7. Remove the heater control knobs and remove the center panel.
8. Remove the heater control mounting screws and push the control panel into the instrument panel.

9. Disconnect the harnesses below the center of the instrument panel.
10. Remove the radio.
11. Remove the mounting screws across the bottom of the instrument panel.
12. Remove the bolt covers across the top of the instrument panel and remove the bolts.
13. Remove the defroster ductwork from the heater unit.
14. Carefully remove the instrument panel from the vehicle.
15. Remove the instrument panel frame and the control panel from the vehicle.
16. Raise the vehicle and support safely. Disconnect the heater hoses from the heater core tubes.
17. Label and disconnect all cables from the heater case. Remove the heater case mounting bolts. Tilt the case away from the bracket and remove it from the vehicle.
18. Disassemble the heater case and remove the heater core.

To install:

19. Install the heater core to the heater case.

20. Install the assembled case to the vehicle, making sure the floor pan seal is seated properly.

21. Connect the heater hoses to the core tubes. Make sure the hoses are not twisted and that the clamps are not touching other parts.

22. Install the instrument panel frame and position the heater control panel.

23. Install the instrument panel and all related parts. Adjust the control cables if necessary.

24. Install the combination switch, if it was removed. Install the steering wheel and column covers.

25. Fill the system with coolant.

26. Connect the negative battery cable, run the vehicle until the thermostat opens and fill the radiator completely.

27. Check for leaks. Once the vehicle has cooled, recheck the coolant level.

28. Check the entire climate control system and all gauges for proper operation.

Rear Heater Core

1. Disconnect the negative battery cable.
2. Drain the coolant.
3. Disconnect the heater hoses from the core tubes.
4. Remove the air duct assembly from the heater case.
5. Remove the blower motor cover and remove the blower motor.
6. Remove the upper half of the case.
7. Remove the heater core from the case.

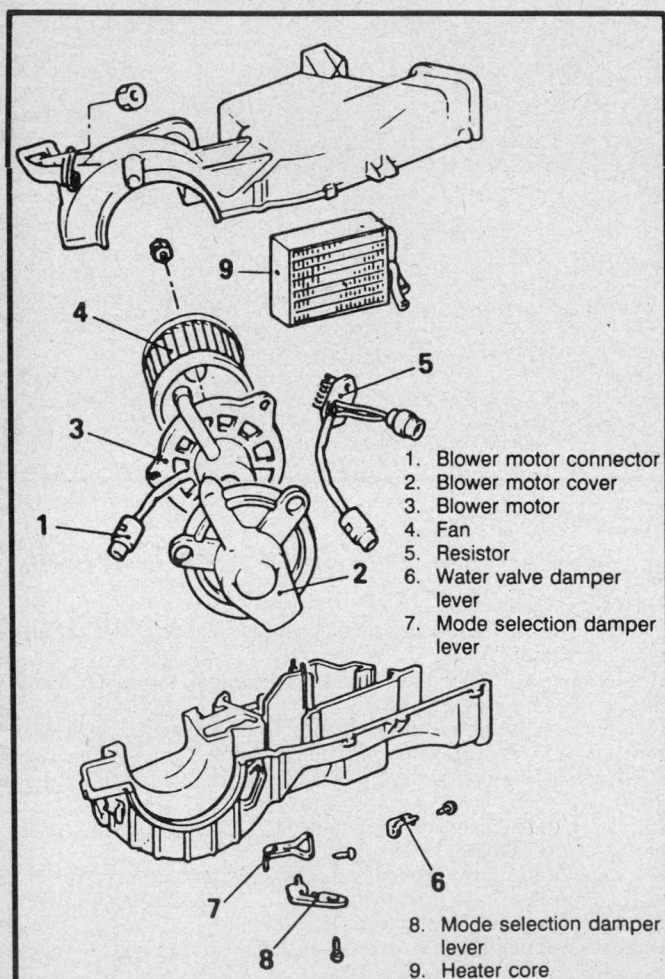

1. Blower motor connector
2. Blower motor cover
3. Blower motor
4. Fan
5. Resistor
6. Water valve damper lever
7. Mode selection damper lever
8. Mode selection damper lever
9. Heater core

Rear heater assembly—Van

8. The installation is the reverse of the removal procedure. When attaching the upper half of the case, make sure the duct seals do not get dislodged.

9. Fill the system with coolant.

10. Connect the negative battery cable, run the vehicle until the thermostat opens and fill the radiator completely.

11. Check for leaks. Once the vehicle has cooled, recheck the coolant level.

12. Check the rear heater system proper operation.

Water Pump

Removal and Installation

2.0L AND 2.4L ENGINES

1. Disconnect the negative battery cable.

2. Drain the antifreeze. On the Van, remove the seat under frame.

3. Remove the upper radiator shroud.

4. Remove the air conditioning compressor tensioner pulley, if equipped and remove all belts.

5. Remove the cooling fan assembly along with the water pump pulley.

6. Disconnect the radiator hose from the water pump.

7. Remove the crankshaft pulley(s).

8. Remove the timing belt(s).

9. The water pump bolts are different lengths, so note their positions before removing them. Remove the water pump mounting bolts and remove the pump from the block and the water pipe connection. Remove the O-ring from the water pipe connection.

To install:

10. Thoroughly clean and dry the mating surfaces of the block and water pump. Install a new O-ring to the water pipe connection.

11. Install the water pump with a new gasket to the block and torque the bolts (except the bolt that goes through the alternator bracket) to 10 ft. lbs. (13 Nm). Torque the aforementioned bolt to 17 ft. lbs. (23 Nm).

12. Install the timing belt(s) and covers.

13. Install the crankshaft pulley(s).

14. Connect the radiator hose to the water pump.

15. Install the water pump pulley and cooling fan assembly.

16. Install the air conditioning compressor tensioner pulley, if equipped and install and adjust the belts.

17. Install the upper radiator shroud.

18. Fill the system with coolant.

19. Connect the negative battery cable, run the vehicle until the thermostat opens and fill the radiator completely.

20. Check for leaks. Once the vehicle has cooled, recheck the coolant level.

21. Install the seat underframe and all related parts, if it was removed.

2.6L ENGINE

1. Disconnect the negative battery cable.

2. Drain the antifreeze.

3. Remove the upper radiator shroud, if equipped.

4. Remove the cooling fan assembly along with the water pump pulley.

5. Remove all belts.

6. Disconnect the radiator hose and heater hose from the water pump.

7. The water pump bolts are different lengths, so note their positions before removing them. Remove the water pump retaining bolts and remove the water pump from the timing chain cover.

8. The installation is the reverse of the removal procedure. Torque the water pump and pulley bolts to 10 ft. lbs. (13 Nm).

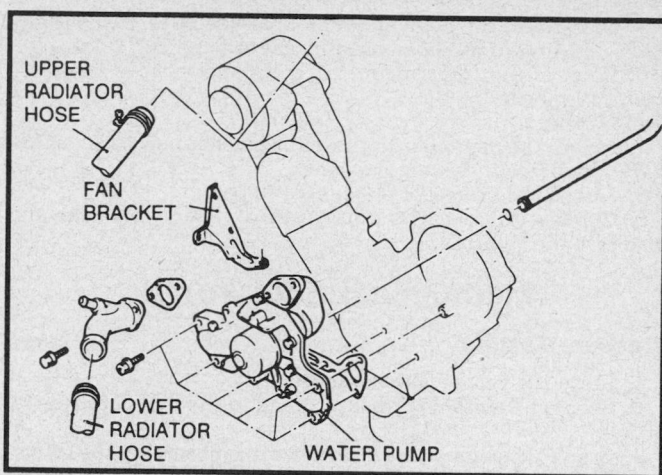

Water pump assembly—3.0L engine

3.0L ENGINE

1. Disconnect the negative battery cable.
2. Drain the antifreeze. Remove the upper radiator hose and the upper radiator shroud.
3. Remove the cooling fan assembly along with the water pump pulley. Remove all belts.
4. Remove the power steering pump from the bracket and remove the bracket.
5. Remove the tensioner pulley bracket, the air conditioning compressor and its bracket.
6. Remove the cooling fan bracket assembly. Remove the crankshaft pulley and flange.
7. Remove the timing belt covers. If the same timing belt will be reused, mark the direction of the timing belt's rotation, for installation in the same direction. Make sure the engine is positioned so the No. 1 cylinder is at the TDC of its compression stroke and the sprockets timing marks are aligned with the engine's timing mark indicators.
8. Loosen the timing belt tensioner bolt and remove the belt. Position the tensioner as far away from the center of the engine as possible and tighten the bolt. Remove the water pump mounting bolts, separate the pump from the water inlet pipe and remove the pump from the engine. Remove the water inlet fitting from the pump.
To install:
9. Thoroughly clean and dry the mating surfaces of the block

and water pump. Install a new O-ring to the water inlet pipe. Install the pump and water inlet fitting with new gaskets to the engine and water pipe. Torque the water pump mounting bolts to 20 ft. lbs. (27 Nm).
10. If not already done, position both camshafts so the marks line up with those on the alternator bracket and inner timing cover. Rotate the crankshaft so the timing mark aligns with the mark on the oil pump.
11. Install the timing belt on the crankshaft sprocket and while keeping the belt tight on the tension side (right side), install the belt on the front camshaft sprocket.
12. Install the belt on the water pump pulley, then the rear camshaft sprocket and the tensioner.
13. Rotate the front camshaft counterclockwise to tension the belt between the front camshaft and the crankshaft. If the timing marks came out of line, repeat the procedure.
14. Install the crankshaft sprocket flange.
15. Loosen the tensioner bolt and allow the spring to tension the belt.
16. Turn the crankshaft 2 full turns in the clockwise direction only until the timing marks align again. Now that the belt is properly tensioned, torque the tensioner lock bolt to 21 ft. lbs. (29 Nm).
17. Install the timing belt covers and all related parts.
18. Fill the cooling system.
19. Connect the negative battery cable, run the vehicle until the thermostat opens and fill the radiator completely.
20. Check for leaks. Once the vehicle has cooled, recheck the coolant level.

Thermostat

Removal and Installation

1. Disconnect the negative battery cable. Drain the coolant down to thermostat level or below.
2. Disconnect the engine coolant temperature switch connector, if equipped.
3. Remove the thermostat housing.
4. Remove the thermostat and discard the gasket.
5. Clean the housing mating surfaces and use a new gasket.
6. The installation is the reverse of the removal procedure.

Cooling System Bleeding

All engines are equipped with self-bleeding thermostats. Cooling system bleeding is not necessary in any vehicles when servicing the cooling system.

FUEL SYSTEM

Fuel System Precaution

Relieving Fuel System Pressure

1. Disconnect the fuel pump harness connector.
2. Start the engine and allow the engine to run itself out of fuel.
3. Once the engine has stalled, turn the key to the **OFF** position and connect the connector.
4. Disconnect the negative battery cable so the pressure cannot build up until work has been completed.

Fuel Filter

Removal and Installation
CARBURETED ENGINE

1. Disconnect the negative battery cable.
2. Raise the vehicle and support safely, if necessary.
3. Remove the air cleaner assembly, if necessary. Remove the fuel filter from its bracket. Inspect the hoses carefully.
4. Install the new filter, hoses and clamps if damaged.

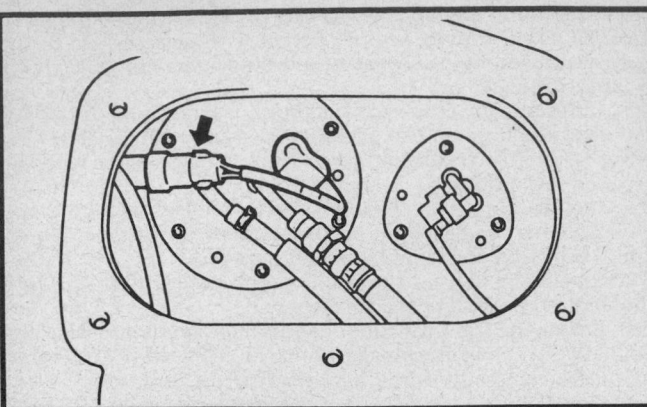

Fuel pump harness connector at the rear of the fuel tank—Montero and Raider

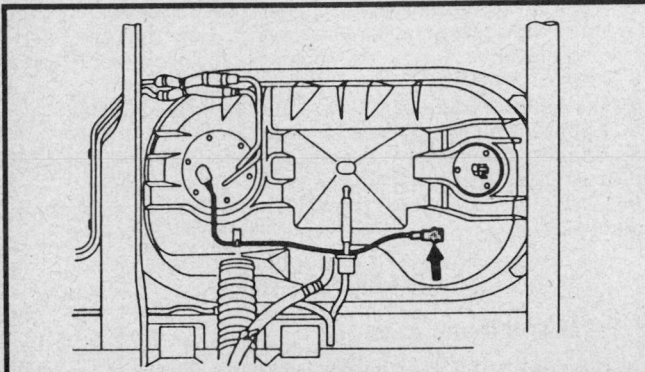

Fuel pump harness connector at the rear of the fuel tank—Pick-Up and Ram 50

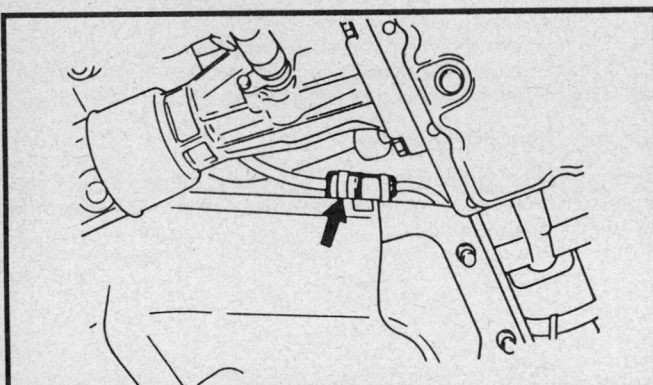

Fuel pump harness connector at the left of the transmission extension housing—Van

5. Connect the negative battery cable, start the engine and check for leaks.

FUEL INJECTED ENGINE

------- CAUTION -------

Do not use conventional fuel filters, hoses or clamps when servicing this fuel system. They are not compatible with the injection system and could fail, causing personal injury or damage to the vehicle. Use only replacemenmt parts specifically designed for fuel injection.

1. Relieve the fuel pressure.
2. Disconnect the negative battery cable.
3. Raise the vehicle and support safely.
4. Remove the fuel filter protector plate, if equipped.

5. Disconnect the main and high pressure lines. Remove any other fuel hose that is damaged in any way.
6. Remove the filter mounting bolts and remove the filter from the vehicle.
To install:
7. Install the new filter to the vehicle using new gaskets. Replace any hoses that were damaged.
8. Install the protector plate, if equipped.
9. Connect the negative battery cable, check for leaks and road test the vehicle.

Mechanical Fuel Pump

Pressure Testing

1. Raise the vehicle and support safely.
2. Connect a suitable pressure gauge to the fuel pump outlet fitting.
3. Crank the engine several times while observing the gauge.
4. The pump should develop 3–4 psi of pressure.

Removal and Installation

1. Disconnect the negative battery cable.
2. Disconnect the fuel lines from the pump and plug them.

NOTE: There is a fuel pump pushrod in the 2.0L engine. When removing or installing the pump, be careful not to drop the pushrod because it will most likely drop down to the oil pan.

Also, it may be necessary to remove the rear thermostat housing bolt and/or the valve cover on the 2.6L engine to remove and install the pump.

3. Remove the fuel pump retaining bolts or nuts and remove the pump from the engine. Remove the pushrod, if equipped.
4. Clean and dry the mounting surfaces, bolts and bolt holes.
5. The installation is the reverse of the removal procedure. Use new gaskets and a new insulator.
6. Connect the negative battery cable, start the engine and check for leaks.

Electric Fuel Pump

Pressure Testing

1. Relieve the fuel pressure.
2. Disconnect the negative battery cable.
3. Cover the high pressure fuel hose hose with a clean shop rag to prevent fuel spray from residual pressure in the line. Disconnect the high pressure fuel hose at the delivery pipe.
4. Connect the proper fuel pressure gauge and accompanying special adaptor tools to the delivery pipe.
5. If not already done, place the key in the **OFF** position. Connect the negative battery cable.

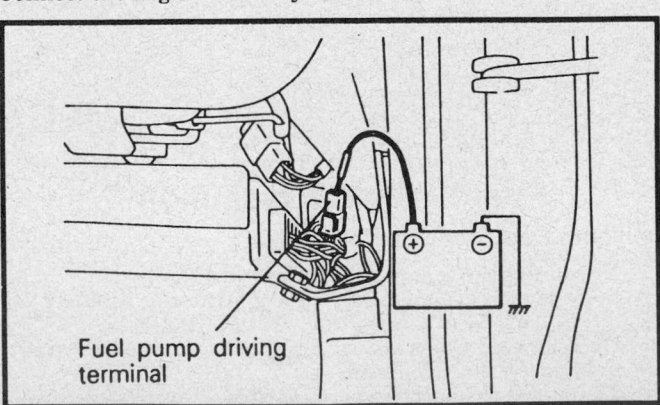

Fuel pump activation terminal—Montero and Raider

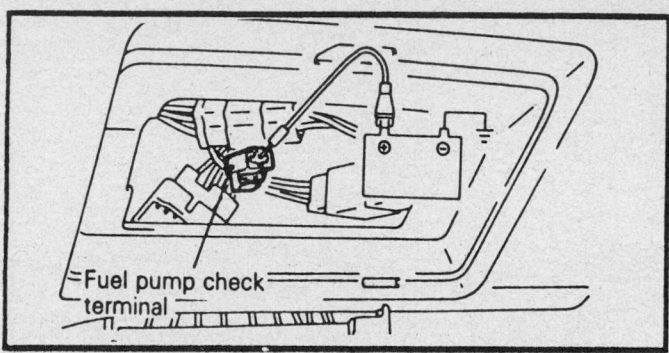

Fuel pump activation terminal located behind the fuse box—Pick-Up and Ram 50

Fuel pump activation terminal—Van

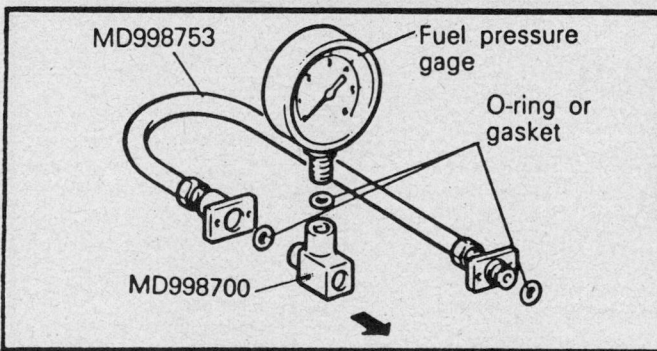

Fuel pressure testing equipment—except Van. The hose is not used on Pick-Up and Ram 50 with 2.4L engine

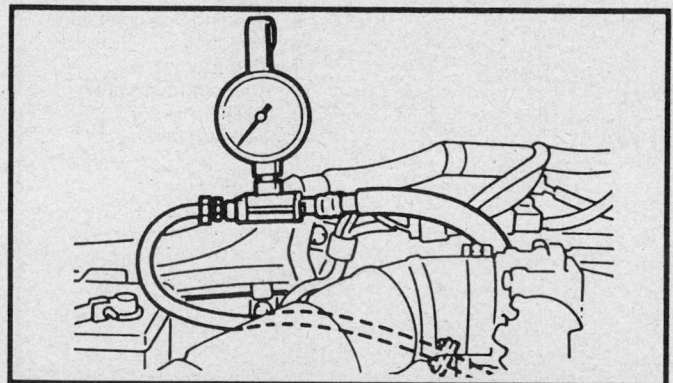

Fuel pressure gauge installation—3.0L engine

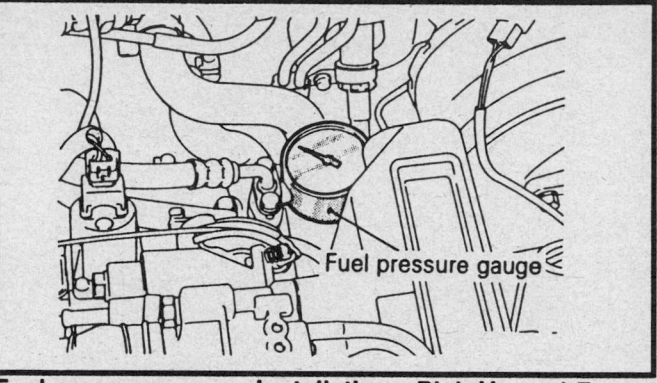

Fuel pressure gauge installation—Pick-Up and Ram 50 with 2.4L engine

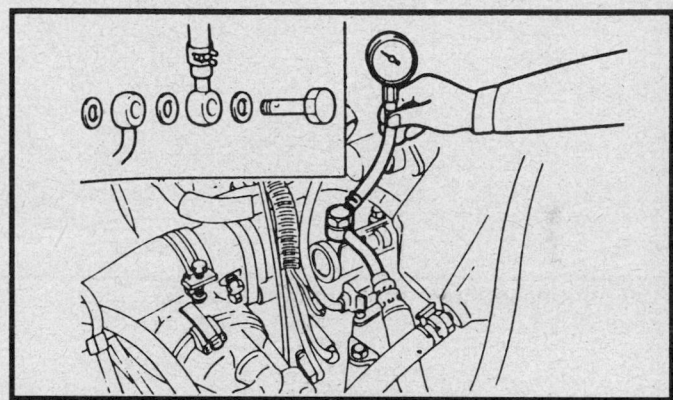

Fuel pressure gauge installation—Van

6. Connect a jumper wire from the fuel pump activation terminal to the positive battery post. This will pressurize the system so that the fuel pump installation assembly can be inspected for leaks. If a leak is found, repair it before proceeding.

7. Disconnect the jumper wire to stop the fuel pump.

8. Start the engine and allow it to idle.

9. Measure the pressure during idling. The specification for all applications is 38 psi.

10. Disconnect and plug the vacuum hose from the fuel pressure regulator.

11. With the hose disconnected, the pressure should increse to about 50 psi.

12. Race the engine a few times to make sure the fuel pressure does not deviate from specifications.

13. Press on the return hose while racing the engine to make sure there is pressure in the hose. Reconnect the vacuum hose.

14. Stop the engine and allow pressure to remain in the system. There should be no decrease in pressure for at least 2 minutes.

15. Relieve the fuel pressure.

16. Remove the fuel pressure measuring equipment.

17. Connect the high pressure fuel hose to the delivery pipe using nw O-rings where necessary.

18. Connect the jumper wire from the fuel pump activation terminal to the positive battery post inspect the system for leaks.

19. Road test the vehicle.

Removal and Installation

MONTERO AND RAIDER

1. Relieve the fuel pressure.
2. Disconnect the negative battery cable.
3. Remove the pump and sending unit access panel.

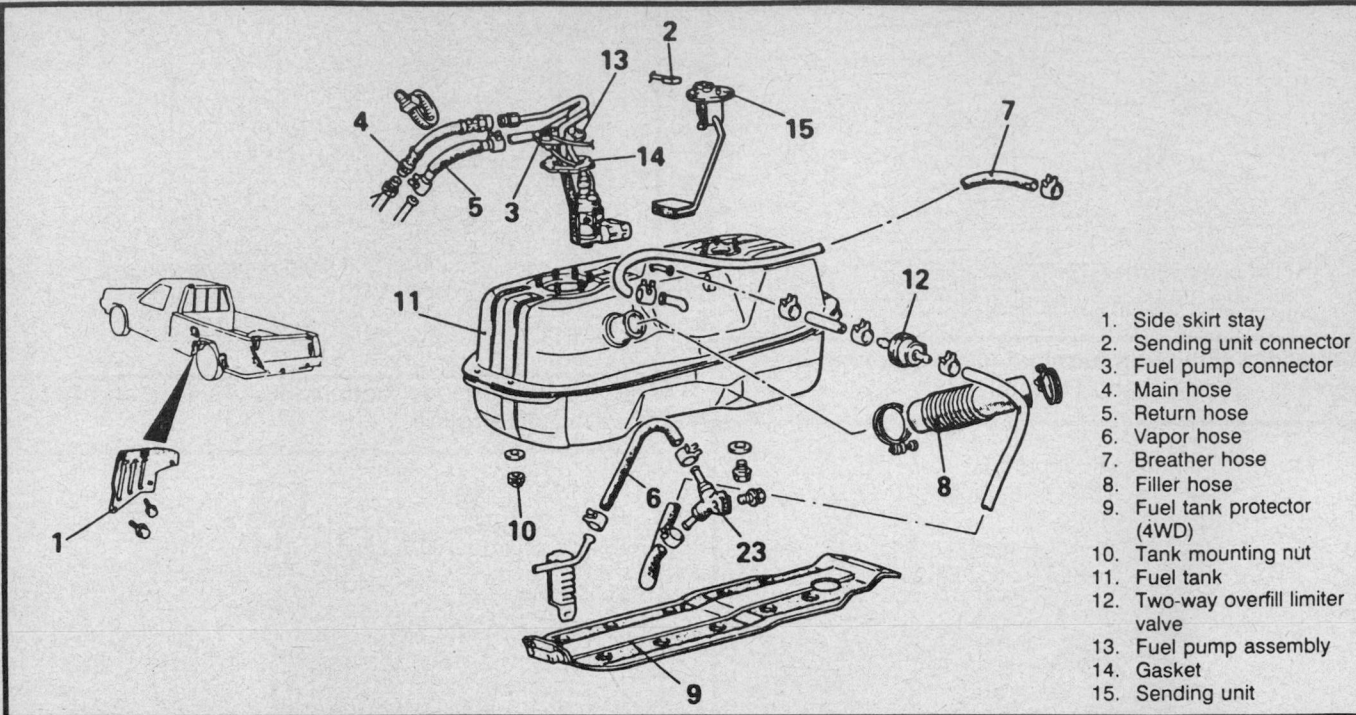

1. Side skirt stay
2. Sending unit connector
3. Fuel pump connector
4. Main hose
5. Return hose
6. Vapor hose
7. Breather hose
8. Filler hose
9. Fuel tank protector (4WD)
10. Tank mounting nut
11. Fuel tank
12. Two-way overfill limiter valve
13. Fuel pump assembly
14. Gasket
15. Sending unit

Fuel tank assembly—Pick-Up and Ram 50

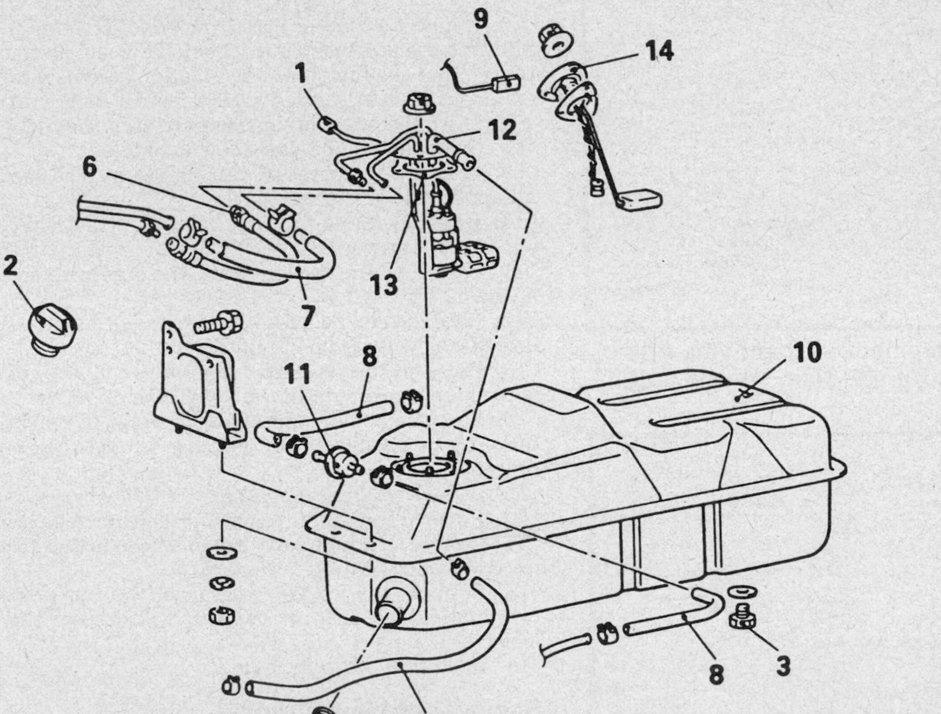

1. Fuel pump connector
2. Filler cap
3. Drain plug
4. Filler hose
5. Leveling hose
6. Main hose
7. Return hose
8. Vapor hose
9. Sending unit connector
10. Fuel tank
11. Two-way valve
12. Fuel pump assembly
13. Gasket
14. Sending unit

Fuel tank assembly—Van

4. Cover the high pressure fuel hose with a clean shop rag to prevent fuel spray from residual pressure in the line. Disconnect the fuel hose and pipe from the pump.

5. Remove the fuel pump mounting screws and remove the pump from the tank.

6. The installation is the reverse of the removal procedure.

PICK-UP, RAM 50 AND VAN

1. Relieve the fuel pressure.
2. Disconnect the negative battery cable.
3. Raise the vehicle and support safely. Remove protective plates, if equipped.
4. Using the proper equipment, drain the fuel tank.
5. Disconnect all hoses, tubes and connectors that can be reached without lowering the tank.
6. Place a transmission jack or equivalent under the center of the tank and apply slight pressure.
7. Remove the retaining bolts and nuts and lower the tank.
8. Lower the tank enough to reach in and disconnect any remaining hoses, tubes and connectors.
9. Remove the tank. Remove the pump retaining screws and remove the pump from the tank.

To install:
10. Clean the seal area of the tank. Install a new gasket.
11. Install the pump in the same position as originally installed.
12. Install the retaining screws and torque them to 15 inch lbs.
13. Install the fuel tank and all related parts.
14. Connect the negative battery cable. Connect the jumper wire from the fuel pump activation terminal to the positive battery post inspect the system for leaks.
15. Road test the vehicle.

Carburetor

Removal and Installation

1. Disconnect the negative battery cable. Drain the radiator because the choke control element is water activated.
2. Remove the air cleaner assembly.
3. Remove and install the fuel tank cap to relieve any pressure in the tank.
4. Matchmark all vacuum hoses and electrical connectors and remove them from the carburetor.
5. Disconnect the throttle, cruise control, choke and kickdown cables and linkages, if equipped.
6. Disconnect and plug the fuel inlet line.
7. Remove the mounting bolts and remove the carburetor from the intake manifold.

To install:
8. Thoroughly clean and dry the mounting surface of the manifold and install a new base gasket.
9. Install the mounting bolts and tighten them alternately to compress the base gasket evenly. Final torque should be 12 ft. lbs. (16 Nm).
10. Connect the fuel line.
11. Connect the throttle, cruise control, choke and kickdown cables and linkages, if equipped.
12. Install all vacuum hoses and electrical connectors in their proper locations.
13. Install the air cleaner.
14. Fill the radiator.
15. Connect the negative battery cable, start the engine and perform all necessary adjustments.

Idle Speed Adjustment

1. Start the engine and allow it to reach normal operating temperature. Before checking or adjusting the idle speed, check ignition timing and adjust if necessary.

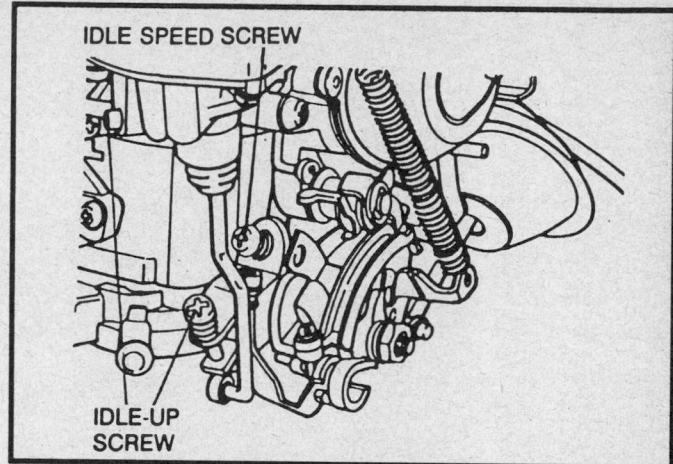

Carburetor adjusting screw locations

2. Turn all lights and accessories **OFF**. Connect a tachometer to the engine.
3. Open the throttle and run at 2500 rpm for 10 seconds. Allow the engine to idle for 2 minutes.
4. Check the idle speed. If the tachometer indicates rpm is not at specifications, turn the idle speed screw until the correct idle speed is obtained.
5. Once the idle speed is set, turn the air conditioning on to its coldest position, if equipped.
6. With the compressor running, set the idle to 900 rpm by turning the idle-up screw.

Idle Mixture Adjustment

1. Drill a 2mm pilot hole in the casting around the idle mixture screw. Drive out the concealment plug.
2. Run the engine until at normal operating temperature.
3. Check and adjust the idle speed and ignition timing.
4. Turn the engine **OFF.**
5. Disconnect the negative battery cable for 5 seconds, then reconnect it.
6. Disconnect the oxygen sensor connector.
7. Open the throttle and run at 2500 rpm for 10 seconds. Allow the engine to idle for 2 minutes.
8. Using a suitable emissions tester, adjust the idle mixture screw until the CO at idle is below 0.30% and the idle is smooth.
9. Turn the engine **OFF.**
10. Connect the oxygen sensor connector.
11. Reinstall the concealment plug in the idle mixture screw hole.

Service Adjustments

For all carburetor service adjustment procedures and Specifications, please refer to "Carburetor Service" in the Unit Repair section.

Fuel Injection

Idle Speed Adjustment

The idle speed is automatically regulated by the idle speed control system. Do not attempt any adjustments or the fuel injection system may get out of calibration.

Idle Mixture Adjustment

There is no idle mixture adjustment provided with any Mitsubishi fuel injection system.

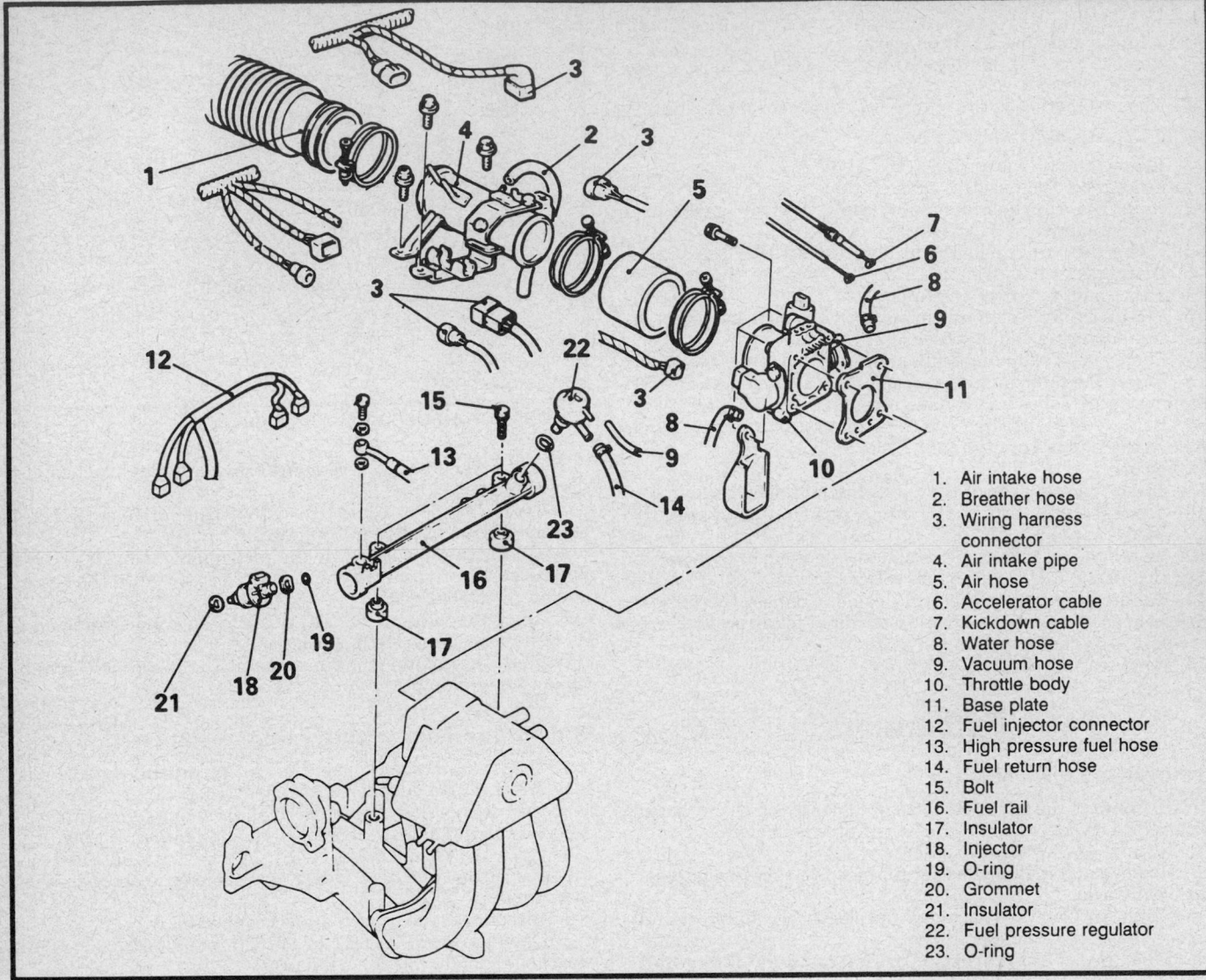

1. Air intake hose
2. Breather hose
3. Wiring harness connector
4. Air intake pipe
5. Air hose
6. Accelerator cable
7. Kickdown cable
8. Water hose
9. Vacuum hose
10. Throttle body
11. Base plate
12. Fuel injector connector
13. High pressure fuel hose
14. Fuel return hose
15. Bolt
16. Fuel rail
17. Insulator
18. Injector
19. O-ring
20. Grommet
21. Insulator
22. Fuel pressure regulator
23. O-ring

Throttle body, fuel rail, injector and related parts — 2.4L engine

Fuel Injector

Removal and Installation

2.4L ENGINE

1. Relieve the fuel pressure.
2. Disconnect negative battery cable.
3. Drain the antifreeze. Remove the throttle body.
4. Remove the boost hose from opposite end of air plenum.
5. Cover the high pressure fuel hose with a clean shop rag to prevent fuel spray from residual pressure in the line. Disconnect the high pressure fuel hose from the fuel rail.
6. Remove the fuel return line and vacuum hose from the fuel pressure regulator.
7. Disconnect the electrical connectors from the injectors.
8. Remove the fuel rail retaining bolts.
9. Lift the rail with injectors attached up and away from the engine. Do not drop injectors during removal. If an injector should fall and hit the floor or other hard surface, it should not be reused.
10. Remove the injector from the rail with a gentle pull. Remove the lower insulator.

To install:

11. Install a new grommet and O-rings onto the injector. Coat the O-rings with a light coating of gasoline.
12. Install the injector to the rail, making sure that injector turns freely. If it does not turn, check for a jammed O-ring and re-insert.
13. Replace the insulators in the intake manifold. Install the fuel rail with injectors onto the manifold. Make sure the rubber bushings are correctly seated in the installation holes.
14. Tighten fuel rail retaining bolts to 18 ft. lbs. (10 Nm).
15. Install the fuel return line and vacuum hose to the fuel pressure regulator.
16. Connect the electrical connectors to the injectors.
17. Replace O-ring and connect the high pressure fuel line to delivery pipe.
18. Connect the boost hose to air plenum.
19. Install the throttle body using a new base gasket.
20. Refill the radiator. Connect the negative battery cable.
21. Connect the jumper wire from the fuel pump activation terminal to the positive battery post inspect the system for leaks.

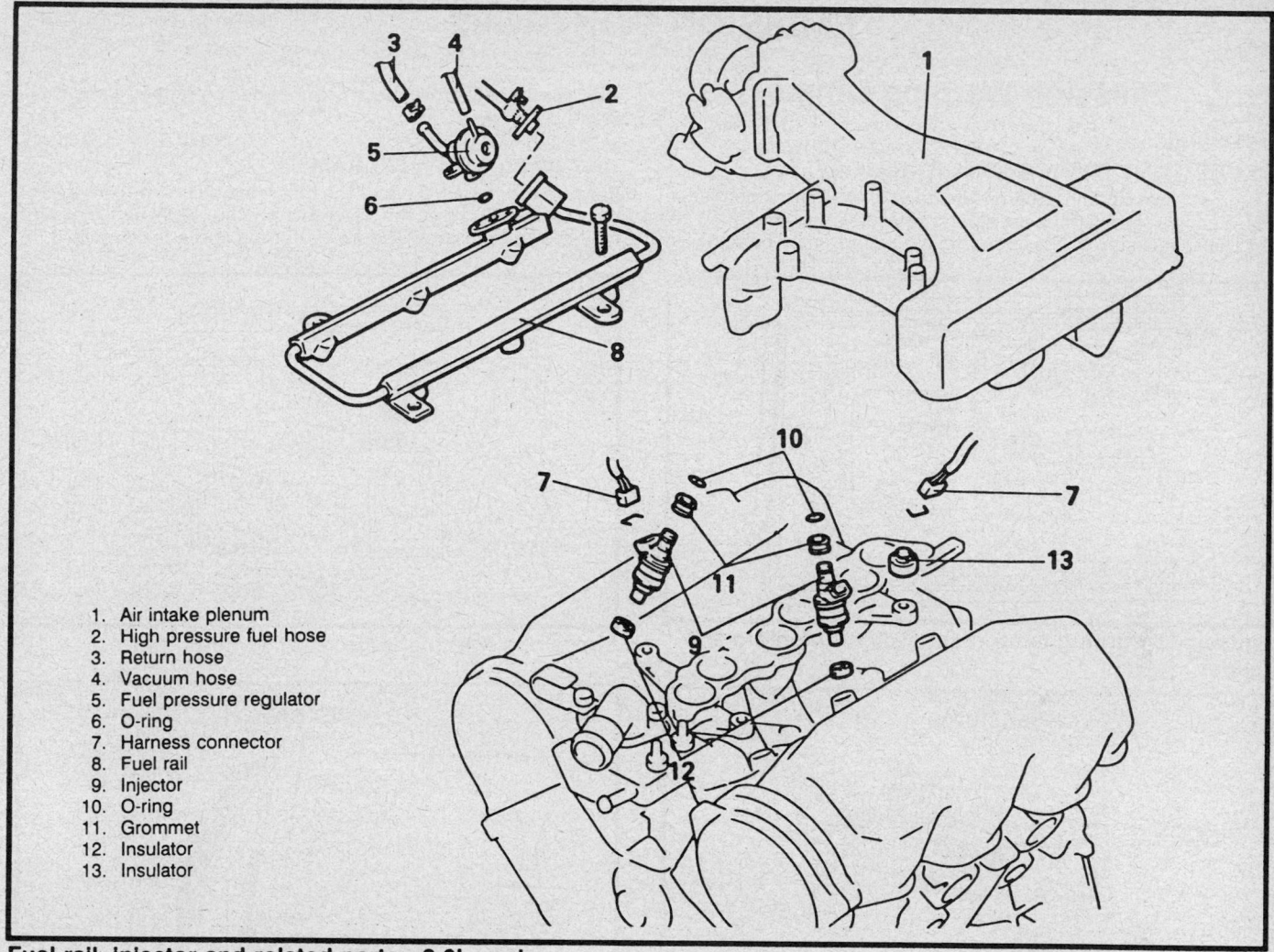

1. Air intake plenum
2. High pressure fuel hose
3. Return hose
4. Vacuum hose
5. Fuel pressure regulator
6. O-ring
7. Harness connector
8. Fuel rail
9. Injector
10. O-ring
11. Grommet
12. Insulator
13. Insulator

Fuel rail, injector and related parts—3.0L engine

3.0L ENGINE

1. Relieve the fuel pressure.
2. Disconnect negative battery cable.
3. Remove the air intake hose from the throttle body.
4. Disconnect all wires, hoses and linkages to the throttle body.
5. Disconnect the EGR temperature sensor wire.
6. Remove the ignition coil.
7. Remove the engine oil filler neck bracket.
8. Unbolt the EGR tube from the air intake plenum.
9. Disconnect the PCV hose and vacuum hose cluster from the plenum.
10. Remove the plenum to engine brackets.
11. Unbolt the air intake plenum assembly from the intake manifold and remove.
12. Cover the high pressure fuel hose with a clean shop rag to prevent fuel spray from residual pressure in the line. Disconnect the high pressure fuel hose from the fuel rail.
13. Remove the fuel return line and vacuum hose from the fuel pressure regulator.
14. Remove electrical connectors from the injectors.
15. Remove the fuel rail retaining bolts.
16. Lift the rail with injectors attached up and away from the engine. If an injector should fall and hit the floor or other hard surface, it should not be reused.
17. Remove the injectors from the fuel rail with a gentle pull. Remove the lower insulator.

To install:

18. Install a new grommet and O-ring onto injector. Coat the O-ring with light coating of gasoline.
19. Install the injectors into the rail, making sure that injector turns freely. If it does not turn, check for a jammed O-ring and re-insert.
20. Replace the seats in the intake manifold. Install new rubber bushings onto mounting points of fuel rail. Install the assembled fuel rail with injectors onto the manifold.
21. Tighten the fuel rail bolts to 8 ft. lbs. (10 Nm).
22. Connect the electrical connectors to the injectors.
23. Connect the fuel return hose and the vacuum hose to the pressure regulator.
24. Using a new O-ring coated lightly with gasoline, install the high pressure fuel line.
25. Install air intake plenum and all related parts.
26. Connect the negative battery cable.
27. Connect the jumper wire from the fuel pump activation terminal to the positive battery post inspect the system for leaks.

EMISSION CONTROLS

Emission Warning Lamps

Resetting

EXCEPT 1987–90 PICK-UP AND RAM 50

The reset switch is located on the back of the instrument cluster. Remove the instrument cluster to access the switch. To reset the timer, simply flip the switch. The bulb may be removed after the 150,000 mile check is completed on Montero and Raider only.

1987–90 PICK-UP AND RAM 50

Remove the glass in from of the instrument cluster to access the reset switch. To reset the timer, simply flip the switch. The bulb may be removed after the 120,000 mile check is completed.

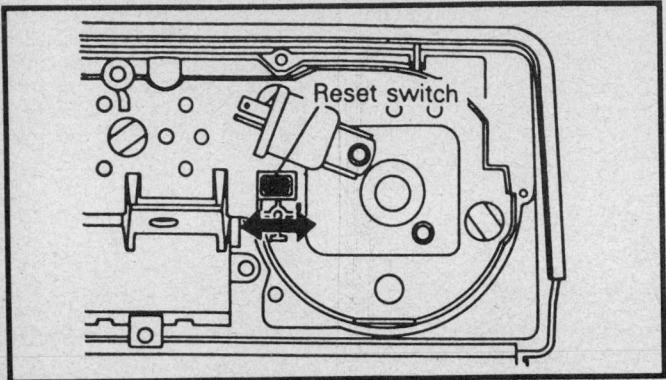

Emissions warning lamp reset switch—Montero and Raider

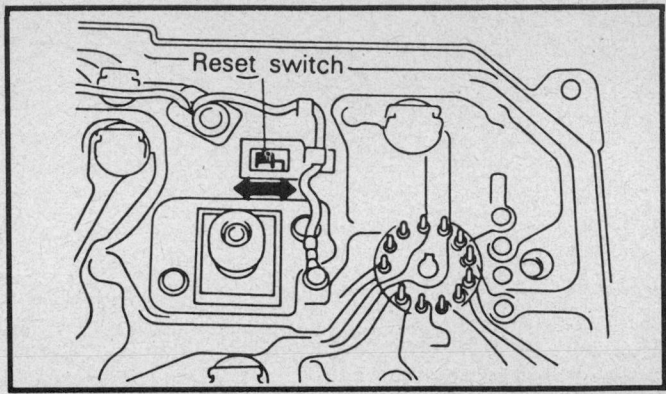

Emissions warning lamp reset switch—Van

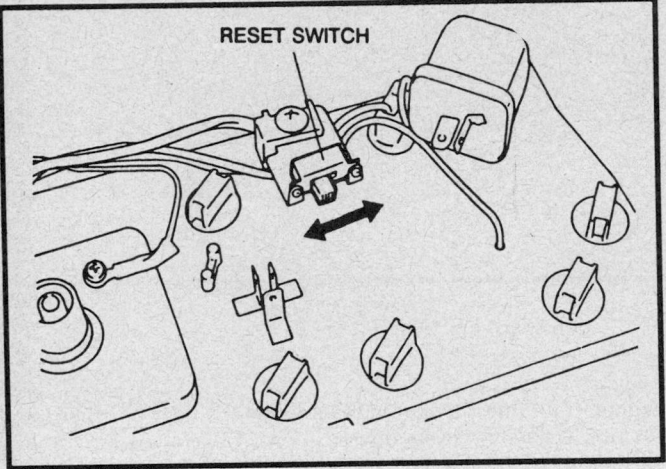

Emissions warning lamp reset switch—1986 Pick-Up and Ram 50

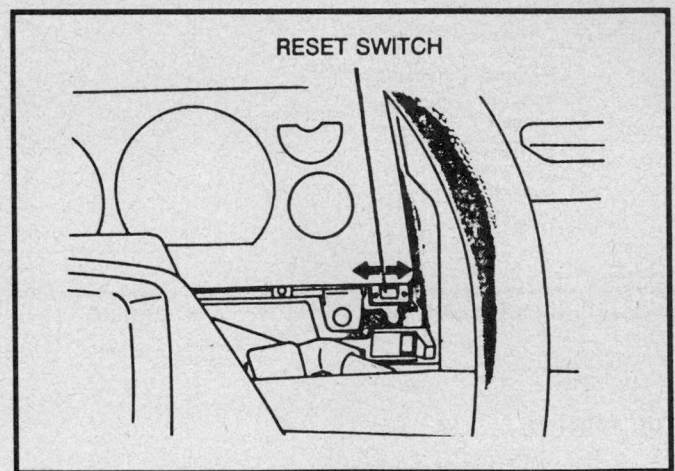

Emissions warning lamp reset switch—1987–90 Pick-Up and Ram 50

ENGINE MECHANICAL

NOTE: Disconnecting the negative battery cable on some vehicles may interfere with the functions of the on board computer systems and may require the computer to undergo a relearning process, once the negative battery cable is reconnected.

Engine

Removal and Installation

EXCEPT VAN

1. Relieve the fuel pressure if the vehicle is equipped with fuel injection. Disconnect the negative battery cable from the battery and from the engine.

2. Matchmark and remove the hood. Remove the oil dipstick.

3. Raise the vehicle and support safely. Remove the engine under cover. Drain the engine oil and coolant.

4. Remove the starter. Remove the lower radiator hose.

5. Remove the exhaust pipe from the exhaust manifold(s).

6. If the vehicle is equipped with a manual transmission, remove the transmission and all related parts.

7. If the vehicle is equipped with an automatic transmission, remove the inspection plate, matchmark the flex plate to the converter, remove the torque converter bolts and push the

13. Throttle position sensor connector
14. Ignition coil connector
15. Power transistor connector
16. EGR temperature sensor connector
17. Coolant temperature sending unit connector
18. Coolant temperature sensor connector
19. Thermo switch connector (automatic transmission only)
20. Oxygen sensor connector
21. Alternator connector
22. Oil pressure sending unit connector
23. Coolant temperature switch connector (automatic transmission only)
24. Ground cable
25. Emission control vacuum hose
26. Brake booster vacuum hose
27. Ground cable
28. I.S.C. connector
29. Motor position sensor connector
30. Engine controller wiring harness
31. Heat shield
32. Engine mount bolt

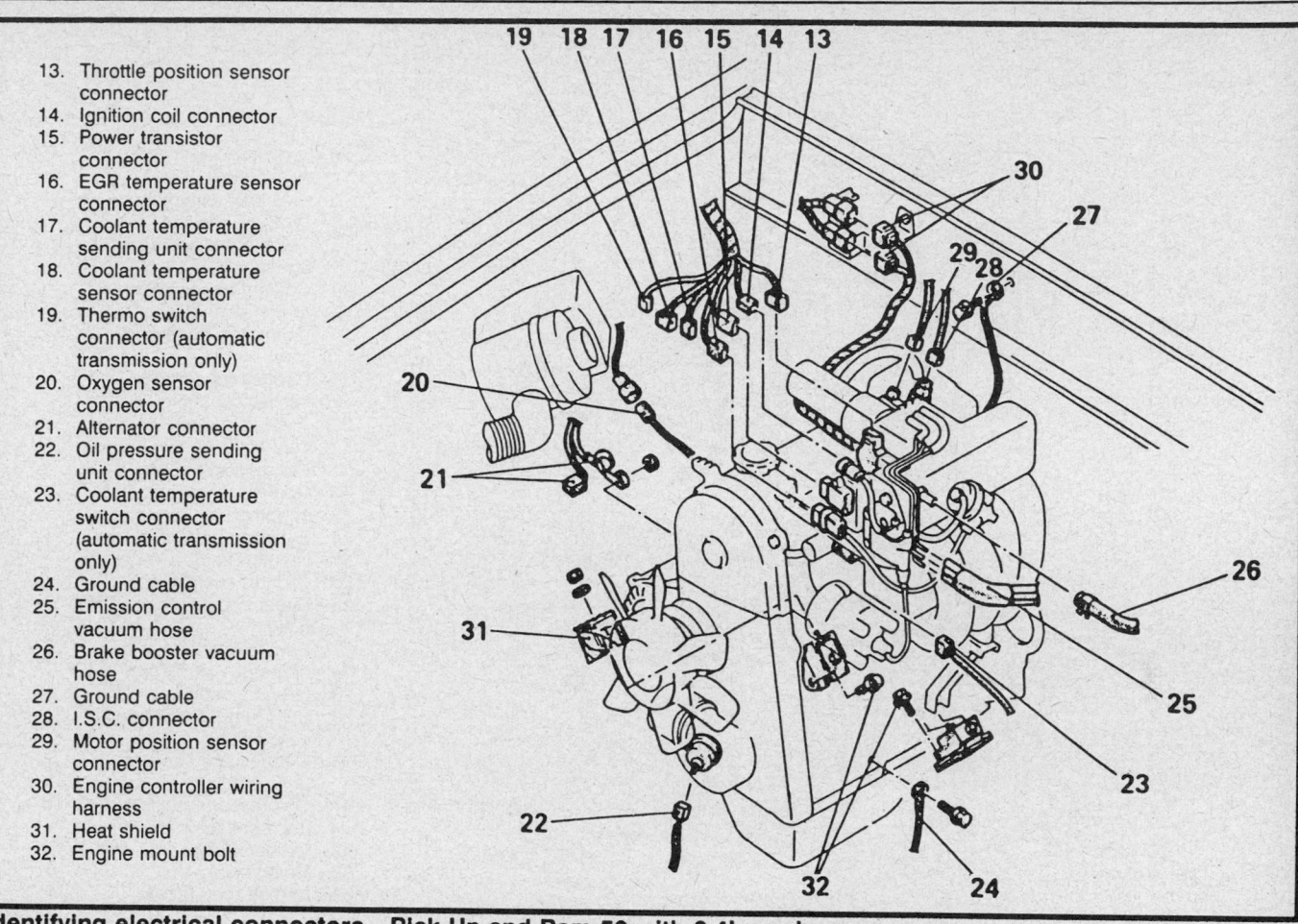

Identifying electrical connectors—Pick-Up and Ram 50 with 2.4L engine

torque converter backwards as far as it will go. Remove the lower bell housing bolts. Lower the vehicle.

8. If the vehicle is equipped with a carburetor, remove the air cleaner assembly. Remove all ductwork and air intake hoses. Disconnect all linkages and cables from the carburetor or throttle body.

9. Cover the fuel line connections with a clean shop rag and disconnect and plug the fuel lines.

10. Without releasing the refrigerant, unbolt the air conditioning compressor from the engine and position it to the side, if equipped.

11. Remove the radiator and shroud. Remove the fan and all related parts. Disconnect the heater hoses.

12. Without disconnecting the lines, unbolt the power steering pump from its brackets and position it to the side, if equipped.

13. Remove the alternator. Remove the ignition coil and power transistor assembly, if equipped.

14. Label and disconnect all remaining electrical connectors, vacuum hoses and check for any other items preventing engine removal.

15. Attach an engine removal device to the engine support eyes on the engine.

16. If the vehicle is equipped with an automatic transmission, support the transmission with a floor jack, or equivalent. Remove the remaining bell housing bolts.

17. Remove the engine mount nuts and remove the engine from the vehicle slowly and carefully.

To install:

18. Lower the engine into position and install the engine

mount nuts. Torque the nuts to 20 ft. lbs. (27 Nm). Install the upper bell housing bolts. Remove the engine removal device. Install the oil dipstick.

19. Raise the vehicle and support safely.

20. Install the remaining bell housing bolts.

21. If the vehicle is equipped with a manual transmission, install the transmission and all related parts.

22. If the vehicle is equipped with an automatic transmission, align the torque converter and flex plate and install the bolts. Install the inspection plate and starter.

23. Install the exhaust pipe to the exhaust manifold(s) using new gaskets. Install the lower radiator hose. Lower the vehicle.

24. Connect the heater hoses.

25. Make sure the negative battery cable is not connected to the battery. Connect the engine side of the negative cable to the engine. Install the alternator, power steering pump and all brackets.

26. Install the air conditioning compressor.

27. Connect all linkages and cables to the carburetor or throttle body.

28. Install the ignition coil and power transistor assembly, if equipped. Connect all electrical connectors, vacuum hoses, etc. that were disconnected during the engine removal procedure.

29. Install the fan and all related parts. Adjust all belt tensions, if required.

30. Install the radiator, shroud and upper hose.

31. Install the air cleaner assembly, ductwork and air intake hoses.

32. Fill the engine with the specified amount of oil and fill the radiator with coolant.

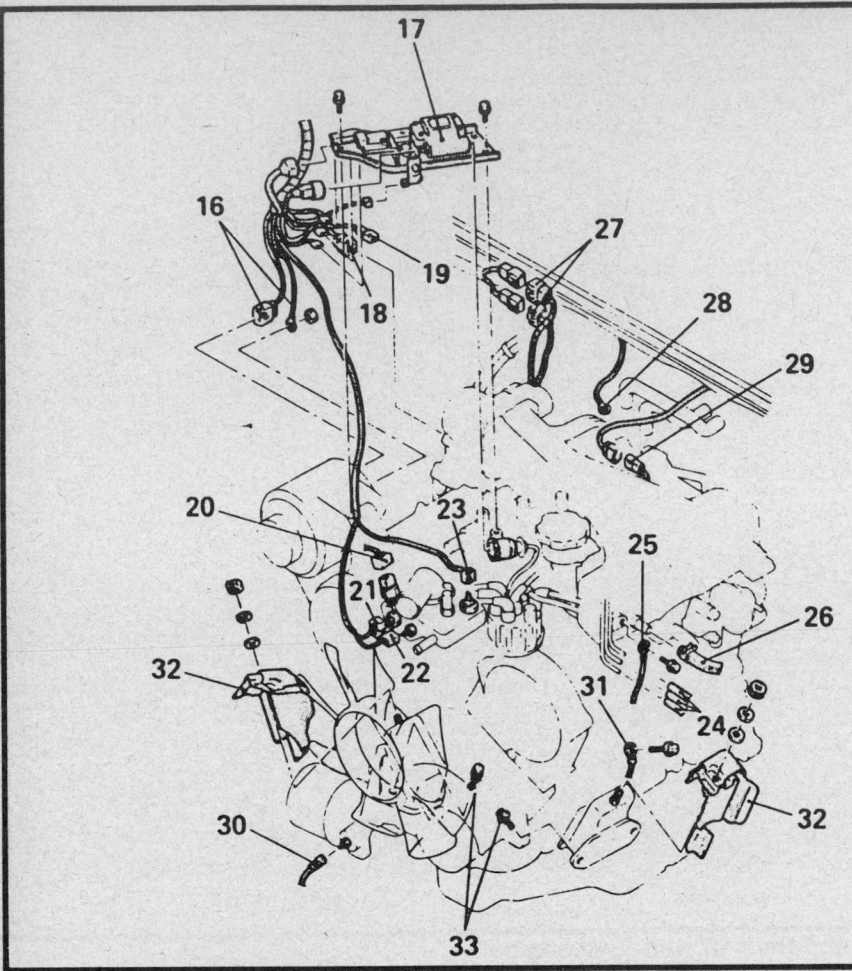

16. Alternator connector
17. Ignition coil and power transistor assembly
18. I.S.C. connector
19. Throttle position sensor connector
20. Coolant temperature switch connector (automatic transmission only)
21. Coolant temperature sensor connector
22. Thermo switch connector (automatic transmission only)
23. Coolant temperature sending unit connector
24. Emission control vacuum hose
25. Ground cable
26. Brake booster vacuum hose
27. Engine controller wiring harness
28. Ground cable
29. EGR temperature sensor connector
30. Oil pressure sending unit connector
31. Oil pressure sending unit connector
32. Ground cable
33. Heat shield
34. Engine mount bolt

Identifying electrical connectors—3.0L engine

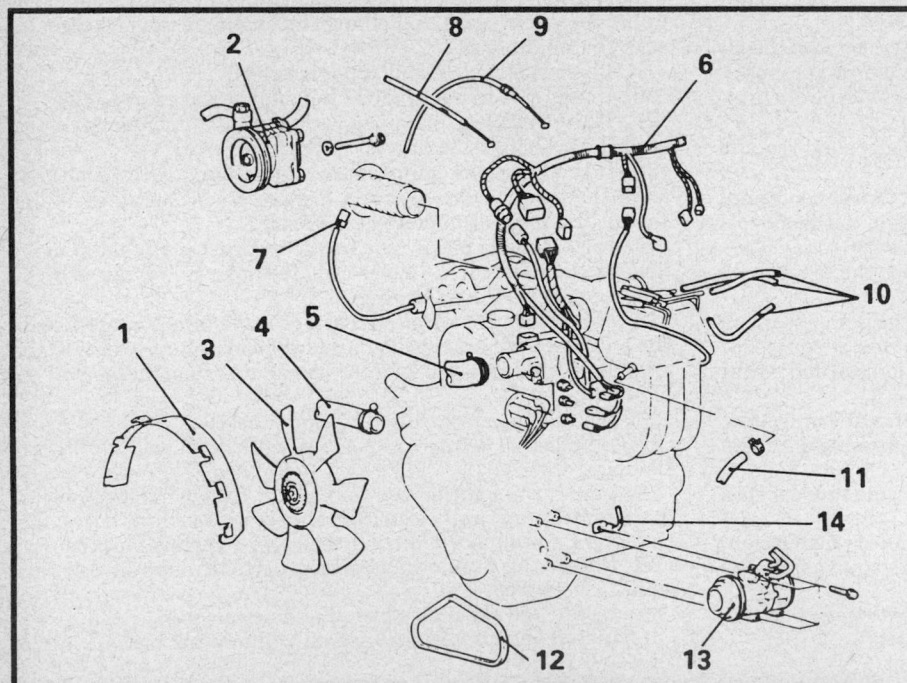

1. Fan shroud
2. Power steering pump
3. Fan
4. Lower radiator hose
5. Upper radiator hose
6. Engine controller wiring harness
7. Oxygen sensor connector
8. Accelerator cable
9. Kickdown cable
10. Vacuum hose cluster
11. Brake booster vacuum hose
12. Air conditioning compressor belt
13. Compressor
14. Ground cable

Identifying electrical connectors—Van

33. Connect the negative battery cable and connect the jumper wire from the fuel pump activation terminal, if equipped, to the positive battery post to inspect the system for leaks.

34. Check the automatic transmission fluid level, if equipped. Set all adjustments to specifications.

34. Install and align the hood.

VAN

─────────── CAUTION ───────────

The engine is removed from the bottom of the Van. Before attempting to remove the engine, obtain the special OTC support fixture, or equivalent, specifically designed for this operation. Do not attempt to remove the engine using a conventional transmission jack. Serious personal injury or damage to the engine or transmission may result if improper equipment is used because transmission jacks are not rated at the proper weight capacity for engine removal.

─────────────────────────────────

1. Remove the seat underframe.
2. Relieve the fuel pressure.
3. Disconnect the negative battery cable.
4. Drain the antifreeze. Remove the upper radiator hose.
5. Remove the radiator shroud, cooling fan and all drive belts.
6. Without disconnecting the lines, unbolt the power steering pump from its brackets and position it to the side.
7. Without releasing the refrigerant, unbolt the air conditioning compressor from the engine and position it to the side, if equipped.
8. Unbolt the battery ground cable from the block.
9. Remove the air intake hose from the throttle body.
10. Disconnect all linkages and cables from the throttle body.
11. Remove the alternator. Label and disconnect all remaining electrical connectors and vacuum hoses and check for any other items preventing engine removal that are only accessible from above the engine.
12. Raise the vehicle and support safely.
13. Matchmark the nut to the threads and remove both strut bars. Remove the driveshaft.
14. Remove the starter.

15. Disconnect the speedometer cable from the transmission. Disconnect the transmission harness connector.
16. Disconnect the transmission ground cable.
17. Remove the header pipe.
18. Disconnect the oil pressure sending unit wire.
19. Disconnect the transmission cooler lines.
20. Cover the fuel line connections with a clean shop rag and disconnect and plug the fuel lines.
21. Disconnect the transmission gear selector cable.
22. Disconnect and plug the heater hoses.
23. Support the engine safely and firmly with the proper adaptor and support fixture assembly.
24. Remove the rear engine mount installation bolt.
25. Remove the engine to crossmember installation bolts and nuts.
26. Carefully remove the engine and transmission assembly from the vehicle.

To install:
27. Raise the engine and transmission assembly into position and install to the vehicle. Install the engine to crossmember bolts and torque the nuts to 65 ft. lbs. (88 Nm).
28. Install the rear engine mount installation bolt and a new nut and torque the nut to 65 ft. lbs. (88 Nm).
29. Connect the heater hoses and secure the hose clamps.
30. Connect the transmission gear selector cable, speedometer cable, harness connector, ground cable and cooler lines.
31. Install the driveshaft and torque the nuts to 40 ft. lbs. (54 Nm).
32. Install the starter.
33. Connect the fuel lines.
34. Connect the oil pressure sending unit wire.
35. Install the header pipe using a new gasket.
36. Install the strut bars and tighten the nuts until the matchmarks line up. Lower the vehicle.
37. Install the alternator.
38. Connect all electrical connectors and vacuum hoses that are accessible from above the engine.
39. Connect all linkages and cables to the throttle body.

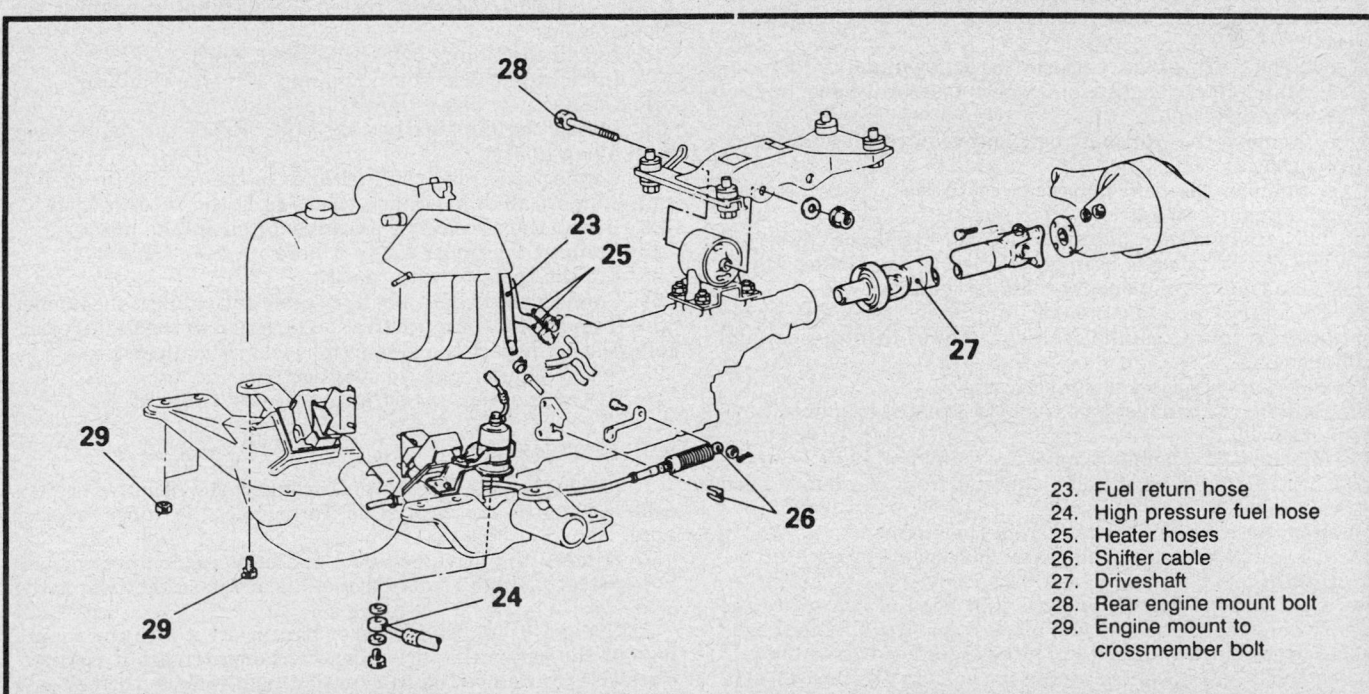

23. Fuel return hose
24. High pressure fuel hose
25. Heater hoses
26. Shifter cable
27. Driveshaft
28. Rear engine mount bolt
29. Engine mount to crossmember bolt

Engine mounting components – Van

40. Make sure the ground cable is not touching the battery post and connect the ground cable to the block.
41. Install the power steering pump and air conditioning compressor.
42. Install the drive belts, cooling fan and radiator shroud.
43. Install the air intake hose to the throttle body.
44. Fill the engine with the specified amount of oil and fill the radiator with coolant.
45. Connect the negative battery cable and connect the jumper wire from the fuel pump activation terminal to the positive battery post to inspect the system for leaks.
46. Check the automatic transmission fluid level. Set all adjustments to specifications.
47. Install the seat underframe.

Cylinder Head

Removal and Installation

2.0L, 2.4L AND 2.6L ENGINES

1. On the Van, remove the seat underframe. Rotate the engine around so the No. 1 cylinder is at TDC. If the engine is fuel injected, relieve the fuel pressure.
2. Drain the cooling system. Remove the upper radiator hose and disconnect the heater hoses.
3. Remove the dipstick bracket bolt.
4. Remove the air cleaner assembly or air intake hose.
5. Disconnect all linkages and cables from the throttle body. Disconnect and plug the fuel lines to the carburetor or fuel rail. Remove the valve cover.
6. On the 2.0L and 2.4L engines, perform the following:
   a. Without disconnecting the lines, unbolt the power steering pump from its brackets and position it to the side, if equipped.
   b. Remove the timing belt upper cover.
   c. Align the timing mark, if it is not already aligned. Secure the timing belt to the sprocket with a sturdy wire tie.
   d. Remove the camshaft bolt.
   e. Remove the sprocket from the camshaft and allow it to rest on the lower cover. If this is not possible, tie it to a fabricated device so the belt remains taut and the timing is not lost.
7. On the 2.6L engine, perform the following:
   a. Matchmark the distributor gear to its drive gear and remove the distributor.
   b. Remove the camshaft bolt and remove the distributor drive gear.
   c. Remove the camshaft gear (with the chain installed) from the camshaft and allow it to rest on the holder just below it. This will hold the valve timing. Do not crank the engine until the distributor has been reinstalled or the timing will be lost and timing components could be damaged.
8. Disconnect and label all vacuum lines, hoses and wiring connectors from the manifolds, carburetor or throttle body and cylinder head.
9. Raise the vehicle and support safely.
10. Remove the exhaust pipe from the exhaust manifold. Lower the vehicle.
11. On the 2.6L engine, remove the small end bolts from the head first. Remove head bolts, starting from the outside and working inward.
12. Remove the cylinder head from the engine.
13. Clean the cylinder head gasket mating surfaces.

To install:
14. On the 2.6L engine, apply a thin bead of sealant to the seam where the chain case and block meet. Install a new head gasket to the block and position the cylinder head assembly with all head bolts and washers. Torque the bolts in sequence to 30 ft. lbs. (41 Nm). Repeat the sequence increasing the torque to 50 ft. lbs. (68 Nm). Repeat the sequence a third time, increasing the

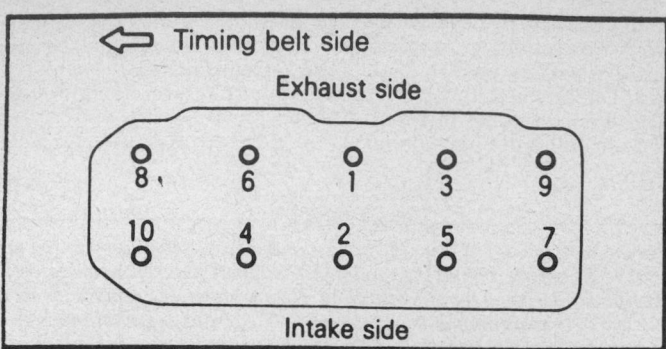

Cylinder head bolt torque sequence—2.0L and 2.4L engines

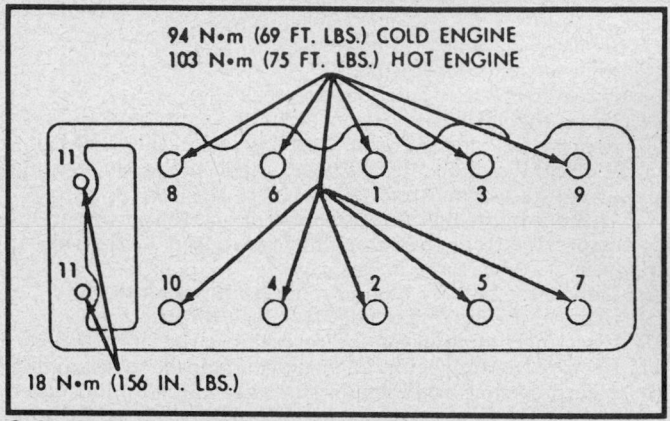

Cylinder head bolt torque sequence—2.6L engine

torque to a final value of 69 ft. lbs. (94 Nm). On the 2.6L engine, tighten the small end bolts to 13 ft. lbs. (18 Nm) last.
15. Install the camshaft gear or sprocket. On the 2.6L engine, install the distributor drive gear, bolt and washer. Torque the bolt to 40 ft. lbs. (54 Nm). Install the distributor, aligning the matchmarks.
16. Install the timing belt cover, if equipped.
17. Install the power steering pump, if it was removed.
18. Connect the heater hoses.
19. Install the dipstick bracket bolt. Install the valve cover with a new gasket.
20. Connect and plug the fuel lines to the carburetor or fuel rail. Connect all linkages and cables from the throttle body.
21. Install the air cleaner assembly or air intake hose.
22. Connect the upper radiator hose.
23. Fill the radiator with coolant.
24. Connect the negative battery cable and connect the jumper wire from the fuel pump activation terminal to the positive battery post to inspect the system for leaks, if equipped.
25. Set all adjustments to specifications.
26. Install the seat underframe, if it was removed.

3.0L ENGINE

1. Relieve the fuel pressure. Disconnect the negative battery cable. Drain the cooling system. Disconnect the upper radiator hose.
2. Remove the drive belts, air conditioning compressor and power steering pump from the mounts and position them to the side.
3. Using a ½ in. drive breaker bar, insert it into the square hole of the serpentine drive belt tensioner, rotate it counterclockwise (to reduce the belt tension) and remove the belt.
4. Remove the alternator.
5. Remove the crankshaft pulley and the torsional damper.

6. To remove the timing belt, perform the following procedures:

    a. Remove the covers. Rotate the crankshaft to position the No. 1 cylinder on the TDC of its compression stroke; the crankshaft sprocket timing mark should align with the oil pan timing indicator and the camshaft sprockets timing marks (triangles) should align with the rear timing belt covers timing marks.

    b. Mark the timing belt in the direction of rotation for reinstallation purposes.

    c. Loosen the timing belt tensioner and remove the timing belt.

NOTE: When removing the timing belt from the camshaft sprocket, make sure the belt does not slip off of the other camshaft sprocket. Support the belt so it can not slip off of the crankshaft sprocket and opposite side camshaft sprocket.

7. Remove the air intake hose.

8. Label and disconnect the spark plug wires and vacuum hoses.

9. Remove the valve cover.

10. If removing the left cylinder head, matchmark the distributor rotor to the distributor housing and the housing to distributor extension locations. Remove the distributor and the distributor extension. Also, remove the EGR pipe.

11. Remove the air intake plenum and intake manifold assembly.

12. Remove the exhaust manifold.

13. Remove the cylinder head bolts starting from the outside and working inward.

14. Remove the cylinder head from the engine.

15. Clean the gasket mounting surfaces.

To install:

16. Install the new cylinder head gaskets over the dowels on the engine block.

17. Install the cylinder heads on the engine and torque the cylinder head bolts in sequence using 3 even steps, to 70 ft. lbs. (95 Nm).

18. Install the intake and exhaust manifolds.

19. Install the EGR pipe with a new gasket, if it was removed.

20. Install the distributor and extension, if they were removed.

21. Install the timing belt and all related items. When installing the timing belt over the camshaft sprocket, use care not to allow the belt to slip off the opposite camshaft sprocket.

21. Make sure the timing belt is installed on the camshaft sprocket in the same position as when removed.

22. Install the alternator and power steering pump.

23. Install the air conditioning compressor and belts.

24. Connect the upper radiator hose.

25. Fill the radiator with coolant.

26. Connect the negative battery cable and connect the jumper wire from the fuel pump activation terminal to the positive battery post to inspect the system for leaks, if equipped.

27. Set all adjustments to specifications.

Jet Valve Lash

Adjustment

2.0L AND 2.6L ENGINES

1. Run the engine until at normal operating temperature. Disconnect the negative battery cable and remove the valve cover.

2. In sequence, check that the head bolts are torqued to 75 ft. lbs. (103 Nm).

3. Position the piston at TDC on the compression stroke.

4. Loosen the jet valve adjuster locknut.

5. Adjust the valve clearance by turning the adjusting screw a

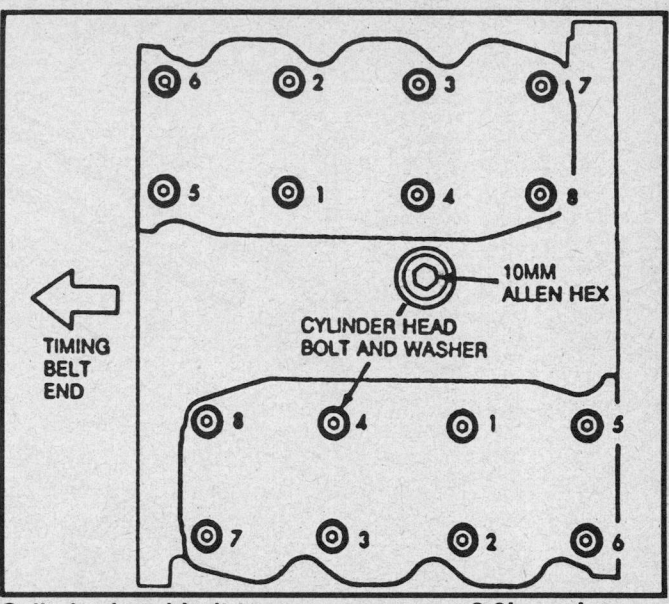

Cylinder head bolt torque sequence—3.0L engine

little at a time while measuring the clearance with a feeler gauge.

6. The jet valve clearance specification on a hot engine is 0.010 in. (0.25mm).

7. Tighten the locknut securely while holding the adjustment screw stationary. Recheck the clearance after the locknut has been tightened.

8. Repeat the procedure for the remaining jet valves.

9. Install the valve cover with a new gasket.

Rocker Arms and Shafts

Removal and Installation

2.0L, 2.4L AND 2.6L ENGINE

1. Disconnect the negative battery cable.

2. Remove the valve cover.

3. Have a helper hold the rear of the camshaft down during removal. Then install the rear cap loosely to hold the camshaft in position.

4. Loosen the camshaft cap bolts but do not remove them from the caps. Remove the caps, arms, shafts and bolts all as an assembly. Take the proper precautions so that the hydraulic lifters do not fall out of the rocker arms.

5. Disassemble the unit keeping all parts in the order of removal and repair as required.

NOTE: On the 2.0L and 2.4L engine, the rocker arms have identification marks on them. Arms with 1–3 on them should only be used on cylinders 1 or 3. Arms with 2–4 on them should only be used on cylinders 2 and 4. The arms on the 2.6L engine are not cylinder specific.

6. The installation is the reverse of the removal procedure. Make sure the arrows on the caps are all pointing to the front of the engine. Torque the cap bolts first to 85 inch lbs. (10 Nm), then to 175 inch lbs. (18 Nm) in the following order: No. 3 cap, No. 2 cap, No. 4 cap, Front cap, Rear cap.

3.0L ENGINE

1. Disconnect the negative battery cable. Remove the air cleaner assembly.

2. Remove the valve cover.

3. Using the auto lash adjuster retainer tools MD998443 or

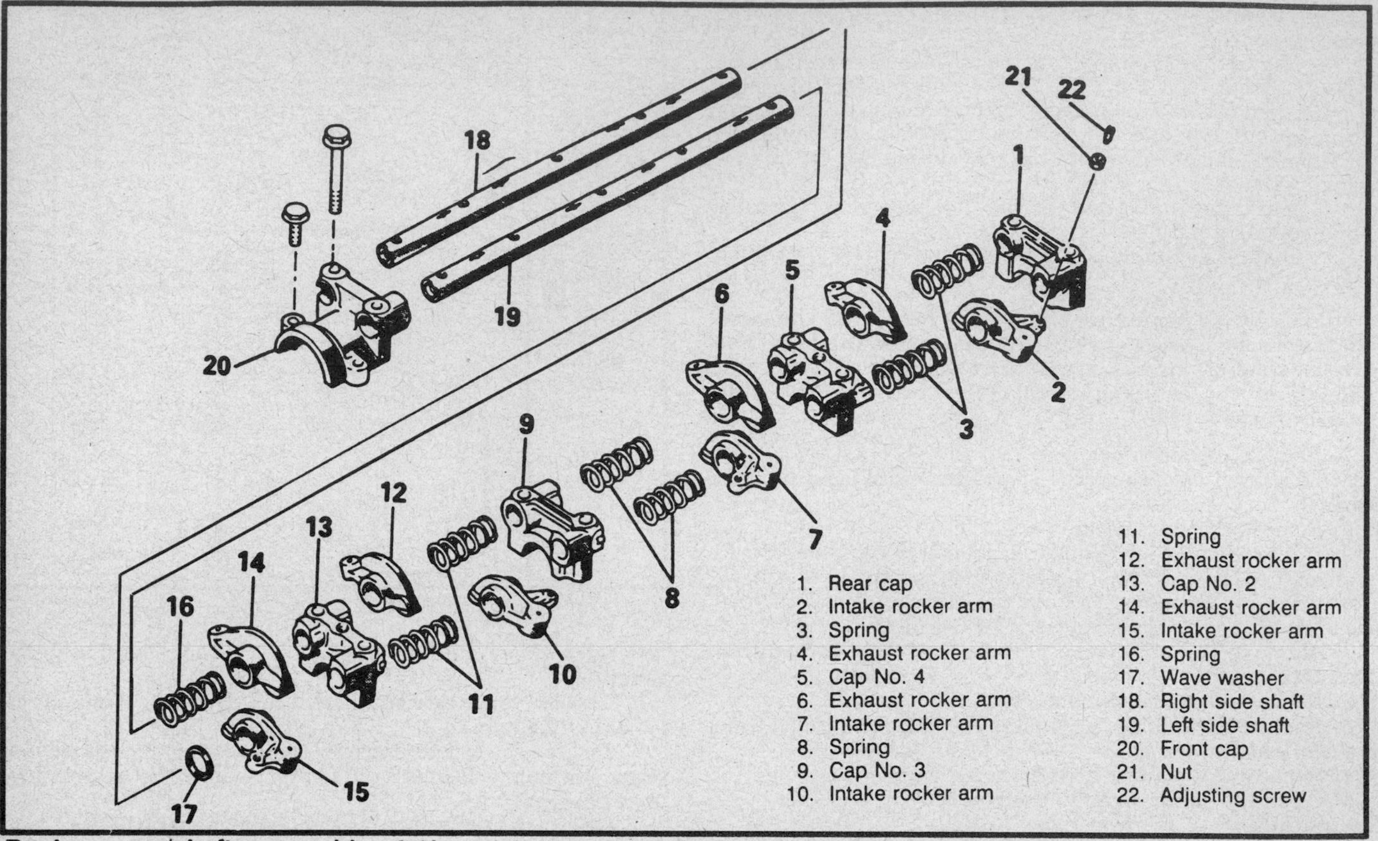

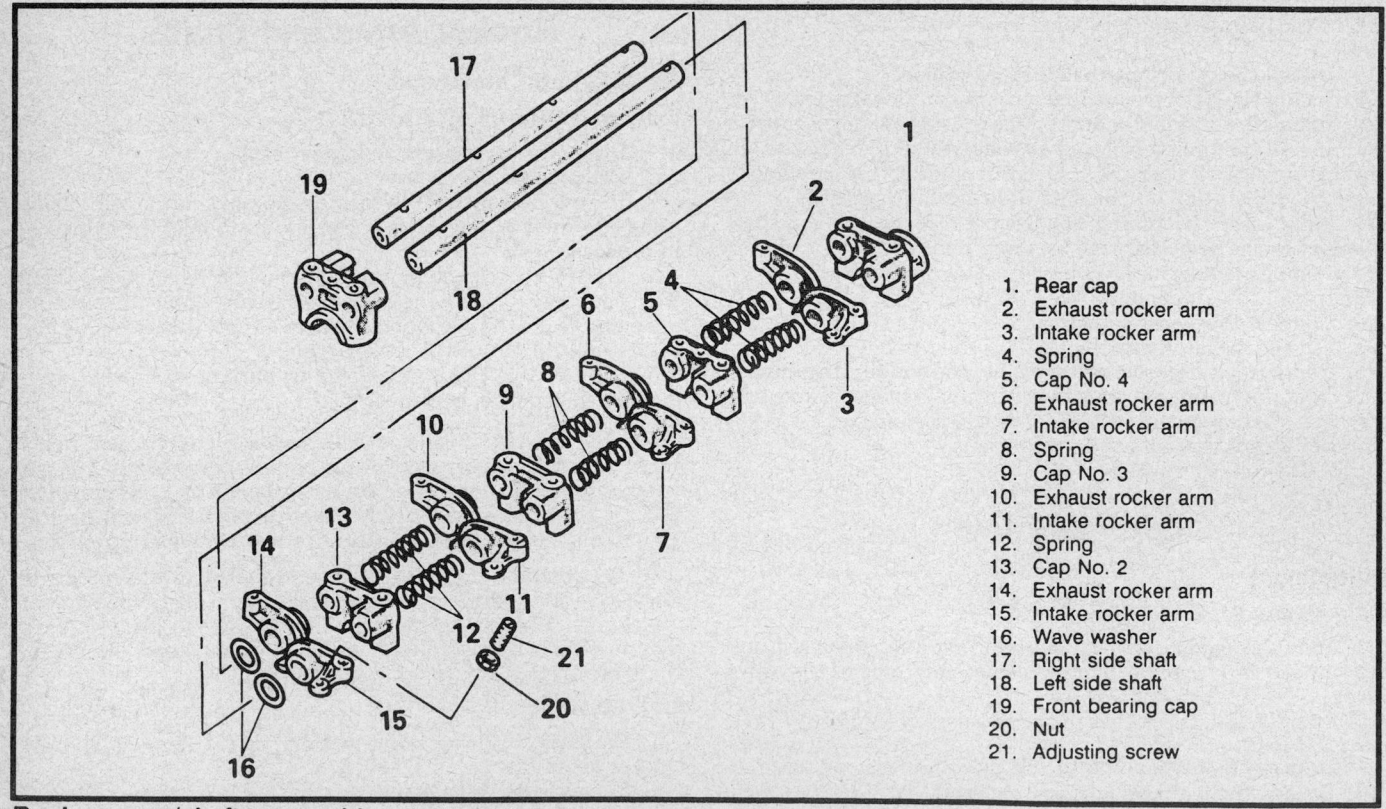

1. Rear cap
2. Intake rocker arm
3. Spring
4. Exhaust rocker arm
5. Cap No. 4
6. Exhaust rocker arm
7. Intake rocker arm
8. Spring
9. Cap No. 3
10. Intake rocker arm
11. Spring
12. Exhaust rocker arm
13. Cap No. 2
14. Exhaust rocker arm
15. Intake rocker arm
16. Spring
17. Wave washer
18. Right side shaft
19. Left side shaft
20. Front cap
21. Nut
22. Adjusting screw

Rocker arms/shafts assembly—2.0L and 2.4L engines. Note that 2.4L rocker arms are not equipped with jet valve extensions

1. Rear cap
2. Exhaust rocker arm
3. Intake rocker arm
4. Spring
5. Cap No. 4
6. Exhaust rocker arm
7. Intake rocker arm
8. Spring
9. Cap No. 3
10. Exhaust rocker arm
11. Intake rocker arm
12. Spring
13. Cap No. 2
14. Exhaust rocker arm
15. Intake rocker arm
16. Wave washer
17. Right side shaft
18. Left side shaft
19. Front bearing cap
20. Nut
21. Adjusting screw

Rocker arms/shafts assembly—2.6L engine

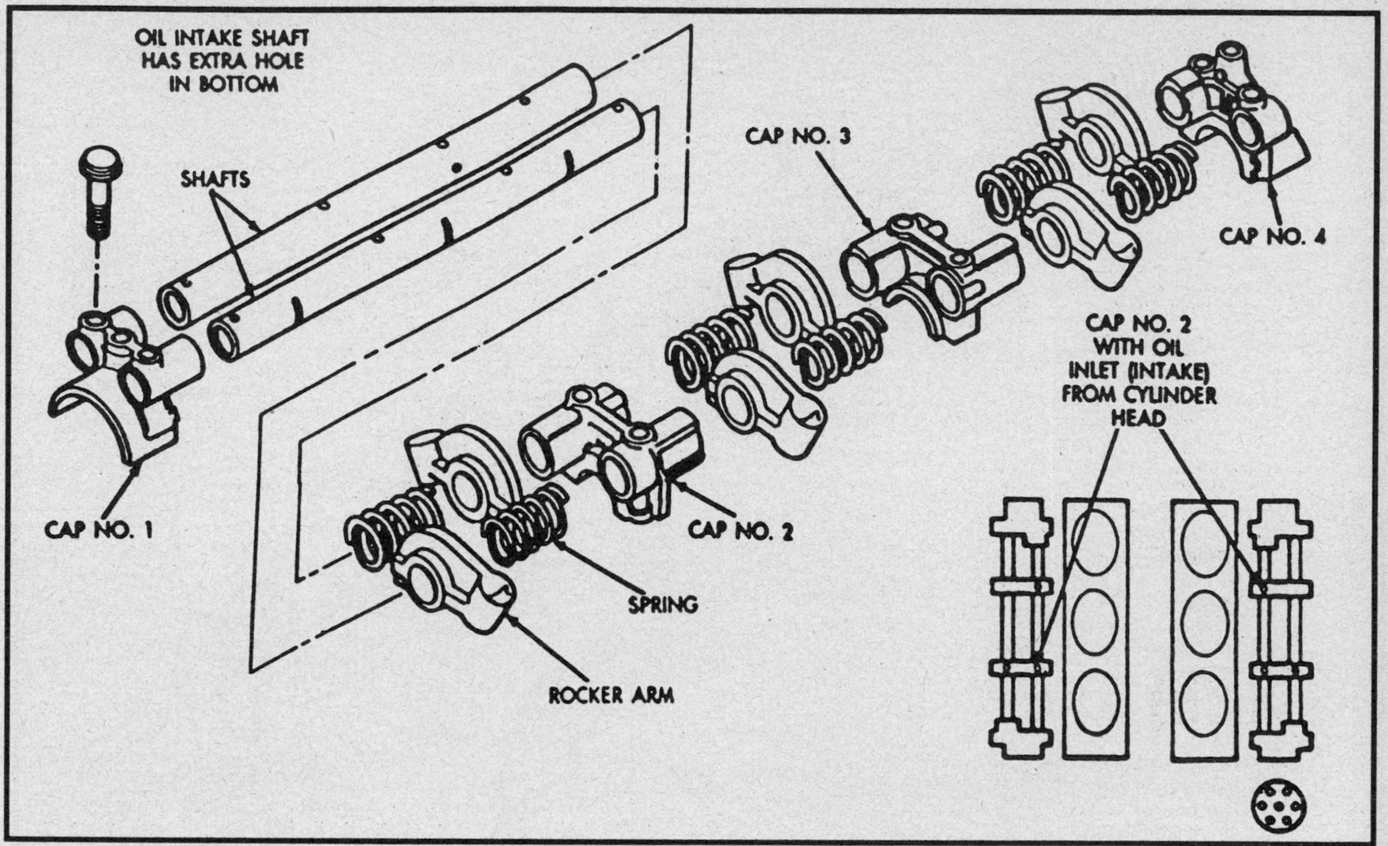

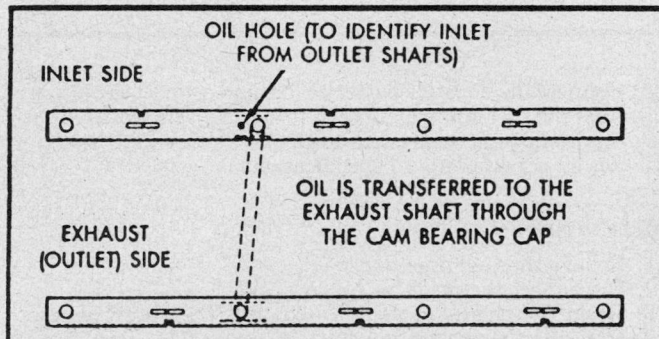

OIL INTAKE SHAFT HAS EXTRA HOLE IN BOTTOM

SHAFTS

CAP NO. 3

CAP NO. 4

CAP NO. 2 WITH OIL INLET (INTAKE) FROM CYLINDER HEAD

CAP NO. 1

CAP NO. 2

SPRING

ROCKER ARM

Rocker arms/shafts assembly—3.0L engine

OIL HOLE (TO IDENTIFY INLET FROM OUTLET SHAFTS)

INLET SIDE

OIL IS TRANSFERRED TO THE EXHAUST SHAFT THROUGH THE CAM BEARING CAP

EXHAUST (OUTLET) SIDE

Identifying rocker shafts—3.0L engine

equivalent, install them on the rocker arms to keep the lash adjusters from falling out.

4. On the right side cylinder head, remove the distributor extension.

5. Have a helper hold the rear end of the camshaft down. If the rear of the camshaft cannot be held down, the belt will dislodge and the valve timing will be lost. Loosen the camshaft cap bolts but do not remove them from the caps. Remove the caps, arms, shafts and bolts all as an assembly.

6. Disassemble the unit keeping all parts in order and repair as required.

7. The installation is the reverse of the removal procedure. Apply a drop of sealant to the rear edge of the rear cap. Torque the cap bolts first to 85 inch lbs. (19 Nm), then to 180 inch lbs. (19 Nm) in the following order: No. 3 cap, No. 2 cap, No. 1 cap, No. 4 cap.

Intake Manifold

Removal and Installation

2.0L AND 2.6L ENGINES

1. Disconnect the negative battery cable.
2. Remove the air cleaner assembly. Remove the dipstick bracket bolt from the thermostat housing.
3. Drain the cooling system. Disconnect the heater hoses from the manifold.
4. Disconnect the upper radiator hose from the thermostat housing.
5. Remove and plug the fuel lines to the carburetor.
6. Disconnect and label the vacuum lines, hoses and wiring connectors from the manifold and carburetor.
7. Disconnect all the linkages from the carburetor.
8. Remove the manifold nuts and bolts and remove the manifold from the engine.
9. The installation is the reverse of the removal procedure. Torque the intake manifold nuts and bolts to 12 ft. lbs. (17 Nm).

2.4L ENGINE

1. Relieve the fuel pressure.
2. Disconnect the negative battery cable.
3. Drain the engine coolant. Disconnect the upper radiator hose from the thermostat housing.
4. Remove the air intake hoses and the air intake pipe.
5. Disconnect all wires, hoses and linkages to the throttle body.
6. Remove the ignition coil.
7. Disconnect the brake booster hose and vacuum hose cluster from the air intake plenum.

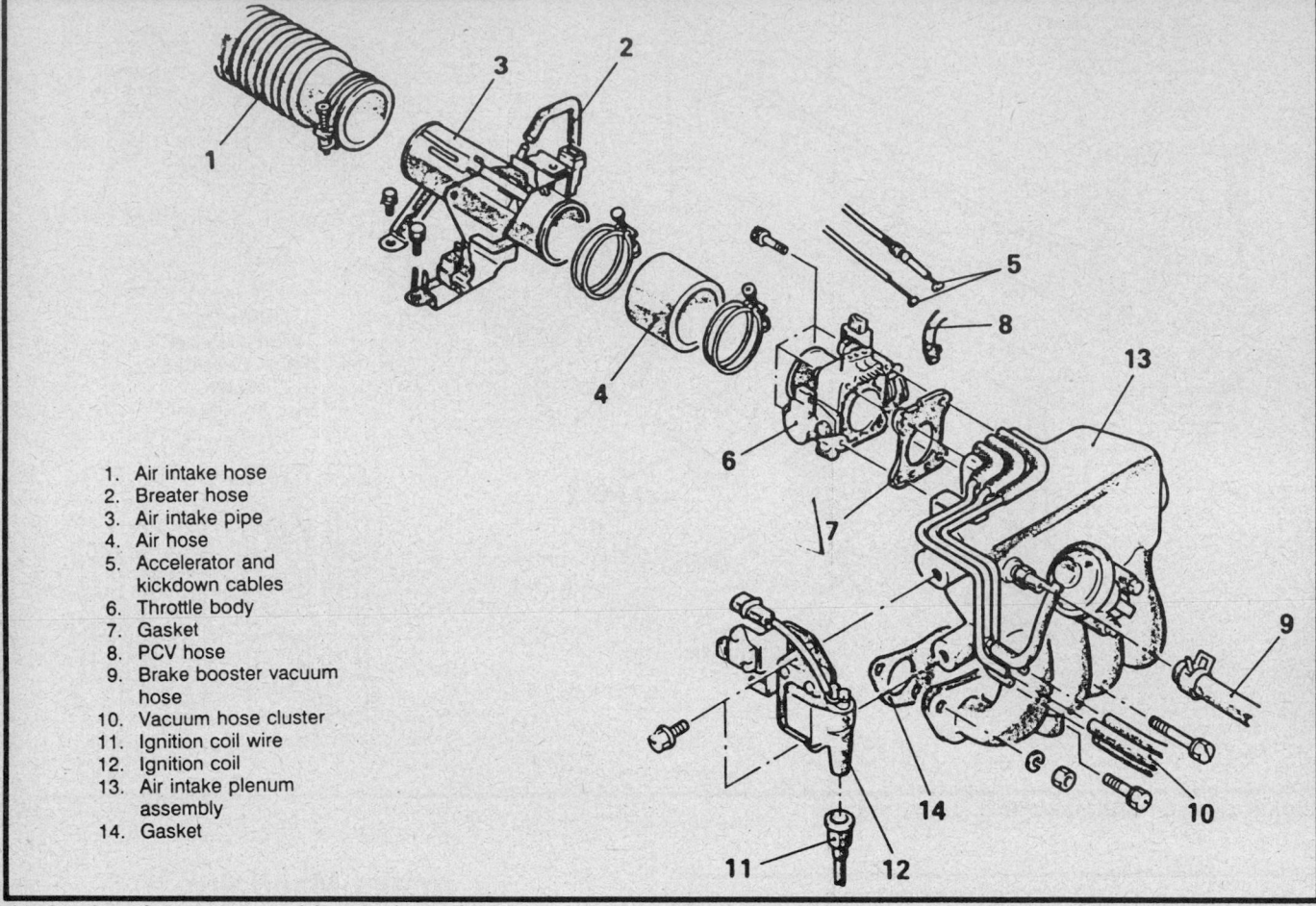

1. Air intake hose
2. Breater hose
3. Air intake pipe
4. Air hose
5. Accelerator and kickdown cables
6. Throttle body
7. Gasket
8. PCV hose
9. Brake booster vacuum hose
10. Vacuum hose cluster
11. Ignition coil wire
12. Ignition coil
13. Air intake plenum assembly
14. Gasket

Air intake plenum assembly—2.4L engine

8. Unbolt the air intake plenum from the intake manifold and remove the plenum from the engine.
9. Cover the fuel line with a clean shop rag and disconnect the fuel lines from the fuel rail. Keep the line covered or plugged.
10. Remove the fuel rail assembly with injectors.
11. Disconnect the heater hose from the manifold.
12. Disconnect the wires to the engine coolant switches.
13. Matchmark the rotor to the housing and remove the distributor.
14. Unbolt the intake manifold from the cylinder head and remove from the engine.
15. Thoroughly clean and dry the mating surfaces of the manifold and cylinder head.
To install:
16. Using a new gasket, install the intake manifold to the head. Starting from the middle and working outward, torque the retaining nuts to 12 ft. lbs. (16 Nm).
17. Connect the wires to the engine coolant switches. Install the distributor.
18. Install the fuel rail assembly to the manifold and connect the fuel line using a new O-ring.
19. Connect the heater hose to the manifold.
20. Install the air intake plenum with a new gasket. Torque the retaining bolts to 12 ft. lbs. (16 Nm).
21. Connect the vacuum hoses cluster, brake booster hose and all wires, hoses and linkages to the throttle body.
22. Install the ignition coil.
23. Install the air intake pipe and hoses.
24. Connect the upper radiator hose.
25. Fill the radiator with coolant.

26. Connect the negative battery cable and connect the jumper wire from the fuel pump activation terminal to the positive battery post to inspect the system for leaks.
27. Set all adjustments to specifications.

3.0L ENGINE

1. Relieve the fuel pressure.
2. Disconnect the negative battery cable.
3. Drain the engine coolant. Disconnect the upper radiator hose from the thermostat housing.
4. Remove the air intake hose from the throttle body.
5. Disconnect all wires, hoses and linkages to the throttle body.
6. Disconnect the EGR temperature sensor wire.
7. Remove the ignition coil.
8. Remove the engine oil filler neck bracket.
9. Unbolt the EGR tube from the air intake plenum.
10. Disconnect the PCV hose and vacuum hose cluster from the plenum.
11. Remove the plenum to engine brackets.
12. Unbolt the air intake plenum assembly from the intake manifold and remove.
13. Cover the fuel lines with a clean shop rag and disconnect the fuel lines from the fuel rail. Keep the lines covered or plugged.
14. Remove the fuel rail with injectors.
15. Disconnect the upper radiator hose from the thermostat housing and disconnect the bypass hose. Disconnect the wires to the coolant temperature switches around the housing.

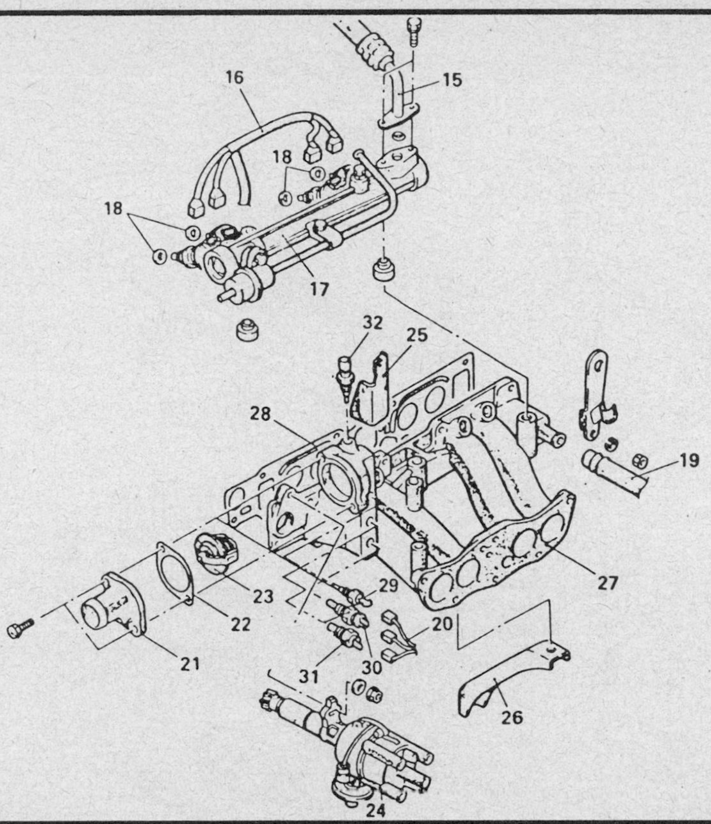

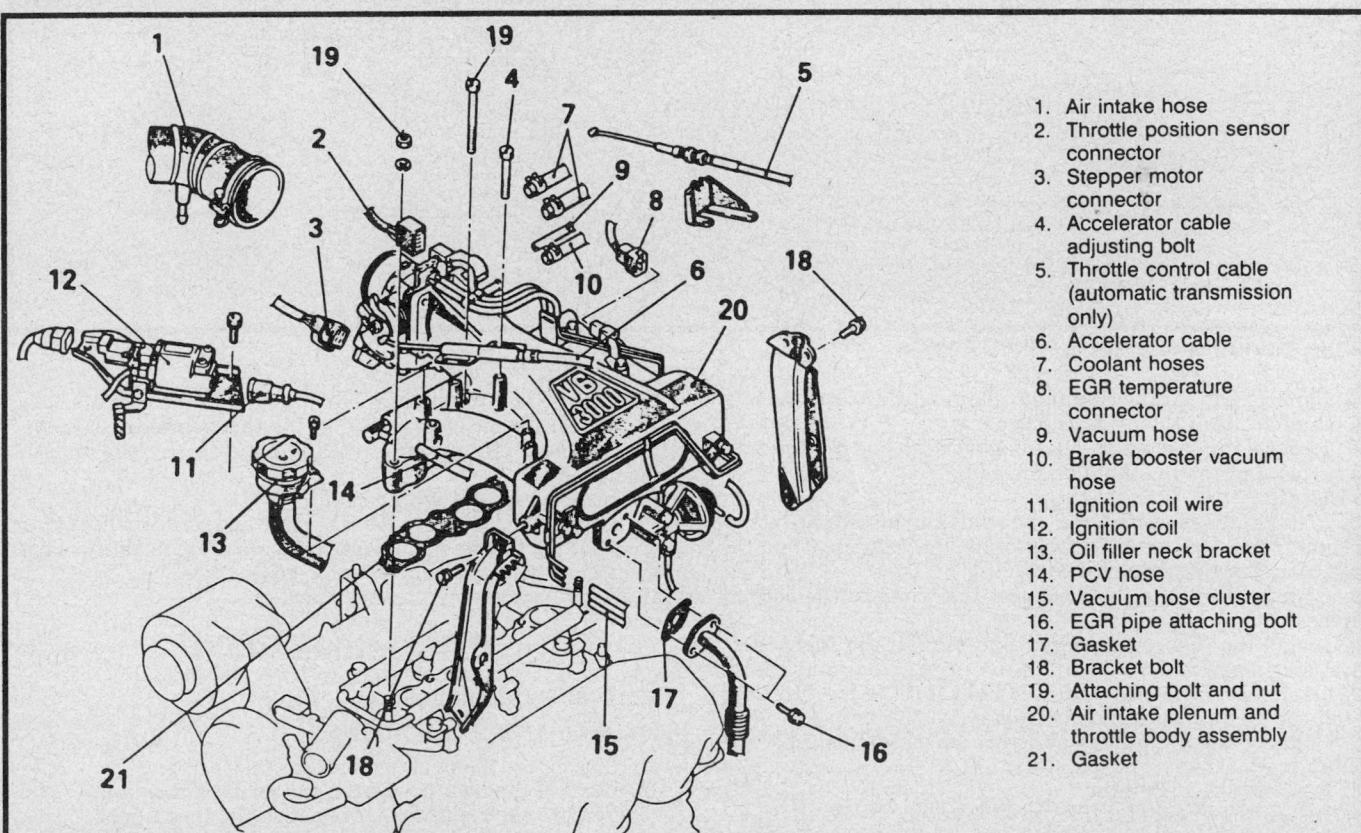

15. High pressure fuel hose
16. Injector harness connector
17. Fuel rail
18. Insulator
19. Heater hose
20. Wiring harness connector
21. Coolant outlet fitting
22. Gasket
23. Thermostat
24. Distributor
25. Plenum bracket
26. Intake manifold bracket
27. Intake manifold
28. Gasket
29. Thermo switch (automatic transmission only)
30. Coolant temperature sensor
31. Coolant temperature sending unit
32. Coolant temperature switch (automatic transmission only)

Intake manifold assembly—2.4L engine

1. Air intake hose
2. Throttle position sensor connector
3. Stepper motor connector
4. Accelerator cable adjusting bolt
5. Throttle control cable (automatic transmission only)
6. Accelerator cable
7. Coolant hoses
8. EGR temperature connector
9. Vacuum hose
10. Brake booster vacuum hose
11. Ignition coil wire
12. Ignition coil
13. Oil filler neck bracket
14. PCV hose
15. Vacuum hose cluster
16. EGR pipe attaching bolt
17. Gasket
18. Bracket bolt
19. Attaching bolt and nut
20. Air intake plenum and throttle body assembly
21. Gasket

Air Intake plenum assembly—3.0L engine

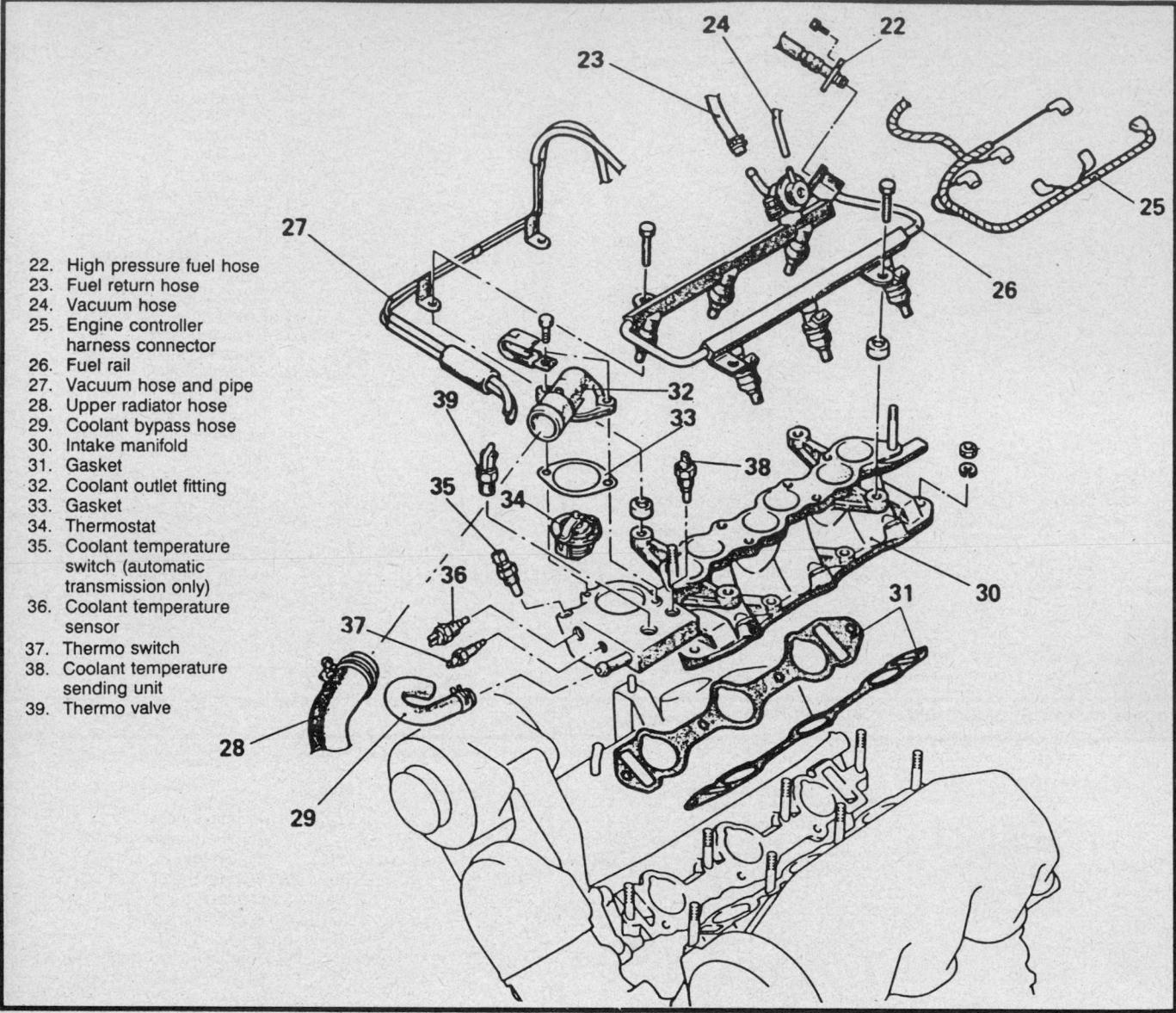

22. High pressure fuel hose
23. Fuel return hose
24. Vacuum hose
25. Engine controller harness connector
26. Fuel rail
27. Vacuum hose and pipe
28. Upper radiator hose
29. Coolant bypass hose
30. Intake manifold
31. Gasket
32. Coolant outlet fitting
33. Gasket
34. Thermostat
35. Coolant temperature switch (automatic transmission only)
36. Coolant temperature sensor
37. Thermo switch
38. Coolant temperature sending unit
39. Thermo valve

Intake manifold assembly—3.0L engine

16. Remove the intake manifold retaining nuts and remove the manifold from the cylinder heads.

17. Remove the gaskets and thoroughly clean and dry the mating surfaces of the manifold and heads.

To install:

18. Position the manifold over the studs and install the retaining nuts. Torque them to 12 ft. lbs. (16 Nm), starting from the center and working outward.

19. Connect the hoses and connect the wires to the coolant switches.

20. Install the fuel rail assembly and connect the fuel hoses.

21. Using a new gasket, install the air intake plenum to the intake manifold. Torque the nuts and bolts to 12 ft. lbs. (16 Nm). Install the plenum to engine brackets.

22. Connect the PCV hose and vacuum hose cluster to the plenum.

23. Connect the EGR tube.

24. Install the engine oil filler neck bracket.

25. Install the ignition coil assembly.

26. Connect the EGR temperature sensor wire.

27. Connect all wires, hoses and linkages to the throttle body.

28. Install the air intake hose to the throttle body.

29. Connect the upper radiator hose to the thermostat housing.

30. Fill the radiator with coolant.

31. Connect the negative battery cable and connect the jumper wire from the fuel pump activation terminal to the positive battery post to inspect the system for leaks.

32. Set all adjustments to specifications.

Exhaust Manifold

Removal and Installation

2.0L, 2.4L AND 2.6L ENGINES

1. Disconnect the negative battery cable.
2. Remove the heat cowl from the exhaust manifold.
3. Remove the aspirator valve assembly, if equipped.
4. Raise the vehicle and support safely. Disconnect the exhaust pipe fromt he manifold. Lower the vehicle

5. Disconnect the oxygen sensor connector or ground cable, if equipped.

6. Remove the manifold mounting nuts and remove the manifold from the engine.

7. Remove the gasket and replace it with a new one.

8. The installation is the reverse of the removal procedure. Torque the manifold mounting nuts to 13 ft. lbs. (18 Nm) starting from the middle and working outward.

9. Start the engine and check for exhaust leaks.

3.0L ENGINE

1. Disconnect the negative battery cable. Raise and safely support the vehicle.

2. Disconnect the exhaust pipe from the exhaust manifolds.

3. Remove the heat shield.

4. If removing the left side manifold, remove the EGR tube.

5. If removing the right side manifold, remove the alternator bracket.

6. Remove the manifold attaching nuts and remove the manifold.

7. Remove the gasket and replace it with a new one.

8. The installation is the reverse of the removal procedure. When installing, the numbers 1–3–5 on the gaskets are used with the right side cylinders and 2–4–6 are on the gasket for the left side cylinders. Torque the manifold nuts to 14 ft. lbs. (19 Nm).

9. Start the engine and check for exhaust leaks.

Timing Chain Case Cover

Removal and Installation

2.6L ENGINE

1. Disconnect the negative battery cable.

2. Drain the cooling system.

3. Remove the shroud, fan, belts and radiator as required.

4. Remove the power steering pump, alternator, air conditioning compressor and accompanying brackets, as required.

5. Remove the valve cover. Matchmark the distributor gear to its drive gear and remove the distributor.

6. Remove the 2 small front bolts from the cylinder head which screw into and seal the top of the timing cover.

7. Remove the crankshaft bolt and pull off the crankshaft pulley.

8. Raise the vehicle and support safely. Remove the engine undercover. Remove the bolts that attach the front of the oil pan to the chain case cover.

NOTE: As soon as the timing cover gasket seal is broken, antifreeze will start pouring out from the water jacket extension in the cover. Place a large drainpan under the work area or the floor will get soaked with antifreeze.

9. Remove the remaining timing cover retaining bolts. Position a drainpan under the timing cover and separate the cover from the block. When the antifreeze has stopped draining, remove the cover. If the oil pan gasket was damaged during this operation, drain the oil and remove the oil pan.

To install:

10. Thoroughly clean and dry all sealing surfaces.

11. Replace the adjuster window gasket.

12. Carefully pry the crankshaft oil seal out of the cover without scratching the seal bore. Install a new seal using a suitable seal driver or installer.

13. Apply a thin coat of silicone sealer to the top of the timing chain cover to seal the head gasket extension. Install the cover to the block using new gaskets.

14. Install all cover bolts with the appropriate brackets in place. Torque the bolts to 10 ft. lbs. (13 Nm).

15. Install the crankshaft pulley. Thoroughly clean and dry

the crankshaft pulley bolt and apply a very thin bead of Loctite® to the threads. Torque the bolt to 87 ft. lbs. (118 Nm).

16. Install the oil pan with a new gasket, if it was removed.

17. Thoroughly clean and dry the 2 end bolts that attach the chain cover to the head. Install them and torque to 13 ft. lbs. (18 Nm).

18. Install the distributor aligning the matchmarks.

19. Install the valve cover with a new gasket.

20. Install the power steering pump, alternator, air conditioning compressor and any remaining brackets. Install the fan and adjust the belt tensions.

21. Install the radiator and shroud, if they were removed.

22. Refill the cooling system and fill the engine with oil.

23. Connect the negative battery cable, road test the vehicle and check for leaks.

Front Cover Oil Seal

Replacement

2.6L ENGINE

1. Disconnect the negative battery cable.

2. Remove the accessory drive belts.

3. Remove the crankshaft pulley.

4. Carefully pry the crankshaft oil seal out of the cover without scratching the seal bore.

5. Install a new seal using a suitable seal driver or installer.

6. Thoroughly clean and dry the crankshaft pulley bolt and apply a very thin bead of Loctite® to the threads. Torque the bolt to 87 ft. lbs. (118 Nm).

7. The installation is the reverse of the removal procedure.

Timing Chain and Gears

Adjustment

2.6L ENGINE

The timing chain is not manually adjustable because spring tension along with oil pressure push the tensioner out to automatically take up slack on the chain. However, if there is noise coming from the chain case, it is possible that the silent chain is loose. To adjust the silent chain:

1. Disconnect the negative battery cable.

2. Remove the adjuster window on the chain case cover located below and to the left of the water pump.

3. Simultaneously apply pressure down on the adjuster protrusion and loosen the adjuster bolt.

4. Hold steady pressure down on the protrusion and tighten the bolt.

5. Reseal the window with silicone sealer or a new gasket and install.

Removal and Installation

2.6L ENGINE

1. If possible, position the engine so that the No. 1 piston is at TDC on the compression stroke. Disconnect the negative battery cable. Drain the coolant.

2. Remove the timing chain case cover.

3. Remove the 3 silent shaft chain guides. Label each bolt as it is removed. The bolts are of different lengths and styles and must be re-installed in the correct locations.

4. Remove the flange bolts from the right silent shaft and oil pump gears and carefully remove the chain with all 3 gears. Watch for the aligning keys on the oil pump shaft and right silent shaft. If the chain is removed individually, remove the gears afterward.

NOTE: The 2 gears are identical, but the oil pump drive sprocket is installed with the concave side toward the engine while the right silent shaft sprocket has the concave side out.

5. The timing chain tensioner maintains constant spring pressure on the chain. To prevent it from popping out of the oil pump it must be fastened in place. Run a piece of wire around the plunger and the left side of the oil pump. Remove the remaining chain guides.

6. Remove the camshaft gear bolt and pry the distributor drive gear from the cam gear. Remove the cam gear from the camshaft and allow it to sit on the gear holder below it. Rotate the camshaft so the spring pin is at the 12 o'clock position.

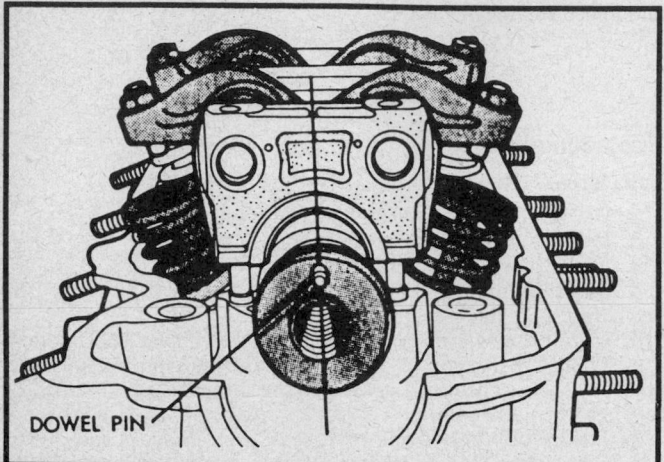

DOWEL PIN

Camshaft position for chain installation—2.6L engine

7. Unbolt the holder and remove the chain with both gears. Remove the tensioner and spring from the oil pump.

8. Inspect all gears, guides and the chains themselves for wear and replace as required.

To install:

9. Assemble the new timing chain with the gears. Both the crankshaft sprocket and the camshaft sprocket have a small dot on their faces. Assemble the chain and sprockets so that each dot aligns with the plated links on the chain. Both sets of marks and links must align.

10. Turn the crankshaft as required so that the installed positions of the respective gears are correct.

11. Install the new tensioner and spring in the bore of the oil pump and hold it down with a piece of wire. Make sure the tensioner is equipped with the black washer on the shaft. If the washer is missing, the chain will slap.

12. Install the crankshaft gear to the crankshaft and install the cam gear holder while holding the gear up in place. Allow the cam gear to rest on the holder.

13. Lift the cam gear into place against the camshaft, install the distributor drive gear and install the bolt. Make certain the sprocket engages the guide pin correctly. Tighten the bolt to 40 ft. lbs. (55 Nm).

14. Remove the wire holding the tensioner plunger and allow it to tension the chain. Install the right side guide.

15. Assemble the silent shaft gear, the oil pump gear and the silent shaft chain. Again, each sprocket is marked with a dot which must be aligned with the plated links on the chain. The sprocket for the silent shaft mounts with the concave side facing out (away from the engine block) and the sprocket for the oil pump mounts with the concave side facing the engine block.

16. Install the silent chain with gears onto the shafts. Turn the oil pump shaft and right silent shaft as required to keep the marks aligned.

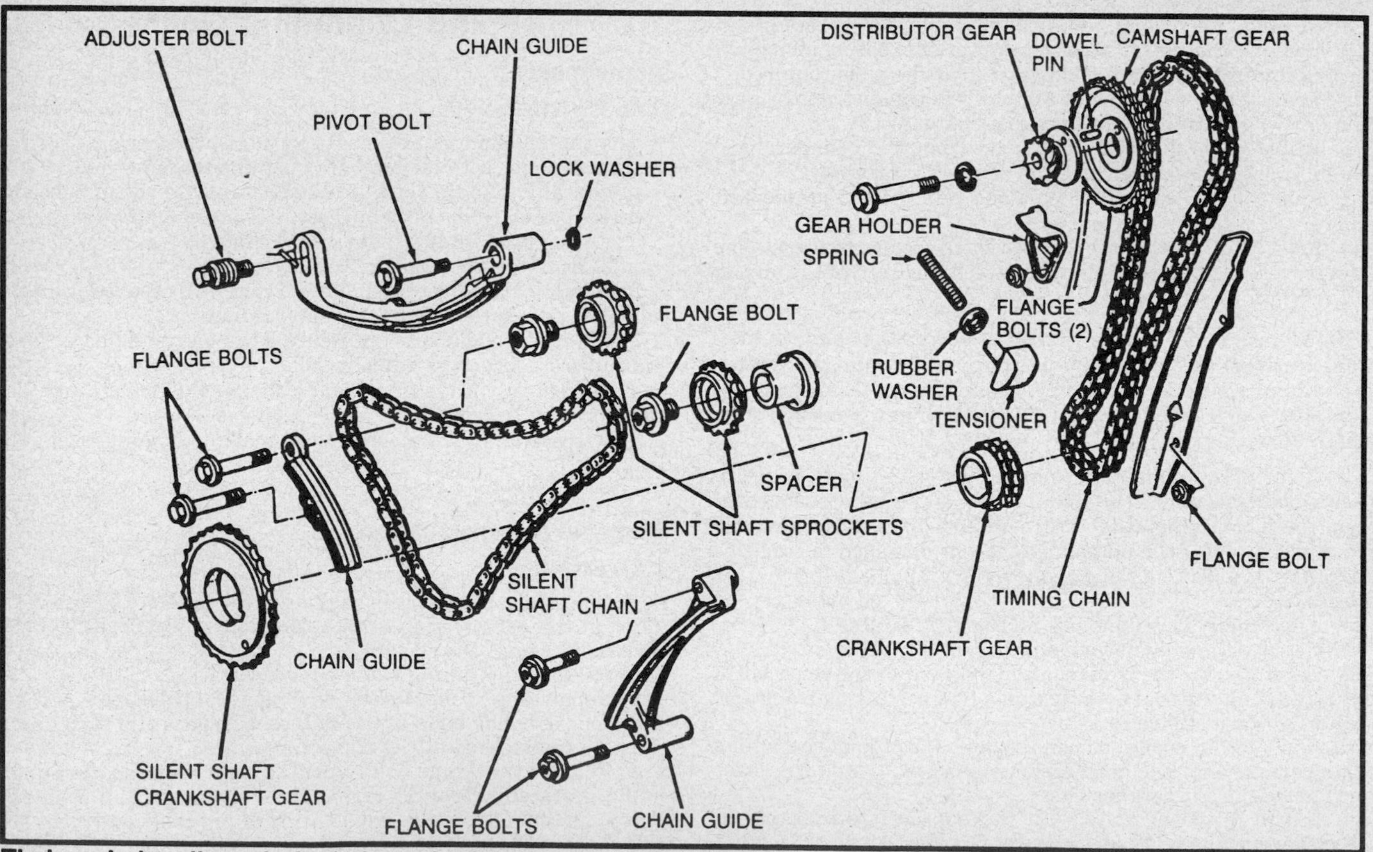

Timing chain, silent shaft chain and related parts—2.6L engine

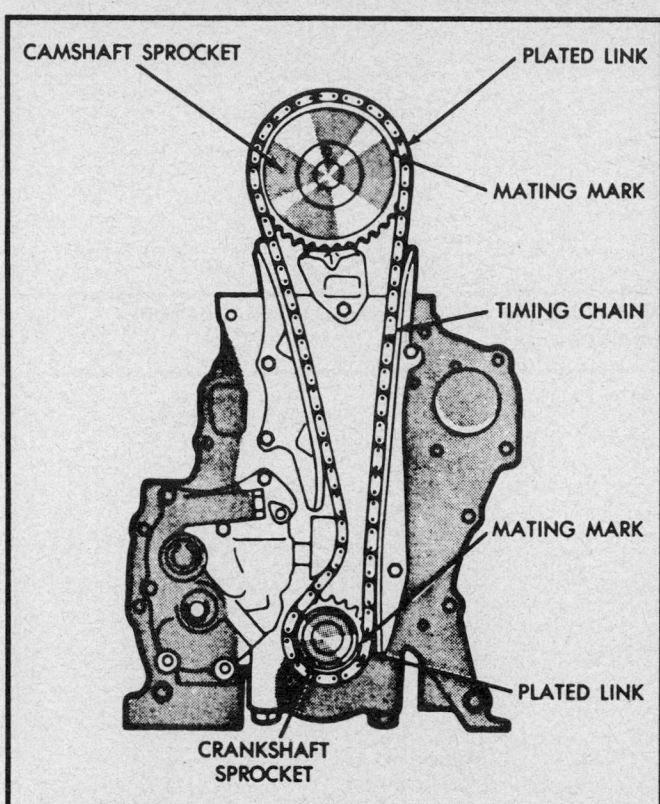

Timing chain installation—2.6L engine

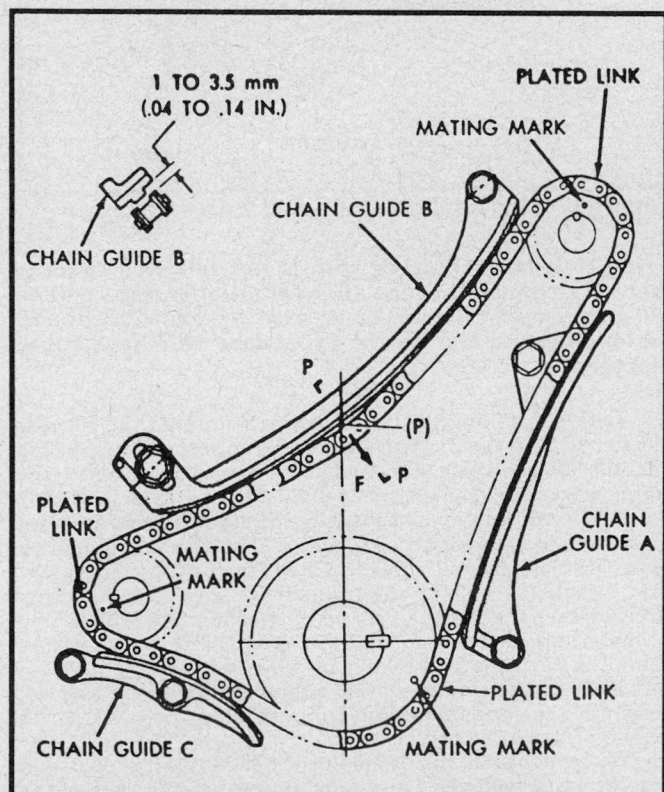

Silent shaft chain installation—2.6L engine

17. Install the chain guides. Make sure the lock washer is installed between the tensioner guide pivot bolt and the timing chain guide under it. Torque all 10mm flanged bolts to 8 ft. lbs. (11 Nm). Adjust the upper guide so that when the chain is pulled downward at the center, the clearance between the chain and the guide is 0.008–0.031 in. (0.20–0.80mm). Torque the tensioner guide locking bolt to 14 ft. lbs. (19 Nm).

18. Install the gear retaining bolts to the oil pump and right silent shaft. Torque the bolts to 25 ft. lbs. (34 Nm).

19. Install the timing chain case cover and all related parts.

20. Refill the cooling system and fill the engine with oil.

21. Connect the negative battery cable, road test the vehicle and check for leaks.

Timing Belt Front Cover

Removal and Installation

2.0L AND 2.4L ENGINES

1. Disconnect the negative battery cable. Remove the spark plug wires from the tree on the upper cover.

2. Drain the cooling system. Remove the shroud, fan, belts and radiator as required.

3. Remove the power steering pump, alternator, air conditioning compressor, tension pulley and accompanying brackets, as required.

4. Remove the upper front timing belt cover.

5. Remove the water pump pulley and the crankshaft pulley(s).

6. Remove the lower timing belt cover to engine screws and remove the cover.

7. The installation is the reverse of the removal procedure. Make sure the packing is positioned in the inner grooves of the covers properly when installing.

3.0L ENGINE

1. Disconnect the negative battery cable.

2. Drain the coolant.

3. Remove the upper radiator shroud.

4. Remove the fan, belts and fan pulley.

5. Without disconnecting the lines, remove the power steering pump from its bracket and position it to the side. Remove the pump brackets.

6. Remove the belt tensioner pulley bracket.

7. Without releasing the refrigerant remove the air conditioning compressor from its bracket and position it to the side. Remove the bracket.

8. Remove the cooling fan bracket.

9. Remove the crankshaft pulley bolt and the pulley from the crankshaft.

10. Remove the timing belt cover bolts and the upper and lower covers from the engine.

11. The installation is the reverse of the removal procedure. Make sure the packing is positioned in the inner grooves of the covers properly when installing. Torque the crankshaft pulley bolt to 110 ft. lbs. (150 Nm).

Timing Belt and Tensioner

Adjustment

2.0L AND 2.4L ENGINES

1. Disconnect the negative battery cable.

2. Remove the timing belt cover.

3. Adjust the silent shaft (inner) belt first. Loosen the pulley center bolt so the pulley may be moved.

4. Move the pulley up by hand so the center span of the long side of the belt deflects about ¼ inch.

5. Hold the pulley tightly so that the pulley itself does not ro-

tate when the bolt is tightened. Tighten the bolt to 15 ft. lbs. (20 Nm). If the pulley has moved, the belt will be too tight.

6. Check the timing (outer) belt tension.

7. To adjust the timing (outer) belt, first loosen the tensioner pulley bolts.

8. Allow the spring to take up the slack. Check that the the deflection of the longest span (between the camshaft and oil pump sprockets) is about ½ inch. Do not manually overtighten the belt or it will howl.

9. Tighten the lower pulley bolts first to 35 ft. lbs. (47 Nm), then the upper bolt to the same value.

10. Install the covers and all related parts.

3.0L ENGINE

1. Loosen the bolt that holds the timing belt tensioner in place.

2. Allow the spring to pull the tensioner in automatically.

3. Tighten the tensioner locking bolt.

Removal and Installation

2.0L AND 2.4L ENGINES

1. If possible, crank the engine around so that the No. 1 piston is at TDC.

2. Disconnect the negative battery cable.

3. Remove the timing belt covers. If the belt(s) are to be re-used, mark the direction of rotation on the belt.

4. Remove the timing (outer) belt tensioner and remove the belt. Unbolt the tensioner from the block and remove.

5. Remove the outer crankshaft sprocket and flange.

6. Remove the silent shaft (inner) belt tensioner and remove the belt. Unbolt the tensioner from the block and remove.

To install:

7. Align the timing mark of the silent shaft belt sprockets on the crankshaft and silent shaft with the marks on the front case. Wrap the silent shaft belt around the sprockets so that there is not slack in the upper span of the belt and the timing marks are still in line.

8. Install the tensioner initially so that the actual center of the pulley is above and to the left of the installation bolt.

9. Move the pulley up by hand so the center span of the long side of the belt deflects about ¼ inch.

10. Hold the pulley tightly so that the pulley itself does not rotate when the bolt is tightened. Tighten the bolt to 15 ft. lbs. (20 Nm). If the pulley has moved, the belt will be too tight.

11. Install the timing belt tensioner fully toward the water pump and temporarily tighten the bolts. Place the upper end of the spring against the water pump body. Align the timing marks of the cam, crankshaft and oil pump sprockets with their corresponding marks on the front case or head.

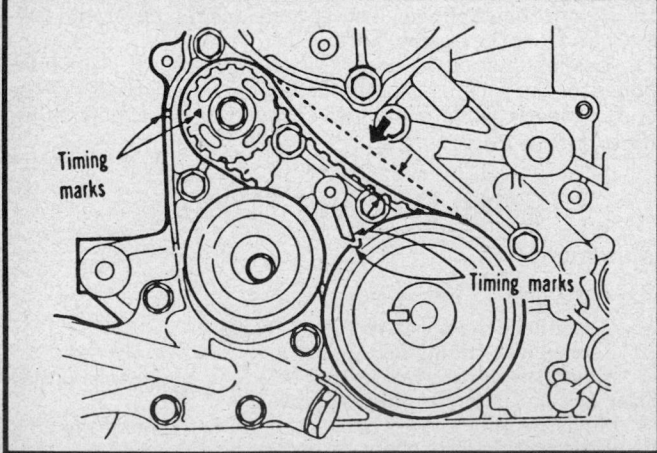

Silent shaft belt installation—2.0L and 2.4L engines

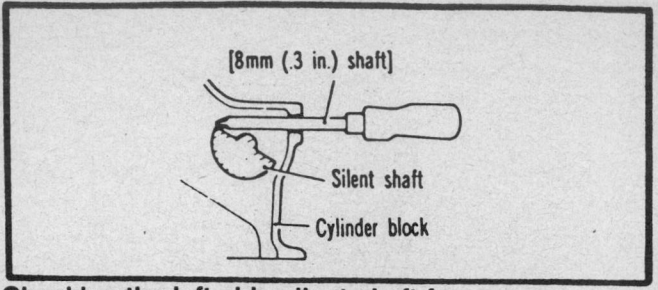

Checking the left side silent shaft for proper positioning

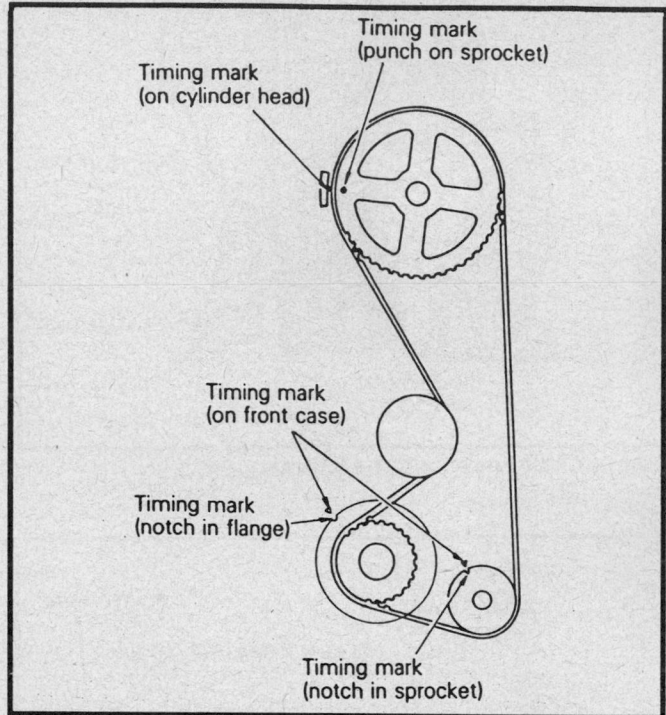

Timing belt installation—2.0L and 2.4L engines

NOTE: If the following step is not followed exactly, there is a chance that the silent shaft alignment will be 180 degrees off. This will cause a noticeable vibration in the engine and the entire procedure will have to be repeated.

12. Before installing the timing belt, ensure that the left side silent shaft is in the correct position. To do so, remove the plug from the left side of the block and insert a suitable tool. With the timing marks still aligned, the tool must be able to go in at least 2⅓ in. If it can only go in about 1 in. turn the oil pump sprocket 1 complete revolution, recheck and realign the timing marks. Leave the tool in place to hold the silent shaft while continuing.

13. Install the belt to the crankshaft sprocket, oil pump sprocket, then the camshaft sprocket, in that order. While doing so, make sure there is no slack between the sprockets except where the tensioner will take it up when released.

14. Recheck the timing marks' alignment. If all are aligned, loosen the tensioner mounting bolt and allow the tensioner to apply tension to the belt.

15. Remove the tool that is holding the silent shaft in place and turn the crankshaft clockwise a distance equal to 2 teeth of the camshaft sprocket. This will allow the tensioner to automatically tension the belt the proper amount.

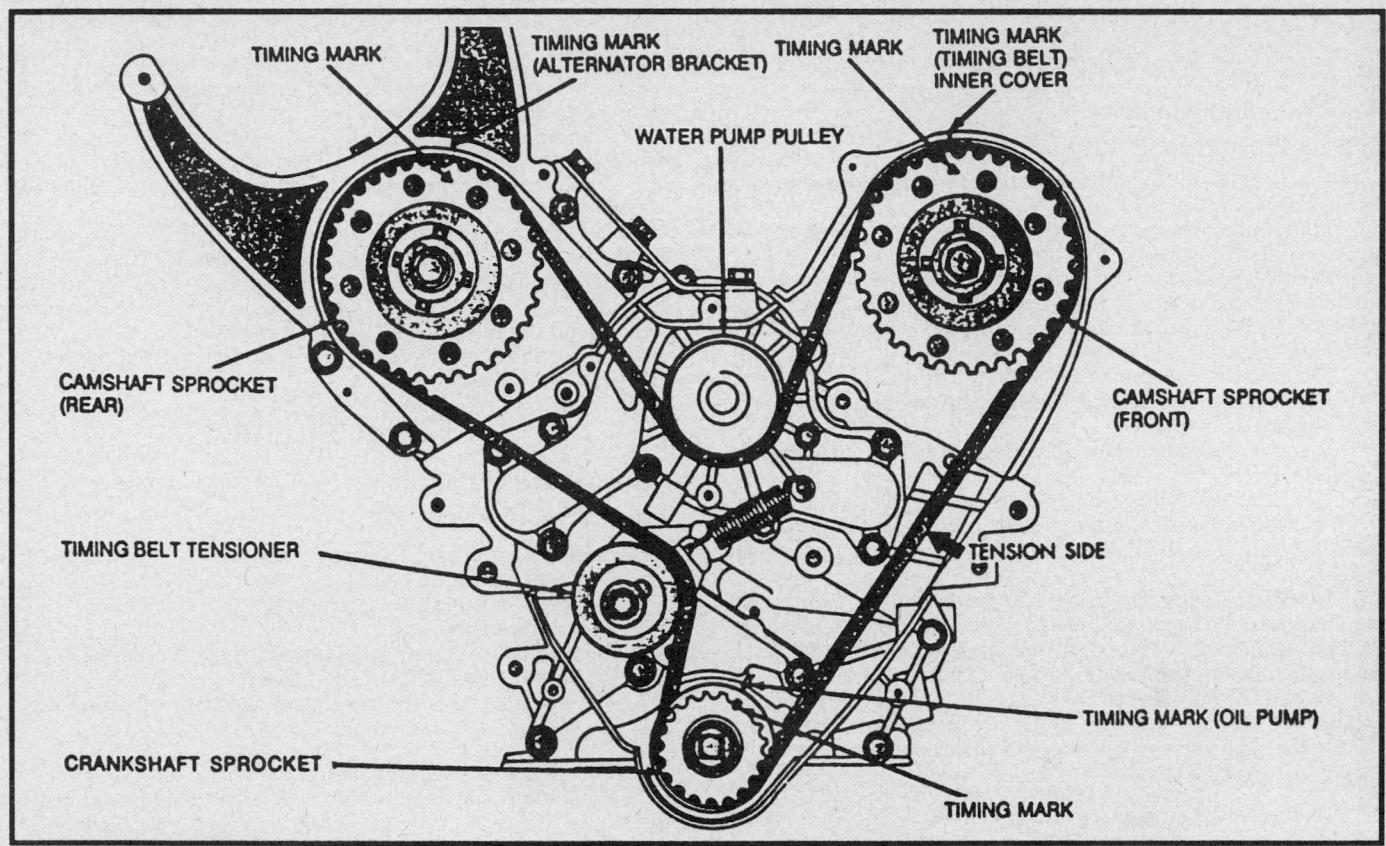

Timing belt installation—3.0L engine

NOTE: Do not manually move the tensioner any more than the spring does; this will overtighten the belt and will cause a howling noise.

16. Tighten the lower mounting bolt, then tighten the upper spacer bolt.

17. To verify that belt tension is correct, check that the the deflection of the longest span (between the camshaft and oil pump sprockets) is about ½ inch.

18. Install the timing belt covers and all related parts.

19. Connect the negative battery cable and road test the vehicle.

3.0L ENGINE

1. If possible, position the engine so that the No. 1 cylinder is at TDC. Disconnect the negative battery cable. Remove the timing covers from the engine.

2. If the same timing belt will be reused, mark the direction of the timing belt's rotation, for installation in the same direction. Make sure the engine is positioned so the No. 1 cylinder is at the TDC of it's compression stroke and the sprockets timing marks are aligned with the engine's timing mark indicators.

3. Loosen the timing belt tensioner bolt and remove the belt. If not removing the tensioner, position it as far away from the center of the engine as possible and tighten the bolt.

4. If the tensioner is being removed, paint the outside of the spring to ensure that it is not installed backwards. Unbolt the tensioner and remove it along with the spring.

To install:

5. Install the tensioner, if removed and hook the upper end of the spring to the water pump pin and the lower end to the tensioner in exactly the same position as originally installed. If not already done, position both camshafts so the marks line up with those on the alternator bracket (rear bank) and inner timing

cover (front bank). Rotate the crankshaft so the timing mark aligns with the mark on the oil pump.

6. Install the timing belt on the crankshaft sprocket and while keeping the belt tight on the tension side (right side), install the belt on the front camshaft sprocket.

7. Install the belt on the water pump pulley, then the rear camshaft sprocket and the tensioner.

8. Rotate the front camshaft counterclockwise to tension the belt between the front camshaft and the crankshaft. If the timing marks came out of line, repeat the procedure.

9. Install the crankshaft sprocket flange.

10. Loosen the tensioner bolt and allow the spring to tension the belt.

11. Turn the crankshaft 2 full turns in the clockwise direction only until the timing marks align again. Now that the belt is properly tensioned, torque the tensioner lock bolt to 21 ft. lbs. (29 Nm).

12. Install the timing belt covers and all related parts.

13. Connect the negative battery cable and road test the vehicle.

Timing Sprockets

Removal and Installation

1. Disconnect the negative battery cable.

2. Remove the timing belt(s).

3. To remove the camshaft sprocket, hold the sprocket with a suiatable holding tool and remove the retaining bolt and washer.

4. To remove the crankshaft sprocket, remove the bolt, if equipped and remove the sprocket from the crankshaft.

5. To remove a silent shafts sprocket, remove the retaining bolt and pry the sprocket from its mounting shaft.

6. The installation is the reverse of the removal procedure.

Camshaft

Removal and Installation

2.0L AND 2.4L ENGINES

1. Disconnect the negative battery cable. Remove the valve cover and the upper timing belt cover.
2. Matchmark the rotor to the distributor housing and remove the distributor.
3. Secure the belt to the sprocket and hold the sprocket up with a fabricated device to keep the belt taut. If timing is lost, it will have to be reset. Remove the camshaft sprocket from the camshaft.
4. Remove the camshaft cap bolts evenly and gradually.
5. Remove the caps, shafts, rocker arms and bolts together as an assembly.
6. Remove the camshaft with the front seal from the engine.

To install:

7. Install a new roll pin to the camshaft. Lubricate the camshaft and install with the front seal in place. Install the camshaft in position so the hole in the sprocket will line up with the roll pin.
8. Install the caps, shafts and arms assembly. Tighten the camshaft bearing cap bolts in the following order to 85 inch lbs. (10 Nm): No. 3, No. 2, No. 4, front cap, rear cap. Repeat the sequence increasing the torque to 175 inch lbs. (19 Nm).
9. Install the sprocket to the camshaft, engaging the roll pin. Torque the bolt to 70 ft. lbs. (95 Nm). Install the distributor.
10. Install the valve cover and all related parts.

2.6L ENGINE

1. Disconnect the negative battery cable.
2. Remove the valve cover.
3. Remove the camshaft gear retaining bolt and matchmark the distributor gear to its drive gear.
4. Remove the distributor. Pry the distributor drive gear off of the cam gear.
5. Remove the cam gear from the camshaft and allow it to rest on the holder below it.
6. Remove the camshaft cap bolts evenly and gradually.
7. Remove the caps, shafts, rocker arms and bolts together as an assembly.
8. Remove the camshaft with the rear seal from the engine.

To install:

9. Install a new roll pin to the camshaft. Lubricate the camshaft and install with the rear seal in place. Install the camshaft in position so the hole in the gear will line up with the roll pin.
10. Install the rocker caps, shafts and arms assembly. Tighten the camshaft bearing cap bolts in the following order to 85 inch lbs. (10 Nm): No. 3, No. 2, No. 4, front cap, rear cap. Repeat the sequence increasing the torque to 175 inch lbs. (19 Nm).
11. Install the gear to the camshaft engaging the roll pin. Install the distributor drive gear and install the bolt and washer. Torque the bolt to 40 ft. lbs. (54 Nm). Install the distributor.
12. Install the valve cover and all related parts.

3.0L ENGINE

1. Disconnect the negative battery cable. Remove the valve cover.
2. Remove the timing belt and remove the sprocket from the camshaft.
3. Install auto lash adjuster retainers MD998443 or equivalent on the rocker arms.
4. If removing the left side camshaft, remove the distributor and the distributor extension.
5. Remove the camshaft bearing caps but do not remove the bolts from the caps. Remove the rocker arms, rocker shafts and bearing caps, as an assembly.
6. Remove the camshaft from the cylinder head.

7. Inspect the bearing journals on the camshaft, cylinder head and bearing caps.

To Install:

8. Lubricate the camshaft journals and camshaft with clean engine oil and install the camshaft in the cylinder head.
9. Align the camshaft bearing caps with the arrow mark (depending on cylinder numbers) and in numerical order.
10. Apply sealer at the ends of the bearing caps and install the assembly.
11. Torque the bearing cap bolts, in the following sequence: No. 3, No. 2, No. 1 and No. 4 to 85 inch lbs. (10 Nm).
12. Repeat the sequence increasing the torque to 175 inch lbs. (18 Nm).
13. Install the distributor, if it was removed.
14. Install the sprocket, timing belt and all related parts.
15. Install the valve cover.

Silent Shafts

Removal and Installation

2.0L AND 2.4L ENGINES

1. Disconnect the negative battery cable.
2. Remove the timing belts.
3. Remove the timing belt sprockets.
4. Remove the front case.
5. Remove the oil pump components.
6. Remove the shafts from the block.
7. The installation is the reverse of the removal procedure.

2.6L ENGINE

1. Disconnect the negative battery cable.
2. Matchmark the silent chain to the gears and remove the chain.
3. Remove the oil pump. The right side silent shaft will come out with the pump. To remove the shaft from the pump, remove the retaining bolt from the pump and remove the shaft from the pump.
4. Remove the left silent shaft gear and spacer. Remove the thrust plate retaining screws and remove the thrust plate by installing two $\frac{1}{32}$ in. screws into the threaded holes and pulling the plate out.
5. Remove the silent shaft.
6. Install a new O-ring to the thrust plate.
7. The installation is the reverse of the removal procedure. Torque the silent shaft retaining bolts to 25 ft. lbs. (34 Nm).
8. Connect the negative battery cable and road test the vehicle.

Piston and Connecting Rod

Positioning

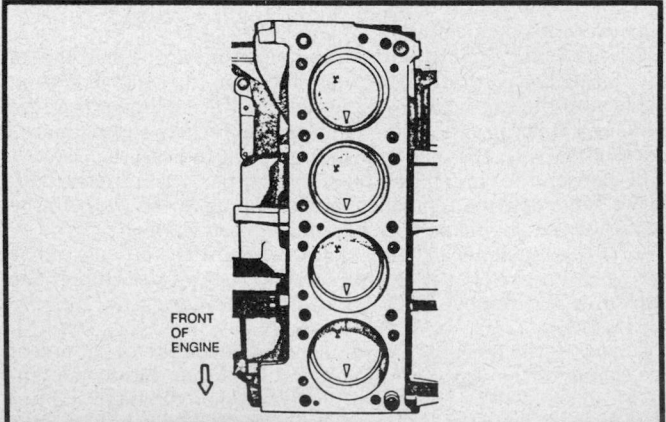

FRONT OF ENGINE

Piston positioning—2.6L engine

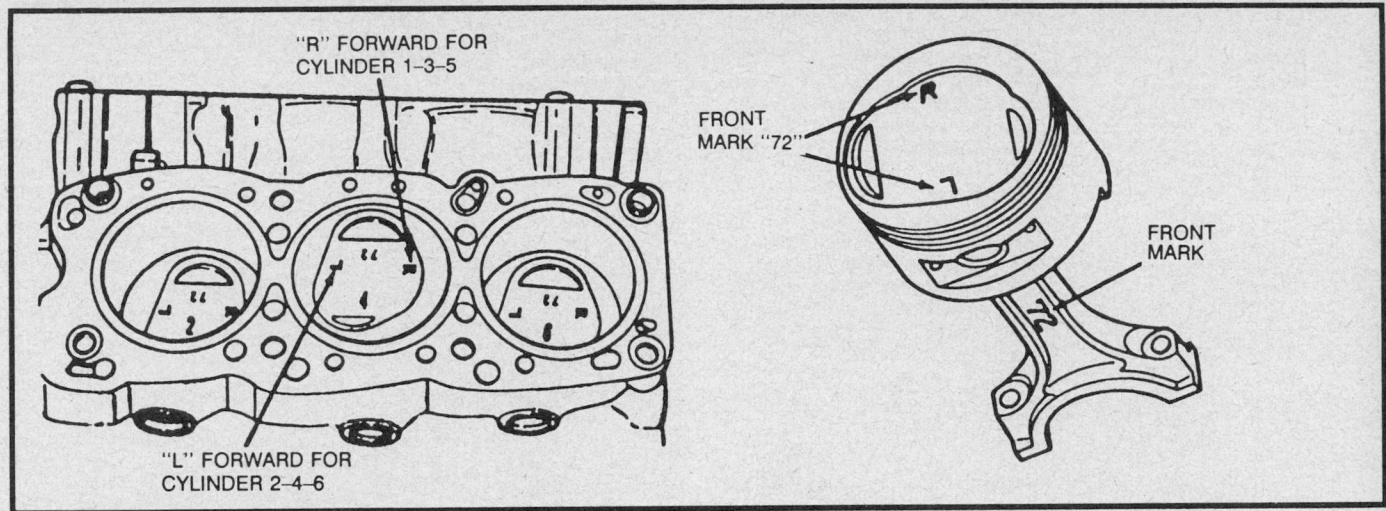

Piston positioning—3.0L engine

ENGINE LUBRICATION

Oil Pan

Removal and Installation

1. Disconnect the negative battery cable.
2. Raise the vehicle and support safely.
3. Remove the skid plate(s), engine undercover, air guide plate, cross shaft plate as required.
4. Remove the front exhaust pipe, if necessary.
5. Remove steering linkage components as required.
6. On some vehicles, unbolt the motor mounts and raise the engine safely using the proper equipment.
6. Drain the engine oil from the pan.
7. Disconnect the fluid level sensor wire, if equipped. Remove the attaching bolts and remove the pan.
8. The installation is the reverse of the removal procedure.

Oil Pump

Removal and Installation

2.0L AND 2.4L ENGINES

1. Disconnect the negative battery cable. Remove the timing belt covers, timing belts and sprockets with the right side silent shaft sprocket spacer.
2. Raise the vehicle and support safely. Drain the oil and remove the oil filter. Remove the oil pan and gasket. Remove the oil pump pickup and gasket.
3. Remove the oil pressure relief plunger plug and gasket. Remove the spring and plunger from the oil filter bracket.
4. Remove the 4 bracket mounting bolts and remove the oil filter mount and gasket.
5. Using special tool MD998162, remove the cap and gasket that cover the oil pump driven gear shaft. This is located on the right side of the front case at the front of the engine, just above the protruding drive gear shaft.
6. Using a long socket, remove the retaining bolt from the oil pump driven gear located behind the plug removed earlier.
7. Remove the front case mounting bolts and remove the case from the block.

8. Completely remove the case gasket from the block.
To install:
9. Prime the pump by pouring fresh oil into the pump intake and turning the driveshaft until oil comes out the pressure port. Repeat a few times until no air bubbles are present. Replace all seals on the case assembly.
10. Install a special seal guide to the crankshaft, MD998285 or equivalent so the smaller diameter faces outward. Coat the outer diameter of the seal with clean engine oil.
11. Install a new front case gasket and install the front case by carefully positioning the crankshaft seal over the seal guide and lining up all bolt holes. Install and tighten the bolts to 17 ft. lbs. (23 Nm).
12. Remove the plug from he left side of the block. Hold the left side silent shaft by inserting a suitable tool in the plug hole and torque the driven gear bolt to 26 ft. lbs. (35 Nm). Using a new O-ring, install the plug cover.
13. Install the oil filter mounting bracket gasket. Install the mounting bracket and bolts; torque the oil filter mounting bracket bolts to 12 ft. lbs. (16 Nm).
14. Clean or replace the oil pickup screen. Install with a new gasket.
15. Install the oil pan using a new gasket.
16. Install the timing sprockets, belts and covers.
17. Fill the engine with the proper amount of engine oil.
18. Connect the negative battery cable and check for proper oil pressure and leaks.

2.6L ENGINE

1. Disconnect the negative battery cable. Remove the dipstick.
2. Raise the vehicle and support safely. Drain the engine coolant and oil. Remove the oil pan and timing chain cover. Rotate the engine until all 3 silent chain gear marks are in a position to matchmark them to the corresponding chain link. Using different color paint, matchmark the chain to the gears. Remove the silent shaft chain. The lower guide bolts are also oil pump mounting bolts.
3. Remove the oil pump mounting bolts and remove the

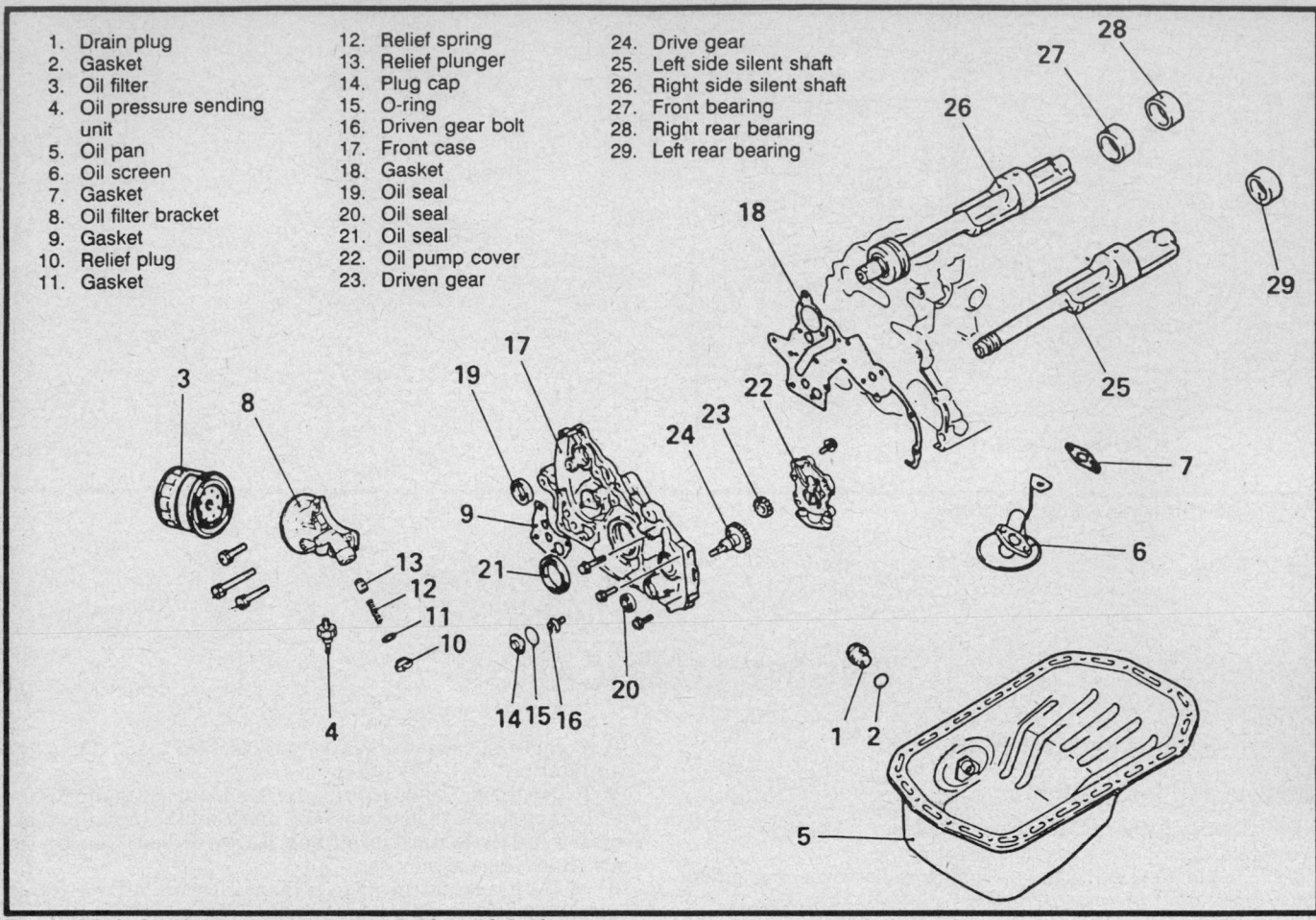

1. Drain plug
2. Gasket
3. Oil filter
4. Oil pressure sending unit
5. Oil pan
6. Oil screen
7. Gasket
8. Oil filter bracket
9. Gasket
10. Relief plug
11. Gasket
12. Relief spring
13. Relief plunger
14. Plug cap
15. O-ring
16. Driven gear bolt
17. Front case
18. Gasket
19. Oil seal
20. Oil seal
21. Oil seal
22. Oil pump cover
23. Driven gear
24. Drive gear
25. Left side silent shaft
26. Right side silent shaft
27. Front bearing
28. Right rear bearing
29. Left rear bearing

Engine lubrication components — 2.0L and 2.4L engines

pump with the timing chain tensioner and the right side silent shaft.

4. Remove the silent shaft and its key from the oil pump.

To install:

5. Remove the gasket material from the block.

6. Prime the pump by pouring fresh oil into the pump intake and turning the driveshaft until oil comes out the pressure port. Repeat a few times until no air bubbles are present.

7. Install the silent shaft key to the oil pump and install the silent shaft itself to the pump.

8. Install the timing chain tensioner and spring to its bore it the pump. Make sure the rubber washer is installed on the tensioner and is not damaged. If it is, the timing chain will make noise.

9. Install the new gasket to the pump and install the pump to the block engaging the tensioner with the timing chain. Make sure the dowels are seated in their bores. Torque the mounting bolts to 13 ft. lbs. (18 Nm).

10. Install the silent shaft chain aligning the matchmarks.

11. Remove the oil pickup and clean or replace, as required. Reinstall with a new gasket.

12. Install the timing chain cover, oil pan and all related parts.

13. Install the dipstick. Fill the engine with the proper amount of oil.

14. Connect the negative battery cable and check the oil pressure.

3.0L ENGINE

1. Disconnect the negative battery cable. Remove the dipstick.

2. Raise the vehicle and support safely. Remove the timing belt, drain the engine oil and remove the oil pan from the engine. Remove the oil pickup.

3. Remove the oil pump mounting bolts and remove the pump from the front of the engine. Note the different length bolts and their position in the pump for installation.

To install:

4. Clean the gasket mounting surfaces of the pump and engine block.

5. Prime the pump by pouring fresh oil into the pump and turning the rotors or, using petroleum jelly, pack the inside of the oil pump. Using a new gasket, install the oil pump on the engine and torque all bolts to 11 ft. lbs. (15 Nm).

6. Install the balancer and crankshaft sprocket to the end of the crankshaft.

7. Clean out the oil pickup or replace as required. Replace the oil pickup gasket ring and install the pickup to the pump.

8. Install the timing belt, oil pan and all related parts.

9. Install the dipstick. Fill the engine with the proper amount of oil.

10. Connect the negative battery cable and check the oil pressure.

Checking

2.0L AND 2.4L ENGINES

1. Remove the oil pump cover from the front case.

2. Check the case and gear cover for stepped wear from the gears.

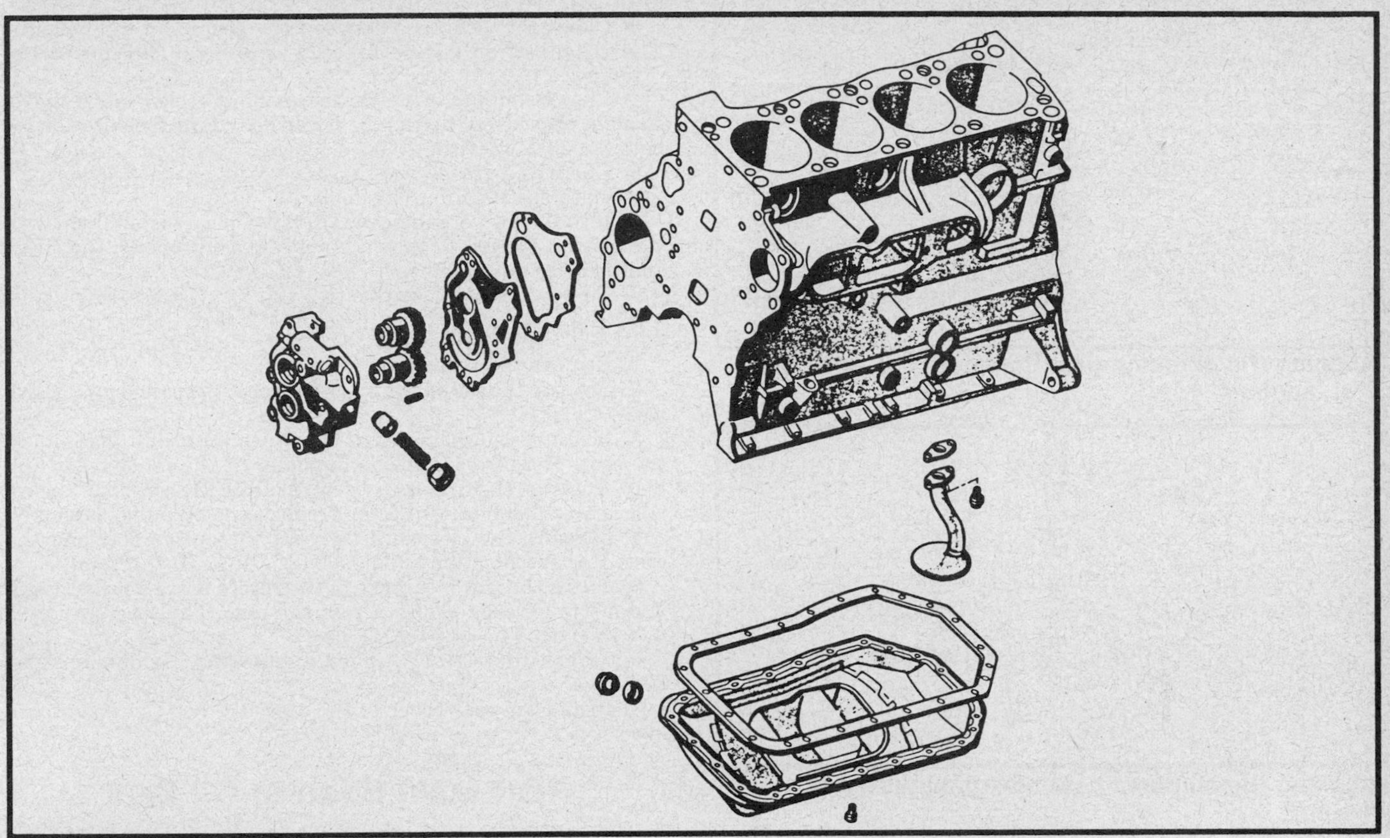

Engine lubrication components – 2.6L engine

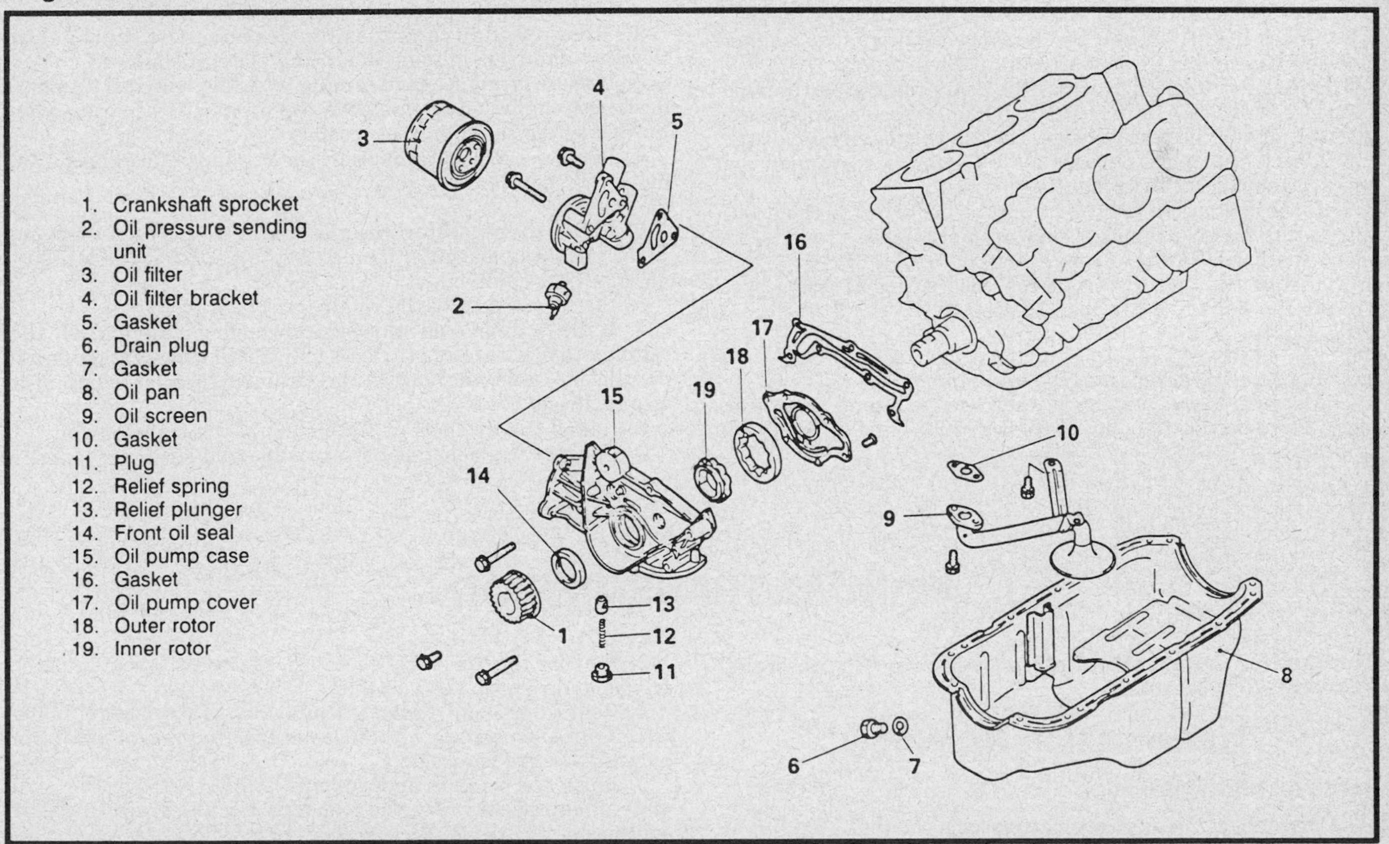

1. Crankshaft sprocket
2. Oil pressure sending unit
3. Oil filter
4. Oil filter bracket
5. Gasket
6. Drain plug
7. Gasket
8. Oil pan
9. Oil screen
10. Gasket
11. Plug
12. Relief spring
13. Relief plunger
14. Front oil seal
15. Oil pump case
16. Gasket
17. Oil pump cover
18. Outer rotor
19. Inner rotor

Engine lubrication components – 3.0L engine

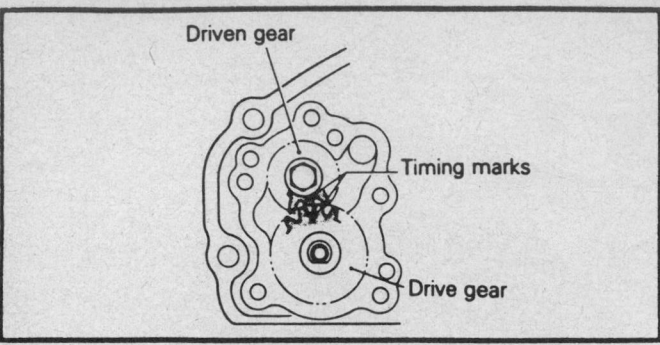

Aligning the oil pump gear timing marks—2.0L and 2.4L engines

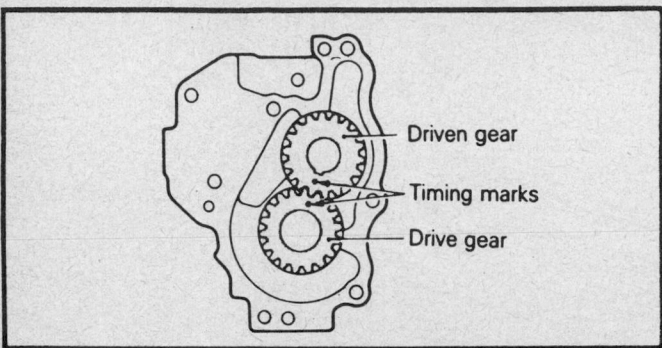

Aligning the oil pump gear timing marks—2.6L engine

3. Measure the drive gear tip clearance between the teeth and the case. The specification is 0.006–0.010 in. (0.16–0.25mm).

4. Check the driven gear tip clearance in the similar manner. The specification is 0.005–0.010 in. (0.13–0.25mm).

5. Place a straightedge across the gears resting on the opposite sides of the case. If a 0.010 in. (0.25mm) feeler gauge can be inserted under the straightedge, replace the assembly.

6. Check the relief plunger for freedom of movement and check he spring for deformation and rust.

7. If the gears were removed from the body, install them with the mating marks aligned. If they are not aligned properly, the silent shaft will be out of time.

8. Install the gear cover to the case using a new gasket. Torque the bolts to 12 ft. lbs. (16 Nm).

2.6L ENGINE

1. Remove the cover from the oil pump.

2. Measure the clearance between the gears and their bearings. The specification for both is 0.0008–0.0020 in. (0.02–0.05mm).

3. Check the clearance between the gears and the housing. The specification for both gears is 0.004–0.006 in. (0.11–0.15mm).

4. Check endplay of the gears using a feeler gauge and a straight edge placed across the pump body. The specification for both is 0.002–0.004 in. (0.04–0.11mm).

5. Check the pressure relief valve for damage. The spring's freelength specification is 1.85 in. (47.00mm).

6. If the gears were removed from the body, install them with the mating aligned. If they are not aligned properly, the silent shaft will be out of time.

7. Torque the cover screws to 13 ft. lbs. (18 Nm).

3.0L ENGINE

1. Remove the rear cover.

2. Remove the pump rotors and inspect the case for excessive wear.

3. Measure the diameter of the inner rotor hub that sits in the case. Measure the inside diameter of the inner rotor hub bore. Subtract the first measurement from the second; if the result is over 0.006 in. (0.15mm), replace the oil pump assembly.

4. Measure the clearance between the outer rotor and the case. The specification is 0.004–0.007 in. (0.10–0.18mm).

5. Check the side clearance of the rotors using a feeler gauge and a straightedge placed across the case. The specification is 0.0015–0.0035 in. (0.04–0.09mm).

6. Check the relief plunger and spring for damage and breakage.

7. Install the rear cover to the case.

Rear Main Bearing Oil Seal

Removal and Installation

1. Disconnect the negative battery cable.

2. Remove the transmission. Remove the flywheel or flexplate and transmission mounting plate, if equipped.

3. If there is any leakage coming from the rear seal retainer, drain the engine oil and remove the oil pan, if necessary. Remove the rear main oil seal retainer.

4. Remove the separator from the retainer, if equipped. Remove the seal from the retainer.

To install:

5. Install the separator with the hole at the 6 o'clock position. Lightly coat the seal outer diameter with Loctite® Stud N' Bearing Mount, or equivalent.

6. Install the seal to the retainer.

7. If the retainer was removed, thoroughly clean and dry the retainer to block sealing surfaces and install a new gasket or apply silicone sealer and install the retainer. Install the pan, if it was removed.

8. Install the flywheel or flexplate and the transmission.

9. Connect the negative battery cable and check for leaks.

MANUAL TRANSMISSION

For further information, please refer to "Professional Transmission Manual".

Transmission Assembly

Removal and Installation

1. Disconnect the negative battery cable.

2. Place the shifter(s) in the nuetral position.

3. Remove the console, if equipped. Remove the boot retainer screws and remove the boot.

4. Remove the shift lever assembly out of the control housing. Cover the opening with a clean towel to prevent dirt from entering the transmission.

5. Raise the vehicle and support safely. Remove the skid plate, if equipped. Drain the transmission and transfer cae, if equipped.

6. Matchmark and remove the driveshaft(s) from the vehicle.

Install a suitable plug in the transfer case adaptor to prevent leakage.

7. Disconnect the speedometer cable from the transmission or transfer case. Remove the slave cylinder or disconnect the clutch cable.

8. Disconnect the reverse lamp lamp switch.

9. Remove the starter and the bell housing cover.

10. Support the weight of the engine using a jack stand with a block of wood to protect the oil pan.

11. Using the proper equipment, support the weight of the transmission safely.

12. Remove the transfer case bracket, if equipped and remove the crossmember.

13. Remove the bellhousing bolts remove the transmission assembly from the vehicle.

To install:

14. Lubricate the pilot bushing and input shaft splines very lightly with high temperature lubricant.

15. Mount the transmission securely on a suitable transmission jack and lift it in place until the input shaft is centered in the clutch housing opening. Roll the transmission forward until the input shaft splines fully engage with the clutch disc.

16. Install the transmission to clutch housing bolts. Torque the bolts to 35 ft. lbs. (47 Nm).

17. Jack the assembly up into position and install the transmission crossmember and transfer case bracket, if equipped. Torque the frame bolts to 50 ft. lbs. (68 Nm). Remove the transmission and engine support fixtures.

18. Install the starter and torque the mounting bolt to 20 ft. lbs. (27 Nm). Install the bellhousing cover.

20. Connect the reverse light switch and clip all wiring to the transmission case.

21. Connect the speedometer cable.

22. Install the driveshaft(s).

23. Install the slave cylinder or connect the clutch cable, using a new cotter pin.

24. Fill the transmission and transfer case with the proper amount of SAE 80W or 75W/85W hypoid gear oil with an API classification of GL–4 or highter.

25. Install the skip plate, if equipped. Lower the vehicle.

26. Install the shift lever assembly, boot and console.

27. Connect the negative battery cable and check the transmission and transfer case for proper operation. Make sure the reverse lights come on when in the reverse gear.

Linkage Adjustment

Since this transmission uses a directly engaging shift mechanism, there are no provisions for adjustment.

CLUTCH

Clutch Assembly

Removal and Installation

1. Disconnect the negative battery cable.
2. Raise the vehicle and support safely.
3. Remove the transmission and transfer case, if equipped.
4. Remove the clutch cover and disc from the flywheel. Sand, machine or replace the flywheel as required.

To install:

5. Apply a very light coating of anti-sieze compound to the input shaft and clutch disc splines. Install a new release bearing.
6. Raise the clutch cover and disc into place and use a suitable clutch aligning tool or spare input shaft to center the disc. Apply Loctite® to the threads and tighten all of the bolts finger tight.
7. The cover bolts must be turned gradually, evenly and to the proper torque to avoid distorting the cover. Torque the bolts to 15 ft. lbs. (20 Nm).
8. Install the transmission and transfer case, if equipped.
9. Connect the negative battery cable and check the clutch for proper operation.

Clutch Cable

Removal and Installation

1. Disconnect the negative battery cable.
2. Turn the cable adjusting wheel counterclockwise to provide enough play to remove the cable end from the clutch lever inside the vehicle. Remove the cable from the lever.
3. Raise the vehicle and support safely.
4. Remove the cotter pin from the lever on the transmission.
5. Remove the clutch cable from the vehicle.
6. The installation is the reverse of the removal procedure. Make sure the insulator is positioning properly.

Pedal Height/Free-Play Adjustment

1. Measure the distance from the face of the pedal pad to the floorboard. This distance should be about 6½–7 in.
2. If the pedal height is not correct, adjust the pedal stopper to contact the pedal at the correct spot.
3. Check the pedal's free-play. The specification is about 1 in.
4. Adjust the clutch cable by turning the star shaped adjusting wheel on the firewall. Turning the wheel counterclockwise will increase the amount of free-play in the pedal and vice-versa.

Clutch Master Cylinder

Removal and Installation

1. Disconnect the negative battery cable. Remove as much fluid as possible from the clutch master cylinder reservior.
2. Remove the cotter pin and remove the clevis pin from the clutch pedal.
3. Disconnect and plug the fluid line from the clutch master cylinder.
4. Remove the mounting nuts and remove the cylinder from the firewall.
5. Remove the reservoir from the cylinder.
5. The installation is the reverse of the removal procedure.
6. Bleed the system.

Clutch Slave Cylinder

Removal and Installation

1. Disconnect the negative battery cable.
2. Raise the vehicle and support safely.
3. Remove the eye bolt and washer from the slave cylinder.

4. Remove the mounting bolts and remove the slave cylinder from the transmission case.

5. Replace the eye-bolt washer.

6. The installation is the reverse of the removal procedure.

7. Bleed the system.

Bleeding the Hydraulic Clutch System

CAUTION

When bleeding, keep the facial area well away from the slave cylinder area. Spewing fluid may cause facial and/or visual damage.

---

1. Fill the clutch master cylinder with fresh DOT3 brake fluid.

2. Have a helper sit in the vehicle. Raise the vehicle and support safely.

3. Remove the bleeder screw cap.

4. If the system is empty, the most efficient way to get fluid down to the cylinder is to loosen the bleeder about ½–¾ turn, place a finger firmly over the bleeder and have the helper pump the brakes slowly until fluid pressure is felt at the bleeder. Once fluid is at the bleeder, close it before the pedal is released.

NOTE: If the pedal is pump rapidly, the fluid will churn and create small air bubbles, which are difficult and time consuming to remove from the system. These air bubble will eventually congregate and will result in a spongy pedal.

5. Once fluid has been pumped to the slave cylinder, open the bleeder screw, have the helper depress the clutch pedal, lock the bleeder and have the helper release the pedal. Wait 15 seconds and repeat the procedure (including the 15 second wait) until no air bubbles emanate from the bleeder. Remember to close the bleeder each time before the pedal is released. If the bleeder is left open when the pedal is released, air will be induced into the system.

6. If a helper is not available, connect a small hose to the bleeder, submerge the other end in a clean container of fresh brake fluid placed in a position that is visible from the driver's seat and pump the pedal until no more air comes out of the tube.

AUTOMATIC TRANSMISSION

For further information, please refer to "Professional Transmission Manual".

Transmission Assembly

Removal and Installation

1. Disconnect the negative battery cable.

2. Remove the transfer shifter boot, if equipped.

3. Raise the vehicle and support safely.

4. Remove the skid plate, if equipped. Drain the transmission and transfer case, if equipped.

5. Matchmark and remove the driveshaft(s).

6. Disconnect the speedometer cable from the transmission or transfer case.

7. Disconnect the shifter linkage or cable.

8. Unplug all transmission electrical connectors.

9. Unbolt the exhaust pipe from the manifold and remove the bracket from the case.

10. Remove the filler neck and dipstick.

11. Remove the torque converter inspection plate. Remove the torque converter bolts.

12. Remove the starter.

13. Disconnect and plug the oil cooler lines.

14. Using a suitable transmission jack, support the transmission and unbolt the transmission from the crossmember.

15. Remove the crossmember on all vehicles except Van, because the transmission hangs from the mount on that vehicle.

16. Lower the transmission down slightly and unbolt the transfer shifter from the transfer case, if equipped.

17. Remove the bellhousing bolts and brackets.

18. Pull the transmission assembly backwards to clear the dowels and remove it from the vehicle.

To install:

19. Install the transmission assembly to the engine using the dowels as guides. Install the bellhousing bolts and torque to 35 ft. lbs. (47 Nm).

20. Install the transfer shifter, if equipped. Jack the assembly up into position and install the rear crossmember or mounting hardware. Torque the crossmember to frame bolts to 50 ft. lbs. (68 Nm). Torque the through bolt and nut on Van to 60 ft. lbs. (81 Nm).

21. Apply Loctite® to the threads and install the torque converter bolts. Torque the bolts to 25 ft. lbs. (34 Nm). Install the inspection plate.

22. Install the filler tube with a new O-ring and the dipstick.

23. Install the exhaust pipe to the manifold and install the brackets.

24. Connect all previously disconnected switches.

25. Connect the shifter linkage or cable and the throttle cable.

26. Install the driveshaft(s). Fill the transfer case with hypoid gear oil with an API classification of GL–4 or higher.

27. Connect the throttle cable.

28. Install the skid plate, if equipped. Lower the vehicle.

29. Install the transfer shifter boot, if equipped.

30. Fill the transmission with the proper amount of Dexron®II.

31. Connect the negative battery cable, start the engine and run through the gears. Add fluid until the transmission is properly filled.

32. Check the operation of the neutral safety switch and make sure the reverse lights come on in the **R** detent.

33. Road test the vehicle and check for leaks.

Shift Linkage Adjustment

1. On the Van, remove the floor console. Position the shifter in the **N** detent.

2. Loosen the nut or bolt on the shifter linkage or cable.

3. Make sure the lever on the transmission is in the **N** detent and the needle in the indicator is also in the **N** position. Jiggle the selector rod to settle the assembly in position. If the rod is equipped with a notch, it should be at the 6 o'clock position.

4. Tighten the adjusting bolt or nut and check for proper assembly.

5. Check the operation of the neutral safely switch.

6. Liberally lubricate all pivoting points within the system.

Throttle Cable Adjustment

1. Depress the accelerator fully and make sure the throttle valve opens all the way. Adjust as required.

2. Measure the distance between the end of the rubber boot and the stopper on the cable at wide open throttle.

3. The specification for carbureted engines is 2.05–2.09 in.

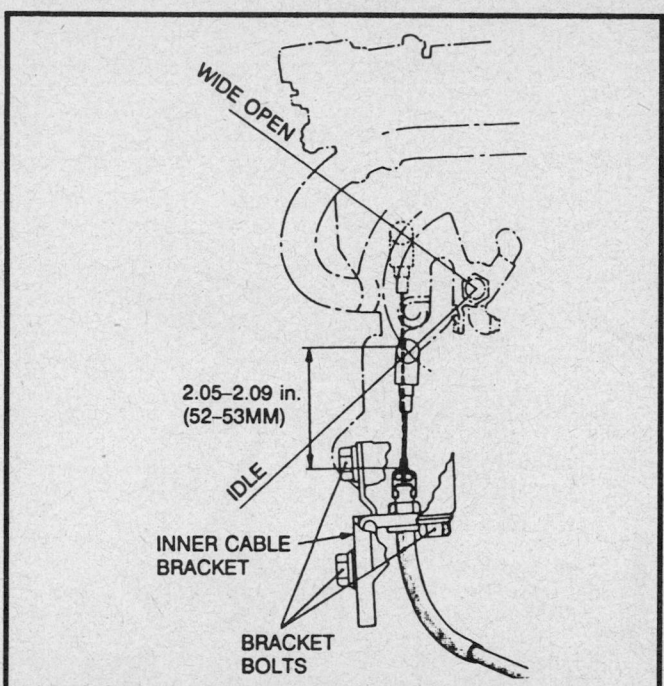

Throttle cable adjustment—carbureted engine

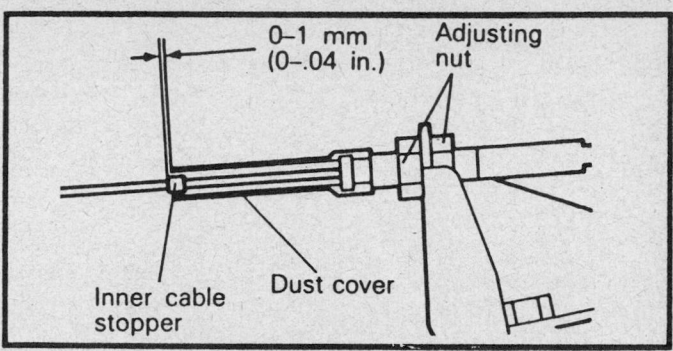

Throttle cable adjustment—fuel injected engine

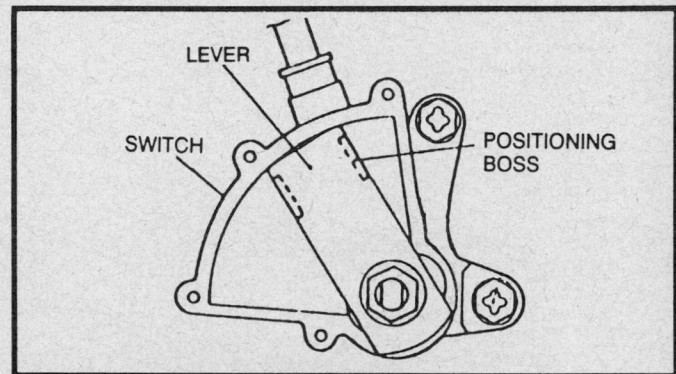

Neutral safety switch adjustment

(52–52mm) and for fuel injected engines is 0–0.04 in. (0–1mm).

4. Adjust the cable on carbureted engines by moving the bracket. Adjust the cable itself on fuel injected engines.

5. Road test the vehicle and check for proper shift points.

Neutral Safety Switch Adjustment

NOTE: Some vehicles are not equipped with an adjustable switch.

1. Adjust the shifter linkage.

2. Raise the vehicle and support safely. Place the shifter in the **N** detent. Loosen the mounting bolts.

3. Align the lever with the positioning boss.

4. Hold in position and tighten the bolts.

5. Check the switch and the reverse lights for proper operation.

TRANSFER CASE

For further information, please refer to "Professional Transmission Manual".

Transfer Case Assembly

Removal and Installation

1. Disconnect the negative battery cable.

2. Remove the transmission and transfer case assembly from the vehicle.

3. Remove the roll pin that retains the shift changer to the control shaft.

4. Remove the selector plunger from the right side of the case.

5. Remove the selector spring and plunger or steel ball.

6. Remove the transfer case to transmission attaching nuts and remove from the transmission.

7. The installation is the reverse of the removal procedure.

Linkage Adjustment

Since this transfer case uses a directly engaging shift mechanism, there are no provisions for adjustment.

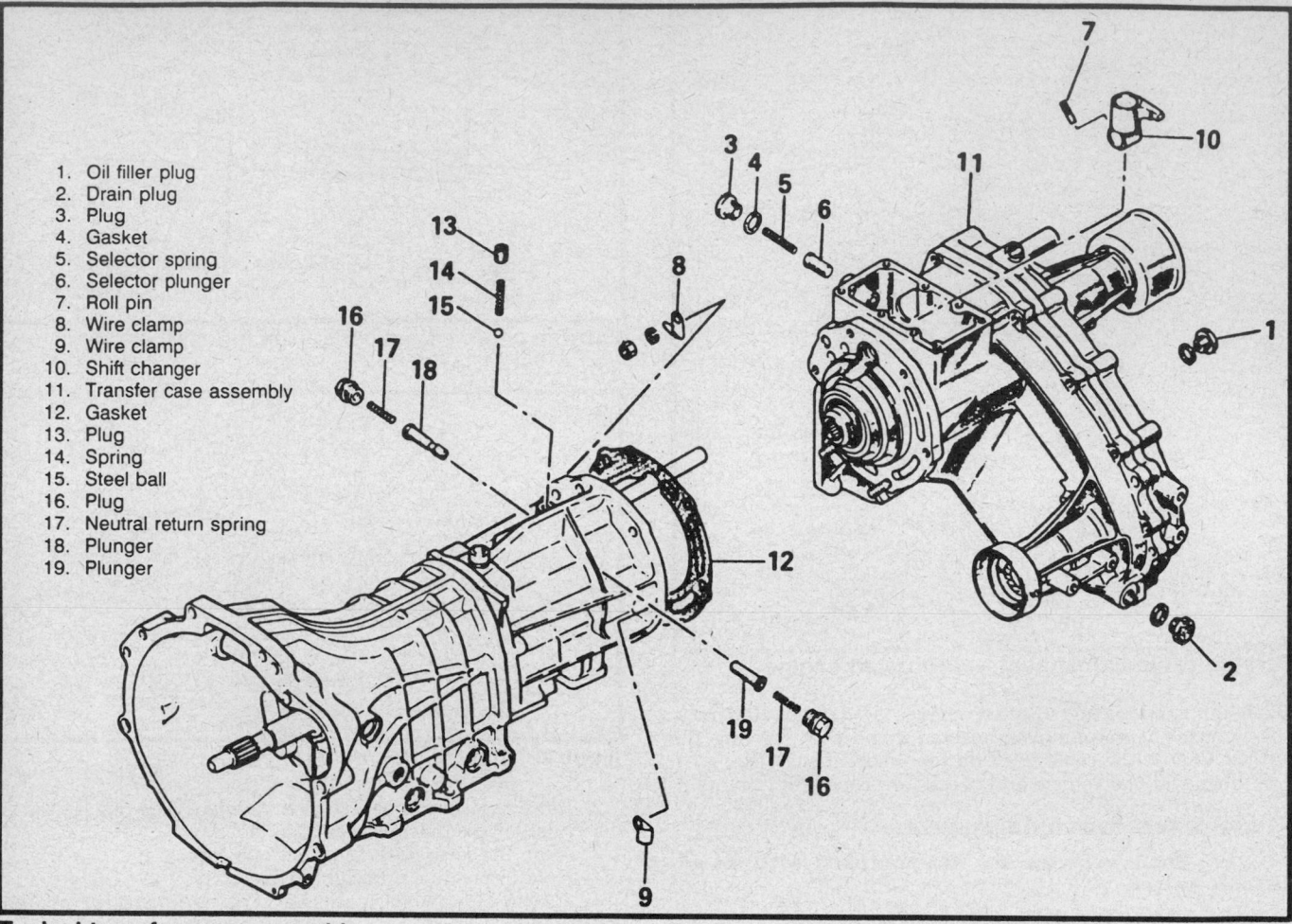

1. Oil filler plug
2. Drain plug
3. Plug
4. Gasket
5. Selector spring
6. Selector plunger
7. Roll pin
8. Wire clamp
9. Wire clamp
10. Shift changer
11. Transfer case assembly
12. Gasket
13. Plug
14. Spring
15. Steel ball
16. Plug
17. Neutral return spring
18. Plunger
19. Plunger

Typical transfer case assembly

DRIVE AXLE

Driveshaft and U-Joints

Removal and Installation

1. Raise the vehicle and support safely. Remove the skid plate, if equipped.

2. Matchmark the driveshaft and the drive pinion gear shaft yoke.

3. Remove the nuts and bolts attaching the driveshaft to the yoke. Pry the shaft from the yoke.

3. Remove the center bearing mounting nuts and bolts.

4. Fluid may run from the rear of the extension housing or transfer case when the shaft is removed, so position a suitable drain pan under the area.

5. Remove the driveshaft from the transmission or transfer case.

6. The installation is the reverse of the removal procedure. Torque the driveshaft to yoke nuts to 40 ft. lbs. (54 Nm). Torque the center bearing retaining nuts to 30 ft. lbs. (41 Nm).

Front Axle Shaft

Removal and Installation

Before beginning, place the free-wheeling hub in the free condition by placing the transfer lever in the **2H** position and moving in reverse for about 6 or 7 feet.

1. Raise the vehicle and support safely. Remove the tire and wheel assembly.

2. Remove the front brake caliper assembly and position it to the side.

3. Remove the free wheeling hub cover assembly and remove the snapring from the axle shaft.

4. Remove the snapring and shim. Remove the knuckle and front hub together as a unit.

5. If removing the left side shaft, simply pull the shaft out of the differential carrier assembly. When pulling the left shaft from the differential carrier assembly, be careful that the shaft splines do not damage the oil seal.

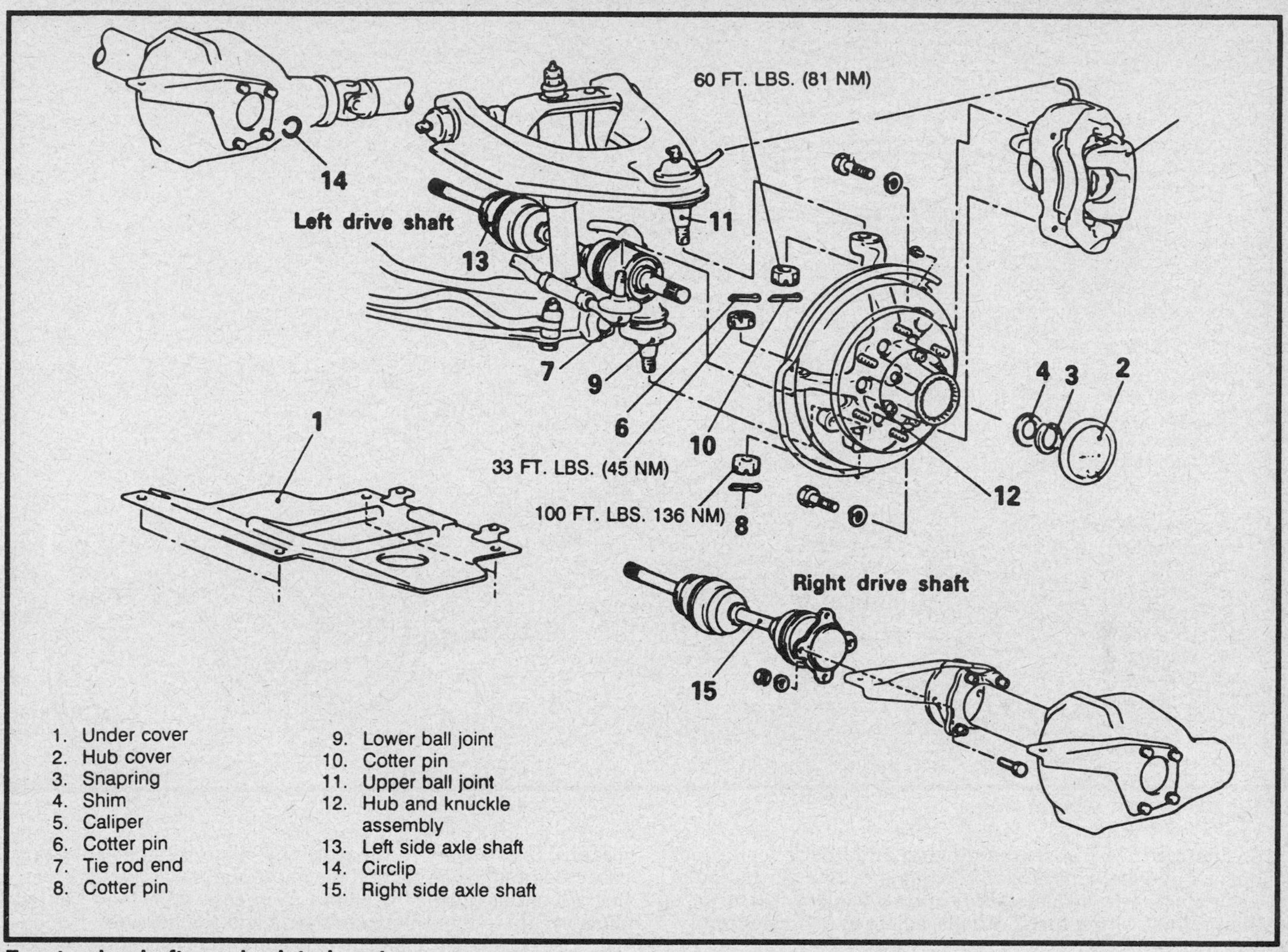

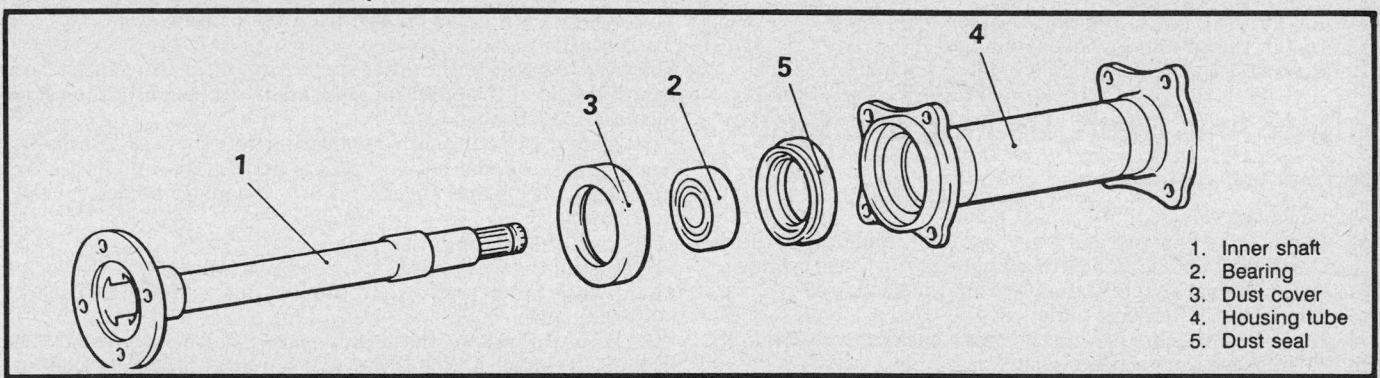

60 FT. LBS. (81 NM)

14

Left drive shaft

13

11

7 9

6

10

33 FT. LBS. (45 NM)

100 FT. LBS. 136 NM) 8

4 3 2

12

1

Right drive shaft

15

1. Under cover
2. Hub cover
3. Snapring
4. Shim
5. Caliper
6. Cotter pin
7. Tie rod end
8. Cotter pin

9. Lower ball joint
10. Cotter pin
11. Upper ball joint
12. Hub and knuckle assembly
13. Left side axle shaft
14. Circlip
15. Right side axle shaft

Front axle shafts and related parts

3 2 5 4

1

1. Inner shaft
2. Bearing
3. Dust cover
4. Housing tube
5. Dust seal

Inner axle shaft and tube

6. On 1986 Pick-Up or Ram 50 only, raise the right lower suspension arm and remove the right shock absorber if removing the right side shaft.

7. Disconnect the right shaft from the inner shaft assembly and remove the shaft. Remove the inner shaft from the housing tube and the housing tube from the differential housing.

8. Press the bearing and seal off of the inner shaft and remove the dust seal from the tube.

To install:

9. Using tool MB990955, install a new dust seal to the tube and coat the lip with grease.

10. Using a suitable long steel pipe, install a new dust cover to the inner shaft and coat the inside with grease. Press the bearing onto the shaft using tool MD990560 and a press.

11. Install a new circlip on the splines of the left side shaft or inner right shaft.

12. Drive the shafts into the differential carrier assembly with a plastic hammer. Be careful not to damage the lip of the oil seal.

13. Install the right outer shaft to the inner shaft and torque the nuts to 40 ft. lbs. (54 Nm). Install the right shock absorber, if it was removed.

14. Install the knuckle and front hub assembly.

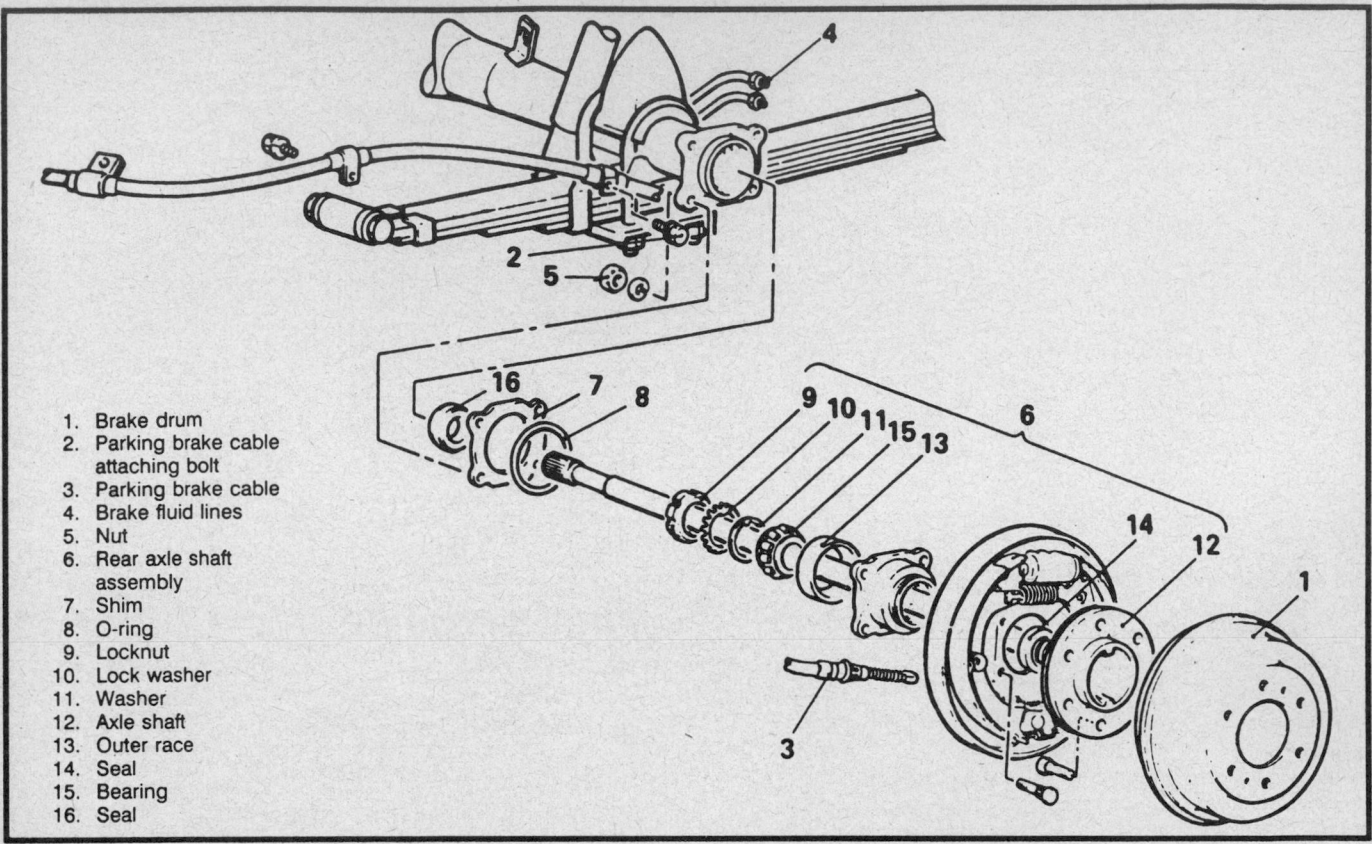

1. Brake drum
2. Parking brake cable attaching bolt
3. Parking brake cable
4. Brake fluid lines
5. Nut
6. Rear axle shaft assembly
7. Shim
8. O-ring
9. Locknut
10. Lock washer
11. Washer
12. Axle shaft
13. Outer race
14. Seal
15. Bearing
16. Seal

Rear axle shaft assembly

15. Install the shim and snapring and check for proper endplay. Set a dial indicator so the pin is resting on the end of the axle shaft. The endplay specification is 0.008–0.020 in. (0.2–0.5mm). If not within specifications, adjust by adding or removing shims.
16. Install the hub cover.
17. Install the front brake caliper assembly
18. Install the tire and wheel assembly.
19. Road test the vehicle.

Rear Axle Shaft, Bearing and Seal

Removal and Installation

1. Raise the vehicle and support safely.
2. Remove the rear tire and wheel assembly and brake drum.
3. Disconnect and plug the brake line(s) at the wheel cylinder. Disconnect the parking brake cable from the shoes and remove the cable from the backing plate.
4. Remove the 4 nuts behind the brake backing plate holding the bearing case to the axle housing assembly.
5. Remove the backing plate, bearing case and the axle shaft as an assembly. If this is not possible by hand, use a slide hammer to remove the assembly.
6. Remove the O-ring and the bearing preload shims. Save the preload shims for reassembly.
7. Remove the oil seal from the axle tube with a hooked slide hammer.
8. To remove the axle shaft bearing, remove the notched locknut with tool MB990785–01 or a brass drift.
9. Remove the lock washer and flat washer.
10. Screw the locknut back on to the axle shaft about 3 turns.
11. If tool MB990787–01 is not available, it will be necessary to fabricate a metal plate that fits over the axle shaft and butts the

locknut. Drill 4 holes in the plate that align with the 4 bearing case studs and fit the plate. Refit 2 nuts and washers to the bearing case studs diagonally across from each other and tighten them evenly to free the bearing case and the bearing.
12. Use a hammer and drift to remove the bearing outer race from the bearing case.
13. Remove the outer oil seal from the bearing case.

To install:

14. Apply grease to the outer surface on the bearing outer race and to the lip of the outer oil seal and drive them into the bearing case from each side.
15. Slide the bearing case and bearing over the rear axle shaft. Apply grease on the bearing rollers and fit the inner race by pressing it into place. Be careful not to damage or deform the dust cover.
16. Pack the bearing with grease.
17. Install the washer, the crowned lock washer and the locknut in that order and torque the locknut to 130–159 ft. lbs. (176–220 Nm)
18. Bend the tab on the lock washer into the groove on the locknut. If the tab and the groove do not line up, slightly tighten the locknut until they do.
19. Drive the new inner oil seal into place after greasing it and refit the assembly. Install a new O-ring, install the shims and apply silicone rubber sealant to the face of the bearing case.
20. Install the entire assembly to the axle housing. Torque the retaining nuts to 40 ft. lbs. (54 Nm).
21. Check the axle shaft endplay. If it is not between 0.002–0.008 in. (0.05–0.20mm), proceed with the axle shaft endplay adjustment procedure.
22. If the endplay is within specifications, install all removed brake parts and bleed the system.
23. Install the tire and wheel assembly and road test the vehicle. Check for leaks.

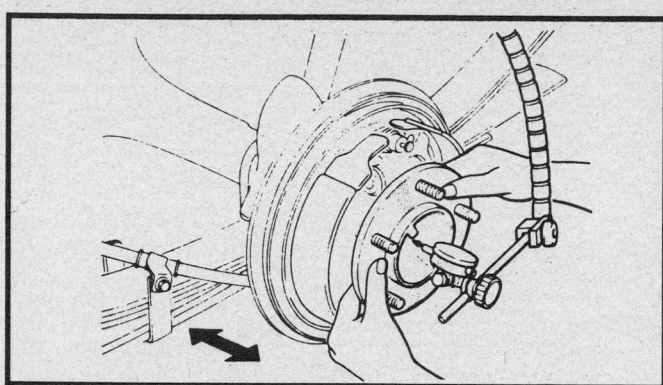

Measuring axle shaft endplay

Endplay Adjustment Procedure

1. Begin with the left side rear axle assembly and insert a 0.04 in. (1mm) shim between the bearing case and the axle shaft housing. Torque the nuts to specification.

2. Install the right side axle assembly into the right side housing without its shim and O-ring. Torque the 4 nuts to about 50 inch. lbs.

3. Using a feeler gauge, measure the gap between the bearing case and the axle housing face.

4. Remove the axle shaft and select a shim or shims that is the equal to the sum of the clearance measured in Step 3 plus 0.002–0.008 in. (0.05–0.20mm) and install them on the housing. Install the O-ring and apply sealant.

5. Install the axle assembly and torque the nuts to 40 ft. lbs. (54 Nm).

6. Measure the endplay and complete the installation procedure.

Front Wheel Hub, Knuckle and Bearings

Removal and Installation
2WD VEHICLE

1. Raise the vehicle and support safely. Remove the tire and wheel assembly.

2. Remove the brake caliper, pads and adaptor and position them out of the way.

3. Remove the grease cap.

4. Remove the cotter pin, castellated nut and washer. Remove the outer bearing.

5. Remove the front hub/rotor assembly from the steering knuckle. Remove the grease seal and inner bearing from the hub. Remove the splash shield.

6. Remove the nuts and bolts that attach the hub to the rotor and separate them. Clean out all of the old grease from the inside of the hub.

7. Remove the shock and stabilizer bar from the lower control arm, if equipped.

8. Support the lower control arm. Compress the coil spring with the special spring compressor, if equipped. Separate the ball joints and tie rod end from the knuckle.

9. Remove the steering knuckle.

To install:

10. Install the knuckle to the ball joint studs. Torque all ball joint nuts except the upper nut on Pick-Up and Ram 50 to 100 ft. lbs. (136 Nm). Torque the aforementioned nut to 60 ft. lbs. (82 Nm). Install new cotter pins. Remove the spring compressor, if it was used. Install the shock.

11. Connect the stabilizer bar to the lower control arm. Tighten the nut until the bushing is the same diameter as the washer.

12. Connect the tie rod end to the knuckle. Torque the nut to 30 ft. lbs. (41 Nm). Install a new cotter pin.

13. Assemble the rotor and front hub. Torque the nuts to 40 ft. lbs. (54 Nm).

14. Apply wheel bearing grease to the inside of the front hub.

15. Pack the inner bearing and install to the hub.

16. Install a new oil seal into the hub so it is flush with the hub end face.

17. Install the assembly onto the steering knuckle, pack and install the outer bearing.

18. Install the washer and castellated nut. Spin the rotor and torque the nut to 22 ft. lbs. (30 Nm), loosen completely and re-tighten to 6 ft. lbs. (8 Nm) while turning the wheel.

19. Install a new cotter pin and install the grease cap.

20. Install the brake hardware and bleed the system if it was opened.

21. Install the tire and wheel assembly and road test the vehicle.

Automatic Hub, Front Axle Hub, Knuckle and Bearings

Removal and Installation

1. Before beginning, place the free-wheeling hub in the free condition by placing the transfer lever in the **2H** position and moving in reverse for about 6 or 7 feet. Raise the vehicle and support safely. Remove the tire and wheel assembly.

2. Remove the front brake caliper, pads and adaptor and position them out of the way.

3. Remove the hub cover.

4. Remove the snapring and shim.

5. Remove the automatic free-wheeling hub retaining bolts and remove the hub.

6. Remove the lock washer. Remove the locknut with special tool MB990954 or equivalent.

7. Remove the front hub and brake rotor assembly, with the inner and outer bearings.

8. Remove the outer bearing, oil seal, inner bearing and races.

9. Remove the nuts and bolts that hold the front hub and brake rotor together and separate them.

10. Support the lower control arm with a jack. Separate the ball joints and tie rod end from the knuckle. Once the ball joints have been released, lower the control arm slowly.

11. Remove the steering knuckle.

12. Remove the oil seal and spacer. If damaged, drive out the needle bearing from the spindle end of the knuckle.

To install:

13. Use either Mitsubishi tool MB990985 or Chrysler tool C–4178 to press the new needle bearing into the knuckle. Lubricate the rollers and install the spacer with the chamfered side facing the center of the vehicle. Install a new seal until it is flush with the knuckle end face and lubricate the lip.

14. Install the knuckle to the ball joint studs. Torque all ball joint nuts except the upper nut on Pick-Up and Ram 50 to 100 ft. lbs. (136 Nm). Torque the aforementioned nut to 60 ft. lbs. (82 Nm). Install new cotter pins.

15. Connect the tie rod end to the knuckle. Torque the nut to 30 ft. lbs. (41 Nm). Install a new cotter pin.

16. Clean out all of the old grease from inside the front hub.

17. Bolt the rotor and front hub together. Torque the nuts to 40 ft. lbs. (54 Nm). Install new races and apply wheel bearing grease to the inside of the front hub.

18. Pack the inner bearing and install to the race.

19. Install a new oil seal into the front hub so it is flush with the front hub end face.

20. Install the assembly onto the steering knuckle, pack and install the outer bearing. Using special tool MB990954 or equivalent, which fits standard torque wrenches, torque the locknut

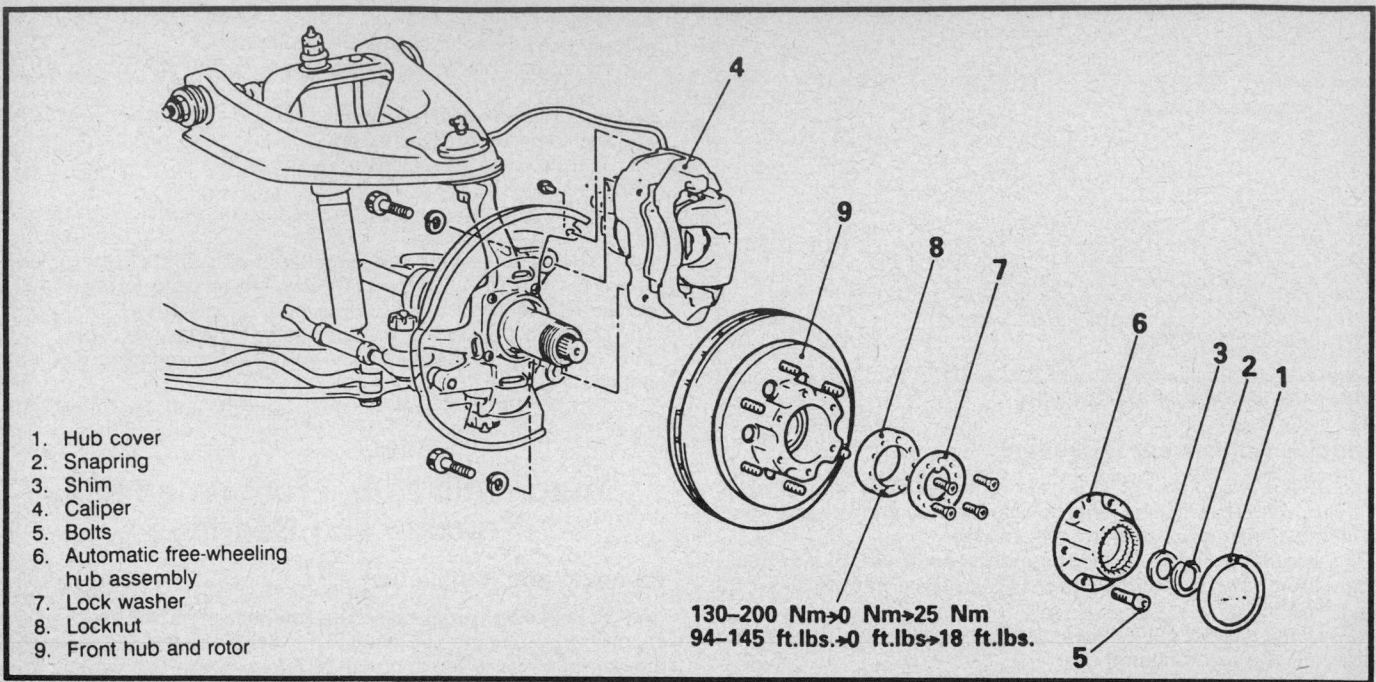

1. Hub cover
2. Snapring
3. Shim
4. Caliper
5. Bolts
6. Automatic free-wheeling
   hub assembly
7. Lock washer
8. Locknut
9. Front hub and rotor

130–200 Nm→0 Nm→25 Nm
94–145 ft.lbs.→0 ft.lbs→18 ft.lbs.

Front hub and automatic hub assembly—4WD vehicles

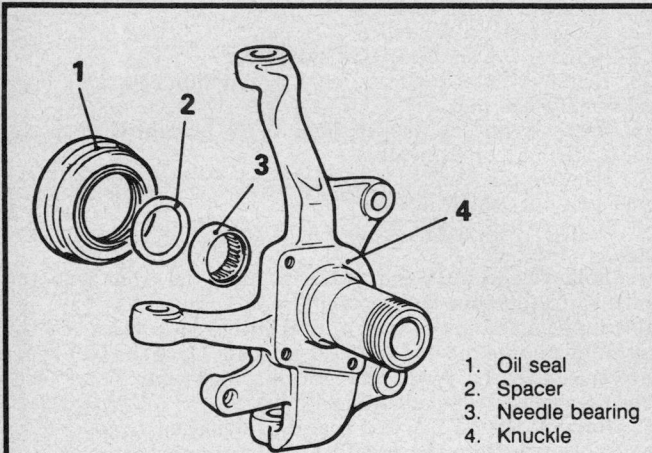

1. Oil seal
2. Spacer
3. Needle bearing
4. Knuckle

Steering knuckle, needle bearing, spacer and seal—4WD vehicle

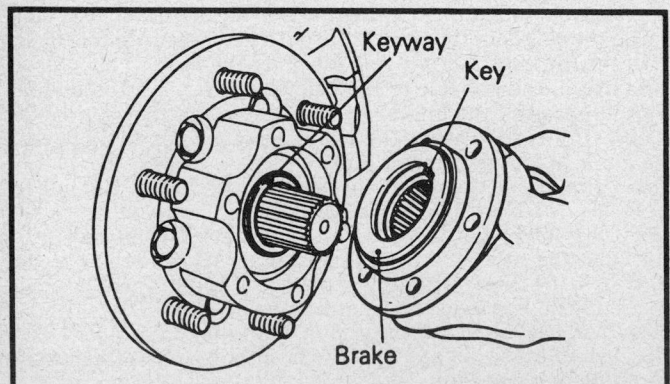

Keyway

Key

Brake

Aligning the key in the automatic hub with the keyway in the spindle

to 95–145 ft. lbs. (130–200 Nm). Loosen the locknut completely, then retorque to 18 ft. lbs. (25 Nm). To complete the procedure, position the torque wrench at the 3 o'clock position and loosen the nut the equivalent of 1 hour (30 degrees).

21. Install the lock washer. If the lock washer and locknut holes do not align, align the holes by loosening the nut slightly.

22. Before installing the automatic hub assembly, measure the turning force of the front hub. If the measured value does not meet specifications (2.5–11.5 inch lbs.), retorque the locknut. Also check the hub for an endplay of no more than 0.002 in. (0.05mm).

23. Apply a very thin even coating of sealant to the free wheeling hub surface of the front hub. Carefully align the key of the free-wheeling hub brake with the keyway of the knuckle spindle and install the automatic hub assembly. The mounting surfaces of the automatic hub and the front hub must be perfectly flush before the mounting bolts are torqued.

24. Torque the automatic hub mounting bolts to 40 ft. lbs. (54 Nm).

25. Check the front hub turning resistance again. If the difference between the reading in Step 16 and this reading is more than 8.7 inch lbs., repair or replace the automatic hub, as required.

26. Install the shim and snapring. Rotate the axle shaft forward and backward and stop at a position midway between 2 heavy spots where there is a heavy feeling.

27. Set a dial indicator so the pin is resting on the end of the axle shaft. The endplay specification is 0.008–0.020 in. (0.2–0.5mm). If not within specifications, adjust by adding or removing shims.

28. Install the hub cover.

29. Install the brake hardware and install the wheel and tire assembly.

30. Road test the vehicle.

Pinion Seal

Removal and Installation

1. Raise the vehicle and support safely.
2. Matchmark and remove the driveshaft.

3. Check the turning torque of the pinion before proceeding. It should be 3.5–4.5 inch lbs. (0.4–0.5 Nm). This is the torque that must be reached during installation of the pinion nut.

4. Using a suitable pinion flange holding tool, remove the pinion nut and washer.

5. Remove the companion flange from the drive pinion.

6. Pry the pinion seal out of the differential carrier.

7. Clean and inspect the sealing surface of the housing.

To install:

8. Using a seal driver, drive the new seal into the housing until the flange on the seal is flush with the carrier.

9. With the seal installed, the pinion bearing preload must be set.

10. Tighten the pinion nut, while holding the flange, until the turning torque is the same as before removal of the nut. The final pinion nut torque must be 137–181 ft. lbs. (190–250 Nm).

11. Align the matchmarks and install the drive shaft.

12. Check the level of the differential lubricant when finished.

Differential Case

Removal and Installation
FRONT DIFFERENTIAL

1. Raise the vehicle and support safely. Remove the under cover.

2. Remove all 3 front axle shafts.

3. Drain the front differential and remove the cover.

4. Remove the bearing cap retaining bolts, matchmark and remove the caps.

5. Carefully pry the differential case out of the housing, being careful not to drop the outer races.

6. Label any loose parts as they are removed from the assembly.

To install:

7. Install the differential case to the housing.

8. Install the caps aligning the matchmarks made previously. Torque the retaining bolts evenly and gradually to 45 ft. lbs. (61 Nm).

9. Thoroughly clean the sealing surfaces of the cover and the differential housing. Reseal the cover and install to the housing.

10. Install the axle shafts.

11. Level the vehicle and fill the differential with Hypoid gear oil with an API classification of at least GL–5, until it spills out the fill hole.

12. Install the under cover and lower the vehicle.

13. Perform a road test and check the differential for leaks.

Differential Carrier

Removal and Installation
REAR DIFFERENTIAL

1. Raise the vehicle and support safely.

2. Drain the rear differential.

3. Remove the rear tire and wheel assemblies and brake drums.

4. Remove the axle shafts.

5. Matchmark and remove the driveshaft.

6. Remove the differential carrier retaining nuts and remove the carrier from the axle housing.

7. The installation is the reverse of the removal procedure. Torque the carrier retaining nuts to 22 ft. lbs. (27 Nm).

Front Differential Housing

Removal and Installation

1. Raise the vehicle and support safely.

2. Remove the under cover and drain the differential.

3. Remove the hubs, knuckles and axle shafts as complete assemblies.

4. Remove the inner shaft.

5. Matchmark and remove the front driveshaft.

6. Support the differential housing with a jack.

7. Remove the differential mounting brackets.

8. Remove the front suspension crossmember.

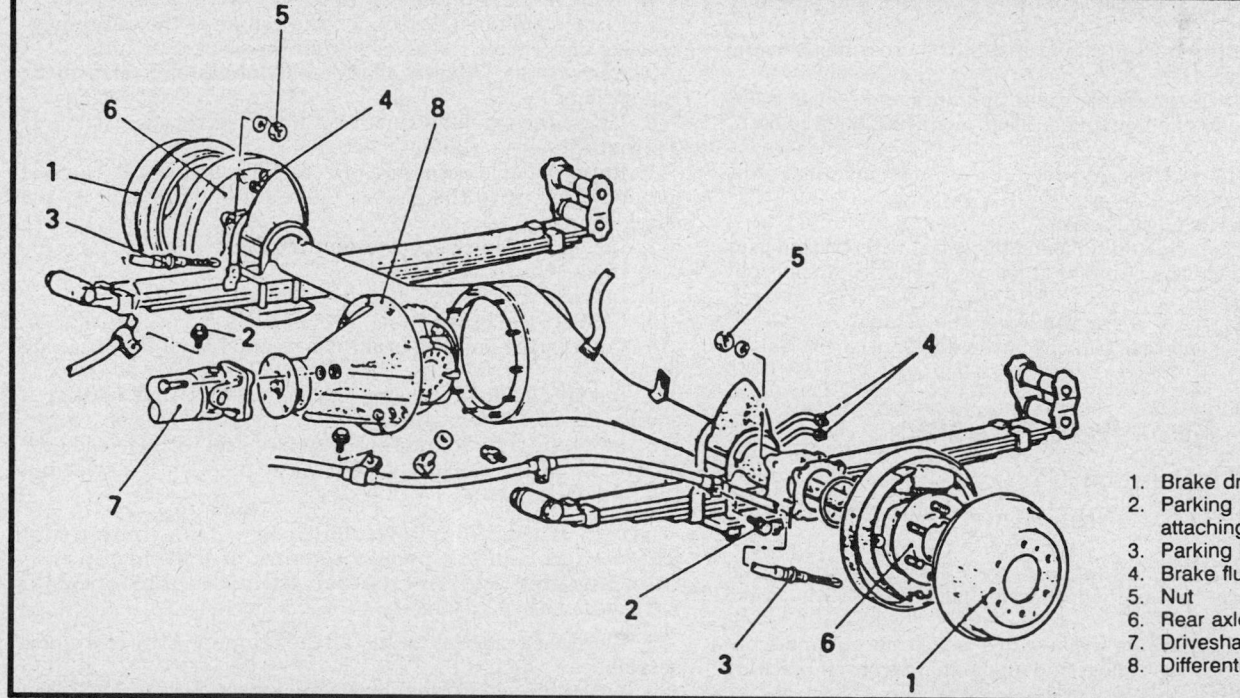

1. Brake drum
2. Parking brake cable attaching bolt
3. Parking brake cable
4. Brake fluid lines
5. Nut
6. Rear axle shaft
7. Driveshaft
8. Differential carrier

Differential carrier removal and installation

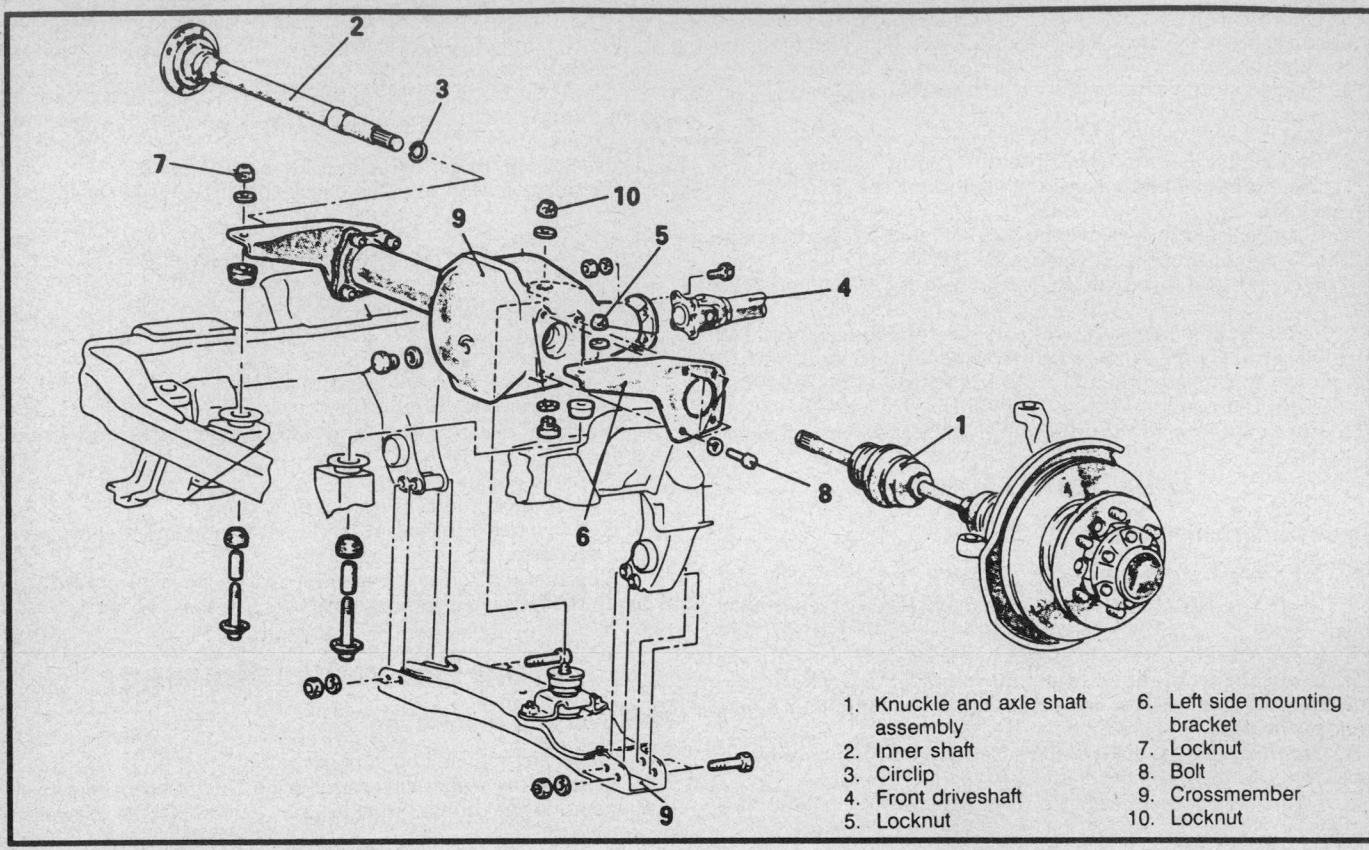

1. Knuckle and axle shaft assembly
2. Inner shaft
3. Circlip
4. Front driveshaft
5. Locknut
6. Left side mounting bracket
7. Locknut
8. Bolt
9. Crossmember
10. Locknut

Front axle removal and installation

9. Lower the differential housing and remove it from the vehicle.

To install:

10. Mount the housing safely on a suitable jack and raise into position.

11. Lubricate the bushings and install the crossmember and housing brackets.

12. Torque all crossmember mounting nuts and bolt to 80 ft. lbs. (109 Nm) and the housing bracket mounting bolts to 65 ft. lbs. (88 Nm).

13. Replace the circlips and install the inner axle and axle, knuckle and hub assemblies.

14. Install the front driveshaft.

15. Level the vehicle and fill the differential with Hypoid gear oil with an API classification of at least GL–5, until it spills out the fill hole.

16. Install the under cover and lower the vehicle.

17. Perform a road test and check the differential for leaks.

Rear Axle Housing

Removal and Installation

EXCEPT MONTERO AND RAIDER WITH COIL SPRINGS

1. Raise the vehicle and support safely. Drain the differential

2. Remove the tire and wheel assemblies. Remove the brake drums.

3. Remove the parking brake cable attaching bolts, disconnect the cables from the shoes and unclip them from the backing plates.

4. Disconnect the brake hose at the T-fitting.

5. Remove the load sensing proportioning valve spring support, if equipped.

6. Disconnect the breather hose, if equipped.

7. Matchmark and remove the driveshaft.

8. Place a suitable jack under the center of the differential housing and unbolt the shocks from their lower mounts.

9. Remove the U-bolts, shackle assemblies and remove the leaf springs.

10. Lower the axle and remove it from the vehicle.

To install:

11. Raise the axle assembly into position and install the leaf springs. Make sure the shackle nuts are on the inside of the shackles.

12. Install the lower shock mounting bolts.

13. Install the driveshaft.

14. Install the breather hose, if equipped.

15. Connect the brake hose.

16. Connect the parking brake cables and install the retaining bolts.

17. Install the load sensing spring support and spring, if equipped.

18. Level the vehicle and fill the differential with Hypoid gear oil with an API classification of at least GL–5, until it spills out the fill hole.

NOTE: If the vehicle is equipped with a limited slip differential, add the proper amount of limited slip friction modifier additive before filling the differential with gear oil.

19. Bleed the rear brakes. Install the drums and tire and wheel assemblies.

20. Lower the vehicle so that the full weight of the vehicle is on the ground. Unload any excess weight that is weighing down the

rear of the vehicle. Adjust the load sensing proportioning valve lever so that the distance from the proportioning valve lever to the spring support is about 7 in.

21. Road test the vehicle and check for leaks.

MONTERO AND RAIDER WITH COIL SPRINGS

1. Raise the vehicle and support safely. Drain the differential.
2. Remove the tire and wheel assemblies. Remove the brake drums.
3. Remove the parking brake cable attaching bolts, disconnect the cables from the shoes and unclip them from the backing plates.
4. Disconnect the brake hose at the T-fitting.
5. Disconnect the breather hose.
7. Matchmark and remove the driveshaft.
8. Remove the rear stabilizer bar attaching bolts, links and bushings.
9. Place a suitable jack under the center of the differential housing and remove the rear trailing arm, if equipped.
10. Remove the lateral rod.
11. Unbolt the shocks from their lower mounts.
12. Lower the axle housing enough to remove the coil springs and the stabilizer bar.
13. Lower the axle assembly and remove it from the vehicle.

To install:

14. With the coil springs and stabilizer bar in place, raise the axle assembly into place and install the lower shock mounting bolts.

15. Install the lateral rod but do not tighten the nuts yet.
16. Assemble the trailing arm with its front mounting spacers, bushings and nuts. Make sure the washer's concave side faces away from the bushings. Install the trailing arm and torque the rear mount nuts to 90 ft. lbs. (122 Nm). Do not tighten the front mounting nuts yet.
17. Install the stabilizer bar and tighten the mounting nuts until the diameter of the bushing is the same as the diameter of the washers.
18. Install the driveshaft and breather hose.
19. Connect the parking brake cables and install the retaining bolts.
20. Level the vehicle and fill the differential with Hypoid gear oil with an API classification of at least GL–5, until it spills out the fill hole.

NOTE: If the vehicle is equipped with a limited slip differential, add the proper amount of limited slip friction modifier additive before filling the differential with gear oil.

21. Bleed the rear brakes. Install the drums and tire and wheel assemblies.
20. Lower the vehicle so that the full weight of the vehicle is on the ground. Torque the lateral rod mounting nuts to 90 ft. lbs. (122 Nm) and the front trailing arm mounting nuts to 100 ft. lbs. (150 Nm).
21. Road test the vehicle and check for leaks.

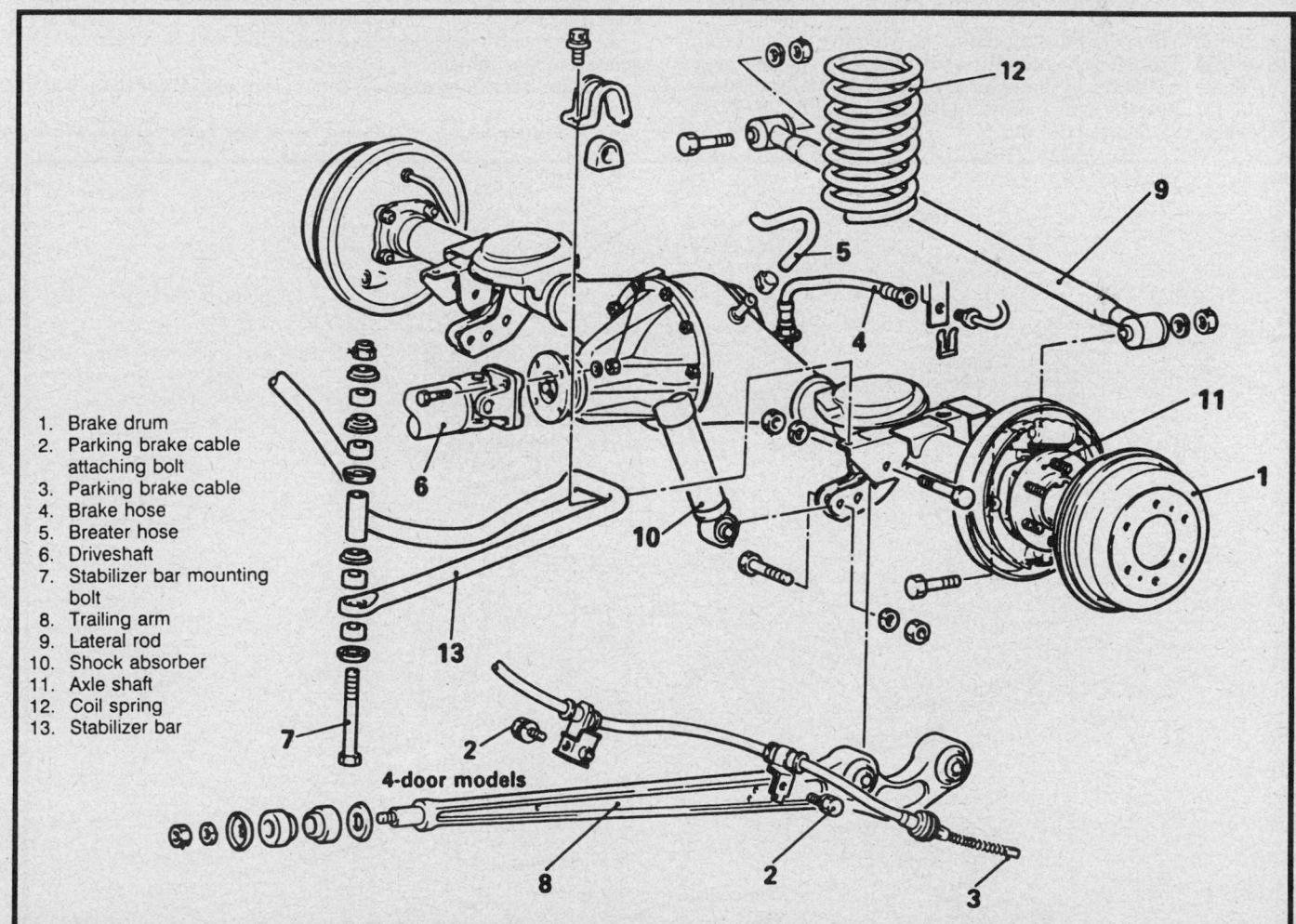

1. Brake drum
2. Parking brake cable attaching bolt
3. Parking brake cable
4. Brake hose
5. Breater hose
6. Driveshaft
7. Stabilizer bar mounting bolt
8. Trailing arm
9. Lateral rod
10. Shock absorber
11. Axle shaft
12. Coil spring
13. Stabilizer bar

Rear axle assembly—Montero and Raider with coil springs

STEERING

Steering Wheel

Removal and Installation

1. Disconnect the negative battery cable.
2. Remove the center pad.
3. Remove the steering wheel hold-down nut. Matchmark the steering wheel to the shaft.
4. Using a suitable steering wheel puller, pull the steering wheel off of the shaft.
5. The installation is the reverse of the removal procedure.

Manual Rack and Pinion Steering Gear

Removal and Installation

VAN

1. Disconnect the negative battery cable.
2. Raise the vehicle and support safely. Remove the under cover.
3. Remove the front tire and wheel assemblies.
4. Remove the cotter pins, castellated nuts and tie rod ends from the steering knuckles.
5. Disconnect the intermediate shaft from the steering gear yoke.
6. Remove the gear housing clamps and remove the gear from the vehicle. Transfer the mounting insulators to the new gear.
7. The installation is the reverse of the removal procedure. Torque the steering gear mounting bolt to 60 ft. lbs. (81 Nm).
8. Align the front end.

Adjustment

With the rack removed from the vehicle, total pinion torque can be checked and adjusted. Remove the boots before attempting to adjust because they will create an additional drag.

1. Attach special tool MB990228–01 to the pinion shaft and rotate the pinion with an inch lb. torque wrench. Turn the pinion 180 degrees to the right and left to measure.
2. The specification is 5–10 inch lbs.
3. If not within specifications, loosen the large locknut below the shaft and tighten the adjust cover until the proper turning torque is reached.
4. If the proper torque is not obtained after tightening the adjust cover 60 degrees, disassemble the unit and replace worn parts.

Manual Steering Gear

Removal and Installation

1. Disconnect the negative battery cable. Raise the vehicle and support safely.
2. Remove the pinch bolt the that holds the steering column shaft to the steering gear main shaft.
3. Remove the cotter pin, castellated nut and remove the steering linkage from the pitman arm.
4. Remove the steering gear mounting nuts and remove the gear from the vehicle.
5. Matchmark and remove the pitman arm from the pitman shaft.
6. The installation is the reverse of the removal procedure.

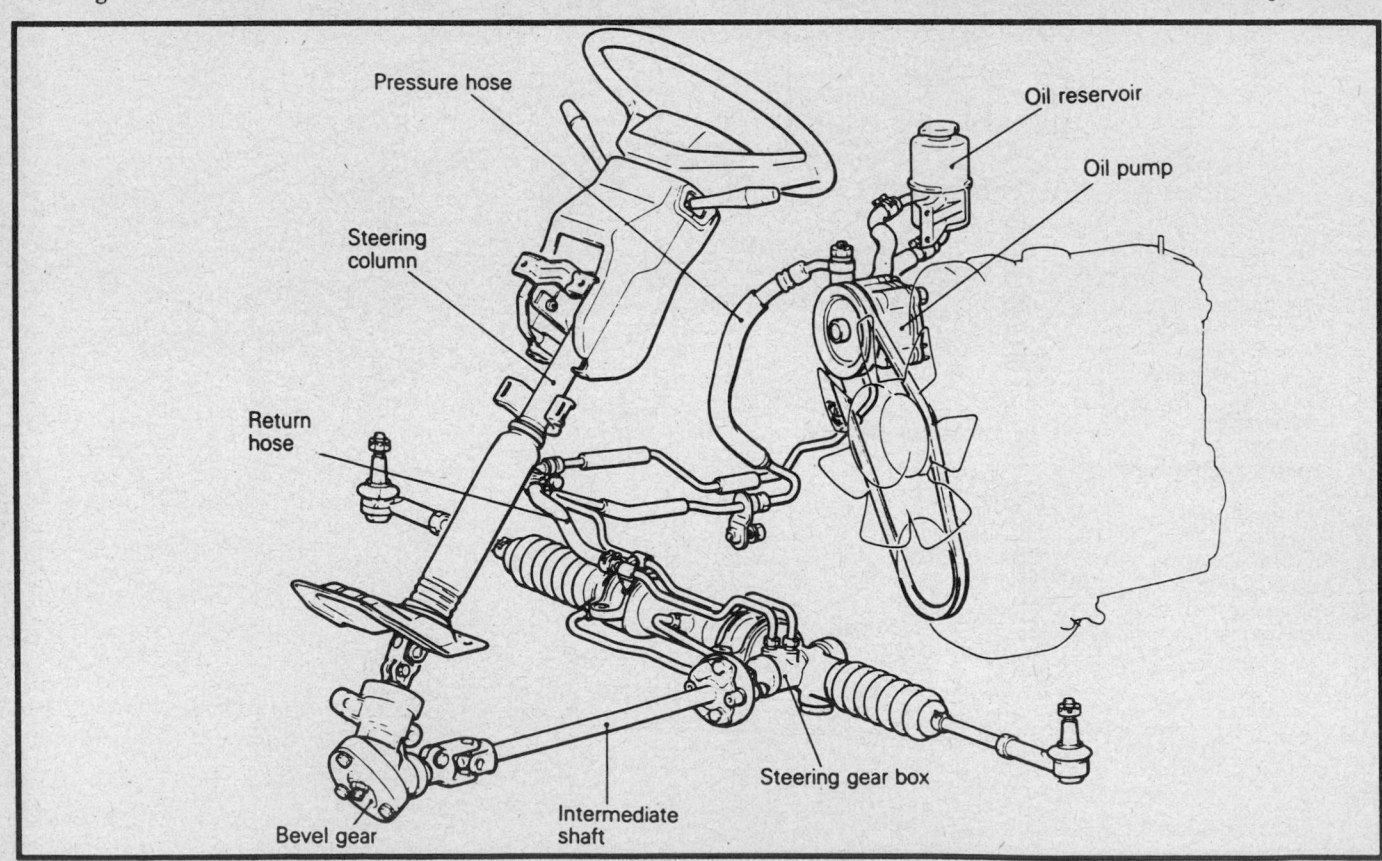

Power steering components—Van

Torque the pitman arm nut to 100 ft. lbs. (136 Nm) and the gear's mounting nuts to 35 ft. lbs. (47 Nm).

7. Align the front end.

Adjustment

1. With the gear removed from the vehicle and the pitman arm installed, move the pitman arm back and forth 5 times to mesh the gears sufficiently.

2. Measure the steering gear backlash by setting up a dial indicator with the pin resting on the side of the end of the pitman arm. Make sure the backlash with all internal gears in the straight ahead position.

3. The backlash should be no more than 0.02 in. (0.5mm). Adjust the adjusting screw to obtain the proper backlash.

Power Rack and Pinion Steering Gear

Removal and Installation

1. Disconnect the negative battery cable.

2. Raise the vehicle and support safely. Remove the under cover.

3. Remove the front tire and wheel assemblies.

4. Remove the cotter pins, castellated nuts and tie rod ends from the steering knuckles.

5. Disconnect the intermediate shaft from the steering gear yoke.

6. Disconnect and plug the fluid lines from the fittings on the rack.

7. Remove the gear housing clamps and remove the gear from the vehicle. Transfer the mounting insulators to the new gear and replace the O-rings on the the fluid lines.

8. The installation is the reverse of the removal procedure.

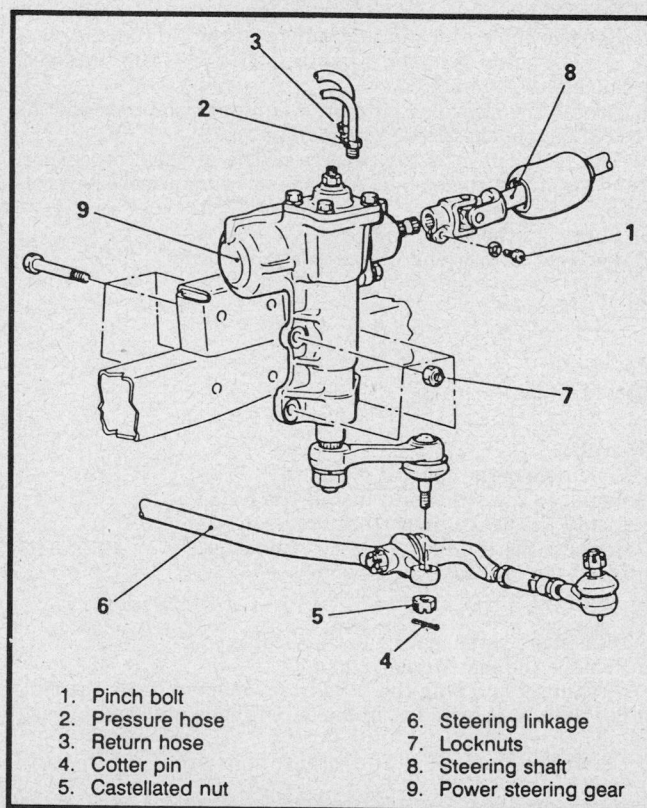

1. Pinch bolt
2. Pressure hose
3. Return hose
4. Cotter pin
5. Castellated nut
6. Steering linkage
7. Locknuts
8. Steering shaft
9. Power steering gear

Power steering gear and related parts — Montero, Raider, Pick-Up and Ram 50

Torque the steering gear mounting bolt to 60 ft. lbs. (81 Nm).

9. Fill and bleed the system.

10. Align the front end as required.

Adjustment

With the rack removed from the vehicle, total pinion torque can be checked and adjusted. Remove the boots before attempting to adjust because they will create an additional drag.

1. Attach special tool MB990228–01 to the pinion shaft and rotate the pinion with an inch lb. torque wrench. Turn the pinion 180 degrees to the right and left to measure.

2. The specification is 6–12 inch lbs.

3. If not within specifications, loosen the large locknut below the shaft and tighten the adjust cover until the proper turning torque is reached.

4. If the proper torque is not obtained after tightening the adjust cover 60 degrees, disassemble the unit and replace worn parts.

Power Steering Gear

Removal and Installation

1. Disconnect the negative battery cable. Raise the vehicle and support safely.

2. Fold back the dust boot which covers the steering shaft joint, if equipped. Remove the pinch bolt the that holds the steering column shaft to the steering gear main shaft.

3. Remove the cotter pin, castellated nut and remove the steering linkage from the pitman arm.

4. Disconnect and plug the fluid lines from the steering gear.

4. Remove the steering gear mounting nuts and remove the gear from the vehicle.

5. Matchmark and remove the pitman arm from the pitman shaft.

6. The installation is the reverse of the removal procedure. Torque the pitman arm nut to 100 ft. lbs. (136 Nm) and the gear's mounting nuts to 28 ft. lbs. (38 Nm) on 2WD vehicles and 45 ft. lbs. (61 Nm) on 4WD vehicles.

7. Fill and bleed the system.

8. Align the front end.

Adjustment

1. Attach special tool MB990228–01 to the mainshaft and rotate the pinion with an inch lb. torque wrench to measure the starting torque.

2. The specification is 4–11 inch lbs.

3. If not within specifications, loosen the adjusting screw locknut and adjust the locknut until the proper starting torque is reached.

4. Tighten the adjusting bolt locknut.

Bevel Gear and Intermediate Shaft

Removal and Installation

VAN

1. Disconnect the negative battery cable. Raise the vehicle and support safely.

2. Remove the pinch bolt that holds the steering column shaft to the bevel gear input shaft.

3. Remove the pinch bolt and remove the intermediate shaft from the bevel gear output shaft.

4. Remove the mounting bolts and remove the bevel gear from the vehicle.

5. Disconnect the intermediate shaft from the steering gear yoke and remove the shaft. Inspect the rubber coupling for damage.

6. The installation is the reverse of the removal procedure. Torque the bevel gear mounting bolt to 35 ft. lbs. (47 Nm).

Power Steering Pump

Removal and Installation

1. Disconnect the negative battery cable.
2. Position a drain pan under the power steering pump.
3. Disconnect the fluid lines from the pump and plug them.
4. Remove the front bracket attaching bolts and remove the belt from the pulley.
5. Remove the pump from the vehicle.
6. The installation is the reverse of the removal procedure.
7. Adjust the belt tension.
8. Fill and bleed the system.

Belt Adjustment
EXCEPT 3.0L ENGINE

1. Loosen the pump mounting bolts.
2. Using a suitable pry bar, move the pump away from the engine.
3. With the pump moved enough so that the belt deflects about ¼–½ in. under a 10 lb. load, tighten the bolts.

3.0L ENGINE

1. Loosen the tensioner pulley locknut.
2. Tighten the adjuster bolt until the belt deflects about ¼–½ in. under a 10 lb. load
3. Tighten the tensioner lock bolt.

System Bleeding
EXCEPT VAN

1. Fill the reservoir with Dexron®II.
2. Raise the front end of the vehicle.
3. Disconnect the ignition coil wire.
4. Simultaneously crank the engine and turn the steering wheel from lock to lock. Repeat this several times.

NOTE: If the bleeding procedure is done with the engine running, high speed rotation of the pump will churn the fluid and create air bubbles filling the system with air. Bleed the system while cranking the engine only.

5. Lower the front end.

6. Connect one end of a suitable vinyl tube to the breather plug on the steering box and place the other a container.
7. Start the engine and allow it to idle.
8. Loosen the breather plug and turn the steering wheel from lock to lock continuously until no more air bubbles appear in the fluid coming out the tube.

NOTE: Do not hold the steering wheel all the way against the stop for more than 5 seconds.

9. After the bleeding is done, tighten the breather plug and refill the reservoir.

VAN

1. Fill the reservoir with Dexron®II. Disconnect the ignition coil wire.
2. Simultaneously crank the engine and turn the steering wheel from lock to lock. Repeat this several times.

NOTE: If the bleeding procedure is done with the engine running, high speed rotation of the pump will churn the fluid and create air bubbles filling the system with air. Bleed the system while cranking the engine only.

3. Start the engine and allow it to idle.
4. Turn the steering wheel from lock to lock until no more bubbles are visible in the fluid reservoir.
5. Confirm that the fluid is not milky and that there is very little change in the fluid level when the steering wheel is turned.
6. If the fluid level rises when the engine is turned off, there is still air present in the system.

Tie Rod Ends

Removal and Installation

1. Raise the vehicle and support safely.
2. Remove the cotter pin and nut from the tie rod end.
3. Using a suitable puller, remove the tie rod from the steering knuckle or center link.
4. Loosen the sleeve clamp nut, if equipped and unscrew the tie rod end from the sleeve or inner tie rod.
5. The installation is the reverse of the removal procedure. Torque the stud nuts to 33 ft. lbs. (45 Nm) and install a new cotter pin.
6. Lubricate the front end.
7. Perform a front end alignment as required.

BRAKES

For all brake system repair and service procedure not detained below, please refer to "Brakes" in the Unit Repair section.

Master Cylinder

Removal and Installation
EXCEPT VAN

1. Disconnect the negative battery cable. Disconnect the fluid level sensor connector.
2. Disconnect and plug the brake lines from the master cylinder.
3. Remove the nuts attaching the master cylinder to the power booster.
4. Remove the master cylinder from the mounting studs.
5. Remove the fluid reservoir from the cylinder.

To install:
6. Bench bleed the master cylinder.
7. Install to the studs and install the nuts.
8. Install the brake lines to the master cylinder.
9. Connect the fluid level sensor connector.
10. Bleed the brakes, if necessary.

VAN

1. Disconnect the negative battery cable.
2. Remove the instrument cluster.
3. Disconnect and plug the fluid hoses that run from the reservoir to the actual cylinder. Make sure fluid is not leaking past the plugs.
4. Disconnect and plug the brake lines from the master cylinder.
5. Remove the nuts attaching the master cylinder to the power booster.
6. Remove the master cylinder from the mounting studs.

To install:
7. Bench bleed the master cylinder.
8. Install to the studs and install the nuts.
9. Install the brake lines to the master cylinder.
10. Connect the fluid hoses to the cylinder.
11. Install the instrument cluster.
12. Bleed the brakes, if necessary.
13. Check the operation of all brake warning indicators on the instrument cluster.

Proportioning Valve

Removal and Installation
MONTERO AND RAIDER

1. Disconnect the negative battery cable.
2. Raise the vehicle and support safely.
3. Identify and disconnect the brake lines from the valve.
4. Disconnect the wires to the valve, if any.
5. Remove the proportioning valve from the vehicle.
6. The installation is the reverse of the removal procedure.
7. Bleed the brakes in the following order:
   a. Right rear
   b. Right front
   c. Left front

Load Sensing Proportioning Valve

Removal and Installation
PICK-UP, RAM 50 AND VAN

1. Disconnect the negative battery cable.
2. Raise the vehicle and support safely.
3. Identify and disconnect the brake lines from the valve.
4. Remove the mounting bolts and remove the valve leaving the spring hanging from the lever.

To install:
5. Install the valve to the vehicle engaging the spring.
6. Connect the brake lines.
7. Bleed the brakes in the following order:
   a. Right rear
   b. Load sensing proportioning valve
   c. Right front
   d. Left front
7. Lower the vehicle so that the full weight of the vehicle is on the ground. Unload any excess weight that is weighing down the rear of the vehicle. Adjust the load sensing proportioning valve lever so that the distance from the proportioning valve lever to the spring support is about 7 in.

Power Brake Booster

Removal and Installation
EXCEPT VAN

1. Disconnect the negative battery cable. Disconnect the vacuum hose from the booster.
2. Remove the nuts attaching the master cylinder to the booster and move the master cylinder to the side.
3. From inside of the vehicle, remove the clevis pin that secures the booster pushrod to the brake pedal.
4. Remove the nuts that attach the booster to the dash panel and remove it from the vehicle.
5. The installation is the reverse of the removal procedure.

VAN

1. Disconnect the negative battery cable.
2. Remove the driver's lap heater duct.
3. Remove the upper and lower column covers.
4. Disconnect the column electrical connectors.

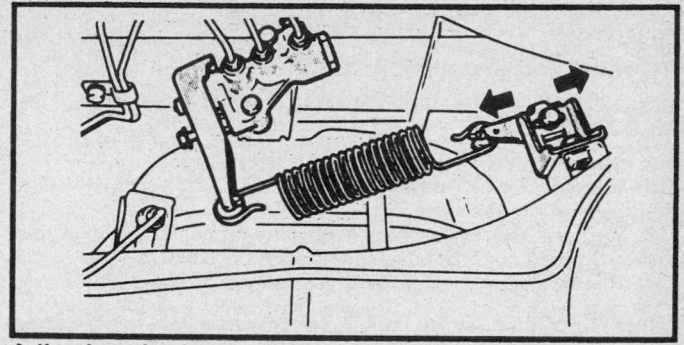
Adjusting the load sensing proportioning valve

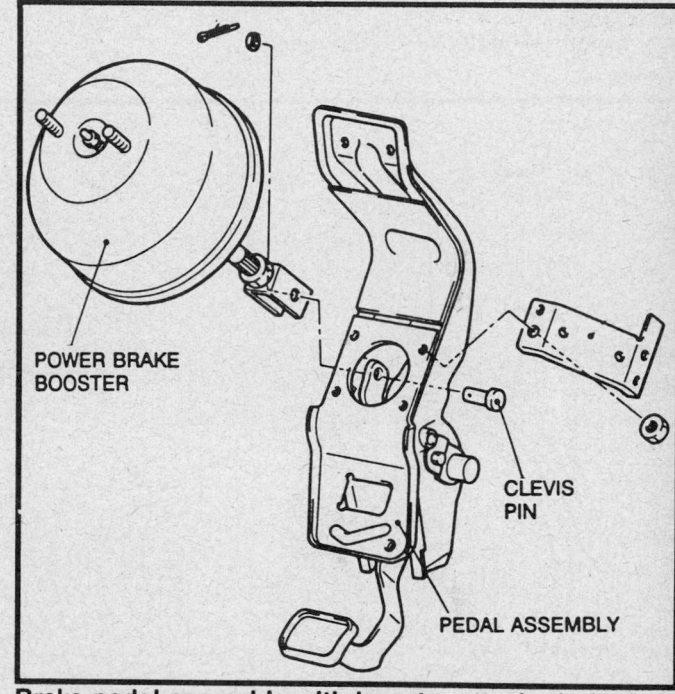

POWER BRAKE BOOSTER

CLEVIS PIN

PEDAL ASSEMBLY

Brake pedal assembly with booster attached—Van

5. Raise the vehicle and support safely. Remove the pinch bolt that retains the column shaft to the bevel gear input shaft. Lower the vehicle.
6. Remove the master cylinder.
7. Disconnect the stop lamp switch connector.
8. Disconnect the vacuum hose from the booster.
9. Remove the entire brake pedal assembly (with its bracket) with the booster attached.
10. Remove the clevis pin that secures the booster pushrod to the brake pedal.
11. Remove the nuts that attach the booster to the brake pedal bracket.

To install:
12. Install the booster to the bracket and attach the pushrod to the brake pedal. Install the clevis pin and install a new cotter pin.
13. Install the assembly to the vehicle. Connect the vacuum hose.
14. Install the master cylinder and connect the stop lamp switch.
15. Install the column and install the pinch bolt.
16. Install the upper and lower covers and the lap duct.
17. Bleed the brakes.

Brake Caliper

Removal and Installation

1986–87 MONTERO AND RAIDER AND 1986 PICK-UP AND RAM 50

1. Raise the vehicle and support safely.
2. Remove the tire and wheel assembly. Disconnect the brake line from the brake hose.
3. Remove the cotter pins from the upper slider pad and knock the pad out. Remove the pad support plate.
4. Repeat the above for the lower slider pad and plate.

NOTE: There is no need to remove the anti-rattle springs to complete this operation.

5. Remove the caliper from the adaptor.
6. Disconnect the brake line from the caliper.

To install:

7. Install the brake line to the caliper.
8. Thoroughly clean, dry and lubricate the slider pads with a very thin application of anti-seize compound.
9. Make sure all anti-rattle and -squeal clips and pads are in place.
10. Install the caliper to the adaptor and install the pad plates and pads. Make sure they are installed the correct way. Compare to the other side to confirm. Install the cotter pins.
11. Connect the brake line to the hose.
12. Bleed the brakes.
13. Install the tire and wheel assembly.
14. Road test the vehicle.

EXCEPT 1986–87 MONTERO AND RAIDER AND 1986 PICK-UP AND RAM 50

1. Raise the vehicle and support safely.
2. Remove the tire and wheel assembly. Disconnect the brake line from the caliper.
3. Label and remove the 2 mounting bolts.
4. Lift the caliper off of the adaptor.

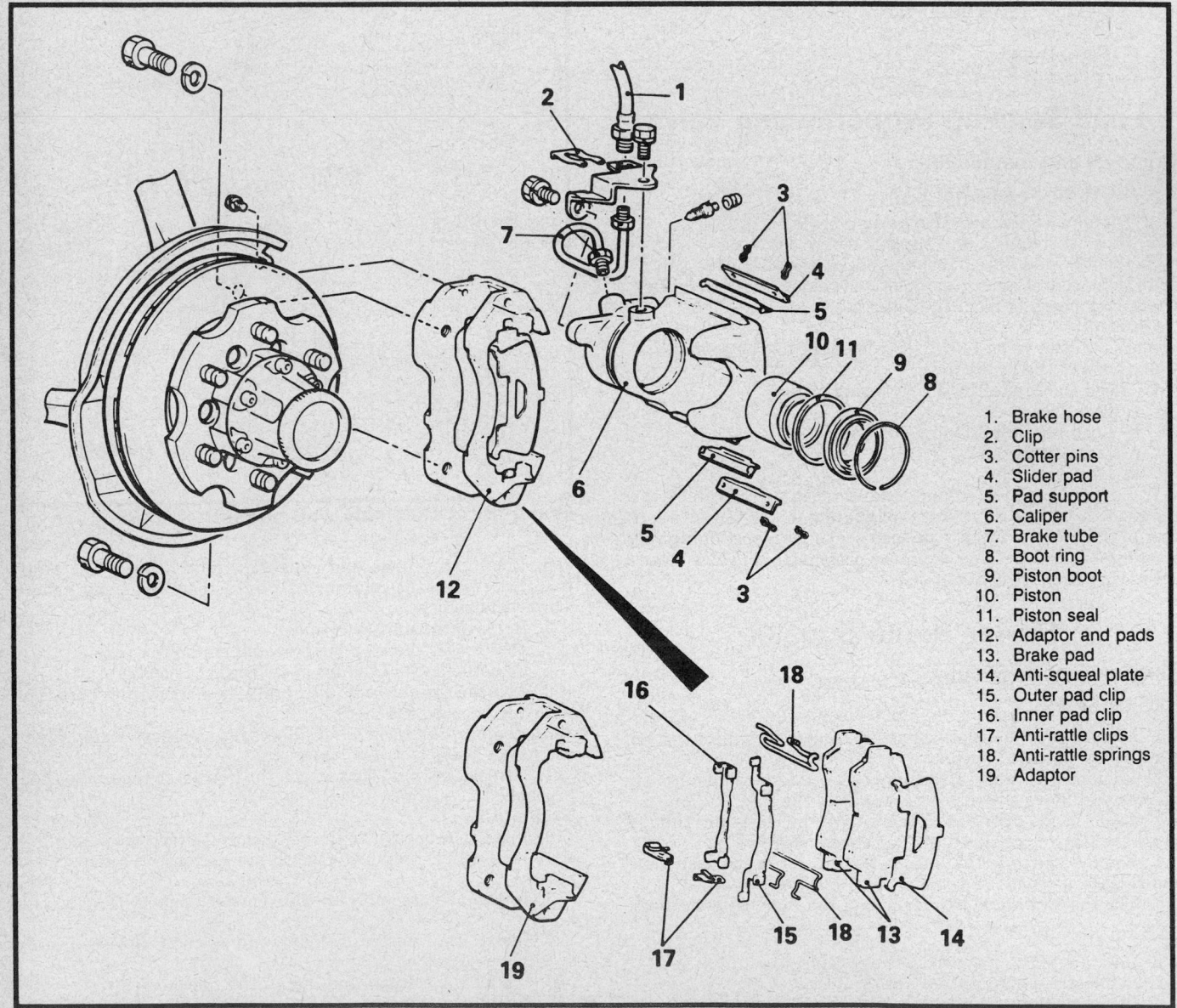

1. Brake hose
2. Clip
3. Cotter pins
4. Slider pad
5. Pad support
6. Caliper
7. Brake tube
8. Boot ring
9. Piston boot
10. Piston
11. Piston seal
12. Adaptor and pads
13. Brake pad
14. Anti-squeal plate
15. Outer pad clip
16. Inner pad clip
17. Anti-rattle clips
18. Anti-rattle springs
19. Adaptor

Front brakes—1986–87 Montero and Raider and 1986 Pick-Up and Ram 50

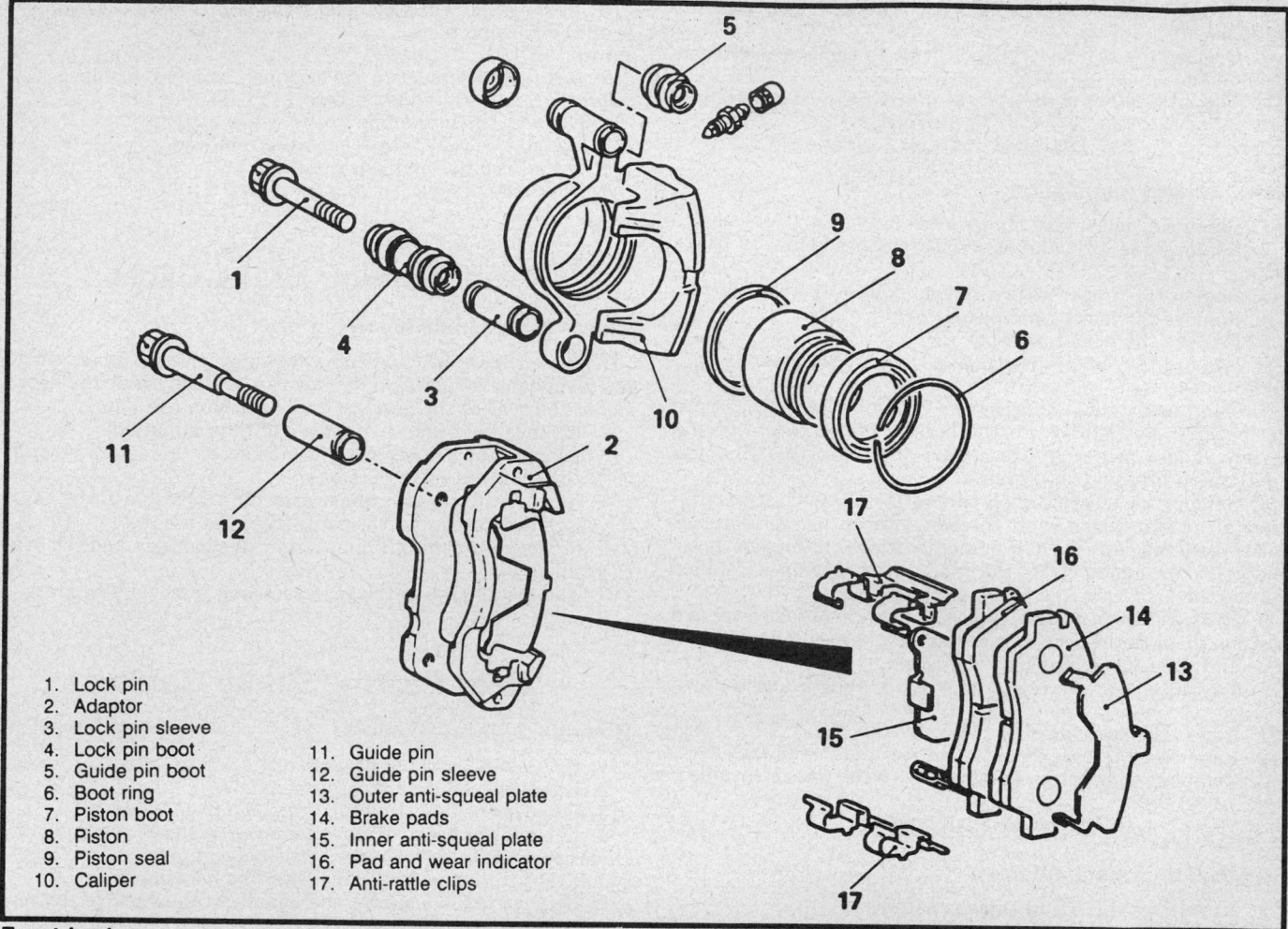

1. Lock pin
2. Adaptor
3. Lock pin sleeve
4. Lock pin boot
5. Guide pin boot
6. Boot ring
7. Piston boot
8. Piston
9. Piston seal
10. Caliper
11. Guide pin
12. Guide pin sleeve
13. Outer anti-squeal plate
14. Brake pads
15. Inner anti-squeal plate
16. Pad and wear indicator
17. Anti-rattle clips

Front brakes—except 1986–87 Montero and Raider and 1986 Pick-Up and Ram 50

5. The installation is the reverse of the removal procedure. Make sure all anti-rattle and -squeal clips and pads are in place. Torque the guide pin bolt to 35 ft. lbs. (47 Nm) and the lock pin bolt to 30 ft. lbs. (41 Nm).

6. Bleed the brakes and road test the vehicle.

Disc Brake Pads

Removal and Installation

1. Remove some of the fluid from the master cylinder.
2. Raise the vehicle and support safely. Remove the tire and wheel assemblies.
3. Remove the caliper.
4. Remove the pads from the adaptor.

To install:

5. Use a large C-clamp to compress the piston back into the caliper bore.
6. Install the pads to the adaptor with all anti-rattle and -squeal clips and pads in place.
8. Install the caliper.
9. Refill the master cylinder.
10. Bleed the brakes if the brake lines were opened.

Brake Rotor

Removal and Installation

1. Raise the vehicle and support safely.

2. Remove the tire and wheel assembly.
3. Remove the caliper and brake pads.
4. Remove the caliper adaptor.
5. If the vehicle is equipped with 4WD, remove the automatic hub, the shim, lock washer and locknut.
6. If the vehicle is 2WD, remove the dust cap, cotter pin, nut lock, nut, washer and outer bearing.
7. Remove the front hub and rotor assembly and unbolt the rotor from the hub.

To install:

8. Install the rotor to the hub and torque the attaching nuts and bolts to 40 ft. lbs. (54 Nm).
9. Install the assembly and retaining parts to the spindle.
10. Install the caliper adaptor. Torque the bolts to 70 ft. lbs. (95 Nm).
11. Install the brake pads and caliper, making sure all anti-rattle and -squeal clips and pads in place.
12. Bleed the brakes if the brake lines were opened.
13. Install the tire and wheel assembly and road test the vehicle.

Brake Drums

Removal and Installation

1. Raise the vehicle and support safely.
2. Remove the tire and wheel assembly.

3. Remove the drum retaining screw with an impact driver if equipped.

4. Remove the drum. If it is difficult to remove the drum, back off the adjusting wheel.

5. The installation is the reverse of the removal procedure.

Brake Shoes

Removal and Installation

1. Raise the vehicle and support safely.

2. Remove the tire and wheel assemblies and the brake drums.

3. Remove the upper return spring along with the adjuster.

4. Remove the lower retaining spring.

5. Remove the hold-down springs.

6. Remove the shoes, disengaging the parking brake lever.

To install:

7. Thoroughly clean and dry the backing plate. To prepare the backing plate, lubricate the bosses, anchor contacts and wheel cylinder piston grooves where the top of the shoe fits lightly with lithium based grease.

8. Remove, clean and dry all parts still on the old shoes. Lubricate the star wheel shaft threads with anti-sieze lubricant and transfer all parts to their proper locations on the new shoes. Make sure the longer end of the upper return spring is installed toward the shoe with the parking brake lever.

9. Spread the shoes apart, engage the parking brake lever and position them on the backing plate so the wheel cylinder pins engage and the anchor pins hold the shoes.

10. Install the lower retaining spring and the hold-down springs.

11. Adjust the star wheel.

12. Remove any grease from the linings and install the drum.

13. Complete the brake adjustment with the wheels installed.

Wheel Cylinder

Removal and Installation

1. Raise the vehicle and support safely.

2. Remove the wheel, drum and brake shoes.

3. Remove the brake line from the wheel cylinder.

4. Remove the wheel cylinder bolts and remove the cylinder from the backing plate.

To install:

5. Install the cylinder to the backing plate and install the retaining bolts. Torque the bolts to 14 ft. lbs. (19 Nm).

6. Connect the brake line to the wheel cylinder.

7. Install all brake parts that were removed.

8. Install the tire and wheel assembly.

9. Bleed the brakes.

Front Parking Brake Cable

Removal and Installation

1. Raise the vehicle and support safely, except Van. Remove the front cable adjusting nut. This can be done inside the vehicle, at the rear of the parking brake lever on the Van.

2. Remove the brake lever cover, if floor mounted.

3. Remove the pin securing the cable to the equalizer and slide the cable out of the bracket.

4. Remove the pin or retainer attaching the cable to the handle assembly. Disengage the cable from the handle.

5. Remove the cable grommet from the floor pan and remove the cable.

6. The installation is the reverse of the removal procedure.

Rear Parking Brake Cable

Removal and Installation

1. Release the parking brakes fully.

2. Raise the vehicle and support safely.

3. Remove the adjusting nut from the front cable.

4. Remove the brake drums. Remove the shoes, if necessary. Disconnect the cable from the lever and compress the cable retainer tabs to remove the cable from the backing plate.

5. Remove the cable from the equalizer and remove the retaining bolts from the frame.

6. The installation is the reverse of the removal procedure.

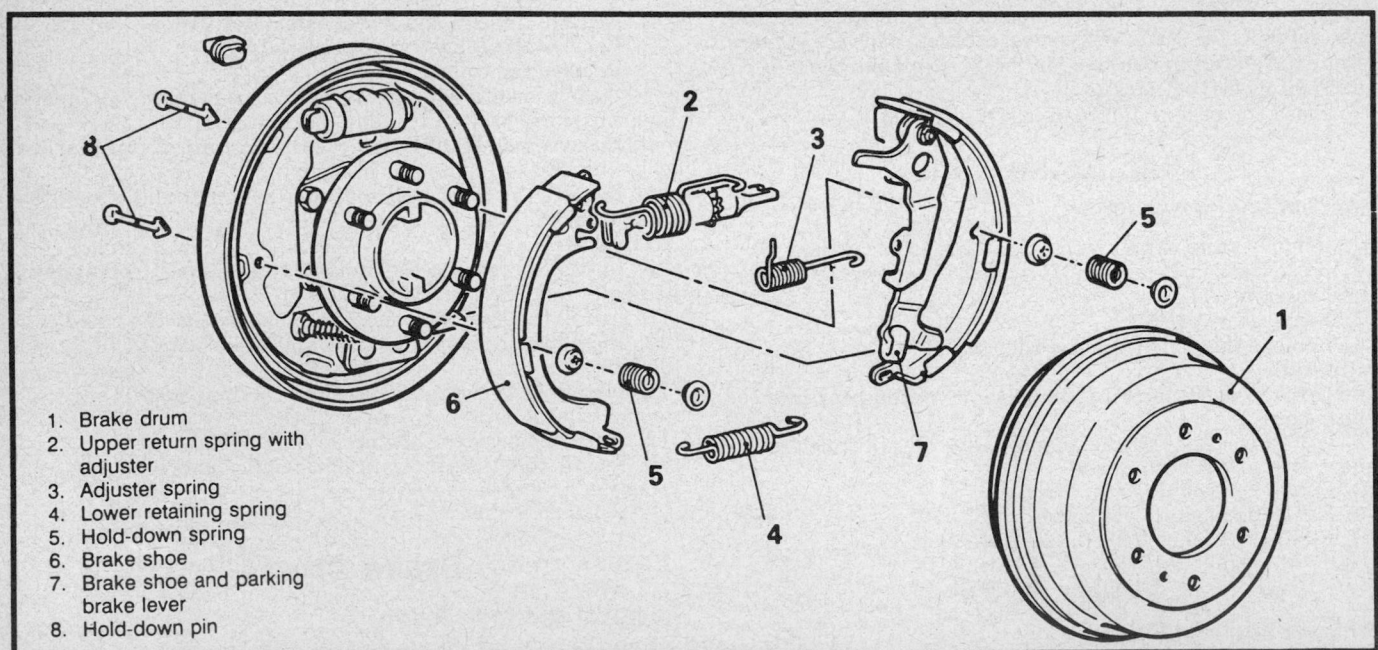

1. Brake drum
2. Upper return spring with adjuster
3. Adjuster spring
4. Lower retaining spring
5. Hold-down spring
6. Brake shoe
7. Brake shoe and parking brake lever
8. Hold-down pin

Rear brake shoes and hardware

Adjustment

1. Release the parking brakes fully.
2. Raise the vehicle and support safely.
3. Adjust the rear brakes.
4. Loosen the adjusting nut until there is slack in all the cables.
5. Rotate the rear wheels and tighten the cable adjusting nut until there is a slight drag at the wheels.

6. Continue to rotate the rear wheels and loosen the nut until all drag is eliminated.
7. Back off the nut an additional 2 turns.
8. Apply and release the parking brake several times. Upon the least release, verify that there is no drag at the wheels. The pedal should be able to be pulled 4–7 notches.
9. To check the operation, make sure the parking brake holds on an incline.

FRONT SUSPENSION

Shock Absorbers

Removal and Installation

1. Support the vehicle safely and raise enough to so there is room to get to the upper shock mount.
2. Remove the upper shock nut, washer and bushing. Raise the vehicle fully and support safely.
3. Remove the lower mounting bolt(s) and remove the shock from the vehicle.
4. The installation is the reverse of the removal procedure.

Coil Spring

Removal and Installation

2WD PICK-UP AND RAM 50

1. Raise the vehicle and support safely.
2. Remove the shock absorber.
3. Disconnect the stabilizer bar from the lower control arm.
4. Install spring compressor tool MB990792, or equivalent to the coil spring and to compress the spring.
5. Remove the cotter pin and lower ball joint nut.
6. Release the lower ball joint taper using ball stud loosening Chrysler tool C–3564–A or Mitsubushi tool MB990809–01.
7. Remove the tool and remove the ball stud from the control arm. Release the compressor tool from the coil spring.
8. Pull the arm down and remove the spring with the rubber isolation pad from the vehicle.

To install:

9. Install the spring with the rubber isolator. Install the compressor tool and compress it enough so the lower ball joint can be inserted through the knuckle.
10. Torque the lower ball joint nut to 100 ft. lbs. (136 Nm). Install a new cotter pin. Remove the spring compressor.
11. Connect the sway bar to the lower control arm, if equipped.
12. Install the shock absorber.

Torsion Bar

Removal and Installation

4WD VEHICLE

1. Raise the vehicle and support safely. Remove the under cover.
2. Support the lower control arm at a point away from where the torsion bar attaches to the arm.
3. Fold the dust covers back and slide them away from the ends of the bar.
4. If the bars are to be reused, matchmark the torsion bar at both ends to the anchor and identify left from right.
5. Paint or measure the distance of the exposed threads of the rear mounting bolt down to the nut to aid in adjustment when

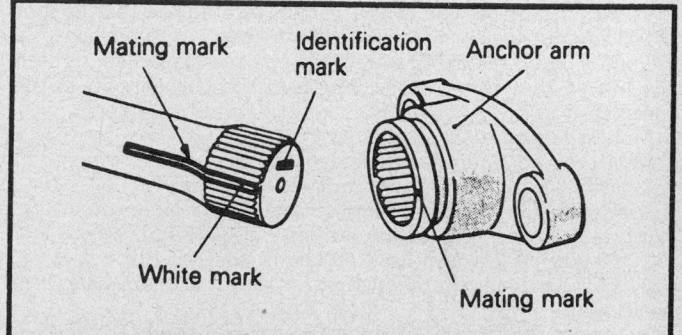

Aligning the front of the torsion bar with the front anchor—Except Van

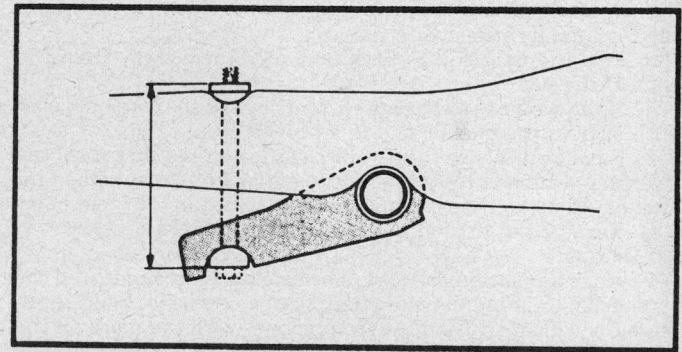

Measure this distance when installing the torsion bar to the rear anchor—Except Van

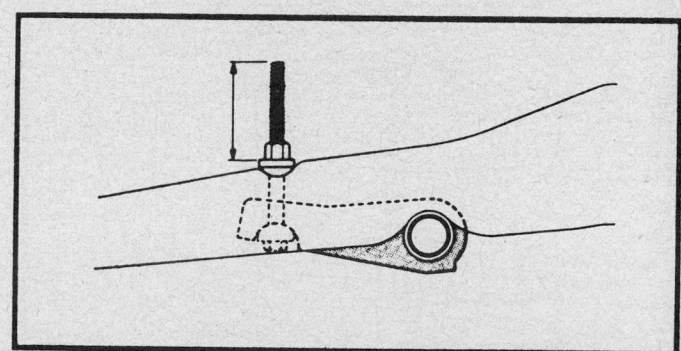

Measure this distance to initially set the riding height—Except Van

installing. Remove the rear anchor arm mounting nut and bolt.

6. Remove the torsion bar from the front anchor arm.

To install:

7. If the bar is being reused, lubricate the ends and install the torsion bar aligning the matchmarks. If a new bar is being used, align the white stripe on the front splines with the mark on the anchor. There is a mark on the front of the torsion bar to differentiate between left and right. Do not install the bar with the mark facing the rear.

8. Install the torsion bar to the rear anchor so that the length of the mounting bolt from the nut to the head of the bolt is the specified length with the rebound bumper in contact with the crossmember. Reposition the bar as required to met the specifications. The specifications are:

Montero and Raider (left side)—5.3–5.6 in.
Montero and Raider (right side)—4.9–5.2 in.
Pick-Up and Ram 50 (left side)—5.5–5.8 in.
Pick-Up and Ram 50 (right side)—5.3–5.6 in.

9. To initially set the riding height, tighten the rear anchor mounting nut to the same point at which it was removed if the old bar is being reused. If a new bar has been installed, tighten the nut so that the exposed length of the bolt threads is the specification:

Montero and Raider (left side)—2.4 in.
Montero and Raider (right side)—2.8 in.
1986 Pick-Up and Ram 50 (left side)—3.0 in.
1986 Pick-Up and Ram 50 (right side)—2.7 in.
1987–90 Pick-Up and Ram 50 (left side)—3.9 in.
1987–90 Pick-Up and Ram 50 (right side)—3.4 in.

10. Fill the dust covers with grease and fold them back into position.

11. Adjust the torsion to the correct riding height.

VAN

1. Raise the vehicle and support safely. Remove the under cover.

2. Support the lower control arm at a point away from where the torsion bar attaches to the arm.

3. Fold the dust covers back and slide them away from the ends of the bar.

4. If the bars are to be reused, matchmark the torsion bar at both ends to the anchor and identify left from right.

5. Paint or measure the distance of the exposed threads of the rear mounting bolt up to the nut to aid in adjustment when installing. Remove the rear anchor arm mounting nut and bolt.

6. Remove the torsion bar from the front anchor arm.

To install:

7. If the bar is being reused, lubricate the ends and install the torsion bar aligning the matchmarks. If a new bar is being used, align the white stripe on the front splines with the mark on the anchor. There is a mark on the rear of the torsion bar to differ-

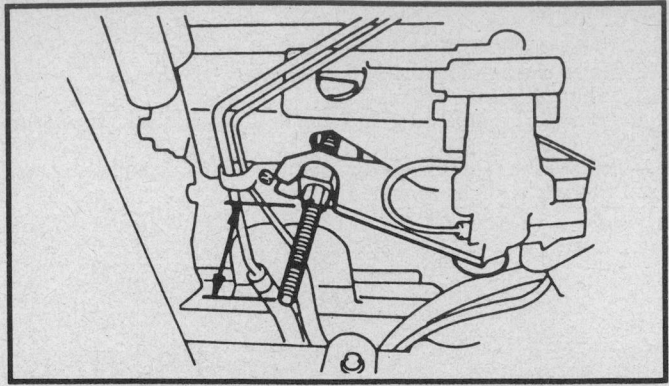

Measure this distance to initially set the riding height—Van

entiate between left and right. Do not install the bar with the mark facing the front.

8. Install the torsion bar to the rear anchor so that the length of the mounting bolt from the nut to the head of the bolt is 1.4 in. for Van or 1.0 in. for Panel Van. Reposition the bar as required to meet the specifications.

9. To initially set the riding height, tighten the rear anchor mounting nut to the same point at which it was removed if the old bar is being reused. If a new bar has been installed, tighten the nut so that the exposed length of the bolt threads is 2.5 in.

10. Fill the dust covers with grease and fold them back into position.

11. Adjust the torsion bar to the correct riding height.

Adjusting the Torsion Bar (Setting the Riding Height)

1. Lower the vehicle so that its full weight is on the ground. If there is any excess weight in the vehicle, unload it.

2. To set the riding height, measure the distance from the rebound bumper to its stopper bracket on the frame. Adjust the torsion bar nut until that distance is the specification:

Montero and Raider—2.8 in.
1986 Pick-Up and Ram 50—2.8 in.
1987–90 Pick-Up and Ram 50—3.1 in.
Van—2.0 in.

3. If, after adjusting the riding height, the exposed portion of the adjusting bolt is protruding up or down so far that it interferes with any front suspension component or is hanging down too low, the bar must be removed and repositioned.

4. Road test the vehicle and remeasure the riding height. Readjust if necessary.

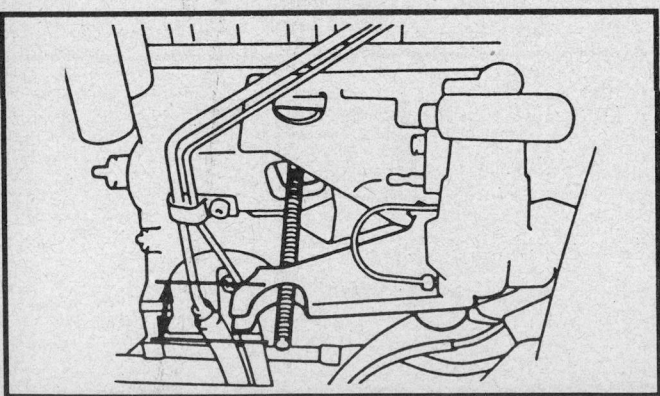

Measure this distance when installing the torsion bar to the anchor—Van

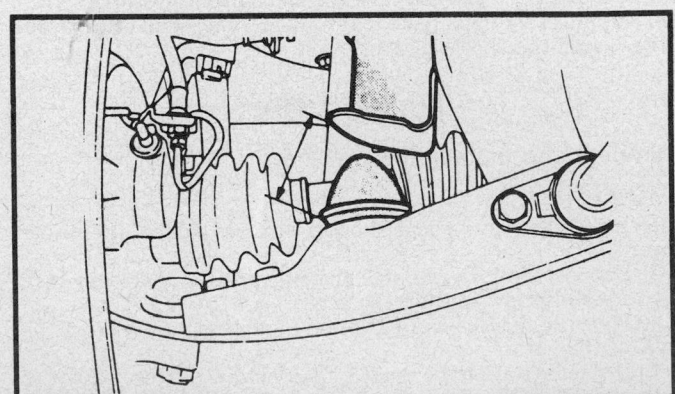

Measure this distance to set the riding height—Except Van

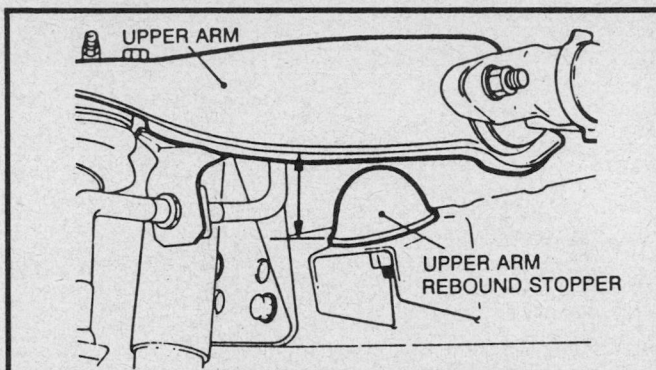

Measure this distance to set the riding height—Van

Upper Ball Joint

Inspection

With the control arm removed, check the starting torque required to turn the ball stud. The specification for all vehicles is 7–30 inch lbs.

Removal and Installation

EXCEPT VAN

NOTE: The upper ball joint and upper control arm must be replaced as an assembly on 1987–90 Pick-Up and Ram 50.

1. Raise the vehicle and support safely. Remove the upper control arm.
2. Remove the ring and boot from the ball joint. Remove the snapring.
3. Remove the ball joint from the control arm using tool sets MB990800 and MB990799.

To install:

3. Align the mating mark on the upper ball joint with the mark on the arm.
4. Press the ball joint in using the same tools that were used to remove the ball joint.
5. Install the snapring If the snapring is loose, install a new one.
6. Fill the boot with grease and install the boot and ring.
7. Install the upper control arm.
8. Lubricate the ball joint with a grease gun.
9. Adjust the riding height, if equipped with a torsion bar and align the front end.

VAN

1. Raise the vehicle and support safely. Remove the upper control arm.
2. Remove the ball joint retaining bolts and remove the ball joint from the arm.
3. The installation is the reverse of the removal procedure. Torque the ball joint retaining bolts to 40 ft. lbs. (54 Nm) and the ball stud nut to 100 ft. lbs. (136 Nm). Install a new cotter pin.
4. Lubricate the ball joint with a grease gun.
5. Adjust the riding height, if equipped with a torsion bar and align the front end.

Lower Ball Joint

Inspection

EXCEPT VAN

With the control arm removed, check the up and down endplay

of the ball stud. If it exceeds 0.02 in. (0.5mm), the ball joint should be replaced.

VAN

With the control arm removed, check the starting torque required to turn the ball stud. The specification is 9–30 inch lbs.

Removal and Installation

NOTE: The lower ball joint and lower control arm must be replaced as an assembly on the Van.

1. Raise the vehicle and support safely. Remove the lower control arm.
2. Remove the ball joint retaining nuts and bolts and remove the ball joint from the arm.
3. The installation is the reverse of the removal procedure. Torque the ball joint retaining nuts and bolts to 50 ft. lbs. (68 Nm) on 4WD vehicles or 28 ft. lbs. (38 Nm) on 2WD vehicles. Torque the ball stud nut to 100 ft. lbs. (136 Nm) and install a new cotter pin.
4. Lubricate the ball joint with a grease gun.
5. Adjust the riding height, if equipped with a torsion bar and align the front end.

Upper Control Arm

Removal and Installation

2WD PICK-UP AND RAM 50

1. Raise the vehicle and support safely. Remove the tire and wheel assembly.
2. Remove the shock absorber.
3. Install Mitsubishi spring compressor tool MB990792 or Chrysler tool DD–1278, or equivalent to the coil spring to compress the spring.
4. Remove the cotter pin and upper ball joint nut.
5. Suspend the rotor assembly with a wire so there is not excessive pull on the brake hose.
6. Release the upper ball joint taper using Mitsubishi tool MB990809–01 or Chrysler tool C–3564–A, or equivalent.
7. Remove the tool and remove the ball stud from the knuckle.
8. Loosen the pivot bar retaining nuts and bolts, identify and remove the alignment shims, remove the nuts and bolts and remove the arm from the vehicle.

To install:

9. Install the arm to the frame rail bracket, install the shims in their original locations and install the retaining nuts and bolts. Torque the nuts initially to about 40 ft. lbs. (54 Nm).
10. Torque the ball joint nut to 60 ft. lbs. (81 Nm). Install a new cotter pin. Remove the spring compressor.
11. Install the shock absorber.
12. Align the front end. When all settings are at specifications, torque the pivot bar retaining bolts to 80 ft. lbs. (109 Nm).

MONTERO, RAIDER AND 4WD PICK-UP AND RAM 50

1. Raise the vehicle and support safely. Remove the skid plate.
2. Remove the shock absorber.
3. Turn the torsion bar adjustment nut counterclockwise to relieve all tension from the torsion bar. Disconnect the brake hose from the brake line and remove the hose from the bracket.
4. Remove the cotter pin from the upper ball stud.
5. Release the upper ball joint taper using Mitsubishi tool MB990809–01 or Chrysler tool C–3564–A, or equivalent. Remove the tool. Remove the ball stud from the steering knuckle.
6. Loosen the pivot bar retaining nuts and bolts, identify and remove the alignment shims, remove the nuts and bolts and remove the arm from the vehicle.
7. Remove the arm from the vehicle.

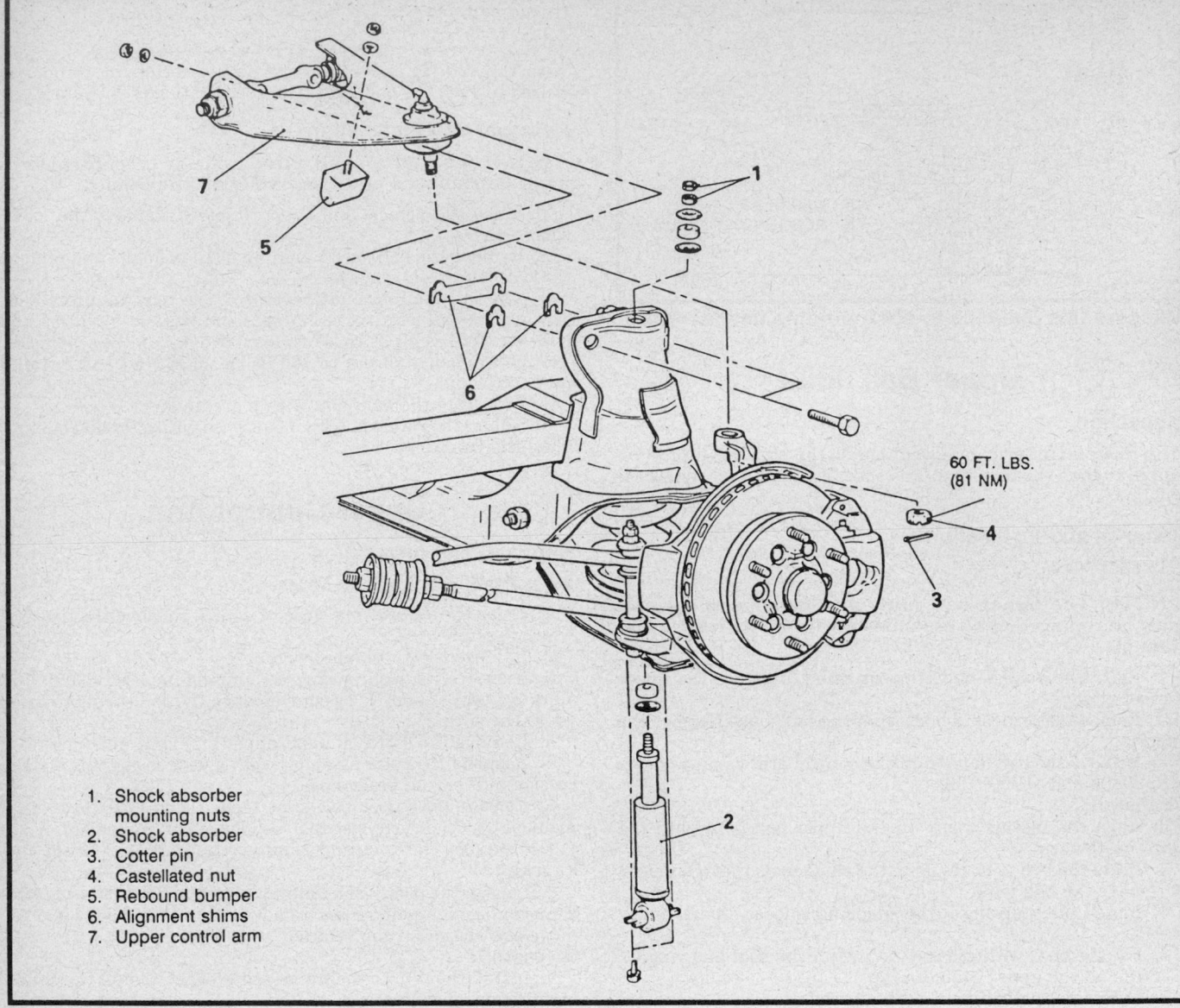

1. Shock absorber mounting nuts
2. Shock absorber
3. Cotter pin
4. Castellated nut
5. Rebound bumper
6. Alignment shims
7. Upper control arm

Front suspension components—2WD Pick-Up and Ram 50

To install:

8. Position the arm at the frame rail bracket.

9. Install the shims in their original locations and install the retaining nuts and bolts. Torque the nuts initially to about 40 ft. lbs. (54 Nm).

10. Insert the upper ball stud in the steering knuckle arm bore and install the nut. Torque the nut to 60 ft. lbs. (81 Nm) and install a new cotter pin. Install the shock absorber and attach the brake hose.

11. Turn the torsion bar adjustment nut clockwise to apply a load on the bar.

12. Lower the vehicle.

13. Set the riding height and align the front end.

VAN

1. Raise the vehicle and support safely.

2. Remove the rubber splash shield. Remove the shock absorber.

3. Turn the torsion bar adjustment nut counterclockwise to relieve all tension from the torsion bar. Remove the nuts and bolts that attach the front torsion bar anchor to the upper control arm.

4. Suspend the rotor assembly with a wire so there is not excessive pull on the brake hose. Remove the cotter pin from the upper ball stud.

5. Release the upper ball joint taper using Mitsubishi tool MB990809–01, or equivalent. Remove the tool. Remove the ball stud from the steering knuckle.

6. Remove the pivot bar retaining nuts and bolts and remove the arm from the vehicle.

7. Remove the arm from the vehicle.

To install:

8. Position the arm at the frame rail bracket.

9. Install the retaining nuts and bolts. Torque the nuts to 100 ft. lbs. (136 Nm).

10. Insert the upper ball stud in the steering knuckle arm bore and install the nut. Torque the nut to 100 ft. lbs. (136 Nm) and install a new cotter pin. Install the shock absorber.

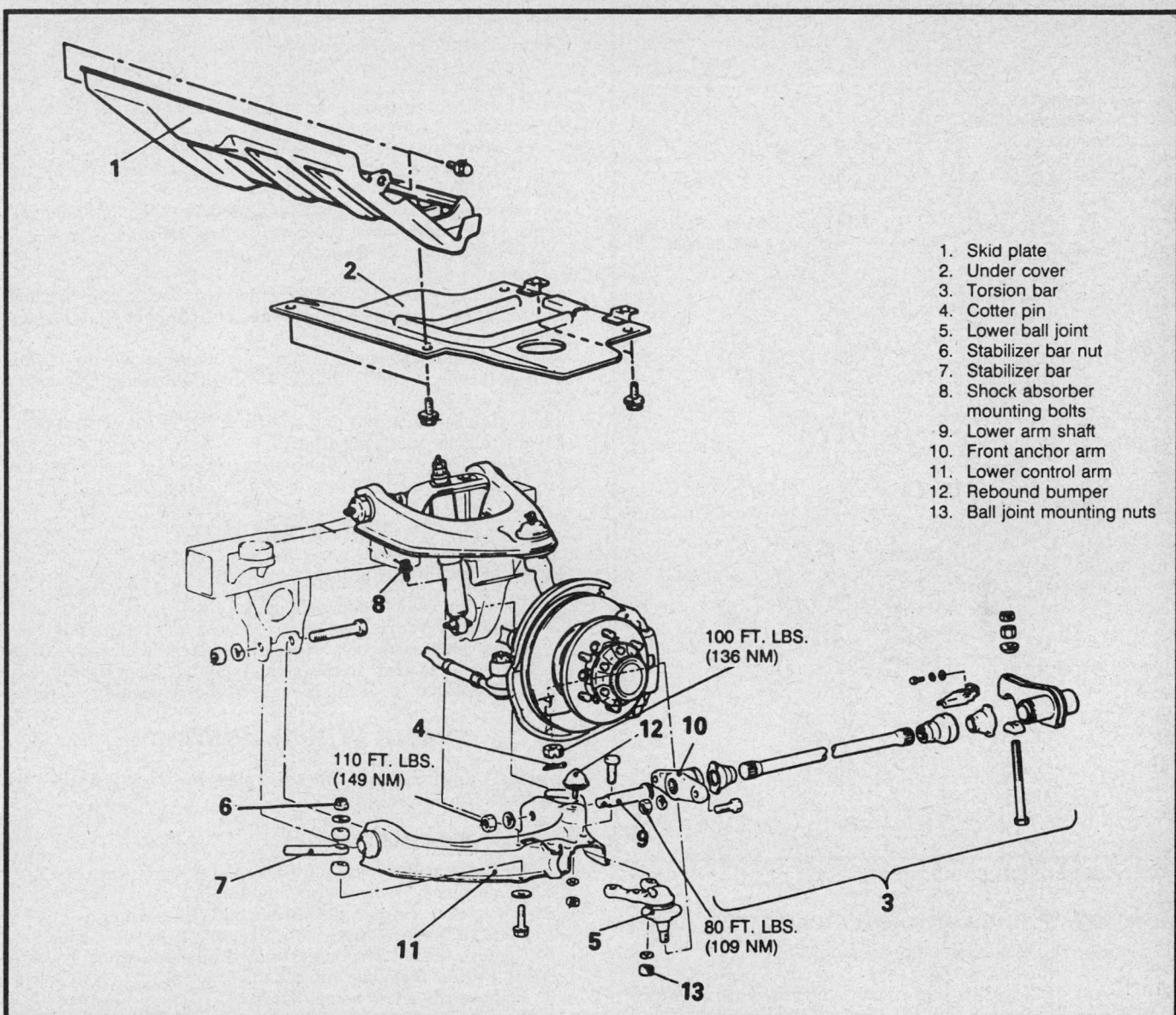

1. Skid plate
2. Under cover
3. Torsion bar
4. Cotter pin
5. Lower ball joint
6. Stabilizer bar nut
7. Stabilizer bar
8. Shock absorber mounting bolts
9. Lower arm shaft
10. Front anchor arm
11. Lower control arm
12. Rebound bumper
13. Ball joint mounting nuts

100 FT. LBS. (136 NM)

110 FT. LBS. (149 NM)

80 FT. LBS. (109 NM)

Front suspension components—4WD vehicles

11. Turn the torsion bar adjustment nut clockwise to apply a load on the bar.
12. Lower the vehicle.
13. Set the riding height and align the front end.

Lower Control Arm

Removal and Installation

2WD PICK-UP AND RAM 50

1. Raise the vehicle and support safely.
2. Remove the shock absorber.
3. Disconnect the sway bar and strut bar from the lower control arm.
4. Install Mitsubishi spring compressor tool MB990792 or Chrysler tool DD–1278, or equivalent to the coil spring and compress the spring.
5. Remove the cotter pin and lower ball joint nut.
6. Release the lower ball joint taper using Mitsubishi tool MB990809–01 or Chrysler tool C–3564–A, or equivalent.

7. Remove the tool and remove the ball stud from the knuckle. Remove the spring compressor.
8. Pull the arm down and remove the spring with the rubber isolation pad from the vehicle. Remove the lower arm shaft mounting nuts and remove the arm from the vehicle.
To install:
9. Install the arm to the crossmember finger tight. Install the spring with the rubber isolators. Install the compressor tool and compress it enough so the lower ball joint can be inserted through the knuckle.
10. Torque the lower ball joint nut to 100 ft. lbs. (136 Nm). Install a new cotter pin. Remove the spring compressor.
11. Connect the sway bar and strut bar to the lower control arm.
12. Install the shock absorber.
13. Lower the vehicle completely. When the weight of the vehicle is completely off of the lifting apparatus, torque the lower control arm to crossmember mounting nut to 50 ft. lbs. (68 Nm).
14. Align the front end.

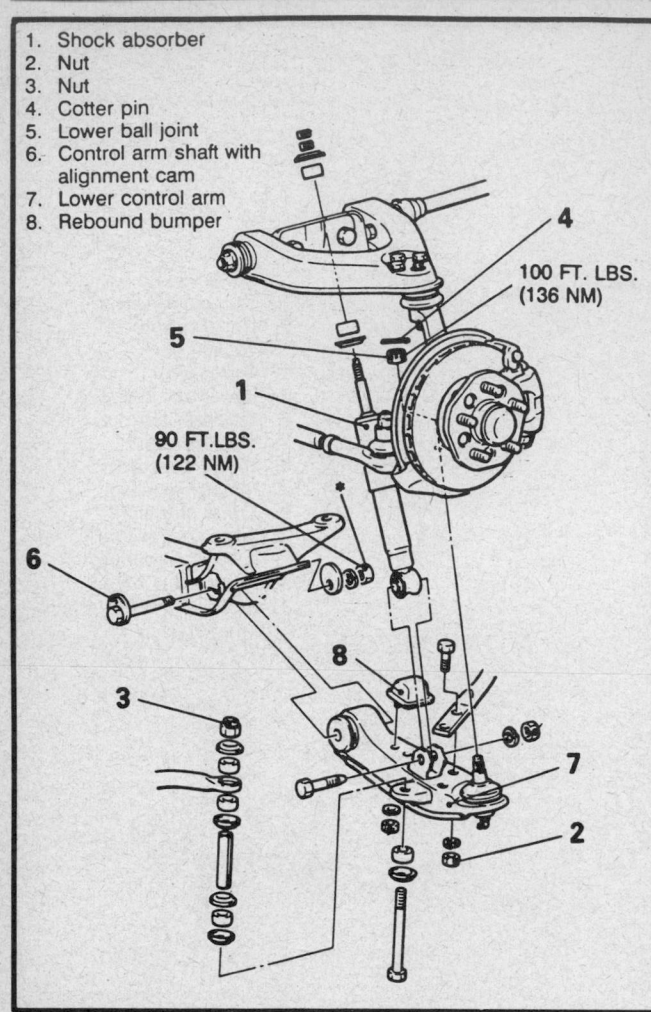

1. Shock absorber
2. Nut
3. Nut
4. Cotter pin
5. Lower ball joint
6. Control arm shaft with alignment cam
7. Lower control arm
8. Rebound bumper

100 FT. LBS. (136 NM)

90 FT.LBS. (122 NM)

Front suspension components – Van

MONTERO, RAIDER AND 4WD PICK-UP AND RAM 50

1. Raise the vehicle and support safely.
2. Remove the skid plate.
3. Remove the torsion bar, anchors and lower arm shaft.
4. Remove the shock absorber lower attaching bolt.
5. Disconnect the stabilizer bar from the lower control arm.
6. Remove the cotter pin and the nut from the lower ball stud. Separate the lower ball stud from the steering knuckle using a suitable puller.
7. Remove the pivot bolts and remove the arm from the vehicle.

To install:

8. Install the new control arm to the vehicle.
9. Install the pivot bolts, but do not torque yet.
10. Insert the ball stud into the steering knuckle bore. Install the nut, torque to 100 ft. lbs. (136 Nm) and install a new cotter pin.
11. Attach the stabilizer bar to the control arm and install the shock mount bolts.
12. Install the torsion bar and turn the adjustment bolt clockwise to apply a load to the bar.
13. Lower the vehicle so the weight of the vehicle is completely off of the lifting apparatus.
14. Torque the pivot nuts to 110 ft. lbs. (149 Nm).
15. Set the riding height and align the front end.

VAN

1. Raise the vehicle and support safely.
2. Remove the under cover.
3. Remove the shock absorber.
4. Disconnect the strut bar and stabilizer bar from the lower control arm.
5. Remove the cotter pin and the nut from the lower ball stud. Separate the lower ball stud from the steering knuckle using a suitable puller.
6. Matchmark the head of the cam bolt to the alignment reference plate and remove the bolt, washer and nut.
7. Remove the arm from the vehicle.

To install:

8. Install the arm to the crossmember and install the bolt aligning the matchmarks. Torque the nut to about 40 ft. lbs. (54 Nm).
9. Insert the ball stud into the steering knuckle bore. Install the nut, torque to 100 ft. lbs. (136 Nm) and install a new cotter pin.
10. Install the strut bar and stabilizer bar to the control arm.
11. Install the shock absorber.
12. Align the front end. When all setting are at specifications, torque the lower arm pivot bolt nut to 110 ft. lbs. (149 Nm).

Stabilizer Bar

Removal and Installation

1. Raise the vehicle and support safely.
2. Remove the front sway bar brackets and retainers.
3. Remove the sway bar support brackets and bushings from the lower control arm. Remove the sway bar from the vehicle.
4. The installation is the reverse of the removal procedure.

Front Wheel Bearings

For 4WD applications, please refer to "Drive Axles" in the Unit Repair section.

Removal and Installation

1. Raise the vehicle and support safely.
2. Remove the tire and wheel assembly.
3. Remove the caliper, disc brake pads and adaptor.
4. Remove the dust cap.
5. Remove the cotter pin, castelated nut lock, wheel bearing nut and washer from the spindle.
6. Remove the outer wheel bearing.
7. Remove the hub and rotor assembly with the inner wheel bearing from the spindle. Remove the grease seal.

To install:

8. Lubricate and install the inner wheel bearing. Install a new grease seal.
9. Install the hub and rotor assembly to the spindle.
10. Lubricate and install the outer wheel bearing, washer and nut. When the bearing preload is properly set, install the nut lock and a new cotter pin.
11. Install the grease cap.
12. Install the brake pads and caliper.
13. Install the wheel.

Adjustment

1. Tighten the wheel bearing nut to 22 ft. lbs. (30 Nm) while turning the rotor.
2. Loosen the wheel bearing adjusting nut completely.
3. Tighten the nut to 6 ft. lbs. (8 Nm).
4. Check the wheel bearing endplay. The specification is 0.0001–0.003 in.
5. Install the nut lock and cotter pin.

REAR SUSPENSION

Shock Absorber

Removal and Installation

1. Raise the vehicle and support safely. If the vehicle is equipped with rear coil springs, support the rear axle using the proper equipment.
2. Remove the bolts that attach the shock to the frame or bracket.
3. Remove the shock from the vehicle.
4. The installation is the reverse of the removal procedure.

Coil Springs

Removal and Installation

MONTERO AND RAIDER WITH 3.0L ENGINE

1. Raise the vehicle and support safely. Remove the parking bake cable attaching bolt.
2. Using the proper equipment, support the weight of the axle.

3. Remove the bolt that attaches the lateral rod to the body.
4. Remove the lower shock mounting bolts.
5. Lower the axle and remove the coil springs with their seats.
6. The installation is the reverse of the removal procedure.

Leaf Springs

Removal and Installation

1. Raise the vehicle and support safely. Remove the parking bake cable attaching bolt.
2. Using the proper equipment, support the weight of the axle.
3. Remove the nuts, washers and U-bolts attaching the springs to the axle housing. Remove the seat and spacer.
4. Remove the spring shackle bolts, shackle and spring front bolt.
5. Remove the springs from the vehicle.
6. The installation is the reverse of the removal procedure. Make sure all mounting nuts are on the inside of the springs.

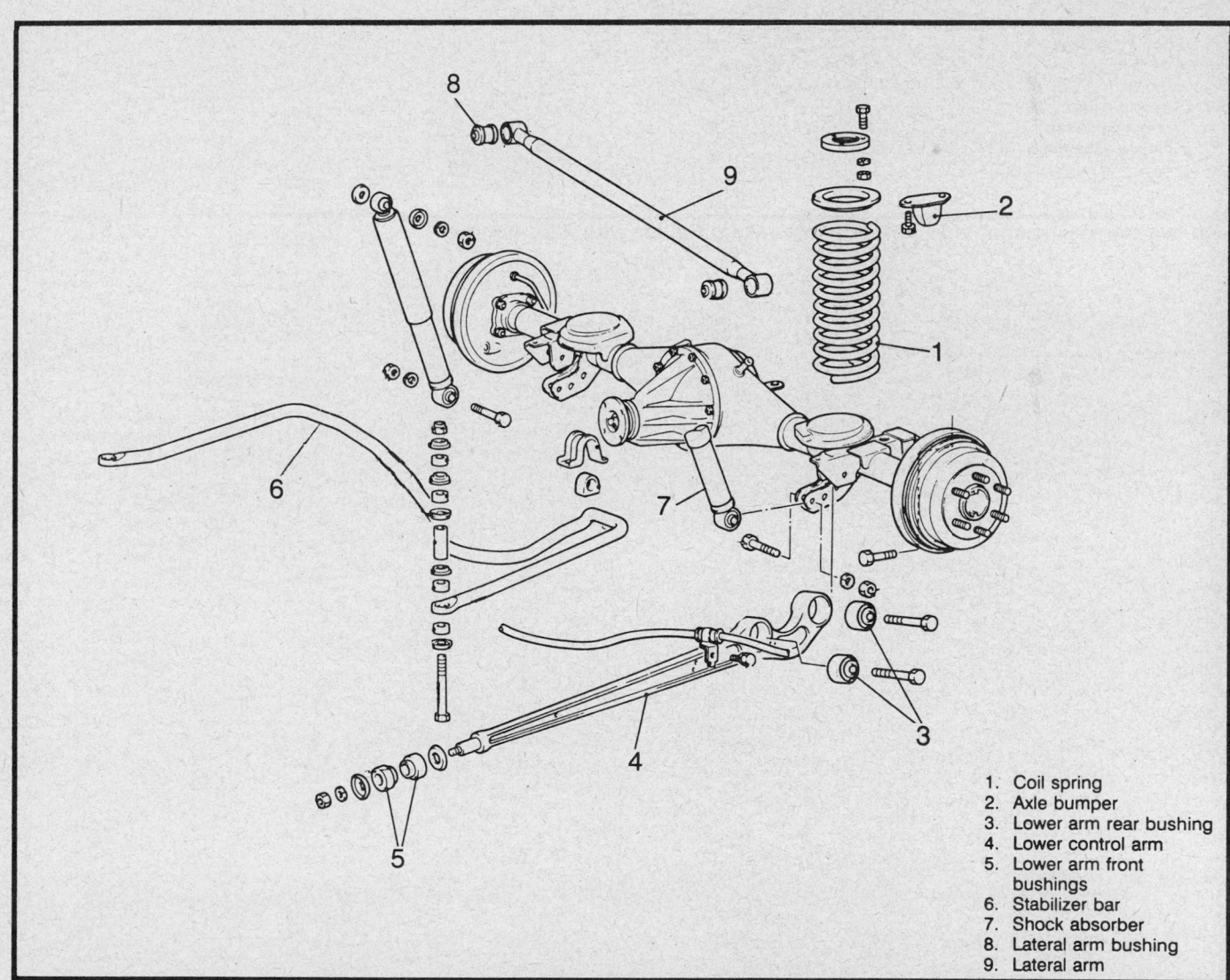

1. Coil spring
2. Axle bumper
3. Lower arm rear bushing
4. Lower control arm
5. Lower arm front bushings
6. Stabilizer bar
7. Shock absorber
8. Lateral arm bushing
9. Lateral arm

Coil spring rear suspension components—Ram Raider with 3.0L engine

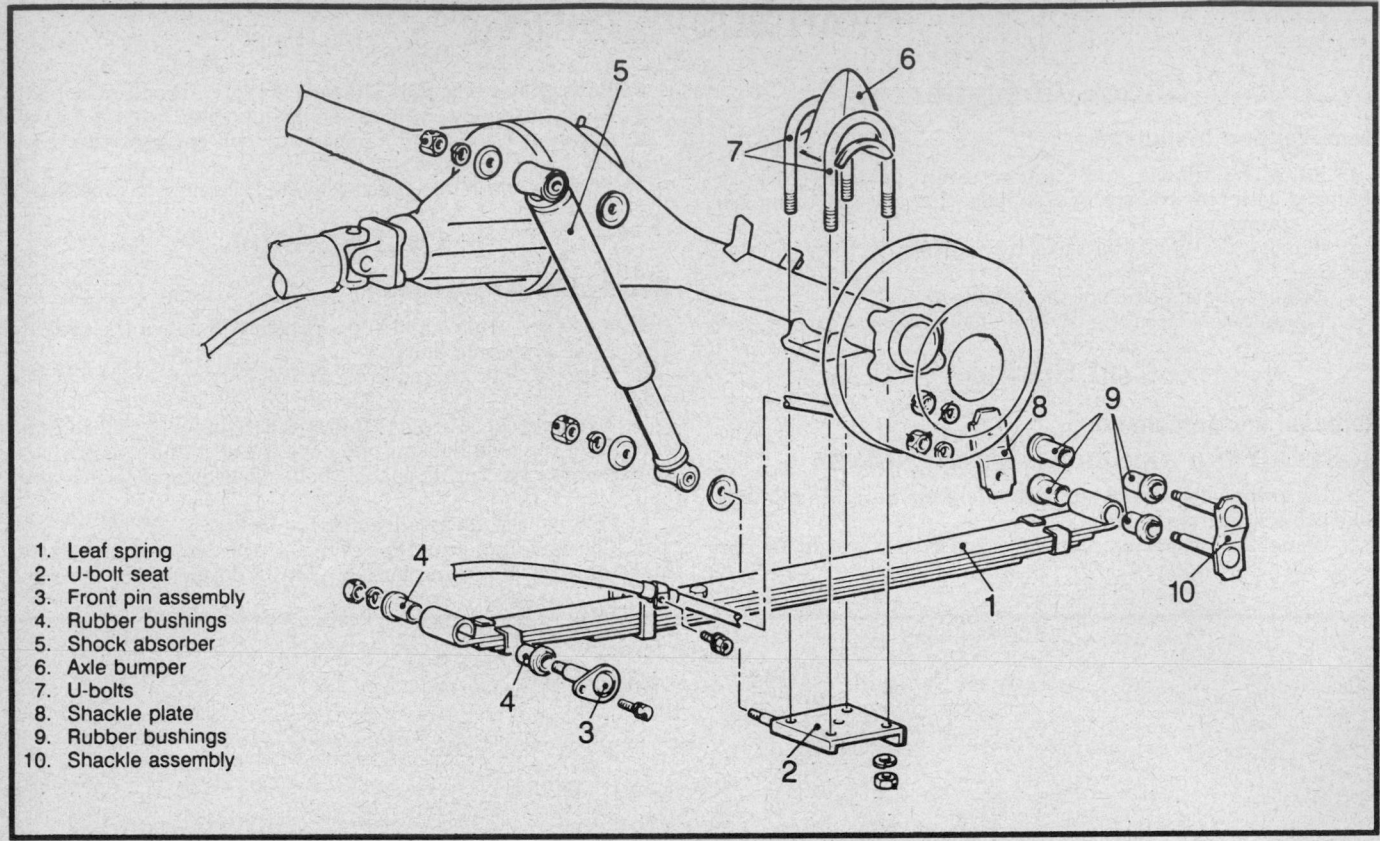

1. Leaf spring
2. U-bolt seat
3. Front pin assembly
4. Rubber bushings
5. Shock absorber
6. Axle bumper
7. U-bolts
8. Shackle plate
9. Rubber bushings
10. Shackle assembly

Leaf spring rear suspension components — Ram Raider with 2.6L engine

SPECIFICATIONS

ENGINE IDENTIFICATION

Year	Model	Engine Displacement cu. in. (cc/liter)	Engine Series Identification	No. of Cylinders	Engine Type
1986	P'up	119 (1950/2.0)	G200Z	4	OHC
	P'up	138 (2254/2.3)	4ZD1	4	OHC
	P'up	137 (2238/2.2)	C223 ①	4	OHV
	P'up	137 (2238/2.2)	C223T ②	4	OHV
	Trooper II	138 (2254/2.3)	4ZD1	4	OHC
	Trooper II	137 (2238/2.2)	C223T ②	4	OHV
1987	P'up	119 (1950/2.0)	G200Z	4	OHC
	P'up	138 (2254/2.3)	4ZD1	4	OHC
	P'up	137 (2238/2.2)	C223 ①	4	OHV
	P'up	137 (2238/2.2)	C223T ②	4	OHV
	Trooper II	138 (2254/2.3)	4ZD1	4	OHC
	Trooper II	137 (2238/2.2)	C223T ②	4	OHV
1988	Pick-Up	138 (2254/2.3)	4ZD1	4	OHC
	Pick-Up	156 (2559/2.6)	4ZE1	4	OHC
	Trooper II	156 (2559/2.6)	4ZE1	4	OHC
1989–90	Amigo	138 (2254/2.3)	4ZD1	4	OHC
	Amigo	156 (2559/2.6)	4ZE1	4	OHC
	Pick-Up	138 (2254/2.3)	4ZD1	4	OHC
	Pick-Up	156 (2559/2.6)	4ZE1	4	OHC
	Trooper/Trooper II	156 (2559/2.6)	4ZE1	4	OHC
	Trooper/Trooper II	173 (2828/2.8)	CPC	6	OHV

OHC—Overhead Cam ① Diesel
OHV—Overhead Valves ② Turbocharged Diesel

GENERAL ENGINE SPECIFICATIONS

Year	Model	Engine Displacement cu. in. (cc)	Fuel System Type	Net Horsepower @ rpm	Net Torque @ rpm (ft. lbs.)	Bore × Stroke (in.)	Compression Ratio	Oil Pressure @ rpm
1986	P'up	119 (1950)	2 bbl	82 @ 4600	101 @ 3000	3.42 × 3.23	8.4:1	57 @ 1400
	P'up	138 (2254)	2 bbl	96 @ 4600	123 @ 2600	3.52 × 3.54	8.3:1	57 @ 3000
	P'up	137 (2238)	①	58 @ 4300	93 @ 2200	3.46 × 3.62	21:1	55 @ 1400
	P'up	137 (2238)	②	80 @ 4000	128 @ 2200	3.46 × 3.62	21:1	55 @ 1400
	Trooper II	138 (2254)	2 bbl	96 @ 4600	123 @ 2600	3.52 × 3.54	8.3:1	57 @ 3000
	Trooper II	137 (2238)	②	80 @ 4000	128 @ 2200	3.46 × 3.62	21:1	55 @ 1400
1987	P'up	119 (1950)	2 bbl	82 @ 4600	101 @ 3000	3.42 × 3.23	8.4:1	57 @ 1400
	P'up	138 (2254)	2 bbl	96 @ 4600	123 @ 2600	3.52 × 3.54	8.3:1	57 @ 3000
	P'up	137 (2238)	①	58 @ 4300	93 @ 2200	3.46 × 3.62	21:1	55 @ 1400
	P'up	137 (2238)	②	80 @ 4000	128 @ 2200	3.46 × 3.62	21:1	55 @ 1400
	Trooper II	138 (2254)	2 bbl	96 @ 4600	123 @ 2600	3.52 × 3.54	8.3:1	57 @ 3000
	Trooper II	137 (2238)	②	80 @ 4000	128 @ 2200	3.46 × 3.62	21:1	55 @ 1400

GENERAL ENGINE SPECIFICATIONS

Year	Model	Engine Displacement cu. in. (cc)	Fuel System Type	Net Horsepower @ rpm	Net Torque @ rpm (ft. lbs.)	Bore × Stroke (in.)	Compression Ratio	Oil Pressure @ rpm
1988	Pick-Up	138 (2254)	2 bbl	96 @ 4600	123 @ 2600	3.52 × 3.54	8.3:1	57 @ 3000
	Pick-Up	156 (2559)	MPFI	120 @ 4600	146 @ 2600	3.65 × 3.74	8.3:1	57–71 @ 4000
	Trooper II	156 (2559)	MPFI	120 @ 4600	146 @ 2600	3.65 × 3.74	8.3:1	57–71 @ 4000
1989–90	Amigo	138 (2254)	2 bbl	96 @ 4600	123 @ 2600	3.52 × 3.54	8.3:1	57 @ 3000
	Amigo	156 (2559)	MPFI	120 @ 4600	146 @ 2600	3.65 × 3.74	8.3:1	57–71 @ 4000
	Pick-Up	138 (2254)	2 bbl	96 @ 4600	123 @ 2600	3.52 × 3.54	8.3:1	57 @ 3000
	Pick-Up	156 (2559)	MPFI	120 @ 4600	146 @ 2600	3.65 × 3.74	8.3:1	57–71 @ 4000
	Trooper/Trooper II	156 (2559)	MPFI	120 @ 4600	146 @ 2600	3.65 × 3.74	8.3:1	57–71 @ 4000
	Trooper/Trooper II	173 (2828)	TBI	N.A.	N.A.	3.50 × 2.99	8.9:1	30–55 @ 2000

① Diesel
② Turbocharged Diesel

GASOLINE ENGINE TUNE-UP SPECIFICATIONS

Year	Model	Engine Displacement cu. in. (cc)	Spark Plugs Type	Spark Plugs Gap (in.)	Ignition Timing (deg.) MT	Ignition Timing (deg.) AT	Compression Pressure (psi)	Fuel Pump (psi)	Idle Speed (rpm) MT	Idle Speed (rpm) AT	Valve Clearance ① In.	Valve Clearance ① Ex.
1986	P'up	119 (1950)	BPR6ES11	0.040	6B	6B	—	3.5	②	900	0.006	0.010
	P'up	138 (2254)	BPR6ES11	0.040	6B	6B	—	3.5	②	—	0.006	0.010
	Trooper II	138 (2254)	BPR6ES11	0.040	6B	6B	—	3.5	②	—	0.006	0.010
1987	P'up	119 (1950)	BPR6ES11	0.040	6B	6B	—	3.5	②	900	0.006	0.010
	P'up	138 (2254)	BPR6ES11	0.040	6B	6B	—	3.5	②	②	0.006	0.010
	Trooper II	138 (2254)	BPR6ES11	0.040	6B	6B	—	3.5	②	900	0.006	0.010
1988	Pick-Up	138 (2254)	R42XLS	0.040	6B	6B	—	3.5	900	900	0.006	0.010
	Pick-Up	156 (2559)	R42XLS	0.040	12B	12B	—	43	900	900	0.008	0.008
	Trooper II	156 (2559)	R42XLS	0.040	12B	12B	—	43	900	900	0.008	0.008
1989	Amigo	138 (2254)	R42XLS	0.040	6B	6B	—	3.5	900	900	0.006	0.010
	Amigo	156 (2559)	R42XLS	0.040	12B	12B	—	43	900	900	0.008	0.008
	Pick-Up	138 (2254)	R42XLS	0.040	6B	6B	—	3.5	900	900	0.006	0.010
	Pick-Up	156 (2559)	R43XLS	0.040	12B	12B	—	43	900	900	0.008	0.008
	Trooper/Trooper II	156 (2559)	R43XLS	0.040	12B	12B	—	43	900	900	0.008	0.008
	Trooper/Trooper II	173 (2828)	R43TSK	0.045	10B	10B	—	9–13	③	③	④	④
1990						See underhood specifications						

① Cold
② 800—Federal
   900—California
③ Refer to underhood specifications sticker
④ Zero lash, plus 1¹⁄₂ turns

DIESEL ENGINE TUNE-UP SPECIFICATIONS

Year	Model	Engine Displacement cu. in. (cc)	Valve Clearance [5] Intake (in.)	Valve Clearance [5] Exhaust (in.)	Intake Valve Opens (deg.) [4]	Injection Pump Setting (deg.)	Injection Nozzle Pressure (psi) New	Injection Nozzle Pressure (psi) Used	Idle Speed (rpm)	Cranking Compression Pressure (psi)
1986	P'up	137 (2238)	0.016	0.016	16	[3]	1493	—	[2]	441
	P'up	137 (2238) [1]	0.016	0.016	16	10	1920	—	[2]	441
	Trooper II	137 (2238) [1]	0.016	0.016	16	10	1920	—	[2]	441
1987	P'up	137 (2238)	0.016	0.016	16	[3]	1493	—	[2]	441
	P'up	137 (2238) [1]	0.016	0.016	16	10	1920	—	[2]	441
	Trooper II	137 (2238) [1]	0.016	0.016	16	10	1920	—	[2]	441

[1] Turbocharged
[2] 750 rpm—manual transmission
   850 rpm—automatic transmission
[3] 15° BTDC—Federal
   13° BTDC—California
[4] BTDC
[5] Cold

CAPACITIES

Year	Model	Engine Displacement cu. in. (cc)	Engine Crankcase with Filter	Engine Crankcase without Filter	Transmission (pts.) 4-Spd	Transmission (pts.) 5-Spd	Transmission (pts.) Auto.	Drive Axle (pts.)	Fuel Tank (gal.)	Cooling System (qts.)
1986	P'up	119 (1950)	4.1	3.8	2.6	3.3	—	3.2 [8]	13.2 [9]	8.5
	P'up	138 (2254)	4.1	3.8	2.6	3.3	13.4	3.2 [8]	13.2 [9]	8.5
	P'up	137 (2238) [1]	6.7	5.7	2.6	3.3	12.6	3.2 [8]	21.5	9.5 [10]
	P'up	137 (2238) [2]	6.7	5.7	2.6	3.3	12.6	3.2 [8]	21.5	11.2
	Trooper II	138 (2254)	4.1	3.8	—	9.7 [11]	—	3.2 [8]	13.2 [9]	8.5
	Trooper II	137 (2238) [2]	6.7	5.7	—	9.7 [11]	—	3.2 [8]	21.5	11.2
1987	P'up	119 (1950)	4.1	3.8	2.6	3.3	—	3.2 [8]	13.2 [9]	8.5
	P'up	138 (2254)	4.1	3.8	2.6	3.3	13.4	3.2 [8]	13.2 [9]	8.5
	P'up	137 (2238) [1]	6.7	5.7	2.6	3.3	12.6	3.2 [8]	21.5	9.5 [10]
	P'up	137 (2238) [2]	6.7	5.7	2.6	3.3	12.6	3.2 [8]	21.5	11.2
	Trooper II	138 (2254)	4.1	3.8	—	9.7 [11]	—	3.2 [8]	13.2 [9]	8.5
	Trooper II	137 (2238) [2]	6.7	5.7	—	9.7 [11]	—	3.2 [8]	21.5	11.2
1988	Pick-Up	138 (2254)	4.2	3.8	—	3.2	13.8	3.2 [7]	[4]	9.5
	Pick-Up	156 (2559)	5.2	4.8	—	6.2 [3]	13.8	3.8 [7]	4	9.5
	Trooper II	156 (2559)	4.4	4.0	—	6.2 [3]	24.0 [5]	4.0 [6]	21.9	8.5
1989–90	Amigo	138 (2254)	4.2	3.8	—	3.2	13.8	3.2 [7]	[4]	9.5
	Amigo	156 (2559)	5.2	4.8	—	6.2 [3]	13.8	3.8 [7]	[4]	9.5
	Pick-Up	138 (2254)	4.2	3.8	—	3.2	13.8	3.2 [7]	[4]	9.5
	Pick-Up	156 (2559)	5.2	4.8	—	6.2 [3]	13.8	3.8 [7]	[4]	9.5
	Trooper/Trooper II	156 (2559)	5.2	4.8	—	7.4 [3]	24.0 [5]	4.0 [6]	21.9	8.5
	Trooper/Trooper II	173 (2828)	4.5	4.0	—	7.4 [3]	24.0 [5]	4.0 [6]	21.9	8.5

[1] Diesel
[2] Turbocharged Diesel
[3] Transfer case—3.0 pts.
[4] Short wheel base—14.0 gal.
   Long wheel base—19.8 gal.
[5] Transfer case—2.4 pts.
[6] Front axle—3.4 pts.
[7] Front axle—3.2 pts.
[8] Front axle—2.1 pts.
[9] Optional fuel tank—19.1 gal.
[10] Automatic transmission—11.2 qts.
[11] With transfer case

FIRING ORDERS

NOTE: To avoid confusion, always replace spark plug wires one at a time.

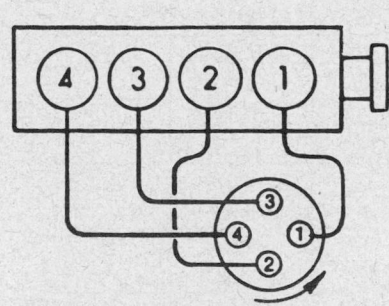

**Isuzu (G200) 119 (2.0L)
Engine firing order:
1-3-4-2 Distributor
rotation: counter-clockwise**

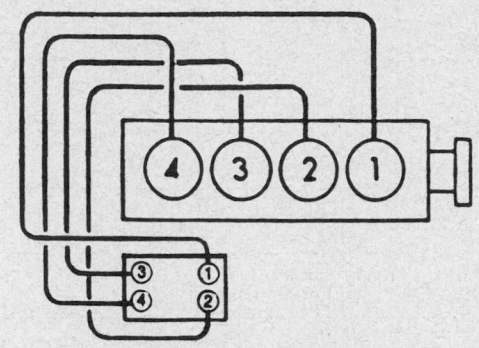

**Isuzu (4ZD1) 138 (2.3L) and
(4ZE1) 156 (2.6L) Engine
firing order: 1-3-4-2 Distributor
rotation: counter-clockwise**

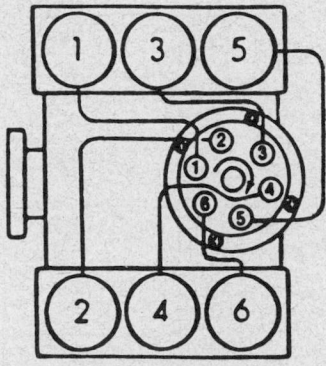

**GM (Chevrolet) 173 (2.8L)
Engine firing order:
1-2-3-4-5-6 Distributor
rotation: clockwise**

CAMSHAFT SPECIFICATIONS

| Year | Engine Displacement cu. in. (cc) | Journal Diameter | | | | | Lobe Lift | | Bearing Clearance | Camshaft End Play |
		1	2	3	4	5	In.	Ex.		
1986	119 (1950)	1.339	1.339	1.339	1.339	1.339	NA	NA	0.0030– 0.0043	0.008 ①
	138 (2254)	1.339	1.339	1.339	1.339	1.339	NA	NA	0.0026– 0.0043	0.008 ①
	137 (2238)	1.890	1.890	1.890	—	—	NA	NA	0.0020	0.008 ①
1987	119 (1950)	1.339	1.339	1.339	1.339	1.339	NA	NA	0.0030– 0.0043	0.008 ①
	138 (2254)	1.339	1.339	1.339	1.339	1.339	NA	NA	0.0026– 0.0043	0.008 ①
	137 (2238)	1.890	1.890	1.890	—	—	NA	NA	0.0020	0.008 ①
1988	138 (2254)	1.339	1.339	1.339	1.339	1.339	NA	NA	0.0026– 0.0043	0.008 ①
	156 (2559)	1.339	1.339	1.339	1.339	1.339	NA	NA	0.0026– 0.0043	0.008 ①
1989–90	138 (2254)	1.339	1.339	1.339	1.339	1.339	NA	NA	0.0026– 0.0043	0.008 ①
	156 (2559)	1.339	1.339	1.339	1.339	1.339	NA	NA	0.0026– 0.0043	0.008 ①
	173 (2828)	1.8678– 1.8815	1.8678– 1.8815	1.8678– 1.8815	1.8678– 1.8815	—	0.262	0.273	0.0010– 0.0040	NA

NA—Not available
① Limit

CRANKSHAFT AND CONNECTING ROD SPECIFICATIONS

Year	Engine Displacement cu. in. (cc)	Crankshaft				Connecting Rod		
		Main Brg. Journal Dia.	Main Brg. Oil Clearance	Shaft End-play	Thrust on No.	Journal Diameter	Oil Clearance	Side Clearance
1986	119 (1950)	2.2016–2.2022	0.0008–0.0025	0.0024–0.0094	3	1.9262–1.9268	0.0007–0.0029	NA
	138 (2254)	2.2032–2.2038	0.0006–0.0026	0.0024–0.0099	3	1.9276–1.9282	0.0004–0.0026	NA
	137 (2238)	2.3591–2.3594	0.0011–0.0033	0.0039	3	2.0835–2.0839	0.0016	NA
1987	119 (1950)	2.2016–2.2022	0.0008–0.0025	0.0024–0.0094	3	1.9262–1.9268	0.0007–0.0029	NA
	138 (2254)	2.2032–2.2038	0.0006–0.0026	0.0024–0.0099	3	1.9276–1.9282	0.0004–0.0026	NA
	137 (2238)	2.3591–2.3594	0.0011–0.0033	0.0039	3	2.0835–2.0839	0.0016	NA
1988	138 (2254)	2.2032–2.2038	0.0006–0.0026	0.0024–0.0099	3	1.9276–1.9282	0.0004–0.0026	0.0078–0.0130
	156 (2559)	2.2032–2.2038	0.0009–0.0020	0.0024–0.0099	3	1.9276–1.9282	0.0008–0.0020	0.0078–0.0130
1989–90	138 (2254)	2.2032–2.2038	0.0006–0.0026	0.0024–0.0099	3	1.9276–1.9282	0.0004–0.0026	0.0078–0.0130
	156 (2559)	2.2032–2.2038	0.0009–0.0020	0.0024–0.0099	3	1.9276–1.9282	0.0008–0.0020	0.0078–0.0130
	173 (2828)	2.6473–2.6483	0.0016–0.0033	0.0020–0.0080	3	1.9983–1.9993	0.0013–0.0026	0.0060–0.0170

NA—Not available

PISTON AND RING SPECIFICATIONS

Year	Engine Displacement cu. in. (cc)	Piston Clearance	Ring Gap			Ring Side Clearance		
			Top Compression	Bottom Compression	Oil Control	Top Compression	Bottom Compression	Oil Control
1986	119 (1950)	0.0018–0.0026	0.0140–0.0200	0.0140–0.0200	0.008–0.035	0.0010–0.0024	0.0010–0.0024	0.0008
	138 (2254)	0.0018–0.0026	0.0120–0.0180	0.0100–0.0160	0.008–0.028	0.0010–0.0024	0.0010–0.0024	—
	137 (2238)	0.0014–0.0022	0.0079–0.0158	0.0079–0.0158	0.0079–0.0158	0.0018–0.0028	0.0012–0.0021	0.0008–0.0021
1987	119 (1950)	0.0018–0.0026	0.0140–0.0200	0.0140–0.0200	0.008–0.035	0.0010–0.0024	0.0010–0.0024	0.0008
	138 (2254)	0.0018–0.0026	0.0120–0.0180	0.0100–0.0160	0.008–0.028	0.0010–0.0024	0.0010–0.0024	—
	137 (2238)	0.0014–0.0022	0.0079–0.0158	0.0079–0.0158	0.0079–0.0158	0.0018–0.0028	0.0012–0.0021	0.0008–0.0021
1988	138 (2254)	0.0008–0.0016	0.0120–0.0180	0.0100–0.0160	0.008–0.028	0.0010–0.0024	0.0010–0.0024	—
	156 (2559)	0.0010–0.0018	0.0120–0.0180	0.0240–0.0280	0.008–0.028	0.0010–0.0024	0.0008–0.0022	—
1989–90	138 (2254)	0.0008–0.0016	0.0120–0.0180	0.0240–0.0280	0.008–0.028	0.0010–0.0024	0.0010–0.0024	—
	156 (2559)	0.0010–0.0018	0.0120–0.0180	0.0240–0.0280	0.008–0.028	0.0010–0.0024	0.0010–0.0024	—
	173 (2828)	0.0170–0.0430	0.0098–0.0196	0.0098–0.0196	0.0020–0.0550	0.0011–0.0027	0.0015–0.0037	0.0078 MAX

VALVE SPECIFICATIONS

Year	Engine Displacement cu. in. (cc)	Seat Angle (deg.)	Face Angle (deg.)	Spring Test Pressure (lbs.)	Spring Installed Height (in.)	Stem-to-Guide Clearance (in.)		Stem Diameter (in.)	
						Intake	Exhaust	Intake	Exhaust
1986	119 (1950)	45	45	55	1.60	0.0009–0.0022	0.0015–0.0031	0.315	0.315
	138 (2254)	45	45	184	1.62	0.0009–0.0012	0.0015–0.0031	0.315	0.315
	137 (2238) ①	45	45	③	④	0.0015–0.0027	0.0025–0.0037	0.315	0.315
	137 (2238) ②	45	45	③	④	0.0015–0.0027	0.0025–0.0037	0.315	0.315
1987	119 (1950)	45	45	55	1.60	0.0009–0.0022	0.0015–0.0031	0.315	0.315
	138 (2254)	45	45	184	1.62	0.0009–0.0012	0.0015–0.0031	0.315	0.315
	137 (2238) ①	45	45	③	④	0.0015–0.0027	0.0025–0.0037	0.315	0.315
	137 (2238) ②	45	45	③	④	0.0015–0.0027	0.0025–0.0037	0.315	0.315
1988	138 (2254)	45	45	56	1.62	0.0009–0.0022	0.0015–0.0031	0.315	0.315
	156 (2559)	45	45	56	1.62	0.0009–0.0022	0.0015–0.0031	0.315	0.315
1989–90	138 (2254)	45	45	56	1.62	0.0009–0.0022	0.0015–0.0031	0.315	0.315
	156 (2559)	45	45	56	1.62	0.0009–0.0022	0.0015–0.0031	0.315	0.315
	173 (2828)	46	45	215	1.72	0.0010–0.0027	0.0010–0.0027	0.341–0.342	0.341–0.342

① Diesel
② Turbocharged Diesel
③ Inner—12–14
  Outer—43–49
④ Inner—1.45
  Outer—1.53

TORQUE SPECIFICATIONS

Year	Engine Displacement cu. in. (cc)	Cylinder Head Bolts	Main Bearing Bolts	Rod Bearing Bolts	Crankshaft Pulley Bolts	Flywheel Bolts	Manifold		Spark Plugs
							Intake	Exhaust	
1986	119 (1950)	⑥	65–80	42–45	76–98	72–80	14–18	14–18	10–17
	138 (2254)	⑤	65–80	42–45	76–98	40–47	14–18	14–18	10–17
	137 (2238) ①	③	116–130	58–65	124–151	83–90	10–17	10–17	—
	137 (2238) ②	④	116–130	58–65	124–151	83–90	13–17	13–17	—
1987	119 (1950)	⑥	65–80	42–45	76–98	72–80	14–18	14–18	10–17

TORQUE SPECIFICATIONS

Year	Engine Displacement cu. in. (cc)	Cylinder Head Bolts	Main Bearing Bolts	Rod Bearing Bolts	Crankshaft Pulley Bolts	Flywheel Bolts	Manifold Intake	Manifold Exhaust	Spark Plugs
1987	138 (2254)	⑤	65–80	42–45	76–98	40–47	14–18	14–18	10–17
	137 (2238) ①	③	116–130	58–65	124–151	83–90	10–17	10–17	—
	137 (2238) ②	④	116–130	58–65	124–151	83–90	13–17	13–17	—
1988	138 (2254)	⑤	65–80	42–45	79–102	40–47	14–18	14–18	10–17
	156 (2559)	⑤	65–80	42–45	79–102	40–47	14–18	14–18	10–17
1989–90	138 (2254)	⑤	65–80	42–45	79–102	40–47	14–18	14–18	10–17
	156 (2559)	⑤	65–80	42–45	79–102	40–47	14–18	14–18	10–17
	173 (2828)	40	70	39	70	52	23	25	22

① Diesel
② Turbocharged Diesel
③ 1st pass—40–47
  2nd pass—54–61
④ 1st pass—33–40
  2nd pass—120–150 degrees
⑤ 1st pass—58
  2nd pass—65
  3rd pass—80
⑥ 1st pass—42
  2nd pass—65
  3rd pass—80

BRAKE SPECIFICATIONS

Year	Model	Lug Nut Torque (ft. lbs.)	Master Cylinder Bore	Brake Disc Minimum Thickness	Brake Disc Maximum Runout	Standard Brake Drum Diameter	Minimum Lining Thickness Front	Minimum Lining Thickness Rear
1986	P'up	58–87	0.874	0.668	0.005	10.0	0.039	0.039
	Trooper II	①	0.874	0.668	0.005	10.0	0.039	0.039
1987	P'up	58–87	0.874	0.668	0.005	10.0	0.039	0.039
	Trooper II	①	0.874	0.668	0.005	10.0	0.039	0.039
1988	Pick-up	①	②	③	0.005	10.0	0.039	0.039
	Trooper II	①	1.000	③	0.005	—	0.039	0.039
1989–90	Amigo	①	②	③	0.005	10.0	0.039	0.039
	Pick-Up	①	②	③	0.005	10.0	0.039	0.039
	Trooper/ Trooper II	①	1.000	③	0.005	—	0.039	0.039

① Aluminum wheel: 80–94
  Steel wheel: 58–87
② 0.938 in.—2.3L engine
  1.000 in.—2.6L engine
③ Front: 0.826
  Rear: 0.432

WHEEL ALIGNMENT

Year	Model	Caster Range (deg.)	Caster Preferred Setting (deg.)	Camber Range (deg.)	Camber Preferred Setting (deg.)	Toe-in (in.)	Steering Axis Inclination (deg.)
1986	P'up 2WD	$0-1P$	$1/2P$	$0-1P$	$1/2P$	0.08	$7^{1/2}$
	P'up 4WD	$1/6N-5/6P$	$1/3P$	$1/12P-11/12P$	$7/12P$	0	$7^{1/2}$
	Trooper II	$0-1P$	$1/2P$	$1/12P-11/12P$	$7/12P$	0	$7^{1/2}$
1987	P'up 2WD	$0-1P$	$1/2P$	$0-1P$	$1/2P$	0.08	$7^{1/2}$
	P'up 4WD	$1/6N-5/6P$	$1/3P$	$1/12P-11/12P$	$7/12P$	0	$7^{1/2}$
	Trooper II	$2P-3P$	$2^{1/2}P$	$0-1P$	$1/2P$	0.08	10
1988	Pick-Up 2WD	$1P-2P$	$1^{1/2}P$	$1/2N-1^{1/2}P$	$1/2P$	0.08	10
	Pick-Up 4WD	$1^{1/4}P-2^{1/4}P$	$1^{3/4}P$	$1/2N-1^{1/2}P$	$1/2P$	0.08	10
	Trooper II	$2P-3P$	$2^{1/2}P$	$0-1P$	$1/2P$	0.08	10
1989-90	Amigo 2WD	$1^{3/4}P-3^{1/4}P$	$2^{1/2}P$	$0-1P$	$1/2P$	0.08	10
	Amigo 4WD	$1^{3/4}P-3^{1/4}P$	$2^{1/2}P$	$0-1P$	$1/2P$	0.08	10
	Pick-Up 2WD	$1P-2P$	$1^{1/2}P$	$1/2N-1^{1/2}P$	$1/2P$	0.08	10
	Pick-Up 4WD	$1^{1/4}P-2^{1/4}P$	$1^{3/4}P$	$1/2N-1^{1/2}P$	$1/2P$	0.08	10
	Trooper/Trooper II	$2P-3P$	$2^{1/2}P$	$0-1P$	$1/2P$	0.08	10

ENGINE ELECTRICAL

NOTE: Disconnecting the negative battery cable on some vehicles may interfere with the functions of the on board computer systems and may require the computer to undergo a relearning process, once the negative battery cable is reconnected.

Distributor

Removal and Installation
UNDISTURBED ENGINE

1. Disconnect the negative battery cable.
2. Disconnect and label the spark plug wires at the distributor cap.
3. Remove the distributor cap from the distributor. Disconnect and label the distributor wiring.
4. Using a piece of chalk, matchmark the rotor to the distributor housing and the housing to the engine.

5. Remove the distributor hold-down nut, the clamp and lift the distributor from the engine.

NOTE: When removing the distributor, it may be necessary to rotate the distributor shaft slightly to disengage it from the drive gear.

To install:
6. Lower the distributor into the engine and align the rotor and distributor housing to the matchmarks.
7. Check and/or adjust the ignition timing when finished.

DISTURBED ENGINE

1. If the engine was disturbed while the distributor was removed, remove the No. 1 spark plug.
2. Rotate the crankshaft in the normal direction of rotation until compression is felt at the spark plug hole.
3. Continue rotating the engine in the same direction while observing the timing marks at the indicator line up when No. 1 cylinder is at TDC.

4. Install the distributor and align the rotor with the No. 1 lug on the distributor cap.

5. Check and/or adjust the ignition timing when finished.

Ignition Timing

Adjustment

EXCEPT 2.8L ENGINE

NOTE: On the 2.0L and 2.3L engines, be sure to set the air gap in the distributor before timing the engine.

The timing marks are located near the front crankshaft pulley and consist of a pointer with graduations attached to the engine block and a mark on the crankshaft pulley.

1. Check and correct the air gap in the distributor.

2. Locate and clean the timing marks on the crankshaft pulley and the front of the engine.

3. Using an inductive pick-up timing light, connect it to the No. 1 spark plug wire. Attach a timing light to the ignition coil.

4. If the distributor is equipped with a vacuum advance, disconnect and plug the vacuum line.

5. Make sure all wires from the timing light and tachometer are clear of the fan and belts. Start the engine.

6. Adjust the idle to the correct rpm.

7. Aim the timing light at the timing marks. Adjust the distributor until the timing marks are aligned.

8. Tighten the distributor mounting bolt and check the timing again.

9. Turn the engine **OFF** and remove the timing light and tachometer. Connect the distributor vacuum line.

2.8L ENGINE

1. Set the parking brake and block the drive wheels.

2. Operate the engine to normal operating temperatures and turn the air conditioning **OFF**, if equipped.

3. Verify that the Check Engine light is not turned **ON**.

4. Place the Electronic Spark Timing (EST) into the bypass mode by disconnect the timing connector.

NOTE: The EST is a single wire connector, located under the center console in the passenger compartment. Do not disconnect the 4-wire connector from the distributor.

5. Using an inductive pick-up timing light, connect it to the No. 1 spark plug wire.

6. Check and/or adjust the engine speed to 800 rpm.

7. Loosen the distributor hold-down bolt and turn the distributor until the timing mark, on the crankshaft pulley, is aligned with the 10 degree BTDC timing mark on the timing cover.

8. Tighten the distributor hold-down bolt.

9. Reconnect the timing connector and clear the ECM trouble code(s).

Air Gap Setting

On the 2.0L and 2.3L engines, the air gap setting in the distributor should be checked and adjusted before the ignition timing is adjusted.

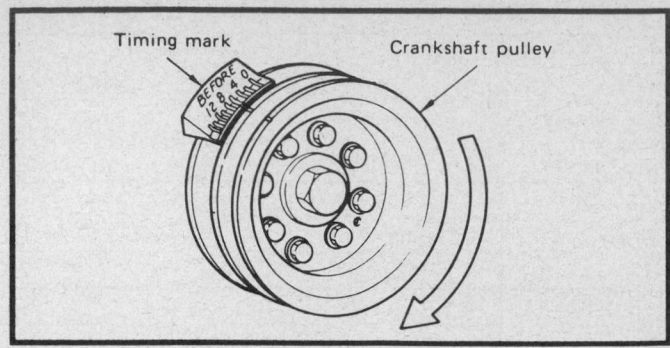

View of the ignition timing marks

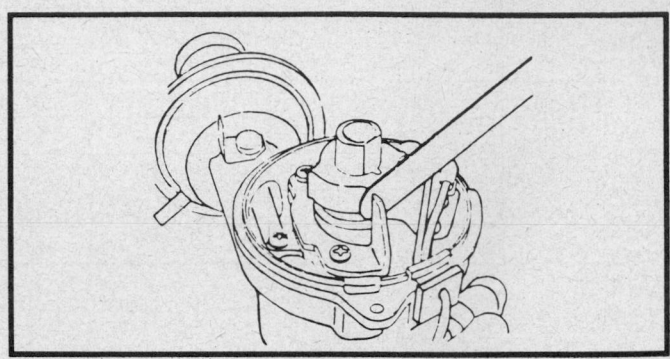

Adjusting the air gap—2.0L and 2.3L engines

Adjustment

1. Remove the distributor cap, O-ring and rotor.

2. Use a feeler gauge to measure the air gap at the pick up coil projection. The gap should be 0.008–0.016 in. (2.0L engine) or 0.012–0.020 in. (2.3L engine); adjust it, if necessary.

3. Loosen the screws and move the signal generator until the gap is correct. Tighten the screws and recheck the gap.

NOTE: The electrical parts in this system are not repairable. If found to be defective, they must be replaced.

Alternator

For further information, please refer to "Electrical" in the Unit Repair section.

Belt Tension Adjustment

EXCEPT 2.8L ENGINE

1. Loosen the alternator pivot bolt.

2. Rotate the alternator to produce a belt deflection of 0.40 in. (10mm).

3. Tighten the alternator pivot bolt.

2.8L ENGINE

The 2.8L engine uses a singe serpentine belt to drive all engine accessories. The belt tension is maintained by a spring loaded tensioner. The belt tensioner has the ability to control the belt tension over a broad range of belt lengths. However, there are limits to which the tensioner can compensate for varying lengths.

Removal and Installation

EXCEPT 2.8L ENGINE

1. Disconnect the negative battery cable. If equipped with an

air pump, it may be necessary to remove it.

2. Disconnect and label the alternator wiring.

3. Remove the alternator pivot bolt on the lower part of the alternator. Remove the drive belt from the pulley.

4. Remove the alternator mounting bolt(s) and the alternator from the engine.

To install:

5. Install the alternator.

6. Adjust the belt tension and tighten the alternator mounting bolts.

7. Reconnect the alternator's wiring connectors. Connect the negative battery cable.

2.8L ENGINE

1. Disconnect the negative battery cable.

2. Remove the terminal plug and the battery lead from the rear of the alternator.

3. Remove the drive belt.

4. Remove the air pump bracket bolt from the rear of the alternator.

5. Remove the mounting bolts from the front of the alternator and the alternator from the vehicle.

To install:

6. Install the alternator and the mounting bolts.

7. Install the drive belt.

8. Torque the lower mounting bolt to 26 ft. lbs. (35 Nm), the upper mounting bolt to 18 ft. lbs. (25 Nm) and the air pump bracket bolt to 18 ft. lbs. (25 Nm).

9. Connect the terminal connector and the battery lead to the rear of the alternator. Reconnect the negative battery cable.

Voltage Regulator

For further information, please refer to "Electrical" in the Unit Repair section.

An external voltage regulator is used only with the 2.0L engine.

Adjustment

1. Remove the regulator from the vehicle and remove the regulator cover.

2. If the points are pitted, clean them carefully with fine emery paper.

3. Check and adjust the core gap first and then the point gap.

4. Adjust the core gap by loosening the screws attaching the contact set to the yoke. Move the contact set up or down as required. The standard core gap is 0.024–0.039 in. Tighten the attaching screw.

5. Adjust the point gap by loosening the screw attaching the upper contact. Move the upper contact up or down as required. The standard point gap is 0.012–0.016 in.

6. Adjust the regulated voltage by turning the adjusting screw. Turn the adjusting screw in to increase voltage and out to reduce voltage. When the correct adjustment is obtained, secure the adjusting screw by tightening the locknut. The regulated voltage is 13.8–14.8V.

7. Install the regulator cover, reconnect the electrical leads and install the regulator.

Removal and Installation

1. Disconnect the negative battery cable.

2. Disconnect and label the electrical leads at the regulator.

3. Remove the 2 regulator mounting screws and remove the regulator.

To install:

4. Install the voltage regulator.

5. Connect the electrical leads to the regulator.

6. Connect the negative battery cable.

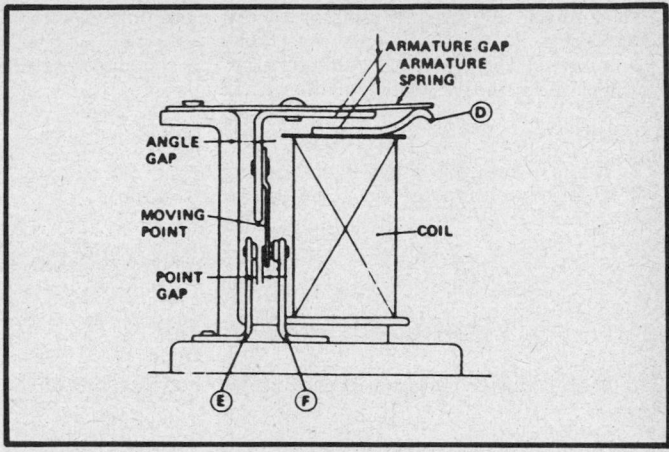

Adjusting the voltage regulator

Starter

For further information, please refer to "Electrical" in the Unit Repair section.

Removal and Installation

EXCEPT 2.8L ENGINE

1. Disconnect the negative battery cable.

2. If equipped, it may be necessary to disconnect and remove the EGR pipe.

3. Disconnect and label the starter wiring at the starter.

4. Remove the starter-to-engine bolts and the starter from the vehicle.

To install:

4. Installation the starter to the engine.

5. Connect the electrical connectors to the starter.

6. If the EGR pipe was removed, install it.

7. Connect the negative battery cable.

2.8L ENGINE

1. Disconnect the negative battery cable.

2. Raise and safely support the vehicle.

3. Label and disconnect the electrical connectors from the starter.

4. Remove the starter-to-engine mounting bolts.

5. Lower the starter from the engine. If any shims are present, keep them for reinstallation purposes.

To install:

6. Install the starter and shims, if equipped, to the engine. Torque the bolts to 30 ft. lbs. (40 Nm).

7. Reconnect the electrical connectors to the starter.

8. Lower the vehicle.

9. Connect the negative battery cable.

Diesel Glow Plugs

Removal and Installation

1. Disconnect the negative battery cable.

2. Remove the electrical connector from the sensing resistor.

3. Remove the sensing resistor from the glow plug connector.

4. Disconnect the electrical connector from the glow plug terminals.

5. Remove the glow plugs from the engine.

NOTE: Even if 1 glow plug is found to be defective, replace the others.

6. Install the glow plugs to the engine.

7. Connect the electrical connector to the glow plug terminals.

8. Connect the sensing resistor to the glow plug electrical connector.

9. Connect the electrical connector to the sensing resistor. Connect the negative battery cable.

Testing

1. Remove the glow plugs from the engine.
2. Using an ohmmeter, set it on the 5V DC scale.

3. Touch 1 lead to the glow plug's electrical terminal and the other lead to the glow plug's tip; the resistance should be 1.0 ohm at room temperature.

NOTE: If no continuity exists, the heat wire is broken and must be replace.

4. Replace the glow plugs.

CHASSIS ELECTRICAL

Heater Blower Motor

The heater blower motor is located under the right side of the dash.

Removal and Installation

1. Disconnect the negative battery cable.
2. Disconnect and label the blower motor electrical leads.
3. Remove the blower-to-heater unit screws and lower the blower motor assembly.

To install:

4. Install the heater blower motor, into the heater unit and install the screws.
5. Connect the electrical connectors to the heater blower motor.
6. Connect the negative battery cable.

Windshield Wiper Motor

Removal and Installation

1. Disconnect the negative battery cable.
2. Disconnect the electrical connector from the wiper motor.
3. Remove the wiper motor bracket-to-chassis bolts.
4. Disconnect the wiper motor from the wiper linkage at the ball joint.

To install:

5. Connect the wiper motor to the wiper linkage at the ball joint.
6. Install the wiper motor-to-chassis bolts.
7. Connect the electrical connector to the wiper motor.
8. Connect the negative battery cable.

Windshield Wiper Switch

Removal and Installation

**EXCEPT PICK-UP 1988–90
AND AMIGO**

The windshield wiper switch is a part of the combination switch located on the steering column.

**PICK-UP 1988–90
AND AMIGO**

The windshield wiper switch is a part of the switch cluster located on the left side of the instrument cluster.

1. Disconnect the negative battery cable.
2. Remove the instrument cluster-to-dash screws.
3. Pull the instrument cluster forward and disconnect the electrical connector from the switch cluster.
4. From the rear of the instrument cluster, loosen the switch cluster-to-instrument cluster bolts.
5. Separate the windshield wiper switch from the switch cluster.

To install:

6. Install the windshield wiper switch to the switch cluster.
7. Tighten the switch cluster-to-instrument cluster bolts.

1. Solenoid valve
2. Diaphragm assembly
3. Door spring and lever
4. Blower motor assembly
5. Thermo sensor assembly
6. Seal
7. Attaching parts
8. Left side case
9. Right side case
10. Blower motor housing
11. Blower motor fan

Exploded view of the heater blower motor

8. Connect the electrical connector to the switch cluster.
9. Install the instrument cluster.
10. Connect the negative battery cable.

Instrument Cluster

Removal and Installation

**EXCEPT PICK-UP 1988–90
AND AMIGO**

1. Disconnect the negative battery cable.
2. Remove the steering wheel.
3. Remove the knob from the light switch.
4. Remove the cover-to-instrument panel screws and the cover.
5. Remove the instrument panel-to-dash screws and pull the panel forward.
6. Disconnect the electrical connectors and the speedometer cable from the rear of the instrument panel.
7. Remove the instrument panel from the vehicle.

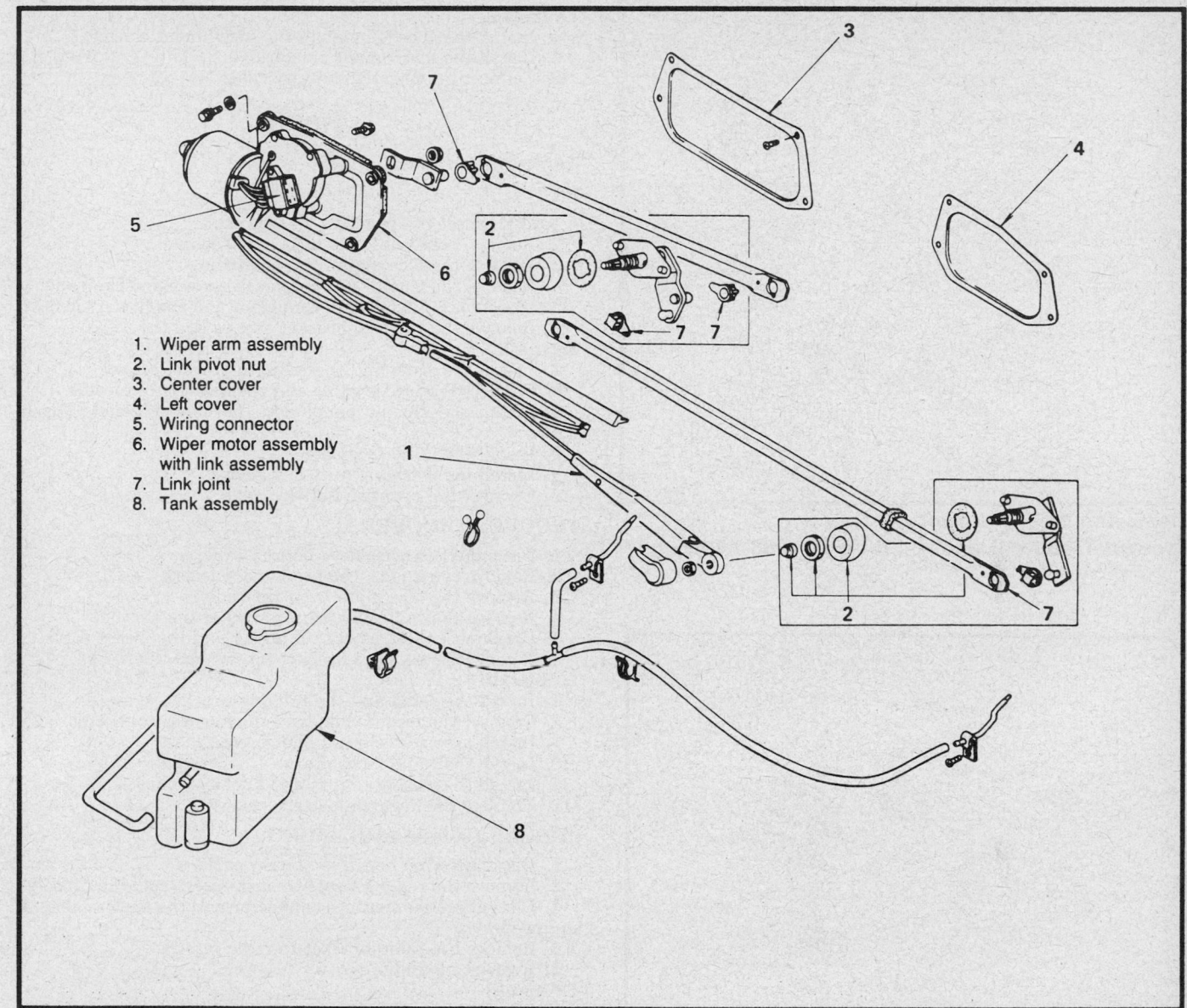

1. Wiper arm assembly
2. Link pivot nut
3. Center cover
4. Left cover
5. Wiring connector
6. Wiper motor assembly with link assembly
7. Link joint
8. Tank assembly

Exploded view of the wiper motor and linkage assembly

To install:
8. Connect the speedometer cable and the electrical connectors to the rear of the instrument cluster.
9. Install the instrument cluster to the dash.
10. Install the cover to the instrument cluster.
11. Install the knob to the light switch.
12. Install the steering wheel.
13. Connect the negative battery cable.

PICK-UP 1988–90 AND AMIGO

Tilt Steering Wheel

1. Disconnect the negative battery cable.
2. Move the steering wheel to the fully down position.
3. Remove the instrument cluster-to-dash screws and pull the instrument cluster forward.

4. Disconnect the electrical connectors and the speedometer cable from the instrument cluster.

To install:
5. Connect the speedometer cable and electrical connectors to the instrument cluster.
6. Install the instrument cluster to the dash.
7. Connect the negative battery cable.

Except Tilt Steering Wheel

1. Disconnect the negative battery cable.
2. Remove the steering wheel and the steering wheel cowl.
3. Remove the instrument cluster-to-dash screws and pull the instrument cluster forward.
4. Disconnect the electrical connectors and the speedometer cable from the instrument cluster.

To install:
5. Connect the speedometer cable and electrical connectors to

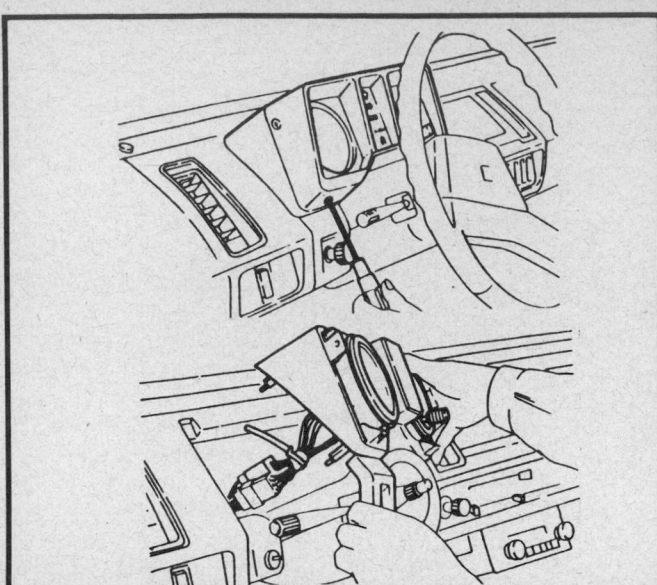

Removing the instrument cluster—
Trooper/Trooper II shown—Pick-Up 1986–87 similar

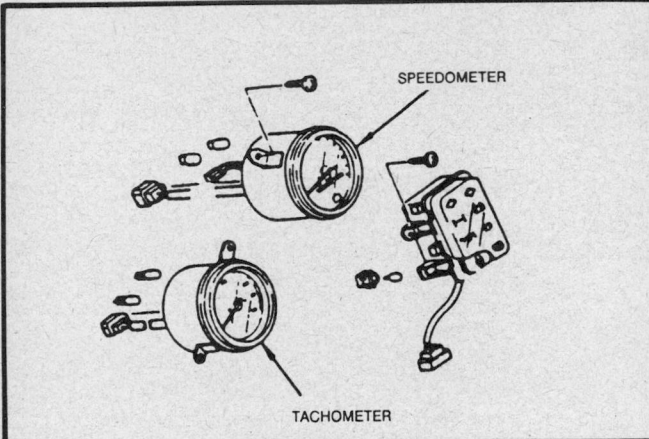

Exploded view of the speedometer—
Trooper/Trooper II

the instrument cluster.
6. Install the instrument cluster to the dash.
7. Install the steering column cowl and the steering wheel.
8. Connect the negative battery cable.

Speedometer

Removal and Installation

EXCEPT TROOPER/TROOPER II

The speedometer is a part of the instrument cluster.

TROOPER/TROOPER II

1. Disconnect the negative battery cable.
2. Remove the instrument cluster.
3. Remove the speedometer from the instrument cluster.

To install:
4. Install the speedometer to the instrument cluster.
5. Install the instrument cluster.
6. Connect the negative battery cable.

Radio

Removal and Installation

P'UP

1. Disconnect the negative battery cable.
2. Remove the knobs, the nuts and washers.
3. Remove the face plate from the radio.
4. Remove the cluster panel-to-dash screws and the panel.
5. Disconnect the harness connector and the feeder cable.
6. Remove the radio-to-bracket screws and the radio.

To install:
7. Install the radio and the radio-to-bracket screws.
8. Connect the feeder cable and the harness connector.
9. Install the cluster panel and the cluster panel-to-dash screws.
10. Install the radio faceplate.
11. Install the washers, nuts and knobs.
12. Connect the negative battery cable.

TROOPER/TROOPER II

1. Disconnect the negative battery cable.
2. Remove the knobs, the nuts and washers.
3. Remove the face plate from the radio.
4. Remove the radio shroud screws and the shroud.
5. Disconnect the harness connector and the feeder cable.
6. Remove the radio-to-bracket screws and the radio.

To install:
7. Install the radio and the radio-to-bracket screws.
8. Connect the feeder cable and the harness connector.
9. Install the radio shroud and screws.
10. Install the radio faceplate.
11. Install the washers, nuts and knobs.
12. Connect the negative battery cable.

PICK-UP 1988–90 AND AMIGO

1. Disconnect the negative battery cable.
2. Remove the radio console-to-dash screws and the console.
3. Disconnect the harness connector and the feeder cable, if equipped.
4. Remove the radio bracket-to-radio screws.
5. Remove the radio.

To install:
6. Install the radio and the radio bracket-to-radio screws.
7. Connect the harness connector and the feeder cable, if equipped.
8. Install the console and the radio console-to-dash screws.
9. Connect the negative battery cable.

Headlight Switch

Removal and Installation

EXCEPT PICK-UP 1988–90 AND AMIGO

The headlight switch is located on the lower left side of the dash.
1. Disconnect the negative battery cable.
2. Remove the headlight switch knob.
3. Disconnect and label the headlight switch wiring under the dashboard.
4. Remove the headlight switch locknut and the switch from the dash.

To install:
5. Install the switch to the dash and secure with the locknut.
6. Connect the electrical connector to the headlight switch.
7. Install the headlight switch knob.

8. Connect the negative battery cable.

PICK-UP 1988–90 AND AMIGO

The push button headlight switch, is a part of the switch cluster located on the left side of the dash.

1. Disconnect the negative battery cable.
2. Remove the instrument cluster-to-dash screws.
3. Pull the instrument cluster forward and disconnect the electrical connector from the switch cluster.
4. From the rear of the instrument cluster, loosen the switch cluster-to-instrument cluster bolts.
5. Separate the headlight switch from the switch cluster.
To install:
6. Install the headlight switch to the switch cluster.
7. Tighten the switch cluster-to-instrument cluster bolts.
8. Connect the electrical connector to the switch cluster.
9. Install the instrument cluster.
10. Connect the negative battery cable.

Dimmer Switch

The dimmer switch is a part of the combination switch located on the steering column.

Turn Signal Switch

The turn signal switch is a part of the combination switch located on the steering column.

Combination Switch

Removal and Installation

P'UP

1. Disconnect the negative battery cable.
2. From the rear of the steering wheel, remove the horn pad screw and lift the horn pad upward to remove it.
3. Disconnect the electrical connector from the horn pad.
4. Remove the steering wheel-to-steering column nut.
5. Matchmark the steering wheel to the steering shaft for reinstallation purposes.

NOTE: Never apply a blow to the steering wheel shaft with a hammer or other impact tool, to remove the steering wheel, for the steering shaft may become damaged.

6. Using a steering wheel puller, press the steering wheel from the steering column.

NOTE: Use steering wheel puller J-29752 (LS model) or J-24292-B (except LS model).

7. Remove the contact ring.
8. Remove the steering column covers.
9. Disconnect the electrical connector from the combination switch.
10. Remove the combination switch-to-steering column screws and the switch.
To install:
11. Install the combination switch to the steering column and secure it with screws.
12. Connect the combination switch electrical connector.
13. Install the steering column covers.
14. Install the contact ring.
15. Align the steering wheel-to-steering column matchmarks and torque the nut to 18–25 ft. lbs.
16. Connect the electrical connector to the horn pad.
17. Install the horn pad and the horn pad screw.
18. Connect the negative battery cable.

EXCEPT P'UP

1. Disconnect the negative battery cable.

2. From the rear of the steering wheel, remove the horn pad screw and lift the horn pad upward to remove it.
3. Remove the steering wheel-to-steering column nut.
4. Matchmark the steering wheel to the steering shaft for reinstallation purposes.

NOTE: Never apply a blow to the steering wheel shaft with a hammer or other impact tool, to remove the steering wheel, for the steering shaft may become damaged.

5. Using a steering wheel puller, press the steering wheel from the steering column.
6. Remove the contact ring.
7. Remove the steering column covers.
8. Disconnect the electrical connector from the combination switch.
9. Remove the combination switch-to-steering column screws and the switch.
To install:
10. Install the combination switch to the steering column and secure it with screws.
11. Connect the combination switch electrical connector.
12. Install the steering column covers.
13. Install the contact ring.
14. Align the steering wheel-to-steering column matchmarks and torque the nut to 22–29 ft. lbs.
15. Install the horn pad and the horn pad screw.
16. Connect the negative battery cable.

Ignition Lock/Switch

Removal and Installation

EXCEPT PICK-UP 1988–90 AND AMIGO

Ignition switch

The ignition switch is located on the lower right side of the dash.

1. Disconnect the negative battery cable.
2. Disconnect and label the ignition switch wiring under the dashboard.
4. Remove the ignition switch locknut and the switch from the dash.
To install:
5. Install the ignition switch to the dash and secure with the locknut.
6. Connect the electrical connector to the ignition switch.
7. Connect the negative battery cable.

Ignition Lock

1. Remove the combination switch.
2. Remove the ignition lock-to-steering column clamp bolts and the ignition lock.
To install:
3. Install the ignition lock to the steering column and secure with bolts.
4. Install the combination switch.

PICK-UP 1988–90 AND AMIGO

1. Disconnect the negative battery cable.
2. From the rear of the steering wheel, remove the horn pad screw and lift the horn pad upward to remove it.
3. Remove the steering wheel-to-steering column nut.
4. Matchmark the steering wheel to the steering shaft for reinstallation purposes.

NOTE: Never apply a blow to the steering wheel shaft with a hammer or other impact tool, to remove the steering wheel, for the steering shaft may become damaged.

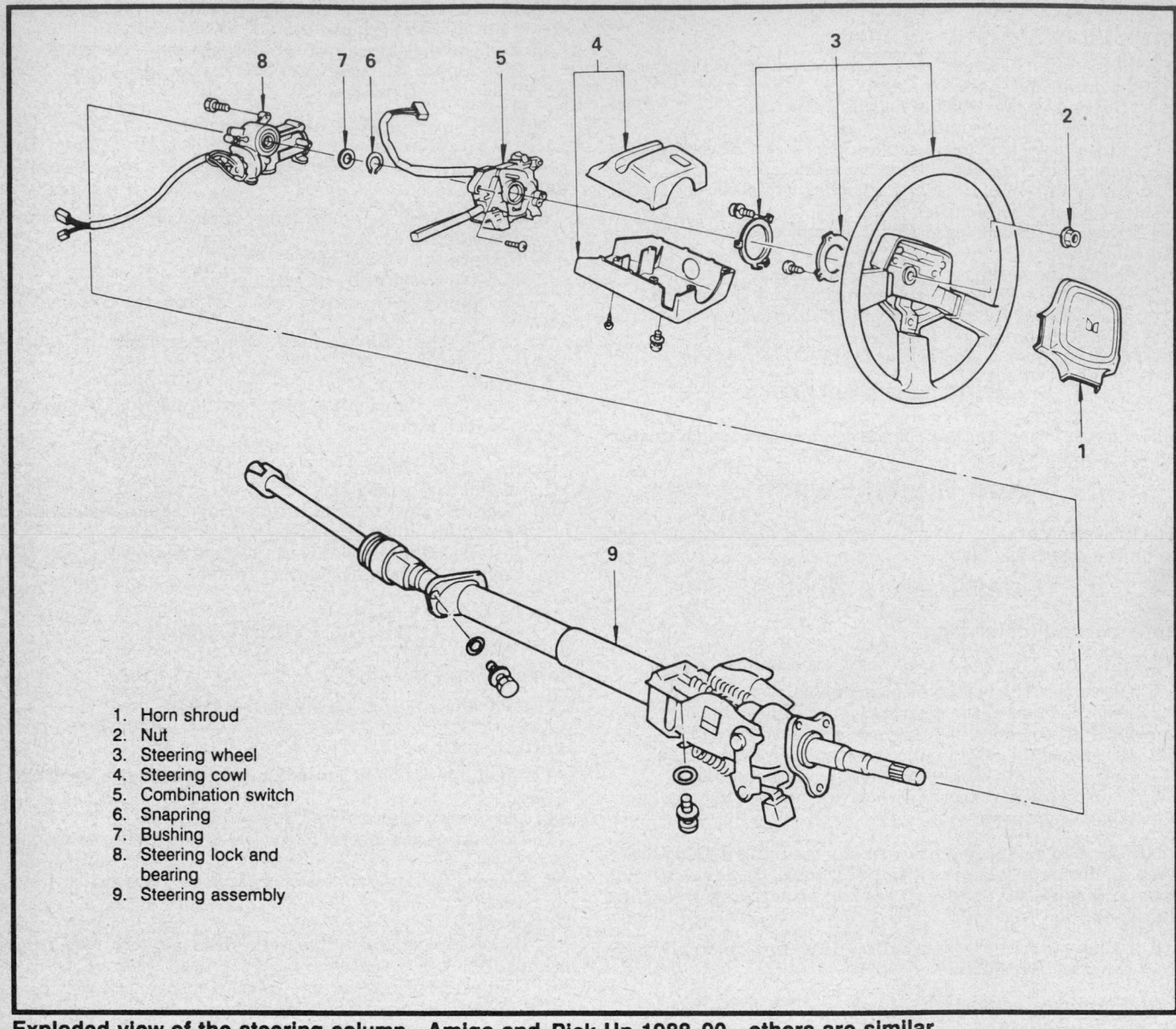

1. Horn shroud
2. Nut
3. Steering wheel
4. Steering cowl
5. Combination switch
6. Snapring
7. Bushing
8. Steering lock and bearing
9. Steering assembly

Exploded view of the steering column—Amigo and Pick-Up 1988–90—others are similar

5. Using a steering wheel puller, press the steering wheel from the steering column.

6. Remove the contact ring.

7. Remove the steering column covers.

8. Disconnect the electrical connector from the combination switch.

9. Remove the combination switch-to-steering column screws and the switch.

10. Remove the ignition lock/switch-to-steering column snapring and bushing.

11. Disconnect the electrical connector from the ignition lock/switch assembly.

12. Remove the ignition lock/switch-to-steering column bolts and the lock/switch assembly.

To install:

13. Install the ignition lock/switch-to-steering column bolts, the bushing and the snapring.

14. Install the combination switch to the steering column and secure it with screws.

15. Connect the combination switch electrical connector.

16. Install the steering column covers.

17. Install the contact ring.

18. Align the steering wheel-to-steering column matchmarks and torque the nut to 22–29 ft. lbs.

19. Install the horn pad and the horn pad screw.

20. Connect the negative battery cable.

Stoplight Switch

Removal and Installation

1. Disconnect the negative battery cable.

2. Locate the stoplight switch on the brake pedal support.
3. Disconnect the electrical connector from the stoplight switch.
4. Remove the locknut and the stoplight switch.
To install:
5. Install the switch on the support and adjust the switch so there is 0.020–0.040 in. (0.5–1.0mm) clearance between the switch and the brake pedal.
6. Torque the locknut to 11–18 ft. lbs.
7. Connect the wiring to the switch and the negative battery cable.
8. Check the operation of the switch.

ENGINE COOLING

Radiator

Removal and Installation

1. Disconnect the negative battery cable.
2. Drain the cooling system.
3. Remove the upper, lower and reservoir hoses from the radiator.
4. Remove the fan shroud-to-radiator bolts and the shroud.
5. Remove the radiator-to-chassis bolts and the radiator.
To install:
6. Install the radiator and the radiator-to-chassis bolts.
7. Install the fan shroud and the shroud-to-radiator bolts.
8. Reconnect the radiator hoses.
9. Refill the cooling system.
10. Connect the negative battery cable.

Heater Core

Removal and Installation
EXCEPT PICK-UP 1988–90 AND AMIGO

1. Disconnect the negative battery cable.
2. Place a drain pan under the heater hoses at the heater core. Remove the heater hoses from the heater core, securing the heater hoses in a raised position to prevent further loss of coolant. Plug the heater core tubes to prevent spillage of coolant in the passenger compartment when removing.
3. Remove the instrument panel-to-chassis screws and the panel.
4. If equipped with air conditioning, perform the following procedures:
   a. Properly discharge the air conditioning system.
   b. Remove the evaporator-to-compressor and receiver tank flare nuts.
   c. Remove the vacuum hose.
   d. Disconnect the connectors from the evaporator relay.
   e. Remove the evaporator-to-chassis nuts and the evaporator.
5. If not equipped with air conditioning, remove the heater unit assembly-to-blower unit assembly duct.
6. Remove the air ducts from the heater unit assembly.
7. Disconnect the mechanical and electrical connectors from the heater unit relay.
8. Remove the heater unit assembly-to-chassis nuts and the assembly.
To install:
9. Install the heater unit assembly and secure with the nuts.
10. Connect the mechanical and electrical connectors to the heater unit relay.
11. Install the air ducts to the heater unit assembly.
12. If not equipped with air conditioning, install the heater unit assembly-to-blower unit assembly duct.
13. If equipped with air conditioning, perform the following procedures:

Fuses and Circuit Breakers

Location

The main fuse box is located at the lower left side of the instrument panel.
The fuse/relay box is located at the right side of the engine compartment with the main fuse installed in it.
Fusible links are in a box located beside the battery.

   a. Install the evaporator and the evaporator-to-chassis nuts.
   b. Connect the connectors to the evaporator relay.
   c. Install the vacuum hose.
   d. Install the evaporator-to-compressor and receiver tank flare nuts.
14. Evacuate and recharge the air conditioning system.
15. Install the panel and secure with the instrument panel-to-chassis screws.
16. Install the heater hoses to the heater core.
17. Connect the negative battery cable.
18. If equipped with air conditioning, recharge the air conditioning system.

PICK-UP 1988–90 AND AMIGO

1. Disconnect the negative battery cable.
2. Place a drain pan under the heater hoses at the heater core. Remove the heater hoses from the heater core, securing the heater hoses in a raised position to prevent further loss of coolant. Plug the heater core tubes to prevent spillage of coolant in the passenger compartment when removing.
3. Remove the instrument panel-to-chassis screws and the panel.
4. Disconnect electrical connectors from the resistor.
5. Remove the evaporator-to-compressor and receiver tank flare nuts.
6. Properly discharge the air conditioning system.
7. Remove the evaporator-to-chassis nuts and the evaporator.
8. Remove the side ventilator air ducts.
9. Remove the heater unit assembly-to-chassis nuts and the assembly.
To install:
10. Install the heater unit assembly and secure with the nuts.
11. Install the side ventilator air ducts.
12. Install the evaporator and the evaporator-to-chassis nuts.
13. Connect the electrical connector to the resistor.
14. Install the evaporator-to-compressor and receiver tank flare nuts.
15. Install the instrument panel and secure with the panel-to-chassis screws.
16. Install the heater hoses to the heater core.
17. Connect the negative battery cable.
18. Recharge the air conditioning system.

Water Pump

Removal and Installation

1. Disconnect the negative battery cable.
2. Remove the undercover, if equipped, and drain the cooling system.
3. Remove the drive belt from the water pump pulley.
4. If equipped with a diesel engine, remove the coolant hose from the pump body.

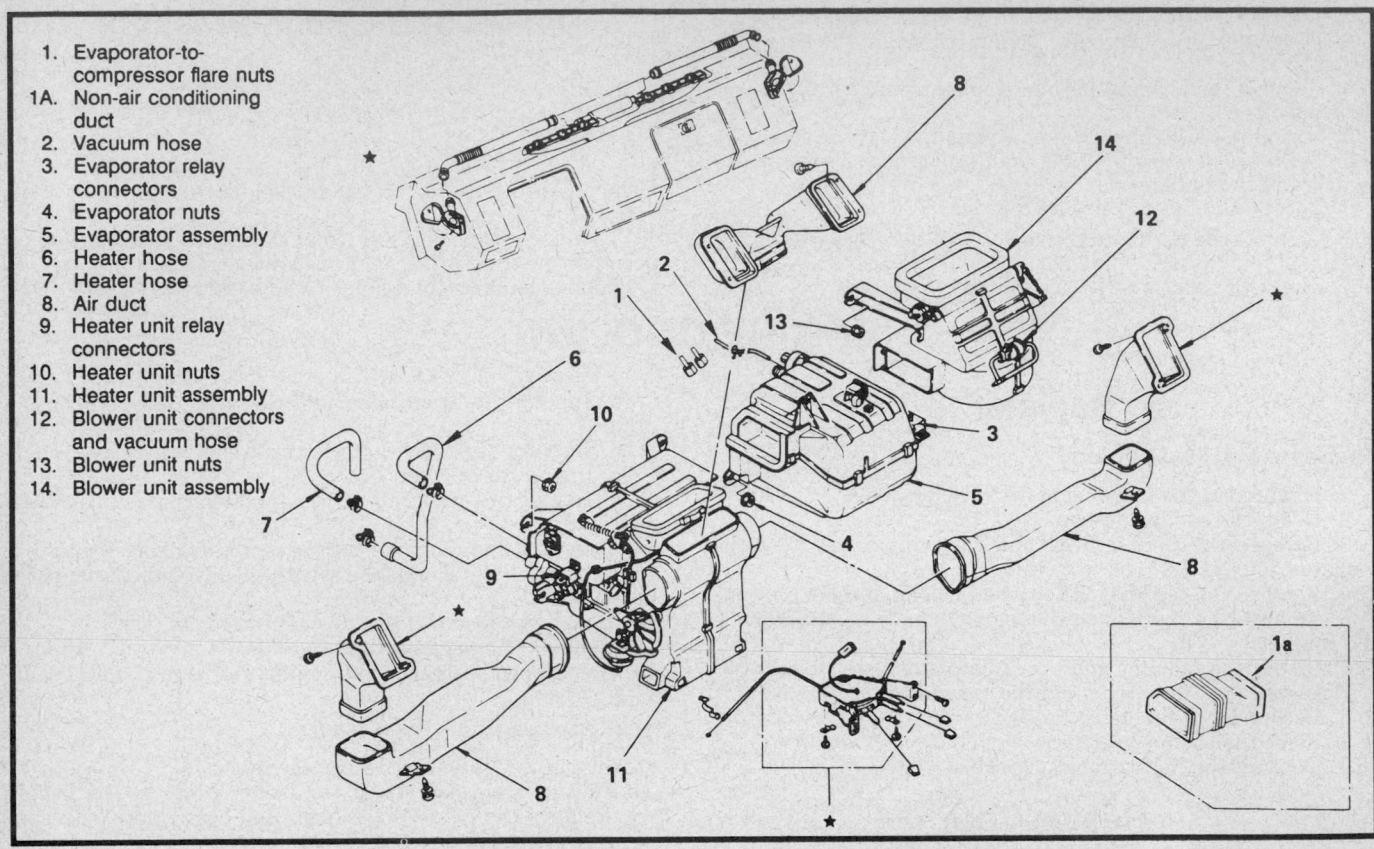

1. Evaporator-to-compressor flare nuts
1A. Non-air conditioning duct
2. Vacuum hose
3. Evaporator relay connectors
4. Evaporator nuts
5. Evaporator assembly
6. Heater hose
7. Heater hose
8. Air duct
9. Heater unit relay connectors
10. Heater unit nuts
11. Heater unit assembly
12. Blower unit connectors and vacuum hose
13. Blower unit nuts
14. Blower unit assembly

Exploded view of the heater/air conditioning system—except Amigo and Pick-Up 1989–90

5. Remove the fan blade and pulley from the pump hub.
6. Remove the water pump-to-engine bolts, the water pump and gasket.
7. Clean and inspect the mounting surfaces of the water pump and engine.
To install:
8. Install a new gasket and the water pump; torque the water pump-to-engine bolts to 17–19 ft. lbs. (2.0L engine), 10–17 ft. lbs. (2.3L and 2.6L engines) or 24–38 ft. lbs. (2.2L diesel engine).
9. Install the fan blade and pulley to the water pump.
10. If equipped with a diesel engine, connect the water hose to the pump.
11. Install and adjust the drive belt.
12. Refill the cooling system and install the undercover, if equipped.
13. Connect the negative battery cable.
14. Operate the engine to normal operating temperatures and check for leaks.

Thermostat

Removal and Installation
GASOLINE ENGINE
The thermostat is located, under the thermostat housing, on top of the intake manifold at the front of the engine.
1. Disconnect the negative battery cable.
2. Drain the cooling system. Disconnect the upper radiator hose from the thermostat housing.
3. Remove the air cleaner assembly.

4. Remove the thermostat housing from the intake manifold.
5. Remove the gasket and the thermostat.
To install:
6. Install the thermostat, with the spring facing the engine.
7. Using a new gasket, install the thermostat housing.
8. Connect the radiator hose to the thermostat housing and refill the cooling system.
9. Install the air cleaner.
10. Connect the negative battery cable.
11. Operate the engine until normal operating temperatures are reached and check the thermostat operation.

DIESEL ENGINE
The thermostat is located, under the thermostat housing, at upper front of the engine.
1. Disconnect the negative battery cable.
2. Drain the cooling system.
3. Disconnect the electrical connectors from the thermostat housing.
4. Remove the upper thermostat housing-to-lower housing bolts and the upper housing.
5. Remove the gasket and the thermostat.
6. Clean the gasket mounting surfaces.
To install:
7. Install the thermostat, with the spring facing the engine.
8. Using a new gasket, install the upper thermostat housing and torque the upper housing-to-lower housing bolts to 10–17 ft. lbs.
9. Connect the electrical connectors.
10. Connect the radiator hose to the thermostat housing and

refill the cooling system.

11. Connect the negative battery cable.

12. Operate the engine until normal operating temperatures are reached and check the thermostat operation.

GASOLINE FUEL SYSTEM

Fuel System Service Precaution

Disconnect the negative battery cable. Keep a Class B dry chemical fire extinguisher available. Always relieve the fuel pressure before disconnecting a fuel line. Wrap a shop cloth around the fuel line when disconnecting a fuel line. Always use new O-rings. Do not replace the fuel pipes with fuel hoses. Always us a back-up wrench when opening or closing a fuel line.

Relieving Fuel System Pressure

CARBURETED ENGINE

1. Release the fuel vapor pressure in the fuel tank by removing the fuel tank cap and reinstalling it.

2. Cover the fuel line with an absorbent shop cloth and loosen the connection slowly to release the fuel pressure gradually.

FUEL INJECTED ENGINE

1. Allow the engine to cool. Then, remove the fuel pump fuse from the fuse block.

2. Crank the engine, it will start and run until the fuel supply

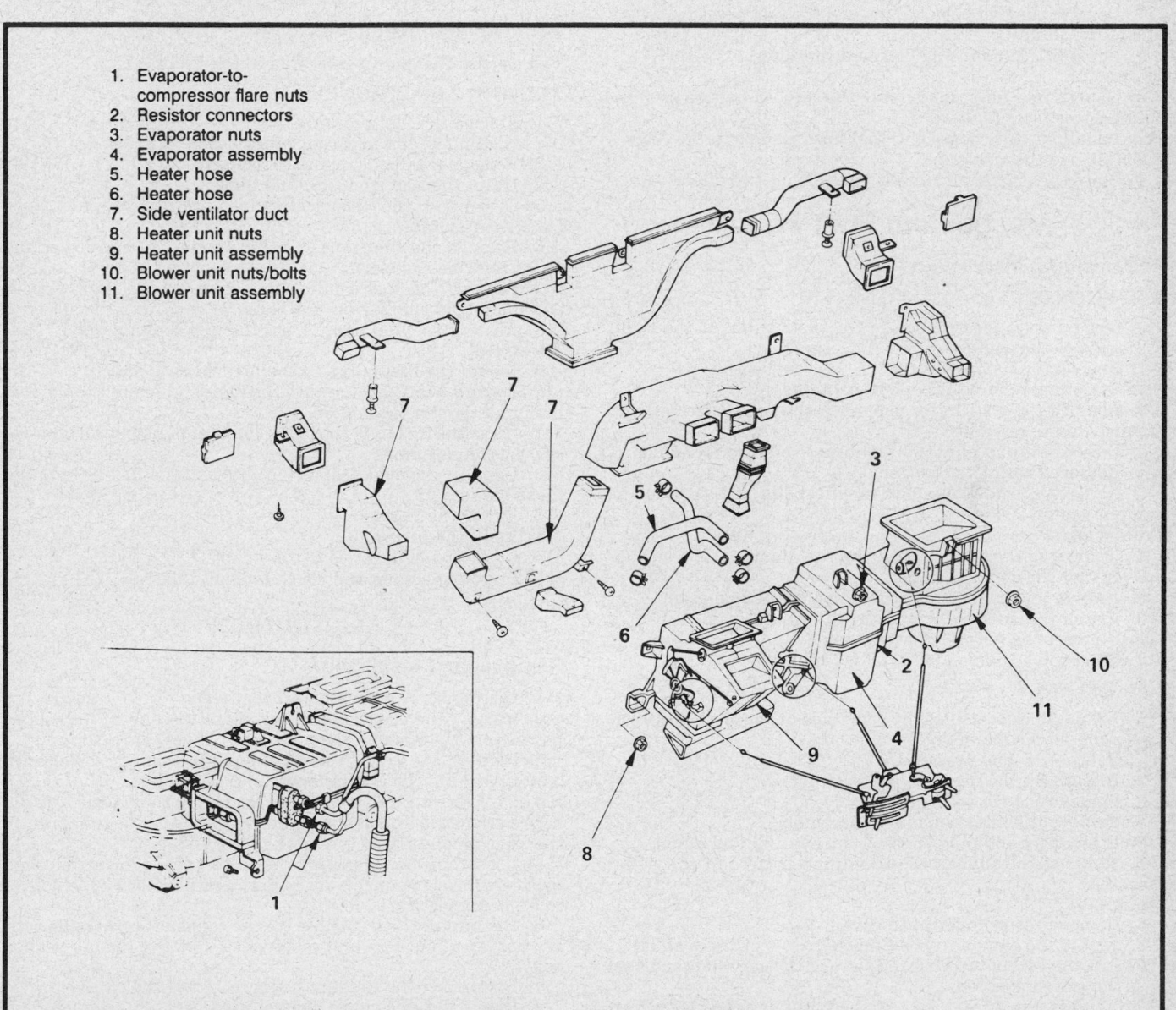

1. Evaporator-to-compressor flare nuts
2. Resistor connectors
3. Evaporator nuts
4. Evaporator assembly
5. Heater hose
6. Heater hose
7. Side ventilator duct
8. Heater unit nuts
9. Heater unit assembly
10. Blower unit nuts/bolts
11. Blower unit assembly

Exploded view of the heater/air conditioning system—Amigo and Pick-Up 1989–90

remaining in the fuel lines is exhausted. When the engine stops, engage the starter again for 3.0 seconds to assure dissipation of any remaining pressure.

3. With the ignition **OFF**, replace the fuel pump fuse.

Fuel Filter

On the P'UP, Amigo and Pick-Up, the fuel filer is located directly in front of the fuel tank. On the Trooper/Trooper II, the fuel filter is located along the inner side of the right frame rail, near the rear of the vehicle.

Removal and Installation

1. Properly relieve the fuel system pressure.
2. Raise and safely support the vehicle.
3. Using 2 pairs of vise grips, pinch off the fuel line on each side of the fuel filter.
4. Remove the fuel hose clamps and the fuel hoses from each side of the filter.
5. Remove the mounting bolt and the filter.

To install:

6. Using a new filter, install it to the vehicle; be sure its directional arrow faces forward.
7. Install the fuel hoses and fuel hose clamps to the filter.
8. Remove the vise grips.
9. Start the engine and check for leaks at the filter.

Mechanical Fuel Pump

Removal and Installation

2.0L ENGINE

The fuel pump is located beside the distributor at the right, front side of the engine.

1. Relieve the fuel pressure.
2. Disconnect the negative battery cable.
3. Remove the distributor cap, with the wires attached and the distributor assembly.
4. Disconnect and plug the fuel lines from the fuel pump.
5. Remove the engine hanger.
6. Remove the fuel pump-to-engine bolts and remove the pump assembly.

To install:

7. Using a new gasket, install the fuel pump on the engine.
8. Install the engine hanger.
9. Unplug and connect the fuel lines to the fuel pump.
10. Install the distributor and the distributor cap.
11. Connect the negative battery cable.
12. Start the engine and check for fuel leaks.

2.3L ENGINE

The fuel pump is located at the right side of the engine, directly under the intake manifold.

1. Relieve the fuel pressure.
2. Disconnect the negative battery cable.
3. Remove the air cleaner assembly.
4. Remove the intake manifold assembly.
5. Disconnect and plug the fuel lines at the fuel pump.
6. Remove the fuel pump-to-engine bolts and the pump assembly.

To install:

7. Remove the cylinder head cover.
8. Rotate the engine to position the No. 4 cylinder at TDC.
9. Lift the fuel pump pushrod toward the camshaft and hold it in the raised position.
10. Using a new gasket, install the fuel pump on the engine; torque the bolts to 15–25 ft. lbs. (20–4 Nm).
11. Connect the fuel hoses to the fuel pump.
12. Using a new gasket, install the intake manifold.
13. Install the air cleaner assembly.

14. Connect the negative battery cable.
15. Start the engine and check for fuel leaks.

Electric Fuel Pump

Pressure Testing

1. Relieve the fuel pressure.
2. Disconnect the fuel line near the engine and install fuel pressure gauge T-connector in the line.
3. Connect the fuel pressure gauge to the T-connector.
4. Start the engine and check the fuel pressure; it should be 43 psi (2.6L engine) or 9–13 psi (2.8L engine).
5. After checking, turn the engine **OFF**.
6. Relieve the fuel pressure.
7. Remove the pressure gauge from the fuel line and reconnect the fuel line.
8. Start the engine and check for leaks.

Removal and Installation

The electric fuel pump is located in the fuel tank.

2.6L AND 2.8L ENGINES

1. Relieve the fuel pressure.
2. Disconnect the negative battery cable.
3. Raise and safely support the vehicle.
4. Drain the fuel from the fuel tank.
5. Disconnect the electrical connectors and the fuel lines from the fuel tank.
6. Remove the fuel tank-to-vehicle supports and lower the tank from the vehicle.
7. Remove the fuel sending unit cover-to-fuel tank screws and lift the assembly from the tank.
8. Remove the fuel pump from the fuel sending unit.

To install:

9. Install the fuel pump to the fuel sending unit.
10. Using a new gasket, install the fuel sending unit to the fuel tank and tighten the screws.
11. Raise the fuel tank into the vehicle and install the tank-to-chassis connectors.
12. Connect the electrical connectors and the fuel lines to the fuel sending unit.
13. Lower the vehicle.
14. Refill the fuel tank.
15. Connect the negative battery cable.
16. Start the engine and check for fuel leaks.

Carburetor

Removal and Installation

1. Disconnect the negative battery cable.
2. Remove the air cleaner wing nut and disconnect the rubber hoses from the clips on the air cleaner cover.
3. Remove the bracket bolts, if equipped, at the air cleaner and remove the air cleaner cover and filter element.
4. Disconnect the hot air hose (to the hot air duct), the air hose to the air pump at the air cleaner and the vacuum hose at the joint nipple side of the intake manifold.
5. Loosen the bolt clamping the air cleaner to the carburetor. Separate the air cleaner body from the carburetor but do not remove it completely.
6. Disconnect the PCV hose (to the camshaft cover), the rubber hoses to the check and relief valve. Remove the air cleaner body.
7. Disconnect the vacuum hoses from the EGR valve.
8. Disconnect the choke control wire.
9. Disconnect the lead from the throttle solenoid.
10. Disconnect the throttle linkage return spring.
11. Disconnect the accelerator linkage.
12. Disconnect the fuel line at the carburetor.

13. Remove the carburetor-to-manifold nuts and the carburetor.

To install:

14. Using a new gasket, install the carburetor to the intake manifold.

15. Connect the fuel line and the accelerator linkage to the carburetor.

16. Connect the throttle linkage return spring, the throttle solenoid lead, the choke control wire and the vacuum hoses to the EGR and the PCV.

17. Install the air cleaner and any necessary hoses.

18. Start the engine and check for fuel leaks.

Idle Speed Adjustment

1. Firmly set the parking brake and block the drive wheels.
2. Place the transmission in **N**.
3. Operate the engine until it reaches normal operating temperatures. Be sure the choke is fully open and the air cleaner is installed. If equipped, turn the air conditioning **OFF**.
4. Disconnect and plug the distributor vacuum, the canister purge and EGR vacuum lines. Shut off the vacuum to the idle compensator by bending the rubber hose.
5. Turn the throttle adjusting screw to the required idle speed.
6. If equipped with air conditioning, turn air conditioning control to **MAX COLD** and the blower on **HIGH**.
7. Open throttle to approximately ⅓ opening and allow it to close.

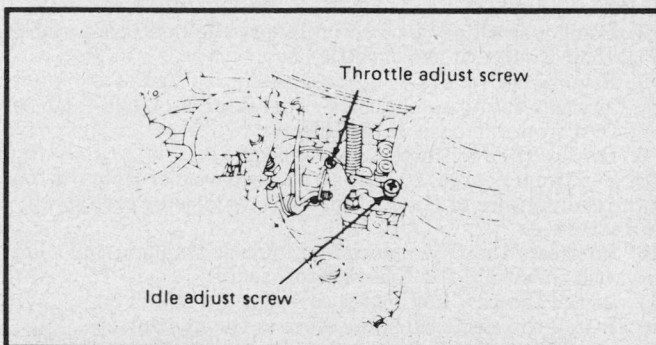

View of the idle and throttle adjusting screws—carbureted models

NOTE: **The speed-up solenoid should reach full travel.**

8. Adjust the speed-up solenoid screw to 850–950 rpm.

Idle Mixture Adjustment

FEDERAL 1986–87

1. Firmly set the parking brake and block the drive wheels.
2. Place the transmission in **N**.
3. Remove the carburetor assembly.
4. Using a drill, drill a hole through the sealing plug covering the idle mixture screw and pry the plug from the carburetor.
5. Reinstall the carburetor.
6. Operate the engine until it reaches normal operating temperatures. Be sure the choke is fully open and the air cleaner is installed. If equipped, turn the air conditioning **OFF**.
7. Disconnect and plug the distributor vacuum, the canister purge and EGR vacuum lines. Shut off the vacuum to the idle compensator by bending the rubber hose.
8. Turn the throttle adjusting screw until the engine speed is 750–850 rpm (manual transmission) or 850–950 rpm (automat-

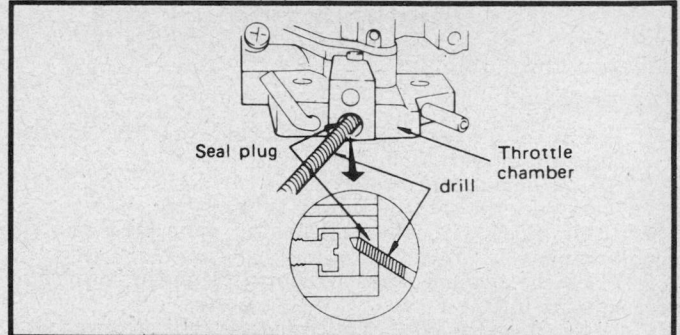

Removing the sealing plug from the idle mixture screw—carbureted models

ic transmission).

9. Turn the idle mixture screw all the way in and back out 3 turns.

10. Turn the throttle adjusting screw until the engine speed is 800 rpm (manual transmission) or 900 rpm (automatic transmission).

11. Adjust the idle mixture screw to achieve the maximum speed.

12. Reset the throttle adjusting screw until the engine speed is 850 rpm (manual transmission) or 950 rpm (automatic transmission).

13. Turn the idle mixture screw counter-clockwise (lean) until the engine speed is 750–850 rpm (manual transmission) or 850–950 rpm (automatic transmission).

14. Reinstall a mixture adjustment plug.

EXCEPT FEDERAL 1986–87

1. Firmly set the parking brake and block the drive wheels.
2. Place the transmission in **N**.
3. Remove the carburetor assembly.
4. Using a drill, drill a hole through the sealing plug covering the idle mixture screw and pry the plug from the carburetor.
5. Reinstall the carburetor.
6. Operate the engine until it reaches normal operating temperatures. Be sure the choke is fully open and the air cleaner is installed. If equipped, turn the air conditioning **OFF**.
7. Disconnect and plug the distributor vacuum, the canister purge and EGR vacuum lines. Shut off the vacuum to the idle compensator by bending the rubber hose.
8. Connect a dwell meter (4 cyl. scale) or duty meter to the duty monitor lead.
9. Turn the idle mixture screw all the way in and back out 1½ turns.
10. Turn the throttle adjusting screw until the engine speed is 950 rpm (1986–87) or 900 rpm (1988–90).
11. Adjust the idle mixture screw to achieve an average dwell of 36 degrees or duty of 40 percent.

NOTE: **The dwell or duty reading specified is the average of the most constant variation.**

12. Reset the throttle adjusting screw until the engine speed is 850–950 rpm.
13. Reinstall a mixture adjustment plug.

Service Adjustments

For all carburetor service adjustment procedures and Specifications, please refer to "Carburetor Service" in the Unit Repair section.

Fuel Injection

Idle Speed Adjustment

2.6L ENGINE

1. Firmly set the parking brake and block the drive wheels.
2. Place the transmission in **N**.
3. Set the engine tachometer.
4. Make sure the throttle valve is fully closed.
5. If equipped with air conditioning, turn **OFF** the air conditioning.
6. Place the manual transmission in **N** or the automatic transmission in **P**.
7. Disconnect the electrical connector from the vacuum switching valve (VSV) on the pressure regulator; the idle speed should 850–950 rpm.
8. If the idle speed is not correct, turn the adjusting screw **A** on the throttle body.

2.8L ENGINE

The idle speed is controlled by the ECM and no adjustment is necessary or possible.

Idle Mixture Adjustment

No idle mixture adjustment is necessary or possible.

Location of the vacuum switching valve (VSV) electrical connector—2.6L engine

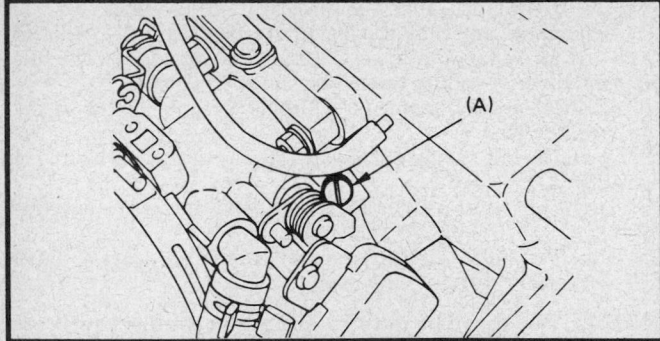

View of the throttle body adjusting screw to alter the idle speed—2.6L engine

Fuel Injector

Removal and Installation

2.6L ENGINE

The engine is equipped 4 fuel injectors, with one located at each cylinder.

1. Relieve the fuel pressure.
2. Disconnect the negative battery cable.
3. Label and disconnect the electrical connectors from the fuel injectors.
4. Disconnect the fuel rail from the fuel system.
5. Remove the fuel rail from the intake manifold; pull the fuel rail with the injectors connected from the intake manifold.
6. Separate the fuel injectors from the fuel rail.

To install:

7. Replace the fuel injector O-rings.
8. Install the fuel injectors to the fuel rail.
9. Lubricate the fuel injector O-rings with automatic transmission fluid and press them, with the fuel rail, into the intake manifold.
10. Install the fuel rail-to-intake manifold bolts.
11. Connect the fuel rail to the fuel system.
12. Connect the electrical connectors to the fuel injectors.
13. Connect the negative battery cable.
14. Turn the ignition switch **ON** and check for fuel leaks at the fuel rail.

2.8L ENGINE

The engine is equipped with 2 fuel injectors, both are located in the throttle body.

1. Relieve the fuel pressure.
2. Disconnect the negative battery cable.
3. Remove the air cleaner.
4. At the injector electrical connectors, squeeze the 2 tabs together and pull them straight upward.
5. Remove the fuel meter cover and leave the cover gasket in place.
6. Using a small pry bar, carefully pry the injectors upward until they are free of the throttle body.
7. Remove the small O-ring from the nozzle end of the injector. Carefully rotate the injector's fuel filter back-and-forth to remove it from the base of the injector.
8. Discard the fuel meter cover gasket.
9. Remove the large O-ring and back-up washer from the top of the counterbore of the fuel meter body injector cavity.

To install:

10. Lubricate the O-rings with automatic transmission fluid and push them into the fuel injector cavities.
11. Install the new fuel meter cover gasket and cover.
12. Install the electrical connectors to the injectors.
13. Install the air cleaner and connect the negative battery cable.

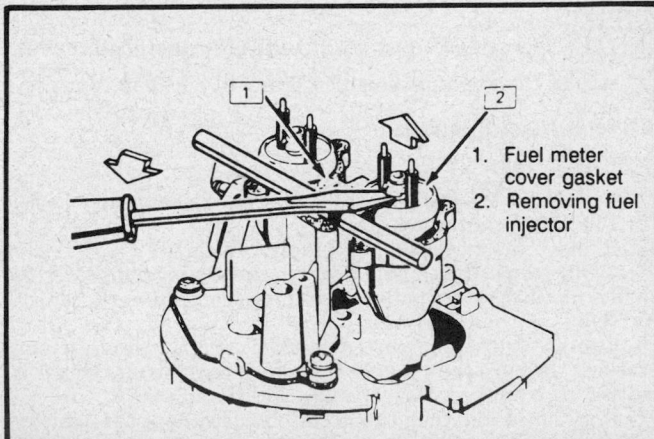

1. Fuel meter cover gasket
2. Removing fuel injector

Removing the fuel injectors from the throttle body—2.8L engine

DIESEL FUEL SYSTEM

Fuel System Service Precaution

Disconnect the negative battery cable. Keep a Class B dry chemical fire extinguisher available. Always relieve the fuel pressure before disconnecting a fuel line. Wrap a shop cloth around the fuel line when disconnecting a fuel line. Always use new O-rings. Do not replace the fuel pipes with fuel hoses. Always us a back-up wrench when opening or closing a fuel line.

Fuel Filter

The fuel filter is located near the battery.

Removal and Installation

1. Properly relieve the fuel system pressure. Disconnect the negative battery cable.
2. Disconnect the water separator sensor wire from the connector.
3. Using a filter wrench, remove the fuel filter.

NOTE: When removing the fuel filter, be careful not to spill the fuel from the cartridge.

4. Drain the fuel cartridge and remove the sensor from the cartridge.

To install:

5. Lubricate the new sensor O-ring with diesel fuel and install the sensor onto the cartridge.
6. Lubricate the cartridge O-ring with diesel fuel. Install the cartridge until the O-ring contacts the sealing surface face, then, tighten the cartridge ⅔ of a turn with a filter wrench.
7. Connect the electrical connector to the sensor.
8. Depress the priming pump, located on top of the cartridge, 30–40 times to fill the cartridge.

NOTE: The pumping force will increase as the filter becomes filled.

9. Start the engine and check for leakage around the sealing portions.

Draining Water From the System

1. Using a 0.2L (0.05 gal) container, place it at the end of the vinyl hose, located under the drain plug of the separator.
2. Loosen the drain plug 5 turns.
3. Depress the priming pump about 10 times until the water is drained from the filter.
4. Tighten the drain plug.
5. Depress the priming pump several times.
6. Start the engine and check for leakage around the drain plug.
7. Make sure the **FILTER** light remains out.

Diesel Injection Pump

Removal and Installation

1. Disconnect the negative battery cable.
2. Remove the timing belt cover.
3. Remove the fuel lines and disconnect the electrical connectors from the fuel injector.
4. Using a pry bar, remove the tension spring from the timing belt tensioner.

NOTE: When removing the tension spring, avoid using excessive force for the spring may become distorted.

5. Remove the tensioner pulley bolt and the pulley.
6. Remove the timing belt and discard it.

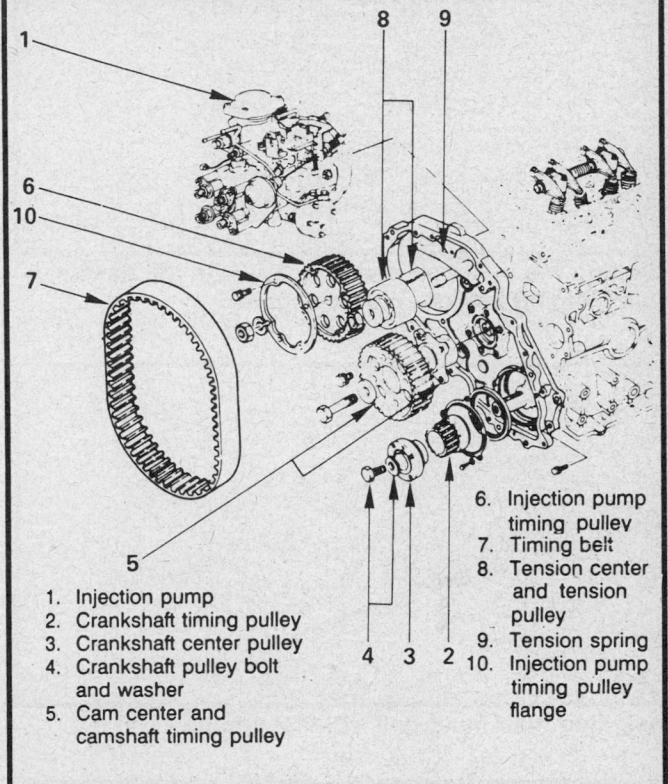

1. Injection pump
2. Crankshaft timing pulley
3. Crankshaft center pulley
4. Crankshaft pulley bolt and washer
5. Cam center and camshaft timing pulley
6. Injection pump timing pulley
7. Timing belt
8. Tension center and tension pulley
9. Tension spring
10. Injection pump timing pulley flange

Exploded view of the injection pump and pulley assembly—diesel engine

7. Using a 6mm, 1.25 pitch bolt, install the threaded portion into the threaded hole in the timing pulley housing through the hole in the pulley to prevent the pulley from turning.
8. Remove the injection pump pulley-to-shaft bolts.
9. Using a wheel puller, connect it to the injection pump pulley and press it from the shaft.
10. Remove the injection pump bracket-to-timing pulley housing bolts, the rear injection pump-to-bracket bolts and the injection pump.

To install:

11. Install the injection pump. Tighten the injection pump-to-timing pulley housing bolts and leave the rear pump-to-bracket bolts semi-tight.
12. Install the injection pump pulley by aligning it with the key groove and torque the bolt to 42–52 ft. lbs.
13. Rotate the crankshaft to bring the No. 1 piston to TDC of the compression stroke.
14. Align the timing marks on the injection pump pulley with the camshaft pulley; the marks must be facing each other.
15. Using a new timing belt, install it in the following sequence: crankshaft pulley, camshaft pulley and the injection pump pulley; the slack must be between the injection pump and camshaft pulleys.
16. Install the tension center and the tension pulley so the end of the tension center is fitted against both pins on the timing pulley housing.
17. Hand tighten the nut so the tension pulley can be rotated freely.

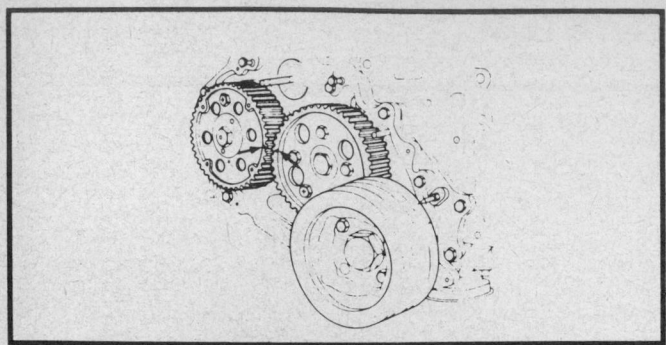

Aligning the injection pump pulley with the camshaft pulley timing marks – diesel engine

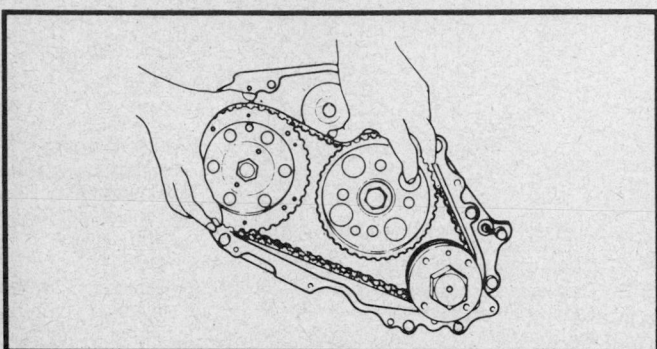

Installing the timing belt – diesel engine

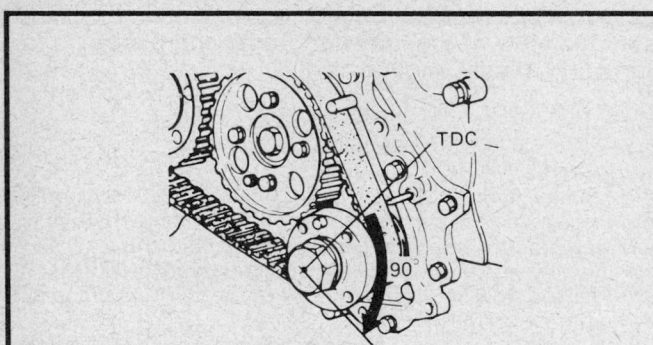

Turning the cranshaft 90 degrees beyond TDC – diesel engine

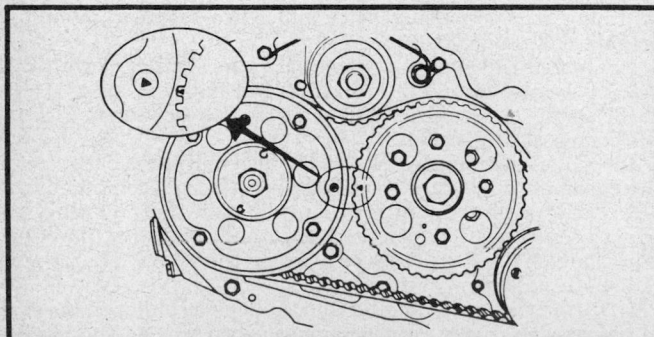

Aligning the injection pump flange with the camshaft pulley timing marks – diesel engine

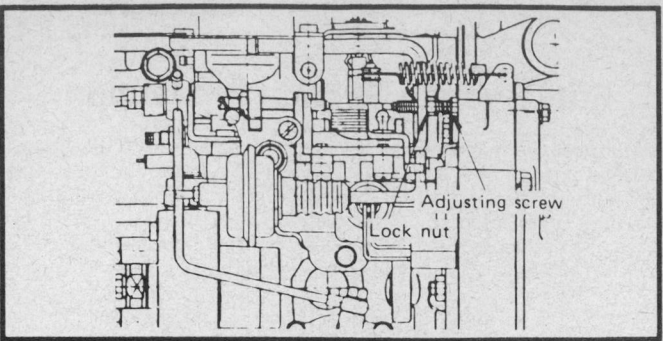

View of the slow idle speed adjusting screw and locknut – diesel engine

18. Install the tension spring and semi-tighten the pulley nut to 22–36 ft. lbs.

19. Rotate the crankshaft 2 full turns clockwise to seat the belt and further turn the crankshaft 90 degrees beyond TDC to settle the injection pump.

20. Loosen the tension pulley nut to take up the timing belt slack. Tighten the tension pulley nut to 79–94 ft. lbs.

21. Install the injection pump pulley flange; the hole in the outer circumference of the flange should be aligned with the triangular timing mark on the injection pump pulley.

22. Rotate the crankshaft 2 full turns clockwise to bring the No. 1 piston to TDC of the compression stroke. Make sure the triangular timing mark on the timing pulley is aligned with the hole in the flange, then, measure the timing belt tension; it should be 33–55 lbs.

23. Install the timing belt cover.

24. Connect the negative battery cable.

Idle Speed Adjustment

SLOW IDLE

1. Firmly, set the parking brake and block the drive wheels.
2. Place the transmission in **N**.
3. Operate the engine until it reaches normal operating temperatures.
4. Turn the air conditioning **OFF** and be sure the air cleaner is installed.
5. Connect a tachometer to the fuel injection pump connector and check the idle speed; it should be 700–800 rpm.
6. If the idle speed is not correct, loosen the locknut and turn the adjusting screw in and out until the speed is correct, then, tighten the locknut.
7. Turn the engine **OFF**. Remove the tachometer and wheel blocks.

FAST IDLE

1. Firmly, set the parking brake and block the drive wheels.
2. Place the transmission in **N**.
3. Operate the engine until it reaches normal operating temperatures.
4. Turn the air conditioning **OFF** and be sure the air cleaner is installed.
5. Disconnect both vacuum hoses from the vacuum switch valve.
6. Using a short, 4mm pipe, install it between the vacuum hoses.
7. Connect a tachometer to the fuel injection pump connector and check the fast idle speed; it should be 900–950 rpm.
8. If the idle speed is not correct, loosen the locknut (4) and turn the adjusting screw (3) until the fast idle speed is correct, then, tighten the locknut (4).
9. Turn the engine **OFF**. Remove the tachometer and wheel blocks.

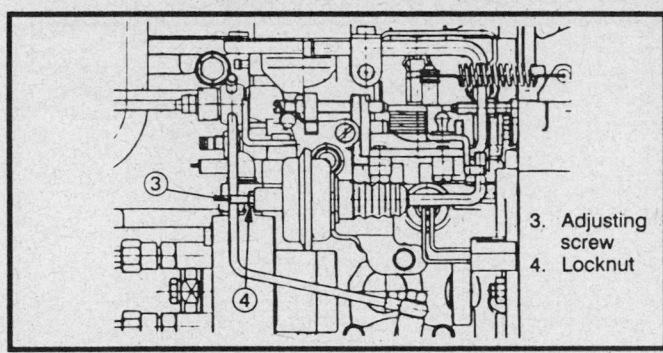

View of the fast idle speed adjusting screw and locknut – diesel engine

3. Adjusting screw
4. Locknut

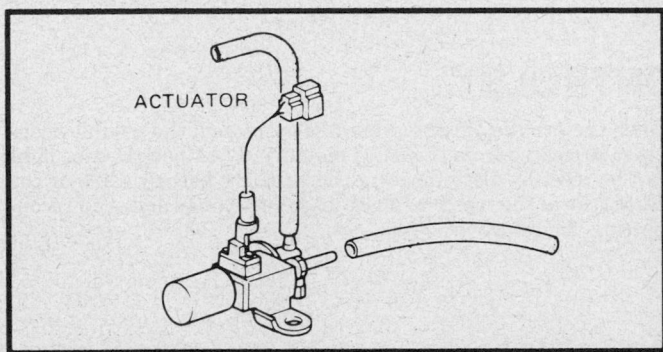

View of the vacuum switch and hoses – fast idle adjustment – diesel engine

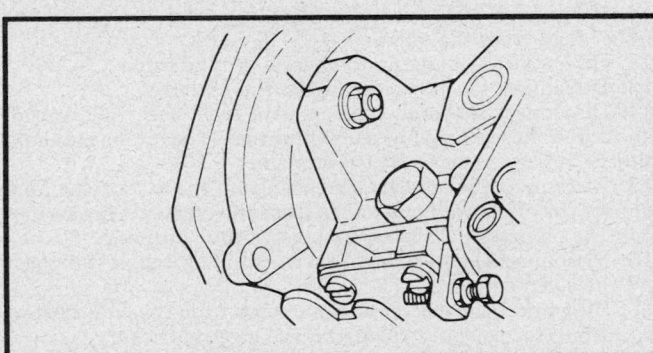

View of the injection pump-to-bracket alignment marks – diesel engine

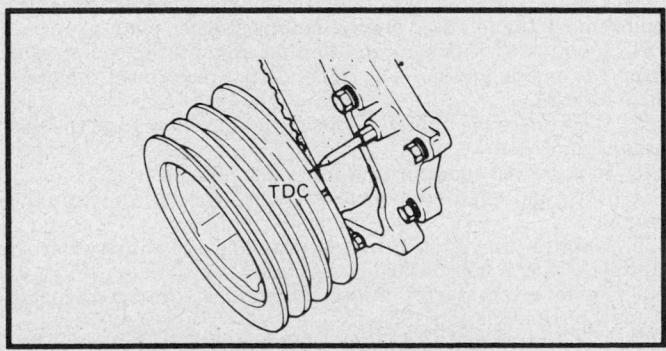

View of the timing marks – diesel engine

10. Remove the pipe from the vacuum hoses and reconnect the hoses to the vacuum switch.

Diesel Injection Timing

Adjustment

1. Make sure the notched line on the injection pump flange is aligned with the notched line on the injection pump's front bracket.
2. Rotate the crankshaft to bring the No. 1 piston to TDC; the timing pointer should be aligned with the timing notch on the crankshaft pulley.
3. Remove the timing pulley housing cover and check that the timing belt is properly tensioned and the timing marks on the pulleys are aligned.
4. Disconnect the injection pipe from the injection pump, remove the distributor head screw and install a static timing gauge.
5. Adjust the lift to approximately 0.04 in. (1mm) from the plunger.

NOTE: Use a wrench to hold the delivery holder when loosening the sleeve nuts on the side of the injection pipe.

6. Rotate the crankshaft to position the No. 1 cylinder to 45–60 degrees BTDC, then, calibrate the dial indicator to zero.
7. Rotate the crankshaft, in the normal direction of rotation, to 10 degrees BTDC and read the dial indicator; the standard reading should be 0.020 in. (0.5mm).
8. If the reading is not correct, loosen the injection pump-to-bracket flange nuts and move the pump to a position where the reading is 0.020 in. (0.5mm) and tighten the nuts.
9. Remove the static timing gauge, install the injection pipe and plug to the injection pump.

Fuel Injector

Removal and Installation

1. Relieve the fuel system pressure.
2. Remove the fuel pressure line(s) and return line(s) from the fuel injector(s).
3. Remove the fuel injector(s) from the engine.
4. Remove the O-rings from the fuel injector.

To install:

5. Using new O-rings, lubricate them in diesel fuel and install them onto the fuel injector(s).
6. Install the fuel injector(s) into the engine.
7. Using new O-rings, install the fuel pressure line(s) and return line(s) onto the fuel injector(s).

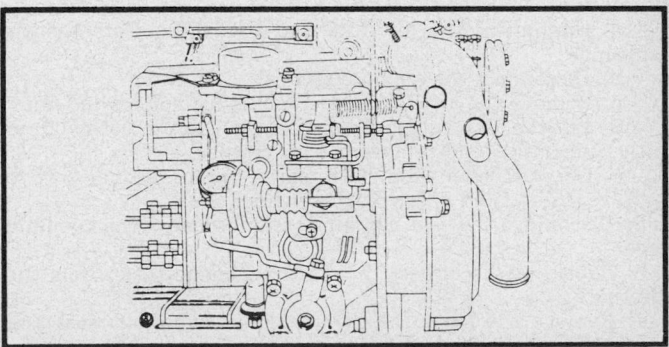

View of the static timing gauge install on the injection pump – diesel engine

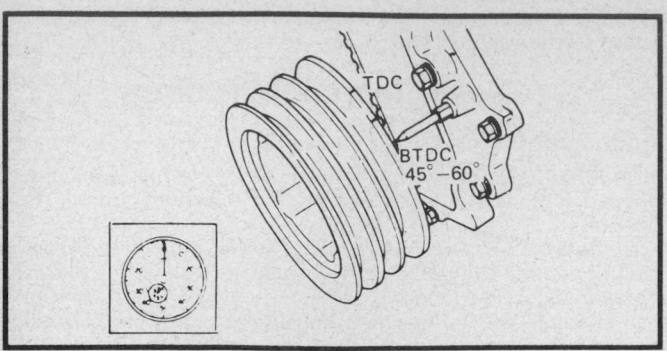

View of the timing marks with the No. 1 piston at 45–60 degrees BTDC—diesel engine

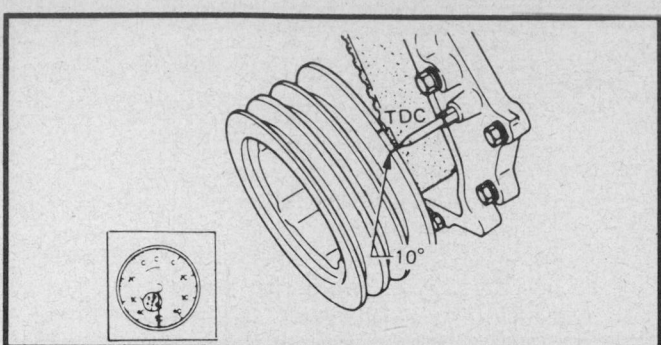

View of the timing marks with the No. 1 piston at 10 degrees BTDC—diesel engine

EMISSION CONTROLS

Please refer to "Professional Emission Component Application Guide".

Emission Warning Lamps

Resetting

Once the problem in the system is corrected, the trouble codes must be cleared from the ECM memory. The Check Engine light can be reset by disconnecting the negative battery cable or the ECM fuse at the fuse box for at least 10 seconds and then reconnecting the cable.

GASOLINE ENGINE MECHANICAL

NOTE: Disconnecting the negative battery cable on some vehicles may interfere with the functions of the on board computer systems and may require the computer to undergo a relearning process, once the negative battery cable is reconnected.

Engine

Removal and Installation

2WD VEHICLES

1986–87

1. Disconnect both battery cables, the negative cable first.
2. Matchmark the hood-to-hinges and remove the hood.
3. Remove the undercover, if equipped. Open the drain plugs on the radiator and the cylinder and drain the cooling system.
4. Remove the air cleaner by performing the following procedures:
    a. Disconnect the air duct and PCV hose from the air cleaner.
    b. Disconnect the air hose from the AIR pump.
    c. Remove the air cleaner-to-bracket bolts and wing nut.
    d. Lift the air cleaner, disconnect the vacuum hose(s) from the under side and remove the air cleaner.
    e. Using a clean shop cloth, cover the air cleaner port to prevent dirt from entering the engine.
5. Disconnect the TCA hot air hose and remove the manifold cover.
6. Label and disconnect the electrical connector(s) from the alternator.
7. Remove the exhaust pipe-to-exhaust manifold nuts and separate the pipe from the manifold.
8. Loosen the clutch cable adjusting nut and relieve the tension, if equipped with a manual transmission.
9. Disconnect the heater hoses from the heater core.

10. If equipped with an oxygen sensor, disconnect the electrical connector.
11. If equipped with a vacuum switching valve, disconnect the rubber hose from the valve.
12. Disconnect the engine-to-chassis ground cable.
13. Disconnect the fuel hoses from the carburetor.
14. Disconnect the high-tension wire from the ignition coil, the vacuum hose from the rear connector of the intake manifold and the rubber hoses from the canister.
15. Disconnect the accelerator cable from the carburetor. Disconnect the electrical connectors from the starter, the thermo-unit, the oil pressure switch and distributor harness.
16. Disconnect the hose from the vacuum switch, if equipped, and the solenoid valve.
17. Disconnect the electrical connectors from the EFE heater, the carburetor solenoid valve and the electric choke.
18. From the rear of the engine, disconnect the back-up light switch and transmission wiring at the connector.
19. Using an engine hoist, connect it to the engine hangers and support the engine.
20. Remove the engine-to-mount nut. Raise the engine slightly and remove the left side engine mount stopper plate.
21. If equipped with air conditioning, remove the compressor from the engine and move it aside; do not disconnect the pressure hoses.
22. Disconnect the upper and lower radiator hoses and the reservoir tank hose.
23. Remove the radiator and fan blade assembly.
24. Raise and safely support the vehicle. Drain the oil from the engine.
25. Remove the clutch return spring and the clutch cable, if equipped with a manual transmission.
26. Remove the starter motor. Disconnect the speedometer from the transmission.
27. Matchmark and remove the driveshaft. Remove the transmission mount bolts. Remove gearshift lever assembly.

28. Lift the engine slightly. Remove the exhaust pipe bracket from the transmission and the engine-to-mount nuts.

29. Make certain that all lines, hoses, cables and wires have been disconnected from the engine and frame.

30. Lift the engine/transmission assembly from the vehicle with the front of the engine raised slightly.

31. Remove the transmission-to-engine bolts and the transmission from the engine.

To install:

32. Lower the engine/transmission assembly into the vehicle, align it with the mounts and install the nuts/bolts.

33. Install the gearshift lever assembly and the driveshaft.

34. Connect the speedometer cable to the transmission. Install the starter motor.

35. If equipped with a manual transmission, install the clutch cable and clutch return spring.

36. Lower the vehicle. Install the fan blade assembly and the radiator.

37. Connect the upper and lower radiator hoses and the reservoir tank hose.

38. If equipped with air conditioning, install the compressor to the engine.

39. Install the left side engine mount stopper plate, lower the engine slightly and install the engine-to-mount nut.

40. Remove the engine hoist.

41. Connect the electrical connector to the back-up light switch and transmission wiring connector at the rear of the engine.

42. Connect the electrical connectors to the EFE heater, the carburetor solenoid valve and the electric choke.

43. Connect the hose to the vacuum switch, if equipped, and the solenoid valve.

44. Connect the accelerator cable to the carburetor. Connect the electrical connectors to the starter, the thermo-unit, the oil pressure switch and distributor harness.

45. Connect the high-tension wire to the ignition coil, the vacuum hose to the rear connector of the intake manifold and the rubber hoses to the canister.

46. Connect the fuel hoses to the carburetor.

47. Connect the engine-to-chassis ground cable.

48. If equipped with a vacuum switching valve, connect the rubber hose to the valve.

49. If equipped with an oxygen sensor, connect the electrical connector.

50. Connect the heater hoses to the heater core.

51. Tension the clutch cable and tighten the adjusting nut, if equipped with a manual transmission.

52. Install the exhaust pipe-to-exhaust manifold nuts.

53. Connect the electrical connector(s) to the alternator.

54. Install the manifold cover and connect the TCA hot air hose.

55. Install the air cleaner by performing the following procedures:

  a. Lower the air cleaner and connect the vacuum hose(s) to the underside.

  b. Install the air cleaner-to-bracket bolts and wing nut.

  c. Connect the air hose to the AIR pump.

  d. Connect the air duct and PCV hose to the air cleaner.

56. Refill the cooling system with the proper coolant and the crankcase with engine oil. Check and adjust the clutch pedal freeplay, if equipped with a manual transmission.

57. Install the hood and connect both battery cables, the positive cable first.

58. Adjust the belt tension. Start the engine, check for leaks.

59. Check and/or adjust the idle speed and ignition timing.

1988–90

1. Relieve the fuel pressure. Disconnect both battery cables, the negative cable first. Remove the battery.

2. Matchmark the hood-to-hinges and remove the hood.

3. Remove the undercover, if equipped. Open the drain plugs on the radiator and the cylinder and drain the cooling system.

4. Remove the air cleaner (2.3L engine) or air cleaner duct and hose (2.6L engine). Using a clean shop cloth, cover the air cleaner port to prevent dirt from entering the engine.

5. Label and disconnect the necessary hoses, electrical connectors, control cables and control rods from the engine.

6. Label and disconnect the following items:

  a. Air switch valve hose.

  b. Oxygen sensor wire.

  c. Vacuum switch valve hose.

  d. Thermal vacuum switching valve hose.

  e. Pressure regulator vacuum hose.

  f. Canister hose.

  g. ECM harness.

  h. Fuel hose(s).

7. Remove the clutch return spring (if equipped), the clutch control cable (if equipped), the back-up light switch connector and the speedometer cable from the transmission.

8. Remove the radiator grille from the deflector panel.

9. Disconnect the upper and lower radiator hoses and the reservoir tank hose.

10. Remove the fan shroud, fan blade assembly and the radiator.

11. If equipped with air conditioning, remove the compressor from the engine and move it aside; do not disconnect the pressure hoses.

12. Remove the gear shift lever by performing the following procedures:

  a. Place the gear shift lever in **N**.

  b. Remove the front console from the floor panel.

  c. Pull the shift lever boot and grommet upward.

  d. Remove the shift lever cover bolts and the shift lever.

13. Raise and safely support the vehicle. Remove the front wheels.

14. Drain the oil from the engine and the transmission fluid.

15. If equipped with an automatic transmission, perform the following procedures:

  a. Remove the oil level gauge and the tube.

  b. Disconnect the shift select control link rod from the select lever.

  c. Disconnect the downshift cable from the transmission.

  d. Disconnect and plug the fluid coolant lines from the transmission.

16. If equipped with a 1-piece driveshaft, remove the driveshaft flange-to-pinion nuts, lower the driveshaft and pull it from the transmission.

17. If equipped with a 2-piece driveshaft, perform the following procedures:

  a. Remove the rear driveshaft flange-to-pinion nuts.

  b. Remove the rear driveshaft flange-to-front driveshaft flange bolts and the rear driveshaft.

  c. Remove the center bearing-to-chassis bolts, move the front driveshaft rearward and from the transmission.

18. Remove the starter-to-engine bolts and the starter.

19. Remove the exhaust pipe-to-exhaust manifold nuts, the exhaust pipe bracket-to-transmission bolts, the front exhaust pipe-to-2nd exhaust pipe bolts and the front exhaust pipe from the vehicle.

20. Attach an engine hanger to the rear of the exhaust manifold.

21. Using an engine hoist, connect it to the engine hangers and support the engine.

22. If equipped with a manual transmission, perform the following procedures:

  a. Using a transmission jack, place it under the transmission; do not support it.

  b. Remove the rear mount-to-transmission nuts.

  c. Remove the rear mount-to-crossmember nuts/bolts and the mount.

NOTE: Further removal of the transmission may require an assistant.

d. Remove the clutch cover and the transmission-to-engine bolts.

e. Move the transmission rearward into the crossmember and floor pan area; the transmission may rest on the crossmember.

f. Lower the front of the transmission toward the jack.

g. Firmly, grasp the transmission the rear cover while the assistant raises the jack toward the transmission.

h. Carefully lower the transmission onto the jack and center it.

i. Lower the jack and move the transmission rearward.

23. If equipped with an automatic transmission, perform the following procedures:

NOTE: Removal of the transmission will require an assistant.

a. Remove the torque converter-to-flex plate bolts through the starter hole.

b. Using a transmission jack, place it under the transmission; do not support it.

c. Remove the rear mount-to-transmission nuts.

d. Remove the rear mount-to-crossmember nuts/bolts and the mount.

e. Remove the transmission-to-engine bolts.

f. Move the transmission rearward into the crossmember and floor pan area; the transmission may rest on the crossmember.

g. Lower the front of the transmission toward the jack.

h. Firmly, grasp the transmission the rear cover while the assistant raises the jack toward the transmission.

i. Carefully, lower the transmission onto the jack and center it.

j. Lower the jack and move the transmission rearward.

24. Remove the engine-to-mount nuts/bolts.

25. Using the hoist, slowly, lift the engine; be sure to hold the front of the engine higher than the rear.

26. Place the engine on a work stand.

To install:

27. Using the hoist, slowly, lower the engine into the vehicle; be sure to hold the front of the engine higher than the rear.

28. Install the engine-to-mount nuts/bolts.

29. If equipped with an automatic transmission, perform the following procedures:

NOTE: Installation of the transmission will require an assistant.

a. Raise the transmission into position.

b. Raise the rear of the transmission and move it into position on the crossmember.

c. Move the transmission forward and engage it with the engine.

d. Install the engine-to-transmission bolts.

e. Install the mount and the rear mount-to-crossmember nuts/bolts.

f. Install the rear mount-to-transmission nuts.

g. Install the torque converter-to-flex plate bolts through the starter hole.

30. If equipped with a manual transmission, perform the following procedures:

NOTE: Installation of the transmission may require an assistant.

a. Raise the transmission into position.

b. Raise the rear of the transmission and move it into position on the crossmember.

c. Move the transmission forward and engage it with the engine.

d. Install the engine-to-transmission bolts.

e. Install the mount and the rear mount-to-crossmember nuts/bolts.

f. Install the rear mount-to-transmission nuts.

31. Remove the engine hoist and the engine hanger from the rear of the exhaust manifold.

32. Install the front exhaust pipe, exhaust pipe-to-exhaust manifold nuts, the exhaust pipe bracket-to-transmission bolts, the front exhaust pipe-to-2nd exhaust pipe bolts.

33. Install the starter and the starter-to-engine bolts.

34. If equipped with a 2-piece driveshaft, perform the following procedures:

a. Install the front driveshaft into the transmission and the center bearing-to-chassis bolts.

b. Install the rear driveshaft and the rear driveshaft flange-to-front driveshaft flange bolts.

c. Install the rear driveshaft flange-to-pinion nuts.

35. If equipped with a 1-piece driveshaft, install the driveshaft into the transmission and the driveshaft flange-to-pinion nuts.

36. If equipped with an automatic transmission, perform the following procedures:

a. Connect the fluid coolant lines to the transmission.

b. Connect the downshift cable to the transmission.

c. Connect the shift select control link rod to the select lever.

d. Install the oil level gauge and the tube.

37. Install the front wheels and lower the vehicle.

38. Install the gear shift lever by performing the following procedures:

a. Install the shift lever and the shift lever cover bolts.

b. Push the grommet and shift lever boot downward.

c. Install the front console to the floor panel.

39. If equipped with air conditioning, install the compressor to the engine.

40. Install the radiator, the fan blade assembly and the fan shroud.

41. Connect the upper and lower radiator hoses and the reservoir tank hose.

42. Install the radiator grille to the deflector panel.

43. Install the clutch return spring (if equipped), the clutch control cable (if equipped), the back-up light switch connector and the speedometer cable to the transmission.

44. Connect the following items:

a. Air switch valve hose.

b. Oxygen sensor wire.

c. Vacuum switch valve hose.

d. Thermal vacuum switching valve hose.

e. Pressure regulator vacuum hose.

f. Canister hose.

g. ECM harness.

h. Fuel hose(s).

45. Connect the necessary hoses, electrical connectors, control cables and control rods to the engine.

46. Install the air cleaner (2.3L) or air cleaner duct and hose (2.6L).

47. Refill the engine, the transmission and the cooling system. Install the undercover, if equipped.

48. Install the hood.

49. Install the battery and connect both battery cables, the positive cable first.

50. Adjust the belt tension. Start the engine, check for leaks.

51. Check and/or adjust the idle speed and ignition timing.

4WD VEHICLES

1986–87

1. Disconnect both battery cables, the negative cable first.

2. Matchmark the hood-to-hinges and remove the hood.

3. Remove the undercover. Open the drain plugs on the radiator and the cylinder and drain the cooling system.

4. Remove the air cleaner by performing the following procedures:

a. Disconnect the air duct and PCV hose from the air cleaner.

b. Disconnect the air hose from the AIR pump.

c. Remove the air cleaner-to-bracket bolts and wing nut.

d. Lift the air cleaner, disconnect the vacuum hose(s) from the underside and remove the air cleaner.

e. Using a clean shop cloth, cover the air cleaner port to prevent dirt from entering the engine.

5. Disconnect the TCA hot air hose and remove the manifold cover.

6. Label and disconnect the electrical connector(s) from the alternator.

7. Remove the exhaust pipe-to-exhaust manifold nuts and separate the pipe from the manifold.

8. Loosen the clutch cable adjusting nut and relieve the tension, if equipped with a manual transmission.

9. Disconnect the heater hoses from the heater core.

10. If equipped with an oxygen sensor, disconnect the electrical connector.

11. If equipped with a vacuum switching valve, disconnect the rubber hose from the valve.

12. Disconnect the engine-to-chassis ground cable.

13. Disconnect the fuel hoses from the carburetor.

14. Disconnect the high-tension wire from the ignition coil, the vacuum hose from the rear connector of the intake manifold and the rubber hoses from the canister.

15. Disconnect the accelerator cable from the carburetor. Disconnect the electrical connectors from the starter, the thermo-unit, the oil pressure switch and distributor harness.

16. Disconnect the hose from the vacuum switch, if equipped, and the solenoid valve.

17. Disconnect the electrical connectors from the EFE heater, the carburetor solenoid valve and the electric choke.

18. From the rear of the engine, disconnect the back-up light switch and transmission wiring at the connector.

19. Using an engine hoist, connect it to the engine hangers and support the engine.

20. Remove the engine-to-mount nut. Raise the engine slightly and remove the left side engine mount stopper plate.

21. If equipped with air conditioning, remove the compressor from the engine and move it aside; do not disconnect the pressure hoses.

22. Disconnect the upper and lower radiator hoses and the reservoir tank hose.

23. Remove the radiator and fan blade assembly.

24. Raise and support the vehicle safely. Drain the oil from the engine.

25. Remove the starter motor and the flywheel cover pan.

26. Remove the bell housing-to-engine bolts and support the transmission.

27. Lift the engine slightly. Remove the exhaust pipe bracket from the transmission and the engine-to-mount nuts.

NOTE: Make certain that all lines, hoses, cables and wires have been disconnected from the engine and frame.

28. Lift the engine from the vehicle with the front of the engine raised slightly to clear the transmission input shaft.

To install:

29. Lower the engine into the vehicle, align it transmission assembly and install the nuts/bolts.

30. Install the starter motor and the flywheel cover pan.

31. If equipped with a manual transmission, install the clutch cable and clutch return spring.

32. Lower the vehicle. Install the fan blade assembly and the radiator.

33. Connect the upper and lower radiator hoses and the reservoir tank hose.

34. If equipped with air conditioning, install the compressor to the engine.

35. Install the left side engine mount stopper plate, lower the engine slightly and install the engine-to-mount nut.

36. Remove the engine hoist.

37. Connect the electrical connector to the back-up light switch and transmission wiring connector at the rear of the engine.

38. Connect the electrical connectors to the EFE heater, the carburetor solenoid valve and the electric choke.

39. Connect the hose to the vacuum switch, if equipped, and the solenoid valve.

40. Connect the accelerator cable to the carburetor. Connect the electrical connectors to the starter, the thermo-unit, the oil pressure switch and distributor harness.

41. Connect the high-tension wire to the ignition coil, the vacuum hose to the rear connector of the intake manifold and the rubber hoses to the canister.

42. Connect the fuel hoses to the carburetor.

43. Connect the engine-to-chassis ground cable.

44. If equipped with a vacuum switching valve, connect the rubber hose to the valve.

45. If equipped with an oxygen sensor, connect the electrical connector.

46. Connect the heater hoses to the heater core.

47. Tension the clutch cable and tighten the adjusting nut, if equipped with a manual transmission.

48. Install the exhaust pipe-to-exhaust manifold nuts.

49. Connect the electrical connector(s) to the alternator.

50. Install the manifold cover and connect the TCA hot air hose.

51. Install the air cleaner by performing the following procedures:

a. Lower the air cleaner and connect the vacuum hose(s) to the underside.

b. Install the air cleaner-to-bracket bolts and wing nut.

c. Connect the air hose to the AIR pump.

d. Connect the air duct and PCV hose to the air cleaner.

52. Refill the cooling system with the proper coolant and the crankcase with engine oil. Check and adjust the clutch pedal freeplay, if equipped with a manual transmission.

53. Install the hood and connect both battery cables, the positive cable first.

54. Adjust the belt tension. Start the engine, check for leaks.

55. Check and/or adjust the idle speed and ignition timing.

1988–90

1. Relieve the fuel pressure. Disconnect both battery cables, the negative cable first. Remove the battery.

2. Matchmark the hood-to-hinges and remove the hood.

3. Remove the undercover, if equipped. Open the drain plugs on the radiator and the cylinder and drain the cooling system.

4. Remove the air cleaner (2.3L engine) or air cleaner duct and hose (2.6L engine). Using a clean shop cloth, cover the air cleaner port to prevent dirt from entering the engine.

5. Label and disconnect the necessary hoses, electrical connectors, control cables and control rods from the engine.

6. Label and disconnect the following items:

a. Air switch valve hose.

b. Oxygen sensor wire.

c. Vacuum switch valve hose.

d. Thermal vacuum switching valve hose.

e. Pressure regulator vacuum hose.

f. Canister hose.

g. ECM harness.

h. Fuel hose(s).

7. Remove the clutch return spring (if equipped), the clutch control cable (if equipped), the back-up light switch connector and the speedometer cable from the transmission.

8. Remove the radiator grille from the deflector panel.

9. Disconnect the upper and lower radiator hoses and the reservoir tank hose.

10. Remove the fan shroud, fan blade assembly and the radiator.

11. If equipped with air conditioning, remove the compressor from the engine and move it aside; do not disconnect the pressure hoses.

12. If equipped with a 2.8L engine, perform the following procedures:

   a. Remove the power steering pump-to-engine brackets and move the pump aside.

   b. Remove the spark plug wire from the No. 1 spark plug.

   c. Remove the distributor cap with the No. 1 spark plug wire.

   d. Remove the ignition coil.

13. Remove the gear shift lever by performing the following procedures:

   a. Place the gear shift lever in **N**.

   b. Remove the front console from the floor panel.

   c. Pull the shift lever boot and grommet upward.

   d. Remove the shift lever cover bolts and the shift lever.

14. Remove the transfer shift lever by performing the following procedures:

   a. Place the transfer shift lever in **H** (except 2.8L engine) or **2H** (2.8L engine).

   b. Pull the shift lever boot and dust cover upward.

   c. Remove the shift lever retaining bolts.

   d. Pull the shift lever from the transfer case.

15. Raise and safely support the vehicle. Remove the front wheels. Drain the oil from the engine.

16. Drain the transmission and transfer case fluid.

17. If equipped with an automatic transmission, perform the following procedures:

   a. Remove the oil level gauge and the tube.

   b. Disconnect the shift select control link rod from the select lever.

   c. Disconnect the downshift cable from the transmission.

   d. Disconnect and plug the fluid coolant lines from the transmission.

18. If equipped with a 1-piece driveshaft, remove the driveshaft flange-to-pinion nuts, lower the driveshaft and pull it from the transmission.

19. If equipped with a 2-piece driveshaft, perform the following procedures:

   a. Remove the rear driveshaft flange-to-pinion nuts.

   b. Remove the rear driveshaft flange-to-front driveshaft flange bolts and the rear driveshaft.

   c. Remove the center bearing-to-chassis bolts, move the front driveshaft rearward and from the transmission.

20. Remove the front driveshaft's splinded yoke flange-to-transfer case bolts and separate the front driveshaft from the transfer case; do not allow the splined flange to fall away from the driveshaft.

21. Remove the starter-to-engine bolts and the starter.

22. If equipped with a clutch slave cylinder, remove it from the transmission and move it aside.

23. Remove the exhaust pipe-to-exhaust manifold nuts, the exhaust pipe bracket-to-transmission bolts, the front exhaust pipe-to-2nd exhaust pipe bolts and the front exhaust pipe from the vehicle.

24. Attach an engine hanger to the rear of the exhaust manifold.

25. Using an engine hoist, connect it to the engine hangers and support the engine.

26. If equipped with a 2.8L engine, remove the catalytic converter and the parking brake cable bracket.

27. Remove the transmission/transfer case assembly by performing the following procedures:

   a. Using a transmission jack, place it under the transmission and support the assembly.

   b. Remove the rear mount-to-transmission nuts.

   c. Remove the rear mount-to-side mount member nuts/bolts and the mount.

   d. Remove the transmission-to-engine bolts.

   e. Move the transmission assembly rearward.

   f. Carefully lower the transmission.

28. Remove the engine-to-mount nuts/bolts.

29. Using the hoist, slowly, lift the engine; be sure to hold the front of the engine higher than the rear.

30. Place the engine on a work stand.

To install:

31. Using the hoist, slowly, lower the engine into the vehicle; be sure to hold the front of the engine higher than the rear.

32. Install the engine-to-mount nuts/bolts.

33. Install the transmission/transfer assembly by performing the following procedures:

   a. Raise the transmission into position.

   b. Move the transmission forward and engage it with the engine.

   c. Install the engine-to-transmission bolts.

   d. Install the rear mount and the rear mount-to-side mount member nuts/bolts.

   e. Install the rear mount-to-transmission nuts.

   f. Remove the transmission jack.

34. If equipped with a 2.8L engine, install the catalytic converter and the parking brake cable bracket.

35. Remove the engine hoist and the engine hanger from the rear of the exhaust manifold.

36. Install the front exhaust pipe, exhaust pipe-to-exhaust manifold nuts, the exhaust pipe bracket-to-transmission bolts, the front exhaust pipe-to-2nd exhaust pipe bolts.

37. If equipped with a clutch slave cylinder, install it onto the transmission.

38. Install the starter and the starter-to-engine bolts.

39. Install the front driveshaft's splinded yoke flange-to-transfer case bolts.

40. If equipped with a 2-piece driveshaft, perform the following procedures:

   a. Install the front driveshaft into the transmission and the center bearing-to-chassis bolts.

   b. Install the rear driveshaft and the rear driveshaft flange-to-front driveshaft flange bolts.

   c. Install the rear driveshaft flange-to-pinion nuts.

41. If equipped with a 1-piece driveshaft, install the driveshaft into the transmission and the driveshaft flange-to-pinion nuts.

42. If equipped with an automatic transmission, perform the following procedures:

   a. Connect the fluid coolant lines to the transmission.

   b. Connect the downshift cable to the transmission.

   c. Connect the shift select control link rod to the select lever.

   d. Install the oil level gauge and the tube.

43. Install the front wheels and lower the vehicle.

44. Install the transfer shift lever by performing the following procedures:

   a. Position the shift lever into the transfer case.

   b. Install the shift lever retaining bolts.

   c. Push the dust cover and the shift lever boot downward.

45. Install the gear shift lever by performing the following procedures:

   a. Install the shift lever and the shift lever cover bolts.

   b. Push the grommet and shift lever boot downward.

   c. Install the front console to the floor panel.

46. If equipped with a 2.8L engine, perform the following procedures:

   a. Install the ignition coil.

   b. Install the distributor cap with the No. 1 spark plug wire.

   c. Install the spark plug wire from the No. 1 spark plug and reconnect the wires to the distributor cap.

d. Install the power steering pump-to-engine brackets.

47. If equipped with air conditioning, install the compressor to the engine.

48. Install the radiator, the fan blade assembly and the fan shroud.

49. Connect the upper and lower radiator hoses and the reservoir tank hose.

50. Install the radiator grille to the deflector panel.

51. Install the clutch return spring (if equipped), the clutch control cable (if equipped), the back-up light switch connector and the speedometer cable to the transmission.

52. Connect the following items:
   a. Air switch valve hose.
   b. Oxygen sensor wire.
   c. Vacuum switch valve hose.
   d. Thermal vacuum switching valve hose.
   e. Pressure regulator vacuum hose.
   f. Canister hose.
   g. ECM harness.
   h. Fuel hose(s).

53. Connect the necessary hoses, electrical connectors, control cables and control rods to the engine.

54. Install the air cleaner (2.3L engine) or air cleaner duct and hose (2.6L engine).

55. Refill the engine, the transmission, the transfer case and the cooling system. Install the undercover, if equipped.

56. Install the hood.

57. Install the battery and connect both battery cables, the positive cable first.

58. Adjust the belt tension. Start the engine, check for leaks.

59. Check and/or adjust the idle speed and ignition timing.

Cylinder Head

Removal and Installation

2.0L ENGINE

1. Disconnect the negative battery cable. Remove the rocker cover.

2. Remove the EGR pipe clamp bolt at the rear of the cylinder head.

3. Raise and support the vehicle safely. Disconnect the exhaust pipe at the exhaust manifold.

4. Lower the vehicle and drain the cooling system.

5. Disconnect the heater hoses at the intake manifold and at the rear of the cylinder head. Remove the air conditioning compressor and/or power steering pump with hoses attached and support them aside.

6. Disconnect the accelerator linkage and fuel line at the carburetor. Disconnect and label the electrical connections, spark plug wires and vacuum lines at the cylinder head.

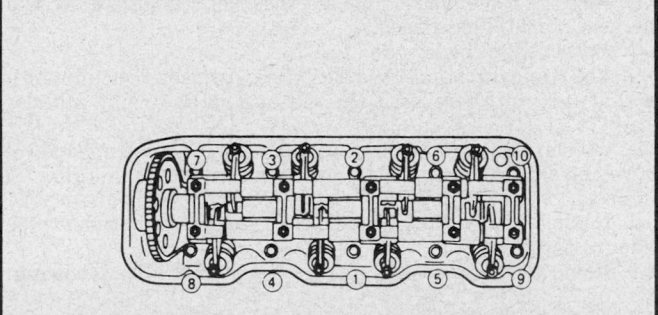

View of the cylinder head bolt torquing sequence — 2.0L engine

7. Rotate the engine until the No. 4 cylinder is in the firing position. Remove the distributor cap and mark the rotor to housing relationship. Remove distributor and the fuel pump.

8. Lock the timing chain adjuster by depressing and turning the automatic adjuster side pin 90 degrees clockwise.

9. Remove the timing sprocket-to-camshaft bolt and remove the sprocket from the camshaft.

NOTE: Keep the sprocket on the chain damper and chain.

10. Disconnect the AIR hose and the check valve at the exhaust manifold.

11. Remove the cylinder head to timing cover bolts.

12. Starting with the outer bolts and working inward, remove the cylinder head bolts.

13. Remove the cylinder head, intake and exhaust manifold as a unit.

To install:

14. To install, use a new gasket and install the cylinder head on the engine.

15. Torque the bolts to 57 ft. lbs. in the 1st step and to 65–79 ft. lbs. in the final step.

16. Install the timing chain by performing the following procedures:
   a. Install the timing sprocket and pinion gear with the groove side toward the front cover. Align the key grooves with the key on the crankshaft, then drive into position.
   b. Confirm that the No. 1 piston is at TDC. If not, turn the crankshaft so the key is turned toward the cylinder head side (No. 1 and No. 4 pistons at top dead center).
   c. Install the timing chain by aligning the mark plate on the chain with the mark on the crankshaft timing sprocket. The side of the chain with the mark plate is on the front side and the side of the chain with the most links between the mark plates is on the chain guide side.
   d. Install the camshaft timing sprocket so the mark side of the sprocket faces forward and so the triangular mark aligns with the chain mark plate.

NOTE: Keep the timing chain engaged with the camshaft timing sprocket until the sprocket is installed on the camshaft.

17. Install the front cover assembly, using a new gasket and sealer.

18. Connect the AIR hose and the check valve at the exhaust manifold.

19. Connect the accelerator linkage and fuel line to the carburetor. Connect the electrical connections, the spark plug wires and the vacuum lines.

20. Connect the heater hoses to the intake manifold and the rear of the cylinder head. Install the air conditioner compressor and/or power steering pump.

21. Connect the exhaust pipe to the exhaust manifold.

22. Install the EGR pipe clamp bolt to the rear of the cylinder head.

23. Install the rocker arm cover and connect the negative battery cable.

24. Start the engine and check for leaks.

2.3L AND 2.6L ENGINES

1. Relieve the fuel pressure. Disconnect the negative battery cable. Drain the cooling system.

2. Remove the drive belts from the power steering pump, the air pump, the air conditioning compressor (if equipped) and the cooling fan.

3. Rotate the engine to position the No. 1 cylinder on TDC.

4. Remove the distributor cap, high tension cables and the distributor.

5. Remove the exhaust manifold-to-exhaust pipe bolts.

6. Label and disconnect the electrical connectors and vacuum hoses which may be in the way.

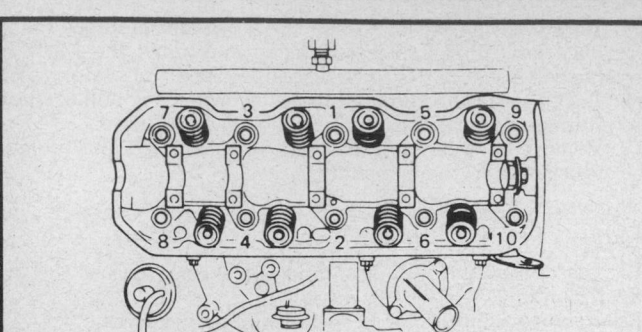

View of the cylinder head bolt torquing sequence— 2.3L and 2.6L engines

7. On the 2.3L engine, remove the carburetor.

8. Remove the coolant hoses, the radiator and the cooling fan assembly.

9. Remove the crankshaft pulley bolt and the pulley.

10. Remove the upper and lower timing belt covers, the tension spring and the timing belt.

11. Remove the camshaft pulley bolt, the pulley and the camshaft boss.

12. Remove the timing belt guide plate and the cylinder head front plate.

13. Remove the rocker arm cover and gasket.

14. Remove the cylinder head-to-engine bolts, the cylinder head and gasket.

15. Clean the gasket mounting surfaces.

To install:

16. Using a new gasket, install the cylinder head and torque the bolts, in sequence to 57 ft. lbs. in the 1st step and to 65–79 ft. lbs. in the final step.

17. Install the camshaft pulley.

18. Using a new gasket, install the rocker arm cover.

19. Align the camshaft pulley mark with the mark on the front plate. Make sure the keyway on the crankshaft if facing upward, aimed at the pointer on the engine block.

20. Install the timing belt in the following order: crankshaft pulley, the oil pump pulley, the camshaft and the tensioner.

21. Install the timing belt covers, using a new gasket.

22. Install the crankshaft pulley.

23. Install the cooling fan assembly, the radiator and the coolant hoses.

24. On the 2.3L engine, install the carburetor.

25. Connect the electrical connectors and vacuum hoses.

26. Install the exhaust manifold-to-exhaust pipe bolts.

27. Install the distributor, the distributor cap, and the high tension cables.

28. Install the drive belts to the power steering pump, the air pump, the air conditioning compressor (if equipped) and the cooling fan.

29. Disconnect the negative battery cable. Refill the cooling system.

30. Start the engine and check for leaks.

2.8L ENGINE

Left Side

1. Relieve the fuel pressure. Disconnect the negative battery cable. Drain the cooling system.

2. Remove the intake manifold.

3. Raise and safely support the vehicle.

4. Disconnect the exhaust pipe from the exhaust manifold and remove the exhaust manifold-to-cylinder head bolts.

5. Remove the dipstick tube from the engine.

6. Lower the vehicle.

7. Loosen the rocker arm nuts, turn the rocker arms and remove the pushrods; keep the pushrods in the same order as removed.

8. Remove the cylinder head bolts in stages and in the reverse order of torquing.

9. Remove the cylinder head; do not pry on the head to loosen it.

10. Clean the gasket mounting surfaces.

To install:

11. Position a new cylinder head gasket over the dowel pins with the words **This Side Up** facing upwards. Carefully, guide the cylinder head into place.

12. Install the pushrods; make sure the lower ends are in the lifter heads. Torque the rocker arm nuts to 14–20 ft. lbs. (20–27 Nm).

13. Install the intake manifold.

14. Install the dipstick tube to the engine.

15. Install the exhaust manifold-to-cylinder head bolts and the exhaust pipe-to-exhaust manifold nuts.

16. Refill the cooling system. Start the engine and check for leaks.

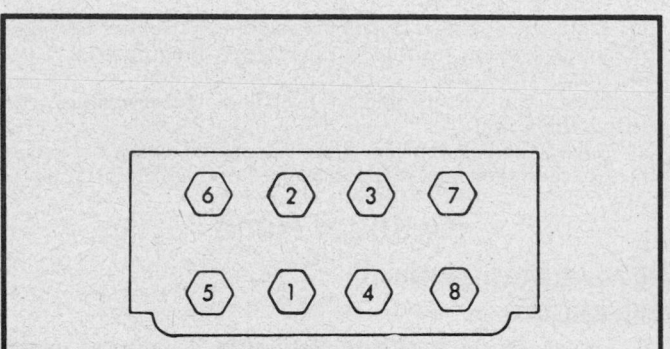

View of the cylinder head bolt torquing sequence— 2.8L engine

Right Side

1. Relieve the fuel pressure. Disconnect the negative battery cable. Drain the cooling system.

2. Remove the intake manifold.

3. If equipped, remove the cruise control servo bracket, the air management valve and hose.

4. Raise and safely support the vehicle.

5. Disconnect the exhaust pipe from the exhaust manifold and remove the exhaust manifold-to-cylinder head bolts.

6. Remove the exhaust pipe at crossover, the crossover and the heat shield, if equipped.

7. Lower the vehicle.

8. Label and disconnect the electrical wiring and vacuum hoses that may interfere with the removal of the right cylinder head.

9. Loosen the rocker arm nuts, turn the rocker arms and remove the pushrods; keep the pushrods in the same order as removed.

10. Remove the cylinder head bolts in stages and in the reverse order of torquing.

11. Remove the cylinder head; do not pry on the head to loosen it.

12. Clean the gasket mounting surfaces.

To install:

13. Position a new cylinder head gasket over the dowel pins with the words **This Side Up** facing upwards. Carefully, guide

the cylinder head into place.

14. Install the pushrods; make sure the lower ends are in the lifter heads. Torque the rocker arm nuts to 14–20 ft. lbs. (20–27 Nm).

15. Install the intake manifold.

16. Install the exhaust pipe at crossover, the crossover and the heat shield, if equipped.

17. Install the exhaust manifold-to-cylinder head bolts and the exhaust pipe-to-exhaust manifold nuts.

19. Connect the electrical wiring and vacuum hoses to the right cylinder head.

20. If equipped, install the cruise control servo bracket, the air management valve and hose.

21. Refill the cooling system. Start the engine and check for leaks.

Valve Lash

Adjustment

2.0L, 2.3L AND 2.6L ENGINES

NOTE: The valves are adjusted with the engine COLD. It is best to allow an engine to sit overnight before beginning a valve adjustment. While all valve adjustments must be made as accurately as possible, it is better to have the valve adjustment slightly loose rather than slightly tight. A burned valve may result from overly tight valve adjustments.

1. Remove the rocker arm cover and discard the gasket.

2. Make sure both the cylinder head and camshaft retaining bolts are tightened to the proper torque.

3. Rotate the crankshaft pulley until the No. 1 piston is at TDC of the compression stroke.

NOTE: To make sure the piston is on the correct stroke, remove the spark plug and place a finger over the hole. Feel for air being forced out of the spark plug hole. Both valves on No. 1 cylinder will be closed. Stop turning the crankshaft when the TDC timing mark on the crankshaft pulley is directly aligned with the timing mark pointer.

4. With the No. 1 piston at TDC of the compression stroke, adjust the clearances of the following valves:
Intake: 1 and 2
Exhaust: 1 and 3

5. Adjust the clearance by loosening the locknut and turning the adjusting screw. Retightening the locknut when the proper thickness feeler gauge passes between the camshaft or valve stem and has a slight drag when the clearance is corrected.

6. Rotate the crankshaft 1 complete revolution (360 degrees) to position the No. 4 piston at TDC of its compression stroke and adjust the clearances of the following valves:
Intake: 3 and 4
Exhaust: 2 and 4

7. After adjustment, use a new gasket, sealant and install the rocker arm cover.

2.8L ENGINE

1. Remove the valve covers.

2. Rotate the crankshaft until the No. 1 cylinder is on the TDC of its compression stroke.

NOTE: When the notch on the damper pulley is aligned with the 0 timing mark and the rocker arms of the No. 1 cylinder do not move, the engine is at the TDC of the compression stroke of the No. 1 cylinder.

3. With the engine at TDC of the No. 1 cylinder, adjust the following valves:
Exhaust: 1, 2 and 3

Adjusting the valves—2.0L, 2.3L and 2.6L engines

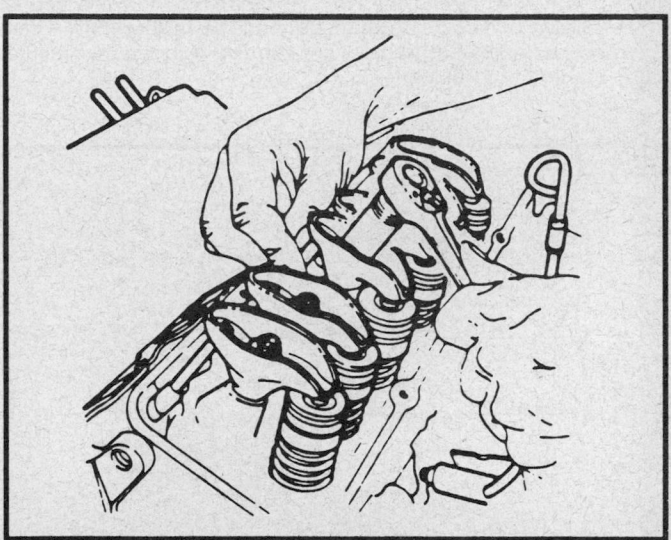
Adjusting the valves—2.8L engine

Intake: 1, 5 and 6

4. Back out the adjusting nut until lash is felt.

5. Tighten the adjusting nut until the lash is removed, then, turn the nut 1½ additional turns to center the lifter plunger.

6. Rotate the engine 1 complete revolution and reposition the notch on the damper pulley with the **0** mark on the timing tab; this is the No. 4 cylinder firing position.

7. With the engine at TDC of the No. 4 cylinder, adjust the following valves:
Exhaust: 4, 5 and 6
Intake: 2, 3 and 4

8. Back out the adjusting nut until lash is felt.

9. Tighten the adjusting nut until the lash is removed, plus, turn the nut 1½ additional turns to center the lifter plunger.

10. Using a new gasket and sealant, install the rocker arm covers.

Rocker Arms/Shafts

Removal and Installation

2.0L, 2.3L AND 2.6L ENGINES

1. Disconnect the negative battery cable. Remove the rocker cover.

2. Loosen the rocker arm shaft bracket nuts a little at a time, in sequence, starting with the outer nuts.

3. Remove the nuts from the rocker arm shaft brackets. Remove shaft assembly.

4. To disassemble the rockers and shafts; remove the spring from the rocker arm shaft, the rocker brackets and arms. Keep parts in order for reassembly.

5. Before installing apply a generous amount of clean engine oil to the rocker arm shaft, rocker arms and valve stems.

To install:

6. Install the longer shaft on the exhaust valve side and the shorter shaft on the intake side so the aligning marks on the shafts are turned on the front side of the engine.

7. Assemble the rocker arm shaft brackets and rocker arms to the shafts so the cylinder number, on the upper face of the brackets, points toward the front of the engine.

8. Align the mark on the No. 1 rocker arm shaft bracket with the mark on the intake and exhaust valve side rocker arm shaft.

9. Make certain the amount of projection of the rocker arm shaft beyond the face of the No. 1 rocker arm shaft bracket, is longer on the exhaust side shaft than on the intake shaft when the rocker arm shaft stud holes are aligned with the rocker arm shaft bracket stud holes.

10. Place the rocker arm shaft springs in position between the shaft bracket and rocker arm.

11. Check that the punch mark on the rocker arm shaft is facing upward, then, install the rocker arm shaft bracket assembly onto the cylinder head studs. Align the mark on the camshaft with the mark on the No. 1 rocker arm shaft bracket.

12. Torque the rocker arm shaft brackets-to-cylinder head nuts to 16 ft. lbs. and bolts to 6 ft. lbs.

NOTE: Hold the rocker arm springs while torquing the nuts to prevent damage to the spring. Start with the center nut and work outward.

13. Adjust the valves and install the camshaft cover, with a new gasket and sealer. Check the ignition timing.

2.8L ENGINE

1. Disconnect the negative battery cable.
2. Remove the rocker arm covers.
3. Remove the rocker arm nut, the pivot balls, the rocker arm and the pushrods. Keep all components separated so they may be reinstalled in the same location.

NOTE: The intake and exhaust pushrods are of different lengths.

To install:

4. Install the pushrods in their original location; be sure the lower ends are seated in the lifter.
5. Coat the bearing surfaces of the rocker arms and pivot balls with Molykote or equivalent.
6. Install the rocker arm nuts and torque them to 14–20 ft. lbs. (20–27 Nm).
7. Adjust the valve lash.

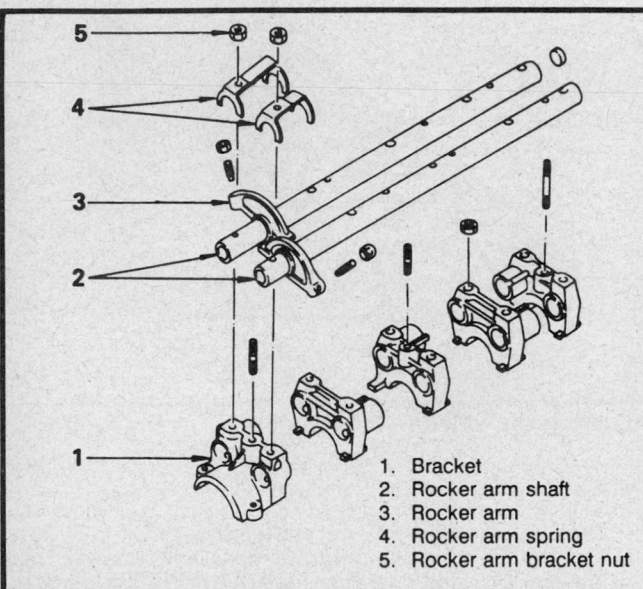

1. Bracket
2. Rocker arm shaft
3. Rocker arm
4. Rocker arm spring
5. Rocker arm bracket nut

Exploded view of the rocker arm/shaft assembly— 2.0L, 2.3L and 2.6L engines

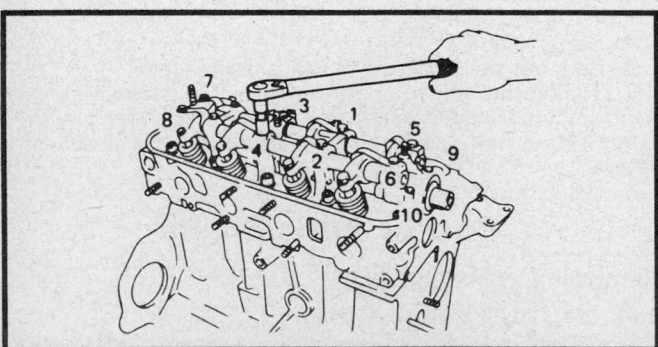

View of the rocker arm/shaft assembly torquing sequence—2.0L, 2.3L and 2.6L engines

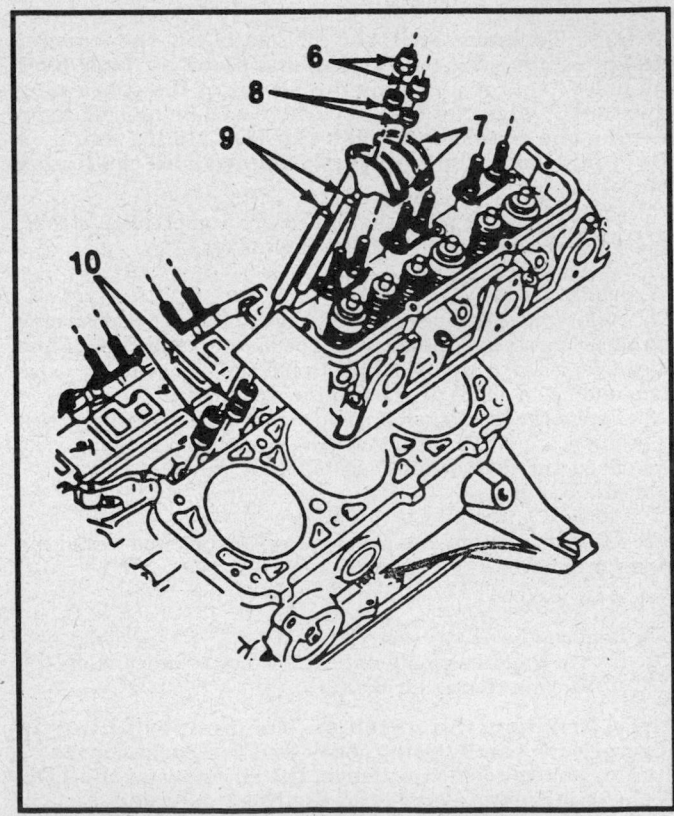

Exploded view of the cylinder head/rocker arm assembly—2.8L engine

Intake Manifold

Removal and Installation

2.0L AND 2.3L ENGINES

1. Relieve the fuel pressure. Disconnect the negative battery cable and remove the air cleaner assembly.
2. Remove the EGR pipe clamp bolt at the rear of the cylinder head.
3. Raise and support the vehicle safely. Remove the EGR pipe from the intake and exhaust manifolds.
4. Remove the EGR valve and bracket assembly from the intake manifold.
5. Lower the vehicle and drain the cooling system.
6. Remove the upper coolant hoses from the manifold.
7. Disconnect the accelerator linkage, vacuum lines, electrical wiring and fuel line from the intake manifold.
8. Remove the intake manifold mounting nuts and remove the manifold from the cylinder head.
9. Remove the lower heater hose while holding the manifold away from the engine. Remove the manifold from the vehicle.

To install:

10. Connect the lower heater hose to the manifold. Using a new gasket, install the intake manifold.
11. Connect the accelerator linkage, vacuum lines, electrical wiring and fuel line to the intake manifold.
12. Connect the upper coolant hose to the intake manifold.
13. Install the EGR valve and bracket assembly to the intake manifold.
14. Install the EGR pipe to the intake and exhaust manifolds. Lower the vehicle.
15. Install the EGR pipe clamp bolt to the rear of the cylinder head.
16. Install the air cleaner and connect the negative battery cable.

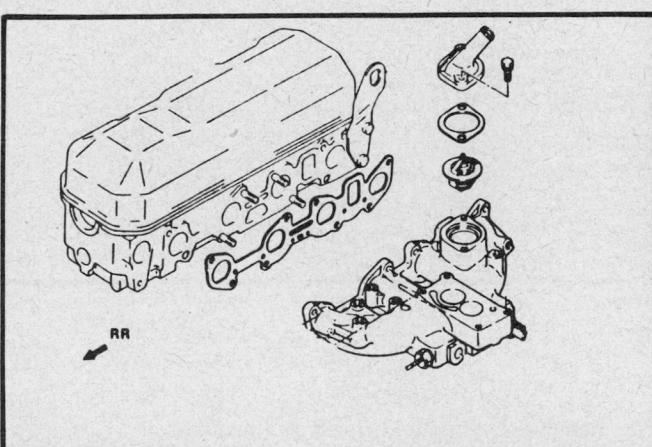

Exploded view of the intake manifold—2.0L and 2.3L engines

2.6L ENGINE

1. Relieve the fuel pressure. Disconnect the negative battery cable and remove the air duct.
2. Drain the cooling system. Remove the upper coolant hoses from the manifold.
3. Remove the air regulator rubber hose from the intake plenum.
4. Remove the EGR valve and bracket assembly from the intake manifold.

5. Disconnect the accelerator linkage, vacuum lines, electrical wiring and fuel line from the throttle body.
6. Remove the throttle body-to-plenum nuts and the throttle body.
7. Remove the plenum-to-intake manifold bolts and the plenum.
8. Remove the intake manifold-to-cylinder head nuts and the manifold from the cylinder head.

To install:

9. Using a new gasket, install the intake manifold to the cylinder head.
10. Using a new gasket, install the plenum to the intake manifold.
11. Using a new gasket, install the throttle body to the plenum.
12. Connect the accelerator linkage, vacuum lines, electrical wiring and fuel line.
13. Install the EGR valve and bracket assembly to the intake manifold.
14. Install the air regulator rubber hose to the intake plenum.
15. Install the upper coolant hoses to the manifold.
16. Install the air duct. Connect the negative battery cable. Refill the cooling system.

2.8L ENGINE

1. Relieve the fuel pressure. Disconnect the negative battery cable.
2. Remove the air cleaner. Drain the cooling system.
3. Label and disconnect the wires and hoses from the TBI unit and the intake manifold.
4. Disconnect and plug the fuel lines from the TBI unit.
5. Disconnect the accelerator cables from the TBI unit.
6. Disconnect the ignition wires from the spark plugs and the wires from the coil.
7. Remove the distributor cap with the wires.
8. Mark the location of the rotor to the distributor housing and the distributor housing to the intake manifold.
9. Remove the distributor hold-down clamp and the distributor.
10. Label and disconnect the EGR vacuum line and the emission hoses.
11. Remove the pipe brackets from the rocker arm covers.
12. Remove the rocker arm covers.
13. Remove the upper radiator hose and the heater hose.
14. Disconnect the electrical connectors from the coolant sensors.
15. Remove the intake manifold nuts/bolts, the manifold and gaskets.
16. Clean the gasket mounting surfaces.

To install:

17. Using RTV sealant, apply an ⅛ in. bead to the front and rear of the block; make sure no water or oil is present.
18. Using new gaskets, marked right and left side, apply a ¼ in. bead of sealant to hold them in place and install them onto the cylinder heads; the gaskets may have to be cut to be installed around the pushrods.
19. Install the intake manifold and torque the nuts/bolts, in sequence, to 23 ft. lbs. (31 Nm) and retorque using the same sequence.

NOTE: Make sure the areas between the case ridges and the intake manifold are completely sealed.

20. Install the heater hose and the radiator to the manifold.
21. Using new gaskets, install the rocker arm covers.
22. Connect the electrical connectors to the coolant sensors.
23. Install the pipe brackets.
24. Align the matchmarks and install the distributor and the distributor cap.
25. Connect the fuel lines and the accelerator cables to the TBI unit.

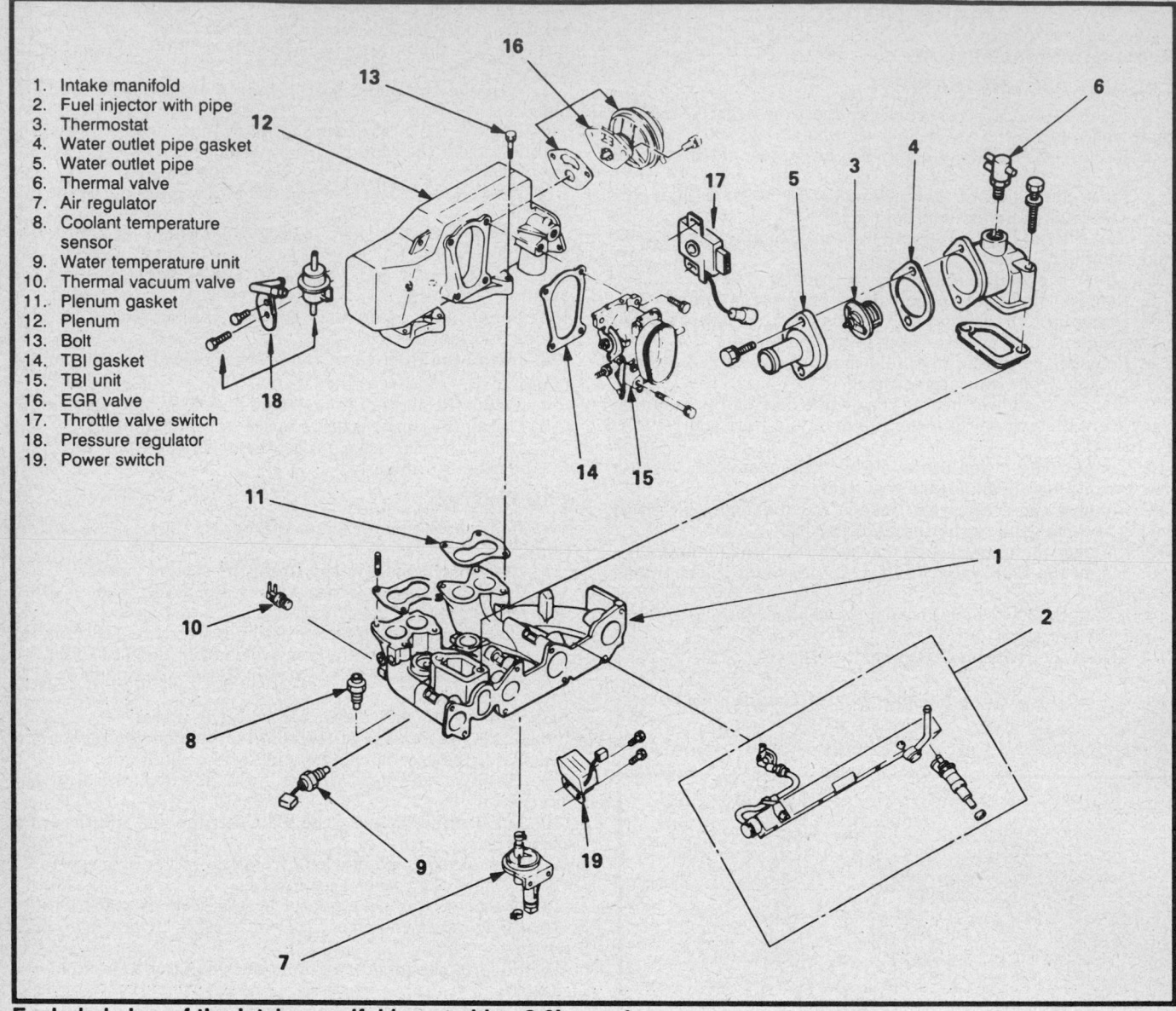

1. Intake manifold
2. Fuel injector with pipe
3. Thermostat
4. Water outlet pipe gasket
5. Water outlet pipe
6. Thermal valve
7. Air regulator
8. Coolant temperature sensor
9. Water temperature unit
10. Thermal vacuum valve
11. Plenum gasket
12. Plenum
13. Bolt
14. TBI gasket
15. TBI unit
16. EGR valve
17. Throttle valve switch
18. Pressure regulator
19. Power switch

Exploded view of the intake manifold assembly—2.6L engine

26. Connect all the wires and vacuum hoses.
27. Install the air cleaner. Connect the negative battery cable. Refill the cooling system.

Exhaust Manifold

Removal and Installation

2.0L AND 2.3L ENGINES

1. Disconnect the negative battery cable and remove the air cleaner assembly.
2. Remove the EGR pipe clamp bolt at the rear of the cylinder head.
3. Raise and safely support the vehicle. Remove the EGR pipe from the intake and exhaust manifolds.
4. Disconnect the exhaust pipe from the exhaust manifold. Disconnect the electrical connector from the oxygen sensor.

5. Remove the manifold shield and heat stove.
6. Remove the manifold retaining nuts and remove the manifold from the engine.
To install:
7. Using a new gasket, install the exhaust manifold and torque the nuts to 14–18 ft. lbs.
8. Install the heat stove and shield.
9. Connect the exhaust pipe to the exhaust manifold. Connect the electrical connector to the oxygen sensor.
10. Install the EGR pipe to the intake and exhaust manifolds and lower the vehicle.
11. Install the EGR pipe clamp bolt to the rear of the cylinder head.
12. Install the air cleaner. Connect the negative battery cable.

2.6L ENGINE

1. Disconnect the negative battery cable and remove the air

duct.

2. Remove the hoses from the air pump.

3. Remove the air pump bolts, remove the drive belt and the air pump.

4. Remove the EGR pipe clamp bolt at the rear of the cylinder head.

5. Raise and safely support the vehicle. Remove the EGR pipe from the intake and exhaust manifolds. If necessary, remove the dipstick and tube.

6. Disconnect the exhaust pipe from the exhaust manifold. Disconnect the electrical connector from the oxygen sensor.

7. Remove the manifold shield.

8. Remove the manifold-to-cylinder head nuts and the manifold from the engine.

To install:

9. Using a new gasket, install the exhaust manifold and torque the nuts to 16 ft. lbs.

10. Install the heat shield. If the dipstick was removed, install the tube and the dipstick.

11. Connect the exhaust pipe to the exhaust manifold. Connect the electrical connector to the oxygen sensor.

12. Install the EGR pipe to the intake and exhaust manifolds and lower the vehicle.

13. Install the EGR pipe clamp bolt to the rear of the cylinder head.

14. Install the air duct. Connect the negative battery cable.

2.8L ENGINE

1. Disconnect the negative battery cable.

2. Raise and safely support the vehicle.

3. Remove the exhaust pipe from the manifold.

4. Lower the vehicle and remove the rear manifold bolts.

5. On the right side, remove the diverter valve, the heat shield, the AIR pump bracket and alternator bracket.

6. On the left side, remove the heat stove tube and the power steering bracket.

7. Remove the exhaust manifold-to-cylinder head bolts and the manifold.

8. Clean the gasket mounting surfaces.

To install:

9. Using a new gasket, install the exhaust manifold-to-cylinder head bolts and torque the bolts to 25 ft. lbs. (34 Nm).

10. On the left side, install the power steering bracket and heat stove tube.

11. On the right side, install the AIR pump bracket, the alternator bracket, the diverter valve and the heat shield.

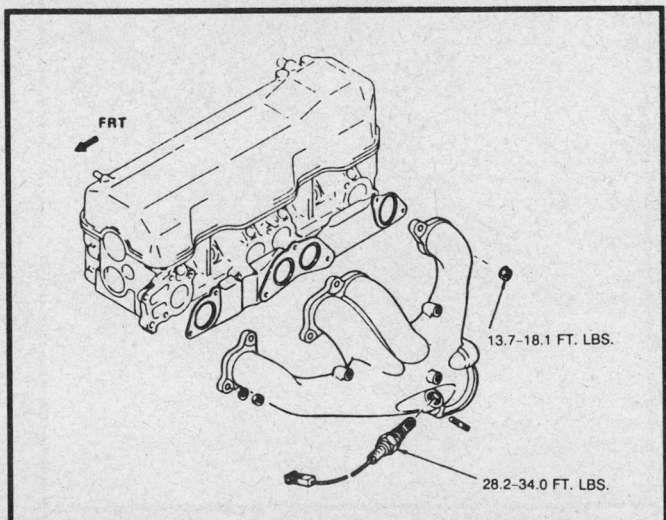

13.7–18.1 FT. LBS.

28.2–34.0 FT. LBS.

Exploded view of the exhaust manifold—2.0L and 2.3L engines

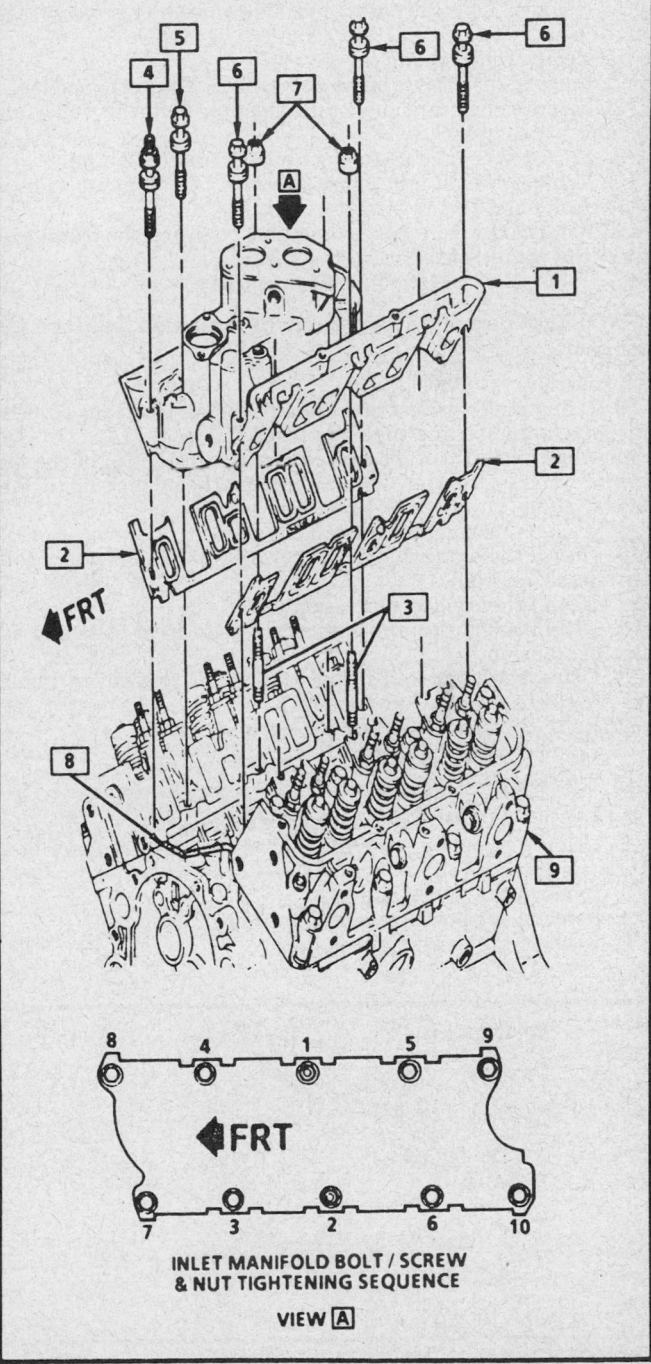

1. Intake manifold
2. Gaskets
3. Studs
4. Bolt/screw studs
5. Bolt/screw assembly
6. Bolt/screw assembly
7. Nut/washer assembly
8. Sealant
9. Cylinder head assembly

INLET MANIFOLD BOLT / SCREW & NUT TIGHTENING SEQUENCE

VIEW A

Exploded view of the intake manifold assembly—2.8L engine

12. Raise and safely support the vehicle.
13. Install the exhaust pipe-to-manifold bolts.
14. Lower the vehicle and connect the negative battery cable.

Timing Chain Front Cover

Removal and Installation

2.0L ENGINE

1. Disconnect the negative battery cable.
2. Drain the cooling system.
3. Disconnect the radiator hoses and remove the radiator.
4. Remove the air cleaner and the rocker arm cover.
5. Remove the alternator and air conditioning compressor drive belts.
6. Remove the cooling fan.
7. Raise and safely support the vehicle. Drain the engine.
8. Remove the crankshaft pulley center bolt, the pulley and balancer assembly.
9. Remove the oil pan-to-engine bolts and the oil pan.
10. Remove the oil pump pick-up tube, the oil pump-to-front cover bolts and the oil pump.
11. Remove the front cover-to-engine bolts and the front cover from the engine and discard the gasket.
12. Clean the gasket mounting surfaces.

NOTE: When the front cover is removed, replace the oil seal.

To install:

13. Using a new gasket and sealant, install the front cover to the engine and torque the bolts to 18 ft. lbs.
14. Align the oil pump's slotted shaft with the tip of the distributor and install the oil pump. Install the oil pick-up tube to the oil pump.
15. Using a new gasket, install the oil pan.
16. Install the crankshaft balancer assembly, pulley and bolt. Lower the vehicle.
17. Install the cooling fan assembly.
18. Install the alternator and compressor drive belts and adjust the tension.
19. Using a new gasket, install the rocker arm cover. Install the air cleaner.
20. Refill the crankcase and the cooling system.
21. Connect the negative battery cable.

2.8L ENGINE

1. Disconnect the negative battery cable.
2. Drain the cooling system. Remove the lower radiator hose from the front cover.
3. Remove the water pump.
4. Remove the power steering bracket, if equipped.
5. Remove the crankshaft pulley.

6. Remove the front cover-to-engine bolts and the cover and discard the gasket.
7. Clean the gasket mounting surfaces.

NOTE: When the front cover is removed, replace the oil seal.

To install:

8. Using a new gasket and sealant, install the front cover.
9. Install the water pump and the lower radiator hose.
10. Install the crankshaft pulley.

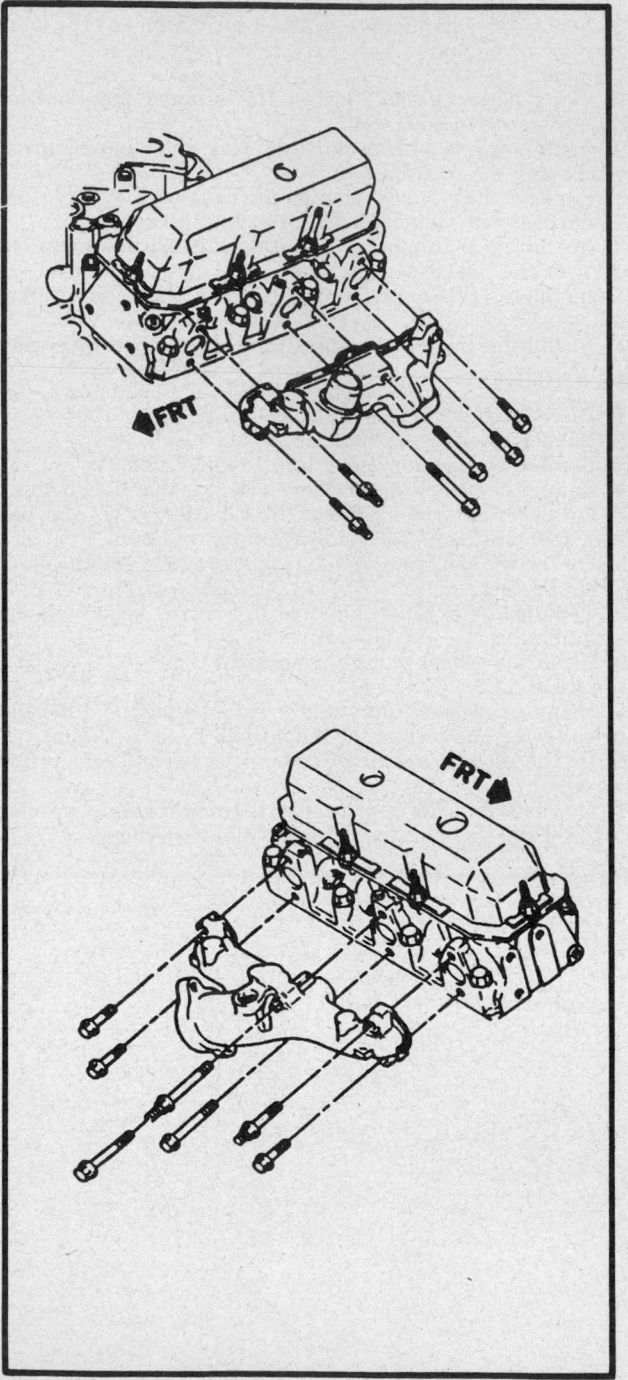
Exploded view of the exhaust manifolds – 2.8L engine

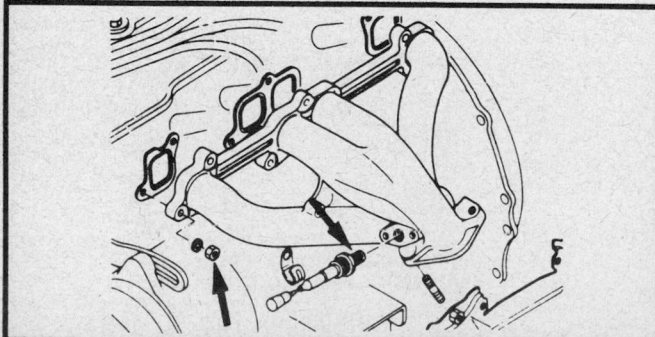
Exploded view of the exhaust manifold – 2.6L engine

11. Install the power steering pump bracket, if equipped.

12. Install the drive belt(s).

13. Connect the negative battery cable and refill the cooling system.

Front Cover Oil Seal

Replacement

2.0L ENGINE

1. Disconnect the negative battery cable.
2. Drain the cooling system.
3. Disconnect the radiator hoses and remove the radiator.
4. Remove the alternator and compressor drive belts.
5. Remove the cooling fan.
6. Remove the crankshaft pulley center bolt, the pulley and balancer assembly.
7. Using a small pry bar and care not to damage the crankshaft and cover sealing surfaces, carefully, pry out the timing cover seal.

To install:

8. Using engine oil, lubricate the new seal and tap it into the front cover.
9. Install the balancer assembly, the pulley and the center bolt.
10. Install the cooling fan and the drive belts.
11. Install the radiator and connect the hoses.
12. Refill the cooling system and connect the negative battery cable.

2.8L ENGINE

1. Disconnect the negative battery cable.
2. Remove the crankshaft pulley.
3. Using a small pry bar, pry the oil seal from the front cover; be careful not to damage the sealing surface or the crankshaft.
4. Using an oil seal installation tool, lubricate the new seal with engine oil and drive it into the front cover; be careful not to cut the seal lip.
5. Install the crankshaft pulley.
6. Connect the negative battery cable.

Timing Chain and Sprockets

Removal and Installation

2.0L ENGINE

1. Disconnect the negative battery cable. Rotate the engine until No. 1 piston is at TDC on the compression stroke.
2. Remove the rocker arm cover, the front cover and the oil pan.
3. Depress or lock the shoe of the automatic chain adjuster in the retracted position.
4. Remove the camshaft sprocket-to-camshaft bolts and the sprocket.
5. Remove the timing chain from the timing sprockets.
6. Using a puller, remove the sprocket and the pinion gear from the crankshaft.
7. Remove the bolt or E-clip and remove the automatic chain adjuster.
8. Inspect the adjuster pin, arm, wedge and rack teeth. Replace assembly if worn. Remove the chain tensioner.
9. Check the timing chain for wear.
10. Check the tensioner pins for wear or damage and replace if necessary.
11. Replace the chain tensioner and adjuster using the E-clips or bolt.

To install:

12. Install the timing sprocket and pinion gear with the groove side toward the front cover. Align the key grooves with the key on the crankshaft, then, drive into position.

13. Confirm the No. 1 piston is at TDC; if not, turn the crankshaft so the key is turned toward the cylinder head side (No. 1 and No. 4 pistons at top dead center).

14. Install the timing chain by aligning the mark plate on the chain with the mark on the crankshaft timing sprocket. The side of the chain with the mark plate is on the front side and the side of the chain with the most links between the mark plates is on the chain guide side.

15. Install the camshaft timing sprocket so the mark side of the sprocket faces forward and so the triangular mark aligns with the chain mark plate.

NOTE: Keep the timing chain engaged with the camshaft timing sprocket until the sprocket is installed on the camshaft.

16. Using a new gasket and sealant, install the front cover assembly.
17. Install the rocker arm cover and oil pan.
18. Refill the cooling system and the crankcase.
19. Connect the negative battery cable.

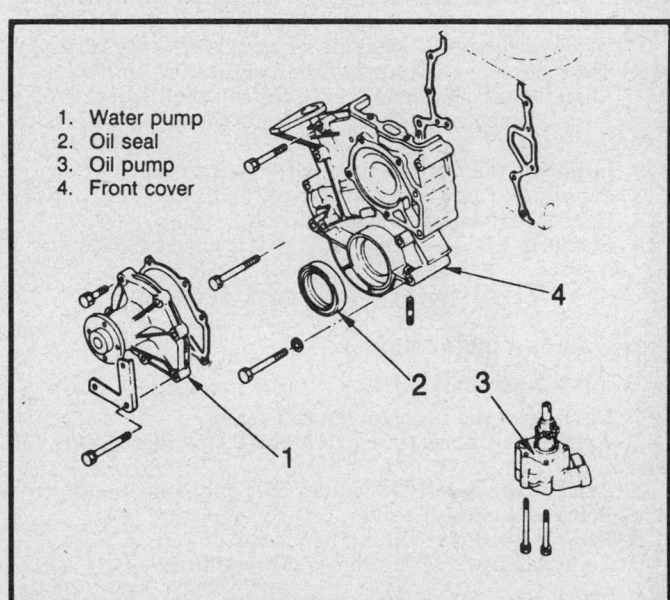

1. Water pump
2. Oil seal
3. Oil pump
4. Front cover

Exploded view of the front cover assembly—2.0L engine

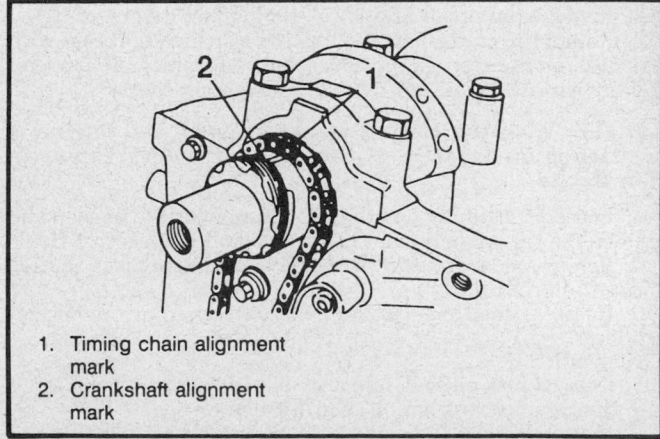

1. Timing chain alignment mark
2. Crankshaft alignment mark

Aligning the timing chain the crankshaft sprocket— 2.0L engine

2.8L ENGINE

1. Disconnect the negative battery cable.
2. Rotate the crankshaft to position the No. 1 cylinder at the TDC of its compression stroke.
3. Remove the front cover.
4. Inspect the sprocket for chipped teeth and wear.
5. Inspect the timing chain for wear; if the chain can be pulled out more than 0.374 in. (9.5mm) from the damper, replace the chain.
6. Remove camshaft sprocket-to-camshaft bolts, the sprocket and the timing chain; if necessary, use a mallet to tap the sprocket from the camshaft.
7. Using a puller tool, press the crankshaft sprocket from the crankshaft.

To install:

8. Using an installation tool and a hammer, drive the crankshaft sprocket onto the crankshaft; make sure the timing mark faces outward.
9. Using Molykote or equivalent, lubricate the camshaft sprocket thrust surface and install the timing chain onto the sprocket.
10. While holding the camshaft sprocket and chain vertically, align the marks on the camshaft and crankshaft sprockets.
11. Align the camshaft dowel with the camshaft sprocket hole. Install the camshaft sprocket and torque the bolts to 17 ft. lbs. (23 Nm).
12. Lubricate the timing chain with engine oil.
13. Install the front cover and crankshaft pulley.
14. Connect the negative battery cable.
15. Start the engine, then, check and/or adjust the timing.

Timing Belt Front Cover

Removal and Installation

2.3L AND 2.6L ENGINES

1. Disconnect the negative battery cable.
2. Remove all accessory drive belts and the cooling fan assembly.
3. Remove the crankshaft pulley bolt and pulley.
4. Remove the upper timing belt cover.
5. Remove the lower timing belt cover.
6. To install, reverse the removal procedures.

Oil Seal Replacement

2.3L AND 2.6L ENGINES

1. Disconnect the negative battery cable. Remove the cranshaft pulley.
2. Remove the upper and lower timing belt covers.
3. Rotate the crankshaft to align the camshaft sprocket with the mark on the rear timing cover and the crankshaft sprocket keyway with the mark on the oil seal retainer cover.

NOTE: With the timing marks aligned, the engine is positioned on the TDC of the No. 4 cylinder's compression stroke.

4. Loosen the timing belt tensioner and relax the tension and remove the timing belt from the crankshaft sprocket.
5. Remove the crankshaft sprocket bolt, the sprocket, the key and deflector shield.
6. Using a small pry bar, pry the oil seal from the oil seal retainer.

To install:

7. Using a new oil seal, lubricate it with engine oil and tap it into the retainer with an oil seal installation tool.
8. Install the defelector, the key, the crankshaft sprocket and bolt.
9. With the crankshaft sprocket aligned with the timing mark, install the timing belt.

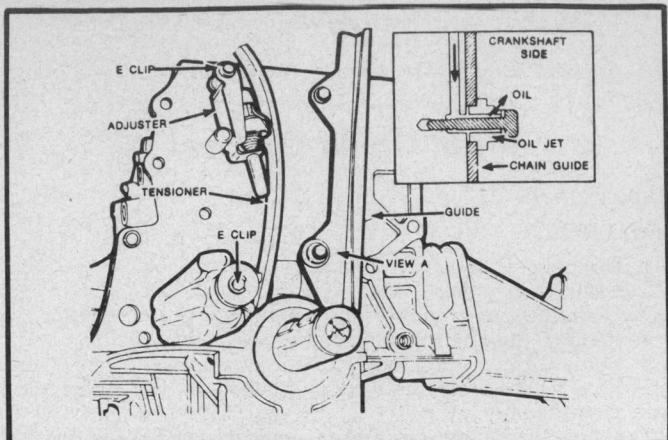

View of the timing chain adjuster—2.0L engine

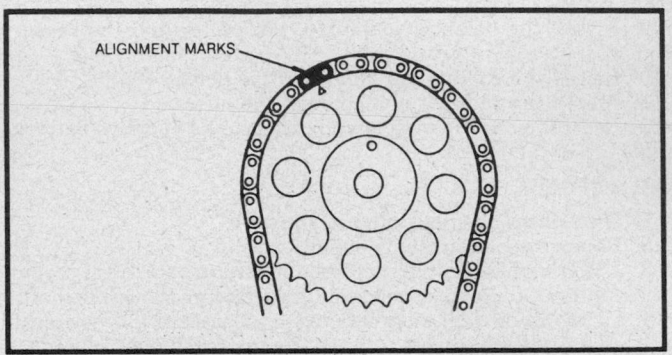

Aligning the timing chain with the camshaft sprocket—2.0L engine

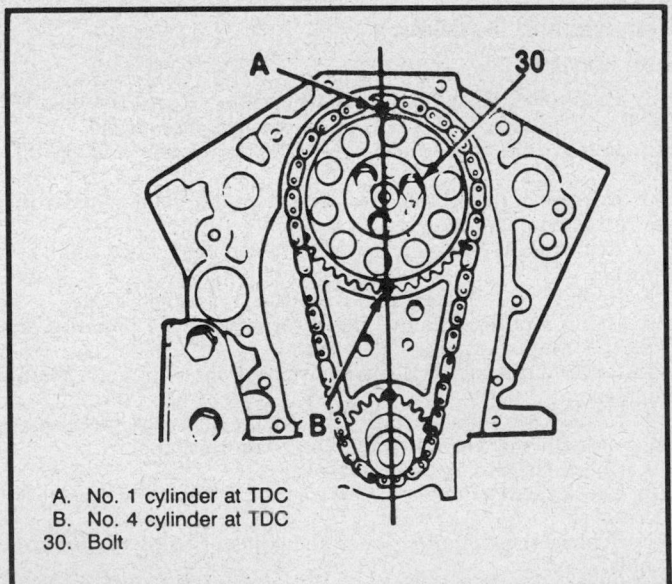

A. No. 1 cylinder at TDC
B. No. 4 cylinder at TDC
30. Bolt

View of the timing chain alignment marks—2.8L engine

10. Apply the tensioner pulley spring pressure to the timing belt.

11. Rotate the crankshaft 2 complete revolutions in the opposite direction of rotation and realign the timing marks.

12. Loosen the tensioner pulley bolt to allow the spring to adjust the correct tension. Torque the tensioner pulley bolt to 14 ft. lbs.

13. Install the timing covers and the crankshaft pulley.

14. To complete the installation, reverse the removal procedures.

Timing Belt and Tensioner

Adjustment

2.3L AND 2.6L ENGINES

1. Disconnect the negative battery cable. Remove the cranshaft pulley.

2. Remove the upper and lower timing belt covers.

3. Loosen the timing belt tensioner and relax the belt tension.

4. Apply the tensioner pulley spring pressure to the timing belt.

5. Rotate the crankshaft 2 complete revolutions in the opposite direction of rotation and realign the timing marks.

6. Loosen the tensioner pulley bolt to allow the spring to adjust the correct tension. Torque the tensioner pulley bolt to 14 ft. lbs.

7. Install the timing covers and the crankshaft pulley.

8. To complete the installation, reverse the removal procedures.

Removal and Installation

2.3L AND 2.6L ENGINES

1. Disconnect the negative battery cable. Remove the cranshaft pulley.

2. Remove the upper and lower timing belt covers.

3. Rotate the crankshaft to align the camshaft sprocket with the mark on the rear timing cover and the crankshaft sprocket keyway with the mark on the oil seal retainer cover.

NOTE: With the timing marks aligned, the engine is positioned on the TDC of the No. 4 cylinder's compression stroke.

4. Loosen the timing belt tensioner and relax the tension and remove the timing belt from the crankshaft sprocket.

To install:

5. With the crankshaft and the camshaft sprockets aligned with the timing marks, install the timing belt. Install the timing belt using the following sequence: the crankshaft sprocket, the oil pump sprocket and the camshaft sprocket.

6. Apply the tensioner pulley spring pressure to the timing belt.

7. Rotate the crankshaft 2 complete revolutions in the opposite direction of rotation and realign the timing marks.

8. Loosen the tensioner pulley bolt to allow the spring to adjust the correct tension. Torque the tensioner pulley bolt to 14 ft. lbs.

9. Install the timing covers and the crankshaft pulley.

10. To complete the installation, reverse the removal procedures.

Timing Sprockets

Removal and Installation

2.3L AND 2.6L ENGINES

Camshaft Sprocket

1. Disconnect the negative battery cable.

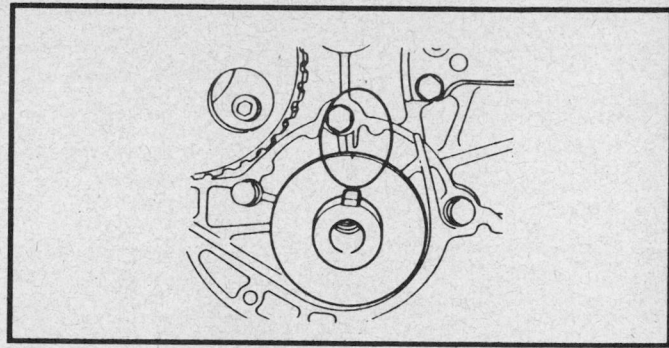

View of the crankshaft sprocket alignment mark—2.3L and 2.6L engines

2. Remove the timing belt.

3. Remove the camshaft sprocket-to-camshaft bolt and the sprocket.

NOTE: It may be necessary to use a mallet to tap the sprocket from the camshaft.

4. Remove and replace the camshaft oil seal.

To install:

5. Align the camshaft sprocket-to-rear plate timing marks. With the crankshaft sprocket aligned with the timing mark, install the timing belt.

6. Apply the tensioner pulley spring pressure to the timing belt.

7. Rotate the crankshaft 2 complete revolutions in the opposite direction of rotation and realign the timing marks.

8. Loosen the tensioner pulley bolt to allow the spring to adjust the correct tension. Torque the tensioner pulley bolt to 14 ft. lbs.

9. Install the timing covers and the crankshaft pulley.

10. To complete the installation, reverse the removal procedures.

Crankshaft Sprocket

1. Disconnect the negative battery cable.

2. Remove the timing belt.

3. Remove the crankshaft sprocket-to-crankshaft bolt. Using a puller, press the sprocket from the crankshaft.

4. Remove and replace the crankshaft oil seal.

To install:

5. Align the crankshaft sprocket-to-oil seal retainer plate timing marks.

6. With the camshaft sprocket aligned with its timing mark, install the timing belt.

7. Apply the tensioner pulley spring pressure to the timing belt.

8. Rotate the crankshaft 2 complete revolutions in the opposite direction of rotation and realign the timing marks.

9. Loosen the tensioner pulley bolt to allow the spring to adjust the correct tension. Torque the tensioner pulley bolt to 14 ft. lbs.

10. Install the timing covers and the crankshaft pulley.

11. To complete the installation, reverse the removal procedures.

Camshaft

Removal and Installation

2.0L ENGINE

1. Disconnect the negative battery cable.

2. Remove the rocker arm cover.

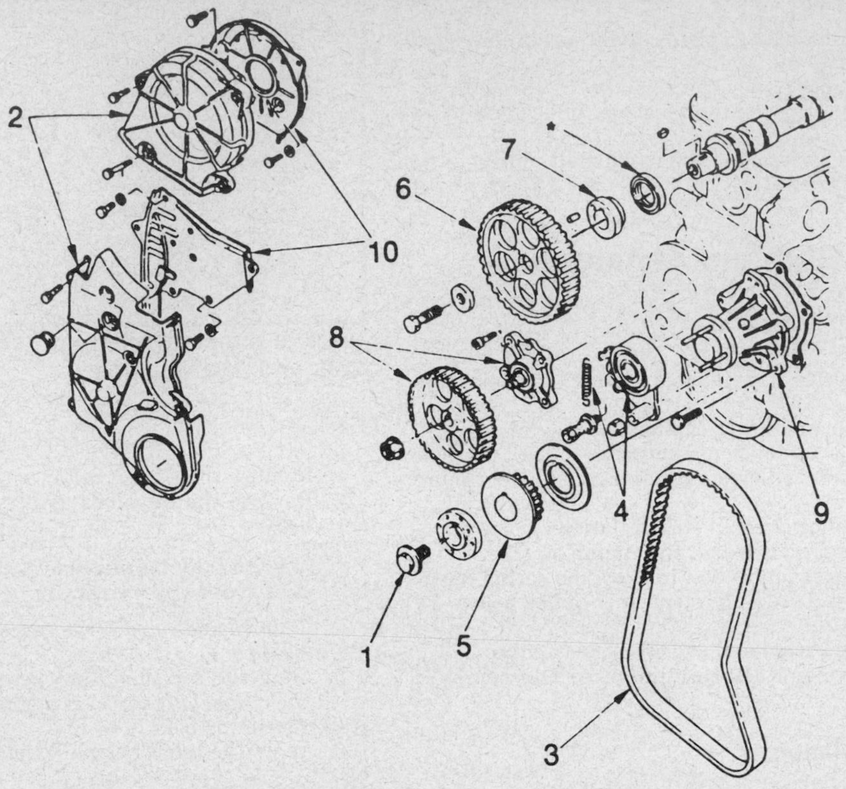

1. Crankshaft pulley bolt
2. Timing belt cover
3. Timing belt
4. Tensioner pulley and spring
5. Crankshaft timing sprocket
6. Camshaft timing sprocket
7. Camshaft boss
8. Oil pump and pulley
9. Water pump
10. Rear timing belt covers

Exploded view of the timing belt assembly—2.3L and 2.6L engines

3. Rotate the engine until the No. 4 cylinder is at TDC (top dead center) on the compression stroke. Remove the distributor cap and mark the rotor to housing position.

4. Release the tension on the automatic timing chain adjuster by performing the following procedures:

a. Using a small pry bar, depress the lock lever on the automatic adjuster rearward.

b. Push on the automatic adjuster shoe and lock it into the retracted position by releasing the lever.

5. Remove the camshaft sprocket-to-camshaft bolt, the sprocket and suspend the assembly on the wire; allow the chain to remain on the sprocket.

6. Remove the rocker arm brackets-to-cylinder head bolts and the rocker arm bracket assembly from the cylinder head.

7. Remove the camshaft from the cylinder head.

To install:

8. Lubricate the camshaft with engine oil and install it onto the cylinder head.

9. Install the rocker arm assembly onto the cylinder head and torque the bolts to 16 ft. lbs.

10. Align the camshaft sprocket hole with camshaft dowel pin and install the sprocket. Torque the camshaft sprocket-to-camshaft bolt to 50–65 ft. lbs.

11. Set the automatic adjuster by turning the adjuster slide pin 90 degrees counter-clockwise with a small pry bar.

12. Adjust the valve lash.

13. Install the rocker arm cover and make sure the alignment marks are aligned.

14. To complete the installation, reverse the removal procedures. Start the engine and check and/or adjust the timing.

2.3L AND 2.6L ENGINES

1. Disconnect the negative battery cable.

2. Rotate the crankshaft to position the No. 4 cylinder on the TDC of its compression stroke.

3. Remove the distributor cap and move it aside. Matchmark the rotor to the distributor housing and the distributor housing to the engine. Remove the distributor.

4. Remove the rocker arm cover, the timing belt cover and the timing belt.

5. Remove the rocker arm assembly-to-cylinder head bolts,

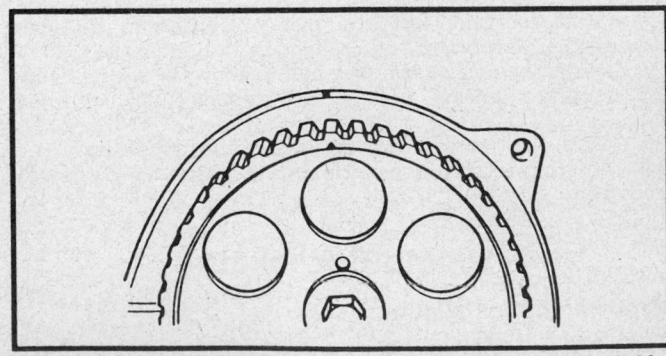

View of the camshaft sprocket alignment mark—2.3L and 2.6L engines

the rocker arm assembly and the camshaft. If necessary, remove the camshaft sprocket-to-camshaft bolt and the sprocket.

To install:

6. Lubricate the camshaft with engine oil and position it onto the cylinder head.

7. Install the rocker arm assembly and torque the bolts to bolts to 6 ft. lbs. (8 Nm) and the nuts to 16 ft. lbs. (22 Nm).

8. Align the timing marks and install the timing belt.

9. Using a new gasket, install the rocker arm cover.

10. Install the timing belt cover.

11. Align the matchmarks and install the distributor to the cylinder head.

12. To complete the installation, reverse the removal procedures.

13. With the timing marks aligned, start the engine, then, check and/or adjust the engine timing.

2.8L ENGINE

1. Relieve the fuel pressure. Disconnect the negative battery cable.

2. Remove the timing cover and the camshaft sprocket.

3. Remove the upper fan shroud and the radiator.

4. Disconnect the fuel line(s), the accelerator linkage, the vacuum hoses and electrical connectors from the throttle body unit.

5. Remove the rocker arm covers.

6. Loosen the valves, rotate them 90 degrees and remove the pushrods; be sure to keep them aligned so they may be installed in their original positions.

7. Remove the intake manifold.

8. Using a hydraulic lifter removal tool, pull the valve lifters from the engine.

9. Using 3 long bolts, thread them into the camshaft holes. Grasp the bolts and carefully, pull the camshaft from the front of the engine.

NOTE: All the camshaft bearing journals are the same diameter; exercise care in removing the camshaft so the bearings do not become damaged.

10. Lubricate the camshaft with engine oil and install it into the engine.

11. Using a hydraulic lifter installation tool, install the hydraulic lifters into the engine.

12. Using new gaskets and sealant, install the intake manifold.

13. Install the pushrods and the rocker arms.

14. Install the camshaft sprocket, the timing chain and the front cover; be sure the timing marks are aligned.

15. Adjust the valves.

16. Using new gaskets, install the rocker arm covers.

17. To complete the installation, reverse the removal procedures. Refill the cooling system.

18. Start the engine and allow it to reach normal operating temperatures. Check and/or adjust the timing.

Piston and Connecting Rod

Positioning

DIESEL ENGINE MECHANICAL

NOTE: Disconnecting the negative battery cable on some vehicles may interfere with the functions of the on board computer systems and may require the computer to undergo a relearning process, once the negative battery cable is reconnected.

Engine

Removal and Installation

2WD VEHICLES

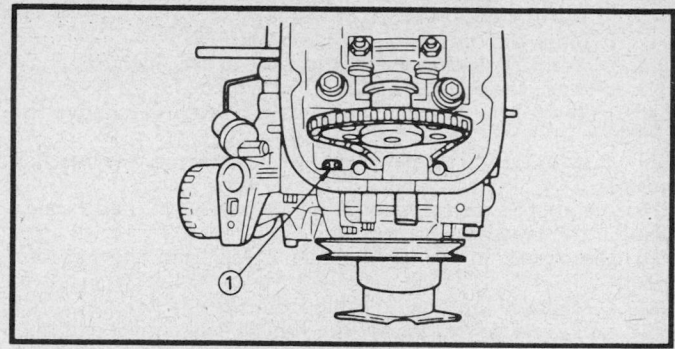

Location of the automatic chain adjuster—2.0L engine

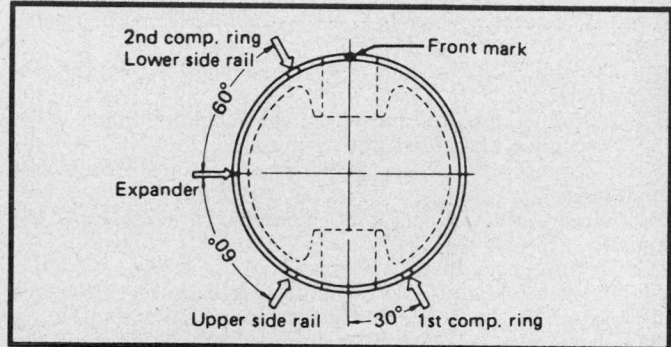

Positioning of the piston and compression rings— 2.0L, 2.3L and 2.6L engines

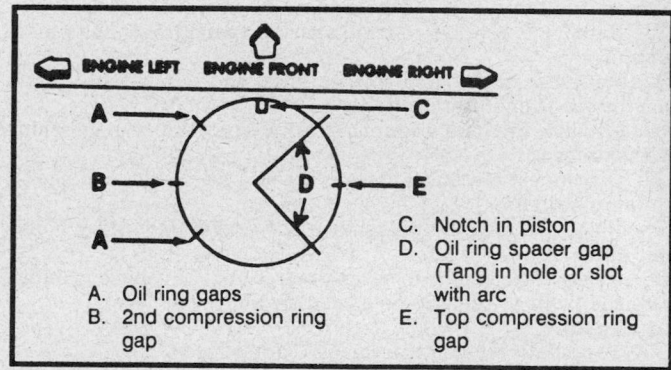

Positioning of the piston and compression rings— 2.8L engine

1. Matchmark hinges to the hood and remove the hood.

2. Disconnect the battery cables, negative first and remove the battery from the vehicle.

3. Drain the cooling system.

4. Remove the air cleaner assembly as follows: Remove the intake silencer. Remove the bolts mounting the air cleaner and loosen the clamp bolt. Lift the air cleaner slightly and disconnect the breather hose. Remove the air cleaner assembly.

5. Disconnect the upper radiator hose at the engine.

6. Loosen the air conditioning compressor drive belts by mov-

ing the power steering pump or idler.

7. Remove the cooling fan and fan shroud.

8. Disconnect the lower radiator hose at the engine.

9. Remove the radiator grille.

10. Remove the radiator attaching bolts and remove the radiator.

11. Disconnect the accelerator control cable from the injection pump.

12. If equipped with air conditioning, disconnect the air conditioning compressor control cable.

13. Disconnect and plug the fuel hoses from the injection pump.

14. Disconnect the ground cable from the engine.

15. Raise and safely support the vehicle. Disconnect and label the transmission wiring. Drain the engne oil.

16. Disconnect the vacuum hose from the fast idle actuator.

17. Disconnect the fuel cut solenoid wiring.

18. Disconnect the air conditioning compressor wiring, sensing resistor and thermoswitch connectors.

19. Disconnect the heater hoses extending from the heater unit from the dash panel side.

20. Disconnect the hose for power brake booster from the vacuum pump.

21. Disconnect vacuum hose from the vacuum pump.

22. Disconnect the alternator wiring.

23. Disconnect the exhaust pipe from the exhaust manifold at the flange.

24. Remove the exhaust pipe mounting bracket from the engine.

25. Disconnect and label the starter motor wiring.

26. Pull the gearshift lever boot upwards on the lever. Remove the 2 gearshift lever bolts and the lever.

27. Disconnect speedometer and ground cables from the transmission.

28. Matchmark and remove the driveshaft.

29. Remove the clutch fork return spring from the clutch fork.

30. Disconnect clutch cable from the hooked portion of clutch fork and pull it out forward through the stiffener bracket.

31. Remove 2 bracket-to-transmission rear mount bolts and nuts.

32. Raise the engine and transmission and remove the crossmember-to-frame bracket bolts.

33. Remove the rear mounting nuts from the transmission rear extension.

34. Disconnect electrical connectors at CRS switch and backup lamp switch.

35. Raise the engine and remove the engine mounting bolts and nuts.

36. Remove the engine towards the front of the vehicle making sure the front of the engine is slightly above the level.

To install:

37. To install, reverse the removal procedures.

38. Refill the cooling system and the crankcase with engine oil. Check and adjust the clutch pedal freeplay.

38. Adjust the fan belt tension. Start the engine, run at idle and check for leakage. Adjust the ignition timing and engine idle speed.

4WD VEHICLES

1. Matchmark the hinges to the hood and remove the hood.

2. Disconnect the battery cables, negative first and remove the battery from the vehicle.

3. Drain the cooling system and remove the upper and lower radiator hoses.

4. Remove the intake silencer. Remove the air cleaner mounting bolts and loosen the clamp bolt. Lift the air cleaner slightly and disconnect the breather hose. Remove the air cleaner assembly.

5. Loosen the air conditioning compressor drive belts by moving the power steering pump or idler.

6. Remove the cooling fan and fan shroud.

7. Remove the radiator grille, the radiator bolts and the radiator.

8. Disconnect the accelerator control cable from the injection pump side.

9. If equipped with air conditioning, disconnect the air conditioner compressor control cable.

10. Disconnect and plug the fuel hose from the injection pump.

11. Disconnect the ground cable from the cylinder body.

12. Disconnect the transmission wiring.

13. Disconnect the vacuum hose from the fast idle actuator.

14. Disconnect the fuel cut solenoid wiring.

15. Disconnect the air conditioning compressor switch wiring, sensing resistor and the thermoswitch connectors.

16. Disconnect the heater hoses from the heater unit from the dash.

17. Disconnect the vacuum hoses from the vacuum pump.

18. Disconnect and label the alternator wiring.

19. Raise and safely support the vehicle. Drain the engine oil.

20. Disconnect the exhaust pipe from the exhaust manifold at the flange.

21. Remove the exhaust pipe mounting bracket from the engine back plate.

22. Disconnect and label the starter motor wiring. Remove the starter motor.

23. Pull the transmission/transfer case gearshift lever boots upward on each lever. Remove the gearshift lever bolts.

24. Remove return spring from transfer gear shift lever and the levers.

25. Remove the transmission/transfer case assembly.

26. Raise the engine slightly and remove the engine mounting bolts and nuts.

27. To remove the engine, check to make certain all the parts have been removed or disconnected frame the engine that are fastened to the frame side. Remove the engine toward front of the vehicle with the front part of the engine raised slightly above the level.

To install:

28. To install, reverse the removal procedures.

29. Refill the cooling system and the crankcase with engine oil. Check and adjust the clutch pedal freeplay.

30. Adjust the fan belt tension. Start the engine, run at idle and check for leakage.

31. Adjust the ignition timing and idle speed.

Cylinder Head

Removal and Installation

1. Relieve the fuel pressure. Disconnect the negative battery cable. Drain the cooling system.

2. Remove the cooling fan assembly and the drive belt. Remove the alternator and bracket.

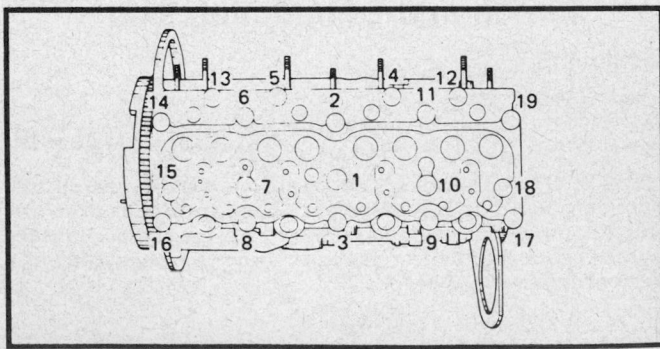

View of the cylinder head bolt torque sequence—2.2L diesel engine

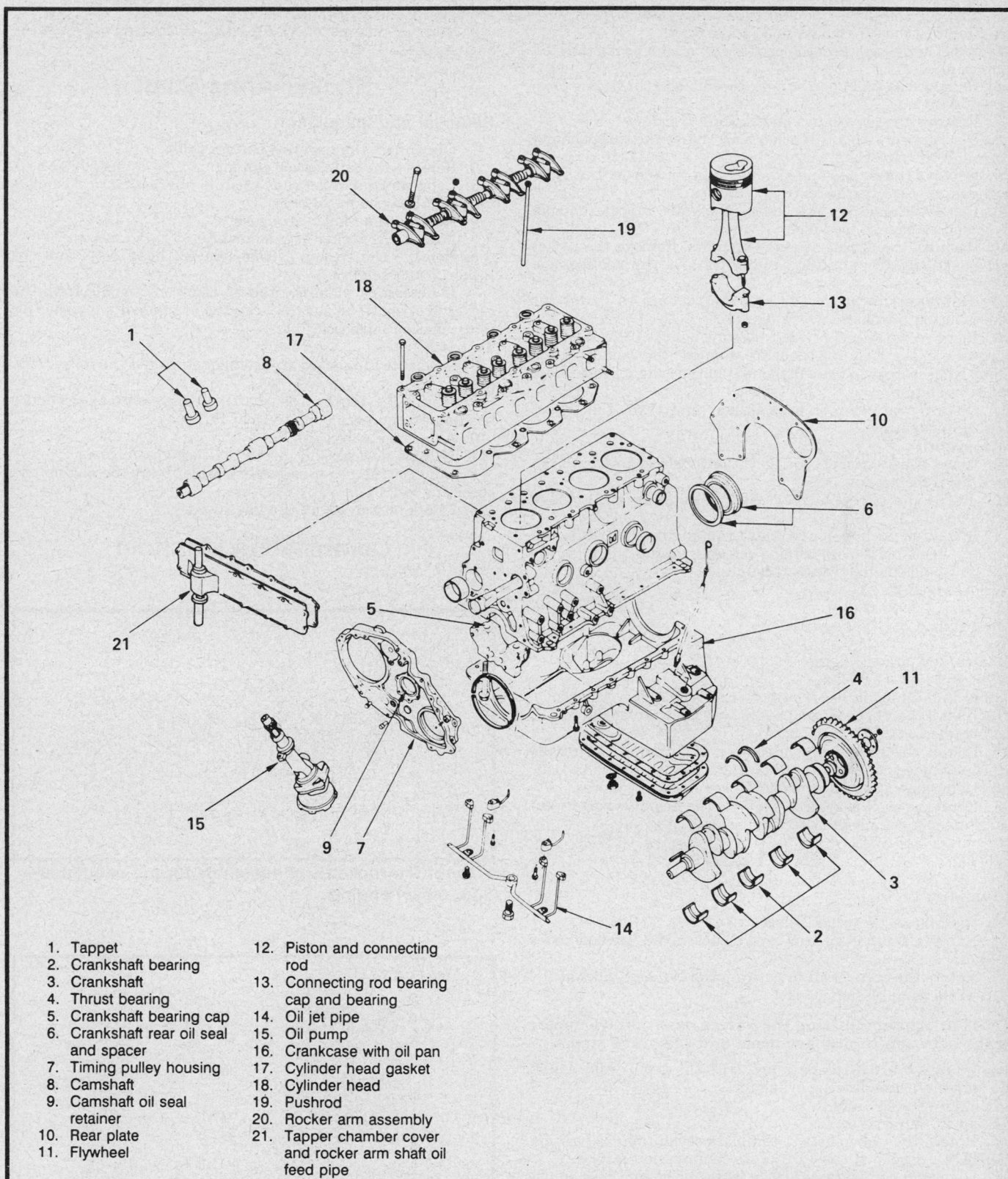

1. Tappet
2. Crankshaft bearing
3. Crankshaft
4. Thrust bearing
5. Crankshaft bearing cap
6. Crankshaft rear oil seal and spacer
7. Timing pulley housing
8. Camshaft
9. Camshaft oil seal retainer
10. Rear plate
11. Flywheel
12. Piston and connecting rod
13. Connecting rod bearing cap and bearing
14. Oil jet pipe
15. Oil pump
16. Crankcase with oil pan
17. Cylinder head gasket
18. Cylinder head
19. Pushrod
20. Rocker arm assembly
21. Tapper chamber cover and rocker arm shaft oil feed pipe

Exploded view of the engine components — 2.2L diesel engine

3. Remove the upper radiator hose and heater hose(s).
4. Remove the air cleaner and intake duct.
5. Label and disconnect the necessary vacuum hoses and electrical connectors.
6. Remove the fuel injector pipe, the clip and the nozzle holder assembly.
7. Remove the glow plugs and sensing resister.
8. If equipped with a turbocharger, remove the turbocharger cover and the turbocharger.
9. Remove the intake and exhaust manifolds from the cylinder head; discard the gaskets.
10. Remove the rocker arm cover, the valve tappet chamber cover and rocker oil feed pipe.
11. Back off the rocker arm adjustments. Remove the rocker arm assembly-to-cylinder head bolts and the rocker arm assembly.
12. Remove the pushrods and keep them in order for reinstallation purposes.
13. Remove the cylinder head-to-engine bolts, a little at a time, by reversing the torquing sequence. Remove the cylinder head; it may be necessary to use a mallet to tap the cylinder head loose from the engine.
14. Discard the cylinder head gasket and clean the gasket mounting surfaces.
To install:
15. Using a new gasket, position it onto the engine with the work **TOP** facing upwards.
16. Refill the turbocharger with clean engine oil before installation.
17. Install the cylinder head onto the engine. Lubricate the cylinder head bolts with engine oil and torque them, in sequence, using the following procedure:
Turbocharged Engine
1st step: 33–40 ft. lbs.
2nd step: 120–150 degrees

Non-turbocharged Engine
1st step: 40–47 ft. lbs.
2nd step: 54–61 ft. lbs. (new bolt) or 61–69 ft. lbs. (used bolt)
18. Install the pushrods and make sure they are positioned in the tappets.
19. Install the rocker arm assembly and torque the rocker arm-to-cylinder head bolts to 9–17 ft. lbs. Adjust the valve lash.
20. Using new gaskets, reverse the removal procedures.
21. Refill the cooling system. Connect the negative battery cable. Start the engine and check for leaks.

Valve Lash

Adjustment

1. Disconnect the negative battery cable.
2. Remove the rocker arm cover. Loosen the valve adjuster locknuts.
3. Rotate the crankshaft to position the No. 1 cylinder at the TDC of its compression stroke.

NOTE: When adjusting the valves, position the feeler gauge between the rocker arms and the valve stems.

4. Using a 0.016 in. feeler gauge, with the engine cold, adjust the valves of the following cylinders:
Instake valves: 1 and 2
Exhaust valves: 1 and 3
5. Rotate the crankshaft, 1 complete revolution, to position the No. 4 cylinder at the TDC of its compression stroke.
6. Using a 0.016 in. feeler gauge, with the engine cold, adjust the valves of the following cylinders:
Instake valves: 3 and 4
Exhaust valves: 2 and 4
7. Tighten the valve adjustment locknuts.
8. Using a new gasket, install the rocker arm cover. Connect

the negative battery cable.
9. Start the engine, check for leaks. Check and/or adjust the engine speed.

Rocker Arms/Shaft

Removal and Installation

1. Disconnect the negative battery cable.
2. Remove the air cleaner and air duct, if equipped.
3. Label and disconnect any vacuum line or electrical connector which may be in the way.
4. Remove the rocker arm cover.
5. Loosen the rocker arm adjusters.
6. Remove the rocker arm-to-cylinder head bolts and the rocker arm assembly.
7. If necessary, slide the rocker arm components from the rocker arm shaft; be sure to keep the components in order for reinstallation purposes.
To install:
8. Assemble the rocker arm components onto the rocker arm shaft.
9. Install the rocker arm shaft assembly onto the cylinder head and torque the bolts to 9–17 ft. lbs.
10. Adjust the valve lash.
11. Using a new gasket, install the rocker arm cover.
12. Connect the negative battery cable. Start the engine and check for leaks.
13. Check and/or adjust the idle speed.

Combination Manifold

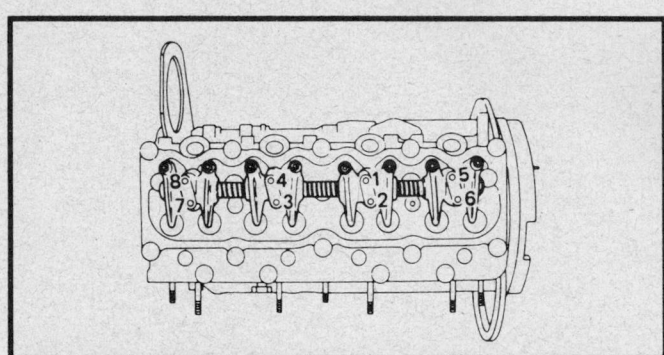

View of the rocker arm assembly torque sequence— 2.2L diesel engine

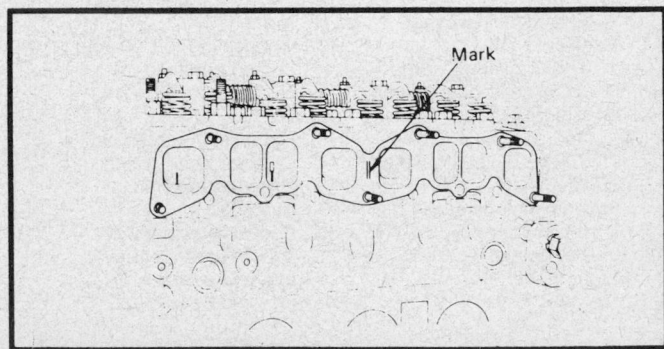

Positioning the intake/exhaust manifold gasket—2.2L diesel engine

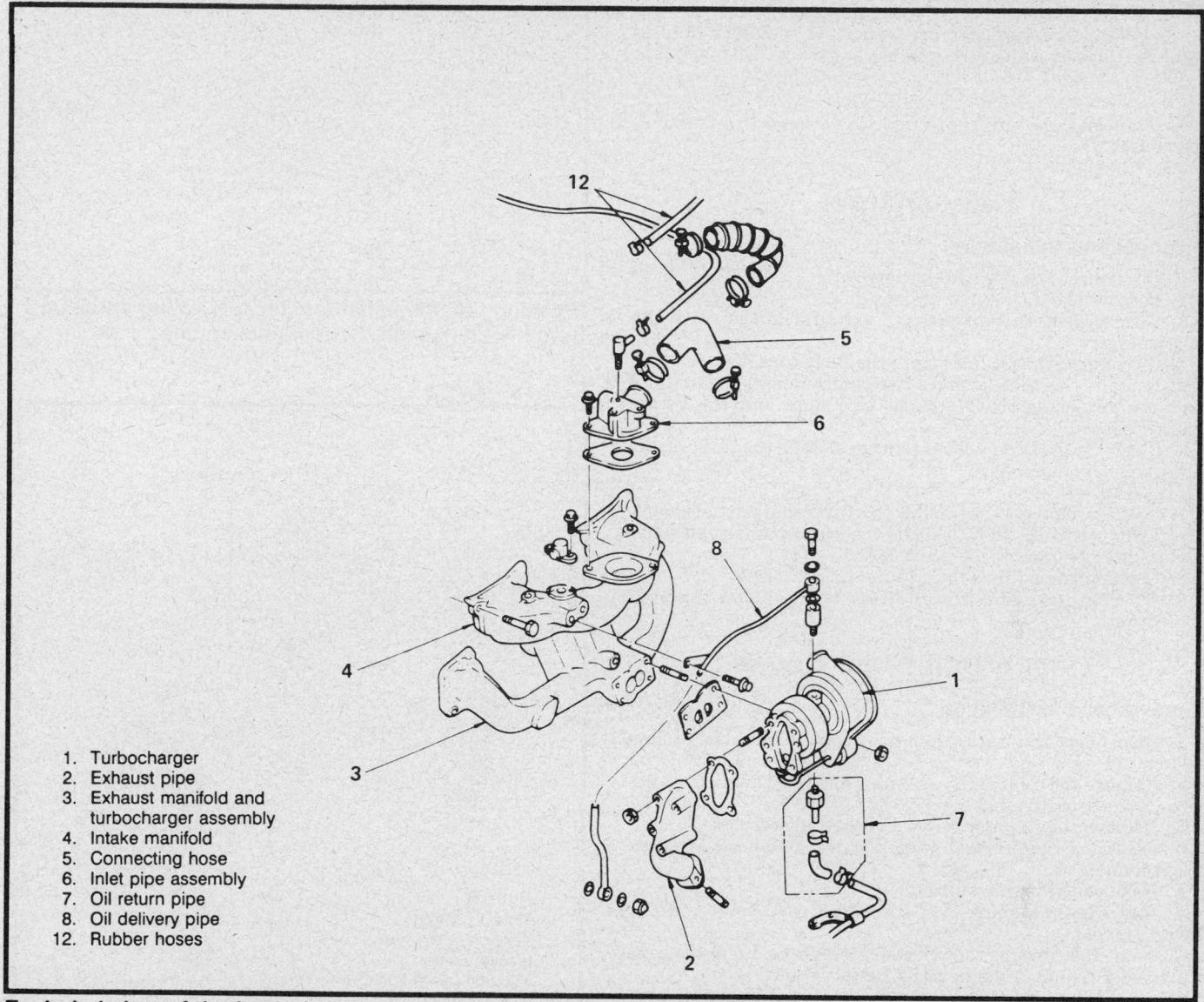

1. Turbocharger
2. Exhaust pipe
3. Exhaust manifold and turbocharger assembly
4. Intake manifold
5. Connecting hose
6. Inlet pipe assembly
7. Oil return pipe
8. Oil delivery pipe
12. Rubber hoses

Exploded view of the intake/exhaust manifold and turbocharger assembly – 2.2L diesel engine – non-turbocharger manifold is similar

Although the intake and exhaust manifolds are individual parts, they must be remove at the same time so the 1-piece gasket may be replaced.

Removal and Installation

1. Disconnect the negative battery cable.
2. Remove the air cleaner and air duct, if necessary.
3. Disconnect the accelerator cable from the throttle body.
4. Label and disconnect the necessary vacuum hoses and electrical connectors.
5. If not equipped with a turbocharger, disconnect the exhaust manifold from the exhaust pipe.
6. If equipped with a turbocharger, perform the following procedures:
  a. Disconnect the intake and exhaust hoses from the turbocharger.
  b. Disconnect the oil lines from the turbocharger.

  c. Remove the turbocharger-to-exhaust manifold nuts, the turbocharger assembly-to-exhaust pipe nuts and the turbocharger assembly.
7. Remove the intake manifold-to-cylinder head bolts and the intake manifold.
8. Remove the exhaust manifold-to-cylinder head bolts, the exhaust manifold and discard the gasket.
9. Clean the gasket mounting surfaces.
To install:
10. Using a new gasket, install it onto the cylinder head with the center mark facing outward and upward.
11. Install the exhaust and intake manifolds onto the cylinder head and torque the nuts/bolts to 10–17 ft. lbs. (non-turbocharged engine) or 13–17 ft. lbs. (turbocharged engine).
12. If not equipped with a turbocharger, install the exhaust manifold to the exhaust pipe.
13. If equipped with a turbocharger, perform the following procedures:

a. Refill the turbocharger with clean engine oil.

b. Install the turbocharger-to-exhaust manifold nuts to 16–23 ft. lbs. and the turbocharger assembly-to-exhaust pipe nuts to 16–23 ft. lbs.

c. Connect the oil feed lines to the turbocharger.

14. To complete the installation, reverse the removal procedures.

Turbocharger

Removal and Installation

1. Disconnect the negative battery cable.
2. Remove the air cleaner and air duct.
3. Disconnect the intake and exhaust hoses from the turbocharger.
4. Disconnect the oil lines from the turbocharger.
5. Remove the turbocharger-to-exhaust manifold nuts, the turbocharger assembly-to-exhaust pipe nuts and the turbocharger assembly.
6. Clean the gasket mounting surfaces. Refill the turbocharger with clean engine oil.

To install:

7. Using a new gasket, install the turbocharger-to-exhaust manifold nuts to 16–23 ft. lbs. and the turbocharger assembly-to-exhaust pipe nuts to 16–23 ft. lbs.
8. Connect the oil feed lines to the turbocharger.
9. To complete the installation, reverse the removal procedures.

Timing Belt Front Cover

Removal and Installation

1. Disconnect the negative battery cable. Drain the cooling system.
2. Remove the cooling fan assembly and the drive belt(s). Remove the alternator and bracket.
3. Remove the radiator hoses and the radiator.
4. Label and disconnect the necessary vacuum hoses and electrical connectors.
5. Remove the crankshaft pulley.
6. Remove the timing belt cover-to-engine bolts and the cover.
7. To install, reverse the removal procedures. Refill the cooling system. Connect the negative battery cable.
8. Start the engine, allow it to reach normal operating temperatures and check for leaks.

Oil Seal Replacement

1. Disconnect the negative battery terminal. Drain the cooling system.
2. Remove the timing belt.
3. Remove the crankshaft sprocket bolt.

NOTE: To remove the crankshaft sprocket bolt, it may be necessary to remove the starter or the flywheel cover plate to lock the flywheel; otherwise, it may be difficult to keep the crankshaft from turning.

4. Using a puller tool press the crankshaft center and timing sprocket from the crankshaft.
5. Remove the oil seal retainer-to-rear timing cover bolts and the retainer.
6. Using a small pry bar, pry the oil seal from engine housing; be careful not to damage the crankshaft or the oil seal mounting surface.

To install:

7. Using a new oil seal, lubricate the seal lips with engine oil and install it into the engine using a seal installation tool.
8. Install the oil seal retainer.

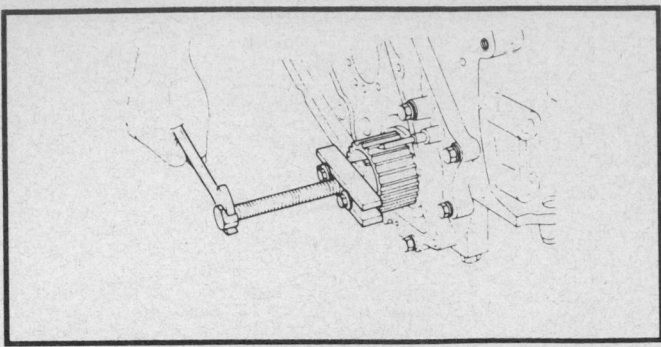

Pressing the crankshaft center and timing sprocket from the crankshaft—2.2L diesel engine

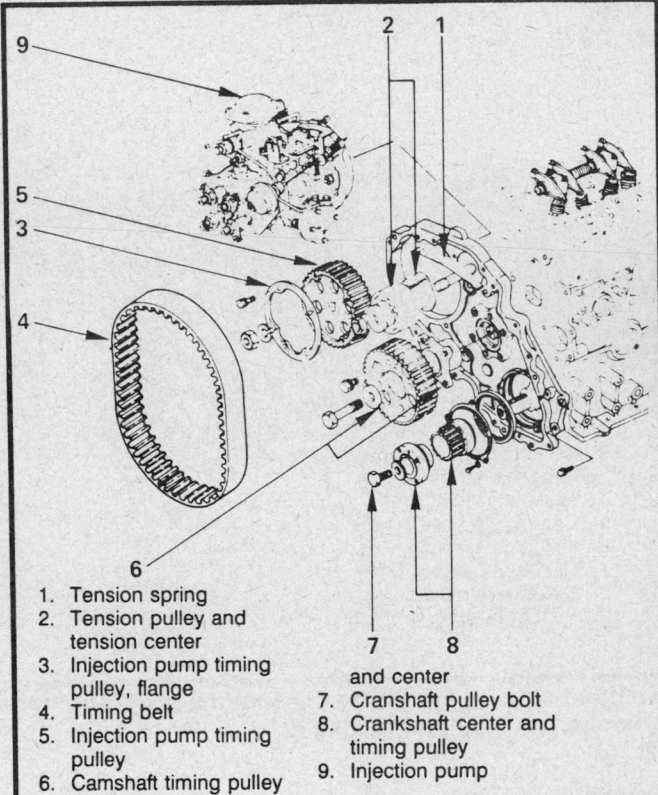

1. Tension spring
2. Tension pulley and tension center
3. Injection pump timing pulley, flange
4. Timing belt
5. Injection pump timing pulley
6. Camshaft timing pulley
   and center
7. Cranshaft pulley bolt
8. Crankshaft center and timing pulley
9. Injection pump

Exploded view of the timing belt assembly—2.2L diesel engine

9. Install the crankshaft center and timing sprocket to the crankshaft.
10. Install the timing belt.
11. To complete the installation, reverse the removal procedures.
12. Refill the cooling system. Start the engine, check and/or adjust the timing and check for leaks.

Timing Belt and Tensioner

Adjustment

1. Disconnect the negative battery cable. Drain the cooling system.

2. Remove the timing belt cover and temporarily install the crankshaft pulley.

3. Rotate the crankshaft until the No. 1 cylinder is at the TDC of its compression stroke; make sure the alignment mark on the crankshaft pulley is aligned with timing indicator. Make sure the timing marks on the camshaft sprocket and the injection pump sprocket are facing each other at their closest point.

NOTE: Any timing belt slack will be absorbed between the injection pump sprocket and camshaft sprocket.

4. Adjust the timing belt tensioner pulley so the end of the tension center is fitted against the 2 pins on the timing pulley housing; hand tighten the nut, so the tension pulley can be rotated freely.

5. Make sure the tension spring is installed correctly. Torque the tension pulley nut to 22–36 ft. lbs.

6. Rotate the crankshaft 2 complete revolutions in the clockwise direction. Further, turn the crankshaft 90 degrees beyond TDC to settle the injection pump.

7. Loosen the tension pulley nut to allow the timing belt slackness to be taken up, then, tighten the tension pulley nut to 79–94 ft. lbs.

NOTE: Never attempt to rotate the crankshaft counterclockwise.

8. Using a belt tension gauge, measure the belt tension between the injection pump sprocket and the crankshaft sprocket; it should be 33–55 lbs.

9. To complete the installation, reverse the removal procedures.

Removal and Installation

1. Disconnect the negative battery cable. Drain the cooling system.

2. Remove the timing belt cover. Remove the injection pump sprocket flange.

3. Using a pry bar, remove the tension spring from the timing belt tensioner.

NOTE: When removing the tension spring, avoid using excessive force for the spring may become distorted.

4. Remove the tensioner pulley bolt and the pulley.

5. Remove the timing belt and discard it.

To install:

6. Rotate the crankshaft to bring the No. 1 piston to TDC of the compression stroke.

7. Align the timing marks on the injection pump sprocket with the camshaft sprocket; the marks must be facing each other.

8. Using a new timing belt, install it in the following sequence: crankshaft sprocket, camshaft sprocket and the injection pump sprocket; the slack must be between the injection pump and camshaft sprockets.

9. Install the tension center and the tension pulley so the end of the tension center is fitted against both pins on the timing pulley housing.

10. Hand tighten the nut so the tension pulley can be rotated freely.

11. Install the tension spring and semi-tighten the pully nut to 22–36 ft. lbs.

12. Rotate the crankshaft 2 full turns clockwise to seat the belt and further turn the cranshaft 90 degrees beyond TDC to settle the injection pump.

13. Loosen the tension pulley nut to take up the timing belt slack. Tighten the tension pulley nut to 79–94 ft. lbs.

14. Install the injection pump sprocket flange; the hole in the outer circumference of the flange should be aligned with the triangular timing mark on the injection pump sprocket.

15. Rotate the crankshaft 2 full turns clockwise to bring the No. 1 piston to TDC of the compression stroke. Make sure the triangular timing mark on the timing sprocket is aligned with the hole in the flange, then, measure the timing belt tension; it should be 33–55 lbs.

16. Install the timing belt cover.

17. To complete the installation, reverse the removal procedures.

18. Connect the negative battery cable.

Timing Sprockets

Removal and Installation

INJECTION PUMP SPROCKET

1. Disconnect the negative battery cable. Drain the cooling system.

2. Remove the timing belt cover. Remove the injection pump sprocket flange.

3. Using a pry bar, remove the tension spring from the timing belt tensioner.

NOTE: When removing the tension spring, avoid using excessive force for the spring may become distorted.

4. Remove the tensioner pulley bolt and the pulley.

5. Remove the timing belt and discard it.

6. Using a 6mm, 1.25 pitch bolt, install the threaded portion into the threaded hole in the timing sprocket housing through the hole in the sprocket to prevent the sprocket from turning.

7. Remove the injection pump sprocket-to-shaft bolts.

8. Using a wheel puller, connect it to the injection pump sprocket and press it from the shaft.

To install:

9. Install the injection pump sprocket by aligning it with the key groove and torque the bolt to 42–52 ft. lbs.

10. Rotate the crankshaft to bring the No. 1 piston to TDC of the compression stroke.

11. Align the timing marks on the injection pump sprocket with the camshaft sprocket; the marks must be facing each other.

12. Using a new timing belt, install it in the following sequence: crankshaft sprocket, camshaft sprocket and the injection pump sprocket; the slack must be between the injection pump and camshaft sprockets.

13. Install the tension center and the tension pulley so the end of the tension center is fitted against both pins on the timing pulley housing.

14. Hand tighten the nut so the tension pulley can be rotated freely.

15. Install the tension spring and semi-tighten the pulley nut to 22–36 ft. lbs.

16. Rotate the crankshaft 2 full turns clockwise to seat the belt and further turn the crankshaft 90 degrees beyond TDC to settle the injection pump.

17. Loosen the tension pulley nut to take up the timing belt slack. Tighten the tension pulley nut to 79–94 ft. lbs.

18. Install the injection pump sprocket flange; the hole in the outer circumference of the flange should be aligned with the triangular timing mark on the injection pump sprocket.

19. Rotate the crankshaft 2 full turns clockwise to bring the No. 1 piston to TDC of the compression stroke. Make sure the triangular timing mark on the timing sprocket is aligned with the hole in the flange, then, measure the timing belt tension; it should be 33–55 lbs.

20. Install the timing belt cover.

21. To complete the installation, reverse the removal procedures.

22. Connect the negative battery cable. Refill the cooling system.

CAMSHAFT SPROCKET

1. Disconnect the negative battery cable.
2. Remove the timing belt cover. Remove the injection pump sprocket flange.
3. Using a pry bar, remove the tension spring from the timing belt tensioner.

NOTE: When removing the tension spring, avoid using excessive force for the spring may become distorted.

4. Remove the tensioner pulley bolt and the pulley.
5. Remove the timing belt and discard it.
6. Using a 6mm, 1.25 pitch bolt, install the threaded portion into the threaded hole in the camshaft sprocket housing through the hole in the sprocket to prevent the sprocket from turning.
7. Using a wheel puller, connect it to the camshaft sprocket and press it from the camshaft.
To install:
8. Install the camshaft sprocket and torque the camshaft sprocket-to-camshaft bolt to 72–87 ft. lbs.
9. Rotate the crankshaft to bring the No. 1 piston to TDC of the compression stroke.
10. Align the timing marks on the injection pump sprocket with the camshaft sprocket; the marks must be facing each other.
11. Using a new timing belt, install it in the following sequence: crankshaft sprocket, camshaft sprocket and the injection pump sprocket; the slack must be between the injection pump and camshaft sprockets.
12. Install the tension center and the tension pulley so the end of the tension center is fitted against both pins on the timing pulley housing.
13. Hand tighten the nut so the tension pulley can be rotated freely.
14. Install the tension spring and semi-tighten the pulley nut to 22–36 ft. lbs.
15. Rotate the crankshaft 2 full turns clockwise to seat the belt and further turn the crankshaft 90 degrees beyond TDC to settle the injection pump.
16. Loosen the tension pulley nut to take up the timing belt slack. Tighten the tension pulley nut to 79–94 ft. lbs.
17. Install the injection pump sprocket flange; the hole in the outer circumference of the flange should be aligned with the triangular timing mark on the injection pump sprocket.
18. Rotate the crankshaft 2 full turns clockwise to bring the No. 1 piston to TDC of the compression stroke. Make sure the triangular timing mark on the timing sprocket is aligned with the hole in the flange, then, measure the timing belt tension; it should be 33–55 lbs.
19. Install the timing belt cover.
20. To complete the installation, reverse the removal procedures.
21. Connect the negative battery cable. Refill the cooling system.

CRANKSHAFT SPROCKET

1. Disconnect the negative battery cable. Drain the cooling system.
2. Remove the timing belt cover.
3. Using a pry bar, remove the tension spring from the timing belt tensioner.

NOTE: When removing the tension spring, avoid using excessive force for the spring may become distorted.

4. Remove the tensioner pulley bolt and the pulley.
5. Remove the timing belt and discard it.
6. Remove the crankshaft sprocket bolt.

NOTE: To remove the crankshaft sprocket bolt, it may be necessary to remove the starter or the flywheel cover

plate to lock the flywheel; otherwise, it may be difficult to keep the crankshaft from turning.

7. Using a puller tool press the crankshaft center and timing sprocket from the crankshaft.
To install:
8. Install the crankshaft center and timing sprocket to the crankshaft and install the bolt.
9. Rotate the crankshaft to bring the No. 1 piston to TDC of the compression stroke.
10. Align the timing marks on the injection pump sprocket with the camshaft sprocket; the marks must be facing each other.
11. Using a new timing belt, install it in the following sequence: crankshaft sprocket, camshaft sprocket and the injection pump sprocket; the slack must be between the injection pump and camshaft sprockets.
12. Install the tension center and the tension pulley so the end of the tension center is fitted against both pins on the timing pulley housing.
13. Hand tighten the nut so the tension pulley can be rotated freely.
14. Install the tension spring and semi-tighten the pulley nut to 22–36 ft. lbs.
15. Rotate the crankshaft 2 full turns clockwise to seat the belt and further turn the crankshaft 90 degrees beyond TDC to settle the injection pump.
16. Loosen the tension pulley nut to take up the timing belt slack. Tighten the tension pulley nut to 79–94 ft. lbs.
17. Install the injection pump sprocket flange; the hole in the outer circumference of the flange should be aligned with the triangular timing mark on the injection pump sprocket.
18. Rotate the crankshaft 2 full turns clockwise to bring the No. 1 piston to TDC of the compression stroke. Make sure the triangular timing mark on the timing sprocket is aligned with the hole in the flange, then, measure the timing belt tension; it should be 33–55 lbs.
19. Install the timing belt cover.
20. To complete the installation, reverse the removal procedures.
21. Connect the negative battery cable. Refill the cooling system.

Camshaft

Removal and Installation

1. Disconnect the negative battery cable.
2. Drain the crankcase. Remove the oil pan and the oil pump.
3. Remove the timing belt cover, the timing belt, the camshaft sprocket.
4. Remove the rocker arm assembly, the pushrods and the valve lifters; be sure to keep the parts in order for reinstallation purposes.
5. Remove the camshaft retainer-to-engine bolts and the retainer. Using a small pry bar, pry the oil seal from the cylinder block.
6. Screw a bolt into the camshaft and carefully remove the camshaft from the front of the engine; be careful not to damage the bearing surfaces.
7. Inspect the camshaft for wear, scoring and/or damage; if necessary, replace it.
To install:
8. Lubricate the camshaft with engine oil and insert it into the front of the engine.
9. Using a new oil seal, lubricate the seal lips with engine oil and install it into the engine.
10. Install the camshaft retainer and the camshaft sprocket.
11. Install the oil pump and the oil pan.
12. Install the valve lifters, the pushrods and the rocker arm assembly.

13. Install and adjust the timing belt. Install the timing belt cover.

14. Rotate the crankshaft to bring the No. 1 piston to TDC of the compression stroke and adjust the valve lash.

15. To complete the installation, reverse the removal procedures.

16. Refill the cooling system and the crankcase.

17. Connect the negative battery cable. Start the engine, allow it to reach normal operating temperatures.

18. Check and/or adjust the idle speed and timing.

Piston and Connecting Rod

Positioning

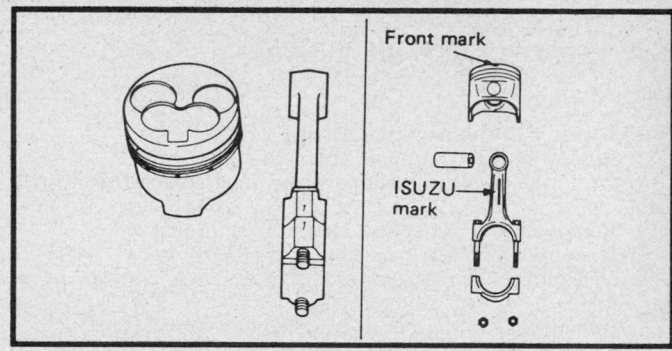

Positioning of the piston and connecting rod—2.2L diesel engine

ENGINE LUBRICATION

Oil Pan

Removal and Installation

2.0L AND 2.3L ENGINES—1986–87

NOTE: On 4WD gasoline engines, the engine must be removed before removing the oil pan.

1. Disconnect the negative battery cable.
2. Raise and safely support the vehicle.
3. Drain the engine oil.
4. Remove the front splash shield, if equipped.
5. If equipped with a crossmember, remove it.
6. Disconnect the relay rod at the idler arm and lower the relay rod.
7. Remove the left side bellhousing bracket.
8. Disconnect the vacuum line from the oil pan.
9. Remove the oil pan bolts and remove the oil pan.
10. Clean the gasket mounting surfaces.
11. Using a new gasket and sealant, install the oil pan. Torque the oil pan-to-engine bolts to 35–51 inch lbs. (2.0L engine) or 11–15 ft. lbs. (2.3L engine).
12. To complete the installation, reverse the removal procedure. Refill the crankcase.

2.2L DIESEL ENGINE—1986–87

Upper Oil Pan

1. Disconnect the negative battery cable.
2. Remove the engine from the vehicle.
3. Drain the engine oil. Remove the dipstick and the dipstick tube.
4. Remove the upper oil pan-to-engine bolts and the oil pan.
5. Clean the gasket mounting surfaces.
6. Using a new gasket and sealant, install the oil pan. Torque the oil pan-to-engine bolts to 10–17 ft. lbs.
7. To complete the installation, reverse the removal procedure. Refill the crankcase.

Lower Oil Pan

1. Raise and safely support the vehicle.
2. Drain the crankcase.
3. Remove the lower oil pan-to-upper oil pan bolts and the lower pan.
4. Clean the gasket mounting surfaces.
5. Using a new gasket and sealant, install the lower oil pan and torque the bolts to 24–96 inch lbs.

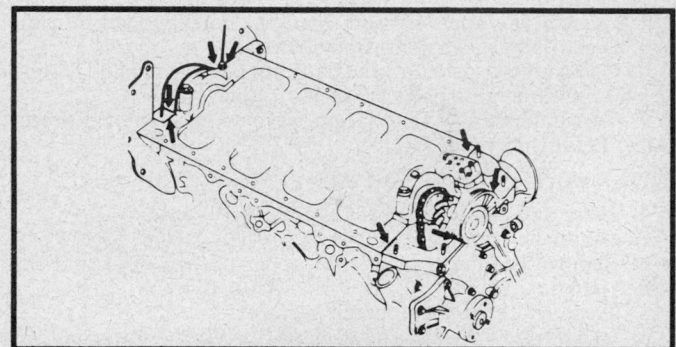

Use sealant at the indicated points when installing the pan gasket—2.0L and 2.3L engines—1986–87

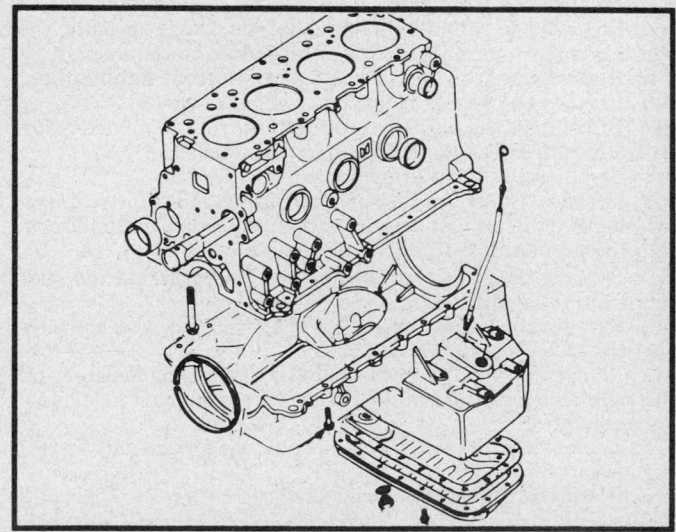

Exploded view of the upper and lower oil pans—2.2L diesel engine

6. Refill the crankcase.

2.3L AND 2.6L ENGINES—1988–90

2WD Vehicles

1. Disconnect the negative battery cable.
2. Raise and safely support the vehicle.
3. Drain the engine oil. Remove the dipstick and the dipstick tube.
4. Remove the front splash shield, if equipped.
5. If equipped with a crossmember, remove it.
6. Disconnect the relay rod at the idler arm and lower the relay rod.
7. Remove the oil pan bolts and remove the oil pan.
8. Clean the gasket mounting surfaces.
9. Using a new gasket and sealant, install the oil pan. Torque the oil pan-to-engine bolts to 48–72 inch lbs.
10. To complete the installation, reverse the removal procedure. Refill the crankcase.

4WD Vehicles—Upper Oil Pan

1. Disconnect the negative battery cable.
2. Remove the engine from the vehicle.
3. Drain the engine oil. Remove the dipstick.
4. Remove the upper oil pan-to-engine bolts and the oil pan.
5. Clean the gasket mounting surfaces.
6. Using a new gasket and sealant, install the oil pan. Torque the oil pan-to-engine bolts to 13–22 ft. lbs.
7. To complete the installation, reverse the removal procedure. Refill the crankcase.

4WD Vehicles—Lower Oil Pan

1. Raise and safely support the vehicle.
2. Drain the crankcase.
3. Remove the lower oil pan-to-upper oil pan bolts and the lower pan.
4. Clean the gasket mounting surfaces.
5. Using a new gasket and sealant, install the lower oil pan and torque the bolts to 47–94 inch lbs.
6. Refill the crankcase.

2.8L ENGINE

1. Disconnect the negative battery cable.
2. Remove the dipstick. Raise and safely support the vehicle. Drain the crankcase.
3. Remove the front skid plate and the crossmember.
4. Remove the exhaust pipe-to-catalytic converter bolts, the exhaust pipe-to-manifolds bolts and the Y-exhaust pipe.
5. Remove the front driveshaft from the front differential.
6. Remove the braces from the flywheel cover.
7. Disconnect the electrical connectors from the starter. Remove the starter-to-engine bolts and the starter.
8. Remove the flywheel inspection cover.
9. Matchmark the pitman arm-to-pitman shaft for reassembly. Remove the pitman arm-to-pitman arm shaft nut and separate the pitman arm from the pitman shaft.
10. Remove the idler arm-to-shaft nut and separate the idler arm from the shaft.
11. Remove the rubber hose from the front axle vent and support the axle housing assembly.
12. Remove both bolts from the left axle housing isolator and the right axle housing isolator, then, lower the front axle housing assembly.
13. Remove the oil pan-to-engine bolts, the oil pan and discard the gasket.
14. Clean the gasket mounting surfaces.
To install:
15. Using a new gasket and sealant, install the oil pan. Torque both rear pan-to-engine bolts to 18 ft. lbs. (25 Nm) and the other bolts/nuts/studs to 7 ft. lbs. (10 Nm).
16. To complete the installation, reverse the removal proce-

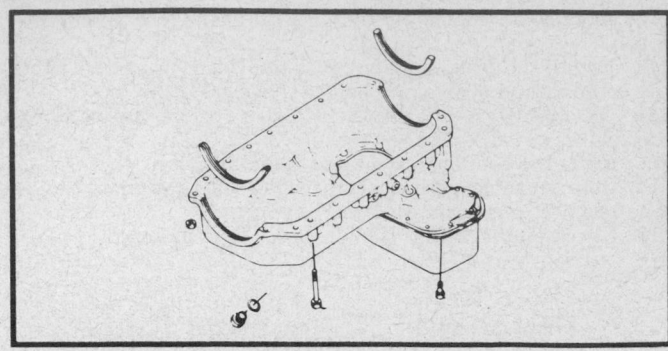

Exploded view of the oil pan used with 4WD—2.3L and 2.6L engines—1988–90

dures. Torque the following fasteners:
  Pitman arm-to-pitman shaft nut—159 ft. lbs. (215 Nm)
  Idler arm-to-shaft nut—86 ft. lbs. (117 Nm)
  Front drive axle shaft bolts—46 ft. lbs. (62 Nm)
17. Refill the crankcase. Connect the negative battery cable.
18. Start the engine and check for leaks.

Oil Pump

Removal and Installation

2.0L ENGINE

The oil pump is located in the oil pan and is attached to the front cover.
1. Disconnect the negative battery cable. Raise and safely support the vehicle.
2. Rotate the crankshaft to position the No. 1 or No. 4 cylinder at the TDC of its compression stroke.
3. Drain the crankcase and remove the oil pan.
4. Remove the oil pick-up-to-engine bolt and the oil pick-up tube from the oil pump.
5. Remove the oil pump-to-front cover bolts and the oil pump.
To install:
6. Turn the punch mark on the oil pump drive gear toward the oil filter and align the center of the oil pump' drive gear with the mark on the oil pump case.
7. Insert the oil pump into the front cover.

NOTE: When installing the oil pump, turn the oil pump shaft so the drive gear engages with the drive pinion. When installed, the punch mark on the drive gear should be facing the main bearings and the shaft tang must be engaged with the distributor shaft.

8. To complete the installation, reverse the removal procedures.
9. Refill the crankcase. Connect the negative battery cable.
10. Start the engine and check for leaks.

2.3L AND 2.6L ENGINES

The oil pump is attached to the front, lower right side of the engine and is driven by the timing belt.
1. Remove the upper and lower timing belt covers.
2. Remove the timing belt from the crankshaft and oil pump sprockets.
3. Remove the oil pump sprocket-to-oil pump nut and the sprocket from the oil pump.
4. Using a 6mm Allen wrench, remove the oil pump-to-engine bolts and the oil pump.
To install:
5. Using petroleum jelly, pack the oil pump.

6. Using a new O-ring, install the oil pump and torque the bolts to 10–17 ft. lbs.

7. Install the sprocket to the oil pump and torque the nut to 48–62 ft. lbs.

8. Align the timing marks on the camshaft and crankshaft sprockets and install the timing belt.

9. To complete the installation, reverse the removal procedures.

2.8L ENGINE

The oil pump is attached to the cylinder block and is located in the oil pan.

1. Disconnect the negative battery cable. Raise and safely support the vehicle.

2. Drain the crankcase. Remove the oil pan.

3. Remove the oil pump-to-engine bolts and the oil pump.

To install:

4. Align the oil pump shaft with the hexagon socket and install the pump. Torque the oil pump-to-engine bolts to 30 ft. lbs. (41 Nm).

5. Install the oil pan.

6. To complete the installation, reverse the removal procedures.

7. Connect the negative battery cable. Start the engine and check for leaks.

2.2L DIESEL ENGINE

1. Disconnect the negative battery cable.

2. Remove the engine from the vehicle.

3. Remove the oil pan.

4. Remove the oil pipe from the oil pump. Remove the oil pump-to-engine bolts and the oil pump.

5. Clean the gasket mounting surfaces.

6. Using a new gasket, install the oil pump and connect the oil pipe to the oil pump. Install and torque the oil pan-to-engine bolts to 10–17 ft. lbs.

7. To complete the installation, reverse the removal procedure. Refill the crankcase.

Checking

2.0L ENGINE

1. Visually inspect the oil pump for wear, damage or other abnormal conditions.

2. Remove the oil pump cover from the bottom of the oil pump.

3. Using a feeler gauge, measure the clearance between the pump body and the vane; it should be 0.0063–0.0086 in. (0.16–0.22mm), if not, replace the entire pump assembly.

4. Using a feeler gauge, measure the clearance between the rotor and the vane; it should be 0.0051–0.0059 in. (0.13–0.15mm), if not, replace the rotor set: pin, shaft, rotor and vane.

5. Place a straight edge across the bottom of the pump and a feeler gauge between the straight edge and the rotor; the clearance between the rotor/vane-to-cover should be 0.0011–0.0035 in. (0.03–0.09mm), if not, replace the rotor set: pin, shaft, rotor and vane.

6. Using a feeler gauge, measure the clearance between the pump body and the rotor shaft; it should be less than 0.0079 in. (0.2mm), if not, replace the entire pump assembly.

2.3L AND 2.6L ENGINES

1. Visually inspect the oil pump for wear, damage or other abnormal conditions.

2. Insert the oil pump vane into the cylinder block.

3. Place a straight edge across the oil pump opening and a feeler gauge between the straight edge and the vane; the clearance between the vane-to-cylinder block surface should be 0.002–0.004 in. (0.04–0.09mm), if not, replace the vane.

4. Using a feeler gauge, measure the side clearance between

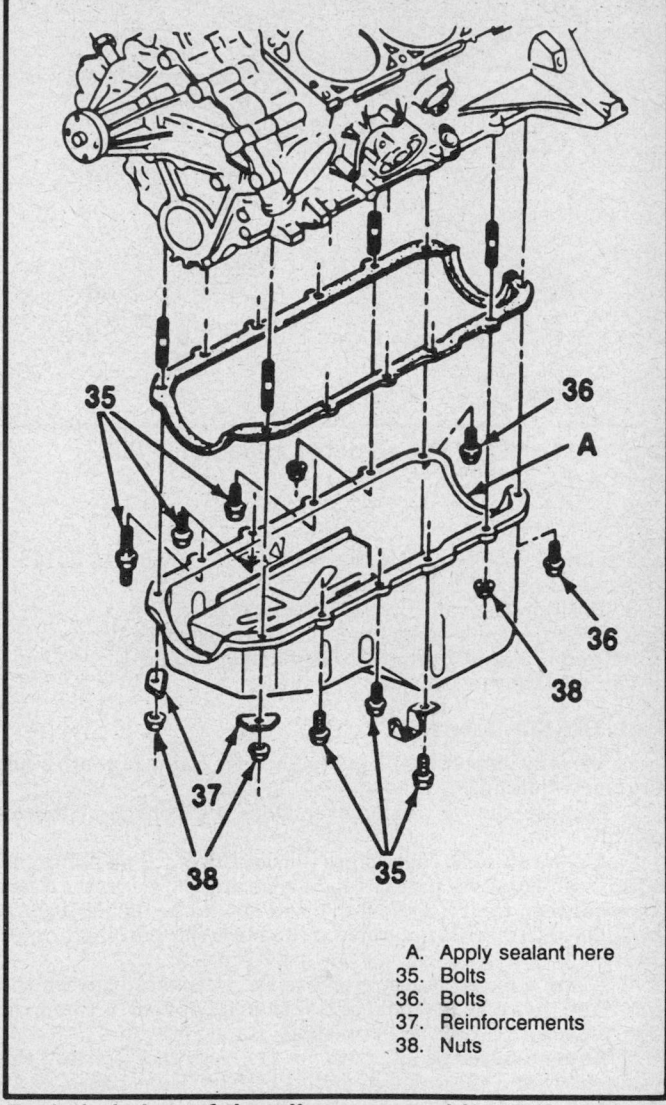

A. Apply sealant here
35. Bolts
36. Bolts
37. Reinforcements
38. Nuts

Exploded view of the oil pan assembly — 2.8L engine

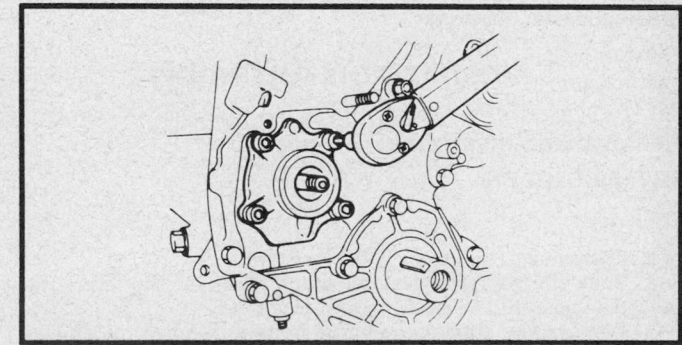

View of the oil pump — 2.3L and 2.6L engines

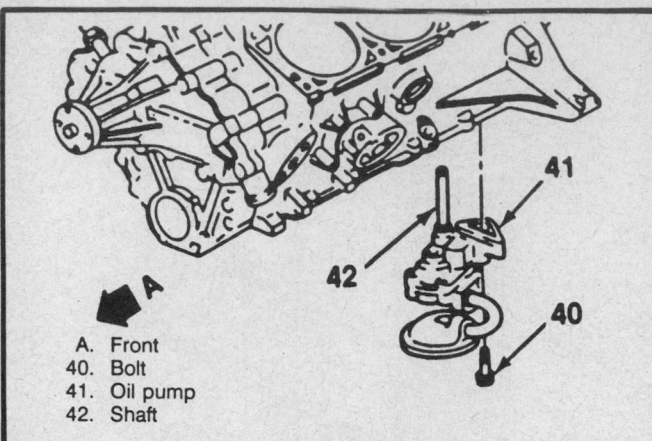

A. Front
40. Bolt
41. Oil pump
42. Shaft

Exploded view of the oil pump assembly — 2.8L engine

the cylinder block and the vane; it should be 0.009–0.0014 in. (0.24–0.36mm), if not, replace the vane.

5. Position the vane onto the rotor shaft.

6. Using a feeler gauge, measure the clearance between the rotor and the vane; it should be 0.005–0.006 in. (0.13–0.15mm), if not, replace the rotor and/or vane.

2.2L DIESEL ENGINE

1. Visually inspect the oil pump for wear, damage or other abnormal conditions.

2. Remove the oil pump cover from the bottom of the oil pump.

3. Place a straight edge across the bottom of the oil pump and a feeler gauge between the straight edge and the rotor; the clearance between the rotor/vane-to-cover should be 0.0008–0.0028 in. (0.02–0.07mm), if not, replace the rotor set: pin, shaft, rotor and vane.

4. Using a feeler gauge, measure the clearance between the rotor and the vane; it should be less than 0.0055 in. (0.14mm), if not, replace the rotor set: pin, shaft, rotor and vane.

5. Using a feeler gauge, measure the clearance between the pump body and the vane; it should be 0.0079–0.0106 in. (0.2–0.27mm), if not, replace the entire pump assembly.

6. Using a feeler gauge, measure the clearance between the pump body and the rotor shaft; it should be less than 0.0079 in. (0.2mm), if not, replace the entire pump assembly.

NOTE: When necessary to replace the pinion and shaft, install the shaft in the pump body and set the pinion on the shaft. Drill a hole through the pinion and shaft using a 5mm drill, then, install and stake the pin.

Rear Main Bearing Oil Seal

Removal and Installation
LIP TYPE SEAL

2.0L Engine

1. Disconnect the negative battery cable. Raise and safely support the vehicle.

2. Drain the engine oil and remove the oil pan.

3. If equipped with an automatic transmission, remove the transmission. If equipped with a manual transmission, remove the transmission and clutch assembly.

4. Remove the starter without disconnecting the wires and secure it aside.

5. Remove the flywheel-to-crankshaft bolts and the flywheel.

6. Remove the rear main seal retainer-to-engine bolts and the retainer.

7. Carefully, remove the oil seal, using a small pry bar; work the tool around the diameter of the seal until the seal begins to lift out. Use care not to damage the seat and area around the seal.

8. Fill the space between the seal lips with grease and lubricate the seal lips with clean engine oil. Install the new oil seal.

9. To complete the installation, reverse the removal procedures.

Except 2.0L Engine

1. Disconnect the negative battery cable. Raise and safely support the vehicle.

2. If equipped with an automatic transmission, remove the transmission. If equipped with a manual transmission, remove the transmission and clutch assembly.

3. Remove the starter without disconnecting the wires and secure it aside.

4. Remove the flywheel-to-crankshaft bolts and the flywheel.

5. Using a small pry bar, carefully, remove the oil seal work the tool around the diameter of the seal until the seal begins to lift out. Use care not to damage the seat and area around the seal.

6. Using a new oil seal, lubricate the seal lips with clean engine oil.

7. Using an oil seal installation tool, install the new oil seal.

8. To complete the installation, reverse the removal procedures.

MANUAL TRANSMISSION

For further information, please refer to "Professional Transmission Manual".

Transmission Assembly

Removal and Installation
2WD VEHICLES

1986–87

1. Disconnect the negative battery cable.

2. Slide the gearshift lever boot upwards on the lever. Remove the gearshift lever bolts and the lever.

3. Remove the starter-to-engine bolts and move the starter aside.

4. Raise and safely support the vehicle. Disconnect the exhaust pipe hanger from the transmission.

5. Drain the transmission. Disconnect the speedometer cable and ground cable. Matchmark and remove the driveshaft.

6. Remove the clutch fork return spring and the clutch cable.

7. Remove the flywheel cover plate.

8. Remove the frame bracket-to-transmission rear mount bolts and nuts.

9. Raise the engine/transmission assembly and remove the crossmember-to-frame bracket bolts.

10. Remove the rear mounting nuts from the transmission rear extension.

11. Lower the engine/transmission assembly and support the rear of the engine.

12. Disconnect the electrical connector from the back-up light switch.

13. Remove the transmission-to-engine bolts.

14. Move the transmission rearward and disengage it form the clutch. Tip the front of the transmission downward and remove it.

To install:

15. To install, position the transmission in the vehicle and slide it forward, guiding the input shaft into the pilot bearing.

16. Install the transmission-to-engine bolts.

17. Raise and lower the engine/transmission assembly and install the crossmember frame bracket and rear mount.

18. Install the flywheel cover.

19. Align the driveshaft matchmarks and install it.

20. Connect the speedometer cable, the ground cable and the exhaust pipe hanger.

21. Connect the clutch cable and adjust the shift fork.

22. Connect the electrical connector to the back-up light switch. Refill the transmission with lubricant.

23. Lower the vehicle and install the starter assembly.

24. Connect the negative battery cable.

25. Install the gearshift lever and adjust the clutch cable.

26. Check the transmission operation.

1988–90

1. Disconnect the negative battery cable.

2. Remove the undercover, if equipped.

3. Remove the air cleaner (2.3L engine) or air cleaner duct and hose (2.6L engine). Using a clean shop cloth, cover the air cleaner port to prevent dirt from entering the engine.

4. Label and disconnect the necessary hoses and electrical connectors.

5. Remove the clutch return spring, the clutch control cable, the back-up light switch connector and the speedometer cable from the transmission.

6. Remove the gear shift lever by performing the following procedures:

    a. Place the gear shift lever in **N**.

    b. Remove the front console from the floor panel.

    c. Pull the shift lever boot and grommet upward.

    d. Remove the shift lever cover bolts and the shift lever.

7. Raise and safely support the vehicle. Remove the front wheels.

8. Drain the transmission fluid.

9. If equipped with a 1-piece driveshaft, remove the driveshaft flange-to-pinion nuts, lower the driveshaft and pull it from the transmission.

10. If equipped with a 2-piece driveshaft, perform the following procedures:

    a. Remove the rear driveshaft flange-to-pinion nuts.

    b. Remove the rear driveshaft flange-to-front driveshaft flange bolts and the rear driveshaft.

    c. Remove the center bearing-to-chassis bolts, move the front driveshaft rearward and from the transmission.

11. Remove the starter-to-engine bolts and the starter.

12. Remove the exhaust pipe-to-exhaust manifold nuts, the exhaust pipe bracket-to-transmission bolts, the front exhaust pipe-to-2nd exhaust pipe bolts and the front exhaust pipe from the vehicle.

13. Attach an engine hanger to the rear of the exhaust manifold.

14. Using an engine hoist, connect it to the engine hangers and support the engine.

15. Using a transmission jack, place it under the transmission; do not support it.

16. Remove the rear mount-to-transmission nuts.

17. Remove the rear mount-to-crossmember nuts/bolts and the mount.

NOTE: Further removal of the transmission may require an assistant.

18. Remove the clutch cover and the transmission-to-engine bolts.

19. Move the transmission rearward into the crossmember and floor pan area; the transmission may rest on the crossmember.

20. Lower the front of the transmission toward the jack.

21. Firmly, grasp the transmission the rear cover while the assistant raises the jack toward the transmission.

22. Carefully, lower the transmission onto the jack and center it.

23. Lower the jack and move the transmission rearward.

To install:

NOTE: Installation of the transmission may require an assistant.

24. Raise the transmission into position.

25. Raise the rear of the transmission and move it into position on the crossmember.

26. Move the transmission forward and engage it with the engine.

27. Install the engine-to-transmission bolts.

28. Install the mount and the rear mount-to-crossmember nuts/bolts.

29. Install the rear mount-to-transmission nuts.

30. Remove the engine hoist and the engine hanger from the rear of the exhaust manifold.

31. Install the front exhaust pipe, exhaust pipe-to-exhaust manifold nuts, the exhaust pipe bracket-to-transmission bolts, the front exhaust pipe-to-2nd exhaust pipe bolts.

32. Install the starter and the starter-to-engine bolts.

33. If equipped with a 2-piece driveshaft, perform the following procedures:

    a. Install the front driveshaft into the transmission and the center bearing-to-chassis bolts.

    b. Install the rear driveshaft and the rear driveshaft flange-to-front driveshaft flange bolts.

    c. Install the rear driveshaft flange-to-pinion nuts.

34. If equipped with a 1-piece driveshaft, install the driveshaft into the transmission and the driveshaft flange-to-pinion nuts.

35. Install the front wheels and lower the vehicle.

36. Install the gear shift lever by performing the following procedures:

    a. Install the shift lever and the shift lever cover bolts.

    b. Push the grommet and shift lever boot downward.

    c. Install the front console to the floor panel.

37. Install the clutch return spring, the clutch control cable, the back-up light switch connector and the speedometer cable to the transmission.

38. Connect the necessary hoses and electrical connectors.

39. Install the air cleaner (2.3L) or air cleaner duct and hose (2.6L).

40. Refill the transmission. Install the undercover, if equipped.

41. Connect the negative battery cable.

4WD VEHICLES

1986–87

4WD vehicles require that the transmission and transfer case be removed as an assembly.

1. Disconnect the negative battery cable.

2. Slide the shift lever boots upward and unbolt each lever.

3. Remove the return spring from the transfer case shift lever and remove both levers.

4. Raise and safely support the vehicle. Label and disconnect the starter wiring. Remove the starter-to-engine bolts and the starter.

5. Disconnect the exhaust pipe from the manifold and disconnect the pipe support from the transmission.

6. Drain the transmission. Matchmark and remove the driveshaft.

7. Disconnect the speedometer cable and ground strap from the transmission.

8. Matchmark and remove the front and rear driveshaft from the transfer case.

9. Disconnect the clutch return spring.

10. Disconnect the clutch cable from the clutch fork.

11. Remove the flywheel cover.

12. Remove the transmission rear crossmember bolts.

13. Raise the engine/transmission assembly and remove the rear crossmember-to-frame bolts.

14. Remove the rear mounting bolts from the transfer case.

15. Remove the side case from the transmission.

16. Remove the stud bolt from the transfer case.

17. Lower the engine/transmission assembly and support the rear of the engine.

18. Disconnect the CRS switch and back-up light switch.

19. Remove the shifter cover and gasket from the transfer case.

20. Remove the transmission-to-engine bolts. When removing the transmission, turn the side case fitting face down and pull the case straight back until it is free of the clutch. Lower the front of the transmission and remove it.

21. To install, reverse the removal procedures.

1988-90

1. Disconnect the negative battery cable.

2. Remove the undercover, if equipped.

3. Remove the air cleaner (2.3L engine) or air cleaner duct and hose (2.6L engine). Using a clean shop cloth, cover the air cleaner port to prevent dirt from entering the engine.

4. Label and disconnect the necessary hoses and electrical connectors.

5. Remove the clutch return spring, the clutch control cable, the back-up light switch connector and the speedometer cable from the transmission.

6. Remove the gear shift lever by performing the following procedures:

    a. Place the gear shift lever in **N**.

    b. Remove the front console from the floor panel.

    c. Pull the shift lever boot and grommet upward.

    d. Remove the shift lever cover bolts and the shift lever.

7. Remove the transfer shift lever by performing the following procedures:

    a. Place the transfer shift lever in **H** (except 2.8L engine) or **2H** (2.8L engine).

    b. Pull the shift lever boot and dust cover upward.

    c. Remove the shift lever retaining bolts.

    d. Pull the shift lever from the transfer case.

8. Raise and safely support the vehicle with jackstands at the front and rear of the vehicle. Remove the front wheels.

9. Drain the transmission and transfer case fluid.

10. If equipped with a 1-piece driveshaft, remove the driveshaft flange-to-pinion nuts, lower the driveshaft and pull it from the transmission.

11. If equipped with a 2-piece driveshaft, perform the following procedures:

    a. Remove the rear driveshaft flange-to-pinion nuts.

    b. Remove the rear driveshaft flange-to-front driveshaft flange bolts and the rear driveshaft.

    c. Remove the center bearing-to-chassis bolts, move the front driveshaft rearward and from the transmission.

12. Remove the front driveshaft's splinded yoke flange-to-transfer case bolts and separate the front driveshaft from the transfer case; do not allow the splined flange to fall away from the driveshaft.

13. Remove the starter-to-engine bolts and the starter.

14. If equipped with a clutch slave cylinder, remove it from the transmission and move it aside.

15. Remove the exhaust pipe-to-exhaust manifold nuts, the exhaust pipe bracket-to-transmission bolts, the front exhaust pipe-to-2nd exhaust pipe bolts and the front exhaust pipe from the vehicle.

16. Attach an engine hanger to the rear of the exhaust manifold.

17. Using an engine hoist, connect it to the engine hangers and support the engine.

18. If equipped with a 2.8L engine, remove the catalytic converter and the parking brake cable bracket.

19. Using a transmission jack, place it under the transmission and support the assembly.

20. Remove the rear mount-to-transmission nuts.

21. Remove the rear mount-to-side mount member nuts/bolts and the mount.

22. Remove the transmission-to-engine bolts.

23. Move the transmission assembly rearward.

24. Carefully lower the transmission.

To install:

25. Raise the transmission into position.

26. Move the transmission forward and engage it with the engine.

27. Install the engine-to-transmission bolts.

28. Install the rear mount and the rear mount-to-side mount member nuts/bolts.

29. Install the rear mount-to-transmission nuts.

30. Remove the transmission jack.

31. If equipped with a 2.8L engine, install the catalytic converter and the parking brake cable bracket.

32. Remove the engine hoist and the engine hanger from the rear of the exhaust manifold.

33. Install the front exhaust pipe, exhaust pipe-to-exhaust manifold nuts, the exhaust pipe bracket-to-transmission bolts, the front exhaust pipe-to-2nd exhaust pipe bolts.

34. If equipped with a clutch slave cylinder, install it onto the transmission.

35. Install the starter and the starter-to-engine bolts.

36. Install the front driveshaft's splinded yoke flange-to-transfer case bolts.

37. If equipped with a 2-piece driveshaft, perform the following procedures:

    a. Install the front driveshaft into the transmission and the center bearing-to-chassis bolts.

    b. Install the rear driveshaft and the rear driveshaft flange-to-front driveshaft flange bolts.

    c. Install the rear driveshaft flange-to-pinion nuts.

38. If equipped with a 1-piece driveshaft, install the driveshaft into the transmission and the driveshaft flange-to-pinion nuts.

39. Install the front wheels and lower the vehicle.

40. Install the transfer shift lever by performing the following procedures:

    a. Position the shift lever into the transfer case.

    b. Install the shift lever retaining bolts.

    c. Push the dust cover and the shift lever boot downward.

41. Install the gear shift lever by performing the following procedures:

    a. Install the shift lever and the shift lever cover bolts.

    b. Push the grommet and shift lever boot downward.

    c. Install the front console to the floor panel.

42. Install the clutch return spring, the clutch control cable, the back-up light switch connector and the speedometer cable to the transmission.

43. Connect the necessary hoses and electrical connectors.

44. Install the air cleaner (2.3L) or air cleaner duct and hose (2.6L).

45. Refill the transmission and the transfer case. Install the undercover, if equipped.

46. Install the negative battery cable.

Linkage Adjustment

No adjustments are possible on the transmission or transfer case linkage.

CLUTCH

Clutch Assembly

Removal and Installation

1. Raise and support the vehicle safely.
2. On 2WD vehicles, remove the transmission. On 4WD models, remove the transmission and transfer case as an assembly.
3. Matchmark the clutch assembly to the flywheel so the clutch assembly can be reassembled in the same position.
4. Loosen the pressure plate-to-flywheel bolts, 1 turn at a time in an alternating sequence, until the spring tension is relieved to avoid distorting or bending the pressure plate.
5. Using a clutch alignment tool, support the pressure plate and cover assembly and remove the bolts and clutch assembly.
To install:
6. Apply a thin coat of grease to the pressure plate fingers, diaphragm spring, clutch cover grooves and the drive bosses on the pressure plate.
7. Apply a thin coat of lubricant to the splines in the clutch disc.
8. Using a clutch alignment tool, assemble the clutch disc and pressure plate onto the flywheel.
9. Align the matchmarks and install the pressure plate-to-flywheel bolts and torque the bolts to 12–14 ft. lbs. Remove the aligning tool.
10. On 2WD vehicles, install the transmission. On 4WD models, install the transmission and transfer case as an assembly.
11. To complete the installation, reverse the removal procedures. Adjust the clutch cable linkage.

Pedal Height Adjustment

The clutch pedal height is the distance from the center of the clutch pedal pad to the cowl.
1. Locate the clutch switch at the top of the clutch pedal under the dash.
2. Loosen the switch-to-clutch pedal bracket.
3. Adjust the clutch switch to obtain a clutch pedal height of 6.9–7.2 in. (P'UP with mechanical clutch), 7.4–7.8 in. (P'UP with hydraulic hydraulic), 7.28–7.68 in. (Pick-Up and Amigo) or 9.15–9.55 in. (Trooper/Trooper II).
4. After adjusting the pedal height, tighten the clutch switch adjusting nut.

Clutch Cable

Removal and Installation

1. Loosen the clutch cable lock and adjusting nuts. Remove the clutch cable clip in the engine compartment.
2. Raise and safely support the vehicle. Remove the spring from the shift fork end.
3. Disconnect the cable end from the shift fork and pull the cable assembly through the bracket.
4. Lower the vehicle enough to disengage the hooked part of the clutch pedal from the cable eye. Pull the cable assembly towards the engine compartment and remove the cable from the vehicle.

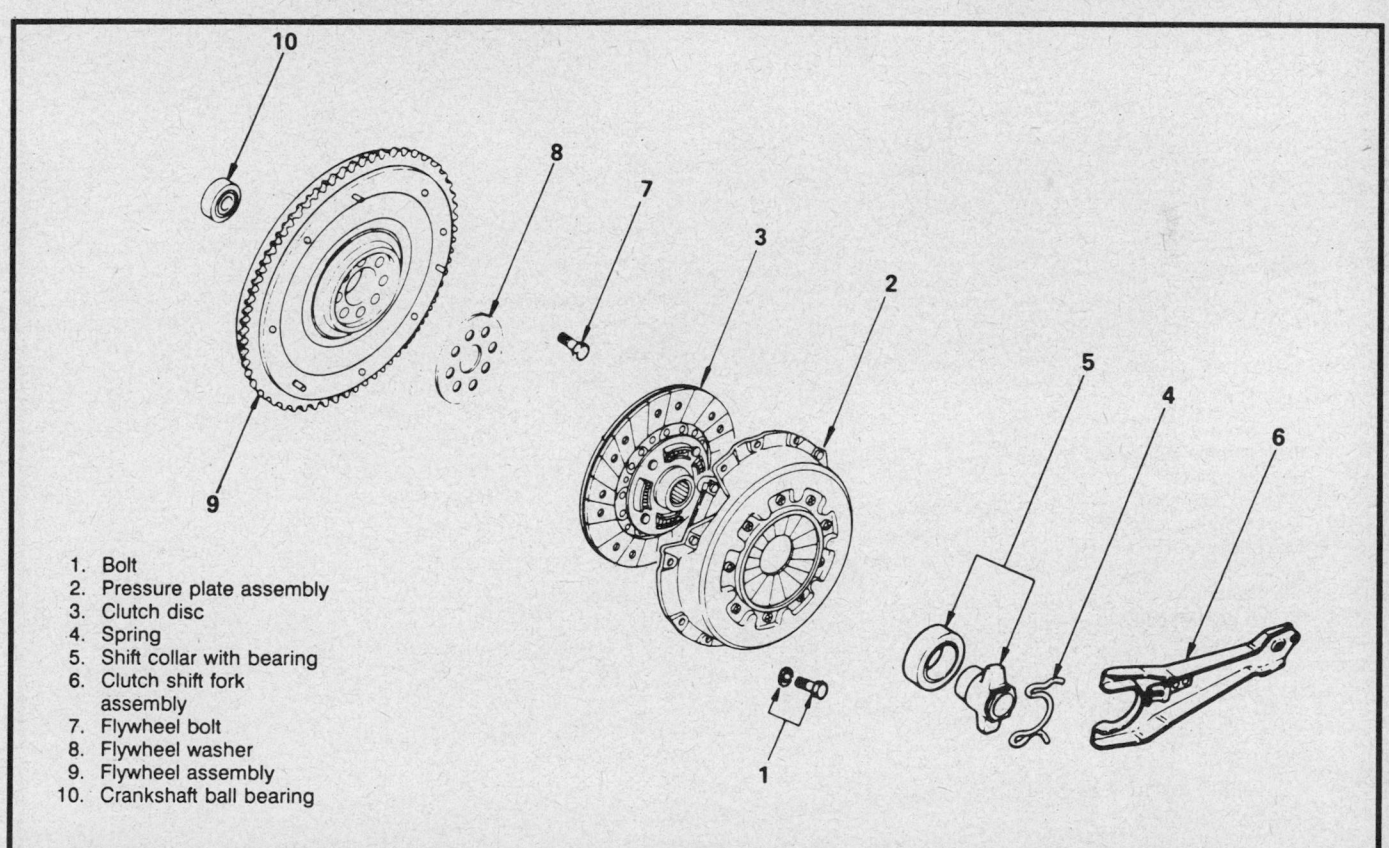

1. Bolt
2. Pressure plate assembly
3. Clutch disc
4. Spring
5. Shift collar with bearing
6. Clutch shift fork assembly
7. Flywheel bolt
8. Flywheel washer
9. Flywheel assembly
10. Crankshaft ball bearing

Exploded view of the clutch assembly

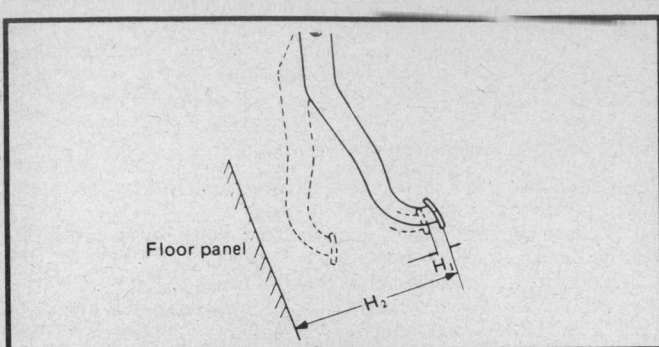

Measuring the clutch pedal height

5. To install, reverse the removal procedures. Adjust the cable when finished.

Adjustment

1. Pull the outer cable, located under the hood, forward as far as possible and secure it.
2. Turn the adjusting nut inward it touches the damper rubber washer, located at the firewall.
3. Depress and release the clutch pedal 3 times.
4. Tighen the adjusting nut again.
5. Pull the outer cable forward again and fully tighten the adjusting nut.
6. Loosen the nut to provide a 1/8 in. clearance between the adjusting nut and the damper washer.

7. Release the outer cable and tighten the locknut to secure the adjusting nut.

Clutch Master Cylinder

The clutch master cylinder is located on the firewall inside the engine compartment.

Removal and Installation

1. Disconnect the negative battery cable. Remove the hudraulic line from the clutch master cylinder.
2. Disconnect the master cylinder pushrod from the clutch pedal.
3. Remove the master cylinder-to-firewall nuts and remove the master cylinder.
4. To install, reverse the removal procedures. Torque the master cylinder-to-firewall nuts to 8–15 ft. lbs. (12–20 Nm).
5. Using new washers, torque the hydraulic line-to-master cylinder bolt to 22–29 ft. lbs. (30–39 Nm).
6. Bleed the hydraulic clutch system.

Clutch Slave Cylinder

The clutch slave cylinder is attached to the bell housing.

Removal and Installation

1. Disconnect the negative battery cable. Remove the hudraulic line from the clutch slave cylinder.
2. Remove the slave cylinder-to-bell housing bolts and remove the slave cylinder.
3. To install, reverse the removal procedures.

1. Clutch cable lock and adjusting nuts
2. Clutch cable clip
3. Return spring from shift fork end
4. Assist spring
5. Clutch damper
6. Clutch control cable
7. Clutch pedal

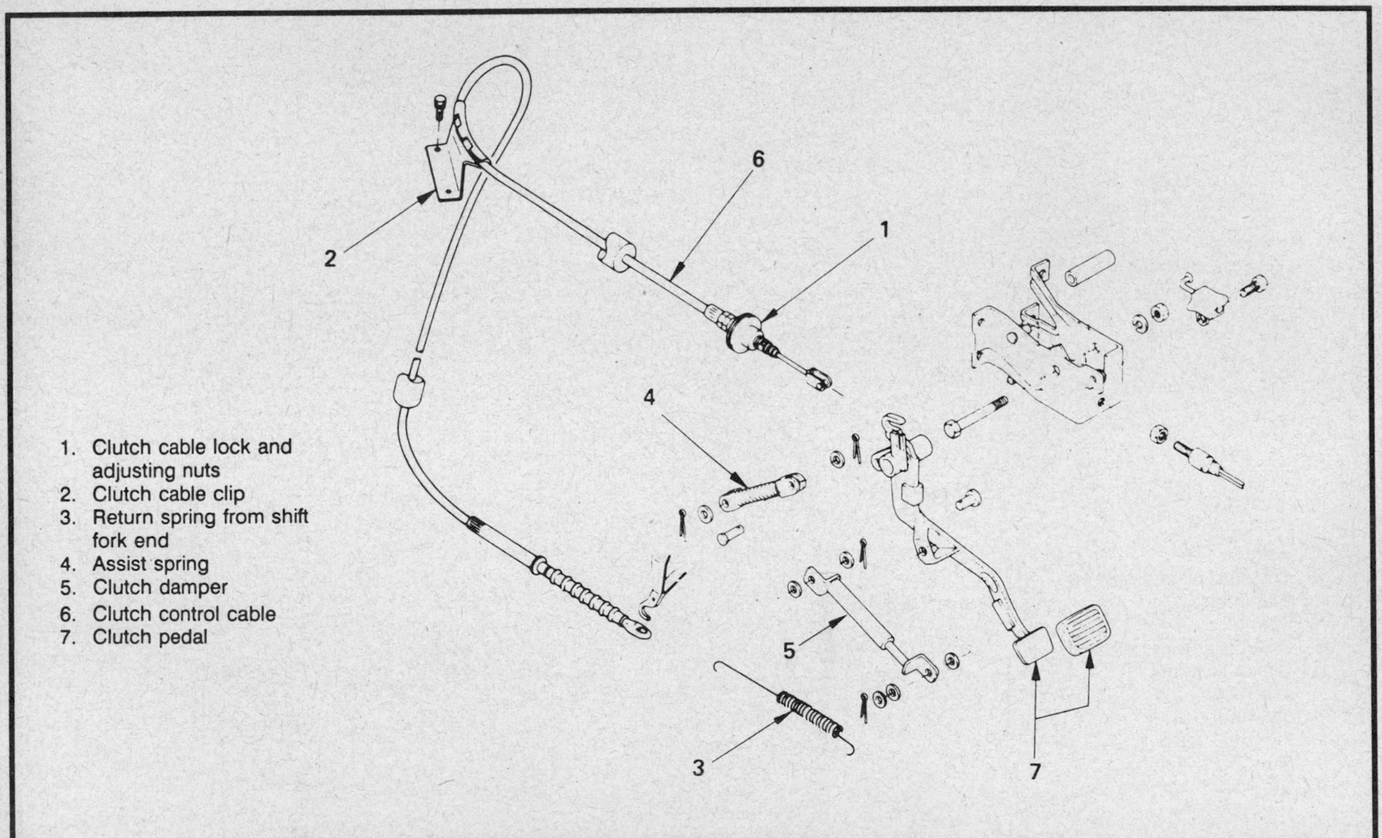

Exploded view of the clutch cable assembly

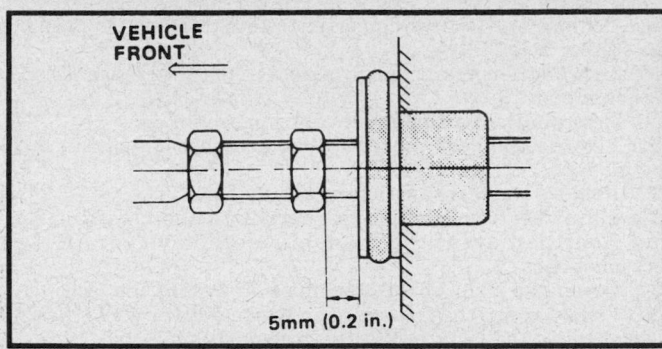

VEHICLE
FRONT

5mm (0.2 in.)

View of the clutch cable adjustment

4. Using new washers, torque the hydraulic line-to-slave cyl-

inder fitting to 11–17 ft. lbs. (16–25 Nm).
5. Bleed the hydraulic clutch system.

Bleeding the Hydraulic Clutch System

1. Firmly, set the parking brake.
2. Check the reservoir fluid level and refill, if necessary.
3. At the slave cylinder, remove the rubber cap from the bleeder screw.
4. Using a vinyl tube, connect it to the bleeder screw and submerge the other end in a transparent container of brake fluid.
5. Have an assistant pump the clutch pedal several times and hold it.
6. Loosen the bleeder screw and allow the air bubble fluid to flow into the container, then, tighten the bleeder screw.
7. Release the clutch pedal.
8. Repeat this operation until the fluid is clear of air bubbles.
9. Refill the reservoir. Remove the vinyl tube and replace the rubber cap on the bleeder screw.

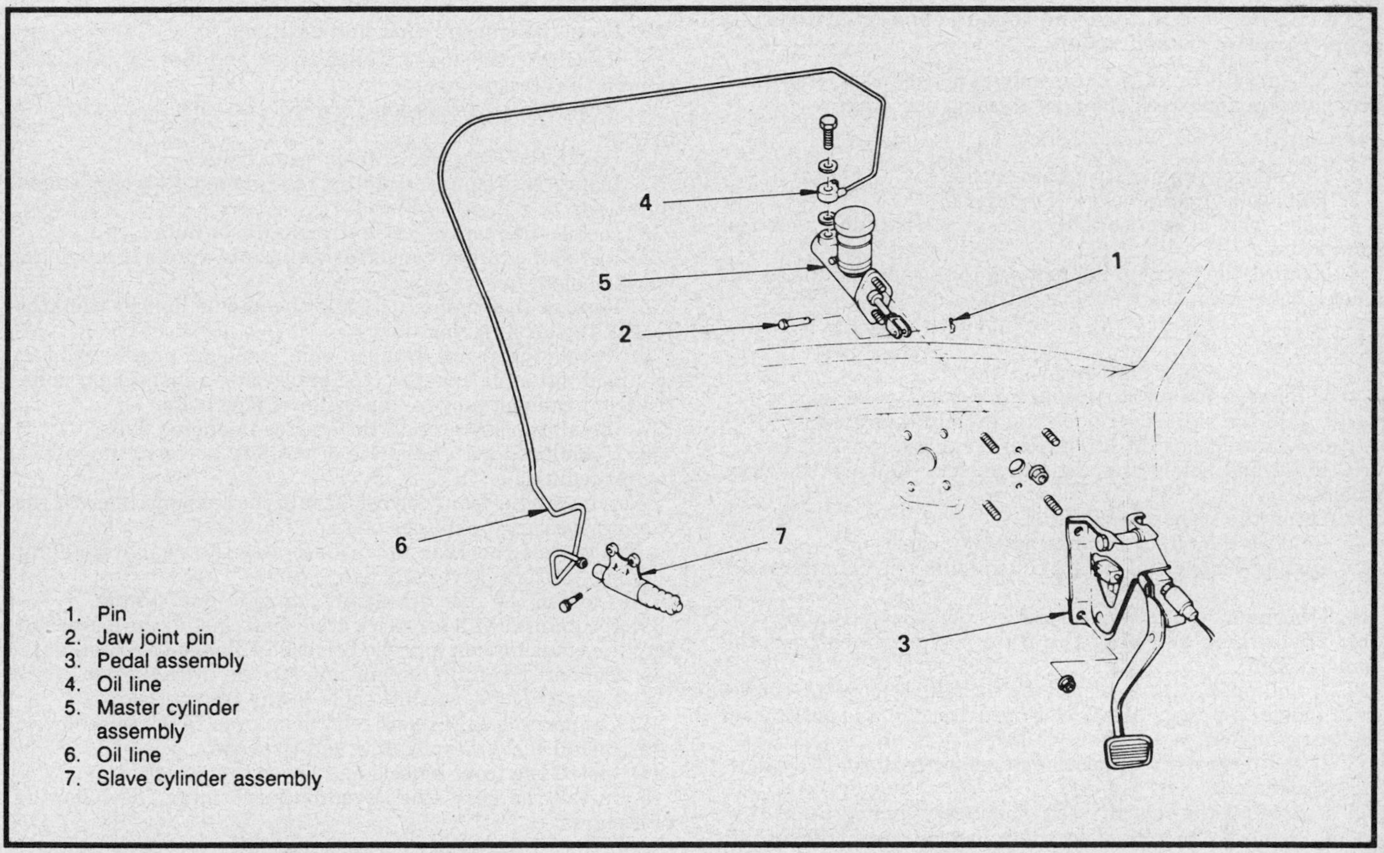

1. Pin
2. Jaw joint pin
3. Pedal assembly
4. Oil line
5. Master cylinder
   assembly
6. Oil line
7. Slave cylinder assembly

Exploded view of the hydraulic system

AUTOMATIC TRANSMISSION

For further information, please refer to "Professional Transmission Manual".

Transmission Assembly

Removal and Installation

2WD VEHICLES
1986–87

1. Disconnect the negative battery cable. Raise and safely support the vehicle.
2. Remove the undercover, if equipped.
3. Remove the transmission dipstick assembly. Drain the transmission fluid. Disconnect and plug the oil cooler lines from the transmission.
4. Remove the torque converter cover. Matchmark the torque converter-to-flywheel location and remove the torque converter-to-flywheel bolts; rotate the torque converter to expose the bolts.

5. Remove the exhaust pipe-to-exhaust manifold nuts and separate the pipe from the manifold.

6. Disconnect the shift lever control rod from the transmission shift lever.

7. Disconnect the back-up light switch and transmission wiring from the transmission.

8. Using an engine hoist, connect it to the engine hangers and support the engine.

9. Raise and safely support the vehicle.

10. Remove the starter motor. Disconnect the speedometer from the transmission.

11. Matchmark and remove the driveshaft. Remove the transmission-to-crossmember bolts.

12. Lift the engine/transmission slightly and remove the transmission frame bracket from the crossmember. Remove the rear mount from the crossmember. Remove the exhaust pipe bracket from the transmission.

13. Support the transmission.

14. Remove the bell housing-to-engine bolts and the transmission from the vehicle.

NOTE: Be careful that the torque converter does not drop from the transmission.

15. To install, reverse the removal procedures. Refill the transmission and check the transmission operation.

1988–90

1. Disconnect the negative battery cable.
2. Remove the undercover, if equipped.
3. Label and disconnect the necessary hoses and electrical connectors.
4. Remove the back-up light switch connector and the speedometer cable from the transmission.
5. Remove the gear shift lever by performing the following procedures:
   a. Place the gear shift lever in **N**.
   b. Remove the front console from the floor panel.
   c. Pull the shift lever boot and grommet upward.
   d. Remove the shift lever cover bolts and the shift lever.
6. Raise and safely support the vehicle. Remove the front wheels.
7. Drain the transmission fluid.
8. Remove the oil level gauge and the tube.
9. Disconnect the shift select control link rod from the select lever.
10. Disconnect the downshift cable from the transmission.
11. Disconnect and plug the fluid coolant lines from the transmission.
12. If equipped with a 1-piece driveshaft, remove the driveshaft flange-to-pinion nuts, lower the driveshaft and pull it from the transmission.
13. If equipped with a 2-piece driveshaft, perform the following procedures:
   a. Remove the rear driveshaft flange-to-pinion nuts.
   b. Remove the rear driveshaft flange-to-front driveshaft flange bolts and the rear driveshaft.
   c. Remove the center bearing-to-chassis bolts, move the front driveshaft rearward and from the transmission.
14. Remove the starter-to-engine bolts and the starter.
15. Remove the exhaust pipe-to-exhaust manifold nuts, the exhaust pipe bracket-to-transmission bolts, the front exhaust pipe-to-2nd exhaust pipe bolts and the front exhaust pipe from the vehicle.
16. Attach an engine hanger to the rear of the exhaust manifold.
17. Using an engine hoist, connect it to the engine hangers and support the engine.

NOTE: Removal of the transmission will require an assistant.

18. Remove the torque converter-to-flex plate bolts through the starter hole.

19. Using a transmission jack, place it under the transmission; do not support it.

20. Remove the rear mount-to-transmission nuts.

21. Remove the rear mount-to-crossmember nuts/bolts and the mount.

22. Remove the transmission-to-engine bolts.

23. Move the transmission rearward into the crossmember and floor pan area; the transmission may rest on the crossmember.

24. Lower the front of the transmission toward the jack.

25. Firmly, grasp the transmission the rear cover while the assistant raises the jack toward the transmission.

26. Carefully, lower the transmission onto the jack and center it.

27. Lower the jack and move the transmission rearward.

To install:

NOTE: Installation of the transmission will require an assistant.

28. Raise the transmission into position.

29. Raise the rear of the transmission and move it into position on the crossmember.

30. Move the transmission forward and engage it with the engine.

31. Install the engine-to-transmission bolts.

32. Install the mount and the rear mount-to-crossmember nuts/bolts.

33. Install the rear mount-to-transmission nuts.

34. Install the torque converter-to-flex plate bolts through the starter hole.

35. Remove the engine hoist and the engine hanger from the rear of the exhaust manifold.

36. Install the front exhaust pipe, exhaust pipe-to-exhaust manifold nuts, the exhaust pipe bracket-to-transmission bolts, the front exhaust pipe-to-2nd exhaust pipe bolts.

37. Install the starter and the starter-to-engine bolts.

38. If equipped with a 2-piece driveshaft, perform the following procedures:
   a. Install the front driveshaft into the transmission and the center bearing-to-chassis bolts.
   b. Install the rear driveshaft and the rear driveshaft flange-to-front driveshaft flange bolts.
   c. Install the rear driveshaft flange-to-pinion nuts.

39. If equipped with a 1-piece driveshaft, install the driveshaft into the transmission and the driveshaft flange-to-pinion nuts.

40. Connect the fluid coolant lines to the transmission.

41. Connect the downshift cable to the transmission.

42. Connect the shift select control link rod to the select lever.

43. Install the oil level gauge and the tube.

44. Install the front wheels and lower the vehicle.

45. Install the gear shift lever by performing the following procedures:
   a. Install the shift lever and the shift lever cover bolts.
   b. Push the grommet and shift lever boot downward.
   c. Install the front console to the floor panel.

46. Install the back-up light switch connector and the speedometer cable to the transmission.

47. Connect the necessary hoses and electrical connectors.

48. Refill the transmission. Install the undercover, if equipped.

49. Connect the negative battery cable.

50. Start the engine, check for leaks.

4WD VEHICLES
1988–90

1. Disconnect the negative battery cable.

2. Remove the undercover, if equipped.

3. Remove the air cleaner (2.3L engine) or air cleaner duct and hose (2.6L engine). Using a clean shop cloth, cover the air cleaner port to prevent dirt from entering the engine.

4. Label and disconnect the necessary hoses and electrical connectors.

5. Remove the back-up light switch connector and the speedometer cable from the transmission.

6. Remove the gear shift lever by performing the following procedures:

   a. Place the gear shift lever in **N**.
   b. Remove the front console from the floor panel.
   c. Pull the shift lever boot and grommet upward.
   d. Remove the shift lever cover bolts and the shift lever.

7. Remove the transfer shift lever by performing the following procedures:

   a. Place the transfer shift lever in **H** (except 2.8L engine) or **2H** (2.8L engine).
   b. Pull the shift lever boot and dust cover upward.
   c. Remove the shift lever retaining bolts.
   d. Pull the shift lever from the transfer case.

8. Raise and safely support the vehicle with jackstands at the front and rear of the vehicle. Remove the front wheels.

9. Drain the transmission and transfer case fluid.

10. Remove the oil level gauge and the tube.

11. Disconnect the shift select control link rod from the select lever.

12. Disconnect the downshift cable from the transmission.

13. Disconnect and plug the fluid coolant lines from the transmission.

14. If equipped with a 1-piece driveshaft, remove the driveshaft flange-to-pinion nuts, lower the driveshaft and pull it from the transmission.

15. If equipped with a 2-piece driveshaft, perform the following procedures:

   a. Remove the rear driveshaft flange-to-pinion nuts.
   b. Remove the rear driveshaft flange-to-front driveshaft flange bolts and the rear driveshaft.
   c. Remove the center bearing-to-chassis bolts, move the front driveshaft rearward and from the transmission.

16. Remove the front driveshaft's splinded yoke flange-to-transfer case bolts and separate the front driveshaft from the transfer case; do not allow the splined flange to fall away from the driveshaft.

17. Remove the starter-to-engine bolts and the starter.

18. Remove the exhaust pipe-to-exhaust manifold nuts, the exhaust pipe bracket-to-transmission bolts, the front exhaust pipe-to-2nd exhaust pipe bolts and the front exhaust pipe from the vehicle.

19. Attach an engine hanger to the rear of the exhaust manifold.

20. Using an engine hoist, connect it to the engine hangers and support the engine.

21. If equipped with a 2.8L engine, remove the catalytic converter and the parking brake cable bracket.

22. Using a transmission jack, place it under the transmission and support the assembly.

23. Remove the rear mount-to-transmission nuts.

24. Remove the rear mount-to-side mount member nuts/bolts and the mount.

25. Remove the transmission-to-engine bolts.

26. Move the transmission assembly rearward.

27. Carefully lower the transmission.

To install:

28. Raise the transmission into position.

29. Move the transmission forward and engage it with the engine.

30. Install the engine-to-transmission bolts.

31. Install the rear mount and the rear mount-to-side mount member nuts/bolts.

32. Install the rear mount-to-transmission nuts.

33. Remove the transmission jack.

34. If equipped with a 2.8L engine, install the catalytic converter and the parking brake cable bracket.

35. Remove the engine hoist and the engine hanger from the rear of the exhaust manifold.

36. Install the front exhaust pipe, exhaust pipe-to-exhaust manifold nuts, the exhaust pipe bracket-to-transmission bolts, the front exhaust pipe-to-2nd exhaust pipe bolts.

37. Install the starter and the starter-to-engine bolts.

38. Install the front driveshaft's splinded yoke flange-to-transfer case bolts.

39. If equipped with a 2-piece driveshaft, perform the following procedures:

   a. Install the front driveshaft into the transmission and the center bearing-to-chassis bolts.
   b. Install the rear driveshaft and the rear driveshaft flange-to-front driveshaft flange bolts.
   c. Install the rear driveshaft flange-to-pinion nuts.

40. If equipped with a 1-piece driveshaft, install the driveshaft into the transmission and the driveshaft flange-to-pinion nuts.

41. Connect the fluid coolant lines to the transmission.

42. Connect the downshift cable to the transmission.

43. Connect the shift select control link rod to the select lever.

44. Install the oil level gauge and the tube.

45. Install the front wheels and lower the vehicle.

46. Install the transfer shift lever by performing the following procedures:

   a. Position the shift lever into the transfer case.
   b. Install the shift lever retaining bolts.
   c. Push the dust cover and the shift lever boot downward.

47. Install the gear shift lever by performing the following procedures:

   a. Install the shift lever and the shift lever cover bolts.
   b. Push the grommet and shift lever boot downward.
   c. Install the front console to the floor panel.

48. Install the back-up light switch connector and the speedometer cable to the transmission.

49. Connect the necessary hoses and electrical connectors.

50. Install the air cleaner (2.3L) or air cleaner duct and hose (2.6L).

51. Refill the transmission and the transfer case. Install the undercover, if equipped.

52. Install the negative battery cable.

Shift Linkage Adjustment

1986–87

1. Loosen the control rod locknuts so the trunnion will slide on the control rod.

2. Turn the manual shaft on the transmission fully clockwise, viewed from the left side of the transmission, then, back it off to the 3rd stop and set it in the **N** position.

3. While holding the shaft in this position, move the shift lever to the **N** position.

4. Push the shift shift, with the shift control lower lever rearward to remove play and tighten the adjusting nuts.

5. Road test the vehicle and check for proper operation of the transmission in all ranges.

1988–90

1. Loosen the shift linkage adjusting nut.

2. Push the shift lever fully rearward.

3. Return the shift lever 2 notches to the **N** position.

4. While holding the selector lever lightly toward the **R** range side, tighten the shift linkage nut.

Throttle Linkage Adjustment

GASOLINE ENGINE

1986–87

1. Loosen the throttle valve control cable adjusting nuts.
2. Check that the carburetor throttle adjusting screw is in contact with the stopper for normal idling.

NOTE: If the adjusting screw is not resting on the stopper, the fast idle mechanism is working and setting of the adjusting screw should be adjusted to obtain normal idling.

3. To obtain normal idling, perform the following procedures:
   a. Disconnect the battery ground cable.
   b. Remove the air cleaner cover.
   c. Fully depress the accelerator pedal to place the choke in the wide open position and release the pedal; do not depress the pedal again.
   d. Check the the throttle adjusting screw is in contact with the stopper.
   e. Install the air cleaner.
   f. Connect the battery cable.
4. Remove the rubber boot from the outer cable and turn the adjusting nuts to adjust the outer cable setting to 0.032–0.059 in. (0.8–1.5mm) and tighten the adjusting nuts; the setting is the distance between the outer cable end and the inner cable stopper.
5. After adjusting, check that the inner cable stroke, from the closed position of the throttle valve to the wide open position is 1.30–1.36 in. (32.9–33.9mm).
6. Install the rubber boot onto the outer cable.

1988–90

1. Depress the accelerator pedal all the way and check that the throttle valve opens fully.

NOTE: If the valve does not open fully, adjust the accelerator link.

2. Fully depress the accelerator.
3. Loosen the adjustment nuts.
4. Adjust the cable housing so the distance between the end of the boot and stopper on the cable is the 0.03–0.06 in. (0.8–1.5mm).
5. Tighten the adjusting nuts.
6. Recheck the adjustment.

DIESEL ENGINE

1. Loosen the throttle valve control cable adjusting nuts.
2. Fully depress the accelerator pedal to place the injection pump lever in contact with the maximum speed adjusting screw and hold the lever in that position.

NOTE: If the injection pump lever is not in contact with the adjusting screw, adjust the accelerator linkage.

3. Turn the outer cable adjusting nuts to adjust the outer cable setting to 0.032–0.059 in. (0.8–1.5mm) and tighten the adjusting nuts; the setting is the distance between the upper face of the rubber boot, on the end of the outer cable, and the inner cable stopper.
4. After adjusting, check that the inner cable stroke, from the normal idling position the maximum speed position is 1.30–1.36 in. (32.9–33.9mm).

NOTE: Normal idling position can not be obtained with the air conditioner operating and the engine coolant temperature higher than 59°F (15°C).

Neutral Safety Switch Adjustment

This adjustment is necessary only if the engine will start with the shift selector in any range except **N** or **P**.
   1. Loosen the neutral start switch bolt and set the shift selec-

tor into the **N** range.
   2. Align the groove and the neutral basic line.
   3. Hold it in position and torque the bolt to 9 ft. lbs.

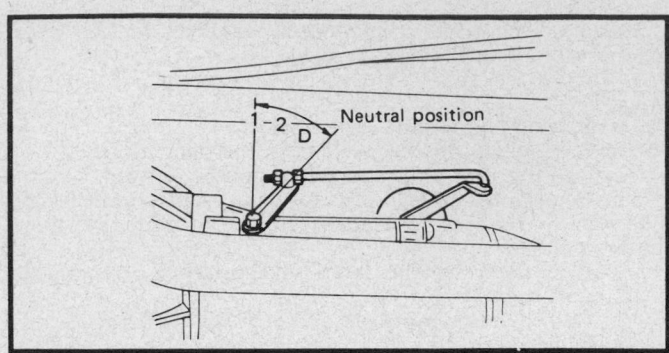

Adjusting the automatic transmission shift linkage— 1986–87

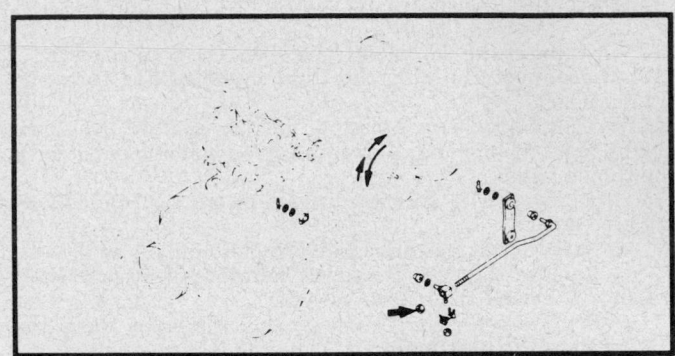

Adjusting the automatic transmission shift linkage— 1988–90

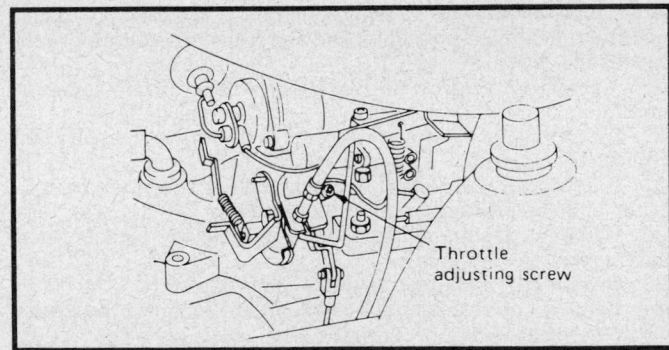

Location the throttle adjusting screw—1987–88 gasoline engine

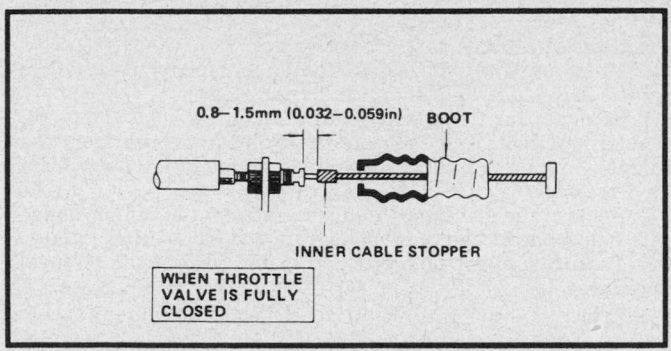

View of the throttle cable adjustment—1987–88 gasoline engine

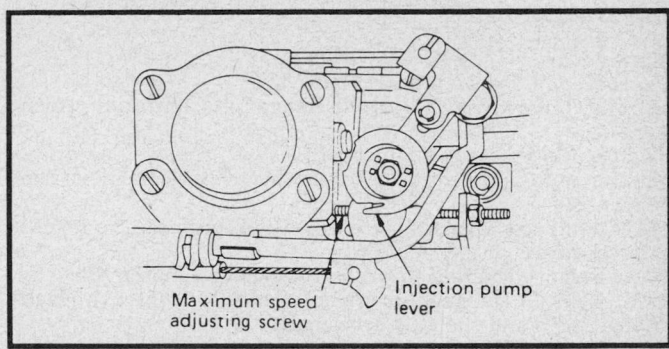

View of the injection pump maximum speed adjusting screw—diesel engine

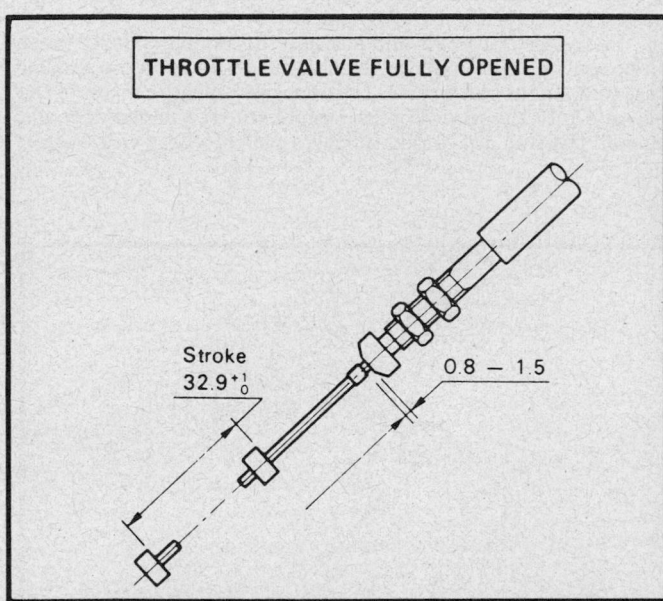

View of the throttle cable adjustment—1988–90 gasoline engine

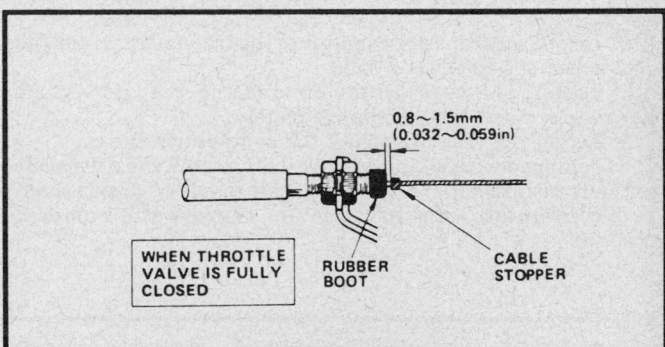

View of the throttle cable adjustment—diesel

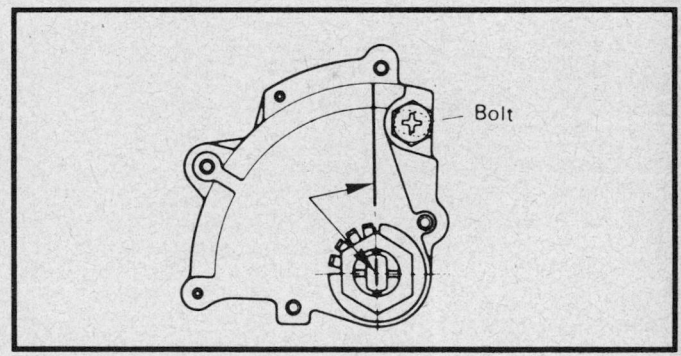

View of the neutral start switch

TRANSFER CASE

Transfer Case Assembly

Removal and Installation

The transfer case is an integral part of the transmission housing. Although the 2 cases can be separated, the transfer case should be removed with the transmission. The transfer case linkage is not adjustable.

DRIVE AXLE

Driveshaft and U-Joints

Removal and Installation

2WD DRIVESHAFT

1. Raise and support the vehicle safely.
2. Matchmark the driveshaft to the yokes.
3. Remove the driveshaft retaining bolts and remove the driveshaft.
4. To install, reverse the removal procedures.

4WD DRIVESHAFT

Rear

1. Raise and safely support the vehicle.
2. Matchmark the driveshaft flange-to-differential pinion flange.
3. If equipped with a 1-piece driveshaft, remove the driveshaft flange-to-pinion nuts, lower the driveshaft and pull it from the transmission.
4. If equipped with a 2-piece driveshaft, perform the following procedures:
   a. Remove the rear driveshaft flange-to-pinion nuts.
   b. Remove the rear driveshaft flange-to-front driveshaft flange bolts and the rear driveshaft.
   c. Remove the center bearing-to-chassis bolts, move the front driveshaft rearward and from the transmission.

To install:

5. If equipped with a 2-piece driveshaft, perform the following procedures:
   a. Install the front driveshaft into the transmission and the center bearing-to-chassis bolts.
   b. Install the rear driveshaft and the rear driveshaft flange-to-front driveshaft flange bolts.
   c. Install the rear driveshaft flange-to-pinion nuts.
6. If equipped with a 1-piece driveshaft, install the driveshaft into the transmission and the driveshaft flange-to-pinion nuts.
5. To complete the installation, reverse the removal procedures.

Front

1. Raise and safely support the vehicle.
2. Matchmark the driveshaft flange-to-transfer case flange and the driveshaft-to-differential pinion flange.
3. Remove the front driveshaft's splinded yoke flange-to-transfer case bolts and separate the front driveshaft from the transfer case; do not allow the splined flange to fall away from the driveshaft.
4. Remove the driveshaft flange-to-differential pinion flange bolts and separate the driveshaft from the front differential.
5. To install, align the matchmarks and reverse the removal procedures.

U-Joints

1. Raise and support the vehicle safely. Remove the driveshaft.
2. If the front yoke is to be disassembled, matchmark the driveshaft and sliding splined yoke so that driveline balance is preserved upon reassembly. Remove the snaprings that retain the bearing caps.
3. Select 2 press components, with 1 small enough to pass through the yoke holes for the bearing caps and the other large enough to receive the bearing cap.
4. Use a vise or a press and position the small and large press components on either side of the U-joint. Press in on the smaller press component so it presses the opposite bearing cap out of the yoke and into the larger press component. If the cap does not come all the way out, grasp it with a pair of pliers and work it out.

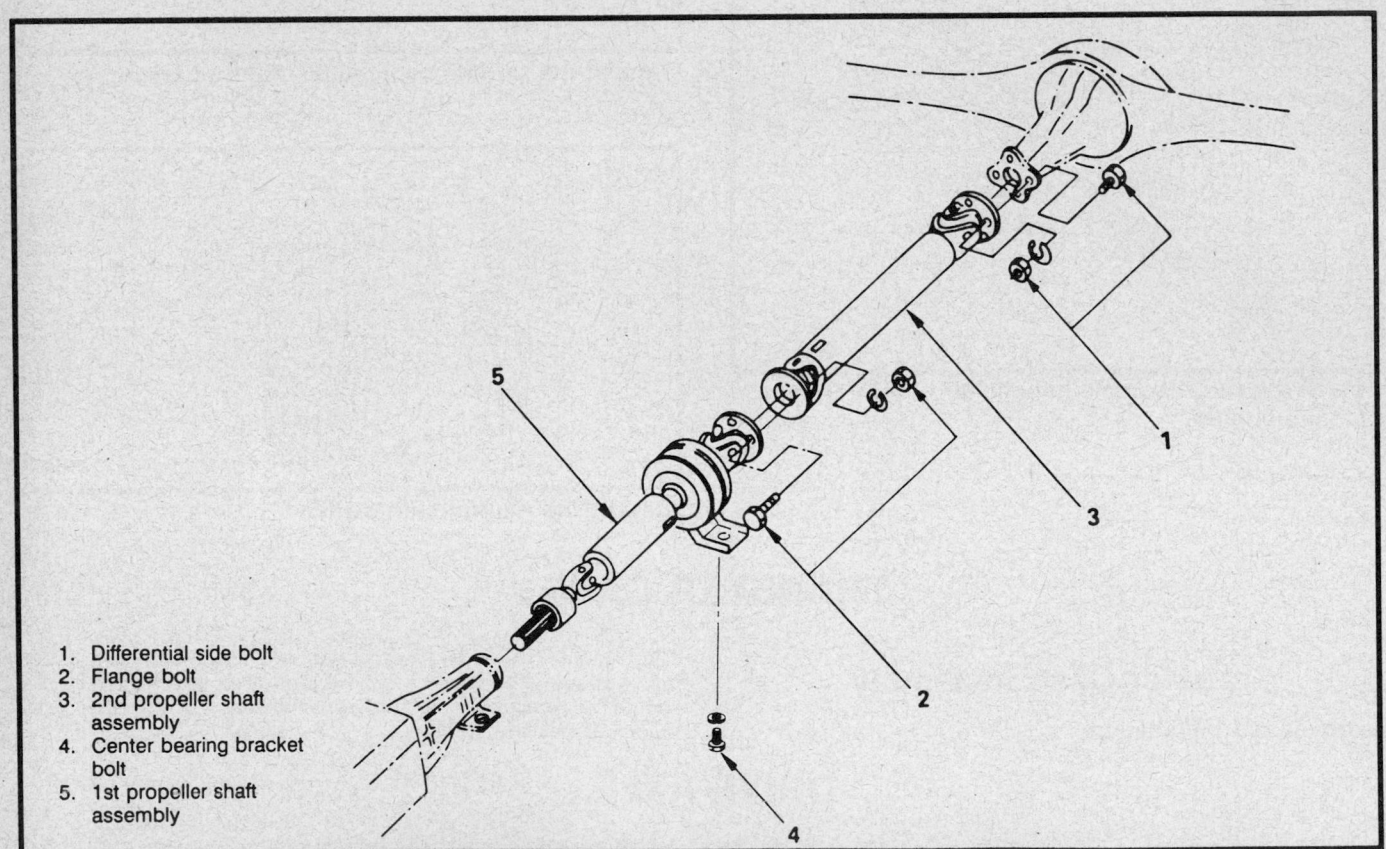

1. Differential side bolt
2. Flange bolt
3. 2nd propeller shaft assembly
4. Center bearing bracket bolt
5. 1st propeller shaft assembly

Exploded view of the rear driveshaft assembly—1986–87 similar

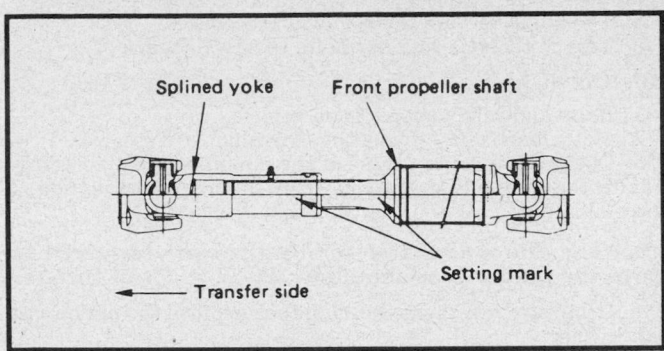

View of the front driveshaft—4WD

5. Reverse the position of the press components so that the smaller press component presses on the cross. Press the other bearing cap out of the yoke.

6. Repeat the procedure on the other bearings.

7. To install, grease the bearing caps and needles thoroughly if they are not pregreased. Start a new bearing cap into a side of the yoke. Position the cross in the yoke.

NOTE: Some U-joints have a grease fitting that must be installed in the joint before assembly. When installing the fitting, make sure that once the driveshaft is installed in the vehicle that the fitting is accessible to be greased at a later date.

8. Select 2 press components small enough to pass through the yoke holes. Put the press components against the cross and the cap and press the bearing cap ¼ in. below the surface of the yoke. If there is a sudden increase in the force needed to press the cap into place, or if the cross starts to bind, the bearings are cocked. They must be removed and restarted in the yoke. Failure to do so will cause premature bearing failure.

9. Install a new snapring.

10. Start the new bearing into the opposite side. Place a press component on it and press in until the opposite bearing contacts the snapring.

11. Install a new snapring. It may be necessary to grind the facing surface of the snapring slightly to permit easier installation.

12. Install the other bearings in the same manner.

13. Check the joint for free movement. If binding exists, smack the yoke ears with a brass or plastic faced hammer to seat the bearing needles. If binding still exists, disassemble the joint and check to see if the needles are in place. Do not strike the bearings unless the shaft is supported firmly. Do not install the driveshaft until free movement exists at all joints.

Front Axle Shaft, Bearing and Seal

Removal and Installation

AXLE SHAFT

1. Raise and safely support the vehicle.

2. Disconnect the front driveshaft from the differential.

3. Remove the wheels and skid plate.

4. Loosen the torsion bar completely with the height control adjusting bolts.

5. Remove the strut bars.

6. Disconnect the stabilizer bars from the lower control arms.

7. Remove the caliper assemblies and wire them to the frame; do not disconnect the brake lines.

8. Remove the ball joints from the tie rods.

9. Disconnect the upper control arms from the frame; make sure to note the number and positions of the shims.

10. Remove the steering link ends from the lower control arms.

11. Disconnect the shock absorbers from the lower control arms.

12. Disconnect the lower control arms from the frame.

13. Remove the locking hub.

14. Remove the rotors and upper links.

15. Remove the pitman arm and idler arm along with the steering linkage assembly.

16. Support the differential housing and lower it clear of the vehicle. Take care to avoid damaging the Birfield joints.

17. Drain the differential case and remove the 4 bolts attaching the axle mounting bracket to the case.

18. Pull the shaft assemblies from the case on both sides.

19. To install, reverse the removal procedures.

20. Check the level of the axle lubricant and bleed the brake system when finished.

AXLE SHAFT SEAL

1. Raise and safely support the vehicle. Remove the wheel assembly.

2. Remove the axle from the housing.

3. Remove the seal from the housing.

4. Clean and inspect the sealing surfaces of the housing and axle.

5. Using a seal installer tool, drive the new seal into the housing with the lip of the seal facing the housing.

6. Lightly coat the lip of the seal with oil and install the axle in the housing.

7. To complete the installation, reverse the removal procedures.

8. Check the level of the axle lubricant when finished.

AXLE SHAFT BEARINGS

1. Raise and safely support the vehicle.

2. Remove the axle shaft from the housing.

3. Support the axle shaft and remove the bearing retainer locknut and washer.

4. Remove the retainer, bearing and seal from the axle shaft.

5. To install, reverse the removal procedures.

6. Always replace the seal and lock washer when removing the axle shaft from the housing. Torque the bearing retainer nut to 188–195 ft. lbs.

WHEEL BEARINGS

1. Place the transfer case in **2H**. Raise and safely support the vehicle.

2. Remove the free wheeling hub cover assembly.

3. Remove the snapring and shims from the spindle.

4. Remove the free wheeling hub body and lock washer.

5. Remove the outer roller bearing assembly from the hub with a finger.

6. Using a brass or wood drift, drive out the inner bearing assembly along with the oil seal. Replace the seal.

7. Wash all parts in a non-flammable solvent.

8. Check all parts for cracks or wear. Thoroughly lubricate all bearing parts with a high-temperature wheel bearing grease. Remove any excess. Apply about 2 ounces of the grease to the hub.

To install:

9. Lightly coat the spindle with the same grease.

10. Place the inner bearing into the hub race and install a new seal and retaining ring.

11. Carefully install the hub on the spindle and install the outer bearing.

12. Install the spindle nut.

13. While rotating the hub, tighten the hub so the wheel can just be turned by hand.

14. Turn the hub 2–3 turns and back off the nut just enough so it can be loosened with the fingers.

15. Finger-tighten the nut so all play is taken up at the

bearing.

16. Attach a pull scale to a lug nut and check the amount of pull needed to start the wheel turning. Initial pull should be 2.6–4.0 lbs. When performing this test, make sure the brake pads are not touching the rotor. If the rotating torque is not correct, tighten the spindle nut until it is.

17. Install the snapring and shims, gasket and cover. Torque the cover bolts to 14 ft. lbs.

Rear Axle Shaft, Bearing and Seal

Removal and Installation

AXLE SHAFT

1. Raise and safely support the vehicle.
2. Remove the rear wheel assembly and brake drum.
3. Remove the 4 axle retainer bolts.
4. Using a slide hammer on the axle, pull the axle out of the housing.

5. To install, reverse the removal procedures.
6. Torque the axle retainer bolts to 51–58 ft. lbs.

PINION SEAL

1. Raise and safely support the vehicle.
2. Matchmark and remove the driveshaft.
3. Check the turning torque of the pinion before proceeding. This is the torque that must be reached during installation of the pinion nut.

NOTE: The amount of turning torque required to move the pinion gear should be 20–30 ft. lbs of torque.

4. Using a pinion flange holding tool, remove the pinion nut and washer.
5. Remove the pinion flange from the pinion gear.
6. Pry the pinion seal out of the differential carrier.
7. Clean and inspect the sealing surface of the carrier.

To install:

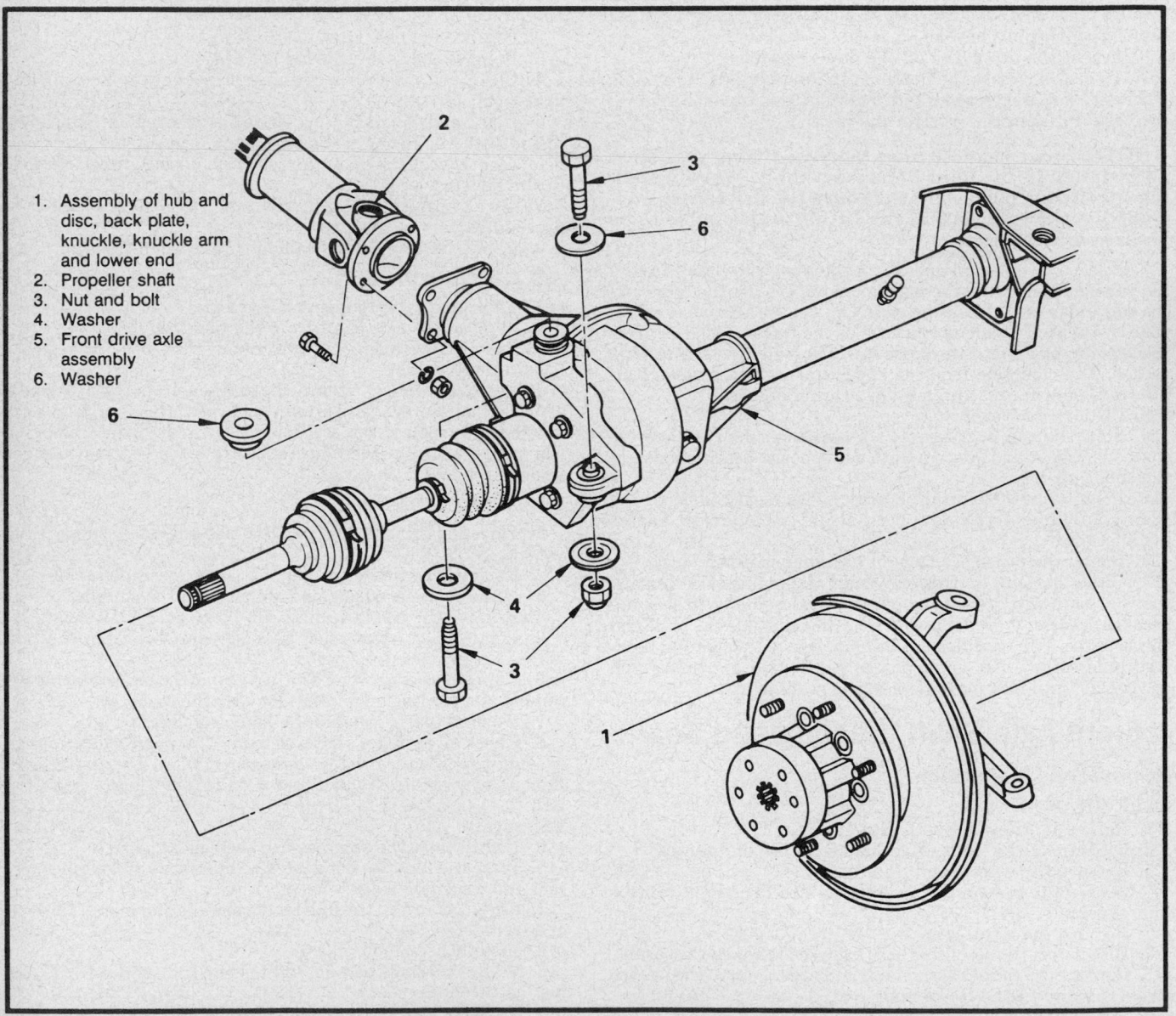

1. Assembly of hub and disc, back plate, knuckle, knuckle arm and lower end
2. Propeller shaft
3. Nut and bolt
4. Washer
5. Front drive axle assembly
6. Washer

Exploded view of the front axle assembly—4WD

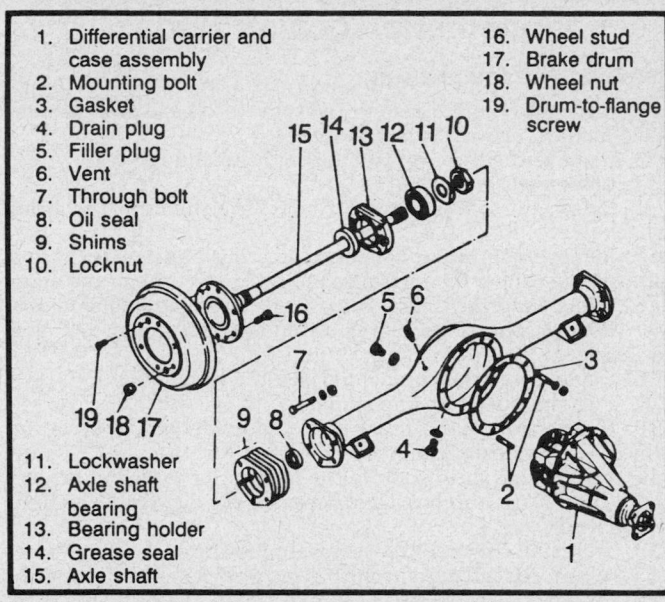

1. Differential carrier and case assembly
2. Mounting bolt
3. Gasket
4. Drain plug
5. Filler plug
6. Vent
7. Through bolt
8. Oil seal
9. Shims
10. Locknut
11. Lockwasher
12. Axle shaft bearing
13. Bearing holder
14. Grease seal
15. Axle shaft
16. Wheel stud
17. Brake drum
18. Wheel nut
19. Drum-to-flange screw

Exploded view of the rear axle assembly

8. Using a seal driver tool, drive the new seal into the carrier until the flange on the seal is flush with the carrier.

9. With the seal installed, the pinion bearing preload must be set.

10. Tighten the pinion nut while holding the flange, until the turning torque is the same as before removal of the nut.

11. Align the matchmarks and install the driveshaft.

12. Check the level of the differential lubricant when finished.

AXLE SHAFT SEAL

1. Raise and safely support the vehicle.
2. Remove the axle shaft from the housing.
3. Support the axle shaft and remove the bearing retainer locknut.
4. Remove the retainer, bearing and seal from the axle shaft.
5. Using a seal driver tool, remove the seal and install the new seal in the retainer.
6. To install, reverse the removal procedures.
7. Torque the bearing retainer nut to 188–195 ft. lbs.
8. Check the level of the axle lubricant when finished.

Front Wheel Hub, Knuckle and Bearings

Removal and Installation

1. Raise and safely support the vehicle. Remove the wheel assembly.
2. Remove the brake caliper and support it on a wire. Remove the rotor and dust shield.
3. If equipped with 4WD, remove the axle shaft from the hub.
4. Remove the tie rod end-to-steering knuckle nut and separate the tie rod from the steering knuckle.
5. Support the lower control arm and separate the steering knuckle from the lower ball joint.
6. Separate the steering knuckle from the upper ball joint.
7. Remove the steering knuckle from the vehicle.
8. To install, reverse the removal procedures.
9. Torque the ball joint nuts to 75 ft. lbs.

1. Bolt
2. Brake caliper
3. Hub cap
4. Split pin
5. Nut retainer
6. Hub nut
7. Lock washer
8. Outer bearing
9. Hub and disc assembly
10. Oil seal
11. Inner bearing and outer race
12. Bolt
13. Wheel pin

Exploded view of the front wheel assembly — 2WD Pick-UP

Manual Locking Hubs

Removal and Installation

1. Place the transfer case in the **2H** position. Raise and safely the vehicle.
2. Set the hubs in the **FREE** position.
3. Remove the hub cover bolts and the hub cover.
4. While pushing the follower toward the knob, turn the clutch assembly clockwise and then remove the clutch assembly from the knob.
5. Remove the snapring and the knob from the cover. Do not loose the detent ball.
6. Remove the ball and spring from the knob.
7. Remove the X-ring from the knob by pressing it off.

NOTE: Do not use a sharp instrument to remove this ring because it may scratch the ring.

8. Remove the compression spring, retaining spring and the follower from the clutch assembly.
9. Remove the retaining spring from the clutch assembly by turning it counterclockwise.
10. Remove the snapring and the inner assembly from the body.
11. Separate the ring, inner and spacer by removing the snapring.
12. To install, reverse the removal procedures. Apply grease to the X-ring, the inner cover and the outside circumference of the knob.

Automatic Locking Hubs

Removal and Installation

1. Move the transfer case shift lever into **2H** and move the vehicle forward and rearward about 3 ft.
2. Remove the hub cap-to-housing bolts and the cap.
3. Loosen the wheel nuts
4. Raise and safely support the vehicle. Remove the front wheel(s).
5. Remove the brake caliper-to-steering knuckle bolts and support the caliper on a wire; do not disconnect the brake hose.
6. Using snapring pliers, remove the snapring and shims.
7. Remove the drive clutch assembly, the inner cam and lockwasher.
8. Using a hub nut wrench, loosen the hub nut.
9. Pull the hub from the spindle.
10. If necessary, use a brass drift and a hammer to drive the wheel bearings from the hub.
11. If removing the disc from the hub, scribe matchmarks, remove the disc-to-hub bolts and separate the disc from the hub.
To install:
12. To install, reverse the removal procedures.
13. When installing the hub nut, perform the following procedures:
    a. Torque the hub nut to 22 ft. lbs. and loosen the nut.
    b. Using a spring gauge, connect it to the stud bolt at 90 degrees.
    c. Retorque the hub nut until the spring gauge measures a

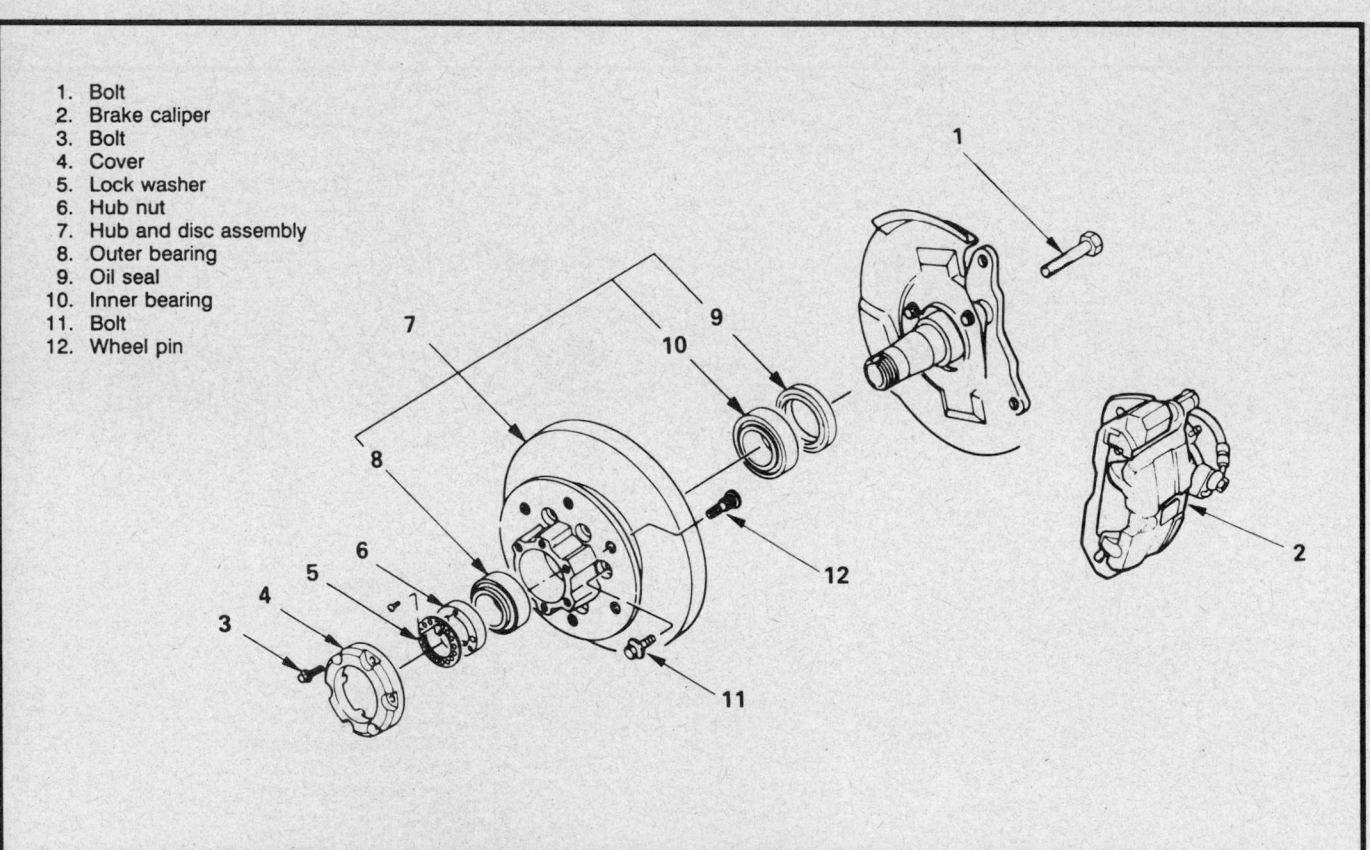

1. Bolt
2. Brake caliper
3. Bolt
4. Cover
5. Lock washer
6. Hub nut
7. Hub and disc assembly
8. Outer bearing
9. Oil seal
10. Inner bearing
11. Bolt
12. Wheel pin

Exploded view of the front wheel assembly—2WD Amigo

bearing preload of 4.4–5.5 lbs. (new bearing and oil seal) or 2.6–4.0 lbs. (used bearing and new oil seal).

14. Adjust the snapring clearance by performing the following procedures:

a. Install the special adjusting tool onto the hub until it comes in contact with the lock washer.

b. Using a feeler gauge, measure the clearance **t** between the hub and the snapring groove on the axle shaft.

c. If the clearance is larger than the snapring groove, install shims on the shaft so clearance **t** is 0–0.039 in. (0–0.1mm).

15. To complete the installation, reverse the removal procedures. Apply Loctite® to the hub cap bolts and torque the hub cap-to-hub assembly bolts to 43 ft. lbs. (60 Nm).

Pinion Seal

Removal and Installation

1. Raise and safely support the vehicle. If necessary, remove the skid plate.

2. Matchmark and remove the front driveshaft.

3. Check the turning torque of the pinion before proceeding. This is the torque that must be reached during installation of the pinion nut.

NOTE: The amount of turning torque required to move the pinion gear should be 20–30 ft. lbs of torque.

4. Using a pinion flange holding tool, remove the pinion nut and washer.

5. Remove the pinion flange from the pinion gear.

6. Pry the pinion seal out of the differential carrier.

7. Clean and inspect the sealing surface of the carrier.

To install:

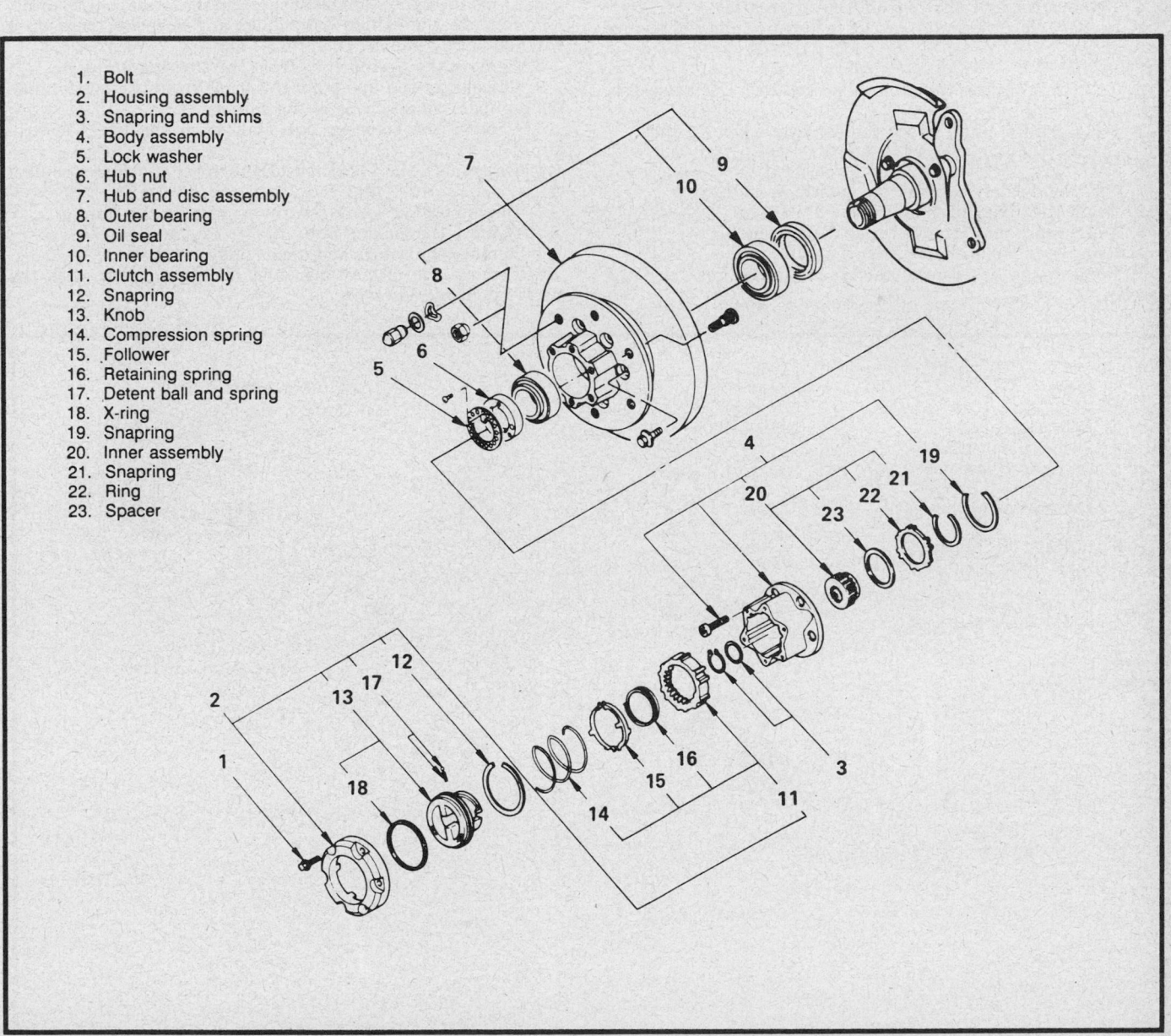

1. Bolt
2. Housing assembly
3. Snapring and shims
4. Body assembly
5. Lock washer
6. Hub nut
7. Hub and disc assembly
8. Outer bearing
9. Oil seal
10. Inner bearing
11. Clutch assembly
12. Snapring
13. Knob
14. Compression spring
15. Follower
16. Retaining spring
17. Detent ball and spring
18. X-ring
19. Snapring
20. Inner assembly
21. Snapring
22. Ring
23. Spacer

Exploded view of the manual locking hub assembly — 4WD

8. Using a seal driver tool, drive the new seal into the carrier until the flange on the seal is flush with the carrier.

9. With the seal installed, the pinion bearing preload must be set.

10. Tighten the pinion nut while holding the flange, until the turning torque is the same as before removal of the nut.

11. Align the matchmarks and install the driveshaft.

12. Check the level of the differential lubricant when finished.

Differential Carrier

Removal and Installation

FRONT DRIVE AXLE

1. Raise and safely support the vehicle.
2. Drain the differential oil.
3. Matchmark and remove the front driveshaft.
4. Remove the axle shafts from the differential.
5. Remove the differential carrier mounting bolts and remove the carrier.

To install:

6. To install, reverse the removal procedures. Use a new gasket when installing.
7. Fill the differential to the correct level when finished.

REAR DRIVE AXLE

1. Raise and safely support the vehicle.
2. Drain the differential oil.
3. Matchmark and remove the rear driveshaft.
4. Remove the axle shafts from the differential.
5. Remove the differential carrier mounting bolts and the carrier.

To install:

6. To install, reverse the removal procedures. Use a new gasket when installing.
7. Fill the differential to the correct level when finished.

Axle Housing

Removal and Installation

FRONT HOUSING

1. Raise and safely support the vehicle.
2. Matchmark and disconnect the front driveshaft from the differential.
3. Remove the wheels and skid plate.
4. Loosen the torsion bar completely with the height control adjusting bolts.
5. Remove the strut bars.
6. Disconnect the stabilizer bars from the lower control arms.
7. Remove the caliper assemblies and suspend them on a wire; do not disconnect the brake lines.
8. Remove the tie rod ends from the steering knuckles.
9. Disconnect the upper control arms from the frame; note the number and positions of the shims.
10. Remove the steering link ends from the lower control arms.
11. Disconnect the shock absorbers from the lower control arms.
12. Disconnect the lower control arms from the frame.
13. Remove the locking hub.
14. Remove the rotors and upper links.
15. Remove the pitman arm and idler arm along with the steering linkage assembly.

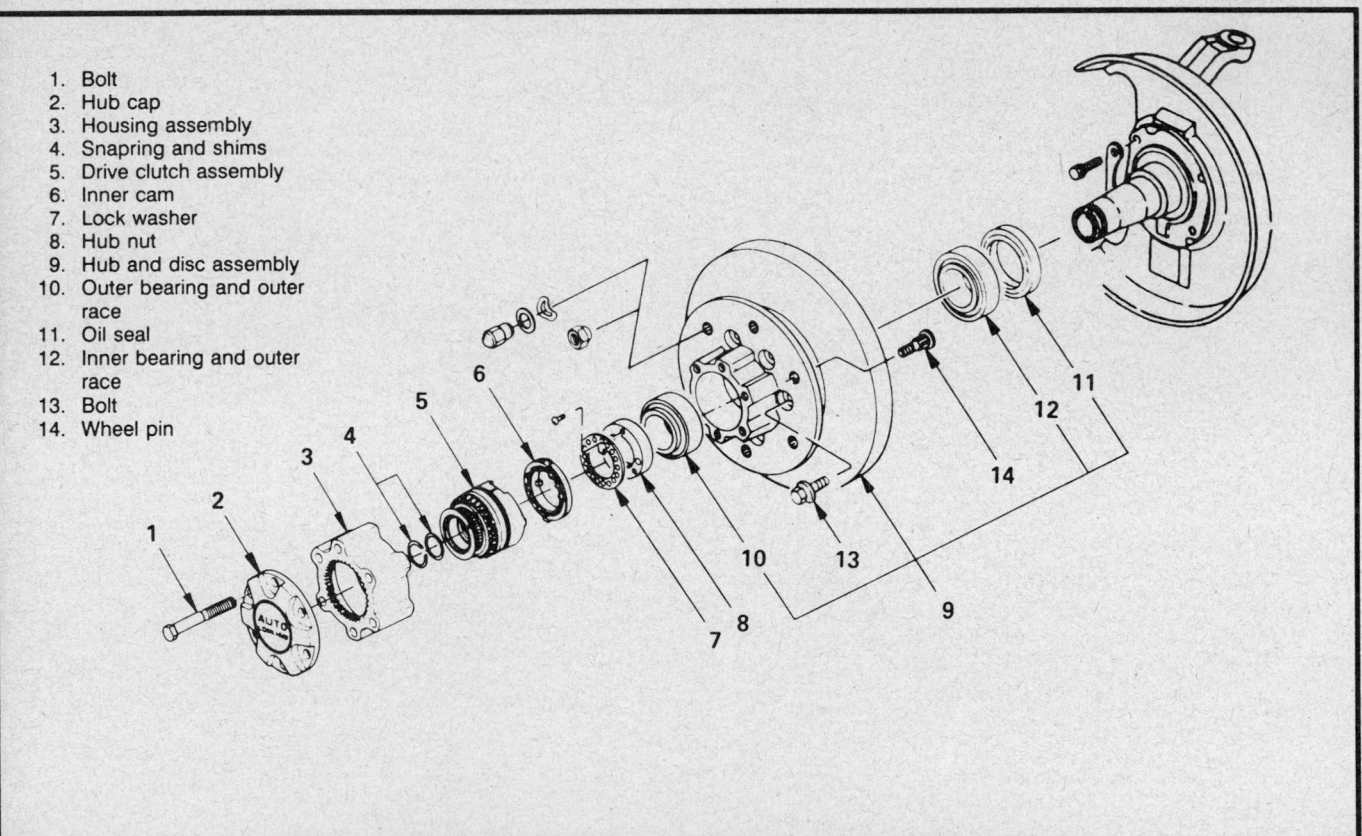

1. Bolt
2. Hub cap
3. Housing assembly
4. Snapring and shims
5. Drive clutch assembly
6. Inner cam
7. Lock washer
8. Hub nut
9. Hub and disc assembly
10. Outer bearing and outer race
11. Oil seal
12. Inner bearing and outer race
13. Bolt
14. Wheel pin

Exploded view of the automatic locking hub assembly — 4WD

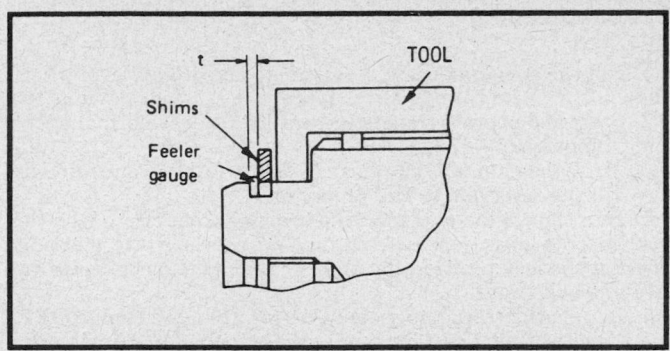

Using a feeler gauge to measure the shim clearance on the automatic locking hub assembly—4WD

16. Support the differential housing and lower it clear of the vehicle. Take care to avoid damaging the Birfield joints.

17. To install, reverse the removal procedures. Check the level of the axle lubricant when finished.

REAR HOUSING

1. Raise and safely support the vehicle. Remove the rear wheels.
2. Disconnect the shock absorbers from the spring plates.
3. Disconnect and plug the brake lines on the rear axle housing.
4. Disconnect the parking brake cables from the rear axle housing.
5. Support the rear axle housing and remove the housing to leaf spring U-bolts.
6. Remove the rear axle housing from the vehicle.
To install:
7. To install, reverse the removal procedures.
8. Torque the housing U-bolts to 36–43 ft. lbs. and the shock absorber bolts to 27–30 ft. lbs.
9. Bleed the brake system and check the level of the axle lubricant when finished.

STEERING

Steering Wheel

Removal and Installation

1. Disconnect the negative battery cable.
2. From the rear of the steering wheel, remove the horn pad screw. Pry the horn pad upward from the steering wheel.
3. Remove the steering wheel-to-steering column nut.
4. Matchmark the steering wheel-to-steering shaft.
5. Using a steering wheel puller, press the steering wheel from the steering shaft.
6. To install, align the matchmarks and reverse the removal procedures. Torque the steering wheel nut to 18–25 ft. lbs. for 1986–87 or 22–29 ft. lbs. (30–39 Nm) for 1988–90.

Manual Steering Gear

Removal and Installation

1. Disconnect the negative battery cable. Raise and safely support the vehicle. Remove the skid plate, if equipped.
2. Remove pitman arm nut and washer. Matchmark the pitman arm-to-pitman shaft.
3. Using a puller tool, press the pitman arm from the pitman shaft.
4. Remove the steering gear-to-steering shaft clamp bolt.
5. Remove the steering gear-to-frame bolts and the steering gear from vehicle.
To install:
6. Place the steering gear in position and install and tighten the mounting bolts.
7. Install the steering gear-to-steering shaft clamp bolt and torque to 29–40 ft. lbs. (40–49 Nm).
8. Torque the steering column mounting bolts to 13 ft. lbs.
9. Install the pitman arm-to-pitman shaft and torque the nut to 145–174 ft. lbs. (196–236 Nm).
10. Install the skid plate, if equipped.
11. Lower the vehicle.

Adjustment

1. Position the front wheel in the straight ahead position.
2. Loosen the locknut on the adjusting screw of the steering unit.
3. Turn the adjusting screw clockwise to decrease the free-play or counterclockwise to increase it.
4. With the steering wheel free-play set at 0.4–1.2 in. (10–30mm), torque the locknut to 15–22 ft. lbs. (20–29 Nm).

Power Steering Gear

Removal and Installation

1. Raise and safely support the vehicle. Remove the skip plate, if equipped.
2. Remove pitman arm nut and washer. Matchmark the pitman arm-to-pitman shaft.
3. Using a puller tool, press the the pitman arm from the pitman shaft.
4. Disconnect and plug the power steering lines at the steering gear.
5. Remove the steering gear-to-steering shaft clamp bolt.
6. Remove the steering gear-to-frame bolts and the steering gear from vehicle.
To install:
7. Place the steering gear in position and install and tighten the mounting bolts.
8. Install steering gear-to-steering shaft bolts and torque to 29–40 ft. lbs. (40–49 Nm).
9. Torque steering column mounting bolts to 13 ft. lbs.
10. Install the pitman arm to the pitman shaft. Install washer and torque nut to 145–174 ft. lbs. (196–236 Nm).
11. Install the skid plate, if equipped.
12. Lower the vehicle. Refill and bleed the power steering system.

Adjustment

1. Position the front wheel in the straight ahead position.
2. Loosen the locknut on the adjusting screw of the steering unit.
3. Turn the adjusting screw clockwise to decrease the free-play or counterclockwise to increase it.
4. With the steering wheel free-play set at 0.4 in. (10mm), torque the locknut to 26–35 ft. lbs. (37–47 Nm).

Power Steering Pump

Removal and Installation

1. Disconnect the negative battery cable.

2. Disconnect and plug the inlet and outlet fluid lines from the power steering pump.

3. Remove the drive belt from the pump.

4. Remove the pump-to-bracket bolts and the pump from the brackets.

5. To install, reverse the removal procedures.

6. Connect the negative battery cable. Refill and bleed the power steering system.

Belt Adjustment

1. Loosen the power steering pump adjusting bolts.

2. Using finger pressure, between the idler pulley and the power steering pump pulley, check the belt deflection; it should be 0.4 in. (10mm).

3. With the power steering pump adjusted to the correct belt deflection, tighten the pump bolts.

System Bleeding

1. Fill the power steering reservoir to the proper level when cold.

2. Start and operate the engine until it reaches normal operating temperatures.

3. Turn the engine **OFF** and check the fluid level. If necessary, fill the reservoir to the proper level.

4. Run the engine and turn the steering wheel from lock-to-lock, in both directions, 3–4 times; do not hold the steering wheel at the lock position for more than 5 seconds or temperature rise will result.

5. Return the steering wheel to center, turn the engine **OFF** and allow the fluid to sit for 5 minutes before adding any more.

6. If necesary, repeat the bleeding procedure until the air bubbles are removed from the system.

7. Fill the system to the proper level when finished.

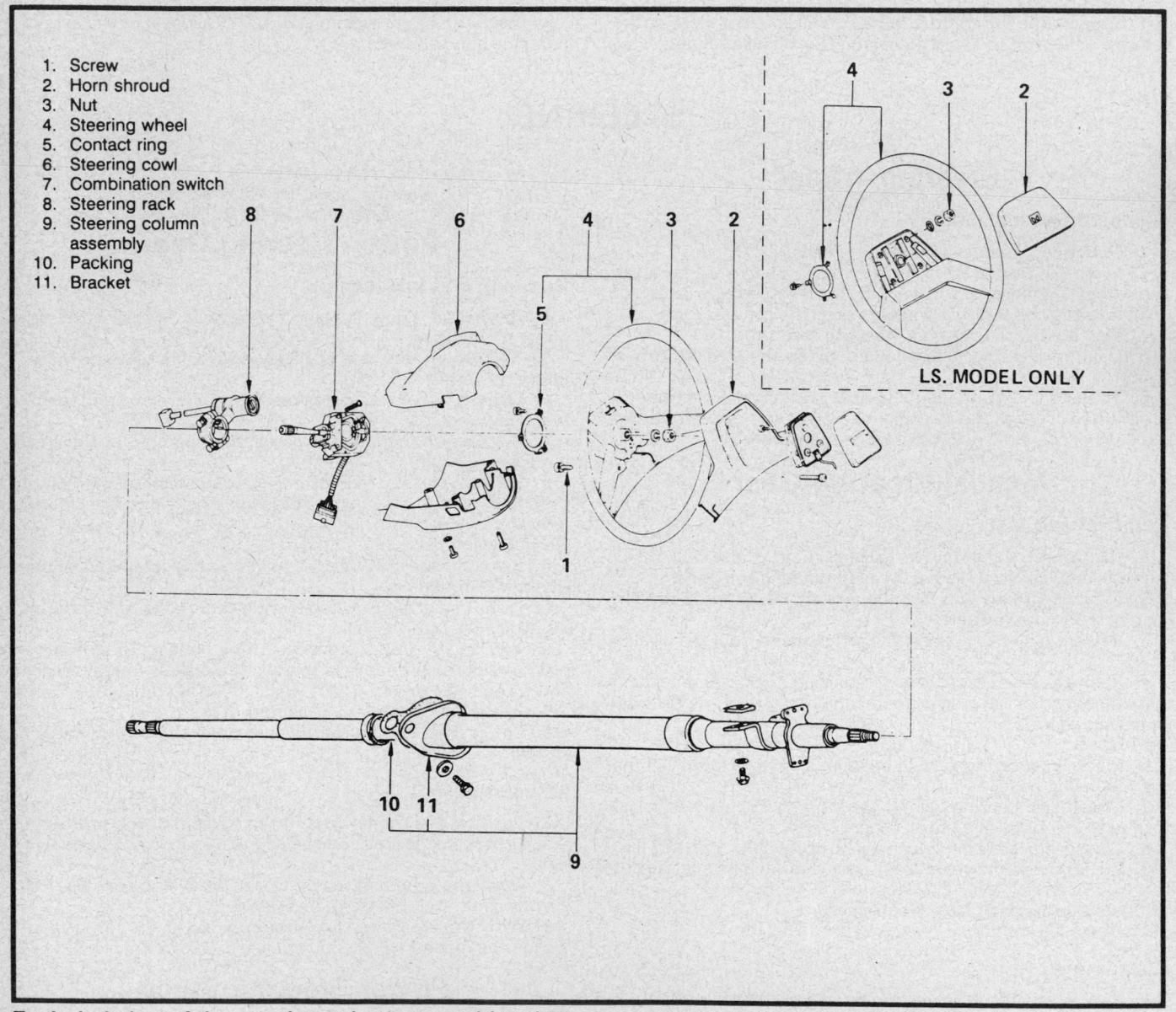

1. Screw
2. Horn shroud
3. Nut
4. Steering wheel
5. Contact ring
6. Steering cowl
7. Combination switch
8. Steering rack
9. Steering column assembly
10. Packing
11. Bracket

LS. MODEL ONLY

Exploded view of the steering column assembly— 1986–87

Tie Rod Ends

Removal and Installation

1. Raise and safely support the vehicle.
2. Matchmark the tie rod ends to the tie rod shaft for reinstallation purposes.
3. Remove the cotter pin and nut from the tie rod end and loosen the clamping bolts on the sleeve.
4. Using a tie rod end puller, separate the tie rod from the steering knuckle.
5. Unscrew the tie rod while counting the number of turns required to remove it.
6. Check the tie rod end for damage and replace it, if necessary.

To install:

7. Install the tie rod end in the sleeve the same number of turns as when removing it.
8. Install the tie rod end in the steering knuckle. Install the nut and new cotter pin.
9. Check the toe in when finished.

Intermediate Rod and Tie Rods

Removal and Installation

1. Raise and safely support the vehicle.
2. Remove cotter pin from the ball studs connecting tie rods-to-intermediate rod and the steering damper. Remove the castellated nuts. Using a ball joint separator tool, separate the parts.
3. Remove the nut and lockwasher on ball stud connecting the intermediate rod to idler arm. Using a ball joint separator tool, separate the intermediate rod from the idler arm.

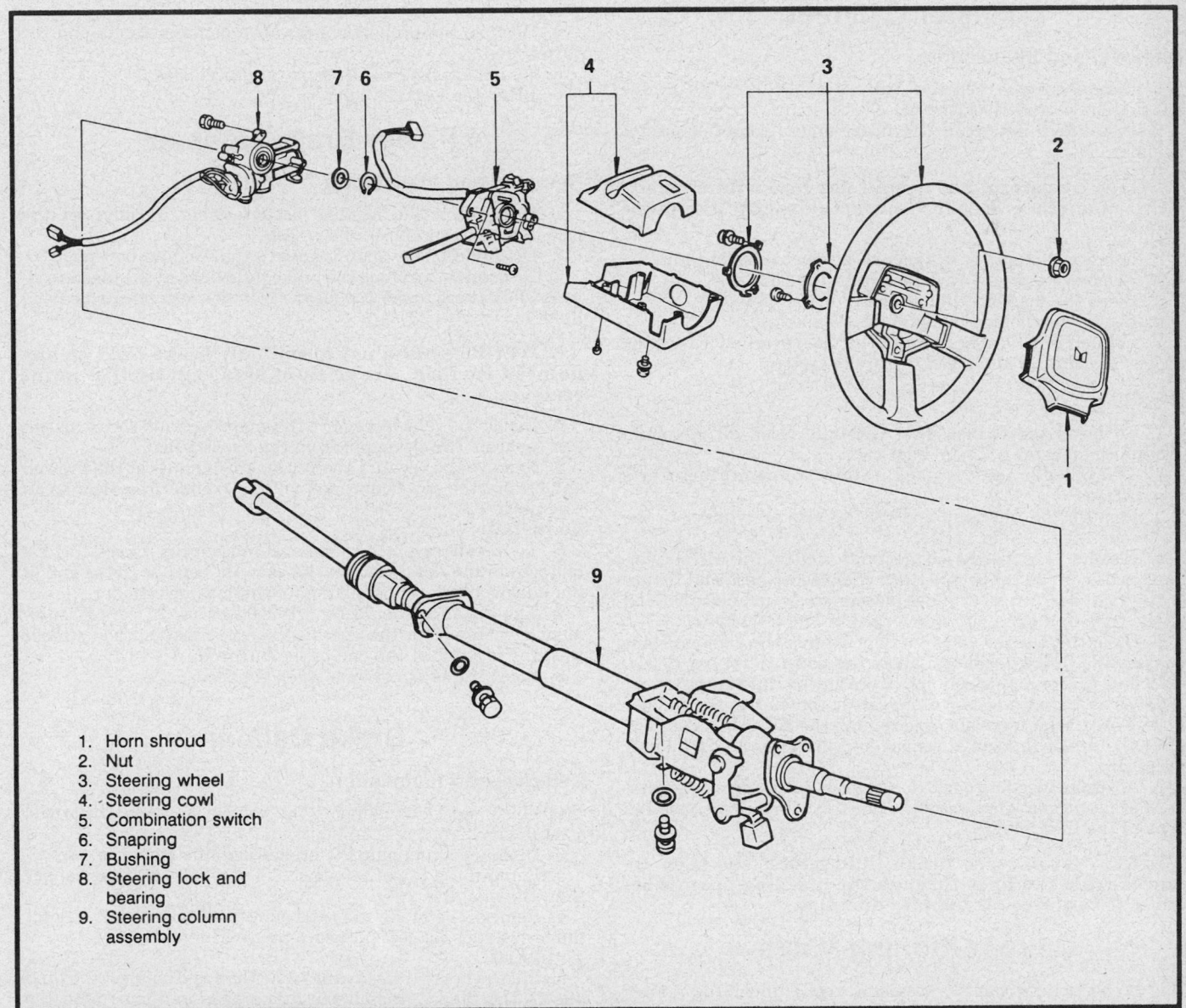

1. Horn shroud
2. Nut
3. Steering wheel
4. Steering cowl
5. Combination switch
6. Snapring
7. Bushing
8. Steering lock and bearing
9. Steering column assembly

Exploded view of the steering column assembly— 1988–90

4. Remove the intermediate rod with tie rods.

5. If the tie rod is replaced, disconnect the intermediate rod from tie rod.

To install:

6. Make sure the threads on the ball studs and nuts are clean and smooth.

7. Install the intermediate rod-to-idler arm and torque the nut to 50 ft. lbs.

8. Raise the end of the rod and install it on the pitman arm.

Torque the nut to 44 ft. lbs. Tighten the nut just enough to insert cotter pin and install new cotter pin.

9. Install intermediate rod to steering damper end. Torque nut to 87 ft. lbs., then, advance nut just enough to insert cotter pin and install new cotter pin.

10. Install the tie rods to adapter, torque nut to 44 ft. lbs., then, advance nut just enough to insert cotter pin and install new cotter pin and lubricate tie rod ball studs.

BRAKES

For all brake system repair and service procedures not detailed below, please refer to "Brakes" in the Unit Repair section.

Master Cylinder

Removal and Installation

1. Disconnect the negative battery cable. Firmly, set the parking brake and block the wheels.

2. Disconnect and plug the brake lines from the master cylinder.

NOTE: Be careful not to spill any brake fluid on any painted surface. Brake fluid acts exactly like paint remover.

3. Remove the master cylinder-to-power brake unit nuts.

4. Remove the master cylinder from the booster.

5. Bleed the master cylinder before installing.

6. Install the master cylinder onto the booster.

7. Connect the fluid lines, refill the master cylinder with the proper brake fluid and bleed the brake system.

Bleeding

1. To bleed the brakes, first carefully clean all dirt from around the master cylinder filler cap.

2. If a bleeder tank is used, follow the manufacturer's instructions.

3. Remove the filler cap and fill the master cylinder to the lower edge of the filler neck.

4. Clean off the bleeder connections at all of the wheel cylinders or disc brake calipers. Attach the bleeder hose and fixture to the right rear wheel cylinder bleeder screw and place the end of the tube in a glass jar, submerged in brake fluid.

5. Open the bleeder valve ½–¾ of a turn. Have an assistant depress the brake pedal and allow the pedal to return slowly. Continue this pumping action to force any air out of the system.

6. When bubbles cease to appear at the end of the bleeder hose, close the bleeder valve and remove the hose. Check the level of the brake fluid in the master cylinder and add fluid, if necessary.

7. After the bleeding operation at each caliper or wheel cylinder has been completed, refill the master cylinder reservoir and replace the filler plug.

NOTE: Never reuse brake fluid which has been removed from the lines through the bleeding process because it contains air bubbles and dirt.

Proportioning Valve

The proportioning valve is located directly under the master cylinder.

Removal and Installation

1. Disconnect the negative battery cable. Firmly, set the

parking brake and block the wheels.

2. Disconnect the electrical connector from the proportioning valve.

3. Disconnect and plug the fluid lines from the proportioning valve.

4. Remove the proportioning valve-to-chassis bolts and the valve.

5. To install, reverse the removal procedures.

6. Bleed the brake system.

Power Brake Booster

Removal and Installation

1. Disconnect the negative battery cable. Firmly, set the parking brake and block the wheels.

2. Disconnect the vacuum hose to the vacuum booster.

3. Disconnect and plug the brake fluid lines at the master cylinder. Place rags under the master cylinder to catch any leaking fluid.

NOTE: Be careful not to spill any brake fluid on any painted surface. Brake fluid acts exactly like paint remover.

4. Inside the vehicle, remove the snapring from the clevis pin and separate the clevis pin from the brake pedal.

5. Remove the vacuum booster mounting nuts at the firewall and lift out the power unit and master cylinder/reservoir as an assembly.

To install:

6. To install, reverse the removal procedures. Check the distance from the flange face of the vacuum booster to the end of the push-rod before installation of the master cylinder.

7. The distance should be 0.709–0.717 in. If the measurement deviates from the specified range, make an adjustment with the locknut at the end of the pushrod.

8. Bleed the brake system when finished.

Brake Caliper

Removal and Installation

1. Raise and safely support the vehicle. Remove the wheel assembly.

2. Disconnect and plug the brake fluid line from the caliper.

3. Remove the brake caliper mounting bolts and the caliper from the mount.

4. Remove the brake pads and clips from the caliper. Inspect the brake pads for wear; replace them, if necessary.

To install:

5. Fill the brake caliper with brake fluid and connect the fluid line to the caliper. Install the brake pads and clips onto the caliper.

6. Install the caliper on the mounting bracket.

7. Install the wheel assembly. Bleed the brake system and lower the vehicle.

Disc Brake Pads

Removal and Installation

FRONT

1. Raise and safely support the vehicle. Remove the wheel assembly.
2. Remove the brake caliper mounting bolts and remove the caliper without disconnecting the brake fluid line. Support the caliper so it does not hang on the brake line.
3. Remove the brake pads and retaining clips from the caliper.
4. Using a C-clamp, press the brake caliper piston into the caliper until it bottoms out.

To install:

5. Install the new brake pads and clips in the caliper and install the caliper in the mounting bracket.
6. Install the wheel assembly. Check the brake fluid level.

7. Pump the brake pedal until pressure is felt before moving the vehicle.

REAR

1. Raise and safely support the vehicle. Remove the wheel assembly.
2. Remove the brake caliper mounting bolts and remove the caliper without disconnecting the brake fluid line. Support the caliper so it does not hang on the brake line.
3. Remove the brake pads and retaining clips from the caliper.
4. Turn the adjusting screw to retract the caliper piston to its lowest position.

To install:

5. Install the new brake pads and clips in the caliper and install the caliper in the mounting bracket.
6. Install the wheel assembly. Check the brake fluid level.
7. Pump the brake pedal until pressure is felt before moving the vehicle.

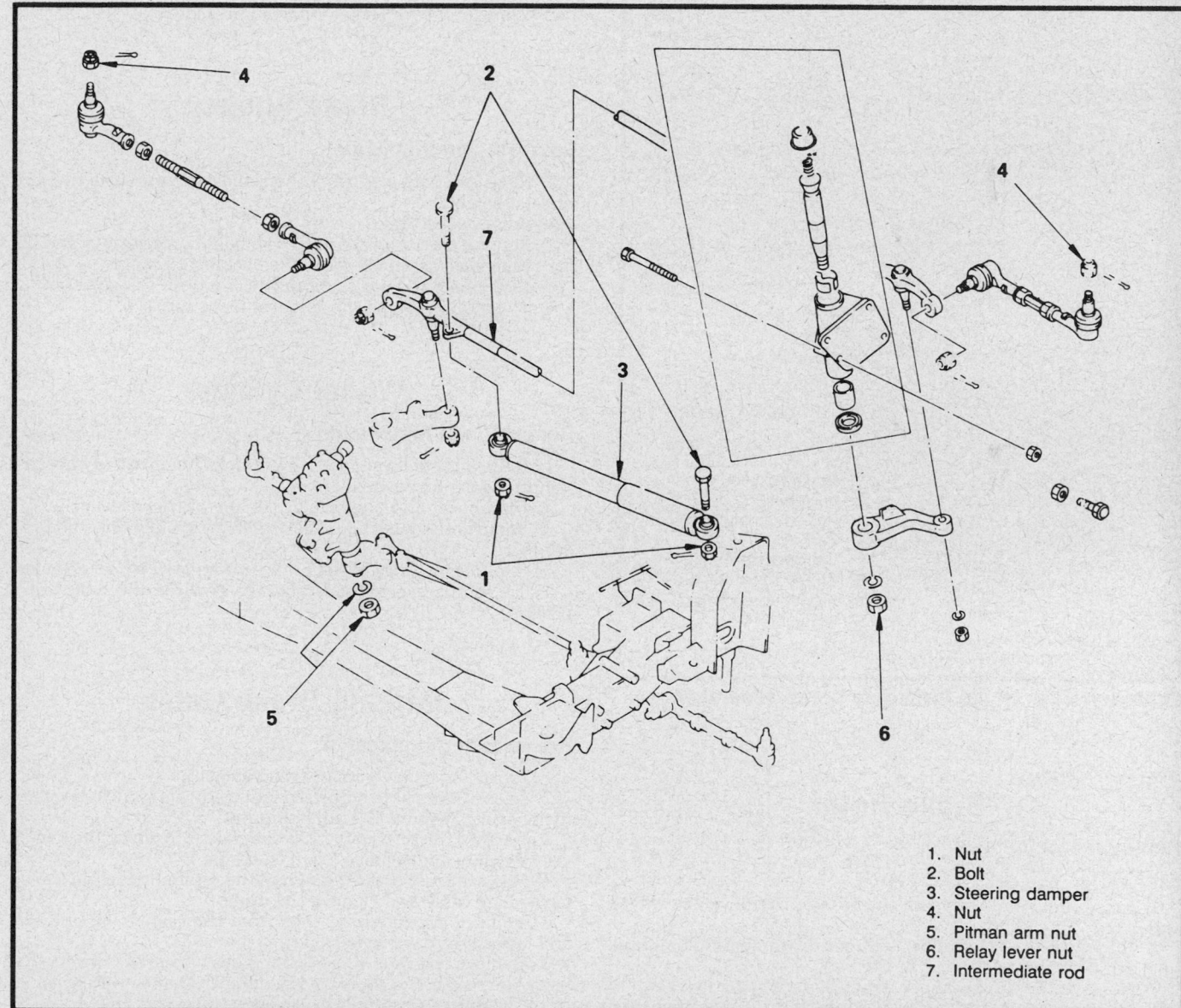

1. Nut
2. Bolt
3. Steering damper
4. Nut
5. Pitman arm nut
6. Relay lever nut
7. Intermediate rod

Exploded view of the steering linkage assembly

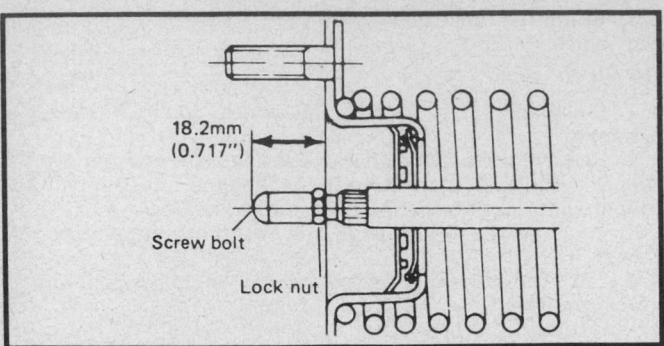

View of the power booster pushrod adjustment

18.2mm
(0.717")

Screw bolt

Lock nut

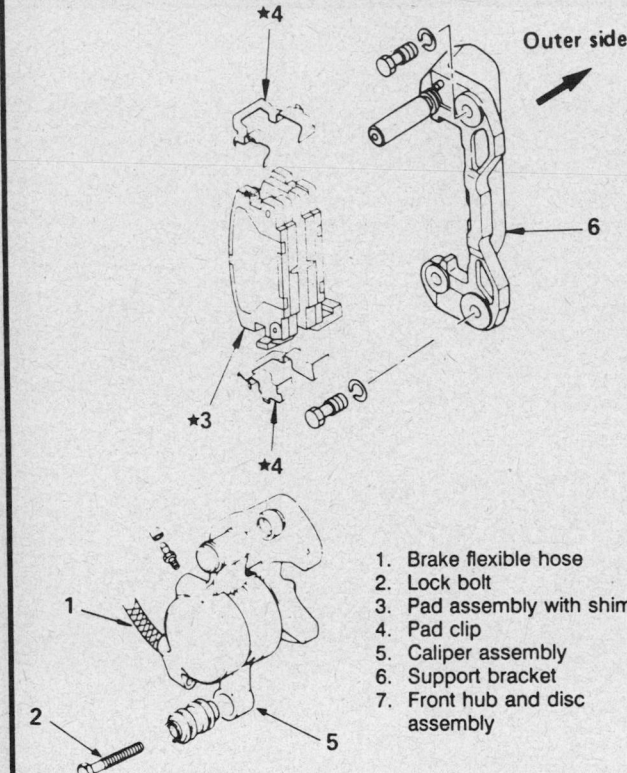

Outer side

1. Brake flexible hose
2. Lock bolt
3. Pad assembly with shim
4. Pad clip
5. Caliper assembly
6. Support bracket
7. Front hub and disc assembly

Exploded view of the front disc brake assembly

Brake Rotor

Removal and Installation

FRONT

1. Raise and safely support the vehicle. Remove the wheel assembly.
2. Remove the brake caliper without disconnecting the fluid line. Support the caliper out of the way.
3. Remove the brake caliper from the mounting bracket.
4. Remove the dust cover, cotter pin and locknut from the rotor.
5. Place a hand over the outer wheel bearing in the rotor and remove the rotor from the spindle.
6. To install, reverse the removal procedures.
7. Adjust the wheel bearings.

REAR

1. Raise and safely support the vehicle. Remove the wheel assembly.
2. Remove the brake caliper without disconnecting the fluid line. Support the caliper out of the way.
3. Remove the brake caliper from the mounting bracket.
4. Remove the rotor from the axle shaft.
5. To install, reverse the removal procedures.

Brake Drums

Removal and Installation

1. Raise and safely support the vehicle.
2. Remove the wheel and the brake drum.
3. To install, reverse the removal procedures.

Brake Shoes

Removal and Installation

1. Raise and safely support the vehicle. Remove the tire and wheel assembly.
2. Remove the brake drum.
3. Remove the return springs, the hold-down springs and lift the brake shoe assembly from the backing plate.
4. Disconnect the parking brake cable from the adjuster.
5. To install, reverse the removal procedures.

Wheel Cylinder

Removal and Installation

1. Raise and safely support the vehicle. Remove the wheel assembly, brake drums and shoes.
2. Disconnect and plug the brake line at the wheel cylinder.
3. Remove the wheel cylinder-to-backing plate bolts and the cylinder.
4. Cap the openings of the brake line and the wheel cylinder.
5. To install, reverse the removal procedures. Bleed the brake system.

Parking Brake Cable

Removal and Installation

1. Raise and safely support the vehicle.
2. Loosen the cable adjusting nut and remove the lever return spring. Remove the adjusting nut.
3. Remove the cotter pin from the retaining pin on the 2nd lever assembly and remove the front cable.
4. Remove the 2 cotter pins from the retaining pins on the intermediate cable and remove the cable.
5. Remove the retaining clips from the rear fixing brackets and lower the rear brake cables.
6. Remove the rear wheel assemblies and brake drums. Remove the rear brake shoes and disconnect the rear brake cables from the lever in the rear brake shoes.
7. To install, reverse the removal procedures. Adjust the cables when finished.

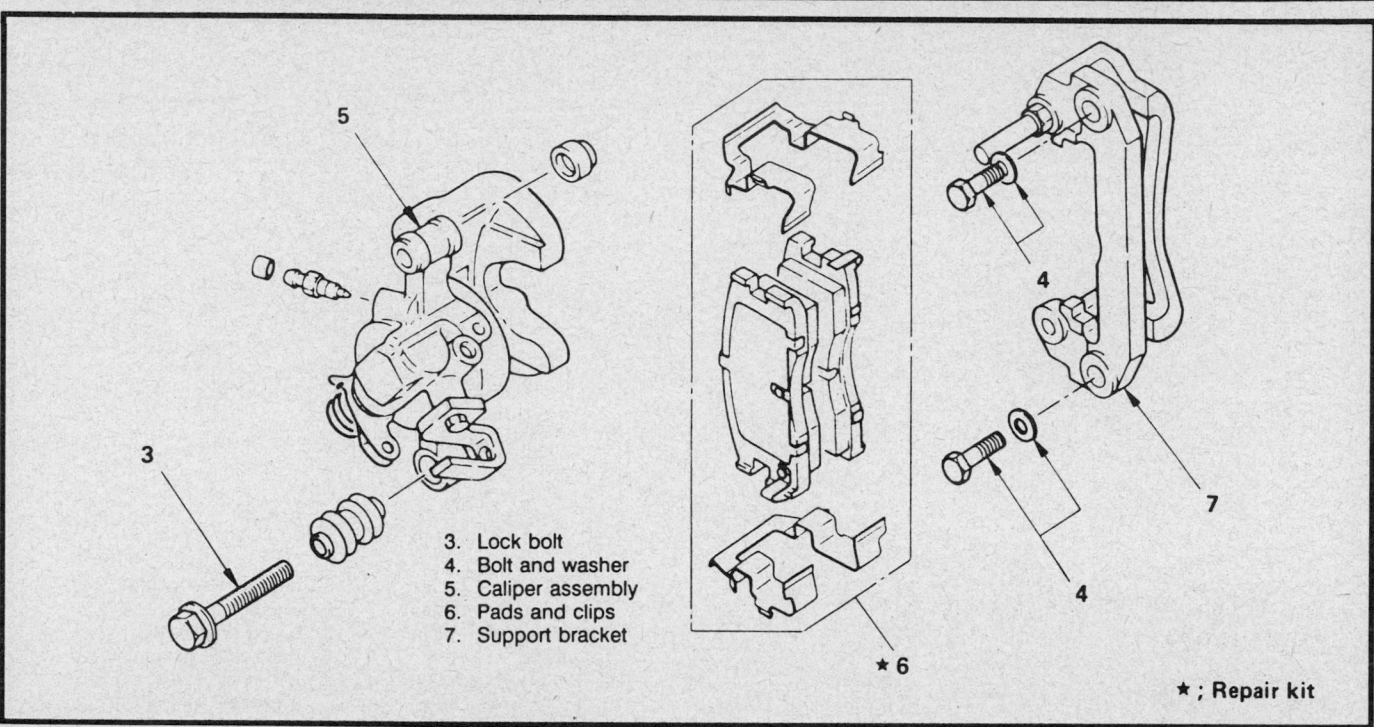

3. Lock bolt
4. Bolt and washer
5. Caliper assembly
6. Pads and clips
7. Support bracket

★ ; Repair kit

Exploded view of the rear disc brake assembly

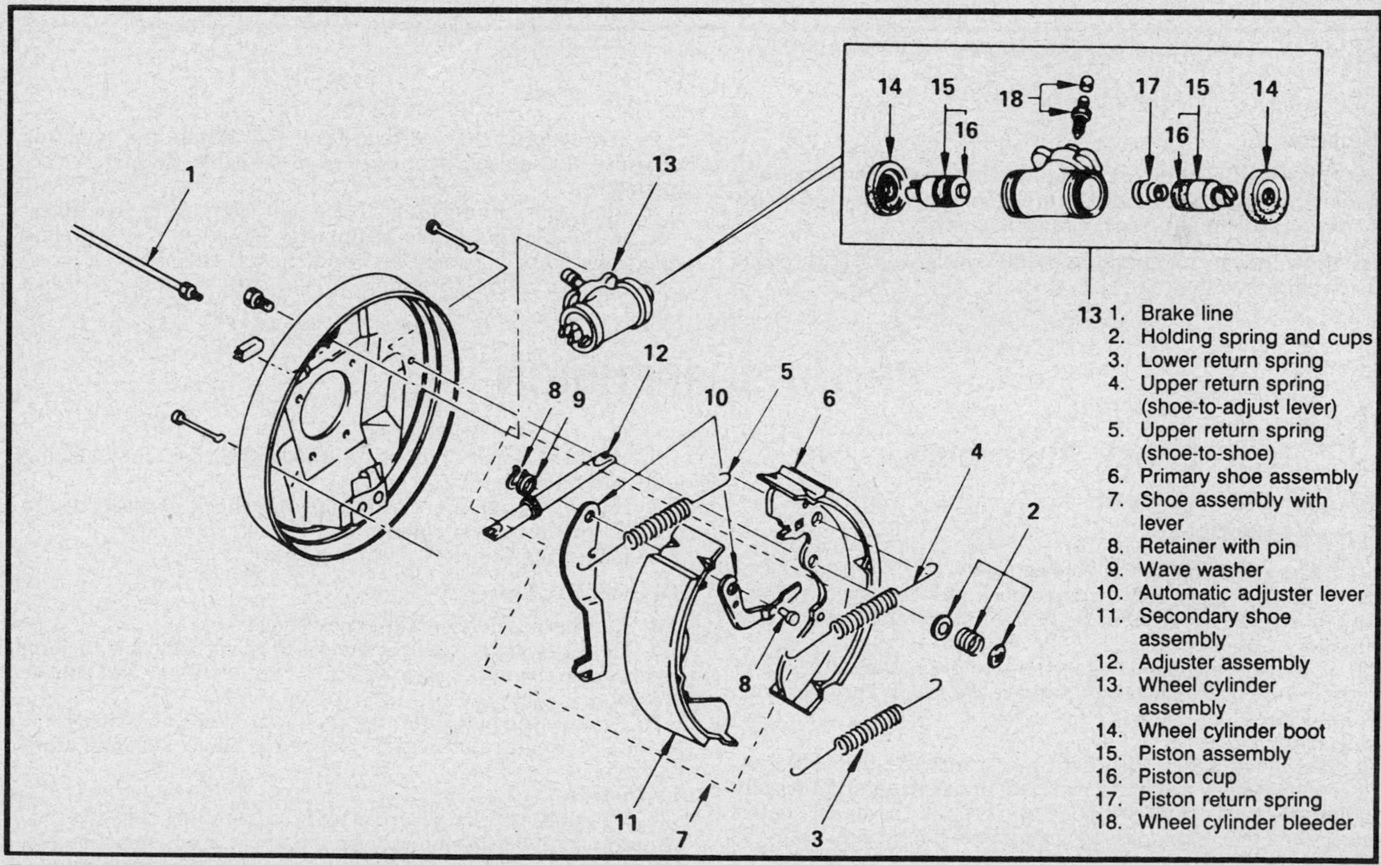

1. Brake line
2. Holding spring and cups
3. Lower return spring
4. Upper return spring (shoe-to-adjust lever)
5. Upper return spring (shoe-to-shoe)
6. Primary shoe assembly
7. Shoe assembly with lever
8. Retainer with pin
9. Wave washer
10. Automatic adjuster lever
11. Secondary shoe assembly
12. Adjuster assembly
13. Wheel cylinder assembly
14. Wheel cylinder boot
15. Piston assembly
16. Piston cup
17. Piston return spring
18. Wheel cylinder bleeder

Exploded view of the rear brake drum/shoe assembly

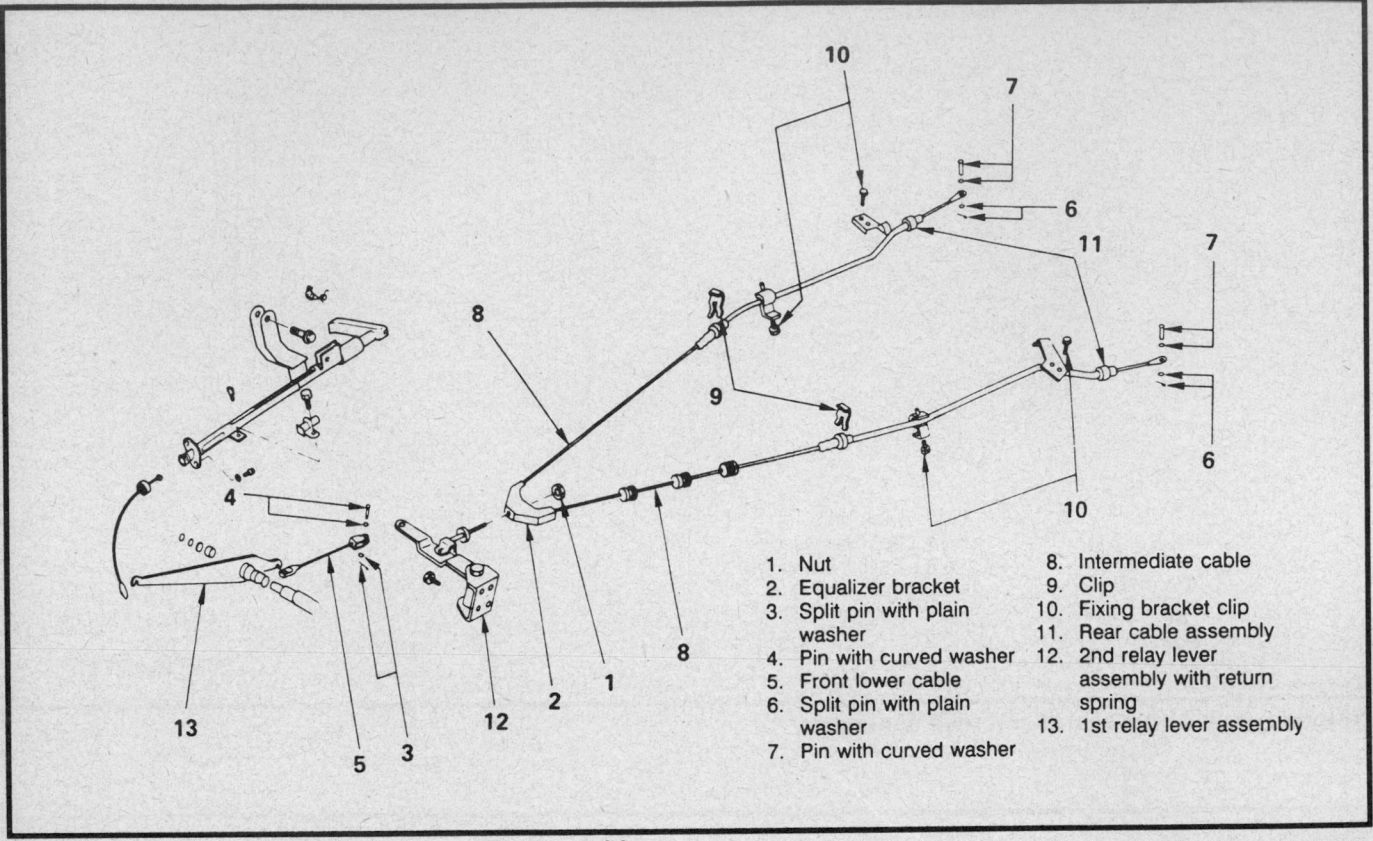

Exploded view of the parking brake cable assembly

1. Nut
2. Equalizer bracket
3. Split pin with plain washer
4. Pin with curved washer
5. Front lower cable
6. Split pin with plain washer
7. Pin with curved washer
8. Intermediate cable
9. Clip
10. Fixing bracket clip
11. Rear cable assembly
12. 2nd relay lever assembly with return spring
13. 1st relay lever assembly

Adjustment

NOTE: Adjustment of the parking brake is necessary every time the rear brake cables are disconnected or after overhauling the rear brake assembly.

1. Fully, release the parking brake lever and check the cable for free movement.

2. Firmly, grab the 2nd relay lever rod. Rotate the adjusting nut until all the slack is removed from the cable. Tighten the adjusting nut.

3. Apply the parking brake to the fully set position 3–4 times.

4. If the parking brake is properly adjusted, the traveling range should be between 12–14 notches. If the travel is incorrect, readjust to specifications.

FRONT SUSPENSION

Shock Absorbers

Removal and Installation

2WD VEHICLES

1. Raise and support the vehicle safely.

2. Hold the upper stem of the shock absorber from turning and remove the upper stem retaining nut, retainer and rubber grommet.

3. Remove the bolt retaining the lower shock absorber pivot to the lower control arm and remove the shock absorber from the vehicle.

To install:

4. Install the shock absorber by first installing the lower retainer and rubber grommet over the upper stem and then, installing the shock fully extended up through the upper control arm so the upper stem passes through the mounting hole in the frame bracket.

5. Install the upper rubber grommet, retainer and attaching nut over the shock absorber upper stem.

6. Hold the upper stem of the shock absorber from turning and tighten the retaining nut.

7. Install the retainers attaching the shock absorber lower pivot to the lower control arm and tighten them.

8. Lower the vehicle.

4WD VEHICLES

1. Raise and safely support the vehicle.

2. Hold the upper stem of the shock absorber from turning and remove the upper stem retaining nut, retainer and rubber grommet.

3. Remove the bolt retaining the lower shock absorber pivot to the lower control arm and remove the shock absorber from the vehicle.

To install:

4. Install the shock absorber by first installing the lower retainer and rubber grommet over the upper stem and then, installing the shock fully extended up through the upper control arm so the upper stem passes through the mounting hole in the frame bracket.

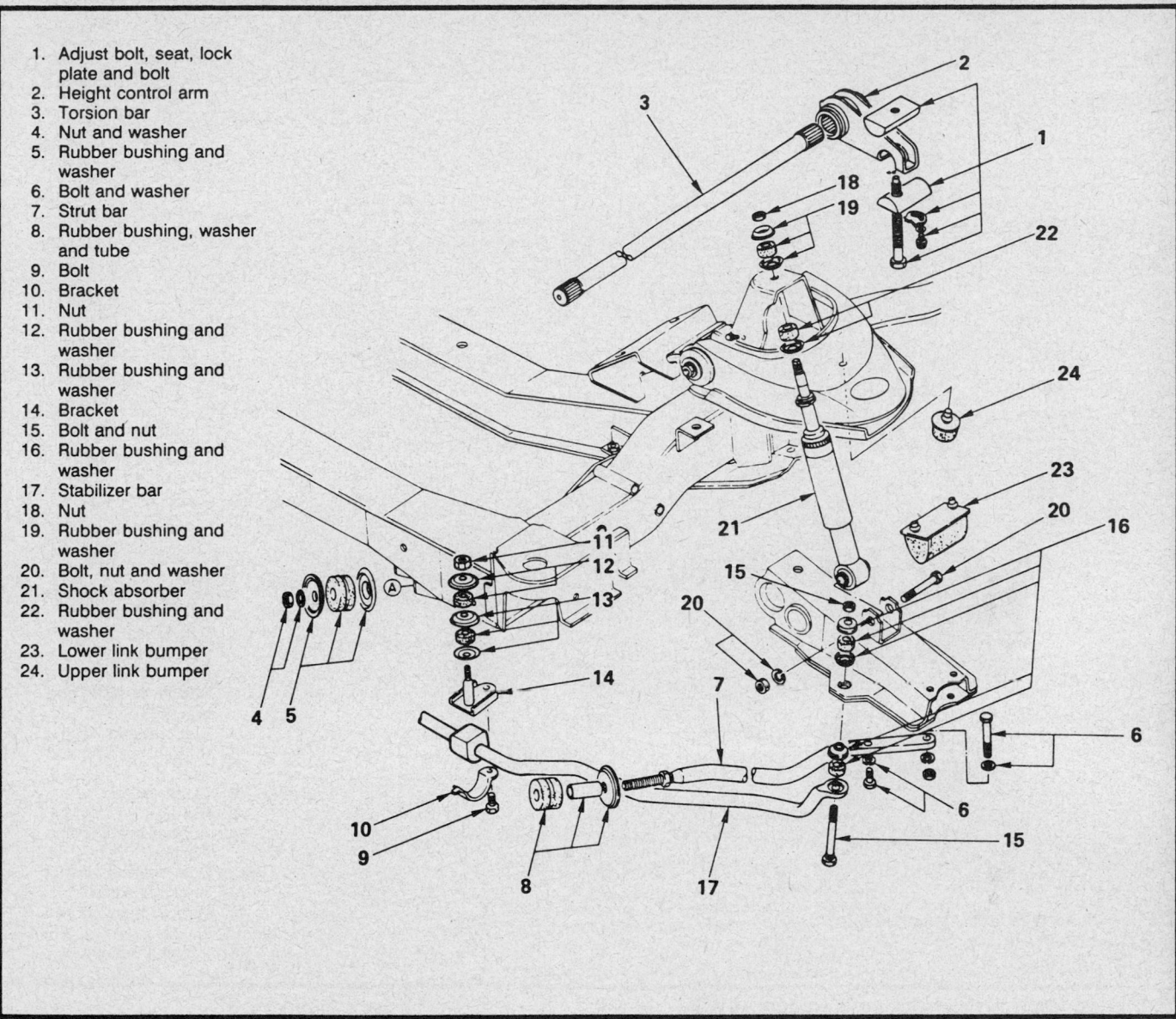

1. Adjust bolt, seat, lock plate and bolt
2. Height control arm
3. Torsion bar
4. Nut and washer
5. Rubber bushing and washer
6. Bolt and washer
7. Strut bar
8. Rubber bushing, washer and tube
9. Bolt
10. Bracket
11. Nut
12. Rubber bushing and washer
13. Rubber bushing and washer
14. Bracket
15. Bolt and nut
16. Rubber bushing and washer
17. Stabilizer bar
18. Nut
19. Rubber bushing and washer
20. Bolt, nut and washer
21. Shock absorber
22. Rubber bushing and washer
23. Lower link bumper
24. Upper link bumper

Exploded view of the front suspension—2WD

5. Install the upper rubber grommet, retainer and attaching nut over the shock absorber upper stem.
6. Hold the upper stem of the shock absorber from turning and tighten the retaining nut.
7. Install the retainers attaching the shock absorber lower pivot to the lower control arm and tighten them.
8. Lower the vehicle.

Torsion Bars

Removal and Installation
2WD VEHICLES
1. Raise and safely support the vehicle.
2. Remove the adjusting bolt from the height control arm.
3. Mark the location and remove the height control arm from the torsion bar and the third crossmember.
4. Mark the location and withdraw the torsion bar from the lower control arm.

To install:
5. To install, apply a generous amount of grease to the serrated ends of the torsion bar.
6. Hold the rubber bumpers in contact with the lower control arm. Raise the vehicle up under the lower control arm to accomplish this.
7. Insert the front end of the torsion bar into the control arm.
8. Install the height control arm in position so it's end is reaching the adjusting bolt. Be sure to lubricate the part of the height control arm that fits into the chassis with grease.
9. Install a new cotter pin in the control arm.
10. Turn the adjusting bolt to the location marked before removal.
11. Lower the vehicle and check the vehicle height.

4WD VEHICLES
1. Raise and safely support the vehicle.
2. Remove the adjusting bolt from the height control arm.
3. Mark the location and remove the height control arm from

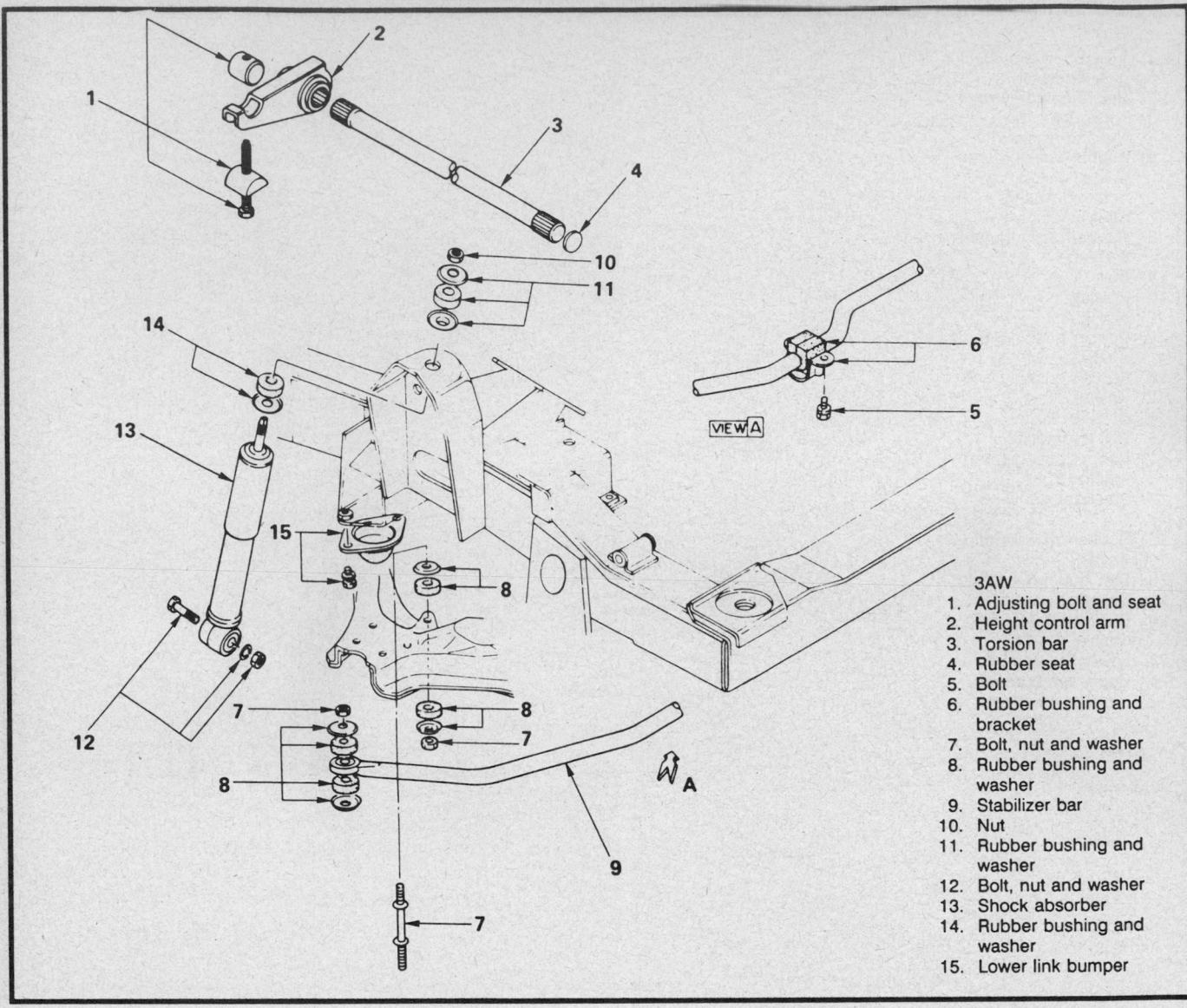

Exploded view of the front suspension — 4WD

3AW
1. Adjusting bolt and seat
2. Height control arm
3. Torsion bar
4. Rubber seat
5. Bolt
6. Rubber bushing and bracket
7. Bolt, nut and washer
8. Rubber bushing and washer
9. Stabilizer bar
10. Nut
11. Rubber bushing and washer
12. Bolt, nut and washer
13. Shock absorber
14. Rubber bushing and washer
15. Lower link bumper

VIEW A

the torsion bar and the 3rd crossmember.

4. Mark the location and withdraw the torsion bar from the lower control arm.

To install:

5. To install, apply a generous amount of grease to the serrated ends of the torsion bar.

6. Hold the rubber bumpers in contact with the lower control arm. Raise the vehicle up under the lower control arm to accomplish this.

7. Insert the front end of the torsion bar into the control arm.

8. Install the height control arm in position so it's end is reaching the adjusting bolt. Be sure to lubricate the part of the height control arm that fits into the chassis with grease.

9. Install a new cotter pin in the control arm.

10. Turn the adjusting bolt to the location marked before removal.

11. Lower the vehicle and check the vehicle height.

Upper Ball Joints

Inspection

Grasp the top of the front wheel and pull it in and out several times to check for excessive movement of the ball joint; if no movement exist, the joint is in good shape.

Removal and Installation

1. Raise and safely support the vehicle. Remove the wheel and tire assembly.

2. Remove the tension from the torsion bar.

3. Remove the upper ball joint-to-steering knuckle nut.

4. Using a ball joint separator tool, separate the upper ball joint from the steering knuckle.

5. Remove the upper ball joint-to-upper control arm bolts and the ball joint.

6. To install, reverse the removal procedures. Torque the upper ball joint-to-upper control arm bolts to 21–25 ft. lbs. (29–35 Nm) and the upper ball joint-to-steering knuckle nut to 72–87 ft. lbs. (96–117 Nm) for 2WD or to 65–80 ft. lbs. (88–108 Nm) for 4WD.

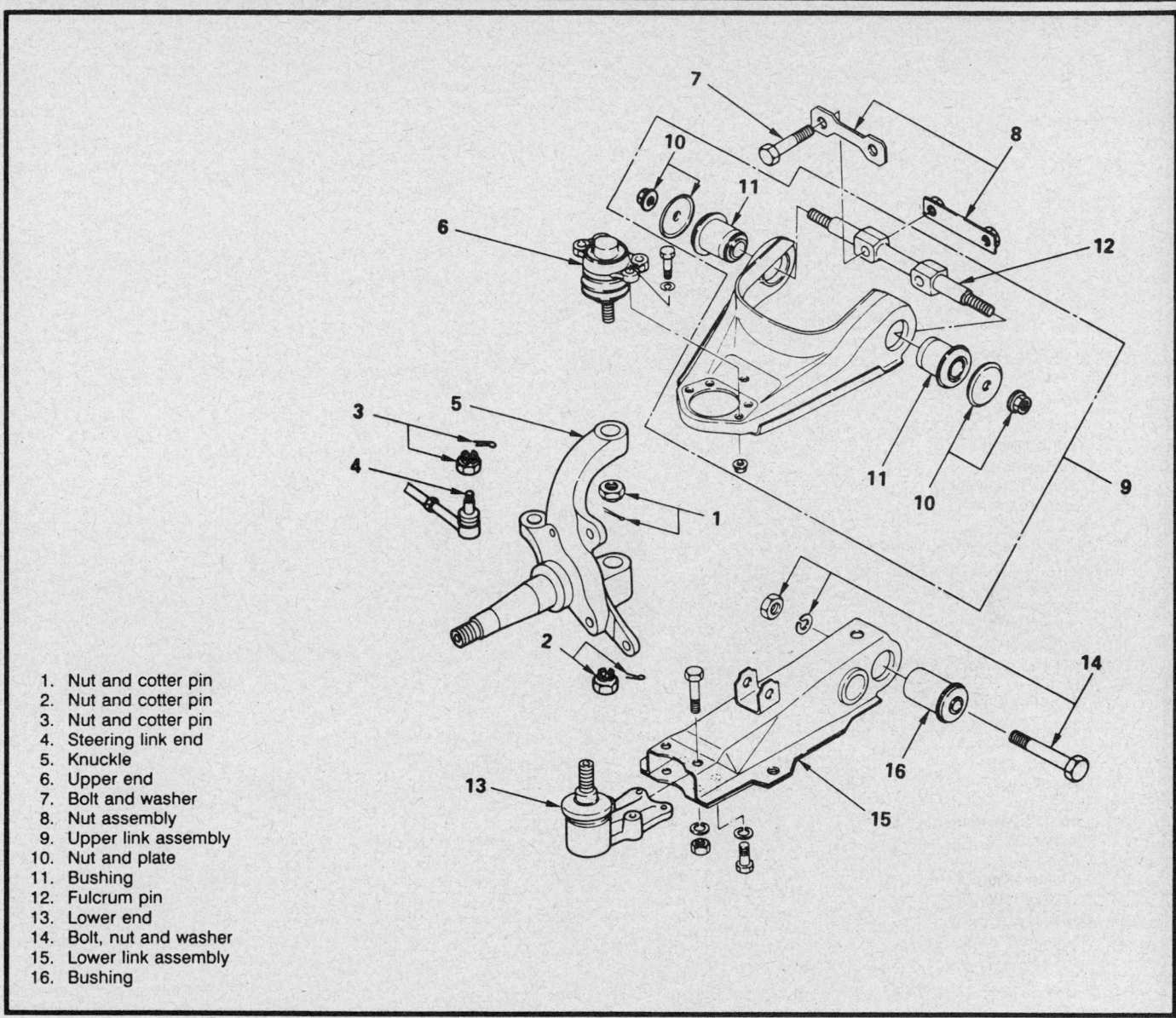

1. Nut and cotter pin
2. Nut and cotter pin
3. Nut and cotter pin
4. Steering link end
5. Knuckle
6. Upper end
7. Bolt and washer
8. Nut assembly
9. Upper link assembly
10. Nut and plate
11. Bushing
12. Fulcrum pin
13. Lower end
14. Bolt, nut and washer
15. Lower link assembly
16. Bushing

Exploded view of the steering knuckle and control arm assembly—2WD

7. Adjust the tension on the torsion bar and lower the vehicle.

Lower Ball Joints

Inspection

1. Raise and safely support the front of the vehicle.
2. Using a large pry bar, place it under the front wheel and try to pry the wheel upwards.
3. If excessive upward movement or clunking is noticed, the ball joint is damaged and requires replacement.

Removal and Installation

1. Raise and safely support the vehicle.
2. Remove the wheel and tire assembly.
3. Release the torsion bar tension.
4. Remove the cotter pin and castellated nut which retains the ball joint to the steering knuckle.
5. Remove the lower ball joint-to-lower control arm and strut rod.

6. Remove the ball joint.
To install:
7. Install the lower ball joint by mounting the joint to the lower control arm and torque the bolts to 45–56 ft. lbs. (61–76 Nm) for 2WD or to 68–83 ft. lbs. (93–113 Nm) for 4WD.
8. Install the ball joint stud into the steering knuckle and install the castellated nut and torque it to 101–116 ft. lbs. (137–157 Nm) for 2WD or to 87–111 ft. lbs. (117–137 Nm) for 4WD and just enough additional torque to align the cotter pin hole with a castellation on the nut. Install a new cotter pin.
9. Lubricate the lower ball joint through the grease fitting.
10. Adjust the torsion bar tension.
11. Install the wheel assembly and lower the vehicle.

Upper Control Arms

Removal and Installation

NOTE: The upper control arm and ball joint are replaced as an assembly.

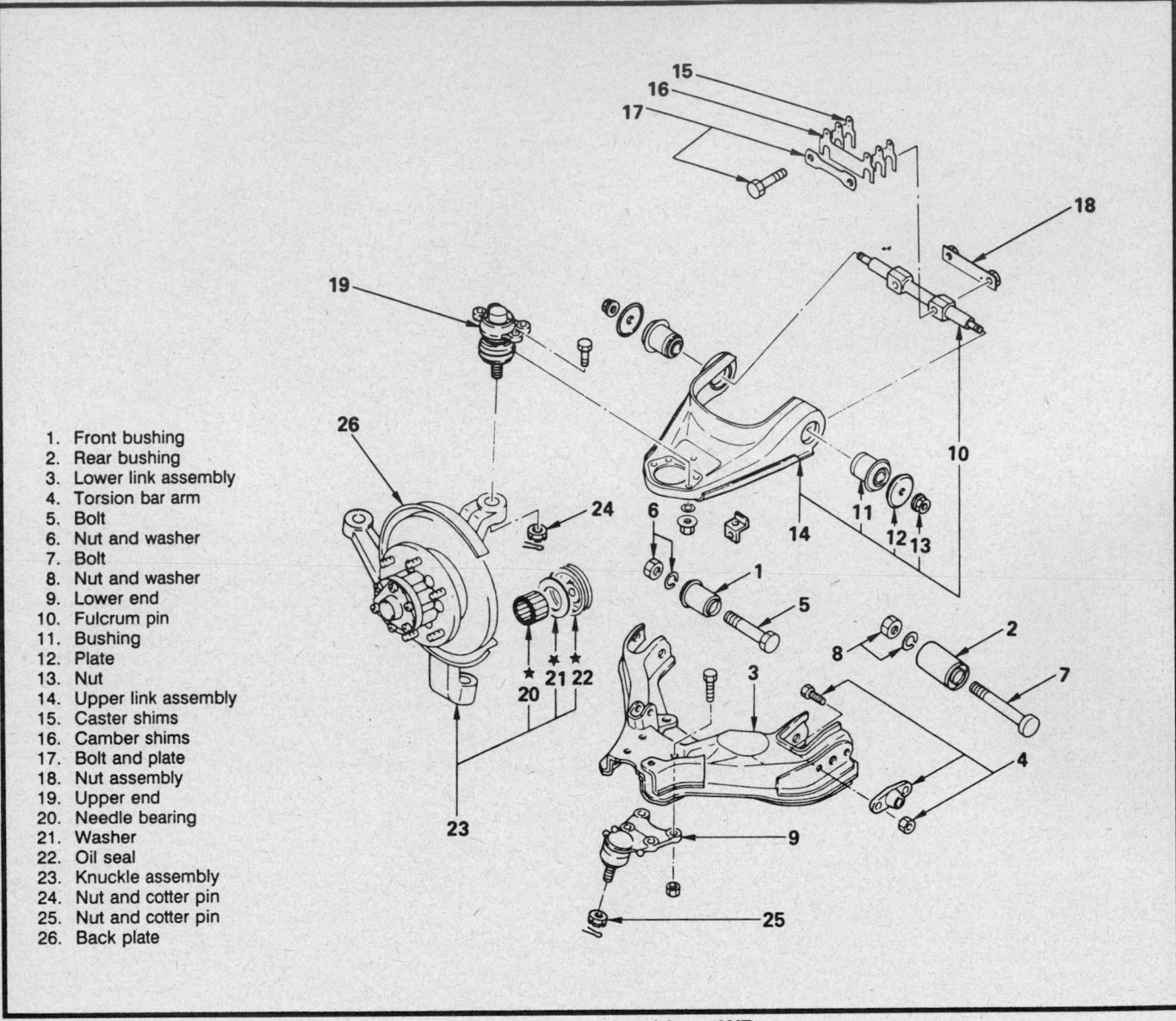

1. Front bushing
2. Rear bushing
3. Lower link assembly
4. Torsion bar arm
5. Bolt
6. Nut and washer
7. Bolt
8. Nut and washer
9. Lower end
10. Fulcrum pin
11. Bushing
12. Plate
13. Nut
14. Upper link assembly
15. Caster shims
16. Camber shims
17. Bolt and plate
18. Nut assembly
19. Upper end
20. Needle bearing
21. Washer
22. Oil seal
23. Knuckle assembly
24. Nut and cotter pin
25. Nut and cotter pin
26. Back plate

Exploded view of the steering knuckle and control arm assembly—4WD

1. Raise and safely support the vehicle on the lower control arms.

2. Remove the wheel and tire assembly.

3. Remove the cotter pin nut fastening the upper control arm and upper ball joint assembly and disconnect the upper control arm from the steering knuckle.

NOTE: Do not allow the steering knuckle to hang by the flexible brake line. Wire the steering knuckle up to the frame temporarily.

4. Remove the bolts from the upper pivot shaft and remove the upper control arm from the bracket. Be sure to note the position and number of shims used for adjusting the camber and caster angles when removing the upper control arm. The shims must be replaced in their original position.

5. To remove the pivot shaft and bushings from the upper control arm assembly, remove the bushing nuts from the pivot shaft by loosening them alternately, then remove the pivot shaft.

To install:

6. To install the upper control arm and ball joint assembly, first install the pivot shaft boots to the pivot shaft.

7. Fill the internal part of the bushings with grease and screw the bushings into the pivot shaft. Be sure to screw the right-side and the left-side bushings alternately into the pivot shafts carefully avoiding getting grease on the outer face of the bushings. Tighten the nuts to 250 ft. lbs.

NOTE: Be sure that the control arm and bushings are centered properly and that the control arm rotates with resistance but not binding on the pivot shaft when tightened to the proper torque.

To install:

8. Install the grease fittings and lubricate the parts with grease through the grease fittings.

9. Install the ball joint stud through the steering knuckle. Install the castellated nut and tighten it to 75 ft. lbs. and just enough additional torque to install the cotter pin. Use a new cotter pin.

10. Mount the upper control arm to the chassis frame and install the shims in their original positions between the pivot shaft and bracket. Tighten the pivot shaft attaching nuts to 55 ft. lbs.

NOTE: Tighten the thinner shim pack's nut first for improved shaft-to-frame clamping force and torque retention.

11. Install the dust cover.

12. Install the wheel assembly and lower the vehicle.

Lower Control Arms

Removal and Installation

1. Raise and safely support the vehicle.

2. Remove the wheel and tire assembly.

3. Remove the strut bar by removing the frame side bracket and the double nuts, washer and the rubber bushing from the front side of the strut bar. Remove the strut bar-to-lower control arm bolts and remove the bar.

4. Disconnect the stabilizer bar from the lower control arm.

5. Remove the torsion bar.

6. Disconnect the shock absorber from the lower control arm.

7. Remove the lower ball joint from the lower control arm joint.

8. Remove the retaining nut and drive out the bolt holding the lower control arm to the chassis with a soft metal drift. Remove the lower control arm from the vehicle.

To install:

9. To install the lower control arm, install the lower ball joint to the lower control arm. Tighten the retaining nuts to 45 ft. lbs.

10. Mount the lower control arm to the frame. Drive the bolt into position carefully. Use care not to damage the serrated portions. Tighten the nut on the end of the pivot bolt to 135 ft. lbs.

11. Install the stabilizer bar to the lower control arm.

12. Place the washers and bushings on the strut rod and install it through the frame bracket. Install the second set of washers and bushings on the strut rod together with the lockwashers and nut. Leave the nut loose temporarily.

13. Install the strut rod to the lower control arm and tighten the bolts to 45 ft. lbs.

14. Assemble the lower ball joint to the steering knuckle.

15. Install the wheel assembly and lower the vehicle.

16. Tighten the 1st strut bar-to-chassis frame attaching nut to 175 ft. lbs. and the 2nd locknut to 55 ft. lbs. with the vehicle on the ground.

Front Wheel Bearings—2WD

Removal and Installation

1. Raise and safely support the vehicle. Remove the wheel assembly. Remove the hub assembly.

2. Remove the outer roller bearing assembly from the hub. Pry out the inner bearing lip seal and remove the inner bearing assembly.

3. Wash all parts in a cleaning solvent and dry with compressed air.

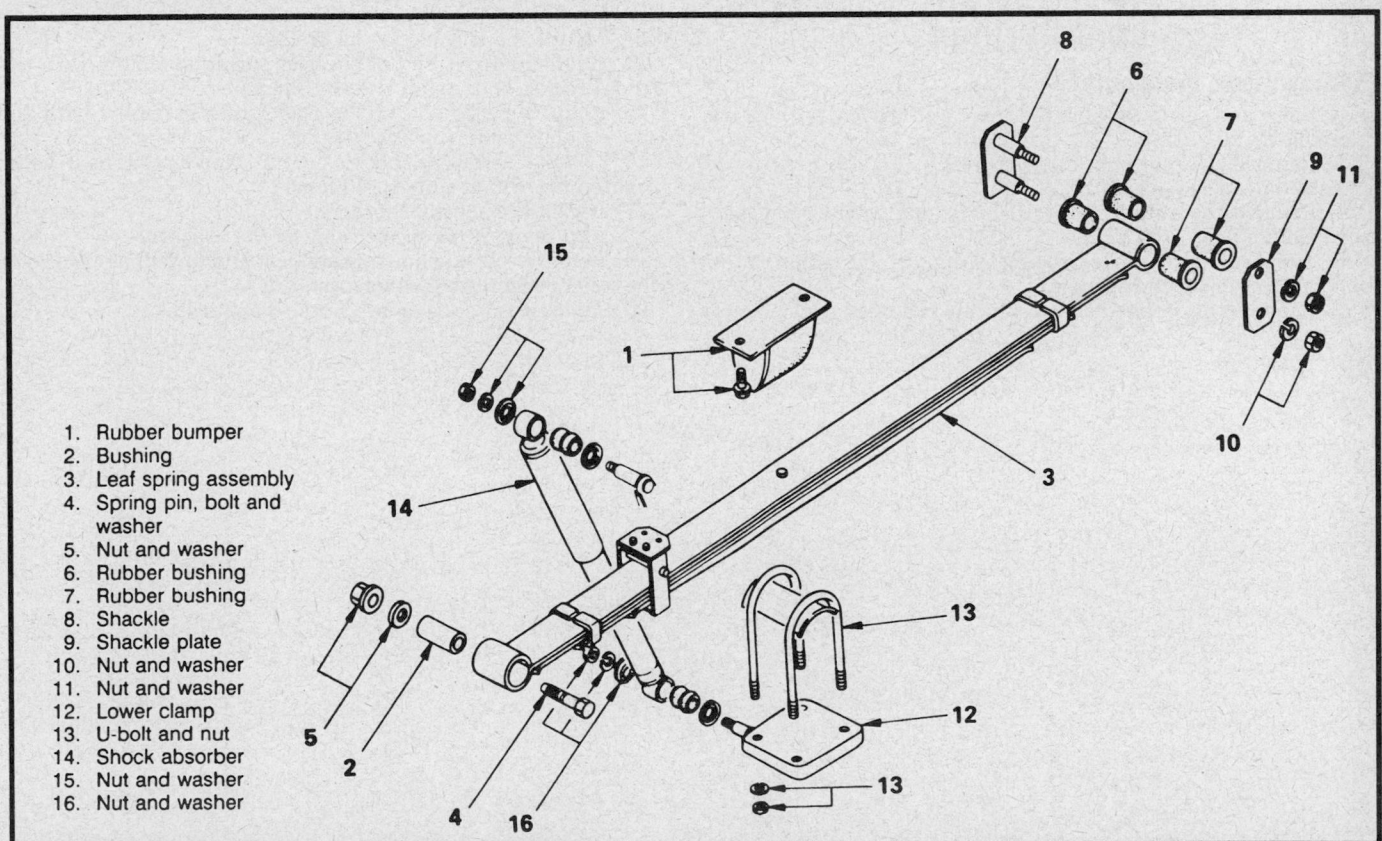

1. Rubber bumper
2. Bushing
3. Leaf spring assembly
4. Spring pin, bolt and washer
5. Nut and washer
6. Rubber bushing
7. Rubber bushing
8. Shackle
9. Shackle plate
10. Nut and washer
11. Nut and washer
12. Lower clamp
13. U-bolt and nut
14. Shock absorber
15. Nut and washer
16. Nut and washer

Exploded view of the rear suspension assembly

4. Check the bearings for pitting or scoring. Also check for smooth rotation and lack of noise.

To install:

5. Thoroughly lubricate the bearings with new wheel bearing lubricant.

6. Apply a light coat of lubricant to the spindle and inside surface of the hub.

7. Place the inner bearing in the race of the hub and install a new grease seal.

8. Install the hub assembly on the spindle.

9. Install the outer wheel bearing, washer and adjust nut.

10. Adjust the wheel bearings.

11. Install the dust cap on the hub.

12. Install the brake caliper and support assembly.

13. Install the wheel assembly.

Adjustment

1. With the wheel raised, remove the hub cap and dust cap and then remove the cotter pin and nut retainer from the end of the spindle.

2. While rotating the wheel, tighten the spindle nut to 22 ft. lbs.

3. Turn the hub 2–3 turns and loosen the nut just enough so it can be turned by hand.

4. Turn the nut all the way hand tight and check to be sure the hub has no freeplay.

5. Measure the starting torque by pulling a wheel hub stud with a pull scale. Tighten the spindle nut so the pull scale reads 1.1–2.6 lbs. when the hub begins to rotate.

NOTE: Make sure the brake pads are not in contact with the drum when measuring rotating torque.

6. Install the nut retainer, new cotter pin, dust cap and hub cap.

REAR SUSPENSION

Shock Absorbers

Removal and Installation

1. Raise and safely support the vehicle.

2. Remove the shock absorber-to-lower mount nut, washers and bushings.

3. Remove the shock absorber-to-chassis nut, washers and bushings.

4. Remove the shock absorber.

5. To install, reverse the removal procedures.

Leaf Springs

Removal and Installation

1. Raise and safely support the vehicle so the leaf springs are hanging freely.

2. Remove the rear shock absorbers.

3. Remove the parking brake cable clips.

4. Remove the nuts from the U-bolts holding the springs to the axle housing.

5. Support the rear axle housing to remove the weight of the axle housing from the springs.

6. Remove the front and rear shackle pin nuts.

7. Drive out the rear shackle pin by using a hammer and drift. Lower the rear end of the leaf spring assembly to the floor.

8. Drive out the front shackle pin and remove the leaf spring assembly rearward.

9. Remove the shackle pin from the rear spring bracket and remove the shackle.

10. Check the leaf springs for cracks, wear and broken leaves. Replace any leaves found to be cracked, broken, fatigued or seriously worn.

11. Check the shackles for bending and the pins for wear.

12. Check the U-bolts for distortion or other damage.

To install:

13. Mount the shackle to the bracket.

14. Align the front end of the leaf spring assembly with the front bracket and install the shackle pin.

15. Align the rear end of the leaf spring assembly with the shackle and install the shackle pin.

16. Loosely install the shackle pin nuts and install the U-bolts. Tighten the U-bolt nuts to 40 ft. lbs.

17. Install the shock absorbers.

18. Clip the parking brake cable to the bracket.

19. Remove the axle housing support and lower the vehicle so the weight is on the leaf springs.

20. Tighten the shackle pin nuts to 130 ft. lbs.

SPECIFICATIONS

ENGINE IDENTIFICATION

Year	Model	Engine Displacement cu. in. (cc/liter)	Engine Series Identification	No. of Cylinders	Engine Type
1986	B2000	122 (1998/2.0)	FE	4	OHC
1987	B2200	133 (2184/2.2)	F2	4	OHC
	B2600	156 (2555/2.6)	G54B	4	OHC
1988	B2200	133 (2184/2.2)	F2	4	OHC
	B2600	156 (2555/2.6)	G54B	4	OHC
1989–90	B2200	133 (2184/2.2)	F2	4	OHC
	B2600i	159 (2606/2.6)	G6	4	OHC
	MPV	159 (2606/2.6)	G6	4	OHC
	MPV	181 (2954/3.0)	JE	6	OHC

GENERAL ENGINE SPECIFICATIONS

Year	Model	Engine Displacement cu. in. (cc)	Fuel System Type	Net Horsepower @ rpm	Net Torque @ rpm (ft. lbs.)	Bore × Stroke (in.)	Compression Ratio	Oil Pressure @ rpm
1986	B2000	122 (1998)	2bbl	80 @ 4500	110 @ 2500	3.395 × 3.700	8.6:1	60 @ 2000
1987	B2200	133 (2184)	2bbl	85 @ 4500	118 @ 2500	3.395 × 3.700	8.6:1	60 @ 2000
	B2600	156 (2555)	2bbl	105 @ 5000	139 @ 2500	3.586 × 3.858	8.7:1	57 @ 2000
1988	B2200	133 (2184)	2bbl	85 @ 4500	118 @ 2500	3.395 × 3.700	8.6:1	60 @ 2000
	B2600	156 (2555)	2bbl	105 @ 5000	139 @ 2500	3.586 × 3.858	8.7:1	57 @ 2000
1989–90	B2200	133 (2184)	2bbl	85 @ 4500	118 @ 2500	3.395 × 3.700	8.6:1	60 @ 2000
	B2600i	159 (2606)	MPI	121 @ 4600	149 @ 3500	3.622 × 3.858	8.4:1	60 @ 2000
	MPV	159 (2606)	MPI	121 @ 4600	149 @ 3500	3.622 × 3.858	8.4:1	60 @ 2000
	MPV	181 (2954)	MPI	150 @ 5000	165 @ 4000	3.540 × 3.050	8.5:1	60 @ 2000

MPI—Multi Port Injection

GASOLINE ENGINE TUNE-UP SPECIFICATIONS

Year	Model	Engine Displacement cu. in. (cc)	Spark Plugs Type	Gap (in.)	Ignition Timing (deg.) MT	AT	Compression Pressure (psi)	Fuel Pump (psi)	Idle Speed (rpm) MT	AT	Valve Clearance In.	Ex.
1986	B2000	122 (1998)	BPR-5E5	.031	6B	—	164	4–5	850	—	0.012	0.012
1987	B2200	133 (2184)	BPR-5E5	.031	6B	6B	171	3–4	825	825	Hyd.	Hyd.
	B2600	156 (2555)	BUR-6EA11	.039	7B	7B	171	3–4	825	825	Hyd.	Hyd.
1988	B2200	133 (2184)	BPR-5ES	.031	6B	6B	171	3–4	825	825	Hyd.	Hyd.
	B2600	156 (2555)	BUR-6EA11	.039	7B	7B	171	3–4	825	825	Hyd.	Hyd.
1989–90	B2200	133 (2184)	BPR-5ES	.031	6B	6B	171	3–4	825	825	Hyd.	Hyd.
	B2600i	159 (2606)	ZFR-5A11	.039	5B ①	5B ①	171	64–85	750 ①	770 ①	Hyd.	Hyd.
	MPV	159 (2606)	ZFR-5A11	.039	5B ①	5B ①	171	64–85	750 ①	770 ①	Hyd.	Hyd.
	MPV	181 (2954)	ZFR-5A11	.041	11B ①	11B ①	164	64–85	800 ①	800 ①	Hyd.	Hyd.

①With test connector grounded

FIRING ORDERS

NOTE: To avoid confusion, always replace the spark plug wires one at a time.

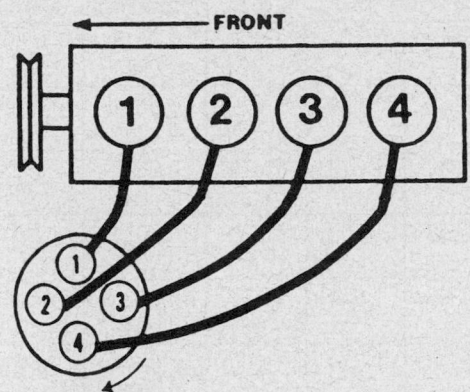

**1998cc and 2184cc engines
Firing order: 1–3–4–2
Distributor rotation: clockwise**

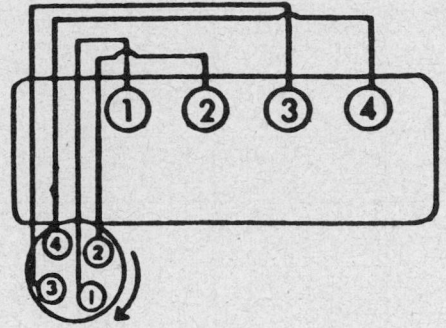

**2555cc and 2606cc engines
Firing order: 1–3–4–2
Distributor rotation: clockwise**

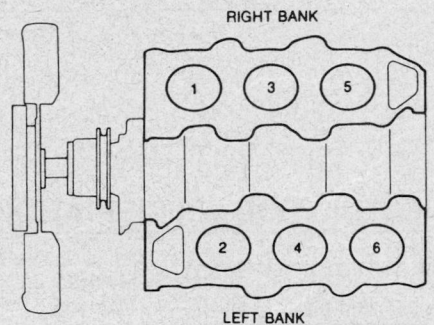

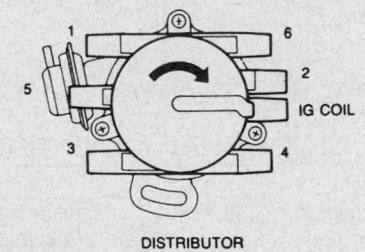

**2954cc engine
Firing order: 1–2–3–4–5–6
Distributor rotation: clockwise**

CAPACITIES

Year	Model	Engine Displacement cu. in. (cc)	Engine Crankcase with Filter	Engine Crankcase without Filter	Transmission (pts.) 4-Spd	Transmission (pts.) 5-Spd	Transmission (pts.) Auto.	Drive Axle (pts.)	Fuel Tank (gal.)	Cooling System (pts.)
1986	B2000	122 (1998)	4.5	4.0	3.0	2.6	—	2.8	①	7.9
1987	B2200	133 (2184)	5.0	4.5	3.6	4.2	—	2.8	②	7.9
	B2600	156 (2555)	5.0	4.5	—	③	8.4	2.8	②	7.9
1988	B2200	133 (2184)	5.0	4.5	3.6	4.2	—	2.8	②	7.9
	B2600	156 (2555)	5.0	4.5	—	③	8.4	2.8	②	7.9
1989–90	B2200	133 (2184)	5.0	4.5	3.6	4.2	—	2.8	②	7.9
	B2600i	159 (2606)	5.0	4.5	—	③	8.4	3.6	②	7.9
	MPV	159 (2606)	5.0	4.5	—	③	8.4	3.6	②	7.9
	MPV	181 (2954)	5.5	5.5	—	5.2	15.4	3.6	18.5	9.9

① Long bed—14.6 gals.
  Short bed—15.6 gals.
② Long bed—17.4 gals.
  Short bed—14.8 gals.

③ 2WD—6.0 pts.
  4WD—6.8 pts.

CAMSHAFT SPECIFICATIONS

Year	Engine Displacement cu. in. (cc)	Journal Diameter					Lobe Lift		Bearing Clearance	Camshaft End Play
		1	2	3	4	5	In.	Ex.		
1986	122 (1998)	1.2578	1.2567	1.2567	1.2567	1.2578	1.500	1.500	0.0014–0.0031	0.004
1987	133 (2184)	1.2578	1.2567	1.2567	1.2567	1.2578	1.500	1.500	0.0014–0.0031	0.004
	156 (2555)	1.3362	1.3362	1.3362	1.3362	1.3362	1.670	1.670	0.0020–0.0040	0
1988	133 (2184)	1.2578	1.2567	1.2567	1.2567	1.2578	1.500	1.500	0.0014–0.0031	0.004
	156 (2555)	1.3362	1.3362	1.3362	1.3362	1.3362	1.670	1.670	0.0020–0.0040	0
1989–90	133 (2184)	1.2578	1.2567	1.2567	1.2567	1.2578	1.500	1.500	0.0014–0.0031	0.004
	159 (2606)	1.1791	1.1780	1.1780	1.1780	1.1791	1.640	1.640	0.0014–0.0033	0.004
	181 (2954)	1.9272	1.9264	1.9264	1.6272	—	1.618	1.626	0.0024–0.0045	0

CRANKSHAFT AND CONNECTING ROD SPECIFICATIONS

Year	Engine Displacement cu. in. (cc)	Crankshaft				Connecting Rod		
		Main Brg. Journal Dia.	Main Brg. Oil Clearance	Shaft End-play	Thrust on No.	Journal Diameter	Oil Clearance	Side Clearance
1986	122 (1998)	2.3618	0.0012–0.0019	0.0031–0.0071	3	2.0079	0.0010–0.0026	0.0039–0.0098
1987	133 (2184)	2.3602	0.0012–0.0019	0.0031–0.0071	3	2.0059	0.0011–0.0026	0.0043–0.0102
	156 (2555)	2.3618	0.0008–0.0020	0.0020–0.0070	3	2.0878	0.0008–0.0024	0.0039–0.0098
1988	133 (2184)	2.3602	0.0012–0.0019	0.0031–0.0071	3	2.0059	0.0011–0.0026	0.0043–0.0102
	156 (2555)	2.3618	0.0008–0.0020	0.0020–0.0070	3	2.0878	0.0008–0.0024	0.0039–0.0098
1989–90	133 (2184)	2.3602	0.0012–0.0019	0.0031–0.0070	3	2.0059	0.0011–0.0026	0.0043–0.0102
	159 (2606)	2.3602	0.0010–0.0017	0.0031–0.0070	3	2.0059	0.0011–0.0026	0.0039–0.0102
	181 (2954)	2.4390	0.0010–0.0015	0.0030–0.0110	3	2.0748	0.0009–0.0016	0.0070–0.0130

VALVE SPECIFICATIONS

Year	Engine Displacement cu. in. (cc)	Seat Angle (deg.)	Face Angle (deg.)	Spring Test Pressure (lbs.)	Spring Installed Height (in.)	Stem-to-Guide Clearance (in.)		Stem Diameter (in.)	
						Intake	Exhaust	Intake	Exhaust
1986	122 (1998)	45	45	①	②	0.0101–0.0114	0.0114–0.0127	0.3161–0.3167	0.3159–0.3165
1987	133 (2184)	45	45	①	②	0.0101–0.0114	0.0114–0.0127	0.3161–0.3167	0.3159–0.3165
	156 (2555)	45	45	72 @ 1.591	1.961	0.0063–0.0147	0.1270–0.0224	0.3130–0.3140	0.3120–0.3130
1988	133 (2184)	45	45	①	②	0.0101–0.0114	0.0114–0.0127	0.3161–0.3167	0.3159–0.3165
	156 (2555)	45	45	72 @ 1.591	1.961	0.0063–0.0147	0.1270–0.0224	0.3130–0.3140	0.3120–0.3130
1989–90	133 (2184)	45	45	①	②	0.0101–0.0114	0.0114–0.0127	0.3161–0.3167	0.3159–0.3165
	159 (2606)	45	45	72 @ 1.591	③	0.0063–0.0152	0.0076–0.0165	0.2744–0.2750	0.2742–0.2748
	181 (2954)	45	45	58 @ 1.555	1.732	0.0010–0.0024	0.0012–0.0026	0.2744–0.2750	0.3159–0.3165

① Inner—96 @ 1.720 in.
　Outer—96 @ 2.008 in.
② Inner—1.681 in.
　Outer—1.984 in.
③ Inner—1.929 in.
　Outer—1.988 in.

PISTON AND RING SPECIFICATIONS

Year	Engine Displacement cu. in. (cc)	Piston Clearance	Ring Gap			Ring Side Clearance		
			Top Compression	Bottom Compression	Oil Control	Top Compression	Bottom Compression	Oil Control
1986	122 (1998)	0.0014–0.0030	0.0079–0.0118	0.0059–0.0118	0.0118–0.0354	0.0012–0.0028	0.0014–0.0028	Snug
1987	133 (2184)	0.0014–0.0030	0.0079–0.0118	0.0059–0.0118	0.0118–0.0354	0.0012–0.0028	0.0014–0.0028	Snug
	156 (2555)	0.0008–0.0024	0.0118–0.0178	0.0098–0.0157	0.0118–0.0236	0.0020–0.0035	0.0008–0.0024	0.0098
1988	133 (2184)	0.0014–0.0030	0.0079–0.0118	0.0059–0.0118	0.0118–0.0354	0.0012–0.0028	0.0014–0.0028	Snug
	156 (2555)	0.0008–0.0024	0.0118–0.0178	0.0098–0.0157	0.0118–0.0236	0.0020–0.0035	0.0008–0.0024	0.0098
1989–90	133 (2184)	0.0014–0.0030	0.0079–0.0118	0.0059–0.0118	0.0118–0.0354	0.0012–0.0028	0.0014–0.0028	Snug
	159 (2606)	0.0023–0.0029	0.0079–0.0138	0.0098–0.0157	0.0079–0.0276	0.0012–0.0028	0.0012–0.0028	0.0059
	181 (2954)	0.0019–0.0026	0.0078–0.0138	0.0059–0.0138	0.0079–0.0276	0.0012–0.0028	0.0012–0.0028	0.0059

TORQUE SPECIFICATIONS

Year	Engine Displacement cu. in. (cc)	Cylinder Head Bolts	Main Bearing Bolts	Rod Bearing Bolts	Crankshaft Pulley Bolts	Flywheel Bolts	Manifold		Spark Plugs
							Intake	Exhaust	
1986	122 (1998)	59–64	61–65	37–41	9–12	71–76	14–19	16–21	16–21
1987	133 (2184)	59–64	61–65	48–51	9–12	71–76	14–19	16–21	16–21
	156 (2555)	①	61–65	33–35	80–94 ②	94–101	11–14	11–14	16–21
1988	133 (2184)	59–64	61–65	48–51	9–12	71–76	14–19	16–21	16–21
	156 (2555)	①	61–65	33–35	80–94 ②	94–101	11–14	11–14	16–21
1989–90	133 (2184)	59–64	61–65	48–51	9–12	71–76	14–19	16–21	16–21
	159 (2606)	③	61–65	48–51	130–145 ②	67–72	14–19	16–21	16–21
	181 (2954)	④	⑤	⑥	116–123 ②	76–81	14–19	16–21	16–21

① Torque cold to 59–64 ft. lbs.; then hot to 72–79 ft. lbs.
② Crankshaft damper bolt
③ Bolts 1 through 10—59–64 ft. lbs. All others—12–17 ft. lbs.
④ Tighten in 3 steps: Step 1—14 ft. lbs. Step 2—90 degree turn Step 3—90 degree turn
⑤ Tighten in 3 steps: Step 1—14 ft. lbs. Step 2—90 degree turn Step 3—45 degree turn
⑥ Tighten to 22 ft. lbs. then an additional 90 degrees

BRAKE SPECIFICATIONS

Year	Model	Lug Nut Torque (ft. lbs.)	Master Cylinder Bore	Brake Disc		Standard Brake Drum Diameter	Minimum Lining Thickness	
				Minimum Thickness	Maximum Runout		Front	Rear
1986	B2000	65–87 ①	0.875	0.709	0.0016	10.240	0.118	0.040
1987	B2200	65–87 ①	0.875	0.709	0.0016	10.240	0.118	0.040
	B2600	65–87 ①	0.875	0.787	0.0016	10.240	0.118	0.040
1988	B2200	65–87 ①	0.875	0.709	0.0016	10.240	0.118	0.040
	B2600	65–87 ①	0.875	0.787	0.0016	10.240	0.118	0.040
1989–90	B2200	65–87 ①	0.875	0.709	0.0016	10.240	0.118	0.040
	B2600i	65–87 ①	0.875	0.787	0.0016	10.240	0.118	0.040
	MPV	65–87 ①	0.937	0.866	0.0040	10.236	0.118	0.040

① Sport wheels—87–105 ft. lbs.

WHEEL ALIGNMENT

Year	Model	Caster		Camber		Toe-in (in.)	Steering Axis Inclination (deg.)
		Range (deg.)	Preferred Setting (deg.)	Range (deg.)	Preferred Setting (deg.)		
1986	B2000	0–1²⁄₃P ①	1⁵⁄₆P	¹⁄₃P–1¹⁄₃P	³⁄₄P	0–¹⁄₄P	NA
1987	B2200	0–1²⁄₃P ①	1⁵⁄₆P	¹⁄₃P–1¹⁄₃P	³⁄₄P	0–¹⁄₄P	NA
	B2600-2WD	0–1²⁄₃P ①	1⁵⁄₆P	¹⁄₃P–1¹⁄₃P	³⁄₄P	0–¹⁄₄P	NA
	B2600-4WD	0–1²⁄₃P ②	1⁵⁄₆P	¹⁄₂P–1¹⁄₂P	1P	0–¹⁄₄P	NA
1988	B2200	0–1²⁄₃P ①	1⁵⁄₆P	¹⁄₃P–1¹⁄₃P	³⁄₄P	0–¹⁄₄P	NA
	B2600-2WD	0–1²⁄₃P ①	1⁵⁄₆P	¹⁄₃P–1¹⁄₃P	³⁄₄P	0–¹⁄₄P	NA
	B2600-4WD	0–1²⁄₃P ②	1⁵⁄₆P	¹⁄₂P–1¹⁄₂P	1P	0–¹⁄₄P	NA
1989–90	B2200	0–1²⁄₃P ①	1⁵⁄₆P	¹⁄₃P–1¹⁄₃P	³⁄₄P	0–¹⁄₄P	NA
	B2600-2WD	0–1²⁄₃P ①	1⁵⁄₆P	¹⁄₃P–1¹⁄₃P	³⁄₄P	0–¹⁄₄P	NA
	B2600-4WD	0–1²⁄₃P ②	1⁵⁄₆P	¹⁄₂P–1¹⁄₂P	1P	0–¹⁄₄P	NA
	MPV	4¹¹⁄₁₆P–6³⁄₁₆P	5⁷⁄₁₆	³⁄₈N–1¹⁄₈P	³⁄₈P	¹⁄₃₂P–⁹⁄₃₂P	NA

① If equipped with power steering—1¹⁄₃P–2¹⁄₃P
② If equipped with power steering—2³⁄₄P

ENGINE ELECTRICAL

NOTE: Disconnecting the battery cable on some vehicles may interfere with the functions of the on board computer systems and may require the computer to undergo a relearning process, once the negative battery cable is disconnected.

Distributor

Removal and Installation

1. Disconnect the negative battery cable. Remove the distributor cap without removing the spark plug wires from the cap.
2. Disconnect the vacuum hose from the distributor.
3. Remove the rubber plug from the timing belt cover. Scribe matchmarks on the distributor body and the engine to indicate their positions.
4. Scribe another mark on the distributor body indicating the position of the rotor. On 1998cc engines, scribe a mark on the cam pulley and on the indicator inside the timing belt cover to mark the position of the pulley relative to the indicator.
5. Disconnect and tag the primary wires from the distributor.
6. Remove the distributor locknut and washers.
7. Remove the distributor from the engine.

To install:

8. Align the matchmarks made during the removal.
9. Install the distributor with the rotor pointing in the same direction as when removed.
10. Align the distributor body to engine matchmarks. Install the locknut and washer.
11. Connect the wires and vacuum hose to the distributor. Install the distributor cap.
12. Start the engine and adjust the ignition timing.
13. With the timing correct, tighten the locknut and recheck the timing.
14. If the engine was disturbed while the distributor was removed:

 a. Rotate the crankshaft until No. 1 cylinder is at TDC.

This can be determined by removing the No. 1 spark plug, placing a finger over the spark plug hole while turning the engine and feeling for compression.

 b. Continue rotating the engine, until the TDC mark on the crankshaft pulley is aligned with the timing pointer.
 c. Install the distributor into the engine with the rotor pointing to the No.1 plug on the distributor cap.
 d. Install the distributor locknut, start the engine and correct the ignition timing.

Ignition Timing

Adjustment

1. Before starting the engine, clean and mark the timing marks.
2. Disconnect and plug the vacuum line at the distributor.

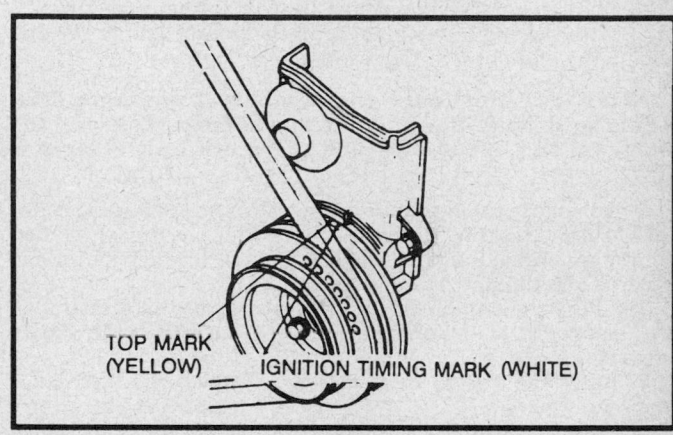

Timing mark location—1998cc and 2184cc engines

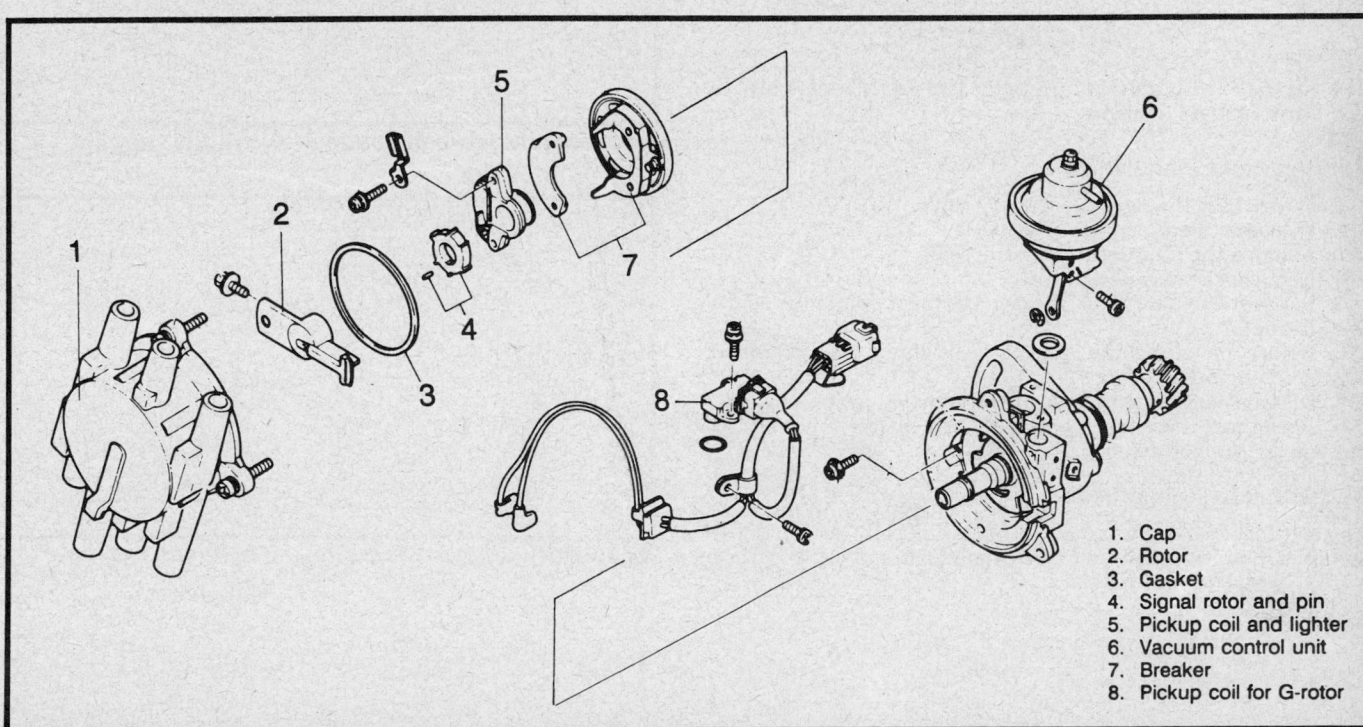

1. Cap
2. Rotor
3. Gasket
4. Signal rotor and pin
5. Pickup coil and lighter
6. Vacuum control unit
7. Breaker
8. Pickup coil for G-rotor

Distributor assembly—2954cc engine shown, others similar

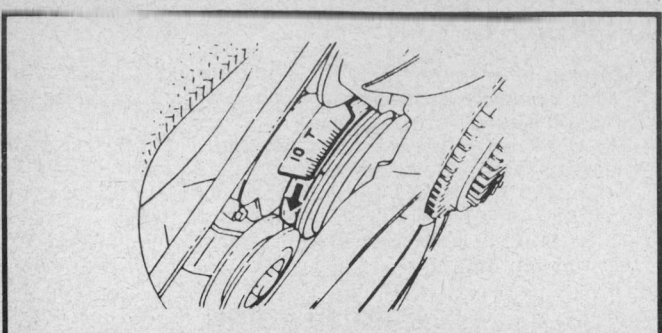

Timing mark location—2555cc, 2606cc and 2954cc engines

3. Connect a timing light and tachometer to the engine according to their manufacturer's instructions.

4. Start the engine and adjust the idle to the correct rpm.

5. With the engine running, point the timing light at the timing marks and observe the reading.

NOTE: All 4 cylinder engines have 2 timing marks. Looking straight down on the marks from the front, the mark on the left is TDC and the mark on the right is BTDC.

6. Adjust the timing if necessary, by loosening the distributor lock bolt and rotating the distributor. When the proper ignition timing is obtained, tighten the lock bolt on the distributor and recheck the timing.

7. Check the centrifugal advance mechanism by accelerating the engine to 2,000 rpm and making sure that the timing advances.

8. Reset the idle to specifications. Connect the distributor vacuum hose.

9. Stop the engine and remove the tachometer and timing light.

Alternator

For further information, please refer to "Electrical" in the Unit Repair section.

Removal and Installation

1. Disconnect the negative battery cable.
2. Disconnect and tag the alternator wiring.
3. Remove the alternator adjusting bolt.
4. Remove the drive belt.
5. Support the alternator, remove the pivot bolt, and remove the alternator.
6. Before installing the alternator, tighten the alternator mount to engine bolts.
7. Installation is the reverse of the removal procedure.
8. Reconnect the alternator wiring and negative battery cable. Adjust the belt tension.

Belt Tension Adjustment

The belt tension is adjusted at the adjusting bolt. Loosen the alternator mounting bolt and turn the adjusting belt to achieve the correct tension. The belt tension can be checked using the deflection method.

The correct deflection should be 0.28–0.32 in. (7–8mm) on the 1998cc, 2184cc, 2555cc and 2606cc for a new belt, 0.32–0.36 in (8–9mm) for a used belt. The deflection for the 2954cc engine should be, 0.17–0.20 in. (4.4–5mm) for a new belt and 0.20–0.22 in. (5–6mm) for a used belt.

Starter

For further information, please refer to "Electrical" in the Unit Repair section.

Removal and Installation

1. Disconnect the negative battery cable.
2. Remove the air cleaner and air intake tube.
3. Disconnect the positive battery cable from the starter solenoid.
4. Remove the ignition switch wire from the solenoid terminal.
5. Raise and support the vehicle safely.
6. Support the starter and remove the starter mounting bolts and nuts.
7. Tilt the drive end of the starter downwards and remove the starter.
8. Installation is the reverse of the removal procedure.
9. Torque the starter mounting bolts to 23–34 ft. lbs., except on the 2954cc engine. Tighten the mounting bolts on the 2954cc engine to 27–38 ft. lbs.

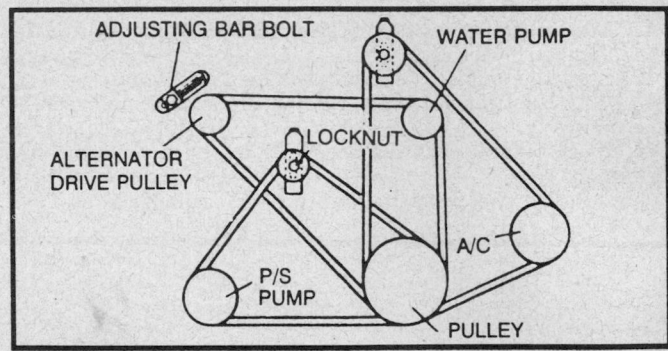

Accessory drive belt routing—4 cylinder engine

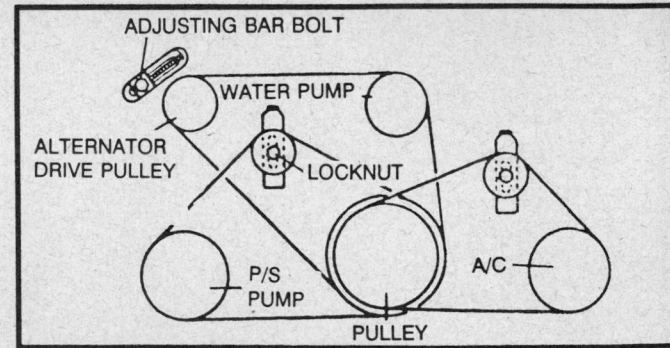

Accessory drive belt routing—6 cylinder engine

CHASSIS ELECTRICAL

Heater Blower Motor

Removal and Installation

1. Disconnect the negative battery cable.
2. Remove the passenger side lower instrument panel cover.
3. Disconnect the blower wiring.
4. Remove the blower motor mounting nuts and remove the blower motor.
5. Installation is the reverse of the removal procedure.

Windshield Wiper Motor

Removal and Installation

EXCEPT MPV

1. Disconnect the negative battery cable. Remove the wiper arm/blade assembly.
2. Remove the rubber seal from the leading edge of the cowl.
3. Unbolt and remove the cowl.
4. Remove the access hole covers.
5. Remove the bolts holding the wiper shaft drives.
6. Matchmark the position of the wiper crank arm in relation to the face of the wiper motor. Disconnect the wiper linkage from the wiper motor crank arm.
7. Remove the wiper linkage.
8. Unbolt and remove the wiper motor. Disconnect the wiring harness.
9. Installation is the reverse of removal. Make sure that the parked height of the wiper arms, measured from the blade tips to the windshield moulding is 0.787 in. (20mm). Torque the arm retaining nuts to 8–10 ft. lbs.

MPV

1. Disconnect the negative battery cable. Remove the wiper arms.
2. Remove the drive link nuts from the top of the cowl.
3. Working under the hood, disconnect the negative battery cable.
4. Remove the motor and linkage mounting bolts and lift out the assembly.
5. After removal, separate the linkage from the motor.

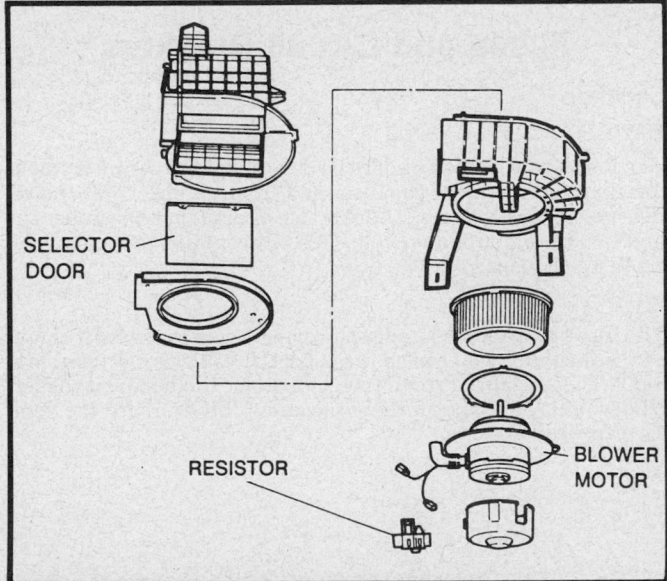

SELECTOR DOOR

RESISTOR

BLOWER MOTOR

Blower motor assembly—exploded view

6. Installation is the reverse of removal. When installing the wiper arms, make sure that the at rest position leaves a gap of 30mm between the blade tips and the lower windshield moulding.

Instrument Cluster

Removal and Installation

1. Disconnect the negative battery cable.
2. Reach behind the cluster and disconnect the speedometer cable.
3. Remove the screws attaching the cluster hood and carefully lift the hood off.
4. Remove the screw attaching the cluster pod to the dash panel and pull the pod outwards gradually. Reach behind the pod and disconnect the wiring connectors.
5. Remove the trip meter knob and on clusters with a tachometer, the clock adjust knob.
6. Remove the screws retaining the lens cover and lift off the cover.
7. Remove the screws retaining the cluster bezel and lift off the bezel.
8. Lift out the warning light plate.
9. Remove any gauges at this time.
10. Installation is the reverse of the removal procedure.

Combination Switch

Removal and Installation

1. Disconnect the negative battery cable.
2. Matchmark and remove the steering wheel.
3. Remove the steering column shroud.
4. Disconnect and tag the electrical connectors at the base of the steering column.
5. Pull the headlight switch knob off the shaft.
6. Remove the snapring which retains the switch on the steering shaft. Pull the turn signal canceling cam off the shaft.
7. Remove the switch mounting bolt at the bottom of the switch. Remove the switch from the steering column.
8. Installation is the reverse of removal. Check the operation of the switch before installing the steering wheel.

Ignition Lock

Removal and Installation

1. Disconnect the negative battery cable.
2. Matchmark and remove the steering wheel.
3. Remove the steering column cover.
4. Disconnect and tag the multiple connectors at the base of the combination switch.
5. Remove the switch retaining snapring. Pull the turn signal indicator cancelling cam off the shaft.
6. Remove the switch retaining bolt and remove the switch from the steering column.

NOTE: Make a groove on the head of the bolts attaching the steering lock body to the column shaft using the proper tool.

7. Remove the ignition lock attaching bolts. Remove the ignition lock.
8. Install and tighten the ignition lock bolts until the heads of the bolts break off.
9. The remainder of the installation is the reverse of the removal procedure.

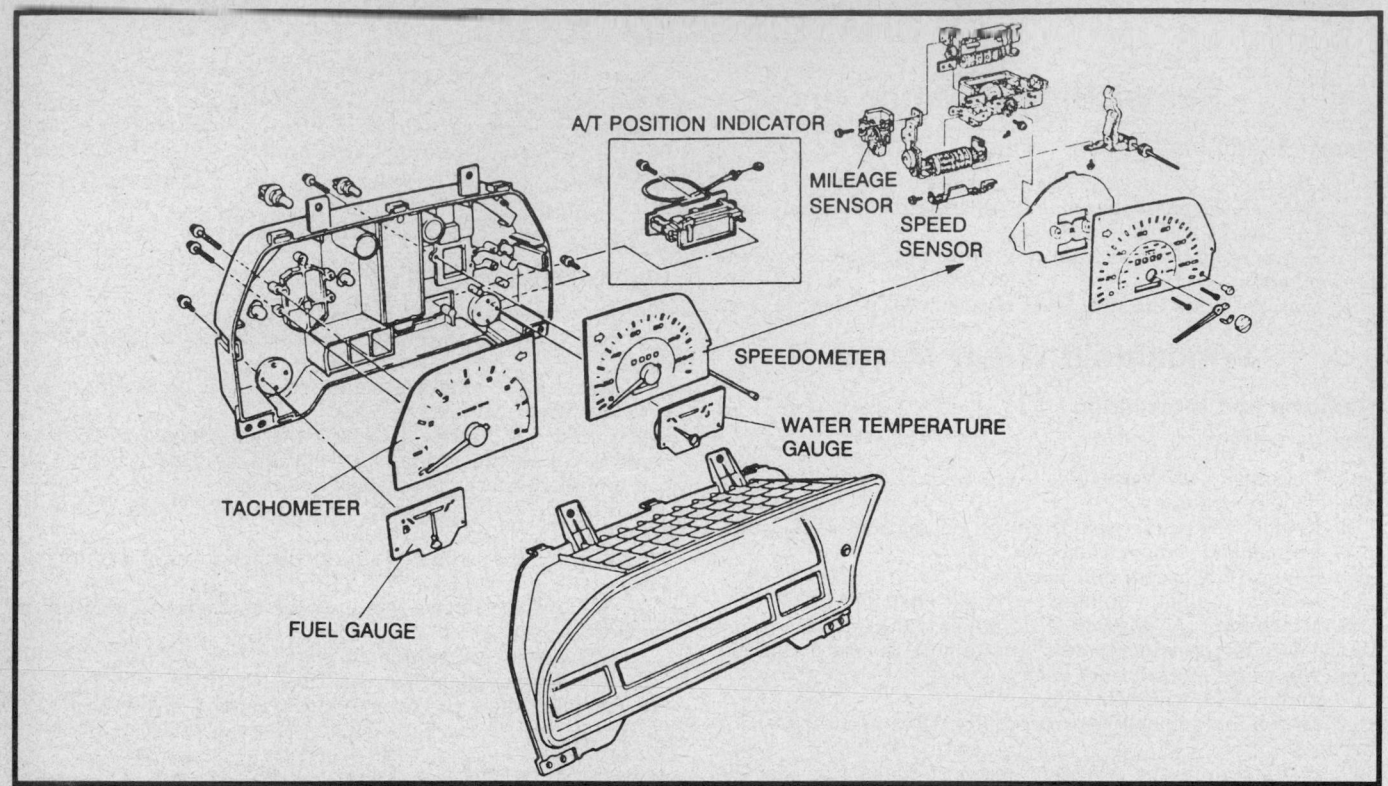

Instrument cluster removal—MPV shown, others similar

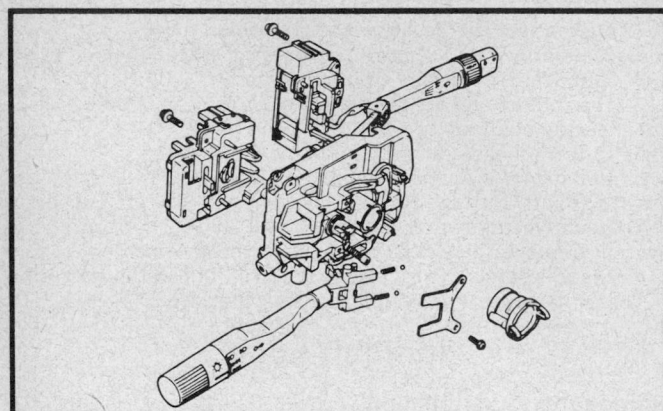

Combination switch—exploded view

Ignition Switch

Removal and Installation

1. Disconnect the negative battery cable.
2. Remove the steering column covers.
3. Disconnect the wiring harness connector at the switch.
4. Remove the switch mounting screws and remove the switch.
5. Installation is the reverse of the removal procedure.

Stoplight Switch

Removal and Installation

1. Disconnect the negative battery cable.
2. Remove the electrical connector from the stoplight switch.
3. Remove the switch retaining locknuts and pull the switch from the brake pedal bracket.
4. Install the switch in position and install the locknuts and connector.
5. Adjust the switch by turning it until it contacts the top of the brake pedal arm. Tighten the locknuts.

Fuses and Circuit Breakers

Location

EXCEPT MPV

The fuse box is located under the drivers side of the instrument panel, it contains all of the fuses and circuit breakers for the vehicles electrical systems. There is also a small fuse box under the hood, on the right fender well. This box contains the main vehicle fuses (2 fuses).

MPV

The fuse box is located under the drivers side of the instrument panel, it contains all of the fuses for the vehicles electrical systems. There is also a small fuse box under the hood, on the left fender well. This box contains the circuit breakers for the vehicle electrical systems.

ENGINE COOLING

Radiator

Removal and Installation

EXCEPT MPV

1. Disconnect the negative battery cable. Drain the cooling system.
2. If equipped, remove the fan shroud.
3. Remove the fan. Don't lay the fan, if equipped with a fan clutch, on its side. Fluid will be lost and the fan clutch will have to be replaced.
4. Disconnect the upper and lower radiator hoses.
5. Disconnect the coolant reservoir hose.
6. On vehicles with automatic transmission, disconnect and plug the cooler lines.
7. Unbolt and remove the radiator.

To install:

8. Install the radiator against the supports and tighten the mounting bolts.
9. Install the hoses on the radiator. Tighten the clamps.
10. Install the fan.
11. If equipped, install the fan shroud.
12. Refill the cooling system with the specified amount and type of coolant. Run the engine and check for leaks.

MPV

1. Disconnect the negative battery cable. Drain the cooling system.
2. Remove the fresh air duct.
3. Disconnect the upper and lower radiator hoses.
4. Disconnect the coolant reservoir hose.

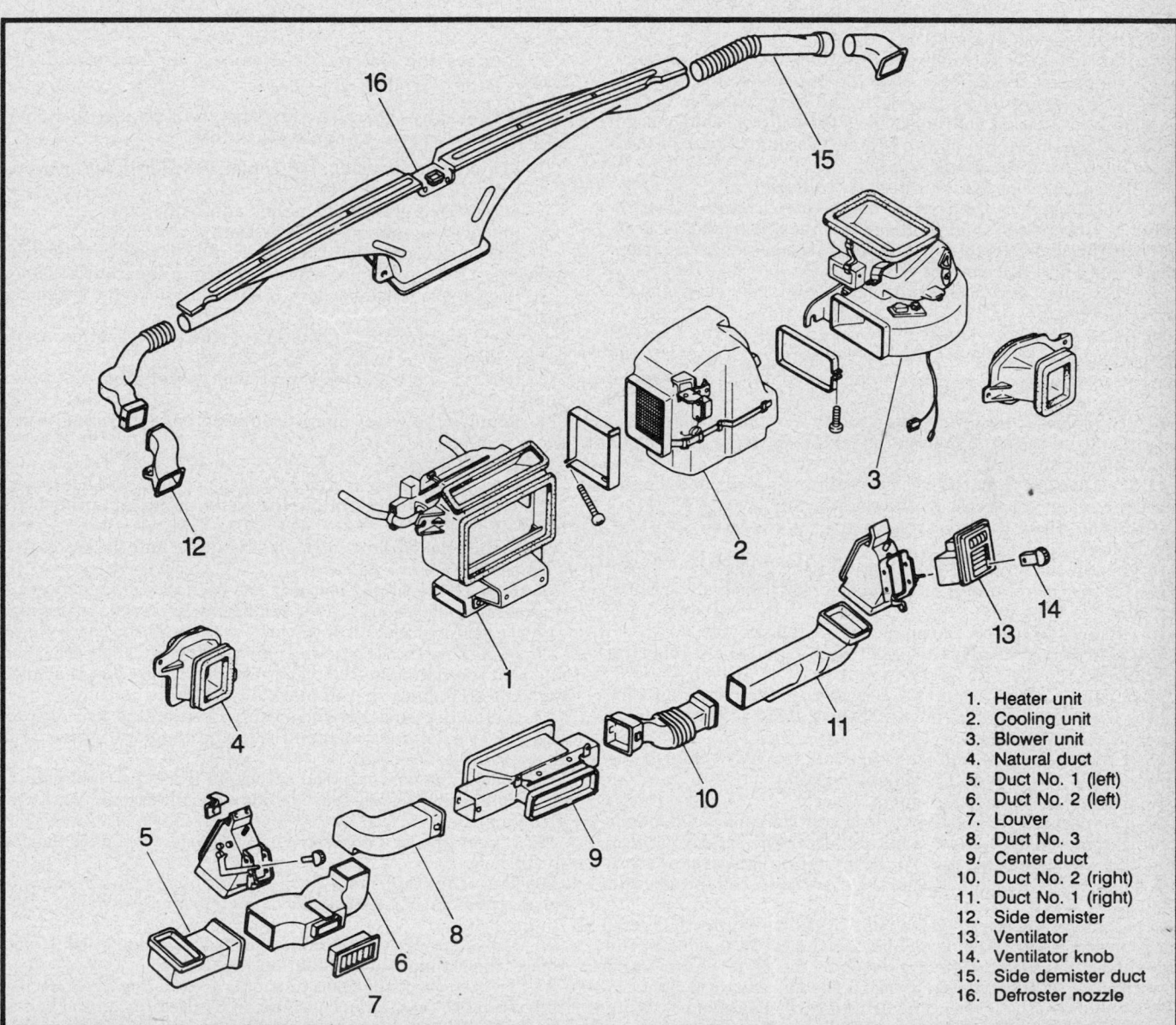

1. Heater unit
2. Cooling unit
3. Blower unit
4. Natural duct
5. Duct No. 1 (left)
6. Duct No. 2 (left)
7. Louver
8. Duct No. 3
9. Center duct
10. Duct No. 2 (right)
11. Duct No. 1 (right)
12. Side demister
13. Ventilator
14. Ventilator knob
15. Side demister duct
16. Defroster nozzle

Heater and defroster assembly — exploded view

5. On vehicles with automatic transmission, disconnect and plug the cooler lines.

6. Remove the fan shroud.

7. Remove the fan. Don't lay the fan, if equipped with a fan clutch, on its side. Fluid will be lost and the fan clutch will have to be replaced.

8. Unbolt and remove the radiator.

To install:

9. Install the radiator against the supports and tighten the mounting bolts.

10. Install the hoses and cooler lines on the radiator. Tighten the clamps.

11. Install the fan.

12. Install the fan shroud.

13. Refill the cooling system with the specified amount and type of coolant. Run the engine and check for leaks.

Heater Core

Removal and Installation

1. Disconnect the negative battery cable.

2. Drain the cooling system.

3. Remove the water valve shield at the left side of the heater.

4. Disconnect the 2 hoses from the left side of the heater.

5. At the heater-defroster door, at the water valve and at the outside recirculation door, disengage the control cable housing from the mounting clip on the heater. Disconnect each of the 3 cable wires from the crank arms.

6. Disconnect the fan motor electrical lead.

7. Working inside the engine compartment, remove the 2 retaining nuts and the single bolt and washer which hold the heater to the firewall. A retaining bolt inside the passenger compartment must also be removed.

8. Disconnect the 2 defroster ducts from the heater and remove the heater.

9. With the heater assembly removed, remove the 5 screws and separate the halves of the heater assembly. To replace the heater core, loosen the hose clamps and slide the heater core from the case.

10. To replace the blower motor, loosen the fan retaining nut. Lightly tap on the nut to loosen the fan. Remove the fan and nut from the motor shaft.

11. Remove the 3 motor-to-case retaining screws and disconnect the bullet connector to the resistor and ground screw.

12. Rotate the motor and remove it from the case.

To install:

13. Install the motor in the case, rotating it slightly.

14. Install the retaining screws and connect the bullet connector and ground wire.

15. Install the fan on the shaft and install the nut.

16. Assemble the halves together and install the 5 retaining screws.

17. Install the heater on the dash so that the heater duct indexes with the air intake duct and the 2 mounting studs enter their respective holes.

18. From the engine side of the firewall, install the nuts on the mounting studs. Install the mounting bolt.

19. Connect the defroster ducts.

20. Connect the heat-defrost door control cable to the door crank arm. Set the control lever (upper) in the **HEAT** position and turn the crank arm toward the mounting clip as far as it will go. Engage the cable housing in the clip and install the screw in the clip.

21. Connect the water valve control cable wire to the crank arm on the water valve lever. Locate the cable housing in the mounting clip. Set the control lever in the **HOT** position and pull the valve plunger and lever to the full outward position. This will move the lever crank arm toward the cable mounting clip as far as it will go. Tighten the clip and screw.

22. Insert the outside-recirculation door control cable into the hole in the door crank arm. Bend the wire over and tighten the screw. Set the center control lever in the **REC** position and turn the door crank arm toward the mounting clip as far as it will go. Engage the cable housing in the clip and install the screw in the clip.

23. Connect the fan motor electrical lead.

24. Connect the 2 hoses to the heater core tubes, at the left side of the heater and tighten the clamp.

25. Install the water valve shield and tighten the 3 screws on the left side of the heater.

26. Refill the cooling system and connect the negative battery cable.

27. Run the engine and check for leaks. Check the operation of the heater.

Water Pump

Removal and Installation

1998cc AND 2184cc ENGINES

1. Disconnect the negative battery cable. Drain the cooling system.

2. Remove the distributor. Remove the fan shroud, fan blades, pulley, hub and bracket.

NOTE: Always store the fan clutch in an upright position after removal to avoid fluid loss.

3. Remove the alternator. Disconnect the air injection pipes.

4. Remove the drive belts.

5. Remove the crankshaft pulley and baffle plate.

6. Remove the upper and lower timing belt covers.

7. Rotate the crankshaft so that the **A** mark on the camshaft pulley is at the top, aligned with the notch in the front housing.

8. Loosen the tensioner lock bolt and remove the tensioner spring.

9. Mark the direction of rotation of the timing belt for installation. Remove the belt.

10. Remove the water inlet pipe and gasket from the water pump.

11. Remove the water pump mounting bolts and remove the water pump.

To install:

12. Use a new O-ring coated with clean coolant and a new gasket coated with sealer. Torque the water pump mounting bolts to 14–19 ft. lbs.

13. Install the coolant inlet pipe, using a new gasket coated with sealer.

14. Replace the timing belt if it has been contaminated by oil or grease, or shows any sign of damage, wear, cracks or peeling.

15. To ease installation of the belt, remove all the spark plugs.

16. Make sure that the timing mark on the camshaft is aligned and that the timing mark on the crankshaft sprocket is aligned with the triangular shaped mark on the front housing.

17. Install the tensioner and spring. Position the tensioner all the way to the intake manifold side and temporarily secure it there with the lock bolt.

18. Install the belt onto the sprockets from the right side. If the original belt is being reused, follow the directional mark previously made.

19. Loosen the lock bolt so that the tensioner applies tension to the belt.

20. Turn the crankshaft 2 full revolutions in the direction of normal rotation. This will apply equal tension to all points of the timing belt.

26. Make sure that the timing marks are still aligned. If not, repeat the timing belt installation procedure.

27. Tighten the timing belt tensioner lock bolt to 30–35 ft. lbs.

28. Measure the timing belt tension by pressing on the belt at the midpoint of the longest straight run. Belt deflection should be 11–13mm. If not, repeat the belt adjustment procedure.

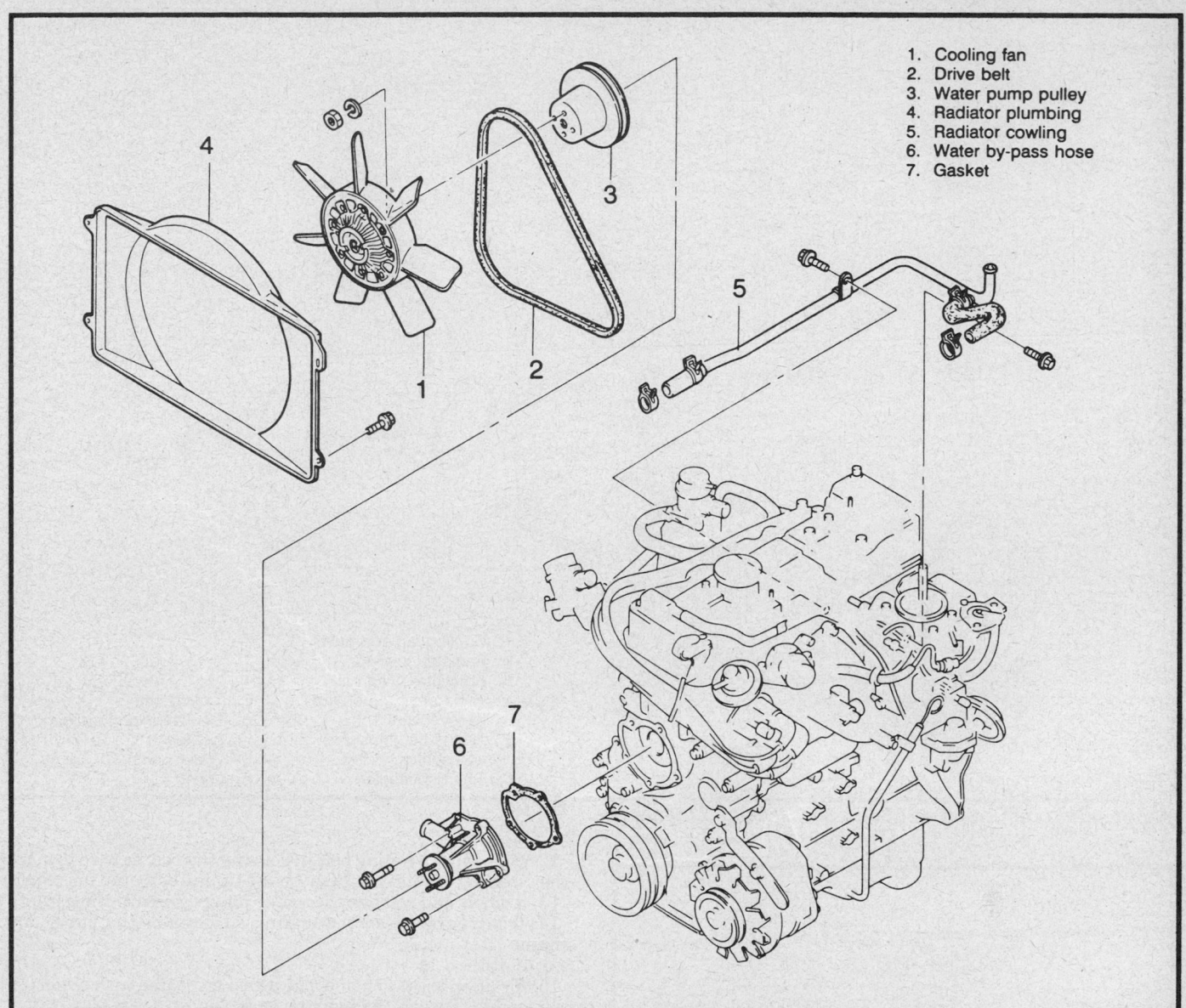

1. Cooling fan
2. Drive belt
3. Water pump pulley
4. Radiator plumbing
5. Radiator cowling
6. Water by-pass hose
7. Gasket

Water pump mounting—1998cc and 2184cc engines

29. The remainder of the installation is the reverse of removal procedure.

2555cc AND 2606cc ENGINES

1. Disconnect the negative battery cable. Drain the cooling system.
2. Remove the water pump drive belt. Remove the cooling fan and belt pulley.
3. Remove the fan shroud. Remove the water bypass hose.
4. Disconnect the lower radiator hose at the water pump.
5. Remove the water pump mounting bolts and remove the water pump.
6. Clean and inspect the water pump sealing surface of the engine.

To install:

7. Using a new gasket, install the water pump on the engine and torque the bolts to 14–19 ft. lbs.
8. Connect the lower radiator hose and water bypass hose.
9. Install the drive belt pulley, cooling fan and drive belt.
10. Adjust the drive belt tension. Install the fan shroud.

11. Fill the cooling system, run the engine and check for leaks.

2954cc ENGINE

1. Position the engine at TDC on the compression stroke.
2. Properly relieve the fuel system pressure.
3. Disconnect the negative battery cable. Remove the air cleaner assembly.
4. Drain the cooling system. Remove the spark plug wires.
5. Remove the fresh air duct assembly. Remove the cooling fan and radiator cowling. Remove the accessory drive belts.
6. Remove the air conditioning compressor idler pulley. If necessary, remove the compressor and position it to the side.
7. Remove the crankshaft pulley and baffle plate. Remove the coolant bypass hose.
8. Remove the upper radiator hose.
9. Remove the timing belt cover assembly retaining bolts and remove the timing belt cover assembly and gasket.
10. Turn the crankshaft to align the mating marks of the pulleys.
11. Remove the upper idler pulley.

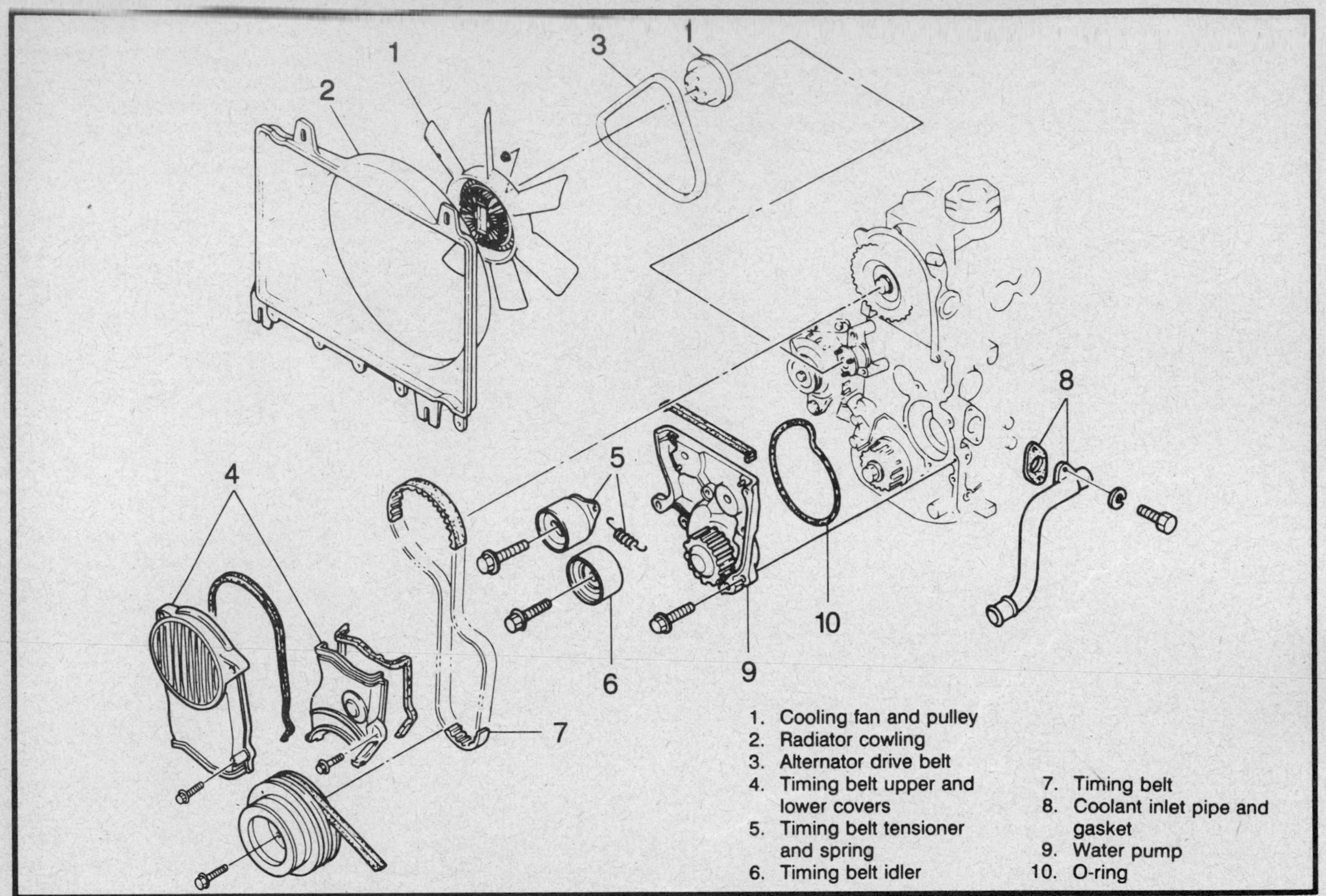

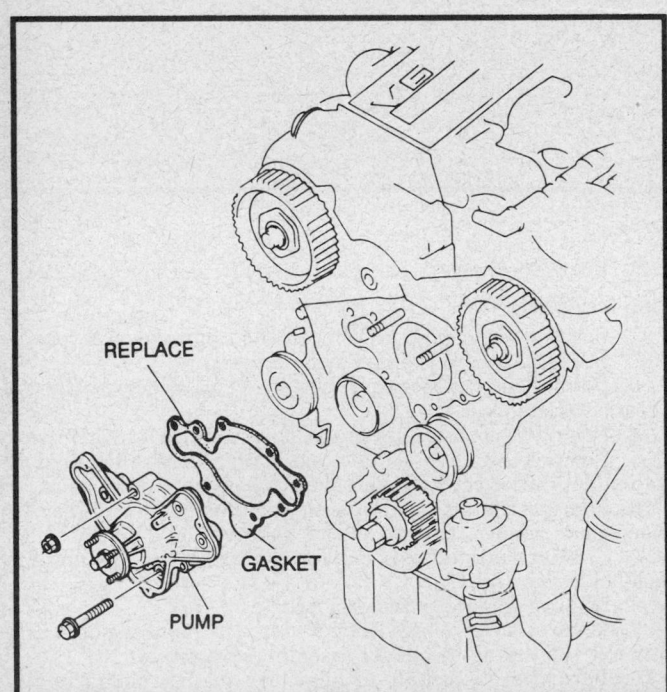

1. Cooling fan and pulley
2. Radiator cowling
3. Alternator drive belt
4. Timing belt upper and lower covers
5. Timing belt tensioner and spring
6. Timing belt idler
7. Timing belt
8. Coolant inlet pipe and gasket
9. Water pump
10. O-ring

Water pump mounting—2555cc and 2606cc engines

Water pump mounting—2954cc engine

12. Remove the timing belt. If reusing the belt be sure to mark the direction of rotation. Remove the timing belt auto tensioner.
13. Unbolt and remove the water pump. Discard the gasket.
14. Thoroughly clean the mating surfaces of the pump and engine.

To install:

15. Position the pump and a new gasket, coated with sealer, on the engine. Torque the bolts to 19 ft. lbs.
16. Install the timing belt.
17. Install the timing belt cover assembly and new gasket. Install the timing belt cover assembly retaining bolts.
18. Install the upper radiator hose. Install the coolant bypass hose.
19. Install the crankshaft pulley and baffle plate. Install the compressor.
20. Install the air conditioning compressor idler pulley and install and adjust the drive belts.
21. Install the cooling fan and radiator cowling.
22. Install the fresh air duct assembly. Install the spark plug wires.
23. Fill the cooling system. Install the air cleaner assembly.
24. Connect the negative battery cable.

Thermostat

Removal and Installation
EXCEPT MPV WITH 2954cc ENGINE

1. Disconnect the negative battery cable. Drain the cooling

system down below the thermostat housing. Disconnect the coolant temperature sending unit wire.

2. Remove the coolant outlet elbow. If equipped, position the vacuum control valve out of the way. The vacuum control valve is not used on California vehicles.

3. Disconnect the coolant bypass hose from the thermostat housing.

4. Remove the thermostat and housing from the engine.

5. Note the position of the jiggle pin and remove the thermostat from the housing.

6. Clean and inspect the sealing surfaces of the housing and engine.

To install:

7. Position the thermostat in the housing with the jiggle pin up. Coat the new gasket with sealer and install it on the thermostat housing.

8. Install the thermostat housing using a new gasket with sealer. Torque the bolts to 20 ft. lbs.

9. Install the coolant outlet elbow and vacuum control valve, if equipped.

10. Connect the bypass and radiator hoses.

11. Connect the temperature sending unit wire.

12. Fill the cooling system with the proper coolant. Run the engine, check the coolant level and check for leaks.

MPV WITH 2954cc ENGINE

NOTE: The thermostat housing is located on the lower part of the engine at the end of the lower radiator hose.

1. Raise and safely support the vehicle.
2. Drain the cooling system.
3. Remove the lower radiator hose.
4. Unbolt and remove the housing and thermostat.
5. Install a new thermostat in the housing and position the housing on the engine. Torque the bolts to 19 ft. lbs.
6. Install the lower hose.
7. Fill the cooling system.

Cooling System Bleeding

After working on the cooling system, even to replace the ther-

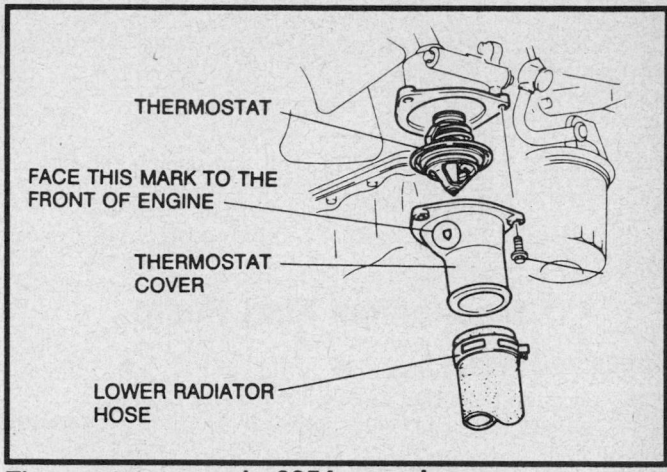

Thermostat removal – 2954cc engine

mostat, it must be bled. Air trapped in the system will prevent proper filling and leave the radiator coolant level low, causing a risk of overheating.

1. To bleed the system, start with the system cool, the radiator cap off and the radiator filled to about an inch below the filler neck.

2. Start the engine and run it at slightly above normal idle speed. This will insure adequate circulation. If air bubbles appear and the coolant level drops, fill the system with an antifreeze/water mixture to bring the level back to the proper level.

3. Run the engine this way until the thermostat opens. When this happens, coolant will move abruptly across the top of the radiator and the temperature of the radiator will suddenly rise.

4. At this point, air is often expelled and the level may drop quite a bit. Keep refilling the system until the level is near the top of the radiator and remains constant.

5. If the vehicle has an overflow tank, fill the radiator right up to the filler neck. Replace the radiator filler cap.

FUEL SYSTEM

Fuel System Service Precaution

When working with the fuel system certain precautions should be taken; always work in a well ventilated area, keep a dry chemical (Class B) fire extinguisher near the work area. Always disconnect the negative battery cable and do not make any repairs to the fuel system until all the necessary steps for repair have been reviewed.

Relieving Fuel System Pressure

Fuel in the system remains under pressure, even with the ignition turned **OFF**. The fuel pressure must be relieved before performing any service on the fuel system.

1. Start the engine.
2. Disconnect the airflow meter connector.
3. After the engine stalls, turn **OFF** the ignition switch.
4. Reconnect the airflow meter.

Priming the Fuel System

After the system pressure has been relieved, the system must be re-pressurized.

1. Connect the terminals of the test connector.

2. Turn the ignition switch **ON** for 10 seconds and check for leaks.

3. Turn the igntion switch **OFF** and disconnect the jumper.

Fuel Filter

Removal and Installation

EXCEPT MPV

The fuel filter is located at the rear of the vehicle, on the left side frame rail.

1. On fuel injected vehicles, relieve the fuel system pressure.
2. Disconnect the negative battery cable.
3. Raise and safely support the vehicle.
4. Disconnect the lines from the fuel filter and remove the filter retaining bolts.
5. Remove the filter.
6. Install the new filter in position and connect the fuel lines. Make sure the filter is installed correctly.
7. Lower the vehicle. On fuel injected vehicles, pressurize the fuel system.
8. Connect the negative battery cable.

MPV

The fuel filter is located on top of the engine, next to the pulsation damper.

1. Relieve the fuel system pressure.
2. Disconnect the negative battery cable.
3. Remove the fuel lines from the filter.
4. Remove the filter mounting bolt and remove the filter.
5. Install the new filter in position and connect the fuel lines. Make sure to install the filter in the correct direction.
6. Pressurize the fuel system and connect the negative battery cable.

Mechanical Fuel Pump

Pressure Testing

1. Disconnect the fuel line from the carburetor.
2. Connect a fuel pressure gauge in the line between the carburetor.
3. Plug the fuel pump return outlet.
4. Check the fuel pressure while the engine is idling. Correct fuel pressure should be 4–5 psi.

Removal and Installation

1. Disconnect the negative battery cable. Disconnect and plug the inlet, outlet and return hoses at the fuel pump.
2. Remove the fuel pump mounting bolts and remove the fuel pump, insulator and gaskets.
3. Clean and inspect the mounting surfaces of the fuel pump and engine.
4. Using a new gasket with sealer, install the fuel pump on the engine and tighten the bolts to 11–14 ft. lbs.
5. Connect the fuel lines, run the engine and check for leaks.

Electric Fuel Pump

Pressure Testing

1. Turn the ignition switch **OFF**. Relieve the fuel system pressure.
2. Disconnect the main fuel hose and connect a pressure gauge in line.
3. Connect the **B** and **D** terminals of the fuel pump control unit with a jumper wire.
4. Turn the ignition switch **ON** and check the fuel pressure. Correct pressure is 3–4 psi. at idle.

Removal and Installation

EXCEPT MPV

1. Disconnect the negative battery cable. Relieve the fuel system pressure. Raise and support the vehicle safely.
2. Disconnect the fuel pump and sending unit wires at the connector, next to the tank.

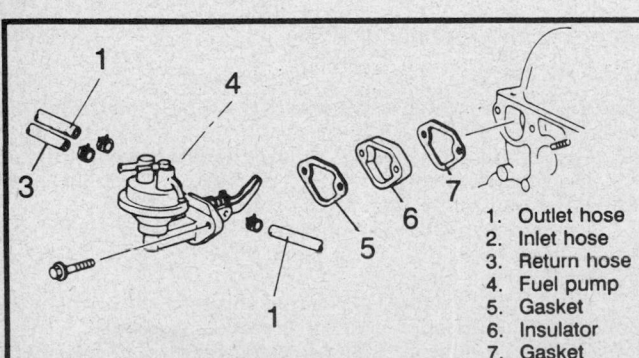

1. Outlet hose
2. Inlet hose
3. Return hose
4. Fuel pump
5. Gasket
6. Insulator
7. Gasket

Mechanical fuel pump mounting

3. Remove the fuel tank drain plug and drain the fuel into approved containers. With the fuel tank drained, support the tank.
4. Remove the fuel tank mounting straps and lower the tank enough to disconnect the fuel hoses. Disconnect the fuel filler hose at the fuel tank.
5. Disconnect and tag the fuel hoses at the fuel pump.
6. Remove the fuel tank from the vehicle.
7. Remove the fuel pump and float assembly from the tank.
8. Installation is the reverse of the removal procedure. Check the fuel pump operation when finished.

MPV

1. Relieve the fuel system pressure. Disconnect the negative battery cable.
2. Remove the rear seat cushion and lift the carpeting. Disconnect the electrical connector located near the pump cover. Remove the attaching screws and remove the cover.
3. Note the hookup locations of the fuel hoses. Disconnect fuel supply and return hoses and plug them. Remove the attaching screws and remove the pump/gauge unit assembly and gasket. If the gasket appears worn, replace it.
4. Unscrew and disconnect the electrical connectors for the pump from the assembly. Loosen the screw at the clamp which holds the pump in position. Loosen the clamps and remove the hose connecting the outlet of the pump to the assembly. Remove the pump. Use a new connecting hose between the pump outlet and the top of the pump/gauge assembly.
To install:
5. Install the pump into its mounting bracket and connect the fuel outlet hose to the pump. Secure the outlet hose with the clamps.
6. Support the pump by hand and install the retaining screw that holds the pump in place in the bracket. Connect the electrical connector to the pump. Install the pump/gauge assembly and secure with the attaching screws.
7. Connect fuel inlet and outlet lines to their respective connections. Check the fuel lines and the pump wiring to make sure that they are tight and in place. Use tie straps as required to secure the fuel hoses and the wiring.
8. Install the fuel pump cover and connect the connector to it. Install the rear seat cushion and reposition the carpeting.
9. Connect the negative battery cable and re-pressurize the fuel system.

Carburetor

Removal and Installation

1. Disconnect the negative battery cable. Remove the air cleaner and air inlet duct.
2. Disconnect the accelerator shaft from the throttle lever.
3. Disconnect and plug the fuel supply and return lines.
4. Disconnect the leads from the throttle solenoid and deceleration valve at the quick-disconnects.
5. Disconnect the carburetor to distributor vacuum line.
6. Disconnect the throttle return spring.
7. Disconnect the choke cable and if equipped, the cruise control cable.
8. Remove the carburetor attaching nuts from the intake manifold studs and remove the carburetor.
To install:
9. Install a new carburetor gasket on the manifold.
10. Install the carburetor and tighten the carburetor attaching nuts.
11. Connect the throttle return spring.
12. Connect the accelerator shaft to the throttle shaft.
13. Connect the electrical leads to the throttle solenoid and deceleration valve.
14. Connect the distributor vacuum line.
15. Connect the fuel supply and return lines.

16. Connect and adjust the choke cable and if equipped, the cruise control cable.

17. Install the air cleaner and air inlet duct. Connect the negative battery cable.

18. Run the engine and check for fuel leaks.

Idle Speed Adjustment

Check that the ignition timing, spark plugs, carburetor float level, etc. are all in normal operating condition. Turn off all lights and other unnecessary electrical loads.

1. Connect a tachometer to the engine.

2. Start and allow the engine to reach normal operating temperature. Check the idle speed and adjust it to the specification by turning the throttle adjusting screw. The idle speed should be 800–850 rpm in **N** or **P**.

Idle Mixture Adjustment

1. Start the engine and allow it to reach normal operating temperature, let the engine run at idle.

2. Connect a dwellmeter (90 degrees, 4 cylinder) to the brown/yellow wire in the check connector of the A/F solenoid valve.

3. Check the idle mixture at specified idle speed. The idle mixture should be 20–70 degrees. If the idle mixture is not within specifiactions, adjust the idle mixture as follows:

    a. To adjust the idle mixture, remove the carburetor and take out the spring pin. Reinstall the carburetor.

    b. Be sure that the air cleaner is installed and the idle compensator is closed.

    c. Warm up the engine and run it at idle speed.

    d. Connect a tachometer to the engine.

    e. Connect a dwellmeter (90 degrees, 4 cylinder) to the brown/yellow wire in the check connector of the A/F solenoid valve and read the meter. The standard value should be 27–45 degrees (at idle).

    f. If the reading obtained is not within the specified range, adjust the idle mixture by turning the mixture adjust screw.

NOTE: If the adjustment cannot be made, it is probably because of a faulty oxygen sensor, or because of either a broken wire or a short in the wiring between the oxygen sensor and the control unit.

    g. Tap in the spring pin.

Service Adjustments

For all carburetor service adjustment procedures and specifications, please refer to "Carburetor Service" in the Unit Repair section.

Fuel Injection

Idle Speed and Mixture Adjustments

The idle speed and misture are controlled by the electronic control unit and are not adjustable.

Fuel Injector

Removal and Installation

2606cc ENGINE

1. Relieve the fuel system pressure. Disconnect the negative battery cable.

2. Remove the air chamber.

3. Disconnect the vacuum hose.

4. Disconnect the fuel lines.

5. Remove the pressure regulator and delivery pipe.

6. Disconnect the injector wiring.

7. Pull off the injectors. Discard the grommets and O-rings.

8. Installation is the reverse of removal. Torque the delivery

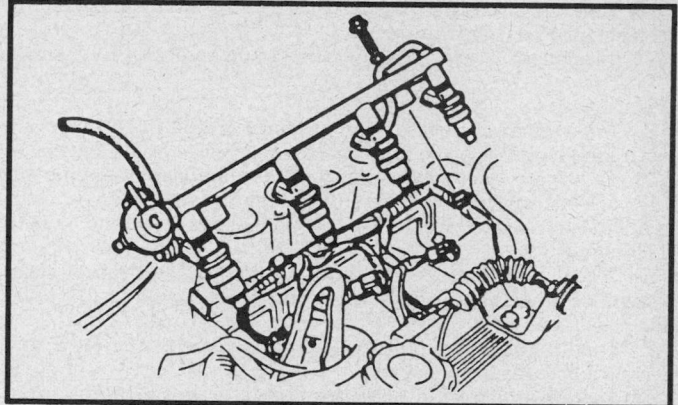
Fuel rail removal—2555cc and 2606cc engines

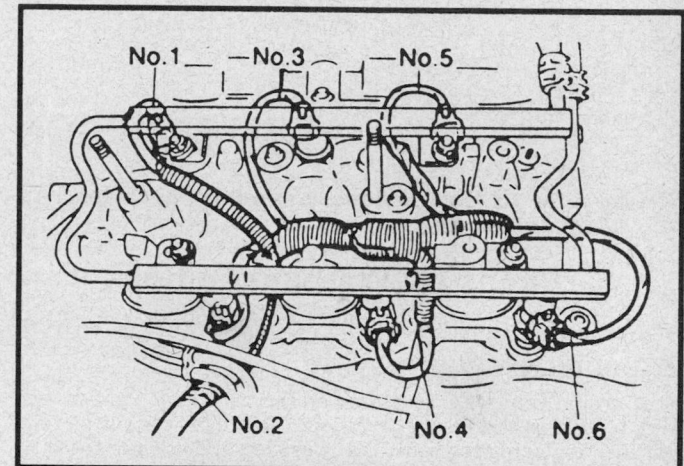
Fuel rail removal—2954cc engine

pipe bolts to 15 ft. lbs. Always use new O-rings coated with clean engine oil.

9. Re-pressurize the fuel system.

2954CC ENGINE

1. Perform fuel system pressure release procedure.

2. Disconnect the negative battery cable.

3. Loosen clamps securing air cleaner to throttle body hose and remove hose.

4. Remove the throttle cable and transmission kickdown linkage.

5. Remove harness connector from throttle position sensor (TPS), and automatic idle speed (AIS) motor.

6. Label and remove vacuum hoses from throttle body. Remove PCV and brake booster hoses from air intake plenum.

7. Remove EGR tube to intake plenum.

8. Remove electrical connection from charge temperature and coolant temperature sensor.

9. Remove vacuum connection from pressure regulator and air intake connection from manifold.

10. Remove fuel hoses to fuel rail connection.

11. Remove air intake plenum to manifold bolts (8) and remove air intake plenum and gaskets.

NOTE: Whenever air intake plenum is remove, cover intake manifold properly to avoid objects from entering cylinder head.

12. Disconnect fuel injector wiring harness from engine wiring harness.

13. Remove pressure regulator attaching bolts and remove pressure regulator from rail.

14. Remove fuel rail attaching bolts and remove fuel rail.

To install:

15. Make certain injector are properly seated in receiver cup with lock rings in place and injector discharge holes are clean.

16. Lubricate injector O-rings with a clean drop of engine oil.

17. Install injector rail assembly making sure each injector seats in their respective ports. Torque fuel rail attaching bolts to 115 inch lbs.

18. Lubricate pressure regulator O-ring with a drop of clean engine oil and install regulator to fuel rail. Torque nuts to 77 inch lbs.

19. Install hold down bolts on fuel supply and return tube, and vacuum crossover tube.

20. Install and torque pressure regulator hose clamps to 10 inch lbs.

21. Reconnect injector wiring harness.

22. Reconnect vacuum hoses to fuel pressure regulator and fuel rail.

23. Set the air intake plenum gasket in place with beaded sealer in the **UP** position.

24. Install air intake plenum and tighten (8) attaching screws to 115 inch lbs.

25. Reconnect fuel line to fuel rail and tighten clamps to 10 inch lbs.

26. Reconnect EGR tube to intake plenum and torque nuts to 200 inch lbs.

27. Reconnect electrical wiring to charge temperature sensor, coolant temperature sensor, TPS and AIS motor.

28. Reconnect vacuum connection to throttle body and air intake plenum.

29. Install accelerator cable and transmission kickdown cable.

30. Install air cleaner to throttle body hose and tighten clamps.

31. Reconnect negative battery cable. Re-pressurize the fuel system.

EMISSION CONTROLS

Please refer to "Professional Emission Component Application Guide".

Emission Warning Lamps

Resetting

CARBURETED VEHICLES

Carbureted vehicles incorporate an service engine light to indicate a fault in the feedback system. This light cannot be reset without repairing the fault in the system and erasing the trouble codes.

FUEL INJECTED VEHICLES

Fuel injected vehicles (except California) incorporate a mileage sensor that keeps track of the vehicle mileage in conjunction with the odometer. The mileage sensor, at 80,000 miles, will il-

luminate the Malfunction Indicator Light (MIL). At this time the oxygen sensor must be replaced.

After replacing the oxygen sensor, reset the MIL using the following procedure:

1. Disconnect the negative battery cable.
2. Remove the instrument cluster.
3. Remove the screw in the middle of the circuit board, from the hole marked **NO** and install it in the hole marked **NC**.
4. Install the instrument cluster.
5. Connect the battery cable and turn the ignition **ON**. Make sure the MIL is out.

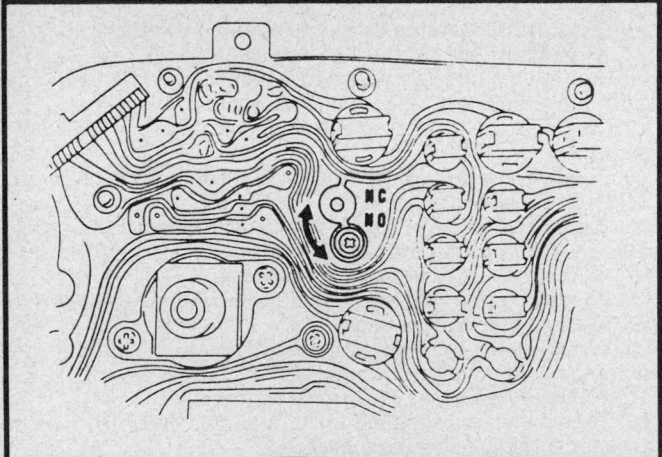

Maintenance reset screw location—on the rear of the instrument cluster

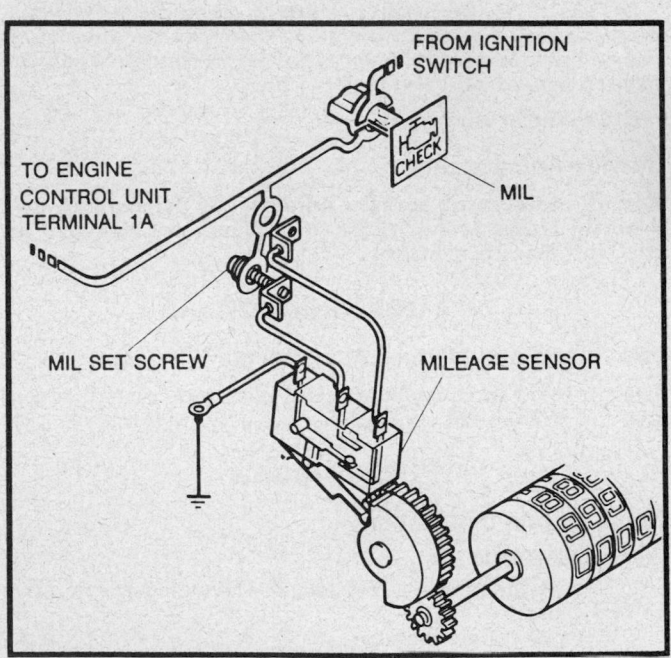

Maintenance timer assembly

ENGINE MECHANICAL

NOTE: Disconnecting the battery cable on some vehicles may interfere with the functions of the on board computer systems and may require the computer to undergo a relearning process, once the negative battery cable is disconnected.

Engine

Removal and Installation

EXCEPT MPV

1. Disconnect the battery ground.
2. Drain the cooling system.
3. Remove the air cleaner. Remove the oil pressure sending unit.
4. Remove the fan and shroud. Remove the accelerator cable.
5. Remove the fuel line. Remove the heater hoses.
6. Remove the brake vacuum hose.
7. Remove the 3-way solenoid valve and vacuum sensor. Remove the duty solenoid valve. Remove the vacuum switch.
8. Remove the canister hoses. Disconnect the engine harness coupler and remove the engine ground wire.
9. Remove the upper and lower radiator hoses. Remove the radiator and condenser.
10. Remove the secondary air pipe. Disconnect the exhaust pipe.
11. Remove the air conditioning compressor and mounting bracket. Do not disconnect the lines.
12. Remove the power steering pump. Remove the starter.
13. Raise and safely support the vehicle. Drain the engine oil. Remove the gusset plates. Remove the rear undercover.
14. Support the transmission with a suitable jack.
15. Attch an suitable lifting device to the engine lifting eyes. Take up the weight of the engine.
16. Remove the flywheel-to-converter nuts on vehicles with automatic transmission.
17. Remove the engine-to-transmission bolts. Remove the engine mount nuts.
18. Pull the engine forward to disengage it from the transmission. Raise the engine and remove it from the vehicle.

To install:

19. Lower the engine into the vehicle.
20. Install the engine-to-transmission bolts. Torque the bolts to 38 ft. lbs.
21. Install the engine mount nuts. Torque the nuts to 35 ft. lbs.
22. Install the flywheel-to-converter nuts on vehicles with automatic transmission. Torque the bolts to 35 ft. lbs.
23. Remove the engine lifting device. Remove the transmission floor jack.
24. Install the rear undercover. Install the gusset plates. Install the starter.
25. Install the power steering pump, the air conditioning compressor and mounting bracket.
26. Connect the exhaust pipe. Install the secondary air pipe.
27. Install the condenser and the radiator. Install the upper and lower radiator hoses.
28. Install the engine ground wire. Connect the engine harness coupler.
29. Install the canister hoses. Install the vacuum switch.
30. Install the duty solenoid valve. Install the 3-way solenoid valve and vacuum sensor.
31. Install the brake vacuum hose. Install the heater hoses and the fuel line.
32. Install the accelerator cable.
33. Install the fan and shroud. Install the oil pressure sending unit.
34. Install the air cleaner.

35. Fill the engine with the correct amount of oil.
36. Fill the cooling system.
37. Connect the negative battery cable and install the hood.

MPV

1. Disconnect the negative battery cable. Drain the cooling system.
2. Remove the starter.
3. Remove the battery. Remove the air duct.
4. Remove the engine undercover. Remove the upper and lower radiator hoses.
5. Remove the fan and shroud. On vehicles with automatic transmission, remove the cooler lines.
6. Remove the radiator and condenser.
7. Disconnect the air flow sensor connector.
8. Remove the accessory belts. Remove the air cleaner.
9. Remove the heater hoses. Remove the accelerator cable.
10. Remove the brake vacuum hose. Remove the canister hoses.
11. Relieve the fuel system pressure and remove the fuel lines.
12. Remove the alternator. Properly discharge the air conditioning system. Remove the air conditioning compressor and mounting bracket.
13. Remove the power steering pump. Disconnect the emissions harness connectors.
14. Remove the engine ground wire. Remove the engine shroud upper panel.
15. Disconnect the exhaust pipe.
16. Remove the lower grille panel. Remove the grille.
17. Raise and safely support the vehicle. Drain the engine oil Remove the engine shroud plate.
18. Support the transmission with a floor jack.
19. Attach a suitable lfitng device to the engine lifting eyes. Take up the weight of the engine.
20. Remove the flywheel-to-converter nuts on vehicles with automatic transmission.
21. Remove the engine-to-transmission bolts.
22. Remove the engine mount nuts.
23. Pull the engine forward to disengage it from the transmission. Raise the engine and remove it from the vehicle.

To install:

24. Lower the engine into the vehicle.
25. Install the engine-to-transmission bolts. Torque to 35 ft. lbs.
26. Install the engine mount nuts. Torque to 35 ft. lbs.
27. Install the flywheel-to-converter nuts on trucks with automatic transmission. Torque to 35 ft. lbs.
28. Remove the engine lifting device. Remove the transmission floor jack.
29. Install the engine shroud upper plate.
30. Install the grille. Install the lower grille panel.
31. Connect the exhaust pipe. Install the engine shroud upper panel.
32. Install the engine ground wire. Connect the emissions harness connectors.
33. Install the power steering pump. Install the air conditioning compressor and mounting bracket.
34. Install the alternator. Install the fuel lines.
35. Install the canister hoses. Install the brake vacuum hose.
36. Install the accelerator cable. Install the heater hose and install the air cleaner.
37. Install the accessory belts.
38. Connect the air flow sensor connector. Install the condenser and radiator.
39. On vehicles with automatic transmission, install the cooler lines.
40. Install the fan and shroud. Install the upper and lower radiator hoses.

41. Install the engine undercover. Install the air duct.
42. Install the battery. Install the starter.
43. Fill the crankcase with the correct amount of oil.
44. Fill the cooling system.
45. Connect the negative battery cable.

Cylinder Head

Removal and Installation

1998cc AND 2184cc ENGINES

1. Disconnect the negative battery cable and drain the cooling system.

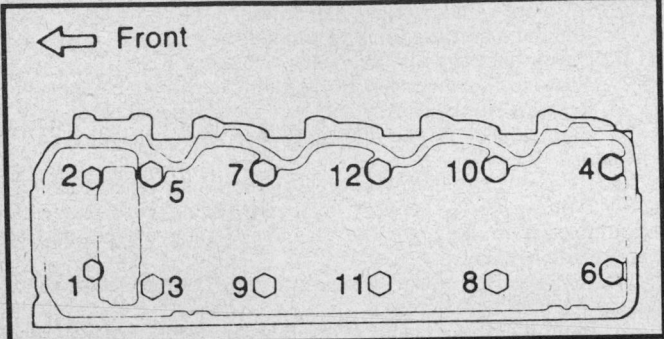

Cylinder head bolt removal sequence—2555cc engine

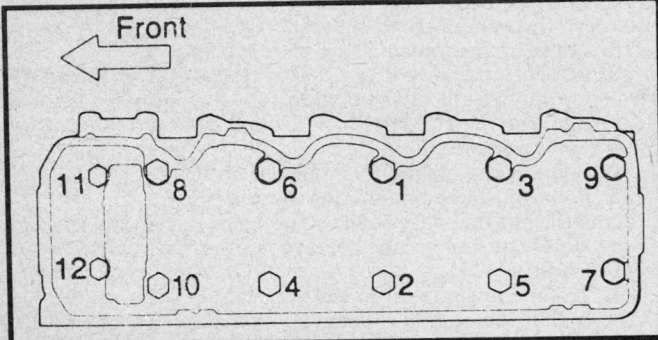

Cylinder head bolt installation sequence—2555cc engine

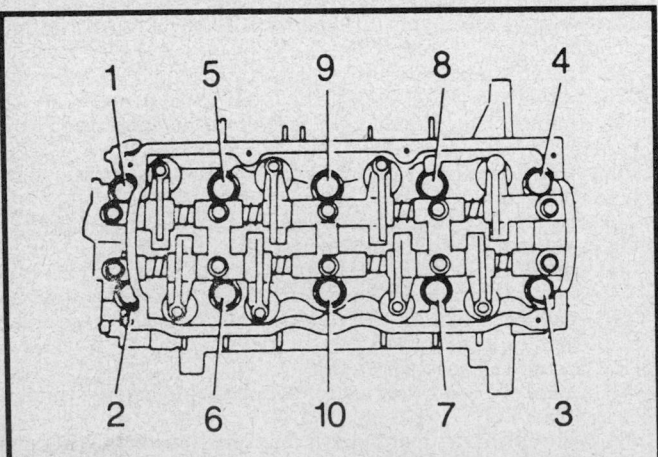

Cylinder head bolt removal sequence—1998cc and 2184cc engines

2. Disconnect the spark plug wires and remove the spark plugs.
3. Disconnect the accelerator cable. If equipped with automatic transmission, disconnect the throttle cable.
4. Remove the air intake pipe.
5. Remove the air cleaner and fuel hose. Cover the fuel hose to prevent leakage.
6. Remove the upper radiator hose, water bypass hose, heater hose, and brake vacuum hose.
7. Remove the 3-way and EGR solenoid valve assemblies.
8. Disconnect the engine harness connector and ground wire.
9. Remove the vacuum chamber and exhaust manifold insulator.
10. Remove the EGR pipe and exhaust pipe.
11. Remove the exhaust manifold.
12. Remove the intake manifold bracket and the intake manifold.
13. Remove the distributor.
14. Loosen the air conditioning compressor and bracket, position it off to the side and tie it out of the way.
15. Remove the upper timing belt cover and the timing belt tensioner spring. Remove the timing belt.
16. Remove the cylinder head cover and cover gasket.
18. Loosen the cylinder head bolts in the proper sequence and remove the cylinder head and head gasket.

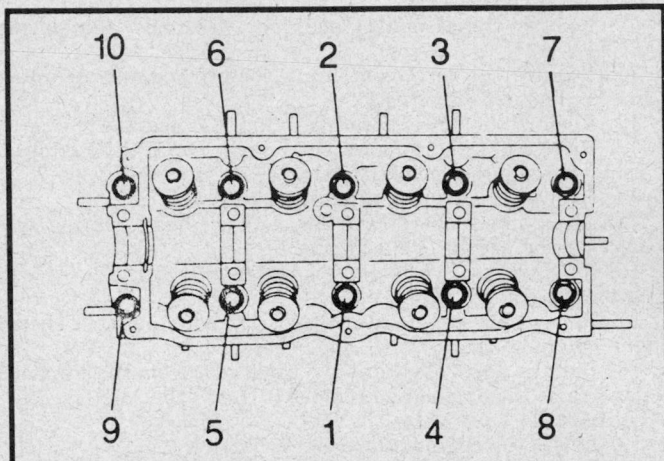

Cylinder head bolt installation sequence—1998cc and 2184cc engines

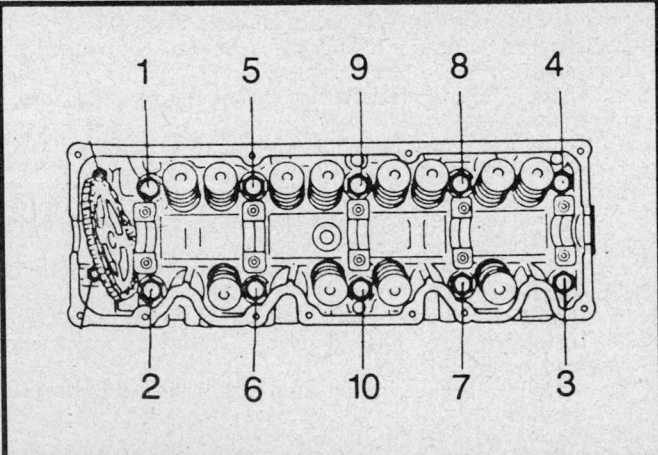

Cylinder head bolt removal sequence—2606cc engine

To install:

19. Thoroughly clean the cylinder head and cylinder block contact surfaces to remove any dirt or oil. Check the cylinder head for warpage and cracks. The maximum allowable contact distortion is 0.15mm (0.038 in.). Inspect the cylinder head bolts for damaged threads and make sure they are free from grease and dirt.

20. Lay the new gasket on the surface of the block.

21. Set the cylinder head on the gasket.

22. Coat the bolt threads and seat surfaces with clean engine oil and torque the bolts in the proper sequence to the correct torque.

23. Apply a suitable sealant to the 4 corners of the cylinder head and install the cover with a new gasket. Torque the cover nuts to 52–69 inch lbs.

24. Make sure that the camshaft pulley and front housing timing marks are still aligned and install the timing belt.

25. Complete the remainder of the installation by reversing the removal procedure. Fill the cooling system to the proper level and connect the negative battery cable.

2555cc AND 2606cc ENGINES

1. Disconnect the battery and drain the cooling system. Relieve the fuel system pressure.

2. Remove the air cleaner assembly.

3. Disconnect the upper radiator hose and heater hose.

4. Disconnect the vacuum hoses and electrical wiring.

5. Separate the throttle linkage.

6. Remove carburetor-to-valve cover bracket. On fuel injected vehicles, remove the throttle body bracket.

7. Disconnect the spark plug wires after marking them for reinstallation. Remove the distributor.

8. Remove the fuel lines. Plug the line leading to the gas tank to prevent fuel leakage.

9. Remove the engine valve cover.

10. Remove the water pump belt and pulley.

11. Rotate crankshaft until No. 1 piston is at the top of its compression stroke (both valves closed).

12. Draw a mark on the timing chain in line with the timing mark on the camshaft sprocket.

13. Remove the camshaft sprocket bolt, sprocket and distributor drive gear. Maintain adequate tension on the sprocket and chain assembly to prevent the chain from disengaging the crankshaft sprocket.

14. Raise the vehicle and disconnect air feeder hoses.

15. Remove the power steering pump and set aside.

16. Remove the dipstick tube and engine ground wire.

17. Remove the exhaust manifold shield.

18. Separate the exhaust manifold from converter.

19. Remove the cylinder head bolts in the correct sequence. Head bolts should be loosened in sequence to prevent head warpage.

20. Remove the cylinder head with intake manifold still attached.

To install:

21. Install a new cylinder head gasket. Install the cylinder head assembly.

22. Install the cylinder head bolts and torque in sequence to the correct torque. Torque cylinder head to chain case cover bolts (2) to 13 ft. lbs.

23. From beneath the vehicle connect the converter to exhaust manifold.

24. Connect the air feeder hoses.

25. Install the exhaust manifold shield.

26. Install the power steering pump.

27. Install the dipstick tube and engine ground wire.

28. Install the camshaft sprocket and chain assembly with marks previously made. Install the distributor drive gear and sprocket bolt, tighten sprocket bolt to 54 Nm (40 ft. lbs.).

29. Install the water pump pully and belt.

30. Install the engine valve cover.

31. Install the fuel pump and fuel lines.

32. Install the distributor and connect spark plug wires.

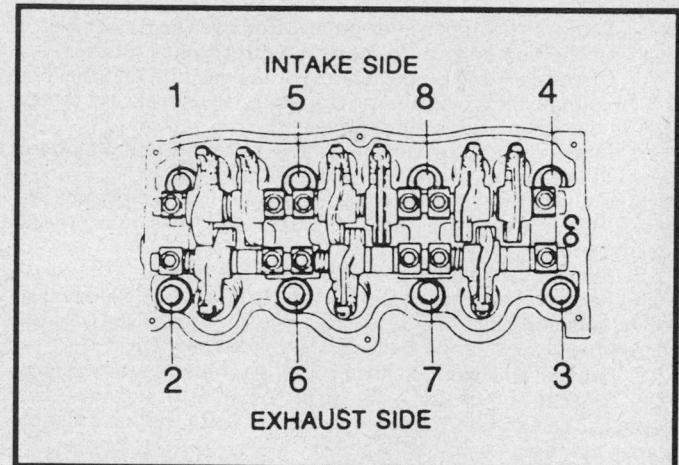

Cylinder head bolt removal sequence—2954cc engine

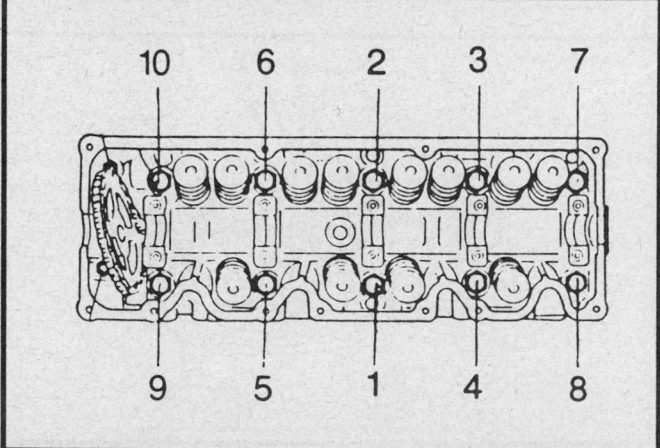

Cylinder head bolt installation sequence—2606cc engine

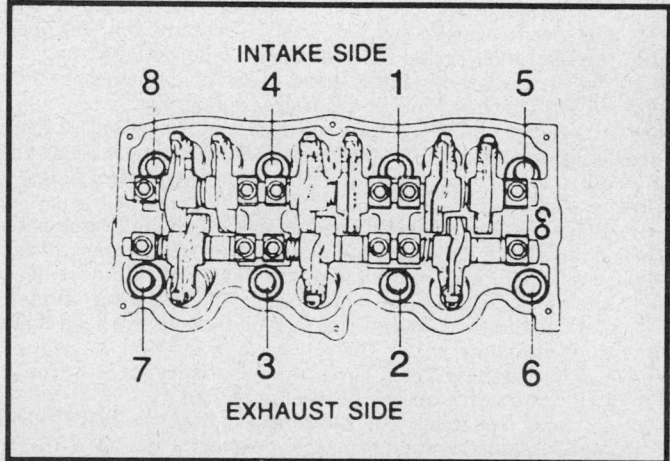

Cylinder head bolt installation sequence—2954cc engine

33. Install the carburetor-to-valve cover bracket. Install the throttle body bracket, on fuel injected vehicles.

34. Install the throttle linkage.

35. Install the vacuum hoses and electrical wiring.

36. Install the upper radiator hose and heater hose.

37. Install the air cleaner.

38. Connect battery cable and refill cooling system.

2954cc ENGINE

1. Position the engine at TDC on the compression stroke.

2. Properly relieve the fuel system pressure.

3. Disconnect the negative battery cable.

4. Remove the air cleaner assembly. Drain the cooling system.

6. Remove the spark plug wires. Remove the fresh air duct assembly.

8. Remove the cooling fan and radiator cowling. Remove the drive belts.

9. Remove the air conditioning compressor idler pulley. If necessary, remove the compressor and position it to the side.

10. Remove the crankshaft pulley and baffle plate.

12. Remove the coolant bypass hose. Remove the upper radiator hose.

13. Remove the timing belt cover assembly retaining bolts. Remove the timing belt cover assembly and gasket.

14. Turn the crankshaft to align the mating marks of the pulleys.

15. Remove the upper idler pulley. Remove the timing belt. If reusing the belt be sure to mark the direction of rotation.

16. Disconnect and plug canister, brake vacuum and fuel hoses. If equipped with automatic transmission, disconnect the automatic transmission vacuum hose.

17. Remove the 3-way soleniod valve assembly and disconnect all engine harness connector and grounds.

18. If equipped with automatic transmission, remove the dipstick. Disconnect the required vacuum hoses. Disconnect the accelerator linkage.

19. Remove the distributor and the EGR pipe.

20. Remove and discard the O-rings from the extension manifolds and purchase new ones. Remove the intake manifold by loosening the retaining bolts in the proper sequence.

21. Remove the cylinder head cover, gasket and seal washers.

22. Remove the center exhaust pipe insulator and pipe. Disconnect the exhaust manifold retaining bolts. Remove the exhaust manifold with insulator.

23. Remove the seal plate.

24. Remove the cylinder head retaining bolts in the proper sequence in 2 or 3 stages. Remove the cylinder head from the vehicle.

25. Thoroughly clean the cylinder head and cylinder block contact surfaces to remove any dirt or oil. Check the cylinder head for warpage and cracks. The maximum allowable warpage is 0.10mm. Inspect the cylinder head bolts for damaged threads and make sure they are free from grease and dirt.

26. Check the oil control plug projection at the cylinder block. Projection should be 0.53–0.57mm. If correct, apply clean engine oil to a new O-ring and position it on the control plug.

To install:

27. Place the new cylinder head gasket on the left bank with the **L** mark facing up. Place the new cylinder head gasket on the right bank with the **R** mark facing up. Install the cylinder head onto the block. Tighten the head bolts in the following manner:

   a. Coat the threads and the seating faces of the head bolts with clean engine oil.

   b. Torque the bolts in the proper sequence to 14 ft. lbs.

   c. Paint a mark on the head of each bolt.

   d. Using this mark as a reference, tighten the bolts in the proper sequence an additional 90 degrees.

   e. Repeat Step d.

28. Install the seal plate. Install the exhaust manifold with insulator.

29. Connect the exhaust manifold retaining bolts. Install the center exhaust pipe insulator and pipe.

30. Install the cylinder head cover, gasket and seal washers.

31. Install the intake manifold and torque the bolts to specification in the proper sequence. Install the O-rings from the extension manifolds.

32. Install the distributor and the EGR pipe.

33. If equipped with automatic transmission, install the dipstick. Connect the required vacuum hoses. Connect the accelerator linkage.

34. Install the 3-way soleniod valve assembly and connect all engine harness connector and grounds.

35. Connect the canister, brake vacuum and fuel hoses. If equipped with automatic transmission, connect the automatic trasmossion vacuum hose.

36. Install the timing belt.

37. Make sure that all the timing marks are aligned properly.

48. Install the upper idler pulley and torque the mounting bolt to 27–38 ft. lbs.

39. Install the upper idler pulley. Install the timing belt cover assembly and new gasket.

40. Install the upper radiator hose. Install the coolant bypass hose.

41. Install the crankshaft pulley and baffle plate.

42. Install the compressor. Install the air conditioning compressor idler pulley.

43. Install the accessory drive belts. Install the cooling fan and radiator cowling.

44. Install the fresh air duct assembly. Install the spark plug wires.

45. Fill the cooling system. Install the air cleaner assembly.

46. Connect the negative battery cable.

Valve Lash

Adjustment

1998cc ENGINE

1. Run the engine until normal operating temperature is reached.

2. Turn off the engine and remove the rocker cover.

3. Torque the cylinder head bolts to 60–64 ft. lbs.

4. Rotate the crankshaft so that the No.1 cylinder is at TDC. This can be determined, by removing the spark plug from the No.1 cylinder and placing a finger over the spark plug hole while rotating the engine. When compression is felt, the No. 1 cylinder is on the compression stroke. Rotate the engine with a wrench on the crankshaft pulley and stop it at TDC of the compression stroke on the No. 1 cylinder, as confirmed by the alignment of the TDC mark in the crankshaft pulley and the timing pointer.

Adjusting the valve clearance—1998cc and 2184cc engines, others similar

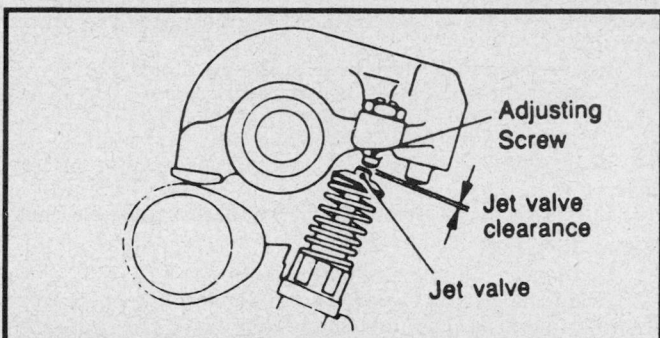

Adjusting the jet valve clearance—2555cc and 2606cc engines

5. Check the valve clearances with by inserting a feeler gauge between the end of the valve stem and the rocker arm. The clearance can be checked for Nos. 1 and 2 intake valves and Nos. 1 and 3 exhaust valves.

6. If the valve clearance is incorrect, loosen the adjusting screw locknut and adjust the clearance by turning the adjusting screw with the feeler blade inserted. Hold the adjusting screw in the correct position and tighten the locknut. Recheck the clearence.

7. Rotate the crankshaft, in the normal direction of rotation, until No. 4 piston is at TDC compression. Adjust Nos. 3 and 4 intake valves and Nos. 2 and 4 exhaust valves.

8. Install the rocker arm cover and torque the nuts to 18 inch lbs.

2555cc AND 2606cc ENGINES

NOTE: These engines, are equipped with hydraulic valve lash adjusters. The engines have a third valve called a Jet Valve located beside the intake valve of each cylinder. The Jet valve works off the intake valve rocker arm and injects a swirl of air into the combustion chamber to promote more complete burning of fuel. The Jet Valve must be adjusted on all engines, whether or not the engine has hydraulic lash adjusters. On engines equipped with hydraulic lash adjusters, only the Jet valve must be adjusted. When adjusting valve clearances, the jet valve must be adjusted before the intake valve.

1. Start the engine and allow it to reach normal operating temperature (170–190°F).

2. Stop the engine and remove the air cleaner. Remove the rocker cover.

3. Disconnect the coil-to-distributor wire at the coil.

4. Watch the rocker arms for No. 1 cylinder and rotate the crankshaft until the exhaust valve is closing and the intake valve has just started to open. At this point, No. 4 cylinder will be at top dead center (TDC), commencing its firing stroke.

5. Loosen the locknut on cylinder No. 4 intake valve and back off the intake valve adjusting screw 2 or more turns.

6. Loosen the locknut on the jet valve adjusting screw.

7. Turn the jet valve adjusting screw counterclockwise and insert a 0.006 in. feeler gauge between the jet valve stem and the adjusting screw.

8. Tighten the adjusting screw until it touches the feeler gauge. Take care not to press in the valve while adjusting because the jet valve spring is very weak.

NOTE: If the adjusting screw is tight, special care must be taken to avoid pressing down on the jet valve when adjusting the clearance or a false reading will result.

9. Tighten the locknut securely while holding the rocker arm

adjusting screw with a suitable tool, to prevent it from turning.

10. Make sure that a 0.006 in. feeler gauge can just be inserted between the jet valve and the rocker arm.

11. Adjust No. 4 cylinder's intake valve to 0.006 in. and exhaust valve to 0.010 in. Tighten the adjusting screw locknuts and recheck each clearance.

12. Perform Step 4 in conjunction with the chart to adjust the remaining 3 cylinders.

13. Install the rocker cover and all other components. Run the engine and check for oil leaks at the valve cover.

2954cc ENGINE

This engine has hydraulic lash adjusters and no adjustment is needed.

Rocker Arms and Shafts

Removal and Installation

1998cc AND 2184cc ENGINES

1. Disconnect the negative battery cable.
2. Disconnect the accelerator cable from the carburetor.
3. Disconnect the air bypass valve cable.
4. Disconnect and tag the spark plug wires. Remove the wires from the spark plug wire clips on the rocker covers and position them out of the way.
5. Remove the rocker cover and discard the gasket.
6. Remove the rocker arm shaft attaching bolts evenly and remove the rocker arm shafts.
7. Install the rocker arm assemblies on the cylinder head. Torque the bolts to 13–20 ft. lbs.
8. Check and adjust the valve adjustment.
9. Clean the mating surfaces of the cylinder head and rocker cover.
10. Install the rocker cover with a new gasket. Torque the bolts to 24–36 inch lbs.
11. Install the spark plug wires on the spark plugs. Place the wires in the clips on the rocker cover. Connect the choke and air bypass valve cable.
12. Start the engine and check for leaks.
13. Allow the engine to reach operating temperature, torque the cylinder head bolts to 60–64 ft. lbs. and adjust the valves lash with the engine hot.

2555cc AND 2606cc ENGINES

NOTE: Eight special holders are needed, tool No. MD998443 or equivalent, to retain the hydraulic lash adjusters when the valve train is disassembled.

1. Relieve the fuel system pressure. Disconnect the negative battery cable. Remove the rocker cover. Loosen the camshaft sprocket bolt until it can be turned by hand. The timing mark on the sprocket ends up on the extreme right of the sprocket bolt as viewed from the front. The TDC mark on the front crankshaft pulley must line up with the timing scale on the front cover.

2. Remove the camshaft sprocket bolt without allowing the tension on the timing chain or belt to be lost. Place the sprocket in the sprocket holder of the front cover or lower timing belt cover. Make sure not to loose tension on the belt/chain. Make sure also that the crankshaft is not turned throughout the work. If equipped with hydraulic lash adjusters, put the special clips on the 8 hydraulic adjusters at the outer ends of all 8 rocker arms. Note that these clips go over the lash adjusters that actuate the large intake valves, not on the small adjusting screw for the smaller jet valves.

3. Loosen, but do not remove the camshaft bearing cap bolts. After all bolts have been loosened, remove them and, holding the ends so the assembly stays together, remove the rocker shaft assembly from the cylinder head. The rearmost cam bearing cap is not associated with the rocker shafts and need not be removed.

4. Keep all parts in original order.

To install:

5. Assemble the parts of the rocker assembly as follows:

a. Install left and right side rocker shafts into the front bearing cap. Notches in the ends of the shaft must be upward. Install the bolts for the front cap to retain the shafts in place. Note that the left rocker shaft is longer than the right rocker shaft.

b. Install the wave washer onto the left rocker shaft with the bulge forward. Then, coat the inner surfaces of the rockers and the upper bearing surfaces of the bearing caps with clean engine oil and assemble rockers, springs and the remaining bearing caps in the order in which removed. Note that the intake rockers are the only ones with the jet valve actuators. Note also that the rockers are labeled for cylinders 1–3 and 2–4 because the direction that the jet valve actuator faces, changes.

c. Use mounting bolts to hold the caps in place after each is assembled. When the assembly is complete, install it onto the head and start all mounting bolts into the head and tighten finger tight.

6. Torque the attaching bolts for the rocker assembly 14–15 ft. lbs. working from the center outward.

7. Without removing tension from the timing chain or belt, lift the sprocket out of the holder and position it against the front of the cam. Make sure the locating tang on the sprocket goes into the hole in the front of the cam.

8. Torque the bolt to 58–72 ft. lbs.

9. Adjust the valve lash.

9. Apply sealant to the top surface of the semicircular seals in the head and then install the valve cover.

2954cc ENGINE

1. Relieve the fuel system pressure. Disconnect the negative battery cable. Remove the rocker cover.

2. Loosen the rocker shaft bolts, going in reverse of the torquing sequence in several stages.

3. Remove the rocker shaft assembly and bolts as an assembly. Stuff a rag in the drain hole to prevent the valve keepers from falling into the oil pan.

4. During the installation, make sure all the spherical valve operators at the outer ends of the rocker levers are positioned so the flat surface is against the top of the valve stem.

5. Position the rocker assembly toward the exhaust side of the engine so that the exhaust valve rocker arms are offset 1mm from the centers of the valve stems.

6. Torque the head bolts in several stages using the correct torque sequence. Torque the rocker bolts in sequence to 14–19 ft. lbs. Be careful not to catch the rocker arm shaft spring between the shaft and the mounting boss during installation.

Intake Manifold

Removal and Installation

1998cc AND 2184cc ENGINES

1. Disconnect the negative battery cable. Drain the cooling system.

2. Remove the air cleaner.

3. Remove the accelerator linkage.

4. Disconnect the choke cable. Disconnect and plug the fuel line. Plug the fuel line.

5. Disconnect the PCV valve hose.

6. Disconnect the heater return hose and bypass hose.

7. Remove the intake manifold-to-cylinder head attaching nuts.

8. Remove the manifold and carburetor as an assembly.

9. Clean the gasket mating surfaces.

To install:

10. Install a new gasket and the manifold on the studs. Torque the attaching nuts to specification, working from the center outward.

11. Connect the PCV valve hose to the manifold.

12. Connect the bypass and heater return hoses.

13. Install the accelerator linkage.

14. Connect the fuel line and choke cable.

15. Replace the air cleaner. Connect the negative battery cable.

16. Fill the cooling system. Run the engine and check for leaks.

2555cc ENGINE

1. Disconnect the negative battery cable.

2. Drain the cooling system and disconnect the hoses from the water pump to the intake manifold.

3. Disconnect the carburetor air horn adapter and move it aside.

4. Disconnect the vacuum hoses and throttle linkage from the carburetor.

5. Disconnect the fuel inlet line at the fuel filter.

6. Remove the fuel filter and fuel pump and move it aside.

7. Remove the intake manifold retaining nuts and washers and remove the manifold.

8. Remove old gasket. Clean cylinder head and manifold gasket surface. Check for cracks or warpage. Install a new gasket on cylinder head.

To install:

9. Install the manifold to the cylinder head. Install the mounting nuts and tighten to the correct specification. Tighten from the inside nuts working outward.

10. Install the fuel pump and filter.

11. Install the carburator air horn.

12. Install the throttle control cable.

13. Install the cooling system hose from water pump to manifold.

14. Install the vacuum hoses.

15. Connect the negative battery cable.

2606cc ENGINE

1. Relieve the fuel system pressure. Disconnect the negative battery cable.

2. Drain the cooling system.

3. Disconnect the water hoses and plug them.

4. Disconnect the air inlet duct from the air cleaner and disconnect the air flow meter connector.

5. Label and disconnect all vacuum hoses connected to the manifold.

6. Remove the air cleaner, air cleaner element, air flow meter and air funnel.

7. Disconnect the bypass air control (BAC) valve connector, water hoses and remove the valve.

8. Disconnect the throttle sensor connector and the accelerator cable. Remove the throttle body and gasket.

9. Label and disconnect all remaining hoses, pipes, sensors and wires connected to the manifold.

10. Remove the wiring harness bracket.

11. Disconnect the air intake pipe.

12. Remove the manifold attaching nuts and lift the manifold straight up from the studs.

To install:

13. Install a new gasket on the studs, coated with sealer.

14. Install the manifold on the studs. Torque the manifold bolts to 18 ft. lbs. in 2 even steps of 9 ft. lbs. each.

15. Connect the air intake pipe.

16. Install the wiring harness bracket.

17. Connect all remaining hoses, pipes, sensors and wires at to the manifold.

18. Install the throttle body and gasket.

19. Connect the throttle sensor connector and the accelerator cable.

20. Install the BAC valve. Connect the bypass air control valve connector and water hoses.

21. Install the air cleaner, air cleaner element, air flow meter and air funnel.
22. Connect all remaining vacuum hoses at to the manifold.
23. Connect the air inlet duct from the air cleaner and connect the air flow meter connector.
24. Connect the water hoses. Fill the cooling system.
26. Connect the negative battery cable.

2954cc ENGINE

1. Relieve the fuel system pressure. Disconnect the negative battery cable. Disconnect the water hoses.
2. Disconnect the air inlet duct from the air cleaner and disconnect the air flow meter connector.
3. Locate the 2 solenoid valves (TICS and purge air control) that are bolted to the front of the air cleaner. Disconnect the vacuum hoses and label them.
4. Remove the air cleaner, air cleaner element, air flow meter and air funnel.
5. Disconnect the bypass air control (BAC) valve connector, water hoses and remove the valve.
6. Disconnect the throttle sensor connector and the accelerator cable. Remove the throttle body and gasket.
7. Disconnect all vacuum hoses, EGR pipe, EGR position sensor connector, water hose and ground wire.
8. Remove the wiring harness bracket.
9. Disconnect the air intake pipe from the dynamic chamber with the gasket.
10. Mark the extension manifolds RIGHT and LEFT for assembly reference as they are not interchangable. Remove the extension manifolds with their gaskets from the dynamic chamber.
11. Disconnect the intake air thermo sensor connector, vacuum hoses and ground connectors.
12. Remove the attaching nuts and lift the dynamaic chamber straight up from the intake manifold studs. Drain the radiator at this time and disconnect all remaining connectors, fuel hoses, water hoses.

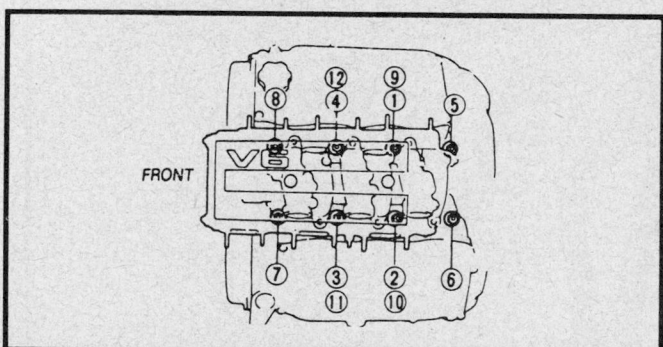

Intake manifold removal sequence—2954cc engine

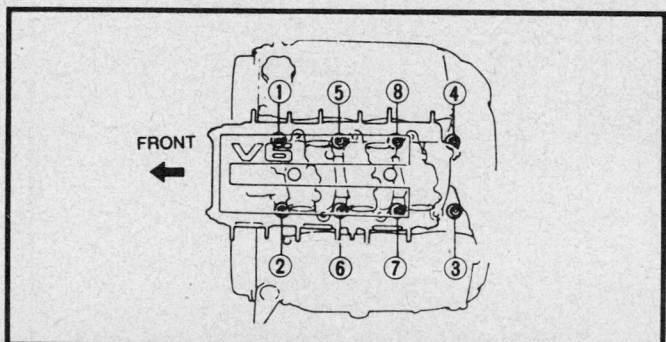

Intake mainfold installation sequence—2954cc engine

13. Loosen the intake manifold nuts in 2 stages, in the correct sequence. Lift the intake manifold from the engine and remove the intake manifold gaskets. Insert clean rags in the intake ports or cover them with masking tape to prevent anything from falling into the engine.
14. Visually inspect the intake manifold for cracks, warpage or any other type of damage and replace as necessary. Remove all gasket material from the seating surface on the manifold and the engine. Forward of one of the studs that secure the dynamic chamber is an O-ring that seal the manifold to the chamber. Remove this O-ring and replace it with a new one.
To install:
15. Place the new intake manifold gaskets onto the cylinder block and lower the manifold over the gaskets. Install the intake manifold washers with the white paint marks facing up. Install the retaining nuts and torque the nuts in stages to the correct torque and in the proper sequence.
16. Install connectors, fuel hoses, water hoses and vacuum hoses.
17. Install the dynamic chamber. Torque the retaining nuts to 14–18 ft. lbs.
18. Install the intake air thermo sensor ground connectors and vacuum hoses.
19. Install the extension manifolds with new gaskets and new O-rings.
20. Install the intake air pipe with new gaskets and wiring bracket.
21. Install the ground wire, water hose, EGR position connector, EGR pipe and vacuum hoses.
22. Install the throttle body with new gasket, accelerator cable and throtle sensor connector. Check the deflection of the accelerator cable. If not within 0.04–0.12 in. (1–3mm), adjust with the nuts on the cable bracket.
23. Install the BAC valve, water hoses and connector.
24. Install the air funnel, air hoses, air flow meter, filter element and air cleaner.
25. Install the TICS and purge control soleniod valves, air flow meter connector, vacuum chamber and air duct.
26. Make sure that all hose connections are tight and fill the cooling system to the proper level. Connect the negative battery cable. Start the engine and check for leaks.

Exhaust Manifold

Removal and Installation

1. Raise and support the vehicle safely.
2. Disconnect the exhaust pipe from the exhaust manifold. Remove the exhaust manifold heat shield. On the 2954cc and 2606cc engine disconnect the wire to the oxygen sensor.
3. Remove the exhaust manifold mounting nuts and remove the manifold.
4. To install, apply a light film of grease to the exhaust manifold mating surfaces before installation.
5. Install the manifold on the studs and install the mounting nuts. Torque the attaching nuts to the correct specification.
6. Install a new exhaust pipe gasket. Connect the exhaust pipe to the exhaust manifold and torque the nuts to the correct specification.

Timing Chain Front Cover

Removal and Installation

2555cc AND 2606cc ENGINES

1. Relieve the fuel system pressure. Disconnect the negative battery cable.
2. Remove the air cleaner assembly.
3. Remove the accessory drive belts.
4. Remove the alternator mounting bolts and remove alternator.

5. Remove the power steering mounting bolts and set power steering pump aside.

6. Remove the air conditioning compressor mounting bolts and set compressor aside.

7. Raise and safely support the vehicle. Remove right inner splash shield.

8. Drain the engine oil.

9. Remove the crankshaft pulley.

10. Lower the vehicle and place a suitable jack under the engine with a piece of wood between jack and lifting point.

11. Raise the jack until contact is made with the engine. Relieve pressure by jacking slightly and remove the center bolt from the right engine mount. Remove right engine mount.

12. Remove the engine oil dipstick.

13. Remove the engine valve cover.

14. Remove the front (2) cylinder head to timing chain cover bolts.

15. Raise and safely support the vehicle. Remove the oil pan retaining bolts and lower the oil pan.

16. Remove the screws holding the timing indicator and engine mounting plate.

17. Remove the bolts holding the timing chain case cover and remove cover.

18. Clean and inspect chain case cover for crack or other damage.

To install:

19. Position a new timing chain case cover gasket on case cover. Trim as required to assure fit at top and bottom.

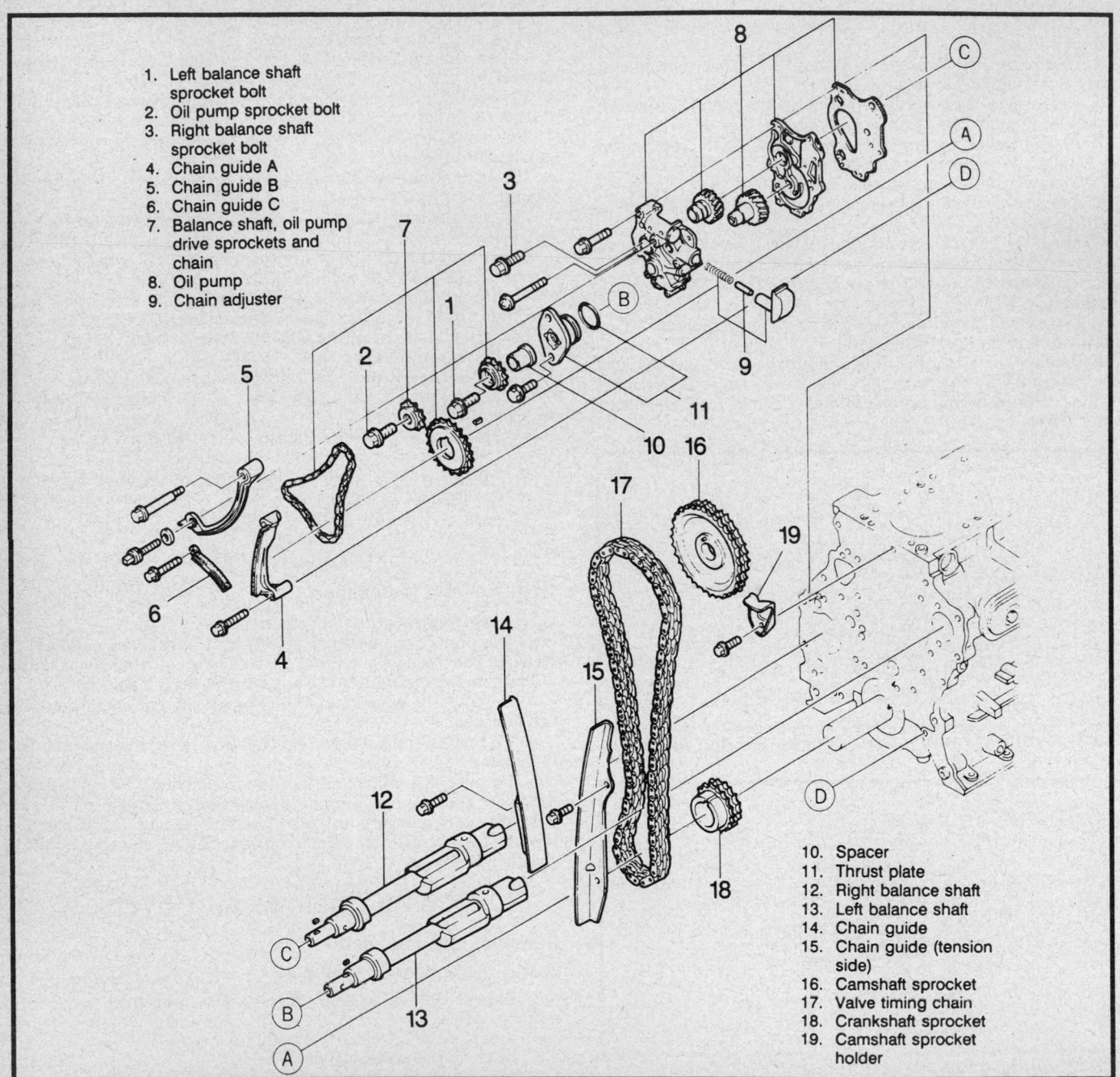

1. Left balance shaft sprocket bolt
2. Oil pump sprocket bolt
3. Right balance shaft sprocket bolt
4. Chain guide A
5. Chain guide B
6. Chain guide C
7. Balance shaft, oil pump drive sprockets and chain
8. Oil pump
9. Chain adjuster
10. Spacer
11. Thrust plate
12. Right balance shaft
13. Left balance shaft
14. Chain guide
15. Chain guide (tension side)
16. Camshaft sprocket
17. Valve timing chain
18. Crankshaft sprocket
19. Camshaft sprocket holder

Timing case and chain assembly—2555cc and 2606cc engines

20. Coat the cover gasket with sealant. Install chain case cover and tighten mounting bolts to 13 ft. lbs.

21. Install the (2) front cylinder head to timing chain case cover mounting bolts and tighten to 13 ft. lbs.

22. Install the engine oil pan tighten screws to 53 inch lbs.

23. Install the engine mounting plate and timing indicator.

24. Install the crankshaft pulley.

25. Install the right engine mount, lower engine and install right engine mount center bolt.

26. Install the engine valve cover.

27. Install the engine oil dipstick.

28. Install the air conditioner compressor.

29. Install the power steering pump.

30. Install the alternator.

31. Install the accessory drive belts.

32. Fill the engine crankcase with recommended engine oil.

33. Install the air cleaner assembly.

34. Connect the negative battery cable.

Front Cover Oil Seal

Replacement

2555cc AND 2606cc ENGINE

NOTE: The front cover oil seal can be removed and a new one installed without removing the front cover.

1. Disconnect the negative battery cable.

2. Drain the cooling system.

3. Disconnect the upper and lower radiator hoses and remove the radiator.

4. Remove the drive belt(s).

5. Remove the crankshaft pulley.

6. Pry the front oil seal from the front cover.

7. Clean the pulley and seal area.

To install:

8. Press a new front seal into position (flush).

9. Install the crankshaft pulley and torque the bolt to specifications.

10. Install the drive belt(s) and adjust the tension.

11. Install the radiator and connect the upper and lower hoses. Fill the cooling system.

12. Start the engine and check for leaks.

13. Install the hood.

Timing Chain and Gears

Removal and Installation

2555cc AND 2606cc ENGINES

NOTE: These engines are equipped with 2 silent shafts which cancel the vertical vibrating force of the engine and the secondary vibrating forces, which include the sideways rocking of the engine due to the turning direction of the crankshaft and other rolling parts. The secondary vibrating forces can be cancelled if forces equivalent in magnitude but opposite in direction are produced. In these engines, the opposite force is produced by silent shafts located in the upper left and lower right sides in the front of the cylinder block. The shafts are driven by a duplex chain and are turned by the crankshaft. The silent shaft chain assembly is mounted in front of the timing chain assembly and must be removed to service the timing chain.

1. Disconnect the negative battery cable. Relieve the fuel system pressure.

2. Drain the radiator and remove it from the vehicle.

3. Remove the cylinder head.

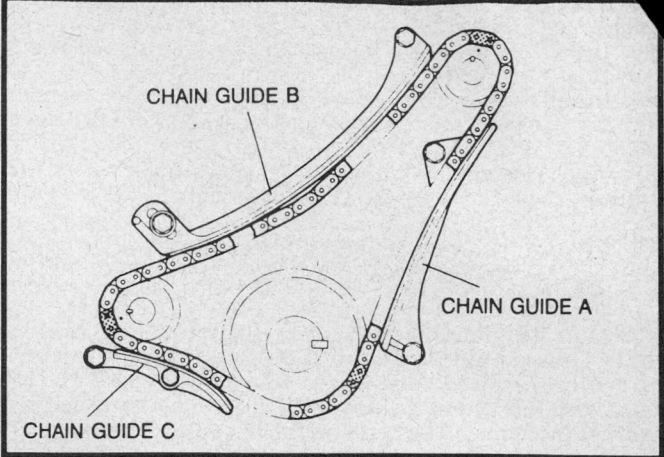

Timing chain guide location—2555cc and 2606cc engines

4. Remove the cooling fan, spacer, water pump pulley and belt.

5. Remove the alternator. Remove the water pump.

6. Raise and support the vehicle safely. Drain the engine oil.

7. Remove the oil pan and screen. Remove the crankshaft pulley.

8. Lower the vehicle. Remove the timing case cover.

9. Remove the chain guides from the outer chain.

10. Remove the locking bolts from the chain sprockets.

11. Remove the crankshaft sprocket, silent shaft sprocket and the outer chain.

12. Remove the crankshaft and camshaft sprockets and the timing chain.

13. Remove the camshaft sprocket holder and the chain guides, both left and right.

14. Remove the tensioner.

15. Remove the sleeve from the oil pump. Remove the oil pump by first removing the bolt locking the oil pump driven gear and the right silent shaft, then remove the oil pump mounting bolts. Remove the silent shaft from the engine block.

NOTE: If the bolt locking the oil pump and the silent shaft is hard to loosen, remove the oil pump and the shaft as a unit.

16. Remove the left silent shaft thrust washer and remove the shaft from the engine block.

17. Install the right silent shaft into the engine block.

18. Install the oil pump assembly. Do not loose the woodruff key from the end of the silent shaft. Torque the oil pump mounting bolts to 6–7 ft. lbs.

19. Tighten the silent shaft and the oil pump driven gear mounting bolt.

NOTE: The silent shaft and the oil pump can be installed as a unit, if necessary.

20. Install the left silent shaft into the engine block.

21. Install a new O-ring on the thrust plate and install the unit into the engine block, using a pair of bolts without heads, as alignment guides.

NOTE: If the thrust plate is turned to align the bolt holes, the O-ring may be damaged.

22. Remove the guide bolts and install the regular bolts into the thrust plate and tighten securely.

23. Rotate the crankshaft to bring No. 1 piston to TDC.

24. Install the cylinder head.

the sprocket holder and the right and left chain

stall the tensioner spring and sleeve on the oil pump

27. Install the camshaft and crankshaft sprockets on the timing chain, aligning the sprocket punch marks to the plated chain links.

28. While holding the sprocket and chain as a unit, install the crankshaft sprocket over the crankshaft and align it with the keyway.

29. Keeping the dowel pin hole on the camshaft in a vertical position, install the camshaft sprocket and chain on the camshaft.

NOTE: The sprocket timing mark and the plated chain link should be at the 2–3 o'clock position when correctly installed. The chain must be aligned in the right and left chain guides with the tensioner pushing against the chain. The tension for the inner chain is predetermined by spring tension.

30. Install the crankshaft sprocket for the outer chain.

31. Install the 2 silent shaft sprockets and align the punched mating marks with the plated links of the chain.

32. Holding the 2 shaft sprockets and chain, install the outer chain in alignment with the mark on the crankshaft sprocket. Install the shaft sprockets on the silent shaft and the oil pump driver gear. Install the lock bolts and recheck the alignment of the punch marks and the plated links.

33. Temporarily install the chain guides.

34. Tighten right chain guide securely.

35. Tighten bottom chain guide securely.

36. Adjust the position of the top chain guide, after shaking the right and left sprockets to collect any chain slack, so that when the chain is moved toward the center, the clearance between the chain guide and the chain links will be approximately $9/64$ inch. Tighten the top chain guide bolts.

37. Install the timing chain cover using a new gasket, being careful not to damage the front seal.

38. Using a new gasket, install the oil screen and oil pan. Torque the bolts to 4.5–5.5 ft. lbs.

39. Install the crankshaft pulley, alternator and accessory belts and the distributor.

40. Install the oil pressure switch, if removed. Connect the negative battery cable.

41. Install the fan blades, radiator, fill the cooling system and run the engine. Check for oil and water leaks.

Timing Belt Front Cover

Removal and Installation
1998cc AND 2184cc ENGINES

1. Disconnect the negative battery cable.
2. Remove the distributor.
3. Remove the fan and radiator shroud.
4. Remove the alternator.
5. Disconnect the air injection pipes.
6. Remove the fan pulley, hub and bracket.
7. If so equipped, remove the air conditioning compressor drive belt.

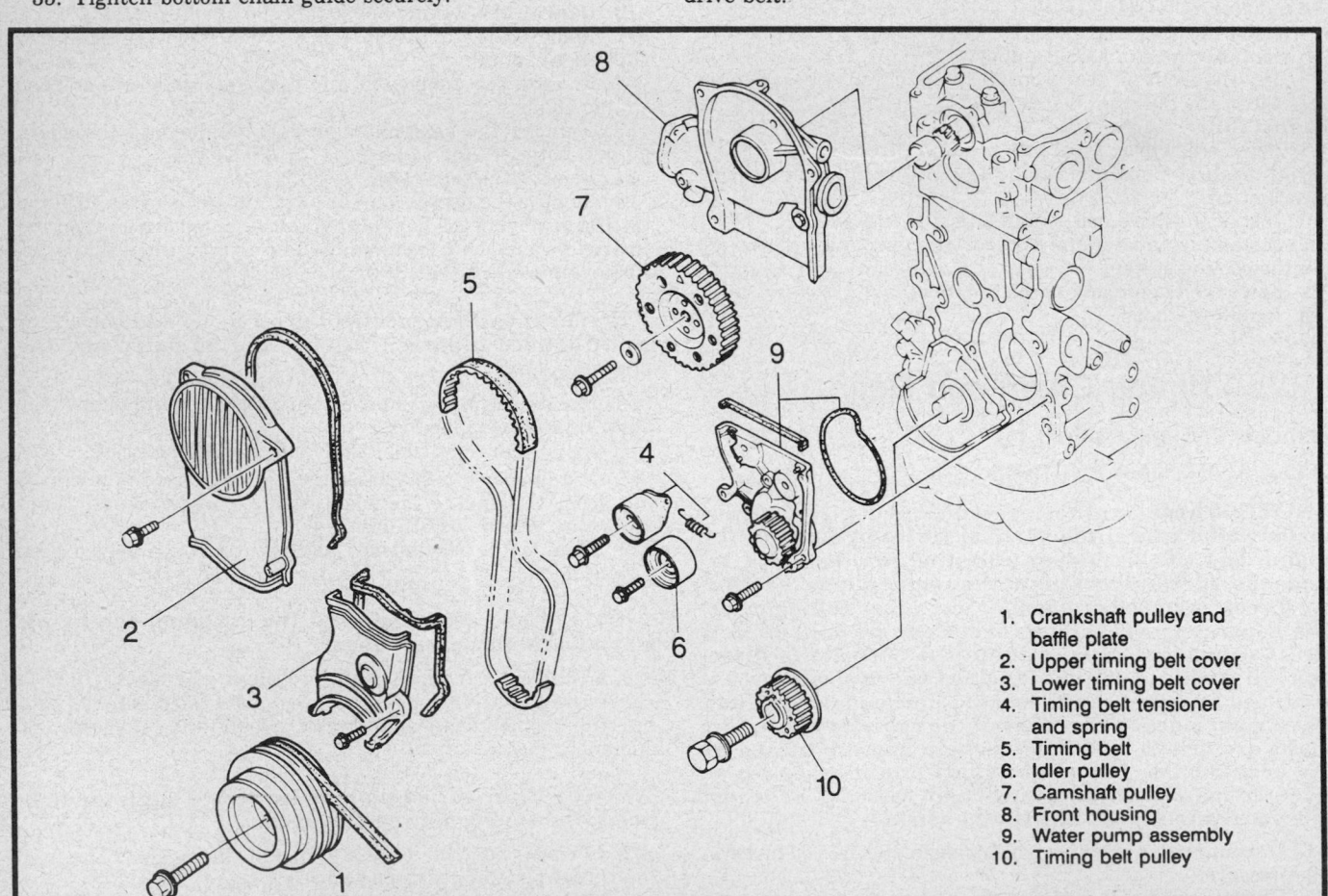

1. Crankshaft pulley and baffle plate
2. Upper timing belt cover
3. Lower timing belt cover
4. Timing belt tensioner and spring
5. Timing belt
6. Idler pulley
7. Camshaft pulley
8. Front housing
9. Water pump assembly
10. Timing belt pulley

Timing belt and cover assembly—1998cc and 2184cc engines

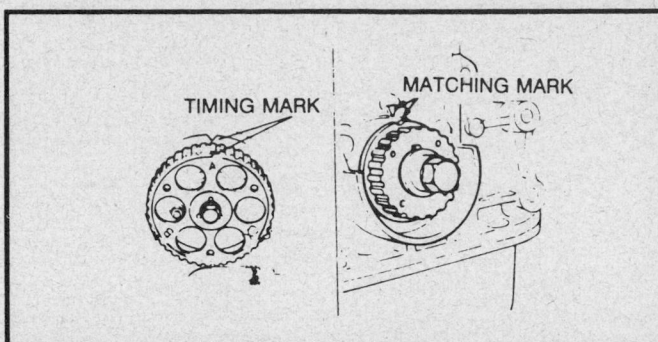

Timing sprocket alignment—1998cc and 2184cc engines

8. If so equipped, remove the power steering pump drive belt.
9. Remove the crankshaft pulley and baffle plate.
10. Remove the upper, then the lower, belt covers.

To install:
11. Install the upper, then the lower, belt covers.
12. Install the crankshaft pulley and baffle plate.
13. Install the power steering pump drive belt.
14. Install the air conditioning compressor drive belt.
15. Install the fan pulley, hub and bracket.
16. Connect the air injection pipes.
17. Install the alternator.
18. Install the fan and radiator shroud.
19. Install the distributor.
20. Connect the negative battery cable.

2954cc ENGINE

1. Position the engine at TDC on the compression stroke. Properly relieve the fuel system pressure.
2. Disconnect the negative battery cable. Remove the air cleaner assembly.3. Drain the cooling system and remove the spark plug wires.
4. Remove the fresh air duct assembly. Remove the cooling fan and radiator cowling. Remove the drive belts.
5. Remove the air conditioning compressor idler pulley. If necessary, remove the compressor and position it to the side.
6. Remove the crankshaft pulley and baffle plate.
7. Remove the coolant bypass hose. Remove the upper radiator hose.
8. Remove the timing belt cover assembly retaining bolts. Remove the timing belt cover assembly and gasket.
9. Installation is the reverse of the removal procedure.

Timing Belt and Tensioner

Removal and Installation

1998cc AND 2184cc ENGINE

1. Disconnect the negative battery cable.
2. Drain the cooling system.
3. Remove the distributor cap, with the wires attached and remove the distributor.
4. Remove the fan shroud and fan.
5. Disconnect and tag the alternator wiring and remove the alternator.
6. Disconnect the air injection pipes from the engine.
7. Remove the fan pulley, hub and bracket.
8. If equipped, remove the air conditioning compressor drive belt.
9. If equipped, remove the power steering pump drive belt.
10. Remove the crankshaft pulley and baffle plate.
11. Remove the upper and lower timing belt covers.
12. Turn the crankshaft so that the **A** mark on the camshaft

pulley is at the top, aligned with the notch in the front housing.
13. Loosen the timing belt tensioner lock bolt and remove the tensioner spring.
14. Mark the forward rotation of the belt for installation. Remove the belt.
15. Unbolt and remove the front housing.
16. Carefully, drive the camshaft seal from the housing.

To install:
17. Coat the outside of a new seal with clean engine oil and press it into place in the front housing.
18. Coat the seal lip with clean engine oil. Install the front housing, using a new gasket. Torque the bolts to 14–19 ft. lbs.
19. Replace the timing belt if it has been contaminated by oil or grease, or shows any sign of damage, wear, cracks or peeling.
20. To ease installation of the belt, remove all the spark plugs.
21. Make sure that the timing mark on the camshaft is aligned and that the timing mark (notch) on the crankshaft sprocket is aligned with the triangular shaped mark on the front housing.
22. Install the tensioner and spring, positioning the tensioner all the way to the intake manifold side and temporarily secure it there with the lock bolt.
23. Install the belt onto the sprockets from the right side. If the original belt is being reused, follow the directional mark previously made.
24. Loosen the lock bolt so that the tensioner applies tension to the belt.
25. Turn the crankshaft 2 full revolutions in the direction of normal rotation. This will apply equal tension to all points of the belt.
26. Make sure that the timing marks are still aligned. If not, repeat the belt installation procedure.
27. Tighten the tensioner lock bolt to 30–35 ft. lbs.
28. Measure the timing belt tension by pressing on the belt at the midpoint of the longest straight run. Belt deflection should be 11–13mm. If not, repeat the belt adjustment procedure, above.
29. Installation of all other parts is the reverse of removal. Torque the belt cover bolts to 80 inch lbs.; the fan bracket bolts to 40 ft. lbs. When installing the drive belts on the various accessories, check the belt deflection.

2954cc ENGINE

1. Position the engine at TDC on the compression stroke.
2. Properly relieve the fuel system pressure. Disconnect the negative battery cable.
3. Remove the air cleaner assembly. Drain the cooling system and remove the spark plug wires.
4. Remove the fresh air duct assembly. Remove the cooling fan and radiator cowling. Remove the drive belts.
5. Remove the air conditioning compressor idler pulley. If necessary, remove the compressor and position it to the side.
6. Remove the crankshaft pulley and baffle plate. Remove the coolant bypass hose. Remove the upper radiator hose.
7. Remove the timing belt cover assembly retaining bolts. Remove the timing belt cover assembly and gasket. Turn the crankshaft to align the mating marks of the pulleys.
8. Remove the upper idler pulley. Remove the timing belt. If reusing the belt be sure to mark the direction of rotation. Remove the timing belt auto tensioner.

To install:
9. To install the timing belt, first the automatic tensioner must be loaded. To load the tensioner, place a flat washer on the bottom of the tensioner body to prevent damage to the body and position the unit on an arbor press. Press the rod into the tensioner body. Do not use more than 2000 lbs of pressure. Once the rod is fully inserted into the body, insert a suitable **L** shaped pin or a small Allen wrench through the body and the rod to hold the rod in place.
10. Remove the unit from the press and install onto the block and torque the mounting bolt to 14–19 ft. lbs. Leave the pin in place, it will be removed later.

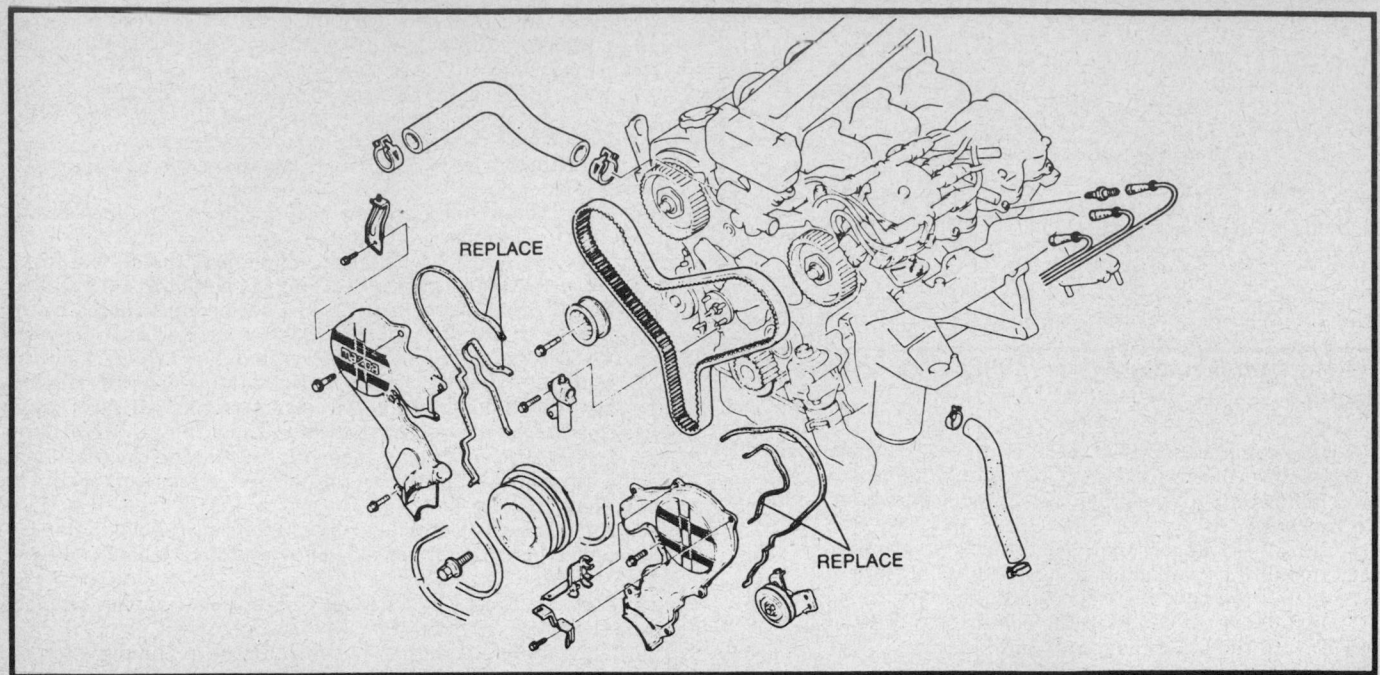

Timing belt and components—2954cc engine

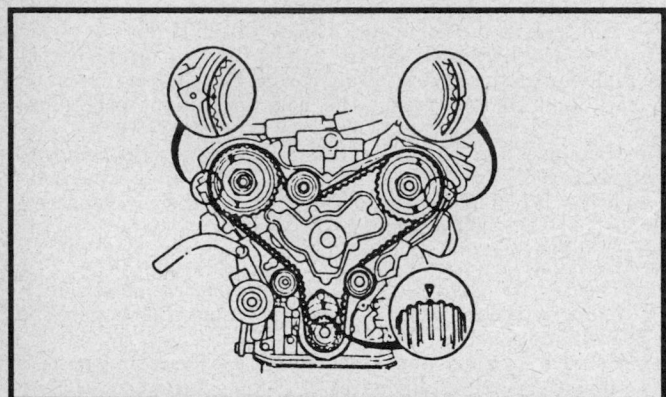

Timing sprocket alignments—2954cc engine

11. Make sure that all the timing marks are aligned properly. With the upper idler pulley removed, hang the timing belt on each pulley. Install the upper idler pulley and torque the mounting bolt to 27–38 ft. lbs.

12. Rotate the crankshaft twice in the normal direction of rotation to align all the timing marks.

13. Make sure all the marks are aligned correctly. If not, repeat Step 8.

14. Remove the pin from the auto tensioner. Again turn the crankshaft twice in the normal direction of rotation and make sure that all the timing marks are aligned properly.

15. Check the timing belt deflection by applying 22 lbs. of force. If the deflection is not 0.20–0.28 in. (5–6mm), repeat the adjustment procedure.

NOTE: Excessive belt deflection is caused by auto tensioner failure or an excessively stretched timing belt.

16. Complete the installation of the remaining components in reverse of the removal procedure. Fill the cooling system to the proper level. Adjust the accessory drive belt tension. Check and/or adjust the ignition timing.

Camshaft

Removal and Installation
1998cc AND 2184cc ENGINES

1. Disconnect the negative battery cable.
2. Drain the cooling system.
3. Remove the distributor.
4. Remove the fan shroud and fan.
5. Remove the alternator.
6. Disconnect the air injection pipes.
7. Remove the fan pulley, hub and bracket.
8. If equipped, remove the A/C compressor and power steering drive belts.
9. Remove the crankshaft pulley and baffle plate.
10. Remove the upper and lower timing belt covers.
12. Turn the crankshaft so that the **A** mark on the camshaft pulley is at the top, aligned with the notch in the front housing.
13. Loosen the tensioner lock bolt and remove the tensioner spring.
14. Mark the forward rotation of the belt for installation. Remove the belt.
15. Insert a bar through the hole in the camshaft sprocket to hold it in position and remove the sprocket bolt.
16. Disconnect the accelerator cable, if necessary.
17. If equipped, disconnect the air bypass valve cable.
18. Disconnect the spark plug wires. Remove the wires from the spark plug wire clips on the rocker covers and position them out of the way.
19. Remove the rocker cover and discard the gasket.
20. Remove the rocker arm shaft attaching bolts evenly in the correct order and remove the rocker arm shafts.
21. Remove the camshaft rear seal cap.
22. Lift out the camshaft.
23. Inspect the camshaft for wear, heat scoring or obvious damage. Replace it if necessary. Check the lobes and journals for wear.

To install:
24. Coat the camshaft with clean engine oil and install it in position, making sure that the lug on the nose of the shaft is at the 12:00 o'clock position.

25. Apply a thin coat of sealant to the areas shown and install the rocker shaft assembly. Torque the bolts evenly, in the order shown, to 15–20 ft. lbs. Install the camshaft sprocket. Torque the camshaft sprocket bolt to 40–45 ft. lbs.

26. Replace the belt if it has been contaminated by oil or grease, or shows any sign of damage, wear, cracks or peeling.

27. To ease installation of the belt, remove all the spark plugs.

28. Make sure that the timing mark on the camshaft is aligned as described above, and that the timing mark (notch) on the crankshaft sprocket is aligned with the triangular shaped mark on the front housing.

29. Install the tensioner and spring, positioning the tensioner all the way to the intake manifold side and temporarily secure it there with the lock bolt.

30. Install the belt onto the sprockets from the right side. If the original belt is being reused, follow the directional mark previously made.

31. Loosen the lock bolt so that the tensioner applies tension to the belt.

32. Turn the crankshaft 2 full revolutions in the direction of normal rotation. This will apply equal tension to all points of the belt.

33. Make sure that the timing marks are still aligned. If not, repeat the belt installation procedure.

34. Tighten the tensioner lock bolt to 30–35 ft. lbs.

35. Measure the timing belt tension by pressing on the belt at the midpoint of the longest straight run. Belt deflection should be 11–13mm. If not, repeat the belt adjustment procedure, above.

36. Check the valve adjustment and reset, if necessary.

37. Clean the mating surfaces of the cylinder head and rocker cover.

39. Install the rocker cover with a new gasket. Torque the bolts to 24–36 inch lbs.

40. Install the spark plug wire on the plugs. Place the wires in the clips on the rocker cover. Connect the choke and air bypass valve cable.

41. Installation of all other parts is the reverse of removal. Torque the belt cover bolts to 80 inch lbs.; the fan bracket bolts to 40 ft. lbs.

41. The remainder of the installation is the reverse of the removal procedure.

2555cc AND 2606cc ENGINE

The camshaft on these engines is removed with the rocker shaft assemblies.

1. Disconnect the negative battery cable. Relieve the fuel system pressure.

2. Remove the valve cover assembly.

3. Remove the rocker arms and shafts.

4. Lift the camshaft from the cylinder head.

5. Installation is the reverse of removal.

2954cc ENGINE

1. Relieve the fuel system pressure. Disconnect the negative battery cable. Remove the cylinder heads from the engine.

2. Engage the camshaft sprocket with a suitable holding tool and loosen the retaining bolt. Pull the sprocekt from the end of the camshaft.

3. Insert the end of a flat tipped prybar between the camshaft oil seal and gently pry the seal from the cylinder head bore. Be careful not to damage the seal bore. Discard the seal.

4. Loosen the rocker arm shaft retaining bolts. Loosen the bolts gradually and in several stages. Remove the rocker arm and shaft assemblies.

NOTE: Do not remove the hydraulic lash adjusters unless it is absolutely necessary to do so. The lash adjusters are sealed in the rocker arms by an O-ring. If this O-ring is disturbed or damaged, the lash adjusters may leak. If

they are removed, make sure that a new O-ring(s) is installed and that the oil reservoirs in the rocker arms are filled with clean engine oil.

5. Measure the camshaft endplay, this will determine if the thrust plate or the camshaft have to be replaced.

6. Remove the thrust plate and slowly and carefully withdraw the camshaft from the cylinder head. Clean off the lobe and journal surfaces and proceed to the insection section.

To install:

7. Apply a liberal coating of clean engine oil to the surfaces of the cam lobes, bearing and journal surfaces. Slowly and carefully insert the camshaft into the cylinder head. Install the camsahft thrust plate and torque the retaining bolt to 6–8 ft. lbs.

8. Wipe down the surface of the seal bore with a clean rag and coat the lip of the new oil seal with clean engine oil. Install the seal into the cylinder head using a socket or a length of pipe that closely approximates the diameter of the seal as an installation tool. Tap the seal evenly into the seal bore.

9. Coat the surfaces of the rocker arm and the rocker arm shafts with clean engine oil. Install the rocker shafts in their original positions. The intake side shaft has twice as many oil holes as the exhaust side. Torque the rocker shaft bolts to 14–19 ft. lbs. in the proper sequnce in several stages. When tightening the rocker shaft bolts, makes sure the rocker arm shaft spring does not get pinched between the shaft and the mounting boss.

10. Complete the installation of the cylinder head by reversing the removal procedure.

Silent Shafts

Removal and Installation

2555cc AND 2606cc ENGINES

1. Disconnect the negative battery cable. Relieve the fuel system pressure.

2. Drain the radiator and remove it from the vehicle.

3. Remove the cylinder head.

4. Remove the cooling fan, spacer, water pump pulley and belt.

5. Remove the alternator. Remove the water pump.

6. Raise and support the vehicle safely. Drain the engine oil.

7. Remove the oil pan and screen. Remove the crankshaft pulley.

8. Remove the timing case cover.

9. Remove the chain guides from the front chain.

10. Remove the locking bolts from the chain sprockets.

11. Remove the crankshaft sprocket, silent shaft sprocket and the outer chain.

12. Remove the crankshaft and camshaft sprockets and the timing chain.

13. Remove the camshaft sprocket holder and the chain guides, both left and right.

14. Remove the tensioner.

15. Remove the sleeve from the oil pump. Remove the oil pump by first removing the bolt locking the oil pump driven gear and the right silent shaft, then remove the oil pump mounting bolts. Remove the silent shaft from the engine block.

NOTE: If the bolt locking the oil pump and the silent shaft is hard to loosen, remove the oil pump and the shaft as a unit.

16. Remove the left silent shaft thrust washer and remove the shaft from the engine block.

17. Install the right silent shaft into the engine block.

18. Install the oil pump assembly. Do not lose the woodruff key from the end of the silent shaft. Torque the oil pump mounting bolts to 6–7 ft. lbs.

19. Tighten the silent shaft and the oil pump driven gear mounting bolt.

NOTE: The silent shaft and the oil pump can be installed as a unit, if necessary.

20. Install the left silent shaft into the engine block.

21. Install a new O-ring on the thrust plate and install the unit into the engine block, using a pair of bolts without heads, as alignment guides.

NOTE: If the thrust plate is turned to align the bolt holes, the O-ring may be damaged.

22. Remove the guide bolts and install the regular bolts into the thrust plate and tighten securely.

23. Rotate the crankshaft to bring No. 1 piston to TDC.

24. Install the cylinder head.

25. Install the sprocket holder and the right and left chain guides.

26. Install the tensioner spring and sleeve on the oil pump body.

27. Install the camshaft and crankshaft sprockets on the timing chain, aligning the sprocket punch marks to the plated chain links.

28. While holding the sprocket and chain as a unit, install the crankshaft sprocket over the crankshaft and align it with the keyway.

29. Keeping the dowel pin hole on the camshaft in a vertical position, install the camshaft sprocket and chain on the camshaft.

NOTE: The sprocket timing mark and the plated chain link should be at the 2–3 o'clock position when correctly installed. The chain must be aligned in the right and left chain guides with the tensioner pushing against the chain. The tension for the inner chain is predetermined by spring tension.

30. Install the crankshaft sprocket for the outer chain.

31. Install the 2 silent shaft sprockets and align the punched mating marks with the plated links of the chain.

32. Holding the 2 shaft sprockets and chain, install the outer chain in alignment with the mark on the crankshaft sprocket. Install the shaft sprockets on the silent shaft and the oil pump driver gear. Install the lock bolts and recheck the alignment of the punch marks and the plated links.

33. Temporarily install the chain guides, side (A), top (B) and bottom (C).

34. Tighten side (A) chain guide securely.

35. Tighten bottom (B) chain guide securely.

36. Adjust the position of the top (B) chain guide, after shaking the right and left sprockets to collect any chain slack, so that when the chain is moved toward the center, the clearance between the chain guide and the chain links will be approximately $9/64$ inch. Tighten the top (B) chain guide bolts.

37. Install the timing chain cover using a new gasket, being careful not to damage the front seal.

38. Using a new gasket, install the oil screen and oil pan. Torque the bolts to 4.5–5.5 ft. lbs.

39. Install the crankshaft pulley, alternator and accessory belts and the distributor.

40. Install the oil pressure switch, if removed. Connect the negative battery cable.

41. Install the fan blades, radiator, fill the cooling system and run the engine. Check for oil and water leaks.

Piston and Connecting Rod

Positioning

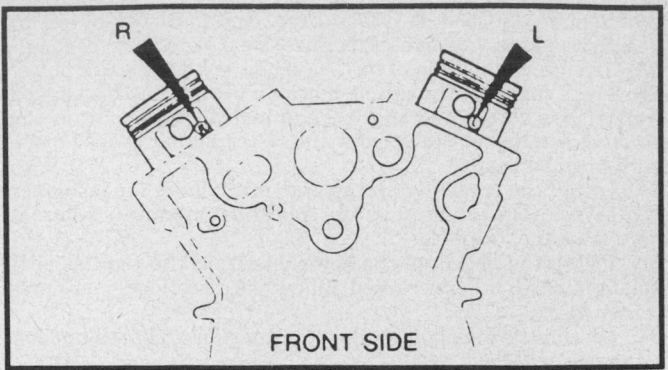

Install the pistons with the L and R marks facing the front of the engine – 2954cc engine

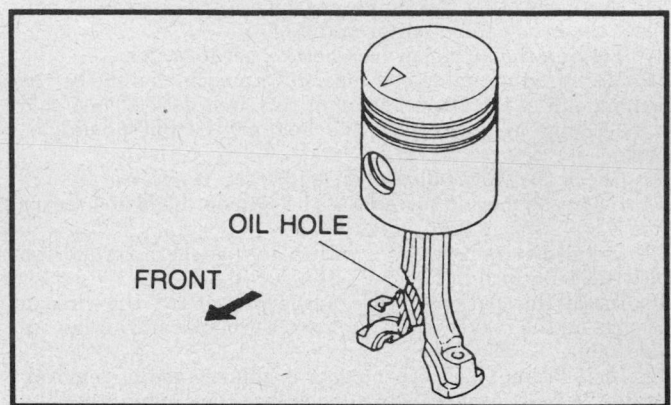

Install the piston with the oil flow port and the arrow facing the front of the engine – 2555cc and 2606cc engines

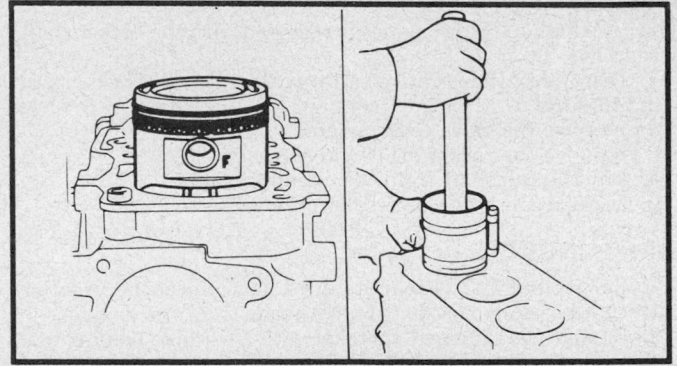

Install the piston with the F mark facing the front of the engine – 1998cc and 2184cc engines

ENGINE LUBRICATION

Oil Pan

Removal and Installation

EXCEPT 2954cc ENGINE

1. Disconnect the negative battery cable.
2. Raise and support the vehicle safely. Drain the engine oil.
3. On 4WD models, remove the skid plate.
4. Support the front of the engine near the crankshaft pulley.
5. Remove the crossmember.
6. Remove the cotter pin and nut. Using a puller, disconnect the idler arm from the center link.
7. Remove the engine mount gusset plates from the sides of the engine.
8. Remove the bell housing front cover.
9. Remove the oil pan retaining bolts and remove the oil pan.

To install:

10. Clean all the gasket surfaces.
11. Clean the oil pan, oil pump pickup tube and oil pump screen.
12. Install a new oil pan gasket coated with oil resistant sealer.Tighten the pan bolts to 5–9 ft. lbs.
13. The remainder of the installation is the reverse of the removal procedure. Torque the idler arm nut to 25–30 ft. lbs. and the bell housing cover to 15–20 ft. lbs.

2954cc ENGINE

1. Disconnect the negative battery cable. Raise and support the vehicle safely.
2. Drain the engine oil and the cooling system
3. Remove the engine under cover.
4. Remove the oil pan retaining bolts.

5. With a scraper or suitable prying tool, separate the oil pan from the block and remove it. Some oil pans may or may not have a gasket.

NOTE: Be careful not to bend the oil pan when separating it from the block.

6. On oil pans with a gasket, apply sealer to the joints between the front cover and the block and the rear main seal housing and the block. On gasketless oil pans, apply a continuous bead of sealant to the oil pan flange around the inside of the bolt holes and overlap the ends.
7. Raise the oil pan onto the block and install the retaining bolts. Torque the bolts to 69–95 inch lbs.
8. Install the engine undercover and lower the vehicle. Fill the crankcase to the proper level. Start the engine and check for leaks.

Oil Pump

Removal and Installation

1998cc AND 2184cc ENGINES

1. Disconnect the negative battery cable.
2. Drain the cooling system.
3. Remove the distributor.
4. Remove the fan shroud and fan.
5. Remove the alternator.
6. Disconnect the air injection pipes.
7. Remove the fan pulley, hub and bracket.
8. If equipped, remove the air conditioning compressor drive belt.

TIMING BELT PULLEY

OIL PUMP

BAFFLE PLATE

STRAINER

OIL PAN

Oil pump and pan removal—1998cc and 2184cc engines

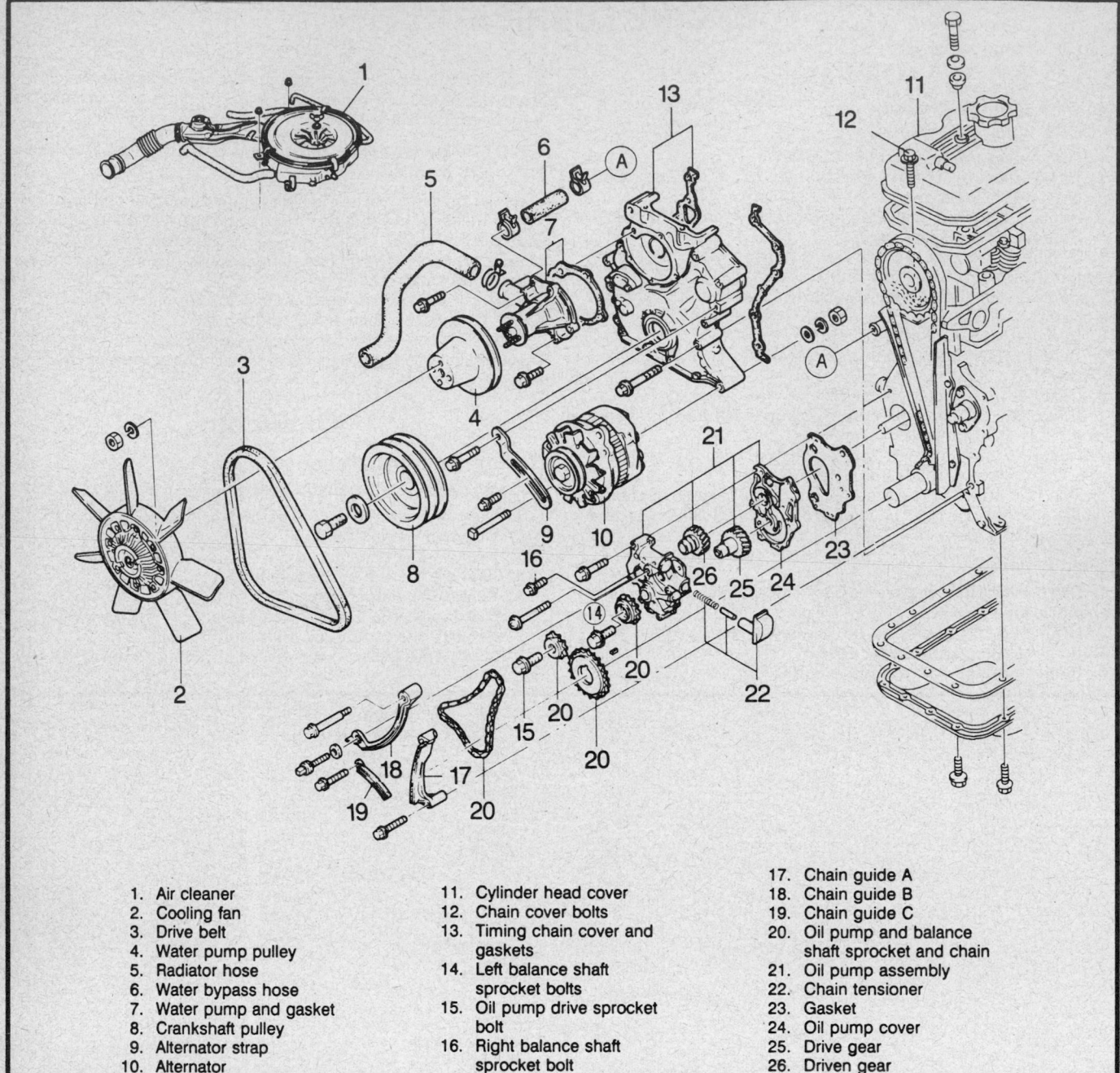

Exploded view of the oil pump and related components — 2555cc and 2606cc engines

1. Air cleaner
2. Cooling fan
3. Drive belt
4. Water pump pulley
5. Radiator hose
6. Water bypass hose
7. Water pump and gasket
8. Crankshaft pulley
9. Alternator strap
10. Alternator
11. Cylinder head cover
12. Chain cover bolts
13. Timing chain cover and gaskets
14. Left balance shaft sprocket bolts
15. Oil pump drive sprocket bolt
16. Right balance shaft sprocket bolt
17. Chain guide A
18. Chain guide B
19. Chain guide C
20. Oil pump and balance shaft sprocket and chain
21. Oil pump assembly
22. Chain tensioner
23. Gasket
24. Oil pump cover
25. Drive gear
26. Driven gear

9. If equipped, remove the power steering pump drive belt.

10. Remove the crankshaft pulley and baffle plate.

11. Remove the upper, then the lower, belt covers.

12. Turn the crankshaft so that the **A** mark on the camshaft pulley is at the top, aligned with the notch in the front housing.

13. Loosen the tensioner lock bolt and remove the tensioner spring.

14. Mark the forward rotation of the belt for installation. Remove the belt.

15. Unbolt and remove the crankshaft sprocket.

16. Raise and safely support the vehicle. Drain the engine oil.

17. Remove the skid plate.

18. Support the front of the engine at the crankshaft pulley.

19. Remove the crossmember.

20. Remove the cotter pin and nut and, with a puller, disconnect the idler arm from the center link.

21. Remove the engine mount gusset plates from the sides of the engine.

22. Remove the bell housing front cover.

23. Remove the oil pan.

24. Remove the oil pick-up tube.

25. Remove the oil pump.

To install:

26. Apply a thin coating of grease to the O-ring and install it in its recess in the pump body.

27. Apply a thin bead of RTV silicone sealer to the pump mounting surface.

28. Coat the oil seal lip with clean engine oil and install the pump. Torque the bolts to 14–19 ft. lbs.

29. Clean all the gasket surfaces. Straighten the portion of the pan rim that may be bent.

30. Clean the oil pan, oil pump pickup tube and oil pump screen.

31. Using a new gasket, install the oil pan on the engine. Tighten the oil pan bolts to 5–9 ft. lbs.

32. Install all other parts in reverse order of removal. Torque the idler arm nut to 25–30 ft. lbs. and the bell housing cover to 15–20 ft. lbs.

33. Replace timing the belt if it has been contaminated by oil or grease, or shows any sign of damage, wear, cracks or peeling.

34. To ease installation of the belt, remove all the spark plugs.

35. Make sure that the timing mark on the camshaft is aligned and that the timing mark (notch) on the crankshaft sprocket is aligned with the triangular shaped mark on the front housing.

36. Install the tensioner and spring, positioning the tensioner all the way to the intake manifold side and temporarily secure it there with the lock bolt.

37. Install the belt onto the sprockets from the right side. If the original belt is being reused, follow the directional mark previously made.

38. Loosen the lock bolt so that the tensioner applies tension to the belt.

39. Turn the crankshaft 2 full revolutions in the direction of normal rotation. This will apply equal tension to all points of the belt.

40. Make sure that the timing marks are still aligned. If not, repeat the belt installation procedure.

41. Tighten the tensioner lock bolt to 30–35 ft. lbs.

42. Measure the timing belt tension by pressing on the belt at the midpoint of the longest straight run. Belt deflection should be 11–13mm. If not, repeat the belt adjustment procedure.

43. The remainder of the installation is the reverse of the removal procedure. Torque the timing belt cover bolts to 80 inch lbs. and the fan bracket bolts to 40 ft. lbs. When installing the drive belts on the various accessories, check the belt deflection.

2555cc AND 2606cc ENGINES

1. Disconnect the negative battery cable. Relieve the fuel system pressure.

2. Drain the radiator and remove it from the vehicle.

3. Remove the cylinder head.

4. Remove the cooling fan, spacer, water pump pulley and belt.

5. Remove the alternator. Remove the water pump.

6. Raise and support the vehicle safely. Drain the engine oil.

7. Remove the oil pan and screen. Remove the crankshaft pulley.

8. Remove the timing case cover.

9. Remove the chain guides from the outer chain.

10. Remove the locking bolts from the chain sprockets.

11. Remove the crankshaft sprocket, silent shaft sprocket and the outer chain.

12. Remove the crankshaft and camshaft sprockets and the timing chain.

13. Remove the camshaft sprocket holder and the chain guides, both left and right.

14. Remove the tensioner.

15. Remove the sleeve from the oil pump. Remove the oil pump by first removing the bolt locking the oil pump driven gear and the right silent shaft, then remove the oil pump mounting bolts.

To install:

16. Install the oil pump assembly. Do not lose the woodruff key from the end of the silent shaft. Torque the oil pump mounting bolts to 6–7 ft. lbs.

17. Tighten the silent shaft and the oil pump driven gear mounting bolt.

NOTE: **The silent shaft and the oil pump can be installed as a unit, if necessary.**

18. Install the left silent shaft into the engine block.

19. Install a new O-ring on the thrust plate and install the unit into the engine block, using a pair of bolts without heads, as alignment guides.

NOTE: **If the thrust plate is turned to align the bolt holes, the O-ring may be damaged.**

20. Remove the guide bolts and install the regular bolts into the thrust plate and tighten securely.

21. Rotate the crankshaft to bring No. 1 piston to TDC.

22. Install the cylinder head.

23. Install the sprocket holder and the right and left chain guides.

24. Install the tensioner spring and sleeve on the oil pump body.

25. Install the camshaft and crankshaft sprockets on the timing chain, aligning the sprocket punch marks to the plated chain links.

26. While holding the sprocket and chain as a unit, install the crankshaft sprocket over the crankshaft and align it with the keyway.

27. Keeping the dowel pin hole on the camshaft in a vertical position, install the camshaft sprocket and chain on the camshaft.

NOTE: **The sprocket timing mark and the plated chain link should be at the 2–3 o'clock position when correctly installed. The chain must be aligned in the right and left chain guides with the tensioner pushing against the chain. The tension for the inner chain is predetermined by spring tension.**

28. Install the crankshaft sprocket for the outer chain.

29. Install the 2 silent shaft sprockets and align the punched mating marks with the plated links of the chain.

30. Holding the 2 shaft sprockets and chain, install the outer chain in alignment with the mark on the crankshaft sprocket. Install the shaft sprockets on the silent shaft and the oil pump driver gear. Install the lock bolts and recheck the alignment of the punch marks and the plated links.

31. Temporarily install the chain guides.

32. Tighten side chain guide securely.

33. Tighten bottom chain guide securely.

34. Adjust the position of the top chain guide, after shaking the right and left sprockets to collect any chain slack, so that when the chain is moved toward the center, the clearance between the chain guide and the chain links will be approximately $9/64$ inch. Tighten the top chain guide bolts.

35. Install the timing chain cover using a new gasket, being careful not to damage the front seal.

36. Using a new gasket, install the oil screen and oil pan. Torque the bolts to 4.5–5.5 ft. lbs.

37. Install the crankshaft pulley, alternator and accessory belts and the distributor.

38. Install the oil pressure switch, if removed. Connect the negative battery cable.

39. Install the fan blades and radiator. Fill the cooling system and run the engine. Check for oil and water leaks.

40. Adjust the ignition timing.

2954cc ENGINE

1. Disconnect the negative battery cable. Raise and support the vehicle safely.

2. Drain the engine oil and the cooling system.

3. Remove the timing belt and the timing belt pulley and key. Remove the thermostat and gasket.

4. Remove the oil pan, oil strainer and O-ring.

5. Unbolt and remove the oil pump and gasket.

6. To install, press in a new oil seal and coat the seal lip with

clean engine oil. Use a new gasket, O-ring and sealant as required. Torque the oil pump retaining bolts to 14–19 ft. lbs.

Checking

SIDE CLEARANCE

Lay a straightedge across the pump body and, using a feeler gauge, measure between the gear faces and straightedge. If the clearance exceeds 0.10mm (0.003937 in.), replace the pump.

OUTER GEAR TO PUMP BODY CLEARANCE

Insert a feeler gauge between the outer gear and the pump body. If the clearance exceeds 0.20mm (0.00787 in.), replace the gear or pump body.

Rear Main Oil Seal

Removal and Installation

1998cc AND 2184cc ENGINES

1. Raise and safely support the vehicle. Remove the transmission.
2. On manual transmission equipped vehicles, remove the clutch assembly.
3. Remove the flywheel or drive plate.
4. Remove the end plate.
5. The seal is located in the rear cover. Remove the rear cover. Discard the gasket.
6. Place the cover on a hard, flat surface. Drive the old seal from the rear cover.
7. Apply clean engine oil to the outer rim of the new seal and the seal bore in the rear cover. Press the new seal into place.
8. Coat the seal lip with clean engine oil. Install the rear cover and new gasket. Torque the bolts to 72–102 inch lbs., (6–8.5 ft. lbs.).
9. Using a suitable tool, cut away the part of the gasket that projects below the rear cover.
10. Install the end plate. Torque the bolts to 14–22 ft. lbs.
11. On manual transmission models, install the flywheel, clutch and transmission. On automatic transmission models, install the drive plate and transmission.
12. The remainder of the installation is the reverse of the removal procedure.

2555cc AND 2606cc ENGINES

NOTE: **The rear main bearing oil seal is located in a housing on the rear of the engine. To replace the seal, remove the transmission and work from underneath the vehicle.**

1. Raise and safely support the vehicle. On manual transmission models, remove the transmission, clutch and flywheel. On automatic transmission models, remove the transmission and flywheel. Remove the oil seal housing from the rear of the engine.
2. Remove the separator from the housing.
3. Pry out the old seal.
4. Lightly oil the replacement seal. The oil seal should be installed so that the seal plate fits into the inner contact surface of the seal case. Install the separator with the oil holes facing down.
5. Install the flywheel, clutch and transmission. Check the engine oil level when finished.

2954cc ENGINE

1. Raise and support the vehicle safely. Remove the transmission from the vehicle.
2. If equipped with manual transmission, remove the clutch pressure plate and flywheel.
3. If equipped with automatic transmission, remove the flywheel assembly.
4. Drain the engine oil.
5. Remove the rear main seal cover retaining bolts. Remove the rear main seal cover. Remove the seal from the rear cover.
6. Installation is the reverse of the removal procedure. Apply clean engine oil to the seal before pressing it into the cover.
7. After installing the rear cover cut away the portion of the gasket that projects out toward the oil pan side.

MANUAL TRANSMISSION

For further information, please refer to "Professional Transmission Manual".

Transmission Assembly

Removal and Installation

B2000 AND B2200

1. Disconnect the negative battery cable.
2. Remove the gearshift knob and shift console attaching screws. Remove the console.
3. Remove the shift lever to extension housing attaching bolts and remove the shift lever.
4. Raise and support the vehicle safely.
5. Drain the transmission oil.
6. Matchmark and remove the driveshaft.
7. Disconnect the speedometer cable from the transmission.
8. Remove the starter motor.
9. Disconnect and tag the back-up light switch wiring at the transmission.
10. Disconnect the parking brake return spring and parking brake cables.
11. Remove the clutch slave cylinder.
12. Remove the transmission front support bracket.

13. Disconnect the exhaust pipe at the transmission and manifold.
14. Support the transmission and engine separately.
15. Remove the transmission crossmember.
16. Lower the transmission to gain access to the top bolts and remove the transmission to engine bolts.
17. Pull the transmission straight back, away from the engine and remove transmission from the vehicle.
18. Installation is the reverse of the removal procedure.
20. Torque the transmission to engine bolts to 60–65 ft. lbs. and the gearshift lever bolts to 6–8 ft. lbs.
21. Check and fill the transmission to the proper level when finished.

B2600

NOTE: **Although the transmission and transfer case are separate units, they share a similar mounting and sealing surface. It is recommended that they be removed as a unit and separated once removed from the vehicle.**

1. Disconnect the negative battery cable.
2. Remove the knobs from the transfer case and transmission shifters.
3. Remove the console box, if equipped.

4. Remove the insulator plate and shifter boot.
5. Remove the shift levers.
6. Raise and support the vehicle safely. Drain the tranfer case and transmission oil.
7. Remove the transmission and transfer case under covers. Remove the starter.
8. Disconnect and remove the exhaust pipe from the manifold and catalytic converter.
9. Matchmark and remove the front and rear driveshafts.
10. Disconnect the speedometer cable, 4WD switch and back-up light switch wires from the transmission/transfer case.
11. Remove the slave cylinder without disconnecting the fluid line. Support the slave cylinder out of the way.
12. Remove the transmission/transfer case gusset plates. Support the transmission. Properly support the engine.
13. Raise the transmission/transfer case and remove the crossmember.
14. Remove the transmission and transfer case as an assembly.
15. Installation is the reverse of the removal procedure.
16. Align the matchmarks on the driveshafts during installation.
17. Check and fill the transmission and transfer case after installation.

MPV
1. Disconnect the battery ground cable.
2. Raise and support the vehicle safely.
3. Drain the transmission fluid.
4. Remove the shifter knob and boot.
5. Shift the transmission into **N** and unbolt and remove the shifter.
6. Disconnect the speedometer cable at the extension housing.
7. Disconnect the electrical connectors at the transmission.
8. Matchmark and remove the driveshaft. Stuff a rag in the double offset joint to prevent damage to the boot from the driveshaft.
9. On the 2606cc engine, unbolt the transmission side support plate from the transmission.
10. Remove the starter.

11. Remove the clutch release cylinder and hyudraulic line bracket. It is not necessary to disconnect the hydraulic line. Remove the bellhousing inspection plate.
12. Disconnect the exhaust pipe at both the engine and the support bracket.
13. Remove the converter heat shield. Remove the side support plates and support the transmission with a transmission jack.
14. Remove the transmission-to-crossmember bolts. Remove the crossmember.
15. Support the engine with a suitable jack. Remove the transmission-to-engine bolts.
16. Pull the transmission straight back on the jack until the mainshaft clears the clutch. Lower the transmission and pull it out from under the vehicle.

To install:
17. Raise the unit and position it under the vehicle.
18. Push the transmission straight forward on the jack until the mainshaft enter the clutch and the transmission engages the locating studs on the engine.
19. Install the transmission-to-engine bolts. Torque the bolts to 45 ft. lbs.
20. Install the starter. Install the crossmember. Torque the bolts to 50 ft. lbs.
21. Install the transmission-to-crossmember bolts. Torque the bolts to 45 ft. lbs. Remove the engine support. Remove the transmission jack.
22. Connect the exhaust pipe at both the engine and the support bracket.
23. Install the transmission side support plate. Install the clutch release cylinder and bracket.
24. Connect the speedometer cable at the extension housing. Connect the elctrical wiring.
25. Install the driveshaft. Install the bellhousing inspection plate.
26. Install the heat shield and install the shifter.
27. Install the floor console. Install the shifter knob and boot.
28. Fill the transmission with fluid.
29. Connect the battery ground cable.

CLUTCH

Clutch Assembly

Removal and Installation

1. Raise and safely support the vehicle. Remove the transmission. If the clutch is being reused, matchmark the pressure plate to the flywheel to insure proper balance during installation.
2. Loosen the bolts holding the clutch cover to the flywheel. Loosen the bolts evenly a turn or 2 at a time.
3. Support the clutch assembly and remove the mounting bolts. Remove the clutch disc.
4. Using a clutch alignment tool, install the pressure plate and disc on the flywheel.
5. Install the clutch-to-flywheel bolts.
6. Tighten the bolts evenly a few turns at a time.
7. Torque the bolts to 13–20 ft. lbs.
8. Remove the alignment tool.
9. Apply a light film of lubricant to the release bearing, release lever contact area on the release bearing hub and input shaft bearing retainer.
10. Install the transmission.
11. Check the operation of the clutch and if necessary, adjust the pedal free-play and the release lever.

Pedal Height/Free-Play Adjustment

1. Measure the distance from the top of the clutch pedal pad to the carpet.
2. The measurement for the pedal height, should be approximately 208–218mm.
3. If the mesurement is not within specification, adjust the pedal by loosening and turning the clutch switch in the bracket.
4. Check the free-play by pressing the pedal by hand until resistance is felt.
5. Measure the distance, it should be 5.5–17.4mm.
6. If the distance is not within specification, loosen the locknut on the actuator rod and turn the actuator rod unitl the measurement is correct.
7. Recheck the measurement. Tighten the locknut.

Clutch Master Cylinder

Removal and Installation

1. Disconnect the negative battery cable. Disconnect and plug the fluid outlet line at the fitting on the master cylinder.

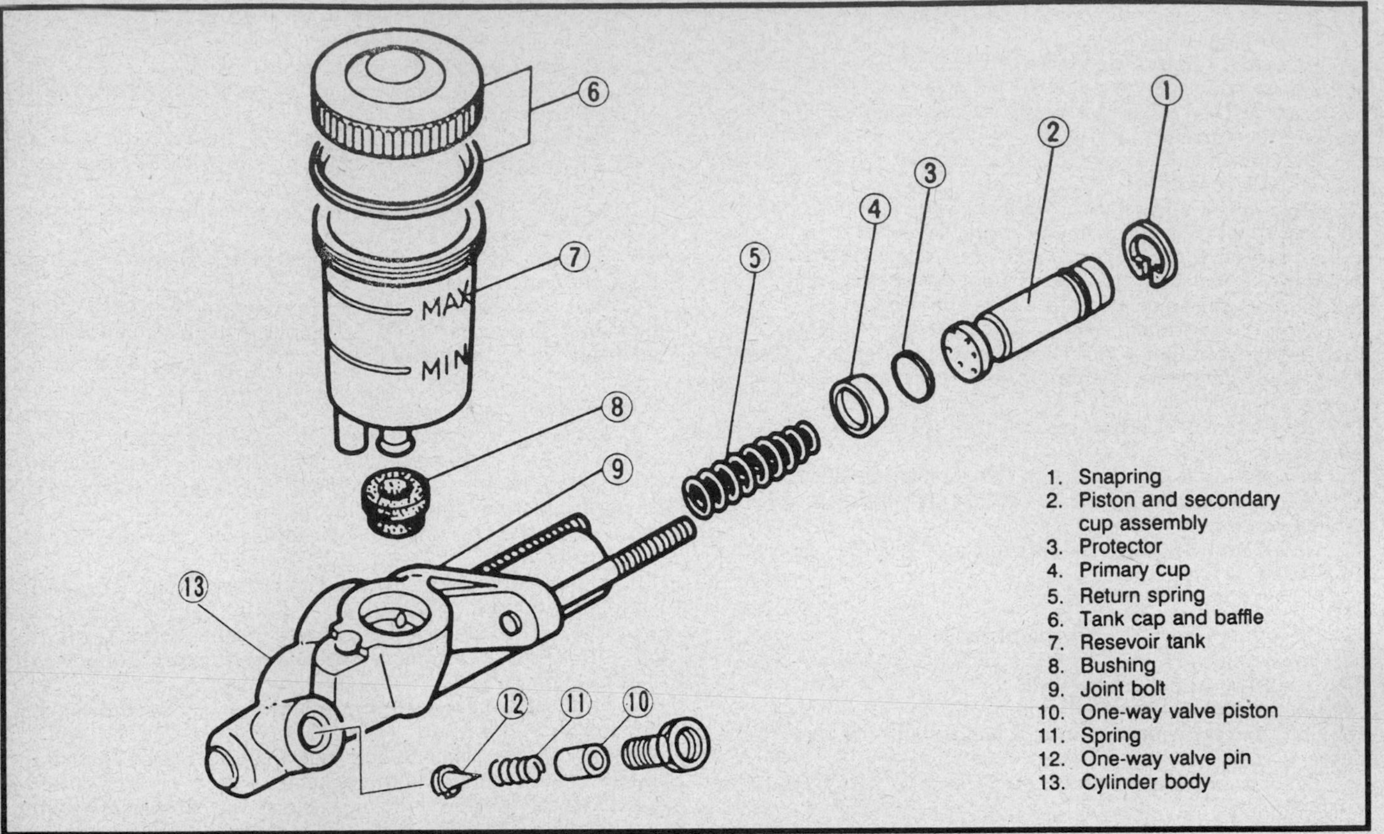

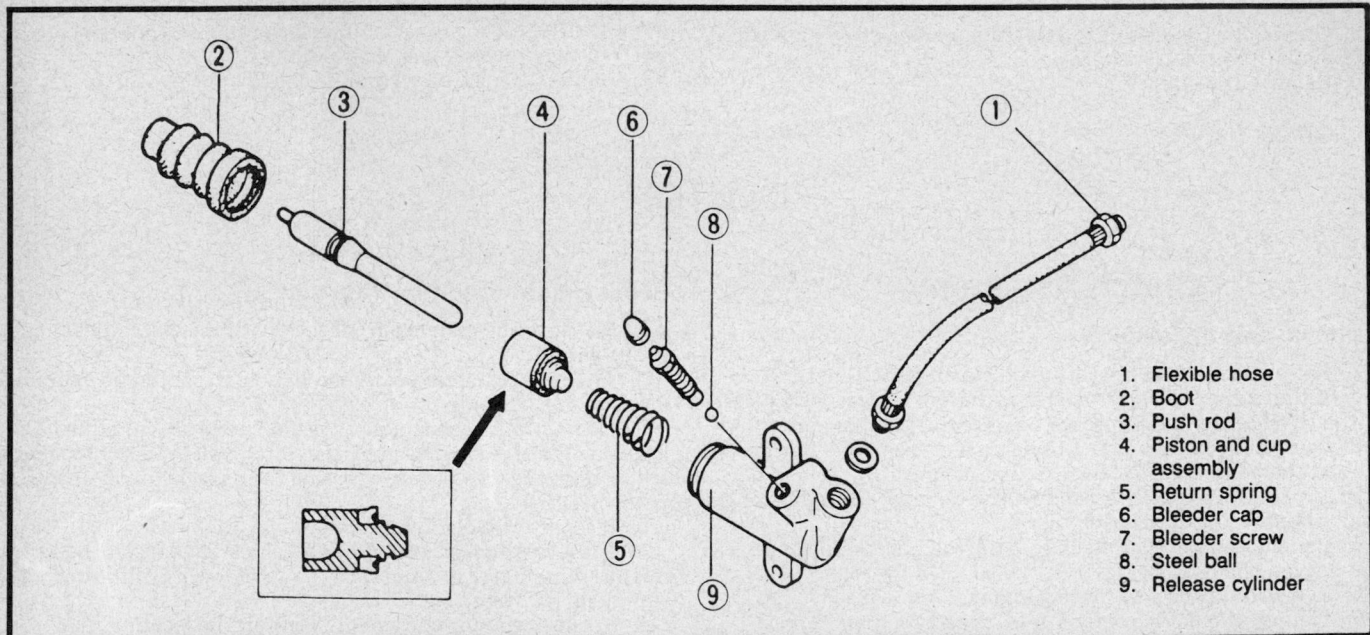

1. Snapring
2. Piston and secondary cup assembly
3. Protector
4. Primary cup
5. Return spring
6. Tank cap and baffle
7. Resevoir tank
8. Bushing
9. Joint bolt
10. One-way valve piston
11. Spring
12. One-way valve pin
13. Cylinder body

Exploded view of the clutch master cylinder

1. Flexible hose
2. Boot
3. Push rod
4. Piston and cup assembly
5. Return spring
6. Bleeder cap
7. Bleeder screw
8. Steel ball
9. Release cylinder

Exploded view of the clutch slave cylinder

2. Remove the nuts and bolts mounting the master cylinder to the firewall.
3. Remove the master cylinder from the firewall.
4. Start the pedal pushrod into the master cylinder and position the master cylinder on the firewall.

5. Install the mounting nuts and bolts. Torque the nuts to 12–17 ft. lbs.
6. Connect the fluid outlet line to the master cylinder fitting.
7. Bleed the hydraulic clutch system.
8. Check the clutch pedal free-play and adjust if necessary.

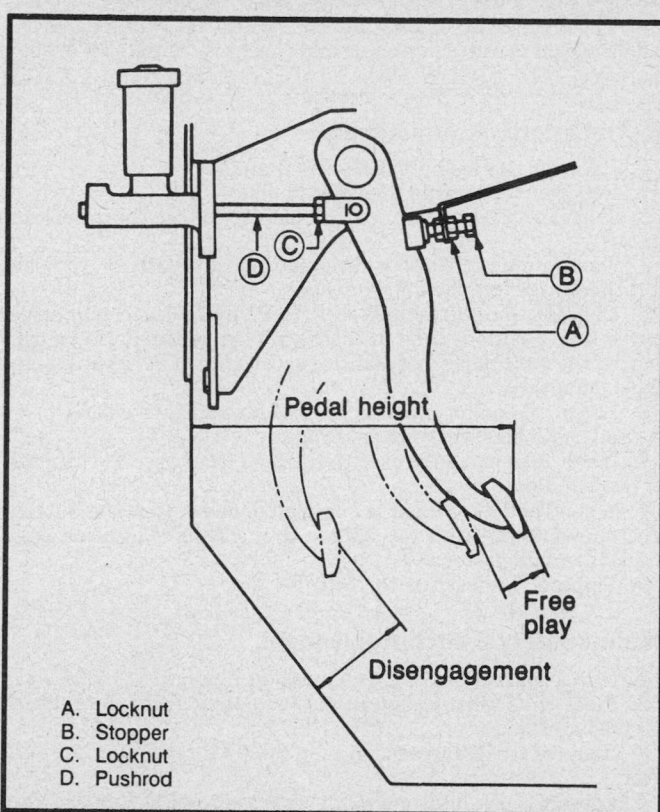

Clutch pedal height and free-play adjustment points

A. Locknut
B. Stopper
C. Locknut
D. Pushrod

Clutch Slave Cylinder

Removal and Installation

1. Disconnect the negative battery cable. Raise and support the vehicle safely.
2. Disconnect the fluid line from the slave cylinder.
3. Pull off the hose retaining clip and remove the hose from the bracket. Cap the pipe to prevent fluid loss.
4. Remove the slave cylinder.
5. Installation is the reverse of removal.
6. Torque the slave cylinder mounting bolt to 12–17 ft. lbs.
7. Bleed the clutch system when finished.

Bleeding the Hydraulic Clutch System

1. To bleed the system, remove the rubber cap from the bleeder valve and attach a rubber hose to the valve.
2. Submerge the other end of the hose in a large jar of clean brake fluid.
3. Open the bleeder valve. Depress the clutch pedal and allow it to return slowly.
4. Continue slowly pumping clutch pedal and watch the jar of brake fluid.
5. When the fluid is clear of air bubbles, close the bleeder valve and remove the tube.
6. Check and fill the reservoir during and after the procedure.

NOTE: If the fluid in the reservoir runs out during the procedure, the entire procedure must be repeated. After the bleeding operation is finished, install the cap on the bleeder valve and fill the master cylinder to the proper level. Always use fresh DOT 3 brake fluid. Do not use the fluid that was in the jar for bleeding, since it may contain air and/or dirt.

AUTOMATIC TRANSMISSION

For further information, please refer to "Professional Transmission Manual".

Transmission Assembly

Removal and Installation

1. Disconnect the negative battery cable.
2. Raise and support the vehicle safely.
3. Drain the transmission fluid. After the fluid has drained, install a few bolts to hold the pan in place, temporarily.
4. Remove the exhaust pipe bracket bolt from the right side of the converter housing.
5. Remove the exhaust pipe flange bolts from the rear of the resonator or catalytic converter and disconnect the pipe.
6. Matchmark and remove the driveshaft from the rear axle flange.
7. Remove the driveshaft center bearing support. Lower the driveshaft and remove it from the transmission.
8. Disconnect the speedometer cable.
9. Disconnect the shift rod from the manual lever.
10. Remove the vacuum hose from the diaphragm. Disconnect the electrical connectors from the downshift solenoid and inhibitor switch and remove their wires from the clip.
11. Disconnect and plug the cooler lines from the radiator at the transmission.
12. Remove the access cover from the lower front of the converter housing.
13. Matchmark the drive plate (flywheel) and torque converter

for reassembly. Remove the 4 bolts holding the torque converter to the drive plate.
14. Remove the bolts connecting the crossmember to the transmission.
15. Support the transmission. Remove the crossmember to frame bolts and remove the crossmember. Properly support the engine.
16. Make sure that the transmission is securely supported.
17. Lower the transmission enough to remove the starter.
18. Remove the converter housing to engine bolts.
19. Remove the fluid filler tube.
20. Make sure that the converter is engaged in the transmission during removal.
21. Lower the transmission and converter as an assembly. Be careful not to let the converter fall out.

To install:

22. To install, make sure that the converter is properly installed in the transmission.
23. Raise the transmission into place. Install the converter housing to engine bolts and torque the bolts in 2 stages to 23–34 ft. lbs.
24. Lower the transmission slightly and install the starter.
25. Install the fluid filler tube with a new O-ring.
26. Raise the transmission slightly and install the crossmember to the frame. Tighten the bolts to 23–34 ft. lbs.
27. Lower the transmission and install the transmission to crossmember bolts. Tighten to 23–34 ft. lbs.
28. Align the matchmarks made earlier on the torque con-

verter and drive plate. Install the 4 attaching bolts and torque to 25–36 ft. lbs. in 3 stages.

29. Install the access cover. Remove the support.

30. Connect the cooler lines.

31. Install the electrical connectors to the switch and solenoid and replace the wires in the clip. Install the diaphragm vacuum hose.

32. Connect the shift rod to the lever.

33. Connect the speedometer cable.

34. Insert the driveshaft into the transmission. Install the center bearing support. Bolt the driveshaft to the rear of the axle flange.

35. Connect the exhaust pipe to the catalytic converter, using a new gasket. Reinstall the exhaust pipe clamp onto the converter housing and torque the bolt to 10–15 ft. lbs.

36. Install a new pan gasket and the fluid pan.

37. Lower the vehicle. Connect the negative battery cable. Fill the transmission through the dipstick tube with the specified fluid, being careful not to overfill. Run the engine and check for leaks.

Shift Linkage Adjustment

1. Put the gearshift lever in **N**.

2. Raise and support the vehicle.

3. Disconnect the clevis from the lower end of the selector lever operating arm.

4. Move the transmission manual lever to **N**, the 3rd detent position from the rear of the transmission.

5. Loosen the 2 clevis retaining nuts and adjust the clevis so that it freely enters the hole of the lever. Tighten the retaining nuts to secure the adjustment.

6. Connect the clevis to the lever and attach it with the spring washer, flat washer and retaining clip.

7. Lower the vehicle and check the operation of the transmission in all gears.

Kickdown Switch Adjustment

1. Turn the ignition switch to the **ON** position.

2. Loosen the kickdown switch attaching nut (the switch is located just above the accelerator pedal) and adjust the switch to engage when the accelerator pedal is depressed about $^7/_8$ of the way. The downshift solenoid will click when the switch engages.

3. Tighten the attaching nut and check the switch for proper operation.

Neutral Interlock Adjustment

1. Back off the locknut below the handle.

2. Position the shifter in either **N** or **D**.

3. Turn in the handle until no play is felt at the interlock button.

4. Turn the handle one additional turn if necessary, to position the button on the driver's side.

5. Depress the button and shift to **P**. If the lever cannot be moved to **P** position, turn in the handle an additional turn, repeating the shift move and additional turn, until Park can be engaged smoothly.

6. From this point, shift through the various positions, confirming that the shifter works properly.

7. If the lever can be shifted to **R** from either **P** or **N**, turn out on the handle.

8. When the adjustment is completed, check that the button protrudes 6.0mm from the handle in the **N** or **P** position. Recheck the shift pattern.

9. Tighten the locknut to 15 ft. lbs.

Neutral Safety Switch Adjustment

1. Check and adjust the transmission linkage.

2. Place the transmission in **N** (3rd detent from the rear of the transmission).

3. Remove the transmission manual lever retaining nut and lever.

4. Loosen the inhibitor switch attaching bolts. Remove the screw from the alignment pin hole at the bottom of the switch.

5. Rotate the switch and insert an alignment pin, 0.059 in. diameter into the alignment pin hole and internal rotor.

6. Tighten the 2 switch attaching bolts and remove the alignment pin.

7. Reinstall the alignment pin hole screw in the switch body.

8. Install the manual lever.

9. Check the operation of the switch. The engine should only start with the transmission selector lever in **N** or **P**.

TRANSFER CASE

Transfer Case Assembly
Removal and Installation

The transfer case and transmission are connected together and share a common seal between them. It is recommended by the manufacturer that they be removed from the vehicle as an assembly and then separated for repairs.

DRIVE AXLE

Driveshaft and U-Joints
Removal and Installation
B2000, B2200 AND MPV

1. Raise and support the vehicle safely. Matchmark the driveshaft with the rear flange. Remove the bolts attaching the driveshaft to the rear flange and remove the driveshaft.

2. On 2-piece units, remove the center support bearing bracket from the underbody.

3. Pull the driveshaft rearward and out of the transmission.

4. Installation is the reverse of removal. Align the matchmarks made during removal. Torque the rear flange bolts to 39–47 ft. lbs. and the center bearing bracket nuts to 27–38 ft. lbs.

B2600 FRONT

1. Raise and support the vehicle safely.

2. Matchmark the driveshaft to the front differential flange.

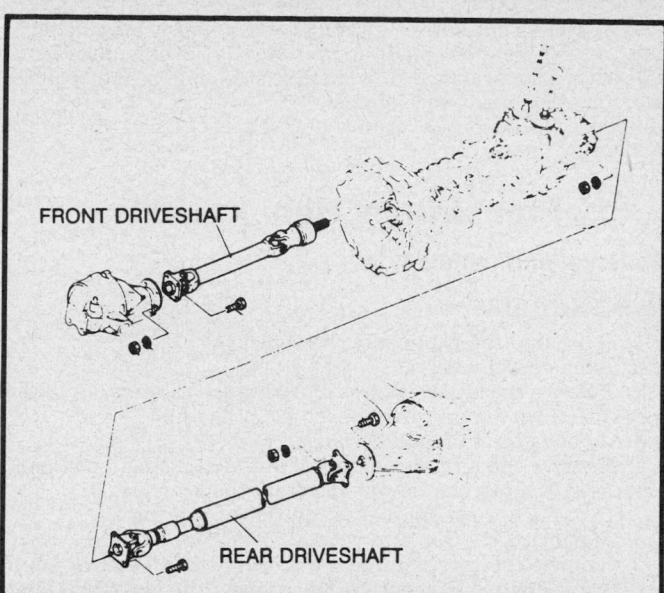

Typical driveshaft types—B2000, B2200 and B2600

3. Remove the driveshaft from the differential and top of the transfer case.
4. Installation is the reverse of the removal procedure.
5. Torque the mounting bolts to 39–47 ft. lbs.

B2600 REAR

1. Raise and support the vehicle safely.
2. Matchmark the front and rear flange to the driveshaft.
3. Support the driveshaft.
4. Remove the front and rear driveshaft flange bolts and center bearing mount.
5. Remove the driveshaft and center bearing as an assembly.
6. Installation is the reverse of the removal procedure.
7. Torque the flange bolts to 36–43 ft. lbs and the bearing mount bolts to 27–36 ft. lbs.

Center Bearing

Removal and Installation

B2600 AND MPV

1. Raise and support the vehicle safely.
2. Matchmark and remove the rear driveshaft.
3. Unbolt and remove the center bearing from the front portion of the rear driveshaft.
4. Install the center bearing on the driveshaft.
5. Install the bearing and driveshaft in the vehicle.
6. Torque the bearing mounting bolts to 27–36 ft. lbs and the flange bolts to 36–43 ft. lbs.

Front Axle Shaft

Removal and Installation

B2600

1. Raise and support the vehicle safely. Remove the tire and wheel assembly.
2. Remove the locking hub assembly.
3. Remove the brake caliper and the mount without disconnecting the fluid line. Support the caliper out of the way.
4. Disconnect the stabilizer bar and shock absorber from the lower control arm.
5. Disconnect the tie rod end from the steering knuckle.

6. Remove the circlip and spacer from the hub end of the axleshaft.
7. Support the lower control arm.
8. Remove the upper and lower ball joint cotter pins and nuts.
9. Separate the ball joints from the control arms.
10. Remove the steering knuckle and hub assembly.
11. Remove the engine under cover.
12. Carefully, remove the axleshaft from the differential end. Use care not to damage the oil seal or dust cover.
13. Remove the axleshaft from the vehicle.
14. Installation is the reverse of the removal procedure.

Front Output Shaft Seal and Bearing

Removal and Installation

B2600

1. Raise and support the vehicle safely. Remove the left wheel and tire assembly.
2. Remove the left side axle shaft. Remove the output shaft.
3. Remove the O-ring from the retainer. Remove the circlip from the retainer side of the output shaft.

NOTE: The next procedures require the use of a press. Certain adapters must also be used, to remove and install the bearing and seal.

4. Press out the output shaft, bearing and seal assembly from the retainer.
5. Remove the oil seal.
6. Press the bearing off of the output shaft.
7. Clean and inspect the output shaft.
8. Press the oil seal in the retainer using tool 49 M005 796 or equivalent.
9. Coat the lip of the oil seal with engine oil.
10. Press the output shaft into the bearing.

NOTE: When pressing the output shaft into the bearing, only support the inner race of the bearing. If an extreme amount of binding occurs, STOP. The output shaft must be pressed into the bearing straight.

11. Press the output shaft and bearing into the retainer.
12. Install the oil seal in the retainer.
13. Install a new circlip on the output shaft at the retainer.
14. Install a new O-ring on the retainer.
15. Install the output shaft into the differential.
16. Install the left side axleshaft.
17. The remainder of the installation is the reverse of the removal procedure.

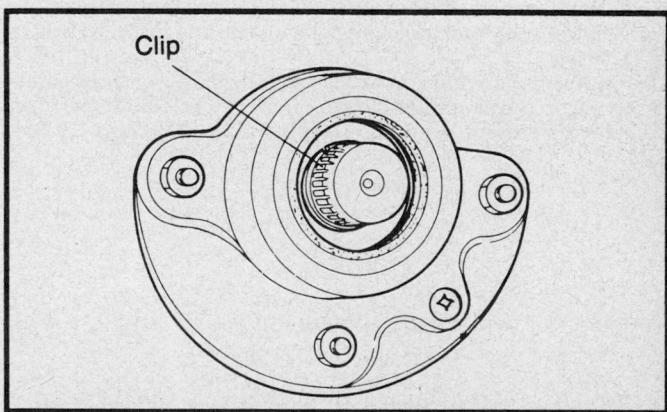

Output shaft seal retaining clip location

Rear Axle Shaft, Bearing and Seal

Removal and Installation

1. Raise and support the vehicle safely.
2. Remove the tire and wheel assembly and brake drum.
3. Remove the brake shoes.
4. Remove the parking brake cable retainer.
5. Disconnect and plug the brake lines at the wheel cylinders.
6. Remove the bolts securing the backing plate and bearing housing.
7. Slide the axle shaft from the axle housing. Be careful to avoid damaging the oil seal with the axle shaft.
8. If the seal in the axle housing is damaged in any way, it must be replaced. The seal can be removed using a slide hammer and adapter.
9. Remove 2 of the backing plate bolts, diagonally from each other.
10. Using a grinding wheel, grind down the bearing retaining collar in one spot, until about 5mm remains above the axle shaft. Using a suitable tool, break the collar. Be careful to avoid damaging the shaft.
11. Using a press or puller, remove the hub and bearing assembly from the shaft. Remove the spacer from the shaft.
12. Remove the bearing and seal from the hub.
13. Using a suitable tool, remove the race from the hub.
14. Check all parts for wear or damage.

NOTE: If either race is being replaced, both must be replaced.

15. Remove the race in the axle housing with a slide hammer and adapter.
16. The outer race must be installed using an arbor press. The inner race can be driven into place in the axle housing. Pack the hub with wheel bearing grease.
17. Tap a new oil seal into the axle housing until it is flush with the end of the housing. Coat the seal lip with wheel bearing grease.
18. Install a new spacer on the shaft with the larger flat surface up.
19. Install a new seal in the hub.
20. Thoroughly pack the bearing with clean wheel bearing grease.
21. Place the bearing in the hub and, using a press, press the hub and bearing assembly onto the shaft.
22. Press the new collar onto the shaft. The press pressure for the collar is critical. Press pressures should be 9,240–13,420 lbs. (4,200–6,100 kg).
23. Install one shaft in the housing being very careful to avoid damaging the inner seal.
24. If only on shaft was being serviced, the other must now be removed to check bearing play on the serviced axle. If both shafts were removed, leave the other one out temporarily.
25. Tighten the backing plate bolts on the one installed axle to 80 ft. lbs.
26. Mount a dial indicator on the backing plate, with the pointer resting on the axle shaft flange. Check the axle shaft end play. Standard bearing play should be 0.026–0.037 in. (0.65–0.95mm).
27. If play is not within specifications, shims are available.
28. Install the other shaft and torque the backing plate bolts. Check the play as on the first shaft. Play should be 0.002–0.010 in. If not, correct it with shims.
29. Install the brake drums and wheels. Bleed the brake system.

Front Wheel Hub, Knuckle

Removal and Installation

2WD VEHICLES

1. Raise and safely support the vehicle.
2. Remove the wheels.
3. Remove the brake calipers. Suspend the calipers out of the way with a wire. Don't disconnect the brake line.
4. Remove the hub and bearings.
5. Remove the tie rod-to-knuckle nut, and, using a ball joint separator, remove the tie rod end from the knuckle.
7. Install a spring compressor on the coil spring.
8. Support the lower arm with a floor jack.
9. Remove the cotter pin and nut from the lower ball joint, and, using a ball joint separator, disconnect the lower ball joint from the knuckle.
10. Remove the cotter pin and nut from the upper ball joint, and, using a ball joint separator, disconnect the upper ball joint from the knuckle.
11. Pull the knuckle and spindle assembly from the control arms.
12. The knuckle arm may now be removed.
13. Clean and inspect all parts for wear or damage. Replace parts as necessary.
To install:
14. Secure the knuckle in a vise and install the knuckle arm. Torque the bolts to 70–74 ft. lbs.
15. Installation of the knuckle assembly is the reverse of removal. Observe the following torques:
    Upper ball joint-to-knuckle – 35–38 ft. lbs.
    Lower ball joint-to-knuckle – 116 ft. lbs.
    Tie rod end-to-knuckle – 22–29 ft. lbs.

4WD VEHICLES

1. Raise and support the vehicle safely. Remove the tire and wheel assembly.
2. Remove the locking hub assembly.
3. Remove the brake caliper and the mount without disconnecting the fluid line. Support the caliper out of the way.
4. Disconnect the stabilizer bar and shock absorber from the lower control arm.
5. Disconnect the tie rod end from the steering knuckle.
6. Remove the circlip and spacer from the hub end of the axle shaft.
7. Support the lower control arm. Using a puller, remove the hub and rotor assembly from the steering knuckle.
8. Remove the upper and lower ball joint cotter pins and nuts.
9. Separate the ball joints from the control arms.
10. Remove the dust shield. Remove the steering knuckle.

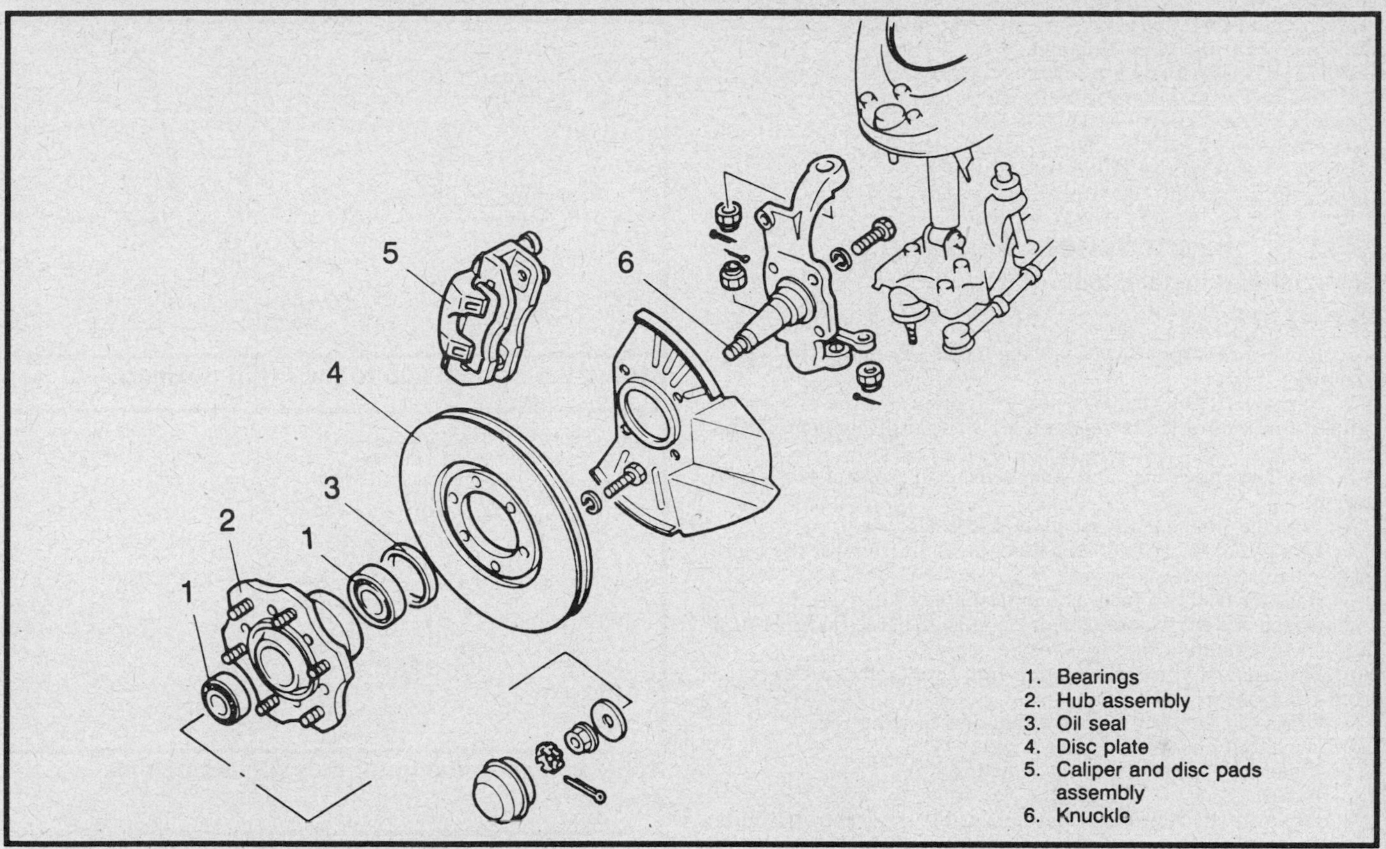

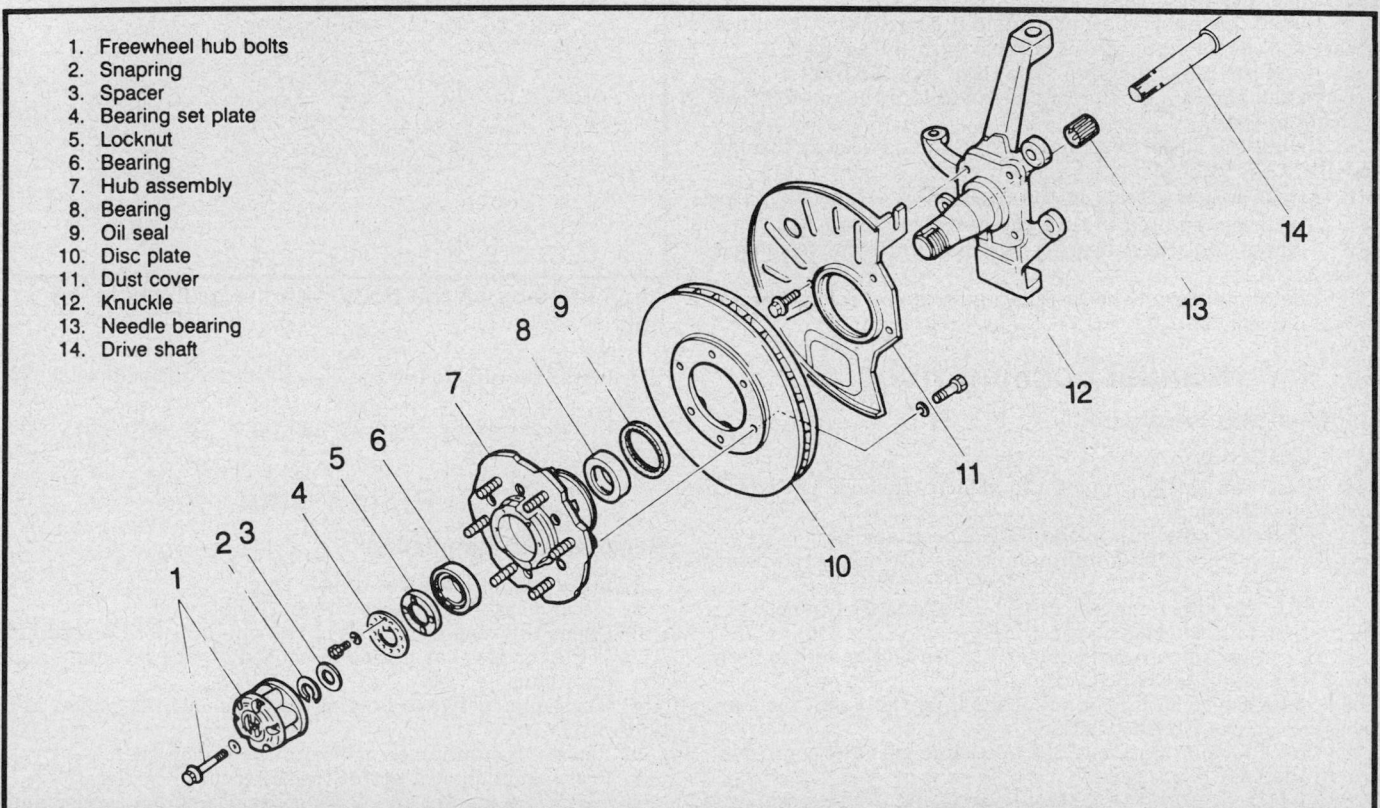

1. Bearings
2. Hub assembly
3. Oil seal
4. Disc plate
5. Caliper and disc pads assembly
6. Knuckle

Front hub and rotor assembly — 2WD vehicles

1. Freewheel hub bolts
2. Snapring
3. Spacer
4. Bearing set plate
5. Locknut
6. Bearing
7. Hub assembly
8. Bearing
9. Oil seal
10. Disc plate
11. Dust cover
12. Knuckle
13. Needle bearing
14. Drive shaft

Front hub and rotor assembly — 4WD vehicles

11. Installation is the reverse of the removal procedure. Adjust the wheel bearing when finished.

12. Observe the following torques during installation:
Upper ball joint nut—22–38 ft. lbs.
Lower ball joint nut—87–115 ft. lbs.
Tie rod nut—23–43 ft. lbs.
Brake caliper mount bolts—65–80 ft. lbs.
Locking hub bolts—22–25 ft. lbs.

Front Wheel Bearings

Removal and Installation

4WD VEHICLES

1. Raise and support the vehicle safely. Remove the wheel assembly.

2. Remove the locking hub assembly. Remove the disc brake caliper and mount from the spindle, without disconnecting the brake line.

3. Remove the circlip and spacer from in front of the wheel bearing.

4. Remove the bearing set plate and set screw.

5. Using tool 49 S231 635 or its equivalent, remove the bearing lock nut counterclockwise.

6. Remove the hub from the axle shaft.

7. Check the hub for cracks or damage. Check the inner and outer bearings and races for wear.

8. Matchmark the rotor to the hub and, remove the rotor from the hub.

9. Drive out the inner grease seal and bearing race.

10. Drive out the outer bearing race.

11. Clean and inspect the inside of the hub.

To install:

12. Drive in the inner and outer bearing races into the hub. Make sure that they are fully seated in the hub.

13. Thoroughly pack the new wheel bearings in high temperature wheel bearing grease.

14. Install the inner wheel bearing in the hub. Drive the inner grease seal in the hub until it is flush with the surface.

15. Align the matchmarks on the rotor and the hub.

16. Install the hub on the spindle and place the outer wheel bearing in the hub.

17. Install the wheel bearing lock nut and adjust the turning torque of the hub.

18. Attach a spring scale to the wheel stud on the hub. The frictional force required to turn the hub should be 1.3–2.6 lbs.

19. Tighten the wheel bearing lock nut until the reading is correct.

20. The remainder of the installation is the reverse of the removal procedure.

Manual Locking Hubs

Removal and Installation

4WD VEHICLES

1. Raise and safely support the vehicle. Remove the wheel and tire assemblies.

2. Set the locking hub in the **FREE** position.

3. Remove the locking hub mounting bolts and remove the locking hub.

4. With the hub removed, install 2 bolts and nuts opposite each other to hold the hub together.

5. Check for smooth operation of the control handle in both the **FREE** and **LOCK** positions.

6. Check for smooth rotation of the inner hub with the control lever in the **FREE** position.

7. Check for no rotation of the inner hub with the control lever in the **LOCK** position.

8. To install, place the control lever in the **FREE** position.

9. Lightly grease the inner splines of the hub.

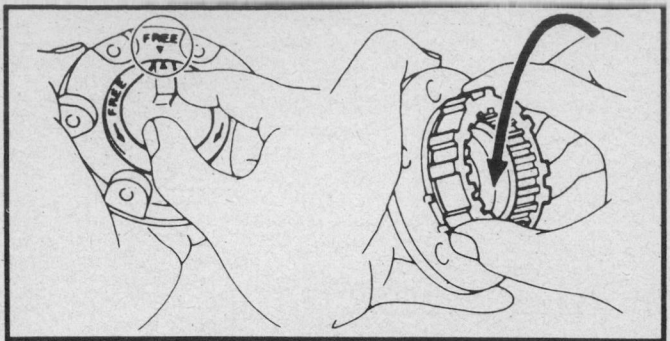

Setting the manual hub to the FREE position

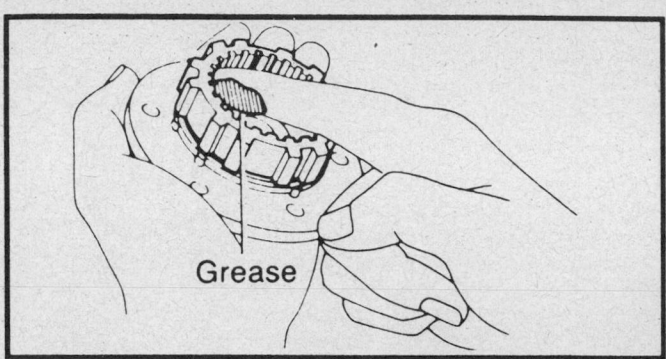

Apply grease to the inner hub splines before assembly

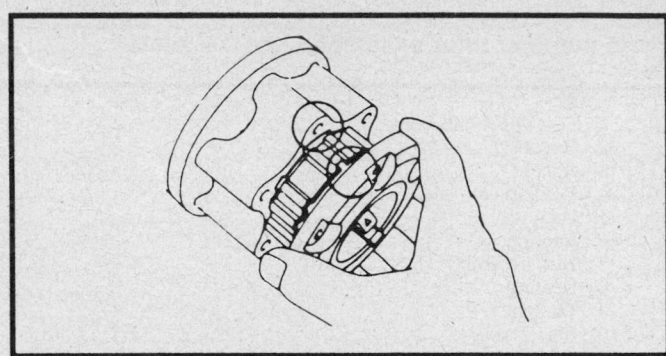

Align the tabs on the body with the grooves in the hub

10. Install the hub on the vehicle and torque the bolts to 22–25 ft. lbs.

11. Install the wheel assembly and check the operation of the hub.

Pinion Seal

Removal and Installation

1. Raise and support the vehicle safely.

2. Matchmark and remove the driveshaft.

3. Check the turning torque of the pinion before proceding. This is the torque that must be reached during installation of the pinion nut.

4. Using pinion flange holding tool, remove the pinion nut and washer.

5. Remove the pinion flange from the pinion gear.

6. Pry the pinion seal out of the differential carrier.

7. Clean and inspect the sealing surface of the carrier and flange.

8. Using a seal driver, drive the new seal into the carrier until the flange on the seal is flush with the carrier.

9. With the seal installed, the pinion bearing preload must be set.

10. Tighten the pinion nut while holding the flange, until the turning torque is the same as before removal of the nut.

11. Align the matchmarks and install the driveshaft.

12. Check the level of the differential lubricant when finished.

Differential Carrier

Removal and Installation

FRONT

1. Raise and support the vehicle safely. Remove the wheel and tire assemblies.

2. Remove the engine undercover. Drain the differential oil.

3. Matchmark and remove the front driveshaft.

4. Remove both axle shafts from the differential.

5. Remove the differential to housing mounting nuts and remove the differential.

6. Clean and inspect the sealing surfaces of the differential and housing.

7. Install the differential in the housing and torque the nuts to 17–20 ft. lbs.

8. The remainder of the installation is the reverse of the removal procedure.

9. Fill the differential to the proper level with SAE 80W–90 oil when finished.

REAR

1. Raise and support the vehicle safely. Remove the tire and wheel assemblies.

2. Drain the differential fluid. Install the plug after all of the fluid has drained.

3. Remove the axle shafts.

4. Matchmark and remove the driveshaft.

5. Remove the carrier to differential housing bolts and remove the carrier assembly from the housing.

To install:

6. Clean the carrier and axle housing mating surfaces.

7. If the differential originally used a gasket between the carrier and the differential housing, replace the gasket. If the unit had no gasket, apply a thin film of oil-resistant silicone sealer to the mating surfaces of both the carrier and the housing and al-

low the sealer to set according to the manufacturer's instructions.

8. Place the carrier assembly into the housing and install the carrier to housing bolts. Torque the bolts to 12–17 ft. lbs.

9. Install the axle shafts. Align the matchmarks and install the driveshaft.

10. Install the brake drums and wheel assemblies.

11. Fill the differential with the proper amount of SAE 80W–90 fluid.

Axle Housing

Removal and Installation

FRONT

1. Raise and safely support the vehicle. Remove the tire and wheel assemblies.

2. Remove the engine under cover. Drain the differential oil.

3. Matchmark and remove the front driveshaft.

4. Matchmark and disconnect the right side axle shaft from the differential.

5. Support the axle housing.

6. Remove the sub-frame mounting bolts and allow the sub-frame to hang down.

7. Remove the axle housing mounting bolts and remove the axle housing from the vehicle.

8. Installation is the reverse of the removal procedure.

9. Observe the following torques during installation:
Sub-frame bolts—59–75 ft. lbs.
Axle housing mounting bolts—41–59 ft. lbs.
Driveshaft bolts—36–43 ft. lbs.

REAR

1. Raise and support the vehicle safely. Remove the tire and wheel assemblies.

2. Disconnect the brake fluid line at the junction.

3. Disconnect the shock absorbers from the lower mounts.

4. Matchmark and remove the driveshaft.

5. Remove the lower spring plate nuts and washers.

6. Remove the U-bolts from the spring plates.

7. Remove the axle housing from the vehicle.

8. Installation is the reverse of the removal procedure.

9. Torque the spring plate nuts to 88–100 ft. lbs. on 4WD vehicles and to 47–58 ft. lbs. on 2WD vehicles.

10. Torque the lower shock absorber bolts to 47–58 ft. lbs. for all models.

11. Bleed the brake system when finished.

STEERING

Steering Wheel

Removal and Installation

1. Disconnect the battery ground.

2. Pull the steering wheel pad straight up to remove it, then remove the horn button and contact.

3. Remove the horn contact spring.

4. Matchmark the steering wheel and shaft.

5. Remove the wheel attaching nut and remove the wheel with a steering wheel puller.

6. Installation is the reverse of removal. Align the marks and tighten the nut to 35 ft. lbs.

Manual Steering Gear

Removal and Installation

1. Raise and support the vehicle safely.

2. Remove the pinch bolt securing the wormshaft to the steering shaft coupling.

3. Remove the cotter pin and nut securing the pitman arm to the center link and separate the pitman arm from the center link.

4. Remove the steering gear mounting bolts and remove the steering gear from the frame.

5. If removing pitman arm from the sector shaft, matchmark their positions in relation to each other.

6. Installation is the reverse of the removal procedure. Observe the following torques during installation:

Steering gear-to-frame—40 ft. lbs.

Wormshaft-to-steering shaft yoke—28 ft. lbs.

Pitman arm-to-sector shaft—139 ft. lbs.

Pitman arm-to-center link—30 ft. lbs.

Power Steering Gear

Removal and Installation

B2000, B2200 AND B2600

1. Raise and support the vehicle safely.

2. Remove the pinch bolt securing the wormshaft to the steering shaft coupling.

3. Remove the cotter pin and nut securing the pitman arm to the center link and separate the pitman arm from the center link.

4. Disconnect the fluid lines from the gear and allow the fluid to drain.

5. Remove the steering gear mounting bolts and remove the steering gear from the frame.

6. If removing pitman arm from the sector shaft, matchmark their positions in relation to each other.

7. Installation is the reverse of the removal procedure. Observe the following torques during installation:

Steering gear-to-frame—40 ft. lbs.

Wormshaft-to-steering shaft yoke—28 ft. lbs.

Pitman arm-to-sector shaft—139 ft. lbs.

Pitman arm-to-center link—30 ft. lbs.

8. Bleed the steering system.

MPV

1. Raise and safely support the vehicle.

2. Remove the tire and wheel assembly.

3. Place a drain pan under the steering gear hose connections.

4. Loosen the tie rod end ball stud nut and separate the tie rod end from the knuckle arm with a separator tool. Disconnect the ends.

5. Remove the steering shaft-to-pinion shaft coupling bolt.

6. Matchmark the pressure line connection and disconnect it.

7. Disconnect the return line.

8. On vehicles with automatic transmission, remove the change counter assembly from the protector plate mounting bolt.

9. Support the steering gear assembly with a floor jack under the lower bracket.

10. Remove the steering gear-to-frame bracket mounting bolts.

11. Lower the steering gear and linkage assembly from the vehicle.

12. Remove the steering gear-to-lower bracket clamp bolts, remove the clamps and rubber isolators.

To install:

13. Install the steering gear-to-lower bracket clamp bolts, clamps and rubber isolators. When tightening the bolts, tighten them in this order:

driver's side front

passenger's side front

driver's side rear

passenger's side rear

Torque the bolts to 69 ft. lbs.

14. Raise the steering gear and linkage assembly into position.

15. Install the steering gear-to-frame bracket mounting bolts. Torque the bolts to 69 ft. lbs.

16. Remove the floor jack.

17. On vehicles with automatic transmission, install the change counter assembly from the protector plate mounting bolt.

18. Connect the return line.

19. Connect the pressure line and torque it to 35 ft. lbs.

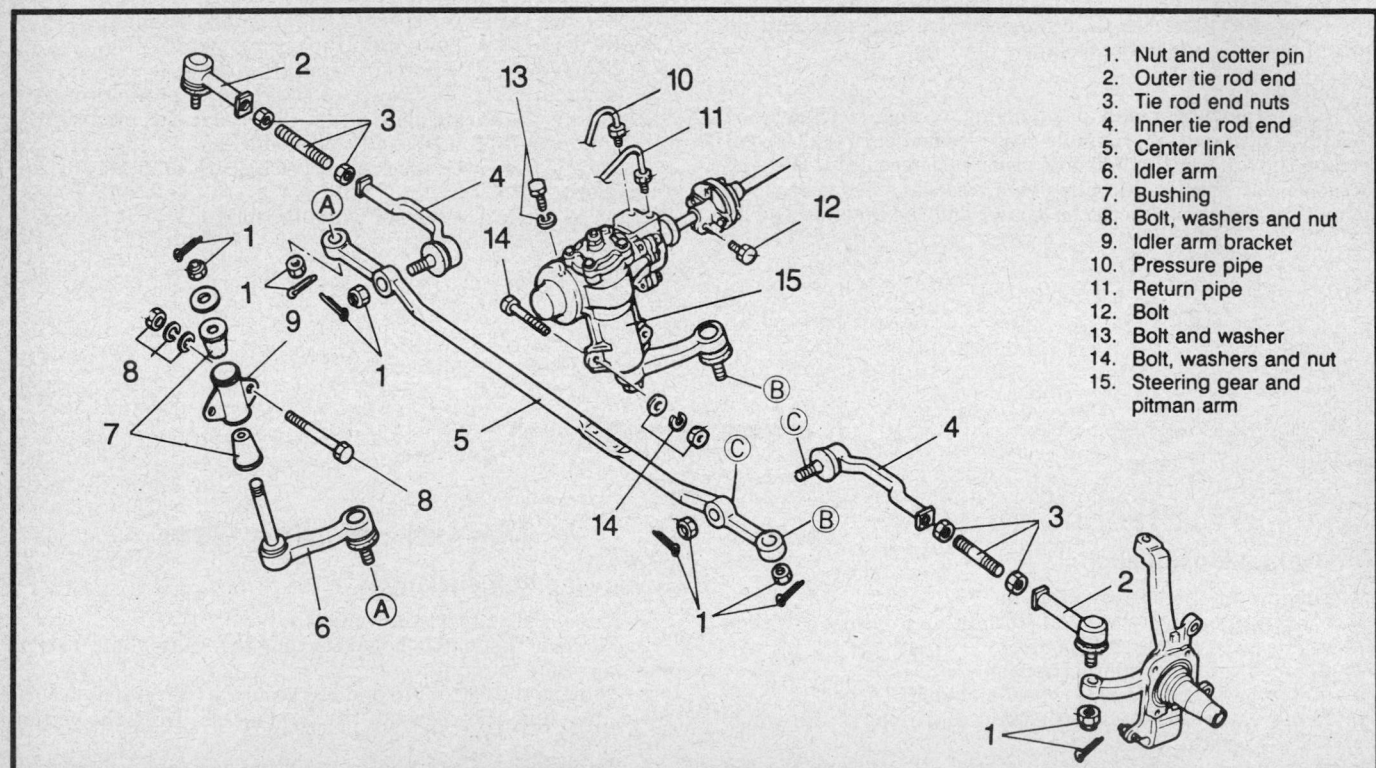

1. Nut and cotter pin
2. Outer tie rod end
3. Tie rod end nuts
4. Inner tie rod end
5. Center link
6. Idler arm
7. Bushing
8. Bolt, washers and nut
9. Idler arm bracket
10. Pressure pipe
11. Return pipe
12. Bolt
13. Bolt and washer
14. Bolt, washers and nut
15. Steering gear and pitman arm

Steering gear and linkage—manual steering

1. Cotter pin
2. Nut
3. Tie rod end and steering knuckle
4. Fixing bolt
5. Pressure pipe
6. Return hose
7. Steering bracket mounting bolts
8. Steering gear and linkage bracket assembly
9. Mounting bracket bolts
10. Mounting bracket and rubbers
11. Steering gear and linkage
12. Steering brackets

Power steering rack and linkage—MPV

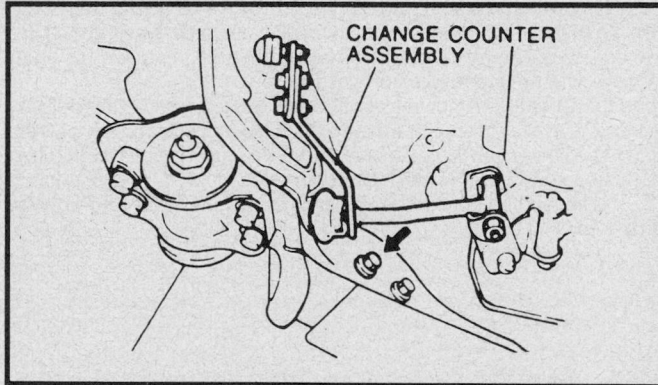

Removing the change counter assembly—MPV

20. Install the steering shaft-to-pinion shaft coupling bolt. Torque the bolt to 20 ft. lbs.
21. Connect the ends. Tighten the ball stud nuts to 58 ft. lbs. Always use a new cotter pin on the ball stud nut. Always advance the nut to align the cotter pin hole. Never back it off.
22. Install the wheels.
23. Fill the steering system and bleed it of air.

Power Steering Pump

Removal and Installation

EXCEPT MPV

1. Disconnect the negative battery cable.
2. Remove the power steering pump pulley nut.
3. Loosen the drive belt tensioner pulley and remove the belt.
4. Remove the pulley from the pump.
5. Disconnect and plug the fluid lines at the pump.
6. Remove the pump bracket bolts and remove the pump from the vehicle.

7. Installation is the reverse of the removal procedure. Adjust the drive belt tension. Fill and bleed the power steering system when finished.

MPV

1. Disconnect the negative battery cable. Loosen the idler pulley locknut.
2. Loosen the pump adjusting bolt.
3. Remove the drive belt.
4. Remove the pump pulley nut. Using a puller, remove the pulley.
5. Disconnect the pressure switch wiring connector.
6. Place a drain pan under the pump.
7. Matchmark the pressure line connection and disconnect it.
8. Remove the pressure line bracket bolt.
9. Disconnect the return line.
10. Remove the pump-to-bracket bolts and lift out the pump.
11. Installation is the reverse of removal. Observe the following torques:
   Mounting bolts to 34 ft. lbs.
   Pressure line connection to 35 ft. lbs.
   Pressure line bracket bolt to 17 ft. lbs.
   Pulley bolt to 43 ft. lbs.
   Adjusting bolt to 35 ft. lbs.
   Idler pulley locknut to 38 ft. lbs.

System Bleeding

1. Check and fill the power steering fluid level.
2. Start and run the engine at idle. Turn the steering wheel lock-to-lock, several times. Turn the engine off, check and fill the fluid.
3. Start and run the engine at idle and turn the wheel lock-to-lock several times again.
4. Place the wheels in the straight ahead position and shut off the engine.
5. Allow the fluid to settle in the system for a few minutes and check the fluid level again.
6. Check for the presence of foaming in the fluid. Repeat the

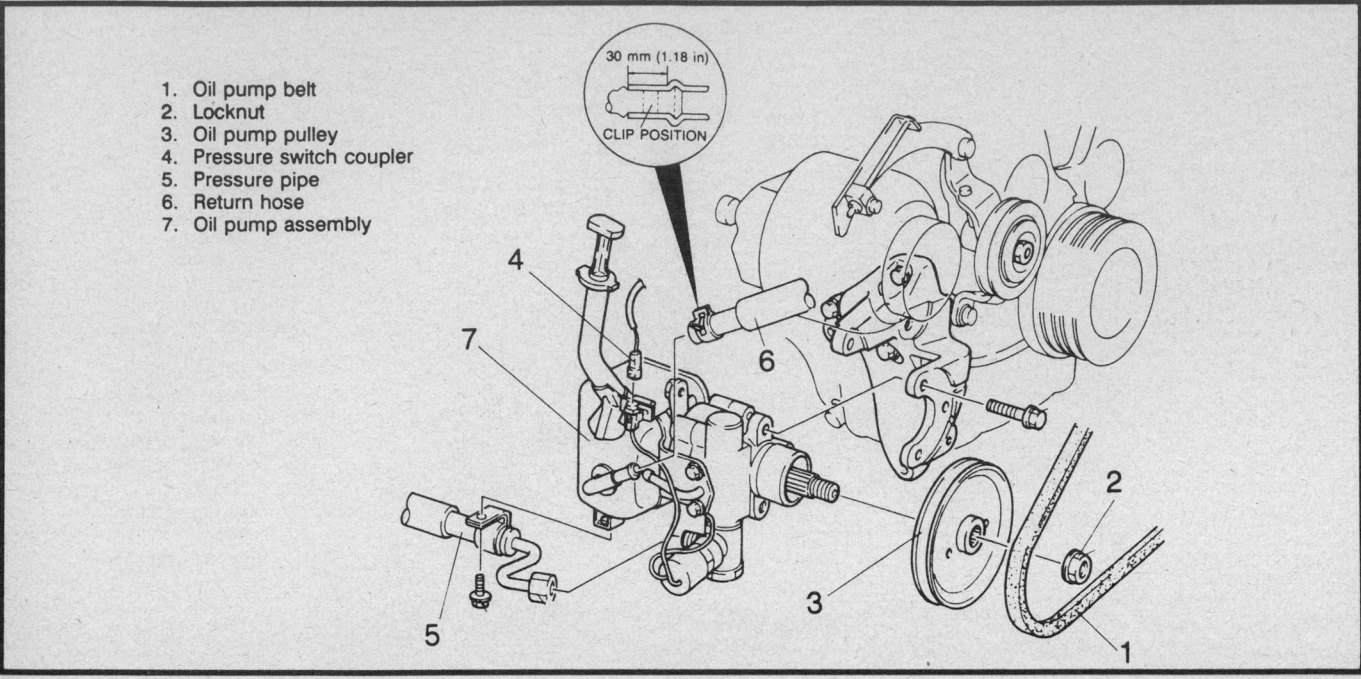

1. Oil pump belt
2. Locknut
3. Oil pump pulley
4. Pressure switch coupler
5. Pressure pipe
6. Return hose
7. Oil pump assembly

30 mm (1.18 in)

CLIP POSITION

Power steering pump mounting

procedure until the fluid is clear and remains at the same level, with the engine off.

Tie Rod Ends

Removal and Installation

1. Raise and supporet the vehicle safely. Remove the tire and wheel assembly. Loosen the tie rod jam nuts.
2. Remove and discard the cotter pin from the ball socket end and remove the nut.
3. Disconnect the ball socket stud from the center link. Remove the stud from the kingpin steering arm.

4. Unscrew the tie rod end from the threaded sleeve, counting the number of threads until it is off. The threads may be left or right hand threads. Tighten the jam nuts to 58 ft. lbs.
5. To install, lightly coat the threads with grease and turn the new end in as many turns as were required to remove it. This will give the approximate correct toe-in.
6. Install the ball socket studs into center link and kingpin steering arm. Tighten the nuts to 30 ft. lbs. Install a new cotter pin. If the cotter pin hole does not line up, tighten the nut to install the cotter pin. Never loosen the nut.
7. Tighten the tie rod clamps or jam nuts. Check and adjust the toe in.

BRAKES

For all brake system repair and service procedures not covered below, please refer to "Brakes" in the Unit Repair section.

Master Cylinder

Removal and Installation

1. Disconnect the negative battery cable. Disconnect and plug the brakes lines at the master cylinder.
2. Disconnect the fluid level sensor coupling.
3. Remove the master cylinder mounting bolts and remove the master cylinder from the power booster.
4. Installation is the reverse of the removal procedure. Torque the mounting nuts to 15 ft. lbs.

Proportioning Bypass Valve

Removal and Installation

1. Raise and safely support the vehicle.

2. Disconnect and cap the brake lines at the valve.
3. Remove the attaching bolts. Remove the valve.
4. Installation is the reverse of removal.
5. Bleed the system.

Load Sensing Proportioning Valve

Removal and Installation
MPV

1. Raise and support the vehicle safely.
2. Remove the nut attaching the bracket to the axle housing.
3. Disconnect the brake lines at the valve.
4. Remove the valve attaching bolts. Remove the valve.
5. Installation is the reverse of removal. Install the valve first, then the axle bracket.
6. When installing the axle bracket, position it so that the length of the spring, measured between the 2 collars, is 150.5mm, with no extra load in the vehicle.
7. Bleed the brake system.

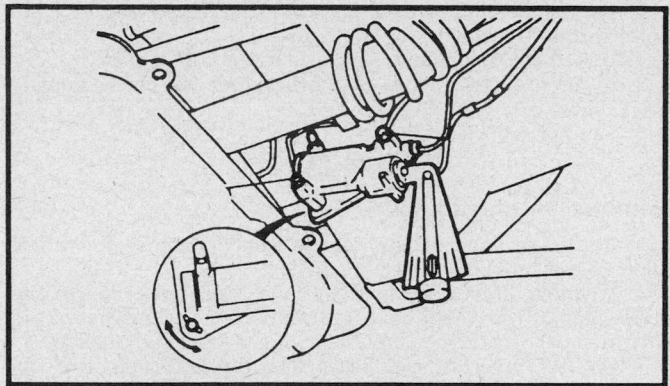

Checking the load sensing G-valve

Load Sensing G-Valve

Removal and Installation

1. Raise and support the vehicle safely.
2. Disconnect and cap the brake lines.
3. Remove the valve mounting bolts. Remove the valve.
4. Install the new valve, tighten the bolts, connect the brake lines and bleed the system.
5. Adjust the inclination angle of the valve:
   a. Place the vehicle on level ground.
   b. Make sure that there is no cargo in the vehicle.
   c. Fill the tires to the recommended inflation pressure.
   d. Attach angle gauge 49 U043 003, or equivalent, to the valve. The correct angle should be 7° ± 1½° for the B-series; 8½° ± 1° for the MPV. If not:
   e. Loosen the mounting bolts and move the valve until the angle is correct.
   f. Tighten the bolts.

Power Brake Booster

Removal and Installation
EXCEPT MPV

1. Disconnect the negative battery cable. Disconnect and plug the master cylinder fluid lines and remove the master cylinder from the booster.
2. Disconnect the booster pushrod at the brake pedal.
3. Remove the power brake booster mounting nuts and remove the booster from the firewall.
4. Installation is the reverse of the removal procedure.
5. Check the clearance between the master cylinder piston and the power booster pushrod. Clearance should be 0.004–0.020 in. If not, adjust the clearance at the pushrod.
6. Tighten the power brake booster mounting nuts to 17 ft. lbs.
7. Bleed the brake system when finished.

MPV

1. Disconnect the negative battery cable. Remove the wiper arms.
2. Remove the drive link nuts from the top of the cowl.
3. Working under the hood, disconnect the battery ground cable.
4. Remove the wiper motor and linkage mounting bolts and lift out the assembly.
5. Remove the master cylinder.
6. Disconnect the pushrod at the pedal.
7. Disconnect the vacuum line at the booster.
9. Unbolt and remove the power booster from the firewall.

To install:
10. Check the clearance between the master cylinder piston and the power booster pushrod. Clearance should be zero, but the piston should not depress the pushrod. Adjust the clearance at the pushrod.

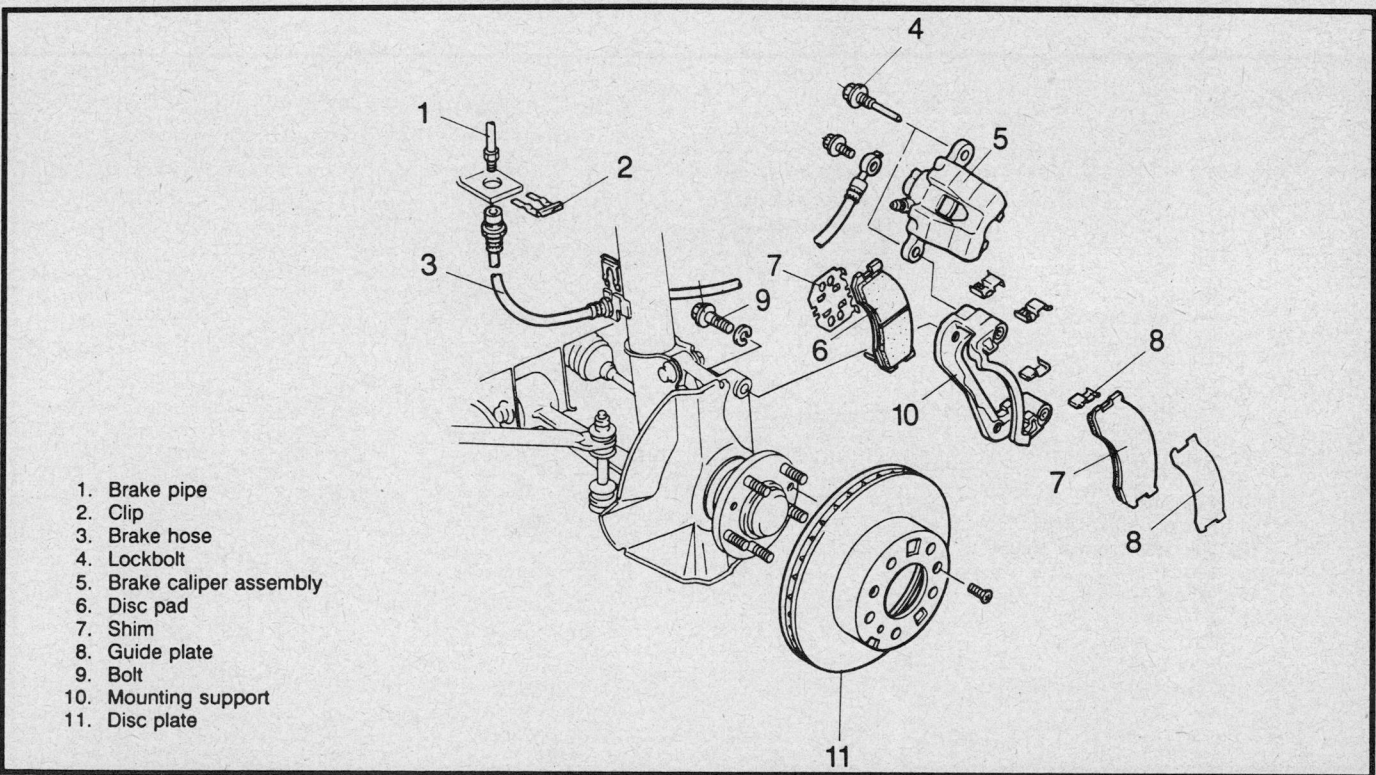

1. Brake pipe
2. Clip
3. Brake hose
4. Lockbolt
5. Brake caliper assembly
6. Disc pad
7. Shim
8. Guide plate
9. Bolt
10. Mounting support
11. Disc plate

Disc brake assembly—typical

11. Position a new mounting gasket, coated with sealant, on the firewall.

12. Position the vacuum unit on the firewall and install the nuts. Torque the mounting nuts to 19 ft. lbs.

13. Connect the pushrod at the pedal.

14. Connect the vacuum line.

15. Install the master cylinder.

16. Install the wiper motor and linkage. When installing the wiper arms, make sure that the at-rest position gives a gap of 30mm between the blade tips and the lower windshield moulding.

17. Bleed the brakes.

Brake Caliper

Removal and Installation

1. Raise and support the vehicle safely. Remove the wheel and tire assembly.

2. Disconnect and plug the brake fluid line at the caliper.

3. Remove the bottom lock pin bolt from the caliper and pivot the caliper upwards.

4. Remove the brake pads and shims from the caliper.

5. Remove the upper caliper pivot bolt and remove the caliper from the mount.

6. Installation is the reverse of the removal procedure. Bleed the brake caliper when finished.

Disc Brake Pads

Removal and Installation

1. Raise and support the vehicle safely. Remove the wheel and tire assembly.

2. Remove the bottom lock pin bolt fom the caliper and pivot the caliper upwards.

3. Remove the brake pads and shims.

4. Push the caliper piston inwards until it is fully seated.

5. Install the brake pads and shims in the caliper.

6. Install the caliper to the mount and install the lock pin bolt. Torque the bolt to 23–30 ft. lbs.

7. Install the wheel assembly and lower the vehicle.

8. Pump the brake pedal until pressure is felt before moving the vehicle.

Brake Rotor

Removal and Installation

1. Raise and support the vehicle safely. Remove the wheel and tire assembly.

2. Without disconnecting the brake fluid line, remove the brake caliper from the mount and support the caliper out of the way. Remove the caliper mount from the steering knuckle.

3. On 2WD vehicles, remove the dust cap, cotter pin, nut and washer from the hub. On 4WD vehicles, remove the locking hub, spacer, bearing plate and lock nut.

4. Remove the brake rotor assembly from the vehicle.

5. If only the rotor is being replaced, remove the hub to rotor mounting bolts and install the hub on the new brake rotor.

6. Installation is the reverse of the removal procedure.

7. Adjust the wheel bearings when finished.

Brake Drums

Removal and Installation

1. Loosen the lug nuts on the rear wheels.

2. Raise and safely support the vehicle.

3. Remove the lug nuts and the rear tire and wheel.

4. Be sure that the parking brake is fully released.

5. Remove the bolts or screws which secure the drum to the rear axle shaft flange or center locknut.

NOTE: If the drum will not come off easily, screw the drum securing bolts into the 2 tapped holes in the drum. Tighten the bolts evenly in order to force the drum away from the flange.

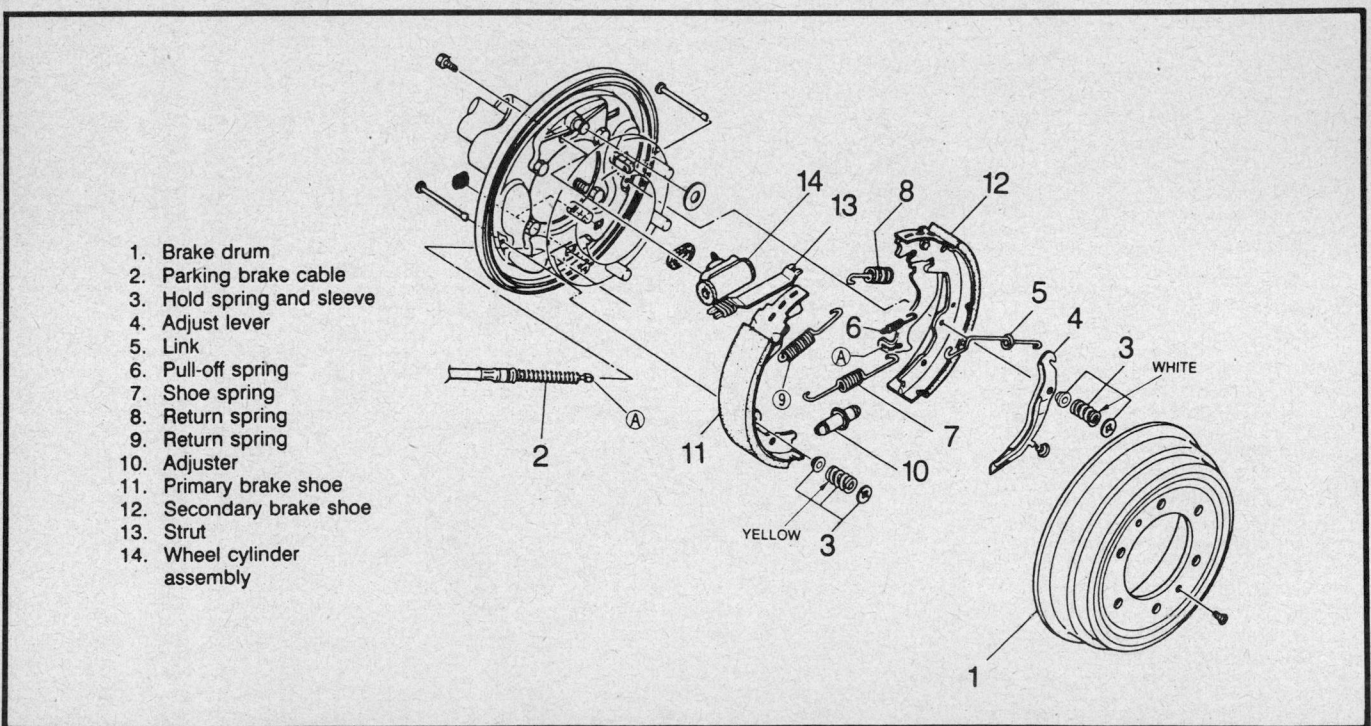

1. Brake drum
2. Parking brake cable
3. Hold spring and sleeve
4. Adjust lever
5. Link
6. Pull-off spring
7. Shoe spring
8. Return spring
9. Return spring
10. Adjuster
11. Primary brake shoe
12. Secondary brake shoe
13. Strut
14. Wheel cylinder assembly

Drum brake assembly—typical

6. Remove the brake drum.

7. Installation is the reverse of the removal procedure.

8. Adjust the shoes after installation is completed.

Brake Shoes

Removal and Installation
EXCEPT MPV

1. Raise and safely support the vehicle. Remove the tire and wheel assembly. Remove the brake drum. Make sure that the parking brake is fully released.

2. Remove the return springs from the upper side of the shoe using a brake spring removal tool.

3. Remove the return springs from the lower side of the shoes.

4. Remove the shoe retaining spring by compressing the retaining spring while turning the pin 90 degrees.

5. Withdraw the primary shoes and the parking brake link.

6. Disengage the parking brake lever from the secondary shoes by unfastening its retaining clip.

7. Remove the secondary shoe.

8. Inspect the linings and replace them if they are badly burned or worn.

9. Replace the linings if they are saturated with oil or grease.

To install:

10. Lubricate the threads of the adjusting screw, the sliding surfaces of the shoes, and the backing plate flanges with a small quantity of grease.

11. Install the eye of the parking brake cable through the parking brake lever which has previously been installed on the secondary shoe and secured with its retaining clip.

12. Fit the link between the shoes.

13. Engage the shoes with the slots in the anchor (adjusting screw) and the wheel cylinder.

14. Fasten the shoes to the backing plate with the retaining springs and pins.

15. Install the shoe return springs with the tool used during removal.

16. Install the drums and adjust the shoes.

17. Install the tire and wheel assembly.

MPV

1. Raise and safely support the vehicle.

2. Remove the tire and wheel assembly. Remove the brake drum.

3. Disconnect the parking brake cable. Remove the hold-down spring assemblies.

4. Remove the self-adjusting lever. Remove the lever link.

5. Remove the pull-off spring.

6. Remove the lower shoe-to-shoe spring. Remove the 2 upper return springs.

7. Remove the star wheel adjuster. Remove the brake shoes and strut.

8. Remove the parking brake cable lever.

9. Inspect the shoes for cracks, heat checking or contamination by oil or grease.

10. Lubricated the threads of the starwheel with lithium based or silicone based grease. Apply a small dab of lithium or silicone based grease to the pads on which the brake shoes ride.

To install:

11. Position the brake shoes on the backing plate. Connect the parking brake.

12. Install the hold-down spring assemblies. Install the strut and star-wheel adjuster.

13. Install the 2 upper return springs. Install the lower spring.

14. Install the pull-off spring. Install the lever link and self-adjusting lever.

15. Install the brake drum.

16. Working through the hole in the backing plate, turn the star-wheel screw with a brake adjusting spoon until the wheel is locked, that is, it can't be turned by hand.

17. Back off the adjuster 8–10 clicks, or until the wheel is free to rotate.

NOTE: The adjustment should be the same on both wheels.

18. Adjust the parking brake.

19. Operate the brake pedal a few times. If the brakes feel at all spongey, bleed the system.

Wheel Cylinder

Removal and Installation

1. Raise and support the vehicle safely. Remove the tire and wheel assembly.

2. Remove the brake drum. Inspect the brake components for signs of damage from leaking brake fluid. Replace if necessary.

3. Disconnect and plug the brake line at the wheel cylinder.

4. Remove the 2 wheel cylinder mounting bolts and remove the wheel cylinder from the backing plate by spreading the brake shoes apart. If necessary, remove the brake shoes from the vehicle.

5. Spread the brake shoes apart and install the new wheel cylinder on the backing plate.

6. Torque the mounting bolts to 7–9 ft. lbs.

7. Install the brake line in the wheel cylinder and torque the flare nut to 10–13 ft. lbs.

8. Install the brake drum and wheel assembly. Bleed the wheel cylinder.

9. Check the system operation before moving the vehicle.

Parking Brake Cable

Removal and Installation
FRONT

1. Raise and support the vehicle safely.

2. Remove the front cable adjusting nut.

3. Separate the front cable from the equalizer and remove the jam nut.

4. Remove the return spring and boot from the cable housing.

5. Pull the lower cable housing forward and out of the slotted frame bracket. Slip the cable shaft sideways through the slot until the cable and housing are free of the bracket.

6. Disengage the upper cable connector from the brake lever by removing the clevis pin and retainer.

7. Remove the upper cable housing retaining clip and pull the upper cable and housing from the slotted bracket on the firewall.

8. Push the upper cable, cable housing and dust shield grommet through the firewall opening and into the engine compartment.

9. Remove the cable and housing.

10. Installation is the reverse of the removal procedure. Adjust the parking brake cable when finished.

REAR

1. Raise and support the vehicle safely.

2. Remove the pin and disconnect the equalizer from the clevis.

3. Disconnect the right side cable from the left cable.

4. Remove the rear wheels, brake drums and brake shoes.

5. Disengage the cables from the brake shoe levers.

6. Remove the cable housing retainer from the backing plate.

7. Pull the return spring to release the retainer plate from the end of the housing.

8. Loosen the cable housing to frame bracket locknut and re-

move the forward end of the cable housing from the frame bracket.

9. Remove the cable housing retaining clip bolts.

10. Disengage the cable housing to frame tension springs and pull the cable out of the backing plate.

11. Installation is the reverse of the removal procedure.

12. Adjust the cable when finished.

Adjustment

1. Adjust the rear brake shoes before attempting to adjust the parking brake.

2. Use the adjusting nut to adjust the length of the front cable so that the rear brakes are locked when the parking brake lever is pulled out 11–13 notches.

3. After adjustment, apply the parking brake several times. Release the parking brake and make sure that the rear wheels rotate without dragging. If they drag, repeat the adjustment.

NOTE: If the parking brake cable is replaced, prestretch it by applying the parking brake hard 3 or 4 times before attempting adjustment.

FRONT SUSPENSION

Shock Absorbers

Removal and Installation

EXCEPT MPV

1. Raise and support the vehicle safely. Remove the tire and wheel assembly.

2. Remove the upper shock absorber mounting nut, washers and bushings.

3. Compress the shock absorber to a level under the upper control arm.

4. Remove the lower shock absorber mounting bolt and nut.

5. Remove the shock absorber from the vehicle.

6. Installation is the reverse of the removal procedure.

7. Torque the lower shock absorber bolt and nut to 40–59 ft. lbs.

8. Torque the upper shock absorber nut to 17–25 ft. lbs. or, until there is a of 7mm of thread protruding from the shock absorber threads.

MacPherson Strut

Removal and Installation

MPV

1. Raise and safely support the vehicle.

2. Remove the tire and wheel assembly.

3. Unclip the brake line from the strut.

4. Remove the lower strut bolts.

5. Remove the rubber cap from the upper end of the strut.

6. Remove the 4 upper end mounting nuts.

7. Remove the strut from the vehicle.

8. Installation is the reverse of removal.

9. The mounting block is installed at the upper end with the white mark on the block facing the front-inside direction.

10. Torque the lower mounting bolts to 85 ft. lbs.; the upper nuts to 25 ft. lbs.

Torsion Bar

Removal and Installation

4WD VEHICLES

1. Raise and support the vehicle safely. Remove the tire and wheel assembly.

2. Support the torsion bar. Matchmark the torsion bar anchor bolt to the torsion bar and remove the torsion bar anchor bolt.

3. Matchmark the torsion bar to the anchor plate and remove the anchor plate from the body. Remove the torsion bar to torque plate bolts. Remove the torsion bar from the plate.

4. Support the lower control arm and remove the lower ball

joint cotter pin and nut. Disconnect the shock absorber from the lower control arm.

5. Separate the lower ball joint from the steering knuckle.

6. Remove the front torsion bar to lower control arm bolt. Remove the torsion bar.

7. Installation is the reverse of the removal procedure. Alignment the matchmarks made during the removal.

8. Torque the ball joint nut to 87–115 ft. lbs. and the torsion bar anchor plate to 55–69 ft. lbs. Torque the shock absorber bolt to 40–59 ft. lbs.

9. Check and adjust the vehicle ride height if necessary, when finished.

Torsion Bar and Lower Control Arm

Removal and Installation

2WD VEHICLES EXCEPT MPV

1. Raise and support the vehicle safely, with the front suspension hanging freely.

2. Remove the tire and wheel assembly.

3. Remove the cotter pin and nut from the lower ball joint.

4. Remove the lower shock absorber mounting bolt.

5. Matchmark the anchor arm bolt and anchor swivel. Remove the bolt and swivel.

NOTE: The matchmarks made determine and are critical to, the vehicles ride height. Failure to do so, will result in having to set the vehicles ride height when finished.

6. Matchmark the torsion bar and anchor arm. Matchmark the torsion bar and torque plate.

7. Remove the anchor arm and torsion bar from the torque plate. Separate the anchor arm from the torsion bar.

8. Remove the torque plate.

9. Remove the lower control arm to frame bolt. Separate the lower arm from the frame bracket with bushing puller/installer 49 0727 575 or its equivalent.

10. Disconnect and remove the tension rod from the lower control arm.

NOTE: Do not change the position of the double nut at the rear of the tension rod bushing. It will affect the vehicles caster alignment.

11. Remove the stabilizer bar bolt, bushing, retainer and nut. Remove the stabilizer bar.

12. Separate the lower ball joint from the knuckle. Remove the lower control arm.

13. Inspect all parts for wear or damage. Replace any suspect parts. Using a spring scale and adapter 49 0180 510B or equivalent, check the ball joint preload. Pull scale reading should be

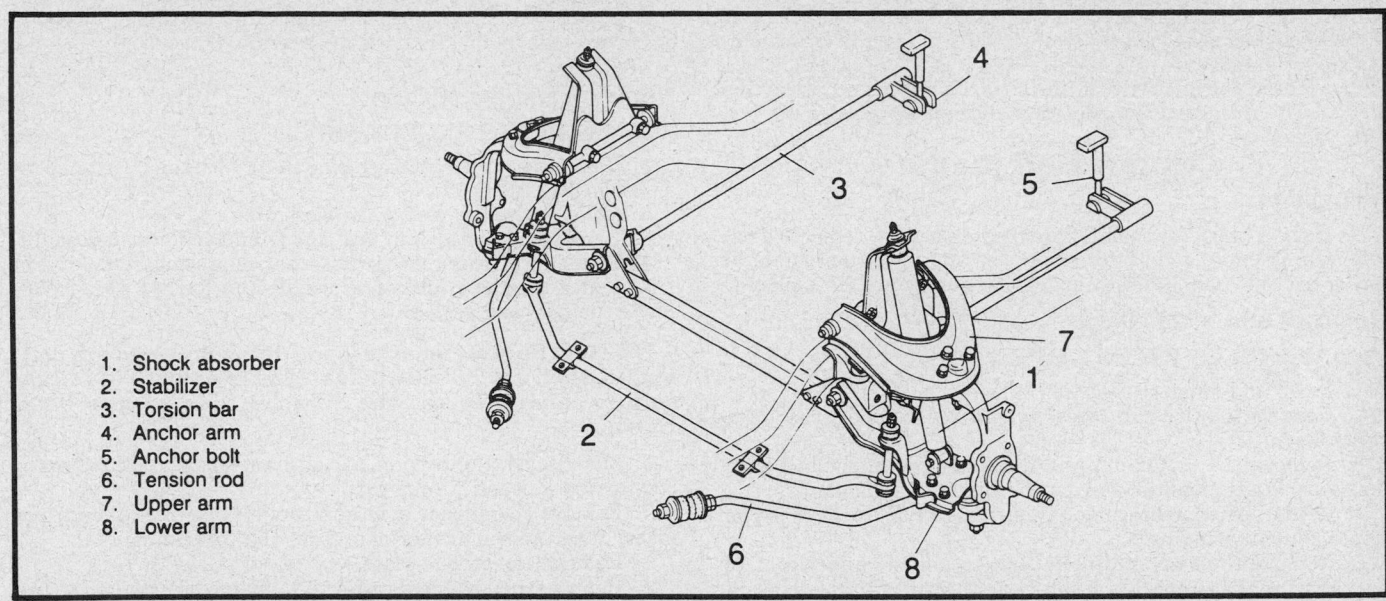

1. Shock absorber
2. Stabilizer
3. Torsion bar
4. Anchor arm
5. Anchor bolt
6. Tension rod
7. Upper arm
8. Lower arm

Front suspension assembly—B2000 and B2200

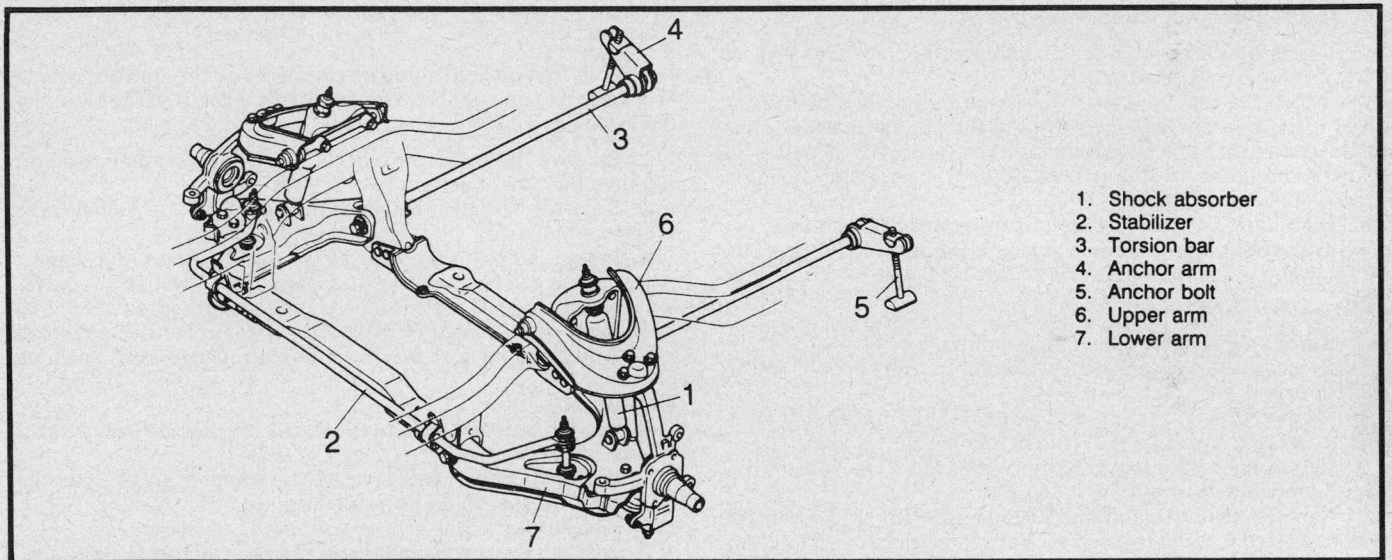

1. Shock absorber
2. Stabilizer
3. Torsion bar
4. Anchor arm
5. Anchor bolt
6. Upper arm
7. Lower arm

Front suspension assembly—B2600

39.6 lbs. or less. Measure the preload after first shaking the ball joint stud to make sure it is free.

14. Install the lower arm on the frame bracket and hand tighten the nut.

15. Install the lower ball joint on the knuckle and torque the nut to 115 ft. lbs. Install the cotter pin.

16. Tighten the lower arm to frame nut to 115 ft. lbs.

17. Position the torque plate and tighten the bolt to 68 ft. lbs.

18. Coat the splines on the torsion bar with grease. Check the ends of the torsion bar. The bars are marked L for left and R for right. Align the matchmarks and install the torsion bar in the torque plate.

19. Coat the splines on the torsion bar with grease. Align the matchmarks and install the anchor arm on the torsion bar.

20. Install the anchor bolt and swivel and tighten the bolt until the matchmarks are mated.

21. Install the tension rod. Torque the bushing end nut to 90 ft. lbs.; the lower arm end bolts to 85 ft. lbs.

22. Install the stabilizer bar. Torque the bolt to 19 ft. lbs.

23. Install the shock absorber bolt. Torque the bolt to 55–59 ft. lbs.

24. Install the wheel assembly and lower the vehicle to the ground.

25. Retorque the lower arm to frame bracket nut.

26. Check the front and rear tire pressures. Set the pressures to what are specified on the vehicle rating plate, except for P-metric radials. Set them at the maximum pressure shown on the side wall.

27. Measure the distance from the center of the wheel hub to the lip of the fender. This is the ride height. Proper ride height is obtained when the difference between the left and the right side is less than 10mm. Adjust the ride height by turning the anchor bolt.

NOTE: If the torsion bar anchor bolt was not matchmarked, the matchmarks were lost, or new, unmarked torsion bar is being installed, follow this procedure to obtain the correct ride height.

28. Install the anchor arm on the torsion bar so that there is 125mm between the lowest point on the arm and the crossmember directly above it.

29. Tighten the anchor bolt until the anchor arm contacts the swivel. Then, tighten the bolt an additional 45mm travel.

Upper Ball joints

Inspection

1. Inspect the dust seals. If cracked or brittle, replace them.
2. Check end play of both the upper and lower ball joints. If either exceeds 0.0039 in., it is defective and must be replaced.

Removal and Installation

2WD VEHICLES EXCEPT MPV

1. Raise and support the vehicle safely.
2. Remove the tire and wheel assemblies. Support the lower control arm.
3. Remove the cotter pin and nut from the upper ball joint and separate the ball joint from the upper control arm.
4. Remove the bushings and dust seals from the ends of the upper control arm shaft.
5. Remove the nuts and bolts that retain the upper control arm shaft to the support bracket. Note the number and location of the shims under the nuts.

NOTE: These shims must be installed in their exact locations for proper wheel alignment.

6. Check all parts for wear or damage. Replace any suspect parts.
7. Check the ball joint preload with a pull scale and adapter 49 0180 510B or equivalent. Move the ball joint stud a few times to make sure that it is free, then take the reading. The pull scale reading should be 40 lbs. or less. Replace if necessary, using a press.
8. Installation is the reverse of the removal procedure.
9. Torque the upper control arm shaft mounting bolts to 60–68 ft. lbs. and the ball joint nut to 30–37 ft. lbs.

4WD VEHICLES

1. Raise and support the vehicle safely.
2. Remove the tire and wheel assembly. Support the lower control arm.
3. Remove the cotter pin and nut from the upper ball joint and separate the ball joint from the upper control arm.
4. Remove the bushings and dust seals from the ends of the upper control arm shaft.
5. Remove the nuts and bolts that retain the upper control arm shaft to the support bracket. Note the number and location of the shims under the nuts.

NOTE: These shims must be installed in their exact locations for proper wheel alignment.

6. Check all parts for wear or damage. Replace any suspect parts.
7. Check the ball joint preload with a pull scale and adapter 49 0180 510B or its equivalent. Move the ball joint stud a few times to make sure that it is free, then take the reading. The pull scale reading should be 40 lbs. or less.
8. Remove the ball joint mounting bolts. Using a press, remove the upper ball joint from the control arm.
9. Installation is the reverse of the removal procedure.
10. Torque the upper control arm shaft mounting bolts to 60–68 ft. lbs. and the ball joint nut to 30–37 ft. lbs. Check the front end alignment if necessary.

Lower Ball Joints

Inspection

1. Inspect the dust seals. If cracked or brittle, replace them.

2. Check end play of both the upper and lower ball joints. If either exceeds 0.0039 in., it is defective.

Removal and Installation

2WD VEHICLES EXCEPT MPV

1. Raise and support the vehicle safely, with the front suspension hanging freely.
2. Remove the tire and wheel assembly.
3. Remove the cotter pin and nut from the lower ball joint.
4. Remove the lower shock absorber mounting bolt.
5. Matchmark the anchor arm bolt and anchor swivel. Remove the bolt and swivel.

NOTE: The matchmarks made determine and are critical to, the vehicles ride height. Failure to do so, will result in having to set the vehicles ride hieght when finished.

6. Matchmark the torsion bar and anchor arm. Matchmark the torsion bar and torque plate.
7. Remove the anchor arm and torsion bar from the torque plate. Separate the anchor arm from the torsion bar.
8. Remove the torque plate.
9. Remove the lower control arm to frame bolt. Separate the lower arm from the frame bracket with bushing puller/installer 49 0727 575 or its equivalent.
10. Disconnect and remove the tension rod from the lower control arm.

NOTE: Do not change the position of the double nut at the rear of the tension rod bushing. It will affect the vehicles caster alignment.

11. Remove the stabilizer bar bolt, bushing, retainer and nut. Remove the stabilizer bar.
12. Separate the lower ball joint from the knuckle. Remove the lower control arm.
13. Inspect all parts for wear or damage. Replace any suspect parts. Using a spring scale and adapter 49 0180 510B or equivalent, check the ball joint preload. Pull scale reading should be 39.6 lbs. or less. Measure the preload after first shaking the ball joint stud to make sure it is free. Replace if necessary, using a press.

To install:

14. Install the lower arm on the frame bracket and hand tighten the nut.
15. Install the lower ball joint on the knuckle and torque the nut to 115 ft. lbs. Install the cotter pin.
16. Tighten the lower arm to frame nut to 115 ft. lbs.
17. Position the torque plate and tighten the bolt to 68 ft. lbs.
18. Coat the splines on the torsion bar with grease. Check the ends of the torsion bar. The bars are marked **L** for left and **R** for right. Align the matchmarks and install the torsion bar in the torque plate.
19. Coat the splines on the torsion bar with grease. Align the matchmarks and install the anchor arm on the torsion bar.
20. Install the anchor bolt and swivel and tighten the bolt until the matchmarks are mated.
21. Install the tension rod. Torque the bushing end nut to 90 ft. lbs.; the lower arm end bolts to 85 ft. lbs.
22. Install the stabilizer bar. Torque the bolt to 19 ft. lbs.
23. Install the shock absorber bolt. Torque the bolt to 55–59 ft. lbs.
24. Install the wheel assembly and lower the vehicle to the ground.
25. Retorque the lower arm to frame bracket nut.
26. Check the front and rear tire pressures. Set the pressures to what are specified on the vehicle rating plate, except for P-metric radials. Set them at the maximum pressure shown on the side wall.
27. Measure the distance from the center of the wheel hub to

the lip of the fender. This is the ride height. Proper ride height is obtained when the difference between the left and the right side is less than 10mm. Adjust the ride height by turning the anchor bolt.

NOTE: If the torsion bar anchor bolt was not matchmarked, the matchmarks were lost, or new, unmarked torsion bar is being installed, follow this procedure to obtain the correct ride height.

28. Install the anchor arm on the torsion bar so that there is 125mm between the lowest point on the arm and the crossmember directly above it.
29. Tighten the anchor bolt until the anchor arm contacts the swivel. Then, tighten the bolt an additional 45mm travel.

4WD VEHICLES

1. Raise and support the vehicle safely. Remove the tire and wheel assembly.
2. Matchmark and remove the torsion bar from the control arm.
3. Disconnect the stabilizer bar from the lower control arm. Note the position of the stabilizer bar bushings.
4. Support the lower control arm and remove the front pivot bolt.
5. Remove the lower control arm from the frame.
6. Remove the lower ball joint to control arm mounting bolts. Using a press, remove the ball joint from the control arm.
To install:
7. Using a press, install the new ball joint in the control arm. The remainder of the installation is the reverse of the removal procedure.
8. Observe the follwing torques during installation:
Lower control arm front pivot bolt 87–115 ft. lbs.
Lower control arm rear bolt 115–145 ft. lbs.
Shock absorber lower bolt 40–59 ft. lbs.
Torsion bar torque plate bolts 55–69 ft. lbs.
9. Check and adjust the vehicle ride height, if necessary. Correct ride height, measured from the center line of the wheel to the top of the front fender well, should be 17.01 in. for short beds and 16.85 in. for long beds.

Upper Control Arms

Removal and Installation

EXCEPT MPV

1. Raise and support the vehicle safely.
2. Remove the tire and wheel assemblies. Support the lower control arm.
3. Remove the cotter pin and nut from the upper ball joint and separate the ball joint from the upper control arm.
4. Remove the bushings and dust seals from the ends of the upper control arm shaft.
5. Remove the nuts and bolts that retain the upper control arm shaft to the support bracket. Note the number and location of the shims under the nuts.

NOTE: These shims must be installed in their exact locations for proper wheel alignment.

6. Check all parts for wear or damage. Replace any suspect parts.
7. Check the ball joint preload with a pull scale and adapter 49 0180 510B or equivalent. Move the ball joint stud a few times to make sure that it is free, then take the reading. The pull scale reading should be 40 lbs. or less.
8. Installation is the reverse of the removal procedure.
9. Torque the upper control arm shaft mounting bolts to 60–68 ft. lbs. and the ball joint nut to 30–37 ft. lbs.

Lower Control Arm

Removal and Installation

2WD VEHICLES EXCEPT MPV

1. Raise and support the vehicle safely, with the front suspension hanging freely.
2. Remove the tire and wheel assembly.
3. Remove the cotter pin and nut from the lower ball joint.
4. Remove the lower shock absorber mounting bolt.
5. Matchmark the anchor arm bolt and anchor swivel. Remove the bolt and swivel.

NOTE: The matchmarks made determine and are critical to, the vehicles ride height. Failure to do so, will result in having to set the vehicles ride hieght when finished.

6. Matchmark the torsion bar and anchor arm. Matchmark the torsion bar and torque plate.
7. Remove the anchor arm and torsion bar from the torque plate. Separate the anchor arm from the torsion bar.
8. Remove the torque plate.
9. Remove the lower control arm to frame bolt. Separate the lower arm from the frame bracket with bushing puller/installer 49 0727 575 or its equivalent.
10. Disconnect and remove the tension rod from the lower control arm.

NOTE: Do not change the position of the double nut at the rear of the tension rod bushing. It will affect the vehicles caster alignment.

11. Remove the stabilizer bar bolt, bushing, retainer and nut. Remove the stabilizer bar.
12. Separate the lower ball joint from the knuckle. Remove the lower control arm.
13. Inspect all parts for wear or damage. Replace any suspect parts. Using a spring scale and adapter 49 0180 510B or equivalent, check the ball joint preload. Pull scale reading should be 39.6 lbs. or less. Measure the preload after first shaking the ball joint stud to make sure it is free. Replace if necessary.
To install:
14. Install the lower arm on the frame bracket and hand tighten the nut.
15. Install the lower ball joint on the knuckle and torque the nut to 115 ft. lbs. Install the cotter pin.
16. Tighten the lower arm to frame nut to 115 ft. lbs.
17. Position the torque plate and tighten the bolt to 68 ft. lbs.
18. Coat the splines on the torsion bar with grease. Check the ends of the torsion bar. The bars are marked **L** for left and **R** for right. Align the matchmarks and install the torsion bar in the torque plate.
19. Coat the splines on the torsion bar with grease. Align the matchmarks and install the anchor arm on the torsion bar.
20. Install the anchor bolt and swivel and tighten the bolt until the matchmarks are mated.
21. Install the tension rod. Torque the bushing end nut to 90 ft. lbs.; the lower arm end bolts to 85 ft. lbs.
22. Install the stabilizer bar. Torque the bolt to 19 ft. lbs.
23. Install the shock absorber bolt. Torque the bolt to 55–59 ft. lbs.
24. Install the wheel assembly and lower the vehicle to the ground.
25. Retorque the lower arm to frame bracket nut.
26. Check the front and rear tire pressures. Set the pressures to what are specified on the vehicle rating plate, except for P-metric radials. Set them at the maximum pressure shown on the side wall.
27. Measure the distance from the center of the wheel hub to the lip of the fender. This is the ride height. Proper ride height is obtained when the difference between the left and the right side

is less than 10mm. Adjust the ride height by turning the anchor bolt.

NOTE: If the torsion bar anchor bolt was not matchmarked, the matchmarks were lost, or new, unmarked torsion bar is being installed, follow this procedure to obtain the correct ride height.

28. Install the anchor arm on the torsion bar so that there is 125mm between the lowest point on the arm and the crossmember directly above it.
29. Tighten the anchor bolt until the anchor arm contacts the swivel. Then, tighten the bolt an additional 45mm travel.

4WD VEHICLES

1. Raise and support the vehicle safely. Remove the tire and wheel assembly.
2. Matchmark and remove the torsion bar from the control arm.
3. Disconnect the stabilizer bar from the lower control arm. Note the position of the stabilizer bar bushings.
4. Support the lower control arm and remove the front pivot bolt.
5. Remove the lower control arm from the frame.
6. Installation is the reverse of the removal procedure.
7. Observe the follwing torques during installation:
Lower control arm front pivot bolt 87–115 ft. lbs.
Lower control arm rear bolt 115–145 ft. lbs.
Shock absorber lower bolt 40–59 ft. lbs.
Torsion bar torque plate bolts 55–69 ft. lbs.
8. Check and adjust the vehicle ride height, if necessary. Correct ride height, measured from the center line of the wheel to the top of the front fender well, should be 17.01 in. for short beds and 16.85 in. for long beds.

MPV

1. Raise and safely support the vehicle.
2. Remove the tire and wheel assembly.
3. Remove the caliper and suspend it out of the way. It's not necessary to disconnect the brake line.
4. Remove the compression rod.
5. Disconnect the tie rod end, using a separator.
6. Support the lower arm with a floor jack and disconnect the lower end of the strut.
7. Remove the lower ball joint nut and separate it from the knuckle using a separator.
8. Remove the lower arm-to-frame bolt and remove the arm.
9. Check all parts for wear or damage and replace if necessary.

NOTE: The ball joint is part of the arm. If either is bad, the entire assembly must be replaced.

To install:

10. Install the lower arm. Torque the arm-to-frame bolt to 108 ft. lbs.
11. Connect the lower ball joint and knuckle. Torque the nut to 116 ft. lbs. Install a new cotter pin. Never back-off the nut to align the cotter pin hole. Always advance it.
12. Connect the lower end of the strut. Torque the bolts to 86 ft. lbs.
13. Connect the tie rod end. Torque the nut to 58 ft. lbs. Never back-off the nut to align the cotter pin hole. Always advance it.
14. Install the compression rod.
15. Install the caliper.
16. Install the wheels.

Stabilizer Bar

Removal and Installation

EXCEPT MPV

1. Raise and safely support the vehicle.
2. Unbolt the stabilizer bar-to-frame clamps.
3. Unbolt the stabilizer bar from the lower control arms. Keep all the bushings, washers and spacers in order.
4. Check all parts for wear or damage and replace anything which looks suspicious.
5. Installation is the reverse of removal. Tighten all fasteners lightly, then torque them to specifications with the wheels on the ground.
6. The correct torque is:
Stabilizer bar-to-control arm nut—34 ft. lbs.
Stabilizer-to-frame clamp bolts—16 ft. lbs.

MPV

1. Raise and safely support the vehicle.
2. Remove the splash shield.
3. Disconnect the end links at the compression rods.
4. Remove the clamp bolts. Lift out the stabilizer bar.
5. Inspect all parts for wear and/or damage. Replace as necessary.
6. Installation is the reverse of removal. The end link bushings have alignment marks on the bar. Torque the clamp bolts to 45 ft. lbs. Tighten the end link bolts until 13mm ± 1mm of thread is visible above the nut.

Tension Rod

Removal and Installation

EXCEPT MPV

1. Raise and safely support the vehicle. Remove the under engine splash shield.
2. Unbolt the tension rod from the lower arm and frame and remove it.

NOTE: Don't change the position of the double nut at the rear of the tension rod bushing, since it would affect caster.

3. Install the tension rod. Torque the bushing end nut to 90 ft. lbs.; the lower arm end bolts to 85 ft. lbs.

Compression Rod

Removal and Installation

MPV

1. Raise and safely support the vehicle.
2. Disconnect the stabilizer link at the compression rod.
3. Remove the compression rod-to-lower arm bolts.
4. Remove the compression rod end nut and washer.
5. Unbolt the compression rod fluid-filled bushing and remove the bushing and washers.
6. Check the bushing for signs of leakage. Replace it if leaking or damaged.
7. Installation is the reverse of removal. Observe the following torques:
Fluid-filled bushing bolts—76 ft. lbs.
Compression rod end nut—127 ft. lbs.
Compression rod-to-lower arm—93 ft. lbs.
8. Tighten the stabilizer bar end link bolt until 13mm of thread is visible above the nut.

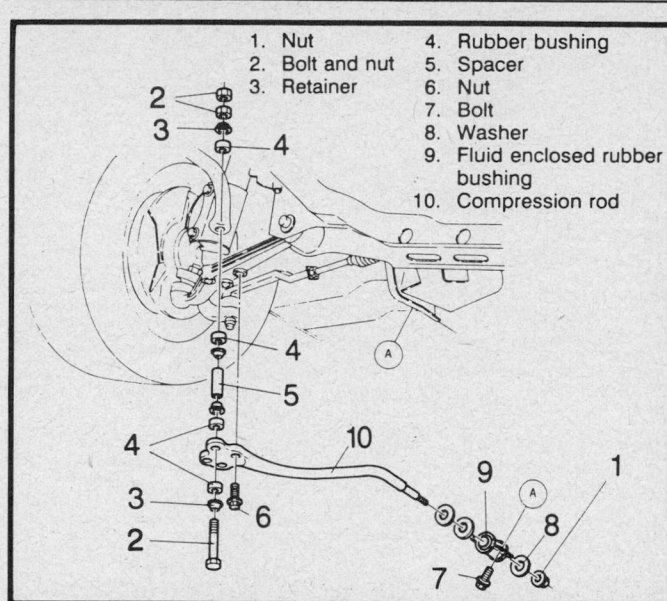

1. Nut
2. Bolt and nut
3. Retainer
4. Rubber bushing
5. Spacer
6. Nut
7. Bolt
8. Washer
9. Fluid enclosed rubber bushing
10. Compression rod

Compression rod mounting—MPV

Front Wheel Bearings

Removal and Installation

2WD VEHICLES

1. Raise and support the vehicle safely.
2. Remove the tire and wheel assembly.
3. Remove the grease cap, cotter pin, hub nut and flat washer.
4. Without disconnecting the brake line from the caliper, remove the caliper and support it out of the way. Place a hand over the outer wheel bearing and remove the hub from the spindle.

5. Remove the spacer, inner seal and inner bearing. Discard the seal.
6. Thoroughly clean the inside of the hub with solvent. Allow to dry completely before proceeding.
7. Inspect the bearings for wear, damage, heat discoloration or other signs of fatigue. If they are at all suspect, replace them.

NOTE: When replacing wheel bearings, replace the bearings and races as a set. Never mix bearings and races.

8. To replace the races, carefully press them out of the hub.
9. Coat the outside of the new races with clean wheel bearing grease and drive them into place until they are seated in the hub. Make certain that they are completely seated.
10. Pack the inside of the hub with clean wheel bearing grease.
11. Pack each bearing with clean grease, making sure that it is thoroughly packed.
12. Install the inner bearing and seal. Drive the seal into place carefully until it is seated to the same depth as when removed.
13. Install the spacer and the hub on the spindle.
14. Install the outer bearing, flat washer and hub nut.
15. Adjust the wheel bearing.
16. Install the nut cap, cotter pin and grease cap. Install the wheel assembly.

Adjustment

1. Raise and support the vehicle safely.
2. Remove the tire and wheel assembly. Without disconnecting the brake line, remove the disc brake caliper. Support the caliper out of the way.
3. Attach a spring scale to a wheel stud on the hub.
4. Pull the scale horizontally and check the force needed to start the hub turning. The force should be 1.3–2.4 lbs. If the reading is not correct, adjust the bearing.
5. To adjust, remove the grease cap and cotter pin.
6. Tighten or loosen the hub nut until the correct pull rating is obtained.
7. Align the cotter pin holes and insert a new cotter pin. Install the grease cap and wheel assembly.

REAR SUSPENSION

Shock Absorber

Removal and Installation

1. Raise and support the vehicle safely.
2. Remove the tire and wheel assemblies.
3. Support the rear axle with a suitable jack.
4. Unbolt and remove the shock absorber at each end.
5. On MPV equipped with air ride suspension, disconnect the air line from the shock absorber.
6. Installation is the reverse of removal. Torque the bolts to 57 ft. lb.

Coil Springs

Removal and Installation

MPV

1. Raise and safely support the vehicle.
2. Remove the splash shields.
3. Support the rear axle with a floor jack.
4. Remove the stabilizer bar.
5. Disconnect the height sensor or rebound spring bracket at the differential.

6. Disconnect the parking brake cable at the differential bracket.
7. Disconnect the shock absorbers at the axle and swing them out of the way.
8. Disconnect the brake line at the axle and plug the line.
9. Lower the axle slowly until the springs are free. Remove them.
10. Installation is the reverse of removal. Install all fasteners hand tight. Lower the vehicle to the ground, then torque all fasteners: Note the following torques:
   Shock absorber— 76 ft. lbs.
   Height sensor—104 in. lbs.
   Rebound spring bracket— 19 ft. lbs.
   Stabilizer bar clamp—38 ft. lbs.
   Parking brake cable clamp—19 ft. lbs.

Leaf Spring

Removal and Installation

EXCEPT MPV

1. Raise and support the vehicle so that the leaf spring is hanging freely.

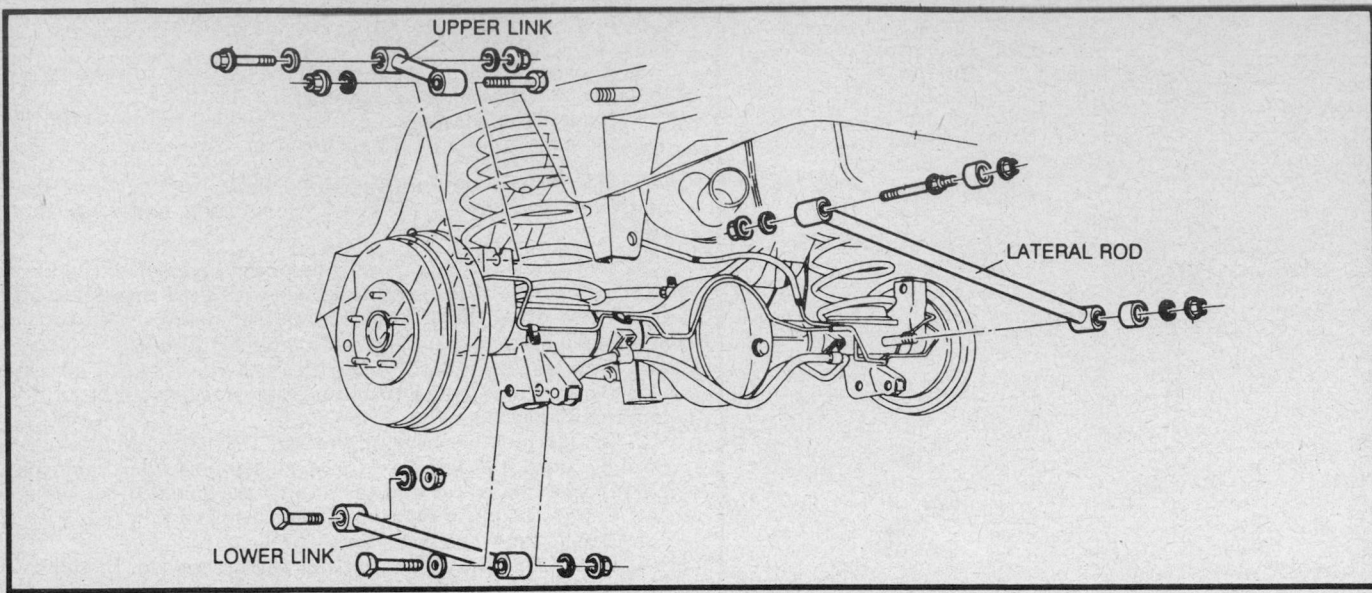

Rear suspension components—MPV

2. Support the rear axle to remove the weight from the spring.
3. Disconnect the lower shock absorber mount.
4. Remove the spring U-bolts and plate.
5. Remove the spring rear pivot bolt.
6. Remove the front shackle nuts and shackle.
7. Remove the spring from the vehicle.
8. Installation is the reverse of the removal procedure. Torque the spring rear shackle-to-frame nut to 47–58 ft. lbs.; the rear shackle-to-spring nut to 72 ft. lbs.; the U-bolt nuts to 47–58 ft. lbs. (88–100 ft. lbs. 4WD) and the front spring pin nut to 18 ft. lbs.

Upper Link

Removal and Installation

MPV

1. Raise and safely support the vehicle.
2. Unbolt the link at the frame and axle. Remove it.
3. Installation is the reverse of removal. Hand tighten the bolts, lower the vehicle to the ground, then torque the bolts to 127 ft. lbs.

Lower Link

Removal and Installation

MPV

1. Raise and safely support the vehicle.
2. Unbolt the link at the frame and axle. Remove the link.
3. Installation is the reverse of removal. Hand tighten the bolts, lower the vehicle to the ground, then torque the bolts to 127 ft. lbs.

Lateral Rod

Removal and Installation

MPV

1. Raise and safely support the vehicle.
2. Unbolt the rod at the frame and axle. Remove the rod.
3. Installation is the reverse of removal. The rod is installed

with the stamped mark towards the body. Hand tighten the bolts, lower the vehicle to the ground, then torque the bolts to 127 ft. lbs.

Height Sensor

Removal and Installation

MPV

1. Raise and safely support the vehicle.
2. Lower the spare tire about 300mm (12 in.).
3. Disconnect the wiring.
4. Remove the bolts and remove the sensor.
5. Installation is the reverse of removal. Torque the bolts to 20 ft. lbs.

Adjustment

1. Measure the length of the height sensor between the 2 locknuts on the sensor rod. Length should be 55mm.
2. If not, loosen the 2 nuts and turn the center section to adjust the length.

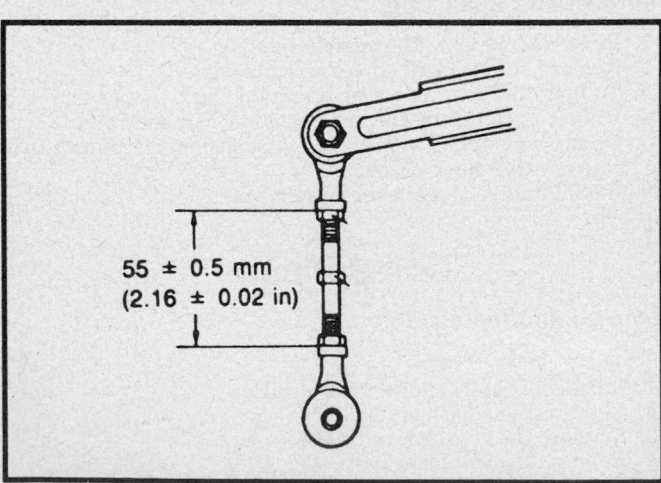

55 ± 0.5 mm
$(2.16 \pm 0.02$ in)

Ride height sensor adjustment points—MPV

SPECIFICATIONS

ENGINE IDENTIFICATION

Year	Model	Engine Displacement cu. in. (cc/liter)	Engine Series Identification (VIN)	No. of Cylinders	Engine Type
1986	Pick-Up 2WD	146 (2389/2.4)	Z24i	4	OHC
	Pick-Up 2WD	152 (2488/2.5)	SD25	4	OHV
	Pick-Up 2WD	181 (2960/3.0)	VG30i	6	DOHC
	Pick-Up 4WD	146 (2389/2.4)	Z24i	4	OHC
	Pick-Up 4WD	181 (2960/3.0)	VG30i	6	DOHC
1987	Van	146 (2389/2.4)	Z24i	4	OHC
	Pick-Up 2WD	146 (2389/2.4)	Z24i	4	OHC
	Pick-Up 2WD	152 (2488/2.5)	SD25	4	OHV
	Pick-Up 2WD	181 (2960/3.0)	VG30i	6	DOHC
	Pick-Up 4WD	146 (2389/2.4)	Z24i	4	OHC
	Pick-Up 4WD	181 (2960/3.0)	VG30i	6	DOHC
	Pathfinder	146 (2389/2.4)	Z24i	4	OHC
	Pathfinder	181 (2960/3.0)	VG30i	6	DOHC
1988	Van	146 (2389/2.4)	Z24i	4	OHC
	Pick-Up 2WD	146 (2389/2.4)	Z24i	4	OHC
	Pick-Up 2WD	181 (2960/3.0)	VG30i	6	DOHC
	Pick-Up 4WD	146 (2389/2.4)	Z24i	4	OHC
	Pick-Up 4WD	181 (2960/3.0)	VG30i	6	DOHC
	Pathfinder	146 (2389/2.4)	Z24i	4	OHC
	Pathfinder	181 (2960/3.0)	VG30i	6	DOHC
1989	Pick-Up 2WD	146 (2389/2.4)	Z24i	4	OHC
	Pick-Up 2WD	181 (2960/3.0)	VG30i	6	DOHC
	Pick-Up 4WD	146 (2389/2.4)	Z24i	4	OHC
	Pick-Up 4WD	181 (2960/3.0)	VG 30i	6	DOHC
	Pathfinder 2WD	181 (2960/3.0)	VG30i	6	DOHC
	Pathfinder 4WD	146 (2389/2.4)	Z24i	4	OHC
	Pathfinder 4WD	181 (2960/3.0)	VG30i	6	DOHC
1990	Axxess 2WD	146 (2389/2.4)	KA24E	4	OHC
	Axxess 4WD	146 (2389/2.4)	KA24E	4	OHC
	Pick-Up 2WD	146 (2389/2.4)	KA24E	4	OHC
	Pick-Up 2WD	181 (2960/3.0)	VG30E	6	DOHC
	Pick-Up 4WD	146 (2389/2.4)	KA24E	4	OHC
	Pick-Up 4WD	181 (2960/3.0)	VG30E	6	DOHC
	Pathfinder	181 (2960/3.0)	VG30E	6	DOHC

OHC—Overhead cam
OHV—Overhead valves
DOHC—Dual overhead cam

GENERAL ENGINE SPECIFICATIONS

Year	Model	Engine Displacement cu. in. (cc)	Fuel System Type	Net Horsepower @ rpm	Net Torque @ rpm (ft. lbs.)	Bore × Stroke (in.)	Compression Ratio	Oil Pressure @ rpm
1986	Pick-Up	146 (2389)	EFI	103 @ 4800	134 @ 2800	3.50 × 3.78	8.3:1	55 @ 3000
	Pick-Up	152 (2488)	DFI	70 @ 4000	115 @ 2000	3.50 × 3.94	21.4:1	60 @ idle
	Pick-Up	181 (2960)	EFI	152 @ 5200	162 @ 3600	3.43 × 3.27	9.0:1	60 @ 3200
1987	Van	146 (2389)	EFI	103 @ 4800	134 @ 2800	3.50 × 3.78	8.3:1	55 @ 3000
	Pick-Up	146 (2389)	EFI	103 @ 4800	134 @ 2800	3.50 × 3.78	8.3:1	55 @ 3000
	Pick-Up	152 (2488)	DFI	70 @ 4000	115 @ 2000	3.50 × 3.94	21.4:1	60 @ idle
	Pick-Up	181 (2960)	EFI	152 @ 5200	162 @ 3600	3.43 × 3.27	9.0:1	60 @ 3200
	Pathfinder	146 (2389)	EFI	103 @ 4800	134 @ 2800	3.50 × 3.78	8.3:1	55 @ 3000
	Pathfinder	181 (2960)	EFI	152 @ 5200	162 @ 3600	3.43 × 3.27	9.0:1	60 @ 3200
1988	Van	146 (2389)	EFI	103 @ 4800	134 @ 2800	3.50 × 3.78	8.3:1	55 @ 3000
	Pick-Up	146 (2389)	EFI	103 @ 4800	134 @ 2800	3.50 × 3.78	8.3:1	55 @ 3000
	Pick-Up	181 (2960)	EFI	152 @ 5200	162 @ 3600	3.43 × 3.27	9.0:1	60 @ 3200
	Pathfinder	146 (2389)	EFI	103 @ 4800	134 @ 2800	3.50 × 3.78	8.3:1	55 @ 3000
	Pathfinder	181 (2960)	EFI	152 @ 5200	162 @ 3600	3.43 × 3.27	9.0:1	60 @ 3200
1989	Pick-Up	146 (2389)	EFI	103 @ 4800	134 @ 2800	3.50 × 3.78	8.3:1	55 @ 3000
	Pick-Up	181 (2960)	EFI	152 @ 5200	162 @ 3600	3.43 × 3.27	9.0:1	60 @ 3200
	Pathfinder	146 (2389)	EFI	103 @ 4800	134 @ 2800	3.50 × 3.78	8.3:1	55 @ 3000
	Pathfinder	181 (2960)	EFI	152 @ 5200	162 @ 3600	3.43 × 3.27	9.0:1	60 @ 3200
1990	Axxess	146 (2389)	MFI	138 @ 5600	148 @ 4400	3.50 × 3.78	8.6:1	65 @ 3000
	Pick-Up	146 (2389)	MFI	138 @ 5600	148 @ 4400	3.50 × 3.78	8.6:1	65 @ 3000
	Pick-Up	181 (2960)	MFI	153 @ 4800	180 @ 4000	3.43 × 3.27	9.0:1	60 @ 3200
	Pathfinder	146 (2389)	MFI	138 @ 5600	148 @ 4400	3.50 × 3.78	8.6:1	65 @ 3000
	Pathfinder	181 (2960)	MFI	153 @ 4800	180 @ 4000	3.43 × 3.27	9.0:1	60 @ 3200

EFI—Electronic fuel injection
DFI—Diesel fuel injection
MFI—Multi fuel injection

GASOLINE ENGINE TUNE-UP SPECIFICATIONS

Year	Model	Engine Displacement cu. in. (cc)	Spark Plugs Type	Gap (in.)	Ignition Timing (deg.) MT	Ignition Timing (deg.) AT	Compression Pressure (psi)	Fuel Pump (psi)	Idle Speed (rpm) MT	Idle Speed (rpm) AT	Valve Clearance In.	Valve Clearance Ex.
1986	Pick-Up	146 (2389)	BPR5ES ①	0.033	5	5	173	36	900	650 ②	0.010	0.012
	Pick-Up	181 (2960)	BCPR5ES-11	0.041	12	12	173	36	800	700 ②	Hyd.	Hyd.
1987	Van	146 (2389)	BPR5ES ①	0.033	10	10	173	36	800	700 ②	0.008	0.009
	Pick-Up	146 (2389)	BCPR5ES-11	0.033	10	10	173	36	900	650 ②	0.008	0.009
	Pick-Up	181 (2960)	BPR5ES ①	0.041	12	12	173	36	800	700 ②	Hyd.	Hyd.
	Pathfinder	146 (2389)	BPR5ES ①	0.033	10	10	173	36	900	650 ②	0.008	0.009
	Pathfinder	181 (2960)	BCPR5ES-11	0.041	12	12	173	36	800	700 ②	Hyd.	Hyd.
1988	Van	146 (2389)	BPR5ES ①	0.033	10	10	173	36	800	700 ②	0.008	0.009
	Pick-Up	146 (2389)	BPR5ES ①	0.033	10	10	173	36	800	650 ②	0.008	0.009
	Pick-Up	181 (2960)	BCPR5ES-11	0.041	12	12	173	36	800	700 ②	Hyd.	Hyd.
	Pathfinder	146 (2389)	BPR5ES ①	0.033	10	10	173	36	800	650 ②	0.008	0.009
	Pathfinder	181 (2960)	BCPR5ES-11	0.041	12	12	173	36	800	700 ②	Hyd.	Hyd.

GASOLINE ENGINE TUNE-UP SPECIFICATIONS

Year	Model	Engine Displacement cu. in. (cc)	Spark Plugs Type	Gap (in.)	Ignition Timing (deg.) MT	AT	Compression Pressure (psi)	Fuel Pump (psi)	Idle Speed (rpm) MT	AT	Valve Clearance In.	Ex.
1989	Pick-Up	146 (2389)	BPR5ES	0.033	10	10	173	36	800	650 ②	0.008	0.009
	Pick-Up	181 (2960)	BCPR5ES-11	0.041	12	12	173	36	800	700 ②	Hyd.	Hyd.
	Pathfinder	146 (2389)	BPR5ES	0.033	10	10	173	36	800	650 ②	0.008	0.009
	Pathfinder	181 (2960)	BCPR5ES-11	0.041	12	12	173	36	800	700 ②	Hyd.	Hyd.
1990	Axxess	146 (2389)	ZFR5E-11	0.033	15	15	175	33	650	650 ②	Hyd.	Hyd.
	Pick-Up	146 (2389)	ZFR5E-11	0.041	15	15	192	33	800	800 ③	Hyd.	Hyd.
	Pick-Up	181 (2960)	BKR6EY	0.033	15	15	173	33	750	750 ②	Hyd.	Hyd.
	Pathfinder	146 (2389)	ZFR5E-11	0.041	15	15	192	33	800	800 ③	Hyd.	Hyd.
	Pathfinder	181 (2960)	BKR6EY	0.033	15	15	173	33	750	750 ②	Hyd.	Hyd.

① Intake and exhaust sides
② Transmission in drive
③ Transmission in neutral

DIESEL ENGINE TUNE-UP SPECIFICATIONS

Year	Engine Displacement cu. in. (cc)	Valve Clearance Intake (in.)	Exhaust (in.)	Intake Valve Opens (deg.)	Injection Pump Setting (deg.)	Injection Nozzle Pressure (psi) New	Used	Idle Speed (rpm)	Cranking Compression Pressure (psi)
1986	152 (2488)	0.014	0.014	NA	7°BTDC	1493–1607	1422–1493	700–750 ①	427
1987	152 (2488)	0.014	0.014	NA	7°BTDC	1493–1607	1422–1493	700–750 ①	427

NA—Not available
① F.I.C.D. Off

FIRING ORDER

NOTE: To avoid confusion, always replace spark plug wires one at a time.

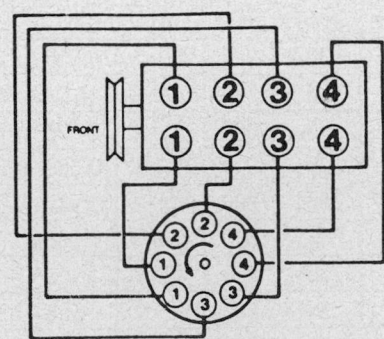

Nissan (Z24i) 146 (2.4L)
Firing order: 1-3-4-2
Distributor rotation: counterclockwise

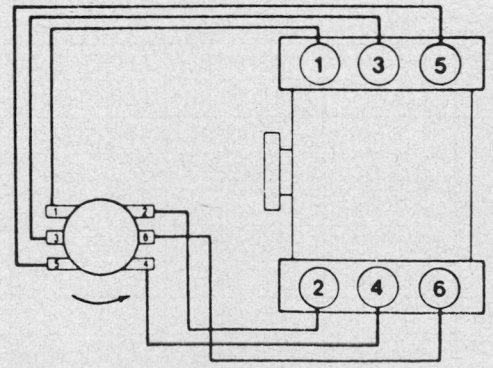

Nissan (VG30i) 181 (3.0L)
Firing order: 1-2-3-4-5-6
Distributor rotation: counterclockwise

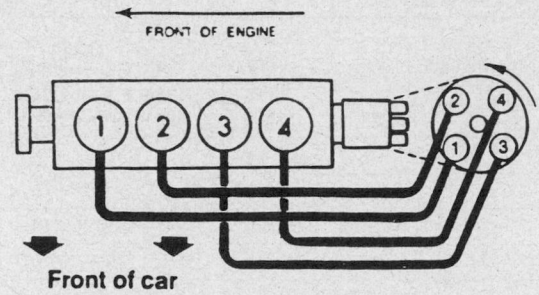

Nissan (VG30E) 181 (3.0L)
Firing order: 1-2-3-4-5-6
Distributor rotation: counterclockwise

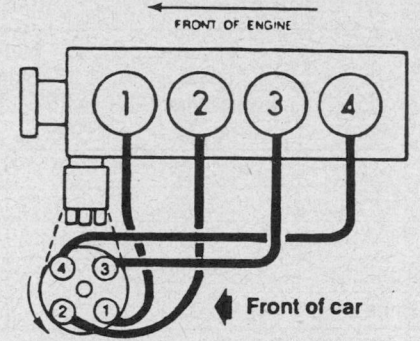

Nissan (KA24E) 146 (2.4L)
Firing order: 1-3-4-2
Distributor rotation: counterclockwise

Nissan (SD25) 152 (2.5L)
Firing order: 1-3-4-2

CAPACITIES

Year	Model	Engine Displacement cu. in. (cc)	Engine Crankcase with Filter	without Filter	Transmission (pts.) 4-Spd	5-Spd	Auto.	Drive Axle (pts.)	Fuel Tank (gal.)	Cooling System (qts.)
1986	Pick-Up	146 (2389)	4.0	3.5	—	③	14.8	⑤	21.1	9.0
	Pick-Up	152 (2488)	7.9	7.1	—	③	—	⑤	21.1	13.0
	Pick-Up	181 (2960)	①	②	—	④	14.8	⑤	21.1	11.0
1987	Van	146 (2389)	4.4	3.9	—	4.25	14.8	2.8	17.1	9.6
	Pick-Up	146 (2389)	4.0	3.5	—	③	14.8	⑤	21.1	9.0
	Pick-Up	152 (2488)	7.9	7.1	—	③	—	⑤	21.1	13.0
	Pick-Up	181 (2960)	①	②	—	④	14.8	⑤	21.1	11.0
	Pathfinder	146 (2389)	4.0	7.1	—	③	14.8	⑤	21.1	9.0
	Pathfinder	181 (2960)	①	②	—	④	14.8	⑤	21.1	11.0
1988	Van	146 (2389)	4.4	3.9	—	4.25	14.8	2.8	17.1	9.6
	Pick-Up	146 (2389)	⑥	⑦	3.6	③	14.8	⑤	15.9	9.0
	Pick-Up	181 (2960)	①	②	—	④	14.8	⑤	21.1	10.5
	Pathfinder	146 (2389)	⑥	⑦	3.6	③	14.8	⑤	15.9	9.0
	Pathfinder	181 (2960)	①	②	—	④	14.8	⑤	21.1	10.5
1989	Pick-Up	146 (2389)	⑥	⑦	3.6	③	14.8	⑤	15.9	9.0
	Pick-Up	181 (2960)	①	②	—	④	14.8	⑤	21.1	10.5
	Pathfinder	146 (2389)	⑥	⑦	3.6	③	14.8	⑤	15.9	9.0
	Pathfinder	181 (2960)	①	②	—	④	14.8	⑤	21.1	10.5

CAPACITIES

Year	Model	Engine Displacement cu. in. (cc)	Engine Crankcase with Filter	Engine Crankcase without Filter	Transmission (pts.) 4-Spd	Transmission (pts.) 5-Spd	Transmission (pts.) Auto.	Drive Axle (pts.)	Fuel Tank (gal.)	Cooling System (qts.)
1990	Axxess	146 (2389)	3.8	3.4	—	10.0	15.8	2.1	—	8.0
	Pick-Up	146 (2389)	⑩	⑪	—	③	16.8	⑤	15.9	⑨
	Pick-Up	181 (2960)	①	②	—	④	16.8 ⑫	⑤	21.1	⑧
	Pathfinder	146 (2389)	⑩	⑪	—	③	16.8	⑤	15.9	⑨
	Pathfinder	181 (2960)	①	②	—	④	16.8 ⑫	⑤	21.1	⑧

① 2WD—4.25
　4WD—3.6
② 2WD—3.9
　4WD—3.1
③ 2WD—4.3
　4WD—8.5
④ 2WD—5.1
　4WD—7.6

⑤ 4WD front—4 cyl.—R180A—2.8
　4WD front—V6—R200A—3.1
　4WD rear—4 cyl.—C200—2.8
　2WD—4 cyl.—H190A—3.1
　2WD or 4WD rear—V6—H233B—5.9
⑥ 2WD—4.0
　4WD—4.5
⑦ 2WD—3.5
　4WD—4.0

⑧ 2WD—11.4
　4WD—12.4
⑨ 2WD—8.6
　4WD—9.5
⑩ 2WD—4.1
　4WD—3.5
⑪ 2WD—3.8
　4WD—3.1
⑫ 4WD—18.0

CAMSHAFT SPECIFICATIONS

All measurements given in inches.

Year	Engine Displacement cu. in. (cc)	Journal Diameter 1	Journal Diameter 2	Journal Diameter 3	Journal Diameter 4	Journal Diameter 5	Lobe Lift In.	Lobe Lift Ex.	Bearing Clearance	Camshaft End Play
1986	146 (2389)	1.2961–1.2968	1.2961–1.2968	1.2961–1.2968	1.2961–1.2968	1.2961–1.2968	NA	NA	0.0024–0.0041	0.008
	152 (2488)	1.7887–1.7892	1.7282–1.7287	1.6228–1.6233	—	—	NA	NA	①	0.0031–0.0110
	181 (2960)	1.8472–1.8480	1.8472–1.8480	1.8472–1.8480	1.8472–1.8480	—	NA	NA	0.0024–0.0041	0.0012–0.0024
1987	146 (2389)	1.2961–1.2968	1.2961–1.2968	1.2961–1.2968	1.2961–1.2968	1.2961–1.2968	NA NA	NA NA	0.0024–0.0041	0.008
	152 (2488)	1.7887–1.7892	1.7282–1.7287	1.6228–1.6233	—	—	NA	NA	①	0.0031–0.0110
	181 (2960)	1.8472–1.8480	1.8472–1.8480	1.8472–1.8480	1.8472–1.8480	—	NA	NA	0.0024–0.0041	0.0012–0.0024
1988	146 (2389)	1.2961–1.2968	1.2961–1.2968	1.2961–1.2968	1.2961–1.2968	1.2961–1.2968	NA	NA	0.0024–0.0041	0.008
	181 (2960)	1.8866–1.8874	1.8472–1.8480	1.8472–1.8480	1.8472–1.8480	1.6701–1.6709	NA	NA	0.0018–0.0035	0.0012–0.0024
1989	146 (2389)	1.2961–1.2968	1.2961–1.2968	1.2961–1.2968	1.2961–1.2968	1.2961–1.2968	NA	NA	0.0024–0.0041	0.008
	181 (2960)	1.8866–1.8874–	1.8472–1.8480	1.8472–1.8480	1.8472–1.8480	1.6701–1.6709	NA	NA	0.0018–0.0035	0.0012–0.0024
1990	146 (2389)	1.2967–1.2974	1.2967–1.2974	1.2967–1.2974	1.2967–1.2974	1.2967–1.2974	NA	NA .	0.0018–0.0035	0.0028–0.0059
	181 (2960)	1.8866–1.8874–	1.8472–1.8480	1.8472–1.8480	1.8472–1.8480	1.6701–1.6709	NA	NA	0.0024–0.0041	0.0012–0.0024

NA—Not available
① Front—0.0009–0.0040
　Center—0.0015–0.0045
　Rear—0.0009–0.0040

CRANKSHAFT AND CONNECTING ROD SPECIFICATIONS

All measurements are given in inches.

Year	Engine Displacement cu. in. (cc)	Crankshaft Main Brg. Journal Dia.	Crankshaft Main Brg. Oil Clearance	Crankshaft Shaft End-play	Crankshaft Thrust on No.	Connecting Rod Journal Diameter	Connecting Rod Oil Clearance	Connecting Rod Side Clearance
1986	146 (2389)	2.3599–2.3604	①	0.0020–0.0071	③	1.9670–1.9675	0.0005–0.0021	0.008–0.012
	152 (2488)	2.7916–2.7921	0.0014–0.0034	0.0024–0.0055	4	2.0832–2.0837	0.0014–0.0032	0.004–0.008
	181 (2960)	2.4790–2.4793	0.0011–0.0022	0.0020–0.0067	4	1.9670–1.9675	0.0004–0.0020	0.0079–0.0138
1987	146 (2389)	2.3599–2.3604	①	0.0020–0.0071	3	1.9670–1.9675	0.0005–0.0021	0.008–0.012
	152 (2488)	2.7916–2.7921	0.0014–0.0034	0.0024–0.0055	4	2.0832–2.0837	0.0014–0.0032	0.004–0.008
	181 (2960)	2.4790–2.4793	0.0011–0.0022	0.0020–0.0067	4	1.9670–1.9675	0.0004–0.0020	0.0079–0.0138
1988	146 (2389)	2.3599–2.3604	①	0.0020–0.0071	3	1.9670–1.9675	0.0005–0.0021	0.008–0.012
	181 (2960)	2.4790–2.4793	0.0011–0.0022	0.0020–0.0067	4	1.9670–1.9675	0.0006–0.0021	0.0079–0.0138
1989	146 (2389)	2.3599–2.3604	①	0.0020–0.0071	3	1.9670–1.9675	0.0006–0.0019	0.008–0.012
	181 (2960)	2.4790–2.4793	0.0011–0.0022	0.0020–0.0067	4	1.9670–1.9675	0.0006–0.0021	0.0079–0.0138
1990	146 (2389)	2.5057–2.5060	0.0008–0.0019	0.0020–0.0071	3	2.3603–2.3612	0.0004–0.0014	0.008–0.016
	181 (2960)	2.4790–2.4793	0.0011–0.0022	0.0020–0.0067	4	1.9667–1.9675	0.0006–0.0021	0.0079–0.0138

① No. 1 and 5—0.0008–0.0024
No. 2, 3 and 4—0.0008–0.0030

VALVE SPECIFICATIONS

Year	Engine Displacement cu. in. (cc)	Seat Angle (deg.)	Face Angle (deg.)	Spring Test Pressure (lbs.)	Spring Installed Height (in.)	Stem-to-Guide Clearance (in.) Intake	Stem-to-Guide Clearance (in.) Exhaust	Stem Diameter (in.) Intake	Stem Diameter (in.) Exhaust
1986	146 (2389)	45	45.5	②	①	0.0008–0.0021	0.0016–0.0029	0.3136–0.3142	0.3128–0.3134
	152 (2488)	45	45.5	73	1.56	0.0006–0.0018	0.0016–0.0028	0.3138–0.3144	0.3128–0.3134
	181 (2960)	45	45.5	③	④	0.0008–0.0021	0.0012–0.0018	0.2742–0.2748	0.3136–0.3138
1987	146 (2389)	45	45.5	②	①	0.0008–0.0021	0.0016–0.0029	0.3136–0.3142	0.3128–0.3134
	152 (2488)	45	45.5	73	1.56	0.0006–0.0018	0.0016–0.0028	0.3138–0.3144	0.3128–0.3134
	181 (2960)	45	45.5	③	④	0.0008–0.0021	0.0012–0.0018	0.2742–0.2748	0.3136–0.3138
1988	146 (2389)	45	45.5	②	①	0.0008–0.0021	0.0016–0.0029	0.3136–0.3142	0.3128–0.3134
	181 (2960)	45	45.5	③	④	0.0008–0.0021	0.0016–0.0029	0.3136–0.3142	0.3128–0.3134

VALVE SPECIFICATIONS

Year	Engine Displacement cu. in. (cc)	Seat Angle (deg.)	Face Angle (deg.)	Spring Test Pressure (lbs.)	Spring Installed Height (in.)	Stem-to-Guide Clearance (in.)		Stem Diameter (in.)	
						Intake	Exhaust	Intake	Exhaust
1989	146 (2389)	45	45.5	②	①	0.0008–0.0021	0.0016–0.0029	0.3136–0.3142	0.3128–0.3134
	181 (2960)	45	45.5	③	④	0.0008–0.0021	0.0016–0.0029	0.2742–0.2748	0.3128–0.3134
1990	146 (2389)	45	45.5	⑤	⑥	0.0008–0.0021	0.0016–0.0029	0.2742–0.2748	0.3128–0.3134
	181 (2960)	45	45.5	③	④	0.0008–0.0021	0.0012–0.0021	0.2742–0.2748	0.3136–0.3138

① Outer—1.58 in.
   Inner—1.34 in.
② Outer—51 lbs.
   Inner—24 lbs.
③ Outer—118 lbs.
   Inner—57 lbs.
④ Outer—1.18 in.
   Inner—0.98 in.
⑤ Outer intake—136 lbs.
   Outer exhaust—144 lbs.
   Inner intake—64 lbs.
   Inner exhaust—74 lbs.
⑥ Outer intake—1.48 in.
   Outer exhaust—1.34 in.
   Inner intake—1.28 in.
   Inner exhaust—1.15 in.

PISTON AND RING SPECIFICATIONS

All measurements are given in inches.

Year	No. Cylinder Displacement cu. in. (liter)	Piston Clearance	Ring Gap			Ring Side Clearance		
			Top Compression	Bottom Compression	Oil Control	Top Compression	Bottom Compression	Oil Control
1986	146 (2389)	0.0010–0.0018	0.011–0.015	0.010–0.014	0.008–0.023	0.0016–0.0029	0.0012–0.0025	NA
	152 (2488)	0.0020–0.0028	0.012–0.017	0.008–0.013	0.006–0.012	0.0024–0.0039	0.0016–0.0031	0.0008–0.0024
	181 (2960)	0.0010–0.0018	0.008–0.013	0.007–0.017	0.008–0.029	0.0016–0.0029	0.0012–0.0025	0.0006–0.0073
1987	146 (2389)	0.0010–0.0018	0.011–0.015	0.010–0.014	0.008–0.023	0.0016–0.0029	0.0012–0.0025	NA
	152 (2488)	0.0020–0.0028	0.012–0.017	0.008–0.013	0.006–0.012	0.0024–0.0039	0.0016–0.0031	0.0008–0.0024
	181 (2960)	0.0010–0.0018	0.008–0.013	0.007–0.017	0.008–0.029	0.0016–0.0029	0.0012–0.0025	0.0006–0.0073
1988	146 (2389)	0.0010–0.0018	0.011–0.015	0.010–0.014	0.008–0.023	0.0016–0.0029	0.0012–0.0025	NA
	181 (2960)	0.0010–0.0018	0.008–0.017	0.007–0.017	0.008–0.029	0.0016–0.0029	0.0012–0.0025	0.0006–0.0075
1989	146 (2389)	0.0010–0.0018	0.011–0.015	0.010–0.014	0.008–0.023	0.0016–0.0029	0.0012–0.0025	NA
	181 (2960)	0.0010–0.0018	0.008–0.017	0.007–0.017	0.008–0.029	0.0016–0.0029	0.0012–0.0025	0.0006–0.0075
1990	146 (2389)	0.0008–0.0016	0.012–0.020	0.017–0.027	0.008–0.027	0.0016–0.0031	0.0012–0.0028	0.0026–0.0053
	181 (2960)	0.0010–0.0018	0.008–0.017	0.007–0.017	0.008–0.029	0.0016–0.0029	0.0012–0.0025	NA

NA—Not available

TORQUE SPECIFICATIONS
All readings in ft. lbs.

Year	Engine Displacement cu. in. (cc)	Cynlinder Head Bolts	Main Bearing Bolts	Rod Bearing Bolts	Crankshaft Pulley Bolts	Flywheel Bolts	Manifold Intake	Exhaust	Spark Plugs
1986	146 (2389)	58	36	36	102	108	14	14	18
	152 (2488)	94	125	50	228	68	12	12	—
	181 (2960)	44	70	36	62	76	①	14	18
1987	146 (2389)	58	36	36	102	108	14	14	18
	152 (2488)	94	125	50	228	68	12	12	—
	181 (2960)	44	70	36	62	76	①	14	18
1988	146 (2389)	58	36	36	102	108	14	14	18
	181 (2960)	44	70	62	62	76	①	14	18
1989	146 (2389)	58	36	30	102	108	14	14	18
	181 (2960)	44	70	62	62	76	①	14	18
1990	146 (2389)	58	36	②	108	72	14	14	18
	181 (2960)	44	70	30	94	76	③	14	18

① Bolt—12–14
Nut—17–20
② 10–12 ft. lbs., plus, 60–65 degrees
③ Bolts—12–14
Nuts—17–20

BRAKE SPECIFICATIONS
All measurements in inches unless noted

Year	Model	Lug Nut Torque (ft. lbs.)	Master Cylinder Bore	Brake Disc Minimum Thickness	Maximum Runout	Standard Brake Drum Diameter	Minimum Lining Thickness Front	Rear
1986	Pick-Up	98	①	③	0.0028	②	0.079	0.059
1987	Van	78	1.000	0.945	0.0028	10.24	0.079	0.059
	Pick-Up	98	①	③	0.0028	②	0.079	0.059
	Pathfinder	98	①	③	0.0028	②	0.079	0.059
1988	Van	78	1.000	0.945	0.0028	10.24	0.079	0.059
	Pick-Up	98	①	③ ④	0.0028	②	0.079	0.059
	Pathfinder	98	①	③ ④	0.0028	②	0.079	0.059
1989	Pick-Up	98	①	③ ④	0.0028	⑤	0.079	0.059
	Pathfinder	98	①	③ ④	0.0028	⑤	0.079	0.059
1990	Van	78	0.938	0.787	0.0028	⑥	0.079	0.059
	Pick-Up	98	0.938	③ ④	0.0028	⑦	0.079	0.059
	Pathfinder	98	0.938	③ ④	0.0028	10.24	0.079	0.059

① 2WD light duty—LT26B: 0.938 and 1.000 in.
Except 2WD light duty—LT26B: 0.938 in.
② 2WD light duty—LT26B: 10.24 in.
2WD light duty—LT26B: 8.66 in.
③ 2WD with 4 cylinder—CL28VA: 0.787 in.
Except 2WD with 4 cylinder—CL28VD: 0.945 in.
④ Sports package—AD14VB—0.630 in.
⑤ 2WD with 4 cylinder—LT26B—10.24 in.
2WD/4WD heavy duty—DS25B and DS25C—10.00 in.
Sports package—AD14VB—11.26 in.
Sports package—DS19HB—7.48 in.
⑥ 2WD—5 passenger: 9.00 in.
4WD and 2WD—7 passenger: 10.24 in.
⑦ Except 4WD Pick-Up—LT26B: 10.24 in.
4WD Pick-Up—LT30A: 11.61 in.

19–9

WHEEL ALIGNMENT

Year	Model	Caster Range (deg.)	Caster Preferred Setting (deg.)	Chamber Range (deg.)	Chamber Preferred Setting (deg.)	Toe-in (in.)	Steering Axis Inclination (deg.)
1986	Pick-Up 2WD	1/6N–5/6P	1/3P	1/12N–11/12P	11/24P	0.16	—
	Pick-Up 4WD	5/6P–15/6P	11/12P	1/6P–11/6P	2/3P	0.16	—
1987	Van	1P–2P	11/2P	1/4N–3/4P	1/4P	0	9–10
	Pick-Up 2WD	1/6N–5/6P	1/3P	1/12N–11/12P	11/24P	0.16	—
	Pick-Up 4WD	5/6P–15/6P	11/12P	1/6P–11/6P	2/3P	0.16	—
	Pathfinder 2WD	1/6N–5/6P	1/3P	1/12N–11/12P	11/24P	0.16	—
	Pathfinder 4WD	5/6N–15/6P	11/12P	1/6P–11/6P	2/3P	0.16	—
1988	Van	3/4P–21/4P	11/2P	1/2N–1P	1/4P	0.04	9–10
	Pick-Up 2WD	1/6N–5/6P	1/3P	1/12N–11/12P	11/24P	0.12	9
	Pick-Up 4WD	5/16P–15/6P	11/12P	1/6P–11/6P	2/3P	0.16	8
	Pathfinder 2WD	1/6N–5/6P	1/3P	1/12N–11/12P	11/24P	0.12	9
	Pathfinder 4WD	5/6P–15/6P	11/12P	1/6P–11/6P	2/3P	0.16	8
1989	Pick-Up 2WD	1/6N–5/6P	1/3P	1/12N–11/12P	11/24P	0.12	9
	Pick-Up 4WD	5/6P–15/6P	11/12P	1/6P–11/6P	2/3P	0.16	8
	Pathfinder	5/6P–15/6P	11/12P	1/6P–11/6P	2/3P	0.16	8
1990	Van 2WD	1/4N–11/4P	1/2P	1/3N–1P	1/3P	0.08	14
	Van 4WD	1/12N–15/12P	2/3P	7/12N–11/12P	1/6P	0.08	14
	Pick-Up 2WD	1/6N–5/6P	1/3P	1/12N–11/12P	11/24P	0.16	9
	Pick-Up 4WD	5/6P–15/6P	11/12P	1/6P–11/6P	2/3P	0.16	8
	Pathfinder	5/6P–15/6P	11/12P	1/6P–11/6P	2/3P	0.16	8

ENGINE ELECTRICAL

NOTE: Disconnecting the negative battery cable on some vehicles may interfere with the functions of the on board computer systems and may require the computer to undergo a relearning process, once the negative battery cable is reconnected.

Distributor

Removal and Installation

1. Disconnect the negative battery cable.
2. Disconnect the distributor cap retaining clips and remove the distributor cap with the plug wires attached.
3. Using a piece of chalk, make alignment marks on the distributor-to-engine and rotor-to-distributor locations; the alignment marks are used for reinstallation.
4. Disconnect the distributor electrical harness connector.
5. Remove the distributor-to-engine bolt and lift the distributor assembly from the engine.
6. If the engine was undisturbed, install the distributor, align the matchmarks and reverse the removal procedures. Check and/or adjust the timing.
7. If the crankshaft was turned, the engine disturbed in any

manner (while the distributor was removed) or alignment marks were not drawn, perform the following procedures:
   a. Remove the No. 1 cylinder spark plug.
   b. Turn the crankshaft until the No. 1 piston is positioned on the Top Dead Center (TDC) of the compression stroke.

NOTE: To determine the TDC of the compression stroke, place your thumb over the spark plug hole and feel the air being forced from the cylinder. Stop turning the crankshaft when the timing marks, used to time the engine, are aligned.

   c. Oil the distributor housing-to-cylinder block surface.
   d. Install the distributor so the rotor points toward the No. 1 spark plug terminal tower of the distributor cap (when installed).
   e. When the distributor shaft has reached the bottom of the hole, move the rotor back and forth slightly until the driving lug on the end of the shaft enters the slots cut in the end of the oil pump shaft and the distributor assembly slides down into place.
8. To complete the installation, reverse the removal procedures. Check and/or adjust the ignition timing.

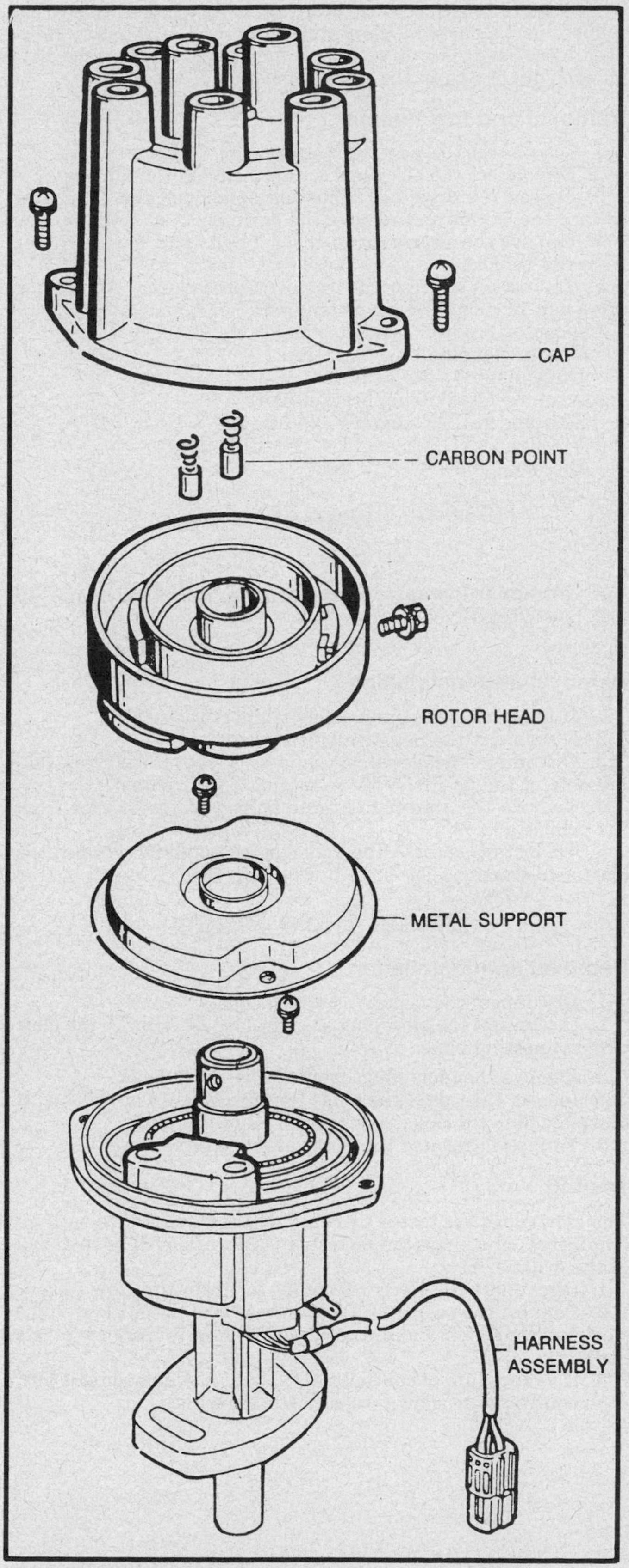

Ignition Timing

Adjustment

GASOLINE ENGINE

The ignition timing is controlled by the ECM.

1. Locate the timing marks on the crankshaft pulley and the front of the engine.

2. Clean the timing marks.

3. Using chalk or white paint, color the mark on the crankshaft pulley and the mark on the scale which will indicate the correct timing when aligned with the notch on the crankshaft pulley.

4. Attach a tachometer to the engine.

5. Attach a timing light to the engine, according to the manufacturer's instructions.

6. If equipped with air conditioning, turn it **OFF**.

7. Check to make sure all of the wires clear the fan, then, start the engine and allow it to reach normal operating temperatures.

8. Block the front wheels and set the parking brake. Shift the transmission into **NEUTRAL** for manual transmission or **D** for

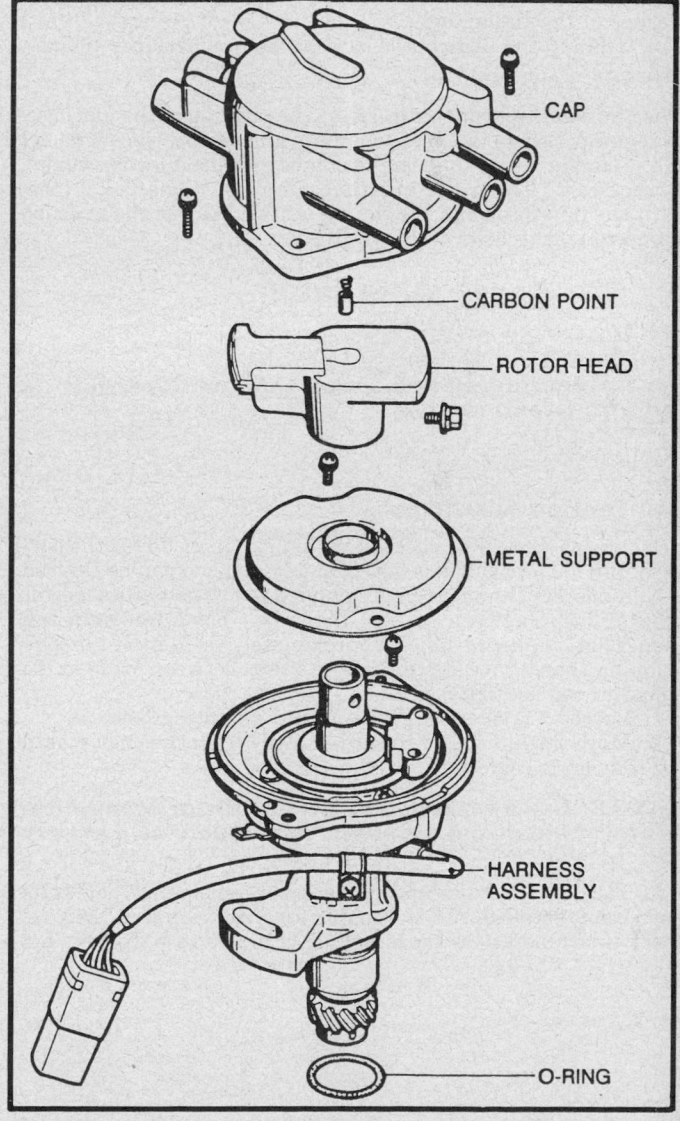

Exploded view of the distributor—2.4L engine

Exploded view of the distributor—3.0L engine

automatic transmission; do not stand in front of the vehicle when making adjustments.

9. Perform the following procedures:

a. Race the engine at 2000 rpm for about 2 minutes under a no-load condition; make sure all of the accessories are turned **OFF**.

b. Run the engine at idle speed.

c. Race the engine 2–3 times under no-load, then, run it for 1 minute at idle.

10. Adjust the idle to the correct setting.

11. Aim the timing light at the timing marks. If the marks on the pulley and the engine are aligned when the light flashes, the timing is correct. Turn the engine **OFF** and remove the tachometer and the timing light. If the marks are not in alignment, proceed with the following steps.

12. Turn the engine **OFF**.

13. Loosen the distributor lockbolt just enough so the distributor can be turned with a little effort.

14. Start the engine. Keep the wires of the timing light clear of the fan.

15. With the timing light aimed at the pulley and the marks on the engine, turn the distributor in the direction of rotor rotation to retard the spark or in the opposite direction to advance the spark. Align the marks on the pulley and the engine with the flashes of the timing light.

16. Tighten the distributor lockbolt and recheck the timing.

DIESEL ENGINE

The ignition timing is controlled by the position of the fuel injection pump. Locate the injection pump and inspect the alignment of the timing marks (one on the engine and the injection pump). If necessary, loosen the injection pump-to-engine bolts, then, turn the pump to align the timing marks. Torque the injection pump-to-engine bolts to 14–18 ft. lbs.

Alternator

For further information, please refer to "Electrical" in the Unit Repair section.

Belt Tension Adjustment

Belt tension should be checked with a gauge made for the purpose. If a tension gauge is not available, tension can be checked with moderate thumb pressure applied to the belt at its longest span midway between pulleys. If the belt has a free span less than 12 in., it should deflect approximately 1/8–1/4 in. If the span is longer than 12 in., deflection can range between 1/8–3/8 in. To adjust or replace belts:

1. Loosen the alternator's pivot and mounting bolts.

2. Move the alternator toward or away from the engine until the tension is correct.

NOTE: Use a wooden hammer handle or broomstick, as a lever but do not use anything metallic, such as a pry bar.

3. Tighten the bolts and recheck the tension. If new belts have been installed, run the engine for a few minutes, then, recheck and readjust as necessary. It is better to have belts too loose than too tight, because overtight belts will lead to bearing failure, particularly in the water pump and alternator. However, loose belts place an extremely high impact load on the driven component due to the whipping action of the belt.

Removal and Installation

1. Disconnect the negative battery cable.

2. Disconnect the electrical connector from the alternator.

3. Loosen the drive belt adjusting bolt, push the alternator toward the engine and remove the drive belt.

4. Remove the alternator-to-bracket bolts and the alternator from the vehicle.

5. To install, reverse the removal procedures. Adjust the drive belt tension. Torque as follows:

Alternator-to-lower bracket bolt
Gasoline engine—27–37 ft. lbs.
Diesel engine—20–27 ft. lbs.
Alternator-to-adjusting bracket bolt
Z24i and KA24E engines—6–8 ft. lbs.
VG30i and VG30E engines—10–12 ft. lbs.
Diesel engine—8–10 ft. lbs.

Starter

For further information, please refer to "Electrical" in the Unit Repair section.

Removal and Installation

1. If necessary, raise and safely support the vehicle.

2. Disconnect the negative battery cable.

3. Disconnect the electrical connectors from the starter, taking note of the positions for reinstallation purposes.

4. Remove the starter-to-engine bolts and the starter from the vehicle.

5. To install, reverse the removal procedures. Torque the starter-to-transmission bolts to 29–36 ft. lbs.

Diesel Glow Plugs

Removal and Installation

1. Disconnect the negative battery cable.

2. Disconnect the glow plug electrical leads. Remove the glow plug connecting plate.

3. Remove the glow plugs from the cylinder head.

4. Inspect the tips of the plugs for any evidence of melting. If one glow plug tip looks bad, replace all of the plugs.

5. To install, reverse the removal procedures.

Testing

The glow plugs are tested by checking their resistance with an ohmmeter. The plugs can be tested either removed or installed in the cylinder head.

1. Disconnect the electrical connector from the glow plug.

2. Connect the positive (+) ohmmeter lead to the glow plug's electrical connector and the negative (−) lead to the glow plug's body.

3. If a minimum of continuity is shown, the glow plug is OK; if no continuity is shown, replace the glow plug.

CHASSIS ELECTRICAL

Heater Blower Motor

Removal and Installation

VAN
Front Unit

1. Disconnect the negative battery cable.
2. Remove the package tray or glove box.
3. Disconnect the electrical connector from the blower motor.
4. Remove the blower motor-to-housing screws and the blower motor.
5. To install, reverse the removal procedures.

Rear Unit

1. Disconnect the negative battery cable.
2. Remove the rear heater unit cover panel.
3. Disconnect the electrical connector from the blower motor.
4. Remove the blower motor-to-housing screws and the blower motor.
5. To install, reverse the removal procedures.

EXCEPT VAN

The blower motor is accessible from under the right side of the instrument panel.

1. Disconnect the negative battery cable.

NOTE: On the Axxess, it may be necessary to remove the glove box or package tray.

2. Disconnect the electrical connector from the blower motor.
3. Remove the blower motor-to-heater unit screws and the blower motor from the unit.
4. To install, reverse the removal procedures.

Windshield Wiper Motor

Removal and Installation

FRONT

1. Disconnect the negative battery cable.
2. Remove the wiper blades and arms as an assembly from the pivots. The arms are retained to the pivots by nuts; remove the nuts and pull the arms straight off.
3. Remove the cowl top grille screws (from the front edge) and pull the grille forward to disengage the rear tabs.
4. Remove the wiper motor arm-to-connecting rod stop ring.
5. From under the instrument panel, disconnect the electrical connector from the wiper motor harness.
6. Remove the wiper motor-to-cowl screws and the wiper motor from the vehicle.

NOTE: If the motor has been run, be sure the motor is in the PARK position before installing the wiper arms. To do this, turn the ignition switch ON and cycle the motor 3–4 times. Turn the motor OFF and allow the motor to return to the PARK position.

7. To install, reverse the removal procedures. The wiper arms should be installed so the blades are 0.98 in. (25mm) for Pick-Up and Pathfinder, 1.12 in. (55mm) driver's side and 0.20 in. (5mm) passenger's side for Van or 1.62 in. (40mm) for Axxess, above and parallel to the windshield molding.

NOTE: If the motor has been run, be sure the motor is in the PARK position before installing the wiper arms. To do this, turn the ignition switch ON and cycle the mo-

tor 3–4 times. Turn the motor OFF and allow the motor to return to the PARK position.

REAR EXCEPT PICK-UP

1. Disconnect the negative battery cable.
2. From the rear door, remove the wiper blade/arm as an assembly from the pivot. The arm is retained to the pivots by a nut; remove the nut and pull the arm straight off.
3. From inside the rear door, remove wiper motor cover plate.
4. Remove the wiper motor arm-to-connecting rod stop ring.
5. Disconnect the electrical connector from the rear wiper motor harness.
6. Remove the wiper motor-to-rear door screws and the wiper motor from the vehicle.

NOTE: If the wiper motor has been run, be sure the motor is in the PARK position before installing the wiper arms. To do this, turn the ignition switch ON and cycle the motor 3–4 times. Turn the motor OFF and allow the motor to return to the PARK position.

7. To install, reverse the removal procedures.

Windshield Wiper Switch

The windshield wiper switch is a part of the combination switch located on the steering column.

Removal and Installation

1. Disconnect the negative battery cable.
2. Remove the shell covers-to-steering column screws and the covers from the steering column.
3. Disconnect the windshield wiper switch electrical connector.
4. Remove the windshield wiper switch-to-combination switch screws and the windshield wiper switch from the steering column.
5. To install, reverse the removal procedures.

Instrument Cluster

Removal and Installation

1. Disconnect the negative battery cable.
2. Remove the instrument cluster bezel screws and the bezel.
3. Remove the instrument cluster-to-dash screws and pull the cluster assembly forward.
4. Disconnect the electrical connectors from the rear of the instrument cluster.
5. To install, reverse the removal procedures.

Headlight Switch

The headlight switch is a part of the combination switch located on the steering column.

Removal and Installation

1. Disconnect the negative battery cable.
2. Remove the shell covers-to-steering column screws and the covers from the steering column.
3. Disconnect the headlight/turn signal switch electrical connector.
4. Remove the headlight/turn signal switch-to-combination switch screws and the headlight/turn signal switch from the steering column.

5. To install, reverse the removal procedures.

Dimmer Switch

The dimmer switch is a part of the combination switch located on the steering column.

Removal and Installation

1. Disconnect the negative battery cable.
2. Remove the shell covers-to-steering column screws and the covers from the steering column.
3. Disconnect the dimmer switch electrical connector.
4. Remove the dimmer switch-to-combination switch screws and the dimmer switch from the steering column.
5. To install, reverse the removal procedures.

Turn Signal Switch

The turn signal switch is a part of the combination switch located on the steering column.

Removal and Installation

1. Disconnect the negative battery cable.
2. Remove the shell covers-to-steering column screws and the covers from the steering column.
3. Disconnect the turn signal switch electrical connector.
4. Remove the turn signal switch-to-combination switch screws and the turn signal switch from the steering column.
5. To install, reverse the removal procedures.

Combination Switch

The combination switch consists of the headlight, windshield wiper/washer, turn signal and dimmer switches.

NOTE: The switches can be removed from the combination switch base without removing the base.

Removal and Installation

1. Disconnect the negative battery cable.
2. Remove the horn pad and the steering wheel nut. Using the puller tool, press the steering wheel from the steering column.
3. Disconnect the wiring harness from the clip which retains it to the lower instrument panel.
4. Disconnect the electrical connectors from the combination switch.
5. Remove the steering column shell cover screws and the covers (upper and lower).
6. Loosen the combination switch-to-steering column screw and remove the switch assembly.

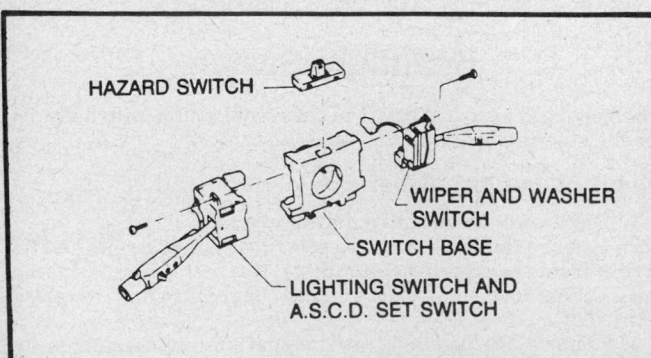

HAZARD SWITCH

WIPER AND WASHER SWITCH

SWITCH BASE

LIGHTING SWITCH AND A.S.C.D. SET SWITCH

Exploded view of the combination switch

7. To install, align the hole in the steering column with the protrusion on the switch body and reverse the removal procedures.

Ignition Lock/Switch

Removal and Installation

1. Disconnect the negative battery cable.
2. From the upper steering column, remove the shell cover screws and the covers.
3. Disconnect the electrical connector from the rear of the ignition switch.
4. Using a drill, remove the self-shear type screws from the ignition switch.
5. Remove the screws and the ignition switch.
6. To install, reverse the removal procedures. Torque the shear-type screws until the heads shear.

Stoplight Switch

The stop light switch is attached to a bracket at the top of the brake pedal.

Removal and Installation

1. Disconnect the negative battery cable.
2. From under the dash, disconnect the electrical connector from the stop light switch.
3. Loosen and remove the locknut from the stop light switch.
4. Unscrew the stop light switch from the brake pedal bracket.

NOTE: To adjust the stop light switch, the engine must be running.

5. To install, reverse the removal procedures. Perform the brake pedal height and freeplay adjustments. Torque the stop light switch locknut to 9–11 ft. lbs.

Adjustment

To perform this procedure the engine must be running.
1. Depress the brake pedal until pushrod resistance is felt.
2. Using a 0.012–039 in. feeler gauge, measure stop light switch-to-brake pedal gap.
3. If necessary, disconnect the electrical connector from the stop light switch, loosen the stop light switch locknut and adjust the stop light switch.
4. After adjustment, torque the stop light switch locknut to 9–12 ft. lbs.

Clutch Switch

The clutch switch is normally attached to a bracket that is mounted to the upper portion of the clutch pedal bracket.

Removal and Installation

1. Disconnect the negative battery cable.
2. Disconnect the electrical connector from the clutch switch.
3. Loosen the locknut and unscrew the switch from the bracket.
4. To install, screw the clutch switch into the bracket until the following pedal height is established:
Pick-Up and Pathfinder
 Z24i, KA24E and SD25 engines – 9.29–9.69 in. (236–246mm)
 VG30i and VG30E engines – 8.94–9.33 in. (227–237mm)
Van
 Z24i engine – 6.97–7.25 in. (177–184mm)
Axxess
 KA24E engine – 6.97–7.36 in. (177–187mm)

NOTE: The pedal height is the distance from the floor board to the front center of the clutch pedal.

5. Torque the clutch switch locknut to 9–11 ft. lbs. (12–15 Nm).

6. Connect the negative battery cable.

Clutch Interlock Switch

The clutch interlock switch is normally attached to a bracket that is mounted to the cowl.

Removal and Installation

1. Disconnect the negative battery cable.
2. Disconnect the electrical connector from the clutch interlock switch.
3. Loosen the locknut and unscrew the switch from the bracket.
4. To install, use a feeler gauge and screw the clutch interlock switch into the bracket.
5. Fully, depress the clutch pedal and adjust the gap between the clutch pedal stopper bracket and the threaded end of the clutch interlock switch to:

Pick-Up, Pathfinder and Van
  0.012–0.039 in. (0.3–1.0mm)

Axxess
  0.059–0.138 in. (1.5–3.5mm)

6. Torque the clutch interlock switch locknut to 9–11 ft. lbs. (12–15 Nm).
7. Connect the negative battery cable.

Fuses and Circuit Breakers

Location

The fuse block is located under the left side of the dash for 1986–87 Pick-Up, 1986–87 Pathfinder, Van and 1990 Axxess or under the right side of the steering column for the 1988–90 Pick-Up and Pathfinder or under a cover panel located on the left side of the steering column.

Fusible links are located at the right front fender for 1986–87 Pick-Up and Pathfinder.

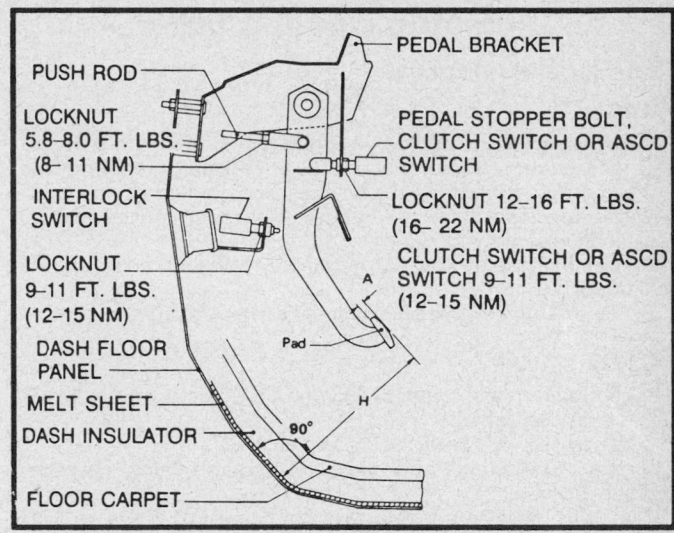

View of the clutch pedal and clutch switch adjustments – typical

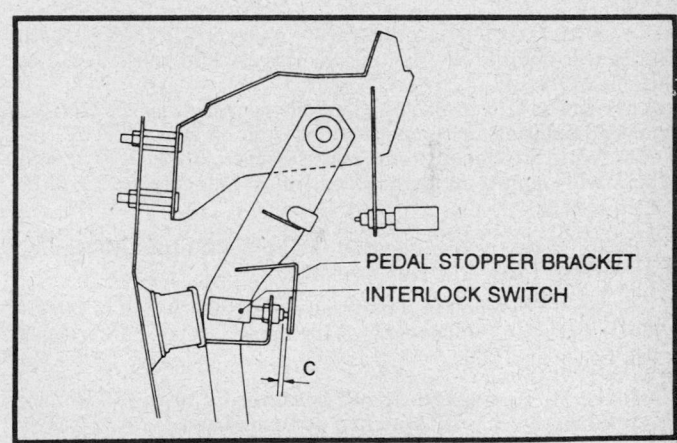

View of the clutch interlock switch adjustment – Typical

ENGINE COOLING

Radiator

Removal and Installation
AXXESS

1. Disconnect the negative battery cable.
2. Disconnect the electrical connectors from the cooling fans.
3. Remove the fan shroud-to-chassis bolts and the shroud.
4. Raise and safely support the vehicle.
5. Drain the cooling system.
6. Remove the upper and lower cooling hoses from the radiator. Remove the reservoir hose from the radiator. If necessary, remove the coolant reservoir.
7. If equipped with an automatic transaxle, disconnect and plug oil coolant lines from the radiator.
8. Remove the upper radiator-to-chassis bolts and lift the radiator from the vehicle.

9. To install, reverse the removal procedures. Refill the cooling system.
10. Start the engine, allow it to reach normal operating temperatures and check for leaks.

EXCEPT AXXESS

1. Disconnect the negative battery cable.
2. Drain the engine cooling system.
3. On the Van, remove the upper radiator hoses and radiator cap assembly. On all except Van, remove the upper and lower radiator hoses.
4. If equipped with an automatic transmission, disconnect and plug the transmission oil cooler lines at the radiator.
5. Remove the radiator shroud and the radiator.
6. To install, reverse the removal procedures.
7. If equipped with an automatic transmission, check and/or refill the transmission. Refill the cooling system.

Electric Cooling Fan

Removal and Installation

AXXESS

1. Disconnect the negative battery cable.
2. Disconnect the electrical connectors from the cooling fans.
3. Remove the fan shroud-to-chassis bolts and the shroud.
4. Remove fan blade assembly-to-fan motor nut(s) and the fan blade assembly(s).
5. Remove the cooling fan motor(s)-to-shroud bolts and the fan motor(s).
6. To install, reverse the removal procedures.

Testing

The cooling fans are controlled by the ECU; testing must be performed on the vehicle.

1. Turn the air conditioning switch **OFF**.
2. Start the engine and allow it to reach normal operating temperatures.

   a. With the coolant temperature below 201°F (94°C), both fans will not operate.

   b. With the coolant temperature at 203°F–210°F (95°C–99°C), 1 fan will operate at low speed; relay 1 will be turned **ON**.

   c. With the coolant temperature above 212°F (100°C), both fans will operate at high speed; relay 1 and relay 2 will be turned **ON**.

3. Turn the air conditioning and blower fan switches **ON**; the evaporator outlet air temperature should be over 46°F (8°C).

   a. With the coolant temperature below 201°F (94°C), both fans will operate at high speed; relay 1 and relay 2 will be turned **ON**.

NOTE: If the vehicle speed is above 50 mph (80 km/h), the cooling fans will not operate.

   b. With the coolant temperature at 203°F–210°F (95°C–99°C), both fans will operate at high speed; relay 1 and relay 2 will be turned **ON**.

NOTE: If the vehicle speed is above 50 mph (80 km/h), the cooling fans will operate at low speed.

   c. With the coolant temperature above 212°F (100°C), both fans will operate at high speed; relay 1 and relay 2 will be turned **ON**.

4. With the air conditioning and blower fan switches turned **ON** and the evaporator outlet air temperature at 37°F–46°F (3°C–8°C).

   a. With the coolant temperature below 201°F (94°C), 1 fan will operate at low speed; relay 1 will be turned **ON**.

NOTE: If the vehicle speed is above 50 mph (80 km/h), the cooling fans will not operate.

   b. With the coolant temperature at 203°F–210°F (95°C–99°C), 1 fan will operate at low speed; relay 1 will be turned **ON**.

   c. With the coolant temperature above 212°F (100°C), both fans will operate at high speed; relay 1 and relay 2 will be turned **ON**.

Heater Core

Removal and Installation

1. Disconnect the negative battery cable.
2. Drain the cooling system to a level below the heater core.
3. Disconnect the heater hose from the engine.
4. Remove the console box and instrument assembly.
5. Disconnect the electrical connectors from the heater unit. Disconnect the air intake control cable from the blower unit.

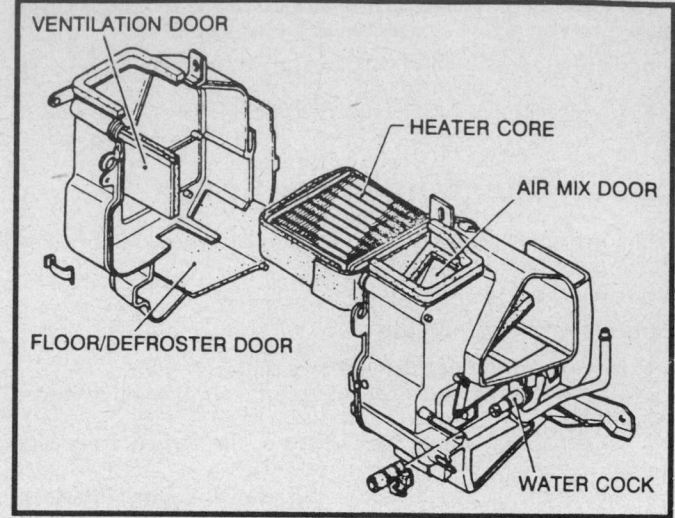

Exploded view of a typical heater core assembly

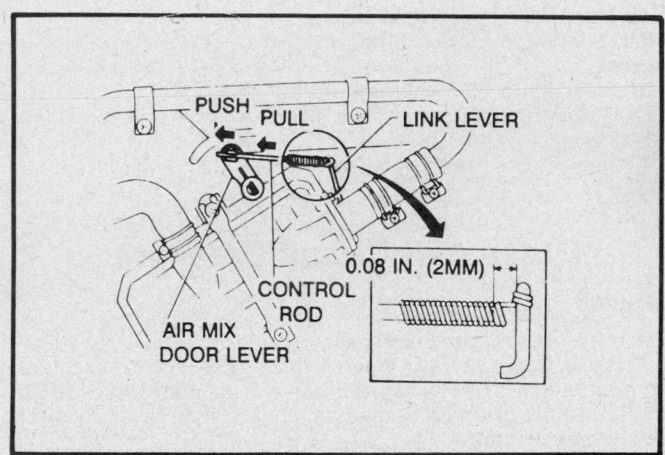

View of the water cock control rod adjustment— except Axxess

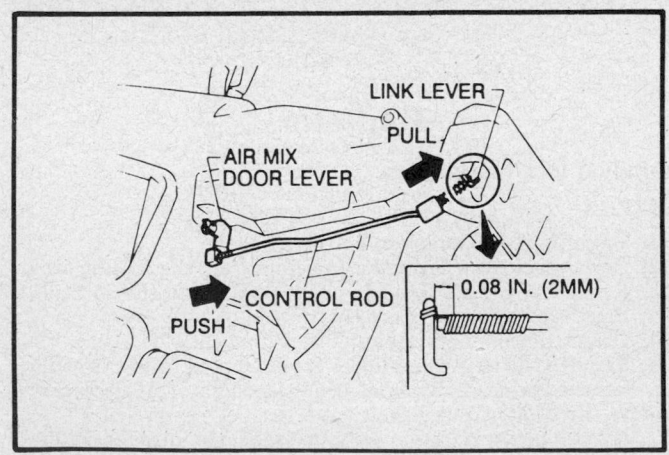

View of the water cock control rod adjustment— Axxess

6. Remove the blower unit. Remove the evaporator unit nuts/bolts but do not remove the unit.

7. Remove the heater assembly and separate the core from the assembly.

8. To install, reverse the removal procedures. Adjust the heater control cable for proper operation. Refill the cooling system. Operate the engine until normal operating temperatures are reached, then, check for leaks.

Water Pump

Removal and Installation

AXXESS

1. Disconnect the negative battery cable.

2. Position a clean drain pan under the radiator, remove the drain plug, remove the radiator cap and drain the engine coolant.

3. If necessary, remove the upper radiator hose.

4. Loosen the alternator-to-bracket bolts, move the inward and remove the drive belt.

5. Remove the drive pulley-to-water pump bolts and the pulley.

6. Remove the water pump-to-water pump housing bolts and the pump with the gasket.

7. Clean the gasket mounting surfaces.

8. To install, use a new gasket, sealant (if necessary) and reverse the removal procedures. Torque the water pump-to-water pump housing bolts to 12–15 ft. lbs. (16–21 Nm), the drive pulley-to-water pump bolts to 5.1–5.8 ft. lbs. (7–8 Nm). Adjust the drive belt tension. Refill the cooling system. Run the engine until normal operating temperatures are reached, then, inspect for leaks.

EXCEPT AXXESS

1. Disconnect the negative battery cable.

2. Position a clean drain pan under the radiator, open the drain cocks, remove the radiator cap and drain the engine coolant. If equipped with a diesel engine, remove the bypass hose from the pump.

NOTE: If equipped with a diesel engine, open the drain cocks on the engine. After draining the coolant, remove the thermostat coolant hose from the water pump.

3. Remove the upper radiator shroud screws and the shroud.

4. Loosen the alternator-to-bracket bolts, move the inward and remove the drive belt.

NOTE: If equipped with power steering, remove the drive belt.

5. Remove the fan-to-water pump bolts and the fan.

6. Remove the water pump-to-engine bolts and the pump with the fan pulley, coupling and gasket.

7. Clean the gasket mounting surfaces.

8. To install, use a new gasket, sealant (if necessary) and reverse the removal procedures. Torque as follows:

Water pump-to-engine bolts
  6mm bolts, 2.4L engine – 3–7 ft. lbs.
  8mm bolts, 2.4L engine – 7–12 ft. lbs.
  3.0L engine – 12–15 ft. lbs.
  8mm bolts, 2.5L diesel engine – 7–9 ft. lbs.
  10mm bolts, 2.5L diesel engine – 14–18 ft. lbs.

9. Adjust the drive belt tension. Refill the cooling system. Run the engine until normal operating temperatures are reached, then, inspect for leaks.

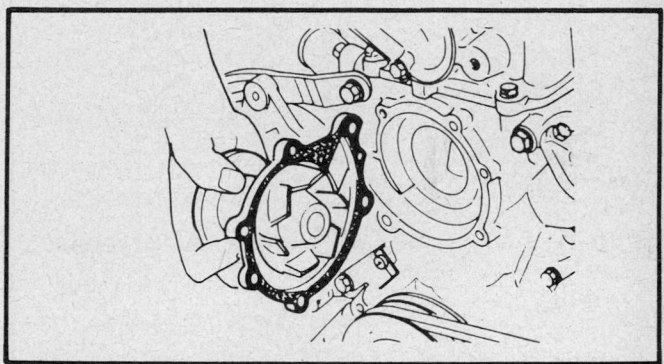

View the water pump assembly – 2.4L engine – except Axxess

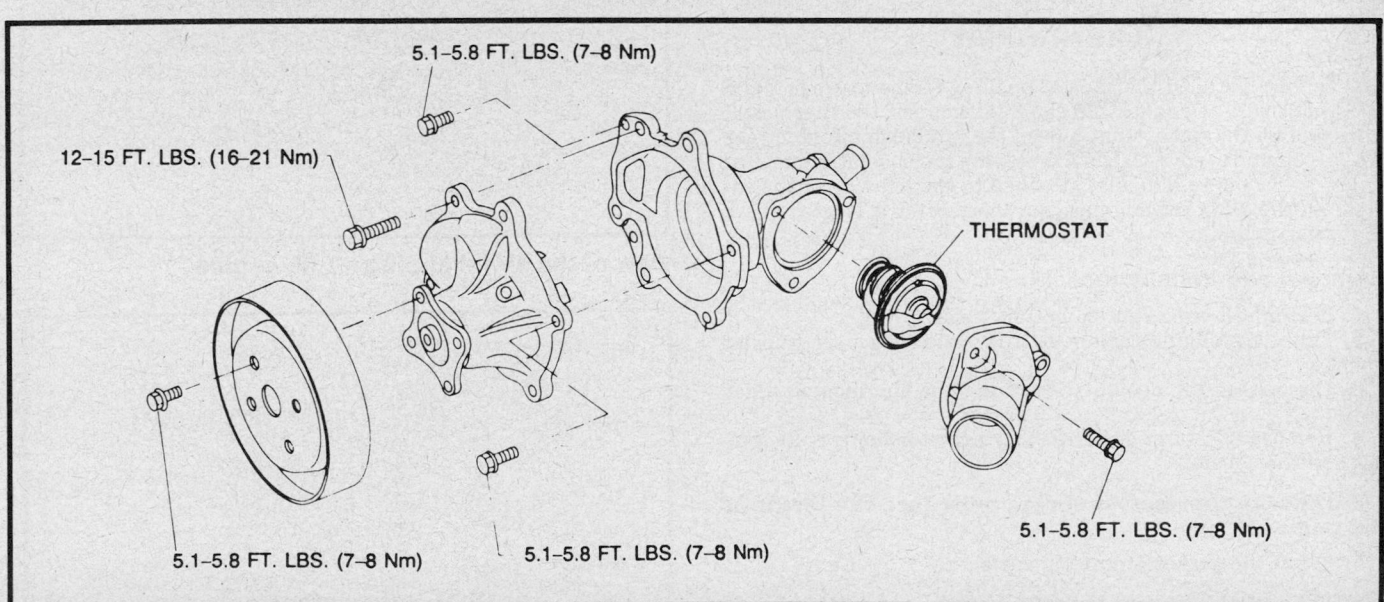

Exploded view the water pump assembly – 1990 2.4L engine – Axxess

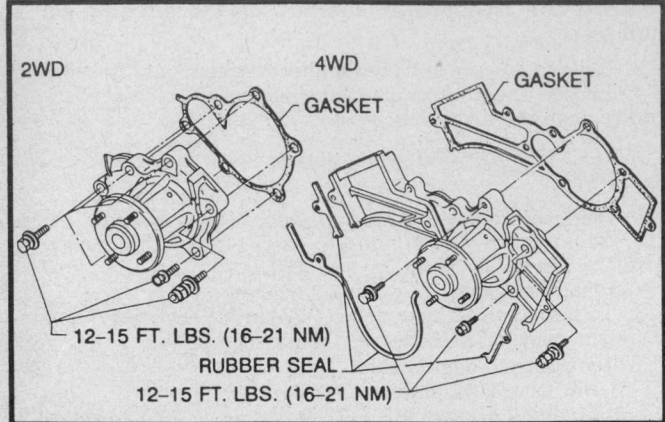

Exploded view of the water pump assemblies—3.0L engine

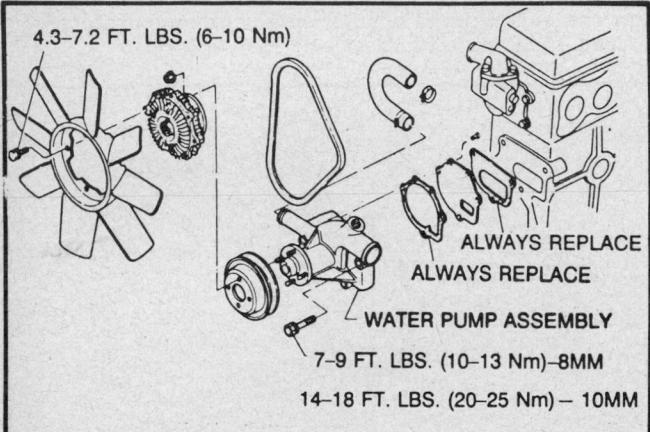

Exploded view of the water pump assembly—2.5L diesel engine

Thermostat

The factory-installed thermostat opening temperature is 180°F (USA) or 190°F (Canada). On the Z24i engines, the thermostat is located on the right, front-side of the intake manifold; on the KA24E engine used with the Axxess, the thermostat is enclosed in the water pump housing, attached to the left side of the engine; on the all other engines, the thermostat is located above the water pump.

Removal and Installation

1. Disconnect the negative battery cable.
2. Drain the engine coolant to a level below the thermostat housing.
3. Disconnect the coolant hose from the thermostat water outlet.
4. Remove the water outlet-to-thermostat housing bolts, gasket and thermostat.

NOTE:The thermostat spring must face the inside of the engine.

5. Clean the gasket mounting surfaces.

NOTE: If the thermostat, is equipped with an air bleed or jiggle valve, be sure to position it in the upward direction.

6. To install, use a new gasket, sealant (if necessary) and reverse the removal procedures. Torque as follows:
  Water outlet-to-thermostat housing bolts
  Z24i, VG30i and VG30E engines—12–15 ft. lbs. (16–21 Nm)
    KA24E engine—5.1–5.8 ft. lbs. (7–8 Nm)
    SD25 diesel engine—7–9 ft. lbs.

Cooling System Bleeding

1. Move the temperature control lever fully, to the **HOT** position.
2. If the radiator drain cock was opened or the engine drain plug was remove, close the drain cock and/or install the drain plug.
3. Fill the radiator.
4. Operate the engine until it warms up, stop it and allow it to cool down.
5. If equipped with an air relief plug, open it to bleed of the trapped air.
6. Repeat the refilling, warming and cooling operation 2–3 times.
7. Make sure the radiator is filled to the tank neck. Fill the reservoir to the **MAX** level.

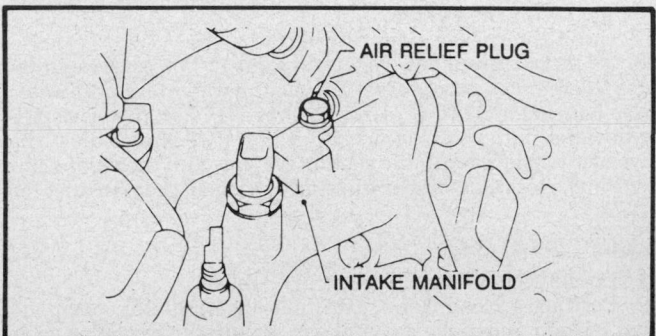

View of the air relief plug—2.4L engine—except Axxess

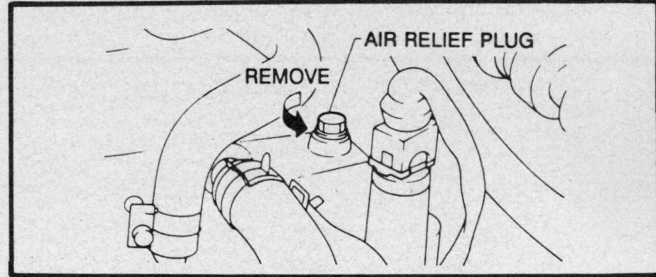

View of the air relief plug—3.0L engine

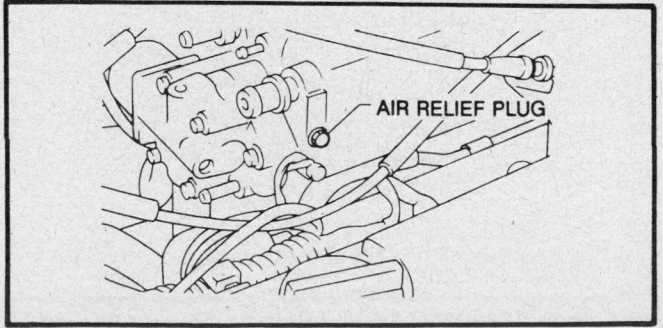

View of the air relief plug—1990 2.4L engine—Axxess

GASOLINE FUEL SYSTEM

Fuel System Service Precaution

Disconnect the negative battery cable. Keep a Class B dry chemical fire extinguisher available. Always relieve the fuel pressure before disconnecting a fuel line. Wrap a shop cloth around the fuel line when disconnecting a fuel line. Always use new O-rings. Do not replace the fuel pipes with fuel hoses. Always us a back-up wrench when opening or closing a fuel line.

Relieving Fuel System Pressure

1. From the fuse box, remove the fuel pump fuse.
2. Start the engine and allow it to run.
3. After the engine stalls, crank it 2–3 times to make sure the pressure is released.
4. Turn the ignition switch **OFF** and replace the fuse.

Fuel Filter

Removal and Installation

AXXESS

The fuel filter is located under the driver's side and attached to the chassis; it is concealed by a cover plate.
1. Relieve the fuel pressure.
2. Disconnect the negative battery cable.
3. Raise and safely support the vehicle.
4. Remove the fuel filter cover plate.
5. Loosen the hose clamps at the fuel inlet and outlet lines and slide each line off the filter nipples.
6. Remove the fuel filter.
7. Replace the fuel filter; be sure to use new hose clamps and the fuel filter arrows are facing the front of the vehicle.

EXCEPT AXXESS

The fuel filter is located in the right side of the engine compartment besided to the engine.
1. Release the fuel pressure.
2. Disconnect the negative battery cable.
3. Loosen the hose clamps at the fuel inlet and outlet lines and slide each line off the filter nipples.
4. Remove the fuel filter.
5. Replace the fuel filter; be sure to use new hose clamps and the fuel filter arrows are facing the engine.

Electric Fuel Pump

The fuel pump is located in the fuel tank which must be removed to remove the fuel pump.

Pressure Testing

1. Disconnect the hose from the pump outlet at the pump.
2. Connect a length of hose to the outlet. The hose should have an inside diameter of ¼ in. (6mm). The diameter of the hose is important for accurate measurements.
3. Raise the end of the hose above the level of the pump. Turn the ignition switch **ON** and catch the gasoline in a graduated container. Pump output should be 1400cc in a minute or less.

Removal and Installation

1. Relieve the fuel pressure. Disconnect the negative battery cable.
2. Siphon the fuel from the fuel tank.

NOTE: If fuel tank is equipped with a drain plug, remove the plug and drain the fuel into a proper fuel container.

3. Raise and safely support the vehicle.
4. Disconnect the fuel lines and the electrical connector(s) from the fuel pump assembly.

NOTE: For 4WD models, remove the fuel tank protector from the bottom of the fuel tank.

5. Remove the fuel tank filler tube-to-vehicle bolts (Pick-Up) or nuts (Van) and the outer plate.
6. Remove the fuel tank-to-chassis connectors and lower the tank from the vehicle.
7. Remove the fuel pump assembly-to-tank screws and lift the assembly from the tank.
8. To install, use a new fuel pump assembly-to-tank O-ring and reverse the removal procedures. Torque the fuel pump assembly-to-tank screws to 18–24 inch lbs. and the fuel tank protectors-to-chassis bolts to 20–26 ft. lbs. Refill the fuel tank.

Fuel Injection

Idle Speed Adjustment

1. Visually inspect the air cleaner for clogging, the hoses/ducts for leaks, the EGR valve operation, the electrical connectors, the gaskets, the throttle valve and throttle sensor operation and the AIV hose.

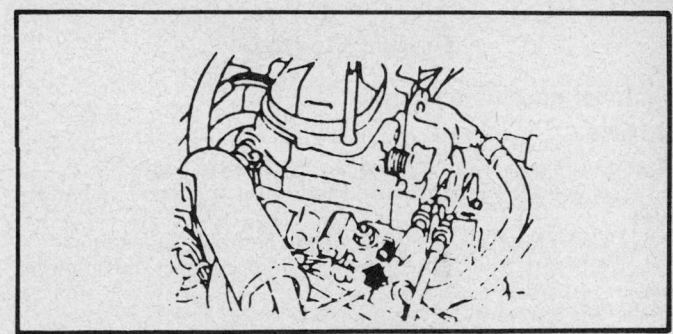

Location of the idle speed screw—1986–89 3.0L engine—1986–89 2.4L engine similar

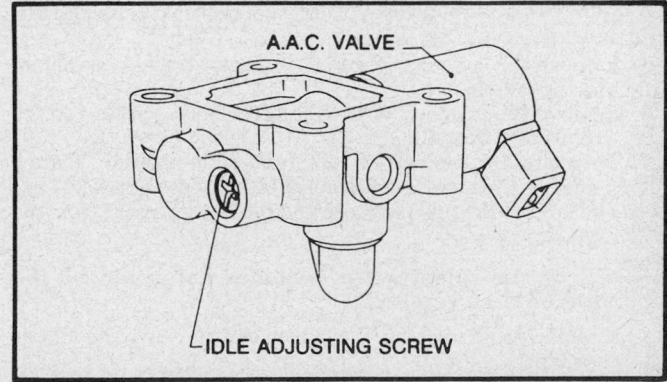

Location of the idle adjusting screw—1990 3.0L engine

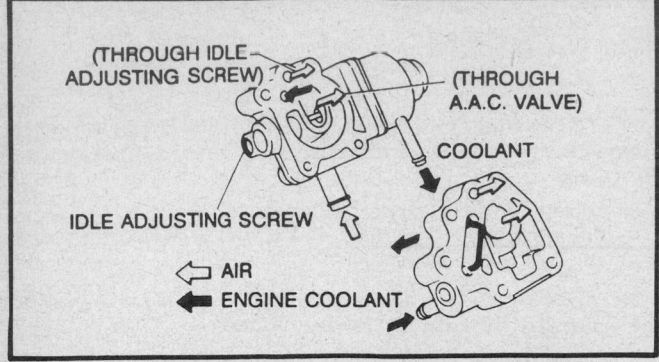

Location of the idle adjusting screw—1990 2.4L engine

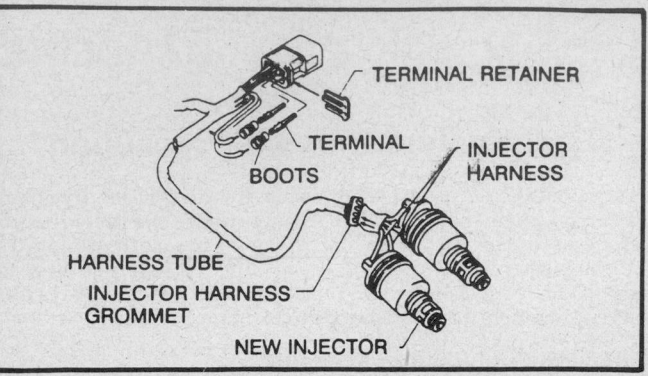

View of a typical 1986–89 fuel injector assembly

2. Set the parking brake and place the gear selector in **N**. Start the engine and allow it to reach normal operating temperatures.

3. Operate the engine, under no-load, for 2 minutes at about 2000 rpm.

4. Race the engine 2–3 times (under no-load) and operate it at idle speed for 1 minute.

5. If equipped with an automatic transmission, place the gear selector in **D**. Check and/or adjust the idle speed.

6. Using a timing light, check and/or adjust the ignition timing.

NOTE: If the ignition timing is not correct, turn the distributor to the correct value, then, reperform the idle speed adjustment until both values are correct.

Fuel Injector

Removal and Installation

1986–89

Dual fuel injectors are located in the throttle body.

1. Relieve the fuel pressure. Disconnect the negative battery cable.

2. Drain about 1⅛ qt. (1L) of coolant from the engine.

3. From the throttle body, remove or disconnect the following items:
   a. Air cleaner
   b. Electrical connectors from the throttle sensor, idle switch, fuel injectors, air flow meter and the Automatic Speed Control Device (ASCD), if equipped
   c. Accelerator cable
   d. Fuel and coolant hoses

4. Remove the throttle body-to-intake manifold nuts and the throttle body.

5. Remove the rubber seal and the injector harness grommet from the throttle body.

6. Remove the injector cover-to-injector body screws and the cover from the throttle body.

7. Turn the throttle valve to the fully open position. Place a hollow pipe, with the inside diameter of not less than 0.217 in., on the bottom of the fuel injectors and tap the injectors from the throttle body.

NOTE: If the injector tip becomes deformed by the pipe, it should be replaced.

8. If replacing an injector with a new one, perform the following operation:
   a. Disconnect the faulty injector wires from the electrical connector, then, cut the injector wires from the metal terminals and pull the injector wiring from the harness tube.

b. Using a new injector(s), install it into the harness tube and connect new terminals to the injector wires.

NOTE: Be sure to install a new electrical harness grommet every time a new injector is installed.

   c. Install the terminals into the electrical harness connector.
To install:

9. To install, use new O-rings (on the fuel injectors) and push the injectors into the throttle body until the O-rings are fully seated.

NOTE: Invert the throttle body to make sure the injector tips are properly seated.

10. Using silicone sealant, apply it to the injector harness grommet.

NOTE: An airtight seal is essential to ensure a stable and proper idling condition.

11. Using locking sealant, coat the injector cover screw threads, install the injector cover-to-throttle body screws. Torque the injector cover screws in a criss-cross pattern to 1.5–2.5 ft. lbs.

12. Using silicone sealant, coat the top of the throttle body and install the air cleaner rubber seal.

NOTE: Do not install the air cleaner until the air cleaner seal (silicone sealant) has hardened.

13. Install the throttle body and torque the throttle body-to-intake manifold nuts to 9–13 ft. lbs.

14. To complete the installation, reverse the removal procedures. Refill the cooling system. Start the engine, then, check for leaks and proper idling conditions. Stop the engine and check for dripping fuel on the throttle valve.

1990
2.4L Engine

The engine is equipped 4 fuel injectors, with one located at each cylinder.

1. Relieve the fuel pressure.

2. Disconnect the negative battery cable.

3. Label and disconnect the electrical connectors from the fuel injectors.

4. Disconnect the fuel rail from the fuel system.

5. Remove the fuel rail from the intake manifold; pull the fuel rail with the injectors connected from the intake manifold.

6. Separate the fuel injectors from the fuel rail.
To install:

7. Replace the fuel injector O-rings.

8. Install the fuel injectors to the fuel rail.

9. Lubricate the fuel injector O-rings with automatic transmission fluid and press them, with the fuel rail, into the intake manifold.

10. Install the fuel rail-to-intake manifold bolts.

11. Connect the fuel rail to the fuel system.

12. Connect the electrical connectors to the fuel injectors.

13. Connect the negative battery cable.

14. Turn the ignition switch **ON** and check for fuel leaks at the fuel rail.

3.0L Engine

The engine is equipped 6 fuel injectors, with one located at each cylinder.

1. Relieve the fuel pressure.

2. Disconnect the negative battery cable.

3. Remove the air cleaner from the throttle body.

4. Label and disconnect the vacuum hoses, electrical connectors and throttle cable from the throttle body/intake manifold collector assembly.

5. Remove the intake manifold collector-to-intake manifold bolts and the collector.

6. Disconnect the electrical connector(s) from the fuel injector(s).

7. Remove the fuel injector-to-fuel tube assembly clamp bolts and the clamp.

8. Pull the fuel injector from the fuel tube assembly. Remove and discard the O-rings.

To install:

9. Replace the fuel injector O-rings.

10. Lubricate the fuel injector O-rings with automatic transmission fluid and press them, into the fuel tube assembly.

11. Connect the electrical connectors to the fuel injectors.

12. Using a new gasket, install the intake manifold collector-to-intake manifold bolts. Torque the bolts to 13–16 ft. lbs. (18–22 Nm).

13. Connect the electrical connectors, the vacuum lines and the accelerator cable.

14. Install the air cleaner to the throttle body.

15. Connect the negative battery cable.

16. Turn the ignition switch **ON** and check for fuel leaks at the fuel rail.

DIESEL FUEL SYSTEM

Fuel System Service Precaution

Disconnect the negative battery cable. Keep a Class B dry chemical fire extinguisher available. Always relieve the fuel pressure before disconnecting a fuel line. Wrap a shop cloth around the fuel line when disconnecting a fuel line. Always use new O-rings. Do not replace the fuel pipes with fuel hoses. Always us a back-up wrench when opening or closing a fuel line.

Fuel Filter

There is a fuel filter and a sedimentor/fuel heater. Both units are found in the rear, right side of the engine compartment, connected to a bracket attached to the firewall.

Removal and Installation

1. Place a rag under the filter and the remove the fuel line.

2. Drain the fuel from the filter.

3. Unscrew the fuel filter from the bracket head.

4. Clean the fuel filter mounting surface on the bracket.

5. To install, use a new fuel filter, lubricate the rubber gasket with diesel fuel, screw it onto the bracket until it is snug and tighten it an additional ⅔ turn.

6. Bleed the fuel system, start the engine and check for leaks.

Draining Water From the System

NOTE: When the fuel filter warning light or buzzer turns ON, the water in the fuel filter must be drained immediately.

1. Raise the hood and position a small pan under the filter to catch the water.

2. Reach under the fuel filter and loosen the drain valve, 4–5 turns, until the water begins to flow; do not remove the drain valve/connector.

3. Depress the priming handle, located on top of the filter bracket, to speed the water removal from the filter. Pump the priming handle until only fuel is being removed from the system.

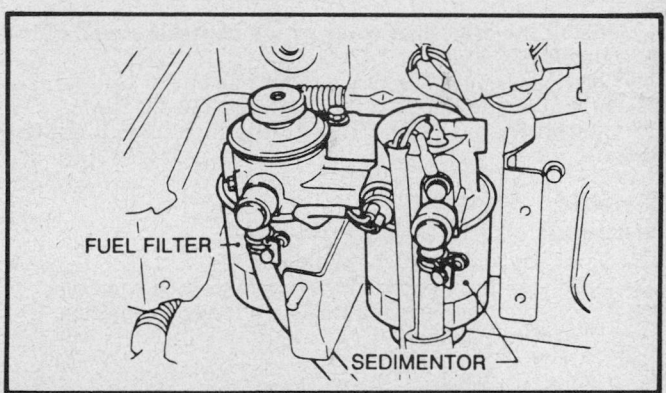
View of the fuel filter and sedimentor—2.5L diesel engine

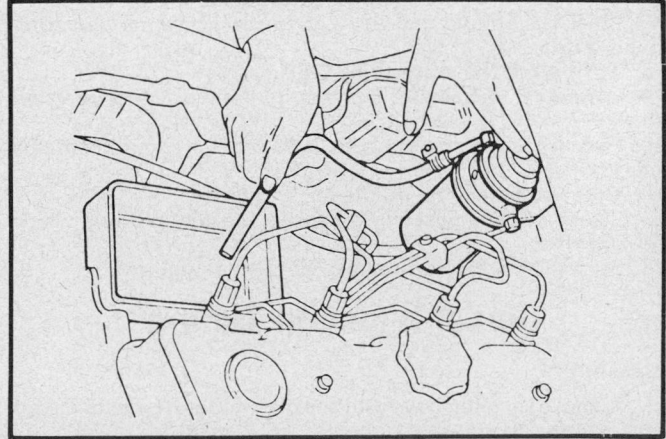
Location of the priming handle and air vent—2.5L diesel engine

Diesel Injection Pump

Removal and Installation

1. Relieve the fuel pressure. Disconnect the negative battery cable.
2. Rotate the crankshaft to position the No. 1 cylinder on the TDC of its compression stroke.
3. Disconnect the injection tubes. Plug the nozzle openings and be careful not to damage the spill tube.
4. Lable and disconnect the fuel cut solenoid harness.
5. Disconnect the accelerator wire, the overflow hose and the fuel inlet hose. Additionally, disconnect the cold start device water line and the fuel return hose; plug it also.
6. Loosen the bolts and remove the injection pump drive gear cover.
7. Loosen the drive gear nut and remove the gear with a 2-arm puller.
8. Loosen the mounting nuts/bolts and remove the injection pump with the injection tubes still attached.

To install:

9. Check that the No. 1 piston is still at TDC and position the injection pump so the pump flange aligns with the **Y** mark on the front cover. Install the drive gear and tighten the nut to 43–51 ft. lbs. (59–69 Nm).

NOTE: Be careful not to allow the key to fall into the front cover and be absolutely certain that the Y marks are aligned.

10. Install the drive gear cover with a new gasket and adjust the plunger lift.
11. Tighten the injection pump mounting nut to 14–18 ft. lbs. (20–25 Nm) and the bolts to 12–16 ft. lbs. (16–22 Nm).
12. Install the injection tubes to the injectors. Bleed the system.

Idle Speed Adjustment

1. Release the cold start device system.
2. Check and/or adjust the timing.
3. Make sure the injection nozzles are in good condition.
4. Make sure the following items are in good condition:
   a. Throttle chamber
   b. Air cleaner unclogged
   c. Glow system
   d. Engine oil and coolant levels
   e. Valve clearance
   f. Air intake system
5. Firmly, engage the parking brake, block the wheels and move the shift lever into the **N** position.
6. Turn the air conditioner and headlights **OFF**.
7. Start the engine and allow it to reach normal operating temperatures.
8. Turn all of the accessories **OFF**.
9. Connect a tachometer's pickup to the No. 1 fuel injection tube.
10. Operate the engine at about 2000 rpm for about 2 minutes under no-load.
11. Operate the engine at idle for 1 minutes.
12. Check and/or adjust the idle speed; the idle speed should be 650–800 rpm.
13. Stop the engine and remove the test equipment.

Diesel Injection Timing

Adjustment

1. Remove the plug bolt from the distributor head and install a dial gauge.
2. Rotate the cold start device linkage clockwise and install a block of wood or paper (15mm) between the linkage and the device.

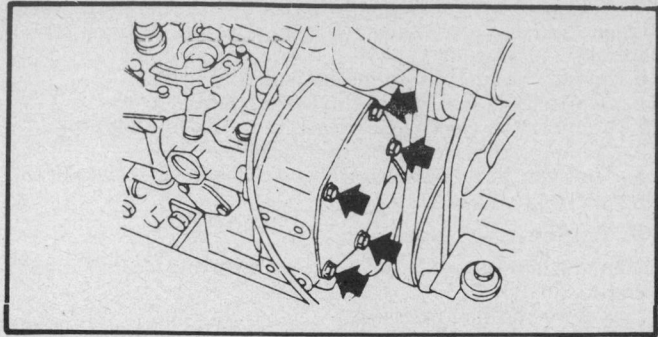

Removing the drive gear cover—2.5L diesel engine

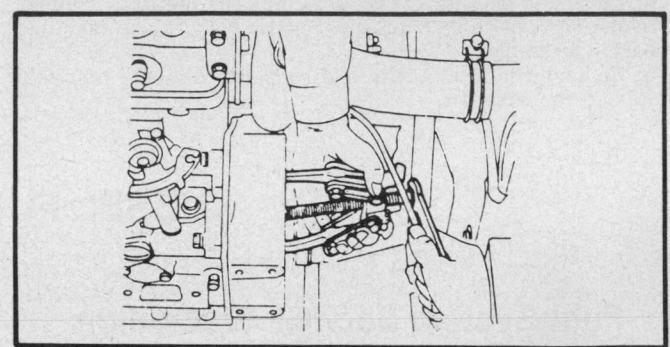

Removing the drive gear nut—2.5L diesel engine

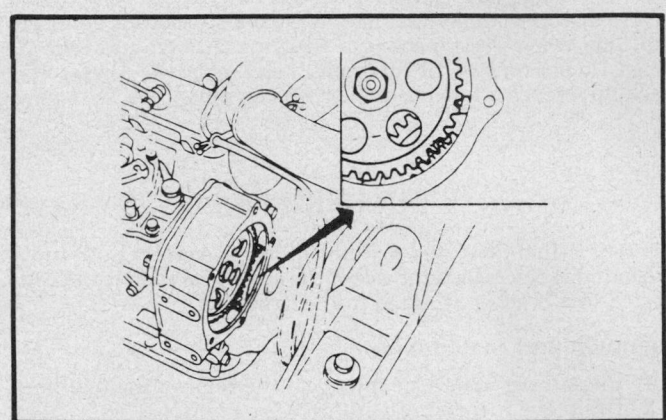

Checking that the Y marks on the gears are aligned—2.5L diesel engine

FRONT COVER MARK

TOP MARK

Aligning the crankshaft timing marks—2.5L diesel engine

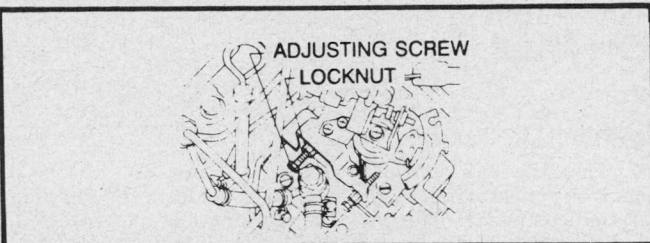

View of the idle speed adjusting screw—2.5L diesel engine

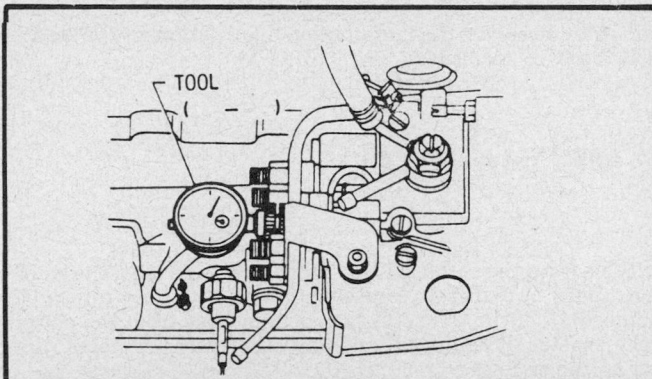

Install a dial gauge in the plug hole to check the plunger lift—2.5L diesel engine

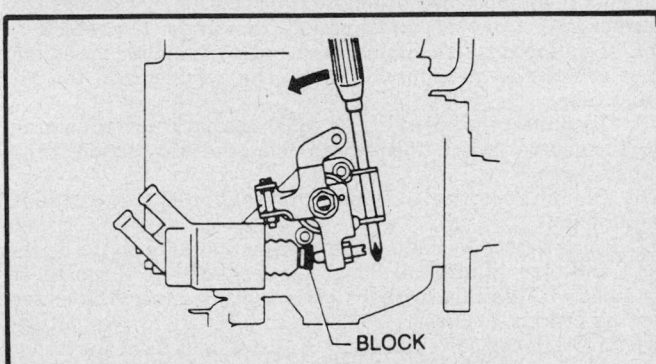

Fabricate a wooden block about 15mm thick—2.5L diesel engine

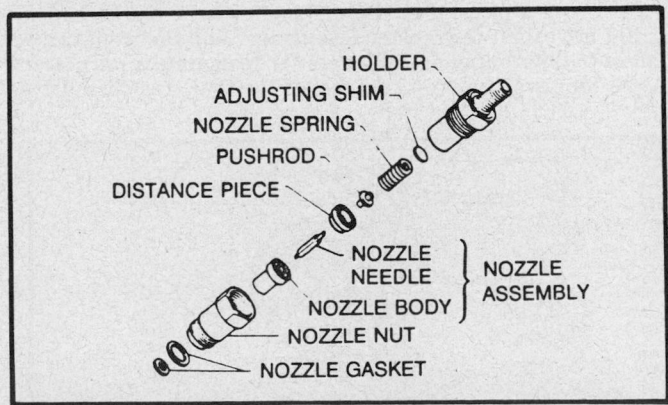

Exploded view of the injection nozzle—2.5L diesel engine

3. Set the No. 1 piston at TDC of the compression stroke and rotate the crankshaft counterclockwise 20–25 degrees. Check the gauge in this position and reset it to zero.

4. Rotate the crankshaft clockwise until the No. 1 piston is at TDC and read the gauge; the plunger lift should be 0.0374–0.0390 in. (0.95–0.99mm).

5. Adjust the plunger lift by rotating the injection pump until it is within range. Clockwise to decrease the measurement and counterclockwise to increase.

6. Tighten the injection pump mounting bolts. Disconnect the dial gauge and install the plug bolt with a new washer; torque it to 10–14 ft. lbs. (14–20mm).

Fuel Injector

Removal and Installation

1. Relieve the fuel pressure.
2. Disconnect the negative battery cable.
3. Loosen the injection lines at the pump and nozzles and remove and plug the lines.
4. Unscrew the injector and holder from the cylinder head.
5. Secure the nozzle holder in a vise and remove the locknut.
6. Remove the nipple.
7. Remove the nozzle holder body from the nozzle nut.
8. Remove the spacer collar and pushrod.
9. Remove the nozzle holder body from the vise, the nozzle spring and adjusting shims.

NOTE: The adjusting shims may be removed with a piece of wire but great care must be taken to avoid damage to the nozzle tip.

10. Clean fuel oil may be used to clean all parts. Inspect all parts for damage and good fit.
11. Assemble the nozzle in the reverse order of disassembly.
12. To install, reverse the removal procedures. Torque the nozzles and lines to 50–65 ft. lbs.

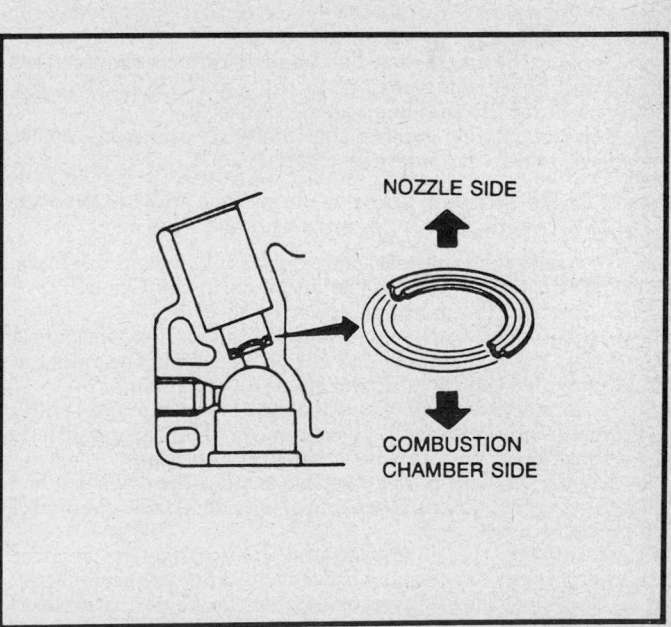

Installing the nozzle gasket—2.5L diesel engine

EMISSION CONTROLS

Please refer to "Professional Emission Component Application Guide".

Emission Warning Lamp

The check engine light is located on the instrument panel of California vehicles only and indicates an emission performance malfunction.

Resetting

1. Turn the ignition switch **ON**.
2. If the check engine light turns **ON**, perform the self-diagnosis procedures to determine the malfunction.
3. Turn the ignition switch **OFF**.
4. Locate and repair the malfunction.

NOTE: When the malfunction is repaired, the check engine light will stay OFF.

5. After 50 starts, the malfunction information will be erased from the ECU memory.

GASOLINE ENGINE MECHANICAL

NOTE: Disconnecting the negative battery cable on some vehicles may interfere with the functions of the on board computer systems and may require the computer to undergo a relearning process, once the negative battery cable is reconnected.

Engine

Removal and Installation

PICK-UP AND PATHFINDER

1. Disconnect the negative battery cable.

NOTE: On some vehicles, it may be necessary to remove the battery.

2. Using a scribing tool, mark the location of the hood hinges on the body and remove the hood.
3. If equipped with fuel injection, remove the fuel pump fuse from the fuse panel, operate the engine until it stalls, crank the engine to make sure it will not start.
4. Remove the air cleaner. Label and disconnect the electrical wiring and hoses which may be in the way. Using a shop rag, wrap it around the fuel line and disconnect it.
5. Raise and safely support the vehicle. If equipped, remove the splash pan from under the engine.

NOTE: Be sure to place a clean rag in the throttle body to prevent dirt from entering the engine.

6. To remove the radiator, perform the following procedures:
 a. Drain the engine coolant into a clean container.
 b. Remove the upper and lower radiator hoses.
 c. If equipped with an automatic transmission, disconnect and plug the transmission oil cooler lines from the radiator.
 d. Remove the radiator shroud and the radiator.
7. If equipped with air conditioning, loosen the idler pulley nut and the adjusting bolt, then, remove the compressor and move it aside; do not disconnect the pressure hoses.
8. If equipped with power steering, remove the drive belt and the power steering pump, then, move it aside; do not disconnect the pressure hoses.
9. Disconnect the engine ground cable from the cylinder head. Disconnect the parking brake cable from the brake lever.
10. Disconnect the electrical leads from the starter, alternator, distributor, the high-tension ignition coil cable, the oil pressure and temperature sending units.
11. Disconnect the heater hose from the engine-side, accelera-

tor cable from the throttle body. Disconnect and label the emission hoses or wires to the carbon canister, air pump (if equipped), fuel cut solenoid; the vacuum hose from the power brake booster (if equipped) and any other wires or hoses running to the engine.
12. Raise and safely support the vehicle.
13. If equipped with a manual transmission, lift the rubber shifter boot and remove the shift control linkage from the transmission. If equipped an automatic transmission, disconnect the selector lever from the transmission from under the vehicle.
14. If equipped with a manual transmission, remove the clutch slave cylinder-to-transmission bolts, the cylinder and the exhaust tube.
15. Disconnect the speedometer cable, the back-up light wiring and the neutral switch (if equipped) from the rear section of the transmission.
16. Disconnect the exhaust pipe(s) from the exhaust manifold(s).
17. Using a piece of chalk, make alignment marks on the driveshaft and rear differential flange for realignment purposes. If equipped with a center driveshaft bearing, disconnect the center bearing bracket-to-chassis bolts. Disconnect the driveshaft-to-differential flange, lower and pull the driveshaft from the transmission extension housing (2WD) or transfer case (4WD). Using a clean shop rag, plug the rear end of the transmission or transfer case to prevent fluid loss.
18. If equipped with 4WD, perform the following procedures:
 a. Using a piece of chalk, make alignment marks on the front driveshaft-to-transfer case flanges and the front driveshaft-to-differential drive flanges for realignment purposes.
 b. Remove the front driveshaft-to-transfer case drive

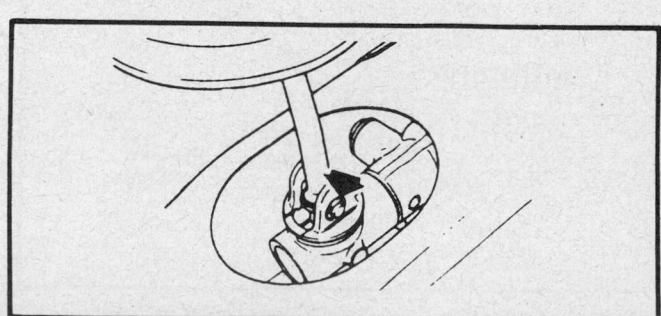

Removing the C-clip and pin from the shift lever

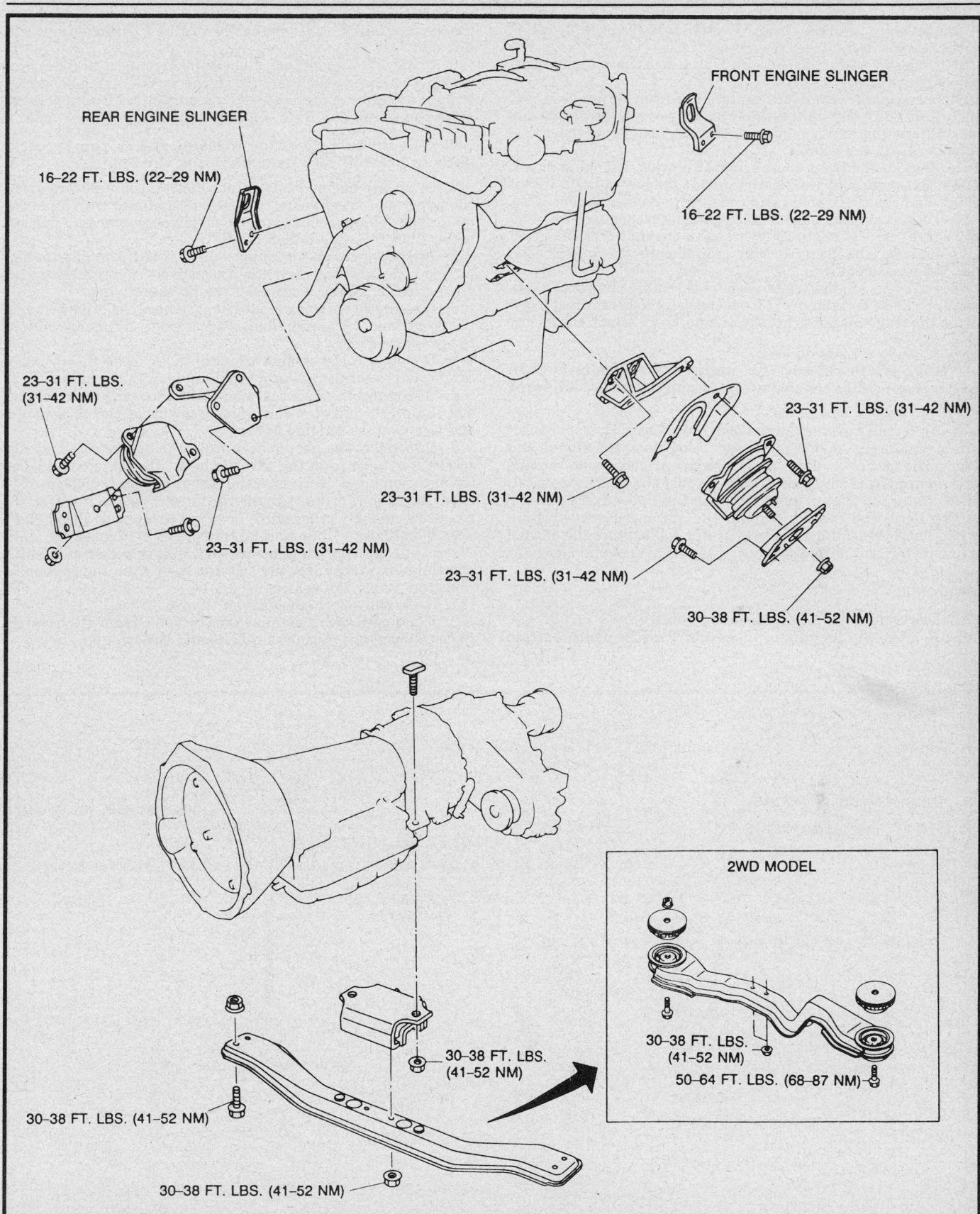

REAR ENGINE SLINGER

16–22 FT. LBS. (22–29 NM)

FRONT ENGINE SLINGER

16–22 FT. LBS. (22–29 NM)

23–31 FT. LBS. (31–42 NM)

23–31 FT. LBS. (31–42 NM)

23–31 FT. LBS. (31–42 NM)

23–31 FT. LBS. (31–42 NM)

23–31 FT. LBS. (31–42 NM)

30–38 FT. LBS. (41–52 NM)

2WD MODEL

30–38 FT. LBS. (41–52 NM)

30–38 FT. LBS. (41–52 NM)

30–38 FT. LBS. (41–52 NM)

30–38 FT. LBS. (41–52 NM)

50–64 FT. LBS. (68–87 NM)

View of the engine/transmission mounts – 3.0L engine – Pick-Up and Pathfinder

flange bolts and the front driveshaft-to-front differential, then, remove the front driveshaft.

19. Using a vertical lifting hoist, attach it to the engine and lift the engine slightly.

20. **If equipped with 4WD, remove the front differential rear** mounting bolts, the front differential carrier mounting bolt and the differential crossmember-to-chassis bolts and the crossmember from the vehicle.

21. Remove the front engine mount bracket-to-engine mount bolts (left side) and the engine mount-to-chassis bolts (right-side). Remove the transmission mount-to-crossmember bolts.

22. Using a vertical hoist, take the engine/transmission assembly weight off the engine supports and the rear crossmember.

23. Remove the transmission crossmember-to-chassis bolts and the crossmember.

24. Pull the engine/transmission assembly forward, then, carefully raise and remove it from the vehicle. If necessary, separate the transmission from the engine, then, attach the engine to a work stand.

NOTE: When raising the engine/transmission assembly, be especially careful not to bump it against adjacent parts.

25. To install, reverse the removal procedures. Do not connect any parts to the engine or transmission until the engine and transmission are in place on the engine/transmission mounts and secured by the mounting bolts. Secure the rear support 1st, then, the front engine mounts, using the upper bolt hole as a guide. Refill the cooling system, the automatic transmission with Dexron®II. Adjust the accelerator cable. Start the engine, allow it to reach normal operating temperatures and check for leaks.

VAN

1. Disconnect the negative battery cable.
2. Remove the fuel pump fuse from the fuse panel, operate the engine until it stalls, crank the engine to make sure it will not start.

3. Remove the air cleaner. Label and disconnect the electrical wiring and hoses which may be in the way. Using a shop rag, wrap it around the fuel line and disconnect it. If equipped, remove the splash pan from under the engine.

NOTE: Be sure to place a clean rag in the throttle body to prevent dirt from entering the engine.

4. Drain the engine coolant into a clean container. Remove the upper and lower radiator hoses. If equipped with an automatic transmission, disconnect and plug the transmission oil cooler lines from the radiator.

5. If equipped with air conditioning, loosen the idler pulley nut and the adjusting bolt, then, remove the compressor and move it aside; do not disconnect the pressure hoses.

6. If equipped with power steering, remove the drive belt and the power steering pump, then, move it aside; do not disconnect the pressure hoses.

7. Disconnect the engine ground cable from the cylinder head. Disconnect the parking brake cable from the brake lever.

8. Disconnect the electrical leads from the starter, alternator, distributor, the high-tension ignition coil cable, the oil pressure and temperature sending units.

9. Disconnect the heater hose from the engine-side and the accelerator cable from the throttle body. Disconnect and label the emission hoses or wires to the carbon canister, fuel cut solenoid; the vacuum hose from the power brake booster (if equipped) and any other wires or hoses running to the engine.

10. If equipped with a manual transmission, remove the shift control linkage from the transmission. If equipped an automatic transmission, disconnect the selector lever from the transmission from under the vehicle.

11. Raise and safely support the vehicle.

12. If equipped with a manual transmission, remove the clutch slave cylinder-to-transmission bolts and the cylinder.

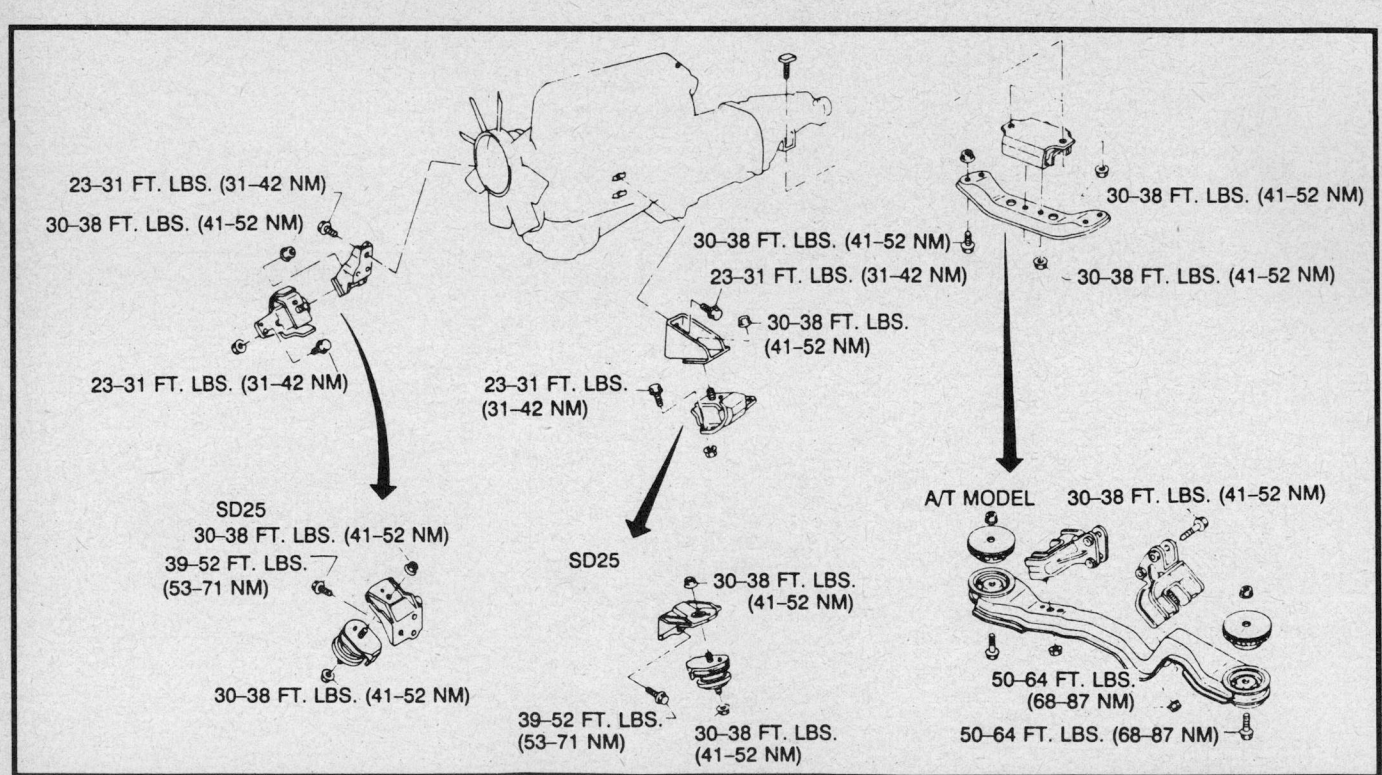

View of the engine/transmission mounts—2.4L engine and 2.5L diesel engine—Pick-Up and Pathfinder

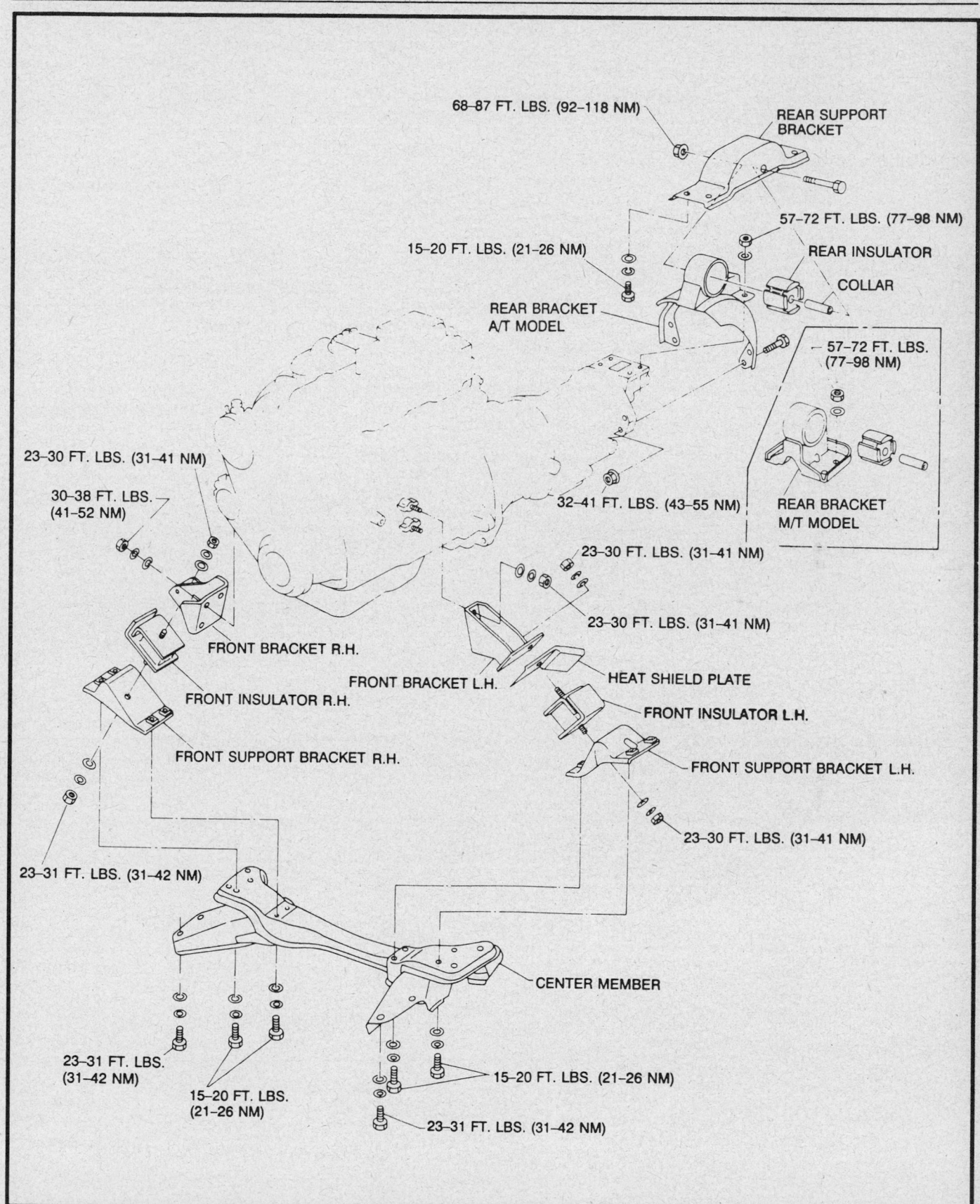

68–87 FT. LBS. (92–118 NM)

REAR SUPPORT BRACKET

57–72 FT. LBS. (77–98 NM)

15–20 FT. LBS. (21–26 NM)

REAR INSULATOR

COLLAR

REAR BRACKET A/T MODEL

57–72 FT. LBS. (77–98 NM)

REAR BRACKET M/T MODEL

23–30 FT. LBS. (31–41 NM)

30–38 FT. LBS. (41–52 NM)

32–41 FT. LBS. (43–55 NM)

23–30 FT. LBS. (31–41 NM)

23–30 FT. LBS. (31–41 NM)

FRONT BRACKET R.H.

FRONT BRACKET L.H.

HEAT SHIELD PLATE

FRONT INSULATOR R.H.

FRONT INSULATOR L.H.

FRONT SUPPORT BRACKET R.H.

FRONT SUPPORT BRACKET L.H.

23–30 FT. LBS. (31–41 NM)

23–31 FT. LBS. (31–42 NM)

CENTER MEMBER

23–31 FT. LBS. (31–42 NM)

15–20 FT. LBS. (21–26 NM)

15–20 FT. LBS. (21–26 NM)

23–31 FT. LBS. (31–42 NM)

View of the engine/transmission mounts—2.4L engine—Van

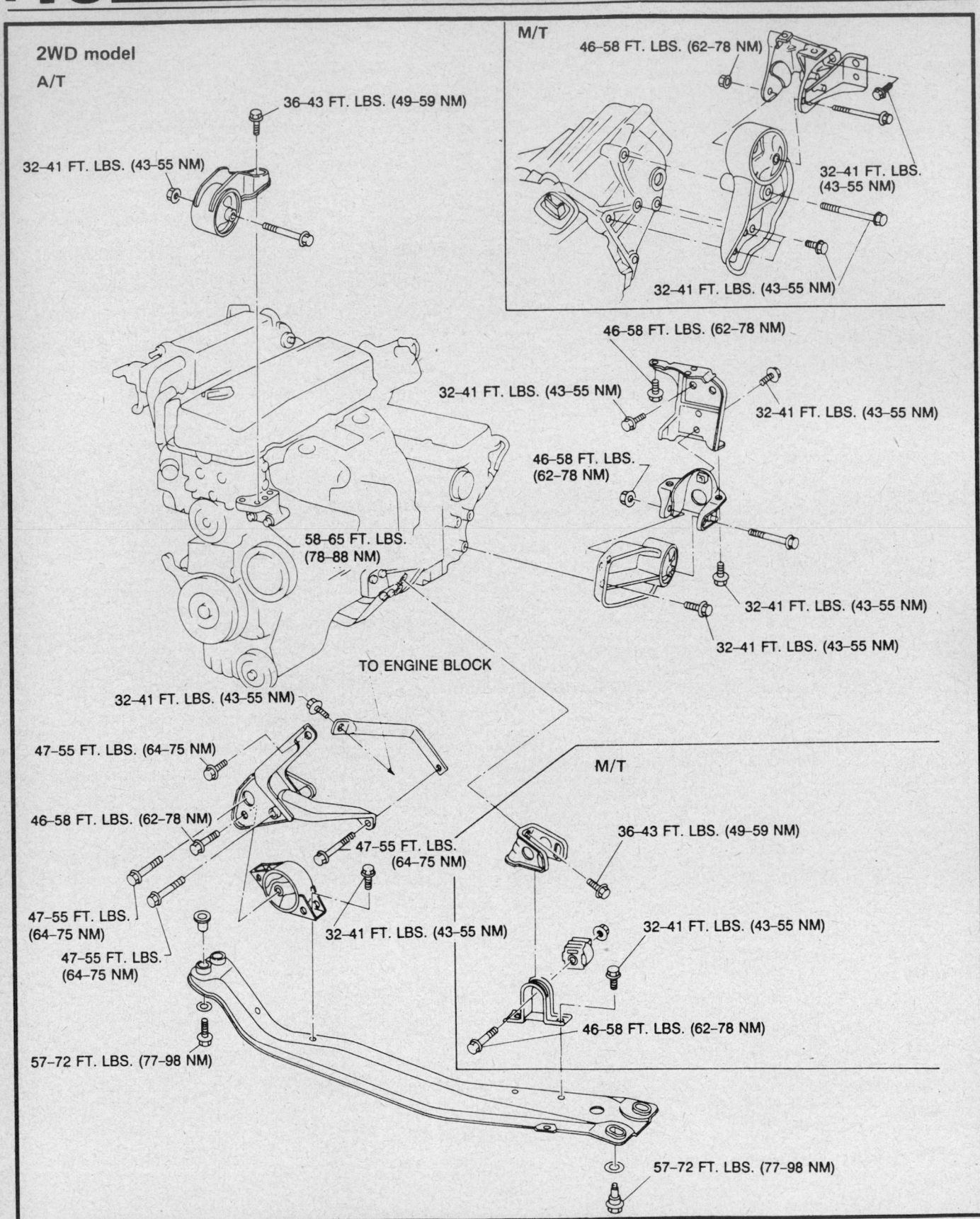

2WD model
A/T

36–43 FT. LBS. (49–59 NM)

32–41 FT. LBS. (43–55 NM)

M/T

46–58 FT. LBS. (62–78 NM)

32–41 FT. LBS. (43–55 NM)

32–41 FT. LBS. (43–55 NM)

46–58 FT. LBS. (62–78 NM)

32–41 FT. LBS. (43–55 NM)

32–41 FT. LBS. (43–55 NM)

46–58 FT. LBS. (62–78 NM)

58–65 FT. LBS. (78–88 NM)

32–41 FT. LBS. (43–55 NM)

32–41 FT. LBS. (43–55 NM)

TO ENGINE BLOCK

32–41 FT. LBS. (43–55 NM)

47–55 FT. LBS. (64–75 NM)

46–58 FT. LBS. (62–78 NM)

47–55 FT. LBS. (64–75 NM)

47–55 FT. LBS. (64–75 NM)

47–55 FT. LBS. (64–75 NM)

32–41 FT. LBS. (43–55 NM)

57–72 FT. LBS. (77–98 NM)

M/T

36–43 FT. LBS. (49–59 NM)

32–41 FT. LBS. (43–55 NM)

46–58 FT. LBS. (62–78 NM)

57–72 FT. LBS. (77–98 NM)

View of the engine/transmission mounts—2.4L engine—Axxess 2WD

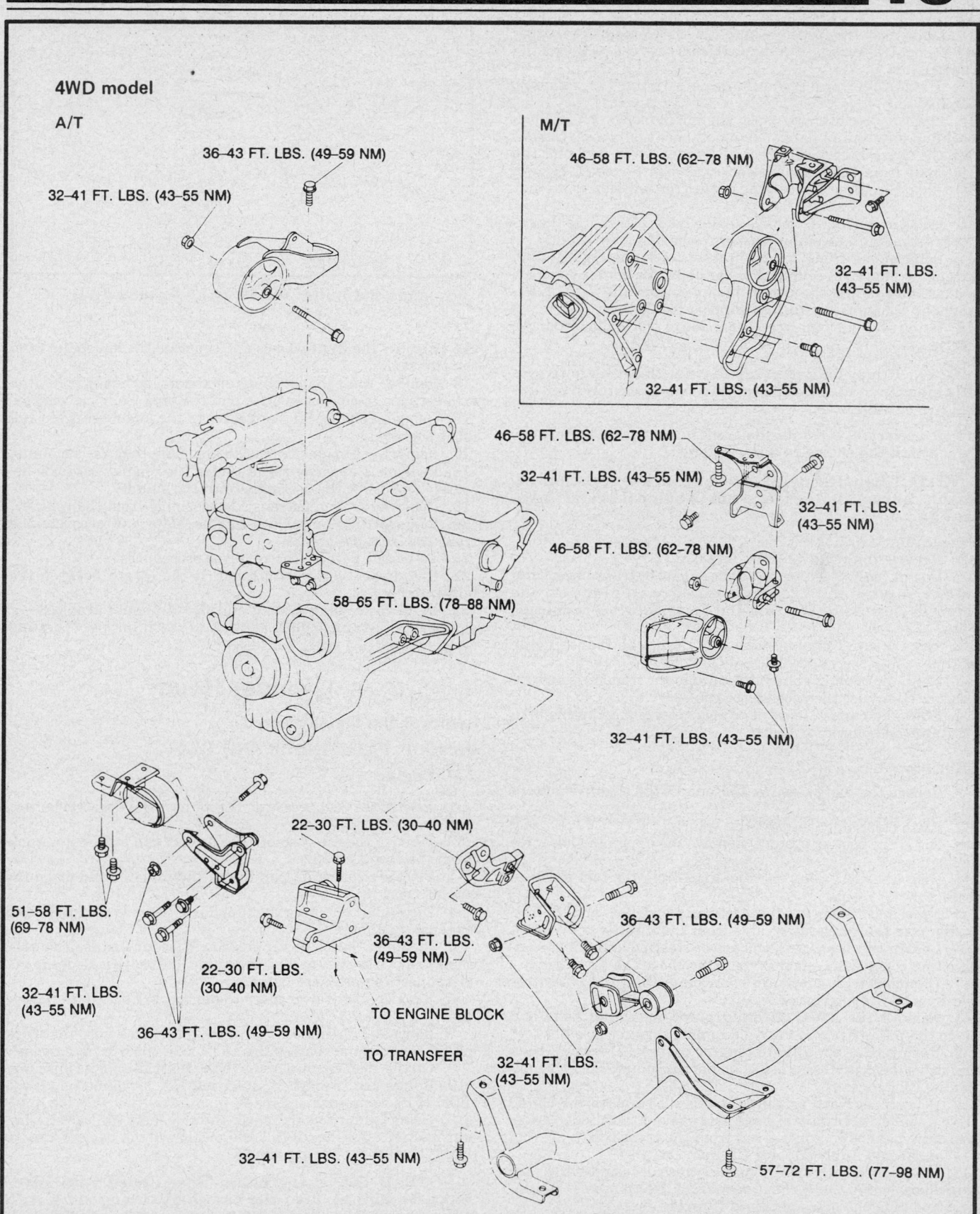

4WD model

A/T

36–43 FT. LBS. (49–59 NM)

32–41 FT. LBS. (43–55 NM)

M/T

46–58 FT. LBS. (62–78 NM)

32–41 FT. LBS. (43–55 NM)

32–41 FT. LBS. (43–55 NM)

46–58 FT. LBS. (62–78 NM)

32–41 FT. LBS. (43–55 NM)

32–41 FT. LBS. (43–55 NM)

46–58 FT. LBS. (62–78 NM)

58–65 FT. LBS. (78–88 NM)

32–41 FT. LBS. (43–55 NM)

51–58 FT. LBS. (69–78 NM)

32–41 FT. LBS. (43–55 NM)

22–30 FT. LBS. (30–40 NM)

36–43 FT. LBS. (49–59 NM)

22–30 FT. LBS. (30–40 NM)

36–43 FT. LBS. (49–59 NM)

36–43 FT. LBS. (49–59 NM)

TO ENGINE BLOCK

TO TRANSFER

32–41 FT. LBS. (43–55 NM)

32–41 FT. LBS. (43–55 NM)

57–72 FT. LBS. (77–98 NM)

View of the engine/transmission mounts—2.4L engine—Axxess 4WD

13. Disconnect the speedometer cable, the back-up light wiring and the neutral switch (if equipped) from the rear section of the transmission.

14. Disconnect the exhaust pipe(s) from the exhaust manifold(s).

15. Using a piece of chalk, make alignment marks on the driveshaft and differential flange for realignment purposes. Disconnect the driveshaft-to-differential flange, lower and pull the driveshaft from the transmission extension housing. Using a clean shop rag, plug the rear end of the transmission to prevent fluid loss.

16. Using an under the vehicle engine hoist, attach it to the engine/transmission assembly and raise the assembly slightly.

17. Remove the front engine bracket-to-engine mount nuts, the engine mount-to-center member bolts, the center member-to-chassis bolts and the center member from the vehicle. Remove the transmission-to-rear support bracket nut/bolt.

18. Using an under the vehicle lift, lower the engine from the vehicle.

NOTE: It may be necessary to raise the vehicle to provide clearance to slide the engine/transmission from under the vehicle.

19. If necessary, separate the transmission from the engine, then, attach the engine to a work stand.

NOTE: When removing the engine/transmission assembly, be especially careful not to bump it against adjacent parts.

To install:

20. Reverse the removal procedures.

21. Do not connect any parts to the engine or transmission until the engine and transmission are in place on the engine/transmission mounts and secured by the mounting bolts.

22. Secure the rear support 1st, then, the front engine mounts, using the upper bolt hole as a guide.

23. Refill the cooling system, the automatic transmission with Dexron®II. Adjust the accelerator cable.

24. Start the engine, allow it to reach normal operating temperatures and check for leaks.

AXXESS

1. Relieve the fuel pressure. Disconnect the negative battery cable.

2. Raise and safely support the vehicle.

3. Drain the cooling system. Remove the upper and lower radiator hoses.

4. Disconnect the plug the fuel lines from the fuel pressure regulator.

5. Label and disconnect the electrical connectors and the hoses. Remove the accelerator cable from the throttle body.

6. Loosen the alternator, the power steering and the air conditioning compressor pivot bolts and remove the drive belts.

7. Disconnect the electrical connectors from the alternator and remove the alternator.

8. Remove the power steering pump mounting bolts and move the pump aside; do not disconnect the pressure lines.

9. Remove the air conditioning compressor-to-engine bolts and move the compressor aside; do not disconnect the air conditioning coolant lines.

10. If equipped with a manual transaxle, remove the clutch slave cylinder-to-transaxle bolts and move the cylinder aside. Disconnect the shift control rod from the transaxle.

11. Raise and safely support the vehicle.

12. If equipped with an automatic transaxle, remove the shift control cable and the throttle wire from the transaxle. Disconnect and plug the oil cooler lines from the radiator.

13. If equipped with 4WD, remove the driveshaft from the transfer case.

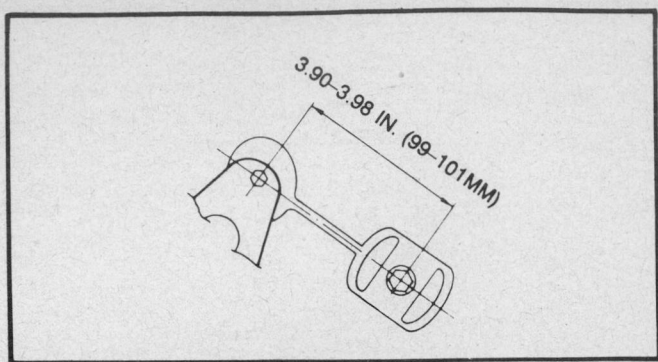

Adjusting the buffer rod length—Axxess 4WD

14. Remove the front wheels and separate the halfshafts from the transaxle.

15. Remove the exhaust pipe-to-exhaust manifold bolts, the exhaust pipe-to-converter bolts and the pipe from the vehicle.

16. Using an engine lift, connect it to the engine slingers and lift it slightly.

17. Remove the engine/transaxle assembly-to-chassis mounts.

18. Position a movable stand under the engine/transaxle assembly and lower the assembly onto the stand.

19. Remove the engine/transaxle assembly from the vehicle.

20. Remove the transaxle-to-engine bolts and separate the transaxle from the engine.

21. To install, reverse the removal procedures.

22. If equipped with a 4WD, adjust the length between the buffer rod bolts.

23. Refill the cooling system and the automatic transaxle, if equipped. Start the engine, allow it to reach normal operating temperatures and check for leaks.

Cylinder Head

Removal and Installation

PICK-UP, PATHFINDER AND VAN

2.4L Engine

1. Relieve the fuel pressure. Disconnect the negative battery cable.

2. Remove the air cleaner. Disconnect the accelerator cable from the throttle body.

3. Place a clean drain pan under the radiator and drain the engine coolant.

4. Disconnect and plug the fuel lines. Remove the intake and exhaust manifolds.

5. If equipped with power steering, disconnect the drive belt, then, remove the power steering pump and move it aside; do not disconnect the pressure hoses.

6. Remove the valve cover-to-engine bolts and the valve cover.

7. Lable and disconnect the spark plug wires from the spark plugs. Remove the spark plugs to protect them from damage.

8. On the 1990 engines, remove the fuel rail and the injectors.

9. Rotate the crankshaft until the No. 1 cylinder is on the TDC of its compression stroke.

10. Using paint or chalk, mark the camshaft sprocket-to-timing chain relationship; if this is done, it will not be necessary to locate the factory timing marks.

NOTE: If the timing chain is equipped with silver links, be sure to align the camshaft timing mark with the silver link.

11. Remove the camshaft sprocket-to-camshaft bolt and the

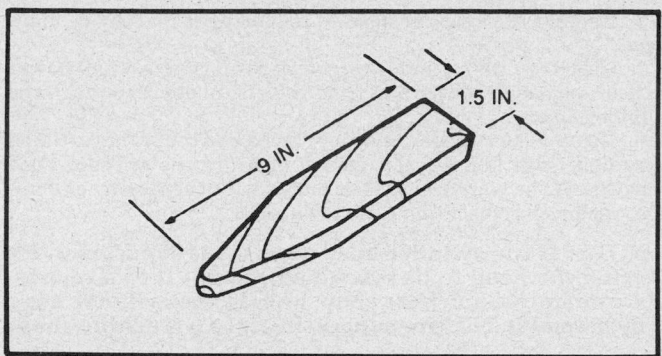

Dimensions for fabricating a wooden wedge used to support the timing chain—2.4L engine

Removing the camshaft sprocket and chain—2.4L engine

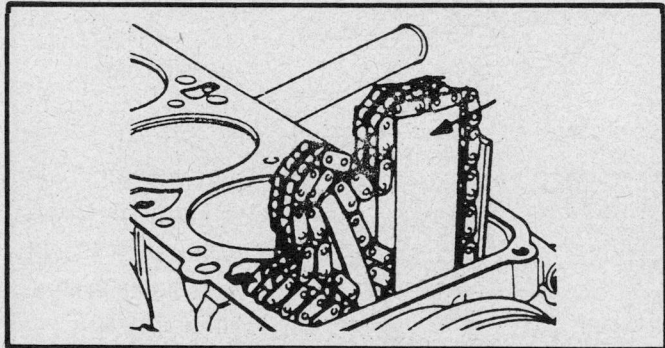

Support the timing chain with a wedge—2.4L engine

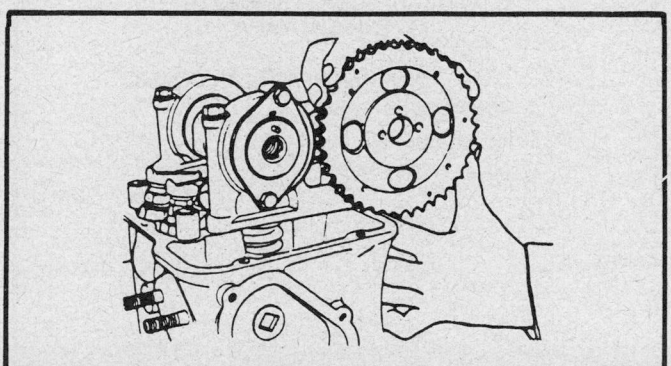

Install the camshaft sprocket with camshaft pin facing upwards—2.4L engine

camshaft sprocket. Using the timing chain tool, wedge and support the timing chain; this will be necessary to keep the chain from falling into the front cover.

12. Remove the cylinder head-to-engine bolts and the cylinder head; be sure to remove the cylinder head-to-front cover bolts. It may be necessary to tap the head lightly with a copper or brass mallet to loosen it.

13. Clean the gasket mounting surfaces. Inspect the cylinder head for warpage; the difference must be less than 0.0059 in.

To install:

14. To install the cylinder head, use a new gasket and torque the cylinder head-to-engine bolts, in sequence, using 5 steps:
   1st—22 ft. lbs. (29 Nm)
   2nd—58 ft. lbs. (78 Nm)
   3rd—loosen all bolts
   4th—22 ft. lbs. (29 Nm)
   5th—54–61 ft. lbs. (74–83 Nm)

15. Install the camshaft sprocket together with the timing chain to the camshaft; make sure the timing marks are aligned. Torque the camshaft sprocket-to-camshaft bolt to 87–116 ft. lbs.

16. To complete the installation, reverse the removal procedures. It is always wise to drain the crankcase oil after the cylinder head has been installed to avoid coolant contamination. Start the engine and allow it to reach normal operating temperatures, then, check for leaks.

3.0L Engine, Left Side

1. Disconnect the negative battery cable.
2. Remove the timing belt, the left exhaust manifold and the intake manifold.

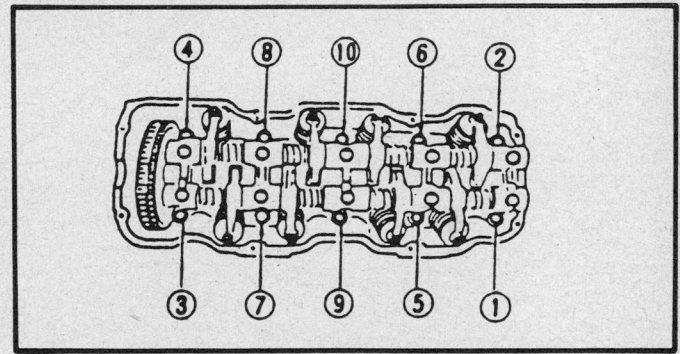

Cylinder head bolt loosening sequence—2.4L engine

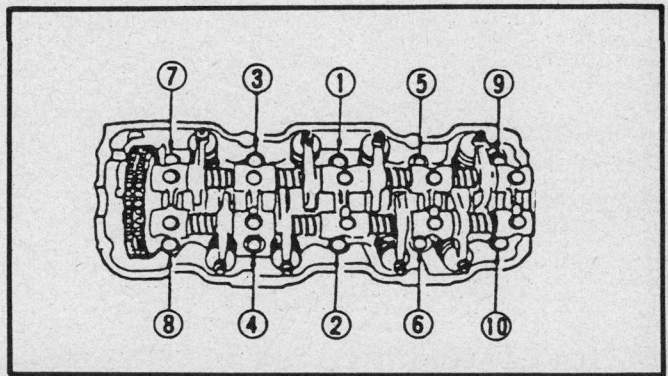

Cylinder head bolt torquing sequence—2.4L engine 1986–89

NOTE: Before removing the timing belt, be sure to mark the position of the timing belt-to-camshaft sprockets and the timing belt-to-crankshaft sprocket, then, place an arrow on the timing belt in the direction or rotation. Do not rotate the crankshaft after the timing belt has been removed.

3. Remove the camshaft sprocket-to-camshaft bolt and the camshaft sprocket, then, remove the rear timing belt cover-to-cylinder head bolts.

4. Remove the distributor cap, then, using a piece of chalk, align the rotor-to-distributor housing and the distributor housing-to-cylinder head. Remove the distributor-to-cylinder head bolt and the distributor.

5. Remove the valve cover from the left cylinder head.

NOTE: It may be necessary to remove the valve lifter guide-to-cylinder head bolts and the valve lifter guide to provide access to the cylinder head bolts. When removing the valve lifter guide, be sure to secure the valve lifters with a safety wire, to keep them in their original positions.

5. Remove the cylinder head-to-engine bolts and the cylinder head.

7. Clean the gasket mounting surfaces. Using a small power wire brush, clean the carbon from the piston depressions in the cylinder head.

8. Inspect the cylinder head for cracks and other flaws. Using a straight-edge and a feeler gauge, measure the cylinder head warpage. If the warpage exceeds 0.004 in. or there is other damage, repair or replace the cylinder head.

NOTE: If the cylinder head warpage is significant, requiring the head to be machined, submit it to a reputable automotive machine shop; be sure the cylinder head is disassembled before submitting it to a machine shop.

To install:

9. Use a new gasket and reverse the removal procedures. Torque as follows:

Cylinder head-to-engine bolts (in sequence) in five steps
- 1st — 22 ft. lbs.
- 2nd — 43 ft. lbs.
- 3rd — loosen all bolts
- 4th — 22 ft. lbs.
- 5th — 40–47 ft. lbs.

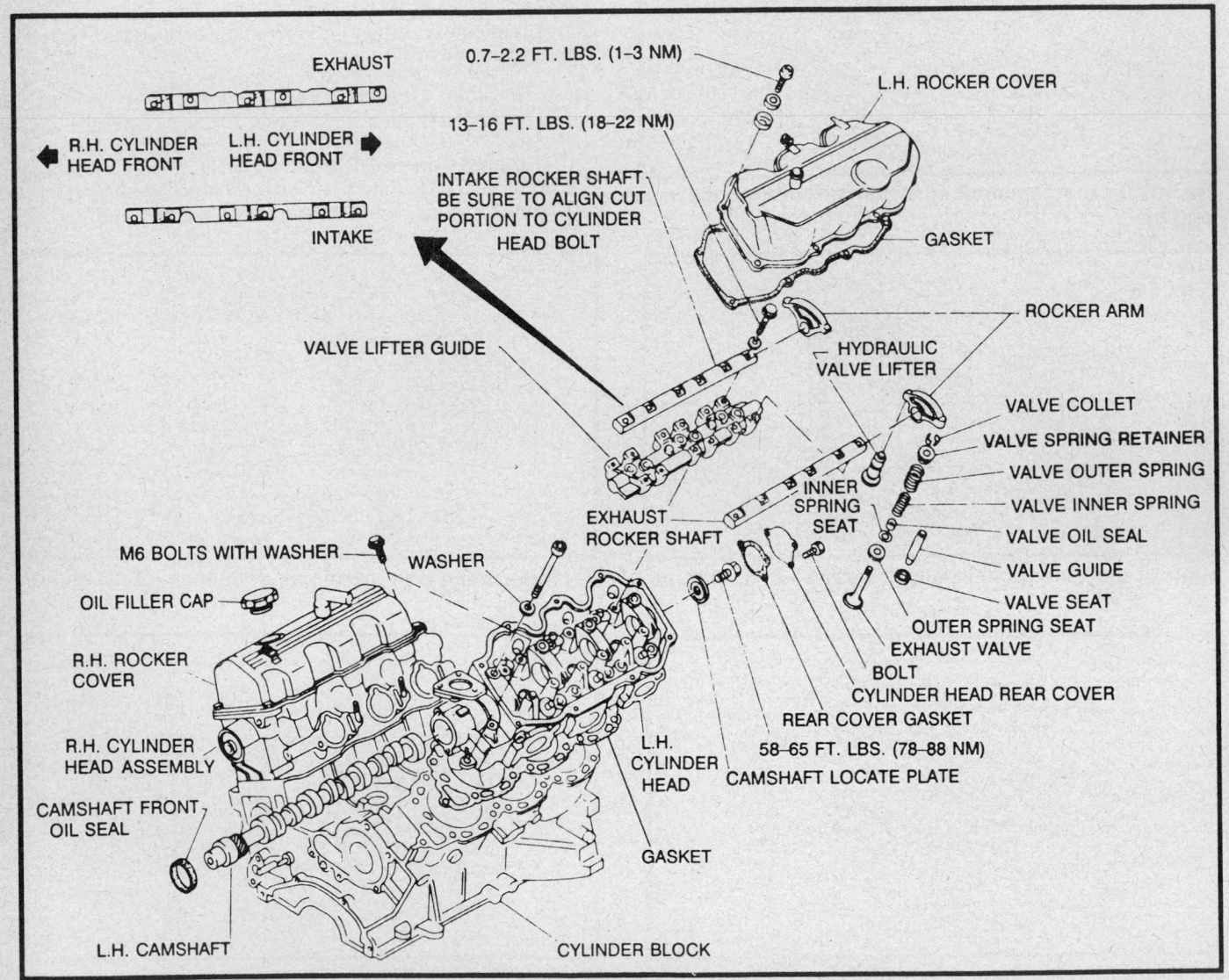

Exploded view of the cylinder head assembly—3.0L engine

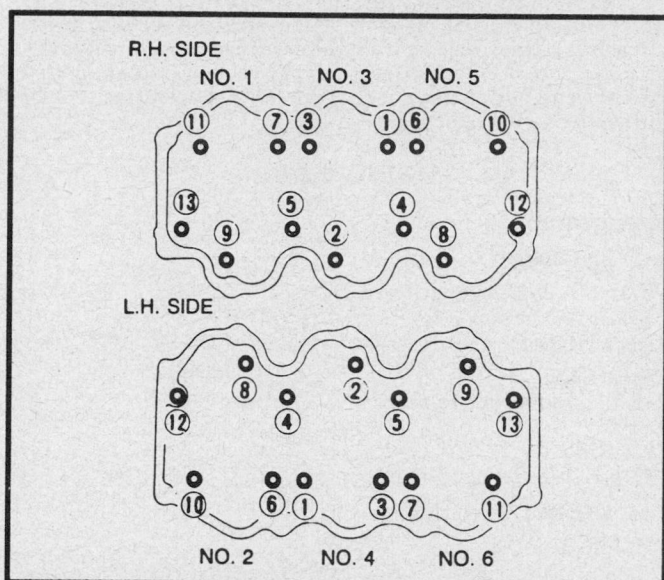

View of the cylinder head torquing sequence — 3.0L engine

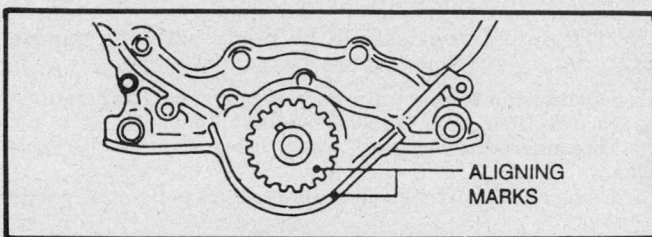

Aligning the crankshaft sprocket marks — 3.0L engine

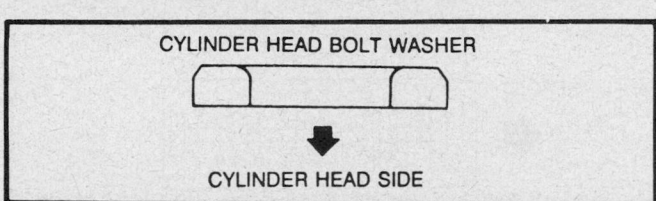

Install the cylinder head bolt washers this way — 3.0L engine

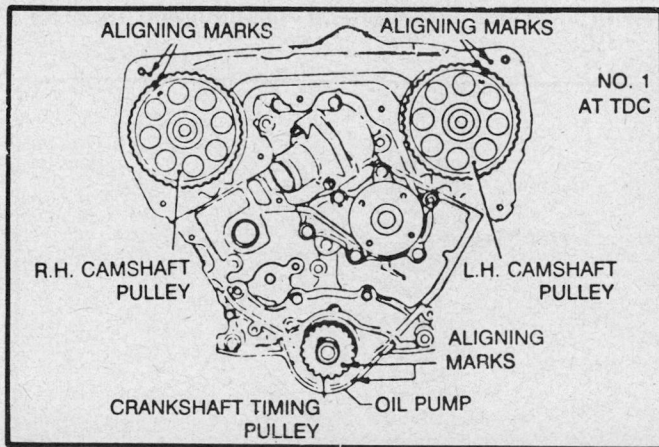

View of the camshaft sprocket timing marks — 3.0L engine

10. To complete the installation, use new gaskets and reverse the removal procedures. Torque as follows
   Valve lifter guide-to-cylinder head bolts — 13–16 ft. lbs.
   Valve cover-to-cylinder head bolts — 9–25 inch lbs.
   Exhaust manifold-to-cylinder head nuts — 13–16 ft. lbs.
   Intake manifold-to-cylinder head nuts — 17–20 ft. lbs. or bolts to 12–14 ft. lbs.
   Camshaft sprocket-to-camshaft nut — 58–65 ft. lbs.
11. Refill the cooling system. Start the engine, allow it to reach normal operating temperatures and check for leaks.

3.0L Engine, Right Side

1. Disconnect the negative battery cable.
2. Remove the timing belt, the right exhaust manifold and the intake manifold.

NOTE: Before removing the timing belt, be sure to mark the position of the timing belt-to-camshaft sprockets and the timing belt-to-crankshaft sprocket, then, place an arrow on the timing belt in the direction or rotation. Do not rotate the crankshaft after the timing belt has been removed.

3. Remove the camshaft sprocket-to-camshaft bolt and the camshaft sprocket, then, remove the rear timing belt cover-to-cylinder head bolts.
4. Remove the valve cover from the right cylinder head.

NOTE: It may be necessary to remove the valve lifter guide-to-cylinder head bolts and the valve lifter guide to provide access to the cylinder head bolts. When removing the valve lifter guide, be sure to secure the valve lifters with a safety wire, to keep them in their original positions.

5. Remove the cylinder head-to-engine bolts and the cylinder head.
6. Clean the gasket mounting surfaces. Using a small power wire brush, clean the carbon from the piston depressions in the cylinder head.
7. Inspect the cylinder head for cracks and other flaws. Using a straight-edge and a feeler gauge, measure the cylinder head warpage. If the warpage exceeds 0.004 in. or there is other damage, repair or replace the cylinder head.

NOTE: If the cylinder head warpage is significant, requiring the head to be machined, submit it to a reputable automotive machine shop; be sure the cylinder head is disassembled before submitting it to a machine shop.

To install:

8. Use a new gasket and reverse the removal procedures. Torque as follows:
   Clinder head-to-engine bolts (in sequence) in five steps
      1st — 22 ft. lbs.
      2nd — 43 ft. lbs.
      3rd — loosen all bolts
      4th — 22 ft. lbs.
      5th — 40–47 ft. lbs.
9. To complete the installation, use new gaskets and reverse the removal procedures. Torque as follows:
   Valve lifter guide-to-cylinder head bolts — 13–16 ft. lbs.
   Valve cover-to-cylinder head bolts — 9–25 inch lbs.
   Exhaust manifold-to-cylinder head nuts — 13–16 ft. lbs.
   Intake manifold-to-cylinder head nuts — 17–20 ft. lbs. or bolts to 12–14 ft. lbs.
   Camshaft sprocket-to-camshaft nut — 58–65 ft. lbs.
10. Refill the cooling system. Start the engine, allow it to reach normal operating temperatures and check for leaks.

AXXESS

2.4L Engine

1. Releive the fuel pressure. Disconnect the negative battery cable.
2. Remove the intake and exhaust manifolds.
3. Place a clean drain pan under the radiator and drain the engine coolant.
4. Disconnect and plug the fuel lines.
5. Disconnect the electrical connectors from the distributor and remove the distributor cap.
6. Remove the intake and exhaust manifolds.
7. If equipped with power steering, disconnect the drive belt, then, remove the power steering pump and move it aside; do not disconnect the pressure hoses.
8. Remove the valve cover-to-engine bolts and the valve cover.
9. Lable and disconnect the spark plug wires from the spark plugs. Remove the spark plugs to protect them from damage.
10. Remove the fuel rail and the injectors.
11. Rotate the crankshaft until the No. 1 cylinder is on the TDC of its compression stroke.
12. Using paint or chalk, mark the camshaft sprocket-to-timing chain relationship; if this is done, it will not be necessary to locate the factory timing marks.

NOTE: If the timing chain is equipped with silver links, be sure to align the camshaft timing mark with the silver link.

13. Remove the camshaft sprocket-to-camshaft bolt and the camshaft sprocket. Using the timing chain tool, wedge and support the timing chain; this will be necessary to keep the chain from falling into the front cover.
14. Remove the cylinder head-to-engine bolts and the cylinder head; be sure to remove the cylinder head-to-front cover bolts. It may be necessary to tap the head lightly with a copper or brass mallet to loosen it.
15. Clean the gasket mounting surfaces. Inspect the cylinder head for warpage; the difference must be less than 0.0059 in.

To install:
16. To install the cylinder head, use a new gasket and torque the cylinder head-to-engine bolts, in sequence, using 5 steps:
   1st—22 ft. lbs. (29 Nm)
   2nd—58 ft. lbs. (78 Nm)
   3rd—loosen all bolts
   4th—22 ft. lbs. (29 Nm)
   5th—54–61 ft. lbs. (74–83 Nm)
17. Install the camshaft sprocket together with the timing chain to the camshaft; make sure the timing marks are aligned. Torque the camshaft sprocket-to-camshaft bolt to 87–116 ft. lbs.

18. To complete the installation, reverse the removal procedures. It is always wise to drain the crankcase oil after the cylinder head has been installed to avoid coolant contamination. Start the engine and allow it to reach normal operating temperatures, then, check for leaks.

Valve Lash

Arrangement

2.4L ENGINE
I–E–E–I–I–E–E–I (front-to-rear)

3.0L ENGINE

Right Side
E–I–E–I–E–I (front-to-rear)

Left Side
I–E–I–E–I–E (front-to-rear)

2.5L DIESEL ENGINE
E–I–I–E–E–I–I–E

Adjustment

2.4L ENGINE (1986–89)

NOTE: Adjustment should be made with the engine hot.

1. Operate the engine until normal operating temperatures are reached, then, turn **OFF** the engine.
2. Disconnect the negative battery cable. Remove the valve cover.
3. Using a socket wrench on the crankshaft pulley bolt, rotate

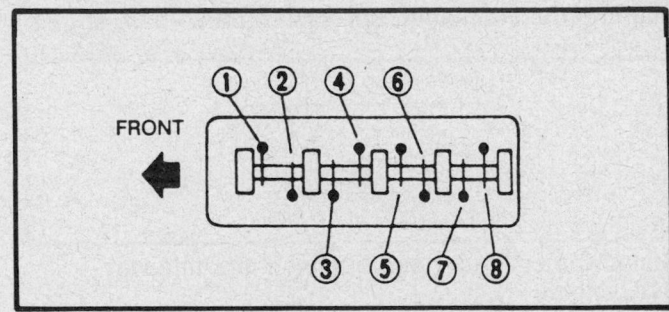

View of the valve arrangement—2.4L engine 1986–89

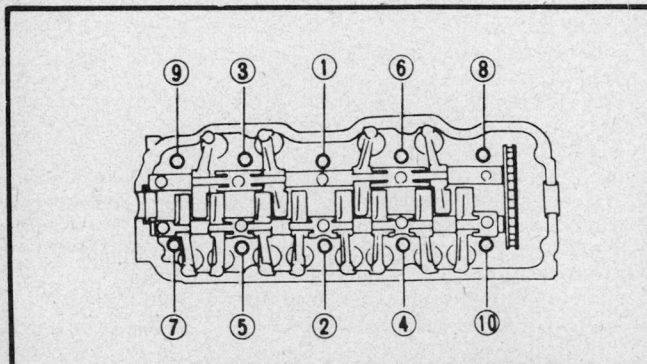

Cylinder head bolt torquing sequence—2.4L engine 1990

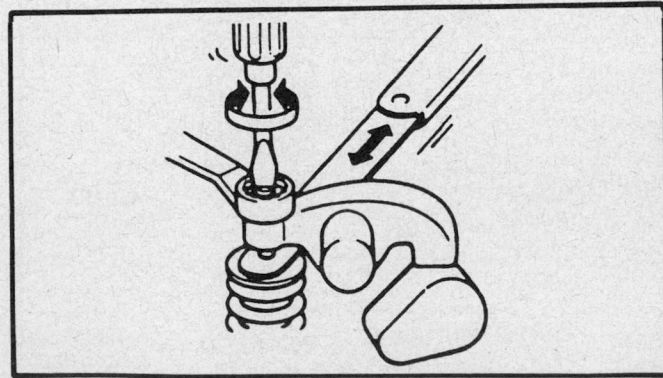

Adjusting the valves—2.4L engine 1986–89

the crankshaft until the No. 1 cylinder is on the TDC of the compression stroke.

NOTE: To check for the No. 1 TDC position, remove the No. 1 spark plug, place a thumb over the hole, rotate the crankshaft until the compression pressure can be felt in the cylinder.

4. Using a wrench, flat-bladed tool and a feeler gauge, check and/or adjust the valves No. 1, 2, 4 and 6.
5. Rotate the crankshaft 180 degrees to position the No. 4 cylinder on the TDC of its compression stroke.
6. With the No. 4 cylinder at the TDC of its compression stroke, adjust the valves No. 3, 5, 7 and 8.
7. Clean the gasket mounting surfaces.
8. After adjustment, use new gaskets, sealant (if necessary) and reverse the removal procedures. Torque the locknut to 12–16 ft. lbs.

Rocker Arms/Shafts

Removal and Installation

2.4L ENGINE

1. Disconnect the negative battery cable.
2. Disconnect any hoses and wires which may interfer with the removal of the valve cover.
3. Remove the valve cover-to-cylinder head bolts and the valve cover.
4. Remove the rocker arm/shaft assembly-to-cylinder head bolts.

NOTE: When removing the rocker/arm shaft bolts, do not remove the No. 1 and No. 5 bracket bolts from the rocker arm bracket or the rocker bracket will spring from the rocker shaft.

5. If separating the rocker arms from the rocker arm shafts, be sure to keep them in order for reinstallation purposes.
6. Clean the gasket mounting surfaces.

NOTE: Be aware that the rocker arm shafts are different in construction and must be install in their original positions.

7. To install, use new gaskets, sealant, if necessary and reverse the removal procedures. Torque the rocker arm/shaft assembly-to-cylinder head bolts to 11–18 ft. lbs. Adjust the valve clearances on the 1986–89 engines.

3.0L ENGINE

1. Relieve the fuel pressure. Disconnect the negative battery cable.
2. Disconnect any hoses and wires which may interfere with the removal of the valve cover.
3. Remove the valve cover-to-cylinder head bolts and the valve cover.
4. Remove the rocker arm/shaft assemblies-to-cylinder head bolts and the rocker arm/shaft assemblies; if necessary, separate the rocker arms from the rocker arm shaft.

NOTE: If separating the rocker arms from the rocker arm shaft, be sure to keep them in order for reinstallation purposes.

5. Clean the gasket mounting surfaces.

NOTE: Be aware that the rocker arm shafts are different in construction and must be install in their original positions.

6. To install, use new gaskets, sealant, if necessary and reverse the removal procedures. Torque the rocker arm shaft-to-cylinder head bolts to 13–16 ft. lbs. and the valve cover-to-cylinder head bolts to 9–25 inch lbs.

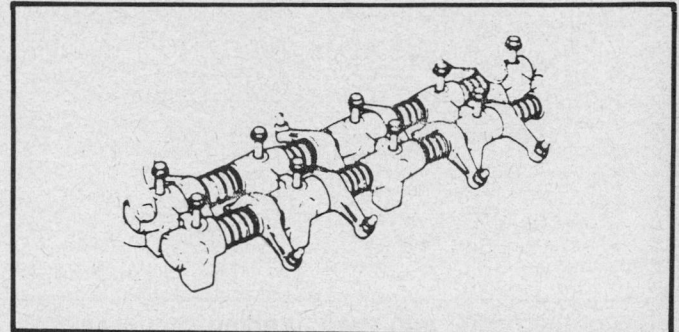

View of the rocker arm assembly—2.4L engine 1986–89

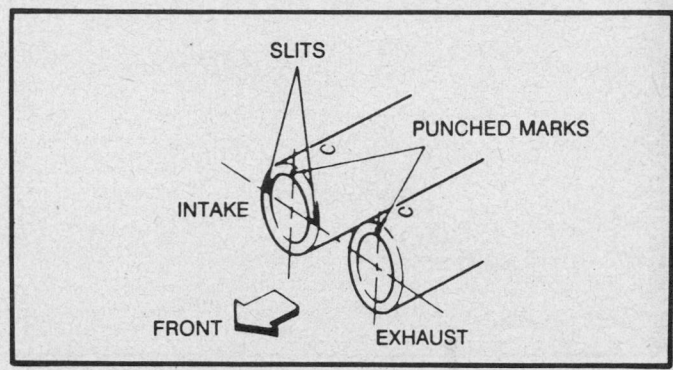

View of the rocker arm shaft positioning indicators—2.4L engine 1986–89

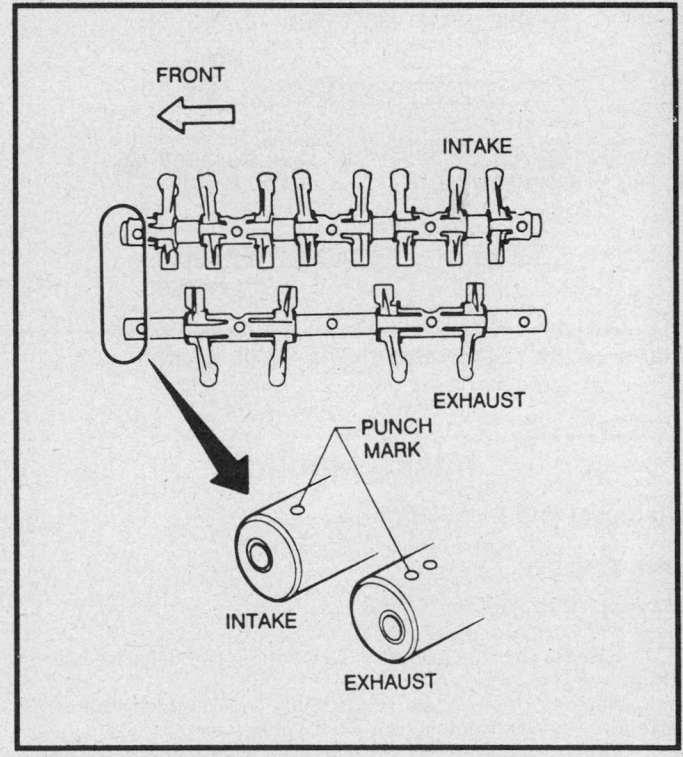

View of the rocker arm assembly and shaft positioning indicators—2.4L engine 1990

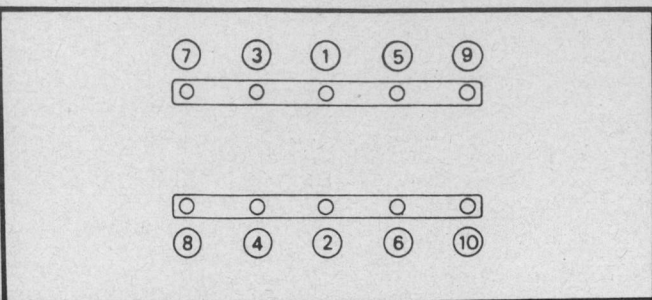

View of the rocker arm shaft torquing sequence— 2.4L engine

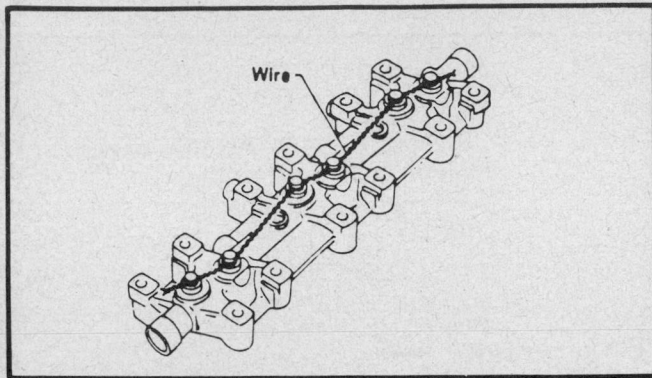

Using a wire to hold the valve lifter in place—3.0L engine

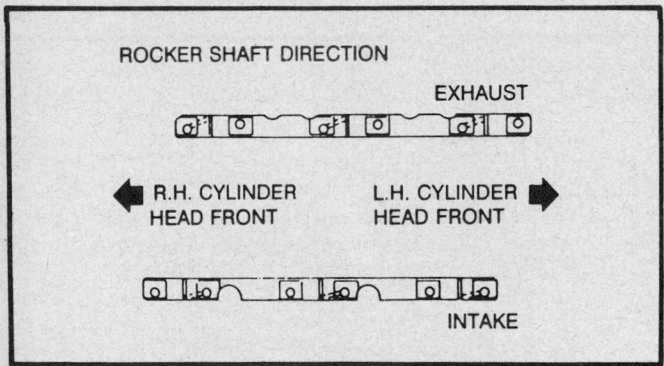

View of the rocker arm shafts—3.0L engine

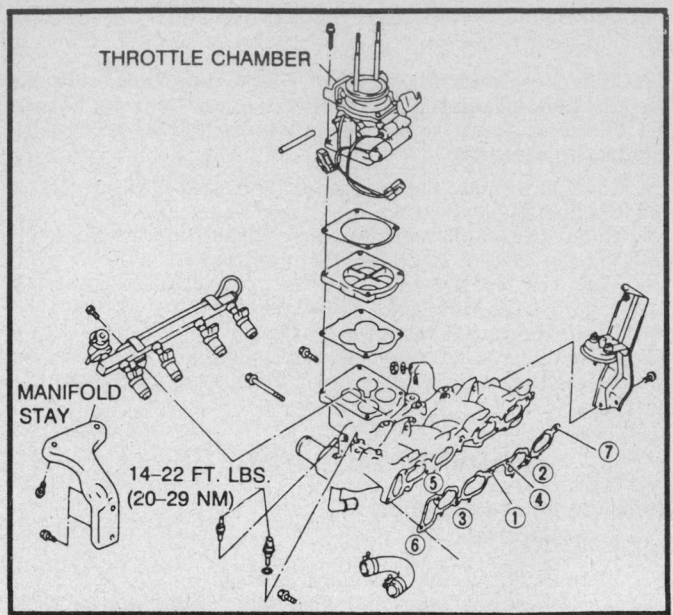

Exploded view of the intake manifold assembly—2.4L engine 1990—except Axxess

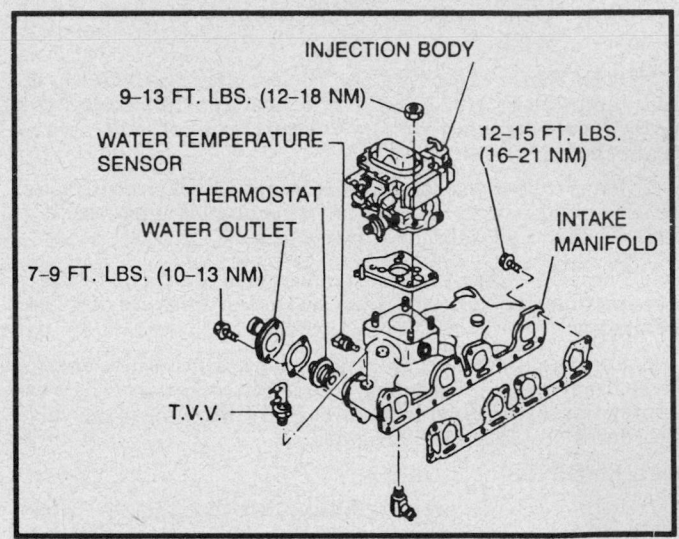

Exploded view of the intake manifold assembly—2.4L engine 1986—89

Intake Manifold

Removal and Installation

2.4L ENGINE
Except 1990 Axxess

1. Release the fuel pressure. Disconnect the negative battery cable.
2. Remove the air cleaner assembly together with all of the attending hoses. Remove the EGR tube.
3. Label and disconnect the electrical wiring and hoses which may be in the way. Using a shop rag, wrap it around the fuel line and disconnect it.
4. Drain the engine coolant to a level below the thermostat

housing, then, disconnect the upper coolant hose from the thermostat housing.
5. Disconnect the throttle linkage and vacuum lines from the throttle body.

NOTE: The throttle body can be removed from the manifold at this point or it can be removed as an assembly with the intake manifold.

6. Remove the throttle body-to-intake manifold nuts, the throttle body and the heater mixture.
7. On the 1990 model, remove the fuel rail with the injectors and the intake manifold stays.
8. Remove the intake manifold-to-engine bolts and the intake manifold.
9. Clean the gasket mounting surfaces.
10. To install, use a new gaskets and reverse the removal pro-

cedures. Torque the intake manifold-to-engine bolts (working from the center in an outwards direction — using 2 progressive steps) to 12–15 ft. lbs. (16–21 Nm) and the throttle body-to-intake manifold nuts 9–13 ft. lbs. (12–18 Nm). Refill the cooling system. Start the engine, allow it to reach normal operating temperatures and check for leaks.

1990 Axxess

1. Release the fuel pressure. Disconnect the negative battery cable.
2. Remove the air duct from the throttle body. Remove the EGR tube.
3. Label and disconnect the electrical wiring and hoses which may be in the way. Using a shop rag, wrap it around the fuel line and disconnect it.
4. Drain the engine coolant to a level below the thermostat housing, then, disconnect the upper coolant hose from the thermostat housing.
5. Disconnect the throttle linkage and vacuum lines from the throttle body.
6. Remove the throttle body-to-intake manifold collector bolts and the throttle body.
7. Remove the intake manifold stays.
8. Remove the fuel rail with the injectors.
9. Remove the intake manifold collector-to-intake manifold, the collector and the gasket.

10. Remove the intake manifold-to-engine bolts and the intake manifold.
11. Clean the gasket mounting surfaces.
12. To install, use a new gaskets and reverse the removal procedures. Torque the intake manifold-to-engine bolts (working from the center in an outwards direction — using 2 progressive steps) to 12–15 ft. lbs. (16–21 Nm), the intake manifold collector-to-intake manifold bolts to 12–15 ft. lbs. (16–21 Nm) and the throttle body-to-intake manifold collector bolts, using 2 passes, to 13–16 ft. lbs. (18–22 Nm). Refill the cooling system. Start the engine, allow it to reach normal operating temperatures and check for leaks.

3.0L ENGINE

1986–89 All Vehicles

1. Remove the fuel pump fuse from the fuse block.
2. Start the engine and allow it to run until it stalls. After it has stalled, crank it 2–3 times, then, turn **OFF** the ignition switch and reinstall the fuel pump fuse.
3. Disconnect the negative battery cable. Drain the cooling system to a level below the intake manifold.
4. Remove the air cleaner. Disconnect the accelerator linkage from the throttle body.
5. Remove the upper radiator hose from the water outlet housing and the exhaust tube from the EGR valve. If necessary,

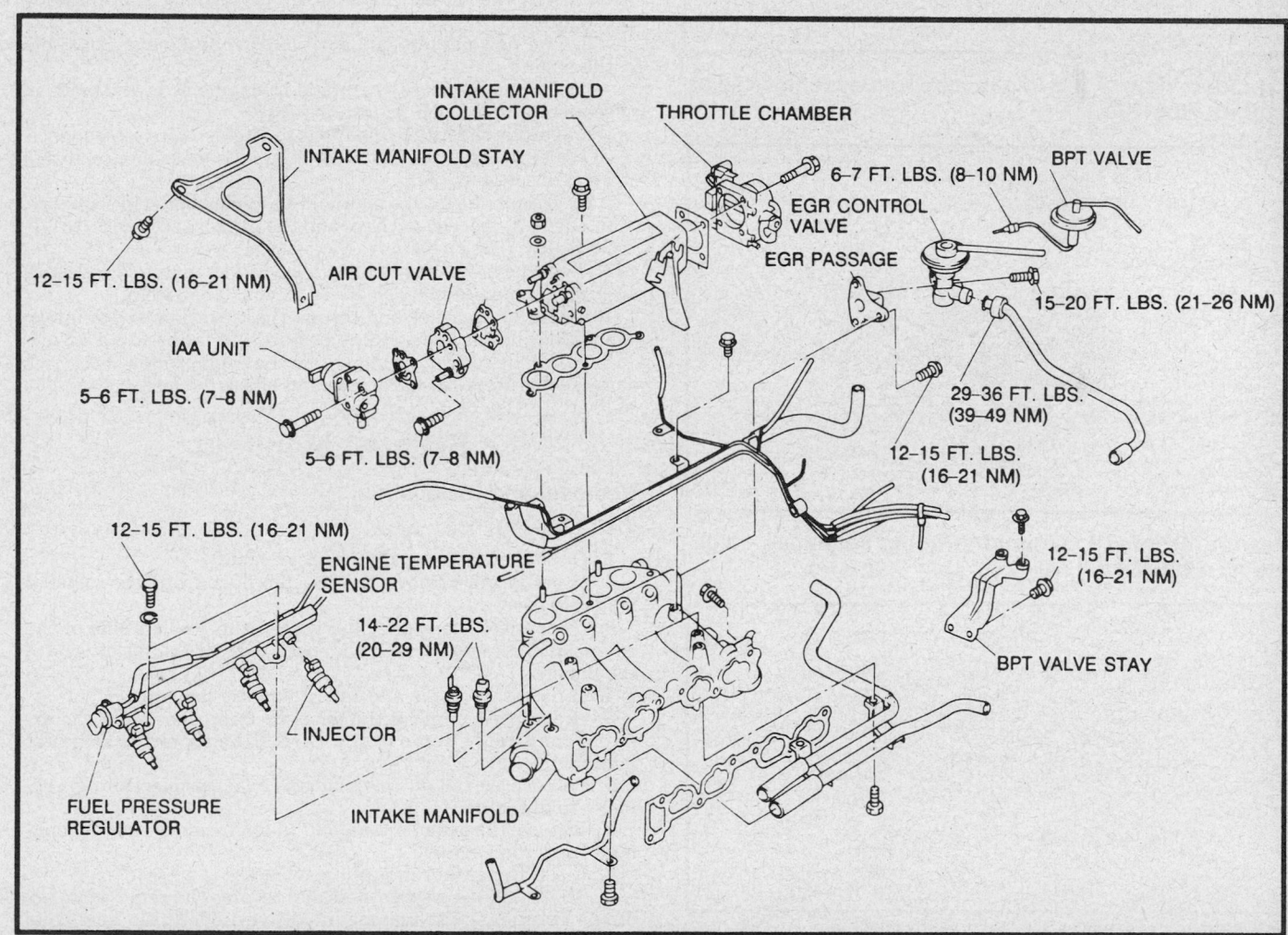

Exploded view of the intake manifold assembly — 2.4L engine 1990 — Axxess

remove the EGR valve-to-intake manifold nuts and the EGR valve.

6. Using a shop rag, wrap it around the fuel line and disconnect it from the throttle body. Remove the throttle body-to-intake manifold nuts, the throttle body and the heater mixture assembly.

7. Remove the intake manifold-to-engine bolts and the intake manifold.

8. Clean the gasket mounting surfaces.

To install:

9. Use new gaskets and reverse the removal procedures. Torque as follows:

Intake manifold-to-engine bolts—12–14 ft. lbs.

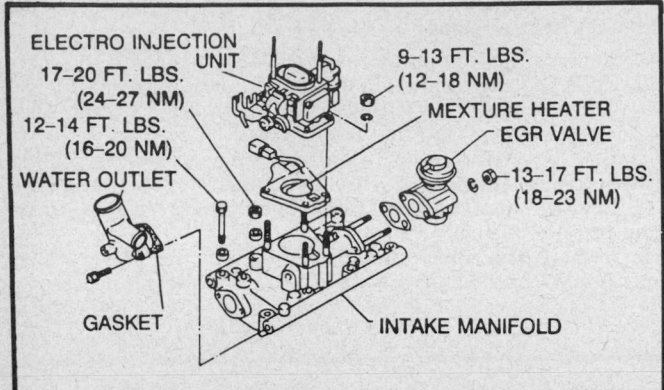

Exploded view of the intake manifold assembly—3.0L engine 1986–89

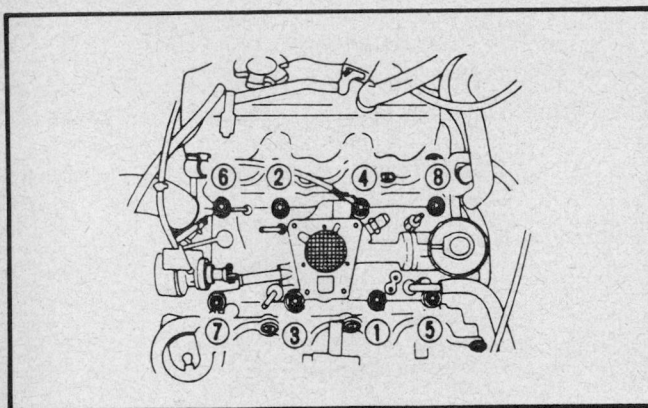

View of the intake manifold torquing sequence—3.0L engine 1986–89

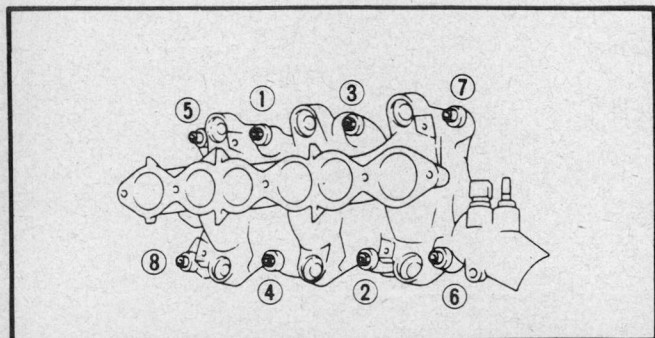

View of the intake manifold torquing sequence—3.0L engine 1990

Intake manifold-to-engine nuts—17–20 ft. lbs.
EGR valve-to-intake manifold nuts—13–17 ft. lbs.
Throttle body-to-intake manifold nuts—9–13 ft. lbs.

10. Refill the cooling system. Start the engine, allow it to reach normal operating temperatures and check for leaks.

1990 All Vehicles

1. Release the fuel pressure.

2. Disconnect the negative battery cable. Drain the cooling system to a level below the intake manifold.

3. Remove the air duct from the throttle body. Disconnect the accelerator linkage from the throttle body.

4. Remove the upper radiator hose from the water outlet housing and the exhaust tube from the EGR valve. If necessary, remove the EGR valve-to-intake manifold nuts and the EGR valve.

5. Using a shop rag, wrap it around the fuel line and disconnect it from the fuel rail. Remove the throttle body-to-intake manifold collector bolts and the throttle body.

6. Remove the intake manifold collector-to-intake manifold bolts and the collector.

7. Remove the fuel rail, with the injectors, from the intake manifold.

8. Remove the intake manifold-to-engine bolts and the intake manifold.

9. Clean the gasket mounting surfaces.

To install:

10. Install the intake manifold by performing the following procedures:

   a. Use new gaskets and position the intake manifold onto the engine.

   b. Torque the intake manifold-to-engine nuts and bolts, in sequence, to 2.2–3.6 ft. lbs. (3–5 Nm).

   c. Torque the intake manifold-to-engine bolts, in sequence, to 12–14 ft. lbs. (16–20 Nm) and the nuts, in sequence, to 17–20 ft. lbs. (24–27 Nm).

   d. Torque the intake manifold-to-engine bolts, in sequence, to 12–14 ft. lbs. (16–20 Nm) and the nuts, in sequence, to 17–20 ft. lbs. (24–27 Nm).

11. Use a new gasket and torque the intake manifold collector-to-intake manifold bolts to 13–16 ft. lbs. (18–22 Nm).

12. Use a new gasket and torque the throttle body-to-intake manifold collector bolts, in 2 steps, to 13–15 ft. lbs. (18–22 Nm).

13. Refill the cooling system. Start the engine, allow it to reach normal operating temperatures and check for leaks.

Exhaust Manifold

Removal and Installation

2.4L ENGINE

1. Disconnect the negative battery cable.

2. If equipped, remove the hot air duct from the exhaust manifold cover.

3. Disconnect the spark plug wires from the left side of the engine; if necessary, remove the spark plugs from the left side of the engine.

4. If necessary, raise and safely support the vehicle.

5. If equipped, remove the air induction tubes from the exhaust manifold. Remove the EGR tube from the exhaust manifold.

6. Remove the hot air cover and the exhaust pipe from the exhaust manifold.

7. Remove the exhaust manifold-to-engine nuts and the manifold from the engine.

8. Clean the gasket mounting surfaces.

9. To install, use new gaskets and reverse the removal procedures. Torque the exhaust manifold-to-cylinder head nuts/bolts to 12–15 ft. lbs. (working from the center to the ends) in 2 progressive steps.

3.0L ENGINE
Left Side

1. Disconnect the negative battery cable.
2. Remove the hot air tube from the exhaust manifold cover. Remove the exhaust manifold cover-to-exhaust manifold bolts and cover.
3. Remove the EGR and the AIR tubes from the exhaust manifold.

NOTE: If the alternator is in the way, remove the drive belt and the alternator.

4. Raise and safely support the vehicle.
5. Remove the exhaust pipe-to-exhaust manifold nuts and separate the exhaust pipe from the manifold.
6. Remove the exhaust manifold-to-cylinder head bolts and the manifold from the engine.
7. Clean the gasket mounting surfaces.
8. To install, use new gaskets and reverse the removal procedures. Torque the exhaust manifold-to-cylinder head nuts to 13–16 ft. lbs. and the exhaust pipe-to-exhaust manifold bolts to 16–20 ft. lbs.

Right side

1. Disconnect the negative battery cable.
2. Remove the upper/lower exhaust manifold cover-to-exhaust manifold bolts and covers.
3. Remove the AIR tube from the exhaust manifold.
4. Raise and safely support the vehicle.

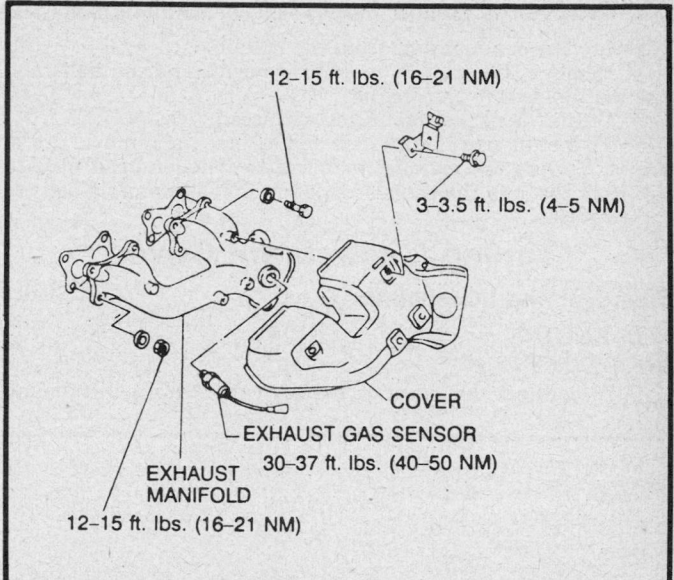

View of the torquing sequence of the exhaust manifolds—2.4L engine

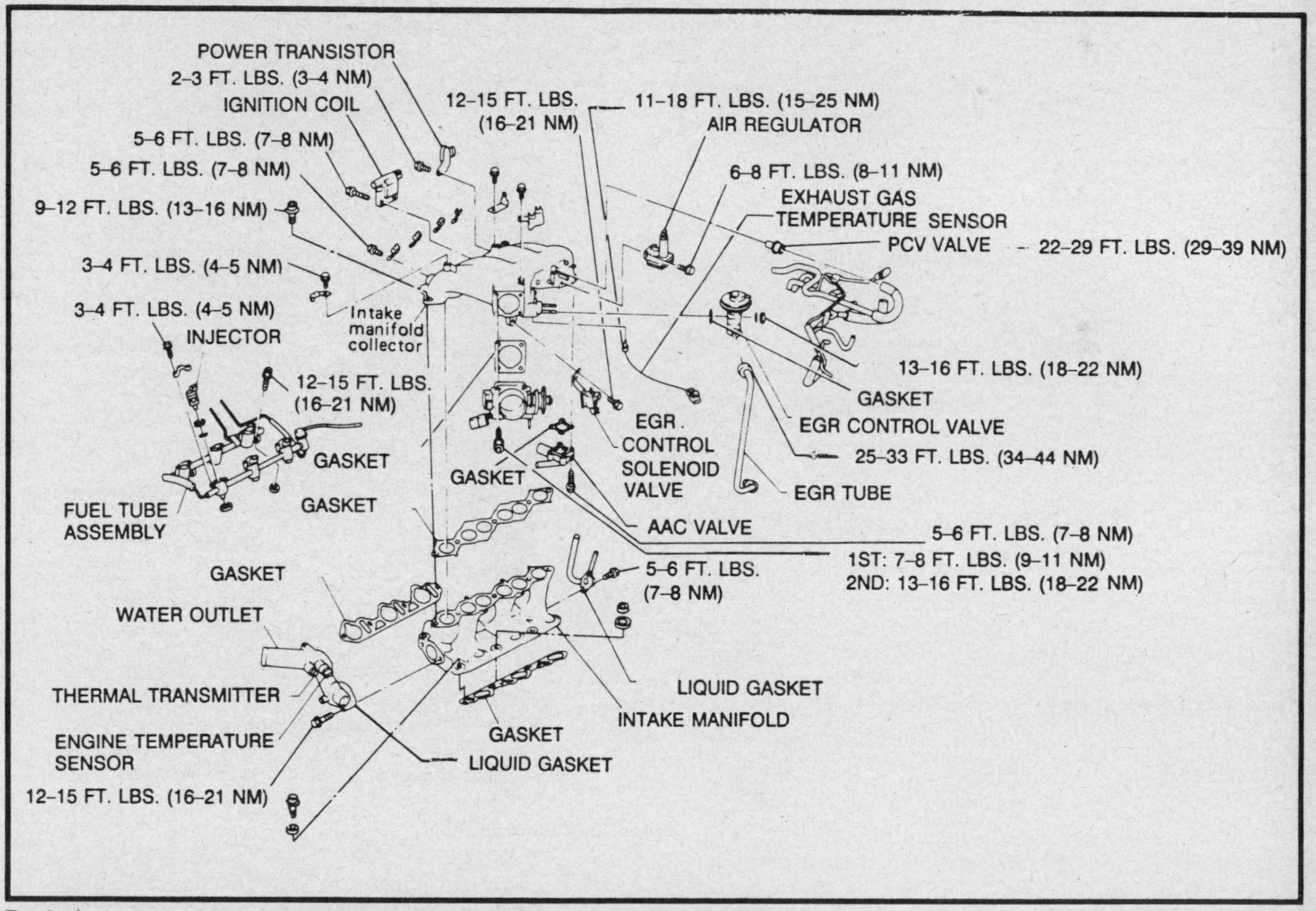

Exploded view of the intake manifold assembly—3.0L engine 1990

5. Remove the exhaust pipe-to-exhaust manifold bolts and separate the exhaust pipe from the manifold.
6. Remove the exhaust manifold-to-cylinder head bolts and the manifold from the engine.
7. Clean the gasket mounting surfaces.
8. To install, use new gaskets and reverse the removal procedures. Torque the exhaust manifold-to-cylinder head nuts to 13–16 ft. lbs. and the exhaust pipe-to-exhaust manifold bolts to 16–20 ft. lbs.

Timing Chain Front Cover

Removal and Installation

2.4L ENGINE
Except Axxess

1. Disconnect the negative battery cable. Drain the cooling

R.H. EXHAUST MANIFOLD
FRONT
1
6
3
4
5
2
L.H. EXHAUST MANIFOLD
FRONT
1
6
3
4
5
2

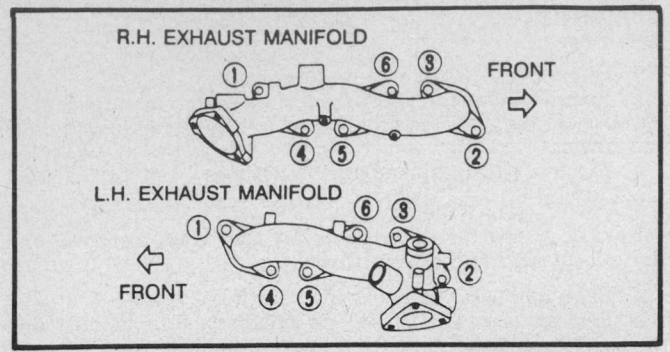

View of the torquing sequence of the exhaust manifolds – 3.0L engine

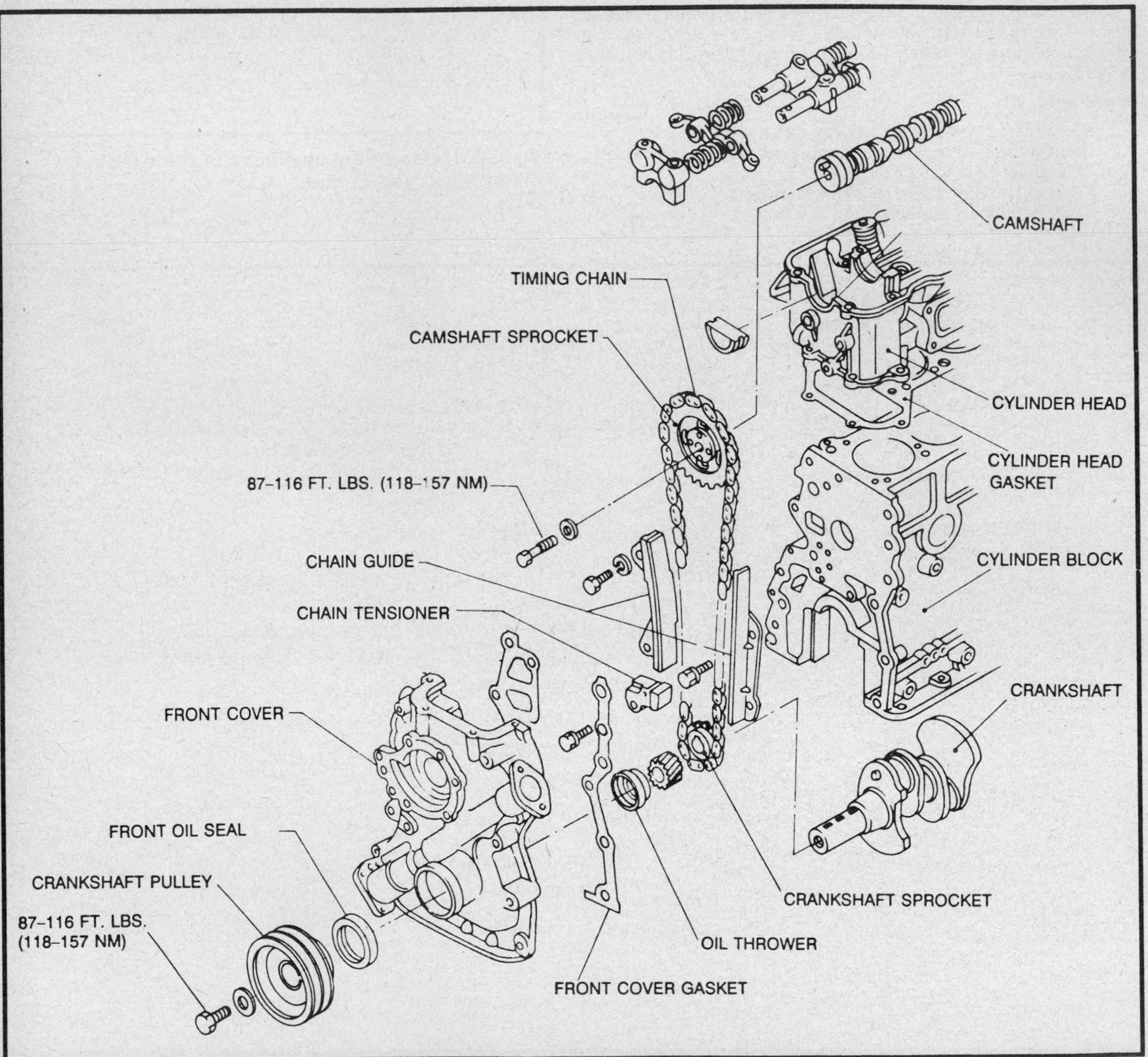

CAMSHAFT
TIMING CHAIN
CAMSHAFT SPROCKET
CYLINDER HEAD
CYLINDER HEAD GASKET
87–116 FT. LBS. (118–157 NM)
CHAIN GUIDE
CYLINDER BLOCK
CHAIN TENSIONER
CRANKSHAFT
FRONT COVER
FRONT OIL SEAL
CRANKSHAFT PULLEY
87–116 FT. LBS. (118–157 NM)
CRANKSHAFT SPROCKET
OIL THROWER
FRONT COVER GASKET

Exploded view of the timing chain assembly – 2.4L engine 1986–89 – except Axxess

system. Remove the upper and lower coolant hoses from the engine, then, the radiator.

2. Loosen the alternator adjusting bolt and remove the drive belt. Remove the alternator bracket-to-engine bolts and move the alternator aside.

3. If equipped with air conditioning, remove the drive belt. If necessary, remove the air conditioning bracket-to-engine bolts, then, move the air conditioning compressor and bracket.

4. If equipped with power steering, remove the drive belt.

5. Rotate the crankshaft to position the No. 1 cylinder on TDC of it's compression stroke.

6. Remove the distributor cap. Matchmark the rotor to the distributor housing and the distributor housing to the timing chain cover. Remove the distributor hold-down bolt and the distributor.

7. Remove the oil pump-to-timing cover bolts, the oil pump and its drive spindle.

8. Remove the cooling fan-to-water pump bolts, the fan, the fan coupling, if equipped and the water pump pulley.

9. Remove the crankshaft pulley-to-crankshaft bolt and the crankshaft pulley.

10. Remove the timing chain cover-to-cylinder head bolts, the timing chain cover-to-engine bolts, the timing chain cover-to-oil pan bolts and the cover.

11. Cut the exposed timing cover-to-oil pan gasket from the oil pan gasket.

12. Clean the gasket mounting surfaces.

To install:

NOTE: Whenever the timing cover is removed, replace the oil seal.

13. To install, use new gaskets, sealant, if necessary and re-

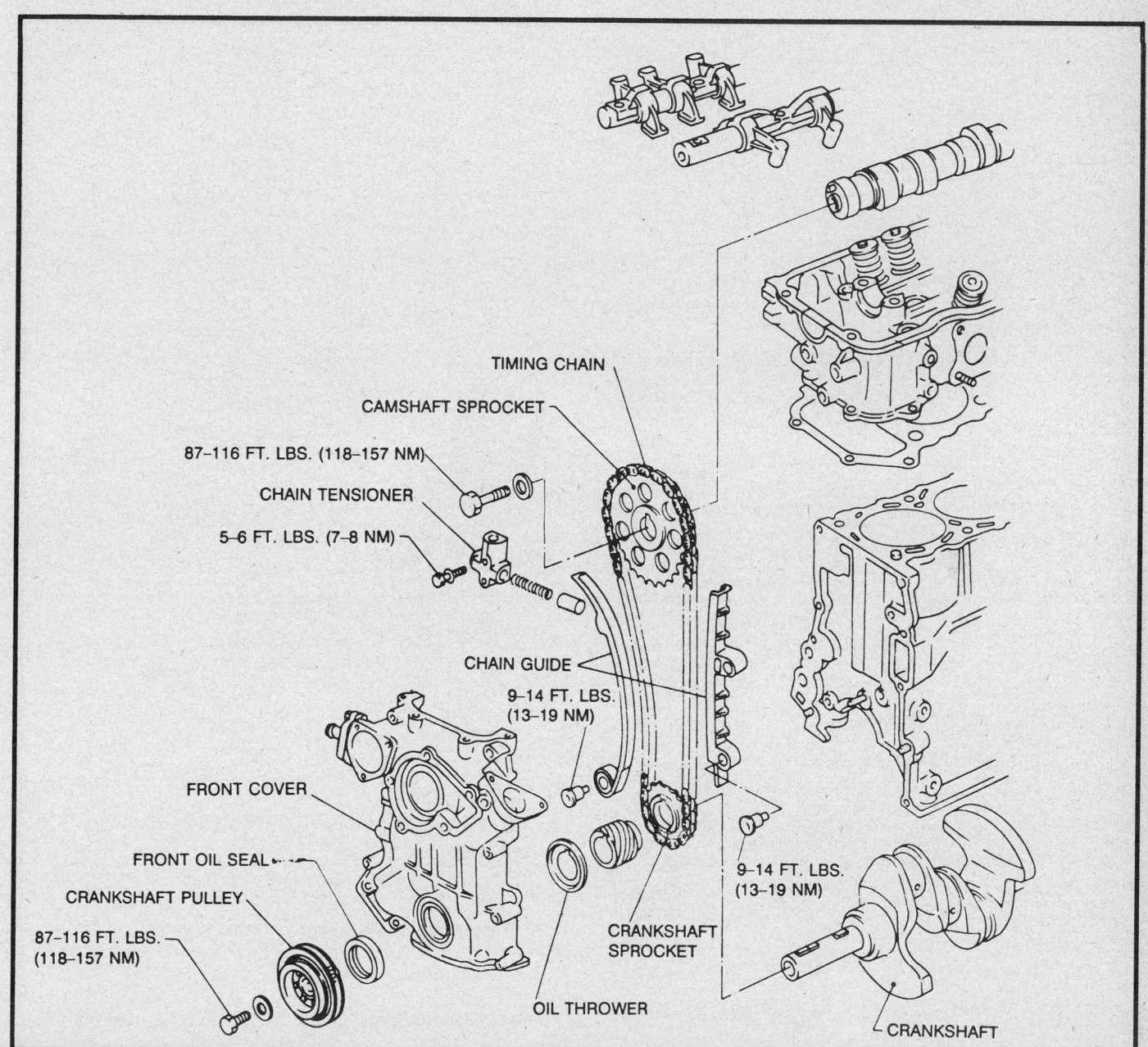

Exploded view of the timing chain assembly — 2.4L engine 1990 — except Axxess

verse the removal procedures. Cut the portions needed from a new oil pan gasket and top front cover gasket.

NOTE: Before installing the oil pump, place the gasket over the shaft and make sure the drive spindle mark (faces) aligns with the oil pump hole.

14. Apply a light coating of oil to the crankshaft oil seal and carefully mount the timing cover to the front of the engine and install all of the mounting bolts. Torque as follows:
   Ttiming cover-to-engine bolts
      8mm bolts – 7–12 ft. lbs. (10–16 Nm)
      6mm bolts – 3–7 ft. lbs. (4–10 Nm)
   Oil pan-to-timing cover bolts – 4–6 ft. lbs. (6–8 Nm)
   Oil pump-to-timing cover bolts – 8–11 ft. lbs. (11–15 Nm)
   Crankshaft pulley bolt – 87–116 ft. lbs. (118–157 Nm).

15. Refill the cooling system. Check and/or adjust the ignition timing.

Axxess

1. Disconnect the negative battery cable. Drain the cooling system. Remove the upper and lower coolant hoses from the engine, then, the radiator.
2. Loosen the alternator adjusting bolt and remove the drive belt. Remove the alternator bracket-to-engine bolts and move the alternator aside.
3. If equipped with air conditioning, remove the drive belt. If necessary, remove the air conditioning bracket-to-engine bolts, then, move the air conditioning compressor and bracket.
4. If equipped with power steering, remove the drive belt.
5. Rotate the crankshaft to position the No. 1 cylinder on TDC of it's compression stroke.
6. Raise and safely support the vehicle. Drain the crankcase.

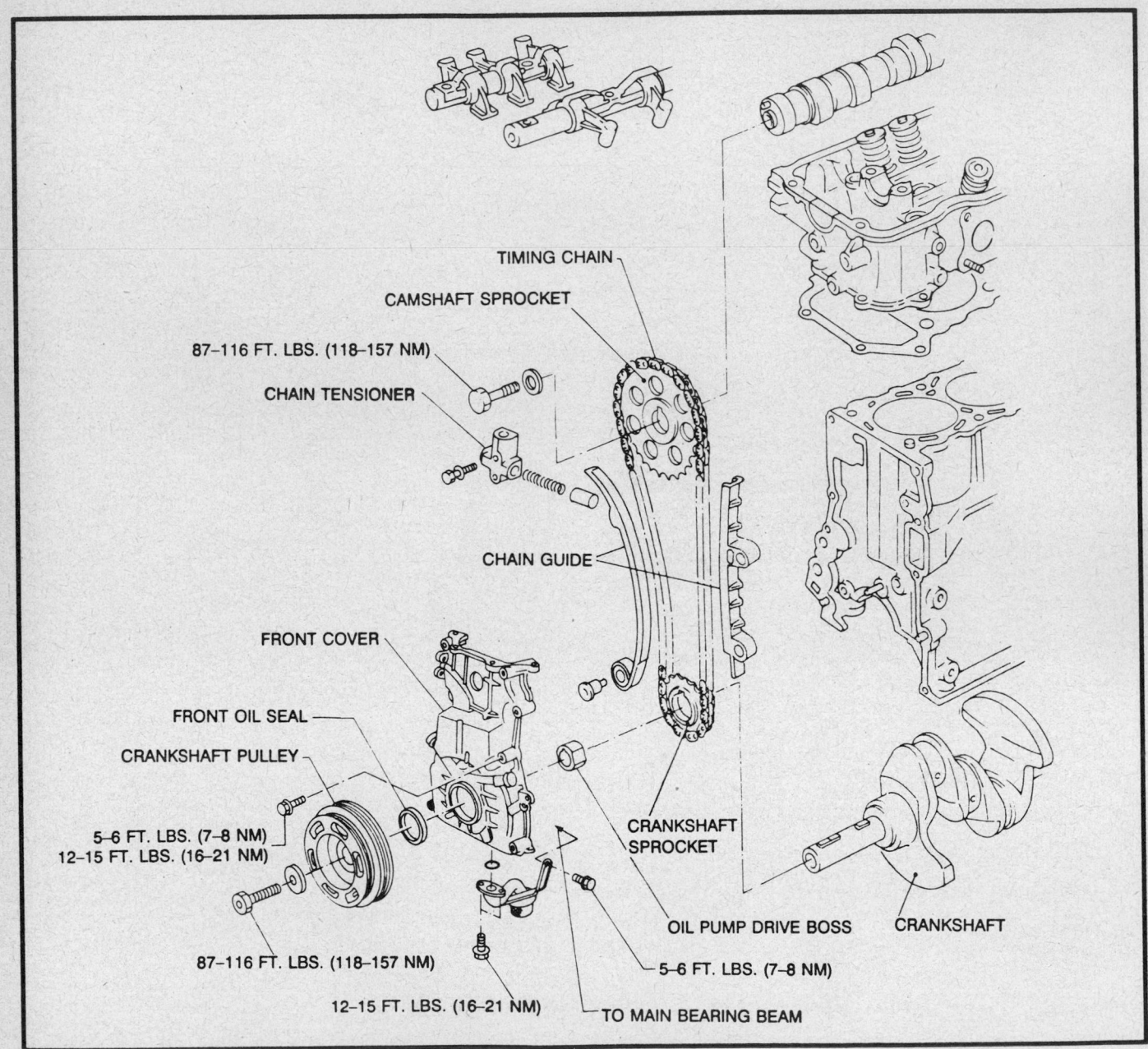

TIMING CHAIN

CAMSHAFT SPROCKET

87–116 FT. LBS. (118–157 NM)

CHAIN TENSIONER

CHAIN GUIDE

FRONT COVER

FRONT OIL SEAL

CRANKSHAFT PULLEY

5–6 FT. LBS. (7–8 NM)
12–15 FT. LBS. (16–21 NM)

CRANKSHAFT SPROCKET

87–116 FT. LBS. (118–157 NM)

OIL PUMP DRIVE BOSS

CRANKSHAFT

5–6 FT. LBS. (7–8 NM)

12–15 FT. LBS. (16–21 NM)

TO MAIN BEARING BEAM

Exploded view of the timing chain assembly – 2.4L engine 1990 – Axxess

7. Remove the oil pan-to-engine bolts and the oil pan. Remove the oil pump pickup tube-to-timing chain cover bolts.

8. Remove the cooling fan-to-water pump bolts, the fan, the fan coupling, if equipped and the water pump pulley.

9. Remove the crankshaft pulley-to-crankshaft bolt and the crankshaft pulley.

10. Remove the timing chain cover-to-cylinder head bolts, the timing chain cover-to-engine bolts and the timing chain cover.

11. Cut the exposed timing cover-to-oil pan gasket from the oil pan gasket.

12. Clean the gasket mounting surfaces.

To install:

NOTE: Whenever the timing cover is removed, replace the oil seal.

13. To install, use new gaskets, sealant, if necessary and reverse the removal procedures. Cut the portions needed from a new oil pan gasket and top front cover gasket.

14. Apply a light coating of oil to the crankshaft oil seal and carefully mount the timing cover to the front of the engine and install all of the mounting bolts. Torque as follows:

Timing cover-to-engine bolts
8mm bolts — 12–15 ft. lbs. (16–21 Nm)
6mm bolts — 5–6 ft. lbs. (7–8 Nm)
Oil pump pickup tube-to-timing cover bolts — 12–15 ft. lbs. (16–21 Nm)
Crankshaft pulley bolt — 87–116 ft. lbs. (118–157 Nm).

15. Refill the cooling system. Check and/or adjust the ignition timing.

Front Cover Oil Seal

Replacement

2.4L ENGINE

1. Disconnect the negative battery cable.
2. Remove the crankshaft pulley.
3. Using a small pry bar, pry the front oil seal from the timing cover.
4. Using an oil seal Installation tool, oil the lips of the new seal and drive the new oil seal into the timing cover until it seats.
5. To complete the installation, reverse the removal procedures. Torque the crankshaft pulley-to-crankshaft bolt to 87–116 ft. lbs. (118–157 Nm). Refill the cooling system. Start the engine, allow it reach normal operating temperatures and check for leaks.

Timing Chain and Sprockets

Removal and Installation

2.4L ENGINE

NOTE: Before attempting this procedure, rotate the crankshaft to position the No. 1 piston on the TDC of its compression stroke.

1. Disconnect the negative battery cable. Drain the cooling system.
2. Remove the timing chain cover.
3. Remove the valve cover-to-cylinder head bolts and the valve cover.

NOTE: With the No. 1 piston at TDC of its compression stroke, the timing marks on the camshaft sprocket and crankshaft sprocket should align with the silver links, if equipped of the timing chain; if no silver marks, paint alignment marks on the chain.

4. Remove the camshaft sprocket-to-camshaft bolt and the sprocket along with the chain.

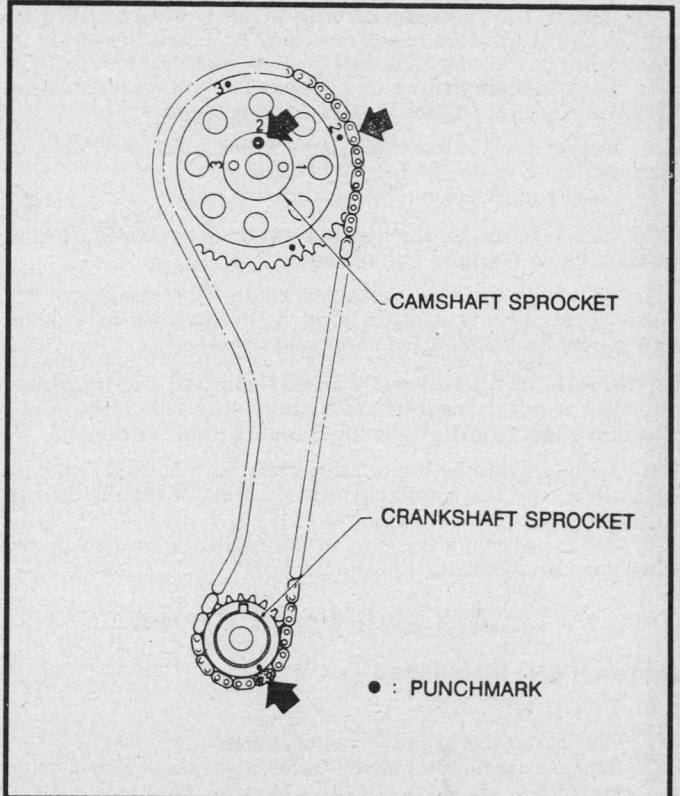

CAMSHAFT SPROCKET

CRANKSHAFT SPROCKET

● : PUNCHMARK

View of the timing chain and sprocket matchmarks — 2.4L engine 1986–89

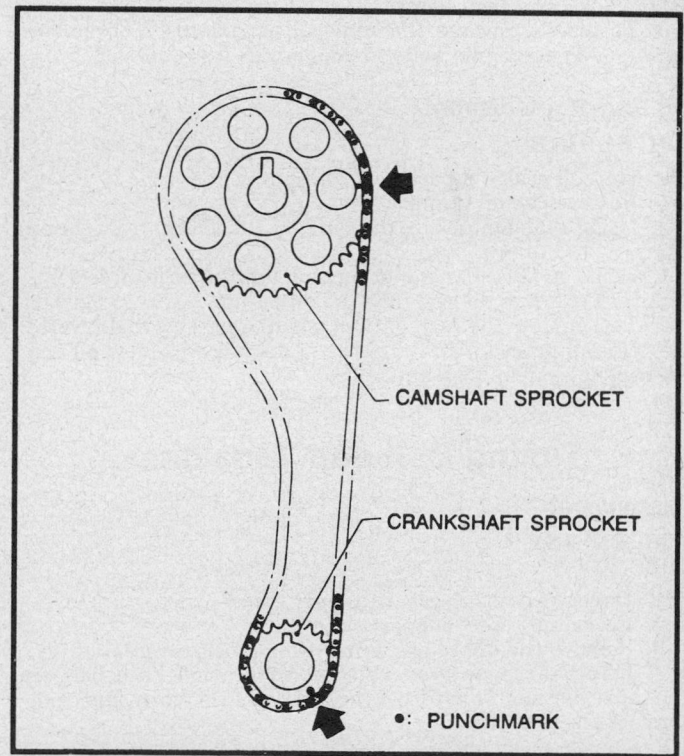

CAMSHAFT SPROCKET

CRANKSHAFT SPROCKET

●: PUNCHMARK

View of the timing chain and sprocket matchmarks — 2.4L engine 1990

NOTE: When removing the timing chain, hold it where the chain tensioner contacts it. When the chain is removed, the tensioner will come apart. Hold on to it and don't lose any the parts. There is no need to remove the chain guide unless it is being replaced.

5. Inspect the timing chain for cracked links, wear and/or damage; if necessary, replace the chain.
6. Clean the gasket mounting surfaces.

NOTE: Whenever the timing cover is removed, it is a good idea to replace the oil seal.

7. To install, use new gaskets, sealant, if necessary and reverse the removal procedures. Cut the portions needed from a new oil pan gasket and top front cover gasket.

NOTE: If equipped with an exterior oil pump, place the gasket over the shaft and make sure the drive spindle mark (faces) aligns with the oil pump hole.

8. Apply a light coating of oil to the crankshaft oil seal and carefully mount the timing cover to the front of the engine and install all of the mounting bolts.
9. Refill the cooling system and the crankcase on the Axxess. Check and/or adjust the ignition timing.

Timing Belt Front Cover

Removal and Installation

3.0L ENGINE

1. Disconnect the negative battery cable.
2. Remove the radiator shroud, the fan-to-water pump bolts and the fan.
3. Loosen and remove the alternator, the power steering, if equipped, the air conditioning, if equipped and the drive belts.
4. Raise and safely support the vehicle.
5. Remove the upper/lower timing belt covers-to-engine to engine bolts and the covers.
6. To install, reverse the removal procedures. Torque the timing cover-to-engine bolts to 26–42 inch lbs.

Oil Seal Replacement

3.0L ENGINE

The front oil seal is a part of the oil pump.
1. Remove the oil pump.
2. Using a medium size pry bar, pry the oil seal from the oil pump.
3. Using an oil seal installation tool, lubricate the oil seal lips and drive the new oil seal into the oil pump.
4. To complete the installation, use new gaskets and reverse the removal procedures. Refill the crankcase with new oil and the cooling system with antifreeze.

Timing Belt and Tensioner

Adjustment

3.0L ENGINE
1986–87

1. Disconnect the negative battery cable.
2. Raise and safely support the vehicle.
3. Remove the upper and lower timing belt covers.
4. Using a hexagon wrench, loosen the tensioner lock bolt, set the tensioner and slowly turn the tensioner clockwise and counterclockwise 2–3 times.

NOTE: If the coarse tensioner stud has been removed, be sure to apply locking sealer to the threads before installing it.

5. Tighten the tensioner locknut to 32–43 ft. lbs. (43–58 Nm). Tighten the rocker arm shaft retaining bolts (in 2–3 stages) to 13–16 ft. lbs. (18–22 Nm).

NOTE: Before tightening, be sure to set the camshaft lobe at the position where the lobe is not lifted.

6. Install the upper and lower timing belt covers.
7. To complete the installation, reverse the removal procedures.

1988–90

1. Disconnect the negative battery cable.
2. Raise and safely support the vehicle.
3. Remove the upper and lower timing belt covers.
4. While keeping the tensioner steady, loosen the locknut with a hexagon wrench.
5. Turn the tensioner approximately 70–80 degrees clockwise with the wrench and tighten the locknut.
6. Turn the crankshaft clockwise several times and slowly set the No. 1 piston to TDC of the compression stroke.
7. Apply 22 lbs. of pressure (push it in) to the center span of the timing belt between the right side camshaft sprocket and the tensioner pulley and loosen the tensioner locknut.
8. Using a 0.0138 in. (0.35mm) feeler gauge (the actual width of the blade must be ½ in.), slowly turn the crankshaft clockwise. The timing belt should move approximately 2½ teeth. Tighten the tensioner locknut, turn the crankshaft slightly and remove the feeler gauge.
9. Slowly, rotate the crankshaft clockwise several times and set the No. 1 piston to the TDC of its compression stroke.
10. Install the upper and lower timing belt covers.
11. To complete the installation, reverse the removal procedures.

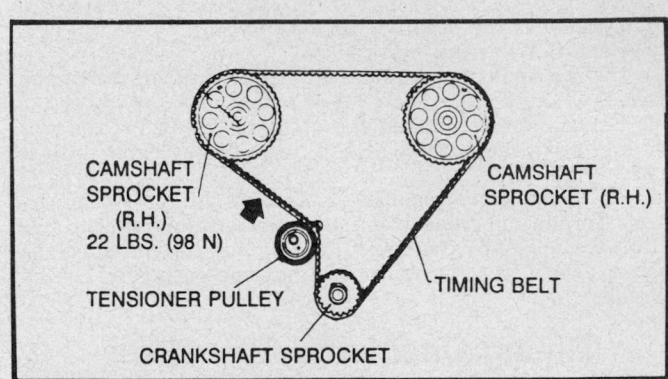

Checking the timing belt tension—3.0L engine 1988–90

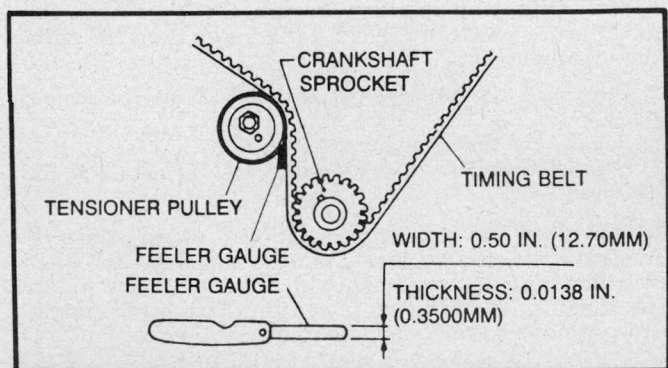

Positioning the feeler gauge—3.0L engine 1988–90

Removal and Installation

3.0L ENGINE

1. Disconnect the negative battery cable.
2. Raise and safely support the vehicle.
3. Place a clean drain pan under the radiator and drain the engine coolant into the pan.
4. Remove the radiator shroud, the fan-to-water pump bolts and the fan.
5. Remove the upper/lower coolant hoses and the radiator.
6. Loosen and remove the alternator, the power steering, if equipped, the air conditioning, if equipped and the drive belts.
7. Using a socket wrench on the crankshaft bolt, rotate the crankshaft to position the No. 1 piston on the TDC of its compression stroke.

NOTE: Make sure the sprocket alignment marks are aligned with rear timing plate and the oil pump housing.

8. Remove the upper/lower timing belt covers-to-engine bolts and the covers.
9. Using a piece of chalk or paint, mark the camshaft sprocket-to-timing belt and crankshaft sprocket-to-timing belt alignment marks; also, mark the direction of timing belt rotation (if reusing the belt).
10. Loosen the timing belt tensioner and remove the return spring. Remove the timing belt from the sprockets.

NOTE: It is good practice to remove and replace the crankshaft oil seal when the crankshaft sprocket is removed.

To install:

11. Clean the gasket mounting surfaces. Inspect the timing belt and the sprockets for cracks, wear and/or damage.
12. To install, align the timing marks, use new gaskets, sealant, if necessary and reverse the removal procedures. Adjust the timing belt tension.
13. Torque the crankshaft sprocket-to-crankshaft bolt to 90–98 ft. lbs. and the timing cover-to-engine bolts to 26–42 inch lbs.
14. Refill the cooling system. Start the engine, allow it to reach normal operating temperatures and check for leaks. Check and or adjust the ignition timing.

Timing Sprockets

Removal and Installation

3.0L ENGINE

1. Disconnect the negative battery cable.
2. Place a clean drain pan under the radiator and drain the engine coolant into the pan.
3. Remove the radiator shroud, the fan-to-water pump bolts and the fan.
4. Remove the coolant hoses and the radiator.
5. Loosen and remove the alternator, the power steering, if equipped, the air conditioning, if equipped and the drive belts.
6. Using a socket wrench on the crankshaft bolt, rotate the crankshaft to position the No. 1 piston on the TDC of its compression stroke.

NOTE: Make sure the sprocket alignment marks are aligned with rear timing plate and the oil pump housing.

7. Remove the upper/lower timing belt covers-to-engine bolts and the covers.
8. Using a piece of chalk or paint, mark the camshaft sprocket-to-timing belt and crankshaft sprocket-to-timing belt alignment marks; also, mark the direction of timing belt rotation (if reusing the belt).
9. Loosen the timing belt tensioner and remove the return spring. Remove the timing belt from the sprockets.

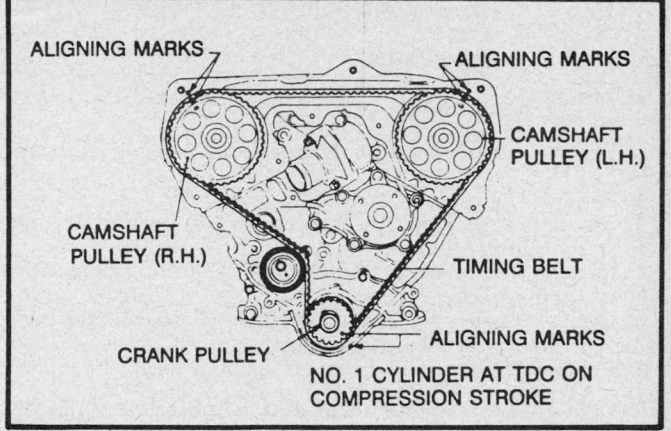

View of the timing belt and sprocket alignment marks – 3.0L engine

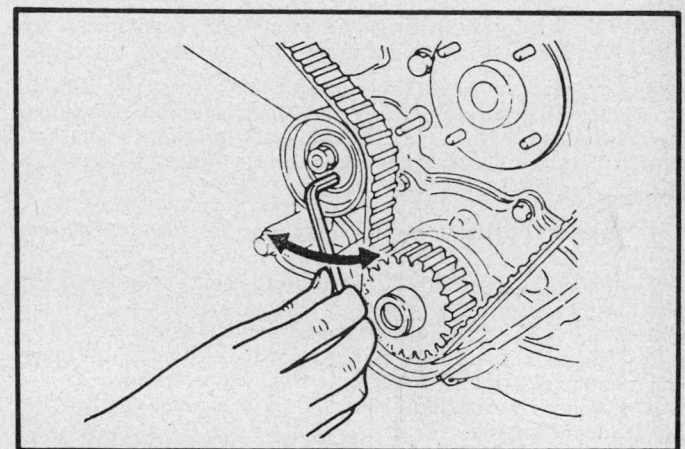

Adjusting the tensioner pulley – 3.0L engine

10. Remove the crankshaft sprocket by performing the following procedures:
    a. Remove the crankshaft pulley-to-crankshaft bolt.
    b. Using a wheel puller tool, press the crankshaft pulley from the crankshaft.
    c. Remove the crankshaft pulley plate and the crankshaft sprocket.

NOTE: It is good practice to remove and replace the crankshaft oil seal when the crankshaft sprocket is removed.

11. Remove the camshaft sprocket(s) by performing the following procedures:
    a. Remove the valve cover(s)-to-cylinder head bolts and the valve covers.
    b. Remove the camshaft sprocket-to-camshaft bolt and the camshaft sprocket.
12. Clean the gasket mounting surfaces. Inspect the timing belt and the sprockets for cracks, wear and/or damage.
13. To install, align the timing marks, use new gaskets, sealant, if necessary and reverse the removal procedures. Torque the camshaft sprocket(s)-to-camshaft bolt(s) to 58–65 ft. lbs., the crankshaft sprocket-to-crankshaft bolt to 90–98 ft. lbs. and adjust the timing belt tension.
14. Torque the timing cover-to-engine bolts to 26–42 inch lbs. Refill the cooling system. Start the engine, allow it to reach normal operating temperatures and check for leaks. Check and or adjust the ignition timing.

Camshaft

Removal and Installation

2.4L ENGINE
Except Axxess

1. Release the fuel pressure. Disconnect the negative battery cable.
2. Remove the rocker arm cover.
3. Rotate the crankshaft to position the No. 1 cylinder on the TDC of its compression stroke.
4. Remove the timing chain cover and the timing chain from the camshaft sprocket.
5. Remove the rocker arm/shaft assembly-to-cylinder head bolts and the rocker arm/shaft assembly.
6. Remove the camshaft from the cylinder head.

NOTE: Be sure to keep the disassembled parts in order for reinstallation purposes.

7. Inspect the camshaft for wear and/or damage, if necessary, replace the camshaft.

NOTE: When installing the camshaft, position it on the cylinder head with its dowel pin pointing upward.

8. To install, lubricate the camshaft and reverse the removal procedures. Torque the rocker arm/shaft assembly-to-cylinder head bolts to 11–18 ft. lbs., the camshaft sprocket-to-camshaft bolt to 87–116 ft. lbs. Readjust the valve clearances, if necessary.

Axxess

1. Release the fuel pressure. Disconnect the negative battery cable.
2. Rotate the crankshaft to position the No. 1 cylinder on the TDC of its compression stroke.
3. Remove the distributor cap and move it aside.
4. Using chalk, matchmark the rotor to the distributor housing and the distributor housing to the cylinder head.
5. Remove the distributor hold-down clamp and the distributor from the engine.
6. Remove the rocker arm cover.
7. Remove the timing chain cover and the timing chain from the camshaft sprocket.
8. Remove the rocker arm/shaft assembly-to-cylinder head bolts and the rocker arm/shaft assembly.
9. Remove the camshaft from the cylinder head.

NOTE: Be sure to keep the disassembled parts in order for reinstallation purposes.

10. Inspect the camshaft for wear and/or damage, if necessary, replace the camshaft.

NOTE: When installing the camshaft, position it on the cylinder head with its dowel pin pointing upward.

11. To install, lubricate the camshaft and reverse the removal procedures. Torque the rocker arm/shaft assembly-to-cylinder head bolts to 11–18 ft. lbs., the camshaft sprocket-to-camshaft bolt to 87–116 ft. lbs.

3.0L ENGINE

1. Relieve the fuel pressure. Disconnect the negative battery cable.
2. Drain the cooling system.
3. Remove the rocker shafts with the rocker arms; loosen the bolts in 2–3 stages.
4. Remove the hydraulic valve lifters and lifter guide.

NOTE: Hold the valve lifters with a wire so they will not drop from the lifter guide. Place identification marks on the lifters to avoid mixing them up.

5. From the rear of the cylinder head, remove the cylinder

head rear cover the camshaft bolt and the locating plate.
6. Remove the camshaft and the camshaft oil seal through the front of the cylinder head.

To install:

7. Clean the gasket mounting surfaces.
8. Install the camshaft by performing the following procedures:
   a. Install the camshaft.
   b. Apply engine oil to the camshaft oil seal and install it in place.
   c. Adjust the camshaft endplay with the correct locating plate.
9. Install the camshaft pulley(s).

NOTE: The right side and the left side camshaft pulleys are different parts. Install them in their correct positions. The right side pulley has a R3 identification mark and the left side has an L3.

10. To complete the installation, use new gaskets, sealant, if necessary and reverse the removal procedures.
11. Adjust the timing belt. Refill the cooling system. Start the engine, allow it to reach operating temperatures and check for leaks.

Piston and Connecting Rod

Positioning

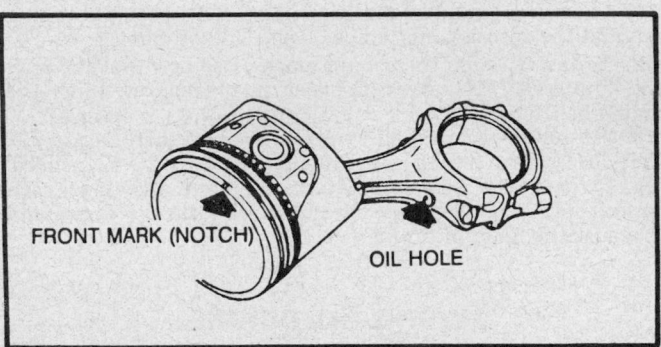

View of the piston/rod identification and positioning—2.4L engine

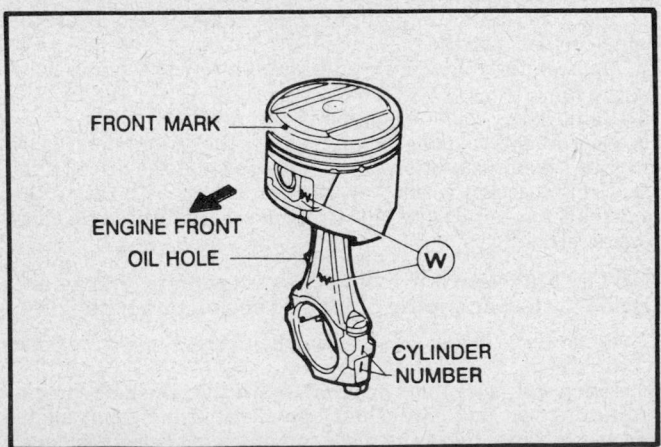

View of the piston/rod identification and positioning—3.0L engine

DIESEL ENGINE MECHANICAL

NOTE: Disconnecting the negative battery cable on some vehicles may interfere with the functions of the on board computer systems and may require the computer to undergo a relearning process, once the negative battery cable is reconnected.

Engine

Removal and Installation

1. Disconnect the negative battery cable. Raise and safely support the vehicle.
2. Remove the engine undercover.
3. Disconnect the windshield washer hose and remove the hood; scribe matchmarks around the hinges for easy installation.
4. Drain the engine oil and the engine cooling system.
5. If equipped with an automatic transmission, drain the fluid.
6. Disconnect the air cleaner hose and remove the air cleaner.
7. Remove the radiator shroud and the radiator.

NOTE: If equipped with an automatic transmission, disconnect and plug the oil cooler lines at the radiator.

8. Remove the coupling fan.
9. Disconnect both heater hoses from the engine.
10. Remove the drive belts.
11. If equipped, remove the power steering pump from it's bracket and move it aside; do not disconnect the pressure lines. Disconnect the ground strap from the bracket.
12. If equipped with air conditioning, loosen the drive belt and remove the air conditioning compressor and move it aside; do not disconnect the coolant lines.
13. Disconnect the shift control from the transmission.
14. On 4WD models, disconnect the starter leads and remove the starter. On 2WD models, disconnect the starter motor leads.
15. Disconnect the speedometer cable. Label and disconnect any electrical leads from the transmission.
16. If equipped with a manual transmission, remove the clutch release cylinder and its bracket from the transmission. Position it aside with disconnecting the hydraulic lines.
17. Remove the bolts and disconnect the exhaust pipe from the manifold.
18. On 4WD models, matchmark the front driveshaft to the transfer case flange and remove the front driveshaft.
19. On 4WD models, carefully, slide a floor jack under the front differential carrier and remove the front mounting bolt. Remove the rear mounting bolts and crossmember and slowly lower the carrier.
20. On 4WD models, remove the transmission-to-engine bracket mounting nuts.
21. On 4WD models, remove the mounting bolts from the front engine mounts.
22. Attach an engine hoist chain to the lifting brackets on the engine and raise the engine enough to ease the weight on the front and rear engine mount insulators.
23. On 4WD models, remove the front differential carrier.
24. On 2WD models, matchmark the rear driveshaft-to-transmission flange and remove the driveshaft; be sure to plug the hole in the extension housing.
25. On 2WD models, remove the transmission-to-rear engine mount bracket bolts.
26. On 2WD models, remove the transmission crossmember.
27. On 4WD models, remove the transmission-to-engine mounting bolts.

28. Tighten the engine hoist chain and carefully lift the engine (4WD) or engine/transmission (2WD) assembly up and out of the vehicle; be careful not to bump into anything as the engine is removed from the engine compartment.

To install:

29. Lower the engine/transmission assembly into the engine compartment.
30. Raise the transmission onto the crossmember with a floor jack.
31. Align the holes in the engine mounts and the frame, install the bolts and remove the engine hoist chain.
32. On 4WD models, install the transmission-to-engine mounting bolts. Torque the 16mm and 25mm bolts to 22–29 ft. lbs. (29–39 Nm).
33. On 2WD models, install the transmission member.
34. On 2WD models, install the transmission-to-rear engine mount bracket bolts and torque to 30–38 ft. lbs. (41–52 Nm).
35. On 2WD models, install the rear driveshaft to the transmission flange.
36. On 4WD models, install the front differential carrier.
37. On 4WD models, install the mounting bolts for the front engine mounts and torque to 30–38 ft. lbs. (41–52 Nm) for the right side and 39–52 ft. lbs. (53–71 Nm) for the left side.
38. On 4WD models, install the transmission-to-engine bracket mounting nuts and torque to 30–38 ft. lbs. (41–52 Nm).
39. On 4WD models, align the matchmarks on the front driveshaft to those on the transfer case flange and install the front driveshaft.
40. Connect the exhaust pipe to the manifold.
41. Install the clutch release cylinder and its bracket to the transmission.
42. Connect the speedometer cable. Connect any electrical leads to the transmission.
43. On 4WD models, connect the starter leads and install the starter. On 2WD models, connect the starter leads.
44. Install the air conditioning compressor and drive belt.
45. Install the power steering pump and its bracket, if equipped; be sure to connect the ground strap to the bracket.
46. Install the drive belts.
47. Connect the heater hoses and the coupling fan.
48. Install the radiator and shroud. If equipped with an automatic transmission, unplug oil cooler lines and connect them to the radiator.
49. Refill the engine and the automatic transmission.
50. Install and adjust the hood. Install the undercover.
51. Connect the negative battery cable, start the engine, allow it to reach normal operating temperatures and check for leaks.

Cylinder Head

Removal and Installation

1. Relieve the fuel pressure. Disconnect the negative battery cable.
2. Remove the air cleaner.
3. Remove the crankcase vent hose and remove the intake and exhaust manifolds; these are bolted together.
4. Remove the alternator, bracket and belts.
5. Disconnect the coolant hose between the head and oil cooler.
6. Remove the fuel filter assembly.
7. Disconnect and plug the injection lines from the pump and the injectors.
8. Remove the bypass hoses between the coolant pump and the thermostat housing.

9. Remove the fan.
10. Remove the rocker arm cover and the rocker arm shaft assembly.
11. Remove the pushrods and keep them in order.
12. Remove the fuel return lines.
13. Remove the injection nozzles from the cylinder head.
14. Remove the cylinder head bolts, gradually, in sequence.
15. Remove the cylinder head from the block. On occasions, the precombustion chambers may fall out, especially it the head is bumped or handled roughly. Take care that they are returned to their original positions, it this occurs.

To install:
16. Remove the head gasket and O-rings.
17. Clean and inspect all parts.
18. Using a straight edge and a feeler gauge, check the head for warpage; maximum warpage is 0.0079 in. (0.2mm).

NOTE: If refinishing the head, do not remove more than 0.011 in. (0.28mm).

19. Using a new cylinder head gasket, place it on the block with the stainless steel inset side facing upward.
20. Install new O-rings around the water and oil passages.
21. Position the cylinder head onto the block.
22. Install the cylinder head bolts by performing the following procedures:
   a. Lubricate the head bolts with engine oil.
   b. Torque the large bolts to 59–78 ft. lbs. (43–58 Nm).
   c. Torque the small bolts to 14–22 ft. lbs. (20–29 Nm).
   d. Torque the large bolts to 87–94 ft. lbs. (118–127 Nm).
   e. Torque the small bolts to 33–40 ft. lbs. (44–54 Nm).
23. Install the pushrods, pressing down and turning them to be sure of proper seating.
24. Install the rocker arm shaft assembly and torque the bolts, in sequence, to 18 ft. lbs. from the center to each end.
25. Install the injection nozzles.
26. Install the remaining components as they were removed.

Valve Lash

Adjustment

NOTE: The engine must be warm before the valves can be adjusted.

1. Disconnect the negative battery cable.
2. Remove the rocker arm cover.
3. Rotate the crankshaft to position the No. 1 cylinder on TDC of its compression stroke.
4. Loosen the adjusting screw locknuts.
5. Using a 0.014 in. (0.35mm) feeler gauge, adjust the valve clearance of valves No. 1, 2, 3 and 5.
6. Rotate the crankshaft 1 complete revolution to position the No. 4 cylinder on TDC of its compression stroke.
7. Using a 0.014 in. (0.35mm) feeler gauge, adjust the valve clearance of valves No. 4, 6, 7 and 8.
8. After adjustment, torque the locknuts to 14–18 ft. lbs. (20–25 Nm).
9. Install the rocker arm cover and connect the negative battery cable.

Rocker Arms/Shafts

Removal and Installation

1. Disconnect the negative battery cable.
2. Remove the rocker arm cover.
3. Remove the rocker arm shaft-to-cylinder head bolts; work from the center toward the outer ends.
4. Lift the shaft assembly from the cylinder head. Remove the cotter pin, the washer and the outer spring from the end of the shaft.
5. Slide the rocker arm and bracket off the shaft.

NOTE: It may be necessary to immerse the assembly in water heated to 160°F (71°C) for a few minutes to free the rocker arms; never hammer them off.

6. Install the rocker arms and brackets onto the shaft and install the spring, a new washer and cotter pin to the outer ends of the shaft.
7. Position the shaft/arm assembly onto the cylinder head and torque the mounting bolts, using 2–3 stages, to 14–18 ft. lbs. (20–22 Nm).

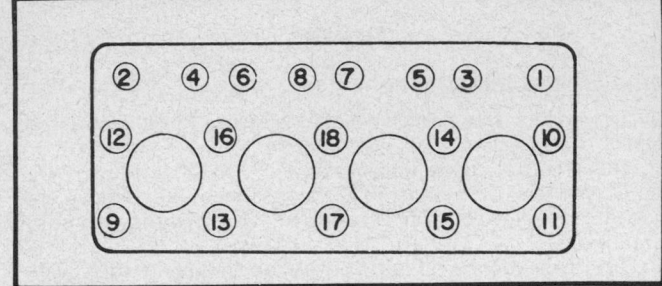

Cylinder head bolt removal sequence—2.5L diesel engine

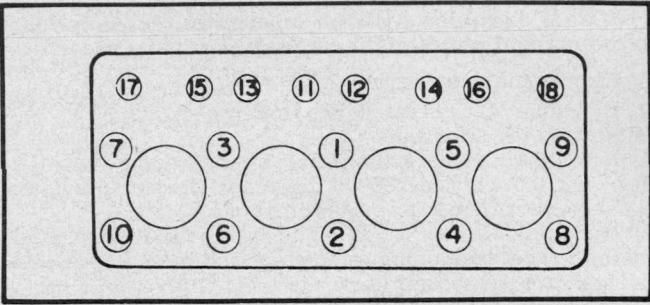

Cylinder head bolt torquing sequence—2.5L diesel engine

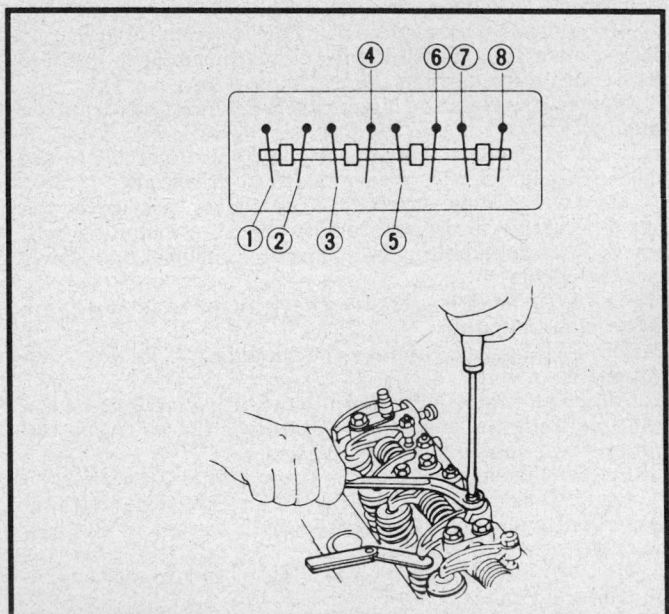

View of the valve locations and torquing sequence—diesel engine

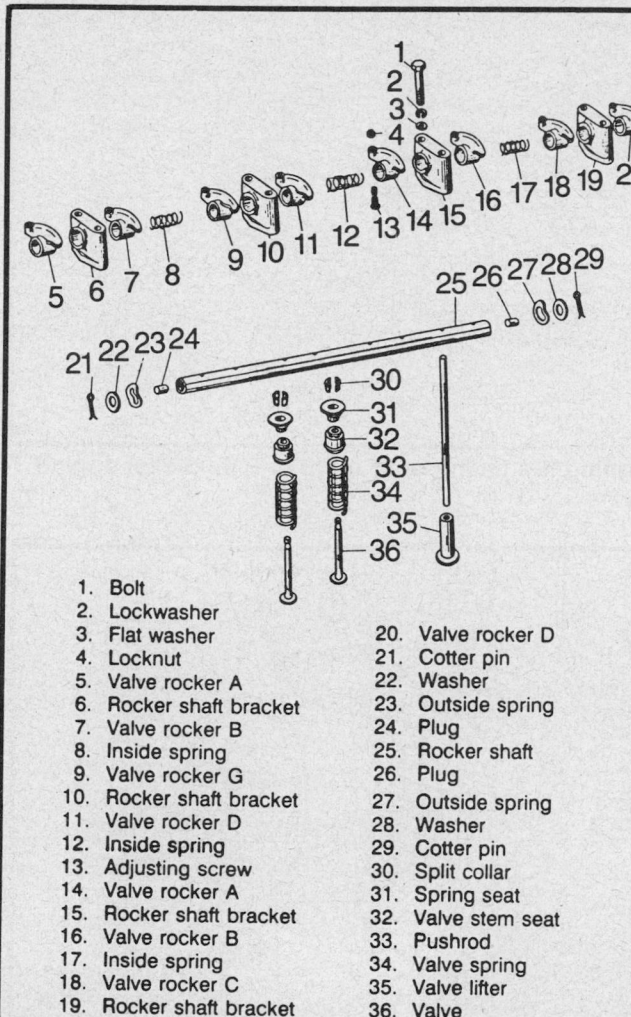

1. Bolt
2. Lockwasher
3. Flat washer
4. Locknut
5. Valve rocker A
6. Rocker shaft bracket
7. Valve rocker B
8. Inside spring
9. Valve rocker G
10. Rocker shaft bracket
11. Valve rocker D
12. Inside spring
13. Adjusting screw
14. Valve rocker A
15. Rocker shaft bracket
16. Valve rocker B
17. Inside spring
18. Valve rocker C
19. Rocker shaft bracket
20. Valve rocker D
21. Cotter pin
22. Washer
23. Outside spring
24. Plug
25. Rocker shaft
26. Plug
27. Outside spring
28. Washer
29. Cotter pin
30. Split collar
31. Spring seat
32. Valve stem seat
33. Pushrod
34. Valve spring
35. Valve lifter
36. Valve

Exploded view of the rocker arm/shaft assembly—2.5L diesel engine

Combination Manifold

Removal and Installation

NOTE: To remove the gasket, it is necessary to remove the exhaust manifold.

1. Disconnect the negative battery cable.
2. Drain the cooling system.
3. Label and disconnect the lines and hoses from the throttle chamber, dropping resistor and breather. On California models, disconnect the EGR pipe from the valve.
4. Disconnect and remove the dashpot from the intake manifold, except California models, or exhaust manifold, for California models.
5. Remove the intake manifold-to-cylinder head bolts and the manifold.
6. Remove the exhaust manifold-to-exhaust pipe bolts. Remove the exhaust manifold-to-cylinder head bolts and the manifold.
7. Clean the gasket mounting surfaces.
8. Using a new gasket, install the exhaust manifold and the intake manifold; torque the bolts in 2–3 steps.

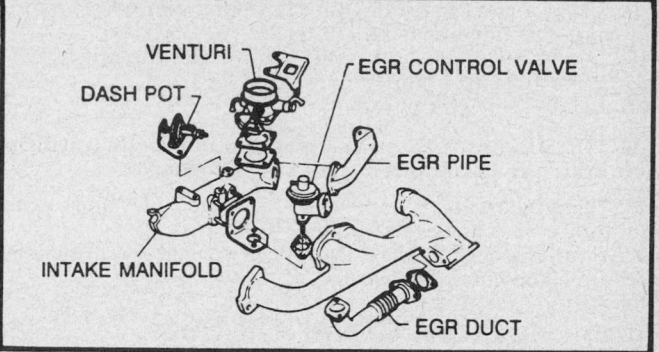

Exploded view of the intake and exhaust manifolds—2.5L diesel engine

9. To complete the installation, reverse the removal procedures.
10. Refill the cooling system. Start the engine and check for leaks.

Timing Gear Front Cover

Removal and Installation

1. Disconnect the negative battery cable.
2. Remove the drive belts, the fan and the pulley.
3. Remove the water pump bypass hose and allow the cooling system to drain below the level of the water pump.
4. Remove the water pump-to-engine bolts and the water pump; discard the gasket.
5. Using a 41mm socket, remove the crankshaft pulley nut.
6. Using a mallet, drive the pulley from the crankshaft.
7. Remove the timing gear cover-to-engine bolts and the cover.

To install:

8. Clean the gasket mounting surfaces.

NOTE: When the timing gear cover is removed, the front seal should be replaced.

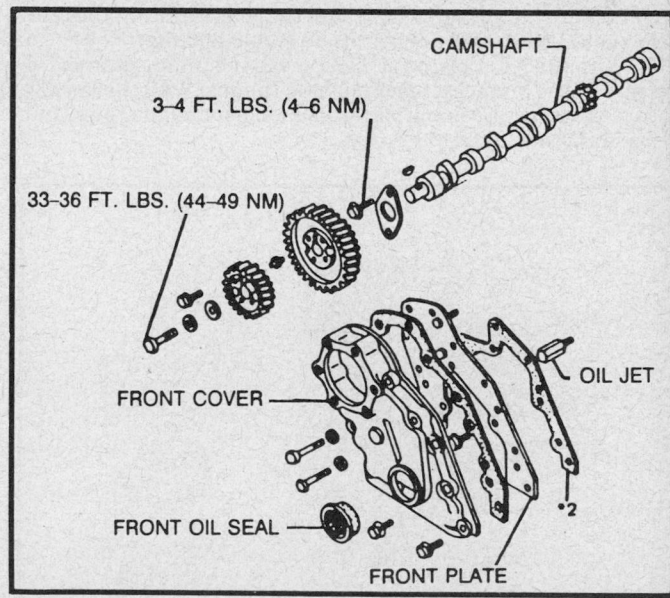

Exploded view of the timing gear cover and camshaft assembly—2.5L diesel engine

9. Using a new gasket, install the timing gear cover; torque the cover-to-engine bolts to 7–9 ft. lbs. (10–13 Nm).

10. Install the crankshaft pulley and torque the nut to 217–239 ft. lbs. (294–324 Nm).

11. Install the water pump.

NOTE: Do not tighten the water pump bolts until the belt adjuster is installed with the alternator.

12. Install the water pump bypass hose, the pulley and cooling fan. Refill the cooling system.

13. Start the engine, allow it to reach normal operating temperatures and check for leaks.

Front Cover Oil Seal

Replacement

1. Disconnect the negative battery cable. Drain the cooling system.

2. Remove the front cover.

3. Using a small prybar, pry the old seal from the cover.

4. Lubricate the new seal with engine oil and press it into the front cover; be sure the flat side faces forward and the lip faces the engine.

5. Install the front cover.

6. Refill the cooling system.

Timing Gears

Removal and Installation

1. Disconnect the negative battery cable. Drain the cooling system.

2. Remove the front cover.

3. Remove the timing gear round nut.

4. Using a timer extractor tool, thread the tool into the timer weight holder. Remove the timing gear assembly by threading the extractor tool bolt.

5. Unbolt and remove the camshaft gear set.

6. Remove the oil slinger. Unbolt the crankshaft gear and remove it with a 2-armed gear puller.

To install:

7. Install the camshaft gear.

8. Install the crankshaft gear and oil slinger while carefully aligning the timing marks. Measure the gear backlash; the backlash should be 0.0028–0.0079 in. (0.071–0.200mm).

9. With the No. 1 piston at TDC, mesh the timing gear and idler gear at the **Y** marks. After aligning the gear with the keyway, secure the timer assembly with a lockwasher and the round nut. Torque the nut to 50–58 ft. lbs.

Aligning the timing gear marks — 2.5L diesel engine

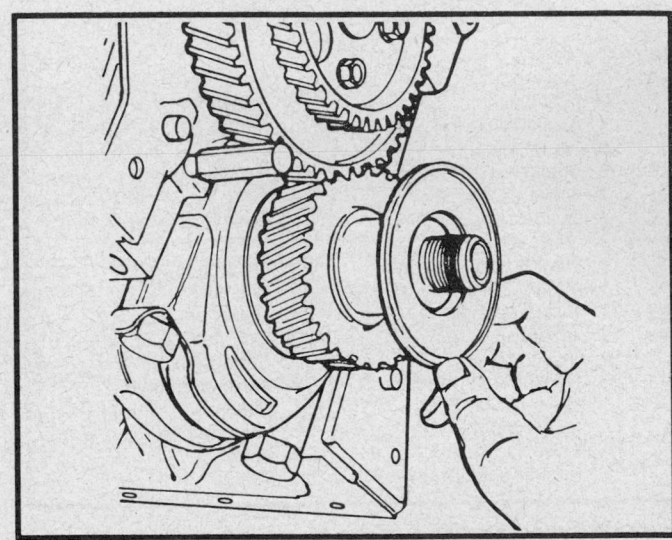

Installing the oil slinger — 2.5L diesel engine

Removing the timer gear — 2.5L diesel engine

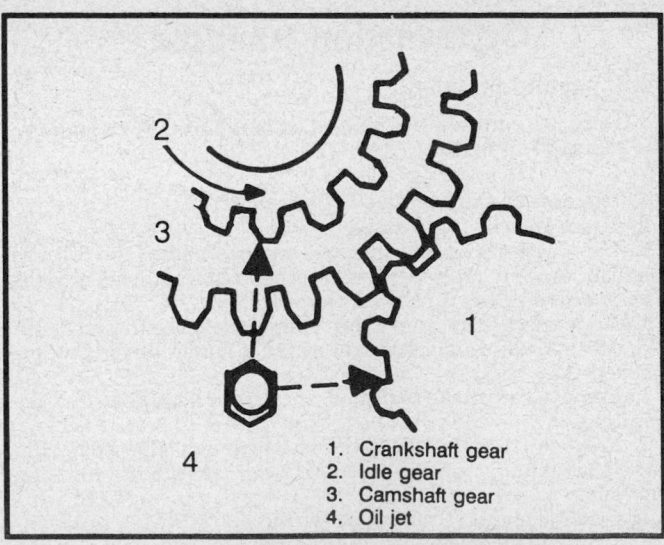

1. Crankshaft gear
2. Idle gear
3. Camshaft gear
4. Oil jet

Orientation of the oil jet — 2.5L diesel engine

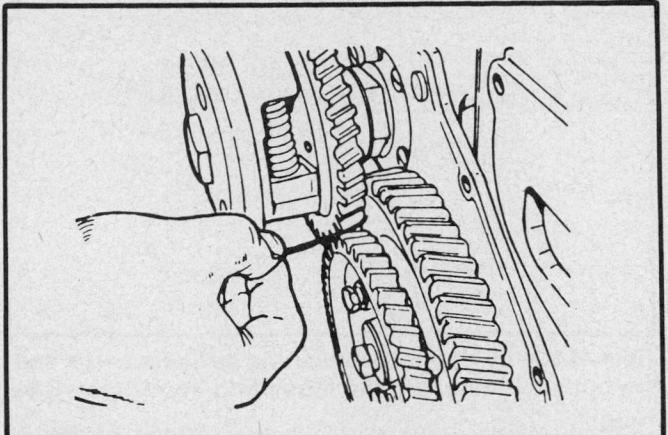

Measuring the timing gear backlash—2.5L diesel engine

10. Install the timing gear cover.

NOTE: If the gear case oil jet was removed, install it in the same relationship.

11. To complete the installation, reverse the removal procedures.

Camshaft

Removal and Installation

1. Disconnect the negative battery cable. Drain the cooling system.
2. Remove the cylinder head.
3. Remove the valve lifters and mark them for reassembly.
4. Remove the front case and timing gear cover.
5. Remove the tachometer drive support nuts.
6. Remove the timer round nut.
7. Thread the timer extractor tool into the timer weight holder. Remove the timer assembly by tightening the extractor bolt.
8. Remove the oil pump drive spindle.
9. Remove the camshaft locating plate bolts and carefully slide the camshaft from the engine.
10. Coat the camshaft with clean engine oil and carefully slide it into the block. Install the locating plate.
11. Install the oil pump drive spindle by aligning the oil pump

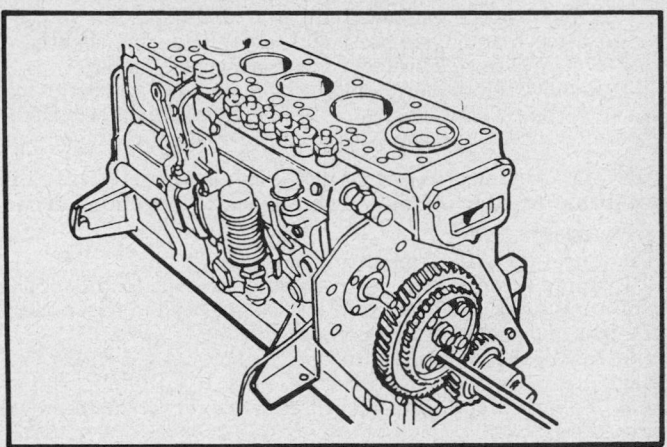

Removing the camshaft locating bolts—2.5L diesel engine

driveshaft groove and the camshaft oil pump drive gear with the spindle.

Piston and Connecting Rod

Positioning

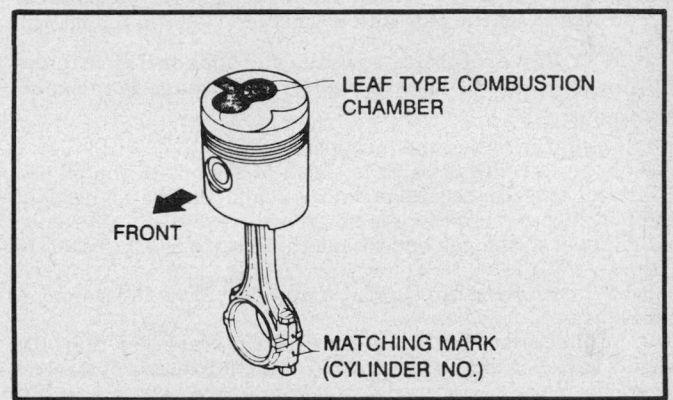

View of the piston and connecting rod locating points—2.5L diesel engine

ENGINE LUBRICATION

Oil Pan

Removal and Installation

2.4L ENGINE
Except Axxess

1. Raise and safely support the vehicle.
2. Remove the engine undercover and drain the engine oil.
3. On 4WD models, perform the following procedures:
   a. Remove the bolt from the front differential carrier member.
   b. Position a floor jack under the front differential carrier and remove the mounting bolts.
   c. Remove the transmission-to-rear engine mount bracket nuts.

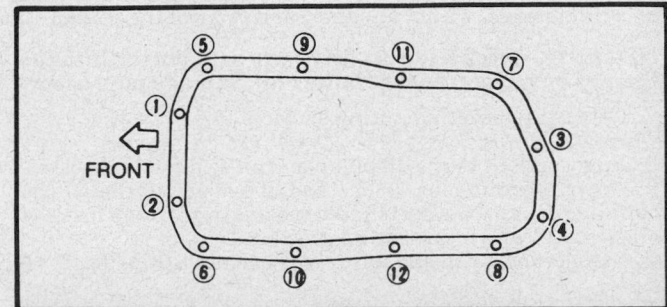

View of the oil pan bolt torquing sequence—2.4L engine

d. Remove the engine mount nuts and bolts.

e. Attach an engine hoist and raise the engine slightly.

4. On 2WD models, remove the front crossmember.

5. Remove the oil pan-to-engine bolts. Insert a seal cutter tool between the cylinder block and the oil pan and tap it around the circumference of the pan with a hammer. Remove the oil pan.

NOTE: Be careful not to drive the seal cutter into the oil pump or rear oil seal retainer as damage may occur.

To install:

6. Clean the gasket mounting surfaces.

7. Apply a continuous ⅛ in. bead of sealant to the oil pan mounting surface; be sure to trace sealant bead to the inside of the bolt holes where there is no groove.

8. Install the oil pan and torque the bolts to 4–5 ft. lbs. (4–7 Nm).

9. To complete the installation, reverse the removal procedures.

10. Wait at least 30 minutes and refill the crankcase. Start the engine and allow it to reach normal operating temperatures and check for leaks.

Axxess

1. Raise and safely support the vehicle.

2. Drain the engine oil.

3. Remove the front exhaust tube and the front side gusset.

4. On 2WD models, remove the crossmember.

5. Remove the oil pan-to-engine bolts. Insert a seal cutter tool between the cylinder block and the oil pan and tap it around the circumference of the pan with a hammer. Remove the oil pan.

NOTE: Be careful not to drive the seal cutter into the oil pump or rear oil seal retainer as damage may occur.

To install:

6. Clean the gasket mounting surfaces.

7. Apply a continuous ⅛ in. bead of sealant to the oil pan mounting surface; be sure to trace sealant bead to the inside of the bolt holes where there is no groove.

8. Install the oil pan and torque the bolts to 5–7 ft. lbs. (7–10 Nm).

9. To complete the installation, reverse the removal procedures.

10. Wait at least 30 minutes and refill the crankcase. Start the engine and allow it to reach normal operating temperatures and check for leaks.

2.5L DIESEL ENGINE

1. Raise and safely support the vehicle.

2. Remove the undercover and drain the engine oil.

3. Remove the stabilizer bar bracket bolts.

4. Remove the front crossmember.

5. Remove the idler arm.

6. Remove the oil pan-to-engine bolts, insert a seal cutter tool between the cylinder block and the oil pan, tap the tool around the circumference, with a hammer, and remove the oil pan.

NOTE: Be careful not to drive the seal cutter into the oil pump or rear oil seal retainer for damage may occur.

7. Clean the gasket mounting surfaces.

To install:

8. Apply sealant to the oil pump and oil seal retainer gasket.

9. Apply a continuous ⅛ in. bead of sealant to the oil pan mounting surface; be sure to trace sealant bead to the inside of the bolt holes where there is no groove.

10. Install the oil pan and torque the bolts to 5–6 ft. lbs. (7–10 Nm).

11. To complete the installation, reverse the removal procedures.

12. Wait at least 30 minutes and refill the crankcase. Start the

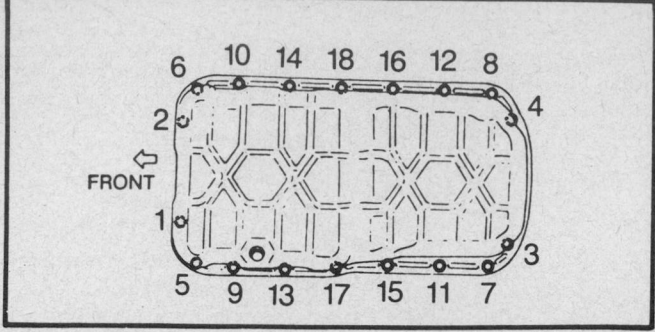

View of the oil pan bolt loosening sequence—torque the bolts by reversing the loosening sequence—3.0L engine

engine and allow it to reach normal operating temperatures and check for leaks.

3.0L ENGINE

1. Raise and safely support the vehicle.

2. Remove the undercover and drain the engine oil.

3. On 2WD models, remove the stabilizer bar bracket bolts.

4. On 4WD models, remove the front driveshaft and disconnect the halfshafts at the transfer case. Position a floor jack under the front differential carrier and remove the mounting bolts.

5. On 2WD models, remove the front crossmember.

6. Remove the idler arm and the starter motor.

7. On 4WD models, remove the transmission-to-rear engine mount bracket nuts and the engine mount nuts/bolts.

8. Remove the engine gussets.

9. On 4WD models, attach a hoist to the engine and raise the engine slightly.

10. Remove the oil pan-to-engine bolts, insert a seal cutter tool between the cylinder block and the oil pan, tap the tool around the circumference, with a hammer, and remove the oil pan.

NOTE: Be careful not to drive the seal cutter into the oil pump or rear oil seal retainer for damage may occur.

11. Clean the gasket mounting surfaces.

To install:

12. Apply sealant to the oil pump and oil seal retainer gasket.

13. Apply a continuous ⅛ in. bead of sealant to the oil pan mounting surface; be sure to trace sealant bead to the inside of the bolt holes where there is no groove.

14. Install the oil pan and torque the bolts to 4–5 ft. lbs. (4–7 Nm).

15. To complete the installation, reverse the removal procedures.

16. Wait at least 30 minutes and refill the crankcase. Start the engine and allow it to reach normal operating temperatures and check for leaks.

Oil Pump

Removal and Installation

2.4L ENGINE
Except Axxess

The oil pump is an external type, mounted to the right side of the crankshaft pulley.

1. Disconnect the negative battery cable.

2. Rotate the crankshaft to position the No. 1 cylinder on the TDC of the compression stroke.

3. If equipped with a splash pan, remove it. If necessary, remove the stabilizer bar.

4. Remove the oil pump-to-housing bolts and the oil pump from the engine.

5. Clean the gasket mounting surfaces.

6. To install, use a new gasket, fill the oil pump with engine oil, align the drive spindle punch mark with the oil hole on the oil pump, then, insert the oil pump into the housing until the driveshaft tang fits into the distributor shaft notch. Torque the oil pump-to-engine housing bolts to 8–11 ft. lbs. Start the engine and check for leaks.

Axxess

The oil pump rides on the crankshaft and is attached to the front cover.

1. Disconnect the negative battery cable.

2. Raise and safely support the vehicle. Drain the cooling system.

3. Drain the engine oil.

4. Remove the oil pan and the front cover.

5. Remove the oil pump cover-to-front cover bolts, the cover and the oil pump gears.

NOTE: When the oil pump is removed, replace the oil seal.

6. Inspect and/or replace the oil pump gears.

7. Using petroleum jelly, pack the oil pump cavity and reverse the removal procedures.

2.5L DIESEL ENGINE

1. Disconnect the negative battery cable.

2. Raise and safely support the vehicle. Drain the engine oil.

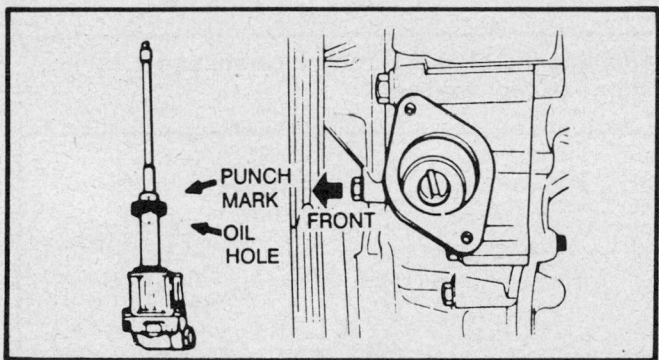

View of the oil pump and front cover—2.4L engine—except Axxess

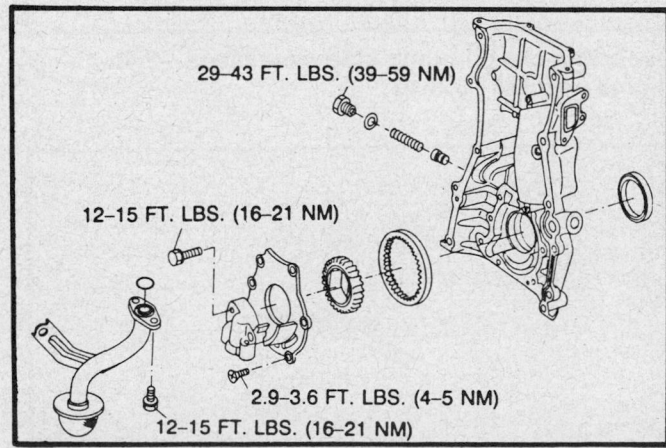

Exploded view of the oil pump assembly—2.4L engine—Axxess

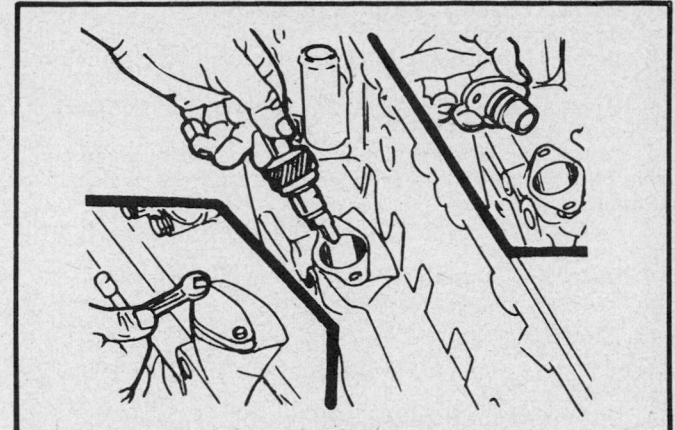

Removing the oil pump spindle—2.5L diesel engine

View of the oil pump—2.5L diesel engine

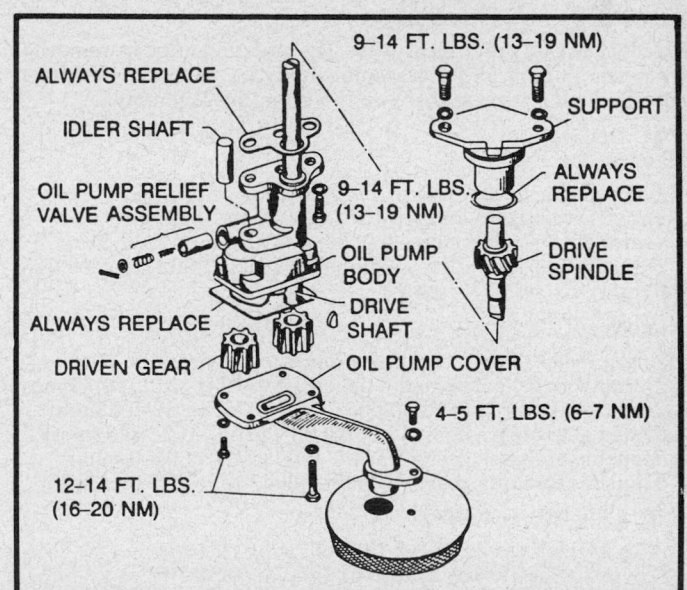

Exploded view of the oil pump assembly—2.5L diesel engine

3. Remove the oil pump drive spindle.

4. Remove the oil pan.

5. Remove the oil pump-to-engine bolts and the oil pump; discard the gasket.

6. Using a new gasket, install the oil pump. Torque the bolts to 9–14 ft. lbs. (13–19 Nm).

7. Install the drive spindle by aligning it with the oil pump driveshaft groove in the cylinder block and the camshaft oil pump drive gear.

8. Place a new O-ring on the spindle support and bolt it to the block.

9. Install the oil pan and refill the engine with oil.

10. Start the engine and check for leaks.

3.0L ENGINE

The oil pump is mounted at the front of the engine behind the crankshaft pulley.

1. Disconnect the negative battery cable.

2. Raise and safely support the vehicle. Drain the cooling system and the crankcase.

3. Remove the oil pan and the timing belt.

4. Remove the crankshaft timing sprocket using a wheel puller and the timing belt plate.

5. Remove the oil pump strainer and the pickup tube from the oil pump.

6. Remove the oil pump-to-engine bolts and the oil pump from the engine.

7. Clean the gasket mounting surfaces.

NOTE: When the oil pump is removed, replace the oil seal.

8. To install, use new gaskets, silicone sealant, pack the oil pump cavity with petroleum jelly and reverse the removal procedures. Torque as follows:
Oil pump-to-engine 6mm bolts
  2WD—4.3–5.1 ft. lbs.
  4WD—4.6–6.1 ft. lbs.
Oil pump-to-engine 8mm bolts
  2WD—9–12 ft. lbs.
  4WD—16–22 ft. lbs.
Pickup tube-to-oil pump bolts—12–15 ft. lbs.
Pickup tube bracket-to-engine bolt—4.6–6.1 ft. lbs.

Checking

To check the oil pump clearances, the oil pump must be removed from the engine and disassembled. If the parts do not meet specifications, replace them or the oil pump assembly.

2.4L ENGINE
Except Axxess

Using a feeler gauge, check the following clearances:
  Inner rotor tip-to-outer rotor—0.0047 in. (0.12mm) max.
  Outer rotor-to-housing—0.0059–0.0083 in. (0.15–0.21mm)
  Side clearance (with gasket)—0.0016–0.0031 in. (0.04–0.07mm)

Axxess

Using a feeler gauge, check the following clearances:
  Pump body-to-outer gear—0.0043–0.0079 in. (0.11–0.20mm)
  Inner gear-to-cressent—0.0087–0.0130 in. (0.22–0.33mm)
  Outer gear-to-cressent—0.0083–0.0126 in. (0.21–0.32mm)
  Housing-to-inner gear—0.0020–0.0035 in. (0.05–0.09mm)
  Housing-to-outer gear—0.0020–0.0043 in. (0.05–0.11mm)

2.5L DIESEL ENGINE

Using a feeler gauge, check the following clearances:
  Cover-to-shaft—less than 0.020 in. (0.50mm)
  Gear backlash—less than 0.020 in. (0.50mm)
  Housing-to-side gear—0.0059 in. (0.15mm) max.
  Housing-to-gear tooth—0.0098 in. (0.25mm) max.

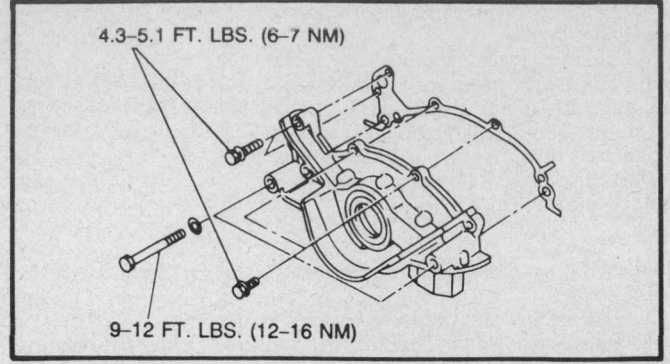

4.3–5.1 FT. LBS. (6–7 NM)

9–12 FT. LBS. (12–16 NM)

Exploded view of the oil pump housing—3.0L engine

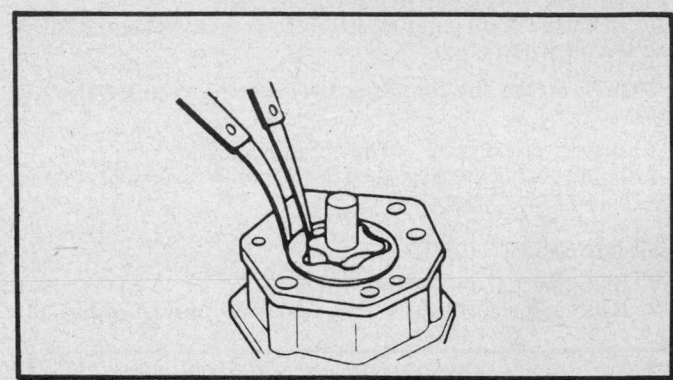

Inspecting the oil pump rotor clearances—2.4L engine—except Axxess

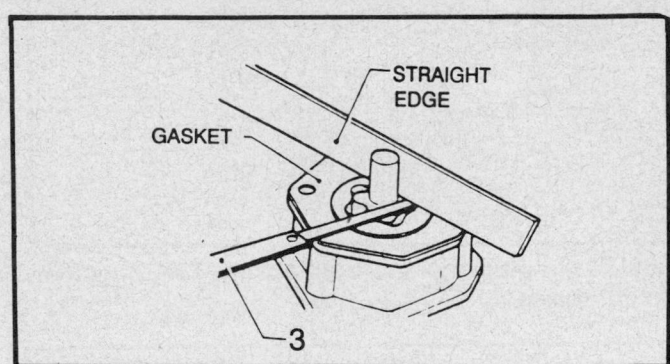

STRAIGHT EDGE

GASKET

3

Inspecting the oil pump side clearances—2.4L engine—except Axxess

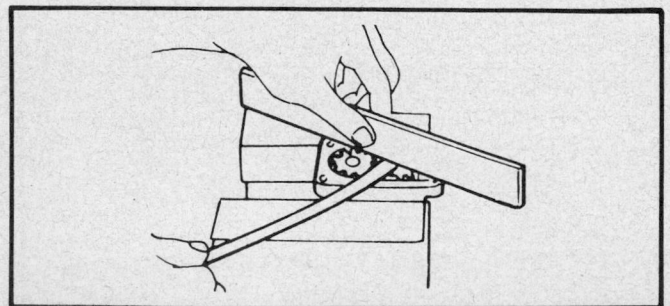

Inspecting the cover-to-side gear clearances—2.5L diesel engine

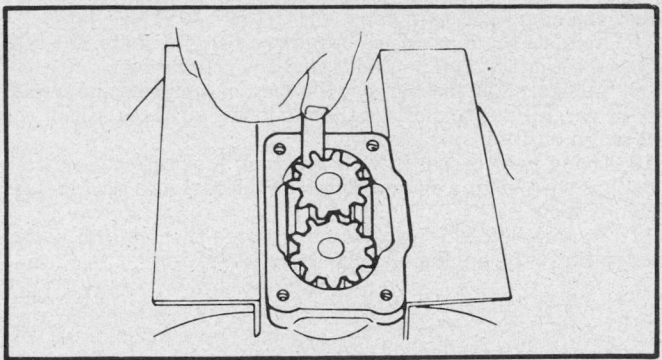

Inspecting the housing-to-gear tooth clearances – 2.5L diesel engine

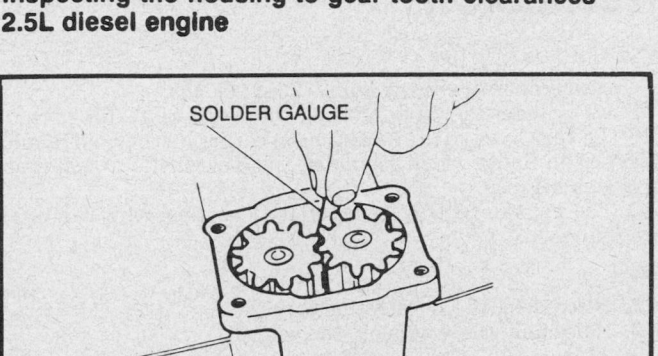

Inspecting the gear backlash – 2.5L diesel engine

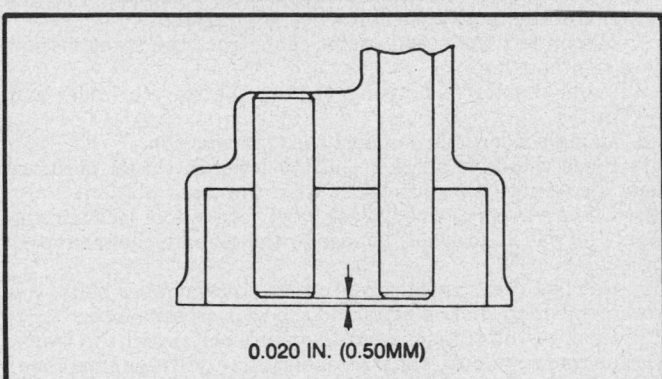

0.020 IN. (0.50MM)

Inspecting the cover-to-shaft clearances – 2.5L diesel engine

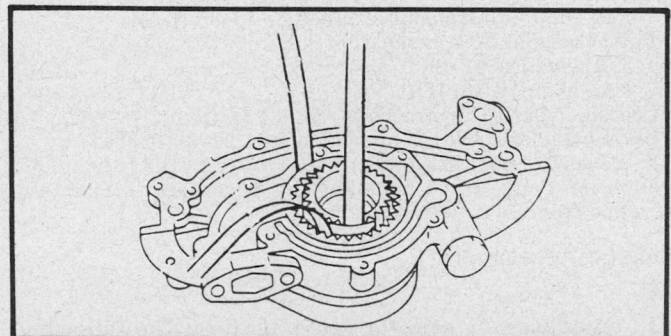

Inspecting the oil pump rotor clearances – 3.0L engine and 2.4L Axxess engine

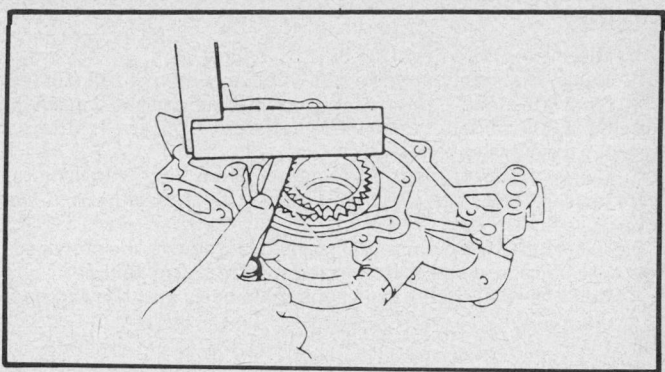

Inspecting the oil pump side clearances – 3.0L engine and 2.4L Axxess engine

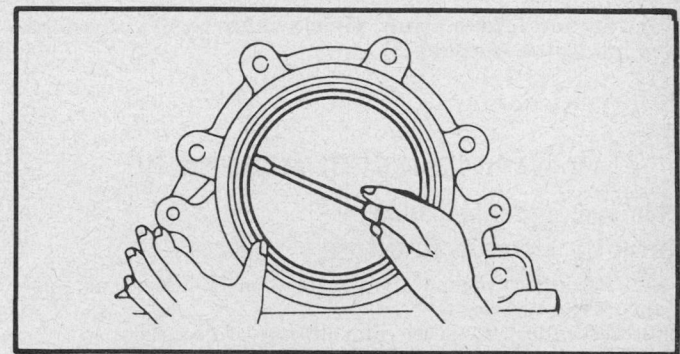

Removing the rear oil seal from the retainer – typical

3.0L ENGINE

Using a feeler gauge, check the following clearances:
Pump body-to-outer gear – 0.0043–0.0079 in. (0.11–0.20mm)
Inner gear-to-cressent – 0.0047–0.0091 in. (0.12–0.23mm)
Outer gear-to-cressent – 0.0083–0.0126 in. (0.22–0.33mm)
Housing-to-inner gear – 0.0020–0.0035 in. (0.05–0.09mm)
Housing-to-outer gear – 0.0020–0.0043 in. (0.05–0.11mm)

Rear Main Bearing Oil Seal

Removal and Installation

EXCEPT AXXESS

1. Disconnect the negative battery cable.
2. Raise and safely support the vehicle. Remove the starter.
3. Remove the transmission from the vehicle.
4. If equipped with a manual transmission, remove the clutch-to-flywheel bolts and the clutch assembly from the vehicle.
5. Remove the flywheel-to-crankshaft bolts and the flywheel from the engine.
6. Remove the rear oil seal retainer-to-engine bolts, the rear oil seal retainer-to-oil pan bolts and the retainer.
7. Using a small pry bar, pry the rear oil seal from the retainer; be careful not to damage the mounting surfaces. Clean the oil seal mounting surfaces.
8. Using the oil seal installation tool, lubricate the new oil seal lips with engine oil and drive the the seal into the retainer until it seats.
9. To complete the installation, reverse the removal procedures. Start the engine and check for leaks.

AXXESS

1. Disconnect the negative battery cable.
2. Raise and safely support the vehicle. Remove the starter.
3. On 2WD models, remove the halfshafts from the transaxle.
4. On 4WD models, remove the halfshaft from the transaxle/transfer case assembly.
5. Remove the transaxle-to-engine bolts, the transaxle-to-transfer case bolts for 4WD, and lower the transaxle from the vehicle.
6. If equipped with a manual transaxle, remove the clutch-to-flywheel bolts and the clutch assembly from the vehicle.
7. Remove the flywheel-to-crankshaft bolts and the flywheel from the engine.
8. Remove the rear oil seal retainer-to-engine bolts, the rear oil seal retainer-to-oil pan bolts and the retainer.
9. Using a small pry bar, pry the rear oil seal from the retainer; be careful not to damage the mounting surfaces. Clean the oil seal mounting surfaces.
10. Using the oil seal installation tool, lubricate the new oil seal lips with engine oil and drive the the seal into the retainer until it seats.
11. To complete the installation, reverse the removal procedures. Start the engine and check for leaks.

MANUAL TRANSMISSION

For further information, please refer to "Professional Transmission Manual".

Transmission Assembly

Removal and Installation

PICK-UP AND PATHFINDER

1. Disconnect the negative battery cable. Raise and safely support the vehicle.
2. Disconnect the accelerator linkage, if necessary.
3. Remove the driveshaft from the transmission (2WD) or transfer case (4WD); be sure to plug the driveshaft opening to keep the transmission/transfer case oil from draining out. If equipped with 4WD, remove the transfer case-to-front differential driveshaft; it may be necessary to remove the front differential carrier/crossmember.
4. If necessary, disconnect the exhaust pipe from the exhaust manifold.
5. Disconnect the electrical connectors from the back-up light switch and the neutral switch wires, if equipped.
6. Disconnect the speedometer cable from the transmission extension housing.
7. From the clutch housing, remove the slave cylinder and the starter.
8. Using a floor jack, support the transmission. On 4WD models, remove the transfer case-to-transmission bolts and the transfer case.
9. Place the transmission shifting lever in the N position, then, remove the console box, the E-ring and the shift lever. On the 4WD models, remove the transfer case shift lever.
10. Using a block of wood, place it between a floor jack and the engine oil pan to prevent damage to the oil pan, then, support the engine.
11. Remove the transmission-to-rear crossmember bolts, the crossmember-to-chassis bolts and the rear crossmember.
12. Remove the transmission-to-engine bolts, pull the transmission rearward until the pilot shaft is free of the engine, then, lower the transmission from the vehicle.
13. Clean the engine-to-transmission mounting surfaces.

To install:

14. Lightly grease the input shaft splines and reverse the removal procedures.
15. Torque as follows:
Upper engine-to-transmission bolts—29–36 ft. lbs.
Bottom engine-to-transmission bolts
3.0L engine—22–29 ft. lbs.
2.4L engine—14–18 ft. lbs.
2.5L diesel engine—7–9 ft. lbs.
Crossmember-to-chassis bolts—23–31 ft. lbs.
Slave cylinder-to-clutch housing bolts—22–30 ft. lbs.
16. Be sure to align the marks made earlier on the U-joint and differential flange when installing the driveshaft, to maintain driveline balance.
17. To complete the installation, reverse the removal procedures.

VAN

1. Disconnect the negative battery cable.
2. Raise and safely support the vehicle.
3. Remove the driveshaft from the transmission; be sure to plug the driveshaft opening to keep the transmission oil from draining out.
4. Disconnect the exhaust pipe from the exhaust manifold.
5. Disconnect the electrical connectors from the back-up light switch and the neutral switch wires, if equipped.
6. Disconnect the speedometer cable from the transmission extension housing.
7. From the clutch housing, remove the slave cylinder and the starter.
8. Using a floor jack, support the transmission.
9. Place the transmission shifting lever in the N position, then, disconnect the shift cables from the transmission.
10. Using a block of wood, place it between a floor jack and the engine oil pan to prevent damage to the oil pan, then, support the engine.
11. Remove the transmission-to-rear crossmember bolts, the crossmember-to-chassis bolts and the rear crossmember.
12. Remove the transmission-to-engine bolts, pull the transmission rearward until the pilot shaft is free of the engine, then, lower the transmission from the vehicle.
13. Clean the engine-to-transmission mounting surfaces.
14. To install, lightly grease the input shaft splines and reverse the removal procedures. Torque as follows:
Upper engine-to-transmission bolts—29–36 ft. lbs.
Bottom engine-to-transmission bolts
3.0L engine—22–29 ft. lbs.
2.4L engine—14–18 ft. lbs.
Crossmember-to-chassis bolts—23–31 ft. lbs.
Slave cylinder-to-clutch housing bolts—22–30 ft. lbs.
15. Be sure to align the marks made earlier on the U-joint and differential flange when installing the driveshaft, to maintain driveline balance.

Linkage Adjustment

VAN

1. To adjust the selector cable, perform the following procedures:
a. Remove the console cover, then, loosen the adjuster locknut.

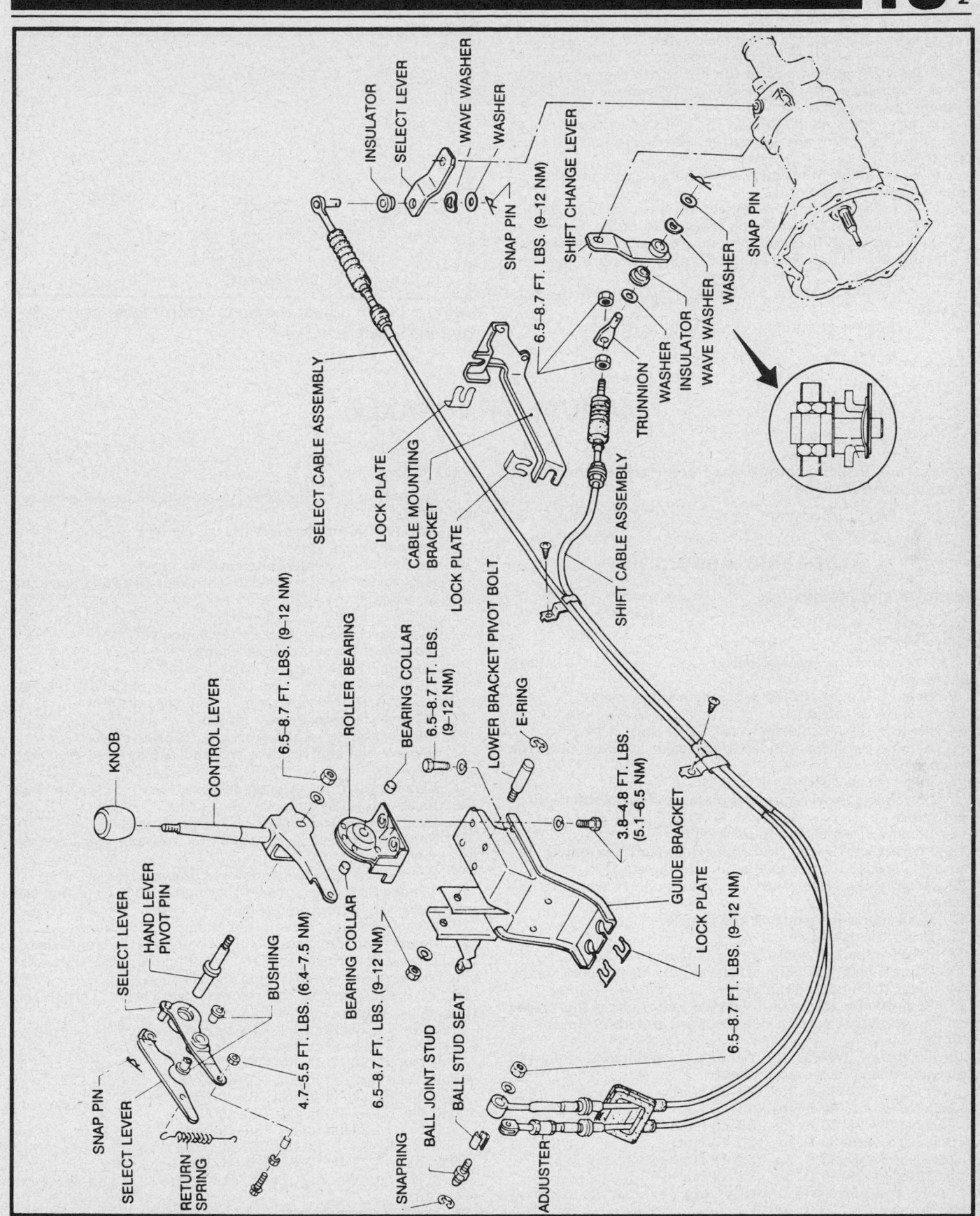

Exploded view of the shift change lever assembly – Van

b. Raise and support the vehicle safely.

c. Working under the vehicle, position the shift change lever (on the transmission) to the 3rd or 4th gear position.

d. From inside the vehicle, adjust the selector cable length using the adjuster.

e. After adjustment, tighten the adjuster locknut.

2. To adjust the shifter cable, perform the following procedures:

a. From under the vehicle, loosen the trunnion-to-shift cable locknut.

b. Remove the shift cable trunnion from the cross shaft.

c. Position the transmission cross shaft in the **N** position.

d. Using a 0.16 in (4mm) pin, insert it (as vertical as possible) into the adjustment holes of both the control lever and roller bearing.

e. Adjust the trunnion position and install it into the cross shaft.

f. Torque the trunnion locknut to 9–12 ft. lbs.

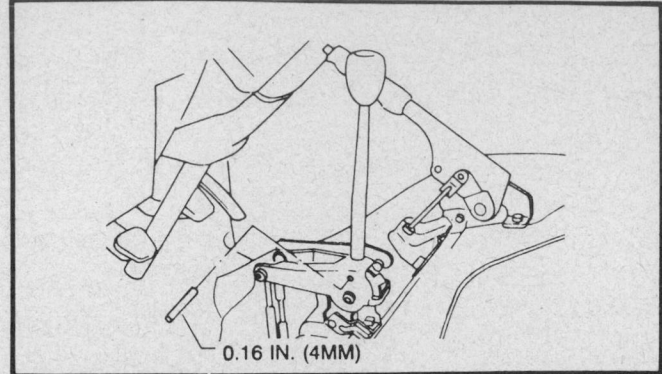

0.16 IN. (4MM)

Using a pin to adjust the shift control lever and roller bearing — Van

MANUAL TRANSAXLE

For further information, please refer to "Professional Transmission Manual".

Transaxle Assembly

Removal and Installation

AXXESS
2WD Model

1. Disconnect the negative battery cable. Remove the battery and bracket.
2. Remove the air cleaner with the air flow meter.
3. Remove the air duct.
4. Remove the air injection vent (AIR) unit.
5. Remove the slave cylinder-to-transaxle bolts and move the cylinder aside.
6. Remove the clutch hose clamp.
7. Disconnect the speedometer pinion and the position switch connectors.
8. Remove the breather hose clamp.
9. Disconnect the electrical connectors from the starter. Remove the starter-to-transaxle bolts and the starter.
10. Remove the shift control rod and support rod from the transaxle.
11. Raise and safely support the vehicle.
12. Drain the transaxle.
13. Remove the halfshafts from the transaxle.
14. Using a floor jack, support the engine; do not position the jack under the oil pan drain plug.
15. Remove the transaxle-to-engine bolts, using the proper equipment, move the transaxle rearward and lower it from the vehicle.
16. To install, reverse the removal procedures. Torque the transaxle-to-engine bolts as follows:
 Bolt No. 1 – 29–36 ft. lbs. (39–49 Nm)
 Bolt No. 2 – 22–30 ft. lbs. (30–40 Nm)
 Bolt No. 3 – 22–30 ft. lbs. (30–40 Nm)
 Bolt No. 4 – 22–30 ft. lbs. (30–40 Nm)
 Bolt No. 5 – 29–36 ft. lbs. (39–49 Nm)
 Bolt No. 6 – 29–36 ft. lbs. (39–49 Nm)
17. To complete the installation, reverse the removal procedures.
18. Refill the transaxle.

4WD Model

1. Disconnect the negative battery cable. Remove the battery and bracket.
2. Remove the air cleaner with the air flow meter.
3. Remove the air duct.
4. Remove the air injection vent (AIV) unit.
5. Remove the slave cylinder-to-transaxle bolts and move the cylinder aside.
6. Remove the clutch hose clamp.
7. Disconnect the position switch connector.
8. Remove the breather hose clamp.
9. Disconnect the negative battery cable.
10. Disconnect the electrical connectors from the starter. Remove the starter-to-transaxle bolts and the starter.
11. Remove the speedometer pinion.
12. Remove the driveshaft from the transfer case.
13. Remove the shift control rod and support rod from the transaxle.
14. Remove the front exhaust tube.
15. Raise and safely support the vehicle.
16. Drain the transaxle and the transfer case.
17. Remove the halfshafts from the transaxle/transfer case assembly.
18. Remove the left side transverse link and gusset.
19. Using a floor jack, support the engine; do not position the jack under the oil pan drain plug.
20. Remove the rear mount and engine front mount.
21. Remove the transaxle-to-engine bolts and the transaxle-to-transfer case bolts, using the proper equipment, move the transaxle rearward and lower it from the vehicle.
22. To install, reverse the removal procedures. Torque the transaxle-to-engine bolts as follows:
 Bolt No. 1 – 29–36 ft. lbs. (39–49 Nm)
 Bolt No. 2 – 22–30 ft. lbs. (30–40 Nm)
 Bolt No. 3 – 29–36 ft. lbs. (39–49 Nm)
 Bolt No. 4 – 22–30 ft. lbs. (30–40 Nm)
 Bolt No. 5 – 22–30 ft. lbs. (30–40 Nm)
 Bolt No. 6 – 22–30 ft. lbs. (30–40 Nm)
 Bolt No. 7 – 29–36 ft. lbs. (39–49 Nm)
 Bolt No. 8 – 29–36 ft. lbs. (39–49 Nm)
 Bolt No. 9 – 22–30 ft. lbs. (30–40 Nm)
23. To complete the installation, reverse the removal procedures.
24. Refill the transaxle.
25. Check and/or adjust the front wheel alignment.

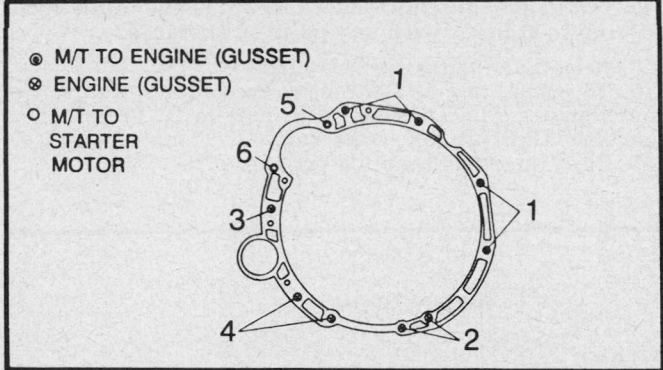

- ⊛ M/T TO ENGINE (GUSSET)
- ⊗ ENGINE (GUSSET)
- ○ M/T TO STARTER MOTOR

View of the transaxle bolt torquing sequence—2WD Axxess

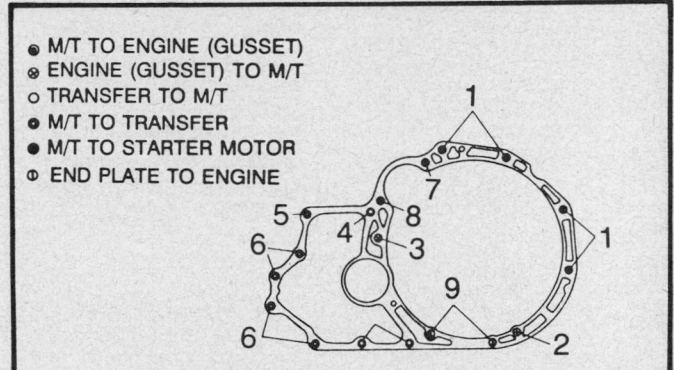

- ⊛ M/T TO ENGINE (GUSSET)
- ⊗ ENGINE (GUSSET) TO M/T
- ○ TRANSFER TO M/T
- ● M/T TO TRANSFER
- ⬤ M/T TO STARTER MOTOR
- ⊕ END PLATE TO ENGINE

View of the transaxle bolt torquing sequence—4WD Axxess

CLUTCH

Clutch Assembly

Removal and Installation

1. Disconnect the negative battery cable. Raise and safely support the vehicle.
2. Remove the transmission (except Axxess) or the transaxle (Axxess).
3. Using a piece of chalk, paint or a center punch, mark the clutch assembly-to-flywheel relationship so it can be reassembled in the same position from which it is removed.
4. Using a clutch aligning tool, insert it into the clutch disc hub.
5. Loosen the clutch cover-to-flywheel bolts, a turn at a time in an alternating sequence, until the spring tension is relieved to avoid distorting or bending the clutch cover. Remove the clutch assembly.
6. Inspect the flywheel for scoring, roughness or signs of overheating. Light scoring may be cleaned up with emery cloth, but any deep grooves or scoring warrant replacement or refacing (if possible) of the flywheel. If the clutch facings or flywheel are oily, inspect the transmission/transaxle front cover oil seal, the pilot bushing and engine rear seals, etc. for leakage; replace any leaking seals before replacing the clutch.
7. If the crankshaft pilot bushing is worn, replace it. Install it using a soft hammer. The factory supplied part does not have to be oiled, but check the procedure if you are using an aftermarket part. Inspect the clutch cover for wear or scoring and replace it, if necessary.

NOTE: The pressure plate and spring cannot be disassembled; replace the clutch cover as an assembly.

8. Inspect the clutch release bearing. If it is rough or noisy, it should be replaced. The bearing can be removed from the sleeve with a puller; this requires a press to install the new bearing. After installation, coat the sleeve groove, the release lever contact surfaces, the pivot pin/sleeve and the release bearing-to-transmission/transaxle contact surfaces with a light coat of grease. Be careful not to use too much grease, which will run at high temperatures and get onto the clutch facings. Reinstall the release bearing on the lever.
9. Apply a thin coat of grease to the pressure plate wire ring, diaphragm spring, clutch cover grooves and the pressure plate drive bosses.
10. Apply a thin coat of Lubriplate® to the splines in the driven plate. Slide the clutch disc onto the splines and move it back and forth several times. Remove the disc and wipe off the excess lubricant. Be very careful not to get any grease on the clutch facings.
11. Assemble the clutch cover and the clutch plate on the clutch alignment arbor.
12. To complete the installation, align the clutch assembly-to-flywheel alignment marks and reverse the removal procedures; three dowels are used to locate the clutch cover on the flywheel. Torque as follows:

Clutch cover-to-flywheel bolts (in an alternating sequence, one turn at a time)—16–22 ft. lbs.
Transmission/transaxle-to-engine bolts—29–36 ft. lbs.
Clutch slave cylinder-to-transmission/transaxle bolts—22–30 ft. lbs.

Pedal Height/Free-Play Adjustment

The pedal height is the distance from the top of the clutch pedal to the floor board (without the carpet).
The pedal freeplay is the distance the clutch pedal pad moves

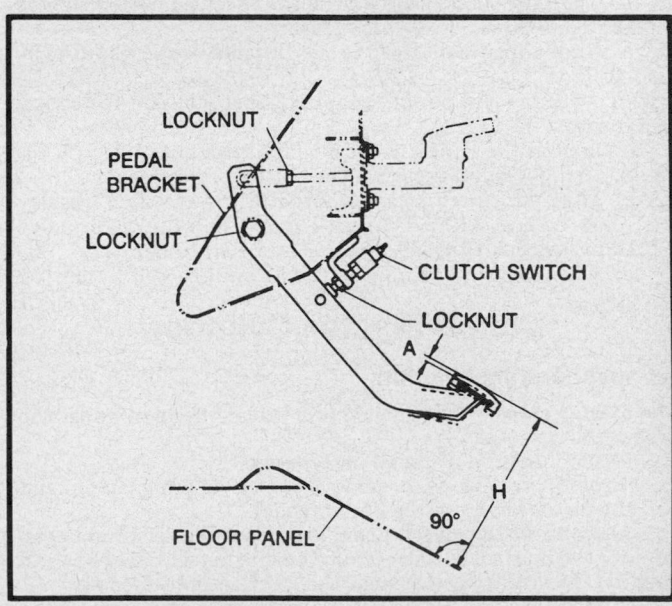

View of the clutch pedal assembly—Van

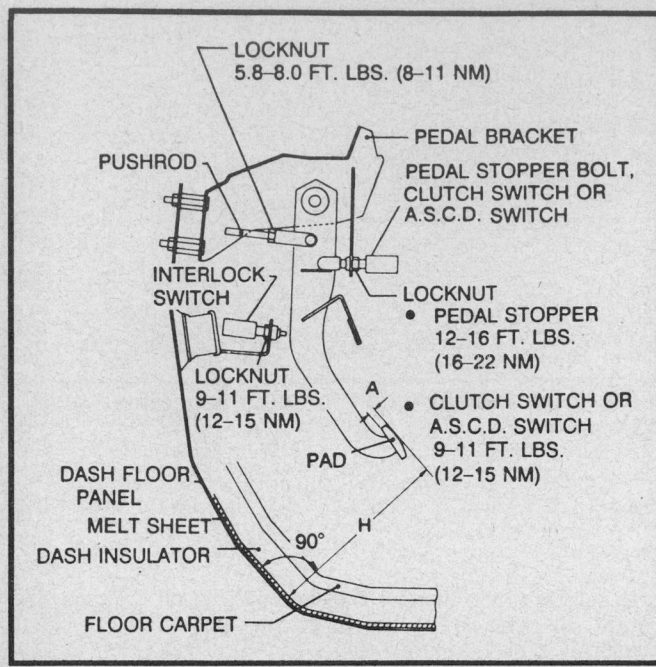

View of the clutch pedal assembly—except Van

NOTE: Take precautions to keep brake fluid from coming in contact with any painted surfaces.

5. Remove the clutch master cylinder.

6. To install, reverse the removal procedures. Torque the clutch master cylinder-to-cowl bolts/nuts to 12–14 ft. lbs. for Van or to 5.8–8.7 ft. lbs. except Van.

7. Bleed the clutch hydraulic system.

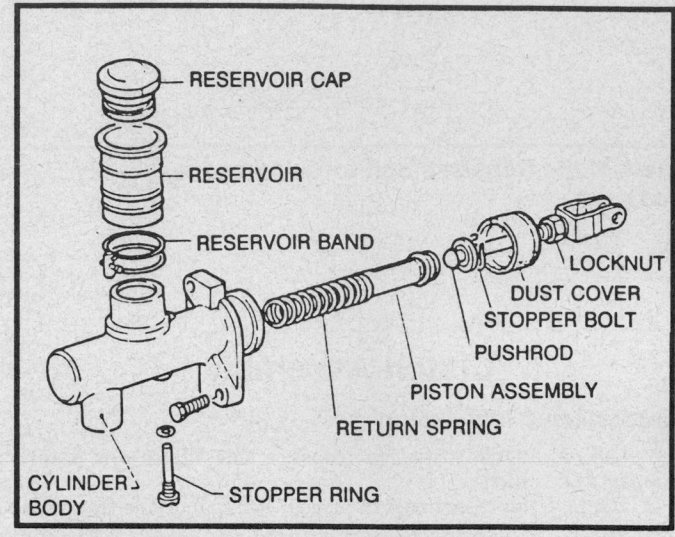

Exploded view of a typical clutch master cylinder

from the released position to the point where resistance is felt.

1. To adjust the pedal height on all models except the Van, perform the following procedure:

    a. From under the dash, loosen the pedal stopper locknut.

    b. Turn the pedal stopper until the specified pedal height is obtained: 9.29–9.69 in. (2.4L and 2.5L engines, except Axxess), 8.94–9.33 in. (3.0L engine, except Axxess) or 6.97–7.36 in. (Axxess).

    c. After adjustment, torque the pedal stopper locknut to 12–16 ft. lbs.

2. To adjust the pedal height on the Van, perform the following procedure:

    a. From under the dash, loosen the clutch switch locknut.

    b. Turn the clutch switch until the specified pedal height is obtained: 6.97–7.36 in. (117–187mm).

    c. After adjustment, torque the clutch switch locknut to 9–11 ft. lbs.

3. To adjust the pedal freeplay, perform the following procedures:

    a. Loosen the clutch pedal, pushrod locknut.

    b. Using a ruler, measure the clutch pedal freeplay.

    c. Turn the clutch pedal pushrod to the specified freeplay is: 0.04–0.06 in. (1986–89 Pick-Up and Pathfinder) or 0.04–0.12 in. (except 1986–89 Pick-Up and Pathfinder).

    d. After adjustment, torque the locknut to 6–9 ft. lbs.

Clutch Master Cylinder

Removal and Installation

The master cylinder is attached to a bracket located under the dash.

1. Disconnect the negative battery cable.

2. From under the dash, remove the clevis pin snap pin and pull the clevis pin from the clutch pedal.

3. Disconnect the clutch pedal arm from the pushrod clevis. Remove the dust cover (boot) from the master cylinder body and pushrod. It will not go through the cowl without tearing.

4. Disconnect and plug the hydraulic line from the clutch master cylinder.

Clutch Slave Cylinder

Removal and Installation

1. Disconnect the negative battery cable.

2. If necessary, raise and safely support the vehicle.

3. Remove the slave cylinder-to-clutch housing bolts and the pushrod from the shift fork.

4. Disconnect and plug the hydraulic hose from the slave cylinder, then, remove the cylinder from the vehicle.

5. To install, reverse the removal procedures. Torque the slave cylinder-to-clutch housing bolts to 22–30 ft. lbs.

6. Bleed the clutch hydraulic system.

Bleeding the Hydraulic Clutch System

1. Check and refill the clutch fluid reservoir to the full mark, if necessary. During the bleeding process, continue to check and replenish the reservoir to prevent the fluid level from getting lower than ½ full.

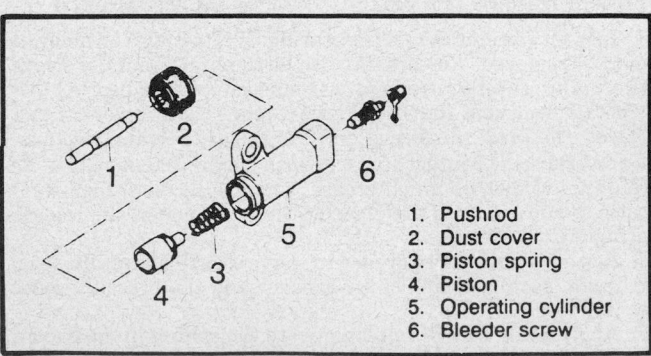

1. Pushrod
2. Dust cover
3. Piston spring
4. Piston
5. Operating cylinder
6. Bleeder screw

Exploded view of a typical clutch slave cylinder

2. Connect a clear vinyl hose to the bleeder screw on the slave cylinder. Immerse the other end of the hose in a clear jar ½ filled with brake fluid.

3. Have an assistant pump the clutch pedal several times and hold it down. Loosen the bleeder screw slowly.

4. Tighten the bleeder screw and release the clutch pedal gradually. Repeat this operation until the air bubbles disappear

from the brake fluid being expelled out through the bleeder screw.

5. When the air is completely removed, securely tighten the bleeder screw and replace the dust cap.

6. Check and refill the master cylinder reservoir as necessary.

7. Depress the clutch pedal several times to check the operation of the clutch and check for leaks.

AUTOMATIC TRANSMISSION

For further information, please refer to "Professional Transmission Manual".

Transmission Assembly

Removal and Installation

2WD MODELS

1. Disconnect the negative battery cable.
2. Raise and safely support the vehicle.
3. If equipped with a 3.0L engine, remove the front exhaust tube.
4. Remove the oil filler tube from the transmission; be sure to plug the opening on the transmission. Disconnect and plug the oil cooler lines at the transmission.
5. Matchmark the driveshaft U-joint and differential flange, then, disconnect them from the differential. If the driveshaft is equipped with a center bearing, remove the center bearing bracket-to-chassis bolts and the driveshaft assembly. Plug the transmission extension housing to keep the fluid from leaking out.
6. Remove the torsion bar springs.
7. Remove the speedometer cable.
8. Remove the automatic transmission control linkage from the selector lever.
9. Disconnect the electrical harness connectors from the transmission.
10. Disconnect the electrical connectors and remove the starter.
11. If equipped with a 3.0L engine, remove the gusset securing the engine to the transmission.
12. Remove the torque converter housing dust cover. Using a piece of chalk, matchmark the converter with the drive plate for reassembly; the unit was balanced at the factory. Remove the torque converter-to-drive plate (flywheel) bolts; using a wrench on the crankshaft pulley bolt, rotate the crankshaft to expose the hidden torque converter bolts.
13. Using a floor jack and a block of wood (placed under the oil pan), support the engine. Using a transmission jack, support transmission.

NOTE: When supporting the engine with a block of wood, do not position the wood under the oil drain plug.

14. Remove the rear engine mount-to-crossmember bolts, the crossmember-to-chassis bolts and the crossmember.
15. Remove the transmission-to-engine bolts, then, slide the torque converter toward the transmission and secure it in place. Move the transmission rearward, lower and remove it from the vehicle.

To install:

16. Using a dial indicator, check the drive plate runout. Turn the crankshaft one full revolution. Maximum allowable runout is 0.020 in., if beyond specifications, replace the drive plate.

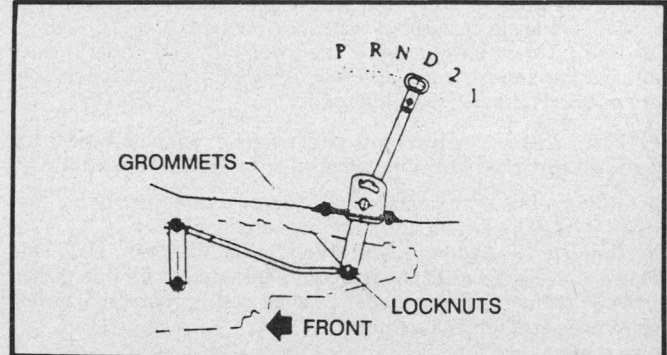

View of the automatic transmission shift linkage — except Axxess

17. To install, use new gaskets (where necessary), align the torque converter-to-drive plate matchmarks and reverse the removal procedures.

NOTE: When installing the torque converter, be sure to align the notch in the converter with the projection on the oil pump.

18. To complete the installation, reverse the removal procedures. Torque as follows:
Torque converter-to-drive plate bolts – 29–36 ft. lbs.

NOTE: Rotate the engine a few turns to make sure the transmission rotates freely without binding.

Upper engine-to-transmission bolt
Pick-Up and Pathfinder – 29–36 ft. lbs.
Van – 22–36 ft. lbs.
Lower engine-to-transmission bolts for Van – 20–24 ft. lbs.
19. Check and/or refill the transmission with clean fluid. Adjust the shift linkage, the back-up light operation and the neutral switch.

4WD MODELS

1. Disconnect the negative battery cable.
2. Raise and safely support the vehicle.
3. If equipped with a 3.0L engine, remove the front exhaust tube.
4. Remove the oil filler tube from the transmission; be sure to plug the opening on the transmission. Disconnect and plug the oil cooler lines at the transmission.
5. Matchmark the driveshaft U-joint and differential flange, then, disconnect them from the differential. If the driveshaft is equipped with a center bearing, remove the center bearing bracket-to-chassis bolts and the driveshaft assembly. Plug the transfer case housing to keep the fluid from leaking out.
6. Remove the transfer control linkage from the transfer

case.

7. Remove the torsion bar springs and the 2nd crossmember.

8. Remove the speedometer cable.

9. Remove the automatic transmission control linkage from the transmission.

10. Disconnect the electrical harness connectors from the transmission.

11. Disconnect the electrical connectors and remove the starter.

12. If equipped with a 3.0L engine, remove the gusset securing the engine to the transmission.

13. Remove the torque converter housing dust cover. Using a piece of chalk, matchmark the converter with the drive plate for reassembly; the unit was balanced at the factory. Remove the torque converter-to-drive plate (flywheel) bolts; using a wrench on the crankshaft pulley bolt, rotate the crankshaft to expose the hidden torque converter bolts.

14. Using a floor jack and a block of wood (placed under the oil pan), support the engine. Using a transmission jack, support the transmission/transfer case assembly.

NOTE: When supporting the engine with a block of wood, do not position the wood under the oil drain plug.

15. Remove the rear engine mount-to-crossmember bolts, the crossmember-to-chassis bolts and the crossmember.

16. Remove the transmission-to-engine bolts, then, slide the torque converter toward the transmission and secure it in place. Move the transmission/transfer case assembly rearward, lower and remove it from the vehicle.

To install:

17. Using a dial indicator, check the drive plate runout. Turn the crankshaft one full revolution. Maximum allowable runout is 0.020 in., if beyond specifications, replace the drive plate.

18. Using new gaskets (where necessary), align the torque converter-to-drive plate matchmarks and reverse the removal procedures.

NOTE: When installing the torque converter, be sure to align the notch in the converter with the projection on the oil pump.

19. To complete the installation, reverse the removal procedures. Torque as follows:
   Torque converter-to-drive plate bolts to 29–36 ft. lbs.

NOTE: Rotate the engine a few turns to make sure the transmission rotates freely without binding.

   Upper engine-to-transmission bolt
   Pick-Up and Pathfinder – 29–36 ft. lbs.
   Van – 22–36 ft. lbs.
   Lower engine-to-transmission bolts for Van – 20–24 ft. lbs.

20. Check and/or refill the transmission with clean fluid. Adjust the shift linkage, the back-up light operation and the neutral switch.

Shift Linkage Adjustment

PICK-UP AND PATHFINDER
2WD Floor Shift Models

1. Place the shift selector in the **P** position.
2. Raise and safely support the vehicle.
3. From under the vehicle, loosen the shift lever locknuts.
4. Tighten the rear locknut **X** until it touches the trunnion; pulling the selector lever toward the **R** position (without pushing the button). Back off the rear locknut **X** a complete revolution, adjust the front locknut **Y** and torque the locknuts to 5.8–8.0 ft. lbs.
5. After adjustment, move the selector lever through the ranges to make sure it moves smoothly.

2WD Column Shift Models

1. Place the shift selector in the **P** position.

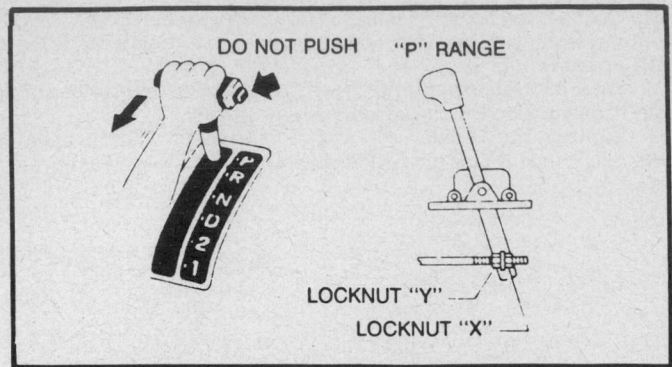

View of the 2WD floor shift model automatic transmission shifter adjustment – Pick-Up and Pathfinder

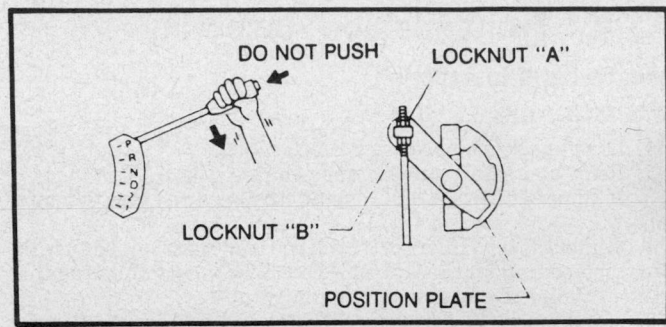

View of the 2WD column shift model automatic transmission shifter adjustment – Pick-Up and Pathfinder

2. Raise and safely support the vehicle.
3. From under the vehicle, loosen the shift lever locknuts.
4. Tighten the front locknut **A** until it touches the trunnion; pulling the selector lever toward the **R** position (without pushing the button). Back off the front locknut **A** 2 complete revolutions, adjust the rear locknut **B** and torque the locknuts to 5.8–8.0 ft. lbs.
5. After adjustment, move the selector lever through the ranges to make sure it moves smoothly.

4WD Floor Shift Models

1. Place the shift selector in the **P** position.
2. Raise and safely support the vehicle.
3. Remove the console cover.
4. Loosen the turn buckle locknuts.
5. Tighten the turn buckle until it aligns with the inner cable; pulling the selector lever toward the **R** position (without pushing the button). Back off the turn buckle a complete revolution, torque the locknuts to 3.3–4.3 ft. lbs.
6. After adjustment, move the selector lever through the ranges to make sure it moves smoothly.

VAN

1. Place the shift selector in the **P** position.
2. Raise and safely support the vehicle.
3. From under the vehicle, loosen the shift lever locknuts.
4. Tighten the front locknut **X** until it touches the trunnion; pulling the selector lever toward the **R** position (without pushing the button). Back off the front locknut **X** a ¼ revolution, adjust the rear locknut **Y** and torque the locknuts to 7–9 ft. lbs.
5. After adjustment, move the selector lever through the ranges to make sure it moves smoothly.

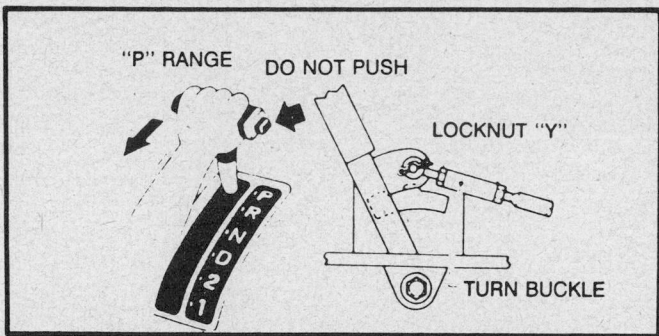

View of the 4WD floor shift model automatic transmission shifter adjustment – Pick-Up and Pathfinder

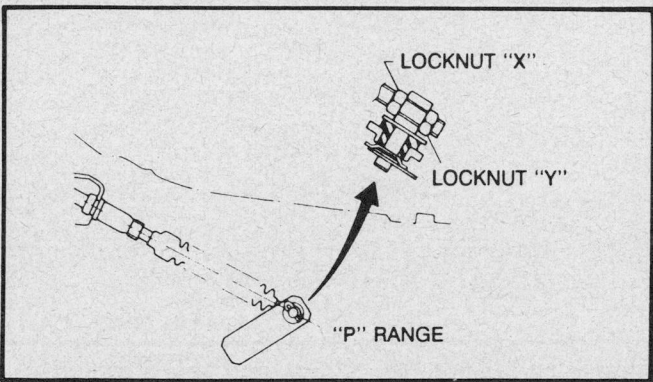

View of the floor shift model automatic transmission shifter adjustment – Van

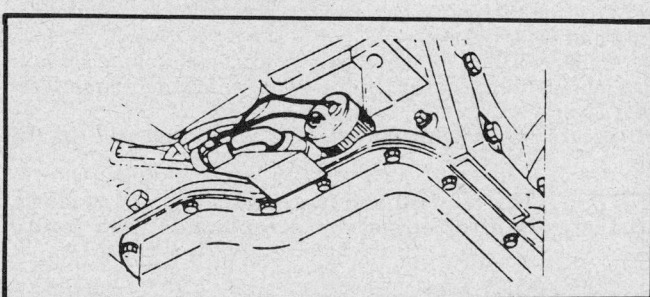

View of the downshift solenoid – 71B transmission 1986–89

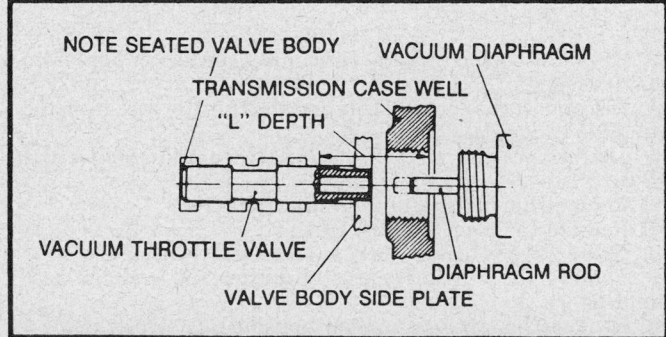

Cross-sectional view of the vacuum diaphragm – 71B transmission 1986–89

Kickdown Switch Adjustment
1986–89 VEHICLES WITH 71B TRANSMISSION

A kickdown switch is located inside the vehicle at the upper post of the accelerator pedal. It purpose is to provide transmission downshifting when the accelerator pedal is fully depressed; a click can be heard just before the pedal bottoms out.

With the ignition switch in the **ON** position and the engine **OFF**, when the accelerator pedal is depressed fully, the kickdown switch contacts should be closed and the downshift solenoid activated, emitting a clicking sound. If the components fail to operate in this manner, check for continuity 1st at the switch and then at the solenoid if the switch checks out as being satisfactory. Replace either of the components as necessary.

Vacuum Modulator Adjustment
1986–89 VEHICLES WITH 71B TRANSMISSION

1. Raise and safely support the vehicle.
2. Remove the vacuum modulator from the transmission.
3. Using a depth gauge, measure the L depth; be sure the vacuum throttle valve is pushed into the valve body as far as possible.
4. Select the correct length rod and install it into the vacuum modulator.
5. Using a new O-ring, install the modulator into the transmission.

Measured depth "L" mm (in)	Rod length mm (in)	Part number
Under 25.55 (1.0059)	29.0 (1.142)	31932-X0103
25.65 - 26.05 (1.0098 - 1.0256)	29.5 (1.161)	31932-X0104
26.15 - 26.55 (1.0295 - 1.0453)	30.0 (1.181)	31932-X0100
26.65 - 27.05 (1.0492 - 1.0650)	30.5 (1.201)	31932-X0102
Over 27.15 (1.0689)	31.0 (1.220)	31932-X0101

Vacuum diaphragm rod selection chart – 71B transmission 1986–89

Throttle Linkage Adjustment
1990 VEHICLES WITH RL4R01A TRANSMISSION

1. Press the lock plate and move the adjusting tube in the direction **T**.
2. Return the lock plate.
3. Quickly, move the throttle drum from P_2-to-P_1.
4. Ensure the throttle wire stroke **L** is within specified range between full throttle and idle; the throttle wire stroke **L** should be 1.50–1.65 in. (38–42mm).

NOTE: Adjust the throttle wire stroke when the throttle wire/accelerator wire is installed. Place marks on the throttle wire to facilitate measuring the wire stroke.

5. If the throttle wire stroke is not adjusted, the following problems may arise:
    a. When full-open position P_1 of the throttle drum is closer to the direction **T**, the kickdown range will greatly increase.
    b. When the full-open position P_1 of the throttle drum is closer to the direction **U**, the kickdown range will not occur.
6. After properly adjusting the throttle wire, make sure the parting line is as straight as possible.

Neutral Safety Switch Adjustment

The neutral safety switch is located on the transmission shift selector lever. The switch operates the back-up lights and controls

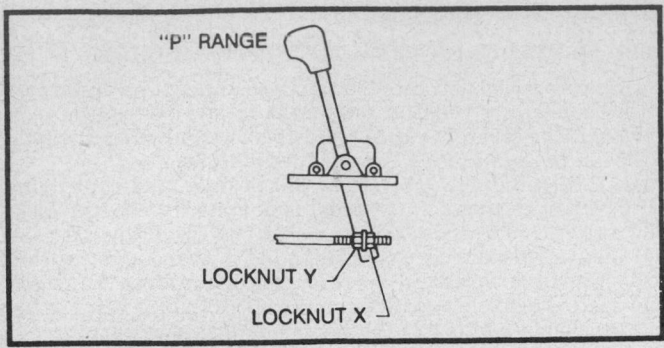

View of the throttle wire adjustment—RL4R01A transmission—1990

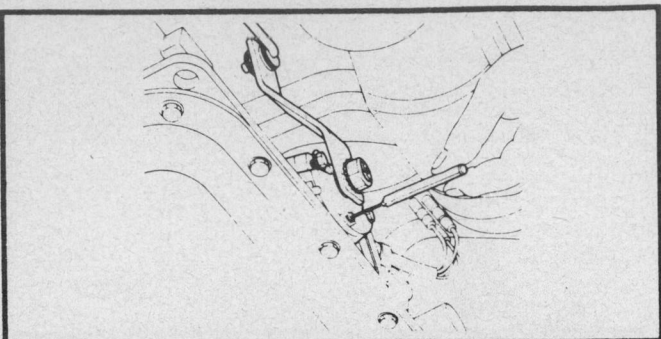

Using a pin to align the neutral start safely switch—71B transmission 1986–89

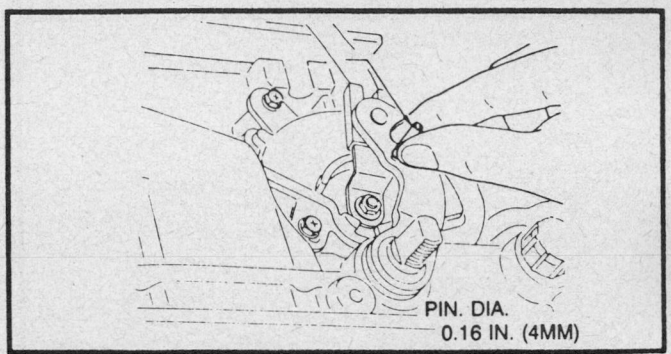

Using a pin to align the neutral start safety switch—except 71B transmission 1986–89

the operation of the starter. The starter should only operate when the transmission is in **P** or **N**.

1986–89 VEHICLES WITH 71B TRANSMISSION

1. Unscrew the securing nut of the shift selector lever and the switch-to-transmission screws.
2. Position the shift selector to the **N** position (in vertical position and detent clicks). Move the switch slightly aside so the screw hole will be aligned with the pin hole of the shift selector lever.
3. Using a 0.080 in. (2mm) diameter alignment pin, place it in the alignment holes of the neutral start switch and the shift selector lever.

NOTE: A No. 47 drill bit will substitute for the pin gauge.

4. Secure the switch body with the screws and pull out the pin.

NOTE: If the neutral safety switch does not perform satisfactorily after adjustment, replace it with a new one.

EXCEPT 1986–89 VEHICLES WITH 71B TRANSMISSION

1. Unscrew the securing nut of the shift selector lever and the switch-to-transmission screws.

2. Position the shift selector to the **N** position (in vertical position and detent clicks).
3. Using a 0.16 in. (4mm) diameter alignment pin, place it in the alignment holes of the neutral start switch and the shift selector lever.
4. Secure the switch body with the screws and pull out the pin.

NOTE: If the neutral safety switch does not perform satisfactorily after adjustment, replace it with a new one.

AUTOMATIC TRANSAXLE

For further information, please refer to "Professional Transmission Manual".

Transaxle Assembly

Removal and Installation

2WD MODELS

1. Disconnect the negative battery cable. Remove the battery and the bracket.
2. Remove the air duct.

3. Drain the cooling system. Disconnect the heater hose from the dash panel.
4. Disconnect the control cable and the throttle wire from the automatic transaxle.
5. Disconnect the electrical connectors and remove the starter.
6. Remove the halfshafts from the transaxle.
7. Remove the front exhaust tube.
8. Using a transmission jack, support the transaxle.
9. Remove the crossmember, the buffer rod and the rear mounting.
10. Remove the torque converter housing dust cover. Using a piece of chalk, matchmark the converter with the drive plate for reassembly; the unit was balanced at the factory. Remove the torque converter-to-drive plate (flywheel) bolts; using a wrench

on the crankshaft pulley bolt, rotate the crankshaft to expose the hidden torque converter bolts.

11. Reinstall the center member to support the engine when removing the transaxle.

12. Insert a wooden block between the engine oil pan and the center member.

13. Remove the left side transaxle mount.

14. Remove the transaxle-to-engine bolts and lower the transaxle from the vehicle.

15. To install, reverse the removal procedures. Torque the transaxle-to-engine bolts to:

    a. Bolts No. 1—29–33 ft. lbs. (39–44 Nm)
    b. Bolts No. 2—29–33 ft. lbs. (39–44 Nm)
    c. Bolts No. 3—22–30 ft. lbs. (30–40 Nm)

16. To complete the installation, reverse the removal procedures. Road test the vehicle.

4WD MODELS

1. Disconnect the negative battery cable. Remove the battery and the bracket.

2. Remove the air duct.

3. Drain the cooling system. Disconnect the heater hose from the dash panel.

4. Disconnect the control cable and the throttle wire from the automatic transaxle.

5. Disconnect the electrical connectors and remove the starter.

6. Remove the halfshafts from the transaxle.

7. Remove the front exhaust tube.

8. Matchmark the driveshaft U-joint and differential flange, then, disconnect them from the differential. If the driveshaft is equipped with a center bearing, remove the center bearing bracket-to-chassis bolts and the driveshaft assembly. Plug the transfer case housing to keep the fluid from leaking out.

9. Remove the buffer rod.

10. Remove the torque converter housing dust cover. Using a piece of chalk, matchmark the converter with the drive plate for reassembly; the unit was balanced at the factory. Remove the torque converter-to-drive plate (flywheel) bolts; using a wrench on the crankshaft pulley bolt, rotate the crankshaft to expose the hidden torque converter bolts.

11. From under the intake manifold, remove the gusset-to-transfer case bolts.

12. Using a socket wrench and a long extension, remove the gusset-to-intake manifold bolts and the gusset.

13. Using a transmission jack, support the transaxle.

14. Remove the rear transfer case mount and the left side transaxle mount.

15. Remove the transaxle-to-engine bolts and lower the transaxle/transfer case assembly from the vehicle.

16. To install, reverse the removal procedures. Torque the transaxle-to-engine bolts to:

    a. Bolts No. 1—29–33 ft. lbs. (39–44 Nm)
    b. Bolts No. 2—29–33 ft. lbs. (39–44 Nm)

17. To complete the installation, reverse the removal procedures. Road test the vehicle.

Shift Linkage Adjustment

1. Remove the center console.

2. Position the shift selector lever into the **P** range.

3. Connect the control cable end to the manual lever of the transaxle unit.

4. Move the selector lever from **P** to **1** range and return to **P**; make sure the lever can move smoothly and without sliding noise.

5. At the bottom of the shift lever, loosen the locknuts **Y** and **X**.

6. Make sure the manual lever on the transaxle is locked into the **P** range.

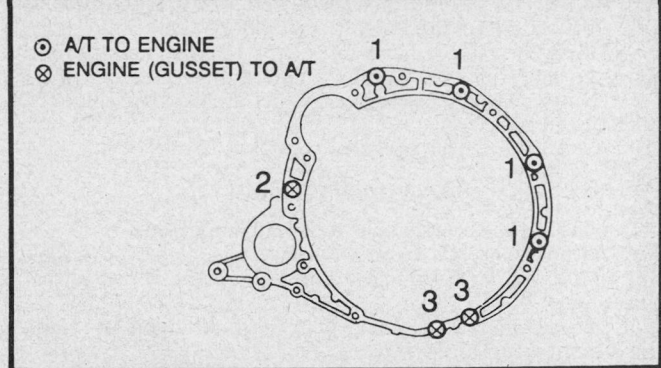

View of the automatic transaxle-to-engine bolt torquing sequence—2WD Axxess

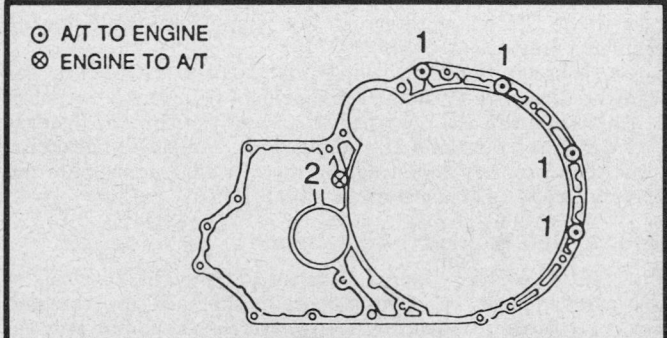

View of the automatic transaxle-to-engine bolt torquing sequence—4WD Axxess

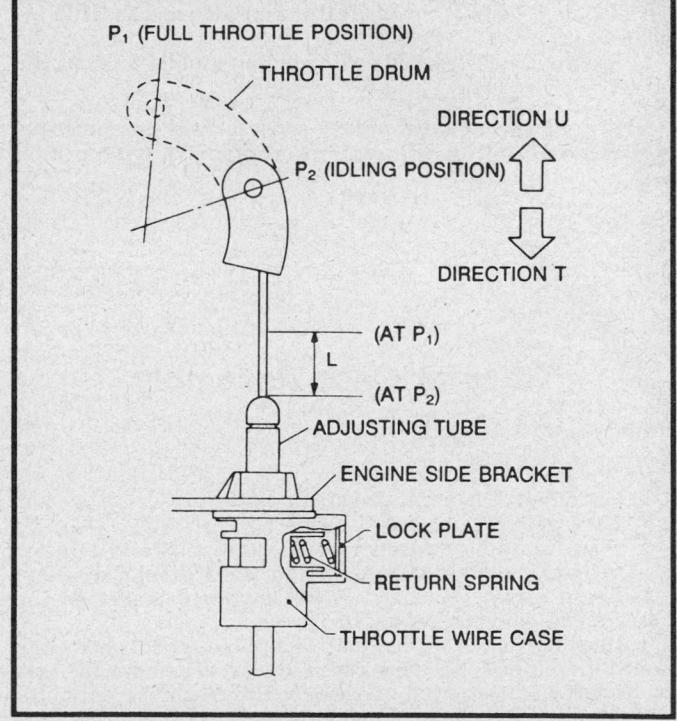

View of the shift lever adjustment locknuts—Axxess

7. Adjust the locknut **X** until it touches the trunnion and tighten the locknut to 12–16 ft. lbs. (16–22 Nm).

8. Move the selector lever from **P** to **1** range; make sure the lever can move smoothly and without sliding noise.

9. Using grease, apply to the contact areas of the selector lever and the select rod.

10. Install the center console.

Throttle Linkage Adjustment

1. Loosen the throttle wire locknuts **A** and **B**.

2. With the throttle drum set at P_1 (fully open), move the fitting **Q** fully in the **T** direction and tighten the **B** nut in the **U** direction.

3. Loosen the **B** 2¾–3¼ turns in the **T** direction and tighten the **A** nut, securely.

4. Make sure the throttle wire stroke **L** is 1.54–1.69 in. (39–43mm) between full throttle and idle.

NOTE: Adjust the throttle wire stroke when the throttle wire/accelerator wire is installed. Place marks on the throttle wire to facilitate measuring the wire stroke.

5. If the throttle wire stroke is not adjusted, the following problems may arise:

  a. When full-open position P_1 of the throttle drum is closer to the direction **T**, the kickdown range will greatly increase.

  b. When the full-open position P_1 of the throttle drum is closer to the direction **U**, the kickdown range will not occur.

6. After properly adjusting the throttle wire, make sure the parting line is as straight as possible.

Neutral Safety Switch Adjustment

The neutral safety switch is attached to the right, rear side of the cylinder head. The switch operates the back-up lights and controls the operation of the starter. The starter should only operate when the transmission is in **P** or **N**.

1. Loosen the neutral safely switch-to-engine bolts.

2. Position the shift selector to the **N** position (in vertical position and detent clicks).

3. Using a 0.16 in. (4mm) diameter alignment pin, place it in the alignment holes of the neutral start switch and the shift selector lever.

4. Secure the switch body with the screws and pull out the pin.

NOTE: If the neutral safety switch does not perform satisfactorily after adjustment, replace it with a new one.

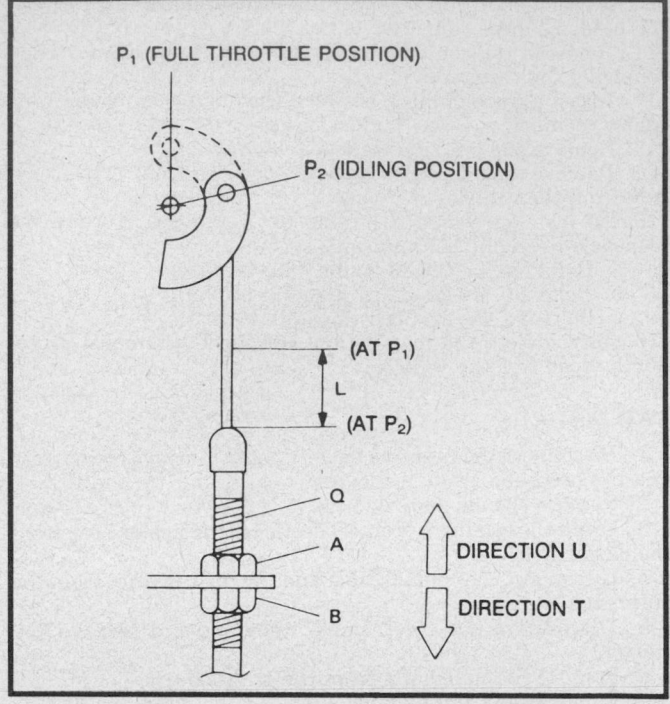

View of the throttle wire adjustment—Axxess

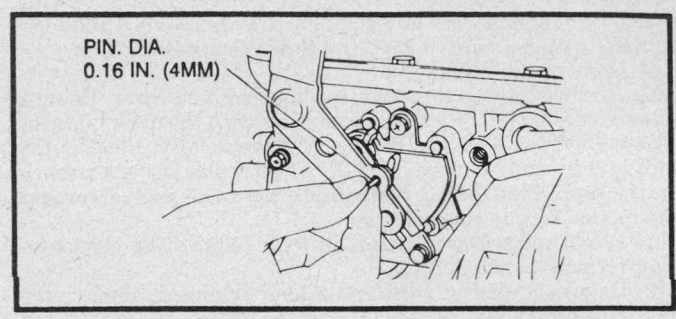

Using a pin to align the neutral start safety switch— Axxess

TRANSFER CASE

Transfer Case Assembly

Removal and Installation

EXCEPT AXXESS

1. Disconnect the negative battery cable.

2. Raise safely support the vehicle.

3. Place a drain pan under the transmission and transfer case, remove the drain plug and drain the oil from the cases.

4. Using a piece of chalk, make alignment marks on the transfer case and differential flanges.

5. Remove the front driveshaft-to-differential nuts/bolts, the front differential-to-transfer case nuts/bolts. Remove the rear driveshaft-to-differential nuts/bolts, the rear differential-to-transfer case nuts/bolts. Remove the differentials from the vehicle.

6. Remove the torsion bar springs from the front lower control arms.

7. Remove the crossmember-to-chassis bolts (located under the transfer case) and the crossmember.

8. From under the vehicle, remove the transfer control lever-to-transfer case nut, then, separate the lever from the transfer case.

9. Using a floor jack, support the transfer case.

10. Remove the transfer case-to-transmission bolts, move the transfer case rearward and lower it to the floor.

11. To install, reverse the removal procedures. Torque the transfer case-to-transmission bolts to 23–30 ft. lbs. (31–41 Nm), the transfer control lever-to-transfer case nut to 18–22 ft. lbs. (25–30 Nm), the crossmember-to-chassis bolt to 43–58 ft. lbs. (59–78 Nm). Refill the transfer case and transmission with new fluid.

AXXESS

1. Disconnect the negative battery cable.
2. If equipped with a manual transaxle, remove the breather clamp from the transfer case.
3. Remove the transaxle/transfer case assembly from the vehicle.
4. Remove the transfer case-to-transaxle bolts and the transfer case.

To install:

5. Using multi-purpose grease, lubricate the transaxle's oil seal on the tranfer case side.
6. Using sealant, apply it around the ring gear oil seal on the transfer case.

NOTE: Be careful not to damage the transaxle oil seal when inserting the spline portion of the transfer ring gear and placing the shaft into the transaxle.

7. Torque the transfer case-to-transaxle bolts to 22–30 ft. lbs. (30–40 Nm).
8. To complete the installation, reverse the removal procedures.
9. Refill the transfer case with gear oil.
10. Test the vehicle by performing the following procedures:
   a. Position the vehicle so all 4 wheels are not touching the ground and are free to turn.
   b. Position the transfer case into the 4WD position.
   c. Make sure the rear wheels are turning.

NOTE: Never test drive the vehicle with the transfer case in the 2WD position.

11. Lower the vehicle.

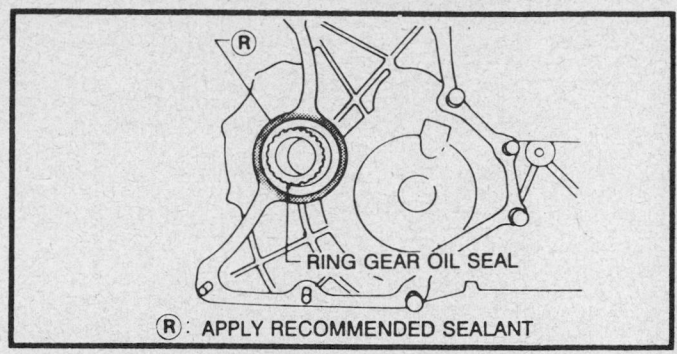

Applying sealant to the transfer case—Axxess

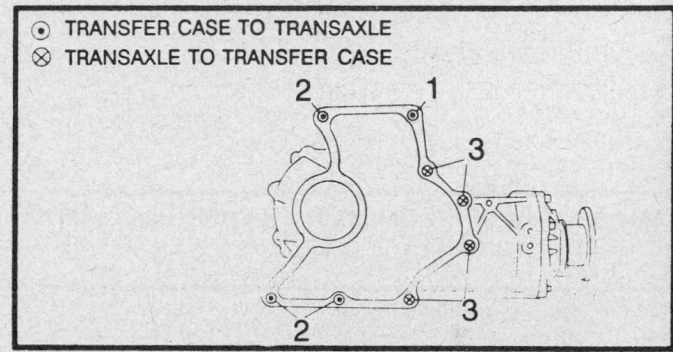

View of the transfer case bolt torquing sequence—Axxess

DRIVE AXLE

Halfshaft

Removal and Installation

EXCEPT AXXESS

Halfshaft are used only on vehicles equipped with 4WD.
1. Raise and safely support the vehicle.
2. Depress the brake pedal and remove the halfshaft-to-differential flange bolts.
3. Remove the locking hub assemblies.
4. Remove the snapring and drive clutch. Disconnect the tie rod from the steering knuckle.
5. Remove the upper ball joint-to-upper control arm bolts.
6. Remove the lower shock absorber-to-lower control arm nut/bolt.
7. Remove the lower ball joint-to-lower control arm bolts; using a floor jack, support the lower control arm.
8. Remove the steering knuckle assembly with the halfshaft and secure the assembly in a vise.
9. Using a hammer and a block of wood, tap the halfshaft from the steering knuckle.

NOTE: Upon installation, apply chassis lube to all bearing surfaces, make sure the spacer is in place and adjust the halfshaft endplay (by using various thicknesses of snaprings) to 0.004–0.012 in.

10. To install, reverse the removal procedures. Torque the halfshaft-to-differential flange bolts to 25–33 ft. lbs. (34–44 Nm), the locking hub-to-wheel hub bolts to 18–25 ft. lbs. (25–34 Nm), the lower ball joint-to-lower control arm nuts/bolts to 35–45 ft. lbs. (47–61 Nm) and the upper ball joint-to-upper control arm bolts to 12–15 ft. lbs. (16–21 Nm).

AXXESS
2WD Models

1. Remove the grease cap. Depress the brake pedal and remove the wheel bearing locknut.
2. Raise and safely support the vehicle. Remove the wheel assembly.
3. Remove the brake caliper-to-steering knuckle bolts and support the assembly on a wire; do not disconnect the pressure hose.
4. Remove the tie rod end-to-steering knuckle cotter pin and nut. Using a tie rod end removal tool, separate the tie rod end from the steering knuckle.
5. Turn the steering knuckle forward. Using a mallet, tap the halfshaft from the hub; be sure to cover the boots with a shop cloth to prevent damaging them.

NOTE: If equipped with an automatic transaxle, remove the right halfshaft first.

6. If equipped with a support bearing, use a prybar to separate the right halfshaft from the transaxle.
7. If equipped with a manual transaxle, pry the right halfshaft from the transaxle.
8. If equipped with an automatic transaxle, insert a prybar through the transaxle, tap it with a mallet to tap the left halfshaft from the transaxle.

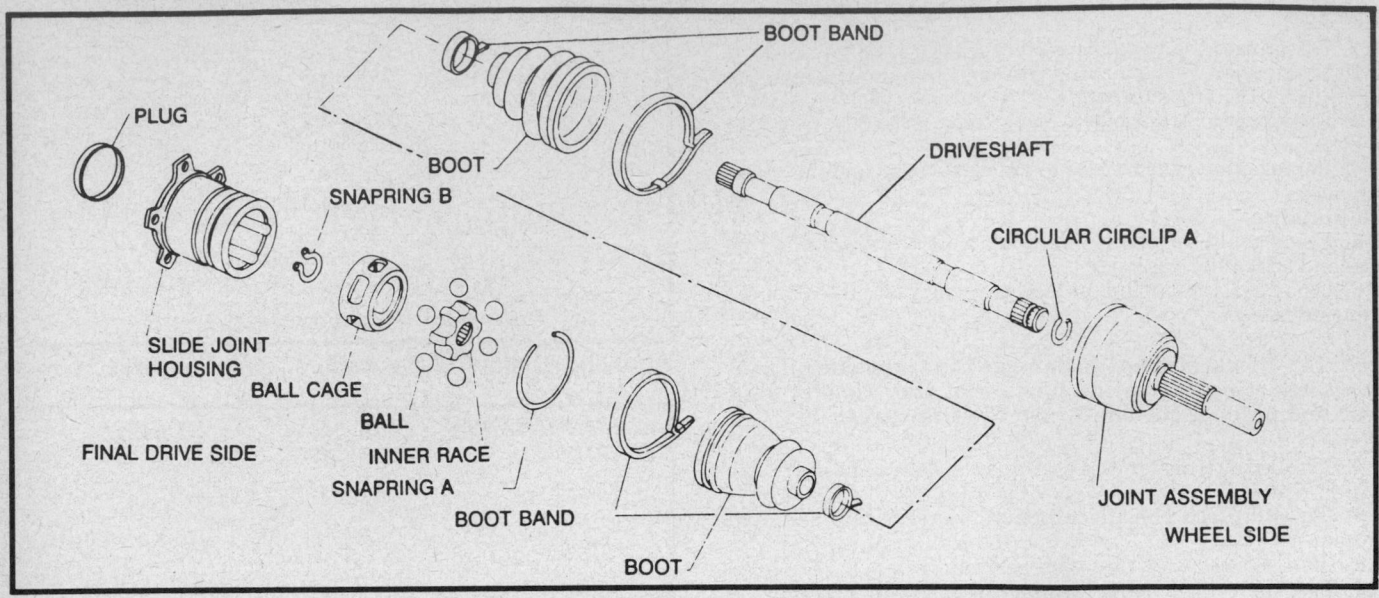

BOOT BAND

PLUG

BOOT

SNAPRING B

DRIVESHAFT

CIRCULAR CIRCLIP A

SLIDE JOINT
HOUSING

BALL CAGE

BALL

INNER RACE

SNAPRING A

FINAL DRIVE SIDE

BOOT BAND

BOOT

JOINT ASSEMBLY

WHEEL SIDE

Exploded view of the halfshaft assembly used with the 3.0L engine—Pick-Up and Pathfinder

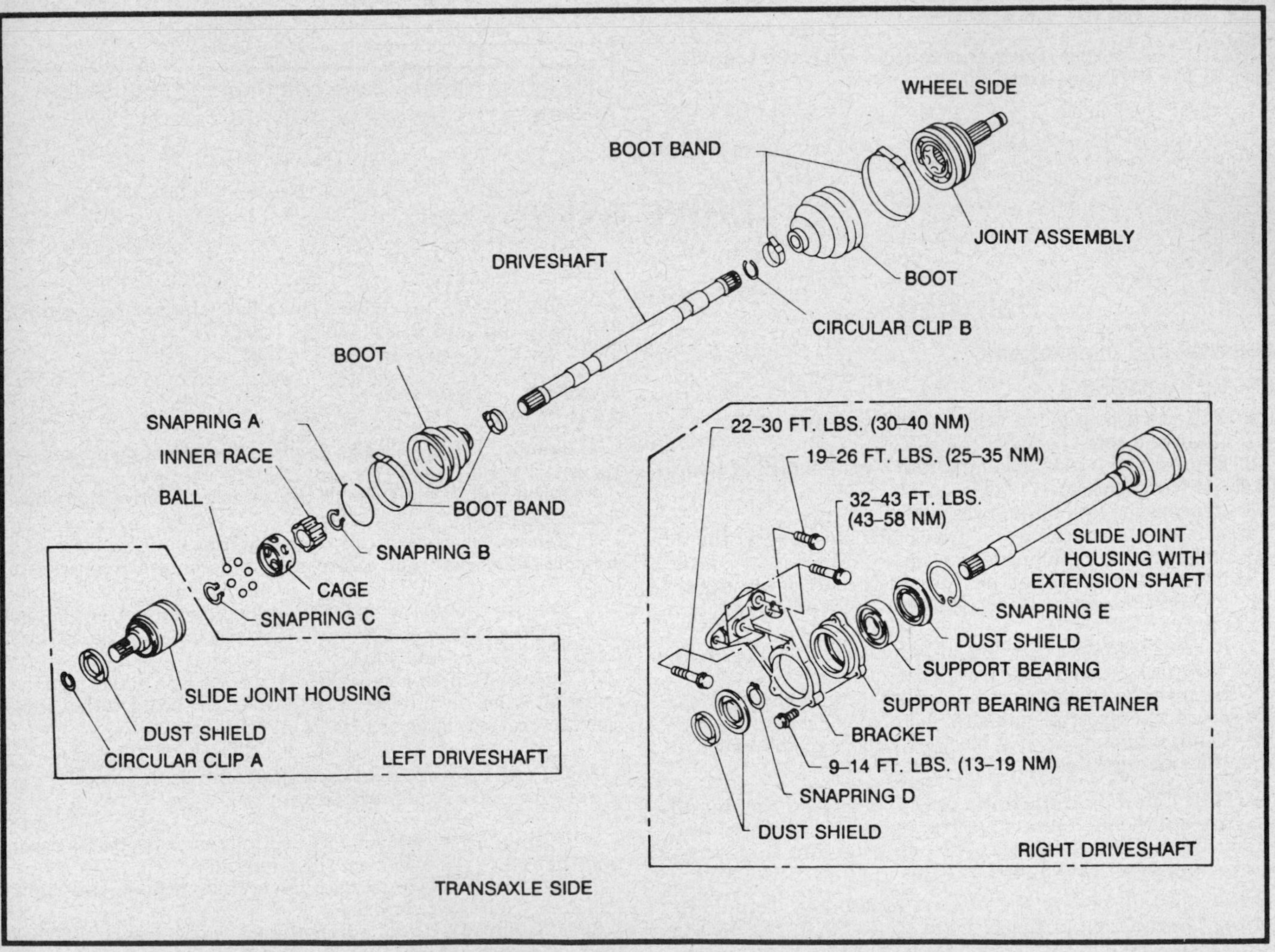

WHEEL SIDE

BOOT BAND

DRIVESHAFT

JOINT ASSEMBLY

BOOT

CIRCULAR CLIP B

BOOT

SNAPRING A

INNER RACE

BALL

BOOT BAND

SNAPRING B

CAGE

SNAPRING C

SLIDE JOINT HOUSING

DUST SHIELD

CIRCULAR CLIP A

LEFT DRIVESHAFT

TRANSAXLE SIDE

22–30 FT. LBS. (30–40 NM)

19–26 FT. LBS. (25–35 NM)

32–43 FT. LBS. (43–58 NM)

SLIDE JOINT
HOUSING WITH
EXTENSION SHAFT

SNAPRING E

DUST SHIELD

SUPPORT BEARING

SUPPORT BEARING RETAINER

BRACKET

9–14 FT. LBS. (13–19 NM)

SNAPRING D

DUST SHIELD

RIGHT DRIVESHAFT

Exploded view of the halfshaft assembly—2WD Axxess

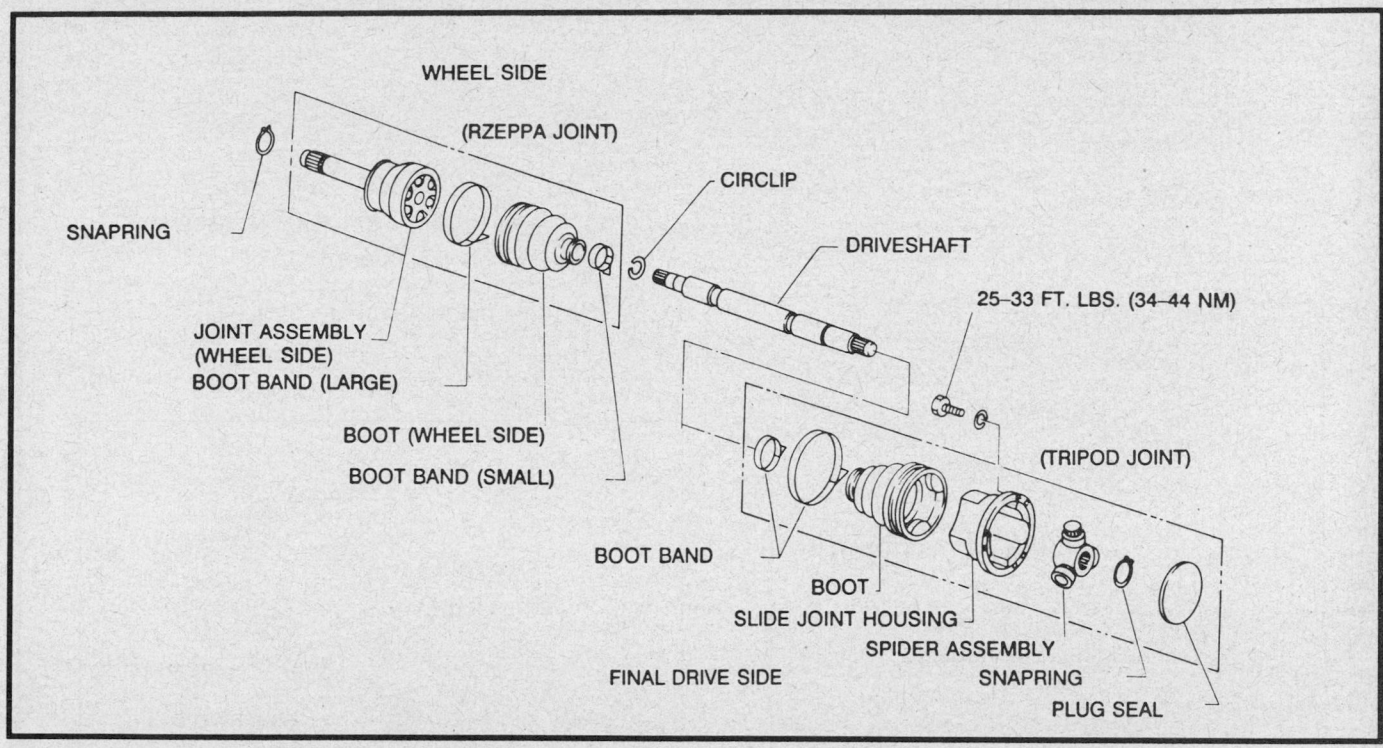

Exploded view of the halfshaft assembly used with the 2.4L engine—Pick-Up and Pathfinder

NOTE: It is a good idea to replace the halfshaft-to-transaxle seals when the halfshaft is removed.

9. To install the halfshaft, press it into the transaxle until the shaft and side gear mesh and the circular clip is seated.
10. To complete the installation, reverse the removal procedures. Torque the wheel bearing locknut to 174–231 ft. lbs. (235–314 Nm).

4WD Models

FRONT HALFSHAFT

1. Remove the grease cap. Depress the brake pedal and remove the wheel bearing locknut.
2. Raise and safely support the vehicle. Remove the wheel assembly.
3. Remove the brake caliper-to-steering knuckle bolts and support the assembly on a wire; do not disconnect the pressure hose.
4. Remove the tie rod end-to-steering knuckle cotter pin and nut. Using a tie rod end removal tool, separate the tie rod end from the steering knuckle.
5. Turn the steering knuckle forward. Using a mallet, tap the halfshaft from the hub; be sure to cover the boots with a shop cloth to prevent damaging them.

NOTE: If equipped with an automatic transaxle, remove the right halfshaft first.

6. If not equipped with a support bearing, use a prybar to separate the right halfshaft from the transaxle.
7. Remove the bearing support bolts and the right halfshaft from the vehicle.

NOTE: It is a good idea to replace the halfshaft-to-transaxle seals when the halfshaft is removed.

8. To install the halfshaft, press it into the transaxle until the shaft and side gear mesh and the circular clip is seated.

9. To complete the installation, reverse the removal procedures. Torque the wheel bearing locknut to 174–231 ft. lbs. (235–314 Nm).

REAR HALFSHAFT

1. Remove the grease cap, the cotter pin and loosen the wheel bearing locknut.
2. Raise and safely support the vehicle.
3. Using a drift and a hammer, lightly separate the halfshaft from the knuckle; be sure to drive it inward.
4. Using shop cloths, cover the halfshaft boots to prevent damaging them.
5. Remove the parallel link-to-knuckle bolt and the radius rods-to-knuckle bolts.
6. Pull the knuckle outward and remove the halfshaft from it.
7. While supporting the halfshaft, use a prybar to separate the halfshaft from the differential.
8. To install, insert the halfshaft into the differential until the circlip snaps into position.
9. To complete the installation, reverse the removal procedures. Torque the radius rods-to-knuckle bolts to 58–72 ft. lbs. (78–98 Nm), the parallel link-to-knuckle bolt to 58–72 ft. lbs. (78–98 Nm) and the hub nut to 174–231 ft. lbs. (235–314 Nm).

Driveshaft and U-Joints

Removal and Installation

EXCEPT AXXESS AND VAN

2WD Model With One Piece Driveshaft

1. Raise and safely support the vehicle.
2. Using a piece of chalk, make alignment marks on the differential-to-driveshaft flange.
3. Remove the driveshaft-to-differential flange bolts, lower the differential and pull it from the transmission.

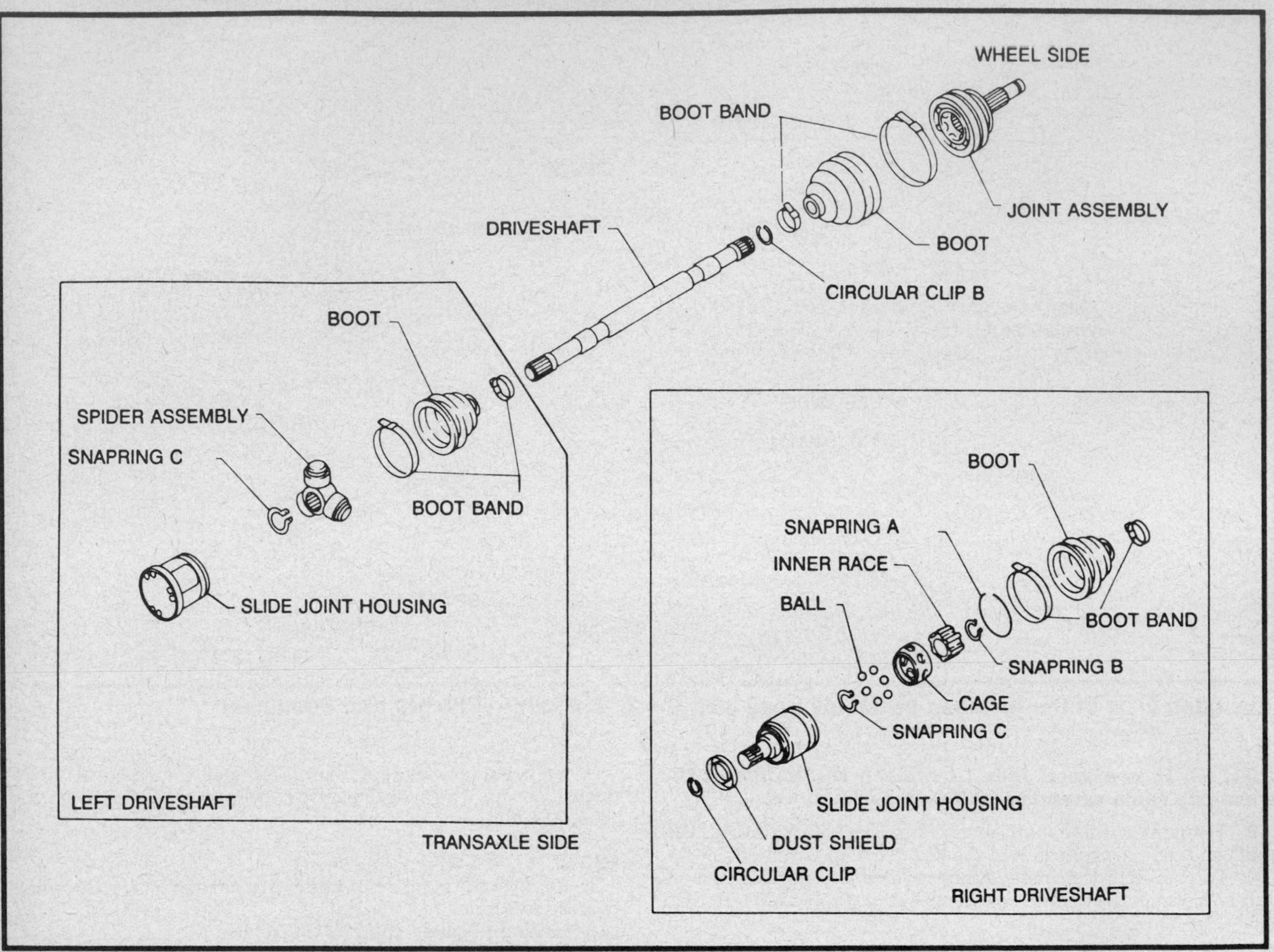

WHEEL SIDE

BOOT BAND

DRIVESHAFT

JOINT ASSEMBLY

BOOT

CIRCULAR CLIP B

BOOT

SPIDER ASSEMBLY

SNAPRING C

BOOT BAND

SLIDE JOINT HOUSING

LEFT DRIVESHAFT

TRANSAXLE SIDE

BOOT

SNAPRING A

INNER RACE

BALL

BOOT BAND

SNAPRING B

CAGE

SNAPRING C

SLIDE JOINT HOUSING

DUST SHIELD

CIRCULAR CLIP

RIGHT DRIVESHAFT

Exploded view of the halfshaft assembly—4WD Axxess

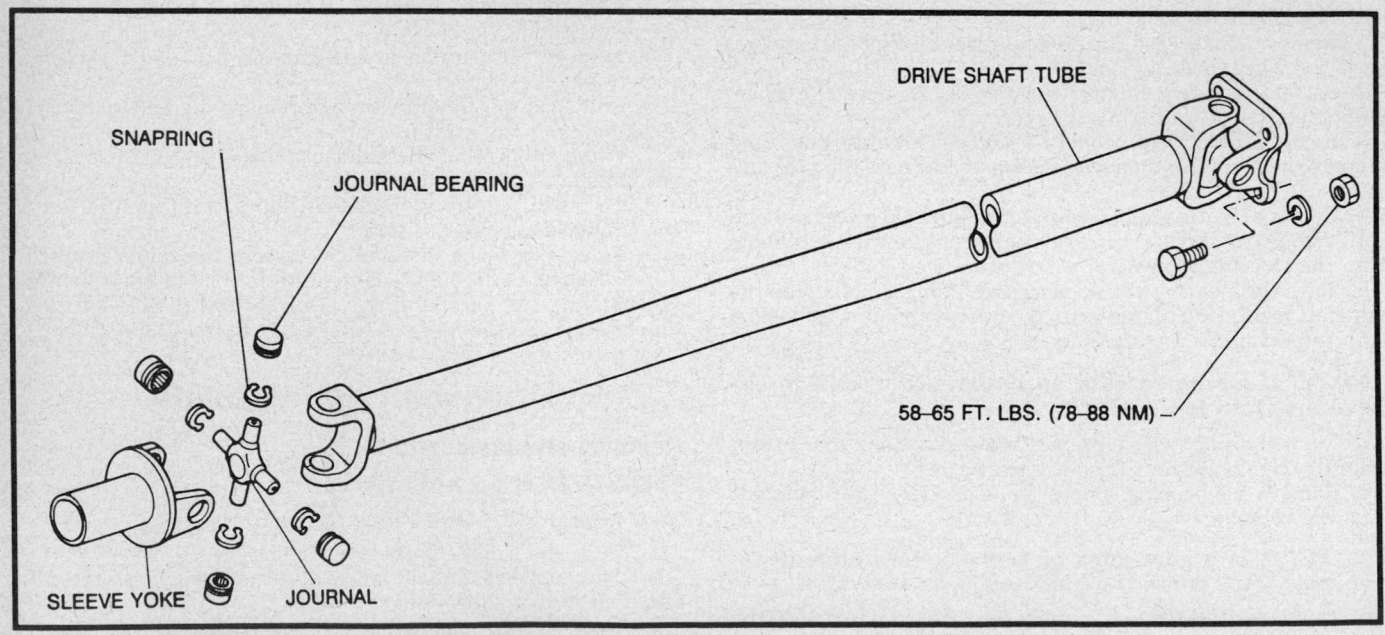

DRIVE SHAFT TUBE

SNAPRING

JOURNAL BEARING

58–65 FT. LBS. (78–88 NM)

SLEEVE YOKE

JOURNAL

Exploded view of a typical 1-piece driveshaft—except Axxess

4. To install, insert the sleeve yoke into the transmission, align the matchmarks and reverse the removal procedures. Torque the driveshaft-to-differential flange nuts/bolts to 29–33 ft. lbs. (39–44 Nm) for model 3S63 or 58–65 ft. lbs. (78–88 Nm) model 3S80.

5. Lower the vehicle.

2WD Model With Two Piece Driveshaft

1. Raise and safely support the vehicle.
2. Using a piece of chalk, make alignment marks on the differential-to-driveshaft flange.
3. Remove the driveshaft-to-differential flange nuts/bolts and the center bearing flange-to-chassis nuts/bolts.
4. Lower and remove the rear driveshaft from the vehicle.
5. Using a clean rag, plug the rear of the transmission to keep the oil from leaking out.
6. If necessary, separate the front section of the driveshaft from the rear section.

NOTE: Replace the transmission rear oil seal when the driveshaft is removed.

7. To install, align the matchmarks and reverse the removal procedures. Torque as follows:
Center bearing-to-chassis bolts to 12–16 ft. lbs. (16–22 Nm)
Driveshaft-to-differential flange nuts/bolts
   Model 3S63 – 29–33 ft. lbs. (39–44 Nm)
   Model 3S80 – 58–65 ft. lbs. (78–88 Nm)

8. If the center bearing was separated from the front driveshaft, torque as follows:
Companion flange-to-front driveshaft nut – 174–203 ft. lbs. (235–275 Nm)
   Rear driveshaft-to-center bearing flange nuts/bolts
     Model 3S63 – 17–24 ft. lbs. (24–32 Nm)
     Model 3S71H – 29–33 ft. lbs. (39–44 Nm)
     Model 3S80 – 58–65 ft. lbs. (78–88 Nm)

4WD Model Front Driveshaft

1. Raise and safely support the vehicle.
2. Using a piece of chalk, make alignment marks on the front driveshaft-to-front differential flange and the front driveshaft-to-transfer case flange.
3. Remove the front driveshaft-to-front differential flange nuts/bolts and the front driveshaft flange.
4. Remove the front driveshaft from the vehicle.
5. To install, align the matchmarks and reverse the removal procedures. Torque the front driveshaft-to-front differential flange and the front driveshaft-to-transfer case flange nuts/bolts to 29–33 ft. lbs. (39–44 Nm).

4WD Model With Rear Driveshaft (One Piece)

1. Using a piece of chalk, make alignment marks on the rear driveshaft-to-rear differential flange.
2. Remove the rear differential-to-driveshaft nuts/bolts.
3. Move the driveshaft rearward (disconnecting it from the

View of the rear drive and suspension assembly – 4WD Axxess

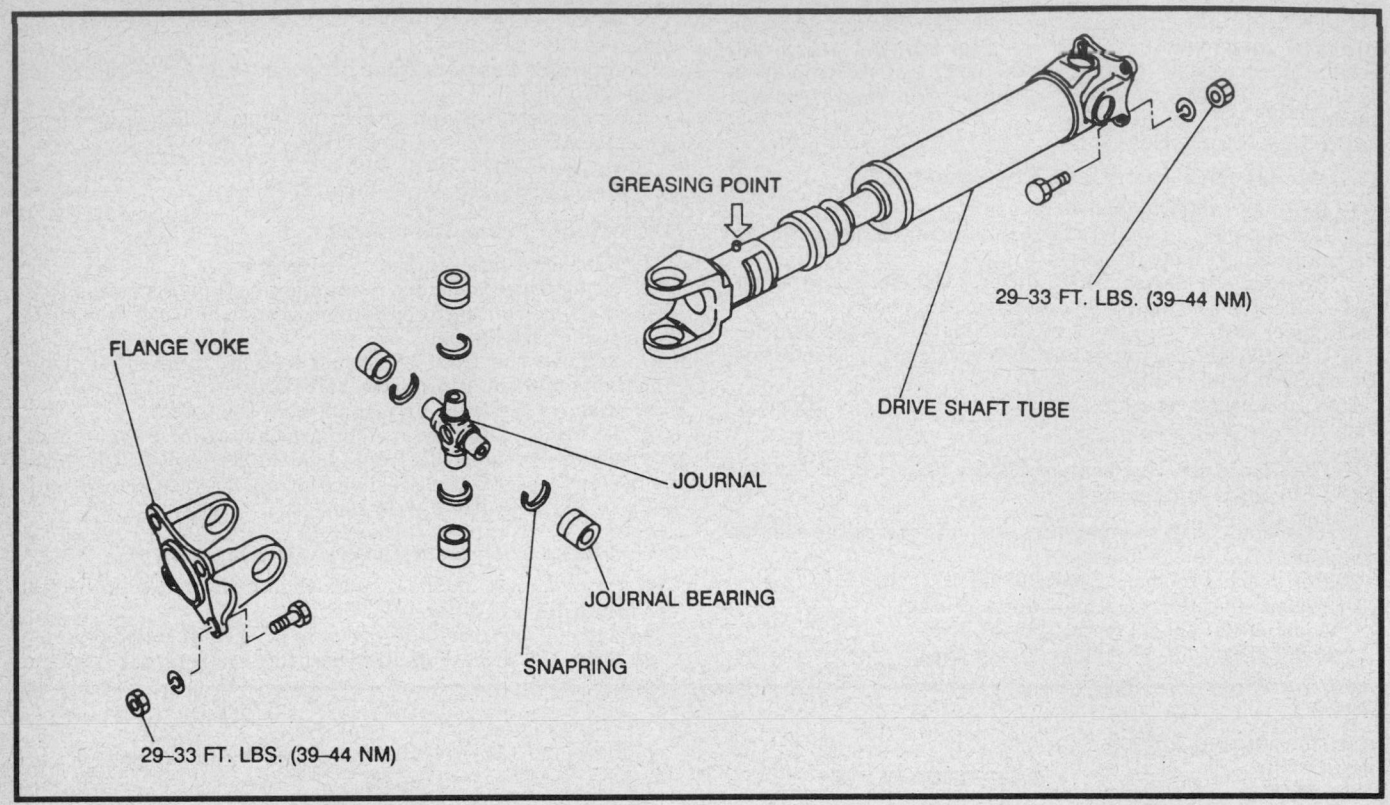

GREASING POINT

29–33 FT. LBS. (39–44 NM)

FLANGE YOKE

DRIVE SHAFT TUBE

JOURNAL

JOURNAL BEARING

SNAPRING

29–33 FT. LBS. (39–44 NM)

Exploded view of a front driveshaft—except Axxess

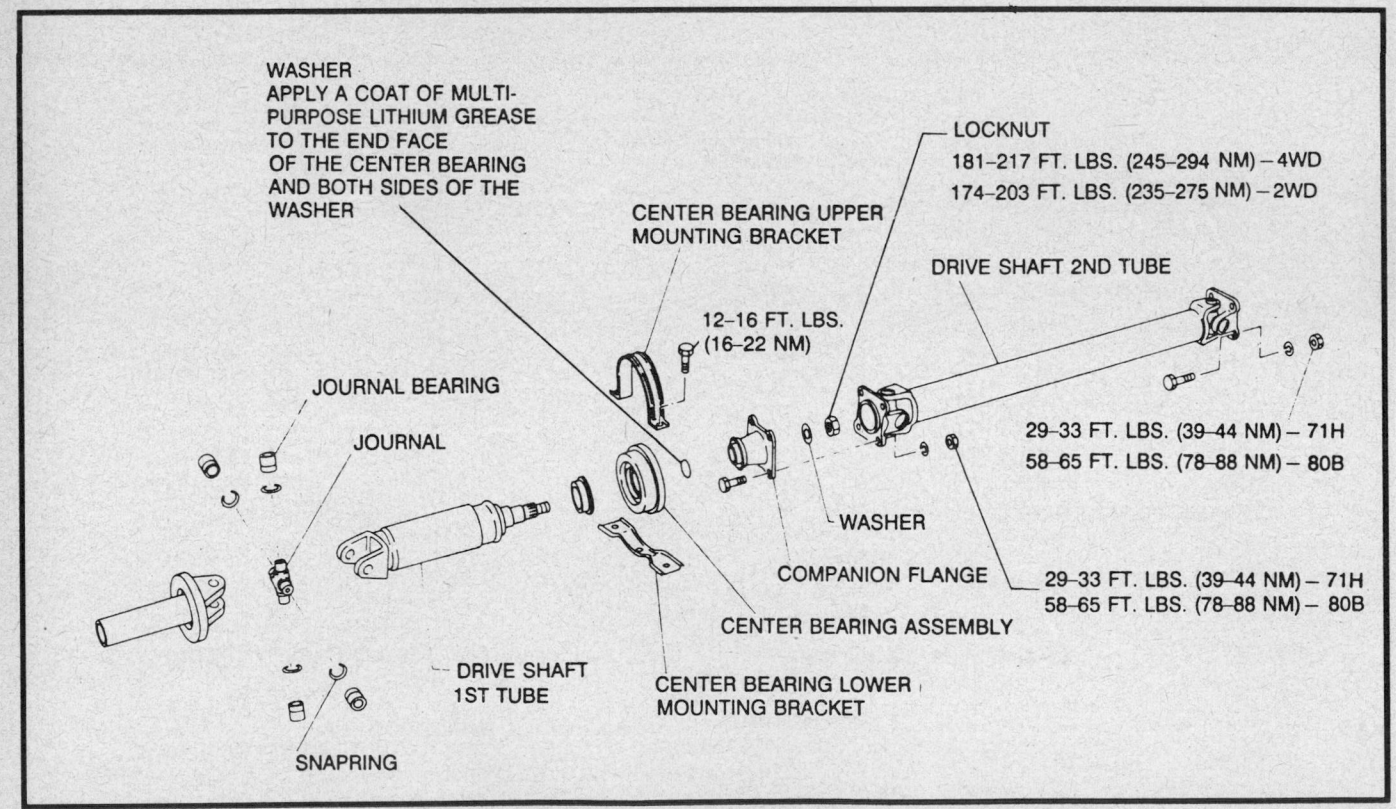

WASHER
APPLY A COAT OF MULTI-PURPOSE LITHIUM GREASE TO THE END FACE OF THE CENTER BEARING AND BOTH SIDES OF THE WASHER

LOCKNUT
181–217 FT. LBS. (245–294 NM)—4WD
174–203 FT. LBS. (235–275 NM)—2WD

CENTER BEARING UPPER MOUNTING BRACKET

DRIVE SHAFT 2ND TUBE

12–16 FT. LBS. (16–22 NM)

JOURNAL BEARING

JOURNAL

29–33 FT. LBS. (39–44 NM) — 71H
58–65 FT. LBS. (78–88 NM) — 80B

WASHER

COMPANION FLANGE

29–33 FT. LBS. (39–44 NM) — 71H
58–65 FT. LBS. (78–88 NM) — 80B

CENTER BEARING ASSEMBLY

DRIVE SHAFT 1ST TUBE

CENTER BEARING LOWER MOUNTING BRACKET

SNAPRING

Exploded view of a typical 2-piece driveshaft—except Axxess

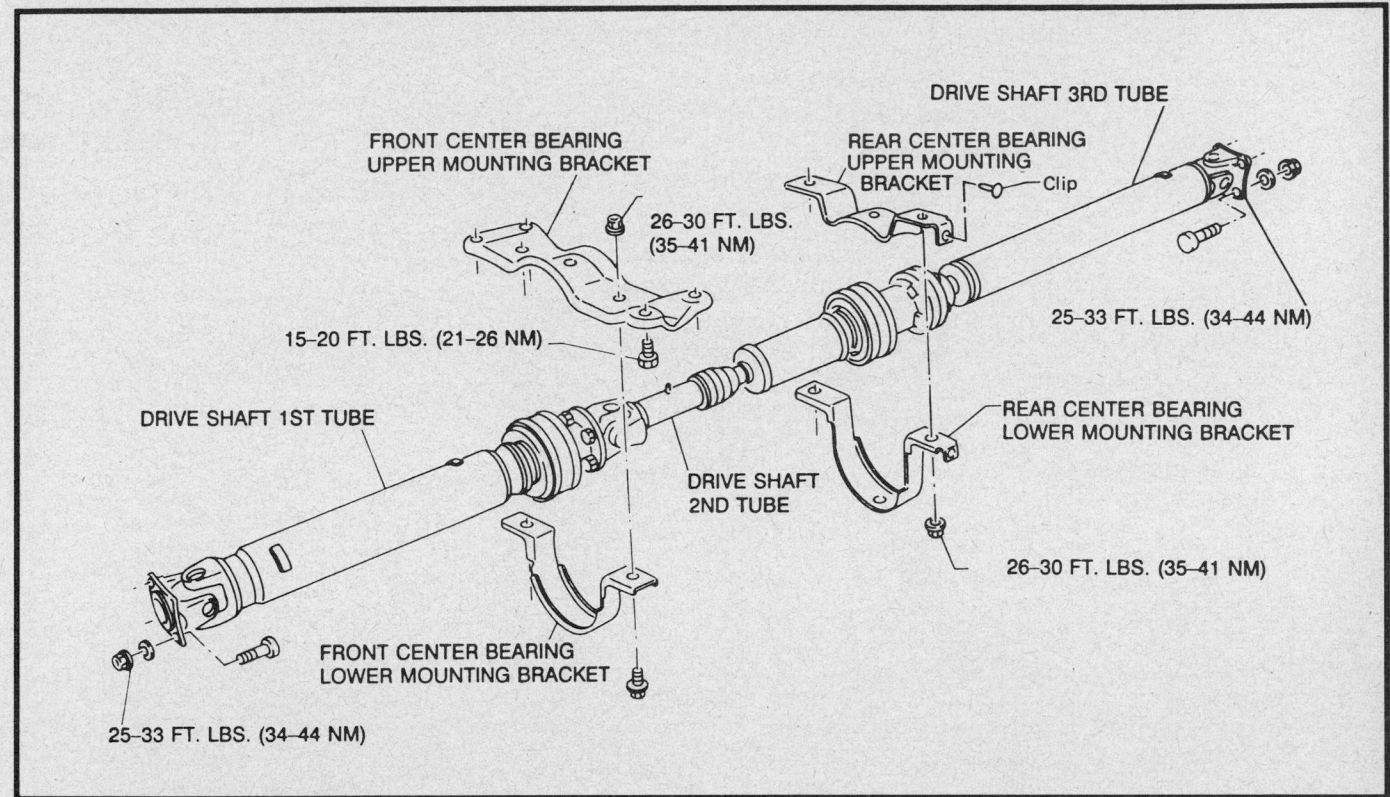

DRIVE SHAFT 3RD TUBE

FRONT CENTER BEARING
UPPER MOUNTING BRACKET

REAR CENTER BEARING
UPPER MOUNTING
BRACKET — Clip

26–30 FT. LBS.
(35–41 NM)

25–33 FT. LBS. (34–44 NM)

15–20 FT. LBS. (21–26 NM)

REAR CENTER BEARING
LOWER MOUNTING BRACKET

DRIVE SHAFT 1ST TUBE

DRIVE SHAFT
2ND TUBE

26–30 FT. LBS. (35–41 NM)

FRONT CENTER BEARING
LOWER MOUNTING BRACKET

25–33 FT. LBS. (34–44 NM)

View of the driveshaft—Axxess

transfer case), be sure to plug the rear of the transfer case to keep the oil from leaking from it.

4. To install, use a new transfer case oil seal, align the matchmarks and reverse the removal procedures. Torque the driveshaft flange-to-differential flange nuts/bolts to 58–65 ft. lbs. (78–88 Nm).

4WD Model Rear Driveshaft (Two Piece)

1. Raise and safely support the vehicle.
2. Using chalk, matchmark the driveshaft flange-to-differential flange and, if necessary, the driveshaft flange-to-center bearing flange.
3. Remove the driveshaft-to-differential flange bolts and the center bearing-to-chassis bolts, then, lower the differential from the vehicle.
4. If necessary, remove the driveshaft-to-center bearing flange bolts and the rear driveshaft.
5. If necessary, separate the center bearing flange from the front driveshaft.
6. To install, reverse the removal procedures. Torque as follows:
Front driveshaft-to-center bearing flange nut to 181–217 ft. lbs. (245–294 Nm).
Center bearing flange-to-rear driveshaft bolts to 58–65 ft. lbs. (78–88 Nm).
Center bearing-to-chassis bolts to 12–16 ft. lbs. (16–22 Nm).
Driveshaft-to-differential flange bolts to 58–65 ft. lbs. (78–88 Nm).

VAN

1. Raise and safely support the vehicle.
2. Using a piece of chalk, make alignment marks on the differential-to-driveshaft flange so the driveshaft can be reinstalled in the same position.

3. Remove the driveshaft-to-differential flange nuts/bolts.
4. Lower and remove the driveshaft from the vehicle.
5. Using a clean rag, plug the rear of the transmission to keep the oil from leaking out.

NOTE: Replace the transmission rear oil seal when the driveshaft is removed.

6. To install, align the matchmarks and reverse the removal procedures. Torque the driveshaft-to-differential flange nuts/bolts to 29–33 ft. lbs. (39–44 Nm).

AXXESS

The rear driveshaft is used only on vehicles equipped with 4WD.

1. Raise and safely support the vehicle.
2. Matchmark the driveshaft flange-to-differential flange and the driveshaft flange-to-transfer case flange.
3. Remove the driveshaft flange-to-differential flange bolts and the driveshaft flange-to-transfer case flange bolts.
4. Support the driveshaft.
5. Remove the front and rear center bearing bracket-to-chassis bolts and lower the driveshaft from the vehicle.
6. To install, align the matchmarks and reverse the removal procedures. Torque the driveshaft flange bolts to 25–33 ft. lbs. (34–44 Nm) and the front/rear center bearing bracket-to-chassis bolts to 26–30 ft. lbs. (35–41 Nm).

Rear Axle Shaft, Bearing and Seal

Removal and Installation

PICK-UP

Single Rear Wheels

1. Block the front wheels. Raise and safely support the vehicle.

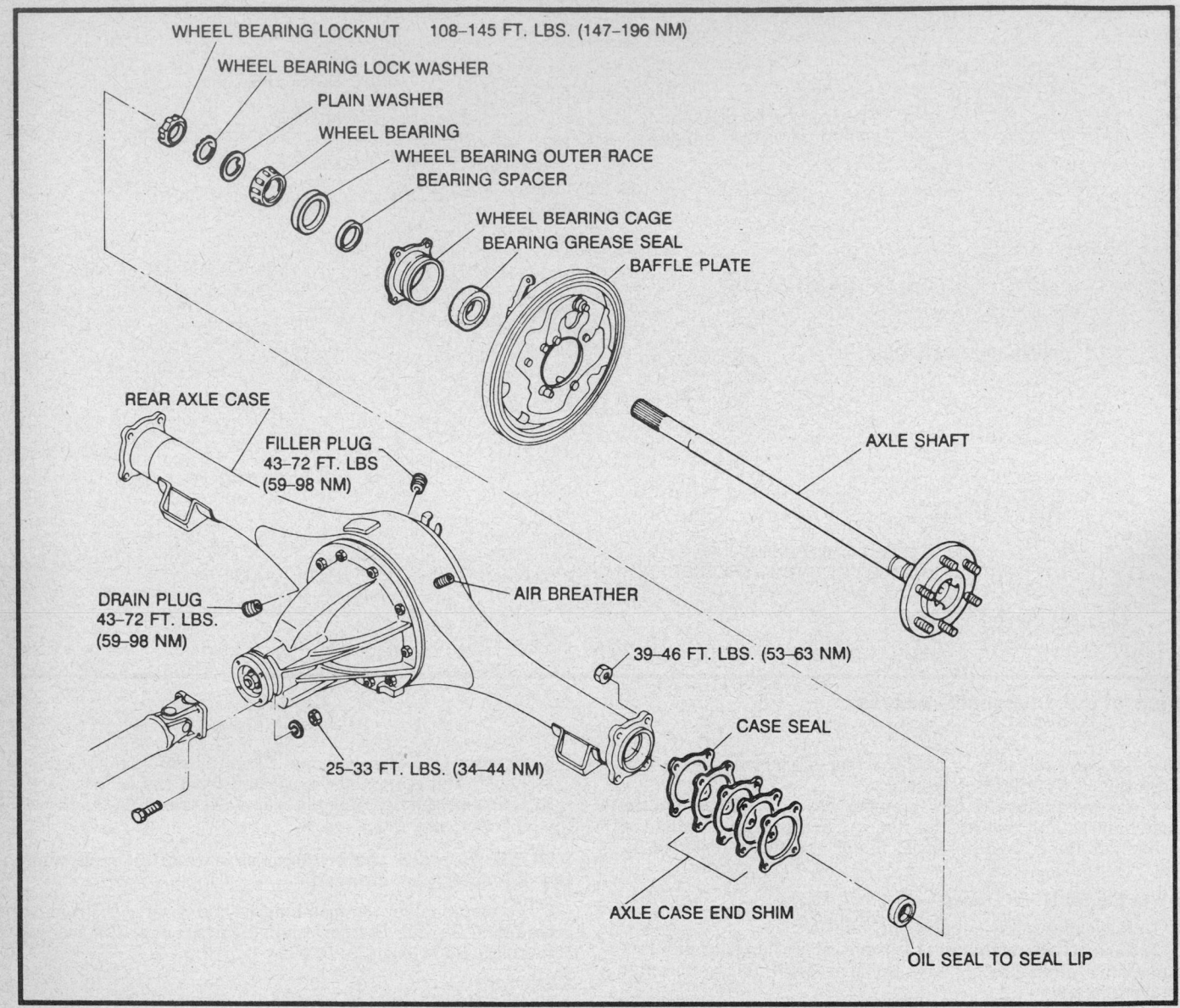

WHEEL BEARING LOCKNUT   108–145 FT. LBS. (147–196 NM)
WHEEL BEARING LOCK WASHER
PLAIN WASHER
WHEEL BEARING
WHEEL BEARING OUTER RACE
BEARING SPACER
WHEEL BEARING CAGE
BEARING GREASE SEAL
BAFFLE PLATE
REAR AXLE CASE
FILLER PLUG
43–72 FT. LBS.
(59–98 NM)
AXLE SHAFT
DRAIN PLUG
43–72 FT. LBS.
(59–98 NM)
AIR BREATHER
39–46 FT. LBS. (53–63 NM)
CASE SEAL
25–33 FT. LBS. (34–44 NM)
AXLE CASE END SHIM
OIL SEAL TO SEAL LIP

Exploded view of the rear axle assembly—single rear wheels—Pick-Up and Pathfinder

2. Using a floor jack, support the differential. Remove the rear wheel/tire assembly.

3. If equipped with rear drum brakes, perform the following procedures:

   a. Remove the brake drum.

   b. Disconnect the parking brake cable from the brake shoes.

   c. Disconnect and plug the brake tube from wheel cylinder.

   d. Remove the brake shoe assembly.

4. If equipped with rear disc brakes, perform the following procedures:

   a. Disconnect the parking brake cable from the caliper.

   b. Remove the caliper-to-knuckle bolts and suspend the caliper on a wire.

   c. Remove the rotor disc.

5. From the rear of the backing plate, remove the backing plate-to-axle housing nuts.

6. Using the rear axle stand tool and the slide hammer puller, pull the axle shaft/backing plate assembly from the axle housing.

NOTE: When the axle shaft has been removed, the oil seal should be replaced.

7. To replace the wheel bearing, perform the following procedures:

   a. At the rear of the backing plate, unbend and discard the lockwasher.

   b. Using a brass drift and a hammer, loosen and remove the locknut.

   c. Using a shop press, press the axle shaft from the backing plate and the bearing from the shaft.

   d. Remove the seal and the bearing cup.

8. To install the wheel bearing assembly, perform the following procedures:

   a. Using a new oil seal, lubricate the seal lips and install the new bearing cup.

   b. Grease the area between the seal and cup.

   c. Place the bearing cage and spacer onto the axle shaft,

then, fit the bearng, tapping it into place with a soft drift and light hammer blows.

d. Place the flat bearing lockwasher over the locknut and install a new locknut. Torque the locknut to 108 ft. lbs. (147 Nm).

e. Continue tightening until grooves align with the lockwasher tabs; the nut can be tightened to 145 ft. lbs. (196 Nm).

f. Bend the lockwasher tabs into place.

g. Lubricate the bearing and recess in the axle housing with wheel bearing grease. Coat the axle splines with gear oil. Coat the seal surface of the shaft with grease.

9. Using a dial indicator, adjust the axle shaft endplay using shims between the backing plate and the axle housing. The endplay should be 0.0008–0.0059 in. (servicing one axle) or 0.0118–0.0354 in. (1st axle) and 0.0008–0.0059 in. (2nd axle).

10. To complete the installation, reverse the removal procedures. Torque the backing plate-to-axle housing nuts to 39–46 ft. lbs. (53–63 Nm). Adjust the axle shaft endplay. Bleed the brake system.

Dual Rear Wheels

1. Block the front wheels. Raise and safely support the rear of the vehicle.

2. Using a floor jack, support the differential. Remove the rear wheel/tire assembly.

3. Remove the brake drum. Disconnect the parking brake cable from the brake shoes.

4. Disconnect and plug the brake tube from wheel cylinder.

5. From the rear of the backing plate, remove the backing plate-to-axle housing nuts.

6. Using the rear axle stand tool and the slide hammer puller, pull the axle shaft/backing plate assembly from the axle housing.

NOTE: When the axle shaft has been removed, the oil seal should be replaced.

7. Remove the attaching screws and detach the lockwasher from the rear wheel bearing nut.

8. Remove the rear wheel bearing nut.

9. Using a brass drift, drive out the bearing and seal.

To install:

10. Using 90W gear oil, lubricate the axle shaft splines and the oil seal lips.

11. Install new bearing races with an installation drift and pack the hub with chassis lube.

12. Pack each bearing and O-ring with chassis lube.

13. Install the bearings and axle shaft; be careful not to damage the seal with the shaft. Always use new seals. Make sure the axle shaft endplay is 0.08mm.

14. Torque the wheel bearing locknut to 123–145 ft. lbs. (167–196 Nm), the backing plate nuts to 62–80 ft. lbs. (84–108 Nm) and the wheel hub studs to 181–217 ft. lbs. (245–294 Nm).

15. To adjust the endplay, perform the following procedure:

a. Turn the wheel hub (in both directions) several times.

b. Loosen the locknut.

c. Retorque the locknut to 0.4–1.1 ft. lbs., then, turn the wheel hub (in both directions) several times.

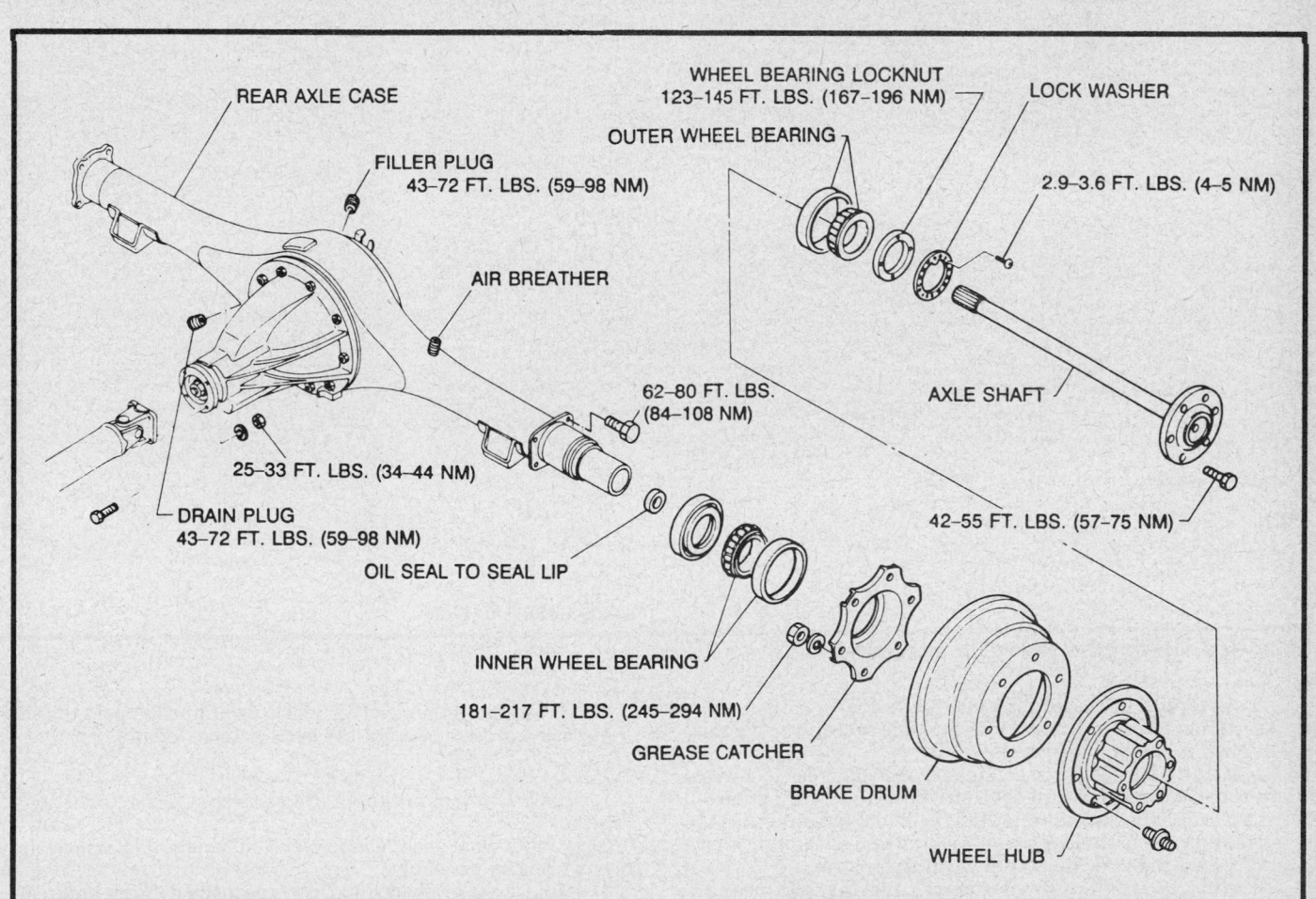

Exploded view of the rear axle assembly — dual rear wheels — Pick-Up 1986–88

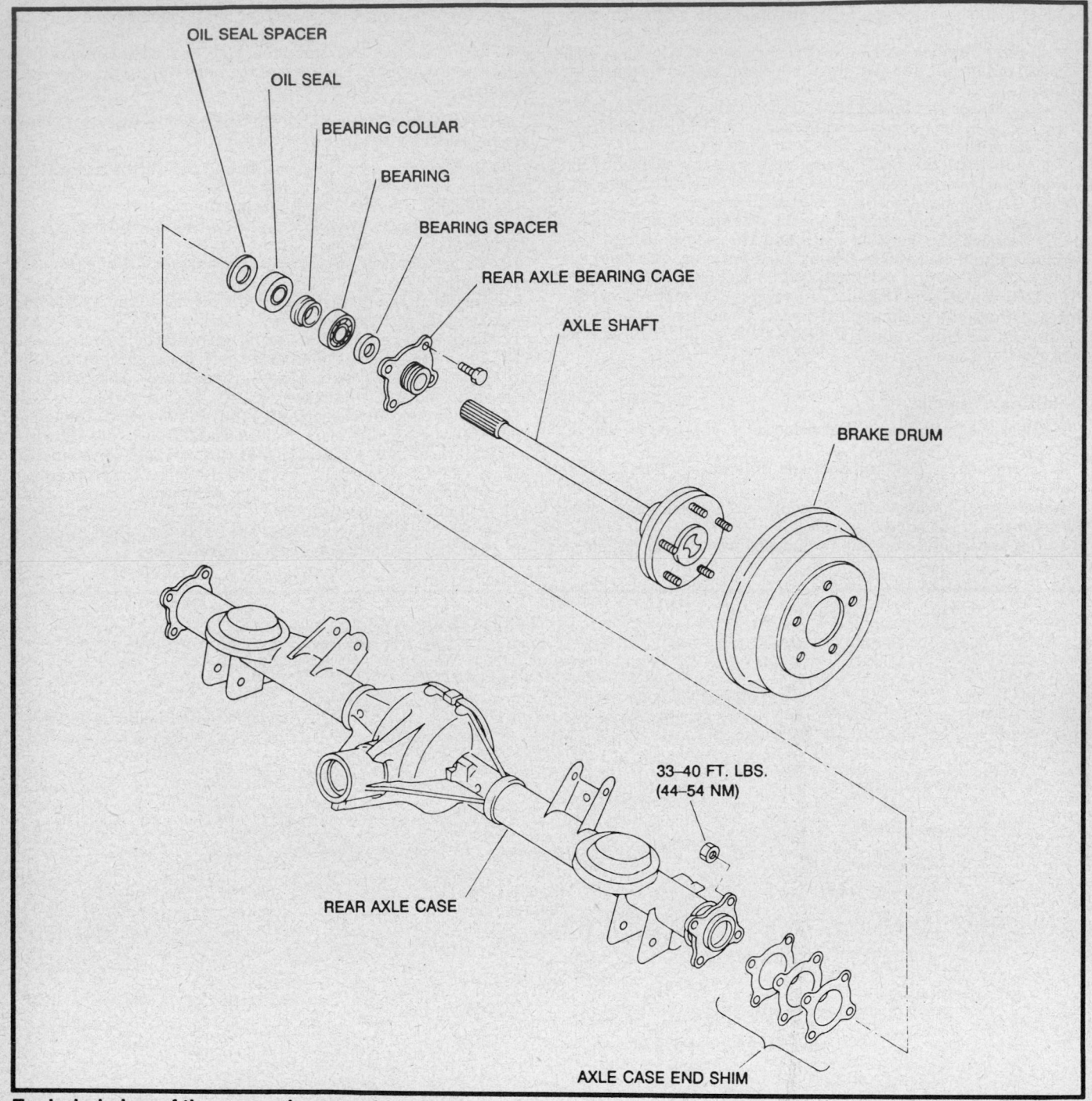

OIL SEAL SPACER

OIL SEAL

BEARING COLLAR

BEARING

BEARING SPACER

REAR AXLE BEARING CAGE

AXLE SHAFT

BRAKE DRUM

33–40 FT. LBS.
(44–54 NM)

REAR AXLE CASE

AXLE CASE END SHIM

Exploded view of the rear axle assembly—Van

d. Retorque the locknut to 0.4–1.1 ft. lbs.

e. Using a dial indicator, measure the wheel bearing axial endplay; it should be zero play.

f. Using a spring gauge connected at 90 degrees to a wheel stud, measure and record the 1st wheel hub turning force.

g. Torque the locknut another 15–30 degrees and turn the wheel hub (in both directions) several times, then, measure and record the 2nd wheel hub turning force.

h. Subtract the 1st measurement from the 2nd measurement; the result is the preload force which should be 1.59–4.72 lbs.

i. If the correct preload force is not obtained, repeat the adjustment procedure until the correct force is obtained.

VAN

1. Block the front wheels. Raise and safely support the vehicle.

2. Using a floor jack, support the differential. Remove the rear wheel/tire assembly.

3. Remove the brake drum. Disconnect the parking brake cable from the brake shoes.

4. Disconnect and plug the brake tube from wheel cylinder.

5. From the rear of the backing plate, remove the backing plate-to-axle housing nuts.

6. Using the rear axle stand tool and the slide hammer puller, pull the axle shaft/backing plate assembly from the axle housing.

NOTE: When the axle shaft has been removed, the oil seal should be replaced.

7. To install, lubricate the oil seal lips and reverse the removal procedures. Torque the backing plate-to-axle housing nuts to 33–40 ft. lbs. Bleed the brake system.

8. Adjust the endplay by performing the following procedures:

   a. Using a dial indicator, measure the axle shaft endplay; it must be 0–0.004 in.

   b. If not, select the correct shim thickness.

   c. Install the shim(s) between the rear axle bearing cage and the axle housing.

9. To complete the installation, reverse the removal procedures.

Front Wheel Hub, Knuckle and Bearings

Removal and Installation

EXCEPT AXXESS AND VAN
2WD Models

1. Raise and safely support the vehicle.
2. Remove the front wheels.
3. Disconnect the brake hose from the knuckle at the bracket.
4. Remove the brake caliper and suspend it on a wire.
5. Remove the wheel hub cup, the cotter pin, the adjusting cap and hub nut.
6. Remove the wheel hub and rotor assembly.
7. Remove the hub from the rotor assembly.
8. Remove the outer bearing cover with fingers and the inner bearing cove by prying out the grease seal. Discard the seal.
9. If it is necessary to replace the bearing outer race, drive it out from the hub with a brass drift and mallet. Evenly, tap the bearing outer race through the hole inside the hub.
10. Remove the baffle plate.

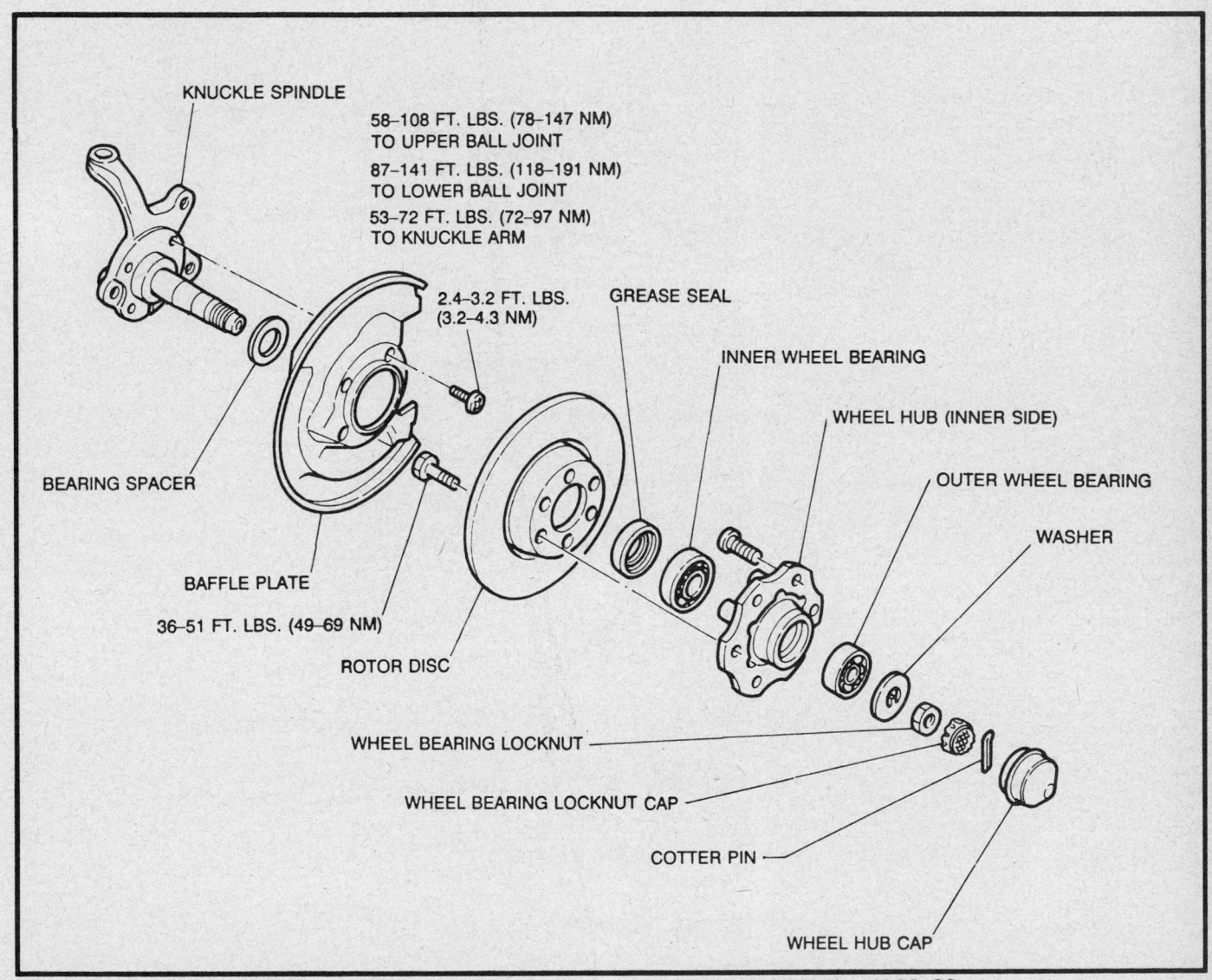

KNUCKLE SPINDLE

58–108 FT. LBS. (78–147 NM) TO UPPER BALL JOINT

87–141 FT. LBS. (118–191 NM) TO LOWER BALL JOINT

53–72 FT. LBS. (72–97 NM) TO KNUCKLE ARM

2.4–3.2 FT. LBS. (3.2–4.3 NM)

GREASE SEAL

INNER WHEEL BEARING

WHEEL HUB (INNER SIDE)

OUTER WHEEL BEARING

WASHER

BEARING SPACER

BAFFLE PLATE

36–51 FT. LBS. (49–69 NM)

ROTOR DISC

WHEEL BEARING LOCKNUT

WHEEL BEARING LOCKNUT CAP

COTTER PIN

WHEEL HUB CAP

Exploded view of the front wheel assembly—2WD Pick-Up and 2WD Pathfinder 1986–88

11. Loosen but do not remove the upper and lower ball joint tightening nut.

12. Separate the upper and lower ball joint from the knuckle spindle.

13. Using a jack, raise the lower control arm (link) and remove the ball joint tightening nut.

14. Separate the knuckle spindle from the upper and lower control arms (links).

15. Using a brass bar, drive the inside wheel bearing race and grease seal from the wheel hub.

16. Invert the wheel hub, then, drive the outside wheel bearing race from the wheel hub.

17. Remove the needle bearing and grease seal from the rear of the steering knuckle.

18. Clean all of the parts in solvent and blow dry with compressed air.

19. Inspect the parts for damage and/or wear; if necessary, replace the damaged parts.

To install:

20. Using the bearing outer race driver kit tool, drive the new bearing races into the wheel hub until they seat. Using multi-purpose grease, pack the inside of the wheel hub.

21. Force multi-purpose grease into each wheel bearing. Place the inside wheel bearing into the rear of the wheel hub, then, lubricate the new grease seal lips with grease and drive it into the wheel hub until it is flush with the wheel hub.

22. At the rear of the steering knuckle, lubricate and replace the needle bearing assembly. Install a new grease seal.

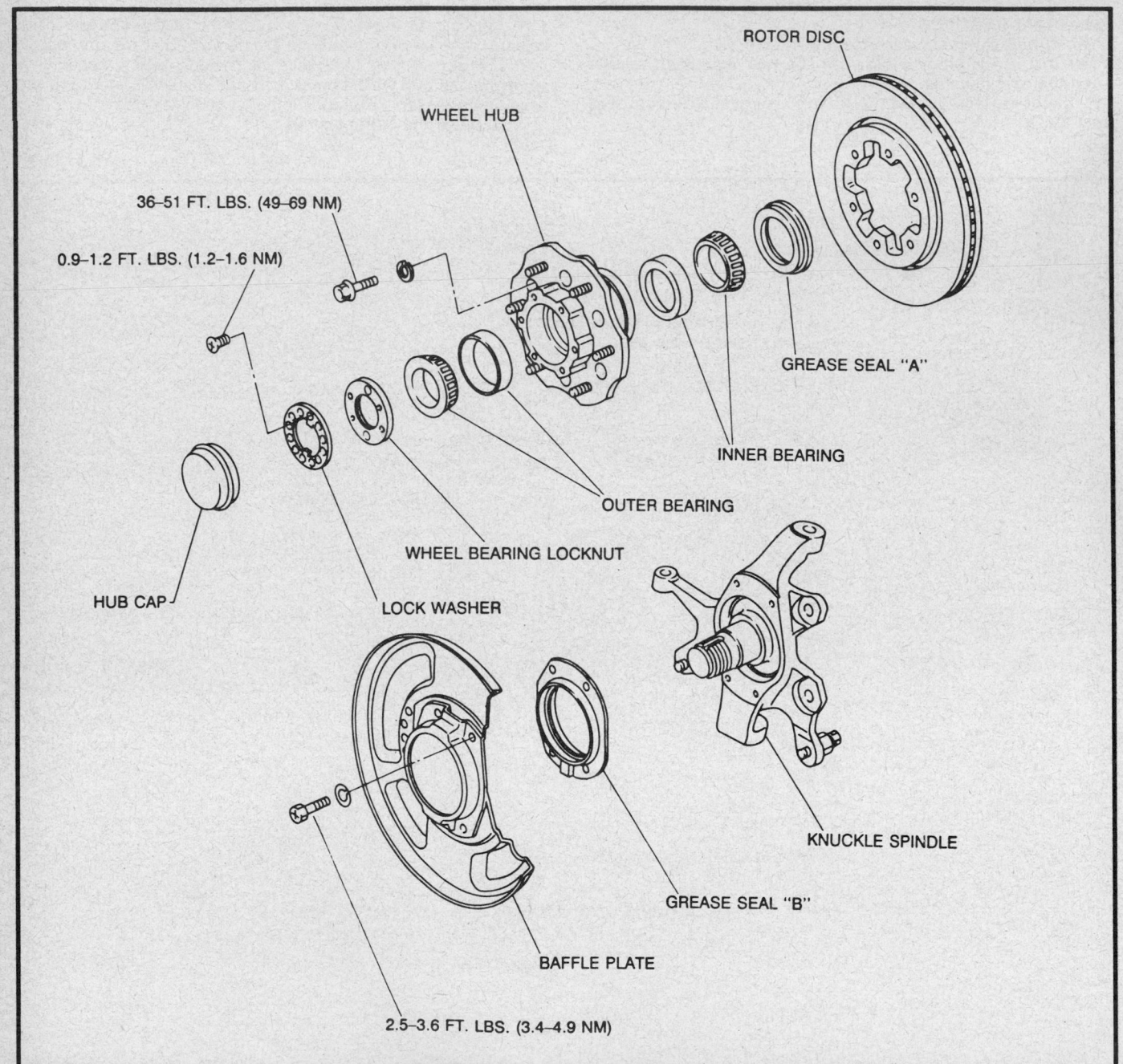

Exploded view of the front wheel assembly—2WD Pathfinder 1989–90

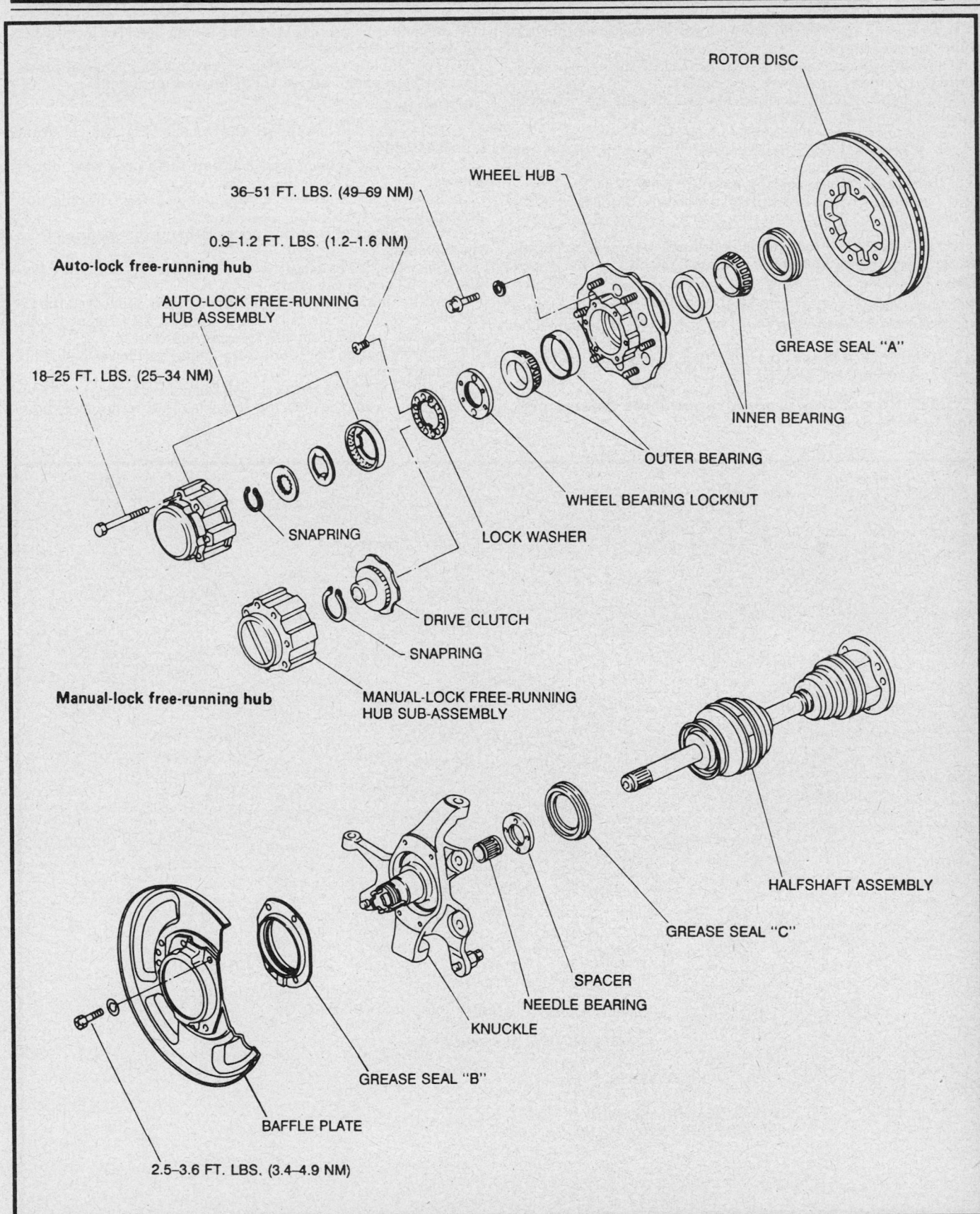

ROTOR DISC

36–51 FT. LBS. (49–69 NM)

WHEEL HUB

0.9–1.2 FT. LBS. (1.2–1.6 NM)

Auto-lock free-running hub

AUTO-LOCK FREE-RUNNING
HUB ASSEMBLY

GREASE SEAL "A"

18–25 FT. LBS. (25–34 NM)

INNER BEARING

OUTER BEARING

WHEEL BEARING LOCKNUT

SNAPRING

LOCK WASHER

DRIVE CLUTCH

SNAPRING

Manual-lock free-running hub

MANUAL-LOCK FREE-RUNNING
HUB SUB-ASSEMBLY

HALFSHAFT ASSEMBLY

GREASE SEAL "C"

SPACER

NEEDLE BEARING

KNUCKLE

GREASE SEAL "B"

BAFFLE PLATE

2.5–3.6 FT. LBS. (3.4–4.9 NM)

Exploded view of the front wheel assembly—4WD Pick-Up and 4WD Pathfinder

23. To install, reverse the removal procedures, except for the following exceptions:

a. While jacking up the lower link, install the knuckle spindle to the upper and lower ball joints.

b. When installing the knuckle arm, torque the retaining bolts to 53–72 ft. lbs.

c. Install the front hub wheel bearings.

d. When attaching the disc rotor to the hub, torque the bolts to 36–51 ft. lbs.

24. Torque the wheel bearing locknut to 58–72 ft. lbs.

25. Loosen the wheel bearing locknut and retorque it to 58–72 ft. lbs.

NOTE: Before checking the wheel bearing preload, make sure the brake pads are not touching the brake disc.

26. Turn the wheel hub several times in both directions. Using a spring scale, measure the wheel bearing preload; it should be 1.59–4.72 lbs.

27. If the preload force is too light, turn the locknut 15–30 degrees and recheck the preload force.

NOTE: Repeat this procedure until the correct preload force is met.

28. When the correct preload force is met, bend the lockwasher tab to secure the locknut.

29. To complete the installation, reverse the removal procedures. Check and/or adjust the front end alignment.

4WD Models

1. Raise and safely support the vehicle. Remove the front wheel assembly.

2. Remove the calipers and suspend them on a wire, out of the way.

3. Remove the auto-lock or manual-lock free running hub assembly.

4. Using a pair of snapring pliers, remove the snapring from the halfshaft.

5. Separate the halfshaft from the steering knuckle by tapping on the end of the shaft.

6. At the tie rod end, remove the cotter pin and loosen the tie rod-to-steering knuckle nut. Using the ball joint removal tool, separate the tie rod from the steering knuckle.

7. Loosen, but do not remove the upper and lower ball joint-to-knuckle nuts.

8. Using a ball joint removal tool, separate the upper and lower ball joints from the steering knuckle; be sure not to remove the ball joint nuts.

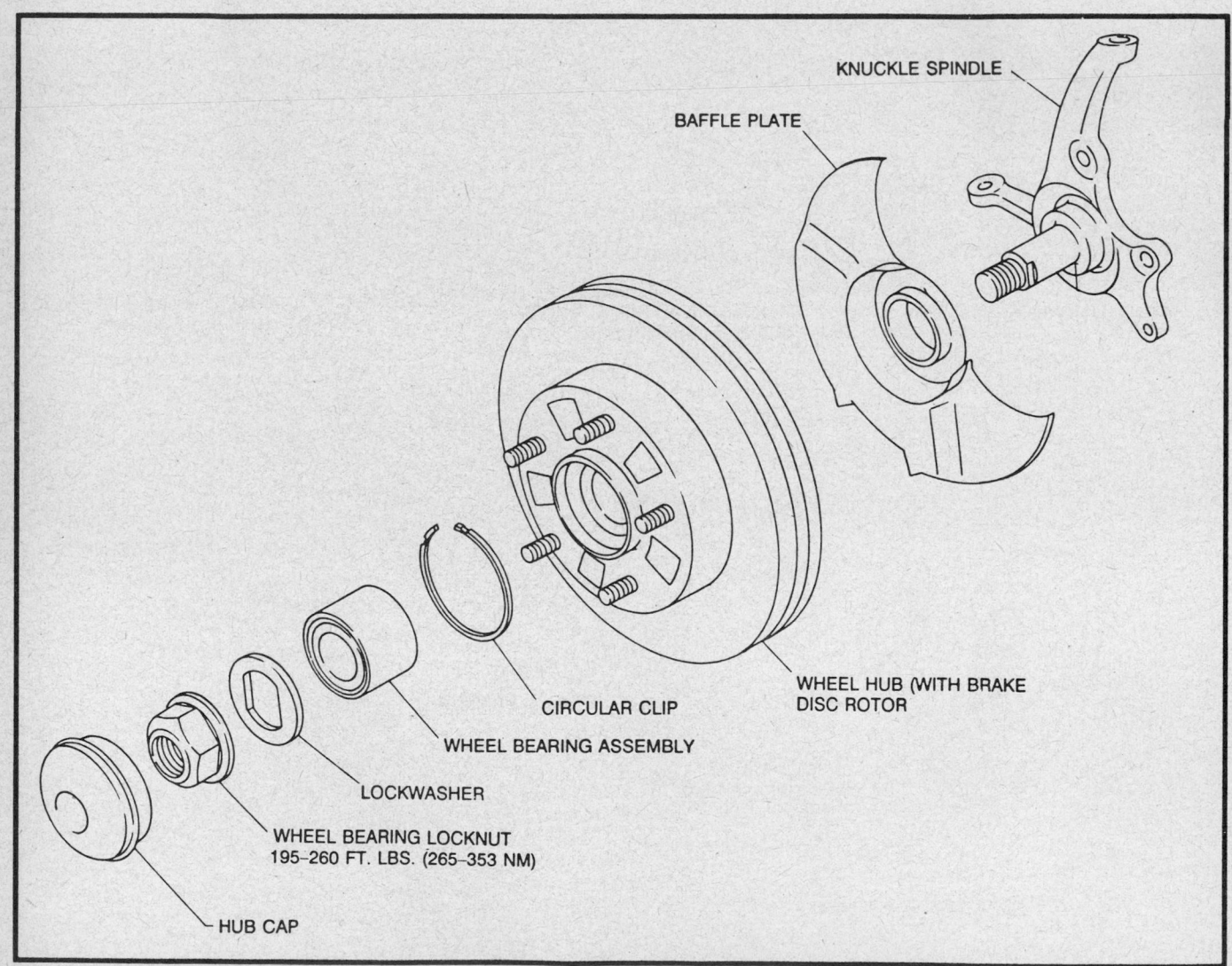

KNUCKLE SPINDLE

BAFFLE PLATE

WHEEL HUB (WITH BRAKE DISC ROTOR)

CIRCULAR CLIP

WHEEL BEARING ASSEMBLY

LOCKWASHER

WHEEL BEARING LOCKNUT
195–260 FT. LBS. (265–353 NM)

HUB CAP

Exploded view of the front wheel assembly—Van

9. Support the lower control arm with a floor jack and remove the ball joint nuts.

10. Remove the steering knuckle from the upper/lower control arms.

11. Using a small pry bar, remove the snapring and lockwasher from the front wheel hub.

12. Using the locknut wrench socket, remove the locknut from the front wheel hub.

13. Separate the front wheel hub/rotor disc from the steering knuckle.

14. Separate the front wheel hub from the brake rotor.

15. Inspect the wheel bearings; if necessary, replace them.

16. When installing, refer to the following notes:

a. When installing the needle bearing into the knuckle spindle, apply multi-purpose grease and make sure the needle bearing is facing in the proper direction.

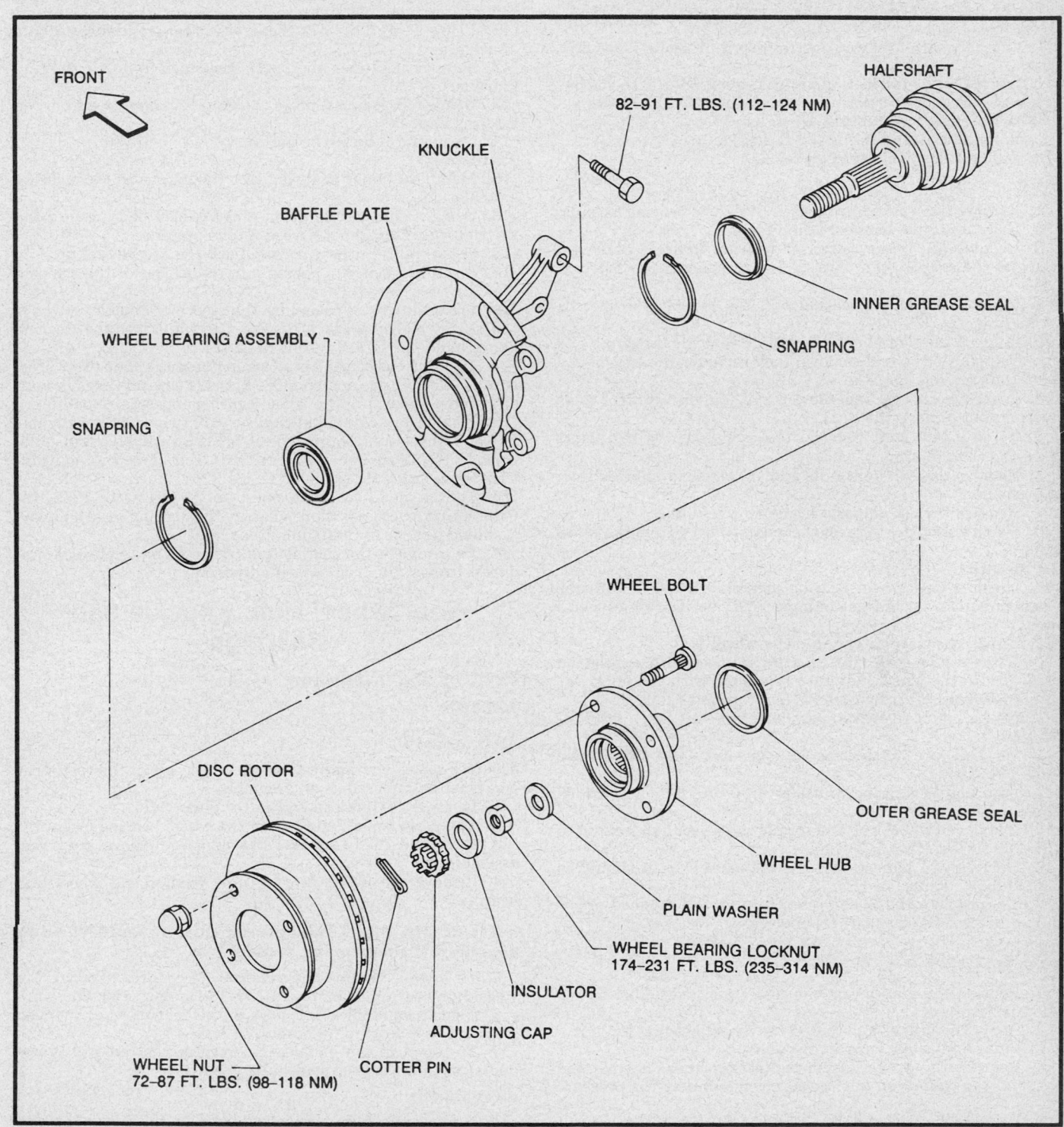

FRONT

HALFSHAFT

82–91 FT. LBS. (112–124 NM)

KNUCKLE

BAFFLE PLATE

INNER GREASE SEAL

SNAPRING

WHEEL BEARING ASSEMBLY

SNAPRING

WHEEL BOLT

DISC ROTOR

OUTER GREASE SEAL

WHEEL HUB

PLAIN WASHER

WHEEL BEARING LOCKNUT
174–231 FT. LBS. (235–314 NM)

INSULATOR

ADJUSTING CAP

COTTER PIN

WHEEL NUT
72–87 FT. LBS. (98–118 NM)

Exploded view of the front wheel assembly—Axxess

b. With the lower control arm jacked up, install the knuckle spindle to the upper and lower ball joints.

c. Adjust the wheel bearing preload.

d. When installing the axle shaft, never reuse the snapring, and check the axial endplay.

17. To install, reverse the removal procedures. Torque as follows:

Steering knuckle arm-to-steering knuckle bolts — 53–72 ft. lbs.

Upper ball joint-to-upper control arm nuts/bolts — 12–15 ft. lbs.

Lower ball joint-to-lower control arm nuts/bolts — 28–38 ft. lbs.

Upper ball joint-to-steering knuckle nut — 58–108 ft. lbs.
Lower ball joint-to-steering knuckle nut — 87–123 ft. lbs.
Wheel bearing locknut — 58–72 ft. lbs.
Locking hub assembly — 18–25 ft. lbs.

18. Adjust the wheel bearing preload.

VAN

1. Remove the hub cap and loosen the wheel bearing locknut.
2. Raise and safely support the vehicle.
3. Remove the brake caliper-to-steering knuckle bolts and suspend the caliper on a wire; do not disconnect the pressure hose.
4. Remove the wheel bearing nut, the lockwasher and the wheel hub.
5. Remove the tie rod end-to-steering knuckle cotter pin and nut. Using a tie rod end removal tool, separate the tie rod end from the steering knuckle.
6. Loosen both the upper/lower ball joints-to-control arms nuts; do not remove the nuts.
7. Using a ball joint removal tool, separate the ball joints from the control arms.
8. Remove the ball joint nuts and the steering knuckle from the vehicle.
9. Remove the circular clip from the wheel hub.
10. Using a shop press, press the wheel bearing from the wheel hub.

To install:

11. Using a new wheel bearing assembly, press it into the wheel hub until it seats; do not force the wheel bearing beyond 3 tons.
12. Install the circular clip into the wheel hub.
13. Using a new seal, lubricate the seal lips with grease and press it into the wheel hub until it is flush with the hub.
14. Install the steering knuckle and torque as follows:

Upper ball joint-to-steering knuckle nut — 40–72 ft. lbs. (54–98 Nm)

Lower ball joint-to-steering knuckle nut — 124–141 ft. lbs. (169–191 Nm)

Tie rod end-to-steering knuckle nut — 40–72 ft. lbs. (54–98 Nm).

15. Install the wheel hub and torque the wheel hub locknut to 195–260 ft. lbs. (265–353 Nm).
16. Using a dial indicator, check the axial play; it should be 0.0020 in. (0.05mm) or less.
17. To complete the installation, reverse the removal procedures. Inspect the front wheel alignment.

AXXESS
2WD Models

1. Remove the grease cap, the cotter pin, the adjusting cap and insulator.
2. Apply the brakes and loosen the wheel bearing locknut.
3. Raise and safely support the vehicle.
4. Remove the brake caliper-to-steering knuckle bolts and suspend the caliper on a wire; do not disconnect the pressure hose.
5. Remove the tie rod end-to-steering knuckle cotter pin and nut. Using a tie rod end removal tool, separate the tie rod end from the steering knuckle.

6. Using a hammer and a drift, tap the halfshaft from the wheel hub.
7. Remove the lower ball joint-to-control arm nuts and the steering knuckle-to-strut nuts/bolts.
8. Remove the steering knuckle from the vehicle.
9. Using a shop press, press the wheel hub from the steering knuckle.
10. Using a shop press, press the bearing race from the wheel hub and remove the grease seal.
11. Using a pry bar, pry the grease seal from the steering knuckle.
12. Remove the inner and outer snaprings from the steering knuckle.
13. Using a shop press, press the outer bearing race from the steering knuckle.
14. Clean and inspect the parts.

To install:

15. Install the inner snapring into the groove in the steering knuckle.
16. Using a shop press, press a new wheel bearing into the steering knuckle; do not exceed 3 tons pressure.
17. Using multi-purpose grease, pack the grease seal lip.
18. Install the outer snapring into the groove of the steering knuckle.
19. Press the grease seals into the steering knuckle.
20. Using a shop press, press the wheel hub into the steering knuckle; do not exceed 3 tons pressure.
21. To check the bearing preload, increase the shop press pressure to 3.5–5.0 tons and spin the knuckle several times in both directions; make sure the wheel bearings operate smoothly.
22. Install the steering knuckle; be sure to insert the halfshaft into the wheel hub. Torque the steering knuckle-to-strut nuts/bolts to 82–91 ft. lbs. (112–124 Nm), the lower ball joint-to-transverse link nuts to 56–80 ft. lbs. (76–109 Nm).
23. Torque the wheel hub locknut to 174–231 ft. lbs. (235–314 Nm). Using a dial indicator, measure the bearing axial endplay; it should be 0.0020 in. (0.05mm) or less.
24. To complete the installation, reverse the removal procedures. Inspect the front wheel alignment.

Rear Wheel Hub, Knuckle and Bearings

Removal and Installation
AXXESS

2WD Models

The rear knuckle and wheel spindle are a part of the rear strut and must be replaced as an assembly.

1. Remove the hub cap and cotter pin.
2. Apply the brakes and loosen the wheel bearing locknut.
3. Raise and safely support the vehicle. Remove the wheel assembly.
4. Remove the wheel bearing nut, washer and wheel hub bearing.

NOTE: The wheel hub bearing must be replaced as an assembly, if the bearing is defective.

5. To install, reverse the removal procedures. Torque the wheel hub bearing assembly to 137–188 ft. lbs. (186–255 Nm).
6. Using a dial indicator, measure the bearing axial endplay; it should be 0.0020 in. (0.05mm) or less.
7. To complete the installation, reverse the removal procedures. Inspect the rear wheel alignment.

4WD Models

1. Remove the hub cap, cotter pin, the adjusting cap and insulator.

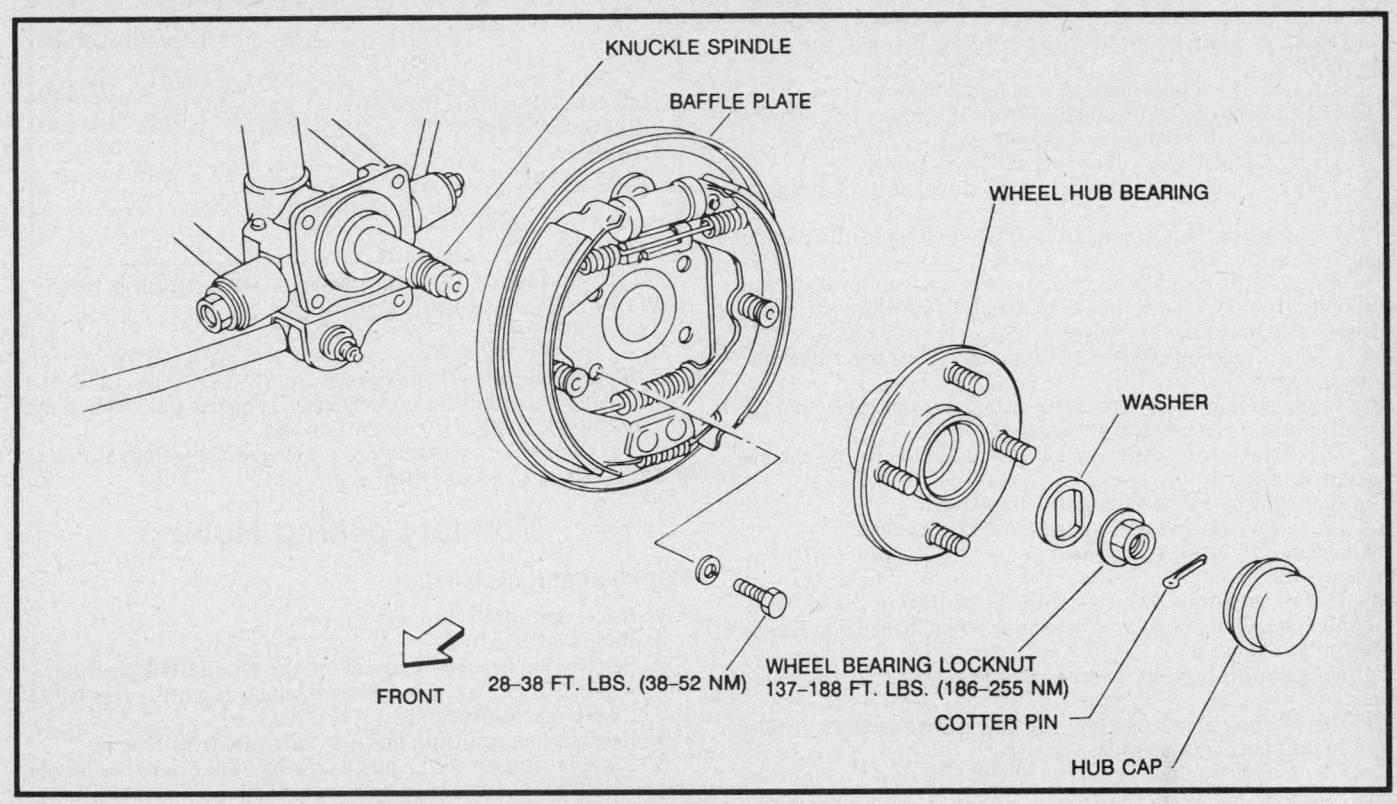

KNUCKLE SPINDLE

BAFFLE PLATE

WHEEL HUB BEARING

WASHER

FRONT

28–38 FT. LBS. (38–52 NM)

WHEEL BEARING LOCKNUT
137–188 FT. LBS. (186–255 NM)

COTTER PIN

HUB CAP

Exploded view of the rear wheel assembly—2WD Axxess

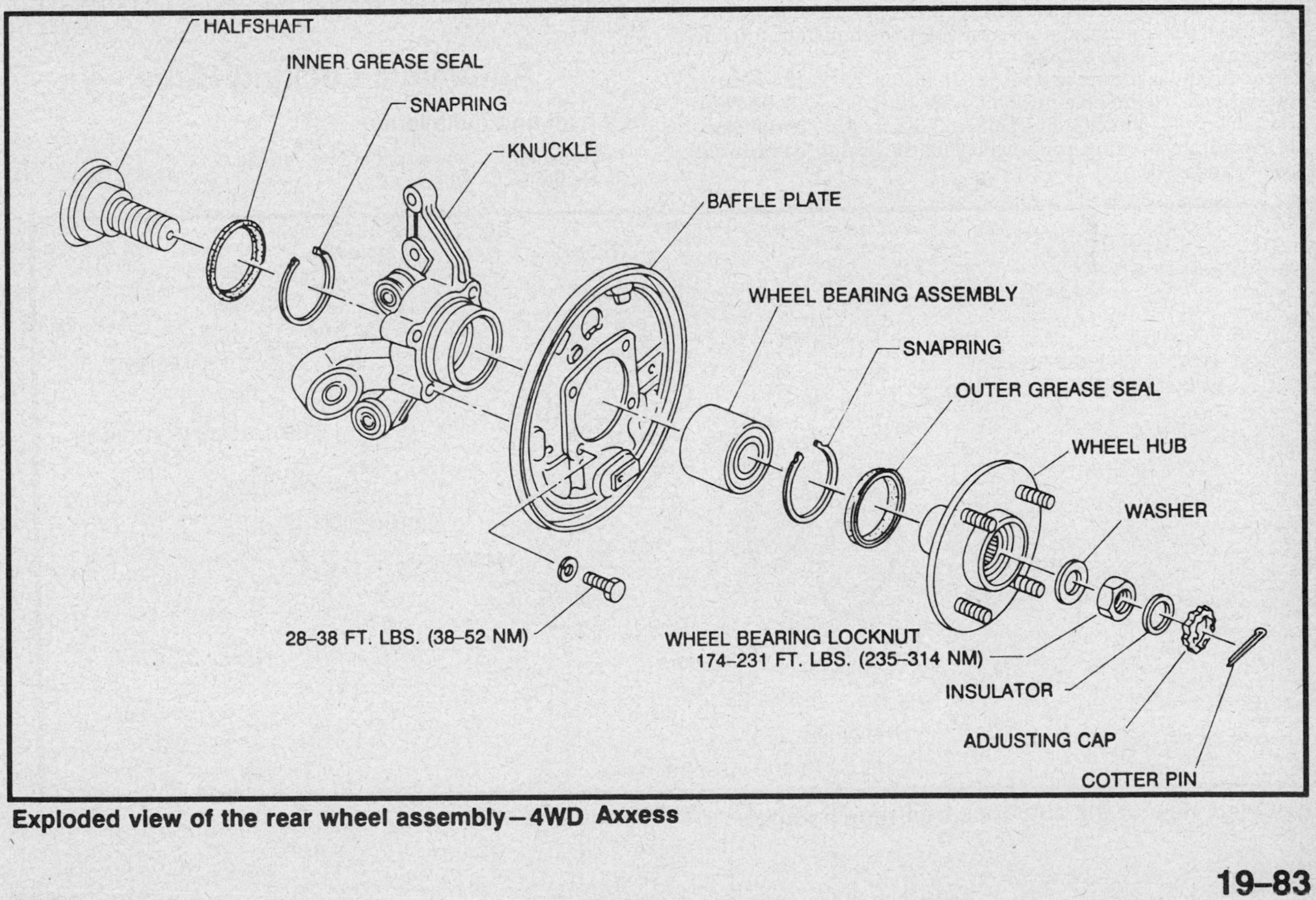

HALFSHAFT

INNER GREASE SEAL

SNAPRING

KNUCKLE

BAFFLE PLATE

WHEEL BEARING ASSEMBLY

SNAPRING

OUTER GREASE SEAL

WHEEL HUB

WASHER

28–38 FT. LBS. (38–52 NM)

WHEEL BEARING LOCKNUT
174–231 FT. LBS. (235–314 NM)

INSULATOR

ADJUSTING CAP

COTTER PIN

Exploded view of the rear wheel assembly—4WD Axxess

2. Apply the brakes and loosen the wheel bearing locknut.

3. Raise and safely support the vehicle. Remove the wheel assembly.

4. Remove the wheel bearing nut and washer.

5. Disconnect the hydraulic line from the wheel cylinder and parking brake cable from the brake shoes.

6. Using shop cloths, cover the halfshaft boots.

7. Using a mallet, tap the halfshaft to separate it from the wheel hub.

8. Remove the radius rods-to-knuckle bolts and the parallel link-to-knuckle bolt.

9. Support the knuckle and remove the strut-to-knuckle nuts and bolts. Remove the knuckle assembly from the vehicle and position the assembly in a vise.

10. Using a piece of pipe and a hammer, drive the wheel hub from the knuckle.

11. Using a shop press, press the outside, inner race from the wheel hub and remove the grease seal.

12. Drive the inside, inner race from the knuckle and remove the grease seal.

13. Remove the inner and outer snaprings.

14. Drive the bearing outer race from the knuckle.

15. Clean and inspect the parts.

To install:

16. Install the inner snapring into the groove in the knuckle.

17. Using a shop press, press the new wheel bearing assembly into the knuckle.

18. Using multi-purpose grease, pack the lip of the new grease seals.

19. Install the outer snapring into the groove of the knuckle.

20. Install both grease seals.

21. Using a shop press, press the wheel hub into the knuckle; do not exceed 3 tons pressure.

22. To check the bearing preload, increase the shop press pressure to 3.5–5.0 tons and spin the knuckle several times in both directions; make sure the wheel bearings operate smoothly.

23. Install the knuckle; be sure to insert the halfshaft into the wheel hub. Torque as follows:

Strut-to-knuckle nuts/bolts—82–91 ft. lbs. (112–124 Nm)
Radius rods-to-knuckle nut/bolt—58–72 ft. lbs. (78–98 Nm)
Parallel rod-to-knuckle nut/bolt—58–72 ft. lbs. (78–98 Nm).

24. Install the parking brake cable and the pressure line to the wheel cylinder.

Exploded view of the manual-lock free-running hub— 4WD Pick-Up and 4WD Pathfinder

25. Torque the wheel hub locknut to 174–231 ft. lbs. (235–314 Nm). Using a dial indicator, measure the bearing axial endplay; it should be 0.0020 in. (0.05mm) or less.

26. To complete the installation, reverse the removal procedures. Inspect the rear wheel alignment.

Manual Locking Hubs

Removal and Installation

1. Raise and safely support the vehicle.

2. Remove the wheels.

3. Set the knob of the manual lock to the **FREE** position.

4. Using a Torx® wrench, remove the locking hub cover while the brake pedal is depressed.

5. Remove the snapring and pull out the drive clutch.

6. Install the drive clutch and snapring; make sure the hub is in the **FREE** position.

7. Install the hub cover and tighten the bolts to 18–25 ft. lbs. (25–34 Nm).

8. Install the wheels, remove the stands and lower the vehicle.

Automatic Locking Hubs

Removal and Installation

1. Raise and safely support the vehicle.

2. Remove the wheels.

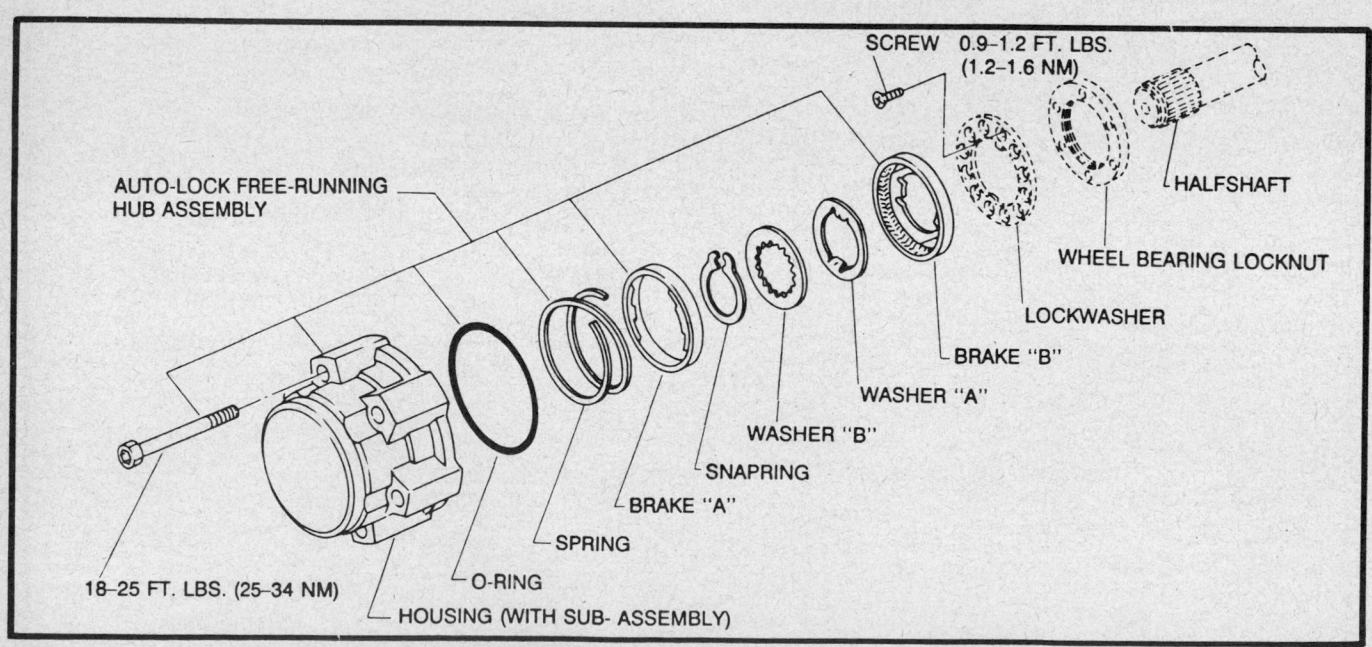

Exploded view of the auto-lock free-running hub— 4WD Pick-Up and 4WD Pathfinder

3. Set the knob of the auto lock to the **FREE** position.

4. Using a Torx® wrench, remove the locking hub cover while the brake pedal is depressed.

5. Remove the snapring.

6. Remove washer **B**, washer **A** and brake **B**.

7. Make sure the hub is in the **FREE** position and install washer **B**, washer **A** and brake **B**.

8. Install the snapring.

9. Install the hub cover and torque the bolts to 18–25 ft. lbs. (25–34 Nm).

10. Install the wheels, remove the stands and lower the vehicle.

Pinion Seal

Removal and Installation

PICK-UP AND PATHFINDER

The pinion oil seal on Models H190A, H233B and C200 differentials must not be replaced for they use a collapsible spacer.

1. Raise and safely support the vehicle.

2. Remove the driveshaft.

3. Using a socket wrench and the differential flange holding tool, hold the differential flange and the remove the differential pinion nut.

4. Using a wheel puller tool, pull the pinion flange from the differential.

5. Using a small pry bar, pry the oil seal from the differential.

6. Using the oil seal driver tool (Model R180A and H190A differentials), lubricate the new oil seal lips with multi-purpose grease and drive the new seal into the differential housing until it is flush the end of the housing.

7. Using a soft hammer, tap the pinion flange onto the pinion shaft.

8. Using a socket wrench and the differential flange holding tool (Model H233B), hold the differential flange and torque the pinion flange nut as follows:

Model R180 – 123–145 ft. lbs.
Model R190A – 94–217 ft. lbs.
Model H233B – 145–181 ft. lbs.

9. To complete the installation, reverse the removal procedures.

VAN

1. Raise and safely support the vehicle. Remove the driveshaft.

2. Using a socket wrench and the differential flange holding tool, hold the differential flange and the remove the differential pinion nut.

3. Using a wheel puller tool, pull the pinion flange from the differential.

4. Using a small pry bar, pry the oil seal from the differential.

5. Using the oil seal driver tool, lubricate the new oil seal lips with multi-purpose grease and drive the new seal into the differential housing until it is flush the end of the housing.

6. Using a soft hammer, tap the pinion flange onto the pinion shaft.

7. Using a socket wrench and the differential flange holding tool, hold the differential flange and torque the pinion flange nut to 94 ft. lbs.

8. Turn the pinion flange, in both directions, several times to set the bearings. Using a small torque wrench, measure the pinion preload; it should be 9.5–14.8 inch lbs. If the preload value is not obtained, repeat the pinion torquing procedure.

AXXESS
4WD Models

1. Raise and safely support the vehicle.

2. Remove the driveshaft.

3. Using a spanner wrench and a socket wrench, remove the drive pinion nut.

4. Using a wheel puller tool, press the companion flange from the differential.

5. Using an oil seal remover tool, press the oil seal from the differential.

To install:

6. Using a new oil seal, lubricate it with multi-purpose grease.

7. Using an oil seal installation tool, drive the new oil seal into the differential.

8. Install the companion flange and torque the drive pinion nut to 123–145 ft. lbs. (167–196 Nm).

9. Install the driveshaft and lower the vehicle.

Differential Carrier

Removal and Installation

PICK-UP AND PATHFINDER (4WD)
Front

1. Raise and safely support the vehicle. Drain the differential.

2. Separate the halfshafts from the front differential.

3. Remove the front driveshaft from the front differential and transfer case.

4. Remove the front engine mounting bolts and raise the engine.

5. Support the differential assembly.

6. Remove the differential crossmember-to-chassis bolts and lower the differential with the crossmember. Remove the assembly from the vehicle.

7. Remove differential-to-crossmember bolts and the crossmember.

8. To install, reverse the removal procedures. Torque the differential-to-front insulator bracket nut/bolt to 50–64 ft. lbs., the differential-to-front crossmember nuts to 50–64 ft. lbs. Inspect the front differential oil level.

9. Install the front driveshaft and halfshafts. Lower the vehicle.

Rear
EXCEPT MODELS C200 DIFFERENTIAL

1. Raise and safely support the vehicle.

2. Disconnect the driveshaft from the differential carrier.

3. Drain all fluid from the differential carrier and remove the axle shafts.

4. Remove the differential carrier-to-axle housing bolts and the carrier.

5. Install the differential carrier and torque the bolts to 12–18 ft. lbs. (17–25 Nm); be sure the gasket on the H233B model is installed in the correct position.

6. Install the axle shafts and connect the driveshaft.

7. Lower the vehicle and fill the differential with gear oil.

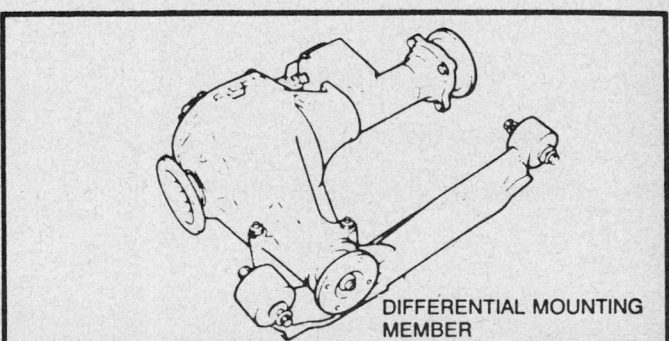

DIFFERENTIAL MOUNTING MEMBER

View of the front differential assembly – 4WD Pick-Ups and 4WD Pathfinder

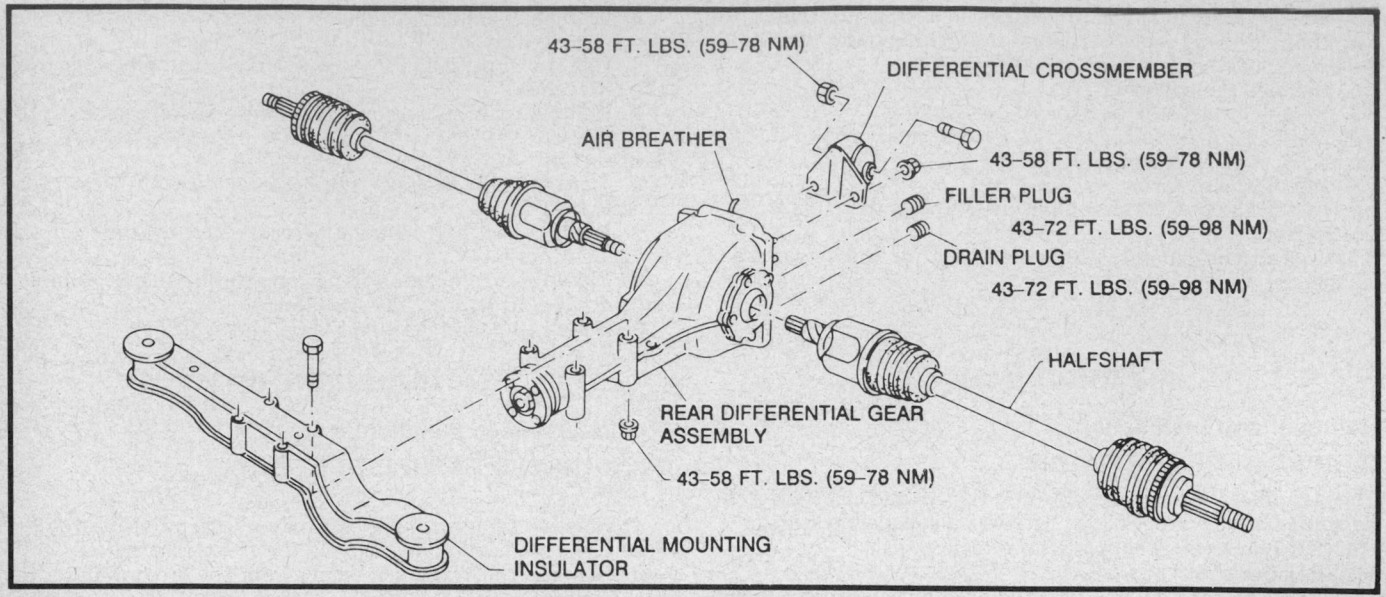

43–58 FT. LBS. (59–78 NM)

DIFFERENTIAL CROSSMEMBER

AIR BREATHER

43–58 FT. LBS. (59–78 NM)

FILLER PLUG

43–72 FT. LBS. (59–98 NM)

DRAIN PLUG

43–72 FT. LBS. (59–98 NM)

HALFSHAFT

REAR DIFFERENTIAL GEAR ASSEMBLY

43–58 FT. LBS. (59–78 NM)

DIFFERENTIAL MOUNTING INSULATOR

Exploded view of the differential carrier assembly — 4WD Axxess

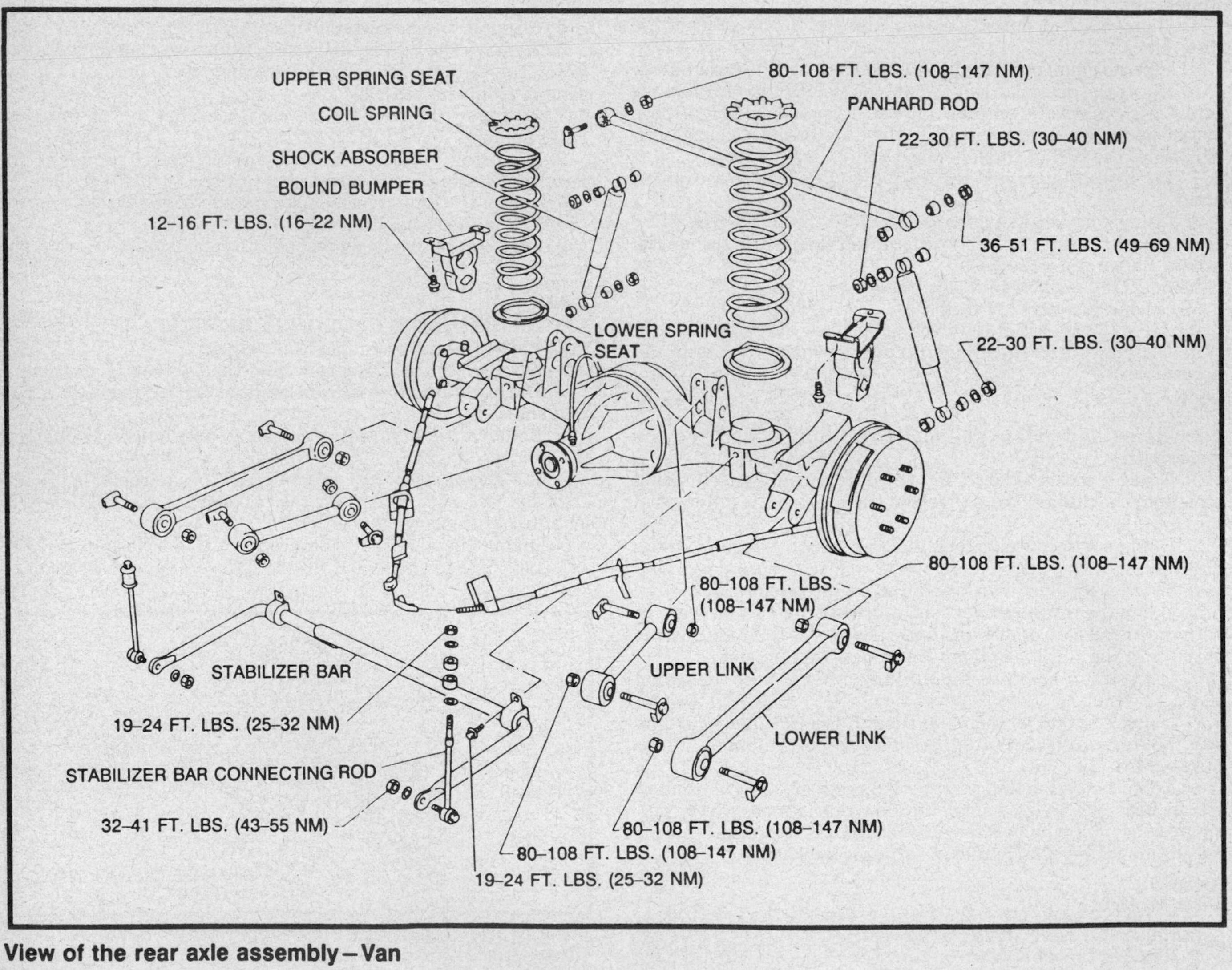

UPPER SPRING SEAT

COIL SPRING

SHOCK ABSORBER

BOUND BUMPER

12–16 FT. LBS. (16–22 NM)

80–108 FT. LBS. (108–147 NM)

PANHARD ROD

22–30 FT. LBS. (30–40 NM)

36–51 FT. LBS. (49–69 NM)

22–30 FT. LBS. (30–40 NM)

LOWER SPRING SEAT

80–108 FT. LBS. (108–147 NM)

80–108 FT. LBS. (108–147 NM)

UPPER LINK

STABILIZER BAR

LOWER LINK

19–24 FT. LBS. (25–32 NM)

STABILIZER BAR CONNECTING ROD

32–41 FT. LBS. (43–55 NM)

80–108 FT. LBS. (108–147 NM)

80–108 FT. LBS. (108–147 NM)

19–24 FT. LBS. (25–32 NM)

View of the rear axle assembly — Van

AXXESS

A differential carrier is used only with 4WD models.
1. Raise and safely support the vehicle.
2. Remove the driveshaft. Separate the halfshafts from the differential carrier.
3. Disconnect the breather hose from the differential carrier.
4. Using a floor jack, support the differential carrier.
5. Remove the differential mounting insulator-to-chassis bolt and the differential carrier-to-crossmember bolts.
6. If necessary, remove the differential crossmember-to-chassis bolts and the crossmember.
7. Lower the differential carrier from the vehicle.
8. To install, reverse the removal procedures. Torque the differential mounting insulator-to-chassis bolt to 43–58 ft. lbs. (59–78 Nm) and the differential carrier-to-crossmember bolts to 43–58 ft. lbs. (59–78 Nm).
9. Connect the driveshaft and halfshafts. Lower the vehicle.

Axle Housing

Removal and Installation

PICK-UP AND PATHFINDER

1. Block the front wheels.
2. Raise and safely support the vehicle. Using a floor jack, position it under the differential and support its weight.
3. Remove the rear wheel/tire assemblies.
4. Using a piece of chalk, make alignment marks on the driveshaft and differential flanges. Remove the driveshaft-to-differential flange nuts/bolts and separate the driveshaft from the differential.
5. If equipped drum brakes, remove the brake drum and disconnect the parking brake cable from the brake assembly. If

equipped with disc brakes, disconnect the parking brake cable from the caliper.
6. Disconnect and plug the brake line from the wheel cylinders or calipers. Disconnect the brake line from the differential clips.
7. Remove the lower shock absorber-to-rear spring pad nut and separate the shock absorber from the rear spring pad.
8. Remove the rear spring pad-to-differential (U-bolt) nuts, the U-bolts and the spring pads.
9. With the rear differential disconnect from the vehicle, move the floor jack to pass it out through either side of the vehicle; pass it out above the springs.
10. To install, reverse the removal procedures. Torque as follows:
   Differential-to-rear spring pad (U-bolts) nuts — 65–72 ft. lbs.
   Lower shock absorber-to-rear spring pad nut — 22–30 ft. lbs.
   Driveshaft-to-differential flange nuts/bolts — 25–33 ft. lbs.
11. Adjust the parking brake. Bleed the rear brake system.

VAN

1. Block the front wheels.
2. Raise and safely support the vehicle. Using a floor jack, position it under the differential and support its weight.
3. Remove the rear wheel/tire assemblies.
4. Using a piece of chalk, make alignment marks on the driveshaft and differential flanges. Remove the driveshaft-to-differential flange nuts/bolts and separate the driveshaft from the differential.
5. Remove the brake drum and disconnect the parking brake cable from the brake assembly.
6. Disconnect and plug the main brake line from the differential junction block.
7. Remove the sway bar-to-chassis nuts/bolts and the sway

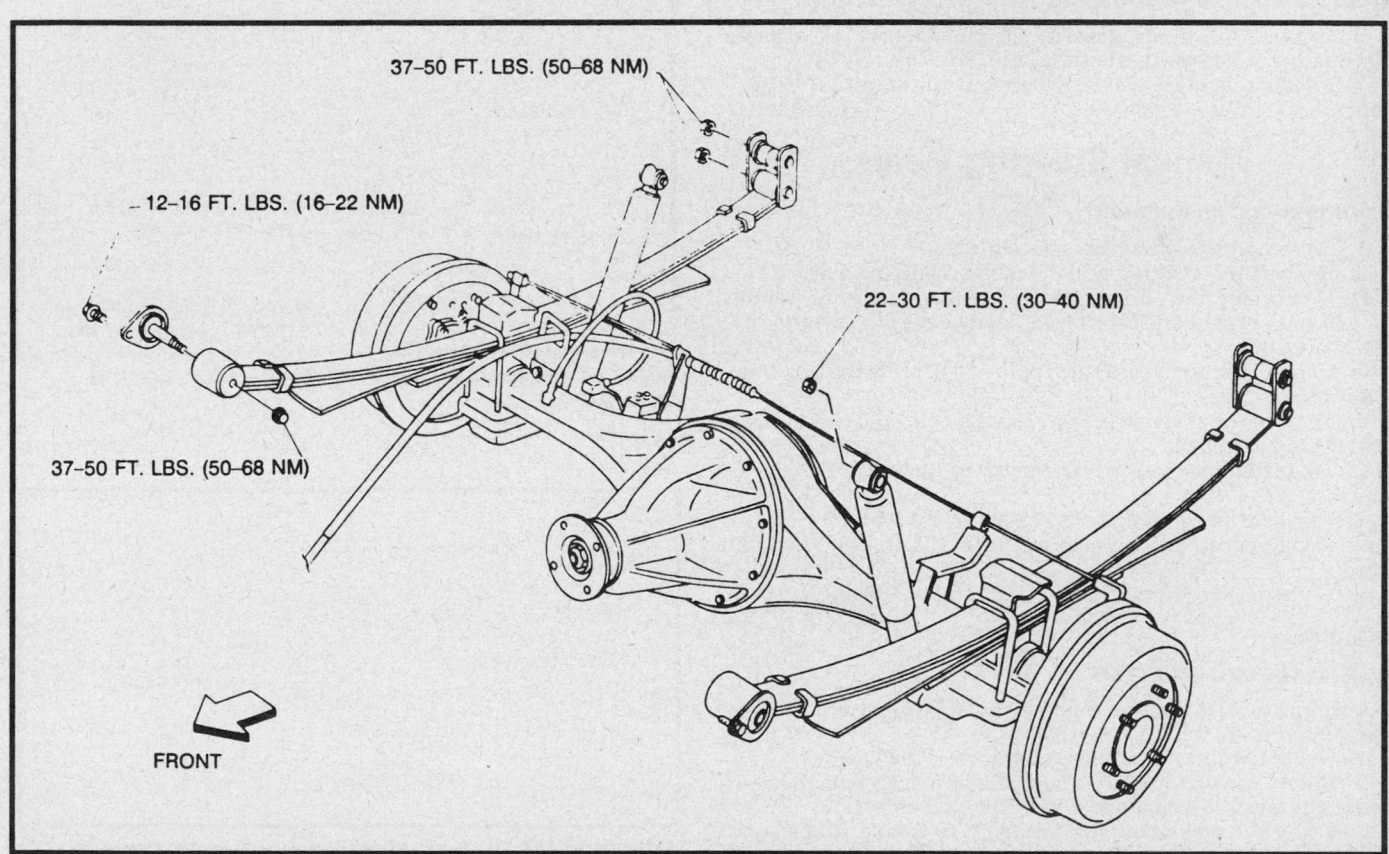

View of the typical rear axle assembly—Pick-Up and Pathfinder

bar-to-differential nuts/bolts and the sway bar from the vehicle.

8. Remove the upper shock absorber-to-chassis nut from inside the vehicle.

NOTE: The upper shock absorber nuts are located inside the vehicle.

9. Remove the panhard rod-to-chassis nut/bolt and lower the rod.

10. Remove the upper and lower links-to-chassis nuts/bolts, then, separate the links from the chassis supports.

11. Lower the differential. Remove the coil spring assemblies and the differential from the vehicle.

12. To install, temporarily tighten all of the links, lower the vehicle to the ground, bounce the vehicle several times and reverse the removal procedures. Torque as follows:

Lower and upper links-to-chassis nuts/bolts—80–94 ft. lbs.
Shock absorber-to-chassis nuts/bolts—12–18 ft. lbs.
Panhard rod-to-chassis nut/bolt—80–94 ft. lbs.
Sway bar-to-chassis nuts/bolts—10–14 ft. lbs.
Sway bar-to-differential—5.8–7.2 ft. lbs.
Driveshaft-to-differential nuts/bolts—25–33 ft. lbs.

STEERING

Steering Wheel

Removal and Installation

1. Position the steering wheel in the straight ahead position.
2. Disconnect the negative battery cable.
3. Remove the horn pad by unscrewing the screws from the rear of the steering wheel crossbar.
4. Matchmark the top of the steering column shaft and the steering wheel flange.
5. Remove the attaching nut and remove the steering wheel with a puller.

NOTE: Do not strike the shaft with a hammer, for the steering column to collapse.

6. Install the steering wheel so the punchmarks are aligned. Torque the steering wheel nut to 22–29 ft. lbs. (29–39 Nm).
7. Install the horn pad and connect the negative battery cable.

Manual Steering Gear

Removal and Installation

1. Raise and safely support the vehicle.
2. Remove the steering gear-to-rubber coupling bolt.
3. Matchmark the pitman arm and sector shaft and with the wheels in a straight ahead position, remove the idler arm-to-sector shaft nut.
4. Using the steering gear arm puller tool, press the arm from the steering gear.
5. Remove the steering gear-to-chassis bolts and the steering gear from the vehicle.
6. To install, reverse the removal procedures. Torque as follows:

Steerig gear-to-coupling bolt—17–22 ft. lbs. (24–29 Nm)
Steering gear-to-pitman arm nut—94–108 ft. lbs. (127–147 Nm)
Steering gear-to-frame bolts—62–71 ft. lbs. (84–96 Nm)

Adjustment
WORM GEAR PRELOAD

For this procedure, the steering gear must be removed from the and placed in a vise.

1. Using the locknut wrench tool, loosen the locknut.
2. Rotate the worm shaft a few times (in both directions) to settle the worm bearing and check the preload.
3. Using the adjusting plug wrench, the torque wrench and an adapter socket, check the worm bearing preload; it should be 1.7–5.2 inch lbs. (0.20–0.59 Nm).

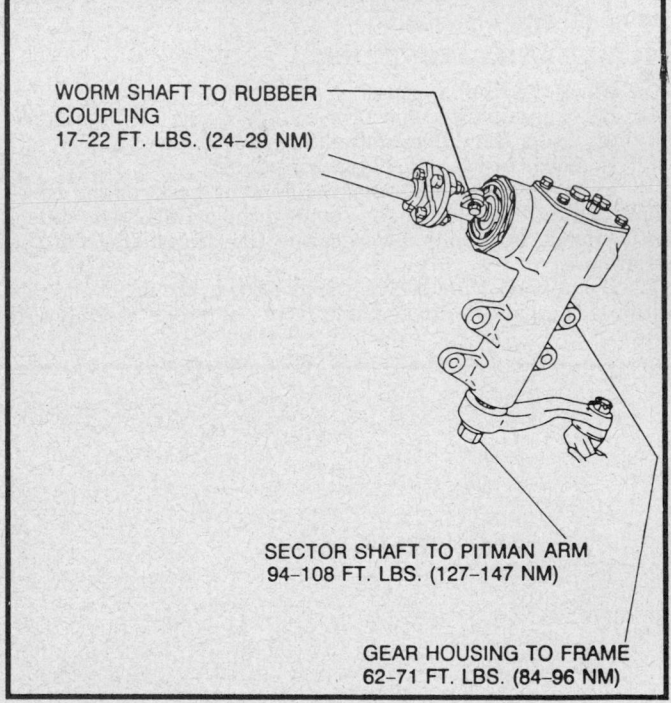

WORM SHAFT TO RUBBER COUPLING 17–22 FT. LBS. (24–29 NM)

SECTOR SHAFT TO PITMAN ARM 94–108 FT. LBS. (127–147 NM)

GEAR HOUSING TO FRAME 62–71 FT. LBS. (84–96 NM)

View of the manual steering gear—Pick-Up and Pathfinder

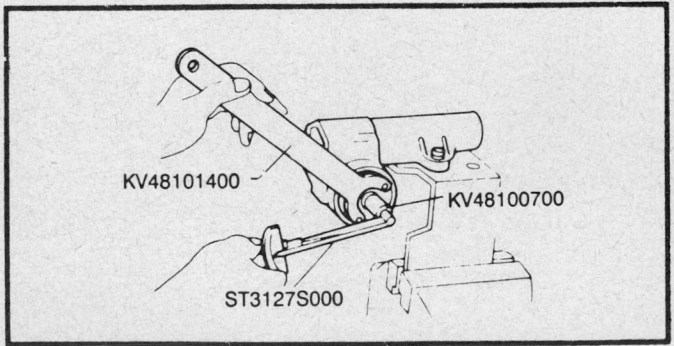

KV48101400   KV48100700   ST3127S000

Adjusting the manual steering worm gear preload—Pick-Up and Pathfinder

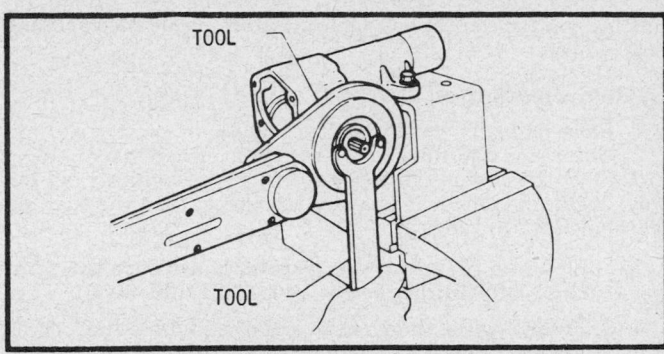

Tightening the manual steering worm gear nut—Pick-Ups and Pathfinder

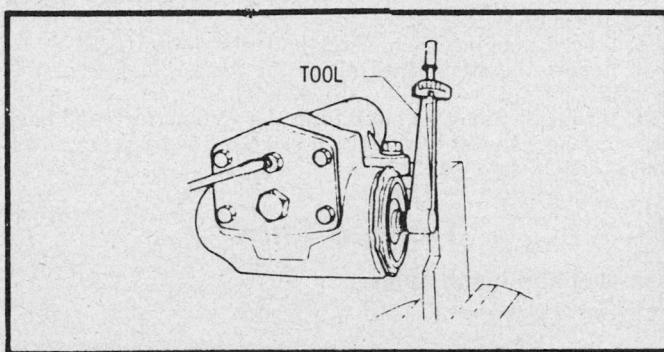

Adjusting the manual steering gear preload—Pick-Ups and Pathfinder

4. If necessary to adjust the worm gear preload, turn the adjusting plug and recheck the preload.

5. With the worm gear preload set, use the adjusting plug wrench, and the locknut wrench, hold the adjusting plug and tighten the locknut.

STEERING GEAR PRELOAD

1. Loosen the adjusting screw locknut.
2. Rotate the worm shaft a few times (in both directions) to settle the worm bearing and check the preload.
3. Set the worm gear in the straight ahead position.
4. Using the torque wrench tool and an adapter socket, check the worm gear preload; it should be 7.4–10.9 inch lbs. (0.83–1.23 Nm) for new parts or 5.2–8.7 inch lbs. (0.59–0.98 Nm) for used parts.
5. If necessary, use a screwdriver, then, turn the adjusting screw to obtain the correct preload.
6. With the preload set, tighten the adjusting screw nut.

Power Steering Gear

Removal and Installation

1. Raise and safely support the vehicle.
2. Remove the wormshaft-to-rubber coupling bolt.
3. Matchmark the idler arm and sector shaft and with the wheels in a straight ahead position, remove the idler arm-to-sector shaft nut.
4. Disconnect the fluid lines from the gear, then, cap the lines and openings in the gear.
5. Using the steering gear arm puller, press the gear arm from the steering knuckle.
6. Remove the steering gear-to-chassis bolts and the steering gear from the vehicle.

7. To install, reverse the removal procedures. Torque as follows:
   Steering gear coupling bolt—17–22 ft. lbs. (49–51 Nm)
   Steering gear-to-pitman arm nut—101–130 ft. lbs. (137–177 Nm)
   Steering gear-to-frame bolts—62–71 ft. lbs. (84–96 Nm).
8. Refill the power steering pump reservoir and bleed the system.

Adjustment

1. Remove the power steering gear and position it in a vise.
2. Loosen the adjusting screw locknut.
3. Set the worm gear in the straight ahead position.
4. Using the torque wrench and an adapter socket, check the turning torque; it should be 0.9–3.5 inch lbs. (0.1–0.4 Nm).
5. If necessary, use a screwdriver, then, turn the adjusting screw to obtain the correct preload.
6. With the preload set, tighten the adjusting screw nut.

Power Steering Rack

Removal and Installation

1. Raise and safely support the vehicle.
2. Remove the wheel assemblies.
3. Remove the tie rod-to-steering knuckle cotter pins and nuts. Using a tie rod end separator tool, separate the tie rod ends from the steering knuckles.
4. Remove the rubber coupling-to-steering rack pinch bolt.
5. Disconnect and plug the power steering lines from the steering rack.
6. Remove the power steering rack-to-chassis bracket bolts and the brackets.
7. Remove the power steering rack from the vehicle.
8. To install, reverse the removal procedures. Torque the power steering rack-to-chassis bracket bolts to 54–72 ft. lbs. (73–97 Nm), the tie rod end-to-steering knuckle nuts to 22–29 ft. lbs. (29–39 Nm); be sure to install new cotter pins.
9. Using new O-rings, install the power steering pressure lines to the steering rack.
10. Refill the power steering pump reservoir and bleed the system.
11. Lower the vehicle.

Adjustment

The power steering rack must be removed from the vehicle and positioned in a vise.
1. Without fluid in the rack, set the gears in the neutral position.
2. Lubricate the adjusting screw with locking sealant and screw it in.
3. Lightly, tighten the locknut.
4. Torque the adjusting screw to 43–52 inch lbs. (4.9–5.9 Nm).
5. Loosen the adjusting screw and retorque it to 0.43–1.74 inch lbs. (0.05–0.20 Nm).
6. Move the rack over its entire stroke several times.
7. Using an inch lb. torque wrench, measure the pinion rotating torque within the range of 180 degrees from the neutral position.
8. Loosen the adjusting screw and retorque it to 43–52 inch lbs. (4.9–5.9 Nm).
9. Loosen the adjusting screw 40–60 degrees.
10. While securing the adjusting screw in position, torque the locknut to 29–43 ft. lbs. (39–59 Nm).
11. Using a spring gauge, connect it to the tie rod end, pull the tie rod to check the frictional sliding force; it should be 27.6–37.5 lbs. (122.6–166.7 N) at neutral point or 27.6–41.9 lbs. (122.6–186.3 N) other than neutral point.

Power Steering Pump

Removal and Installation

1. Disconnect the negative battery cable.
2. Remove the drive belt from the power steering pump.
3. Place a container under the power steering pump, then, disconnect/plug the pressure lines and drain the fluid into the container.
4. Remove the power steering pump-to-engine bolts and the pump from the vehicle.
5. To install, reverse the removal procedures. Adjust the drive belt tension. Bleed the power steering system.

Belt Adjustment

1. Loosen the drive belt adjustment screw.
2. Inspect and adjust the belt deflection:

Axxess
    Used belt — 0.24–28 in. (6–7mm)
    New belt — 0.20–0.24 in. (5–6mm)
Pick-Up and Pathfinder
  2.4L Engine
    Used belt — 0.35–0.43 in. (9–11mm)
    New belt — 0.28–0.35 in. (7–9mm)
  2.5L Engine
    Used belt — 0.55–0.63 in. (14–16mm)
    New belt — 0.47–0.55 in. (12–14mm)
  3.0L Engine
    Used belt — 0.43–0.51 in. (11–13mm)
    New belt — 0.35–0.43 in. (9–11mm)
Van
    Used belt — 0.35–0.39 in. (9–10mm)
    New belt — 0.28–0.35 in. (7–9mm)

3. Adjust the correct belt tension and retorque the adjusting bolt locknut.

System Bleeding

1. Raise and support the vehicle safely.
2. Check and add fluid to the reservoir, if necessary.
3. Start the engine. Turn the steering wheel quickly (all the way), right and left, just touching the stops; turn the steering wheel at least 10 times.

NOTE: When bleeding the system, make sure the temperature of the fluid reaches 140–176°F (60–80°C).

4. Stop the engine, then, check and/or add more fluid.
5. Start and run the engine for 3–5 seconds.
6. Stop the engine, then, check and/or add more fluid.
7. Start the engine. Turn the steering wheel (all the way) right and left, just touching the stops; turn the steering wheel at least 10 times.
8. Stop the engine, then, check and/or add more fluid.
9. Repeat the steps until all of the air is bleed from the system.
10. If the air cannot be bleed from the system, turn and hold the steering wheel at each stop for at least 5 seconds but never more than 15 seconds.

Tie Rod Ends

Removal and Installation

EXCEPT AXXESS

1. Raise and safely support the vehicle. Remove the wheel/tire assembly.

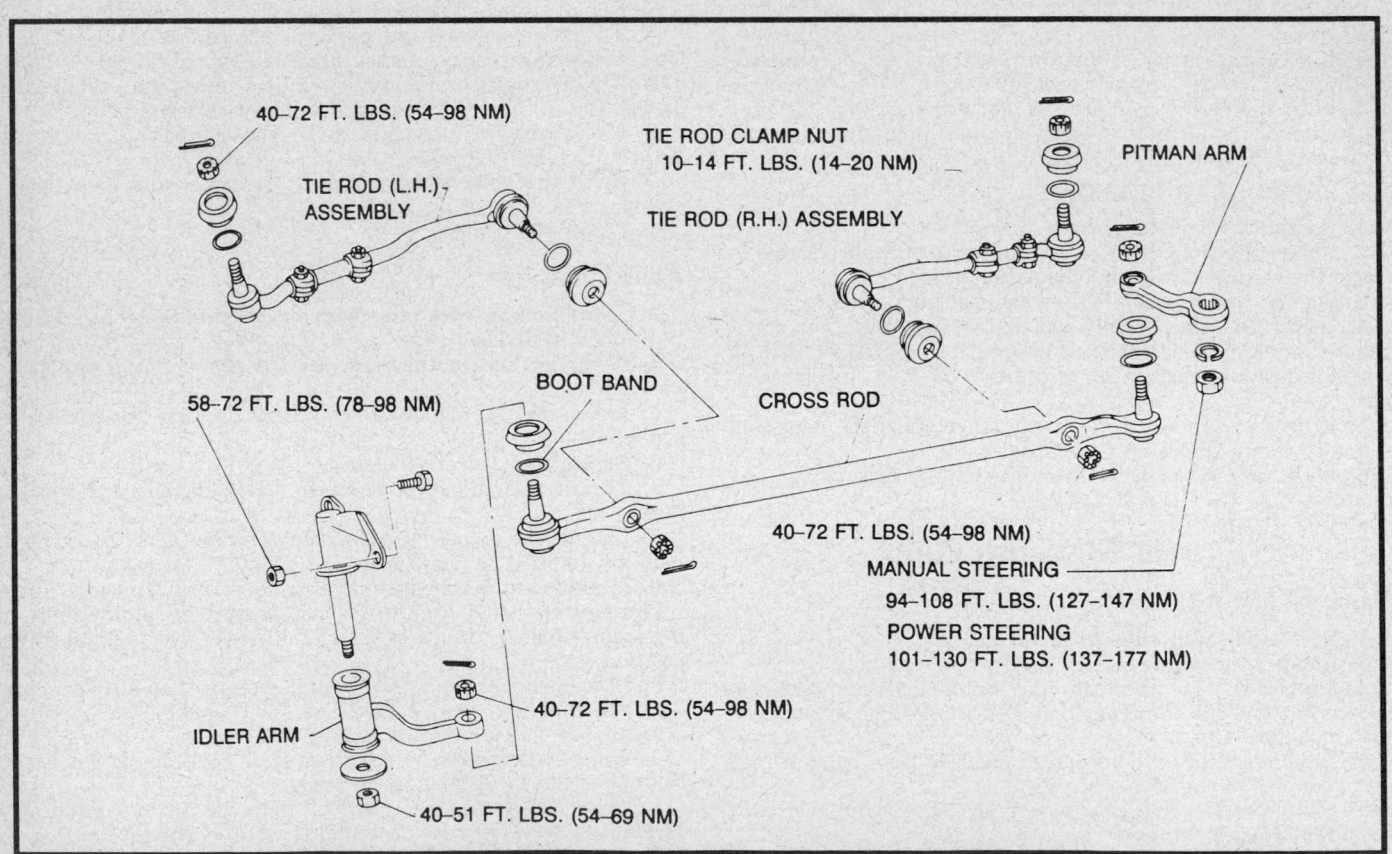

Exploded view of the steering linkage assembly — 2WD Pick-Up and 2WD Pathfinder

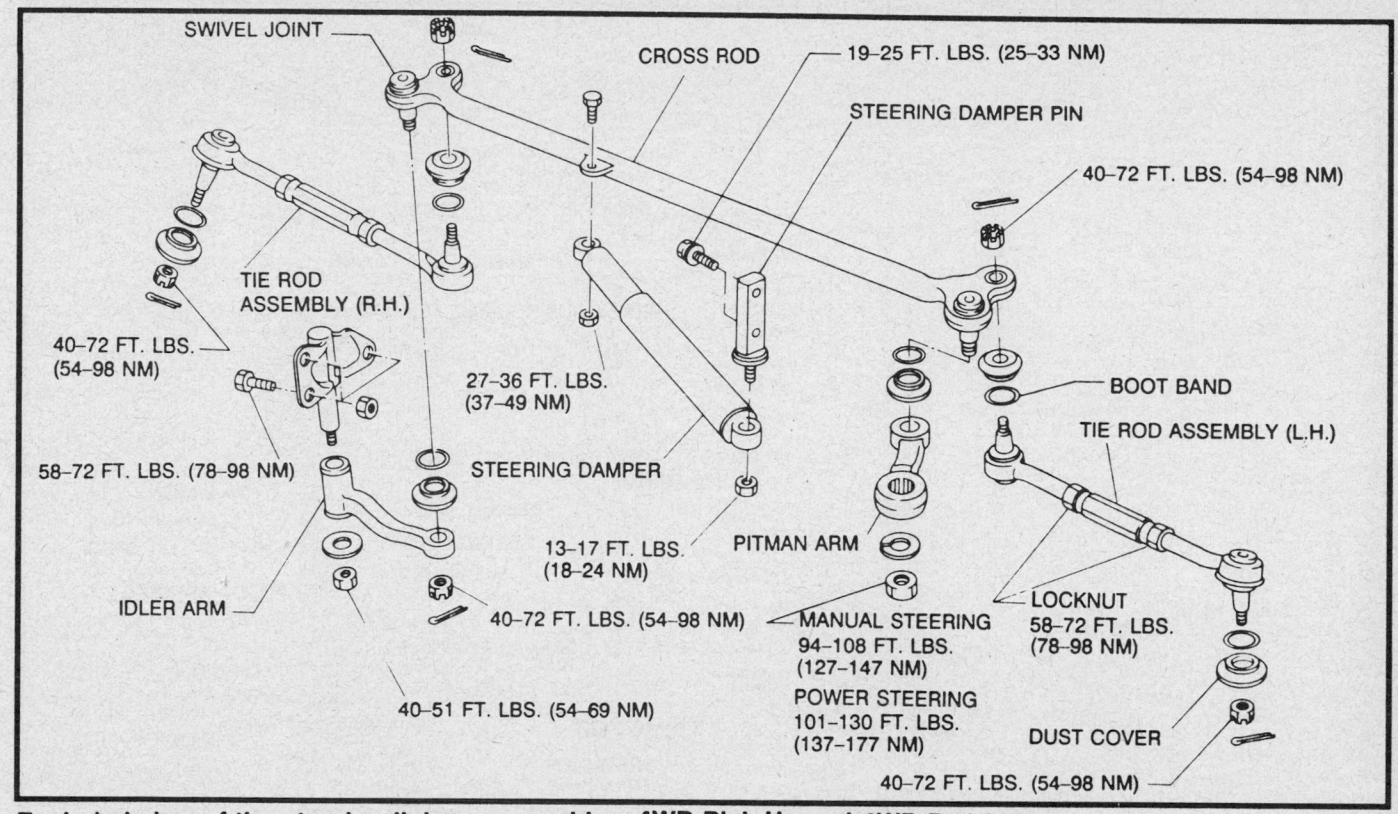

SWIVEL JOINT

CROSS ROD

19–25 FT. LBS. (25–33 NM)

STEERING DAMPER PIN

40–72 FT. LBS. (54–98 NM)

TIE ROD ASSEMBLY (R.H.)

40–72 FT. LBS. (54–98 NM)

58–72 FT. LBS. (78–98 NM)

27–36 FT. LBS. (37–49 NM)

BOOT BAND

TIE ROD ASSEMBLY (L.H.)

STEERING DAMPER

IDLER ARM

13–17 FT. LBS. (18–24 NM)

PITMAN ARM

40–72 FT. LBS. (54–98 NM)

MANUAL STEERING 94–108 FT. LBS. (127–147 NM)

LOCKNUT 58–72 FT. LBS. (78–98 NM)

40–51 FT. LBS. (54–69 NM)

POWER STEERING 101–130 FT. LBS. (137–177 NM)

DUST COVER

40–72 FT. LBS. (54–98 NM)

Exploded view of the steering linkage assembly– 4WD Pick-Up and 4WD Pathfinder

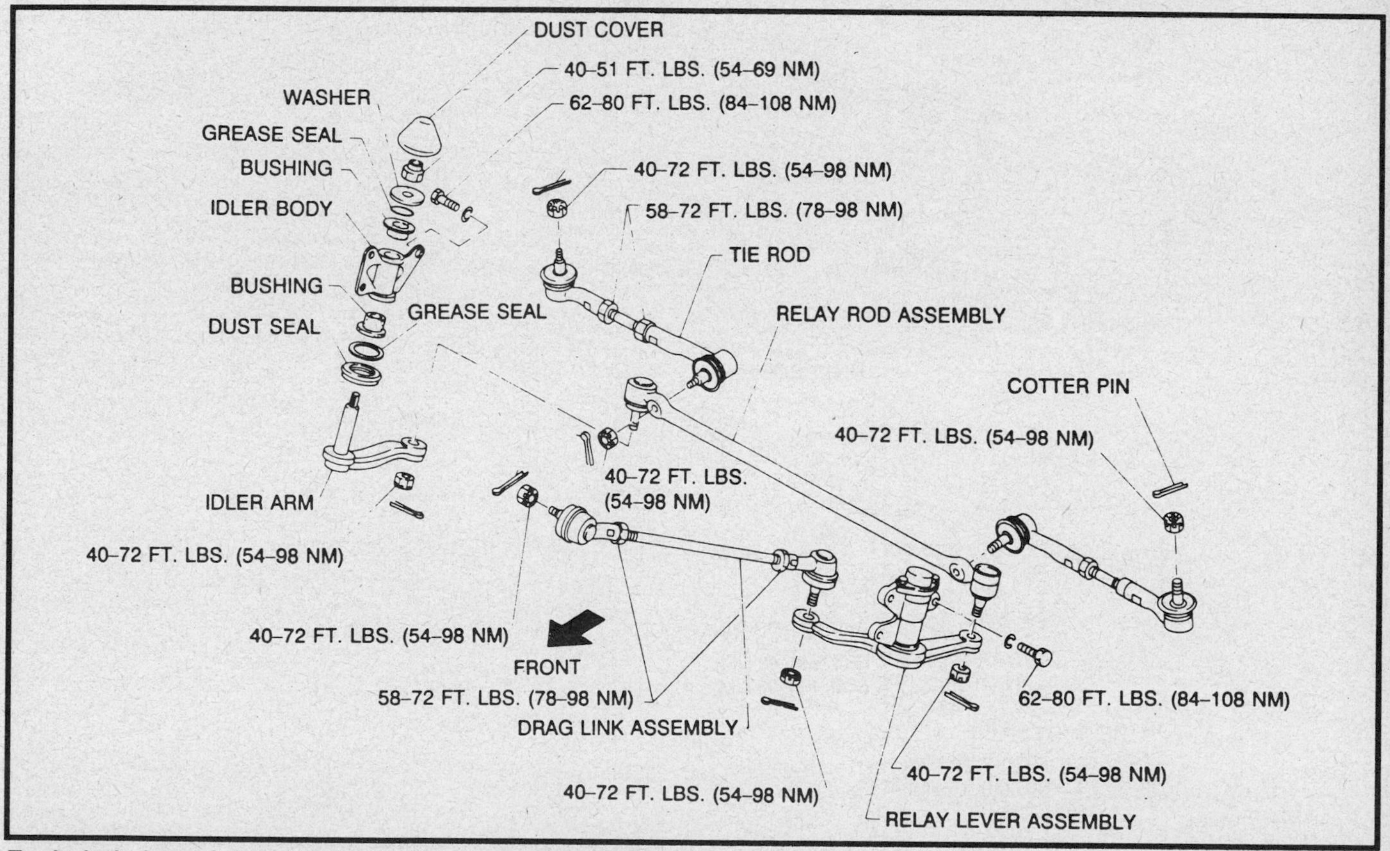

DUST COVER

40–51 FT. LBS. (54–69 NM)

WASHER

62–80 FT. LBS. (84–108 NM)

GREASE SEAL

BUSHING

40–72 FT. LBS. (54–98 NM)

IDLER BODY

58–72 FT. LBS. (78–98 NM)

TIE ROD

BUSHING

DUST SEAL

GREASE SEAL

RELAY ROD ASSEMBLY

COTTER PIN

40–72 FT. LBS. (54–98 NM)

IDLER ARM

40–72 FT. LBS. (54–98 NM)

40–72 FT. LBS. (54–98 NM)

40–72 FT. LBS. (54–98 NM)

FRONT

58–72 FT. LBS. (78–98 NM)

DRAG LINK ASSEMBLY

62–80 FT. LBS. (84–108 NM)

40–72 FT. LBS. (54–98 NM)

40–72 FT. LBS. (54–98 NM)

RELAY LEVER ASSEMBLY

Exploded view of the steering linkage assembly–Van

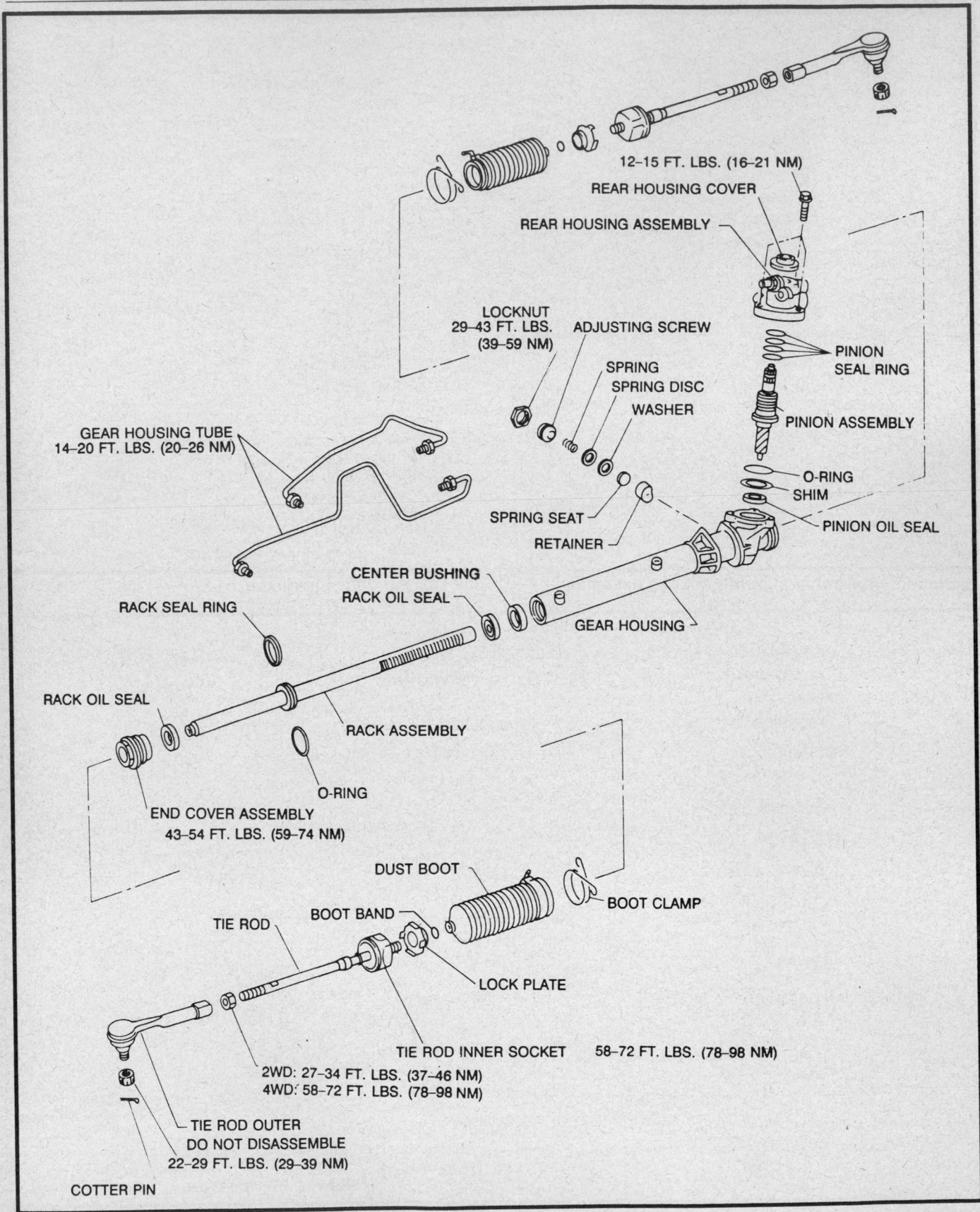

12–15 FT. LBS. (16–21 NM)
REAR HOUSING COVER

REAR HOUSING ASSEMBLY

LOCKNUT
29–43 FT. LBS.
(39–59 NM)

ADJUSTING SCREW

SPRING
SPRING DISC
WASHER

PINION SEAL RING

PINION ASSEMBLY

GEAR HOUSING TUBE
14–20 FT. LBS. (20–26 NM)

SPRING SEAT
RETAINER

O-RING
SHIM
PINION OIL SEAL

CENTER BUSHING
RACK OIL SEAL

GEAR HOUSING

RACK SEAL RING

RACK OIL SEAL

RACK ASSEMBLY

O-RING

END COVER ASSEMBLY
43–54 FT. LBS. (59–74 NM)

DUST BOOT

BOOT BAND

BOOT CLAMP

TIE ROD

LOCK PLATE

TIE ROD INNER SOCKET   58–72 FT. LBS. (78–98 NM)
2WD: 27–34 FT. LBS. (37–46 NM)
4WD: 58–72 FT. LBS. (78–98 NM)

TIE ROD OUTER
DO NOT DISASSEMBLE
22–29 FT. LBS. (29–39 NM)

COTTER PIN

Exploded view of the steering rack assembly— Axxess

2. If removing the tie rod as an assembly, perform the following procedure:

   a. Remove the tie rod-to-cross rod cotter pin (discard it) and nut.

   b. Remove the tie rods-to-steering knuckle cotter pin (discard it) and nut.

   c. Using the ball joint remover tool, press the tie rod from the steering knuckle and the tie rod from the cross rod.

3. If removing a defective tie rod end, perform the following procedure:

   a. Remove the tie rod-to-cross rod/steering knuckle cotter pin (discard it) and nut.

   b. Loosen the tie rod end-to-tie rod clamp or locknut.

   c. Using the ball joint remover tool, press the tie rod from the cross rod/steering knuckle and the tie rod from the cross rod/steering knuckle.

   d. Measure the tie rod end-to-tie rod clamp distance.

   e. Unscrew the tie rod end from the tie rod.

   f. Using a new tie rod end, screw the new tie rod end into the tie rod clamp until the measured distance is the same, then, torque the tie rod clamp bolt to 10–14 ft. lbs. (14–20 Nm) or nut to 58–72 ft. lbs. (78–98 Nm).

4. Inspect the tie rod ball joint for wear; if necessary, replace it.

5. To install, use new cotter pins and reverse the removal procedures.

cedures. Torque the tie rod-to-steering knuckle nut to 40–72 ft. lbs. (54–98 Nm) and the tie rod-to-cross rod nut to 40–72 ft. lbs. (54–98 Nm). Check and/or adjust the front-end alignment.

AXXESS

1. Raise and safely support the vehicle.

2. Remove the wheel assembly.

3. Remove the tie rod end-to-steering knuckle cotter pin and nut. Using a tie rod removal tool, separate the tie rod end from the steering knuckle.

4. Loosen the tie rod-to-tie rod end locknut.

5. While counting the number of turns, remove the tie rod end from the tie rod.

6. To install, screw the tie rod end onto the tie rod the same number of turns necessary to remove it.

7. Install the tie rod end into the steering knuckle. Torque as follows:

Tie rod end-to-steering knuckle nut — 22–29 ft. lbs. (29–39 Nm)

Tie rod end-to-tie rod locknut

   2WD — 27–34 ft. lbs. (37–46 Nm)

   4WD — 58–72 ft. lbs. (78–98 Nm)

8. To complete the installation, reverse the removal procedures. Check and or adjust the front wheel alignment.

BRAKES

For all brake system repair and service procedures not detailed below, please refer to "Brakes" in the Unit Repair section.

Master Cylinder

NOTE: Be careful not to spill brake fluid on the painted surfaces of the vehicle; it will damage the paint.

Removal and Installation

1. Disconnect the negative battery cable.

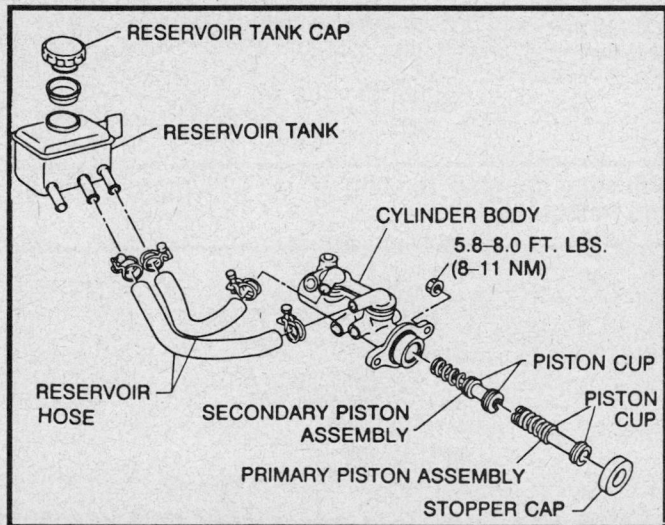

Exploded view of the Axxess master cylinder – Van is similar

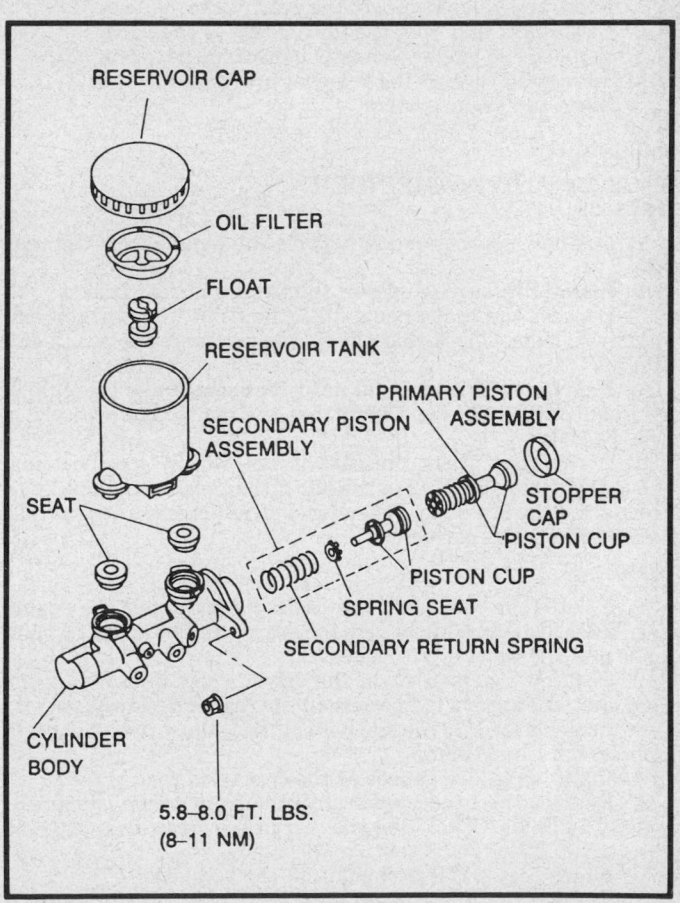

Exploded view of the master cylinder – Pick-Up and Pathfinder

2. Using a syringe, remove the brake fluid from the master cylinder.

3. Disconnect and plug the hydraulic lines at the master cylinder.

4. If equipped, disconnect the level warning switch connector from the master cylinder.

5. Remove the master cylinder mounting bolts, by performing one of the following procedures:

   a. If not equipped with power brakes, remove the master cylinder-to-cowl bolts and the clevis pin from the brake pedal. Remove the master cylinder.

   b. If equipped with power brakes, remove the master cylinder-to-power booster nuts and the master cylinder assembly from the power brake unit.

6. To install, reverse the removal procedures. Torque the master cylinder nuts to 6–8 ft. lbs. and the brake lines-to-master cylinder to 11–13 ft. lbs. Refill the master cylinder with new brake fluid and bleed the brake system.

NOTE: Before tightening the master cylinder mounting nuts or bolts, screw the hydraulic line fitting into the cylinder body a few turns.

Load Sensing Proportioning Valve

The purpose of this valve is to control the fluid pressure applied to the brakes to prevent rear wheel lock-up during weight transfer at high speed stops.

Removal and Installation

1. Raise and safely support the rear of the vehicle.
2. Disconnect and plug the lines going to the valve.
3. Remove the valve-to-chassis bolts and the valve.
4. To install, reverse the removal procedures.
5. Bleed the brake system.

Adjustment

PICK-UP AND PATHFINDER
1986–89

1. Position approximately 220 lbs. of weight over the rear axle.
2. Install pressure gauges at the front and rear brakes.
3. Depress the brake pedal until the front brake is approximately 711 lbs. Check that the rear brake pressure is 327–469 lbs.
4. Depress the brake pedal until the front brake pressure is approximately 1422 lbs. Check that the rear brake pressure is 455–654 lbs.
5. If the rear brake pressure is not within specifications, move the spring bracket to the left if the pressure is high or to the right if the pressure is low. Repeat this process until the rear brake pressure is correct.

1990

1. Ensure the fuel tank, the cooling system and the engine crankcase are filled. Make sure the spare tire, the jack, the hand tools and the mats are installed.
2. Position a person sit in the driver's seat and one on the rear end;, then, have the person on the rear end, slowly, get off.
3. Attach a lever to the stopper bolt and adjust the lenght **L** to approx. 7.44 in. (189mm).
4. Install pressure gauges at the front and rear brakes.
5. Depress the brake pedal until the front brake is approximately 1422 lbs. Check that the rear brake pressure is 327–441 lbs.
6. Slowly, set a 220 lb. weight on the rear axle.
7. Depress the brake pedal until the front brake pressure is approximately 1422 lbs. Check that the rear brake pressure is 711–995 lbs. for except heavy duty or 640–924 for heavy duty.

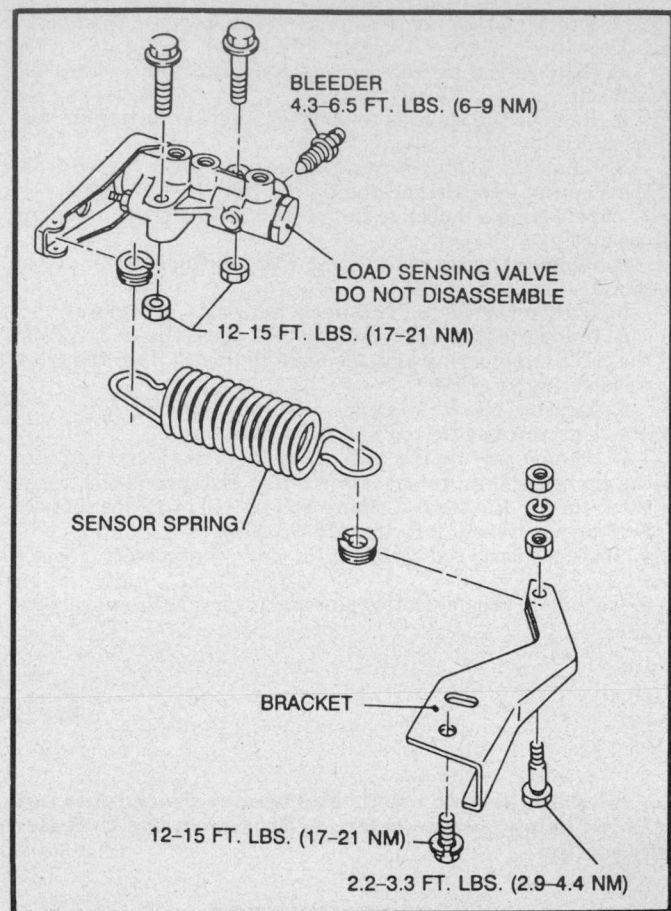

Exploded view of the load sensing valve—Pick-Up and Pathfinder

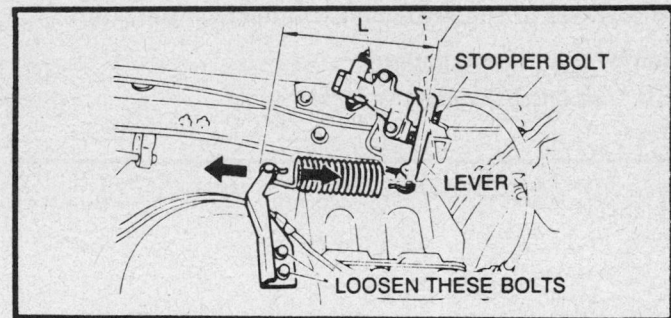

Adjusting the load sensing valve "L" length—Pick-Up and Pathfinder

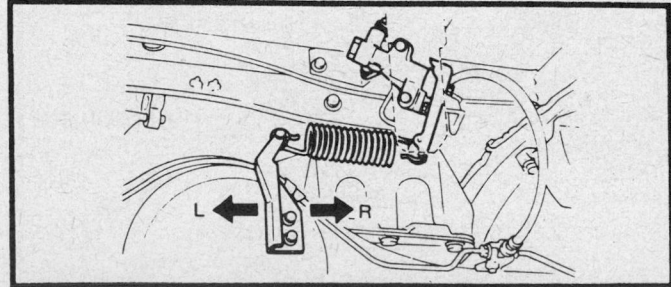

Adjusting the load sensing valve to proper specification—Pick-Up and Pathfinder

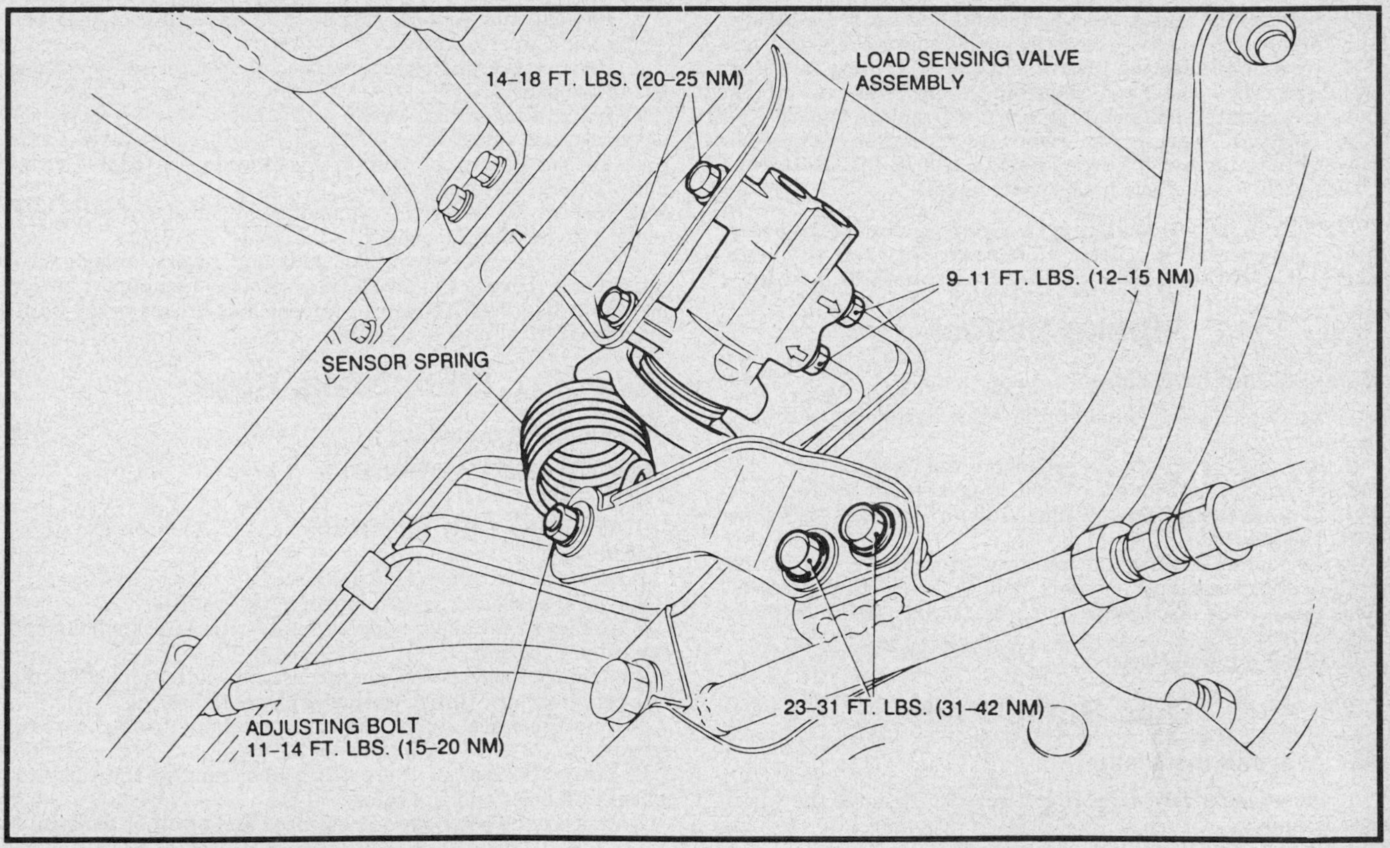

14–18 FT. LBS. (20–25 NM)

LOAD SENSING VALVE ASSEMBLY

9–11 FT. LBS. (12–15 NM)

SENSOR SPRING

23–31 FT. LBS. (31–42 NM)

ADJUSTING BOLT 11–14 FT. LBS. (15–20 NM)

View of the load sensing valve—Axxess

8. If the rear brake pressure is above specification, adjust the bracket in the **L** direction.

9. If the rear brake pressure is below specification, adjust the bracket in the **R** direction.

AXXESS

1. Position a person sit in the driver's seat and position 1544 lbs. over the rear axle.

2. Install pressure gauges at the front and rear brakes.

3. Bleed the air from the front and rear brake lines.

4. Depress the brake pedal until the front brake is approximately 711 lbs. Check that the rear brake pressure is 455–597 lbs. for 2WD, 5 passenger model, 412–555 for 2WD, 7 passenger model, 370–512 lbs. for 4WD, 5 passenger model, 341–483 for 4WD, 7 passenger model.

5. Depress the brake pedal until the front brake pressure is approximately 1422 lbs. Check that the rear brake pressure is 455–597 lbs. for 2WD, 5 passenger model, 412–555 for 2WD, 7 passenger model, 370–512 lbs. for 4WD, 5 passenger model, 341–483 for 4WD, 7 passenger model.

6. If the rear brake pressure is above specification, adjust the bracket in the **A** direction.

7. If the rear brake pressure is below specification, adjust the bracket in the **B** direction.

8. If necesary, repeat the pressure procedure.

9. If the pressure is outside the specified range after the spring length is adjusted, replace the load sensing valve assembly.

Power Brake Booster

Removal and Installation

1. Disconnect the negative battery cable.

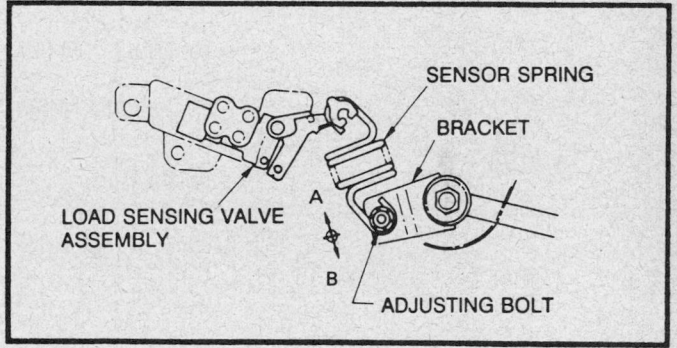

SENSOR SPRING

BRACKET

LOAD SENSING VALVE ASSEMBLY

A

B

ADJUSTING BOLT

View of the load sensing valve—2WD Axxess

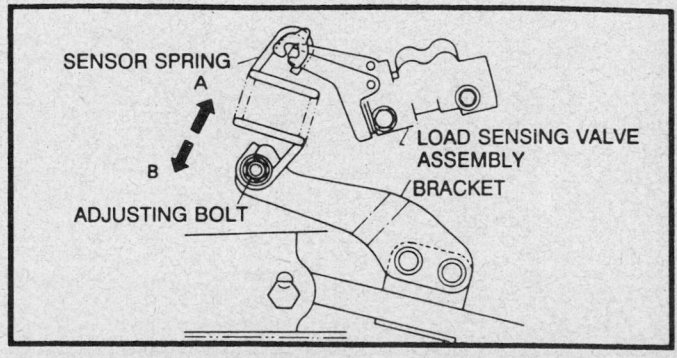

SENSOR SPRING

A

B

LOAD SENSING VALVE ASSEMBLY

BRACKET

ADJUSTING BOLT

View of the load sensing valve—4WD Axxess

2. Remove the master cylinder from the power brake booster.

3. Remove the vacuum hose form the power brake booster.

4. Working under the instrument panel, remove the brake pedal-to-brake booster rod clevis pin. Remove the power brake booster mounting bolts and the booster from the vehicle.

5. To install, reverse the removal procedures. Torque the power brake booster-to-cowl nuts to 5.8–8 ft. lbs. (8–11 Nm). Check and/or adjust the brake pedal height.

NOTE: When installing the power brake booster, make sure there is a little clearance between the push-rod end and the master cylinder piston; 0.40–0.41 in.

Brake Caliper

Removal and Installation

1. Raise and safely support the vehicle. Remove the wheel assembly.

2. Remove the disc brake pads from the caliper.

3. Disconnect and plug the brake hose from the brake caliper.

4. Remove the caliper-to-caliper support bolt and the caliper from the vehicle.

5. To install, reverse the removal procedures. Torque the brake caliper-to-caliper support bolt to 53–72 ft. lbs. (72–97 Nm) except rear disc brakes or 28–38 ft. lbs. (38–52 Nm) rear disc brakes.

6. Bleed the brake system.

Disc Brake Pads

Removal and Installation

1. Raise and safely support the vehicle. Remove the wheel/tire assembly.

2. Remove the bottom caliper-to-caliper support bolt and swing the caliper upward.

3. Remove the pad retainers, the inner/outer retainers and the brake pads.

4. Using a medium C-clamp and a block of wood, place the wood against the caliper piston(s), then, using the C-clamp press the piston into the caliper; this procedure is to make clearance for the new brake pads.

5. Inspect the caliper for signs of fluid leakage; if necessary, replace or rebuild the caliper.

6. To install, use new brake pads and reverse the removal procedures. Torque the brake caliper-to-caliper support bolt to 53–72 ft. lbs. (72–97 Nm) except rear disc brakes or 28–38 ft. lbs. (38–52 Nm) rear disc brakes.

Front Brake Rotor

Removal and Installation
PICK-UP AND PATHFINDER
2WD

1. Raise and safely support the vehicle. Remove the wheel assembly.

2. Remove the calipers; do not disconnect the brake hose. Using a wire, suspend the calipers from the vehicle.

3. Remove the caliper support-to-steering knuckle bolts and the caliper support.

4. Remove the wheel bearing grease cup, cotter pin, adjusting nut cap, hub nut, thrust washer and wheel bearing.

5. Pull the wheel hub/brake rotor assembly from the wheel spindle.

6. From the rear of the brake rotor, remove the rotor-to-wheel hub bolts and the rotor.

7. Inspect the rotor for cracks, wear and/or other damage; if

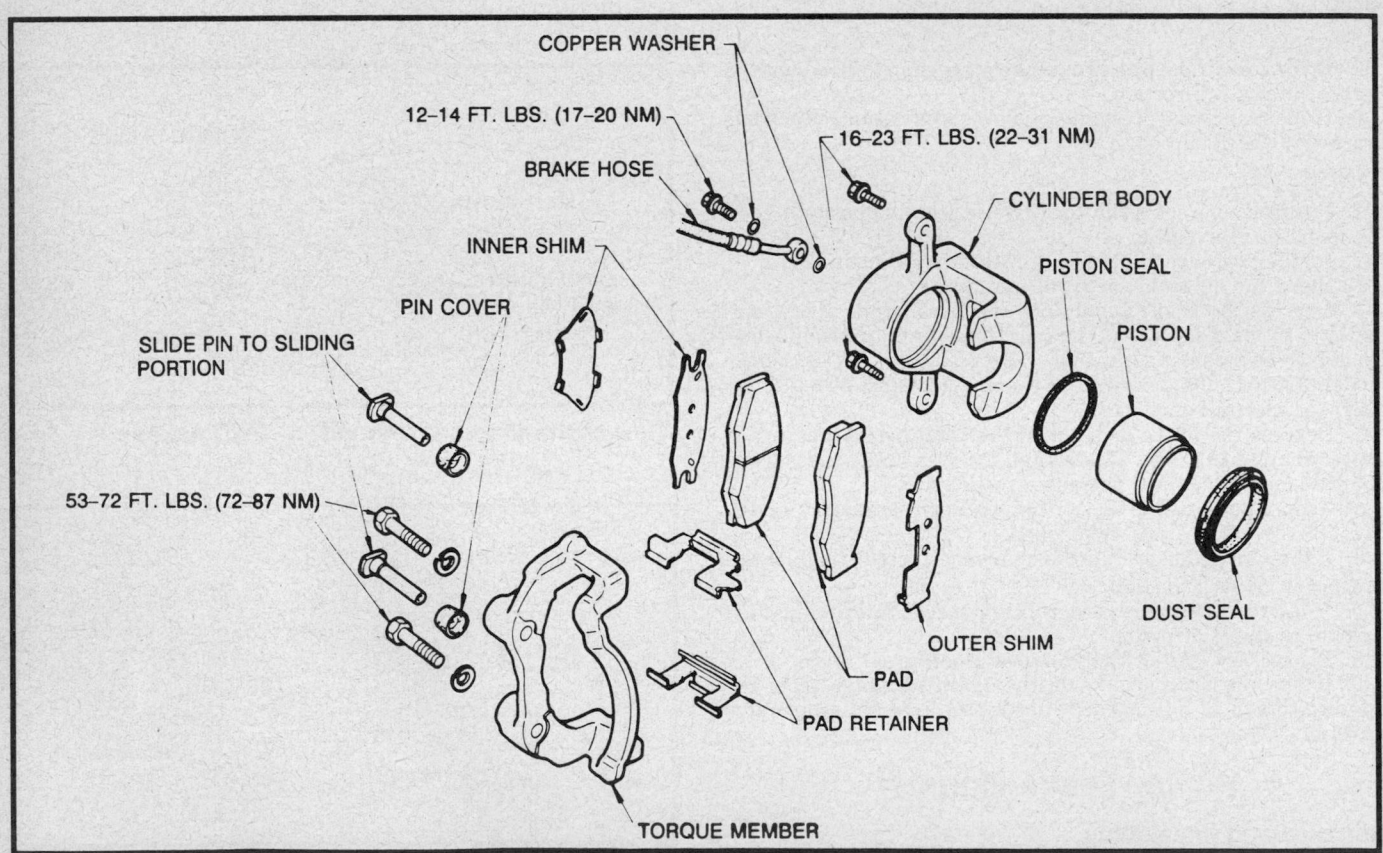

Exploded view of the single piston front disc brake assembly — Pick-Up and Pathfinder

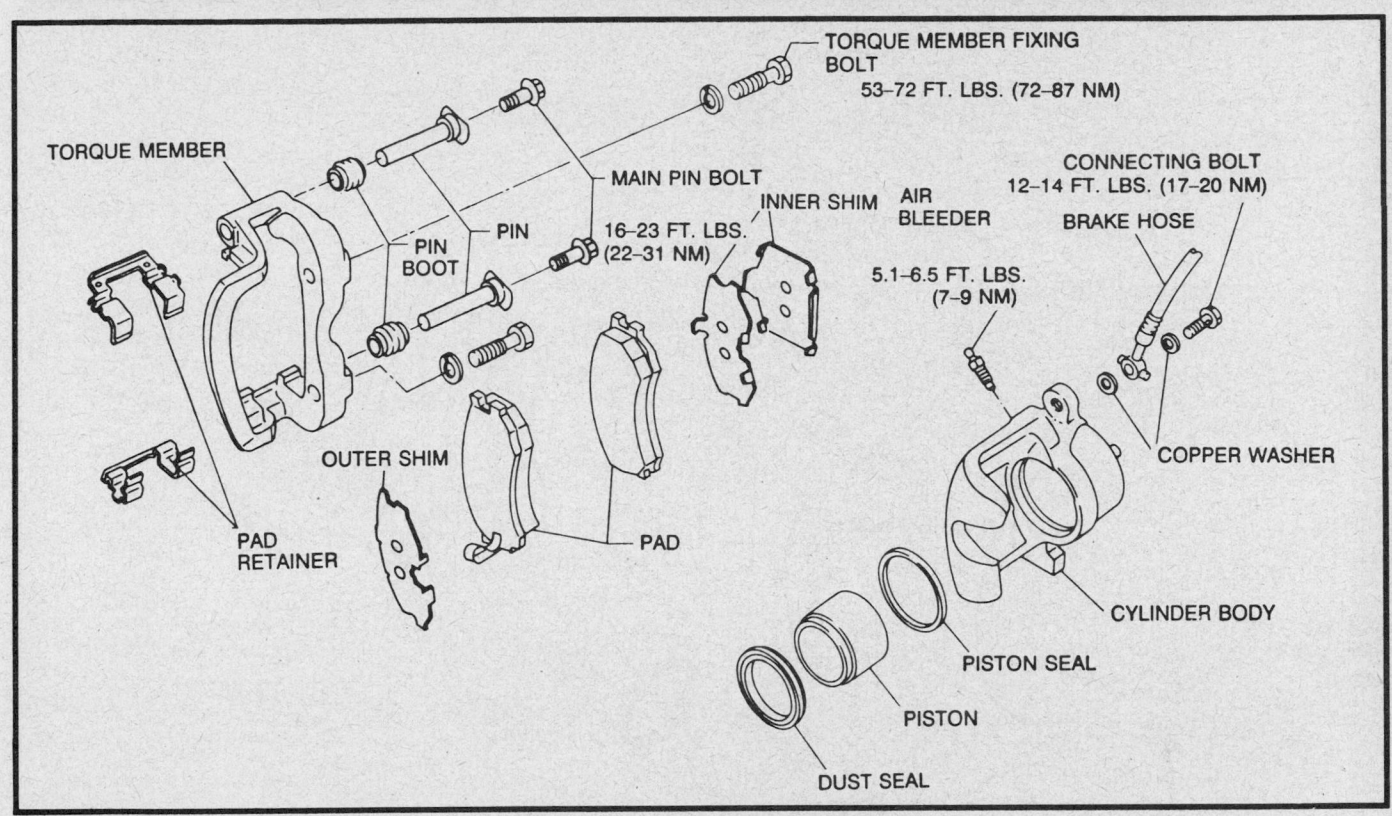

Exploded view of the single piston front disc brake assembly—Axxess

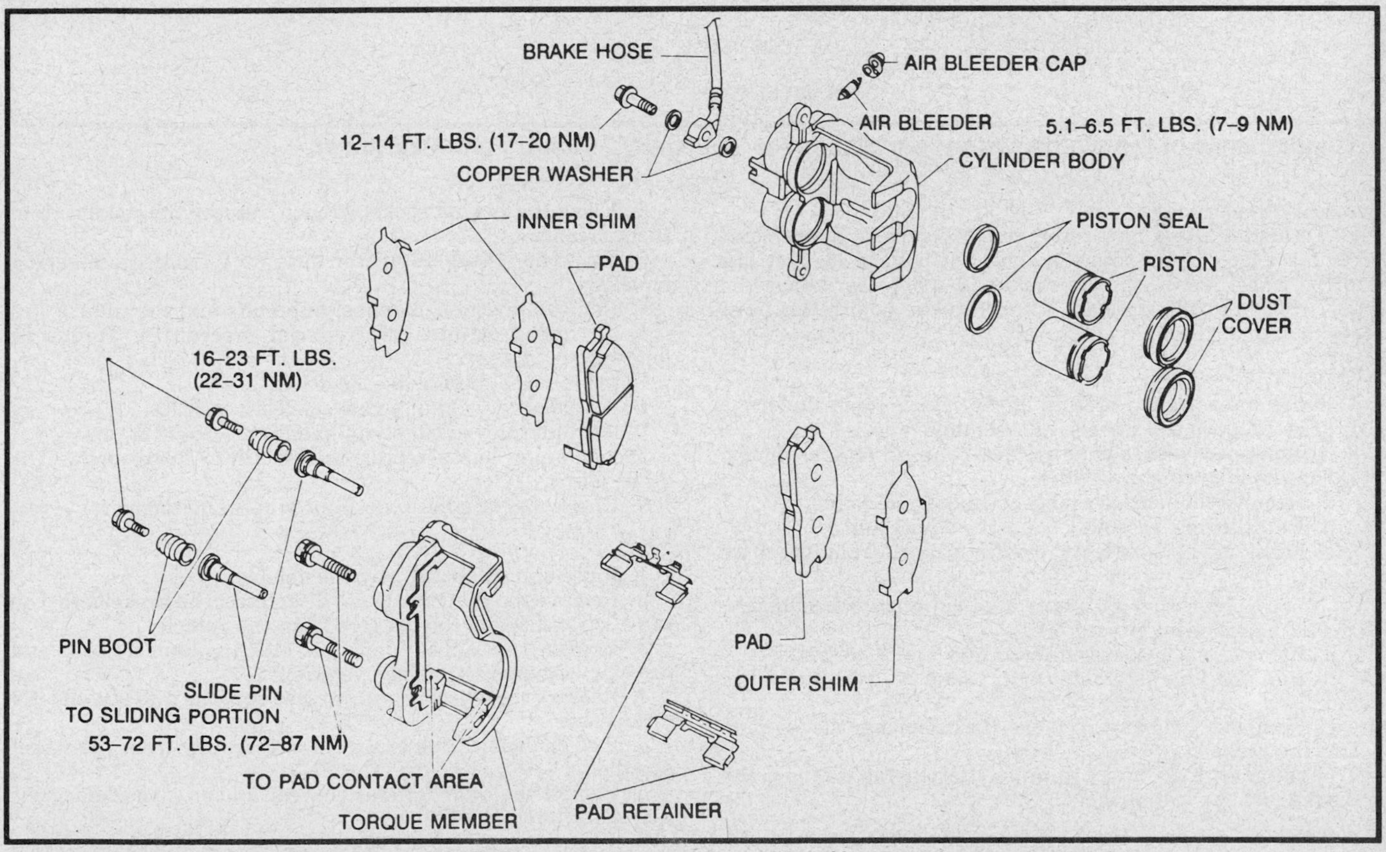

Exploded view of the dual piston front disc brake assembly—Pick-Up, Pathfinder and Van

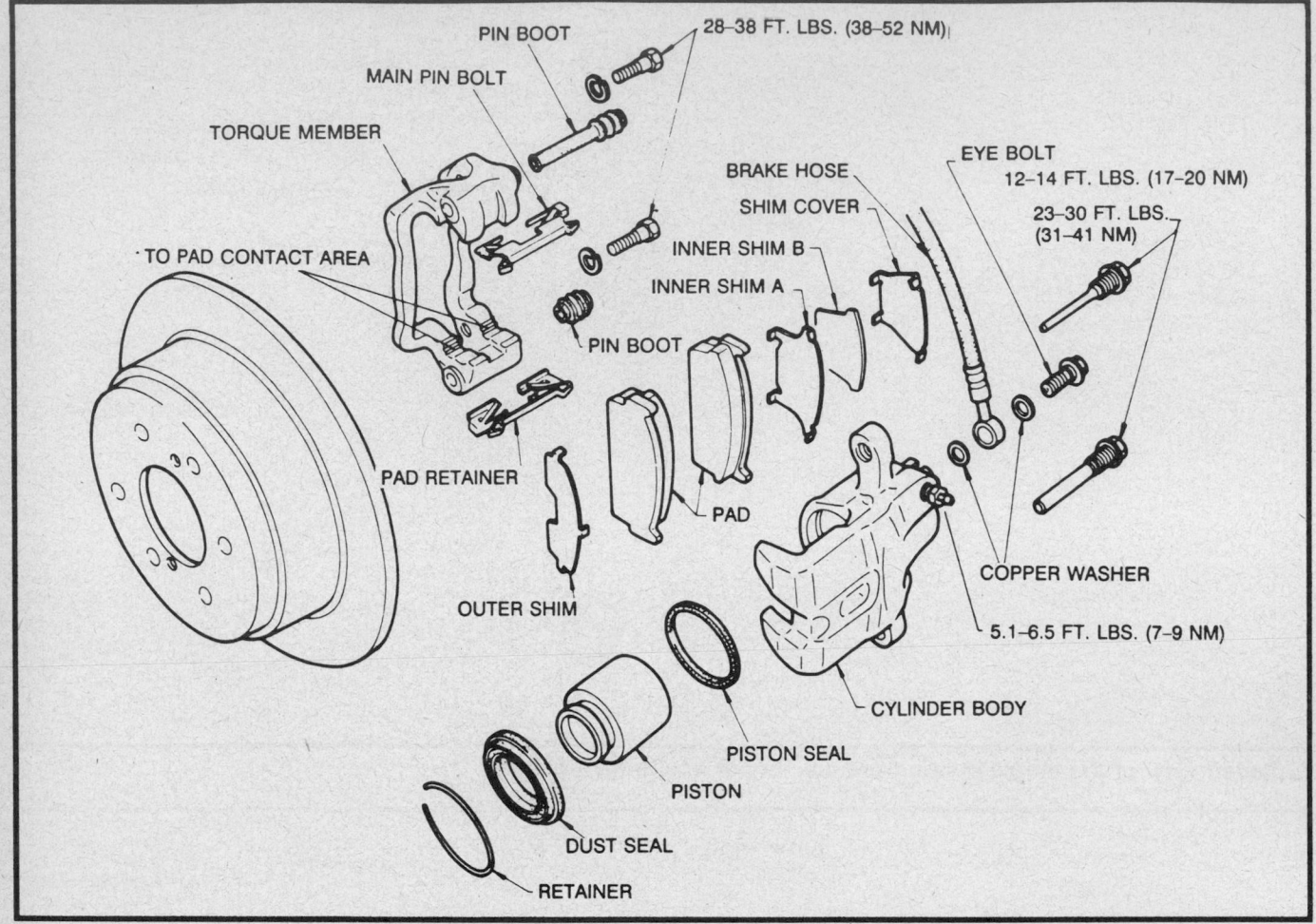

Exploded view of the single piston rear disc brake assembly — Pick-Up and Pathfinder

necessary, replace it.

8. To install, use a new cotter pin and reverse the removal procedures. Torque the rotor-to-wheel hub bolts to 36–51 ft. lbs. and the wheel hub-to-spindle nut to 25–29 ft. lbs. Adjust the front wheel bearing preload. Check and/or adjust the front wheel alignment.

4WD

1. Raise and support the front of the vehicle safely under the axle case. Remove the wheel/tire assembly.

2. If equipped with a manual/free-running lock assembly, perform the following procedure:
   a. Remove the lock assembly-to-hub Torx® bolts.
   b. Pull the lock assembly from the wheel hub.
   c. From the halfshaft, remove the snapring and the drive clutch.

3. If equipped with a automatic/free-running lock assembly, perform the following procedure:
   a. Remove the lock assembly-to-hub Torx® bolts.
   b. Pull the lock assembly (with brake **A**) from the wheel hub.
   c. From the halfshaft, remove the snapring, the washers and the brake **B**.

4. From the halfshaft, remove the thrust washer, the snapring and the lockwasher.

NOTE: To remove the lockwasher (4WD models), remove the lockwasher-to-locknut screw(s).

5. Using the locknut socket wrench, remove the locknut from the halfshaft.

6. Pull the wheel hub/rotor assembly from the steering knuckle.

7. Remove the rotor-to-wheel hub bolts and the rotor.

8. To install, reverse the removal procedures. Torque as follows:
   Rotor-to-wheel hub bolts — 36–51 ft. lbs.
   Lockwasher-to-locknut screw(s) — 9–14 inch lbs.
   Wheel hub/rotor assembly-to-halfshaft — 58–72 ft. lbs.
   Free-running hub assembly-to-wheel hub Torx® bolts — 18–25 ft. lbs.

9. Check and/or adjust the front wheel alignment.

VAN

1. Raise and safely support the vehicle.

2. Remove the calipers; do not disconnect the brake hose. Using a wire, suspend the calipers from the vehicle.

3. Remove the caliper support-to-steering knuckle bolts and the caliper support from the vehicle.

4. Remove the wheel bearing grease cup, the hub nut and the lockwasher.

5. Pull the wheel hub/brake rotor assembly from the wheel spindle.

6. Inspect the rotor for cracks, wear and/or other damage; if necessary, replace it.

7. To install, reverse the removal procedures. Torque the rotor/wheel hub assembly-to-spindle nut to 195–260 ft. lbs. Adjust

the front wheel bearing.

AXXESS

1. Raise and safely support the front of the vehicle.
2. Remove the wheel assembly.
3. Remove the brake caliper assembly and suspend it on a wire.
4. Remove the brake caliper support-to-steering knuckle bolts and the support.
5. Remove the rotor from the wheel hub.
6. To install, reverse the removal procedures.

Rear Brake Rotor

Removal and Installation
PICK-UP AND PATHFINDER

1. Raise and safely support the vehicle.
2. Remove the wheel assembly.
3. Remove the brake caliper assembly and suspend it on a wire.
4. Remove the brake caliper support-to-steering knuckle bolts and the support.
5. Remove the rotor from the hub.
6. To install, reverse the removal procedures.

Brake Drums

Removal and Installation
FRONT

1. Raise and safely support the vehicle. Remove the wheel assembly.
2. Remove the axle hub grease cap.
3. Remove the cotter pin and loosen the hub nut. When the nut is close to the end of the spindle, pull the drum and hub assembly outward. If it does not slide of the brake shoes, loosen the brake shoe adjuster star wheels. Remove the spindle nut, the brake drum/hub, the washer and the wheel bearings.

NOTE: Be careful not to get foreign matter in the wheel bearings. The heavy coating of grease will hold many particles. These will damage the bearing.

4. Inspect and/or replace the brake drum.
5. To install, reverse the removal procedures. Adjust the wheel bearing preload.

REAR

1. Raise and safely support the vehicle.
2. Remove the wheel assembly.
3. Pull the brake drum from the wheel hub.
4. Inspect and/or replace the brake drum.
5. To install, reverse the removal procedures.

Brake Shoes

Removal and Installation

1. Raise and safely support the vehicle. Remove the wheel assembly.
2. Remove the brake drum.
3. Using a pair of pliers, remove the brake shoe hold-down anti-rattle spring retainers. Depress the retainer while rotating it 90 degrees to align the slot in the retainer with the flanged end of the pin. Remove the retainers, springs, spring seats and pins.
4. Move the brake shoes outward against the return springs and remove the parking brake extension link.
5. Disconnect the brake shoe return springs.
6. Remove the brake shoes from the backing plate. The secondary (after) brake shoe must be disconnected from the parking brake toggle lever after withdrawing the toggle lever clevis pin.
7. Remove the rubber boot from behind the brake backing plate and slide the adjuster shim, lockplate and adjuster springs off the back of the adjuster assembly. Remove the adjuster assembly from the backing plate.
8. Clean the backing plate and adjuster assembly so they are free of all dust and dirt.
9. Check the wheel cylinders.

To install:

10. Apply brake grease to the adjuster assembly housing bore, the adjuster wheel and the adjuster screw. Assemble the adjuster assembly with the adjuster screw turned all the way in. Apply brake grease to the sliding surfaces of the adjuster assembly, the brake backing plate and the retaining spring. Install the adjuster assembly to the backing plate.

NOTE: On 4WD models, after install the crank lever on the backing plate, make sure there is no play between the crank lever and the backing plate when pulling the crank lever. If play exists, adjust the bolt A and locknut A.

11. Before assembling the brake shoes to the backing plate, apply grease to the following areas: the brake shoe grooves in the parking brake extension link, the inside surfaces of the anti-rattle (retaining) spring seats and the contact surfaces between the brake backing plate and the brake shoes.
12. Assemble the secondary (after) brake shoe to the parking brake toggle lever and adjust the clearance between the toggle lever and the brake shoe.
13. Assemble the brake shoes to the backing plate. Measure the inner diameter of the brake drum and the outer diameter of the shoes. The shoe outer diameter should be 0.0098–0.0157 in. (0.25–0.40mm) less then the drum inner diameter; if not, adjust it by rotating the star wheel adjuster.
14. Install the brake drum and the wheel.
15. Bleed the brakes, if necessary.
16. Adjust the shoe-to-drum clearance by operating the parking brake lever several times.

Parking Brake Shoes

Rear parking brake shoes are used in combination with rear disc brakes.

Removal and Installation
PICK-UP AND PATHFINDER

1. Fully, release the parking brake.
2. Raise and safely support the vehicle. Remove the wheel assembly.
3. Remove the brake caliper, the brake caliper support and the brake disc/drum assembly.

NOTE: If the disc/drum is difficult to remove, insert 2–8mm × 1.25 screws in the disc/drum holes, tighten the screws to press the disc/drum from the hub.

4. Remove the brake shoe retainers and the springs.
5. Separate the parking brake cable from the from the parking brake lever.
6. Using brake grease, lubricate the shoe adjuster and the backing plate contact points.
7. Turn the shoe adjuster all the way inward.
8. To install, reverse the removal procedures. Adjust the parking brakes by turning the adjuster wheel.

Adjustment

1. Make sure the parking brake lever is fully released.

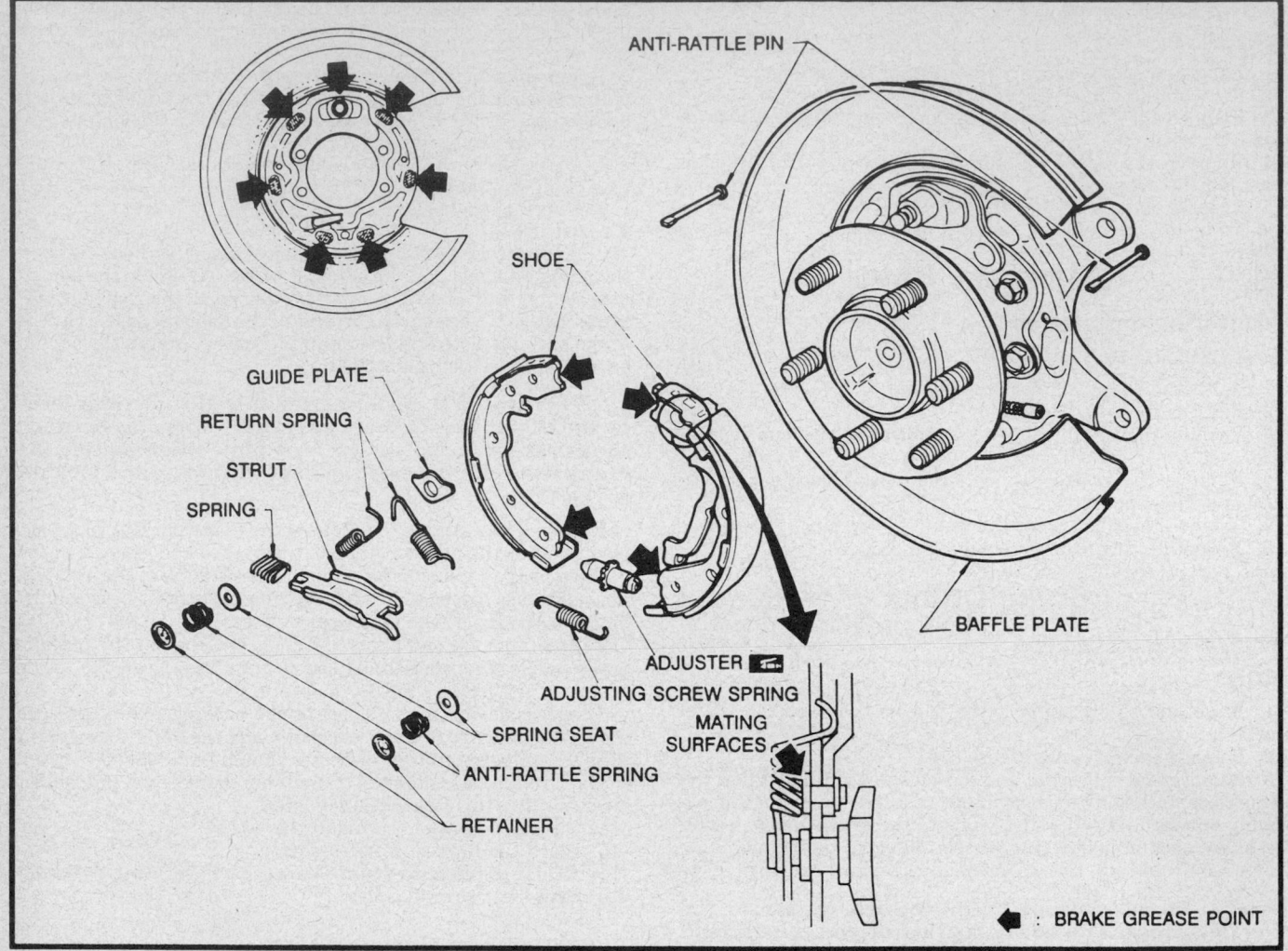

Exploded view of the rear disc/drum parking brake assembly — Pick-Up and Pathfinder

2. From the rear of the backing plate, remove the adjuster hole plug.

3. Using a small prybar, rotate the adjuster wheel until the shoe touches the brake drum.

4. Back off the adjuster wheel 7–8 latches.

5. Install the adjuster hole plug.

6. Make sure there is no drag between the shoes and the brake drum when rotating the disc rotor.

Wheel Cylinder

Removal and Installation

1. Raise and safely support the rear of the vehicle.

2. Remove the wheel, brake drum and brake shoes.

3. Disconnect the brake tube from the rear of the wheel cylinder.

4. Remove the wheel cylinder-to-backing plate bolts and the wheel cylinder from the backing plate.

5. To install, reverse the removal procedures. Torque the wheel cylinder-to-backing plate nuts to bolt to 3.9–5.4 ft. lbs. Bleed the brake hydraulic system.

Parking Brake Cable

Removal and Installation

REAR CABLE(S)

1. Fully release the parking brake control lever.

2. Raise and safely support the vehicle.

3. Loosen the adjusting nut at the adjuster cable lever.

4. Disconnect the cable from the balance lever or adjuster.

5. Disconnect the rear parking brake cable(s) from the parking brake toggle levers of the rear service brake assemblies.

6. Remove the rear parking brake cable brackets-to-chassis bracket screws.

7. Remove parking brake cable(s) from the vehicle.

8. To install, reverse the removal procedures. Apply a light coat of grease to the cables to make sure that they slide properly. Torque the parking brake cable bracket screws to 5.8–8 ft. lbs. Adjust the parking brake cables.

FRONT CABLE

1. Fully release the parking brake control lever.

2. Raise and safely support the vehicle.

3. Loosen the adjusting nut at the adjuster cable lever.

4. Disconnect the cable from the balance lever or adjuster.

5. Remove the front cable bracket-to-chassis bolt(s) and the cable from the vehicle.

6. To install, reverse the removal procedures. Apply a light coat of grease to the cable to make sure it slides properly. Torque the front cable bracket-to-chassis bolt, if equipped to 5.8–8 ft. lbs. Adjust the parking brake cables.

Adjustment

1. Raise and safely support the vehicle.
2. Adjust the rear brakes.

3. From under the vehicle, adjust the parking brake cable locknut(s). Turn the adjusting nut until the parking brake control lever operating stroke is (using 44 lbs. force):

10–12 clicks—console lever—Pick-Up and Pathfinder
10–12 clicks—stick lever—2WD Pick-Up and 2WD Pathfinder
9–11 clicks—stick lever—4WD Pick-Up and 4WD Pathfinder
7–9 clicks—Van
8–9 clicks—2WD Axxess
10–11 clicks—4WD Axxess

4. Release the parking brake and make sure the rear wheels turn freely with no drag.
5. Lower the vehicle.

FRONT SUSPENSION

Shock Absorbers

Removal and Installation

EXCEPT AXXESS

1. Raise and safely support the vehicle. Remove the wheel assembly.

2. While holding the upper stem of the shock absorber, remove the shock absorber-to-chassis nut (Pick-Up and Pathfinder) or nut/bolt (Van), washer and rubber bushing.

3. Remove the lower shock absorber-to-lower control arm nut/bolt (Pick-Up and Pathfinder) or nut (Van) and the shock absorber from the vehicle.

4. To install, use new rubber bushings and reverse the removal procedures. Torque the shock absorber-to-lower control arm nut/bolt to 43–58 ft. lbs. and the shock absorber-to-chassis nut to 12–16 ft. lbs. (Pick-Up and Pathfinder) or nut/bolt to 22–30 ft. lbs. (Van).

MacPherson Strut

Removal and Installation

AXXESS

1. Raise and safely support the vehicle; position support under the front of the frame.

2. Remove the wheel assembly.

3. Matchmark the strut-to-steering knuckle position.

4. Remove the strut-to-steering knuckle nut/bolts.

5. Remove the strut-to-chassis nuts and the strut from the vehicle.

6. To install, reverse the removal procedures. Align the strut-to-steering knuckle matchmarks. Torque the strut-to-chassis nuts to 33–40 ft. lbs. (44–54 Nm) and the strut-to-steering knuckle nuts/bolts to 82–91 ft. lbs. (112–124 Nm).

7. Check and/or adjust the front end alignment.

Leaf Springs

Removal and Installation

VAN

1. Raise and safely support the vehicle; position supports under the frame.

2. Remove the wheel assembly.

3. Remove the lower control arm from one side.

4. From the opposite side, loosen the leaf spring-to-lower control arm bolt.

5. Remove the leaf spring by sliding it from the opposite lower control arm.

6. Inspect the spring for wear and/or cracks; if necessary, re-

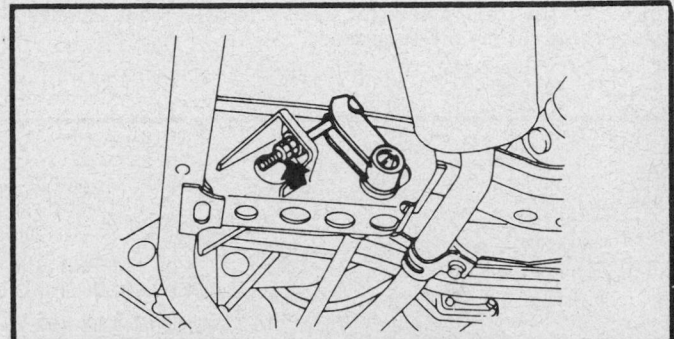

Location of the torsion bar adjustment nut—2WD Pick-Up and 2WD Pathfinder

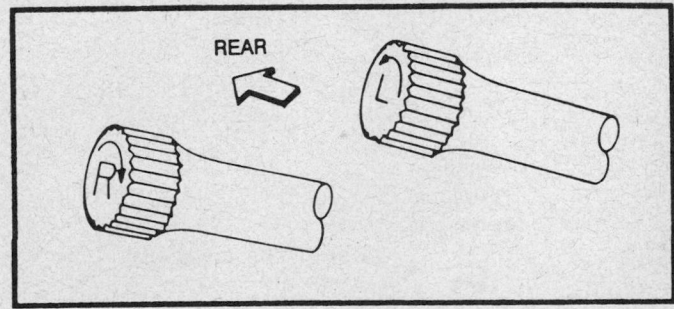

View of the torsion bar serrated ends. Note they are marked and are not interchangeable—Pick-Up and Pathfinder

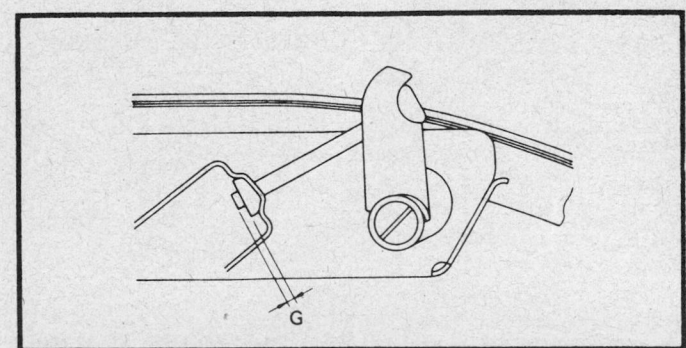

Adjusting the torsion bar anchor arm length—2WD Pick-Up and 2WD Pathfinder

place the spring.

7. To install, reverse the removal procedures.

Torsion Bars

Removal and Installation

PICK-UP AND PATHFINDER
2WD Models

1. Block the rear wheels. Raise and safely support the front of the vehicle with supports placed under the frame. Remove the wheel assemblies.

2. Remove the torsion bar spring adjusting nut.

3. Remove the dust cover and the snapring from the anchor arm.

4. Pull the anchor arm off rearward and remove the torsion bar spring.

5. Remove the torque arm.

To install:

6. Check the torsion bars for wear, cracks or other damage; replace them if they are suspected.

7. Install the torque arm on the lower link (control arm) and torque the bolts to 37–50 ft. lbs. (50–68 Nm).

8. Install the snapring and dust cove on the torsion bar.

9. Coat the splines on the inner end of the torsion bar with chassis lube and install it into the torque arm. The torsion bars are marked **L** and **R** and are not interchangeable.

10. Position a floor jack under the lower link and raise it so the clearance between the link and the rebound bumper is 0.

11. Install the anchor arm so the dimension **G** is 0.24–0.71 in. (6–18mm).

12. Install the snapring to the anchor arm and dust cover. Make sure the snapring is properly installed in the groove of the anchor arm.

13. Tighten the anchor arm adjusting nut until dimension **L** is 1.38 in. (35mm) for heavy duty, cab/chassis and std models or 1.93 in. (49mm) for all other models.

14. Lower the vehicle so it is resting on the wheels and bounce it several times to set the suspension. Turn the anchor bolt adjusting nut so dimension **H** is 4.37–4.53 in. (111–115mm) for 1986–87 models or 4.25–4.65 in. (108–118mm) on 1988–90 models.

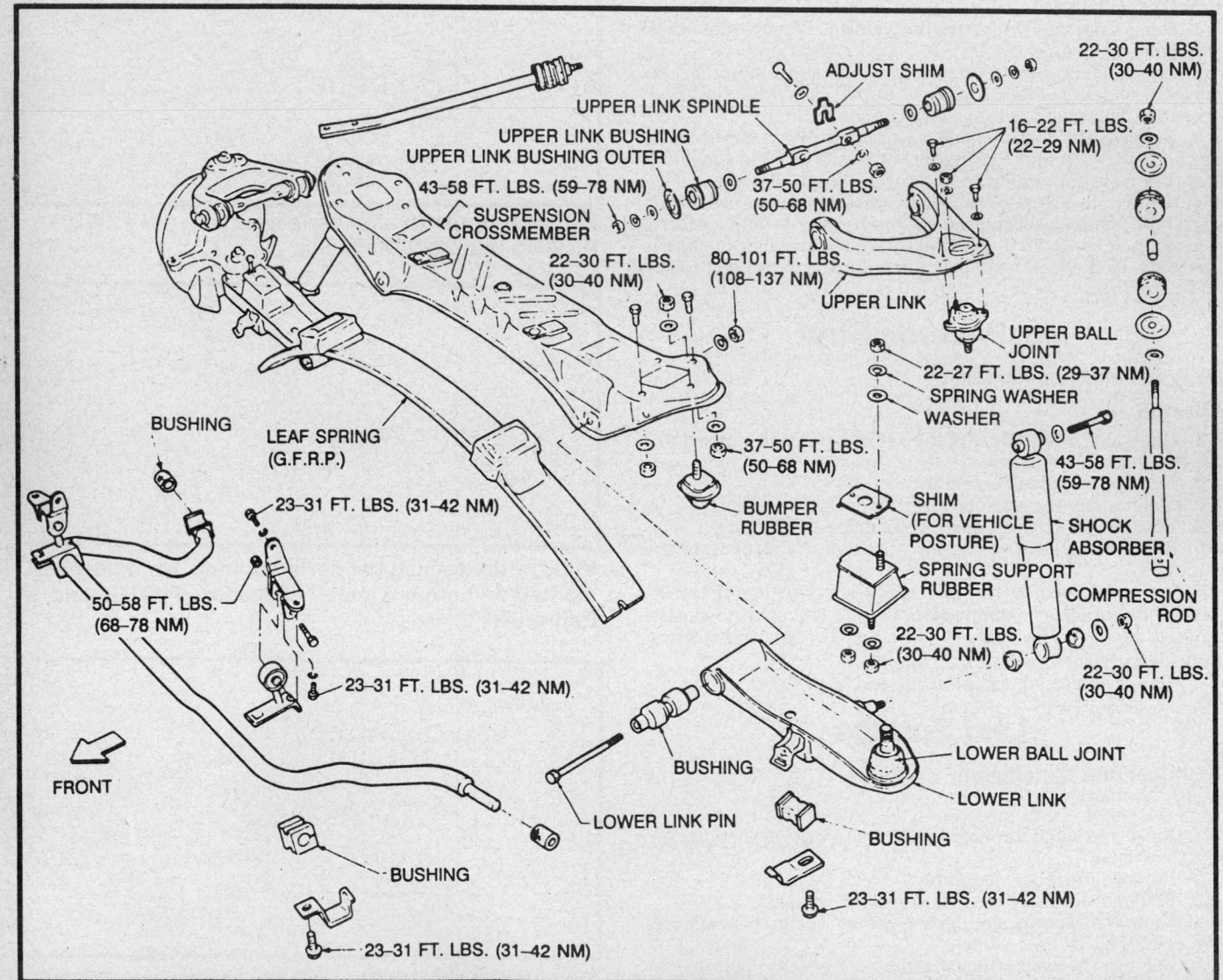

Exploded view of the front suspension system—Van

4WD Models

1. Block the rear wheels. Raise and safely support the front of the vehicle with supports placed under the frame.
2. Remove the torsion bar spring adjusting nut.
3. Pull back the dust boot and remove the anchor arm snapring.
4. Remove the torque arm attaching nuts and withdraw the torsion bar spring forward with the torque arm still attached.
5. Check the torsion bar for wear, cracks or other damage; replace them, if they are suspected.

To install:

6. Coat the splines on the torsion bar with chassis lube and install it in the anchor arm. The torsion bars are marked **L** and **R** and are not interchangeable.
7. Position a floor jack under the lower link (control arm) and raise it so the clearance between the link and the rebound bumper is 0.
8. Install the anchor arm so the dimension **G** is 1.97–2.36 in. (50–60mm).
9. Install the snapring on the anchor arm and pull the dust boot over it.
10. Tighten the anchor arm adjusting nut until dimension **L** is 3.03 in. (77mm).
11. Lower the vehicle so it is resting on the wheels and bounce it several times to set the suspension. Turn the anchor bolt adjusting nut so dimension **H** is 1.73–1.89 in. (44–48mm) for 1986–87 or 1.61–2.01 in. (41–51mm) for 1988–90.

Upper Ball Joints

Inspection

EXCEPT AXXESS

The ball joint(s) should be replaced when play becomes exces-

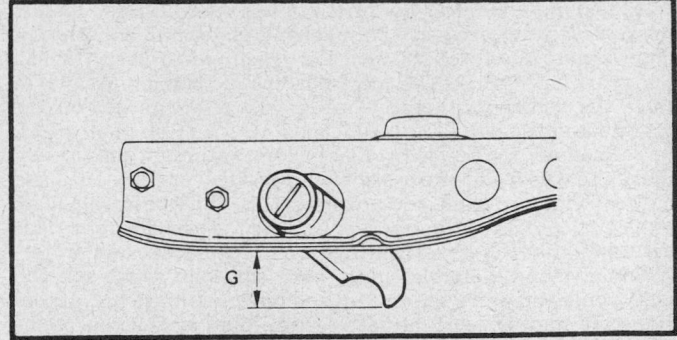

Adjusting the torsion bar anchor arm length—4WD Pick-Up and 4WD Pathfinder

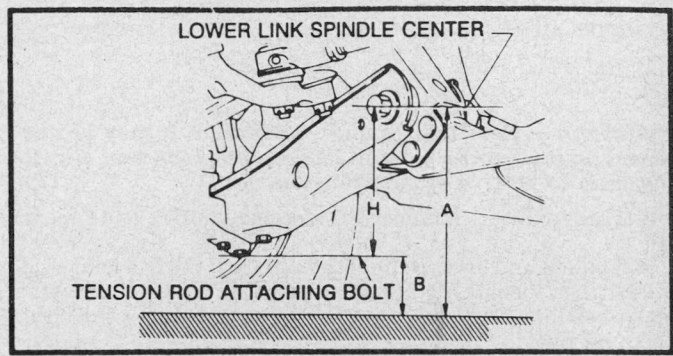

Adjusting the vehicle ride height—2WD Pick-Up and 2WD Pathfinder

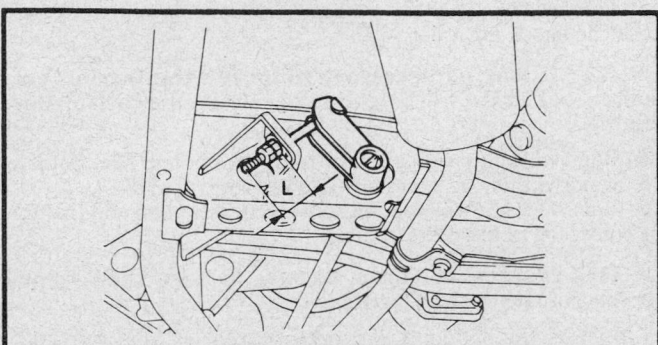

Torquing the torsion bar anchor arm bolt to length—2WD Pick-Up and 2WD Pathfinder

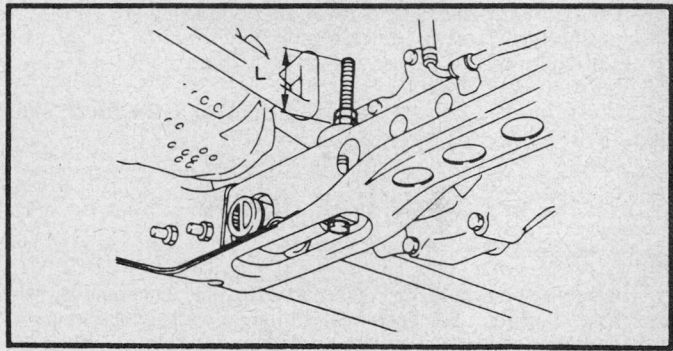

Torquing the torsion bar anchor arm bolt to length—4WD Pick-Up and 4WD Pathfinder

Location of the torsion bar adjustment nut—4WD Pick-Up and 4WD Pathfinder

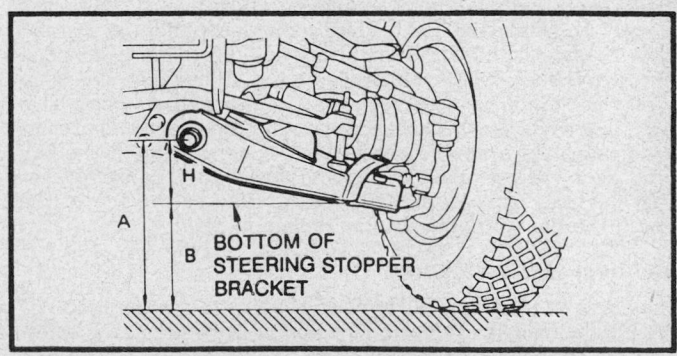

Adjusting the vehicle ride height—4WD Pick-Up and 4WD Pathfinder

sive. The manufacturer does not publish specifications on just what constitutes excessive play, relying instead on a method of determining the force (in inch lbs.) required to keep the ball joint turning. An effective way to determine ball joint play is to raise the vehicle until the wheel is just a few inches off the ground and the ball joint is unloaded, which means not to jack directly under the ball joint. Place a long bar under the tire and move the wheel and tire assembly up and down; place one hand on top of the tire while you are doing this. If there is over ¼ in. of play at the top of the tire, the ball joint is probably bad. This assuming that the wheel bearings are in good shape and properly adjusted. As a double check, have someone watch the ball joint while you move the tire up and down with the bar. If considerable play is seen, besides feeling play at the top of the wheel, the ball joints need to be replaced.

Removal and Installation
EXCEPT AXXESS

1. Raise and safely support the vehicle.
2. Remove the wheel/tire assembly.

NOTE: On the Pick-Up and Pathfinder, it may be necessary to loosen the torsion bar anchor lock and adjusting nuts to relieve spring tension.

3. Place a floor jack under the steering knuckle and support it.
4. Remove and discard the cotter pin from the ball joint stud, then, loosen the nut. Using the ball joint removal tool, press the upper ball joint from the lower control arm. Remove the upper ball joint nut.
5. Remove the upper ball joint-to-upper control arm bolts and the ball joint from the vehicle.
6. To install, use a new ball joint, a new cotter pin and reverse the removal procedures. Torque as follows:
Upper ball joint-to-upper control arm bolts – 12–16 ft. lbs.
Upper ball-to-steering knuckle nut
Pick-Up and Pathfinder – 58–108 ft. lbs.
Van – 40–72 ft. lbs.
7. Check and/or adjust the ride height and the front end alignment.

Lower Ball Joints

Inspection

The ball joint(s) should be replaced when play becomes excessive. The manufacturer does not publish specifications on just what constitutes excessive play, relying instead on a method of determining the force (in inch lbs.) required to keep the ball joint turning. An effective way to determine ball joint play is to raise the vehicle until the wheel is just a few inches off the ground and the ball joint is unloaded, which means not to jack directly under the ball joint. Place a long bar under the tire and move the wheel and tire assembly up and down; place one hand on top of the tire while you are doing this. If there is over ¼ in. of play at the top of the tire, the ball joint is probably bad. This assuming that the wheel bearings are in good shape and properly adjusted. As a double check, have someone watch the ball joint while you move the tire up and down with the bar. If considerable play is seen, besides feeling play at the top of the wheel, the ball joints need to be replaced.

Removal and Installation

The lower control arm ball joint on the 2WD Pick-Up and 2WD Pathfinder models are not removable; if the ball joint is defective, replace the lower control arm.
1. Raise and safely support the vehicle.
2. Remove the wheel/tire assembly.

NOTE: On the Pick-Up and Pathfinder, loosen the torsion bar spring anchor lock and adjusting nuts and remove the anchor arm bolt from the anchor arm. Remove the snapring, then move the anchor arm and torsion bar fully rearward. This procedure is to relieve the spring pressure on the lower control arm.

3. If equipped, it may be necessary to disconnect the sway bar from the lower arm.
4. Disconnect the tension rod from the lower arm.
5. Remove the cotter pin, discard it, from the ball joint stud and loosen the nut.
6. Using the ball joint separator tool, press the ball joint from the steering knuckle.
7. Remove the lower ball joint-to-lower control arm bolts and the ball joint.
8. To install, use a new cotter pin and reverse the removal procedures. Torque as follows:
Ball joint-to-control arm bolts
4WD Pick-Up and 4WD Pathfinder – 35–45 ft. lbs.
Axxess – 56–80 ft. lbs.
Ball joint-to-steering knuckle nut
Pick-Up and Pathfinder – 87–141 ft. lbs.
Axxess – 52–64 ft. lbs.
Van – 124–141 ft. lbs.
9. Check and/or adjust the torsion bar ride height assembly and the front end alignment.

Upper Control Arms

Removal and Installation
PICK-UP AND PATHFINDER

1. Raise and safely support the vehicle.
2. Remove the wheels.
3. Remove the upper shock absorber-to-chassis nut and compress the shock absorber.

NOTE: If may be necessary to loosen the torsion bar anchor lock and adjusting nuts to relieve the torsion bar tension.

4. Remove the upper ball joint-to-upper control arm bolts.
5. Using a floor jack, raise the lower control arm.
6. Remove the upper control arm-to-chassis bolts and the upper control arm from the vehicle.

NOTE: If shims are used, be sure to keep them in order for reinstallation purposes.

7. Inspect the ball joint, if necessary, replace it.
8. To install, replace the shims (if used) in their original locations and reverse the removal procedures. Torque the upper control arm-to-chassis bolts to 80–108 ft. lbs., the ball joint-to-upper control arm bolts to 12–15 ft. lbs. and the upper shock absorber-to-chassis nut to 12–16 ft. lbs. Lower the vehicle and adjust the ride height. Check and/or adjust the front end alignment.

VAN

1. Raise and safely support the vehicle. Remove the wheel assembly.
2. Using a floor jack, support the lower control arm.
3. Remove the upper ball joint-to-upper control arm bolts and separate the ball joint from the upper control arm.
4. Remove the upper control arm-to-chassis bolts and the control arm from the vehicle.

NOTE: If shims are used, be sure to keep them in order for reinstallation purposes.

5. To install, replace the shims (if used) in their original locations and reverse the removal procedures. Torque the upper

control arm-to-chassis bolts to 37–50 ft. lbs. and the upper ball joint-to-upper control arm bolts to 16–22 ft. lbs. Check and/or adjust the front end alignment.

Lower Control Arms

Removal and Installation
PICK-UP AND PATHFINDER
2WD Models

1. Raise and safely support the vehicle.
2. Remove the wheel assembly.
3. Loosen the torsion bar spring anchor lock and adjusting nuts and remove the anchor arm bolt from the anchor arm.
4. Remove the snapring, then, move the anchor arm and torsion bar fully rearward.
5. Remove the lower shock absorber-to-lower control arm nut/bolt.
6. Disconnect the sway bar-to-lower control arm nut and separate the sway bar from the lower control arm.
7. Disconnect the tension rod-to-lower control arm bolts.
8. Remove and discard the cotter pin from the ball joint stud, then, remove the nut. Using the ball joint removal tool, press the ball joint from the knuckle spindle.
9. Remove the lower control arm-to-chassis nut/bolt, tap the pivot shaft from the bushing. Push down on the tension rod and remove the lower control arm.
10. To install, use a new cotter pin and reverse the removal procedures. Torque as follows:
   Lower control arm-to-chassis nut/bolt – 80–108 ft. lbs.
   Tension rod-to-lower control arm bolt – 36–47 ft. lbs.
   Lower ball joint-to-lower control arm nut – 87–141 ft. lbs.
   Shock absorber-to-lower control arm nut/bolt – 43–58 ft. lbs.
   Sway bar-to-lower control arm nut – 12–16 ft. lbs.
11. Check and/or adjust the torsion bar ride height assembly and the front end alignment.

4WD Models

1. Raise and safely support the vehicle.
2. Remove the wheel assembly.
3. Loosen the torsion bar spring anchor lock and adjusting nuts and remove the anchor arm bolt from the anchor arm.
4. Remove the snapring, then, move the anchor arm and torsion bar fully rearward.
5. Remove the lower shock absorber-to-lower control arm nut/bolt.
6. Disconnect the sway bar-to-lower control arm nut and separate the sway bar from the lower control arm.
7. Disconnect the compression rod-to-lower control arm bolts.
8. Remove and discard the cotter pin from the ball joint stud, then, remove the nut. Using the ball joint removal tool, press the ball joint from the knuckle spindle.
9. Remove the lower control arm-to-chassis nut/bolt, tap the pivot shaft from the bushing. Push down on the compression rod and remove the lower control arm.
10. To install, use a new cotter pin and reverse the removal procedures. Torque as follows:
   Lower control arm-to-chassis nut/bolt – 80–108 ft. lbs.
   Compression rod-to-lower control arm nut – 87–108 ft. lbs.
   Lower ball joint-to-lower control arm nut – 87–141 ft. lbs.
   Shock absorber-to-lower control arm nut/bolt – 43–58 ft. lbs.
   Sway bar-to-lower control arm nut – 12–16 ft. lbs.
11. Check and/or adjust the torsion bar ride height assembly and the front end alignment.

VAN

1. Raise and safely support the vehicle.
2. Remove the wheel/tire assembly.
3. From the lower ball joint, remove the cotter pin (discard

it), then, loosen the lower ball joint nut (do not remove it).
4. Remove the tie rod-to-steering knuckle nut, then, install the nut upside-down (to prevent damage to the nut). Using the tie rod removal tool, press the tie rod from the steering knuckle.
5. Using a floor jack, support the steering knuckle assembly.
6. Disconnect the brake caliper from the steering knuckle and support it on a wire; do not disconnect the brake hose.
7. Remove the upper ball joint-to-upper control arm bolts.
8. Using the ball joint removal tool, press the lower ball joint from the lower control arm. Remove the lower ball joint nut and the steering knuckle from the vehicle.
9. Remove the sway bar brackets-to-lower control arm bolts and swing the sway down (away) from the lower control arm.
10. Remove the shock absorber-to-lower control arm nut and the compression rod-to-lower control arm bolts, then, separate the shock absorber and compression rod from the lower control arm.
11. Lower the floor jack to take the spring pressure off the lower control arm.
12. Remove the leaf spring-to-lower control arm nut and support rubber.
13. Remove the lower control arm-to-suspension crossmember nut/bolt and the lower control arm.

NOTE: When installing the leaf spring and spring support rubber, be certain the washer does not protrude beyond the end surface of the leaf spring.

14. To install, reverse the removal procedures. Torque as follows:
   Lower control arm-to-suspension crossmember nut/bolt – 80–101 ft. lbs.
   Leaf spring-to-lower control arm nut – 22–27 ft. lbs.
   Sway bar-to-lower control arm bolt – 23–31 ft. lbs.
   Upper ball joint-to-upper control arm bolts – 16–22 ft. lbs.
   Lower ball joint-to-steering knuckle nut – 124–141 ft. lbs.
   Tie rod-to-steering knuckle nut – 40–72 ft. lbs.
   Compression rod-to-lower control arm bolts – 22–30 ft. lbs.
   Lower shock absorber-to-lower control arm nut – 22–30 ft. lbs.
15. Check and/or adjust the front end alignment.

Sway Bar

Removal and Installation
PICK-UP AND PATHFINDER

1. Raise and safely support the vehicle.
2. If equipped with a splash shield, remove it.
3. From both sides of the vehicle, remove the sway bar-to-lower control arm connecting rod nut, bushings and tube.
4. Remove the sway bar-to-chassis bracket bolts and brackets.

NOTE: On some vehicles, it may be necessary to remove the tension rod in order to remove the sway bar.

5. Remove the sway bar from the vehicle.
6. To install, reverse the removal procedures. Torque the sway bar-to-chassis bracket bolts to 12–16 ft. lbs. and the sway bar-to-lower control arm connecting rod nut/bolt to 16–22 ft. lbs.

VAN

1. Raise and safely support the front of the vehicle.
2. From both sides of the vehicle, remove the sway bar-to-lower control arm bracket bolts and brackets.
3. Remove the sway bar-to-chassis bracket bolts, then, remove the sway bar from the vehicle.
4. **Inspect the bushing for damage; replace them, if necessary.**
5. To install, reverse the removal procedures. Torque the

sway bar-to-chassis bracket bolts to 23–31 ft. lbs. and the sway bar-to-lower control arm bracket bolts to 23–31 ft. lbs.

AXXESS

A stabilizer bar is used on the 2WD models only.

1. Raise and safely support the front of the vehicle.
2. Remove the stabilizer bar-to-connecting rod nut.
3. Remove the stabilizer bar clamp-to-chassis bolts and the stabilizer bar from the vehicle.
4. To install, reverse the removal procedures. Torque the stabilizer bar clamp-to-chassis bolts to 23–31 ft. lbs. (31–42 Nm). and the stabilizer bar-to-connecting rod nuts to 30–38 ft. lbs. (41–51 Nm).

Front Wheel Bearings

For the FWD Axxess, the 4WD Pick-Up and 4WD Pathfinder models, please refer to the Drive Axle section.

Only the front wheel bearings require periodic service. The lubricant to use is high temperature disc brake wheel bearing grease meeting NLGI No.2 specifications. Special tools are not needed for this job, although the use of a torque wrench is strongly recommended for accurate measurement of bearing preload. The most important thing to remember when working with the wheel bearings is that although they are basically durable, in some ways they are remarkably fragile. Mishandling, grit, misalignment, scratches, improper preload, etc. will quickly destroy any roller bearing, no matter how well hardened during manufacture.

Removal and Installation

PICK-UP AND PATHFINDER

1. Loosen the wheel nuts. Raise and safely support the vehicle. Remove the wheel/tire assembly.
2. Remove the brake caliper-to-steering knuckle bolts and suspend the caliper on a wire.
3. Using 2 small pry bars, pry the grease cap from the wheel hub. Remove the cotter pin (discard it), the adjusting cap nut, the adjusting nut, the thrust washer and the outside wheel bearing. Pull the hub/disc assembly from the wheel spindle.

NOTE: It is not necessary to remove the disc from the hub.

4. Using a hammer and a brass drift, drive the inside wheel bearing, the grease seal (discard it) and the inside outer race, then, invert the hub/disc assembly and remove the outside outer race.
5. Using solvent clean all of the parts, then, allow them to air dry or blow them dry with compressed air.

NOTE: Do not use a cloth to dry the parts, you risk leaving bits of lint in the races.

6. Inspect the wheel bearings for wear, cracks, pits, burns, scoring or etc., if necessary, replaced them; do not mix old and new parts.
7. Using multi-purpose grease, coat the wheel bearing parts throughly.
8. Using the wheel bearing race installation tool, drive the races into the wheel hub until they seat.

NOTE: Use care not to cock the bearing cups in the hub. If they are not fully seated, the bearings will be impossible to adjust properly.

9. Using the multi-purpose grease, pack the internal areas of the hub and cups.
10. To pack the wheel bearing with grease, perform the following procedures:
    a. Place a large glob of grease into the palm of one hand.
    b. Using a rolling motion and push the wheel bearing; continue packing until the grease begins to ooze through the roller gaps.
11. Install the inner bearing into its cup in the hub. Drive the new grease seal (bearing side is indicated) into the wheel hub until it is flush.
12. To complete the installation, use a new cotter pin and reverse the removal procedures. Adjust the wheel bearing.

VAN

1. Loosen the wheel lug nuts. Raise and safely support the vehicle. Remove the wheel/tire assembly.
2. Remove the caliper-to-steering knuckle bolts and the caliper. Using a wire, suspend the caliper from the vehicle; do not disconnect the brake hose from the caliper.
3. Remove the grease cap from the wheel hub.
4. Remove the wheel bearing nut and the lockwasher. Pull the rotor/wheel hub from the spindle.
5. Remove the lock ring from the rotor/wheel hub.
6. Using a hydraulic press, press the wheel bearing and grease seal from the rotor/wheel hub assembly.
7. Using a new bearing, press it into the rotor/wheel hub assembly until it seats; use no more than 3 tons pressure. Install a new lock ring into the rotor/wheel hub.
8. **To complete the installation, reverse the removal procedures. Torque the wheel bearing nut to 195–260 ft. lbs.**

Adjustment

The Van does not require an adjustment procedure.

1. Raise and safely support the front of the vehicle. Remove the grease cup, the cotter pin and the adjusting nut retainer.

NOTE: If the wheel bearings have not been replaced, loosen the wheel bearing adjusting nut.

2. Using a torque wrench, torque the wheel bearing nut (while turning the wheel) to 22–29 ft. lbs.
3. Rotate the wheel hub a few more times to snug down the bearings.
4. Retighten the nut to 25–29 ft. lbs. Unscrew the adjusting nut 1/8 turn (45°). Install the locknut (castellated nut) and snug it down against the adjusting nut until one of its grooves aligns with the a spindle hole.

NOTE: The adjusting nut can be tightened up to 15 degrees to allow the locknut holes to align.

5. Install a new cotter pin, bending its ends around the locknut.
6. Check the axial play of the wheel by shaking it back and forth. The bearing freeplay should feel close to zero but the wheel should spin freely.

REAR SUSPENSION

Shock Absorbers

Removal and Installation

1. Raise and safely support the vehicle.
2. Remove the upper shock-to-vehicle nut, the lower shock-to-vehicle nut and the shock from the vehicle.

NOTE: The weight of the vehicle must be on the rear wheels before tightening the shock absorber attaching nuts.

3. To install, reverse the removal procedures. Torque as follows:
   Upper shock-to-vehicle nut
   Pick-Up and Pathfinder—22–30 ft. lbs.
   Van—12–18 ft. lbs.
   Lower shock absorber-to-axle nut
   2WD—Pick-Up and 2WD Pathfinder—12–16 ft. lbs.
   4WD—Pick-Up and 4WD Pathfinder—22–30 ft. lbs.
   Van—53–72 ft. lbs.

MacPherson Strut

Removal and Installation

AXXESS
2WD Model

On the 2WD models, the wheel spindle and knuckle are a part of the strut.

1. Remove the hub cap and cotter pin.
2. Apply the brakes and loosen the wheel bearing locknut.
3. Raise and safely support the vehicle. Remove the wheel assembly.
4. Remove the wheel bearing nut, washer and wheel hub bearing.

NOTE: The wheel hub bearing must be replaced as an assembly, if the bearing is defective.

5. Disconnect and plug the brake line from the wheel cylinder.
6. Remove radius rod-to-knuckle nut/bolt, the stabilizer rod-to-knuckle nut/bolt and the parallel rods-to-knuckle nut/bolt.
7. From inside the vehicle, remove the strut cover.
8. Remove the strut-to-chassis nuts and the strut.

To install:

9. Install strut and the strut-to-chassis nuts and torque to 43–58 ft. lbs. (59–78 Nm).
10. Install the parallel rods-to-knuckle nut/bolt and torque to 65–87 ft. lbs. (88–118 Nm).
11. Install the stabilizer rod-to-knuckle nut/bolt and torque to 43–58 ft. lbs. (59–78 Nm).
12. Install the radius rod-to-knuckle nut/bolt and torque to 65–87 ft. lbs. (88–118 Nm).
13. To install, reverse the removal procedures. Torque the wheel hub bearing assembly to 137–188 ft. lbs. (186–255 Nm).
14. Using a dial indicator, measure the bearing axial endplay; it should be 0.0020 in. (0.05mm) or less.
15. To complete the installation, reverse the removal procedures. Bleed the rear brakes and inspect the rear wheel alignment.

4WD Models

1. Raise and safely support the vehicle. Remove the wheel assembly.
2. Matchmark the strut-to-knuckle location.

3. Support the knuckle and remove the strut-to-knuckle nuts and bolts.
4. From inside the vehicle, remove the strut-to-chassis nuts.
5. Remove the strut from the vehicle.
6. To install, reverse the removal procedures. Torque the strut-to-chassis nuts to 43–51 ft. lbs. (59–69 Nm) and the strut-to-knuckle nuts/bolts to 82–91 ft. lbs. (112–124 Nm).
7. To complete the installation, reverse the removal procedures.
8. Inspect the rear wheel alignment.

Coil Springs

Removal and Installation

VAN

1. Raise and safely support the vehicle.
2. Lower the axle housing and remove the coil spring(s).
3. To install, reverse the removal procedures.

Leaf Springs

Removal and Installation

PICK-UP AND PATHFINDER

——————————— CAUTION ———————————
The leaf springs are under a considerable amount of tension. Be very careful when removing or installing them; they can exert enough force to cause serious injuries.
————————————————————————————————

1. Raise and safely support the vehicle. Using a floor jack, support the axle hosusing.
2. Disconnect the shock absorbers at their lower end.
3. Remove the axle housing-to-spring pad U-bolt nuts and the spring pad.
4. Raise the axle housing to remove the weight off the springs.
5. Remove the spring shackle nuts, drive out the shackle pins and remove the spring from the vehicle.

NOTE: The weight of the vehicle must be on the rear wheels before torquing the front pin, shackle and shock absorber nuts.

6. To install, reverse the removal procedures. Torque as follows:
   Front pin and shackle nuts—83–94 ft. lbs.
   U-bolt nuts—53–72 ft. lbs.
   Shock absorber lower end nut
   2WD—12–16 ft. lbs.
   4WD—22–30 ft. lbs.

Rear Control Arms

Removal and Installation

VAN
Lower Link

1. Raise and safely support the vehicle.
2. Remove the lower link-to-axle housing nut/bolt and the lower link-to-chassis nut/bolt.
3. Remove the lower link from the vehicle.
4. To install, reverse the removal procedures. Torque the lower link-to-chassis nut/bolt to 80–94 ft. lbs. and the lower link-to-axle housing nut/bolt to 80–94 ft. lbs.

Upper Link

1. Raise and safely support the vehicle.
2. Remove the upper link-to-axle housing nut/bolt and the upper link-to-chassis nut/bolt.
3. Remove the upper link from the vehicle.
4. To install, reverse the removal procedures. Torque the upper link-to-chassis nut/bolt to 80–94 ft. lbs. and the upper link-to-axle housing nut/bolt to 80–94 ft. lbs.

Panhard Rod

1. Raise and safely support the vehicle.
2. Remove the panhard rod-to-axle housing nut and the panhard rod-to-chassis nut/bolt.
3. Remove the panhard rod from the vehicle.
4. To install, reverse the removal procedures. Torque the panhard rod-to-chassis nut/bolt to 80–94 ft. lbs. and the panhard rod-to-axle housing nut to 36–50 ft. lbs.

AXXESS
2WD Models With Radius Rod

1. Raise and safely support the vehicle.
2. Remove the wheel assembly.
3. Remove the radius rod-to-knuckle nut and bolt.
4. Remove the radius rod-to-chassis nut/bolt and the rod.
5. To install, reverse the removal procedures. Torque the radius rod-to-chassis nut/bolt to 65–80 ft. lbs. (88–108 Nm) and the radius rod-to-knuckle nut/bolt to 65–80 ft. lbs. (88–108 Nm).
6. To complete the installation, reverse the removal procedures.

2WD Models With Parallel Rods

Dual rods are connected from the chassis to the knuckle.
1. Raise and safely support the vehicle.
2. Remove the wheel assembly.
3. Remove the parallel rods-to-knuckle nut and bolt.
4. Remove the parallel rods-to-chassis nut/bolt and the rods.
5. To install, reverse the removal procedures. Torque the parallel rods-to-chassis nut/bolt to 65–87 ft. lbs. (88–118 Nm) and the parallel rods-to-knuckle nut/bolt to 65–87 ft. lbs. (88–118 Nm).
6. To complete the installation, reverse the removal procedures.

4WD Models With Radius Rod

1. Raise and safely support the vehicle.
2. Remove the wheel assembly.
3. Remove the radius rod-to-knuckle nut and bolt.
4. Remove the radius rod-to-chassis nut/bolt and the rod.
5. To install, reverse the removal procedures. Torque the radius rod-to-chassis nut/bolt to 65–80 ft. lbs. (88–108 Nm) and the radius rod-to-knuckle nut/bolt to 58–72 ft. lbs. (78–98 Nm).
6. To complete the installation, reverse the removal procedures.

4WD With Parallel Rods

Dual rods are connected from the chassis to the knuckle.
1. Raise and safely support the vehicle.
2. Remove the wheel assembly.
3. Remove the parallel rods-to-knuckle nut and bolt.
4. Remove the parallel rods-to-chassis nut/bolt and the rods.
5. To install, reverse the removal procedures. Torque the parallel rods-to-chassis nut/bolt to 58–72 ft. lbs. (78–98 Nm) and the parallel rods-to-knuckle nut/bolt to 58–72 ft. lbs. (78–98 Nm).
6. To complete the installation, reverse the removal procedures.

Rear Wheel Bearings

For RWD models, refer to the drive axle section.

Removal and Installation
AXXESS

1. Remove the hub cap, the grease cap and the cotter pin.
2. Loosen the wheel hub nut; do not remove it.
3. Raise and safely support the vehicle.
4. Remove the wheel assembly and the brake drum.
5. Remove the hub nut, the washer and the wheel hub assembly.

NOTE: If the wheel bearings are defective, replace the entire wheel hub bearing assembly.

6. To install, reverse the removal procedures. Torque the wheel hub nut to 137–188 ft. lbs. (186–255 Nm).

SPECIFICATIONS

ENGINE IDENTIFICATION

Year	Model	Engine Displacement cu. in. (cc/liter)	Engine Series Identification	No. of Cylinders	Engine Type
1986	Samurai	80.8 (1324/1.3)	5	4	SOHC
1987	Samurai	80.8 (1324/1.3)	5	4	SOHC
1988	Samurai	80.8 (1324/1.3)	5	4	SOHC
1989	Samurai	80.8 (1324/1.3)	5	4	SOHC
	Sidekick	79.2 (1298/1.3)	5	4	SOHC
	Sidekick	97.0 (1590/1.6)	0	4	SOHC
	Tracker	97.0 (1590/1.6)	U	4	SOHC
1990	Samurai	79.2 (1298/1.3)	5	4	SOHC
	Sidekick	97.0 (1590/1.6)	0	4	SOHC
	Tracker	97.0 (1590/1.6)	U	4	SOHC

GENERAL ENGINE SPECIFICATIONS

Year	Model	Engine Displacement cu. in. (cc)	Fuel System Type	Net Horsepower @ rpm	Net Torque @ rpm (ft. lbs.)	Bore × Stroke (in.)	Compression Ratio	Oil Pressure @ rpm
1986	Samurai	80.8 (1324)	2 bbl	NA	NA	2.91 × 3.03	8.9:1	42.7–59.7 ①
1987	Samurai	80.8 (1324)	2 bbl	NA	NA	2.91 × 3.03	8.9:1	42.7–59.7 ①
1988	Samurai	80.8 (1324)	2 bbl	NA	NA	2.91 × 3.03	8.9:1	42.7–59.7 ①
1989	Samurai	80.8 (1324)	2 bbl	64 @ 5500	74 @ 3500	NA	8.9:1	NA
	Sidekick	79.2 (1298)	2 bbl	64 @ 5500	73 @ 3500	2.91 × 2.97	8.7:1	NA
	Sidekick	97.0 (1590)	EFI	80 @ 5400	94 @ 3000	2.95 × 3.54	8.9:1	51.2–62.6 ①
	Tracker	97.0 (1590)	EFI	80 @ 5400	94 @ 3000	2.95 × 3.54	8.9:1	51.2–62.6 ①
1990	Samurai	79.2 (1298)	EFI	66 @ 6000	76 @ 3500	NA	9.5:1	NA
	Sidekick	97.0 (1590)	EFI	80 @ 5400	94 @ 3000	2.95 × 3.54	8.9:1	51.2–62.6 ①
	Tracker	97.0 (1590)	EFI	80 @ 5400	94 @ 3000	2.95 × 3.54	8.9:1	51.2–62.6 ①

① @ 3000 rpm.

GASOLINE ENGINE TUNE-UP SPECIFICATIONS

Year	Model	Engine Displacement cu. in. (cc)	Spark Plugs Type	Gap (in.)	Ignition Timing (deg.) MT	AT	Compression Pressure (psi)	Fuel Pump (psi)	Idle Speed (rpm) MT	AT	Valve Clearance In. Ex.
1986	Samurai	80.8 (1324)	BPR5ES	.027–.031	10B	NA	170–199	3–4	800	NA	①
1987	Samurai	80.8 (1324)	BPR5ES	.027–.031	10B	NA	170–199	3–4	800	NA	①
1988	Samurai	80.8 (1324)	BPR5ES	.027–.031	10B	NA	170–199	3–4	800	NA	①
1989	Samurai	80.8 (1324)	NA	NA	NA	NA	NA	NA	NA	NA	NA
	Sidekick	79.2 (1298)	BPR5ES	.027–.031	10B	NA	170–199	34.1–39.8	800	NA	①
	Sidekick	94.0 (1590)	BPR5ES	.027–.031	8B	8B	170–199	34.1–39.8	800	800	①
	Tracker	94.0 (1590)	BPR5ES	.027–.031	8B	8B	170–199	34.1–39.8	800	800	①
1990	Samurai	79.2 (1298)	NA	NA	NA	NA	NA	NA	NA	NA	NA
	Sidekick	94.0 (1590)	BPR5ES	.027–.031	8B	8B	170–199	34.1–39.8	800	800	①
	Tracker	94.0 (1590)	BPR5ES	.027–.031	8B	8B	170–199	34.1–39.8	800	800	①

① Intake
   Cold—0.0051–0.0067 in.
   Hot—0.009–0.011 in.

Exhaust
   Cold—0.0063–0.0079 in.
   Hot—0.0102–0.0118 in.

FIRING ORDERS

NOTE: To avoid confusion, always replace spark plug wires one at a time.

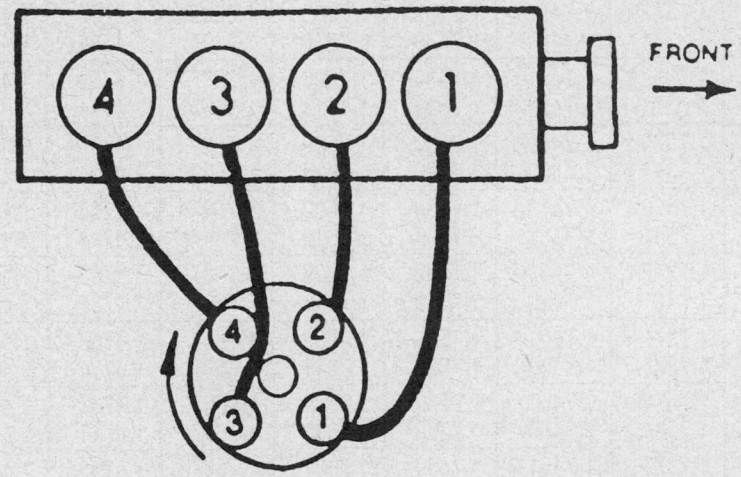

Suzuki 1.3L and 1.6L
Engine firing order: 1–3–4–2
Distributor rotation: clockwise

CAPACITIES

Year	Model	Engine Displacement cu. in. (cc)	Engine Crankcase with Filter	Engine Crankcase without Filter	Transmission (pts.) 4-Spd	Transmission (pts.) 5-Spd	Transmission (pts.) Auto.	Drive Axle (pts.)	Fuel Tank (gal.)	Cooling System (qts.)
1986	Samurai	80.8 (1324)	3.7	3.5	NA	2.7	NA	②	10.6	5.1
1987	Samurai	80.8 (1324)	3.7	3.5	NA	2.7	NA	②	10.6	5.1
1988	Samurai	80.8 (1324)	3.7	3.5	NA	2.7	NA	②	10.6	5.1
1989	Samurai	80.8 (1324)	3.7	3.5	NA	2.7	NA	②	10.6	5.1
	Sidekick	79.2 (1298)	3.7	3.5	NA	3.2	NA	③	11.1	①
	Sidekick	97.0 (1590)	4.5	4.3	NA	3.2	10.8	③	11.1	①
	Tracker	97.0 (1590)	4.5	4.3	NA	3.2	9.8	④	11.1	①
1990	Samurai	79.2 (1298)	3.7	3.5	NA	2.7	NA	②	10.6	5.1
	Sidekick	97.0 (1590)	4.5	4.3	NA	3.2	10.8	③	11.1	①
	Tracker	97.0 (1590)	4.5	4.3	NA	3.2	9.8	④	11.1	①

① Manual transmission—5.6 qts.
Automatic transmission—5.5 qts.
② Front—4.2 pts.
Rear—3.2 pts.
③ Front—2.1 pts.
Rear—4.6 pts.
④ Front—4.6 pts.
Rear—2.1 pts.

CAMSHAFT SPECIFICATIONS

All measurements are given in inches.

Year	Engine Displacement cu. in. (cc)	Journal Diameter 1	Journal Diameter 2	Journal Diameter 3	Journal Diameter 4	Journal Diameter 5	Lobe Lift In.	Lobe Lift Ex.	Bearing Clearance	Camshaft End Play
1986	80.8 (1324)	1.7372–1.7381	1.7451–1.7460	1.7530–1.7539	1.7609–1.7618	1.7687–1.7697	1.4763–1.4724	1.4763–1.4724	.0020–.0036 ①	.0039
1987	80.8 (1324)	1.7372–1.7381	1.7451–1.7460	1.7530–1.7539	1.7609–1.7618	1.7687–1.7697	1.4763–1.4724	1.4763–1.4724	.0020–.0036 ①	.0039
1988	80.8 (1324)	1.7372–1.7381	1.7451–1.7460	1.7530–1.7539	1.7609–1.7618	1.7687–1.7697	1.4763–1.4724	1.4763–1.4724	.0020–.0036 ①	.0039
1989	79.2 (1298)	1.7372–1.7381	1.7451–1.7460	1.7530–1.7539	1.7609–1.7618	1.7687–1.7697	1.4763–1.4724	1.4763–1.4724	.0020–.0036 ①	.0039
	80.8 (1324)	1.7372–1.7381	1.7451–1.7460	1.7530–1.7539	1.7609–1.7618	1.7687–1.7697	1.4763–1.4724	1.4763–1.4724	.0020–.0036 ①	.0039
	97.0 (1590)	1.7372–1.7381	1.7451–1.7460	1.7530–1.7539	1.7609–1.7618	1.7687–1.7697	1.4763–1.4724	1.4763–1.4724	.0020–.0036 ①	.0039
1990	79.2 (1298)	1.7372–1.7381	1.7451–1.7460	1.7530–1.7539	1.7609–1.7618	1.7687–1.7697	1.4763–1.4724	1.4763–1.4724	.0020–.0036 ①	.0039
	80.8 (1324)	1.7372–1.7381	1.7451–1.7460	1.7530–1.7539	1.7609–1.7618	1.7687–1.7697	1.4763–1.4724	1.4763–1.4724	.0020–.0036 ①	.0039
	97.0 (1590)	1.7372–1.7381	1.7451–1.7460	1.7530–1.7539	1.7609–1.7618	1.7687–1.7697	1.4763–1.4724	1.4763–1.4724	.0020–.0036 ①	.0039

① .0059 Limit.

CRANKSHAFT AND CONNECTING ROD SPECIFICATIONS

All measurements are given in inches.

| Year | Engine Displacement cu. in. (cc) | Crankshaft | | | | Connecting Rod | | |
		Main Brg. Journal Dia.	Main Brg. Oil Clearance	Shaft End-play	Thrust on No.	Journal Diameter	Oil Clearance	Side Clearance
1986	80.8 (1324)	①	.0008–.0016 ②	.0044–.0122 ③	3	1.6529–1.6535	.0012–.0019 ④	.0039–.0078 ⑤
1987	80.8 (1324)	①	.0008–.0016 ②	.0044–.0122 ③	3	1.6529–1.6535	.0012–.0019 ④	.0039–.0078 ⑤
1988	80.8 (1324)	①	.0008–.0016 ②	.0044–.0122 ③	3	1.6529–1.6535	.0012–.0019 ④	.0039–.0078 ⑤
1989	79.2 (1298)	①	.0008–.0016 ②	.0044–.0122 ③	3	1.6529–1.6535	.0012–.0019 ④	.0039–.0078 ⑤
	80.8 (1324)	①	.0008–.0016 ②	.0044–.0122 ③	3	1.6529–1.6535	.0012–.0019 ④	.0039–.0078 ⑤
	97 (1590)	⑥	.0012–.0023	.0100–.0149	3	1.7316–1.7323	.0008–.0031	.0039–.0137
1990	79.2 (1298)	①	.0008–.0016 ②	.0044–.0122 ③	3	1.6529–1.6535	.0012–.0019 ④	.0039–.0078 ⑤
	97 (1590)	⑥	.0012–.0023	.0100–.0149	3	1.7316–1.7323	.0008–.0031	.0039–.0137

① Bearing cap stamped
  No. 1—1.7714–1.7716 in.
  No. 2—1.7712–1.7714 in.
  No. 3—1.7710–1.7712 in.
② Maximum clearance—.0023
③ Maximum clearance—.0149
④ Maximum clearance—.0031
⑤ Maximum clearance—.0137
⑥ Bearing cap stamped
  No. 1—2.047–2.0472
  No. 2—2.0468–2.0470
  No. 3—2.0465–2.0468

VALVE SPECIFICATIONS

| Year | Engine Displacement cu. in. (cc) | Seat Angle (deg.) | Face Angle (deg.) | Spring Test Pressure (lbs.) | Spring Installed Height (in.) | Stem-to-Guide Clearance (in.) | | Stem Diameter (in.) | |
						Intake	Exhaust	Intake	Exhaust
1986	80.8 (1324)	45	45	54.7–64.3 @ 1.63 in.	1.9409	.0008–.0019 ①	.0014–.0025 ②	.2742–.2748	.2737–.2742
1987	80.8 (1324)	45	45	54.7–64.3 @ 1.63 in.	1.9409	.0008–.0019 ①	.0014–.0025 ②	.2742–.2748	.2737–.2742
1988	80.8 (1324)	45	45	54.7–64.3 @ 1.63 in.	1.9409	.0008–.0019 ①	.0014–.0025 ②	.2742–.2748	.2737–.2742
1989	79.2 (1298)	45	45	54.7–64.3 @ 1.63 in.	1.9409	.0008–.0019 ①	.0014–.0025 ②	.2742–.2748	.2737–.2742
	80.8 (1324)	45	45	54.7–64.3 @ 1.63 in.	1.9409	.0008–.0019 ①	.0014–.0025 ②	.2742–.2748	.2737–.2742
	97.0 (1590)	45	45	54.7–64.3 @ 1.63 in.	1.9074	.0008–.0019 ①	.0014–.0025 ②	.2742–.2748	.2737–.2742
1990	79.2 (1298)	45	45	54.7–64.3 @ 1.63 in.	1.9409	.0008–.0019 ①	.0014–.0025 ②	.2742–.2748	.2737–.2742
	97.0 (1590)	45	45	54.7–64.3 @ 1.63 in.	1.9074	.0008–.0019 ①	.0014–.0025 ②	.2742–.2748	.2737–.2742

① Maximum clearance—.0027 in.
② Maximum clearance—.0035 in.

PISTON AND RING SPECIFICATIONS

All measurements are given in inches.

Year	Engine Displacement cu. in. (cc)	Piston Clearance	Ring Gap			Ring Side Clearance		
			Top Compression	Bottom Compression	Oil Control	Top Compression	Bottom Compression	Oil Control
1986	80.8 (1324)	.0008–.0015	.0079–.0129 ①	.0079–.0137 ①	.0079–.0275 ②	.0012–.0027	.0008–.0023	NA
1987	80.8 (1324)	.0008–.0015	.0079–.0129 ①	.0079–.0137 ①	.0079–.0275 ②	.0012–.0027	.0008–.0023	NA
1988	80.8 (1324)	.0008–.0015	.0079–.0129 ①	.0079–.0137 ①	.0079–.0275 ②	.0012–.0027	.0008–.0023	NA
1989	79.2 (1298)	.0008–.0015	.0079–.0129 ①	.0079–.0137 ①	.0079–.0275 ②	.0012–.0027	.0008–.0023	NA
	80.8 (1324)	.0008–.0015	.0079–.0129 ①	.0079–.0137 ①	.0079–.0275 ②	.0012–.0027	.0008–.0023	NA
	97.0 (1590)	.0008–.0015	.0079–.0129 ①	.0079–.0137 ①	.0079–.0275 ②	.0012–.0027	.0008–.0023	NA
1990	79.2 (1298)	.0008–.0015	.0079–.0129 ①	.0079–.0137 ①	.0079–.0275 ②	.0012–.0027	.0008–.0023	NA
	97.0 (1590)	.0008–.0015	.0079–.0129 ①	.0079–.0137 ①	.0079–.0275 ②	.0012–.0027	.0008–.0023	NA

① Limit—.0275 in.
② Limit—.0708 in.

TORQUE SPECIFICATIONS

All readings in ft. lbs.

Year	Engine Displacement cu. in. (cc)	Cylinder Head Bolts	Main Bearing Bolts	Rod Bearing Bolts	Crankshaft Pulley Bolts	Flywheel Bolts	Manifold		Spark Plugs
							Intake	Exhaust	
1986	80.8 (1324)	46–50	36–41	24–26	7–9	41–47	13–20	13–20	14–21
1987	80.8 (1324)	46–50	36–41	24–26	7–9	41–47	13–20	13–20	14–21
1988	80.8 (1324)	46–50	36–41	24–26	7–9	41–47	13–20	13–20	14–21
1989	79.2 (1298)	46–50	36–41	24–26	7–9	41–47	13–20	13–20	14–21
	80.8 (1324)	46–50	36–41	24–26	7–9	41–47	13–20	13–20	14–21
	97.0 (1590)	54	36–41	26	8	57–58	17	17	18
1990	79.2 (1298)	46–50	36–41	24–26	7–9	41–47	13–20	13–20	14–21
	97.0 (1590)	54	36–41	26	8	57–58	17	17	18

BRAKE SPECIFICATIONS

All measurements in inches unless noted

Year	Model	Lug Nut Torque (ft. lbs.)	Master Cylinder Bore	Brake Disc Minimum Thickness	Brake Disc Maximum Runout	Standard Brake Drum Diameter	Minimum Lining Thickness Front	Minimum Lining Thickness Rear
1986	Samurai	36–57	NA	.394	.334	8.66	.236 ①	.120 ②
1987	Samurai	36–57	NA	.394	.334	8.66	.236 ①	.120 ②
1988	Samurai	36–57	NA	.394	.334	8.66	.236 ①	.120 ②
1989	Samurai	36–57	NA	.394	.334	8.66	.236 ①	.120 ②
	Sidekick	36–57	NA	.394	.334	8.66	.236 ①	.120 ②
	Tracker	48	NA	.394	.334	8.66	.236 ①	.120 ②
1990	Samurai	36–57	NA	.394	.334	8.66	.236 ①	.120 ②
	Sidekick	36–57	NA	.394	.334	8.66	.236 ①	.120 ②
	Tracker	48	NA	.394	.334	8.66	.236 ①	.120 ②

① Lining plus pad rim
② Lining plus shoe rim

WHEEL ALIGNMENT

Year	Model	Caster Range (deg.)	Caster Preferred Setting (deg.)	Camber Range (deg.)	Camber Preferred Setting (deg.)	Toe-in (in.)	Steering Axis Inclination (deg.)
1986	Samurai	2½P–4½P	3½P	¼P–1¾P	1P	$^5/_{32}$–$^{15}/_{32}$	9
1987	Samurai	2½P–4½P	3½P	¼P–1¾P	1P	$^5/_{32}$–$^{15}/_{32}$	9
1988	Samurai	2½P–4½P	3½P	¼P–1¾P	1P	$^5/_{32}$–$^{15}/_{32}$	9
1989	Samurai	2½P–4½P	3½P	¼P–1¾P	1P	$^5/_{32}$–$^{15}/_{32}$	9
	Sidekick	½P–2½P	1½P	½N–1½P	½P	$^5/_{16}$–¼	NA
	Tracker	½P–2½P	1½P	½N–1½P	½P	$^3/_{32}$–¼	31
1990	Samurai	2½P–4½P	3½P	¼P–1¾P	1P	$^5/_{32}$–$^{15}/_{32}$	9
	Sidekick	½P–2½P	1½P	½N–1½P	½P	$^5/_{16}$–¼	NA
	Tracker	½P–2½P	1½P	½N–1½P	½P	$^3/_{32}$–¼	31

ENGINE ELECTRICAL

NOTE: Disconnecting the battery cable on some vehicles may interfere with the functions of the on board computer systems and may require the computer to undergo a relearning process, once the negative battery cable is disconnected.

Distributor

Removal and Installation

1. Disconnect the negative battery terminal from the battery.
2. Disconnect vacuum hose and electrical connections.

NOTE: Do not bend or twist the spark plug wires to avoid internal damage. Grip the the wire boot when removing or installing the wires.

3. Remove the distributor cap.
4. Mark the rotor position on the distributor housing and the distributor housing position on the engine.
5. Remove the distributor flange bolt and remove the distributor.

NOTE: Do not crank the engine with the distributor removed.

6. If the engine has not been disturbed with the distributor removed, reverse the removal procedure to install.
7. Set the timing to specification.
8. If the engine was accidentally cranked after the distributor was removed (or if the matchmark was not made prior to the removal of the distributor), the following procedure can be used to properly the position the distributor:

a. Rotate the crankshaft in the clockwise position until the specified timing mark on the flywheel aligns with the timing matchmark on the engine.

NOTE: After aligning the 2 marks, remove the cylinder head cover to visually confirm that the rocker arms are not riding on the camshaft cams at No.1 cylinder. If the arms are found to be riding on the cams, turn the crankshaft 360 degrees to realign the 2 marks.

b. Position the rotor to the No.1 cylinder position and install the distributor.
c. Re-attach the vacuum and electrical connections.
d. Adjust the ignition timing.

Ignition Timing

Adjustment

1. Start the engine and warm up to normal operating temperature. Prior to any adjustment, be sure all the electrical accessories are OFF .
2. After warming up, make sure the idle speed is within the proper specification.
3. Connect the timing light to the No.1 cylinder spark plug wire.
4. With the engine running at the specified idle speed, direct the timing light to the crankshaft pulley. If the specified timing mark on the timing tab is aligned with the timing notch on the crankshaft pulley the ignition is properly timed.
5. If the timing is out of adjustment, loosen the distributor flange bolt and turn the distributor housing to advance or retard the timing. Turn the distributor counterclockwise to advance the timing and clockwise to retard the timing.
6. After the adjustment, tighten the flange bolt and recheck the timing.

Alternator

For further information, please refer to "Electrical" in the Unit Repair section.

Belt Tension Adjustment

1. Disconnect the negative battery cable.
2. Loosen the alternator bolt and pivot bolts.
3. Adjust the belt tension to 0.24 – 0.32 in. of deflection using a belt tension guage.

Removal and Installation

1. Disconnect the negative battery cable.
2. Disconnect the wire coupler and white lead wire from the alternator.
3. Remove the charcoal cannister mounting bracket, if neccessary.
4. Remove the alternator mounting bolt and alternator drive belt adjusting bolt.
5. Remove the alternator from the vehicle.
6. Installation is the reverse of the removal procedure. Adjust the drive belt tension.

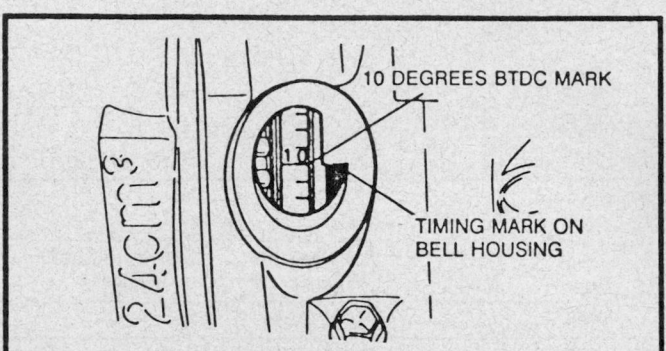

Timing mark alignment — Samurai
The timing marks are visible by removing the rubber plug in the bell housing

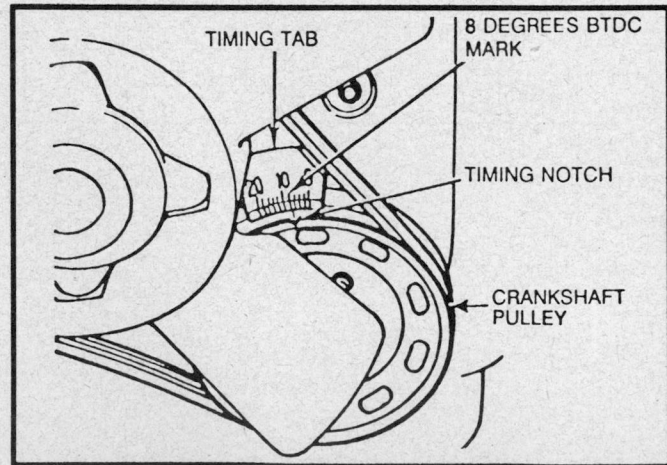

Timing belt marks — Sidekick and Tracker

Starter

For further information, please refer to "Electrical" in the Unit Repair section.

Removal and Installation

1. Disconnect the negative battery cable.

2. Raise and support the vehicle safely.
3. Disconnect the lead wire and battery cable from the starter motor.
4. Support the starter and remove the 2 mounting bolts.
5. Remove the starter.
6. Installation is the reverse of the removal procedure.

CHASSIS ELECTRICAL

Heater Blower Motor

Removal and Installation

SAMURAI

1. Disconnect the negative battery cable. Drain the cooling system.
2. Disconnect the inlet and outlet heater hoses from the heater core.
3. Take off the horn pad and remove the steering wheel retaining nut and remove the steering wheel by using the proper puller.
4. Disconnect and tag the radio and cigar lighter wires. Remove the radio from the vehicle.
5. Remove the ash tray and mounting plate.
6. Disconnect the hood release cable from the release lever.
7. Disconnect and tag the heater control cables and wires at the controls.
8. Remove the heater control lever knobs and facing plate. Loosen the lever case screws.
9. Remove the defroster and side ventilator hoses.
10. Disconnect the lead wires and speedometer cable from the speedometer and remove the lead wires from the heater controls.
11. Disconnect the wiring harness clamps from the instrument panel.
12. Loosen the instrument panel mounting screws and remove the instrument panel.

NOTE: When removing the heater lever case which is fitted in the steering column holder, be very careful not to damage it.

13. Loosen the front door opening stop screws and remove the steering column holder.
14. Disconnect and tag the blower motor and resistor connections at the coupler.
15. Loosen the heater case securing nut on the engine side.
16. Remove the heater assembly from the vehicle.
17. Remove the blower motor from the case.

To install:

18. Install the blower motor in the heater case and replace the heater assembly in the vehicle.
19. Tighten the heater case securing nut on the engine side.
20. Install the blower motor and resistor connections at the coupler.
21. Tighten the front door opening stop screws and replace the steering column holder.
22. Tighten the instrument panel mounting screws and replace the instrument panel.
23. Reconnect the wiring harness clamps to the instrument panel.
24. Reconnect the lead wires and speedometer cable to the speedometer.
25. Install the defroster and side ventilator hoses.
26. Replace the heater control knobs and plate, and tighten the lever case screws.
27. Reconnect the heater control cables at the controls.

28. Reconnect the hood release cable to the release lever.
29. Replace the ash tray and mounting plate.
30. Reconnect the radio and cigar lighter wires. Install the radio in the vehicle.
31. Install the horn pad and replace the steering wheel retaining nut and install the steering wheel.
32. Reconnect the inlet and outlet heater hoses to heater core.
33. Refill the cooling system with the proper coolant. Replace the negative battery cable.

SIDEKICK AND TRACKER

1. Disconnect the negative battery cable.
2. Remove the glove box assembly.
3. Disconnect the blower motor and resistor wire connectors.
4. Disconnect the fresh air control cable from the blower motor case.
5. Loosen, but do not remove the blower housing fastener bolts.
6. Remove the 3 blower motor mounting screws.
7. Remove the blower motor.
8. Installation is the reverse of the removal procedure.

Windshield Wiper Motor

Removal and Installation

SAMURAI SOFT TOP

1. Disconnect the negative battery cable.
2. Remove the wiper linkage to wiper mounting nut.
3. Disconnect the wire connector from the wiper motor.
4. Remove the 3 wiper mounting bolts and remove the wiper motor.
5. Installation is the reverse of the removal procedure.

SAMURAI HARD TOP

NOTE: On hard top models, the windshield frame may have to be removed.

1. Disconnect the negative battery cable.
2. Loosen the weatherstrip bonded to the window body panel and remove the windshield from the vehicle.
3. Remove the wiper linkage to wiper mounting nut.
4. Disconnect the wire connector from the wiper motor.
5. Remove the 3 wiper mounting bolts and remove the wiper motor.
6. Installation is the reverse of the removal procedure.
7. Remove the urethane gum sticking to the glass and the window panel.
8. Use a proper cleaning solvent to clean the glass, the weatherstrip and the window body panel.
9. Assemble the glass into the weatherstrip's glass channel. Do not us soapy water as a lubricant, use a proper cleaning agent as a lubricant.
10. Insert a cord into the weatherstrip's body flange channel and install the glass and weatherstrip assembly to the window body panel.
11. Start the installation from the bottom center of the glass.
12. Position the glass and weatherstrip assembly in the win-

dow panel body opening, with a helper applying pressure from the outside.

13. Pull the weatherstrip over the flange with the cord to install the assembly into position.

14. Tap the glass from the outside to settle into position.

15. Use a proper urethane based bonding agent and fill between the glass and the weatherstrip and also between the window body panel and the weatherstrip.

16. Clean any excess bonding agent with a proper cleaning solvent.

SIDEKICK AND TRACKER

1. Disconnect the negative battery cable.
2. Remove the right and left cowl grilles.
3. Remove the wiper linkage to wiper mounting nut.
4. Disconnect the wire connector from the wiper motor.
5. Remove the 4 wiper mounting bolts and remove the wiper motor.
6. Installation is the reverse of the removal procedure.

Instrument Cluster

Removal and Installation

1. Disconnect the negative battery cable.
2. Remove the lower instrument panel cover.
3. Loosen, but do not remove the 2 upper and 4 lower steering column mounting bolts. Lower and support the steering column, if neccessary.
4. Remove the outer instrument cluster cover.
5. Remove the 4 cluster mounting screws, and slide the cluster outwards.
6. Disconnect the lead wires and speedometer cable from the speedometer.
7. Remove the speedometer.
8. Disconnect and tag the wire connector from the rear of the instrument cluster.
9. Remove the instrument cluster.
10. Installation is the reverse of the removal procedure.

Combination Switch

The combination switch incorporates the turn signal, windshield wiper, dimmer and headlight switches into one switch.

Removal and Installation

1. Disconnect the negative battery cable.
2. Take off the horn button and remove the steering wheel retaining nut and remove the steering wheel.
3. Remove the upper and lower column cover screws and remove the covers.
4. Disconnect the lead wires from the combination switch at the connector.
5. Remove the combination switch assembly screws.
6. Remove the combination switch from the steering column.
7. Installation is the reverse of the removal procedure.

Ignition Switch

1. Disconnect the negative battery cable.
2. Remove the steering wheel from the vehicle.
3. Disconnect the wire connector at the ignition switch.
4. With the ignition switch in the **OFF** position, remove the mounting bolts and remove the switch.
5. Installation is the reverse of the removal procedure.

Ignition Lock

1. Disconnect the negative battery cable.

2. Remove the steering wheel.
3. Disconnect the lead wires to the ignition and combination switches.
4. Disconnect the steering joint by removing the joint bolt.
5. Remove the steering column fastening bolts.
6. Remove the steering column assembly.
7. Using a center punch, loosen and remove the steering lock mounting bolts.
8. Turn the key to **ACC** or **ON** position and remove the steering lock assembly from the steering column.
9. To install the switch position the oblong hole of the steering shaft in the center of the hole in the steering column.
10. Turn the ignition key to the **ACC** or **ON** position and install the steering lock assembly onto the column.
11. Turn the ignition key to the **LOCK** position and remove it.
12. Align the hub on the lock with oblong hole of the steering shaft.
13. Rotate the shaft to assure that the steering shaft is locked.
14. Tighten the 2 new steering lock mounting bolts.
15. Turn the ignition key to the **ACC** or **ON** position and check to be sure that the steering shaft rotates smoothly. Also check the lock mechanism.
16. Install the steering column assembly by attaching the steering joint and joint bolt.
17. Install the steering column fastening bolts.
18. Reconnect the lead wires to the ignition and combination switches.
19. Replace the steering wheel and negative battery cable.

Stoplight Switch

Removal and Installation

1. Disconnect the negative battery cable. Remove the under dash trim panel, if equipped.
2. Push the brake pedal down and remove the stoplight locknut.
3. Disconnect the wire connector at the switch.
4. Remove the switch from the bracket.
5. Install the new switch on the bracket.
6. Adjust the switch so that there is 0.02–0.04 in. clearance between the switch and the brake pedal.
7. Replace the locknut and tighten to 7.5–10.5 ft. lbs.
8. Replace the negative battery cable.

Clutch Switch

Removal and Installation

SIDEKICK AND TRACKER

1. Disconnect the negative battery cable. Remove the under dash trim panel, if equipped.
2. Disconnect the start switch connector beside the clutch pedal bracket.
3. Remove the locknut and start switch.

Fuses and Circuit Breakers

Location

The fuse box is located under the drivers side of the dashboard.

Engine Cooling

Radiator

Removal and Installation

1. Disconnect the negative battery cable.
2. Drain the cooling system.

3. Disconnect and plug the transmission cooler lines, if equipped.

4. Loosen the water pump drive belt tension.

5. Remove cooling fan and radiator shroud.

6. Disconnect the water hoses to the radiator.

7. Remove the radiator retaining bolts and remove the radiator.

8. Replace the radiator mounting bolts and install the radiator.

9. Reconnect the water hoses to the radiator.

10. Install the cooling fan and radiator shroud.

11. Tighten the water pump drive belt to the proper tension.

12. Reconnect the transmission cooler lines, if necessary to the radiator.

13. Refill the cooling system.

14. Reconnect the negative battery cable.

Heater Core

Removal and Installation

SAMURAI

1. Disconnect the negative battery cable. Drain the cooling system.

2. Disconnect the heater hoses from the heater core.

3. Disconnect the radio and cigar lighter lead wires, and remove the radio from the vehicle.

4. Remove the ash tray and mounting plate.

5. Disconnect the hood release cable from the release lever.

6. Disconnect and tag the heater control cables and wires at the controls.

7. Remove the heater control lever knobs and facing plate, and loosen the lever case screws.

8. Remove the defroster and side ventilator hoses.

9. Disconnect the lead wires and speedometer cables from the speedometer.

10. Disconnect the wiring harness from the instrument panel.

11. Loosen the instrument panel mounting screws and remove the instrument panel.

12. Loosen the front door opening stop screws and remove the steering column holder.

13. Disconnect and tag the blower motor and resistor connections at the coupler.

14. Loosen the heater securing nut on the engine side.

15. Remove the heater assembly from the vehicle.

16. Remove the clips holding the heater case together, separate the case and remove the heater core.

To install:

17. Install the heater core into the heater case and replace the clips holding the case together.

18. Install the heater assembly in the vehicle and tighten the securing nut on the engine side.

19. Reconnect the blower motor and resistor connections at the coupler.

20. Replace the steering column holder and tighten the front door opening stop screws.

21. Install the instrument panel and tighten panel mounting screws.

22. Reconnect the wiring harness to the instrument panel.

23. Install the defroster and side ventilator hoses.

24. Tighten the heater control case screws and replace the control knobs and facing plate.

25. Reconnect the heater control cable and wires to the heater control.

26. Reconnect the hood release cable the release lever.

27. Replace the ash tray and mounting plate.

28. Install radio and connect the cigar lighter and radio wires.

29. Reconnect the heater hoses to the heater core

30. Refill the cooling system to the proper with the proper coolant. Replace the negative cable.

SIDEKICK AND TRACKER

1. Disconnect the negative battery cable. Drain the cooling system.

2. Disconnect the heater hose from the heater core.

3. Remove the steering wheel. Disconnect the lead wires from the ignition and combination switches.

4. Disconnect the steering joint, by removing the joint bolt.

5. Remove the steering column fastener bolts and remove the steering column assembly.

6. Disconnect the 2 front screws from the center console.

7. Disconnect the 2 back lock pins from the console.

8. Ease in the shifter boot and lift out the housing and console.

9. Remove the steering wheel housing and instrument cluster.

10. Remove the 3 inspection cover and upper housing cover bolts.

11. Remove the 3 lower housing bolts on the driver's side and remove the center cover dash mount.

12. Remove the glove box and the lower dash screws to remove the handle bar on the passenger's side.

13. Move the hood release bolt lever and remove the center mounting bracket from the radio and ash tray.

14. Disconnect the wiring harness and remove the instrument panel.

15. Disconnect all the wiring connections and cables from the heater controls.

16. Disconnect the defroster duct and speedometer cable retaining bracket from the heater case.

17. Remove the heater assembly and remove the heater core.

To install:

18. Install the heater core and replace the heater assembly.

19. Reconnect the defroster duct and speedometer cable retaining bracket to the heater case.

20. Reconnect the wiring connections and cables to the heater controls.

21. Reconnect the wiring harness and install the instrument panel.

22. Replace the center mounting bracket from the radio and ash tray and realign hood release bolt lever.

23. Replace the handle bar on the passenger's side and install the glove box and lower dash screws.

24. Install the center cover dash mount and replace the 3 lower housing bolts on the driver's side.

25. Install the upper housing and inspection cover bolts.

26. Install the instrument cluster and steering wheel housing.

27. Install center housing and console and connect the 2 back lock pins to the console.

28. Connect the 2 front screws to center console.

29. Install the steering column assembly and replace the steering column fastener bolts.

30. Install the joint bolt and connect the steering joint to the steering column assembly.

31. Connect the lead wires to the ignition and combination switches and install the steering wheel.

32. Connect the heater hoses to the heater core.

33. Refill the cooling system with the proper coolant and replace the negative battery cable.

Water Pump

Removal and Installation

1. Disconnect the negative battery cable.

2. Drain the cooling system.

3. Loosen the drive belt tension and remove the drive belt. If equipped, loosen the air conditioning belt tension and remove the air conditioning belt.

4. Remove the radiator fan shroud mounting bolts and radia-

tor fan mounting bolts. Remove the radiator shroud, fan and water pump pulley from the vehicle.

5. Remove the crankshaft pulley bolts and remove the crankshaft pulley.

NOTE: The crankshaft pulley bolt can be removed without removing the center crankshaft bolt.

6. Remove the timing belt cover mounting bolts and remove the cover.

7. Loosen the timing belt tensioner adjusting bolt and pivot nut. Hold the tensioner to loosen the timing belt and remove the belt from the camshaft pulley.

8. Remove the timing belt tensioner mounting bolts and remove the tensioner plate and spring.

9. Remove the water pump mounting bolts and remove the water pump assembly.

10. On Tracker, it is necessary to remove the dip stick tube and the alternator bracket from the vehicle.

To install:

11. Clean and inspect the surface of the engine before installation.

12. Using a new gasket, install the new water pump on the engine. Torque the mounting bolts to 7.5–9.0 ft. lbs.

13. On Tracker, replace the dip stick tube and the alternator bracket to the vehicle.

14. Install the rubber seals between the water pump to cylinder head and water pump to oil pump.

15. Install the timing belt tensioner plate, tensioner and spring.

16. Align the marks on the timing belt and the camshaft sprocket. Install the timing belt in the same position on the camshaft sprocket as when removed.

17. Adjust the timing belt to be free of any slack. Torque the tensioner bolts to 7.5–9.0 ft. lbs.

18. Install the crankshaft and water pump pulleys. Torque the crankshaft and water pulley bolts to 7.5–9.0 ft. lbs.

19. Install the timing belt cover, cooling fan/clutch, shroud and drive belt. Adjust the belt tension.

20. As required, adjust the intake and exhaust valve lash.

21. Refill the cooling system with the proper coolant and replace the negative battery cable.

Thermostat

Removal and Installation

1. Disconnect the negative battery cable.
2. Drain the cooling system.
3. Disconnect the thermostat cap from the intake manifold and remove the thermostat.
4. Clean and inspect the surfaces of the housing and the engine.
5. Install the new thermostat with the spring facing towards the engine.
6. Install a new gasket and the thermostat cap to the intake manifold.
7. Refill the cooling system with the proper coolant and replace the negative battery cable.

Cooling System Bleeding

In the top portion of the thermostat, an air bleed valve is provided. This valve is for venting air, if any, that is accumulated in the system.

FUEL SYSTEM

Fuel System Service Precaution

When working with the fuel system, certain precautions should be taken; always work in a well ventilated area, keep a dry chemical (Class B) fire extinguisher near the work area. Always disconnect the negative battery cable and do not make any repairs to the fuel system until all the necessary steps for repair have been reviewed.

Relieving Fuel System Pressure

The fuel pressure must be relieved before performing any service on the fuel system.

1. Disconnect the negative battery cable.
2. Remove the fuel filler cap from the fuel filler neck to release the fuel vapor pressure in the fuel tank. Reinstall the fuel cap.
3. Raise and support the vehicle safely.
4. Place an appropriate container under the fuel filter.
5. Cover the plug bolt on the fuel filter inlet union bolt with a rag and loosen the plug bolt slowly to release the fuel pressure gradually.
6. When the pressure has been released, tighten the plug bolt to 7.5 ft. lbs. so that the fuel does not leak.
7. Lower the vehicle.
8. Reconnect the negative battery cable.

Fuel Filter

Removal and Installation

1. Disconnect the negative battery cable.

2. Remove the fuel filler cap to release the fuel vapor pressure in the fuel tank. After releasing pressure, reinstall filler cap.
3. Raise and support the vehicle safely.
4. Release the fuel pressure.
5. Disconnect the inlet and outlet hoses from the fuel filter.
6. Remove the fuel filter from the chassis frame.
7. Installation is the reverse of the removal procedure.

Mechanical Fuel Pump

Removal and Installation

1.3L ENGINE

1. Disconnect the negative battery cable.
2. Remove the fuel filler cap to release the fuel vapor pressure in the fuel tank.
3. Disconnect and tag the fuel inlet, outlet and return hoses from the fuel pump.
4. Remove the fuel pump mounting bolts and remove the fuel pump.
5. Remove the fuel pump mounting rod from the engine and lubricate it with engine oil before installation.
6. Install the lubricated pump rod in the engine.
7. Clean the engine mounting surface and install the fuel pump using a new gasket.
8. Connect the inlet, outlet and return hoses to the fuel pump.
9. Reconnect the negative battery cable. Run the engine and check for leaks when finished.

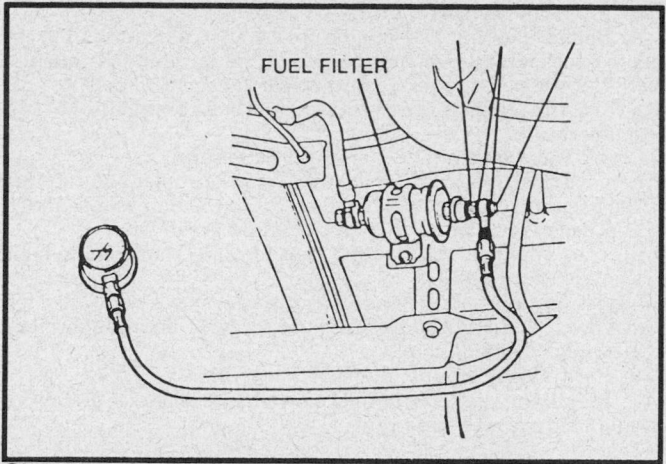

Checking fuel pump pressure—1.6L engine

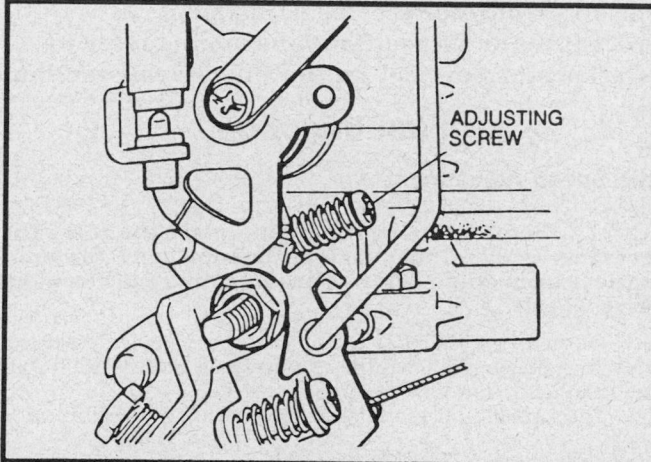

Idle adjustment— 1.3L engine

Electric Fuel Pump

Pressure Testing

1. Remove the fuel filler cap to release the fuel vapor pressure in the fuel tank. Reinstall the cap.
2. Raise and support the vehicle safely.
3. Release the fuel pressure in the fuel feed line.
4. Remove the plug bolt on the fuel filter union bolt and connect the proper fuel pressure gauge to the fuel filter inlet union bolt.

NOTE: If the pressure in the fuel tank is not released prior to system service, the fuel in the fuel tank may be forced out through the fuel hoses during disconnection.

5. Start the engine and warm up to the proper operating temperature.
6. Measure the fuel pressure under each of the following conditions.
   a. At a specified idle speed or with the fuel pump operating and the engine stopped the fuel pressure should read: 34.1–39.8 psi.
   b. Within 1 minute after the fuel pump has stopped the fuel pressure should read: 21.3 psi.
7. Release the fuel pressure and remove the fuel pressure gauge.

8. Install the plug bolt to the fuel filter inlet bolt. Use a new gasket.
9. Start the engine and check for leaks.
10. Lower the vehicle.

Removal and Installation

1.6L ENGINE

The fuel pump is located in the fuel tank. The fuel pump and the fuel gauge sending unit are located on the upper part of the fuel tank.

1. Disconnect the negative battery cable.
2. Remove the rear bumper assembly.
3. Disconnect the fuel gauge sending unit and fuel pump electrical connectors from the fuel tank.
4. Relieve the fuel system pressure.
5. Disconnect the fuel tank filler hose cover, filler hose, and fuel tank inlet valve (breather hose).
6. Disconnect the inlet pipe from the fuel filter and remove the fuel vapor and return hoses.
7. If necessary, drain the fuel from the tank using a hand operating pump.
8. Disconnect the fuel tank protector and remove the fuel tank and cover from the vehicle.
9. Remove the fuel pump from the fuel tank.
10. Install the fuel pump to the fuel tank using a new gasket.
11. Install the fuel tank and cover to the vehicle and connect the fuel tank protector.
12. Replace the fuel vapor and return hoses and connect the inlet pipe to the fuel filter.
13. Reconnect the fuel tank inlet valve (breather hose), filler hose, and fuel tank filler hose cover.
14. Connect the fuel pump and fuel gauge sending sending unit electrical connectors to the fuel tank.
15. Replace the bumper assembly and reconnect the negative battery cable.
16. If necessary, refill the fuel tank with any fuel that had been drained.
17. Start the engine and check for leaks when finished.

Carburetor

Removal and Installation

1. Disconnect the negative battery cable. Drain the cooling system.
2. Remove the air intake case from the carburetor.
3. Disconnect and tag the micro switches, switch vent solenoid valve, fuel cut off valve, vacuum switch valve and mixture control valve (MCSV) lead wires at their couplers.
4. Disconnect the EGR valve bracket from the carburetor.
5. Disconnect the water inlet and outlet hoses from the carburetor.
6. Disconnect the accelerator cable from the carburetor.
7. Relieve the fuel pressure by removing the fuel filler cap and reinstalling it. Remove the fuel inlet hose from the carburetor.
8. Remove the carburetor mounting nuts and remove the carburetor from the intake manifold.
9. Install the carburetor to the intake manifold and replace the mounting nuts. Torque the carburetor mounting nuts to 20 ft. lbs.
10. Install the fuel inlet hose and connect the accelerator cable to the carburetor.
11. Reconnect the water inlet and outlet hoses to the carburetor.
12. Connect the EGR valve bracket to the carburetor.
13. Reconnect the micro switches, switch vent solenoid valve, fuel cut off valve, vacuum switch valve and (MCSV) lead wires to their couplers.
14. Replace the air intake hose to the carburetor.

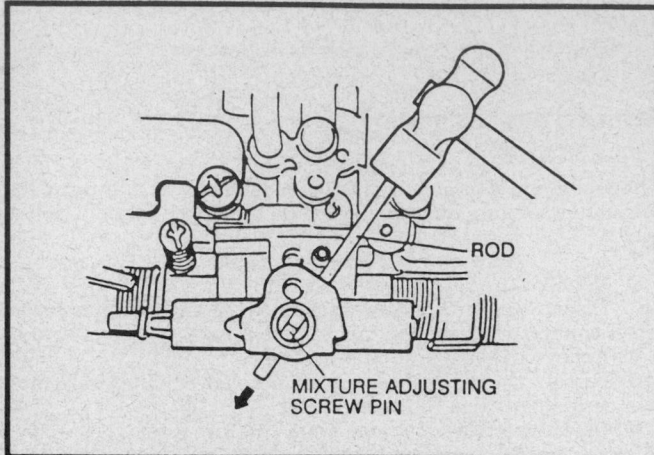

Idle mixture adjustment—1.3L engine

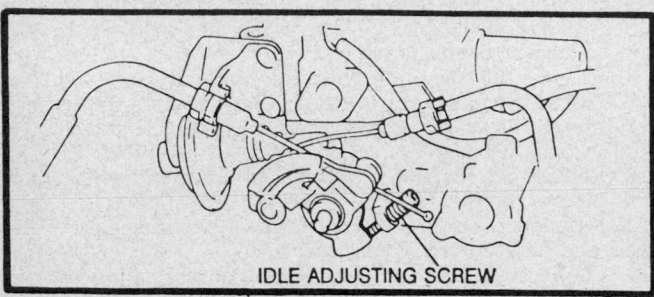

Idle adjustment—1.6L engine

15. Refill the cooling system with the proper coolant and connect the negative battery cable.

Idle Speed Adjustment

NOTE: Before starting the engine, place the gear shift lever in neutral for manual transmission and P for automatic transmission. Set the parking brake and block the drive wheels.

1. Warm up the engine to the normal operating temperature.
2. Check the idle speed to see if within specifications; 750–850 rpm.
3. If idle speed is not within specifications, adjust by turning the idle speed adjusting screw.
4. After idle speed adjustment, check idle-up for operation with the electrical accessories **ON** one at a time.

Idle Mixture Adjustment

1. Remove the carburetor from the intake manifold to gain access to the mixture adjusting screw pin covering the mixture adjusting screw.
2. Drive out the mixture adjusting screw pin using about 0.18 in. thick iron rod.

3. Reinstall the carburetor.
4. Before starting the engine, place the gear shift lever in neutral for manual transmission and **P** for automatic transmission. Set the parking brake and block the drive wheels.
5. Start the engine and warm up to normal operating temperature.
6. Check and adjust the idle speed if necessary.
7. Remove the rubber seal of the dwell check coupler and connect the positive terminal of a dwell meter to the blue and red wire and negative terminal to the black and green wire.
8. Run the engine at 1500–2000 rpm for 30 seconds and adjust the idle speed.
9. Adjust the idle mixture adjusting screw slowly, allowing for the dwell to stabilize after turning screw to obtain a dwell of 10–50 @ 750–850 rpm.
10. Recheck the engine idle speed.
11. Install the rubber seal to the dwell check coupler and drive in idle mixture adjusting pin.

Service Adjustment

For all carburetor service adjustment procedures and Specifications, please refer to "Carburetor Service" in the Unit Repair section.

Fuel Injection

Idle Speed Adjustment

NOTE: Before starting the engine, place the gear shift lever in neutral for manual transmission and P for automatic transmission. Set the parking brake and block the drive wheels.

1. Warm up the engine to the normal operating temperature.
2. Race the engine until the engine speed exceeds 1500 rpm and than let it slow down to idle speed.
3. Check and see if the idle speed is within 750–850 rpm.

Fuel Injector

Removal and Installation

1. Disconnect the negative battery cable.
2. Release the fuel pressure in the fuel feed line.
3. Remove the the air intake case from the throttle body.
4. Remove the fuel feed pipe clamp from the intake manifold and disconnect the fuel feed pipe from the throttle body.
5. Remove the injector cover.
6. Disconnect the injector coupler, release its wire harness from the clamp and remove its grommet from the throttle body.
7. Place a cloth over the injector and a hand on top of it. Using an air gun, blow low pressure compressed air into the fuel inlet port of the throttle body, and the injector can be removed.

NOTE: Be precise about the pressure of the compressed air. Using excessively high pressure may force the injector to jump out and may cause damage, not only to the injector itself but also to other parts.

EMISSION CONTROLS

Please refer to "Professional Emission Component Application Guide".

Emission Warning Lamps

The CHECK ENGINE light automatically comes on at 50,000, 80,000, and 100,000 miles.

Resetting

The lamp reset switch is located on the left side of the dashboard, mounted on the steering column support. The lamp can be reset by moving the switch upwards and then downwards. If the switch remains on after being reset, check the system.

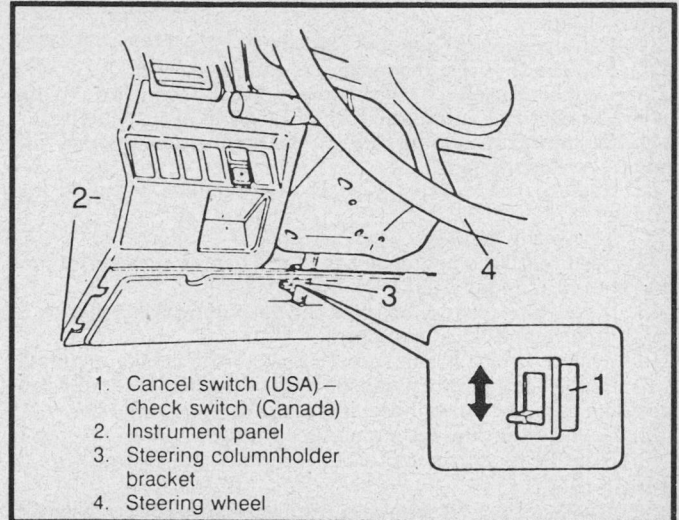

1. Cancel switch (USA) — check switch (Canada)
2. Instrument panel
3. Steering columnholder bracket
4. Steering wheel

Resetting the check engine light

ENGINE MECHANICAL

NOTE: Disconnecting the battery cable on some vehicles may interfere with the functions of the on board computer systems and may require the computer to undergo a relearning process, once the negative battery cable is disconnected.

Engine

Removal and Installation

1. Disconnect the negative and positive cables at the battery.
2. Remove the hood from the vehicle and drain the cooling system.
3. Remove the radiator reservoir tank, fan shroud, cooling fan and radiator.
4. Properly discharge the air conditioning system and remove the air conditioning condenser, if equipped.
5. Remove the air cleaner outlet hose.
6. Disconnect the accelerator and the automatic transmission kickdown cable from the throttle body, if equipped.
7. Disconnect and tag the throttle opener VSV and EGR VSV wires at the coupler.
8. Disconnect and tag the water temperature, oil pressure, air temperature and ground cable wires at the intake manifold.
9. Disconnect and tag the injector, throttle position sensor and idle speed control solenoid valve wires at their couplers, if equipped.
10. Disconnect the PTC heater wires at the coupler for automatic transmission vehicles, if equipped.
11. Disconnect and tag the wires at the starter and alternator.
12. Disconnect and tag the oxygen sensor and distributor wires at their couplers. Remove the coil wire.
13. Remove the starter motor and disconnect the ground wires from the distributor assembly.
14. Remove the fuel tank filler cap to relieve the pressure. Reinstall the cap.
15. Relieve the fuel pressure in the fuel feed line. Disconnect and tag the fuel feed and return hoses.

16. Remove the gear shift lever mounting bolts and remove the shifter.
17. Disconnect the canister purge hose and remove the pressure sensor hose from the fuel filter, if equipped.
18. Disconnect the brake booster hose from the intake manifold.
19. Remove the vacuum hose for the automatic transmission from the intake manifold, if equipped.
20. Disconnect the heater hoses from the heater core outlet pipe and the intake manifold.
21. Raise and safely support the vehicle.
22. Drain the engine oil and remove the exhaust pipe from the exhaust manifold and muffler.
23. Disconnect the clutch cable if equipped with manual transmission.
24. Drain the automatic transmission fluid, if equipped.
25. Disconnect the clutch (torque converter) housing lower plate.
26. Remove the lock drive plate, using the special tool, if equipped with automatic transmission.
27. Lower the vehicle.
28. Remove the nuts and bolts fastening the cylinder block and transmission.
29. Support the transmission, using an appropriate stand or jack.
30. Support the engine from the top using a chain type hoist or equivalent means.
31. Remove the engine mounts with the chassis side mounting brackets.

NOTE: Before lifting the engine, check to ensure all the hoses, wires and cables are disconnected from the engine.

32. Remove the engine assembly from the chassis and transmission by sliding towards the front side and carefully hoist the engine.

To install

33. Install the engine into the engine compartment and connect to the transmission.
34. Replace the engine mounts with the chassis side mounting

brackets. Tighten to 41 ft. lbs.

35. Remove the lifting device.
36. Install the nuts and bolts fastening the cylinder block and transmission.
37. Raise and safely support the vehicle.
38. Replace the lock drive plate, if equipped.
39. Connect the clutch (torque converter) housing lower plate.
40. Connect the automatic transmission lines, if equipped.
41. Reconnect the clutch cable to the bracket, if equipped with manual transmission.
42. Replace the exhaust pipe to the exhaust manifold and muffler.
43. Lower the vehicle.
44. Reconnect the heater hoses to the heater core outlet pipe and the intake manifold.
45. Install the vacuum hose for the automatic transmission to the intake manifold, if equipped.
46. Reconnect the brake booster hose to the intake manifold.
47. Replace the pressure sensor hose to the fuel filter and connect the canister purge hose, if equipped.
48. Replace the fuel return and feed hoses.
49. Install the starter motor and connect the ground wire to the distributor.
50. Replace the coil wire and connect the oxygen sensor and distributor wires to their couplers.
51. Reconnect the wires at the alternator and starter motor.
52. Replace the PTC heater wires at the coupler, if equipped with automatic transmission.
53. Install the idle speed control solenoid valve, throttle position sensor and injector wires at their couplers, if equipped.
54. Connect the ground cable, air temperature, oil pressure and water temperature wires to the intake manifold.
55. Reconnect the throttle opener VSR and EGR VSR wires to their couplers, if equipped.
56. Connect the accelerator cable and the automatic transmission kickdown cable, if equipped, to the throttle body.
57. Replace the air cleaner outlet hose. Refill the engine oil and the transmission oil to the proper level.
58. Replace the air conditioning condenser and properly recharge the air conditioning system, if equipped.
59. Replace the radiator, cooling fan, fan shroud and radiator reservoir tank.
60. Replace the hood and refill the cooling system with the proper coolant.
61. Reconnect the positive and negative battery cables.
62. Adjust the accelerator, clutch and the automatic transmission kickdown cable, if equipped.
63. Before starting the engine, check to see if all the parts disassembled are back in place securely.
64. Start the engine and check the timing. Check for any oil leaks.

Cylinder Head

Removal and installation

1. Disconnect the negative battery cable. Drain the cooling system.
2. Disconnect the air intake case.
3. Disconnect the brake booster hose from the intake manifold and the air valve water hose from the throttle body.
4. Disconnect the accelerator and the automatic transmission kickdown cable, if equipped, from the throttle body.
5. Disconnect and tag the throttle opener VSV and EGR VSV wires at the coupler.
6. Disconnect and tag the water temperature, oil pressure, air temperature sensor and ground cable wires at the intake manifold.
7. Disconnect and tag the injector, throttle position sensor and idle speed control solenoid valve wires at their couplers, if equipped.

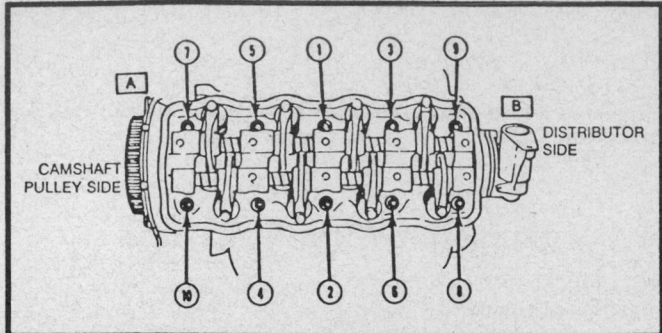

Cylinder head and bolt tightening sequence

8. Disconnect the PTC heater wires at the coupler, if equipped with automatic transmission.
9. Disconnect and tag the oxygen sensor and distributor wires at their couplers. Remove the coil wire.
10. Disconnect the ground wires from the distributor assembly.
11. Remove the fuel tank filler cap to relieve the pressure. Reinstall the cap.
12. Release the fuel pressure in the fuel feed line.
13. Disconnect the fuel feed and return hoses.
14. Disconnect the canister purge hose and remove the pressure sensor hose from the fuel filter, if equipped.
15. Remove the vacuum hose for the automatic transmission from the intake manifold, if equipped.
16. Disconnect the radiator cooling fan, fan shroud, water pump drive belt and water pump pulley.
17. Disconnect the crankshaft pulley, timing belt cover and the timing belt.
18. Raise and safely support the vehicle.
19. Disconnect the exhaust pipe from the exhaust manifold and lower the vehicle.
20. Disconnect the air conditioning compressor adjusting arm, if equipped.
21. Remove the cylinder head cover mounting bolts and remove the cylinder head cover.
22. Loosen all the valve adjusting screw locknuts, turn the adjusting screws back all the way to allow all the valves to close.
23. Remove the intake manifold with the carburetor attached, from the cylinder head.
24. Remove the distributor and distributor housing from the cylinder head.
25. Remove the cylinder head mounting bolts and remove the cylinder head from the engine.
26. Remove any oil and water in the cylinder bores and on top of the pistons.
27. Clean and inspect the sealing surfaces of the cylinder head and the engine block.

To install

28. Install the cylinder head using a new gasket.
29. Replace the cylinder head mounting bolts and tighten to 46–54 ft. lbs.
30. Install the distributor and distributor housing to the cylinder head.
31. Replace the intake manifold with the carburetor attached, to the cylinder head.
32. Tighten all the valve adjusting screw nuts.
33. Adjust the valve lash.
34. Replace the cylinder head cover and connect the air conditioning compressor adjusting arm, if equipped.
35. Raise and safely support the vehicle.
36. Connect the exhaust pipe to the exhaust manifold and safely lower the vehicle.
37. Reconnect the timing belt, timing belt cover and crankshaft pulley.

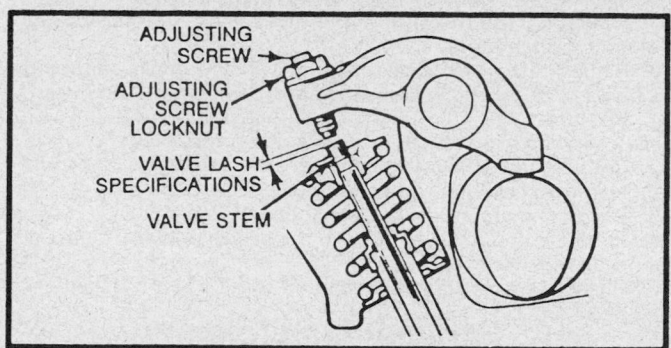

Valve lash adjustment

38. Replace the water pump pulley, water pump drive belt, fan shroud and the radiator cooling fan.
39. Replace the vacuum hose for the automatic transmission to the intake manifold, if equipped.
40. Replace the pressure sensor hose to the fuel filter and connect the canister purge hose, if equipped.
41. Replace the fuel return and feed hoses.
42. Connect the ground wires to the distributor assembly.
43. Replace the coil wire. Connect the oxygen sensor and distributor wires to their couplers.
44. Connect the PTC wires to the coupler.
45. Connect the idle speed control valve, throttle position sensor and injector wires to their couplers, if equipped.
46. Reconnect the ground cable, air temperature, oil pressure and water temperature sensor wires to the intake manifold.
47. Replace the throttle opener VSV and EGR VSV wires to their couplers.
48. Connect the accelerator and the automatic transmission kickdown cables, if equipped, to the throttle body.
49. Replace the air valve water hose to the throttle body and connect the brake booster hose to intake manifold.
50. Reconnect the air intake case.
51. Refill the cooling system with the proper coolant and connect the negative battery.
52. Check for any water and oil leaks when finished.

Valve Lash

Adjustment

Valve lash can be adjusted with the engine hot or cold. Specifications are provided for both adjustments.
1. Remove the air intake case and cylinder head cover.
2. On the 1.3L engine, remove the rubber plug from the transmission case to gain access to the timing marks.
3. Turn the crankshaft clockwise so that;
   a. The **T** mark punched on the flywheel is aligned with the matchmark on the transmission on the 1.3L engine.
   b. The **V** mark on the crankshaft pulley is aligned with the **0** mark on the timing belt cover on the 1.6L engine.
4. Remove the distributor cap and confirm that the rotor is facing the No.1 firing position. If the rotor is out of place, turn the crankshaft 360 degrees.
5. With the engine in this position, check the valve lash at valves 1,2,5 and 7.

NOTE: The valves are adjusted by loosening the locknut on the valve adjuster and turning the adjusting screw to obtain the proper clearance. Once the proper clearance is obtained, the locknut must be torqued to 11–13 ft. lbs. while holding the adjusting screw. Check the clearance after the locknut is torqued.

Clearance should be: Intake;0.13–0.17mm (0.0051–0.0067in.)

COLD, 0.23–0.27mm (0.009–0.011in.) HOT. Exhaust; 0.16–.020mm (0.0063–0.0079in.) COLD, 0.26–0.30mm. (0.0102–0.0118in.) HOT.

6. Rotate the crankshaft 360 degrees, and check the valve lash at valves 3,4,6 and 8.
7. After adjusting and checking all the valves, install the cylinder head cover, distributor cover and intake hose.

Rocker Arms/Shafts

Removal and Installation

NOTE: The rocker arm shafts are not identical and must be kept in the proper order for installation. If the shafts get mixed up before installation, the intake rocker shaft has a 14mm stepped end and the exhaust rocker shaft has a 13mm stepped end. The stepped end of the intake rocker shaft faces the front of the engine and the stepped end of the exhaust rocker shaft faces the rear of the engine.

1. Disconnect the negative battery cable. Drain the cooling system.
2. Remove the front grille (Sidekick and Tracker).
3. Remove the radiator cooling fan and fan shroud. Properly discharge the air conditioning system and remove the air conditioning flexible suction hose, if equipped.
4. Remove the radiator (Sidekick).
5. Remove the water pump drive belt and the water pump pulley.
6. Remove the timing belt outside cover, timing belt and the tensioner.
7. Disconnect the air intake case and remove the cylinder head cover.
8. Remove the camshaft timing belt pulley and timing belt inside cover. Insert the proper size rod into the hole in the camshaft to lock the camshaft and loosen the pulley nut.
9. Loosen all the valve lash adjusting screw locknuts and turn the adjusting screws out all the way.
10. Remove the rocker arm shaft screws.
11. Remove the intake and exhaust rocker arm shafts, rocker arms and springs.
12. Keep all the valve train parts in the order that they were removed.
13. Apply engine oil to the rocker arms, springs and shafts. Install the shafts in the correct direction, into the cylinder head by placing the rocker arms and springs on the shafts as they are installed. With the rocker arms, springs and shafts installed, torque the rocker shaft mounting screws to 7.0–8.5 ft. lbs.

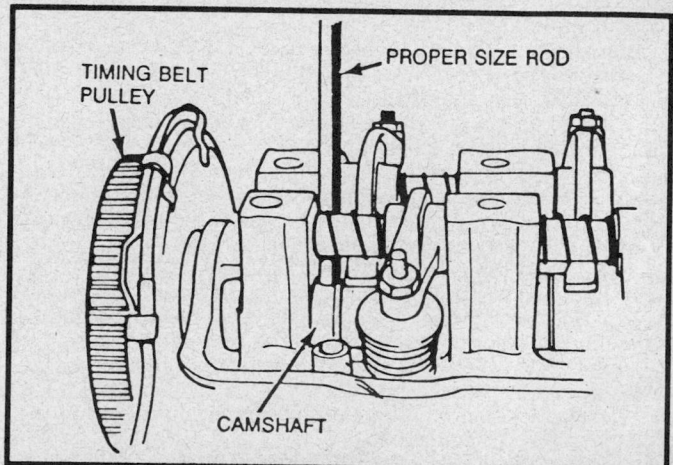

Locking the camshaft in position

14. Install the timing belt pulley and inside cover by locking the camshaft with the proper size rod.

15. With the camshaft locked, tighten the camshaft pulley bolt to 41–46 ft. lbs.

16. The remainder of the installation is the reverse of the removal procedure.

Intake Manifold

Removal and Installation

1. Disconnect the negative battery cable. Drain the cooling system.

2. Remove the air intake case from the manifold.

3. Disconnect the accelerator cable and the automatic transmission kickdown cable, if equipped.

4. Disconnect the injector, throttle position sensor and idle speed control solenoid valve wires at their couplers, if equipped.

5. Disconnect the vacuum hoses from the throttle body and throttle opener. Remove the water hose from the air valve, if equipped.

6. Remove the fuel filler cap to release the fuel pressure in the fuel tank. Reinstall the cap.

7. Release the fuel pressure in the fuel line.

8. Disconnect the fuel line from the throttle body or carburetor and intake manifold.

9. Remove the fuel return hose.

10. Disconnect the throttle body or carburetor from the intake manifold and remove the PCV hose from the cylinder head cover.

11. Disconnect the pressure sensor hose from the fuel filter, if equipped, and remove the brake booster hose from the intake manifold.

12. Disconnect the vacuum hose for the automatic transmission from the intake manifold, if equipped.

13. Remove the VSV (for throttle opener) hose from the intake manifold.

14. Disconnect the water hose from the thermostat cap. Remove the heater inlet and water bypass hose from the intake manifold.

15. Disconnect the hoses at the EGR valve and remove the ground wire from the intake manifold.

16. Disconnect the wire couplers from the air temperature sensor, water temperature sensor, water temperature gauge and PTC heater, if equipped wuth automatic transmission.

17. Disconnect the wire harnesses from their clamps.

18. Remove the intake manifold mounting bolts and remove the intake manifold from the cylinder head.

19. Remove the PCV valve, EGR valve, fuel filter, thermostat from the intake manifold.

20. Clean and inspect the sealing surfaces of the intake manifold and the cylinder head.

To install

21. Install the thermostat, fuel filter, EGR valve and PCV valve to the intake manifold.

22. Using a new gasket, install the intake manifold and tighten the mounting bolts to 13–20 ft. lbs.

23. Reconnect the wiring harnesses to their clamps and fasten the wire couplers to the air temperature sensor, water temperature sensor, water temperature gauge and PTC heater, if equipped with automatic transmission.

24. Reconnect the ground wire to the intake manifold and replace the hoses at the EGR valve.

25. Install the water heater inlet and bypass hose to the intake manifold. Replace the water hose to the thermostat cap.

26. Replace the VSV (for throttle opener) hose to the intake manifold.

27. Connect the automatic transmission vacuum hose to the intake manifold, if equipped.

28. Replace the brake booster hose to the intake manifold and connect the pressure sensor to the fuel filter, if equipped.

29. Reconnect the fuel line to the throttle body or carburetor to the intake manifold.

30. Replace the water hose to the air valve. Connect the vacuum hoses to the throttle body and throttle opener, if equipped.

31. Reconnect the injector, throttle position sensor and idle speed control wires to their couplers, if equipped.

32. Connect the accelerator cable and the automatic transmission kickdown cable, if equipped, to the throttle body.

33. Install the air intake case to the manifold.

34. Refill the cooling system with the proper coolant. Connect the negative battery cable.

35. Check for vacuum, water and oil leaks when finished.

Exhaust Manifold

Removal and Installation

1. Disconnect the negative cable.

2. Raise and safely support the vehicle.

3. Disconnect the exhaust pipe from the exhaust manifold and lower the vehicle.

4. Disconnect the oxygen sensor lead wire at the coupler and remove the air intake case bracket – 1.6L Engine.

5. Disconnect the exhaust manifold upper and lower covers or heat shields from the exhaust manifold.

6. Remove the exhaust manifold mounting bolts and remove the exhaust manifold from the cylinder head.

7. Clean and inspect the sealing surfaces of the exhaust manifold and the cylinder head.

8. Using new gaskets, install the exhaust manifold to the cylinder head and tighten the mounting bolts to 13–20 ft. lbs.

9. The remainder of the installation is the reverse of the removal procedure.

10. Check for exhaust leaks when finished.

Timing Belt Front Cover

Removal and Installation

1. Disconnect the negative battery cable.

2. Remove the radiator cooling fan and fan shroud.

3. If equipped, disconnect the air conditioning compressor drive belt, properly discharge the air conditioning system and remove the air conditioning compressor flexible suction hose.

4. Loosen the alternator mounting bolts and remove the water pump drive belt and pulley.

5. Remove the crankshaft mounting bolts and remove the crankshaft pulley.

NOTE: The crankshaft drive belt pulley can be removed without loosening the center crankshaft bolt.

6. Disconnect the timing belt cover mounting bolts and remove the timing belt cover.

7. Clean and inspect all mounting surfaces.

8. Install the timing belt cover and tighten the bolts to 7.0–9.0 ft. lbs.

9. Install the crankshaft pulley. Replace the 5 mounting bolts and tighten to 7.0–9.0 ft. lbs.

10. Install the water pump drive belt pulley and replace the drive belt .

11. Adjust the belt tension and tighten the alternator mounting bolts.

12. Install the air conditioning flexible suction hose and replace the air conditioning compressor drive belt. Adjust the belt tension and properly recharge the air conditioning system, if equipped.

13. Replace the radiator cooling fan and fan shroud.

14. Connect the negative battery cable.

Oil Seal Replacement

1. Disconnect the negative battery cable.

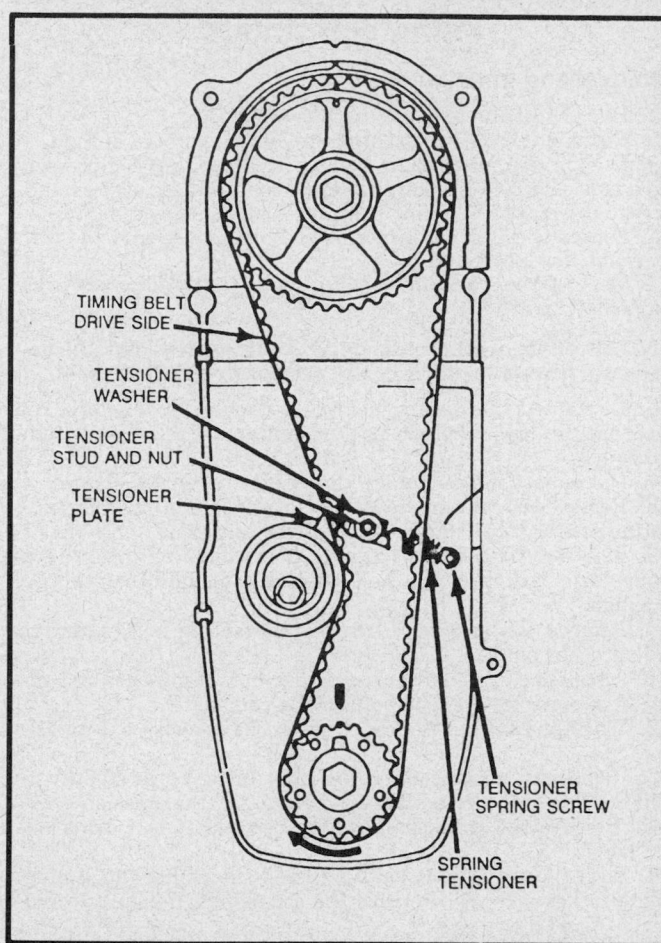

Exploded view of the timing belt and the tensioner assembly

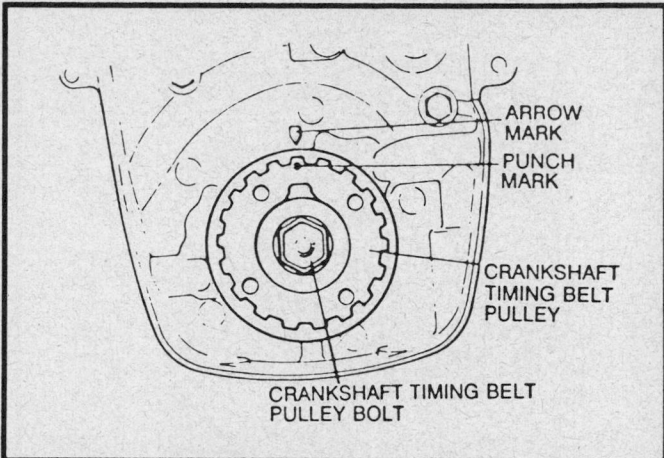

Timing marks on the crankshaft pulley

2. Remove the the timing belt and the crankshaft sprocket.

3. Insert a suitable tool between the crankshaft and the oil seal and pull the seal outwards to remove it.

NOTE: Use care when removing or installing the oil seal, not to damage the crankshaft or the oil pump sealing surfaces.

4. Clean and inspect the surfaces of the crankshaft and the oil pump assembly.

5. Install the crankshaft sleeve, using the proper tool, onto the crankshaft.

6. Install the new seal over the crankshaft and into the oil pump, making sure that the oil seal lip is not upturned.

7. Install the crankshaft sprocket and the timing belt. Check the timing.

8. Connect the negative battery cable.

Timing Belt and Tensioner

Adjustment

1. Disconnect the negative battery cable.

2. Remove the radiator cooling fan and fan shroud.

3. If equipped, disconnect the air conditioning compressor drive belt, properly discharge the air conditioning system and remove the air conditioning compressor flexible suction hose.

4. Loosen the alternator mounting bolts and remove the water pump drive belt and pulley.

5. Remove the crankshaft mounting bolts and disconnect the crankshaft pulley.

NOTE: The crankshaft drive belt pulley can be removed without loosening the center crankshaft bolt.

6. Disconnect the timing belt cover mounting bolts and remove the timing belt cover. Loosen, but do not remove the tensioner bolt.

7. Disconnect the air intake case from the intake manifold.

8. Remove the cylinder head cover and loosen all the valve adjusting screws to permit free rotation of the camshaft.

9. Turn the camshaft pulley clockwise and align the timing marks.

10. Turn the crankshaft clockwise, using a 17mm wrench to crank the timing belt pulley bolt.

11. Align the punch mark on the timing belt pulley with the arrow mark on the oil pump.

12. With the 4 marks aligned, remove any slack from the drive side of the belt. Tighten the tensioner bolt to 17.5–21.5 ft. lbs.

13. To allow the belt to be free of any slack, turn the crankshaft clockwise 2 full rotations. Confirm that the 4 marks are aligned.

14. Replace the timing cover and tighten the bolts to 7.0–8.5 ft. lbs.

15. Adjust the valve lash and install the cylinder head cover, using a new gasket.

16. Connect the air intake case to the throttle body.

17. Install the crankshaft pulley and replace the 5 mounting bolts. Tighten to 7.0–8.5 ft. lbs.

18. Replace the water pump pulley, water pump drive belt and tighten the alternator mounting bolts.

19. Install the air conditioning compressor flexible suction hose and the air compressor belt. Properly recharge the air conditioning system, if equipped.

20. Replace the radiator cooling fan and fan shroud.

21. Connect the negative battery cable.

22. Properly recharge the air conditioning system, if equipped. Run the engine and check for any leaks.

Removal and Installation

1. Disconnect the negative battery cable.

2. Remove the radiator cooling fan and fan shroud.

3. If equipped, disconnect the air conditioning compressor drive belt, properly discharge the air conditioning system and remove the air conditioning compressor flexible suction hose.

4. Loosen the alternator mounting bolts and remove the water pump drive belt and pulley.

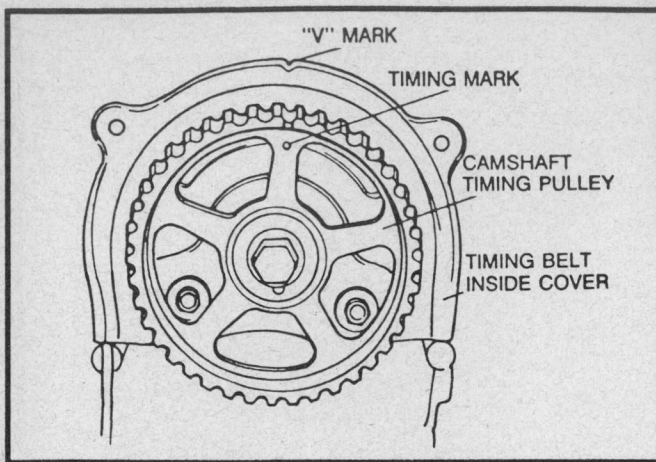

Timing marks on the camshaft pulley

5. Remove the crankshaft mounting bolts and disconnect the crankshaft pulley.

NOTE: The crankshaft drive belt pulley can be removed without loosening the center crankshaft bolt.

6. Disconnect the timing belt cover mounting bolts and remove the timing belt cover. Loosen, but do not remove the tensioner bolt.
7. Disconnect the air intake case from the intake manifold.
8. Loosen the timing belt tensioner adjusting bolt and pivot nut. Hold pressure on the tensioner to loosen the timing belt and remove the timing belt from the camshaft and crankshaft pulleys.
9. Remove the timing belt tensioner, tensioner plate and tensioner spring.

To install

10. Install the timing belt tensioner, plate and spring. Hand tighten the tensioner bolt and stud only at this time.
11. Remove the cylinder head cover and loosen all the valve adjusting screws to permit free rotation of the camshaft.
12. Turn the camshaft pulley clockwise and align the timing marks.
13. Turn the crankshaft clockwise, using a 17mm wrench to crank the timing belt pulley bolt.
14. Align the punch mark on the timing belt pulley with the arrow mark on the oil pump
15. With the 4 marks aligned, remove any slack from the drive side of the belt. Tighten the tensioner bolt to 17.5–21.5 ft. lbs.
16. To allow the belt to be free of any slack, turn the crankshaft clockwise 2 full rotations. Confirm that the 4 marks are aligned.
17. Install the timing cover and tighten the bolts to 7.0–8.5 ft. lbs.
18. Adjust the valve lash and install the cylinder head cover, using a new gasket.
19. Connect the air intake case to the intake manifold.
20. Install the crankshaft pulley and replace the mounting bolts. Tighten to 7.0–8.5 ft. lbs.
21. Replace the water pump pulley, water pump drive belt and tighten the alternator mounting bolts.
22. If equipped, install the air conditioning compressor flexible suction hose and replace the air conditioning compressor belt.
23. Replace the radiator cooling fan and fan shroud.
24. Connect the negative battery cable.
25. If equipped, properly recharge the air conditioning system. Run the engine and check for any leaks.

Timing Sprockets

Removal and Installation

1. Disconnect the negative battery cable.
2. Remove the radiator cooling fan/clutch and fan shroud.
3. If equipped, disconnect the air conditioning compressor drive belt, properly discharge the air conditioning system and remove the air conditioning compressor flexible suction hose.
4. Loosen the alternator mounting bolts and remove the water pump drive belt and pulley.
5. Remove the crankshaft mounting bolts and disconnect the crankshaft pulley.

NOTE: The crankshaft drive belt pulley can be removed without loosening the center crankshaft bolt.

6. Disconnect the timing belt cover mounting bolts and remove the timing belt cover. Loosen, but do not remove the tensioner bolt.
7. Disconnect the air intake case from the throttle body.
8. Remove the cylinder head cover and loosen all the valve adjusting screws to permit rotation of the camshaft.
9. Remove the camshaft timing belt pulley by inserting a proper size rod into the hole in the camshaft to lock the camshaft.
10. Remove the camshaft sprocket mounting bolt, sprocket and sprocket pin.
11. Install the camshaft sprocket pin in the sprocket and replace the sprocket and the bolt on the camshaft.
12. With the camshaft locked, tighten the sprocket bolt to 41–46 ft. lbs.
13. Remove the crankshaft sprocket by using a gear stopper to hold the flywheel (drive plate for automatic transmission vehicles). Remove the crankshaft timing belt pulley bolt, sprocket and key.
14. With the crankshaft locked, install the crankshaft timing belt sprocket and key. Replace the crankshaft pulley bolt and tighten to 47–54 ft. lbs.
15. Align the camshaft and crankshaft timing marks, install the timing belt and tighten the timing belt tensioner.
16. Adjust the valve lash and replace the cylinder head cover.
17. Reconnect the air intake hose to the throttle body.
18. If equipped, install the air conditioning compressor flexible suction hose and replace the air conditioning compressor belt.
19. Install the water pump pulley and replace the water pump drive belt.
20. Replace the radiator cooling fan and fan shroud.
21. Install the water pump pulley and replace the water pump drive belt.
22. Connect the negative battery cable.
23. If equipped, properly recharge the air conditioning system. Run the engine and check for any leaks.

Camshaft

Removal and Installation

1. Disconnect the negative battery cable.

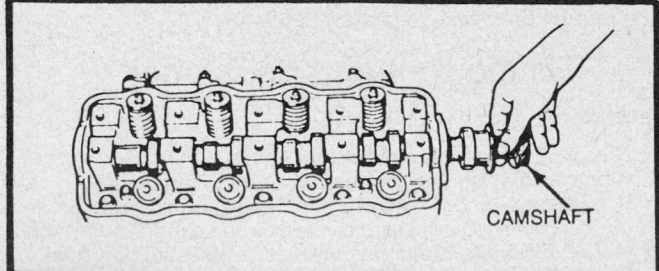

Camshaft removal

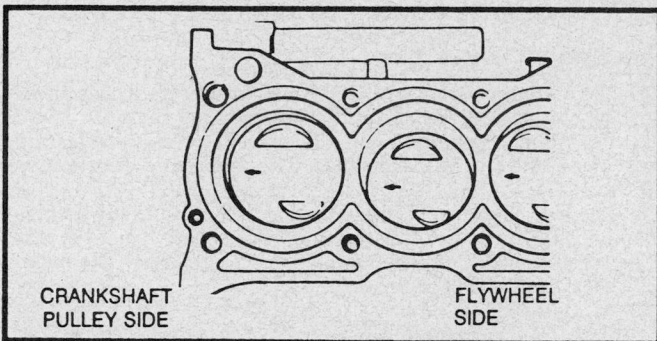

Piston arrow marks to the cylinder head

2. Remove the cylinder head from the engine block. Place in a suitable place to be able to remove the camshaft from the cylinder head.

3. Remove the distributor, intake and exhaust manifold from the cylinder head. Remove the fuel pump on the Samurai.

4. Disconnect the timing belt gear from the camshaft and remove the rocker arms, springs and rocker arm shafts.

5. Keep all the valve train parts in the order that they were removed.

6. Remove the camshaft from the rear of the cylinder head.

7. To install, lubricate the lobes and journals of the camshaft and the oil seal on the cylinder head with engine oil.

8. Install the camshaft to the cylinder head from the transmission side.

Piston and Connecting Rod
Positioning

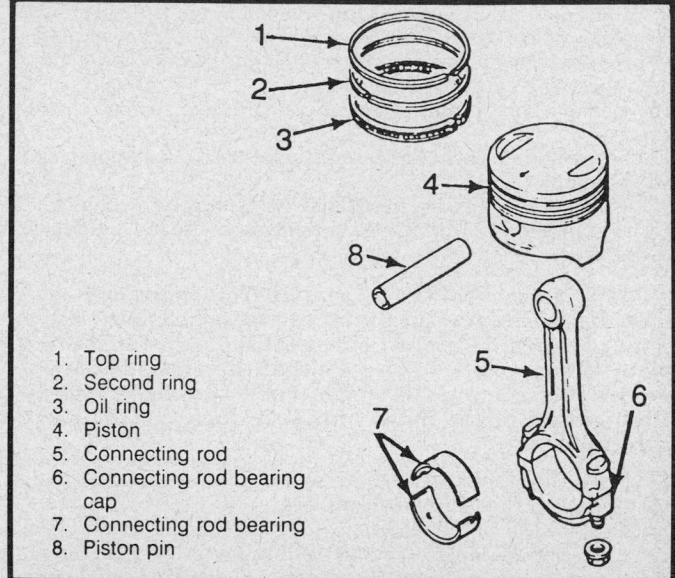

1. Top ring
2. Second ring
3. Oil ring
4. Piston
5. Connecting rod
6. Connecting rod bearing cap
7. Connecting rod bearing
8. Piston pin

Exploded view of the piston and rod assembly

9. For the remainder of the installation use the reverse of the removal procedure.

ENGINE LUBRICATION

Oil Pan

Removal and Installation

1. Raise and safely support the vehicle.

2. On Sidekick and Tracker, drain and remove the front differential assembly from the chassis.

3. Drain the engine oil.

4. Remove the clutch housing lower plate or the torque converter housing lower plate on the Sidekick and Tracker.

5. Remove the oil pan mounting bolts and remove the pan.

6. Clean and inspect the sealing surfaces on the oil pan and the engine block.

7. Using new gaskets, install the oil pan and tighten the oil pan bolts to 7.0–8.5 ft. lbs.

NOTE: Tightening should begin at the center moving outward on both sides.

8. Install the oil drain plug and tighten to 22.0–28.5 ft. lbs.

9. Replace the clutch housing lower plate or the torque converter on the Sidekick and Tracker.

10. Install the front differential assembly to the chassis and fill with differential oil on the Sidekick and Tracker.

11. Lower the vehicle.

12. Refill the engine with engine oil. Run the engine and check for leaks.

Oil Pump

Removal and Installation

1. Disconnect the negative battery cable.

2. Remove the radiator cooling fan, fan shroud, water pump pulley and water pump drive belt.

3. Remove the timing belt outside cover, timing belt and timing belt tensioner.

4. Disconnect the alternator and remove the bracket, if neccessary.

5. If equipped, properly discharge the air conditioning system and remove the air compressor and bracket.

6. Disconnect the crankshaft timing belt pulley and the timing belt guide.

NOTE: To lock the crankshaft, engage a special tool

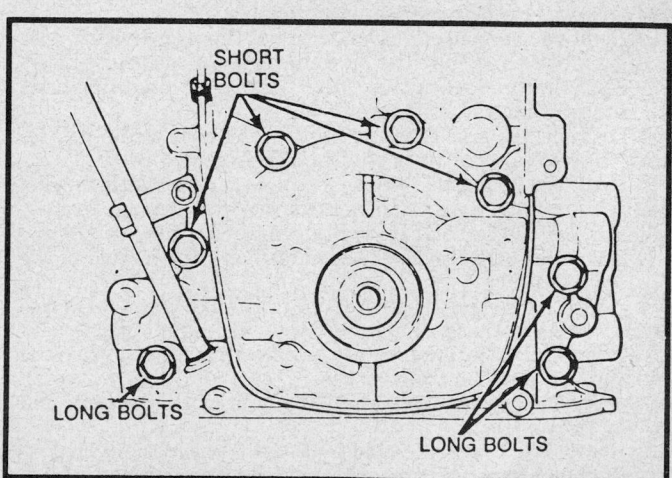

SHORT BOLTS

LONG BOLTS

LONG BOLTS

Oil pump installation

(gear stopper) with the flywheel ring gear (drive plate ring gear for automatic transmission vehicles). With the crankshaft locked, remove the crankshaft timing belt pulley bolt.

7. Raise and safely support the vehicle. Drain the engine oil.
8. Remove the clutch (torque converter) housing lower plate.
9. Remove the oil pan mounting bolts and remove the oil pan. Disconnect the oil pump strainer.
10. Remove the oil pump mounting bolts and remove the oil pump.
11. Clean and inspect the sealing surfaces of the oil pump and the engine block.
12. Using a new gasket, install the oil pump to the engine.
13. Install the No.1 and No.2 mounting bolts and tighten to 7.0–8.5 ft. lbs.

NOTE: To prevent the oil seal lip from being damaged when installing the oil pump to the crankshaft, use a proper seal guide tool when installing. After installing the oil pump, check to be sure that the oil lip is not upturned, then remove the special tool. The edge of the oil pump gasket might bulge out. If it does, cut off bulge with knife.

14. With the crankshaft locked, install the crankshaft timing belt guide and the timing belt pulley.
15. Replace the clutch (torque converter) housing lower plate.
16. If equipped, replace the air conditioning bracket, the air conditioning compressor and properly rechargew the air conditioning system.
17. Replace the alternator and the alternator bracket, if necessary.
18. Reinstall the timing belt tensioner, timing belt and timing belt outside cover.
19. Replace the water pump drive belt, water pump pulley, radiator cooling fan and fan shroud.
20. Refill the engine with engine oil and connect the negative battery cable.
21. Run the engine and check for any leaks.

Checking

With the oil pump removed from the engine, certain clearances must be checked on the oil pump, if it is being reused.
1. The radial clearance is the clearance between the oil pump outer rotor and the oil pump case. The maximum clearance is 0.0122 in.
2. The side clearance is measured with a straightedge across the mounting surface of the oil pump. The measurement is taken between the oil pump gears and the straightedge. The maximum clearance is 0.0059 in.

Rear Main Bearing Oil Seal

Removal and Installation

1. Raise and safely support the vehicle.
2. Support the engine and remove the transmission from the vehicle.
3. Disconnect the clutch and flywheel, for manual transmission vehicles or the drive plate, for automatic transmission vehicles.
4. Using a suitable tool, remove the seal by pulling it outwards. Use care not to damage the sealing surface of the crankshaft.
5. Clean and inspect the sealing surfaces of the crankshaft and seal housing.
6. Using a seal driver, install the new seal into the seal housing with the lip of the seal facing the engine.
7. Install the flywheel and clutch, for manual transmission vehicles or the drive plate, for automatic transmission vehicles.
8. Install the transmission in the vehicle.
9. Lower the vehicle and check all the fluids. Run the engine and check for any leaks.

MANUAL TRANSMISSION

For further information, please refer to "Professional Transmission Manual".

Transmission Assembly

Removal and Installation

1. Disconnect the negative battery cable.
2. Remove the console cover, remove the 4 gear shift boot mounting bolts and slide the boot upwards on the gear shifter.
3. On Samurai, loosen the 3 gear shift lever mounting bolts and remove the gear shift lever.
4. On Sidekick and Tracker, remove the boot clamp and remove the second boot from the shift lever case.
5. Push the gear shift lever control case down with fingers, turn it counterclockwise and remove the shift control lever.
6. Remove the transfer case shift control lever the same way.
7. Disconnect the breather hose and clamp at the rear of the cylinder head.
8. Remove the clamp at the rear of the intake manifold to free up the wiring harness. Disconnect the harness coupler.
9. Raise and safely support the vehicle. Drain the oil from the transmission and the transfer case.
10. Disconnect the starter lead wires and mounting bolts and remove the starter.
11. Remove the fuel line clamp on the transmission. Disconnect the bolts fastening the engine to the transmission.
12. Disconnect the flange bolts from the front driveshaft and remove and mark the shaft.
13. Disconnect the flange bolts from the rear driveshaft and remove and mark the shaft.
14. Disconnect the clutch cable and remove the clutch housing lower plate.
15. Disconnect the center exhaust pipe and remove the nuts from the joint with the engine.
16. Disconnect the speedometer cable from the transfer case.
17. Position a transmission jack and remove the engine rear mounting member from the vehicle. Move the transmission and transfer case rearwards and lower.
18. Disconnect the wiring harness and breather hose at the transmission.
19. Separate the gear shift lever case and transfer case from the transmission. Remove the transmission from the vehicle.
20. Install the gear shift lever case and transfer case to the transmission.
21. Install the transmission wiring harness and breather hose.
22. Raise the transmission and transfer case on the transmission jack and place under the vehicle.
23. Install the engine rear mounting member and tighten the bolts.
24. Connect the speedometer cable to the transfer case and joint with the engine.
25. Remove the transmission jack and replace the center exhaust pipe.
26. Replace the clutch housing lower plate and connect the clutch cable.

27. Install the front and rear driveshaft and replace the flange bolts.

28. Connect the bolts attaching the engine to the transmission and replace the fuel line clamp on the transmission.

29. Install the starter and replace the mounting bolts and the lead wires to the starter.

30. Lower the vehicle. Refill the transmission and transfer case with the recommended gear oil.

31. Connect the wiring coupler and replace the clamp holding the wiring harness at the rear of the intake manifold.

32. Replace the breather hose and clamp at the rear of the cylinder head.

33. Install the transfer case and the gear shift control levers. Replace the gear shift lever boots and the console cover.

34. Connect the negative battery cable. Run the engine and check for any leaks.

35. Observe the following torques during installation: Samurai transmission mount bolts, 13–20 ft. lbs., driveshaft bolts, 17–21 ft. lbs. Sidekick and Tracker engine rear mount bolts, 37 ft. lbs., driveshaft bolts, 37 ft. lbs.

CLUTCH

Clutch Assembly

Removal and Installation

1. Disconnect the negative battery cable.
2. Raise and safely support the vehicle.
3. Support the engine and remove the transmission from the vehicle.
4. Support the pressure plate and remove the 6 pressure plate to flywheel mounting bolts.
5. Remove the pressure plate and the clutch disc from the flywheel.
6. Inspect the condition of the flywheel, pressure plate and clutch disc and replace as necessary.
7. Remove the flywheel mounting bolts and remove the flywheel.
8. Install the new flywheel and replace the mounting bolts, tighten to 41–47 ft. lbs.
9. Inspect the condition of the clutch release bearing and the input shaft bearing and replace if necessary.
10. Align the clutch disc to the flywheel using a clutch disc alignment tool.
11. Install the pressure plate and evenly tighten the pressure plate bolts to 13–20 ft. lbs.

NOTE: Before assembling, make sure that the clutch disc and the pressure plate are clean and dry.

12. With the engine supported, install the transmission in the vehicle.
13. Lower the vehicle. Connect the negative battery cable.
14. Check and adjust the clutch pedal height. Check the clutch operation when finished.

Pedal Height/Freeplay Adjustment

The only adjustment possible is the clutch pedal free play. The free play is adjusted by moving the joint nut on the release bearing arm. Clutch linkage free play should be between 0.8–1.1 in. (Samurai), 0.6–1.1 in. (Sidekick and Tracker).

Clutch Cable
Removal and Installation

1. Disconnect the negative battery cable.

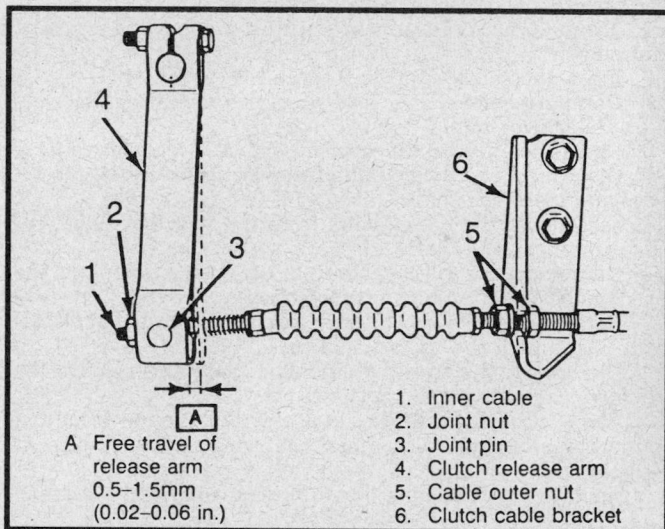

A Free travel of release arm 0.5–1.5mm (0.02–0.06 in.)

1. Inner cable
2. Joint nut
3. Joint pin
4. Clutch release arm
5. Cable outer nut
6. Clutch cable bracket

Clutch cable free travel adjustment

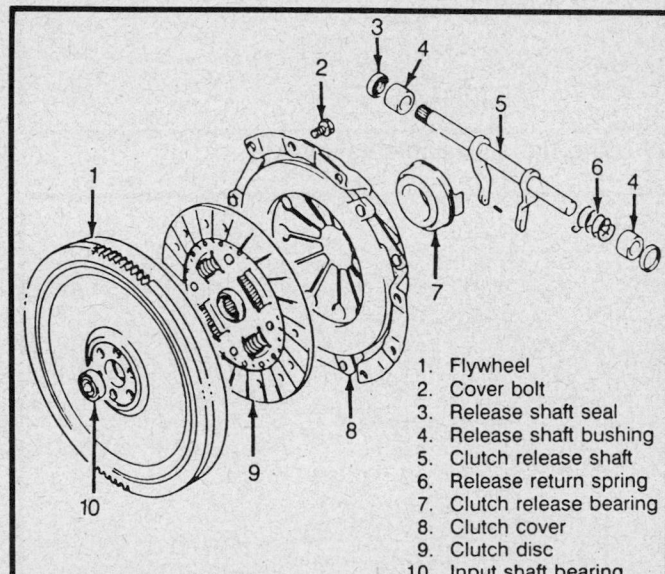

1. Flywheel
2. Cover bolt
3. Release shaft seal
4. Release shaft bushing
5. Clutch release shaft
6. Release return spring
7. Clutch release bearing
8. Clutch cover
9. Clutch disc
10. Input shaft bearing

Exploded view of the clutch assembly

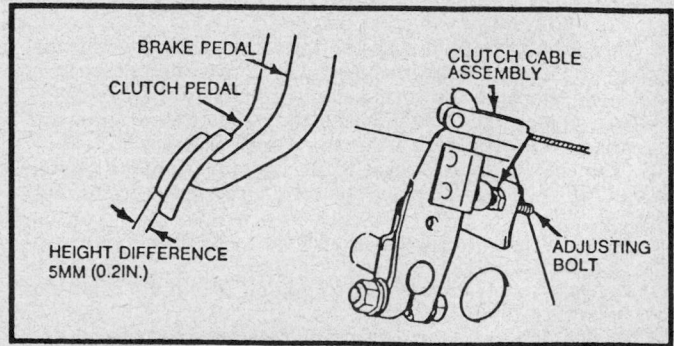

BRAKE PEDAL
CLUTCH PEDAL
CLUTCH CABLE ASSEMBLY
HEIGHT DIFFERENCE 5MM (0.2IN.)
ADJUSTING BOLT

Clutch pedal height adjustment

2. Raise and safely support the vehicle.

3. Disconnect the cable adjusting nuts on the clutch release and remove the adjusting nuts on the cable support bracket.

4. Disconnect the clutch cable from the 3 cable clamps.

5. Remove the clutch cable support bolts. Lower the vehicle.

6. Disconnect the cable hook at the clutch pedal shaft arm and remove the clutch cable.

7. Install the cable after first applying grease to the cable end hook and the joint pin.

8. The remainder of the installation is the reverse of the removal procedure.

Adjustment

Adjust the clutch pedal height by adjusting the bolt located on the pedal bracket so that the clutch pedal exceeds the height of the brake pedal by 5mm (0.2in.). Tighten the locknut.

AUTOMATIC TRANSMISSION

For further information, please refer to "Professional Transmission Manual".

Transmission Assembly

Removal and Installation

1. Disconnect the negative battery cable.

2. Disconnect the transmission shift control lever and remove the transfer case shift control lever knob.

3. Disconnect the breather hose from the clamp at the rear of the cylinder head.

4. Disconnect the wiring harness clamp at the rear end of the intake manifold to free up the harness.

5. Disconnect the wiring harness coupler and remove the detent cable at the throttle body, if equipped.

6. Remove the vacuum modulator hose at the intake manifold.

7. Raise and safely support the vehicle.

8. Disconnect the starter lead wires and mounting bolts, remove the starter motor.

9. Drain the oil from the transmission and transfer case.

10. Disconnect the flange bolts from the front driveshaft, remove and mark the shaft.

11. Disconnect the flange bolts from the rear driveshaft, remove and mark the shaft.

12. Disconnect the select cable from the transmission and the speedometer cable from the transfer cases.

13. Remove the torque converter housing lower plate and disconnect and plug the oil cooler lines.

14. Disconnect the transfer case skid plate and remove the kickdown cable from the transmission.

15. Remove the exhaust bracket at the catalytic converter and at the transmission. Disconnect the center exhaust pipe, if necessary.

16. Remove the transmission to engine retaining bolts and nuts.

17. Support the transmission using a transmission jack or equivalent. Disconnect the transmission crossmember mounting bolts and remove the crossmember.

18. Disconnect the lead wires and breather hose at the transmission and lower the transmission with the transfer case from the vehicle. Remove the torque converter to flywheel bolts.

19. Disconnect the transmission-to-transfer case bolts and separate the transmission from the transfer case.

20. Connect the transfer case to the transmission and tighten the bolts to 20 ft. lbs. Replace the torque converter to flywheel bolts.

21. Raise the transmission, connect the lead wires and breather to the transmission.

22. Replace the transmission to engine retaining bolts and tighten to 62 ft. lbs.

23. Install the transmission cross member and tighten the bolts to 62 ft. lbs.

24. Connect the exhaust bracket to the catalytic converter and the transmission.

25. Reconnect the center exhaust pipe, if necessary.

26. Connect the transfer case skid plate and replace the kickdown cable to the transmission.

27. Replace the torque converter housing lower plate and connect the transmission cooler lines.

28. Reconnect the select cable to the transmission and the speedometer cable to the transfer case.

29. Replace the front and rear driveshafts and tighten the flange bolts to 37 ft. lbs.

30. Install the starter and connect the lead wires to the starter.

31. Lower the vehicle and connect the vacuum modulator hose to the intake manifold.

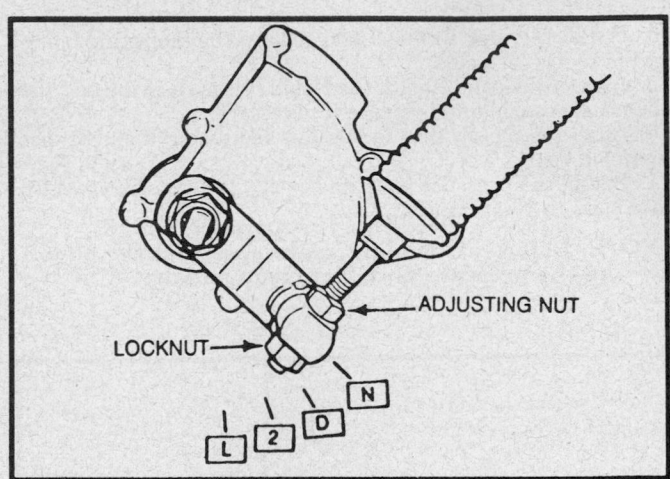

Adjusting the shift cable assembly

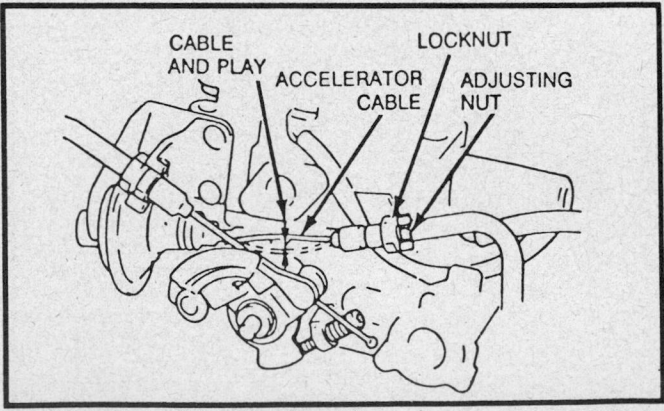

Accelerator cable adjustment

32. Connect the wiring coupler at the rear of the intake manifold and replace the wiring harness clamp in the proper position.

33. Connect the breather hose to the clamp at the rear of the cylinder head.

34. Install the transmission shift control lever and replace the transfer case shift control lever knob.

35. Connect the negative battery cable and refill the transmission. Run the engine and check for leaks.

Shift Linkage Adjustment

1. Adjust the shift cable assembly by moving the shift selector to the **N** position and placing a pin in the selector to hold that position.

2. Put the manual select lever in **L** position and set the cable to the cable bracket with the E-clip.

3. Adjust the manual select lever back to the **N** position and tighten the cable end locknut to 5ft. lbs.

NOTE: When the manual selector is moved to the N position, there should be a little clearance between the lever and the adjusting nut.

Throttle linkage Adjustment

Adjust the cable by loosening the cable locknut and adjust the cable to specifications. The cable endplay should be (0.12–0.20 in.) when the throttle valve is in the idle position.

Detent Cable Adjustment

1. Make sure accelerator play is within specifications.

2. Loosen the kickdown cable nut and adjusting nut.

3. With the accelerator pedal fully depressed and the cable pulled towards the firewall, adjust the locknut-to-bracket clearance to (0.039 in.) by turning the locknut

NOTE: When adjusting the clearance make sure that the adjusting nut does not rub against the bracket.

4. Release the accelerator pedal and adjust the locknut-to-bracket clearance by tightening the adjusting nut. Tighten the locknut securely.

TRANSFER CASE

Transfer Case Assembly

Removal and Installation

1. Disconnect the negative battery cable.
2. Raise and safely support the vehicle.
3. Support the transmission and transfer case using a suitable transmission jack.

4. Disconnect the speedometer cable from the transfer case.

5. Remove the transmission and transfer case from the vehicle.

6. Remove the 10 transmission-to-transfer case mounting bolts and separate the transfer case from the transmission.

7. Installation is the reverse of the removal procedure.

DRIVE AXLE

Halfshaft

Removal and Installation

SIDEKICK AND TRACKER

1. Raise and safely support the vehicle. Drain the transmission.

2. Remove the front wheels and disconnect the locking hubs.

3. Disconnect the halfshaft snaprings and remove the stabilizer bar links.

4. Disconnect the tie rod ends and remove the brake caliper and brake disc. Support the brake caliper.

5. Disconnect the wheel hub and remove the steering knuckle.

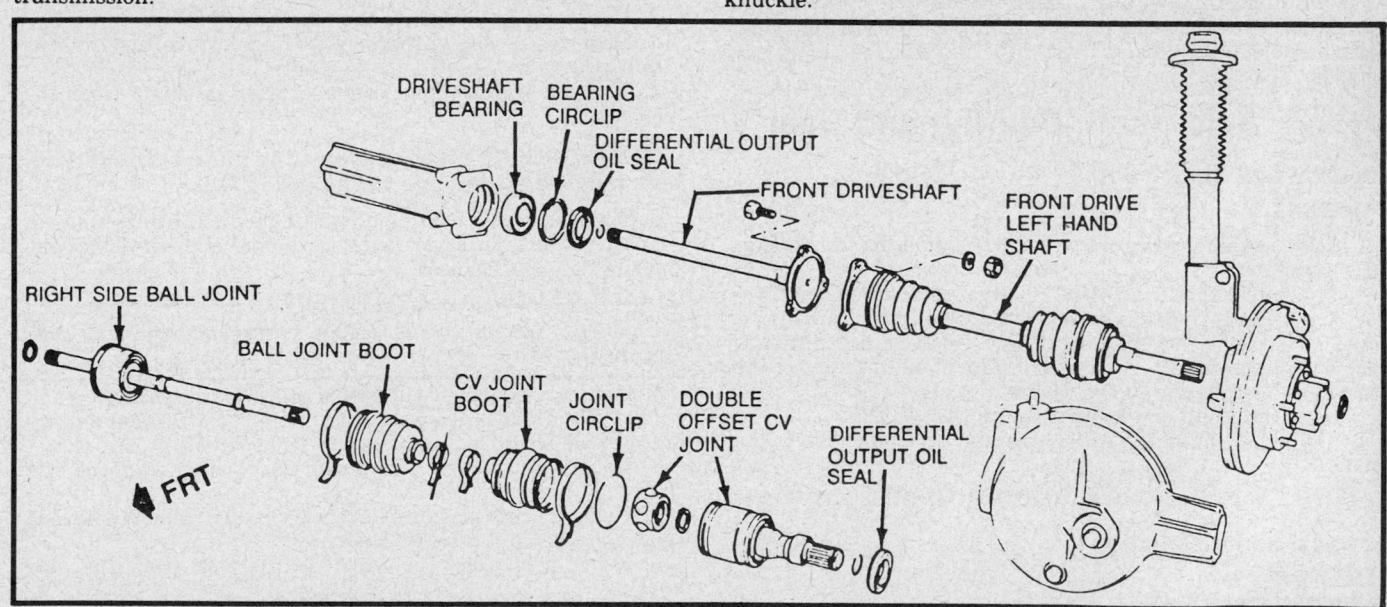

Exploded view of the halfshaft assembly

6. Disconnect the differential side joint snapring and remove the right side halfshaft by prying the joint away from the differential assembly.

7. Disconnect the left side halfshaft bolts and remove the halfshaft from the left inner axle flange.

8. Installation is reverse of the removal procedure.

9. Torque the axle shaft bolts to 37 ft. lbs.

Driveshaft and U-Joints
Removal and Installation

1. Raise and safely support the vehicle.

2. Matchmark the driveshafts to the yokes on the transfer case and the differential.

3. Drain the transfer case oil (when servicing the front driveshaft shaft).

4. Support the driveshaft and remove the attaching bolts.

5. Remove the driveshaft from the vehicle.

6. Install the driveshaft, by aligning the matchmarks to the vehicle.

7. Tighten the mounting bolts to 17–21 ft. lbs. on Samurai and 37 ft. lbs. on Sidekick and Tracker.

8. Refill the transfer case and lower the vehicle.

Front Axle Shaft
Removal and Installation
SAMURAI

1. Raise and safely support the vehicle.

2. Drain the oil in the front differential.

3. Remove the front wheels and disconnect the brake caliper. Support the brake caliper.

4. Disconnect the tie rod end from the steering knuckle. The tie rod end removal may require the use of a puller.

5. Remove the 8 oil seal cover mounting bolts and disconnect the felt pad, oil seal and the retainer from the steering knuckle.

6. Mark the upper and lower king pins. Remove the 4 mounting bolts and disconnect the king pins from the steering knuckle.

7. Remove the axle shaft from the housing with the steering knuckle attached.

8. Transfer the steering knuckle to the new axle.

9. Installation is the reverse of the removal procedure. Refill the front differential with the proper fluid when finished.

10. Observe the following torques during the installation: joint seal bolts, 6.0–8.5 ft. lbs.; tie rod nut, 22–39 ft. lbs.; king- pin bolts, 14–21 ft. lbs.

Front Axle Shaft, Bearing and Seal

Removal and Installation
SAMURAI

1. Raise and safely support the vehicle. Drain the front differential assembly.

2. Disconnect the front wheel hub and remove the bearing.

3. Support the hub and drive out the seal in the hub.

4. Using a seal driver, install the new seal in the hub until it is flush with the hub face. Apply a thin film of oil to the lip of the seal before installation to the vehicle.

5. Install the hub and the bearing to the vehicle.

6. Refill the front differential assembly and safely lower the vehicle.

Rear Axle Shaft, Bearing and Seal

Removal and Installation
SAMURAI

1. Raise and safely support the vehicle. Drain the rear differential assembly.

2. Make sure that the rear brake is released.

3. Remove the rear wheels and remove the rear brake drums from the vehicle.

4. Disconnect the parking brake cables from the levers. Remove the parking brake lever stop plates.

5. Disconnect and plug the brake lines to the wheel cylinders.

6. Remove the backing plate mounting bolts.

7. Remove the rear axles with the backing plates attached using a slide hammer type puller.

8. Using a suitable tool, remove the axle seal from the housing.

9. If the axle, axle bearing or backing plate is being replaced, support the axle in a vise with additional support under the shaft next to the bearing.

CAUTION

Eye protection must be worn during the 3 steps. Failure to do so could cause injury.

---

10. With the axle shaft supported properly, grind the top and bottom of the axle bearing retainer to remove it without damaging the axle shaft.

11. Using a chisel, finish removing the retainer from the axle shaft.

12. Using a press or suitable bearing puller, remove the axle shaft bearing from the axle shaft.

13. Remove the backing plate from the axle shaft.

14. Using a seal driver, install the new seal with the lip facing the housing to the same depth as the old seal.

15. Install the backing plate on the axle shaft and using a press, install the bearing and the retainer on the axle shaft.

16. Install the axle shaft in the housing.

17. Replace the backing plate mounting bolts and connect the brake lines to the wheel cylinders.

18. Replace the parking brake lever plates and connect the brake cables to the parking brake lever.

19. Install the rear brake drums and replace the rear wheels.

20. Adjust the brakes and bleed the brake system.

21. Refill the rear differential and safely lower the vehicle.

SIDEKICK AND TRACKER

1. Raise and safely support the vehicle.

2. Remove the rear wheels and remove the rear brake drums from the vehicle.

3. Drain the gear oil from the rear axle housing.

4. Remove the rear wheel bearing retainer nuts from the rear axle housing.

5. Using a suitable tool, remove the axle shaft from the housing.

NOTE: Do not remove the backing plate with the axle. This may cause damage to the inner seal.

6. If the axle, axle bearing or backing plate is being replaced, support the axle in a vise with additional support under the shaft next to the bearing.

CAUTION

Eye protection must be worn during the 3 steps. Failure to do so could cause injury.

---

7. With the axle shaft supported properly, grind the top and bottom of the axle bearing retainer to remove it without damaging the axle shaft.

8. Using a chisel, finish removing the retainer from the axle shaft.

9. Using a press or suitable bearing puller, remove the axle shaft bearing from the axle shaft.

10. Using a suitable tool, remove the seal from the axle housing.

11. Using a seal driver, install the new seal with the lip facing the housing to the same depth as the old seal.

12. Install the new bearing and the retainer on the axle shaft using a suitable press.

13. Install the axle shaft in to the rear axle housing and replace the rear wheel bearing retaining nuts, tighten to 17 ft. lbs.

14. Replace the rear brake drums and replace the rear tires on the vehicle.

15. Refill the rear axle housing with the proper gear oil and safely lower the vehicle.

Front Wheel Hub, Knuckle and Bearings

Removal and Installation

SAMURAI

1. Raise and safely support the vehicle. Remove the front wheels.

2. Disconnect the locking hub. Remove the caliper mounting bolts and move the caliper out of position with the brake line attached.

NOTE: Do not allow the caliper to hang on the brake hose. Support it by the mounting bracket.

3. Install 2 (8mm) bolts into the threaded holes and tighten evenly. This will remove the rotor from the hub assembly.

4. Remove the front axle shaft cap and the circlip. Remove the drive flange from the steering knuckle.

5. Straighten the bent lock washer and remove the hub nut and washer.

6. Remove the front wheel hub and bearing from the spindle.

7. Remove the oil seal and race from the wheel hub.

8. Clean and inspect the hub and bearing seats. Install the new bearing, race and grease seal in the same position.

9. Loosen the upper and lower king pin bolts, but do not remove the king pins.

10. Disconnect the disc dust cover and remove the spindle.

11. Disconnect the tie rod end from the steering knuckle.

12. Remove the 8 joint seal cover bolts and remove the cover, pad, oil seal and retainer from the knuckle.

13. Mark the upper and lower king pins. Remove the 4 mounting bolts and disconnect the king pins from the steering knuckle.

14. Remove the steering knuckle while noting the upper from the lower king pin positions during the removal of the knuckle.

15. Install the king pin bearings in the new knuckle and install the knuckle to the vehicle.

16. Install the king pins and tighten the mounting bolts to 14–21 ft. lbs.

17. Replace the joint seal cover, pad oil seal and retainer. Tighten the joint seal cover bolts to 6.0–8.5 ft. lbs.

18. Connect the tie rod end to the steering knuckle.

19. Replace the spindle and connect disc dust cover.

20. Install the front wheel hub and bearing to the spindle.

21. Install the front hub nut and lock washer and replace the drive flange to the steering knuckle.

22. Install the front axle cap and circlip. Connect the rotor to the hub assembly.

23. Place the brake caliper into position and replace the caliper mounting bolts.

24. Reconnect the locking hub assembly and replace the front wheels.

25. Lower the vehicle.

SIDEKICK AND TRACKER

1. Disconnect the negative battery cable. Raise and safely support the vehicle.

2. Remove the wheels and disconnect the locking hub assembly.

3. Remove the caliper mounting bracket and position the caliper out of the way. Support the caliper.

4. Disconnect the front wheel bearing lock plate and washer and remove the wheel hub complete with bearings and seals.

5. Remove the oil seal and race from the wheel hub.

6. Clean and inspect the hub and bearing seats. Install the new bearing, race and grease seal in the same position.

7. Support the suspension with a jack and remove the dust cover.

8. Disconnect the spindle by tapping with a hammer.

9. Remove the strut bracket bolts from the steering knuckle.

10. Disconnect the tie rod end from the knuckle and the knuckle from the control arm.

11. Remove the dust seal and the spindle from the knuckle.

12. Install the new seal and the spindle to the knuckle.

13. Connect the knuckle to the ball joint and tighten the nut to 40 ft. lbs.

14. Connect the knuckle to the strut damper and tighten the bolts to 66 ft. lbs.

15. Replace the tie rod end to the knuckle and tighten the nut 30 ft. lbs.

16. Install the spindle and replace the dust cover and remove the jack from under the suspension.

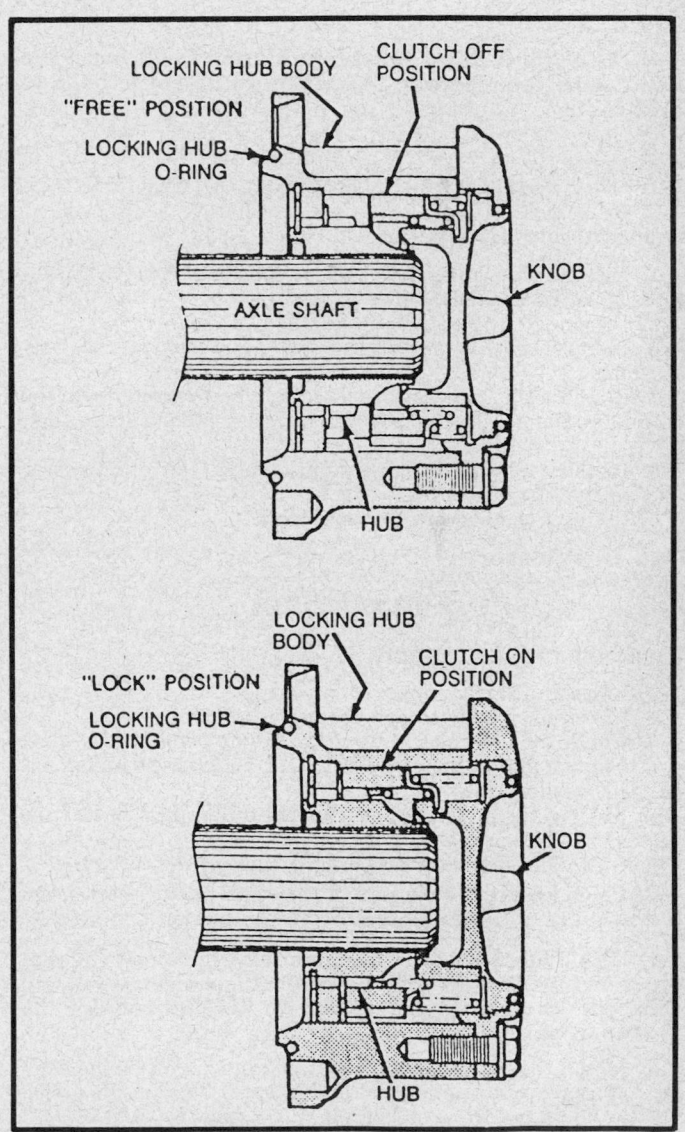

Wheel hub position

17. Install the wheel hub assembly and connect the locking hub.
18. Replace the wheels and lower the vehicle.
19. Connect the negative battery cable.

Manual Locking Hubs

Removal and Installation

1. Disconnect the negative battery cable and remove the locking hub cover.
2. Raise and support the vehicle safely.
3. Remove the locking hub body assembly.

NOTE: The manual locking hubs must not be packed with grease.

4. Install a new O-ring to the locking hub assembly.
5. Install the locking hub body assembly to the wheel hub flange and tighten the hub body bolts to 18 ft. lbs.
6. Install a new gasket in the manual locking hub cover.
7. Replace the locking hub cover and connect the negative battery cable.
8. Lower the vehicle.

NOTE: The O mark on the hub knob must be in the FREE position. Tighten the locking hub cover bolts to (106 in. lb.).

Automatic Locking Hubs

Removal and Installation

1. Disconnect the negative battery cable and remove the automatic locking hub cover.
2. Disconnect the automatic hub body assembly.
3. Install a new O-ring to the automatic locking hub body assembly.
4. Connect the automatic locking hub body assembly to the wheel hub flange. Tighten the hub body assembly bolts to 18 ft. lbs.
5. Install a new gasket in the automatic locking hub cover and replace the hub cover.
6. Connect the negative battery cable.

Pinion Seal

Removal and Installation

1. Raise and safely support the vehicle.
2. Matchmark and remove the driveshaft.
3. Check the turning torque of the pinion before proceeding.
4. Using a pinion flange holding tool, remove the pinion nut and the washer.
5. Remove the pinion flange from the differential carrier and pry out the pinion seal.
6. Clean and inspect the sealing surface of the carrier.
7. Using a seal driver, install the new seal into the carrier until the flange of the seal is flush with the carrier.

NOTE: Tightening the flange nut will preload the pinion bearings. Exceeding the preload specifications will compress the collapsible spacer to far and require the spacer to be replaced.

8. Install the pinion flange and using the pinion flange holding tool, replace the pinion nut and washer. Tighten the pinion nut to the same torque as before.
9. Align the matchmarks and install the driveshaft.
10. Check the level of the differential fluid when finished.

Differential Carrier

Removal and Installation

1. Raise and safely support the vehicle. Drain the oil from the rear differential.
2. Remove the left and right axle shafts.
3. Disconnect the driveshaft.
4. Remove the 4 mounting bolts to the upper rear suspension arm.
5. Support the differential carrier with a proper jack.
6. Remove the differential case nuts and lower the differential assembly from the rear housing.
7. Clean and inspect the sealing surfaces of the carrier and the housing.
8. Using a liquid sealant on the carrier, install the carrier in the housing and tighten the nuts to 13–20 ft. lbs.
9. Replace the 4 mounting bolts to the upper rear suspension arm and tighten to 41 ft. lbs.
10. Connect the rear driveshaft and replace the left and rear axles.
11. Refill the rear differential to the proper level with SAE 75W–90W API GL5 Hypoid Gear Oil.
12. Lower the vehicle.

Front Axle Housing

Removal and Installation
SAMURAI

1. Raise and safely support the vehicle. Remove the rear wheels.
2. Matchmark and remove the front driveshaft.
3. Disconnect and plug the brake lines at the brake calipers.
4. Remove the housing to leaf springs U-bolts and nuts.
5. Slide the housing to one side while tilting the opposite side under the leaf spring.
6. Remove the housing from the vehicle.
7. Installation is the reverse of the removal procedure. Torque the housing U-bolt nuts to 43–57 ft. lbs.
8. Refill the differential with the proper lubricant and bleed the brake system when finished.

Rear Axle Housing

Removal and Installation
SAMURAI

1. Raise and safely support the vehicle. Drain the rear differential assembly.
2. Make sure that the parking brake is in the released position.
3. Remove the rear wheels and remove the rear brake drums from the vehicle.
4. Disconnect the parking brake cables from the levers. Remove the parking brake lever stop plates.
5. Disconnect and plug the brake lines to the wheel cylinders.
6. Remove the backing plate mounting bolts and remove the axle shafts with the backing plates attached.
7. Remove the differential carrier assembly.
8. Remove the brake line from the flexible hose and remove the E-clip.
9. Disconnect the brake clamps and remove the brake lines from the rear housing.
10. Disconnect the driveshaft and remove from the transmission.
11. Disconnect the mounting bolts to the rear suspension arm and remove the housing to leaf spring U-bolts and nuts.
12. Remove shock absorber lower mount bolt.
13. Slide the housing to one side while tilting the opposite side under the leaf spring and remove the housing from the vehicle.

14. Installation is the reverse of the removal procedure. Torque the housing U-bolts to 43–57 ft. lbs.
15. Refill the differential and bleed the brake system when finished.

SIDEKICK AND TRACKER

1. Raise and safely support the vehicle. Drain the rear differential assembly.
2. Make sure that the parking brake is in the released position.
3. Remove the rear wheels and remove the rear brake drums from the vehicle.
4. Disconnect the parking brake cables from the levers. Remove the parking brake lever stop plates.
5. Disconnect and plug the brake lines to the wheel cylinders.
6. Remove the rear wheel bearing retainer nuts and remove the axle shafts from the vehicle. Do not remove the axle shafts with the backing plates attached.
7. Remove the rear axle carrier assembly.
8. Disconnect the brake line from the flexible hose and remove the E-clip. Remove the brake lines from the rear housing.
9. Remove the breather hose from the axle housing and disconnect the rear driveshaft.
10. Support the rear axle housing with a suitable jack.
11. Remove the ball joint bracket from the differential carrier and remove the carrier assembly.

12. Loosen the rear mount nut of the trailing rod. Do not remove it.
13. Disconnect the shock absorber lower mount bolt.
14. Lower the jack to relieve the tension of the coil springs and remove the rear mount bolt of the trailing rod.
15. Remove the rear axle housing.
16. Place the rear axle housing on a jack and install the trailing rod rear mounting bolts. Mount the nuts but do not tighten.
17. Install the coil spring on the spring seat and raise the axle housing.
18. Replace the shock absorber lower mounting bolts. Do not tighten.
19. Install the differential carrier assembly and replace the rear upper ball joint bracket onto the carrier assembly and tighten to 37 ft. lbs.
20. Install the rear driveshaft and remove the jack from under the axle housing.
21. Replace the breather hose and brake lines to axle housing. Tighten them securely.
22. Connect the flexible brake hose to the bracket on the axle housing and secure with the E-clip.
23. Tighten the trailing rod nuts and the shock absorber nuts to 66 ft. lbs.
24. Install the brake line to the flexible hose and replace the axle shafts.
25. Install the brake lines to the wheel cylinders and replace the brake drums.
26. Install the wheels and refill the rear differential assembly.
27. Bleed the brake system and lower the vehicle.

STEERING

Steering Wheel

Removal and Installation

1. Disconnect the negative battery cable.
2. Disconnect the horn button and remove the steering wheel shaft nut.
3. Make matchmarks on the steering wheel and the shaft to use as a guide during reinstallation.
4. Remove the steering wheel, using a suitable steering wheel puller.
5. Install the steering wheel onto the shaft, aligning the matchmarks.
6. Install and tighten the shaft nut to 24 ft. lbs.
7. Install the horn button and connect the negative battery cable.

Manual Steering Gear

Removal and Installation
SAMURAI

1. Remove the steering shaft coupler bolt and disconnect the coupler from the steering box. As required, raise and support the vehicle safely.
2. Remove the radiator under cover and disconnect the ball stud of the drag rod. Remove the steering damper from the pitman arm.
3. Support the steering gear and remove the mounting bolts.
4. Remove the steering gear from the vehicle.
5. Installation is the reverse of the removal procedure.
6. Torque the steering gear mounting bolts to 51–65 ft. lbs., the steering shaft joint flange bolt to 14–21 ft. lbs., the steering damper nut to 25–39 ft. lbs.

SIDEKICK AND TRACKER

1. As required, raise and support the vehicle safely. Disconnect the steering lower shaft mounting bolts.
2. Disconnect the center link end from the pitman arm.
3. Remove the 3 steering gear box mounting bolts.
4. Disconnect the steering lower shaft joint and remove the steering gear.
5. Install the steering gear box by connecting to the lower shaft joint.

NOTE: Align the flat part of the steering gear worm shaft with the bolt hole of the lower shaft joint.

6. Replace the steering gear box mounting bolts and tighten to 50–72 ft. lbs.
7. Attach the center link to the pitman arm and tighten the nut to 22–50 ft. lbs.
8. Connect the lower shaft mounting bolts and tighten to 14–22 ft. lbs.

Adjustment

1. Check the worm shaft to make sure it is free from thrust play.
2. Place the pitman arm in a position that is nearly parallel with the worm shaft.
3. With the pitman arm in this position, the front wheels are in a straight forward position.
4. Measure the worm shaft starting torque from it's straight foward position. The torque should be 0.4–0.7 ft. lbs.
5. Adjust the worm shaft adjusting bolt to specifications.

Power Steering Gear

Removal and Installation

1. Disconnect the negative battery cable.
2. Remove the coolant reservoir tank from the radiator.
3. Disconnect the steering column lower shaft from the gear box.

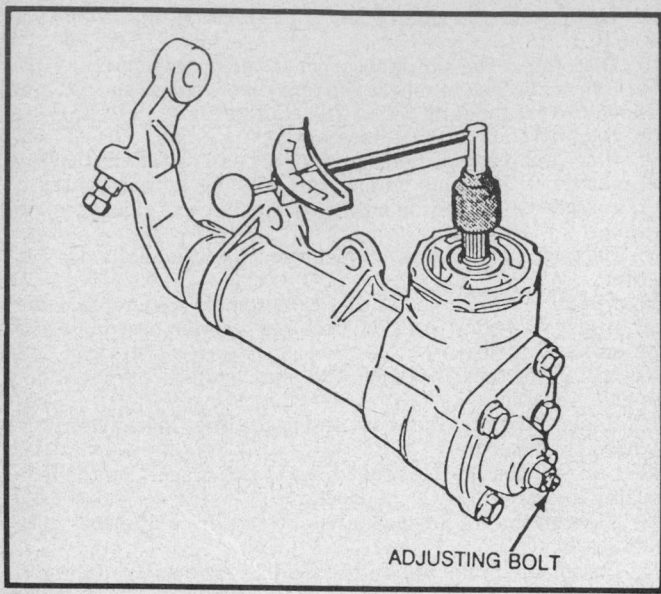

Adjusting the steering gear assembly

4. Raise and safely support the vehicle.

5. Remove the center link nut and lock washer and disconnect the center link from the pitman arm, using a piman arm puller.

6. Lower the vehicle. Remove the pressure hose from the power steering gear assembly and plug.

7. Disconnect the return hose and plug. Remove the 3 power steering gear mounting bolts.

8. Remove the power steering gear. Disconnect the pitman arm from the gear assembly, note the alignment marks.

9. Align the matchmarks on the pitman arm and the power steering gear secter shaft. Install the pitman arm to the gear assembly and tighten the nut to 95 ft. lbs.

10. Install the power steering gear assembly on the vehicle and tighten the mounting bolts to 72 ft. lbs.

11. Connect the power steering pressure and return hoses.

12. Raise and safely support the vehicle.

13. Install the center link to the pitman arm and tighten the nut to 40 ft. lbs. Lower the vehicle.

14. Connect the steering column lower shaft to the gear assembly and tighten the bolts to 29 ft. lbs.

15. Install the coolant reservoir tank to the radiator. Refill the power steering pump.

16. Connect the negative battery cable. Run the engine and operate the power steering. Recheck the fluid level and for any leaks.

Adjustment

1. Check the worm shaft to make sure it is free from thrust play.

2. Place the pitman arm in a position that is nearly parallel with the worm shaft.

3. With the pitman arm in this position, the front wheels are in a straightforward state.

4. Measure the worm shaft starting torque from it's straightfoward state. The torque should be 0.4–0.7 ft. lbs.

5. Adjust the worm shaft adjusting bolt to specifications.

Power Steering Pump

Removal and Installation

NOTE: Before disconnecting the power steering pres-sure and return line at the pump assembly, make sure any dirt or grease is removed.

1. Disconnect the negative battery cable. Remove the coolant reservoir tank from the radiator.

2. Loosen the air conditioning compressor adjusting and pivot bolts, if equipped.

3. Loosen the power steering pump adjusting and mounting bolts, if not equipped with air conditioning.

4. Remove the power steering belt.

5. Disconnect the power steering pressure and return hose and plug.

6. Disconnect the power steering pressure switch lead wire at the switch terminal.

7. Remove the engine oil filter.

8. Remove the power steering pump mounting and adjusting bolts.

9. Remove the power steering pump.

10. Install the power steering pump and replace the pump mounting bolts. Do not tighten.

11. Install the power steering pump pressure switch lead wire to the switch terminal.

12. Replace the power steering pressure and return hoses.

13. Install the power steering belt and tighten the power steering pump mounting bolts to 21 ft. lbs.

14. Tighten the air conditioning mounting bolts to 21 ft. lbs., if equipped.

15. Replace the coolant reservoir tank to the radiator and connect the negative battery cable. Refill the power steering pump.

16. Replace the oil filter and fill the crankcase to the proper level.

17. Run the engine and operate the power steering. Recheck the fluid level and for any leaks.

Belt Adjustment

1. To adjust the power steering belt tension, loosen the adjusting bolt of the air conditioning compressor, if equipped, or that of the power steering pump for vehicles without air conditioning.

2. Adjust the belt tension to (0.24–0.35 in.) deflection, using the proper belt tension guage.

3. Tighten the proper adjusting and mounting bolts to the specified torque.

System Bleeding

1. Raise and support the vehicle safely.

2. Fill the power steering reservoir to the specified level.

3. Run the engine for 3 to 5 minutes, stop it and add fluid if necessary to reach specified level.

4. With the engine stopped, turn the steering wheel to the left and to the right as far as it turns. Repeat a few times and refill the reservoir.

5. With the engine running at idle speed, bleed air from the system by loosening the bleeder valve at the gear assembly.

6. Repeat the stop to stop turn of the steering wheel until all the foam is gone.

7. Tighten the bleed valve securely. Recheck the fluid level in the reservoir.

NOTE: When air bleeding is not complete, it is indicated by a foaming fluid on the level indicator or a humming noise from the power steering pump.

Tie Rod Ends

Removal and Installation

1. Raise and safely support the vehicle and remove the wheels.

2. Remove the tie rod end from the steering knuckle, using a suitable tie rod end remover tool.

3. Mark the tie rod end locknut position on the tie rod thread.
4. Loosen the locknut and remove the tie rod end from the tie rod.
5. Install the tie rod end locknut and the tie rod end to the tie

rod. Align the locknut with the mark on the tie rod thread and tighten the locknut to 48 ft. lbs.
6. Connect the tie rod end to the steering knuckle. Tighten the castle nut until the holes of the split pin are aligned, but only within the specified torque 33 ft. lbs.

BRAKES

Master Cylinder

Removal and Installation

1. Disconnect the negative battery cable. Remove the air cleaner case.
2. Disconnect the reservoir lead wire on the Sidekick and the Samurai.
3. Clean the outside of the reservoir and remove the fluid from the reservoir.
4. Disconnect and plug the brake fluid lines at the master cylinder.
5. Remove the master cylinder to booster mounting bolts and remove the master cylinder.
6. Install the new master cylinder and tighten the mounting bolts to 12 ft. lbs.
7. Install the hydraulic brake lines to the master cylinder and tighten and tighten the flare nuts to 13 ft. lbs.
8. Replace the reservoir lead wire, if equipped.
9. Fill the reservoir with the specified brake fluid. Replace the air cleaner case.
10. Bleed the air from the brake hydraulic system and check the brake pedal play.

Proportioning Valve

Removal and Installation

1. Raise and safely support the vehicle.
2. Disconnect and plug the hydraulic brake lines from the proportioning valve assembly.
3. Remove the proportioning valve from the vehicle body.

NOTE: The proportioning valve should be removed with the spring attached.

4. Install the proportioning valve to the vehicle body and tighten the mounting bolts to 20 ft. lbs.
5. Connect the hydraulic brake lines to the proportioning valve and tighten the flare nuts to 13 ft. lbs.
6. Fill the brake reservoir to the proper level and bleed the brake hydraulic system. Lower the vehicle.

NOTE: Bleed the air from the proportioning valve bleeder valve.

Power Brake Booster

Removal and Installation

1. Disconnect the negative battery cable. Remove the air

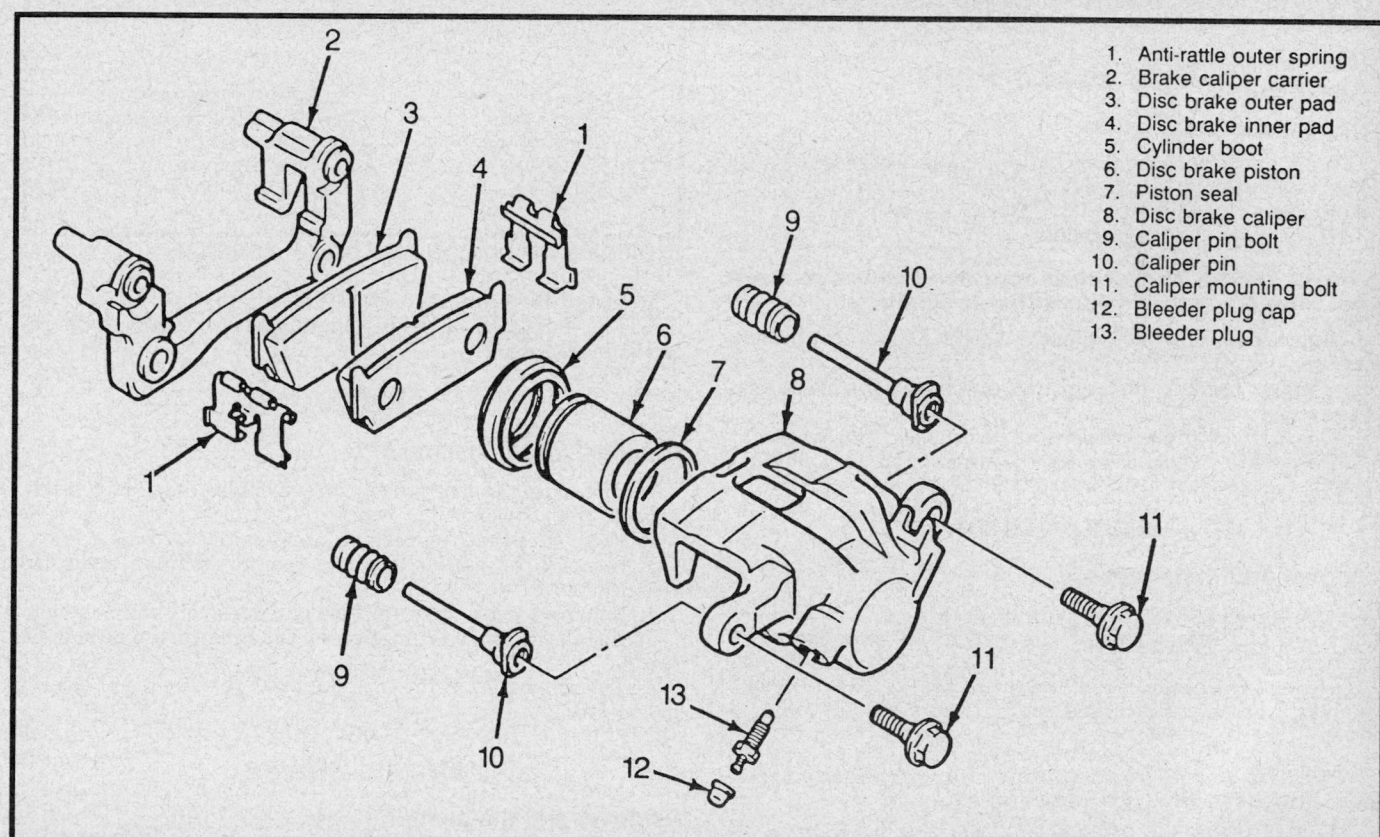

1. Anti-rattle outer spring
2. Brake caliper carrier
3. Disc brake outer pad
4. Disc brake inner pad
5. Cylinder boot
6. Disc brake piston
7. Piston seal
8. Disc brake caliper
9. Caliper pin bolt
10. Caliper pin
11. Caliper mounting bolt
12. Bleeder plug cap
13. Bleeder plug

Exploded view of the front disc brake assembly

cleaner case.

2. Remove the fluid from the brake reservoir and remove the master cylinder.

3. Disconnect the vacuum hose from the booster. Remove the pushrod clevis pin and cotter pin from the brake pedal arm.

4. Disconnect the brake booster mounting nuts and remove the brake booster from the vehicle.

5. Disconnect the pedal attachment from the booster.

6. Connect the pedal attachment to the booster and install the booster to the vehicle. Tighten the mounting nuts to 7.5–11.5 ft. lbs.

7. Install the pushrod clevis pin and cotter pin to the brake pedal arm.

8. Connect the vacuum hose to the booster and install the master cylinder to the booster.

9. Replace the air cleaner case and connect the negative battery cable.

10. Fill the brake reservoir and bleed the brake hydraulic system.

Brake Caliper

Removal and Installation

1. Disconnect the negative battery cable. Raise and safely support the vehicle.

2. Remove the wheels. Disconnect and plug the brake line.

3. Remove the caliper mounting bolts and remove the caliper from the vehicle.

4. Install the caliper on the vehicle. Tighten the mounting bolts to 65 ft. lbs.

5. Connect the hydraulic brake line, using 2 new washers. Replace the front wheels.

6. Lower the vehicle. Connect the negative battery cable.

7. Fill the brake reservoir and bleed the hydraulic brake system.

Disc Brake Pads

Removal and Installation

1. Disconnect the negative battery cable. Raise and safely support the vehicle.

2. Remove the wheels.

3. Disconnect the brake caliper.

NOTE: Do not allow the caliper hang from the brake hose. Support it by the mounting bracket.

4. Remove the disc pads from the caliper. Disconnect the anti rattle springs.

5. Connect the anti rattle springs and install the brake pads on to caliper assembly.

6. Connect the brake caliper and install the front wheels.

7. Lower the vehicle. Connect the negative battery cable.

Brake Rotor

Removal and Installation

1. Disconnect the negative battery cable.

2. Raise and safely support the vehicle. Remove the wheel assembly.

3. Remove the brake caliper mounting bracket, with the caliper and the brake line attached, move it out of the way and support it.

NOTE: Do not allow the caliper hang from the brake hose. Support it by the mounting bracket.

4. Install 2 bolts into the threaded holes in the brake rotor and tighten them evenly. This will remove the rotor from the hub assembly.

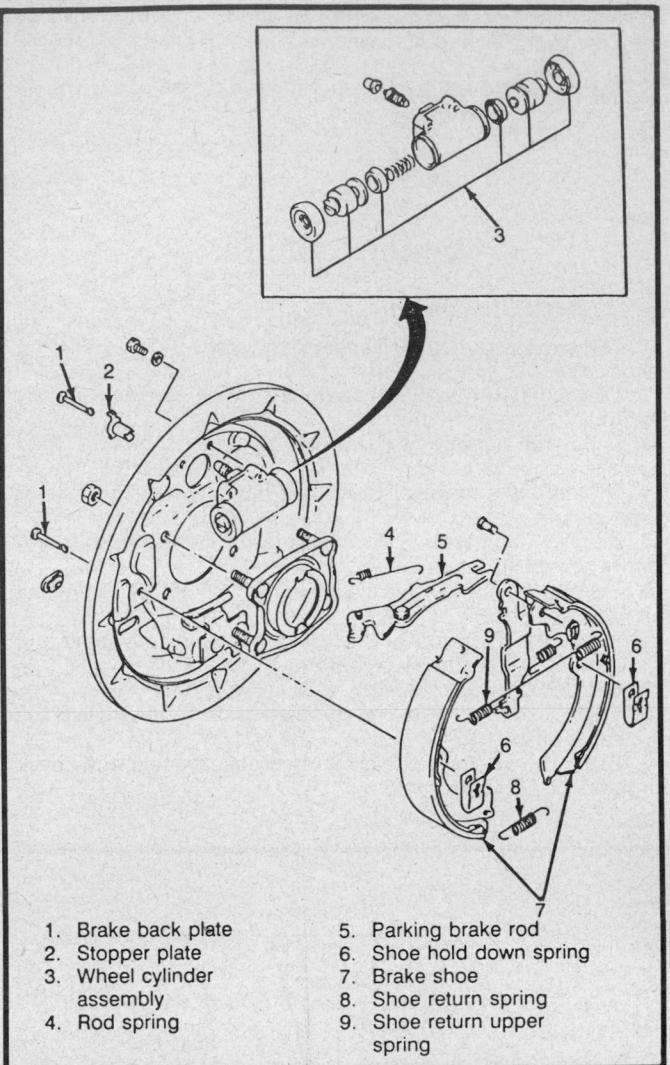

1. Brake back plate	5. Parking brake rod
2. Stopper plate	6. Shoe hold down spring
3. Wheel cylinder assembly	7. Brake shoe
4. Rod spring	8. Shoe return spring
	9. Shoe return upper spring

Exploded view of the rear brake assembly

5. Install the new brake rotor on the hub.

6. The remainder of the installation is the reverse of the removal procedure.

Brake Drums

Removal and Installation

1. Disconnect the negative battery cable. Raise and safely support the vehicle.

2. Make sure that the parking brake is released.

3. Remove the wheels and the rear drum nuts from the vehicle.

4. Remove the brake drum, using a suitable slide hammer.

5. Install the brake drum, tighten the brake drum nuts to 58 ft. lbs.

6. The remainder of the installation is the reverse of the removal procedure.

Brake Shoes

Removal and Installation

1. Disconnect the negative battery cable. Raise and safely support the vehicle.

2. Remove the rear wheels from the vehicle. Remove the rear brake drums.

3. Remove the brake shoe holddown springs.

4. Disconnect the parking brake cable from the parking brake shoe lever and remove the brake shoes.

5. The installation is the reverse of the removal procedure.

Wheel Cylinder

Removal and Installation

1. Disconnect the negative battery cable. Raise and safely support the vehicle.

2. Remove the rear wheels and brake drums from the vehicle.

3. Remove the rear brake shoes and disconnect the brake line from the rear of the wheel cylinder. Plug the brake line.

4. Remove the 2 rear wheel cylinder mounting bolts. Remove the rear wheel cylinder.

5. Install the wheel cylinder and tighten the mounting bolts to 6.0–8.5 ft. lbs.

6. Connect the brake line to the wheel cylinder and install the rear brake shoes.

7. Replace the rear brake drums and the rear wheels.

8. Lower the vehicle. Connect the negative battery cable.

9. Bleed the brake system and check for any leaks when finished.

Parking Brake Cable

Removal and Installation

1. Disconnect the parking brake cable from the parking lever.

2. Raise and safely support the vehicle. Remove the rear wheels and brake drums from the vehicle.

3. Remove the rear brake shoes and disconnect the park brake cable from the park brake shoe lever.

4. Remove the cable from the brake backing plate by squeezing the park brake cable stop ring.

5. Installation is the reverse of the removal procedure.

Adjustment

1. Adjust the parking brake lever by loosening or tightening the self locking nut at the park brake lever.

2. The proper adjustment is when the park brake lever is within 7–9 notches, when the lever is pulled up at 44 lbs.

3. Ckeck the rear drum for dragging after adjustment.

FRONT SUSPENSION

Shock Absorbers

Removal and Installation

1. Raise and safely support the vehicle.

2. Support the axle assembly and remove the upper shock absorber mounting nut.

3. Remove the lower shock absorber mounting nut and remove the shock absorber.

4. Installation is the reverse of the removal procedure.

5. Torque the upper mounting nut to 16–25 ft. lbs. and the lower nut to 23–40 ft. lbs.

MacPherson Strut

Removal and Installation

1. Disconnect the negative battery cable.

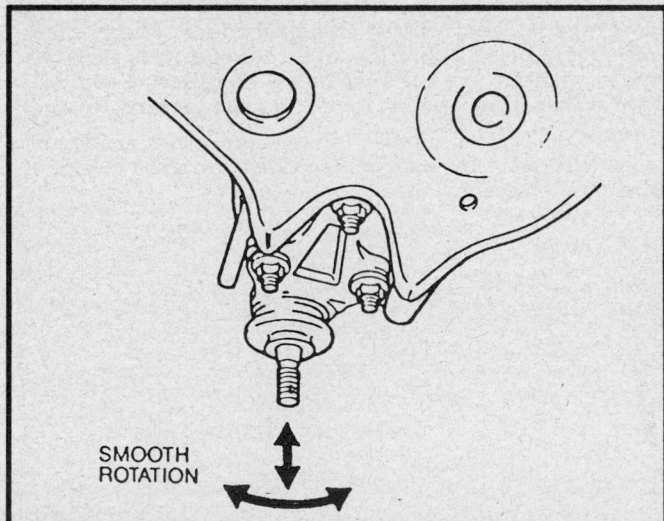

Checking ball joint play

SMOOTH ROTATION

2. Raise and safely support the vehicle. Allow the front suspension to hang free.

3. Remove the front wheel. Disconnect the E-clip mounting the brake hose and remove the brake hose from the strut bracket.

4. Remove the strut bracket to steering knuckle bolts.

5. Lower the vehicle. Remove the strut support nuts, while holding the strut by hand. Remove the strut assembly.

6. Install the strut assembly and tighten the strut support nuts to 18 ft. lbs.

7. Raise and safely support the vehicle.

8. Install the strut bracket to steering knuckle bolts and tighten to 66 ft. lbs.

9. Connect the brake hose to the strut bracket using the E-clip.

10. Replace the front wheels and lower the vehicle.

11. Connect the negative battery cable.

Coil Springs

Removal and Installation

SIDEKICK AND TRACKER

1. Disconnect the negative battery cable.

2. Raise and safely support the vehicle. Allow the front suspension to hang free.

3. Remove the front wheel and the locking hub assembly.

4. Remove the front axle circlip and washer.

5. Remove the brake caliper mounting bracket, with the caliper and the brake line attached, move it out of the way and support it.

6. Remove the brake disc and disconnect the stabilizer link from the control arm.

7. Disconnect the tie rod end and support the lower control arm using a jack.

8. Disconnect the strut bracket and remove the ball joint castle nut.

9. Remove the steering knuckle and the wheel hub assembly while lowering the jack.

10. Remove the coil spring from the vehicle.

11. Installation is the reverse of the removal procedure.

Leaf Springs

Removal and Installation
SAMURAI

1. Disconnect the negative battery cable.
2. Raise and safely support the vehicle. Allow the front suspension to hang free.
3. Remove the stabilizer bar pivot bolt.
4. Support the front axle assembly with an adjustable stand.
5. Remove the leaf spring to spring plate mounting U-bolts.
6. Remove the shackle pin and the nut from the front of the leaf spring.
7. Disconnect the leaf spring bolt and remove the leaf spring.

NOTE: Removal of the leaf spring causes the axle housing to hang. Support it with a safety stand to prevent it from damaging the U-joint of the driveshaft.

8. Installation is the reverse of the removal procedure.
9. Torque the leaf spring and the stabilizer nuts and bolts to 51–65 ft. lbs.

Lower Ball Joints

Inspection
SIDEKICK AND TRACKER

1. Inspect for the smoothness of the rotation.
2. Check the ball stud for damage.
3. Inspect the dust shield for damage.

Removal and Installation
SIDEKICK AND TRACKER

1. Disconnect the negative battery cable. Remove the coil spring from the vehicle.
2. Remove the control arm mounting bolts.
3. Remove the control arm.
4. Disconnect the ball joint from the control arm and remove the ball joint.
5. Install the ball joint to the control arm and tighten the bolts to 63 ft. lbs.
6. Install the control arm to the chassis and tighten the bolts to 74 ft. lbs.
7. Replace the coil spring and connect the negative battery cable.

Lower Control Arms

Removal and Installation
SIDEKICK AND TRACKER

1. Disconnect the negative battery cable. Remove the coil spring from the vehicle.
2. Remove the control arm mounting bolts.

3. Remove the control arm.
4. Install the control arm to the chassis and tighten the bolts to 74 ft. lbs.
5. Replace the coil spring and connect the negative battery cable.

Stabilizer Bar

Removal and Installation

1. Disconnect the negative battery cable. Raise and safely support the vehicle.
2. Disconnect the left and the right stabilizer ball joints from the front control arms on the Sidekick and Tracker.
3. Disconnect the stabilizer bar pivot bolts on the Samurai.
4. Remove the stabilizer bar mount bushing bracket bolts and nuts.
5. Remove the stabilizer bar.
6. Remove the stabilizer links on the Sidekick and Tracker.
7. Install the new stabilizer bar, using new bushings.
8. The remainder of the installation is the reverse of the removal procedure.
9. Torque the stabilizer bar pivot bolts to 51–65 ft lbs. and the mounting bracket nuts to 13–20 ft lbs. (Samurai). Torque the stabilizer link nuts to 21 ft. lbs. and the stabilizer bar bracket bolts and nuts to 37 ft. lbs. (Sidekick and Tracker).

King Pin and Bushings

Removal and Installation
SAMURAI

1. Raise and safely support the vehicle.
2. Remove the steering knuckle from the vehicle.

NOTE: When the steering knuckle is pulled, the lower king pin bearing sometimes falls off.

3. Remove the upper and the lower king pins, mark them. Check the number of shims on each side.
4. Install the new king pin bearings in the steering knuckle holding them in with grease.
5. Install the steering knuckle on the axle assembly.
6. Install the new king pins in the steering knuckle, shim them correctly and torque the bolts to 14–21 ft. lbs.

NOTE: The correct procedure for installing the king pins is to check the turning torque of the spindle while pulling it outwards from the tie rod end hole. A spring type gauge is required for this procedure. The correct force should be 2.20–3.96 lbs. of force require to turn the spindle without the oil seal being installed. Use additional shims, if necessary, to correct the turning torque.

7. With the turning torque of the spindle correct and the oil seal installed, the remainder of the installation is the reverse of the removal procedure.

REAR SUSPENSION

Shock Absorbers

Removal and Installation

1. Raise and safely support the vehicle. Support the rear axle housing.
2. Remove the upper and lower shock absorber mounting bolts.
3. Remove the rear shock absorber.
4. Install the the rear shock absorber.
5. On Sidekick and Tracker, replace the upper mounting bolts and tighten to 21. ft. lbs. Replace the lower mounting bolts and tighten to 63 ft. lbs.
6. On Samurai, tighten the upper and the lower mounting bolts to 25–39 ft. lbs.

Coil Springs

Removal and Installation

SIDEKICK AND TRACKER

1. Raise and safely support the vehicle. Remove the rear wheels.
2. Support the rear axle housing , using a floor jack.
3. Remove the shock absorber lower mounting bolt.
4. Lower the rear axle housing so that the coil spring can be removed.

5. Remove the coil spring from the vehicle.
6. Install the coil spring. The remainder of the installation is the reverse of the removal procedure.

Leaf Springs

Removal and Installation

SAMURAI

1. Raise and safely support the vehicle. Remove the rear wheels.
2. Safely, support the rear axle housing separately.
3. Disconnect the rear shocks and the stabilizer bar from the shackle plate under the rear leaf spring.

NOTE: Do not let the rear axle housing hang on the rear brake hoses or lines.

4. Remove the rear axle housing U-bolts nuts and bolts.
5. Raise the axle housing and remove the shackle plate.
6. Support the leaf spring and disconnect the front and the rear leaf spring mounting bolts.
7. Remove the rear leaf spring. Installation is the reverse of the removal procedure.
8. Torque the front leaf spring bolts to 33–50 ft. lbs., the rear leaf spring bolts to 22–39 ft. lbs., the stabilizer bar bolts to 16–25 ft. lbs. and the shock absorber nuts to 25–39 ft. lbs.

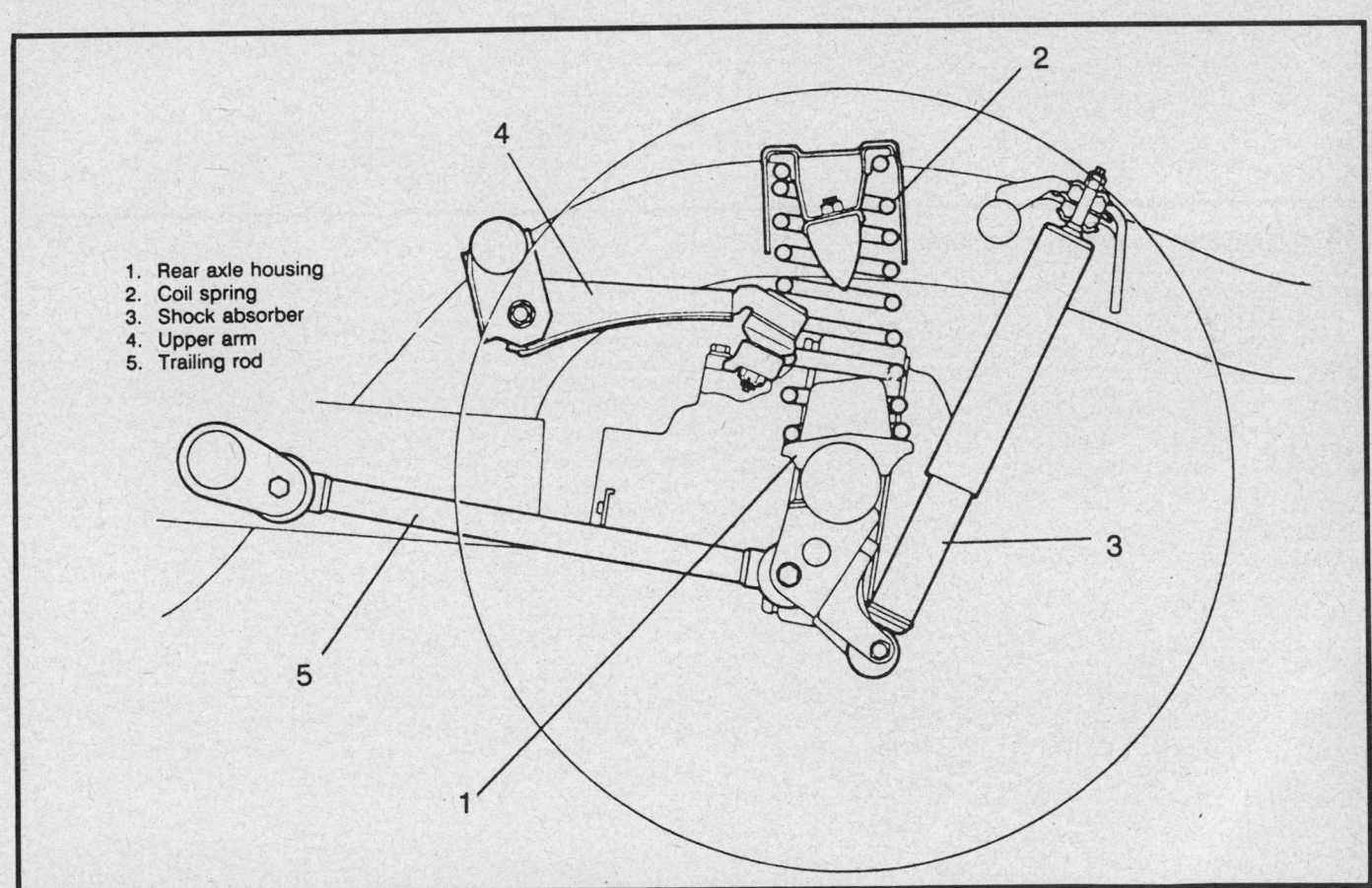

1. Rear axle housing
2. Coil spring
3. Shock absorber
4. Upper arm
5. Trailing rod

Rear suspension assembly—Sidekick and Tracker

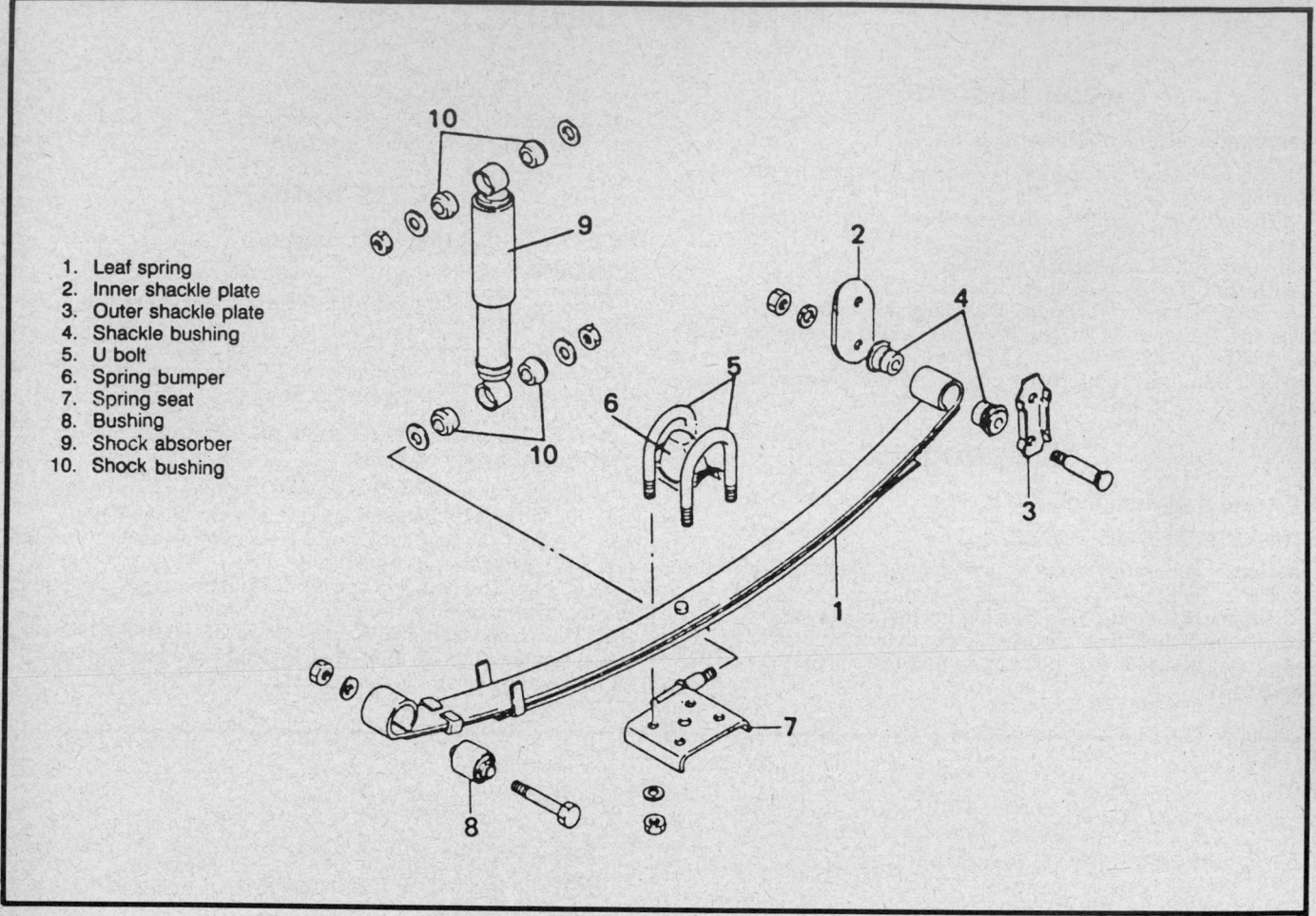

1. Leaf spring
2. Inner shackle plate
3. Outer shackle plate
4. Shackle bushing
5. U bolt
6. Spring bumper
7. Spring seat
8. Bushing
9. Shock absorber
10. Shock bushing

Rear suspension assembly—Samurai

SPECIFICATIONS

ENGINE IDENTIFICATION

Year	Model	Engine Displacement cu. in. (cc/liter)	Engine Series Identification	No. of Cylinders	Engine Type
1986	Pick-Up	144.4 (2366/2.4)	22R	4	OHC
	Pick-Up	144.4 (2366/2.4)	22R-E	4	OHC
	Pick-Up	144.4 (2366/2.4)	22R-TE	4	OHC-Turbo
	4Runner	144.4 (2366/2.4)	22R	4	OHC
	4Runner	144.4 (2366/2.4)	22R-E	4	OHC
	4Runner	144.4 (2366/2.4)	22R-TE	4	OHC-Turbo
	Van	136.5 (2237/2.2)	4Y-E	4	OHC
	Land Cruiser	258.1 (4200/4.0)	2F	6	OHV
1987	Pick-Up	144.4 (2366/2.4)	22R	4	OHC
	Pick-Up	144.4 (2366/2.4)	22R-E	4	OHC
	Pick-Up	144.4 (2366/2.4)	22R-TE	4	OHC-Turbo
	4Runner	144.4 (2366/2.4)	22R	4	OHC
	4Runner	144.4 (2366/2.4)	22R-E	4	OHC
	4Runner	144.4 (2366/2.4)	22R-TE	4	OHC-Turbo
	Van	136.5 (2237/2.2)	4Y-E	4	OHC
	Land Cruiser	258.1 (4200/4.0)	2F	6	OHV
1988	Pick-Up	144.4 (2366/2.4)	22R	4	OHC
	Pick-Up	144.4 (2366/2.4)	22R-E	4	OHC
	Pick-Up	144.4 (2366/2.4)	22R-TE	4	OHC-Turbo
	4Runner	144.4 (2366/2.4)	22R	4	OHC
	4Runner	144.4 (2366/2.4)	22R-E	4	OHC
	4Runner	144.4 (2366/2.4)	22R-TE	4	OHC-Turbo
	Van	136.5 (2237/2.2)	4Y-EC	4	OHC
	Land Cruiser	241.3 (3956/4.0)	3F-E	6	OHV
1989–90	Pick-Up	144.4 (2366/2.4)	22R	4	OHC
	Pick-Up	144.4 (2366/2.4)	22R-E	4	OHC
	Pick-Up	180.5 (2959/3.0)	3VZ-E	6	OHC
	4Runner	144.4 (2366/2.4)	22R-E	4	OHC
	4Runner	180.5 (2959/3.0)	3VZ-E	6	OHC
	Land Cruiser	241.3 (3956/4.0)	3F-E	6	OHV
	Van	136.5 (2237/2.2)	4Y-EC	4	OHC

GENERAL ENGINE SPECIFICATIONS

Year	Model	Engine Displacement cu. in. (cc)	Fuel System Type	Net Horsepower @ rpm	Net Torque @ rpm (ft. lbs.)	Bore × Stroke (in.)	Compression Ratio	Oil Pressure @ rpm
1986	Pick-Up	144.4 (2366)	2 bbl	96 @ 4800	129 @ 2800	3.62 × 3.50	9.3:1	36–71 @ 3000
	Pick-Up	144.4 (2366)	EFI	116 @ 4800	140 @ 2800	3.62 × 3.50	9.3:1	36–71 @ 3000
	Pick-Up	144.4 (2366)	EFI ①	135 @ 4800	173 @ 2800	3.62 × 3.50	7.5:1	36–71 @ 3000
	4Runner	144.4 (2366)	2 bbl	96 @ 4800	129 @ 2800	3.62 × 3.50	9.3:1	36–71 @ 3000
	4Runner	144.4 (2366)	EFI	116 @ 4800	140 @ 2800	3.62 × 3.50	9.3:1	36–71 @ 3000

GENERAL ENGINE SPECIFICATIONS

Year	Model	Engine Displacement cu. in. (cc)	Fuel System Type	Net Horsepower @ rpm	Net Torque @ rpm (ft. lbs.)	Bore × Stroke (in.)	Compression Ratio	Oil Pressure @ rpm
1986	4Runner	144.4 (2366)	EFI ①	135 @ 4800	173 @ 2800	3.62 × 3.50	7.5:1	36–71 @ 3000
	Van	136.5 (2237)	EFI	101 @ 4000	132 @ 3000	3.58 × 3.40	8.8:1	50–70 @ 3000
	Land Cruiser	258.1 (4200)	2 bbl	125 @ 3600	200 @ 1800	3.70 × 4.00	7.8:1	50–70 @ 2000
1987	Pick-Up	144.4 (2366)	2 bbl	96 @ 4800	129 @ 2800	3.62 × 3.50	9.3:1	36–71 @ 3000
	Pick-Up	144.4 (2366)	EFI	116 @ 4800	140 @ 2800	3.62 × 3.50	9.3:1	36–71 @ 3000
	Pick-Up	144.4 (2366)	EFI ①	135 @ 4800	173 @ 2800	3.62 × 3.50	7.5:1	36–71 @ 3000
	4Runner	144.4 (2366)	2 bbl	96 @ 4800	129 @ 2800	3.62 × 3.50	9.3:1	36–71 @ 3000
	4Runner	144.4 (2366)	EFI	116 @ 4800	140 @ 2800	3.62 × 3.50	9.3:1	36–71 @ 3000
	4Runner	144.4 (2366)	EFI ①	135 @ 4800	173 @ 2800	3.62 × 3.50	7.5:1	36–71 @ 3000
	Van	136.5 (2237)	EFI	101 @ 4000	132 @ 3000	3.58 × 3.40	8.8:1	50–70 @ 3000
	Land Cruiser	258.1 (4200)	2 bbl	125 @ 3600	200 @ 1800	3.70 × 4.00	7.8:1	50–70 @ 2000
1988	Pick-Up	144.4 (2366)	2 bbl	96 @ 4800	129 @ 2800	3.62 × 3.50	9.3:1	36–71 @ 3000
	Pick-Up	144.4 (2366)	EFI	116 @ 4800	140 @ 2800	3.62 × 3.50	9.3:1	36–71 @ 3000
	Pick-Up	144.4 (2366)	EFI ①	135 @ 4800	173 @ 2800	3.62 × 3.50	7.5:1	36–71 @ 3000
	4Runner	144.4 (2366)	2 bbl	96 @ 4800	129 @ 2800	3.62 × 3.50	9.3:1	36–71 @ 3000
	4Runner	144.4 (2366)	EFI	116 @ 4800	140 @ 2800	3.62 × 3.50	9.3:1	36–71 @ 3000
	4Runner	144.4 (2366)	EFI ①	135 @ 4800	173 @ 2800	3.62 × 3.50	7.5:1	36–71 @ 3000
	Van	136.5 (2237)	EFI	101 @ 4000	132 @ 3000	3.58 × 3.40	8.8:1	50–70 @ 3000
	Land Cruiser	241.3 (3956)	EFI	154 @ 4000	220 @ 3000	3.70 × 3.74	8.1:1	36–71 @ 4000
1989–90	Pick-Up	144.4 (2366)	2 bbl	103 @ 4800	133 @ 2800	3.62 × 3.50	9.3:1	36–71 @ 3000
	Pick-Up	144.4 (2366)	EFI	116 @ 4800	140 @ 2800	3.62 × 3.50	9.3:1	36–71 @ 3000
	Pick-Up	180.5 (2959)	EFI	150 @ 4800	180 @ 3400	3.44 × 3.23	9.0:1	36–71 @ 4000
	4Runner	144.4 (2366)	EFI	116 @ 4800	140 @ 2800	3.62 × 3.50	9.3:1	36–71 @ 3000
	4Runner	180.5 (2959)	EFI	150 @ 4800	180 @ 3400	3.44 × 3.23	9.0:1	36–71 @ 4000
	Land Cruiser	241.3 (3956)	EFI	154 @ 4000	220 @ 3000	3.70 × 3.74	8.1:1	36–71 @ 4000
	Van	136.5 (2237)	EFI	101 @ 4000	132 @ 3000	3.58 × 3.40	8.8:1	50–70 @ 3000

① Turbocharged

GASOLINE ENGINE TUNE-UP SPECIFICATIONS

Year	Model	Engine Displacement cu. in. (cc)	Spark Plugs Type	Spark Plugs Gap (in.)	Ignition Timing (deg.) MT	Ignition Timing (deg.) AT	Compression Pressure (psi)	Fuel Pump (psi)	Idle Speed (rpm) MT	Idle Speed (rpm) AT	Valve Clearance In.	Valve Clearance Ex.
1986	Pick-Up ①	144.4 (2366)	W16-EXRU	0.031	0 ④	0 ④	142–171	2.1–4.3	700	750	0.008	0.012
	Pick-Up ②	144.4 (2366)	W16-EXRU	0.031	5B ⑤	—	142–171	36–38	750	—	0.008	0.012
	Pick-Up ③	144.4 (2366)	W16-EXRU	0.031	5B ⑤	—	142–171	36–38	800	—	0.008	0.012
	4Runner ①	144.4 (2366)	W16-EXRU	0.031	0 ④	0 ④	142–171	2.1–4.3	700	750	0.008	0.012
	4Runner ②	144.4 (2366)	W16-EXRU	0.031	5B ⑤	—	142–171	36–38	750	—	0.008	0.012
	4Runner ③	144.4 (2366)	W16-EXRU	0.031	5B ⑤	—	142–171	36–38	800	—	0.008	0.012
	Van	136.5 (2237)	P-16R	0.043	12B ⑤	—	128–178	27–31	700	750	Hyd.	Hyd.
	Land Cruiser	258.1 (4200)	W14-EXRU	0.031	7B ④	—	142–171	2.1–4.3	650	—	0.008	0.012

GASOLINE ENGINE TUNE-UP SPECIFICATIONS

Year	Model	Engine Displacement cu. in. (cc)	Spark Plugs Type	Gap (in.)	Ignition Timing (deg.) MT	AT	Com-pression Pressure (psi)	Fuel Pump (psi)	Idle Speed (rpm) MT	AT	Valve Clearance In.	Ex.
1987	Pick-Up ①	144.4 (2366)	W16-EXRU	0.031	0 ④	0 ④	142–171	2.1–4.3	700	750	0.008	0.012
	Pick-Up ②	144.4 (2366)	W16-EXRU	0.031	5B ⑤	—	142–171	36–38	750	—	0.008	0.012
	Pick-Up ③	144.4 (2366)	W16-EXRU	0.031	5B ⑤	—	142–171	36–38	800	—	0.008	0.012
	4Runner ①	144.4 (2366)	W16-EXRU	0.031	0 ④	0 ④	142–171	2.1–4.3	700	750	0.008	0.012
	4Runner ②	144.4 (2366)	W16-EXRU	0.031	5B ⑤	—	142–171	36–38	750	—	0.008	0.012
	4Runner ③	144.4 (2366)	W16-EXRU	0.031	5B ⑤	—	142–171	36–38	800	—	0.008	0.012
	Van	136.5 (2237)	P-16R	0.043	12B ⑤	—	128–178	27–31	700	750	Hyd.	Hyd.
	Land Cruiser	258.1 (4200)	W14-EXRU	0.031	7B ④	7B	142–171	2.1–4.3	650	650	0.008	0.012
1988	Pick-Up ①	144.4 (2366)	W16-EXRU	0.031	0 ④	0 ④	142–171	2.1–4.3	700	750	0.008	0.012
	Pick-Up ②	144.4 (2366)	W16-EXRU	0.031	5B ⑤	—	142–171	36–38	750	—	0.008	0.012
	Pick-Up ③	144.4 (2366)	W16-EXRU	0.031	5B ⑤	—	142–171	36–38	800	—	0.008	0.012
	4Runner ①	144.4 (2366)	W16-EXRU	0.031	0 ④	0 ④	142–171	2.1–4.3	700	750	0.008	0.012
	4Runner ②	144.4 (2366)	W16-EXRU	0.031	5B ⑤	—	142–171	36–38	750	—	0.008	0.012
	4Runner ③	144.4 (2366)	W16-EXRU	0.031	5B ⑤	—	142–171	36–38	800	—	0.008	0.012
	Van	136.5 (2237)	P-16R	0.043	12B ⑤	—	128–178	27–31	700	750	Hyd.	Hyd.
	Land Cruiser	241.3 (3956)	W16-EXRU	0.031	7B ④	7B	142–171	37–46	650	650	0.008	0.014
1989	Pick-Up ①	144.4 (2366)	W16-EXRU	0.031	0 ④	0 ④	142–171	2.1–4.3	700	750	0.008	0.012
	Pick-Up ②	144.4 (2366)	W16-EXRU	0.031	5B ⑤	—	142–171	36–38	750	—	0.008	0.012
	Pick-Up	180.5 (2959)	Q16-RU	0.031	10B	10B	142–171	38–44	800	800	0.012	0.013
	4Runner ②	144.4 (2366)	W16-EXRU	0.031	5B ⑤	—	142–171	36–38	750	—	0.008	0.012
	4Runner	180.5 (2959)	Q16-RU	0.031	10B	10B	142–171	38–44	800	800	0.012	0.013
	Land Cruiser	241.3 (3956)	W16-EXRU	0.031	7B ④	7B	142–171	37–46	650	650	0.008	0.014
	Van	136.5 (2237)	P-16R	0.043	12B ⑤	—	128–178	27–31	700	750	Hyd.	Hyd.
1990					Refer to Underhood Sticker							

① 2 bbl
② EFI
③ Turbocharged
④ 950 rpm
⑤ ''T'' terminal shorted

FIRING ORDERS

NOTE: To avoid confusion, always replace spark plug wires one at a time.

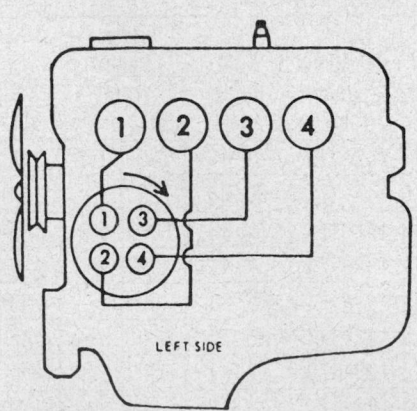

22R, 22R–E, 22R–TE 4Y–E and 4Y–EC engines
Engine firing order: 1–3–4–2
Distributor rotation: clockwise

FIRING ORDERS

NOTE: To avoid confusion, always replace spark plug wires one at a time.

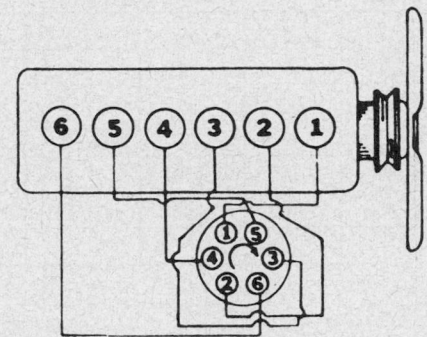

2F and 3F–E engines
Engine firing order: 1–5–3–6–2–4
Distributor rotation: clockwise

3VZ–E engine
Engine firing order: 1–2–3–4–5–6
Distributor rotation: counterclockwise

CAPACITIES

Year	Model	Engine Displacement cu. in. (cc)	Engine Crankcase with Filter	without Filter	Transmission (pts.) 4-Spd	5-Spd	Auto.	Drive Axle (pts.)	Fuel Tank (gal.)	Cooling System (qts.)
1986	Pick-Up ①	144.4 (2366)	4.5	4.0	2.5	2.5	6.9	1.9 ⑦	14.8 ④	8.9
	Pick-Up ②	144.4 (2366)	4.5	4.0	—	3.2	10.9	2.6 ⑦	14.8 ④	8.9
	Pick-Up ③	144.4 (2366)	4.5	4.0	—	3.2	10.9	2.6 ⑦	14.8 ④	8.9
	4Runner ①	144.4 (2366)	4.5	4.0	2.5	2.5	6.9	1.9 ⑦	14.8 ④	8.9
	4Runner ②	144.4 (2366)	4.5	4.0	—	3.2	10.9	2.6 ⑦	14.8 ④	8.9
	4Runner ③	144.4 (2366)	4.5	4.0	—	3.2	10.9	2.6 ⑦	14.8 ④	8.9
	Van	136.5 (2237)	3.7	3.2	—	2.5	6.9	1.5	15.9	7.5
	Land Cruiser	258.1 (4200)	8.2	7.4	3.7	5.2	15.9	2.2 ⑦	22.2 ⑤	17.5 ⑥
1987	Pick-Up ①	144.4 (2366)	4.5	4.0	2.5	2.5	⑧	⑨	⑩	8.9
	Pick-Up ②	144.4 (2366)	4.5	4.0	—	4.1	⑧	⑨	⑩	8.9
	Pick-Up ③	144.4 (2366)	4.5	4.0	—	4.1	⑧	⑨	⑩	8.9
	4Runner ①	144.4 (2366)	4.5	4.0	2.5	2.5	⑧	⑨	⑩	8.9
	4Runner ②	144.4 (2366)	4.5	4.0	—	4.1	⑧	⑨	⑩	8.9
	4Runner ③	144.4 (2366)	4.5	4.0	—	4.1	⑧	⑨	⑩	8.9
	Van	136.5 (2237)	3.7	3.2	—	2.5	6.9	1.5 ⑪	15.9	7.5
	Land Cruiser	258.1 (4200)	8.2	7.4	3.3	5.7	15.9	2.2 ⑦	22.2 ⑤	17.5 ⑥
1988	Pick-Up ①	144.4 (2366)	4.5	4.0	2.5	2.5	⑧	⑨	⑩	8.9
	Pick-Up ②	144.4 (2366)	4.5	4.0	—	4.1	⑧	⑨	⑩	8.9
	Pick-Up ③	144.4 (2366)	4.5	4.0	—	4.1	⑧	⑨	⑩	8.9
	4Runner ①	144.4 (2366)	4.5	4.0	2.5	2.5	⑧	⑨	⑩	8.9
	4Runner ②	144.4 (2366)	4.5	4.0	—	4.1	⑧	⑨	⑩	8.9
	4Runner ③	144.4 (2366)	4.5	4.0	—	4.1	⑧	⑨	⑩	8.9
	Van	136.5 (2237)	3.7	3.2	—	2.5	6.9	1.5 ⑪	15.9	7.5
	Land Cruiser	258.1 (4200)	8.2	7.4	3.3	5.7	15.9	2.2 ⑦	22.2 ⑤	17.5 ⑥

CAPACITIES

Year	Model	Engine Displacement cu. in. (cc)	Engine Crankcase with Filter	Engine Crankcase without Filter	Transmission (pts.) 4-Spd	Transmission (pts.) 5-Spd	Transmission (pts.) Auto.	Drive Axle (pts.)	Fuel Tank (gal.)	Cooling System (qts.)
1989–90	Pick-Up ①	144.4 (2366)	4.5	4.0	2.5	2.5	⑧	⑨	⑩	8.9
	Pick-Up ②	144.4 (2366)	4.5	4.0	—	4.1	⑧	⑨	⑩	8.9
	Pick-Up	180.5 (2959)	4.8	4.4	—	3.2	—	2.5	17.2	⑫
	4Runner	144.4 (2366)	4.5	4.0	—	4.1	⑧	⑨	17.2	⑫
	4Runner	180.5 (2959)	4.8	4.4	—	3.2	⑧	2.5	17.2	⑫
	Van	136.5 (2237)	3.7	3.2	—	2.5	6.9	1.5 ⑪	15.9	7.5
	Land Cruiser	241.3 (3956)	8.2	7.4	3.3	5.7	15.9	2.2 ⑦	22.2 ⑤	17.5 ⑥

① 2 bbl
② EFI
③ Turbocharged
④ 17.2 gallon optional
⑤ 23.8 gallon optional
⑥ Wagon—18.3 qts.
⑦ Front Axle—1.7 pts. for Pick-Up and 4Runner
   3.2 pts. for Land Cruiser
⑧ A43D Automatic Transmission—6.9 qts.
   A340E Automatic Transmission—7.3 qts.
   A340H Automatic Transmission—10.9 qts.

⑨ 2WD
   7.5 in: 1.42 qts.
   8 in: 1.9 qts.
   4WD
   22R and 22R Engines: 2.3 qts.
   22R-TE Engine: 2.5 qts.
⑩ Short bed—13.7 gallons
   Long bed—17.2 gallons
⑪ 4WD—2.0 qts.
⑫ Manual Transmission—11.0 qts.
   Automatic Transmission—10.8 qts.

CAMSHAFT SPECIFICATIONS

All measurements given in inches.

Year	Engine Displacement cu. in. (cc)	Journal Diameter 1	2	3	4	5	Lobe Lift In.	Lobe Lift Ex.	Bearing Clearance	Camshaft End Play
1986	144.4 (2366)	1.2984–1.2992	1.2984–1.2992	1.2984–1.2992	1.2984–1.2992	—	1.6783–1.6891	1.6807–1.6842	0.0004–0.0020	0.0031–0.0071
	136.5 (2237)	1.8291–1.8297	1.8192–1.8199	1.8094–1.8100	1.7996–1.8002	1.7913–1.7929	1.5205–1.5244	1.5208–1.5248	0.0010–0.0032	0.0028–0.0087
	258.1 (4200)	1.8880–1.8888	1.8289–1.8297	1.7699–1.7707	1.7108–1.7116	—	1.5102–1.5142	1.5059–1.5098	0.0010–0.0030	0.0079–0.0103
1987	144.4 (2366)	1.2984–1.2992	1.2984–1.2992	1.2984–1.2992	1.2984–1.2992	—	1.6783–1.6891	1.6807–1.6842	0.0004–0.0020	0.0031–0.0071
	136.5 (2237)	1.8291–1.8297	1.8192–1.8199	1.8094–1.8100	1.7996–1.8002	1.7913–1.7929	1.5205–1.5244	1.5208–1.5248	0.0010–0.0032	0.0028–0.0087
	258.1 (4200)	1.8880–1.8888	1.8289–1.8297	1.7699–1.7707	1.7108–1.7116	—	1.5102–1.5142	1.5059–1.5098	0.0010–0.0030	0.0079–0.0103
1988	144.4 (2366)	1.2984–1.2992	1.2984–1.2992	1.2984–1.2992	1.2984–1.2992	—	1.6783–1.6891	1.6807–1.6842	0.0004–0.0020	0.0031–0.0071
	136.5 (2237)	1.8291–1.8297	1.8192–1.8199	1.8094–1.8100	1.7996–1.8002	1.7913–1.7929	1.5205–1.5244	1.5208–1.5248	0.0010–0.0032	0.0028–0.0087
	241.3 (3956)	1.8880–1.8888	1.8289–1.8297	1.7699–1.7707	1.7108–1.7116	—	1.5102–1.5142	1.5059–1.5098	0.0010–0.0030	0.0079–0.0103
1989–90	144.4 (2366)	1.2984–1.2992	1.2984–1.2992	1.2984–1.2992	1.2984–1.2992	—	1.6783–1.6891	1.6807–1.6842	0.0004–0.0020	0.0031–0.0071
	136.5 (2237)	1.8291–1.8297	1.8192–1.8199	1.8094–1.8100	1.7996–1.8002	1.7913–1.7929	1.5205–1.5244	1.5208–1.5248	0.0010–0.0032	0.0028–0.0087

CAMSHAFT SPECIFICATIONS

All measurements given in inches.

Year	Engine Displacement cu. in. (cc)	Journal Diameter 1	2	3	4	5	Lobe Lift In.	Ex.	Bearing Clearance	Camshaft End Play
1989-90	180.5 (2959)	1.3370–1.3376	1.3370–1.3376	1.3370–1.3376	1.3370–1.3376	—	1.6783–1.6891	1.6807–1.6842	0.0010–0.0030	0.0031–0.0075
	241.3 (3956)	1.8880–1.8888	1.8289–1.8297	1.7699–1.7707	1.7108–1.7116	—	1.5102–1.5142	1.5059–1.5098	0.0010–0.0030	0.0079–0.0103

CRANKSHAFT AND CONNECTING ROD SPECIFICATIONS

All measurements are given in inches.

Year	Engine Displacement cu. in. (cc)	Crankshaft Main Brg. Journal Dia.	Main Brg. Oil Clearance	Shaft End-play	Thrust on No.	Connecting Rod Journal Diameter	Oil Clearance	Side Clearance
1986	144.4 (2366)	2.3616–2.3622	0.0010–0.0022	0.0008–0.0087	3	2.0861–2.0866	0.0010–0.0022	0.0008–0.0087
	136.5 (2237)	2.2829–2.2835	0.0008–0.0020	0.0008–0.0087	3	1.8892–1.8898	0.0008–0.0020	0.0063–0.0123
	258.1 (4200)	①	0.0008–0.0017	0.0024–0.0063	3	2.1252–2.1260	0.0008–0.0024	0.0043–0.0091
1987	144.4 (2366)	2.3616–2.3622	0.0010–0.0022	0.0008–0.0087	3	2.0861–2.0866	0.0010–0.0022	0.0008–0.0087
	136.5 (2237)	2.2829–2.2835	0.0008–0.0020	0.0008–0.0087	3	1.8892–1.8898	0.0008–0.0020	0.0063–0.0123
	258.1 (4200)	①	0.0008–0.0017	0.0024–0.0063	3	2.1252–2.1260	0.0008–0.0024	0.0043–0.0091
1988	144.4 (2366)	2.3616–2.3622	0.0010–0.0022	0.0008–0.0087	3	2.0861–2.0866	0.0010–0.0022	0.0008–0.0087
	136.5 (2237)	2.2829–2.2835	0.0008–0.0020	0.0008–0.0087	3	1.8892–1.8898	0.0008–0.0020	0.0063–0.0123
	241.3 (3956)	①	0.0008–0.0017	0.0024–0.0063	3	2.1252–2.1260	0.0008–0.0024	0.0043–0.0091
1989-90	144.4 (2366)	2.3616–2.3622	0.0010–0.0022	0.0008–0.0087	3	2.0861–2.0866	0.0010–0.0022	0.0008–0.0087
	136.5 (2237)	2.2829–2.2835	0.0008–0.0020	0.0008–0.0087	3	1.8892–1.8898	0.0008–0.0020	0.0063–0.0123
	180.5 (2959)	2.5195–2.5197	0.0009–0.0017	0.0008–0.0098	3	2.1648–2.1654	0.0009–0.0021	0.0059–0.0130
	241.3 (3956)	②	0.0008–0.0017	0.0006–0.0080	3	2.0861–2.0866	0.0008–0.0020	0.0063–0.0118

① No. 1—2.6367–2.6376
No. 2—2.6957–2.6967
No. 3—2.7548–2.7557
No. 4—2.8139–2.8148
② No. 1—2.6367–2.6376
No. 2—2.6957–2.6967
No. 3—2.7548–2.7557
No. 4—2.8139–2.8148

VALVE SPECIFICATIONS

Year	Engine Displacement cu. in. (cc)	Seat Angle (deg.)	Face Angle (deg.)	Spring Test Pressure (lbs.)	Spring Installed Height (in.)	Stem-to-Guide Clearance (in.)		Stem Diameter (in.)	
						Intake	Exhaust	Intake	Exhaust
1986	144.4 (2366)	45 ①	44.5	66	1.909 ②	0.0010–0.0024	0.0012–0.0026	0.3138–0.3144	0.3136–0.3142
	136.5 (2237)	45 ①	44.5	64–77	1.850 ②	0.0010–0.0024	0.0012–0.0026	0.3138–0.3144	0.3136–0.3142
	258.1 (4200)	45	44.5	71.6	1.693	0.0012–0.0024	0.0016–0.0028	0.3140	0.3137
1987	144.4 (2366)	45 ①	44.5	66	1.909 ②	0.0010–0.0024	0.0012–0.0026	0.3138–0.3144	0.3136–0.3142
	136.5 (2237)	45 ①	44.5	64–77	1.850 ②	0.0010–0.0024	0.0012–0.0026	0.3138–0.3144	0.3136–0.3142
	258.1 (4200)	45	44.5	71.6	1.693	0.0012–0.0024	0.0016–0.0028	0.3140	0.3137
1988	144.4 (2366)	45 ①	44.5	66	1.909 ②	0.0010–0.0024	0.0012–0.0026	0.3138–0.3144	0.3136–0.3142
	136.5 (2237)	45 ①	44.5	64–77	1.850 ②	0.0010–0.0024	0.0012–0.0026	0.3138–0.3144	0.3136–0.3142
	241.3 (3956)	45	44.5	71.6	1.693	0.0012–0.0024	0.0016–0.0028	0.3140	0.3137
1989–90	144.4 (2366)	45 ①	44.5	66	1.909 ②	0.0010–0.0024	0.0012–0.0026	0.3138–0.3144	0.3136–0.3142
	136.5 (2237)	45 ①	44.5	64–77	1.850 ②	0.0010–0.0024	0.0012–0.0026	0.3138–0.3144	0.3136–0.3142
	180.5 (2959)	45 ①	44.5	57	1.594	0.0010–0.0024	0.0012–0.0026	0.3138–0.3144	0.3136–0.3142
	241.3 (3956)	45	44.5	71.6	1.693	0.0012–0.0024	0.0016–0.0028	0.3140	0.3137

① Blend the seat with 30° and 60° cutters to center the 45° portion on the valve face.
② Free length

PISTON AND RING SPECIFICATIONS

All measurements are given in inches.

Year	Engine Displacement cu. in. (cc)	Piston Clearance	Ring Gap			Ring Side Clearance		
			Top Compression	Bottom Compression	Oil Control	Top Compression	Bottom Compression	Oil Control
1986	144.4 (2366)	0.0012–0.0020 ①	0.0138–0.0224	0.0098–0.0185	0.0079–0.0323	0.0080 ②	0.0080 ②	0.0080 ②
	136.5 (2237)	0.0026–0.0033	0.0091–0.0189	0.0063–0.0173	0.0051–0.0185	0.0012–0.0028	0.0012–0.0028	0.0012–0.0028
	258.1 (4200)	0.0012–0.0020	0.0079–0.0157	0.0079–0.0157	0.0118–0.0354	0.0012–0.0028	0.0008–0.0024	0.0016–0.0075
1987	144.4 (2366)	0.0012–0.0020 ①	0.0138–0.0224	0.0098–0.0185	0.0079–0.0323	0.0080 ②	0.0080 ②	0.0080 ②
	136.5 (2237)	0.0026–0.0033	0.0091–0.0189	0.0063–0.0173	0.0051–0.0185	0.0012–0.0028	0.0012–0.0028	0.0012–0.0028
	258.1 (4200)	0.0012–0.0020	0.0079–0.0157	0.0079–0.0157	0.0118–0.0354	0.0012–0.0028	0.0008–0.0024	0.0016–0.0075

PISTON AND RING SPECIFICATIONS

All measurements are given in inches.

Year	Engine Displacement cu. in. (cc)	Piston Clearance	Ring Gap			Ring Side Clearance		
			Top Compression	Bottom Compression	Oil Control	Top Compression	Bottom Compression	Oil Control
1988	144.4 (2366)	0.0012–0.0020 ①	0.0138–0.0224	0.0098–0.0185	0.0079–0.0323	0.0080 ②	0.0080 ②	0.0080 ②
	136.5 (2237)	0.0026–0.0033	0.0091–0.0189	0.0063–0.0173	0.0051–0.0185	0.0012–0.0028	0.0012–0.0028	0.0012–0.0028
	241.3 (3956)	0.0012–0.0020	0.0079–0.0157	0.0079–0.0157	0.0118–0.0354	0.0012–0.0028	0.0008–0.0024	0.0016–0.0075
1989–90	144.4 (2366)	0.0012–0.0020 ①	0.0138–0.0224	0.0098–0.0185	0.0079–0.0323	0.0080 ②	0.0080 ②	0.0080 ②
	136.5 (2237)	0.0026–0.0033	0.0091–0.0189	0.0063–0.0173	0.0051–0.0185	0.0012–0.0028	0.0012–0.0028	0.0012–0.0028
	180.5 (2959)	0.0031–0.0039	0.0090–0.0130	0.0150–0.0190	0.0060–0.0160	0.0012–0.0028	0.0012–0.0028	snug
	241.3 (3956)	0.0012–0.0020	0.0079–0.0157	0.0079–0.0157	0.0118–0.0354	0.0012–0.0028	0.0008–0.0024	0.0016–0.0075

① 22R-TE Engine—0.0022–0.0030
② Maximum

TORQUE SPECIFICATIONS

All readings in ft. lbs.

Year	Engine Displacement cu. in. (cc)	Cylinder Head Bolts	Main Bearing Bolts	Rod Bearing Bolts	Crankshaft Pulley Bolts	Flywheel Bolts	Manifold	
							Intake	Exhaust
1986	144.4 (2366)	53–63	69–83	40–47	102–130	73–86	13–19	29–36
	136.5 (2237)	④	58	36	116	61 ③	36	36
	258.1 (4200)	83–98	90–108 ①	35–55	116–145	59–62	28–37 ②	28–37 ②
1987	144.4 (2366)	53–63	69–83	40–47	102–130	73–86	13–19	29–36
	136.5 (2237)	④	58	36	116	61 ③	36	36
	258.1 (4200)	83–98	90–108 ①	35–55	116–145	59–62	28–37 ②	28–37 ②
1988	144.4 (2366)	53–63	69–83	40–47	102–130	73–86	13–19	29–36
	136.5 (2237)	④	58	36	116	61 ③	36	36
	241.3 (3956)	87–93	⑥	40–46	247–259	60–68	⑦	⑦
1989–90	144.4 (2366)	53–63	69–83	40–47	102–130	73–86	13–19	29–36
	136.5 (2237)	④	58	36	116	61 ③	36	36
	180.5 (2959)	⑤	43–47	16–20	176–186	63–67	11–15	25–33
	241.3 (3956)	87–93	⑥	40–46	247–259	60–68	⑦	⑦

① Rear bearing—76–94 ft. lbs.
② California vehicles—37–51 ft. lbs.
③ drive plate—54 ft. lbs.
④ 12 mm bolt—14 ft. lbs.
   14 mm bolt—65 ft. lbs.
⑤ Step 1—27
   Step 2—33
   Step 3—90 degree turn
   Step 4—90 degree turn

⑥ 19 mm bolt—99 ft. lbs.
   17 mm bolt—85 ft. lbs.
⑦ 14 mm bolt—37 ft. lbs.
   17 mm bolt—51 ft. lbs.
   Nut—41 ft. lbs.

BRAKE SPECIFICATIONS
All measurements in inches unless noted.

Year	Model	Lug Nut Torque (ft. lbs.)	Master Cylinder Bore	Brake Disc Minimum Thickness	Brake Disc Maximum Runout	Standard Brake Drum Diameter	Minimum Lining Thickness Front	Minimum Lining Thickness Rear
1986	Pick-Up	65–86	NA	①	0.0059	②	0.039	0.039
	4Runner	65–86	NA	①	0.0059	②	0.039	0.039
	Van	65–86	NA	0.748	0.0059	10.00	0.039	0.039
	Land Cruiser	65–86	NA	0.748	0.0059	11.61	0.040	0.059
1987	Pick-Up	65–86	NA	①	0.0059	②	0.039	0.039
	4Runner	65–86	NA	①	0.0059	②	0.039	0.039
	Van	65–86	NA	0.748	0.0059	10.00	0.039	0.039
	Land Cruiser	65–86	NA	0.748	0.0059	11.61	0.040	0.059
1988	Pick-Up	65–86	NA	①	0.0059	②	0.039	0.039
	4Runner	65–86	NA	①	0.0059	②	0.039	0.039
	Van	65–86	NA	0.748	0.0059	10.00	0.039	0.039
	Land Cruiser	65–86	NA	0.748	0.0059	11.61	0.040	0.059
1989–90	Pick-Up	65–86	NA	①	0.0059	②	0.039	0.039
	4Runner	65–86	NA	①	0.0059	②	0.039	0.039
	Van	65–86	NA	0.748	0.0059	10.00	0.039	0.039
	Land Cruiser	65–86	NA	0.748	0.0059	11.61	0.040	0.059

① 2WD with PD60 Brake Disc—0.945
2WD with FS17 Brake Disc—0.827
4WD—0.748
② 2WD—10.00
4WD—11.64

WHEEL ALIGNMENT

Year	Model	Caster Range (deg.)	Caster Preferred Setting (deg.)	Camber Range (deg.)	Camber Preferred Setting (deg.)	Toe-in (in.)	Steering Axis Inclination (deg.)
1986	Pick-Up 2WD Short Bed	$1/12$N–$1^5/12$P	$2/3$P	$1/4$N–$1^1/4$P	$1/2$P	0–0.08P	10
	Pick-Up 2WD Long Bed	$5/12$P–$1^{11}/12$P	$1^1/6$P	$1/4$N–$1^1/4$P	$1/2$P	0.08P–0.16P	10
	Pick-Up, 4WD and 4Runner	$3/4$P–$2^1/4$P	$1^1/2$P	$1/12$N–$1^5/12$P	$2/3$P	0–0.08P	12
	Van	$2^1/4$P–$3^3/4$P	3P	$3/4$N–$3/4$P	0	0.04N–0.04P	$10^1/2$
	Land Cruiser	$1/2$P–$1^1/2$P	1P	$1/2$–$1^1/2$P	1P	0.04N–0.04P	$9^1/2$
1987	Pick-Up 2WD Short Bed	$1/12$N–$1^5/12$P	$2/3$P	$1/4$N–$1^1/4$P	$1/2$P	0–0.08P	10
	Pick-Up 2WD Long Bed	$5/12$P–$1^{11}/12$P	$1^1/6$P	$1/4$N–$1^1/4$P	$1/2$P	0.08P–0.16P	10
	Pick-Up, 4WD and 4Runner	$3/4$P–$2^1/4$P	$1^1/2$P	$1/12$N–$1^5/12$P	$2/3$P	0–0.08P	12
	Van 2WD	2P–3P	$2^1/2$P	$5/6$N–$5/6$P	$1/12$P	0.04N–0.04P	$10^1/2$
	Van 4WD	$2^1/3$P–$3^1/3$P	$2^5/6$P	$1/3$N–$2/3$P	$1/6$P	0.04N–0.04P	$12^1/2$
	Land Cruiser	$1/2$P–$1^1/2$P	1P	$1/2$–$1^1/2$P	1P	0.04N–0.04P	$9^1/2$
1988	Pick-Up 2WD Short Bed	$1/12$N–$1^5/12$P	$2/3$P	$1/4$N–$1^1/4$P	$1/2$P	0–0.08P	10
	Pick-Up 2WD Long Bed	$5/12$P–$1^{11}/12$P	$1^1/6$P	$1/4$N–$1^1/4$P	$1/2$P	0.08P–0.16P	10
	Pick-Up, 4WD and 4Runner	$3/4$P–$2^1/4$P	$1^1/2$P	$1/12$N–$1^5/12$P	$2/3$P	0–0.08P	12
	Van 2WD	2P–3P	$2^1/2$P	$5/6$N–$5/6$P	$1/12$P	0.04N–0.04P	$10^1/2$

WHEEL ALIGNMENT

Year	Model	Caster Range (deg.)	Caster Preferred Setting (deg.)	Camber Range (deg.)	Camber Preferred Setting (deg.)	Toe-in (in.)	Steering Axis Inclination (deg.)
1988	Van 4WD	2⅓P–3⅓P	2⅚P	⅓N–⅔P	⅙P	0.04N–0.04P	12½
	Land Cruiser	½P–1½P	1P	½–1½P	1P	0.04N–0.04P	9½
1989-90	Pick-Up 2WD Short Bed	1⁄12N–1⁵⁄12P	⅔P	¼N–1¼P	½P	0–0.08P	10
	Pick-Up 2WD Long Bed	⁵⁄12P–1¹¹⁄12P	1⅙P	¼N–1¼P	½P	0.08P–0.16P	10
	Pick-Up, 4WD and 4Runner	¾P–2¼P	1½P	1⁄12N–1⁵⁄12P	⅔P	0–0.08P	12
	Van 2WD	2P–3P	2½P	⅚N–⅚P	1⁄12P	0.04N–0.04P	10½
	Van 4WD	2⅓P–3⅓P	2⅚P	⅓N–⅔P	⅙P	0.04N–0.04P	12½
	Land Cruiser	½P–1½P	1P	½–1½P	1P	0.04N–0.04P	9½

ENGINE ELECTRICAL

NOTE: Disconnecting the battery cable on some vehicles may interfere with the functions of the on board computer systems and may require the computer to undergo a relearning process, once the negative battery cable is disconnected.

Distributor

Removal

2F, 3F–E, 22R, 22R–E, 22R–TE AND 3VZ–E ENGINES

1. Disconnect the negative battery cable. Label and disconnect the high tension cables from the spark plugs. Remove the high tension cable from the coil.

2. Remove the primary wire or the electrical connector and the vacuum line, if equipped from the distributor. Remove the distributor cap spring clips or screws, then the cap.

3. Using a piece of chalk, matchmark the rotor-to-distributor housing and the distributor-to-engine block. This will aid in correct positioning of the distributor during installation.

4. Remove the distributor hold-down clamp bolt and the distributor from the engine.

NOTE: It is easier to install the distributor if the engine timing is not disturbed while it is removed.

4Y–EC AND 4Y–E ENGINES

1. Disconnect the negative battery terminal from the battery.
2. Remove the front-right seat from the vehicle.
3. Remove the engine service hole cover.
4. Disconnect the distributor vacuum advance hoses.
5. Disconnect the high tension cables from the spark plugs.
6. Using a piece of chalk, matchmark the rotor-to-distributor housing and the distributor housing-to-engine.
7. Remove the distributor-to-engine bolt and the distributor from the engine.

Installation—Timing Not Disturbed

ALL ENGINES

1. Insert the distributor into the engine block by aligning the matchmarks made during removal.
2. Engage the distributor drive with the oil pump drive shaft.
3. Install the distributor hold-down clamp, the cap, the high

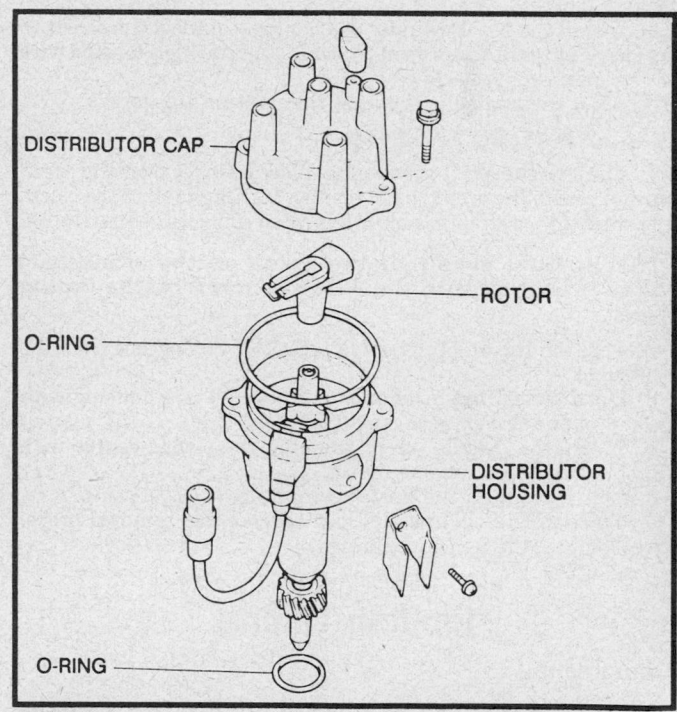

DISTRIBUTOR CAP

ROTOR

O-RING

DISTRIBUTOR HOUSING

O-RING

Distributor assembly—22R, 22R–E and 22R–TE engines

tension wire, the primary wire or the electrical connector and the vacuum line(s).

4. Install the spark plugs cables.

5. Connect the negative battery cable.

Installation—Timing Disturbed

2F, 3F–E, 22R, 22R–E, 22R–TE AND 3VZ–E ENGINES

If the engine has been cranked, dismantled or the timing otherwise lost, proceed as follows:

1. Determine the Top Dead Center (TDC) of the No. 1 cylinder's compression stroke by removing the spark plug from the

No. 1 cylinder and placing a finger or a compression gauge over the spark plug hole.

NOTE: Using a wrench, turn the crankshaft until the compression pressure starts to build up. Continue cranking the engine until the timing marks indicate TDC (0 degrees).

2. Turn the crankshaft to align the timing marks on the 22R–E and 22R–TE engines to 5 degrees BTDC or on the 22R and 3VZ–E engines to 0 degree TDC.

3. Temporarily install the rotor on the distributor shaft so that the rotor is pointing toward the No. 1 terminal of the distributor cap.

4. Using a small prybar, align the slot on the distributor drive (oil pump driveshaft) with the key on the bottom of the distributor shaft.

5. Install the distributor in the block by rotating it slightly (no more than a gear tooth in either direction) until the driven gear meshes with the drive.

NOTE: Oil the distributor drive gear and the oil pump driveshaft end before installation.

6. Temporarily tighten the lock bolt.

7. Remove the rotor, then install the dust cover, the rotor and the distributor cap.

8. Install the primary wire or the electrical connector and the vacuum line(s).

9. Install the No. 1 cylinder spark plug. Connect the cables to the spark plugs in the proper order. Install the high tension wire on the coil.

10. Start the engine and adjust the ignition timing.

4Y–E AND 4Y–EC ENGINES

1. Remove the No. 1 spark plug, place a finger over the opening and rotate the crankshaft, using a turning tool, in the clockwise direction, until pressure is felt, then replace the spark plug.

NOTE: Make sure that the notch on the crankshaft pulley is aligned with the 0 degree mark on the timing plate.

2. Position the oil pump drive rotor slot 30 degrees from the centerline.

3. On the distributor, align the groove on the housing with the pin of the driven gear (the drill mark side).

4. Insert the distributor by aligning the flange center with the bolt hole in the engine block.

5. Lightly tighten the hold-down bolt.

6. To complete the installation, reverse the removal procedures. Adjust the ignition timing.

Ignition Timing

Adjustment

NOTE: The timing mark locations differ between the engines used in the Pick-Up and the 4Runner (22R, 22R–E, 22R–TE and 3VZ–E), the Van (4Y–E, 4Y–EC) and the Land Cruiser (2F and 3F–E). On the 22R, 22R–E, 22R–TE, 4Y–EC, 4Y–E and 3VZ–E engines, the timing marks are located on the crankshaft pulley (painted notch) and the timing cover (plate). On the 2F and 3F–E the timing marks are located on the flywheel (ball) and the bellhousing (pointer).

1. Set the parking brake and block the wheels.

2. Clean off the timing marks and mark them with chalk or paint. The crankshaft may have to rotated to find the marks.

3. Warm the engine to operating temperatures. Connect a tachometer to the engine, then, check and/or adjust the engine idle speed.

Timing mark location – 4Y–E and 4Y–EC engines

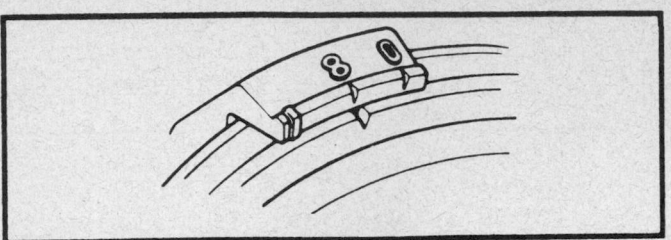

Timing mark location – 22R, 22R–E and 22R–TE engines

Timing mark location – 3VZ–E engine

NOTE: On the 22R, 22R–E, 22R–TE and 3VZ–E engines, connect the positive (+) tachometer terminal either to the negative (–) ignition coil terminal or to the yellow service connector. On the 4Y–EC and 4Y–E engines, connect the positive (+) tachometer to the service connector on the ignition coil/igniter assembly. DO NOT connect it to the distributor side. Improper connections will damage the transistorized igniter. On the 4Y–E, 4Y–EC and 3VZ–E engines, use a service wire to short the engine check connector.

4. Turn off the engine and connect a timing light according to the manufacturer's directions.

5. On the 22R–E and 22R–TE engine, disconnect and short the T and the E_1 connector of the engine check harness (near the front of the vehicle). On all other engines, disconnect and plug the vacuum hose(s) from the distributor vacuum unit.

NOTE: If equipped with a High Altitude Compensation (HAC) system there are 2 vacuum hoses which connect to the distributor. Both must be disconnected and plugged. These systems require an extra step in the timing procedure.

6. Be sure that the timing light wires are clear of the fan and pulleys, then start the engine.

7. Allow the engine to run at the specified idle speed with the shift selector in neutral for manual transmission equipped vehicles or **D** for automatic transmission equipped vehicles.

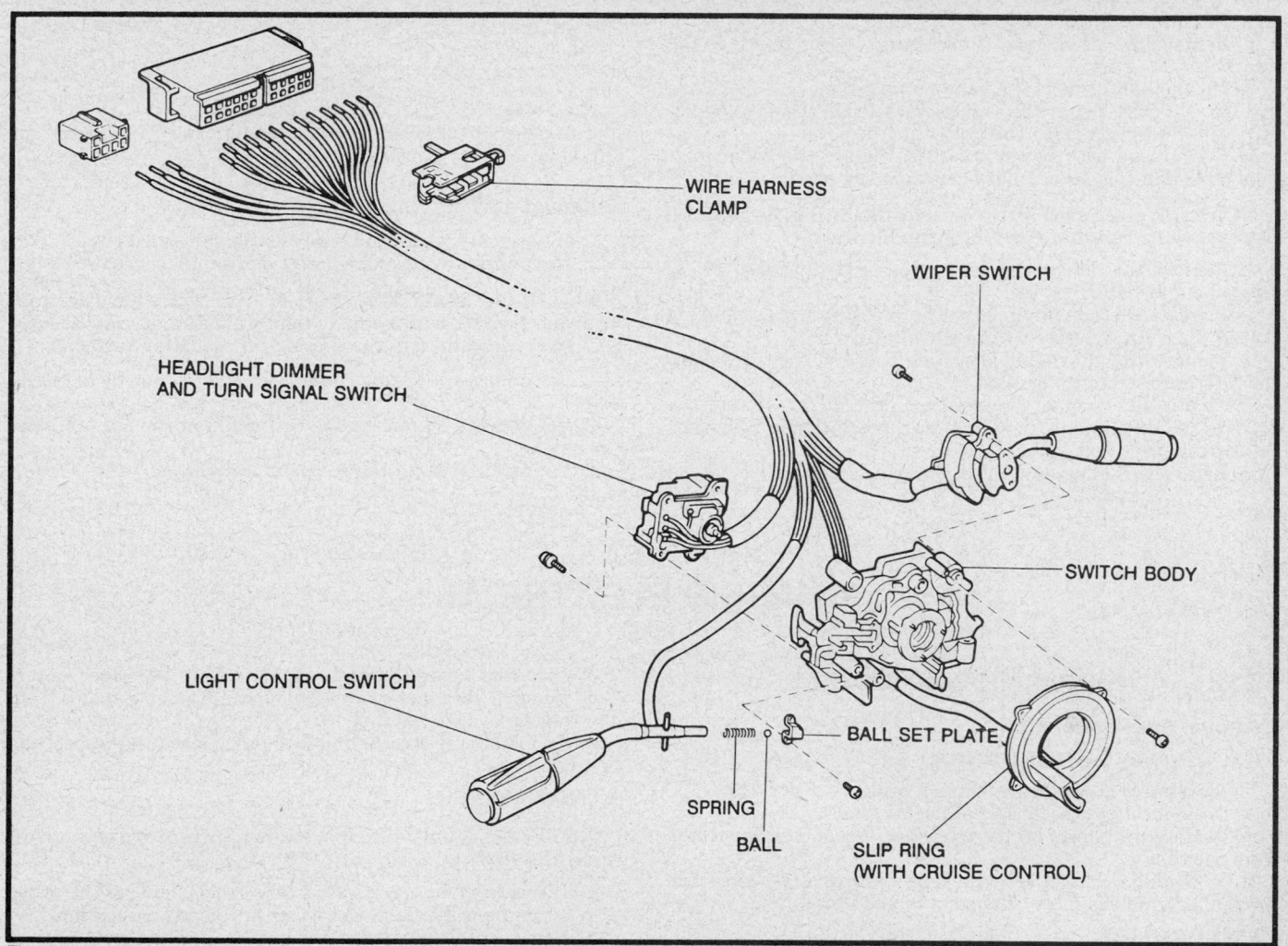

WIRE HARNESS CLAMP

WIPER SWITCH

HEADLIGHT DIMMER AND TURN SIGNAL SWITCH

SWITCH BODY

LIGHT CONTROL SWITCH

BALL SET PLATE

SPRING

BALL

SLIP RING (WITH CRUISE CONTROL)

Typical combination switch assembly

8. Point the timing light at the marks. With the engine at the specified idle, the marks should align.

9. If the timing is incorrect, loosen the bolt at the base of the distributor just enough so that the distributor can be turned. Hold the distributor by its base and turn it slightly to advance or retard the timing as required. Once the marks are seen to align properly, tighten the bolt.

10. After tightening the distributor bolt or adjusting the octane selector, recheck the timing. Turn off the engine, then, disconnect the timing light and connect the vacuum line(s) at the distributor or the electrical T and E$_1$ connector, except on engines with HAC.

11. On engines with HAC after setting the initial timing, reconnect the vacuum hoses at the distributor. Recheck the timing.

12. If the advance is still low, pinch the hose between the HAC valve and the 3 way connector; it should now be to specifications. If not, the HAC valve should be checked for proper operation.

Alternator

For further information, please refer to "Electrical" in the Unit Repair section.

Belt Tension Adjustment

Inspection and adjustment to the alternator drive belt should be performed every 30,000 miles or if the alternator has been removed.

1. Inspect the drive belt to see that it is not cracked or worn. Be sure that its surfaces are free of grease or oil.

2. If not using a belt tension gauge, push down on the belt halfway between the fan and the alternator pulleys, (or crankshaft pulley) with thumb pressure; belt deflection should be 3/8-1/2 in.

3. If using the an appropriate belt tension gauge, position it in the middle of the drive belt and check the belt tension; a new belt should be 170-180 lbs. (Van) or 100-150 lbs. (Pick-Up and 4Runner), a used belt should be 95-135 lbs. (Van) or 60-100 lbs. (Pick-Up and 4Runner).

4. If the belt tension requires adjustment, loosen the adjusting link bolt and move the alternator until the proper belt tension is obtained.

5. Tighten the adjusting link bolt.

Removal and Installation

NOTE: On some engines the alternator is mounted very low. On these engines it may be necessary to remove the gravel shield and work from underneath the vehicle in order to gain access to the alternator.

1. Disconnect the negative battery cable.
2. Remove the air cleaner, if necessary, to gain access to the alternator.
3. On the 22R remove the vane pump pulley.
4. On the 22R–E and 22R–TE engines, drain the engine coolant. If necessary, remove the under engine cover.
5. If equipped with power steering, remove the water inlet pipe bolts and the water inlet hose from the engine.

NOTE: If equipped with air conditioning, it may be necessary to remove the No. 2 fan shroud.

6. Remove the nut or the wiring connector and the wire(s) from the alternator.
7. Remove the adjusting lock, the pivot and the adjusting bolt(s), then the drive belt from the alternator.
8. Remove the alternator attaching bolt and then withdraw the alternator from its bracket.
9. To install, reverse the removal procedures. Rotate the drive belt 8 revolutions (new belt) or 5 revolutions (used belt). Adjust the drive belt tension.
10. Refill the cooling system, if it was drained.

11. Connect the negative battery cable.

Starter

For further information, please refer to "Electrical" in the Unit Repair section.

Removal and Installation

1. If necessary, raise and support the vehicle safely.
2. Disconnect the negative battery terminal from the battery.

NOTE: On some 22R, 22R–E and 22R–TE engines, equipped with an automatic transmission, it may be necessary to remove the transmission oil filler tube.

3. Disconnect the wiring connectors and the wiring from the starter.
4. Remove the starter-to-engine bolts and the starter from the engine.
5. To install, reverse the removal procedures.

CHASSIS ELECTRICAL

Heater Blower Motor

Removal and Installation
PICK-UP, VAN AND 4RUNNER

1. Disconnect the negative battery cable.
2. Disconnect the electrical connector from motor.
3. Remove the blower motor-to-case screws and lift the motor from the case.
4. To install, reverse the removal procedures. Make sure that the seal around the motor flange is in good condition.

LAND CRUISER

1. Disconnect the negative battery cable. Disconnect the electrical connector from the blower motor.
2. Disconnect the flexible tube from the side of the blower motor.
3. Remove the blower motor fasteners and lower the blower motor out of the air inlet duct.
4. To install, reverse the removal procedures. During installation, be sure to position the motor so that the flexible tube can be attached to the motor.

Windshield Wiper Motor

Removal and Installation
PICK-UP, VAN AND 4RUNNER
Front

1. Disconnect the negative battery cable. Disconnect the wiring from the wiper motor. Remove the motor from the fire wall.
2. Remove the nut, then, pry the wiper link from the crank arm.
3. Remove the motor.
4. To install, reverse the removal procedures and inspect he operation.

Rear

1. Disconnect the negative battery cable. At the rear of the vehicle, remove the wiper motor cover panel.
2. Remove the wiper arm from the wiper motor.

3. Disconnect the electrical connector from the wiper motor.
4. Remove the wiper motor-to-door bolts and the motor from the vehicle.
5. To install, reverse the removal procedures and inspect the operation.

LAND CRUISER

NOTE: On these vehicles, the wiper motor is removed with the linkage assembly.

1. Disconnect the negative battery cable. Remove the wiper arm retaining nuts, then, the wiper arm/blade assemblies.
2. Remove both wiper arm pivot covers and the pivot-to-cowl attaching screws.
3. Remove the service hole covers from the cowl area of the engine compartment.
4. Disconnect the wiring from the wiper motor.
5. From the engine compartment, remove the wiper motor plate-to-cowl screws. Withdraw the wiper motor and the linkage from the cowl panel as an assembly.
6. Pry the linkage from of the wiper motor.
7. To install, reverse the removal procedures.

Windshield Wiper Linkage

Removal and Installation
PICK-UP, VAN AND 4RUNNER

1. Disconnect the negative battery cable. Remove the wiper motor.
2. Remove the wiper arms by removing their retaining nuts and working them off their shafts.
3. Remove the wiper shafts nuts/spacers and push the shafts down into the body cavity. Pull the linkage out of the cavity through the wiper motor hole.
4. To install, reverse the removal procedures.

LAND CRUISER

1. Disconnect the negative battery cable. Remove the wiper arm assemblies.
2. Remove the end plate from the pivot housing.
3. Remove the wiper motor with the linkage cable.

4. Separate the wiper motor and the transmission.
5. Remove the linkage cable.
6. To install, reverse the removal procedures.

Winshield Wiper Switch

Removal and Installation

FRONT

1. Disconnect negative battery terminal from the battery.
2. Remove the upper and the lower steering column shrouds.
3. Disconnect the combination switch electrical connector.
4. Remove the terminal from the horn contact.
5. To remove the windshield/wiper switch wires from the electrical connector, place a small prybar into the end of the connector, pry up on the retaining tab and pull the wire(s) from the connector.
6. Remove the windshield/wiper switch-to-combination switch screw and the switch.
7. Installation is the reverse of the removal procedure. To install, place the wire(s) into the electrical connector's slots, place a suitable tool behind the wire terminal and push the wire into the connector until the retaining tab locks it into place.

REAR

If equipped with a rear wiper switch, it will be located in the center of the dash.
1. Disconnect the negative battery cable. Using a small pry bar, pry the rear wiper switch from the center of the dash.
2. Disconnect the electrical connector from the rear of the switch.
3. To install, reverse the removal procedures.

Instrument Cluster

Removal and Installation

PICK-UP, VAN AND 4RUNNER

1. Disconnect the negative battery terminal from the battery.
2. Remove the upper and lower steering column covers.
3. Remove the instrument trim panel screws and the panel.
4. Disconnect the speedometer cable from the speedometer.
5. Remove the instrument panel screws and pull the panel forward. Disconnect the electrical connectors from the back of the panel and remove the panel.
6. To install, reverse the removal procedures.

LAND CRUISER

1. Disconnect the negative battery terminal from the battery.
2. Disconnect the speedometer cable. Remove the instrument panel screws.
3. Loosen the steering column clamp by removing the attaching bolts.
4. Pull out the instrument panel and the speedometer, disconnect the electrical connectors and remove the panel.
5. To install, reverse the removal procedures.

Speedometer

Removal and Installation

1. Disconnect the negative battery cable. Remove the instrument cluster and disconnect the cable from the speedometer.
2. Disconnect the other end of the speedometer cable from the transmission extension housing and pull the cable from its jacket at the transmission end.

NOTE: If the cable is being replace because it is broken, be sure to remove both pieces of the broken cable.

3. Using graphite, lubricate the new speedometer cable and insert it into the cable jacket at the lower end.

4. Connect the speedometer cable to the transmission, then, to the instrument cluster.
5. To complete the installation, reverse the removal procedures.

Headlight Switch

Removal and Installation

1. Disconnect the negative battery terminal from the battery.
2. Remove the upper and lower steering column covers.
3. Disconnect the electrical connector from the combination switch.
4. Remove the headlight switch-to-combination switch screws and the headlight switch from the combination switch.
5. To install, reverse the removal procedures.

Turn Signal Switch

Removal and Installation

1. Disconnect negative battery terminal from the battery.
2. Remove the upper and the lower steering column shrouds.
3. Disconnect the combination switch electrical connector.
4. At the left-rear of the combination switch, remove the mounting screws and the turn signal switch.
5. If necessary to the remove the turn signal switch wires from the electrical connector, place a small prybar into the end of the connector, pry up on the retaining tab and pull the wire(s) from the connector.
6. To install, place the wire(s) into the electrical connector's slots, place a prybar behind the wire terminal and push the wire into the connector until the retaining tab locks it into place.
7. To complete the installation, reverse the removal procedures.

Combination Switch

Removal and Installation

The combination switch is composed of the turn signal, the headlight control, the dimmer, the hazard, the wiper and the washer switches.
1. Disconnect the negative battery cable. Remove the steering wheel.
2. Remove the upper and lower steering column shroud screws and the shrouds.
3. Remove the combination switch screws and the switch from the column.
4. Disconnect the electrical connector from the combination switch. To remove the wires from the electrical connector, perform the following procedures.
   a. Using a small prybar, insert it into the open end between the locking lugs and the terminal.
   b. Pry the locking lugs upward and pull the terminal out from the rear.
   c. To install the terminals, simply push them into the connector until they lock securely in place.
5. To complete the installation, reverse the removal procedures.

Ignition Lock/Switch

Removal and Installation

The ignition lock/switch is located behind the combination switch on the steering column.
1. Disconnect the negative battery terminal from the battery.
2. Remove the upper and lower steering column covers.
3. Disconnect the ignition switch from the electrical connector.

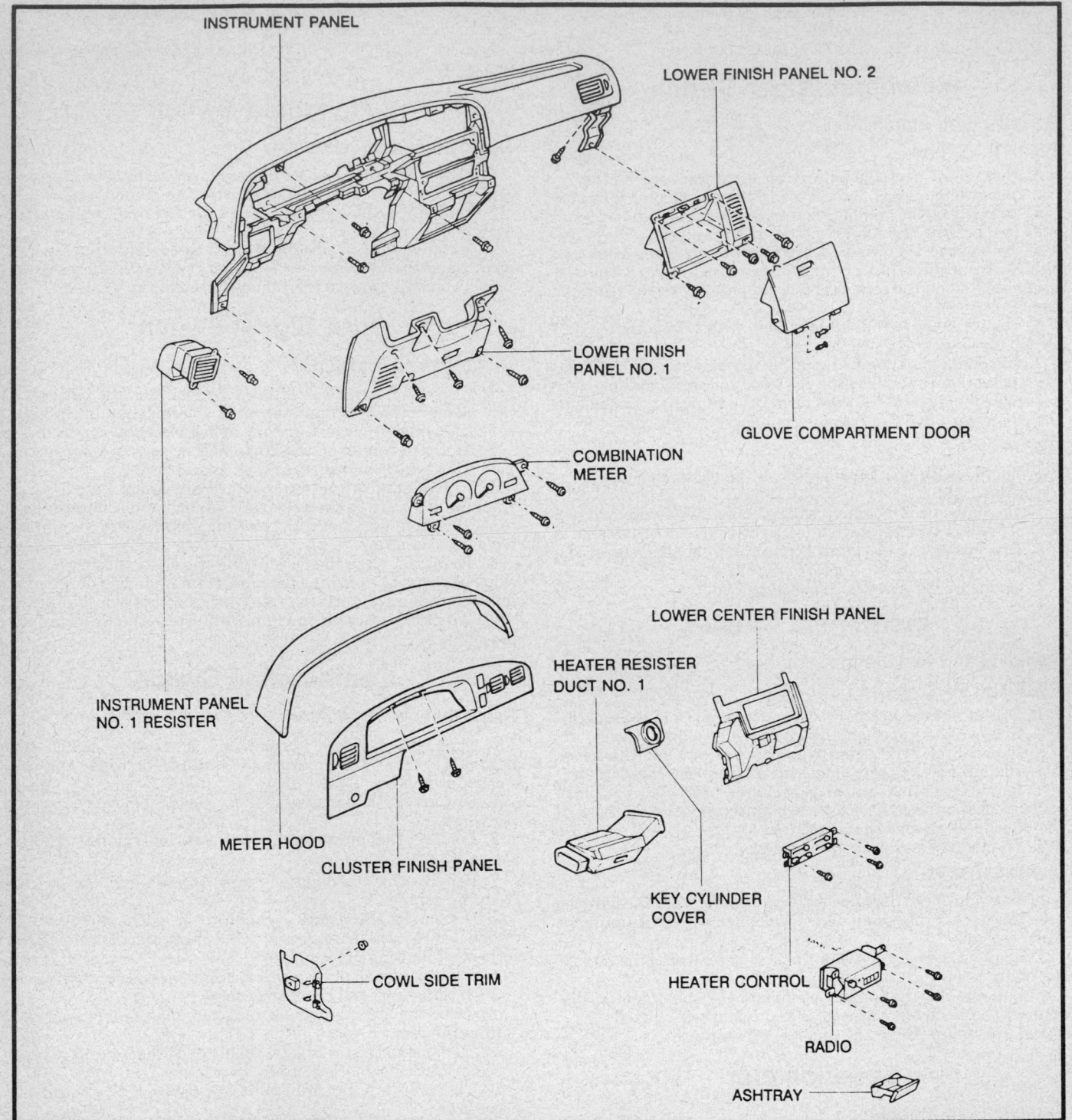

Typical instrument cluster and panel assembly—Pick- Up and 4Runner

4. Using the key in the ignition switch, turn it to the **ACC** position.

5. Using a thin rod, place it into the hole of the cylinder lock housing. Pushing down on the thin rod, pull out the cylinder lock.

6. Remove the unlock warning switch-to-combination switch screws and the unlock warning switch.

7. Remove the ignition switch-to-combination switch screw and the ignition switch.

8. To install, push the ignition switch into the housing and install the screw. Using the key, install cylinder lock into the housing until the retaining tab locks it in place.

9. To complete the installation, reverse the removal procedures.

Stoplight Switch

Removal and Installaion

1. Disconnect the negative battery cable.
2. Remove the electrical connector from the switch.
3. Remove the mounting nut and remove the switch from the bracket.
4. Installation is the reverse of the removal procedure.

Fuses and Circuit Breakers

Location

There are 3 fuse boxes in the Pick-Up, 4Runner and Land Cruiser. One is located in the engine compartment, 1 at the drivers side kick panel and 1 behind the glove box. The Van has a combination fuse box and relay panel, located behind a panel on the passengers side of the instrument panel.

Each fuse box has the fuse numbers and circuits protected on the lid of the box.

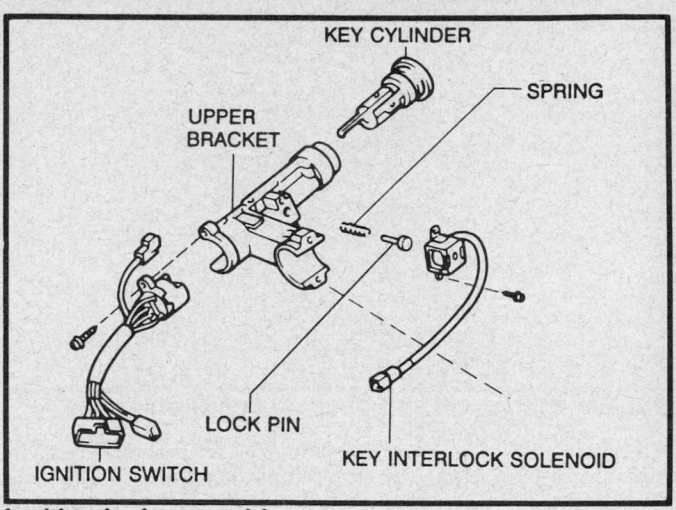

Ignition lock assembly

ENGINE COOLING

Radiator

Removal and Installation

1. Disconnect the negative battery cable. Drain the cooling system.
2. Unfasten the hose clamps and disconnect the hoses from the radiator. On Land Cruiser vehicles equipped with air conditioning, properly discharge the system.
3. Disconnect the transmission cooling lines on vehicles equipped with an automatic transmission.
4. On the 22R–TE engine, disconnect the No. 1 turbocharger cooling line.
5. Remove the fan shrouds, if so equipped.
6. Remove the grille assembly and remove the hood lock from the radiator support. On Land Cruiser vehicles with air conditioning, remove the condenser to radiator bolts.
7. Remove the coolant recovery tank. Unbolt the radiator and remove it from the vehicle.

To install:

8. Install the radiator into position.
9. On Land Cruiser vehicles with air conditioning, install the condensor-to-radiator bolts.
10. Install the hood lock assembly and install the grille.
11. Connect the radiator hoses and the transmission cooler lines.
12. On the 22R–TE engine, connect the turbocharger water line.
13. Install the coolant recovery bottle. Refill the cooling system to the correct level.
14. Run the engine and check for leaks.

Heater Core

Removal and Installation

NOTE: On vehicles equipped with air conditioning, the heater and the air conditioner are completely separate units. Be certain when working under the dashboard that only the heater hoses are disconnected.

------- **CAUTION** -------

The air conditioning hoses are under pressure; if disconnected, the escaping refrigerant will freeze any surface with which it comes in contact, including skin and eyes.

PICK-UP, VAN AND 4RUNNER

1. Disconnect the negative battery terminal from the battery.
2. Drain the cooling system.
3. Remove the glove box, the defroster hoses, the air damper, the air duct and the 2 side defroster ducts.
4. Remove the control unit from the instrument panel.
5. Disconnect the heater hoses from the core tubes.
6. Remove the retaining bolts and lift out the heater unit. At this point, the core may be pulled from the case.
7. To install, reverse the removal procedures. Refill the cooling system.

LAND CRUISER

Front Heater

NOTE: The entire heater unit must be removed to gain access to the heater core. This procedure requires almost complete disassembly of the instrument panel and lowering of the steering column.

1. Disconnect the negative battery terminal from the battery. Remove the glove box and the glove box door.
2. Remove the lower heater ducts. Remove the large heater duct from the passenger side of the heater unit.
3. Remove the ductwork from behind the instrument panel. Remove the radio.
4. Disconnect the wiring connector from the right-side inner portion of the glove opening.
5. Remove the instrument panel pad. Remove the hood release lever. Disconnect the hand throttle control cable.
6. Remove the retaining screw from the left-side of the fuse block.
7. Remove the steering column-to-instrument panel attaching nuts and carefully lower the steering column. Tag and disconnect the wiring as necessary in order to lower the column assembly.

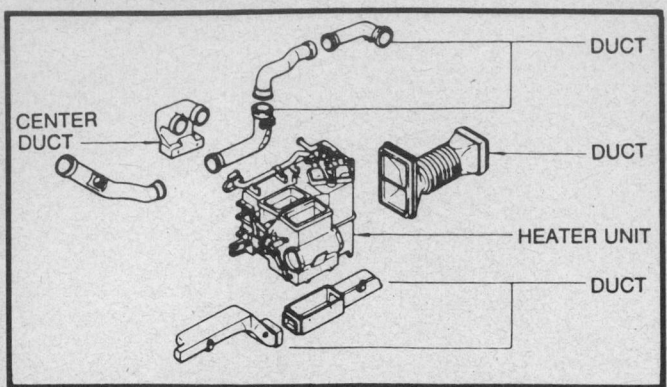

Typical heater unit and ducts – Land Cruiser

8. Disconnect the electrical connector from the rheostat located to the left of the steering column opening.

9. Remove the center dual outlet duct which is attached to the upper portion of the heater unit.

10. Remove the lower instrument panel.

11. Tag and disconnect the hoses from the heater unit. Remove the heater unit-to-firewall fasteners and the heater unit.

12. Remove the heater core-to-heater unit pipe clamps and the heater core retaining clamp, then, withdraw the heater core from the heater unit.

13. To install, reverse the removal procedures. Torque the steering column-to-instrument panel fasteners to 14–15 ft. lbs. Refill the cooling system.

Rear Heater

1. Turn off the water valve and disconnect both hoses from the rear heater core.

2. Disconnect the wiring from the rear heater.

3. Remove the mounting bolts and lift out the core.

4. To install, reverse the removal procedures. Refill the cooling system.

Water Pump

Removal and Installation

22R, 22R–E AND 22R–TE ENGINES

1. Disconnect the negative battery cable. Drain the cooling system.

2. If equipped, remove the fan shroud bolts and the shroud.

3. Loosen the alternator adjusting link bolt and remove the drive belt, then, swing the alternator toward the engine.

4. If equipped with an air pump, air conditioning compressor or power steering pump drive belts, it may be necessary to loosen the adjusting bolt, remove the drive belt(s) and move the component(s) out of the way.

5. Remove the fan from the fluid coupling, the fluid coupling and pulley from the water pump, then, the water pump-to-engine bolts and the pump.

6. Clean the gasket mounting surfaces.

7. To install, use a new gasket, sealant and reverse the removal procedures. Adjust the drive belt(s) tension. Refill the cooling system.

4Y–E AND 4Y–EC ENGINES

1. Disconnect the negative battery cable. Drain the cooling system. Disconnect the drive belt from the water pump.

2. Remove the fan from the fluid coupling and the fluid coupling/pulley from the water pump.

3. Remove the drive belt adjusting bar (from the water pump), the water pump-to-engine bolts and the water pump.

4. Clean the gasket mounting surfaces.

5. To install, use a new gasket, sealant and reverse the removal procedures.

6. Torque the water pump nuts/bolts to 13 ft. lbs., the drive belt adjusting bar to 29 ft. lbs., the pulley/fluid coupling-to-water pump nuts to 10 ft. lbs. and the fan-to-fluid coupling nuts to 10 ft. lbs. Adjust the drive belt tension. Refill the cooling system.

2F AND 3F–E ENGINES

1. Disconnect the negative battery cable.

2. Drain the engine coolant.

3. Remove the accesory drive belt. Loosen the power steering pump mount, idler pulley and adjusting bolts.

4. Disconnect the overflow tank hose.

5. Disconnect the radiator inlet hose and remove the fan shroud.

6. Remove the fan, fluid coupling and the water pump pulley.

7. Remove the alternator. Disconnect the hoses from the water pump.

8. Remove the water pump, power steering idler pulley and bracket as an assembly.

9. Installation is the reverse of the removal procedure. Torque the water pump mounting bolts to 27 ft. lbs. (37 Nm).

3VZ–E ENGINE

1. Disconnect the negative battery cable.

2. Remove the timing belt assembly.

3. Remove the thermostat.

4. Remove the idler pulley.

5. Remove the water pump mounting bolts and remove the water pump.

To install:

6. Clean the mounting surface.

7. Use new seal packing on the water pump and install it in position on the engine.

8. Torque the bolts marked **A** to 13 ft. lbs. (18 Nm) and the bolts marked **B** to 14 ft. lbs. (20 Nm).

9. Install the thermostat and the idler pulley.

10. Install the timing belt assembly.

11. Connect the negative battery cable and refill the cooling system.

Thermostat

Removal and Installation

22R, 22R–E AND 22R–TE ENGINES

1. Disconnect the negative battery cable. Partially drain the cooling system to a level below the thermostat.

NOTE: Unless the upper radiator hose is positioned over one of the thermostat housing (water outlet) bolts, it is not necessary to detach the hose.

2. Remove the mounting bolts, the water outlet and the thermostat from the intake manifold.

3. Clean the gasket mounting surfaces.

4. To install, use a new gasket, sealant and reverse the removal procedures. Refill the cooling system.

NOTE: When installing a new thermostat, be sure that the thermostat is positioned with the spring down.

5. Bleed the cooling system.

4Y–E AND 4Y–EC ENGINES

1. Disconnect the negative battery cable. Drain the cooling system to a level below the thermostat.

2. Disconnect the radiator outlet hose from the thermostat housing.

3. Remove the mounting bolts, the thermostat housing and the thermostat.

4. Clean the gasket mounting surfaces.

5. To install, use a new gasket, sealant and reverse the re-

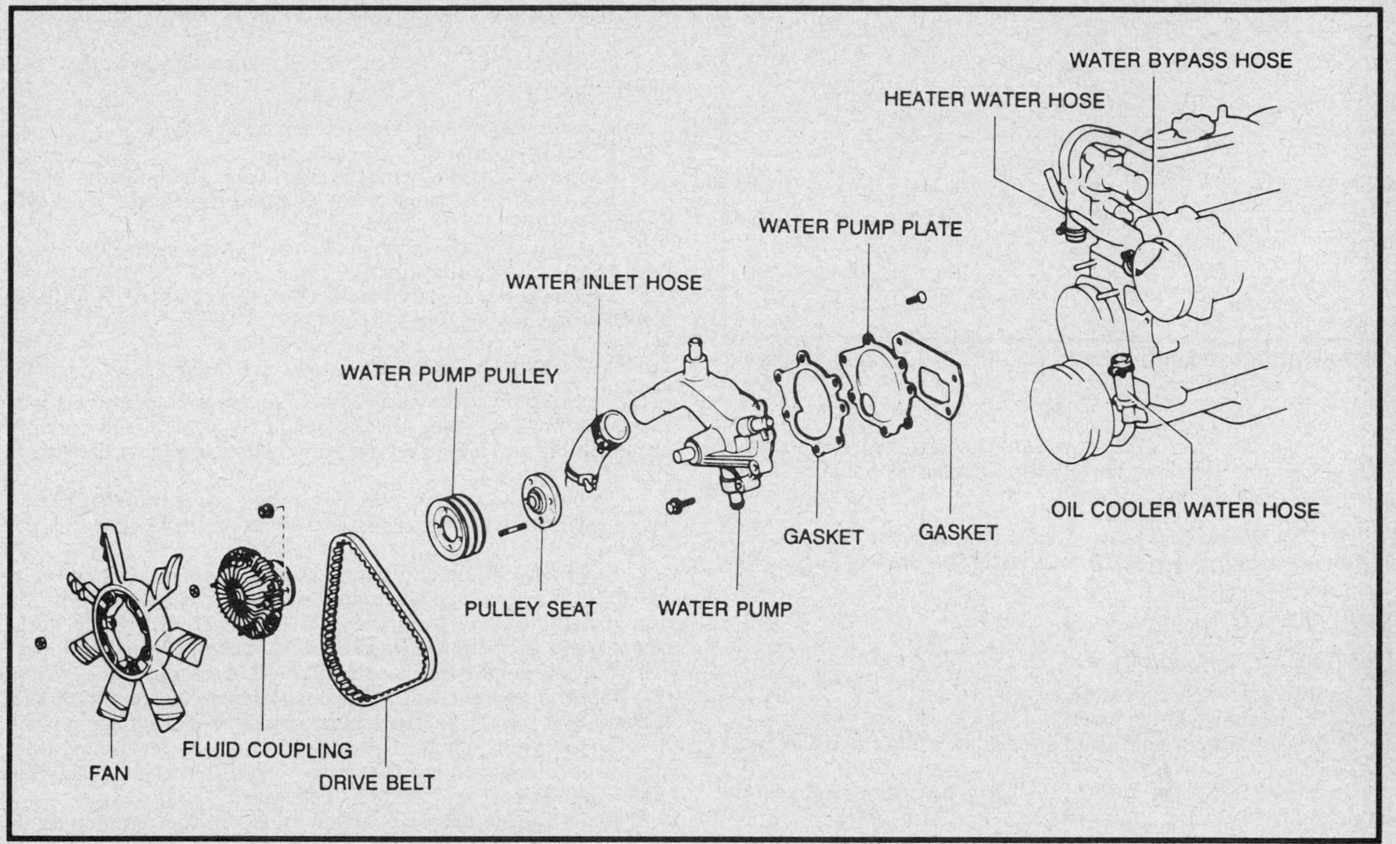

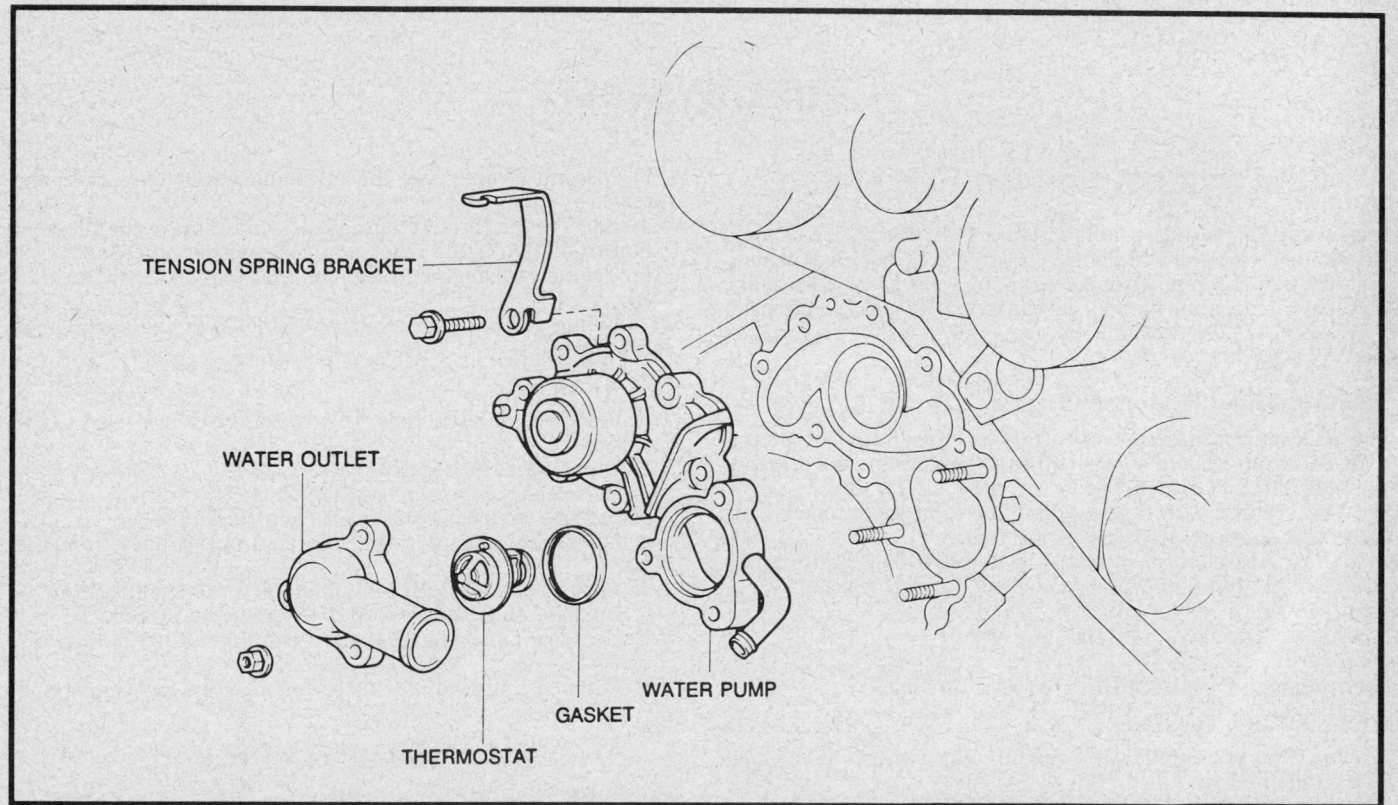

WATER BYPASS HOSE

HEATER WATER HOSE

WATER PUMP PLATE

WATER INLET HOSE

WATER PUMP PULLEY

OIL COOLER WATER HOSE

GASKET   GASKET

PULLEY SEAT   WATER PUMP

FAN

FLUID COUPLING

DRIVE BELT

Water pump assembly—2F and 3F–E engines

TENSION SPRING BRACKET

WATER OUTLET

WATER PUMP

GASKET

THERMOSTAT

Water pump assembly—3VZ–E engine

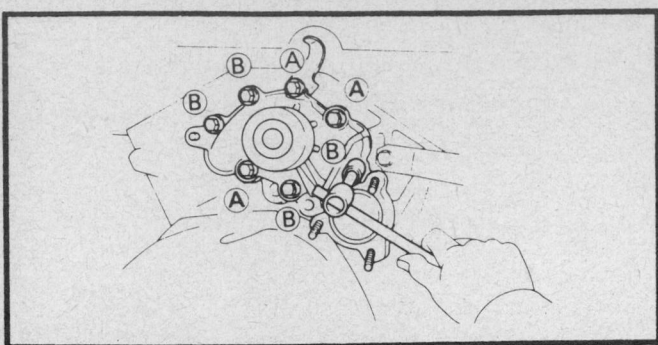

Water pump mounting bolt locations – 3VZ–E engine

moval procedures, making sure that the jiggle valve is placed at the upper-left position. Torque the thermostat housing to 9 ft. lbs. Refill the cooling system.

NOTE: When installing a new thermostat, be sure that the thermostat is positioned with the spring facing the engine block.

6. Bleed the cooling system.

2F AND 3F–E ENGINES

1. Disconnect the negative battery cable.
2. Drain the cooling system.
3. Disconnect the cold start injector wire and the BVSV vacuum lines.
4. Remove the thermostat housing bolts and remove the housing.
5. Remove the thermostat housing.

6. Installation is the revrse of removal. Torque the housng bolts to 13 ft. lbs. (18 Nm).
7. Refill the cooling system. Bleed the cooling system.

3VZ–E ENGINE

1. Disconnect the negative battery cable.
2. Drain the coolant.
3. Remove the radiator outlet hose from the housing.
4. Remove the thermostat housing and thermostat from the engine.
5. Installation is the reverse of the removal procedure. Use a new gasket for installation.
6. Torque the housing bolts to 14 ft. lbs. (20 Nm). Refill and bleed the cooling system.

Cooling System bleeding

After working on the cooling system, even to replace the thermostat, it must be bled. Air trapped in the system will prevent proper filling and leave the radiator coolant level low, causing a risk of overheating.

1. To bleed the system, start with the system cool, the radiator cap off and the radiator filled to about an inch below the filler neck.
2. Start the engine and run it at slightly above normal idle speed. This will insure adequate circulation. If air bubbles appear and the coolant level drops, fill the system with an antifreeze/water mixture to bring the level back to the proper level.
3. Run the engine this way until the thermostat opens. When this happens, coolant will move abruptly across the top of the radiator and the temperature of the radiator will suddenly rise.
4. At this point, air is often expelled and the level may drop quite a bit. Keep refilling the system until the level is near the top of the radiator and remains constant.
5. If the vehicle has an overflow tank, fill the radiator right up to the filler neck. Replace the radiator filler cap.

FUEL SYSTEM

Fuel System Service Precaution

When working with the fuel system certain precautions should be taken; always work in a well ventilated area, keep a dry chemical (Class B) fire extinguisher near the work area. Always disconnect the negative battery cable and do not make any repairs to the fuel system until all the necessary steps for repair have been reviewed.

Relieving Fuel System Pressure

1. Disconnect the negative battery terminal from the battery.
2. Allow the system enough time to bleed off the fuel pressure through the fuel return line.
3. Before disconnecting any fuel line component, place a rag under the item to catch any excess fuel.
4. After installation, install the negative battery terminal, turn **ON** the ignition switch and check for fuel leaks.

Fuel Filter

Removal and Installation
EXCEPT 22R ENGINE

Th fuel filter is located in the engine compartment, at the inlet line to the fuel rail.
1. Disconnect the negative battery cable.
2. Relieve the fuel system pressure.

3. Disconnect and plug the inlet and outlet lines from the filter.
4. Remove the filter retainng bolts and remove the filter.
5. Installation is the reverse of the removal procedure.
6. Use new O-rings and tighten the lines to 22 ft. lbs, (29 Nm).
7. Connect the negative battery cable. Run the engine and check for leaks.

22R ENGINE

The fuel filter is located under the rear of the vehicle, next to the fuel tank.
1. Disconnect the negative battery cable.
2. Raise and safely support the vehicle.
3. Remove the protective cover from the filter.
4. Disconnect and plug the inlet and outlet lines from the filter.
5. Remove the filter retainng bolts and remove the filter.
6. Installation is the reverse of the removal procedure.
7. Use new O-rings and tighten the lines to 22 ft. lbs. (29 Nm).
8. Connect the negative battery cable. Run the engine and check for leaks.

Mechanical Fuel Pump
Pressure Testing

1. Attach a pressure gauge to the pressure side of the fuel

line. On vehicles equipped with a vapor return system, squeeze off the return hose.

2. Run the engine at idle and note the reading on the gauge. Stop the engine and compare the reading with the specification. If the pump is operating properly, the pressure will be as specified and will be constant at idle speed. If the pressure varies or is too high or low, the pump should be repaired or replaced.

3. Remove the pressure gauge.

Flow Test

1. Disconnect the fuel line from the carburetor. Run the fuel line into a suitable measuring container.

2. Run the engine at idle until there is one pint of fuel in the container. One pint should be pumped in 30 seconds or less.

3. If the flow is below minimum, check for a restriction in the line.

Removal and Installation

22R ENGINES

1. Disconnect the negative battery terminal from the battery.

2. Drain the cooling system to a level below the upper radiator hose and remove the upper radiator hose.

3. Remove all 3 lines from the fuel pump, the mounting bolts, the fuel pump and the gasket.

NOTE: The fuel pump is not repairable. It must be replaced as a complete unit.

4. Clean the gasket mounting surfaces.

5. To install, use a new gaskets and reverse the removal procedures. Refill the cooling system. Start the engine and check for leaks.

2F ENGINE

1. Disconnect the negative battery terminal from the battery.

2. Remove and plug the fuel lines at fuel pump. Remove the fuel pump-to-engine bolts and the pump.

3. Clean the gasket mounting surfaces.

4. To install, use a new gasket and reverse the removal procedures. Start the engine and check for fuel leaks.

Electric Fuel Pump

An electric fuel pump is used on all fuel injected engines. The fuel pump is wired into the ignition switch and oil pressure switch circuits. In the event of an oil pressure loss, the fuel pump is turned **OFF** so that the engine will stall, thus preventing engine damage due to the oil pressure loss. The fuel pump will operate only when the ignition switch is turned to the **START** position and when the oil pressure is normal.

Operation Testing

1. Disconnect the electrical clip from the oil pressure switch.

2. Turn the ignition switch to the **ON** position (do not start the engine).

3. Short the **Fp** and the **+B** terminals of the check connector. Check the cold start injector hose for pressure.

4. Check for a smooth flow of gasoline from the fuel filter outlet. If the pump is noisy, it is probably defective. If the pump does not run, check the pump resistor and relay.

5. Disconnect the jumper wire and reconnect the check connector. Turn the ignition switch **OFF**.

Pressure Testing

1. Disconnect the negative battery terminal from the battery and the wiring connector from the cold start injector.

2. Place a container or a shop towel near the end of the delivery tube.

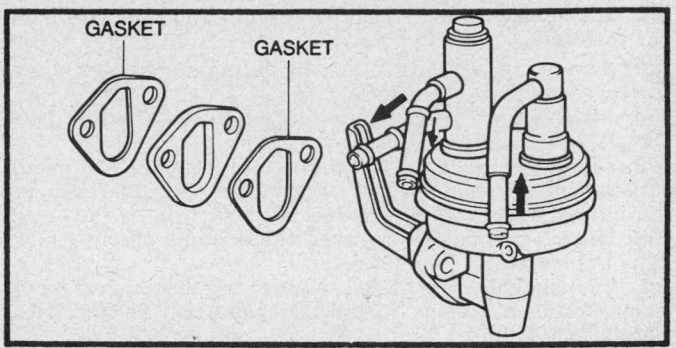

Typical mechanical fuel pump

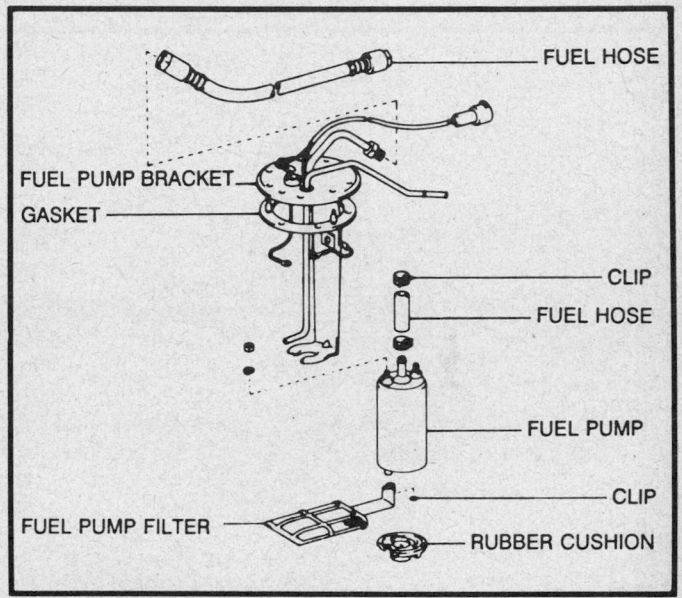

Typical electric fuel pump

3. Slowly loosen the cold start injector union bolt, then, remove the bolt and the gaskets. Drain the fuel line.

4. Using pressure gauge tool No. 09268–45011 or equivalent, connect it in line with the cold start injector. Reconnect the battery cable.

5. Short the **Fp** and **+B** terminals of the check connector wire. Turn the ignition switch to the **ON** position and measure to fuel pump pressure. It should be 33–38 psi. Turn the ignition switch **OFF**.

NOTE: If the pressure is high, replace the pressure regulator; if the pressure is low, check the hoses, the connections, the fuel pump, the fuel filter or the pressure regulator.

6. Remove the jumper wire from the check connector. Start the engine. Disconnect and plug the vacuum sensing hose at the pressure regulator, then, measure the fuel pressure at idle. It should be 33–38 psi.

7. Reconnect the vacuum sensing hose to the pressure regulator. The pressure should now be 27–31 psi.; if not, check the vacuum hose and/or the pressure regulator.

8. Stop the engine and check that the fuel pressure remains at 21 psi. for 5 minutes. If not, check the fuel pump, the pressure regulator and/or the injectors.

Removal and Installation

1. Disconnect the negative battery cable. Drain the fuel tank.

2. Disconnect the electrical connector and the fuel lines from the fuel tank.

3. Remove the inlet tube and mounting bolts/straps, then, the fuel tank from the vehicle.

4. Remove the access plate-to-fuel tank bolts, then, pull out the plate/fuel pump assembly.

5. Disconnect the electrical connectors from the fuel pump. Pull the bracket from the lower-side of the fuel pump, then, remove the fuel pump from the fuel hose.

6. Remove the rubber cushion, the clip and the fuel filter from the bottom of the fuel pump.

7. To install, use new gaskets and reverse the removal procedures. Torque the fuel pump bracket-to-fuel tank to 43 inch lbs. Refill the fuel tank.

Carburetor

Removal and Installation

1. Disconnect the negative battery terminal from the battery.

2. Label and disconnect the emission control hoses. Disconnect the air intake hose. Remove the mounting and butterfly nuts, then, lift the air cleaner from the carburetor.

3. If equipped with an automatic transmission, disconnect the throttle cable or rod. Disconnect the fuel hose, the emission control hose, the PCV hose and the wiring connector(s) from the carburetor.

4. Disconnect the accelerator linkage and the choke pipe (if equipped).

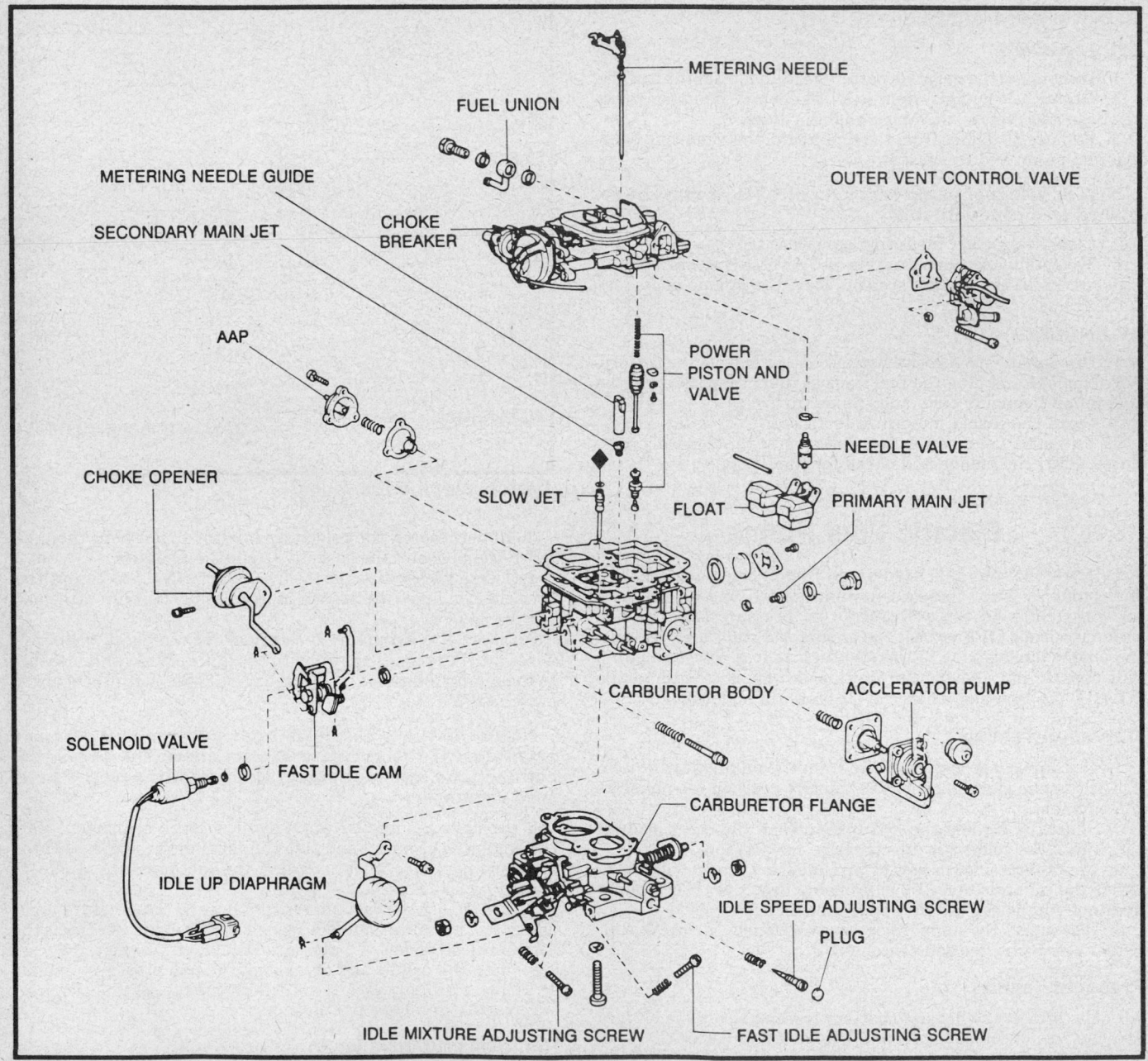

Carburetor components—22R, 22R-E and 22R-TE engines

5. On the 2F engine, disconnect the magnetic valve wire from the coil terminal and the choke cable from the carburetor.

6. Remove the carburetor-to-manifold nuts/bolts and lift it from the manifold.

7. Cover the open manifold with a clean cloth to prevent dirt and small objects from entering into the engine. Clean the gasket mounting surfaces.

8. To install, use a new gasket and reverse the removal procedures. After the engine has been started, check for fuel and vacuum leaks.

Idle Speed and Mixture Adjustment

2F ENGINE

NOTE: Idle mixture adjustments cannot be performed; these adjustments are preset at the factory.

The idle speed and mixture should be adjusted under the following conditions: the air cleaner must be installed, the choke fully opened, the transmission should be in **N**, all accessories should be turned **OFF**, all vacuum lines should be connected and the ignition timing should be set to specification.

1. Start the engine and allow it to reach normal operating temperatures.

2. Check the float setting; the fuel level should be just about even with the spot on the sight glass. If the fuel level is too high or low, adjust the float level.

3. Connect a tachometer in accordance with its manufacturer's instructions. However, connect the tachometer positive (+) lead to the coil's (−) negative terminal or to the igniter's service connector (if provided).

NOTE: Do not connect the tachometer to the distributor side; damage to the transistorized ignition could result. Never allow the tachometer terminal to touch ground for damage to the igniter or the ignition coil could result.

4. Remove the caps from the idle mixture screws. Turn the idle speed adjusting screw to obtain the initial idle speed of 690 rpm (manual transmission).

5. Turn the idle mixture adjusting screw to increase the idle speed as much as is possible.

6. Next, turn the idle speed screw to again obtain the same idle speed figure given in Step 4.

7. If possible, turn the idle mixture screw to increase the idle speed again.

8. Repeat Steps 6 and 7 until the idle mixture adjusting screw will no longer increase the idle speed above the figure specified in Step 4.

9. Slowly turn the idle mixture screw clockwise, until the correct idle speed is reached (this makes the mixture leaner).

10. Disconnect the tachometer and install new idle mixture screw caps.

22R ENGINE

NOTE: The idle mixture screw is preset at the factory and adjustment should not be necessary.

The idle speed should be adjusted under the following conditions: the air cleaner must be installed, the choke fully opened, the transmission should be in **N**, all accessories should be turned **OFF**, all vacuum lines should be connected and the ignition timing should be set to specification.

1. Start the engine and allow it to reach normal operating temperatures.

2. Check the float setting; the fuel level should be just about even with the spot on the sight glass. If the fuel level is too high or low, adjust the float level.

NOTE: Do not connect the tachometer to the distributor side; damage to the transistorized ignition could re-

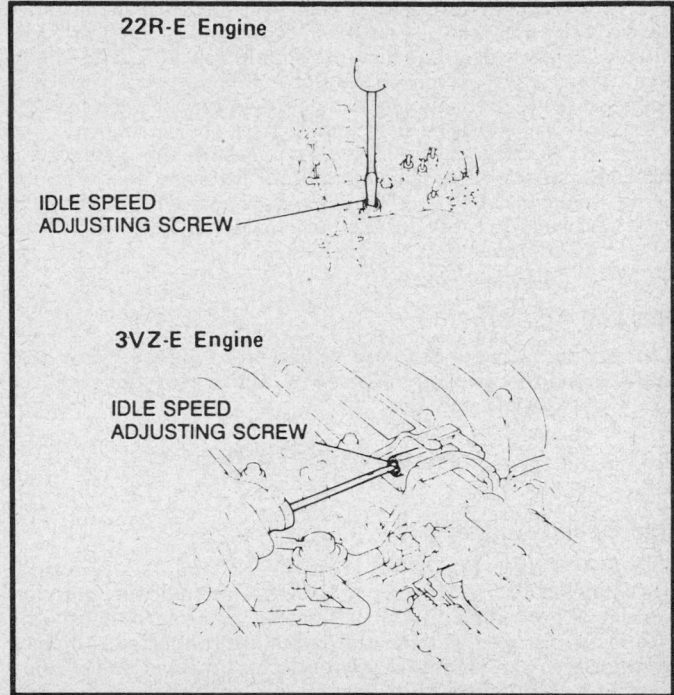

Idle speed adjustment screw location

sult. Never allow the tachometer terminal to touch ground for damage to the igniter or the ignition coil could result.

3. Connect a tachometer in accordance with its manufacturer's instructions. However, connect the tachometer positive (+) lead to the coil's (−) negative terminal or to the igniter's service connector (if provided).

NOTE: If the idle mixture caps have been removed, turn the idle mixture screws to the fully closed position, then, open them 3½ turns.

4. Using a pair of pliers, remove the caps from the idle speed adjusting screw. Turn the idle speed adjusting screw to obtain the correct idle speed: 700 rpm (if equipped with a manual transmission) or 750 rpm (if equipped with an automatic transmission).

5. Disconnect the tachometer and install new idle speed adjusting screw cap.

Float Level Adjustment

22R ENGINE

For this procedure, the air horn must be removed from the carburetor and the gasket removed from the air horn.

1. Position the air horn with the floats facing upward; allow the float to rest by itself.

2. Using tool No. SST 09240–00014 or equivalent, position it between the floats and the air horn; the measurement should be 0.386 in. If adjustment is necessary, bend the tang at the float pivot point.

3. Using a vernier caliper, raise the float and measure the distance between the bottom of the float and the air horn; the distance should be 1.89 in. If adjustment is necessary, bend the tang at the pivot point.

4. After adjustment, replace the air horn onto the carburetor.

2F ENGINE

1. Remove the air horn from the carburetor. Invert the air horn and allow the float to hang towards the air horn.

2. With the air horn gasket removed, measure the distance between the float and the air hron, at the end of the float opposite the needle valve. The distance should be 0.295 in. If adjustment is necessary, remove the flat and bend the tab which is centered between the hinge pivot points. After the adjustment is completed, reinstall the float and recheck the setting.

3. Lift upwards on the float and measure the distance between the needle valve push pin and the lip of the float. The distance should be 0.043 in. If adjustment is necessary, remove the float and bend the tabs located just inside of the hinge points. After the adjustment is completed, reinstall the float and recheck the setting.

Service Adjustments

For all carburetor service adjustment procedures and specifications, please refer to "Carburetor Service" in the Unit Repair section.

Fuel Injection

Idle Speed Adjustment

The 22R–E, 22R–TE, 3F–E, 4Y–E, 4Y–EC and 3VZ–E engines are equipped with a computer activated, electronic fuel injection system. Prior to adjusting the idle speed, make sure that the air cleaner is installed. All vacuum hoses are connected. All pipes and hoses in the air intake system are connected and in good condition. All fuel injection system wiring is connected and in good condition. The engine is at normal operating temperature. All accessories are **OFF**. Transmission selector lever in **N**.

1. Connect the tachometer positive (+) lead to the coil's (−) negative terminal or to the igniter's service connector (if provided).
2. Run the engine at 2500 rpm for 2 minutes.
3. Run the engine at idle and turn the idle speed adjusting screw to obtain the correct idle speed.
4. Disconnect and remove the tachometer.

Cold Start Injector

The EFI engines have a cold start injector located in the intake air chamber which aids in cold weather starting.

Removal and Installation

1. Disconnect the negative battery cable and the cold start injector wire.
2. Place a shop towel or a container under the fuel delivery pipe and drain the fuel from the pipe.
3. Disconnect the fuel pipe from the cold start injector.
4. Remove the mounting bolts and the cold start injector from the intake air chamber.
5. To install, use new gaskets and reverse the removal procedures. Torque the injector bolts to 44–60 inch lbs.

Fuel Pressure Regulator

The fuel pressure regulator is located on the fuel delivery pipe of the fuel system, it maintains a constant fuel pressure in the injection system.

Removal and Installation

1. Disconnect the vacuum sensing hose from the pressure regulator.

NOTE: On the 22R–E and the 22R–TE engines, remove the No. 1 EGR pipe.

2. Place a shop towel or a container under the fuel hose connection and disconnect the fuel return hose from the regulator.

3. Remove the locknut (22R–E, 22R–TE and 3F–E) or the mounting bolts (4Y–E, 4Y–EC and 3VZ–E) and the pressure regulator from the fuel delivery pipe.
4. To install, reverse of removal. Torque the locknut to 22 ft. lbs. (22R–E, 22R–TE and 3F–E) or bolts to 44–60 inch lbs. (4Y–E, 4Y–EC and 3VZ–E). Start the engine and check for fuel leaks.

Fuel Injector

Testing

Each injector may be tested for operation while on the engine, in 2 ways.
1. Listen for a clicking at the injector.
2. Using an ohmmeter, check the continuity at each injector's terminal; the resistance should be 1.5–3.0 ohms.

Removal and Installation

1. Disconnect the negative battery terminal from the battery and the ground strap from the rear side of the engine.
2. Disconnect the accelerator wire. If equipped with an automatic transmission, disconnect the throttle cable from the bracket and the clamp.
3. Disconnect the No. 1 and No. 2 PCV hoses.
4. If equipped with a 22R–TE engine, disconnect the No. 2 PCV hose and the Vacuum Control Valve (VCV).
5. Disconnect the following items:
  a. Brake power booster hose
  b. Air control valve hoses
  c. Vacuum Switching Valve (VSV)
  d. Evaporative emission control hose
  e. EGR vacuum hose and modulator
  f. Pressure regulator hose (2WD)
  g. Fuel pressure-up (VSV) and hose
  h. No. 1 and No. 2 air valve hose from the throttle body
  i. No. 2 and No. 3 water bypass hoses from the throttle body
  j. Cold start injector wire
  k. Throttle position wire

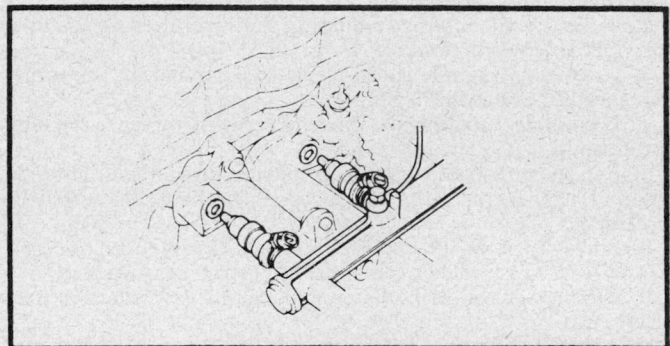

Removing the fuel delivery pipe

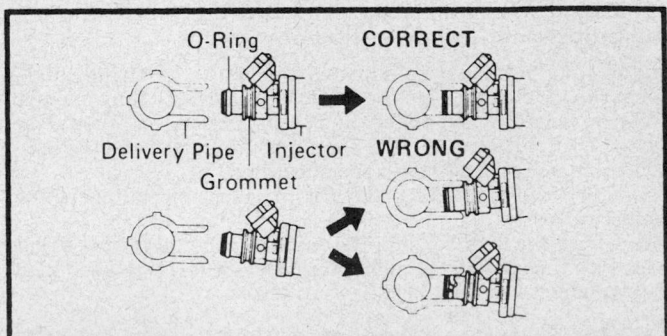

Injector installation into delivery pipe

6. Remove the following items:
  a. Cold start injector-to-plenum chamber bolt.
  b. No. 1 EGR pipe-to-plenum chamber bolts.
  c. Manifold stay-to-plenum chamber bolts.
  d. Fuel hose clamp, 4 bolts, 2 nuts and the bond strap.
  e. The plenum chamber with the throttle body and gaskets.
7. Disconnect the fuel return hose.
8. Disconnect the following wires:
  a. Auxiliary air valve wire
  b. Knock sensor wire
  c. Oil pressure sender gauge/switch
  d. Starter wire (terminal 50)
  e. Transmission wires
  f. Air conditioning compressor wires
  g. Injector wires
  h. Water temperature sender gauge wire
  i. Overdrive temperature switch wire (air conditioning)
  j. Oxygen sensor and igniter wire
  k. Vacuum Switching Valve (VSV) wire (air conditioning)
  l. Cold start injector time switch wire
  m. Water temperature sensor wire
9. Disconnect the fuel hose from the delivery pipe with the pulsation damper and gaskets.
10. Remove the injectors from the engine. Take care in handling the injectors.

NOTE: Injector performance tests are possible but special tools are required. If these tools are unavailable, use the test procedures above.

11. To install, use new O-rings and reverse the removal procedures. Torque the hold-down bolts to 14 ft. lbs. Check for fuel leakage.

NOTE: Each injector should have 4 insulators. Prior to installation, coat the O-rings with clean gasoline. Prior to tightening the hold-down bolts, make sure that the injector rotates smoothly in its bore. If not, the O-rings are twisted.

EMISSION CONTROLS

Please refer to "Professional Emission Component Application Guide".

ENGINE MECHANICAL

Engine

Removal and Installation

22R, 22R–E AND 22R–TE ENGINES

1. Disconnect the negative battery cable.
2. Remove the engine undercover.
3. Disconnect the windshield washer hose and then remove the hood. Scribe matchmarks around the hinges for easy installation.
4. Drain the engine oil. Drain the engine coolant from the radiator and the cylinder block.
5. Drain the automatic transmission fluid on models so equipped.
6. Disconnect the air cleaner hose and then remove the air cleaner.
7. Remove the radiator and shroud. Disconnect the No. 1 turbocharger water line on the 22R–TE.
8. Remove the coupling fan.
9. Disconnect the heater hoses at the engine.
10. On vehicles with automatic transmissions, disconnect the accelerator and throttle cables at their bracket.
11. Disconnect the following:
  a. No. 1 and No. 2 PCV hoses
  b. Brake booster hose
  c. Air control valve hoses
  d. EVAP hose at the canister
  e. Actuator hose on vehicles with cruise control
  f. Vacuum modulator hose at the EGR valve
  g. Air valve hoses at the throttle body and chamber
  h. Two water bypass hoses at the throttle body
  i. Air control valve hose at the actuator
  j. Pressure regulator hose at the chamber
  k. Cold start injector pipe
  l. BVSV hose.
12. Tag and disconnect the cold start injector wire and the throttle position sensor wire.
13. Remove the EGR valve from the throttle chamber.
14. Disconnect the throttle chamber at the stay. Remove the chamber-to-intake manifold mounting bolts and lift off the throttle chamber.
15. Tag and disconnect the following wires:
  a. Cold start injector time switch wire
  b. Water temperature sensor wire
  c. On vehicles with air conditioning: VSV and air conditioning compressor wires
  d. Oxygen sensor wire (22R–TE only)
  e. OD temperature switch wire (with automatic transmission)
  f. Injector wires
  g. Knock sensor connector
  h. Air valve wire
  i. Oil pressure switch wire
  j. Starter wire.
16. Remove the power steering pump from its bracket (if equipped). Disconnect the ground strap from the bracket.
17. On vehicles with air conditioning, loosen the drive belt and remove the air conditioning compressor. Position it out of the way with the refrigerant lines still attached.
18. Disconnect the engine ground straps at the rear and right side of the engine.
19. On vehicles with a manual transmission, remove the shift lever from inside the vehicles.
20. Raise and safely support the vehicle. Drain the engine oil. Remove the rear driveshaft.
21. On vehicles with automatic transmission, disconnect the manual shift linkage at the neutral start switch. On 4WD vehi-

cles with automatic transmission, disconnect the transfer shift linkage.

22. Disconnect the speedometer cable. Be sure not to lose the felt dust protector and washers.

23. Remove the transfer case undercover on 4WD vehicles.

24. Remove the stabilizer bar on 4WD vehicles.

25. Remove the front driveshaft on 4WD vehicles.

26. Remove the No. 1 frame crossmember.

27. Disconnect the front exhaust pipe at the manifold and tail pipe and remove the exhaust pipe.

28. On vehicles with manual transmission, remove the clutch release cylinder and its bracket from the transmission.

29. Remove the No. 1 front floor heat insulator and the brake tube heat insulator on 4WD.

30. On 2WD vehicles, remove the rear engine mount bolts, raise the transmission slightly with a floor jack and then remove the support member mounting bolts.

31. On 4WD vehicles, remove the 4 rear engine mount bolts, raise the transmission slightly with a floor jack and then remove the bolts from the side member and remove the No. 2 frame crossmember.

32. Lower the vehicle. Attach an engine hoist chain to the lifting brackets on the engine. Remove the engine mount nuts and bolts and slowly lift the engine/transmission out of the truck.

To install:

33. Slowly lower the engine assembly into the engine compartment.

34. Raise the transmission onto the crossmember with a floor jack.

35. Align the holes in the engine mounts and the frame, install the bolts and then remove the engine hoist chain.

36. On 2WD vehicles, raise the transmission slightly and align the rear engine mount with the support member and tighten the bolts to 9 ft. lbs. (13 Nm). Lower the transmission until it rests on the extension housing and then tighten the bracket mounting bolts to 19 ft. lbs. (25 Nm).

37. On 4WD vehicles, raise the transmission slightly and tighten the No. 2 frame crossmember-to-side frame bolts to 70 ft. lbs. (95 Nm). Lower the transmission and tighten the rear engine mount bolts to 9 ft. lbs. (13 Nm).

38. On 4WD vehicles, install the brake tube and front floor heat insulators.

39. Install the clutch release cylinder and its bracket to the manual transmission. Tighten the bracket bolts to 29 ft. lbs. (39 Nm) and the cylinder bolts to 9 ft. lbs. (13 Nm).

40. Reconnect the exhaust pipe. Install the No. 1 frame crossmember.

41. On 4WD vehicles, install the front driveshaft, stabilizer bar and the transfer case undercover.

42. Connect the speedometer cable. Connect the transfer shift linkage on 4WD vehicles with automatic transmission.

43. Connect the manual shift linkage to the neutral start switch (automatic transmission only).

44. Install the rear driveshaft. Install the shift lever (manual transmission only).

45. Connect the engine ground straps. Install the air conditioning compressor.

47. Install the power steering pump and connect the ground strap.

48. Connect all of the following wires:
   a. Cold start injector time switch wire
   b. Water temperature sensor wire
   c. On vehicles with air conditioning: VSV and air conditioning compressor wires
   d. Oxygen sensor wire (22R–TE only)
   e. OD temperature switch wire (with automatic transmission)
   f. Injector wires
   g. Knock sensor connector
   h. Air valve wire

i. Oil pressure switch wire
   j. Starter wire

49. Connect all of the following parts:
   a. No. 1 and No. 2 PCV hoses
   b. Brake booster hose
   c. Air control valve hoses
   d. EVAP hose at the canister
   e. Actuator hose on vehicles with cruise control
   f. Vacuum modulator hose at the EGR valve
   g. Air valve hoses at the throttle body and chamber
   h. Two water bypass hoses at the throttle body
   i. Air control valve hose at the actuator
   j. Pressure regulator hose at the chamber
   k. Cold start injector pipe
   l. BVSV hose.

50. Connect the accelerator and throttle cables to the bracket (automatic transmission only).

51. Connect the heater hoses and install the coupling fan. Install the radiator and shroud.

52. Install the air cleaner. Refill the engine with oil and the radiator with coolant. Install the engine undercover.

53. Install and adjust the hood.

54. Connect the battery cable, start the engine and road test the vehicle.

4Y–E AND 4Y–EC ENGINES

1. Disconnect the negative battery terminal from the battery.

2. Remove the right seat and the engine service hole cover.

3. Drain the coolant from the radiator. Remove the reservoir tank, the heater hoses and the radiator.

4. Remove the air cleaner, the breather tube, the brake booster, the charcoal canister and the fuel hoses from the engine.

5. If equipped with power steering, remove the drive belt, the pulley, the woodruff key and the pump from the engine, then, move the pump aside.

NOTE: When removing the power steering pump, do not disconnect the pressure lines unless it is absolutely necessary.

6. Disconnect the accelerator cable with the bracket from the throttle body.

7. Disconnect the following wiring connectors from the: water temperature sender, oil pressure switch, IIA unit, air conditioning compressor, idle-up solenoid, VSV, water temperature switch (automatic transmission), alternator connector and wire, air flow meter and solenoid resistor.

8. Remove the fan shroud, the fan, the fluid coupling and the water pump pulley.

9. From inside the vehicle, remove the center pillar cover, the seat belt retractor and cover, then, disconnect the electrical connectors from the ECU.

10. If equipped with A/C, remove the drive belt and the compressor mounting bolts, then, move the compressor aside.

11. Raise and safely support the vehicle.

12. Drain the engine oil. Remove the driveshaft and the front exhaust pipe.

13. Remove the transmission selector and shift cables, then, the clutch release cylinder (manual transmission).

14. Disconnect the starter wires, the mounting bolts and the starter from the engine.

15. Remove the speedometer cable, the bond cable and the back-up light switch connector.

16. If equipped with a rear heater, disconnect the mode selector and the air mix damper cable from the damper. Disconnect the heater hoses to the rear heater unit.

17. Disconnect the bond cable(s) from the engine mount(s). Remove the engine under cover.

18. Disconnect the oil level sensor and the oil cooler hoses (if equipped with automatic transmission).

19. Place matchmarks on the front strut bar and the rear

mounting nut. Remove the rear nut, the strut bar-to-lower control arm bolts and the strut.

20. Using an engine saddle, place it under the engine and support it. Place a floor jack under the transmission and support it.

NOTE: If equipped with a manual transmission, remove the engine rear mounting bracket from the body. If equipped with automatic transmission, remove the engine mounting member-to-transmission through bolt.

21. Remove the engine mounts-to-body nuts/bolts and lower the engine/transmission assembly, then, remove the engine mounting member from the engine.

22. Remove the transmission from the engine.

23. To install, reverse the removal procedures. Refill the engine with oil and the cooling system with coolant.

2F ENGINE

1. Scribe marks on the hood and hinges to aid in alignment during installation. Remove the hinge bolt from the hood and then remove the hood.

2. Raise and safely support the vehicle. Drain the cooling system and engine oil. Lower the vehicle.

3. Unfasten the radiator grille mounting bolts and remove the grille.

4. Remove the hood latch support rod. Detach the hood latch assembly from the radiator upper bracket. Remove the bracket.

5. Disconnect the heater hose from the radiator.

6. Detach the upper radiator hose at the water outlet housing and the lower hose at water pump.

7. Remove the 6 bolts which secure the radiator and lift the radiator out of the vehicle.

8. Remove the heater hoses from the water valve and heater box. Disconnect the temperature control cable from the water valve.

9. Detach both the battery cables and remove the battery.

10. Remove the wires from the starter solenoid terminal.

11. Detach the fuel lines from the pump and remove the fuel filter assembly.

12. Disconnect the primary wire from the ignition coil.

13. Detach both of the intermediate rods from the shifter shafts (column shift vehicles only).

14. Remove the air cleaner assembly, complete with hoses, from its bracket.

15. Remove the emission control system cables and hoses as necessary.

16. Disconnect the alternator wires.

17. Disconnect the hand throttle, accelerator, and choke linkage from the carburetor.

18. On vehicles equipped with vacuum assisted 4WD engagement, remove the control unit vacuum hose from its manifold fitting.

19. Disconnect the oil pressure and water temperature gauge sender's wiring.

20. Unfasten the downpipe from the exhaust manifold.

21. Detach the parking brake cable from the intermediate lever.

22. Raise and safely support the vehicle. Unbolt the front driveshaft from the flange on the transfer case output shaft.

23. Remove both the left and right engine stone shields. Remove the transmission skidplate.

24. Remove both the cotter pin and disconnect both the high and low range shifter link lever and the high/low shift rod.

25. Remove the high/low range shifter link lever and the high/low shift rod.

26. Disconnect the clutch release fork spring. Remove the clutch release cylinder from its mounting bracket at the rear of the engine.

27. Unfasten the clamp screws and withdraw the vacuum lines from the transfer case control unit vacuum chamber (only on vehicles with vacuum assist 4WD engagement).

28. Remove the 4WD indicator switch assembly.

29. Unfasten the speedometer cable from the transmission.

31. Detach the gearshift rod and gear selector rod from the shift outer lever and the gear selector outer lever respectively.

32. Unbolt the rear engine mounts from the frame. Remove the front engine mounts. Lower the vehicle.

34. Install lifting hooks on the engine lift points and connect a suitable hoist.

35. Lift the engine slightly and toward the front, so the engine/transmission assembly clears the front of the vehicle.

To install:

36. Lower the engine into position in the vehicle.

37. Install the engine mounts and bolts. Attach the gearshift rod and gear selector rod to the shift outer lever and the gear selector outer lever respectively.

38. Install the speedometer cable to the transmission. Install the 4WD indicator switch assembly.

39. Install the vacuum lines to the transfer case control unit vacuum chamber (only on vehicles with vacuum assist 4WD engagement).

40. Connect the clutch release fork spring. Install the clutch release cylinder in its mounting bracket at the rear of the engine.

41. Install the high/low range shifter link lever and the high/low shift rod.

42. Connect both the high and low range shifter link lever and the high/low shift rod. Install the left and right engine stone shields. Install the transmission skid plate.

43. Install the front driveshaft. Attach the parking brake cable to the intermediate lever.

44. Fasten the downpipe to the exhaust manifold. Connect the oil pressure and water temperature gauge sender's wiring.

45. Connect accelerator, and choke linkage to the carburetor. Connect the alternator wires.

46. Connect all hoses and wiring. Connect the shifter rods. Install the battery. Install the water valve and cable.

47. Install the radiator and hoses. Install the hood latch and grille.

48. Install the hood. Refill the cooling system and the crankcase.

3F–E ENGINE

1. Disconnect the negative battery cable. Drain the engine coolant.

2. Scribe matchmarks around the hood hinges and then remove the hood.

3. Remove the battery and its tray.

4. Disconnect the accelerator and throttle cables.

5. Remove the air intake hose, air flow meter and air cleaner assembly.

6. Remove the coolant reservoir tank.

7. Remove the radiator.

8. Tag and disconnect the following wires and connectors:
   a. Oil pressure connector
   b. High tension cord at the coil
   c. Neutral start switch and transfer connectors near the starter
   d. Front differential lock connector
   e. Starter wire and connector
   f. Starter ground strap
   g. O_2 sensor connectors
   h. Alternator wire and connector
   i. Cooling fan connector
   j. Check connector.

9. Disconnect the following hoses:
   a. Heater hoses
   b. Fuel hoses
   c. Transfer case hose
   d. Brake booster hose
   e. Air injection hoses

f. Distributor hose

g. Emission control hoses

10. Remove the glove box, pull out the 4 connectors and then pull the EFI wiring harness from the cowl.

11. Unbolt the power steering pump and position it out of the way with the hoses still connected.

12. Do the same with the air conditioning compressor.

13. Raise the vehicle and remove the transfer case undercover. Drain the engine oil.

14. Remove the front and rear driveshafts.

15. Disconnect the speedometer cable.

16. Disconnect the engine ground strap.

17. Disconnect the 2 vacuum hoses at the diaphragm cylinder underneath the transfer case.

18. Remove the clip and pin and then disconnect the shift rod at the transfer case. Remove the nut, disconnect the washers and the shift lever at the shift rod.

19. Disconnect the transmission control rod.

20. Disconnect the exhaust pipe at the manifold.

21. With a floor jack under the transmission, remove the bolts and nuts that attach the frame crossmember and then remove the crossmember. Lower the vehicle.

22. Attach an suitable engine hoist to the lifting brackets on the engine. Remove the engine mount nuts and bolts and slowly lift the engine/transmission out of the vehicle.

To install:

23. Slowly lower the engine assembly into the engine compartment.

24. Raise the transmission onto the crossmember with a suitable floor jack.

25. Align the holes in the engine mounts and the frame, install the bolts and then remove the engine hoist chain.

26. Raise the transmission slightly and tighten the frame crossmember-to-chassis bolts to 29 ft. lbs. (39 Nm). Tighten the 2 nuts to 43 ft. lbs. (59 Nm).

27. Install the exhaust pipe with a new gasket and tighten the nuts to 46 ft. lbs. (62 Nm).

28. Connect the transmission control rod. Connect the transfer case shift lever.

29. Connect the engine ground strap. Connect the speedometer cable.

30. Install the front and rear driveshafts. Tighten the nuts to 65 ft. lbs. (88 Nm).

31. Install the transfer case undercover. Install the air conditioning compressor. Install the power steering pump and tighten the pulley nut to 35 ft. lbs. (47 Nm).

32. Connect the EFI wiring harness at the ECU. Connect all of the following hoses:

a. Heater hoses

b. Fuel hoses

c. Transfer case hose

d. Brake booster hose

e. Air injection hoses

f. Distributor hose

g. Emission control hoses.

33. Connect all of the following the wires and connectors:

a. Oil pressure connector

b. High tension cord at the coil

c. Neutral start switch and transfer connectors near the starter

d. Front differential lock connector

e. Starter wire and connector

f. Starter ground strap

g. Oxygen sensor connectors

h. Alternator wire and connector

i. Cooling fan connector

j. Check connector

34. Install the radiator and the coolant reservoir tank.

35. Install the air intake hose, air flow meter and air cleaner. Connect the accelerator and throttle cables.

36. Refill the engine with oil and the radiator with coolant. Install the engine undercover. Install the battery.

37. Install and adjust the hood.

38. Install the battery, start the engine and road test the vehicle.

3VZ–E ENGINE

1. Disconnect the battery cables and remove the battery.

2. Remove the engine undercover.

3. Disconnect the windshield washer hose and then remove the hood. Scribe matchmarks around the hinges for easy installation.

4. Drain the engine coolant from the radiator and the cylinder block.

5. Raise and safely support the vehicle. Drain the engine oil. Drain the automatic transmission fluid, on vehicles so equipped.

6. Lower the vehicle. Disconnect the air cleaner hose and then remove the air cleaner.

7. Remove the radiator.

8. Remove all drive belts and then remove the fluid coupling and fan pulley.

9. Tag and disconnect the following wires and connectors:

a. Left side and rear ground straps

b. Alternator connector and wire

c. Igniter connector

d. Oil pressure switch connector

e. ECU connectors

f. VSV connectors

g. Starter relay connector (manual transmission only)

h. Solenoid resistor connector

i. Check connector

j. Air conditioning compressor connector

10. Tag and disconnect the following hoses:

a. Power steering hoses at the gas filter and air pipe

b. Brake booster hose

c. Cruise control vacuum hose (if equipped)

d. Charcoal canister hose at the canister

e. VSV vacuum hoses.

11. Disconnect the accelerator, throttle and cruise control cables where applicable.

12. Unbolt the power steering pump and position it out of the way with the hydraulic lines still connected.

13. Properly discharge the air conditioning system. Remove the air conditioning compressor if equipped.

14. Disaconnect the clutch release cylinder hose (manual transmission only).

15. Disconnect the 2 heater hoses.

16. Disconnect and plug the fuel inlet and outlet lines.

17. Remove the shift levers (manual transmission only).

18. Raise and safely support the vehicle. Remove the rear driveshaft.

19. Disconnect the manual shift linkage (automatic transmission only).

20. Disconnect the speedometer cable, don't lose the felt dust protector and washers.

21. Remove the transfer case undercover. Remove the stabilizer bar.

22. Remove the front driveshaft. Remove the front exhaust pipe.

23. Remove the No. 1 front floor heat insulator and the brake tube heat insulator.

24. Remove the rear engine mount bolts, raise the transmission slightly with a floor jack and then remove the 4 bolts from the side member and remove the No. 2 frame crossmember. Lower the vehicle.

25. Attach an engine hoist chain to the lifting brackets on the engine. Remove the engine mount nuts and bolts and slowly lift the engine/transmission out of the vehicle.

To install:

26. Slowly lower the engine assembly into the engine compartment.

27. Raise the transmission onto the crossmember with a floor jack.
28. Align the holes in the engine mounts and the frame, install the bolts and then remove the engine hoist chain.
29. Raise the transmission slightly and tighten the No. 2 frame crossmember-to-side frame bolts to 70 ft. lbs. (95 Nm). Lower the transmission and tighten the 4 rear engine mount bolts to 9 ft. lbs. (13 Nm).
30. Install the brake tube and front floor heat insulators. Reconnect the exhaust pipe.
31. Install the No. 1 frame crossmember. Install the front driveshaft, stabilizer bar and the transfer case undercover.
32. Connect the speedometer cable. Connect the manual shift linkage (automatic transmission only).
33. Install the rear driveshaft. Install the shift levers (manual transmission only).
34. Install the fuel inlet and outlet lines. Connect the heater hoses.
35. Connect the clutch release cylinder hose. Install the air conditioning compressor.
36. Install the power steering pump and connect the ground strap.
37. Connect the throttle, cruise control and accelerator cables.
38. Connect the following hoses:
a. Power steering hoses at the gas filter and air pipe
b. Brake booster hose
c. Cruise control vacuum hose (if equipped)
d. Charcoal canister hose at the canister
e. VSV vacuum hoses.
39. Install the fan pulley, belt guide, fluid coupling and drive belt. Connect the following wires:
a. Left side and rear ground straps
b. Alternator connector and wire
c. Igniter connector
d. Oil pressure switch connector
e. ECU connectors
f. VSV connectors
g. Starter relay connector (manual transmission only)
h. Solenoid resistor connector
i. Check connector
j. Air conditioning compressor connector
40. Install the air conditioning belt. Install the power steering pump and connect the ground strap.
41. Install the radiator and shroud. Install the air cleaner. Refill the engine with oil and the radiator with coolant.
42. Install the engine undercover. Install the battery. Install and adjust the hood.
43. Install the battery, start the truck and road test it.

Cylinder Head

Removal and Installation

22R ENGINE

1. Disconnect the negative battery cable.
2. Drain the cooling system.
3. Mark all vacuum hoses and disconnect them.
4. Remove the air cleaner assembly, complete with hoses, from the carburetor.

NOTE: Cover the carburetor with a clean shop cloth so that nothing can fall into it.

5. Remove all linkages, fuel lines, etc., from the carburetor, cylinder head, and manifolds. Remove the wire supports.
6. Mark the spark plug leads and disconnect them from the plugs.
7. Matchmark the distributor housing and block. Disconnect the primary lead and remove the distributor.
8. Unfasten the 14mm nuts which secure the cam cover. Remove the cam cover.

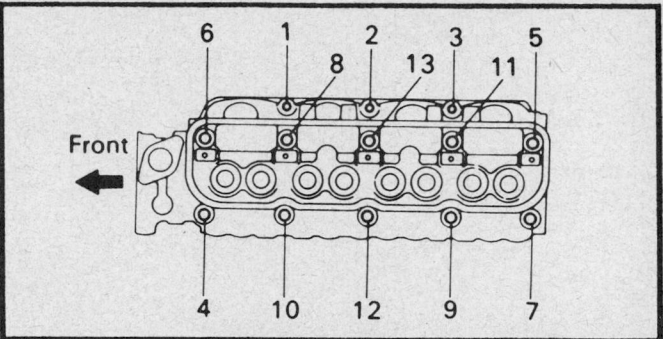
Cylinder head bolt removal sequence—22R, 22R-E and 22R-TE engines

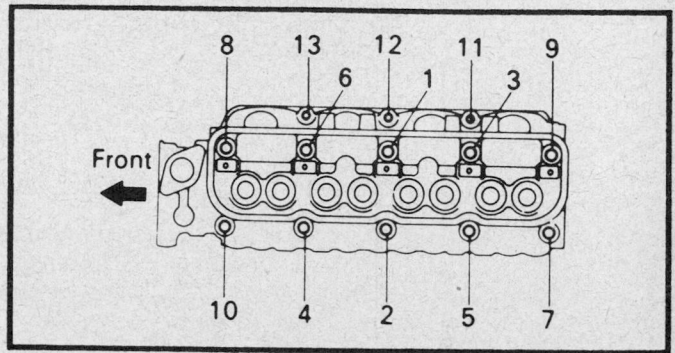
Cylinder head bolt installation sequence—22R, 22R-E and 22R-TE engines

9. Remove the rubber camshaft seals. Turn the crankshaft until the No. 1 piston is at TDC on its compression stroke. Match mark the timing sprocket to the cam chain, and remove the semi-circular lug. Using a 19mm wrench, remove the cam sprocket bolt. Slide the distributor drive gear and spacer off the cam and wire the cam sprocket in place.
10. Remove the timing chain cover 14mm bolt at the front of the head. This must be done before the head bolts are removed. Remove the exhaust pipe flange nuts and disconnect the pipe.
11. Remove the cylinder head bolts in the correct order. Improper removal could cause head damage.
12. Using pry bars applied evenly at the front and the rear of the valve rocker assembly, pry the assembly off its mounting dowels.
13. Lift the head off its dowels. Do not pry it off.
14. Drain the engine oil from the crankcase after the head has been removed, because the oil will become contaminated with coolant while the head is being removed.

To install:

15. Apply liquid sealer to the front corners of the block and install the head gasket.
16. Lower the head over the locating dowels. Do not attempt to slide it into place.
17. Rotate the camshaft so that the sprocket aligning pin is at the top. Remove the wire and hold the cam sprocket. Manually rotate the engine so that the sprocket hole is also at the top. Wire the sprocket in place.
18. Install the rocker arm assembly over its positioning dowels.
19. Tighten the cylinder head bolts evenly, in 3 stages and in the correct order.
20. Install the timing chain cover bolt and tighten it to 7–11 ft. lbs.
21. Remove the wire and fit the sprocket over the camshaft dowel. If the chain won't allow the sprocket to reach, rotate the

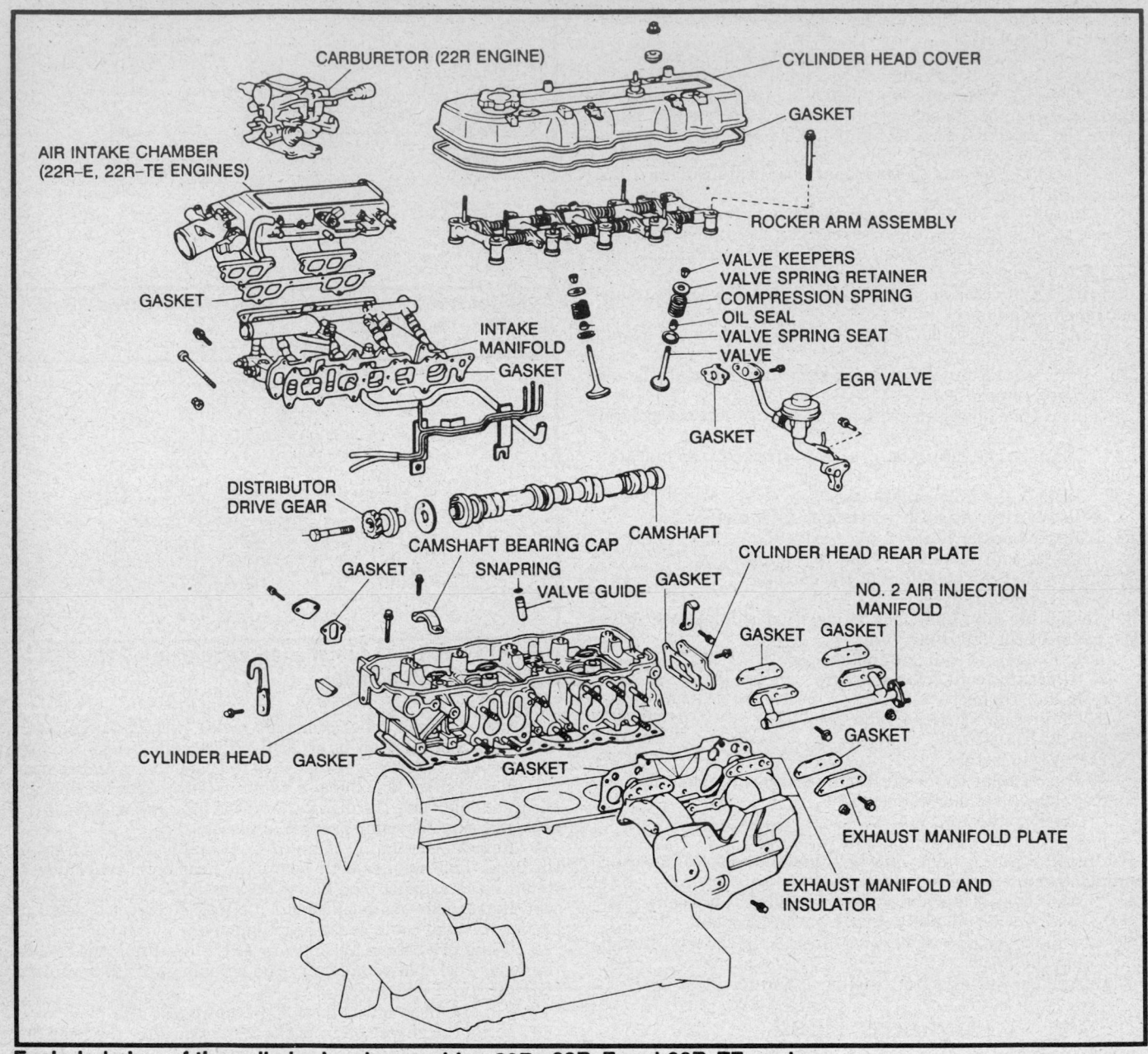

CARBURETOR (22R ENGINE)

CYLINDER HEAD COVER

GASKET

AIR INTAKE CHAMBER
(22R-E, 22R-TE ENGINES)

ROCKER ARM ASSEMBLY

VALVE KEEPERS
VALVE SPRING RETAINER
COMPRESSION SPRING
OIL SEAL
VALVE SPRING SEAT
VALVE

GASKET

INTAKE
MANIFOLD
GASKET

EGR VALVE

GASKET

DISTRIBUTOR
DRIVE GEAR

CAMSHAFT BEARING CAP   CAMSHAFT

GASKET   SNAPRING   CYLINDER HEAD REAR PLATE

VALVE GUIDE   GASKET   NO. 2 AIR INJECTION
MANIFOLD

GASKET   GASKET

CYLINDER HEAD   GASKET   GASKET

GASKET

EXHAUST MANIFOLD PLATE

EXHAUST MANIFOLD AND
INSULATOR

Exploded view of the cylinder head assembly—22R, 22R-E and 22R-TE engines

crankshaft back and forth, while lifting up on the chain and sprocket.

22. Install the distributor drive gear and tighten the crankshaft bolt to 51–65 ft. lbs.

23. Set the No. 1 piston at TDC of its compression stroke and adjust the valves.

24. After completing valve adjustment, rotate the crankshaft 352 degrees, so that the 8 BTDC mark on the pulley aligns with the pointer.

25. Install the distributor.

26. Install the spark plugs and leads.

27. Make sure that the oil drain plug is installed. Fill the engine with oil after installing the rubber cam seals. Pour the oil over the distributor drive gear and the valve rockers.

28. Install the rocker cover and tighten the bolts to 8–11 ft. lbs.

29. Connect all the vacuum hoses and electrical leads which were removed during disassembly. Install the spark plug lead supports. Fill the cooling system. Install the air cleaner.

30. Tighten the exhaust pipe-to-manifold flange bolts to 25–33 ft. lbs.

31. Reconnect the battery. Start the engine and allow it to reach normal operating temperature. Check and adjust the timing and valve clearance. Adjust the idle speed and mixture. Road test the vehicle.

22R-E AND 22R-TE ENGINES

1. Relieve the fuel system pressure. Disconnect the negative battery cable.

2. Drain the coolant from the radiator and the cylinder block. Raise and safely support the vehicle. Drain the engine oil.

3. Remove the turbocharger on the 22R-TE engine.

4. Disconnect and remove the air cleaner hose on the 22R-E engine.

5. Disconnect the oxygen sensor wire. Remove the nuts attaching the manifold to the exhaust pipe and then separate them.

6. Remove the oil dipstick. Remove the distributor with the spark plug leads attached.

7. Disconnect the upper radiator hose and the heater hoses where they attach to the engine and then position them out of the way.

8. Disconnect the actuator cable, the accelerator cable and the throttle cable for the automatic transmission at their bracket.

9. Tag and disconnect the following:
   a. Both PCV vacuum hoses
   b. Brake booster hose
   c. Actuator hose (if equipped with cruise control)
   d. Air control valve hoses
   e. Air control valve.

10. Tag and disconnect the EGR vacuum modulator hoses and then remove the modulator itself along with the bracket.

11. Tag and disconnect the following:
   a. Green and brown BVSV hoses
   b. Vacuum advance hoses
   c. The 2 air valve hoses; one at the throttle body, the other at the air chamber
   d. Air control valve hose (if equipped with air conditioning)
   e. Pressure regulator hose at the air chamber
   f. Cold start injector pipe and wire
   g. Throttle position sensor wire.

12. Remove the bolt holding the EGR valve to the air chamber. Disconnect the chamber from the stay. Remove the air chamber-to-intake manifold bolts and then lift off the chamber with the throttle body.

13. Disconnect the fuel return hose.

14. Tag and disconnect the following:
   a. Water temperature sender gauge wire
   b. Temperature sensor wire
   c. Start injection time switch wire
   d. Fuel injector wires.

15. Remove the pulsation damper. Remove the bolt holding the fuel hose to the delivery pipe and then disconnect and remove the fuel hose.

16. Disconnect the wire and hose and then remove the air valve from the intake manifold.

17. Disconnect the bypass hose at the intake manifold on the 22R–E engine. On the 22R–TE engine, disconnect the oil cooler hose at the manifold.

18. If equipped with power steering, remove the pump and position it out of the way without disconnecting the hydraulic lines.

19. Remove the 4 nuts and then remove the cylinder head cover.

20. Remove the rubber camshaft seals. Turn the crankshaft until the No. 1 piston is at TDC of its compression stroke. Matchmark the timing sprocket to the timing chain and then remove the semi-circular plug. Using a 19mm wrench, remove the camshaft sprocket bolt. Slide the distributor drive gear and spacer off the camshaft and wire the cam sprocket in place.

21. Remove the timing chain cover bolt in front of the cylinder head.

NOTE: This must be done before the cylinder head bolts are removed.

22. Remove the cylinder head bolts gradually, in 2 or 3 stages, in the correct order.

23. Using pry bars applied evenly at the front and rear of the rocker arm assembly, pry the assembly off of its mounting dowels.

24. Lift the cylinder head off of its mounting dowels.

To install:

25. Apply liquid sealer to the front corners of the block and install the head gasket.

26. Lower the head over the locating dowels. Do not attempt to slide it into place.

27. Rotate the camshaft so that the sprocket aligning pin is at the top. Remove the wire and hold the cam sprocket. Manually rotate the engine so that the sprocket hole is also at the top. Wire the sprocket in place.

28. Install the rocker arm assembly over its positioning dowels.

29. Tighten the cylinder head bolts evenly, in 3 stages and in the correct order.

30. Install the timing chain cover bolt and tighten it to 7–11 ft. lbs.

31. Remove the wire and fit the sprocket over the camshaft dowel. If the chain won't allow the sprocket to reach, rotate the crankshaft back and forth, while lifting up on the chain and sprocket.

32. Install the distributor drive gear and tighten the crankshaft bolt to 51–65 ft. lbs.

33. Set the No. 1 piston at TDC of its compression stroke and adjust the valves.

34. After completing valve adjustment, rotate the crankshaft 352 degrees, so that the 8 BTDC mark on the pulley aligns with the pointer.

35. Install the distributor.

36. Install the spark plugs and leads.

37. Make sure that the oil drain plug is installed. Fill the engine with oil after installing the rubber cam seals. Pour the oil over the distributor drive gear and the valve rockers.

38. Install the rocker cover and tighten the bolts to 8–11 ft. lbs.

39. Connect all the vacuum hoses and electrical leads which were removed during disassembly. Install the spark plug lead supports. Fill the cooling system. Install the air cleaner.

40. Tighten the exhaust pipe-to-manifold flange bolts to 25–33 ft. lbs.

41. Reconnect the battery. Start the engine and allow it to reach normal operating temperature. Check and adjust the timing and valve clearance. Adjust the idle speed and mixture. Road test the vehicle.

4Y–E AND 4Y–EC ENGINES

1. Disconnect the negative battery terminal from the battery.

2. Remove the right-front seat and the engine service hole cover.

3. Raise and safely support the vehicle. Drain the engine coolant at the radiator. Drain the engine oil. Lower the vehicle.

4. If equipped with power steering, perform the following:
   a. Remove the air hoses from the air control valve
   b. Drain the fluid from the reservoir tank
   c. Disconnect the return hose from the pump
   d. Disconnect the pressure hose from the pump
   e. Remove the drive belt, the pulley nut, the pulley, the Woodruff key, the mounting bolts and the pump

5. Remove the exhaust pipe and the bracket. Remove the air cleaner pipe and the hoses.

6. Disconnect the accelerator cable with the bracket from the throttle body.

7. Disconnect the water temperature sender gauge connector from the cylinder head.

8. Disconnect the following EFI connectors from the:
   a. The water thermo sensor
   b. The cold start injector time switch
   c. The cold start injector
   d. The air valve
   e. The throttle position sensor
   f. The oxygen sensor
   g. The water temperature switch

9. Disconnect the following hoses from the:
   a. The radiator inlet
   b. The radiator breather

c. The reserve tank
d. The heater outlet
e. The PCV valve
f. The water bypass
g. The brake booster vacuum
h. The charcoal canister
i. Label and disconnect the emission control

10. Remove the throttle body from the air intake chamber.

11. Remove the EGR valve nuts from the intake chamber and the exhaust manifold-to-EGR valve union.

12. Disconnect the cold start injector pipe, the water by-pass hoses and the pressure regulator hose.

13. Using a 12mm offset box wrench, remove the air intake chamber brackets, then, the chamber with the air valve.

14. Remove the wire clamp bolts and the injector connectors from the injectors.

15. Remove the exhaust manifold bracket, the heater pipe bracket, the fuel inlet pipe union bolt from the fuel filter and the fuel outlet hose.

16. Remove the spark plugs and the tubes.

17. Remove the cap nuts, the seal washers, the cylinder head cover and the gasket.

18. Remove the rocker arm shaft assembly nuts/bolts a little at a time, in 3–4 steps. Remove the push rods, keeping them in order.

19. Remove the cylinder head bolts, a little at a time, in 3 passes. Lift the cylinder head off of the engine.

20. Remove the valve lifters from the cylinder block.

To install:

21. Clean the gasket mounting surfaces.

22. To install, use new gaskets and reverse the removal procedures. Torque the cylinder head bolts (in 3 passes) to 65 ft. lbs. (14mm) or 14 ft. lbs. (12mm), the rocker arm shaft-to-cylinder head bolts (in 3 passes) to 17 ft. lbs., the spark plugs to 13 ft. lbs., the air intake chamber bolts to 9 ft. lbs., the throttle body-to-intake chamber to 9 ft. lbs. and the exhaust pipe-to-exhaust manifold to 29 ft. lbs.

23. Adjust the drive belts.

24. Refill the cooling system and the engine with oil.

25. Check and/or adjust the timing.

NOTE: Use special tool No. 09270–71010, or its equivalent, to hold the push rods in position when installing the push rods.

2F ENGINE

1. Disconnect the negative battery cable and drain the cooling system.

2. Remove the air cleaner assembly from its bracket.

3. Detach the accelerator cable from its support on the cylinder head cover and also from the carburetor throttle arm.

4. Remove the choke cable and fuel lines from the carburetor.

5. Remove the water hose bracket from the cylinder head cover.

6. Unfasten the water hose clamps an remove the hoses from the water pump and the water valve. Detach the heater temperature control cable from the water valve.

7. Disconnect the PCV line from the cylinder head cover.

8. Disconnect the vacuum lines, which run from the vacuum switching valve, at the various components of the emission control system.

9. Raise and safely support the vehicle. Drain the engine oil. Unfasten the oil lines from the oil filter and remove the filter assembly from the manifold. Lower the vehicle.

10. Detach the vacuum valve solenoid wire from the coil.

11. Disconnect any remaining lines from the carburetor and remove the carburetor from the manifold.

12. Unfasten the alternator adjusting link and then remove the drive belt and the alternator.

13. Disconnect the distributor vacuum line from the distributor. Remove the wire from its supports on the head.

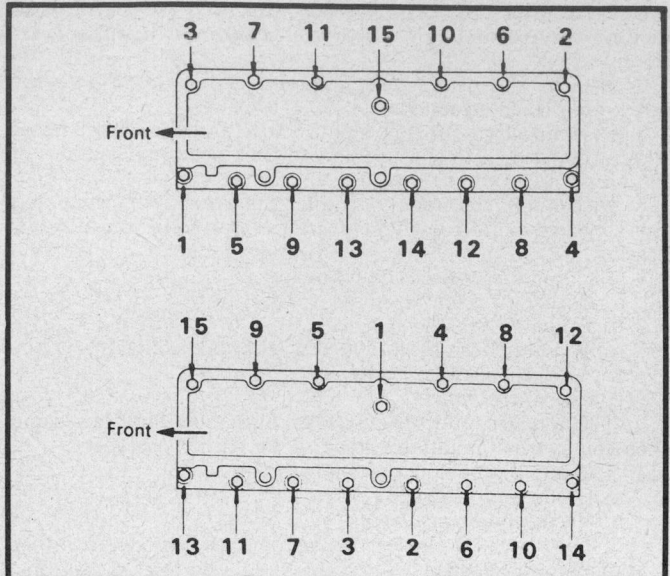

Cylinder head bolt removal sequence and installation sequence – 2F engine

14. Disconnect the carburetor fuel line from the fuel pump. Remove the line.

15. Disconnect the spark plug and coil cables, after marking their respective locations.

16. Unfasten the primary wire from the distributor. Remove the distributor clamp bolts and remove the distributor.

17. Remove the oil gauge sending unit.

18. Remove the coil from its bracket on the cylinder head.

19. Remove the fuel pump.

20. Remove the oil filter tube clamping bolt from the valve lifter (side) cover. Drive the oil filler tube out of the cylinder block

21. Remove the combination intake/exhaust manifold from the cylinder block.

22. Take off the cylinder head cover and its gasket.

23. Unfasten the oil delivery union, spring, and sleeve from the valve rocker shafts.

24. Unfasten the securing nuts and bolts from the valve rocker shaft supports. Withdraw the rocker assembly.

25. Withdraw the pushrods from their bores. Be sure to keep them in the same order in which they were removed.

26. Remove the valve lifter (side) cover and gasket.

27. Withdraw the valve lifters from the block.

NOTE: The valve lifters should be kept, with their respective pushrods, in the sequence in which they were removed.

28. Unfasten the oil delivery union from the oil feel pipe.

29. Loosen the cylinder head bolts in stages, in the correct sequence.

30. Lift off the cylinder head and the gasket.

To install:

31. Clean the gasket mounting surfaces of both the cylinder head and block.

32. Place a new head gasket over the dowels on the block.

33. Lower the cylinder head on to the block.

34. Tighten the bolts, in stages, and in the proper sequence, to the specified torque.

35. Install the oil feed pipe.

36. Install the valve lifters.

37. Install the valve rocker assembly, oil delivery union, spring and connecting sleeve in the head. Tighten the rocker as-

sembly support nuts and bolts to the following torque specifications, in several stages:

   10mm nuts and bolts: 24–30 ft. lbs.

   8mm bolts: 14–22 ft. lbs.

38. Adjust the valves to the cold specifications (each piston TDC of its compression stroke).

NOTE: Adjust the valve clearance again after the engine is assembled and warmed up.

39. The rest of the cylinder head installation is performed in the reverse order of the removal procedure.

3F–E ENGINE

1. Drain the coolant.
2. Disconnect the negative battery cable.
3. Scribe matchmarks around the hood hinges and then remove the hood.
4. Disconnect the accelerator and throttle cables.
5. Remove the air intake hose, air flow meter and air cleaner cap.
6. Unbolt the power steering pump and position it out of the way without disconnecting the hydraulic lines.
7. Unbolt the air conditioning compressor and position it out of the way without disconnecting the refrigerant lines.
8. Remove the power steering pump and air conditioning compressor brackets.
9. Disconnect the high tension leads from the spark plugs and the coil.
10. Disconnect and remove the heater water (oil cooler) pipe.
11. Disconnect the upper radiator hose.
12. Disconnect and plug the fuel lines.
13. Disconnect the exhaust pipe at the manifold.
14. Remove the air pump.
15. Remove the fuel delivery pipe along with the fuel injectors.
16. Remove the air injection manifold.
17. Remove the intake and exhaust manifolds.
18. Disconnect the water bypass hose at the water outlet and then remove the outlet.
19. Remove the spark plugs.
20. Remove the cylinder head cover and its gasket.
21. Loosen the bolts and nuts that attach the rocker shaft assembly in several stages and then remove the rocker shaft.
22. Remove the pushrods.
23. Remove the cylinder head bolts in the reverse of the tightening sequence. Remove the air pump bracket and engine hanger.
24. Lift the cylinder head off of its mounting dowels.

To install:

25. Install the cylinder head on the cylinder block using a new gasket.
26. Lightly coat the threads of the cylinder head bolts with engine oil and then install them into the head. Tighten in several stages, to the correct torque.
27. Install the pushrods in the order that they were removed.
28. Position the rocker shaft assembly on the cylinder head and align the rocker arm adjusting screws with the heads of the pushrods. Tighten the mounting bolts with a 12mm head to 17 ft. lbs. (24 Nm); tighten the bolts with a 14mm head to 25 ft. lbs. (33 Nm).
29. Adjust the valve clearance and install the spark plugs. Install the cylinder head cover and tighten the cap nuts to 78 inch lbs. (8.8 Nm).
30. Install the water outlet and connect the bypass hose. Tighten the bolts to 18 ft. lbs. (25 Nm).
31. Install the intake and exhaust manifolds using a new gasket. Make sure the front mark on the gasket is towards the front of the engine.
32. Install the heat insulators and the manifold stay.
33. Install the air injection manifold and tighten the union nuts and clamp bolts to 15 ft. lbs. (21 Nm).

34. Install the fuel injector/delivery pipe assembly.
35. Install the air pump and connect the air hose.
36. Connect the exhaust pipe to the manifold. Use a new gasket and tighten the bolts to 46 ft. lbs. (62 Nm).
37. Connect the fuel lines and the upper radiator hose.
38. Install the heater water pipe.
39. Connect the high tension cords.
40. Install the air conditioning compressor and the power steering pump. Remember to adjust the belt tension later.
41. Install the air intake hose, the air flow meter and the air cleaner cap.
42. Connect and adjust the accelerator and throttle cables.
43. Connect the battery cable, fill the engine with coolant, start the engine and check for any leaks. Road test the vehicle.

3VZ–E ENGINE

1. Disconnect the negative battery cable.
2. Remove the air cleaner hose and case.
3. Drain the engine coolant.
4. Remove the radiator.
5. Unbolt the power steering pump and position it out of the way with the hoses still attached.
6. Remove all drive belts and then remove the fluid coupling and fan pulley.
7. Tag and disconnect all wires and connectors that will interfere with cylinder head removal.
8. Disconnect the following hoses:
   a. Power steering air hoses
   b. Brake booster hose
   c. Cruise control vacuum hose
   d. Charcoal canister has at the canister
   e. VSV vacuum hose.
9. Disconnect the accelerator, throttle and cruise control cables.
10. Disconnect the clutch release cylinder hose (manual transmission only).
11. Disconnect the heater hoses and the fuel lines.
12. Remove the left side scuff plate and disconnect the O_2 sensor and then remove the front exhaust pipe.
13. Remove the timing belt as detailed later in this chapter.
14. Remove the distributor with the spark plug leads attached; position it out of the way.
15. Remove the air intake chamber.
16. Disconnect the connectors and then remove the engine wire.
17. Remove the Nos. 2 and 3 fuel pipes.
18. Remove the No. 4 timing belt cover.
19. Remove the No. 2 idler pulley and the No. 3 timing belt cover.
20. Disconnect the hose and remove the water bypass outlet.
21. Remove the intake manifold.
22. Remove the exhaust crossover pipe.

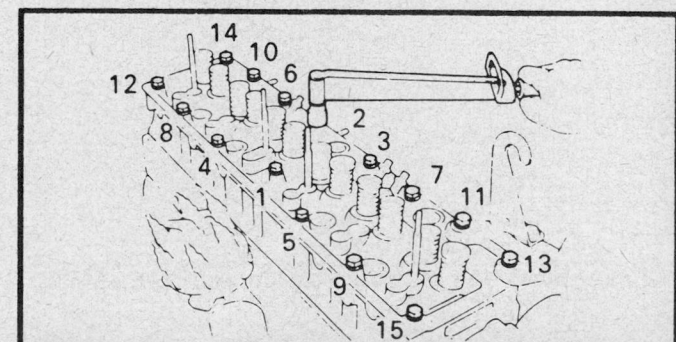

Cylinder head bolt installation sequence – 3F–E engine

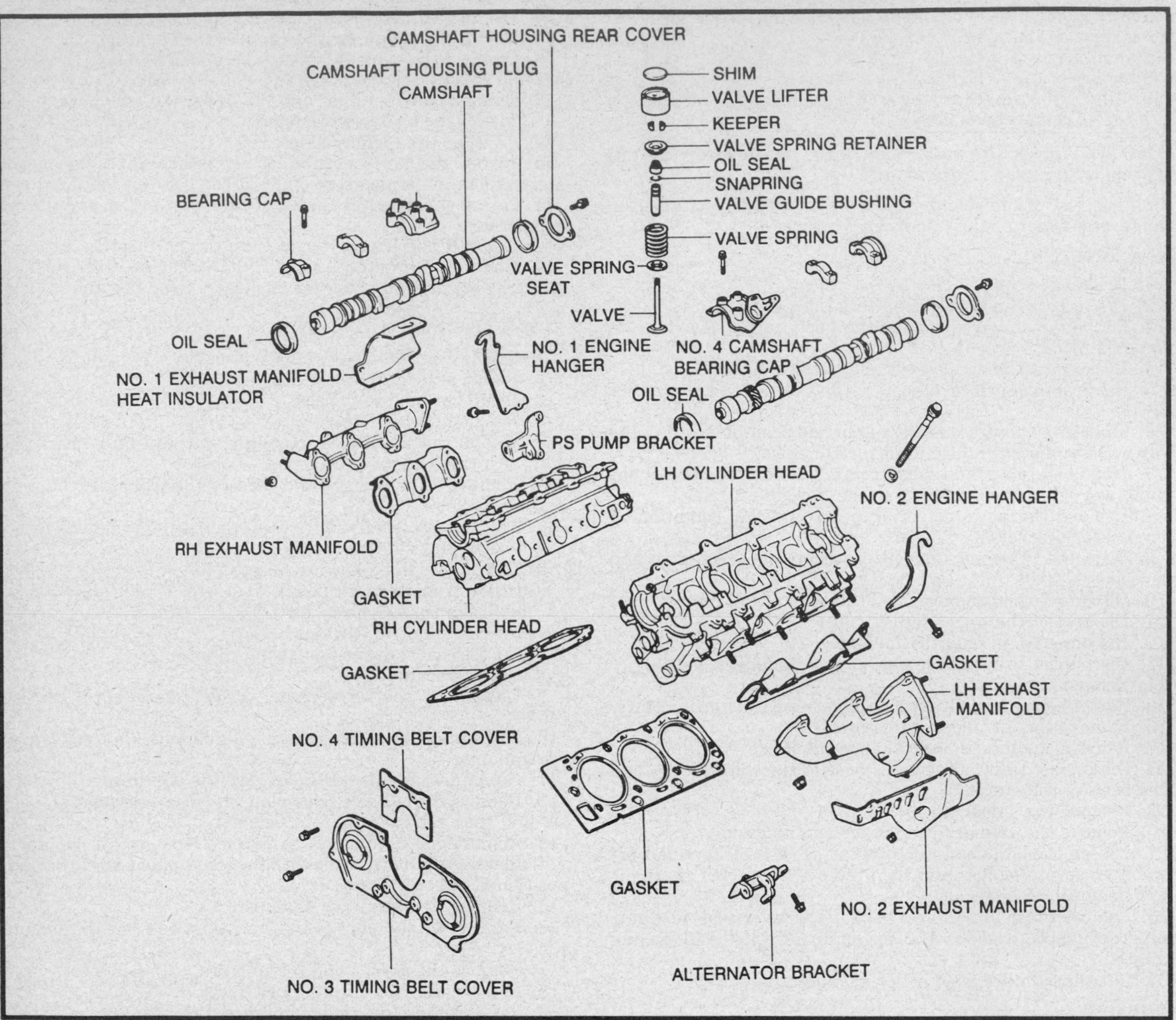

CAMSHAFT HOUSING REAR COVER
CAMSHAFT HOUSING PLUG
CAMSHAFT
SHIM
VALVE LIFTER
KEEPER
VALVE SPRING RETAINER
OIL SEAL
SNAPRING
VALVE GUIDE BUSHING
BEARING CAP
VALVE SPRING
VALVE SPRING SEAT
VALVE
OIL SEAL
NO. 1 ENGINE HANGER
NO. 4 CAMSHAFT BEARING CAP
NO. 1 EXHAUST MANIFOLD HEAT INSULATOR
OIL SEAL
PS PUMP BRACKET
LH CYLINDER HEAD
NO. 2 ENGINE HANGER
RH EXHAUST MANIFOLD
GASKET
RH CYLINDER HEAD
GASKET
GASKET
LH EXHAST MANIFOLD
NO. 4 TIMING BELT COVER
GASKET
NO. 2 EXHAUST MANIFOLD
ALTERNATOR BRACKET
NO. 3 TIMING BELT COVER

Exploded view of the cylinder head assembly – 3VZ-E engine

2
8
6
4
1
5
7
9
3

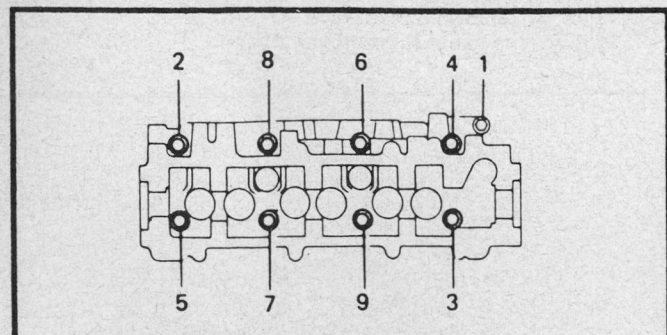

Cylinder head bolt removal sequence–3VZ-E engine

11
9
7
5
1
3
12
10
8
6
2
4

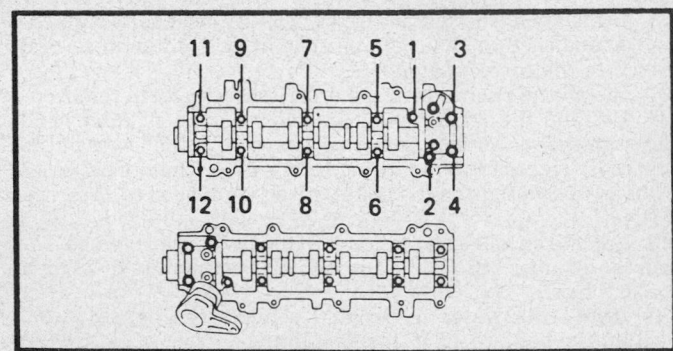

Camshaft bearing cap loosening sequence – 3VZ-E engine

Right side:

23. Remove the reed valve with the No. 1 air injection manifold.
24. Remove the water bypass pipe mounting bolt.
25. Remove the cylinder head cover.
26. Remove the camshaft.
27. Loosen the cylinder head bolts in several stages, in the op-

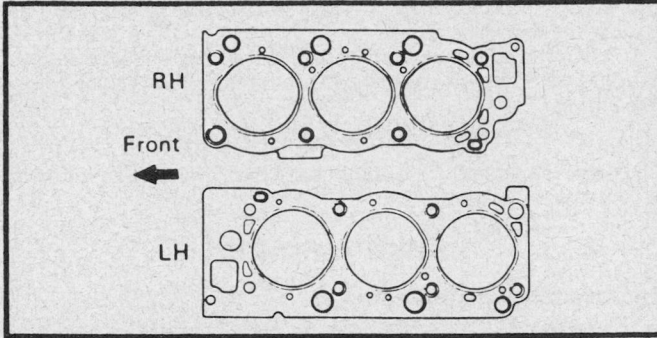

Cylinder head gasket installation – 3VZ–E engine

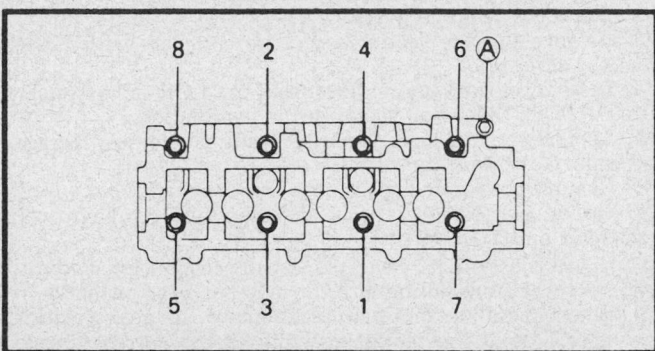

Cylinder head bolt tightening sequence – 3VZ–E engine

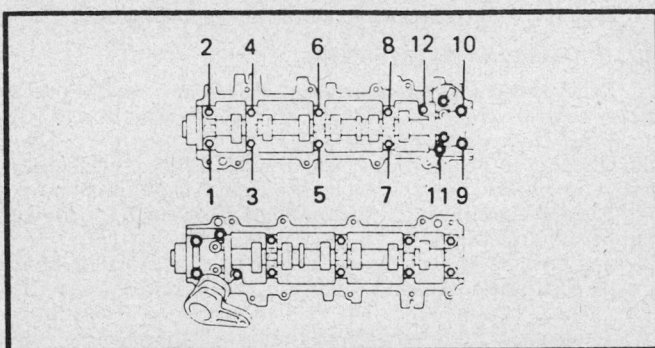

Camshaft bearing cap bolt tightening sequence – 3VZ–E engine

posite order of the tightening sequence. Remove the air pump bracket and engine hanger.

28. Lift the cylinder head off of its mounting dowels, do not pry it off.

Left side:

29. Remove the alternator.

30. Remove the oil dipstick guide tube.

31. Remove the cylinder head cover.

32. Remove the camshaft.

33. Loosen the cylinder head bolts in several stages, in the opposite order of the tightening sequence. Remove the air pump bracket and engine hanger.

34. Lift the cylinder head off of its mounting dowels, do not pry it off.

To install:

35. Install the cylinder head on the cylinder block using a new gasket.

36. Lightly coat the threads of the cylinder head bolts with engine oil and then install them into the head. Tighten them in

several stages, in the correct order. After the initial tightening, mark the front side the the top of the bolt with paint. Tighten the bolts an additional 90 degrees (¼ turn) and check that the mark is now facing the side of the head. Tighten the bolts an additional 90 degrees and check that the mark is now facing the rear of the head. Install the bolt (A) and tighten it to 27 ft. lbs. (37 Nm).

37. Install the camshaft.

38. Install the alternator and the water bypass pipe mounting bolt.

39. Install the reed valve with the No. 1 injection manifold.

40. Install the oil dipstick tube.

41. Install the crossover pipe and tighten it to 29 ft. lbs. (39 Nm).

42. Connect the oxygen sensor wire.

43. Install the intake manifold with new gaskets and tighten the mounting bolts to 29 ft. lbs. (39 Nm).

44. Install the water bypass outlet and tighten the bolts to 13 ft. lbs. (18 Nm).

45. Install the fuel delivery pipes and injectors.

46. Install the No. 2 idler pulley. Install the Nos. 3 and 4 timing belt covers and tighten the bolts to 74 inch lbs. (8.3 Nm).

47. Install the fuel pipes and tighten the union bolts to 22 ft. lbs. (29 Nm).

48. Install the timing belt. Install the cylinder head covers.

49. Install the air intake chamber and tighten the nuts and bolts to 13 ft. lbs. (18 Nm).

50. Install the EGR valve and connect all hoses and lines. Install the distributor and the front exhaust pipe.

51. Connect the fuel lines and heater hoses. Connect the clutch release cylinder hose.

52. Install the power steering pump. Connect all cables (and adjust), hoses and wires previously removed.

53. Install the fan pulley, fluid coupling and drive belts. Install the radiator.

54. Install the air cleaner hose, refill the engine with coolant and connect the battery cable.

Valve Lash

Adjustment

22R, 22R–E AND 22R–TE ENGINES

1. Start the engine and allow it to reach normal operating temperatures (above 175 degrees F).

2. Stop the engine. Remove the air cleaner assembly, the hoses and the bracket, then any cables, hoses, wires and etc., which are attached to the valve cover. Remove the valve cover.

3. Set the No. 1 cylinder to TDC of the compression stroke. Place a wrench on the crankshaft pulley bolt and turn the engine until the notch on the crankshaft pulley is aligned with the 0 degree mark on the timing plate; the engine is at TDC.

NOTE: The rocker arms on cylinder No. 1 should be loose and the rocker arms on cylinder No. 4 should be tight.

4. With the engine hot, the valve clearances are 0.008 in. (intake) and 0.012 in. (exhaust).

NOTE: The clearance is measured with a feeler gauge between the valve stem and the adjusting screw.

5. To adjust the valve clearance, loosen the locknut and turn the adjusting screw until the specified clearance is obtained. Tighten the locknut and check the clearance again. Adjust the intake valves of No. 1 and 2 cylinders; the exhaust valves of No. 1 and 3 cylinders.

6. Turn the crankshaft one full revolution (360 degrees). Adjust the intake valves of No. 3 and 4 cylinders; the exhaust valves of No. 2 and 4 cylinders.

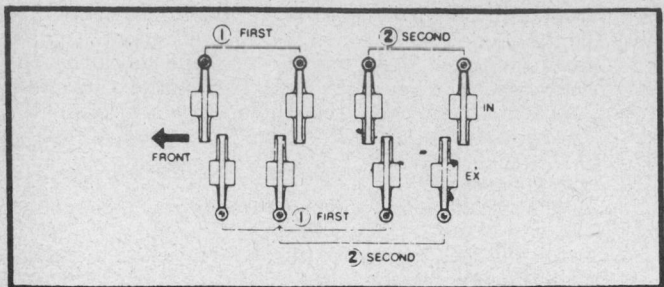

Valve adjustment sequence—22R, 22R–E and 22R–TE engines

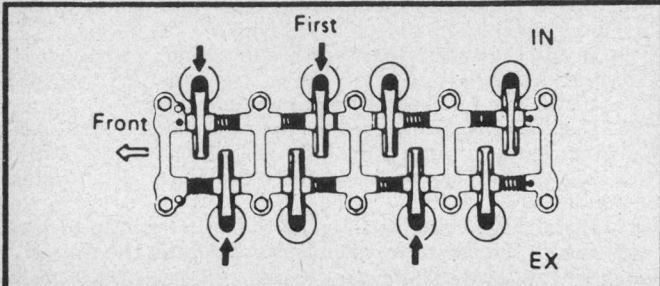

First step of the valve adjustment procedure—22R, 22R–E and 22R–TE engines

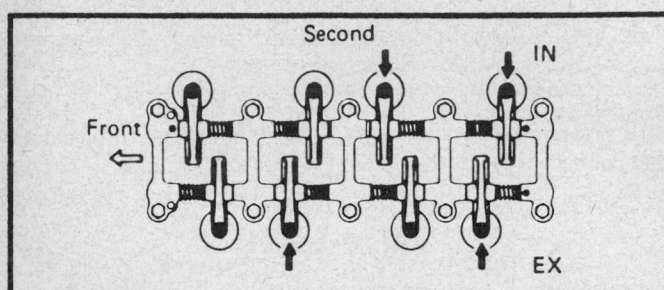

Second step of the valve adjustment procedure—22R, 22R–E and 22R–TE engines

7. To install the components, reverse the removal procedures.

NOTE: **The valves must be initially adjusted with the engine cold. After the initial engine start-up, allow the engine to reach normal operating temperature and adjust the valves to the correct hot clearances.**

2F ENGINE

1. Operate the engine until it reaches normal operating temperatures.
2. Remove the cylinder head cover.
3. Turn the crankshaft until the No. 1 cylinder is on the TDC of the compression stroke. The valves of the No. 1 cylinder must be loose.
4. To adjust the valve clearance, loosen the adjuster locknut and turn the adjusting screw.
5. Using a feeler gauge, check and/or adjust the clearance of valve No. 1, 2, 3, 5, 7 and 9 (numbered from the front).

NOTE: **The intake valve clearance is 0.008 in. (warm); the exhaust valve clearance is 0.014 in. (warm).**

6. Using a wrench on the crankshaft pulley bolt, turn the crankshaft one revolution, aligning the 0 degree mark on the timing pulley with the timing pointer.

7. Adjust the clearance of valve No. 4, 6, 8, 10, 11 and 12 (numbered from the front).
8. With the adjustment complete, install the removed components by reversing the removal procedures. Check and/or adjust the timing.

3F–E, 4Y–E, 4Y–EC AND 3VZ–E ENGINES

The valve tappets of these engines are hydraulic; no adjustment is necessary.

Intake Manifold

Removal and Installation

22R ENGINE

1. Disconnect the negative battery cable.
2. Drain the cooling system.
3. Remove the air cleaner assembly, complete with hoses, from the carburetor.
4. Disconnect the vacuum lines from the EGR valve and carburetor. Mark them first to aid in the installation.
5. Remove the fuel lines, electrical leads, accelerator linkage, and water hose from the carburetor.
6. Remove the water bypass hose from the manifold.
7. Unbolt and remove the intake manifold, complete with carburetor and EGR valve.
8. Cover the cylinder head ports with clean shop cloths to keep anything from falling into the cylinder head or block.
9. When installing the manifold, replace the gasket with a new one. Torque the mounting bolts to the correct torque. Tighten the bolts in several stages working from the inside bolts outward.
10. Connect the bypass line and all other lines and hoses.
11. Install the air cleaner and refill the cooling system.

22R–E AND 22R–TE ENGINES

1. Relieve the fuel system pressure. Disconnect the negative battery cable.
2. Drain the cooling system.
3. Disconnect the air intake hose from both the air cleaner assembly on one end and the air intake chamber on the other.
4. Tag and disconnect all vacuum lines attached to the intake chamber and manifold.
5. Tag and disconnect the wires to the cold start injector, throttle position sensor, and the water hoses from the throttle body.
6. Remove the EGR valve from the intake chamber.
7. Tag and disconnect the actuator cable, accelerator cable and throttle valve cable (if equipped) from the cable bracket on the intake chamber.
8. Unbolt the air intake chamber from the intake manifold and remove the chamber with the throttle body attached.
9. Disconnect the fuel hose from the fuel delivery pipe.
10. Tag and disconnect the air valve hose from the intake manifold.
11. Make sure all hoses, lines and wires are tagged for later installation and disconnected from the intake manifold. Unbolt the manifold from the cylinder head, removing the delivery pipe and injection nozzle with the manifold.

3VZ–E ENGINE

1. Relieve the fuel system pressure. Disconnect the negative battery cable.
2. Drain the cooling system.
3. Disconnect the air intake hose from both the air cleaner assembly on one end and the air intake chamber on the other.
4. Tag and disconnect all vacuum lines attached to the intake chamber and manifold.
5. Disconnect the throttle position sensor connector at the air chamber. Disconnect the PCV hose at the union.

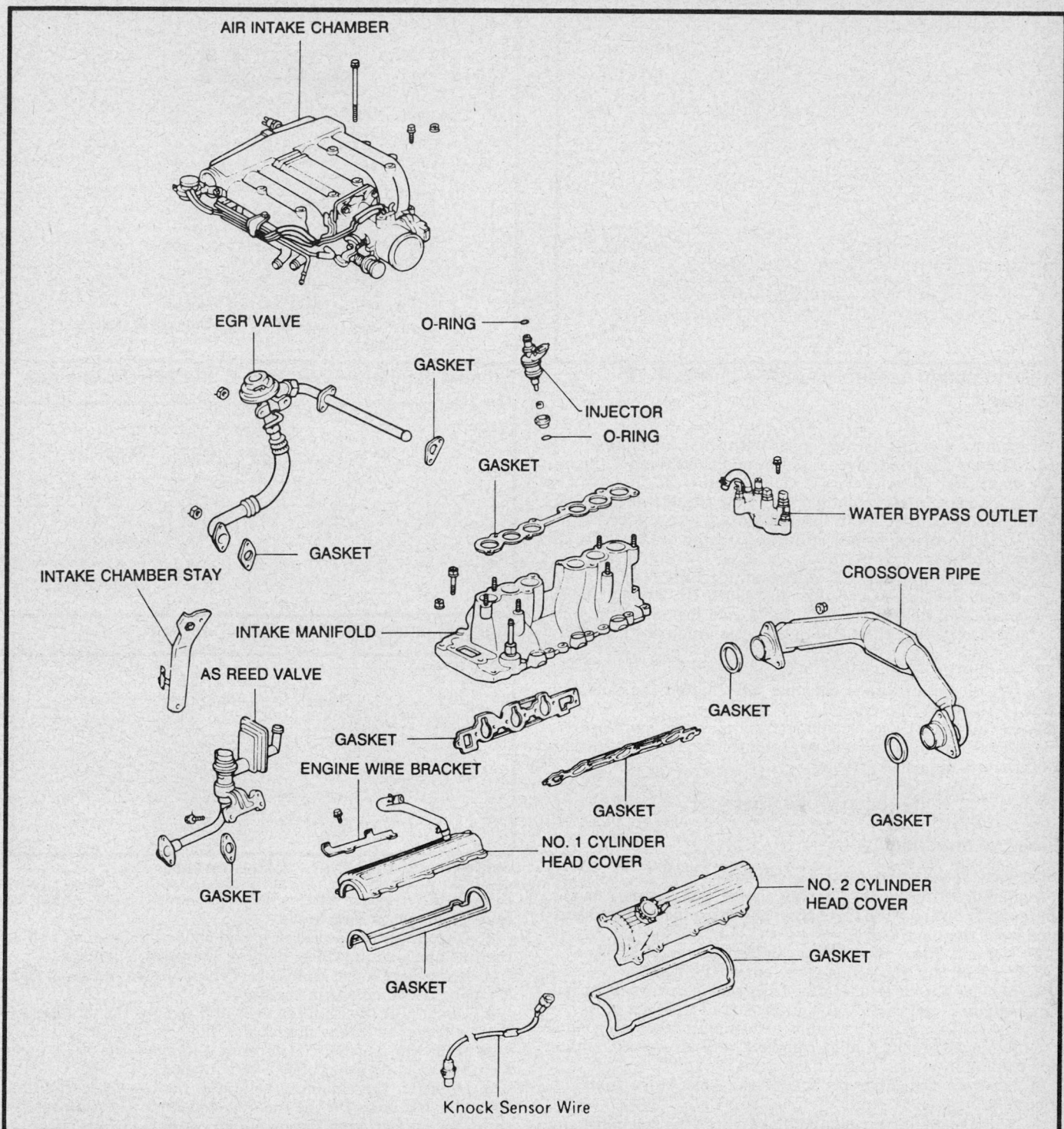

AIR INTAKE CHAMBER

EGR VALVE

O-RING

GASKET

INJECTOR

O-RING

GASKET

WATER BYPASS OUTLET

GASKET

INTAKE CHAMBER STAY

CROSSOVER PIPE

INTAKE MANIFOLD

AS REED VALVE

GASKET

GASKET

GASKET

ENGINE WIRE BRACKET

GASKET

GASKET

GASKET

NO. 1 CYLINDER HEAD COVER

NO. 2 CYLINDER HEAD COVER

GASKET

GASKET

Knock Sensor Wire

Intake manifold assembly — 3VZ–E engine

6. Disconnect the No. 4 water bypass hose at the manifold. Remove the No. 5 bypass hose at the water bypass pipe.

7. Disconnect the cold start injector and the vacuum hose at the fuel filter.

8. Remove the union bolt and gaskets, then remove the cold start injector tube.

9. Disconnect the EGR gas temperature sensor and the EGR vacuum hoses from the air pipe and the vacuum modulator.

10. Remove the EGR valve.

11. Disconnect the No. 1 air hose at the reed valve.

12. Remove the air intake chamber and then remove the engine wire.

13. Remove the union bolts and then remove the No. 2 and 3 fuel pipes.

14. Remove the No. 4 timing belt cover. Remove the the No. 2 idler pulley and the No. 3 timing belt cover.

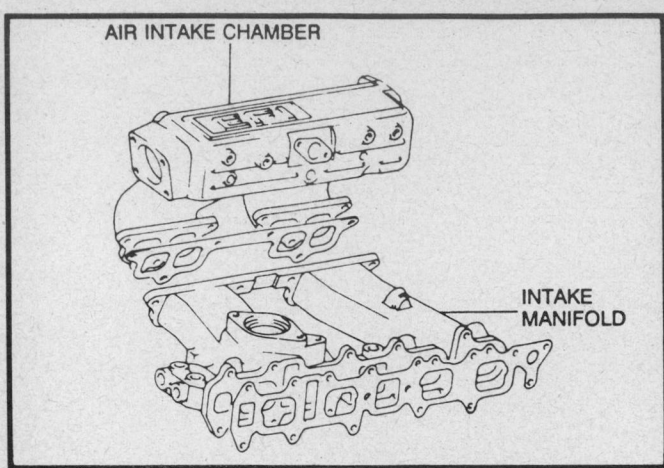

Intake manifold assembly—22R–E and 22R–TE engines

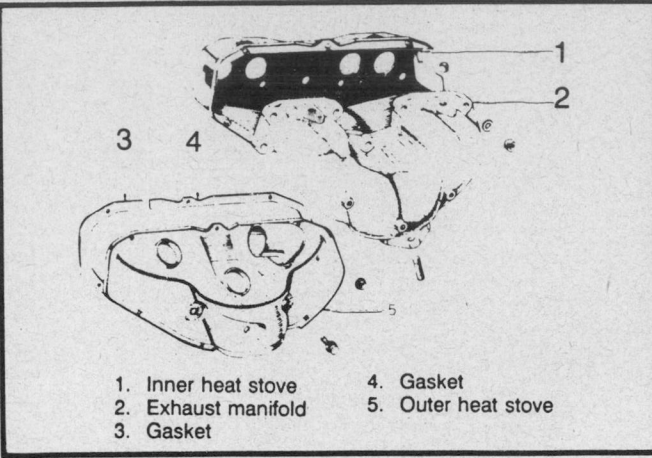

1. Inner heat stove
2. Exhaust manifold
3. Gasket
4. Gasket
5. Outer heat stove

Exhaust manifold—22R, 22R–E and 22R–TE engines

Right exhaust manifold—3VZ–E engine

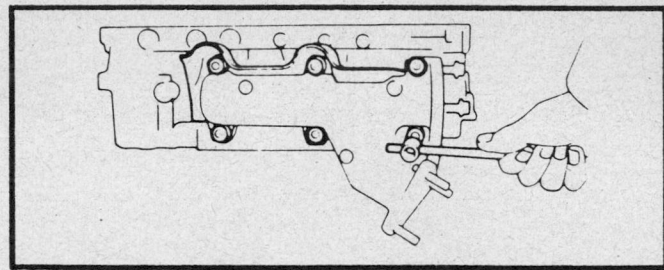

Left exhaust manifold—3VZ–E engine

15. Remove the fuel delivery pipes with their injectors.
16. Remove the water bypass outlet and then remove the intake manifold.
17. Install the intake manifold with new gaskets and tighten the mounting bolts to 29 ft. lbs. (39 Nm).
18. Install the water bypass outlet and tighten the 2 bolts to 13 ft. lbs. (18 Nm).
19. Install the fuel delivery pipes and injectors.
20. Install the No. 2 idler pulley. Install the No. 3 and 4 timing belt covers and tighten the bolts to 74 inch lbs. (8.3 Nm).
21. Install the fuel pipes and tighten the union bolts to 22 ft. lbs. (29 Nm).
22. Install the engine wire.
23. Install the air intake chamber and tighten the nuts and bolts to 13 ft. lbs. (18 Nm).
24. Install the EGR valve and connect all hoses and lines.
25. Install the air cleaner hose, refill the engine with coolant and connect the battery cable.

Exhaust Manifold

Removal and Installation

22R, 22R–E, 22R–TE AND 3VZ–E ENGINES

1. Remove the 3 exhaust pipe flange bolts (turbocharger flange bolts on the 22R–TE engine) and disconnect the exhaust pipe from the manifold.
2. Tag and disconnect the spark plug leads.
3. Position the spark plug wires out of the way.
4. Remove the air cleaner tube from the heat stove on carbureted engines, and remove the outer part of the heat stove.
5. Use a 14mm wrench to remove the manifold securing nuts.
6. Remove the manifold(s), complete with air injection tubes and the inner portion of the heat stove.
7. Separate the inner portion of the heat stove from the manifold.
8. When installing the manifold(s), tighten the retaining nuts to 29–36 ft. lbs., working from the inside out, and in several stages. Install the distributor and set the timing. Tighten the exhaust pipe flange nuts to 25–32 ft. lbs.

Combinaton Manifold

Removal and Installation

2F AND 3F–E ENGINES

1. Relieve the fuel system pressure on the 3F–E engine. Disconnect the negative battery cable. Remove the air cleaner assembly, complete with hoses.
2. Disconnect the accelerator and choke linkages, as well as the fuel and vacuum lines. Remove the throttle linkage.
3. Remove, or move aside, any of the emission control system components which are in the way.
4. Disconnect the oil filter lines and remove the oil filter assembly from the intake manifold. Unfasten the solenoid valve wire from the ignition coil terminal. Remove the EGR pipes from the exhaust gas cooler, if so equipped.
5. Unfasten the retaining bolts and remove the carburetor from the manifold. On the fuel injected engine, disconnect the throttle chamber from the manifold.
6. Loosen the manifold retaining nuts, working from the inside out, in 2 or 3 stages.
7. Remove the intake/exhaust manifold assembly from the cylinder head as a complete unit.
8. When installing the manifolds, always use new gaskets. Tighten the bolts, working from the inside out.

4Y–E AND 4Y–EC ENGINES

1. Relieve the fuel system pressure. Disconnect the negative battery terminal from the battery. Remove the right seat and the engine service hole cover.

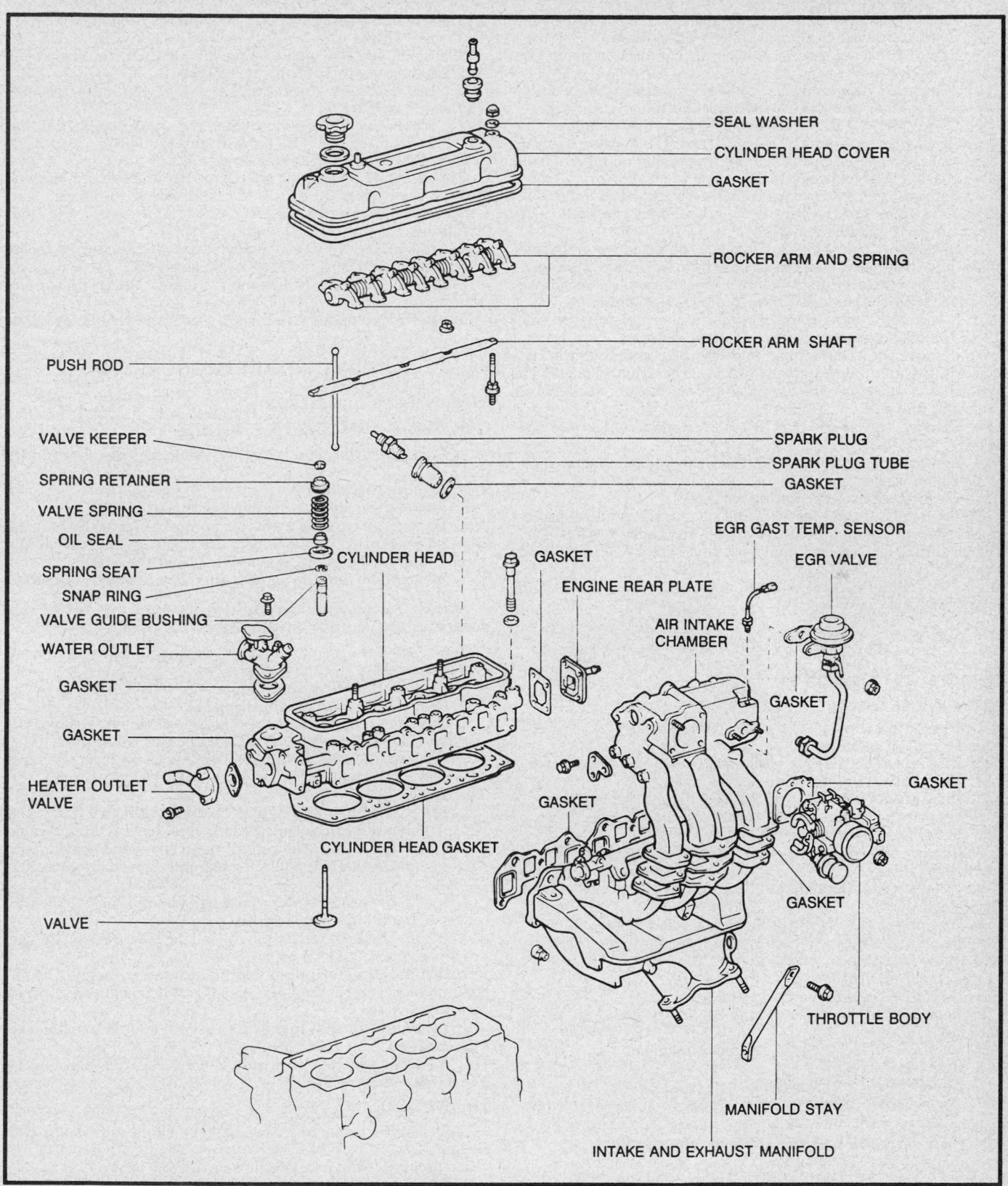

Intake manifold assembly—4Y–E and 4YE–C engines

SEAL WASHER

CYLINDER HEAD COVER

GASKET

ROCKER ARM AND SPRING

ROCKER ARM SHAFT

PUSH ROD

SPARK PLUG

SPARK PLUG TUBE

GASKET

VALVE KEEPER

SPRING RETAINER

VALVE SPRING

OIL SEAL

SPRING SEAT

SNAP RING

VALVE GUIDE BUSHING

WATER OUTLET

GASKET

GASKET

HEATER OUTLET VALVE

CYLINDER HEAD

GASKET

ENGINE REAR PLATE

EGR GAST TEMP. SENSOR

EGR VALVE

AIR INTAKE CHAMBER

GASKET

GASKET

GASKET

GASKET

CYLINDER HEAD GASKET

VALVE

THROTTLE BODY

MANIFOLD STAY

INTAKE AND EXHAUST MANIFOLD

2. Drain the engine coolant to a level below the throttle body.

3. Remove the air cleaner-to-throttle body hose.

4. Remove the accelerator cable with the bracket from the throttle body.

5. Disconnect the air valve connector, the throttle position sensor connector and the O_2 sensor connector.

6. Disconnect the PCV hose from the air intake chamber, the water bypass hoses from the throttle body, the booster vacuum hose and the charcoal canister hose, then label and disconnect the emission control hoses.

7. Remove the throttle body from the air intake chamber, the EGR tube union nut from the exhaust manifold, the EGR valve from the air intake chamber.

8. Disconnect the cold start injector tube, the water bypass hoses and the pressure regulator hose from the intake manifold.

9. Remove the air intake chamber brackets and the air intake chamber with the air valve from the intake manifold.

10. Remove the wire clamp bolt from the fuel injector rail, then, the fuel injector rail from the fuel injectors.

11. Remove the exhaust manifold-to-intake manifold bracket, the exhaust manifold-to-engine bracket, the exhaust pipe from the exhaust manifold, the fuel inlet and outlet tubes union nut from the fuel rail.

12. Remove the spark plug wires, the spark plugs and the tubes.

13. Remove the retaining bolts, then, the intake/exhaust manifolds as an assembly.

14. Clean the gasket mounting surfaces.

15. To install, use new gaskets and reverse the removal procedures. Torque the manifold-to-cylinder head bolts to 36 ft. lbs., the air intake chamber-to-intake manifold bolts to 9 ft. lbs. and the throttle body bolts to 9 ft. lbs. Refill the cooling system. Start the engine, allow it to reach operating temperatures and check for leaks.

Turbocharger

Removal and Installation

22R–TE ENGINE

1. Disconnect the negative battery cable.

2. Drain the coolant.

3. Disconnect the oxygen sensor wire clamp and connector.

4. Disconnect the No. 1 and 3 PCV hoses.

5. Disconnect the No. 1 and 2 turbocharger water hoses.

6. Loosen the clamp on the throttle body, remove the nuts and lift off the air tube assembly.

7. Remove the No. 1 air cleaner hose assembly and the No. 2 air cleaner hose.

8. Remove the exhaust manifold and turbocharger heat insulators.

9. Disconnect the No. 3 turbocharger water hose.

10. Raise and safely support the vehicle. Disconnect the exhaust pipe from the turbine outlet.

11. Remove the turbocharger bracket stay.

12. Disconnect the turbocharger oil pipe.

13. Remove the turbocharger and exhaust manifold as an assembly.

14. Remove the No. 2 turbocharger water pipe.

15. Remove the oil pipe.

16. Remove the No. 1 water pipe.

17. Remove the turbine outlet elbow with the O_2 sensor attached.

18. Disconnect the turbocharger from the manifold.

To install:

19. Pour approximately 20cc of new oil into the oil inlet and then turn the turbocharger impeller wheel so as to wet the bearing.

20. Using a new gasket, attach the turbocharger to the manifold and tighten the nuts to 29 ft. lbs. (39 Nm).

21. Install the turbine outlet elbow and tighten the nuts to 19 ft. lbs. (25 Nm).

22. Install the No. 1 water pipe. Install the turbo oil pipe and tighten the nuts to 14 ft. lbs. (19 Nm).

23. Install the No. 2 water pipe and then mount the assembly to the cylinder head.

24. Install the oil pipe and tighten the union bolt to 20 ft. lbs. (27 Nm). Tighten the nuts to 14 ft. lbs. (19 Nm).

7. Install the turbocharger bracket stay.

25. Connect the exhaust pipe to the turbine outlet elbow and tighten the nuts to 32 ft. lbs. (43 Nm). Lower the truck.

26. Connect the No. 3 water hose and install the heat insulators.

27. Install the No. 2 air cleaner hose with the arrow facing the turbocharger and fasten the clip as shown.

28. Install the air tube assembly. Connect the O_2 sensor and clamp.

29. Refill the engine with coolant, start it and check for leaks.

Timing Chain Front Cover

Removal and Installation

22R, 22R–E AND 22R–TE ENGINES

1. Disconnect the negative battery cable. Remove the cylinder head.

2. Remove the radiator.

3. Remove the alternator. Remove the oil pan.

4. On engines equipped with air pumps, unfasten the adjusting link bolts and the drive belt. Remove the hoses from the pump; remove the pump and bracket from the engine.

5. Remove the fan and water pump as a complete assembly.

NOTE: To prevent the fluid from running out of the fan coupling, do not tip the assembly over on its side.

6. Unfasten the crankshaft pulley securing bolt and remove the pulley with a suitable puller.

7. Remove the water bypass pipe.

8. Remove the fan belt adjusting bar.

9. Disconnect and remove the heater water outlet pipe. On the 22R–TE, remove the No. 3 turbocharger water pipe.

10. Remove the bolts securing the timing chain cover. Remove the cover.

To install:

11. Install the cover and tighten the 8mm bolts to 9 ft. lbs. (13 Nm). Tighten the 10mm bolts to 29 ft. lbs. (39 Nm). Apply sealer to the gaskets for both the timing chain cover and the oil pan.

12. Install the fan belt adjusting bar and tighten it to 9 ft. lbs. (13 Nm).

13. Install the heater water outlet pipe and the No. 3 turbo water hose. Install the water bypass pipe.

14. Install the crankshaft pulley and tighten the bolt to the proper torque.

15. Install the water pump and fluid coupling. Install the air conditioning compressor and then adjust the tension on all drive belts.

16. Install the oil pan. Install the radiator and then install the cylinder head.

17. Refill the engine with oil and coolant. Road test the vehicle and check for leaks.

2F AND 3F–E ENGINES

1. Disconnect the negative battery cable and drain the coolant.

2. Disconnect the accelerator and throttle cables.

3. Remove the air intake hose, air flow meter and air cleaner as an assembly.

4. Loosen the power steering pump drive pulley nut.

5. Remove the fluid coupling with the fan and water pump pulley.

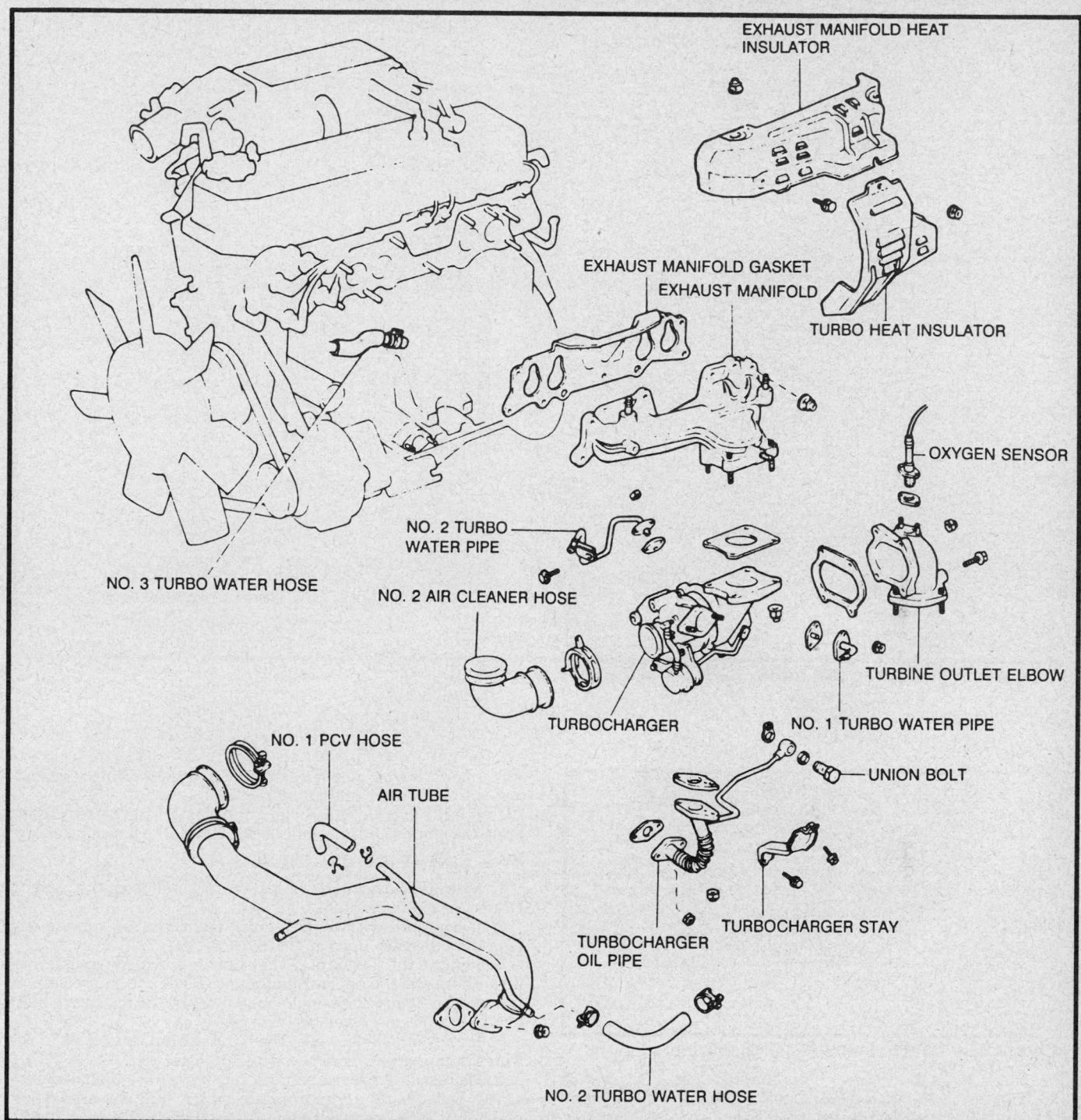

EXHAUST MANIFOLD HEAT INSULATOR

EXHAUST MANIFOLD GASKET

EXHAUST MANIFOLD

TURBO HEAT INSULATOR

OXYGEN SENSOR

NO. 2 TURBO WATER PIPE

NO. 3 TURBO WATER HOSE

NO. 2 AIR CLEANER HOSE

TURBINE OUTLET ELBOW

TURBOCHARGER

NO. 1 TURBO WATER PIPE

NO. 1 PCV HOSE

AIR TUBE

UNION BOLT

TURBOCHARGER STAY

TURBOCHARGER OIL PIPE

NO. 2 TURBO WATER HOSE

Exhaust manifold and turbocharger assembly—22R— TE engine

6. Remove the power steering pump and the air conditioning compressor. Remove their brackets. Remove the power steering pump idler pulley and its bracket.

7. Remove the cylinder head cover. Remove the rocker shaft assembly.

8. Remove the distributor.

9. Remove the pushrod cover and then remove the valve lifters. Be certain that they are kept in order.

10. Loosen the 6 bolts and then slide the power steering pump pulley off the crankshaft.

11. Using special tool 09213–58011 or equivalent and a 46mm socket wrench, remove the crankshaft pulley bolt. Remove the pulley.

12. Remove the oil cooler pipe and its hose.

13. Remove the timing gear cover and gasket.

To install:

14. There are 3 sizes of timing gear cover bolts. Apply adhesive to the two A bolts. Install a new gasket and then position the cover. Finger tighten all bolts. Align the crankshaft pulley set key with the groove of the pulley; gently tap the pulley onto the

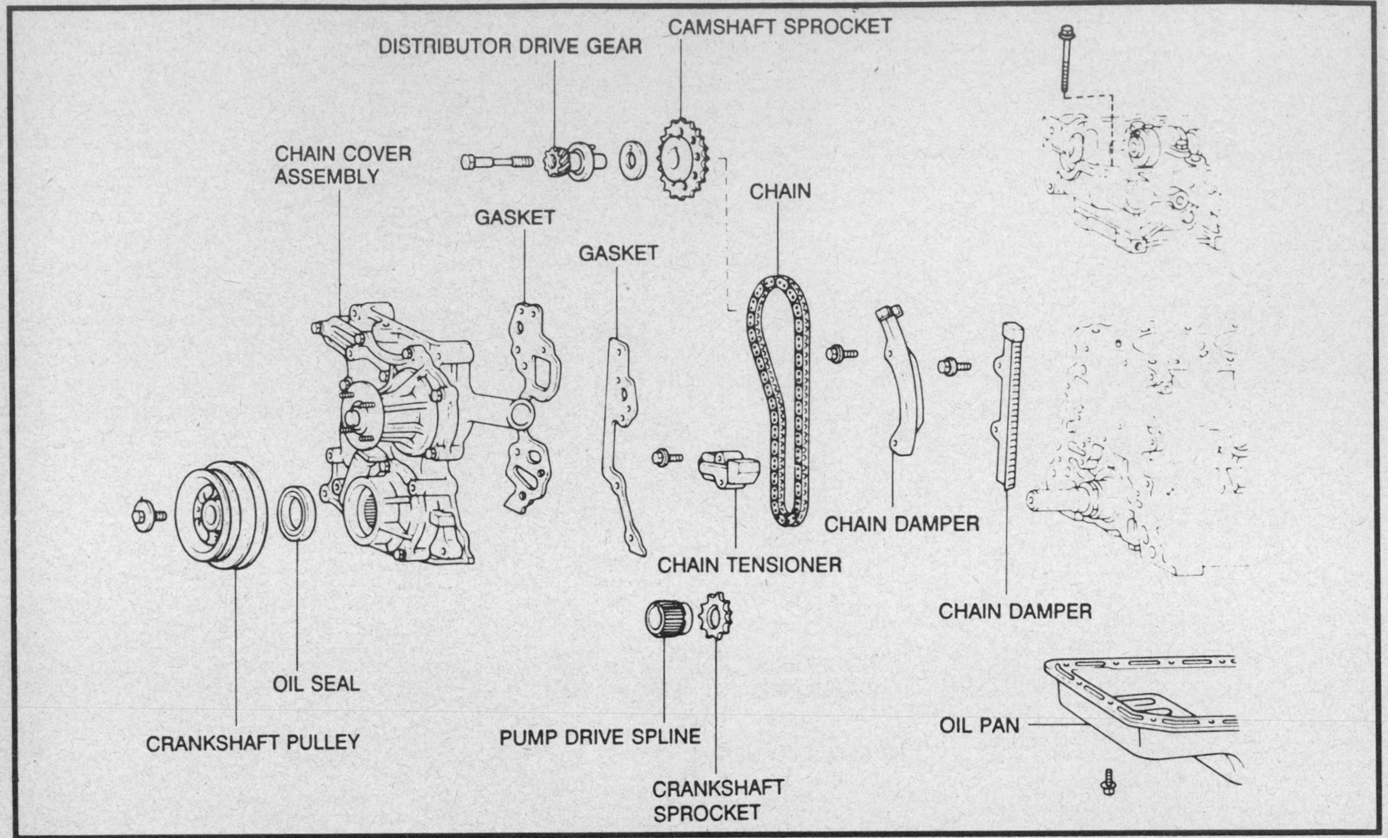

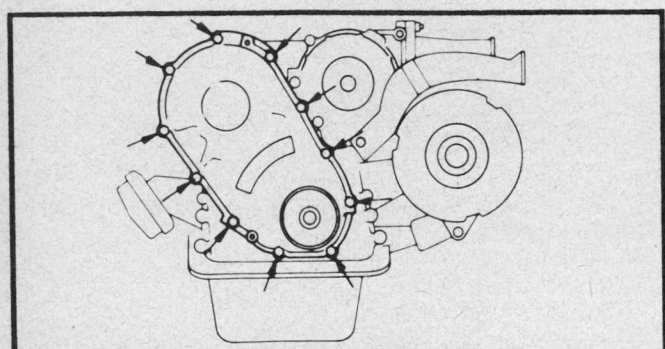

DISTRIBUTOR DRIVE GEAR
CAMSHAFT SPROCKET
CHAIN COVER ASSEMBLY
GASKET
GASKET
CHAIN
CHAIN DAMPER
CHAIN TENSIONER
CHAIN DAMPER
OIL SEAL
CRANKSHAFT PULLEY
PUMP DRIVE SPLINE
CRANKSHAFT SPROCKET
OIL PAN

Timing chain and sprockets—22R, 22R–E and 22R–TE engines

Timing chain cover removal—3F–E engine

crankshaft. Tighten the cover bolts marked **A** to 18 ft. lbs. (25 Nm). Tighten those marked **B** or **C** to 43 inch lbs. (5 Nm). Tighten the pulley bolt to 253 ft. lbs. (343 Nm).

15. Position the power steering pulley on the crankshaft and tighten the bolts to 13 ft. lbs. (18 Nm).

16. Insert the valve lifters into their bores and install the pushrod cover. Tighten the bolts to 35 inch lbs. (4 Nm). Make sure the valve lifters are installed in the same bore that they were removed from.

17. Install the rocker shaft assembly, the cylinder head cover and the distributor.

18. Install the water pump pulley, fluid coupling and fan.

19. Install the power steering pump idler pulley and bracket. Install the power steering pump and air conditioning compressor. Adjust the drive belts.

20. Install the air cleaner assembly and then connect and adjust the accelerator and throttle cables.

21. Fill the engine with coolant and connect the battery cable. Start the engine and check for leaks. Check the ignition timing.

4Y-E AND 4Y-EC ENGINES

1. Disconnect the negative battery terminal from the battery. Drain the cooling system.

2. If equipped with an automatic transmission, remove and plug the oil cooler lines at the radiator.

3. Remove the fan shroud, the radiator hoses, the coolant reservoir hose and the upper radiator bolt. Raise and safely support the vehicle. Remove the engine under cover, the mounting bolts and the radiator. Lower the vehicle.

4. Remove the drive belts, the fan, the fluid coupling and the water pump pulley from the water pump.

5. Using the appropriate tools, remove the crankshaft pulley center bolt. Using an appropriate puller, pull the crankshaft pulley from the crankshaft.

6. Remove the front cover mounting bolts. Using a small pry bar, lift the front cover from the engine.

To install:

7. Using a putty knife, clean the gasket mounting surfaces.

8. Use a new gasket, sealant and reverse the removal procedures.

9. Using a soft faced hammer, drive the crankshaft pulley onto the crankshaft. Torque the crankshaft pulley bolt to 80 ft. lbs.

10. Adjust the drive belts and refill the cooling system.

11. Start the engine, allow it to reach normal operating temperatures and check for leaks.

Front Cover Oil Seal

Replacement

22R, 22R–E AND 22R–TE ENGINES

1. Disconnect the negative battery cable. Remove the crankshaft pulley.
2. Using a small pry bar, pry the oil seal from the oil pump housing.
3. Using the appropriate seal installer, drive the new seal into the oil pump housing. Apply multi-purpose grease to the lip of the new seal.
4. To complete the installation, reverse the removal procedures.

2F AND 3F–E ENGINES

1. Disconnect the negative battery cable. Remove the crankshaft pulley.
2. Using a small pry bar, pry the oil seal from the front cover.
3. Using the appropriate seal installer, drive the new seal into the front cover. Apply multi-purpose grease to the lip of the new seal.
4. To complete the installation, reverse the removal procedures.

4Y–E AND 4Y–EC ENGINES

Front Cover Removed

1. Using a drift punch and a hammer, drive the oil seal from the front cover.
2. Using an appropriate seal installer and a hammer, drive the new oil seal into the front cover.
3. Apply grease to the lip of the new seal.

Front Cover Installed

1. Disconnect the negative battery cable. Remove the crankshaft pulley.
2. Using the appropriate seal remover, pull the oil seal from the front cover.
3. Apply multi-purpose grease to the lip of the new seal.
4. Using the appropriate seal installer and a hammer, drive the new oil seal into the front cover.
5. To complete the installation, reverse the removal procedures.

Timing Chain and Tensioner

Removal and Installation

22R, 22R–E AND 22R–TE ENGINES

1. Disconnect the negative battery cable. Remove the cylinder head and timing chain cover.
2. Separate the chain from the damper and remove the chain, complete with the camshaft sprocket.
3. Remove the crankshaft sprocket and the oil pump drive with a puller.
4. Inspect the chain for wear or damage. Replace it if necessary.
5. Inspect the chain tensioner for wear. If it measures less than 11mm, replace it.
6. Check the dampers for wear. If their measurements are below the following specifications, replace them. The specification for the upper damper is 5.0mm and the lower damper is 4.5mm.
To install:
7. Rotate the crankshaft until its key is at TDC. Slide the sprocket in place over the key.
8. Place the chain over the sprocket so that its single bright link aligns with the mark on the camshaft sprocket.
9. Install the cam sprocket so that the timing mark falls between the two bright links on the chain.
10. Fit the oil pump drive spline over the crankshaft key.

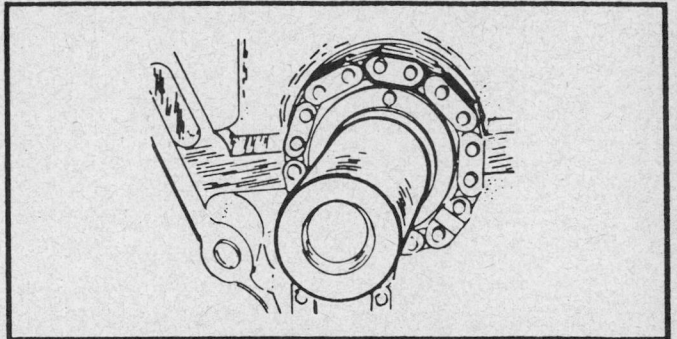

Aligning the crankshaft gear with the single bright link of the timing chain—22R, 22R–E and 22R–TE engines

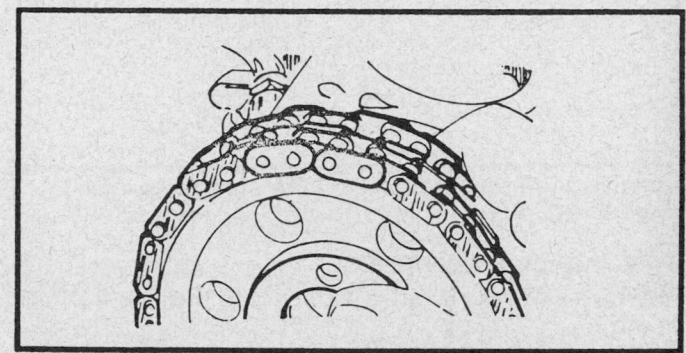

Aligning the camshaft sprocket mark between the 2 bright links of the timing chain—22R, 22R–E and 22R–TE engines

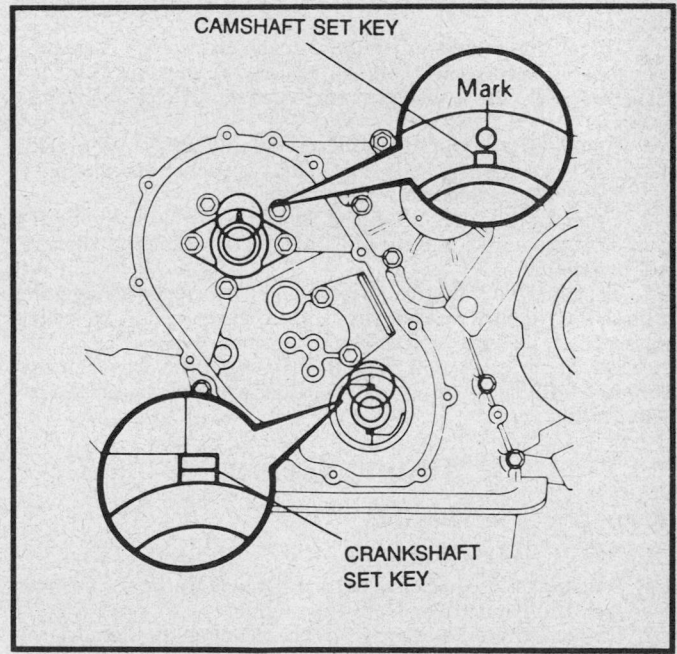

Aligning the timing chain and sprockets—4Y–E and 4YE–C engines

11. Install the timing cover gasket on the front of the block.
12. Rotate the camshaft sprocket counterclockwise to remove the slack from the chain.
13. Install the timing chain cover and cylinder head.

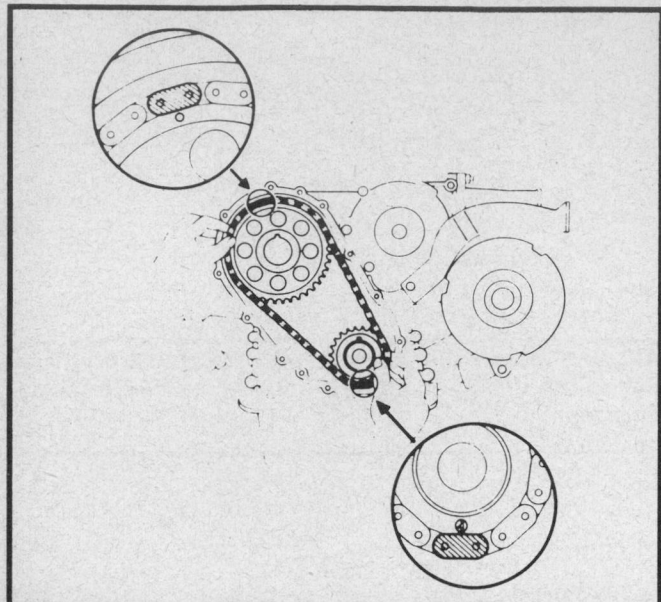

Installing the timing chain on the sprockets—4Y–E and 4Y–EC

4Y–E AND 4Y–EC ENGINES

1. Disconnect the negative battery cable. Remove the front cover.

NOTE: Using a tension gauge, measure the slack of the timing chain, it should be 0.531 in. at 22 lbs. pressure.

2. Remove the mounting bolts and the timing chain tensioner.

3. Install the crankshaft pulley on the cransshaft. Using the proper tools, secure the crankshaft pulley, remove the camshaft mounting bolt with a socket wrench and remove the crankshaft pulley.

4. Using an appropriate puller tool, uniformly remove the camshaft sprocket with the crankshaft sprocket and chain.

5. Clean the gasket mounting surfaces.

6. Upon installation, align the timing chain with the timing marks on the sprockets, then install the sprockets on their respective shafts.

7. To complete the installation, use new gaskets, sealant and reverse the removal procedures. Torque the camshaft mounting bolt to 67 ft. lbs., the timing chain tensioner bolts to 13 ft. lbs., the crankshaft pulley bolt to 80 ft. lbs. Adjust the drive belt tension and refill the cooling system. Check and/or adjust the engine timing.

Timing Gears

Removal and Installation

2F AND 3F–E ENGINES

1. Disconnect the negative battery cable. Remove the cylinder head and the front cover from the engine.

2. Remove the oil slinger from the crankshaft. Remove the camshaft thrust plate retaining bolts, by working through the holes provided in the camshaft timing gear.

3. Remove the camshaft through the front of the cylinder block. Support the camshaft while removing it, so the bearings or the lobes do not become damaged.

NOTE: The timing gear is a press-fit and cannot be removed without removing the camshaft.

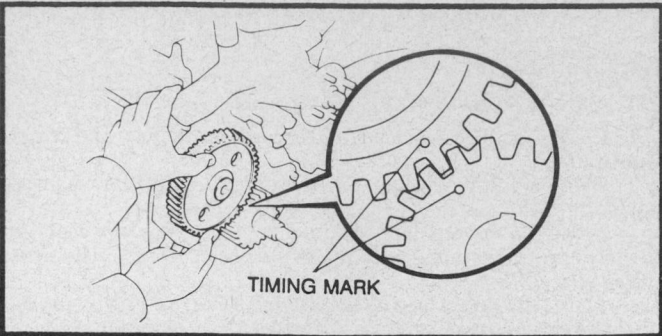

Aligning the timing marks—2F engine

4. Inspect the crankshaft timing gear. Replace it if it has worn or damaged teeth.

5. Remove the sliding key, then, pull the crankshaft timing gear from the crankshaft with a gear puller.

6. Use a large piece of pipe to drive the timing gear onto the crankshaft. Lightly and evenly tap the end of the pipe until the gear is in its original position.

To install:

7. Apply a coat of engine oil to the camshaft journals and bearings, then, insert the camshaft into the block.

8. Align the mating marks on the timing gears. Slip the camshaft into position. Torque the camshaft thrust plate bolts to 14.5 ft. lbs.

9. Using a feeler gauge, check the gear backlash, inserted between the crankshaft and the camshaft timing gears. The maximum backlash should be 0.002–0.005 in.; if it exceeds this, replace one or both of the gears, as required.

10. Using a dial indicator, check the gear run-out. Maximum run-out, for both gears, is 0.008 in.; if not, replace the gear.

11. Install the oil nozzle (if removed) by screwing it in place with a screwdriver and punching it in two places, to secure it.

NOTE: Be sure that the oil hole in the nozzle is pointed toward the timing gear before securing it.

12. To complete the installation, use new gaskets, sealant and reverse the removal procedures.

Timing Belt Front Cover

Removal and Installation

3VZ–E ENGINE

1. Disconnect the negative battery cable and drain the coolant.

2. Remove the radiator and shroud.

3. Remove the power steering belt and pump.

4. Remove the spark plugs.

5. Disconnect the No. 2 and 3 air hoses at the air pipe.

6. Disconnect the No. 1 water bypass hose at the air pipe and then remove the water outlet.

7. Remove the air conditioning belt. Remove the alternator drive belt, fluid coupling, guide and fan pulley.

8. Disconnect the high tension cords and their clamps at the No. 2 (upper) timing belt cover and then remove the cover and its gaskets.

9. Rotate the crankshaft pulley until the groove on its lip is aligned with the **0** on the No. 1 (lower) timing belt cover, this should set the No. 1 cylinder at TDC of its compression stroke. The matchmarks on the camshaft timing pulleys must be in alignment with those on the No. 3 (upper rear) timing cover. If not, rotate the engine 360 degrees (one complete revolution).

10. Remove the crankshaft pulley using a puller.

11. Remove the fan pulley bracket and then remove the No. 1 timing belt cover.

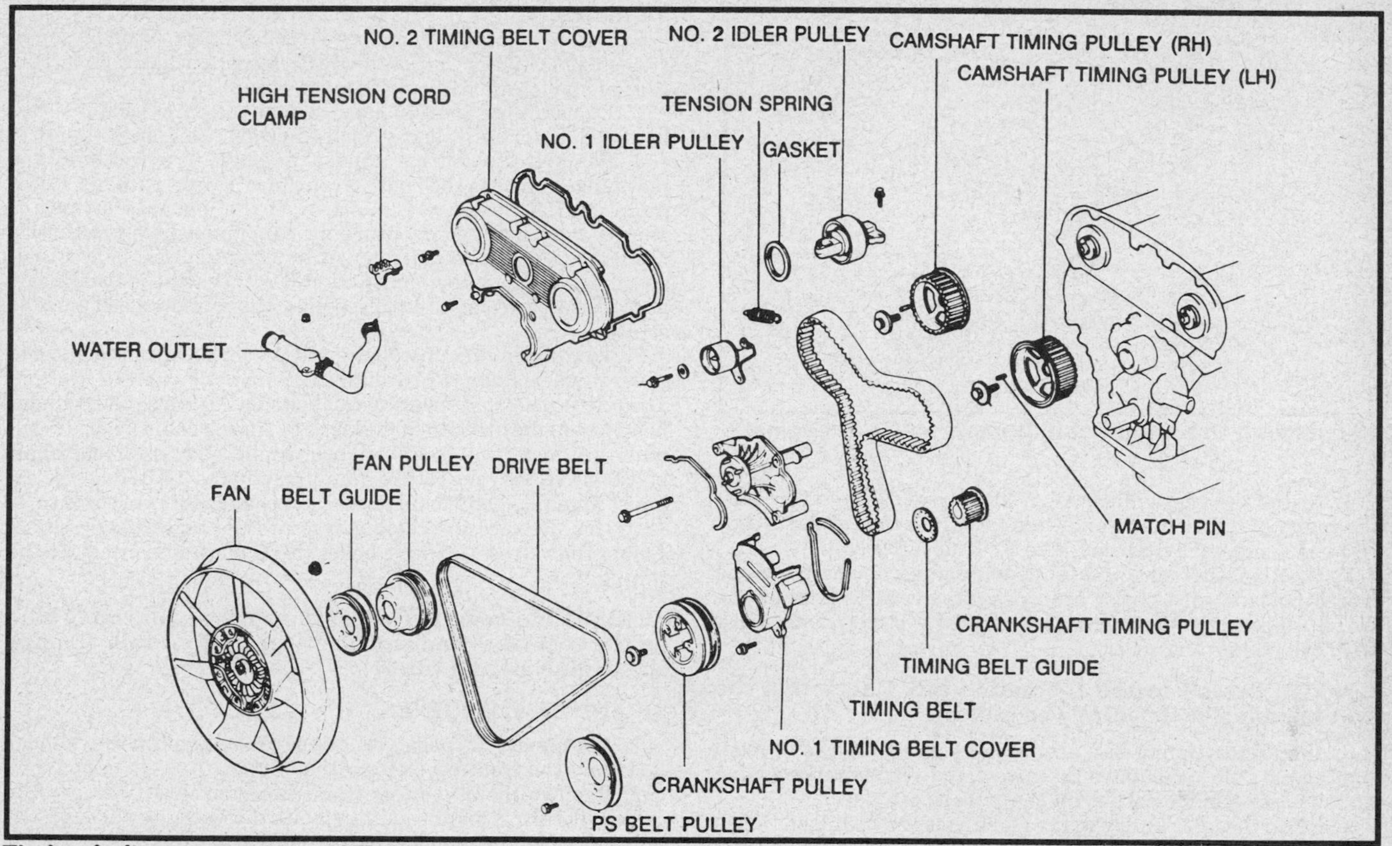

Timing belt components — 3VZ–E engine

To install:

12. Install the No. 1 cover with the 2 gaskets and tighten the bolts to 48 inch lbs. (5.4 Nm).

13. Install the fan pulley bracket and tighten it to 30 ft. lbs. (41 Nm).

14. Install the No. 2 cover and tighten the bolts 48 inch lbs. (5.4 Nm).

15. Position the crankshaft pulley so the groove in the pulley is aligned with the woodruff key in the crankshaft. Tighten the bolt to 181 ft. lbs. (245 Nm).

16. Install the fan pulley, guide, fluid coupling and alternator drive belt. Adjust the belt tension.

17. Install the power steering pump and belt. Install the air conditioning belt. Adjust the belt tension.

18. Install the water outlet and connect the bypass hose. Connect the No. 2 and 3 air hoses.

19. Install the spark plugs. Install the radiator, fill with coolant and road test the vehicle. Check for leaks and check the ignition timing.

Timing Belt and Tensioner

Removal and Installation

3VZ–E ENGINE

1. Disconnect the negative battery cable. Remove the timing belt covers.

2. Draw a directional arrow on the timing belt and matchmark the belt to each of the pulleys. Remove the timing belt guide and then remove the tension spring.

3. Loosen the idler pulley bolt and shift it left as far as it will go. Tighten the set bolt and relieve the tension on the timing belt. Remove the belt.

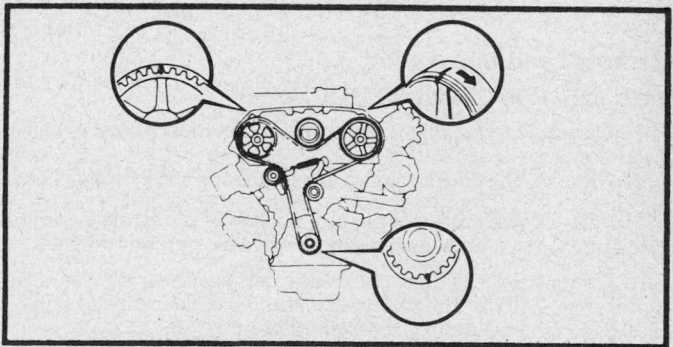

Aligning the timing marks with the rear cover — 3VZ–E engine

Installing the timing belt — 3VZ–E engine

4. Remove the crankshaft and camshaft sprocket timing pulleys. Remove the No. 1 idler pulley.

5. Align the groove in the crankshaft pulley with the key on the crankshaft and press the pulley onto the shaft.

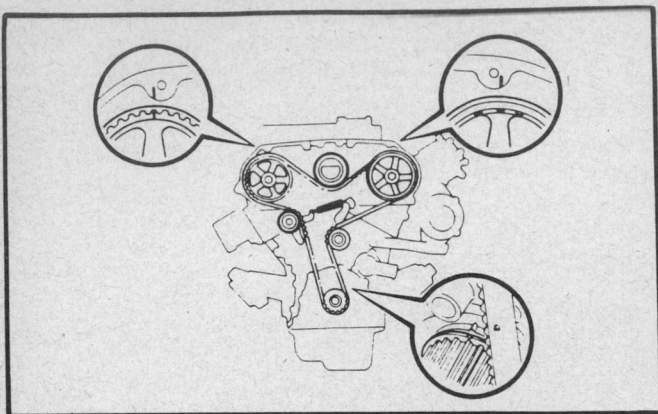

Rechecking the sprocket alignment – 3VZ–E engine

6. Install the idler pulley. Align the groove on the pulley with the cavity of the oil pump and then force it to the left as far as it will go. Temporarily tighten it to 27 ft. lbs. (37 Nm).

7. Position the camshaft pulleys on the camshafts so the match holes in each pulley are in alignment with those on the No. 3 (upper rear) timing cover. Align the pulley matchmark with the one on the cover.

NOTE: Do not install the match pin. Check that the bolt head is not touching the pulley.

8. Install the timing belt around the timing pulleys. If reusing the old belt, make sure the arrow and matchmarks all line up with those made earlier on the pulleys.

9. Move the idler pulley to the right as far as it will go. Install the tension spring and then loosen the pulley bolt until the pulley moves lightly with the tension spring force.

10. Check the valve timing and belt tension by turning the crankshaft 2 complete revolutions clockwise. Check that each pulley aligns with its timing marks. Retighten the idler pulley bolt to 27 ft. lbs. (37 Nm).

11. Remove the camshaft timing pulley bolts and align the match pin hole with the match pin hole in the camshaft. Install the pin and bolt and tighten to 80 ft. lbs. (108 Nm).

12. Remove the crankshaft timing pulley bolt and position the belt guide over the crankshaft pulley so the cupped side is out.

13. Install the timing covers. Connect the negative battery cable.

Camshaft

Removal and Installation

22R, 22R–E AND 22R–TE ENGINES

1. Disconnect the negative battery cable. Remove the cylinder head cover.

2. Remove the rocker arm assembly from the cylinder head.

NOTE: It may be necessary to use a small pry bar to lift the rocker arm assembly from the cylinder head.

3. Using a feeler gauge, measure the thrust bearing clearance at the front of the camshaft; the standard clearance is 0.003–0.007 in., it should not exceed 0.0098 in.

4. Remove the camshaft bearing caps and lift out the camshaft. Keep the bearings in order so that they may be installed in their original position.

5. Check the camshaft journal caps for damage. Clean all of the bearing surfaces, including the caps, cam journal and the cylinder head.

To install:

6. With the camshaft in place on the cylinder head, lay small strips of plastigage® on each of the camshaft journals (at the tops of the journals, facing front-to-rear).

7. Reinstall the journal caps in their original locations (arrows facing forward) and torque the caps to 13–16 ft. lbs.

8. Remove the journal caps and gauge the width of the plastigage® against the chart on the plastigage® package. Maximum journal clearance is 0.004 in. If the journal clearance is greater than specified, measure the cam journal diameters with a micrometer. If the diameter of any cam journal is less than specified, obtain a new camshaft and recheck the journal clearance. If the clearance is still excessive, the cylinder head must be replaced.

9. To complete the installation, use new gaskets, sealant and reverse the removal procedures. Refill the cooling system. Torque the camshaft bearing cap bolts to 14 ft. lbs., the cylinder head-to-engine block to 58 ft. lbs., the timing chain cover-to-cylinder head bolt to 9 ft. lbs., the camshaft sprocket-to-camshaft bolt to 58 ft. lbs., the intake manifold bolts to 14 ft. lbs., the exhaust manifold bolts to 33 ft. lbs. and the rocker arm cover to 7–12 ft. lbs. Replace the cooling system fluid and the engine oil. Adjust the valves, the drive belts, then, check and/or adjust the timing.

NOTE: If a new cam is installed, use an assembly lube on the cam lobes and engine oil on the journals. Change the engine oil and filter.

2F AND 3F–E ENGINES

1. Disconnect the negative battery cable. Remove the cylinder head and the front cover from the engine.

2. Remove the oil slinger from the crankshaft. Remove the camshaft thrust plate retaining bolts, by working through the holes provided in the camshaft timing gear.

3. Remove the camshaft through the front of the cylinder block. Support the camshaft while removing it, so the bearings or the lobes do not become damaged.

4. Inspect the crankshaft timing gear. Replace it if it has worn or damaged teeth.

5. Remove the sliding key, then, pull the crankshaft timing gear from the crankshaft with a gear puller.

6. Use a large piece of pipe to drive the timing gear onto the crankshaft. Lightly and evenly tap the end of the pipe until the gear is in its original position.

To install:

7. Apply a coat of engine oil to the camshaft journals and bearings, then, insert the camshaft into the block.

8. Align the mating marks on the timing gears. Slip the camshaft into position. Torque the camshaft thrust plate bolts to 14.5 ft. lbs.

9. Using a feeler gauge, check the gear backlash, inserted between the crankshaft and the camshaft timing gears. The maximum backlash should be 0.002–0.005 in.; if it exceeds this, replace one or both of the gears, as required.

10. Using a dial indicator, check the gear run-out. Maximum run-out, for both gears, is 0.008 in.; if not, replace the gear.

11. Install the oil nozzle (if removed) by screwing it in place and punching it in 2 places, to secure it.

NOTE: Be sure that the oil hole in the nozzle is pointed toward the timing gear before securing it.

12. To complete the installation, use new gaskets, sealant and reverse the removal procedures.

4Y–E AND 4Y–EC ENGINES

1. Disconnect the negative battery cable. Remove the timing chain from the engine.

2. Remove the right-front seat, the service hole cover and the distributor.

3. Disconnect the cold start injector connector, place a shop towel under the injector tube, then, remove the cold start injector union bolts, the injector and the gaskets. Remove the valve cover, the mounting bolts and the rocker arm assembly.

4. Remove the pushrods, keeping them in order. Using a wire hook or a magnetic finger, remove the valve lifters, keeping them in order.

5. Remove the thrust plate mounting bolts and the plate.

6. While turning the camshaft, slowly pull it out through the front of the engine, making sure not to damage the bearings, the camshaft lobes or the camshaft bearing surfaces.

To install:

7. Install the thrust plate, the camshaft sprocket and bolt onto the camshaft. Using a feeler gauge, measure the thrust bearing clearance, it should be 0.0028–0.0087 in.; if the clearance exceeds 0.012 in., replace the thrust plate.

8. Using a micrometer, check the bearing diameters of the camshaft. Using an internal micrometer, check the camshaft bearing diameters on the engine block.

9. Clean the gasket surfaces.

NOTE: Before installing the valve lifters, coat them with oil.

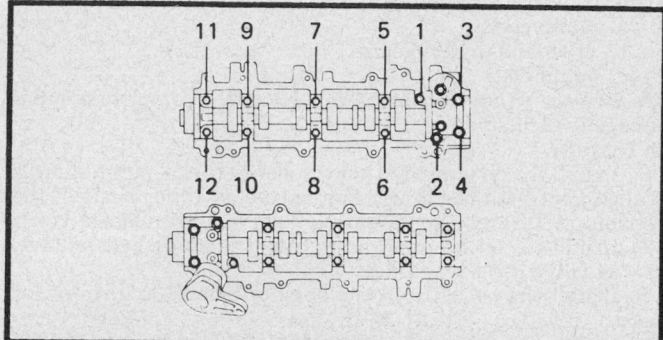

Removing the camshaft bearing bolts

10. Use new gaskets, sealant and reverse the removal procedures. Torque the camshaft thrust bearing plate bolts to 13 ft. lbs., the camshaft sprocket bolt to 67 ft. lbs., the timing chain tensioner bolts to 13 ft. lbs. and the crankshaft pulley bolt to 80 ft. lbs. Adjust the drive belts and refill the cooling system. Check and/or adjust the timing.

3VZ–E ENGINE

1. Disconnect the negative battery cable.
2. Remove the timing belt covers and remove the timing belt.
3. Disconnect all wires and hoses to the air intake chamber.
4. Remove the bolts retraining the air intake chamber and remove the air intake chamber from the intake manifold.
5. Remove the rear timing belt cover.
6. Remove the idler pulley and timing cover.
7. Remove the fuel rail and insjectors from the intake manifold.
8. Remove the cylinder head cover.

9. Remove the camshaft housing rear cover. Loosen the camshaft retaining bolts a little at a time in the correct sequence.

10. Remove the camshaft from the cylinder head.

11. Installation is the reverse of the removal procedure. When installing the bearing caps, make sure the arrow faces the front of the engine. Torque the caps to 12 ft. lbs. (16 Nm) in the correct sequence.

Piston and Connecting Rod

Positioning

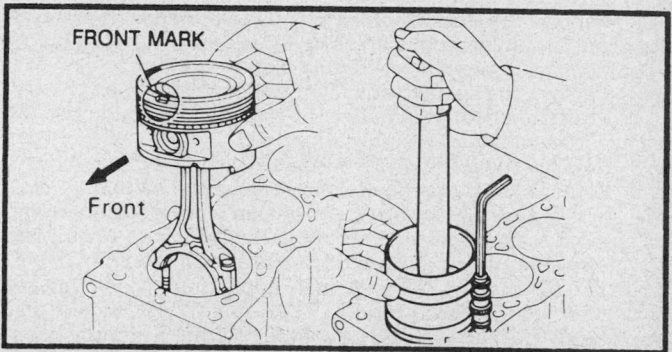

Piston and connecting rod positioning—22R, 22R–E and 22R–TE, 2F, 3F–E, 4Y–E and 4YE–C engines

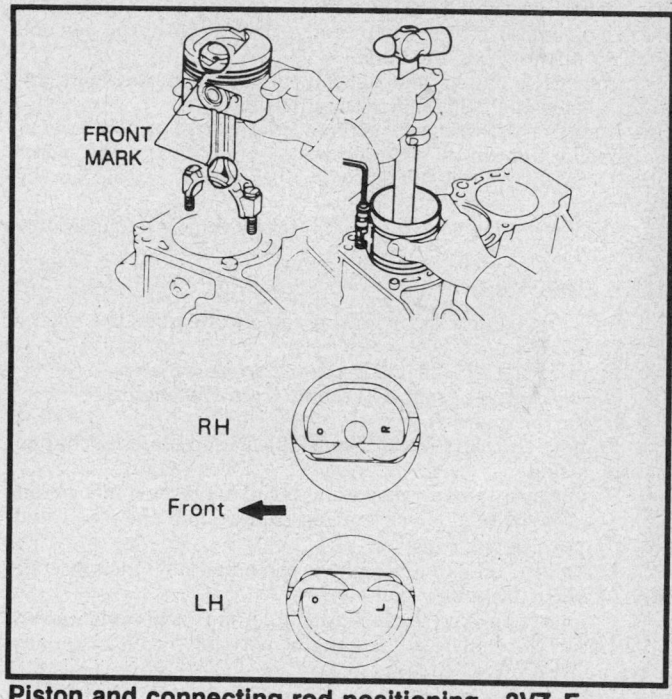

Piston and connecting rod positioning—3VZ–E engine

ENGINE LUBRICATION

Oil Pan

Removal and Installation

PICK-UP, VAN AND 4RUNNER

1. Raise the hood and disconnect the negative battery cable.
2. Raise and safely support the vehicle.
3. Drain the engine oil.
4. Remove the steering relay rod and the tie rods from the idler arm, pitman arm, and steering knuckles.
5. Remove the engine stiffening plates.
6. Remove the splash pans from under the engine.
7. Position a floor jack under the transmission and raise the engine/transmission assembly slightly.
8. Remove the front motor mount attaching bolts.
9. Remove the oil pan bolts and remove the oil pan.
10. Scrape the cylinder block and oil pan mating surfaces clean of any old sealing material. Apply gasket sealer to the oil pan when installing a new gasket. On vehicles with the 22R, 22R–E, 22R–TE, 4Y–E and 4Y–EC engines, apply 5mm bead of gasket sealer; on vehicles with the 2F, 3F–E and 3VZ–E engine, use 3mm bead. The parts should be installed within 5 minutes of applying the sealer.
11. The oil pan bolts should be tightened to 9 ft. lbs. on the 22R, 22R–E, 22R–TE, 4Y–E and 4Y–EC engines; 6 ft. lbs. (bolt), 52 inch lbs. on the 2F, 3F–E and 3V–ZE engines. Tighten the bolts in a circular pattern, starting in the middle of the pan and working out towards the ends.
12. Lower the engine and tighten the motor mount bolts. Install the splash shields and stiffening plates.
13. Install any steering arms removed in Step 4 and then lower the vehicle; tighten all suspension components and the motor mounts to their final torque with the vehicle resting on the ground.
14. Fill the engine with oil, road test the vehicle and check for leaks.

LAND CRUISER

1. Raise and safely support the vehicle. Remove the engine skid plates.
2. Remove the flywheel side cover and skid plate.
3. Disconnect the front driveshaft from the engine.
4. Drain the engine oil.
5. Remove the bolts which secure the oil pan. Remove the pan and its gasket.
6. Scrape away any old gasket material and then apply gasket sealer to the cylinder block mating surface and the No. 1 and No. 4 main bearing caps.
7. Install the oil pan and tighten the bolts to 69 inch lbs. (7.8 Nm). Always use a new pan gasket.
8. Connect the driveshaft, skid plate and flywheel side cover.
9. Lower the vehicle, fill the engine with oil and check for any leaks.

Oil Pump

Removal and Installation

22R, 22R–E AND 22R–TE ENGINES

1. Raise and safely support the vehicle. Drain the oil, and remove the oil pan and the oil strainer and pick-up tube.
2. Remove the drive belts from the crankshaft pulley.
3. Remove the crankshaft bolt, and remove the pulley with a gear puller.
4. Remove the 5 bolts from the oil pump and remove the oil pump assembly.
5. Inspect the drive spline, driven gear, pump body, and timing chain cover for excessive wear or damage. If necessary, replace the gears or pump body or cover. Unbolt the relief valve (the vertical bolt on the pump body) when attached to the engine) and check the pistons, oil passages, and sliding surfaces for burrs or scoring. Inspect the crankshaft front oil seal and replace if worn or damaged.
6. When installing, use a new O-ring if necessary.
7. Apply a sealer to the upper bolt and install the 5 bolts.
8. Install the crankshaft pulley and use a new gasket on the oil strainer and oil pan. Be sure to apply sealer to the corners of the oil pan gasket before installing the pan.

2F AND 3F–E ENGINES

1. Disconnect the negative battery cable. Raise and safely support the vehicle. Remove the oil pan.
2. Remove the oil strainer and unfasten the union nuts on the oil pump pipe.
3. Remove the lock wire and the oil pump retaining bolt and pipe from the engine.
4. Remove the oil pump cover and inspect the following parts for nicks, scoring, grooving, etc.:
   a. pump cover
   b. drive and driven gears
   c. pump body
5. Replace either the damaged parts or the complete pump if damage is excessive.

To install:

6. Install the oil pump so that the slot in the oil pump shaft is in alignment with the protrusion on the governor shaft of the distributor. Tighten the mounting bolts to 13 ft. lbs. (18 Nm).
7. Install the outlet pipe and tighten the union bolt to 33 ft. lbs. (44 Nm); use new gaskets.
8. Install the oil pan, fill the engine with oil and check for leaks.

NOTE: Be sure to check all of the gaskets and replace if necessary.

4Y–E AND 4Y–EC ENGINES

1. Disconnect the negative battery cable. Raise and safely support the vehicle. Remove the oil pan.
2. Remove the oil pump mounting bolts, then pull out the pump assembly.
3. Using a putty knife, clean the gasket mounting surfaces.
4. To install, use new gaskets, sealant and reverse the removal procedures. Torque the oil pump bolts to 13 ft. lbs.

3VZ–E ENGINE

1. Disconnect the negative battery cable.
2. Remove the timing belt.
3. Raise and safely support the vehicle. Remove the engine under cover.
4. Remove the front differential.
5. Drain the oil.
6. Remove the crankshaft timing pulley.
7. Raise the engine slightly and remove the oil pan.
8. Remove the oil strainer. Insert a drift between the cylinder block and the oil pan baffle plate, cut off the sealer and remove the baffle plate.

NOTE: When removing the baffle plate with the drift, do not damage the baffle plate flange.

9. Remove the oil pump and O-ring.

To install:

10. Apply sealer to the oil pump mating surface running the bead on the inside of the bolts holes. Position a new O-ring in the groove in the cylinder block and install the pump so that the

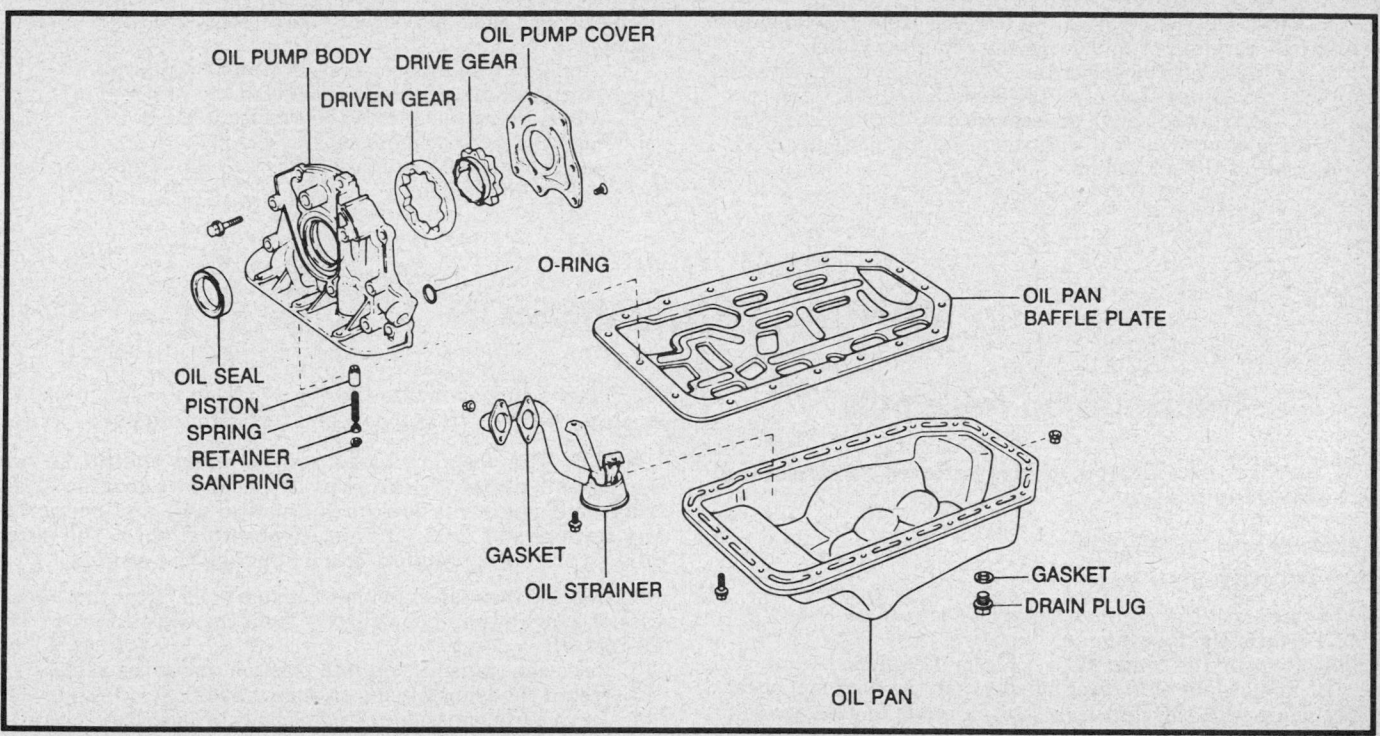

Oil pan and pump assembly—3VZ–E engine

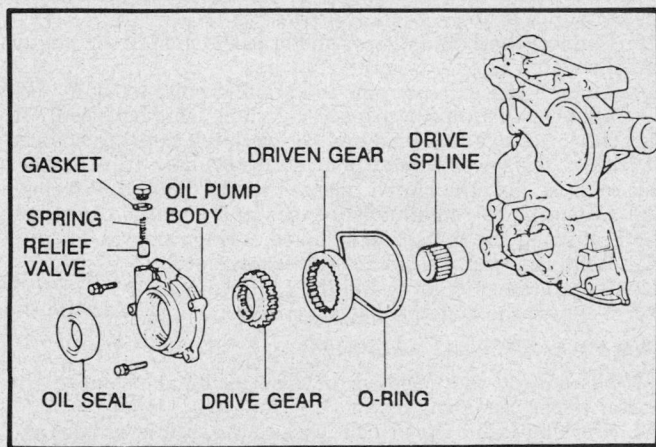

Oil pump assembly—22R, 22R–E and 22R–TE engines

spline teeth of the drive gear engage the large teeth on the crankshaft. Tighten the mounting bolts to 14 ft. lbs. (20 Nm).

11. Remove any old sealer and install the baffle plate with new sealer.

12. Install the oil strainer and tighten the bolts to 61 inch lbs. (7 Nm).

13. Install the oil pan, crankshaft pulley and the timing belt.

14. Install the front differential and the undercovers.

15. Fill the engine with oil and check for leaks.

Rear Main Bearing Oil Seal

Removal and Installation

22R, 22R–E AND 22R–TE ENGINES

1. Raise and safely support the vehicle. Remove the transmis-

sion and the clutch assembly (if equipped). Remove the transfer case, if equipped.

2. Remove the flywheel or the flex plate from the crankshaft. Remove the cover plate from the rear of the engine.

3. Remove oil pan-to-oil seal retaining plate bolts, the oil seal retaining plate-to-engine bolts and oil seal retaining plate.

4. Carefully pry or drive the old seal from the retaining plate. Be careful not to damage the retaining plate.

5. Using an oil seal driver tool, drive the new seal into the oil seal retaining plate, until the surface is flush.

6. Lubricate the lips of the seal with multipurpose grease.

7. Clean the gasket mounting surfaces.

8. To install, use new gaskets and reverse the removal procedures. Adjust the clutch.

2F AND 3F–E ENGINES

1. Raise and safely support the vehicle. Remove the transfer case, the transmission and the clutch assembly.

2. Remove the flywheel from the crankshaft.

3. Using a small pry bar, carefully pry the oil seal from the rear of the crankshaft.

4. Lubricate the lips of the seal with multipurpose grease.

5. Using an oil seal driver tool, drive the new seal into the rear of the crankshaft.

6. Clean the gasket mounting surfaces.

7. To install, reverse the removal procedures. Adjust the clutch.

4Y–E, 4Y–EC AND 3VZ–E ENGINES

1. Raise and safely support the vehicle. Remove the transmission and the clutch assembly (if equipped). Remove the transfer case, if equipped.

2. Remove the flywheel or the flex plate from the crankshaft. Remove the cover plate from the rear of the engine.

3. To replace the oil seal with the retaining plate removed:

a. Remove oil pan-to-oil seal retaining plate bolts, the oil seal retaining plate-to-engine bolts and oil seal retaining plate.

b. Carefully pry or drive the old seal from the retaining plate. Be careful not to damage the retaining plate.

c. Using an oil seal driver tool, drive the new seal into the oil seal retaining plate, until the surface is flush.

d. Lubricate the lips of the seal with multipurpose grease.

4. To replace the oil seal with the retaining plate installed:

a. Cut off the oil seal lip.

b. Using a small pry bar, pry the oil seal from the retaining plate.

c. Apply multi-purpose grease to the new oil seal.

d. Using an oil seal driver tool, drive the new seal into the oil seal retaining plate until the surface is flush.

5. Clean the gasket mounting surfaces.

6. To complete the installation, reverse the removal procedures. Adjust the clutch.

MANUAL TRANSMISSION

Transmission Assembly

For further information, please refer to "Professional Transmission Manual".

Removal and Installation
2WD PICKUP AND VAN

1. Disconnect the negative battery terminal.

2. Perform the following:

a. Remove the center floor console, if equipped.

b. Remove the shift lever handle, then the floor mat or carpet along with the shift lever boot in order to gain access to the shift lever.

c. Using an shift lever removal tool, remove the shift lever.

NOTE: On the Pick-Up, remove the boot and the shift lever from inside the vehicle.

3. Raise and safely support the vehicle. Drain the transmission fluid.

4. Make matchmarks on the driveshaft flange and the differential pinion flange to indicate their relationships; these marks must be aligned during installation.

5. Remove the driveshaft flange bolts and the center support bearing-to-frame bolts (if equipped with a 2-piece driveshaft). Lower the driveshaft out of the vehicle. Using an appropriate tool, insert it into the end of the transmission to prevent oil leakage.

6. On the Van, disconnect the shift and the select cables from the select outer levers, the clips and the cables.

7. Disconnect the back-up lamp switch electrical connector and the speedometer cable from the transmission, then tie the cable out of the way.

8. Disconnect the wiring at the starter. Remove the starter mounting bolts and lower the starter out of the vehicle.

9. Remove the exhaust pipe clamp and the exhaust pipe.

10. If the hydraulic line from the clutch release cylinder is clamped to the frame, remove the clamp retaining bolt. Remove the release cylinder mounting bolts and the fork spring (if equipped). Tie the release cylinder out of the way.

NOTE: It is not necessary to disconnect the hydraulic line from the release cylinder.

11. On column shift vehicles, disconnect the shift selector linkage at the transmission and remove the transmission cross shafts.

12. Support the rear of the transmission with a jack and remove the transmission-to-crossmember bolts, the crossmember-to-frame bolts and the crossmember from the vehicle.

NOTE: When removing the crossmember, raise the rear of the transmission, just enough to take the weight off of the crossmember.

13. Place a support under the engine with a wooden block (¾ in. thick) between the support and the engine oil pan.

NOTE: The wooden block and support should be no more than about ¼ in. away from the engine so that when the engine is lowered, damage will not occur to any underhood components. If possible, shim the support so that the wooden block touches the engine.

14. Remove the transmission-to-engine bolts, draw the transmission rearward and down, away from the engine.

To install:

15. Raise the transmission into position under the vehicle.

16. Install the transmission-to-engine bolts.

17. Torque transmission-to-engine bolts to 53 ft. lbs., the stiffener plate bolts to 27 ft. lbs., the transmission mount/bracket bolts to 19 ft. lbs., the rear engine mount bracket-to-crossmember bolts to 9 ft. lbs.

18. Install the exhaust pipes and brackets. Install the starter and the clutch release cylinder.

19. Tighten the exhaust pipe-to-manifold bolts to 29 ft. lbs., the upper exhaust pipe bracket-to-clutch housing bolts to 27 ft. lbs., the lower exhaust pipe bracket-to-clutch housing bolts to 51 ft. lbs., the lower starter bolt/release cylinder tube bracket bolt to 29 ft. lbs., the clutch release cylinder bolts to 9 ft. lbs.

20. Connect the remaining linkages and connect the driveshaft, aligning the matchmarks made during removal.

21. Refill the transmission to the correct level.

22. Install the shift lever and the center console.

23. Connect the negative battery cable.

4WD PICK-UP AND 4RUNNER

1. Disconnect the negative battery terminal. Remove the starter upper mounting bolt.

2. Working inside the vehicle, pull up the shift lever boot and pull out the shift lever. If equipped with a 22R–E engine, pull up the shift lever boot, then, remove the mounting bolts and pull out the shift lever.

3. Using needle nose pliers, remove the transfer case shift lever snapring and the shift lever.

4. Raise and safely support the vehicle.

5. Drain the lubricant from both the transmission and the transfer case.

6. Make matchmarks on the driveshaft flanges and the differential pinion flanges to indicate their relationships. These marks must be aligned during installation.

7. Remove the driveshaft mounting bolts and remove the front driveshaft assembly.

NOTE: Do not disassemble the front driveshaft to remove it.

8. Using a piece of chalk, place matchmarks on the rear driveshaft and the slip yoke to indicate their relationships; these marks must be aligned during installation.

9. Remove the mounting bolts from the rearward flange of the rear driveshaft. Lower the driveshaft out of the vehicle. Re-

move the mounting bolts from the slip yoke flange, then, remove the flange and yoke assembly.

10. Unbolt the clutch release cylinder and tie it out of the way.

NOTE: It is not necessary to disconnect the hydraulic line from the clutch release cylinder.

11. Disconnect the starter motor electrical connectors. Remove the starter bolts and lower the starter from the vehicle.

12. At the transfer case, disconnect the speedometer cable (tie it out of the way), the back-up light switch connector and the 4WD indicator switch connector.

13. Disconnect the exhaust pipe clamp and the exhaust pipe from the transmission housing.

14. Remove the clutch release cylinder and the tube bracket, then, move the cylinder aside.

NOTE: When removing the clutch release cylinder, do not disassemble the hydraulic line from the cylinder.

15. Remove the crossmember-to-transfer case mounting bolts. Using a jack, raise the transmission and transfer case assembly off of the crossmember. Remove the crossmember-to-frame attaching bolts and remove the crossmember.

16. Place a support under the engine oil pan, with a wooden block (¾ in. thick) between the support and the engine oil pan.

NOTE: The wooden block and support should be no more than about ¼ in. away from the engine so that when the engine is lowered, damage will not occur to any underhood components. If possible, shim the support so that the wooden block touches the engine.

17. Lower the jack until the engine rests on the support.

18. Remove the exhaust pipe bracket and the stiffener plate bolts.

19. Remove the transmission-to-engine bolts, draw the transmission/transfer case assembly rearward and down away from the engine.

20. Remove the transmission-to-transfer case adapter bolts and pull the transfer case from the transmission.

To install:

21. Raise the transmission into position under the vehicle.

22. Install the transmission-to-engine bolts.

23. Torque transmission-to-engine bolts to 53 ft. lbs., the stiffener plate bolts to 27 ft. lbs., the transmission mount/bracket bolts to 19 ft. lbs., the rear engine mount bracket-to-crossmember bolts to 9 ft. lbs.

24. Connect the exhaust pipes and brackets. Install the starter and the clutch release cylinder.

25. Tighten the exhaust pipe-to-manifold bolts to 29 ft. lbs., the upper exhaust pipe bracket-to-clutch housing bolts to 27 ft. lbs., the lower exhaust pipe bracket-to-clutch housing bolts to 51 ft. lbs., the lower starter bolt/release cylinder tube bracket bolt to 29 ft. lbs., the clutch release cylinder bolts to 9 ft. lbs.

26. Connect the remaining linkages and connect the driveshaft, aligning the matchmarks made during removal.

27. Refill the transmission to the correct level.

28. Install the shift lever and the center console.

29. Connect the negative battery cable.

LAND CRUISER

1. Disconnect the negative battery terminal from the battery.

2. Remove the entrance scuff plates from the floor of the interior.

3. Remove both side trim panels from beneath the instrument panel.

4. Remove the center heater duct and the front floor mat or carpet.

5. Remove the handles from both shift levers and the transmission tunnel cover along with the shift lever boots.

6. Disconnect the wiring from both the back-up lamp switch and the 4WD indicator (if equipped).

7. Remove the transmission shift lever.

8. Raise and safely support the vehicle. Remove the transfer case skid plate.

9. Disconnect the speedometer cable from the transfer case and tie it out of the way.

10. Using chalk, place matchmarks on the driveshaft flanges and the differential pinion flanges to indicate their relationships; these marks must be aligned during installation.

11. Remove the driveshaft flanges mounting bolts and the driveshaft assemblies.

12. Disconnect the starter electrical connectors, the mounting bolts and the starter from the vehicle.

13. Remove the clutch release cylinder and move it out of the way.

NOTE: It is not necessary to disconnect the hydraulic line from the release cylinder.

14. Drain the lubricant from both the transmission and the transfer case. Remove the tachometer sensor, if equipped.

15. Remove the crossmember-to-transfer case mounting bolts. Using a jack, raise the transmission and transfer case assembly off the crossmember. Remove the crossmember-to-frame attaching bolts and the crossmember.

16. Place a support under the engine oil pan, with a wooden block (¾ in. thick) between the support and the engine oil pan.

17. Lower the jack until the engine rests on the support.

NOTE: For the next step, it is recommended that an assistant help guide the transmission and transfer case assembly out of the vehicle.

18. Remove the exhaust pipe bracket and the stiffener plate bolts.

19. Remove the transmission-to-engine bolts, then, draw the transmission/transfer case assembly rearward and down away from the engine.

20. To separate the transfer case from the transmission, remove the transfer case mounting bolts and slide the transfer case off the transmission.

To install:

21. Raise the transmission into position under the vehicle.

22. Install the transmission-to-engine bolts.

23. Torque transmission-to-engine bolts to 53 ft. lbs., the stiffener plate bolts to 27 ft. lbs., the transmission mount/bracket bolts to 19 ft. lbs., the rear engine mount bracket-to-crossmember bolts to 9 ft. lbs.

24. Connect the exhaust pipes and brackets. Install the starter and the clutch release cylinder.

25. Tighten the exhaust pipe-to-manifold bolts to 29 ft. lbs., the upper exhaust pipe bracket-to-clutch housing bolts to 27 ft. lbs., the lower exhaust pipe bracket-to-clutch housing bolts to 53 ft. lbs., the lower starter bolt/release cylinder tube bracket bolt to 29 ft. lbs., the clutch release cylinder bolts to 9 ft. lbs.

26. Connect the remaining linkages and connect the driveshaft, aligning the matchmarks made during removal.

27. Refill the transmission to the correct level.

28. Install the shift lever and the center console.

29. Connect the negative battery cable.

CLUTCH

Clutch Assembly

Removal and Installation

1. Raise and safely support the vehicle. Remove the transmission from the vehicle.
2. Make matchmarks on the clutch cover and flywheel, indicating their relationship.
3. Loosen the clutch cover-to-flywheel retaining bolts a turn at a time. The pressure on the clutch disc must be released gradually.
4. Remove the clutch cover-to-flywheel bolts. Remove the clutch cover and the clutch disc.
5. If the clutch release bearing is to be replaced, perform the following:
   a. Remove the bearing retaining clip(s), the bearing and hub.
   b. Remove the release fork and the boot.
   c. The bearing is press fitted to the hub.
   d. Clean all parts and lightly grease the input shaft splines and all of the contact points.
   e. Install the bearing/hub assembly, the fork, the boot and the retaining clip(s) in their original locations.
To install:
6. Inspect the flywheel surface for cracks, heat scoring (blue marks) and warpage.

NOTE: Before installing any new parts, make sure that they are clean. During installation, do not get grease or oil on any of the components, as this will shorten clutch life considerably.

7. Using an clutch alignment tool, position the clutch disc against the flywheel. (Pick-Up and Vans: The short side of the splined section faces the flywheel; Land Cruiser: The long side of the splined section faces the flywheel).
8. Install the clutch cover over the disc and install the bolts loosely. Align the pressure plate-to-flywheel matchmarks. If a new or rebuilt clutch cover assembly is installed, use the matchmark on the old cover assembly as a reference. Torque the pressure plate-to-flywheel bolts to 14 ft. lbs. (using a criss-cross pattern).
9. Install the transmission into the vehicle.

Pedal Height Adjustment

The pedal height measurement is gauged from the angled section of the floorboard to the center of the clutch pedal pad. The correct pedal height is 7.7 in. for Land Cruiser, 6.7–7.3 in. for Van and 6.12 for Pick-Up and 4Runner.

If necessary, adjust the pedal height by loosening the locknut and turning the pedal stop bolt which is located above the pedal towards the drivers seat. Tighten the locknut after the adjustment.

Clutch Master Cylinder

Removal and Installation

PICK-UP, 4RUNNER AND LAND CRUISER

1. Disconnect the negative battery cable. Disconnect the master cylinder pushrod pin from the top of the clutch pedal.
2. Remove the hydraulic line from the master cylinder, being careful not to damage the compression fitting.
3. Remove the master cylinder-to-cowl nuts/ bolts.
4. To install, reverse the removal procedures. Partially tighten the hydraulic line before tightening the master cylinder mounting nut(s). Torque the nuts/bolts to 9 ft. lbs. Bleed the clutch system. Adjust the push rod play clearance.

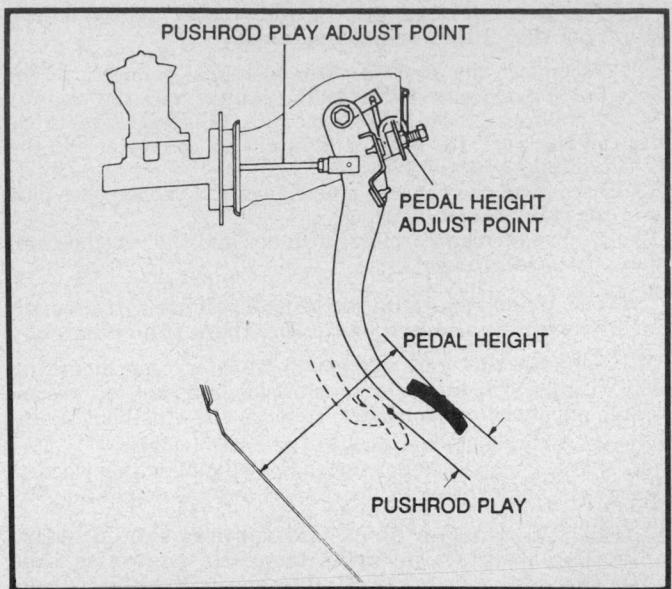

Clutch pedal adjustment points

VAN

1. Disconnect the negative battery terminal from the battery.
2. Remove the reservoir cap from the cluster finish panel, the mounting screws, then, pull the cluster finish panel forward and remove it.
3. Remove the mounting screws and pull the instrument panel forward, then, disconnect the speedometer and the electrical connectors from it.
4. Remove the No. 3, the No. 1 and the No. 2 air ducts.
5. Disconnect and plug the reservoir hose at the master cylinder. Disconnect the clutch line union.
6. Remove the mounting bolts and the master cylinder.
7. To install, reverse the removal procedures. Bleed the clutch system. Adjust the clutch pedal.

Adjustment
PUSHROD

The pedal pushrod play is the distance between the clutch master cylinder piston and the pedal pushrod located above the pedal towards the firewall. Since it is nearly impossible to measure this distance at the source, it must be measured at the pedal pad, preferably with a dial indicator gauge. The push rod play specification is: 0.040–0.200 for Land Cruiser, 0.039–0.197 for Vans, Pick-Ups and 4Runner.

If necessary, adjust the pedal play by loosening the pedal pushrod locknut and turning the pushrod. Tighten the locknut after the adjustment.

FREE PLAY

The free play measurement is the total travel of the clutch pedal from the fully released position to where resistance is felt as the pedal is pushed downward. The free play specification is: 0.20–0.59 for all vehicles.

Clutch Slave Cylinder

Removal and Installation

1. Raise and safely support the vehicle.

2. If equipped, remove the tension spring on the clutch fork.

3. Remove the hydraulic line from the release clinder. Be careful not to damage the fitting.

4. Turn the release cylinder pushrod in sufficiently to gain clearance from the fork.

5. Remove the mounting bolts and withdraw the cylinder.

6. To install, reverse the removal procedures. Bleed the clutch system. Adjust the fork tip clearance.

Bleeding the Hydraulic Clutch System

1. Fill the master cylinder reservoir with brake fluid.

2. Remove the cap and loosen the bleeder screw on the clutch release cylinder. Cover the hole with a finger.

3. Pump the clutch pedal several times. Take the finger off the hole while the pedal is being depressed so that the air in the system can be released. Put a finger back on the hole and release the pedal.

4. When fluid pressure can be felt tighten the bleeder screw.

5. Place a short length of hose over the bleeder screw and the other end in a jar half full of clean brake fluid.

6. Depress the clutch pedal and loosen the bleeder screw. Allow the fluid to flow into the jar.

7. Tighten the plug, then release the clutch pedal.

8. Repeat this procedure until no air bubbles are visible in the bleeder tube.

9. When there are no more air bubbles in the system, tighten the plug fully with the pedal depressed. Replace the plastic cap.

10. Refill the master cylinder to the correct level with brake fluid. Check the system for leaks.

AUTOMATIC TRANSMISSION

For further information, please refer to "Professional Transmission Manual".

Transmission Assembly

Removal and Installation

1. Disconnect the negative battery terminal from the battery. On the Pick-Up and 4Runner, remove the air cleaner assembly.

2. Disconnect the transmission throttle cable from the carburetor linkage or the throttle body.

3. Raise and safely support the vehicle. Drain the transmission fluid.

4. Disconnect the wiring connectors (near the starter) for the neutral start switch and the back-up light switch. If equipped, disconnect the solenoid (overdrive) switch wiring at the same location.

5. Disconnect the starter wiring at the starter. Remove the mounting bolts and the starter from the engine.

6. Make matchmarks on the rear driveshaft flange and the differential pinion flange. These marks must be aligned during installation.

7. Unbolt the rear driveshaft flange. If the vehicle has a 2 piece driveshaft, remove the center bearing bracket-to-frame bolts. Remove the driveshaft from the vehicle.

8. Disconnect the speedometer cable (tie it out of the way) and the shift linkage from the transmission.

9. Disconnect the transmission oil cooler lines at the transmission.

10. Disconnect the exhaust pipe clamp and remove the oil filler tube.

11. Support the transmission, using a jack with a wooden block placed between the jack and the transmission pan. Raise the transmission, just enough to take the weight off of the rear mount.

12. On the Pick-Up and 4Runner, remove the rear engine mount with the bracket and the engine under cover, to gain access to the engine crankshaft pulley. On the Van, remove the fuel tank mounting bolts and support the fuel tank; remove the transmission mount through bolt.

13. Place a wooden block (or blocks) between the engine oil pan and the front frame crossmember.

14. Slowly, lower the transmission until the engine rests on the wooden block.

15. Remove the rubber plug(s) from the service holes located at the rear of the engine in order to gain access to the torque convertor bolts.

16. Rotate the crankshaft (to remove the torque convertor bolts) to access the bolts through the service holes.

17. Obtain a bolt of the same dimensions as the torque convertor bolts. Cut the head off of the bolt and hacksaw a slot in the bolt opposite the threaded end.

NOTE: This modified bolt is used as a guide pin. Two guides pins are needed to properly install the transmission.

18. Thread the guide pin into one of the torque convertor bolt holes. The guide pin will help keep the convertor with the transmission.

19. Remove the stiffener plates from the transmission.

20. Remove the transmission-to-engine bolts, then carefully move the transmission rearward by prying on the guide pin through the service hole.

21. Pull the transmission rearward and lower it (front end down) out of the vehicle.

To install:

22. Apply a coat of multi-purpose grease to the torque convertor stub shaft and the corresponding pilot hole in the flywheel.

23. Install the torque convertor into the front of the transmission. Push inward on the torque convertor while rotating it to completely couple the torque convertor to the transmission.

24. To make sure that the convertor is properly installed, measure the distance between the torque convertor mounting lugs and the front mounting face of the transmission. The proper distance is 0.080 in.

25. Install guide pins into two opposite mounting lugs of the torque convertor.

26. Raise the transmission to the engine, align the transmission with the engine alignment dowels and position the convertor guide pins into the mounting holes of the flywheel.

27. Install and tighten the transmission-to-engine mounting bolts. Torque the bolts to 47 ft. lbs.

28. Remove the convertor guide pins and install the convertor mounting bolts. Rotate the crankshaft as necessary to gain access to the guide pins and bolts through the service holes. Evenly, tighten the convertor mounting bolts to 13 ft. lbs. Install the rubber plugs into the access holes.

29. Install the engine undercover. Raise the transmission slightly and remove the wood block(s) from beneath the engine oil pan.

30. Install the transmission crossmember. Torque the crossmember-to-frame bolts to 26–36 ft. lbs.

31. Lower the transmission onto the crossmember and install the transmission mounting bolts. Torque the bolts to 19 ft. lbs.

32. Install the oil filler tube and connect the exhaust pipe clamp.

33. Connect the oil cooler lines to the transmission and torque the fittings to 25 ft. lbs.

34. To complete the installation, reverse the removal procedures. Adjust the transmission throttle cable. Refill the transmission with Dexron®II fluid. Road test the vehicle and check for leaks.

Shift Linkage Adjustment

1. Loosen the adjustment nut on the transmission shift cable.
2. Push the manual lever of the transmission fully rearward.
3. Move the manual lever back 2 notches, which is the **N** position.
4. Set the gearshift selector lever in the **N** position.
5. Apply a slight amount of forward pressure on the selector lever and tighten the shift cable adjustment nut.

Throttle Linkage Adjustment

1. Remove the air cleaner assembly.
2. Push the accelerator to the floor and check that the throttle valve opens fully; if not, adjust the accelerator link, so that it does.

3. Push back the rubber boot from the throttle cable which runs down to the transmission. Loosen the throttle cable adjustment nuts so that the cable housing can be adjusted.
4. Fully open the carburetor throttle by pressing the accelerator all the way to the floor.
5. Adjust the cable housing so that, with the throttle wide open, the distance between the outer cable end rubber cap to the inner cable stopper is 0–0.04 in.
6. Tighten the nuts and double check the adjustment. Install the rubber boot and the air cleaner.

Neutral Start Switch Adjustment

The neutral safety switch prevents the vehicle from starting unless the gearshift selector is in either the **P** or **N** positions. If the vehicle will start in these positions, adjustment of the switch is required.

1. Loosen the neutral start switch bolt.
2. Place the selector lever in the **N** position.
3. Disconnect the wires from the neutral start switch.
4. Connect an ohmmeter between the terminals of the switch.
5. Adjust the switch until there is continuity between the N and B terminals.
6. Reconnect the wires. Torque the bolt to 48 inch lbs.

TRANSFER CASE

Transfer Case Assembly

Removal and Installation

The transfer case and transmission are connected together. It is recommended by the manufacturer that they be removed from the vehicle as an assembly and then separated for repairs.

DRIVE AXLE

Front Halfshaft

Removal and Installation
4WD PICK-UP, 4RUNNER AND VAN

1. Remove the 4WD hub (with the flange) from the axle hub.
2. Raise and safely support the vehicle. Remove the wheel and tire assembly.
3. Disconnect and plug the brake line from the caliper. Remove the caliper from the axle hub.
4. Using a drift punch and a hammer, drive the lock washer tabs away from the locknut.
5. Remove the locknut from the halfsahft. Remove the lock washer, the adjusting nut, the thrust washer, the outer bearing and the axle hub/disc assembly from the vehicle.
6. Remove the knuckle spindle bolts, the dust seal and the dust cover. Using a brass bar and a hammer, tap the steering spindle from the steering knuckle.
7. Turn the halfshaft until a flat spot on the outer shaft is in the upper position, then pull the halfshaft from the steering knuckle.

8. Using a slide hammer, pull the oil seal from the axle housing.
9. Using a clean shop towel, wipe the grease from inside the steering knuckle housing and the halfshaft.
To install:
10. Using an oil seal installation tool, drive a new oil seal into the axle housing until it seats.
11. Install the halfshaft into the axle housing.
12. Using multi-purpose grease, fill the steering knuckle cavity to about ¾ full.
13. To complete the installation, use new seals/gaskets and reverse the removal procedures.
14. Torque the steering spindle-to-steering knuckle bolts to 38 ft. lbs., the axle hub adjusting nut to 18 ft. lbs., the axle hub locknut to 33 ft. lbs., the free wheel/locking hub nuts to 23 ft. lbs. and the brake caliper to 65 ft. lbs.

NOTE: To install the wheel bearings with the axle hub, torque the adjusting nut to 43 ft. lbs., turn the axle hub (back and forth, several times), loosen the nut and retorque the adjusting nut to 18 ft. lbs.

15. Install the wheel and tire assembly. Lower the vehicle.

Driveshaft and U-Joints

Removal and Installation

4WD VEHICLES EXCEPT
LONG BED PICK-UP AND LAND CRUISER

Rear

1. Raise and safely support the vehicle.
2. Paint a mating mark on the halves of the rear universal joint flange.
3. Remove the bolts which hold the rear flange together.
4. Remove the splined end of the driveshaft from the transmission.

NOTE: Plug the end of the transmission with a rag or dummy flange to avoid losing transmission oil.

5. Remove the driveshaft from under the vehicle.
6. To install, reverse the removal procedures. Grease the splined end of the shaft before installing. Torque bolts to 31 ft. lbs. (Van) or 54 ft. lbs. (Pick-Up and 4Runner).

2WD LONG BED PICK-UP

Rear

1. Raise and safely support the vehicle.
2. Paint mating marks on all 6 flange halves.
3. Remove the bolts attaching the rear universal joint flange to the drive pinion flange.
4. Drop the rear section of the shaft slightly and pull the unit out of the center bearing sleeve yoke.
5. Remove the center bearing support from the crossmember.
6. Unbolt the driveshaft flange from the rear of the transmission and remove driveshaft along with center bearing support.

7. To install, align the matchmarks and reverse the removal procedures. Torque the flange bolts to 54 ft. lbs.

4WD VEHICLES

Front

1. Raise and safely support the vehicle.
2. Matchmark the driveshaft flange at the front axle housing and the transfer case.
3. On Vans, remove the differential support bracket.
4. On Pick-Up and 4Runner, remove the falnge dust cover.
5. Remove the bolts retaining the driveshaft and remove the driveshaft from the vehicle.
6. Install the driveshaft by aligning the matchmarks made during removal.
7. Torque the retaining bolts to 54–58 ft. lbs. (74–78 Nm).

Front Axle Shaft

Removal and Installation

LAND CRUISER

1. Raise and safely support the vehicle. Remove the wheel and tire assembly.
2. Plug the brake master cylinder reservoir to prevent brake fluid leakage from the disconnected brake flexible hose.
3. Remove the outer axle shaft flange cap (automatic locking hub) or the hub cover bolts and the cover (free wheel locking hub) and the shaft snapring from the axle hub.
4. Remove the outer axle shaft flange (automatic locking hub) or the hub ring-to-axle hub bolts, then alternately, screw 2 service bolts into the shaft flange or hub ring and remove the shaft flange or the hub ring with it's gasket.
5. Remove the caliper and disc.

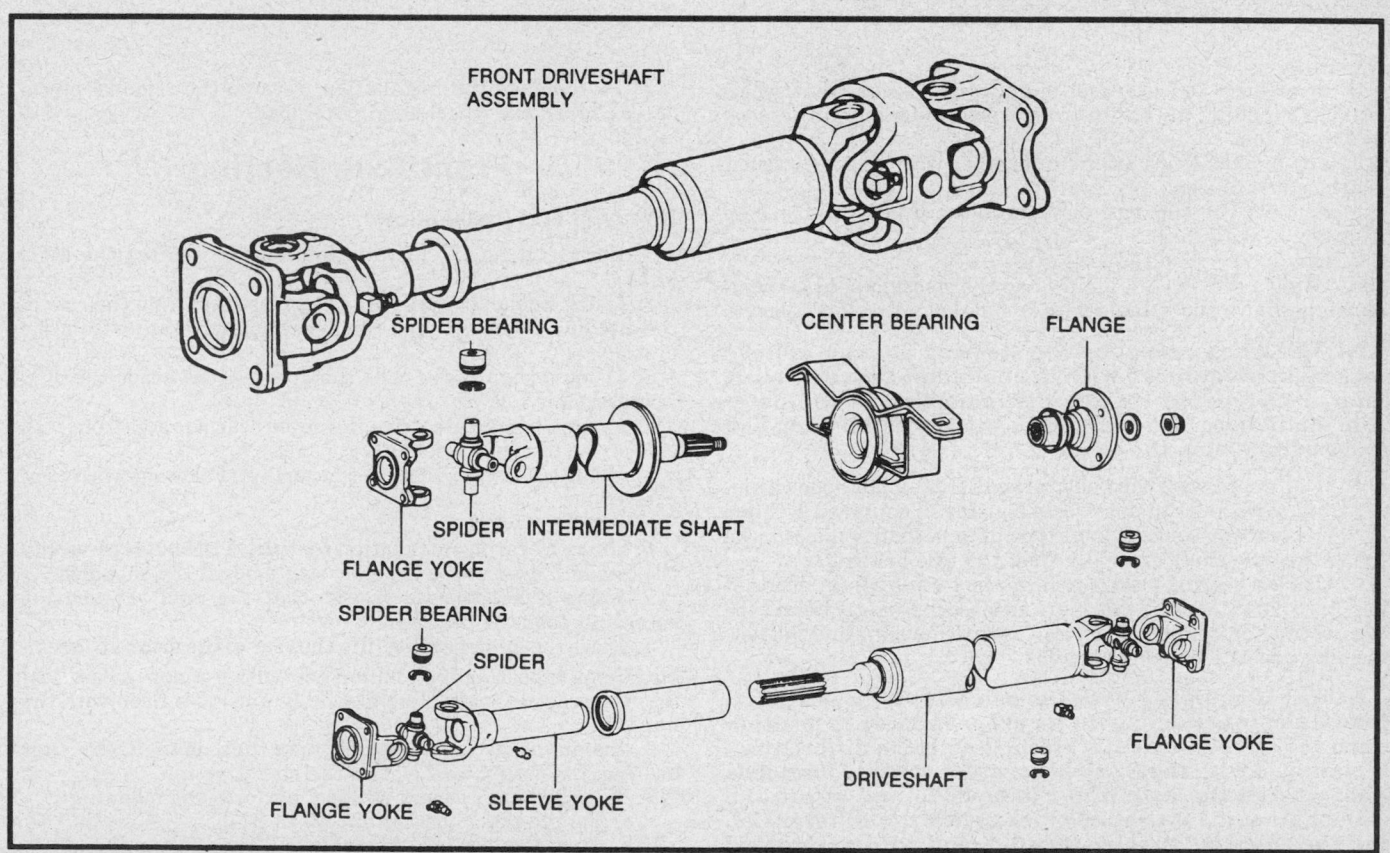

Driveshaft assemblies—Pick-Up and 4Runner

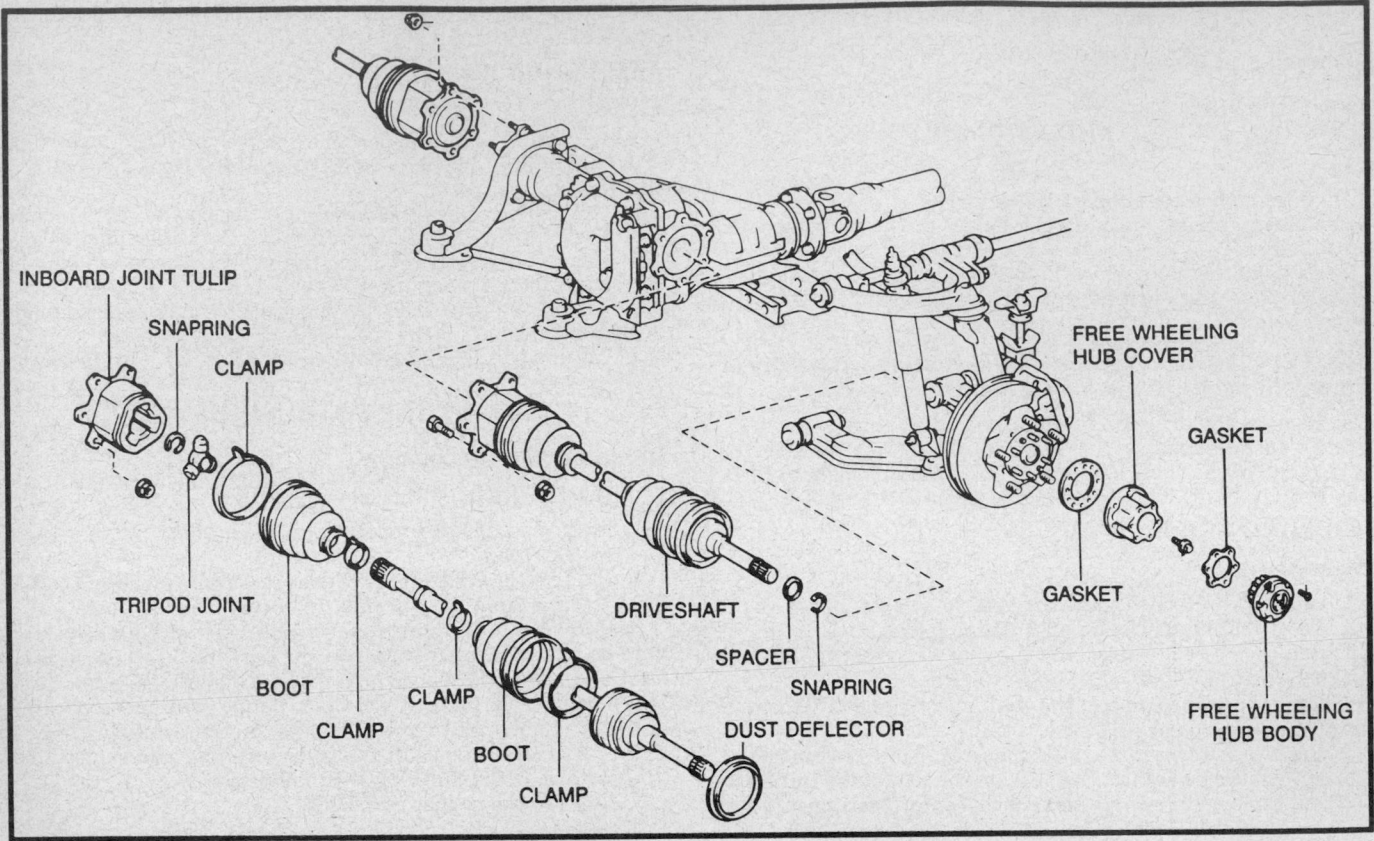

Front drive axle assembly—Pick-Up and 4Runner

6. Straighten the lockwasher and remove the front wheel bearing adjusting nuts with front wheel adjusting nut wrench or similar tool.

7. Remove the front axle hub together with its claw washer, bearings and oil seal.

8. Remove the clip and disconnect the brake flexible hose from the brake tube.

9. Cut and remove the lock wire.

10. Using a soft mallet, lightly, tap the steering knuckle spindle and remove the spindle with it's gasket.

NOTE: When removing the steering knuckle spindle on a vehicle equipped with the ball joint type axle shaft joint, be prepared for the disconnection of the outer axle shaft from the joint. Prevent the shaft joint ball from falling from the joint.

11. If equipped with the ball type axle shaft joint, slide the inner front axle shaft out of the axle housing. If equipped with the Birfield constant velocity joint type of axle shaft joint, remove the entire axle shaft assembly from the axle housing.

12. Using a bearing puller, remove the bushing from inside of knuckle spindle and the axle housing oil seal. Using a metal tube as a seating tool, drive oil seal into the axle housing and the new bushing into the knuckle spindle.

NOTE: If equipped with the ball joint type axle joint, install the inner axle with its proper spacer in position until the splines are fully meshed with the differential. If equipped with the Birfield constant velocity joint axle joint, install the axle into the housing and rotate the axle shaft until its splines mesh with the differential. Fill the steering knuckle about ¾ full with grease and place the joint ball on the inner shaft end.

13. To complete the installation, reverse the removal procedures. Adjust the wheel bearing preload.

Front Axle Bearing

Removal and Installation

1. Raise and safely support the vehicle. Remove the 4WD hubs.

2. Using a small pry bar, pry the grease seal from the rear of the disc/hub assembly, then remove the inner bearing from the assembly.

3. Using a shop cloth, wipe the grease from inside the disc/hub assembly.

4. Using a brass drift, drive the outer bearing races from each side of the disc/hub assembly.

5. Using solvent, clean all of the parts and blow dry with compressed air.

To install:

6. Using a bearing installation tool, drive the outer races into the disc/hub assembly until they seat against the shoulder.

7. Using multi-purpose grease, coat the area between the races and pack the bearings.

8. Place the inner bearing into the rear of the disc/hub assembly. Using a bearing installation tool, drive a new grease seal into the rear of the disc/hub assembly until it is flush with the housing.

9. Install the disc/hub assembly onto the axle shaft, the outer bearing, the thrust washer and the adjusting nut.

10. To adjust the bearing preload, perform the following:

   a. Torque the adjusting nut to 43 ft. lbs.

   b. Turn the disc/hub assembly 2-3 times, from the left to the right.

c. Loosen the adjusting nut until it can be turned by hand.
d. Retorque the adjusting nut to 18 ft. lbs.
e. Install the lock washer and the locknut. Torque the locknut to 33 ft. lbs.
f. Check that the bearing has no play.
g. Using a spring gauge, connect it to a wheel stud, the gauge should be held horizontal, then measure the rotating force, it should be 6–12 lbs.
11. Lower the vehicle.

Rear Axle Shaft and Bearings

Removal and Installation
PICK-UP AND 4RUNNER

1. Loosen the rear wheel lug nuts, then raise and safely support the vehicle. Remove the wheel and tire assembly.
2. Place a pan under the axle, remove the plug and drain the axle housing.
3. For 2WD vehicles, remove the clip/clamp-to-frame bolts and disconnect the parking brake cable from the equalizer. For 4WD vehicles, remove the pin and disconnect the rear parking brake cable from the bell crank.
4. Remove the brake drum securing screw and the drum.
5. Disconnect the brake line from the wheel cylinder and plug it, being careful not to damage the fitting.
6. Remove the brake backing plate-to-axle housing nuts and pull the backing plate with the axle from the axle housing.

NOTE: When removing the axle shaft, be careful not to damage the oil seal.

7. Using a pair of snapring pliers, remove the snapring from the axle shaft.
8. Slip tool No. 09521–25011, or its equivalent, over the axle shaft and fasten it to the backing plate. Using 2 metal blocks and a press, press the axle from the backing plate assembly.
9. If necessary to remove the bearing from backing plate, perform the following:
a. Remove the brake spring, the retracting spring clamp bolt, the lower springs, the shoe strut, the brake shoes and the parking brake lever.
b. Using a slide hammer puller, pull the outer oil seal from the backing plate.
c. Press the bearing from the backing plate.
d. Using the proper installation tools, press the new bearing into the backing plate.
e. Using the proper seal installation tool, press the new oil seal into the backing plate.
f. Reassemble the brake components to the backing plate.
10. Using a slide hammer, pull the oil seal from the axle housing.
To install:
11. Using the installation tool and a hammer, drive a new oil seal into the axle housing.
12. Using a press, press the axle shaft into the backing plate and the bearing retainer. Using snapring pliers, install the snapring onto the axle shaft.
13. Clean the gasket mounting surfaces.
14. To complete the installation, reverse the removal procedures. Torque the backing plate-to-axle housing nuts to 51 ft. lbs. Adjust the brake shoe clearance and bleed the brake system. Refill the axle housing with SAE 90W GL5 gear oil.

VAN

1. Loosen the rear wheel nuts. Raise and safely support the vehicle. Remove the wheel and tire assembly.
2. Working through the hole in the axle flange, remove the backing plate-to-axle housing bolts.
3. Using a slide hammer puller, pull the axle shaft from the housing.

4. Using a grinder, grind down the inner bearing retainer on the axle shaft. Using a chisel and a hammer, cut off the retainer and remove it from the shaft.
5. Using a arbor press, press the bearing from the axle shaft.
6. Using a slide hammer puller, pull the oil seal from the axle housing.
To install:
7. Lubricate the new oil seal with multi-purpose grease. Using the proper seal installation tool and a hammer, drive the new oil seal into the axle housing to a depth of 0.236 in.
8. To install, use new gaskets and reverse the removal procedures. Torque the axle retainer-to-housing bolts to 48 ft. lbs.

LAND CRUISER
Semi-Floating Type

1. Loosen the rear wheel nuts. Raise and safely support the vehicle. Remove the wheel and tire assembly.
2. Place a pan under the axle, remove the plug and drain the oil from the differential.
3. Remove the brake drum and related parts, as follows:
a. Remove the cover from the back of the differential housing.
b. Remove the pin from the differential pinion shaft.
c. Withdraw the pinion shaft and it's spacer from the case.
d. Use a mallet to tap the rear axle shaft toward the differential, then remove the C-lock from the axle shaft.
e. Withdraw the axle shaft from the housing.
4. Using a bearing puller, remove axle bearing and oil seal together from the axle housing. Using a metal tube and a hammer, drive the bearing and the seal into the housing until they seat.

NOTE: Do not mix the parts of the left and right axle shaft assemblies.

5. To complete the installation, reverse the removal procedures. Refill the axle housing with SAE 90W GL5 gear oil.

NOTE: After installing the axle shaft, C-lock, spacer and pinion shaft, measure the clearance between the axle shaft and the pinion shaft spacer with a feeler gauge. The clearance should fall between 0.0024–0.0181 in. If the clearance is not within specifications, use one of the following spacers to adjust it:

a. 1.172–1.173 in.
b. 1.188–1.189 in.
c. 1.204–1.205 in.

Full Floating Type
1. Loosen the rear wheel nuts. Raise and safely support the vehicle. Remove the wheel and tire assembly.
2. Place a pan under the axle, remove the plug and drain the oil from the differential.
3. Remove the rear axle shaft plate nuts.
4. Remove the cone washers from the mounting studs by tapping the slits of the washers with a tapered punch.
5. Install bolts into the 2 unused holes of the axle shaft plate.
6. Tighten the bolts to draw the axle shaft assembly out of the housing.
7. To install, use a new gasket, sealant and reverse the removal procedures. Torque the axle shaft nuts to 21–25 ft. lbs.

Front Wheel Hub, Knuckle and Bearing

Removal and Installation
2WD PICK-UP, 4RUNNER AND VAN

1. Raise and safely support the vehicle. Remove the wheel and tire assembly.

2. Remove the brake caliper (do not disconnect the brake hose from the caliper) and suspend it on a wire.

3. Remove axle hub dust cap, the cotter pin, the nut lock, the adjusting nut, the thrust washer and the outer bearing, then pull the hub/disc assembly from the axle spindle.

4. Remove the backing plate cotter pins and the mounting nuts or bolts, then the backing plate.

5. Remove steering knuckle arm from the back of the steering knuckle.

6. Remove the nuts, the retainers and the bushings, then the shock absorber from the lower control arm.

7. Support the lower arm with a jack and raise to put pressure on spring.

NOTE: Be careful not to unbalance vehicle support stands when jacking up lower arm.

8. Remove cotter pins, then the upper and lower ball joint nuts. Using a ball joint removal tool, separate the ball joints from the steering knuckle.

9. Remove the steering knuckle from the vehicle.

NOTE: Whenever the hub/disc assembly is removed from the vehicle, it is good practice to replace the grease seal.

10. To install, reverse the removal procedures. Torque the upper ball joint nut to 80 ft. lbs. (Pick-Up and 4Runner) or 58 ft. lbs. (Van), the lower ball joint nut to 105 ft. lbs. (Pick-Up and 4Runner) or 76 ft. lbs., the steering knuckle arm-to-steering knuckle bolts to 80 ft. lbs. (Pick-Up and 4Runner) or 61 ft. lbs. (Van), the shock absorber-to-lower control arm nuts to 19 ft. lbs. and the backing plate-to-steering knuckle bolts to 80 ft. lbs. (Pick-Up and 4Runner) or 61 ft. lbs. (Van). Adjust the wheel bearing.

4WD VEHICLES

1. Remove the front axle shaft assembly from the vehicle.

2. Remove the oil seal retainer and the oil seal set from the rear of the steering knuckle.

3. At the drag link end of the steering knuckle arm, remove the cotter pin. Using the proper tool, remove the plug from the drag link, then disconnect the drag link from the steering knuckle arm.

4. Remove the tie-rod-to-steering knuckle, cotter pin and nut. Using the proper ball joint removal tool, separate the tie-rod from the steering knuckle arm..

5. Remove the steering knuckle arm-to-steering knuckle (top) nuts and the steering knuckle-to-bearing cap (bottom) nuts. Using a tapered punch, tap the cone washers slits and remove the washers.

NOTE: Do not mix or lose the upper and lower bearing cap shims.

6. Using a bearing removal tool (without a collar), press the steering knuckle arm with the shims from the steering knuckle.

7. Using a bearing removal tool (without a collar), press the bearing cap with the shims from the steering knuckle.

8. Remove the steering knuckle from the vehicle.

To install:

9. To install the steering knuckle, use a suitable tool to support the upper inner bearing. Using a hammer, tap the steering knuckle arm into the bearing inner race.

10. Using the proper tool, support the lower bearing inner race. Using a hammer, tap the bearing cap into the bearing inner race.

NOTE: When installing the drag link-to-steering knuckle arm, torque the plug all the way, then loosen it 1⅓ turns and secure it with the cotter pin.

11. To install, use gaskets, seals, pack the steering knuckle with multi-purpose grease and reverse the removal procedures.

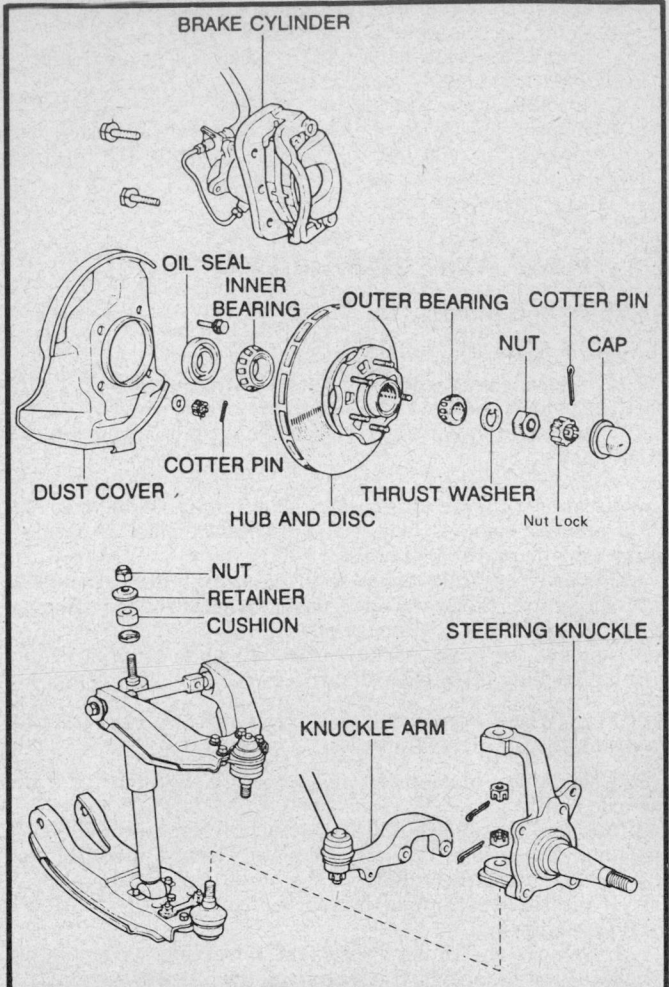

Front hub and steering knuckle—typical 2WD vehicle

Torque the steering knuckle arm-to-steering knuckle nuts to 71 ft. lbs., the bearing cap-to-steering knuckle nuts to 71 ft. lbs., the tie-rod-to-steering knuckle arm nut to 67 ft. lbs., the axle spindle-to-steering knuckle bolts to 38 ft. lbs. Adjust the wheel bearing preload.

NOTE: To test the knuckle bearing preload, attach a spring scale to the tie-rod end hole (at a right angle) in the steering knuckle arm. The force required to move the knuckle from side to side should be 6.6–13 lbs. or 4–5 lbs. (Land Cruiser). If the preload is not correct, adjust by replacing shims.

Locking Hubs

Removal and Installation

1. If equipped with free-wheeling hubs, turn the hub control handle to the **FREE** position.

2. Remove the hub cover bolts and pull off the cover.

3. If equipped with automatic locking hubs, remove the axle bolt with the washer.

4. Using snapring pliers, remove the snapring from the axle shaft.

5. Remove the hub body mounting nuts.

6. Remove the cone washers from the hub body mounting studs by tapping on the washer slits with a tapered punch.

7. Remove the hub body from the axle hub.

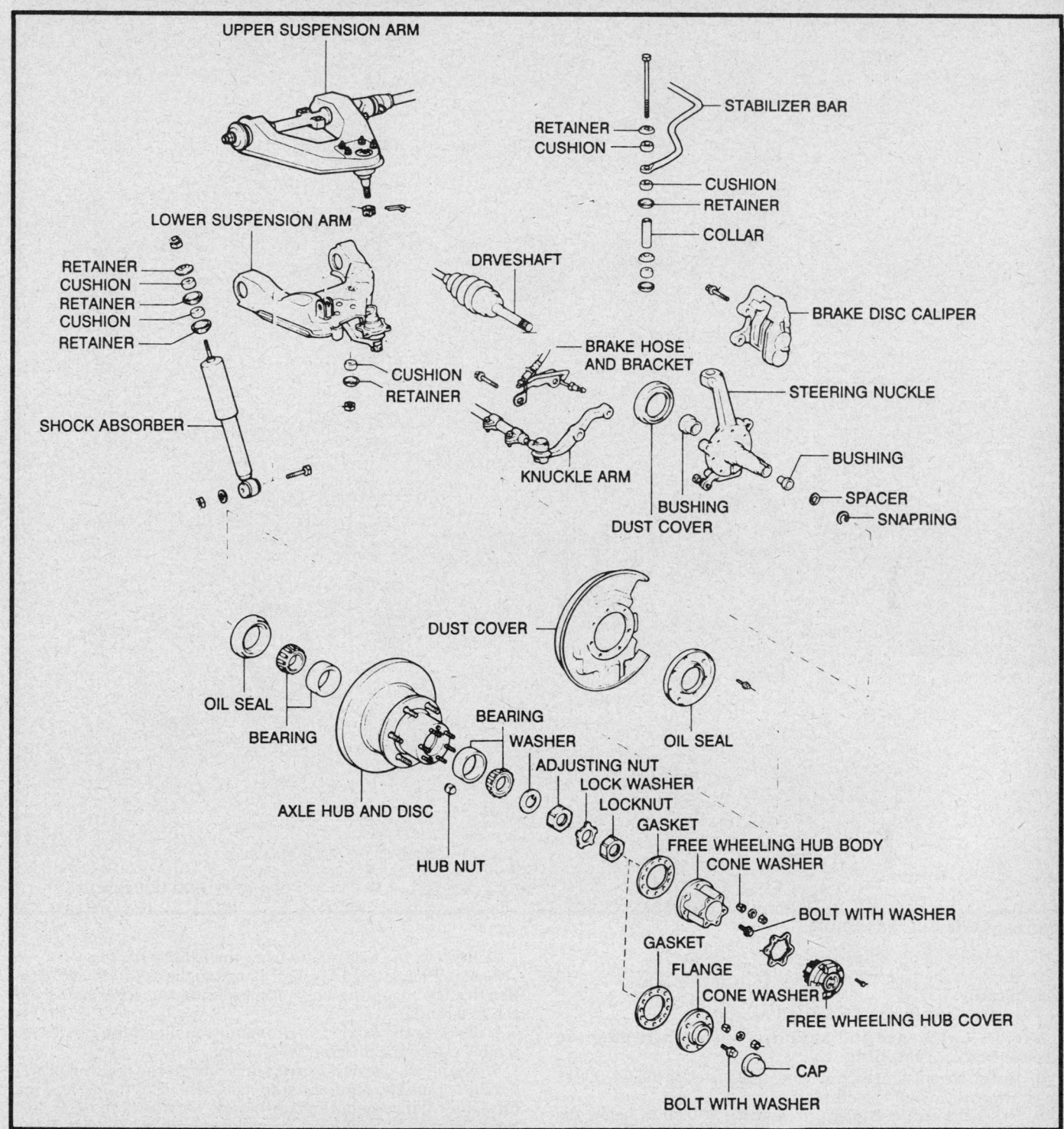

UPPER SUSPENSION ARM

STABILIZER BAR

RETAINER
CUSHION

CUSHION
RETAINER

COLLAR

LOWER SUSPENSION ARM

DRVESHAFT

BRAKE DISC CALIPER

RETAINER
CUSHION
RETAINER
CUSHION
RETAINER

BRAKE HOSE
AND BRACKET

STEERING NUCKLE

CUSHION
RETAINER

BUSHING

SHOCK ABSORBER

KNUCKLE ARM

SPACER
SNAPRING

BUSHING
DUST COVER

DUST COVER

OIL SEAL

BEARING

BEARING
WASHER
ADJUSTING NUT
LOCK WASHER
LOCKNUT
GASKET

OIL SEAL

AXLE HUB AND DISC

HUB NUT

FREE WHEELING HUB BODY
CONE WASHER

BOLT WITH WASHER

GASKET
FLANGE
CONE WASHER

FREE WHEELING HUB COVER

CAP

BOLT WITH WASHER

Front hub and steering knuckle—typical 4WD vehicle

8. Apply multi-purpose grease to the inner hub splines.
9. To install, use new gaskets and reverse the removal procedures. Torque the hub body-to-axle hub nuts to 23 ft. lbs., the plate washer/bolt to 13 ft. lbs. (auto. locking hub) and the hub cover-to-hub body bolts to 7 ft. lbs.

NOTE: To install the snapring onto the axle shaft, install a bolt into the axle shaft, pull it out and install the snapring.

Pinion Seal

Removal and Installaton

1. Raise and safely support the vehicle.
2. Matchmark and remove the driveshaft.
3. Remove the companion flange from the differential.
4. Using puller 09308–10010 or equivalent, remove the oil seal from the housing.

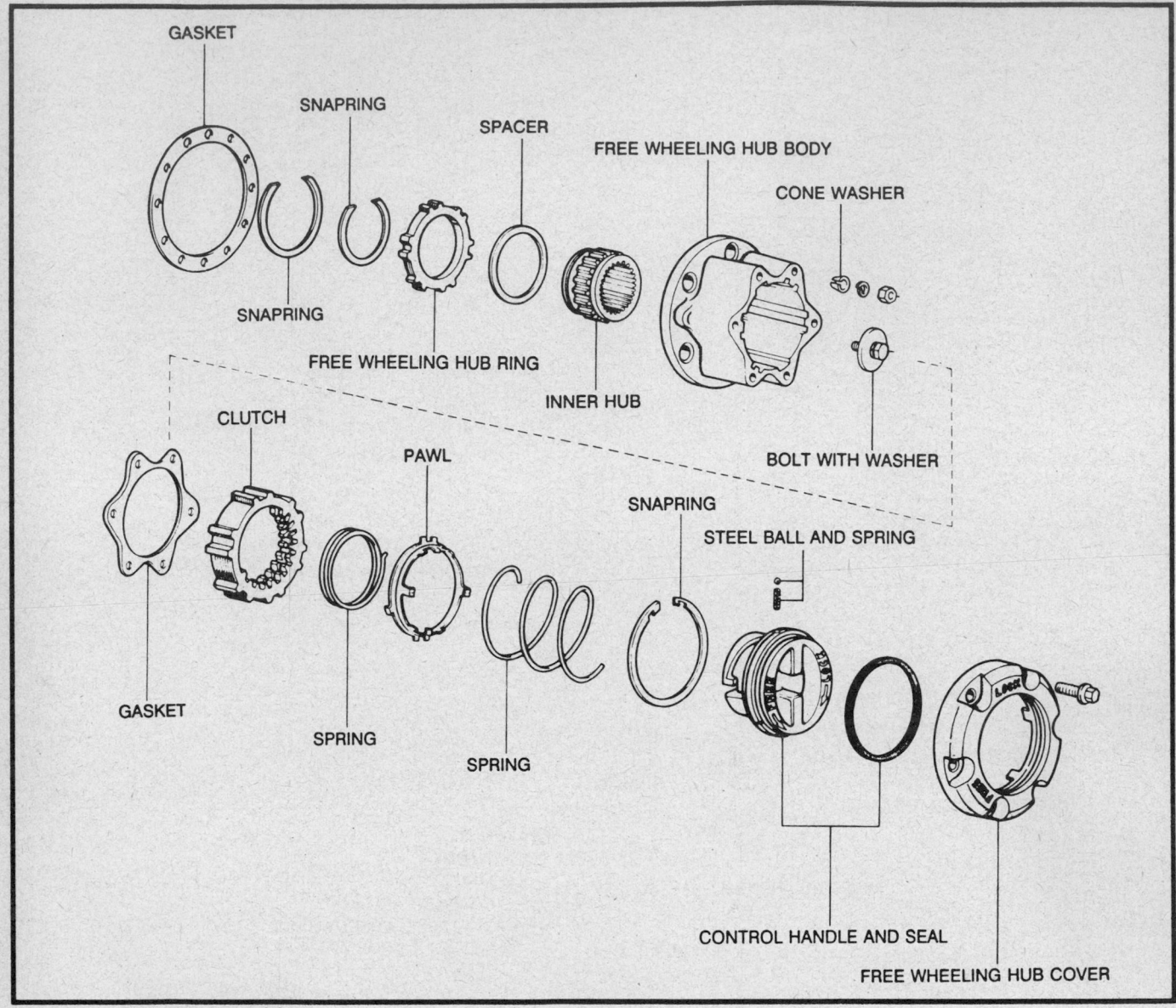

GASKET

SNAPRING

SPACER

FREE WHEELING HUB BODY

CONE WASHER

SNAPRING

FREE WHEELING HUB RING

INNER HUB

BOLT WITH WASHER

CLUTCH

PAWL

SNAPRING

STEEL BALL AND SPRING

GASKET

SPRING

SPRING

CONTROL HANDLE AND SEAL

FREE WHEELING HUB COVER

Manual 4WD hub assembly

5. Remove the oil slinger.

6. Remove the bearing and spacer.

To install:

7. Install the bearing spacer and bearing.

NOTE: Lubricate the seal lips with multi-purpose grease before installing it.

8. Install the oil slinger and using seal installer 09554–30011 or equivalent, install the oil seal.

9. Drive the seal into place, to a depth of 0.59 in below the housing lip for 7.5 in. axles and 0.39 in. below the lip for 8 in. axles.

10. Install the companion flange and install the driveshaft.

11. Lower the vehicle.

Differential Carrier

Removal and Installation

REAR

1. Raise and safely support the vehicle. Drain the lubricant from the differential.

2. Remove the axle shafts from the axle housing.

3. Matchmark the driveshaft flange to the differential flange. Remove the mounting bolts and separate the driveshaft from the differential.

4. Remove the carrier retaining nuts and pull the carrier assembly out of the differential housing.

5. To install, use new gaskets and reverse the removal procedures. Torque the differential-to-axle nuts to 23 ft. lbs. and the driveshaft flange-to-differential flange nuts/bolts to 31 ft. lbs. Refill the axle with 80W–90 gear oil to a level of ¼ in. below the fill hole.

NOTE: Before installing the carrier, apply a thin coat of liquid or silicone sealer to the carrier housing gasket and to the carrier side face of each carrier retaining nut.

FRONT

1. Raise and safely support the vehicle. Drain the lubricant from the differential.

2. Remove the front axle shafts from the axle housing.

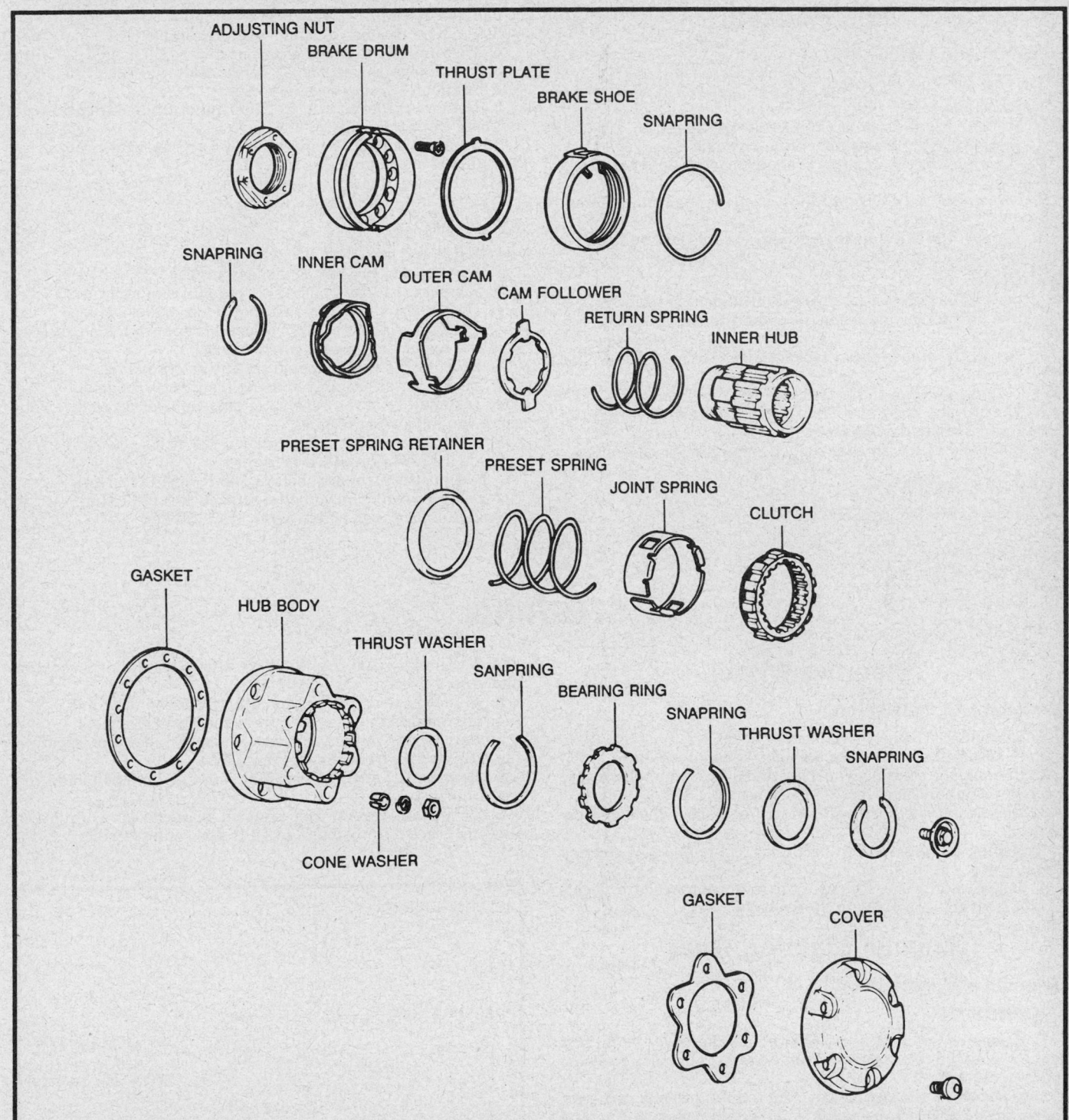

ADJUSTING NUT
BRAKE DRUM
THRUST PLATE
BRAKE SHOE
SNAPRING
SNAPRING
INNER CAM
OUTER CAM
CAM FOLLOWER
RETURN SPRING
INNER HUB
PRESET SPRING RETAINER
PRESET SPRING
JOINT SPRING
CLUTCH
GASKET
HUB BODY
THRUST WASHER
SANPRING
BEARING RING
SNAPRING
THRUST WASHER
SNAPRING
CONE WASHER
GASKET
COVER

Automatic 4WD hub assembly

3. Matchmark the front driveshaft flange to the differential flange. Remove the mounting bolts and separate the driveshaft from the differential.

4. Remove the carrier retaining nuts and pull the carrier assembly out of the differential housing.

5. To install, use new gaskets and reverse the removal procedures. Torque the differential-to-axle nuts to 19 ft. lbs. and the front driveshaft flange-to-differential flange nuts/bolts to 54 ft. lbs. Refill the axle with 80W–90 gear oil to a level of ¼ in. below the fill hole.

NOTE: Before installing the carrier, apply a thin coat of liquid or silicone sealer to the carrier housing gasket and to the carrier side face of each carrier retaining nut.

Axle Housing

Removal and Installation

FRONT – 4WD VEHICLES

1. Raise and safely support the vehicle.
2. Matchmark and remove the front driveshaft.
3. Disconnect the axle shafts from the axle assembly.
4. Disconnect vacuum hoses, if equipped with automatic locking hubs.
5. Disconnect the 4WD indicator. Remove the front differential mounting bolt.
6. Support the axle housing with an suitable jack and remove the rear mounting bolts.

To install:

7. Install the differential in position under the vehicle.
8. Install the rear mounting bolts and torque to 123 ft. lbs. (167 Nm).
9. Install the front mounting bolt and torque to 108 ft. lbs. (147 Nm).
10. Connect vacuum hoses and the 4WD indicator.
11. Install the axle shafts and the driveshaft, aligning matchmarks made during removal.
12. Refill the axle with the coorect oil and lower the vehicle.

REAR – EXCEPT VAN

1. Raise and safely support the vehicle.

2. Remove the tire and wheel assemblies.
3. Support the axle housing with a suitable jack.
4. Disconnect the shock absorber lower bolts.
5. Disconnect the stabilizer bar and lateral rod. Disconnect the brake lines from the axle housing.
6. Remove the leaf spring U-bolts and carefully lower the axle housing from the vehicle.
7. Installation is the reverse of the removal procedure. Torque the shock absorber lower bolts to 19 ft. lbs (25 Nm) on 2WD vehicles and to 47 ft. lbs (64 Nm) on 4WD vehicles. Tighten the U-bolt nuts to 90 ft. lbs (123 Nm).

REAR – VAN

1. Raise and safely support the vehicle.
2. Remove the tire and wheel assemblies.
3. Support the axle housing with a suitable jack.
4. Disconnect the shock absorber lower bolts.
5. Disconnect the stabilizer bar and lateral rod. Also, disconnect the upper and lower control arms.
6. Remove the brake lines from the axle housing.
7. Slowly lower the axle housing from the vehicle.
8. Installation is the reverse of the removal procedure. Observe the folloowing torques:
   a. Shock absorber bottom bolts – 27 ft.lbs (37 Nm) 2WD, 94 ft. lbs (127 Nm) 4WD vehicles.
   b. Upper control arm bolts – 105 ft. lbs. (142 Nm).
   c. Lower control arm bolts – 105 ft. lbs. (142 Nm).
   d. Stabilizer bar bolts – 19 ft. lbs (25 Nm).

STEERING

Steering Wheel

Removal and Installation

1. Disconnect the negative battery cable.
2. Position the wheels in a straight ahead position.
2. Remove the steering wheel center cover, some vehicles use a screw to retain the cover.
3. Disconnect the horn wire. Matchmark the wheel and the shaft.
4. Using an appropriate wheel puller tool remove the steering wheel.
5. Installation is the reverse of the removal procedure. Tighten the steering wheel nut to 25 ft. lbs (34 Nm).

Manual Steering Gear

Removal and Installation

2WD PICK-UP

1. Raise and safely support the vehicle. Remove the pitman arm-to-relay rod cotter pin and nut. Separate the relay rod from the pitman arm.
2. Matchmark the flexible steering coupling-to-steering gear, then remove the lock bolt and separate the steering coupling from the steering gear.
3. Remove the steering gear housing mounting bolts and the gear housing.
4. To install, reverse the removal procedures. Torque the housing-to-frame bolts to 48 ft. lbs., the pitman arm-to-relay rod nut 67 ft. lbs. and the steering gear-to-coupling yoke to 15–20 ft. lbs.

4WD PICK-UP AND 4RUNNER

1. Raise and safely support the vehicle. Remove the stone shield from the gear housing, if equipped.

2. Matchmark the intermediate shaft-to-steering gear and disconnect them.
3. Remove the cotter pin and plug from the drag link.
4. Disconnect the drag link from the pitman arm.
5. Remove the pitman arm nut. Using a puller tool, separate the pitman arm from the steering gear.
6. Remove the steering gear housing-to-frame bolts and the gear housing.
7. To install, reverse the removal procedures. Torque the steering gear-to-frame bolts to 42 ft. lbs., the steering gear-to-

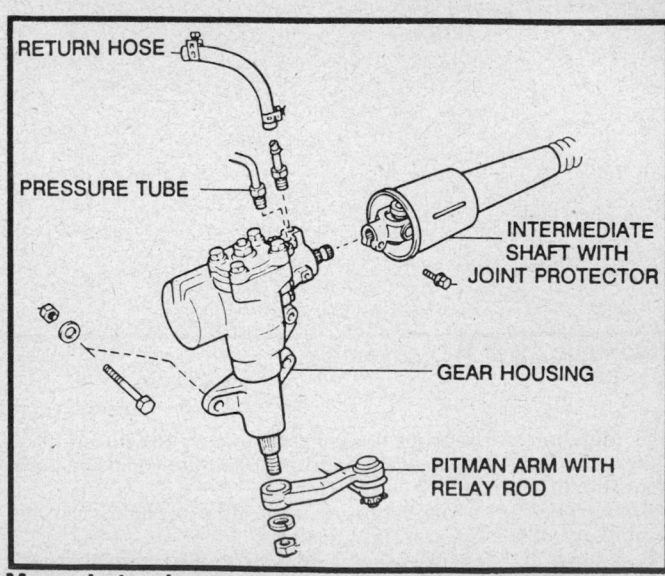

RETURN HOSE

PRESSURE TUBE

INTERMEDIATE SHAFT WITH JOINT PROTECTOR

GEAR HOUSING

PITMAN ARM WITH RELAY ROD

Manual steering gear assembly – all except Van

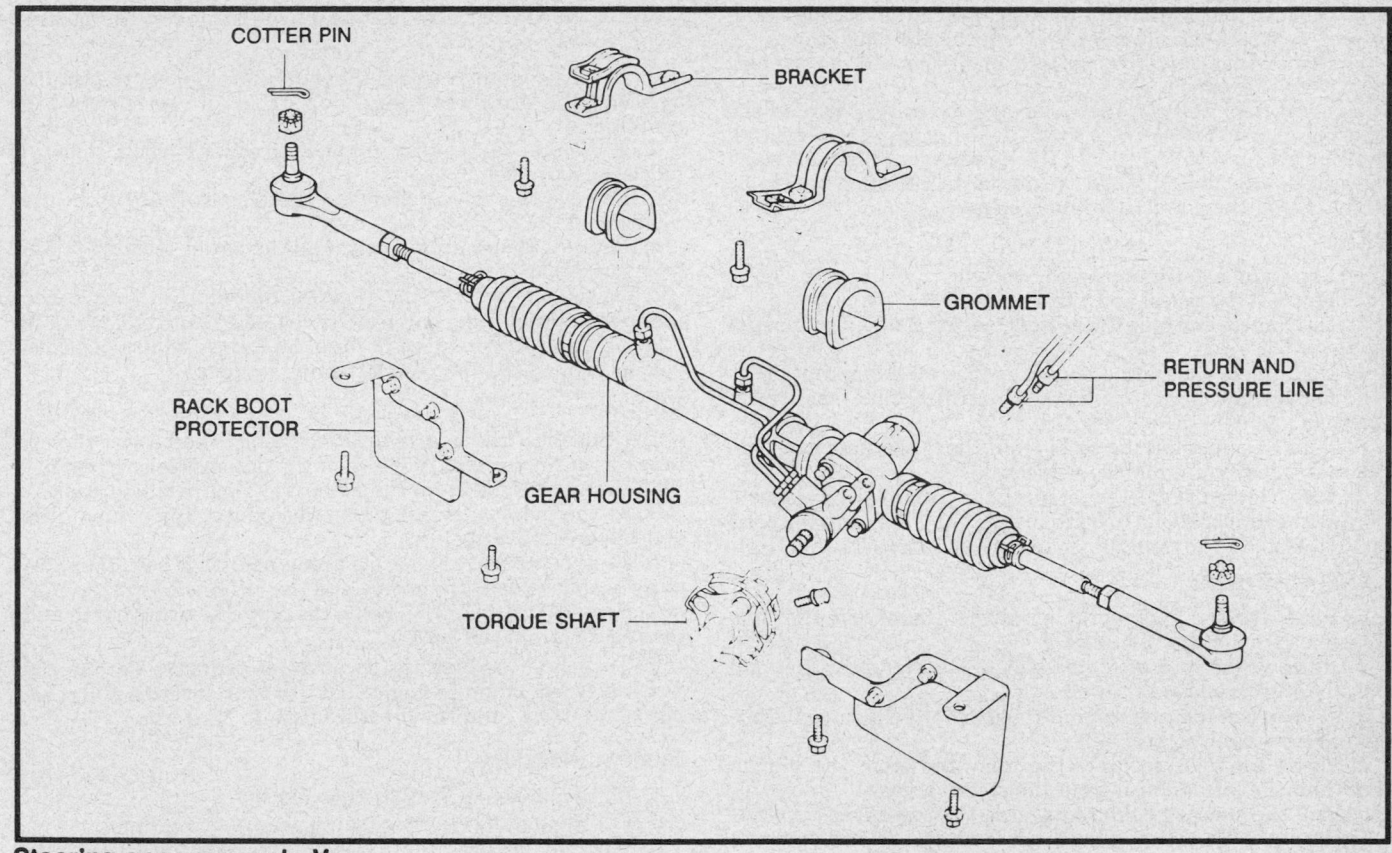

Steering gear removal – Van

intermediate bolts to 29 ft. lbs., the pitman arm-to-steering gear nut to 127 ft. lbs.

> NOTE: When installing the drag link to the pitman arm, tighten the plug completely and loosen it $1\frac{1}{3}$ turns.

VAN

1. Raise and safely support the vehicle.
2. Remove the wheel and tire assemblies.
3. Disconnect the tie rod ends from the steering knuckle.
4. Matchmark and disconnect the intermediate shaft from the gear.
5. Remove the retaining bolts from the 2 brackets and slide the rack out from under the vehicle.
6. Installation is the reverse of the removal procedure. Torque the bracket bolts to 56 ft. lbs (76 Nm), the coupling bolts to 26 ft. lbs. (35 Nm) and the tie rod bolts to 43 ft. lbs. (59 Nm).

LAND CRUISER

1. Raise and safely support the vehicle. Remove the worm yokes from the worm and the main shaft.
2. Remove the intermediate shaft assembly.
3. Remove the pitman arm from the sector shaft.
4. Remove the steering gear-to-frame bolts and the steering gear from the vehicle.
5. To install, reverse the removal procedures. Torque the pitman arm to 119–141 ft. lbs.

> NOTE: The intermediate shaft must be installed with the wheels in a straight ahead position and the steering wheel straight ahead.

Power Steering Gear

Removal and Installation

2WD PICK-UP

1. Raise and safely support the vehicle. Disconnect and plug the pressure line clamp bolts at the steering gear.
2. Matchmark the intermediate shaft-to-steering gear, then, remove the coupling bolt and separate the intermediate shaft from the steering gear.
3. Remove the pitman arm-to-steering gear and the pitman arm-to-relay rod nuts.
4. Using a puller tool, separate the pitman arm from the relay rod and the pitman arm from the steering gear.
5. Remove the steering gear-to-frame bolts and the steering gear from the vehicle.
6. To install, reverse the removal procedures. Torque the steering gear-to-frame bolts to 48 ft. lbs., the pitman arm-to-steering gear nut to 90 ft. lbs., the pitman arm-to-relay rod nut to 67 ft. lbs., the intermediate shaft-to-steering gear bolt to 19 ft. lbs. and the pressure line nuts to 33 ft. lbs. Bleed the power steering system.

4WD PICK-UP AND 4RUNNER

1. Remove the battery and the engine lower gravel shield.
2. Raise and safely support the vehicle. Disconnect and plug the pressure lines at the steering gear.
3. Remove the steering gear stone shield.
4. Matchmark the intermediate shaft-to-steering gear, then remove coupling bolt and the intermediate shaft from the steering gear.

5. Remove the pitman arm-to-steering gear nut. Using a puller tool, separate the pitman arm from the steering gear.

6. Remove the gear housing-to-frame bolts and the steering gear from the vehicle.

7. To install, reverse the removal procedures. Torque the steering gear-to-frame bolts to 42 ft. lbs., the pitman arm-to-steering gear nut to 127 ft. lbs., the intermediate shaft-to-steering gear bolt to 29 ft. lbs. and the pressure line union nuts to 33 ft. lbs. Bleed the power steering system.

VAN

1. Raise and safely support the vehicle.
2. Remove the wheel and tire assemblies.
3. Disconnect and plug the power steering fluid lines from the gear.
4. Disconnect the tie rod ends from the steering knuckle.
5. Matchmark and disconnect the intermediate shaft from the gear.
6. Remove the retaining bolts from the 2 brackets and slide the rack out from under the vehicle.
7. Installation is the reverse of the removal procedure. Torque the bracket bolts to 56 ft. lbs (76 Nm), the coupling bolts to 26 ft. lbs. (35 Nm) and the tie rod bolts to 43 ft. lbs. (59 Nm).

LAND CRUISER

1. Raise and safely support the vehicle. Disconnect the pressure lines from the steering gear.
2. Remove the intermediate shaft-to-steering gear bolt and the steering column-to-firewall bolts.
3. Loosen the steering column-to-dash bolts. Remove the pitman arm-to-steering gear nut.
4. Using a puller, separate the relay rod from the pitman shaft and the pitman arm from the steering gear.
5. Pull the steering column towards the passenger compartment to uncouple the steering shaft from the steering gear.
6. Remove the steering gear-to-frame bolts and the steering gear from the vehicle.
7. To install, reverse the removal procedures. Torque the steering gear-to-frame bolts to 40–63 ft. lbs., the pitman arm-to-steering gear nut to 120–141 ft. lbs., the intermediate shaft-to-steering gear bolt to 22–32 ft. lbs., the pressure hose fitting to 29–36 ft. lbs. and the return hose fitting to 24–30 ft. lbs. Bleed the power steering system.

NOTE: During installation of the hydraulic lines, position each line clear of any surrounding components, then tighten the fittings.

Power Steering Pump

Removal and Installation

PICK-UP, LAND CRUISER AND 4RUNNER

NOTE: Disconnect the air hoses from the air control valve and the high tension wires from the distributor.

1. Disconnect the negative battery cable. Loosen the power steering pump pulley nut.

NOTE: Use the drive belt as a brake to keep the pulley from rotating.

2. Place a container under the pump. Disconnect the return line and the pressure tube, then drain the fluid into the container.
3. Loosen the idler pulley nut and the adjusting bolt, then remove the drive belt.
4. Remove the drive pulley and the Woodruff key from the pump shaft.
5. Remove the mounting bolts and the power steering pump from the vehicle.
6. To install, reverse the removal procedures. Torque the pump pulley mounting bolt to 29 ft. lbs., the pump pulley nut to 32 ft. lbs. and the pressure hoses to 33 ft. lbs. Adjust the drive belt tension. Bleed the power steering system.

VAN

1. Disconnect the negative battery cable. Disconnect the air hoses from the air control valve of the power steering pump.
2. Drain the fluid from the power steering reservoir tank.
3. At the power steering pump, disconnect the return hose and the pressure tube.
4. Loosen the power steering pump adjusting bolt, then, remove the drive belt, the pulley and the woodruff key.
5. Remove the mounting bolts, the power steering pump and the bracket from the vehicle.
6. To install, reverse the removal procedures. Torque the power steering pump-to-engine bolts to 29 ft. lbs., the pulley set nut to 32 ft. lbs. and the pressure tube to 33 ft. lbs.

System Bleeding

1. Raise and safely support the vehicle.
2. Fill the pump reservoir with power steering fluid.
3. With the engine running, rotate the steering wheel from lock to lock several times. Add fluid as necessary.

NOTE: Perform the bleeding procedure until all of the air is bled from the system.

4. The fluid level should not have risen more than $^2/_{10}$ in.; if it does, check the pump.

Tie Rod Ends

Removal and Installation

1. Raise and safely support the vehicle.
2. Remove the wheel and tire assembly.
3. Using a tie rod end puller, disconnect the tie rod from the relay rod.
4. Using a tie rod end puller remove the tie rod from the steering knuckle.
5. Remove the tie rod end from the vehicle.
6. Installation is the reverse of the removal procedure. Tighten the clamp nuts to 19 ft. lbs.(25 Nm) and the knuckle-to-arm nuts to 67 ft. lbs.

BRAKES

For all brake system repair and service procedures not detailed below, please refer to "Brakes" in the Unit Repair section.

Master Cylinder

Removal and Installation

PICK-UP, 4RUNNER AND LAND CRUISER

1. Disconnect the negative battery cable. Using a syringe, remove the brake fluid from the master cylinder.
2. Disconnect and plug the hydraulic lines at the master cylinder.
3. If equipped, disconnect the level warning switch connector from the master cylinder.
4. Remove the master cylinder-to-power booster nuts and the master cylinder assembly from the power brake unit.
5. To install, reverse the removal procedures. Torque the master cylinder mounting bolts to 9 ft. lbs. and the brake lines-to-master cylinder to 11 ft. lbs. Refill the master cylinder with new brake fluid and bleed the brake system.

VAN

1. Disconnect the negative battery terminal from the battery.
2. To expose the master cylinder, perform the following:
   a. Remove the master cylinder reservoir cap, located at the left-side of the instrument panel.
   b. Remove the instrument cluster finish panel and the lower cluster finish panel. Disconnect the electrical connectors and the speedometer cable from the instrument panel, then remove the instrument panel.
   c. Remove the No. 1, 2 and 3 air ducts.
3. Using a syringe, remove the brake fluid from the master cylinder reservoir.
4. Remove the reservoir hoses from the master cylinder. Disconnect and plug the brake lines at the master cylinder.
5. Remove the master cylinder mounting nuts, the vacuum check valve bracket and the master cylinder from the vehicle.
6. To install, reverse the removal procedures. Torque the master cylinder mounting nuts to 9 ft. lbs. and the brake lines-to-master cylinder to 11 ft. lbs. Refill the master cylinder with new brake fluid and bleed the brake system.

Load Sensing Proportioning Valve

Removal and Installation

1. Raise and safely support the vehicle, so that it is level.
2. Disconnect the No. 2 shackle from the bracket.
3. Disconnect and plug the brake lines from the load sensing valve.
4. Remove the load sensing valve bracket from the frame.
5. To install, reverse the removal procedures. Torque the load sensing valve-to-frame bolts to 14 ft. lbs. and the brake tubes to 11 ft. lbs. Bleed the brake system.
6. Adjust the load sensing valve and the rear axle load.
7. Check and/or adjust the length of the No. 2 shackle (distance from the center of the No. 2 shackle-to-shackle bracket bolt to the center of the No. 1 shackle-to-spring bolt): 3.07 in.

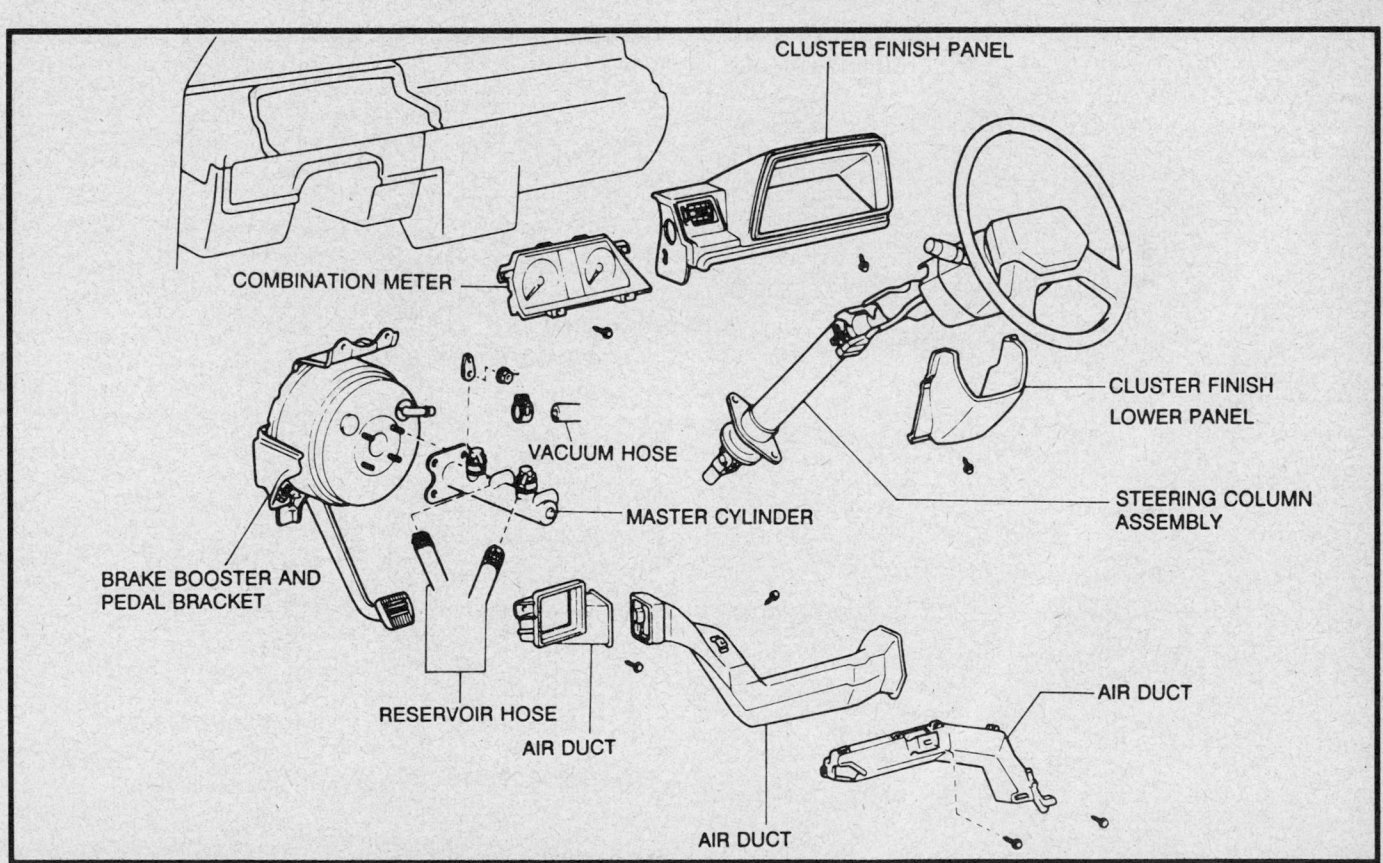

CLUSTER FINISH PANEL

COMBINATION METER

VACUUM HOSE

MASTER CYLINDER

CLUSTER FINISH LOWER PANEL

STEERING COLUMN ASSEMBLY

BRAKE BOOSTER AND PEDAL BRACKET

RESERVOIR HOSE

AIR DUCT

AIR DUCT

AIR DUCT

Removing the brake booster and master cylinder— Van

(2WD Pick-Up and Van) or 4.72 in. (4WD Pick-Up, 4Runner and Land Cruiser).

Power Brake Booster

Removal and Installation

EXCEPT VAN

1. Disconnect the negative battery cable. Separate the master cylinder from the power brake booster.
2. Remove the vacuum hose form the power brake booster.
3. Working under the instrument panel, remove the brake pedal-to-brake booster rod clevis pin. Remove the power brake booster mounting bolts and the booster from the vehicle.
4. To install, reverse the removal procedures. Torque the power brake booster nuts to 9 ft. lbs.

NOTE: When installing a new booster, make sure there is a little clearance between the pushrod end and the master cylinder piston.

VAN

1. Disconnect the negative battery terminal from the battery.
2. To expose the master cylinder, perform the following:
    a. Remove the master cylinder reservoir cap, located at the left-side of the instrument panel.
    b. Remove the instrument cluster finish panel and the lower cluster finish panel. Disconnect the electrical connectors and the speedometer cable from the instrument panel, then remove the instrument panel.
    c. Remove the No. 1, 2 and 3 air ducts.
3. Using a syringe, remove the brake fluid from the master cylinder reservoir.

4. Remove the reservoir hoses from the master cylinder. Disconnect and plug the brake lines at the master cylinder.
5. Remove the master cylinder mounting nuts, the vacuum check valve bracket and the master cylinder from the vehicle.
6. Remove the bolts retaining the brake pedal and booster bracket. Remove the bracket from the vehicle.
7. To install, reverse the removal procedures. Torque the master cylinder mounting nuts to 9 ft. lbs. and the brake lines-to-master cylinder to 11 ft. lbs. Refill the master cylinder with new brake fluid and bleed the brake system.

Brake Caliper

Removal and Installation

1. Raise ands safely support the vehicle.
2. Remove the wheel and tire assembly.
3. Remove the 2 wire clips at the ends of the brake pad pins.
4. Pull out the pads and anti-rattle springs.
5. Lift out the anti squeal shims.
6. Plug the vent hole on the master cylinder cap, to prevent fluid leakage. Disconnect and plug the brake line from the caliper.
7. Remove the 2 caliper mounting bolts and remove the caliper.

To install:

8. Position the caliper and install the mounting bolts. Tighten the caliper mounting bolts to 29 ft. lbs. on 2WD vehicles and to 90 ft. lbs on 4WD vehicles.
9. Install the brake pads. Install the wheel and tire assembly and lower the vehicle.
10. Road test the vehicle.

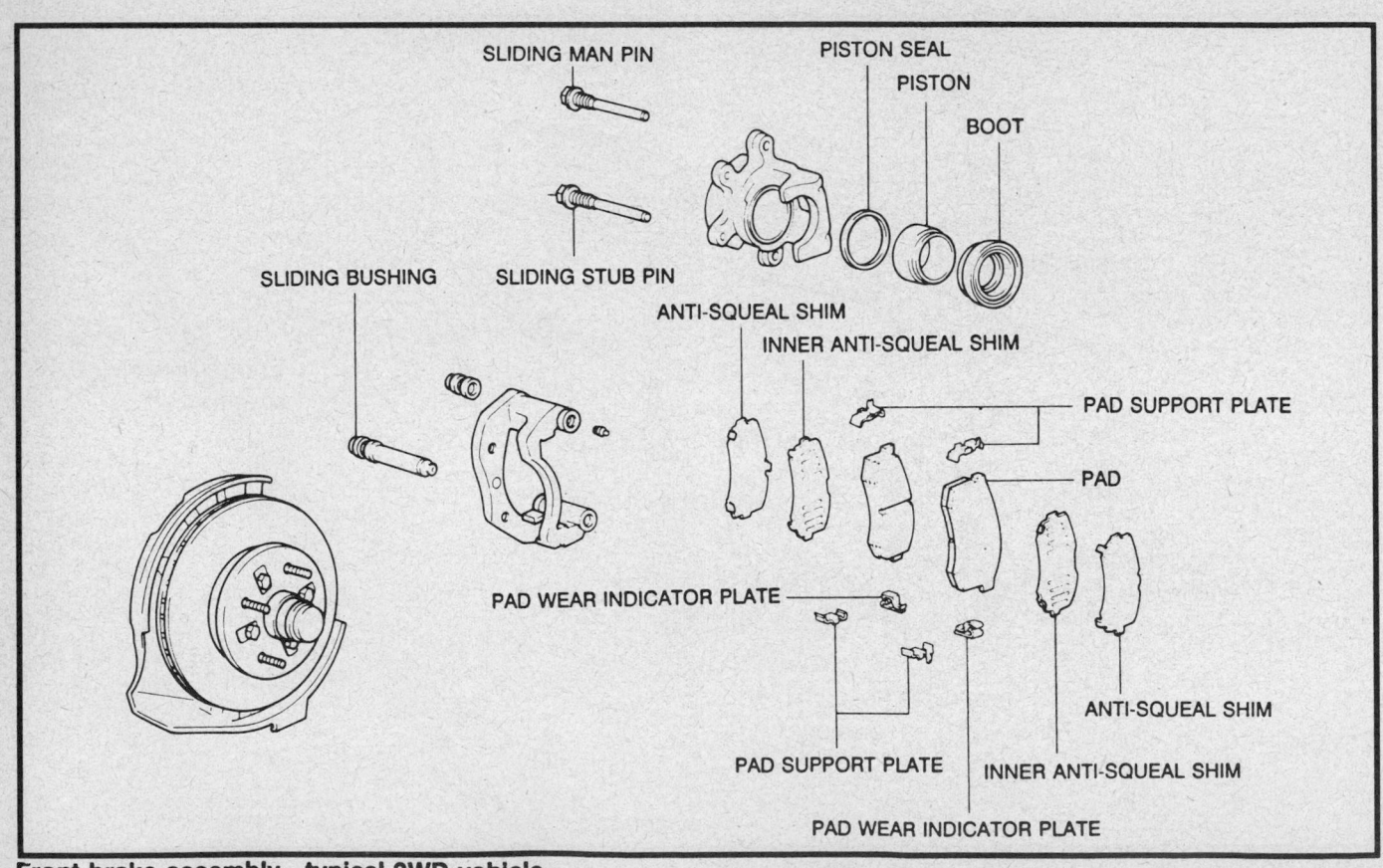

Front brake assembly—typical 2WD vehicle

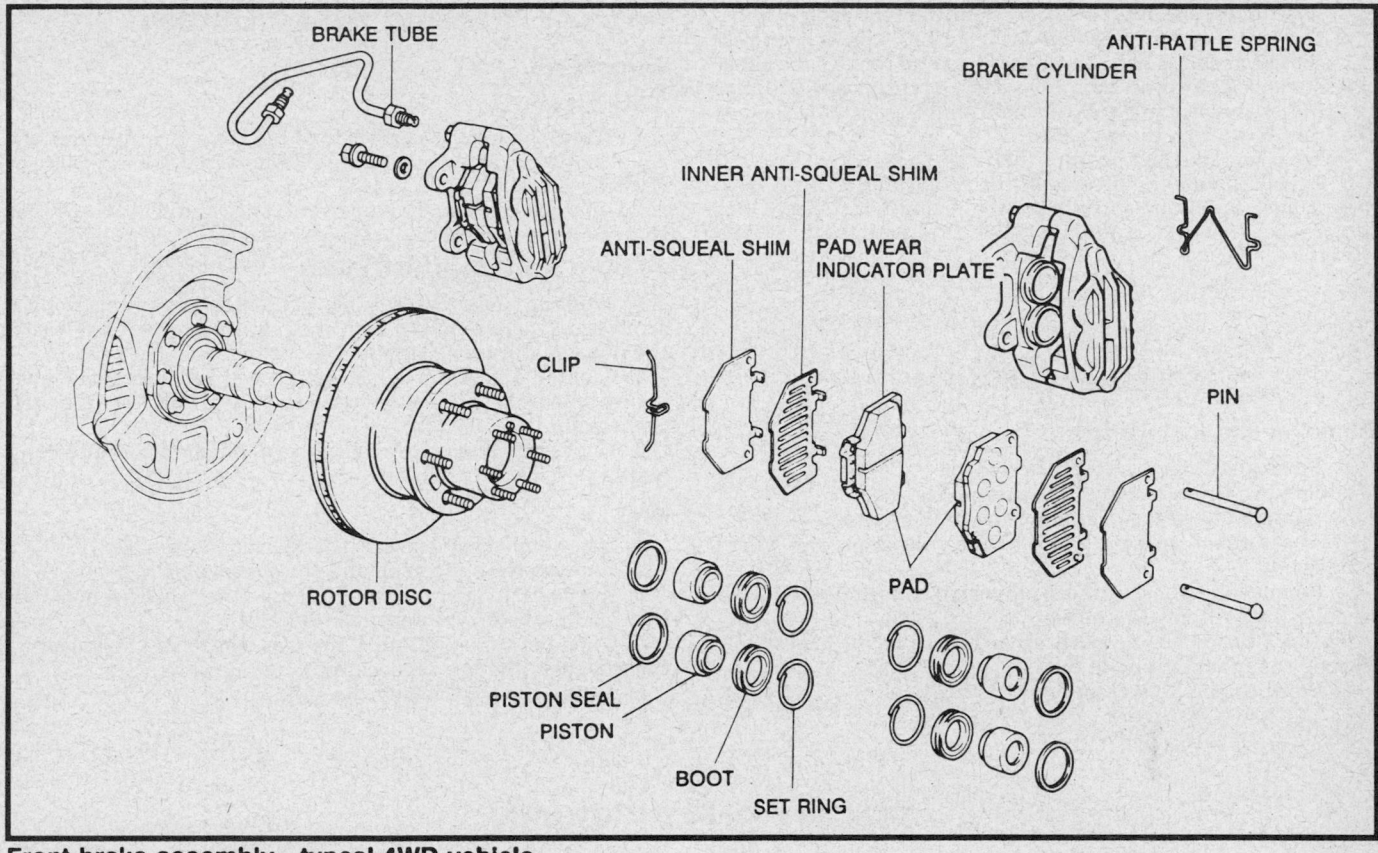

Front brake assembly—typcal 4WD vehicle

Disc Brake Pads

Removal and Installation

2WD VEHICLE

1. Raise and safely support the vehicle.
2. Remove the wheel and tire assembly.
3. Remove the bottom caliper retaining bolt and loosen the top bolt.
4. Pivot the caliper upward and suspend it with wire, do not disconnect the brake line.
5. Remove the anti-squeal springs, brake pads, anti-squeal shims, wear indicator plates and the 4 pad support plates.
6. Installation is the reverse of the removal procedure. Torque the caliper bolts to 29 ft. lbs. (39 Nm).

4WD VEHICLE

1. Raise and safely support the vehicle.
2. Remove the wheel and tire assembly.
3. Remove the brake pad retaining clips, 2 locating pins, anti-rattle spring, brake pads and anti-squeal shims.
4. Installation is the reverse of the removal procedure.

Brake Rotor

Removal and Installation

1. Raise and safely support the vehicle.
2. Remove the wheels and tires.
3. On 2WD vehicles, remove the grease cap, cotter pin and nut from the hub.
4. On 4WD vehicles, remove the bolt retaining the locking

hub assembly and lift it off the hub. Remove the nuts and washer from the inside of the hub.
5. Remove the rotor from the vehicle. Be careful not to drop the bearings from the hub.
6. Installation is the reverse of the removal procedure. Adjust the wheel bearings as required.
7. Bleed the brake system.

Brake Drums

Removal and Installation

1. Raise and safely support the vehicle.
2. Remove the wheel and tire assemblies.
3. Remove the brake drum retaining screws.
4. Remove the drum from the vehicle. If the drum is difficult to remove, release the brake adjusters from behind the drum.
5. Install the drum on the vehicle and install the retaining screws.
6. Install the wheel and tire assemblies.
7. Lower the vehicle. Check the operation of the brakes and adjust as needed.

Brake Shoes

Removal and Installation

1. Raise and safely support the vehicle.
2. Remove the wheel and tire assemblies.
3. Remove the brake drum retaining screws and remove the brake drum.

4. Disconnect the return spring from the rear shoe.

5. Remove the rear shoe hold-down spring, cups and pin. Disconnect the anchor spring from the shoe and remove the shoe.

6. Remove the front shoe hold-down spring, cups and pin. Disconnect the parking brake cable from the lever and remove the front shoe with the adjuster.

7. Remove the adjuster from the front shoe.

8. Installation is the reverse of the removal procedure.

9. Adjust the brake shoes after the drum is installed. Once the vehicle is lowered, pump the brakes several times to seat the shoes.

Wheel Cylinder

Removal and Installation

1. Raise and safely support the vehicle.

2. Remove the wheel and tire assemblies.

3. Remove the brake drum and the brake shoes.

4. Disconnect and plug the brake line from the wheel cylinder.

5. Remove the wheel cylinder mounting bolts and remove the wheel cylinder from the vehicle.

6. Installation is the reverse of the removal procedure. Torque the mounting bolts to 7 ft. lbs. (10 Nm).

7. Bleed the brake system after installation.

Parking Brake Cable

Adjustment

2WD PICK-UP

1. Working under the vehicle, tighten the adjusting nut at the equalizer until the travel is within limits and there is no drag at the rear shoes.

2. Apply the parking brake several times and again check that there is no drag with the brake released.

4WD PICK-UP AND 4RUNNER

1. Working under the vehicle, tighten the bellcrank stopper screw until the play at the rear brake links is gone, then loosen the nut one full turn. Tighten the locknut.

2. Tighten one of the adjusting nuts on the intermediate lever while loosening the other, until the travel is correct. Tighten the locknuts.

3. Confirm that the bellcrank is in contact with the backing plate.

VAN

1. Raise and safely support the rear of the vehicle.

2. Remove the shift knob and the console box.

3. At the parking brake handle, loosen the cable locknut. Pull the hand brake upward about 7–9 clicks.

4. Turn the adjust nut until the rear wheels can no longer be turned, then, tighten the locknut.

5. Install the console and the shift knob.

FRONT SUSPENSION

Shock Absorbers

Removal and Installation

2WD PICK-UP AND VAN

1. Raise and safely support the vehicle. Remove the wheel and tire assembly.

2. Unfasten the double nuts at the top end of the shock absorber. Remove the cushions and the cushion retainers.

3. Remove the shock absorber-to-lower control arm bolts.

4. Compress the shock absorber and remove it from the vehicle.

5. To install, reverse the removal procedures. Torque the shock absorber-to-lower control arm bolts to 13 ft. lbs. and the shock absorber-to-body nuts to 19 ft. lbs.

4WD PICK-UP, 4RUNNER AND VAN

1. Raise and safely support the vehicle. Remove the wheel and tire assembly.

2. Unfasten the double nuts at the top end of the shock absorber. Remove the cushions and the cushion retainers.

3. Remove the shock absorber-to-axle housing bolt.

4. Compress the shock absorber and remove it from the vehicle.

5. To install, reverse the removal procedures. Torque the shock absorber-to-suspension arm nut/bolt to 101 ft. lbs. (Pick-Up and 4Runner) or 70 ft. lbs. (Van) and the shock absorber-to-body nuts to 19 ft. lbs.

LAND CRUISER

1. Raise and safely support the vehicle. Remove the wheel and tire assembly.

2. Remove mounting bolts from the top and the bottom of the shock and remove shock.

3. To install, reverse the removal procedures.

Leaf Springs

Removal and Installation

LAND CRUISER

1. Raise and safely support the vehicle. Support the axle housing with a floor jack. Remove the wheel and tire assembly.

2. Lower the floor jack to take the tension off of the spring. Remove the shock absorber mounting nuts/bolts and the shock absorber.

3. Remove the cotter pins and the nuts from the lower end of the stabilizer link. Detach the link from the axle housing.

4. Remove the spring-to-axle housing U-bolt nuts, the spring bumper and the U-bolt.

5. At the front of the spring, remove the hanger pin bolt. Disconnect the spring from the bracket.

6. Remove the spring shackle retaining nuts and the spring shackle inner plate, then carefully pry out the spring shackle with a pry bar.

7. Remove the spring from the vehicle.

To install:

8. To install, perform the following procedure:

 a. Install the rubber bushings in the eye of the spring.

 b. Align the eye of the spring with the spring hanger bracket and drive the pin through the bracket holes and rubber bushings.

NOTE: Use soapy water as lubricant (if necessary), to aid in pin installation. Never use oil or grease.

 c. Finger-tighten the spring hanger nuts/bolts.

 d. Install the rubber bushings in the spring eye at the opposite end of the spring.

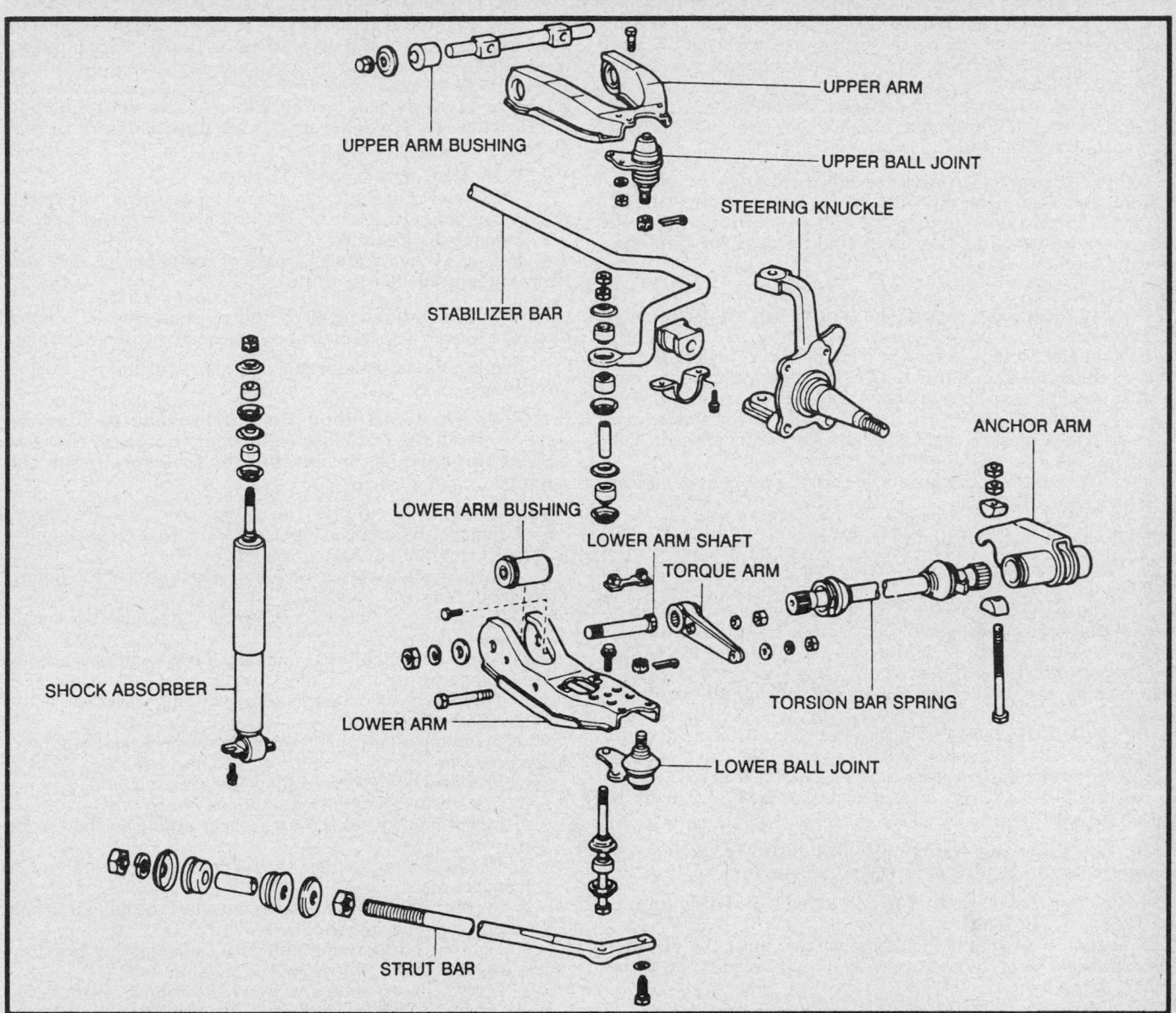

UPPER ARM

UPPER ARM BUSHING

UPPER BALL JOINT

STEERING KNUCKLE

STABILIZER BAR

ANCHOR ARM

LOWER ARM BUSHING

LOWER ARM SHAFT

TORQUE ARM

SHOCK ABSORBER

LOWER ARM

TORSION BAR SPRING

LOWER BALL JOINT

STRUT BAR

Front suspension components – 2WD vehicle

e. Raise the free end of the spring. Install the spring shackle through the bushings and the bracket.

f. Install the shackle inner plate and finger-tighten the retaining nuts.

g. Center the bolt head in the hole which is provided in the spring seat on the axle housing.

h. Fit the U-bolts over the axle housing. Install the spring bumper and the nuts.

9. To complete the installation, reverse the removal procedures. Torque the U-bolt nuts to 90 ft. lbs., the hanger pin-to-frame nut to 67 ft. lbs., the shackle pin nuts to 67 ft. lbs., the shock absorber bolts to 47 ft. lbs.

NOTE: When installing the U-bolts, tighten the nuts so that the length of the bolts are equal.

Torsion Bars

Removal and Installation
2WD PICK-UP AND VAN

These vehicles are equipped with torsion bar front springs.

NOTE: Great care must be taken to make sure springs are not mixed after removal. It is strongly suggested that before removal, each spring be marked with paint, showing front and rear of spring and from which side of the vehicle it was taken. If the springs are installed backwards or on the wrong sides of the vehicle, they could fracture. If replacing the springs, it is not necessary to mark them.

1. Raise and safely support the front of the vehicle.

2. Slide the boot from the rear of torsion bar spring, then paint an alignment mark from the torsion bar spring onto the anchor arm and the torque arm. There are right and left identification marks on the rear end of the torsion bar springs.

3. On the rear torsion bar spring holder, there is a long bolt that passes through the arm of the holder and up through the frame crossmember. Remove the locking nut only from this bolt.

4. Using a small ruler, measure the length from the bottom of the remaining nut to the threaded tip of the bolt and record this measurement.

5. Place a jack under the rear torsion bar spring holder arm and raise the arm to remove the spring pressure from the long bolt. Remove the adjusting nut from the long bolt.

6. Slowly lower jack.

7. Remove the long bolt, the spacers, the anchor arm and the torsion bar spring. The torsion bar should be easily pulled out of the anchor and the torque arms.

NOTE: Inspect all parts for wear damage or cracks. Check the boots for rips and wear. Inspect the splined ends of the torsion bar spring and the splined holes in the rear holder and the front torque arm for damage. Replace as necessary.

To install:

8. Coat the splined ends of the torsion bar with multi-purpose grease.

9. If installing the old torsion bars, perform the following:

   a. Slide the front of the torsion bar spring into the torque arm, making sure that the alignment marks are matched.

   b. Slide the anchor arm onto the rear of the torsion bar spring, making sure that the alignment marks are matched. Install the long bolt and it's spacers.

   c. Tighten the adjusting nut so that it is the same length as it was before removal.

NOTE: Do not install the locknut.

10. When installing a new torsion bar spring, perform the following:

   a. Raise the front of the vehicle, replace the wheel and tire assembly, place a wooden block (7½ in. high) under the front tire. Lower the jack until the clearance between the spring bumper (on the lower control arm) and the frame is ½ in.

   b. Slide the front of the torsion bar spring into the torque arm.

   c. Install the anchor arm into the rear of the torsion bar spring, then the long bolt and the spacers. the distance from the top of the upper spacer to the tip of the threaded end of bolt is 0.310–1.100 in. (½ ton vehicles) or 0.430–1.220 in. (¾ ton vehicles).

NOTE: Make sure the bolt and bottom spacer are snuggly in the holder arm while measuring.

   d. Remove the wooden block and lower the vehicle until it rests on the jackstands.

   e. Install and tighten the adjusting nut until the distance from the bottom of the nut to the tip of the threaded end of the bolt is 2.7–3.5 in.

NOTE: Do not install the locknut.

11. Apply multi-purpose grease to the boot lips, then refit the boots to the torque and the anchor arms.

12. Lower the vehicle to the floor and bounce it several times to settle the suspension. With the wheels on the ground, measure the distance from the ground to the center of the lower control arm-to-frame shaft. Adjust the vehicle height using the adjusting nut on the anchor arm. The height should be approximately 10.31 in.

NOTE: If, after achieving the correct vehicle height, the distance from the bottom of the adjusting nut to the top of the threaded end of the long bolt is not within 2.7–3.5 in., change the position of the anchor arm-to-tension bar spring spline and reassemble.

13. Install and torque the locknut on the long bolt to 61 ft. lbs.

NOTE: Make sure the adjusting nut does not move when tightening locknut.

4WD VAN

NOTE: Great care must be taken to make sure springs

are not mixed after removal. It is strongly suggested that before removal, each spring be marked with paint, showing front and rear of spring and from which side of the vehicle it was taken. If the springs are installed backwards or on the wrong sides of the vehicle, they could fracture. If replacing the springs, it is not necessary to mark them.

1. Raise and safely support the vehicle.

2. Using a piece of chalk, remove the boots, then, matchmark the torsion bar spring, the anchor arm and the torque arm.

3. Remove the locknut.

4. Measure the protruding length of the adjusting arm bolt (from the nut to the end of the bolt).

NOTE: The adjusting arm bolt measurement is used as a reference to establish the chassis ground clearance.

5. Remove the adjusting nut, the anchor arm and the torsion bar spring.

NOTE: When installing the torsion bar springs, be sure to check the left/right indicating marks on the rear end of the springs; be careful not to interchange the springs.

To install:

6. Using molybdenum disulphide lithium base grease, apply a coat to the torsion bar spring splines.

7. If installing a used torsion bar spring, perform the following procedures:

   a. Align the matchmarks and install the torsion bar spring to the torque arm.

   b. Align the matchmarks and install the anchor arm to the torsion bar spring.

   c. Tighten the adjusting nut until the bolt protrusion is the same as it was before.

8. If installing a new torsion bar spring, perform the following procedures:

   a. Make sure the upper and lower arms rebound.

   b. Install the boots onto the torsion bar spring.

   c. Install one end of the torsion bar spring to the torque arm.

   d. Install the torsion bar spring onto the opposite end of the anchor arm.

   e. Finger tighten the adjusting nut until the adjusting bolt protrudes about 1.570 in.

   f. Tighten the adjusting nut until the adjusting bolt protrudes about 2.480 in. (wagon) or 2.400 in. (van).

   g. Install the wheel(s) and lower the vehicle. Bounce the front of the vehicle to stablize the suspension.

9. To adjust the ground clearance, turn the adjusting nut until the center of the cam plate nut (located of the front end of the lower suspension arm) is 10.090 in. (wagon) or 9.940 in. (van) above the ground.

10. After adjusting the ground clearance, torque the locknut to 58 ft. lbs., then, install the boots.

4WD PICK-UP AND 4RUNNER

These vehicles are equipped with torsion bar front springs.

NOTE: Great care must be taken to make sure springs are not mixed after removal. It is strongly suggested that before removal, each spring be marked with paint, showing front and rear of spring and from which side of the vehicle it was taken. If the springs are installed backwards or on the wrong sides of the vehicle, they could fracture. If replacing the springs, it is not necessary to mark them.

1. Raise and safely support the vehicle.

2. Using a piece of chalk, remove the boots. Matchmark the torsion bar spring, the anchor arm and the torque arm.

3. Remove the locknut.

4. Measure the protruding length of the adjusting arm bolt (from the nut to the end of the bolt).

NOTE: The adjusting arm bolt measurement is used as a reference to establish the chassis ground clearance.

5. Remove the adjusting nut, the anchor arm and the torsion bar spring.

NOTE: When installing the torsion bar springs, be sure to check the left/right indicating marks on the rear end of the springs; be careful not to interchange the springs.

To install:

6. Using molybdenum disulphide lithium base grease, apply a coat to the torsion bar spring splines.

7. If installing a used torsion bar spring, perform the following procedures:

a. Align the matchmarks, install the torsion bar spring to the torque arm.

b. Align the matchmarks and install the anchor arm to the torsion bar spring.

c. Tighten the adjusting nut until the bolt protrusion is the same as it was before.

8. If installing a new torsion bar spring, perform the following procedures:

a. Make sure the upper and lower arms rebound.

b. Install the boots onto the torsion bar spring.

c. Install one end of the torsion bar spring to the torque arm.

d. Install the torsion bar spring onto the opposite end of the anchor arm.

e. Finger tighten the adjusting nut until the adjusting bolt protrudes about 1.570 in.

f. Tighten the adjusting nut until the adjusting bolt protrudes about 3.430 in.

g. Install the wheel(s) and remove the jackstands. Bounce the front of the vehicle to stablize the suspension.

9. To adjust the ground clearance, turn the adjusting nut until the center of the cam plate nut (located of the front end of the lower suspension arm) about 11.220 in. above the ground.

10. After adjusting the ground clearance, torque the locknut to 61 ft. lbs., then, install the boots.

Upper Ball Joints

Inspection

1. Raise the lower control arm and check for excess play.

2. If the ball joints are within specifications and a looseness problem still exists, check the other suspension parts (wheel bearings, tie-rods and etc.).

3. The bottom of the tire should not move more than 0.200 in. when the tire is pushed and pulled inward and outward. The tire should not move more than 0.090 in. up and down.

4. If the play is greater than these figures, replace the ball joint.

Removal and Installation

1. Raise and safely support the vehicle. Remove the wheel and tire assembly.

2. Support the lower control arm with a floor jack.

3. Remove the brake caliper and support it out of the way, with a wire.

4. Using a ball joint removal tool, separate the tie-rod end from the knuckle arm.

5. Remove the ball joint-to-control arm mounting bolts and separate the joint from the arm.

6. To install, reverse the removal procedures. Torque the ball joint-to-upper control arm bolts 20 ft. lbs. (2WD Pick-Up), 25 ft.

lbs. (4WD Pick-Up) or 22 ft. lbs. (2WD Van), the ball joint-to-lower control arm bolts to 51 ft. lbs. (Pick-Up) or 49 ft. lbs. (Van), and the lower ball joint-to steering knuckle nut to 25 ft. lbs. (4WD Pick-Up), 76 ft. lbs. (2WD Van) or 83 ft. lbs. (4WD Van).

NOTE: Be sure to grease the ball joints before moving the vehicle.

Lower Ball Joint

Inspection

1. Raise the lower control arm and check for excess play.

2. If the ball joints are within specifications and a looseness problem still exists, check the other suspension parts (wheel bearings, tie-rods and etc.).

3. The bottom of the tire should not move more than 0.200 in. when the tire is pushed and pulled inward and outward. The tire should not move more than 0.090 in. up and down.

4. The upper ball joint should be replaced if a distinct looseness is felt when turning the ball joint stud with the steering knuckle removed.

Removal and Installation

1. Raise and safely support the vehicle. Remove the wheel and tire assembly.

2. Support the lower control arm with a floor jack.

3. Remove the brake caliper and support it out of the way, with a wire.

4. Using a ball joint removal tool, separate the tie-rod end from the knuckle arm.

5. Using a ball joint removal tool, separate the upper ball joint from the steering knuckle.

6. Remove the ball joint-to-control arm mounting bolts and separate the joint from the arm.

7. To install, reverse the removal procedures. Torque the ball joint-to-upper control arm bolts 20 ft. lbs. (2WD Pick-Up), 25 ft. lbs. (4WD Pick-Up) or 22 ft. lbs. (2WD Van), the upper ball joint-to-steering knuckle nut to 80 ft. lbs. (2WD Pick-Up), 105 ft. lbs. (4WD Pick-Up), 58 ft. lbs. (2WD Van) or 83 ft. lbs. (4WD Van).

NOTE: Be sure to grease the ball joints before moving the vehicle.

Upper Control Arm

Removal and Installation

PICK-UP AND 4RUNNER

1. Raise and safely support the vehicle. Remove the wheel and tire assembly.

2. Using a floor jack, support the lower control arm.

3. Remove the upper ball joint-to-upper control arm nuts/bolts, then, disconnect the upper control arm.

4. Remove the upper conrol arm-to-chassis bolts and camber adjusting shims and the upper control arm.

NOTE: When removing the camber adjusting shims, be sure to record their location and thickness of shims, so they may be reinstalled in their original positions.

5. To install, reverse the removal procedures. Torque the upper control arm-to-chassis bolts to 72 ft. lbs. and the upper control arm-to-upper ball joint nuts/bolts to 20 ft. lbs. Check and/or adjust the front wheel alignment.

2WD VAN

1. Raise and safely support the vehicle. Remove the torsion bar spring.

2. Remove the cool air intake duct.

3. Remove the upper control arm-to-upper ball joint nuts/

bolts and separate the upper control arm from the ball joint.

4. Remove the upper control arm-to-chassis bolts and the control arm from the vehicle.

5. To install, reverse the removal procedures. Torque the upper control arm-to-chassis bolts to 65 ft. lbs. (front) and 112 ft. lbs. (rear), then, the upper control arm-to-ball joint nuts/bolts to 22 ft. lbs. Check and/or adjust the front end alignment.

4WD VAN

1. Raise and safely support the vehicle. Remove the torsion bar spring. Lower the vehicle.

2. Remove the front-right seat and the console box. Disconnect the control and shift cables from the shift levers, then, remove the transmission/transfer shifting levers (with retainer).

3. Disconnect the parking brake cable from the brake lever, then, remove the parking brake lever assembly from the vehicle.

4. Disconnect the parking brake cable from the intermediate lever and remove it. Disconnect the shift cable from the transmission and remove it.

5. Remove the seat floor panel.

6. Remove the fan shroud, the radiator mounting bolts/nuts and move it aside; do not drain the coolant. Raise and safely support the vehicle.

7. Remove the shock absorber-to-frame nuts and disconnect the shock absorber from the frame.

8. From the upper ball joint, remove the cotter pin and the nut. Using a ball joint removal tool, press the ball joint from the steering knuckle.

9. Remove the upper control arm-to-chassis bolts and the arm from the vehicle.

10. To install, reverse the removal procedures. Torque the upper control arm-to-chassis bolts to 112 ft. lbs., the upper ball joint-to-steering knuckle nut to 83 ft. lbs.

Lower Control Arm

Removal and Installation

2WD PICK-UP

1. Raise and safely support the vehicle. Remove the torsion bar spring.

2. Remove the shock absorber, the stablizer bar and the strut bar from the lower arm.

3. Remove the shock absorber from the lower arm.

4. From the lower ball joint, remove the cotter pin and the nut. Using a ball joint removal tool, press the ball joint from the lower control arm.

NOTE: If the lower ball joint is not to be replaced, simply unbolt it from the lower control arm. It is not necessary to separate the ball joint from the steering knuckle.

5. Remove the lower control arm shaft nut. Remove the spring torque arm from the other side of the lower control arm, then, remove the lower arm shaft bolt and the lower arm.

6. To install, reverse the removal procedures.

7. Tighten the bolt(s) holding the lower control arm to the frame but do not torque them until the vehicle is on the ground.

8. Torque the ball joint-to-lower control arm nuts/bolts to 51 ft. lbs., the strut bar-to-lower control arm bolts to 70 ft. lbs., the stabilizer bar-to-lower control arm bolts to 9 ft. lbs., the lower shock absorber bolt to 13 ft. lbs., upper shock absorber bolt to 18 ft. lbs. and the lower arm mounting nuts to 166 ft. lbs.

9. Check and/or adjust the front end alignment.

NOTE: Do not torque the control arm bolts fully until the vehicle is lowered and bounced several times; if the bolts are tightened with the control arm(s) hanging, excessive bushing wear will result.

4WD PICK-UP AND 4RUNNER

1. Raise and safely support the vehicle. Remove the shock absorber.

2. Disconnect the stabilizer bar from the lower suspension arm.

3. Remove the lower ball joint-to-lower control arm bolts, then, separate the control arm from the ball joint.

4. Using a piece of chalk, place matchmarks on the front/rear adjusting cams.

5. Remove the nuts and adjusting cams and the lower control arms.

6. To install, reverse the removal procedures. Torque the lower ball joint-to-lower control arm bolts to 20 ft. lbs., the stabilizer bar-to-lower control arm bolts to 19 ft. lbs., the shock absorber-to-lower control arm nut/bolt to 101 ft. lbs.

7. Lower the vehicle to the ground, bounce it a few times, align the matchmarks and torque the adjusting cam nuts to 203 ft. lbs. Check and/or adjust the front wheel alignment.

2WD VAN

1. Raise and safely support the vehicle.

2. Remove the stablizer bar and the strut bar from the lower arm.

3. Remove the shock absorber from the lower arm. If necessary, disconnect the tie-rod end from the steering knuckle.

4. From the lower ball joint, remove the cotter pin and the nut. Using a ball joint removal tool, press the ball joint from the lower control arm.

NOTE: If the lower ball joint is not to be replaced, simply unbolt it from the lower control arm. It is not necessary to separate the ball joint from the steering knuckle.

5. Using a piece of chalk, matchmark the adjusting cam of the lower control arm.

6. Remove the adjusting cam, the nut and the lower control arm.

7. To install, reverse the removal procedures. Align the cam matchmarks and finger tighten the nut. Torque the ball joint-to-lower control arm nuts/bolts to 49 ft. lbs., the lower ball joint-to-steering knuckle nut to 76 ft. lbs., the strut bar-to-lower control arm bolts to 49 ft. lbs., the stabilizer bar-to-lower control arm bolts to 9 ft. lbs., the tie-rod end-to-steering knuckle nut to 43 ft. lbs., the lower shock absorber bolt to 13 ft. lbs., upper shock absorber bolt to 19 ft. lbs. and the adjusting cam nut to 152 ft. lbs. Check and/or adjust the front end alignment.

NOTE: Do not torque the control arm bolts fully until the vehicle is lowered and bounced several times.

4WD VAN

1. Raise and safely support the vehicle.

2. Remove the stablizer bar from the lower control arm.

3. Remove the shock absorber from the lower control arm.

4. From the lower ball joint, remove the cotter pin and the nut. Using a ball joint removal tool, press the ball joint from the lower control arm.

NOTE: If the lower ball joint is not to be replaced, simply unbolt it from the lower control arm. It is not necessary to separate the ball joint from the steering knuckle.

5. Using a piece of chalk, matchmark the adjusting cam of the lower control arm.

6. Remove the adjusting cam, the nut and the lower control arm.

7. To install, reverse the removal procedures. Align the cam matchmarks and finger tighten the nut. Torque the ball joint-to-lower control arm nuts/bolts to 83 ft. lbs., the stabilizer bar-to-lower control arm bolts to 14 ft. lbs., the tie-rod end-to-steering knuckle nut to 43 ft. lbs., the lower shock absorber bolt to 70 ft. lbs. and the adjusting cam nut to 152 ft. lbs. Check and/or adjust the front end alignment.

NOTE: Do not torque the control arm bolts fully until the vehicle is lowered and bounced several times.

REAR SUSPENSION

Shock Absorbers

Removal and Installation

PICK-UP, 4RUNNER AND LAND CRUISER

1. Raise and safely support the vehicle.
3. Remove the upper shock absorber retaining bolts from the upper frame member.
4. Remove the lower end bolt of the shock absorber from the spring seat.
5. Remove the shock absorber from the vehicle.

NOTE: Inspect the shock for wear, leaks or other signs of damage.

6. To install, reverse the removal procedures. Torque the upper bolt to 19 ft. lbs. (2WD vehicle) or 47 ft. lbs. (4WD vehicle) and the lower bolt to 19 ft. lbs. (2WD vehicle) or 47 ft. lbs. (4WD vehicle).

VAN

1. Raise and safely support the vehicle.
2. Remove the shock absorber-to-axle housing bolt.
3. Working inside the vehicle, remove the locknut, the retaining nut, the retainers and the rubber bushings from the top of the shock absorber.

NOTE: When removing the retaining nut, from the top of the shock absorber, it may be necessary to hold the top of the shock to keep it from turning.

4. Remove the shock absorber from the vehicle.
5. To install, reverse the removal procedures. Torque the shock absorber-to-body nut to 16–24 ft. lbs. and the shock absorber-to-axle housing bolt to 27 ft. lbs.

Coil Spring

Removal and Installation

VAN

1. Raise and safely support the vehicle. Support the axle housing with a floor jack. Remove the wheel and tire assembly.
2. Remove the shock absorber-to-axle housing bolt.
3. Remove the stabilizer-to-axle housing bar bushing bracket bolts.
4. Remove the lateral control arm-to-axle housing nut and disconnect the lateral control arm.
5. Lower the floor jack, then remove the coil spring(s) and the insulators.

NOTE: While lowering the axle housing, be careful not to snag the brake line of the parking brake cable.

6. To install, reverse the removal procedures. Torque the shock absorber bolt to 27 ft. lbs., the lateral control arm-to-axle housing nut to 43 ft. lbs. and the stabilizer-to-axle housing bolts to 27 ft. lbs.

NOTE: Before tightening the lateral control arm and the stabilizer nuts/bolts, bounce the vehicle to stabilize the suspension.

Leaf Springs

Removal and Installation

1. Raise and safely support the vehicle. Support the axle housing with a floor jack. Remove the wheel and tire assembly.

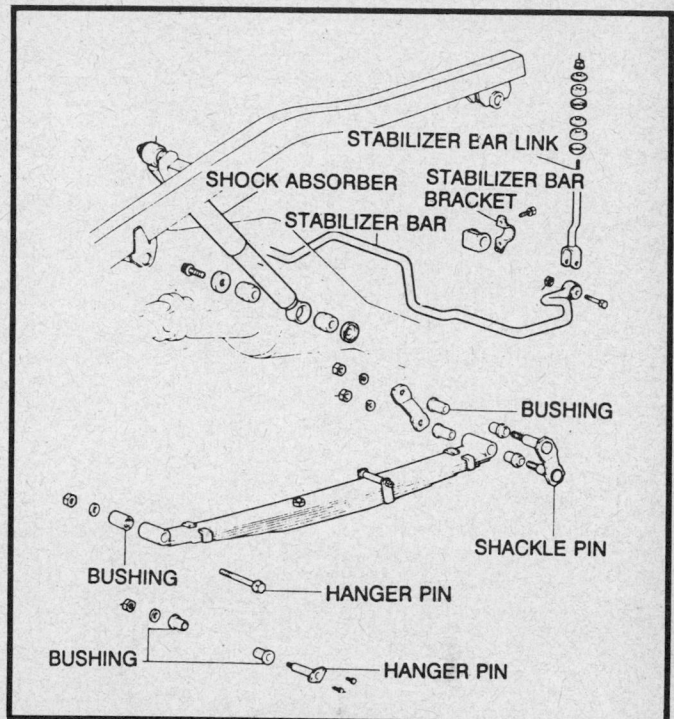

Rear suspension—except Van

2. Lower the floor jack to take the tension off of the spring. Remove the shock absorber mounting nuts/bolts and the shock absorber.
3. Remove the cotter pins and the nuts from the lower end of the stabilizer link. Detach the link from the axle housing.
4. Remove the spring-to-axle housing U-bolt nuts, the spring bumper and the U-bolt.
5. At the front of the spring, remove the hanger pin bolt. Disconnect the spring from the bracket.
6. Remove the spring shackle retaining nuts and the spring shackle inner plate, then carefully pry out the spring shackle with a pry bar.
7. Remove the spring from the vehicle.

To install:

8. To install, perform the following procedure:
   a. Install the rubber bushings in the eye of the spring.
   b. Align the eye of the spring with the spring hanger bracket and drive the pin through the bracket holes and rubber bushings.

NOTE: Use soapy water as lubricant (if necessary), to aid in pin installation. Never use oil or grease.

   c. Finger-tighten the spring hanger nuts/bolts.
   d. Install the rubber bushings in the spring eye at the opposite end of the spring.
   e. Raise the free end of the spring. Install the spring shackle through the bushings and the bracket.
   f. Install the shackle inner plate and finger-tighten the retaining nuts.
   g. Center the bolt head in the hole which is provided in the spring seat on the axle housing.

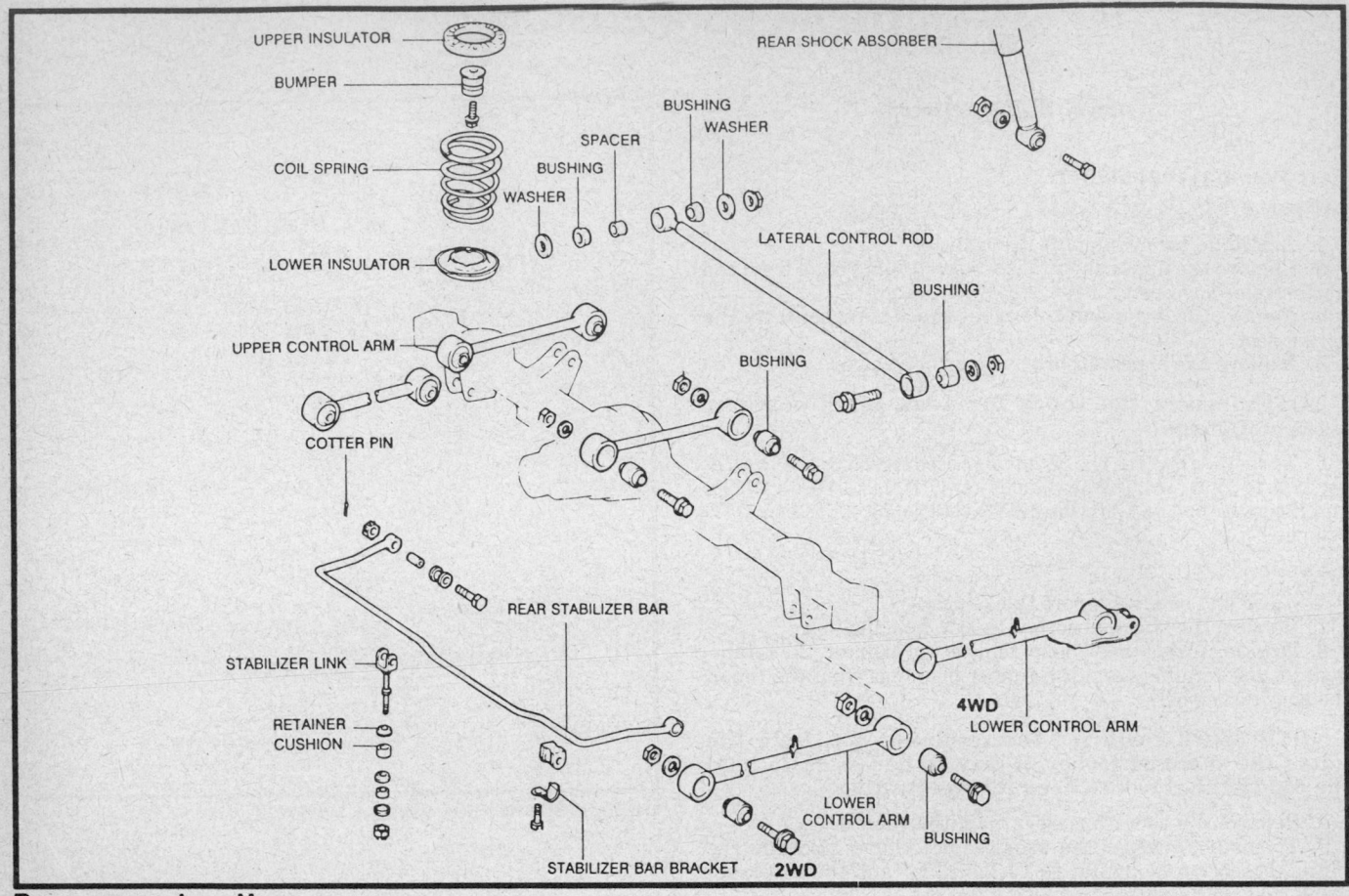

Rear suspension—Van

h. Fit the U-bolts over the axle housing. Install the lower spring seat (2WD vehicle) or spring bumper (4WD vehicle) and the nuts.

9. To complete the installation, reverse the removal procedures. Torque the U-bolt nuts to 90 ft. lbs., the hanger pin-to-frame nut to 67 ft. lbs., the shackle pin nuts to 67 ft. lbs., the shock absorber bolts to 47 ft. lbs. (4WD vehicle).

NOTE: When installing the U-bolts, tighten the nuts so that the length of the bolts are equal.

Rear Control Arms

Removal and Installation

VAN

1. Raise and safely support the vehicle. Place a floor jack under the axle housing to support it.
2. Remove the upper control arm-to-body bolt, the upper control arm-to-axle housing bolt and the upper control arm from the vehicle.
3. Disconnect the brake line from the lower control arm.
4. Remove the lower control arm-to-body bolt, the lower control arm-to-axle housing bolt and the lower control arm from the vehicle.
To install:
5. Install the upper control arm to the body and to the axle housing with the nuts. Do not tighten the nuts.
6. Install the lower control arm to the body and to the axle housing with the nuts. Do not tighten the nuts.
7. Remove the jack and the supports from under the vehicle. Bounce the vehicle to stabilize the suspension.

8. Using the floor jack under the axle housing, raise the vehicle. Place jackstands under the frame but do not let them touch the frame.
9. To complete the installation, torque the upper control arm-to-body bolt to 105 ft. lbs., the upper control arm-to-axle housing bolt to 105 ft. lbs., the lower control arm-to-body bolt to 130 ft. lbs. and the lower control arm-to-axle housing bolt to 105 ft. lbs.

Lateral Control Rod

Removal and Installation

VAN

1. Raise and safely support the vehicle. Place a floor jack under the axle housing and support it.
2. Remove the lateral control rod-to-axle housing nut.
3. Remove the lateral control rod-to-body nut and the control rod from the vehicle.
To install:
4. Raise the axle housing until the frame is just free of the jack.
5. Install the lateral control rod-to-body with the nut. Do not tighten the nut.
6. Install the lateral control rod-to-axle housing in the following order: washer, bushing, spacer, lateral control rod, bushing, washer and nut. Do not tighten the nut.
7. Remove the jack, lower the vehicle to the floor and bounce it to stabilize the suspension.
8. Using the floor jack under the axle housing, raise the vehicle. Torque the lateral control rod-to-body nut to 81 ft. lbs. and the lateral control rod-to-axle housing nut to 43 ft. lbs.

SPECIFICATIONS

ENGINE IDENTIFICATION

Year	Model	Engine Displacement cu. in. (cc/liter)	Engine Series Identification	No. of Cylinders	Engine Type
1986	Vanagon	129 (2109/2.1)	MV	4	OHV
	Vanagon Syncro	129 (2109/2.1)	MV	4	OHV
1987	Vanagon	129 (2109/2.1)	MV	4	OHV
	Vanagon Syncro	129 (2109/2.1)	MV	4	OHV
1988	Vanagon	129 (2109/2.1)	MV	4	OHV
	Vanagon Syncro	129 (2109/2.1)	MV	4	OHV
1989-90	Vanagon	129 (2109/2.1)	MV	4	OHV
	Vanagon Syncro	129 (2109/2.1)	MV	4	OHV

GENERAL ENGINE SPECIFICATIONS

Year	Model	Engine Displacement cu. in. (cc)	Fuel System Type	Net Horsepower @ rpm	Net Torque @ rpm (ft. lbs.)	Bore × Stroke (in.)	Compression Ratio	Oil Pressure @ rpm
1986	Vanagon	129 (2109)	EFI	95 @ 4800	117 @ 3200	3.70 × 2.99	9.0:1	29 @ 2000
1987	Vanagon	129 (2109)	EFI	95 @ 4800	117 @ 3200	3.70 × 2.99	9.0:1	29 @ 2000
1988	Vanagon	129 (2109)	EFI	90 @ 4800	117 @ 3200	3.70 × 2.99	9.0:1	29 @ 2000
1989-90	Vanagon	129 (2109)	EFI	90 @ 4800	117 @ 3200	3.70 × 2.99	9.0:1	29 @ 2000

GASOLINE ENGINE TUNE-UP SPECIFICATIONS

Year	Model	Engine Displacement cu. in. (cc)	Spark Plugs Type	Spark Plugs Gap (in.)	Ignition Timing (deg.) ① MT	Ignition Timing (deg.) ① AT	Compression Pressure (psi)	Fuel Pump (psi) ②	Idle Speed (rpm) MT	Idle Speed (rpm) AT	Valve Clearance In.	Valve Clearance Ex.
1986	Vanagon	129 (2109)	W7CCO	0.028	5BTDC	5BTDC	145-190	29	830-930	830-930	Hyd. ③	Hyd. ③
1987	Vanagon	129 (2109)	W7CCO	0.028	5BTDC	5BTDC	145-190	29	830-930	830-930	Hyd. ③	Hyd. ③
1988	Vanagon	129 (2109)	W7CCO	0.028	5BTDC	5BTDC	145-190	29	830-930	830-930	Hyd. ③	Hyd. ③
1989-90	Vanagon	129 (2109)	W7CCO	0.028	5BTDC	5BTDC	145-190	29	830-930	830-930	Hyd. ③	Hyd. ③

① Check Timing at 2000-25000 RPM
② AT IDLE
③ Must be adjusted when overhauling cylinder head

CAPACITIES

Year	Model	Engine Displacement cu. in. (cc)	Engine Crankcase with Filter	Engine Crankcase without Filter	Transmission (pts.) 4-Spd	Transmission (pts.) 5-Spd	Transmission (pts.) Auto.	Drive Axle (pts.)	Fuel Tank (gal.)	Cooling System (qts.)
1986	Vanagon	129 (2109)	4.2	4.2	3.2 ③	—	12.8	②	15.9 ①	18.5
1987	Vanagon	129 (2109)	4.7	4.7	3.2 ③	—	12.8	②	15.9 ①.	16.9
1988	Vanagon	129 (2109)	4.7	4.7	3.2 ③	—	12.8	②	15.9 ①	16.9
1989-90	Vanagon	129 (2109)	4.8	4.8	3.2 ③	—	12.8	②	15.9 ①	16.9

① Syncro—18.4 gal.
② Front drive axle on Syncro—1.6 pts.
③ Syncro equipped with extra low gear—3.7 pts.

FIRING ORDERS

NOTE: To avoid confusion, always replace spark plug wires one at a time.

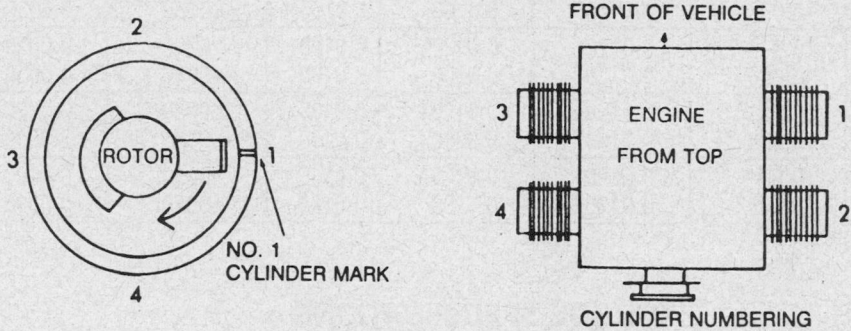

2.1L engine
Engine firing order: 1–4–3–2
Distributor rotation: clockwise

CRANKSHAFT AND CONNECTING ROD SPECIFICATIONS

All measurements are given in inches.

| Year | Engine Displacement cu. in. (cc) | Crankshaft | | | | Connecting Rod | | |
		Main Brg. Journal Dia.	Main Brg. Oil Clearance	Shaft End-play	Thrust on No.	Journal Diameter	Oil Clearance	Side Clearance
1986	129 (2109)	2.126	0.001–0.003	0.003–0.007	3	1.811	0.001–0.003	0.015
1987	129 (2109)	2.126	0.001–0.003	0.003–0.007	3	1.811	0.001–0.003	0.015
1988	129 (2109)	2.126	0.001–0.003	0.003–0.007	3	1.811	0.001–0.003	0.015
1989–90	129 (2109)	2.126	0.001–0.003	0.003–0.007	3	1.811	0.001–0.003	0.015

VALVE SPECIFICATIONS

| Year | Engine Displacement cu. in. (cc) | Seat Angle (deg.) | Face Angle (deg.) | Spring Test Pressure (lbs.) | Spring Installed Height (in.) | Stem-to-Guide Clearance (in.) | | Stem Diameter (in.) | |
						Intake	Exhaust	Intake	Exhaust
1986	129 (2109)	45	45	NA	NA	0.047	0.047	0.313–0.314	0.3508–0.3512
1987	129 (2109)	45	45	NA	NA	0.047	0.047	0.313–0.314	0.3508–0.3512
1988	129 (2109)	45	45	NA	NA	0.047	0.047	0.313–0.314	0.3508–0.3512
1989–90	129 (2109)	45	45	NA	NA	0.047	0.047	0.313–0.314	0.3508–0.3512

NA—Not Available

PISTON AND RING SPECIFICATIONS

| Year | Engine Displacement cu. in. (cc) | Piston Clearance | Ring Gap | | | Ring Side Clearance | | |
			Top Compression	Bottom Compression	Oil Control	Top Compression	Bottom Compression	Oil Control
1986	129 (2109)	0.001–0.008	0.0120–0.0180	0.0120–0.0200	0.0100–0.0160	0.0020–0.0030	0.0020–0.0030	0.0010–0.0020
1987	129 (2109)	0.001–0.008	0.0120–0.0180	0.0120–0.0200	0.0100–0.0160	0.0020–0.0030	0.0020–0.0030	0.0010–0.0020
1988	129 (2109)	0.001–0.008	0.0120–0.0180	0.0120–0.0200	0.0100–0.0160	0.0020–0.0030	0.0020–0.0030	0.0010–0.0020
1989–90	129 (2109)	0.001–0.008	0.0120–0.0180	0.0120–0.0200	0.0100–0.0160	0.0020–0.0030	0.0020–0.0030	0.0010–0.0020

TORQUE SPECIFICATIONS

| Year | Engine Displacement cu. in. (cc) | Cylinder Head Bolts | Main Bearing Bolts | Rod Bearing Bolts | Crankshaft Pulley Bolts | Flywheel Bolts | Manifold | | Spark Plugs |
							Intake	Exhaust	
1986	129 (2109)	①	37 ②	33	257 ③	80	15	15	14
1987	129 (2109)	①	37 ②	33	257 ③	80	15	15	14
1988	129 (2109)	①	37 ②	33	257 ③	80	15	15	14
1989–90	129 (2109)	①	37 ②	33	257 ③	80	15	15	14

① Coat the bolts with sealing compound. Torque in sequence to 7 ft. lbs., then retorque in sequence to 37 ft. lbs.
② Coat with sealing compound before assembling case
③ Triple V-belt pulley only. If equipped with single belt pulley, 44 ft. lbs.

BRAKE SPECIFICATIONS

| Year | Model | Lug Nut Torque (ft. lbs.) | Master Cylinder Bore | Brake Disc | | Standard Brake Drum Diameter | Minimum Lining Thickness | |
				Minimum Thickness	Maximum Runout		Front	Rear
1986	Vanagon	132	NA	0.512	NA	9.921	0.276	0.098
1987	Vanagon	132	NA	0.512	NA	9.921	0.276	0.098
1988	Vanagon	132	NA	0.512	NA	9.921	0.276	0.098
1989–90	Vanagon	132	NA	0.512	NA	9.921	0.276	0.098

WHEEL ALIGNMENT

| Year | Model | Caster | | Camber | | Toe-in (in.) | Steering Axis Inclination (deg.) |
		Range (deg.)	Preferred Setting (deg.)	Range (deg.)	Preferred Setting (deg.)		
1986	Vanagon	7P–7½P	7¼P	½N–½P	0	11/64	NA
	Vanagon Syncro	4 7/16P–4 15/16P	4 11/16P	0–11/16P	11/32P	5/64	NA
1987	Vanagon	7P–7½P	7¼P	½N–½P	0	11/64	NA
	Vanagon Syncro	4 7/16P–4 15/16P	4 11/16P	0–11/16P	11/32P	5/64	NA
1988	Vanagon	7P–7½P	7¼P	½N–½P	0	11/64	NA
	Vanagon Syncro	4 7/16P–4 15/16P	4 11/16P	0–11/16P	11/32P	5/64	NA
1989–90	Vanagon	7P–7½P	7¼P	½N–½P	0	11/64	NA
	Vanagon Syncro	4 7/16P–4 15/16P	4 11/16P	0–11/16P	11/32P	5/64	NA

ENGINE ELECTRICAL

NOTE: Disconnecting the battery cable on some vehicles may interfere with the functions of the on board computer systems and may require the computer to undergo a relearning process, once the negative battery cable is disconnected.

Distributor

Removal and Installation

1. Disconnect the negative battery cable.
2. Disconnect the connector plug at the distributor. Remove the distributor cap and shield.
3. Rotate the engine so that the rotor points to the No. 1 spark plug wire tower on the distributor cap and the timing marks are aligned at **0**. Matchmark the rotor-to-distributor. Also, matchmark the distributor housing to engine relationship.
4. Remove the distributor mounting bolt and lift off the retaining flange. Lift the distributor straight out of the engine.
5. If the engine has not been rotated while the distributor was out, reinstall the distributor in the reverse order of removal. Align the matchmarks made during removal and adjust the ignition timing.
6. If the engine has been rotated while the distributor was out, proceed as follows:

   a. Rotate the engine until the No. 1 cylinder is at TDC on the compression stroke and align the timing marks on **0**. Align the matchmarks and insert the distributor into the engine.

   b. If the oil pump driveshaft does not engage, remove the distributor and turn the pump shaft so that it is parallel to the center line of the crankshaft.

   c. Install the distributor, aligning the marks and reconnect the wiring.

   d. Install the distributor cap.

   e. Run the engine and adjust the ignition timing.

Distributor Driveshaft

Removal and Installation

1. Rotate the engine until No. 1 cylinder is at TDC on the compression stroke. Align the timing marks at **0**.
2. Matchmark and remove the distributor.
3. Remove the spacer spring from the driveshaft.
4. Turn the shaft slowly to the left while withdrawing it from its bore.

NOTE: An extractor tool, 0.583–0.782 in. in diameter must be installed into the driveshaft in order to remove it.

5. Carefully, remove the washer under the shaft.
To install:
6. To install, make sure that the engine is at TDC on the compression stroke for No. 1 cylinder with the timing marks aligned at **0**. Make sure the rotor is pointing to the No. 1 cylinder mark on the edge of the distributor housing.
7. Install the washer on the shaft and insert the shaft into the bore.

NOTE: Due to the slant of the teeth on the drive gears, the shaft must be rotated slightly to the left when it is inserted into the crankcase.

8. When the shaft is properly inserted in the engine, the slot should be about 12 degrees out of parallel with the center line of

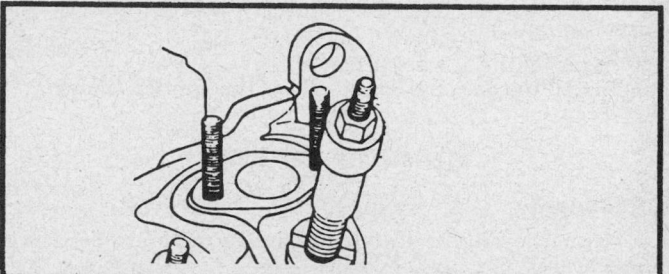
Removing the distributor shaft using a puller

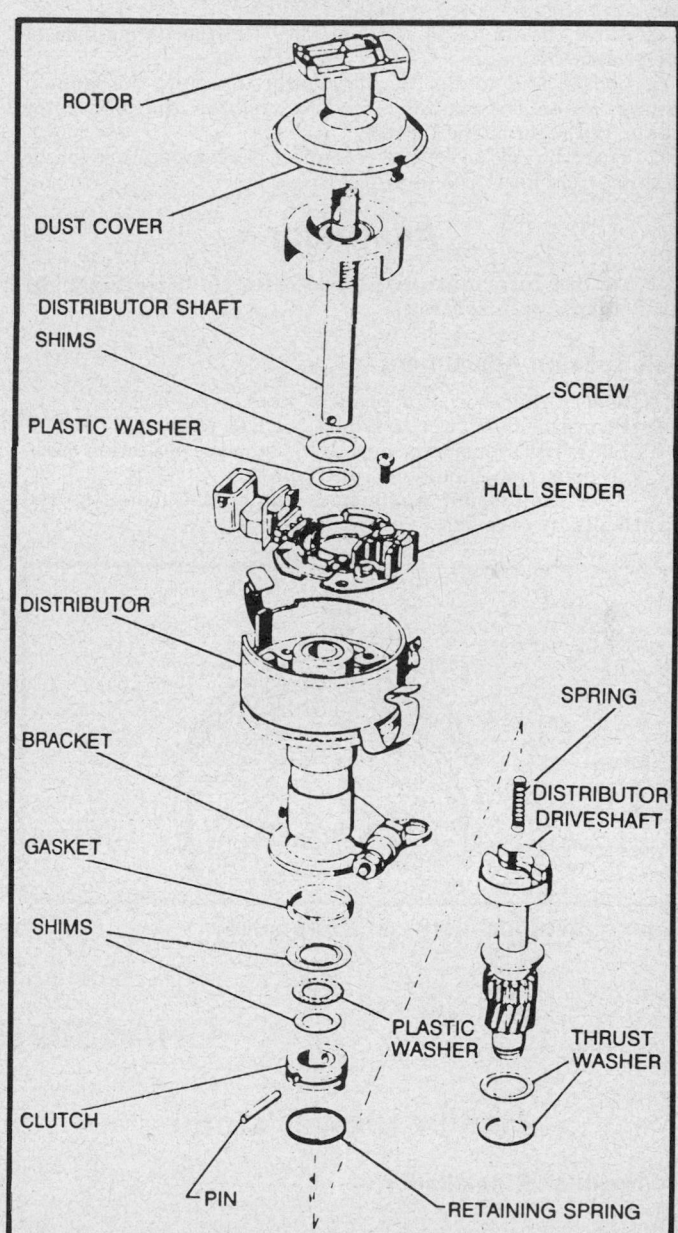
Distributor assembly – exploded view

the engine and the slot offset should be facing outside the engine.

NOTE: Insert the shaft so that the offset slot in the top of the driveshaft is pointing toward the tapped hole in the crankcase. The small segment points toward the water pump.

9. Reinstall the spacer spring.
10. Install the distributor and adjust the ignition timing.

Ignition Timing

Adjustment

1. Run the engine until it reaches normal operating temperature.
2. Disconnect the temperature sensor II connector.
3. Connect a timing light and tachometer. Start the engine and raise the idle speed to 2000–2500 rpm.
4. Allow the engine to settle at idle. Aim the timing light at the crankshaft pulley.
5. Loosen and rotate the distributor to adjust the ignition timing. When the timing is correct, tighten the distributor clamp and recheck the timing.
6. Turn the engine off and reconnect the temperature sensor II connector. Reset the idle speed.

Alternator

For further information, please refer to "Electrical" in the Unit Repair section.

Belt Tension Adjustment

1. Loosen the alternator pivot and mounting bolts.
2. Pivot the alternator to adjust the belt tension.
3. The correct tension is measured using the deflection method. The deflection should be 10–15mm.
4. After the tension is adjusted, tighten the mounting and pivot bolts to 14 ft. lbs.

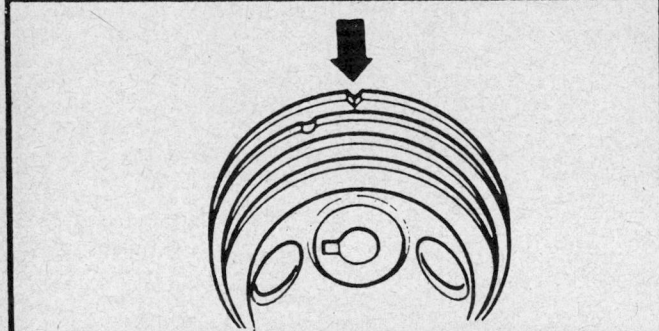

Timing mark location—on triple pulley

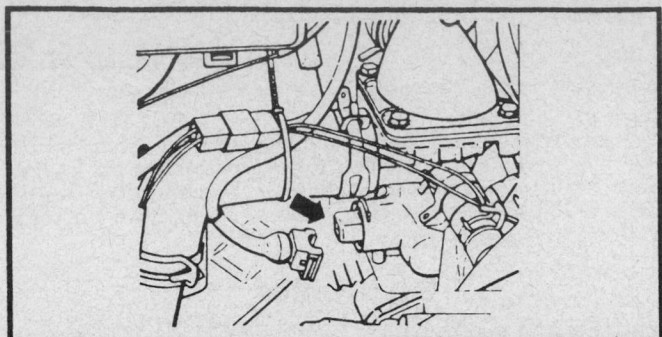

Disconnect the temperature sensor (arrow)

Removal and Installation

1. Disconnect the negative battery cable.
2. Disconnect the alternator wiring at the voltage regulator and alternator.
3. Remove the dipstick and oil filler neck.
4. Loosen the alternator adjusting bolt and remove the drive belt.
5. Remove the right rear engine cover plate and alternator cover plate.
6. Remove the mounting bolt and remove the alternator from above.
7. Installation is the reverse of the removal procedure. Use care to ensure that the rubber grommet on the intake cover for the wiring harness is installed correctly.
8. After installation, adjust the drive belt tension.

Starter

For further information, please refer to "Electrical" in the Unit Repair section.

Removal and Installation

1. Disconnect the negative battery cable.
2. Disconnect and tag the wiring at the starter.
3. Remove the upper starter mounting bolt through the engine compartment.
4. Raise and support the vehicle safely.
5. Remove the lower starter mounting bolt and remove the starter.
To install:
6. Before installing the starter, lubricate the outboard bushing in the nose with grease. Apply sealing compound to the mating surfaces between the starter and transaxle.
7. Locate the starter on the transaxle housing and install the lower mounting bolt.
8. Lower the vehicle and install the upper mounting bolt.
9. Connect the starter wiring and battery cable.

CHASSIS ELECTRICAL

Heater Blower Motor

Removal and Installation

FRONT

1. Disconnect the negative battery cable.

2. Drain the cooling system, using the following procedures:
   a. Open the heater controls.
   b. Open the expansion tank cap.
   c. Position a catch pan under the water pump.
   d. Disconnect the lower coolant hose from the water pump connection pipe and the center coolant hose from the water pump.

e. Drain the system to a level below the heater core.

3. Disconnect the electrical and vacuum cables from the center heater unit, under the instrument panel. Disconnect the air ducts from the hosuing.

4. Remove the heater housing mounting bolts and remove the housing from under the instrument panel.

5. Remove the top cover and remove the blower from the housing.

To install:

6. Install the blower motor in position in the housing and install the cover.

7. Install the heater assembly in position under the instrument panel.

8. Connect the electrical wires and the vacuum lines to the housing. Connect the air ducts to the housing.

9. Connect the negative battery cable and fill the cooling system. Run the engine at 2500 rpm and check that water flows at the breather valve with no bubbles.

10. Check the operation of the blower motor.

AUXILIARY BLOWER

1. Disconnect the negative battery cable.

2. Remove the kick panel from under the rear seat.

3. Remove the 4 bolts retaining the auxiliary heater unit to the floor.

4. Pivot the heater unit outward, do not disconnect the heater hoses or the cables from the housing.

5. Disconnect the blower electrical lead and remove the blower from the housing.

6. Installation is the reverse of the removal procedure.

7. Check the operation of the blower.

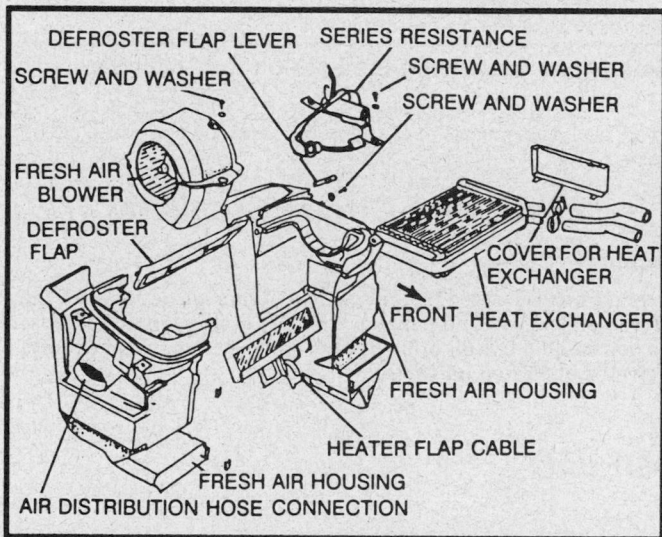

Typical heater assembly

Windshield Wiper Motor

Removal and Installation

1. Place the wiper arms in the park position.

2. Disconnect the negative battery cable.

3. Remove both wiper arms.

4. Remove the glove compartment.

5. Remove the bearing cover and nut from the motor.

6. Remove the heater branch connections under the instrument panel.

7. Disconnect the wiper motor wiring.

8. Remove the wiper motor mounting screws and remove the motor.

To install:

9. Install the wiper motor in position under the instrument panel.

10. Install the bearing cover and nut to the motor.

11. Install the fresh air ducts and reconnect the wiring.

12. Install the glove compartment.

13. Install the wiper arms and connect the negative battery cable.

14. The wiper blades should be 2¾ in. (70mm) from the bottom of the windshield, when correctly installed.

Windshield Wiper Switch

Removal and Installation

1. Disconnect the negative battery cable.

2. Matchmark and remove the steering wheel.

3. Disconnect the combination switch wiring and remove the combination switch.

4. Disconnect the wiper switch wiring and remove the wiper switch.

5. Installation is the reverse of the removal procedure.

6. Align the steering wheel matchmarks during installation.

Instrument Cluster

Removal and Installation

1. Disconnect the negative battery cable.

2. Grasp the rear of the instrument cluster cover, by the 2 recesses, and pull the cover off.

3. Remove the 2 screws retaining the instrument cluster and pull it forward.

4. Disconnect the speedometer cable from the EGR counter and remove the cluster from the vehicle.

5. All instruments can be removed from the rear of the cluster.

6. Installation is the reverse of the removal procedure.

Combination Switch

Removal and Installation

The combination switch incorporates the headlight, turn signal, dimmer and cruise control switches.

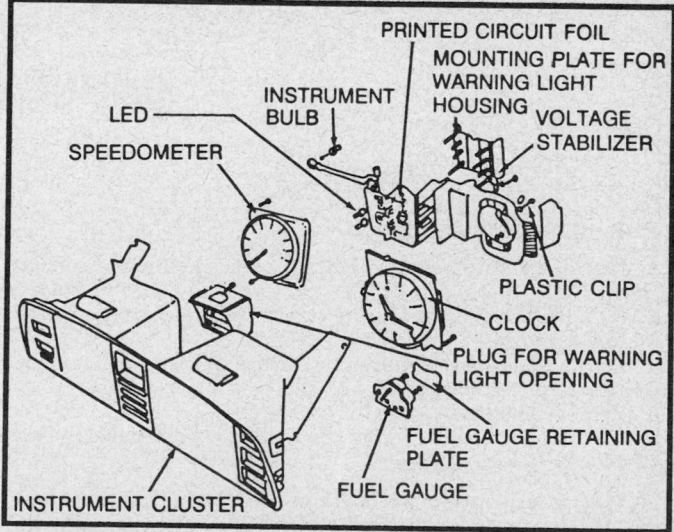

Instrument cluster—exploded view

1. Disconnect the negative battery cable.
2. Matchmark and remove the steering wheel.
3. Pry off the switch cover on the end of the steering column.
4. Disconnect and tag the switch wiring.
5. Remove the switch mounting screws and remove the switch from the steering column.
6. Installation is the reverse of the removal procedure.
7. Align the steering wheel matchmarks during installation. Tighten the steering wheel retaining nut to 36 ft. lbs. (50 Nm).

Ignition Lock/Switch

Removal and Installation

1. Disconnect the negative battery cable.
2. Remove the ignition switch.
3. With the key in the cylinder and turned to the **ON** position, pull the lock cylinder out far enough so the securing pin can be depressed through a hole in the side of the lock cylinder housing.
4. As the pin is depressed, gently push the cylinder into its housing.
5. Make sure the pin engages correctly and that the retainer fits easily in place. Do not force any parts together. When they are correctly aligned, they will fit easily together.
6. Installation is the reverse of the removal procedure.

Stoplight Switch

Removal and Installation

The stoplight switch is located in the side of the master cylinder.
1. Disconnect the negative battery cable.
2. Remove the instrument cluster cover.
3. Remove the instrument cluster from the vehicle.
4. Disconnect the electrical lead from the stoplight switch.
5. Place a rag under the stoplight switch. Remove the switch and quickly plug the opening in the master cylinder.

NOTE: It is important that the switch opening be plugged immediately, to prevent the brake fluid from leaking out and to protect the interior trim components from damage.

To install:
6. Install the switch into the master cylinder and reconnect the electrical lead.
7. Fill the master cylinder to the correct level.
8. Install the instrument cluster and cover.
9. Connect the negative battery cable.

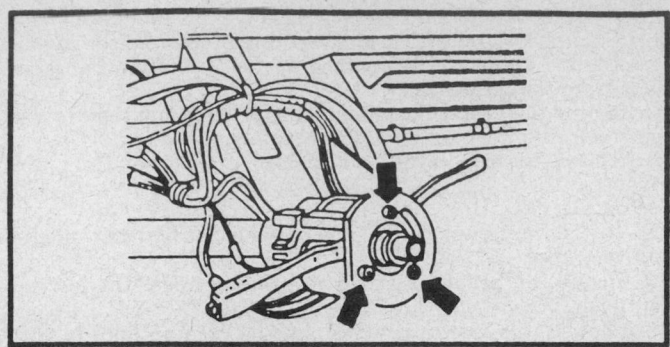

Combination switch mounting

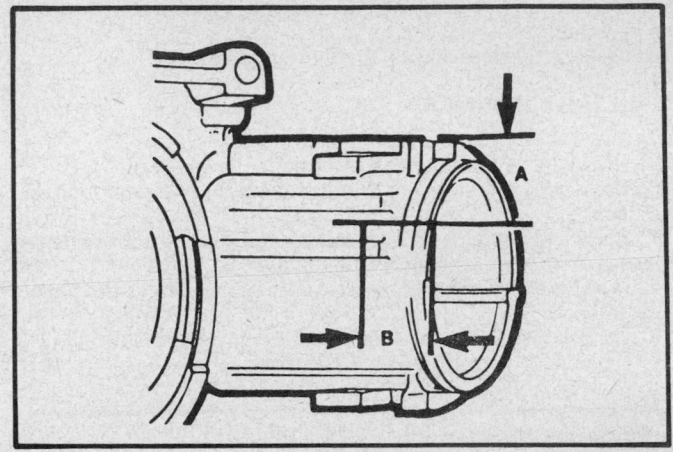

Dimensions for drilling the ignition lock cylinder

10. Check the operation of the switch and the operation of the brake system.

Fuses and Circuit Breakers

Location

The fuse box is located behind a panel, under the left side of the instrument panel. The panel can be removed by lifting it from the bottom and pulling it upward. The fuse ratings and circuits protected are listed on the fuse box cover.

ENGNE COOLING

Radiator

Removal and Installation

1. Disconnect the negative battery cable. Drain the cooling system.
2. Remove the grille retaining screws and remove the grille.
3. Raise and safely support the vehicle.
4. Remove the spare tire from the spare tire tray and remove the spare tire tray bracket.
5. Remove the lower radiator cover.
6. Disconnect the hoses from the radiator and remove the radiator lower bolts.

NOTE: If equipped with air conditioning, the system does not have to be discharged. The condenser can be lowered with the radiator and supported aside.

7. Lower the radiator partially and disconnect the electrical lead from the thermo-time switch.
8. Carefully remove the radiator from the vehicle. If equipped with air conditioning, use care not to kink the refrigerant lines. Remove the condenser-to-radiator bolts and support the condenser aside.
To install:
9. If equipped with air conditioning, attach the condenser to the radiator.
10. Raise the radiator assembly into position and install the lower retaining bolts. Tighten to 11 ft. lbs. (15 Nm).
11. Connect the electrical lead to the thermo-time sensor.
12. Connect the hoses to the radiator. Install the lower radiator cover.
13. Install the spare tire tray bracket and tire. Lower the vehicle.

14. Install the grille assembly. Connect the negative battery cable.

15. Fill and bleed the cooling system.

Electric Cooling Fan

Removal and Installation

1. Disconnect the negative battery cable.
2. Remove the grille assembly.
3. Raise and safely support the vehicle.
4. Remove the spare tire and spare tire bracket.
5. Lower the radiator from the vehicle, it is not necessary to disconnect the hoses from the radiator or to drain the coolant. Support the radiator assembly aside.
6. Disconnect the fan electrical lead and remove the fan retaining bolts.
7. Remove the fan from the vehicle.
8. Installation is the reverse of the removal procedure. Check the operation of the fan.

Heater Core

Removal and Installation

1. Disconnect the negative battery cable.
2. Drain the cooling system.
3. Locate and remove the heater core cover in the side of the heater box.
4. Disconnect the heater hoses from the heater core.

NOTE: It may be necessary to remove the heater box from the vehicle. If so, disconnect and tag the wiring and cables at the heater box.

5. If the unit has a core cover on the side, remove the screws or unclip the cover and remove the core. The core should pull straight out.
6. If the heater box is separated in halfs, remove the heater box clips that hold the halves of the heater box together. Separate the halves and remove the heater core.
7. Installation is the reverse of the removal procedure.

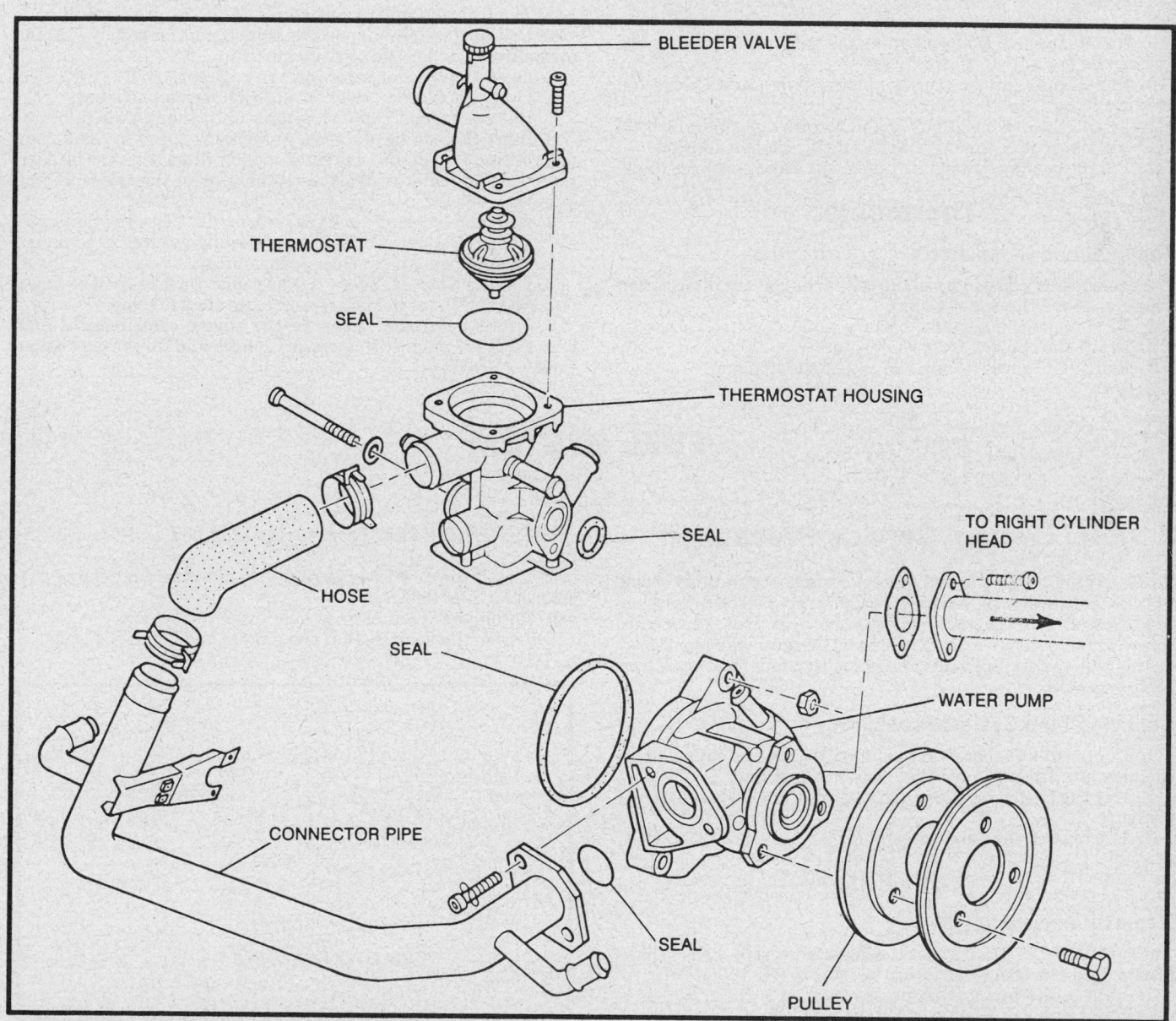

BLEEDER VALVE
THERMOSTAT
SEAL
THERMOSTAT HOUSING
SEAL
TO RIGHT CYLINDER HEAD
HOSE
SEAL
WATER PUMP
CONNECTOR PIPE
SEAL
PULLEY

Water pump assembly—exploded view

8. Fill the cooling system and check the operation of the heater when finished.

9. If the heater box was removed, check the heater controls to insure that there is full travel with the controls.

Water Pump

Removal and Installation

1. Disconnect the negative battery cable. Drain the cooling system. Loosen the water pump pulley bolts.

2. Remove the drive belt and pulley from the water pump.

3. Disconnect the coolant hoses and remove the left side coolant elbow from the water pump.

4. Remove the right side coolant elbow from the pump.

5. Remove the water pump.

To install:

6. Clean and inspect the mounting surfaces of the water pump and engine.

7. Lightly grease the O-ring and install the water pump on the engine. Torque the bolts to 15 ft. lbs.

8. Torque the bolts to 15 ft. lbs.

9. Install the left side coolant elbow with a new O-ring and torque the bolts to 15 ft. lbs.

10. Install the right side coolant elbow with a new O-ring and torque the bolts to 15 ft. lbs.

11. Install the drive belt pulley and torque the retaining bolts to 15 ft. lbs. Install the drive belt. Adjust the belt tension.

12. Fill the cooling system, run the engine and check for leaks.

Thermostat

Removal and Installaton

The thermostat is mounted in the top of the coolant distribution housing, above the water pump.

1. Disconnect the negative battery cable.

2. Drain the coolant from the engine.

3. Remove the hoses from the top of the housing.

4. Remove the housing top retaining bolts and remove the top from the housing.

5. Remove the thermostat from the housing.

To install:

6. Replace the O-ring in the top of the thermostat housing.

7. Install the thermostat in position and install the top of the housing.

8. Tighten the retaining bolts to 15 ft. lbs. Connect the hoses and refill the cooling system.

9. Connect the battery cable and bleed the cooling system.

Bleeding the Cooling System

NOTE: The manufacturer specifies the use of a specially-formulated coolant, part no. ZVW 237 102 in this engine. Anti-freeze other than this may cause corrosion of the cooling system, leading to engine damage.

1. Set the heater control to **MAX** heat.

2. Open the control valve for the auxiliary heater under the rear seat.

3. Remove the radiator grille.

4. Raise and safely support the vehicle approximately 15¾ in. at the front, under the crossmember.

5. Open the bleeder screw on the radiator.

6. Open the bleeder valve in the engine compartment.

7. Fill the coolant expansion tank until the tank is full.

8. Start the engine. Increase the engine speed to 2000 rpm and continue to fill the tank until coolant flows from the bleeder screw on the radiator. Wait until the coolant flowing is free of bubbles.

9. Add more coolant until the tank is full. Close the tank cap.

10. Turn the engine **OFF**. Restart the engine after 20 seconds.

11. At 2000 rpm, open the expansion cap.

12. Close the bleeder screw on the radiator when coolant flows out. Add coolant if necessary and close the tank cap.

13. Close the bleeder screw in the engine compartment and turn **OFF** the engine. If necessary, check and fill the expansion tank.

FUEL SYSTEM

Fuel System Service Precaution

When working with the fuel system certain precautions should be taken; always work in a well ventilated area, keep a dry chemical (Class B) fire extinguisher near the work area. Always disconnect the negative battery cable and do not make any repairs to the fuel system until all the necessary steps for repair have been reviewed.

Relieving Fuel System Pressure

1. Connect an fuel pressure gauge, VW–1318 or equivalent to the pressure fitting at the fuel pressure regulator.

2. Use the switch on the gauge assembly to slowly release the pressure.

3. Disconnect the gauge assembly.

Fuel Filter

Removal and Installation

The fuel filter is located under the right front side of the vehicle, just behind the fuel tank.

1. Relieve the fuel system pressure.

2. Raise and safely support the vehicle.

3. Disconnect the fuel lines from the filter.

4. Remove the filter bracket retaining bolt and remove the filter.

5. Install the new filter in position, note the direction of the arrows for fuel flow.

6. Reconnect the fuel lines and lower the vehicle.

7. Lower the vehicle. Run the engine and check for leaks.

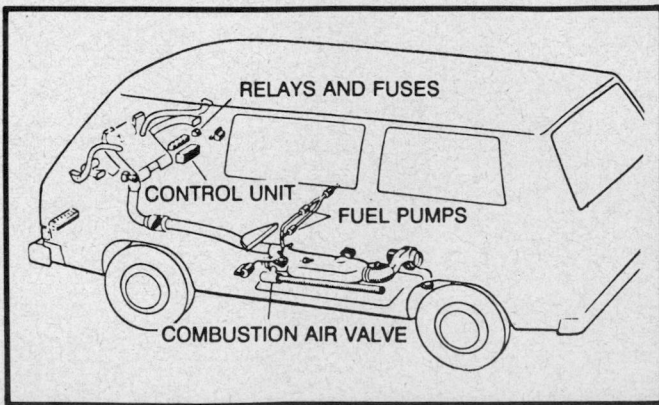

Fuel pump location

Electric Fuel Pump

Pressure Testing

1. Connect fuel pressure gauge VW-1318 or equivalent, to the pressure fitting at the fuel pressure regulator.
2. Run the engine at idle and check the pressure reading. The pressure should be 29 psi. with the vacuum line connected to the regulator and 36 psi. with the vacuum line disconnected.
3. Shut off the engine and wait 10 minutes. If the value is not maintained; check the fuel pump by clamping off the line from the fuel pump to the regulator and observing the gauge. Check the pressure regulator by clamping off the return line to the fuel tank and observing the gauge and check the injectors by clamping the lines from the injectors to the regulator.
4. If the pressure drop stops or slows down the problem is in the tested component.

Adjustment

1. Electric fuel pump pressure is 29 psi.
2. Fuel pump pressure is determined by a pressure regulator which diverts part of the fuel pump output to the gas tank when 29 psi is reached.
3. The regulator, located on the engine firewall, has a screw and locknut on its end.
4. Loosen the locknut and adjust the screw to adjust the pressure.
5. Do not force the screw in or out if it does not turn.

Removal and Installation

1. Relieve the fuel system pressure. Disconnect the negative battery cable.
2. Raise and safely support the vehicle. Disconnect the fuel pump wiring. Pull the plug from the pump, but do not pull on the wiring.
3. Disconnect and plug the fuel hoses.
4. Remove the fuel pump mounting nuts and remove the pump.
5. Reconnect the fuel pump hoses and wiring.
6. Install the pump on the vehicle.

Fuel Injection

Idle Speed Adjustment

1. Run the engine until it reaches normal operating temperature. Turn **OFF** all electrical accessories including the radiator fan. Check that the throttle valve switch is in the closed position at idle. The crankcase breather hose should be removed from the oil vent and plugged. Check to see that the idle stabilizer is operating properly. With the ignition turned **ON**, the valve should vibrate.
2. Connect the tester, VW tool VAG 1367 or equivalent. Using adapter VW 1473, connect the tester VW 1473 or equivalent to the No. 1 terminal of the ignition coil.
3. Connect the CO meter to the left side exhaust pipe.
4. With the ignition switched **OFF**, disconnect the oxygen sensor connector and the idle stabilizer control valve connector.
5. Run the engine at idle speed. After 2 minutes adjust as necessary by turning the adjusting screw on the throttle valve housing. The idle speed should be 880 ± 50 rpm.
6. Check the CO and adjust as necessary. The CO should be 0.3–1.1% If the CO% is above this level use the following procedures.
7. Stop the engine. To adjust the CO, first remove the screw caps. Center punch the plug in the CO adjusting hole. Drill a $3/32$ in. hole in the center of the plug, $9/64$–$5/32$ in. deep. Keep the area clean of metal shavings.
8. Screw a sheet metal screw into the plug and remove the plug by pulling upwards.

9. Start the engine and set the idle speed to 880 ± 50 rpm and the CO content to 0.7% by alternately turning the adjusting screws to obtain the correct specifications.
10. Reconnect the oxygen sensor connector and idle stabilizer connector. Let the engine idle for approximately 2 minutes. Check the CO content and correct if necessary by repeating the above procedure.
11. Stop the engine. Install a new plug until it is flush with the intake air sensor.

Fuel Injector

Removal and Installation

1. Relieve the fuel system pressure.
2. Disconnect the negative battery cable.
3. Remove the electrical connector from the injector.
4. Disconnect the fuel line from the injector.
5. Pull the injector from its bore.
6. Using a new O-ring, install the injector in position.
7. Connect the fuel line and electrical lead.
8. Connect the negative battery cable. Check for leaks around the injector base and at the fuel line.

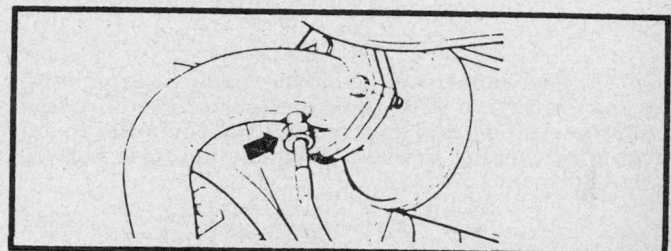

CO meter test connection

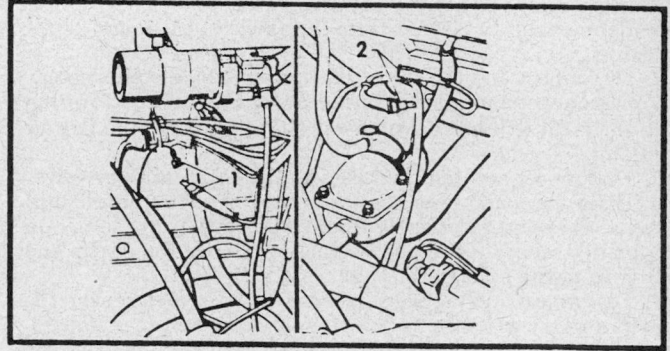

Oxygen sensor (1) and idle stabilizer (2) connection locations

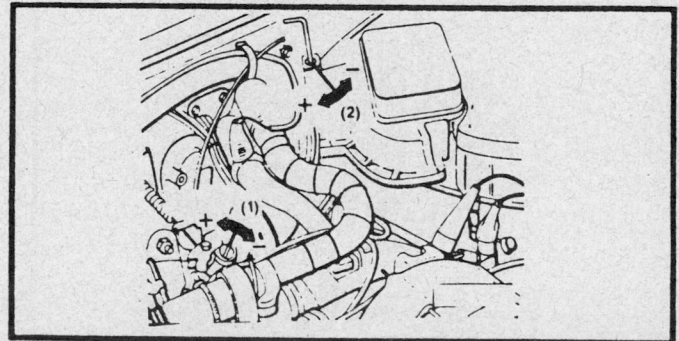

(1) Idle speed adjustment screw and (2) idle mixture adjustment screw locations

EMISSION CONTROLS

Please refer to "Professional Emission Component Application Guide".

Emission Warning Lamps

Resetting

The emission systems incorporates a mileage counter which activates the oxygen sensor warning light on the instrument panel. The counter will illuminate the light at 60,000 mile intervals. The oxygen sensor must be replaced when the light comes on.

The light can reset by locating the counter under the left front dash of the vehicle and depressing the reset button on it.

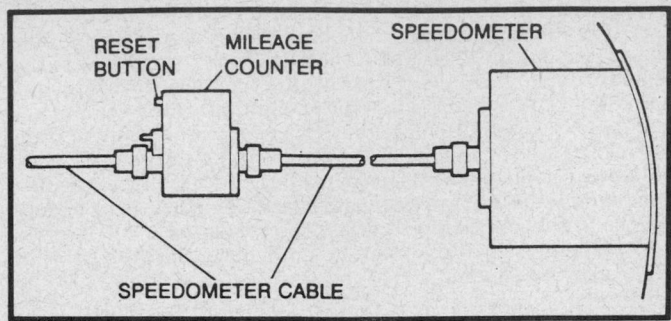

Mileage counter assembly—press button to reset

ENGINE MECHANICAL

NOTE: Disconnecting the battery cable on some vehicles may interfere with the functions of the on board computer systems and may require the computer to undergo a relearning process, once the negative battery cable is disconnected.

Engine

Removal and Installation

1. Disconnect the negative battery cable.
2. Remove the air cleaner from the air flow sensor and air intake duct.
3. Disconnect and tag the alterntor wires at the alternator.
4. Disconnect and tag the connectors at the fuel injectors, the plug at the throttle valve switch and the plug at the auxiliary air regulator.
5. Disconnect and tag the hoses at the charcoal filter valve.
6. Disconnect and plug the fuel hoses near the distributor. Remove the accelerator cable from the throttle valve lever. On automatic transaxle equipped vehicles, remove the circlip and spring from the accelerator rod.
7. Disconnect and tag the connector at the oxygen sensor, the distributor, oil pressure switch, temperature sensor, temperature sender and coolant level warning switch (located at the coolant expsansion tank).

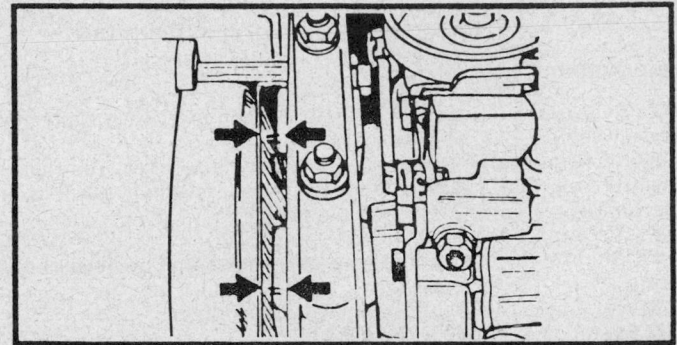

Checking the position of the engine carrier

8. Plug the coolant hoses and open the coolant expansion tank cap. Remove the drain plugs at the cylinder heads and drain the coolant.

NOTE: Always replace the sealing rings underneath the drain plugs during installation.

9. Disconnect the brake booster line and all coolant hoses. Remove the coolant expansion tank.

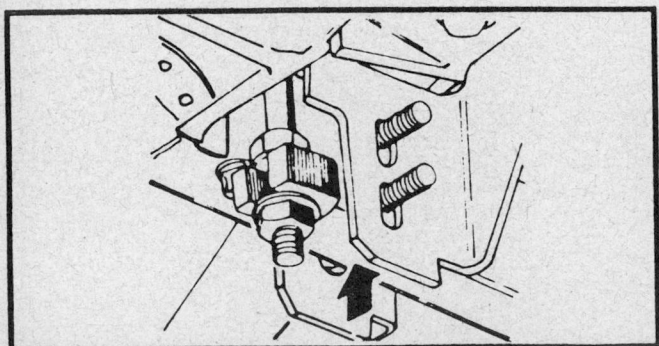

Engine carrier bolts positioned at the top of their elongated holes

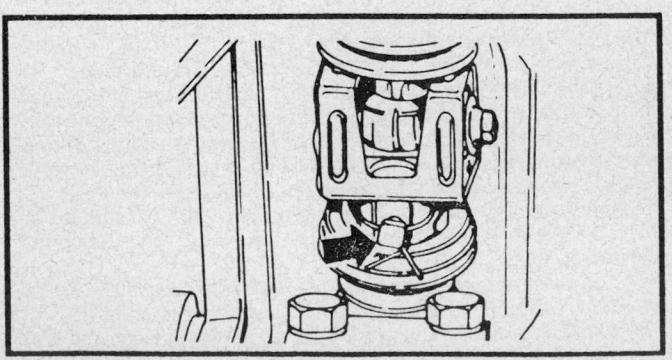

Shift linkage coupling location

10. Raise and support the vehicle safely. Remove the engine-to-transaxle bolts and nuts on both sides.

11. On automatic transaxle equipped vehicles, remove the bolts which attach the torque converter to the drive plate through the hole on the top of the transaxle housing.

12. Disconnect and tag the starter motor wiring.

13. On automatic transaxle equipped vehicles, disconnect the accelerator rod.

14. The vehicle must be raised and safely supported, to remove the engine from under the vehicle.

15. Remove the engine mounting plates from underneath.

16. Loosen the transaxle mounting bolt.

17. Support the underside of the engine.

18. Remove the engine carrier bolts. Carefully lower the engine and transaxle assembly slightly. Keep the wiring harness aside so that it can pass the oil filler tube. Lower the assembly more, to have access to the lower engine mounting bolts. Remove the engine from the transaxle and lower it out of the vehicle.

To install:

19. Check the clutch release bearing for wear and replace if necessary.

20. Lubricate the clutch release bearing and main shaft splines lightly with grease. Do not lubricate the guide sleeve for the release bearing.

21. Raise the engine and transaxle assembly into position. Install the transaxle mounting bolts. Tighten to 22 ft. lbs. Install the mounting bolts for the engine carrier, make sure they are correctly positioned at the top of their holes.

22. Install the torque converter bolts on automatic transaxle equipped vehicles.

23. Connect the accelerator rod and the wiring to the starter. Install the coolant expansion tank and reconnect all coolant lines.

24. Reconnect all electrical leads on the engine. Reconnect all of the fuel lines to the injectors and the fuel pressure regulator.

25. Connect the wiring to the alternator and install the air cleaner assembly.

26. Connect the negative battery cable. Refill the cooling system, using the correct procedure.

27. Run the engine to normal operating temperature and check for leaks. Check the idle speed and transmission operation.

Cylinder Head

Removal and Installation

NOTE: It is not necessary to remove or lower the engine to remove the cylinder heads. Either head can be removed and installed while the engine is in place in the vehicle.

1. Relieve the fuel system pressure. Disconnect the negative battery cable.

2. Drain the coolant from the cooling system using the coolant drain plugs on the bottom of each cylinder head.

3. Install new sealing rings and reinstall the drain plugs.

4. Remove the valve cover and gasket.

5. Remove the rocker arm assembly.

6. Unbolt the intake manifold from the cylinder head. The cylinder head is held in place by 8 studs. The cylinder head also holds the cylinders in place, it will be necessary to hold the cylinders in place after the head is removed.

7. After the rocker arm cover, rocker arm retaining nuts and rocker arm assemblies have been removed, the cylinder head nuts can be removed and the cylinder head lifted off.

8. Before installing the head, make sure all gasket contact areas are completely clean and free of any damage. Apply a thin bead of sealing compound to the gasket surface facing the cylinder head.

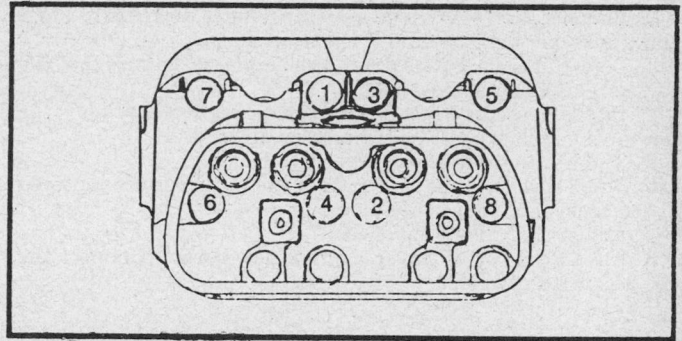

Cylinder head bolt torque sequence

To install:

9. The pushrod tubes should be installed so that the small end faces the cylinder head and so that the seam on the tube is facing upward. Guide the tubes into the hydraulic lifter holes carefully. Always replace the sealing rings.

NOTE: If the pushrod tube rests on the edge of the valve lifter, the basic valve setting will be incorrect and the lifter(s) will be damaged when the engine is started.

10. Install the cylinder head. Coat the cylinder head cap nuts with sealer. Tighten stud No. 1 cap nut just enough so that the remaining 7 cap nuts can be installed.

11. Torque all nuts in sequence to the correct torque.

12. Complete the installation in the reverse order of the removal procedures.

13. Torque the rocker shaft nuts to 18 ft. lbs. Use new rocker cover gaskets.

14. Connect the negative battery cable. Fill the cooling system, run the engine and check for leaks.

Valve Lash

Adjustment

NOTE: No routine valve adjustment is necessary however; the valves must still be adjusted whenever the cylinder heads have been removed. The rocker arms in the Vanagon engines are equipped with conventional locknut-type adjusters.

1. Disconnect the negative battery cable. Remove the rocker arm covers. Unscrew the adjusting screws on the rocker arms so that the ball shaped end is flush with the surface of the rocker arm.

2. Rotate the crankshaft until No. 1 cylinder is at TDC on compression. Both valves should be closed and the mark on the distributor rotor should be in line with the mark on the distributor housing.

3. Turn the adjusting screws in so that they just touch the valve stems.

4. Turn the adjusting screws 2 turns clockwise and tighten the locknuts.

5. Rotate the crankshaft 180 degrees and adjust cylinder No. 2. Repeat the procedure on cylinders 3 and 4 until all valves are adjusted.

6. Install the rocker covers. Connect the negative battery cable.

Rocker Arms/Shafts

Removal and Installation

1. Disconnect the negative battery cable. Pull the clip that retains the rocker cover over the cover and remove the cover.

2. Remove the rocker arm retaining nuts, rocker arm shaft and the rocker arms. Remove the stud seals.

3. Before installing the rocker arm assembly, be sure that the parts are as clean as possible.

4. Install new stud seals. Install the rocker arm assembly, the slot on the rocker shaft support faces upward.

5. Tighten the retaining nuts to 18 ft. lbs.

6. Make sure that the ball ends of the pushrods are centered in the sockets of the rocker arms.

7. Adjust the valve clearance.

8. Install the rocker cover using a new gasket. Connect the negative battery cable.

Intake Manifold

Removal and Installation

1. Relieve the fuel system pressure. Disconnect the negative battery cable. Remove the air cleaner.

2. Remove the pressure switch which is mounted under the right pair of intake manifold pipes. Disconnect the injector wiring.

3. Disconnect the fuel lines to the injectors and remove the fuel injectors.

4. Disconnect the hoses from the intake air distributor to the

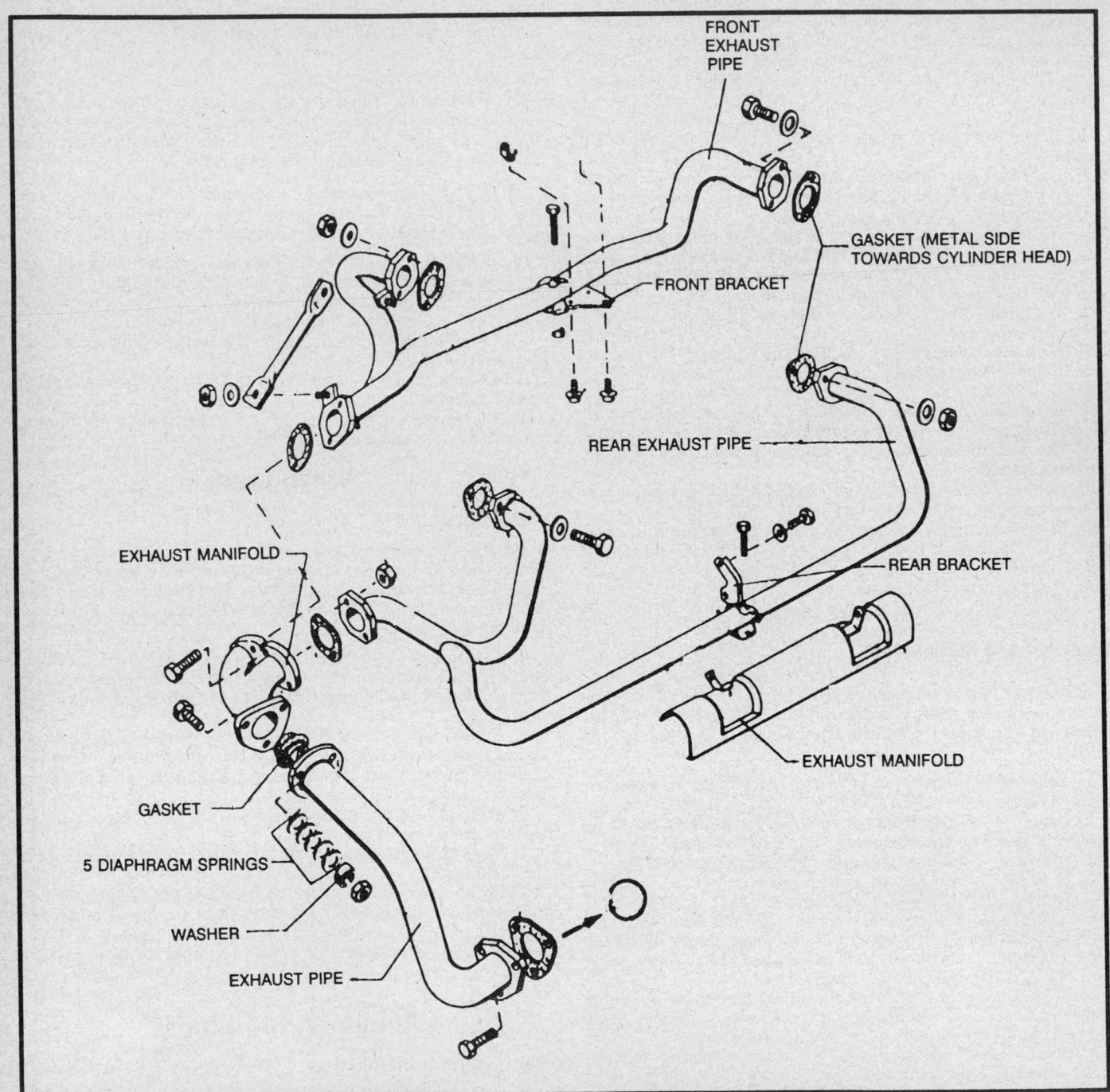

Exhaust system components

manifold pipes.

5. Remove the manifold retaining nuts. Remove the manifold from its mounting.

To install:

6. Using new gaskets, install the manifold in position on the cylinder head.

7. Tighten the intake manifold bolts to 15 ft. lbs. (20 Nm).

8. Connect the hoses from the intake air distributor to the manifold pipes.

9. Install the injectors, using new O-rings. Reconnect the fuel and electrical leads to the injectors.

10. Install the pressure switch to the right manifold.

11. Connect the negative battery cable.

12. Run the engine and check for leaks.

Intake Air Distributor

Removal and Installation

The intake air distributor is located at the center of the engine at the junction of the intake manifold pipes. The throttle valve housing and the air inlet pipes are connected to it.

NOTE: It is not necessary to remove the distributor if only the manifold pipes are to be removed.

1. Disconnect the negative battery cable. Relieve the fuel system pressure. Remove the air cleaner and pressure switch which are located under the right pair of manifold pipes.

2. Push the 4 rubber hoses onto the intake manifold pipes and away from the intake air distributor.

3. Remove the accelerator cable and the throttle valve switch.

4. Disconnect the accelerator cable.

5. Disconnect and tag the leads to the ignition distributor and the pressure sensor.

6. Disconnect the vacuum hose at the auxiliary air regulator.

7. Remove the retaining bolts and remove the throttle valve housing from the crankcase.

To install:

8. Install the air intake distributor in position on the crankcase.

9. Connect the vacuum hoses and auxiliary air regulator. Connect the distributor electrical leads.

10. Connect the accelerator cable and the throttle valve switch.

11. Reposition the rubber hoses from the intake pipes to the air distributor.

12. Install the pressure switch and the air cleaner.

13. Connect the negative battery cable. Check the operation of the accelerator cable and adjust the idle as needed.

Exhaust Manifold

Removal and Installation

1. Disconnect the negative battery cable. Raise and support the vehicle safely. Remove the rear wheel and tire assemblies.

2. Remove the catalytic converter to muffler clamps and bolts.

3. Support the converter/tail pipe assembly and remove the converter to exhaust manifold bolts. Remove the converter.

4. Remove the exhaust manifold to pre-heat pipe bolts.

5. Support the manifold and remove the manifold supporting clamp bolt.

6. Remove the exhaust manifold from the engine.

7. To install, always use new gaskets and O-rings.

8. Installation is the reverse of the removal procedure.

9. Run the engine and check for exhaust leaks.

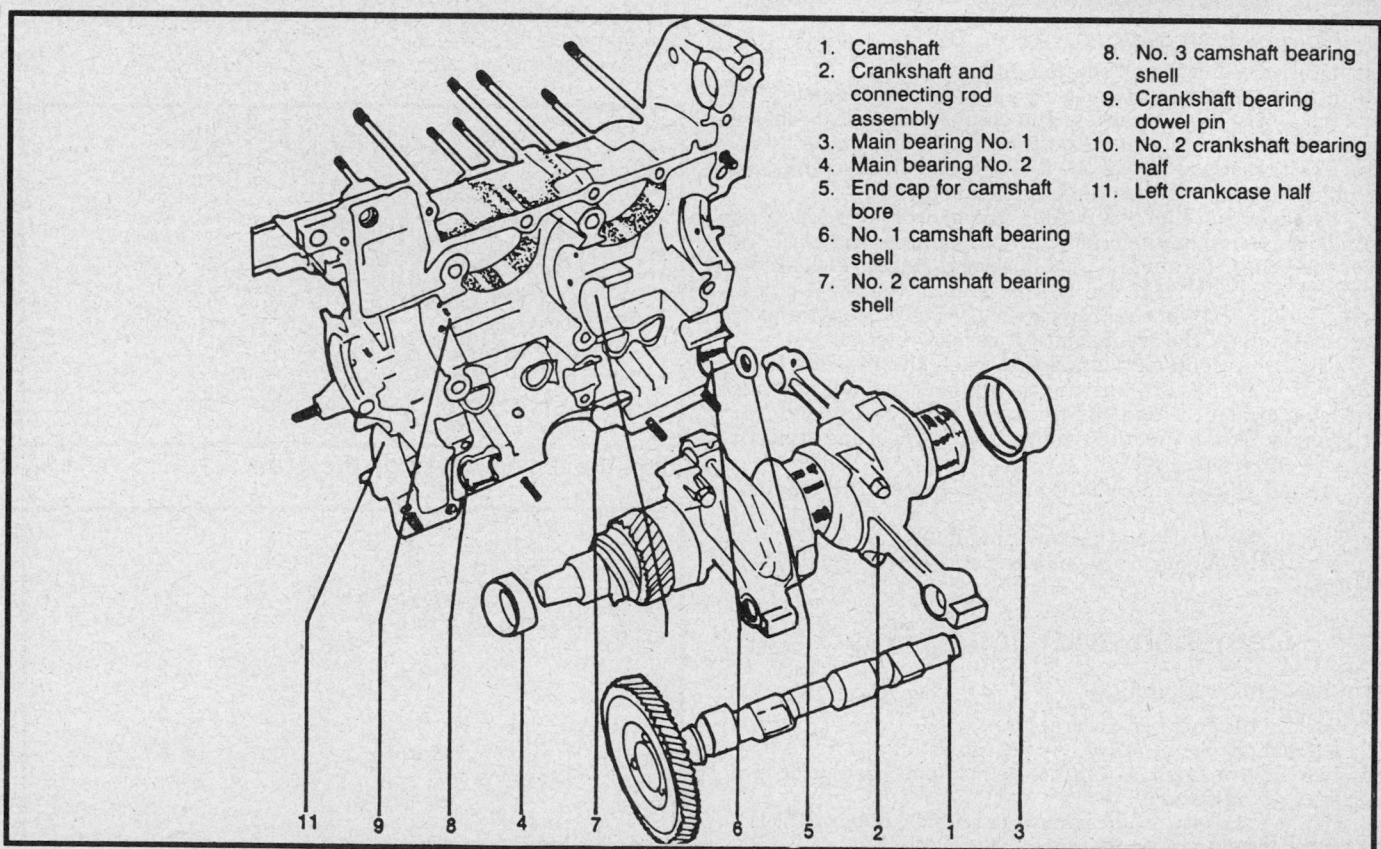

1. Camshaft
2. Crankshaft and connecting rod assembly
3. Main bearing No. 1
4. Main bearing No. 2
5. End cap for camshaft bore
6. No. 1 camshaft bearing shell
7. No. 2 camshaft bearing shell
8. No. 3 camshaft bearing shell
9. Crankshaft bearing dowel pin
10. No. 2 crankshaft bearing half
11. Left crankcase half

Crankcase assembly—exploded view

Crankcase

Disassembly and Assembly

1. Relieve the fuel system pressure.
2. Disconnect the negative battery cable.
3. Remove the engine and position it in a suitable holding fixture.
4. Remove the intake and exhaust manifolds. Remove the cylinder heads, cylinders and pistons.
5. Remove the oil strainer, oil pressure switch and crankcase nuts. Remove the flywheel and oil pump. Matchmark the flywheel so that it can be replaced in the same position.
6. Keep the cam followers in the right crankcase half in position by using a retaining spring.
7. Use a rubber hammer to break the seal between the crankcase halves.

NOTE: Never insert sharp metal tools, wedges, or any prying device between the crankcase halves.

8. After the seal between the crankcase halves is broken, remove the right-hand crankcase half, crankshaft oil seal and the camshaft can now be lifted out of the crankcase half.
9. Remove the cam followers, bearing shells and oil pressure relief valve.
10. Before starting reassembly, check the crankcase for any damage or cracks.
11. Flush and blow out all oil passages. Check the studs for tightness.
12. Install the crankshaft bearing dowel pins and bearing shells for the crankshaft and camshaft. Make sure that the bearing shells with thrust flanges are installed in the proper journal.
13. Install the crankshaft and camshaft after the bearings have been well lubricated. When installing the camshaft and cranshaft, make sure that the timing marks on the timing gears are aligned.
14. Install the oil pressure relief valve.
15. Lubricate and install the cam followers.
16. Install the camshaft end plug using sealing compound.
17. Install the thrust washers and crankshaft oil seal. The oil seal must rest squarely on the bottom of its recess in the crankcase. The thrust washers at the flywheel end of the crankshaft are shims used to set the crankshaft endplay.
18. Spread a thin film of VW AMV 188–000–02 or equivalent, sealing compound on the crankcase joining faces and place the halves together. Torque the nuts in several stages. Tighten the 8mm nut located next to the 122mm stud of the No. 1 crankshaft bearing first. As the crankcase halves are being torqued, continually check the crankshaft for ease of rotation.
19. Crankshaft end-play is checked when the flywheel is installed. It is adjusted by varying the number and thickness of the shims located behind the flywheel. Measure the end-play with a dial indicator mounted against the flywheel and attached firmly to the crankcase.
20. Install the cylinders and pistons. Install the cylinder heads.
21. Install the intake and exhaust manifolds.
22. Install the engine in the vehicle. Connect the negative battery cable.

Camshaft and Timing Gear

Removal and Installation

1. Relieve the fuel system pressure.
2. Disconnect the negative battery cable.
3. Remove the engine from the vehicle and position it in a suitable holding fixture.
4. Remove the intake and exhaust manifolds. Remove the cylinder heads, cylinders and pistons.
5. Disassemble the crankcase.

6. Remove the camshaft and timing gear from the case.
To install:
7. Before reinstalling the camshaft, it should be checked for wear on the lobe surfaces and on the bearing surfaces. In addition, the riveted joint between the camshaft timing gear and the camshaft should be checked for tightness.
8. The camshaft should be checked for a maximum run-out of 0.0015 in.
9. The timing gear should be checked for the correct tooth contact and for wear.
10. If the camshaft bearing shells are worn or damaged, new shells should be fitted. The camshaft bearing shells should be installed with the tabs engaging the notches in the crankcase. Before installing the camshaft, the bearing journals and cam lobes should be generously coated with oil.
11. When the camshaft is installed, care should be taken to ensure that the timing gear tooth marked **0** is located between the teeth of the crankshaft timing gear marked with a center punch.
12. Coat the camshaft end cap with sealant and make sure it is installed in it's original position.
13. The camshaft endplay is measured at the No. 3 bearing on all engines. Endplay is 0.0015–0.005 in. (0.04–0.12mm) and the wear limit is 0.006 in. (0.16mm).
14. Assemble the crankcase and install the cylinders, pistons, cylinder heads, intake and exhaust manifolds.
15. Install the engine in the vehicle. Connect the negative battery cable.

Pistons and Cylinders

Removal and Installation

1. Relieve the fuel system pressure.
2. Disconnect the negative battery cable.
3. Remove the engine from the vehicle and position it in a suitable holding fixture. Remove the intake and exhaust manifolds.
4. Remove the cylinder head(s) and pushrod tubes.

Align the timing marks on the gears

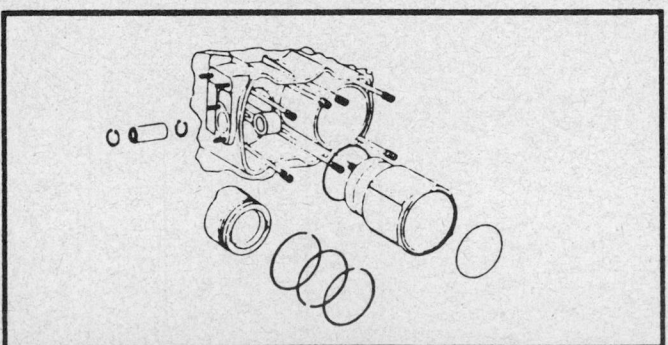

Cylinder and piston assemblies

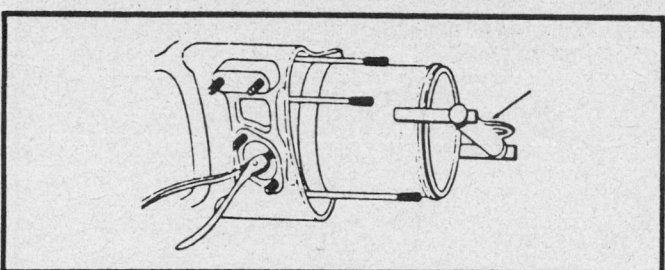

Removing the cylinder using a puller

5. Matchmark the tops of each piston to it's respective cylinder liner. Pistons and liners must be installed in the same locations. Note the boss on the inner side of each liner.

6. Set the piston to be removed at TDC. Using tool 3092 or an equivalent sleeve puller, pull out the cylinder until the piston pin circlip is visible through the coolant passage on the drive belt side of the engine. Remove the circlip.

7. To remove the sleeve, remove the circlip on the flywheel side. Remove the wrist pin through the same coolant passage using wrist pin puller no. 3091 or equivalent.

8. The cylinder block can be removed after the second piston on each side of the crankcase is removed. The block slides off of the cylinder block/cylinder head studs which protrude from the crankcase.

To install:

9. Make sure the cylinder block-to-crankcase mating surfaces are clean. Install the cylinder block onto the crankcase.

10. The sealing rings on the top and bottom sides of the cylinder liners must always be replaced. The cylinder head end ring is a thin green ring and the crankcase end ring is thick and black in color.

11. Lubricate the piston and liner bore with clean engine oil. Install the piston into the cylinder sleeve. The arrow on the piston faces the flywheel side of the engine. The gap on the oil scraper ring must be to the top and the piston ring gaps must be offset by 180 degrees. Install the flywheel-side wrist pin circlip into the piston.

12. Obtain a connecting rod support tool 3090 or equivalent. Note the markings on the tool; R is the right side of the engine, L is the left side of the engine.

13. Push the connecting rod support onto the center stud so that the finger of the tool suports the connecting rod, then secure it with a rubber band to prevent it from slipping. Align the connecting rod so that the piston wrist pin can be installed through the same coolant passage from which it was removed. The crankshaft must be at TDC and the lug on the rod faces UP.

14. Install the piston/sleeve assembly.

15. The piston should be protruding from the bottom of the sleeve just enough so that the entire wrist pin area is exposed. Using tool 3091 or equivalent, install the wrist pin through the coolant passage. Install the other wrist pin clip and slide the liner down into seated position.

16. Repeat this procedure for all cylinders. Install the cylinder head and remaining components in the reverse order of the removal procedure.

Piston and Connecting Rod

Positioning

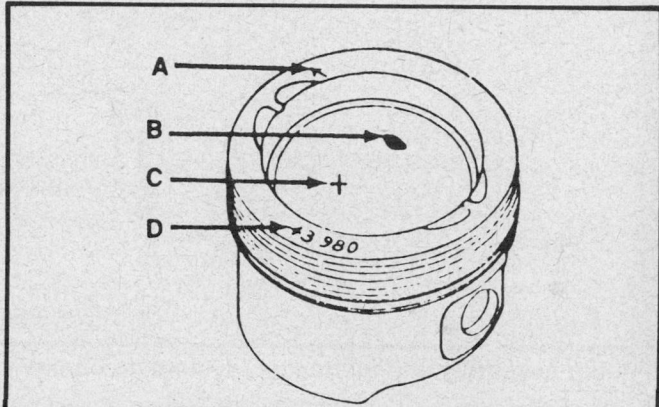

Piston identification and positioning marks:
A = stamped arrow, must face towards the flywheel when the piston is installed;
B = blue paint dot, indicates the matching size;
C = weight group (+ or -);
D = piston size in mm

ENGINE LUBRICATION

Oil Pump

Removal and Installation

1. Relieve the fuel system pressure.
2. Disconnect the negative battery cable.
3. Remove the engine from the vehicle and position it in a suitable holding fixture.
4. Remove the 4 oil pump securing nuts and pry the pump assembly out of the crankcase.
5. To dissasemble the pump, the pump cover must be pressed apart.

To install:

4. Prior to assembly, check the oil pump body for wear, especially the gear seating surface. If the pump body is worn, the result will be loss of oil pressure. Check the driven gear shaft for tightness and if necessary, peen it tightly into place or replace the pump housing. The gears should be checked for excessive wear, backlash and endplay. Maximum endplay without a gas-

ket is 1mm (0.004 in.).

5. The endplay can be checked using a T-square and a feeler gauge. Check the mating surface of the pump body and the crankcase for damage and cleanliness.

6. Install the pump into the crankcase with a new gasket. Do not use any sealing compound.

7. Turn the camshaft several revolutions in order to center the pump body opposite the slot in the camshaft.

8. Tighten the securing nuts.

9. Install the engine and fill the crankcase to the correct level.

Crankshaft Oil Seal

Removal and Installation

1. Relieve the fuel system pressure.
2. Disconnect the negative battery cable.
3. Remove the engine from the vehicle and support it in a suitable holding fixture.

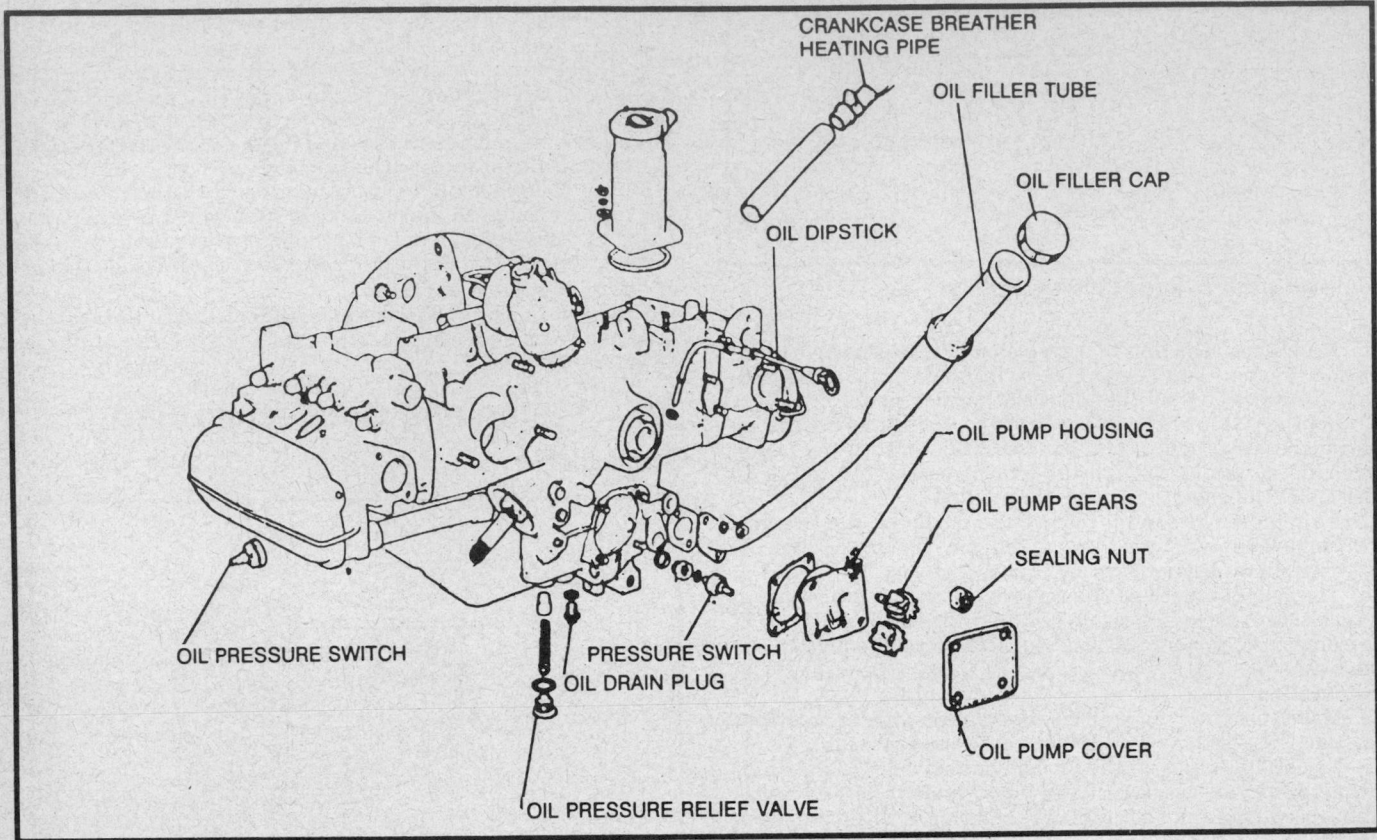

CRANKCASE BREATHER
HEATING PIPE

OIL FILLER TUBE

OIL FILLER CAP

OIL DIPSTICK

OIL PUMP HOUSING

OIL PUMP GEARS

SEALING NUT

OIL PRESSURE SWITCH

PRESSURE SWITCH

OIL DRAIN PLUG

OIL PUMP COVER

OIL PRESSURE RELIEF VALVE

Oil pump assembly and lubrication system components

4. Remove the flywheel. Once the flywheel is removed, inspect the surface on the flywheel joining flange where the seal makes contact.

5. If there is a deep groove or any other damage, the flywheel must be replaced.

6. Remove the oil seal by prying it out of it's bore.

7. Before installing a new seal, clean the crankcase oil seal recess and coat it with sealing compound.

8. Be sure that the seal rests squarely on the bottom of its recess. Make sure that the correct side of the lip of the seal is facing inward, towards the crankcase.

9. Reinstall the flywheel after coating the oil seal contact surface with oil.

NOTE: Be careful not to damage the seal when sliding the flywheel into place.

MANUAL TRANSAXLE

For further information, please refer to "Professional Transmission Manual".

Transaxle Assembly

Removal and Installation

1. Disconnect the negative battery cable.
2. Raise and safely support the vehicle.
3. Remove the top engine-to-transaxle bolts.
4. Remove the rear skid plate on 4WD vehicles.
5. Loosen the side bolts of the transaxle mounting bracket.
6. Remove the driveshaft-to-flange bolts and support the driveshaft aside.
7. Remove the left side halfshaft bolts and support the axle shaft aside.
8. Disconnect the clutch line bracket from the side of the transaxle.

9. Remove the clutch slave cylinder from its bracket and support it aside.
10. Disconnect the backup light switch wiring.
11. Remove the right side halfshaft bolts and support the halfshaft aside.
12. Disconnect the shift linkage from the transaxle. Place a suitable support under the transaxle/engine assembly.
13. Remove the front transaxle mounting bracket and lower the front of the transaxle approximately 6 in.
14. Disconnect the starter cables. Remove the vent hose from the transaxle.
15. Remove the bottom transaxle mounting bolts and pull the transmission off the engine guides.
16. Lower the transaxle from the vehicle.

To install:
17. Raise the transaxle into position.
18. Install the lower transaxle mounting bolts, tighten to 22 ft.

Front differential housing forward mount bolt

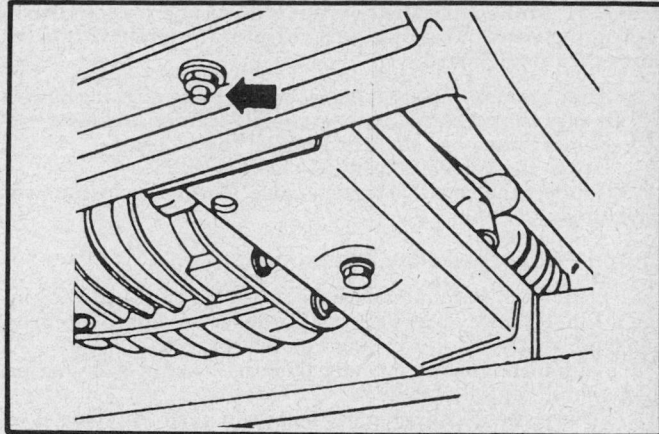
Front differential housing side mount bolts

lbs. (30 Nm).

19. Reconnect the starter cables and install the vent hose. Raise the transaxle and install the front mounting bracket.

20. Connect the shift linkage to the transaxle and connect both halfshafts. Tighten the halfshaft bolts to 26 ft. lbs. (35 Nm).

21. Connect the backup light switch. Install the slave cylinder in its bracket.

22. Connect the clutch line bracket to the transaxle.

23. Connect the driveshaft to the drive flange and tighten the bolts to 26 ft. lbs. (35 Nm).

24. Install the transaxle bracket side mounting bolts.

25. Install the skid plate, if equipped.

26. Install the top transaxle mounting bolts. Tighten to 22 ft. lbs. (30 Nm).

27. Lower the vehicle and connect the battery cable.

28. Check the operation of the transaxle and check the clutch operation.

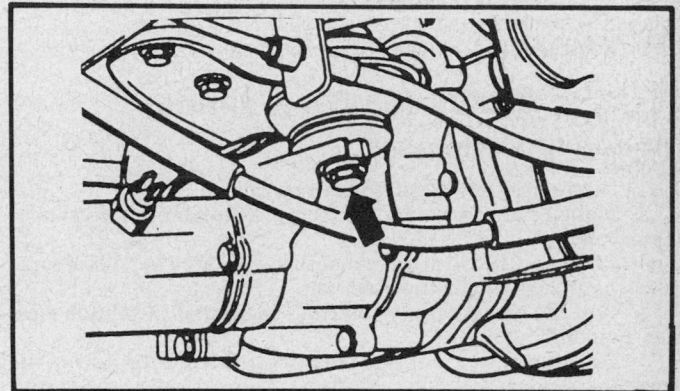
Front transaxle bracket—mounting bolt

CLUTCH

Clutch Assembly

Removal and Installation

1. Disconnect the negative battery cable.
2. Raise and safely support the vehicle.
3. Remove the transaxle from the vehicle.
4. Remove the pressure plate securing bolts a turn at a time until all spring pressure is released.
5. Remove the bolts and remove the clutch assembly.

NOTE: Note which side of the clutch disc faces the flywheel and install the new disc in the same direction.

6. Before installing the new clutch, check the condition of the flywheel. It should not have excessive heat cracks and the friction surface should not be scored or warped. Check the condition of the throw out bearing. If the bearing is worn, replace it.

To install:

7. Lubricate the pilot bearing in the end of the crankshaft with grease.

8. Insert a pilot shaft, used for centering the clutch disc, through the clutch disc and place the disc against the flywheel. The pilot shaft will hold the disc in place.

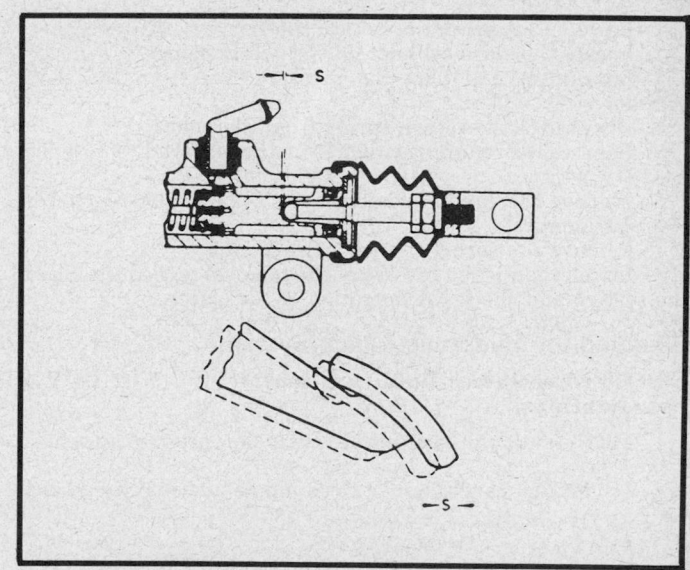
Adjusting the clutch pedal free-play

NOTE: **Make sure the correct side of the clutch disc is facing outward. The disc will rub the flywheel if it is incorrectly positioned.**

9. After making sure that the pressure plate aligning dowels will fit into the pressure plate, gradually tighten the bolts.
10. Remove the pilot shaft and install the transaxle.
11. Lower the vehicle. Bleed the clutch system.
12. Connect the negative battery cable. Check the operation of the clutch.

Clutch Pedal Free-Play Adjustment

1. The clutch pedal should have a free-play of 0.20–0.28 in. and a 7 in. total travel. If either of the above are not to specifications, adjust the master cylinder as follows.
2. Loosen the master cylinder pushrod locknut and shorten the pushrod length slightly.
3. Loosen the master cylinder bolts and push the cylinder as far forward as it will go. Retighten the bolts.
4. Remove the rubber cap from the clutch pedal stop screw and adjust distance to 0.89 in. Install the rubber cap.
5. Lengthen the pushrod as necessary to obtain a pedal free-play of 0.20–0.28 in. Tighten the pushrod locknut.
6. Road test the vehicle to insure proper clutch operation.

Clutch Master Cylinder

Removal and Installation

1. Disconnect the negative battery cable.
2. Siphon the hydraulic fluid from the clutch master cylinder reservoir.
3. Pull back the carpeting from the pedal area and place some absorbent rags under the reservoir.
4. Pull the elbow connection from the top of the clutch master cylinder.
5. Disconnect and plug the pressure line from the rear of the master cylinder.
6. Remove the master cylinder mounting bolts and remove the cylinder from the rear.
7. Installation is the reverse of the removal procedure. Bleed the clutch system when finished.

Clutch Slave Cylinder

Removal and Installation

1. Raise and support the vehicle safely.
2. Locate the slave cylinder on the bell housing.
3. Disconnect and plug the pressure line from the slave cylinder.
4. Disconnect the return spring from the pushrod.
5. Remove the retaining circlip from the boot and remove the boot.
6. Remove the circlip and slide the slave cylinder rearwards from its mount.
7. Remove the spring clip from the mount.
8. Installation is the reverse of the removal procedure. Bleed the system and check the operation of the clutch.

Bleeding the Hydraulic Clutch System

NOTE: **Use brake fluid that meets DOT 3 or DOT 4 specifications.**

1. Fill the clutch fluid reservoir and make sure the cap vent is open.
2. Locate the slave cylinder bleed nipple and remove all dirt

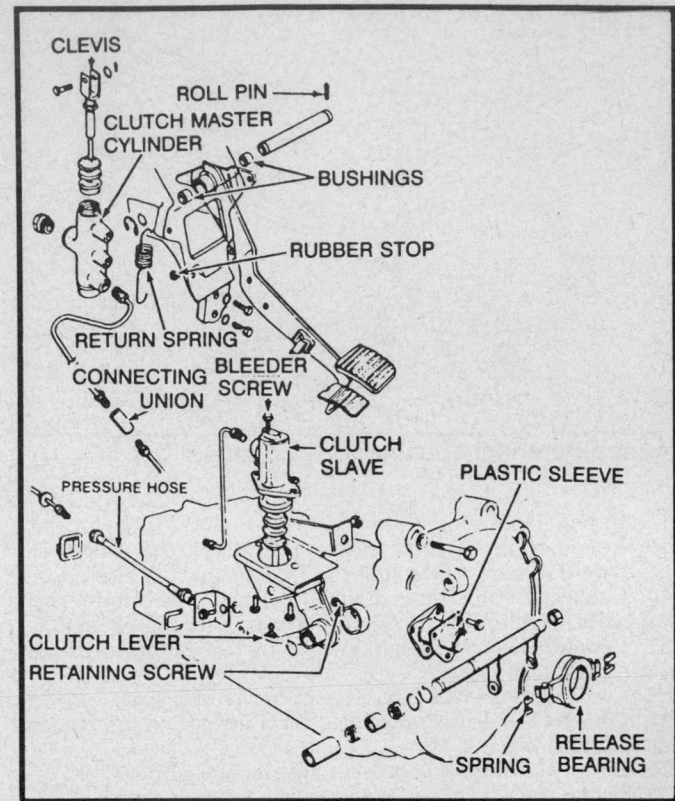

Hydraulic clutch system components

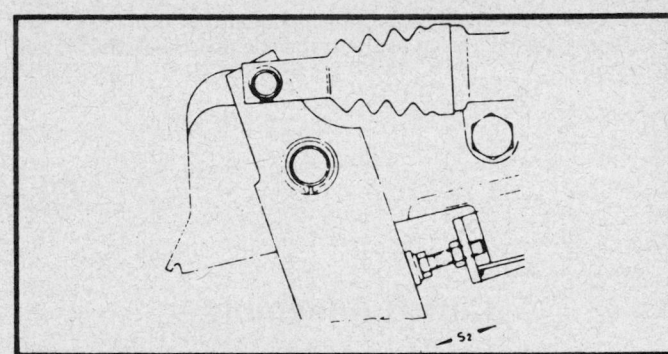

Clutch pedal stop adjusting screw

and grease from the valve. Attach a hose to the nipple and submerge the other end of the hose in a glass jar containing clean brake fluid.

3. Have an assitant operate the clutch pedal. Depresses the clutch pedal slowly to the floor, open the bleeder valve 1 turn. Hold the pedal on the floor until the bleeder valve is closed. Repeat this operation several times until no air bubbles are emitted from the tube.

NOTE: **During the procedure, check the fluid level in the fluid reservoir. Never let the level fall below the ½ full mark.**

4. After bleeding, discard the old fluid and top up the reservoir.

AUTOMATIC TRANSAXLE

For further information, please refer to "Professional Transmission Manual".

Transaxle Assembly

Removal and Installation

1. Disconnect the negative battery cable.
2. Remove the torque converter-to-flywheel bolts through the hole in the top of the transaxle housing. Rotate the crankshaft to bring each bolt into position. Remove the top transaxle-to-engine bolts.
3. Raise and safely support the vehicle.
4. Disconnect both halfshafts from the transaxle, support them aside. On 4WD vehicles, remove engine skid plate and disconnect the front driveshaft at the drive flange.
5. Disconnect the starter wiring and remove the starter.
6. Loosen the transaxle fluid dipstick tube.
7. Disconnect the accelerator linkage and accelerator cable.
8. Remove the circlip from the selector lever.
9. Support the engine with a suitable support bar.
10. Remove the ground strap and selector lever cable. Remove the side mounting bracket.
11. Support the transaxle with a suitable lifting device. Remove the rear transaxle support.
12. Remove the lower transaxle-to-engine bolts. Slowly lower the transaxle out of the vehicle. Use care not to drop the converter from the input shaft.

To install:
13. Raise the transaxle into position under the vehicle. Install the lower transaxle-to-engine bolts and tighten to 22 ft. lbs. (30 Nm).
14. Install the rear transaxle support.
15. Install the ground strap and selector lever cable. Install the side mounting bracket.
16. Remove the engine support bar and connector the selector lever.
17. Connect the accelerator cable and linkage. Attach the dipstick tube.

18. Install the starter. Install the front driveshaft and tighten the flange bolts to 33 ft. lbs. (45 Nm).
19. Connect the halfshafts and tighten the bolts to 33 ft. lbs. (45 Nm).
20. On 4WD vehicles, install the skid plate.
21. Install the upper transaxle bolts, tighten to 22 ft. lbs. (35 Nm).
22. Lower the vehicle and install the converter bolts. Tighten to 22 ft. lbs. (35 Nm).
23. Connect the negative battery cable and check the operation of the transaxle.

Shift Linkage Adjusment

1. Make sure the shift cable is not kinked or bent and that the linkage and cable are properly lubricated.
2. Move the gear shift lever to the **P** position.
3. Loosen the clamp which holds the front and rear halves of the shifting rod together. Loosen the clamping bolts on the transaxle lever.
4. Press the lever on the transaxle rearward, as far as possible. Spring pressure will be felt. The manual valve must be on the stop in the valve body.
5. Holding the transaxle lever against it's stop, tighten the clamping bolt.
6. Holding the rear shifting rod half, push the front half forward to take up any clearance and tighten the clamp bolt.
7. Test the shift pattern.

Neutral Safety Switch Adjustment

1. The combination neutral start and backup light switch is mounted inside the shifter housing.
2. The engine should start in **P** or **N** only and the backup lights should only come on only in **R**.
3. Adjust the switch by loosening the screws and moving it on it's mounts.
4. After any adjustment or replacement, check that the engine starts only with the switch in **P** or **N** and the backup lights come on only in **R**.

DRIVE AXLE

Halfshaft

Removal and Installation

FRONT

1. With the vehicle on the ground, remove the front halfshaft end-nut and washer.
2. Raise and support the vehicle safely. Remove the wheel and tire assembly.
3. Remove the socket head bolts retaining the halfshaft to the differential.
4. Remove the bolts holding the ball joint to the lower control arm.
5. Removing the ball joint from the control arm will give enough clearance to remove the axle shaft. It pulls right out of the steering knuckle.
6. Installation is the reverse of the removal procedure.
7. Always use a new halfshaft end-nut when installing. Tight-

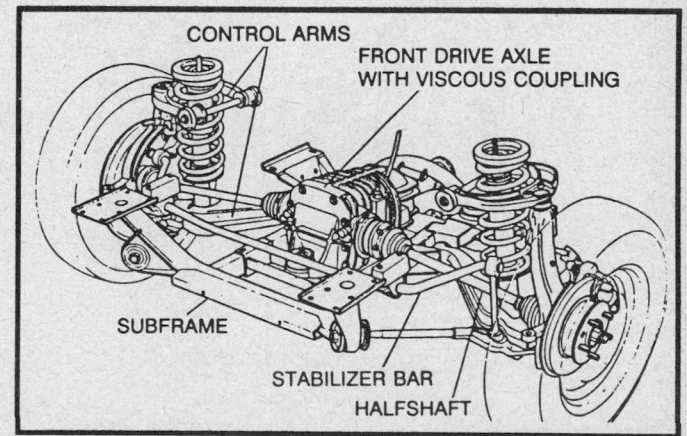

Front suspension and drive assembly—Syncro 4WD

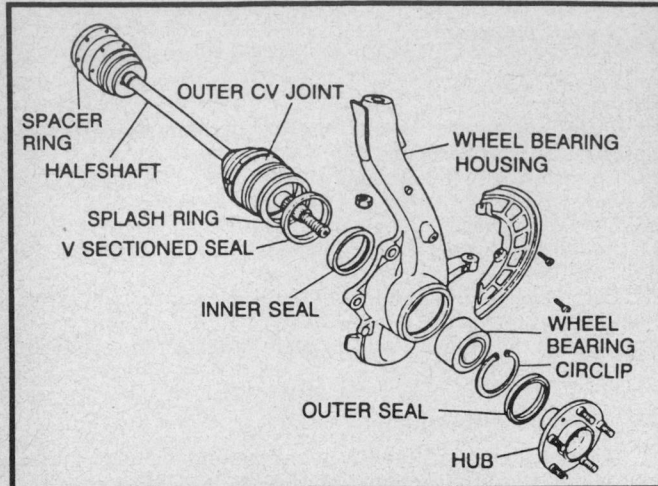

Front halfshaft assembly — exploded view

en the halfshaft to differential bolts to 26 ft. lbs., the ball joint bolts to 22 ft. lbs. and the halfshaft end-nut to 236 ft. lbs.

REAR

1. Raise and support the vehicle safely.
2. Matchmark the halfshaft to the transaxle and to the stub axle.
3. Remove the bolts which secure the halfshaft at each end.
4. Tilt the halfshaft downwards and remove the halfshaft from the vehicle.
4. Install the halfshaft in position, aligning the matchmarks made during removal.
5. Torque the axleshaft bolts to 32 ft. lbs.

Driveshaft and U-Joints

Removal and Installation
SYNCRO 4WD

1. Raise and safely support the vehicle.

2. Matchmark the driveshaft ends to the flanges.
3. Remove the driveshaft retaining bolts and remove the driveshaft from the vehicle.
4. Install the driveshaft in position, aligning the matchmarks.
5. Tgihten the bolts to 33 ft. lbs. (45 Nm).
6. Lower the vehicle.

Front Wheel Bearing and Seal

Removal and Installation
SYNCRO 4WD

1. Remove the outer halfshaft end nut and washer with the vehicle on the ground.
2. Raise and support the vehicle safely. Remove the wheel and tire assembly.
3. Remove the brake caliper from the steering knuckle and support it out of the way.
4. Remove the disc brake rotor from the hub assembly.
5. Remove the ball joint to control arm bolts and separate the ball joint from the control arm.
6. Remove the lower shock absorber mounting bolt.
7. Remove the tie rod end to steering knuckle nut and separate the tie rod from the steering knuckle.
8. While supporting the halfshaft, pull the steering knuckle and hub assembly out away from the vehicle. After separating the halfshaft from the steering knuckle assembly, support it out of the way.
9. Remove the steering knuckle to upper ball joint bolts and remove the steering knuckle assembly from the vehicle.
10. Use a suitable tool on top of parallel rail blocks on an arbor press to support the steering knuckle assembly. Place the steering knuckle and hub assembly on top of tools with the hub facing down.
11. Stack a suitable tool on top of the hub shaft and press the hub from the steering knuckle.
12. Secure the hub in a vise. Using a puller, remove the inner race from the hub shaft.
13. Remove the internal snaprings from the steering knuckle.
14. With the steering knuckle assembly in the same pressing position, stack suitable pressing tools, on the bearing and press the bearing from the steering knuckle.

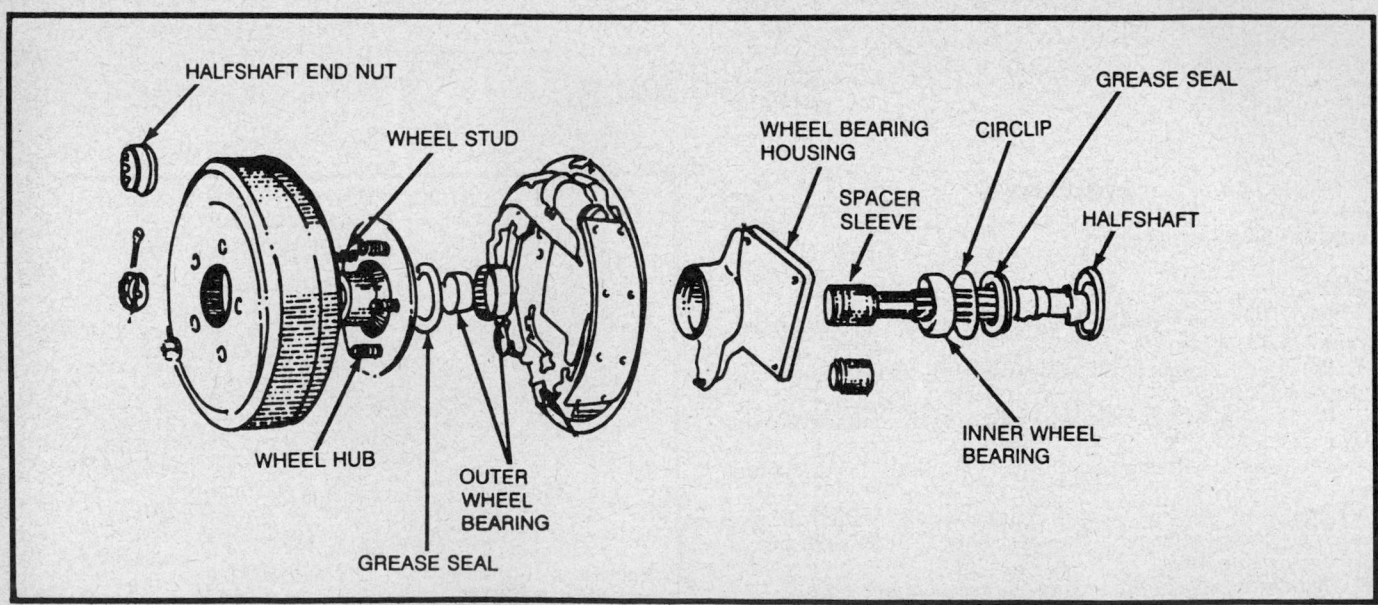

Rear wheel bearing and halfshaft assembly

15. Thoroughly clean all parts. If worn or damaged parts are present, replace them.

To install:

16. Use the same set of tools used to extract the bearing, place the new bearing on the steering knuckle and press it into the steering knuckle until it seats against the bottom retaining ring. Install the other retaining ring.

17. Lift the steering knuckle assembly and place the hub on a flat surface followed by the steering knuckle, it must be facing the same direction.

18. Using suitable pressing tools, stack them on the bearing and press the hub into the steering knuckle assembly.

19. To complete the installation, reverse the removal procedures. Align the matchmarks and torque the steering knuckle bolts to 59 ft. lbs.

20. Torque the control arm to steering knuckle to 32 ft. lbs., the tie rod to the steering knuckle to 22 ft. lbs. and the halfshaft end nut to 236 ft. lbs.

Stub Axle, Bearing and Seal

Removal and Installation

1. Raise and support the vehicle safely.
2. Remove the wheel and tire assembly, grease cap, cotter pin and axle nut.
3. Remove the brake drum and wheel hub.
4. Disconnect and plug the brake line at the wheel cylinder. Remove the brake assembly and backing plate.
5. Remove the 4 wheel bearing housing retaining bolts and remove the wheel bearing housing.
6. Slide the halfshaft out of the bearing housing.
7. Press the stub shaft from the bearing housing using the appropriate tools and a press.
8. Remove the inner and outer grease seals from the bearing housing.
9. Remove the spacer sleeve and the outer bearing.
10. Remove the inner grease seal and circlip. Press out the inner wheel bearing using the proper tools. Remove the spacer sleeve.

To install:

11. Pack new wheel bearings with grease.
12. Install a new spacer sleeve in the inner wheel bearing housing. Press the inner wheel bearing in until it is seated in the bearing housing. Fill the space between the inner and outer bearing with grease. Press the outer bearing into position using the same tools used to place the inner bearing. Install new spacer sleeves, circlip and grease seals.

13. Press the stub axle into the bearing housing.
14. Installation of the halfshaft is the reverse of the removal procedure.
15. Torque the wheel bearing housing to axle housing retaining bolts to 14 ft. lbs.
16. Install the remaining components in the reverse order of the removal procedure.
17. Tighten the brake line hose.
18. Bleed the brake system.

Front Differential

Removal and Installation

SYNCRO 4WD

1. Raise and support the vehicle safely. Remove the skid plate.
2. Loosen, but do not remove, the front differential mounting bolt and the side differential mounting bracket bolts.
3. Matchmark and remove the driveshaft.
4. Disconnect the halfshafts, speedometer cable and vent hose from the differential.
5. Remove the differential rear mounting bolt. Remove the bracket from the frame.
6. Support the differential and remove the front mounting bolts.
7. Carefully lower the differential from the vehicle.

To install:

8. Raise the differential into position.
9. Install the rear mounting bolts, do not tighten. Install the bracket to the frame.
10. Connect the halfshafts, speedometer cable and vent hose.
11. Install the front mounting bolts.
12. Tighten the halfshaft-to-differential bolts to 26 ft. lbs., driveshaft-to-differential bolts to 26 ft. lbs.
13. Tighten the differential mounts and bolts last.
14. Align the driveshaft matchmarks during installation.

STEERING

Steering Wheel

Removal and Installation

1. Disconnect the negative battery cable.
2. Remove the horn pad from the steering wheel. Pull the horn pad up by hand to remove it.
3. Disconnect the electrical lead from the horn pad.
4. Matchmark the steering wheel and the steering shaft.
5. Remove the steering wheel hold-down nut and remove the steering wheel.
6. To install the steering wheel, align the matchmarks made during removal and install the wheel.
7. Tighten the retaining nut to 36 ft. lbs (50 Nm).
8. Install the horn pad. Connect the negative battery cable.

Manual Rack and Pinion

Removal and Installation

1. Raise and safely support the vehicle.

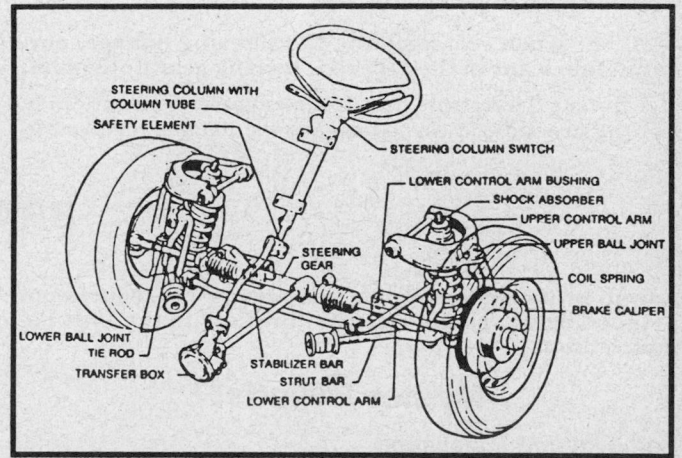

Steering assembly—typical

2. Detach the connecting shaft from the coupling disc.

3. Remove the tie rod retaining nut from the end stud.

4. Using a suitable tie rod removal tool, remove the tie rod end from the bearing housing, being careful not to pull the ball out of its socket.

5. Unscrew the tie rod from the tie rod ends, while counting and recording the number of turns necessary to remove the tie rods.

6. At the steering rod/steering gear junction, pull back the boot and remove the clamping bolts, then separate the steering rod from the steering gear.

7. Remove the steering gear-to-subframe clamp nuts, the clamps and the steering gear assembly from the vehicle.

To install:

8. Install the steering gear in position in the vehicle. Torque the steering gear clamp nuts to 22 ft. lbs.

9. Install the steering rod to the steering gear. Install the boot over the steering rod. Tighten the steering rod bolt to 22 ft. lbs.

10. Install the tie rod into the tie rod end, counting the same number of turns as for removal.

11. Install the tie rods to the bearing housing.

12. Connect the steering rod to the coupling shaft.

Power Rack and Pinion

Removal and Installation

1. Raise and safely support the vehicle.

2. Detach the connecting shaft from the coupling disc.

3. Remove the tie rod retaining nut from the end stud.

4. Using a suitable tie rod removal tool, remove the tie rod end from the bearing housing, being careful not to pull the ball out of its socket.

5. Disconnect and plug the power steering lines from the steering gear housing.

NOTE: Place a drain pan under the power steering pump suction hose to catch the fluid when removing the power steering lines, then discard the fluid.

6. Unscrew the tie rod from the tie rod ends, while counting and recording the number of turns necessary to remove the tie rods.

7. At the steering rod/steering gear junction, pull back the boot and remove the clamping bolts, then separate the steering rod from the steering gear.

8. Remove the steering gear-to-subframe clamp nuts, the clamps and the steering gear assembly from the vehicle.

To install:

9. Use new O-rings at the pressure hose connections and reverse the removal procedures.

NOTE: When reassembling the steering linkage, never put lubricant in the tapered steering gear fluid holes.

10. Torque the pressure hose-to-steering gear fittings to 15 ft. lbs., the steering gear clamp nuts and the steering rod-to-steer-

ing gear retaining bolt to 22 ft. lbs.

11. Fill the reservoir with an approved power steering fluid and bleed the system.

Power Steering Pump

Removal and Installation

1. Disconnect the negative battery cable. Place a pan under the power steering pump when draining the fluid.

2. Remove the suction hose and pressure line from the pump, then drain the fluid into the pan.

3. Loosen the belt tensioning bolt at the front of the bracket and remove the drive belt from the pulley.

4. Remove the pump mounting bolts and remove the pump from the vehicle.

5. Install the pump in position on the engine.

6. Tension the drive belt. Torque the mounting bolts to 15 ft. lbs.

7. Fill the reservoir with approved power steering fluid and bleed the system.

System Bleeding

1. Fill the power steering reservoir to **MAX** with Dexron® II automatic transmission fluid.

2. Raise and safely support the vehicle.

3. With the engine off, rotate the steering wheel from lock to lock.

4. Fill the reservoir to the **MAX** mark.

5. Start the engine several times, truning it off immediately after the engine starts. Add fluid as necessary, maintaining the level at the **MAX** mark.

NOTE: Never let the reservoir run out of fluid. Damage to the pump and/or steering gear may result.

6. When the fluid level no longer drops, start and run the engine. Rotate the steering wheel lock to lock several times. Check that no bubbles appear in the reservoir and that the level remains steady.

7. If air bubbles appear, repeat the procedure until the fluid is clear.

Tie Rod Ends

Removal and Installation

1. Raise and safely support the vehicle. Remove the tie rods from the bearing housing. All tie rod ends are secured by a nut which holds the tapered tie rod end stud into a matching tapered hole.

2. Once the tie rod end stud has been removed, turn the tie rod end out of the adjustment sleeve, while counting the number of turns.

3. When reassembling, install the tie rods in the sleeve the same nunber of turn as when removing.

4. Check and adjust the toe in when finished.

BRAKES

For all brake system repair and service procedures not detailed below, please refer to "Brakes" in the Unit Repair section.

Master Cylinder

Removal and Installation

NOTE: In order to remove the master cylinder reser-

voir, the intrument cluster must first be removed.

1. Disconnect the negative battery cable. Grasp the recesses provided on the back of the instrument cluster frame and pull it forward.

2. Disconnect and tag the wiring leading to the back of the instrument cluster and then remove the cluster.

3. Disconnect and plug the brake lines at the master cylinder.

4. Disconnect the electrical plug from the sending unit for the

brake failure switch.

5. Remove the master cylinder mounting nuts.

6. Lift the master cylinder and reservoir out of the vehicle.

NOTE: Do not depress the brake pedal while the master cylinder is removed.

To install:

7. Position the master cylinder and reservoir assembly onto the mounting studs and install the washers and nuts. Tighten the nuts to 11–14 ft. lbs.

8. Remove the plugs and connect the brake lines to the master cylinder.

9. Connect the wiring to the sending unit for the brake failure switch.

10. Install the instrument cluster. Connect the negative battery cable.

11. Fill the master cylinder and bleed the brake system.

12. Install the instrument cluster cover.

Power Brake Booster

Removal and Installation

1. Disconnect the negative battery cable.

2. Remove the instrument cluster. Remove the steering column covers and remove the steering column bolts (there are 2 shear bolts that retain the column, these must be drilled out and replaced).

3. Remove the glove box and remove the center dash panel. Pull off the heater controls levers.

4. Remove the screws inside the center cover and to the side of the instrument cluster opening.

5. Disconnect the air ducts under the instrument panel. Remove the instrument panel retaining screws at the top of the panel nd at the sides. Remove the instrument panel from the firewall.

6. Disconnect the electrical leads from the stop light switch.

7. Remove the bolts that retain the pedal bracket to the firewall and remove the booster/pedal bracket assembly from the vehicle. Disconnect the pushrod from the pedal assembly.

8. Remove the booster retaining bolts and remove the booster from the bracket.

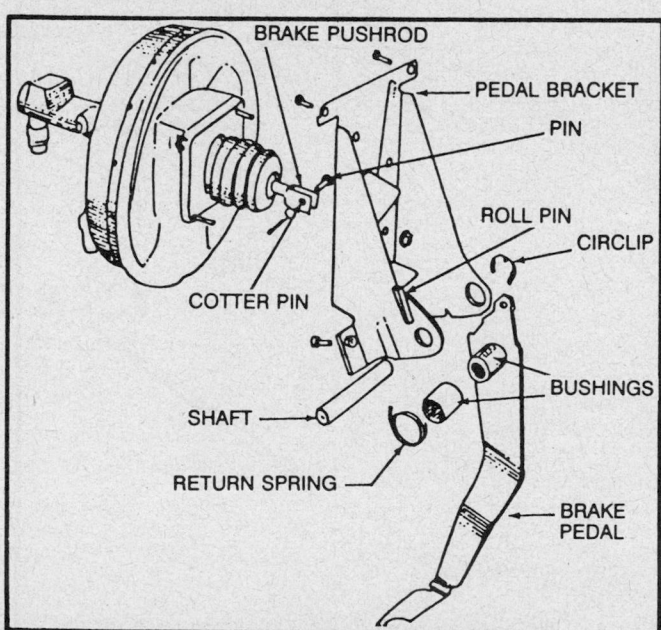

Master cylinder and brake booster mounting

To install:

9. Install the booster to the bracket assembly. Tighten the nuts to 11 ft. lbs. (15 Nm).

10. Install the booster/pedal bracket assembly to the firewall. Connect the pedal to the pushrod and connect the stop light switch lead.

11. Install the instrument panel to the firewall. Use new shear bolts at the steering column.

12. Install the master cylinder.

13. Install the instrument cluster.

14. Bleed the brake system.

15. Connect the negative battery cable and install the instrument cluster hood.

Brake Caliper

Removal and Installation

1. Raise and support the vehicle safely. Remove the wheel and tire assembly.

2. Remove the brake pads from the caliper.

3. Disconnect and plug the brake fluid line at the caliper.

4. Remove the brake caliper mounting bolts and remove the caliper.

To install:

5. Position the caliper on the mount and install the mounting bolts.

NOTE: The upper caliper mounting bolt has a shoulder on the top of the bolt. This bolt must be installed on the top.

6. Torque the mounting bolts to 123 ft. lbs.

7. Connect the brake fluid line to the caliper. Install the brake pads, pins and clips.

8. Fill and bleed the entire brake system.

Disc Brake Pads

Removal and Installation

1. Raise and support the vehicle safely. Remove the wheel and tire assembly.

2. Using a suitable tool, knock out the brake pad retaining pins, inward.

3. Remove the brake pads.

4. Push the caliper piston into the caliper until it bottoms out.

To install:

5. Install the new brake pads and retaining pins. Check that the pins are fully seated in the caliper.

6. Install the wheel and tire assembly.

7. Repeat the procedure for the opposite side. Check the brake fluid level in the reservoir when finished.

8. Depress the brake pedal several times until pressure is felt before moving the vehicle.

Brake Rotor

Removal and Installation

1. Raise and support the vehicle safely. Remove the wheel and tire assembly.

2. Remove the brake pads and pins.

3. Without disconnecting the brake fluid line, remove the brake caliper and mount. Support it aside.

4. Remove the cotter pin and bearing retaning nut. Remove the rotor.

5. Installation is the reverse of the removal procedure.

6. Adjust the wheel bearings.

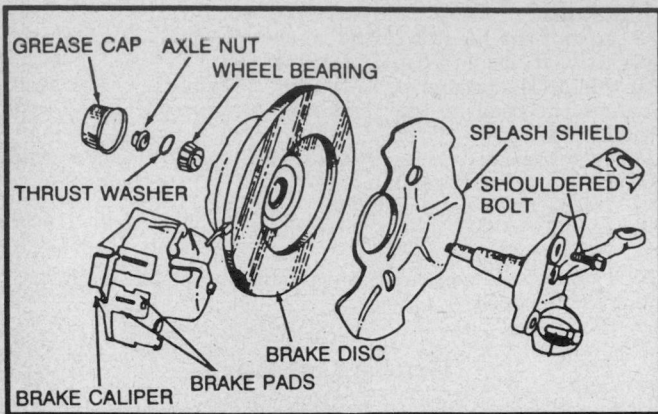

GREASE CAP   AXLE NUT
WHEEL BEARING
THRUST WASHER
SPLASH SHIELD
SHOULDERED BOLT
BRAKE DISC
BRAKE CALIPER   BRAKE PADS

Front rotor and hub assembly—except Syncro 4WD

Brake Drums

Removal and Installation

1. Raise and safely support the vehicle.
2. Remove the wheel and tire assembly.
3. Remove the drum retaining screws.
4. Remove the brake drum.
5. Install the brake drum in position and install the retaining screws. If the drum will not go on easily, turn the brake shoes in with the brake adjuster.
6. Install the wheel and tire assembly.
7. Lower the vehicle.

Brake Shoes

Removal and Installation

1. Raise and safely support the vehicle.
2. Remove the wheel and tire assembly.
3. Remove the brake drum.
4. Remove the brake shoe hold-down springs and pins.
5. Unhook the parking brake lever at the leading brake shoe.
6. Remove the lower return spring and the adjuster spring.
7. Move the brake shoes out of the lower support and unhook the return springs.
8. Remove the brake shoes and the push/adjusting rod.
To install:
9. Install the return springs and adjuster/push rod on the brake shoes.
10. Install the shoes on the backing plate and into the lower support.
11. Pull the top of the brake shoes around the wheel cylinder.
12. Install the hold-down spring and the pins.
13. Install the adjuster spring.
14. Attach the parking brake lever. Install the lower return spring.
15. Trun the brake adjuster to pre-adjust the shoes.
16. Install the brake drum. Install the wheel and tire assembly.
17. Check the adjustment of the brakes.

Wheel Cylinder

Removal and Installation

1. Raise and support the vehicle safely. Remove the wheel and tire assembly. Remove the brake drum and brake shoes.
2. Disconnect and plug the brake line on the rear of the wheel cylinder.
3. Remove the bolts and lockwashers that attach the wheel cylinder to the backing plate and remove the wheel cylinder.
4. Position the new wheel cylinder on the backing plate and install the attaching bolts and lockwashers.
5. Connect the brake line.
6. Install the brake drum, brake shoes, wheel and tire assembly. Bleed the wheel cylinder.

Parking Brake Cable

Removal and Installation

1. Disconnect the cables at the hand brake lever by removing the nuts which secure the cables to the lever. Pull the cables rearward to remove that end from the lever bracket.
2. Raise and support the vehicle safely. Remove the wheel and tire assemblies.
3. Remove the brake drum and detach the cable end from the lever attached to the rear brake shoe.
4. Remove the brake cable bracket from the backing plate and remove the cable from the vehicle.
5. Installation is the reverse of the removal procedure.
6. Adjust the parking brake.

Adjustment

1. Brake cable adjustment is performed at the hand brake lever in the passenger compartment.
2. There is a cable for each rear wheel and there are 2 adjusting nuts at the lever.
3. Loosen the locknut at each cable.
4. Raise and safely support the rear wheel to be adjusted so that it can be turned by hand.
5. Turn the adjusting nut until a very slight drag is felt as the wheel is turned.
6. Back off on the adjusting nut until the lever can be pulled up 3 notches.

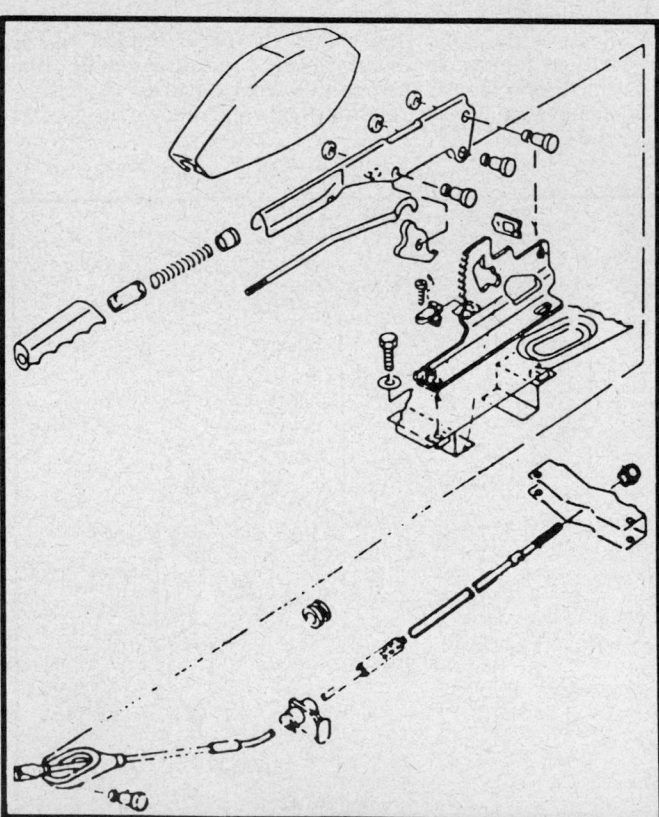

Parking brake lever and cable assemblies

FRONT SUSPENSION

Shock Absorber

Removal and Installation

1. Raise and support the vehicle safely so that the front suspension is hanging freely. Remove the wheel and tire assembly.
2. Support the lower control arm and remove the upper and lower shock absorber mounting bolts, nuts and washers.
3. Remove the shock absorber from the vehicle.
4. Install the shock absorber, rubber boot and stopper.
5. Tighten the upper shock absorber mounting nut until the rubber washer is compressed to the same width as the metal washer.
6. Raise the lower control arm and tighten the lower shock absorber mounting bolt to 23–29 ft. lbs.

7. Install the wheel and tire assembly. Lower the vehicle.

Coil Spring

Removal and Installation

1. Raise and safely support the vehicle.
2. Remove the wheel and tire assembly.
3. Remove the shock absorber.
4. With the shock absorber removed, the coil spring can be removed.
5. Remove the coil spring, noting the position of the rubber stopper.

To install:

6. Install the new coil spring and seat the spring in the lower

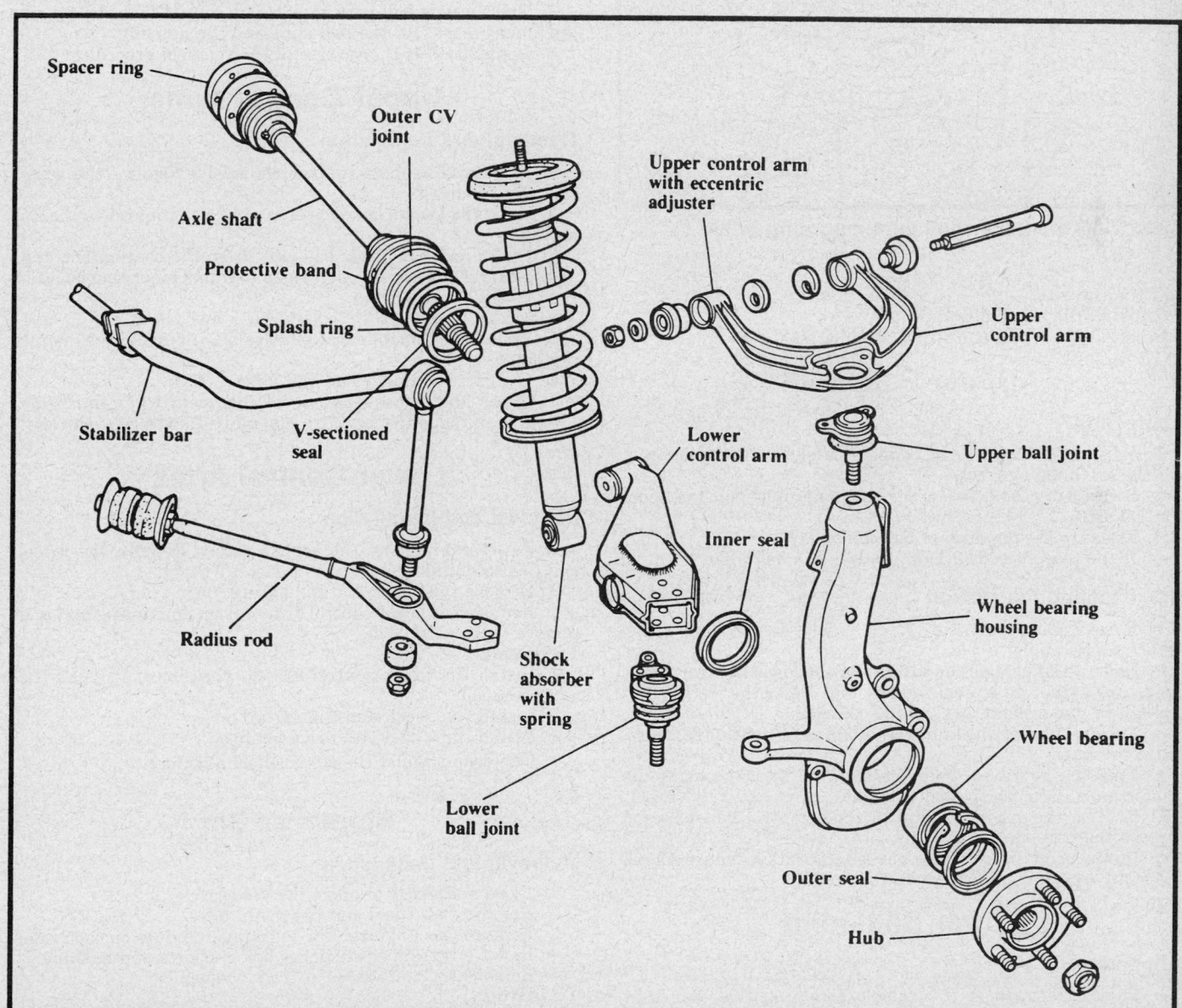

Front suspension components—Syncro 4WD

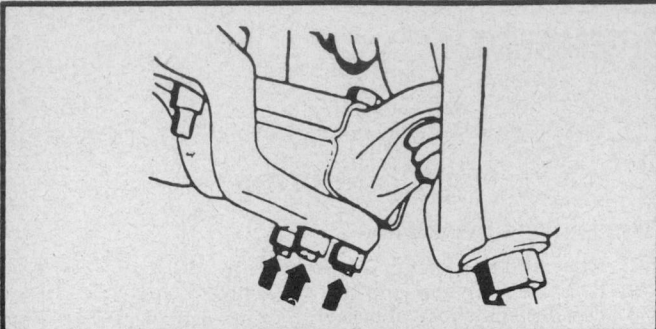

Removing the lower ball joint mounting bolts

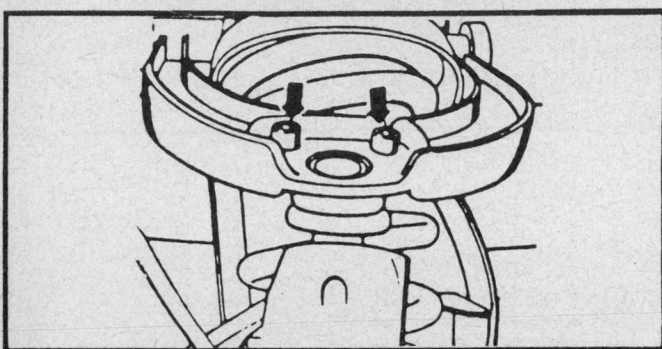

Removing the upper ball joint mounting bolts

control arm seat.

7. Install the shock absorber.
8. Install the wheel and tire assembly.

Upper Ball Joint

Inspection

1. Raise and support the vehicle safely so that the front wheels are hanging freely.
2. Insert a pry bar between the ball joint pinch bolt and upper control arm.
3. Measure the distance of ball joint play.
4. If the play exceeds 0.1 in., replace the ball joint.

Removal and Installation

1. Raise and support the vehicle safely. Remove the wheel and tire assembly.
2. Place an adjustable support under the lower control arm as close to the steering knuckle as possible. Raise the control arm enough to put a slight load on the coil spring.
3. Loosen the steering knuckle-to-ball joint nut but do not remove the nut.
4. Free the ball joint from the steering knuckle, using the proper tools. Remove the ball joint nut.
5. Remove the upper ball joint to upper control arm bolts and remove the ball joint.
6. Installation is the reverse of the removal procedure. Check the front wheel alignment when finished.

Lower Ball Joint

Inspection

1. Raise and support the vehicle safely so that the front wheels are hanging freely.
2. Insert a pry bar between the ball joint pinch bolt and lower

control arm.
3. Measure the distance of ball joint play.
4. If the play exceeds 0.1 in., replace the ball joint.

Removal and Installation

1. Raise and support the vehicle safely. Remove the wheel and tire assembly.
2. Place an adjustable support under the lower control arm as close to steering knuckle as possible and place a slight load on the coil spring.
3. Without disconnecting the brake caliper hose from the caliper, remove the brake caliper and rotor. Support them out of the way.
4. Loosen the upper ball joint-to-steering knuckle nut, but do not remove the nut. Free the upper ball joint from the steering knuckle, using the proper tools and remove the nut.
5. Remove the lower ball joint to lower control arm nut and remove the ball joint from the control arm. Remove the bearing housing.
6. Press the ball joint off of the bearing housing.
7. Press a new ball joint in place on knuckle, observing any alignment marks on the ball joint and the housing.
8. Installation is the reverse of the removal procedure.

Upper Control Arms

Removal and Installation

1. Raise and support the vehicle safely. Remove the wheel and tire assembly.
2. Raise the lower control arm to place a slight load on the coil spring.
3. Disconnect the upper ball joint from the bearing housing.
4. Remove the upper control arm to frame mounting bolt and remove the control arm.
To install:
5. Install the control arm to the frame and install the mounting bolt.
6. Connect the upper ball ball joint.
7. Check and adjust front wheel alignment when finished.
8. Install the wheel and tire assembly. Lower the vehicle.

Lower Control Arms

Removal and Installation

1. Raise and support the vehicle safely. Remove the wheel and tire assembly.
2. Remove the shock and coil spring.
3. Remove the lower control arm to frame mounting bolt and remove the control arm.
To install:
4. Install the lower control arm in position and install the mounting bolt.
5. Install the shock and coil spring.
6. Install the wheel and tire assembly.
7. Check and adjust the front wheel alignment.

Stabilizer Bar

Removal and Installation

1. Raise and safely support the vehicle.
2. Remove the wheel and tire assemblies.
3. Remove the stabilizer bar-to-radius rod nuts on each side.
4. Remove the upper stabilizer bar supports and bushing.
5. Remove the stabilizer bar from the vehicle.
To install:
6. Install the stabilizer in position. Install the upper supports and bushings.

7. Install the stabilizer bar retaining nuts. Tighten to 22 ft. lbs.

8. Install the wheel and tire assembly and lower the vehicle.

Radius Rod

Removal and Installation

1. Raise and safely support the vehicle.
2. Remove the wheel and tire assemblies.
3. Disconnect the stabilizer bar from the radius rod.
4. Remove the front retaining nut from the radius rod. Mark the position of the nut for installation.
5. Remove the rear radius rod mounting nuts from the lower control arm.
6. Remove the radius rod from the vehicle.

To install:

7. Install the radius rod in position. Install the rear retaining nuts.
8. Install the front rod nut, install it to the position marked during removal. Tighten the nut to 111 ft. lbs. (150 Nm).
9. Connect the stabilizer bar to the radius rod.
10. Install the wheel and tire assemblies.
11. Lower the vehicle.

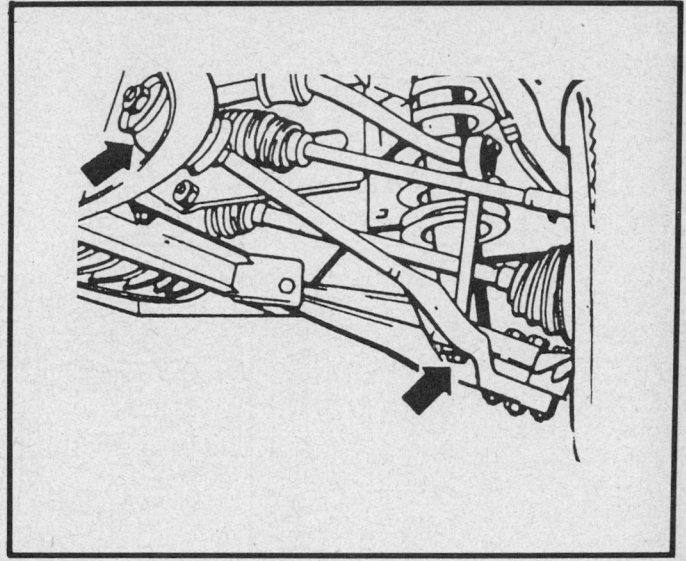

Removing radius rod mounting bolts

REAR SUSPENSION

Shock Absorber

Removal and Installation

1. Raise and safely support the vehicle.
2. Remove the wheel and tire assemblies.
3. Support the trailing arm assembly and remove the upper and lower shock mounting bolts.
4. Remove the shock absorber from the vehicle.
5. Installation is the reverse of the removal procedure.
6. Tighten the shock mounting bolts to 65 ft. lbs.

Coil Springs

Removal and Installation

1. Raise and safely support the vehicle.
2. Remove the wheel and tire assembly.
3. Support the trailing arm and remove the shock absorber.
4. Lower the trailing arm slightly and remove the coil spring.
5. Installation is the reverse of the removal procedure.

Trailing Arms

Removal and Installation

1. Raise and safely support the vehicle.
2. Remove the wheel and tire assemblies.
3. Disconnect and plug the brake line. Remove the the backing plate assembly from the trailing arm. The brake shoes do not need to be removed.
4. Disconnect the halfshaft from the transaxle.
5. Disconnect and remove the shock absorber and the coil spring.
6. Remove the trailing arm pivot bolt and lower the trailing arm from the vehice with the halfshaft attached.

To install:

7. Install the trailing arm in position and install the pivot bolt. Tighten the pivot bolt to 65 ft. lbs.
8. Install the shock absorber and coil spring.
9. Connect the halfshaft to the transaxle.

10. Attach the backing plate assembly to the trailing arm, tighten the retaining bolts to 102 ft. lbs.
11. Connect the brake lines and bleed the brakes.
12. Install the wheel and tire asembly.
13. Road test the vehicle and check the handling.

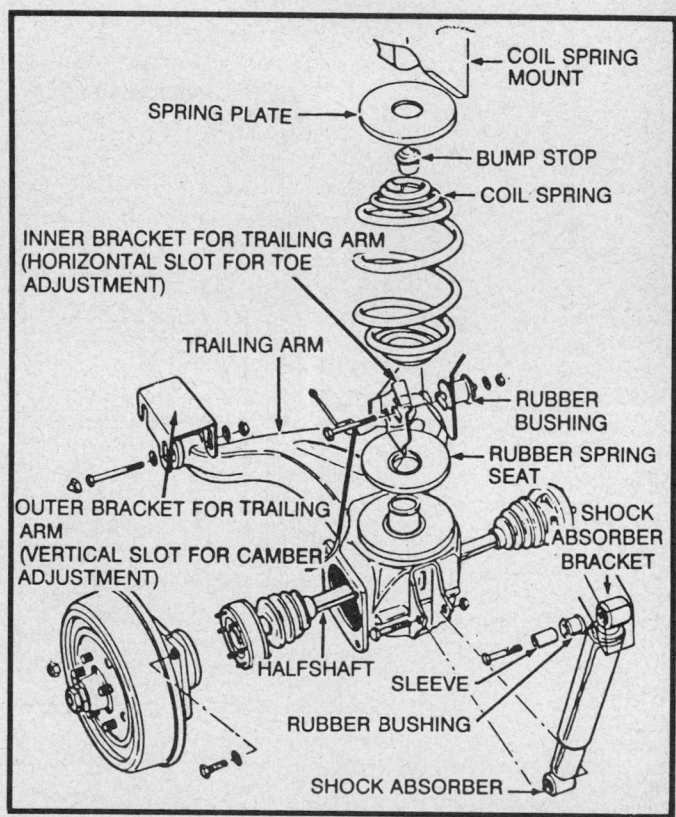

Rear suspension components—Syncro 4WD

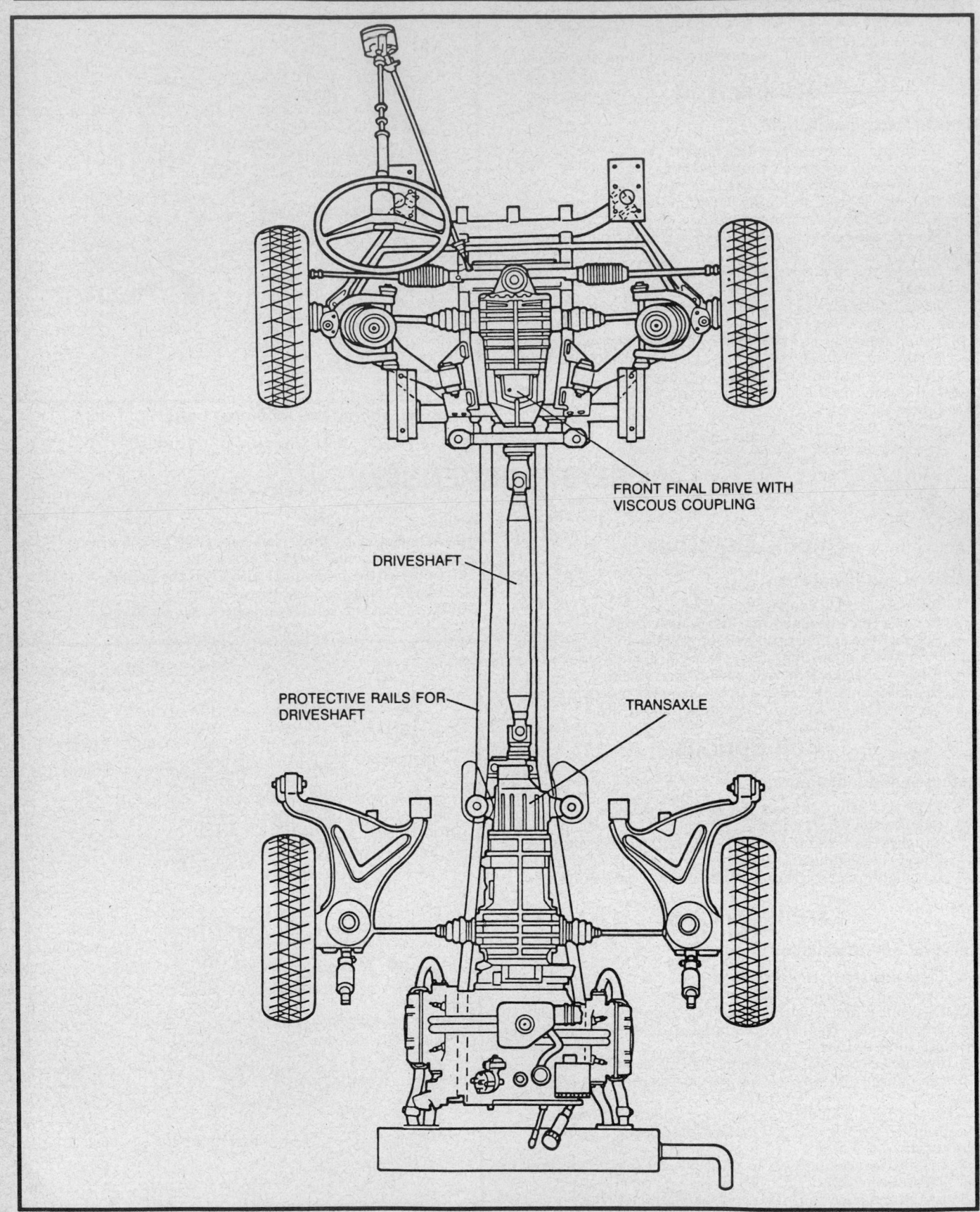

FRONT FINAL DRIVE WITH
VISCOUS COUPLING

DRIVESHAFT

PROTECTIVE RAILS FOR
DRIVESHAFT

TRANSAXLE

Vanagon All Wheel Drive (AWD) layout

ELECTRICAL

Test Instruments

OHMMETER

An ohmmeter is used to measure electrical resistance in a unit or circuit. The ohmmeter has a self-contained power supply. In use, it is connected across (or in parallel with) the terminals of the unit being tested.

AMMETER

An ammeter is used to measure current (amount of electricity) flowing through a unit or circuit. Ammeters are always connected in the line (in series) with the unit or circuit being tested.

VOLTMETER

A voltmeter is used to measure voltage (electrical pressure) pushing the current through a unit or circuit. The meter is connected across the terminals of the unit being tested.

Alternator Testing

IS IT THE ALTERNATOR OR THE VOLTAGE REGULATOR

The first step in diagnosing troubles of the charging system, is to identify the source of failure. Does the fault lie in the alternator or the regulator. The next move depends upon preference or necessity; either repair or replace the offending unit.

Alternator output is controlled by the amount of current supplied to the field circuit of the system.

The alternator is capable of producing substantial current at idle speed. Higher maximum output is also a possibility. This presents a potential danger when testing. As a precaution, a field rheostat should be used in the field circuit when making the following isolation test. The field rheostat permits positive control of the amount of current allowed to pass through the field circuit during the isolation test. Unregulated alternator capacity could ruin the unit.

NOTE: Most manufacturers of precision gauges offer special test connectors, in sets, that will adapt to the leads and connections of any charging system.

There are certain precautionary measures that apply to alternator tests in general. These items are listed in detail to avoid repetition when testing each make of alternator and to encourage a habit of good test procedure.

1. Check alternator drive belt for condition and tension.
2. Disconnect battery cables, check physical, chemical and electrical condition of battery.
3. Be absolutely sure of polarity before connecting any battery in the circuit. Reversed polarity will ruin the diodes.
4. Never use a battery charger to start the engine.
5. Disconnect both battery cables when making a battery recharge hook-up.
6. Be sure of polarity connections when using a booster battery for starting.
7. Never ground the alternator output or battery terminal.
8. Never ground the field circuit between alternator and regulator.
9. Never run any alternator on an open circuit with the field energized.
10. Never try to polarize an alternator, unless directed by the manufacturer of the alternator.
11. Do not attempt to motor an alternator.

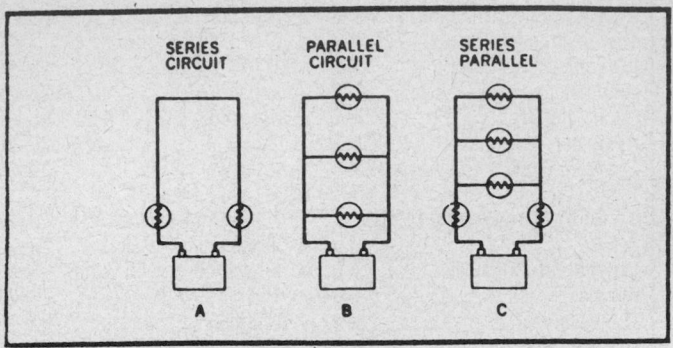

Basic electrical circuits

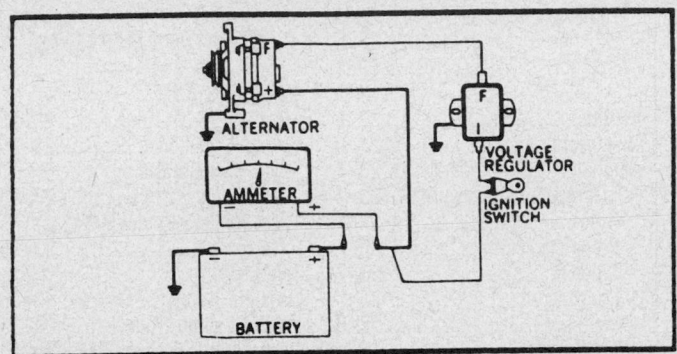

Ammeter connected to test wire—circuit equipped with external voltage regulator

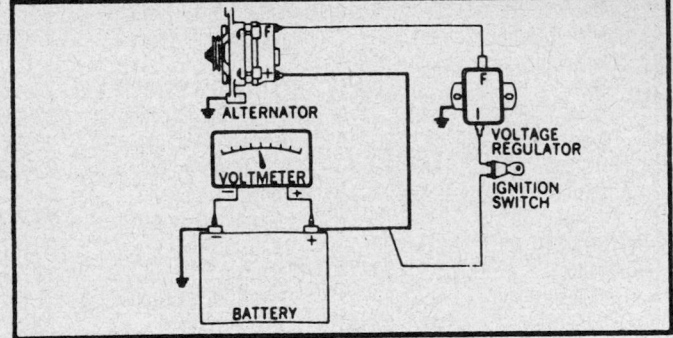

Voltmeter connected in parallel circuit—circuit equipped with external voltage regulator

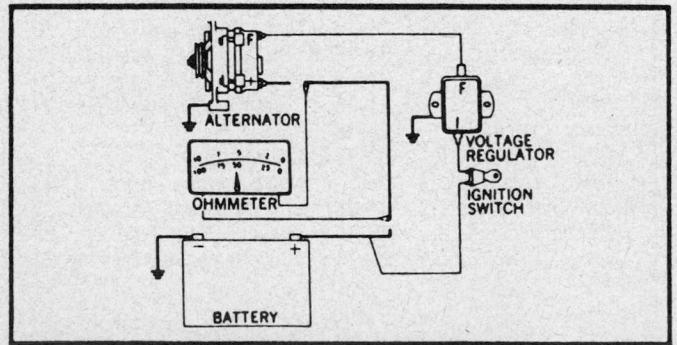

Ohmmeter connected to test wire resistance—circuit equipped with external voltage regulator

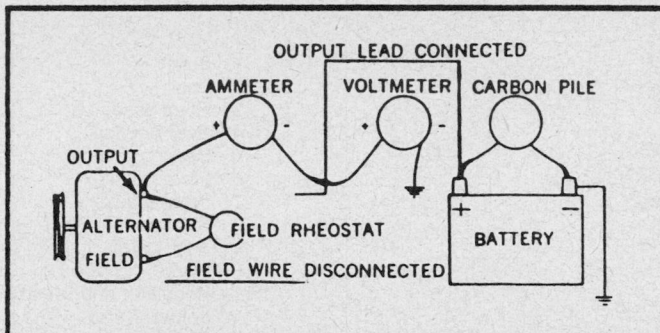

Checking the current output of the charging system

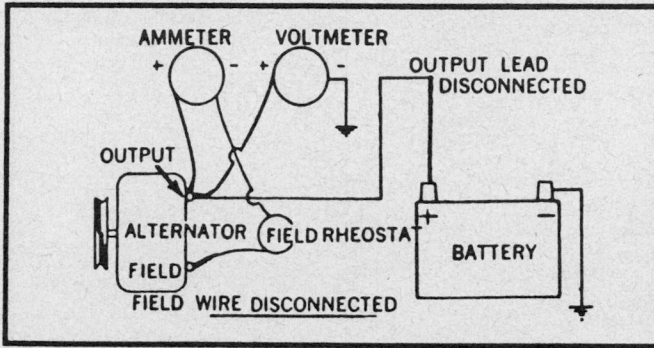

Checking the field current draw

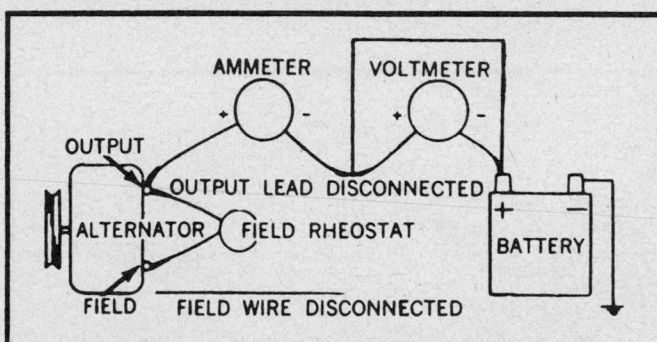

Checking the charging system resistance

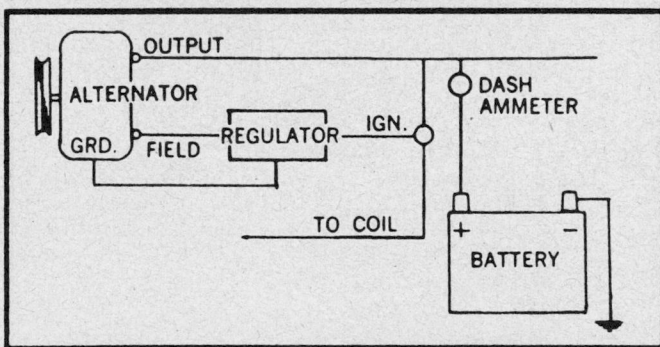

Alternator system with ammeter in the circuit

12. The regulator cover must be in place when taking voltage limiter readings.

13. The ignition switch must be in the **OFF** position when removing or installing the regulator cover.

14. Use insulated tools only to make adjustments to the regulator.

15. When making engine idle speed adjustments, always consider potential load factors that influence engine rpm. To compensate for electrical load, turn **ON** the lights, radio, heater, air conditioner, etc.

DIAGNOSIS OF CHARGING SYSTEM
LOW OR NO CHARGING
1. Blown fuse.
2. Broken or loose fan belt.
3. Voltage regulator not working.
4. Brushes sticking.
5. slipring dirty.
6. Open circuit.
7. Bad wiring connections.
8. Bad diode rectifier.
9. High resistance in charging circuit.
10. Voltage regulator needs adjusting.
11. Grounded stator.
12. Open rectifiers (check all 3 phases).
13. If rectifiers are found blown or open, check capacitor.

NOISY UNIT
1. Damaged rotor bearings.
2. Poor alignment of unit.
3. Broken or loose belt.
4. Open diode rectifiers.

REGULATOR POINTS BURNED OR STUCK
1. Regulator set too high.
2. Poor ground connections.
3. Shorted generator field.
4. Regulator air gap incorrect.

Chrysler Corporation Imports Charging System

ALTERNATOR

Disassembly

1. Place a soldering iron on the bearing box for approximately 3–4 minutes to heat it, then pull out the bolts and insert a flat tip tool between the stator and front bracket and separate them.

NOTE: The bearing box must be heated or the bearing cannot be pulled out.

2. Separate the front and rear sections, being careful not to lose the stopper spring that fits around the circumference of the rear bearing.
3. Remove the pulley nut, then disassemble the pulley, rotor and front bracket.
4. The rear bearing can be removed by using a bearing puller.
5. Remove the nut of the **B** terminal and the insulation bushing. Remove the rectifier retaining screws and the brush holder retaining screw. Separate the rear bracket and stator.
6. Remove the IC regulator.
7. Remove the solder from the rectifier and stator leads.

NOTE: Do not use the soldering iron for more than 5 seconds as the rectifier may be damaged if overheated.

8. The brush may be removed by removing the solder from the pigtail.

ROTOR

Testing

1. Using an ohmmeter, check for continuity at the slip end rings. If there is no continuity, replace the rotor.

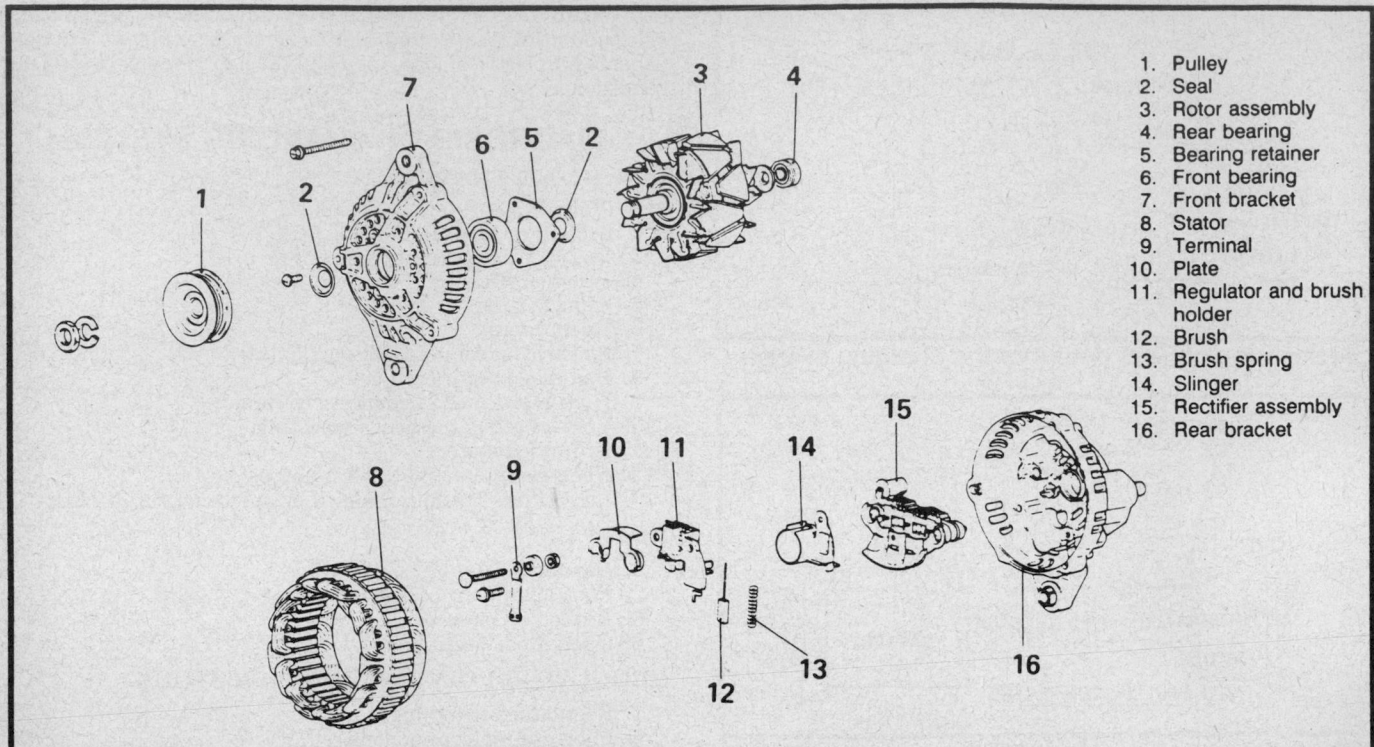

1. Pulley
2. Seal
3. Rotor assembly
4. Rear bearing
5. Bearing retainer
6. Front bearing
7. Front bracket
8. Stator
9. Terminal
10. Plate
11. Regulator and brush holder
12. Brush
13. Brush spring
14. Slinger
15. Rectifier assembly
16. Rear bracket

Exploded view of the Chrysler alternator—2.6L engine

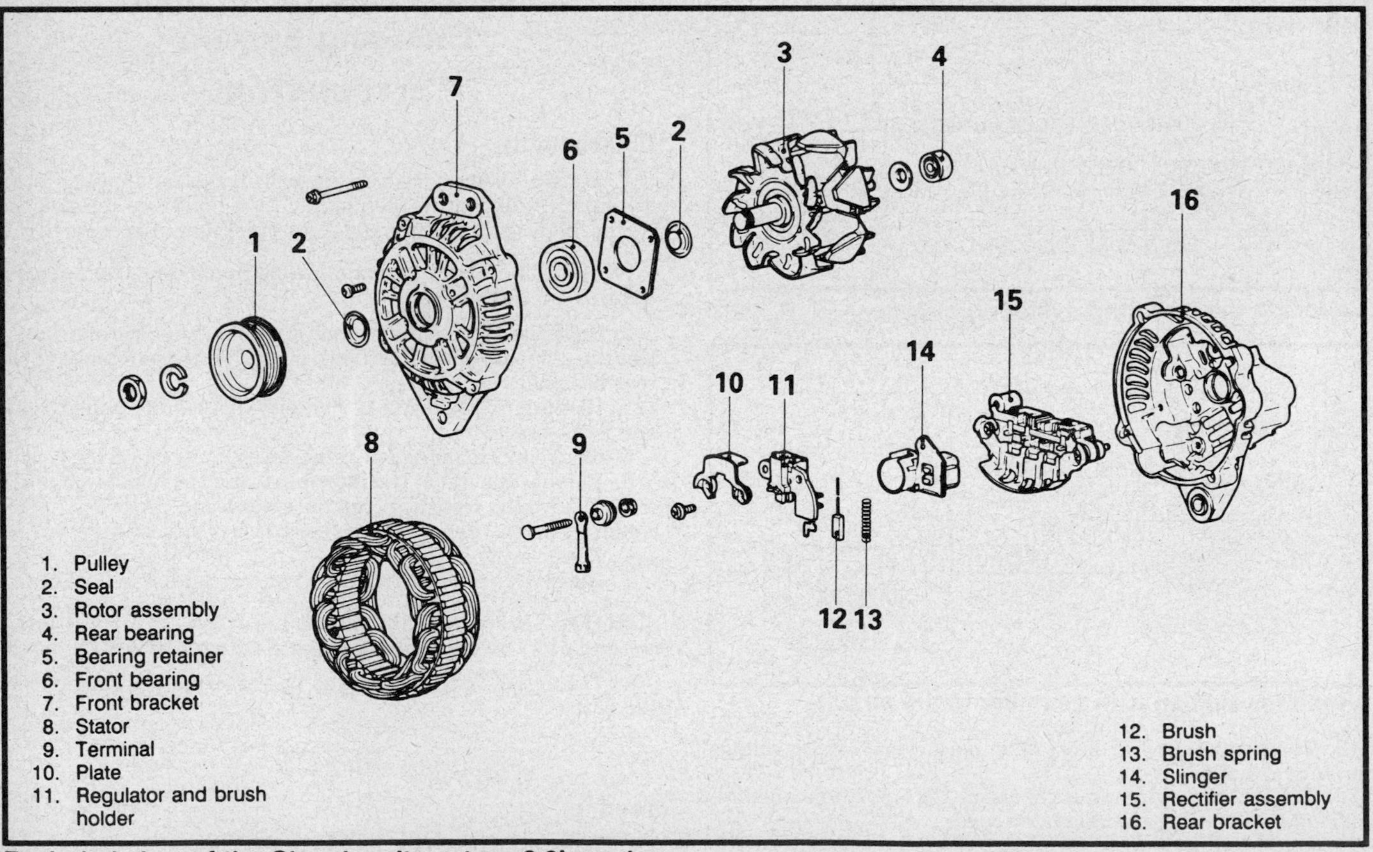

1. Pulley
2. Seal
3. Rotor assembly
4. Rear bearing
5. Bearing retainer
6. Front bearing
7. Front bracket
8. Stator
9. Terminal
10. Plate
11. Regulator and brush holder

12. Brush
13. Brush spring
14. Slinger
15. Rectifier assembly
16. Rear bracket

Exploded view of the Chrysler alternator—3.0L engine

2. Using an ohmmeter, make an insulation test. Check for continuity between the slipring and the rotor core. If continuity exists, replace the rotor.

3. Measure the slipring outer diameter for wear. Mimimum diameter is 1.18 in. (30mm).

STATOR

Testing

1. Using an ohmmeter, make a continuity test between the stator lead wires. If there is no continuity, replace the stator.

2. Using an ohmmeter, make an insulation test between the stator core and the lead wire. If the continuity exists, replace the stator.

DIODE

Testing

1. Using and ohmmeter, perform a continuity test on diodes in both directions.

2. Replace as necessary.

BRUSHES

Testing

1. Check for smooth movement of the brush and clean the brush holder if necessary.

2. Check for brush wear by looking at the wear limit line on the brush and replace if necessary.

Assembly

1. Assembly of the alternator is the reverse of disassembly with the following instructions:

2. When installing the front bearing, use a socket which exactly fits the outer race of the bearing, then use a hand press or vise and press the bearing in evenly. When pressing the rear bearing on, first heat the rear bracket, then press it so that the groove at the bearing circumference is at the slipring side. When soldering a new brush, solder the pigtail so that the wear limit line of the brush projects 0.079–0.118 in. out from the end of the brush holder. Fit the stopper spring into the eccentric groove of the rear bearing circumference. The protruding part of the

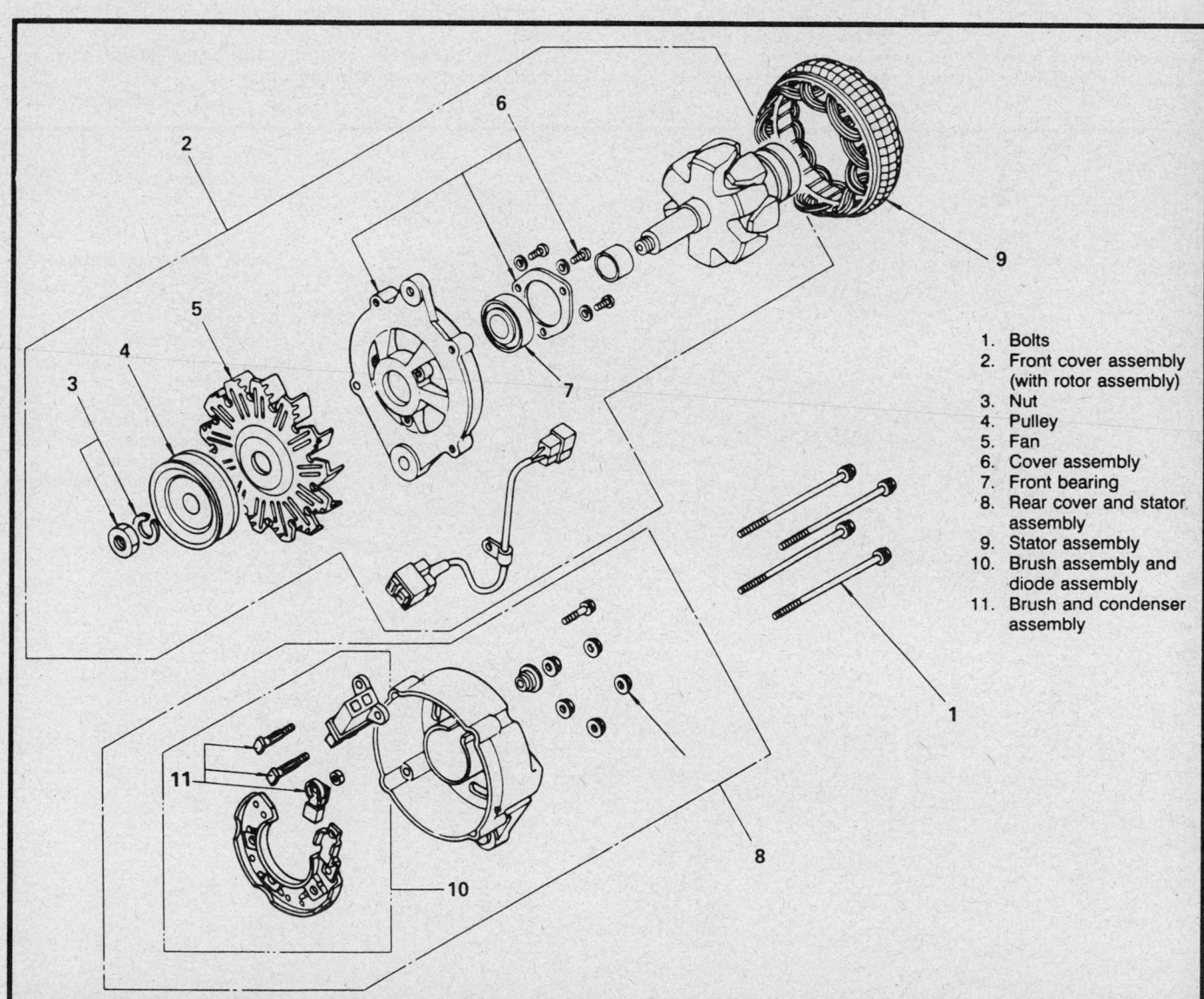

1. Bolts
2. Front cover assembly (with rotor assembly)
3. Nut
4. Pulley
5. Fan
6. Cover assembly
7. Front bearing
8. Rear cover and stator assembly
9. Stator assembly
10. Brush assembly and diode assembly
11. Brush and condenser assembly

Exploded view of the Isuzu alternator — 2.0L gas engine

spring should be fit into the deepest part of the groove. This makes assembly much easier.

3. Before assembly, use a finger to push the brush into the brush holder, then pass a wire through the hole and secure the brush into position. After reassembly, manually turn the pulley to make sure the rotor turns easily.

Isuzu Charging System

Troubleshooting

1. Measure the resistance between **F** and **E** terminals (rotor coil resistance): The rotor coil circuit is normal if resistance measured across the terminals is 5 ohms. If resistance is higher than 5 ohms, the trouble is poor contact between the brushes and commutator. If no continuity exists between terminals **F** and **E**, the trouble is either an open coil rotor circuit, brush sticking or a broken lead wire. If resistance is lower than 5 ohms, it may be an indication of rotor coil layer short or the circuit being grounded.

2. Test the rectifying diodes in the following manner: Connect the positive (+) lead of a tester to the alternator **N** terminal and the tester negative (−) lead to the alternator **A** terminal. If there exists a continuity between terminals, it indicates that 1 or more of the 3 diodes in the positive side are shorted. Connect the positive (+) lead of a tester to the alternator **E** terminal and the tester negative (−) lead to the alternator **N** terminal. If there exists a continuity, it indicates that 1 or more of the 3 diodes in the negative side are shorted.

ALTERNATOR

Disassembly
GASOLINE ENGINE

1. Remove the through bolts and disconnect the lead wires at the connector.

2. Separate the alternator assembly into front and rear sections. The stator should be on the rear side.

3. Carefulley clamp the rotor in a vise and remove the pulley nut, then remove the pulley fan and rotor.

4. Remove the bearing retainer screws, then remove the ball bearing.

5. Remove the rear side nuts, then remove the stator from the rear cover together with the diodes, brush and capacitor.

6. Unsolder the diode-to-stator coil connections, then separate the diodes from the stator together with the brush and capacitor.

7. Remove the screws retaining the brush holder, then remove the diodes, brush and capacitor.

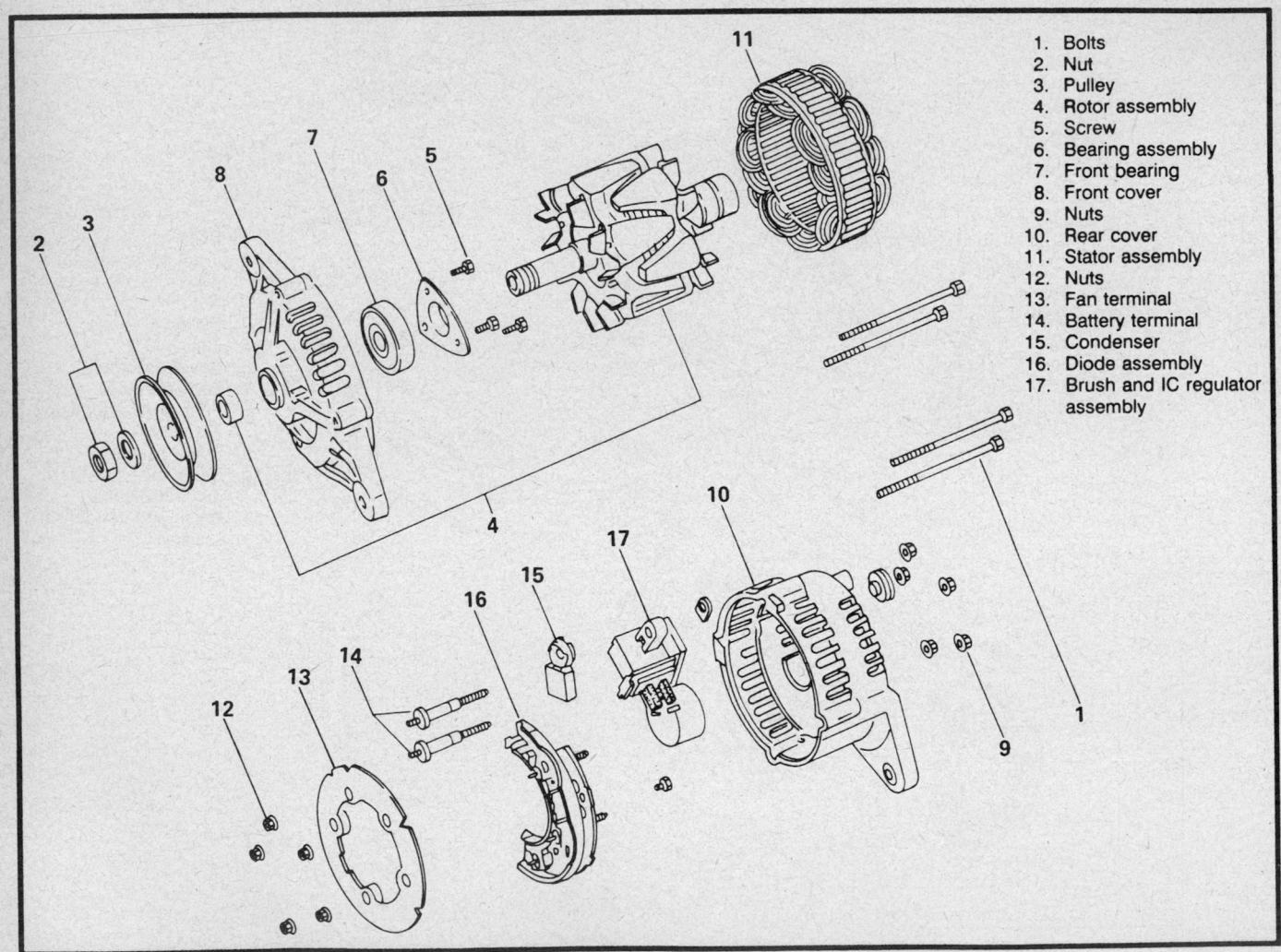

1. Bolts
2. Nut
3. Pulley
4. Rotor assembly
5. Screw
6. Bearing assembly
7. Front bearing
8. Front cover
9. Nuts
10. Rear cover
11. Stator assembly
12. Nuts
13. Fan terminal
14. Battery terminal
15. Condenser
16. Diode assembly
17. Brush and IC regulator assembly

Exploded view of the Isuzu alternator—2.3L gas engine

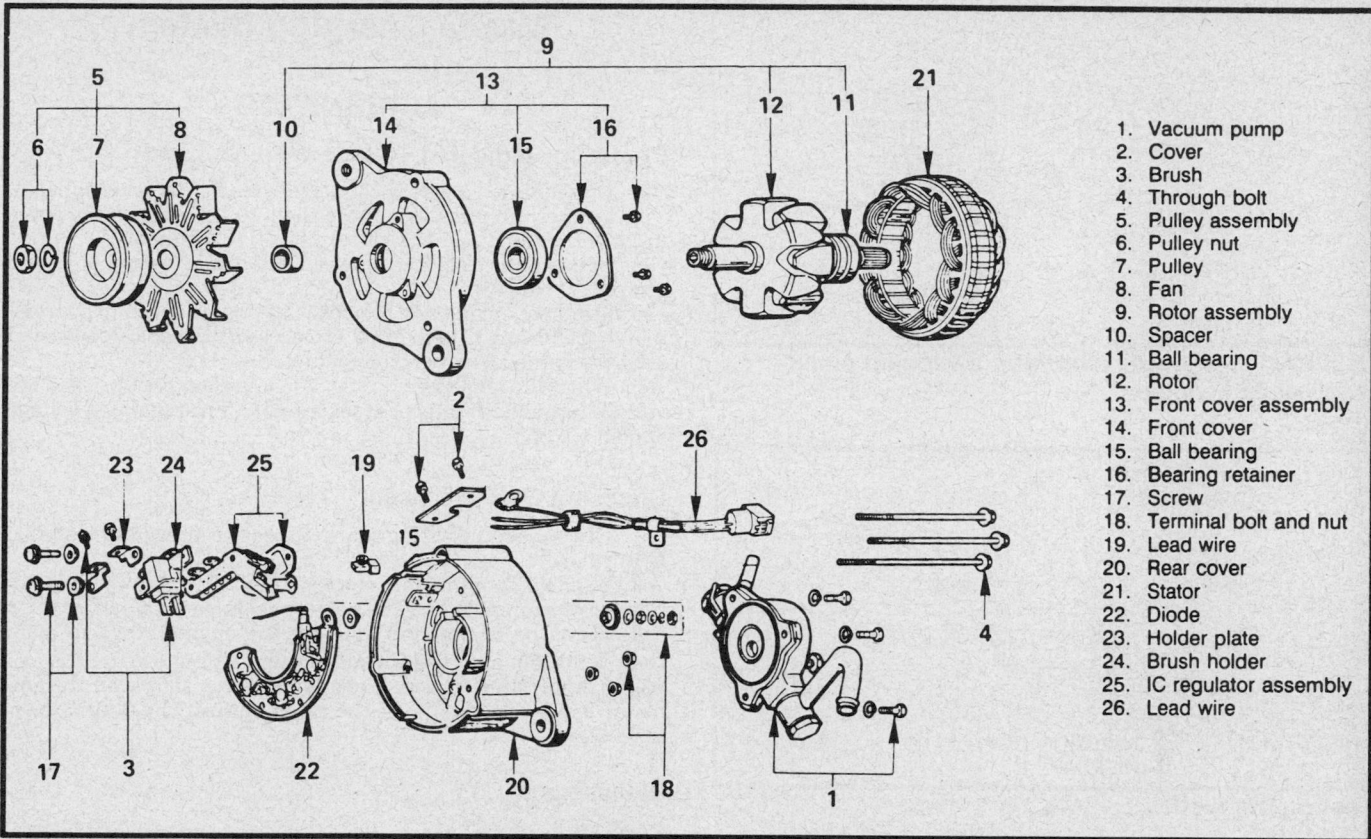

1. Vacuum pump
2. Cover
3. Brush
4. Through bolt
5. Pulley assembly
6. Pulley nut
7. Pulley
8. Fan
9. Rotor assembly
10. Spacer
11. Ball bearing
12. Rotor
13. Front cover assembly
14. Front cover
15. Ball bearing
16. Bearing retainer
17. Screw
18. Terminal bolt and nut
19. Lead wire
20. Rear cover
21. Stator
22. Diode
23. Holder plate
24. Brush holder
25. IC regulator assembly
26. Lead wire

Exploded view of the Isuzu alternator — diesel engine

DIESEL ENGINE

1. If so equipped, remove the vacuum pump attaching bolts, then hold the center plate and remove the vacuum pump in direction in line with the rotor shaft.

2. Remove the brush cover and the brush attaching bolts, then remove the brush from the holder.

3. Remove the through bolts and separate the body into front and rear sections.

NOTE: When separating, be careful so that the stator coils do not come off the rear cover. Do not damage the oil seal when removing the rear cover. Taping the splines could provide some protection.

4. Carefully clamp the rotor assembly in a vise and remove the pulley nut.

5. Separate the pulley front cover and rotor, then remove the spacer and ball bearing.

6. Remove the bearing retaining screws from the front cover, then remove the bearing.

7. Remove the terminal bolt and nut, then remove the lead wire.

8. Remove the nuts securing the **B** terminal and diode holder, then remove the screw inside the stator. Separate the stator and rear cover.

NOTE: Observe the position of the insulation washers for reassembly.

9. Remove the stator, then separate the diodes from the stator by melting the solder on the stator coil, diode and **N** terminal leads. When melting the solder, hold the lead wire with long nose pliers to prevent heat from being transferred to the diodes.

10. Remove the holder plate and brush holder.

11. Melt away the solder on the IC holder plate terminal, then remove the IC regulator assembly.

12. If necessary, the vacuum pump may be disassembled by removing the center plate, exposing the rotor and vane.

ROTOR

Testing

1. Using an ohmmeter, check for continuity at the slip end rings. If there is no continuity, replace the rotor.

2. Using an ohmmeter, make an insulation test. Check for continuity between the slipring and the rotor core. If continuity exists, replace the rotor.

3. Measure the slipring outer diameter for wear. Mimimum diameter is 1.18 in. (30mm).

STATOR

Testing

1. Using an ohmmeter, make a continuity test between the stator lead wires. If there is no continuity, replace the stator.

2. Using an ohmmeter, make an insulation test between the stator core and the lead wire. If the continuity exists, replace the stator.

DIODE

Testing

1. Using and ohmmeter, perform a continuity test on diodes in both directions.

2. Replace as necessary.

BRUSH

Testing

1. Check for smooth movement of the brush and clean the brush holder if necessary.

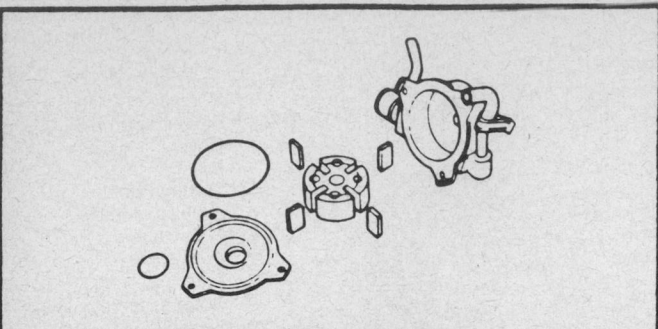

Exploded view of the alternator's vacuum pump— Isuzu diesel engine

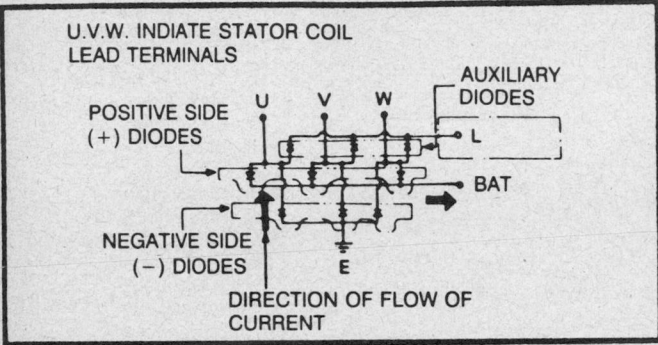

Testing the diodes

2. Check for brush wear by looking at the wear limit line on the brush and replace if necessary.

Assembly

GASOLINE ENGINE

1. Assembly of the alternator is the reverse of disassembly with the following instructions.
2. Before assembling the front and rear sections. insert a wire into the hole in the rear face of the rear cover from the outboard side to support the brush in the raised position, then insert the front section to which the rotor is assembled

DIESEL ENGINE

1. Assembly of the alternator is the reverse of disassembly with the following instructions: Resolder the IC regulator lead wires. To prevent heat from being transfered to the diodes, use long nose pliers to hold the stator coil leads and diode leads and solder as quickly as posible.
2. Carefully clamp the rotor in a vise and torque the pulley nut to 33–43 ft. lbs.
3. Place some type of guide bar through the holes in the front cover and rear cover flange for alignment, then, install the through bolts. Make sure the brush is installed in the brush holder correctly.
4. If the vacuum pump was disassembled, position the rotor, with the serrated boss turned up, on the center plate and housing. Install the vanes into the slits in the rotor. The vanes should be installed with the camfered side turned outward.
5. Install the housing, making sure the O-ring is not projected beyond the slot in the center plate. If the holes in the housing and center plate are not in alignment, adjust by turning the housing slightly, then, tighten the retaining bolts.
6. Add engine oil (around 5cc) through the filler port and make sure the pulley can be turned smoothly by hand.

Mazda Charging System

ALTERNATOR

Checking Regulated Voltage With No Load

1. Disconnect the wiring connected to alternator terminal **B**.
2. Connect an ammeter (more than 40 A) between the alternator terminal **B** and the battery positive terminal.
3. Connect a voltmeter between alternator terminal **L** and ground.
4. Start the engine and increase the engine speed to approximately 2000 rpm. Turn off all unnecessary electrical loads and read the value shown on the ammeter.
5. When the amperage in Step 4 is less than 5 amp., read the voltage (regulated voltage) of terminal **L**. The regulated voltage should be 14.1–14.7 V.

Checking Output Current

1. Disconnect the wiring connected to the alternator terminal **B**.
2. Connect an ammeter (more than 40 amp) between the alternator terminal **B** and the battery positive terminal.
3. Start the engine and increase the engine speed to more than 2500 rpm and read the maximum value shown on the ammeter. Apply all electrical loads. If the value shown on the ammeter is more than 90% of the rated output, the alternator is normal.

Disassembly

1986–88

1. Place a soldering iron on the bearing box for approximately 3–4 minutes to heat it, then pull out the bolts and insert a flat tip tool between the stator and front bracket and separate them.

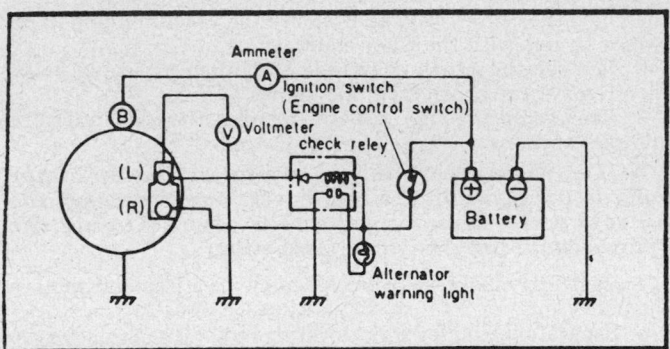

Checking the charging system

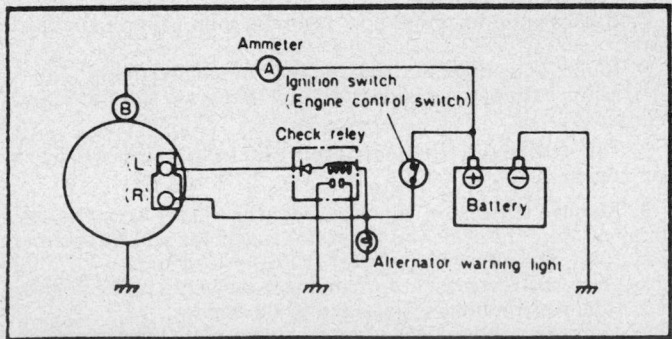

Checking the regulated voltage with no-load

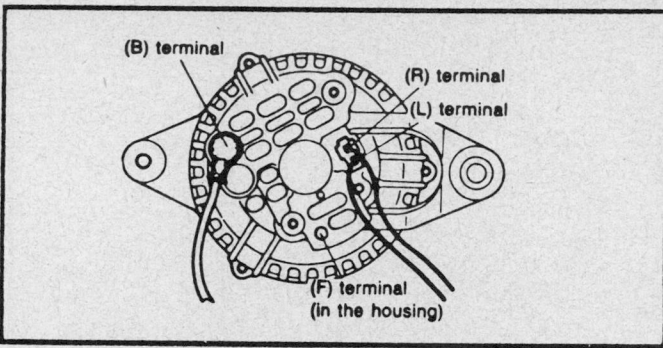

Location of the Mazda alternator terminals

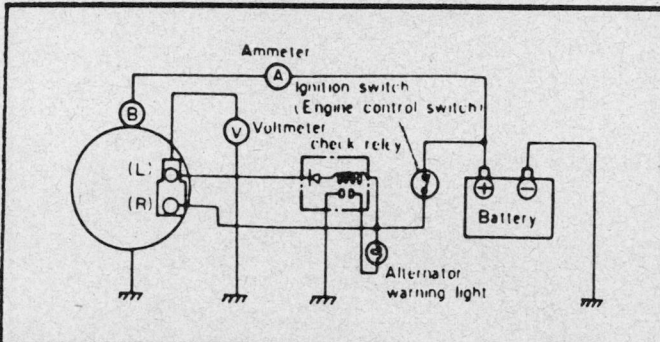

Checking the current output

NOTE: The bearing box must be heated or the bearing cannot be pulled out.

2. Separate the front and rear sections, being careful not to lose the stopper spring that fits around the circumference of the rear bearing.

3. Remove the pulley nut, then disassemble the pulley, rotor and front bracket.

4. The rear bearing can be removed by using a bearing puller.

5. Remove the nut of the **B** terminal and the insulation bushing. Remove the rectifier retaining screws and the brush holder retaining screw and then separate the rear bracket and stator.

6. Remove the IC regulator.

7. Remove the solder from the rectifier and stator leads.

NOTE: Do not use the soldering iron for more than 5 seconds as the rectifier may be damaged if overheated.

8. The brush may be removed by removing the solder from the pigtail.

1989–90

1. Remove the alternator through bolts and separate the rear case/stator assembly from the front case/rotor assembly.

2. Secure the rotor and remove the pulley nut, the washer and the pulley.

3. Pull the rotor from the front case.

4. Remove the front bearing retainer-to-front case bolts, the retainer and the bearing.

5. From the rear case, remove the stator, the brush holder/rectifier assembly-to-rear case nuts/washers, the brush holder assembly and the rectifier.

ROTOR

Testing

1. Using an ohmmeter, check for continuity at the slip end rings. If there is no continuity, replace the rotor.

2. Using an ohmmeter, make a ground test. Check for continuity between the slipring and the rotor core. If continuity exists, replace the rotor.

3. Measure the slipring outer diameter for wear. Mimimum diameter is 1.18 in. (30mm).

STATOR

Testing

1. Using an ohmmeter, make a continuity test between the stator lead wires. If there is no continuity, replace the stator.

2. Using an ohmmeter, make a ground test between the sta-

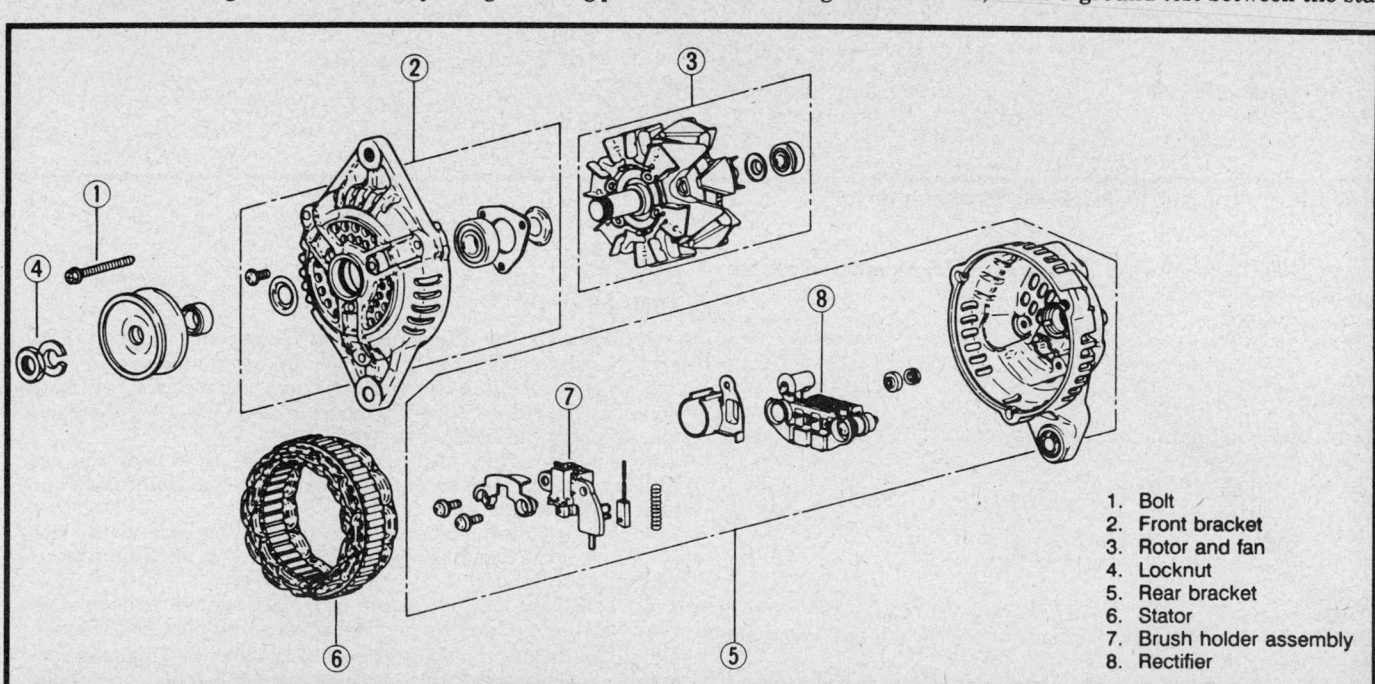

1. Bolt
2. Front bracket
3. Rotor and fan
4. Locknut
5. Rear bracket
6. Stator
7. Brush holder assembly
8. Rectifier

Exploded view of the 1986–88 Mazda alternator

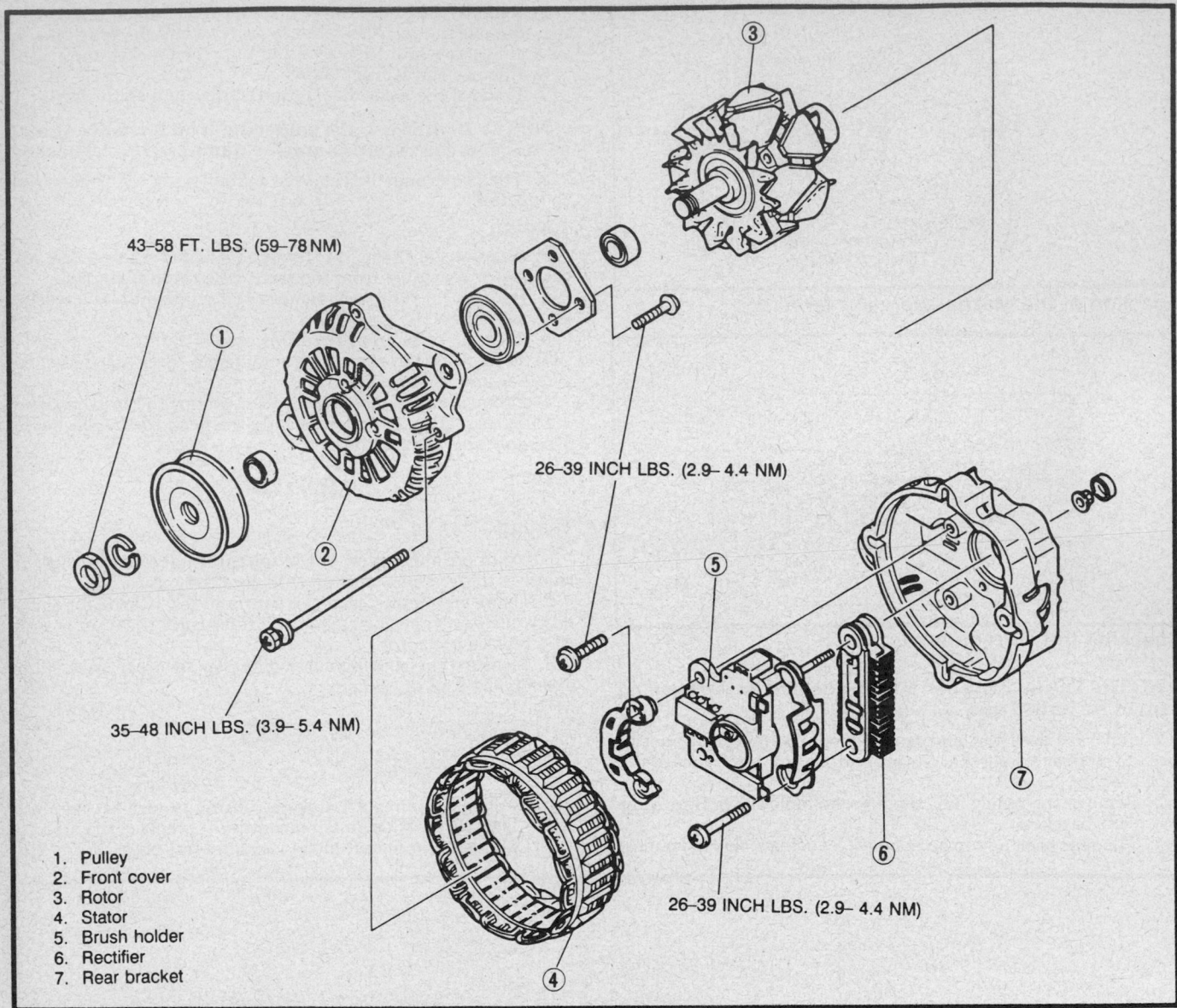

43–58 FT. LBS. (59–78 NM)

26–39 INCH LBS. (2.9– 4.4 NM)

35–48 INCH LBS. (3.9– 5.4 NM)

26–39 INCH LBS. (2.9– 4.4 NM)

1. Pulley
2. Front cover
3. Rotor
4. Stator
5. Brush holder
6. Rectifier
7. Rear bracket

Exploded view of the 1989–90 Mazda alternator

tor core and the lead wire. If the continuity exists, replace the stator.

DIODE

Testing

1. Using and ohmmeter, perform a continuity test on diodes in both directions.
2. Replace as necessary.

BRUSHES

Testing

1. Check for smooth movement of the brush and clean the brush holder, if necessary.
2. Check for brush wear by looking at the wear limit line on the brush and replace, if necessary.

Assembly

1986–88

1. Assemble the alternator by reversing the order of disassembly, while observing the following instructions:
2. When installing the front bearing, use a socket which exactly fits the outer race of the bearing, then use a hand press or vise to press the bearing in evenly.
3. When pressing the rear bearing on, first heat the rear bracket, then press it so the groove at the bearing circumference is at the slipring side.
4. When soldering a new brush, solder the pigtail so the wear limit line of the brush projects 0.079–0.118 in. out from the end of the brush holder.
5. Install the stopper spring into the eccentric groove of the rear bearing circumference. The protruding part of the spring should be fit into the deepest part of the groove; this makes assembly much easier.
6. Before assembly, use a finger to push the brush into the

brush holder, then, pass a wire through the hole in the brush holder and secure the brush into position.

7. After assembly, manually turn the pulley to make sure the rotor turns easily.

1989–90

1. Install the front bearing into the front cover.
2. Install the front bearing retainer and torque the bolts to 26–39 inch lbs. (2.9–4.4 Nm).
3. Install the rotor into the front case. Install the pulley and torque the nut to 43–58 ft. lbs. (58–78 Nm).
4. Install the rectifier, the brush holder assembly and stator to the rear housing. Torque the bolts to 26–39 inch lbs. (2.9–4.4 Nm).
5. Using a wire, depress the brushes into the brush holder and secure them in place.
6. Assemble the alternator halves.
7. Install the through bolts and torque to 35–48 ft. lbs. (3.9–5.4 Nm).
8. Remove the wire securing the brushes.
9. Manually, turn the pulley to make sure the rotor turns easily.

Mitsubishi Charging System

ALTERNATOR

Troubleshooting (On Vehicle)

1. Place the ignition switch in the **OFF** position.
2. Disconnect the battery ground cable.
3. Disconnect the cable from terminal **B** of the alternator and connect an ammeter between the terminal **B** and the cable.
4. Connect a voltmeter between terminal **B** (+) and ground (−).
5. Set the engine tachometer.
6. Connect the battery ground cable to the battery. The voltmeter should indicate the battery voltage.
7. Start the engine.

8. Turn **ON** the lamps, accelerate the engine to the speed specified and measure the output current. Check it against the specifications.

Disassembly

1. Remove alternator from vehicle.
2. Remove the through bolts from the alternator body.
3. Insert an appropriate pry tool between the front bracket and stator. Pry the front bracket away from the stator. Remove the front bracket along with the rotor.

NOTE: If the tool is inserted too deeply, the stator coil might be damaged.

4. Hold the rotor in a vise and remove the pulley nut. Then remove the pulley, fan, spacer and seal. Remove the rotor from the front bracket and remove the seal.
5. Unsolder the rectifier from the stator coil lead wires and remove the stator assembly.

NOTE: Make sure the solder is removed quickly (in less than 5 seconds). If a diode is heated to more than 150°C, it might be damaged.

6. Remove the condenser from terminal **B**.
7. Unsolder the plates **B** and **L** from the rectifier assembly.
8. Remove the mounting screw and terminal **B** bolt and remove the electronic voltage regulator and brush holder. The regulator and brush holder cannot be separated.
9. Remove the rectifier assembly.
10. When only a brush or brush spring is to be replaced, it is not necessary to remove the stator, etc. Raise the brush holder assembly and unsolder the wire pigtail of the brush and remove the brush.

NOTE: Be very careful when bending the plates B and L so as not to disturb the rectifier moulding.

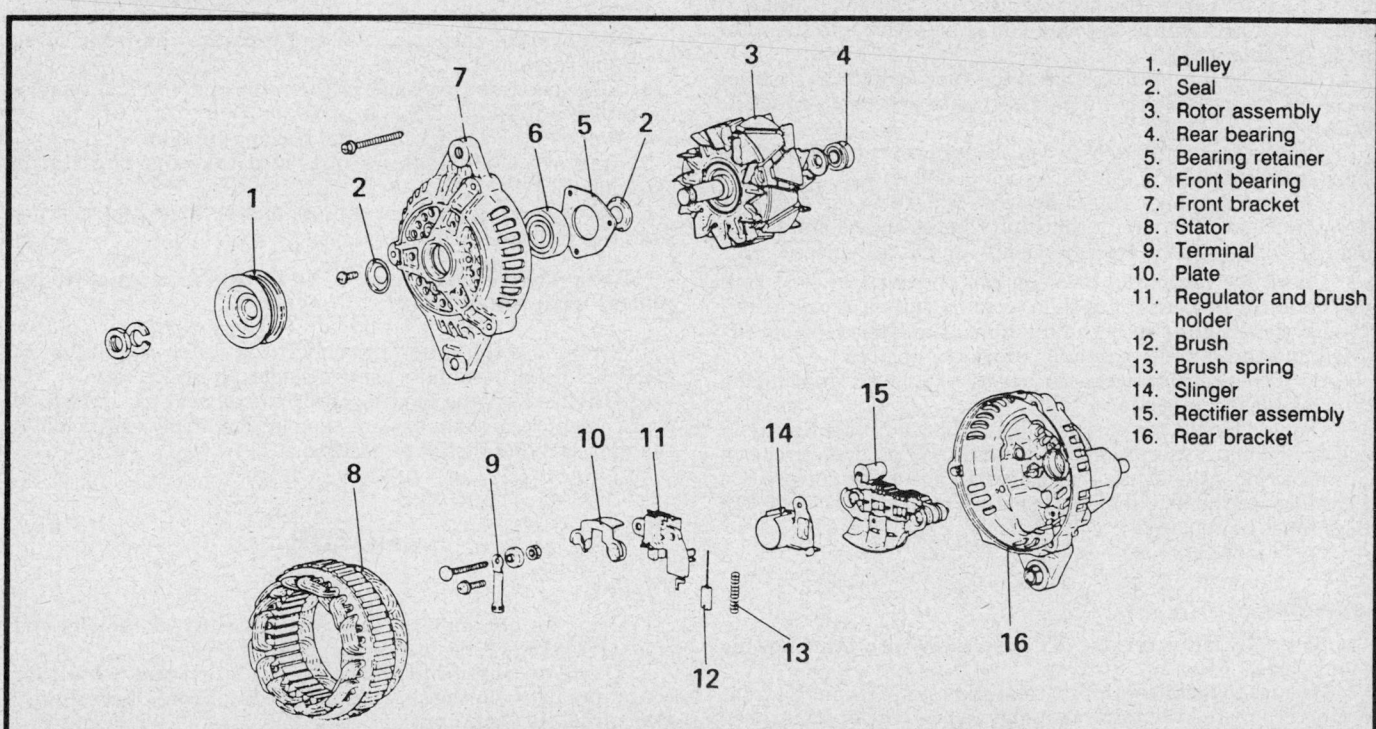

1. Pulley
2. Seal
3. Rotor assembly
4. Rear bearing
5. Bearing retainer
6. Front bearing
7. Front bracket
8. Stator
9. Terminal
10. Plate
11. Regulator and brush holder
12. Brush
13. Brush spring
14. Slinger
15. Rectifier assembly
16. Rear bracket

Exploded view of the Mitsubishi alternator – 2.6L engine

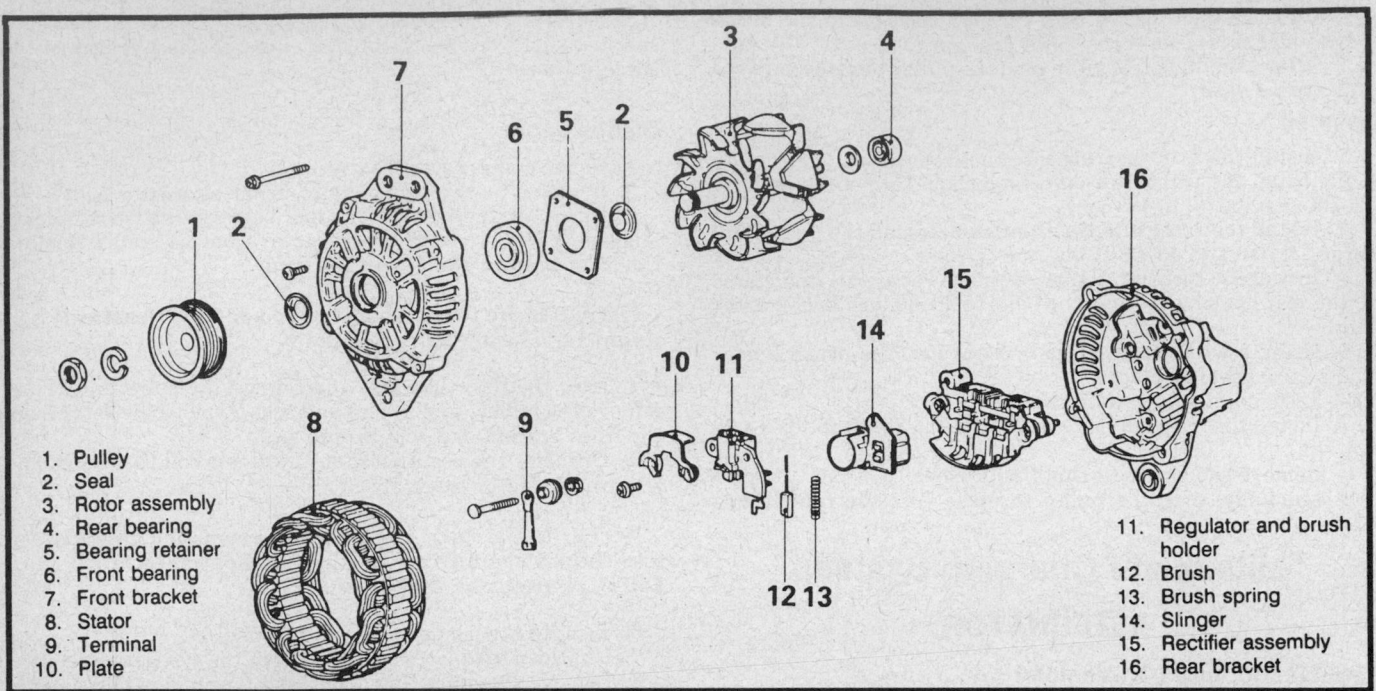

1. Pulley
2. Seal
3. Rotor assembly
4. Rear bearing
5. Bearing retainer
6. Front bearing
7. Front bracket
8. Stator
9. Terminal
10. Plate

11. Regulator and brush holder
12. Brush
13. Brush spring
14. Slinger
15. Rectifier assembly
16. Rear bracket

Exploded view of the Mitsubishi alternator—3.0L engine

Testing

1. Check the outside circumference of the slipring for dirtiness and roughness. Clean or polish with armature paper, if required. A badly damaged slipring or a slipring worn down beyond the service limit should also be replaced. The service limit for the slipring outside diameter is 1.268 in.

2. Check for continuity between the field coil and slipring. If there is not continuity, the field coil is defective and the rotor must be replaced.

3. Check for continuity between the slipring and the shaft (or core). If there is continuity, the rotor assembly must be replaced.

4. Check for continuity between the leads of the stator coil. If there is no continuity, the stator coil is defective.

5. Check for an open circuit between the stator coil leads and the stator core. If there is continuity between the stator core and the coil leads, the stator assembly must be replaced.

6. Check for continuity between the positive (+) heat sink and the stator coil lead connection terminal with a circuit tester. If there is continuity in both directions, the diode is short circuited and the rectifier assembly must be replaced.

7. Perform Step 6 between the negative (−) heat sink and the stator coil lead connection.

8. Using a circuit tester, check the 3 diodes for continuity in both directions. If there is either continuity or an open circuit in both directions, the diode is defective and must be replaced.

9. Measure the length of the brush. If it is worn below 0.315 in., it must be replaced.

Assembly

1. Assembly is the reverse of disassembly with the following instructions:

2. Be sure to install both the front and rear seals on the front bearing. To install the rotor assembly in the rear bracket, push the brushes into the brush holder, insert a wire to hold them in the raised position and install the rotor. Remove the wire.

Nissan Charging System

ALTERNATOR

Disassembly

1. On diesel engine models only, remove the vacuum pump.

2. Remove the through bolts and separate the front cover from the rear cover.

3. Place the rear cover side of the rotor in a vise and remove the pulley nut and pulley.

4. Remove the screws from the bearing retainer.

5. Remove the attaching nuts and take out the stator assembly.

6. Use a bearing puller or a press and pull the rear bearing from the rotor assembly.

NOTE: The bearing cannot be reused and must be replaced with a new one.

7. To remove the stator, disconnect the stator coil lead wires from the diode terminals, using a soldering iron.

8. On diesel engine models, check the oil seal for leakage. If replacement is needed, pry out the old seal, apply engine oil to the new seal and install in position.

ROTOR

Testing

1. Using an ohmmeter, check for continuity at the slip end rings. If there is no continuity, replace the rotor.

2. Using an ohmmeter, make an insulation test. Check for continuity between the slipring and the rotor core. If continuity exists, replace the rotor.

3. Measure the slipring outer diameter for wear. Mimimum diameter is 1.18 in. (30mm).

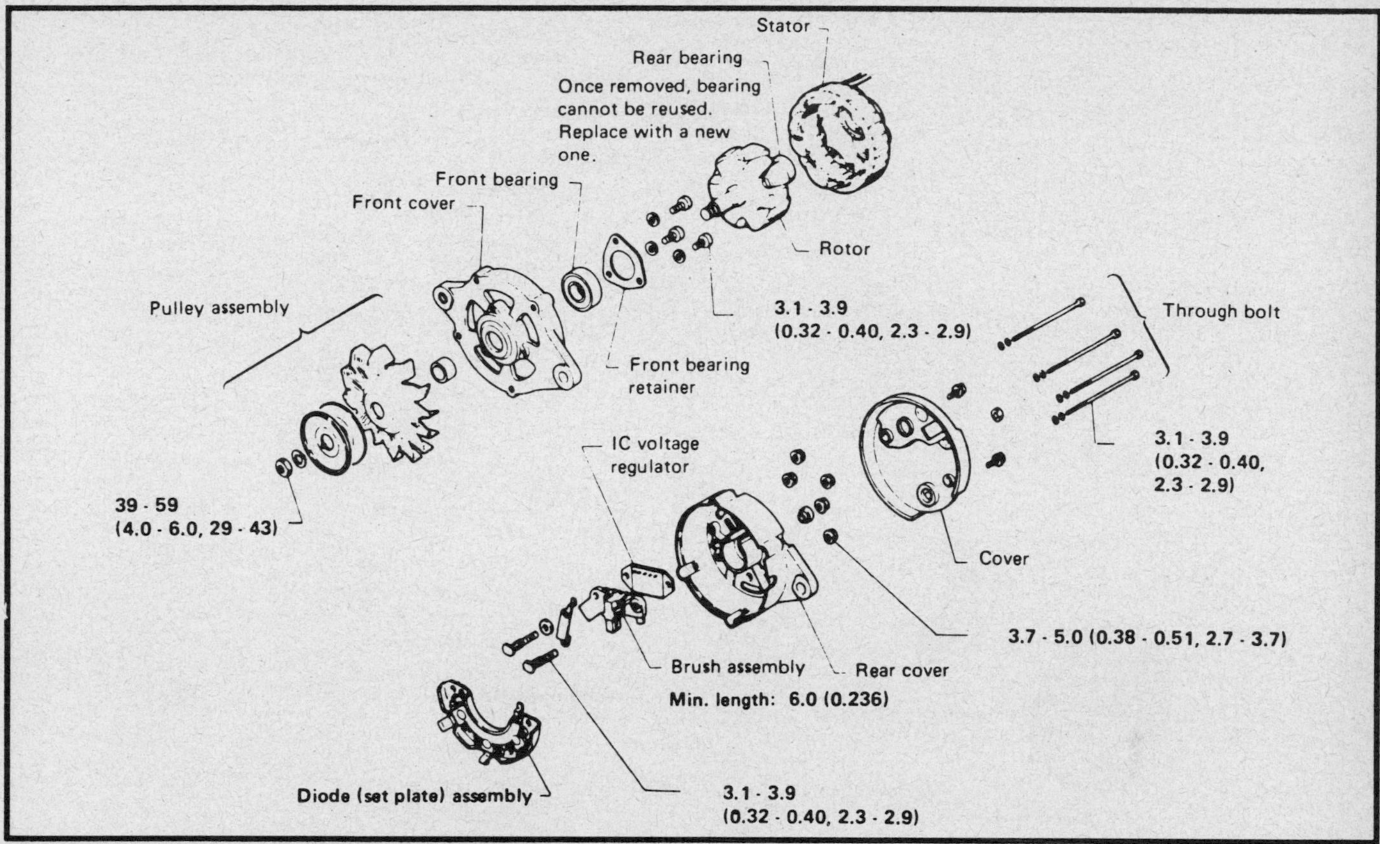

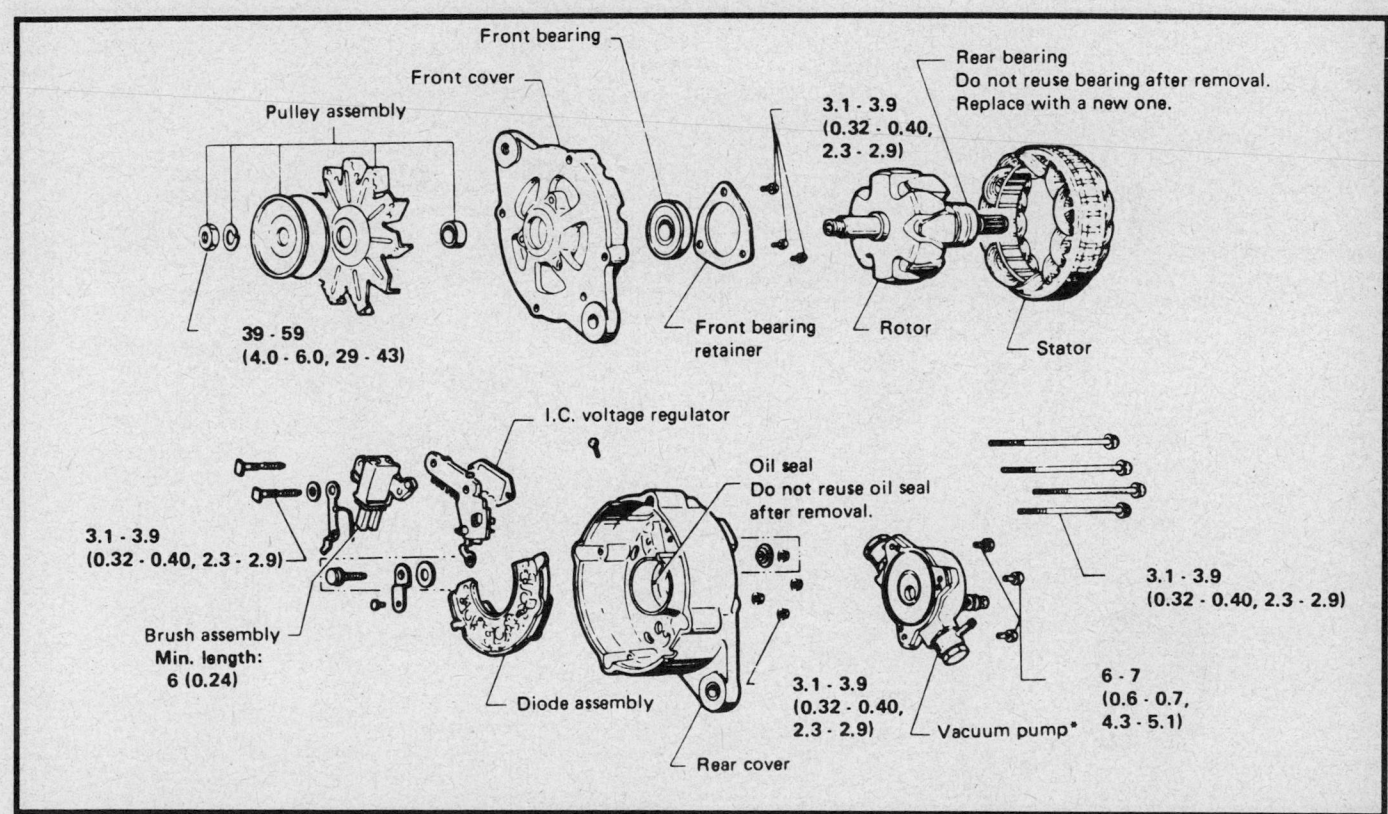

Stator

Rear bearing
Once removed, bearing cannot be reused. Replace with a new one.

Rotor

Front bearing
Front cover

3.1 - 3.9
(0.32 - 0.40, 2.3 - 2.9)

Through bolt

Pulley assembly

Front bearing retainer

3.1 - 3.9
(0.32 - 0.40, 2.3 - 2.9)

IC voltage regulator

39 - 59
(4.0 - 6.0, 29 - 43)

Cover

3.7 - 5.0 (0.38 - 0.51, 2.7 - 3.7)

Brush assembly
Min. length: 6.0 (0.236)

Rear cover

Diode (set plate) assembly

3.1 - 3.9
(0.32 - 0.40, 2.3 - 2.9)

Exploded view of the 1986–89 Nissan alternator—gas engines

Front bearing
Front cover

Rear bearing
Do not reuse bearing after removal. Replace with a new one.

Pulley assembly

3.1 - 3.9
(0.32 - 0.40, 2.3 - 2.9)

39 - 59
(4.0 - 6.0, 29 - 43)

Front bearing retainer

Rotor

Stator

I.C. voltage regulator

Oil seal
Do not reuse oil seal after removal.

3.1 - 3.9
(0.32 - 0.40, 2.3 - 2.9)

3.1 - 3.9
(0.32 - 0.40, 2.3 - 2.9)

Brush assembly
Min. length:
6 (0.24)

Diode assembly

3.1 - 3.9
(0.32 - 0.40, 2.3 - 2.9)

Vacuum pump*

6 - 7
(0.6 - 0.7, 4.3 - 5.1)

Rear cover

Exploded view of the Nissan alternator—diesel engine

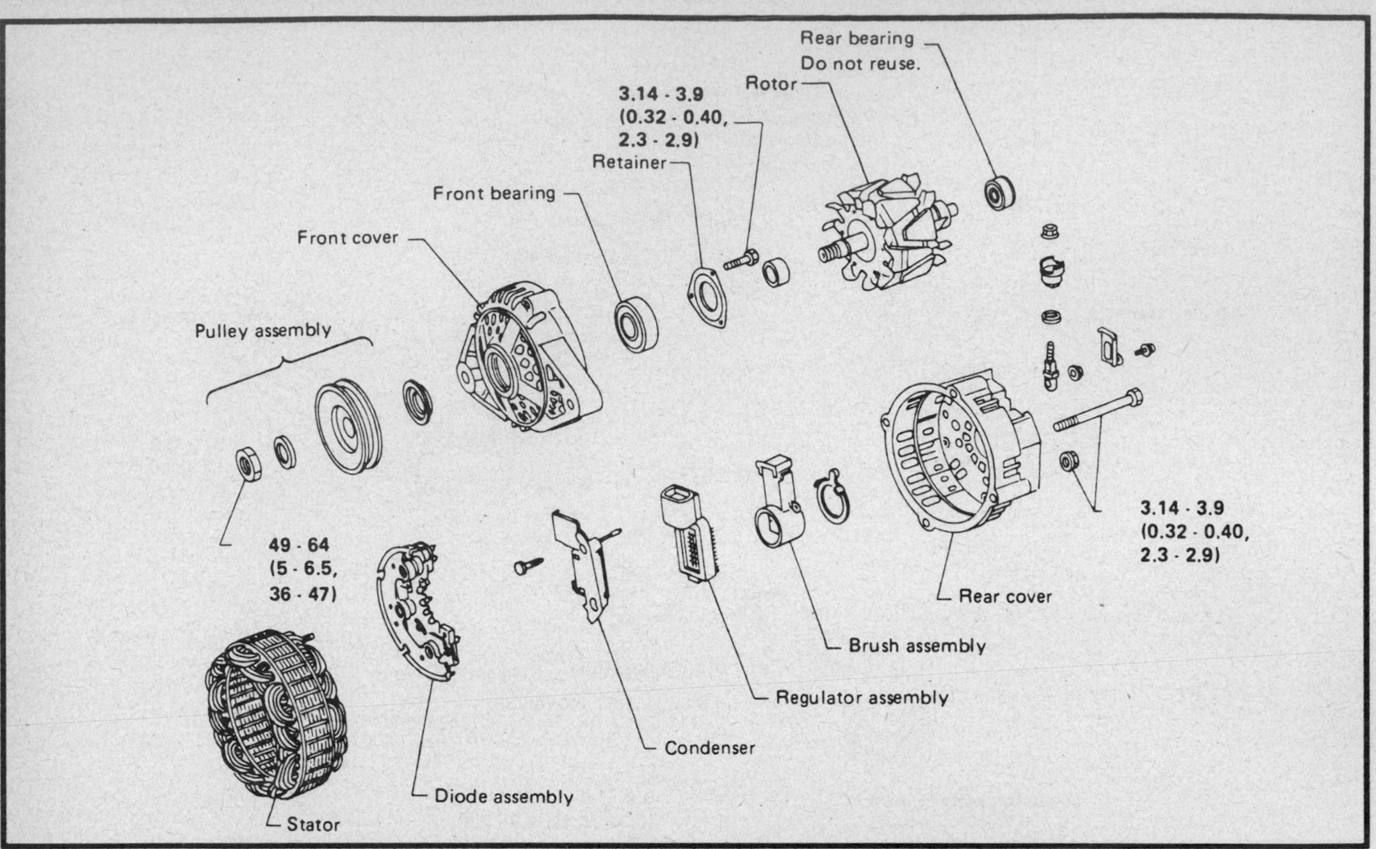

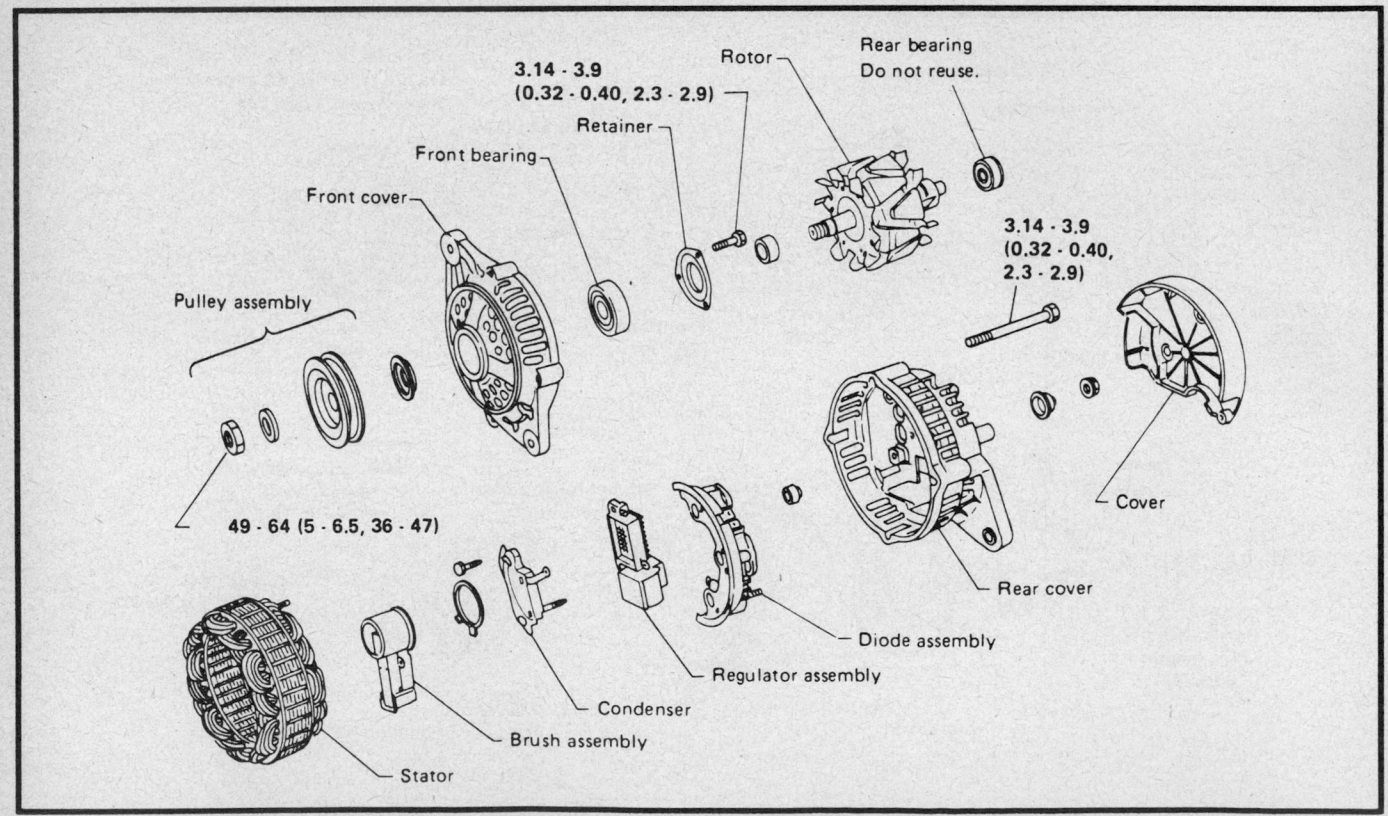

Rear bearing
Do not reuse.
Rotor

**3.14 - 3.9
(0.32 - 0.40,
2.3 - 2.9)**

Retainer

Front bearing

Front cover

Pulley assembly

**3.14 - 3.9
(0.32 - 0.40,
2.3 - 2.9)**

Rear cover

Brush assembly

Regulator assembly

**49 - 64
(5 - 6.5,
36 - 47)**

Condenser

Diode assembly

Stator

Exploded view of the 1990 Nissan alternator—Pick-Up and Pathfinder with 2.4L engine

Rear bearing
Do not reuse.
Rotor

**3.14 - 3.9
(0.32 - 0.40, 2.3 - 2.9)**

Retainer

Front bearing

Front cover

**3.14 - 3.9
(0.32 - 0.40,
2.3 - 2.9)**

Pulley assembly

Cover

49 - 64 (5 - 6.5, 36 - 47)

Rear cover

Diode assembly

Regulator assembly

Condenser

Brush assembly

Stator

Exploded view of the 1990 Nissan alternator—Pick-Up and Pathfinder with 3.0L engine

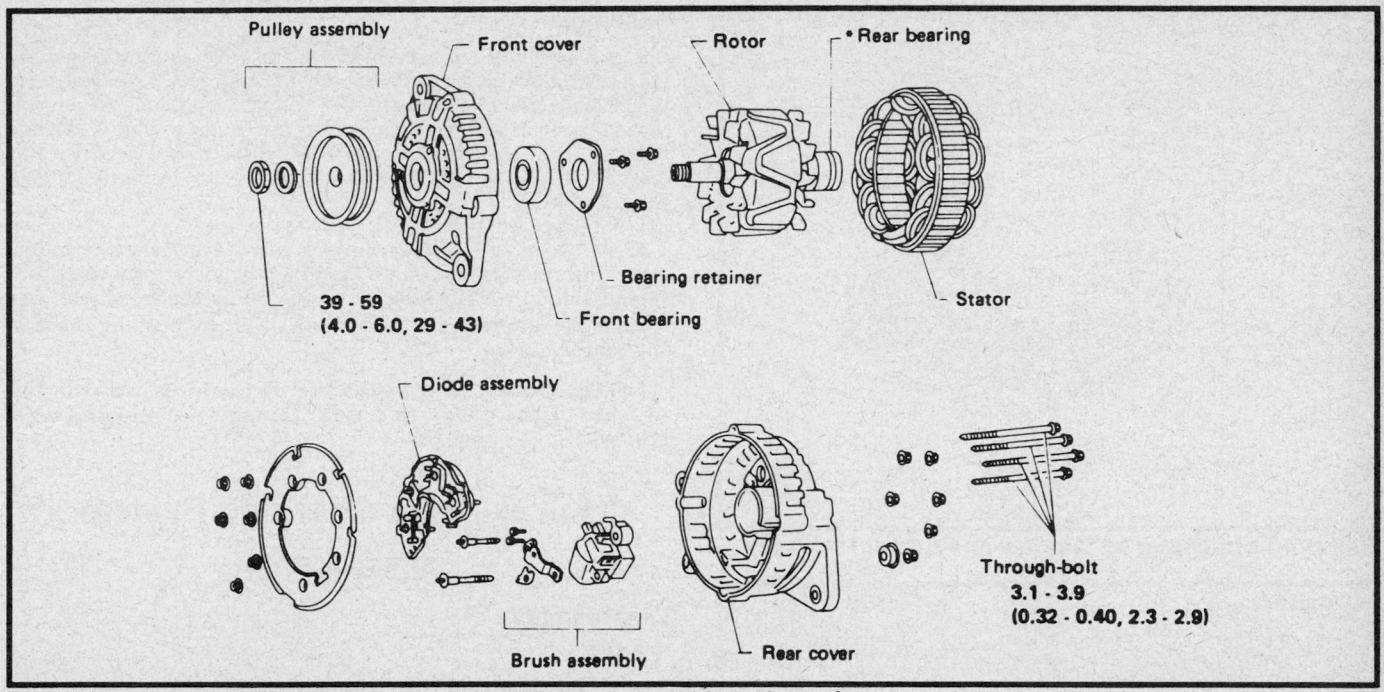

Exploded view of the 1990 Nissan alternator—Axxess with 2.4L engine

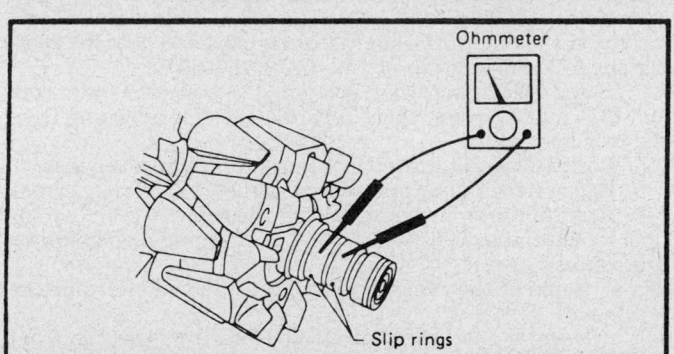

Performing the rotor continuity test

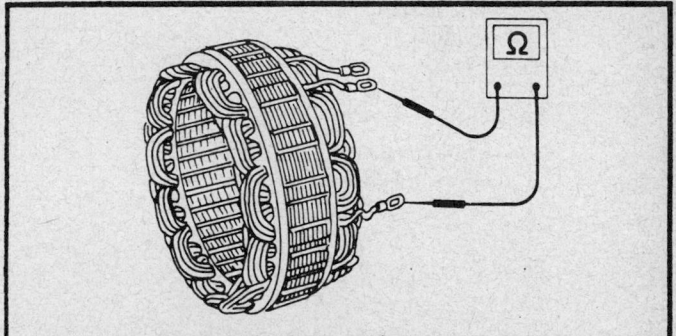

Performing the stator continuity test

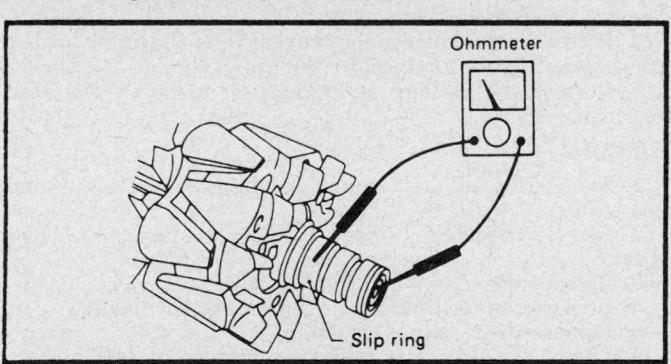

Performing the rotor ground test

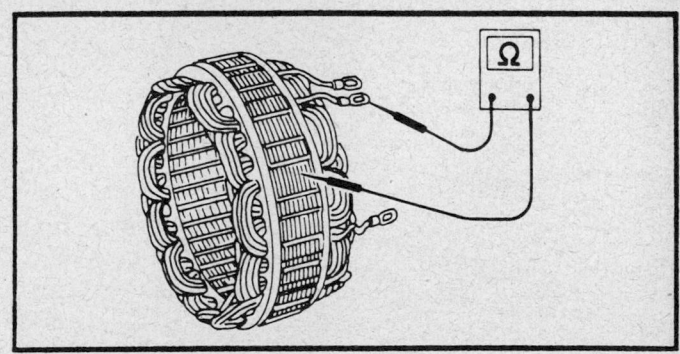

Performing the stator ground test

STATOR

Testing

1. Using an ohmmeter, make a continuity test between the stator lead wires. If there is no lead wires, replace the stator.

2. Using an ohmmeter. make an insulation test between the stator core and the lead wire. If the continuity exists, replace the stator.

DIODE

Testing

1. Using an ohmmeter, perform a continuity test on diodes in both directions.

2. Replace diodes as necessary.

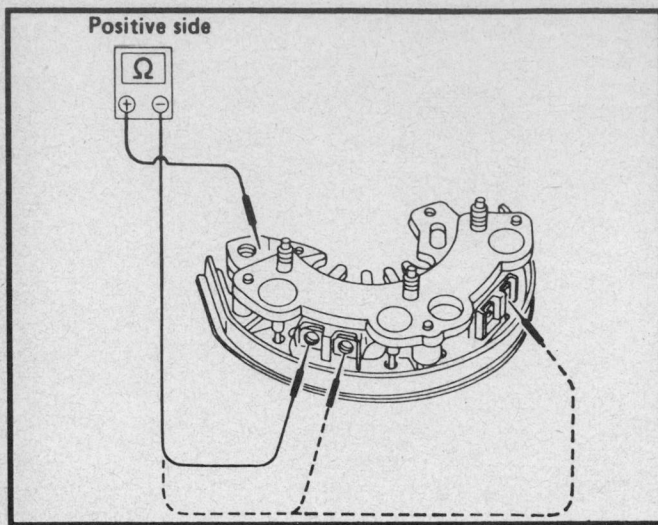

Using an ohmmeter to test the positive side diodes

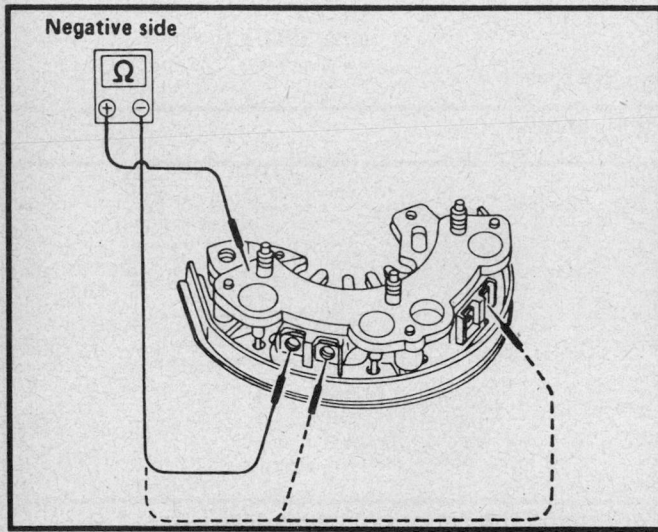

Using an ohmmeter to test the negative side diodes

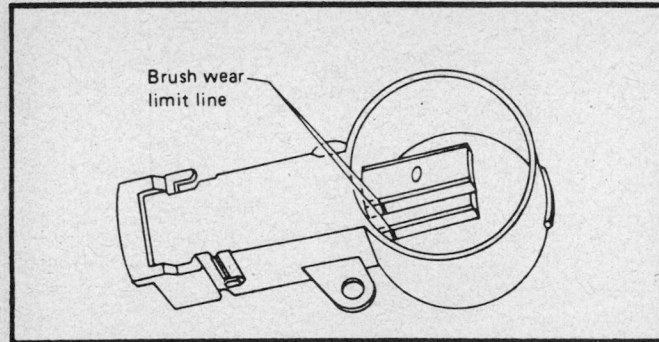

View of the brush wear limit lines

BRUSH

Testing

1. Check for smooth movement of the brush and clean the brush holder if necessary.
2. Check for brush wear at the wear limit line on the brush and replace if necessary.

Assembly

1. Assembly of the alternator is the reverse of disassembly with the following instructions: Solder each stator coil lead wire to the diode assembly terminal as quickly as possible. When soldering the brush lead wire, position the brush so that it extends 0.43 in. from the brush holder and wrap the coil lead wire at least 1.5 times around the terminal groove. Solder the outside of the terminal.
2. Tighten the pulley nut to 29–43 ft. lbs.
3. Before installing the front and rear sides of the alternator, push the brush up and retain the brush by inserting a wire from the outside into a lift hole. After installing the front and rear sides of the alternator, pull the brush lift by pushing towards the center.

NOTE: Do not pull brush lift by pushing towards the outside of the cover as it will damage the slipring as it slides.

Suzuki/GEO Charging System
ALTERNATOR

Disassembly
TRACKER

1. Place alignment matchmarks on the cases.
2. Remove the through bolts from the generator.
3. Using a 200W soldering iron, position it against the bearing box at the rear of the alternator housing and heat the bearing box to a temperature of 122–140°F (50–60°C).
4. Using a medium prybar, position it between the stator core and the front housing, then, separate the front housing from the rear housing.
5. Position the rotor/front housing into a soft jawed vise.
6. Remove the pulley nut and the pulley.
7. Remove the front housing from the rotor.
8. Remove the front bearing by performing the following procedures:
    a. Remove the front bearing retainer screws and the retainer.
    b. Using a shop press, press the bearing from the front housing.
9. Remove the stator-to-rear housing screws, the battery terminal nut and the stator.
10. If necessary to remove the brushes from the brush holder, use a soldering iron to unsolder the brush wire(s).
11. Remove the rectifier and condensor assembly from the rear housing.

SAMURAI

1. Remove the nut and terminal insulator, then, the nuts and end cover.
2. Remove the screws, the brush holder and the brush holder cover.
3. Remove the screws and the IC regulator.
4. Remove the rectifier holder screws and the holder.
5. Remove the terminal insulator.
6. Loosen the alternator pulley nut and the pulley.

NOTE: To prevent damage to the rotor shaft, do not loosen the pulley nut more than ½ turn.

7. Remove the nuts from the rear end frame. Using a puller, remove the rear end frame.
8. Remove the rotor from the drive end frame.
9. If necessary, remove the front bearing by removing the screws from the bearing retainer.
10. If necessary, remove the rear bearing by using a puller. Remove the rear bearing with the cover from the rotor shaft.

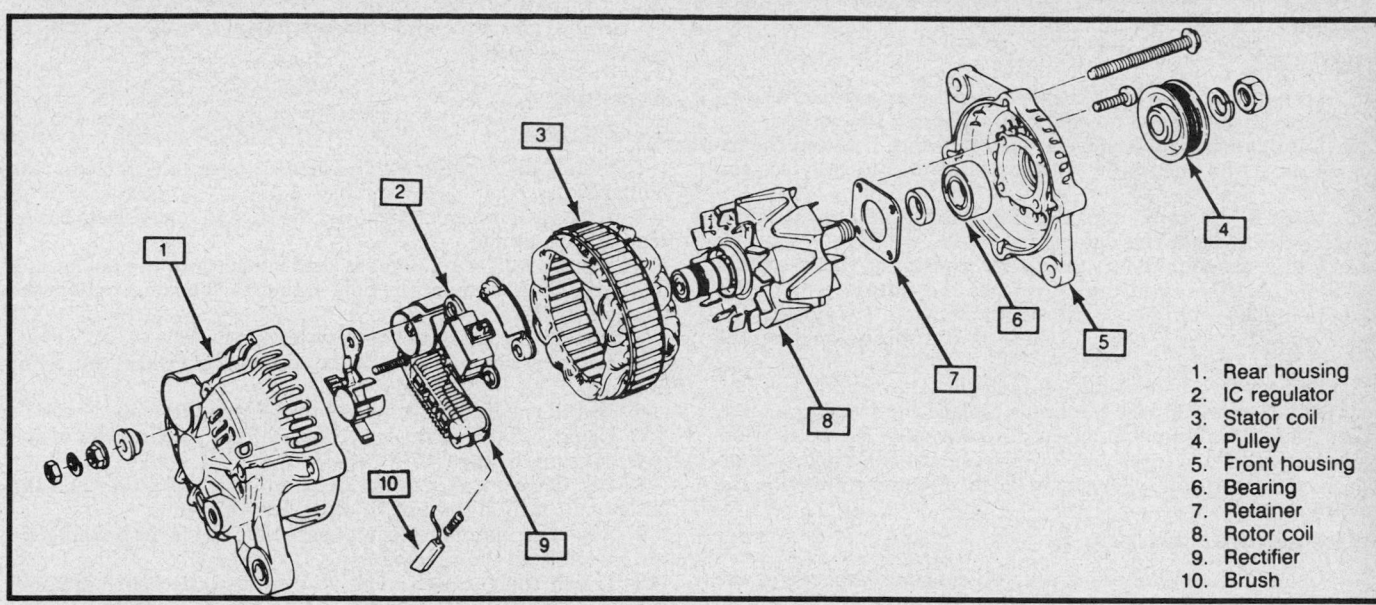

1. Rear housing
2. IC regulator
3. Stator coil
4. Pulley
5. Front housing
6. Bearing
7. Retainer
8. Rotor coil
9. Rectifier
10. Brush

Exploded view of the GEO Tracker alternator

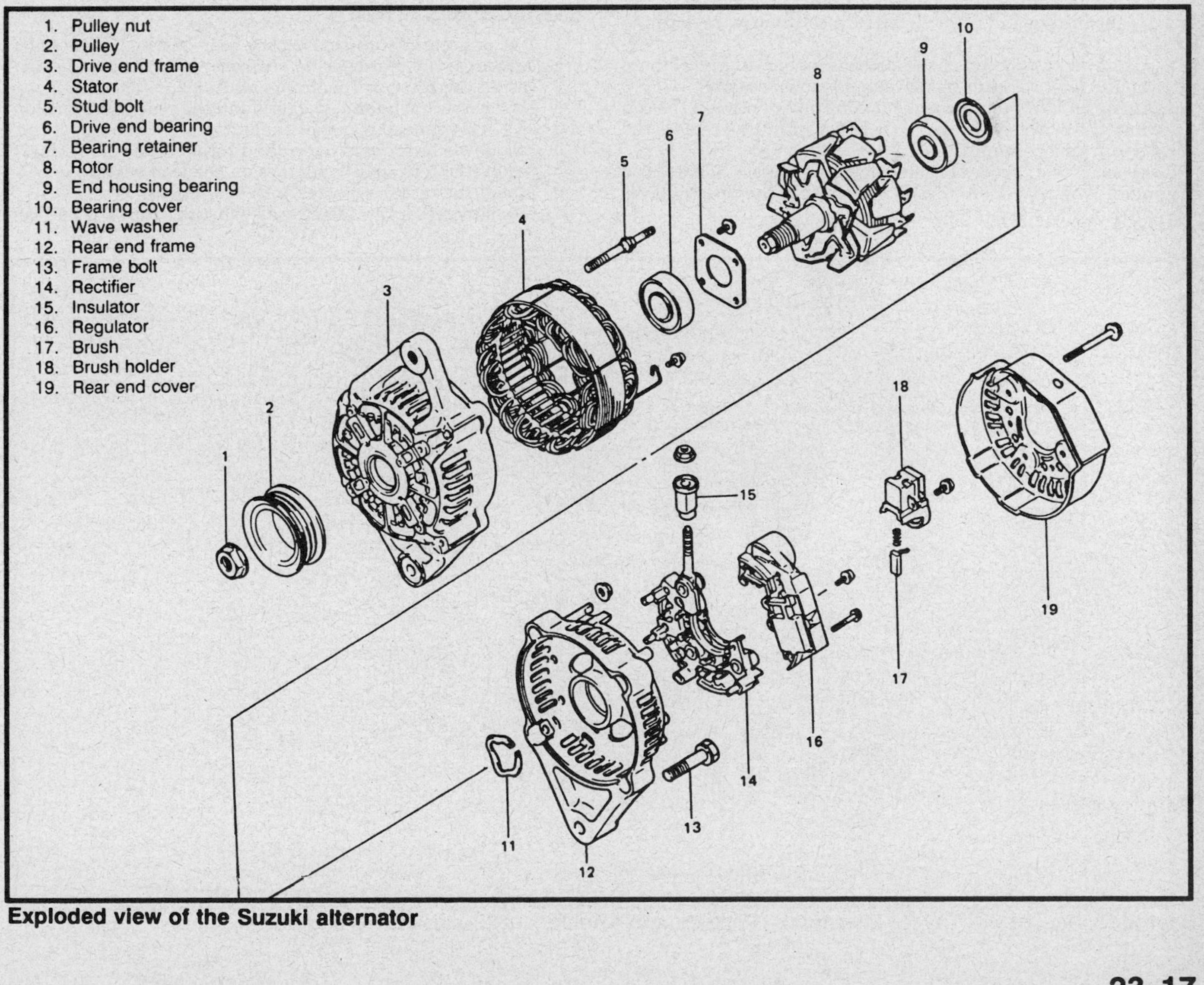

1. Pulley nut
2. Pulley
3. Drive end frame
4. Stator
5. Stud bolt
6. Drive end bearing
7. Bearing retainer
8. Rotor
9. End housing bearing
10. Bearing cover
11. Wave washer
12. Rear end frame
13. Frame bolt
14. Rectifier
15. Insulator
16. Regulator
17. Brush
18. Brush holder
19. Rear end cover

Exploded view of the Suzuki alternator

Testing

TRACKER

1. Using an ohmmeter, check the resistance between the rotor sliprings; if there is no continuity, replace the rotor.

2. Using an ohmmeter, check the resistance between the rotor slipring and the rotor; if there is continuity, replace the rotor.

3. Inspect the rotor sliprings for scoring or roughness; if rough or scored, replace the rotor.

4. Using an ohmmeter, check for continuity between the leads; if there is no continuity, replace the stator.

5. Using an ohmmeter, check for continuity between the leads and the stator core; if there is continuity, replace the stator.

6. Inspect the brushes for wear; the brush wear limit is 0.55 in. (14mm), if worn past the limit, replace the brushes.

7. Using an ohmmeter, check for continuity, in both directions, between the upper and lower rectifier bodies and each diode lead; if continuity exists in both directions, replace the rectifier.

SAMURAI AND SIDEKICK

1. Using an ohmmeter, check for continuity between the ssliprings. Standard resistance is 2.8–3.0 ohms; if there is no continuity, replace the rotor.

2. Using an ohmmeter, check that there is no continuity between the slipring and rotor; if there is continuity, replace the rotor.

3. Using an ohmmeter, check all leads for continuity. If there is no continuity, replace the drive end frame assembly.

4. Using an ohmmeter, check for continuity between the coil leads and the drive end frame; if there is continuity, replace the drive end frame assembly.

5. Measure the exposed brush length and replace, if necesary. Minimum length is 0.200 in. Also check that the brush moves smoothly in the brush holder.

6. Inspect the front and rear bearings for roughness and replace, if necessary.

Assembly

TRACKER

1. Install the rectifier and condensor assembly into the rear housing.

2. If the brushes were removed, be sure to solder them to the regulator terminal.

3. Using a stiff wire, depress the brushes into the holder and insert the wire, through the hole in the rear housing, to hold the brushes in place.

4. Install the stator to the rear housing.

5. Using a shop press, press the bearing into the front housing.

6. Install the bearing retainer to the front housing.

7. Using a 200W soldering iron, heat the bearing box of the rear housing to 122–140°F (50–60°C).

8. Install the rotor into the front housing, the pulley and the pulley nut; torque the nut to 48 ft. lbs. (65 Nm).

9. Align the matchmarks and assemble the front housing/rotor assembly to the rear housing.

10. Install the through bolts and remove the brush support wire.

11. Make sure the rotor turn freely within the assembly.

SAMURAI AND SIDEKICK

1. If it is necessary to replace the rear bearing, use a shop press and press the rear bearing and cover onto the rotor shaft.

2. Install the rotor to the drive end frame.

3. Using a plastic hammer, lightly tap the rear end frame on the drive end frame and install the nuts.

4. Install the alternator pulley and torque to 37–47 ft. lbs.

5. Install the terminal insulators on the lead wires.

6. Install the rectifier holder with the screws.

7. If it is necessary to install a new brush, unsolder and re-

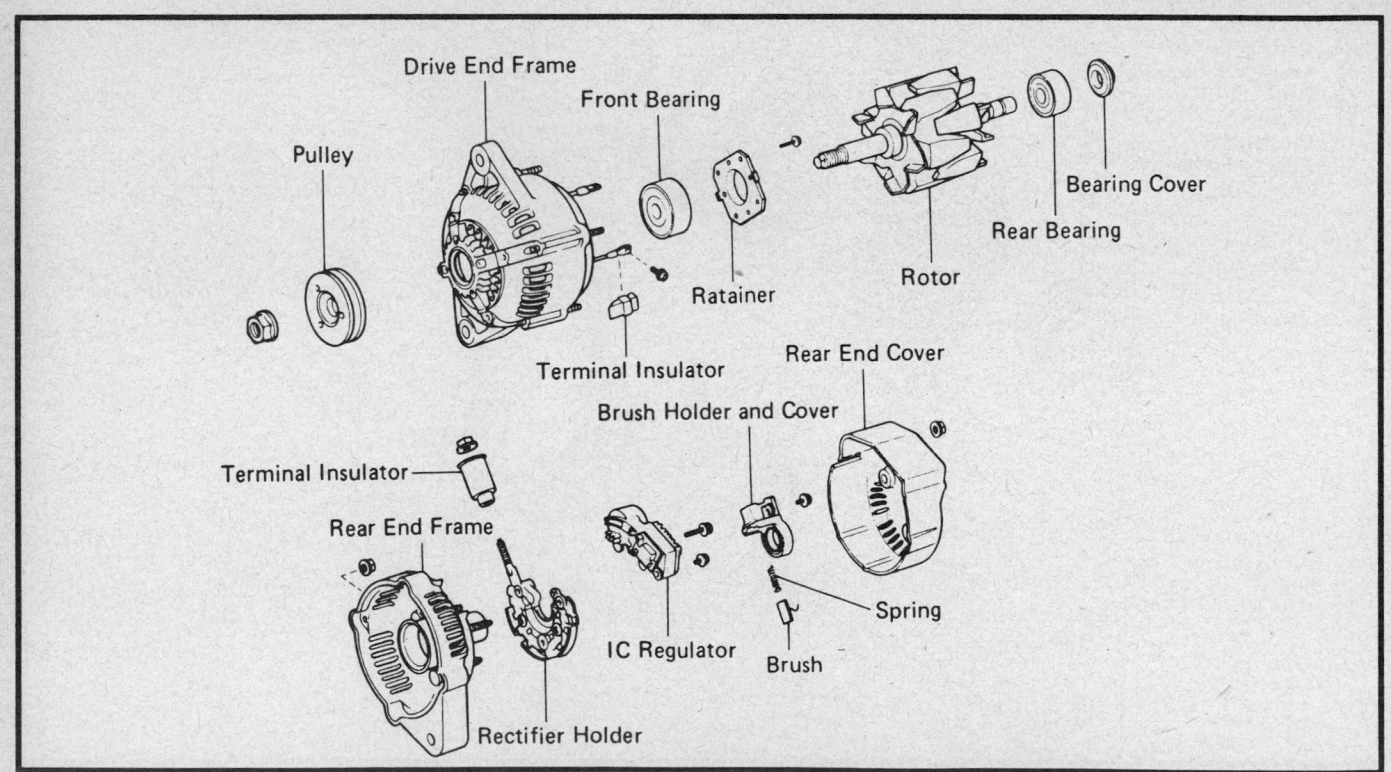

Exploded view of the Toyota alternator—Pick-Up and 4Runner—22R and 22R-E engines

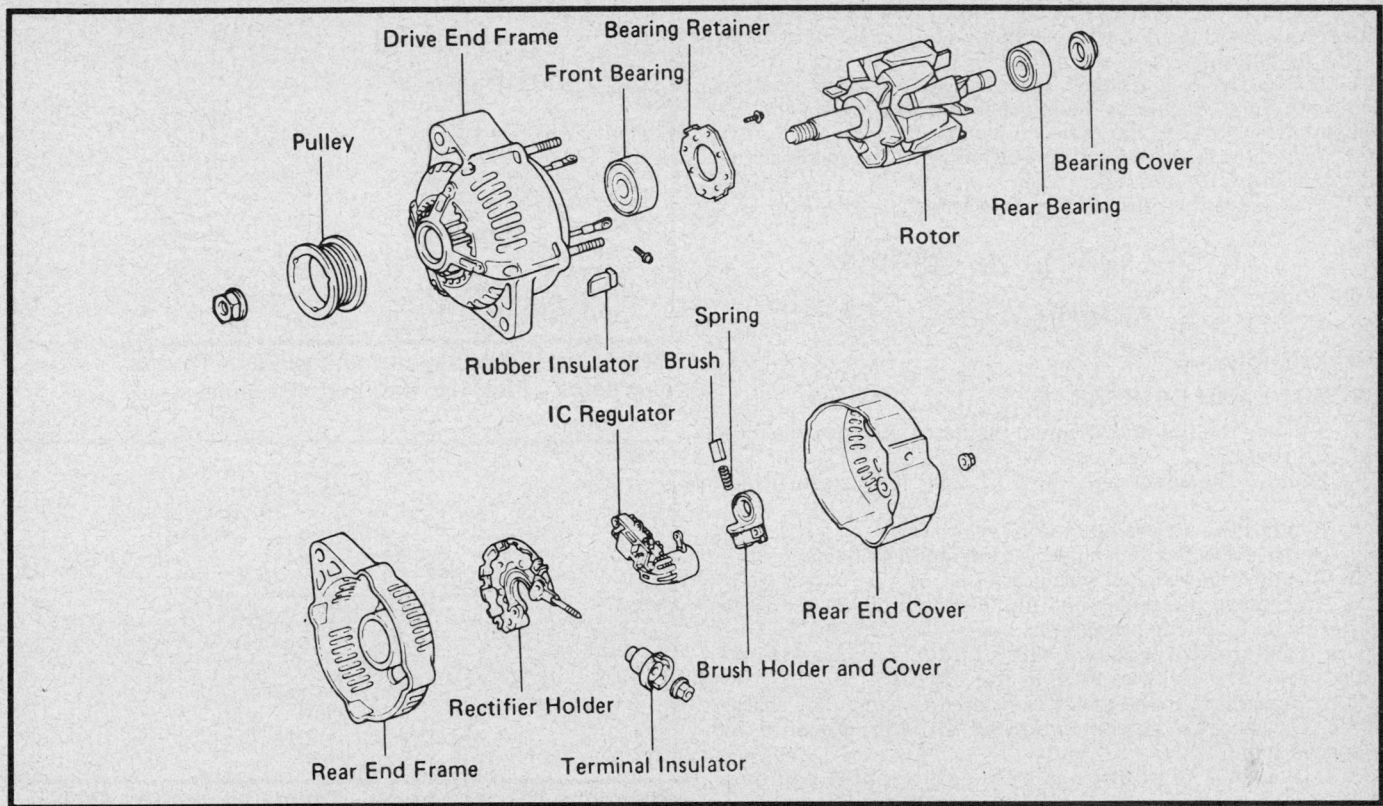

Exploded view of the Toyota alternator—Pick-Up and 4Runner—3VZ-E engine

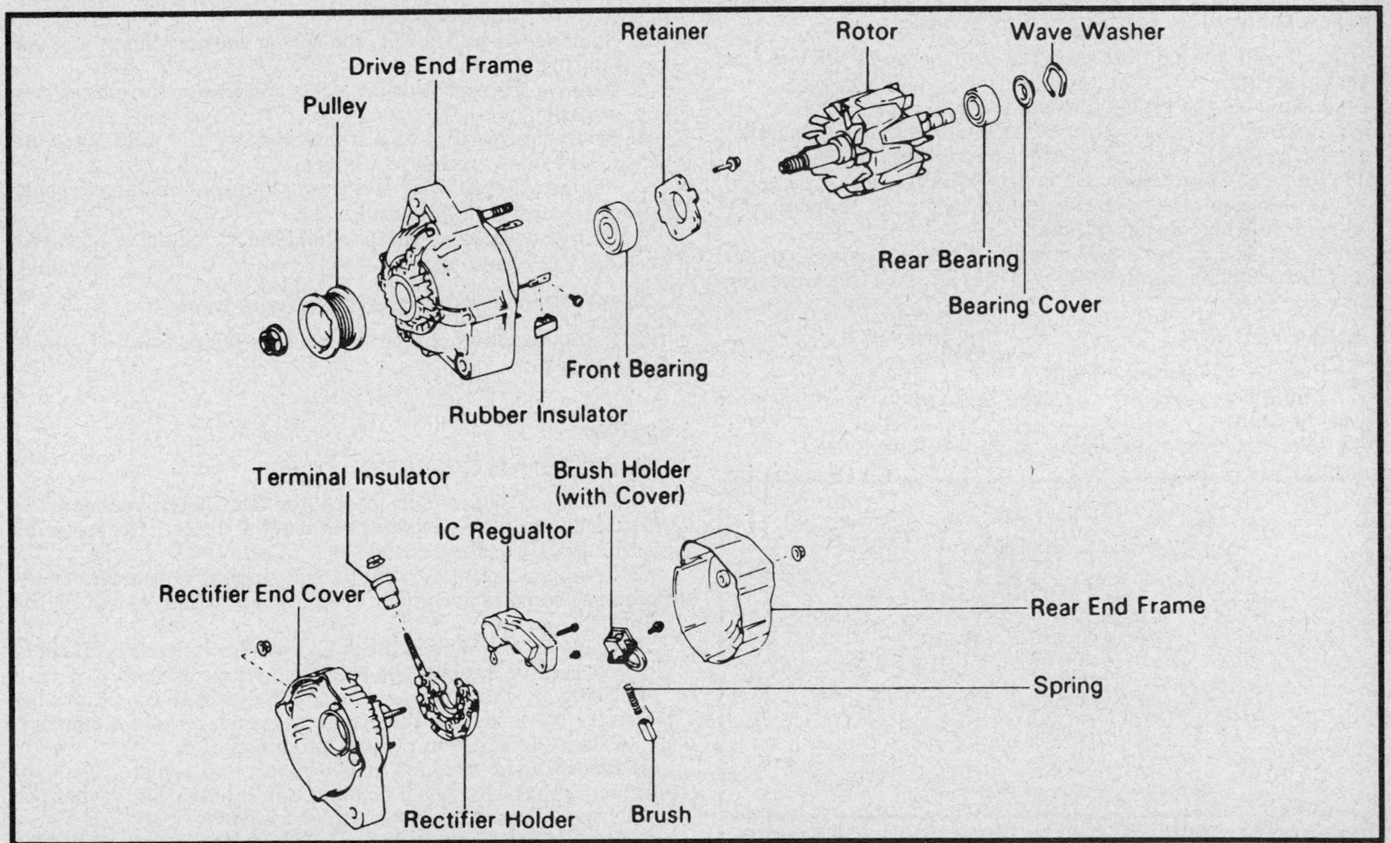

Exploded view of the Toyota alternator—Van

move the brush and spring. Put the new brush wire through the spring and insert it into the brush holder. Solder the wire to the brush holder and cut off any excess.

8. Install the brush holder with the IC regulator and the screws to the IC regulator. Install the retaining screws and the brush holder cover to the rear end frame.

9. Install the end cover with the retaining nuts and install the terminal insulator and nut.

10. Make sure the rotor rotates smoothly.

Toyota Charging System

ALTERNATOR

Disassembly

EXCEPT LAND CRUISER

1. Remove the nut and terminal insulator. Remove the nuts and end cover.

2. Remove the screws, the brush holder and brush holder cover.

3. Remove the screws and the IC regulator.

4. Remove the rectifier holder screws and the holder.

5. Remove the terminal insulator(s).

6. To remove the pulley and nut, use tool 09820–63010 to perform the following procedure:

    a. Hold the tool at point **A** with a torque wrench and tighten at point **B** clockwise to 29 ft. lbs. (39 Nm).

    b. Confirm that the tool **A** is secured to the pulley shaft.

    c. Grip tool **C** in a vise and install the alternator into the special tool **C**.

    d. Loosen the pulley nut by turning tool **A** counterclockwise.

NOTE: To prevent damage to the rotor shaft, do not loosen the pulley nut more than ½ turn.

    e. Turn the tool at point **B** and remove all the tool components.

    f. Remove the pulley nut and the pulley.

7. Remove the nuts from the rear end frame. Using a puller, tool 09286–46011, remove the rear end frame.

8. Remove the rotor from the drive end frame.

9. If necessary, remove the front bearing by removing the screws from the bearing retainer.

10. If necessary, remove the rear bearing by using a puller, tool 09820–00020. Remove the rear bearing with the cover from the rotor shaft.

LAND CRUISER

1. Remove the through bolts.

2. Using a prybar, pry the drive end frame/rotor assembly from the stator.

3. Mount the rotor assembly into a soft jawed vise.

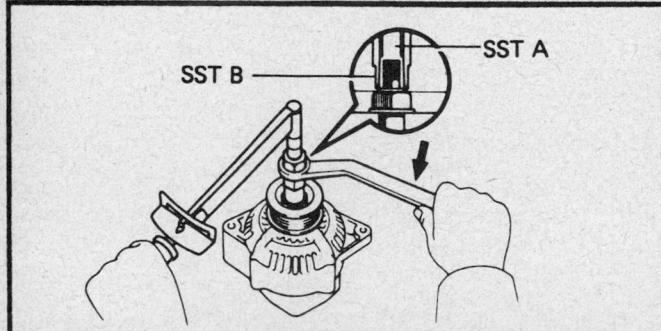

Installing the removal tool to the rotorshaft—Toyota alternator—Pick-Up, Van and 4Runner

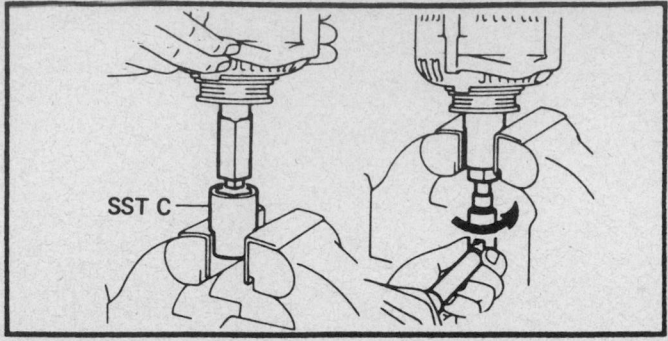

Removing the pulley nut and pulley—Toyota alternator—Pick-Up, Van and 4Runner

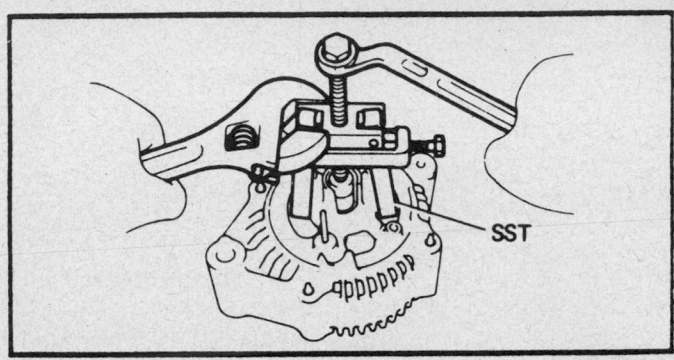

Removing the rear frame—Toyota alternator—Pick-Up, Van and 4Runner

4. Remove the pulley nut, the spring washer, the pulley and fan from the rotor.

5. Remove the spacer collar, drive end frame, the spacer ring and snapring.

6. From the rectifier end frame, remove the nuts, the condenser and the terminal insulators.

7. Remove the rectifier end frame and the insulator washer from the rectifier holder stud.

8. Using needle-nose pliers to hold the IC regulator terminal, unsolder the terminals.

NOTE: Protect the rectifiers from heat.

9. Using needle-nose pliers to hold the stator coil lead, unsolder the leads.

Testing

EXCEPT LAND CRUISER

1. Using an ohmmeter, check for continuity between the ssliprings; standard resistance is 2.8–3.0 ohms. If there is no continuity, replace the rotor.

2. Using an ohmmeter, check that there is no continuity between the slipring and rotor. If there is continuity, replace the rotor.

3. Using an ohmmeter, check all leads for continuity. If there is no continuity, replace the drive end frame assembly.

4. Using an ohmmeter, check that there is no continuity between the coil leads and the drive end frame. If there is continuity, replace the drive end frame assembly.

5. Measure the exposed brush length and replace, if necessary; minimum length is 0.059 in. (1.5mm). Also check that the brush moves smoothly in the brush holder.

6. Inspect the front and rear bearings for roughness and replace if necessary.

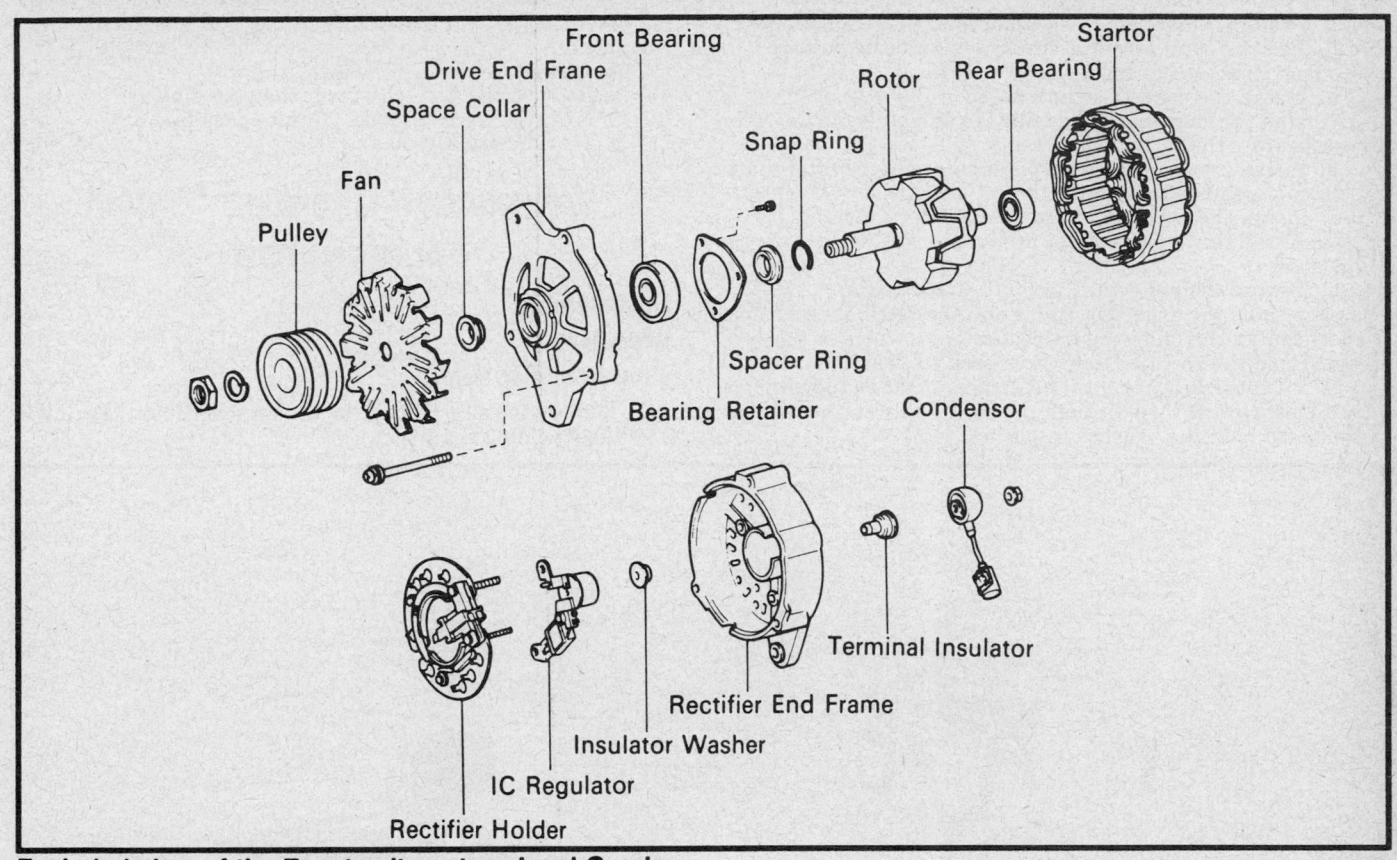

Exploded view of the Toyota alternator — Land Crusier

LAND CRUISER

1. Using an ohmmeter, check for continuity between the ssliprings; standard resistance is 2.8–3.0 ohms. If there is no continuity, replace the rotor.

2. Using an ohmmeter, check that there is no continuity between the slipring and rotor. If there is continuity, replace the rotor.

3. Using an ohmmeter, check all leads for continuity; if there is no continuity, replace the stator.

4. Using an ohmmeter, check that there is no continuity between the coil leads and the stator core; if there is continuity, replace the stator.

5. Measure the exposed brush length and replace, if necessary; minimum length is 0.217 in. (5.5mm). Also check that the brush moves smoothly in the brush holder.

6. Inspect the front and rear bearings for roughness and replace if necessary.

7. Using an ohmmeter, inspect the diodes of the rectifier assembly; good diodes will show continuity in one direction and no continuity in the other direction.

Assembly

EXCEPT LAND CRUISER

1. If it is necessary to replace the rear bearing, use bearing installation and press the rear bearing and cover onto the rotor shaft.

2. Install the rotor to the drive end frame.

3. Using a plastic hammer, lightly tap the rear end frame on the drive end frame and install the nuts.

4. Install the pulley in the following manner:

   a. Using the pulley onto the rotor shaft and tighten the pulley nut by hand.

   b. Using tool 09820–63010, hold it at point **A** with a torque wrench and tighten tool **B** clockwise to 29 ft. lbs. (39 Nm).

   c. Confirm tool **A** is secured to the pulley shaft.

   d. Grip special tool **C** in a vise and then install the alternator to tool **C**.

   e. To torque the pulley nut, turn tool **A** and tighten to 81 ft. lbs. (110 Nm).

   f. Turn tool **B** and remove all the tool components.

5. Install the terminal insulators on the lead wires.

6. Install the rectifier holder with the screws.

7. If it is necessary to install a new brush, unsolder and remove the brush and spring. Put the new brush wire through the spring and insert it into the brush holder. Solder the wire to the brush holder and cut off any excess.

8. Install the brush holder with the IC regulator and install the screws to the IC regulator. Install the retaining screws and the brush holder cover to the rear end frame.

9. Install the end cover with the retaining nuts and install the terminal insulator and nut. Make sure the rotor rotates smoothly.

LAND CRUISER

1. Using needle-nose pliers to hold the stator coil lead, solder the leads.

NOTE: Protect the rectifiers from heat.

2. Using needle-nose pliers to hold the IC regulator terminal, solder the terminals.

3. Install the rectifier end frame-to-rectifier holder by performing the following procedures:

   a. Position the insulator washer onto the positive (+) stud of the rectifier holder.

   b. Position both cushions onto the brush holder and alternator terminal.

c. Position the rectifier end frame onto the rectifier holder.

d. Position both terminal insulators onto the positive (+) studs of the rectifier holder.

e. Install the condensor and nuts.

4. Install the drive end frame, the fan and pulley to the rotor by performing the following procedures:

a. Install the snapring and spacer ring onto the rotor shaft.

b. Position the rotor into the soft jawed vise.

c. Install the drive end frame and spacer collar.

d. Install the fan, the pulley and spring washer onto the rotor shaft.

e. Torque the pulley nut to 65 ft. lbs. (88 Nm).

5. Assemble the drive end frame and the rectifier end frame by performing the following procedures:

a. Bend the rectifier lead wires back to clear the rotor.

b. Push the brushes into the holder, as far as they will go, and insert a stiff wire through the access hole, in the rectifier frame, to hold the brushes in place.

c. Assemble the drive end frame and the rectifier end frame.

d. Install the through bolts.

e. Remove the stiff wire from the access hole.

f. Turn the rotor to make sure it turns freely.

g. Seal the access hole.

Volkswagen Charging System

ALTERNATOR

Disassembly

BOSCH

45 Amp and 65 Amp

1. Remove the alternator from the vehicle. Mount the unit in a suitable holding fixture.

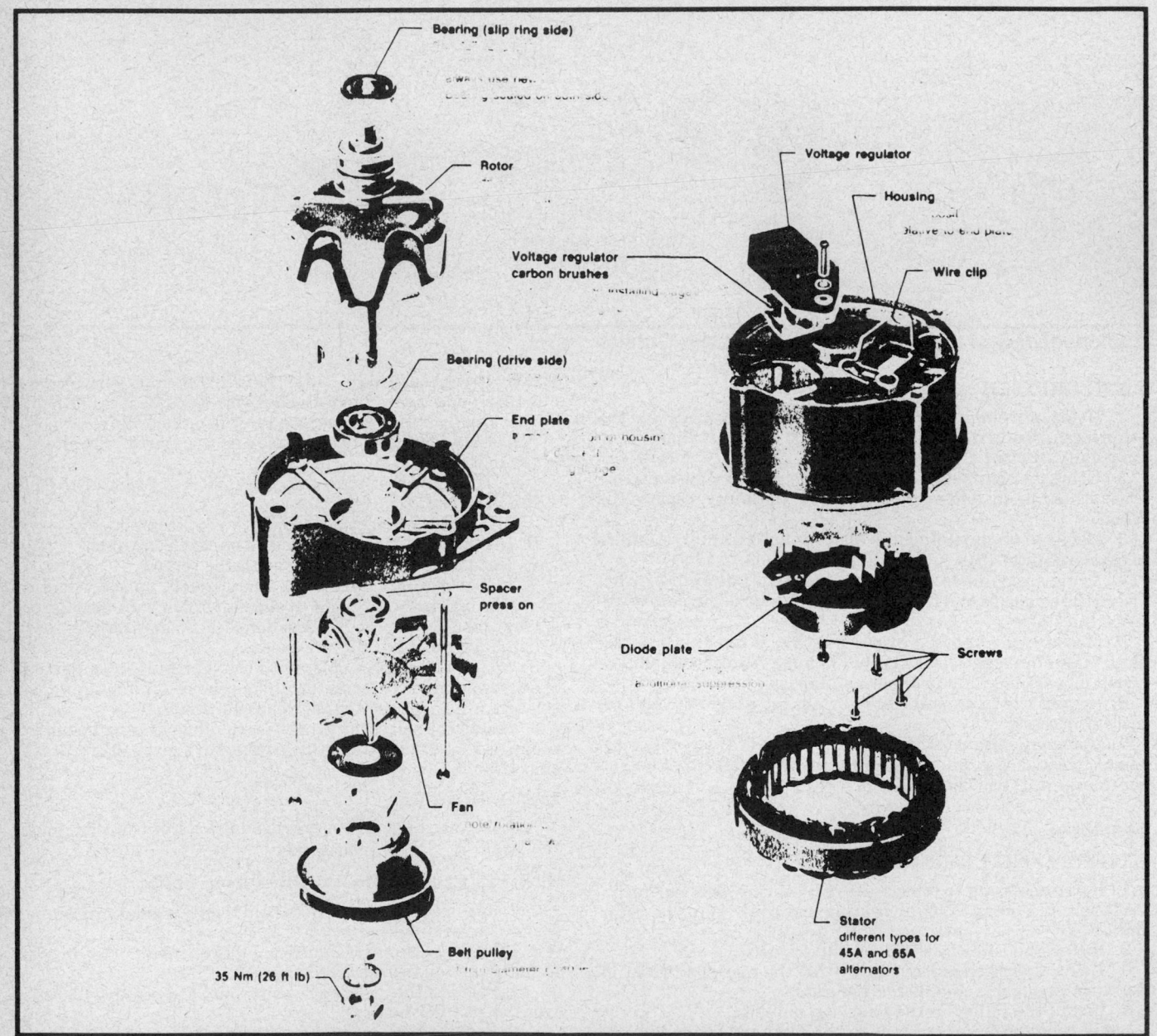

Exploded view of the Bosch 45 amp and 65 amp alternators—Volkswagen

2. Hold the alternator pulley and remove the pulley retaining nut.

3. Remove the pulley lockwasher, pulley fan spacer and pulley from the alternator assembly.

4. Remove the Woodruff® key from the rotor shaft.

5. From the rear of the alternator remove the brush holder retaining screws. Remove the brush holder.

6. To test the inner and outer brush circuits, use an ohmmeter and touch 1 test probe to the inner brush and the other test probe to the brush terminal. If continuity does not exist replace the brush assembly. Repeat the same test for the outer brush circuit.

7. Disconnect the capacitor electrical connection and remove the capacitor retaining screw. Remove the capacitor from its mounting on the alternator.

8. Remove the ground stud nut and stud washer.

9. Remove the alternator through bolts that retain the unit together.

10. Using the proper tool, separate the stator and the drive end shield.

11. To test the positive and negative rectifiers use tool C–3929–A or equivalent.

NOTE: Do not break the plastic cases of the rectifiers. These cases are for protection against corrosion. Be sure to always touch the test probe to the metal pin of the nearest rectifier.

12. Position the rear end shield and the stator assembly on an insulated surface. Connect the test lead clip to the alternator battery output terminal.

13. Plug in tool C–3829–A or equivalent. Touch the metal pin of each of the positive rectifiers with the test probe.

14. Reading for satisfactory rectifiers will be 1¾ amperes or more. Reading should be approximately the same and meter needle must move in the same direction for all 3 rectifiers.

15. When some rectifiers are good and 1 is shorted, the reading taken at good rectifiers will be low and the reading at shorted rectifiers will be 0. Disconnect stator lead to rectifiers reading 0 and retest. Reading of good rectifiers will now be within satisfactory range.

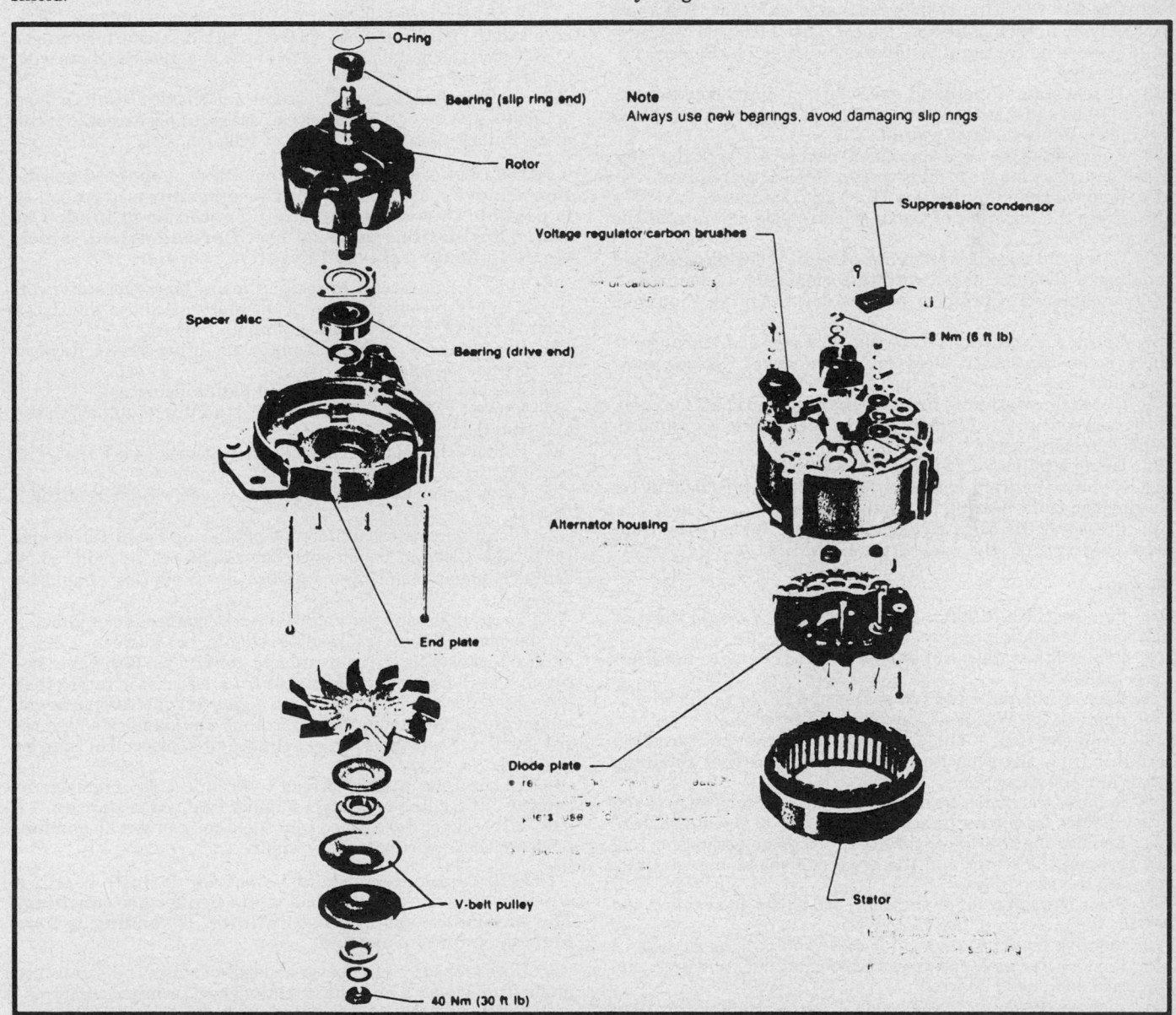

Exploded view of the Bosch 90 amp alternator – Volkswagen

16. When a rectifier is open, it will read approximately 1 ampere and good rectifiers will read within satisfactory range.

17. To test the negative rectifiers, connect the test clip of tool C–3829–A to the rectifier end housing.

18. Touch the metal pin of each of the negative rectifiers with the test probe.

19. Test specifications are the same and test results will be approximately same as for positive case rectifiers except that the meter will read on opposite side of scale.

NOTE: If a negative rectifier shows a shorted condition, remove stator from rectifier assembly and retest. It is possible that a stator winding could be grounded to stator laminations or to an rectifier end shield which would indicate a shorted negative rectifier.

20. Remove the battery (B+) stud nut, stud lockwasher, stud flatwasher and stud insulator.

21. Remove the rectifier assembly retaining screws. Remove the stator assembly along with the rectifier unit. Unsolder the stator to rectifier leads.

22. Check for continuity between stator coil leads. Press test probe firmly to each of 3 phase (stator) lead terminals separately. If there is no continuity, stator coil is defective. Replace stator assembly.

23. To test stator for ground, check for continuity between stator coil leads and stator coil frame. If there is continuity stator is grounded. Replace stator assembly.

24. Remove the rear bearing oil and dust seal. Check the rotor bearing surface for wear and scoring. Replace as required.

25. Remove the inner battery (B+) stud insulator.

26. Press the rotor out of the drive end shield and remove the spacer.

27. Check outside circumference of slipring for dirtiness and roughness. Clean or polish with fine sandpaper, if required. A badly roughened slipring or a worn down slipring should be replaced.

28. Check for continuity between field coil and sliprings. If there is no continuity, field coil is defective. Replace rotor assembly.

29. Check for continuity between sliprings and shaft (or core). If there is continuity, it means that coil or slipring is grounded. Replace rotor assembly.

30. Using a puller remove the rotor bearing.

31. Remove the front bearing from the drive end shield by removing the front bearing retaining screws.

32. Press out the drive end shield bearing. Remove the front drive bearing from the front drive end shield.

90 Amp

1. Remove the alternator from the vehicle. Position the unit in a suitable holding fixture.

2. Remove the pulley nut and lockwasher. Remove the alternator pulley.

3. Remove the pulley to fan spacer and pulley fan.

4. Remove the Woodruff key from the rotor shaft.

5. From the rear of the alternator disconnect the electrical terminal from the capacitor. Remove the capacitor retaining screw and the capacitor.

6. Remove the brush holder retaining screw and remove the brush holder from its mounting on the rear of the alternator.

7. Remove the alternator through bolts. Using a suitable tool pry between the stator and the drive end shield and carefully separate the assembly.

8. Press the rotor out of the drive end shield and remove the spacer. Remove the pulley fan spacer.

9. Remove the front alternator drive end bearing screws.

10. Remove the drive end shield bearing retainer and press out the drive end shield bearing.

11. Remove the front drive bearing from the front of the drive end shield.

12. To test the positive and negative rectifiers use tool C–3929–A or equivalent.

NOTE: Do not break the plastic cases of the rectifiers. These cases are for protection against corrosion. Be sure to always touch the test probe to the metal pin of the nearest rectifier.

13. Position the rear end shield and the stator assembly on an insulated surface. Connect the test lead clip to the alternator battery output terminal.

14. Plug in tool C–3829–A or equivalent. Touch the metal pin of each of the positive rectifiers with the test probe.

15. Reading for satisfactory rectifiers will be 1¾ amperes or more. Reading should be approximately the same and meter needle must move in same direction for all 3 rectifiers.

16. When some rectifiers are good and 1 is shorted, the reading taken at good rectifiers will be low and the reading at shorted rectifiers will be 0. Disconnect stator lead to rectifiers reading 0 and retest. Reading of good rectifiers will now be within satisfactory range.

17. When a rectifier is open it will read approximately 1 ampere and the good rectifiers will read within satisfactory range.

18. Touch the metal pin of each of the negative rectifiers with the test probe.

19. Test specifications are the same and the test results will be approximately same as for positive case rectifiers except that the meter will read on opposite side of scale.

NOTE: If a negative rectifier shows a shorted condition remove stator from rectifier assembly and retest. It is possible that a stator winding could be grounded to stator laminations or to an rectifier end shield, which would indicate a shorted negative rectifier.

20. Unsolder the stator to rectifier leads. Mark the stator coil frame, to aid in reinstallation of the stator. Remove the stator from the rectifier end shield assembly.

21. Remove the 3 rectifier assembly mounting screws. Remove the rectifier assembly.

22. Remove the inner battery (B+) stud insulator.

23. Remove the D+ stud insulator, stud nut, stud flatwasher and stud insulating washer.

24. Remove the rear bearing oil and dust seal. Check the rotor bearing surface for scoring.

25. Using puller C–4068 or equivalent, remove the rear rotor bearing.

26. Check outside circumference of slipring for dirtiness and roughness. Clean or polish with fine sandpaper, as required. A badly roughened slipring or a worn down slipring should be replaced.

27. To check for an open rotor field coil, connect an ohmmeter to sliprings. Ohmmeter reading should be between 1.5–2.0 ohms on rotor coils at room ambient conditions. Resistance between 2.5–3.0 ohms would result from alternator rotors that have been operated on vehicle at higher engine compartment temperatures. Readings above 3.5 ohms would indicate high resistance rotor coils and further testing or replacement may be required.

28. To check for a shorted field coil connect an ohmmeter to sliprings. If reading is below 1.5 ohms field coil is shorted.

29. To check for a grounded rotor field coil connect an ohmmeter from each slipring to rotor shaft.

NOTE: Ohmmeter should be set for infinite reading when probes are apart and 0 when probes are touching. The ohmmeter should read infinite. If reading is 0 or higher, rotor is grounded.

30. Check for continuity between leads of stator coil. Press test probe firmly to each of 3 phase (stator) lead terminals separately. If there is no continuity, stator coil is defective. Replace stator assembly.

31. To test the stator for ground check for continuity between the stator coil leads and the stator coil frame. If there is no continuity the stator is grounded and must be replaced.

32. To test the inner and outer brush circuit, use an ohmmeter and touch 1 test probe to the inner brush and the other test probe to the brush terminal. If continuity does not exist replace the brush assembly. Repeat the same procedure for the outer brush.

Assembly

45 Amp and 65 Amp

1. Be sure to check all parts for wear and replace the defective components as required.
2. Install the rear rotor bearing oil and dust seal.
3. Install the inner alternator battery terminal insulator.
4. Solder the stator leads to the rectifier assembly; be sure to use needle nose pliers as a heat sink.
5. Position the stator and rectifier assembly. Install the rectifier mounting screws, both terminal insulators, the insulator washer, the insulator lockwasher and the insulator nut.
6. Position and press the front bearing into the drive end shield. Install the bearing retainer.
7. Position the drive end shield and spacer over the rotor. Press the drive end shield onto the rotor.
8. Install the rectifier end shield over the drive end shield. Install the through bolts and tighten.
9. Install the capacitor and terminal plug onto the alternator assembly.
10. Push the brushes into the brush holder and install the brush holder onto the alternator assembly.
11. Install the Woodruff key into the shaft and the fan over the shaft.

12. Install the drive pulley-to-fan spacer, the pulley, the lockwasher and the nut over the shaft. Secure the pulley and tighten the nut.

90 Amp

1. Be sure to check all parts for wear and replace the defective components as required.
2. Install the rear rotor bearing oil and dust seal.
3. Install the inner alternator battery B + terminal insulator.
4. Position the rectifier assembly. Install the rectifier mounting screws, the insulator, the insulator washer, the insulator lockwasher and the insulator nut.
5. Position the stator assembly into the rectifier end shield. Align the scribe marks on the stator and the rectifier end shield.
6. Solder the stator leads to the rectifier assembly; be sure to use needle nose pliers as a heat sink.
7. Position and press the front bearing into the drive end shield. Install the bearing retainer and the pulley fan spacer onto the drive end shield.
8. Position the drive end shield and spacer over the rotor. Using a socket wrench, press the drive end shield onto the rotor.
9. Install the rectifier end shield and stator assembly into the drive end shield and rotor assembly. Install the through bolts and tighten.
10. Push the brushes into the brush holder and install the brush holder onto the alternator assembly.
11. Install the capacitor and terminal plug onto the alternator assembly.
12. Install the Woodruff key into the shaft and the fan over the shaft.
13. Install the drive pulley-to-fan spacer, the pulley, the lockwasher and the nut over the shaft. Secure the pulley and tighten the nut.

SWITCHES AND SOLENOIDS

Magnetic Switches

Magnetic switches serve only to make contact for the starter motor. Usually, such switches are located on the inner fender panel, although they are found mounted on the starter in a few cases.

MAGNETIC SWITCHES WITH TWO CONTROL TERMINALS

On this type of magnetic switch current is supplied from the ignition switch or transmission neutral button to 1 of the magnetic switch control terminals. The other control terminal is connected to the transmission neutral safety switch (on the transmission) where it is grounded.

MAGNETIC SWITCHES WITH IGNITION RESISTOR BYPASS TERMINALS

All normally use a magnetic switch with a single control terminal. The second terminal is an ignition resistor bypass terminal.

SOLENOIDS WITHOUT RELAYS

This type of starter solenoid is always mounted on the starter. Makes electrical contact for the starter and pulls the starter and drive clutch into mesh with the flywheel. The Chrysler reduction gear starter has this solenoid embodied in the starter housing.

There is only 1 control terminal on the solenoid and the ignition bypass terminal is usually marked **R** or **IGN**, if it is used.

SOLENOIDS WITH SEPARATE RELAYS

The solenoid itself is always mounted on the starter. In addition to making contact for the starter, it also pulls the starter drive clutch gear into mesh with the flywheel. A single control terminal is used on the solenoid itself. The relay is usually found mounted to the inner fender panel or on the firewall.

SOLENOIDS WITH BUILT-IN RELAYS

These units are always mounted on the starter and are connected, through linkage, to the starter drive clutch. The relay portion is built into and integral with the front end of the solenoid assembly.

NEUTRAL SAFETY SWITCHES

The purpose of the neutral safety switch is to prevent the starter from cranking the engine except when the transmission is in neutral or park.

On some vehicles, the neutral safety switch is located on the transmission. It serves to ground the solenoid or magnetic switch, whichever is used.

On other vehicles, the neutral safety switch is located on the steering column, where it contacts the shift mechanism within the steering column or on the shift linkage when a console is used.

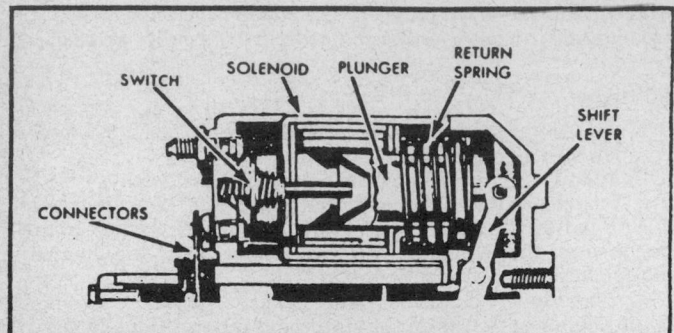

Sectional view of the starter solenoid mounted on a starter motor

Some manual transmission models have a clutch linkage safety switch to prevent starter operation unless the clutch pedal is depressed.

On most vehicles, the neutral safety switch and the backup light switch are combined into a single switch mechanism.

Troubleshooting Neutral Safety Switches Quick Test

If the starter fails to function and the neutral safety switch is to be checked, a jumper can be placed across its terminals. If the starter then functions, the safety switch is defective.

In the case of neutral safety switches with 1 wire, the wire must be grounded for testing purposes. If the starter works with the wire grounded, the switch is defective.

NEUTRAL SAFETY SWITCH/BACK-UP LIGHT SWITCH

When the neutral safety switch is built in combination with the back-up light switch, the quickest way to determine which terminals are for the back-up lights is to take a test lamp/jumper wire and cross from a hot wire to a neutral wire. The wires which light the back-up lamps should be ignored when testing the neutral safety switch. Once the back-up light wires have been located, jump the other pair of wires to test the neutral safety switch. If the starter functions only when the jumper is placed across both wires, the neutral safety switch is defective or requires adjustment.

STARTING SYSTEMS

Starter Motor Testing

The starter circuit should be divided and tested in 4 separate phases:

1. Cranking voltage check
2. Amperage draw
3. Voltage drop on grounded side
4. Voltage drop on battery side

NOTE: The battery must be in good condition for this test to have significance. To accurately check battery condition, use equipment designed to measure its capacity under a load. Instructions accompanying the equipment should be followed.

CRANKING VOLTAGE

Connect voltmeter leads to prods tapped into the battery posts

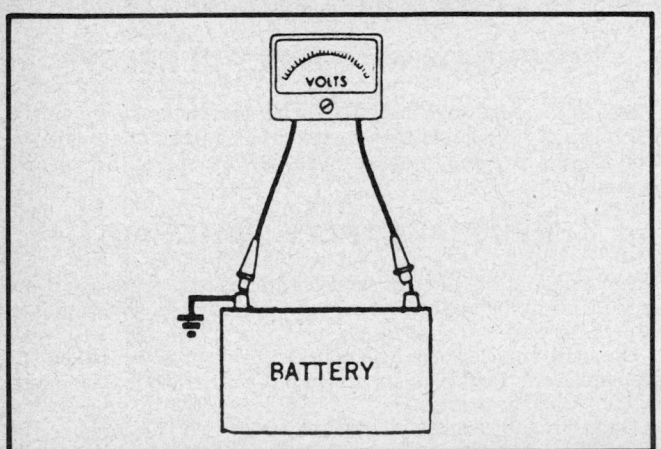

Voltmeter connected to battery for cranking voltage test

(observe polarity and reverse meter leads if necessary). Remove the high tension wire from the distributor cap and ground it to prevent engine starting. With electronic ignition, disconnect the control box harness from the distributor. Turn the key to the start position. Observe both voltmeter reading and cranking speed. The cranking speed should be even and at a satisfactory rate of speed, with a voltmeter reading of at least 9.6 volts for 12 volt systems.

AMPERAGE DRAW

The amount of current the starter motor draws is usually (but not always) associated with the mechanical problems involved in cranking the engine. (Mechanical trouble in the engine, frozen or worn starter parts, misaligned starter or starter components, etc.) Because starter motor amperage draw is directly influenced by anything restricting the free turning of the engine or starter, it is important that the engine and all components be at operating temperatures.

To measure starter current draw, remove the high tension wire from the center of the distributor cap and ground it. With electronic ignition, disconnect the control box harness from the distributor. A very simple and inexpensive starter current indicator is available. This indicator is an induction type gauge and shows, without disconnecting any wires, starter current draw.

Place the yoke of the meter directly over the insulated starter supply cable (cable must be straight for a minimum of 2 in.). Close the starter switch for about 20 seconds, watch the meter dial and record the average reading. If the indicator swings in the wrong direction, reverse the position of the meter.

The cranking amperage draw can vary from 150–400 amperes, depending on the engine size, engine compression and starter type.

NOTE: When starter specifications are not available, average starter draw amperage can be derived from testing a like starter unit, known to be operating satisfactorily.

More accurate equipment is available from many manufac-

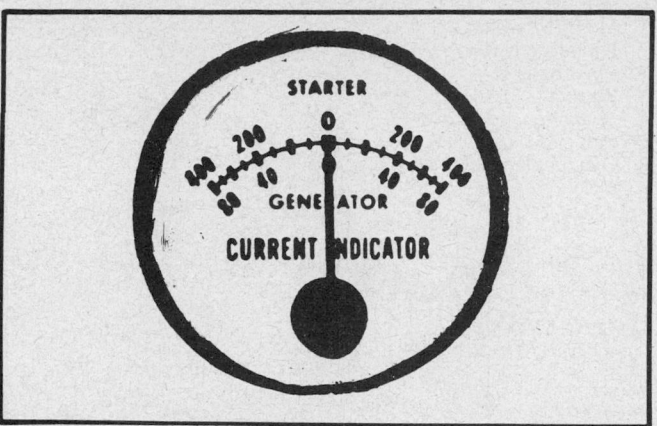

Starter current indicator

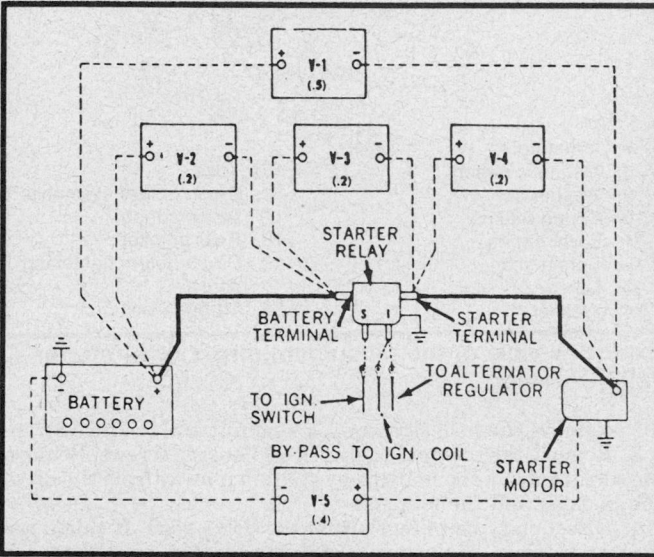

Starter cable resistance tests

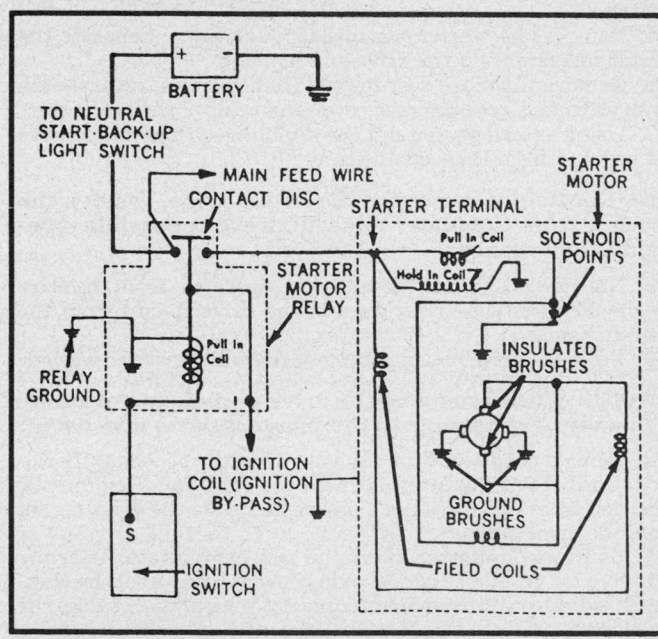

Positive engagement starter circuits

turers. This equipment consists of a combination voltmeter, ammeter and carbon pile rheostat. When using this equipment, follow the equipment manufacturer's procedures and recommendations.

High amperage and lazy performance would suggest an excessively tight engine, friction in the starter or starter drive, grounded starter field or armature.

Normal amperage and lazy performance suggest high resistance or possibly poor connections somewhere in the starter circuit.

Low amperage and lazy or no performance suggest battery condition poor, bad cables or connections along the line.

VOLTAGE DROP ON GROUNDED SIDE

With a voltmeter on the 3 volt scale and without disconnecting any wires, connect negative test lead of the voltmeter to a prod secured in the grounded battery post. The positive test lead is connected to a cleaned, bare metal portion of the starter motor housing. Close the starter switch and note the voltmeter reading. If the reading is the same as battery reading, the ground circuit is open somewhere between the battery and the starter. In many cases, the reading will be very small. The reading shown will indicate voltage drop (loss) between battery ground post and starter housing. The drop should not exceed 0.2 volts. If the voltage drop is above the specified amount, the next step is to isolate and correct the cause. It can be a bad cable or connection anywhere in the battery-to-starter ground circuit. A check of this type should progress along the various points of possible trouble between the battery ground post and the starter motor housing until the trouble spot has been located.

VOLTAGE DROP ON BATTERY SIDE

Bad starter cranking may result from poor connections or faulty components of the battery or hot phase of the starter motor circuit. To check this phase of the circuit, without disconnecting any wires, connect a lead of a voltmeter to a prod secured in the hot post of the battery and the other voltmeter lead to the field terminal of the starting motor. The meter should be set to the 16–20 volt scale. Before closing the starter switch, the voltmeter reading will be that of the battery. After closing the starter switch, change the selector on the voltmeter to the 3 volt scale. With a jumper wire between the relay battery terminal and the relay starter switch terminal, crank the engine. If the starting motor cranks the engine, the relay (solenoid) is operating.

While the engine is being cranked, watch the voltmeter. It should not register more than 0.5 volts. If more than this, check each part of the circuit for voltage drop to isolate the trouble, (high resistance).

Without disturbing the voltmeter-to-battery hook-up, move the free voltmeter lead to the battery terminal of the relay (solenoid) and crank the engine. The voltmeter should show no more than 0.1 volts.

If this reading is correct, move the same voltmeter lead to the starting motor terminal of the relay (solenoid). While the engine is being cranked, the voltmeter should show no more than 0.3 volts. If it does, the trouble lies in the relay.

If the reading is correct, the trouble is in the cable or connections between the relay and the starting motor.

Diagnosis
STARTER WON'T CRANK ENGINE

1. Dead battery.
2. Open starter circuit, such as:
   a. Broken or loose battery cables.
   b. Inoperative starter motor solenoid.

c. Broken or loose wire from starter switch to solenoid.
d. Poor solenoid or starter ground.
e. Bad starter switch.

3. Defective starter internal circuit, such as:
a. Dirty or burnt commutator.
b. Stuck, worn or broken brushes.
c. Open or shorted armature.
d. Open or grounded fields.

4. Starter motor mechanical faults, such as:
a. Jammed armature end bearings.
b. Bad bearing, allowing armature to rub fields.
c. Bent shaft.
d. Broken starter housing.
e. Bad starter worm or drive mechanism.
f. Bad starter drive or flywheel driven gear.

5. Engine hard or impossible to crank such as:
a. Hydrostatic lock caused by water or other liquid in combustion chamber.
b. Crankshaft seizing in bearings.
c. Piston or ring seizing.
d. Bent or broken connecting rod.
e. Seizing of connecting rod bearing.
f. Flywheel jammed or broken.

STARTER SPINS FREE, WON'T ENGAGE

Sticking or broken drive mechanism.

Chrysler Corporation Import Starter System
DIRECT DRIVE TYPE

Disassembly and Assembly

MITSUBISHI
1986

1. Position the assembly in the soft jawed vise. Disconnect the field coil wire from the solenoid terminal.
2. Remove the solenoid-to-starter screws and the solenoid.
3. Remove the through bolts and the commutator end frame cover. Remove both brushes and the brush plate. Slide the field frame from the armature.
4. Remove the shift lever pivot bolt, the rubber gasket and plate.
5. Press the stop collar from the snapring and remove the snapring, stop collar and clutch.
6. Brushes that are worn less than ½ the length of new brushes or oil soaked should be replaced; new brushes are $^{11}/_{16}$ in. long.

To Assemble:

7. Do not immerse the starter clutch unit in cleaning solvent; lubricant will be washed from inside the clutch.
8. Place the drive unit on the armature shaft and while holding the armature, rotate the pinion. The drive pinion should rotate smoothly in 1 direction only. The pinion may not rotate easily but as long as it rotates smoothly it is in good condition. If the clutch unit does not function properly or if the pinion is worn, chipped or burred replace the unit.
9. To assemble, lubricate the bushings/splines and reverse the disassembly procedures.
10. Install the clutch, stop collar, lock ring and shaft fork on the armature.
11. Install the armature assembly and shift fork in the drive end housing.
12. To complete the installation, reverse the removal procedures.

FORD
1987-90

1. Position the starter in a soft jawed vice.

1. Magnetic switch tightening screw
2. Front bracket
3. Washer
4. Snapring
5. Stopring
6. Overrunning clutch and pinion
7. Armature
8. Magnetic switch
9. Washer set
10. Spring retainer
11. Lever spring
12. Spring seat
13. Lever
14. Washer
15. Yoke
16. Brush holder assembly
17. Brush spring
18. Rear bracket
19. Brush holder tightening screw
20. Through bolt

Exploded view of the Mitsubishi direct drive starter—1986 Chrysler

2. Remove the field strap-to-solenoid nut and the field strap.
3. Remove the solenoid-to-drive end housing screws. Remove the solenoid from the housing by guiding it away from the drive end housing and the plunger.
4. Disconnect the plunger from the drive yoke. If shims are present between the solenoid and the starter, save them for reinstallation; the shims determine the starter pinion depth clearance.
5. Remove the starter housing through bolts. Separate the starter housing from the drive end housing.
6. Remove the rear cover-to-field frame screws, separate the strap grommet from the rear cover and remove the rear cover.
7. Using a small pry bar, lift the retaining springs and remove the brushes from their channels.

NOTE: Before removing the brush plate, remove the brushes from the plate; this will prevent possible damage to the brushes.

8. Note the position of the yoke and separate it from the drive pinion. Remove the armature and the drive pinion from the drive housing.
9. From the drive housing, remove the yoke, seal and washer.

NOTE: When removing the drive pinion, do not clamp it in a vise, for damage to the internal parts may occur.

10. Using a deep socket or equivalent, drive the armature collar towards the armature to expose the snapring. Remove the snapring from the armature's groove and slide the drive pinion from the armature.
11. Using an ohmmeter, check the each commutator-to-armature core for grounds; there should be no movement of the ohmmeter indicator. If the ohmmeter indicates a ground, replace the armature.
12. Inspect the commutator burn spots, scored surface and/or

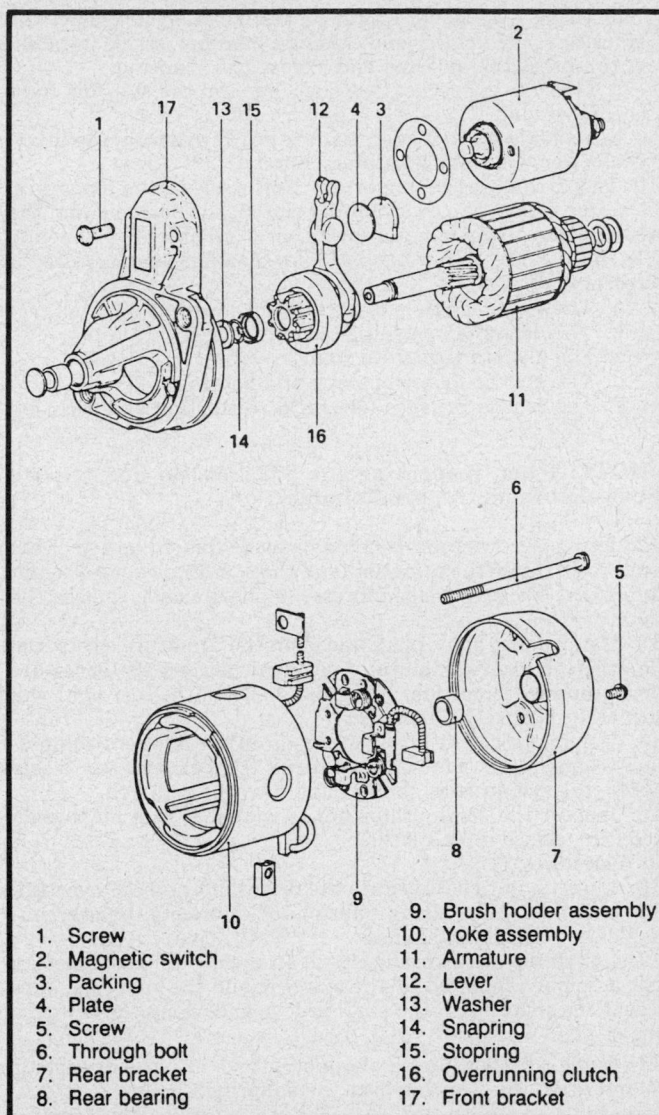

1. Screw
2. Magnetic switch
3. Packing
4. Plate
5. Screw
6. Through bolt
7. Rear bracket
8. Rear bearing
9. Brush holder assembly
10. Yoke assembly
11. Armature
12. Lever
13. Washer
14. Snapring
15. Stopring
16. Overrunning clutch
17. Front bracket

Exploded view of the Ford direct drive starter—1987-90 Chrysler

dirt. Using a set of V-blocks and a dial indicator, check the commutator runout. If the runout is greater than 0.002 in., refinish the commutator or replace the armature.

13. Using a micrometer, check the commutator's outer diameter; if it is less than 1.220 in., replace the armature.

NOTE: Never use emery cloth to clean the commutator face.

14. Inspect the depth of the insulating material between the commutator segments; it should be greater than 0.008 in. If necessary to undercut the insulating material, use a broken hacksaw blade and scrap the material to a depth of 0.020-0.031 in.

15. If the armature core shows signs of scuffing, the bushings are probably worn and need replacement.

16. Inspect the field coil for corrosion, insulation burnt/bare spots and/or deterioration; if necessary, replace the field coil housing assembly.

17. Using an ohmmeter, check the field strap connector-to-brushes for continuity; if there is no continuity, replace the field coil housing assembly.

18. Using an ohmmeter, check for continuity between the field strap connector and the field coil housing; if there is continuity, replace the field coil housing assembly. When performing this test, be certain the brushes and wires are not touching the housing.

19. Measure the brush lengths for wear, if they are near or beyond 0.453 in., replace the brushes.

20. To inspect the drive pinion, perform the following procedures:

a. Inspect the drive pinion teeth for excessive wear or milling. If either condition exists, the drive pinion and flywheel (manual) or flexplate (automatic) must be replaced.

b. To check the one-way clutch, try to turn the drive pinion in both directions; it should turn freely one-way and lock up the other way.

To Assemble:

21. Lubricate the armature splines with Lubriplate® 777 or equivalent. Install the drive pinion and the locking collar on the armature. Install the snapring and pull the collar over the snapring to secure it.

22. Using Lubriplate® 777 or equivalent, lubricate the shift fork and install it into the drive end housing. Engage the armature assembly into the drive end housing and couple the shift fork with the drive pinion.

23. Position the drive end housing into a soft jawed vise (nose down) and install the plug and seal into the housing recess.

24. Lower the field coil housing over the armature and seat it onto the drive end housing; position the housing so the field strap is on the solenoid side.

25. Install the washers onto the armature. Load the brushes into the brush plate holders. With the brushes pull all the way back in the holders, position the brush springs on the brush sides.

26. Install the brush plate over the commutator. Push the brushes toward the commutator until the springs snap onto the brush ends. Make sure the brush wires do not contact any metal parts.

27. Seat the field strap grommet and the rear cover. Install the through bolts and torque them to 55-75 ft. lbs. Install the solenoid and shims, if equipped.

28. To check the pinion depth, perform the following procedures:

a. If the field strap was connected to the solenoid terminal, disconnect it.

b. Using a 12 volt battery, attach the negative (−) terminal to the solenoid's M-terminal and the positive (+) terminal to the solenoid's S-terminal; this will energize the solenoid.

NOTE: When energizing the solenoid, do not engage it for more than 20 seconds. Between each engagement, allow it to cool for at least 3 minutes.

c. Using a feeler gauge and the solenoid energized, check the drive pinion-to-collar gap; it should be 0.020-0.080 in. If necessary, add or subtract shims between the solenoid and drive end housing until the desired depth is achieved.

REDUCTION DRIVE TYPE

Disassembly and Assembly
MITSUBISHI

NOTE: Do not place the stator frame in a vise or strike it with a hammer for damage to the permanent magnets could occur.

1. Disconnect the coil wire from the solenoid.
2. Remove the solenoid-to-front end frame screws and the solenoid.
3. Loosen, do not remove the commutator shield-to-brush holder screws.

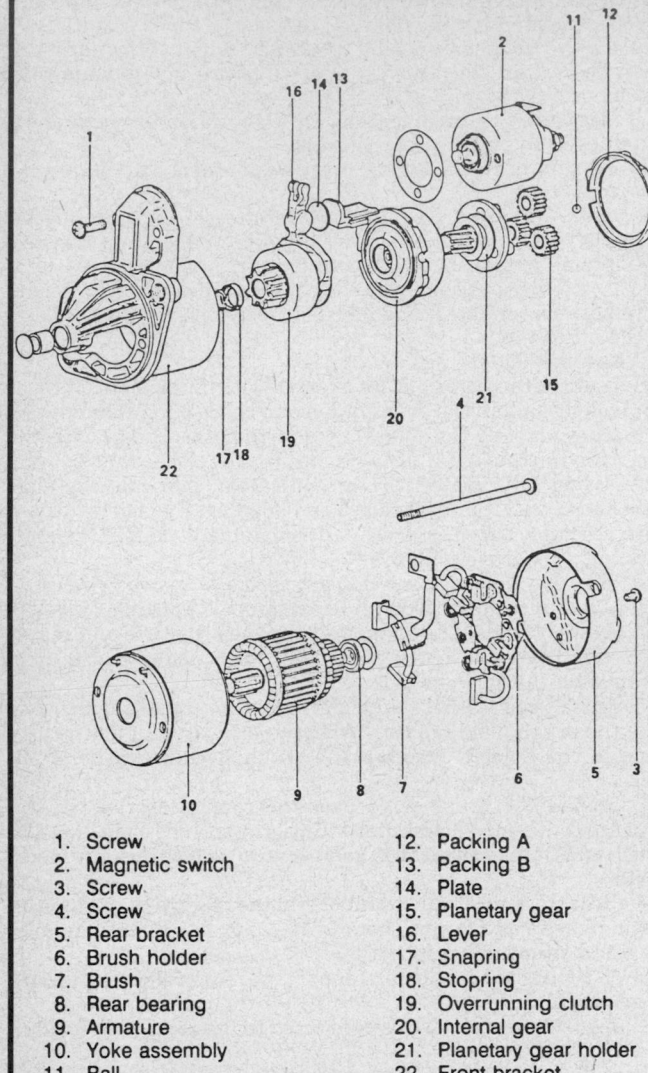

1.	Screw	12.	Packing A
2.	Magnetic switch	13.	Packing B
3.	Screw	14.	Plate
4.	Screw	15.	Planetary gear
5.	Rear bracket	16.	Lever
6.	Brush holder	17.	Snapring
7.	Brush	18.	Stopring
8.	Rear bearing	19.	Overrunning clutch
9.	Armature	20.	Internal gear
10.	Yoke assembly	21.	Planetary gear holder
11.	Ball	22.	Front bracket

Exploded view of the Mitsubishi reduction drive starter—Chrysler

4. Remove the through bolts, the rubber retainer (under solenoid) and the coin washer.

NOTE: When removing the output shaft assembly, do not loose the armature shaft ball.

5. Remove the stator frame, the commutator shield and output shaft assembly as a unit. Separate the clutch fork from the output shaft assembly.

6. From the stator frame, pull the output shaft assembly forward, then, push the armature and commutator shield to the rearward.

7. Remove the commutator shield-to-brush holder plate screws and the shield; do not remove the brush holder assembly.

8. Using a 22mm socket, slide it up against the commutator, slide the brush holder assembly onto the socket and position the socket/brush holder assembly aside.

9. To disassemble the output shaft assembly, perform the following procedures:

   a. Remove the rubber packing ring and the gears.

   b. Using a 17mm socket, position it into the armature end of the driveshaft and position the assembly in the vertical position, resting on the socket.

c. Using a 12 point 14mm socket, position it against the stopring (on the clutch end). Using a hammer, strike the socket to unseat the stopring and expose the snapring.

d. Remove the socket, the snapring and the stopring from the driveshaft.

e. Using fine sandpaper, remove any burrs from the driveshaft. Remove the overruning clutch.

10. Using compressed air or dry cloths, clean the armature, the stator frame, the overrunning clutch, the solenoid and the brush holder. Using mineral spirits, clean all other components.

11. Inspect the following parts for damage and replace, if necessary:

   a. The stator frame and permanent magnets

   b. The driveshaft bushing (armature side)

   c. The planetary gear set and driveshaft

   d. The starter motor bushing and bearing

   e. The carbon brushes for cracks, distortion and wear below 0.354 in.

NOTE: When inspecting the brushes, do not remove the socket from the brush holder.

12. Using a growler and a hacksaw blade (placed on top of the armature), rotate the armature and check it for a shorted condition. If the hacksaw blade vibrates, a short exists; replace the armature.

13. Using a test light, place a lead on the armature's core and the other on each commutator segment, inspect the armature for a grounded condition. If a ground exists, the test light will turn **ON**; replace the armature.

14. Using a test light, place the leads on the adjacent commutator segments. If the test light turns **ON** between any 2 segments, the armature is shorted and must be replaced.

15. Inspect the commutator out-of-round, if it is more than 0.001 in., reface it on a lathe.

To Assemble:

16. Using motor oil, lubricate the driveshaft and the overruning clutch bushing. Using Lubriplate®, lubricate the overrunning clutch spiral cut splines.

17. Install the overrunning clutch on the driveshaft/planetary gear assembly, followed by the stopring and the snapring; sure to seat the snapring in the shaft groove and crimp the it with a pair of pliers.

18. Using a battery terminal puller, attach it to the driveshaft tip and press the stopring over the snapring.

NOTE: When installing the stopring, be careful not to scratch the driveshaft.

19. Install the clutch fork, with the assembled planetary gear set, lubricated with lithium grease, into the front end housing; make sure the locating lugs are properly seated in the front end housing.

20. Install the coin washer and the rubber fork retainer.

21. Install the rubber backing ring by placing the largest rubber lug at the top.

22. Install the brush holder onto the armature's commutator; make sure the brushes and brush holders are seated in the holder. Inspect the flex washer and install the commutator shield onto the armature. Install the brush holder screws but do not tighten them.

23. Install the armature assembly into the stator frame and seat the wire grommet into the frame.

24. Be sure the armature spline gear is seated in the planetary gear seat with the armature shaft ball in place. Seat the armature shaft in the shaft bushing bore; rotate the stator frame to align the tabs on the drive housing frame.

25. Install the through bolts and torque to 28 inch lbs. Torque the brush holder screws to 18 inch lbs.

26. To complete the assembly, reverse the disassembly procedures.

Isuzu Starting System

NON-REDUCTION TYPE

Disassembly and Assembly

1. Position the starter in a soft jawed vise. Disconnect the field coil wire from the solenoid terminal.

2. Remove the solenoid mounting screws and work the solenoid from the shift fork. Remove the bearing cover, the armature shaft lock, the washer, the spring and the seal.

3. Remove the commutator end frame cover through bolts, the cover, the brushes and the brush plate.

4. Slide the field frame from over the armature. Remove the shift lever pivot bolt, the rubber gasket and the metal plate.

5. Remove the armature assembly and the shift lever from the drive end housing. Press the stop collar from the snapring, then remove the snapring, the stop collar and the clutch assembly.

6. If the brushes are worn more than ½ the length of new brushes or are oil-soaked, should be replaced; the new brushes are 0.630 in. long.

7. Do not immerse the starter clutch unit in cleaning solvent as the solvent will wash the lubricant from the clutch. Place the drive unit on the armature shaft, then, while holding the armature, rotate the pinion.

NOTE: The drive pinion should rotate smoothly in one direction only. The pinion may not rotate easily but as long as it rotates smoothly it is in good condition. If the clutch unit does not function properly or if the pinion is worn, chipped or burred, replace the unit.

To Assemble:

8. Lubricate the armature shaft and splines with lubricant.

9. Install the clutch, the stop collar, the lock ring and the shift fork onto the armature.

10. Install the armature assembly into the drive end housing.

11. Install the field frame housing over the armature and onto the drive end housing.

12. Position the brushes into the brush holder and position the brush holder over the armature's commutator.

13. Install the commutator end housing and the through bolts.

14. Install the cap end gasket, the armature brake spring, the armature plate and the commutator end cap.

REDUCTION GEAR TYPE

Disassembly and Assembly

1. Position the starter in a soft jawed vise. Remove the nut and disconnect the motor wire from the magnetic switch terminal.

2. Remove the through bolts and pull the field frame (with the armature) from the magnetic switch assembly.

3. Remove the starter housing to magnetic switch assembly bolts and separate the housing from the assembly. Remove the pinion gear, the pinion retainer/bearings and the clutch assembly.

4. Using a magnetic finger, remove the spring and the steel ball from the hole in the clutch assembly shaft. Remove the field frame end cover.

5. Using a small pry bar, separate the brush springs, then remove the brushes from the brush holder and pull the brush holder from the field frame.

6. Remove the armature from the field frame. Using an ohmmeter, make sure there is no continuity between the commutator and the armature coil core. If there is continuity, replace the armature.

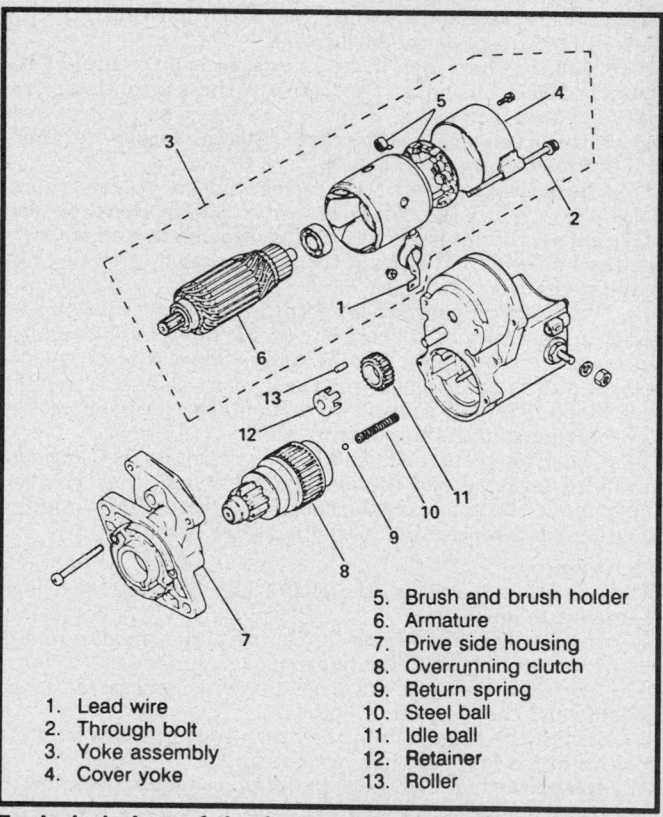

1. Magnetic switch lead
2. Solenoid switch assembly
3. Dust cover and snapring
4. Rear cover assembly
5. Brush holder assembly
6. Field coil assembly
7. Armature assembly with shift lever
8. Pinion stop clip
9. Pinion assembly

Exploded view of the Isuzu non-reduction drive starter – 2.0L engine

1. Lead wire
2. Through bolt
3. Yoke assembly
4. Cover yoke
5. Brush and brush holder
6. Armature
7. Drive side housing
8. Overrunning clutch
9. Return spring
10. Steel ball
11. Idle ball
12. Retainer
13. Roller

Exploded view of the Isuzu reduction drive starter – 2.3L engine

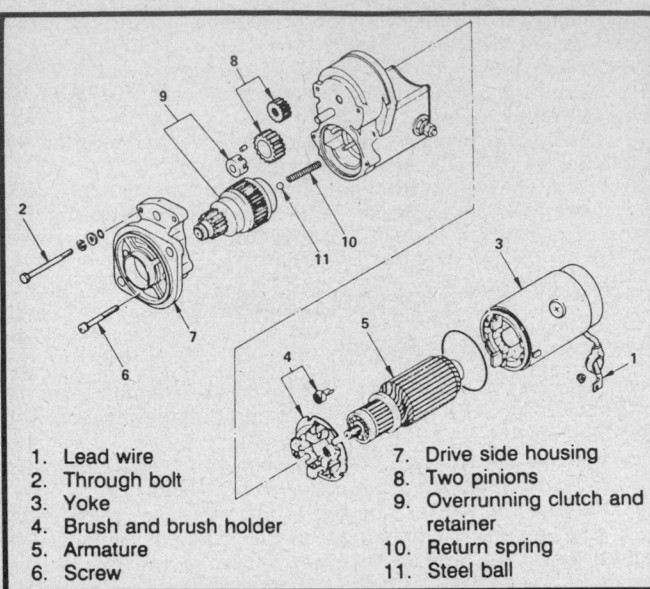

1. Lead wire
2. Through bolt
3. Yoke
4. Brush and brush holder
5. Armature
6. Screw
7. Drive side housing
8. Two pinions
9. Overrunning clutch and retainer
10. Return spring
11. Steel ball

Exploded view of the Isuzu reduction drive starter— 2.2L diesel engine

7. Using an ohmmeter, check for continuity between the commutator segments. If there is no continuity between any of the segments, replace the armature.

8. If the commutator is dirty, burnt or the runout exceeds 0.002 in., use a lathe to reface the surface; do not machine the diameter to less than 1.140 in. diameter.

9. Using an ohmmeter, make sure there is continuity between the lead wire and the brush lead of the field coil. If there is no continuity, replace the field frame.

10. Using an ohmmeter, make sure there is no continuity between the field coil and the field frame. If there is continuity, replace the field frame.

11. If the brush length is less than 0.394 in., replace the brush and dress with emery cloth.

12. Check the gear teeth for wear or damage, if damaged, replace them. Turn the clutch assembly pinion clockwise and make sure it rotates freely, try to turn the pinion counterclockwise and make sure it locks. If the pinion does not respond correctly, replace it.

13. While applying inward force on the bearings, turn each by hand; if resistance or sticking is noticed, replace the bearings. To replace the bearings, use the tool 09286–46011 or equivalent, to pull the bearing(s) from the armature shaft. Using the tool 09285–76010 or equivalent, and an arbor press, press the new bearing(s) onto the armature shaft.

14. Using an ohmmeter, check for continuity between the grounded terminal and the insulated terminal, then between the grounded terminal and the housing. If there is no continuity in either case, replace the magnetic switch assembly.

To Assemble:

15. Lubricate the gears, the shafts and bearings with high temperature grease.

16. Install the over-running clutch, the pinion and the retainers with the rollers into the housing.

17. Install the spring to the magnetic switch and assembly the housing and the magnetic switch.

18. Install the brushes into the brush holder; make sure the positive brush leads are not grounded.

19. Install the rear end frame to the yoke, engage the tab with the wire grommet and install the cover.

20. Install the yoke to the magnetic switch, engage the tab on the yoke with the magnetic switch notch.

21. To complete the installation, reverse the removal procedures.

Mazda Starting System

NON-REDUCTION TYPE

Disassembly and Assembly

1. Remove the starter from the engine.
2. Disconnect the field strap from the solenoid.
3. Remove the screws attaching the solenoid to the drive end housing. Disengage the solenoid plunger hook from the shift fork and remove the solenoid.
4. Remove the shift fork pivot bolt, nut and lockwasher.
5. Remove the through bolts and separate the drive end housing from the starter frame. At the same time, disengage the shift fork from the drive assembly.
6. Remove the brush end bearing cover-to-brush end cover screws.
7. Remove the C-washer, washer and spring from the brush end of the armature shaft.
8. Pull the brush end cover from the starter frame.
9. Slide the armature from the starter frame and brushes.
10. Slide the drive stop-ring retainer toward the armature and remove the stop-ring. Slide the retainer and drive assembly off the armature shaft.
11. Remove the field brushes from the brush holder and separate the brush holder from the starter frame.

To Assemble:

12. Position the drive assembly on the armature shaft.
13. Position the drive stop-ring retainer on the armature shaft and install the drive stop-ring. Slide the stop-ring retainer over the stop-ring to secure the stop-ring on the shaft.
14. Position the armature in the starter frame. Install the

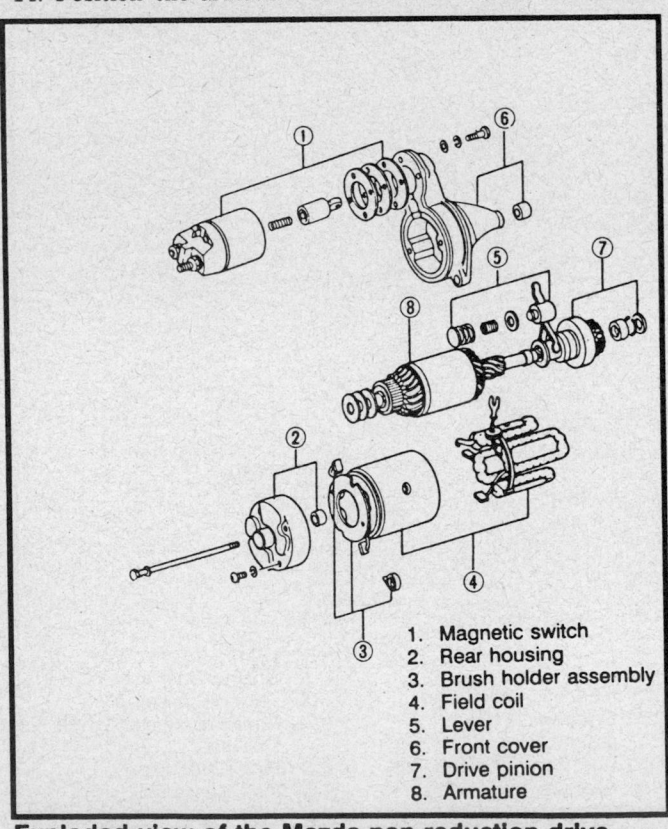

1. Magnetic switch
2. Rear housing
3. Brush holder assembly
4. Field coil
5. Lever
6. Front cover
7. Drive pinion
8. Armature

Exploded view of the Mazda non-reduction drive starter

brush holder on the armature and starter frame. Install the brushes in the brush holder.

15. Install the drive end housing on the armature shaft and starter housing. Engage the shift fork with the starter drive assembly as the drive end housing is moved toward the starter frame.

16. Install the brush end cover on the starter frame making sure that the rear tabs of the brush holder are aligned with the through-bolt holes.

17. Install the through-bolts.

18. Install the rubber washer, spring, washer and C-washer on the armature shaft at the brush end. Install the brush end bearing cover on the brush end cover and install the attaching screws. If the brush end cover is not properly positioned, the bearing cover screws cannot be installed.

19. Align the shift fork with the pivot bolt hole and install the pivot bolt, lockwasher and nut. Tighten the nut securely.

20. Position the solenoid on the drive end housing. Be sure that the solenoid plunger hook is engaged with the shift fork.

21. Install both solenoid retaining screws and washers.

22. Apply 12 volts to the solenoid **S** terminal (ground the **M** terminal) and check the clearance between the starter drive and the stop-ring retainer. The clearance should be 0.080–0.200 in. If not, the solenoid plunger is not properly adjusted. The clearance can be adjusted by inserting an adjusting shim between the solenoid body and drive end housing.

23. Install the field strap and tighten the nut.

24. Install the starter. Check the operation of the starter.

COAXIAL REDUCTION TYPE

Disassembly and Assembly

1. Position the starter in a soft jawed vise. Disconnect the field coil wire from the solenoid terminal.

2. Remove the solenoid mounting screws and work the solenoid from the shift fork. Remove the bearing cover, the armature shaft lock, the washer, the spring and the seal.

3. Remove the commutator end frame cover through bolts, the cover, the brushes and the brush plate.

4. Slide the field frame from over the armature. Remove the shift lever pivot bolt, the rubber gasket and the metal plate.

5. Remove the armature assembly and the shift lever from the drive end housing. Press the stop collar from the snapring, then remove the snapring, the stop collar and the clutch assembly.

6. If the brushes are worn more than ½ the length of new brushes or are oil-soaked, should be replaced; the new brushes are 0.630 in. long.

7. Do not immerse the starter clutch unit in cleaning solvent as the solvent will wash the lubricant from the clutch. Place the drive unit on the armature shaft, then, while holding the armature, rotate the pinion.

NOTE: The drive pinion should rotate smoothly in one direction only. The pinion may not rotate easily but as long as it rotates smoothly it is in good condition. If the clutch unit does not function properly or if the pinion is worn, chipped or burred, replace the unit.

To Assemble:

8. Lubricate the armature shaft and splines with lubricant.

9. Install the clutch, the stop collar, the lock ring and the shift fork onto the armature.

10. Install the armature assembly into the drive end housing.

11. Install the field frame housing over the armature and onto the drive end housing.

12. Position the brushes into the brush holder and position the brush holder over the armature's commutator.

13. Install the commutator end housing and the through bolts.

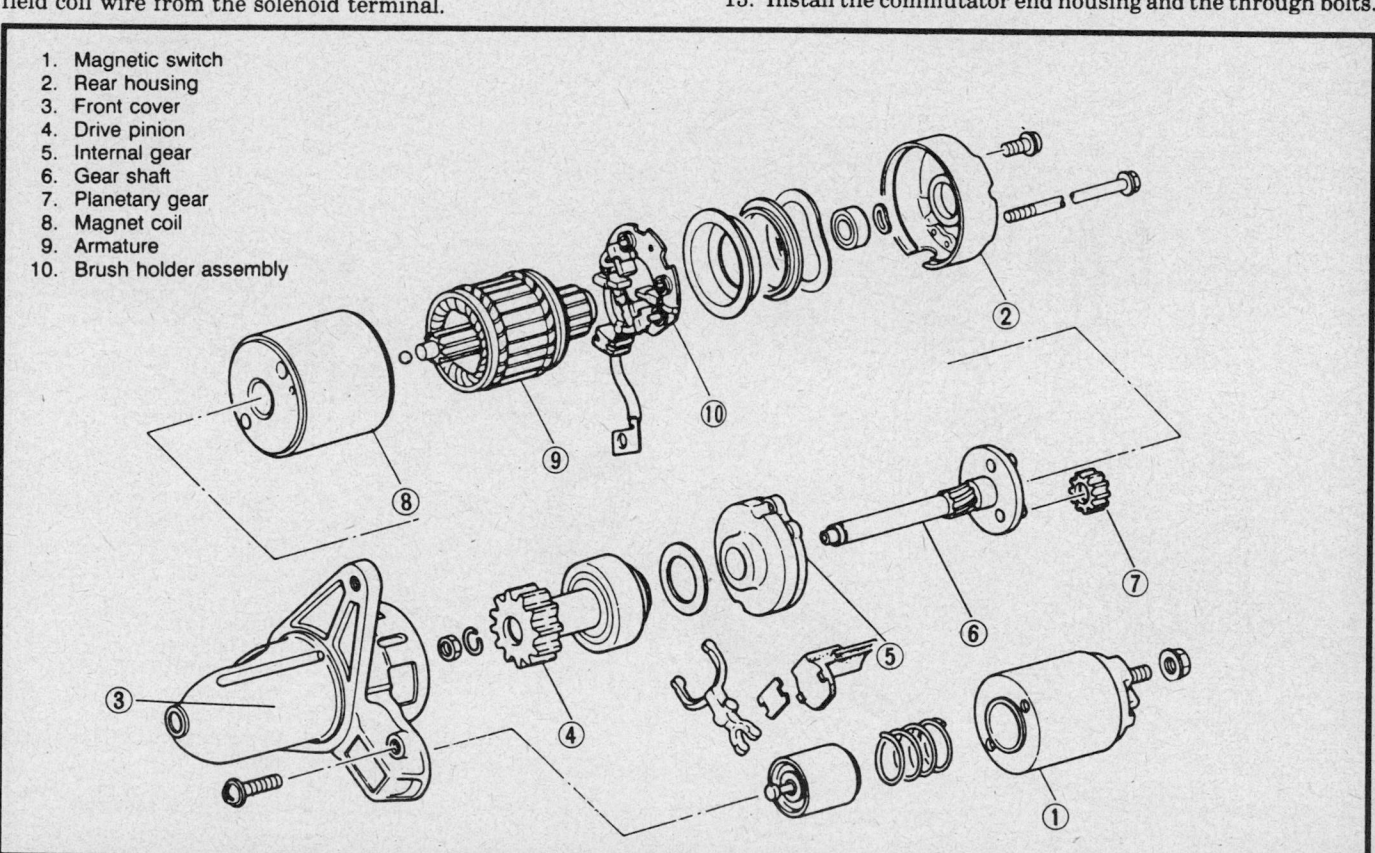

1. Magnetic switch
2. Rear housing
3. Front cover
4. Drive pinion
5. Internal gear
6. Gear shaft
7. Planetary gear
8. Magnet coil
9. Armature
10. Brush holder assembly

Exploded view of the Mazda coaxial reduction drive starter

14. Install the cap end gasket, the armature brake spring, the armature plate and the commutator end cap.

NON-COAXIAL REDUCTION TYPE

Disassembly and Assembly

1. Remove the starter from the vehicle. Position the unit in a soft jawed vise.

2. Remove the field connector nut, the solenoid switch screws and the solenoid.

3. If equipped with shims between the solenoid and the drive end housing, retain these for installation purposes.

4. Remove the starter through bolts and the brush holder bolts. Remove the commutator end frame from the armature and bearing assembly. Remove the field frame assembly and the armature from the center housing.

5. Pry back each brush spring so that each brush can be backed away from the armature about ¼ in. Release the spring to hold the brushes in the backed out position, then remove the armature from the field frame and brush holder.

6. Remove the shaft cover-to-center housing screws and the shaft cover. Remove the C-shaped washer and plate. Remove the center housing bolts, the center housing shim and thrust washers.

7. Remove the reduction gear, the spring holder and the lever springs.

8. To remove the drive pinion, perform the following procedures:

   a. Using a ⅝ in. socket, slide it over the shaft against the stopper.

   b. Using the socket as a driving tool, tap it with a hammer to move the stopper off the ring.

   c. Remove the stopper and the drive pinion.

9. Remove the pinion shaft and the lever assembly. Note the direction of the lever and the lever holders.

10. Clean all parts in the proper cleaning solution. Inspect all parts for wear and damage; replace or repair defective components as required. Inspect all bearings for wear, roughness or dryness; replace damaged bearings with new ones.

11. Inspect the armature commutator. If the commutator is rough, it should be refinished on a lathe; do not turn the commutator to less than 1.480 in. outside diameter.

12. With the brush holder assembly still attached to the field frame, test the field coils for open. Using a test lamp, place a test lead on the field coil connector and the other test lead on the positive (+) brush.

13. The test light should turn ON. If the test light fails to light, the field coil is open; the field coil must be replaced. Repeat the test on the other positive brush.

14. To test the field coil for ground, place a test light lead on the field coil connector and the other lead on the field frame; the test light should stay OFF. If the test light turns ON, the field coils are grounded to the field frame assembly; the field frame must be replaced.

To Assemble:

15. To replace the brushes, remove the positive brushes from the brush holder, the brush holder and the negative brush assembly from the field frame.

16. Cut the old brush leads off of their mountings as close to brush connection point as possible. Solder the new brushes as required. Careful installation of the positive side is necessary to

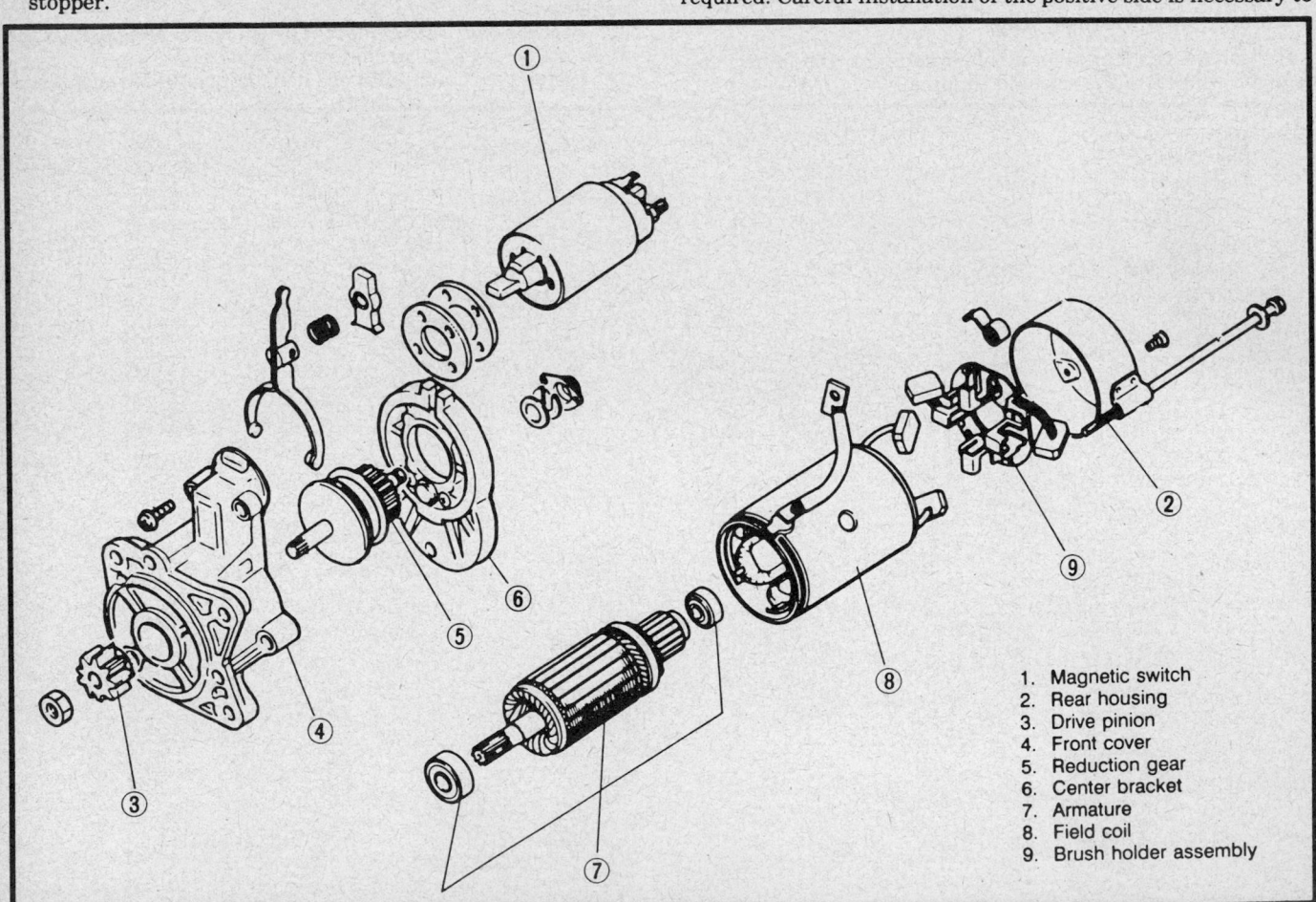

1. Magnetic switch
2. Rear housing
3. Drive pinion
4. Front cover
5. Reduction gear
6. Center bracket
7. Armature
8. Field coil
9. Brush holder assembly

Exploded view of the Mazda non-coxial reduction drive starter

prevent grounding of the brush connection point having no insulation.

17. Reinstall the positive and negative brushes in the brush holder assembly and position the assembly in the starter housing.

18. In order to replace the drive end bearing, it will be necessary to press the bearing out of the drive end housing using a press. Replace the armature commutator end bearing and the armature drive end bearing.

19. To assemble, reverse the disassembly procedures. Be sure to check all parts for wear and damage; repair or replace defective parts.

20. If either the drive end housing, pinion shaft, reduction gear, shim washers or center housing were replaced, it will be necessary to check the endplay for the pinion shaft. Install the plate and C-shaped washer onto the end of the pinion shaft.

21. With the drive end housing mounted in a soft jawed vise, measure the endplay. Insert feeler gauge between C-washer and cover plate, pry the pinion shaft in the axial direction to check the endplay; it should be 0.004–0.020 in.

22. If the endplay is not correct, remove the plate, C-shaped washer, center bracket and add or remove the shim thrust washers to adjust the endplay and recheck.

NOTE: Shim thrust washers are available in 2 thicknesses 0.010 in. and 0.020 in.

23. When the starter has been disassembled or the solenoid switch has been replaced, it is necessary to check the pinion position. Pinion position must be correct to prevent the top of the lever from rubbing on the clutch collar during cranking.

24. Connect the positive lead of a 12 volt battery to the "S" terminal on the switch and momentarily connect the other to the starter frame. This will shift the pinion into cranking position and will retain it until the battery is disconnected. Do not leave engaged more than 30 seconds at a time.

25. Using a dial indicator (with pinion engaged), push the pinion shaft back by hand and measure the amount of pinion shaft movement; the clearance should be 0.020–0.080 in.

26. If the amount does not fall within limits, adjust it by adding or removing the shims which are located between the switch and the front bracket; adding shims decreases the amount of the movement. Solenoid switch shims are available in 2 thicknesses 0.020 in. and 0.010 in.

Mitsubishi Starting System

DIRECT DRIVE TYPE

Disassembly and Assembly

1. Remove the wire connecting the starter solenoid to the starter.

2. Remove the starter solenoid-to-starter drive housing screws and the solenoid.

3. Remove both long through bolts from the rear of the starter and separate the armature yoke from the armature.

4. Carefully remove the armature and the starter drive engagement lever from the front bracket, noting the way they are positioned along with the attendant spring and spring retainer.

5. Loosen both screws and remove the rear bracket.

6. Tap the stopper ring at the end of the drive gear engagement shaft in towards the drive gear to expose the snapring. Remove the snapring.

7. Pull the stopper, drive gear and overrunning clutch from the end of the shaft.

8. Inspect the pinion and spline teeth for wear or damage. If the engagement teeth are damaged, visually check the flywheel ring gear through the starter hole to insure that it is not damaged. It will be necessary to turn the engine over by hand to completely inspect the ring gear.

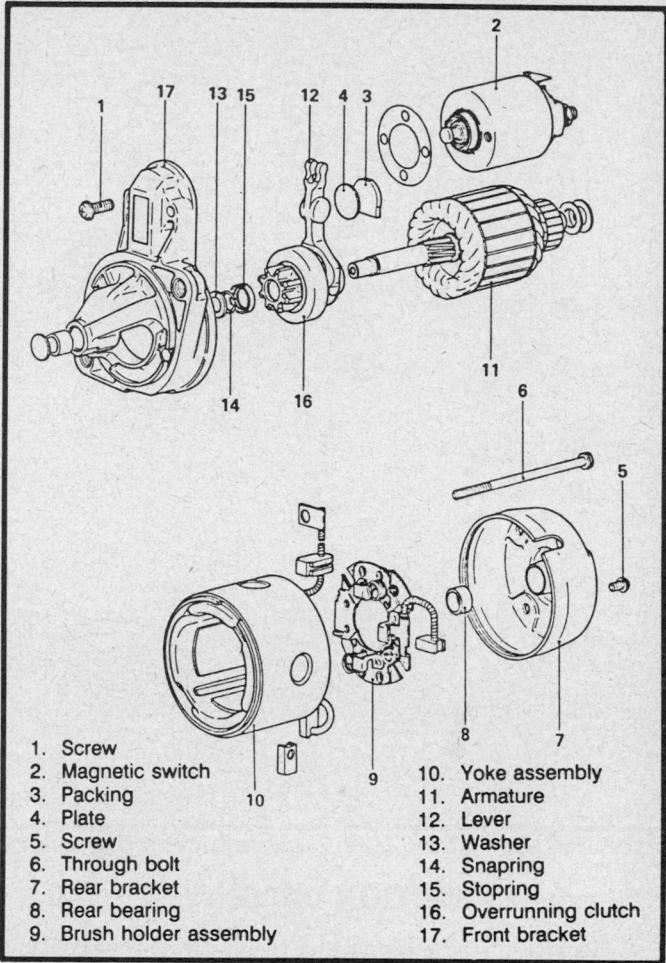

1. Screw	10. Yoke assembly
2. Magnetic switch	11. Armature
3. Packing	12. Lever
4. Plate	13. Washer
5. Screw	14. Snapring
6. Through bolt	15. Stopring
7. Rear bracket	16. Overrunning clutch
8. Rear bearing	17. Front bracket
9. Brush holder assembly	

Exploded view of the Mitsubishi direct drive starter

9. Check the brushes for wear. Their service limit length is 0.453 in. Replace if necessary.

To Assemble:

10. Install the spring retainer and spring on the armature shaft.

11. Install the overrunning clutch assembly on the armature shaft.

12. Fit the stopper ring with its open side facing out on the shaft.

13. Install a new snapring and, using a gear puller, pull the stopper ring into place over the snapring.

14. Fit the small washer on the front end of the armature shaft.

15. Fit the engagement lever into the overrunning clutch and refit the armature into the front housing.

16. Fit the engagement lever spring and spring retainer into place and slide the armature yoke over the armature. Position the yoke with the spring retainer cut-out space in line with the spring retainer.

NOTE: Make sure the brushes are seated on the commutator.

17. Replace the rear bracket and retainer screws.

18. Install the through bolts in the end of the yoke.

19. Refit the starter solenoid, fitting the plunger over the engagement lever. Install the screws and connect the wire running from the starter yoke to the starter solenoid.

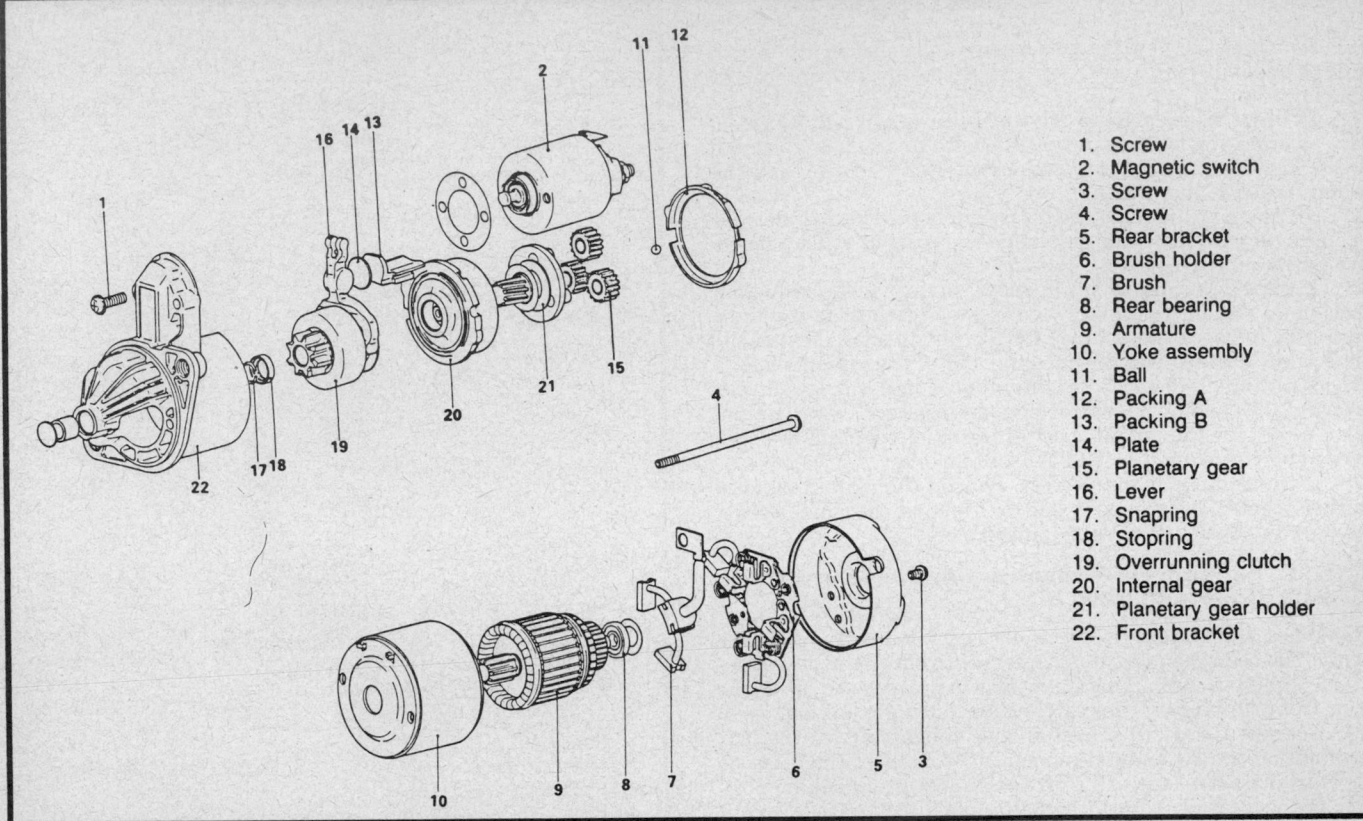

1. Screw
2. Magnetic switch
3. Screw
4. Screw
5. Rear bracket
6. Brush holder
7. Brush
8. Rear bearing
9. Armature
10. Yoke assembly
11. Ball
12. Packing A
13. Packing B
14. Plate
15. Planetary gear
16. Lever
17. Snapring
18. Stopring
19. Overrunning clutch
20. Internal gear
21. Planetary gear holder
22. Front bracket

Exploded view of the Mitsubishi reduction drive starter

REDUCTION DRIVE TYPE

1. Remove the wire connecting the starter solenoid to the starter.

2. Remove the solenoid screws, pull it out, unhook and disengage it from the engagement lever.

3. Remove the through bolts in the end of the starter and the bracket screws. Pull off the rear bracket.

NOTE: Since the conical spring washer is contained in the rear bracket, be sure to take it out.

4. Remove the yoke and brush holder assembly while pulling the brush upward.

5. Pull the armature assembly out of the mounting bracket.

6. In the side of the mounting bracket that the armature fits into, there is a small dust cap held by screws. Remove it and remove the snapring and washer under it.

7. Remove the remaining bolts in the mounting bracket and split the reduction case.

NOTE: Several washers will come out when the case is split. These adjust the endplay for the pinion shaft. Do not lose them.

8. Remove the reduction gear, lever and lever spring from the front bracket.

9. Using a brass drift or deep socket, knock the stopper ring on the end of the shaft in toward the pinion. Remove the snapring. Remove the stopper, pinion and pinion shaft assembly.

10. Remove the ball bearings at both ends of the armature.

NOTE: The ball bearings are pressed in the front bracket and are not replaceable. Replace them together with the bracket.

11. Inspect the pinion and spline teeth for wear or damage. If the engagement teeth are damaged, visually check the flywheel ring gear through the starter hole to insure that it is not damaged also. It will be necessary to turn the engine over by hand to completely inspect the ring gear.

12. Check the brushes for wear. Their service limit length is 0.453 in. Replace if necessary.

13. Assembly is the reverse of disassembly. Be sure to replace all adjusting and thrust washers. When replacing the rear bracket, fit the conical spring pinion washer with its convex side facing out. Make sure the brushes seat on the commutator.

Nissan Starting System

NON-REDUCTION GEAR TYPE

Disassembly and Assembly

MITSUBISHI

1. Position the assembly in the soft jawed vise. Disconnect the field coil wire from the solenoid terminal.

2. Remove the solenoid-to-starter screws and the solenoid from the shifting fork.

3. Remove the through bolts and the commutator end frame cover. Remove the 2 brushes and the brush plate. Slide the field frame from the armature.

4. Remove the shift lever pivot bolt, the rubber gasket and plate.

5. Remove the snapring, the clutch assembly and the drive end housing from the armature.

6. Press the stop collar from the snapring and remove the snapring, stop collar and clutch.

7. Brushes that are worn less than ½ the length of new

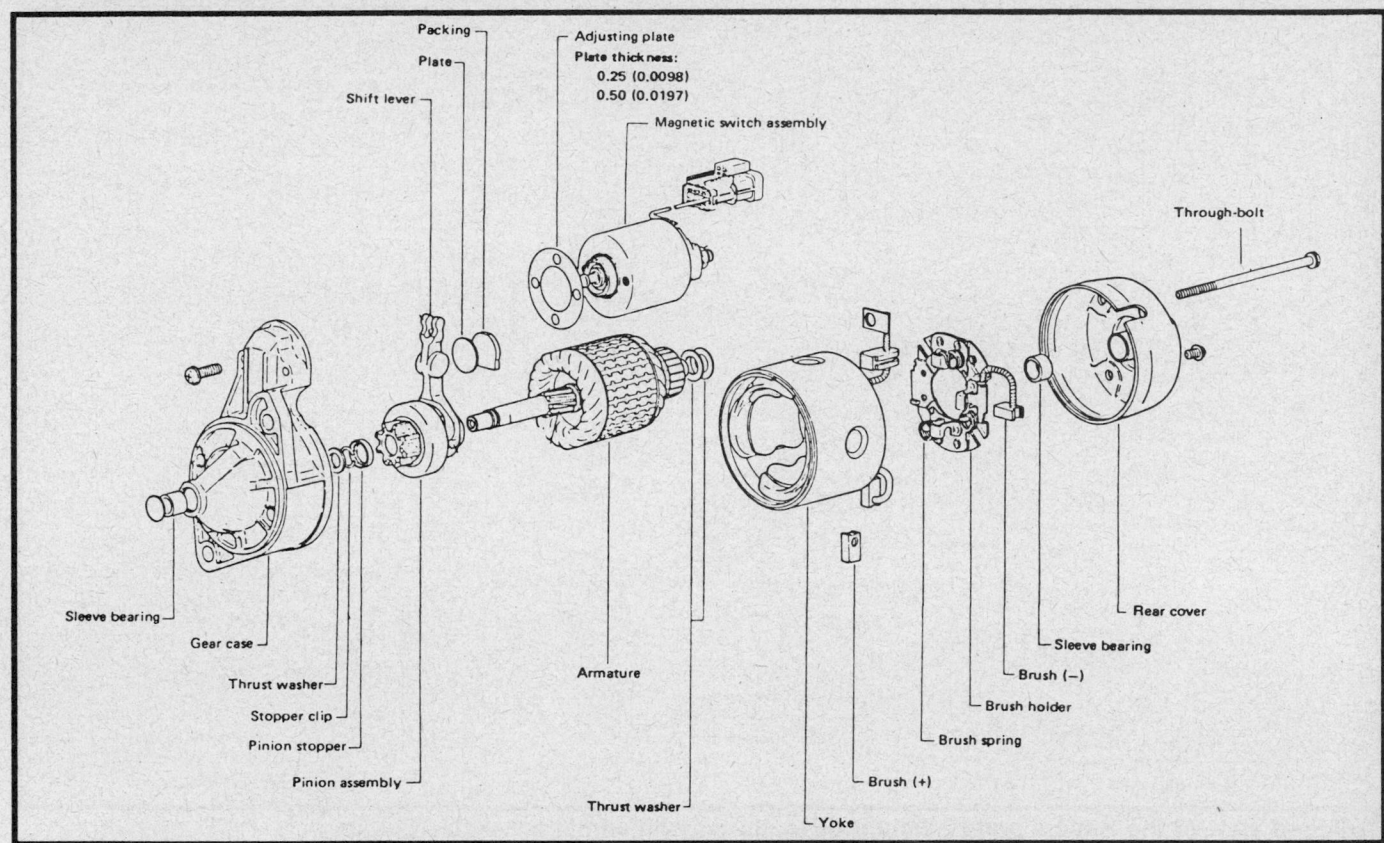

Exploded view of the Mitsubishi non-reduction drive starter — Nissan

brushes or oil soaked should be replaced; new brushes are $^{11}/_{16}$ in. long.

To Assemble:

8. Do not immerse the starter clutch unit in cleaning solvent; lubricant will be washed from inside the clutch.

9. Place the drive unit on the armature shaft and while holding the armature, rotate the pinion. The drive pinion should rotate smoothly in one direction only. The pinion may not rotate easily but as long as it rotates smoothly it is in good condition. If the clutch unit does not function properly or if the pinion is worn, chipped or burred replace the unit.

10. To assemble, lubricate the bushings/splines and reverse the disassembly procedures.

11. Install the clutch, stop collar, lock ring and shaft fork on the armature.

12. Install the armature assembly and shift fork in the drive end housing. Check the endplay, it should be 0.002–0.021 in.

HITACHI

1. Support the starter in a soft jawed vise.

2. Remove the rear mounting bracket-to-starter nuts, the bracket and the plastic cap.

3. Disconnect the field wire from the solenoid.

4. Remove the solenoid-to-starter nuts and the solenoid.

5. From the end cover, remove the nuts, the through bolts and the end cover.

6. Using a pin punch at the drive end housing, drive the yoke axle pin from the housing.

7. At the positive brushes, move the brush spring clips to the side of the brushes and pull the brushes away from the armature. Carefully pull the field housing from the drive end housing.

8. Remove the pinion yoke and armature from the drive end housing.

9. Using a deep socket which fits over the armature shaft, tap the stop collar (driving it toward the armature) to expose the snapring. Remove the snapring from the groove and slide it from the shaft.

NOTE: When removing the snapring, be careful not to bend or distort it.

10. Remove the stop collar, the drive pinion and the support plate.

11. Using compressed air or a brush, clean the drive pinion, the drive end frame, the armature, the field coils and the starter frame; all other parts can be cleaned in solvent.

12. Inspect the condition of the starter parts, perform the following procedures:

a. Check for broken wires or badly soldered connections.

b. Replace any bushings which are scored or badly worn.

c. If the armature's commutator more than 0.005 in. out of round, reface it on a lathe.

NOTE: Never use emery cloth to clean a commutator.

d. The drive pinion should be free of excessive wear or damage.

e. If the brushes are cracked, broken, distorted or worn to less than 0.314 in., replace them.

f. Using a growler and a hacksaw blade (placed on top of the armature), rotate the armature and check it for a shorted condition. If the hacksaw blade vibrates, a short exists; replace the armature.

g. Using a test light, place a lead on the armature's core and the other on each commutator segment, inspect the armature for a grounded condition. If a ground exists, the test light will turn **ON**; replace the armature.

h. Using a test light, check for continuity between the posi-

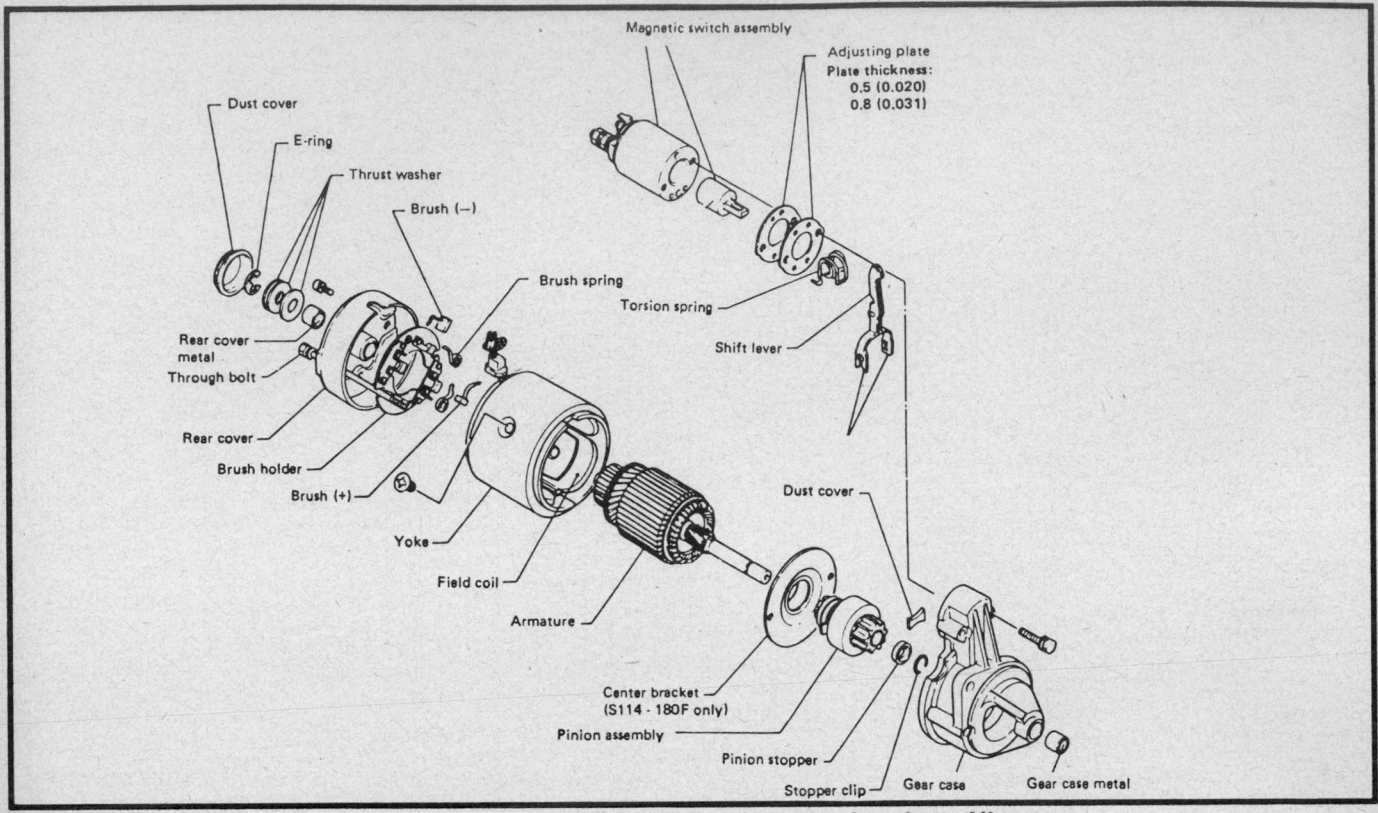

Exploded view of the Hitachi non-reduction drive starter with center bracket—Nissan

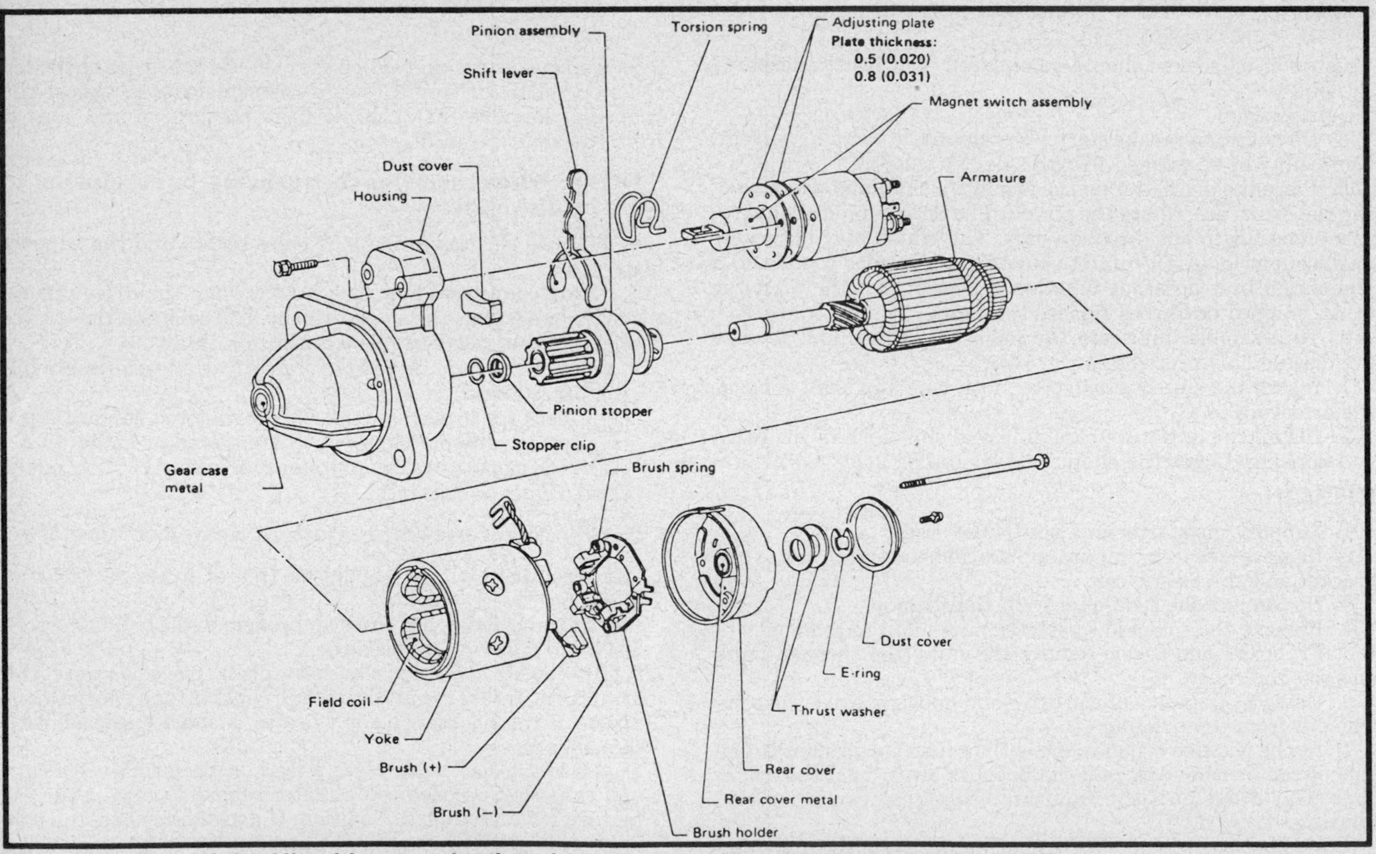

Exploded view of the Hitachi non-reduction drive starter without center bracket—Nissan

tive brushes; if no continuity exists, replace the winding. Repeat this test for the negative windings.

   i. Using a test light, place a lead on the coil housing and the other on each coil lead, make sure there is NO continuity; if continuity exists, replace the winding(s).

To Assemble:

13. Lubricate the necessary parts and place the support plate onto the armature, followed by the drive pinion and the stop collar. Carefully slide the snapring into the armature groove. Slide the stop collar over the snapring until it locks.

14. Position the armature and pinion yoke into the drive end housing. Install the pinion yoke axle pin.

15. Install the coil housing over the armature and onto the drive end housing. Position the brush holder onto the coil housing. Install the brushes and secure the brush springs.

16. Install the solenoid to the drive end housing. Position the field wire grommet to the coil housing and connect field wire to the solenoid.

17. Install the end cover to the coil housing and the install the through bolts/nuts. Install the armature brake assembly, the plastic cover and the mounting bracket.

REDUCTION GEAR TYPE

Disassembly and Assembly

MITSUBISHI

NOTE: Do not place the stator frame in a vise or strike it with a hammer for damage to the permanent magnets could occur.

1. Disconnect the coil wire from the solenoid.
2. Remove the solenoid-to-front end frame screws and the solenoid.

3. Loosen, do not remove the commutator shield-to-brush holder screws.
4. Remove the through bolts, the rubber retainer (under solenoid) and the coin washer.

NOTE: When removing the output shaft assembly, do not loose the armature shaft ball.

5. Remove the stator frame, the commutator shield and output shaft assembly as a unit. Separate the clutch fork from the output shaft assembly.
6. From the stator frame, pull the output shaft assembly forward, then, push the armature and commutator shield to the rearward.
7. Remove the commutator shield-to-brush holder plate screws and the shield; do not remove the brush holder assembly.
8. Using a 22mm socket, slide it up against the commutator, slide the brush holder assembly onto the socket and position the socket/brush holder assembly aside.
9. To disassemble the output shaft assembly, perform the following procedures:

   a. Remove the rubber packing ring and the gears.

   b. Using a 17mm socket, position it into the armature end of the driveshaft and position the assembly in the vertical position, resting on the socket.

   c. Using a 12 point 14mm socket, position it against the stopring (on the clutch end). Using a hammer, strike the socket to unseat the stopring and expose the snapring.

   d. Remove the socket, the snapring and the stopring from the driveshaft.

   e. Using fine sandpaper, remove any burrs from the driveshaft. Remove the overruning clutch.

10. Using compressed air or dry cloths, clean the armature, the stator frame, the overrunning clutch, the solenoid and the brush holder. Using mineral spirits, clean all other components.

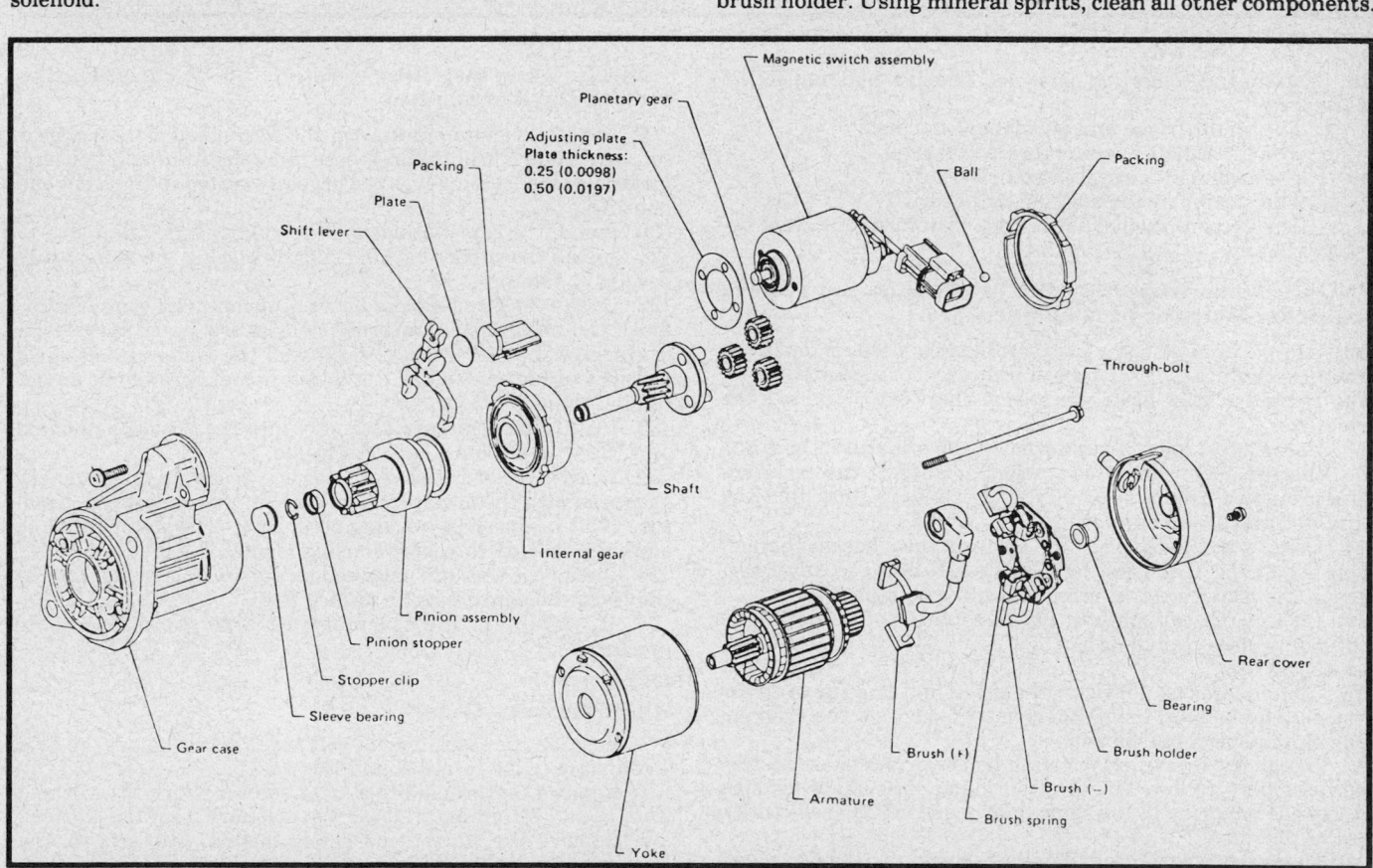

Exploded view of the Mitsubishi reduction drive starter—Nissan Pick-Up and Pathfinder

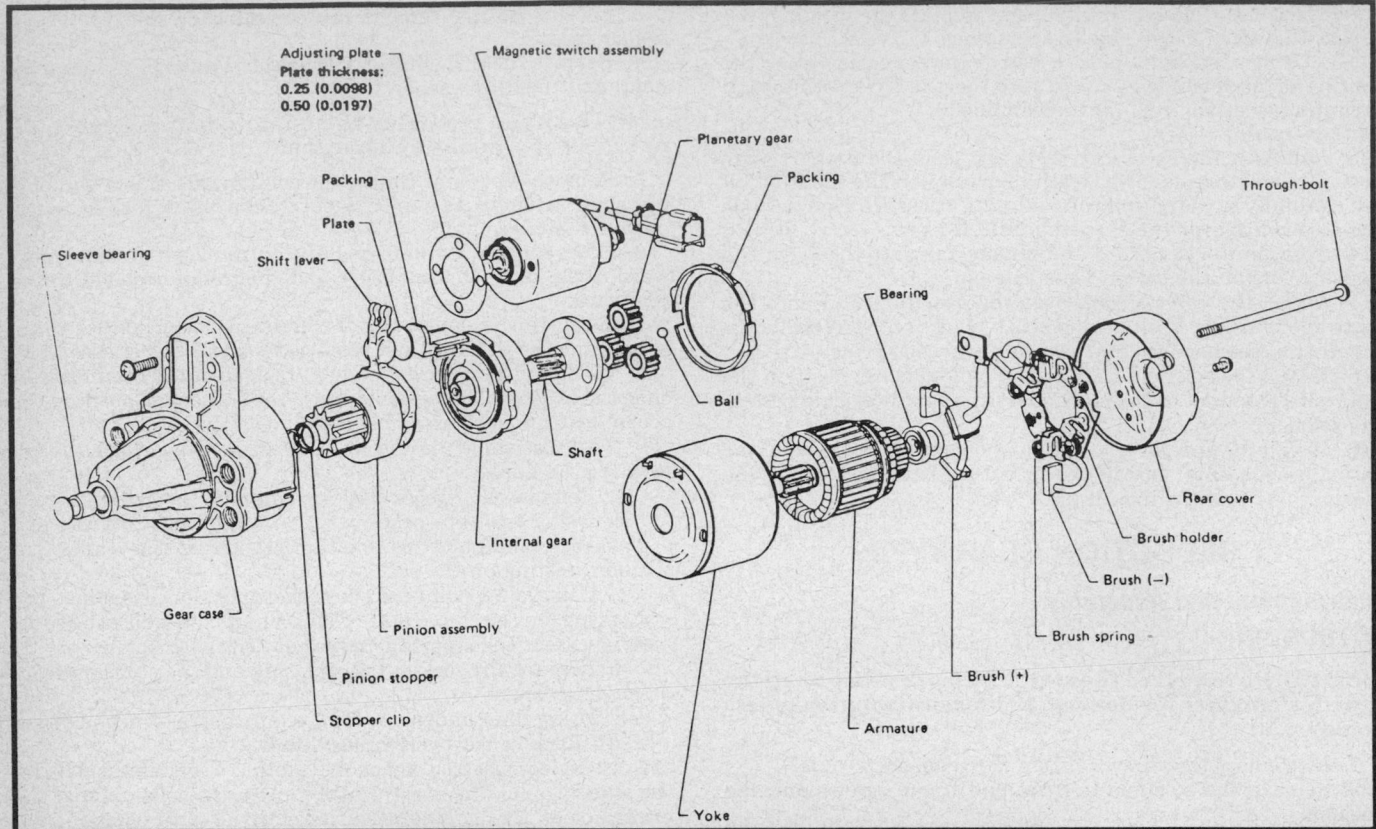

Exploded view of the Mitsubishi reduction drive starter—Nissan Axxess

11. Inspect the following parts for damage and replace, if necessary:
    a. The stator frame and permanent magnets
    b. The driveshaft bushing (armature side)
    c. The planetary gear set and driveshaft
    d. The starter motor bushing and bearing
    e. The carbon brushes for cracks, distortion and wear below 0.354 in.

NOTE: When inspecting the brushes, do not remove the socket from the brush holder.

12. Using a growler and a hacksaw blade (placed on top of the armature), rotate the armature and check it for a shorted condition. If the hacksaw blade vibrates, a short exists; replace the armature.

13. Using a test light, place a lead on the armature's core and the other on each commutator segment, inspect the armature for a grounded condition. If a ground exists, the test light will turn **ON**; replace the armature.

14. Using a test light, place the leads on the adjacent commutator segments. If the test light turns **ON** between any 2 segments, the armature is shorted and must be replaced.

15. Inspect the commutator out-of-round, if it is more than 0.001 in., reface it on a lathe.

To Assemble:

16. Using motor oil, lubricate the driveshaft and the overrunning clutch bushing. Using Lubriplate®, lubricate the overrunning clutch spiral cut splines.

17. Install the overrunning clutch on the driveshaft/planetary gear assembly, followed by the stopring and the snapring; sure to seat the snapring in the shaft groove and crimp the it with a pair of pliers.

18. Using a battery terminal puller, attach it to the driveshaft tip and press the stopring over the snapring.

NOTE: When installing the stopring, be careful not to scratch the driveshaft.

19. Install the clutch fork, with the assembled planetary gear set, lubricated with lithium grease, into the front end housing; make sure the locating lugs are properly seated in the front end housing.

20. Install the coin washer and the rubber fork retainer.

21. Install the rubber backing ring by placing the largest rubber lug at the top.

22. Install the brush holder onto the armature's commutator; make sure the brushes and brush holders are seated in the holder. Inspect the flex washer and install the commutator shield onto the armature. Install the brush holder screws but do not tighten them.

23. Install the armature assembly into the stator frame and seat the wire grommet into the frame.

24. Be sure the armature spline gear is seated in the planetary gear seat with the armature shaft ball in place. Seat the armature shaft in the shaft bushing bore; rotate the stator frame to align the tabs on the drive housing frame.

25. Install the through bolts and torque to 28 inch lbs. Torque the brush holder screws to 18 inch lbs.

26. To complete the assembly, reverse the disassembly procedures.

HITACHI
With Planetary Gears

1. Position the assembly in a soft jawed vise. Remove the field terminal nut, the terminal and the washer.

2. Remove the solenoid-to-starter screws. Work the solenoid from the shift fork and remove the solenoid from the starter.

3. Remove the starter end shield bushing cap screws, the starter end shield bushing cap, the end shield bushing and C-washer.

4. Remove the starter end shield bushing washer and seal.

5. Remove the starter through bolts, the starter end shield and the brush plate.

6. Slide the field frame from the starter and over the armature. Remove the armature assembly from the drive end housing.

7. Remove the rubber seal from the drive end housing. Remove the starter drive gear train.

8. Remove the dust plate. Press the stop collar from the snapring. Using snapring pliers, loosen the snapring.

9. Remove the output shaft snapring, the clutch stopring collar and the clutch assembly from the starter.

10. Remove the clutch shift lever bushing, the clutch shift lever and the C-clip retainer.

11. Remove the retaining washer, the sun and the planetary gears from the annulus gear.

12. To assemble, lubricate the necessary parts and reverse the disassembly procedures. Replace all defective components as required.

Without Planetary Gears

1. Remove the starter from the vehicle. Position the unit in a soft jawed vise.

2. Remove the field coil screw, the field frame through bolts and separate the field frame assembly from the drive gear assembly. Separate the armature and the commutator end frame from the field frame.

3. Remove the solenoid screws and the solenoid from the drive housing.

4. Remove the retaining ring, shift lever shaft and housing through bolts. Separate the drive assembly, drive housing and gear assembly.

5. To remove the overrunning clutch from the armature shaft, perform the following procedures:

a. Remove the washer or collar from the armature shaft.

b. Using a ⅝ in. deep socket, slide it over the shaft and against the retainer. Use the socket as a driving tool, tap the socket with a hammer to move the retainer off of the snapring.

c. Remove the snapring from the groove in the shaft; if the snapring is distorted, replace it.

d. Remove the retainer and the clutch assembly from the armature shaft.

6. To replace the starter brushes, remove the brush holder pivot pin which positions the insulated and the ground brushes. Remove the brush spring.

7. Inspect armature commutator, shaft and bushings, overrunning clutch pinion, brushes and springs for discoloration, damage or wear; replace the damaged parts (if necessary). Check the armature shaft fit in drive housing bushing; the shaft should fit snugly in the bushing. If the bushing is worn, it should be replaced.

8. Inspect armature commutator. If commutator is rough, it should be refinished on a lathe; do not undercut or turn to less than 1.650 in. O.D. Inspect the points where the armature conductors join the commutator bars to make sure they have a good connection. A burned commutator is usually evidence of a poor connection.

9. Using a growler and holding hacksaw blade over armature core while armature is rotated, check the armature for short circuits; if the saw blade vibrates, the armature is shorted.

10. Using a test lamp, place a lead on the shunt coil terminal and the other lead to a ground brush. The test should be made from both ground brushes to insure continuity through both brushes and leads. If the lamp fails to light, the field coil is open and will require replacement.

11. Using a test lamp, place a lead on the series coil terminal and the other lead on the insulated brush. If the lamp fails to

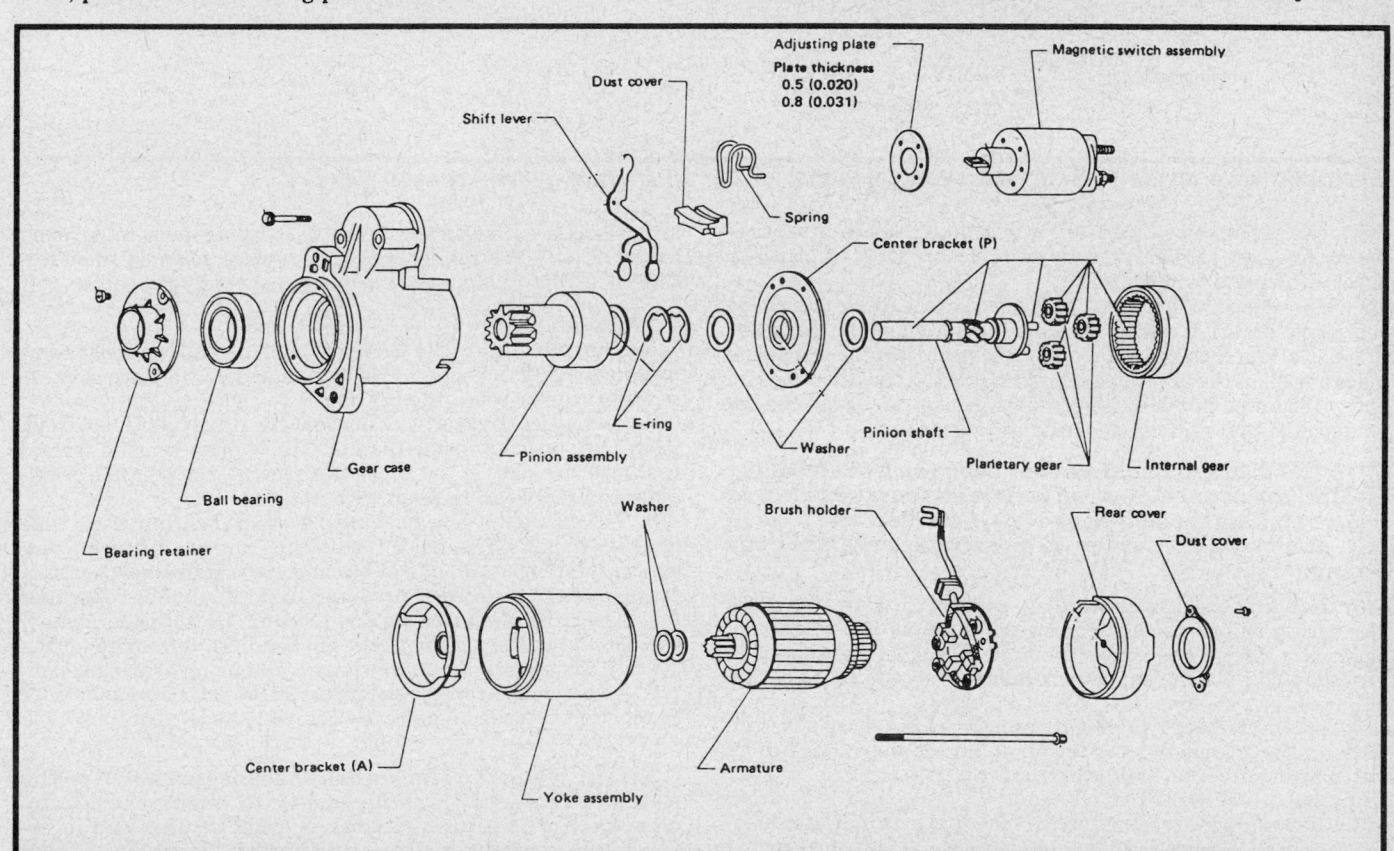

Exploded view of the Hitachi reduction drive starter with planetary gears—Nissan Pick-Up and Pathfinder

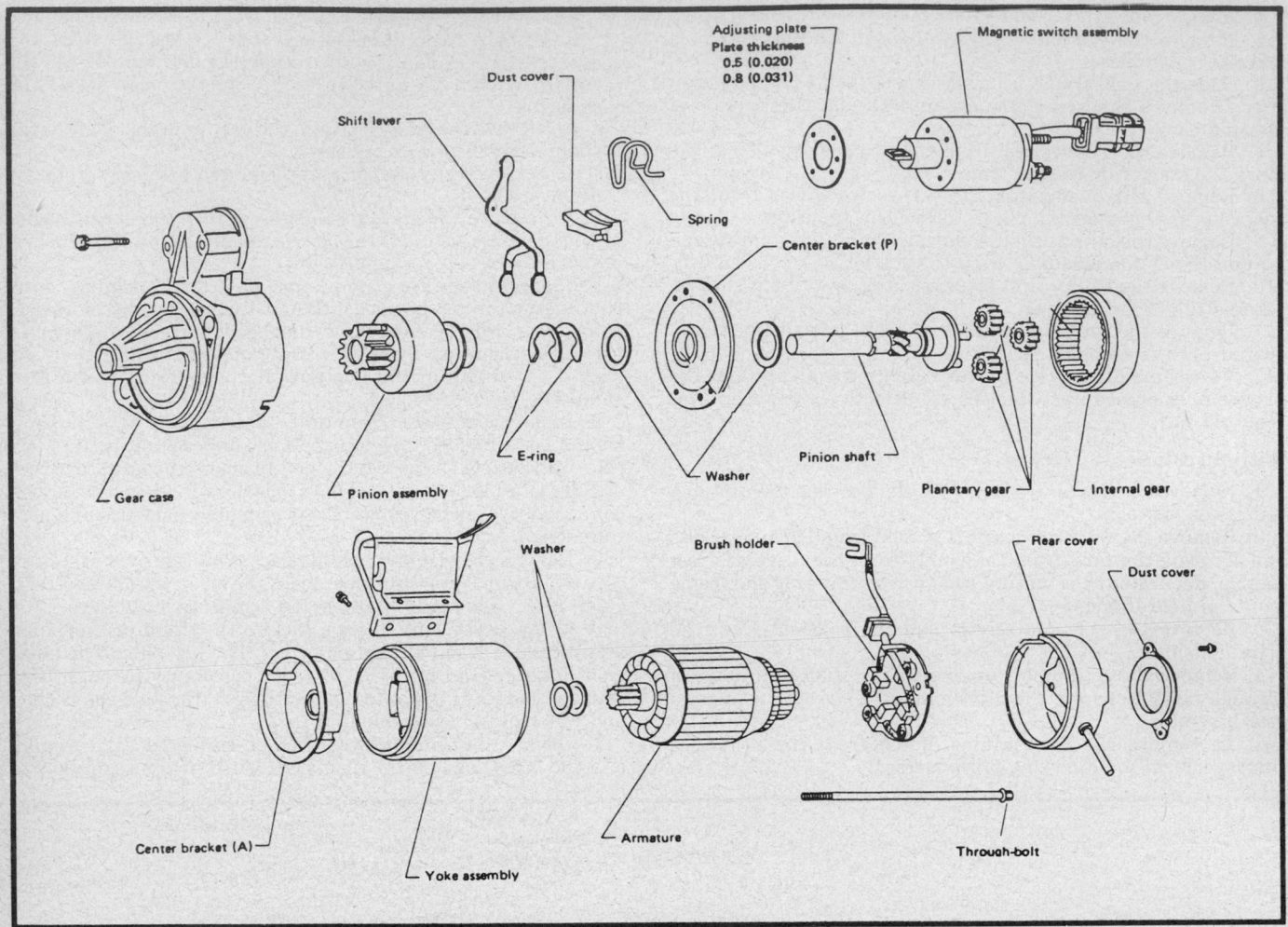

Exploded view of the Hitachi reduction drive starter with planetary gears—Nissan Axxess

light, the series coil is open and will require repair or replacement. The test should be made from each insulated brush to check brush and lead continuity.

12. If equipped with a shunt coil, separate the series and shunt coil strap terminals during this test; do not allow the strap terminals to touch the case or other ground. Using a test lamp, place a lead on the grounded brush holder and the other lead on either insulated brush. If the lamp lights, a grounded series coil is indicated and must be repaired or replaced.

NOTE: **If the solenoid has not been removed from the starter, the connector strap terminals must be removed before making the following tests. Complete the tests as fast as possible in order to prevent overheating the solenoid.**

13. To check the starter winding, connect an ammeter in series with a 12 volt battery, the switch terminal and to ground. Connect a carbon pile across the battery. Adjust the voltage to 10 volts and note the ammeter reading; it should be 14.5–16.5 amperes.

14. To check both windings, connect as for previous test. Ground the solenoid motor terminal, adjust the voltage to 10 volts and note the ammeter reading; it should be 41–47 amperes.

15. Current draw readings above specifications indicate shorted turns or a ground in the windings of the solenoid; the solenoid should be replaced. Current draw readings under specifica-

tions indicate excessive resistance. No reading indicates an open circuit. Check the connections and replace solenoid (if necessary). Current readings will decrease as windings heat up.

To Assemble:

16. The roller bearing in the drive housing and the roller bearings in the gear housing must be replaced (if they are dry); do not lubricate or reuse the bearings.

17. To replace the gear housing bearing, use a tube or solid cylinder that just fits inside the housing to push bearing toward the armature side. In the opposite direction, use the tube or cylinder to press bearing flush with housing.

18. To replace the gear housing driveshaft bearing, use a tube or collar that just fits inside the housing and press bearing out; press against the open end of bearing. To install a new bearing, press against the closed end, using a thin wall tube or collar that fits in space between bearing and housing. Do not press against the flat end of the bearing; this will bend the thin metal of the bearing. As required, replace the drive housing bearing.

19. To assemble, reverse the disassembly procedures. Be sure to replace or repair all defective components as required.

NOTE: **When the starter has been disassembled or the solenoid replaced, it is necessary to check the pinion clearance. The pinion clearance must be checked in order to prevent the buttons on the shift lever yoke from rubbing on the clutch collar during engine cranking.**

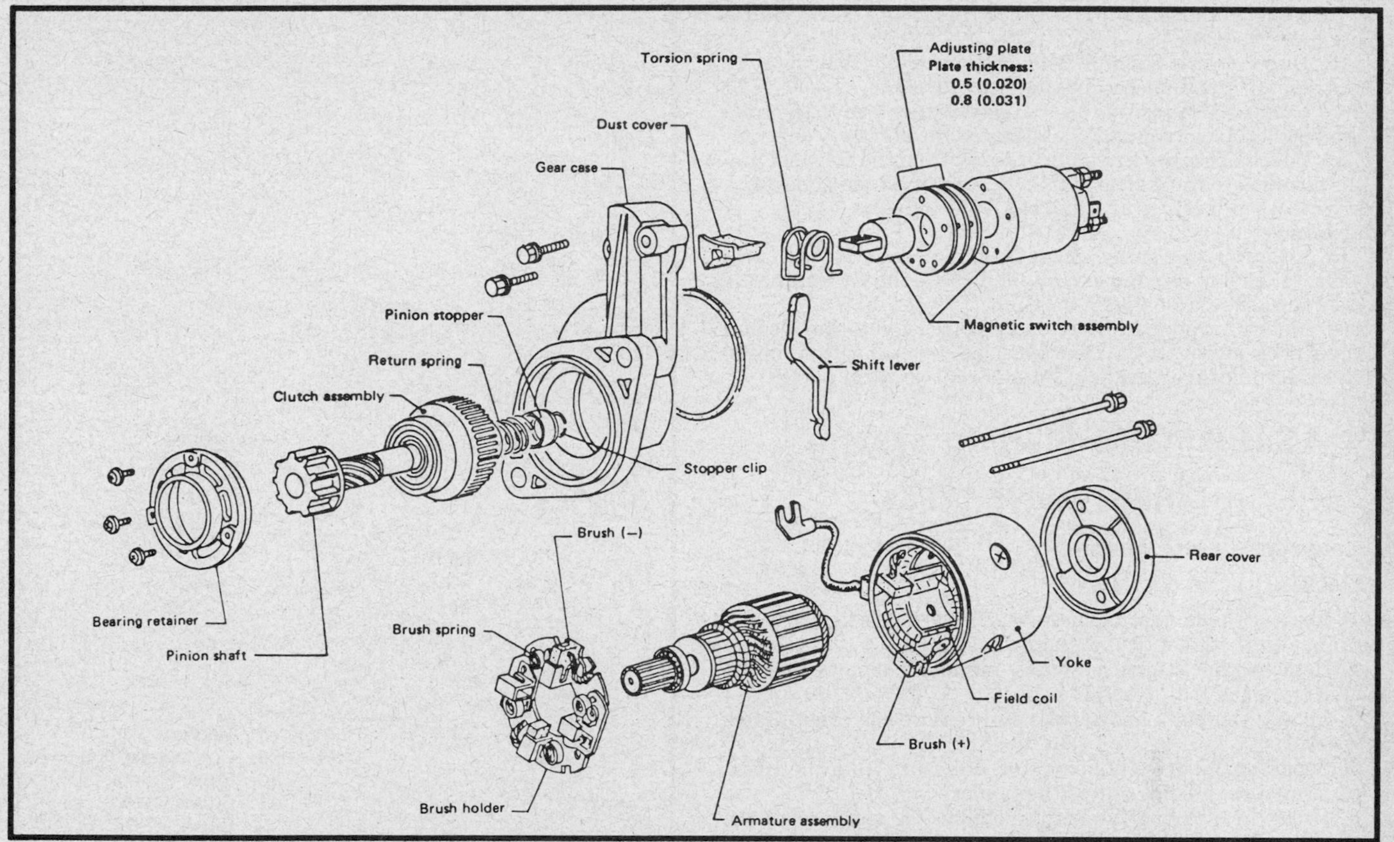

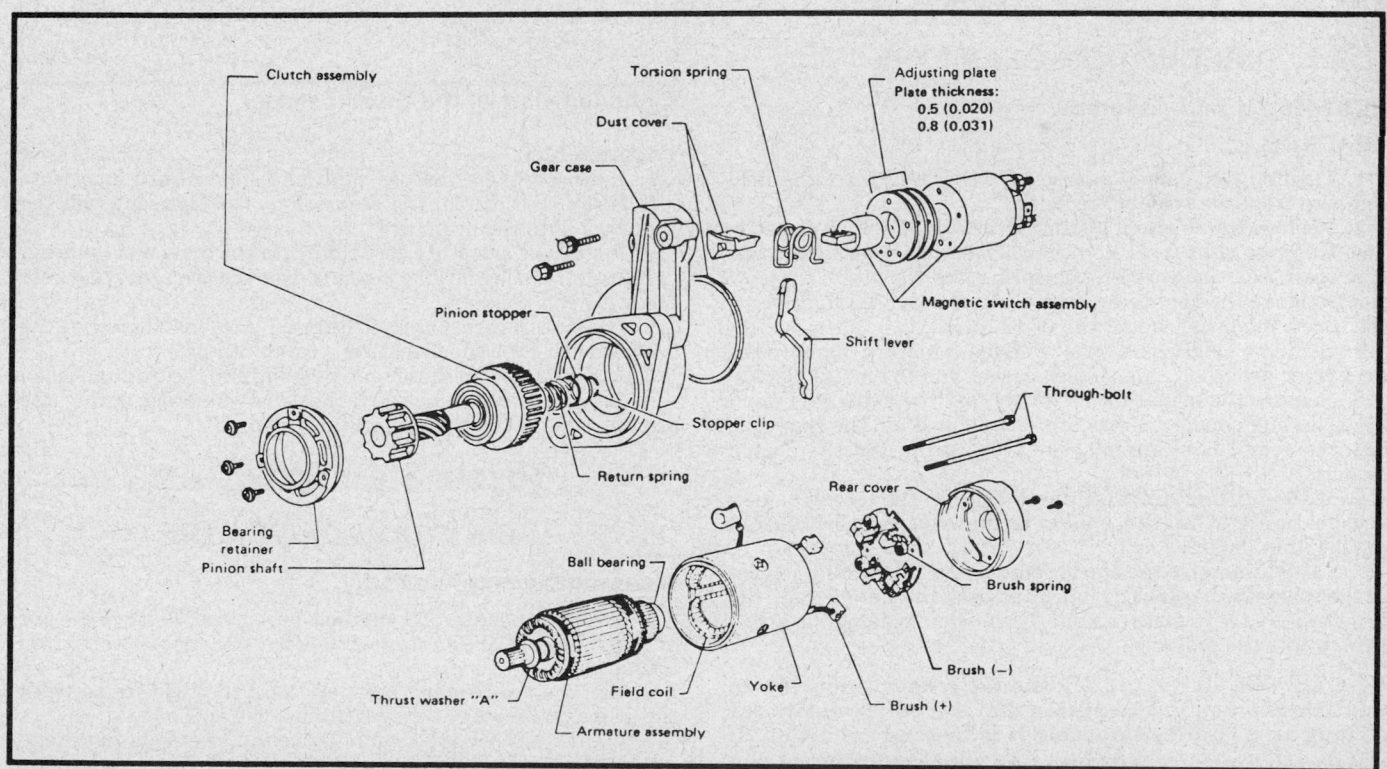

Torsion spring

Adjusting plate
Plate thickness:
0.5 (0.020)
0.8 (0.031)

Dust cover

Gear case

Pinion stopper

Return spring

Clutch assembly

Magnetic switch assembly

Shift lever

Stopper clip

Brush (−)

Rear cover

Brush spring

Bearing retainer

Pinion shaft

Yoke

Field coil

Brush (+)

Brush holder

Armature assembly

Exploded view of the Hitachi reduction drive starter with front mounted brush holder — Nissan

Clutch assembly

Torsion spring

Adjusting plate
Plate thickness:
0.5 (0.020)
0.8 (0.031)

Dust cover

Gear case

Pinion stopper

Magnetic switch assembly

Shift lever

Stopper clip

Through-bolt

Return spring

Rear cover

Bearing retainer

Brush spring

Pinion shaft

Ball bearing

Brush (−)

Brush (+)

Thrust washer "A"

Field coil

Yoke

Armature assembly

Exploded view of the Hitachi reduction drive starter with rear mounted brush holder — Nissan

20. To check the pinion clearance, perform the following procedures:

a. Disconnect the motor field coil connector from the solenoid motor terminal and insulate the terminal.

b. Connect the positive (+) 12 volt battery lead to the solenoid switch terminal and the other to the starter frame.

c. Touch a jumper lead momentarily from the solenoid motor terminal to the starter frame; this will shift the pinion into cranking position and retain it until the battery is disconnected.

d. Using a feeler gauge, push the pinion back as far as possible, to take up any movement, and check the clearance; the clearance should be 0.010–0.140 in.

e. Means for adjusting pinion clearance is not provided on the starter motor. If the clearance does not fall within limits, check for improper installation and replace worn parts.

Suzuki/GEO Starting System

DIRECT DRIVE TYPE

Dissassembly and Assembly

SAMURAI

1. Remove the nut securing the end of the field coil lead to the terminal on the head of the magnetic switch.

2. Remove the magnetic switch mounting screws and the switch from the motor body.

3. Loosen the bolts and screws and remove the commutator end cover.

4. Separate the drive housing and armature from the yoke.

5. Draw the brushes out of the holder.

6. Draw the stopring toward the clutch side and remove the armature ring and slide off the overrunning clutch.

7. To assemble, reverse the disassembly procedures. Replace brushes that are worn more than 0.450 in. New brushes are 0.670 in.

REDUCTION GEAR TYPE

Disassembly and Assembly

TRACKER

1. Position the starter in a soft jawed. Disconnect the field coil wire from the solenoid terminal.

2. Remove the solenoid mounting screws and work the solenoid from the shift fork. Remove the bearing cover, the armature shaft lock, the washer, the spring and the seal.

3. Remove the commutator end frame cover through bolts, the cover, the brushes and the brush plate.

4. Slide the field frame from over the armature. Remove the shift lever pivot bolt, the rubber gasket and the metal plate.

5. Remove the armature assembly and the shift lever from the drive end housing. Press the stop collar from the snapring, then remove the snapring, the stop collar and the clutch assembly.

6. If the brushes are worn more than ½ the length of new brushes or are oil-soaked, should be replaced; the new brushes are 0.630 in. long.

7. Do not immerse the starter clutch unit in cleaning solvent as the solvent will wash the lubricant from the clutch. Place the drive unit on the armature shaft, then, while holding the armature, rotate the pinion.

NOTE: The drive pinion should rotate smoothly in one direction only. The pinion may not rotate easily but as long as it rotates smoothly it is in good condition. If the clutch unit does not function properly or if the pinion is worn, chipped or burred, replace the unit.

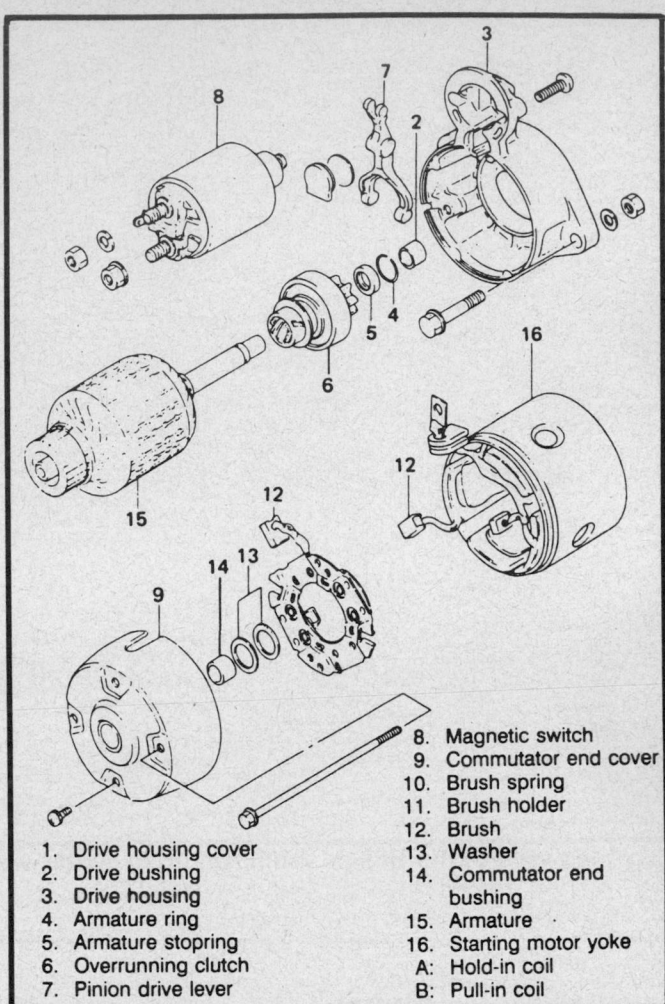

1. Drive housing cover	8. Magnetic switch
2. Drive bushing	9. Commutator end cover
3. Drive housing	10. Brush spring
4. Armature ring	11. Brush holder
5. Armature stopring	12. Brush
6. Overrunning clutch	13. Washer
7. Pinion drive lever	14. Commutator end bushing
	15. Armature
	16. Starting motor yoke
	A: Hold-in coil
	B: Pull-in coil

Exploded view of the Suzuki starter

To Assemble:

8. Lubricate the armature shaft and splines with lubricant.

9. Install the clutch, the stop collar, the lock ring and the shift fork onto the armature.

10. Install the armature assembly into the drive end housing.

11. Install the field frame housing over the armature and onto the drive end housing.

12. Position the brushes into the brush holder and position the brush holder over the armature's commutator.

13. Install the commutator end housing and the through bolts.

14. Install the cap end gasket, the armature brake spring, the armature plate and the commutator end cap.

Toyota Starting System

REDUCTION DRIVE TYPE

Disassembly and Assembly

1. Position the assembly in a soft jawed vise. Remove the nut and disconnect the motor wire from the magnetic switch terminal.

2. Remove the through bolts and pull the field frame (with the armature) from the magnetic switch assembly.

3. On the 1.0 KW type, remove the felt seal from the armature shaft; on the 1.4 KW type, remove the field frame to magnetic switch assembly O-ring.

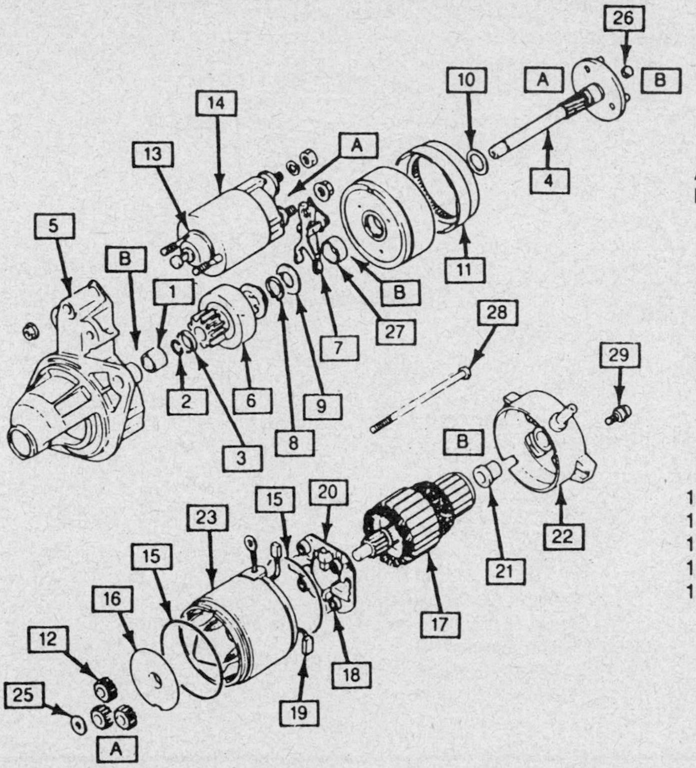

A. Apply grease
B. Do not wash or lubricate spare parts have been lubricated
1. Needle bearings
2. Snapring
3. Pinion stopring
4. Planetary carrier shaft
5. Drive housing assembly
6. Overrunning clutch assembly
7. Shift lever
8. C-clip
9. Washer
10. Washer
11. Internal gear
12. Planetary gear
13. Boot
14. Starter solenoid
15. O-ring
16. Plate
17. Armature
18. Brush spring
19. Brush
20. Brush holder assembly
21. Bushing
22. Commutator end housing assembly
23. Frame and field assembly
24. Center bearing and shock absorber assembly
25. Washer
26. Bushing
27. Bushing
28. Housing bolt
29. Screw with O-ring

Exploded view of the GEO Tracker starter

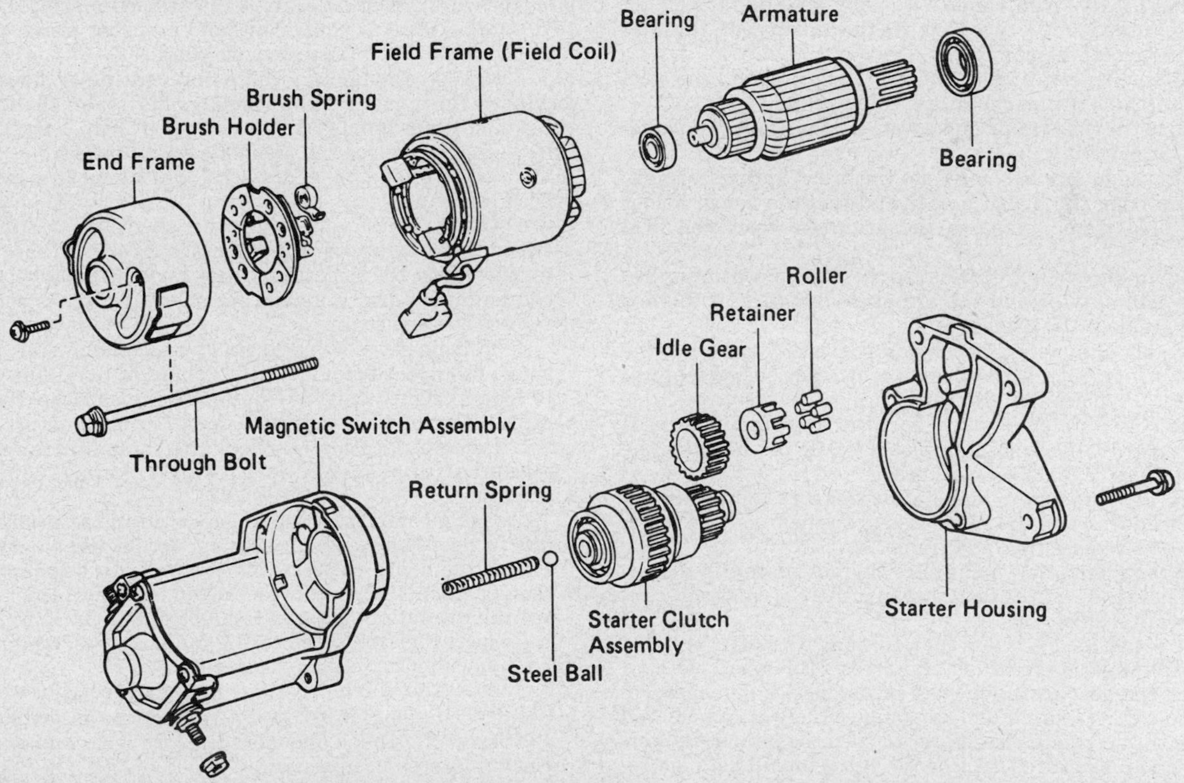

Exploded view of the 1.0 KW Nippondenso starter— Toyota

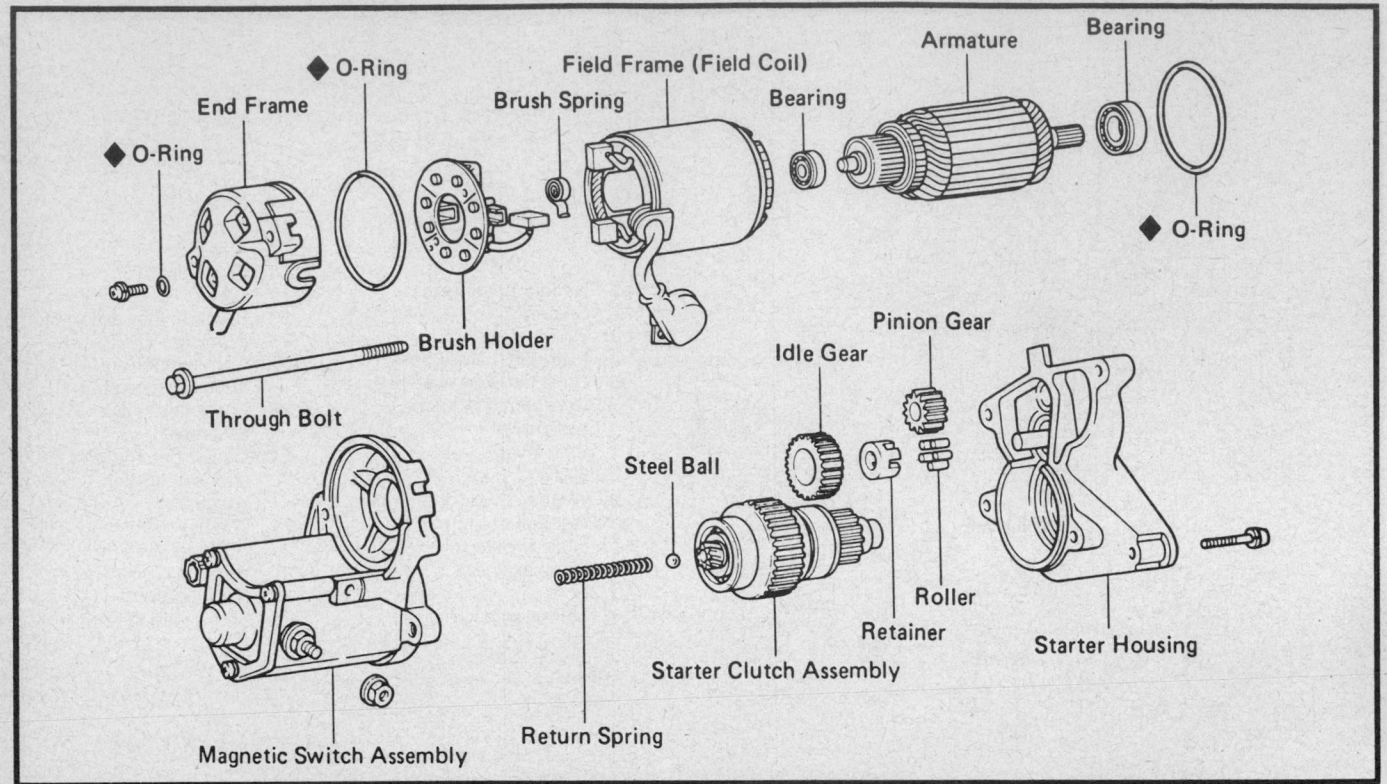

Exploded view of the 1.4 KW and 1.6 KW Nippondenso starters—Toyota

4. Remove the starter housing to magnetic switch assembly bolts and separate the housing from the assembly.

5. On the 1.0 KW type, remove the idler gear and the clutch assembly. On the 1.4 KW type, remove the pinion gear, the idler gear and the clutch assembly.

6. Using a magnetic finger, remove the spring and the steel ball from the hole in the clutch assembly shaft.

7. Remove the field frame end cover. On the 1.4 KW type, remove the large O-ring.

8. Using a small pry bar, separate the brush springs, remove the brushes from the brush holder and pull the brush holder from the field frame. Remove the armature from the field frame.

9. Using an ohmmeter, make sure there is no continuity between the commutator and the armature coil core; if there is continuity, replace the armature.

10. Using an ohmmeter, check for continuity between the commutator segments. If there is no continuity between any of the segments, replace the armature.

11. If the commutator is dirty, burnt or the runout exceeds 0.0020 in., use a lathe to clean the surface; do not machine the diameter to less than 1.14 in. diameter.

12. Using an ohmmeter, make sure there is continuity between the lead wire and the brush lead of the field coil; if there is no continuity, replace the field frame.

13. Using an ohmmeter, make sure there is no continuity between the field coil and the field frame; if there is continuity, replace the field frame.

14. If the brush length is less than 0.335 in. (1.0 KW) or 0.394 in. (1.4 KW), replace the brush and dress with emery cloth.

15. Check the gear teeth for wear or damage, if damaged, replace them. Turn the clutch assembly pinion clockwise and make sure that it rotates freely, try to turn the pinion counterclockwise and make sure that it locks. If the pinion does not respond correctly, replace it.

16. While applying inward force on the bearings, turn each by hand; if resistance or sticking is noticed, replace the bearings. To replace the bearings, use the tool 09286–46011 or equivalent, to pull the bearing(s) from the armature shaft. Using the tool 09285–76010 or equivalent, and an arbor press, press the new bearing(s) onto the armature shaft.

17. Using an ohmmeter, check for continuity between the grounded terminal and the insulated terminal, then between the grounded terminal and the housing. If there is no continuity in either case, replace the magnetic switch assembly.

18. To inspect the armature, perform the following procedures:

   a. Using digital volt-ohmmeter, check for continuity between the commutator's segments and core; if there is continuity, replace the armature. Check for continuity between the commutator's segments and the shaft; it there is continuity, replace the armature.

   b. Using a set of V-blocks and a dial micrometer, measure the commutator's runout; if the runout is more than 0.002 in. (0.05mm), lightly turn the commutator on a lathe. If the commutator's runout is excessive, replace the armature.

   c. Using a micrometer, check the commutator's outer diameter; if it is less than 1.14 in. (29mm), replace the armature.

   d. Using commutator sand paper, clean the commutator's face of burnt spots and/or scoring; do not use emery cloth.

   e. If the depth between the commutator segments is less than 0.008 in. (0.2mm), use a broken hacksaw blade to undercut the insulating material to 0.008–0.024 in. (0.2–0.6mm).

19. Inspect the armature bearing for looseness, binding or abnormal noise; if necessary, replace it.

20. Inspect the clutch/drive assembly gear teeth for wear, milling and/or chipping; if necessary, replace the assembly.

21. Inspect the pinion and idler gears for wear and/or damage; replace the gears if, necessary.

22. Inspect the brushes for wear by measuring the amount of useable brush remaining; the wear limit is 0.39 in. (10.0mm).

Check the brushes for free movement in the brush holder; if necessary, clean the brush channels.

To Assemble:

23. Lubricate the gears, shafts and bearings with high temperature grease. Install the armature into the frame and field assembly.

24. Position the brushes into the brush holder.

25. Install a new O-ring onto the frame and field assembly.

26. Install the commutator end housing and screws.

27. Install the pinion gear, the idler gear bearing, the idler gear and the clutch/drive assembly; be sure to mesh the idler gear with the clutch and drive assembly during installation.

28. Install the spring into the solenoid assembly.

29. Install the drive housing to the solenoid screws.

30. Using a new O-ring, install it onto the drive housing side of the field frame assembly.

31. Align the matchmarks and install the field frame assembly onto the drive housing. Install and torque the through bolts to 33 ft. lbs. (45 Nm).

32. Install the lead wire to the starter solenoid terminal and torque the nut to 26 ft. lbs. (35 Nm).

Volkswagen Starting System

DIRECT DRIVE TYPE

Disassembly and Assembly

1. Position the assembly in the soft jawed vise. Disconnect the field coil wire from the solenoid terminal.

2. Remove the solenoid-to-starter screws and the solenoid, for automatic transmissions, and work the solenoid plunger, for automatic transmissions, from the shifting fork.

3. Remove the end shield bearing cap screws, the cap and washers.

4. Remove the through bolts and the commutator end frame cover. Remove the 2 brushes and the brush plate. Slide the field frame from the armature.

5. Remove the shift lever pivot bolt, the rubber gasket and plate.

6. For the automatic transmission models, remove the armature assembly and shift lever from the drive end housing. For the manual transmission models, press the stop collar from the

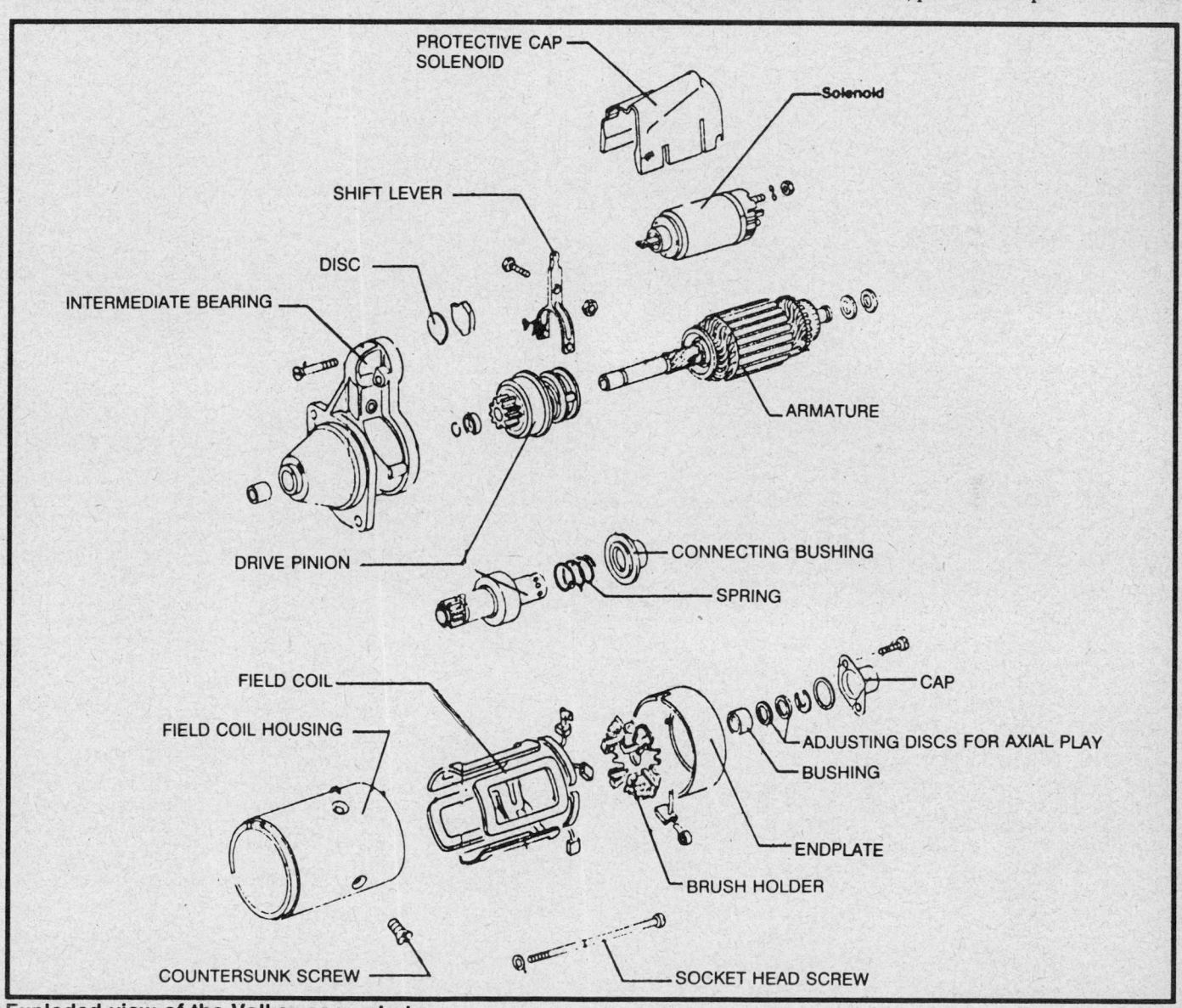

Exploded view of the Volkswagon starter

snapring. Remove the snapring, the clutch assembly and the drive end housing from the armature.

7. For the automatic transmission model, press the stop collar from the snapring and remove the snapring, stop collar and clutch.

8. Brushes that are worn less than ½ the length of new brushes or oil soaked should be replaced; new brushes are $^{11}/_{16}$ in. long.

9. Do not immerse the starter clutch unit in cleaning solvent; lubricant will be washed from inside the clutch.

10. Place the drive unit on the armature shaft and while holding the armature, rotate the pinion. The drive pinion should rotate smoothly in 1 direction only. The pinion may not rotate easily but as long as it rotates smoothly it is in good condition. If the clutch unit does not function properly or if the pinion is worn, chipped or burred replace the unit.

11. To assemble, lubricate the bushings/splines and reverse the disassembly procedures.

12. On the automatic transmission models, install the clutch, stop collar, lock ring and shaft fork on the armature. On the manual transmission models, install the drive end housing on the armature, the clutch, stop collar and snapring on the armature.

13. On the automatic transmission models, install the armature assembly and shift fork in the drive end housing. Install the shim and armature shaft lock. Check the endplay, it should be 0.002–0.021 in.

CHRYSLER IMPORT/MITSUBISHI

Electronic Ignition System

GENERAL INFORMATION

The ignition system consists of a battery, distributor (built-in igniter), ignition coil, spark plugs, high tension cable, ignition switch and connection wires.

The distributor contains a signal generator (signal rotor and pick-up, the latter being built into the igniter), primary current controller (igniter), timing controller (governor and vacuum controller) and distributor (rotor and distributor cap).

IGNITION COIL

Testing

1. Using a suitable ohmmeter, measure resistance. It should be 1.1–1.3 ohms. An open or short circuited coil should be replaced.

2. Check the case for cracks or damage, particularly around the tower. If there are any cracks present, replace the coil.

3. Check for any fluid (oil) leaks. If there are any leaks present, replace coil.

Removal and Installation

1. Disconnect the negative battery cable. Disconnect the high tension wire from the coil.

2. Disconnect the wires from the positive and negative terminals.

3. Remove the 2 coil attaching bolts and remove the coil.

4. Installation is the reverse of the removal and Installation

CENTRIFUGAL TIMING DEVICE

Testing

1. Connect an tachometer and timing light to the engine.
2. Set the parking brake, start the engine and run at idle.
3. Disconnect the vacuum hose from vacuum controller.
4. While slowly increasing engine speed, check timing advance. Timing should advance smoothly as the engine speed increases. If the timing does not change smoothly, check the following possible causes:

   a. Timing advance too large—check for deteriorated or weakened governor spring

   b. Timing advance too sudden, not proportional to rpm increase—check for broken spring or binding internally.

   c. Timing advance too small or hysteresis (lag or delay) too large—check governor weight and cam operations.

5. If any symptoms are observed, disassemble and check distributor.

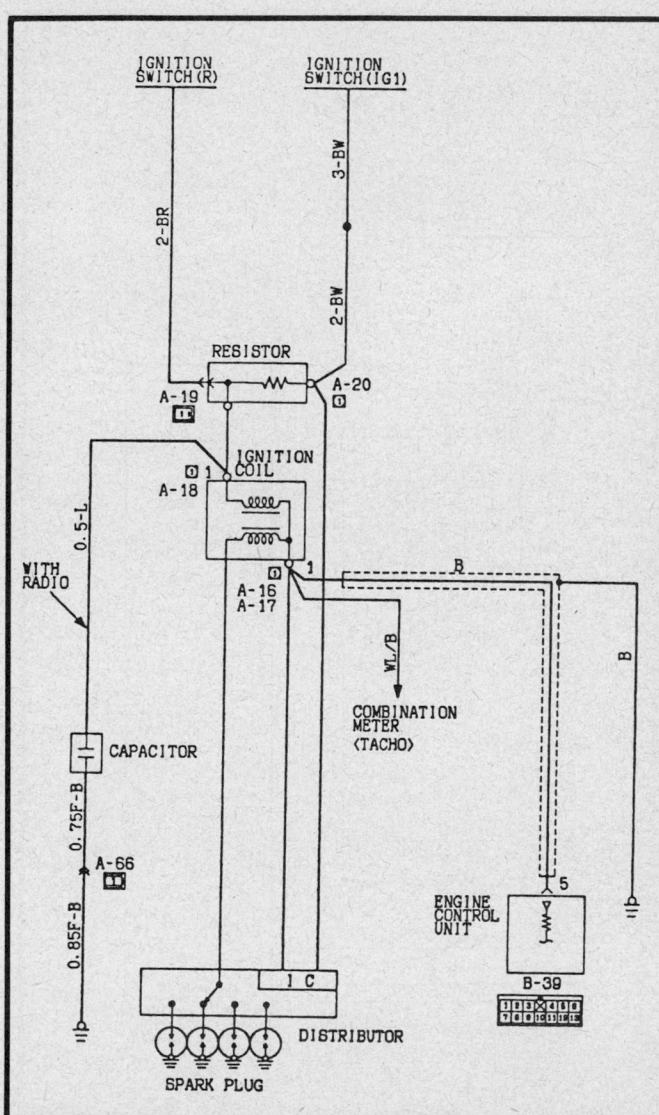

Ignition system schematic—Mitsubishi 2.6L engine

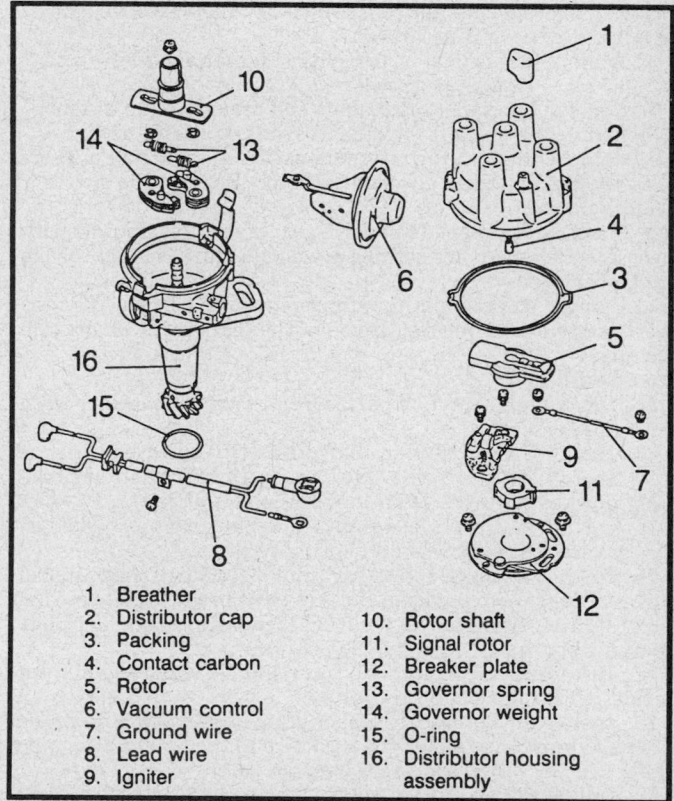

1. Breather	10. Rotor shaft
2. Distributor cap	11. Signal rotor
3. Packing	12. Breaker plate
4. Contact carbon	13. Governor spring
5. Rotor	14. Governor weight
6. Vacuum control	15. O-ring
7. Ground wire	16. Distributor housing
8. Lead wire	assembly
9. Igniter	

Distributor assembly—Mitsubishi 2.6L engine

6. After checking, turn ignition switch **OFF**, reconnect hose and remove tachometer and timing light.

VACUUM TIMING DEVICE

Testing

1. Connect an tachometer and timing light.
2. Set the parking brake, start the engine and run at idle.
3. Disconnect vacuum hose from vacuum controller and connect a vacuum pump to controller.
4. Apply vacuum to vacuum controller gradually and check timing advance. Timing should advance smoothly as negative pressure increases. If not, check below:
    a. Timing advance too large—check for weakened vacuum controller spring
    b. Timing advance too sharp—check for broken spring
    c. Timing advance too small—check for breaker base not operating correctly
    d. No timing advance at all—check for broken diaphragm
5. If any symptoms are observed, disassemble and check distributor or advance unit.

DISTRIBUTOR

Disassembly and Assembly
MITSUBISHI DISTRIBUTOR

1. Disconnect the negative battery cable. Remove the distributor and lightly clamp the assembly into vise equipped with soft jaws.
2. Pull rotor from rotor shaft.
3. Remove the 2 vacuum controller retaining screws.
4. Remove the link of controller from the pin on breaker base, then remove the vacuum controller.
5. Remove the 2 igniter retaining screws and remove igniter. Be sure to remove the lead wire.
6. Remove the signal rotor shaft tightening screw and 2 breaker plate retaining screws.
7. Remove the signal rotor shaft and breaker plate assembly.
8. Remove the signal rotor shaft from the signal rotor.
9. Remove the 2 spring retainers with a suitable pair of pliers and then remove the 2 governor springs. Remove the governor weights.
10. Mark the location of the drive gear on the distributor shaft. Place drive the gear on a soft base (wooden block) so that roll pin can be removed.
11. Using a suitable pin punch, remove the roll pin. Remove the drive gear and washer. Remove the distributor shaft from housing.
To assemble:
12. Clean and inspect all parts, replace any damaged or worn parts as necessary.
13. Install the distributor shaft into distributor housing.
14. Install the drive gear into the distributor shaft at previously marked location. Then install a new roll pin.
15. Install the governor weights onto the governor plate. Install governor the springs and spring retainer.
16. Install the signal rotor shaft into distributor shaft. Install the breaker plate to housing. Be sure to fit breaker plate so that the projection fits into the groove. Tighten the 2 breaker plate retaining screws.
17. Install the signal rotor to rotor shaft. Fit the signal rotor so that spring pin fits on rotor shaft.
18. Install the igniter to breaker plate and install 2 retaining screws. Connect one end of the lead wire to the igniter attaching screw and the other end to breaker plate.
19. Adjust the air gap between signal rotor and pick up of igniter. Air gap should be: 0.008–0.015 in. (0.2–0.4mm)

20. Connect the vacuum control link to breaker plate and tighten the 2 retaining screws.
21. Install the rotor to rotor shaft.

NIPPON DENSO DISTRIBUTOR

1. Disconnect the negative battery cable. Remove the distributor. Lightly clamp the distributor assembly into vise equipped with soft jaws.
2. Pull the rotor from rotor shaft.
3. Remove the vacuum controller attaching screw.
4. Remove the link of the controller from the pin on breaker base, then remove the vacuum controller.
5. Remove the 2 igniter retaining screws and remove igniter. Be sure to remove the lead wire.
6. Remove the screws and signal generator with igniter. Remove the 2 breaker plate retaining screws and remove breaker plate assembly.
7. Remove the 2 governor springs. Remove the cap and signal rotor shaft tightening screw.
8. Remove the signal rotor shaft.
To assemble:
9. Clean and inspect all parts, replace any damaged or worn parts as necessary.

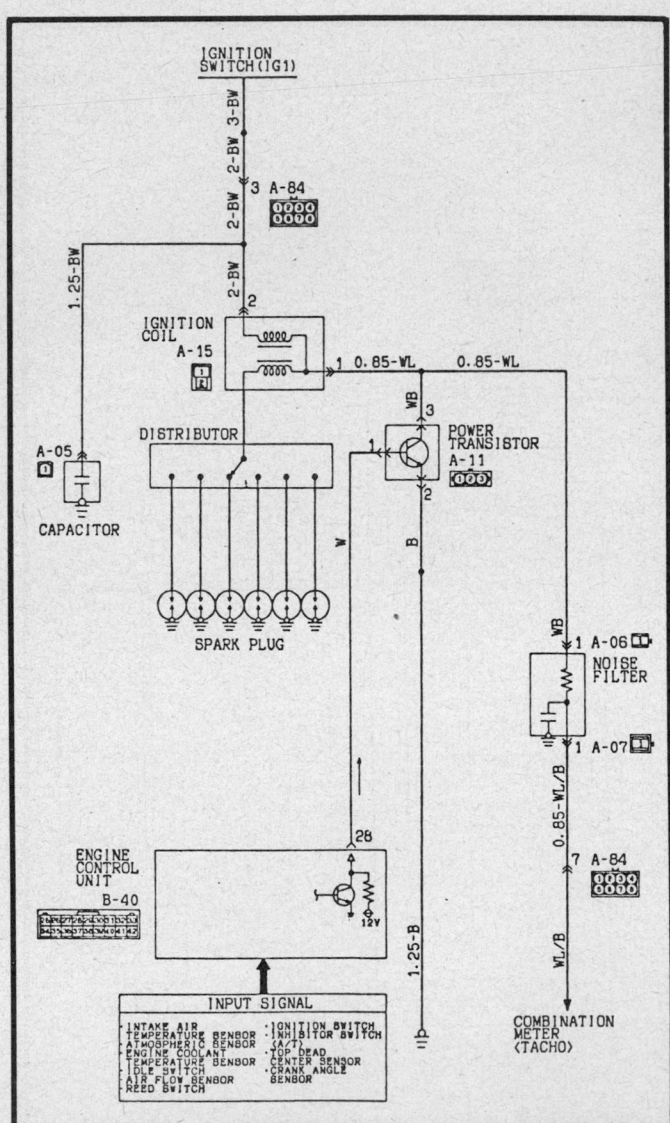

Ignition system schematic – Mitsubishi 3.0L engine

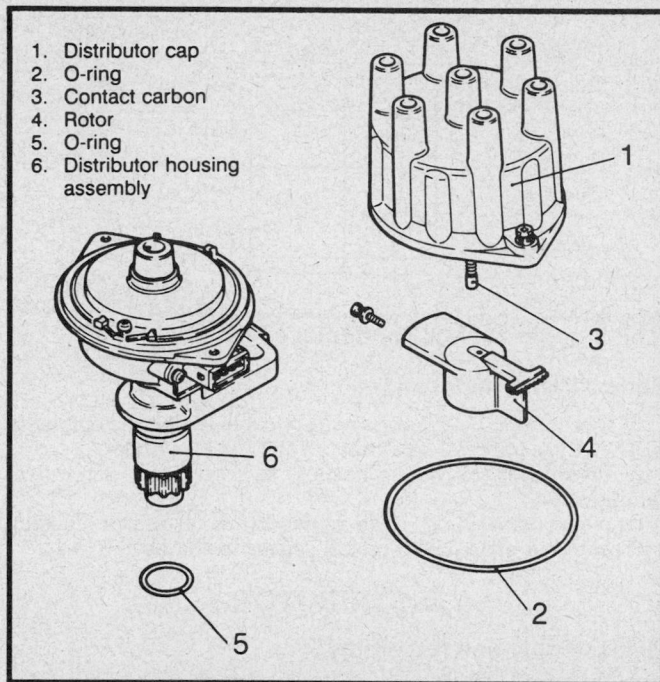

1. Distributor cap
2. O-ring
3. Contact carbon
4. Rotor
5. O-ring
6. Distributor housing assembly

Distributor assembly — Mitsubishi 3.0L engine

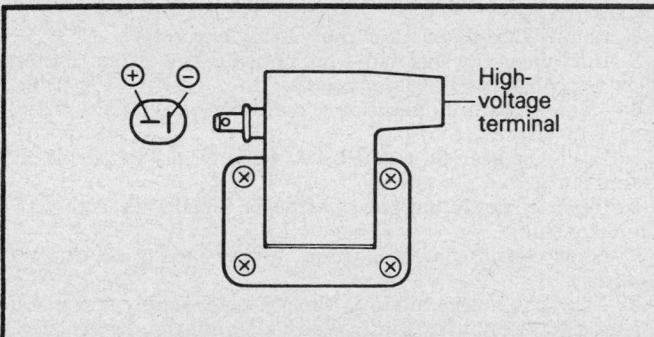

High-voltage terminal

Checking ignition coil voltage — Mitsubishi 3.0L engine

10. Install the signal rotor shaft into distributor shaft.
11. Install the signal rotor shaft tightening screw and cap.
12. Install the governor springs.
13. Install the breaker plate assembly.
14. Install the breaker plate retaining screws. Tighten 2 signal generator screws temporarily.
15. Adjust the air gap between signal rotor and signal generator. Air gap should be 0.031 in. (0.8mm).
16. Install the signal generator and 2 screws.
17. Install the igniter and 2 screws.
18. Connect the vacuum controller link to breaker plate and tighten the vacuum controller retaining screw.
19. Install the rotor to rotor shaft.

Electronic Control Ignition Timing (ECIT) System

GENERAL INFORMATION

Ignition timing is controlled by the electronic control ignition timing (ECIT) system. The standard ignition timing data for engine operating conditions are programmed into the fuel injec-tion computer (ECU) at the time of manufacture. The computer uses these pre-planned values to maintain the best engine timing under all operating conditions. This results in improved economy and lowered emissions.

The engine conditions (rpm, load, coolant temperature, barometric pressure and others) are detected by the various sensors. Signals from these sensors are compared to the standard ignition timing data within the computer. Optimum timing is computed and signals to interrupt the primary current are sent to the power transistor. The ignition coil is activated, and the ignition timing is in this way controlled.

IGNITION COIL

Testing

1. Label and disconnect all wiring to coil, including the high tension cable.
2. Measure the primary coil resistance across the positive and negative terminals of ignition coil. Correct resistance for all of the single coil systems — 0.72–0.88 ohms.
3. Measure the secondary coil resistance between ignition coil positive terminal and high voltage terminal. Correct resistance for all systems using a single coil — 10.3–13.9 kilo-ohm.
4. Replace coil if any resistance is not to specification.

Removal and Installation

1. Disconnect the negative battery cable.
2. Disconnect the high tension wire from the coil.
3. Disconnect the connector at the end of the coil.
4. Remove the coil mounting bolt and remove the coil from the vehicle.
5. Install the coil in position and tighten the mounting bolt to 15–21 ft. lbs. (20–30 Nm).
6. Reconnect the electrical leads. Connect the negative battery cable.

POWER TRANSISTOR

Testing

NOTE: This test must be done with a known good ignition coil.

EXCEPT 1990 MONTERO AND PICK-UP

1. Connect a 12 volt supply to the positive terminal of the ignition coil and power supply negative to ground.

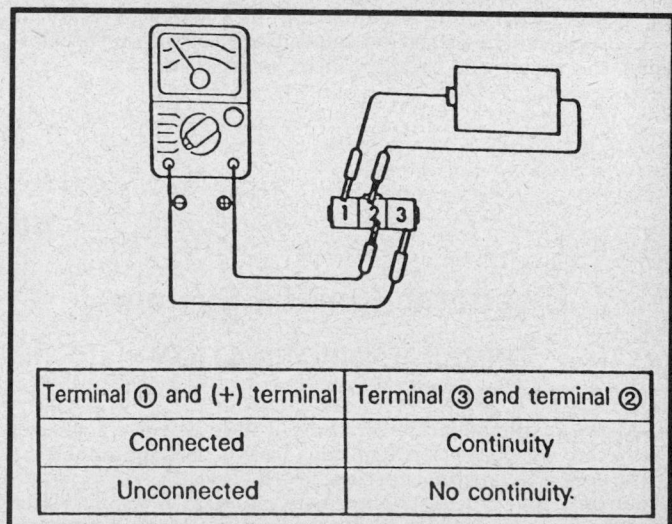

Terminal ① and (+) terminal	Terminal ③ and terminal ②
Connected	Continuity
Unconnected	No continuity.

Checking power transistor — Mitsubishi 3.0L engine

2. Connect the jumper wire between the ignition coil negative terminal and the power transistor connector terminal No. 3.

3. Connect the jumper wire between the power transistor connector terminal No. 2 and ground.

4. Connect the ohmmeter positive probe to ground.

5. Hold the high tension cable 0.3 in. (7mm) from a good metal ground. Using the ohmmeter negative probe, momentarily contact the power transistor connector terminal No. 1; a spark should emit from the ignition coil high tension cable.

6. If no spark is discharged, replace the power transistor and retest.

1990 MONTERO AND PICK-UP

1. Connect the negative terminal of a 1.5 volt dry cell to terminal No. 2 of the power transistor.

2. Connect an ohmmeter between terminals 2 and 3. Connect the positive terminal of the 1.5 volt source to terminal No. 1 on the connector; when the connection is made, the ohmmeter should show continuity. No continuity should exist when voltage is removed from terminal No. 1.

3. If any test condition is not met, replace the power transistor.

CRANKSHAFT ANGLE SENSOR

The crankshaft angle sensor, if not within the distributor, is on the end of the camshaft. It detects the position of each piston and converts those data to pulse signals which are input to the engine control unit. The ECU then computes rpm and regulates both injection timing and ignition timing.

Power for the crank angle sensor is supplied from the ignition switch and is grounded to the vehicle body. The ECU sends a 5 volt signal to the sensor, which returns an interrupted signal to the computer. The pattern of interruption or pulsing is read by the ECU.

Testing

1. With engine off, disconnect external sensor lead and connect voltmeter between terminal 2 of wire harness (not sensor lead) and ground.

2. With the ignition **ON**, meter should show supply voltage, approximately 12 volts.

3. Connect voltmeter between terminal 4 of wire harness and ground.

4. With ignition **ON**, meter should show ECU control voltage, 4.8–5.2 volts.

5. Connect ohmmeter between terminal 1 of wire harness and ground. Continuity should exist.

6. If any voltage or ground condition is not within specifications, the wiring and circuitry must be repaired.

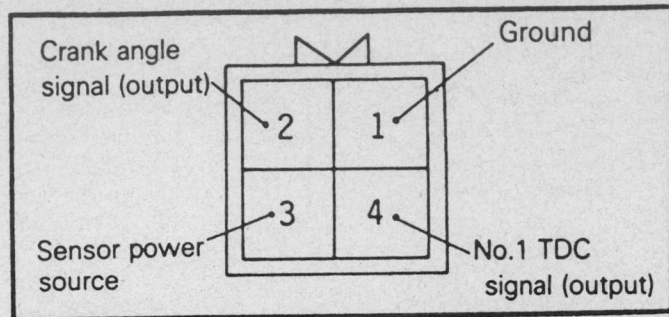

Crank angle sensor connector — Mitsubishi 3.0L

Removal and Installation

1. Disconnect the negative battery cable. Bring the engine to TDC of the compression stroke on the No. 1 cylinder.

2. Disconnect the wiring harness to sensor and remove retaining bolts.

3. When reinstalling, align punch mark on sensor housing with notch in plate., then install sensor to the head.

DISTRIBUTOR

Disassembly and Assembly

1. Disconnect the negative battery cable. Remove the distributor from the vehicle. Support the distributor in a suitable holding fixture.

2. Remove the distributor cap, O-ring and rotor.

3. Disconnect the lead wire from housing. Not all distributors allow the wiring to be disconnected.

4. Make a position identifying mark for driven gear on the distributor shaft.

5. Place the gear on a soft base (wood block) and drive out spring pin with a pin punch.

6. Remove the O-ring and distributor housing assembly.

To assemble:

7. After cleaning or inspection, install O-ring on housing assembly.

8. Align the marks made at time of disassembly and install the gear to distributor shaft. When aligning the driven gear's mating mark and the housing's mating mark, set the shaft so that the rotor locating notch (top of the shaft) is positioned as shown. Align the pin hole and drive a new spring pin. Install the pin so that the slot is at a right angle relative to the shaft.

9. Connect the wire harness to the housing if it was disconnected.

10. Install the rotor, O-ring and cap. Reinstall the distributor.

ISUZU

Electronic Ignition System

GENERAL INFORMATION

EXCEPT 2.8L ENGINE

There are 2 types of ignition systems used on Isuzu vehicles: one uses a conventional centrifugal advance type distributor and the other uses a fully transistorized type distributor.

Conventional type distributors are made up of the distribtor shaft, rotor shaft, rotor head, breaker assembly, reluctor, governor flyweight, pinion gear and vacuum control unit.

Transistorized distributors consist of dust bushing, rotor, pinion and a crank angle sensor built into the distributor housing. The crank angle sensor uses a photo-electric pick-up to measure piston position and engine speed.

2.8L ENGINE

The computer controlled Electronic Spark Timing (EST) ignition system used on the 2.8L engine consists of the battery, distributor, engine control switch, spark plugs, primary and secondary wiring.

The computer, or Electronic Control Module (ECM), monitors the information from the engine sensor network. The ECM

1. Distributor cap
2. Distributor rotor
3. Distributor lead wire
4. Vacuum control
5. Reluctor
6. Breaker plate, magnet and unit
7. Distributor magnet
8. Distributor unit
9. Breaker plate
10. Housing gasket
11. Roll pin
12. Pinion gear and gasket
13. Distributor shaft
14. Rotor shaft
15. Governor flywheel and spring
16. Distributor housing

Distributor assembly—Isuzu 2.2L engine

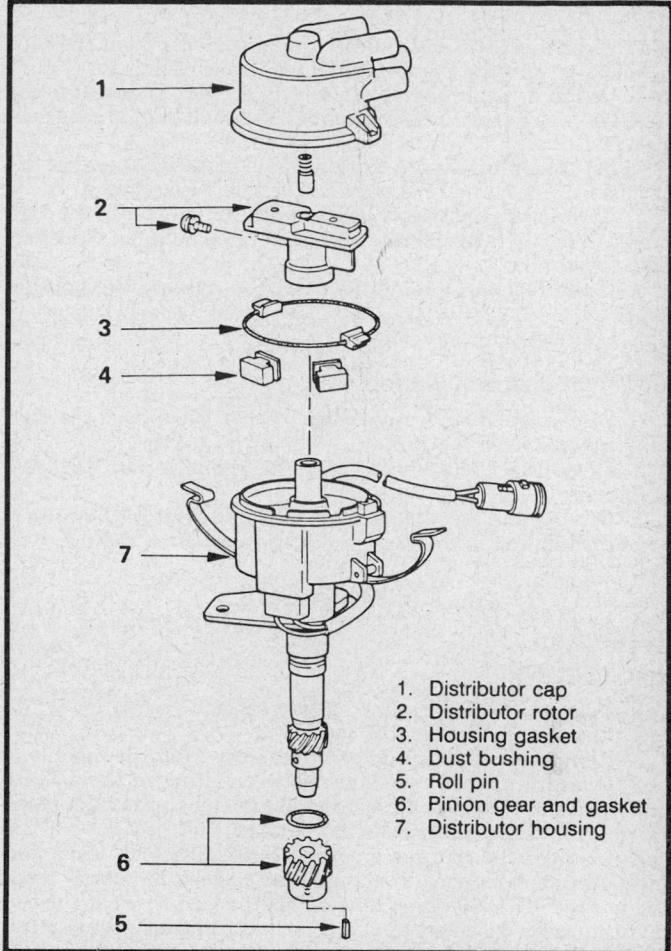

1. Distributor cap
2. Distributor rotor
3. Housing gasket
4. Dust bushing
5. Roll pin
6. Pinion gear and gasket
7. Distributor housing

Distributor assembly—Isuzu 2.5L engine

uses this information to calculate the proper spark timing and tell the distributor when to make timing modifications.

The distributor does not have centrifugal advance weights, springs or a vacuum advance unit.

The 2.8L engine is equipped with Electronic Spark Control (ESC). At the heart of the ESC system is the knock sensor which is mounted to the engine block. The knock sensor is connected to the electronic spark control module which is located on the right fender panel in the engine compartment or on a bracket mounted to the block. In response to engine knock, the sensor transmits a signal to the electronic spark module ("half function box"). The spark control module sends the signal to the ECM which in turn tells the distributor to retard the spark timing up to 20 degrees to reduce spark knock in the engine.

IGNITION COIL

Testing

EXCEPT 2.8L ENGINE

1. Disconnect the wiring along with the ignition coil and high tension cable at the connector.

2. Using a suitable ohmeter, measure the resistance of the coil across the appropriate coil terminals. The resistance should be as follows:
  a. Primary coil resistance
    2.2L engine—1.2–1.4 ohms
    2.5L engine—0.81–0.99 ohms

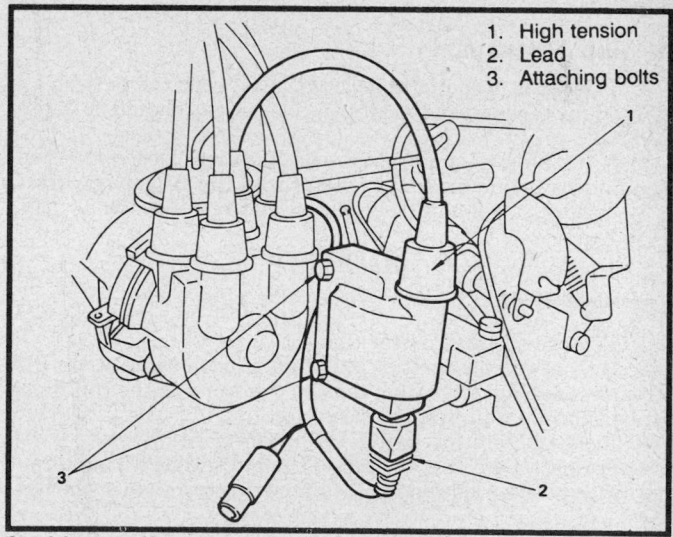

1. High tension
2. Lead
3. Attaching bolts

Ignition coil mounting—Isuzu engines

  b. Secondary coil resistance
    2.2L engine—8.6–13.0 kilo-ohms
    2.5L engines—7.5–13.5 kilo-ohms
  c. Insulation resistance
    2.2L and 2.5L engines—more than 10 mega-ohms.

2.8L ENGINE

1. Disconnect the distributor wire and wiring from the coil.
2. Make sure the metal ground surface is clean.
3. Connect an ohmmeter to the coil. Set the ohmmeter to the high ohms scale and measure the resistance. It should read infinite resistance.
4. Set the ohmmeter to the low ohms scale and measure the resistance. It should read very low or zero resistance.
5. Reverse the ohmmeter leads. Set the ohmmeter to the high ohms scale and measure the resistance. It should not read infinite resistance.
6. If the resistance is not as described, replace the ignition coil.
7. Connect the coil wiring.

Removal and Installation

1. Disconnect the negative battery cable. Disconnect the high tension wire from the coil.
2. Disconnect the wires from the positive and negative terminals.
3. Remove the 2 coil attaching bolts and remove the coil.
4. Installation is the reverse of the removal procedure.

PICK-UP COIL

Testing

2.8L ENGINE

1. Disconnect the negative battery cable.
2. Remove the distributor cap.
3. Disconnect the pick-up coil connector from the module.
4. Measure the coil resistance between either of the pick-up coil leads and the housing. Set the ohmmeter to the high ohms range. Infinite resistance should be read.
5. Connect the ohmmeter probes across the coil leads and measure the resistance. It should read a constant, steady reading in the 500–1000 ohms range. Flex the lead wires at the coil and connector by hand to check for intermittent opens in the wiring.
6. If the resistance readings are not within specifications, replace the coil.

Air Gap Adjustment

1. Insert the proper size feeler gage between the pick-up coil projections to measure the air gap. The air gap should be 0.012–0.020 in.
2. If the air gap is not within specification, loosen the 2 adjusting screws and move the igniter until the air gap is correct.
3. Tighten the 2 adjusting screws and re-check the air gap.

IGNITER

Testing

1. Remove the distributor cap.
2. Disconnect the ignition coil high tension cable at the distributor side. Move the high tension cable end to the coil fixing screw and maintain a 5mm clearance.
3. Place the ignition switch to the **ON** position.
4. Connect a 1.5 volt dry cell to the red igniter wiring terminal at the positive side and the white wiring terminal at the negative side.

NOTE: Do not apply voltage to the igniter for more than 3 seconds at a time to avoid destroying the power transistor in the igniter.

5. The igniter is normal when sparks are generated between the high tension cable and ground when one connected wiring (or probe) is disconnected.
6. If the igniter fails this test (no sparks), replace it.

7. Reconnect all disconnected wiring and install all removed parts.

DISTRIBUTOR

Disassembly and Assembly

2.2L ENGINE

1. Disconnect the negative battery cable. Remove the distributor from the vehicle and support it in a suitable holding fixture. Remove the distributor cap retaining screw.
2. Remove the distributor cap and rotor.
3. Remove the carbon points from the cap.
4. Remove distributor packing gasket and packing.
5. Remove the distributor lead wire.
6. Remove the ground terminal and vacuum control mounting screw. Remove the vacuum control unit.
7. Remove the reluctor as follows:
   a. Pry loose the reluctor outer cover.
   b. Using 2 small pry bars or equivalent, slide the pry bars into the lower side of the reluctor and pull it free.
8. Remove the breaker plate, magnet and distributor unit assembly.
9. Remove the roll pin, pinion gear and gasket as follows:
   a. File off the staked end of the roll pin.
   b. From the opposite side, drive the roll pin from the gear set using a suitable drill press.
   c. Pull the pinion gear and gasket from the distributor shaft.
10. Remove the distributor shaft and rotor shaft.
11. Remove the governor springs. Release the snap ring and remove the governor weights.

To assemble:

12. Clean and inspect all parts, replace any damaged or worn parts as necessary.
13. Inspect the distributor cap for cracking, burning, corrosion and wear.
14. Check the ventilator, electrode, center contact piece and spring.
15. The carbon length limit is 0.087 in. (2.2mm) or less.
16. Apply a vacuum to the vacuum advance controller and check to see that it is operating smoothly.
17. To reassemble, follow the disassembly procedure in the reverse order. When installing the pinion gear roll pin make sure to stake it on both sides after it is in place. Be sure to carefully align the rotor shaft notches and the shaft notches when installing the rotor shaft. Also when installing the igniter and breaker assembly, align the scribe mark on the breaker plate and the housing. When installing the reluctor, the roll pin notch and the reluctor notch must be parallel when the roll pin is inserted into the reluctor.
18. Inspect the air gap, by using a feeler gauge. Measure the gap between the signal rotor and the pick-up coil projection. The air gap should be 0.008–0.0016 in.
19. If an air gap adjustment is needed, loosen the 2 screws and move the igniter until the proper specified gap (0.012–0.020) is reached. Then tighten the 2 screws and recheck the air gap.
20. Also check the governor function by turning the rotor both to the right and the left. The rotor should spin freely in both directions.

2.5L ENGINE

1. Disconnect the negative battery cable. Remove the distributor from the vehicle and support it in a suitable holding fixture. Remove the distributor cap assembly.
2. Remove the rotor set screw (if so equipped) and remove the rotor.
3. Remove the distributor packing gasket and packing.
4. Remove the distributor ventilation bushings. Remove the distributor bracket bolts and remove distributor body assembly.
5. Remove the distributor base plate O-ring and discard it.

To assemble:

6. Clean and inspect all parts, replace any damaged or worn parts as necessary.

7. Inspect the distributor cap for cracking, burning, corrosion and wear.

8. Remove the 2 screws of the fixing rotor plate cover, then remove it. Using a soft brush, clean the rotor plate in the angle signal port area while blowing some air over it.

NOTE: The distributor body assembly is of an integral design and cannot be disassembled. The entire assembly must be replaced if service becomes necessary.

9. Assembly is the reverse of the disassembly procedure.

2.8L ENGINE

There are no serviceable components in the distributor used with this engine.

MAZDA

Electronic Ignition System

GENERAL DESCRIPTION

The Mazda electronic ignition system, uses a solid state ignition system with conventional distributor. This system is used on the B series Pick-Ups. The principal components of the ignition system are the spark plugs, ignition coil and distributor. The distributor has a rotor, a module, a signal rotor, a vacuum advance, a centrifugal advance, igniter and ignition coil.

The pick-up coil is used to generate the ignition signal and consists of a signal rotor, a magnet and a signal generator. The pole piece is attached to the distributor shaft, and the magnet and the pick-up coil are attached to the pick-up coil base plate.

When the distributor shaft rotates, the magnetic flux passing through the pick-up coil varies due to the change in the air gap between the pick-up coil and the pole piece. As a result, the alternating current voltage is induced in the pick-up coil. The induced voltage turns the module on and off which switches the ignition coil primary current off. Thus, the high voltage is induced in the secondary winding of the ignition coil and ignition sparks are generated at the spark plugs.

IGNITION COIL

Testing

Before checking the coil, start and run the engine as to get the coil to normal operating temperature.

1. Using a suitable ohmmeter, check the primary resistance. Primary resistance should be as follows:

    1986–1988 models and 1989–90 B2200 – 1.0–1.3 ohms
    1989–90 B2600 – Terminal – 0.77–0.95 ohms
    1990 MPV with 4 cylinder engine – 0.9–1.1 Kilo-ohms
    1990 MPV with 6 cylinder engine – 0.81–0.99 ohms

2. Using a suitable ohmmeter, check the secondary resistance. Secondary resistance should be as follows:

    1986–1988 B2000, B2200 and 1989–90 models – 6–30 Kilo-ohms
    1988–90 B2600 – 10–20 Kilo-ohms
    1990 MPV – 6–30 Kilo-ohms

3. Measure the insulation resistance between the primary terminal and the casing. Be sure to use a 500 volt megger resistance range for this measurement. Insulation resistance should be 10 Mega-ohms or more.

Removal and Installation

1. Disconnect the negative battery cable. Disconnect the high tension wire from the coil.

2. Disconnect the wires from the positive and negative terminals.

3. Remove the 2 coil attaching bolts and remove the coil.

4. Installation is the reverse of the removal and Installation

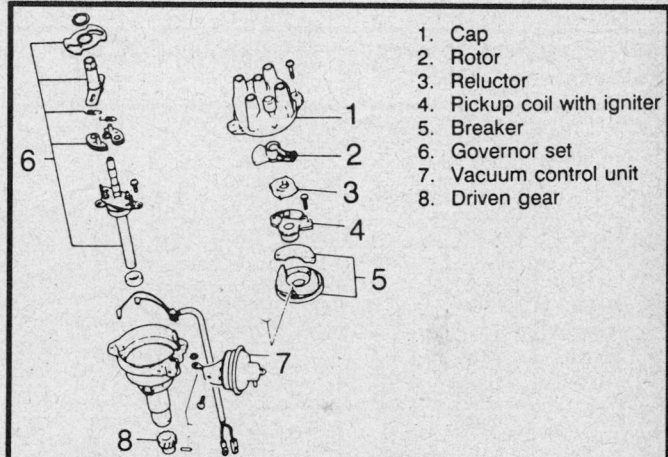

1. Cap
2. Rotor
3. Reluctor
4. Pickup coil with igniter
5. Breaker
6. Governor set
7. Vacuum control unit
8. Driven gear

Distirbutor assembly – Mazda B Series

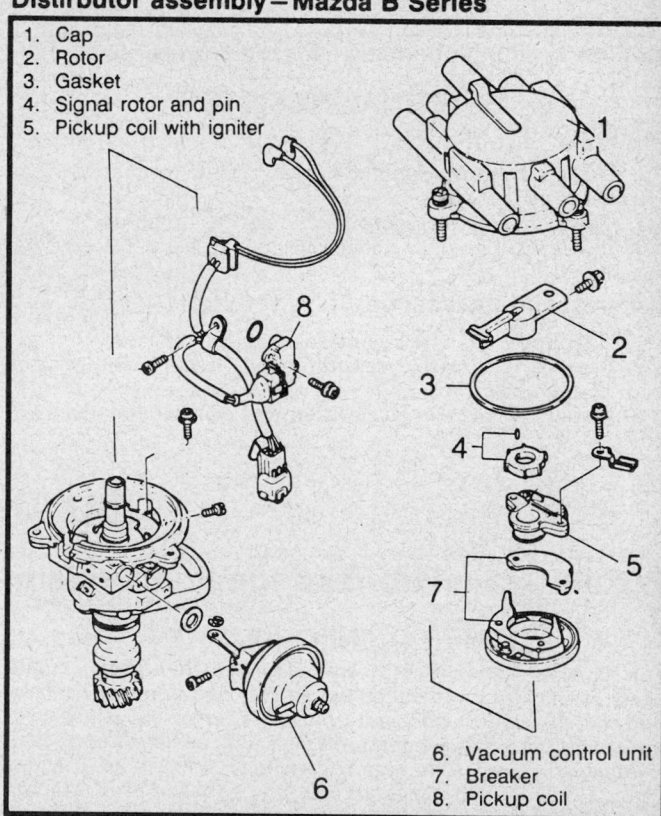

1. Cap
2. Rotor
3. Gasket
4. Signal rotor and pin
5. Pickup coil with igniter

6. Vacuum control unit
7. Breaker
8. Pickup coil

Distirbutor assembly – Mazda MPV

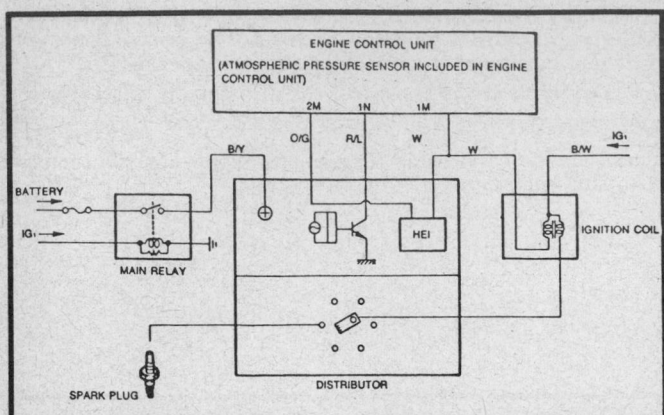

Ignition system schematic — Mazda 2.0L, 2.2L and 2.6L engines

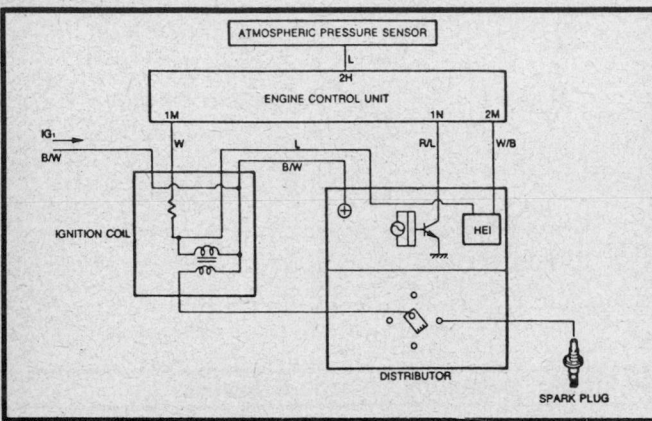

Ignition system schematic — Mazda 3.0L engine

EXTERNAL RESISTOR

Testing

1. Using a suitable ohmmeter, measure the resistance of the external resistor.
2. The standard resistance should be 1.0–1.5 ohms.
3. If specifications are not as specified, replace the external resistor.

Removal and Installation

1. Disconnect the electrical leads from the resistor.
2. Remove the resistor retaining bolt. Remove the resistor from the vehicle.
3. Install the resistor in position and connect the electrical leads.

VACUUM ADVANCE

Testing

1. Start the engine and allow to reach normal operating temperature.
2. Connect a timing light and tachometer to the engine. Check that the idle speed and ignition timing are within specification. Remove the tachometer.
3. Disconnect and plug the vacuum hoses from the vacuum controller. Run the engine at idle.
4. Connect a suitable hand operated vacuum pump to the vacuum controller. Using the timing light, check the advance on the crankshaft pulley while applying vacuum.

PICK-UP COIL WITH IGNITER

Testing

1. Using a suitable ohmmeter measure the resistance of the pick-up coil.
2. Pick-up coil resistance should be 900–1200 ohms.
3. If specifications are not as specified, replace the pick-up coil with igniter.

DISTRIBUTOR

Disassembly and Assembly

1. Disconnect the negative battery cable. Remove the distributor from the vehicle. Place the distributor assembly into a suitable holding fixture. Remove the cap and rotor.
2. Using 2 small pry bars or equivalent, remove the reluctor and/or signal rotor and pin.
3. Remove the pick-up coil attaching screws, then remove the pick-up coil from the distributor. Remove the governor assembly.
4. Remove the vacuum controller and the breaker plate assembly.
5. Using a suitable drift, remove the distributor drive gear pin, then the drive gear. Remove the shaft from the distributor housing.

To assemble:

6. Clean and inspect all parts, replace any damaged or worn parts as necessary.
7. Inspect the distributor cap for cracking, burning, corrosion and wear.
8. On B2600 series, align the top of reluctor with the pick-up coil protrusion and check the air gap.
9. The air gap should be 0.031 in. If the air gap is not within specification, loosen the pick-up coil mounting bolt and move the pick-up coil until the air gap is within specification. Tighten the mounting bolts and recheck.
10. On all models, to reassemble, follow the disassembly procedure in the reverse order.

SUZUKI/GEO

Suzuki Transistorized Ignition System

GENERAL INFORMATION

The ignition system is fully transistorized. The basic components of the system includes the battery, ignition switch, ignition coil, distributor and spark plugs. The distributor has a rotor, an ignitor, a signal generator, a vacuum advancer and a centrifugal advancer. The signal generator consists of a signal rotor, a magnet and a pick-up coil. The signal rotor is attached to the distributor shaft and the magnet and pick-up coil are attached to the generator

When the distributor shaft rotates, the air gap between the pick-up coil and the signal rotor changes. As a result, the magnetic flux passing through the pick-up coil varies and creates an alternating current voltage to be induced in the pick-up coil. The voltage signal turns on and off the ignitor which switches off the

ignition coil primary circuit. When the ignition coil primary circuit is interrupped, a high voltage is induced in the secondary winding of the ignition coil and an ignition spark is generated at the spark plugs via the rotor and high tension wires. A brief description of the system components follows:

Distributor—the distributor acts basically as a rotory switch. It connects the high voltage from the ignition coil secondary winding to the spark plugs via the rotor, distributor cap and high tension wires. The distributor shaft, from its driven gear end to the rotor carrying end, is a 2 piece shaft connected together through the timing advancer.

Vacuum Advancer—the vacuum advance mechanism, attached to the distributor, is a vacuum controlled device which assist in ignition timing advancement. When vacuum in the carburetor gets high, the pressure acting on the diaphragm overcomes the spring force in the vacuum advancer and a controller rod attached to the diaphragm is pulled. The controller rod in turns pulls the generator base plate counter to the direction of distributor shaft rotation to advance the ignition timing.

Centrifugal advancer—the centrifugal advancer, located inside the distributor, is essentially a flyweight mechanism which assist in ignition timing advancement. Timing advancement is accomplished by twisting the top shaft piece (slightly ahead) relative to the bottom shaft piece in the same direction of distributor shaft rotation. The twisting movement is produced by the speed dependent radial movememts of the 2 flyweights.

Ignition coil—the ignition coil is basically a step-up transformer. The primary and secondary windings are so close to each other that any fluxuation in the primary current induces a very large voltage in the secondary winding. The ignition coil has 3 terminals, 1 high tension terminal and 2 low tension terminals.

IGNITION COIL

Testing

1. Disconnect the negative battery cable and remove the ignition coil.
2. Measure the primary coil resistance between the positive and negative terminals.

NOTE: Measure the readings when the ignition coil is approximately 68°F (20°C).

3. The primary coil resistance should be 1.35–1.65 ohms.
4. Measure the secondary coil resistance between the positive and the high tension terminals.
5. The secondary coil resistance should be 11.0–14.5 kiloohms.
6. If any readings are not within specification, replace the ignition coil.

Removal and Installation

1. Disconnect the negative battery cable.
2. Remove the high tension wire and the lead wires from the coil.
3. Remove the cil mounting bolts and remove the coil from the vehicle.
4. Install the coil in position in the vehicle. Connect the lead and high tension wires.
5. Connect the negative battery cable.

SIGNAL GENERATOR (PICK-UP COIL)

Testing

1. Disconnect the negative battery cable.
2. Remove the distributor cap, ignitor dust cover, ignitor and signal generator.
3. Disconnect and tag the electrical leads from the ignitor.

NOTE: Never connect the signal generator electrical leads reversely. Reverse connection may cause damage to the generator and ignitor.

4. Measure the resistance across the signal generator (pick-up coil) electrical leads. The signal generator (pick-up coil) resistance should be within 130–190 ohms.
5. If the resistance is not within specification, replace the signal generator.
6. Install the signal generator and adjust the signal rotor air gap.

IGNITER

Testing

1. Disconnect the negative battery cable.
2. Remove the distributor cap, ignitor dust cover, ignitor and generator.
3. Disconnect and tag the electrical leads from the ignitor.

NOTE: Never connect the signal generator electrical leads reversely. Reverse connection may cause damage to the generator and ignitor. Under no circumstances should the ohmmeter be connected reversely. Also, try not to allow the ohmmeter to be connected longer than 2–3 seconds.

4. Connect an ohmmeter (set at 1–10 ohm range), a test lamp and a 12 volt battery to the ignitor as indicated.
5. If the test lamp illuminates after all connections are made, it indicates that the ignitor is satisfactory.
6. If the test lamp fails to illuminate after all connections are made, replace the ignitor.
7. Reconnect the electrical wires of the generator to the ignitor. After the generator and ignitor have been assembled, adjust the air gap.

SIGNAL ROTOR AIR GAP

Checking

1. Disconnect the negative battery cable.
2. Remove the distributor cap, rotor and ignitor dust cover.
3. Using a feeler gauge, measure the air gap between the signal rotor tooth and the generator. The signal rotor air gap should be 0.008–0.016 in. (0.2–0.4mm).
4. If the air gap is out of specification, adjustment is necessary. Adjust the air gap as follows:
   a. Remove the ignitor.
   b. Loosen the signal generator retaining screws.

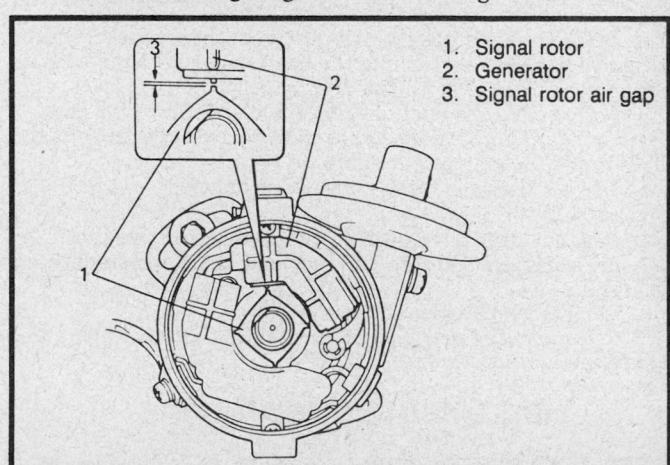

1. Signal rotor
2. Generator
3. Signal rotor air gap

Adjusting the signal rotor air gap—Suzuki 1.3L, 1.6L engines

c. Move the signal generator and adjust the air gap to specification.

d. After adjustment, tighten the signal generator retaining screws and recheck the air gap.

5. Install the ignitor, rotor and distributor.

VACUUM AND CENTRIFUGAL ADVANCER

Testing

1. Disconnect the negative battery cable.
2. Remove the distributor cap.
3. Disconnect the vacuum hose from the 3-way joint and connect a vacuum pump gauge.
4. Apply vacuum and check that the vacuum gauge needle remains constant; then, release the vacuum.
5. Check that the generator base plate moves smoothly. If the plate does not move smoothly, check the base plate or vacuum controller.
6. To check the centrifugal advancer, turn the rotor clockwise by finger and release it.
7. Check that the rotor returns smoothly counterclockwise by spring force.
8. If defective, replace the distributor.

DISTRIBUTOR

Disassembly and Assembly

1. Remove the ignitor and signal generator.
2. Remove the vacuum controller and then the generator base plate.
3. Remove the vacuum controller retaining screw and the vacuum controller rod snap washer. Remove the 2 base plate retaining screws and remove the base plate. Check the base plate for smooth rotation. If it does not rotate smoothly, replace it.

To Assemble:

4. Position the generator base plate into the distributor housing while aligning the 4 clips on the base plate into the grooves of the distributor case.
5. Install the 2 base plate retaining screws.
6. Install the vacuum controller; then, install the snap washer and retaining screw.
7. Install the generator assembly and adjust the signal rotor air gap to specification.
8. Install the ignitor to distributor housing.

DISTRIBUTOR DRIVEN GEAR

Removal and Installation

1. Disconnect the negative battery cable.
2. Before removing the distributor from the engine, check for excessive backlash by turning the shaft back and forth with its driven gear in mesh with the driving gear.
3. Remove the distributor from the distributor gear case.
4. Grind off both caulked ends of the driven gear set pin and drive it out the distributor shaft.
5. Inspect the gear teeth for wear or damage.

To Install:

6. Position the driven gear on the distributor shaft.
7. Fit a new set pin into the gear and shaft and caulk it on both ends.
8. Reinstall the distributor.
9. Reconnect the negative battery cable, start the engine and adjust the ignition timing.

DISTRIBUTOR GEAR CASE

Removal and Installation

1. Disconnect the negative battery cable.
2. Remove the distributor from the distributor gear case.

3. Before removing the distributor gear case, place an oil container under the gear case. Remove the distributor gear case retaining bolts and remove the gear case.
4. Remove the O-ring from the gear case and discard it.

To install:

4. Lubricate the new O-ring with clean engine oil and install it into the gear case.
5. Position the gear case on the cylinder head and install the retaining bolts.
6. Install the distributor into the gear case.
7. Reconnect the negative battery cable.
8. Check and adjust the engine oil level, as necessary.
9. Start the engine and adjust the ignition timing.

Geo Electronic Ignition System

GENERAL INFORMATION

The Geo Tracker uses a solid state ignition system with conventional distributor. The principal components of the ignition system are the spark plugs, ignition coil and distributor. The distributor has a rotor, a module, a pole piece, a vacuum advance, a centrifugal advance and ignition coil.

The signal generator (pick-up coil) is used to generate the ignition signal and consists of a signal rotor (pole piece), a magnet and a signal generator (pick-up coil). The pole piece is attached to the distributor shaft, and the magnet and the pick-up coil are attached to the pick-up coil base plate.

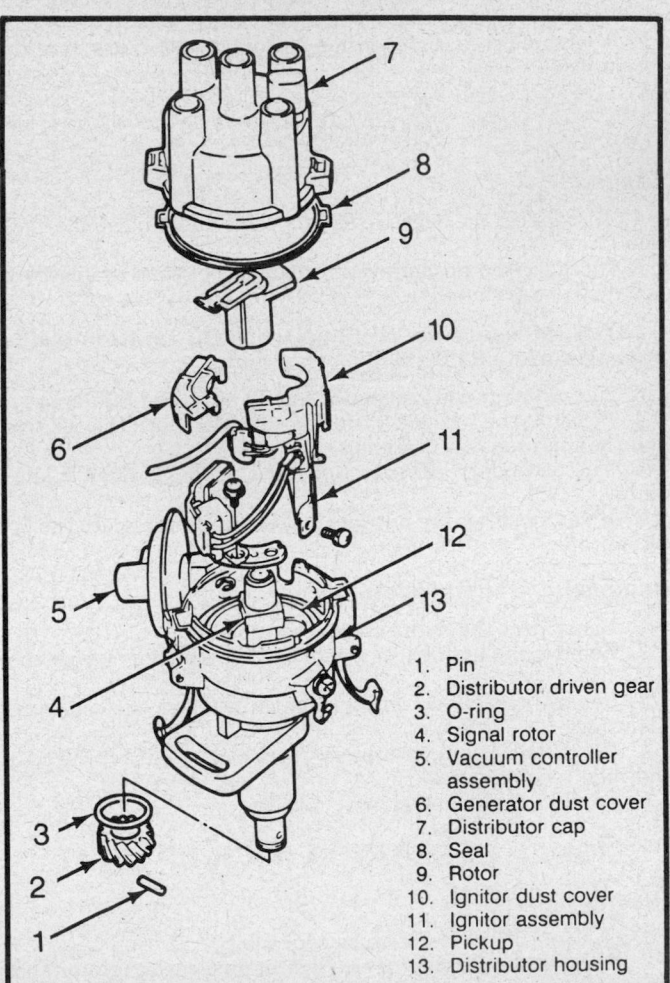

1. Pin
2. Distributor driven gear
3. O-ring
4. Signal rotor
5. Vacuum controller assembly
6. Generator dust cover
7. Distributor cap
8. Seal
9. Rotor
10. Ignitor dust cover
11. Ignitor assembly
12. Pickup
13. Distributor housing

Distributor assembly—Geo Tracker

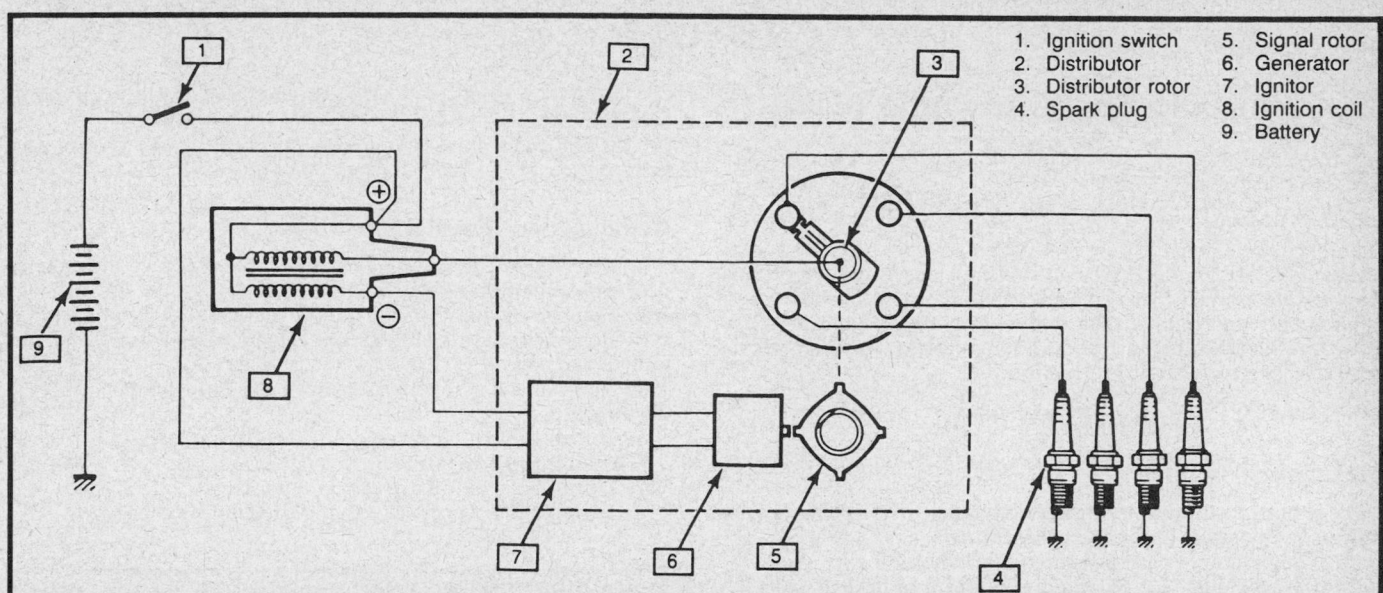

1. Ignition switch
2. Distributor
3. Distributor rotor
4. Spark plug
5. Signal rotor
6. Generator
7. Ignitor
8. Ignition coil
9. Battery

Ignition system schematic—Geo Tracker

When the distributor shaft rotates, the magnetic flux passing through the pick-up coil varies due to the change in the air gap between the pick-up coil and the pole piece. As a result, the alternating current voltage is induced in the pick-up coil. The induced voltage turns the module on and off which switches the ignition coil primary current off. Thus, the high voltage is induced in the secondary winding of the ignition coil and ignition sparks are generated at the spark plugs.

VACUUM ADVANCE UNIT.

Testing

Check to see if the diaphragm functions normally when applying about 16 in. Hg (400mm Hg) of vacuum to the main and sub diaphragm.

PICK-UP COIL

Testing

Measure the resistance of the pick-up coil by connecting the negative probe to the red wire and the positive probe to the white wire. The standard resistance should be 130–190 ohms. If not, replace the pick-up coil.

Removal and Installation

1. Disconnect the negative battery cable. Mark the position of the distributor.
2. Remove the distributor from the vehicle.
3. Remove the cap, rotor and dust cover.
4. Disconnect the wiring harness.
5. Remove the module.
6. Disconnect the vacuum advance link from the generator assembly.
7. Remove the screws and pick-up coil.

To install:

8. Install the pick-up coil and slightly tighten the retaining screws.
9. Measure the air gap between the pick-up coil and timer core using a thickness gauge. The thickness should be 0.008–0.015 in. (0.2–0.4mm). Tighten the pick-up screws.
10. Install the distributor into the vehicle and adjust timing.

IGNITION COIL

Testing

INPUT VOLTAGE

With the ignition switch **ON**, measure the voltage between the positive terminal of the coil and ground. The value should be 12 volts.

PRIMARY RESISTANCE

With the ignition switch **OFF**, disconnect the coil terminal and measure the resistance between the positive terminal and the negative terminal. The standard resistance should be 1.06–1.43 ohms (Tracker 1.35–1.65 ohms).

SECONDARY RESISTANCE

With the ignition switch **OFF**, disconnect the coil terminal and measure the resistance between the positive terminal and the high voltage terminal. The standard resistance should be 10,800–16,200 ohms (Tracker 11,000–14,500 ohms).

MODULE

Connect an ohmmeter, bulb and 12 volt battery to the module. Set the ohmmeter at the 1–10 ohm range, connect the negative probe to the red wire terminal of the module and connect the positive probe to the white wire terminal. If the bulb LIGHTS, the module is satisfactory. If no light, replace the module. Do not reverse the ohmmeter connections.

TOYOTA

Electronic Spark Advance (ESA) System

GENERAL INFORMATION

The electronic control unit is programmed with data for optimum ignition timing under any and all operating conditions. Using data provided by the sensors which monitor various engine functions (rpm, intake air volume, engine temperature, etc.) the electronic control unit (microcomputer triggers the spark at precisely the right instant.

PRIMARY COIL

Resistance Testing

1. Using a suitable ohmmeter, measure the resistance between the positive and negative terminals.
2. The primary coil resistance (cold) should be:
   1986–89 Van – 4Y-EC engine – 1.2–1.5 ohms
   1986–1988 Pick-Up, Land Cruiser, 4Runner – 0.4–0.5 ohms
   1987–90 Pick-Up, Land Cruiser, 4Runner – 22R series engine – 0.4–0.5 ohms

1989–90 Pick-Up, 4Runner – 3VZ-E engine – 0.4–0.5 ohms
3. If the resistance is not within specifications replace the coil.

Removal and Installation

1. Disconnect the negative battery cable. Remove the distributor cap, packing and rotor.
2. Remove the ignition coil dust cover and dust proof packing.
3. Remove the nuts and disconnect the wires from the terminals of the coil.
4. Remove the screws and remove the ignition coil.

To Install:
5. Install the coil and replace the retaining screws.
6. Install the wires to coil.
7. Install the coil dust cover and packing.
8. Install the rotor, packing and distributor cap.

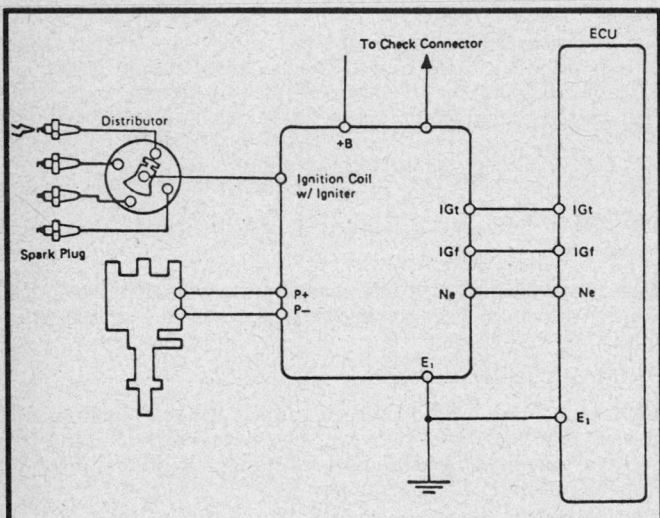

ESA ignition system schematic – Toyota 22R series engines

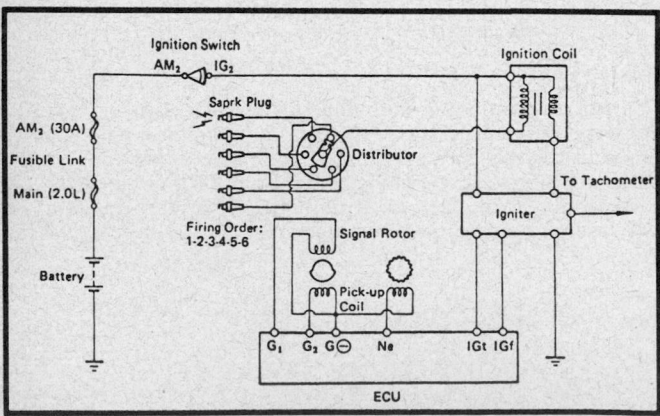

ESA ignition system schematic – Toyota 3VZ-E engine

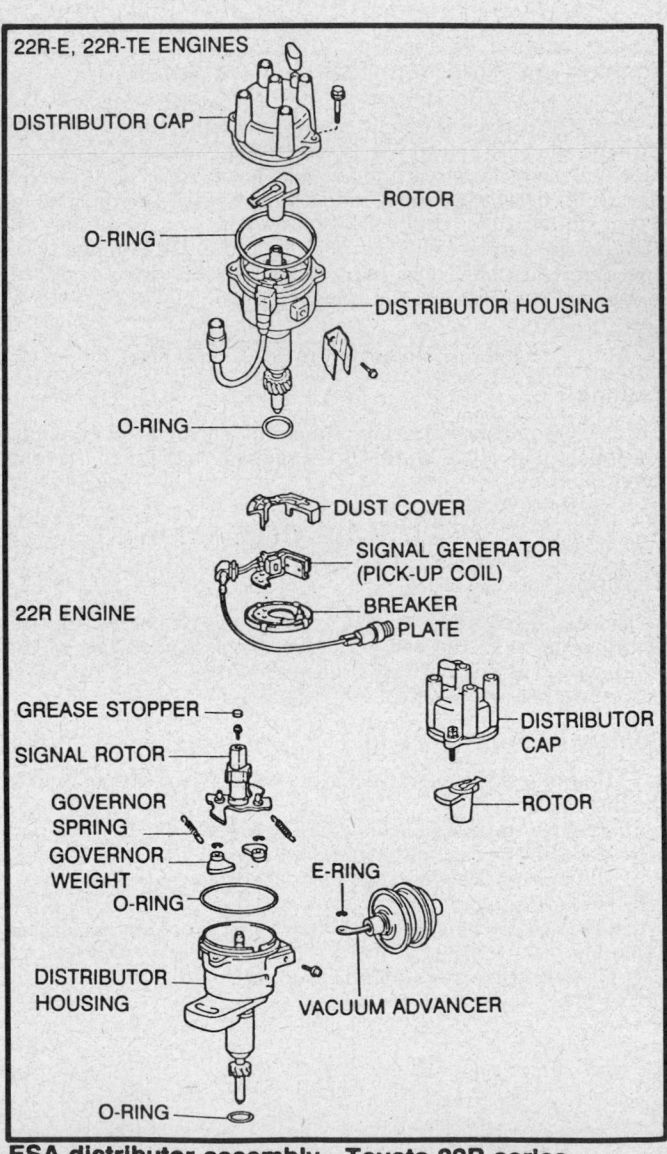

ESA distributor assembly – Toyota 22R series engines

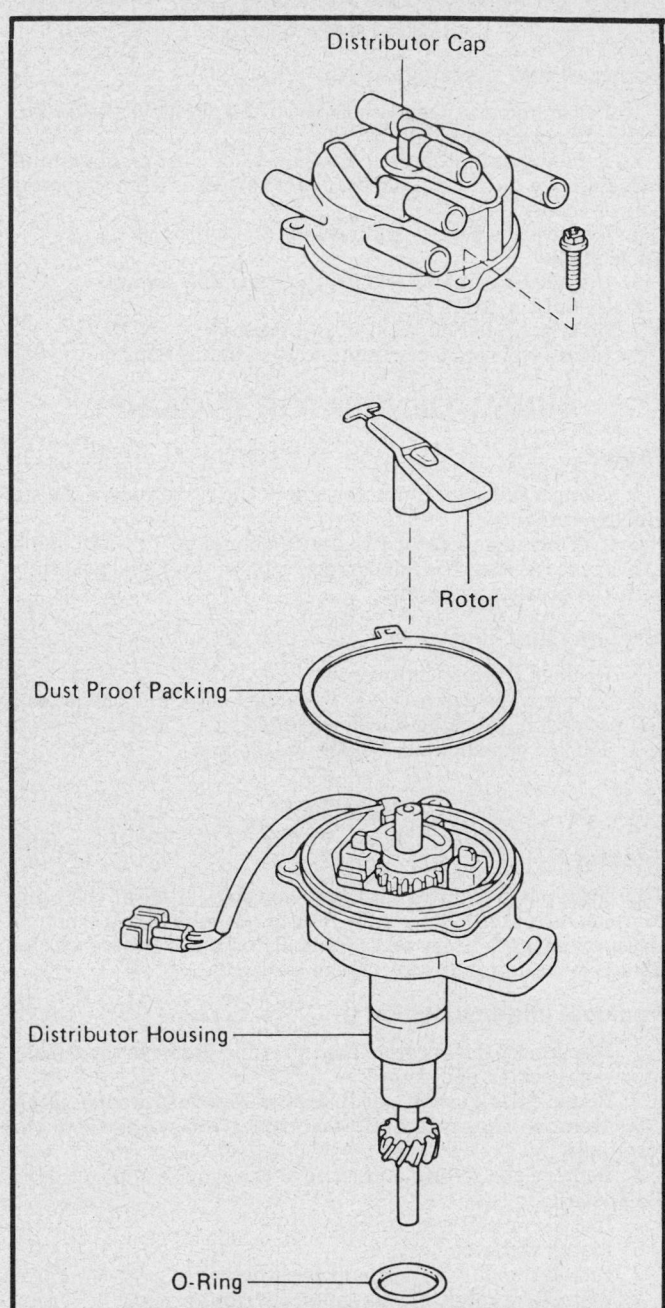

ESA distributor assembly – Toyota 3VZ-E engine

SECONDARY COIL RESISTANCE

Testing

1. Using a suitable ohmmeter, measure the resistance between the positive terminal and the high tension terminal.
2. The secondary coil resistance (cold) should be:
   1986–89 Van – 4Y-EC – 7.7–10.4 Kilo-ohms
   1986–90 Pick-Up, Land Cruiser, 4Runner – 8.5–11.5 Kilo-ohms
   1988–90 Pick-Up, 4Runner – 22R series engine – 11.4–15.6 Kilo-ohms
   1989–90 Pick-Up, 4Runner – 3VZ-E engine – 10.2–13.8 Kilo-ohms
3. If not within specifications, replace the coil.

SIGNAL GENERATOR (PICK-UP)

Testing

1. Using a suitable ohmmeter, check the resistance of the signal generator coils.
2. All signal generator pick-up resistances should be 140–180 ohms.
3. If the resistance is not correct, replace the necessary signal generator with the breaker assembly, as needed.

Air Gap Checking

1. Remove the distributor cap.
2. Measure the gap between the signal rotor and the pick-up coil projection, by using a feeler gauge.
3. The air gap should be 0.008 to 0.0016 in. (0.2–0.4mm).

DISTRIBUTOR

Disassembly and Assembly

1. Disconnect the negative battery cable. Support the distributor in a suitable holding fixture. Remove the cap, rotor, dust cover and O-ring.
2. Remove the screw and ground strap. Remove the 2 screws and pull out the signal generator (pick-up coil).
3. Remove the screw and E-ring. Pull out the vacuum advance diaphragm.
4. Remove the 2 screws and pull out the stationary plate and generator.
5. Remove the governor springs.
6. Pry out the grease stopper, remove the screws at the end of the governor shaft and pull off the signal rotor.
7. Use a suitable tool to remove the E-rings and pull off the governor weights.

To assemble:

8. Before reassembling, lightly coat the governor shaft with grease.
9. Using a suitable tool, install the governor weights with the E-rings.
10. Install the signal rotor on the governor shaft with the cut-out part positioned at the right side of the governor shaft stopper pin.
11. Apply grease to the end of the governor shaft and push on the grease stopper.
12. Install the governor springs.
13. Fit the 4 clips on the breaker plate into the housing slots, then install the 2 hold-clips with 2 screws.
14. Insert the vacuum advance diaphragm with a gasket into the distributor and place the lever hole over the plate pin. Install and tighten the vacuum advance diaphragm screw.
15. Align the rotor tooth with the pick-up coil, then make sure the air gap measurement is 0.008–0.016 in.
16. Install the dust cover O-ring and rotor.

Integrated Ignition Assembly (IIA)
GENERAL INFORMATION

The Integrated Ignition Assembly (IIA) is a typical electronic ignition system. The major components consist of an integral ignition coil, signal generator (pick-up), igniter, vacuum and governor weight advance system and a rotor and distributor cap distribution system.

PRIMARY COIL RESISTANCE

Testing

1. Using a suitable ohmmeter, measure the resistance between the positive and negative terminals.

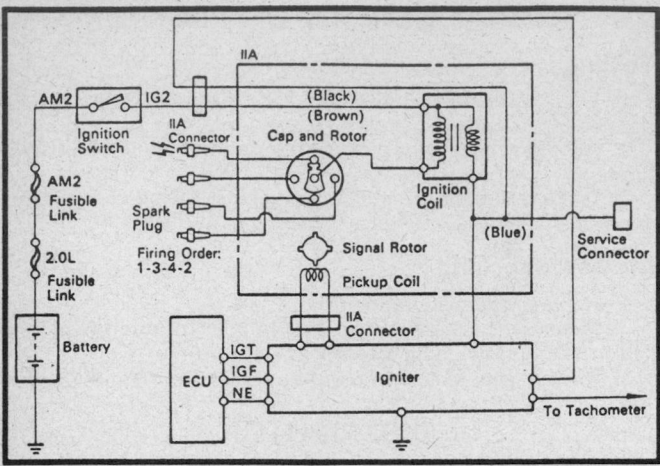

IIA ignition system schematic – Toyota 4Y-E and 4Y-EC engines

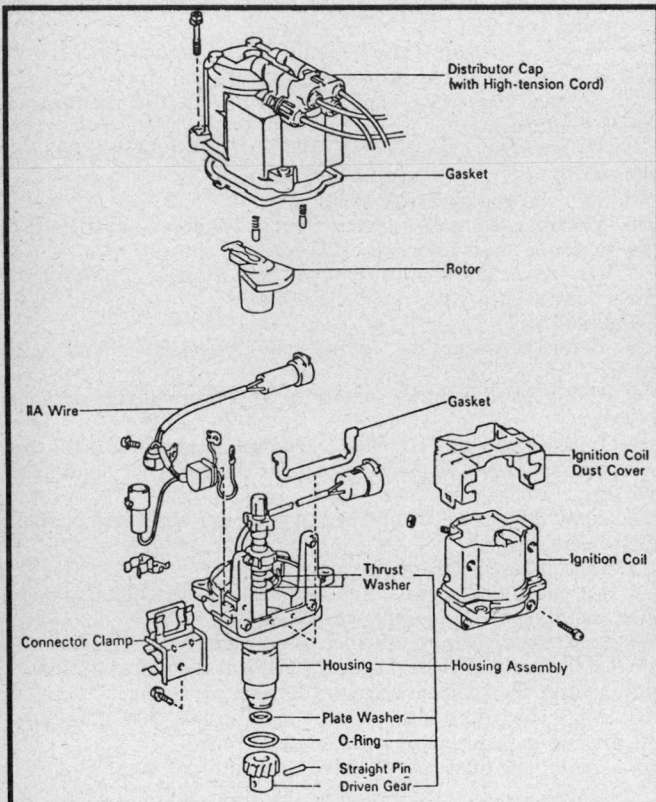

IIA distributor assembly – Toyota 4Y-E and 4Y-EC engines

2. The primary coil resistance (cold) should be 1.2–1.5 ohms.
3. If the resistance is not within specifications replace the coil.

SECONDARY COIL RESISTANCE

Testing

1. Using a suitable ohmmeter, measure the resistance between the positive terminal and the high tension terminal.
2. The secondary coil resistance (cold) should be 7.7–10.4 kilo-ohms.
3. If not within specifications, replace the coil.

IGNITION COIL

Removal and Installation

1. Disconnect the negative battery cable. Remove the distributor cap, packing and rotor.
2. Remove the ignition coil dust cover and dust proof packing.
3. Remove the nuts and disconnect the wires from the terminals of the coil.
4. Remove the screws and remove the ignition coil.

To Install:

5. Install the coil and replace the retaining screws.
6. Install the wires to coil.
7. Install the coil dust cover and packing.
8. Install the rotor, packing and distributor cap.

SIGNAL GENERATOR (PICK-UP)

Testing

1. Using a suitable ohmmeter, check the resistance of the signal generator.
2. The signal generator resistance should be 140–180 ohms.
3. If the resistance is not correct, replace the signal generator with the breaker assembly.

Air Gap Checking

1. Remove the distributor cap.
2. Measure the gap between the signal rotor and the pick-up coil projection, by using a feeler gauge.
3. The air gap should be 0.008 in. (0.2mm).

IGNITER

Testing

The igniter is not directly tested, however, if all of the other components in the system test OK and the vehicle still is not operating, the igniter may be at fault. Replace the igniter whith a known good unit and recheck the system.

Removal and Installation

1. Disconnect the negative battery cable. Remove the distributor cap, packing and rotor.
2. Remove the ignition coil dust cover and dust proof packing.
3. Remove the nuts and disconnect the wires from the terminals.
4. Remove the screws and remove the igniter and coil.

To Install:

5. Install the coil and igniter.
6. Install the wires.
7. Install the dust covers and packing.
8. Install the rotor, packing and distributor cap.

DISTRIBUTOR

Disassembly and Assembly

1. Disconnect the negative battery cable. Remove the distributor from the vehicle. Support the distributor in a suitable holding fixture. Remove the distributor cap without disconnecting the high tension cords.
2. Remove the rotor and the coil dust cover.
3. Remove the nuts and disconnect the wires from the terminals of the ignition coil, then remove the 4 screws, ignition coil and gasket.
4. Remove the distributor wire and connector lamp.
5. To remove the driven gear, use a grinder and carefully grind the head off the pin, then with a punch and a hammer, tap out the pin. Remove the drive gear and plate washer.

6. Remove the governor shaft and thrust washer.

To assemble:

7. Before assembly, lightly coat the governor shaft with high temperature grease, then slide the thrust washer onto the shaft and push the shaft into the housing.

8. Slide the plate washer and the new driven gear onto the governor shaft, then align the drill mark on the driven gear (not the driven gear pin hole) with the groove of the housing.

NOTE: Make sure the governor shaft cutout is positioned properly.

9. Install a new pin and measure the governor shaft thrust clearance. If clearance is not within 0.0059–0.0197 in., adjust with thrust washers, which are available. Secure the ends of the pin in a vise.

10. The remainder of the assembly is the reverse of disassembly. Coat the new O-rings with a light coat of oil.

VOLKSWAGEN

Map Controlled Hall Effect System

GENERAL INFORMATION

The map controlled ignition system operates on the principle of a timing map programmed into the Electronic Control Unit (ECU). Information on engine load, speed and coolant temperature are provided to the ECU in the form of voltage signals. In the ECU these signals are processed so that the ignition coil is controlled at its No. 1 terminal using the information from the ignition timing map.

The distributor contains a Hall effect switch, which is activated by a trigger wheel with 4 openings in it, one for each cylinder. The distributor has no vacuum or centrifugal advance. From the signal generated by the Hall effect switch, the ECU can determine engine speed and crankshaft position.

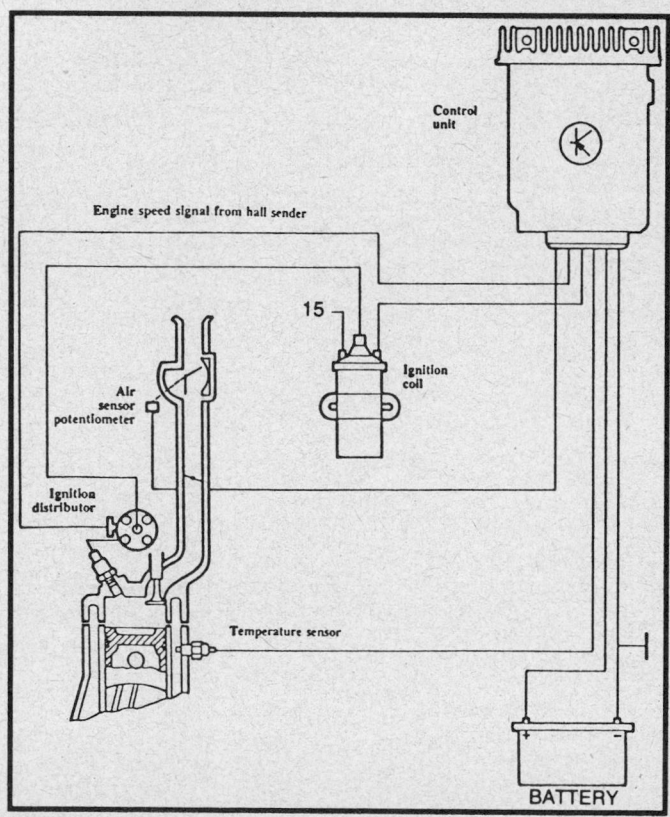

Ignition system diagram – Volkswagen

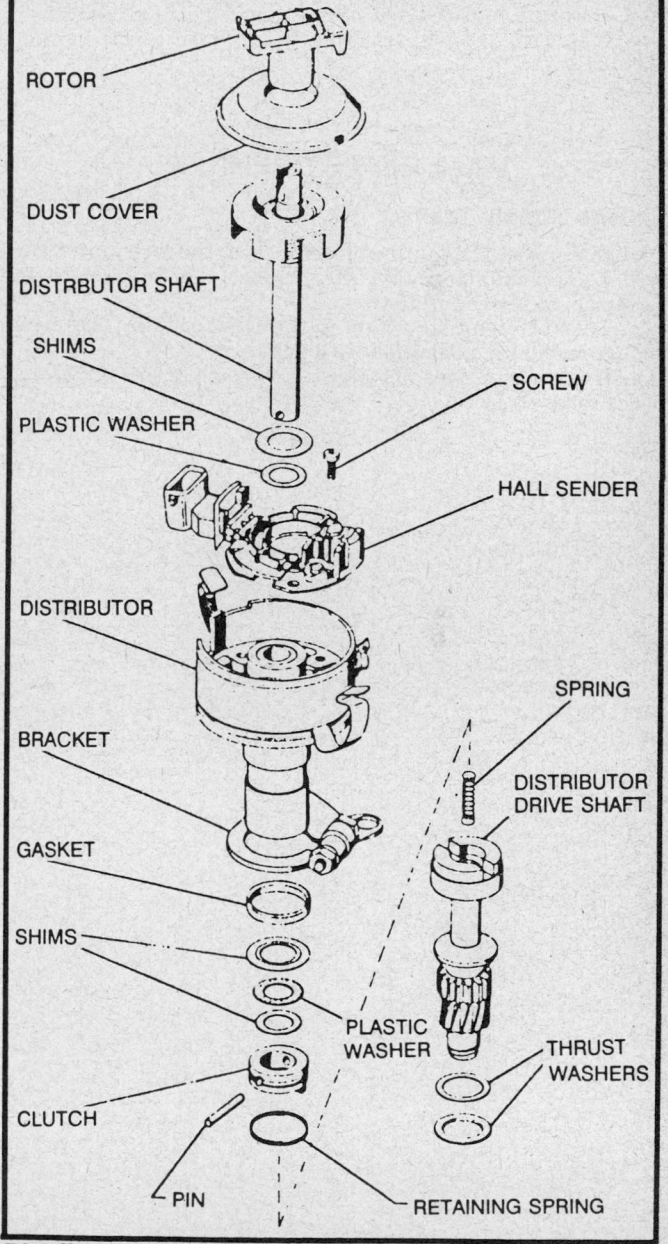

Distributor assembly – Volkswagen

IGNITION COIL

Resistance Testing

1. Remove the electrical connector from the coil.
2. Check the primary resistance between terminals 1 and 15. Correct primary resistance should be 0.5–0.8 ohms.
3. Check the secondary resistance between terminals 4 and 15. Correct secondary resistance should be 2.4–3.5 kilo-ohms.
4. If the resistance is incorrect, replace the coil.

Removal and Installation

1. Disconnect the negative battery cable.
2. Disconnect the electrical leads and high tension wire from the coil.
3. Remove the coil mounting bolt and remove the coil from the vehicle.
4. Install the coil in position and reconnect the wiring. Coils that are being replaced and have a gray stripe marking them, should be replaced with coils having a green stripe marking them.

HALL EFFECT SENDER

Voltage Supply Testing

1. Disconnect the mutli-connector from the distributor.
2. Using a suitable multi-meter, connect it between the outer terminals of the connector.
3. Turn the ignition switch to the **ON** position. The meter should register a minimum of 10 volts.
4. If the meter does not register correctly, the control unit needs to be replaced.

Function Test

1. Check for voltage on the positive terminal 15 of the ignition coil. There should be voltage with the ignition **ON**.
2. Ground a high tension coil wire.
3. Connect a test light between the positive terminal 15 and negative terminal 1.
4. Crank the engine with the starter for approximately 5 seconds. The test light should flicker.
5. If the light does not flicker, replace the ignition distributor.

DISTRIBUTOR

Disassembly and Assembly

1. Disconnect the negative battery cable.
2. Remove the distributor from the vehicle and support it in a suitable holding fixture.
3. Remove the distributor cap and rotor.
4. Remove the dust cover from the Hall effect sender.
5. Remove the roll pin from the distributor shaft clutch. Remove the clutch and shims from the shaft. Note the position of the shims.
6. Pull the shaft from the body.
7. Remove the Hall effect sender retaining screw and remove it from the distributor body.

To assemble:

8. Clean the distributor body and all of the components.
9. Install the Hall effect sender in position.
10. Install the distibutor shaft into position in the distributor body. Install the shims in the correct location.
11. Install the distributor clutch in position and install a new roll pin.
12. Install the dust cover, cap and rotor.
13. Install the distributor into the vehicle. Connect the negative battey cable.

GENERAL INFORMATION

Hydraulic System Basics

CAUTION

When servicing brake parts, do not create dust by grinding the linings or by blowing them clean with compressed air. Many brake parts contains asbestos fibers which can become airborne if dust is generated during brake servicing. Continuously breathing this dust can cause serious bodily harm. A dampened cloth or a spray bottle with water should be used to remove brake dust prior to work. Equipment is also commercially available for safe brake servicing.

The hydraulic system controls the braking operation and consists of a master cylinder, hydraulic lines and hoses, control valves and calipers and/or wheel cylinders. When the brake pedal is depressed, the master cylinder forces brake fluid regulated by the proportioning valve to the calipers and/or cylinders, via lines and hoses. Rubber seals throughout the system contain the fluid and prevent leakage.

Return springs in the master cylinder help the brake pedal return to the original unapplied position. Check valves (in most cases) regulate the return flow of the fluid to the master cylinder. Other valves, such as the metering valve, proportioning valve, or combination valve, regulate the flow of fluid to the caliper/wheel cylinder, to achieve even and efficient braking.

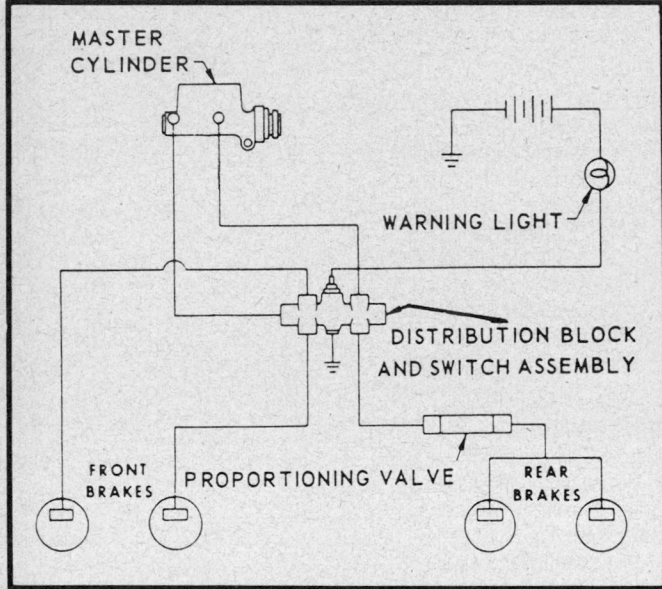

Typical brake system schematic

Dual Braking Systems

The dual system uses a tandem master cylinder, consisting of 2 separate pistons in a single cylinder bore. Dual brake lines split the calipers and/or wheel cylinders into 2 groups, each actuated by a separate master cylinder piston. In event of failure of 1 of the systems, the other should provide enough braking power to safely stop the vehicle. The dual system usually includes a red warning light on the instrument panel which is activated by a pressure differential valve. The valve is sensitive to any loss of

hydraulic pressure that might result from a braking failure on either side of the system.

Light trucks are equipped with either a front/rear wheel split or a diagonally split system. On front/rear systems, the front wheels are connected to one circuit while the rear wheels are connected to the other circuit. Diagonally split systems have diagonally opposite wheels connected to each circuit.

Brake Fluid

Approved DOT3 heavy duty type brake fluid retains the correct consistency throughout the widest range of temperature variation, will not affect rubber cups or seals, helps protect the metal parts of the brake system against failure and has a high boiling point to assure long trouble free brake operation when properly maintained.

Never use brake fluid from a container that has been used for any other liquid. Mineral oil, alcohol, antifreeze, or cleaning solvents, even in very small quantities, will contaminate brake fluid. Contaminated brake fluid will cause rubber parts within the hydraulic system to swell or deteriorate. Always return the cap to the fluid container after using the brake fluid. This will prevent the fluid from absorbing moisture from the surrounding air, which will lower its boiling point. Do not use brake fluid that has been sitting in an unopened container for an extending amount of time.

Hydraulic Line Repair

Steel tubing is used for the hydraulic lines between any 2 parts that do not move independant of one another, like the master cylinder and the front brake tube connector, or along the axle tubes between the brake tee and the rear brake cylinders. Brake hoses provide a flexible connection between the tube and a part that moves independantly, like the hose that connects the brake tube to the front brake calipers or the tube that runs along the body of the vehicle conneted by hose down to the axle.

BRAKE TUBING

If a section of the brake tube becomes damaged, the entire section should be replaced with tubing of the same type, size, shape, and length. Copper tubing should not be used in the hydraulic system. When bending brake tubing to fit the frame or axle contours, be careful not to kink or crack the tube.

All brake tubing should be double flared to provide good leak proof connections. Always clean the inside of a new brake tube with clean isopropyl alcohol before installing.

BRAKE HOSE

All flexible brake hoses should be carefully inspected often. They should be replaced if they show any signs of softening, cracking, swelling or other damage.

When installing a new brake hose, make sure it is not twisted and is positioned to avoid contact with other vehicle components under any suspension condition.

Hydraulic Control Valves

PRESSURE DIFFERENTIAL VALVE

The valve activates a panel warning lamp in event of pressure loss failure. As pressure fails in one split system, the other sys-

tem's normal pressure causes a piston in the switch to compress a spring and move until an electrical circuit is completed lighting the dash lamp. Normally, the spring balanced piston automatically recenters when the brake pedal is released, thus flashing the warning lamp only during brake application and will recenter automatically after repairs are successfully completed and the system is properly bled.

METERING VALVE

Often used on vehicles equipped with front disc and rear drum brakes, the metering valve improves braking balance during light brake applications by preventing application of the front disc brakes unitl the pressure to the rear brakes overcomes the tension of the rear brake shoe return springs. Thus, when the front brake pads contact the rotor the rear brakes shoes move outward to contact the brake drum at approximately the same time.

The metering valve should be inspected whenever the brakes are serviced. A slight amount of moisture inside the boot does not indicate a defective valve, however a great deal of fluid indicates a faulty valve and replacement is recommended. Make sure to install the brake lines in the correct ports when installing a new valve, crossed lines will cause the hydraulic system to malfunction.

PROPORTIONING VALVE

The proportioning valve is used to transmit full inpout pressure to the rear brakes up to a certain point (the split point). Beyond the split point, it reduces the amount of pressure to the rear brakes according to a certain ratio, which is built into the valve. On light pedal applications, equal braking pressure is transmitted to to the front and rear brakes. During heavier brake applications, however, the pessure delivered to the rear brakes is lower than that at the front brakes to prevent rear wheel lockup and skidding.

Whenever the brakes are serviced, the valve should be inspected. To check valve operation, install hydraulic gauges ahead of and behind the valve and determine that it has an operative transition point above which rear brake pressure is proportioned. If the valve is leaking replacement is required.

COMBINATION VALVE

A valve combining two or three functions (metering, proportioning, and/or brake warning) may be used. The combination valve is usually mounted under the hood close to the master cylinder, where the brake lines can be easily routed to the front and rear wheels. The combination valve is a non-serviceable unit, and if found to be malfunctioning, must be replaced as a unit.

Disc Brakes

CALIPERS

Caliper disc brakes can be divided into 3 types: dual piston floating caliper, single piston floating caliper and single piston sliding caliper. On the floating caliper types, the inner pad is hydraulically pushed into contact with the disc, while the reaction force generated is used to pull the outer pad into contact with the other side of the disc, made possible by allowing the caliper to move slightly along the axle's center line. Two pistons may be used to accomodate more severe braking requirements on heavier vehicles. All disc brake systems are self-adjusting and have no provision for amnual adjustment.

With the sliding caliper type, the caliper assembly slides along the smooth and lubricated surface of a key or stopper (nomenclature varies between manufacturers) which is held stationary by cotter pins or retaining bolts. The caliper is held against the key or stopper with 1 or 2 support springs.

One of the recent developments in brake equipment materials includes the use of aluminum calipers for the purpose of saving weight. A vast array of anti-rattle springs, clips and anti-squeal pads and shims are used by manufacturers to prevent the pads from making any undesirable noises. In addition, most brake pads are comprised of semi-metallic materials for improved stopping power. Unfortunately, these pads often produce an annoying brake squeal as they are used, but the squeal itself should not reduce the stopping ability of the pads. If the pad kit includes plates or shims, use them when servicing the disc brakes. Aftermarket spreads and sprays are also available to quiet noisy pads. It is always a good idea to replace calipers in pairs.

ROTORS

Rotors provide the surface upon which the brake pads stop the vehicle. It is important to inspect the rotor carefully. Manufacturers differ some on permissable runout (warpage) of the rotor, but excessive runout can usually be felt as a pulsation at the brake pedal regardless of the specification. A wobble pump effect is created when the rotor is not perfectly flat and the pad hits a high spot forcing fluid back into the master cylinder. This alternating pressure causes a pulsation which is felt at the pedal when the brakes are applied. An excessive amount of runout can cause the pads to be out of adjustment because they cannot hold themselves against the rotor at all times. It is always a good idea to replace rotors in pairs.

To check the actual runout of the rotor, fist tighten the spindle nut to remove all endplay. Fasten a dial indicator on the suspension on a convenient location so the pin contacts the rotor surface about 1 in. from its outer edge. Set the dial at 0 and check the runout while turning the rotor 1 full revolution. If the

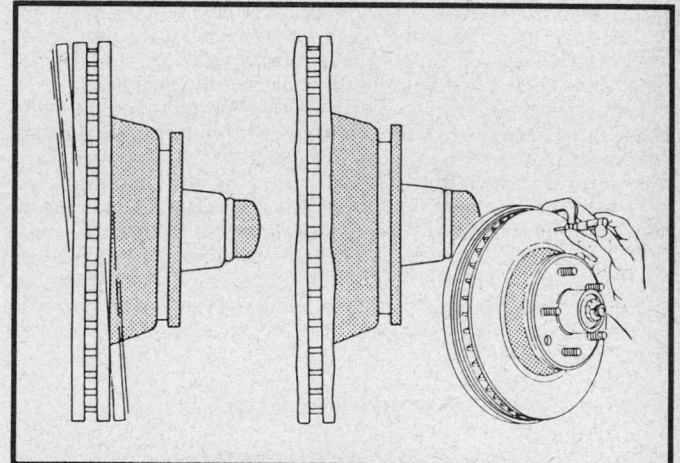

Excessive runout of parallelism

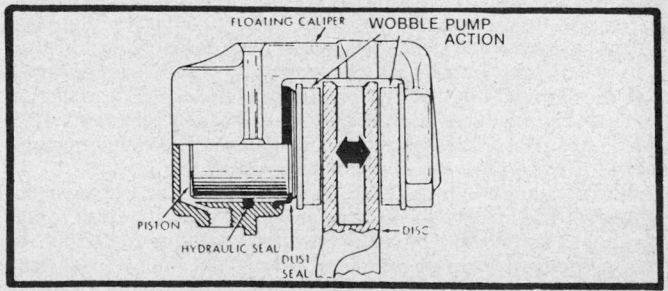

Wobble pump action resulting from a warped rotor

rotor is warpe beyond limits, the rotor should be replace. Rotors the are not warped beyond the specification can be resurfaced, as long as the final thickness is not below the minumum thickness requirement of the rotor.

Lateral Runout: The wobbly movement of the rotor from side to side as it rotates. Excessive lateral runout causes the rotor faces to knock bask the pads and can cause brake chatter, shudder or vibration.

Parallelism (lack of): This refers to the amount of variation in the thickness of the rotor. Excessive variation of parallelism can cause a pulsating pedal, front end vibrations or grabbing condiions; a condition comparable to an out-of-round brake drum. Check parallelism with a micrometer. Measure the thickness of the rotor a 8 or more equally spaced locations on the rotor, equally distant from the outer edge, preferably at the midpoint of the braking surface. A lack of parallelism results if the difference between the highest and lowest measurement is beyond the parallelism specification.

Surface or Micro-inch finish, flatness and smoothness: These terms all refer to the degree of perfection of the flat surfaces on each side fo the rotor. Visually inspecting the rotor, the machined surface should have a fine ground polish with a swirling pattern to reduce brake squeal.

DISC BRAKE PADS

The brake pads are the tools that the vehicle uses to stop, so they should be inspected very carefully. Pads should be replaced only in sets (both sides of the same axle) if any of the pads is damaged, cracked, burnt, or separated from the plate that it is glued or riveted to. Replace the pads if any of their lining is worn down to $1/16$ in. thickness. If the lining is allowed to wear beyond this point, severe and costly damage to the rotor may result. Note that individual state inspection guidelines take precedence over these general recommendation.

Floating caliper type disc brake pads may wear at an angle; the measurement should always be taken at the narrowest end of the taper. Tapered lining should be replaced if the amount of tapering exceeds $1/8$ in. from end to end and the cause of the taper should be investigated and repaired, if possible.

To prevent potentially costly paint damage, remove some brake fluid from the master fluid reservoir and install the reservoir cover before servicing the pads. When installing new pads, the caliper piston is forced back into its bore and fluid is pushed back into the master cylinder. The fluid could spill and remove paint from any painted surface that it comes in contact with.

When the caliper is removed from its mouning adaptor, do not allow it to dangle by the brake hose. This can damage the hose and create a dangerous situation. Always rest the caliper on a suspensiion member of suspent it from the frame with a wire or rope.

Drum Brakes

WHEEL CYLINDERS

The wheel cylinder performs in response to the master cylinder. It receives fluid from the hydraulic tube through its inlet port. As the pressure increases, the wheel cylinder cups and pistons are forced apart. As a result, the hydraulic pressure is converted into mechanical force acting on the brake shoes. The variation in wheel cylinder size (diameter) is one of the factors controlling the distribution of braking force in a vehicle. Bleeder screws are provided to remove air or vapor trapped in the system.

Wheel cylinders may need reconditioning or replacement whenever the brake shoes are replaced or when required to correct a leak condition. On many designs, the wheel cylinders can be diassembled without removing them from the backing plate. On some designs, however, the cylinder is mounted in an indention in the backing plate or a cylinder piston stop is welded to the backing plate. When servicing brakes of this type, the cylinder must be removed from the backing plate before being disassembled.

Leaks which coat the boot and the cylinder with fluid, or result in a dropped reservoir fluid level, or dampen and stain the brake linings are dangerous. Such leaks can cause the brakes to grab or fail and should be immediately corrected. A leakage, not immediately apparent, can be detected by pulling back the cylinder boot. A small amount of fluid seepage dampening the interior of the boot is normal, however a dripping boot is not. Unless other conditions causing a brake to pull, grab, or drag becomes obvious, the wheel cylinder is a suspect and should be included in general reconditioning. It is always a good idea to service wheel cylinders in pairs.

Cylinder binding may be caused by rust, deposits, grime, or swollen cups due to fluid contamination, or by a cup wedged into an excessive piston clearance. If the clearance between the pistons and the bore wall exceeds allowable values, a condition called heel drag may exist. It can result in rapid cup wear and can cause the pistons to retract very slowly when the brakes are released. A ring of a hard, crystal like substance is sometimes noticed in the cylinder bore where the piston stops after the brakes are released.

BRAKE DRUMS

The condition of the brake drum surface is equally as important as the surface of the lining. All drum braking surfaces should be clean, smooth, free of hark spots, heat damage, scoring and forign material embedded in the braking surface. The drum should not be out-of-round, bell mouthed or barrel shaped. Drums should be checked with a drum micrometer before resurfacing to see if it within over-size limits. If the drum is within safe limints, it should be machined to true the drum surface and to remove any contamination in the surface from previous linings and road matter. Too much metal removed from the drum is unsafe and may result in brake fade due to the thin drum not being able to absorb the heat generated, vibration from ensuing drum distortion and generally unsafe conditions.

Brake drum runout should not exceed 0.005 in. Drums machined to more than 0.060 in. oversize are unsafe and should be replaced. It is always good practice to replace drums on both whels at the same time to ensure even braking.

If the drums are in good condition, smooth up any slight scoring by sanding with coarse sand paper, then polishing with emery cloth. If deep scores or grooves are present, machine the drums to restore them to good operating condition.

DRUM BRAKE SHOES

The brake shoes should also be inspected very carefully. Shoes should be replaced only in sets (both sides of the same axle) if any of the shoes are bent, damaged, cracked, burnt, or separated from the plate that it is glued or riveted to. Replace the shoes if any of their lining is worn down to $1/16$ in. thickness. If the lining is allowed to wear beyond this point, severe and costly damage to the drum may result. Note that individual state inspection guidelines take precedence over these general recommendation.

Rear brakes with weak return springs may create a bell-mouthed condition which causes the shoes to wear at an angle; if so the measurement should always be taken at the narrowest end of the taper. Tapered linings should be replaced if the amount of tapering is excessive and the cause of the taper should be investigated and repaired, if possible.

Disassemble and assemble one side at a time to prevent improper assembly. This will also provide a model that can be refered if the installation doen not look right. Always complete the brake shoe adjustment with the wheels installed and adjust the parking brake cable last.

STAR AND SCREW ADJUSTER

Star and screw self-adjusters are used on most late-model vehicles. This system requires manual adjustment only when the shoes have been replaced, when the star wheel has been disturbed or when the star wheel is not operating properly.

As the star wheel is turned, it expands or contracts the shoes accordingly.

In most cases, the brakes can be initially adjusted by removing the drum, measuring the internal diameter of the drum and setting the shoes to slightly less than that measurement. Normally, the brakes will self-adjust when the vehicle is backed up and the brakes are firmly applied.

CHRYSLER IMPORTS/MITSUBISHI

NOTE: When cleaning brake system components, use only brake fluid or denatured isopropyl alcohol. Never use a mineral-based solvent such as gasoline or paint thinner; these fluids will leave a residue that may swell and deteriorate rubber parts within the system. All alcohol must be removed from the system when the work is done because alcohol mixed with brake fluid lowers its boiling point.

Do not hone any aluminum bores. There is a hard anodized coating on the aluminum which will be removed if honed. This will allow the aluminum to wear quickly and will damage the component.

Master Cylinder Service

Disassembly and Assembly

1. Remove the brake fluid reservoir retainer screw, if equipped and remove the reservoir and seals or remove the reservoir unions and seals.
2. Push the primary piston in and remove the stopper bolt and gasket.
3. Hold the pistons in and remove the snapring.

NOTE: Do not disassemble either piston assembly as the individual parts are not serviceable.

4. Let the primary piston spring out and remove the primary piston assembly.
5. Remove the secondary piston assembly. This may be accomplished by carefully blowing low pressure compressed air through the secondary side outlet port if it does not come out easily.
6. Remove the brake line connector block and washers.

To assemble:
7. Coat the master cylinder bore and secondary and primary piston seals liberally with brake fluid.
8. Install both assemblies to the master cylinder.
9. Push the pistons in and install a new snapring.
10. Hold the pistons in and install the stopper bolt with a new gasket.
11. Install the brake fluid reservoir or unions with new seals. Install the reservoir retaining screw, if equipped.
12. Install the connector block with new washers.

Brake Booster Service

The brake boosters installed on these vehicles are not serviceable. If the unit is defective, replace the entire assembly.

Caliper Service

Disassembly and Assembly

1. Remove the bleeder screw.
2. Drain the brake fluid from the caliper.
3. Remove the dust boot ring and the dust boot.
4. Position a shop rag opposite the top of the piston. Apply

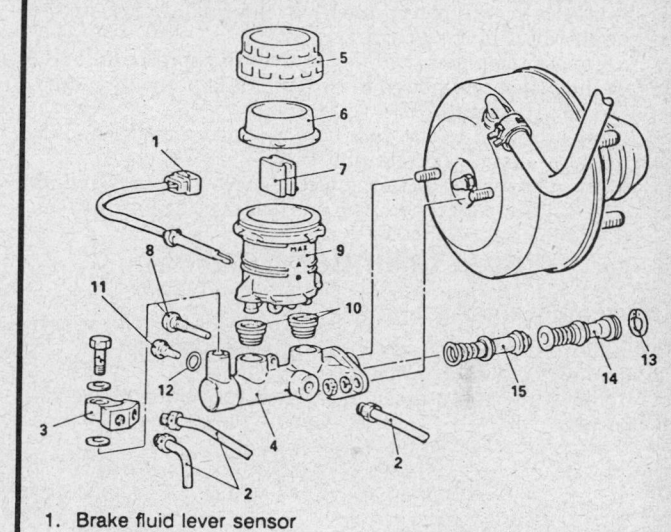

1.	Brake fluid lever sensor connector	8.	Reservoir retainer screw
2.	Brake tube	9.	Reservoir
3.	Brake line connector block	10.	Reservoir seals
4.	Master cylinder	11.	Piston stopper bolt
5.	Reservoir cap	12.	Gasket
6.	Diaphragm	13.	Snapring
7.	Float	14.	Primary piston assembly
		15.	Secondary assembly

Chrysler/Mitsubishi master cylinder

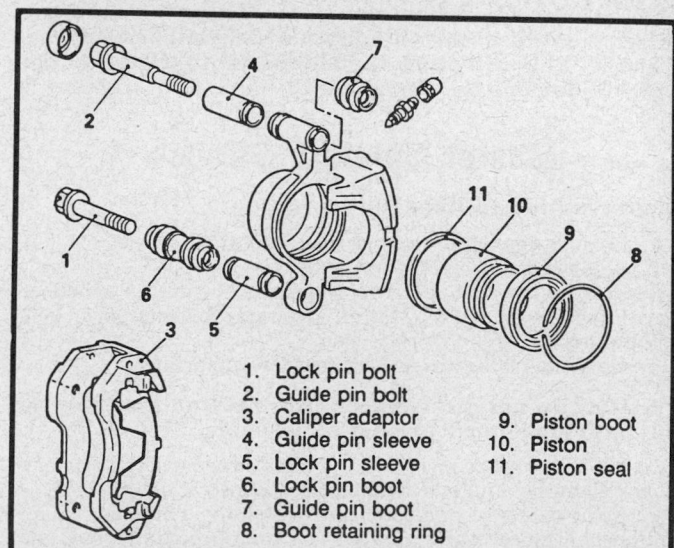

1.	Lock pin bolt		
2.	Guide pin bolt		
3.	Caliper adaptor	9.	Piston boot
4.	Guide pin sleeve	10.	Piston
5.	Lock pin sleeve	11.	Piston seal
6.	Lock pin boot		
7.	Guide pin boot		
8.	Boot retaining ring		

Chrysler/Mitsubishi caliper

low pressure compressed air to the fluid inlet and carefully blow the piston out of the bore.

CAUTION

Do not put fingers where the piston will land when it is blown out of the caliper. The force of the piston can crush fingers and cause personal injury.

5. Remove the piston seal from inside the bore.
To assemble:
6. Blow out all fluid passages with low pressure compressed air.
7. Slight corrosion or rust can be removed with commutator paper or crocus cloth. Replace pistons that are pitted, scored, peeling or otherwise damaged.
8. Lubricate the caliper bore with brake fluid. Lubricate the seal and install it in the groove.
9. Lubricate the piston and install it to the bore until it bottoms. If the piston will not go in by hand, it is probably cocked. Remove it and reinstall.
10. Apply lubricant to the dust boot mounting groove and install the boot. Install the retaining ring.
11. Apply rust penetrant to the bleeder screw threads and install to the caliper. Tighten it until it is just snug against its seat.

Wheel Cylinder Service

Disassembly and Assembly

1. Remove the bleeder screw, if equipped.
2. Remove both rubber boots.
3. Remove the piston assemblies, each consisting of the piston and cup.

4. Remove the piston cups from the pistons, being careful not to scratch the piston.
5. Remove the return spring.
6. Hone the cylinder bore if it is not damaged, to provide a smooth sealing surface. Wash and dry the bore after honing.
To assemble:
7. Lubricate the cylinder bore with brake fluid.
8. Lubricate the new piston cups and install them to the pistons, with their lips facing upward. Install the assemblies to the cylinder.
9. Apply lubricant to the boot mounting groove and install the boot.
10. Apply rust penetrant to the bleeder screw threads and install to the wheel cylinder. Tighten it until it is just snug against its seat.

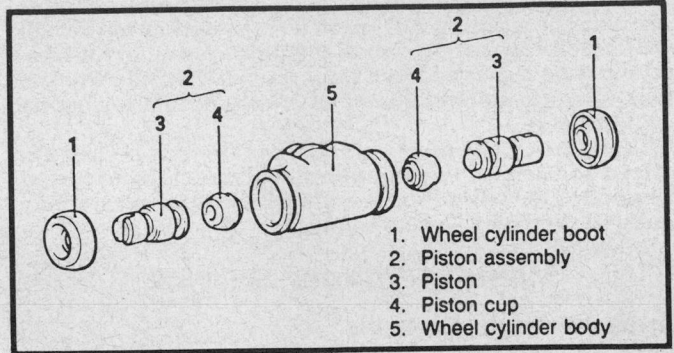

1. Wheel cylinder boot
2. Piston assembly
3. Piston
4. Piston cup
5. Wheel cylinder body

Chrysler/Mitsubishi wheel cylinder

ISUZU

NOTE: When cleaning brake system components, use only brake fluid or denatured isopropyl alcohol. Never use a mineral-based solvent such as gasoline or paint thinner; these fluids will leave a residue that may swell and deteriorate rubber parts within the system. All alcohol must be removed from the system when the work is done because alcohol mixed with brake fluid lowers its boiling point.

Do not hone any aluminum bores. There is a hard anodized coating on the aluminum which will be removed if honed. This will allow the aluminum to wear quickly and will damage the component.

Master Cylinder Service

Disassembly and Assembly

1. Remove the brake fluid reservoir retainer screw.
2. Remove the reservoir and seals.
3. Remove the dust seal from the end of the master cylinder.
4. Push the primary piston in and remove the stopper bolt and gasket.
5. Hold the pistons in and remove the snapring.

NOTE: Do not disassemble either piston assembly as the individual parts are not serviceable.

6. Let the primary piston spring out and remove the primary piston assembly and end washer, if equipped.
7. Remove the secondary piston assembly. This may be accomplished by carefully blowing low pressure compressed air through the secondary side outlet port if it does not come out easily.

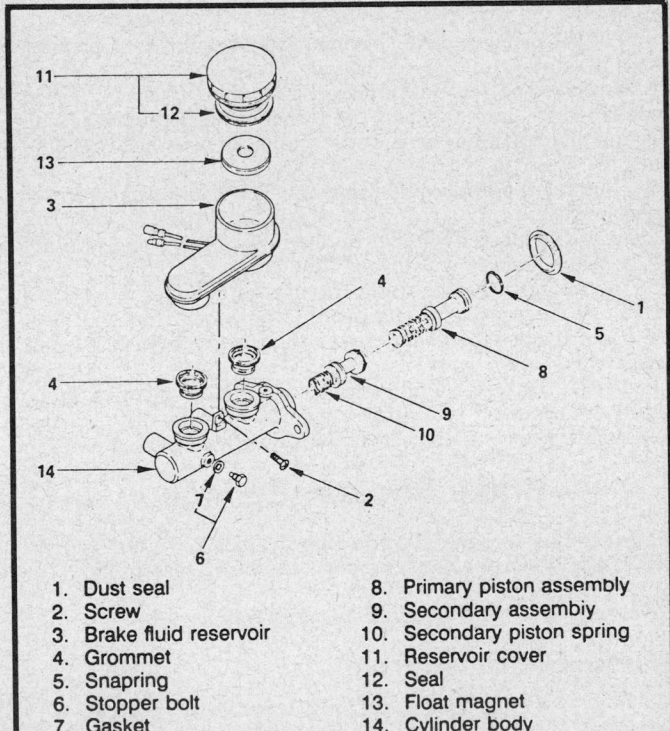

1. Dust seal
2. Screw
3. Brake fluid reservoir
4. Grommet
5. Snapring
6. Stopper bolt
7. Gasket
8. Primary piston assembly
9. Secondary assembiy
10. Secondary piston spring
11. Reservoir cover
12. Seal
13. Float magnet
14. Cylinder body

Isuzu master cylinder

To assemble:

8. Coat the master cylinder bore and secondary and primary piston seals liberally with brake fluid. Install both assemblies to the master cylinder.

9. Push the pistons in and install a new snapring.

10. Hold the pistons in and install the stopper bolt with a new gasket.

11. Install the brake fluid reservoir with new seals. Install the reservoir retaining screw.

Brake Booster Service

SINGLE VACUUM SERVO

Disassembly and Assembly

EXCEPT 1988–90 PICK-UP AND AMIGO WITH 2.6L ENGINE AND 1988–90 TROOPER II

1. Remove the clevis yoke and locknut from the actuator rod. Remove the low vacuum switch (diesel only).

2. Pry out the servo retainer and seal from the front of the shell.

3. Remove the rubber boot.

───────── CAUTION ─────────

The rear shell is spring loaded. Loosen it slowly and carefully or personal injury may result.

4. Matchmark the front and rear shells. Using wrench J–9504–01 and holder J–34250, separate the 2 shells slowly. Remove the servo spring.

5. Remove the entire diaphragm plate assembly.

6. Pry out the servo retainer, bearing and valve body seal from the rear shell.

7. Using a knife, cut the vacuum servo diaphragm and remove. Make sure not to damage the valve body when cutting.

8. Remove the servo retainer from the valve body.

9. Remove the vacuum filter and silencers from the valve body.

10. Push in the actuating rod and remove the rod stopper key. Remove the actuating rod assembly.

11. Remove the reaction disc, valve body, diaphragm plate and pushrod assembly.

To assemble:

12. Install the new actuating rod assembly to the valve body. Push the rod in and install the rod stopper key.

13. Install the new vacuum silencers and filter.

14. Install the new retainer to the rear shell.

15. Install the diaphragm plate and carefully attach the new vacuum servo diaphragm to the valve body.

16. Apply silicone grease to the new reaction disc and install to the valve body. Install the pushrod and spring.

17. Apply silicone grease to the rear shell seal and install.

18. Mount the holding tool J–34350 in a vise and mount the front shell on the tool. Assemble the entire diaphragm plate assembly to the rear shell. Install the bearing and new retainer.

19. To assemble the unit, connect a vacuum source to the vacuum intake pipe on the front shell. Using the matchmarks as guides, apply vacuum and assemble the unit using tool J–9504–01. Make sure the bent area of the of the diaphragm does not drop against the front and rear shell engaging areas.

20. Rotate the rear shell clockwise until the notch on the rear shell is fully against the stopper. Tighten until the matchmarks are perfectly aligned.

21. Install the new rubber boot, locknut and clevis yoke.

22. Apply silicone grease to the last seal and install to the front shell. Install the remaining retainer over the seal.

23. Install the low vacuum switch, if equipped.

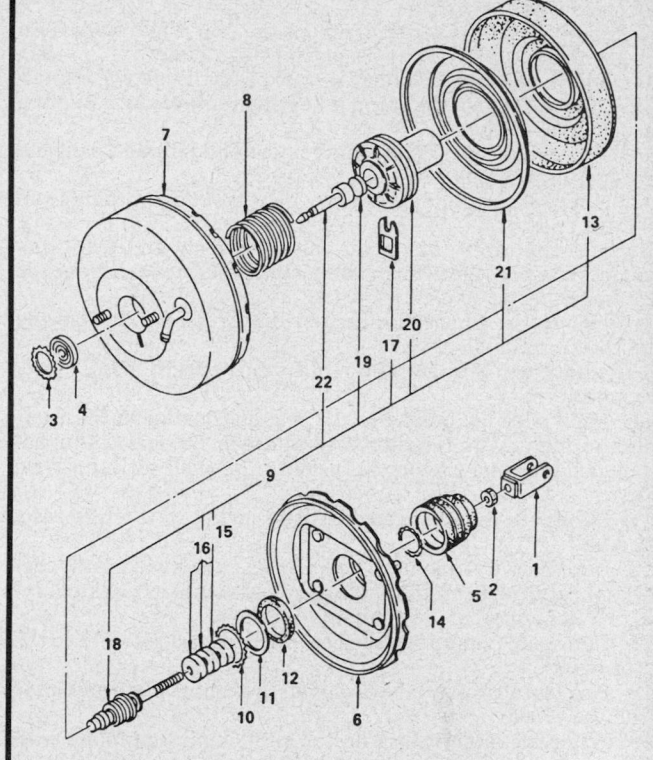

1. Clevis yoke	12. Valve body seal
2. Locknut	13. Vacuum servo diaphragm
3. Servo retainer	14. Servo retainer
4. Seal	15. Vacuum filter
5. Rubber boot	16. Vacuum silencer
6. Rear shell assembly	17. Actuating rod stopper key
7. Front shell assembly	18. Actuating rod
8. Servo spring	19. Reaction disc
9. Diaphragm plate assembly	20. Valve body
10. Servo retainer	21. Diaphragm plate
11. Servo bearing	22. Pushrod assembly

Isuzu single vacuum servo booster

TANDEM VACUUM SERVO

Disassembly and Assembly

1988–90 PICK-UP AND AMIGO WITH 2.6L ENGINE

1. Remove the clevis yoke and locknut from the actuator rod.

2. Remove the rubber boot.

3. Install holding tool J–34350 to the mounting studs and clamp in a vise. Matchmark the front and rear shells. Install wrench J–9504–01 to the rear shell studs.

───────── CAUTION ─────────

The rear shell is spring loaded. Loosen it slowly and carefully or personal injury may result.

4. Connect a vacuum source to the vacuum intake pipe on the front shell. Rotate the lever counterclockwise slightly (about $\frac{1}{20}$ turn). The front shell caulking tab must be aligned with the V-groove on the outside of the rear shell. Exhaust the vacuum and pry the rear shell from the front shell.

5. Remove the retainer, bearing and seal from the rear shell.

6. Remove the retainer and remove the filter and silencers from the actuating rod.

7. Remove the retainer and remove the rear diaphragm from the valve body. Remove the rear diaphragm plate.

8. Remove the C-ring from the valve body. Push the actuating rod down, remove the stopper key and remove the actuating rod from the valve body.

9. Remove the center plate and remove the retainer, seal and bearing from the plate.

10. Remove the retainer and remove the front diaphragm from the valve body.

11. Raise the catch that holds the valve body and front diaphragm plate together. Turn the plate and remove it from the valve body.

12. Remove the pushrod, reaction disc, retainer and spring from the front shell.

13. Remove the retainer and seal from the front shell.

To assemble:

14. Apply silicone grease to the seal and install to the front shell and install the retainer over the seal. Lubricate the diaphragm sliding surfaces on the inside of the shell with the same grease.

15. Lubricate the pushrod stem and install to the hub reaction disc.

16. Lubricate and install a new O-ring to the valve body. Set the diaphragm plate on the valve body and rotate it to install. Install the new front diaphragm and retainer.

17. Lubricate and install the bearing, seal and retainer to the center plate.

18. Use installer J–38595 to install the center plate assembly to the valve body.

19. Align the arrow mark on the rear diaphragm plate with the mark on the valve body and install the plate with a tilting motion. Install a new retainer to the front diaphragm.

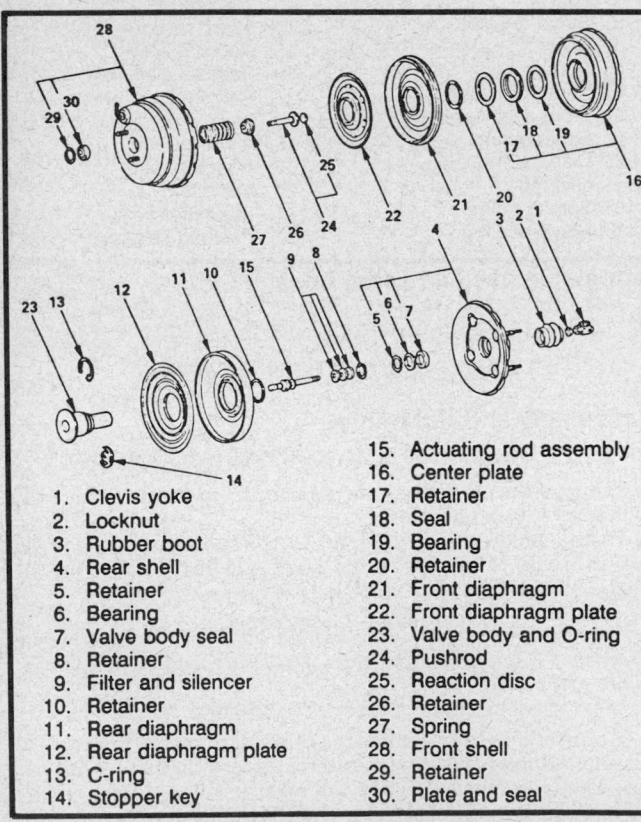

1. Clevis yoke	15. Actuating rod assembly
2. Locknut	16. Center plate
3. Rubber boot	17. Retainer
4. Rear shell	18. Seal
5. Retainer	19. Bearing
6. Bearing	20. Retainer
7. Valve body seal	21. Front diaphragm
8. Retainer	22. Front diaphragm plate
9. Filter and silencer	23. Valve body and O-ring
10. Retainer	24. Pushrod
11. Rear diaphragm	25. Reaction disc
12. Rear diaphragm plate	26. Retainer
13. C-ring	27. Spring
14. Stopper key	28. Front shell
	29. Retainer
	30. Plate and seal

Isuzu tandam vacuum servo–1988–90 Pick-Up and Amigo with 2.6L engine

20. Lubricate and install the actuating rod to the valve body and install the C-ring. Push the actuating rod and install the stopper key.

21. Install the first filter, the silencer then the second filter to the valve body and install the new retainer.

22. Lubricate and install the seal, bearing and retainer to the rear shell.

23. Mount the holding tool J–34350 in a vise and mount the front shell on the tool. Assemble the entire center plate assembly to the rear shell.

24. To assemble the unit, connect a vacuum source to the vacuum intake pipe on the front shell. Using the matchmarks as guides, apply vacuum and assemble the unit using tool J–9504–01. Make sure the bent area of the of the diaphragm does not drop against the front and rear shell engaging areas.

25. Rotate the rear shell clockwise until the notch on the rear shell is fully against the stopper. Tighten until the matchmarks are perfectly aligned.

26. Install the new rubber boot, locknut and clevis yoke.

27. Adjust the pushrod length to 0.7 in. (18.2mm) from the base of the front shell.

1988–90 TROOPER/TROOPER II

1. Remove the clevis yoke and locknut from the actuator rod.

2. Pry out the servo retainer and seal from the front of the shell.

─────────────── **CAUTION** ───────────────

The rear shell is spring loaded. Loosen it slowly and carefully or personal injury may result.

─────────────────────────────────────

3. Matchmark the front and rear shells. Using wrench J–9504–01 and holder J–34250 (holes elongated to fit), separate the 2 shells slowly. Remove the servo spring.

4. Remove the rubber boot.

5. Remove the retainer, bearing and seal from the rear shell.

6. To disassemble the diaphragm assembly, remove the large nut with a 1½ in. wrench.

7. Remove the front diaphragm plate, front diaphragm and center plate.

8. Remove the retainer, center plate seal and bearing from the center plate.

9. Remove the pushrod and carefully pry the key out of the valve body. Remove the key retainer.

10. Rotate the reaction disc hub 90 degrees and release it from the center body. Remove the reaction disc and O-ring.

11. Remove the center body and diaphragm from the rear diaphragm plate.

12. Remove the valve body assembly. Remove the retainer and remove the actuating rod.

13. Remove the retainer and remove the filters and silencer from the rod.

To assemble:

14. Install the valve body to the rear diaphragm plate. Install the retainer with the cutouts to the valve body lugs and install the actuating rod.

15. Install the new rear diaphragm.

16. Install the center body and new lubricated O-ring. Set the retainer against the outer pawl of the reaction and rotate the reaction disc 90 degrees to install.

17. Install the key retainer, push in the actuating rod and install the stopper key.

18. Install the new filter, silencer, second filter and retainer.

19. Install the reaction disc (with the stepped side inward) and pushrod.

20. Lubricate and install the bearing, center plate seal and retainer to the center plate.

21. Install the front diaphragm to its plate and install 1½ in. nut.

22. Lubricate and install the seal, bearing and retainer to the rear shell. Install the new rubber boot.

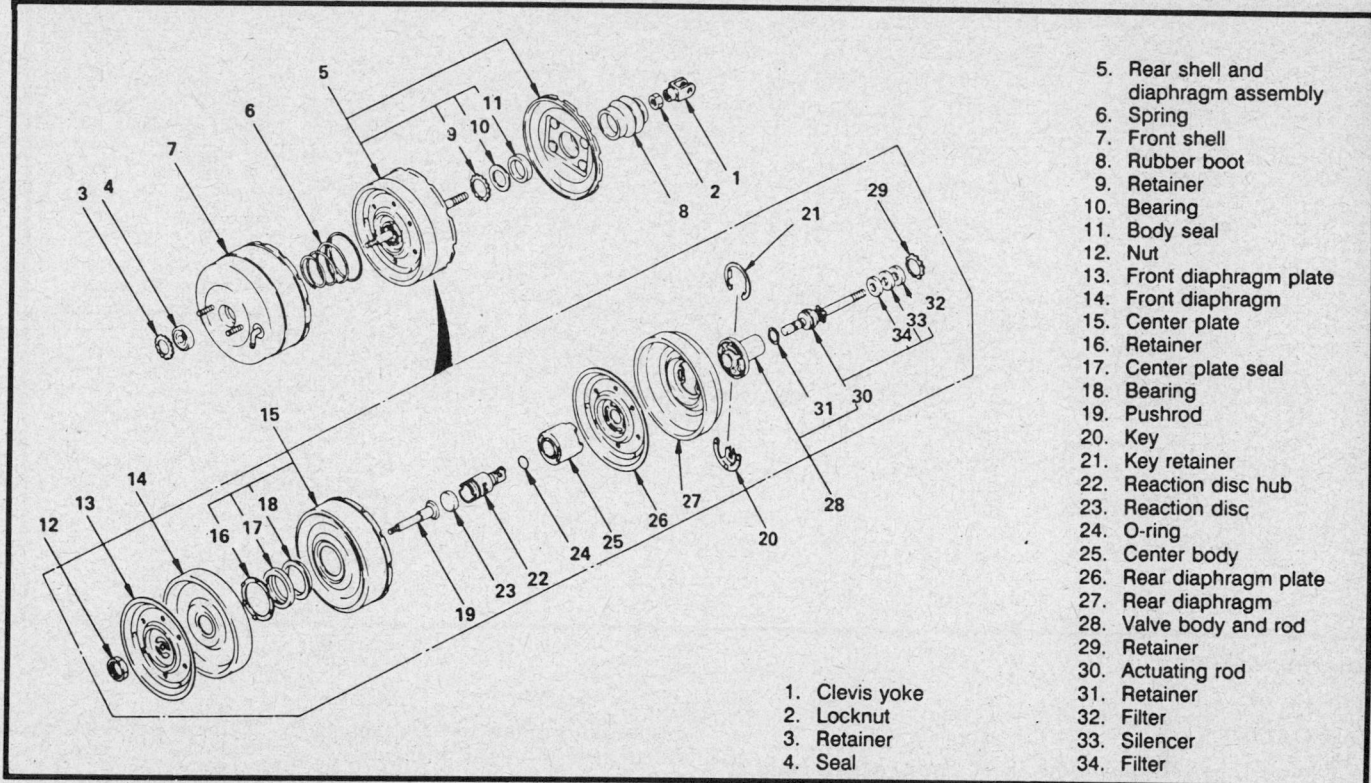

Isuzu tandam vacuum servo – 1988–90 Trooper II

1. Clevis yoke	18. Bearing
2. Locknut	19. Pushrod
3. Retainer	20. Key
4. Seal	21. Key retainer
5. Rear shell and diaphragm assembly	22. Reaction disc hub
6. Spring	23. Reaction disc
7. Front shell	24. O-ring
8. Rubber boot	25. Center body
9. Retainer	26. Rear diaphragm plate
10. Bearing	27. Rear diaphragm
11. Body seal	28. Valve body and rod
12. Nut	29. Retainer
13. Front diaphragm plate	30. Actuating rod
14. Front diaphragm	31. Retainer
15. Center plate	32. Filter
16. Retainer	33. Silencer
17. Center plate seal	34. Filter

23. Mount the holding tool J–34350 in a vise and mount the front shell on the tool. Assemble the entire diaphragm assembly, spring and the rear shell.

24. To assemble the unit, connect a vacuum source to the vacuum intake pipe on the front shell. Using the matchmarks as guides, apply vacuum and assemble the unit using tool J–9504–01. Make sure the bent area of the of the diaphragm does not drop against the front and rear shell engaging areas.

25. Rotate the rear shell clockwise until the notch on the rear shell is fully against the stopper. Tighten until the matchmarks are perfectly aligned.

26. Install locknut and clevis yoke.

27. Apply silicone grease to the last seal and install to the front shell. Install the remaining retainer over the seal.

Caliper Service

Disassembly and Assembly

FRONT CALIPER

1. Remove the bleeder screw.
2. Drain the brake fluid from the caliper.
3. Remove the dust boot ring and the dust boot.
4. Position a shop rag opposite the top of the piston. Apply low pressure compressed air to the fluid inlet and carefully blow the piston out of the bore.

─────── **CAUTION** ───────

Do not put fingers where the piston will land when it is blown out of the caliper. The force of the piston can crush fingers and cause personal injury.

─────────────────────────

5. Remove the piston seal from inside the bore.

To assemble:

6. Blow out all fluid passages with low pressure compressed air.

7. Slight corrosion or rust can be removed with commutator paper or crocus cloth. Replace pistons that are pitted, scored, peeling or otherwise damaged.

8. Lubricate the caliper bore with brake fluid. Lubricate the seal and install it in the groove.

9. Lubricate the piston and install it to the bore until it bottoms. If the piston will not go in by hand, it is probably cocked. Remove it and reinstall.

10. Apply lubricant to the dust boot mounting groove and install the boot. Install the retaining ring.

11. Apply rust penetrant to the bleeder screw threads and install to the caliper. Tighten it until it is just snug against its seat.

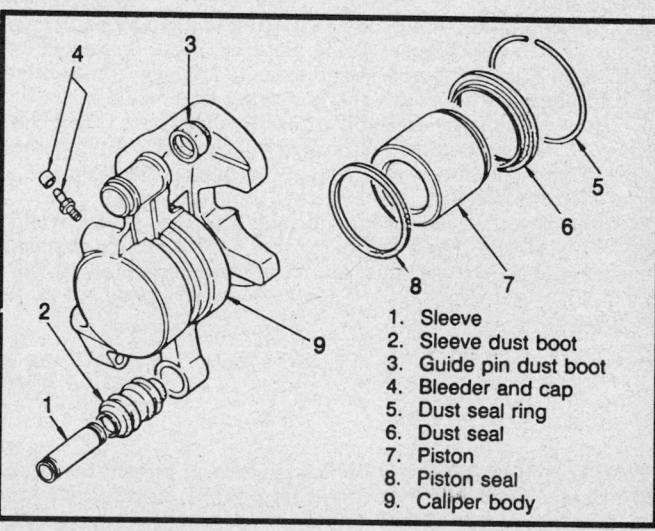

1. Sleeve	
2. Sleeve dust boot	
3. Guide pin dust boot	
4. Bleeder and cap	
5. Dust seal ring	
6. Dust seal	
7. Piston	
8. Piston seal	
9. Caliper body	

Isuzu front caliper

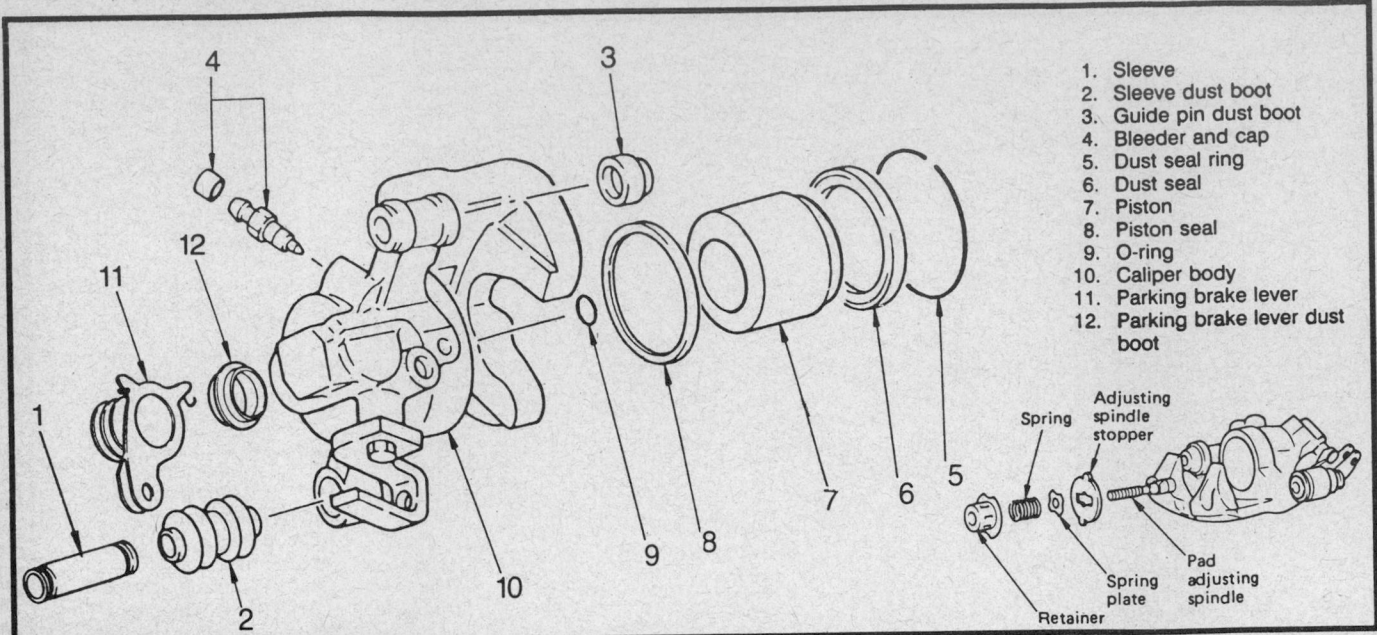

1. Sleeve
2. Sleeve dust boot
3. Guide pin dust boot
4. Bleeder and cap
5. Dust seal ring
6. Dust seal
7. Piston
8. Piston seal
9. O-ring
10. Caliper body
11. Parking brake lever
12. Parking brake lever dust boot

Spring
Adjusting spindle stopper
Spring plate
Retainer
Pad adjusting spindle

Isuzu rear caliper

REAR CALIPER

1. Remove the sleeve and its dust boot. Remove the mounting pin dust boot.
2. Remove the bleeder screw.
3. Drain the brake fluid from the caliper. Remove the dust boot ring and the dust boot.
4. To remove the piston, unscrew it using tool J–37617. Remove the piston seal.
5. Remove the snapring at the bottom of the caliper bore. Pull out the pad adjusting spindle along with the retainer, spring, spring plate and stopper. Remove the O-ring from the spindle.
6. Remove the parking brake link from the bottom of the caliper bore.
7. Remove the parking brake lever, spring and dust boot.
8. Remove the return spring and dust boot.

To assemble:

9. Apply brake system compatible grease to the parking brake link and install.
10. Lubricate and install the new O-ring to the pad adjusting spindle. Attach the stopper, spring plate, spring and retainer to the spindle. Turn the embossed side of the stopper to the outer side and align the cutaways of the stopper and retainer.
11. Insert the spindle assembly into the caliper bore fitting the stopper to the groove at the bottom of the bore. Install the snapring and position it so that the open area between ends aligns with the bleeder.
12. Lubricate the piston seal and install to the groove in the caliper. Install the piston and using tool J–37617, turn the piston clockwise until it bottoms. Align the piston cutouts with the inspection window in the caliper body. If this is not done, the brake pads will wear unevenly.
13. Apply lubricant to the dust boot mounting groove and install the boot. Install the retaining ring.
14. Apply rust penetrant to the bleeder screw threads and install to the caliper. Tighten it until it is just snug against its seat.
15. Install the new parking brake lever dust boot, spring and lever. Torque the retaining bolt to 35 ft. lbs. (47 Nm).

Wheel Cylinder Service

Disassembly and Assembly

1. Remove the bleeder screw.
2. Remove both rubber boots.
3. Remove the pistons from the cylinder.
4. Remove the piston cups.
5. Remove the return spring.
6. Hone the cylinder bore if it is not damaged, to provide a smooth sealing surface. Wash and dry the bore after honing.

To assemble:

7. Lubricate the cylinder bore with brake fluid. Install the return spring.
8. Lubricate the new piston cups and install them to the cylinder. Lubricate and install the pistons.
9. Apply lubricant to the boot mounting groove and install the boot.
10. Apply rust penetrant to the bleeder screw threads and install to the wheel cylinder. Tighten it until it is just snug against its seat.

MAZDA

NOTE: When cleaning brake system components, use only brake fluid or denatured isopropyl alcohol. Never use a mineral-based solvent such as gasoline or paint thinner; these fluids will leave a residue that may swell and deteriorate rubber parts within the system. All alcohol must be removed from the system when the work is done because alcohol mixed with brake fluid lowers its boiling point.

Do not hone any aluminum bores. There is a hard anodized coating on the aluminum which will be removed if honed. This will allow the aluminum to wear quickly and will damage the component.

Master Cylinder Service

Disassembly and Assembly

1. Remove the brake fluid reservoir retainer screw.
2. Remove the reservoir and seals.
3. Remove the dust seal from the end of the master cylinder.
4. Push the primary piston in and remove the stopper bolt and gasket.
5. Hold the pistons in and remove the snapring.
6. Let the primary piston spring out and remove the primary piston assembly and end washer, if equipped.
7. Remove the secondary piston assembly. This may be accomplished by carefully blowing low pressure compressed air through the secondary side outlet port if it does not come out easily.

To assemble:

8. Assemble the secondary piston assembly, if it was disassembled. Coat the master cylinder bore and secondary and primary piston seals liberally with brake fluid. Install both assemblies to the master cylinder.
9. Push the pistons in and install a new snapring.
10. Hold the pistons in and install the stopper bolt with a new gasket.
11. Install the brake fluid reservoir with new seals. Install the reservoir retaining screw.

Brake Booster Service

The brake booster on the MPV is not serviceable. If the unit is defective, replace the entire assembly.

SINGLE DIAPHRAGM

Disassembly and Assembly

2WD PICK-UP

1. Remove the clevis yoke and locknut from the actuator rod.
2. Pry out the servo retainer and seal from the front of the shell.
3. Remove the rubber boot.

— CAUTION —

The rear shell is spring loaded. Loosen it slowly and carefully or personal injury may result.

4. Matchmark the front and rear shells. Using the special tools, separate the 2 shells slowly. Remove the servo spring.
5. Remove the entire diaphragm and plate assembly.
6. Pry out the retainer, bearing and seal from the rear shell.
7. Using a knife, cut the vacuum diaphragm and remove. Make sure not to damage the power piston assembly when cutting.
8. Remove the retainer from the power piston.
9. Remove the vacuum filter and silencers from the power piston.
10. Push in the valve rod and remove the retainer key. Remove the valve rod assembly.
11. Remove the reaction disc, power piston, diaphragm plate and pushrod assembly.

To assemble:

12. Install the new valve rod assembly to the power piston. Push the rod in and install the retainer key.
13. Install the new vacuum silencers and filter.
14. Install the new retainer to the rear shell.

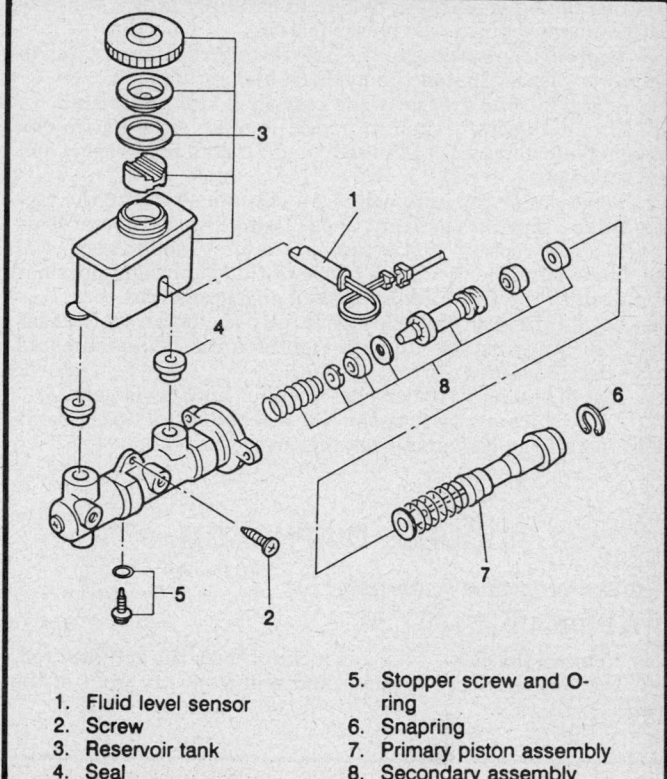

1. Fluid level sensor
2. Screw
3. Reservoir tank
4. Seal
5. Stopper screw and O-ring
6. Snapring
7. Primary piston assembly
8. Secondary assembly

Mazda master cylinder

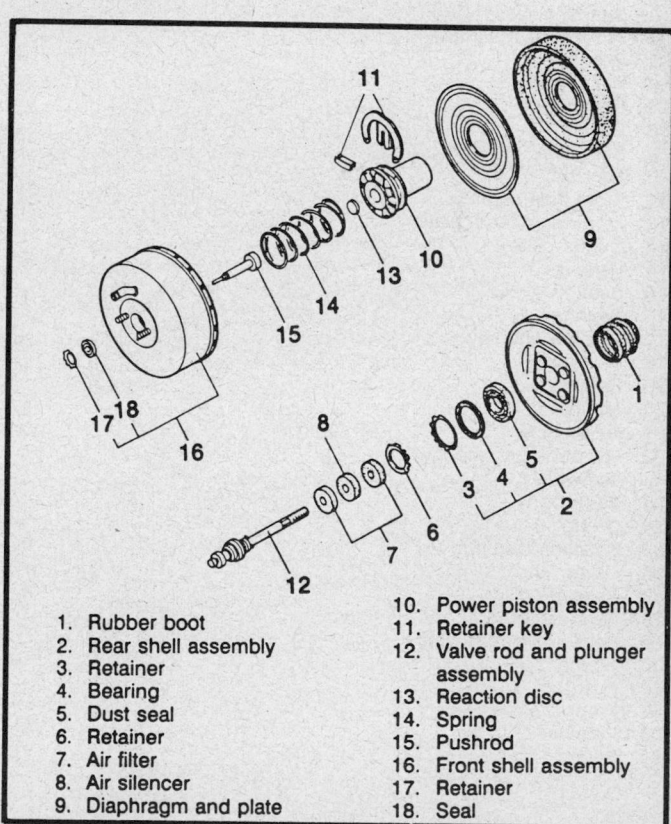

1. Rubber boot
2. Rear shell assembly
3. Retainer
4. Bearing
5. Dust seal
6. Retainer
7. Air filter
8. Air silencer
9. Diaphragm and plate
10. Power piston assembly
11. Retainer key
12. Valve rod and plunger assembly
13. Reaction disc
14. Spring
15. Pushrod
16. Front shell assembly
17. Retainer
18. Seal

Mazda single diaphragm booster

15. Install the diaphragm plate and carefully attach the new vacuum diaphragm to the power piston.

16. Apply silicone grease to the new reaction disc and install to the power piston. Install the pushrod and spring.

17. Apply silicone grease to the rear shell seal and install.

18. Mount the front shell in a vise. Assemble the entire diaphragm plate assembly to the rear shell. Install the bearing and new retainer.

19. To assemble the unit, connect a vacuum source to the vacuum intake pipe on the front shell. Using the matchmarks as guides, apply vacuum and assemble the unit using the special tool. Make sure the bent area of the of the diaphragm does not drop against the front and rear shell engaging areas.

20. Rotate the rear shell clockwise until the notch on the rear shell is fully against the stopper. Tighten until the matchmarks are perfectly aligned.

21. Install the new rubber boot, locknut and clevis yoke.

22. Apply silicone grease to the last seal and install to the front shell. Install the remaining retainer over the seal.

DOUBLE DIAPHRAGM

Disassembly and Assembly

4WD PICK-UP

1. Remove the clevis yoke and locknut from the actuator rod.

2. Pry out the servo retainer and seal from the front of the shell.

─── **CAUTION** ───

The rear shell is spring loaded. Loosen it slowly and carefully or personal injury may result.

3. Matchmark the front and rear shells. Using the special tools, separate the shells. Remove the rubber boot.

4. Clamp holding tool 49–U043–002 in a vise and mount the rear shell assembly to the tool. Uncrimp the reaction disc hub. Remove the locknut using wrench 49–U043–001.

5. Remove the retainer, bearing and seal from the rear shell.

6. Remove the front diaphragm plate, front diaphragm and center plate.

7. Remove the retainer, center plate seal and bearing from the center plate.

8. Remove the pushrod and carefully pry the key out of the valve body.

9. Remove the key retainer.

10. Rotate the reaction disc hub 90 degrees and release it from the center body. Remove the reaction disc and O-ring.

11. Remove the center body and diaphragm from the rear diaphragm plate.

12. Remove the valve body assembly. Remove the retainer and remove the actuating rod.

13. Remove the retainer and remove the filters and silencer from the rod.

To assemble:

14. Install the valve body to the rear diaphragm plate. Install the retainer with the cutouts to the valve body lugs and install the actuating rod.

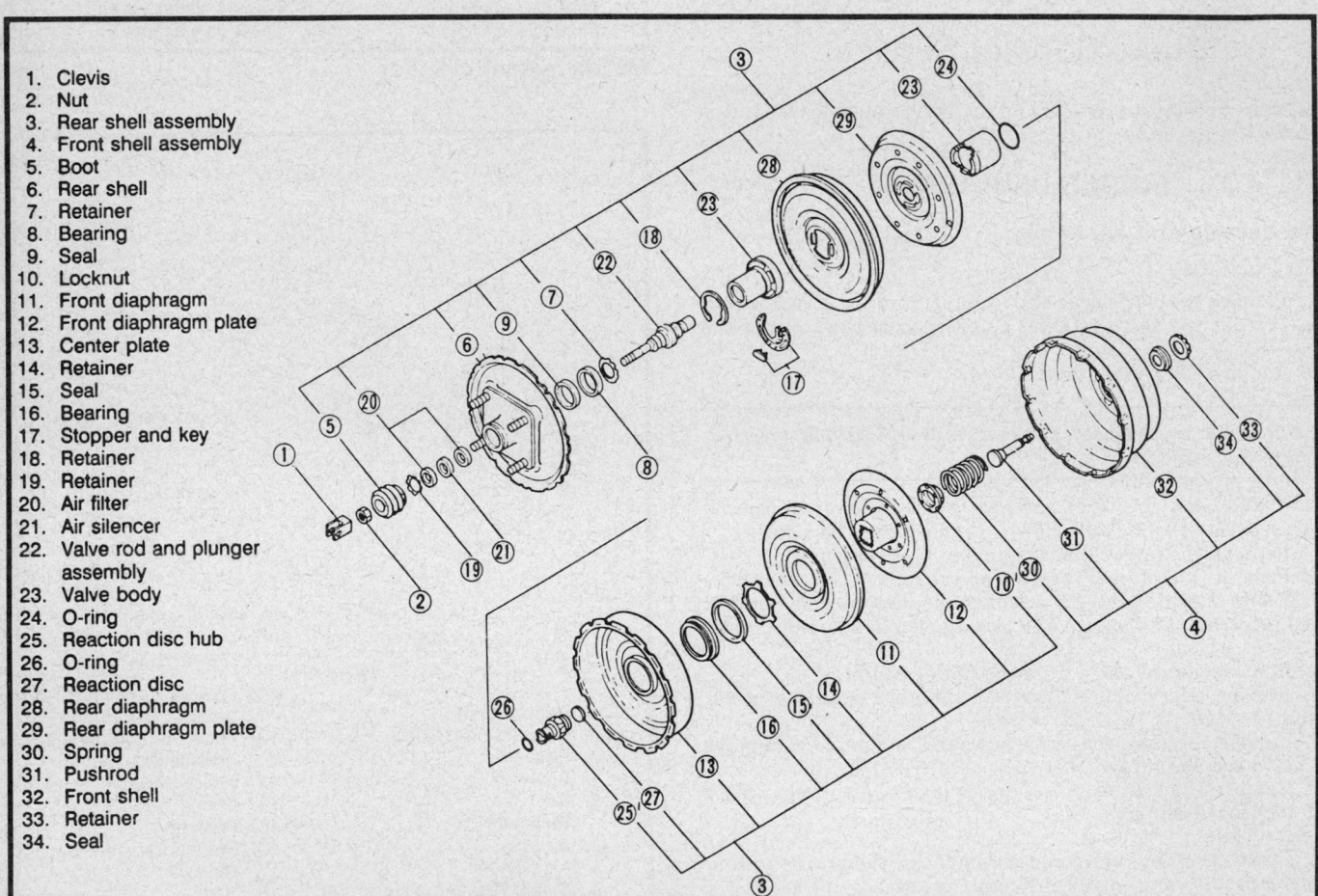

1. Clevis
2. Nut
3. Rear shell assembly
4. Front shell assembly
5. Boot
6. Rear shell
7. Retainer
8. Bearing
9. Seal
10. Locknut
11. Front diaphragm
12. Front diaphragm plate
13. Center plate
14. Retainer
15. Seal
16. Bearing
17. Stopper and key
18. Retainer
19. Retainer
20. Air filter
21. Air silencer
22. Valve rod and plunger assembly
23. Valve body
24. O-ring
25. Reaction disc hub
26. O-ring
27. Reaction disc
28. Rear diaphragm
29. Rear diaphragm plate
30. Spring
31. Pushrod
32. Front shell
33. Retainer
34. Seal

Mazda double diaphragm booster

15. Install the new rear diaphragm.

16. Install the center body and new lubricated O-ring. Set the retainer against the outer pawl of the reaction and rotate the reaction disc 90 degrees to install.

17. Install the key retainer, push in the actuating rod and install the stopper key.

18. Install the new filter, silencer, second filter and retainer.

19. Install the reaction disc (with the stepped side inward) and pushrod.

20. Lubricate and install the bearing, center plate seal and retainer to the center plate.

21. Install the front diaphragm to its plate and install locknut using the special wrench. Crimp the reaction disc hub in the 2 notched grooves of the locknut.

22. Lubricate and install the seal, bearing and retainer to the rear shell. Install the new rubber boot.

23. Align the notches of the rear shell and center plate. Make sure the bent area of the of the diaphragm does not drop against the front and rear shell engaging areas.

24. Push down and rotate the rear shell clockwise until the notch on the rear shell is fully against the stopper. Tighten until the matchmarks are perfectly aligned.

25. Install locknut and clevis yoke.

26. Apply silicone grease to the last seal and install to the front shell. Install the remaining retainer over the seal.

Caliper Service

Disassembly and Assembly

1. Remove the bleeder screw.
2. Drain the brake fluid from the caliper.
3. Remove the dust boot.
4. Position a shop rag opposite the top of the piston. Apply low pressure compressed air to the fluid inlet and carefully blow the piston out of the bore.

CAUTION

Do not put fingers where the piston will land when it is blown out of the caliper. The force of the piston can crush fingers and cause personal injury.

---

5. Remove the piston seal from inside the bore.

To assemble:

6. Blow out all fluid passages with low pressure compressed air.

7. Slight corrosion or rust can be removed with commutator paper or crocus cloth. Replace pistons that are pitted, scored, peeling or otherwise damaged.

8. Lubricate the caliper bore with brake fluid. Lubricate the seal and install it in the groove.

9. Lubricate the piston and install it to the bore until it bottoms. If the piston will not go in by hand, it is probably cocked. Remove it and reinstall.

10. Apply lubricant to the dust boot mounting groove and install the boot.

11. Apply rust penetrant to the bleeder screw threads and install to the caliper. Tighten it until it is just snug against its seat.

Wheel Cylinder Service

Disassembly and Assembly

1. On the left side, remove the bleeder screw and check ball.

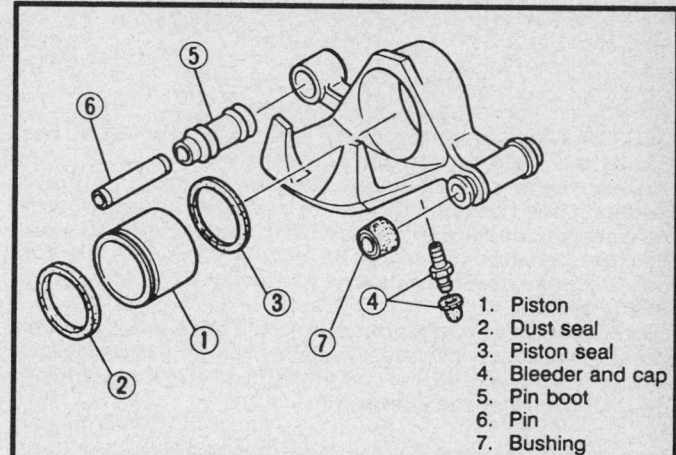

1. Piston
2. Dust seal
3. Piston seal
4. Bleeder and cap
5. Pin boot
6. Pin
7. Bushing

Mazda caliper

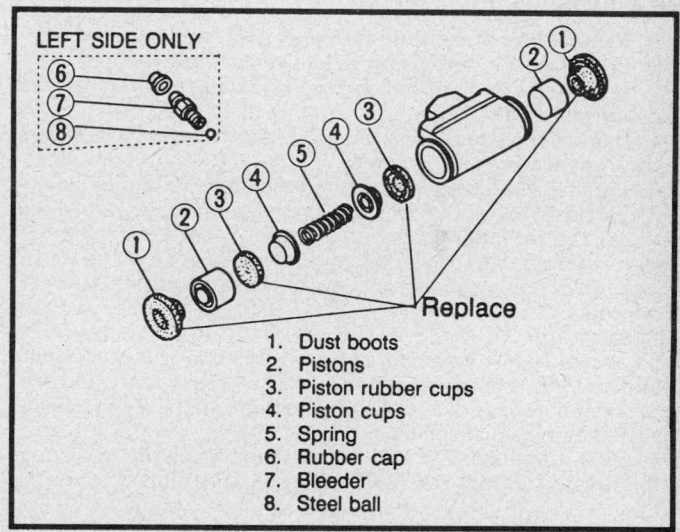

LEFT SIDE ONLY

Replace

1. Dust boots
2. Pistons
3. Piston rubber cups
4. Piston cups
5. Spring
6. Rubber cap
7. Bleeder
8. Steel ball

Mazda wheel cylinder

2. Remove both dust boots.
3. Remove the pistons.
4. Remove the piston cups.
5. Remove the return spring.
6. Hone the cylinder bore if it is not damaged, to provide a smooth sealing surface. Wash and dry the bore after honing.

To assemble:

7. Lubricate the cylinder bore with brake fluid. Install the return spring.

8. Lubricate the new piston cups and install them to the cylinder. Lubricate and install the pistons.

9. Apply lubricant to the boot mounting groove and install the boot.

10. Apply rust penetrant to the bleeder screw threads and install it with the check ball to the wheel cylinder. Tighten until just snug.

NISSAN

NOTE: When cleaning brake system components, use only brake fluid or denatured isopropyl alcohol. Never use a mineral-based solvent such as gasoline or paint thinner; these fluids will leave a residue that may swell and deteriorate rubber parts within the system. All alcohol must be removed from the system when the work is done because alcohol mixed with brake fluid lowers its boiling point.

Do not hone any aluminum bores. There is a hard anodized coating on the aluminum which will be removed if honed. This will allow the aluminum to wear quickly and will damage the component.

Master Cylinder Service

Disassembly and Assembly

1. Remove the brake fluid reservoir and seals or hoses.
2. Push the primary piston in and remove the stopper cap.
3. Let the primary piston spring slowly out and remove the primary piston assembly.
4. Inspect the stopper cap carefully. If either claw is damaged in any way, replace it.
5. Remove the secondary piston assembly. This may be accomplished by carefully blowing low pressure compressed air through the secondary side outlet port if it does not come out easily. Disassemble the secondary piston on Pick-Up and Pathfinder only. The secondary pistons on Axxess and Van are not serviceable.

To assemble:

6. Assemble the secondary piston assembly, if it was disassembled. Coat the master cylinder bore and secondary and primary piston seals liberally with brake fluid. Install both assemblies to the master cylinder.
7. Push the pistons in and install the stopper cap.
8. Install the fluid reservoir and seals, if equipped.

Brake Booster Service

The brake boosters installed on these vehicles are not serviceable. If the unit is defective, replace the entire assembly.

Caliper Service

SINGLE PISTON TYPE

Disassembly and Assembly

1. Remove the bleeder screw.
2. Drain the brake fluid from the caliper.
3. Remove the dust seal ring (rear caliper only) and the dust seal.
4. Position a shop rag opposite the top of the piston. Apply low pressure compressed air to the fluid inlet and carefully blow the piston out of the bore.

――――――― CAUTION ―――――――

Do not put fingers where the piston will land when it is blown out of the caliper. The force of the piston can crush fingers and cause personal injury.

―――――――――――――――――――

5. Remove the piston seal from inside the bore.

To assemble:

6. Blow out all fluid passages with low pressure compressed air.

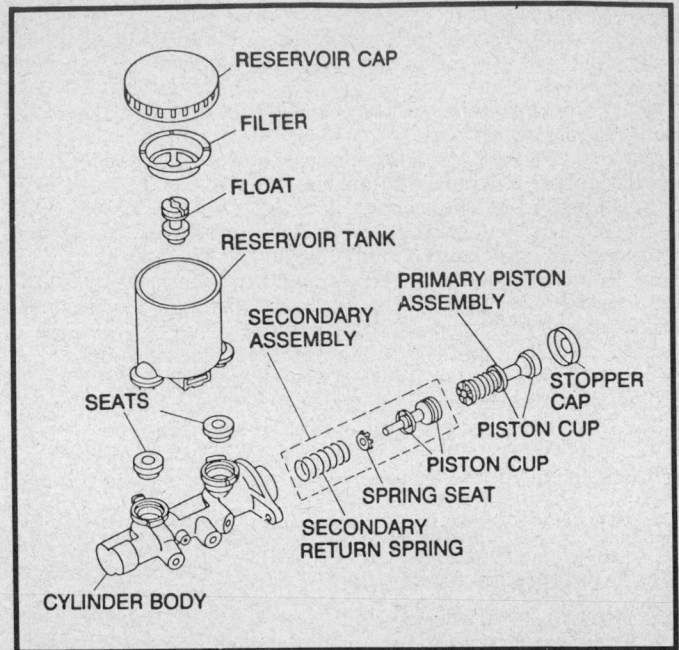

Nissan master cylinder—Pick-Up and Pathfinder

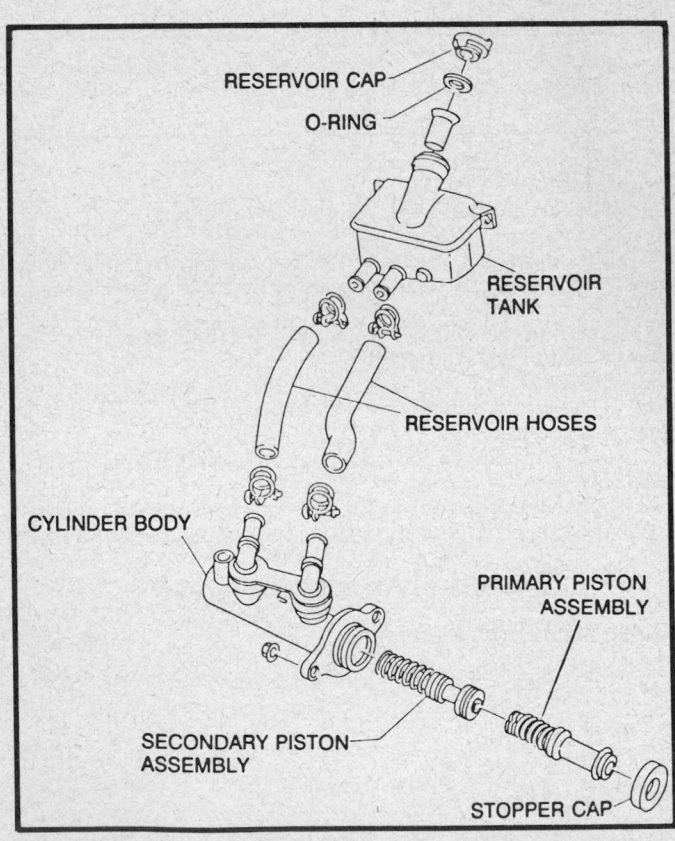

Nissan master cylinder—Van and Axxess

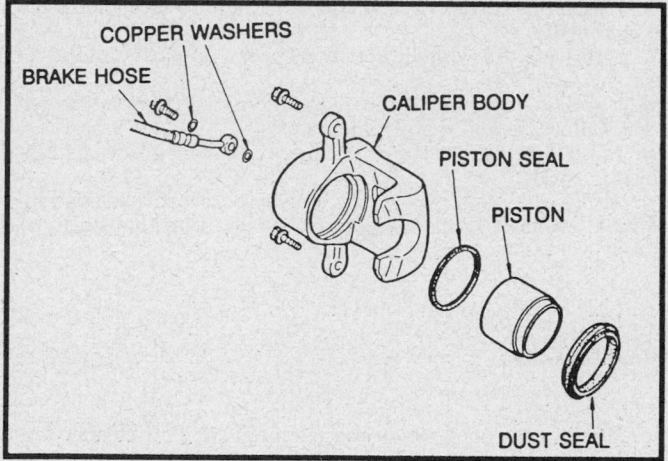

Nissan single piston front caliper

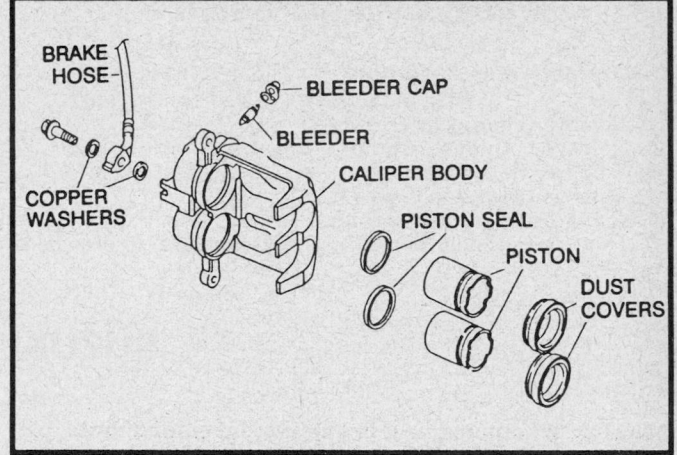

Nissan double piston caliper

7. Slight corrosion or rust can be removed with commutator paper or crocus cloth. Replace pistons that are pitted, scored, peeling or otherwise damaged.

8. Lubricate the caliper bore with brake fluid. Lubricate the seal and install it in the groove.

9. Lubricate the piston and install it to the bore until it bottoms. If the piston will not go in by hand, it is probably cocked. Remove it and reinstall.

10. Apply lubricant to the dust seal mounting groove and install the seal. Install the retaining ring, if equipped.

11. Apply rust penetrant to the bleeder screw threads and install to the caliper. Tighten it until it is just snug against its seat.

DOUBLE PISTON TYPE

Disassembly and Assembly

1. Remove the bleeder screw.
2. Drain the brake fluid from the caliper.
3. Remove the dust covers.
4. Position a shop rag opposite the top of the piston. Apply low pressure compressed air to the fluid inlet and carefully blow the pistons out of their bores. If both pistons do not come out, install the extracted piston back into its bore just enough to seal; then hold it place with a suitable spacer. Blow out the remaining piston.

—— **CAUTION** ——

Do not put fingers where the piston will land when it is blown out of the caliper. The force of the piston can crush fingers and cause personal injury.

5. Remove the piston seals from inside the bore.
To assemble:
6. Blow out all fluid passages with low pressure compressed air.

7. Slight corrosion or rust can be removed with commutator paper or crocus cloth. Replace pistons that are pitted, scored, peeling or otherwise damaged.

8. Lubricate the caliper bore with brake fluid. Lubricate the seals and install in the grooves.

9. Lubricate the pistons and install them to the bores until they bottom. If either piston will not go in by hand, it is probably cocked. Remove it and reinstall.

10. Apply lubricant to the dust seal mounting grooves and install the seals.

11. Apply rust penetrant to the bleeder screw threads and install to the caliper. Tighten it until it is just snug against its seat.

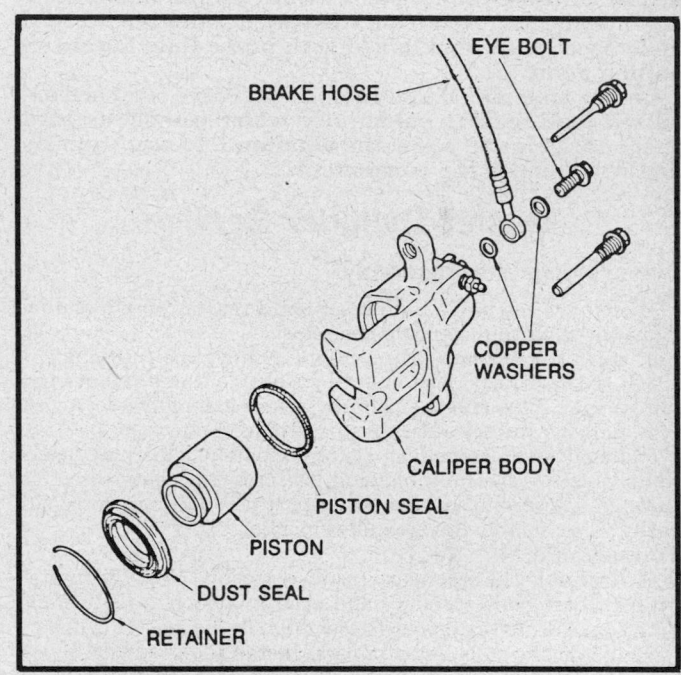

Nissan rear caliper

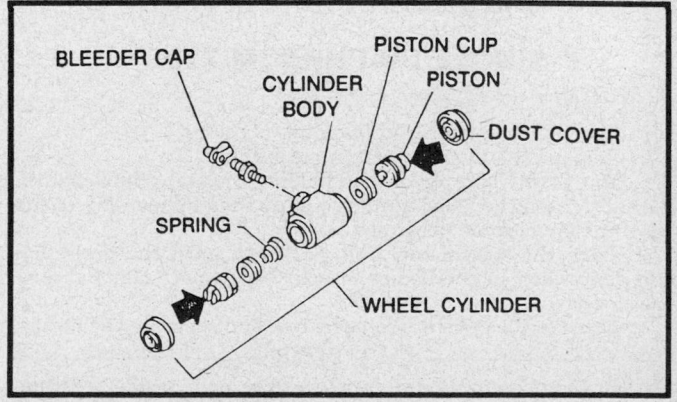

Nissan wheel cylinder

Wheel Cylinder Service

Disassembly and Assembly

1. Remove the bleeder screw.
2. Remove both dust covers.
3. Remove the pistons.
4. Remove the piston cups.
5. Remover the return spring.
6. Hone the cylinder bore if it is not damaged, to provide a smooth sealing surface. Wash and dry the bore after honing.

To assemble:

7. Lubricate the cylinder bore with brake fluid. Install the return spring.
8. Lubricate the new piston cups and install them to the cylinder. Lubricate and install the pistons.
9. Apply lubricant to the dust cover mounting groove and install the cover.
10. Apply rust penetrant to the bleeder screw threads and install to the wheel cylinder. Tighten it until it is just snug against its seat.

SUZUKI AND GEO

NOTE: When cleaning brake system components, use only brake fluid or denatured isopropyl alcohol. Never use a mineral-based solvent such as gasoline or paint thinner; these fluids will leave a residue that may swell and deteriorate rubber parts within the system. All alcohol must be removed from the system when the work is done because alcohol mixed with brake fluid lowers its boiling point.

Do not hone any aluminum bores. There is a hard anodized coating on the aluminum which will be removed if honed. This will allow the aluminum to wear quickly and will damage the component.

Master Cylinder Service

Disassembly and Assembly

1. Remove the brake fluid reservoir screw of roll pin and remove the reservoir. Remove the seals.
2. Push the primary piston in and remove the snapring.
3. Let the primary piston spring slowly out and remove piston stopper, cups and the primary piston assembly.
4. Remove the secondary piston stopper bolt.
5. Remove the secondary piston assembly. This may be accomplished by carefully blowing low pressure compressed air through the secondary side outlet port if it does not come out easily. Disassemble the secondary piston.

To assemble:

6. Assemble the secondary piston assembly. Coat the master cylinder bore and secondary and primary piston seals liberally with brake fluid. Install both assemblies to the master cylinder.
7. Install the cups and stoppers. Install the snapring.
8. Push the pistons in and install the stopper bolt.
9. Install the fluid reservoir and seals.

Brake Booster Service

SINGLE DIAPHRAGM TYPE

SAMURAI

1. Remove the piston rod from the booster.
2. Remove the pushrod clevis and locknut.
3. Mount the booster on the holding tool set 09950–88210. Do not tighten the 2 outer nuts to more than 30 inch lbs. or the booster may become deformed.
4. Turn the special tool bolt clockwise until the projection and depression in the bodies match. Matchmark the bodies at that location.
5. Remove the booster from the tool and separate the bodies.

— CAUTION —
The rear body is spring loaded. Loosen it slowly and carefully or personal injury may result.

6. Remove the boot, air cleaner elements and air cleaner separator from the rear body.
7. Turn the booster piston counterclockwise and remove from the rear body.
8. Push the air valve down and remove the stopper key. Remove the air valve assembly from the booster piston.
9. Remove the diaphragm from the pressure plate.
10. Remove the reaction disc from the booster piston.
11. Remove the seal from the from the rear body.

To assemble:

12. Lubricate and install a new seal to the rear body.
13. Lubricate and install the booster air valve to the booster piston.
14. Compress the valve and install the stopper key.
15. Install the new diaphragm to the pressure plate. Make sure the diaphragm is seated securely in its groove in the pressure plate.

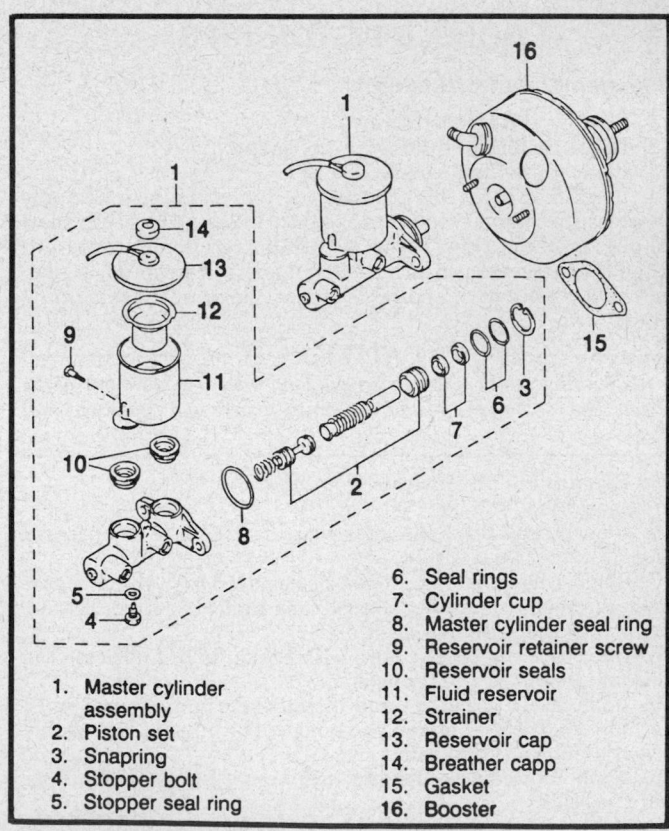

1. Master cylinder assembly	6. Seal rings
2. Piston set	7. Cylinder cup
3. Snapring	8. Master cylinder seal ring
4. Stopper bolt	9. Reservoir retainer screw
5. Stopper seal ring	10. Reservoir seals
	11. Fluid reservoir
	12. Strainer
	13. Reservoir cap
	14. Breather capp
	15. Gasket
	16. Booster

Suzuki master cylinder — Samaral

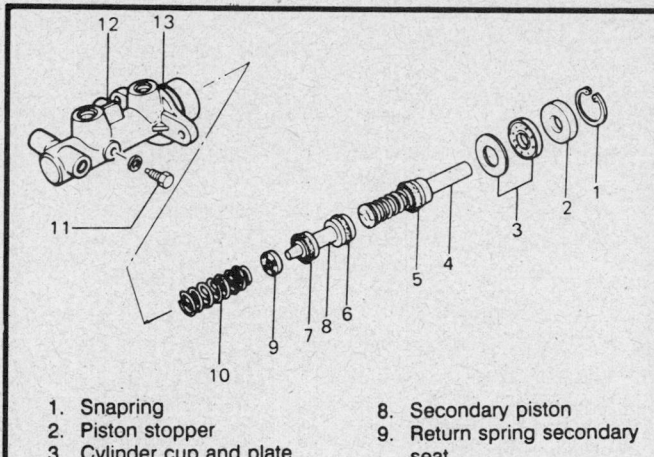

1. Snapring
2. Piston stopper
3. Cylinder cup and plate
4. Primary piston
5. Piston cup
6. Secondary piston pressure cap
7. Piston cup
8. Secondary piston
9. Return spring secondary seat
10. Secondary piston return spring
11. Stopper bolt
12. Cylinder body
13. Seal

Suzuki/Geo master cylinder—Sidekick and Tracker

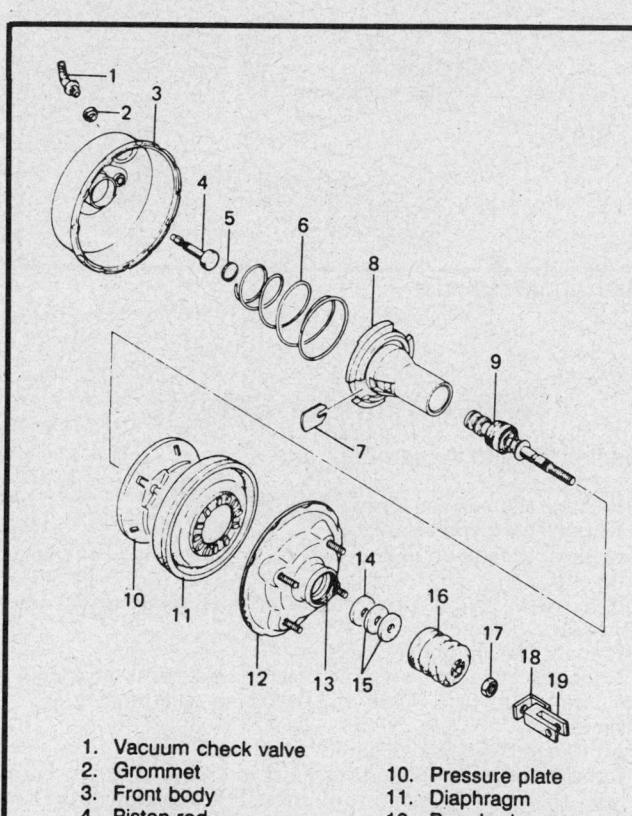

1. Vacuum check valve
2. Grommet
3. Front body
4. Piston rod
5. Reaction disc
6. Booster piston return spring
7. Valve stopper key
8. Booster piston
9. Booster air valve assembly
10. Pressure plate
11. Diaphragm
12. Rear body
13. Seal
14. Air cleaner separator
15. Air cleaner element
16. Rubber boot
17. Nut
18. Bracket
19. Pushrod clevis

Suzuki single diaphragm booster—Samaral

16. Lubricate the face and install the reaction disc to the booster piston.

17. Install the booster piston to the rear body by turning it clockwise into place.

18. Install the new air cleaner separator and elements to the air valve rod.

19. Install the boot to the rear body.

20. Place the front body on the special tool and place the return spring on it large end up.

21. Place the assembled rear body on the return spring and compress. Turn the special bolt counterclockwise until the projection and depression line up.

22. Install the piston rod into the booster piston.

23. Install the locknut and clevis.

SIDEKICK AND TRACKER

1. Remove the pushrod clevis.
2. Remove the locknut.
3. Mount the booster on the holding tool set 09950–88210. Do not tighten the 2 outer nuts to more than 30 inch lbs. or the booster may become deformed.
4. Turn the special tool bolt clockwise until the projection and depression in the bodies match. Matchmark the bodies at that location.
5. Remove the booster from the tool and separate the bodies.

— **CAUTION** —

The rear body is spring loaded. Loosen it slowly and carefully or personal injury may result.

6. Remove the piston rod, boot, air cleaner elements and air cleaner separator from the rear body.
7. Remove the valve stopper key cushion.
8. Push the air valve down and remove the stopper key. Remove the air valve assembly from the booster piston.
9. Remove the diaphragm circular ring from the booster piston. Remove the diaphragm from the pressure plate.
10. Remove the reaction disc from the booster piston.
11. Remove the seal from the from the rear body.

To assemble:

12. Lubricate and install a new seal to the rear body.
13. Install the retainer to the diaphragm. Install the diaphragm to the booster piston and install the new diaphragm circular ring.
14. Lubricate and install the booster air valve to the booster piston. Compress the valve and install the stopper key. Install the cushion to the notch in the stopper.
15. Install the booster piston to the rear body.
16. Install the new air cleaner separator and elements to the air valve rod.
17. Install the boot to the rear body.
18. Lubricate the face and install the reaction disc to the booster piston.
19. Place the front body on the special tool and place the return spring, rod retainer and piston rod on it.
20. Place the assembled rear body on the return spring and compress. Turn the special bolt counterclockwise until the projection and depression line up.
21. Install the piston rod into the booster piston.
22. Install the locknut and clevis.

Caliper Service

Disassembly and Assembly

1. Remove the bleeder screw.
2. Drain the brake fluid from the caliper.
3. Remove the cylinder boot.
4. Position a shop rag opposite the top of the piston. Apply low pressure compressed air to the fluid inlet and carefully blow the piston out of the bore.

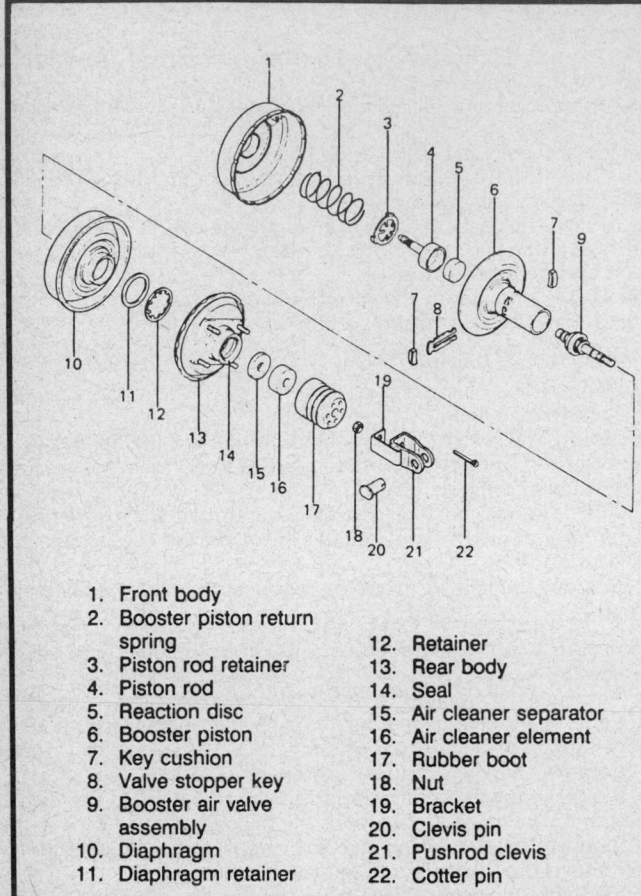

1. Front body
2. Booster piston return spring
3. Piston rod retainer
4. Piston rod
5. Reaction disc
6. Booster piston
7. Key cushion
8. Valve stopper key
9. Booster air valve assembly
10. Diaphragm
11. Diaphragm retainer
12. Retainer
13. Rear body
14. Seal
15. Air cleaner separator
16. Air cleaner element
17. Rubber boot
18. Nut
19. Bracket
20. Clevis pin
21. Pushrod clevis
22. Cotter pin

Suzuki/Geo single diaphragm booster—Sidekick and Tracker

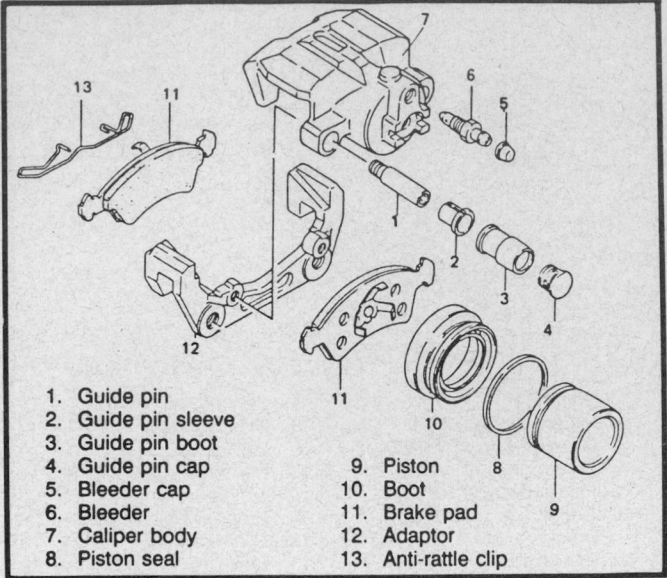

1. Guide pin
2. Guide pin sleeve
3. Guide pin boot
4. Guide pin cap
5. Bleeder cap
6. Bleeder
7. Caliper body
8. Piston seal
9. Piston
10. Boot
11. Brake pad
12. Adaptor
13. Anti-rattle clip

Suzuki caliper

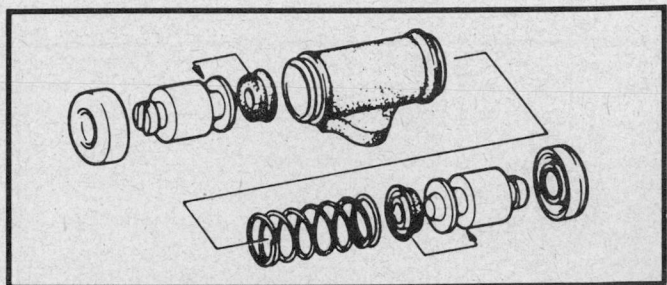

Suzuki wheel cylinder

CAUTION

Do not put fingers where the piston will land when it is blown out of the caliper. The force of the piston can crush fingers and cause personal injury.

5. Remove the piston seal from inside the bore.

To assemble:

6. Blow out all fluid passages with low pressure compressed air.

7. Slight corrosion or rust can be removed with commutator paper or crocus cloth. Replace pistons that are pitted, scored, peeling or otherwise damaged.

8. Lubricate the caliper bore with brake fluid. Lubricate the seal and install it in the groove.

9. Lubricate the piston and install it to the bore until it bottoms. If the piston will not go in by hand, it is probably cocked. Remove it and reinstall.

10. Apply lubricant to the cylinder boot mounting groove and install.

11. Apply rust penetrant to the bleeder screw threads and install to the caliper. Tighten it until it is just snug against its seat.

Wheel Cylinder Service

Disassembly and Assembly

1. Remove the bleeder screw, if equipped.
2. Remove both rubber boots.
3. Remove the piston assemblies, each consisting of the piston and cup.
4. Remove the piston cups from the pistons, being careful not to scratch the piston.
5. Remove the return spring.
6. Hone the cylinder bore if it is not damaged, to provide a smooth sealing surface. Wash and dry the bore after honing.

To assemble:

7. Lubricate the cylinder bore with brake fluid.
8. Lubricate the new piston cups and install them to the pistons, with their lips facing upward. Install the assemblies to the cylinder.
9. Apply lubricant to the boot mounting groove and install the boot.
10. Apply rust penetrant to the bleeder screw threads and install to the wheel cylinder. Tighten until it is just snug against its seat.

TOYOTA

NOTE: When cleaning brake system components, use only brake fluid or denatured isopropyl alcohol. Never use a mineral-based solvent such as gasoline or paint thinner; these fluids will leave a residue that may swell and deteriorate rubber parts within the system. All alcohol must be removed from the system when the work is done because alcohol mixed with brake fluid lowers its boiling point.

Do not hone any aluminum bores. There is a hard anodized coating on the aluminum which will be removed if honed. This will allow the aluminum to wear quickly and will damage the component.

Master Cylinder Service

Disassembly and Assembly

1. Remove the brake fluid reservoir retainer screw, if equipped and remove the reservoir and seals or remove the reservoir unions and seals.
2. Remove the boot. Push the primary piston in and remove the stopper bolt and gasket.
3. Hold the pistons in and remove the snapring.

NOTE: Do not disassemble either piston assembly on the Pick-Up and 4Runner. The individual parts are not serviceable.

4. Let the primary piston spring out and remove the primary piston assembly.
5. Remove the secondary piston assembly. This may be accomplished by carefully blowing low pressure compressed air through the secondary side outlet port if it does not come out easily.

To assemble:

6. Assemble the pistons, if they were disassembled.
7. Coat the master cylinder bore and secondary and primary piston seals liberally with brake fluid.
8. Install both assemblies to the master cylinder.
9. Push the pistons in and install a new snapring.
10. Hold the pistons in and install the stopper bolt with a new gasket. Install a new boot.
11. Install the brake fluid reservoir or unions with new seals. Install the reservoir retaining screw, if equipped.

Brake Booster Service

The brake boosters installed on these vehicles are not serviceable. If the unit is defective, replace the entire assembly.

Caliper Service

SINGLE PISTON TYPE

Disassembly and Assembly

1. Remove the bleeder screw.
2. Drain the brake fluid from the caliper.
3. Remove the boot.
4. Position a shop rag opposite the top of the piston. Apply low pressure compressed air to the fluid inlet and carefully blow the piston out of the bore.

─────── CAUTION ───────

Do not put fingers where the piston will land when it is blown out of the caliper. The force of the piston can crush fingers and cause personal injury.

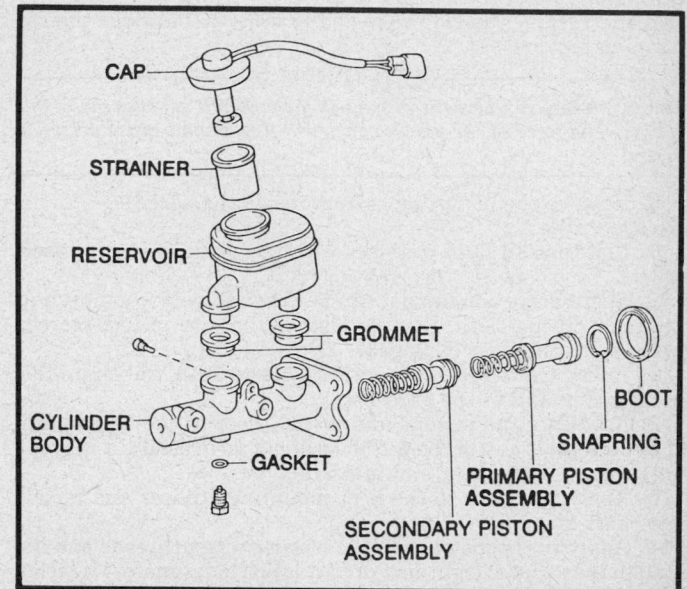

Toyota master cylinder

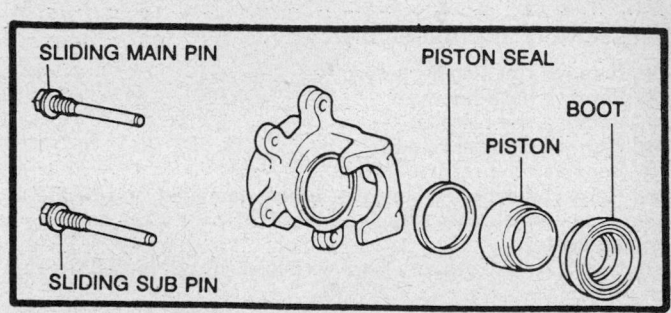

Toyota single piston caliper

5. Remove the piston seal from inside the bore.

To assemble:

6. Blow out all fluid passages with low pressure compressed air.
7. Slight corrosion or rust can be removed with commutator paper or crocus cloth. Replace pistons that are pitted, scored, peeling or otherwise damaged.
8. Lubricate the caliper bore with brake fluid. Lubricate the seal and install it in the groove.
9. Lubricate the piston and install it to the bore until it bottoms. If the piston will not go in by hand, it is probably cocked. Remove it and reinstall.
10. Apply lubricant to the boot mounting groove and install the boot.
11. Apply rust penetrant to the bleeder screw threads and install to the caliper. Tighten it until it is just snug against its seat.

FOUR PISTON TYPE

Disassembly and Assembly

1. Remove the bleeder screw.
2. Drain the brake fluid from the caliper.

3. Remove the boot set rings and boots.

4. Position a suitable block of wood across the caliper and use an old brake pad to keep 1 pair of pistons in their bores. Apply low pressure compressed air to the fluid inlet and carefully blow the pistons out of their bores. Reinsert the piston just enough to seal and reverse the old brake pad in order to blow out the remaining pistons.

CAUTION

Do not put fingers where the piston will land when it is blown out of the caliper. The force of the piston can crush fingers and cause personal injury.
---

5. Remove the piston seals from inside the bore.

To assemble:

6. Blow out all fluid passages with low pressure compressed air.

7. Slight corrosion or rust can be removed with commutator paper or crocus cloth. Replace pistons that are pitted, scored, peeling or otherwise damaged.

8. Lubricate the caliper bore with brake fluid. Lubricate the seals and install in the grooves.

9. Lubricate the pistons and install them to the bores until they bottom. If any of the pistons will not go in easily, it is probably cocked. Remove it and reinstall.

10. Apply lubricant to the boot mounting grooves and install the boots and rings.

11. Apply rust penetrant to the bleeder screw threads and install to the caliper. Tighten it until it is just snug against its seat.

Wheel Cylinder Service

Disassembly and Assembly

1. Remove the bleeder screw.
2. Remove both boots.
3. Remove the pistons.
4. Remove the piston cups.
5. Remover the return spring.
6. Hone the cylinder bore if it is not damaged, to provide a smooth sealing surface. Wash and dry the bore after honing.

To assemble:

7. Lubricate the cylinder bore with brake fluid. Install the return spring.

8. Lubricate the new piston cups and install them to the cylinder. Lubricate and install the pistons.

9. Apply lubricant to the dust cover mounting groove and install the cover.

10. Apply rust penetrant to the bleeder screw threads and install to the wheel cylinder. Tighten it until it is just snug against its seat.

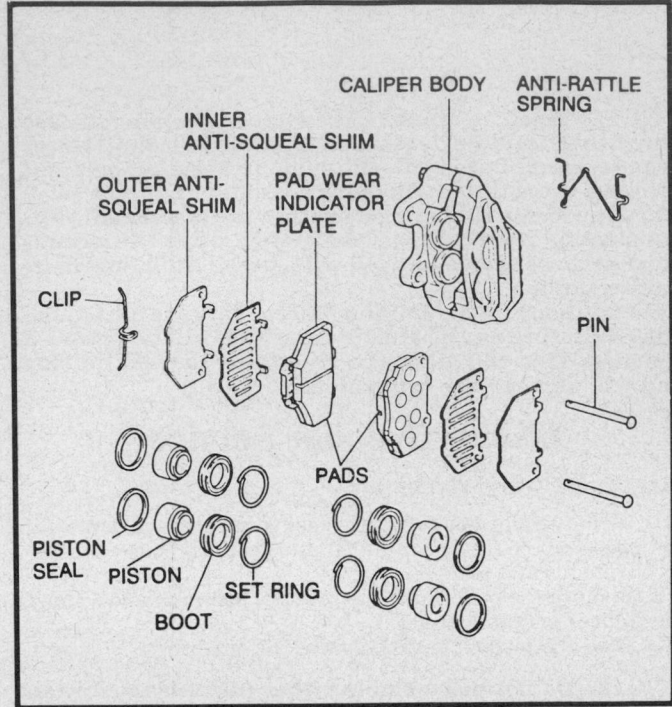

Toyota Four-piston caliper

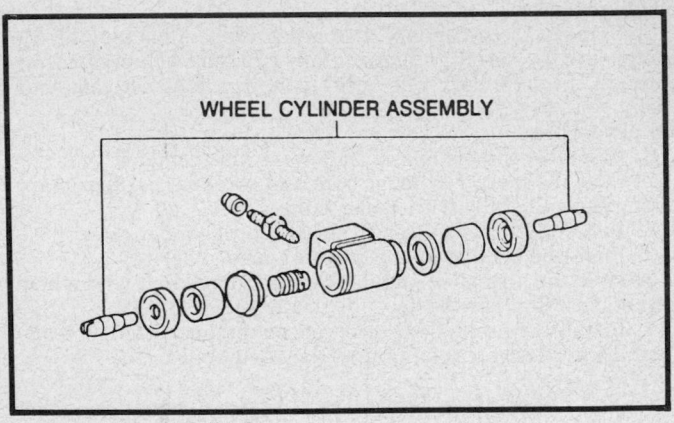

Toyota wheel cylinder

VOLKSWAGEN

NOTE: When cleaning brake system components, use only brake fluid or denatured isopropyl alcohol. Never use a mineral-based solvent such as gasoline or paint thinner; these fluids will leave a residue that may swell and deteriorate rubber parts within the system. All alcohol must be removed from the system when the work is done because alcohol mixed with brake fluid lowers its boiling point.

Master Cylinder Service

Disassembly and Assembly

1. Remove the brake fluid reservoir and seals. Remove the brake light switches, if equipped.

2. Push the primary piston in and remove the stopper bolt and gasket.

3. Hold the pistons in and remove the snapring.

4. Let the primary piston spring out and remove the primary piston assembly.

5. Remove the secondary piston assembly. This may be accomplished by carefully blowing low pressure compressed air through the secondary side outlet port if it does not come out easily.

6. Disassemble the pistons.

To assemble:

7. Assemble the pistons using all parts provided with the kit.

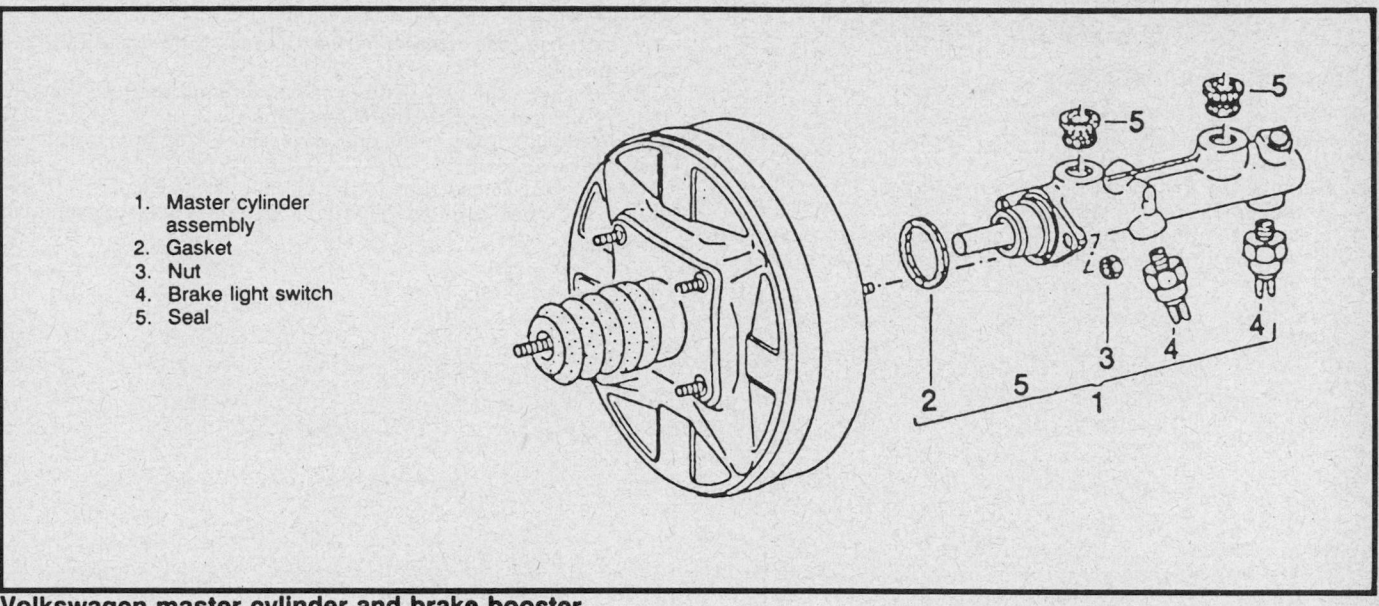

1. Master cylinder assembly
2. Gasket
3. Nut
4. Brake light switch
5. Seal

Volkswagen master cylinder and brake booster

Coat the master cylinder bore and secondary and primary piston seals liberally with brake fluid.

8. Install both assemblies to the master cylinder.
9. Push the pistons in and install a new snapring.
10. Hold the pistons in and install the stopper bolt with a new gasket.
11. Install the brake fluid reservoir and new seals.
12. Install the switches.

Brake Booster Service

These brake boosters are not serviceable. If the unit is defective, replace the entire assembly.

Caliper Service

Disassembly and Assembly

1. Remove the bleeder screw.
2. Drain the brake fluid from the caliper.
3. Remove the dust boot.
4. Position a shop rag opposite the top of the piston. Apply low pressure compressed air to the fluid inlet and carefully blow the piston out of the bore.

─── **CAUTION** ───

Do not put fingers where the piston will land when it is blown out of the caliper. The force of the piston can crush fingers and cause personal injury.

5. Remove the piston seal from inside the bore.
To assemble:
6. Blow out all fluid passages with low pressure compressed air.
7. Slight corrosion or rust can be removed with commutator paper or crocus cloth. Replace pistons that are pitted, scored, peeling or otherwise damaged.
8. Lubricate the caliper bore with brake fluid. Lubricate the seal and install it in the groove.
9. Lubricate the piston and install it to the bore until it bottoms. If the piston will not go in by hand, it is probably cocked. Remove it and reinstall.
10. Apply lubricant to the dust boot mounting groove and install the boot.
11. Apply rust penetrant to the bleeder screw threads and install to the caliper. Tighten it until it is just snug against its seat.

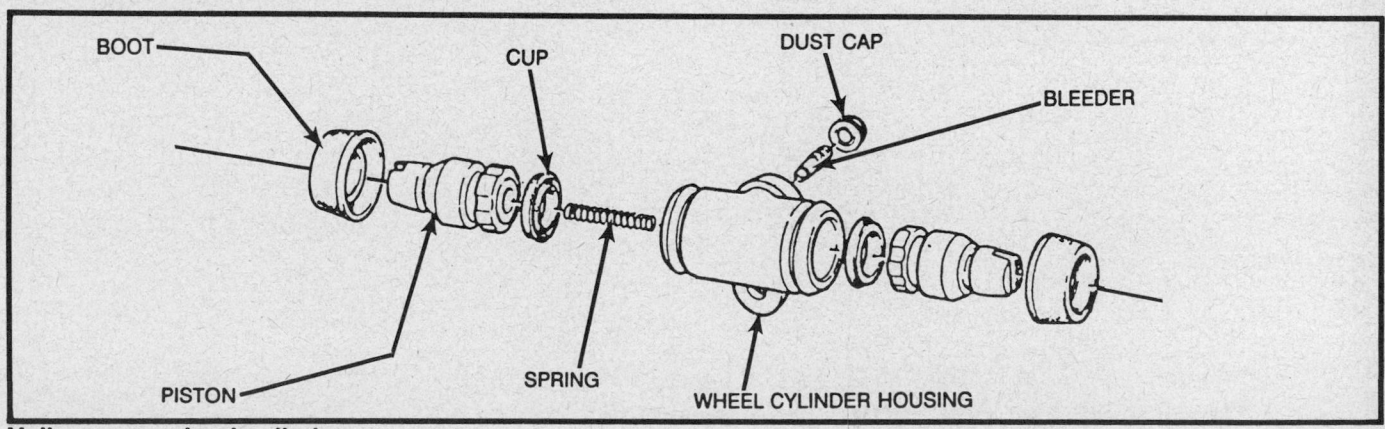

Volkswagen wheel cylinder

Wheel Cylinder Service

Disassembly and Assembly

1. Remove the bleeder screw.
2. Remove both dust covers.
3. Remove the pistons.
4. Remove the piston cups.
5. Remover the return spring.
6. Hone the cylinder bore if it is not damaged, to provide a smooth sealing surface. Wash and dry the bore after honing.

To assemble:

7. Lubricate the cylinder bore with brake fluid. Install the return spring.
8. Lubricate the new piston cups and install them to the cylinder. Lubricate and install the pistons.
9. Apply lubricant to the dust cover mounting groove and install the cover.
10. Apply rust penetrant to the bleeder screw threads and install to the wheel cylinder. Tighten it until it is just snug against its seat.

CARBURETOR IDENTIFICATION

All carburetors are identified by code numbers, either stamped on the attaching flange side, the main body or on a metal tag retained by a bowl cover screw. This identification number is important in order to obtain the correct carburetor replacement or parts and to properly adjust the carburetor when matched to a specific engine.

Carburetor Overhaul Tips

When the carburetor is disassembled, wash all parts (except diaphragms, electric choke units, pump plunger, and any other plastic, leather, fiber, or rubber parts) in clean carburetor solvent. Do not leave parts in the solvent any longer than is necessary to sufficiently loosen the deposits. Excessive cleaning may remove the special finish from the float bowl and choke valve bodies, leaving these parts unfit for service. Rinse all parts in clean solvent and blow them dry with compressed air or allow them to air dry. Wipe clean all cork, plastic, leather, and fiber parts with a clean, lint-free cloth.

Blow out all passages and jets with compressed air and be sure that there are no restrictions or blockages. Never use wire or similar tools to clean jets, fuel passages, or air bleeds. Clean all jets and valves separately to avoid accidental interchange. Check all parts for wear or damage. If wear or damage is found, replace the defective parts. Especially check the following:

1. Check the float needle and seat for wear. If wear is found, replace the complete assembly.
2. Check the float hinge pin for wear and the float(s) for dents or distortion. Replace the float if fuel has leaked into it.
3. Check the throttle and choke shaft bores for wear or an out-of-round condition. Damage or wear to the throttle arm, shaft, or shaft bore will often require replacement of the throttle body. These parts require a close tolerance of fit. Wear may allow air leakage, which could affect starting and idling.
4. Inspect the idle mixture adjusting needles for burrs or grooves. Any such condition requires replacement of the needle, since you will not be able to obtain a satisfactory idle.
5. Test the accelerator pump check valves. They should pass air one way but not the other. Test for proper seating by blowing and sucking on the valve. Replace the valve if necessary. If the valve is satisfactory, wash the valve again to remove breath moisture.
6. Check the bowl cover for warped surfaces with a straight edge.
7. Closely inspect the valves and seats for wear and damage, replacing as necessary.
8. After the carburetor is assembled, check the choke valve for freedom of operation.

Carburetor overhaul kits are recommended for each overhaul. These kits contain all gaskets and new parts to replace those that deteriorate most rapidly. Failure to replace all parts supplied with the kit (especially gaskets) can result in poor performance later.

After cleaning and checking all components, reassemble the carburetor, using new parts and referring to the exploded view. When reassembling, make sure that all screws and jets are tight in their seats, but do not overtighten as the tips will be distorted. Tighten all screws gradually, in rotation. Do not tighten needle valves into their seats. Uneven jetting will result. Always use new gaskets. Be sure to adjust the float level, following the instructions contained in the rebuilding kit, when reassembling.

CHRYSLER IMPORTS AND MITSUBISHI CARBURETORS

CHRYSLER IMPORTS/MITSUBISHI CARBURETORS
(All measurements in inches)

Year	Carburetor Number	Fast Idle Opening	Float Level	Choke Breaker Opening	Throttle Position Sensor (volts)	Dashpot (rpm)
1986	DIDTA-209	0.028	.0394	—	0.25	—
	DIDTA-210	0.031	.0394	—	0.25	—
	DIDTF-205	0.025	.0394	—	0.25	—
	DIDTF-206	0.028	.0394	—	0.25	—
	DIDTF-207	0.028	.0394	—	0.25	—
	DIDTF-208	0.031	.0394	—	0.25	—
1987	DIDEF-400	—	—	①	0.25	2000
	DIDEF-401	—	—	①	0.25	1500
	DIDEF-402	—	—	①	0.25	2000
	DIDEF-403	—	—	①	0.25	1500
	DIDEF-404	—	—	②	0.25	2000
	DIDEF-405	—	—	②	0.25	1500
	DIDEF-406	—	—	②	0.25	2000
	DIDEF-407	—	—	②	0.25	1500
	DIDEF-410	—	—	②	0.25	2000

CHRYSLER IMPORTS/MITSUBISHI CARBURETORS
(All measurements in inches)

Year	Carburetor Number	Fast Idle Opening	Float Level	Choke Breaker Opening	Throttle Position Sensor (volts)	Dashpot (rpm)
1987	DIDEF-411	—	—	②	0.25	1500
	DIDEF-412	—	—	②	0.25	2000
	DIDEF-413	—	—	②	0.25	1500
	DIDEF-420	—	—	①	0.25	2000
	DIDEF-421	—	—	①	0.25	1500
	DIDEF-422	—	—	②	0.25	2000
	DIDEF-432	—	—	②	0.25	1500
1988	DIDEF-400	—	—	①	0.25	2000
	DIDEF-401	—	—	①	0.25	1500
	DIDEF-402	—	—	①	0.25	2000
	DIDEF-403	—	—	①	0.25	1500
	DIDEF-420	—	—	②	0.25	2000
	DIDEF-421	—	—	②	0.25	1500
	DIDEF-429	—	—	②	0.25	2000
	DIDEF-430	—	—	②	0.25	1500
	DIDEF-431	—	—	③	0.25	2000
	DIDEF-432	—	—	③	0.25	1500
	DIDEF-435	—	—	②	0.25	2000
	DIDEF-436	—	—	②	0.25	1500
	DIDEF-437	—	—	②	0.25	2000
	DIDEF-438	—	—	②	0.25	1500
	DIDEF-441	—	—	③	0.25	2000
	DIDEF-442	—	—	③	0.25	1500
	DIDEF-443	—	—	③	0.25	2000
	DIDEF-444	—	—	③	0.25	1500
1989	DIDEF-400	—	—	①	0.25	2000
	DIDEF-401	—	—	④	0.25	1500
	DIDEF-402	—	—	①	0.25	2000
	DIDEF-403	—	—	①	0.25	1500
	DIDEF-420	—	—	①	0.25	2000
	DIDEF-428	—	—	①	0.25	1500
	DIDEF-429	—	—	②	0.25	2000
	DIDEF-430	—	—	②	0.25	1500
	DIDEF-431	—	—	③	0.25	2000
	DIDEF-435	—	—	②	0.25	2000
	DIDEF-436	—	—	②	0.25	1500
	DIDEF-437	—	—	②	0.25	2000
	DIDEF-438	—	—	②	0.25	1500
	DIDEF-441	—	—	③	0.25	2000
	DIDEF-443	—	—	③	0.25	2000

① 1st stage: 0.087-0.094
 2nd stage: 0.114-0.122
② 1st stage: 0.098-0.106
 2nd stage: 0.126-0.133
③ 1st stage: 0.091-0.098
 2nd stage: 0.118-0.126
④ 1st stage: 0.079-0.087
 2nd stage: 0.114-0.122

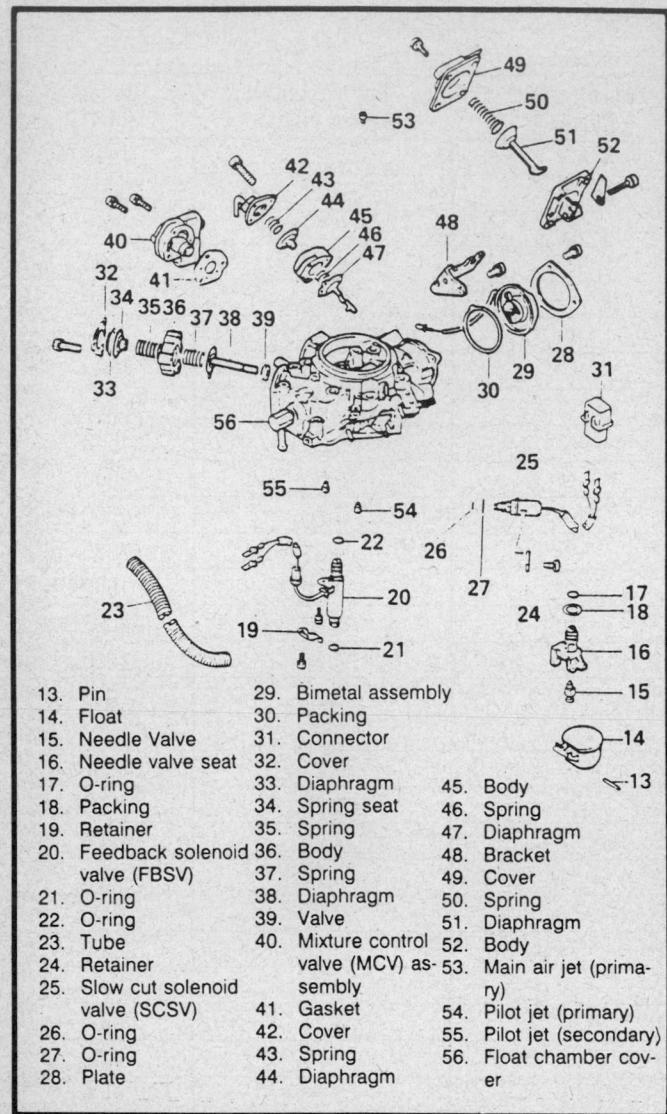

13.	Pin	29.	Bimetal assembly
14.	Float	30.	Packing
15.	Needle Valve	31.	Connector
16.	Needle valve seat	32.	Cover
17.	O-ring	33.	Diaphragm
18.	Packing	34.	Spring seat
19.	Retainer	35.	Spring
20.	Feedback solenoid	36.	Body
	valve (FBSV)	37.	Spring
21.	O-ring	38.	Diaphragm
22.	O-ring	39.	Valve
23.	Tube	40.	Mixture control
24.	Retainer		valve (MCV) as-
25.	Slow cut solenoid		sembly
	valve (SCSV)	41.	Gasket
26.	O-ring	42.	Cover
27.	O-ring	43.	Spring
28.	Plate	44.	Diaphragm

45.	Body
46.	Spring
47.	Diaphragm
48.	Bracket
49.	Cover
50.	Spring
51.	Diaphragm
52.	Body
53.	Main air jet (prima-ry)
54.	Pilot jet (primary)
55.	Pilot jet (secondary)
56.	Float chamber cover

Chrysler/Mitsubishi carburetor upper half exploded view

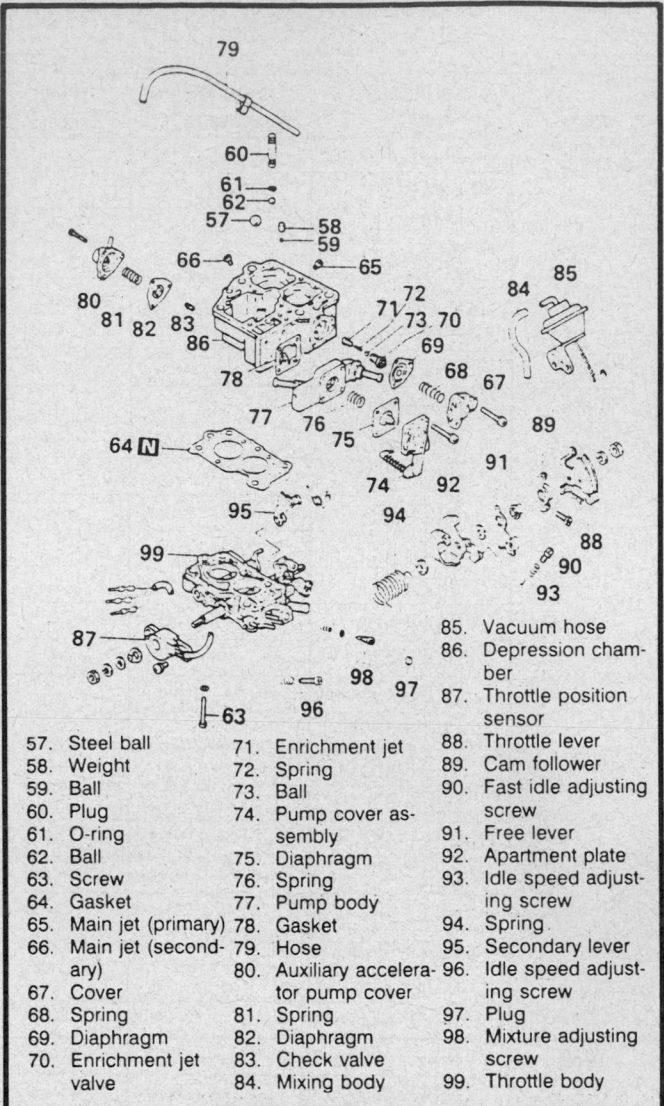

57.	Steel ball	71.	Enrichment jet
58.	Weight	72.	Spring
59.	Ball	73.	Ball
60.	Plug	74.	Pump cover as-
61.	O-ring		sembly
62.	Ball	75.	Diaphragm
63.	Screw	76.	Spring
64.	Gasket	77.	Pump body
65.	Main jet (primary)	78.	Gasket
66.	Main jet (second-ary)	79.	Hose
67.	Cover	80.	Auxiliary accelera-tor pump cover
68.	Spring	81.	Spring
69.	Diaphragm	82.	Diaphragm
70.	Enrichment jet valve	83.	Check valve
		84.	Mixing body

85.	Vacuum hose
86.	Depression cham-ber
87.	Throttle position sensor
88.	Throttle lever
89.	Cam follower
90.	Fast idle adjusting screw
91.	Free lever
92.	Apartment plate
93.	Idle speed adjust-ing screw
94.	Spring
95.	Secondary lever
96.	Idle speed adjust-ing screw
97.	Plug
98.	Mixture adjusting screw
99.	Throttle body

Chrysler/Mitsubishi carburetor lower half exploded view

Float Level Adjustment

1. Invert the float chamber cover assembly without a gasket.
2. Position a float gauge and measure the distance from the bottom of the float to the surface of the float chamber cover.
3. If not within specification the shim under the needle seat must be changed.
4. Adding or removing a shim will change the float level by 3 times the thickness of the shim.

Fast Idle Opening Adjustment

1986

1. With the carburetor at room temperature, insert the diameter drill specified and adjust the fast idle opening by adjustng the fast idle screw.
2. Use a drill diameter of 0.028 in. on vehicles with manual transmission and 0.031 in. with automatic transmission.

Choke Breaker Opening

1. Disconnect the vacuum hose (yellow stripe) from the choke breaker.

Chrysler/Mitsubishi float level adjustment

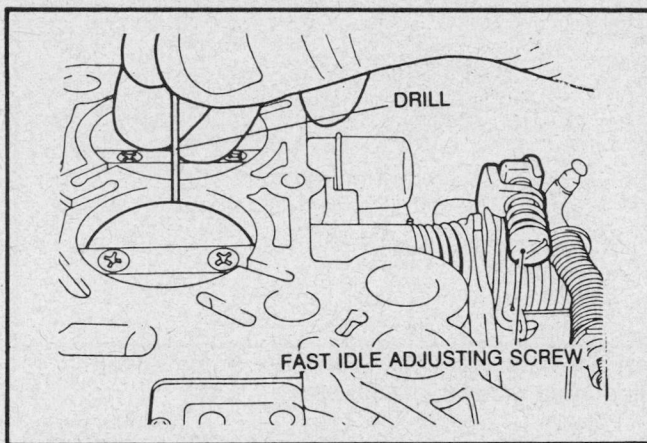

Chrysler/Mitsubishi fast idle opening adjustment

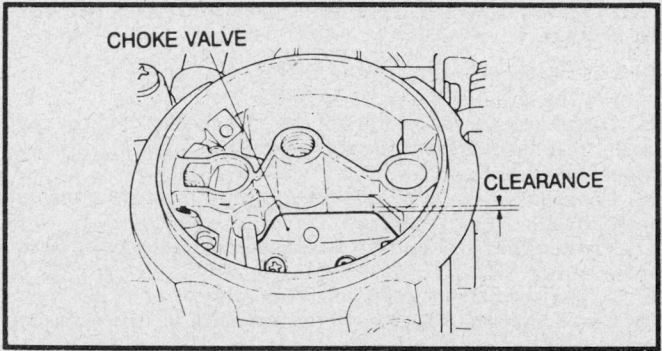

Chrysler/Mitsubishi choke breaker opening measurement

2. With the engine idling, close the choke valve lightly until the choke valve stops.

3. Measure the choke valve to choke bore clearance to see if it is within the 1st stage specification. If necessary, remove the bimetal assembly and adjust the rod end opening to be within the 1st stage specification.

NOTE: When removing the bimetal assembly, put a mark on the electric choke body.

4. Reconnect the vacuum hose (yellow stripe) from the choke breaker and remeasure the choke valve to choke bore clearance.

5. If the clearance is not within the 2nd stage specification, adjust by the adjusting screw.

Throttle Position Sensor Adjustment

1986

1. Warm the engine to normal operating temperature and make sure the fast idle cam is released.

2. Stop the engine, then turn the No. 1 and 2 idle speed adjusting screws counterclockwise enough to close the throttle valve completely. Record the number of turns.

3. Connect a digital type voltmeter between the TPS connectors 2 and 3.

NOTE: Do not disconnect the TPS connector and body harness.

4. Switch the ignition key on and adjust the TPS adjustment screw so that the TPS output is 0.25 volts.

5. Turn the ignition key off.

6. Close the No. 1 and 2 idle speed adjusting screws the same number of turns.

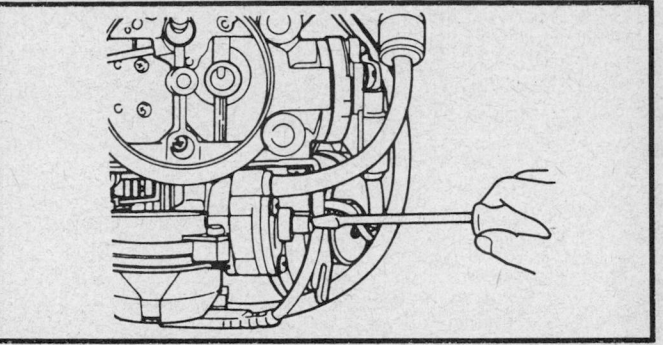

Chrysler/Mitsubishi TPS adjusting screw—1986

1987–89

Montero and Pick-up

1. Loosen the accelerator cable.

2. Turn the No. 1 and 2 idle speed adjusting screws counterclockwise enough to close the throttle valve completely. Record the number of turns. At this time, the fast idle control should have been released (the lever not resting on the fast idle cam).

3. Disconnect the carburetor connectors.

4. Connect the special test harness tool MD998474 between the disconnected connectors.

5. Connect a digital voltmeter between the No. 2 red sensor output terminal and the No. 8 blue sensor (ground) of the carburetors connectors.

6. Turn the ignition switch to **ON** but do not start the engine.

7. Measure the output voltage of the TPS. The standard value is 0.25 volts.

8. If adjustment is necessary, loosen the TPS attaching screw and adjust by turning the TPS to the standard value.

NOTE: Turning the TPS clockwise increases the output voltage.

9. Tighten the No. 1 and 2 idle speed adjusting screws recorded earlier.

10. Remove the voltmeter and the special tool and connect the carburetor's connector.

11. Adjust the play of the accelerator cable.

12. Check that the idle speed is as specified on the Emission Control Label.

Ram 50 and Ram Raider

1. Loosen the accelerator cable.

2. Turn the No. 1 and 2 idle speed adjusting screws counterclockwise enough to close the throttle valve completely. Record the number of turns. At this time, the fast idle control should have been released (the lever not resting on the fast idle cam).

3. Turn the ignition switch to **LOCK**.

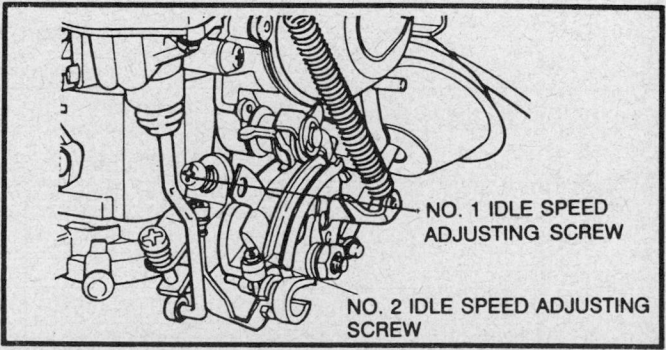

Chrysler/Mitsubishi No. 1 and No. 2 idle speed adjusting screws—1987–89

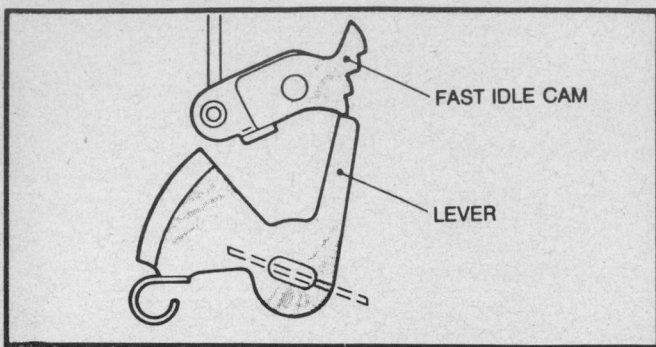

Chrysler/Mitsubishi fast idle cam and lever — 1987–89

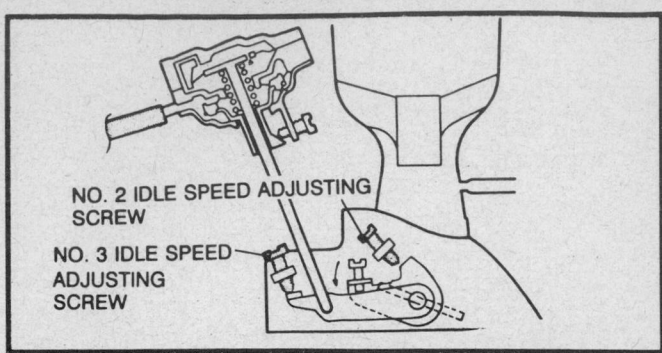

Chrysler/Mitsubishi No. 2 and No. 3 idle speed adjustment screws — 1987–89

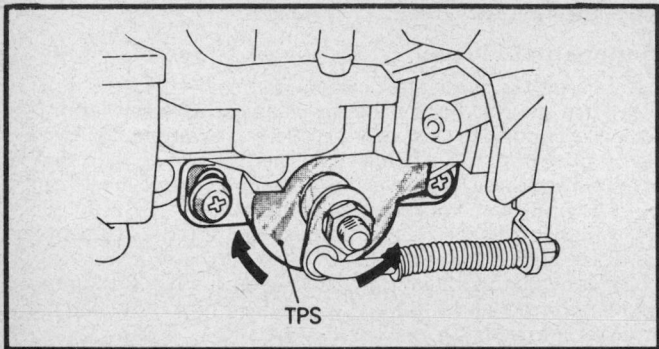

Chrysler/Mitsubishi TPS adjustment — 1987–89

4. Disconnect the large and small harness connector from the engine control unit.

5. Set the check switch of the ECI switch **OFF**.

6. Set the select switch of the ECI checker toool MD998451 to **A**.

7. Connect a carburetor test harness MD998456 to the engine control unit and the harness connectors.

8. Connect a volt meter to the extension terminals of the ECI checker, and then change the extension switch from **CHECK METER** down to the extension position.

9. Set the select switch and the check switch on the ECI checker to **A** and **3** respectively.

10. Turn the ignition switch to **ON** but do not start the engine.

11. Measure the output voltage of the TPS. The standard velue is 0.25 volts.

12. If adjustment is necessary, loosen the TPS attaching screw and adjust by turning the TPS to the standard value.

NOTE: Turning the TPS clockwise increases the output voltage.

13. Set the check switch of the ECI checker to **OFF**.

14. Set the ignition switch to **LOCK**.

15. Disconnect the connectors of the ECI checker and the carburetor test harness from the engine control unit and body side harness connectors.

16. Connect the body side harness connectors to the engine control unit.

17. Tighten the No. 1 and No. 2 idle speed adjusting screws recorded earlier.

18. Adjust the play of the accelerator cable.

19. Check that the idle speed is as specified on the emission control label.

Dashpot Adjustment

1. Make sure the curb idle speed is correct, the engine temperature is at normal operating temperature, lights and accessories off, manual transmission in neutral and automatic transmission in **PARK**.

2. Start the engine and run at idle.

3. Close the throttle valve until the No. 2 idle speed adjusting screw contacts the free lever. Check the engine speed at that moment. If the engine speed is not as specified, adjust the dashpot by turning the No. 3 idle speed adjustment screw.

4. Release the free lever and verify that the engine returns to the idle speed slowly.

ISUZU CARBURETORS

ISUZU CARBURETORS
Stromberg Models

(All measurements in inches)

		Float Level	Primary Throttle Valve	Choke Valve Opening	Unloader	Primary and Secondary Throttle Valve
1986	DCH340-227	0.059	0.050–0.059	—	—	—
	DCH340-228	0.059	0.050–0.059	—	—	—
	DFP340-3	0.059	0.050–0.059	—	—	—
	DFP340-4	0.059	0.050–0.059	—	—	—
	DCR384	0.059	0.050–0.059	—	—	—
	DFP384	0.059	0.050–0.059	—	—	—

ISUZU CARBURETORS
Stromberg Models
(All measurements in inches)

		Float Level	Primary Throttle Valve	Choke Valve Opening	Unloader	Primary and Secondary Throttle Valve
1987	DCH340-227	0.059	0.050–0.059	—	—	—
	DCH340-228	0.059	0.050–0.059	—	—	—
	DFP340-3	0.059	0.050–0.059	—	—	—
	DFP340-4	0.059	0.050–0.059	—	—	—
	DCR384	0.059	0.050–0.059	—	—	—
	DFP384	0.059	0.050–0.059	—	—	—
1988	DFP384-205	0.059	—	0.031–0.050	0.105–0.050	0.272–0.331
1989	DFP384-205	0.059	—	0.031–0.050	0.105–0.050	0.272–0.331
1990	DFP384-205	0.059	—	0.031–0.050	0.105–0.129	0.272–0.331

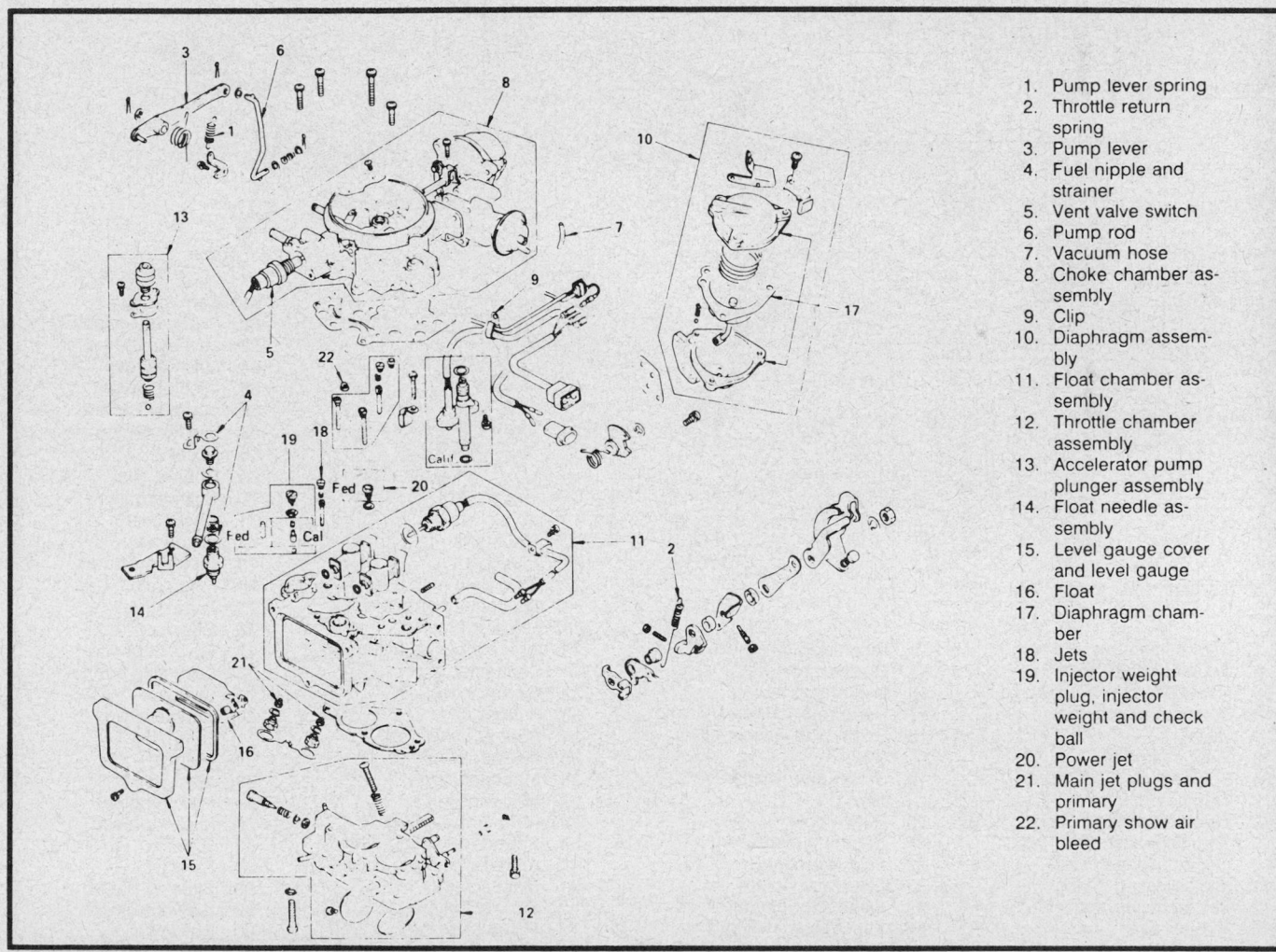

1. Pump lever spring
2. Throttle return spring
3. Pump lever
4. Fuel nipple and strainer
5. Vent valve switch
6. Pump rod
7. Vacuum hose
8. Choke chamber assembly
9. Clip
10. Diaphragm assembly
11. Float chamber assembly
12. Throttle chamber assembly
13. Accelerator pump plunger assembly
14. Float needle assembly
15. Level gauge cover and level gauge
16. Float
17. Diaphragm chamber
18. Jets
19. Injector weight plug, injector weight and check ball
20. Power jet
21. Main jet plugs and primary
22. Primary show air bleed

Isuzu (Stromberg) carburetor disassembled view – 1986–90 models DCR384/DFP384

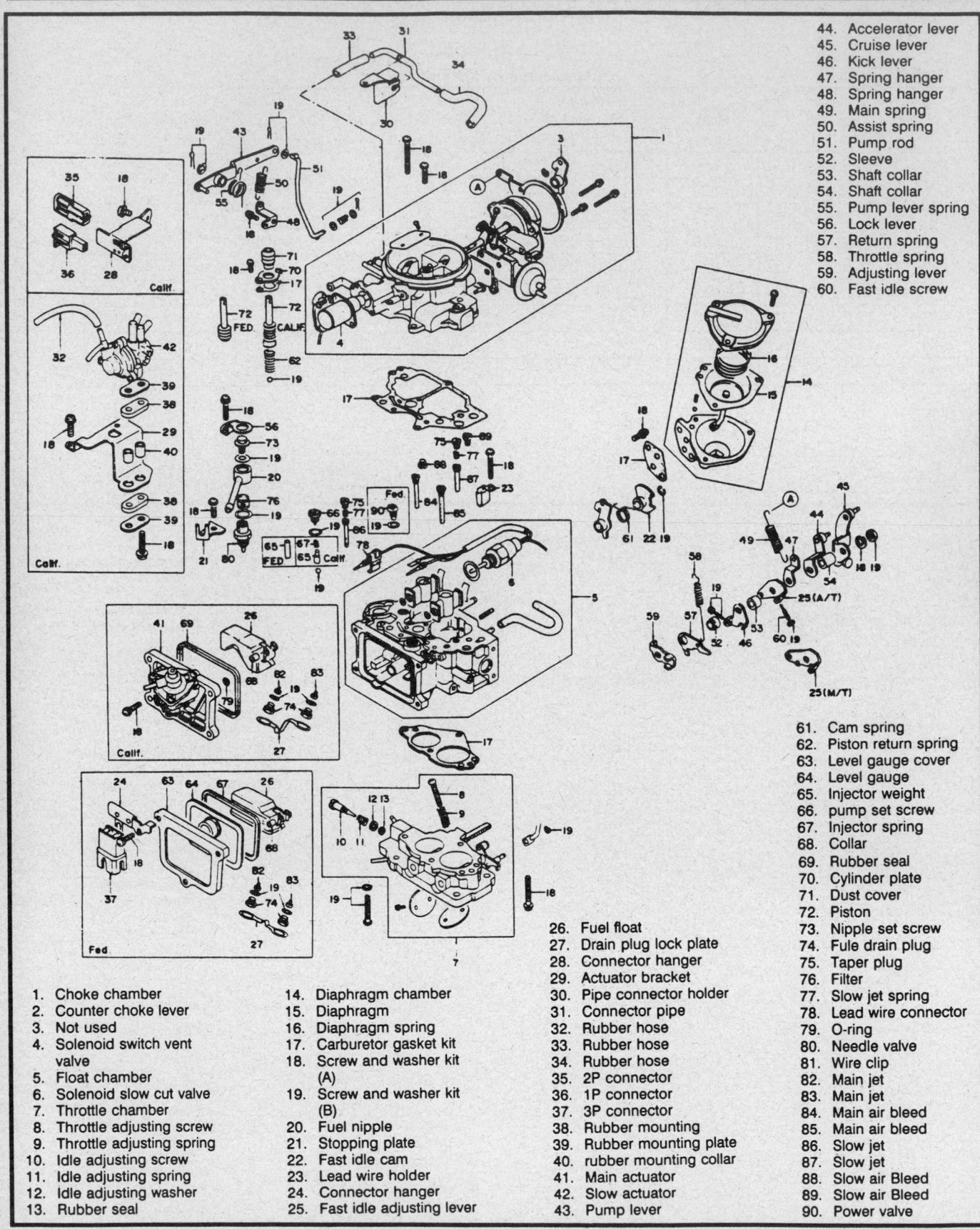

44. Accelerator lever
45. Cruise lever
46. Kick lever
47. Spring hanger
48. Spring hanger
49. Main spring
50. Assist spring
51. Pump rod
52. Sleeve
53. Shaft collar
54. Shaft collar
55. Pump lever spring
56. Lock lever
57. Return spring
58. Throttle spring
59. Adjusting lever
60. Fast idle screw

61. Cam spring
62. Piston return spring
63. Level gauge cover
64. Level gauge
65. Injector weight
66. pump set screw
67. Injector spring
68. Collar
69. Rubber seal
70. Cylinder plate
71. Dust cover
72. Piston
73. Nipple set screw
74. Fule drain plug
75. Taper plug
76. Filter
77. Slow jet spring
78. Lead wire connector
79. O-ring
80. Needle valve
81. Wire clip
82. Main jet
83. Main jet
84. Main air bleed
85. Main air bleed
86. Slow jet
87. Slow jet
88. Slow air Bleed
89. Slow air Bleed
90. Power valve

1. Choke chamber
2. Counter choke lever
3. Not used
4. Solenoid switch vent valve
5. Float chamber
6. Solenoid slow cut valve
7. Throttle chamber
8. Throttle adjusting screw
9. Throttle adjusting spring
10. Idle adjusting screw
11. Idle adjusting spring
12. Idle adjusting washer
13. Rubber seal
14. Diaphragm chamber
15. Diaphragm
16. Diaphragm spring
17. Carburetor gasket kit
18. Screw and washer kit (A)
19. Screw and washer kit (B)
20. Fuel nipple
21. Stopping plate
22. Fast idle cam
23. Lead wire holder
24. Connector hanger
25. Fast idle adjusting lever
26. Fuel float
27. Drain plug lock plate
28. Connector hanger
29. Actuator bracket
30. Pipe connector holder
31. Connector pipe
32. Rubber hose
33. Rubber hose
34. Rubber hose
35. 2P connector
36. 1P connector
37. 3P connector
38. Rubber mounting
39. Rubber mounting plate
40. rubber mounting collar
41. Main actuator
42. Slow actuator
43. Pump lever

Isuzu (Stromberg) carburetor disassembled view 1986–90 model DCH340

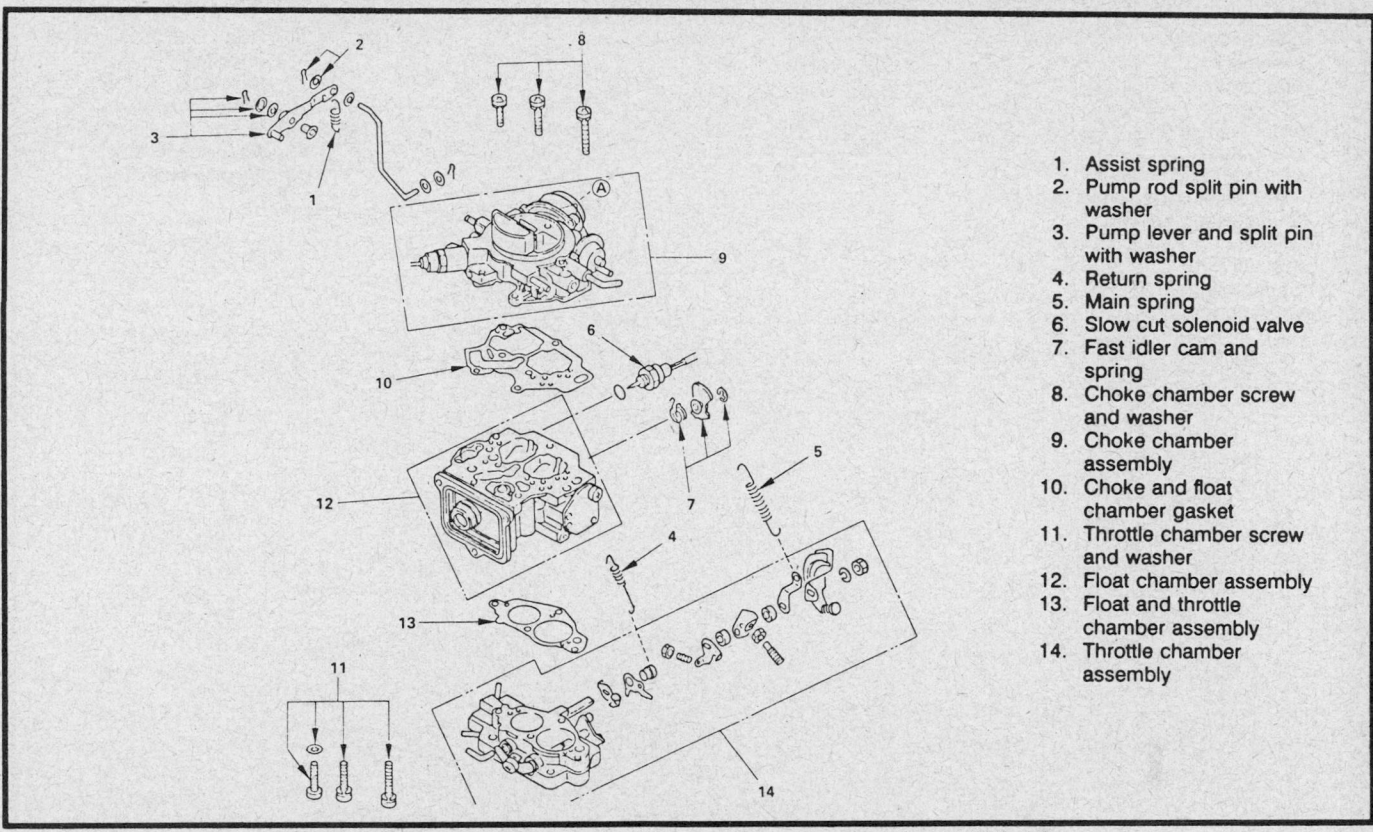

1. Assist spring
2. Pump rod split pin with washer
3. Pump lever and split pin with washer
4. Return spring
5. Main spring
6. Slow cut solenoid valve
7. Fast idler cam and spring
8. Choke chamber screw and washer
9. Choke chamber assembly
10. Choke and float chamber gasket
11. Throttle chamber screw and washer
12. Float chamber assembly
13. Float and throttle chamber assembly
14. Throttle chamber assembly

Isuzu (Stromberg) carburetor disassembled view of the major components — 1988–90

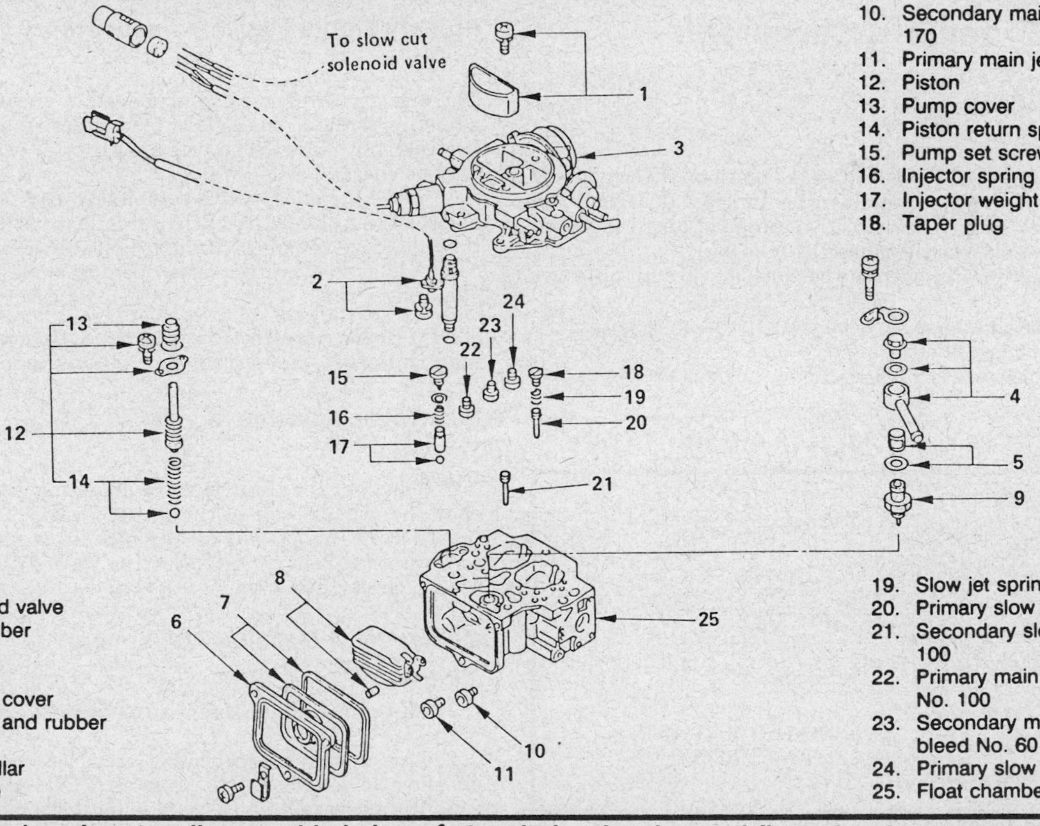

To slow cut solenoid valve

1. Vent cover
2. Duty solenoid valve
3. Choke chamber
4. Fuel nipple
5. Fuel filter
6. Level gauge cover
7. Level gauge and rubber seal
8. Float and collar
9. Needle valve
10. Secondary main jet No. 170
11. Primary main jet No. 88
12. Piston
13. Pump cover
14. Piston return spring
15. Pump set screw
16. Injector spring
17. Injector weight
18. Taper plug
19. Slow jet spring
20. Primary slow jet No. 52
21. Secondary slow jet No. 100
22. Primary main air bleed No. 100
23. Secondary main air bleed No. 60
24. Primary slow air bleed
25. Float chamber

Isuzu (Stromberg) carburetor disassembled view of the choke chamber and float chamber — 1988–90

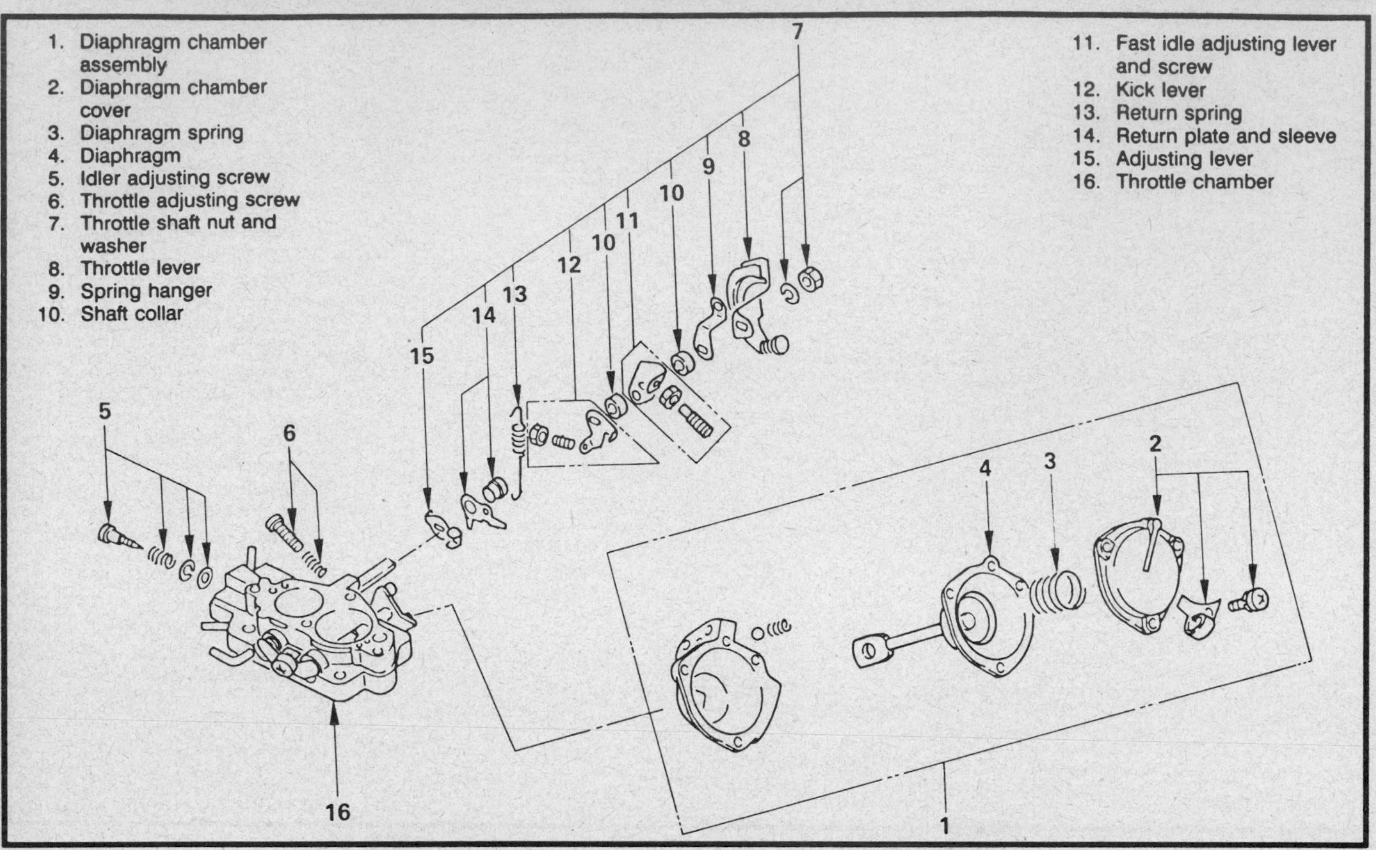

1. Diaphragm chamber assembly
2. Diaphragm chamber cover
3. Diaphragm spring
4. Diaphragm
5. Idler adjusting screw
6. Throttle adjusting screw
7. Throttle shaft nut and washer
8. Throttle lever
9. Spring hanger
10. Shaft collar
11. Fast idle adjusting lever and screw
12. Kick lever
13. Return spring
14. Return plate and sleeve
15. Adjusting lever
16. Throttle chamber

Isuzu (Stromberg) carburetor disassembled view of the throttle chamber—1988–90

Stromberg Carburetor

Float Level Adjustment

1986–90

The fuel level is normal if it is within the mark on the window. If the level is outside the line, adjust by bending the float seat. The needle valve should have an effective stroke of about 0.059 in. The float stroke may be measured as follows:

1. Hold the carburetor with the bottom side up and fully raise the float.
2. Measure the distance between the valve stem (resting at its bottom position) and the float seat.
3. Normal clearance is 0.059 in. Bend the float stopper as necessary to adjust.

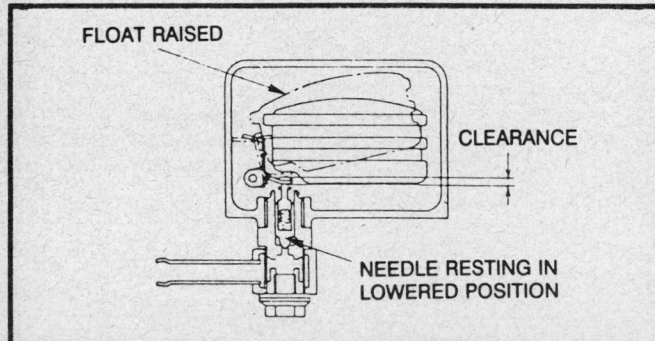

FLOAT RAISED

CLEARANCE

NEEDLE RESTING IN LOWERED POSITION

Isuzu (Stromberg) float level adjustment

Primary Throttle Valve Adjustment

1986–87

The primary throttle valve is opened by means of the fast idle adjusting screw to an angle of 16 degrees when the choke valve is completely closed. The primary throttle valve opening angle may be checked as follows:

1. Close the choke valve completely and measure the clearance between the center of the throttle valve and the wall of the throttle valve chamber. Standard clearance is 0.050–0.059 in.
2. Adjust the throttle valve opening angle with the fast idle adjusting screw.

NOTE: Be sure to turn the throttle stop screw all the way in before measuring the clearance.

Kick Lever Adjustment

1986–87

1. Turn out the throttle valve adjusting screw to completely close the primary side of the throttle valve.
2. Loosen the locknut on the kick lever screw and turn the screw until it is in contact with the return plate.
3. Tighten the locknut.

Choke Valve Opening Adjustment

1988–90

1. Move the fast idle screw tip against the 2nd step of the fast idle cam.
2. Measure the clearance between the choke valve and the choke valve chamber wall.
3. If the clearance measured is not between 0.031–0.050 in., bend the counter lever tang to adjust.

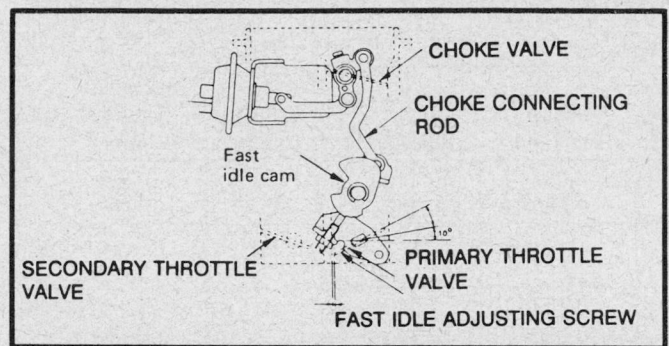

Isuzu (Stromberg) primary throttle valve adjustment—1986–87

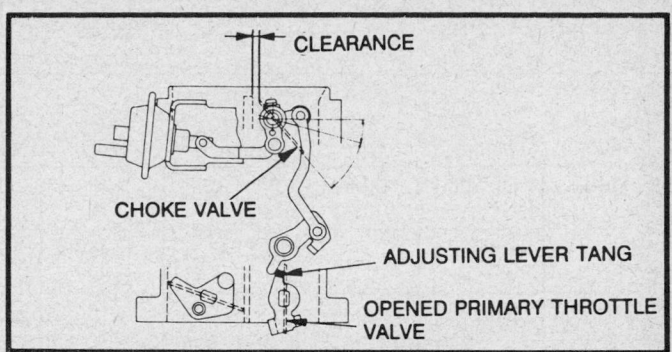

Isuzu (Stromberg) unloader adjustment—1988–90

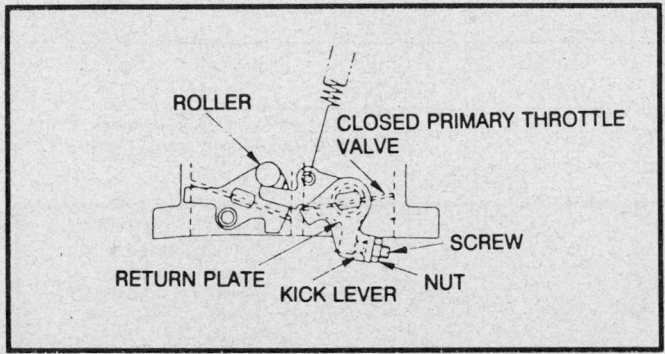

Isuzu (Stromberg) kick lever adjustment—1986–87

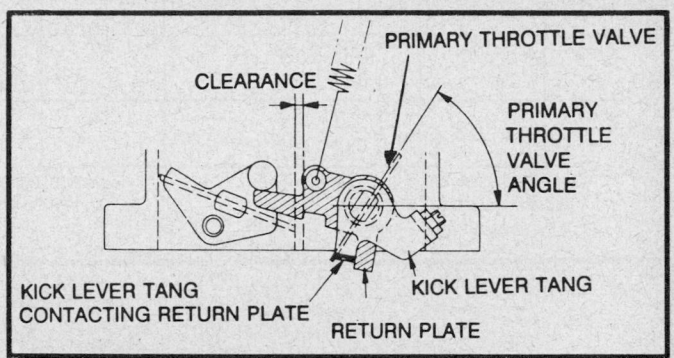

Isuzu (Stromberg) primary and secondary throttle valve adjustment—1988–90

Unloader Adjustment

1988–90

1. Open the primary valve fully.
2. Measure the clearance between the choke valve and the choke valve chamber wall.
3. If the clearance measured is not between 0.105–0.129 in., bend the adjusting lever tang to adjust.

Primary and Secondary Throttle Valve Adjustment

1988–90

1. Slowly open the primary throttle valve until the kick lever tang contacts the return plate.
2. Measure the clearance between the choke valve and the choke valve chamber wall.
3. If the clearance measured is not between 0.272–0.331 in., bend the kick lever tang to adjust.

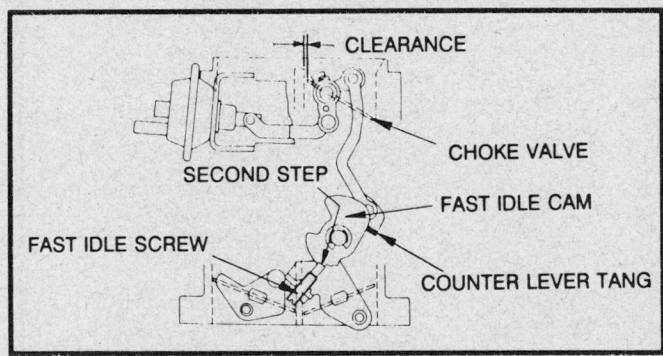

Isuzu (Stromberg) choke valve opening—1988–90

MAZDA CARBURETORS

MAZDA CARBURETORS

(All measurements in inches)

Year	Model	Fast Idle Cam	Fast Idle Opening	Float Level	Choke Valve Opening	Choke Diaphragm	Choke Unloader	Dashpot (rpm)	Secondary Throttle Valve
1986	B-2000	0.029–0.044	—	0.453–0.492	0.023–0.039	0.066–0.084	0.108–0.142	—	0.289–0.325

MAZDA CARBURETORS

(All measurements in inches)

Year	Model	Fast Idle Cam	Fast Idle Opening	Float Level	Choke Valve Opening	Choke Diaphragm	Choke Unloader	Dashpot (rpm)	Secondary Throttle Valve
1987	B-2200	0.033–0.041	—	①	0.024–0.039	0.067–0.085	0.110–0.143		0.289–0.325
	B-2600	—	②	0.748–0.827	—	—	—	③	—
1988	B-2200	0.033–0.041	—	①	0.024–0.045	0.067–0.085	0.110–0.143		0.289–0.325
	B-2600	—	0.026–0.030	0.748–0.827	—	—	—	③	—
1989	B-2200	0.033–0.041	—	①	0.024–0.045	0.067–0.085	0.110–0.143		0.289–0.325
1990	B-2200	0.033–0.041	—	①	0.024–0.045	0.067–0.085	0.110–0.143		0.289–0.325

① Manual transmission: 0.457–0.496
Automatic transmission: 0.421–0.461

② Manual transmission: 0.028
Automatic transmission: 0.031

③ Manual transmission: 1400–1600 rpm
Automatic transmission: 1900–2100 rpm

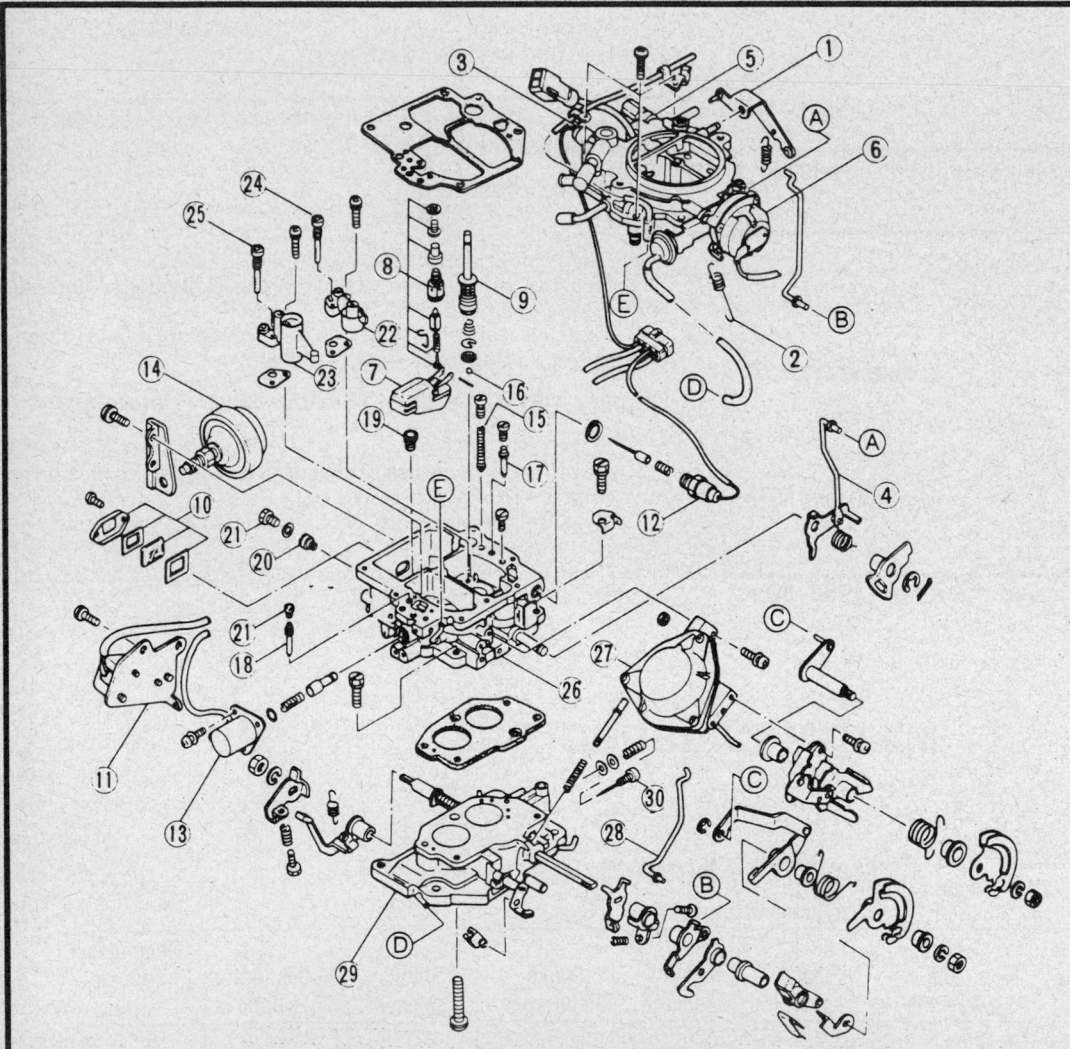

1. Accelerator pump connecting rod
2. Connecting spring
3. Air vent solenoid valve
4. Chock rod
5. Air horn
6. Automatic choke assembly
7. Float
8. Needle valve asssembly
9. Accelerator pump plunger
10. Fuel bowl sight glass
11. Idle switch
12. Slow fuel cut solenoid valve
13. Coasting richer solenoid valve
14. Dashpot
15. Accelerator pump outlet check ball and spring
16. Accelerator pump inlet check ball
17. Primary slow jet
18. Secondary slow jet
19. Primary main jet
20. Secondary main jet
21. Plug
22. Primary venturi and nozzle
23. Secondary venturi and nozzle
24. Primary main air bleed
25. Secondary main air bleed
26. Main body
27. Vacuum Diaphragm
28. Throttle link
29. Throttle body
30. Mixture adjusting screw

Mazda carburetor disassembled view – B2000 and B2200

Float Level Adjustments

B2000 AND B2200

1. Without the gasket turn the air horn upside down and allow the float to lower by its own weight.
2. Measure the clearance between the float and the air horn.
3. Bend the float seat lip until the proper clearance is obtained.
4. Turn the air horn to its normal position and allow the float to lower by its own weight.
5. Measure the clearance between the bottom of the float and the air horn. If the clearance is not between 1.811–1.850 in., bend the float stopper to adjust.

B2600

1. Invert the float chamber cover assembly.
2. Measure the clearance between the bottom of the float to the surface of the float chamber cover without the gasket in place.
3. Add or remove needle valve seat shims to adjust the fuel level to specifications as follows:
   a. Pull out the float lever pin and remove the float.
   b. Remove the needle valve and retainer.
   c. Use pliers and remove the needle valve seat.
   d. Insert the necessary shims for adjustment and reinstall the needle valve, float and float chamber cover.

Choke Diaphragm Adjustment

B2000 AND B2200

1. Using a vacuum pump, apply a vacuum of about 15.7 in.Hg to the choke diaphragm vacuum tube.
2. Push the choke valve lightly to close it and measure the clearance.
3. If the clearance is not within specification, adjust by bending the choke lever.

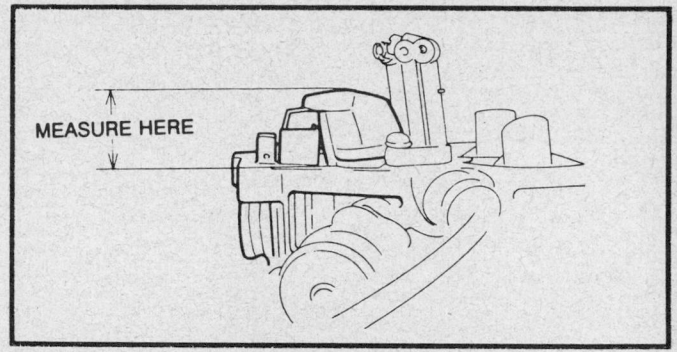

Mazda float level measurement—B2600

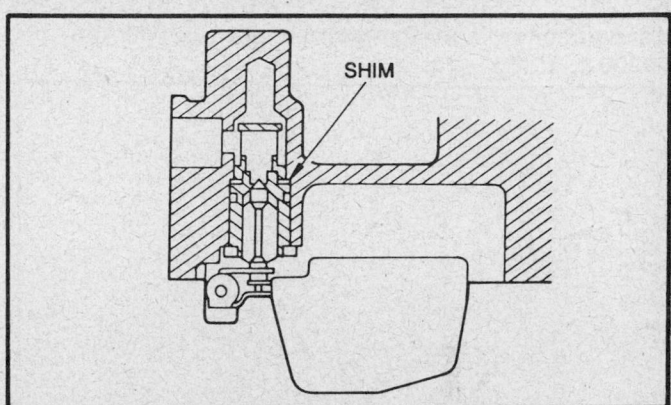

Mazda valve seat shim location—B2600

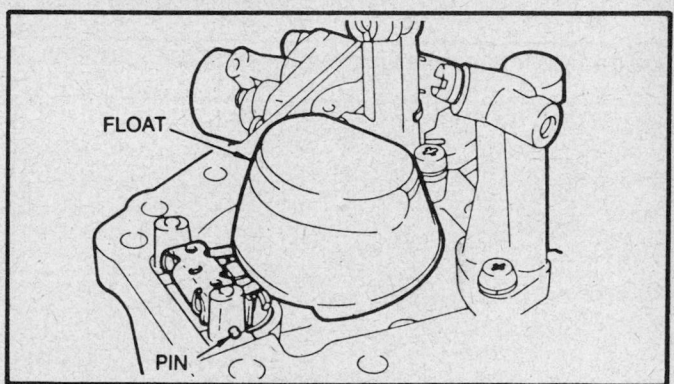

Mazda float and pin—B2600

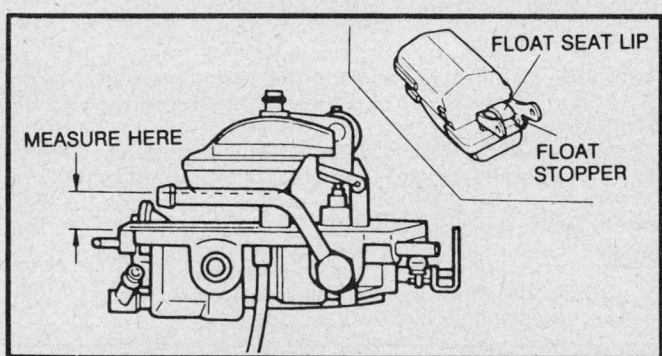

Mazda float level adjustment with the air horn upside down—B2000 and B2200

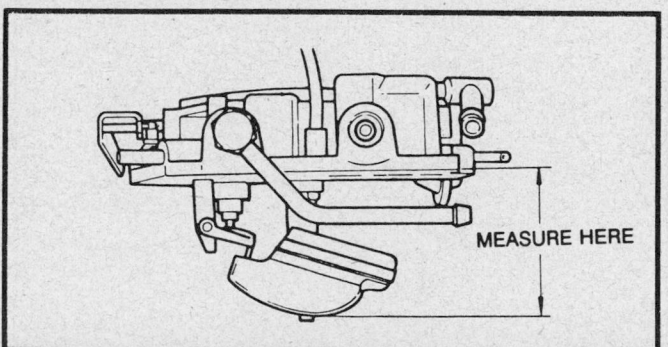

Mazda float level adjustment with the air horn at its normal position—B2000 and B2200

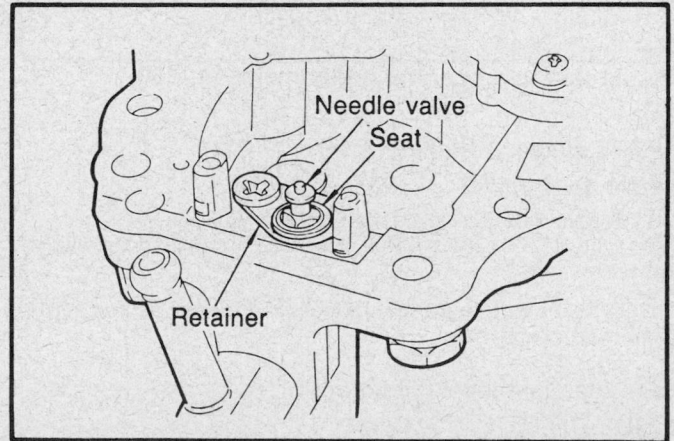

Mazda float needle valve seat and retainer—B2600

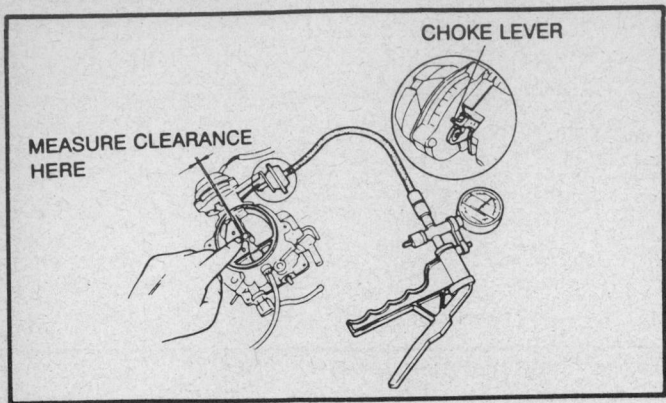

Mazda choke diaphragm adjustment—B2000 and B2200

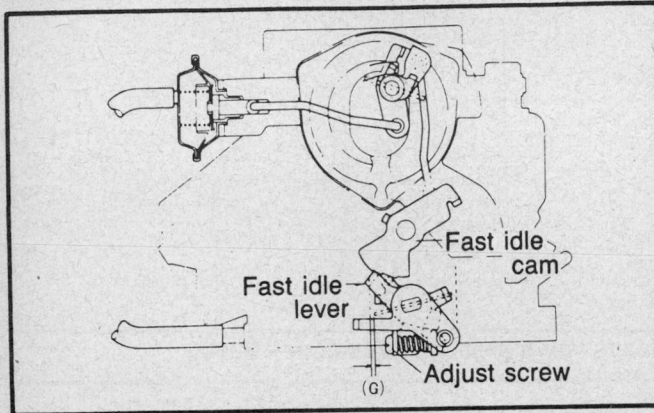

Mazda fast idle cam adjustment—B2000 and B2200

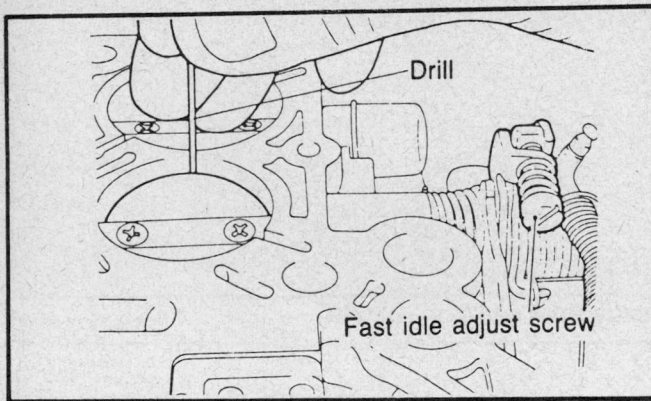

Mazda fast idle opening adjustment—B2600

Fast Idle Cam Adjustment

B2000 AND B2200

1. Set the fast idle cam to the second position.
2. Adjust the throttle valve clearance by turning the adjusting screw.

NOTE: The clearance will become larger as the screw is turned clockwise.

Fast Idle Opening Adjustment

B2600

1. With the carburetor at normal room temperature, insert

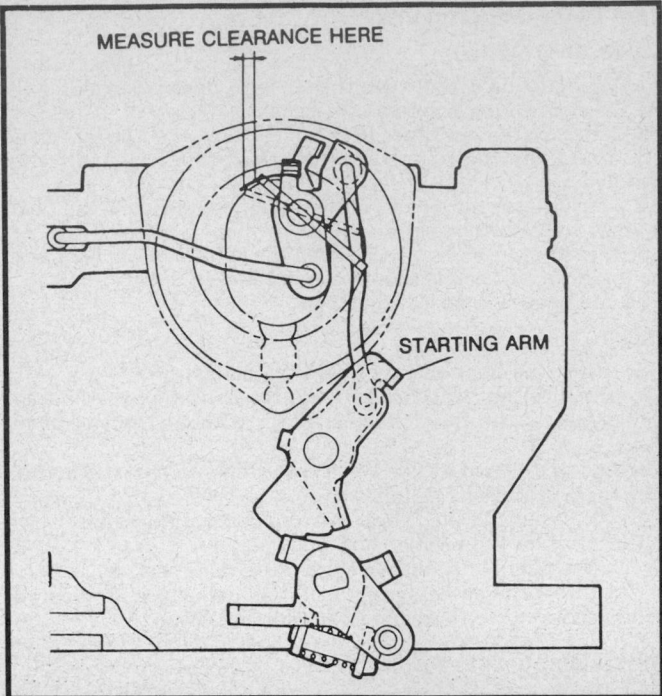

Mazda choke valve clearance adjustment—B2000 and B2200

the specified drill between the choke valve and the choke valve chamber wall.

2. Adjust the fast idle opening by using the fast idle adjusting screw.

Choke Valve Clearance Adjustment

B2000 AND B2200

1. Set the fast idle cam select to the second position.
2. Make sure the choke valve clearance is within specification.
3. Adjust the choke valve clearance by bending the starting arm. If a large adjustment is required, bend the choke rod.

Choke Valve Setting Adjustment

B2600

1. Remove the choke cover. It may be necessary to grind off the rivet heads and replace with locking screws.

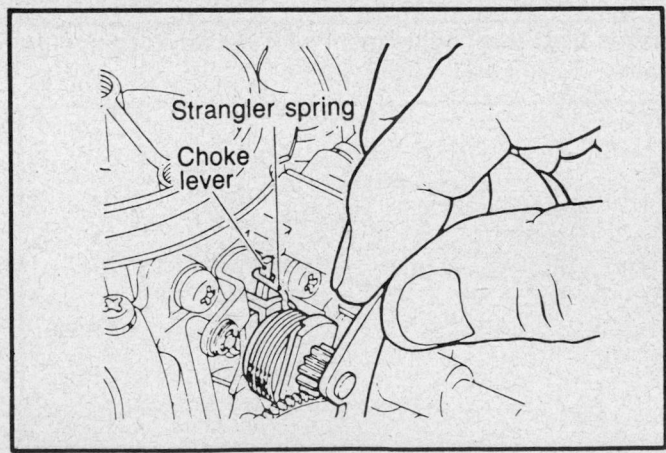

Fit the strangler spring to the choke lever—Mazda B2600

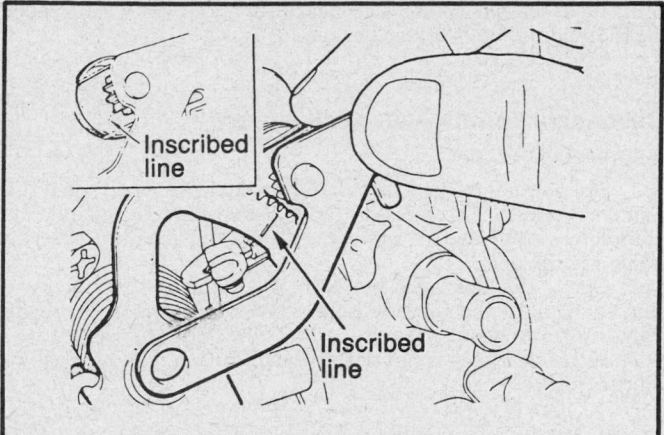

Aligning the cam lever and choke pinion—Mazda B2600

Pinion arm lock screws—Mazda B2600

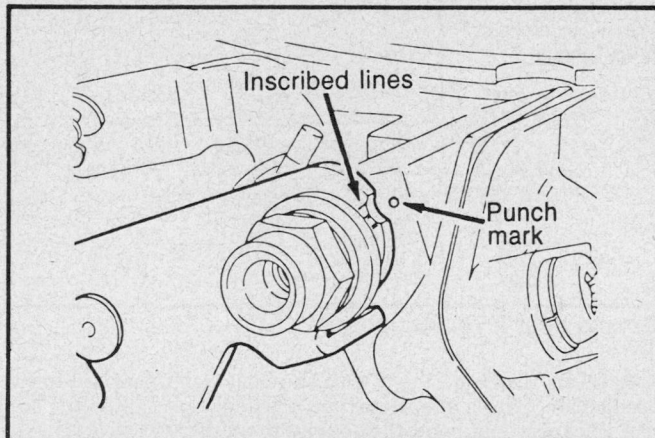

Align the center line with the punch mark—Mazda B2600

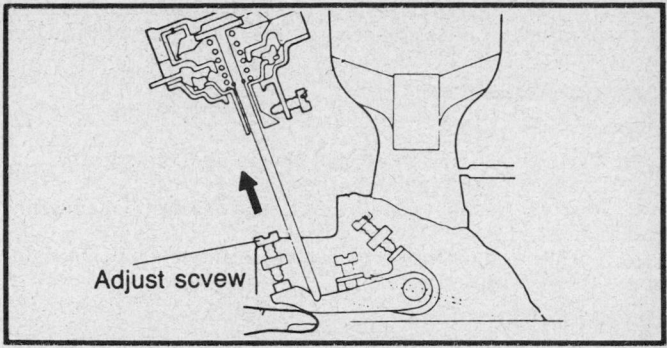

Mazda dashpot adjustment—B2000 and B2200

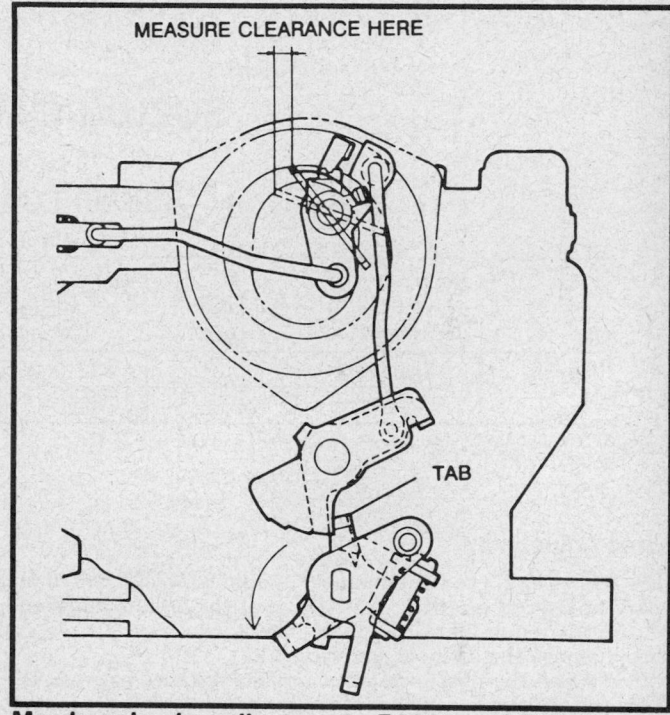

Mazda unloader adjustment—B2000 and B2200

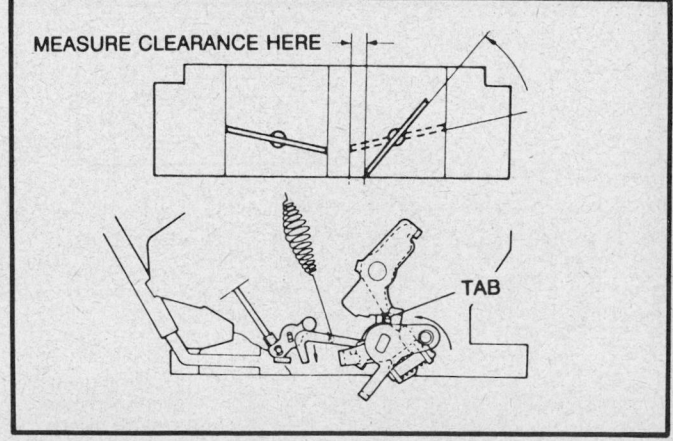

Mazda secondary throttle valve adjustment—B2000 and B2200

2. Remove the 2 lock screws and remove the choke valve pinion assembly.
3. Install the strangler spring to the choke lever.
4. Assemble, aligning the inscribed line or black painted line on the teeth of the choke pinion with the inscribed line on the cam lever.
5. Loosely tighten the new lock screws.
6. Set the choke valve by moving the pinion arm up or down,

align the punch mark on the float chamber cover with the center of the 3 inscribed lines and secure the pinion arm with the lock screws.

Dashpot Adjustment

B2600

1. Warm the engine to normal operating temperature.
2. Connect a tachometer to the engine.
3. Push the dashpot rod up and loosen the dashpot adjusting screw.
4. Turn the adjusting screw clockwise and and set the engine speed to specification.

Unloader Adjustment

B2000 AND B2200

1. Open the primary throttle valve all the way.

2. Measure the choke valve clearance and if not within specification adjust by bending the tab.

Secondary Throttle Valve Adjustment

B2000 AND B2200

1. The secondary throttle valve should start to open when the primary throttle valve opens (50–52 degrees), and should be completely open at the same time that the primary throttle valve is fully open.
2. Check the clearance between the primary throttle valve and the wall of the throttle bore when the secondary throttle valve starts to open.
3. If the clearance is not within specification, bend the tab to adjust.

SUZUKI CARBURETORS

SUZUKI CARBURETORS
(All measurements in inches)

Year	Model	Float Level	Choke Unloader	Fast Idle Clearance	Choke Piston	Choke Valve Clearance
1986–90	Samurai	0.31	0.10–0.12	0.10–0.12	①	0.004–0.023 ②
	Sidekick	0.31	0.10–0.12	0.118–0.137	①	0.004–0.023 ②

① See procedure in text
② At 75°F (25°C)

Float Adjustment

The fuel level in the float chamber should be within the round mark at the center of the level gauge. If the level is not found within the round mark adjust as follows:
1. Remove the air horn and invert it.
2. To find the float level, measure the distance between the float and the mating surface of the air horn without the gasket.
3. If the float level is not to specification, bend the tongue up or down to adjust.

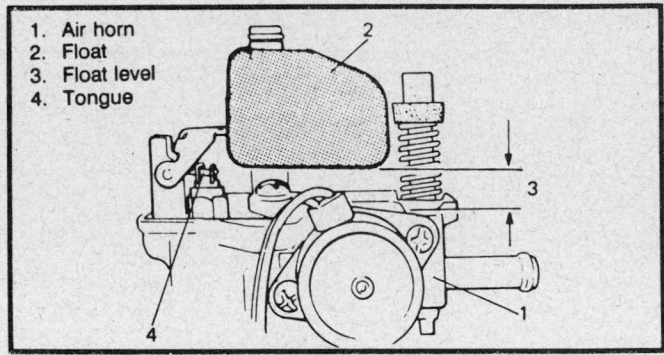

1. Air horn
2. Float
3. Float level
4. Tongue

Suzuki float level adjustment

4. Check the float height with the float weight applied to the needle valve. Use a gauge such as a drill or bolt that is the correct thickness and bend the tongue to adjust.

Choke Valve Clearance Adjustment

1. Check the choke valve for smooth movement.
2. Make sure that the choke valve is closed almost completely when ambient temperature is below 77°F and the engine is cold.
3. Measure the clearance between the choke valve and the carburetor bore.
4. If the clearance is found excessively large or small, check the strangler spring, choke piston and each link in the choke system for smooth operation. Lubricate as necessary.
5. If clearance is still out of specification, remove the carbure-

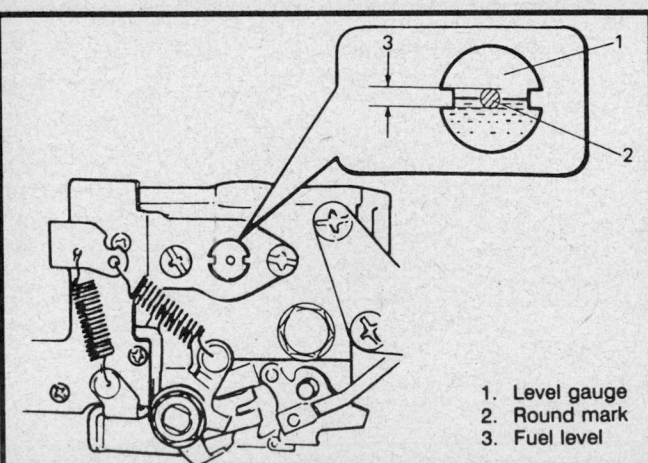

1. Level gauge
2. Round mark
3. Fuel level

Suzuki fuel level adjustment

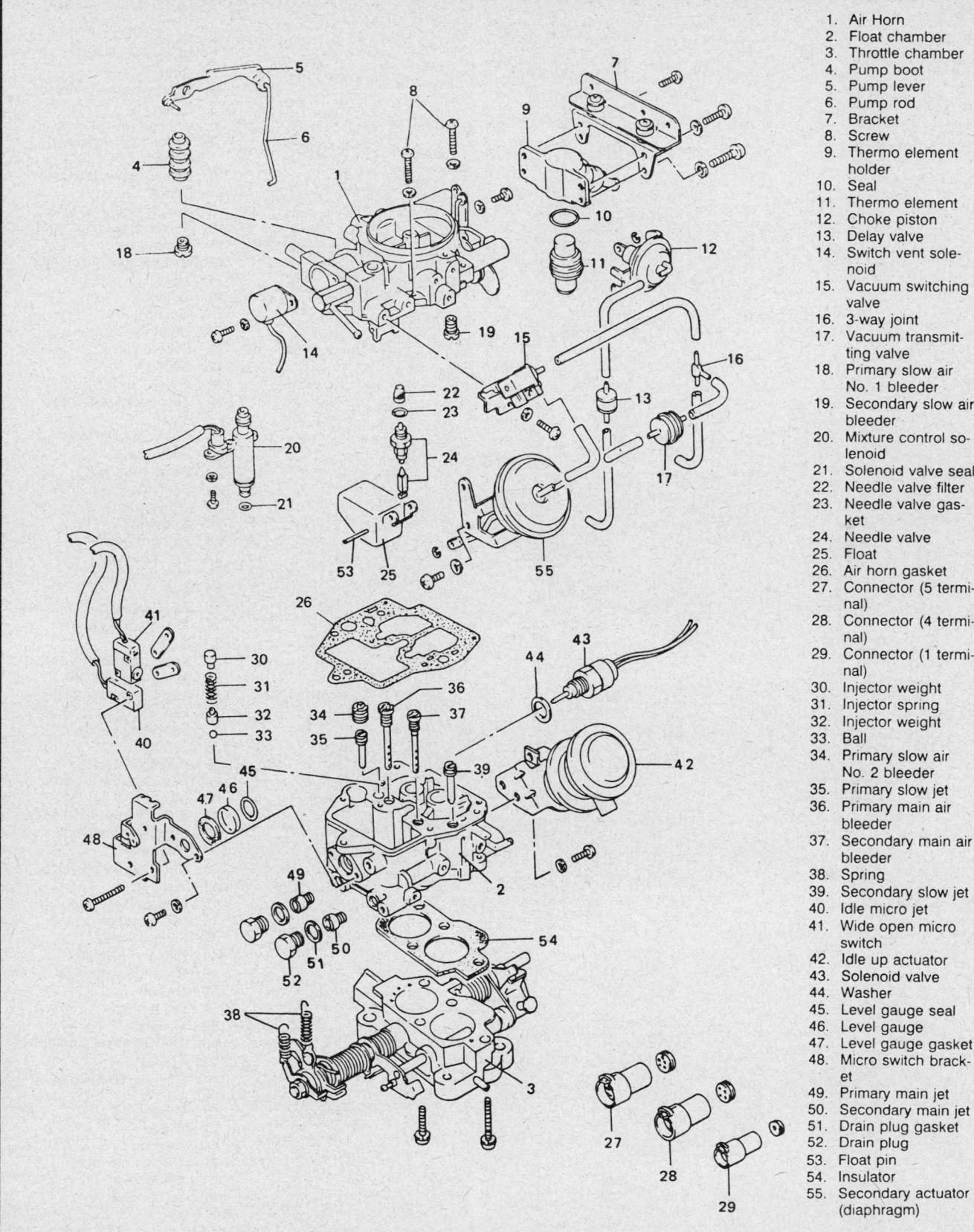

1. Air Horn
2. Float chamber
3. Throttle chamber
4. Pump boot
5. Pump lever
6. Pump rod
7. Bracket
8. Screw
9. Thermo element holder
10. Seal
11. Thermo element
12. Choke piston
13. Delay valve
14. Switch vent solenoid
15. Vacuum switching valve
16. 3-way joint
17. Vacuum transmitting valve
18. Primary slow air No. 1 bleeder
19. Secondary slow air bleeder
20. Mixture control solenoid
21. Solenoid valve seal
22. Needle valve filter
23. Needle valve gasket
24. Needle valve
25. Float
26. Air horn gasket
27. Connector (5 terminal)
28. Connector (4 terminal)
29. Connector (1 terminal)
30. Injector weight
31. Injector spring
32. Injector weight
33. Ball
34. Primary slow air No. 2 bleeder
35. Primary slow jet
36. Primary main air bleeder
37. Secondary main air bleeder
38. Spring
39. Secondary slow jet
40. Idle micro jet
41. Wide open micro switch
42. Idle up actuator
43. Solenoid valve
44. Washer
45. Level gauge seal
46. Level gauge
47. Level gauge gasket
48. Micro switch bracket
49. Primary main jet
50. Secondary main jet
51. Drain plug gasket
52. Drain plug
53. Float pin
54. Insulator
55. Secondary actuator (diaphragm)

Suzuki (Samurai) carburetor exploded view

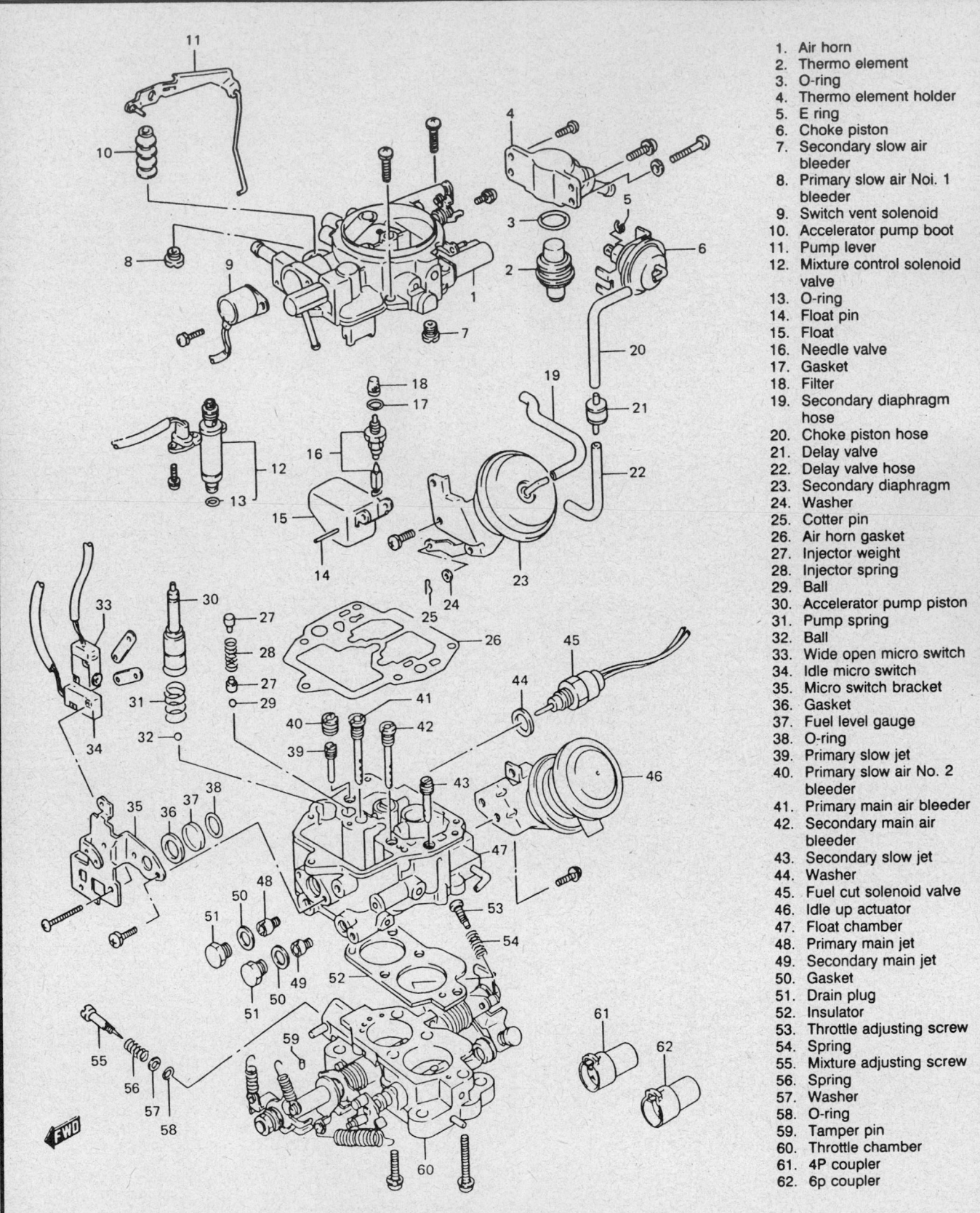

1. Air horn
2. Thermo element
3. O-ring
4. Thermo element holder
5. E ring
6. Choke piston
7. Secondary slow air bleeder
8. Primary slow air Noi. 1 bleeder
9. Switch vent solenoid
10. Accelerator pump boot
11. Pump lever
12. Mixture control solenoid valve
13. O-ring
14. Float pin
15. Float
16. Needle valve
17. Gasket
18. Filter
19. Secondary diaphragm hose
20. Choke piston hose
21. Delay valve
22. Delay valve hose
23. Secondary diaphragm
24. Washer
25. Cotter pin
26. Air horn gasket
27. Injector weight
28. Injector spring
29. Ball
30. Accelerator pump piston
31. Pump spring
32. Ball
33. Wide open micro switch
34. Idle micro switch
35. Micro switch bracket
36. Gasket
37. Fuel level gauge
38. O-ring
39. Primary slow jet
40. Primary slow air No. 2 bleeder
41. Primary main air bleeder
42. Secondary main air bleeder
43. Secondary slow jet
44. Washer
45. Fuel cut solenoid valve
46. Idle up actuator
47. Float chamber
48. Primary main jet
49. Secondary main jet
50. Gasket
51. Drain plug
52. Insulator
53. Throttle adjusting screw
54. Spring
55. Mixture adjusting screw
56. Spring
57. Washer
58. O-ring
59. Tamper pin
60. Throttle chamber
61. 4P coupler
62. 6p coupler

Suzuki (Sidekick) carburetor exploded view

tor from the intake manifold and remove the idle up actuator from the carburetor.

6. Turn the fast idle cam counterclockwise and insert a pin into the holes in the cam and bracket to lock the cam.

7. Using pliers, bend the choke lever up or down. Bending up causes the choke valve to close and down to open.

8. Start the engine and warm it up fully.

9. Stop the engine and check to see if the choke valve is fully open.

10. If the choke valve doesn't open fully, the wax element or its link system is defective. Replace defective parts as necessary.

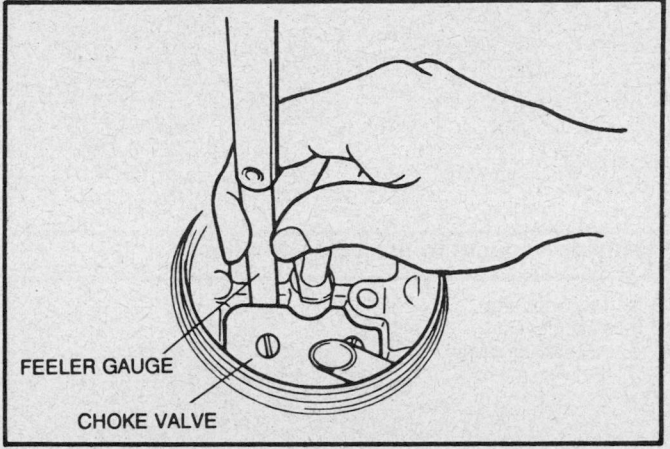

FEELER GAUGE

CHOKE VALVE

Suzuki choke valve to carburetor bore measurement

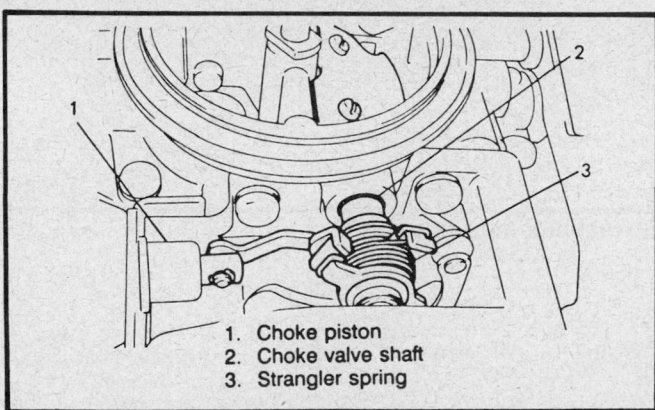

1. Choke piston
2. Choke valve shaft
3. Strangler spring

Suzuki choke linkage

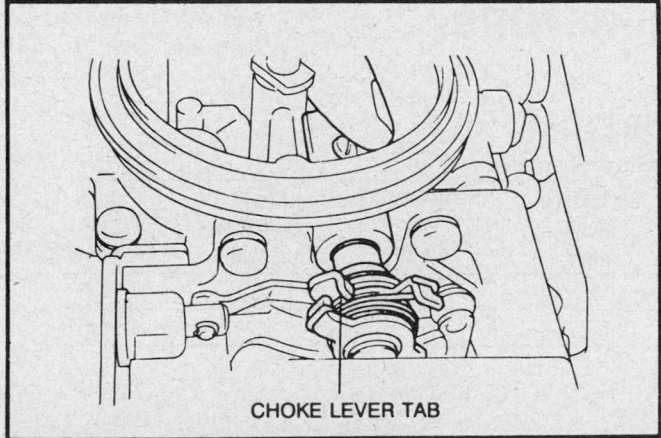

CHOKE LEVER TAB

Suzuki choke lever adjusting tab

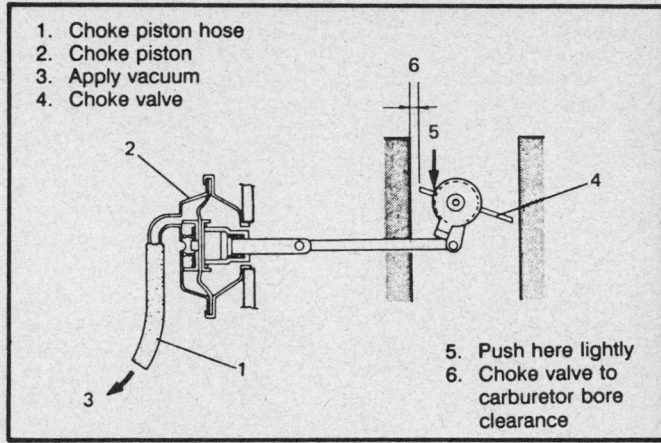

1. Choke piston hose
2. Choke piston
3. Apply vacuum
4. Choke valve

5. Push here lightly
6. Choke valve to carburetor bore clearance

Suzuki choke piston measurement

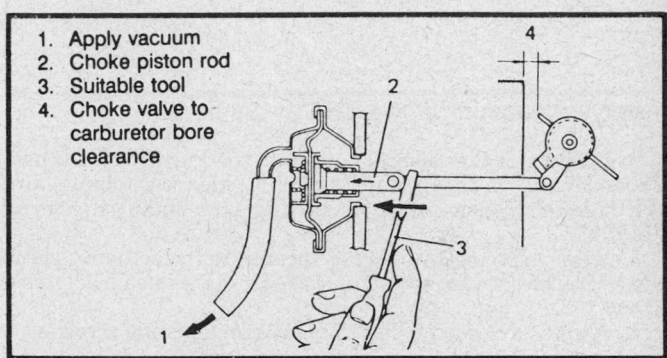

1. Apply vacuum
2. Choke piston rod
3. Suitable tool
4. Choke valve to carburetor bore clearance

Moving the choke piston rod—Suzuki

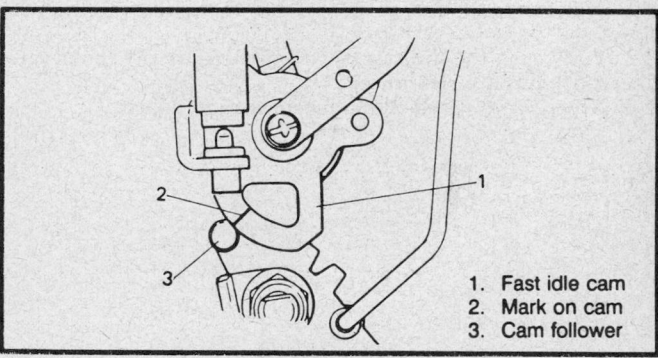

1. Fast idle cam
2. Mark on cam
3. Cam follower

Suzuki cam and cam follower mark

Choke Piston Adjustment

1. Disconnect the choke piston hose at the throttle chamber.

2. While pushing down lightly on the choke valve to its closed position, apply vacuum to the choke piston hose with a vacuum gauge and measure the choke valve to carburetor bore clearance. It should be 0.04–0.05 in. for the Samarai and 0.070–0.078 in. for the Sidekick.

3. With vacuum applied, use a suitable tool and move the choke piston rod in towards the choke piston and check to see if the choke valve to carburetor bore clearance is 0.13–0.14 in. for the Samarai and 0.142–0.163 in. on the Sidekick.

Fast Idle Cam Adjustment

1. Make sure the ambient temperature is between 71–81°F and that the mark on the cam and the center of the cam follower are in alignment.

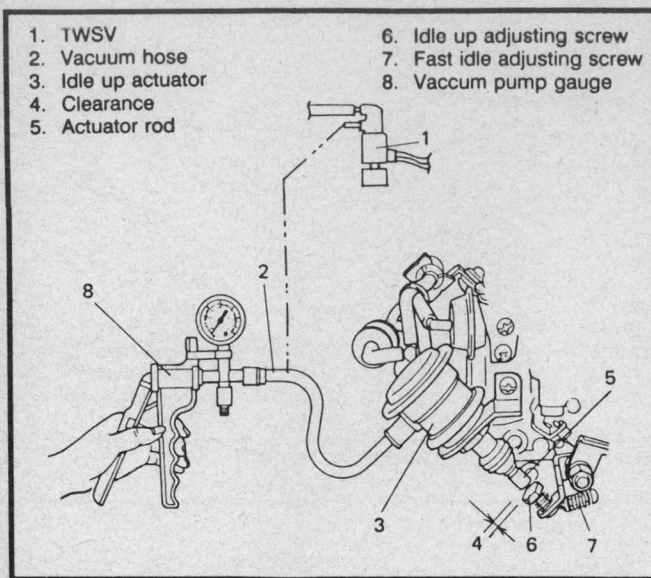

1. TWSV
2. Vacuum hose
3. Idle up actuator
4. Clearance
5. Actuator rod
6. Idle up adjusting screw
7. Fast idle adjusting screw
8. Vaccum pump gauge

Applying vacuum to the TWSV—Samurai

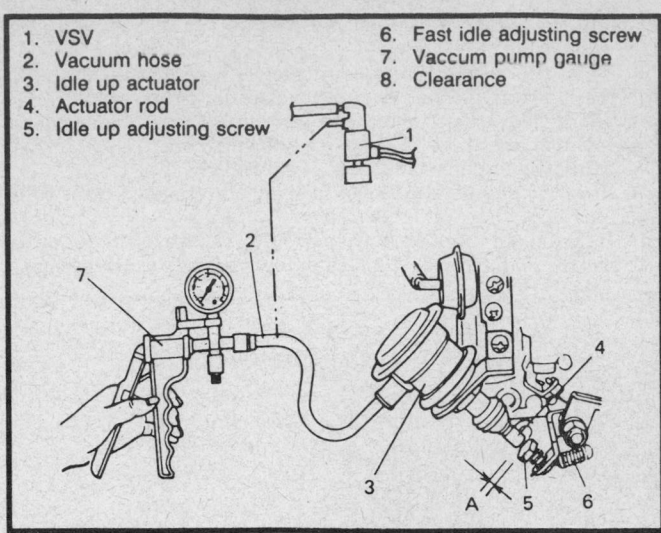

1. VSV
2. Vacuum hose
3. Idle up actuator
4. Actuator rod
5. Idle up adjusting screw
6. Fast idle adjusting screw
7. Vaccum pump gauge
8. Clearance

Applying vacuum to the VSV—Sidekick

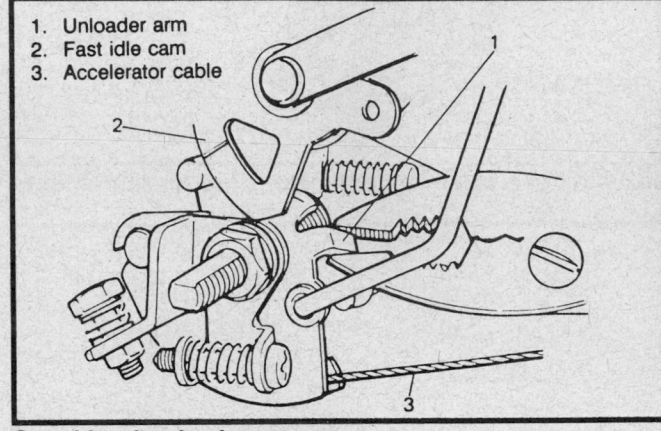

1. Unloader arm
2. Fast idle cam
3. Accelerator cable

Suzuki unloader lever arm

2. Disconnect the vacuum hose from the Three Way Solenoid Valve (TWSV) on the Samurai, or the Vacuum Switching Valve (VSV) on the Sidekick and connect a vacuum pump gauge to its hose.

3. While applying 15 in.Hg of vacuum to the actuator, check the clearance between the actuator rod and the idle up adjusting screw.

4. Adjust as needed using the fast idle adjusting screw.

Unloader Adjustment

1. Make sure the engine is cool and the choke valve is fully closed.

2. Fully open the throttle valve and measure the choke valve to carburetor bore clearance.

3. If necessary, bend the unloader arm to adjust.

TOYOTA CARBURETORS

TOYOTA CARBURETORS
(All measurements in inches or degrees)

Year	Carburetor Number	Float Level	Throttle Valve Angle	Secondary Touch Angle	Fast Idle Angle	Choke Unloader Angle	Idle-Up Angle
1986–88	All	②	90°	59°	23°	45°	16.5°
1989	All	②	90°	59°	①	45°	16.5°

NOTE: Use angle degree tool for angle specifications
① Federal and Canada: 24.5 degrees
   California: 23.0 degrees
② Raised position: 0.386 in.
   Lowered position: 1.89 in.

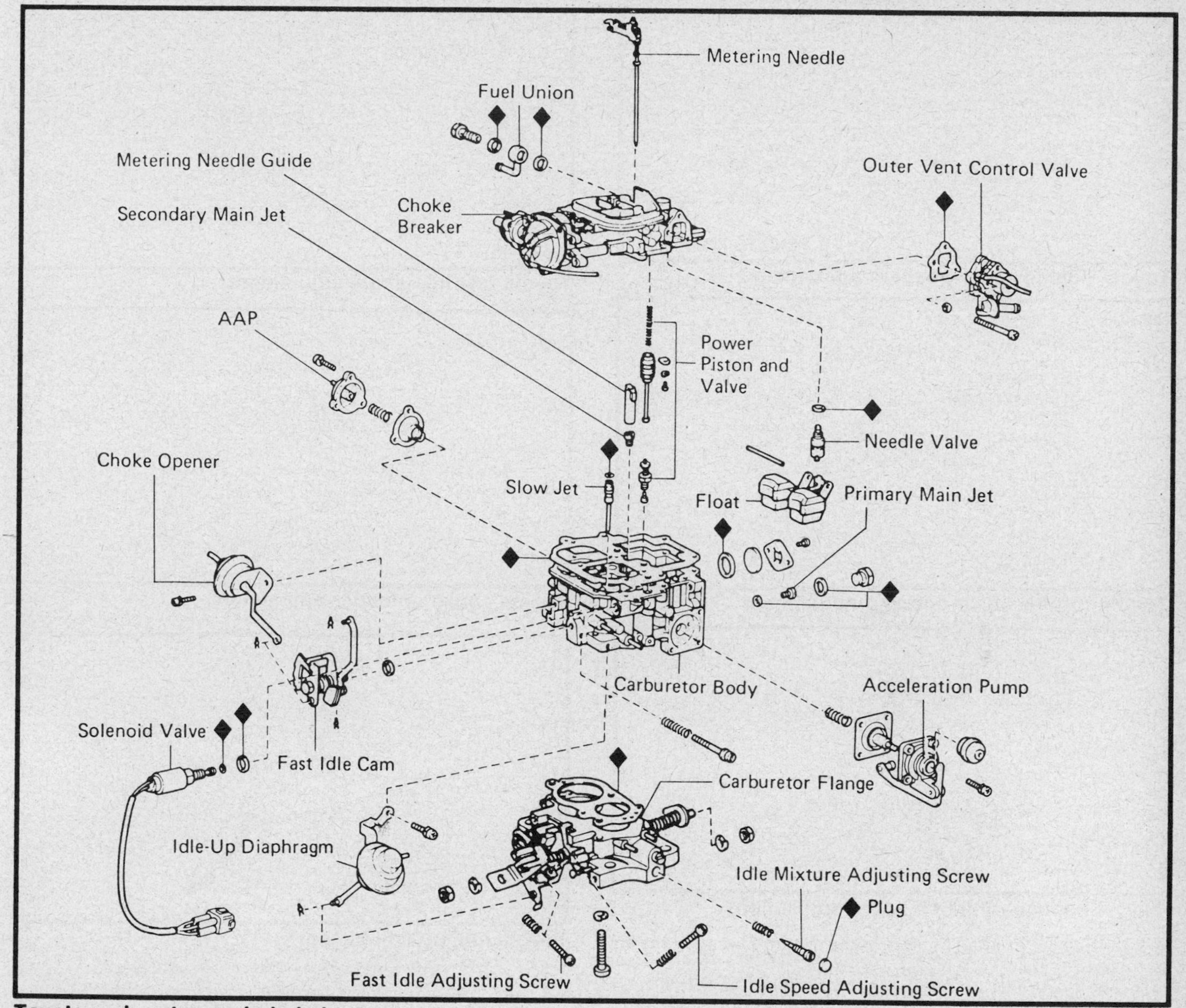

Metering Needle

Fuel Union

Metering Needle Guide

Secondary Main Jet

Choke Breaker

Outer Vent Control Valve

AAP

Power Piston and Valve

Choke Opener

Needle Valve

Slow Jet

Float

Primary Main Jet

Carburetor Body

Acceleration Pump

Solenoid Valve

Fast Idle Cam

Carburetor Flange

Idle-Up Diaphragm

Idle Mixture Adjusting Screw

Plug

Fast Idle Adjusting Screw

Idle Speed Adjusting Screw

Toyota carburetor exploded view

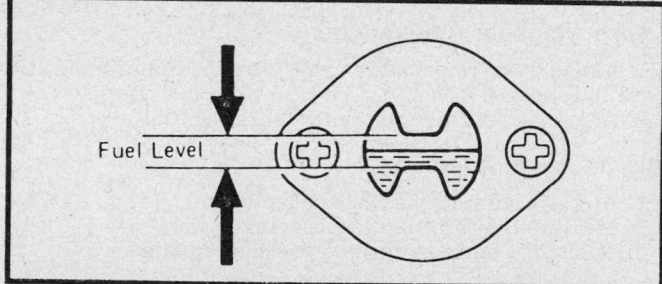

Fuel Level

Toyota float level sight glass

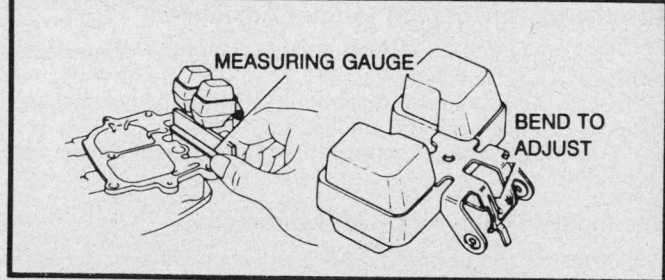

MEASURING GAUGE

BEND TO ADJUST

Toyota float raised position adjustment

Fuel Level

The fuel level is about even with the center of the sight glass.

Float Level Adjustment

1. Allow the float to hang down by its own weight.

2. Measure the clearance between the float top and the air horn without the gasket.

3. The float level (raised position), should be 0.386 in. If necessary, bend the upper portion of the float tab to adjust to specification.

BEND TO ADJUST

Toyota float lowered position adjustment

PRIMARY THROTTLE ARM LEVER

SECONDARY THROTTLE ARM LEVER

Toyota throttle valve opening adjustment

Toyota secondary touch angle adjustment

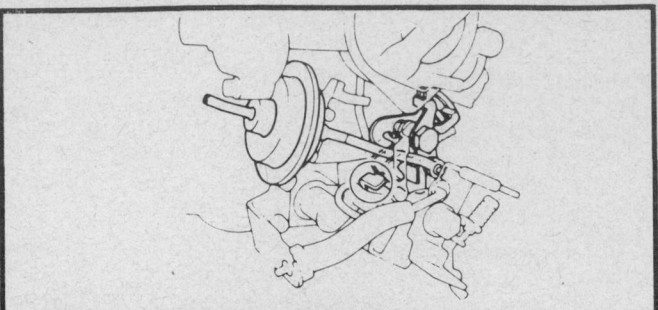

Toyota fast idle angle adjustment

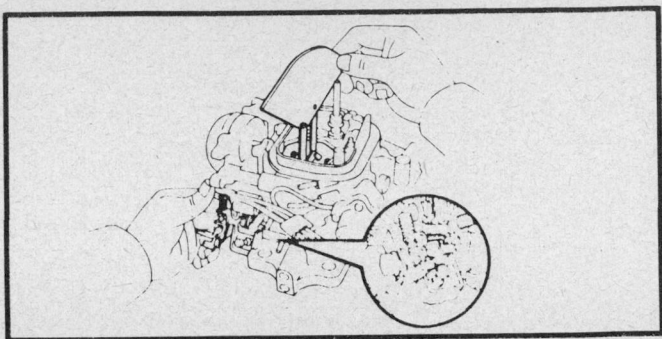

Toyota choke unloader adjustment

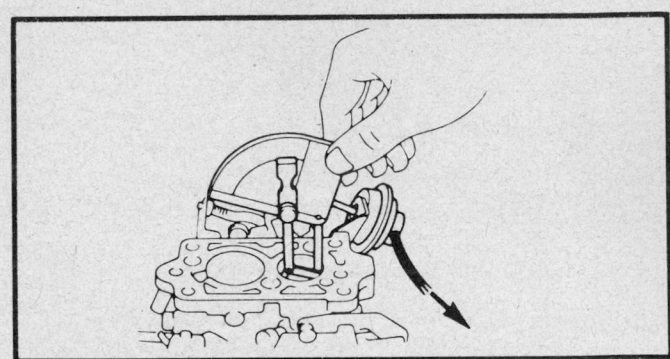

Toyota idle-up adjustment

4. Lift up the float and measure the distance between the air horn and the float bottom.

5. The float level (lowered position), should be 0.189 in. If necessary, bend the lower portion of the float tab to adjust to specification.

Throttle Valve Opening (Angle) Adjustment

1. Measure the full opening angle of the of the primary and secondary throttle valves.

2. Both the primary and secondary throttle valve openings should be 90 degrees from the horizontal plane.

3. Adjust by bending the respective throttle arm levers of either valve.

Secondary Touch Angle Measurement

1. Measure the primary throttle valve opening at the same time the second throttle valve just starts to open.

2. The standard angle is 59 degrees from the horizontal plane.

3. Adjustment is not necessary, this is a rebuilding reference only.

Fast Idle Angle Adjustment

1. Set the throttle shaft lever to the first step of the fast idle cam.

2. Measure the primary throttle valve angle with the choke valve fully closed.

3. Adjust by turning the fast idle adjusting screw.

Choke Unloader Adjustment

1. Measure the choke valve angle with the primary throttle valve fully opened.

2. Adjust by bending the primary throttle arm.

Idle-Up Angle Adjustment

1. Apply vacuum to the idle-up diaphragm.

2. Measure the throttle valve opening angle.

3. Adjust the angle by turning the idle adjusting screw.

Dashpot Adjustment

1. Open the throttle valve until the throttle lever separates from the dashpot end.

2. Release the throttle valve gradually, and check the dashpot touch angle when the throttle lever touches the dashpot end.

3. If the dashpot touch angle is not 24.5 degrees from the horizontal plane, unlock the locknut and adjust the angle by turning the dashpot diaphragm.

CHRYSLER IMPORT/MITSUBISHI MULTI-POINT INJECTION (MPI) SYSTEM

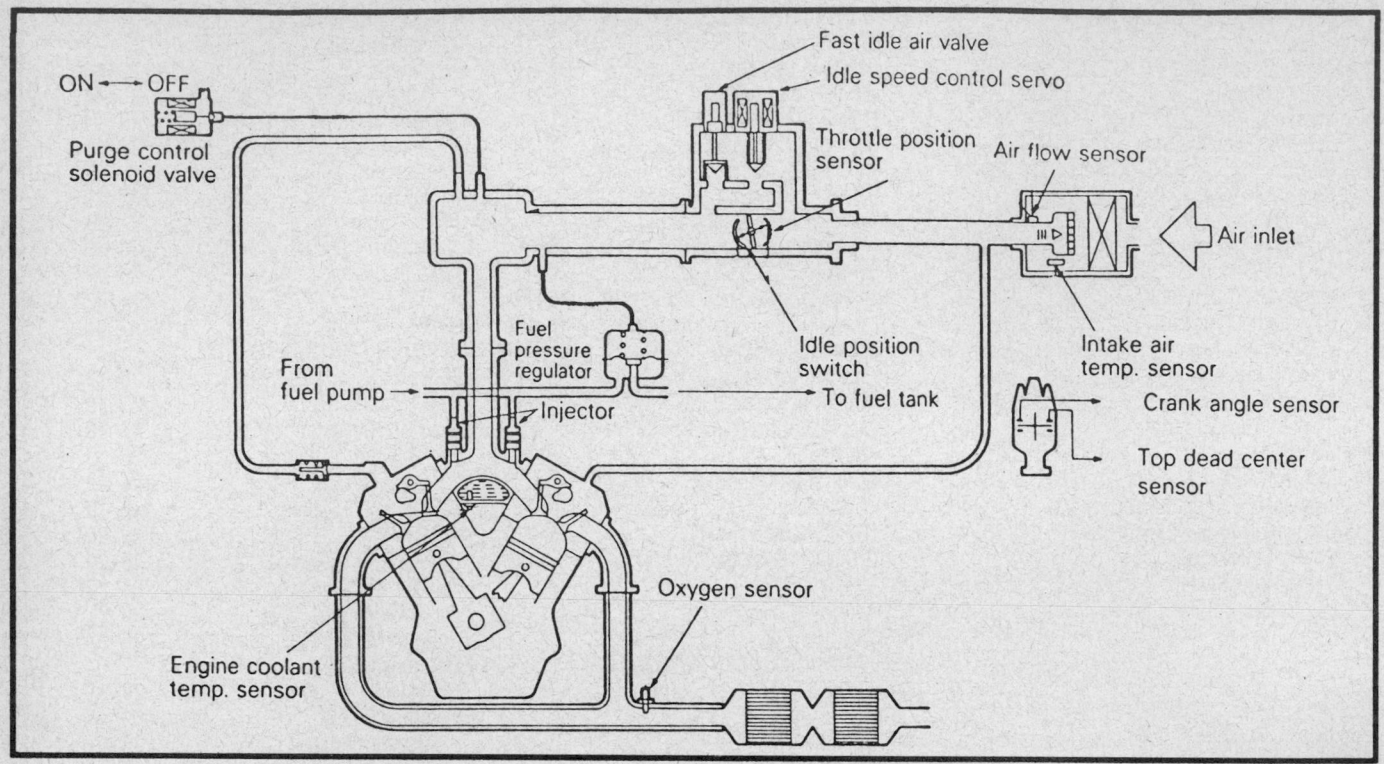

MPI System schematic—Mitsubishi

General Information

The Multi-Point Injection (MPI) system controls the fuel flow, idle speed, and ignition timing. The basic function of the MPI system is to control the air/fuel ratio according to operational conditions through the Electronic Control Unit (ECU), based on data from various sensors. The MPI System is roughly divided into 3 areas—the fuel system, intake system and control system.

FUEL SYSTEM

The fuel is supplied by the electronic in tank fuel pump and is distributed to the respective injectors via the main pipe and fuel filter. The fuel pressure applied to the injector constant and is higher than the pressure in the intake manifold. The pressure is controlled by the pressure regulator. The excess fuel, after its regulation, is returned to the fuel tank through the return pipe.

When an electric current flows in the injector, the injector valve is fully opened to inject the fuel. Since the fuel pressure is constant, the amount of the fuel injected from the injector into the manifold is increased or decreased in proportion to the time the electric current flows. Based on ECU signals, the injectors inject fuel to the cylinder manifold ports in firing order.

INTAKE SYSTEM

The flow rate of the air drawn through the air cleaner is measured by the air flow sensor. The air enters the air intake plenum through the throttle body.

The air is distributed to each cylinder manifold from the air intake plenum. In the manifold, the air is mixed with the fuel from the injectors and is drawn into the cylinder. The air flow rate is controlled according to the degree of the throttle valve and the servo motor openings.

The amount of air drawn during idling is adjusted by the idle speed control (ISC) servo controlled by the ECU. Further, the amount of air drawn during warm-up and deceleration is also controlled by the ISC servo.

CONTROL SYSTEM

The control system is composed of a sensor section, which monitors engine conditions, and an Electronic Control Unit (ECU), which calculates the injection timing and rate according to the signals from the sensors. The sensors convert such conditions as the amount of intake air, amount of oxygen in the exhaust gas, coolant temperature, intake air temperature, engine revolution speed, and driving speed into electric signals, which are sent to the ECU.

Analyzing these signals, the ECU determines the amount of fuel to inject according to driving conditions and drives the injectors. The fuel injection is by sequential injection type, in which four or six injectors are sequentially driven.

During idling, the ISC Servo is driven according to the load to assure stable idling.

SYSTEM OPERATION

The air fuel ratio control is achieved by controlling the driving time of each injector installed at each intake air port. After passing through the in-tank filter, fuel is force-fed by the in-tank pump so as to be sent to the delivery pipe through the main pipe and fuel filter, and is distributed to each injector by the delivery pipe. The fuel pressure applied to the injector is maintained at a

fixed level by the fuel pressure regulator so that it may be higher than the internal pressure of the intake manifold where fuel injection takes place. After pressure regulation, excess fuel is returned to the fuel tank through the return hose. When the injector is energized, the valve inside the injector opens fully to inject the fuel. Since the fuel pressure is kept at a fixed level, supply of fuel injected from the injectors into the intake manifold varies with the energizing time. The injectors inject fuel to each manifold port, in the sequential firing order of each cylinder, according to ECU signals.

System Components

INJECTORS

Description

Injectors are electromagnetic type injection nozzles which inject fuel according to signals calculated and provided by the ECU. When there is continuity at the solenoid coil, the plunger and the needle valve unified with it are pulled and, as a result, fuel is sprayed from the nozzle. Because the stroke of the needle valve is always constant, the amount of fuel spray (injection) is determined by the continuity time of the solenoid coil.

Using a stethoscope or similar tool, check for operating sound as engine idles. Each injector gives a distinct ticking as it opens and closes. Check that the sound occurs at shorter intervals as the engine speed increases. Listen carefully; other injectors may produce similar sound even if the injector being checked is not working.

PRESSURE REGULATOR

Description

The pressure regulator maintains the fuel volume at a fixed amount relative to fuel injection time. As a means to improve precision, the pressure regulator controls the fuel pressure applied to the injectors at a constant pressure relative to the surge tank negative pressure.

Surge tank negative pressure is applied to the diaphragm chamber of the pressure regulator. When the fuel pressure within the pressure regulator reaches a pressure of approximately 36 psi (250 kPa) or higher, extra fuel is bypassed to the return hose and is returned to the fuel tank.

FUEL PULSATION DAMPER

Description

The fuel pulsation damper absorbs the slight fluctuations of fuel pressure which occur when the injectors inject the fuel.

The fuel pressure is constantly maintained by the pressure regulator at a pressure of approximately 36 psi (250 kPa) but slight fluctuations of the fuel pressure do occur when the injector sprays the fuel. The fuel pulsation damper, through the action of the diaphragm, absorbs these minor fluctuations of the fuel pressure to create smoother engine operation..

RESISTOR

Description

The resistor is used to lower the source voltage to a level suitable for the injector. The resistor is connected in series with the injector. It reduces the voltage to approximately ¼ of the source voltage. These resistors protect the injectors from alternator voltage surges and the effects of other components in the vehicle's electrical system.

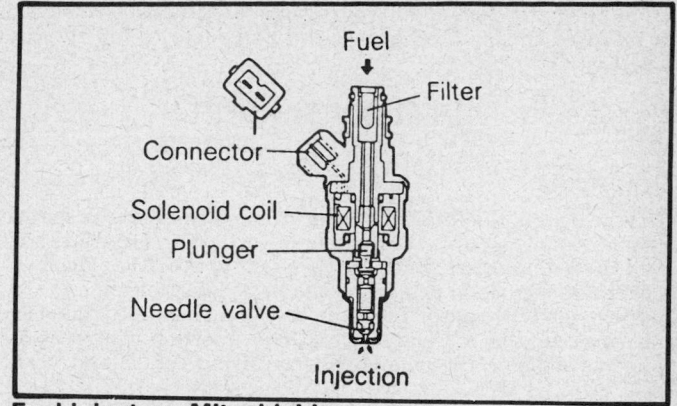

Fuel injector—Mitsubishi

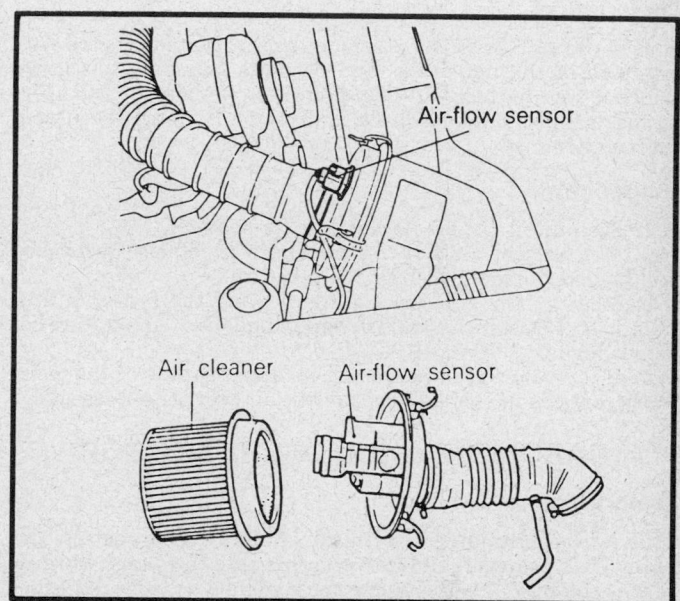

Air flow sensor—Mitsubishi. Note that the barometric pressure sensor and air temperature sensor are built into the air flow sensor

SPARK-ADVANCE SWITCHING SOLENOID DRIVE

Description

The spark-advance switching solenoid is activated in order to advance the ignition timing at high altitudes where the atmospheric pressure is low or during cold weather.

At a barometric pressure of less than 660mm Hg or a water temperature of less than 95°F (35°C), the spark-advance control solenoid is driven, and, by leading the surge tank negative pressure to the boost control, the ignition timing is advanced 5 degrees.

AIR CONDITIONING RELAY CONTROL

Description

The air conditioning relay is switched off, even when the air conditioner switch is switched **ON**, according to the engine rpm and the throttle opening. The air conditioner relay is also switched

off at an engine rpm of 400 rpm or less. Additionally, this relay is switched off for 5 seconds if the ECU detects full throttle acceleration.

AIR FLOW SENSOR

Description

This measures the intake airflow; utilizing the Karman vortex phenomenon, it counts the number of vortices and converts this data to electric pulses which are then sent to the ECU. The ECU uses these signals to determine the basic injection time.

If the air flow sensor fails, the intake air volume cannot be measured and as a result, normal fuel injection control is no longer available. The engine will run using the default value built into the ECU.

INTAKE AIR TEMPERATURE SENSOR

Description

Part of the air flow sensor assembly, this sensor detects the temperature of the intake air, and converts this data to voltage which is sent to the ECU. Based on these signals, the ECU performs air/fuel ratio feedback control and configures usable information.

Inspection

1. Disconnect the air flow sensor connectors.
2. Measure the resistance between its terminals. Resistance will be determined by sensor temperature.
3. Measure the resistance while heating the sensor with a hair drier. Resistance should become smaller as temperature becomes higher.
4. If the value deviates from the standard value or the resistance remains unchanged, replace the air flow sensor assembly.

BAROMETRIC PRESSURE SENSOR

Description

This sensor, also integral with the air flow sensor, detects the barometric pressure, and converts this data to voltage which is sent to the ECU. The ECU uses these signals for correct the fuel injection amount and the ignition timing.

THROTTLE POSITION SENSOR (TPS)

Description

The TPS detects the degree of throttle opening; this data is converted to voltage and is sent to the ECU. The ECU uses these signals to calculate the changes in the degree of throttle opening and to sense the variable speed condition.

IDLE SWITCH

Description

This switch detects the fact that the throttle valve is in the idle position and sends this data as signals to the ECU. The ECU senses that the engine is idling and then controls the fuel injection amount, the ignition timing, the ISC servo, etc.

COOLANT TEMPERATURE SENSOR

Description

This sensor detects the temperature of the engine's coolant, and converts this data to voltage which is sent to the ECU. The ECU

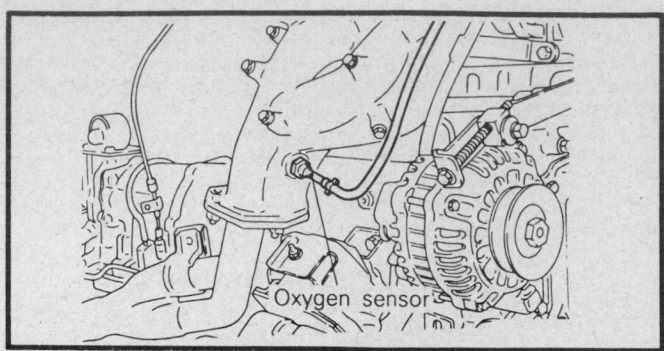

Oxygen sensor location—Mitsubushi Van

uses these signals for correction of the fuel injection amount and the ignition spark advance.

Inspection

1. With temperature sensing portion of engine coolant temperature sensor immersed in hot water, measure its resistance.
2. Resistance should vary according to temperature: resistance should decrease as the temperature increases.
3. Resistance should be close to 0 at boiling point.
4. Replace the sensor if its measurements do not meet specifications.

OXYGEN SENSOR

Description

This sensor measures the amount of oxygen in the exhaust gas, and sends these signals to the ECU. The ECU, based on these signals, performs air/fuel ratio feedback control.

Inspection

1. Before checking, warm the engine until engine coolant temperature reaches 185–205°F (85–95°C). Use an accurate digital voltmeter for testing.
2. Disconnect the oxygen sensor connector and connect a voltmeter to the oxygen sensor connector.
3. With the engine running, observe voltage at idle, then the race engine momentarily. Voltage should increase when the engine is accelerated to approximately 1 volt, then drop as engine returns to idle.
4. If voltage is not correct, or no change occurs during rpm increases, replace the oxygen sensor.

TOP DEAD CENTER (TDC) SENSOR

Description

Built into the distributor, this sensor identifies the reference signal applicable to each cylinder. The disc slit is read by the light-emitting diode and the photo diode; this data is sent from the unit assembly to the ECU as electrical pulses. The ECU uses these signals and the signals from the crankshaft angle sensor to determine the injection timing.

CRANKSHAFT ANGLE SENSOR

Description

Also built into the distributor, this sensor detects the position of the crankshaft (and therefore, the piston). The 360 slits in the disc are read by the light-emitting diode and the photo diode, and this data is sent from the unit assembly to the ECU as electrical pulses.

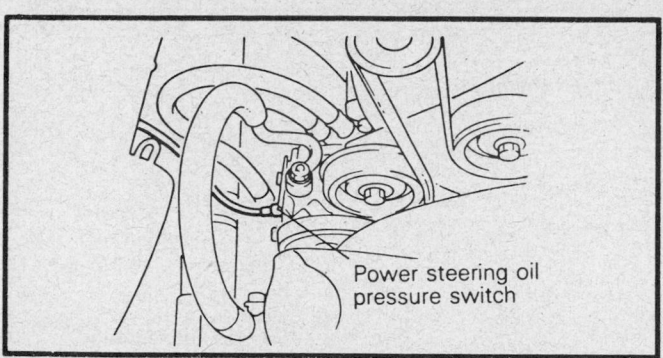

Power steering oil pressure switch—Mitsubishi

POWER STEERING OIL PRESSURE SWITCH

Description

This switch detects a load on the power steering system and increases the idle to compensate.

Inspection

1. Disconnect the power steering oil pressure switch connector.
2. Start the engine and check continuity between the pressure switch terminal and body ground. When the steering wheel is straight ahead, there circuit should be open. With the wheels turned, continuity should exist.
3. If the check result is otherwise than specified, check the oil pump assembly.

IDLE SPEED CONTROL (ISC) SERVO

Description

The ISC system provides the following 4 modes of control:

Start Control: The throttle valve opening is controlled to optimum position for start according to the engine coolant temperature and the altitude (atmospheric pressure).

Fast Idle Control: When the idle switch is on, the engine speed is controlled to a target rpm according to the engine coolant temperature (rpm feedback control). When the idle switch is off, the ISC servo is actuated to move the throttle valve to a target opening position (throttle valve opening position) according to the engine coolant temperature (target opening control).

Idle Control: When the air conditioner switch is turned on or when the transmission is shifted from N to D, the system causes the idle speed to increase to the target rpm according to the load (rpm feedback control).

Dash Pot Control: The system provides dash pot control according to deceleration conditions to alleviate shock at deceleration.

Removal and Installation

1. Disconnect the negative battery cable.
2. Disconnect the throttle return spring from the bracket, if required.
3. Remove the bracket retaining screws and remove the bracket.
4. Disconnect all connectors to the servo assembly.
5. Remove the servo retaining screws and remove the servo assembly and O-ring, if equipped.
6. The installation is the reverse of the removal procedure. Torque the retaining screws to 35 inch lbs.

ISUZU FUEL INJECTION SYSTEM

General Information

SYSTEM OPERATION

MULTI-PORT INJECTION (MPI) I-TEC SYSTEM—2.6L ENGINE

The I-TEC fuel injection control system constantly monitors and controls engine operation, which in turn helps lower emissions while maintaining the fuel economy and driveability. The Electronic Control Unit (ECU) controls the fuel injection and ignition systems.

The fuel injection system basically consists of the following components: the crank angle sensor, the throttle valve switch, the vehicle speed sensor, the coolant temperature sensor, air flow sensor, oxygen sensor, fuel injectors and the ECU.

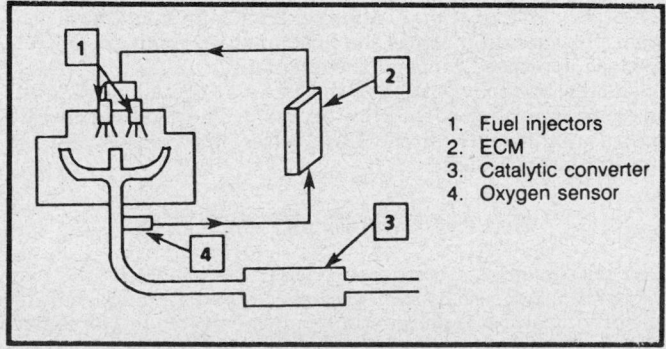

1. Fuel injectors
2. ECM
3. Catalytic converter
4. Oxygen sensor

Closed loop mode—Trooper/Trooper II with 2.8L TBI

THROTTLE BODY INJECTION (TBI) SYSTEM—2.8L ENGINE

The electronic throttle body fuel injection system used on the 2.8L engine is a fuel metering system with the amount of fuel delivered by the throttle body dual injectors, determined by an electronic signal supplied by the Electronic Control Module (ECM). The ECM monitors various engine and vehicle parameters to calculate the fuel delivery time (pulse width) of the injectors. The fuel pulse may be modified by the ECM to account for

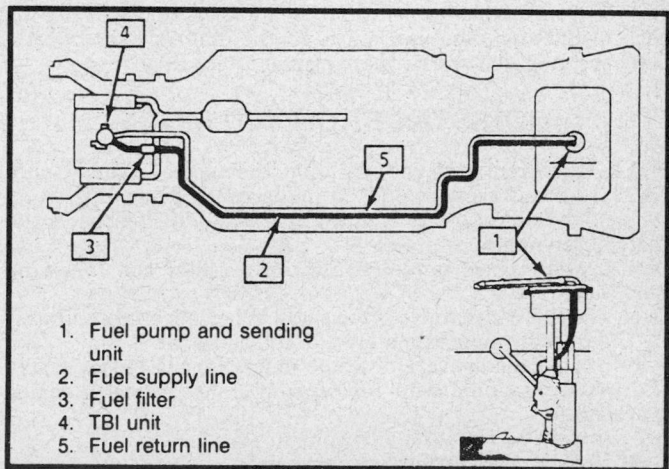

1. Fuel pump and sending unit
2. Fuel supply line
3. Fuel filter
4. TBI unit
5. Fuel return line

Fuel metering system—Trooper/Trooper II with 2.8L TBI

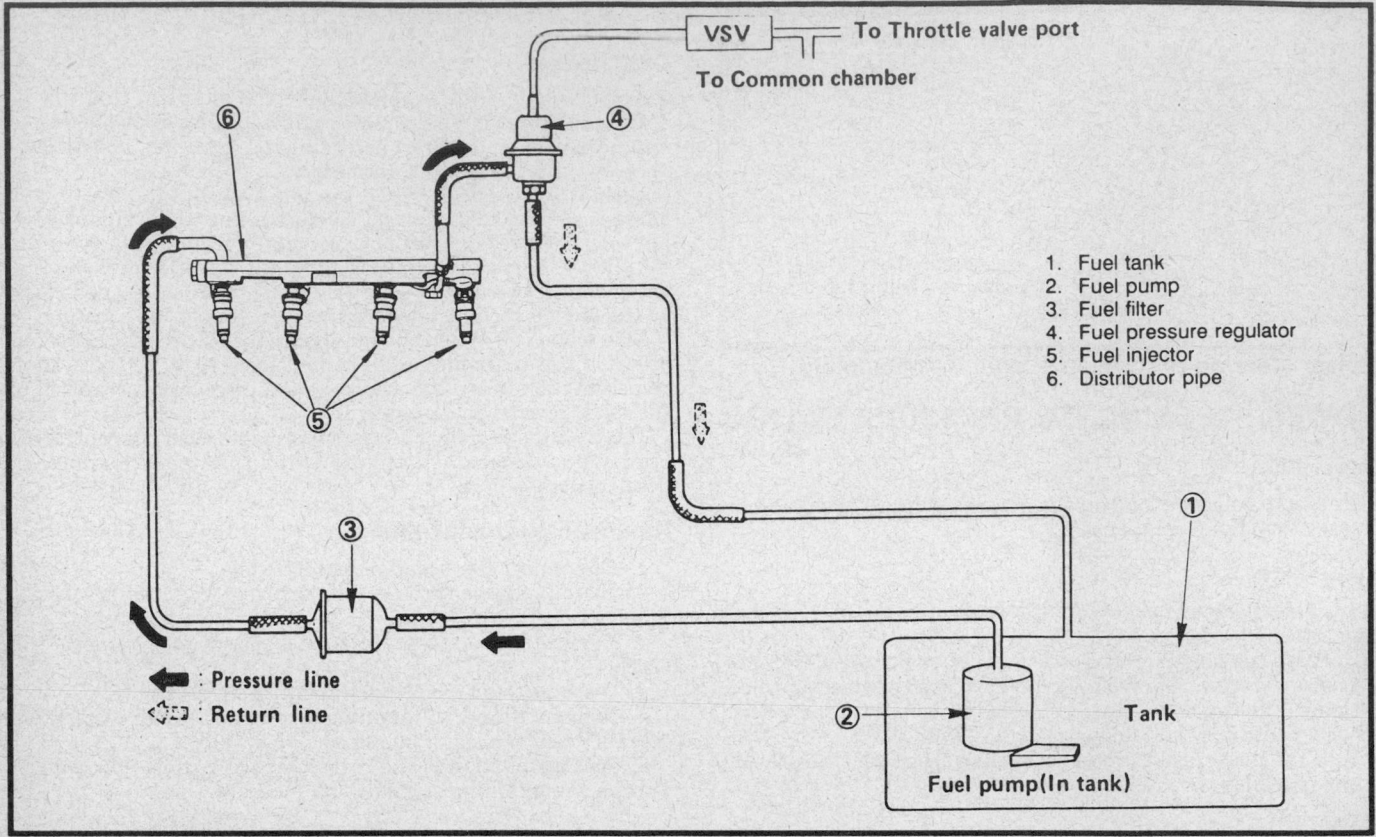

1. Fuel tank
2. Fuel pump
3. Fuel filter
4. Fuel pressure regulator
5. Fuel injector
6. Distributor pipe

System schematic — Isuzu I-TEC system

special operating conditions such as cranking, cold starting, altitude, acceleration and deceleration.

The ECM controls the exhaust emissions by modifying fuel delivery to achieve, as near as possible, an air/fuel ratio of 14.7:1. The injector on-time is determined by various inputs to the ECM. By increasing the injector pulse, more fuel is delivered, enriching the air/fuel ratio. Decreasing the injector pulse leans the air/fuel ratio. Pulses are sent to each injector in synchronized and nonsynchronized modes.

SYNCHRONIZED MODE

In synchronized mode operation, the injector is pulsed once for each distributor reference pulse. In the dual injector throttle body systems, the injectors are pulsed alternately.

NON-SYNCHRONIZED MODE

In non-synchronized mode operation, the injector is pulsed once every 12.5 milliseconds or 6.25 milliseconds depending on its particular calibration. This pulse time is totally independent of distributor reference pulses.
Non-synchronized mode results only under the following conditions:

1. The fuel pulse width is too small to be delivered accurately by the injector (approximately 1.5 milliseconds).
2. During the delivery of prime pulses (prime pulses charge the intake manifold with fuel during or just prior to engine starting).
3. During acceleration enrichment.
4. During deceleration leanout.
The basic TBI unit is made up of 2 major casting assemblies: a throttle body with a valve to control airflow and a fuel body as-

sembly with an integral pressure regulator and fuel injector to supply the fuel. An electronically operated device to control the idle speed and a device to provide information regarding throttle valve position are included as part of the TBI unit.

The Throttle Position Sensor (TPS) is a variable resistor used to convert the degree of throttle plate opening to an electrical signal to the ECM. The ECM uses this signal as a reference point of throttle valve position. In addition, an Idle Air Control (IAC) assembly, mounted in the throttle body is used to control idle speeds. A cone-shaped valve in the IAC assembly is located in an air passage in the throttle body that leads from the point beneath the air cleaner to below the throttle valve. The ECM monitors idle speeds and, depending on engine load, moves the IAC cone in the air passage to increase or decrease air bypassing the throttle valve to the intake manifold for control of idle speeds.

The pressure regulator is a diaphragm-operated relief valve with injector pressure on one side and air cleaner pressure on the other. The function of the regulator is to maintain a constant pressure drop across the injector throughout the operating load and speed range of the engine.

The throttle body portion of the TBI may contain ports located at, above or below the throttle valve. These ports generate the vacuum signals for the EGR valve, MAP sensor, and the canister purge system.

SELF-DIAGNOSIS SYSTEM

The self-diagnosis system is so designed that the circuits handling the input signals from the sensors and output signals for the driving actuator are continuously monitored by the control unit. In the event of a failure, the control unit stores it in memory and operates the **CHECK ENGINE** light on the instrument

panel when the nature of trouble is important, to warn the operator of failure.

The self-diagnosis system is capable of trouble-shooting the electrical circuits in the Closed Loop Emission Control system only and does not cover the trouble in the sensors, actuators or the engine itself.

When a failure has developed in the following systems while driving, the **CHECK ENGINE** light within the instrument panel is operated to warn the driver of a system failure.
1. Air flow sensor system
2. Coolant temperature sensor
3. Fuel injector system
4. Micro computer
5. Oxygen sensor
6. Vehicle speed sensor

When the diagnosis lead in the vicinity of the control unit is connected with the ignition switch in the **ON** position (engine not running), the trouble code stored in the memory is displayed by the **CHECK ENGINE** light.

After completion of the service operation, clear the trouble codes stored in memory by disconnecting the 60A main fuse in the fuse junction block, then check that only Code 12 is displayed.

All the codes stored in memory will be cleared automatically when the 13-pole connector in the control unit is disconnected. Since all the memory will be cleared when number 4 fuse is disconnected, it will be necessary to reset the clock and other electrical equipment.

System Components

AIR CONDITIONING REQUEST SIGNAL

Description

This signal indicates to the ECM that an air conditioning mode is selected at the switch and that the A/C low pressure switch is closed. The ECM controls the A/C and adjusts the idle speed in response to this signal. This signal is only included with the 2.8L engine TBI system.

AIR FLOW SENSOR

Description

The air flow sensor is located in the air cleaner housing assembly. The purpose of the air flow sensor is to measure the volume (rate) of air that is coming into the engine. This sensor generates voltage corresponding to the mass flow of the air drawn through the air cleaner assembly and into the engine. The changing voltage is transformed into a usable electrical signal and sent oto the ECM. The air flow sensor is only included with the 2.6L engine MPI system.

BACK-UP CONTROL SYSTEM

Description

Programmed into the ECU in vehicles equipped with the 2.8L engine only, this useful system is used in case there is a malfunction with the microcomputer within the ECU, the back-up control system works to maintain the necessary functions of the control unit to permit continuous operation of the vehicle.

COOLANT TEMPERATURE SENSOR

Description

2.6L ENGINE

This sensor is located on the engine block, under the intake manifold. It sends the coolant temperature information back to

the ECU. The ECU then uses this information to determine the engine temperature for calculating the required air/fuel mixture.

2.8L ENGINE

The coolant sensor is a thermistor (a resistor which changes value based on temperature) mounted in the engine coolant stream. As the temperature of the engine coolant changes, the resistance of the coolant sensor changes. Low coolant temperature produces a high resistance (100,000 ohms at -40°F/-40°C), while high temperature causes low resistance (70 ohms at 266°F/130°C).

The ECM supplies a 5 volt signal to the coolant sensor and measures the voltage that returns. By measuring the voltage change, the ECM determines the engine coolant temperature. The voltage will be high when the engine is cold and low when the engine is hot. This information is used to control fuel management, spark timing, EGR use, canister purge and other engine operating conditions.

CRANK ANGLE SENSOR

Description

The crank angle sensor is usually located inside the distributor housing on the 2.6L engine. It is used to detect the engine speed and relative position of each piston in its cylinder. Using these parameters, the ECU calculates the proper ignition timing and dwell angle. The ECU then sends a signal to the transistorized ignition coil to create a spark.

CRANKSHAFT AND CAMSHAFT SENSORS

Description

These sensors are mounted on the engine block, near the crankshaft and also near the camshaft on the 2.8L engine. They are used to send a signal through the Direct Ignition System (DIS) module to the ECM. The ECM uses this reference signal to calculate engine speed and crankshaft position.

The engine uses a sensor called a Hall effect switch. With the direct ignition connected to the vehicle electrical system, the system voltage is applied to the Hall effect switch located near the tip of the sensor. A small permanent magnet creates a magnetic field in the Hall effect switch circuit. As the disc with the slots rotates past the sensor tip, the magnetic field in the Hall effect switch changes and a change in the voltage occurs at the Hall effect switch output terminal.

Since this terminal is connected to the ignition module, the module senses this change in voltage and correlates the frequency of the voltage curve to determine the engine speed. The ignition module uses this voltage input to help determine when to close and open the ignition coil primary circuit and fire the spark plug.

ELECTRONIC CONTROL UNIT (ECU)

Description

The ECU is usually located under the instrument panel. The ECU analyzes all electrical data signals from the sensors. It controls the fuel injection system and the ignition system. The ECU has a built in back-up, diagnostic and fail safe control systems.

ELECTRONIC SPARK CONTROL (ESC)

Description

When engines are equipped with ESC in conjunction with electronic spark timing, ESC is used to reduce spark advance under conditions of detonation. A knock sensor signals a separate ESC controller to retard the timing when it senses engine knock. The

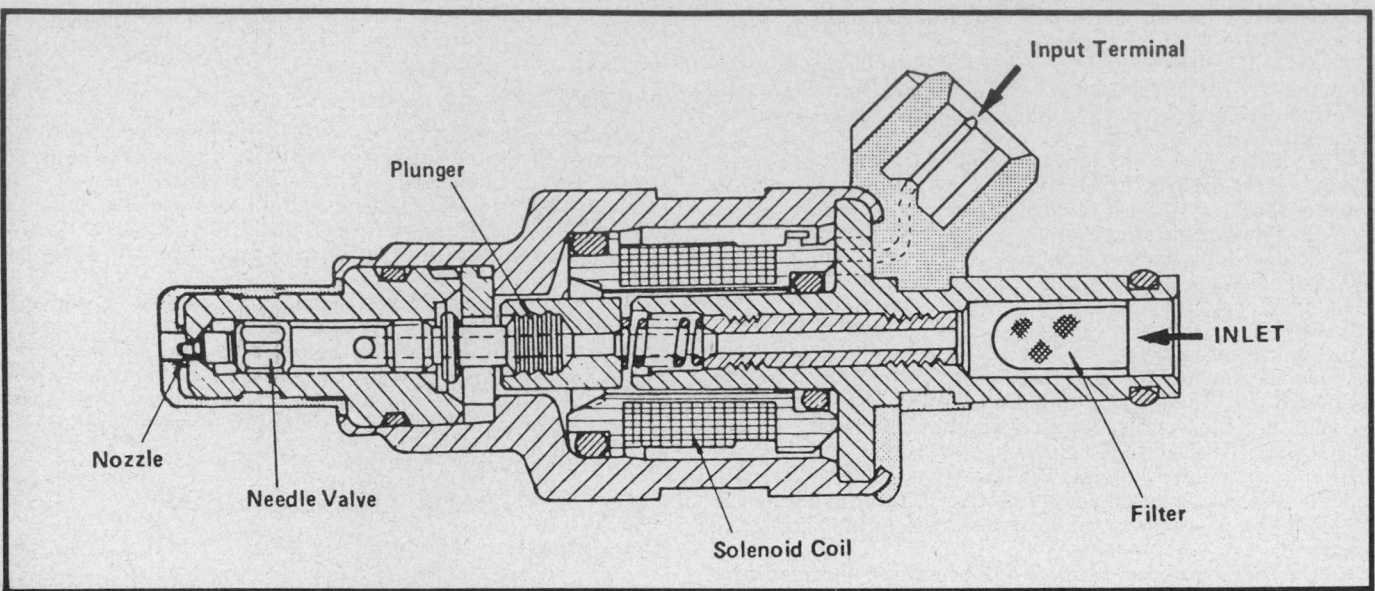

Fuel injector — Isuzu with 2.6L engine

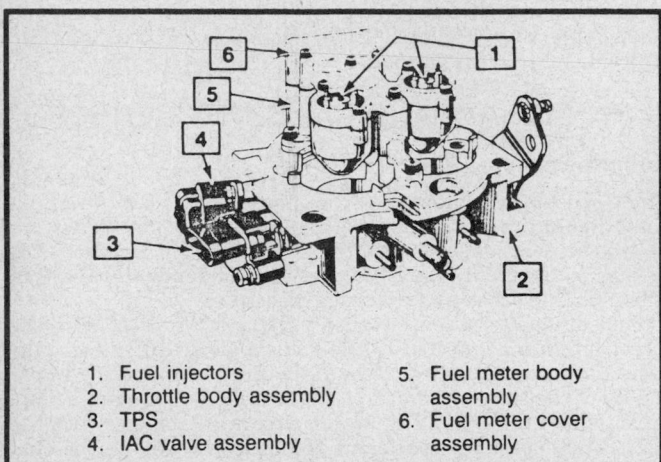

1. Fuel injectors
2. Throttle body assembly
3. TPS
4. IAC valve assembly
5. Fuel meter body assembly
6. Fuel meter cover assembly

Throttle body assembly — Trooper/Trooper II with 2.8L TBI

ESC controller signals the ECM which reduces spark advance until no more signals are received from the knock sensor. Included with the 2.8L TBI electronics.

FUEL INJECTOR

Description

Each fuel injector is a solenoid operated device controlled by the vehicles's controlling unit. The incoming fuel is directed to the lower end of the injector assembly which has a fine screen filter surrounding the injector inlet. The control unit actuates the solenoid, which lifts a normally closed ball valve off a seat. The fuel, under pressure, is injected in a conical spray pattern. The excess fuel passes through a pressure regulator before returning to the vehicle's fuel tank.

Inspection

1. Disconnect the fuel injector harness at the connector. Us-ing a suitable ohmmeter, measure the resistance across the terminals.

2. The standard resistance should be 2–3 ohms.

3. If the injector resistance deviates from the specified range, replace the injector.

4. With the engine running, check the fuel injector operating noise using a metal bar or stethoscope. Normal operation of the injector is indicated when a regular click is heard which varies with engine speed. If a regular click is not heard, the injector is malfunctioning and should be replaced.

5. Test for leakage as follows:

   a. Remove the common chamber assembly. Remove all the injectors with the fuel hoses still connected.

   b. Check for fuel leakage by operating the fuel pump with the battery voltage applied directly to the fuel pump relay terminal.

   c. The leakage should be less than 2 drops per minute.

   d. If the amount of leakage is beyond the set limit, replace the injector.

   e. Install the parts in the reverse order of the removal. Start the engine and check for fuel leaks.

MANIFOLD ABSOLUTE PRESSURE (MAP) SENSOR

Description

Included in the 2.8L engine TBI system, the Manifold Absolute Pressure (MAP) sensor measures the changes in the intake manifold pressure which result from engine load and speed changes. The pressure measured by the MAP sensor is the difference between barometric pressure (outside air) and manifold pressure (vacuum). A closed throttle engine coastdown would produce a relatively low MAP value (approximately 20–35 kPa), while wide-open throttle would produce a high value (100 kPa). This high value is produced when the pressure inside the manifold is the same as outside the manifold, and 100% of outside air (or 100 kPa) is being measured. This MAP output is the opposite of what would be measured on a vacuum gauge. The use of this sensor also allows the ECM to adjust automatically for different altitudes.

The ECM sends a 5 volt reference signal to the MAP sensor. As the pressure changes, the electrical resistance of the sensor also changes. By monitoring the sensor output voltage the ECM

can determine the manifold pressure. A higher pressure, lower vacuum (high voltage) requires more fuel, while a lower pressure, higher vacuum (low voltage) requires less fuel. The ECM uses the MAP sensor to control fuel delivery and ignition timing.

Manifold Air Temperature (MAT) Sensor

Description

The Manifold Air Temperature (MAT) sensor is a thermistor mounted in the intake manifold. A thermistor is a resistor which changes resistance based on temperature. Low manifold air temperature produces a high resistance (100,000 ohms at -40°F/-40°C), while high temperature cause low resistance (70 ohms at 266°F/130°C).

The ECM supplies a 5 volt signal to the MAT sensor through a resistor in the ECM and monitors the voltage. The voltage will be high when the manifold air is cold and low when the air is hot. By monitoring the voltage, the ECM calculates the air temperature and uses this data to help determine the fuel delivery and spark advance. The MAT sensor is also on the 2.8L TBI system only.

OIL PRESSURE SWITCH

Description

The oil pressure switch is mounted on the back of the 2.8L engine engine, just below the intake manifold. Some vehicles use the oil pressure switch as a parallel power supply (with the fuel pump relay) and will provide voltage to the fuel pump after approximately 4 psi (28 kPa) of oil pressure is reached. This switch will also help prevent engine seizure by shutting off the power to the fuel pump and causing the engine to stop when the oil pressure is lower than 4 psi.

OXYGEN SENSOR

Description

2.6L ENGINE

This sensor is usually threaded into the exhaust manifold. The oxygen sensor measures and produces an electrical signal proportional to the amount of the oxygen present in the exhaust gases.

2.8L ENGINE

The exhaust oxygen sensor is mounted in the exhaust system where it can monitor the oxygen content of the exhaust gas stream. The oxygen content in the exhaust reacts with the oxygen sensor to produce a voltage output. This voltage ranges from approximately 100 millivolts (high oxygen – lean mixture) to 900 millivolts (low oxygen – rich mixture).

By monitoring the voltage output of the oxygen sensor, the ECM will determine what fuel mixture command to give to the injector (lean mixture – low voltage – rich command, rich mixture – high voltage – lean command). The oxygen sensor only indicates to the ECM what is happening within the exhaust system; it does not cause things to happen. It is simply a type of gauge: high oxygen content = lean mixture; low oxygen content = rich mixture. The ECM adjusts fuel to keep the system working.

POWER STEERING PRESSURE SWITCH

Description

The power steering pressure switch is used so that the power steering pump load will not effect the engine idle. Turning the steering wheel increases the power steering oil pressure and pump load on the engine. The power steering pressure switch

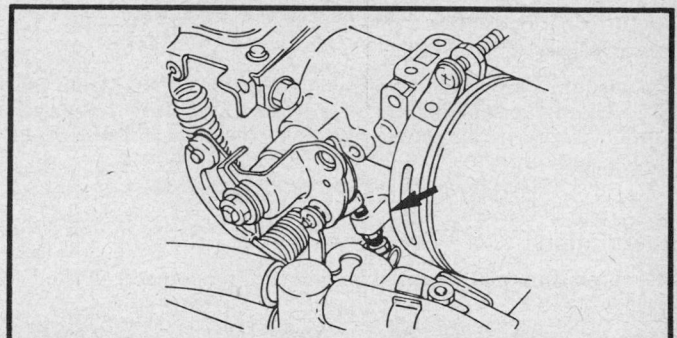

Throttle valve switch and TPS – Isuzu with 2.6L engine

will close before the load can cause an idle problem. This switch is mounted in-line with the power steering fluid on the 2.8L engine only.

THROTTLE POSITION SENSOR (TPS)

Description

The Throttle Position Sensor (TPS) is connected to the throttle shaft and is controlled by the throttle mechanism. A 5 volt reference signal is sent to the TPS from the ECM. As the throttle valve angle is changed (accelerator pedal moved), the resistance of the TPS also changes. At a closed throttle position, the resistance of the TPS is high, so the output voltage to the ECM will be low (approximately 0.5 volts). As the throttle plate opens, the resistance decreases so that, at wide open throttle, the output voltage should be approximately 5 volts. At closed throttle position, the voltage at the TPS should be less than 1.25 volts.

By monitoring the output voltage from the TPS, the ECM can determine fuel delivery based on throttle valve angle (driver demand). The TPS can either be misadjusted, shorted, open or loose. Misadjustment might result in poor idle or poor wide-open throttle performance. An open TPS signals the ECM that the throttle is always closed, resulting in poor performance. A loose TPS indicates to the ECM that the throttle is moving. This causes intermittent bursts of fuel from the injector and an unstable idle. On some vehicles, the TPS is adjustable and therefore can be adjusted to correct any complications caused by a voltage signal that is too high or low.

Inspection

1. Turn the ignition switch to the **ON** position. Remove the water shield cover.
2. Using a suitable voltmeter, place the positive probe into the white color wire harness.
3. Measure the voltage between the white color harness of the throttle position sensor and ground.

NOTE: The throttle position sensor has 3 leads, red for 5 volt power source, white for output and black for ground.

4. The voltage should be higher than 4 volts at idle contact and lower than 2 volts at full contact.

NOTE: Make sure that 5 volts (± 0.5 volts) is measured at the red colored harness before making the voltage check in Step 4.

5. Confirm the difference in the voltage of the idle contact and full contact is 3.6 ± 1 volt.
6. If the throttle position sensor fails any part of this inspection, replace it.

VACUUM SWITCHING VALVE

Description

The vacuum switching valve is controlled by a signal from the ECU. This valve controls the fuel pressure according to the vacuum developed in the intake manifold. Included in the 2.6L I-TEC system only.

VEHICLE SPEED SENSOR

Description

The speed sensor is mounted behind the speedometer in the instrument cluster or on the transmission/speedometer drive gear. It provides electrical pulses to the ECM from the speedometer head. The pulses indicate the road speed. The ECM uses this information to operate several of its parameters.

Some vehicles equipped with digital instrument clusters use a Permanent Magnet (PM) generator to provide the VSS signal. The PM generator is located in the transmission and replaces the speedometer cable. The signal from the PM generator drives a stepper motor which drives the odometer.

A vehicle equipped with a speed sensor, should not be driven without the speed sensor connected, or idle quality may be affected.

MAZDA ELECTRONIC FUEL INJECTION

General Information

INTAKE AIR SYSTEM

The air intake system controls the air that is induced into the engine for efficient operation. The system consists of the air duct work, air cleaner assembly, air flow sensor, throttle body, dynamic chamber, extension manifolds or plenums and intake manifolds. The intake air system may contain the Variable Resonance Induction System (VIRS) and Idle Speed Control (ISC) system for improved engine power and idle smoothness.

Some air flow sensor are equipped with a self-cleaning feature (burn off control system) that momentarily super-heats the hot wire to burn contaminants that may have collected over time. This operation will only occur after the vehicle has been shut off after after being operated.

THROTTLE BODY

Inspection

1. Check the mounting base for warpage and cracks.
2. Check the throttle valve operation. Check the free play of the accelerator cable. Free play should be 0.04–0.12 in. (1–3mm).
3. If freeplay is not as specified, depress the accelerator pedal to the floor and check that the throttle valve is fully opened.
4. Adjust with the adjustment bolt, if necessary.

Removal and Installation

1. Disconnect the negative battery cable.
2. Disconnect the accelerator cable from the throttle linkage.
3. Disconnect the air funnel, then the air hoses and lines from the throttle body. Remove the BAC valve, if equipped.
4. Disconnect all electrical connectors from the throttle body assembly. Remove the throttle body attaching screws.
5. Remove the the throttle body assembly.
6. The installation is the reverse of the removal procedure.

AIR FLOW SENSOR

Removal and Installation

2.6L ENGINE

1. Disconnect the negative battery cable.
2. Disconnect the air flow sensor electrical connector.
3. Loosen the air hose clamps. Remove the mounting bolts.
4. Remove the air flow sensor.
5. The installation is the reverse of the removal procedure.

3.0L ENGINE

1. Disconnect the negative battery cable. Disconnect the high tension leads and connectors.

2. Loosen the hose band and remove the intake hose.
3. Remove the air flow sensor attaching bolts.
4. Turn the air cleaner cover upside down and remove the attaching nuts and remove the air flow sensor.
5. The installation is the reverse of the removal procedure.

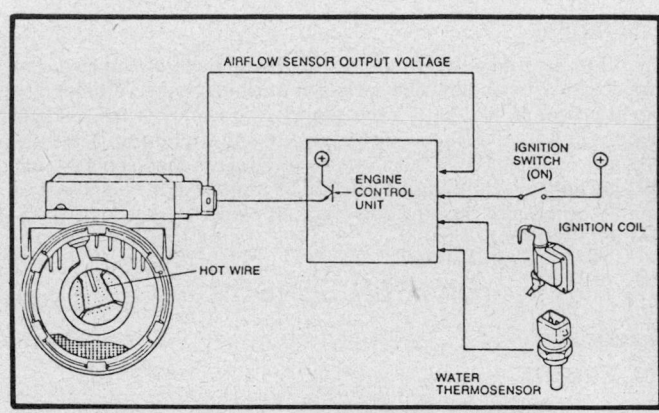

Burn off control system schematic – Mazda

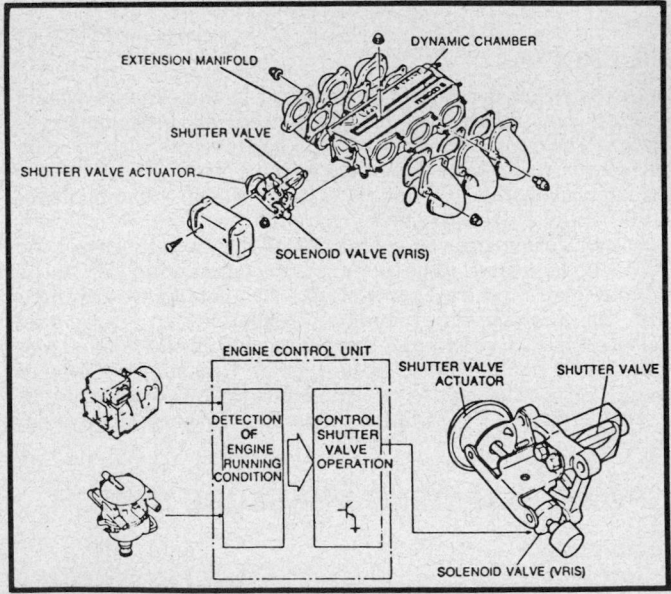

Variable Resonance Induction System (VRIS) schematic – Mazda

IDLE SPEED CONTROL (ISC) SYSTEM

Description

The ISC system controls the intake air amount (detected by the air flow meter), by regulating the amount of bypass air that passes through the throttle body, which is instrumental in maintaining a steady idle speed. The ISC system consists of the Bypass Air Control (BAC) valve and its control system.

VARIABLE RESONANCE INDUCTION SYSTEM (VRIS)

Description

This system is only included in the MPV with the 3.0L engine to enhance low speed torque capabilities. This system consists of the dynamic chamber, shutter valve actuator, extension manifolds, intake manifold and its control system.

The shutter valve is installed on the dynamic chamber and its operation is controlled by engine control unit. The resonance charge uses pressure waves from the intake air caused by the closing and opening of the intake valve. As each cylinder's intake valve operates, it forces air to fill the other cylinders. The engine speed at which this actually takes place is determined by the dynamic chamber capacity and the length of the passage between cylinders.

Inspection

1. Remove the shutter valve actuator.
2. Connect vacuum pump tester to the actuator and confirm that the rod is pulled into the chamber when vacuum is applied.
3. Remove the shutter valve actuator. Replace or repair if the valve rod does not move perfectly smoothly.
4. Disconnect the vacuum hose from the top port of VRIS solenoid valve (mounted on the side of the actuator) that is parallel to the valve. Blow through the other hose (connected to the perpendicular port) and check that air is flowing from the filter end.
5. Disconnect te connector and apply 12 volts and ground to the terminals. Blow through the hose and check that air is flowing through the parallel port.
6. Make sure the in-line check valve is functioning properly.

FUEL SYSTEM

Description

The fuel system supplies the necessary fuel to the injectors to achieve combustion at a constant pressure. Fuel is metered and injected into the intake manifold according to the signals from the engine control unit coming from the various sensors.

The fuel system consists of the fuel pump, fuel filter, distribution pipe, pressure regulator, injectors, transfer pump (4WD vehicles) and a circuit opening relay in 1990.

FUEL INJECTOR

Inspection

1. Start the engine and allow it to reach normal operating temperature.
2. While the engine is idling, touch a sound scope or equivalent to the injector and check for an operating clicking sound.
4. On B2600 and 1990 MPV with 2.6L engine, check the resistance of the injector harness connector. First, disconnect the electrical connector from the fuel injector.
5. Using a suitable ohmmeter, measure the resistance across the fuel injector connector terminals. The ohmmeter values should read 12–16 ohms.

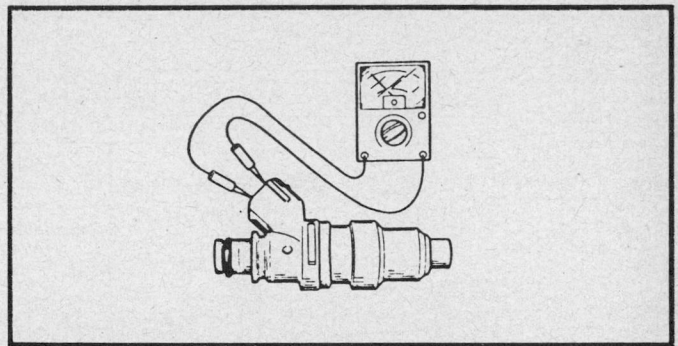

Checking injector resistance – Mazda

6. If the specifications are not as indicated, replace the fuel injector.
7. Repeat for the remaining fuel injectors.

Leak Test

1. Relieve the fuel pressure from the fuel system and disconnect the battery ground cable.
2. Remove the injectors and delivery pipe as an assembly.
3. Firmly attach each injector to the distribution pipe with a piece of wire. Ensure that the injectors are not allowed to move or rotate on the distribution pipe.
4.
5. Connect the battery ground cable. Install a jumper to the test connector (yellow wire).
6. Turn the ignition switch to the **ON** position. Tilt injectors approximately 60 degrees and check the injectors for fuel leakage.
7. After approximately 1 minute, a slight amount of fuel leakage is acceptable. If excessive fuel leaks from any injector, replace it.

ENGINE CONTROL UNIT (ECU)

Description

The ECU, through various input signals, monitors battery voltage, engine rpm, amount of air intake, cranking signal, intake temperature, coolant temperature, oxygen concentration in the exhaust gases, throttle opening, atmospheric pressure gearshift position, clutch engagement, braking, power steering operation and A/C compressor operation.

The ECU controls the operation of the fuel injection system, idle-up system, fuel evaporation system and ignition timing. The ECU has a built in fail-safe mechanism. If a fault is generated while driving, The ECU will substitute pre-programmed values for the faulty one(s). Driving performance will be affected, but the vehicle will still be driveable.

PRESSURE REGULATOR CONTROL (PRC) SYSTEM

By cutting the vacuum to the pressure regulator, this system prevents fuel percolation and eventual loss during idle after the engine is started while it is still hot. The PRC system causes an increase in fuel pressure to overcome the percolating effect.

EVAPORATIVE EMISSION CONTROL (EEC) SYSTEM

This system is controlled by signals sent from the water thermo sensor, intake air thermo sensor, air flow sensor and the engine speed sensor (ignition coil). The ECU calculates the engine operating conditions from the signals, and controls the EEC system

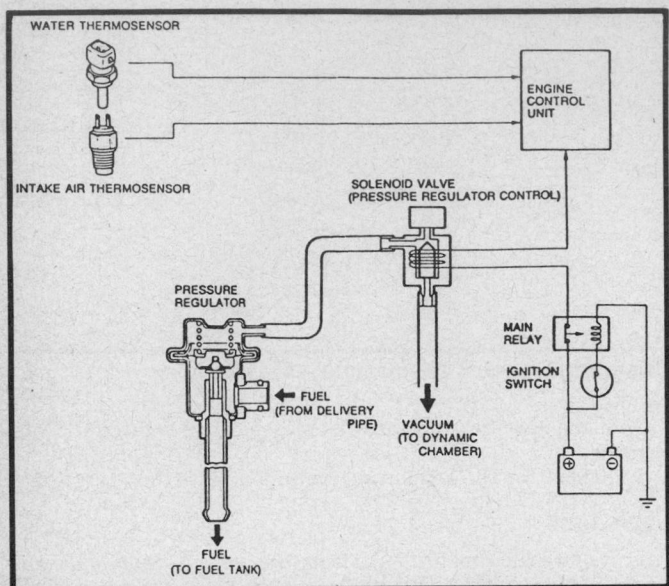

Pressure regulator control system—Mazda

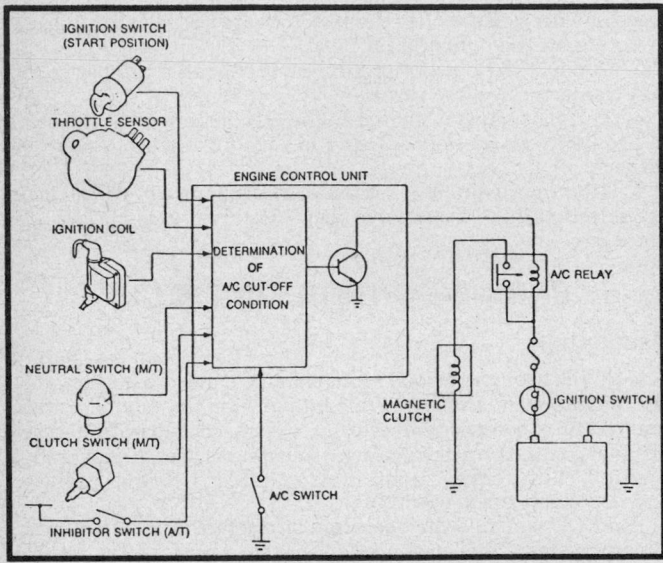

Air conditioning cutoff system schematic—Mazda

by the operation of the solenoid valves for the No. 1 purge control valve and the vacuum switching valve.

DECELERATION CONTROL SYSTEM

Description

This system, only available on the MPV with the 3.0L engine, consists of the fuel cut operation and dashpot unit. The fuel cut feature is used to improve fuel economy and prevent bucking during deceleration. The dashpot prevents the throttle valve from closing suddenly and causing an undesirable braking action.

Dashpot Adjustment

1. Push lightly on the dashpot rod and check that the rod goes into the dashpot slowly. Release the dashpot rod, and check that the rod comes out quickly.
2. Start the engine and allow it to reach normal operating temperature.
3. Stop the engine and connect a suitable tachometer to the engine.
4. Start the engine and slowly increase engine speed to 4000 rpm.
5. Slowly decrease engine rpm, and check that the dashpot rod touches the lever at 3200–3800 rpm.
6. If the touch point is not as specified, loosen the lock nut and adjust.

AIR CONDITIONING CUT-OFF SYSTEM

Description

To improve idle smoothness just after engine start up and acceleration performance, this cut-off system is used. The air conditioning compressor will be turned off when all of the following condition are met:

1. The air conditioning is **ON**.
2. The transmission is in gear and the clutch pedal is released, if equipped with a manual transmission.
3. The automatic transmission is not in **P** or **N**, if so equipped.
4. The throttle valve is at least half opened.
5. The air conditioning is cut off for about 10 seconds after the engine is started.

NISSAN ELECTRONIC CONCENTRATED CONTROL SYSTEM (ECCS)

General Information

The Nissan ECCS is a throttle body or multi-port fuel injection system used on all fuel injected vehicles. The electronic control unit consists of a microcomputer, inspection lamps, a diagnostic mode selector and connectors for signal input and output and for power supply. The Electronic Concentrated Control System (ECCS) computer controls the amount of fuel injected, ignition timing, mixture ratio feedback, idle speed, fuel pump operation, mixture heating, Air Injection Valve (AIV) operation, Exhaust Gas Recirculation (EGR) and vapor canister purge operation.

System Operation

In operation, the on-board computer (control unit) calculates the basic injection pulse width by processing signals from the crank angle sensor and air flow meter. Receiving signals from each sensor which detects various engine operating conditions, the computer adds various enrichments (which are preprogrammed) to the basic injection amount. In this manner, the optimum amount of fuel is delivered through the injectors. The fuel is enriched when starting, during warm-up, when accelerating, when cylinder head temperature is high and when operating under a heavy load. The fuel is leaned during deceleration according to the closing rate of the throttle valve. Fuel shut-off

is accomplished during deceleration, when vehicle speed exceeds 137 mph, or when engine speed exceeds 6400 rpm for about 500 revolutions.

The mixture ratio feedback system (closed loop control) is designed to control the air/fuel mixture precisely to the stoichiometric or optimum point so that the 3-way catalytic converter can minimize CO, HC and NOx emissions simultaneously. The optimum air/fuel fuel mixture is 14.7:1. Some systems use an exhaust gas (oxygen) sensor located in the exhaust manifold to give an indication of whether the fuel mixture is richer or leaner than the stoichiometric point. The control unit adjusts the injection pulse width according to the sensor voltage so the mixture ratio will be within the narrow window around the stoichiometric fuel ratio. The system goes into closed loop as soon as the oxygen sensor heats up enough to register. The system will operate under open loop when starting the engine, when the engine temperature is cold, when exhaust gas sensor temperature is cold, when driving at high speeds or under heavy load, at idle (after mixture ratio learning is completed), during deceleration, if the exhaust gas sensor malfunctions, or when the exhaust gas sensor monitors a rich condition for more than 10 seconds and during deceleration.

Ignition timing is controlled in response to engine operating conditions. The optimum ignition timing in each driving condition is preprogrammed in the computer. The signal from the control unit is transmitted to the power transistor and controls ignition timing. The idle speed is also controlled according to engine operating conditions, temperature and gear position. On manual transmission models, if battery voltage is less than 12 volts for a few seconds, a higher idle speed will be maintained by the control unit to improve charging function.

There is a fail-safe system built into the ECCS control unit. If the output voltage of the air flow meter is extremely low, the ECU will substitute a preprogrammed value for the air flow meter signal and allow the vehicle to be driven as long as the engine speed is kept below 2000 rpm. If the cylinder head temperature sensor circuit is open, the control unit locks the warmup enrichment at a certain amount. This amount is almost the same as that when the cylinder head temperature is between 68–176°F (20–80°C). If the fuel pump circuit malfunctions, the fuel pump relay comes on until the engine stops. This allows the fuel pump to receive power from the relay.

System Components

CRANK ANGLE SENSOR

Description

The crank angle sensor is a basic component of the entire system. It monitors engine speed and piston position and sends other signals which the control unit uses to calculate ignition timing and other functions. The crank angle sensor has a rotor plate and a wave forming circuit. The rotor plate has 360 slits for 1° signals (engine speed) and 4 slits for 180° signals (crank angle). Light emitting diodes (LED's) and photo diodes are built in the wave forming circuit. When the rotor plate passes the space between the LED and the photo diode, the slits of the rotor plate continually cut the light which is sent to the photo diode from the LED, causing rough shaped pulses. These pulses are converted into on-off signals by the wave forming circuit and sent to the control unit as input signals.

AIR FLOW METER

Description

The air flow meter measures the intake air flow rate by taking a part of the entire flow. Measurement are made in such a manner that the control unit receives electrical output signals varied by

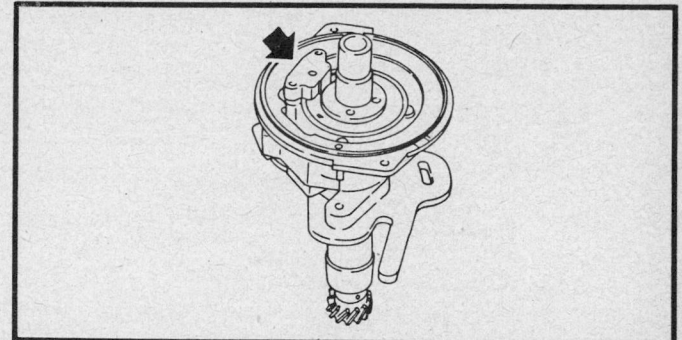

Crank angle sensor in distributor — Nissan

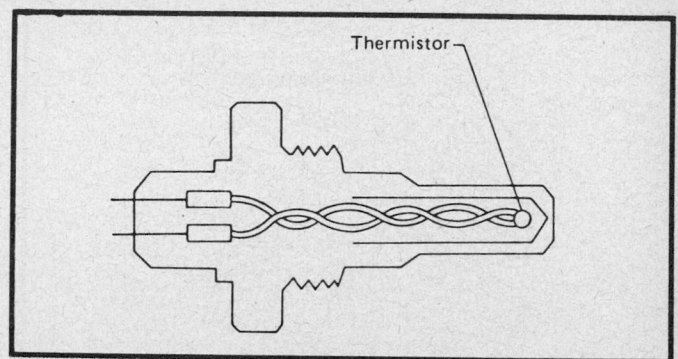

Water temperature sensor — Nissan

the amount of heat emitted from a hot wire placed in the stream of intake air. When intake air flows into the intake manifold through a route around the hot wire, the heat generated by the wire is taken away by the passing air. The amount of heat removed depends on the air flow, but the maximum temperature of the hot wire is automatically controlled, requiring more electrical current to maintain the controlled temperature in the wire as the amount of intake air increases. By measuring the amount of current necessary to maintain the hot wire temperature, the control unit measures the amount of intake air passing the wire and therefore knows the volume of air entering the engine.

Before removing the air flow meter, remove the throttle valve switch. When removing the air flow meter, pull it out vertically, taking care not to bend or damage the plug portion. Never touch the sensor portion with your finger and apply silicone grease to the mating surface between the air flow meter and throttle body when installing to allow heat to escape. Failure to use silicone grease for heat dissipation will result in air flow meter failure.

WATER TEMPERATURE SENSOR

Description

The water temperature sensor, located on the front side of the intake manifold, detects engine coolant temperature and sends signals to the control unit. The air temperature sensor is installed in the air cleaner and senses the temperature of the intake air. The water and air temperature sensors employs a thermistor which is sensitive to changes in temperature. The electrical resistance of this type of thermistor decreases as temperature rises.

EXHAUST GAS SENSOR

Description

The exhaust gas sensor, which is placed in the exhaust pipe,

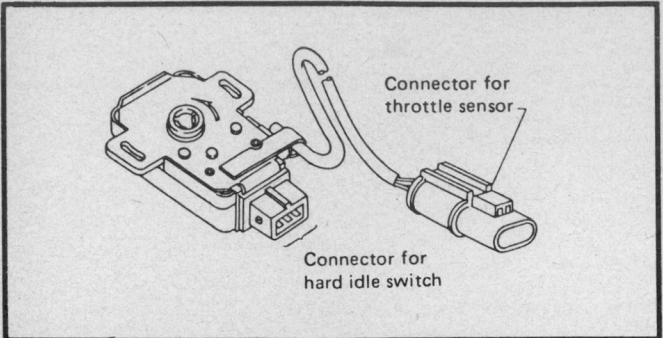

Throttle sensor and hard idle switch—Nissan

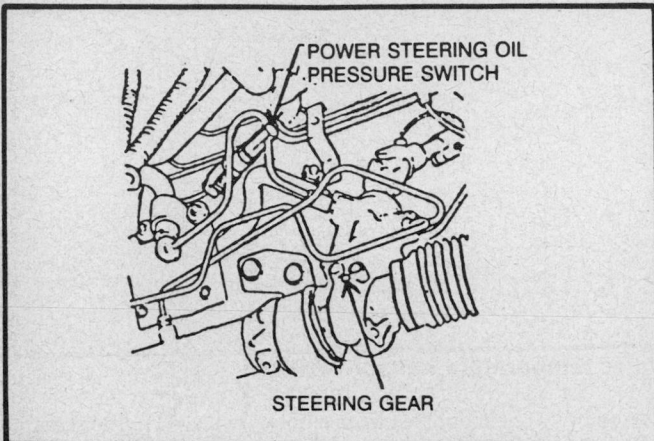

Power steering pressure switch—Axxess

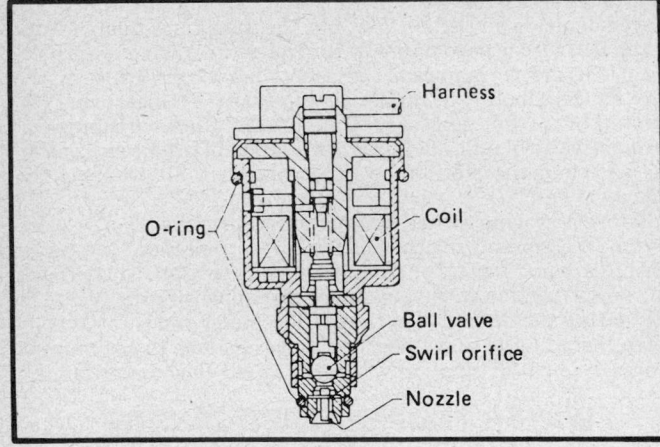

Fuel injector—Nissan with TBI

monitors the amount of oxygen in the exhaust gas. The sensor is made of ceramic titania which changes electrical resistance at the ideal air/fuel ratio (14.7:1). The control unit supplies the sensor with approximately 1 volt and takes the output voltage of the sensor depending on its resistance. The oxygen sensor is equipped with a heater to bring it to operating temperature quickly.

THROTTLE SENSOR/HARD IDLE SWITCH

Description

The throttle sensor/hard idle switch is attached to the throttle body and operates in response to accelerator pedal movement.

This sensor has two functions; it contains an idle switch and throttle position sensor. The idle switch closes when the throttle valve is positioned at idle and opens when it is in any other position. The throttle sensor is a potentiometer which transforms the throttle valve position into output voltage and feeds the voltage signal to the control unit. In addition, the throttle sensor detects the opening or closing speed of the throttle valve and feeds the rate of voltage change to the control unit.

POWER STEERING OIL PRESSURE SWITCH

Description

A power steering oil pressure switch is attached to the power steering high pressure line and detects the power steering load, sending a load signal to the control unit which then sends the idle-up signal to the idle speed control (ISC) valve.

FUEL PRESSURE REGULATOR

Description

A fuel pressure regulator is built into the side of the throttle body. It maintains fuel pressure at a constant 14 psi. Since the injected fuel amount depends on injection pulse duration, it is necessary to keep the fuel pressure constant. The fuel pump with a fuel damper is located in the fuel tank. The pump is an electric, vane roller type.

FUEL INJECTOR

Description

The fuel injector is basically a small solenoid valve. As the control unit sends injection signals to the injector, high pressure fuel, which is supplied to the coil built into the injector, pulls the ball valve back and the fuel is injected onto the throttle valve through the nozzle. The amount of injected fuel is controlled by the computer by means of longer or shorter signals (pulse duration) to the injector. A mixture heater is located between the throttle valve and the intake manifold. This is designed and operated for atomizing fuel in the cold engine start condition. The heater is also controlled by the computer. Injectors make a clicking noise when functioning properly.

MIXTURE HEATER

Description

If equipped, the mixture heater is located between the throttle valve and the intake manifold. This is designed and operated for atomizing fuel in the cold engine start condition. The ECU controls the heater.

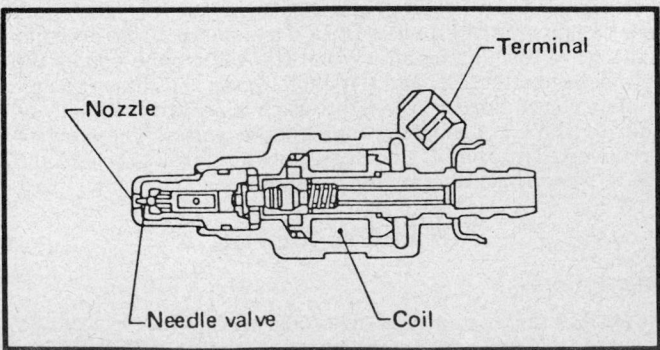

Fuel injector—Nissan with MPFI

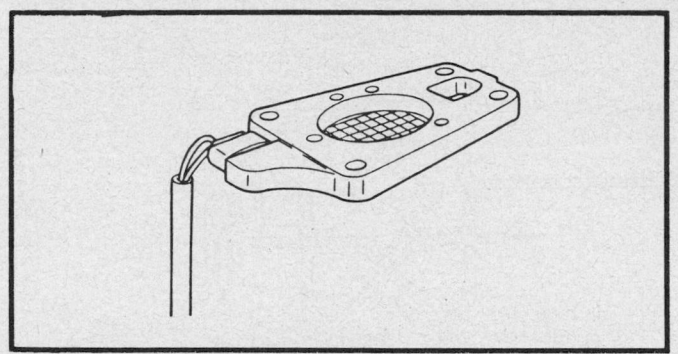

Typical mixture heater—Nissan

IDLE SPEED CONTROL (ISC) VALVE

Description

The idle speed control (ISC) valve is a rotary solenoid valve that receives a pulse signal from the control unit. This pulse signal determines the position of the slider, thereby varying bypass air quantity which raises or lowers the idle speed. The ISC valve has additional functions which include idle-up after cold start (fast idle), idle speed feedback control, idle-up for air conditioner and power steering (fast idle control device) and deceleration vacuum control.

ELECTRONIC CONTROL UNIT (ECU)

Description

The ECU consists of a microcomputer, inspection lamps, a diagnostic mode selector and connectors for signal input and output, and for power supply. The unit has control of the injected fuel amount, ignition timing, mixture ratio feedback, idle speed, fuel pump operation, mixture heating, AIV operation, and EGR and canister purge operation.

SUZUKI/GEO ELECTRONIC FUEL INJECTION (EFI) SYSTEM

General Information

Used in the Suzuki Sidekick and Geo Tracker, the Electronic Fuel Injection (EFI) system supplies the combustion chambers with an air/fuel mixture of optimized ratio under varying driving conditions.

The TBI system consists of a single injector which injects fuel into a throttle body bore. This system consists of 2 major subsystems: An air/fuel delivery system and the electronic control system.

The main components of the air/fuel delivery system consists of the fuel tank, fuel pump, fuel filter, throttle body assembly, fuel feed and return lines, air cleaner and the Idle Speed Control (ISC) solenoid valve.

The electronic control system consists of the Electronic Control Module (ECM), which controls various devices according to signals received from sensors. Functionally, the air/fuel control system is divided into 5 sub-systems. These sub-systems are as follows:

Fuel injection control system
ISC solenoid valve control system
Fuel pump control system
EGR control system (California)
Shift-up indicator light control system, if equipped with manual transmission

Also, vehicles equipped with automatic transmission, the ECM sends a throttle valve opening signal to an automatic transmission control module to control the transmission.

The TBI system includes a self-diagnosis function which is controlled by the ECM. If a fault is detected when the ignition switch is ON and the engine is running, the ECM will response by turning on or flashing the check engine light. The self-diagnosis system includes the following components; however, not all vehicles used every components listed below:

Oxygen Sensor
Water Temperature Sensor (WTS)
Throttle Position Sensor (TPS)
Air temperature sensor (ATS)
Pressure sensor
Ignition signal
EGR system
Idle Switch Circuit
Lock-up Circuit—automatic transmission

5th Switch Circuit—manual transmission only
Central Processing Unit (CPU) of the ECM

When the ignition switch is turned ON and the engine is stopped, the check engine light will light. This is only to check the check engine light bulb and circuit. However, if the self-diagnosis system detects trouble in the EFI system, the ECM will turn ON the check engine light with the engine running to warn the driver of such trouble and at the same time it stroes the trouble area in the ECM backup memory. The check engine light will remain ON as long as the trouble exists but will turn OFF when the normal condition is restored.

The EFI system also includes a fail-safe function. Should a malfunction occur in the EFI system, the ECM will control such functions as the injector, ISC solenoid valve and others on the basic of a standard program pre-stored in the ECM. During a fail-safe condition, the ECM will ignore the failure signal and/or the CPU and thus provide the vehicle with a deminished level of engine performance.

System Operation

When the ignition switch is turn ON, power is supplied to the

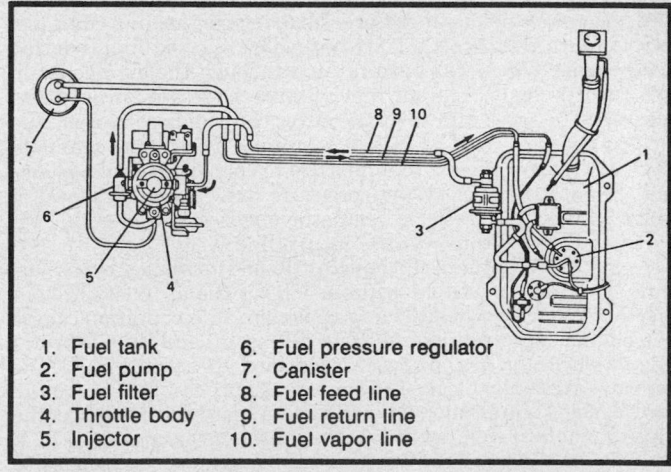

1. Fuel tank
2. Fuel pump
3. Fuel filter
4. Throttle body
5. Injector
6. Fuel pressure regulator
7. Canister
8. Fuel feed line
9. Fuel return line
10. Fuel vapor line

Fuel delivery system schematic—Suzuki/Geo

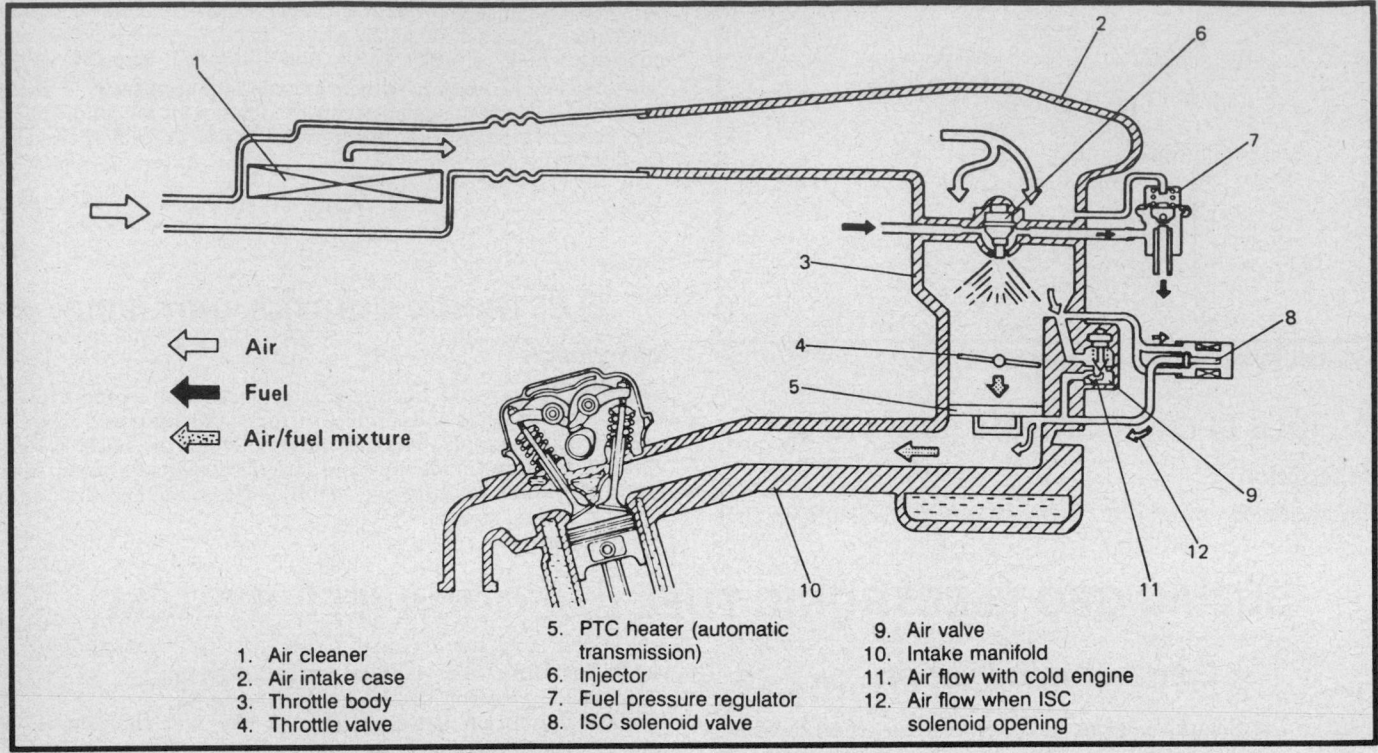

1. Air cleaner
2. Air intake case
3. Throttle body
4. Throttle valve
5. PTC heater (automatic transmission)
6. Injector
7. Fuel pressure regulator
8. ISC solenoid valve
9. Air valve
10. Intake manifold
11. Air flow with cold engine
12. Air flow when ISC solenoid opening

Air ⇦
Fuel ⬅
Air/fuel mixture ⬅

Air and fuel flow schematic—Suzuki/Geo

fuel pump via the fuel pump relay. The fuel pump is activated and the fuel system is pressurized. Simultaneously, an ignition signal is sent from the ignition coil primary circuit. An engine start signal is also sent to the ECM via the engine starter circuit. The ECM uses the engine start signal to determine whether the engine is cranking or not and thus control the fuel injector and fuel pump relay accordingly.

While the engine is cranking, the ECM keeps the Idle Speed Control (ISC) solenoid valve **ON**. This provides the engine with a better start. After the engine has started, the ECM gradually reduces the ISC solenoid valve **ON** time to maintain the specified idle speed.

When the injector (solenoid coil) is energized by the ECM, the needle valve, which is incorporated with the plunger, opens and the injector, which is under pressure, injects fuel in a conic dispersion into the throttle body bore. The injected fuel is mixed with the air which has been filtered through the air cleaner in the throttle body. The air/fuel mixture is drawn through the clearance between the throttle valve, throttle bore and an idle bypass passage into the intake manifold. The intake manifold then distributes the air/fuel mixture to each combustion chamber. Should the fuel system pressure exceed a preset level, a valve in the fuel pressure regulator opens and excess fuel returns to the fuel tank via the return line.

An air valve, located in the throttle body supplies bypass air into the intake manifold without letting the air pass through the throttle valve when the engine is cold. This condition causes the engine speed to increase (fast idle state) and thus provides engine warm-up. As the engine is warmed up, a piston inside the air valve gradually blocks the amount of air passing through the air valve and simultaneously the engine speed is reduced. As the engine coolant temperature reaches approximately 176°F (80°C), the valve is fully open and the engine speed returns to normal idle speed.

The ECM also uses the following signals to compensate for engine speeds and/or fuel injection **ON** time:

Air Conditioning Signal—The ECM uses this signal to determine whether the air conditioner is operating or not and uses it as 1 of the signals for controlling the ISC valve operation.

Battery Voltage—The fuel injector is driven by its solenoid coil based upon the ECM output. However, there is some delay, called "ineffective injection time," which doesn't provide fuel, between the ECM signal and the valve action. The ineffective injection time depends on the battery voltage signal. The ECM takes this information to compensate for fuel injection time.

R, D, 2 or L Range Signal—When in these ranges, the automatic transmission module sends a battery voltage signal to the ECM. The ECM uses this signal as 1 of the signals to control the fuel injector and the ISC solenoid valve.

System Components

ELECTRONIC CONTROL MODULE (ECM)

Description

The ECM consists of a microcomputer, analog/digital converter and an Input/Output unit. The ECM controls the fuel injectors, ISC solenoid valve, fuel pump relay, self-diagnosis and the fail-safe functions.

Removal and Installation

1. Disconnect the negative cable from the battery. Locate the ECM at the underside of the left instrument panel.

2. Remove the retaining bolts from the junction/fuse block. Lower it, as required.

3. Disconnect the connectors from the ECM while releasing the connector locks.

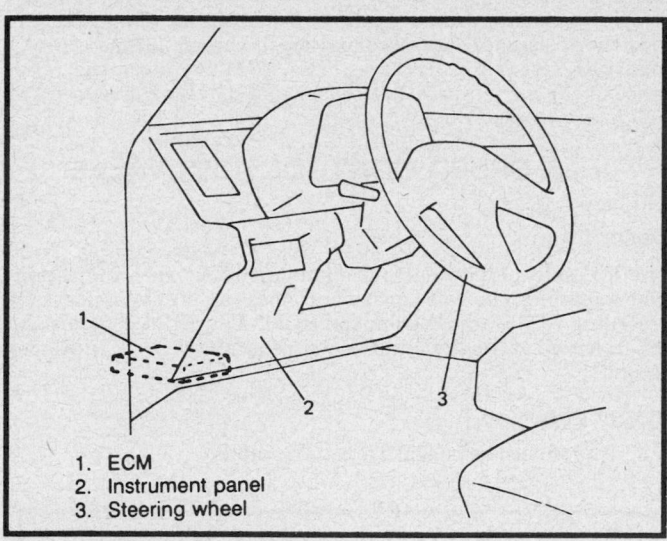

1. ECM
2. Instrument panel
3. Steering wheel

ECM location—Suzuki/Geo

4. Remove the ECM from the vehicle.

To install:

5. Install the ECM to the vehicle and install the electrical connectors securely.

6. Raise the junction/fuse block, as required. Install the retaining bolts.

7. Connect the negative battery cable.

FUEL PUMP

Description

The fuel pump, located in the fuel tank, consists of an armature, magnet, impeller, brush and a check valve. Fuel is drawn into the inlet port of the fuel pump and while under pressure, it is discharged through the outlet port. The fuel pump is also equipped with a check valve to keep the fuel system pressurized when the fuel pump is not operating. The ECM controls fuel pump operation.

THROTTLE BODY

Description

The throttle body consists of the main bore, air and fuel passage, vacuum passage, air induction passage, fuel injector, fuel pressure regulator, throttle valve, air valve and a throttle position sensor.

Removal and Installation

1. Disconnect the negative battery cable.
2. Drain the cooling system.
3. Remove the air intake case, accelerator cable, and the kickdown cable (automatic transmission) from the throttle body.
4. Disconnect and tag all electrical harnesses from the throttle body.
5. Disconnect and tag all vacuum hoses from the throttle body.
6. Remove the water hose from the air valve.
7. Relieve the fuel system pressure.
8. Remove the fuel feed pipe from the throttle body and fuel return hoses from the fuel pressure regulator.
9. Remove the throttle body retaining bolts and remove the throttle body and gasket from the intake manifold. Clean the gasket surfaces.

To install:

10. Install a new gasket on the intake manifold.

11. Position the throttle body on the intake manifold and EGR modulator bracket to the throttle body. Tighten the 4 throttle body retaining bolts 13.5–20 ft. lbs. (18–28 Nm).

12. Install the water hose to the air valve and the fuel return hose to the fuel pressure regulator. Lubricate a new O-ring and install it on the fuel feed pipe. Install the fuel feed pipe to the throttle body.

13. Reconnect the electrical connectors to the injector, TPS and ISC solenoid valve.

14. Reconnect all vacuum hoses to the throttle body and throttle opener.

15. Install the throttle cable to the throttle valve lever and adjust as required. Install the kickdown cable, if it was removed.

16. Install the air intake assembly.

17. Refill the cooling system, connect the negative battery cable, start the engine and check for leaks.

FUEL PRESSURE REGULATOR

Description

The fuel pressure regulator is a diaphragm operated relief valve consisting of a diaphragm, spring and valve. The fuel pressure regulator maintains the fuel pressure to the injector at 25.6 psi (180 kpa) higher than that in the intake manifold at all times. If the pressure increase more than 25.6 psi (180 kpa) higher than the intake manifold pressure, a valve in the regulator opens and excess fuel returns to the fuel tank via the return line.

FUEL INJECTOR

Description

The fuel injector is an electromagnetic type solenoid valve, which injects fuel in the throttle body bore according to a signal from the ECM. The amount of fuel injected at any given time is determined by the length of time (duration) the solenoid coil is energized.

Inspection

1. Disconnect the negative battery cable.
2. Disconnect the injector electrical connector and measure the resistance across the injector. Injector resistance should be 1.0–2.0 ohms at 68°F (20°C).
3. If the resistance reading is not within specification, replace the fuel injector.
4. Reconnect the injector leads and remove the air cleaner assembly without disconnecting the ATS connector.
5. Check that fuel is injected out in a conical shape from the fuel injector when cranking or running the engine.
6. If no fuel is injected, check the wiring harness for continuity and the connector for proper connection.
7. If the fuel in not injected in a conical shape, replace the fuel injector.
8. Check that the fuel injector does not leaks after the engine is stopped. Replace if leakage is visible.
9. Reinstall the air cleaner assembly.

PRESSURE SENSOR

Description

The pressure sensor, consisting of a semi-conductor element, senses pressure changes in the intake manifold and converts it into a signal voltage. As the manifold pressure changes, the electrical resistance of the pressure sensor also changes. The ECM uses the voltage signal from the pressure sensor as one of the signals to control the fuel injectors.

THROTTLE POSITION SENSOR (TPS)

Description

The TPS, connected to the throttle valve shaft, consists of a contact point (idle switch) and a potentiometer which detects throttle valve angle. The throttle position in the idle state is detected by the idle switch, but beyond idle position, it is detected by the output voltage across the the potentiometer. The ECM not only uses the TPS signal to control the injector, but also sends it to the automatic transmission control module, where it is used as 1 of the signals to control the automatic transmission.

Removal and Installation

1. Disconnect the negative battery cable.
2. Remove the air cleaner assembly.
3. Disconnect the TPS electrical connector. Pull out the wire harness terminals from the coupler after unlocking the terminal lock.
4. Remove the TPS from the throttle body.

To install:

5. Fit the TPS to the throttle body in such a way that the sensor adjusting holes are offset slightly counterclockwise from the retaining bolts holes. Then rotate the sensor clockwise so that the sensor adjusting holes align with the mounting bolts holes. Install the retaining bolts finger tight.
6. Connect the TPS connector and check to ensure it is locked securely.
7. Adjust the TPS and tighten the bolts.
8. Reconnect the negative battery cable.

Adjustment

1. Disconnect the negative cable from the battery.
2. Disconnect the throttle opener vacuum hose from the VSV and connect a vacuum pump to the hose.
3. Apply 15 in. Hg of vacuum to the throttle opener to move the throttle valve to the idle position.
4. To close the throttle valve fully, loosen the idle speed adjusting screw, noting the number of turns, until there is clearance between the throttle valve lever and the idle speed adjusting screw. Then, tighten the screw until it just contacts the lever, again noting the number of turns. Subtract the number of turns counted while tightening the screw from that noted previously. The difference represents the number of turns by which the idle speed adjusting screw was actually loosened from the idle position. Use it as a guide when setting it back to the idle position after adjustment.
5. Insert a 0.086 in. (2.2mm) feeler gauge between the throttle valve lever and the idle speed adjusting screw (vehicles equipped with manual transmission). Vehicles equipped with automatic transmission, use a 0.094 in. (2.4mm) feeler gauge.
6. Loosen the TPS retaining bolts and measure the resistance between the terminals.
7. First, turn the TPS fully clockwise and then counterclockwise gradually to find the position where the reading changes from infinity to 0. Then, tighten the TPS retaining bolts to 2.5 ft. lbs. (3.5 Nm).
8. Reconnect the TPS electrical connector and the throttle opener vacuum hose to the VSV.
9. Tighten the idle speed adjusting screw the number of turns recorded in Step 4.
10. Reconnect the negative battery cable. Start the engine and adjust the idle speed.

AIR TEMPERATURE SENSOR (ATS)

Description

The ATS, located on the side of the air cleaner assembly, measures the temperature of the incoming air and converts the air temperature into resistance values. When the air temperature is low, the resistance increases and when the air temperature is high, the resistance decreases. The ECM monitors the resistance of the air temperature sensor and adjusts the amount of fuel injection accordingly.

IDLE SPEED CONTROL (ISC) VALVE

Description

The ISC solenoid regulates the amount of air entering the intake manifold. The valve opens and closes an air bypass passage according to the signal from the ECM. The ECM controls the ISC solenoid valve **ON** and **OFF** time at a rate of 12 times per second.

Inspection

1. Disconnect the negative battery cable.

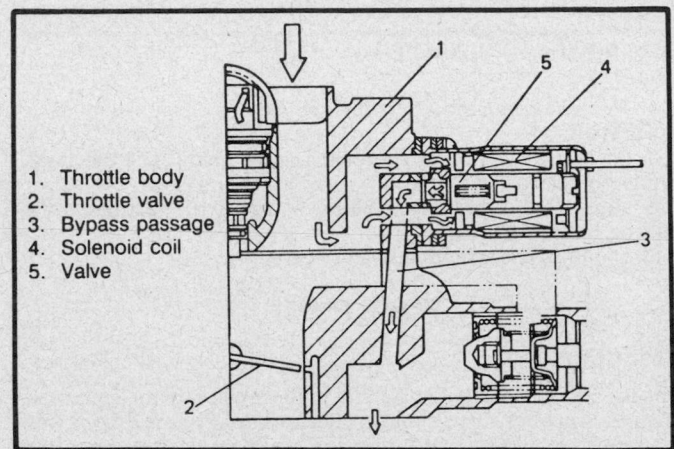

1. Throttle body
2. Throttle valve
3. Bypass passage
4. Solenoid coil
5. Valve

ISC solenoid valve – Suzuki/Geo

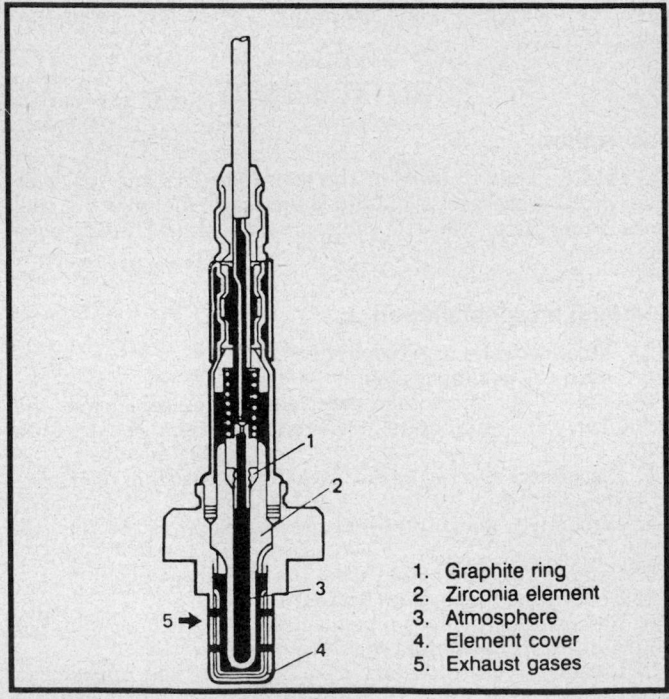

1. Graphite ring
2. Zirconia element
3. Atmosphere
4. Element cover
5. Exhaust gases

Oxygen sensor – Suzuki/Geo

2. Disconnect the ISC solenoid valve connector and measure the resistance across the ISC solenoid valve. The resistance of the ISC solenoid valve should be 5.4–6.6 ohms at 68°F (20°C).

3. If the resistance reading is not within specification, replace the ISC solenoid valve.

4. Reconnect the ISC solenoid valve leads and the negative battery cable.

Removal and Installation

1. Disconnect the negative cable from the battery.

2. Disconnect the ISC solenoid valve connector. Pull out the wire harness terminals from the coupler after unlocking the terminal lock.

3. Remove the ISC solenoid valve and gasket form the throttle body.

NOTE: Do not immersed the ISC solenoid valve in any type of liquid solvent or cleaner, as damage may occur.

To install:

4. Install the ISC solenoid valve to the throttle body using a new gasket. Tighten the ISC solenoid valve retaining screws 2.5 ft. lbs. (3.5 Nm).

5. Connect the ISC solenoid valve connector and check to ensure it is locked securely.

6. Reconnect the negative battery cable.

WATER TEMPERATURE SENSOR (WTS)

Description

The WTS, located at the side of the throttle body, measures the temperature of the engine coolant and signal the ECM with resistance changes. When the coolant temperature is low, the resistance value increases and when the coolant temperature is high, the resistance decreases.

OXYGEN SENSOR

Description

The oxygen sensor, located on the exhaust manifold, detects the concentration of oxygen in the exhaust gases. The sensor zirconia element, generates an electromotive force when a difference in oxygen concentration exists between its faces. A large concentration (lean mixture) difference results in approximately 1 volt and a small difference (rich mixture) results in slightly higher than 0 volt.

TOYOTA COMPUTER CONTROL SYSTEM (TCCS)

FUEL SYSTEM

Description

An electric fuel pump supplies sufficient fuel, under a constant pressure, to the fuel injectors. These injectors inject a metered quantity of fuel into the intake manifold in accordance with signals from the Electronic Control Computer (ECU). Each injector simultaneously injects ½ the fuel required for ideal combustion with each engine revolution.

COLD START INJECTOR

Inspection

1. Unplug the wiring connector on the cold start injector.

2. Using a suitable ohmmeter, check the continuity of both terminals.

3. The ohmmeter reading should be 2–4 ohms, except on the 4Y-EC engine. On the 4Y-EC engine, the resistance should be 3–5 ohms.

4. If the resistance is not as specified, replace the injector.

FUEL INJECTOR

Inspection

1. Unplug the wiring connector on the injector.

2. Using a suitable ohmmeter, check the continuity of both terminals.

3. The ohmmeter reading should be as follows:
   3VZ-E engine—13.8 ohms
   4Y-EC engine—1.1–2.2 ohms
   22R-TE engine—1.6 ohms
   22R-E engine (1986–88)—1.75 ohms
   22R-E engine (1989–90)—13.8 ohms

4. If the resistance is not as specified, replace the injector.

AIR INDUCTION SYSTEM

Description

The air induction system provides sufficient air for the engine

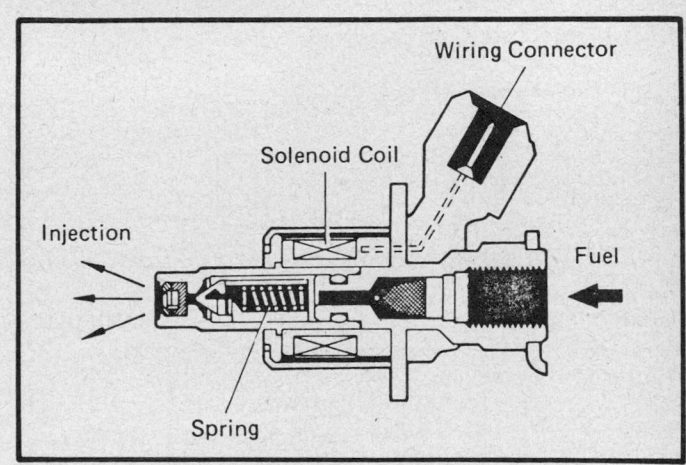

Cold start injector—Toyota

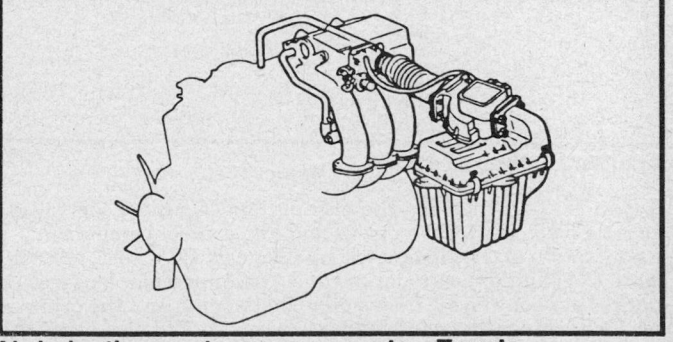

Air induction system components—Toyota

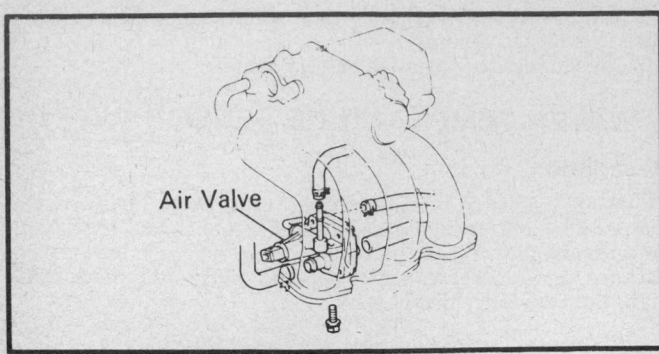

Air valve location—Toyota

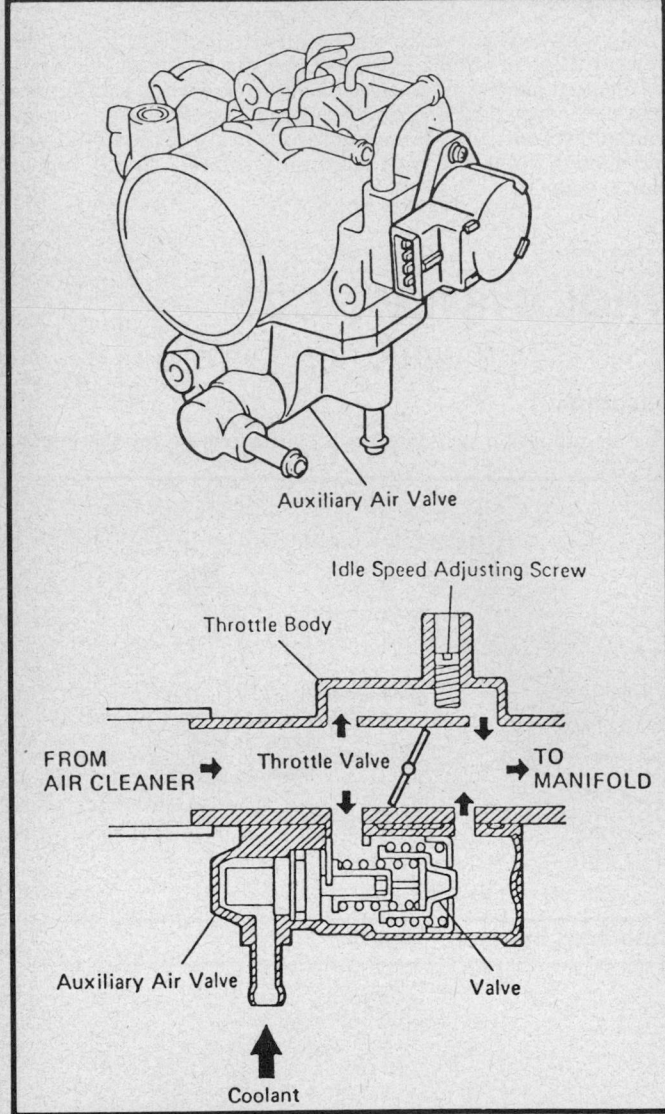

Auxiliary valve—Toyota

operation. This includes the primary and auxiliary air valves, throttle body, air intake device and idle control components.

Seperation of the oil dipstick, oil filler cap, PCV hose, etc. may cause the engine to run out of tune. Disconnection, loosenes or cracks between the air flow meter components and the cylinder head will throw the air induction system off and also cause the engine to run out of tune.

AIR VALVE

Inspection

1986–88 22R-E AND 22R-TE ENGINE

1. With engine coolant temperature below 140°F (60°C), check the engine rpm while pinching the air hose.
2. With the engine cold, the rpm should drop.
3. Allow the engine to reach normal operating temperature.
4. Check engine rpm while pinching the air hose. Engine speed should not drop more than 50 rpm.
5. Using an ohmmeter check the resistance of air valve heating coil.
6. The resistance should be 40–60 ohms, with coolant at normal operating temperature.
7. If the air valve fails any test, replace the valve.

1989–90 22R-E AND 3VX-E ENGINES

1. With engine coolant temperature below 176°F (80°C), check the engine rpm by fully screwing in the idle speed adjusting screw.
2. With the engine cold, the rpm should drop.
3. Allow the engine to reach normal operating temperature.
4. When the idle speed adjusting screw is in, the engine rpm should drop below the idle speed stop.

AUXILIARY AIR VALVE

Description

Some models are equipped with an auxiliary air valve. This air valve operates in the same manner as the main air valve. To remove the auxiliary air valve, the throttle body must first be removed and then the auxiliary air valve can be removed. This valve can be tested in the same manner as the main air valve.

THROTTLE BODY

Removal and Installation

NOTE: Procedures may vary slightly dependent on models and options.

1. Disconnect the negative battery cable.
2. Drain the engine coolant.
3. Disconnect the accelerator cable and throttle cable from the throttle body, if equipped.
4. Remove the air cleaner, air flow meter and air cleaner hose.
5. Disconnect the PCV, vacuum sensing, emission control and water bypass hoses.
6. Disconnect the ISC and TPS connectors.
7. Remove the throttle cable bracket, if equipped.
8. Remove the throttle body retaining bolts.
9. Remove the throttle body.

To install:
10. Install the throttle body with a new gasket.
11. Install the the throttle cable bracket, if equipped.
12. Connect the ISC and TPS connectors.
13. Connect the PCV, vacuum sensing, emission control and water bypass hoses.
14. Install the air cleaner, air flow meter and air cleaner hose.
15. Connect the accelerator cable and throttle cable.
16. Fill the cooling system and connect the negative battery cable.

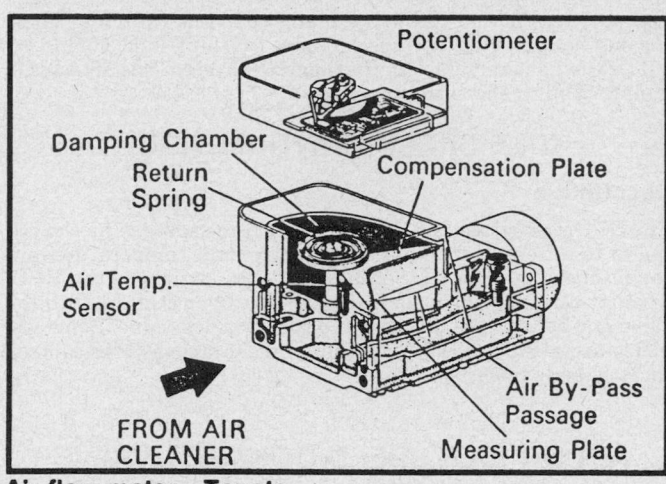

Air flow meter — Toyota

AIR FLOW METER

Removal and Installation

1. Disconnect the negative battery cable.
2. Disconnect the air flow meter connector.
3. Disconnect the vacuum hoses and air cleaner hose. Remove the air cleaner cap, if necessary.
4. Disconnect the air flow meter wiring.
5. Carefully pry off the lock plate in order to gain access to the retaining bolts. Remove the air flow meter retaining bolts and nuts and remove the air flow meter.

To install:

6. Install air flow meter with gasket, lock plate, plate washers and nuts.
7. Install the lock plate on the nut.
8. Install the air cleaner cap and air flow meter assembly.
9. Connect the air flow meter wiring.
10. Connect the negative battery cable.

ELECTRONIC CONTROL SYSTEM

Description

All vehicles are equipped with a Toyota Computer Control System (TCCS) which centrally controls the electronic fuel injection, electronic spark advance, Idle Speed Control (ISC), electronic transmission, if equipped and diagnostics system. The ECU and the TCCS control the following functions:

ELECTRONIC FUEL INJECTION (EFI)

Description

The ECU receives signals from the various sensors indicating changing engine operations conditions such as:

1. Intake air volume
2. Intake air temperature
3. Coolant temperature sensor
4. Engine rpm
5. Acceleration/deceleration
6. Exhaust oxygen content

These signals are utilized by the ECU to determine the injection duration necessary for an optimum air-fuel ratio.

Service Precautions

1. Make sure all EFI harness connectors are fastened securely. A poor connection can cause an extremely high surge voltage in the coil and condenser and result in damage to integrated circuits.

2. Keep the EFI harness at least 4 in. away from adjacent harnesses to prevent an EFI system malfunction due to external electronic feedback.

3. Keep EFI all parts and harnesses dry during service.

4. Before attempting to remove any parts, turn the ignition **OFF** and disconnect the negative battery cable.

5. Always use a 12 volt battery as a power source.

6. Do not disconnect the battery cables with the engine running.

7. Do not depress the accelerator pedal when starting.

8. Do not rev up the engine immediately after starting or just prior to shutdown.

9. Do not apply battery power directly to injectors.

Equipment Mounting Location

The ECU has been designed so that it will not be affected by outside interference. However, the vehicle is equipped with a mobile radio system, it may have an effect on the ECU's performance. The following precautions should be observed to prevent adverse effects:

1. Make sure the antenna mast is located as far from the ECU as possible.

2. Keep the antenna feeder wire at least 8 in. away from the ECU. More precisely, do not wind the antenna feeder cable with any of the wires going to or coming from the ECU.

3. Make sure the radio equipment trimmers are properly adjusted.

4. Ground the equipment directly to the vehicle body only.

5. Do not use powerful mobile radio systems.

6. Do not open the ECU case; if the IC terminals are touched, the IC may be destroyed by static electricity.

ELECTRONIC SPARK ADVANCE (ESA)

Description

The ECU is programmed with data for optimum ignition timing during all operating conditions. Using the data provided by sensors which monitor various engine functions (rpm, intake air volume, coolant temperature, etc.), the microcomputer (ECU) triggers the spark at precisely the right moment.

EGR TEMPERATURE SENSOR

Description

The ECU detects the coolant temperature and controls the EGR operations accordingly. The EGR sensor is available on California vehicles.

Inspection

1. Unplug the wiring connector on the sensor.

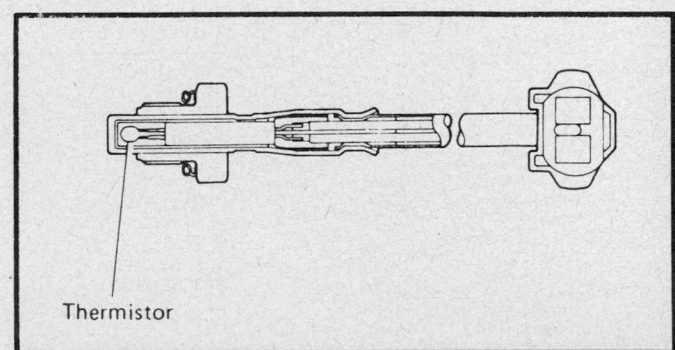

Thermistor

EGR gas temperature sensor — Toyota (California)

2. Using a suitable ohmmeter, check the continuity between the terminals.

3. The ohmmeter reading should be as follows:
69.40–88.50 ohms – 112°F (50°C)
11.89–14.37 ohms – 212°F (100°C)
2.79–3.59 ohms – 302°F (150°C)

4. If the resistance is not as specified, replace the sensor.

FAIL-SAFE AND BACK-UP FUNCTIONS

Description

When an abnormality occurs in any of the ECU input signals, the ECU substitutes nominal values stored in the microcomputer's memory to provide enough driveability to keep the vehicle moving. In the event of serious problems, the ECU may stop the engine.

SELF-DIAGNOSIS

Description

The ECU contains a built-in self diagnosis system by which troubles with the engine signal the engine signal network are detected. The check engine light on the instrument panel informs the driver that a malfunction has been detected. The light goes out automatically when the malfunction has been cleared.

The check engine warning light will come on when the igni-

tion switch is placed **ON** and the engine is not running. When the engine is started, the check engine warning light should go out. If the light remains on, the diagnosis system has detected a malfunction in the system.

IDLE SPEED CONTROL (ISC)

Description

The ECU is programmed with specific engine speed values to respond to different engine conditions (coolant temperature, air conditioner on/off, etc.). Sensors transmit signals to the ECU which controls the flow of air through the bypass of the throttle valve and adjusts the idle speed to the specified value. Some vehicles use a ISC valve while others use an air valve to control throttle body bypass air flow.

AIR OR IDLE SPEED CONTROL VALVE

Removal and Installation

1. Remove the throttle body.
2. Remove the ISC valve screws and remove the ISC valve and gasket.

To install:
3. Install a gasket and the ISC valve to the throttle body.
4. Install the throttle body.

VOLKSWAGEN DIGIFANT SYSTEM

General Information

Using a single control unit, all of the functions of the fuel system, ignition system and oxygen sensor system are controlled to provide optimum mixture and ignition control for improved acceleration, deceleration and driveability.

The Digifant system features a 50mm throttle bore and an idle stabilization system to eliminate the need for a digital idle

stabilizer or auxiliary air regulation. Electronic fuel injection control is based on the measurement of air entering the air intake and engine speed measured by the Hall sender. The coolant temperature sensor provides for correction during cold engine running.

The oxygen sensor, intake air temperature sensor and throttle switch provide the control unit with the required additional measurements to ensure smooth performance under all driving conditions. A seperate control unit is used for the idle stabiliza-

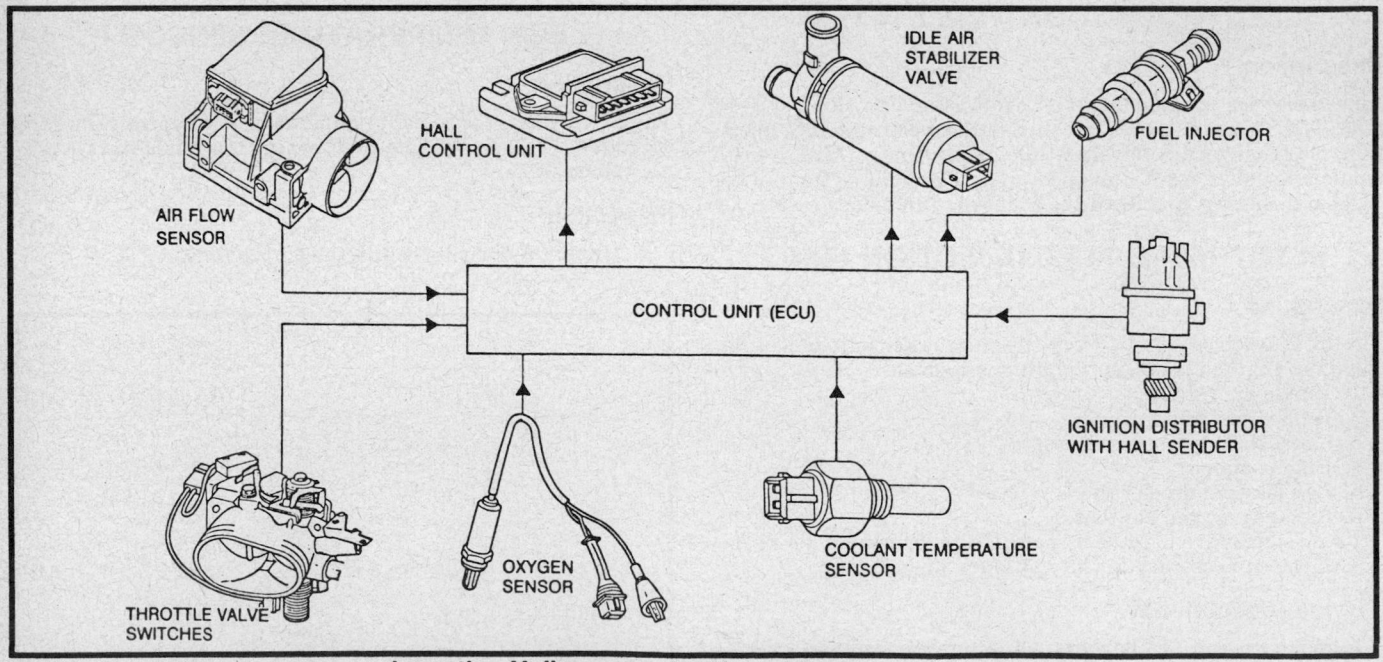

Engine management system schematic – Volkswagen Digifant system

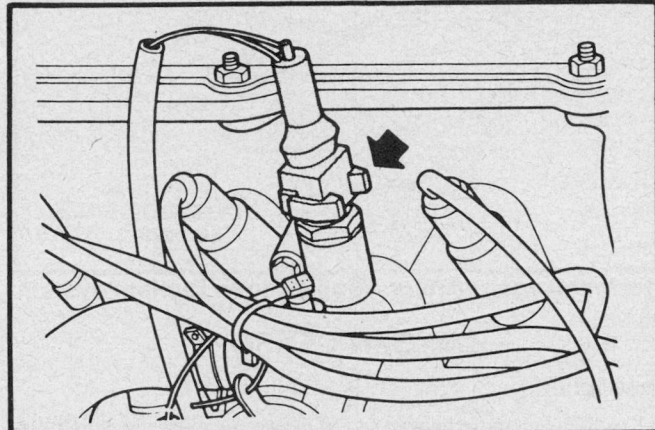

Coolant temperature sensor—Volkswagen Digifant system

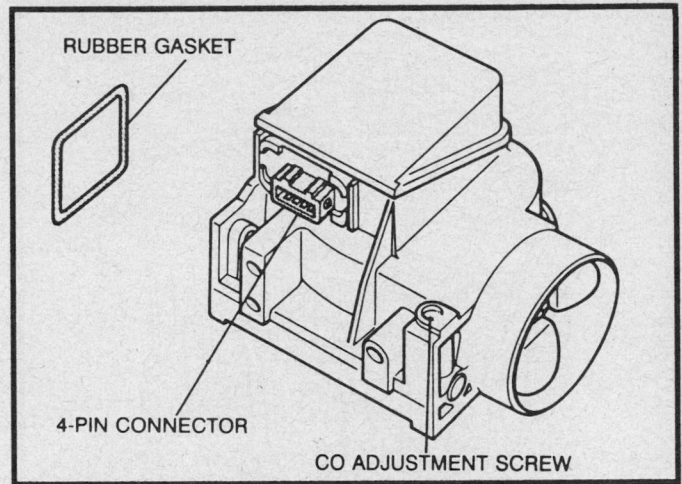

Air flow sensor—Volkswagen Digifant system

tion valve. Ignition timing control is determined by engine speed signal from the Hall sender and a load signal from the air sensor.

System Components

ELECTRONIC CONTROL UNIT (ECU)

Description

The ECU used with the Digifant system incorporates all the functions of the fuel system and ignition system and provides both the actuation signals for the injectors and optimum ignition timing point for all engine operating conditions. Injection duration opening signals are provided based on the following inputs:

  Engine speed
  Intake air volume
  Coolant temperature
  Oxygen content in the exhaust gas
  Battery voltage
  Throttle position
  Intake air temperature

COOLANT TEMPERATURE SENSOR

Description

This sensor is a negative coefficient resistor. The resistance signal it produces is utilized by the ECU to determine the amount of cold start and warm-up enrichment, ignition advance and idle stabilization when the different sensor's functions are activated. The resistance of the sensor should decrease as the temperature of its thermistor increases.

FUEL PUMP

Description

The electronic fuel pump is a roller cell design. Centrifugal force seals the rollers against the walls of the pressure chamber as the rotor spins. Fuel that is trapped between the rollers is pressurized and forces out the delivery port. The pump is designed to be cooled and lubricated by the fuel flowing through it. The pump constantly delivers more fuel than is needed by the engine. Excess fuel is returned to the fuel tank by the fuel regulator.

The regulator also maintains a constant pressure to the injectors. It responds to intake manifold fluctuations and compensates different engine load requirement. When the engine is shut off, the regulator seals the system and maintains a residual pressure to provide for good start up.

FUEL INJECTORS

Description

Digifant fuel injectors are electronically controlled on/off valves. A solenoid activates a needle valve allowing fuel to be forces out the nozzle. All 4 injectors open at the same time and inject fuel directly into the intake manifold near the intake valve. Injection quantity is controlled by the amount of time the injectors stay open. The resistance between the injector's terminals should be 14–18 ohms.

Digifant injectors with a yellow body are not interchangeable with injectors from other non-compatible Volkswagen injection systems.

Inspection

SPRAY PATTERN TEST

1. Remove the fuel injectors in pairs (left bank or right bank). Leave the wires connected to the injectors.
2. Disconnect the other 2 injectors which were not disconnected.
3. Hold the injectors in suitable open container with a paper towel on the bottom.
4. Operate the starter briefly. The spray patterm must be neatly coneshaped. If not, replace the faulty injector.
5. Reinstall the injectors using new O-rings.
6. Repeat the test with the other injectors.

LEAK TEST

1. Disconnect all of injectors.
2. Remove 1 pair of injectors, still connected to the fuel rail, from the manifold.
3. Turn the ignition **ON** for about 5 seconds to pressurize the system.
4. If more than 2 drops of fuel leaks from any injector in 1 minute, replace the injector.
5. Repeat the test with the other pair of injectors.

Air Flow Sensor

Description

The air flow sensor measures the amount of air entering the intake manifold and sends a voltage signal to the ECU accordingly. Intake air opens the air flow sensor flap which actuates a potentiometer to determine the voltage signal. This signal and the engine speed signal are used as principal parameters to determine the injector opening duration and ignition timing. com-

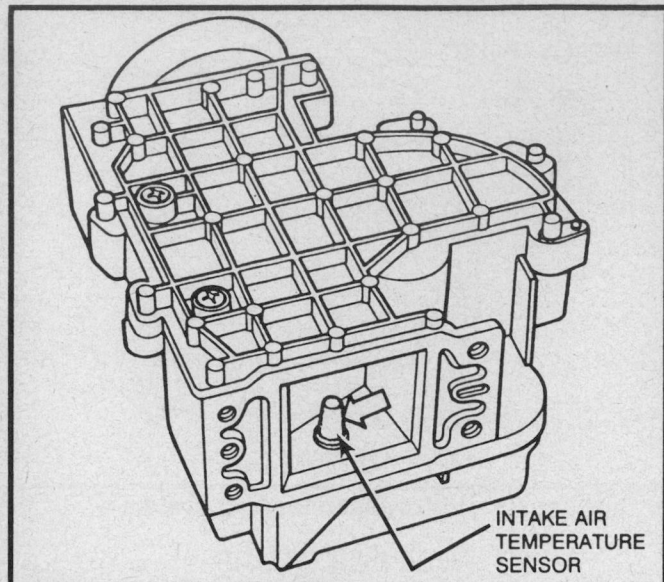

Intake air temperature sensor—Volkswagen Digifant system

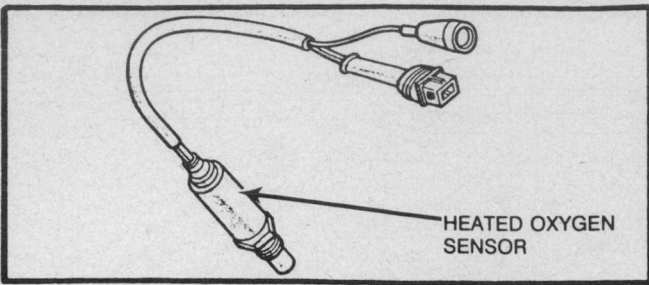

Heated oxygen sensor—Volkswagen Digifant system

pensation flap connected to the air sensor dampens sudden movement of the air sensor flap due to changes in intake air.

INTAKE AIR SENSOR

Description

This sensor is mounted in the air flow sensor housing. Like the coolant temperature sensor, this sensor is a negative coefficient resistor. The resistance signal it produces is utilized by the ECU to modify the fuel injection rate depending on intake air temperature. The resistance of the sensor should decrease as the temperature of its thermistor increases.

THROTTLE SWITCH

Description

Digifant uses a single throttle switch to signal the ECU when the throttle plate fully closed at idle or fully open. The signal enables the ECU to determine that 1 of 3 auxiliary functions (idle stabilization, deceleration fuel shut-off or full load enrichment) is required and activates the appropriate circuit.

The throttle switch is normally open unless actuated. The contact arm is actuated by a cam with 2 eccentrics which attach to the throttle plate shaft. One eccentric closes the the contacts when the plate is closed and the other fulfills the duty at wide open throttle.

Adjustment

1. Loosen the allen head retaining screw slightly.
2. Open the throttle and allow it to slowly return closed.
3. Measure the switch point with a feeler gauge between the the idle stop and idle stop screw. At the point where the switch contact closes, the gap must be 0.002–0.004 in.
4. If not within specification, adjust the position of the switch using the allen head cam screw. Do not tamper with the idle stop screw.
5. Tighten the retaining screw.
6. Connect an ohmmeter to the throttle switch terminals. With the switch must be open at all points except throttle closed and throttle wide open.

OXYGEN SENSOR

Description

The oxygen sensor is comprised of a ceramic material called Zirconium dioxide. The inner and outer surfaces of the ceramic is coated with platinum. The outer platinum surface is exposed to the exhaust gases, while the inside surface is exposed to outside air.

The difference in the amount of oxygen contacting the inner and outer surfaces of the sensor create a pressure differential which results in a small voltage signal ranging from 175–1100mV supplied to the ECU. The amount of voltage supplied is determined by the fuel mixture.

The oxygen sensor is electrically heated to keep it at a constant operating temperature. This ensures continuously accurate sensor reaction regardless of the surrounding conditions. The heated oxygen sensor has 3 leads: 2 for heating it and a signal wire to the ECU. Power is supplied to the heating element all the time when the ignition is on.

Inspection

1. Start the engine, bring it up to operating temperature and allow it to idle for 2 minutes. Hook up an emissions machines or CO reader to the vehicle.
2. Remove and plug the hose from the pressure regulator.
3. The CO should increase briefly, then drop to 0.1–0.3%. If not, proceed to determine whether the problem exists in the oxygen sensor or elsewhere.
4. Turn the engine off and disconnect the oxygen sensor.
5. Restart the engine. Connect the oxygen sensor signal wire to ground. The CO content should rise.
6. If it does not, check the wiring. If no other problems are detected, replace the oxygen sensor.

IDLE STABILIZATION

Description

This system ensures that the idle speed will remain constant at the predetermined level. The system controls the amount of air bypassing the throttle plate. If engine idle speed varies from the value stored in the control unit, the idle stabilizer valve will adjust the volume of air induced into the engine at idle. This action maintains idle speed within certain limits.

The idle stabilizer valve is operated by a control unit located in the engine compartment near the air cleaner intake duct. The control unit receives input values from the following components:

    Throttle switch
    Coolant temperature sensor
    Air condition compressor clutch
    Ignition coil terminal No. 1
    Automatic transmission selector switch
    Power steering pressure switch

Since the idle speed is now automatically adjusted, other regulatory systems are not needed and periodic adjustment is accomplished electronically.

MANUAL STEERING GEAR

MANUAL STEERING—TROUBLESHOOTING

Condition	Cause	Correction
Steering wheel operation is hard (insufficient power assist)	Air in fluid line	Bleed the system
	Twisted or damaged hoses	Correct the hose routing or replace the hoses
	Fluid leakage	Repair or replace
	Malfunction of gear box	Check and replace the gear box if necessary
	Malfunction of oil pump	Check the oil pump pressure and repair oil pump
Rattling noise	Loose installation of oil pump or gear box	Retighten the oil pump or gear box
	Loose oil pump pulley nut	Retighten the oil pump pulley nut
	Interference around column or between pressure hose and other parts	Correct or replace the pressure hose and the parts around the column
	Abnormal noise inside of gear box and oil pump	Replace the gear box or oil pump
Shrill noise	Air sucked into oil pump	Check the oil level and hose clips, bleed the system or replace the oil pump
	Oil pump seizure	Replace the oil pump
Squealing noise	Loose belt	Adjust the belt deflection
	Oil pump seizure	Replace the oil pump
Hissing noise	Air sucked into oil pump	Check the oil level and hose clips, bleed the system
	Damaged to the olive of the gear box port section	Replace the gear box
	Malfunction of return hose	Replace the hose
Droning noise	Loose mounting bolt on oil pump or oil pump bracket	Retighten the pump bracket or pump mounting bolt
	Poor condition of oil pump body	Replace the oil pump
Squeaking noise	Malfunction of steering stopper contact	Check and adjust the steering stopper
	Interference of wheel with vehicle body	Adjust the steering angle
	Malfunction of gear box	Replace the gear box
Oil leakage from hose connection	Improperly tightened flare nut Incorrectly inserted hose Improperly clamped hose	Check and repair or replace
Oil leakage from hose assembly	Damaged or clogged hose Hose connector malfunction	Replace
Oil leakage from reservoir	Improperly welded pipe	Weld the pipes or replace
	Overflow	Bleed the system or adjust the oil level
Oil leakage from oil pump	Malfunction oil pump housing	Replace the oil pump
	Malfunction of O-ring and/or oil seal	Replace the O-ring and oil seal
Oil leakage from gear box	Malfunction of gear box housing (including leakage from air hole)	Replace the gear box
	Malfunction of O-ring and/or oil seal	Replace the O-ring and oil seal

CHRYSLER IMPORT/MITSUBISHI

Recirculating Ball and Nut

Disassembly and Assembly

1. Place the gear assembly in a suitable holding fixture and record the total mainshaft starting torque.
2. Remove the breather plug and drain the gear oil.
3. Remove the upper cover mounting bolts.
4. Loosen the locknut of the adjusting bolt and screw in the the adjusting bolt a couple of turns.
5. Place the mainshaft and the cross-shaft in a center position. Tap the bottom of the cross-shaft with the proper tool to remove the cross-shaft and the upper cover.

NOTE: Do not damage the cross-shaft oil seal.

6. Turn the adjusting bolt and separate the upper cover and the cross-shaft. Keep the spacer.
7. Remove the end cover and the mainshaft adjusting shims. Keep the adjusting shims.
8. Remove the mainshaft assembly and the bearings from the gear housing.

NOTE: Do not disassemble the mainshaft and the ball nut assembly.

9. Remove the cross-shaft and mainshaft oil seal using a suitable pry tool.
10. Inspect all the parts for damage and excessive wear. Check the operation of the ball nut and the mainshaft for a smooth rotation.

NOTE: Do not attempt to move the ball nut to either end of the mainshaft fully.

To assemble:

11. Check the pitman arm for damage or deformation and check the ball stud for looseness.
12. If the ball joint starting torque is below the lower limit, the pitman arm can be reused as long there is no play and it turns smoothly.
13. Lubricate the cross-shaft and mainshaft oil seals and install using the proper tool.
14. Secure the gear housing in a suitable holding device and insert the mainshaft assembly into the gear housing. Hold the mainshaft horizontally.
15. Install the gasket, shim(s) and the end cover to the housing. Tighten the locknut to 11–14 ft. lbs.
16. Measure the mainshaft starting torque with the proper tool. The measured value should be 3–5 inch lbs. except 1986 Ram 50 and 3.1–4.7 inch lbs. on 1986 Ram 50.
17. Adjust the value by increasing or decreasing the assembled thickness of the adjusting shim(s).

18. Remove the end cover and apply a proper sealer to the mating surfaces of the gear housing and the end cover.
19. Reassemble the adjusting shim and the end cover.
20. Mount the adjusting spacer onto the adjusting bolt and insert the adjusting bolt into the "T" groove in the cross-shaft.
21. Measure the gap between the "T" groove in the cross-shaft

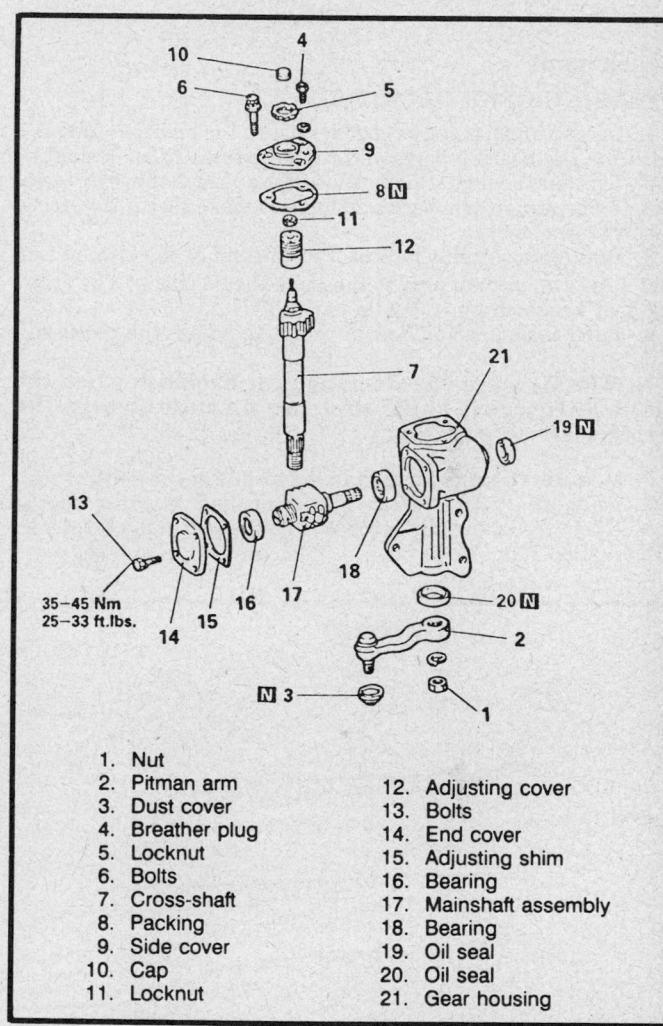

1. Nut	12. Adjusting cover
2. Pitman arm	13. Bolts
3. Dust cover	14. End cover
4. Breather plug	15. Adjusting shim
5. Locknut	16. Bearing
6. Bolts	17. Mainshaft assembly
7. Cross-shaft	18. Bearing
8. Packing	19. Oil seal
9. Side cover	20. Oil seal
10. Cap	21. Gear housing
11. Locknut	

Exploded view of the manual steering gear—except 1986 Ram 50

and the adjusting bolt. The measurement should be 0.002 in. or less.

22. Adjust by using the proper thickness of spacer.

23. Apply a suitable sealer to the adjusting bolt threads in the cross-shaft and install the upper cover onto the cross-shaft.

24. Install the cross-shaft and the packing to the gear housing and tighten the upper cover to 18–25 ft. lbs.

NOTE: Do not apply any sealer to the breather plug mounting hole.

25. Refill the gear assembly with the proper gear oil.

Adjustments

STEERING GEAR BACKLASH

1. Inject a small amount of gear oil into the breather plug and lubricate the bearing parts and the gear teeth of each shaft.

2. Tighten the adjusting bolt until it engages the gear teeth. Rotate the pitman arm back and forth to make sure it is engaged with the gear teeth.

3. Position a suitable indicator at the end of the pitman arm and move the pitman arm to measure the backlash. The steering gear backlash limit is 0.02 in.

4. Turn the adjusting bolt in or out to adjust the backlash.

NOTE: Measure the steering gear backlash when the mainshaft, cross-shaft and the pitman arm in the straight ahead position.

5. Measure the mainshaft starting torque at the neutral position using the proper tool. The mainshaft starting torque should be, 7.7–8.6 inch lbs. except 1986 Ram 50 and 5.6-7.4 inch lbs. on 1986 Ram 50.

Manual Rack and Pinion

Disassembly and Assembly

1. Place the rack assembly in a suitable holding fixture.

2. Loosen the locknut and remove the tie rod end.

3. Lift the tab washer using a suitable tool and remove the tie rod from the rack assembly.

4. Remove the locknut, adjusting cover and remove the rack support from the housing.

5. Remove the dust cover, oil seal, snapring and remove the pinion with the bearing attached, from the housing.

6. Remove the rack from the gear housing in the proper direction.

NOTE: If the rack is pulled out in the wrong direction, the bushing in the gear assembly may be damaged by the rack threads.

7. Remove the stopper ring and using the proper tool, press out the rack bushing from the gear housing.

8. Inspect the rack support, pinion teeth, bearings and the rack bushing for any excessive wear or damage.

9. Pack the rack bushing with a suitable multi-purpose grease.

10. Align the rack bushing retainer with the hole in the gear housing. Match the stopper ring peak with the hole in the housing. Install the rack bushing with the proper tool.

11. Install the rack in the gear housing from the proper direction.

12. Apply a suitable multi-purpose grease to the rack serrations an the surfaces contacting the rack bushing.

13. Install the pinion with the bearing attached in the housing and replace the snapring oil seal and the dust cover.

14. Install the rack support and tighten the locknut to 29–43 ft. lbs.

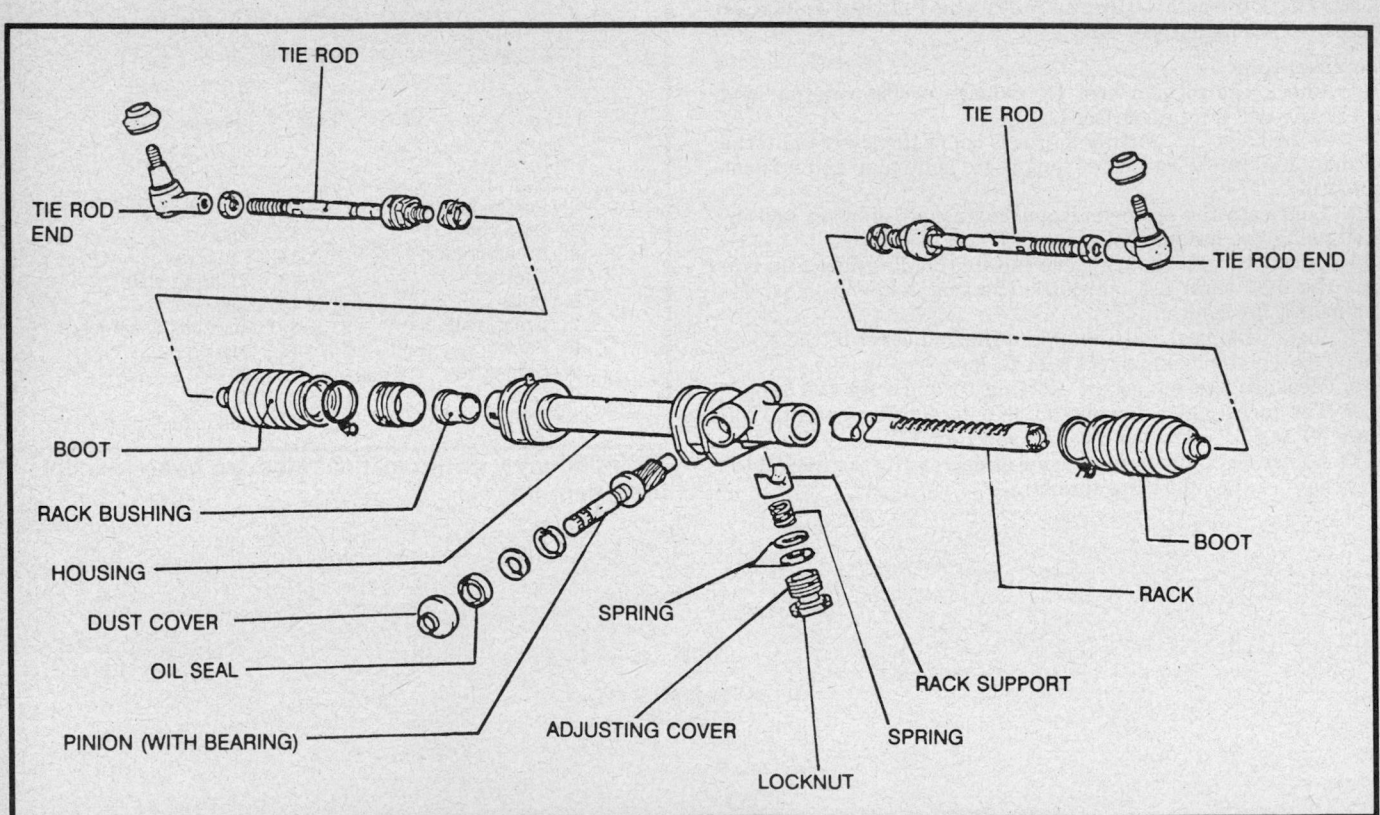

Exlpoded view manual rack and pinion – Chrysler/ Mitsubishi

15. Tighten the adjuster cover to 7 ft. lbs. Rotate the pinion at a rate of 1 turn in 4–6 seconds using the proper tool and measure the pinion torque.

16. The torque should be 5–10 inch lbs. Turn the adjuster cover to reach the specifications. Install the locknut.

17. Measure the total pinion torque rotating 180 degrees in both directions from the neutral position.

18. Adjust the total pinion torque to the highest setting within specifications.

19. Install the tie rod to the rack using the proper tool. Replace the wire clamp to lock the boot in position.

20. Install the tie rod end so that the left and right lengths are 7.0 in. from the edge of the boot to the edge of the locknut. Tighten the locknut to 47–58 ft. lbs.

Adjustments

Total Pinion Torque

1. Using the proper tool, rotate the pinion at a speed of one rotation in 4–6 seconds. Measure the total pinion torque.

2. Remove the boots from the gear housing and turn the pinion 180 degrees in either direction from the neutral position to measure.

3. Adjust to 5–10 inch lbs.

Bevel Gear

Disassembly and Assembly

1. Secure the gear assembly in a proper holding fixture.
2. Remove the locknut using the proper tool.
3. Remove the front cover mounting bolts, adjusting bolt and remove the front cover.
4. Remove the locknut and loosen the rear cover with the proper tool, until the input gear separates from the output gear.
5. Remove both the input gear and the output gear from the housing.
6. Inspect the gear teeth, bearings and the dust cover for any cracks or excessive damage.
7. Install the input and the output gear into the gear housing so that the teeth mesh properly.
8. Tighten the rear cover, using the proper tool. Replace the locknut and tighten to 47–87 ft. lbs. depending on which tool was used.
9. Install the front cover and replace the mounting bolts. Tighten to 12–19 ft. lbs.
10. Install the adjusting bolt and replace the locknut and tighten to 12–19 ft. lbs.

Adjustments

OUTPUT GEAR ROTATIONAL TORQUE

1. Turn the output gear, using the proper tool, at a speed of one rotation every 4–6 seconds. Measure the rotational torque.

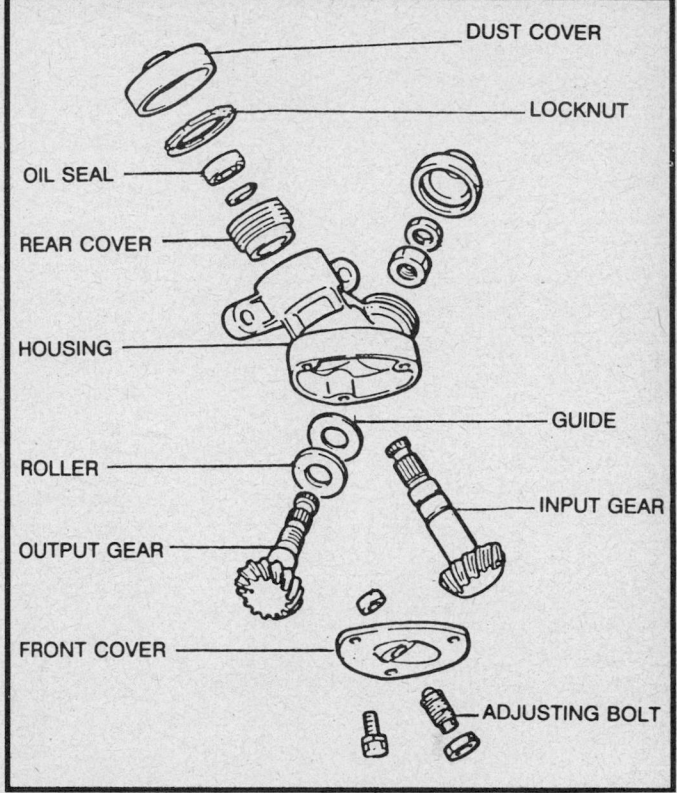

Exploded view of the bevel gear assembly—Chrysler/Mitsubishi

2. Adjust the nut so that the output side gear rotational torque is 0.4–0.9 inch lbs.

3. Tighten the locknut to 47–87 ft. lbs., depending on which tool was used.

TOTAL BEVEL GEAR ROTATIONAL TORQUE

1. Turn the input gear, using the proper tool, at a speed of one rotation every 4–6 seconds. Measure the rotational torque.

NOTE: Return the adjustment bolt to a position where there is no contact with the input side gear.

2. Using the proper tool, tighten the rear cover assembly so that the input side gear rotational torque is 2.2–3.9 inch lbs.

3. Tighten the adjustment bolt so that the total bevel gear rotational torque is 2.6–4.8 inch lbs.

4. Install the locknut and tighten to 47–87 ft. lbs., depending on which tool was used.

ISUZU

Recirculating Ball

Disassembly and Assembly

1. Secure the gear in a suitable holding fixture. Remove the locknut on the side cover.

2. Turn the adjusting screw counterclockwise and remove the side cover mounting bolt.

3. Turn the adjusting screw clockwise with the side cover kept from turning and remove the side cover.

4. Remove the gasket, adjusting screw and adjusting shim.

5. Hold the sector shaft in the straight ahead position and remove it from the gear assembly. Do not remove the sector shaft from the gear assembly with a hammer or any impact tools.

6. Remove the locknut using the proper tool.

7. Remove the end cover using the proper tool and remove the oil seal and O-ring.

8. Remove the ball nut and wormshaft assembly. Hold it in the horizontal position so that the ball nut will not slide out.

9. Remove the bearings, oil seal and the bushing

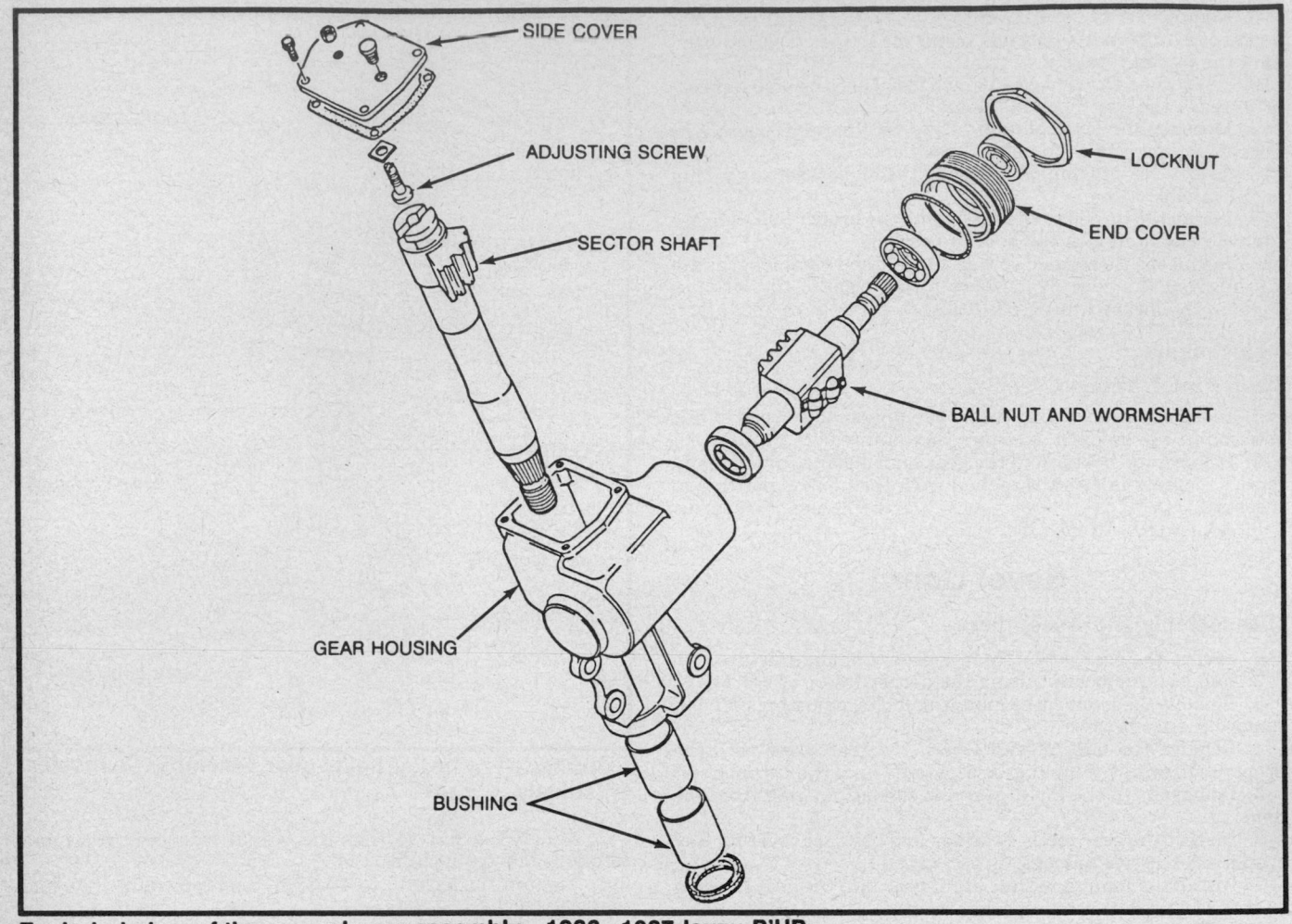

SIDE COVER

ADJUSTING SCREW

SECTOR SHAFT

LOCKNUT

END COVER

BALL NUT AND WORMSHAFT

GEAR HOUSING

BUSHING

Exploded view of the manual gear assembly—1986– 1987 Isuzu P'UP

10. Inspect the parts for any wear or excessive damage.

11. Install the bushing, oil seal and the bearings into the gear housing, using the proper tool.

12. Install the ball nut and the wormshaft assembly, while holding in the horizontal position.

13. Replace the oil seal and the O-ring. Install the end cover.

NOTE: Tape the splines to prevent damage to the oil seal.

14. Adjust the bearing preload with the proper tool to 0.22–0.43 ft. lbs.

15. Replace the locknut and tighten to 116–145 ft. lbs. Recheck the bearing preload.

16. Install the sector shaft by aligning the center tooth of the ball nut with that of the sector shaft.

17. Adjust the clearance to 0.004 in. and check that the adjusting screw turns freely. There are 5 different thickness adjusting shims available.

18. Install the side cover using the proper sealer applied to the mounting surfaces and replace the locknut. Tighten to 14–22 ft. lbs.

Adjustments

BACKLASH PRELOAD

1. Position the sector shaft in a straight ahead position.

2. Turn the adjusting screw to 0.36–0.72 ft. lbs. on the P'UP and 0.22–0.43 ft. lbs. except the P'UP.

3. Lock the adjusting screw with the locknut and tighten to 14–22 ft. lbs.

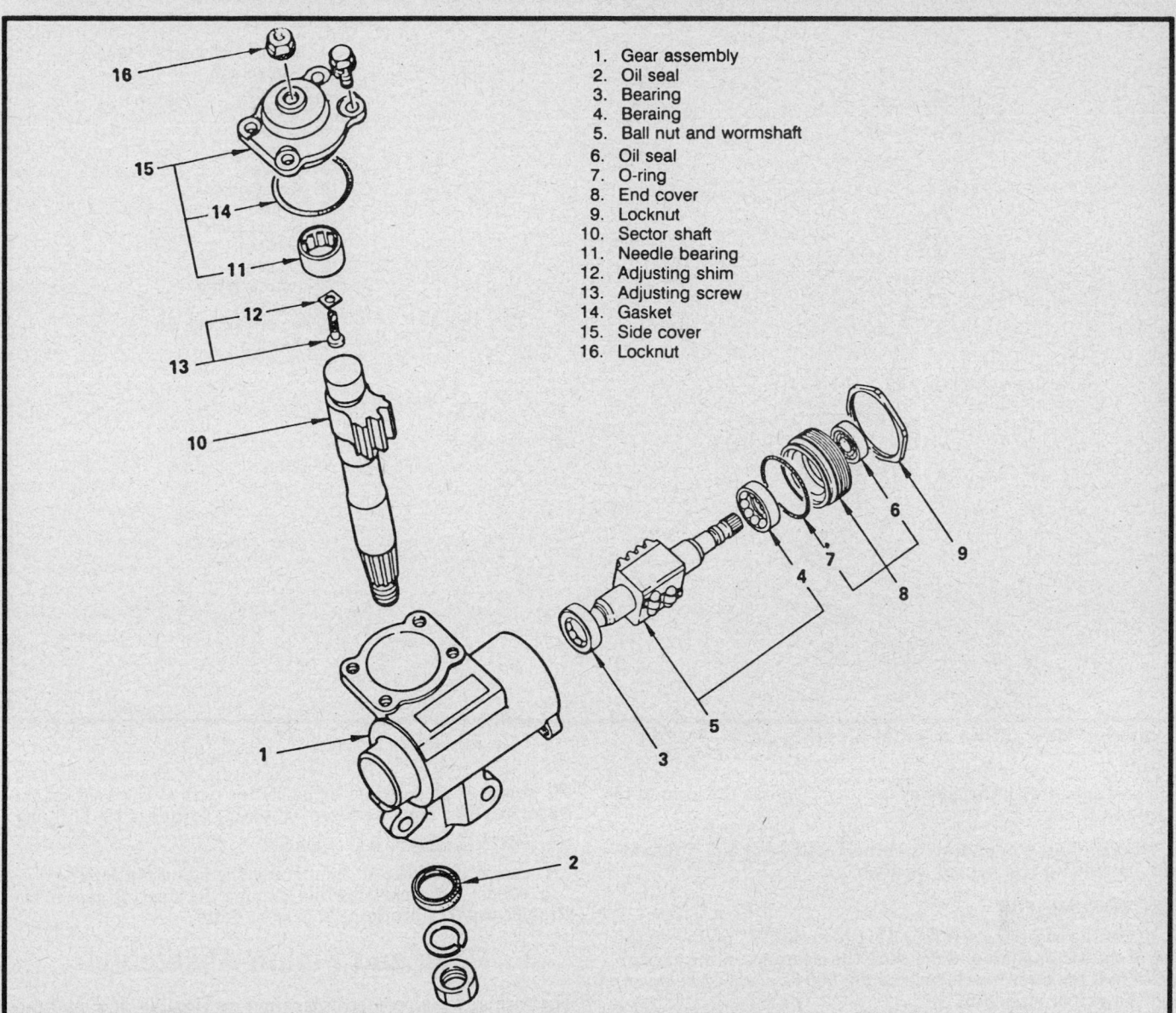

1. Gear assembly
2. Oil seal
3. Bearing
4. Beraing
5. Ball nut and wormshaft
6. Oil seal
7. O-ring
8. End cover
9. Locknut
10. Sector shaft
11. Needle bearing
12. Adjusting shim
13. Adjusting screw
14. Gasket
15. Side cover
16. Locknut

Exploded view of the manual gear assembly— except1986–1987 Isuzu P'UP

MAZDA

Recirculating Ball and Nut

Disassembly and Assembly

1. Secure the gear assembly in a suitable holding fixture. Remove the pitman arm nut and washer and remove the pitman arm using a suitable puller, then remove the seal.
2. Remove the locknut and bolt, then remove the side cover and gasket.
3. Remove the adjusting shim and adjusting screw, then pull out the sector shaft while keeping it in the middle position.
4. Remove the locknut with the proper tool.
5. Remove the oil seal and the adjusting nut with the proper tool.

6. Remove the bearing then the worm ball nut and the bearing at the end of the ball nut.
7. Clean all the parts and check for any damage or excessive wear. Check the rotation of the ball nut assembly to be free of any binding.
8. Apply grease or oil to the lips of all oil seals.
9. Installation is the reverse of the removal procedure.

Adjustments
WORMSHAFT PRELOAD

Preload of the worm ball nut is 0.7–1.3 lbs., using a pull scale (without sector). If an adjustment is to be made loosen the lock-

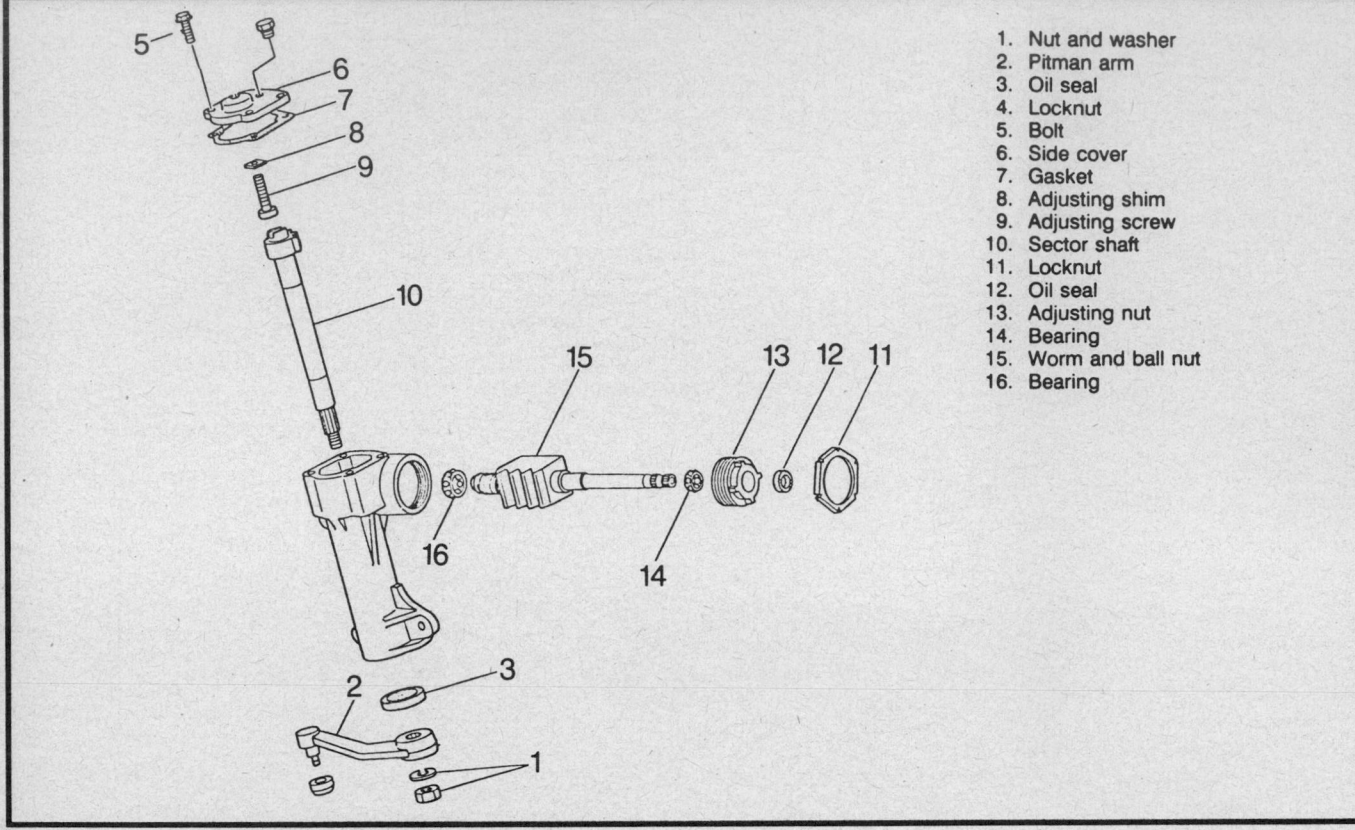

1. Nut and washer
2. Pitman arm
3. Oil seal
4. Locknut
5. Bolt
6. Side cover
7. Gasket
8. Adjusting shim
9. Adjusting screw
10. Sector shaft
11. Locknut
12. Oil seal
13. Adjusting nut
14. Bearing
15. Worm and ball nut
16. Bearing

Exploded view of the manual steering gear—Mazda

nut and adjust with the adjusting screw. Tighten the locknut to 116–144 ft. lbs.

NOTE: The wormshaft preload will be 1.3–2.4 lbs. after installing the sector shaft.

SECTOR SHAFT

1. Set the adjusting screw and shim, in the "T" groove on the top of the sector shaft and measure the clearance in the axial direction. If the clearance is more than 0.004 in., adjust by selecting the proper size shim.
2. When installing the sector shaft, make sure the teeth of

the sector shaft mesh with the center part of the teeth of the worm ball nut. The side cover tightening torque is 12–17 ft. lbs.

STEERING GEAR BACKLASH

1. Adust the backlash by turning the adjusting screw.
2. Adjust the backlash while keeping the steering gear in the straight forward position. Backlash: 0mm

Rack and Pinion Assembly

The rack and pinion assembly is not serviceable. If a malfunction occurs, replace with a new unit.

NISSAN

Recirculating Ball and Nut—B56S

Disassembly and Assembly

1. Secure the gear assembly in a suitable holding fixture.
2. Place the worm gear in a straight ahead position.
3. Remove the sector shaft with the sector cover.

NOTE: Do not remove the sector shaft needle bearings. If neccessary, replace the gear housing.

4. Loosen the adjusting plug locknut with the proper tool.
5. Remove the worm gear with the worm bearing.

NOTE: Do not allow the ball nut to run down to either

end of the worm. Do not detach the ball nut from the wormshaft assembly.

6. Fill the space between the sealing lips of the sector shaft and the adjusting plug oil seals with multi-purpose grease.
7. Inspect the parts for any damage or excessive wear. The ball nut must rotate smoothly on the worm gear.
8. Install the worm gear assembly with the worm gear into the gear housing.
9. Adjust the worm bearing preload with the proper tool.
10. Apply a suitable sealant around the locknut inner surface and tighten the locknut to 181–231 ft. lbs.
11. Turn the worm gear several times to break in the worm bearing. Check the steering gear preload.

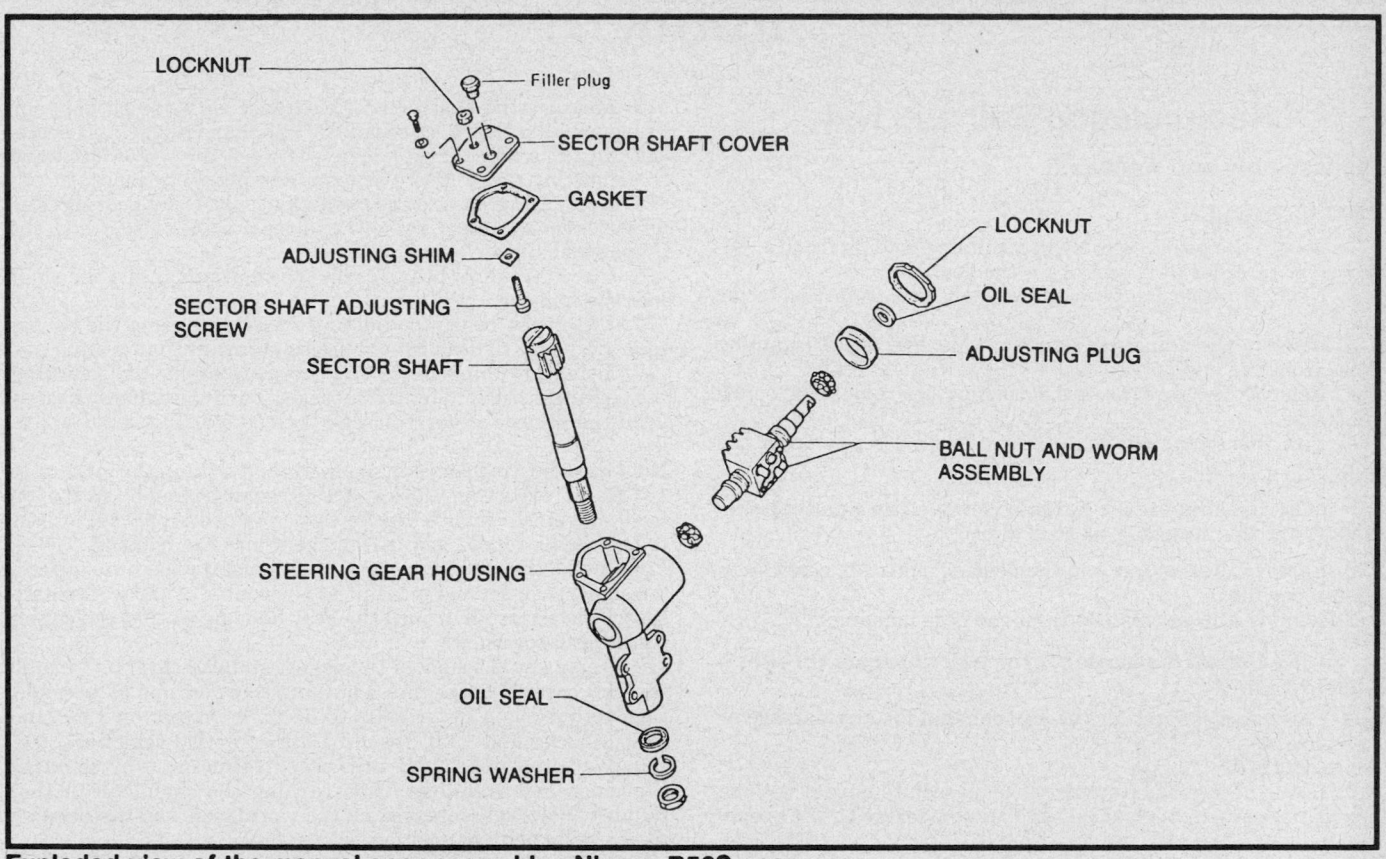

Exploded view of the manual gear assembly—Nissan B56S gear

12. Install the oil seal with the proper tool.
13. Measure the total preload and check the backlash.

Adjustments

WORM BEARING PRELOAD

1. Turn the adjusting plug in the tighten direction.
2. Rotate the wormshaft a few turns in both directions and measure the preload.

3. The preload should read—1.7–5.2 inch lbs., without seals. The steering gear total preload with seals should read 7.4–10.9 inch lbs. for a new gear and 5.2–8.7 inch lbs. for a used gear.

STEERING GEAR BACKLASH

Measure the backlash at the pitman arm top end in a straight ahead position. The backlash should read 0.004 in. or less for a new gear and 0.012 in. or less for a used gear.

SUZUKI/GEO

The steering gear assembly is not serviceable. If a malfunction occurs, replace with a new unit.

TOYOTA

Recirculating Ball and Nut

Disassembly and Assembly

2WD VEHICLES

1. Secure the gear assembly in a suitable holding fixture. Remove the oil filler plug and drain the gear oil.
2. Using a puller, remove the pitman arm from the sector shaft.
3. Remove the adjusting screw locknut and the 3 retaining bolts from the end cover.
4. Remove the end cover by turning the adjusting screw clockwise.
5. Pull the sector shaft and the adjusting screw from the housing.

   NOTE: On some later models remove the needle bearings from the housing at this time.

6. Remove the locknut and the bearing adjusting screw with the proper tool.
7. Remove the wormshaft from the gear housing.

   NOTE: Do not disassemble the ball nut from the steering wormshaft.

8. Clean and inspect all the components for any damage or excessive wear.

To assemble:

9. If it is neccessary to replace the oil seal, remove it with an appropriate prying tool, then install a new seal with the proper tool.
10. If it is neccessary to replace the outer race in the gear housing use the proper tool to remove it then install a new one.
11. If it is neccessary to replace the outer race for the adjusting nut, perform the following: Remove the oil seal with an appropriate prying tool. Using the proper tool remove the outer race from the nut. Using the proper tool, install a new race and then a new seal into the nut.
12. If neccessary, remove the inner races from the shaft with a press, then using the proper tool, press the new ones into the shaft.

13. Measure the shaft thrust clearance with the proper tool. The maximum clearance should be less than 0.0020 in. If neccessary, install a new thrust washer between the sector shaft and the adjusting screw to provide the minimum clearance.
14. Apply MP grease to the bushing needle, roller bearings and oil seals. If neccessary, remove and replace the oil seal with the proper tool.
15. Place the worm bearings on the shaft and insert the shaft into the housing.
16. Install the bearing adjusting screw and using the proper tool, gradually tighten the adjusting screw until it is snug.
17. Using a torque wrench and the same special tool, measure the bearing preload in both directions. Turn the adjusting screw until the preload is correct. The preload starting is 2.6–4.3 ft. lbs.
Hold the adjusting screw in position then tighten the locknut to 177 ft. lbs. except on 1989 and 1990 vehicles and 80 ft. lbs. on 1989 and 1990 vehicles. Recheck the preload. Apply MP grease to the needle rollers and install them into the housing.
18. Install the adjusting screw and thrust washer onto the sector shaft, then set the ball nut at the center of the wormshaft. Insert the sector shaft into the gear housing so that the center teeth mesh together.
19. Apply liquid sealer to the gasket and end cover and install the end cover. Loosen the adjusting screw as far as possible, then torque the 4 cover bolts to 36 ft. lb. except on 1989 and 1990 vehicles and 13 ft. lbs. on 1989 and 1990 vehicles.
20. Place the wormshaft in the neutral position by counting the total shaft rotations, then turning the shaft half of that number. Place matchmarks on the wormshaft and the housing to show the neutral position.
21. Using a torque wrench and special tool, turn the adjusting screw while measuring the preload until it is correct. Make sure the wormshaft is in the neutral position. The preload is 6.9–9.1 inch lbs.
22. Apply liquid sealer to the locknut, then hold the screw with a suitable tool and tighten the locknut to 20 ft. lbs. Recheck the preload.
23. Measure the sector shaft backlash. There should be no backlash within 100 degrees of the right and left sides from the neutral position.

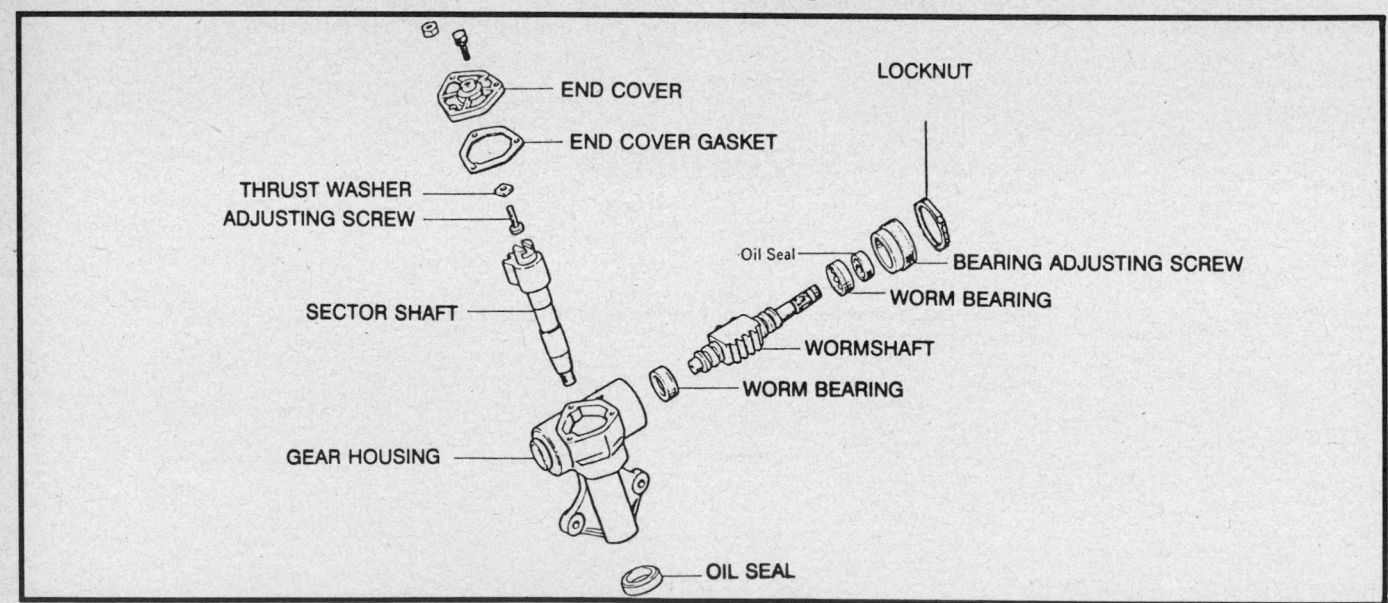

Exploded view of the manual gear assembly—Toyota 2WD vehicle

24. Install the pitman arm and replenish with gear oil. Install the filler plug.

4WD VEHICLES

1. Secure the gear assembly in a suitable holding fixture and drain the oil.

2. Using a puller, remove the pitman arm from the sector shaft, if neccessary.

3. Remove the adjusting screw locknut and 4 retaining bolts from the end cover.

4. Remove the end cover by turning the adjusting screw clockwise.

5. Remove the sector shaft by tapping on it with a suitable tool to remove it.

6. Remove the locknut and the bearing adjusting screw with the proper tool.

7. Remove the wormshaft from the gear housing.

NOTE: Do not disassemble the ball nut from the steering wormshaft.

8. Clean and inspect all the components for any damage or excessive wear.

To assemble:

9. If it is neccessary to replace the oil seal, remove it with an appropriate prying tool, then install a new seal with the proper tool.

10. If it is neccessary to replace the outer race in the gear housing use the proper tool to remove it then install a new one.

11. If it is neccessary to replace the outer race from the adjusting nut, remove the oil seal with an appropriate prying tool. Using the proper tool remove the outer race from the nut. Using the proper tool, install a new race and then a new seal into the nut.

12. If neccessary remove the inner races from the shaft with a press, then using the proper tool, press the new ones into the shaft.

13. Measure the shaft thrust clearance with the proper tool. The maximum clearance should be less than 0.0020 in. If necessary, install a new thrust washer between the sector shaft and the adjusting screw to provide the minimum clearance.

14. Apply MP grease to the bushing needle, roller bearings and oil seals. If neccessary, remove and replace the oil seal with the proper tool.

15. Place the worm bearings on the shaft and insert the shaft into the housing.

16. Install the bearing adjusting screw and using the proper tool, gradually tighten the adjusting screw until it is snug.

17. Using a torque wrench and the same special tool, measure the bearing preload in both directions. Turn the adjusting screw until the preload is correct. The preload starting torque is 3.0–4.3 inch lbs.
Hold the adjusting screw in position then tighten the locknut to 80 ft. lbs. Recheck preload. Apply MP grease to the needle rollers and install them into the housing.

18. Install the adjusting screw and thrust washer onto the sector shaft, then set the ball nut at the center of the wormshaft. Insert the sector shaft into the gear housing so that the center teeth mesh together.

19. Apply liquid sealer to the gasket and end cover and install the end cover. Loosen the adjusting screw as far as possible, then torque the four cover bolts to 72 ft. lbs.

20. Place the wormshaft in the neutral position by counting the total shaft rotations, then turning the shaft half of that number. Place matchmarks on the wormshaft and housing to show the neutral position.

25. Using a torque wrench and special tool, turn the adjusting screw while measuring the preload until it is correct. Make sure the wormshaft is in the neutral position. The preload is 6.9–9.5 inch lbs.

26. Apply liquid sealer to the locknut, then hold the screw with a suitable tool and tighten the locknut to 33 ft. lbs. Recheck the preload.

27. Measure the sector shaft backlash. There should be no backlash within 100 degrees of the right and left sides from the neutral position.

Manual Rack and Pinion

Disassembly and Assembly

1. Secure the gear assembly in a suitable holding fixture.

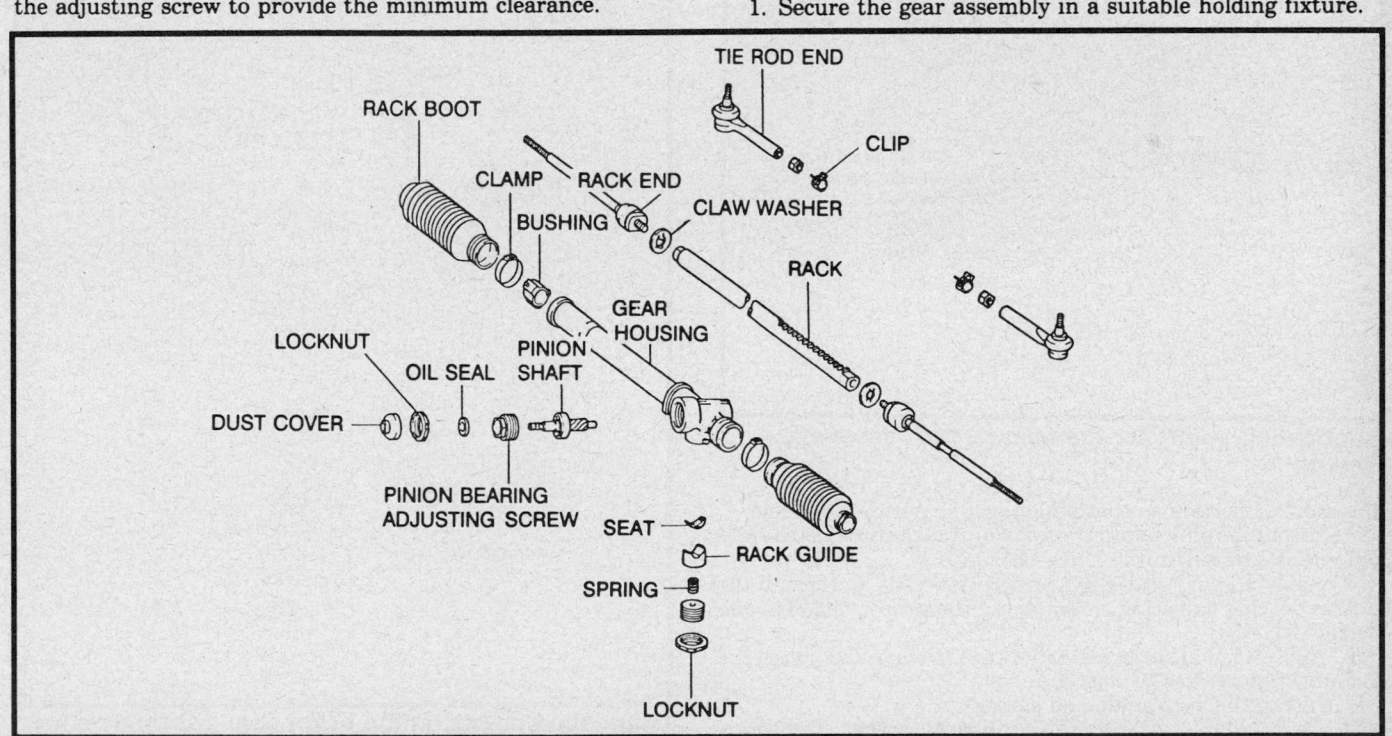

Exploded view of the manual rack and pinion – Toyota

2. Loosen the locknut and place matchmarks on the tie rod ends and the rack ends.

3. Remove the clips, clamps and the rack boots.

4. Unstake the claw washers. Remove the rack ends and the claw washers.

5. Remove the rack ends with the proper tool. Mark the left and right ends.

6. Remove the rack guide spring clamp with the proper tool and remove the rack guide spring.

7. Remove the rack guide and the rack seat.

8. Remove the pinion bearing adjusting screw locknut and remove the pinion bearing adjusting screw.

9. Fully pull the rack from the rack side and remove the pinion together with the upper bearing.

NOTE: Be careful not to damage the serrations.

10. Remove the rack from the pinion side without revolving it.

NOTE: If the rack is pulled from the tube, there is a possibility of damaging the bushing with the rack teeth surface.

11. Inspect the rack for runout and teeth damage. The maximum runout is 0.012 in. Do not use a wire brush when cleaning.

12. If neccessary, replace the rack bushing with the proper tool.

13. If neccessary, replace the pinion seal with the proper tool.

To assemble:

14. Pack these rack components with molybdenum disulphide lithium base grease.

15. Install the rack into the housing from the pinion side. Set

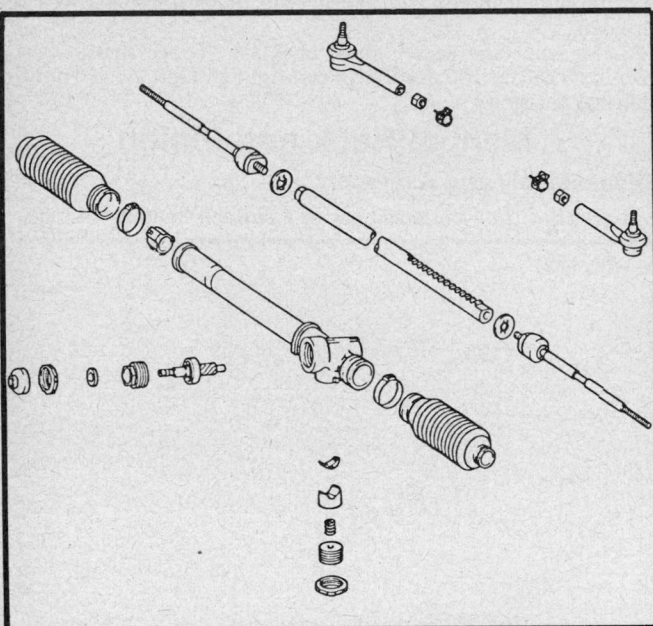

Lubrication points for the manual rack assembly—Toyota

the notched portion so that pinion can be positioned inside.

16. Install the pinion into the housing. Make sure that the pinion end is securely in the lower bearing.

17. Apply a liguid sealer to the screw threads and install the pinion bearing adjusting screw, using the proper tool. Tighten to 15–18 ft. lbs.

18. Apply a liguid sealer to the locknut threads and install the locknut, tighten to 67–83 ft. lbs.

19. Install the rack guide and spring.

20. Apply a liguid sealer to the spring cap threads. Temporarily install the spring cap and mesh the rack with the pinion.

21. Using the proper tool, torque the rack guide spring cap to 18 ft. lbs. Return the rack guide spring cap 30 degrees.

22. Adjust the total preload, using a suitable torque wrench, to 4.3–11.3 inch lbs.

23. Apply a liguid sealer to the locknut threads and the housing surface. Tighten the locknut to 41–51 ft. lbs.

24. Install the dust cover.

25. Install the claw washers and align the claw of the claw washer with the rack groove.

26. Install the rack ends, using the proper tool and tighten to 61 ft. lbs. Stake the claw washers.

27. Install the rack boots. The left and right boots are different. Be careful not to interchange them.

28. Install the clamps and the clips. Stake the clamps to bend upward.

29. Screw the locknuts and the tie rod ends onto the rack ends until the matchmarks are aligned.

Bevel Gear

Disassembly and Assembly

1. Secure the gear in a suitable holding fixture.

2. Remove both dust covers and the adjusting screw locknut.

3. Remove the adjusting screw with the proper tool and pull out the spring.

4. Remove the housing cover bolts and remove the housing cover.

5. Loosen the locknut and adjusting bolt. Remove the plate set bolts and plate.

6. Take out the adjusting bolt seat, spring and spring holder. Wipe the grease off the gear teeth.

7. Inspect the tooth contact between the No. 1 and No. 2 bevel gear.

8. Push in the No. 2 bevel gear and pull out the No. 1 bevel gear and thrust washer.

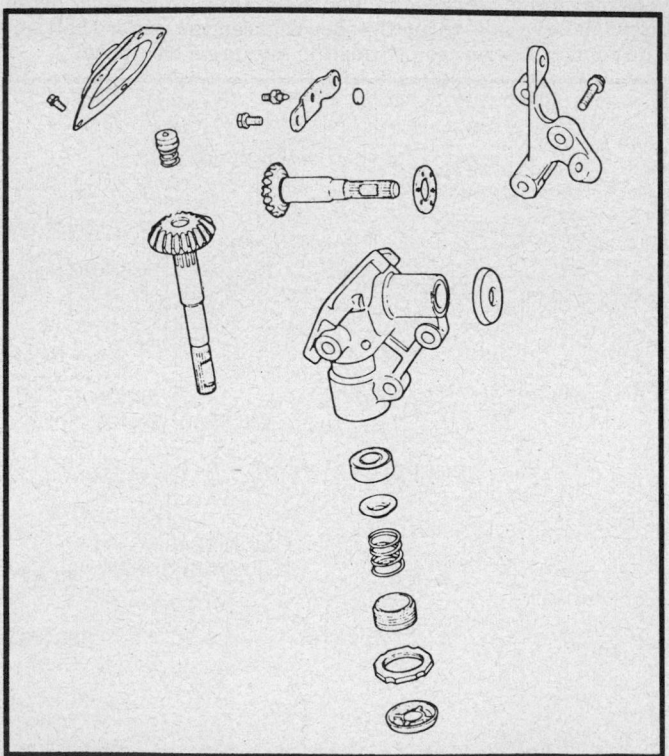

Lubrication points on the bevel gear assembly—Toyota

9. Tap out the No. 2 bevel gear and remove the bearing spring retainer.

10. Inspect all the components for any damage or excessive wear.

To assemble:

11. If neccessary, replace the No. 1 bevel gear oil seal. Remove and replace, using the proper tool.

12. If neccessary, replace the No. 2 bevel gear oil seal. Remove and replace, using the proper tool.

13. Pack these components with molybdenum disulphide lithium base grease.

14. Insert the No. 2 gear into the housing. Use a suitable tool to press in the bearing.

15. Install the thrust washer to the No. 1 bevel gear.

16. Install the No. 1 bevel gear into the housing.

NOTE: Line up the cutout portion of the No. 1 and No. 2 bevel gear.

17. Install the spring with the spring holder to the No. 2 bevel gear.

18. Install the plate with the 2 bolts and tighten to 69 inch lbs.

19. Install the adjusting bolt seat. Screw in the adjusting bolt until it touches the seat.

20. Using the proper tool adjust the No. 1 bevel gear preload. Adjust to 0.7–1.3 inch lbs.

21. Hold the adjusting bolt and install the locknut, tighten to 7 ft. lbs.

22. Install the spring retainer into the housing

23. Install the spring to the adjusting screw and apply a sealant to the threads of the adjusting screw.

24. Install the adjusting screw to the housing.

25. Using the proper tool, tighten the adjusting screw until the No. 1 and No. 2 bevel gears backlash is 0. Turn the No. 1 bevel gear left and right 5 times and snug it.

26. Loosen the adjusting screw to set the total preload; total preload should be 1.3–3.5 inch lbs.

NOTE: When loosening the adjusting screw make sure that the backlash is not more than 0.0142 in.

27. Install the adjusting screw locknut and tighten to 64 ft. lbs. Pack molybdenum disulphide lithium base grease into the gear housing.

28. Apply the proper sealant to the contact surface of the housing cover and install the cover. Tighten the bolts to 69 inch lbs.

29. Install both dust covers.

VOLKSWAGEN

The power rack and pinion steering gear is not adjustable or serviceable, it must be replaced as a complete unit.

POWER STEERING GEAR

POWER STEERING—TROUBLESHOOTING

Condition	Cause	Correction
Steering wheel operation is hard (insufficient power assist)	Air in fluid line	Bleed the system
	Twisted or damaged hoses	Correct the hose routing or replace the hoses
	Fluid leakage	Repair or replace
	Malfunction of gear box	Check and replace the gear box if necessary
	Malfunction of oil pump	Check the oil pump pressure and repair oil pump
Rattling noise	Loose installation of oil pump or gear box	Retighten the oil pump or gear box
	Loose oil pump pulley nut	Retighten the oil pump pulley nut
	Interference around column or between pressure hose and other parts	Correct or replace the pressure hose and the parts around the column
	Abnormal noise inside of gear box and oil pump	Replace the gear box or oil pump
Shrill noise	Air sucked into oil pump	Check the oil level and hose clips, bleed the system or replace the oil pump
	Oil pump seizure	Replace the oil pump
Squealing noise	Loose belt	Adjust the belt deflection
	Oil pump seizure	Replace the oil pump

POWER STEERING—TROUBLESHOOTING

Condition	Cause	Correction
Hissing noise	Air sucked into oil pump	Check the oil level and hose clips, bleed the system
	Damaged to the olive of the gear box port section	Replace the gear box
	Malfunction of return hose	Replace the hose
Whistling noise	Malfunction of gear box port section	Replace the gear box
Droning noise	Loose mounting bolt on oil pump or oil pump bracket	Retighten the pump bracket or pump mounting bolt
	Poor condition of oil pump body	Replace the oil pump
Squeaking noise	Malfunction of steering stopper contact	Check and adjust the steering stopper
	Interference of wheel with vehicle body	Adjust the steering angle
	Malfunction of gear box	Replace the gear box
Vibration	Air suction	Bleed the system
	Malfunction of gear box	Replace the gear box
Excessive play of steering wheel	Excessive play in steering gear box	Repair
	Loose steering gear mounting bolts	Retighten
	Loose or worn stud of tie rod end	Retighen or replace as necessary
Steering wheel operation is hard (insufficient power assist)	Loose belt	Adjust the belt tension
	Damaged belt	Replace the belt
	Low fluid level	Refill with fluid

CHRYSLER IMPORT/MITSUBISHI

Recirculating Ball and Nut

Disassembly and Assembly

1. Secure the gear assembly in a suitable holding device and loosen the adjusting bolt locknut and remove it.
2. With the gear in neutral position, tap the bottom of the cross-shaft with a plastic hammer to remove the cross-shaft.
3. Remove the side cover bolts and screw in the adjusting bolt a couple turns.
4. Remove the valve housing nut with the proper tool.
5. Remove the valve housing bolts and take out the valve housing and rack piston, holding the rack piston to avoid turning it.
6. Be careful not to let the rack piston fall off of the shaft.
7. To remove the rack piston, turn it counterclockwise.

NOTE: There are 26 steel balls in the rack piston which will probably fall out when removed from the shaft. Do not lose them.

8. To disassemble the rack piston, remove the circular holder, the circulator, the steel balls, the seal ring and the O-ring. Do not disassemble the rack piston end cap.
9. Loosen the top cover and remove it and the input wwormshaft from the valve housing.
10. Remove wormshaft thrust plate, thrust needle roller bearing, the seal rings and the O-rings.
11. Screw in the adjusting bolt at the tip of the cross-shaft and remove the side cover.

NOTE: There are 33 needle bearing rollers which may fall out when the cross-shaft is removed. Do not lose them.

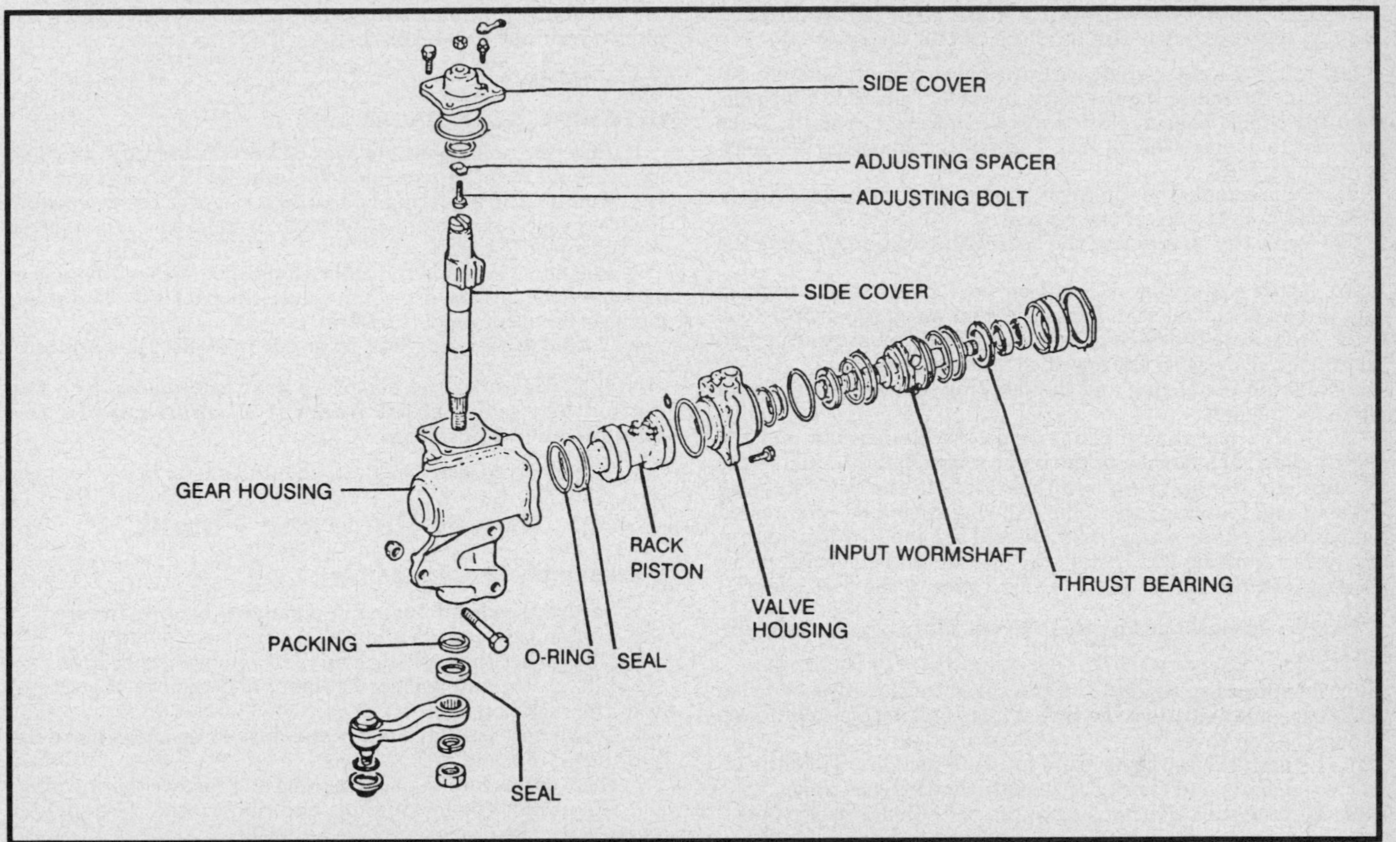

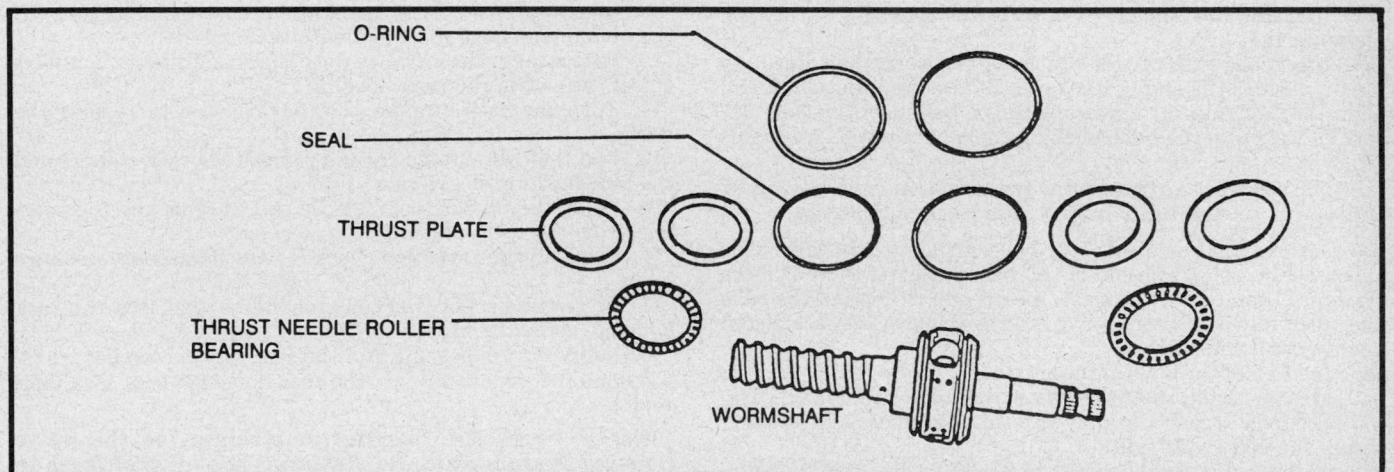

Exploded view of recirculating ball and nut type gear — Chrysler/Mitsubishi

Exploded view of the input wormshaft assembly — Chrysler/Mitsubishi

12. Remove the O-ring, needle bearings, adjusting bolt and adjusting plate from the side cover.

NOTE: If no oil leaks through the threads of the adjusting bolt, do not remove the sealing at the rear of the needle bearing seat.

13. Remove the seal ring and O-ring from the valve housing.
14. Remove the ball bearing and oil seal from the top cover, using a suitable tool.
15. Remove the oil seal and seal ring from the gear housing using a suitable tool.

16. Clean and inspect all parts for wear or damage. Always use new gaskets and oil seals and coat indicated parts with Dexron®II before installing.
17. Apply a thin coat of multi-purpose grease to the bearing race in the side cover and insert the 33 roller bearings. Apply a dab of grease to bottom of the side cover. Be careful not to disturb the needle bearings.
18. Install the side cover O-ring.
19. With the adjusting bolt and adjusting plate inserted in the top of the cross-shaft, measure the clearance between the bolt head and the cross-shaft. It should be 0.002 in. or less. Adjust clearance by replacing with an appropriate adjusting spacer.

NOTE: Install the adjusting plate with its chamfered side in contact with the surface of the cross-shaft.

20. Align the cross-shaft with the side cover and install. Attach them by tightening the adjusting bolt. Take care not to disturb the needle bearings while installing the cross-shaft. Make sure not to damage the oil seal. Tighten the adjusting bolt locknut temporarily.

21. To assemble the top cover, apply a thin coat of multipurpose grease to the lip of the oil seal.

22. Press the oil seal and the bearing into position, using the proper tool.

23. Apply a thin coat of multi-purpose grease to the packing and the lip of the oil seal. Press them in, using the proper tool.

24. Lubricate the O-ring, seal ring, needle roller bearing and the thrust plate with the specified transmission fluid.

25. Install the O-ring and the seal ring (in that order) to the input wormshaft.

26. Install the thrust plate, thrust needle bearing and the thrust plate in that order to the input wormshaft.27. Install the O-rings and the seal ring into their seats in the valve housing without using undue force. The seal ring should be compressed into a heart shape when fit.28. Install the input wormshaft in the valve housing.29. Install the thrust plate, needle roller bearing and the thrust plate in that order to the top cover.

NOTE: Install the thinner thrust plate on the top cover side.

30. Temporarily, tighten the top cover to the valve housing. Take care not to disturb the thrust plate and needle roller bearing in the top cover.

31. Tighten the top cover bolts to 12–16 inch lbs. Turn the input wormshaft and check for smooth rotation and noise.

32. Tighten the valve housing nut to 130–166 ft. lbs. Do not allow the top cover to rotate while tightening the nut.

33. Measure the starting preload of the input wormshaft. It should be from 2.2–5.6 inch lbs. If not, adjust by loosening the valve housing nut. Install the O-ring and seal ring to the rack piston in that order.

34. Insert the rack piston into the input wormshaft until the piston reaches the end of its travel. Rotate the input shaft and align the ball running surface with the ball insertion hole. Insert 19 balls into the hole, pushing them lightly with a suitable tool.

NOTE: Do not rotate the wormshaft on rack piston at this point or the balls might enter other grooves.

35. After installing all 19 of the balls, make sure the last ball is about 1/2 in. below the end of the rack piston. If there is more clearance than that, it probably means one or more of the balls has fallen into a different worm groove. Remove the rack piston and reinstall the balls.

36. Insert 7 of the balls in the circulator, holding them in place with grease. Install the circulator and tighten to 2.6–3.2 ft. lbs.

37. Secure the gear assembly in a suitable holding fixture and install the ball screw unit.

38. Tighten the valve housing to 33–39 ft. lbs. After installation, rotate the input wormshaft to move the rack piston to the neutral (center) position. Be careful not to damage the seal ring when installing the rack piston.

39. Install the cross-shaft assembly (with side cover) in to the gear housing and tighten the side cover to 33–39 ft. lbs. When installing the cross-shaft, apply a thin coat of ATF to the teeth and shaft of the rack piston and multi-purpose grease to the oil seal lip. Do not rotate the side cover during installation to prevent damage to the O-ring. Wrap tape around the splined end of the cross-shaft to prevent damage to the seals.

40. Measure the total starting torque of the input wormshaft to neutral position (center), using the proper tool. Make sure the ball screw operates smoothly throughout its entire travel. Starting torque should be between 4.4–7.8 inch lbs.

41. Install the pitman arm on the cross-shaft and tighten the pitman arm nut to 94–108 ft. lbs.

Adjustments
STEERING GEAR BACKLASH

1. Inject a small amount of gear oil into the breather plug and lubricate the bearing parts and the gear teeth of each shaft.

2. Tighten the adjusting bolt until it engages the gear teeth. Rotate the pitman arm back and forth to make sure it is engaged with the gear teeth.

3. Position a suitable indicator at the end of the pitman arm and move the pitman arm to measure the backlash. The steering gear backlash limit is 0.02 in.

4. Turn the adjusting bolt in or out to adjust the backlash.

NOTE: Measure the steering gear backlash when the mainshaft, cross-shaft and the pitman arm in the straight ahead position.

5. The steering gear backlash should be 0.02 in.

Power Rack and Pinion

Disassembly and Assembly

1. Secure the rack housing in a suitable holding fixture.

2. Loosen the locknut and remove the tie rod end.

3. Disconnect the bellows band and remove the bellows.

4. Lift up the tab washer caulking and remove the tie rod from the rack housing

5. Disconnect the tab washer and dust cover and remove the feed tubes from the rack.

6. Disconnect the end plug caulking and remove the end plug.

7. Disconnect the locking nut and remove the rack support cover, using the proper tool.

8. Take out the rack support spring and remove the rack support.

9. Remove the snapring, using the proper tool, and pull out the pinion and valve assembly with the oil seals

10. Rotate the rack clockwise until the end of the circlip comes out of the slot in the rack housing.

11. Turn the rack stopper counterclockwise to remove the circlip.

12. Pull the rack out slowly and remove the rack stopper and the rack bushing at the same time.

13. Using the proper tool, remove the oil seals and the bearings from the rack housing.

14. Clean all the parts and check for any damage or excessive wear.

15. Press the backup washer and the oil seal into the rack housing, using the proper tool.

16. Lubricate the bearing and the seal with the proper transmission fluid and install into the rack housing, using a suitable tool.

NOTE: Press the bearing in straight, as the valve housing is aluminum. Be sure that the oil seal faces in the correct direction.

17. Lubricate the oil seal for the rack bushing and install the oil seal until it touches the rack bushing end.

18. Apply a coating of multi-purpose grease to the rack teeth. Align the oil seal center with the rack and slowly insert the rack from the power cylinder side.

19. Wrap the end of the rack with a vinyl tape, lubricate with transmission fluid and install the rack bushing and the rack stopper.

NOTE: Do not allow the oil seal retainer to slip out.

20. Align the rack stopper mark with the cylinder hole and install the circlip while turning the rack stopper clockwise.

21. Press fit the oil seal, using the proper tool.

22. Apply the proper sealant to the threaded part of the end plug and install the end plug.

23. Secure the threaded part of the end plug at 2 places, using a suitable punch.

24. Adjust the total pinion torque and install the tie rods to the rack and fold the tab washer into position.

Adjustments

TOTAL PINION TORQUE

1. Position the rack at it's center.

2. Tighten the rack support cover to 11 ft. lbs., using the proper tool.

3. In the neutral position, rotate the pinion shaft clockwise, one turn in 4–6 seconds. Return the rack support cover 30–60 degrees and adjust the torque to 6–12 inch lbs.

4. Lock the rack cover support with the locknut.

Bevel Gear Assembly

Disassembly and Assembly

1. Secure the gear assembly in a proper holding fixture.

2. Remove the locknut using the proper tool.

3. Remove the front cover mounting bolts, adjusting bolt and remove the front cover.

4. Remove the locknut and loosen the rear cover with the proper tool, until the input gear separates from the output gear.

5. Remove both the input gear and the output gear from the housing.

6. Inspect the gear teeth, bearings and the dust cover for any cracks or excessive damage.

7. Install the input and the output gear into the gear housing so that the teeth mesh properly.

8. Tighten the rear cover, using the proper tool. Replace the locknut and tighten to 47–87 ft. lbs. depending on which tool was used.

9. Install the front cover and replace the mounting bolts. Tighten to 12–19 ft. lbs.

10. Install the adjusting bolt and replace the locknut and tighten to 12–19 ft. lbs.

Adjustments

OUTPUT GEAR ROTATIONAL TORQUE

1. Turn the output gear, using the proper tool, at a speed of one rotation every 4–6 seconds. Measure the rotational torque.

2. Adjust the nut so that the output side gear rotational torque is 0.4–0.9 inch lbs.

3. Tighten the locknut to 47–87 ft. lbs., depending on which tool was used.

TOTAL BEVEL GEAR ROTATIONAL TORQUE

1. Turn the input gear, using the proper tool, at a speed of one rotation every 4–6 seconds. Measure the rotational torque.

NOTE: Return the adjustment bolt to a position where there is no contact with the input side gear.

2. Using the proper tool, tighten the rear cover assembly so that the input side gear rotational torque is 2.2–3.9 inch lbs.

3. Tighten the adjustment bolt so that the total bevel gear rotational torque is 2.6–4.8 inch lbs.

4. Install the locknut and tighten to 47–87 ft. lbs., depending on which tool was used.

ISUZU

Integral Gear

Disassembly and Assembly

P'UP

1. Secure the gear in a suitable holding fixture. Remove the dust cover, retaining ring and back up ring.

2. Clean the faces of the stub shaft extended outward and plug the hose fitting on the inlet side. Remove the oil seal by applying compressed air through the hole in the outlet side.

3. Remove the adjusting screw locknut and turn the adjusting screw counterclockwise to remove the preload between the sector gear and the rack piston. Remove the top cover bolts.

4. Hold the top cover stationary, turn the adjusting screw clockwise to raise and free the cover, then remove the cover.

5. Remove the O-ring and needle bearing.

6. Position the stub shaft in a straight ahead position and remove the sector shaft.

NOTE: Do not use a hammer or any impact tools to remove the sector shaft.

7. Remove the ball nut and valve housing assembly.

NOTE: Always keep the ball nut and valve housing assembly in the horizontal position, or the rack piston will fall off onto the end of the worm, causing the rack piston to slip out of the wormshaft and the balls to fall out.

8. Remove the dust seal and ring from the gear housing.

9. Apply a thin coat of grease to the lips of all seals and O-rings.

To assemble:

10. Install the seal ring and dust seal into the the gear housing.

11. Install the needle bearing into the housing, using the proper tool.

12. Install the both O-rings and the seal ring onto the ball nut and valve assembly.

13. Install the ball nut and valve assembly and tighten the valve housing retaining bolts to 27–30 ft. lbs.

NOTE: Be careful not to drop the O-ring fitted to the oil passage in the valve housing. Keep the ball screw and valve housing assembly in a horizontal position.

14. Install the oil seal using the proper tool, then install the back up ring and retaining ring. Turn the face with the rounded edge (outer circumference) to the oil seal.

15. Install the dust cover.

16. Tape the sector shaft serration to protect the seal ring from damage, then align the center tooth of the ball nut with that of the sector shaft and install the sector shaft.

17. Install the needle bearing, O-ring and top cover. Tighten the top cover bolts to 29–39 ft. lbs.

18. Install the locknut and adjust the backlash between the sector gear and ball nut.

Adjustments

WORM GEAR AND BALL NUT BACKLASH

1. Rotate the worm gear to a straight ahead position.

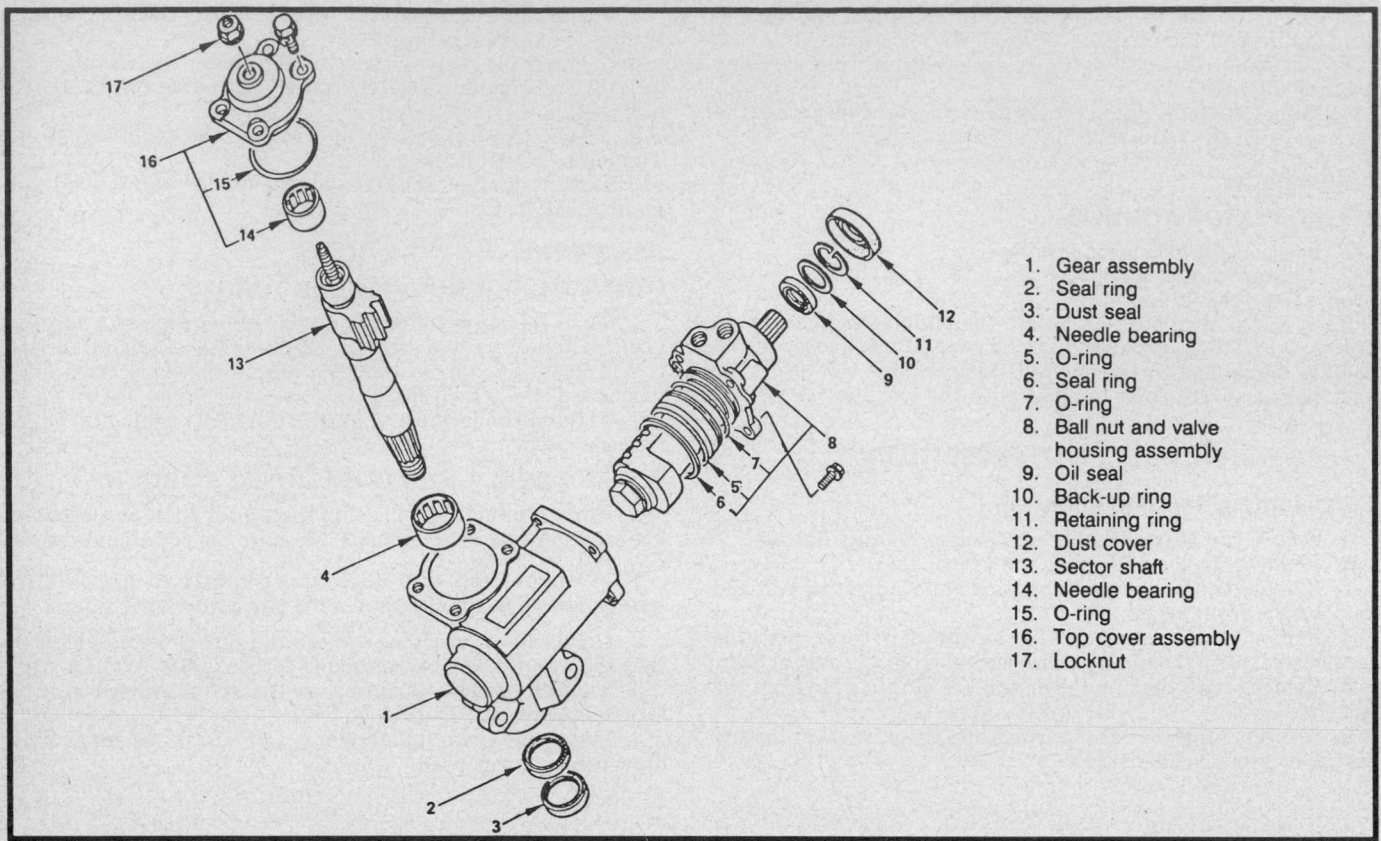

1. Gear assembly
2. Seal ring
3. Dust seal
4. Needle bearing
5. O-ring
6. Seal ring
7. O-ring
8. Ball nut and valve housing assembly
9. Oil seal
10. Back-up ring
11. Retaining ring
12. Dust cover
13. Sector shaft
14. Needle bearing
15. O-ring
16. Top cover assembly
17. Locknut

Exploded view of the integral gear assembly— P'UP

2. Set the wormshaft backlash to below 4 inch lbs. with the sector shaft adjusting screw.

3. Measure the wormshaft backlash with the worm gear turned 450 degrees in both directions.

4. The worm gear backlash in these positions should be 0.8–1.6 inch lbs. lower than in the straight ahead position.

5. Lock the sector shaft adjusting screw with the locknut. Tighten the locknut to 25–35 ft. lbs.

MAZDA

Recirculating Ball and Nut

Disassembly and Assembly

1. Secure the gear assembly in a suitable holding fixture.

2. Plug the openings of all pipe installation fittings and clean the exterior of the gear assembly.

3. Remove the locknut and the pitman arm, using the proper puller.

4. Loosen the locknut and side cover mounting bolts. Remove the side cover.

5. Place the sector shaft in the middle position and tap the lower end of the shaft, using the proper tool.

6. Remove the sector shaft from the gear housing.

7. Remove the dust cover and pry out the oil seal with the proper tool.

8. Remove the dust cover, snapring, washer and pry out the oil seal with the proper tool.

9. Loosen the mounting bolts and remove the valve and piston assembly.

10. Remove the O-ring and the piston seal ring.

11. Clean all the parts and check for any damage or excessive wear.

To assemble:

12. Apply the proper fluid to the lips of the oil seals and all the sliding surfaces.

13. Insert the valve and piston assembly into the gear housing. Tighten the mounting bolts to 28–36 ft. lbs.

NOTE: Do not scratch the O-ring and the seal ring on the piston against the side of the housing.

14. Install the dust cover and the oil seal into the proper groove using a suitable seal installer tool.

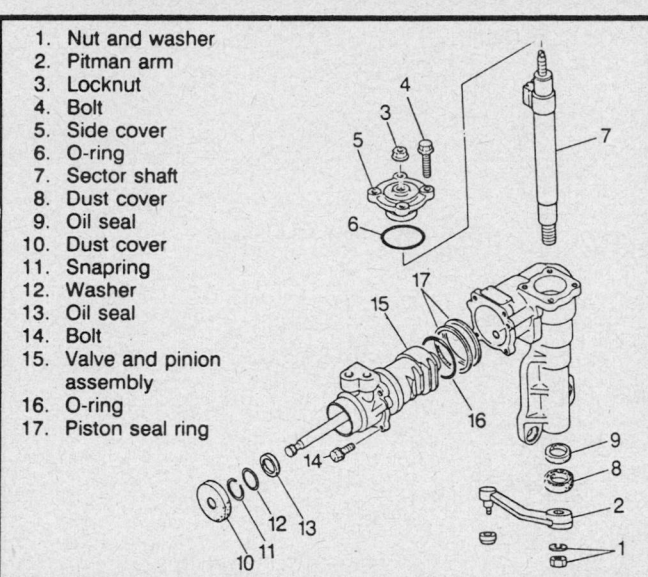

1. Nut and washer
2. Pitman arm
3. Locknut
4. Bolt
5. Side cover
6. O-ring
7. Sector shaft
8. Dust cover
9. Oil seal
10. Dust cover
11. Snapring
12. Washer
13. Oil seal
14. Bolt
15. Valve and pinion assembly
16. O-ring
17. Piston seal ring

Exploded view of the recirculating ball and nut gear assembly — Mazda

15. Insert the sector shaft and replace the side cover. Tighten the mounting bolts to 29–36 ft. lbs.

16. Install the pitman arm and tighten the locknut to 108–130 ft. lbs.

Adjustments
WORMSHAFT PRELOAD

1. Place the wormshaft in the center position.
2. Set the sector shaft adjusting screw so that the preload is 1.3–2.0 lbs.
3. The preload at the center position must be 0.4–0.9 lbs. higher than the preload when the wormshaft is turned 360 degrees to the left and the right.
4. Tighten the sector screw locknut to 25–35 ft. lbs.

Power Rack and Pinion

The power rack and pinion assembly is not adjustable or serviceable, must be replaced as an entire unit.

NISSAN

Recirculating Ball and Nut—PB56S

Disassembly and Assembly

1. Secure the gear assembly in suitable holding fixture.
2. Remove the adjusting screw locknut and replace the O-ring.
3. Set the stub shaft in a straight ahead position. The straight ahead position is where the stub shaft is turned 2.14 turns from the lock position.
4. Disconnect the sector shaft cover bolt.

NOTE: Do not loosen the adjusting screw locknut. Turning the locknut at this time could cause damage to the O-ring resulting in an oil leak.

5. Draw out the sector shaft and knock out the end of the sector shaft approximately 0.79 in.
6. Connect a roll of plastic film to the sector shaft. (1mm thick, length and width approximately 8 in.).
7. Attach the plastic film to the two bearings located inside the gear housing while simultaneously pulling out the sector shaft so that the bearings will not drop into the housing.
8. Carefully pry out the dust seal so that it will not damage the inner side of the gear housing.
9. Remove the snapring, back-up ring and the oil seal.
10. Remove the O-ring, using the proper tool.
11. Loosen the rear housing bolts. Do not remove.
12. Turn the stub shaft counterclockwise, slightly.
13. Remove the rear housing with the worm gear assembly attached.

NOTE: When the worm assembly is removed, the piston may turn and come off under its own weight. Hold the piston to prevent it from turning. If piston to rear housing clearance exceeds 1.28 in. after loosening, the recirculating ball will be out of groove of worm; do not reinstall the piston but replace the entire assembly.

14. Turn the worm assembly upside down and lightly tap the stub shaft end. Remove the rear housing.
15. Remove the oil seal and the O-rings with the proper tools.
To assemble:
16. Apply a multi-purpose grease to the lips between the rear housing seal and the intermediate cover.
17. Apply a thin coat of a proper grease to the new O-rings and install on both sides of the intermediate cover.
18. Position the rear housing onto the intermediate cover with the worm gear assembly.

NOTE: Make sure that the O-rings are not protruding. Do not separate the worm and stub shaft. Wrap vinyl tape around the serration of the stub shaft to prevent the oil seal from being damaged.

19. Install the worm gear assembly with the rear housing and the intermediate cover attached, into the gear housing.
20. Tighten the rear housing bolts in criss-cross fashion to 20–24 ft. lbs.
21. Apply a thin coat of the proper grease to the new adjusting screw llocknut O-ring and insert it into the groove.
22. Apply a thin coat of grease to the new oil seal and dust seal then press in the new seal and the back-up ring with the proper tool.
23. Install a new snapring into the gear housing. Turn the snapring to make sure it fits into the groove and always install the snapring with its rounded edges facing the oil seal.
24. Press in a new dust seal.
25. Apply a thin coat of grease to a new O-ring then fit the O-ring into the sector shaft cover.
26. Set the piston rack at a straight ahead position. Turn the piston rack about 10–15 degrees toward yourself. This is for the smooth insertion of the sector gear.
27. Wrap vinyl tape around serration area of sector shaft to prevent damage to the oil seal lip during insertion.
28. With the plastic film wrapped around the sector shaft and insert the sector shaft into the gear housing. Gradually remove

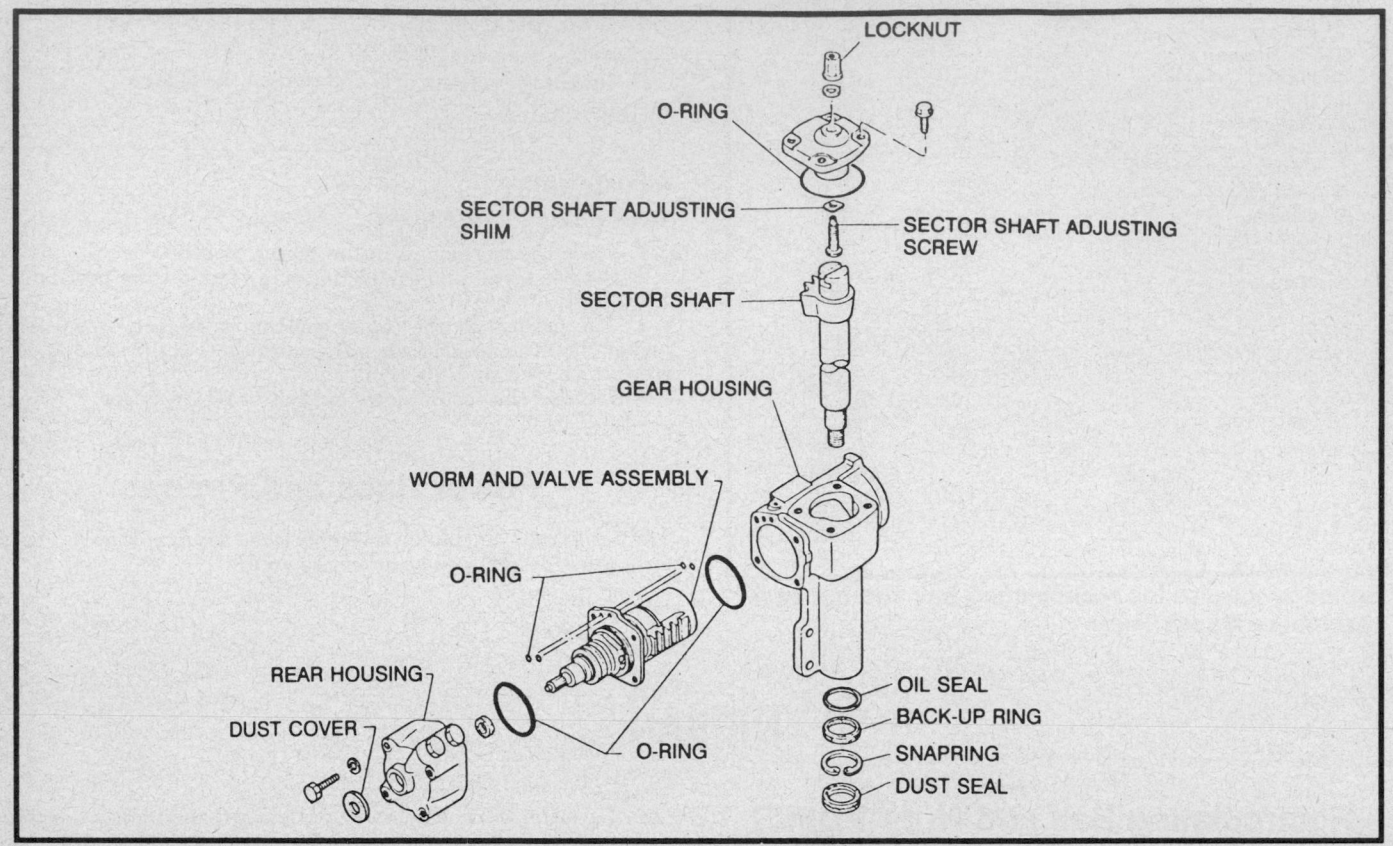

Exploded view of the power steering gear assembly—Nissan PB56S gear

the plastic film being careful not to drop the bearings into the gear housing.

29. Tighten the sector shaft cover bolts to 20–24 ft. lbs. in a criss-cross pattern.

Adjustments
TURNING TORQUE

1. Measure the turning torque at a 360 degrees position.
2. Turn the stub shaft all the way to the right and left several times.
3. Measure the turning torque at 360 degrees position from the straight ahead position. (6.1–10.4 inch lbs.). If it is beyond specification, the gear must be replaced as an assembly.
4. Measure the turning torque at a straight ahead position.
5. Set the worm gear in a straight ahead position. This position is where the stub shaft is turned 2.13 turns from the lock position.
6. Measure the turning torque at this position it should be 0.9–3.5 inch lbs., higher than at 360 degrees.
7. After the adjustment is completed, tighten the locknut to 25–30 ft. lbs. If the turning torques are not within specifications, replace the gear assembly.

Rcirculating Ball and Nut PB48S

Disassembly and Assembly

1. Secure the gear in suitable holding fixture.
2. Remove the adjusting screw locknut and replace the O-ring.
3. Set the stub shaft in a straight ahead position. The straight ahead position is where the stub shaft is turned 2.14 turns from the lock position.
4. Disconnect the sector shaft cover bolt.

NOTE: Do not loosen the adjusting screw locknut. Turning the locknut at this time could cause damage to the O-ring resulting in an oil leak.

5. Draw out the sector shaft and knock out the end of the sector shaft approximately 0.79 in.
6. Connect a roll of plastic film to the sector shaft. (1mm thick, length and width approximately 8 in.).
7. Attach the plastic film to the bearings located inside the gear housing while simultaneously pulling out the sector shaft so that the bearings will not drop into the housing.
8. Remove the torx screws, then remove the rear housing together with the worm gear assembly.

NOTE: When the worm assembly is removed, the piston may turn and come off under its own weight. Hold the piston to prevent it from turning. If piston to rear housing clearance exceeds 1.38 in. after loosening, the recirculating ball will be out of groove of worm; do not reinstall the piston but replace the entire assembly.

9. Remove the O-rings.
10. Remove the snapring, then the rear cover.
11. Remove the O-ring then the oil seal.

To assemble:
12. Apply a thin coat of grease to a new adjusting screw llocknut O-ring and insert it into the groove.
13. Apply a thin coat of grease to the new oil seal and dust seal then press in the new seal and the special washer.
14. Install a new snapring into the gear housing. Turn the snapring to make sure it fits into the groove and always install the snapring with its rounded edges facing the oil seal.
15. Press in a new dust seal.
16. Apply a thin coat of grease to a new O-ring then fit the O-ring into the sector shaft cover.

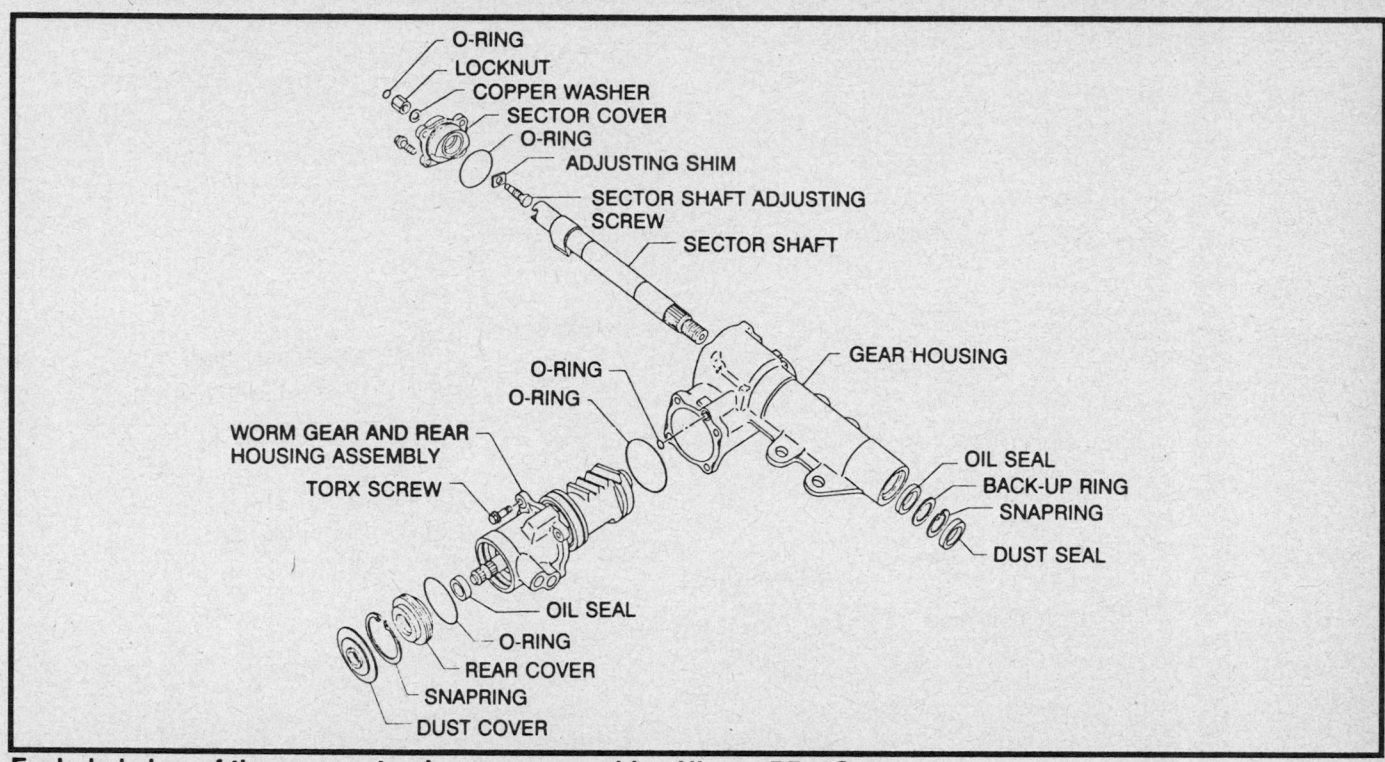

O-RING
LOCKNUT
COPPER WASHER
SECTOR COVER
O-RING
ADJUSTING SHIM
SECTOR SHAFT ADJUSTING SCREW
SECTOR SHAFT
GEAR HOUSING
O-RING
O-RING
WORM GEAR AND REAR HOUSING ASSEMBLY
TORX SCREW
OIL SEAL
BACK-UP RING
SNAPRING
DUST SEAL
OIL SEAL
O-RING
REAR COVER
SNAPRING
DUST COVER

Exploded view of the power steering gear assembly—Nissan PB48S gear

17. Set the piston rack at a straight ahead position. Turn the piston rack about 10 degrees to 15 degrees toward yourself. This is for smooth insertion of the sector gear.

18. Wrap vinyl tape around serration area of sector shaft to prevent damage to the oil seal lip during insertion.

19. With the plastic film wrapped around the sector shaft insert the sector shaft into the gear housing. Gradually remove the plastic film being careful not to drop the bearings into the gear housing.

20. Tighten the sector shaft cover bolts to 20–24 ft. lbs. in a criss-cross pattern.

21. Apply a thin coat of grease to new rear housing O-ring then install.

22. Gradually insert the worm gear and rear housing assembly into the gear housing, being careful not to damage the oil seal and O-rings.

23. Install and tighten the torx screws in a criss-cross pattern to 20–24 ft. lbs.

24. Install a new O-ring and oil seal.

25. Install the rear cover then the snapring. Turn the ssnapring to make sure it fits into the groove and always install the snapring with its rounded edge facing the rear cover.

26. Select suitable adjusting shims and adjust the endplay between the sector shaft and adjusting screw. Endplay should be 0.0004–0.0012 in.

Power Rack and Pinion PR26SC Type

Disassembly and Assembly

1. Secure the gear assembly in a suitable holding device and drain the fluid.

2. Prior to disassembling, measure the pinion rotating torque. Record the pinion rotating torque as a reference.

3. Remove the pinion gear being careful not to damage the pinion gear when removing the pinion seal ring.

4. Remove the tie rod outer sockets and boots.

5. Loosen the tie rod inner socket by prying up on the staked portion. Remove the inner socket.

6. Remove the adjusting screw, spring, spring seat and lift out the retainer.

7. Remove the rear housing cover and assembly. Remove the pinion assembly.

8. Drill the staked portion of the gear housing with a drill of 0.079–0.098 in. diameter, until the staking is eliminated.

9. Remove the end cover, using the proper tool. Draw out the rack assembly.

10. Remove the rack seal ring. Heat the ring with approximately 104°F of heat to remove.

NOTE: Be careful not to damage the rack.

11. Remove the center bushing and the rack oil seal using the proper tool. Do not scratch the inner surfaces of the pinion housing.

To assemble:

12. Heat the rack seal ring and install it onto the rack, using your hand.

13. Compress the rack seal ring into position and secure it on the rack with the proper tool. Always insert the tool from the rack side.

14. Place a plastic film into the rack oil seal to prevent damage to the rack teeth.

15. Insert the rack oil seal into position and remove plastic film. Make sure the lips of the oil seal face each other.

16. Install the center bushing and the rack oil seal with rack assembly.

17. Replace the end cover assembly and tighten 43–54 ft. lbs., using the proper tool.

18. Set the rack in a neutral position.

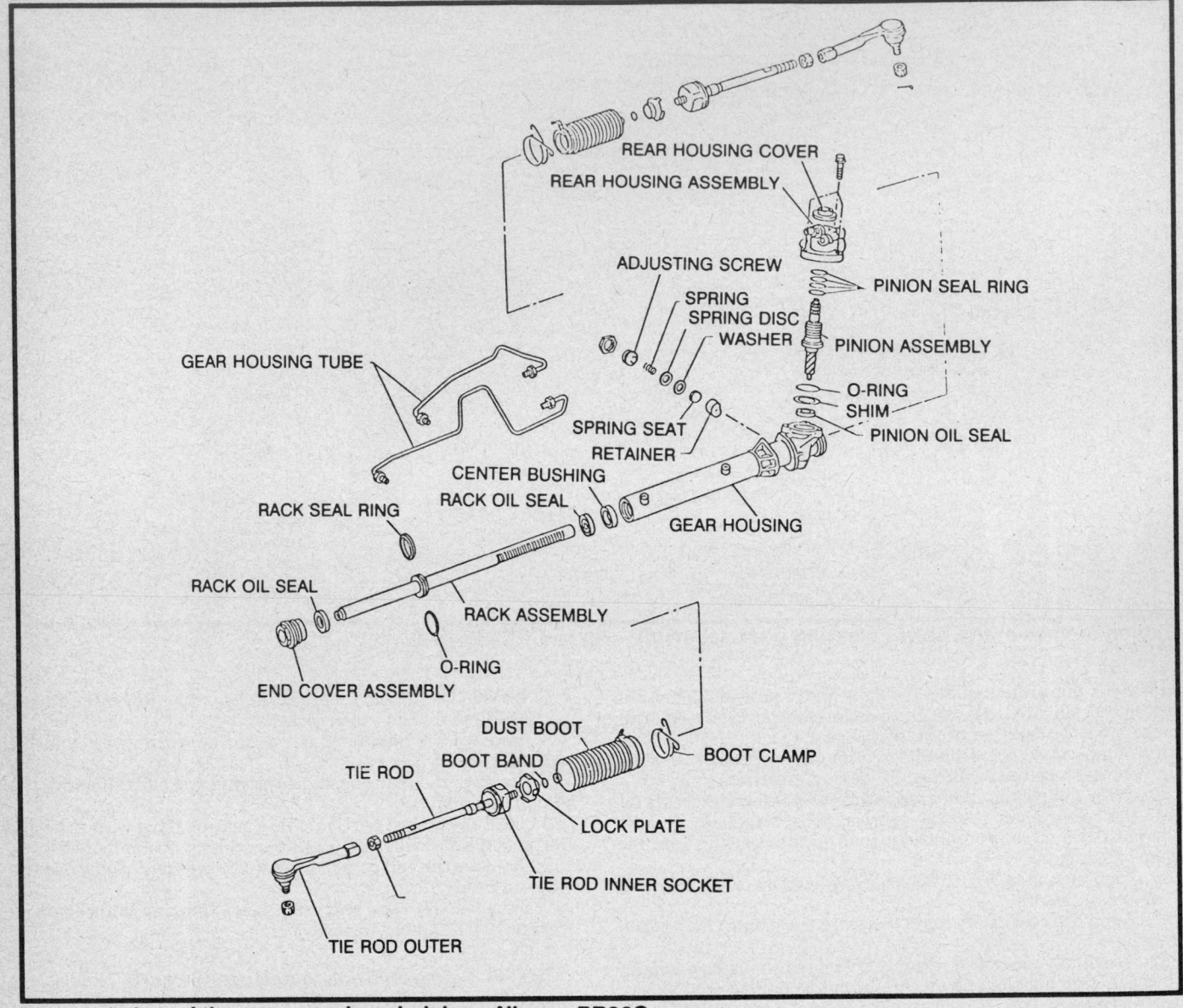

Exploded view of the power rack and pinion—Nissan PR26C gear

19. Lubricate the lip of the oil seal with a multi-purpose grease install the new oil seal to the housing, using the proper tool.

20. Install the pinion bearing adjusting shims, using the number of shims that were removed.

21. Heat the pinion seal and install on pinion gear assembly. Make sure that the pinion seal ring is properly settled in the valve groove.

22. Lubricate oil seal lip and needle bearing roller. Install the pinion assembly to the punion housing of the gear housing.

NOTE: Be careful not to damage the pinion oil seal.

23. Lubricate the rear oil seal with a multi-purpose grease and install the seal into the rear housing, using the proper tool.

24. Install the rear cover cap being careful not to damage the worm ring and the oil seal.

25. Install the retainer spring and the adjusting screw temporarily.

26. Install the new lock plate and screw the inner socket into the rack and tighten to 58–72 ft. lbs. Cinch the 2 places of the lock plate at the racks groove.

27. Install the outer tie rod and tighten the locknut to 27–34 ft. lbs. on the 2WD vehicle and 58–72 ft. lbs. on the 4WD vehicle.

28. Coat the surfaces between the tie rod and the boot with grease and install the boot.

29. Install the boot clamps, making sure that the clamps do not contact the boot.

Adjustments

PINION ROTATING TORQUE

1. Set the gears to neutral without fluid in the gear. Lightly tighten the adjusting screw.

2. Tighten the adjusting screw to 43–52 inch lbs.

3. Loosen the adjusting screw, then retighten the screw to 0.43–1.74 inch lbs.

4. Move the rack over it's entire stroke several times.

5. Measure the rotating pinion torque within a range of 180 degrees from the neutral position. Stop the gear at the point of maximum torque.

6. Loosen the adjusting screw, then retighten to 43–52 inch lbs.

7. Loosen the adjusting screw by 40–60 degrees and tighten the locknut to 29–43 ft. lbs.

8. Check the steering gear for the rack sliding frictional force;

a. Around the neutral point of the rack stroke the frictional force should be 27.6–37.5 lbs. pus or minus 0.217in.

b. Except for the neutral point it should be 27.6–41.9 lbs.

9. Measure the pinion rotating torque within a range of plus or minus 100 degrees from the neutral point. The average rotating torque is 6.9–11.3 inch lbs. The maximum rotating torque is 16 inch lbs. and the minimum is 5.2 inch lbs.

SUZUKI/GEO

The power steering gear assembly is not serviceable. If a malfunction occurs, replace with a new unit.

TOYOTA

Recirculating Ball and Nut

Disassembly and Assembly

1986–1988 VEHICLES

1. Secure the gear housing in a suitable holding fixture.

2. Remove the bolts and lift out the solenoid valve. Remove the O-ring on 2WD vehicles.

3. Remove the pitman arm, using the proper tool.

4. Remove the adjusting screw locknut and the mounting bolts. Screw in the adjusting and remove the end cover.

5. Tap on the cross-shaft end with the proper tool and remove the cross-shaft.

6. Remove the cap screws from the housing. Hold the piston nut so that it cannot move and turn the wormshaft clockwise.

7. Remove the valve body and piston assembly. Remove the O-ring.

NOTE: Make sure that the power piston does not come off the wormshaft.

8. Pull out the power piston nut, using the proper tool. Do not lose the ball.

9. Hold the adjusting screw with the proper tool and remove the locknut.

10. Remove the adjusting screw and the bearings with the proper tool.

11. Remove the O-ring and take out the wormshaft.

12. Remove the thrust bearing, plate washer, teflon ring. Pry out the O-ring.

13. Pry out the seal from the pitman arm end of the housing and remove the snapring, using the proper tool.

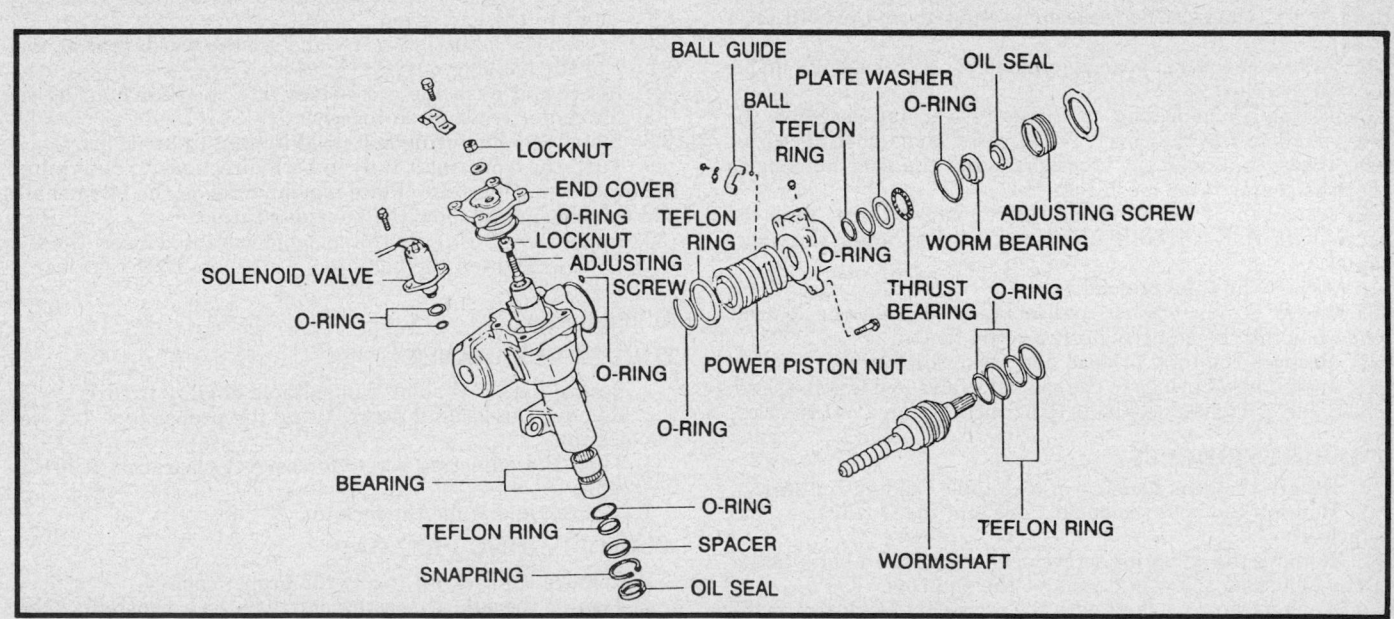

Exploded view of the power steering gear assembly – except 1989–90 Toyota

14. Remove the metal spacer, teflon ring and the O-ring. Drive out the bearings with the proper tool.

15. Inspect the cross-shaft adjusting screw clearance, using the proper tool to measure the clearance. The thrust clearance should be; 0.0012–0.0020 in.

16. Clean all the components and inspect for damage or excessive wear.

To assemble:

17. Install the top bearing, using the proper tool, with the long flange facing out. Drive the bearing in flush with the inside casting surface.

18. Install the lower bearing, using the proper tool, with the long flange facing out. Make sure that the bearing is properly seated.

19. Install the new O-ring, metal spacer and the snapring, using the proper tool.

20. Install the teflon ring into the housing.

NOTE: The teflon ring must be squeezed before inserting the sector shaft or damage may result.

21. Drive the new seal into the gear housing, using the proper tool.

22. If neccessary, drive out the adjusting screw oil seal and replace with a new seal, using a suitable tool.

23. If neccessary, replace the control valve teflon ring.

24. Coat all the components with power steering fluid.

25. Secure the valve body in a suitable holding fixture. Install a new O-ring and teflon ring, using the proper tool.

26. Install the wormshaft with the thrust bearing and the plate washer to the valve body.

27. Install a new O-ring and bearing to the control valve with the proper tool.

28. Temporarily tighten the adjusting screw and locknut.

29. Insert the piston nut about 0.59 in. from the wormshaft end, align the ball transfer surface with the ball hole.

30. Insert the balls one at a time into the holes and turn the wormshaft a little with each insertion. Then securely insert the 33 balls into the piston.

31. Install 11 balls to the ball guide and apply MP grease to the ball guide so that the balls do not fall out. Be careful not to damage the ball guide.

32. Install the ball guide clamp and tighten to 26 inch lbs. Check that the power piston nut rotates smoothly.

33. Replace new O-rings to the gear housing and the valve body. Install the valve body assembly and tighten the bolts to 34 ft. lbs.

34. Adjust the worm bearing preload. The preload should be; 3.5–5.6 inch lbs.

35. Install a new O-ring on the end cover and assemble the cross-shaft to the end cover. Fully loosen the adjusting screw.

36. Insert and push the cross-shaft into the gear housing so that the center teeth mesh together.

37. Install the 4 cap bolts and tighten to 34 ft. lbs. Turn the wormshaft fully in both directions to determine the exact center.

38. Adjust the total preload.

39. Install a new washer and locknut. Tighten the locknut while holding the adjusting screw to 34 ft. lbs.

40. Recheck the total preload and stake the locknut.

41. Install new O-rings to the solenoid valve and install the solenoid valve. Tighten the bolts to 52 inch lbs. on 2WD vehicles.

1989–1990 VEHICLES

1. Secure the gear housing in a suitable holding fixture.

2. Remove the bolts, solenoid valve and the O-rings on 2WD vehicles.

3. Remove the adjusting screw locknut and the 4 bolts. Screw in the adjusting screw and remove the end cover.

4. Tap on the cross-shaft with the proper tool and remove the cross-shaft.

5. Remove the plunger guide nut, using the proper tool.

6. Remove the spring, plunger, plunger guide and pry out the O-ring.

7. Remove the cap bolts from the housing.

8. Turn the wormshaft clockwise while holding the power piston nut so it cannot move. Pull out the valve body and the power piston assembly.

NOTE: Make sure that the power piston nut does not come off the wormshaft.

9. Remove the O-ring, using the proper tool.

10. Secure the valve body in a suitable holding fixture. Move the worm gear up and down to check the ball clearance. The maximum clearance is 0.0059 in.

11. Secure the cross-shaft in a suitable holding fixture and check the adjusting screw thrust clearance. The thrust clearance is 0.0012–0.0020 in.

12. Pry out the oil seal and remove the snapring with the proper tools.

13. Remove the metal spacer, teflon ring and the O-ring. Press out the bearing.

To assemble:

14. Install a new lower bearing with the proper tool so that it is positioned 0.909 in. away from the housing inner end surface.

15. Install a new upper bearing with the proper tool so that it aligns with the housing end surface.

16. Install a new O-ring, metal spacer and replace the snapring.

17 Insert a new teflon ring into the housing.

NOTE: The teflon ring must be squeezed before installing the sector shaft or damage may result.

18. Drive a new seal into the housing, using the proper tool.

19. If neccessary, replace the control valve teflon ring. Be careful not to damage or over expand the teflon ring.

20. If neccessary, replace the union seat.

21. Install the O-rings to the gear housing and the valve body. Install the 4 bolts and tighten 34 ft. lbs.

22. Check the worm gear preload. The preload should be; 2.6–4.8 inch lbs.

23. Install the plunger, plunger guide and the spring.

24. Install a new O-ring to the plunger guide nut. Replace the nut and tighten to 15 ft. lbs.

25. Install a new O-ring on the end cover and assemble the cross-shaft to the end cover.

26. Loosen the adjusting screw and set the worm gear at the center of the housing.

27. Insert and push the cross-shaft into the gear housing so that the center teeth mesh together.

28. Install the mounting bolts and tighten to 34 ft. lbs.

29. Turn the wormshaft fully in both directions to determine the exact center position. Place matchmarks on the wormshaft and the housing to show the neutral position.

30. Install new O-rings to the solenoid valve and insert the solenoid valve. Tighten the bolts to 7 ft. lbs. on 2WD vehicles.

Adjustments

THRUST CLEARANCE

1. Secure the cross-shaft in a suitable holding fixture.

2. Remove the locknut stake, using the proper tool. Loosen the locknut.

3. Turn the adjusting screw for correct clearance; 0.0012–0.0020 in.

4. Tighten and stake the locknut.

WORM BEARING PRELOAD

1. Remove the locknut, using the proper tool.

2. Tighten the adjusting screw and turn the wormshaft to the right and the left to snug the bearing.

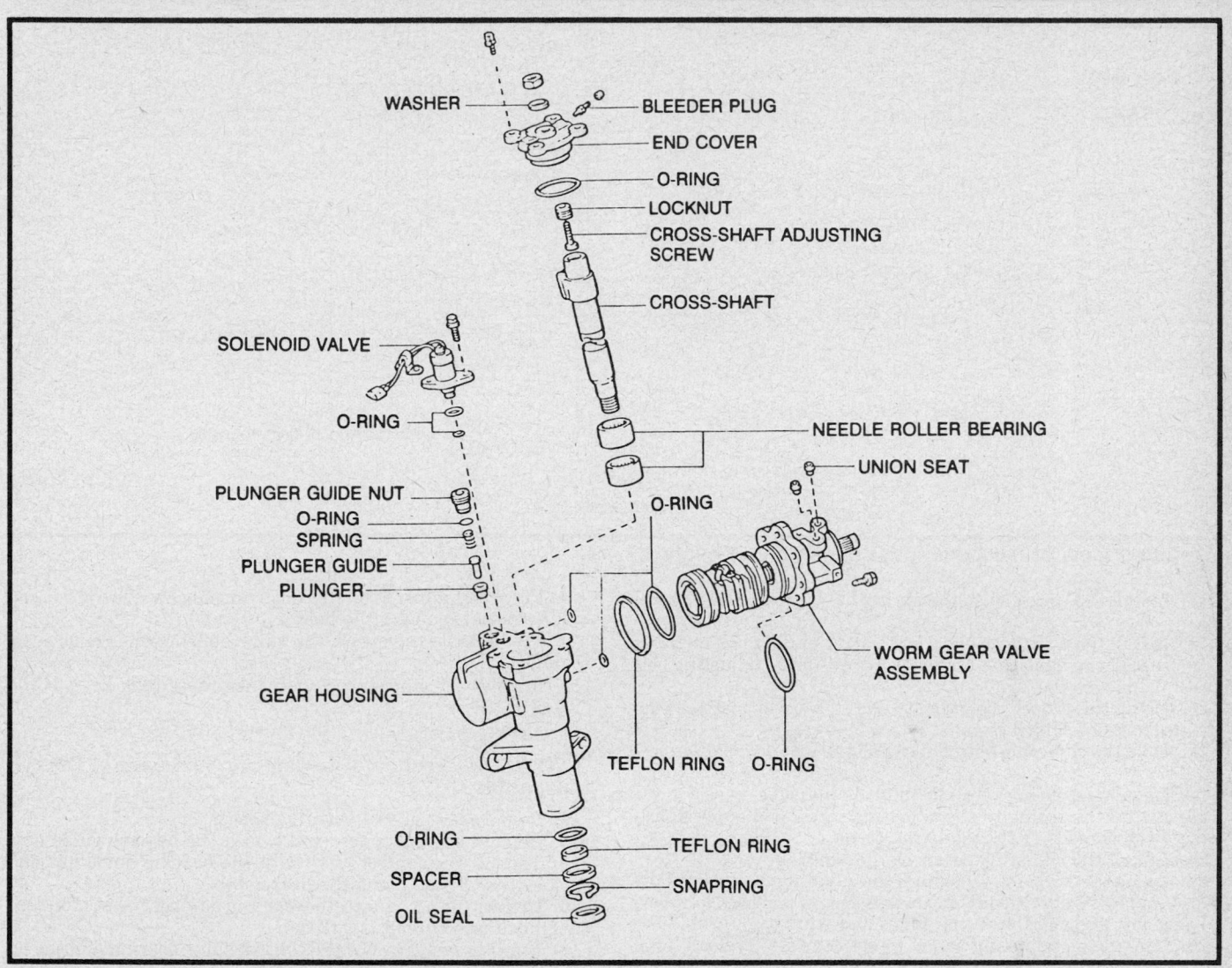

Exploded view of the power steering gear assembly—1989–90 Toyota

3. Slightly, loosen the adjusting screw.
4. Tighten the adjusting screw with the proper tool until the preload is correct. The preload should be 3.5–5.6 inch lbs. for 1986–1988 vehicles and 2.6–4.8 inch lbs. for 1988–1990 vehicles.

TOTAL PRELOAD

1. Install a suitable meter on the center wormshaft.
2. Turn the adjusting screw until the preload is correct.
3. The total preload should be 1.7–2.6 inch lbs. for 1986–1988 vehicles and 4.3–8.3 inch lbs. for 1988–1990 vehicles.

Bevel Gear

Disassembly and Assembly

1. Secure the gear in a suitable holding fixture.
2. Remove both dust covers and the adjusting screw locknut.
3. Remove the adjusting screw with the proper tool and pull out the spring.
4. Remove the housing cover bolts and remove the housing cover.
5. Loosen the locknut and adjusting bolt. Remove the plate set bolts and plate.

6. Take out the adjusting bolt seat, spring and spring holder. Wipe the grease off the gear teeth.
7. Inspect the tooth contact between the No. 1 and No. 2 bevel gear.
8. Push in the No. 2 bevel gear and pull out the No. 1 bevel gear and thrust washer.
9. Tap out the No. 2 bevel gear and remove the bearing and spring retainer.
10. Inspect all the components for any damage or excessive wear.

To assemble:

11. If neccessary, replace the No. 1 bevel gear oil seal. Remove and replace, using the proper tool.
12. If neccessary, replace the No. 2 bevel gear oil seal. Remove and replace, using the proper tool.
13. Pack these components with molybdenum disulphide lithium base grease.
14. Insert the No. 2 gear into the housing. Use a suitable tool to press in the bearing.
15. Install the thrust washer to the No. 1 bevel gear.
16. Install the No. 1 bevel gear into the housing.

NOTE: Line up the cutout portion of the No. 1 and No. 2 bevel gear.

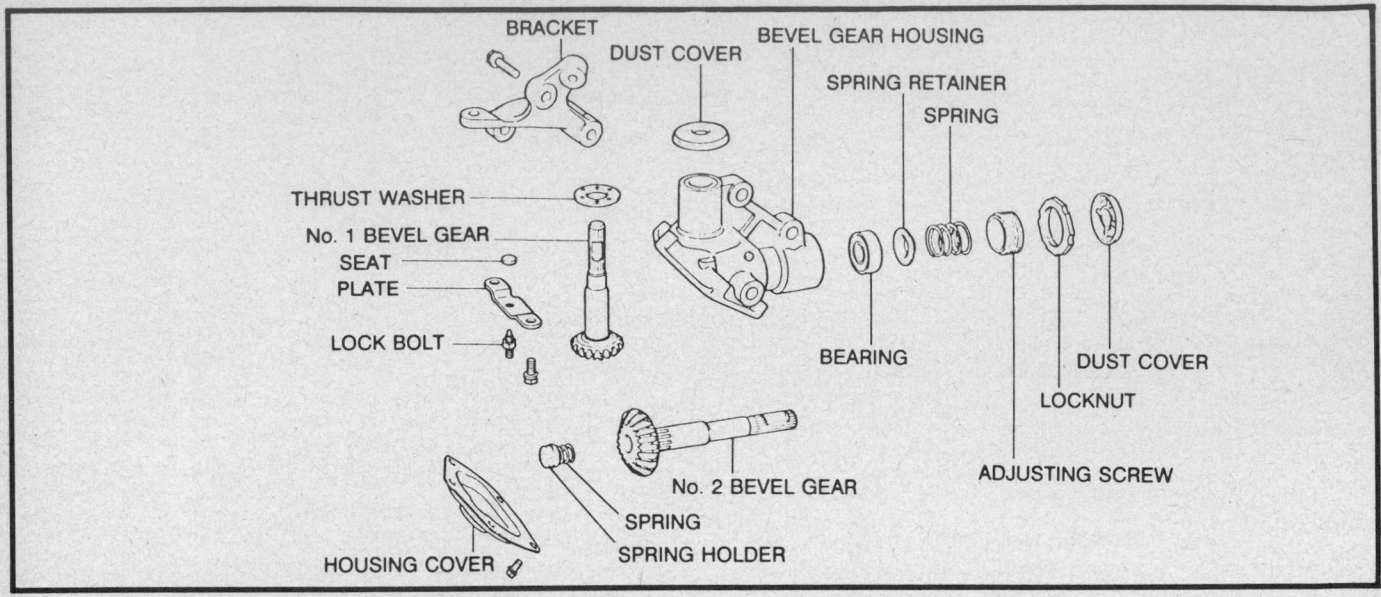

Exploded view of the bevel gear assembly—Toyota

17. Install the spring with the spring holder to the No. 2 bevel gear.

18. Install the plate with the 2 bolts and tighten to 69 inch lbs.

19. Install the adjusting bolt seat. Screw in the adjusting bolt until it touches the seat.

20. Using the proper tool adjust the No. 1 bevel gear preload. Adjust to 0.7–1.3 inch lbs.

21. Hold the adjusting bolt and install the locknut, tighten to 7 ft. lbs.

22. Install the spring retainer into the housing

23. Install the spring to the adjusting screw and apply a sealant to the threads of the adjusting screw.

24. Install the adjusting screw to the housing.

25. Using the proper tool, tighten the adjusting screw until the No. 1 and No. 2 bevel gears backlash is zero. Turn the No. 1 bevel gear left and right a couple times and snug it.

26. Loosen the adjusting screw to set the total preload; total preload should be 1.3–3.5 inch lbs.

NOTE: When loosening the adjusting screw make sure that the backlash is not more than 0.0142 in.

27. Install the adjusting screw locknut and tighten to 64 ft. lbs. Pack molybdenum disulphide lithium base grease into the gear housing.

28. Apply the proper sealant to the contact surface of the housing cover and install the cover. Tighten the bolts to 69 inch lbs.

29. Install the 2 dust covers.

Power Rack and Pinion

Disassembly and Assembly

1. Secure the gear housing in a suitable holding fixture.

2. Remove the left and the right turn pressure tubes with the proper tool.

3. Loosen the locknuts and make matchmarks on the tie rod ends and the rack ends. Remove the tie rod ends and the locknuts.

4. Remove the clips, clamps and the rack boots.

5. Unstake the claw washers to remove the rack ends and the claw washers.

6. Remove the rack guide spring cap locknut, using the proper tool.

7. Remove the rack guide, spring and the seat.

8. Place matchmarks on the valve housing and the rack housing. Remove the mounting bolts.

9. Pull out the valve with the valve housing and remove the O-ring.

10. Remove the stopper nut with the proper tool. Pry out the O-ring.

11. Using a press, remove the oil seal and the rack.

NOTE: Be careful not to damage the inside of the cylinder tube.

12. Remove the oil seal with the spacer.

13. Remove the dust cover and loosen the bearing guide nut.

14. Tap out the control valve with the bearing guide nut and remove the O-ring, using the proper tool.

15. Inspect the rack for teeth wear and damage. Check for runout; maximum runout is 0.012 in.

16. If neccessary, replace the control valve bearing and the oil seal. Press out the oil seal and the bearing, using the proper tool.

To assemble:

17. Coat the lip of the oil seal with power steering fluid and install into the control valve housing.

18. Press the new bearing into the control valve housing with the proper tool.

19. If neccessary, replace the bearing nut guide oil seal. Use the proper tool to tap out and press in the new seal.

20. If neccessary, replace the teflon ring and the O-ring. Pry out the teflon ring and the O-ring.

NOTE: Be careful not to damage the steering rack.

21. Install a new O-ring and teflon ring. Coat the teflon ring with power steering fluid and snug it down with your fingers.

22. If neccessary, replace the control valve teflon rings. Use the proper tool to remove and install the rings.

23. If neccessary, replace the union seat. Use the proper tool to remove and install the seat.

To assemble:

24. Coat these points on the rack assembly with molybdenum disulphide lithium base grease.

25. Coat the oil seal lip with power steering fluid. Install the oil seal and the spacer into the rack housing, using the proper tool.

26. Place the protective sleeve onto the rack, coat the sleeve with power steering fluid.

27. Insert the rack into the cylinder and remove the protective sleeve.

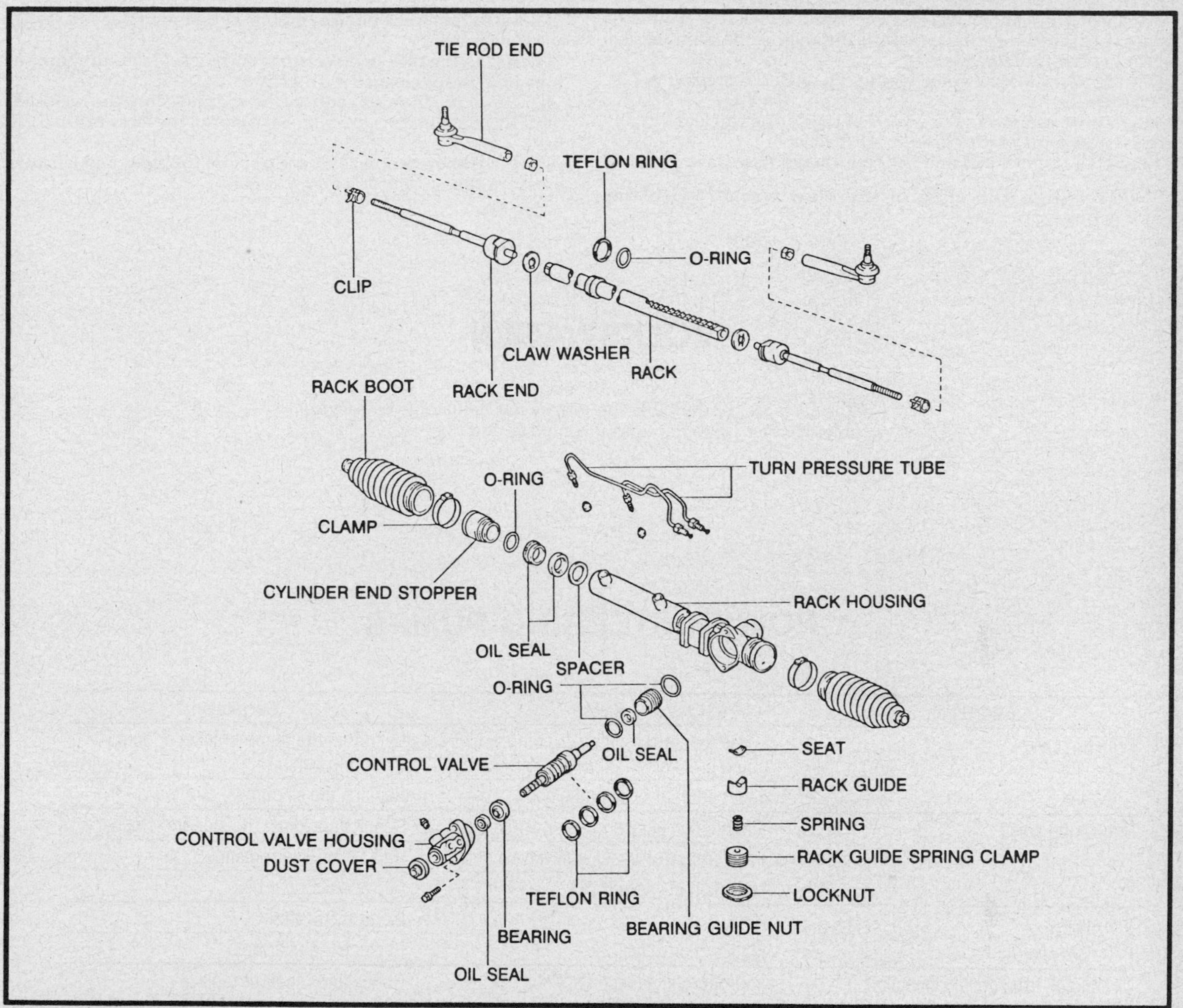

TIE ROD END

TEFLON RING

CLIP

O-RING

CLAW WASHER

RACK

RACK BOOT

RACK END

TURN PRESSURE TUBE

CLAMP

O-RING

CYLINDER END STOPPER

RACK HOUSING

OIL SEAL

SPACER

O-RING

OIL SEAL

CONTROL VALVE

SEAT

RACK GUIDE

SPRING

CONTROL VALVE HOUSING

DUST COVER

RACK GUIDE SPRING CLAMP

LOCKNUT

TEFLON RING

BEARING

BEARING GUIDE NUT

OIL SEAL

Exploded view of the power rack and pinion assembly—Toyota

28. Coat the oil seal with power steering fluid and wrap vinyl tape in the steering rack end.

29. Install the oil seal by pushing it into the cylinder, without tilting.

30. Install a new O-ring to the end stopper, tighten to 58 ft. lbs. Stake the housing and the stopper.

31. Coat the teflon ring and the O-ring with power steering fluid. Install the O-ring to the control valve housing. Push the control valve into the housing.

32. Install the bearing guide nut with the proper tool and tighten to 18 ft. lbs.

33. Stake the nut and install the dust cover.

34. Install a new O-ring to the valve housing. Align the marks on the valve housing and the rack housing.

35. Install the control valve and tighten the bolts to 13 ft. lbs.

36. Install the rack guide, seat and rack guide spring.

37. Apply a sealant to the threads of the spring cap and install the rack guide spring cap.

38. Using the proper tool, torque the rack guide spring cap to 18 ft. lbs. Return the rack guide spring cap 30 degrees.

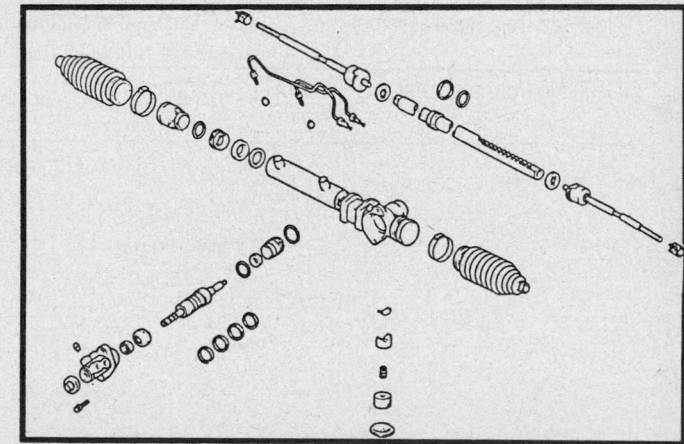

Lubrication points on the power rack assembly—Toyota

39. Turn the control valve shaft right and left a couple of times. Loosen the spring cap until the rack guide compression spring is not functioning.

40. Tighten the rack guide spring cap until the preload is 7.8–11.3 inch lbs.

41. Apply a sealant to the screws of the spring cap locknut. Install the locknut and tighten to 41 ft. lbs.

42. Stake the locknut and the cap. Install new claw washers.

NOTE: Align the claw of the claw washer with the rack groove.

43. Install the rack ends and tighten them to 65 ft. lbs. Stake the claw washer.

44. Install the rack boots, clamps and clips. Make sure that the tube hole is not clogged with grease.

45. Screw the locknuts and the tie rod ends onto the rack ends until the matchmarks are aligned. Tighten the locknuts to 51 ft. lbs.

46. Install new union seats and replace the right and left turn pressure tubes, tighten to 14 ft. lbs.

VOLKSWAGEN

The rack and pinion steering gear is not adjustable or serviceable, it must be replaced as a complete unit.

POWER STEERING PUMPS

Condition	Cause	Correction
Droning noise	Loose mounting bolt on oil pump or oil pump bracket	Retighten the pump bracket or pump mounting bolt
	Poor condition of oil pump body	Replace the oil pump
Squeaking noise	Malfunction of steering stopper contact	Check and adjust the steering stopper
	Interference of wheel with vehicle body	Adjust the steering angle
	Malfunction of gear box	Replace the gear box
Vibration	Air suction	Bleed the system
	Malfunction of gear box	Replace the gear box
Oil leakage from hose connection	Improperly tightened flare nut Incorrectly inserted hose Improperly clamped hose	Check and repair or replace
Oil leakage from hose assembly	Damaged or clogged hose Hose connector malfunction	Replace
Oil leakage from reservoir	Improperly welded pipe	Weld the pipes or replace
	Overflow	Bleed the system or adjust the oil level

Condition	Cause	Correction
Oil leakage from oil pump	Malfunction oil pump housing	Replace the oil pump
	Malfunction of O-ring and/or oil seal	Replace the O-ring and oil seal
Oil leakage from gear box	Malfunction of gear box housing (including leakage from air hole)	Replace the gear box
	Malfunction of O-ring and/or oil seal	Replace the O-ring and oil seal

CHRYSLER IMPORTS/MITSUBISHI

Vane Type Pump

Disassembly and Assembly

RAM 50 AND MITSUBISHI PICK-UP

1. Secure the pump assembly in a suitable holding fixture. Drain the fluid from the pump.
2. Remove the pump cover mounting bolts and remove the pump cover.
3. Lossen and remove the suction port assembly and remove the pressure fitting.

NOTE: On vehicles with the reservoir attached, remove the mounting bolts and remove the reservoir.

4. Remove the cam ring, vanes, O-ring, side plate assembly and the dowel pins.
5. Remove the shaft assembly snapring, the protector
6. Press out the shaft from the bearing and remove the shaft.

NOTE: Do not allow the shaft to drop.

7. Remove the oil seal with the proper tool. Remove the suction connector.
8. Remove the connector at the top of the pump body and remove the flow control valve assembly and flow control spring.

NOTE: Do not disasssemble the flow control valve.

9. Clean and check all parts for any wear or excessive damage. Always use new gaskets and lubricate all the parts with Dexron®II before assembling.

To assemble:
10. Check the amount of play between the pump shaft and the pump body. The clearance should be 0.008 in.
11. Install the flow control valve spring, flow control valve and the connecter into the pump body. Tighten the connector to 51–58 ft. lbs.
12. Install the seal into the pump body, using a suitable seal installer.

13. Press the shaft into the bearing with the proper tool.
14. Lubricate the vanes with the proper fluid and install the vanes on the rotor. Position the vanes with the rounded edge facing the cam ring.
15. When installing the cam ring, align the dowel pins of the pump body with the knock holes of the cam ring. Install so that the cam ring's punch mark is at the pump body side.
16. Install the pump cover and tighten the mounting bolts to 24–31 ft. lbs.
17. Install the suction connector and tighten to 10-13 ft. lbs.

EXCEPT RAM 50 AND MITSUBISHI PICK-UP

1. Secure the pump assembly in a suitable holding fixture. Drain the fluid.
2. Disconnect the suction connector and remove the O-ring.
3. Disconnect the top connector and remove the O-ring

NOTE: On vehicles with the reservoir attached, remove the mounting bolts and remove the reservoir.

4. Remove the flow control valve and the flow control spring from the pump housing. Do not disassemble the control valve.
5. Loosen the pump cover mounting bolts and remove the pump cover.
6. Remove the cam case, O-ring and the cam ring.
7. Remove the vanes and the snapring from the rotor. Remove the rotor.
8. Tap the side of the shaft and remove the pulley assembly.
9. Remove the oil seal, using the proper tool.
10. Clean and inspect the parts for any wear and excessive damage.

To assemble:
11. Install the vanes to the rotor grooves. Measure the gap between the vane and the rotor groove. The distance should be 0.0024 in.
12. Install the seal into the pump body, using the proper tool.
13. Lubricate the rotor with the proper fluid and install the rotor with the punch mark side facing the pump cover.
14. Lubricate the vanes and the cam ring with the proper fluid.

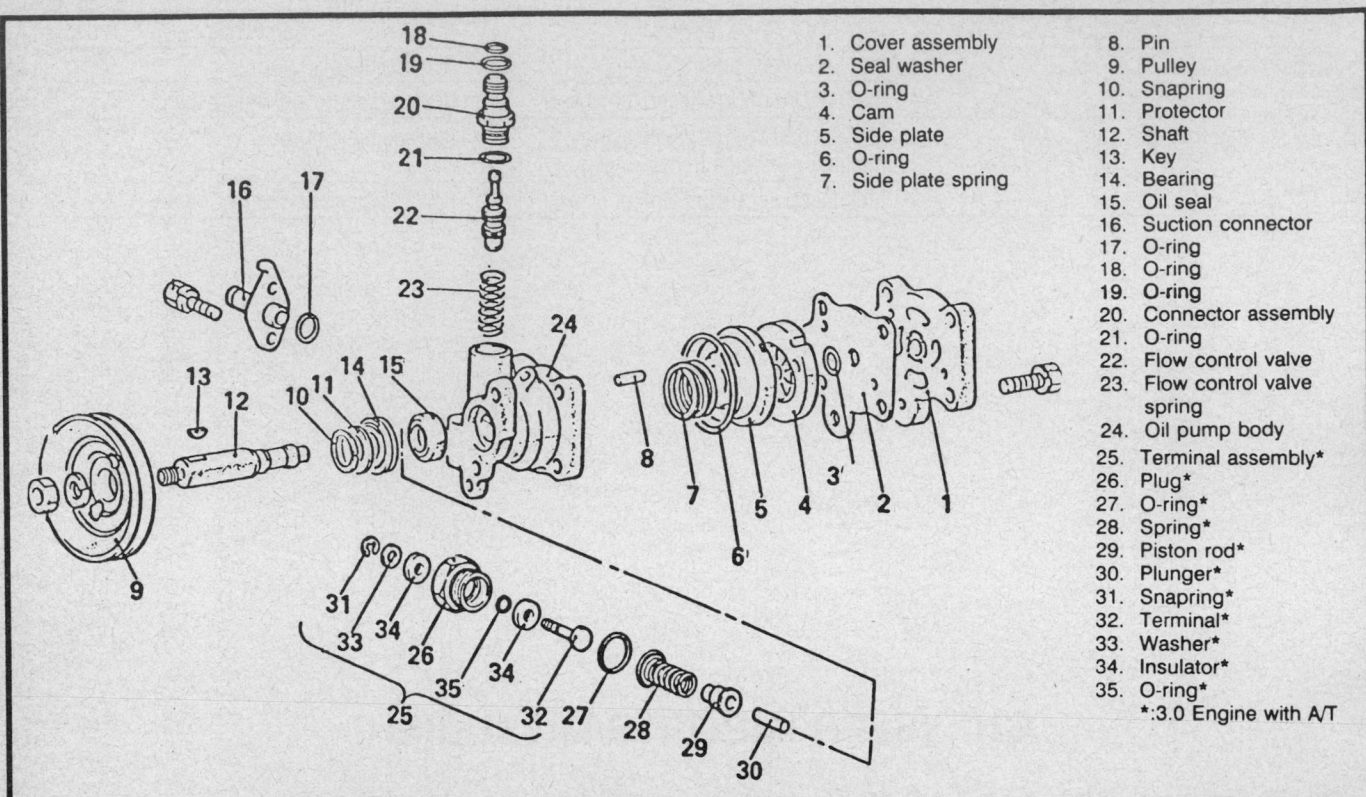

1. Cover assembly
2. Seal washer
3. O-ring
4. Cam
5. Side plate
6. O-ring
7. Side plate spring
8. Pin
9. Pulley
10. Snapring
11. Protector
12. Shaft
13. Key
14. Bearing
15. Oil seal
16. Suction connector
17. O-ring
18. O-ring
19. O-ring
20. Connector assembly
21. O-ring
22. Flow control valve
23. Flow control valve spring
24. Oil pump body
25. Terminal assembly*
26. Plug*
27. O-ring*
28. Spring*
29. Piston rod*
30. Plunger*
31. Snapring*
32. Terminal*
33. Washer*
34. Insulator*
35. O-ring*
*:3.0 Engine with A/T

Exploded view of the power steering pump—Ram 50 and Mitsubishi Pick-Up

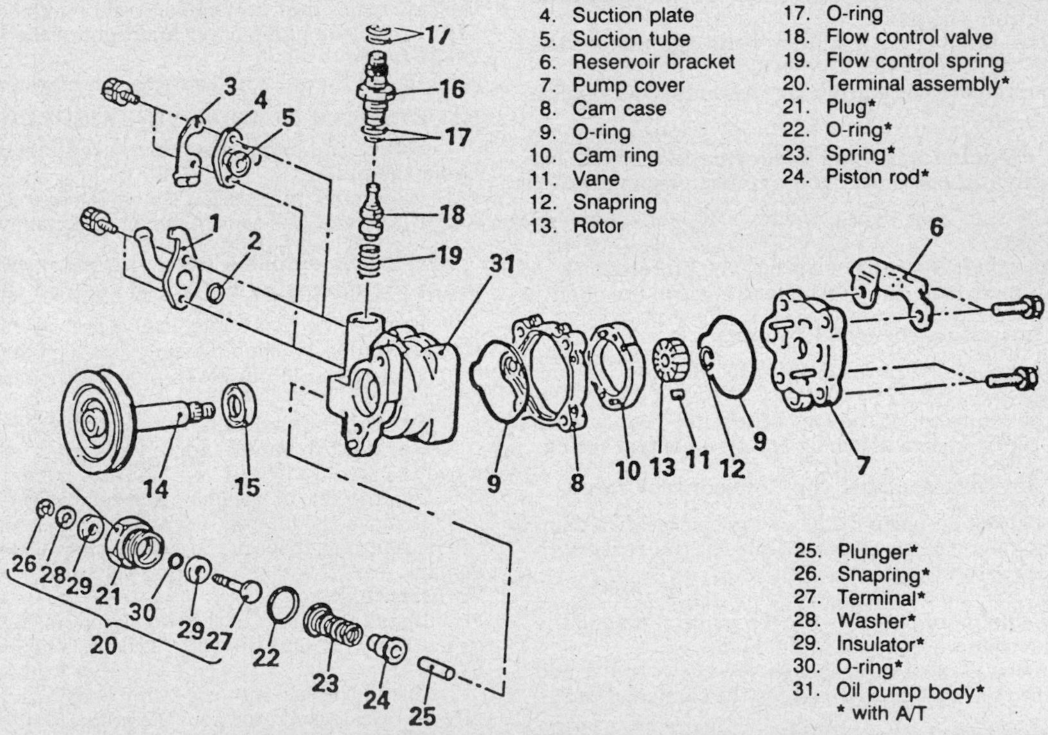

1. Suction connector
2. O-ring
3. Plate
4. Suction plate
5. Suction tube
6. Reservoir bracket
7. Pump cover
8. Cam case
9. O-ring
10. Cam ring
11. Vane
12. Snapring
13. Rotor
14. Pulley
15. Oil seal
16. Connector
17. O-ring
18. Flow control valve
19. Flow control spring
20. Terminal assembly*
21. Plug*
22. O-ring*
23. Spring*
24. Piston rod*
25. Plunger*
26. Snapring*
27. Terminal*
28. Washer*
29. Insulator*
30. O-ring*
31. Oil pump body*
* with A/T

Exploded view of the power steering pump—except Ram 50 and Mitsubishi Pick-Up

15. Align the dowel pins of the pump body with the dowel holes of the cam ring.

16. Install the vanes to the rotor with the round edge facing the cam ring.

17. Install the flow control valve, spring, O-ring and the top connector. Tighten the connector to 29–43 ft. lbs.

18. Install the cam case, O-ring and the cam ring.

19. Replace the pump cover and tighten the mounting bolts to 13–16 ft. lbs.

20. Install the oil seal, using the proper tool. Replace the pulley.

21. Replace and tighten the suction connector to 4–7 ft. lbs.

ISUZU

Vane Type pump

Disassembly and Assembly

C223 AND G200Z ENGINES

1. Secure the pump in suitable holding fixture. Remove the pulley, using the proper tool.

2. Remove the end plate retaining ring, using the proper tool, then remove the end plate.

3. Remove the pressure plate spring.

4. Remove the pump cartridge and shaft.

5. Remove the pressure plate.

6. Remove the cam.

7. Remove the retaining ring, then remove the rotor vane thrust plate and dowel pins.

8. Remove the O-rings from the pump housing.

9. Remove the control valve assembly.

10. Remove the oil seal from the housing, using the proper tool.

11. Clean all the parts and inspect for any wear or excessive damage.

To assemble:

12. Install the oil seal into the housing, using the proper seal installer tool.

13. Install the O-rings and the control valve assembly.

14. Insert the shaft and the pump cartridge. Install the vanes with the curved side facing the inner side of the cam. Set the side plate in the in the correct direction.

15. Insert the pressure plate spring and install the end plate.

16. Install the end plate retaining ring, using the proper tool to press the ring into position.

17. Install the pulley using a suitable tool.

4ZD1 ENGINE

1986–1988 Vehicles

1. Secure the pump assembly in a suitable holding fixture. Remove the pulley, using the proper tool.

2. Remove the connector, O-ring, flow control valve assembly and spring from the body.

3. Lossen the cover mounting bolts and remove the cover.

4. Remove the cam case and the O-ring.

5. Remove the snapring, using the proper tools, then remove the cartridge asembly, shaft assembly and the oil seal.

6. Clean all the parts and inspect for any damage or excessive wear.

7. Install the oil seal with the suitable tool.

8. Install the cartridge and shaft assembly with the specified rotor position facing up.

9. Align the holes of the cam ring to the slots of the body. The round end of the vane should be matched to the inner surface of the cam ring.

10. When installing the spacer and snapring, make sure the outer diameter of the snapring is less than 0.038 in.

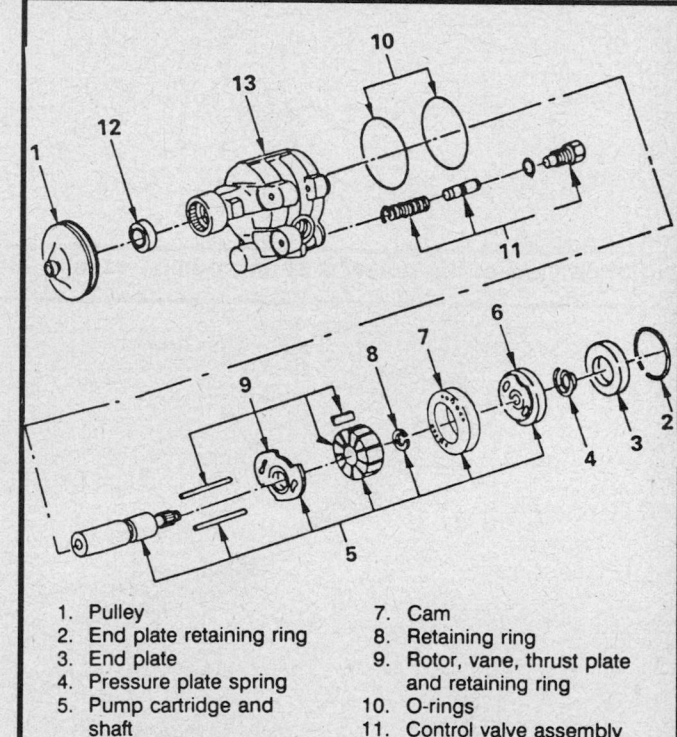

1. Pulley	7. Cam
2. End plate retaining ring	8. Retaining ring
3. End plate	9. Rotor, vane, thrust plate and retaining ring
4. Pressure plate spring	
5. Pump cartridge and shaft	10. O-rings
	11. Control valve assembly
6. pressure plate	12. Oil seal
	13. Pump housing

Exploded view of the power steering pump—Isuzu C223 and G200Z engines

4ZE1 AND 4ZD1 ENGINES

1988–1990 Vehicles

1. Secure the pump in a suitable holding fixture.

2. Disconnect the connector and remove the O-ring.

3. Remove the flow control valve assembly and spring.

4. Loosen the mounting bolts and remove the cover and gasket.

5. Disconnect the pin and remove the cartridge assembly and the pressure plate.

6. Remove the snapring with a suitable tool and remove the shaft assembly.

7. Remove the bearing from the shaft.

8. Remove the retaining ring, oil seal and the O-rings.

9. Loosen the bolts and remove the hose connecting pipe—4ZE1 engines.

10. Clean all the parts and inspect for any damage or excessive wear.

11. Install the hose connecting pipe and tighten the bolts to 13–18 ft. lbs. on the 4ZE1 engine.

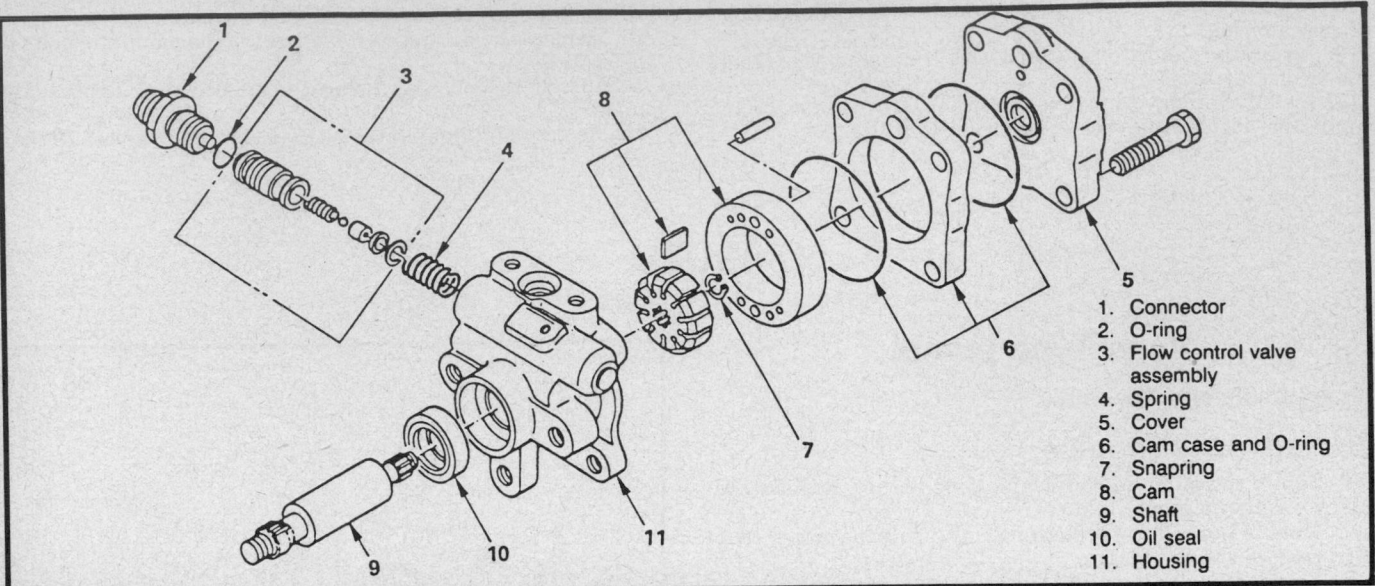

Exploded view of the power steering pump—except 1989–90 Isuzu with 4ZD1 engine

1. Connector
2. O-ring
3. Flow control valve assembly
4. Spring
5. Cover
6. Cam case and O-ring
7. Snapring
8. Cam
9. Shaft
10. Oil seal
11. Housing

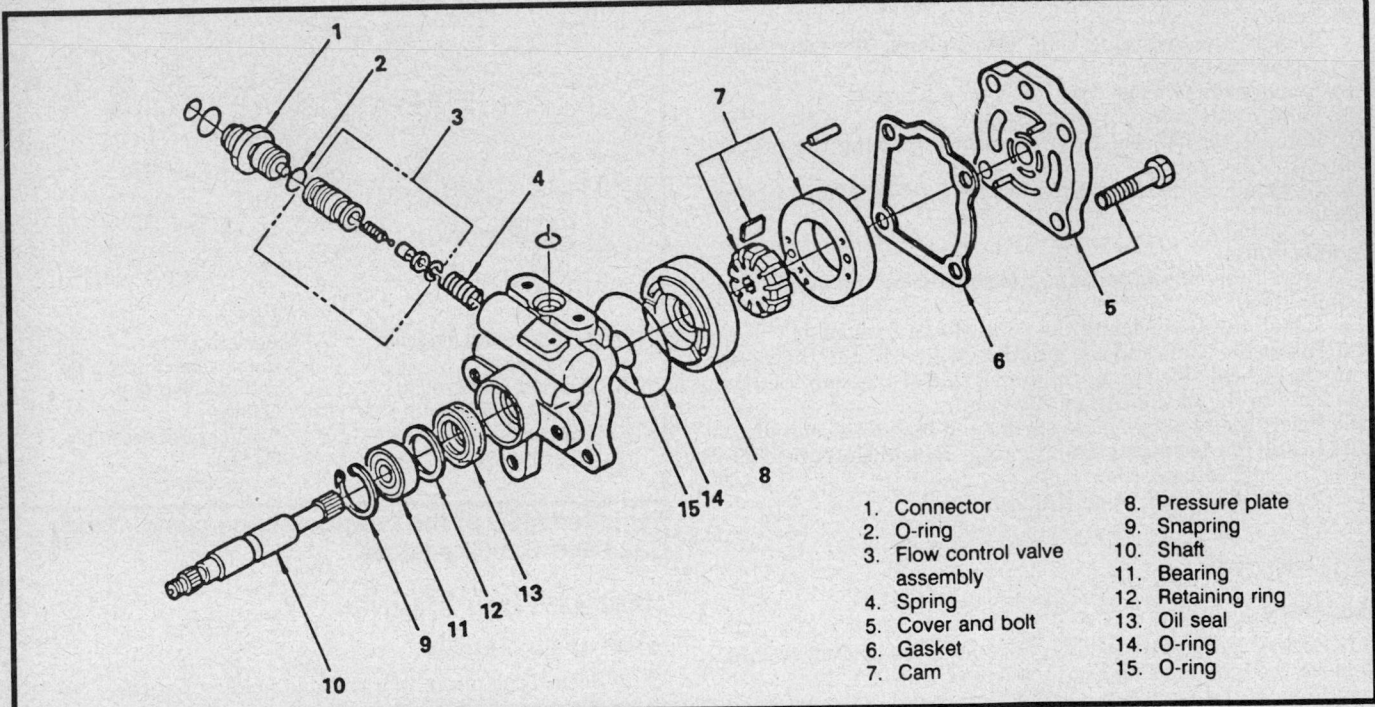

Exploded view of the power steering pump—1989–90 Isuzu with 4ZD1 engine

1. Connector
2. O-ring
3. Flow control valve assembly
4. Spring
5. Cover and bolt
6. Gasket
7. Cam
8. Pressure plate
9. Snapring
10. Shaft
11. Bearing
12. Retaining ring
13. Oil seal
14. O-ring
15. O-ring

12. Install the gasket and the cover. Tighten the bolts to 36–43 ft. lbs.

13. Insert the cartridge assembly with the rotor specified mark facing up.

14. Align the holes of the cam ring to the slots in the body. The round end of the vane should be matched to the inner surface of the cam ring.

15. Install the oil seal, using the proper tool.

16. Install the retaining ring, shaft and bearing and replace the snapring.

17. Insert the flow control spring and valve assembly. Tighten the connector to 36–43 ft. lbs.

CPC ENGINE

1. Secure the pump in a suitable holding fixture. Remove pulley with a suitable tool.
2. Remove the connector, pump mounting bolts and the O-rings.
3. Drain the oil from the reservoir and remove the reservoir.
4. Remove the magnet and the end retaining ring with the proper tool.
5. Remove the end plate and take out the pressure plate spring, pump cartridge and shaft assembly.
6. Remove the pressure plate, cam and retaining ring.
7. Remove the rotor, vanes, thrust plate and dowel pins.
8. Remove the O-rings and take out the control valve assembly.

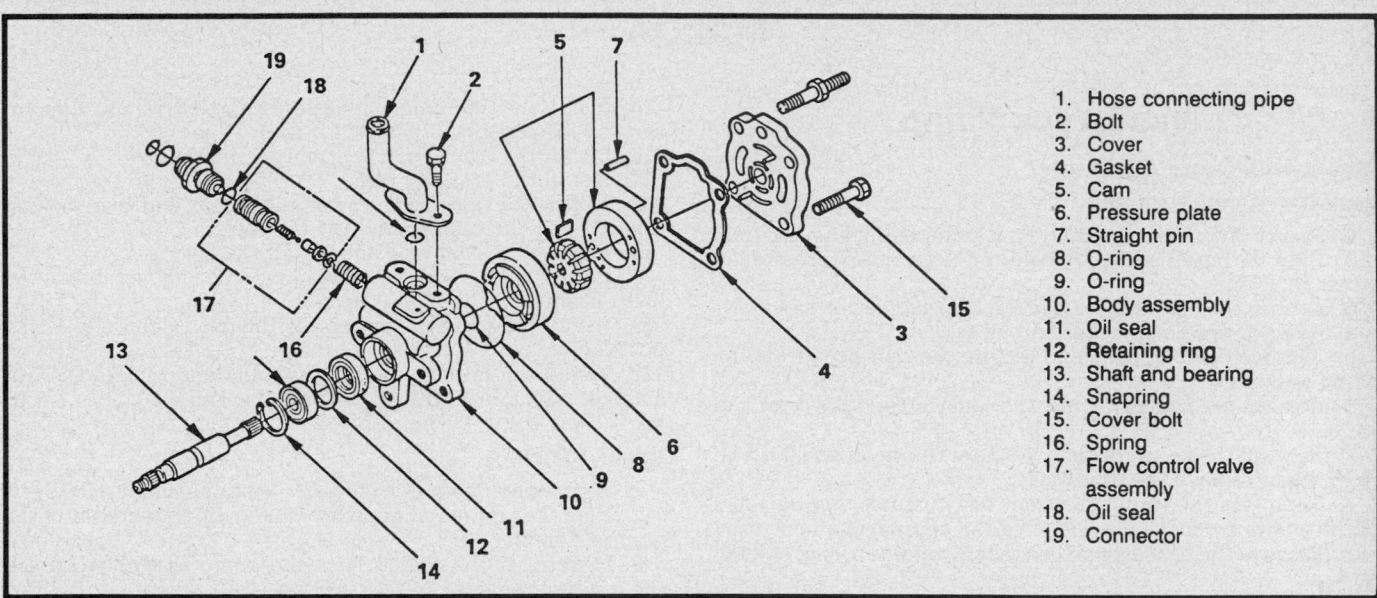

Exploded view of the power steering pump—Isuzu 4ZE1 engine

1. Hose connecting pipe
2. Bolt
3. Cover
4. Gasket
5. Cam
6. Pressure plate
7. Straight pin
8. O-ring
9. O-ring
10. Body assembly
11. Oil seal
12. Retaining ring
13. Shaft and bearing
14. Snapring
15. Cover bolt
16. Spring
17. Flow control valve assembly
18. Oil seal
19. Connector

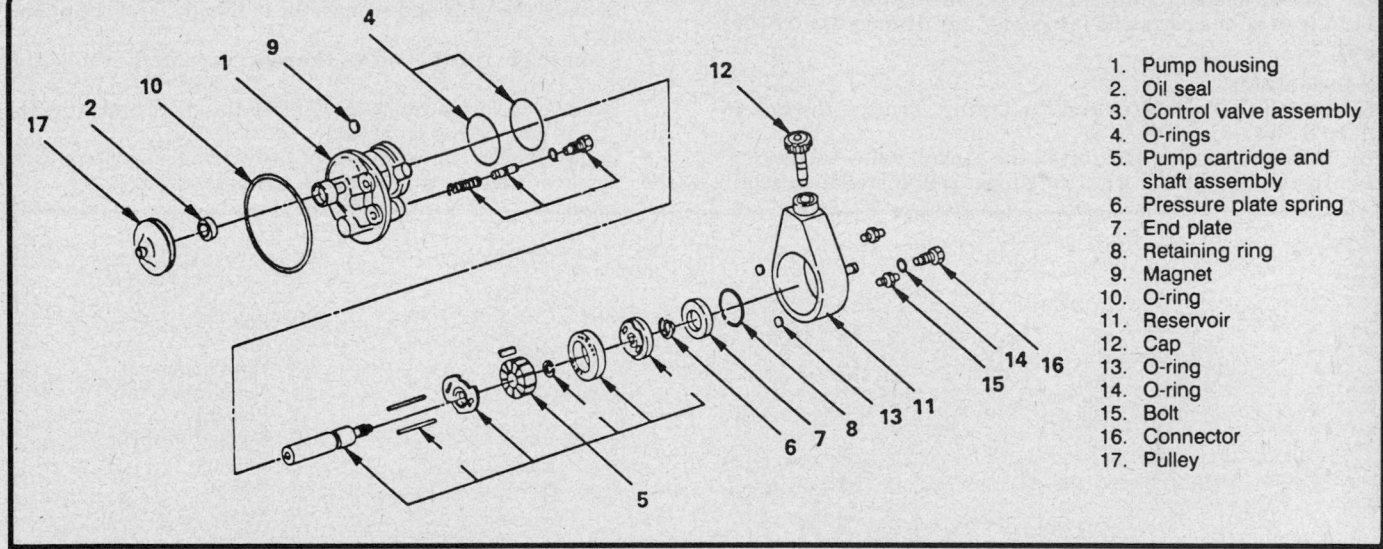

Exploded view of the power steering pump—Isuzu CPC engine

1. Pump housing
2. Oil seal
3. Control valve assembly
4. O-rings
5. Pump cartridge and shaft assembly
6. Pressure plate spring
7. End plate
8. Retaining ring
9. Magnet
10. O-ring
11. Reservoir
12. Cap
13. O-ring
14. O-ring
15. Bolt
16. Connector
17. Pulley

9. Remove the oil seal from the pump housing with proper tool.
10. Clean all the parts and inspect for any damage or excessive wear.

NOTE: Never remove the welch plug on top of the pump body.

To assemble:
11. Install the oil seal into the housing, using the proper seal installer tool.
12. Install the O-rings and the control valve assembly.

13. Insert the shaft and the pump cartridge. Install the vanes with the curved side facing the inner side of the cam. Set the side plate in the in the correct direction.
14. Insert the pressure plate spring and install the end plate.
15. Install the end plate retaining ring, using the proper tool.
16. Install the magnet into the pump housing and replace the O-rings.
17. Install the reservoir and replace the pump mounting bolts. Tighten to 26 ft. lbs.
18. Install the connector and tihgten to 55 ft. lbs.
19. Install the pulley with the proper tool.

MAZDA

Vane Type Pump

Disassembly and Assembly

EXCEPT B2600 SERIES

1. Secure the pump assembly in a suitable holding fixture.
2. Plug the pipe installation hole and clean the exterior of the pump assembly.
3. Loosen the bolt and remove the hose connector assembly.
4. Remove the nut, washer and oil tank.
5. Remove the long bolts and remove the rear body from the pump assembly.
6. Remove the rubber O-ring, the cam ring and the rotor and vanes.
7. Remove the pressure plate. Remove the small and large O-rings, then remove the front body.
8. Compress the clip in the front body using snapring pliers then remove from the groove using the appropriate tool.
8. Remove the bearing and driveshaft, retaining ring and the oil seal.
9. Remove the control valve and O-ring assembly and take out the spring.
10. Loosen the bolt and remove the connector and O-ring.
11. Clean all the parts and inspect for any damage or excessive wear.

To assemble:

12. Install the connector and the O-ring. Tighten the bolt to 13–18 ft. lbs.
13. Insert the spring and install the control valve and O-ring.
14. Install the oil seal with the proper seal installation tool.

15. Install the retaining ring, bearing and driveshaft, then insert the snapring with the proper tool.
16. Install the front body and replace the O-rings.
17. Install the pressure plate.
18. Attach the vanes to the rotor with the round edge making contact with the cam. Install the rotor.
19. Replace the cam ring and install the O-ring.
20. Place the rear body into the pump housing and install the bolts. Tighten to 13–22 ft. lbs.
21. Install the oil tank and replace the nut. Tighten to 12–14 ft. lbs.
22. Install the hose connector assembly and replace the nut and bolt. Tighten the nut to 22–25 ft. lbs. and the bolt to 4–7 ft. lbs.

B2600 SERIES

1. Secure the pump assembly in a suitable holding fixture.
2. Plug the pipe installation hole and clean the exterior of the pump assembly.
3. Disconnect the switch from the pump assembly. Loosen the nut and remove the rear bracket.
4. Remove the nut and remove the pulley with the proper tool.
5. Remove the bolts and remove the rear body from the pump assembly.
6. Remove the rubber O-ring, the cam ring and the rotor and vanes.
7. Remove the pressure plate. Remove the small and large O-rings, then remove the front body.
8. Compress the clip in the front body using snapring pliers then remove from the groove using the appropriate tool.

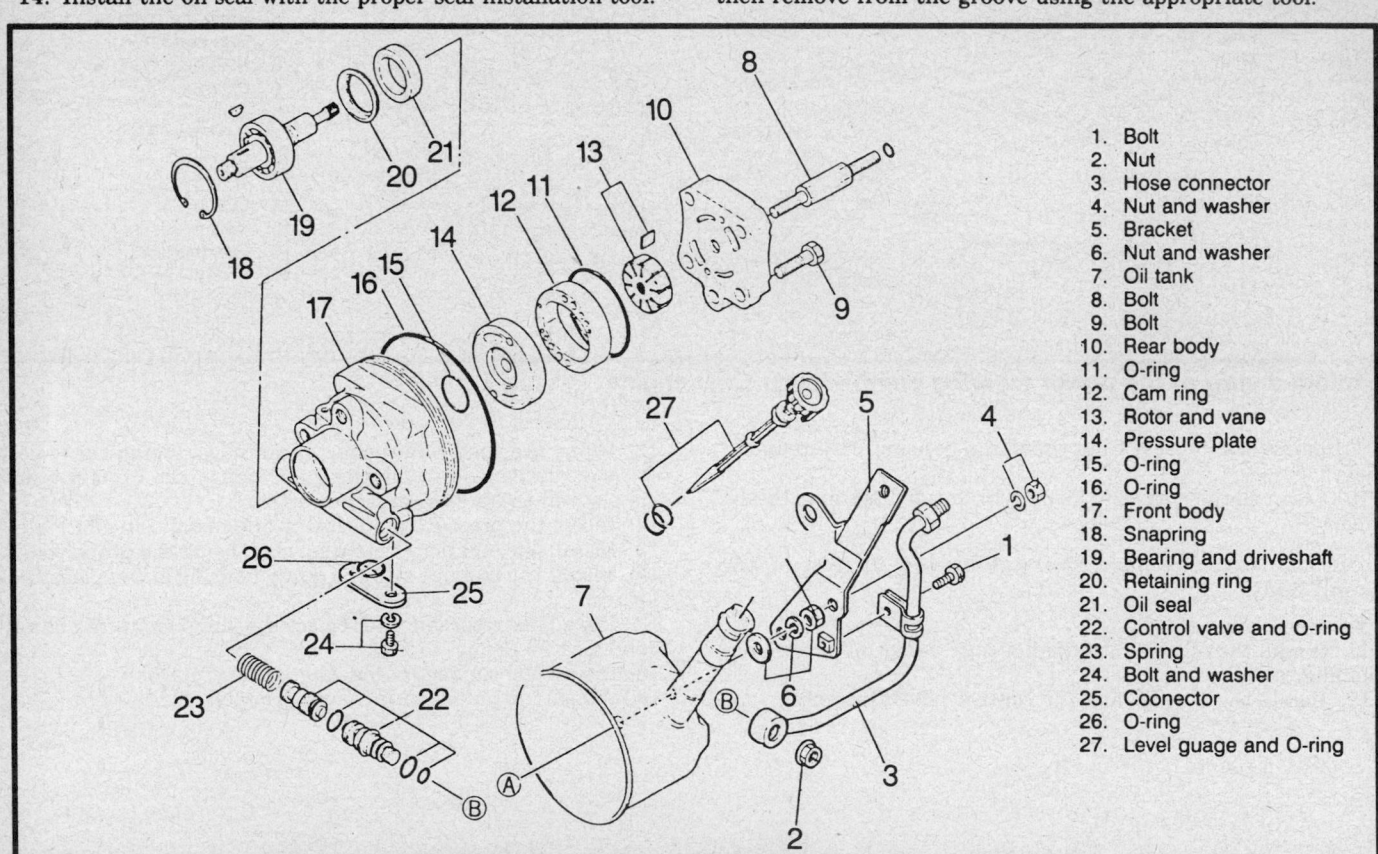

1. Bolt
2. Nut
3. Hose connector
4. Nut and washer
5. Bracket
6. Nut and washer
7. Oil tank
8. Bolt
9. Bolt
10. Rear body
11. O-ring
12. Cam ring
13. Rotor and vane
14. Pressure plate
15. O-ring
16. O-ring
17. Front body
18. Snapring
19. Bearing and driveshaft
20. Retaining ring
21. Oil seal
22. Control valve and O-ring
23. Spring
24. Bolt and washer
25. Coonector
26. O-ring
27. Level guage and O-ring

Exploded view of the power steering pump—except Mazda B2600

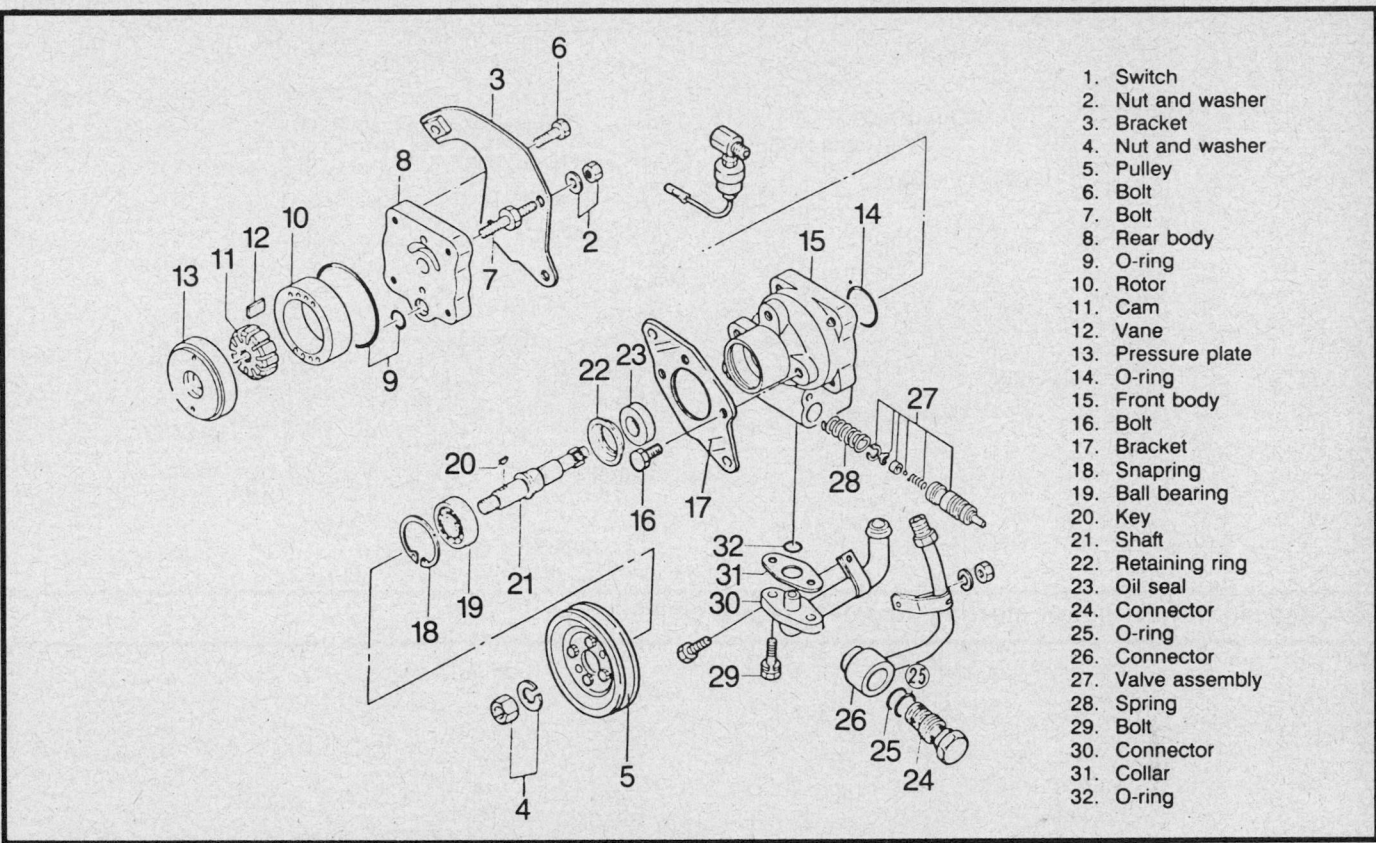

1. Switch
2. Nut and washer
3. Bracket
4. Nut and washer
5. Pulley
6. Bolt
7. Bolt
8. Rear body
9. O-ring
10. Rotor
11. Cam
12. Vane
13. Pressure plate
14. O-ring
15. Front body
16. Bolt
17. Bracket
18. Snapring
19. Ball bearing
20. Key
21. Shaft
22. Retaining ring
23. Oil seal
24. Connector
25. O-ring
26. Connector
27. Valve assembly
28. Spring
29. Bolt
30. Connector
31. Collar
32. O-ring

Exploded view of the power steering pump – Mazda B2600

8. Remove the bearing and driveshaft, retaining ring and the oil seal.

9. Remove the O-ring and both connectors.

10 Remove the control valve and O-ring assembly and take out the spring.

11. Loosen the bolt and remove the connector, collar and O-ring.

12. Clean all the parts and inspect for any damage or excessive wear.

To assemble:

13. Install the connector, collar and the O-ring.

14. Insert the spring and install the control valve and O-ring.

15. Install the oil seal with the proper seal installation tool.

16. Insert the O-ring and replace both connectors.

17. Install the retaining ring, bearing and driveshaft, then insert the snapring with the proper tool.

18. Install the front body and replace the O-rings.

19. Install the pressure plate

20. Attach the vanes to the rotor with the round edge making contact with the cam. Install the the rotor.

21. Replace the cam ring and install the O-ring.

22. Place the rear body into the pump housing and install the bolts.

23. Install the pulley and replace the nut. Tighten to 29–43 ft. lbs.

24. Replace the rear bracket and install the switch into the pump housing.

NISSAN

Vane Type Pump

Disassembly and Assembly

VG, SD AND Z ENGINES

1. Secure the pump in a suitable holding fixture.

2. Inscribe matching marks on the rear cover and the housing.

3. Loosen the rear cover mounting bolts and remove the rear cover.

4. Remove the O-ring from the cam case, using the proper tool.

5. Remove the cam case and the O-ring.

6. Remove the rotor, making sure that the vane does not come off the rotor.

7. Remove the snapring with the proper tool and lift out the pulley shaft. Note the direction of the rotor.

8. Remove the oil seal with the proper tool, making sure not to damage casing.

9. Remove the connector, making sure not to drop the spool.

10. Remove the suction pipe, then remove the O-ring.

11. Clean all the parts and inspect for any damage or excessive wear.

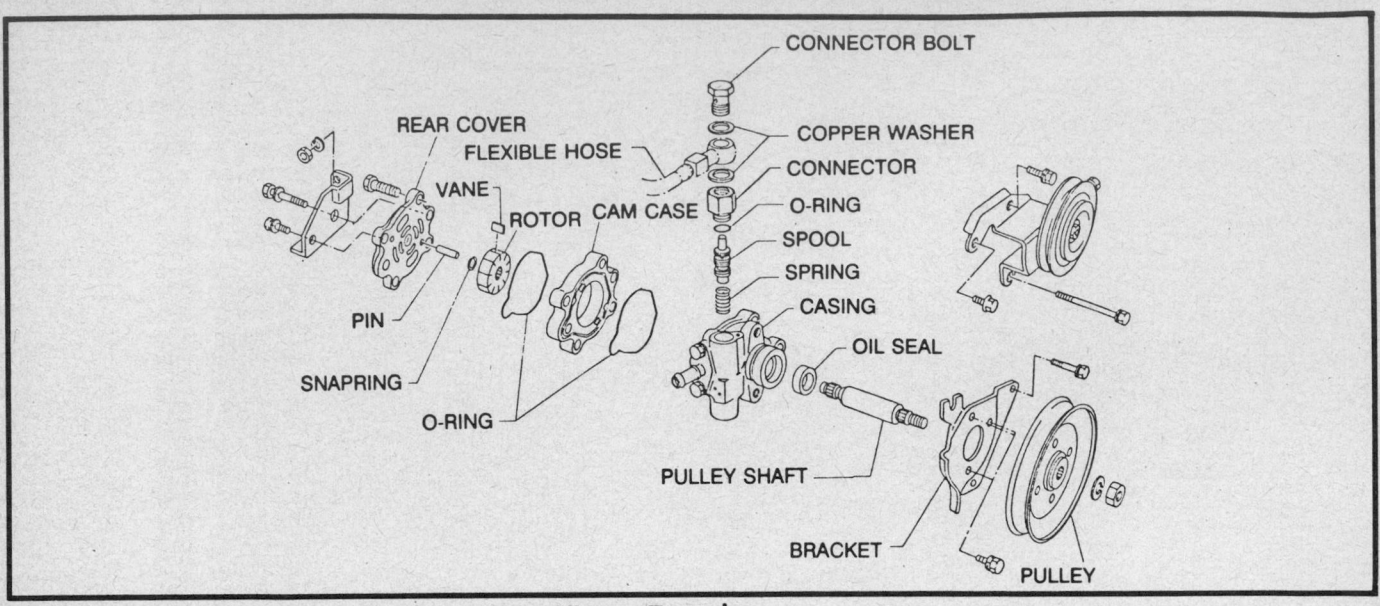

Exploded view of the power steering pump—Nissan Z engine

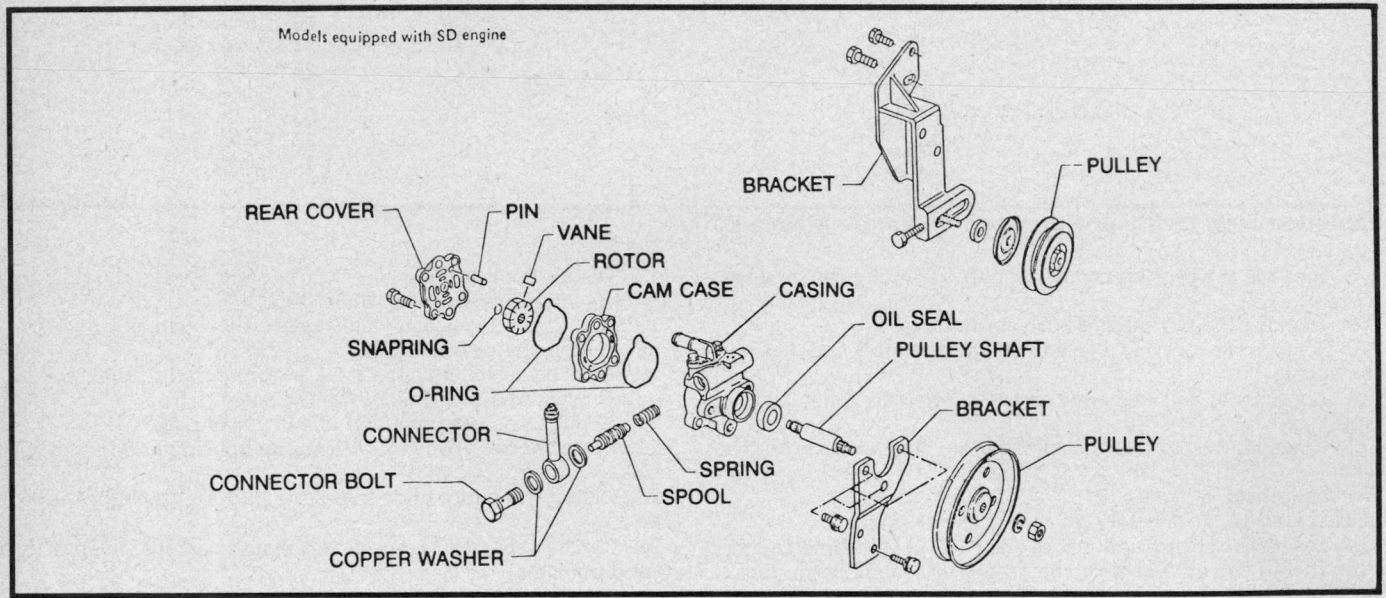

Exploded view of the power steering pump—Nissan SD engine

To assemble:

12. Lubricate the O-rings and the oil seals with power steering.

13. Install the O-ring and replace the suction pipe.

14. Install the spool and replace the connector. Tighten to 51–58 ft. lbs.

15. Replace the oil seal with the proper tool.

16. Insert the pulley shaft and replace the snapring using the proper tool.

17. Install the rotor with the punch mark facing the front housing and the portion without the punch mark faces the cam side.

18. Insert the O-ring and replace the cam case.

19. Install the rear cover and tighten the mounting bolts to 28–38 ft. lbs.

KA24E ENGINE

1. Secure the pump in a suitable holding fixture.

2. Remove the snapring, using the proper tool, then draw the pulley shaft out.

3. Remove the oil seal, being careful not to damage the housing.

4. Remove the connector. Be careful not to drop the control valve.

5. Loosen the rear housing mounting bolts and remove the rear housing.

6. Remove the pins from the pin grooves and remove the cam ring, rotor and vanes as a unit.

7. Clean and inspect each component for damage or excessive wear.

8. Lubricate all the components with power steering fluid.

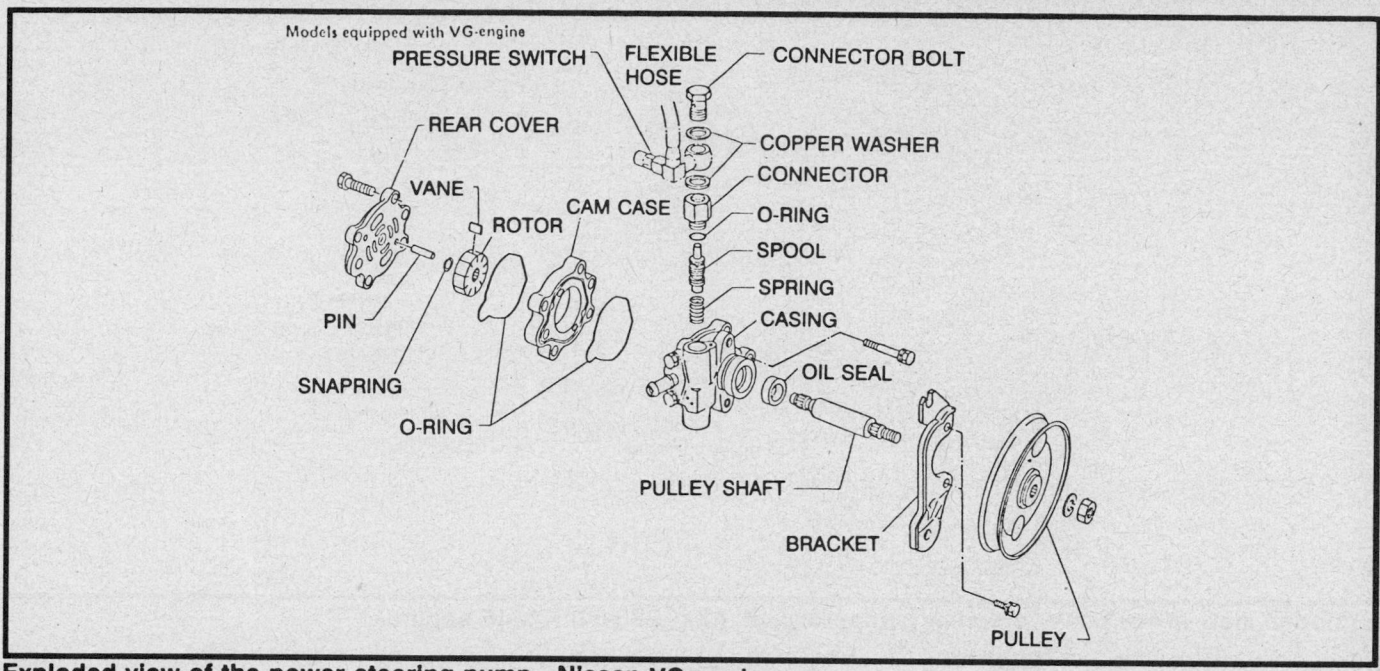

Exploded view of the power steering pump—Nissan VG engine

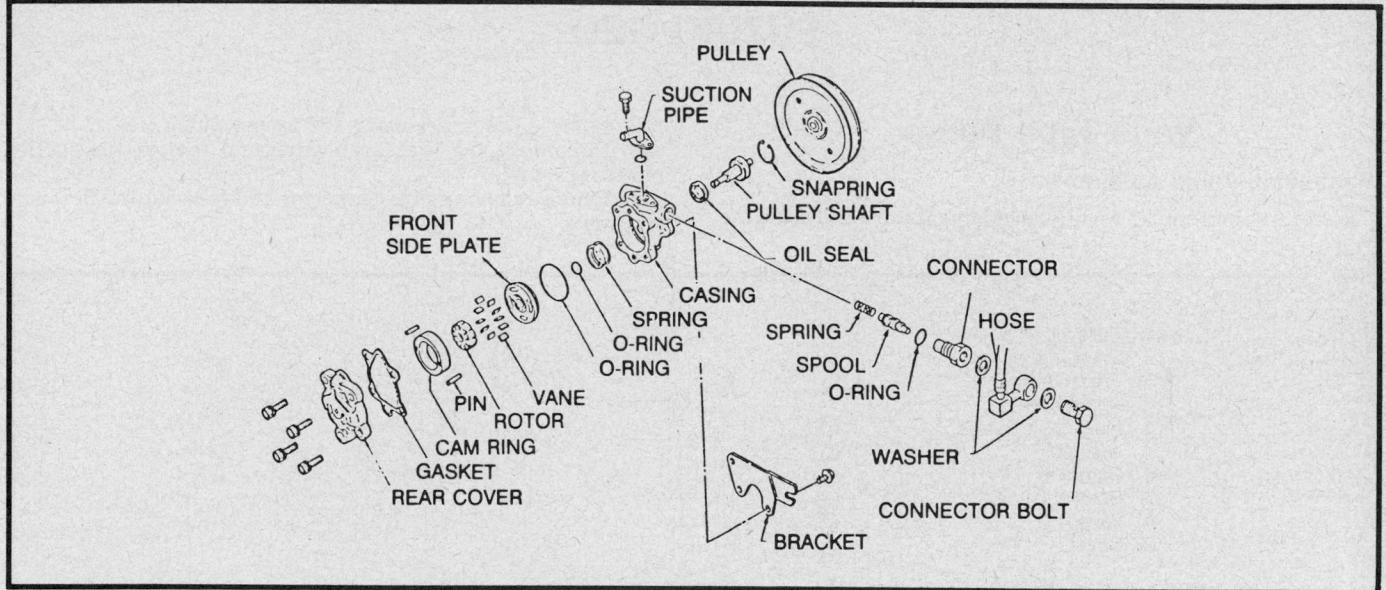

Exploded view of the power steering pump—AXXESS with KA24E engine

9. Assemble the vanes to the rotor with the rounded surface of the vanes facing the cam ring side.

10. Insert the pins into the grooves of the front housing and the front side plate.

11. Install the cam ring. Replace the rear cover and tighten the mounting bolts to 23–31 ft. lbs.

12. Insert the control valve and replace the connector. Tighten to 51–58 ft. lbs.

13. Insert the pulley shaft and replace the snapring with the proper tool.

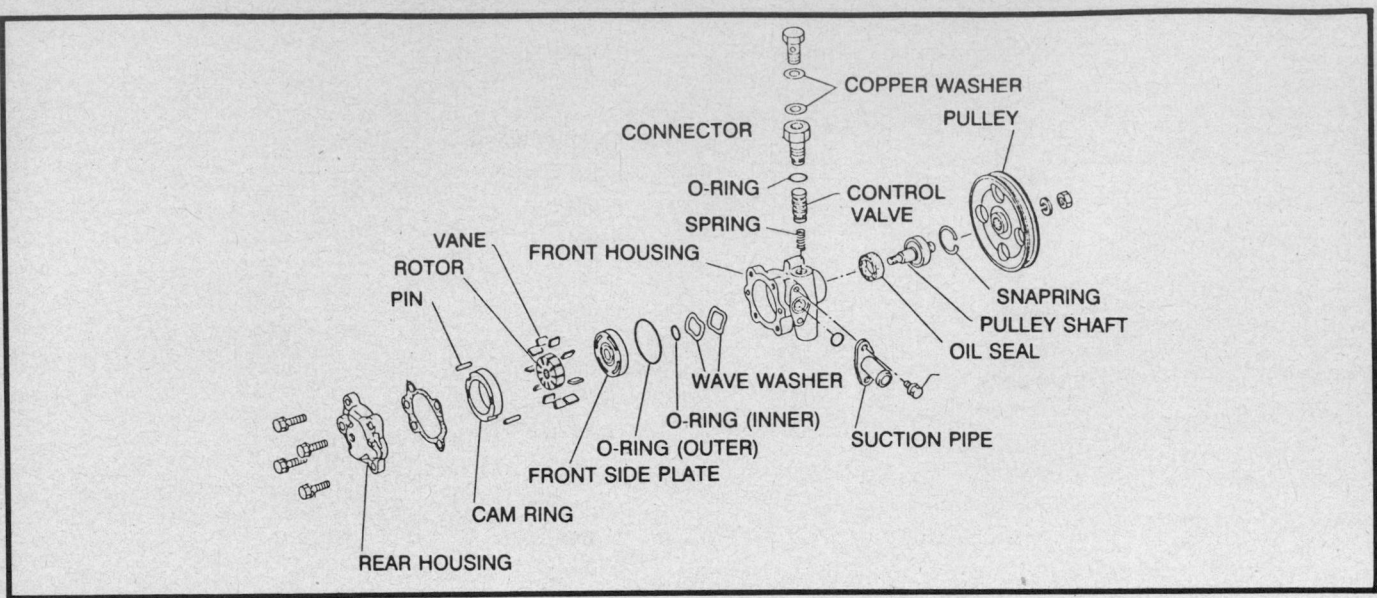

Exploded view of the power steering pump—except AXXESS with KA24E engine

SUZUKI/GEO

Vane Type Pump

Disassembly and Assembly

1. Secure the pump in a suitable holding fixture and drain the fluid.

2. Remove the puller using the proper puller.
3. Disconnect the pressure switch and remove the suction pipe connector.
4. Remove the pressure connector and take out the flow control valve.

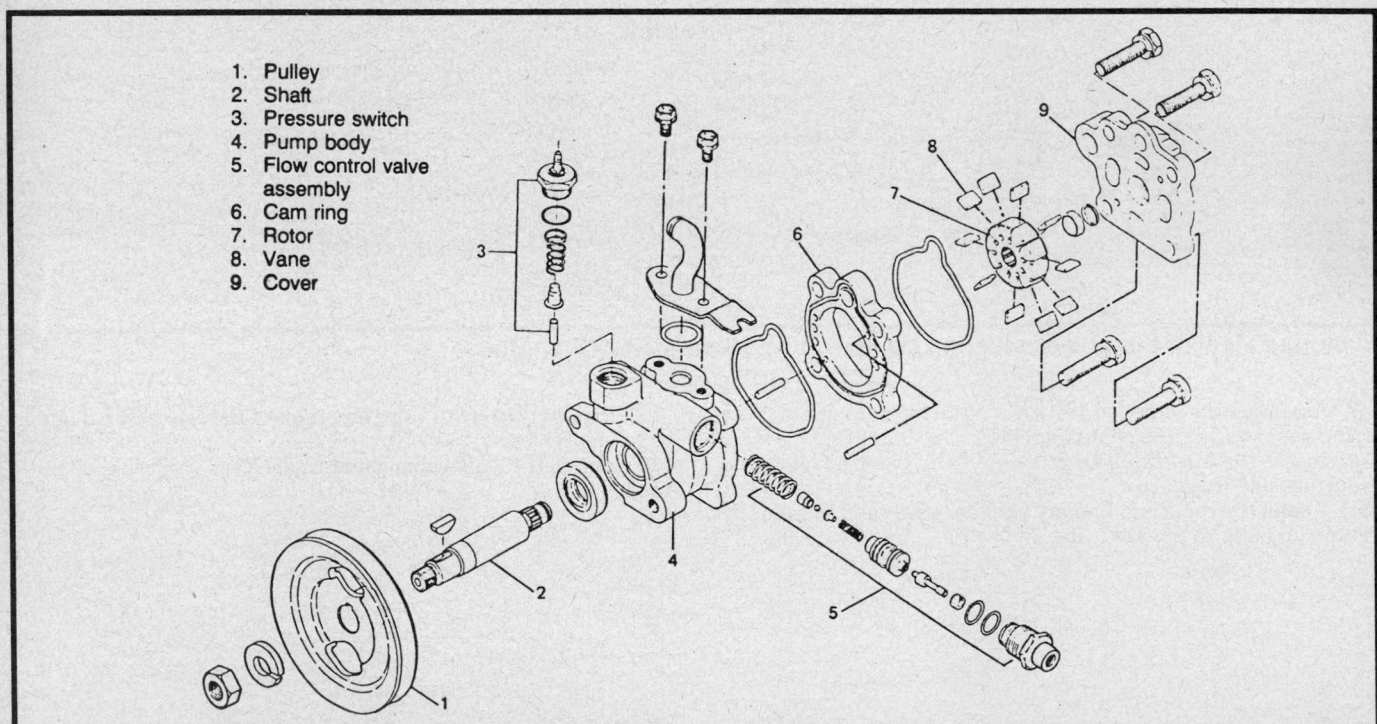

1. Pulley
2. Shaft
3. Pressure switch
4. Pump body
5. Flow control valve assembly
6. Cam ring
7. Rotor
8. Vane
9. Cover

Exploded view of the power steering pump—Suzuki/ Geo

5. Remove the pump cam ring and remove the rotor snapring, using the proper tool.
6. Remove the rotor and the vanes.
7. Remove the pump shaft and pry out the shaft oil seal with a suitable seal remover.
8. Clean and inspect all the parts for damage or excessive wear.

To assemble:
9. Lubricate all the parts with the proper power steering fluid.
10. Insert the shaft oil seal with the proper tool.

11. Install the pump shaft and the rotor and vanes, with the vanes facing the proper direction.
12. Install the O-ring seals and replace the cam ring. Tighten the cam bolts to 15 ft. lbs.
13. Install the flow control valve and replace the pressure connector. Tighten the connector bolts to 43 ft. lbs.
14. Install the suction pipe connector and tighten the bolts to 7.4 ft. lbs.
15. Install the pressure switch and tighten to 21 ft. lbs.
16. Install the pump pulley and replace the nut. Tighten the nut to 32 ft. lbs.

TOYOTA

Vane Type Pump

Disassembly and Assembly

1. Secure the pump in a suitable holding fixture.
2. Remove the air control valve from the rear housing on the 22R–E engine.
3. Remove the suction port union from the rear housing—exc. Land Cruiser.
4. Remove the reservoir tank and the O-ring on the Land Cruiser.
5. Place matchmarks on the front and rear housing.
6. Remove the 4 front housing bolts, then using the proper tool, tap off the front housing. Be careful that the vane plates, rotor and cam ring do not fall out.
7. Remove the cam ring, rotor and vane plates.

NOTE: Be careful not to scratch the cam ring, rotor or vane plates.

8. Secure the front housing in a suitable holding fixture. Pry off the oil seal using the proper tool.
9. Remove the snapring, using the proper tool. Using a plastic hammer, lightly tap the rotor shaft out of the front housing.
10. Tap the bottom end of the rear housing and remove the rear plate and spring.
11. Temporarily install a bolt to the plug. Push the bolt and remove the ssnapring with the proper tool.
12. Pull out the bolt and remove the plug. Remove the spring and flow control valve by hand.

NOTE: Be careful not to drop, scratch or nick the valve.

13. Remove the pressure port union.
14. Check the front housing bushing for wear or damage. If wear or damage is found, the entire housing must be replaced.
15. Check the oil clearance between the bushing and rotor shaft. Maximum oil clearance is 0.0028 in. except Land Cruiser and 0.0012 in. on Land Cruiser.
16. If neccessary, replace the rotor shaft bearing.
  a. Remove the snapring with the proper tool. Using a suitable press, press out the old bearing and press in the new one.
  b. Install the snapring with the proper tool.
17. Measure the cam ring thickness. Check that the difference between the rotor and cam ring is less than the maximum 0.0024 in. If the difference is excessive, replace the cam ring with one having the same letter as the rotor.
18. Check the vane plates for wear or scratches.
19. Measure the clearance between the vane plate and the rotor groove. Maximum clearance is 0.0024 in. except Land Cruiser and 0.0012 in. for Land Cruiser.
20. Check the flow control valve for wear or damage. If neces-

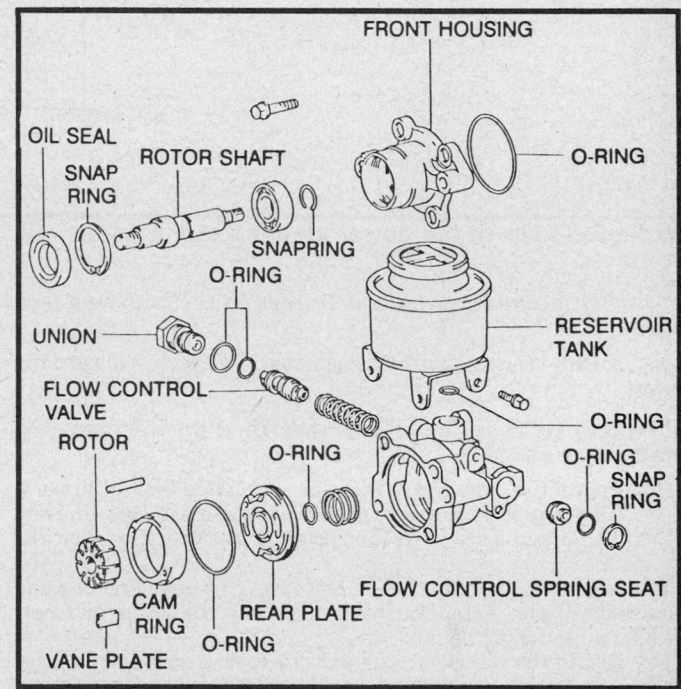

Exploded view of the power steering pump—1986–88 Land Cruiser

sary, replace the valve with one having the same letter on the rear housing.
21. Check that the flow control valve spring is within 1.85–1.97 in. If not replace it.

To assemble:
22. Install the flow control valve, spring, plug and snapring.

NOTE: Make sure the letter inscribed on the flow control valve matches the letter stamped on the rear of the pump body.

23. Install the pressure port union and tighten to 51 ft. lbs.
24. Install the rotor shaft to the front housing by tapping it with the proper tool.
25. Install the snapring to the front housing with the proper tool.
26. Apply a light coat of MP grease to the oil seal lip, then using the proper tool, install the oil seal.
27. Install the O-ring except on Land Cruiser.
28. Align the fluid passages of the cam ring and front housing, and install the cam ring.

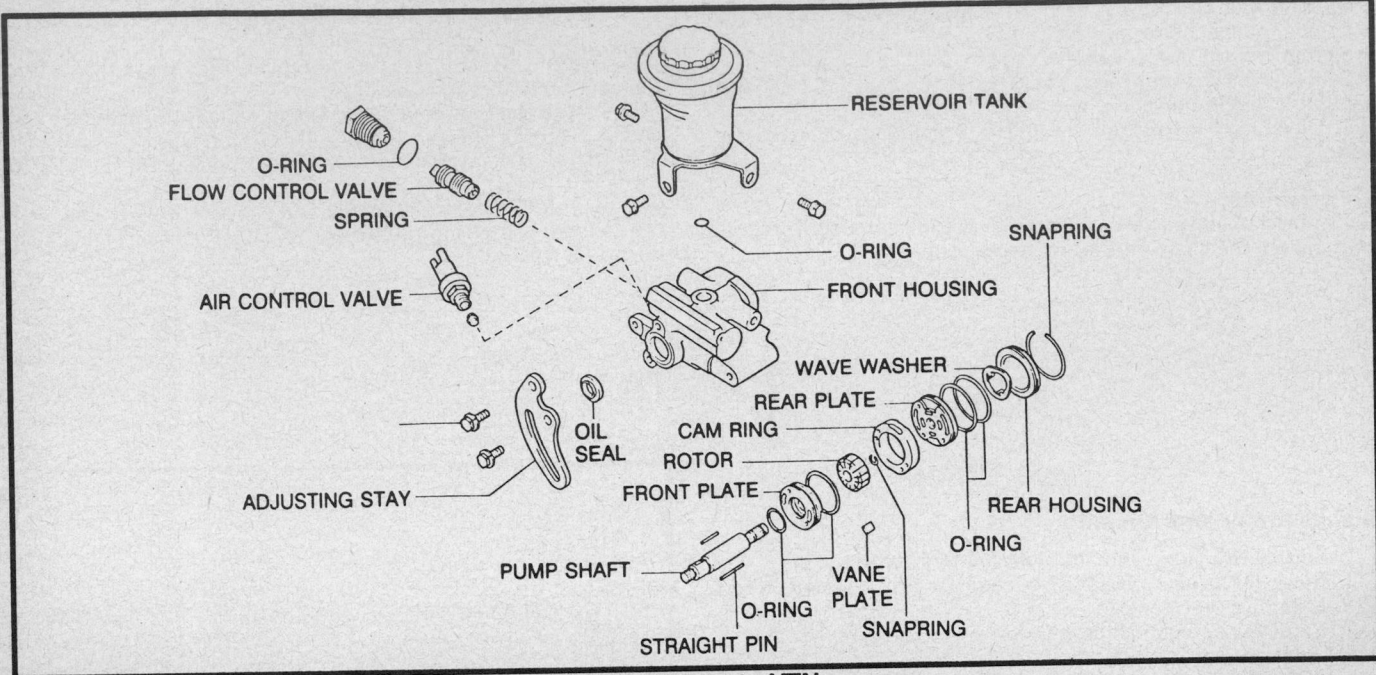

Exploded view of the power steering pump—1989–90 Toyota VZN pump

NOTE: Make sure that the letters on the cam ring face upward.

29. Install the rotor with the camfered end facing toward the front.

NOTE: Be sure the letters inscribed on the cam ring and rotor match.

30. Install the vane plates with the round end facing outward.

31. Align the fluid passages of the rear plate and cam ring and install the rear plate with the spring. Place the spring on the rear plate.

32. Align the matchmarks on the front and rear housing and assemble them. Temporarily, tighten the the front and rear housing mounting bolts.

33. Install the reservoir tank and the O-ring on Land Cruiser.

34. Secure the rear housing in a suitable holding fixture, then tighten the housing bolts evenly to 34 ft. lbs. Tighten the reservoir tank bolts to 9 ft. lbs. on Land Cruiser.

35. Insert the union to the rear housing and tighten to 9 ft. lbs.

36. Install the air control valve to the rear housing and tighten to 27 ft. lbs. on the 22R-E engine.

37. Check that the rotor shaft rotates smoothly. Check the rotating torque; the rotating torque should be lees than 2.4 inch lbs.

VZN Series Pump

Disassembly and Assembly

1. Secure the pump in a suitable holding fixture.
2. Remove the air control valve and take out the union seat.
3. Remove the mounting bolts and lift off the reservoir tank. Remove the O-ring from the reservoir tank.
4. Remove the pressure port union and remove the O-ring from the union.
5. Remove the flow control valve and the spring from the housing.
6. Remove the snapring with the proper tool and tap out the rear housing. Pry out the O-ring from the rear housing.

7. Tap the end of the shaft with the proper tool and remove the rear plate. Pry out the O-ring from the rear plate.
8. Remove the pump shaft with the cam ring and vane plates from the front housing.
9. Remove the cam ring and the 10 plates from the pump shaft. Remove the longer straight pin from the front housing.
10. Remove the snapring with the proper tool and remove the rotor and front plate from the pump shaft.
11. Remove both O-rings and the straight pin from the front plate.
12. Remove the bolts and the adjusting stay.
13. Check the oil clearance with the proper tool. The maximum clearance is 0.0028 in.
14. Measure the clearance between the rotor groove and the vane plate. The maximum clearance is 0.0011 in.
15. Inspect the control valve for damage or leakage. Measure the free length of the spring. The spring free length should be 1.38–1.46 in.
16. If neccessary, replace the oil seal with the proper tool.

To assemble:

17. Coat all the sliding surfaces with power steering fluid.
18. Install the adjusting stay and tighten the bolts to 30 ft. lbs.
19. Install the shorter front pin to the front plate and install new O-rings to the front plate.
20. Install the front plate to the pump shaft.
21. Install the rotor to the pump shaft with the inscribed mark facing out. Install the snapring with the proper tool.
22. Coat the oil lip with MP grease and install the longer straight pin to the front housing. Align the hole of the front plate with the straight pin and tap in the pump shaft with the proper tool.
23. Align the oval hole of the cam ring with the longer straight pin and insert the cam ring with the inscribed mark facing out.
24. Install the 10 vane plates with the round end facing outward.
25. Install a new O-ring to the rear plate and align the holes of the rear plate with the pins. Install the rear plate.
26. Install the washer and the O-ring to the rear housing.
27. Tap in the rear housing with the proper tool and install the snapring.

28. Check that the shaft rotates smoothly. Temporarily, install the pulley nut and check the rotating torque. The rotating torque should be 2.4 inch lbs. or less.

29. Install the spring and the valve into the housing and install a new O-ring in the groove of the pressure port union.

30. Install the port union and tighten to 51. ft. lbs.

31. Install a new O-ring to the reservoir tank.

32. Install the reservoir tank to the housing and replace the bolts. Tighten the 12mm bolts to 9 ft. lbs. and the 14mm bolts to 30 ft. lbs.

33. Install a new union seat to the housing.

34. Install the air control valve and tighten the bolts to 27 ft. lbs.

RN Series Pump

Disassembly and Assembly

1. Secure the pump in a suitable holding fixture.

2. Remove the air control valve and the union seat on the 22R-E engine.

3. Remove the bolts and remove the suction port union. Pry out the O-ring from the union.

4. Remove the front housing bolts.

5. Place matchmarks on the front and rear housing. Tap off the front housing with the proper tool.

NOTE: Be careful that the vane plates, rotor and the cam ring do not fall out.

6. Remove the cam ring, rotor and vane plates, do not scratch.

7. Secure the front housing in a suitable holding fixture.

8. Pry out the oil seal and remove the snapring with the proper tools.

9. Tap the rotor shaft out of the housing.

10. Tap the bottom end of the rear housing and remove the rear plate and spring.

11. Remove the pressure port union and pry out the O-rings from the union and the housing.

12. Remove the flow control valve and spring.

13. Temporarily, install a bolt to the spring seat. Push the bolt and remove the snapring with the proper tool.

14. Pull out the bolt and remove the spring seat. Pry out the O-ring from the spring seat.

15. Check the oil clearance between the bushing and the rotor shaft. The maximum oil clearance is 0.0028 in.

16. Measure the cam thickness. Check that the difference between the rotor and the cam ring is less than 0.0024 in.

17. Measure the clearance between the vane plate and the rotor groove. The maximum clearance is 0.0024 in.

18. Check the flow control valve for wear or damage. If necessary, replace the valve with one having the same letter on the rear housing.

19. Check that the flow control valve spring is within 1.85–1.97 in. If not replace it.

To assemble:

20. Install a new O-ring to the spring seat. Insert the spring seat into the housing, install the snapring.

21. Install a new O-ring to the housing. Insert the spring and control valve to the housing. Make sure that the letter marked on the flow control valve matches the letter marked on the rear of the pump body.

22. Install a new O-ring to the pressure port union. Replace the union and tighten the bolts to 51 ft. lbs.

23. Install the rotor shaft into the front housing by tapping on it with the proper tool. Install the snapring to the front housing.

24. Apply a light coat of MP grease to the oil seal lip and install the oil seal with the proper tool.

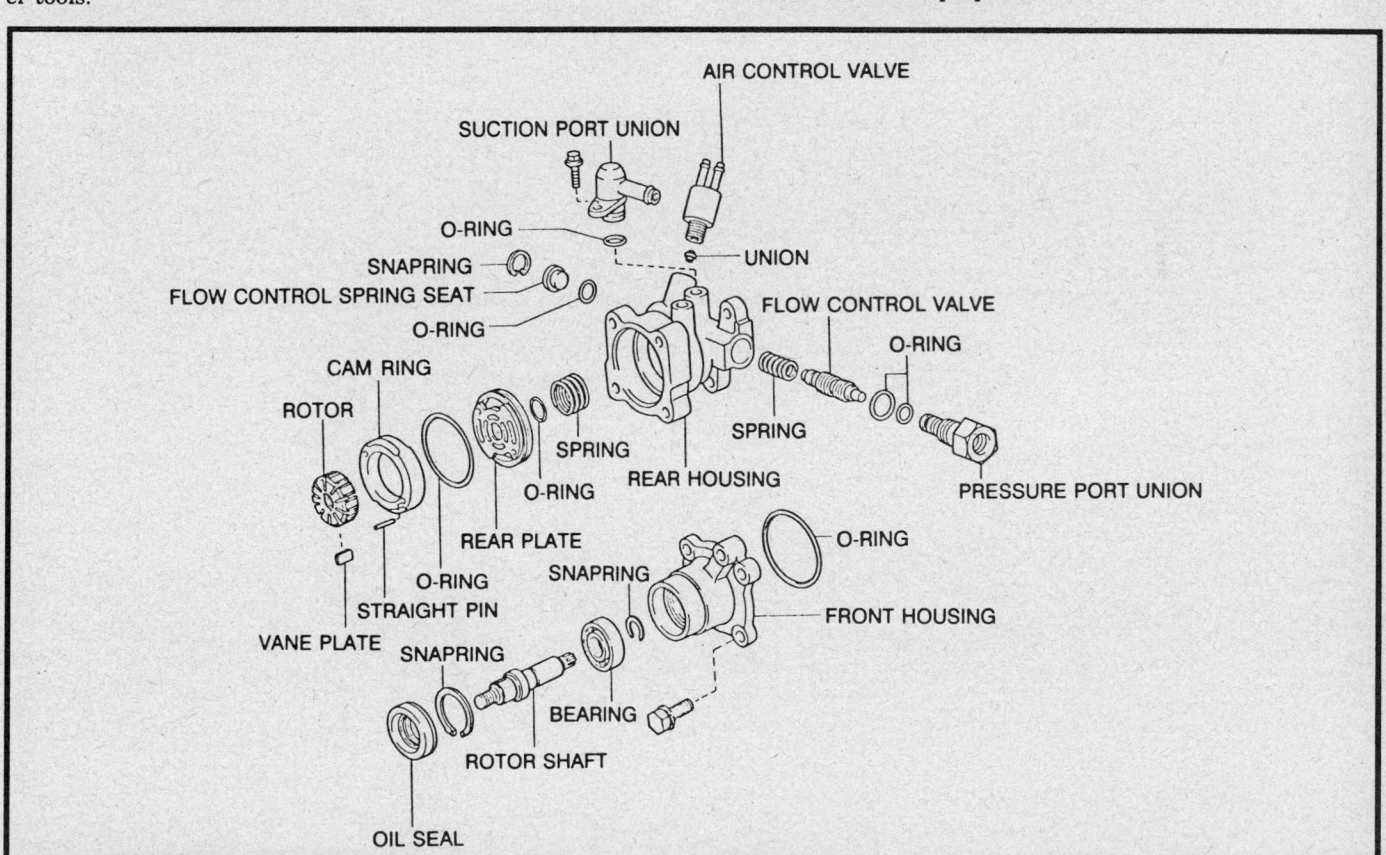

Exploded view of the power steering pump—1989–90 Toyota RN pump

25. Install a new O-ring.
26. Align the fluid passages of the rear plate with the cam ring and install the rear plate. Place the spring on the rear plate.
27. Align the matchmarks on the front and rear housing and assemble the housings. Tighten the housing bolts evenly to 34 ft. lbs.

28. Install the suction port union and tighten to 9 ft. lbs.
29. Install a new union seat and the air control valve on the 22R-E engine.
30. Check that the rotor shaft rotates smoothly and that the rotational torque is 2.4 inch lbs. or less.

VOLKSWAGEN

Vane Type Pump

Disassembly and Assembly

1. Secure the pump in a suitable holding fixture.
2. Loosen the end housing bolts and remove the end hosing.
3. Remove the spring, pressure/flow limiting valve and valve retainer, using the proper tool.
4. Remove the seal support with the proper tool and lift out the valve plate. Remove the stator.
5. Press the rotor down and remove the circlip from the groove in the housing with the proper tool.
6. Remove the rotor and the O-ring from the front housing.

NOTE: Be careful not to let the vanes fall out.

7. Loosen the front housing cover bolts and remove the pump shaft with the flange. Remove the shaft seal with the proper tool.
8. Clean all the components and check for damage or excessive wear. Coat all the sealing components with power steering fluid.

9. Install the shaft seal with the proper tool. Make sure the seal bottoms.
10. Install the pump shaft with the flange and tighten the bolts to 14 ft. lbs.
11. Install the O-ring and the rotor to the shaft. Replace the circlip.

The circlip must fit properly in the groove and be secured by the rotor.

12. Install the stator with the long pins facing downward.
13. Install the valve plate, seal and the seal support, using the proper tool.
14. Insert the pressure/flow limiting valve and replace the valve retainer with the proper tool.
15. Install the valve retainer with the angled ends positoned in the housing slot. Press down the angled ends with the proper tool.
16. Install the end cover and replace the bolts, tighten to 14 ft. lbs.

GENERAL INFORMATION

Wheel Alignment

For a vehicle to have safe steering control with a minimum of tire wear, certain established rules must be followed. These rules fix the values of planes, angles and radii relative to each other and to vehicle and tire dimensions. Some factors are built in, with no provision for adjustment; others are adjustable within limits. The entire system depends upon all value factors, separately and combined. It is therefore difficult to change some of the established settings without influencing others.

This system is called steering geometry or wheel alignment and requires a complete check of all the factors involved. Definitions of these factors and the effect each has on the vehicle are as follows.

WHEEL POSITIONING

Always check steering wheel alignment in conjunction with and at the same time as toe-in. In fact, the steering wheel spoke position, with the vehicle on a straight section of highway, may be the first indication of front end misalignment.

If the vehicle has been wrecked, or indicates any evidence of steering gear or linkage disturbance, the pitman arm should be disconnected from the sector shaft. The steering wheel (or gear) should be turned from extreme right to extreme left to determine the halfway point in its turning scope. This will be the spot on the gear that is in action during straight ahead driving and in which position the steering gear should be adjusted. With the steering wheel in the straight ahead position and the steering gear adjusted to zero lash status, reconnect the pitman arm.

CAMBER ANGLE

Camber is the amount that the front wheels are inclined outward or inward at the top. Camber is spoken of, and measured, in degrees from the perpendicular. The purpose of the camber angle is to take some of the load off the spindle outboard bearing.

CASTER ANGLE

Caster is the amount that the king pin (or in the case of vehicles

without king pins, the knuckle support pivots) is tilted towards the back or front of the vehicle. Caster is usually spoken of, and measured, in degrees. Positive caster means that the top of the king pin is tilted toward the back of the vehicle. Positive caster is indicated by a plus sign.

Negative caster is exactly the opposite; the top of the king pin is tilted toward the front of the vehicle. This is generally indicated by a minus sign. Negative caster is sometimes referred to as reverse caster.

The effect of positive caster is to cause the vehicle to steer in the direction in which it tends to go. Positive caster in the front wheels may cause the vehicle to steer down off a crowned road or steer in the direction of a cross wind. For this reason, a number of our modern vehicles are arranged with negative caster so that the opposite is true, which is that the vehicle tends to steer up a crowned road and into a cross wind.

Caster angle specifications are based on the vehicle load limits, which will usually result in a level frame. Since load requirements may vary, the frame does not always remain level and must be considered when determining the correct caster angle.

Because of their naturally straight running characteristics, front wheel drive vehicles are not overly sensitive to caster, therefore caster is not adjustable.

To measure the caster angle, the vehicle should be on a smooth and level surface. Place a bubble protractor on the frame rail and measure the degree of frame tilt and in what direction, either front or rear.

Two methods of determining caster angles are used. The first method is to determine the caster angle from the wheel with alignment equipment, and the second method is to obtain the desired caster angle from the specification charts. The frame angle is then added to or subtracted from the caster angles as necessary.

METHOD ONE

1. Determine the frame angle.
   a. If the frame is high at rear, than the frame angle is negative.
   b. If the frame is low at rear, than the frame angle is positive.
2. Determine the caster angle at the wheel with the alignment checking equipment.
3. Add or subtract frame angle to determine caster angle.
   a. Negative frame angle is added to positive caster angle.
   b. Positive frame angle is subtracted from positive caster angle.
   c. Negative frame angle is subtracted from negative caster angle.
   d. Positive frame angle is added to negative caster angle.
4. Determine the correct caster angle and the specified caster angle. Correct the vehicle caster, as required.

METHOD TWO

1. Measure the frame angle.
   a. If the front of the frame is down than the frame angle is positive.
   b. If the front of the frame is up than the frame angle is negative.
2. From the specifications, determine the specified or desired caster setting.
3. Add or subtract the frame angle from the specified caster setting.
   a. Positive frame angle is subtracted from the specified setting.
   b. Negative frame angle is added to the specified caster setting.
4. Using wheel alignment equipment, obtain the measured caster angle from the wheel and determine the corrected specified setting.

KING PIN INCLINATION ANGLE

In addition to the caster angle, the king pins, if equipped, (or knuckle support pivots) are also inclined toward each other at the top. This angle is known as king pin inclination and is usually spoken of, and measured, in degrees.

The effect of king pin inclination is to cause the wheels to steer in a straight line, regardless of outside forces such as crowned roads, cross winds, etc., which may tend to make the vehicle steer at a tangent. As the spindle is moved from extreme right to extreme left it apparently rises and falls. The spindle reaches its highest position when the wheels are in the straight ahead position. In actual operation, the spindle cannot rise and fall because the wheel is in constant contact with the ground.

Therefore, the vehicle itself will rise at the extreme right turn and come to its lowest point at the straight ahead position, and again rise for an extreme left turn. The weight of the vehicle will tend to cause the wheels to come to the straight ahead position, which is the lowest position of the vehicle itself.

KING PIN INCLUDED ANGLE

Included angle is the name given to that angle which includes king pin inclination and camber. It is the relationship between the centerline of the wheel and the centerline of the king pin (or the knuckle support pivots). This angle is built into the knuckle (spindle) forging and will remain constant throughout the life of the vehicle, unless the spindle itself is damaged.

When checking a vehicle on the front end alignment machine, always measure king pin inclination as well as camber unless some provision is made on the stand for checking condition of the spindle. Where no such provision is made, add the king pin inclination inclination to the camber for each side of the vehicle. These totals should be exactly the same, regardless of how far from the norm the readings may be.

Since the most common cause of a bent spindle is striking the curb when parking, which causes the spindle to bend upward, the side having the greater included angle usually has the bent spindle. It will be found impossible to achieve good alignment and minimum tire wear unless the bent spindle is replaced.

TOE-IN

Toe-in is the amount that the front wheels are closer together at the front than they are at the back. This dimension is usually measured, in inches or fractions of an inch.

Generally speaking, the wheels are toed-in because they are cambered. When a vehicle operates with zero degrees camber it will be found to operate with zero toe-in. As the required camber increases, so does the toe-in. The reason for this is that the cambered wheel tends to steer in the direction in which it is cambered. Therefore it is necessary to overcome this tendency by compensating very slightly in the direction opposite to that in which it tends to roll. Caster and camber both have an effect on toe-in. Therefore toe-in is the last component on the front end which should be corrected.

TOE-OUT

When a vehicle is steered into a turn, the outside wheel of the vehicle scribes a much larger circle than the inside wheel. Therefore, the outside wheel must be steered to a somewhat less angle than the inside wheel. This difference in the angle is often called toe-out.

The change in angle from toe-in in the straight ahead position to toe-out in the turn is caused by the relative position of the steering arms to the king pin and to each other.

If a line were drawn from the center of the king pin through the center of the steering arm tie rod attaching hole at each

wheel the lines would be found to cross almost exactly in the center of the rear axle.

If the front end angles, including toe-in, are set correctly, and the toe-out is found to be incorrect, one or both of the steering arms are bent.

TRACKING

While tracking is more a function of the rear axle and frame, it is difficult to align the front suspension when the vehicle does not track straight. Tracking means that the centerline of the rear axle follows exactly the path of the centerline of the front axle when the vehicle is moving in a straight line.

On vehicles that have equal tread, front and rear, the rear tires will follow in exactly the thread of the front tires, when moving in a straight line. However, there are many vehicles whose rear tread is wider than the front tread. On such vehicles, the rear axle tread will straddle the front axle tread an equal amount on both sides, when moving in a straight line.

Perhaps the easiest way to check a vehicle for tracking is to stand directly in back of it and watch it more in a straight line down the street. If the observer will stand as near to the center of the vehicle as possible, he can readily observe, even with the difference in perspective between the front and rear wheels, whether or not they are tracking properly. If the vehicle is found to track incorrectly, the difficulty will be found in either the frame or in the rear axle alignment.

Another more accurate method to check tracking is to park the vehicle on a level floor and drop a plumb line from the extreme outer edge of the front suspension lower A-frame. Use the same drop point on each side of the vehicle. Make a chalk lie where the plumb line strikes the floor. Do the same with the rear axle, selecting a point on the rear axle housing for the plumb line.

Measure diagonally from the left rear mark to the right front mark and from the right rear mark to the left front mark. These diagonal measurements should be the same but a ¼ in. variation is acceptable.

If the diagonal measurements taken are different, measure from the right rear mark to the right front mark and from the left rear to the left front. These measurements should also be the same within ¼ in.

If the diagonal measurements are different, but the longitudinal measurements are the same, the frame is swayed (diamond shaped).

However, in the event that the diagonal measurements are unequal and the longitudinal measurements are also unequal, and the vehicle is tracking incorrectly, the rear axle is misaligned.

If the diagonal and longitudinal measurements are both unequal, but the vehicle appears to track correctly on the street, a kneeback is indicated.

NOTE: A kneeback means that a complete side of the front suspension is bent back. This is often caused by crimping the front wheels against the curb when parking the vehicle, then starting up without straightening the wheels out.

Tire and Wheel Service

TIRE AND WHEEL BALANCE

There are 2 types of tire and wheel balancing procedures. They are the dynamic balance and the static balance.

The dynamic balance is the equal distribution of weight on each side of the centerline, so that when the tire and wheel assembly spins there is no tendency for the assembly to move from side to side. Tire and wheel assemblies that are dynamically unbalanced may cause wheel shimmy.

The static balance is the equal distribution of weight around the wheel. Tire and wheel assemblies that are statically unbalanced cause a bouncing action called wheel tramp. This condition will eventually cause uneven tire wear.

Before the tire and wheel assembly can be properly balanced all deposits of mud, etc. must be removed from the inside of the rim area. Stones and other foreign matter should be removed from the tire tread area. The tire and wheel assembly should be inspected for any signs of external damage. Once these conditions have been met the tire and wheel assembly is ready to be balanced according to manufacturers instructions.

TIRE ROTATION

To ensure that all tires wear evenly tire rotation should be done every 8000 miles. If a tire shows excessive wear the wear problem should be corrected before rotating the tires. If the vehicle is equipped with a temporary spare tire, do not include it in the tire rotation procedure.

TIRE REPLACEMENT

Specialized tools and equipment have been designed for use in the replacement of a tire on multipiece rims. The manufacturers instructions should be followed in the use of the machines in the mounting and dismounting of tires to avoid personal injury.

CHRYSLER IMPORT/MITSUBISHI

Wheel Alignment

Measure the wheel alignment with the vehicle parked on a level ground and with the front wheels place in a straight ahead position. The front suspension, steering system tires and wheels should be serviced to the should be serviced to the proper condition prior to the measurement of the wheel alignment. Use approved wheel alignment equipment for checking the wheel alignment.

Toe-In Adjustment

1. Measure the toe-in with an appropriate toe-in guage.
2. Adjust the toe-in by turning the left and the right tie rod turnbuckles the same amount in opposite directions. The toe-in

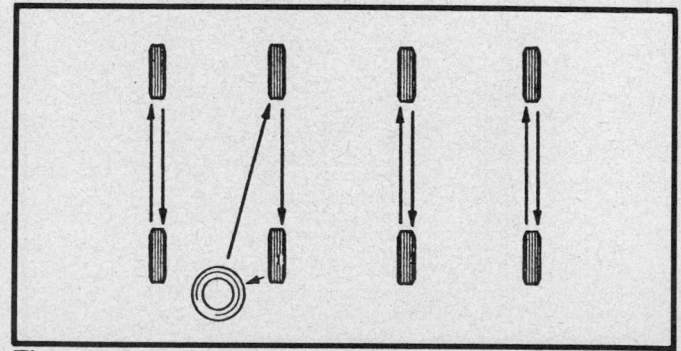

Tire rotation sequence—Chrysler Import/Mitsubishi

value will decrease if the left turnbuckle is turned toward the front of the vehicle and the right one is turned to the rear.

3. Adjust to specifications and tighten the tie rod turnbuckles.

Camber and Caster Adjustment
RAIDER AND MONTERO

1. Adjust the tire inflation pressure to the proper specifications.
2. Remove the front wheeling hub assembly.
3. Loosen the upper arm mounting bolts and adjust by increasing or decreasing the amount of the adjusting shims between the upper arm shaft and the crossmember.
4. Remove the upper arm from the crossmember and turn the upper arm shaft to adjust the caster.

EXCEPT RAIDER AND MONTERO

1. Adjust the tire inflation pressure to the proper specifications.
2. Place the vehicle on a turning radius guage and level the vehicle.
3. Adjust the camber by rotating the lower arm's shaft assembly on the Van.
4. Loosen the upper mounting bolts and increase or decrease the amount of shims between the upper arm shaft and the crossmember to adjust the camber and caster except on the Van.

Wheel Service

Tire Rotation

Rotate the tires periodically to ensure uniform wear of the tires. If the spare wheel is of a different type from the other 4 wheels, the 4 wheel rotation method should be used.

ISUZU

Wheel Alignment

The wheel alignment should be checked periodically to ensure proper wear of the tires and excessive wear of the suspension components.

Toe-In Adjustment

1. Place the front wheels in straight ahead position.
2. Align a suitable toe-in guage with the center height of each wheel at the front end.
3. Apply center marks to each wheel, then take the measurement of distance A between the center marks on each wheel.
4. Slowly, move the vehicle rearward until the center marks reach the rear end position.

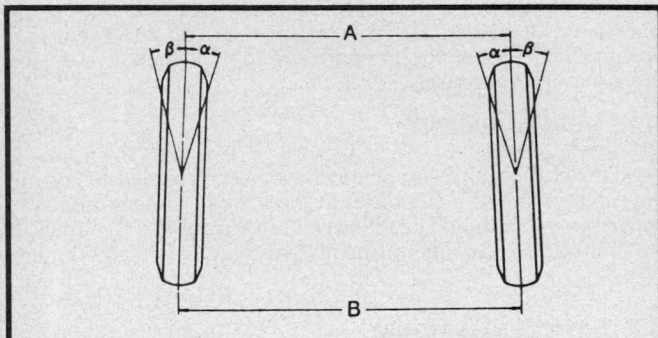

Measuring distance for toe-in adjustment—Isuzu

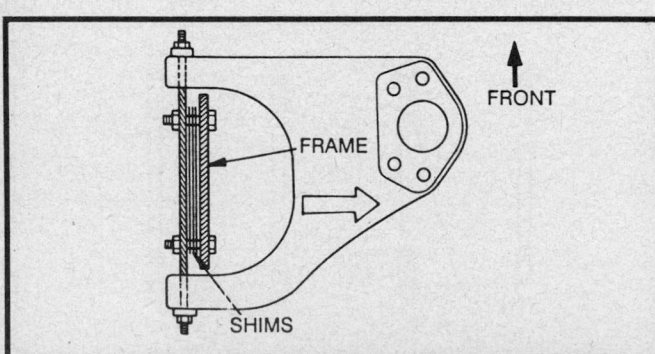

Caster angle adjustment—Isuzu 4WD and Amigo

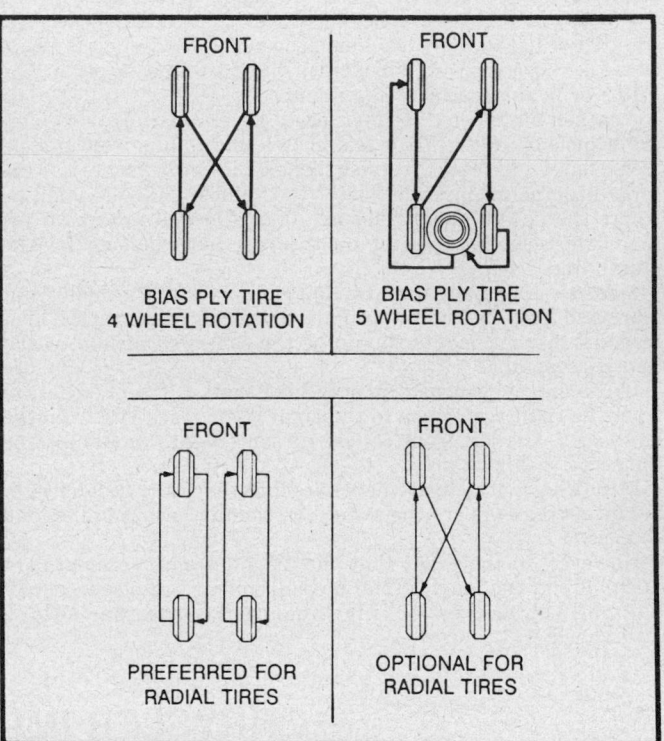

Tire rotation sequence—Isuzu

5. Take the measurement of distance B between the center marks at the rear end.
6. The toe-in equals B minus A.
7. To adjust the toe-in, loosen the locknut on the outer tie rod end and turn the outer track rod the same distance right and left.

Camber and Caster Adjustment

1. The camber angle can be adjusted by the means of camber pins installed in position between the chassis frame and the fulcrum pins. Adding shims decreases the camber angle and removing shims increases the camber angle.
2. The caster angle on the 2WD vehicles can be adjusted by varying the length of the strut bar. Adjust with the locknut. Shims should not be used for this adjustment.

3. The caster angle on the 4WD and Amigo can be adjusted by means of the caster shims installed in position between the frame and fulcrum pins. Adding shims to the front side decreases the caster angle while removing shims increases the angle. Adding shims to the rear side increases the caster angle while removing shims increases the angle.

Steering Angle Adjustment

1. The maximum steering angle on the front wheels can be adjusted with the stopper bolts under the frame side members.
2. Position each front wheel on a suitable turning radius guage in a straight ahead position.

3. Adjust the inside angle of each side with the stopper bolts.

NOTE: The maximum steering angles should be set after adjusting the front wheel alignment.

Wheel Service

Tire Rotation

Rotating the tires evens out tire wear and prolongs the tire life. Tire rotation should be performed every 7500 miles for maximum performance.

MAZDA

Wheel Alignment

Measure the wheel alignment with the vehicle parked on a level ground and with the front wheels place in a straight ahead position. The front suspension, steering system tires and wheels should be serviced to the should be serviced to the proper condition prior to the measurement of the wheel alignment. Use approved wheel alignment equipment for checking the wheel alignment.

Toe-In Adjustment

1. Raise and safely support the front of the vehicle.
2. Turn the wheels by hand, mark a line in the center of each tire tread using a proper scribing tool.
3. Place the front wheels in a straight ahead position and lower the vehicle.
4. Measure the distance between the marked lines at the front and the rear of the wheels.
5. To adjust, loosen the left and the right tie rod locknuts and turn the tie rods by the same degree.
6. Adjust the toe-in after adjusting the steering angle except on the MPV.

Camber and Caster Adjustment

EXCEPT MPV

1. Position the front wheels on a turning radius guage.
2. Remove the front wheel hub on 4 WD vehicles.
3. Remove the wheel cap and the wheel hub nut on 2 WD vehicles. Attach a suitable guage adapter to the hub.
4. Attach a suitable camber and caster guage to the hub or the adapter and measure the camber and the caster.
5. The camber and the caster are adjusted by adding or subtracting the amount of the shims.

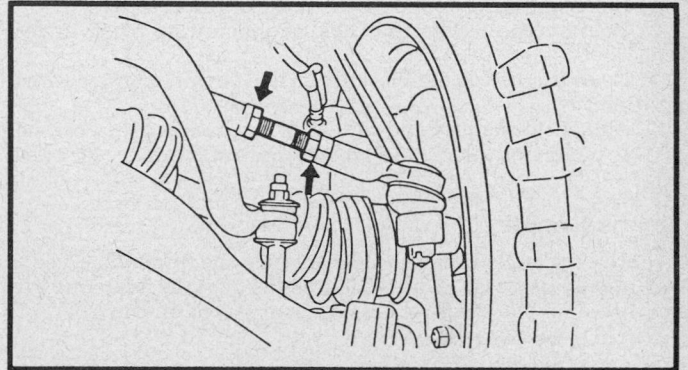

Toe-in adjustment on the vehicle–Mazda B2200 and B2600

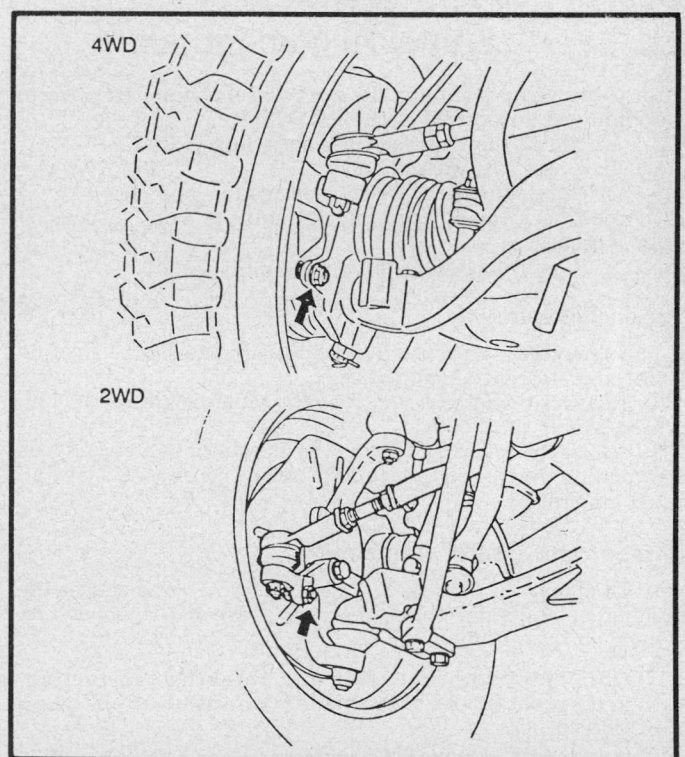

Checking the steering angle – Mazda 2WD and 4WD vehicles

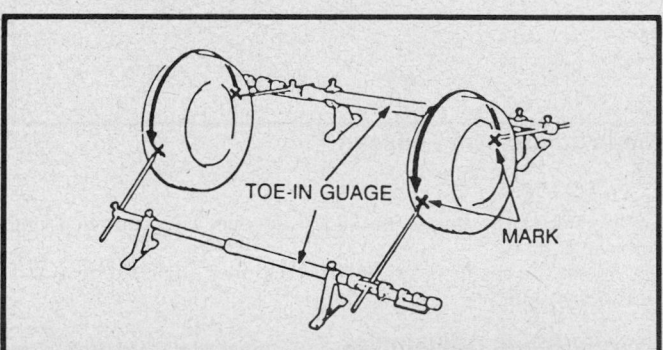

Checking toe-in with a suitable guage – Mazda

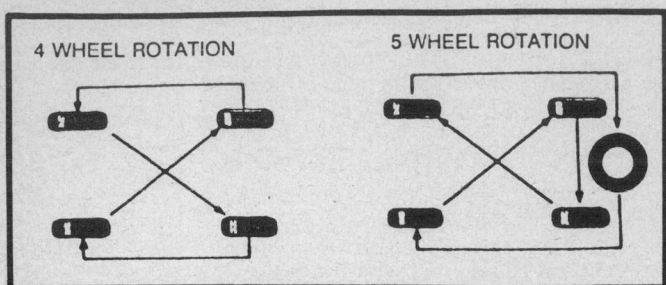

Tire rotation sequence—Mazda

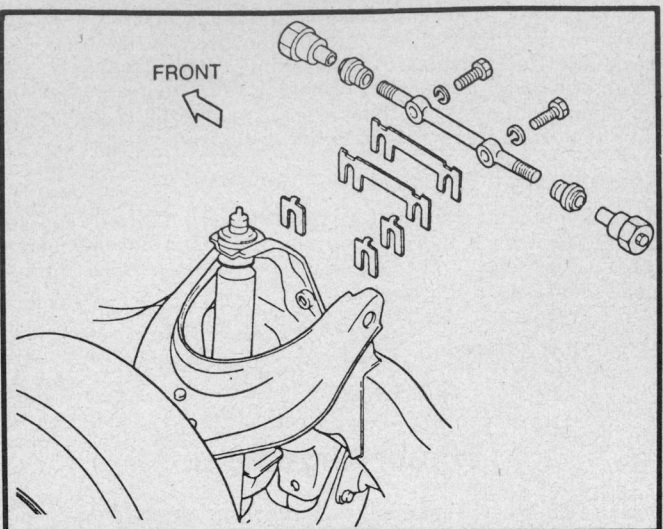

Location of the adjusting shims for the camber and caster—Mazda

MPV

1. Raise and safely support the front of the vehicle.
2. Remove the blocks that hold the mounting block to the fender.
3. Push the mounting block down and turn it to the desired position.
4. Adjust the camber and the caster by changing the position of the mounting block. Retighten the nuts to the specified torque.

Steering Angle

The steering angle is measured by placing the front wheels on a turning radius guage. Adjust the steering angle by adjusting the bolt fitted on the steering knuckle arm except on the MPV.

Wheel Service

Tire Rotation

In order to prolong tire life and assure uniform wear, the tires should be rotated every 3,750 miles. Do not include the temporary spare in the rotation.

NISSAN

Wheel Alignment

Prior to any adjustments to the front wheel alignment, perform a preliminary inspection of the following:

    a. Check the tires for wear and proper inflation.
    b. Check the wheel runout.
    c. Check the front wheel bearings for looseness.
    d. Check the steering linkage and the front suspension for looseness.
    e. Check the operation of the front shocks.

Toe-In Adjustment

1. Draw a line across the tread of the tire and set the steering wheel in a straight ahead position.
2. Measure distance A and B at the same height as the hub center, this is the toe-in.
3. Adjust the toe-in by varying the length of the steering rods and turning the tie-rod tubes clockwise and counterclockwise an equal amount.

Camber and Caster Adjustment

1. To adjust the camber and caster, increase or decrease the number of adjusting shims inserted between the upper link spindle and the frame.

NOTE: The camber, caster and the king pin inclination are preset at the factory and cannot be adjusted on the Axxess.

2. Do not install 3 or more shims at one place.
3. To adjust the camber, equalize the thickness of the front and rear shims by adding or subtracting shim(s)

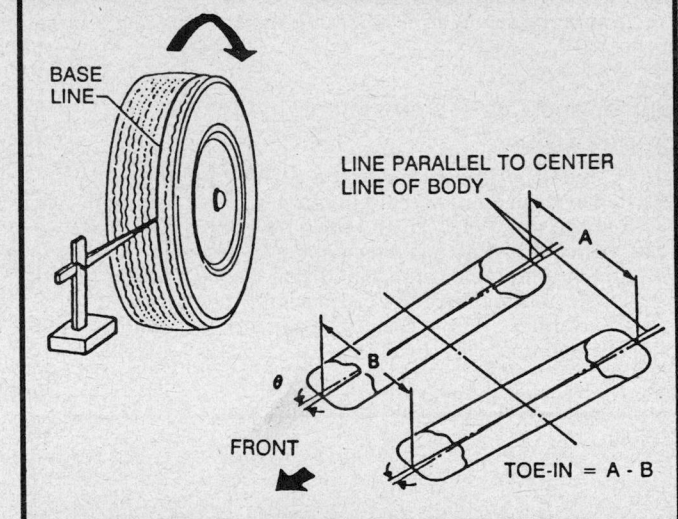

Toe-in adjustment—Nissan

4. To adjust the caster, make a difference between the front and rear shims.
5. When the caster is adjusted the camber angle changes and must be readjusted.

Steering Angle Adjustment

1. Set the wheels in a straight ahead position.

2. Move the vehicle forward until the front wheels rest on the turning radius guage properly.

3. Rotate the steering wheel all the way to the right and the left and check the turning angle.

Wheel Service

Tire Rotation

Do not include the T type spare and small type spares in the rotation. Make sure that the wheel nuts are tightened to specifications when completed.

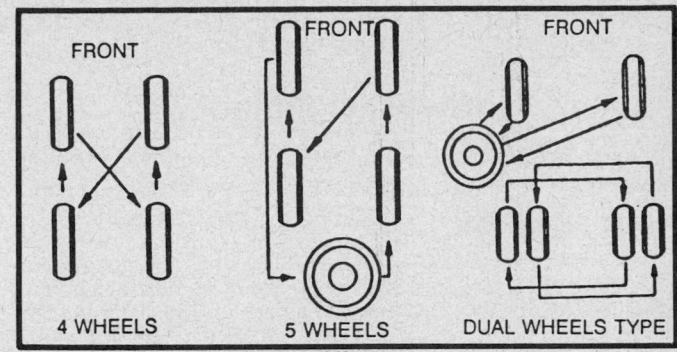

Tire rotation sequence — Nissan

SUZUKI/GEO

Wheel Alignment

The wheel alignment refers to the angular relationship between the front wheels, the front suspension mounting parts and the ground. Generally the only adjustment required is toe-in.

Toe-In Adjustment

The toe is adjusted by changing the tie rod length. Adjust by loosening the locknuts first the rotate the left and the right tie-rod by the same amount. In this adjustment the left and the right tie rod should become equal in length.

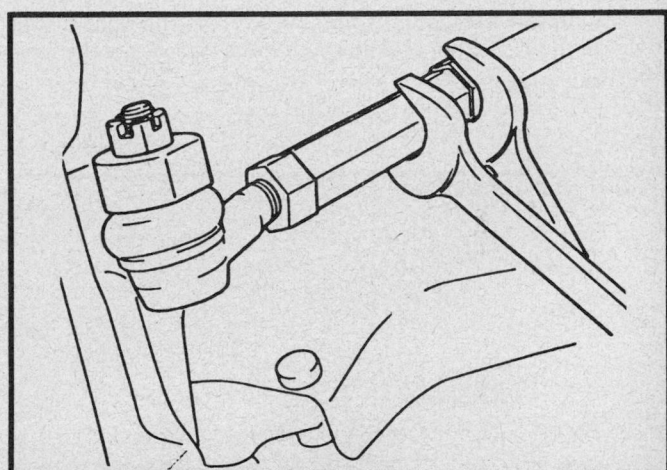

Toe-in adjustment — Suzuki/Geo

Camber and Caster Adjustment

The camber and caster cannot be adjusted for this vehicle. To prevent any possible incorrect reading of the camber or caster, move the front of the vehicle up and down a few times before inspection.

Wheel Service

Tire Rotation

To equalize tire wear, rotate the tire and wheels at 7500 miles and every 15000 miles thereafter. The tire and wheel assemblies should be rotated whenever uneven tire wear is noticed.

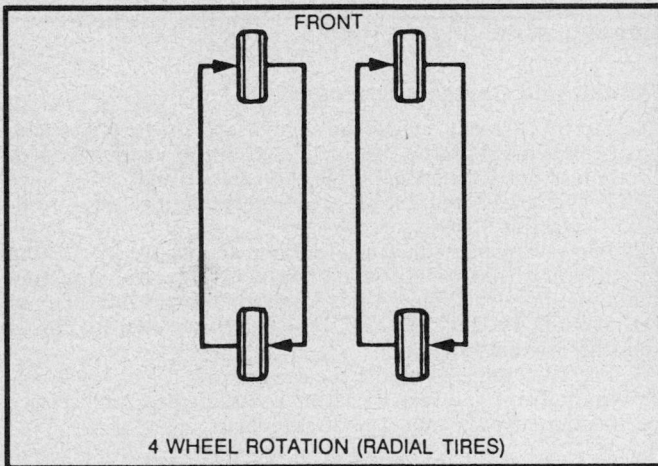

Tire rotation sequence — Suzuki/Geo

TOYOTA

Wheel Alignment

Follow the specific instructions of the equipment manufacturer the wheel alignment.

Toe-In Adjustment

1. Rock the vehicle up and down to stabilize the suspension.
2. Mark the center of each rear tread at spindle height and measure the distance between the marks on the right and left tires.
3. Advance the vehicle until the marks on the rear side of the tires come to the front.

NOTE: The toe-in should be measured at the same point on the tire and at the same level.

4. Measure the distance between the marks on the front side of the tires.
5. Adjust the toe-in by turning the left and the right tie rod tubes an equal amount. Make sure that the tie rods are the same length.

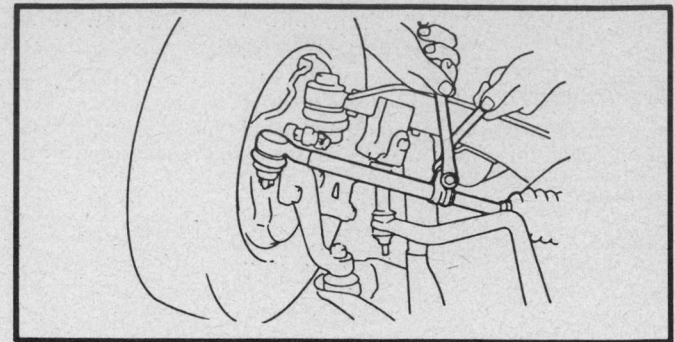
Toe-in adjustment—Toyota

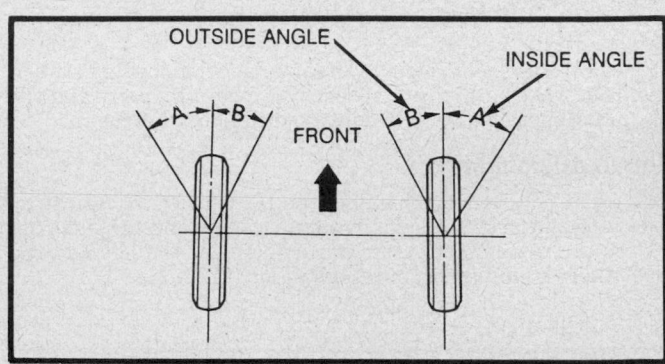
Steering wheel angle—Toyota

Camber and Caster Adjustment

1. For 2WD trucks, adjust the camber and the caster by adding or removing shims on the upper arm. If the steering axis inclination is not as specified after the camber and caster have been properly adjusted, recheck the steering knuckle for bending or looseness.
2. For 2WD vans, adjust the camber and caster by turning the adjusting cam or the strut bar nut. The adjusting cam should not be turned more than 4.5 graduations from the neutral position. Do not turn the strut bar more than 3 threads from the original position.
3. For 4WD vehicles, adjust the camber and the caster by adjusting the front and rear adjusting cams. Refer to the service specifications for the adjustment standards.

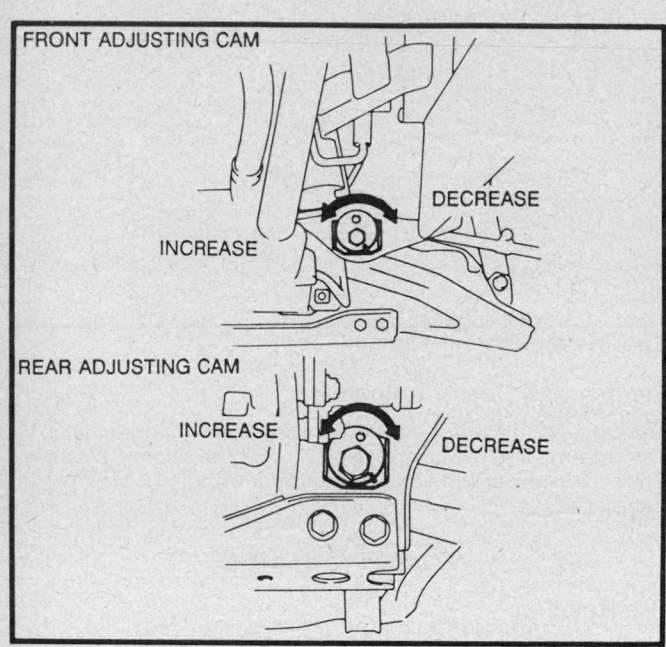
Camber and caster adjustment—Toyota 4WD vehicles

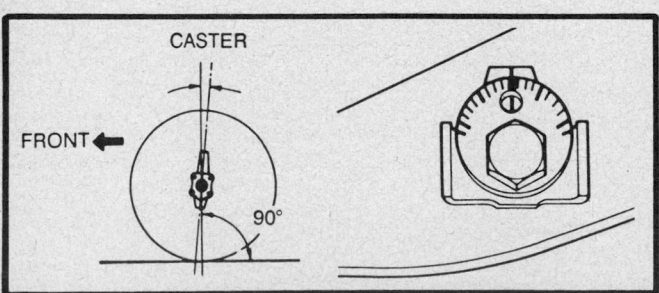
Camber and caster adjustment—Toyota 2WD vans

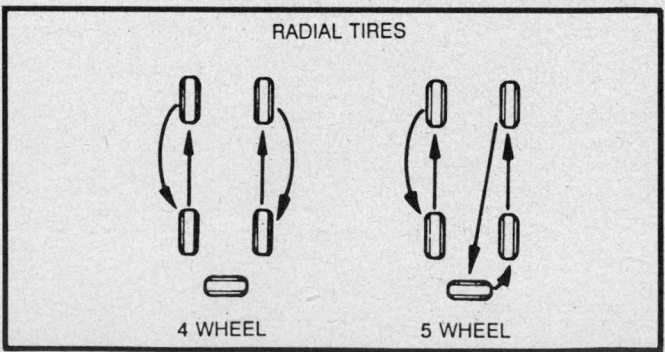
Tire rotation sequence—Toyota

Steering Angle Adjustment

1. Remove the caps of the steering knuckle stopper bolts.
2. Loosen the knuckle stopper bolt locknuts and tighten the stopper bolts by hand.
3. Remove the boot clips and loosen the tie rod end locknuts.
4. Adjust the maximum wheel angle by turning the left and the right tie rod ends an equal amount.

5. Check that the lengths of the left and right tie rod are the same distance

Wheel Service

Tire Rotation

It is recommended that the tires and wheels be rotated every 7500 miles to ensure uniform wear.

VOLKSWAGEN

Wheel Alignment

The vehicle should have been run from 625–1250 miles to let the coil springs settle before performing an alignment. The vehicle should be empty.

Toe-In Adjustment

FRONT WHEELS

1. Place the steering gear in the center position by turning the steering wheel from lock to lock and count the number of turns. Turn the wheel back 1/2 the number of turns.
2. Align the lug on the rubber washer on the pinion shaft with the notch in the steering housing.
3. Loosen the locknuts and turn both tie rods until the desired setting is reached. Retighten the locknuts.
4. Check that the bellows are not twisted after turning the tie rods.
5. The specification of the total toe at the front axle is determined by the ride height of the vehicle.

REAR WHEELS

1. Loosen the outer bolt on the trailing arm.
2. Adjust the camber by moving the trailing arm up or down with the proper tool.
3. Tighten the bolt.

Camber and Caster Adjustment

FRONT WHEELS

1. Adjust the caster by adjusting the length of the radius bar A at location B.
2. To adjust the camber, loosen the nut on the upper control arm shaft. Turn the upper control arm shaft to obtain the desired setting. Tighten the nut.

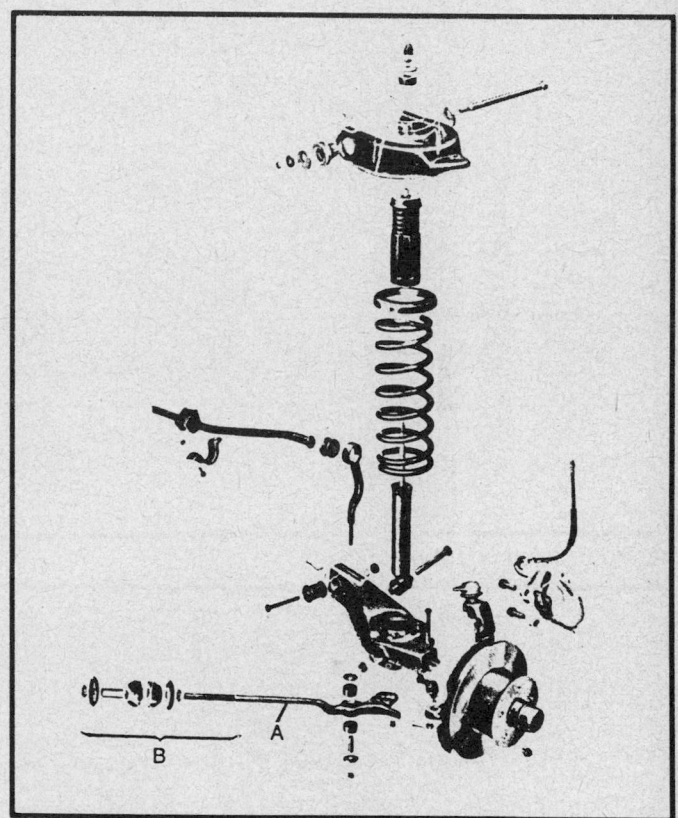

Caster adjustment — Vanagon

REAR WHEELS

1. Loosen the inner bolt on the trailing arm.
2. Adjust the toe by moving the trailing arm to the front or rear, using the proper tool.
3. Tighten the bolt.

Wheel Service

Tire Rotation

It is recommended that the tires and wheels be rotated every 7500 miles to ensure uniform wear. After the rotation torque the wheel nuts diagonally.

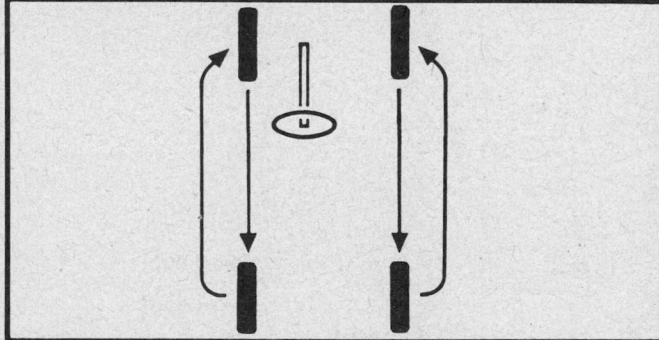

Tire rotation sequence — Vanagon

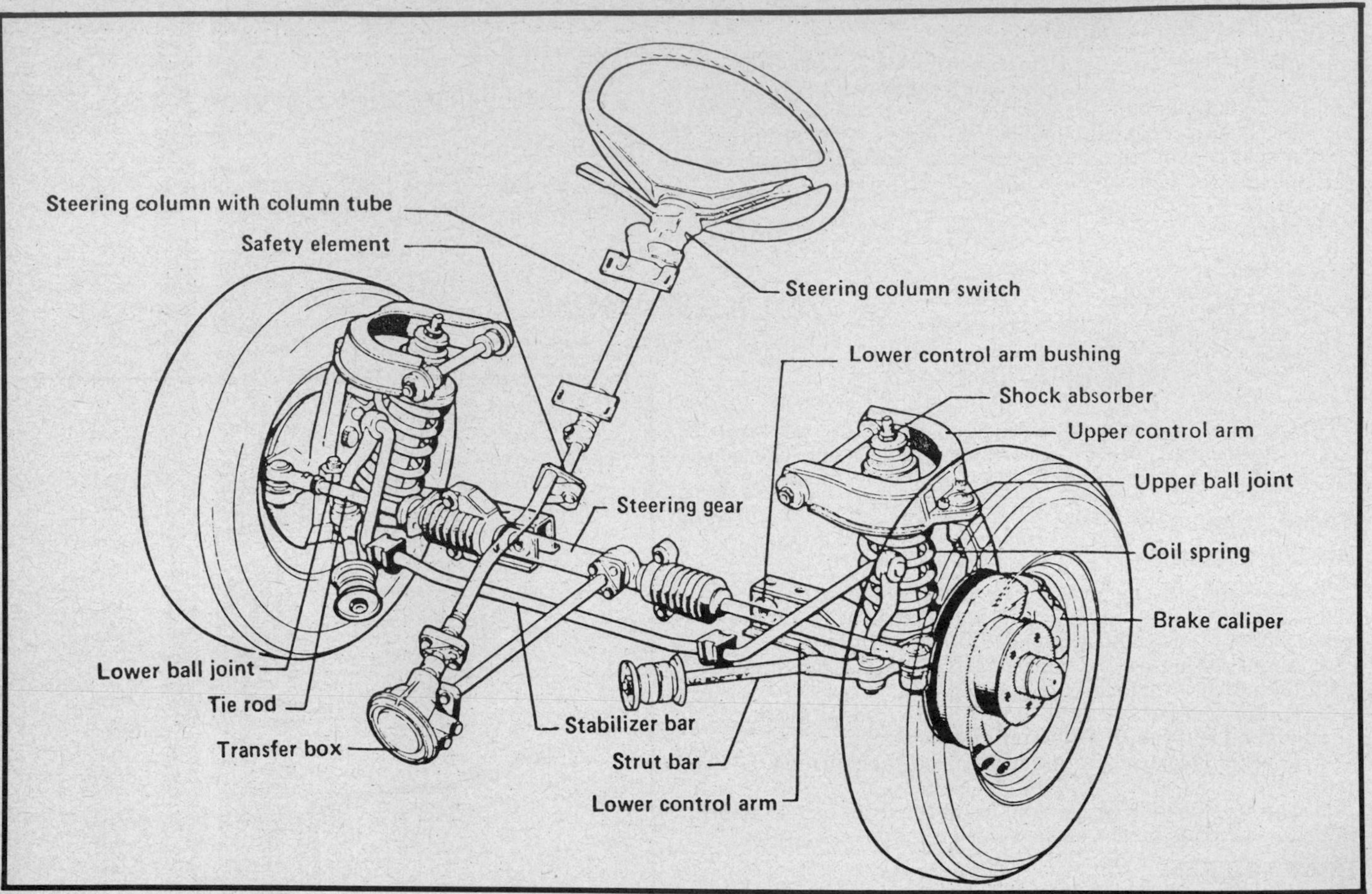

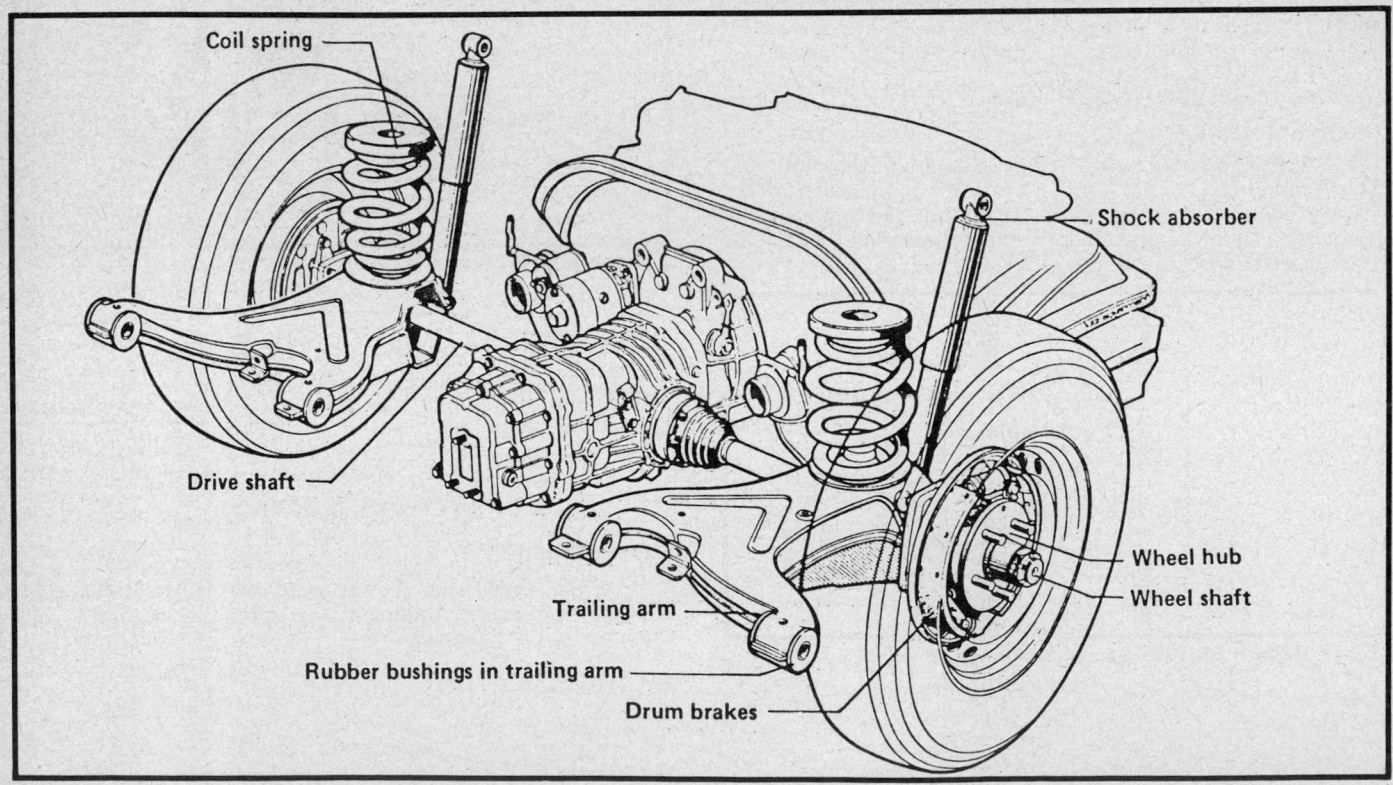

Steering column with column tube
Safety element
Steering column switch
Lower control arm bushing
Shock absorber
Upper control arm
Upper ball joint
Steering gear
Coil spring
Brake caliper
Lower ball joint
Tie rod
Transfer box
Stabilizer bar
Strut bar
Lower control arm

Vanagon front suspension

Coil spring
Shock absorber
Drive shaft
Wheel hub
Wheel shaft
Trailing arm
Rubber bushings in trailing arm
Drum brakes

Vanagon rear suspension

GENERAL INFORMATION

Differential Operation

The differential is an arrangement of gears that permits the wheels to turn at different speeds when cornering and divides the torque between the axle shafts. The differential gears are mounted on a pinion shaft and the gears are free to rotate on this shaft. The pinion shaft is fitted in a bore in the differential case and is at right angles to the axle shafts.

Power flow through the differential is as follows. The drive pinion, which is turned by the driveshaft, turns the ring gear. The ring gear, which is bolted to the differential case, rotates the case. The differential pinion forces the pinion gears against the side gears. In cases where both wheels have equal traction, the pinion gears do not rotate on the pinion shaft, because the input force of the pinion gear is divided equally between the 2 side gears. Consequently the pinion gears revolve with the pin-

ion shaft, although they do not revolve on the pinion shaft itself. The side gears, which are splined to the axle shafts and meshed with the pinion gears, rotate the axle shafts.

Gear Ratios

The drive axle of a vehicle is said to have a certain axle ratio. This number (usually a whole number and a decimal fraction) is actually a comparison of the number of gear teeth on the ring gear and the pinion gear. For example, a 4:11 rear means that theoretically, there are 4:11 teeth on the ring gear and one tooth on the pinion. Actually, on a 4:11 rear, there are 37 teeth on the ring gear and nine teeth on the pinion gear. By dividing the number of teeth on the pinion gear into the number of teeth on the ring gear, the numerical axle ratio (4:11) is obtained.

DIFFERENTIAL DIAGNOSIS

The most essential part of rear axle service is proper diagnosis of the problem. Any gear driven unit will produce a certain amount of noise. Acceptable or normal noise can be classified as a slight noise heard only at certain speeds or under unusual conditions. This noise tends to reach a peak at 40–60 mph depending on the road condition, load, gear ratio and tire size. Frequently, other noises are mistakenly diagnosed as coming from the axle assembly. Vehicle noises from tires, transmission, driveshaft, U-joints and front and rear wheel bearings will often be mistaken as emanating from the front or rear axle assemblies.

External Noise Elimination

It is advisable to make a thorough road test to determine whether the noise originates in the axle assembly or whether it originates from the tires, engine transmission, wheel bearings or road surface. Noise originating from other places cannot be corrected by overhauling the axle assemblies.

Road Noise

Brick roads or rough surfaced concrete, may cause a noise which can be mistaken as coming from the axle assembly. Driving on a different type of road (smooth asphalt or dirt) will determine whether the road is the cause of the noise. Road noise is usually the same on drive or coast conditions.

Tire Noise

Tire noise can be mistaken as axle assembly noises, even though the tires are at fault. Snow tread and mud tread tires or tires worn unevenly will frequently cause vibrations which seem to originate elsewhere; temporarily and for test purposes only, inflate the tires to 40–50 lbs. This will significantly alter the noise produced by the tires, but will not alter noise from the axle assembly. Noises from the axle assembly will normally cease at speeds below 30 mph on coast, while tire noise will continue at lower tone as vehicle speed is decreased. Th axle noise will usually change from drive conditions to coast conditions, while tire noise will not. Do not forget to lower the tire pressure to normal after the test is complete.

Engine and Transmission Noise

Engine and transmission noises also seem to originate in the axle assemblies. Road test the vehicle and determine at which speeds the noise is most pronounced. Stop the vehicle in a quiet place to avoid interfering noises. With the transmission in N position, run the engine slowly through the engine speeds corresponding to the vehicle speed at which the noise was most noticeable. If a similar noise was produced with the vehicle standing still, the noise is not in the axle assemblies, but somewhere in the engine or transmission.

Front Wheel Bearing Noise

Front wheel bearing noises, sometimes confused with axle noises, will not change when comparing drive and coast conditions. While holding the vehicle speed steady, lightly apply the footbrake. This will often cause wheel bearing noise to lessen, as some of the weight is taken off the bearing. Front wheel bearings are easily checked by jacking up the wheels and spinning the wheels. Shaking the wheels will also determine if the wheel bearings are excessively loose.

Axle Assembly Noise

If a logical test of the vehicle shows that the noise is not caused by external items, it can be assumed that the noise originates from the axle assembly. The axle assembly should be tested on a smooth level road to avoid road noise. It is not advisable to test the axle by jacking up the wheels and running the vehicle.

True axle noises generally fall into 2 classes; gear noise and bearing noises and can be caused by a faulty driveshaft, faulty wheel bearings, worn differential or pinion shaft bearings, U-joint misalignment, worn differential side gears and pinions, or mismatched, improperly adjusted, or scored ring and pinion gears.

Rear Wheel Bearing Noise

A rough rear wheel bearing causes a vibration or growl which will continue with the vehicle coasting or in neutral. A brinelled

rear wheel bearing will also cause a knock or click noise. Jack up the rear wheels and spin the wheel slowly, listening for signs of a rough or brinelled wheel bearing.

Differential Side Gear And Pinion Noise

Differential side gears and pinions seldom cause noise since their movement is relatively slight on straight ahead driving. Noise produced by these gears will be more noticeable on turns.

Pinion Bearing Noise

Pinion bearing failures can be distinguished by their speed of rotation, which is higher than side bearings or axle bearings. Rough or brinelled pinion bearings cause a continuous low pitch whirring or scraping noise beginning at low speeds.

Side Bearing Noise

Side bearings produce a constant rough noise, which is slower than the pinion bearing noise.

BEARING DIAGNOSIS

This section will help in the diagnosis of bearing failure and the causes. Bearing diagnosis can be very helpful in determining the cause of axle assembly failure.

When disassembling a axle assembly, the general condition of all bearings should be noted and classified where possible. Proper recognition of the cause will help in correcting the problem and avoiding a repetition of the failure. Some of the common causes of bearing failure are:
1. Abuse during assembly or disassembly.
2. Improper assembly methods.
3. Improper or inadequate lubrication.
4. Bearing contact with dirt or water.
5. Wear caused by dirt or metal chips.

6. Corrosion or rust.
7. Seizing due to overloading.
8. Overheating.
9. Frettage of the bearing seats.
10. Brinelling from impact or shock loading.
11. Manufacturing defects.
12. Pitting due to fatigue.

To avoid damage to the bearing from improper handling, it is best to treat a used bearing the same as a new bearing. Always work in a clean area with clean tools. Remove all outside dirt from the housing before exposing a bearing and clean all bearing seats before installing a bearing. Never spin a bearing, either by hand or with compressed air.

GENERAL SERVICE AND INSPECTION

Cleaning Bearings

Proper bearing cleaning is important. Bearings should always be cleaned separately from other rear axle parts.
1. Soak all bearings in clean kerosene or diesel fuel oil. Ordinary gasoline should not be used. Bearings should not be cleaned in hot solution tank.
2. Slush bearings in cleaning solution until all oil lubricant is loosened. Brush bearings with soft bristled brush until all dirt has been removed. Remove loose particles of dirt by striking flat against a wood block.
3. Rinse bearings in clean fluid. While holding races to prevent rotation, blow dry with compressed air. Do not spin bearings while drying.
4. After bearings have been inspected, lubricate thoroughly with regular axle lubricant; then wrap each bearing in clean cloth until ready to use.

Cleaning Parts

Immerse all parts in suitable cleaning fluid and clean thoroughly. Use a stiff bristle brush as required to remove foreign deposits. Clean all lubricant passages or channels in pinion cage, carrier, caps and retainers. Make certain that interior of housing is thoroughly cleaned. Clean vent plugs and breathers. Small parts such as cap screws, bolts, studs, nuts etc., should be cleaned thoroughly.

Inspection

Magna Flux or equivalent test all steel parts, except ball and roller bearings, to detect presence of wear and cracks.

Bearings

Rotate each bearing and check to see if the rollers are worn, chipped, rough or in any other way damaged. Check the cage to see if it is in any way damaged. If either the bearing rollers or the cage are damaged the bearing must be replaced.

Gears

Examine drive gear and drive pinion, differential pinions and differential side gears carefully, for damaged teeth, worn spots in surface hardening, distortion and where drive gear is attached to differential case with rivets, inspect rivets for looseness, replace loose rivets. Check radial clearances between differential side gears and differential case. Check fit of differential pinions on spider.

Differential Case

Inspect case for cracks, distortion or damage, if in good condition, thoroughly clean case and cover; then assemble case with bolts and mount in lathe centers of block stand. If lathe is not available, install differential side bearings and mount case in differential carrier. Install dial indicator and check differential case run out.

Differential case with drive gear installed is checked in the same manner, except that dial indicator reading must be taken at gear instead of at case flange.

Axle Shafts

Examine splined end of axle shaft for twisted or cracked splines, twisted shaft and worn dowel holes in flange. Install new shafts if necessary.

Install axle shaft assembly in lathe centers and check shaft run out with dial indicator so that indicator shaft end contacts inner surface of flange near outer edge of flange and check flange run out.

Shims

Carefully inspect shims for uniform thickness. Where various thickness of shims are used in a pack, it is recommended that the thickest shims be used between the thin shims.

Thrust Washers

Replace all thrust washers upon installation.

Spider Assembly

Carefully inspect spider componets for wear or defects.

Pinion Bushings

Examine bushings (when used) for excessive wear, looseness, or damage. Check fit or gears on spider for excessive clearance.

Axle Housing Sleeves

Sleeves showing damaged threads, wear, or other damage should be replaced as necessary.

CHRYSLER IMPORT/MITSUBISHI

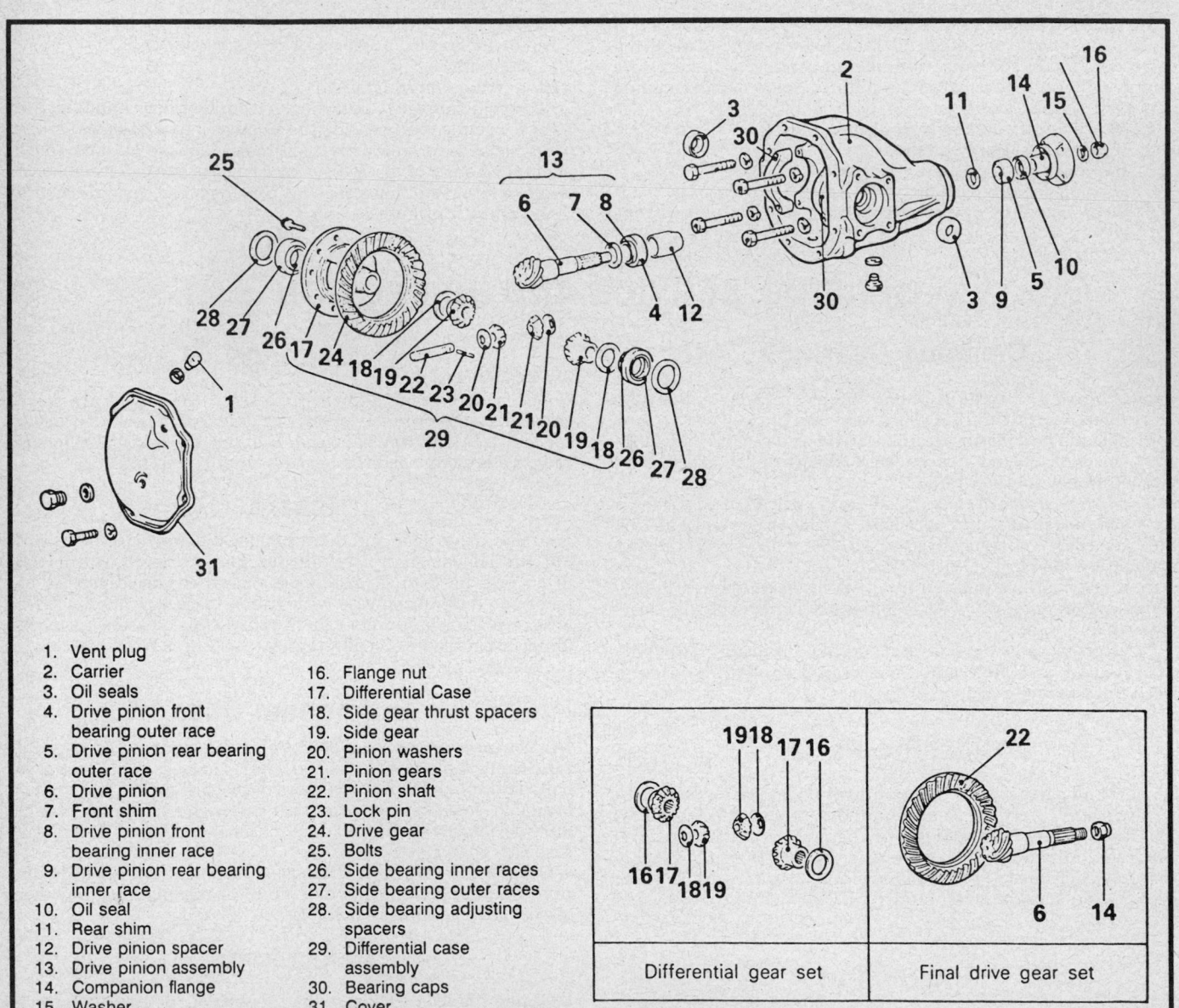

1. Vent plug
2. Carrier
3. Oil seals
4. Drive pinion front bearing outer race
5. Drive pinion rear bearing outer race
6. Drive pinion
7. Front shim
8. Drive pinion front bearing inner race
9. Drive pinion rear bearing inner race
10. Oil seal
11. Rear shim
12. Drive pinion spacer
13. Drive pinion assembly
14. Companion flange
15. Washer
16. Flange nut
17. Differential Case
18. Side gear thrust spacers
19. Side gear
20. Pinion washers
21. Pinion gears
22. Pinion shaft
23. Lock pin
24. Drive gear
25. Bolts
26. Side bearing inner races
27. Side bearing outer races
28. Side bearing adjusting spacers
29. Differential case assembly
30. Bearing caps
31. Cover

Differential gear set

Final drive gear set

Exploded view of front differential assembly—Chrysler Import/Mitsubishi

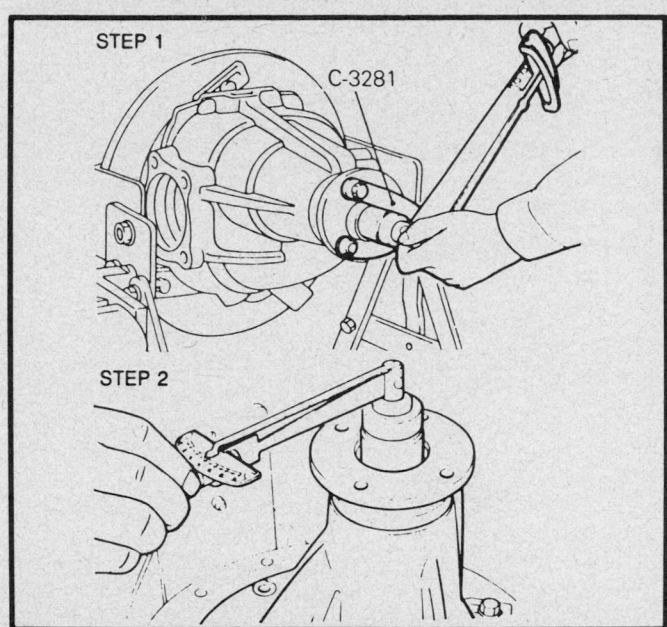

Adjustment of drive pinion preload—front differential carrier

Front Drive Axle

Inspection Before Dissassembly

1. Position the removed differential carrier assembly in a suitable holding fixture. Remove the differential cover.

2. With the drive pinion locked in place, measure the final drive gear (ring gear) backlash with a dial indicator on the drive gear. Measure at 4 points or more on the drive gear. If the backlash is not within the standard valve, adjust it by using the correct side bearing spacer.

3. The final drive gear backlash standard valve is 0.0043–0.0063 in. on all engines.

4. Measure the drive gear runout at the shoulder on the reverse side of the drive gear the limit is 0.0020 in. on all engines.

5. While locking the side gear with a wedge or equivalent, measure the differential gear backlash with a dial indicator on the pinion gear. The standard valve is 0–0.0030 in. The service limit is 0.008 in. on all engines.

6. Check the final drive gear tooth contact by the following steps:

    a. Apply a thin uniform coat of machine blue or equivalent to both surfaces of the drive gear teeth.

    b. Insert a tool between the differential carrier and the differential case and then rotate the companion flange by hand (once in normal direction and once reverse direction) while applying a load to the drive gear so that the revolution torque (about 2.5 ft. lbs.) is applied to the drive pinion.

    c. If the drive gear is rotated too much, contact pattern will become unclear and difficult to read. If a correct pattern cannot be obtained (drive gear and pinion worn beyond allowable limits), replace the drive gear and the drive pinion as a set.

Disassembly and Assembly

1. Position the removed differential carrier assembly in a suitable holding fixture. Remove the differential cover.

2. Matchmark and remove the bearing (carrier) caps and pry out the differential assembly.

3. Remove the differential side bearings. Be sure to keep the right and left bearings and shims separated. Remove side bearings inner and outer races.

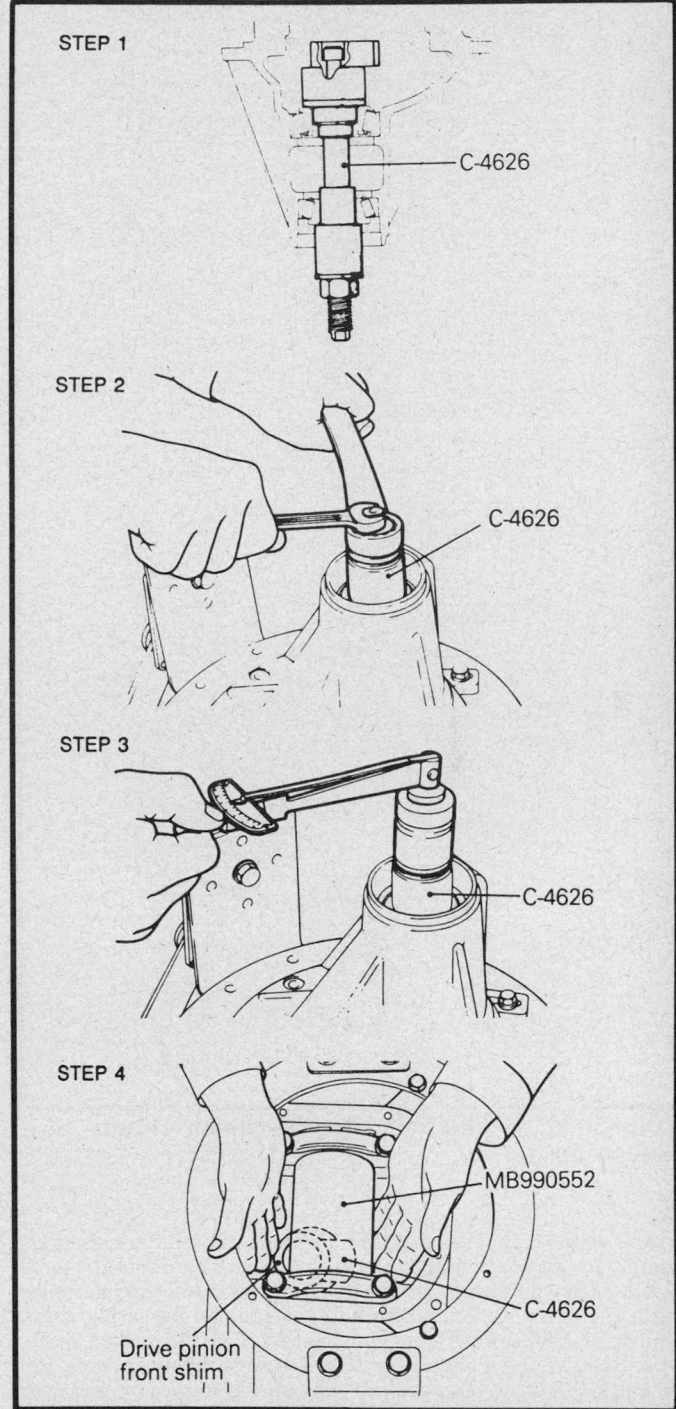

Adjustment of pinion height—front differential carrier

4. Matchmark ring gear assembly and loosen the ring gear mounting bolts in diagonal sequence. Remove the ring gear.

5. Drive the pinion shaft lock pin out from the rear of the ring gear using a punch and remove the pinion shaft assembly.

6. Remove the pinion gears and washers. Remove the side gears with their spacers. Keep left and right side gears and spacers separate. Remove the differential case.

7. Hold the end yoke (companion flange) and remove the self-locking nut and washer. Matchmark for correct installation then remove the companion flange.

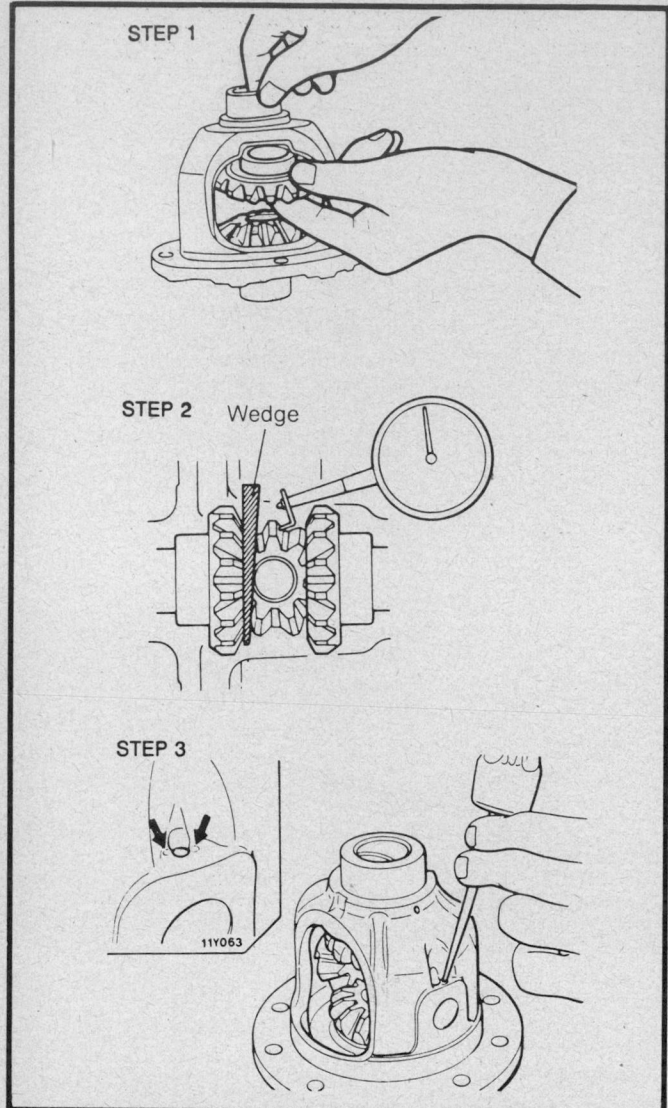

Adjustment of differential gear backlash—front differential carrier

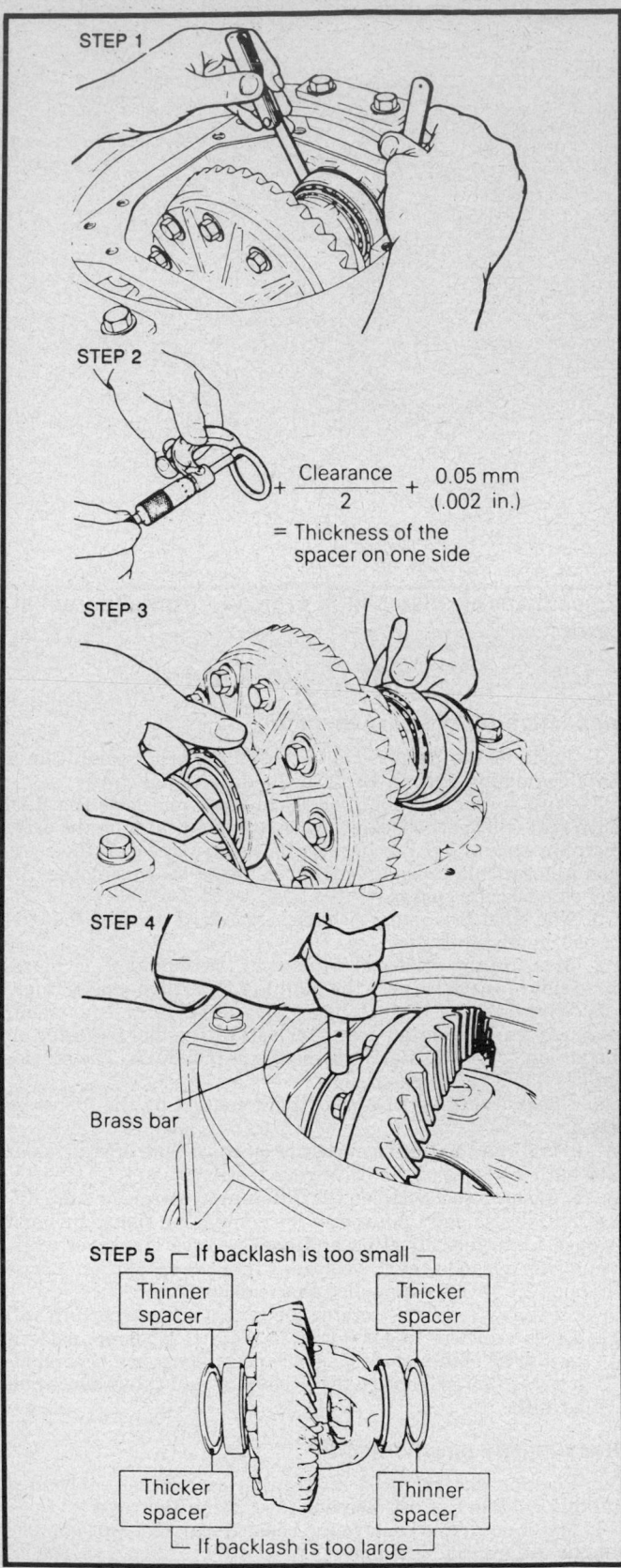

$$+ \frac{\text{Clearance}}{2} + \begin{array}{c}0.05 \text{ mm} \\ (.002 \text{ in.})\end{array}$$
$$= \text{Thickness of the spacer on one side}$$

Brass bar

STEP 5 — If backlash is too small —

Thinner spacer		Thicker spacer
Thicker spacer		Thinner spacer

— If backlash is too large —

Adjustment of final drive backlash—front differential carrier

8. Tap the end of the drive pinion shaft (matchmark shaft assembly for correct installation) with a plastic hammer and force out the drive pinion along with its adjusting shim, the rear inner race, the drive pinion spacer and the preload adjusting shim. The rear bearing inner race can be pressed off the pinion shaft.

9. Remove the front and rear pinion bearing outer races. Remove the oil seals. Remove the vent plug if necessary and gear carrier case.

10. Install the vent plug to the gear carrier case if necessary. Install oil seals.

11. Press the drive pinion front and rear bearing outer races into the differential carrier case. Make sure that the races do not tilt and that they sit fully in the case.

12. At this point of the reassembly, adjust the drive pinion height by following this procedure:

   a. Install special service tool C–4626 and drive pinion front and rear bearing inner races to the gear carrier in the correct sequence.

   b. Gradually tighten the nut of the special tool until the standard valve of the drive pinion turning torque is reached.

c. Measure the drive pinion turning torque without the oil seal installed. The standard valve is 1.30–2.17 inch lbs. of turning torque for all engines except 3.0L engine. The standard valve is 3.47–4.34 inch lbs. of turning torque for 3.0L engine.

d. Because one rotation cannot be made when the special tool is in contact with the gear carrier, move it a few times and after seating the bearing measure the rotation torque.

e. Mount the special service tool MB990552 in the side bearing seat of the gear carrier and then select a drive pinion front height adjusting shim (keep front shims to a minimum) of a thickness which corresponds to the gap between the special tools. Be sure to clean the side bearing seat thoroughly. When mounting the special tool be sure that the cut-out sections are in the correct position and also confirm that the tool is in close contact with the side bearing seat.

f. Install the selected drive pinion front shim(s) to the drive pinion. Using special tool MB990802, press fit the drive pinion front bearing inner race.

13. At this point of the reassembly, adjust the drive pinion preload (turning torque) by following this procedure:

a. Without the oil seal installed insert the drive pinion into the gear carrier and then install from the front side of the carrier, the driver pinion spacer, drive pinion rear shim, drive pinion rear bearing inner race and the companion flange in that order.

b. Tighten the companion flange to 116–159 ft. lbs. on all engines except the 3.0L engine. On the 3.0L engine torque the companion flange to 137–181 ft. lbs. Measure the drive pinion turning torque without the oil seal installed. The standard valve is 1.30–2.17 inch lbs. turning torque for all engines except the 3.0L engine. The standard valve is 3.47–4.34 inch lbs. turning torque for the 3.0L engine.

c. Adjust the turning torque by replacing the drive pinion rear shim(s) or the drive pinion spacer. Reduce number of drive pinion rear shims by replacing drive pinion spacer(s) as necessary.

d. Remove the companion flange and drive pinion once again.

14. Install drive pinion rear bearing inner race. Install oil seal into the gear carrier using suitable tools.

15. Install the drive pinion assembly and companion flange in the correct position. Tighten the companion flange to 116–159 ft. lbs. on all engines except the 3.0L engine. On the 3.0L engine torque the companion flange to 137–181 ft. lbs.

16. Measure the drive pinion turning torque with oil seal installed. The standard valve is 3.04–3.91 inch lbs. of turning torque for all engines except the 3.0L engine. The standard valve for the 3.0L engine is 5.21–6.08 inch lbs. of turning torque.

17. If not within the standard valve, check for faulty installation of the oil seal or wrong torque on the companion flange locking nut.

18. At this point of the reassembly, adjust the differential gear backlash by following this procedure:

a. Install the side gears, side gear thrust spacers, pinion gear and pinion washers into the differential case. Temporarily install the pinion shaft. Do not drive the lock pin in place yet.

b. While locking the side gear with a wedge or equivalent, measure the differential gear backlash with a dial indicator on the pinion gear. The standard valve is 0–0.0030 in. and the service limit is 0.008 in. on all engines.

c. If the differential gear backlash exceeds the limit adjust the backlash by installing thicker side gear thrust spacers. If adjustment is not possible replace the side gears and pinion gears as a set.

19. Align the pinion shaft lock pin hole with the differential case lock pin hole.

20. Drive the lock pin in and stake the pin with a suitable tool in 2 different locations.

21. Install the drive gear onto the differential case with matchmarks in the correct position. Torque (with locking adhesive or equivalent on threads) drive gear attaching bolts to 58–65 ft. lbs. in a diagonal sequence for all engines.

22. Press fit the side bearing inner races to the differential case using suitable tools.

23. At this point of the reassembly, adjust the final drive gear backlash as follows:

a. Install the side bearing adjusting spacers (both sides same size-thin spacers as possible) to the side bearing outer races, then mount ther differential case assembly into the gear carrier.

b. Push the differential case assembly to one side. Measure the clearance between the gear carrier and the side bearing adjusting spacer with a feeler gauge.

c. Measure the thickness of the side bearing adjusting spacers on a side. Select 2 pairs of spacers which correspond to that thickness plus ½ of the clearance plus 0.002 in. and then install one pair each to the drive pinion side and the drive gear side.

24. Install the side bearing adjusting spacers and differential case assembly in the gear carrier.

25. Tap the side bearing adjusting spacers with a brass tool to position them to the side bearing outer races.

26. Align the mating marks on the gear carrier and the bearing caps and tighten the bearing caps to 40–47 ft. lbs. on all engines.

27. Attach a dial indicator to the ring gear teeth and measure the final drive gear backlash at 4 different locations. Final drive gear backlash standard valve is 0.0043–0.0063 in. for all engines. Change the side bearing spacers as necessary for correct adjustment. When increasing the number of side bearing adjusting spacers, use the same number for each side and as few as possible.

28. Measure the ring gear runout in 2 or more locations. Runout should be 0.002 in. or less on all engines.

29. If necessary make a ring gear tooth pattern check. Apply gear oil to all moving parts and use sealant and or gasket when assembling to the axle housing.

Rear Drive Axle

Inspection Before Disassembly

1. Position the removed differential carrier assembly in a suitable holding fixture.

2. With the drive pinion locked in place, measure the final drive gear (ring gear) backlash with a dial indicator on the drive gear. Measure at 4 points or more on the drive gear.

3. The final drive gear backlash standard valve for 2.0L, 2.4 and 2.6L engines is 0.0043–0.0063 in. The standard valve for 3.0L engine is 0.0051–0.0071 in.

4. Measure the drive gear runout at the shoulder on the reverse side of the drive gear the limit is 0.0020 in. on all engines.

5. On a conventional differential asssembly the differential gear backlash must be checked. While locking the side gear with a wedge or equivalent, measure the differential gear backlash with a dial indicator on the pinion gear. The differential gear backlash (conventional) for the 2.0L, 2.4L and 2.6L engines standard valve is 0.0004–0.0030 in. The standard valve (conventional) for the 3.0L engine is 0–0.0030 in. The service limit is 0.008 in. on all engines.

6. Check the final drive gear tooth contact by the following steps:

a. Apply a thin uniform coat of machine blue or equivalent to both surfaces of the drive gear teeth.

b. Insert a tool between the differential carrier and the differential case and then rotate the companion flange by hand (once in normal direction and once reverse direction) while

applying a load to the drive gear so that the revolution torque (about 2.5 ft. lbs.) is applied to the drive pinion.

c. If the drive gear is rotated too much, contact pattern will become unclear and difficult to read. If a correct pattern cannot be obtained (drive gear and pinion worn beyond allowable limits), replace the drive gear and the drive pinion as a set.

Disassembly and Assembly

1. Position the differential assembly in a suitable holding fix-

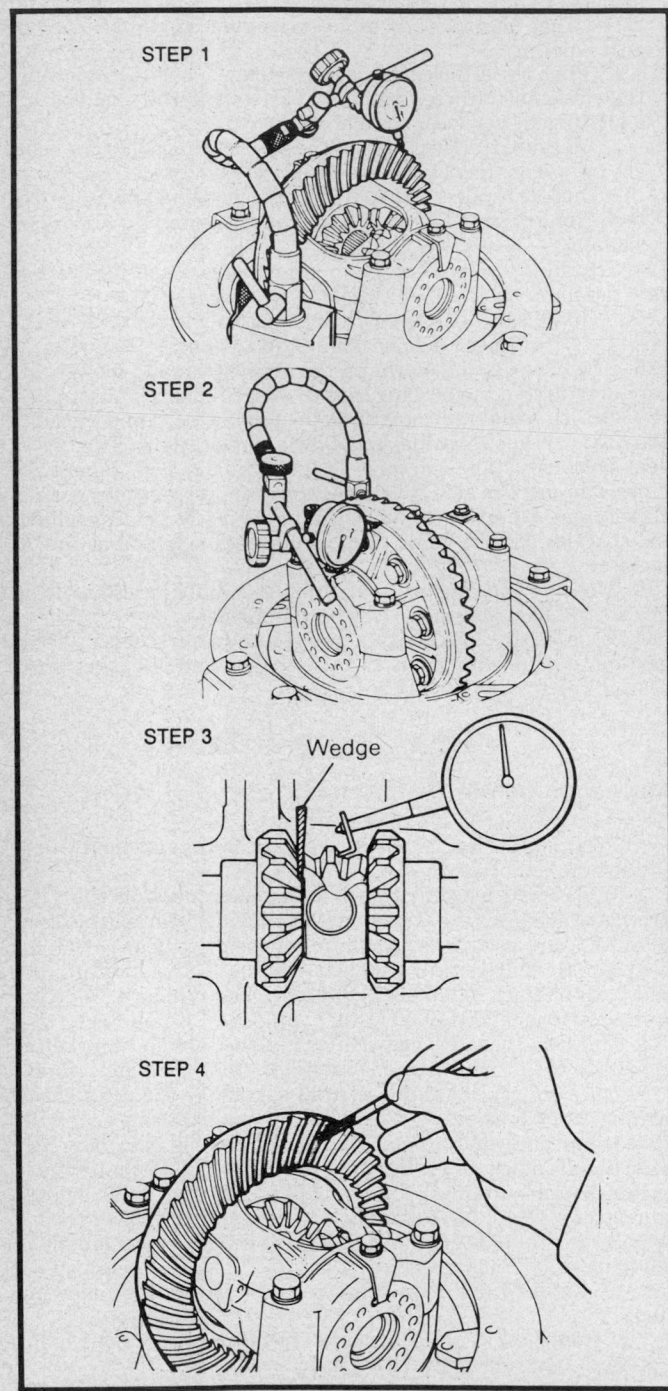

Inspection of rear differentail carrier before disassembly

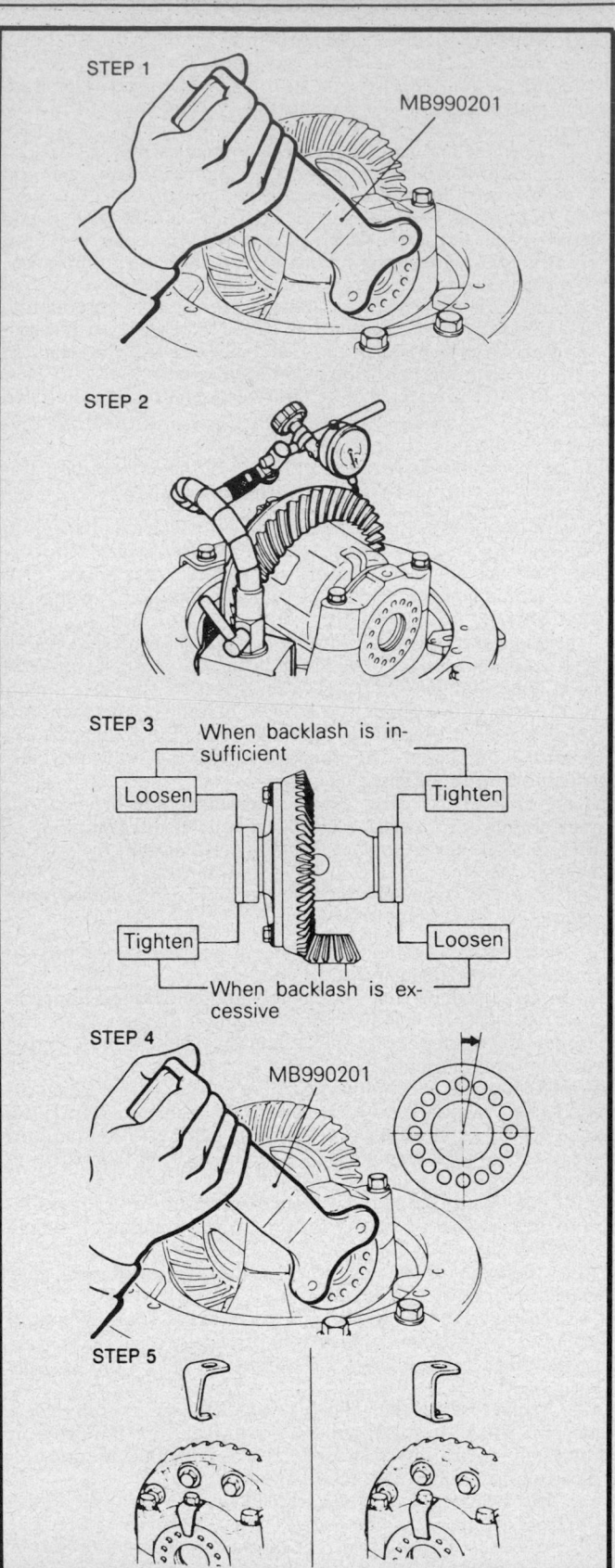

Adjustment of final drive gear backlash—rear differerntial carrier

ture. Remove the lock bolts and plates holding the side bearing nut in place.

2. Remove the side bearing nuts with the special adjusting tool spanner wrench No. MB990201 or equivalent.

3. Matchmark and remove the carrier caps and pry out the differential.

4. Pull off the differential side bearings. Be sure to keep the right and left bearings and shims separated. Remove side bearings inner and outer races.

5. Matchmark ring gear assembly and loosen the ring gear mounting bolts in diagonal sequence. Remove the ring gear.

6. Drive the pinion shaft lock pin out from the rear of the ring

Standard tooth contact pattern

1 Toe
2 Drive-side
3 Heel
4 Coast-side

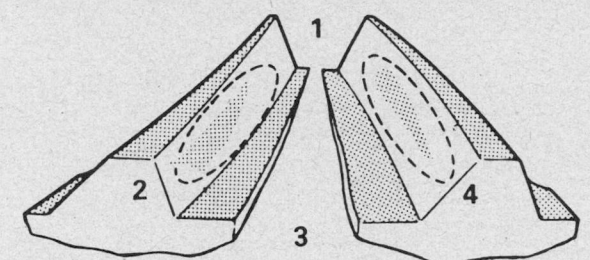

Problem	Solution

Tooth contact pattern resulting from excessive pinion height

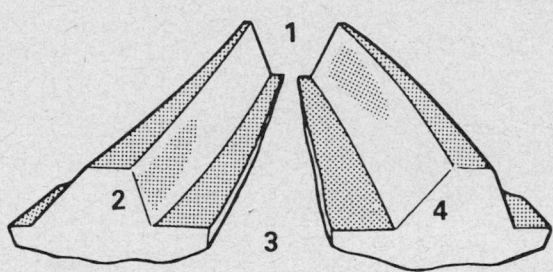 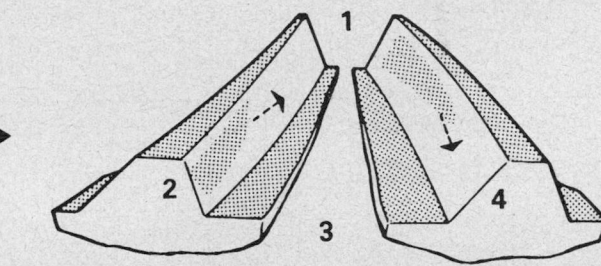

The drive pinion is positioned too far from the center of the drive gear.

Increase the thickness of the pinion height adjusting shim, and position the drive pinion closer to the center of the drive gear.
Also, for backlash adjustment, position the drive gear farther from the drive pinion.

Tooth contact pattern resulting from insufficient pinion height

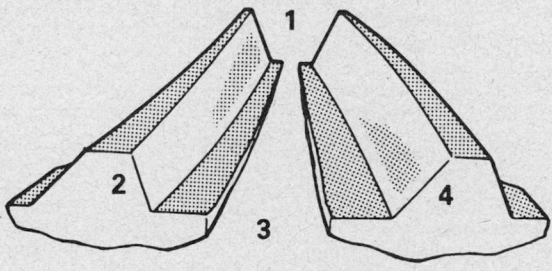 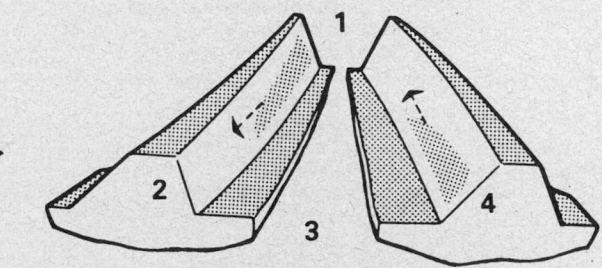

The drive pinion is positioned too close to the center of the drive gear.

Decrease the thickness of the pinion height adjusting shim, and position the drive pinion farther from the center of the drive gear.
Also, for backlash adjustment, position the drive gear closer to the drive pinion.

Differential tooth contact pattern — Chrysler Import/Mitsubishi

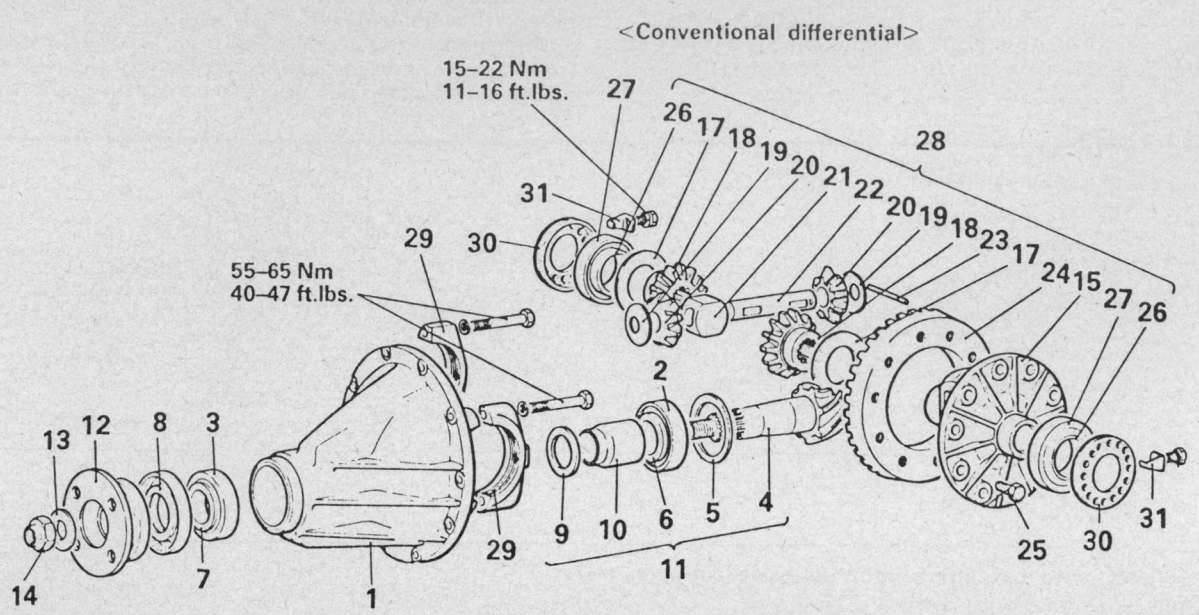

<Conventional differential>

15–22 Nm
11–16 ft.lbs.

55–65 Nm
40–47 ft.lbs.

<Limited slip differential>

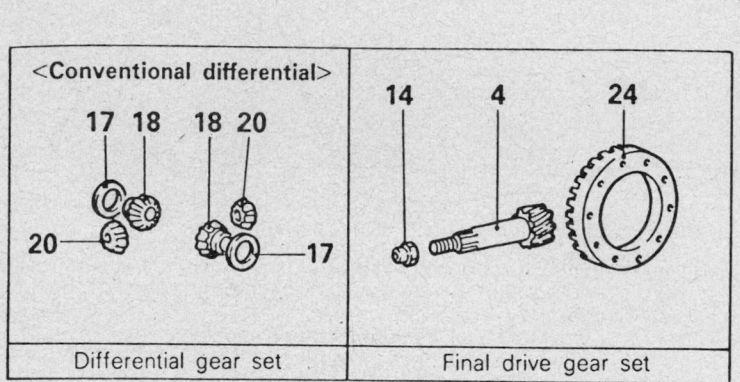

<Conventional differential>

Differential gear set	Final drive gear set

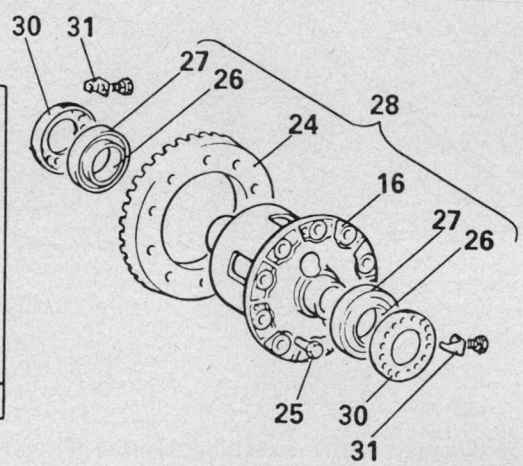

1. Carrier
2. Drive pinion rear bearing outer race
3. Drive pinion front bearing outer race
4. Drive pinion
5. Rear shim
6. Drive pinion rear bearing inner race
7. Drive pinion front bearing inner race
8. Oil seal
9. Front shim
10. Drive pinion spacer
11. Drive pinion assembly
12. Companion flange
13. Washer
14. Flange nut
15. Differential Case

16. Limited slip differential case assembly
17. Side gear thrust spacers
18. Side gear
19. Pinion washers
20. Pinion gears
21. Thrust block
22. Pinion shaft
23. Lock pin
24. Drive gear
25. Bolts
26. Side bearing inner races
27. Side bearing outer races
28. Differential case assembly
29. Bearing caps
30. Side bearing nuts
31. Lock plates

Exploded view of rear differential assembly – Chrysler Import/Mitsubishi

gear using a punch and remove the pinion shaft assembly.

7. Remove the thrust block, pinion gears and washers. Remove the side gears with their spacers. Keep left and right side gears and spacers separate. Remove the differential case.

8. On limited slip differential vehicles, remove limited slip differential case assembly.

9. Hold the end yoke (companion flange) and remove the self-locking nut and washer. Matchmark for correct installation then remove the companion flange.

10. Tap the end of the drive pinion shaft (matchmark shaft assembly for correct installation) with a plastic hammer and force out the drive pinion along with its adjusting shim, the rear inner race, the drive pinion spacer and the preload adjusting shim. The rear bearing inner race can be pressed off the pinion shaft.

11. Remove the front and rear pinion bearing outer races. The front inner race should be removed with its oil seal. Remove the differential carrier case.

NOTE: Do not reuse the old oil seal. If the unit is to be assembled using no replacement parts except oil seals, the same spacers and shims can generally be used. If either pinion bearing or ring gear and drive pinion are being replaced, new shims should be used. Only replace the drive pinion and ring gear in matched sets.

12. Press the drive pinion front and rear bearing outer races into the differential carrier case. Make sure that the races do not tilt and that they sit fully in the case.

13. At this point of the reassembly, adjust the drive pinion height by following this procedure:

   a. Install special service tool MB991169 (use special adapter head tool C–4626 for 3.0L engine only) and drive pinion front and rear bearing inner races to the gear carrier in the correct sequence.

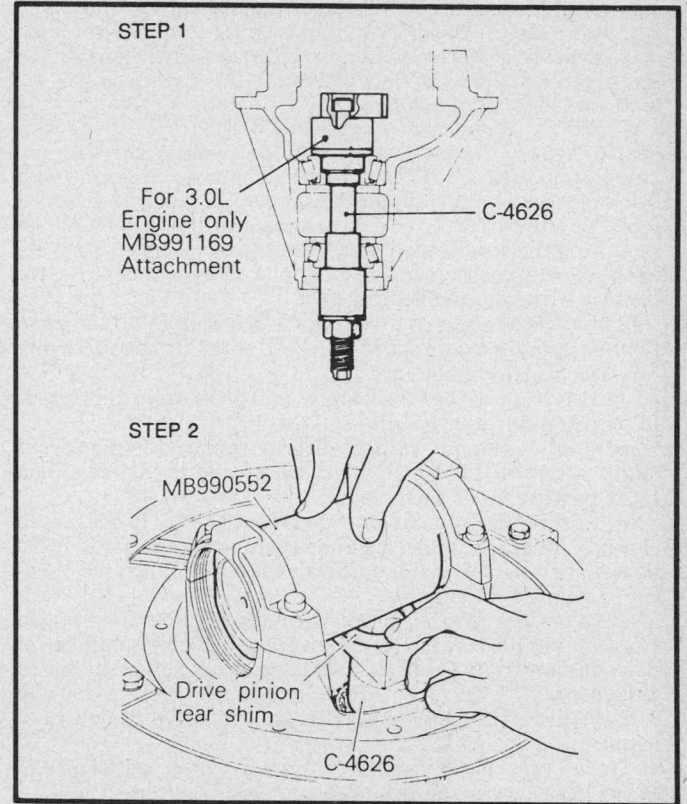

STEP 1

For 3.0L Engine only MB991169 Attachment — C-4626

STEP 2

MB990552

Drive pinion rear shim

C-4626

Adjustment of pinion height – rear differential carrier

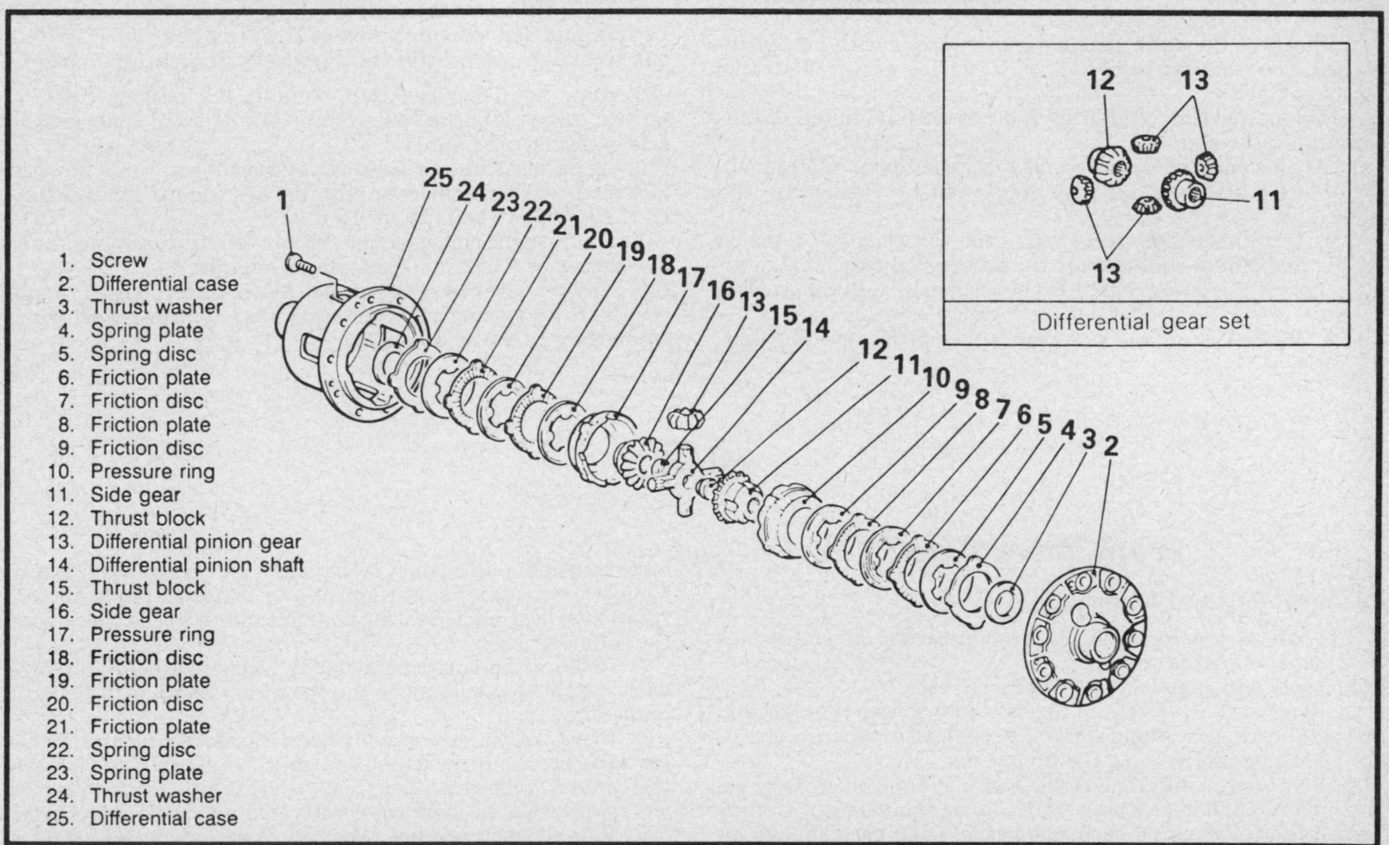

1. Screw
2. Differential case
3. Thrust washer
4. Spring plate
5. Spring disc
6. Friction plate
7. Friction disc
8. Friction plate
9. Friction disc
10. Pressure ring
11. Side gear
12. Thrust block
13. Differential pinion gear
14. Differential pinion shaft
15. Thrust block
16. Side gear
17. Pressure ring
18. Friction disc
19. Friction plate
20. Friction disc
21. Friction plate
22. Spring disc
23. Spring plate
24. Thrust washer
25. Differential case

Differential gear set

Exploded view of limited slip differential carrier – Chrysler Import/Mitsubishi

b. Gradually tighten the nut of the special tool until the standard valve of the drive pinion turning torque is reached.

c. Measure the drive pinion turning torque without the oil seal installed. The standard valve for all engines is 3.5–4.3 inch lbs. of turning torque.

d. Mount the special service tool MB990552 in the side bearing seat of the gear carrier and then select a drive pinion height adjusting shim (keep rear shims to a minimum) of a thickness which corresponds to the gap between the special tools. Be sure to clean the side bearing seat thoroughly. When mounting the special tool be sure that the cut-out sections are in the correct position and also confirm that the tool is in close contact with the side bearing seat.

e. Install the selected drive pinion rear shim(s) to the drive pinion. Using special tool MB990802, press fit the drive pinion rear bearing inner race.

14. At this point of the reassembly, adjust the drive pinion preload (turning torque) by following this procedure:

a. Without the oil seal installed fit the drive pinion front shims between the drive pinion spacer and the drive pinion front bearing inner race.

b. Tighten the companion flange to 137–181 ft. lbs. on all engines. Measure the drive pinion turning torque without the oil seal installed. The standard valve is 3.5–4.3 inch lbs. turning torque for all engines.

c. Adjust the turning torque by replacing the drive pinion front shim(s) or the drive pinion spacer. Reduce number of drive pinion front shims by replacing drive pinion spacer as necessary.

d. Remove the companion flange and drive pinion once again.

15. Install drive pinion front bearing inner race. Install oil seal into the gear carrier using suitable tools.

16. Install the drive pinion assembly and companion flange in the correct position. Torque the companion flange locking nut to 137–181 ft. lbs. on all engines.

17. Measure the drive pinion turning torque with oil seal installed. The standard valve is 5.6–6.5 inch lbs. of turning torque on all engines.

18. On limited slip differential vehicles, install limited slip differential case assembly.

19. At this point of the reassembly (conventional differential), adjust the differential gear backlash by following this procedure:

a. Install the side gears, side gear thrust spacers, pinion gear and pinion washers into the differential case. Temporarily install the pinion shaft. Do not drive the lock pin in place yet.

b. While locking the side gear with a wedge or equivalent, measure the differential gear backlash with a dial indicator on the pinion gear. The differential gear backlash for the 2.0L, 2.4L and 2.6L engines standard valve is 0.0004–0.0030 in. The standard valve for the 3.0L engine is 0–0.0030 in. The service limit is 0.008 in. on all engines.

c. If the differential gear backlash exceeds the limit adjust the backlash by installing thicher side gear thrust spacers. If adjustment is not possible replace the side gears and pinion gears as a set.

20. Install the thrust block. Align the pinion shaft lock pin hole with the differential case lock pin hole.

21. Drive the lock pin in and stake the pin with a suitable tool in 2 different locations.

22. Install the drive gear onto the differential case with matchmarks in the correct position. Torque (with locking adhesive or equivalent on threads) drive gear attaching bolts to 58–65 ft. lbs. on conventional and limited slip differentials in a diagonal sequence.

23. Press fit the side bearing inner races to the differential case using suitable tools.

24. Install the differential case assembly.

25. Install the carrier (bearing) caps with their mating marks in line with the marks on the carriers and finger tighten the 4 set bolts.

26. Install the side bearing nuts and tighten the carrier cap bolts to 40–47 ft. lbs. on all engines.

27. Screw in the side bearing nuts to adjust the final drive gear backlash. Each nut should be tightened to the state just before preloading of the side bearing.

28. Attach a dial indicator to the ring gear teeth and measure the final drive gear backlash in 4 different locations. The final drive gear backlash standard valve for 2.0L, 2.4 and 2.6L engines is 0.0043–0.0063 in. The standard valve for 3.0L engine is 0.0051–0.0071 in.

NOTE: If the backlash has to be adjusted, loosen the bearing nut on the back side of the ring gear and tighten the bearing nut on the teeth side by the same amount.

29. After adjusting backlash, tighten the bearing nuts $\frac{1}{2}$ pitch. One pitch is the space between 2 adjacent holes on the side of the bearing nut.

30. Again measure the backlash and install a 1 or 2 pronged lock plate whichever lines up with the bearing nut holes. Tighten the lock plate bolts to 11–16 ft.lb.

31. Measure the ring gear runout in 2 or more locations. Runout should be 0.002 in. or less on all engines.

32. If necessary make a ring gear tooth pattern check. Apply gear oil to all moving parts and use sealant and or gasket when assembling to the axle housing.

ISUZU

Front Drive Axle

Disassembly and Assembly

1. Position the removed differential carrier assembly in a suitable holding fixture.

2. Mark and remove the side bearing caps.

3. Remove the differential cage assembly. Keep the right and left side bearing races and shims if so equiped in separate groups for reinstallation in same positions.

4. Remove the differential side bearings from the case by using puller J–22888 and plug J–8107–2 or equivalent. Carefully record the thickness of each side bearing and each shim(s) removed for later use in reassembly and keep separated. Puller arms must not pull against roller cage. Use care to position legs against inner race. As bearing is being removed, check for free rotation of bearing. If bearing does not rotate freely, check position of puller legs.

5. Remove the companion flange nut while holding flange with suitable tools. Remove the flange assembly with puller if necessary.

6. Drive the pinion assembly from the carrier using suitable tools and brass punch. The outer (front) bearing will fall loose in the carrier, while the inner (rear) bearing will remain pressed on the drive pinion. Both races will remain in the carrier bores.

7. Remove rear bearing from the drive pinion by use of a press and tool J–22912–01 or equivalent.

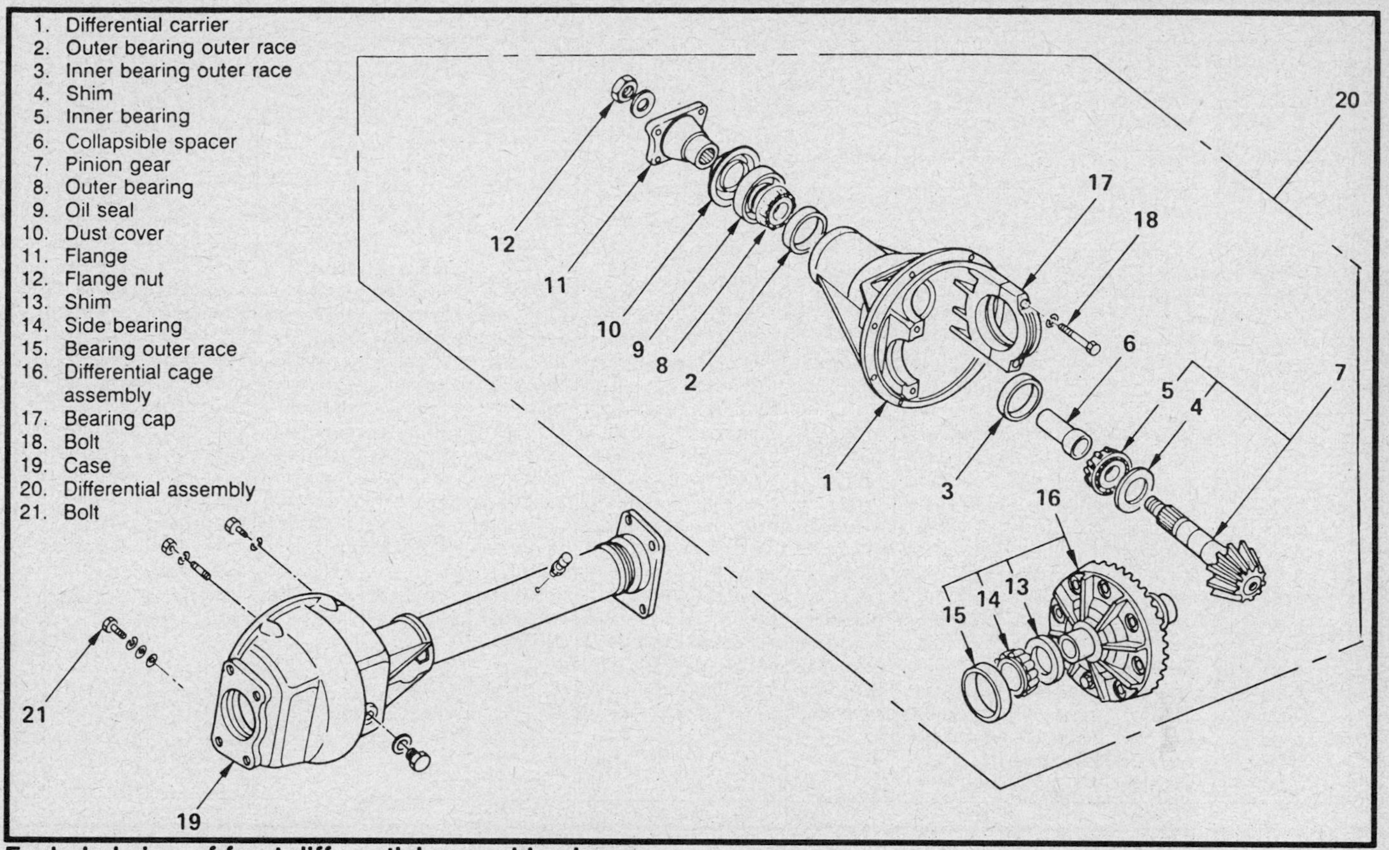

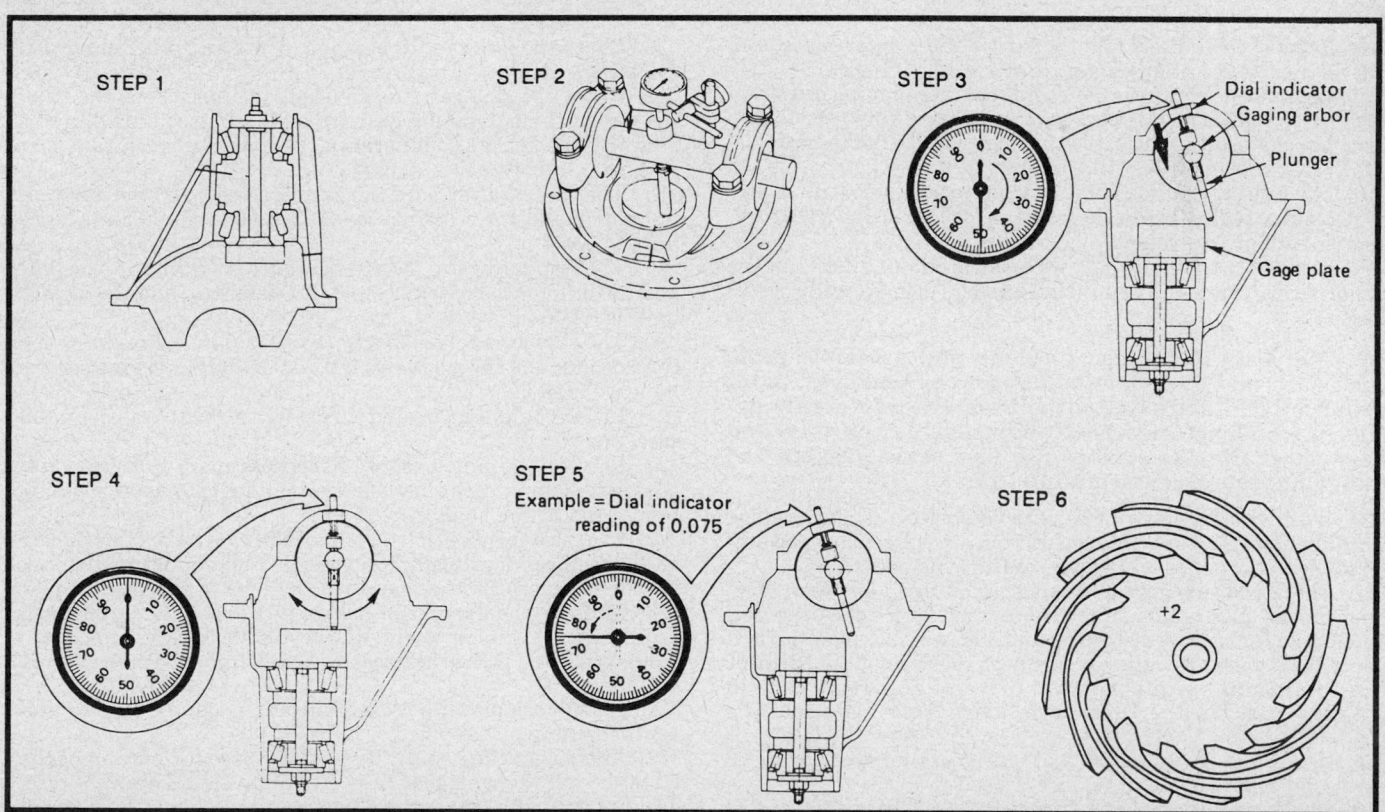

1. Differential carrier
2. Outer bearing outer race
3. Inner bearing outer race
4. Shim
5. Inner bearing
6. Collapsible spacer
7. Pinion gear
8. Outer bearing
9. Oil seal
10. Dust cover
11. Flange
12. Flange nut
13. Shim
14. Side bearing
15. Bearing outer race
16. Differential cage assembly
17. Bearing cap
18. Bolt
19. Case
20. Differential assembly
21. Bolt

Exploded view of front differential assembly—Isuzu

STEP 1

STEP 2

STEP 3
Dial indicator
Gaging arbor
Plunger
Gage plate

STEP 4

STEP 5
Example = Dial indicator reading of 0.075

STEP 6
+2

Adjustment of drive pinion mounting distance

Pinion marking / Dial indicator reading (Inches)	+10	+8	+6	+4	+2	0	-2	-4	-6	-8	-10
0.081											2.18(0.0858)
0.082										2.18(0.0858)	2.20(0.0866)
0.083									2.18(0.0858)	2.20(0.0866)	2.24(0.0882)
0.084								2.18(0.0858)	2.20(0.0866)	2.24(0.0882)	2.26(0.0890)
0.085							2.18(0.0858)	2.20(0.0866)	2.24(0.0882)	2.26(0.0890)	2.28(0.0898)
0.086						2.18(0.0858)	2.20(0.0866)	2.24(0.0882)	2.26(0.0890)	2.28(0.0898)	2.32(0.0914)
0.087					2.18(0.0858)	2.20(0.0866)	2.24(0.0882)	2.26(0.0890)	2.28(0.0898)	2.32(0.0914)	2.34(0.0921)
0.088				2.18(0.0858)	2.20(0.0866)	2.24(0.0882)	2.26(0.0890)	2.28(0.0898)	2.32(0.0914)	2.34(0.0921)	2.36(0.0929)
0.089			2.18(0.0858)	2.20(0.0866)	2.24(0.0882)	2.26(0.0890)	2.28(0.0898)	2.32(0.0914)	2.34(0.0921)	2.36(0.0929)	2.38(0.0937)
0.090		2.18(0.0858)	2.20(0.0866)	2.24(0.0882)	2.26(0.0890)	2.28(0.0898)	2.32(0.0914)	2.34(0.0921)	2.36(0.0929)	2.38(0.0937)	2.42(0.0953)
0.091	2.18(0.0858)	2.20(0.0866)	2.24(0.0882)	2.26(0.0890)	2.28(0.0898)	2.32(0.0914)	2.34(0.0921)	2.36(0.0929)	2.38(0.0937)	2.42(0.0953)	2.44(0.0961)
0.092	2.20(0.0866)	2.24(0.0882)	2.26(0.0890)	2.28(0.0898)	2.32(0.0914)	2.34(0.0921)	2.36(0.0929)	2.38(0.0937)	2.42(0.0953)	2.44(0.0961)	2.46(0.0969)
0.093	2.24(0.0882)	2.26(0.0890)	2.28(0.0898)	2.32(0.0914)	2.34(0.0921)	2.36(0.0929)	2.38(0.0937)	2.42(0.0953)	2.44(0.0961)	2.46(0.0969)	2.48(0.0977)
0.094	2.26(0.0890)	2.28(0.0898)	2.32(0.0914)	2.34(0.0921)	2.36(0.0929)	2.38(0.0937)	2.42(0.0953)	2.44(0.0961)	2.46(0.0969)	2.48(0.0977)	2.52(0.0992)
0.095	2.28(0.0898)	2.32(0.0914)	2.34(0.0921)	2.36(0.0929)	2.38(0.0937)	2.42(0.0953)	2.44(0.0961)	2.46(0.0969)	2.48(0.0977)	2.52(0.0992)	2.54(0.1000)
0.096	2.32(0.0914)	2.34(0.0921)	2.36(0.0929)	2.38(0.0937)	2.42(0.0953)	2.44(0.0961)	2.46(0.0969)	2.48(0.0977)	2.52(0.0992)	2.54(0.1000)	2.56(0.1008)
0.097	2.34(0.0921)	2.36(0.0929)	2.38(0.0937)	2.42(0.0953)	2.44(0.0961)	2.46(0.0969)	2.48(0.0977)	2.52(0.0992)	2.54(0.1000)	2.56(0.1008)	
0.098	2.36(0.0929)	2.38(0.0937)	2.42(0.0953)	2.44(0.0961)	2.46(0.0969)	2.48(0.0977)	2.52(0.0992)	2.54(0.1000)	2.56(0.1008)		
0.099	2.38(0.0937)	2.42(0.0953)	2.44(0.0961)	2.46(0.0969)	2.48(0.0977)	2.52(0.0992)	2.54(0.1000)	2.56(0.1008)			
0.000	2.42(0.0953)	2.44(0.0961)	2.46(0.0969)	2.48(0.0977)	2.52(0.0992)	2.54(0.1000)	2.56(0.1008)				
0.001	2.44(0.0961)	2.46(0.0969)	2.48(0.0977)	2.52(0.0992)	2.54(0.1000)	2.56(0.1008)					
0.002	2.46(0.0969)	2.48(0.0977)	2.52(0.0992)	2.54(0.1000)	2.56(0.1008)						
0.003	2.48(0.0977)	2.52(0.0992)	2.54(0.1000)	2.56(0.1008)							
0.004	2.52(0.0992)	2.54(0.1000)	2.56(0.1008)								
0.005	2.54(0.1000)	2.56(0.1008)									
0.006	2.56(0.1008)										

Shim selection chart—Isuzu front and rear conventional drive axles

8. Remove the oil seal and then drive the 2 outer races from the carrier by use of a brass drift and suitable tools.

9. Remove the ring gear bolts and separate the ring gear from the differential case. Use care when removing ring gear to prevent damage to differential case or ring gear. Do not force a chisel or other tools between the joining faces.

10. Drive out the pinion shaft lock pin with a long drift. It may be necessary to first break the stake on lock pin using a 0.020 diameter drill or equivalent.

11. Remove the pinion shaft with a drift pin and take out the pinion gears, side gears and thrust washers from the differential case.

NOTE: It is important to clean and assemble parts with care and to follow adjustment procedures. Axles which are contaminated with dirt or other foreign material, or which are incorrectly adjusted may be noisy and have short life. Be sure to use new seals, gaskets and flange nut when reassembling axle.

12. Wash the bearings in a suitable solvent. Then examine bearings carefully for wear, separation, cracks, seizure and other abnormal conditions. Replace bearings as necessary.

13. Check the ring gear and drive pinion teeth for wear, chipping, cracks, pitting and abnormal contact. Check the drive pinion splines for cracks, distortion and step wear. Replace parts if needed. Ring gear (torque for ring gear replacement is 73–87 ft. lbs. in diagonal sequence) and drive pinion come only in matched sets. If either item is defective, both parts must be replaced.

14. Check the pinion gears and side gears for wear, chipped teeth and separation and replace if needed.

15. Check and replace the thrust blocks if so equipped and thrust washers, if worn or damaged.

16. Check the lock pin for bending, dents and other abnormal conditions. Replace if necessary.

17. Check the side gear-to-axle shaft fit. Also check the fit of the pinion shaft to pinion gears. Examine the contact surfaces between side gears and differential case and between ring gear and case.

18. The standard valve for the clearance between the differential pinion and the cross pin is 0.002–0.005 in. and the service limit is 0.008 in.

19. The standard valve for the clearance between the side gear and the differential assembly is 0.001–0.004 in. and the service limit is 0.006 in.

20. The standard valve for play (backlash) in splines betwwen the side gear and the axle shaft is 0.001–0.006 in. and the service limit is 0.010 in.

21. Install the side gears and thrust washers in the differential case.

22. Position the pinion gears 180 degrees apart. Roll gears into position, making sure they are in alignment, to allow installation of the pinion shaft.

23. Place the thrust block if equipped between the pinion gears and drive the pinion shaft into position. Make sure that the lock pin hole in cross shaft aligns with the hole in the case.

24. Measure the amount of backlash between the differential gears and the pinion gears. If the backlash is greater than 0.001–0.003 in., make the necessary adjustment with the thrust washers.

25. Install lock pin into cross shaft and stake the cage to prevent loosening of the pin.

26. Apply Loctite or equivalent to the threaded portion of the bolts. Install the ring gear in position on the differential case. Tighten the bolts (always use new retaining bolts) in diagonal sequence to 73–87 ft. lbs.

27. To set pinion depth install the drive pinion front and rear bearing outer races into carrier bores. Use drive handle J–8092 with J–24256 for front bearing race and J–24252 or equivalent for rear bearing race.

28. Lubricate and position the front and rear bearings to be used for final assembly into their respective races.

29. Install gauging plate J–23597–7 and preload stud and pilot J–23597–9 or their equivalent through front and rear bearings and tighten nut snugly.

30. Rotate the bearings to insure proper seating and tighten locknut until 20 inch lbs. of torque are required to rotate new bearings; 8–10 inch lbs. for used bearings.

31. Place discs J–23597–8 onto arbor J–23597–1 or equivalent and place tool into position in side bearing bores.

32. Install bearing caps and torque to 65–72 ft. lbs.

33. Mount dial indicator J–8001 or equivalent on arbor post and preload dial ½ revolution. Tighten indicator in this position.

34. Position the indicator plunger on the gauge plate and slowly swing across until the highest reading is obtained. Zero the indicator on the highest reading of the gauge plate.

35. Carefully swing the plunger off the gauge plate. Note the indicator reading. Recheck to verify the reading. Record the number the dial indicator needle points to. The reading on the dial is the correct dimension for the rear pinion depth shim. Convert the dial indicator reading (inches) to pinion marking (depth code) specification.

36. Record pinion depth code on the head of the drive pinion. The number indicates a necessary change in the pinion mounting distance. A plus number indicates the need for a greater mounting distance (which can be achieved by decreasing the shim thickness). A minus number indicates the need for a smaller mounting distance (which can be achieved by increasing the

shim thickness). If examination reveals no pinion depth code, the pinion is nominal. Determine the proper shim variation to compensate for plus or minus markings.

37. Place the shim on the drive pinion, then install the rear bearing, using J–6133–01 or equivalent. Do not press on roller cage press only on inner race.

38. To set pinion bearing preload place the drive pinion and spacer (always use new spacer) into the carrier.

39. Lubricate, then position the front bearing to be used in final assembly into the carrier. Install new oil seal.

40. Install companion flange to drive pinion. Apply hypoid lubricant to pinion threads. Install new pinion nut and torque to 130–202 ft. lbs. using J–8614–01 or equivalent to hold companion flange.

41. Rotate drive pinion to insure that bearings are seated. Measure the bearing preload by using a torque wrench. Note the scale reading required to rotate the flange.

42. Continue tightening until the correct starting toque is obtained. The standard valve for starting torque is 5.6–9.9 inch lbs. The pinion nut should be tightened only in small increments and the scale should be checked after each small amount of tightening. Exceeding preload specifications may compress the collapsible spacer too far and require its replacement.

43. Install the side bearings to be used in final assembly onto the differential case. Do not install shims at this time. Use J–24244 or equivalent for the first bearing installation.

44. Support case on plug J–8107–2 or equivalent for opposite bearing installation.

45. Install the differential cage assembly into carrier bores.

46. Using 2 sets of feeler gauges, insert a feeler gauge of sufficient thickness between each bearing outer race and the carrier to remover all endplay. Make certain the feeler gauge is pushed to the bottom of the bearing bores.

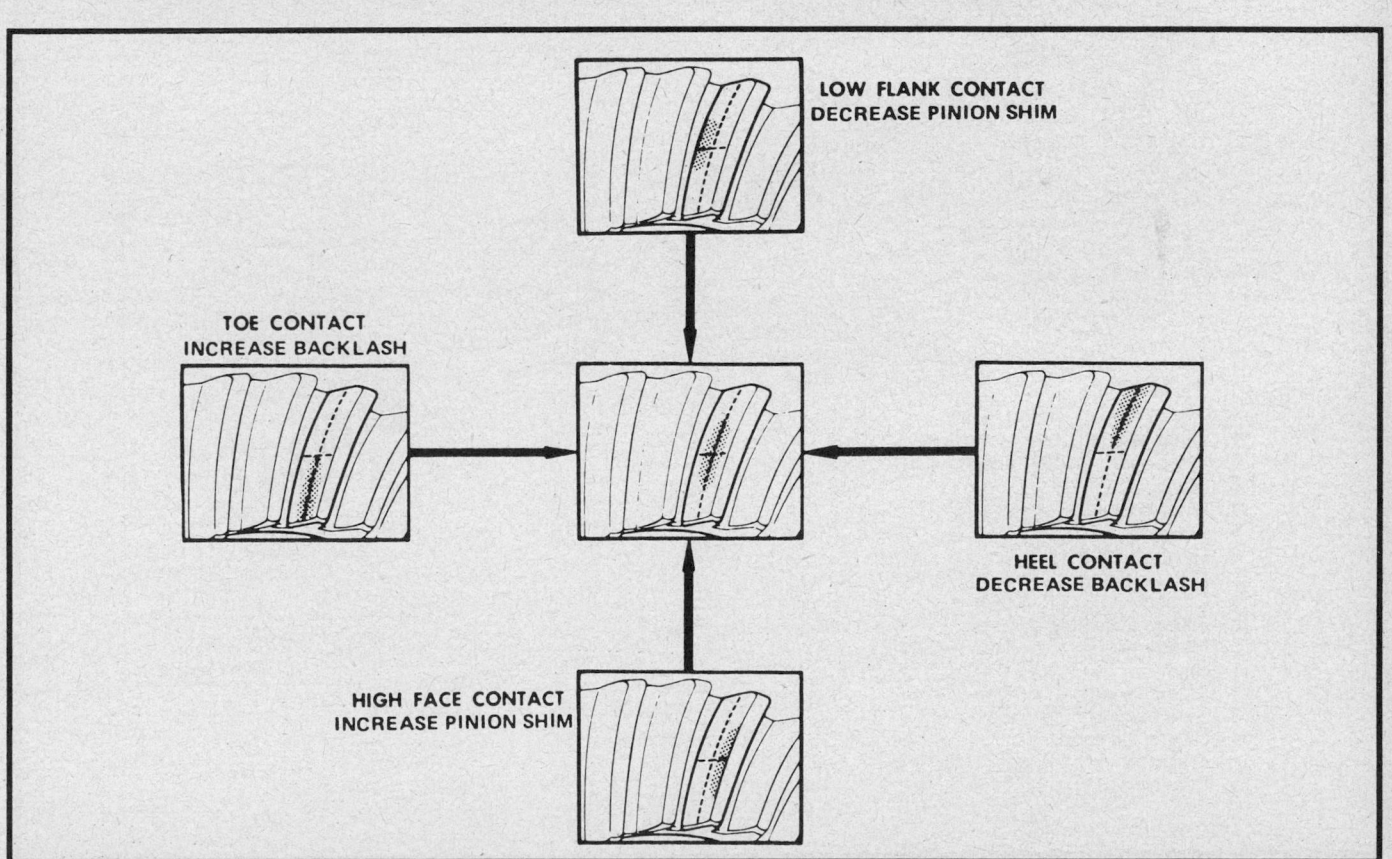

Differential tooth contact pattern — Isuzu

47. Install a dial indicator on the carrier so that the stem of the tool is at a right angle to a tooth on the ring gear.

48. Adjust feeler gauge thickness from side to side until the gear backlash is 0.005–0.007 in.

49. With zero endplay and correct backlash established, remove the feeler gauge. Determine the thickness of the shims (always use new shims) required and add 0.002 in. to each shim pack to provide side bearing preload.

50. Remove the case from the carrier. Carefully remove both side bearings. Install shims as determined behind each bearing, install bearings onto case.

51. Install case onto carrier, tapping carefully into place. Install side bearing caps in original position. Tighten to 65–79 ft. lbs.

52. Measure the run out of the ring gear. If the run out exceeds 0.002 in., correct by replacement.

53. Apply a thin coat of prussian blue or equivalent to the faces of 7–9 teeth of the ring gear. Check the impression of the contact on the ring gear teeth and make the necessary adjustments.

54. Apply gear oil to all moving parts and use sealant and or gasket when assembling to the axle housing.

Rear Drive Axle

Disassembly and Assembly

1. Position the removed differential carrier assembly in a suitable holding fixture. Take tooth pattern check this check will help deteremine what service should be performed on the differential components.

2. Mark and remove the side bearing caps.

3. Remove the differential cage assembly. Keep the right and left side bearing races and shims if so equiped in separate groups for reinstallation in same positions.

4. Remove the differential side bearings from the case by using puller J–22888 and plug J–8107–2 or equivalent (some special tools may be different on the limited slip differential carrier). Carefully record the thickness of each side bearing and each

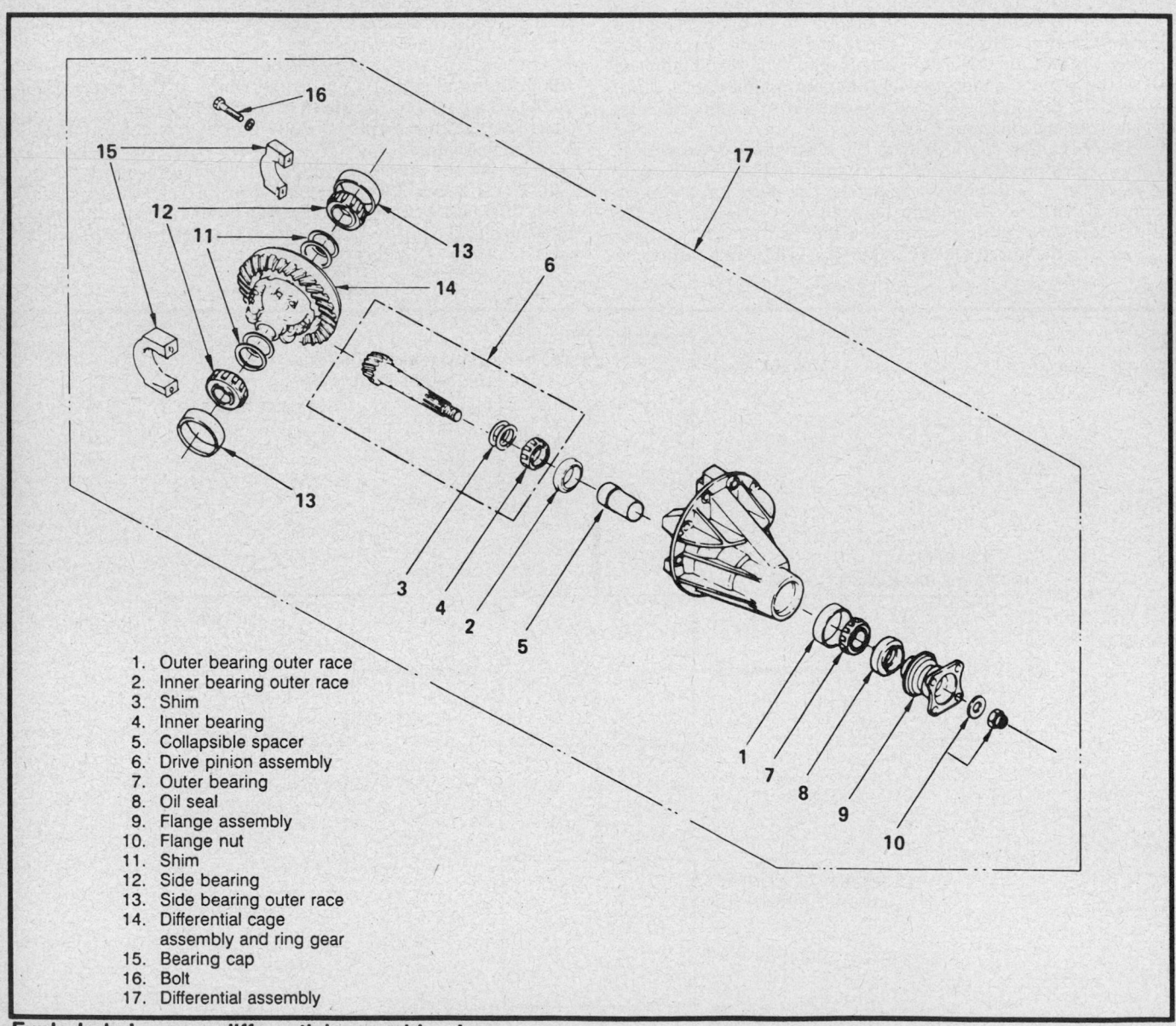

1. Outer bearing outer race
2. Inner bearing outer race
3. Shim
4. Inner bearing
5. Collapsible spacer
6. Drive pinion assembly
7. Outer bearing
8. Oil seal
9. Flange assembly
10. Flange nut
11. Shim
12. Side bearing
13. Side bearing outer race
14. Differential cage assembly and ring gear
15. Bearing cap
16. Bolt
17. Differential assembly

Exploded view rear differential assembly—Isuzu

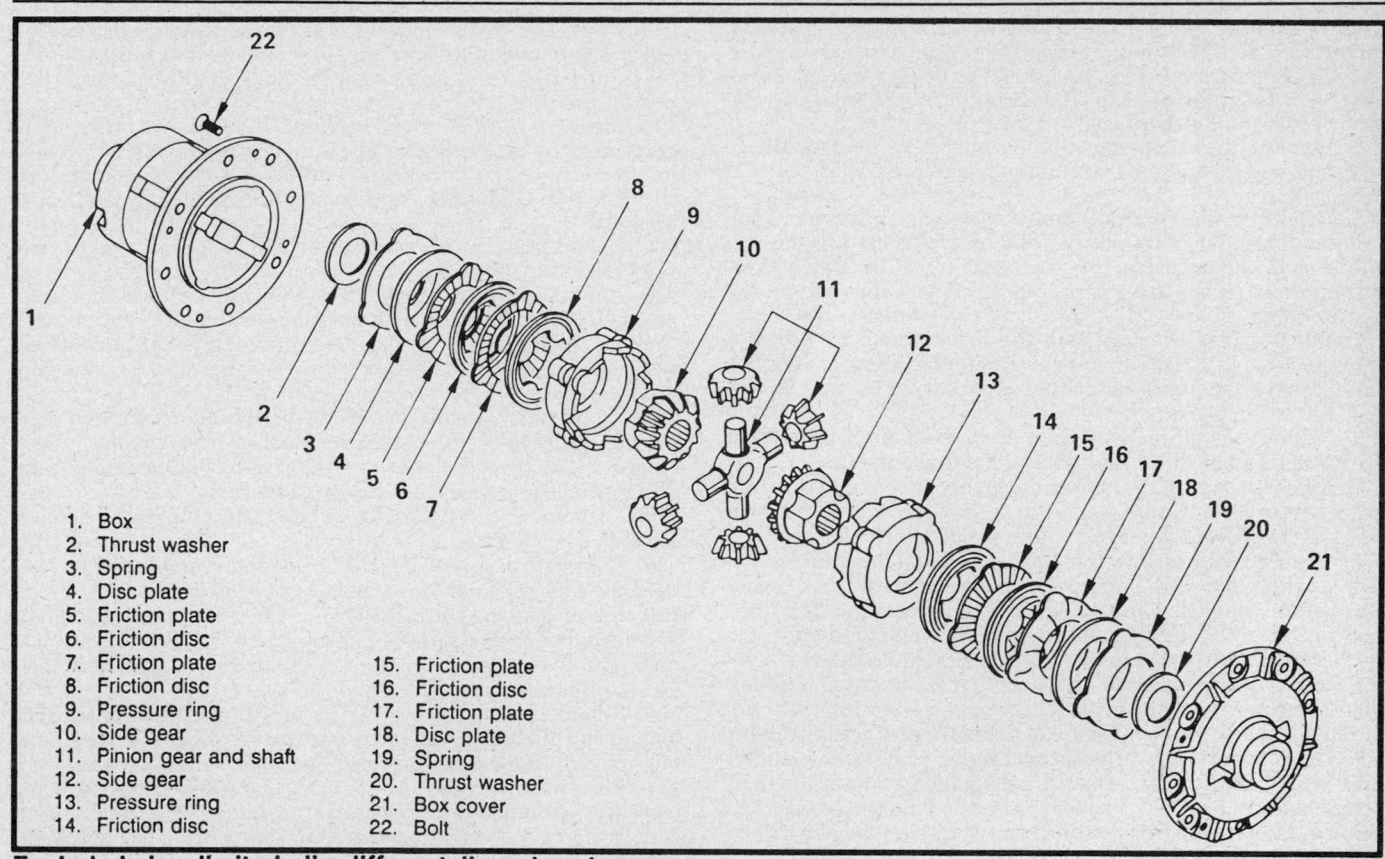

1. Box
2. Thrust washer
3. Spring
4. Disc plate
5. Friction plate
6. Friction disc
7. Friction plate
8. Friction disc
9. Pressure ring
10. Side gear
11. Pinion gear and shaft
12. Side gear
13. Pressure ring
14. Friction disc
15. Friction plate
16. Friction disc
17. Friction plate
18. Disc plate
19. Spring
20. Thrust washer
21. Box cover
22. Bolt

Exploded view limited slip differentail carrier—Isuzu

Pinion marking / Dial indicator reading (Inches)	+10	+8	+6	+4	+2	0	−2	−4	−6	−8	−10
0.073										1.94(0.0764)	1.96(0.0772)
0.074									1.94(0.0764)	1.96(0.0772)	1.98(0.0779)
0.075								1.94(0.0764)	1.96(0.0772)	1.98(0.0779)	2.00(0.0787)
0.076						1.94(0.0764)	1.96(0.0772)	1.98(0.0779)	2.00(0.0787)	2.02(0.0795)	2.04(0.0803)
0.077						1.96(0.0772)	1.98(0.0779)	2.00(0.0787)	2.02(0.0795)	2.04(0.0803)	2.06(0.0811)
0.078				1.94(0.0764)	1.96(0.0772)	1.98(0.0779)	2.00(0.0787)	2.02(0.0795)	2.04(0.0803)	2.06(0.0811)	2.08(0.0819)
0.079			1.94(0.0764)	1.96(0.0772)	1.98(0.0779)	2.00(0.0787)	2.02(0.0795)	2.04(0.0803)	2.06(0.0811)	2.08(0.0819)	2.10(0.0827)
0.080	1.94(0.0764)	1.96(0.0772)	1.98(0.0779)	2.00(0.0787)	2.02(0.0795)	2.04(0.0803)	2.06(0.0811)	2.08(0.0819)	2.10(0.0827)	2.12(0.0835)	2.14(0.0842)
0.081	1.96(0.0772)	1.98(0.0779)	2.00(0.0787)	2.02(0.0795)	2.04(0.0803)	2.06(0.0811)	2.08(0.0819)	2.10(0.0827)	2.12(0.0835)	2.14(0.0842)	2.16(0.0850)
0.082	1.98(0.0779)	2.00(0.0787)	2.02(0.0795)	2.04(0.0803)	2.06(0.0811)	2.08(0.0819)	2.10(0.0827)	2.12(0.0835)	2.14(0.0842)	2.16(0.0850)	2.18(0.0858)
0.083	2.00(0.0787)	2.02(0.0795)	2.04(0.0803)	2.06(0.0811)	2.08(0.0819)	2.10(0.0827)	2.12(0.0835)	2.14(0.0842)	2.16(0.0850)	2.18(0.0858)	2.20(0.0866)
0.084	2.04(0.0803)	2.06(0.0811)	2.08(0.0819)	2.10(0.0827)	2.12(0.0835)	2.14(0.0842)	2.16(0.0850)	2.18(0.0858)	2.20(0.0866)	2.22(0.0874)	2.24(0.0882)
0.085	2.06(0.0811)	2.08(0.0819)	2.10(0.0827)	2.12(0.0835)	2.14(0.0842)	2.16(0.0850)	2.18(0.0858)	2.20(0.0866)	2.22(0.0874)	2.24(0.0882)	2.26(0.0890)
0.086	2.08(0.0819)	2.10(0.0827)	2.12(0.0835)	2.14(0.0842)	2.16(0.0850)	2.18(0.0858)	2.20(0.0866)	2.22(0.0874)	2.24(0.0882)	2.26(0.0890)	2.28(0.0898)
0.087	2.12(0.0835)	2.14(0.0842)	2.16(0.0850)	2.18(0.0858)	2.20(0.0866)	2.22(0.0874)	2.24(0.0882)	2.26(0.0890)	2.28(0.0898)	2.30(0.0906)	2.32(0.0913)
0.088	2.14(0.0842)	2.16(0.0850)	2.18(0.0858)	2.20(0.0866)	2.22(0.0874)	2.24(0.0882)	2.26(0.0890)	2.28(0.0898)	2.30(0.0906)	2.32(0.0913)	2.34(0.0921)
0.089	2.16(0.0850)	2.18(0.0858)	2.20(0.0866)	2.22(0.0874)	2.24(0.0882)	2.26(0.0890)	2.28(0.0898)	2.30(0.0906)	2.32(0.0913)	2.34(0.0921)	2.36(0.0929)
0.090	2.18(0.0858)	2.20(0.0866)	2.22(0.0874)	2.24(0.0882)	2.26(0.0890)	2.28(0.0898)	2.30(0.0906)	2.32(0.0913)	2.34(0.0921)	2.36(0.0929)	
0.091	2.22(0.0874)	2.24(0.0882)	2.26(0.0890)	2.28(0.0898)	2.30(0.0906)	2.32(0.0913)	2.34(0.0921)	2.36(0.0929)			
0.092	2.24(0.0882)	2.26(0.0890)	2.28(0.0898)	2.30(0.0906)	2.32(0.0913)	2.34(0.0921)	2.36(0.0929)				
0.093	2.26(0.0890)	2.28(0.0898)	2.30(0.0906)	2.32(0.0913)	2.34(0.0921)	2.36(0.0929)					
0.094	2.28(0.0898)	2.30(0.0906)	2.32(0.0913)	2.34(0.0921)	2.36(0.0929)						
0.095	2.32(0.0913)	2.34(0.0921)	2.36(0.0929)								
0.096	2.34(0.0921)	2.36(0.0929)									
0.097	2.36(0.0929)										

Shim selection chart—Isuzu rear limited slip differential drive axle

shim(s) removed for later use in reassembly and keep separated. Puller arms must not pull against roller cage. Use care to position legs against inner race. As bearing is being removed, check for free rotation of bearing. If bearing does not rotate freely, check position of puller legs.

5. Remove the companion flange nut while holding flange with suitable tools. Remove the flange assembly with puller if necessary.

6. Drive the pinion shaft assembly from the carrier using suitable tools and brass punch. The outer (front) bearing will fall loose in the carrier, while the inner (rear) bearing will remain pressed on the drive pinion. Both races will remain in the carrier bores.

7. Remove rear bearing from the drive pinion by use of a press and tool J-22912-01 or equivalent on conventional differential carrier. On limited slip differential carrier use special tool J-37452 and a press.

8. Remove the oil seal and then drive the 2 outer races from the carrier by use of a brass drift and suitable tools.

9. Remove the ring gear bolts (diagonal pattern) and separate the ring gear from the differential case. Use care when removing ring gear to prevent damage to differential case or ring gear. Do not force a chisel or other tools between the joining faces.

10. At this point of the reassembly, check the amount of backlash before removal. The standard valve for backlash is 0.001–0.003 in. for conventional differential. The standard valve for backlash is 0.005–0.007 in. for limited slip differential.

11. On conventional differential carrier drive out the pinion shaft lock pin with a long drift. It may be necessary to first break the stake on lock pin using a 0.020 diameter drill or equivalent.

12. On conventional differential carrier remove the pinion shaft with a drift pin and take out the pinion gears, side gears, thrust block and thrust washers from the differential case.

13. On limited slip differential remove the limited slip differential carrier assembly.

14. Wash the bearings in a suitable solvent. Then examine bearings carefully for wear, separation, cracks, seizure and other abnormal conditions. Replace bearings as necessary.

15. Check the ring gear and drive pinion teeth for wear, chipping, cracks, pitting and abnormal contact. Check the drive pinion splines for cracks, distortion and step wear. Replace parts if needed. Ring gear and drive pinion come only in matched sets. If either item is defective, both parts must be replaced.

16. Check the pinion gears and side gears for wear, chipped teeth and separation and replace if needed.

17. Check and replace the thrust blocks on conventional differential and thrust washers, if worn or damaged.

18. On conventional differential check the lock pin for bending, dents and other abnormal conditions. Replace if necessary.

19. Check the clearance between pinion gear and cross pin. The standard valve for the clearance between the differential pinion and the cross pin is 0.002–0.005 in. and the service limit is 0.008 in. on both differential carriers.

20. Check the clearance between the side gear and differential box. The standard valve for the clearance between the side gear and the differential assembly is 0.001–0.004 in. and the service limit is 0.006 in. on conventional carrier. The standard valve for the clearance between the side gear and the differential assembly is 0.002–0.004 in. and the service limit is 0.006 in. on limited slip differential carrier.

21. Check the play in splines betwwen the side gear and axle shafts. The standard valve for play (backlash) in splines betwwen the side gear and the axle shaft is 0.001–0.006 in. and the service limit is 0.010 in. on the conventional differential. The standard valve for play in splines betwwen the side gear and the axle shaft is 0.03–0.15 in. and the service limit is 0.010 in. on the limited slip differential.

22. Install the side gears and thrust washers in the differential case. Position the pinion gears 180 degrees apart. Roll gears into position, making sure they are in alignment, to allow installation of the pinion shaft.

23. Place the thrust block on conventional differential between the pinion gears and drive the pinion shaft into position. Make sure that the lock pin hole in cross shaft aligns with the hole in the case.

24. Measure the amount of backlash between the differential gears and the pinion gears. The standard valve is 0.001–0.003 in. on conventional differential and 0.005–0.007 in. on limited slip differential. Make the necessary adjustment with the thrust washers.

25. Install lock pin into cross shaft and stake the cage to prevent loosening of the pin.

26. Apply Loctite or equivalent to the threaded portion of the bolts. Install the ring gear in position on the differential case. Tighten the bolts (always use new retaining bolts) in diagonal sequence to 73–87 ft. lbs. on conventional and limited slip differentials.

27. To set pinion depth install the drive pinion front and rear bearing outer races into carrier bores. Use drive handle J-8092 with J-24256 (conventional carrier) or J-37262 for limited slip differential carrier for front bearing race and J-24252 (conventional carrier) and J-24252 for limited slip differential carrier for rear bearing race.

28. Lubricate and position the front and rear bearings to be used for final assembly into their respective races.

29. Install gauging plate J-23597-7 and preload stud and pilot J-23597-9 or their equivalent through front and rear bearings and tighten nut snugly. On limited slip differential carriers special tool numbers may change.

30. Rotate the bearings to insure proper seating and tighten locknut until 20 inch lbs. of torque are required to rotate new bearings; 8–10 inch lbs. for used bearings.

31. Place discs J-23597-8 onto arbor J-23597-1 or equivalent (special tool numbers may change on limited slip differential carrier) and place tool into position in side bearing bores. Install bearing caps and torque to 65–72 ft. lbs. on conventional carrier. Torque the bearing caps 73–87 ft. lbs. on limited slip differential carrier.

32. Mount dial indicator J-8001 or equivalent on arbor post and preload dial ½ revolution. Tighten indicator in this position.

33. Position the indicator plunger on the gauge plate and slowly swing across until the highest reading is obtained. Zero the indicator on the highest reading of the gauge plate. Repeat procedure if necessary for correct readings.

34. After zero setting is obtained carefully swing the plunger off the gauge plate. Note the indicator reading. Recheck to verify the reading. Record the number the dial indicator needle points to. The reading on the dial is the correct dimension for the rear pinion depth shim. Convert the dial indicator reading (inches) to the correct pinion marking (depth code) specification.

35. Record pinion depth code on the head of the drive pinion. The number indicates a necessary change in the pinion mounting distance. A plus number indicates the need for a greater mounting distance (which can be achieved by decreasing the shim thickness). A minus number indicates the need for a smaller mounting distance (which can be achieved by increasing the shim thickness). If examination reveals no pinion depth code, the pinion is nominal. Determine the proper shim variation to compensate for plus or minus markings.

36. Place the shim on the drive pinion with chamfered side toward the pinion head then install the rear bearing, using J-6133-01 or equivalent. Do not press on roller cage press only on inner race.

37. To set pinion bearing preload place the drive pinion and spacer (always use new spacer) into the carrier.

38. Lubricate, then position the front bearing to be used in final assembly into the carrier. Install new oil seal.

39. Install companion flange to drive pinion. Apply hypoid lubricant to pinion threads. Install new pinion nut and torque to 130–202 ft. lbs. using J-8614-01 or equivalent to hold companion flange. On limited slip differential carrier torque new pinion

nut to 180–217 ft. lbs. using suitable tools to hold flange.

40. Rotate drive pinion to insure that bearings are seated. Measure the bearing preload by using a torque wrench. Note the scale reading required to rotate the flange.

41. Continue tightening until the correct starting toque is obtained. The standard valve for starting torque is 5.6–9.9 inch lbs. on conventional differential and 6.1–11.3 inch lbs. on limited slip differential carrier. The pinion nut should be tightened only in small increments and the scale should be checked after each small amount of tightening. Exceeding preload specifications may compress the collapsible spacer too far and require its replacement.

42. Install the side bearings to be used in final assembly onto the differential case. Do not install shims at this time. Use J–24244 or equivalent for the first bearing installation (on limited slip differential carrier special tools numbers may be different).

43. Support case on plug J–8107–2 or equivalent for opposite bearing installation.

44. Install the differential cage assembly into carrier bores.

45. Using 2 sets of feeler gauges, insert a feeler gauge of sufficient thickness between each bearing outer race and the carrier to remover all endplay. Make certain the feeler gauge is pushed to the bottom of the bearing bores.

46. Install a dial indicator on the carrier so that the stem of the tool is at a right angle to a tooth on the ring gear.

47. Adjust feeler gauge thickness from side to side until the gear backlash is 0.005–0.007 in. on conventional differential and 0.006–0.008 in. on limited slip differential.

48. With zero endplay and correct backlash established, remove the feeler gauge. Determine the thickness of the shims (always use new shims) required and add 0.002 in. to each shim pack to provide side bearing preload.

49. Remove the case from the carrier. Carefully remove both side bearings. Install shims as determined behind each bearing, install bearings onto case.

50. Install case onto carrier, tapping carefully into place. Install side bearing caps in original position. Tighten bearing caps to 65–79 ft. lbs. on conventional differential carrier and 73–87 ft. lbs. on limited slip differential carrier.

51. Measure the run out of the ring gear. If the run out exceeds 0.002 in., correct by replacement. Apply a thin coat of prussian blue or equivalent to the faces of 7–9 teeth of the ring gear. Check the impression of the contact on the ring gear teeth and make the necessary adjustments.

52. Apply gear oil to all moving parts and use sealant and or gasket when assembling to the axle housing.

MAZDA

Front And Rear Drive Axles

Disassembly and Assembly

1. Position the removed differential carrier assembly in a suitable holding fixture.

2. Apply identification punch marks on the carrier, the differential bearing cap and adjusters for correct reassembly.

3. Remove the adjuster lock plates.

4. Loosen the bolts securing the bearing cap and slowly back off the adjuster slightly to relieve the preload.

5. Remove the nuts, bearing caps and adjusters. Keep each bearing cap with its own adjuster.

6. Lift out the differential assembly and keep each bearing outer race with its own bearing.

7. If the differential bearings are to be replaced, mark for correct installation and remove using a suitable puller.

8. Remove the bolts (in diagonal pattern) and washers retaining the ring gear to the case.

9. Remove the ring gear. On conventional differential position the assembly in a vise or equivalent and remove the lock pin (tap out toward the ring gear side) with a suitable punch (0.16 in. diameter size).

10. On conventional differential remove the pinion shaft and the thrust block. Rotate the differential pinion gears 90 degrees and remove. Remove the differential side gears and thrust washers.

11. On limited slip differential remove the limited slip differential carrier assembly.

12. Using a holding tool, steady the companion flange and remove the nut.

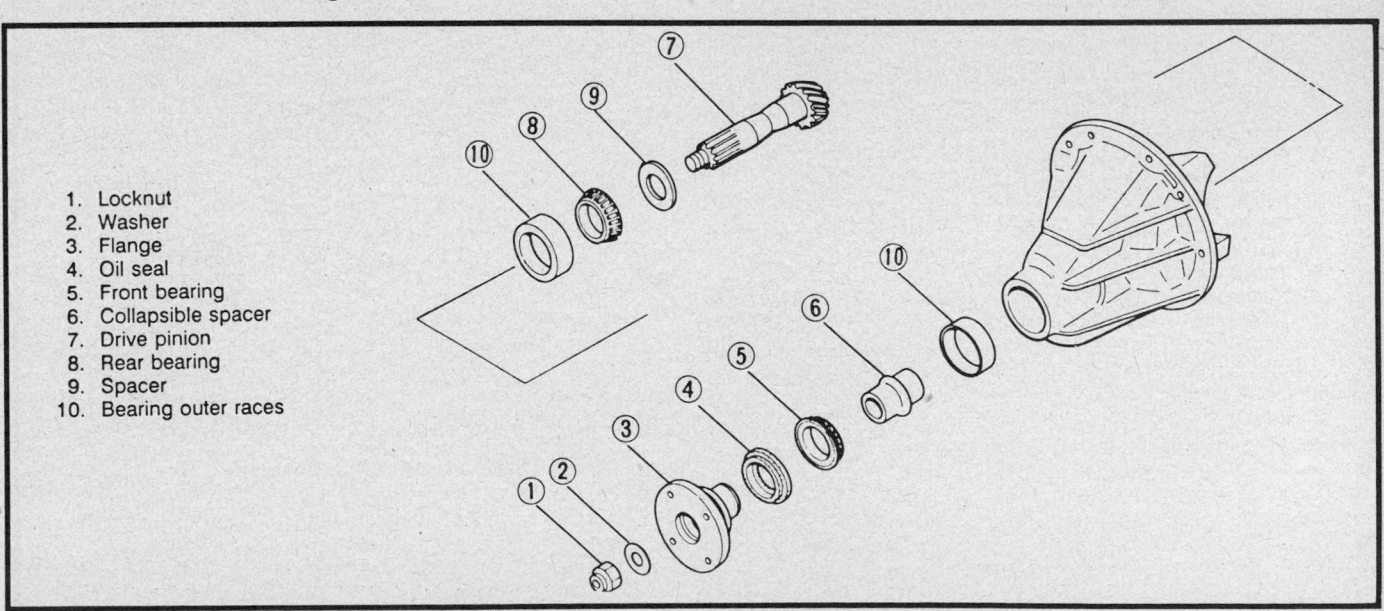

1. Locknut
2. Washer
3. Flange
4. Oil seal
5. Front bearing
6. Collapsible spacer
7. Drive pinion
8. Rear bearing
9. Spacer
10. Bearing outer races

Exploded view of drive pinion assembly—Mazda

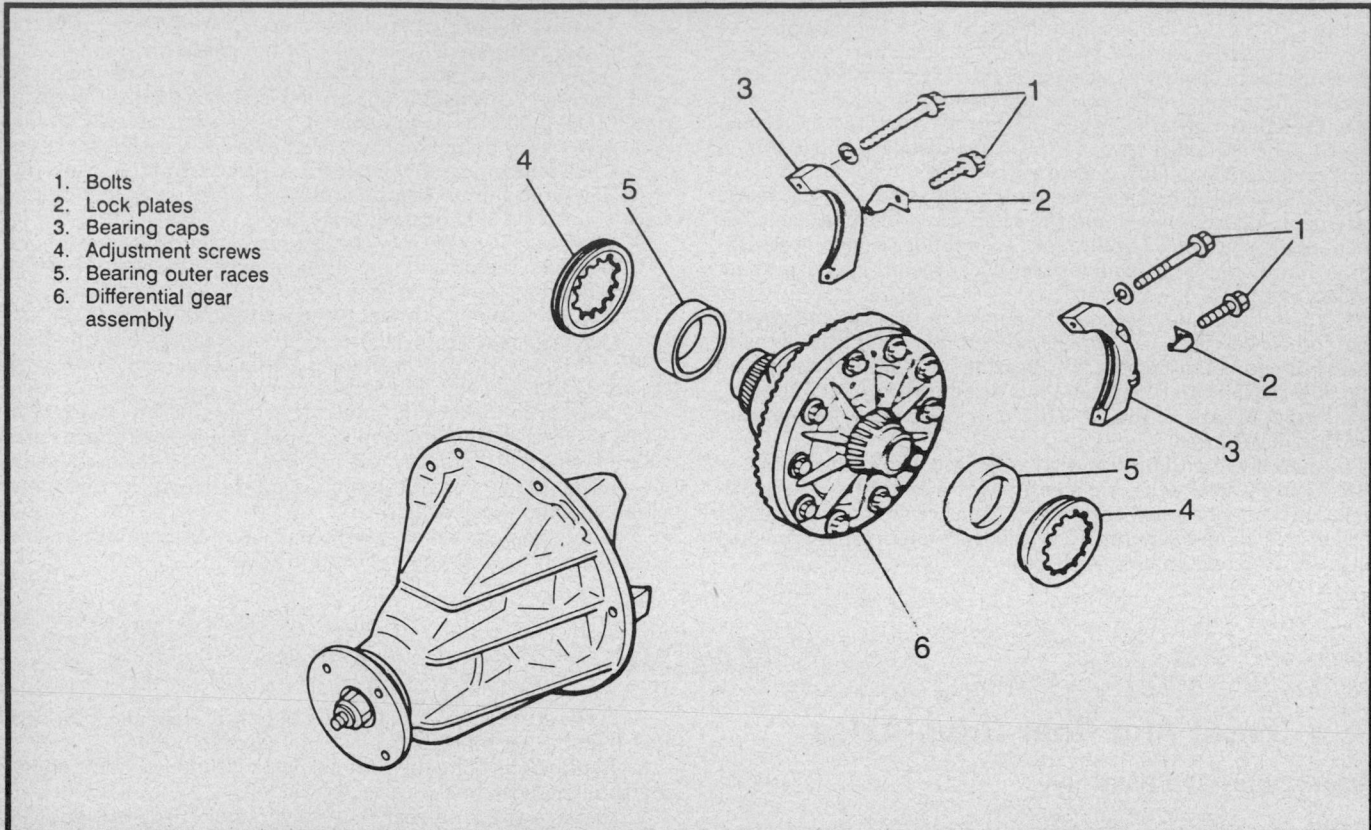

1. Bolts
2. Lock plates
3. Bearing caps
4. Adjustment screws
5. Bearing outer races
6. Differential gear
   assembly

Exploded view of differential carrier—Mazda

1. Bolt
2. Ring gear
3. Pin
4. Pinion shaft
5. Pinion gears
6. Thrust block
7. Side gears
8. Thrust washer
9. Bearings
10. Gear case

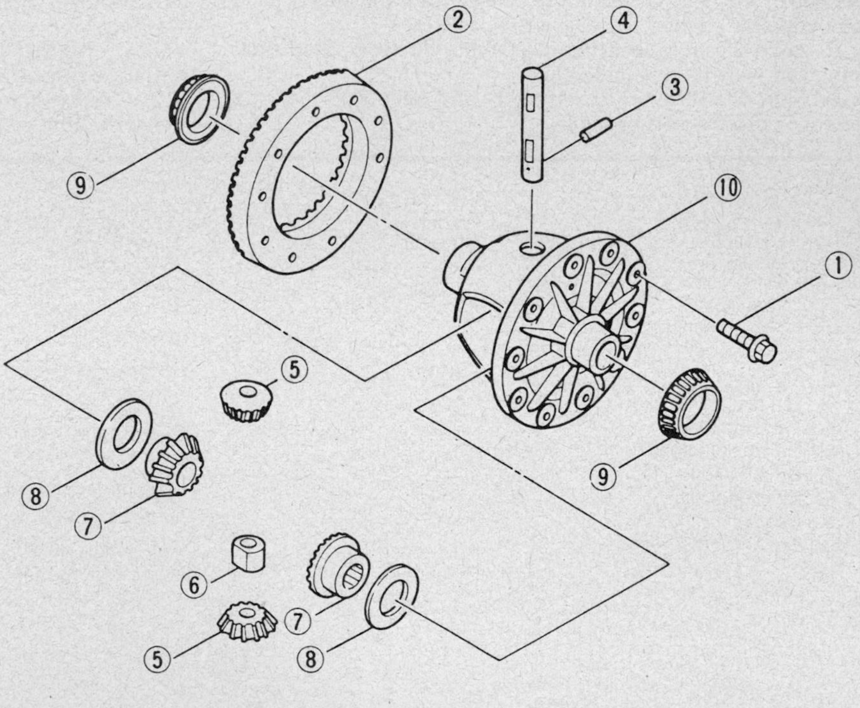

Exploded view standard differential assembly—Mazda

13. Remove the companion flange using suitable puller.

14. Remove the front bearing, drive pinion and rear bearing from the carrier, which may require tapping with a plastic mallet or equivalent. Guide the pinion assembly to avoid damage to any component.

15. Remove the oil seal and the front bearing.

16. The pinion bearing outer races (cups) can be removed (mark for correct installation) from the carrier by tapping out using a drift in the slots provided.

17. Remove the rear bearing from the pinion (support the pinion during bearing removal) using suitable press and separator plate.

18. Check the drive pinion for damaged or worn teeth, damaged bearing journals or splines. Inspect the ring gear again for worn or chipped teeth. If any of the above conditions are found, replace both drive pinion and ring gear as a set.

19. Inspect bearing cones and cups and replace any showing wear, flaking or damage. Replace only in sets. Do not use an old cup with a new bearing or an old bearing with a new cup.

20. Check the companion flange carefully for cracks or worn splines. If either exist, the part should be replaced. Check for rough or scratched oil seal contact surface. If only slight scratches appear, it may be possible to repair with crocus cloth. Otherwise, replace it. Be sure to use a new oil seal when reassembling the carrier.

21. On conventional differential assemble the side gears, thrust washers, thrust block, pinion gears, pinion shaft and lock pin. After installing lock pin stake pin so pin cannot come out of gear case.

22. On conventional differential assemble press the side bearings (correct location) onto the gear case using suitable tools. Adjust the backlash of the side gears and pinion gear as follows:

    a. Position a dial indicator against the pinion gear. Secure one of the side gears.

    b. Move the pinion gear and measure the backlash at the end of the pinion gear.

    c. The standard valve for backlash is 0–0.004 in. on all vehicles. If backlash exceeds the standard valve use suitable thrust washer to adjust.

23. On conventional and limited slip differetial carriers apply thread locking compound install ring gear to differential assembly. Torque the retaining bolts to 51–61 ft. lbs. all vehicles in a diagonal pattern.

24. Press fit the companion flange side bearing outer races using bearing installer set.

25. Press fit the ring gear side bearing outer races using bearing installer set.

NOTE: Special tools are required to check and adjust the pinion height, these include a drive pinion model tool 498531565, a pinion height adjustment gauge body tool 490727570 and a gauge block tool 400305555.

26. At this point of the reassembly, adjust the pinion height as follows:

    a. Fit the spacer, rear bearing and collar onto the drive pinion model. Secure the collar with an O-ring and install in the assembly in the carrier.

    b. Attach the front bearing, collar, companion flange, washer and nut to the drive pinion model. Use the same spacer and nut which were removed at disassembly. Be careful to install collars in their correct position facing in the correct direction.

    c. Tighten the nut until the drive pinion model can be turned by hand without any apparant play.

    d. Install a dial indicator on the pinion height adjustment gauge body. Place the gauge block on top of the drive pinion model and then set the pinion height adjustment gauge body on top of the gauge block.

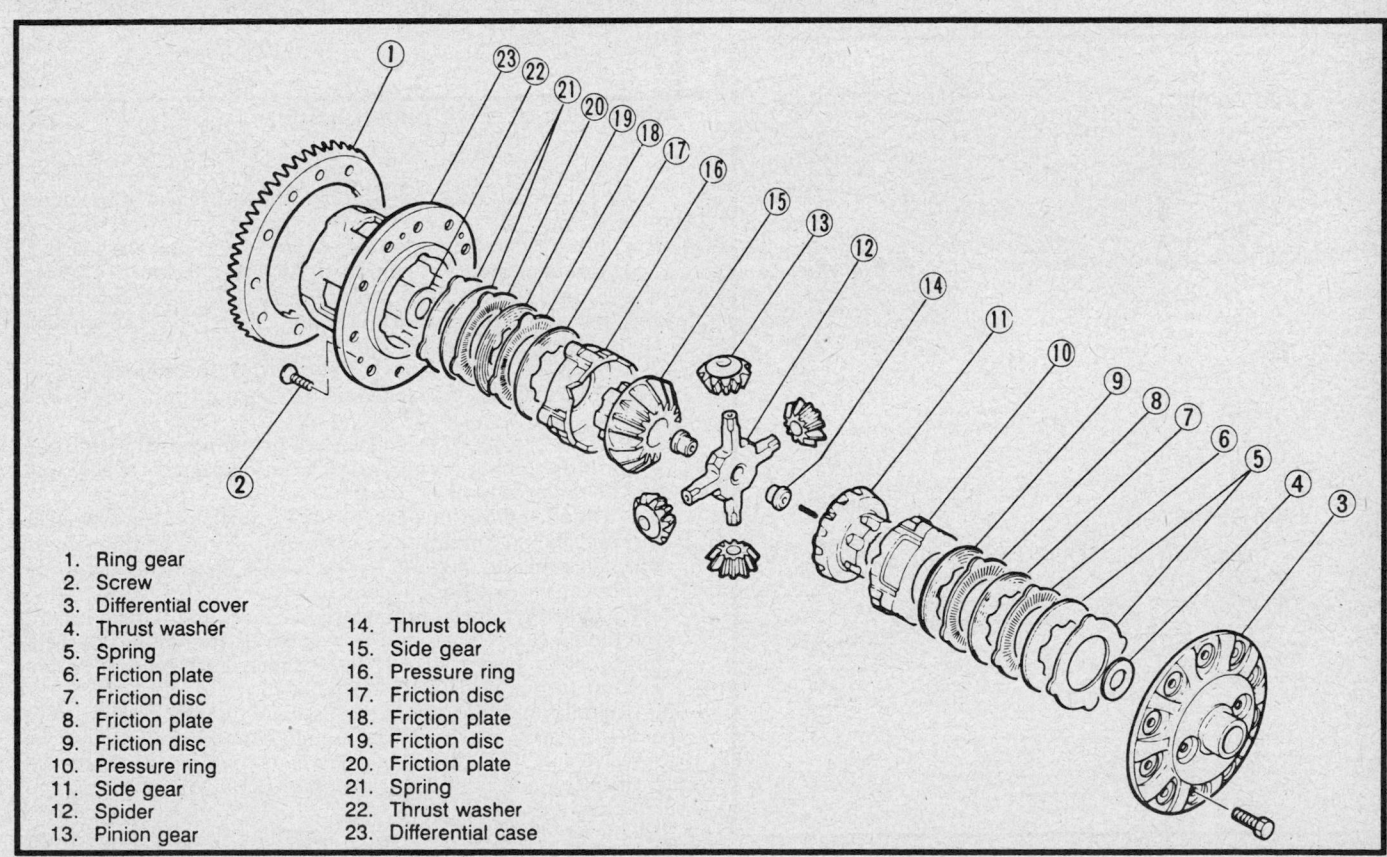

1. Ring gear
2. Screw
3. Differential cover
4. Thrust washer
5. Spring
6. Friction plate
7. Friction disc
8. Friction plate
9. Friction disc
10. Pressure ring
11. Side gear
12. Spider
13. Pinion gear
14. Thrust block
15. Side gear
16. Pressure ring
17. Friction disc
18. Friction plate
19. Friction disc
20. Friction plate
21. Spring
22. Thrust washer
23. Differential case

Exploded view limited slip differential assembly – Mazda

e. Place the measuring probe of the dial indicator so that it contacts the location where the side bearing is installed in the carrier. Zero and set up the indicator to measure the lowest point. Measure both the left and right sides. Add the 2 values (right and left side readings) and divide the total by 2. The standard valve of this specification is 0 in. on all vehicles. Install correct spacer as necessary to adjust pinion height.

27. Install the correct spacer(s) on the pinion shaft (facing in the proper direction) and press the bearing on the pinion shaft.

28. Install the drive pinion, spacer, front bearing, collapsible spacer and companion flange in the carrier and temporarily tighten the locknut. Do Not install the pinion oil seal at this time.

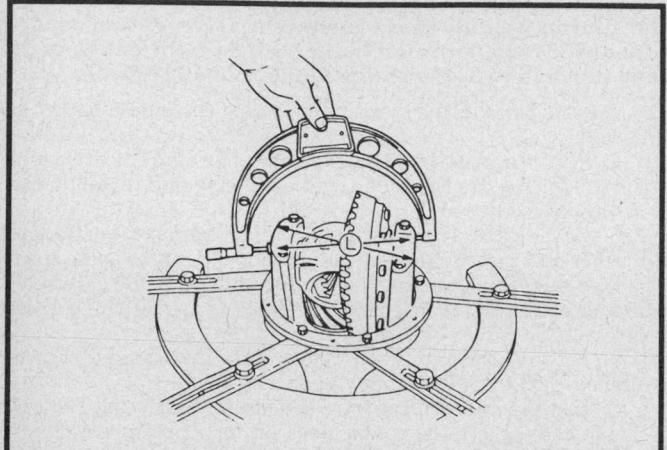

Adjustment of drive pinion and ring gear backlash

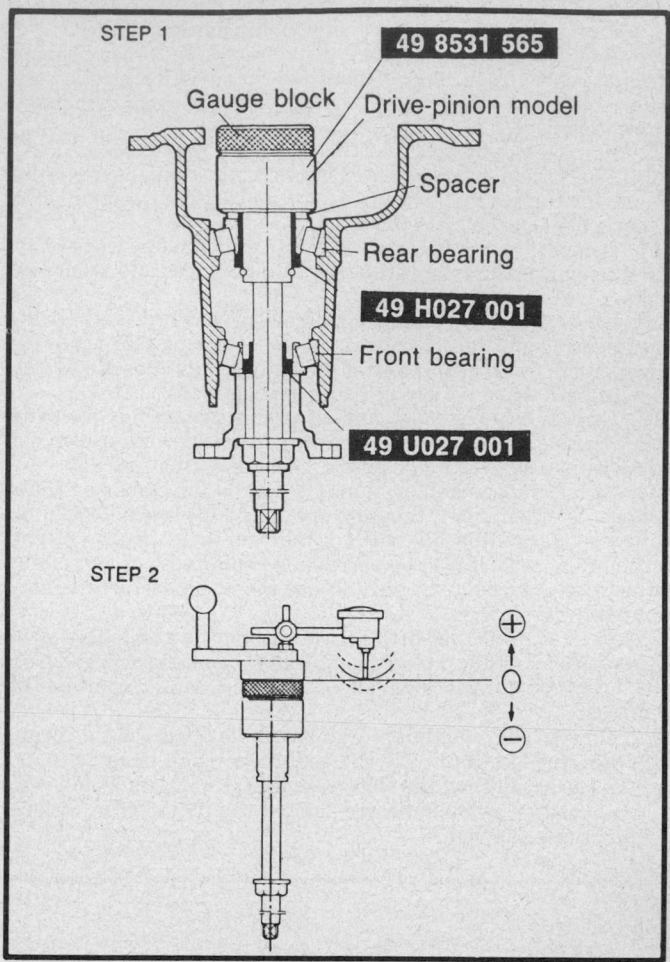

STEP 1

49 8531 565

Gauge block   Drive-pinion model

Spacer

Rear bearing

49 H027 001

Front bearing

49 U027 001

STEP 2

⊕
○
⊖

Adjustment of drive pinion height

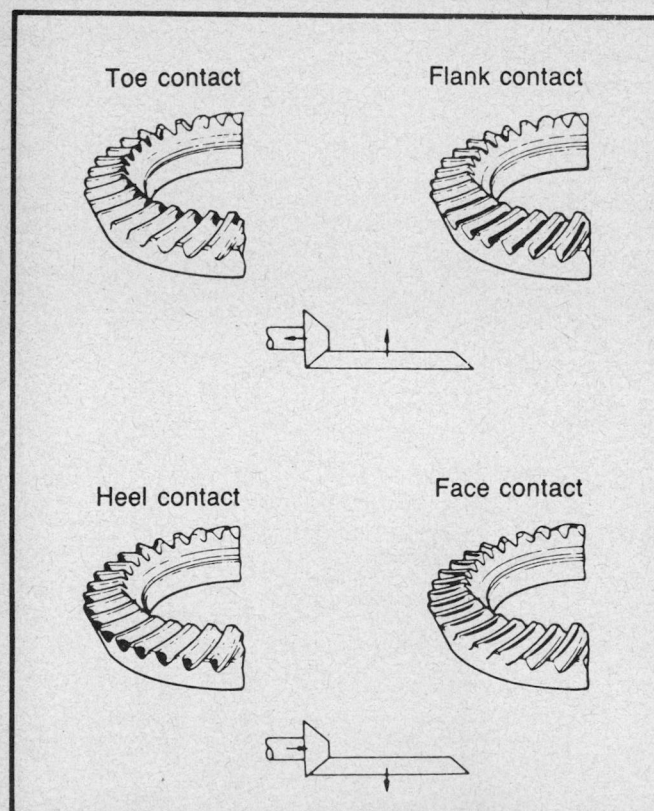

Toe contact   Flank contact

Heel contact   Face contact

Differential tooth contact pattern—Mazda

29. At this point of the reassembly, adjust preload of the drive pinion as follows:

a. Rotate the companion flange by hand to seat the bearing.

b. Use a torque wrench to tighten the locknut. Tighten slowly until the required preload drag of 7.8–12.2 inch lbs. is reached with a locknut torque of 94–130 ft. lbs. for all applications except MPV vehicle.

c. On MPV vehicle, slowly tighten until the preload drag of 11.3–15.6 inch lbs. is reached with a locknut torque of 94–210 ft. lbs.

d. If the specified preload cannot be maintained within the locknut tightening range, install a new collapsible spacer and repeat the process if necessary.

e. On all applications except MPV vehicle remove the locknut and flange. Install the pinion seal, flange and new locknut. Tighten the locknut to the ft. lbs. specification torque giving the correct preload.

f. On MPV vehicle, remove the locknut and flange. Install the pinion seal, flange and new locknut. Retighten the locknut to the preload drag of 13.9–18.2 inch lbs. is reached with a locknut torque of 94–210 ft. lbs.

30. Install the differential gear assembly in the carrier. Note the identification marks on the adjusters and install each to its respective side. Install the bearing caps making sure that the identification marks on the caps correspond with those on the carrier and install the bolts.

31. Loosely tighten the bearing cap mounting bolts and completely tighten the adjustment screws by hand. Then, while

turning the ring gear, alternately tighten the left and right adjustment screws using a suitable tool.

32. At this point of the reassembly, adjust the drive pinion and ring gear backlash and side bearing preload as follows:

    a. Mark the ring gear at 4 points at approximately 90 degree intervals and mount a dial indicator to the carrier flange so that the feeler comes in contact at right angles with one of the ring gear teeth.

    b. Turn both bearing adjusters equally until backlash becomes (standard valve for all vehicles) 0.0035–0.0043 in.

    c. Check the backlash at the other 3 marked points and make sure that minimum backlash is more than 0.002 in. and the difference in the valve of the maximum and minimum backlash is less than 0.0028 in.

    d. After adjusting the backlash, tighten the adjustment screws equally until the distance between both pilot sections on the bearing caps becomes the standard distance. The standard distance is 7.3004–7.3031 in. for B2000 (2WD) and B2200 (2WD) rear axle assemblies and B2600 (4WD) front axle assembly. The standard distance is 8.0484 in. plus or minus 0.028 in. for B2600 (2WD and 4WD) rear axle assemblies and the MPV rear axle assembly. When adjusting the differential bearing preload, care must be taken not to affect the backlash of the drive pinion gear and ring gear.

33. Tighten the bearing caps to the standard valve. The standard valve for B2000 (2WD) and B2200 (2WD) rear axles and B2600 (4WD) front axle assembly is 27–38 ft. lbs. The standard valve for B2600 (2WD and 4WD) rear axle assemblies is 41–59 ft. lbs. The standard valve for the MPV vehicle is 51–61 ft. lbs.

34. Install the adjuster lock plates.

35. Coat both surfaces of 6–8 teeth of the ring gear uniformly with a thin coat of red lead or equivalent.

36. While moving the ring gear back and forth by hand, rotate the drive pinion several times and check the tooth contact.

37. If pattern is not correct readjust the pinion height then the backlash.

38. Apply gear oil to all moving parts and use sealant and or gasket when assembling to the axle housing.

NISSAN

Front Drive Axle

Inspection Before Disassembly

1. Position the removed differential carrier assembly in a suitable holding fixture.

2. Check total preload by turning drive pinion in booth directions several times to set bearings. Using torque wrench or equivalent measure valve. The standard valve for model R180 and R180A differential carriers is 8.7–20 inch lbs. of turning torque. The standard valve for model R200A is 10.9–20.4 inch lbs. of turning torque.

3. Check the backlash of ring gear with a dial indicator at several points. The standard valve for ring gear to drive pinion backlash is 0.0051–0.0071 in., on all vehicles.

4. Check runout of ring gear with a dial indicator. The standard valve is 0.0020 in. of runout for R180A and R200A models. The standard valve is 0.0030 in. of runout for R180 model.

5. Using suitable equipment check differential tooth contact for correct pattern as follows:

    a. Thoroughly clean ring gear and drive pinion teeth.

    b. Sparingly apply red lead or equivalent to 3 or 4 teeth of ring gear drive side.

    c. Hold companion flange steady by hand and rotate the ring gear in both directions.

    d. Interrupt contact marks left on the ring gear assembly. Gear tooth contact pattern check is necessary to verify correct relationship between ring gear and drive pinion.

6. On R180 model, check backlash of side gear. Using a thickness gauge, measure clearance between side gear and differential case. The standard valve is 0.006 in. of side gear clearance.

Disassembly and assembly

1. Position the removed differential carrier assembly in a suitable holding fixture.

2. On R180A and R200A models remove the extension tube and differential side shaft assembly. Remove differential side flanges.

3. Matchmark side retainers and shims (some have retaining bolts) with paint to ensure that they are replaced in proper position during reassembly.

4. Remove the differential case from the final drive housing.

5. Remove the side bearing outer races. Mark all parts for correct installation.

6. Remove the side bearing oil seals using suitable puller.

7. Attach a flange holding wrench or equivalent to hold flange from turning. Loosen the drive pinion nut.

8. Remove the companion flange using suitable puller.

9. Remove the drive pinion together with pinion rear bearing inner cone, drive pinion bearing spacer and pinion bearing adjusting washer.

10. Remove front oil seal and pinion front bearing inner cone.

11. Remove the pinion front and rear bearing outer races with brass drift from housing.

12. Remove the pinion rear bearing inner cone and drive pinion adjusting washer. Remove rear bearing with suitable press and separator plate.

13. Remove side bearing inner race assembly with a puller from the differential carrier. Mark all parts for correct installation.

14. Remove ring gear by spreading out lock straps if so equipped and loosening ring gear bolts in a criss-cross pattern. Remove all retaining bolts.

15. Tap ring gear off gear case using a soft hammer or equivalent. Tap evenly all around to keep ring gear from binding.

16. On R180A model, separate the left and right differential case halves.

17. On R180 and R200A models, drive out pinion mate shaft lock pin with drift pin from ring gear side.

18. Draw out pinion mate shaft and thrust block if so equipped. Rotate pinion mate gears out of case and remove side gears and thrust washers. Put marks on gears and thrust washers so that they can be reinstalled in their original positions from which they were removed.

19. Clean disassembled parts completely. Repair or replace any damaged or faulty parts. If replacing drive pinion or ring gear, replace with a new hypoid gear as a set.

20. On R180A model, assemble the differential carrier as follows:

    a. Measure the clearance between the side gear thrust washer and differential case.

    b. The standard valve for the clearance between side gear thrust washer and differential case is 0.0039–0.0079 in. The clearance can be adjusted with side gear thrust washer.

    c. Apply gear oil to gear tooth surfaces and thrust surfaces and check to see they turn properly.

    d. Install the left and right differential case halves torque retaining bolts to 47–54 ft. lbs. Position the differential case on the ring gear. Apply Locktite or equivalent and tighten

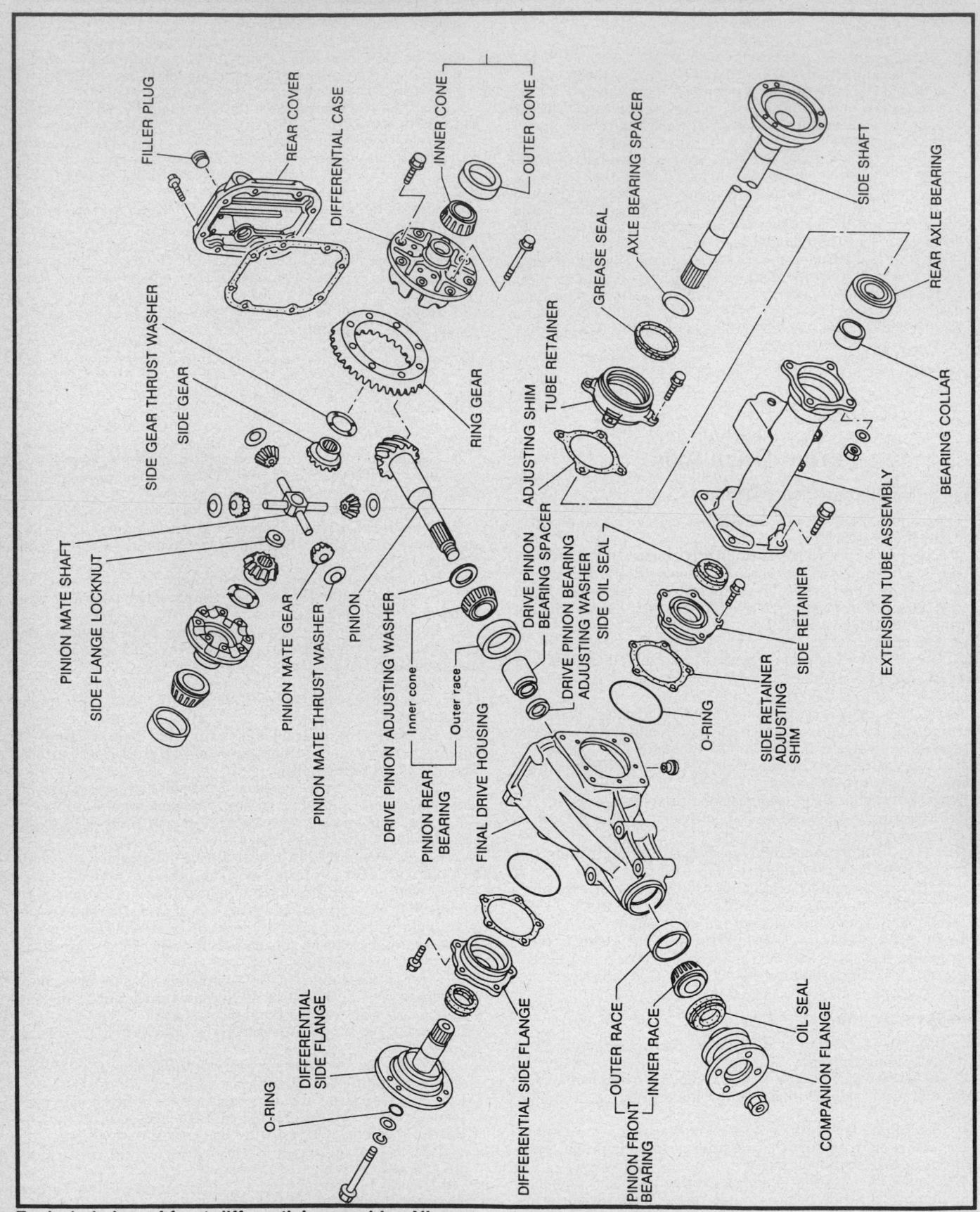

FILLER PLUG

REAR COVER

DIFFERENTIAL CASE

INNER CONE

OUTER CONE

AXLE BEARING SPACER

SIDE SHAFT

REAR AXLE BEARING

GREASE SEAL

ADJUSTING SHIM

TUBE RETAINER

BEARING COLLAR

SIDE GEAR THRUST WASHER

SIDE GEAR

RING GEAR

PINION MATE SHAFT

SIDE FLANGE LOCKNUT

PINION MATE GEAR

PINION MATE THRUST WASHER

PINION

DRIVE PINION ADJUSTING WASHER

Inner cone

Outer race

PINION REAR BEARING

DRIVE PINION BEARING SPACER

DRIVE PINION BEARING ADJUSTING WASHER

SIDE OIL SEAL

O-RING

SIDE RETAINER

SIDE RETAINER ADJUSTING SHIM

SIDE RETAINER

EXTENSION TUBE ASSEMBLY

FINAL DRIVE HOUSING

DIFFERENTIAL SIDE FLANGE

O-RING

DIFFERENTIAL SIDE FLANGE

OUTER RACE

INNER RACE

PINION FRONT BEARING

OIL SEAL

COMPANION FLANGE

Exploded view of front differential assembly – Nissan

ring gear retaining bolts to (criss-cross fashion) 76–90 ft. lbs.

e. Press fit side bearings on the differential case using suitable press and tools.

21. On R180 and R220A models, assemble the differential carrier as follows:

a. Install pinion mate gears, side gears and thrust washers into differential case.

b. Fit pinion mate shaft and thrust block.

c. Adjust clearance between rear face of side gear and thrust washer by selecting side gear thrust washer. The standard valve for clearance on R200A model is 0.0039–0.0079 in. specification. The standard valve for clearance on R180 model is 0–0.006 in. specification.

d. Install pinion mate shaft lock pin using a punch. Make sure lock pin is flush with case.

e. Apply gear oil to gear tooth surfaces and thrust surfaces and check to see they turn properly.

f. On R180 model, place ring gear on differential case and install new lock straps and bolts. Tighten bolts to 88–98 ft. lbs. in a criss-cross fashion, lightly tapping bolt head with a hammer. Then bend up lock straps to lock the bolts in place.

g. Press fit front and rear bearing outer races using suitable tools. Make sure that the bearing races are seated squarely in their respective bores.

h. On R200A model, position the differential case on the ring gear. Apply Locktite or equivalent and tighten ring gear retaining bolts to (criss-cross fashion) 98–112 ft. lbs. Press fit side bearings on the differential case using suitable press and tools.

22. Press fit pinion front and rear bearing outer races into housing with suitable tools on all models as necessary.

23. On all models select pinion bearing adjusting washer and drive pinion bearing spacer as follows:

a. Make sure all parts are clean and that bearings are well lubricate. Assemble the pinion gear bearings into the pinion preload shim selector tool J–34309 or equivalent. Make sure that the front and rear bearings are in the correct position on the special tool (rear bearing first).

b. Install the pinion preload shim selector tool or equivalent into the final drive axle housing. Make sure that the pinion height gauge will make a full turn and tighten the 2 sections by hand. Turn the special tool with bearings installed on it several times to seat the bearings.

c. Measure the turning torque at the end of the tool with a torque wrench. The standard valve for the R180A model is 5.2–8.7 inch lbs. The standard valve for the R200A model is 8.7–11.3 inch lbs. The standard valve for the R180 model is 7.8–14.8. inch lbs.

d. Place correct pinion height adapter (each model has different pinion height adapter) onto the gauge plate and tighten it by hand.

e. Insert the pinion bearing adjusting spacer squarely into the recessed portion of the correct special tool. Select ther correct thickness of the pinion bearing preload adjusting washer using a standard valve plus the distance between spacer and gauge anvil tool. The exact measurement you get with the standard valve and distance between spacer and special tool is the thickness of the adjusting washer required. The standard valve for the R180A model is 0.24 in. and 0.138 in. for the R200A model. The standard valve is 0.118 in. for R180 model.

f. On R180A model position the side bearing discs tool J–25269–4 and arbor firmly in the side bearing bores. On R200A model install tool as previous described and torque the side bearing cap bolts to 65–72 ft. lbs.

g. Select the correct standard pinion height adjusting washer thickness using a standard valve plus the distance between pinion height adapter tool and the arbor. The standard valve for the R180A and R200A models is 0.12 in. On R180 model use the appropriate service tool for this operation and measure the thickness of the lead washer.

Pinion Head Height Number	Add or Remove from the Standard Pinion Height Washer Thickness Measurement
−6	Add 0.06 mm (0.0024 in)
−5	Add 0.05 mm (0.0020 in)
−4	Add 0.04 mm (0.0016 in)
−3	Add 0.03 mm (0.0012 in)
−2	Add 0.02 mm (0.0008 in)
−1	Add 0.01 mm (0.0004 in)
0	Use the selected washer thickness
+1	Subtract 0.01 mm (0.0004 in)
+2	Subtract 0.02 mm (0.0008 in)
+3	Subtract 0.03 mm (0.0012 in)
+4	Subtract 0.04 mm (0.0016 in)
+5	Subtract 0.05 mm (0.0020 in)
+6	Subtract 0.06 mm (0.0024 in)

Drive pinion gear height chart – Nissan

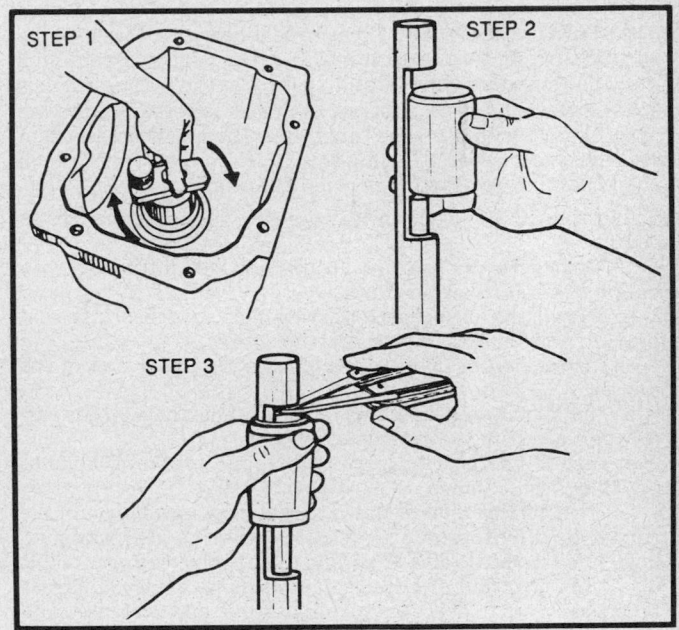

Drive pinion gear preload adjustment

h. Correct the pinion height washer size by referring to the pinion head number. There are 2 numbers on the pinion gear. The first one refers to the pinion and ring gear as a matched set and the number should be the same on the ring gear. The second number is the pinion head height number and it refers to the ideal pinion height for proper operation. Use this number to determine the correct pinion height washer. Select the correct pinion height washer and remove the special tools with pinion bearings from housing.

24. Install pinion height adjusting washer in drive pinion, bevel side toward gear and press fit rear bearing inner race in it, using press and special tools.

25. Lubricate front bearing with gear oil and place it in gear housing.

26. Carefully fit a new oil seal into carrier. Make sure oil seal is flush with end of carrier and apply multi-purpose grease into cavity between lips.

27. Install the drive pinion bearing spacer, pinion bearing adjusting washer and drive pinion in housing.

28. Install companion flange into drive pinion by tapping with a soft hammer or equivalent.

29. Hold companion flange and temporarily tighten pinion nut, until there is no axial play. Ascertain that threaded portion of drive pinion and pinion nut are free from oil or grease. Tighten pinion nut by degrees to the specified preload while checking the preload with torque wrench. Preload with oil seal is 7.8–14.8 inch lbs. for R180 and R180A models and 10.0–15.2 inch lbs. for the R200A model.

30. When checking preload, turn drive pinion in both directions several times set bearing rollers. After preload is reached torque pinion nut to 123–145 ft. lbs. on R180 and R180A models and 137–217 ft. lbs. on R200A model. Preload and final pinion nut torque **MUST** both be attained for correct operation of axle unit.

31. On the R180 and R180A models select the side retaining washer as follows:

   a. Make sure all parts are cleaned and well lubricated with auotmatic transmission fluid.

   b. Install the differentrial carrier and side bearing assembly into the housing.

   c. Install all old bearing preload shims onto side bearing retainer. Install both bearing retainers onto housing and torque retaining bolts to 6.5–7.2 ft. lbs.

   d. Turn carrier several times to seat bearings. Measure the carrier turning torque with a tool at the ring gear retaining bolt. The standard valve of pulling force at the ring gear bolt is 7.7–8.8 ft. lbs. Add or subtract shims as necessary. Increase shim thickness to decrease turning torque and decrease shim thickness to increase turning torque. Record correct shim(s) thickness and remove carrier and bearings.

32. On the R220A model select the side retaining washer as follows:

   a. Make sure all parts are cleaned and well lubricated with auotmatic transmission fluid.

   b. Install the differential carrier with side bearings and bearing races installed into gear housing.

   c. Install side bearing spacer on the ring gear end of the carrier.

   d. Install old preload shims using suitable tools on the carrier end opposite the ring gear.

   e. Install side bearing caps and torque retaining bolts to 65–72 ft. lbs.

   f. Turn carrier several times to seat bearings. Measure the carrier turning torque with a tool at the ring gear retaining bolt. The standard valve of pulling force at the ring gear bolt is 7.7–8.8 ft. lbs. Add or subtract shims as necessary. Increase shim thickness to decrease turning torque and decrease shim thickness to increase turning torque. Record correct shim(s) thickness and remove carrier and bearings.

33. On R180 and R180A model, press fit side bearing outer race into side retainer using suitable tools.

34. Install oil seals. Install differential case assembly. Place side retainer (correct marked position) adjusting shims and O-ring on side retainer and install on housing.

35. On R200A model install differential case assembly with side bearings outer races into housing. Insert the correct bearing adjusting washers between side bearings and housing. Drive in side bearing spacer with suitable tools.

36. Align mark on bearing caps and install caps torque to 65–72 ft. lbs.

37. Measure the ring gear to drive pinion backlash witrh a dial indicator. The standard valve is 0.0051–0.0071 in. If backlash is too small, decrease thickness of right shim and increase thickness of left shim by the same amount. If backlash is to great reverse the above procedure. Never change the toatal amount of shims as it will change the bearing preload.

38. Check total preload with torque wrench, turn drive pinion

several times in both directions to set bearings. The standard valve for total preload is 8.7–20.0 inch lbs. for R180 and R180A models. The standard valve for total preload is 10.9–20.4 inch lbs. for R200A model.

39. On R180 and R180A models if preload is too great, add the same amount of shims to each side. If preload is too small, remove the same amount of shims from each side. Never add or remove a different number of shims for each side as it will change ring gear to drive pinion backlash.

40. On R200A model if preload is too great, remove the same amount of shims from each side. If preload is too small, add the same amount of shims to each side. Never add or remove a different number of shims for each side as it will change ring gear to drive pinion backlash.

41. Recheck ring gear to drive pinion backlash. Check runout of ring gear the standard valve for R180 and R180A models is 0.0031 in. and 0.0020 in. for the R200A model.

42. Check tooth contact pattern as necessary.

43. Install rear cover and gasket on all models. Install extension tube and differential side shaft assembly on R180A and R200A models. Install the side flange in correct position on R180 model.

Rear Drive Axle

Inspection Before Disassembly

1. Position the removed differential carrier assembly in a suitable holding fixture.

2. Check total preload by turning drive pinion in booth directions several times to set bearings. Using torque wrench or equivalent measure valve. The standard valve for model H190A and C220 models is 10–19 inch lbs. of turning torque. The standard valve for H233B model is 8.7–17.4 inch lbs. of turning torque.

3. Check backlash of ring gear with a dial indicator at several points. The standard valve for models H190A and C220 ring gear to drive pinion backlash is 0.0051–0.0071 in. and 0.0059–0.0079 in. for H233B model.

4. Check runout of ring gear with a dial indicator. The standard valve is 0.0031 in. of runout for all models.

5. Using suitable equipment check differential tooth contact for correct pattern as follows:

   a. Thoroughly clean ring gear and drive pinion teeth.

   b. Sparingly apply red lead or equivalent to 3 or 4 teeth of ring gear drive side.

   c. Hold companion flange steady by hand and rotate the ring gear in both directions.

   d. Interrupt contact marks left on the ring gear assembly. Gear tooth contact pattern check is necessary to verify correct relationship between ring gear and drive pinion.

6. On all models, check backlash of side gear. Using a thickness gauge, measure clearance between side gear thrust washer and differential case. The standard valve is 0.039–0.0079 in. of side gear clearance.

Disassembly and assembly

1. Position the removed differential carrier assembly in a suitable holding fixture.

2. Matchmark side bearing caps and shims if so equipped to ensure that they are replaced in proper position during reassembly.

3. On H233B model, remove the side lock fingers and side bearing caps. Remove side bearings with suitable tools.

4. Remove the differential case from the final drive housing. Mark all parts for correct installation.

5. Attach a flange holding wrench or equivalent to hold flange from turning. Remove the drive pinion nut.

6. Remove the companion flange using suitable puller.

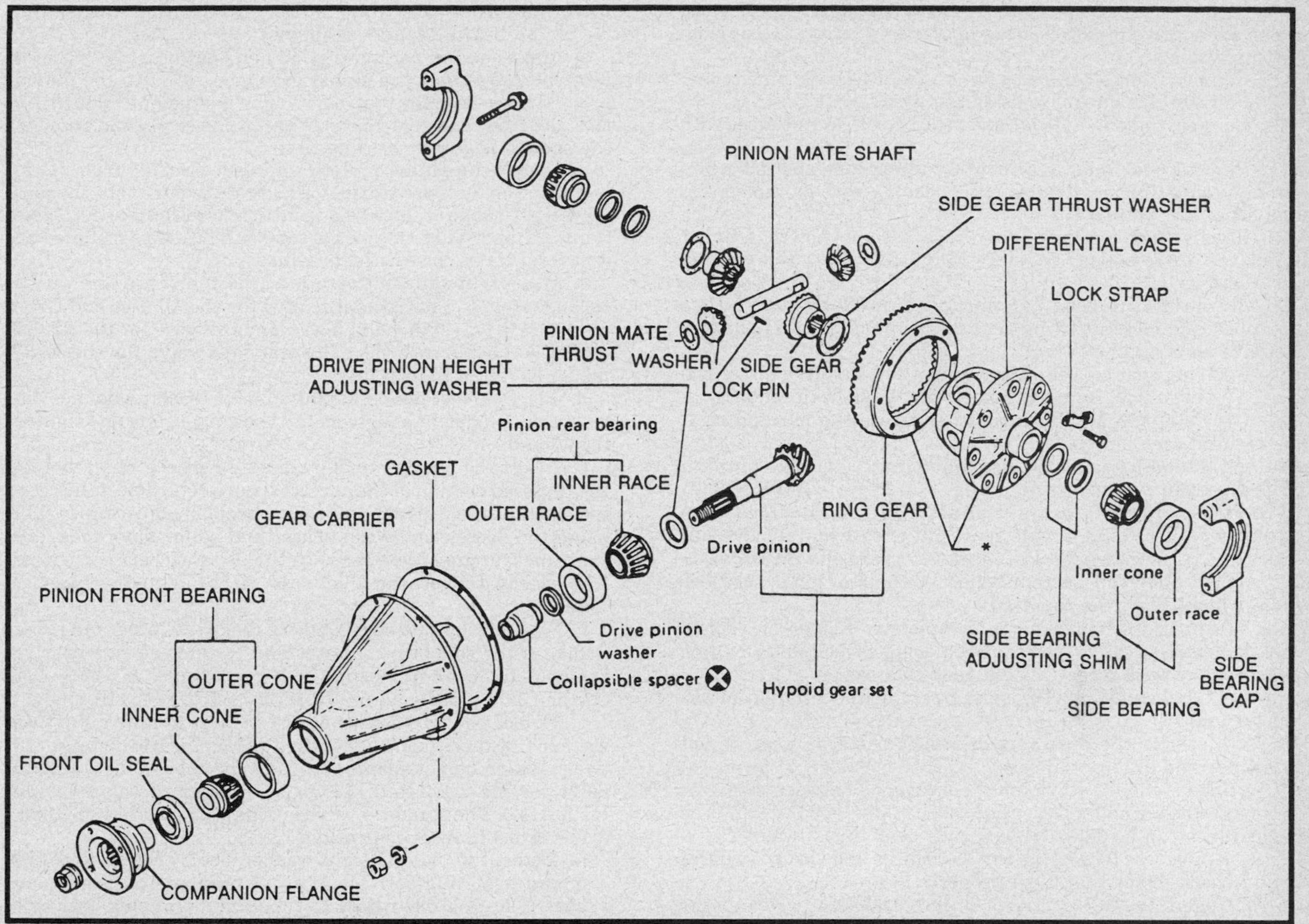

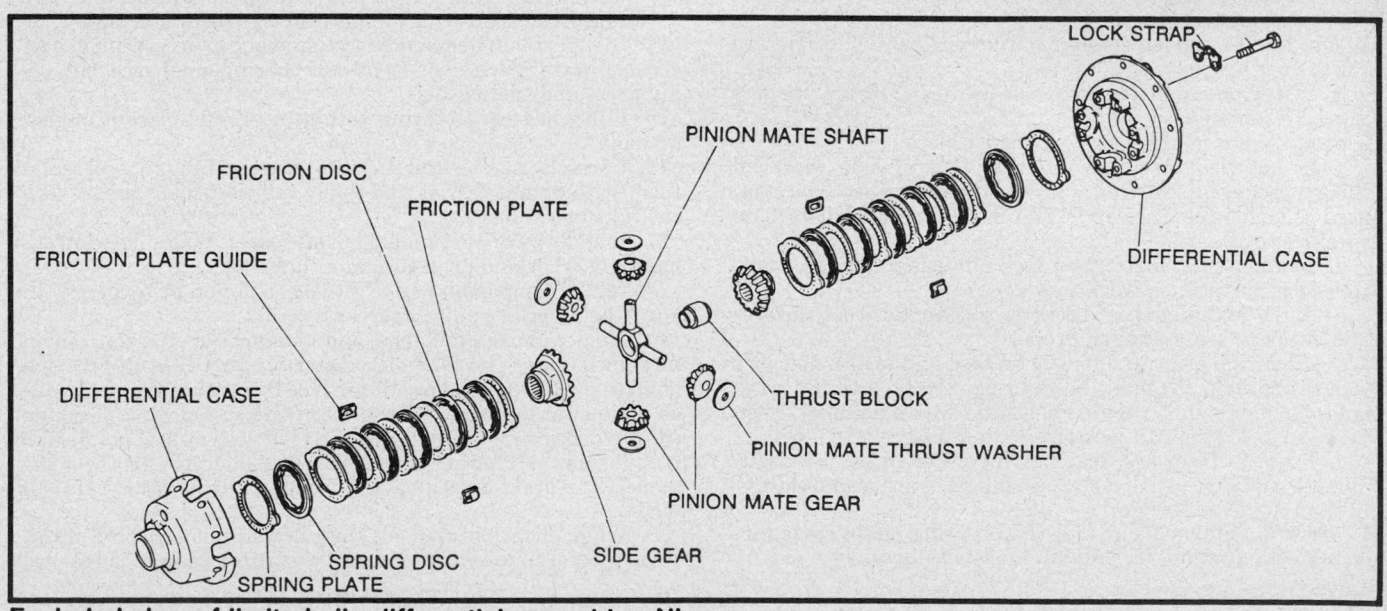

PINION MATE SHAFT

SIDE GEAR THRUST WASHER

DIFFERENTIAL CASE

LOCK STRAP

PINION MATE THRUST WASHER

SIDE GEAR

LOCK PIN

DRIVE PINION HEIGHT ADJUSTING WASHER

Pinion rear bearing

GASKET

INNER RACE

OUTER RACE

GEAR CARRIER

Drive pinion

RING GEAR

Inner cone

Outer race

PINION FRONT BEARING

Drive pinion washer

OUTER CONE

INNER CONE

Collapsible spacer

Hypoid gear set

SIDE BEARING ADJUSTING SHIM

SIDE BEARING

SIDE BEARING CAP

FRONT OIL SEAL

COMPANION FLANGE

*

Exploded view of rear differential assembly — Nissan

LOCK STRAP

FRICTION DISC

FRICTION PLATE

PINION MATE SHAFT

FRICTION PLATE GUIDE

DIFFERENTIAL CASE

DIFFERENTIAL CASE

THRUST BLOCK

PINION MATE THRUST WASHER

SPRING DISC

SPRING PLATE

SIDE GEAR

PINION MATE GEAR

Exploded view of limited slip differential assembly — Nissan

7. Remove the drive pinion together with pinion rear bearing inner cone, drive pinion bearing spacer and pinion bearing adjusting washer.

8. Remove front oil seal and pinion front bearing inner cone.

9. Remove the side oil seals as required.

10. Remove the pinion front and rear bearing outer races with brass drift from housing.

11. Remove the pinion rear bearing inner cone and drive pinion adjusting washer. Remove rear bearing with suitable press and separator plate.

12. Remove side bearing inner race assembly with a puller from the differential carrier. Mark all parts for correct installation.

13. Remove ring gear by spreading out lock straps if so equipped and loosening ring gear bolts in a criss-cross pattern. Remove all retaining bolts.

14. Tap ring gear off gear case using a soft hammer or equivalent. Tap evenly all around to keep ring gear from binding.

15. On C200 and H233B models, separate the left and right differential case halves.

16. On R190A model, drive out pinion mate shaft lock pin with drift pin from ring gear side.

17. Draw out pinion mate shaft and thrust block if so equipped. Rotate pinion mate gears out of case and remove side gears and thrust washers. Put marks on gears and thrust washers so that they can be reinstalled in their original positions from which they were removed.

18. Clean disassembled parts completely. Repair or replace any damaged or faulty parts. If replacing drive pinion or ring gear, replace with a new hypoid gear as a set.

20. On C200 and H233B models, assemble the differential carrier as follows:

a. Measure the clearance between the side gear thrust washer and differential case.

b. The standard valve for the clearance between side gear thrust washer and differential case is 0.0039–0.0079 in. The clearance can be adjusted with side gear thrust washer.

c. Apply gear oil to gear tooth surfaces and thrust surfaces and check to see they turn properly.

d. Install the left and right differential case halves torque retaining bolts to 40–47 ft. lbs. Position the differential case on the ring gear. Apply Locktite or equivalent and tighten ring gear retaining bolts to (criss-cross fashion) 98–112 ft. lbs. bend up lock straps if so equipped.

e. Press fit side bearings on the differential case using suitable press and tools.

21. On R190A model, assemble the differential carrier as follows:

a. Install pinion mate gears, side gears and thrust washers into differential case.

b. Fit pinion mate shaft and thrust block.

c. Adjust clearance between rear face of side gear and thrust washer by selecting side gear thrust washer. The standard valve for clearance on R190A model is 0.0039–0.0079 in. specification.

d. Install pinion mate shaft lock pin using a punch. Make sure lock pin is flush with case.

e. Apply gear oil to gear tooth surfaces and thrust surfaces and check to see they turn properly.

f. Place ring gear on differential case and install new lock straps and bolts. Tighten bolts to 98–112 ft. lbs. in a criss-cross fashion, lightly tapping bolt head with a hammer. Then bend up lock straps to lock the bolts in place.

g. Press fit front and rear bearing outer races using suitable tools. Make sure that the bearing races are seated squarely in their respective bores.

22. Press fit pinion front and rear bearing outer races into housing with suitable tools on all models as necessary.

23. On all models select pinion bearing adjusting washer and drive pinion bearing spacer as follows:

a. Make sure all parts are clean and that bearings are well lubricate. Assemble the pinion gear bearings into the pinion preload shim selector tool J–34309 or equivalent. Make sure that the front and rear bearings are in the correct position on the special tool (rear bearing first).

b. Install the pinion preload shim selector tool or equivalent into the final drive axle housing. Make sure that the pinion height gauge will make a full turn and tighten the 2 sections by hand. Turn the special tool with bearings installed on it several times to seat the bearings.

c. Measure the turning torque at the end of the tool with a torque wrench. The standard valve for the H190A and C200 models is 8.7–11.3 inch lbs. The standard valve for the R233B model is 3.5–7.8 inch lbs. The standard valve for the R180 model is 7.8–14.8. inch lbs.

d. Place correct pinion height adapter (each model has different pinion height adapter) onto the gauge plate and tighten it by hand.

e. Insert the pinion bearing adjusting spacer squarely into the recessed portion of the correct special tool. Select ther correct thickness of the pinion bearing preload adjusting washer using the distance between spacer and gauge anvil tool. The exact measurement you get with the distance between spacer and special tool is the thickness of the adjusting washer required.

f. Position the side bearing discs tool J–25269–4 and arbor firmly in the side bearing bores and torque the side bearing cap bolts to 36–43 ft. lbs. on the H190A model, 65–72 ft. lbs. on the C200 model and 69–76 ft. lbs. on the H233B model.

g. Select the correct standard pinion height adjusting washer thickness using a standard valve plus the distance between pinion height adapter tool and the arbor. The standard valve for the C200 is 0.138 in. The standard valve for the H190A is 0. The standard valve for the H233B is either 0.098, 0.118 or 0.138 in. specification.

h. Correct the pinion height washer size by referring to the pinion head number. There are 2 numbers on the pinion gear. The first one refers to the pinion and ring gear as a matched set and the number should be the same on the ring gear. The second number is the pinion head height number and it refers to the ideal pinion height for proper operation. Use this number to determine the correct pinion height washer. Select the correct pinion height washer and remove the special tools with pinion bearings from housing.

24. Install pinion height adjusting washer in drive pinion, bevel side toward gear and press fit rear bearing inner race in it, using press and special tools.

25. Lubricate front bearing with gear oil and place it in gear housing.

26. Carefully fit a new oil seal into carrier. Make sure oil seal is flush with end of carrier and apply multi-purpose grease into cavity between lips.

27. Install the drive pinion bearing spacer, pinion bearing adjusting washer and drive pinion in housing.

28. Install companion flange into drive pinion by tapping with a soft hammer or equivalent.

29. Hold companion flange and temporarily tighten pinion nut, until there is no axial play. Ascertain that threaded portion of drive pinion and pinion nut are free from oil or grease. Tighten pinion nut by degrees to the specified preload while checking the preload with torque wrench. Preload with oil seal is 9.5–13.9 inch lbs. for H190A model and 9.5–14.8 inch lbs. for the C200 model. The preload with oil seal is 4.3–8.7 inch lbs. for H233B model.

30. When checking preload, turn drive pinion in both directions several times set bearing rollers. After preload is reached

torque pinion nut t0 94–217 ft. lbs. for H190A and C200 models. Torque the pinion nut to 145–181 ft. lbs. on H233B model. Preload and final pinion nut torque must both be attained for correct operation of axle unit.

31. On the H190A model select the side retaining washer as follows:

a. Make sure all parts are cleaned and well lubricated with auotmatic transmission fluid.

b. Remove the side bearings with suitable tools. Install side bearing old shims on the carrier side away from the ring gear.

c. Reinstall carrier side bearings using suitable press.

d. Install the assembly into the housing. Install side bearing caps and torque retaining bolts to 36–43 ft. lbs.

e. Turn carrier several times to seat bearings. Measure the carrier turning torque with a tool at the ring gear retaining bolt. The standard valve of pulling force at the ring gear bolt is 7.7–8.8 ft. lbs. Add or subtract shims as necessary. Increase shim thickness to increase turning torque and decrease shim thickness to decrease turning torque. Record correct shim(s) thickness and remove carrier and bearings.

32. On the C200 model select the side retaining washer as follows:

a. Make sure all parts are cleaned and well lubricated with auotmatic transmission fluid.

b. Install the differential carrier with side bearings and bearing races installed into gear housing.

c. Install side bearing spacer on the ring gear end of the carrier.

d. Install old preload shims using suitable tools on the carrier end opposite the ring gear.

e. Install side bearing caps and torque retaining bolts to 65–72 ft. lbs.

f. Turn carrier several times to seat bearings. Measure the carrier turning torque with a tool at the ring gear retaining bolt. The standard valve of pulling force at the ring gear bolt is 7.7–8.8 ft. lbs. Add or subtract shims as necessary. Record correct shim(s) thickness and remove carrier and bearings.

33. On all models press fit side bearing outer race into side case retainer using suitable tools.

34. On H190A model install differential case assembly with side bearings outer races into housing. On C200 model insert left and right side bearing adjusting washers between side bearing and carrier. Install differential assembly and side bearing spacer using suitable tools.

35. On H233B model install the side bearing adjusters on gear carrier, screw adjusters lightly at this stage.

36. Align mark on bearing caps and install bearing caps torque to 36–43 ft. lbs. on H190A model and 65–72 ft. lbs. on C200 model. On the H223 model do not fully tighten at this point to allow further tightening of side bearing adjusters.

37. On the H190A and C200 models measure the ring gear to drive pinion backlash with a dial indicator. The standard valve is 0.0051–0.0071 in. If backlash is too small, decrease thickness of right shim and increase thickness of left shim by the same amount. If backlash is to great reverse the above procedure. Never change the toatal amount of shims as it will change the bearing preload.

38. On the H233B model tighten both right and left bearing adjusters alternately and measure the backlash and total preload at the same time. The standard valve is 0.0059–0.0079 in. Tighten side bearing caps to 69–76 ft. lbs. and install side lock clip in correct position.

39. On the H190A and C200 models check total preload with torque wrench, turn drive pinion several times in both directions to set bearings. The standard valve for total preload is 10–19 inch lbs. for H190A model and 10–20 inch lbs. for the C200 model.

40. On H190 and C200 models if preload is too great, remove the same amount of shims from each side. If preload is too small, add the same amount of shims to each side. Never add or remove a different number of shims for each side as it will change ring gear to drive pinion backlash.

41. Recheck ring gear to drive pinion backlash. Check runout of ring gear the standard valve for runout is 0.0031 in. on all models.

42. Check tooth contact pattern as necessary. Apply gear oil to all moving parts and use sealant and or gasket when assembling to the axle housing. On the C200 model install rear cover and gasket.

SUZUKI/GEO

Front And Rear Drive Axles

Disassembly and Assembly

1. Position the removed differential carrier assembly in a suitable holding fixture.

2. Mark side differential side bearing caps for correct installation.

3. Remove the bearing side lock plates and bearing caps. Remove bearing adjusters and outer races. Remove ring gear complete assembly.

4. Remove the flange nut using suitable tools to hold flange.

5. Remove the pinion shaft assembly from the carrier. Remove the pinion shaft oil seal using suitable tools.

6. Remove the outer pinion bearing from the differential carrier.

7. Remove the outer and inner pinion bearing races from the differential carrier.

8. Remove the ring gear bolts and remove the ring gear from the differential assembly.

9. Drive out spring pin (3 spring pins are used on 4 pinion type rear assembly) and remove the differential side gears, selective shims, pinion gears, thrust washers and cross shafts.

10. Remove the collapsible spacer and inner pinion bearing using tool and suitable press. Discard the collapsible spacer.

11. Clean disassembled parts completely. Repair or replace any damaged or faulty parts. If replacing drive pinion or ring gear, replace as a set. All taper roller bearings and races must be replaced as a set.

12. Install the differential side gears, thrust washers, cross shaft and side gears with the correct selective shim in the differential case.

13. Measure the differential side gear endplay. The standard valve is 0.005–0.14 in. select the correct shim to obtain the standard valve.

14. Drive the spring pin (3 spring pins are used on 4 pinion type rear assembly) for the differential side pinion shaft until it is flush with the case surface.

15. When correct endplay is obtained install the ring gear to differential case. Torque the ring gear (special) retaining bolts to 70 ft. lbs.

16. Install the right and left side differential bearings using suitable tools. Hold one side bearing when installing the other side bearing to prevent damage to any component.

17. Install pinion gear inner bearing race into the differential case using suitable tool and a press.

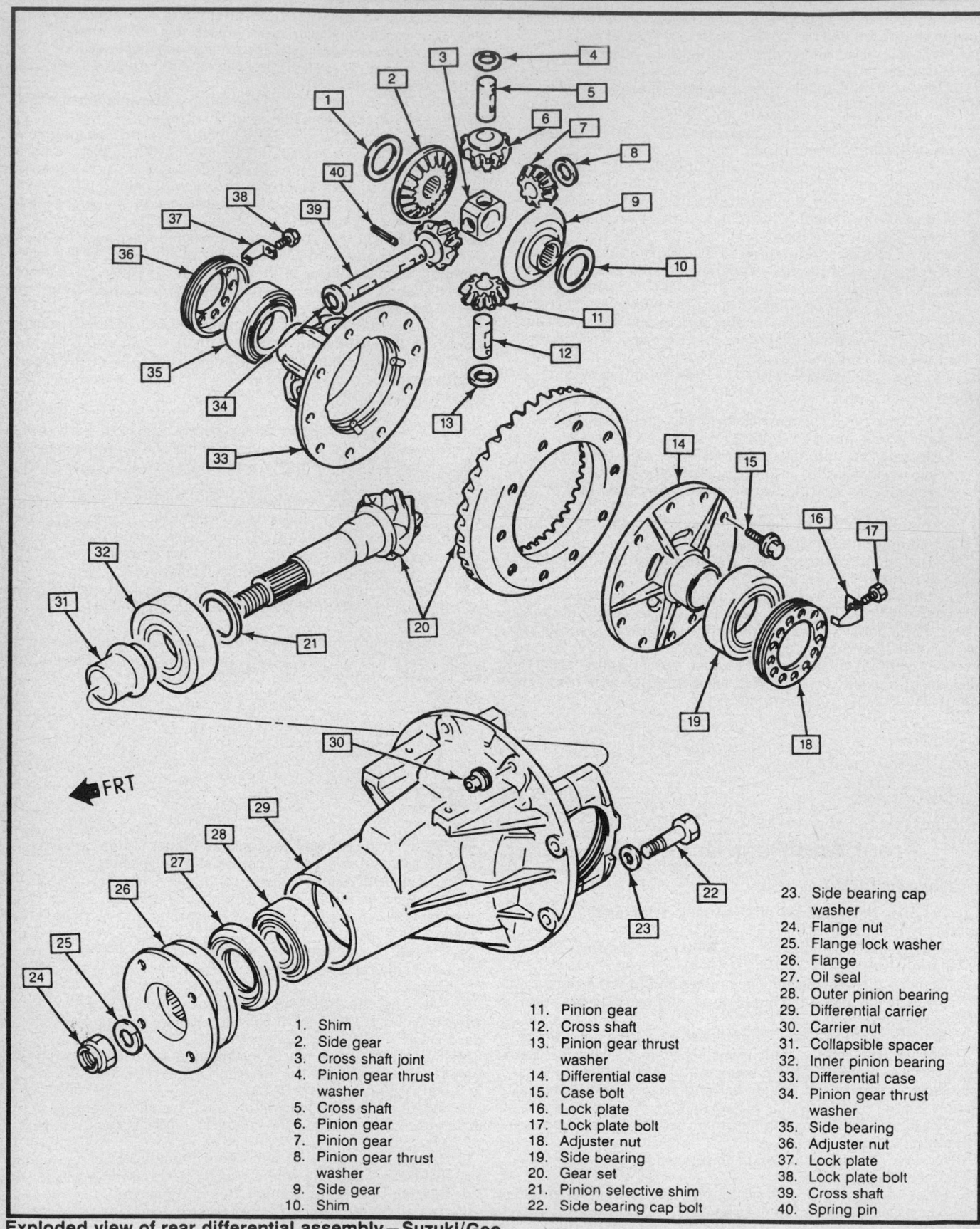

Exploded view of rear differential assembly—Suzuki/Geo

1. Shim
2. Side gear
3. Cross shaft joint
4. Pinion gear thrust washer
5. Cross shaft
6. Pinion gear
7. Pinion gear
8. Pinion gear thrust washer
9. Side gear
10. Shim
11. Pinion gear
12. Cross shaft
13. Pinion gear thrust washer
14. Differential case
15. Case bolt
16. Lock plate
17. Lock plate bolt
18. Adjuster nut
19. Side bearing
20. Gear set
21. Pinion selective shim
22. Side bearing cap bolt
23. Side bearing cap washer
24. Flange nut
25. Flange lock washer
26. Flange
27. Oil seal
28. Outer pinion bearing
29. Differential carrier
30. Carrier nut
31. Collapsible spacer
32. Inner pinion bearing
33. Differential case
34. Pinion gear thrust washer
35. Side bearing
36. Adjuster nut
37. Lock plate
38. Lock plate bolt
39. Cross shaft
40. Spring pin

18. Install pinion gear outer bearing race into the differential case using suitable tool and a press.

19. At this point of the reassembly, set pinion depth. The pinion setting gauge provides in effect a nominal or zero pinion as reference.

20. Lubricate inner and outer pinion bearings with axle lubricant. While holding pinion bearings in the correct position install the pinion depth gauge.

21. Tighten depth gauge stud nut to 18 inch lbs. Rotate the gauge plate several times to seat the bearings. Retighten the locknut on stud of tool to 18 inch lbs.

22. Install special tool side bearing discs and arbor in the correct position in the side bearing bores of the housing.

23. Rotate the gauge plate until the correct area are parallel with the 2 side bearing discs.

24. Position a dial indicator rod over the lower step (94mm) of the gauging plate for front drive axle. Position a dial indicator rod over the higher step (97mm) of the gauging plate for rear drive axle.

25. Connect the dial indicator to the arbor and position gauge shaft over the dial indicator rod.

26. Install the side bearing caps and torque the bolts to 63 ft. lbs.

27. Position the dial indicator to the zero setting. Slowly rotate the arbor on the lower step (94mm) front drive axle or higher step (97mm) rear driver axle of the gauge plate to determine the point of the greatest deflection. At this point reset the dial indicator to zero setting.

28. Slowly rotate the arbor until the dial indicator is no longer on the gauge plate.

29. Record the dial indicator reading. This reading indicates the selective shim required for the correct pinion depth. The selective shims range from 0.012–0.050 in.

30. Install the correct pinion shim on the pinion gear shaft.

31. Assembly the inner pinion bearing on the pinion gear shaft using suitable press plate and press.

32. Install new collapsible spacer on the pinion gear shaft.

33. Install the outer pinion bearing in the differential carrier using suitable tools.

34. Apply lubricant to the oil seal lip. Install the new pinion oil seal using a suitable seal installer or equivalent.

35. Install pinion flange, pinion washer and nut. Hold the pinion flange (suitable flange holding tool) while frequently rotating pinion to seal pinion bearings. Tighten pinion flange nut (little at a time) until endplay is taken up. Measure preload with torque wrench the standard valve for all applications is 11 inch

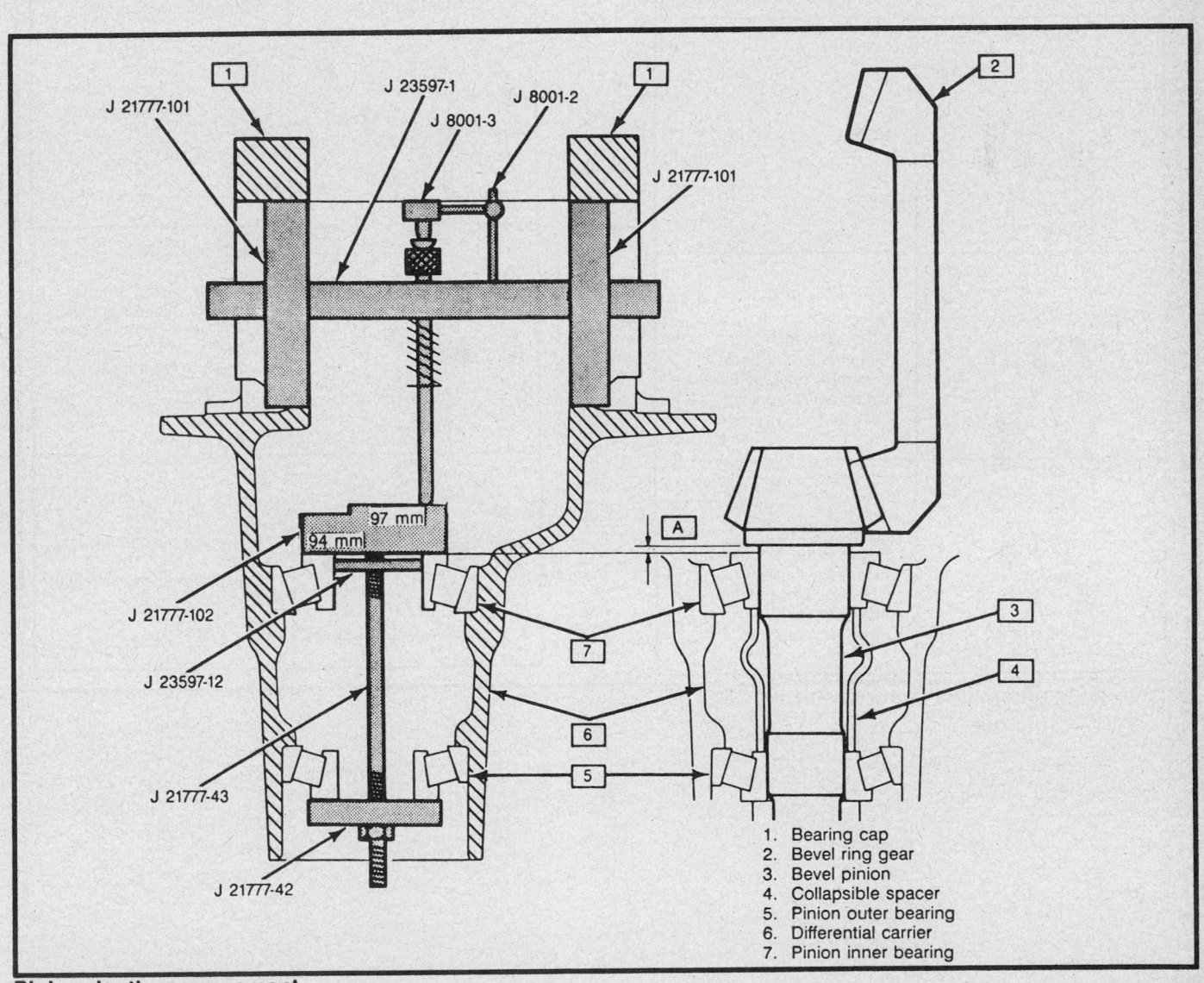

1. Bearing cap
2. Bevel ring gear
3. Bevel pinion
4. Collapsible spacer
5. Pinion outer bearing
6. Differential carrier
7. Pinion inner bearing

Pinion depth measurement

lbs. of starting torque not rotating torque. Exceeding preload specification will compress the collapsible spacer.

36. After final preload has be reached rotate the pinion several times to make sure the bearings have been seated. Recheck the preload specification.

37. Install the ring gear and differential carrier assembly, side bearing outer races, bearing adjusters and bearing caps to housing. Align all identification marks.

38. Rotate pinion gear to ensure the side bearings seat. Tighten bearing caps 15 ft. lbs. on the front and rear drive axle assembly.

39. Using suitable tool turn the bearing adjusters to push side bearings lightly from outside so that outer races are in contact with inner races. Apply a small amount of lubricant to bearings. With dial indicator installed to differential carrier and carrier at 0.0 backlash (ring gear fully engaged into pinion gear) set or check preload. The differential side bearing preload is 0.002–0.006 in.

40. Rotate pinion gear to ensure the side bearings seat. Tight-

en bearing caps to 44 ft. lbs. on the front drive axle assembly and 63 ft. lbs. on the rear drive axle assembly.

41. Check backlash using a dial indicator installed to the differential ring gear. The standard valve for all applications is 0.008–0.015 in. If adjustment is necessary loosen one adjuster nut and tighten the opposite nut an equal amount. This will move the ring gear away from or toward the pinion gear and maintain side bearing preload.

42. When turning the side bearing adjusters the final movement must be made in the tightening direction to ensure correct side bearing preload.

43. Install the side bearing lock plates. Torque the side bearing lock plate bolts to 25 ft. lbs.

44. Paint the ring gear with suitable marking compound and rotate the pinion flange to obtain a tooth mesh contact pattern.

45. Inspect pattern contact and adjust or service the assembly as required. After all adjustments and correct pattern contact is obtained stake the pinion flange locknut.

46. Apply gear oil to all moving parts and use sealant and or gasket when assembling to the axle housing.

Differential tooth contact pattern—Suzuki/Geo

TOYOTA

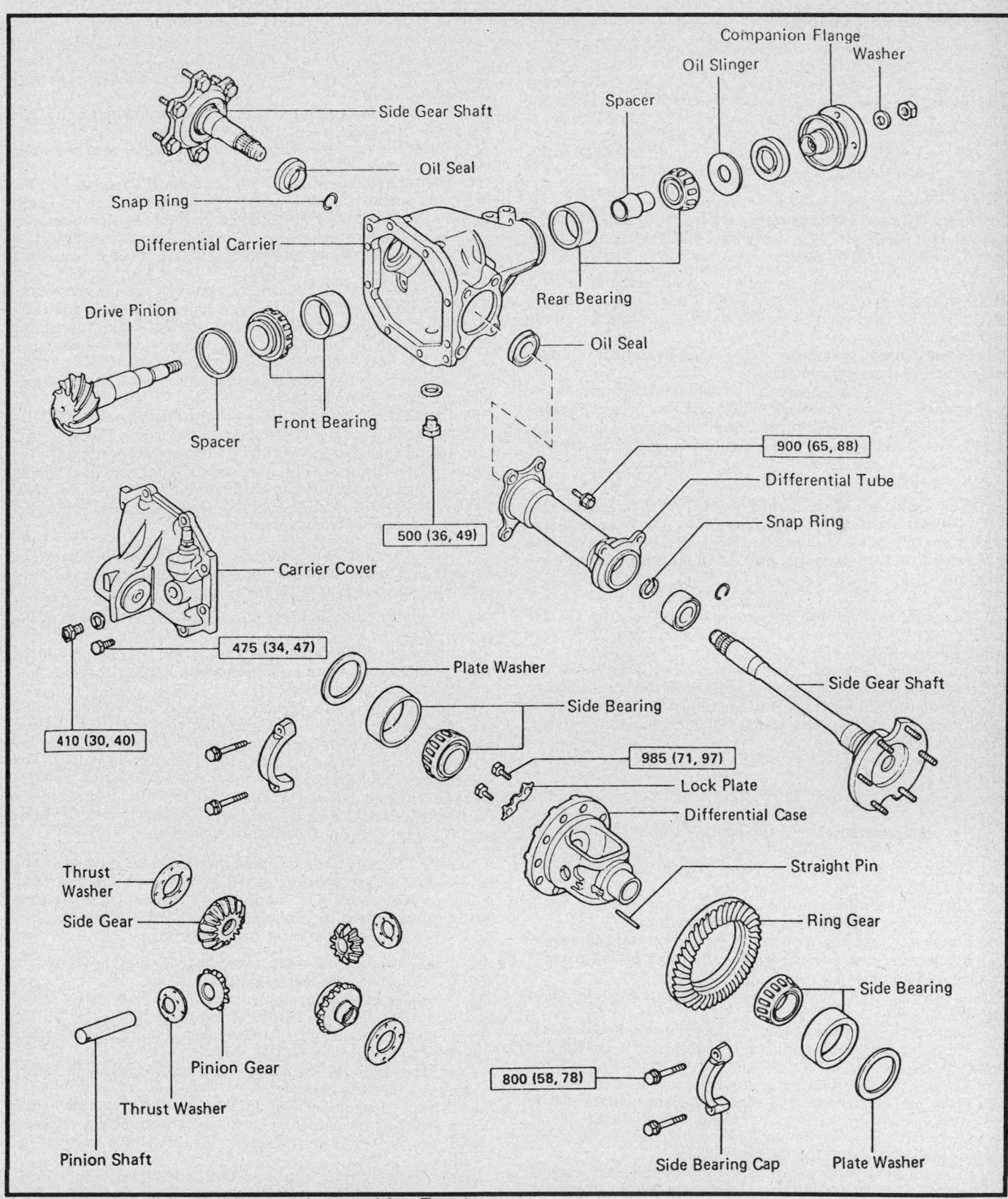

Exploded view of front differential assembly—Toyota

Front and Rear Drive Axles

Disassembly and Assembly

1. Position the removed differential carrier assembly in a suitable holding fixture.

2. Measure the side gear backlash while holding one pinion gear toward the case. The standard valve is 0.0020–0.0079 in. on all except Land Cruiser. The standard valve for Land Cruiser is 0.0008–0.0079 in.

3. Check ring gear runout. Maximum runout is 0.0028 in. on all except Land Criuser. The standard valve for Land Cruiser is 0.0039 in.

NOTE: On rear axle assembly with 7½ in. ring gear the runout is 0.0028. On rear axle assembly with 8 in. ring gear the runout is 0.0039 in.

4. Hold drive pinion flange check ring gear backlash (several different locations). The standard valve is 0.0051–0.0071 in. on all except Land Criuser. The standard valve for Land Cruiser is 0.0059–0.0079 in.

5. Inspect tooth contact between ring gear and drive pinion using suitable marking compound.

6. Using a torque wrench measure the (starting) preload of the backlash between the drive pinion and ring gear. The standard valve is 5.2–8.7 inch lbs. for all vehicles except Land Cruiser and vans. The standard valve specification for Land Cruiser is 6.1–8.7 inch lbs. and 4.3–6.9 inch lbs. for vans.

NOTE: On rear axle assembly with 7½ in. ring gear the drive pinion preload is 5.2–8.7 inch lbs. On rear axle assembly with 8 in. ring gear 2 pinion type the drive pinion preload is 7.8–11.3 inch lbs. and 4.3–6.9 inch lbs. on 4 pinion type.

7. The total preload specification standard valve is 1.6–3.0 inch lbs. for all vehicles except Land Cruiser and vans. The standard valve specification for Land Cruiser is 3.5–5.2 inch lbs. and 2.6–4.3 inch lbs. for vans. This measurement is total preload (starting) also adding drive pinion preload to the specification.

8. Loosen the the staked part of the flange retaining nut. Remove the nut using a suitable tool to hold flange. Remove flange using a puller or equivlent.

9. Remove the companion flange oil seal and slinger from the housing.

10. Remove the rear bearing spacer and rear bearing from the drive pinion.

11. Put alignment marks on the bearing cap and differential carrier.

12. Remove both bearing caps. Remove both side bearing preload adjusting washers.

13. Remove the differential case with bearing outer races (mark for correct installation) from the carrier.

14. Remove the drive pinion from the differential carrier.

15. Remove the front bearing from the drive pinion using a suitable tool and press.

16. Remove the drive pinion front and rear bearing outer races from the housing.

17. Remove the side bearing from the differential case using suitable puller. Puller jaws must align with notches in the differential case.

18. Remove the ring gear retaining bolts and lock plates.

19. Place matchmarks on the ring gear then using a plastic tool or equivalent separate it from the differential case.

20. Drive out the straight pin and remove the pinion shaft, pinion gears, side gears and thrust washers.

21. Assemble the differential case by installing the correct (check backlash with dial indicator) thrust washer to side gears. Try to select washers of the same thickness for both sides. Install the thrust washer and side gears in the differerntial case.

NOTE: On some rear axle assemblies the differential case splits. The retaining torque for left and right case halves is 35 ft. lbs.

22. Temporarily install the side gear shaft. Measure the side gear backlash the standard valve is 0.0020–0.0079 in. on all vehicles except Land Cruiser. The standard valve for Land Cruiser is 0.0008–0.0079 in.

23. Drive the straight pin through the case and hole in the pinion shaft. Stake the pin and differential case.

24. Clean the contact suface of the differential case before installing the ring gear to the assembly.

25. Heat the ring gear in oil bath to about 212 degrees Fahrenheit then quickly install the ring gear on the differential case. Caution should be used when performing this service operation.

26. Align the matchmarks on the ring gear differential case. Coat the ring gear bolts with gear oil install the lock plates and retaining bolts.

27. After the ring gear cools down enough, torque the retaining bolts uniformly and little at a time. The standard valve torque for ring gear installation is 71 ft. lbs. on all trucks and vans except Land Crusier. The standard valve for Land Cruiser is 81 ft. lbs. Stake the lock plates on all appplications.

28. Using a suitable press plate and press install the side bearings into the differential case.

29. Install the differential case onto the carrier assembly. Install the plate washers where there is no play in the bearings.

30. Install the bearing caps using a dial indicator measure the runout of the ring gear. The standard valve for runout is 0.0028 in. on all except Land Criuser. The standard valve for Land Criuser is 0.0039 in. after runout inspection is performed remove the assembly from the carrier.

NOTE: On rear axle assembly with 7½ in. ring gear the runout is 0.0028. On rear axle assembly with 8 in. ring gear the runout is 0.0039 in.

31. Install the front and rear pinion bearing outer races to the carrier.

32. Install the drive pinion assembly (rear bearing) and front bearing in housing. Install the companion flange with a suitable tool to hold flange in place.

33. Rotate the flange several times to seat the bearing. Adjust the drive pinion preload by tightening the flange nut. Use a torque wrench to measure the preload. The standard valve for preload (starting torque) is 10.4–16.5 inch lbs. on trucks. The standard valve for preload (starting torque) is 8.7–13.9 inch lbs. on vans. The standard valve for preload (starting torque) specification is 11.3–17.4 inch lbs. on Land Crusier. In order to measure the total preload, record this preload specification.

NOTE: On rear axle assembly with 7½ in. ring gear the preload (starting torque) is 10.4–16.5 inch lbs. On rear axle assembly with 8 in. ring gear 2 pinion type the preload (starting torque) specification is 16.5–22.6 inch lbs. and 8.7–13.9 inch lbs. on 4 pinion type.

34. Install the bearing outer races in the correct location. Install the differential case in the carrier.

35. At this point of reassembly, on all front drive axle vehicles except Land Crusier use the following procedure:

a. Insure the ring gear has backlash. Install only the plate washer on the ring gear back side.

b. Snug down on the washer and bearing by pushing the ring gear into the housing.

c. Hold the side bearing boss on the teeth surface of the ring gear and measure the backlash. The standard valve for backlash is 0.0051 in. Select a ring gear plate washers as required.

d. Install both (as required) the adjusting washers and differential case into the carrier.

e. Using a dial indicator, measure the ring gear backlash again to obtain the standard valve. Adjust by either increasing

or decreasing the number of washers on both sides by a equal amount. Insure that ring gear has standard valve of backlash.

36. Adjust the side bearing preload by removing the ring gear adjusting washer and measure the thickness. Using the backlash as a reference specification select a correct washer to obtain the standard valve of backlash (0.0051–0.0071 in.) by increasing or decreasing the washer thickness on both sides by an equal amount.

37. Install the side bearing caps in the correct position. Torque the side bearing cap bolts to 58 ft. lbs.

38. Measure the total preload using a torque wrench. The total preload specification standard valve is 1.6–3.0 inch lbs. for all trucks except for trucks with automatic disconnecting differential assembly which is 3.5–5.2 inch lbs. The standard valve specification for vans 2.6–4.3 inch lbs. This measurement is total preload (starting) also add drive pinion preload to the specification.

39. At this point of reassembly, on rear drive axle vehicles and Land Crusier use the following procedure:

a. Install the adjusting nuts in the correct location in the carrier.

b. Align the marks on the cap and carrier. Insure that bearing caps and adjusting nuts are installed properly.

c. Torque the bearing caps bolts until the spring washers are slightly compressed.

d. Tighten the adjusting nuts (equal amount on both sides) on the ring gear side until the ring gear backlash is 0.0051–0.0071 in. for all trucks and vans rear axle assemblies and 0.0059–0.0079 in. on Land Cruiser.

40. Install the side bearing caps in the correct position. Torque the side bearing cap bolts to 58 ft. lbs.

41. Recheck the ring gear backlash standard valve specification.

42. Measure the total preload using a torque wrench. The total preload specification standard valve is 3.5–5.2 inch lbs. This measurement is total preload (starting) also add drive pinion preload to the specification.

43. On all applications inspect tooth pattern contact between ring gear and drive pinion. Adjust as required.

44. Remove the companion flange and drive pinion bearing. Install new bearing spacer on the drive pinion. Install the bearing.

45. Install oil slinger and new oil seal. The oil seal drive in depth is 0.059 in. for trucks, 0.0079 in. for vans and 0.0039 in. for Land Cruiser.

NOTE: On rear axle assembly with 7½ in. ring gear the oil seal drive depth is 0.059 in. On rear axle assembly with 8 in. ring gear the oil seal drive depth is 0.039 in. specification.

46. Using suitable tools install the companion flange. Coat the threads of the new nut with lubricant or equivalent.

47. The torque specification for the companion flange is 89 ft. lbs. on trucks, 80 ft. lbs. on vans and 181 ft. lbs on Land Cruiser.

NOTE: On rear axle assembly with 7½ in. ring gear the flange torque is 80 ft. lbs. On rear axle assembly with 8 in. ring gear the flange torque is 145 ft. lbs.

48. Check drive pinion bearing preload. The standard valve for preload (starting torque) is 10.4–16.5 inch lbs. on trucks. The standard valve for preload (starting torque) is 8.7–13.9 inch lbs. on vans. The standard valve for preload (starting torque) specification is 11.3–17.4 inch lbs. on Land Crusier.

NOTE: On rear axle assembly with 7½ in. ring gear the preload (starting torque) is 10.4–16.5 inch lbs. On rear axle assembly with 8 in. ring gear 2 pinion type the preload (starting torque) specification is 16.5–22.6 inch lbs. and 8.7–13.9 inch lbs. on 4 pinion type.

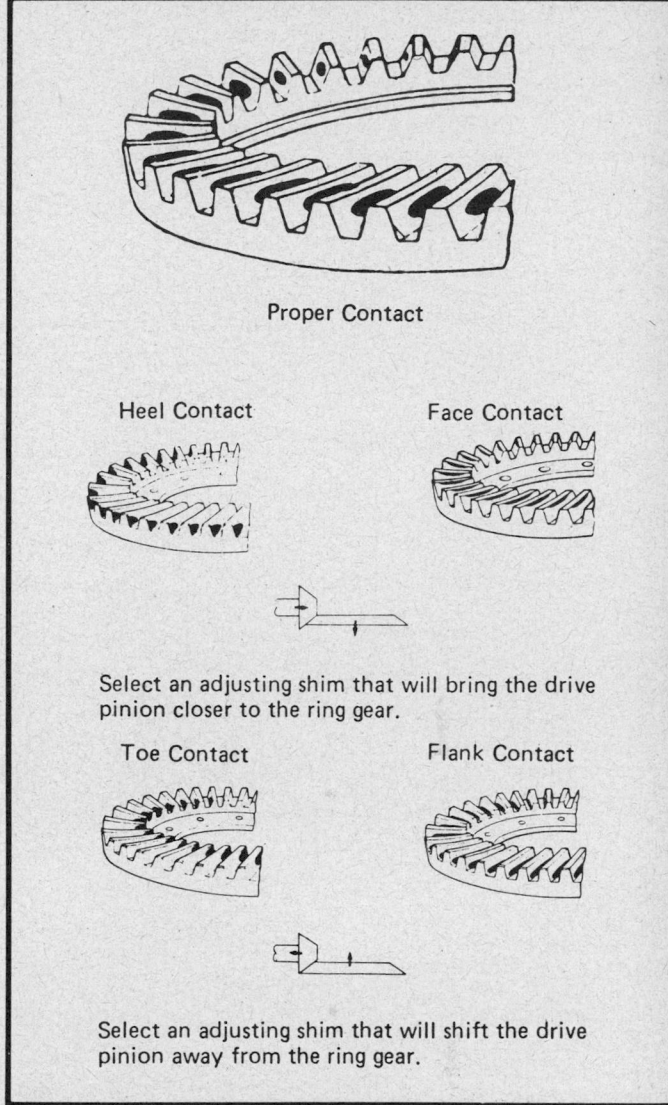

Proper Contact

Heel Contact   Face Contact

Select an adjusting shim that will bring the drive pinion closer to the ring gear.

Toe Contact   Flank Contact

Select an adjusting shim that will shift the drive pinion away from the ring gear.

Differential tooth contact pattern—Toyota

49. If the preload is greater than specification, replace the bearing spacer. If the preload is less than specification, retighten flange nut (little at a time) until preload is reached.

50. The maximum torque on the new companion flange nut is 165 ft. lbs. on trucks, 174 ft. lbs. on vans and 325 ft. lbs on Land Cruiser.

NOTE: On rear axle assembly with 7½ in. ring gear the maximum torque on the new companion flange nut is 174 ft. lbs. On rear axle assembly with 8 in. ring gear the maximum torque is 253 ft. lbs.

51. Recheck total preload and ring gear backlash as necessary. Inspect tooth contact pattern between ring gear and drive pinion.

52. Using a dial indicator measure the runout (vertical and lateral) of companion flange, maximum runout is 0.0039 in. Stake drive pinion nut.

53. On all front drive axle vehicles except Land Cruiser, install a attaching components to axle housing. Install rear cover with suitable sealant or gasket torque retaining bolts to 34 ft. lbs.

54. On rear drive axle vehicles and Land Cruiser vehicles select correct locks, whichever will fit the adjusting nuts. Torque the lock retaining bolts to 9 ft. lbs.

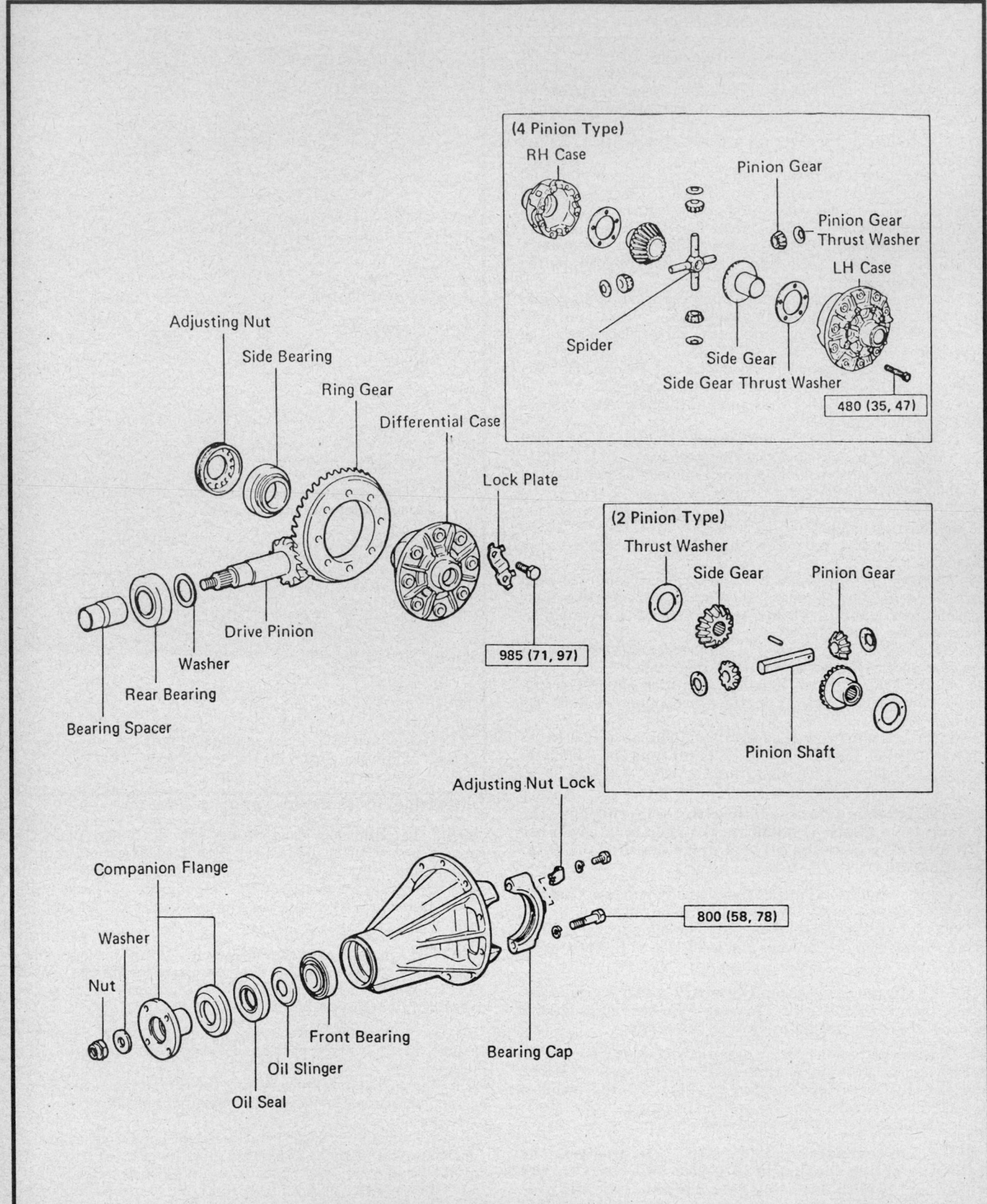

(4 Pinion Type)

RH Case

Pinion Gear

Pinion Gear
Thrust Washer

LH Case

Spider

Side Gear

Side Gear Thrust Washer

480 (35, 47)

Adjusting Nut

Side Bearing

Ring Gear

Differential Case

Lock Plate

Drive Pinion

Washer

Rear Bearing

Bearing Spacer

985 (71, 97)

(2 Pinion Type)

Thrust Washer

Side Gear

Pinion Gear

Pinion Shaft

Adjusting Nut Lock

Companion Flange

Washer

Nut

Oil Seal

Oil Slinger

Front Bearing

Bearing Cap

800 (58, 78)

Exploded view of rear differential assembly—Toyota

Transfer Case

MITSUBISHI

Trouble Diagnosis

SLIPS OUT OF GEAR (HIGH-LOW)

1. Shifting poppet spring weak.
2. Bearing broken or worn.
3. Shifting fork bent.
4. Improper control rod adjustment.

HARD SHIFTING

1. Lack of lubricant.
2. Shift lever binding on shaft.
3. Shifting poppet ball scored.
4. Shifting fork bent.
5. Low tire pressure.

BACKLASH

1. Companion yoke loose.
2. Transfer case loose on mounts.
3. Internal parts excessively worn.

NOISY

1. Low lubricant level.
2. Bearings improperly adjusted or excessively worn.
3. Gears worn or damaged.
4. Improper alignment of driveshafts or U-joints.

OIL LEAKAGE

1. Excessive amount of lubricant in case.
2. Vent clogged.
3. Gaskets or seals leaking.
4. Bearings loose or damaged.
5. Driveshaft yoke mating surfaces scored.

OVERHEATING

1. Excessive or insufficient amount of lubricant.
2. Bearing adjustment too tight.

Removal and Installation

TRANSFER CASE REMOVAL

1. Raise and safely support the vehicle.
2. Drain the oil from the transmission and transfer case.
3. Remove all electrical connections and shifter lever assemblies from the transmission/transfer case.
4. Remove the exhaust system, as needed.
5. Matchmark and remove the front and rear driveshafts.
6. Support the transmission/transfer case with a suitable transmission jack or equivalent and remove all brackets, support members and case protector.
7. Disconnect the speedometer cable or pulse generator.
8. Remove all necessary components to gain access to transmission/transfer case retaining bolts. Remove all retaining bolts and transmission/transfer case assembly.
9. Lower the supported transmission/transfer case assembly and tilt assembly to remove from the vehicle.
10. Remove the transfer case from the transmission assembly.

TRANSFER CASE INSTALLATION

1. Align transfer case with transmission. Install the transfer case assembly to the transmission.
2. Torque the transfer case retaining bolts to specifications. Install the supported transmission/transfer case to the vehicle.
3. Install all necessary components that were removed to gain access to transmission/transfer case retaining bolts.
4. Reconnect the speedometer cable or pulse generator.
5. Install all brackets, support members and case protector. Remove the transmission jack or equivalent.
6. Install the front and rear driveshafts in the correct positions.
7. Install the exhaust system as required.
8. Install all electrical connections and shifter lever assembly to the transmission/transfer case assembly.
9. Refill the transmission and transfer case with the correct amount of the specified oil. Lower the vehicle.
10. Road test the vehicle through each gear range to check for proper operation.

Before Disassembly

Cleanliness is an important factor in the overhaul of the transfer case. Before opening up this unit, the entire outside of the transfer case should be cleaned, preferably with a high pressure washer such as a car wash spray unit. During inspection and reassembly all parts should be thoroughly cleaned with solvent then dried with compressed air. Wiping cloths and rags should not be used to dry parts.

Wheel bearing grease, long used to hold thrust washers and lube parts, should not be used. Lube seals with clean transaxle oil and use ordinary unmedicated petroleum jelly to hold the thrust washers and to ease the assembly of seals, since it will not leave a harmful residue as grease often will. Do not use solvent on neoprene seals, if they are to be reused, or thrust washers.

Before installing bolts into aluminum parts, always dip the threads into clean transmission oil. Antiseize compound can also be used to prevent bolts from galling the aluminum and seizing. Always use a torque wrench to keep from stripping the threads. The internal snaprings should be expanded and the external rings should be compressed, if they are to be reused. This will help insure proper seating when installed.

TRANSFER CASE DISASSEMBLY

1. Remove the 4WD switch from the case. Take out the steel balls behind the switch.
2. Remove the speedometer sleeve clamp and the speedometer sleeve assembly.
3. Remove the rear cover, gasket, wave spring and spacer.
4. Take a $\frac{3}{16}$ in. punch and drive out the spring pin that retains the H-L shift fork. Remove the 2 threaded plugs and remove the poppet springs and balls.
5. Pull out the H-L shift rail. Take out the interlock plunger.
6. Remove the rear bearing snapring from the rear output shaft. Remove the chain cover, oil guide and side cover.
7. Remove the countershaft locking plate and remove the countershaft. Remove the counter gear assembly through the side cover opening. The gear assembly consists of gear, spacers, needle bearings and thrust washers.
8. Remove the snapring, the 2 spring retainers and the spring from the 2W-4W shift rail.
9. Remove the front output shaft, the rear output shaft and the chain (as an assembly) from the transfer case.
10. Remove the 2W-4W shift rail. Remove the H-L shift fork

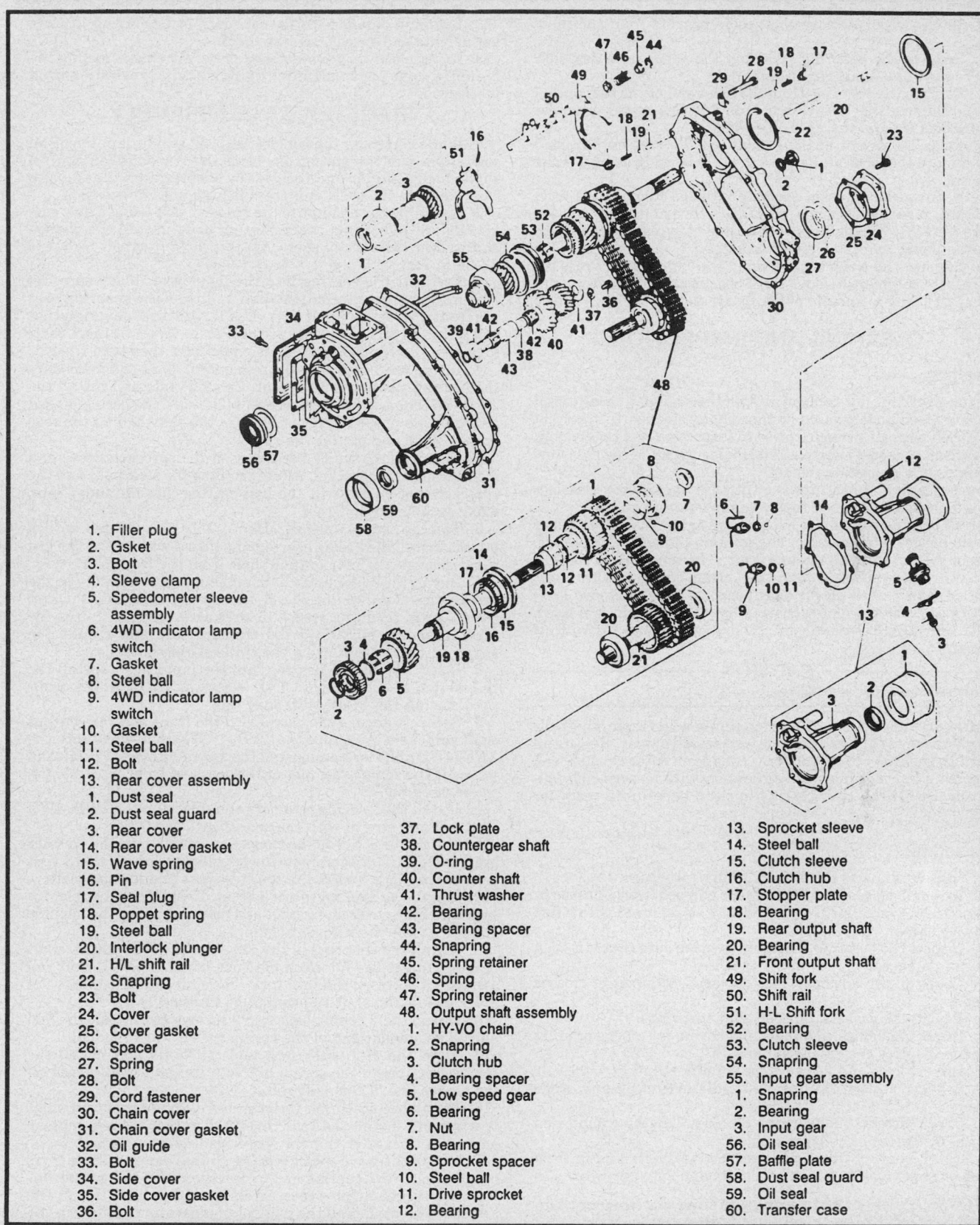

1. Filler plug
2. Gsket
3. Bolt
4. Sleeve clamp
5. Speedometer sleeve assembly
6. 4WD indicator lamp switch
7. Gasket
8. Steel ball
9. 4WD indicator lamp switch
10. Gasket
11. Steel ball
12. Bolt
13. Rear cover assembly
1. Dust seal
2. Dust seal guard
3. Rear cover
14. Rear cover gasket
15. Wave spring
16. Pin
17. Seal plug
18. Poppet spring
19. Steel ball
20. Interlock plunger
21. H/L shift rail
22. Snapring
23. Bolt
24. Cover
25. Cover gasket
26. Spacer
27. Spring
28. Bolt
29. Cord fastener
30. Chain cover
31. Chain cover gasket
32. Oil guide
33. Bolt
34. Side cover
35. Side cover gasket
36. Bolt

37. Lock plate
38. Countergear shaft
39. O-ring
40. Counter shaft
41. Thrust washer
42. Bearing
43. Bearing spacer
44. Snapring
45. Spring retainer
46. Spring
47. Spring retainer
48. Output shaft assembly
1. HY-VO chain
2. Snapring
3. Clutch hub
4. Bearing spacer
5. Low speed gear
6. Bearing
7. Nut
8. Bearing
9. Sprocket spacer
10. Steel ball
11. Drive sprocket
12. Bearing

13. Sprocket sleeve
14. Steel ball
15. Clutch sleeve
16. Clutch hub
17. Stopper plate
18. Bearing
19. Rear output shaft
20. Bearing
21. Front output shaft
49. Shift fork
50. Shift rail
51. H-L Shift fork
52. Bearing
53. Clutch sleeve
54. Snapring
55. Input gear assembly
1. Snapring
2. Bearing
3. Input gear
56. Oil seal
57. Baffle plate
58. Dust seal guard
59. Oil seal
60. Transfer case

Exploded view of transfer case—Mitsubishi

and clutch sleeve. Remove the needle bearing from the input gear.

11. Remove the snapring retaining the input gear assembly and remove the input gear assembly.

12. Remove the snapring from the front end of the rear output shaft. Remove the H-L clutch hub, the low speed gear, the thrust bearing and the needle bearing.

13. Raise the detent of the locknut on the rear output shaft and remove the locknut. Remove the rear bearing using a puller or press.

14. Remove the sprocket spacer and balls. Remove the drive sprocket, 2 needle bearings, sprocket sleeve and steel ball. Remove the 2W-4W clutch sleeve, hub and stop plate. Remove the bearing using a suitable puller or press.

15. Remove the snapring retaining the input gear. Press the shaft from the gear. Remove the 2 bearings from the front output shaft using a suitable puller or press.

CLEANING AND INSPECTION

Cleaning

During overhaul, all components of the transfer case (except bearing assemblies) should be thoroughly cleaned with solvent and dried with air pressure prior to inspection and reassembly. Be sure all gasket sealing material is cleaned off of the case, cover plates and mounting flanges.

Proper cleaning of bearings is of utmost importance. Bearings should always be cleaned separately from other parts.

Soak all bearing assemblies in clean solvent or fuel oil. Bearings should never be cleaned in a hot solution tank. Wash the bearings in solvent until all old lubricant is loosened. Hold races so that bearings will not rotate; then clean bearings with a soft bristled brush until all dirt has been removed. Remove loose particles of dirt by tapping bearing flat against a block of wood. Rinse bearings in clean solvent; then blow bearings dry with air pressure.

—————————— CAUTION ——————————
Do not spin bearings while drying.

After drying, rotate each bearing slowly while examining balls or rollers for roughness, damage, or excessive wear. Replace all bearings that are not in first class condition. After cleaning and inspecting bearings lubricate generously with recommended lubricant. then wrap each bearing in clean paper until ready for reassembly.

Inspection

1. Inspect all parts for discoloration or warpage.

2. Examine all gears and splines for chipped, worn, broken or nicked teeth. Small nicks or burrs may be removed with a fine abrasive stone.

3. Inspect the breather assembly to make sure that it is open and not damaged.

4. Check all threaded parts for damaged, stripped, or crossed threads.

5. Replace all gaskets, oil seals and snaprings.

6. Inspect housings, retainers and covers for cracks or other damage. Replace the damaged parts.

7. Inspect keys and keyways for condition and fit.

8. Inspect shift forks for wear, distortion or any other damage.

9. Check detent ball springs for free length, compressed length, distortion or collapsed coils.

10. Check bearing fit on their respective shafts and in their bores or cups. Inspect bearings, shafts and cups for wear.

NOTE: If either the bearings or cups are worn or damaged, it is advisable to replace both parts.

11. Inspect all bearing rollers or balls for pitting or galling.

12. Examine detent balls for corrosion or brinneling. If shift bar detents show wear, replace them.

13. Replace all worn or damaged parts. When assembling the transfer case, coat all moving parts with recommended lubricant.

TRANSFER CASE ASSEMBLY

1. When replacing the control shaft oil seal or input gear oil seal, drive out the spring pin from the transmission control shaft change shifter and remove the adapter from the transfer case. Remove the seals and press fit new ones in position.

2. Assemble the adapter to the transfer case using a new gasket. Before tightening the mounting bolts, install the change shifter over the control shaft. Adapter mounting bolt torque is 22–30 ft.·lbs.

3. Press fit the bearing into the input gear. Make sure the bearing turns freely after installation. Install the snapring over the front end of the input gear. Use the thickest snapring that will fit in the groove (5 sizes are available). Press fit the 2 bearings over the front output shaft, make sure they turn freely.

4. Install the bearing on the rear output shaft and make sure the bearing turns freely. Mount the stop plate and install the 2WD–4WD clutch hub and sleeve. Make sure they are installed facing in the proper direction. Mount the steel ball on the rear output shaft and mount the sprocket sleeve.

5. Install the 2 needle berarings on the sprocket sleeve and mount the drive sprocket. After installing the steel balls and the sprocket spacer, press fit the ball bearing into the inner race, make sure it moves freely.

6. Tighten the mainshaft locknut and lock the tab with a punch. Install the needle bearing, the thrust washer and the low speed gear on the rear output shaft from the front end.

7. Install the H–L clutch hub, making sure it is facing in the proper direction. Mount the H–L snapring using the thickest one that will fit in the groove (5 sizes are available). Insert the input gear assembly into the transfer case and mount the snapring. Once again using the thickest ring possible.

8. Insert the needle bearing into the input gear. Install the H–L clutch sleeve and shift fork (sleeve facing in proper direction). Install the 2WD–4WD shift rail.

9. Securely engage the chain with the front and rear output shaft sprockets. Assemble the 2WD–4WD clutch sleeve with the 2WD–4WD shift fork and install the assembly over the shift rail while, at the same time, mount the rear and front input shafts, chain assembly.

10. Install the 2 spring retainers and spring on the 2WD–4WD shift rail and secure with the snapring.

11. Install the 2 needle bearings and spacer into the counter gear. Install the assembly in the transfer case with the thrust washers in place. Insert the counter shaft and locking plate.

12. Install the side cover and gasket. Install the oil guide. Install the chain cover and gasket and make sure that the oilguide end fits in the chain cover opening.

13. Install the snapring in the groove of the rear output shaft bearing. Insert the interlock plunger. Insert the H–L shift rail and pass it through the shift fork. The shift fork must be to the 4WD side or the shift rail cannot be inserted.

14. Install the 2 poppet balls and 2 springs and mount the seal plug. The smaller end of the spring goes toward the ball.

15. Align the H–L shift fork and rail holes and install the spring pin. Install the spring pin with its center slit placed on the center line of the shift rail.

16. Install the spacer on the rear end of the rear output shaft bearing and install the rear cover and gasket. Check endplay and use a thicker or thinner spacer as needed.

17. Install the wave spring washer on the rear end of the front output shaft rear bearing and install the cover and gasket. Install the speedometer sleeve assembly and secure. Install the switch and ball. Install the neutral plungers and springs in the hole on top of the adapter and tighten the seal plug. Install the steel ball, resistance spring and plug.

Specifications

TORQUE SPECIFICATIONS

Part	ft. lbs.	Nm
Pulse rotor installation bolt	11–15	15–22
Pulse generator bolt	7–9	10–12
Adapter to transfer case mounting bolts and nuts	22–30	30–42
Chain cover bolt	22–30	30–42
Side cover bolt	5–7	8–10
Rear cover bolt	11–15	15–22
Cover bolt	11–15	15–22
Control housing bolt	11–15	15–22
Oil filler plug	22–25	30–35
Drain plug	22–25	30–35

TORQUE SPECIFICATIONS

Part	ft. lbs.	Nm
Select plunger plug	22–25	30–35
Lock plate bolt	11–15	15–22
Rear output shaft locknut	72–94	100–130
Speedometer sleeve clamp bolt	11–15	15–22
Seal plug	22–30	30–42
4WD indicator light switch	22	30
Transfer mounting bracket to transmission	13–18	18–25
Transfer mounting bracket to body	13–18	18–25
Gear shift lever assembly		
Control housing to transfer case	11–15	15–22
Control housing cover to control housing	7–9	10–12

TRANSFER CASE ENDPLAY SPECIFICATIONS

Assembly	Specification in. (mm.)
Input gear endplay	0–0.002 (0–0.06)
High-Low clutch hub endplay	0–0.003 (0–0.08)
Output shaft bearing endplay	0–0.004 (0–0.1)

ISUZU

Trouble Diagnosis

SLIPS OUT OF GEAR (HIGH-LOW)

1. Shifting poppet spring weak.
2. Bearing broken or worn.
3. Shifting fork bent.
4. Improper control rod adjustment.

HARD SHIFTING

1. Lack of lubricant.
2. Shift lever binding on shaft.
3. Shifting poppet ball scored.
4. Shifting fork bent.
5. Low tire pressure.

BACKLASH

1. Companion yoke loose.
2. Transfer case loose on mounts.
3. Internal parts excessively worn.

NOISY

1. Low lubricant level.
2. Bearings improperly adjusted or excessively worn.
3. Gears worn or damaged.
4. Improper alignment of driveshafts or U-joints.

OIL LEAKAGE

1. Excessive amount of lubricant in case.
2. Vent clogged.
3. Gaskets or seals leaking.
4. Bearings loose or damaged.
5. Driveshaft yoke mating surfaces scored.

OVERHEATING

1. Excessive or insufficient amount of lubricant.
2. Bearing adjustment too tight.

Removal and Installation

TRANSFER CASE REMOVAL

1. Raise and safely support the vehicle.
2. Drain the oil from the transmission and transfer case.
3. Remove all electrical connections and shifter lever assemblies from the transmission/transfer case.
4. Remove the exhaust system as needed.
5. Matchmark and remove the front and rear driveshafts.
6. Support the transmission/transfer case with a suitable transmission jack or equivalent and remove all brackets, support members and case protector.
7. Disconnect the speedometer cable or pulse generator.
8. Remove all necessary components to gain access to transmission/transfer case retaining bolts. Remove all retaining bolts and transmission/transfer case assembly.

9. Lower the supported transmission/transfer case asembly and tilt assembly to remove from the vehicle.

10. Remove the transfer case from the transmission assembly.

TRANSFER CASE INSTALLATION

1. Align transfer case with transmission. Install the transfer case assembly to transmission.

2. Torque the transfer case retaining bolts to specifications. Install the supported transmission/transfer case to the vehicle.

3. Install all necessary components that were removed to gain access to transmission/transfer case retaining bolts.

4. Reconnect the speedometer cable or pulse generator.

5. Install all brackets, support members and case protector. Remove the transmission jack or equivalent.

6. Install the front and rear driveshafts in the correct positions.

7. Install the exhaust system as required.

8. Install all electrical connections and shifter lever assembly to the transmission/transfer case assembly.

9. Refill the transmission and transfer case with the correct amount of the specified oil. Lower the vehicle.

10. Road test the vehicle through each gear range to check for proper operation.

Before Disassembly

Cleanliness is an important factor in the overhaul of the transfer case. Before opening up this unit, the entire outside of the transfer case should be cleaned, preferably with a high pressure washer such as a car wash spray unit. During inspection and reassembly all parts should be thoroughly cleaned with solvent then dried with compressed air. Wiping cloths and rags should not be used to dry parts.

Wheel bearing grease, long used to hold thrust washers and lube parts, should not be used. Lube seals with clean transaxle oil and use ordinary unmedicated petroleum jelly to hold the thrust washers and to ease the assembly of seals, since it will not leave a harmful residue as grease often will. Do not use solvent on neoprene seals, if they are to be reused, or thrust washers.

Before installing bolts into aluminum parts, always dip the threads into clean transmission oil. Antiseize compound can also be used to prevent bolts from galling the aluminum and seizing. Always use a torque wrench to keep from stripping the threads. The internal snaprings should be expanded and the external rings should be compressed, if they are to be reused. This will help insure proper seating when installed.

TRANSFER CASE DISASSEMBLY

1. Remove the 3 bolts retaining the lock plate.

2. Remove the distance piece below the lock plate.

3. Lightly tap the transfer countershaft assembly out through the fitting hole in the case.

4. From the transfer countershaft, remove the O-ring, thrust washer, countergear, needle roller bearings and thrust washer.

5. Remove the spacer, needle roller bearing and the high/low sleeve from the output shaft.

6. Expand the rear output shaft front bearing snapring and remove the output shaft assembly foreward.

7. Remove the 1⅝ in. (41mm) nut from the output shaft.

8. Using a bench press and special tool J–22912–01 or equivalent, press the bearing off of the front of the input shaft.

9. Remove the spacer, speedometer drive gear and the distance piece.

10. Using a bench press and special tool J–22912–01 or equivalent, press the bearing off of the center of the input shaft.

11. Remove the thrust washer, output gear, needle roller bearing and the 4 × 2/4 × 4 sleeve.

TRANSFER SIDE CASE DISASSEMBLY

1. Remove the detent spring and detent ball.

2. Remove the 2 screw plugs.

3. Remove the spring pin from the shift arm and drive the shift rod toward the output side of the case, remove the shift rods.

4. Remove the 4 × 2/4 × 4 shift arm and shift block.

5. Remove the high/low shift arm.

6. Remove the dowel pin.

7. Position the idler gear shaft by turning in a bolt in the threaded hole at the end of the idler shaft, then remove the thrust washers, idler gear and needle bearing.

8. Remove the 2 thrust washers.

9. Remove the front output shaft cover, then remove the distance piece

10. Set the special tool J–8614–01 or equivalent, to the flanged portion of the front output shaft and loosen and remove the

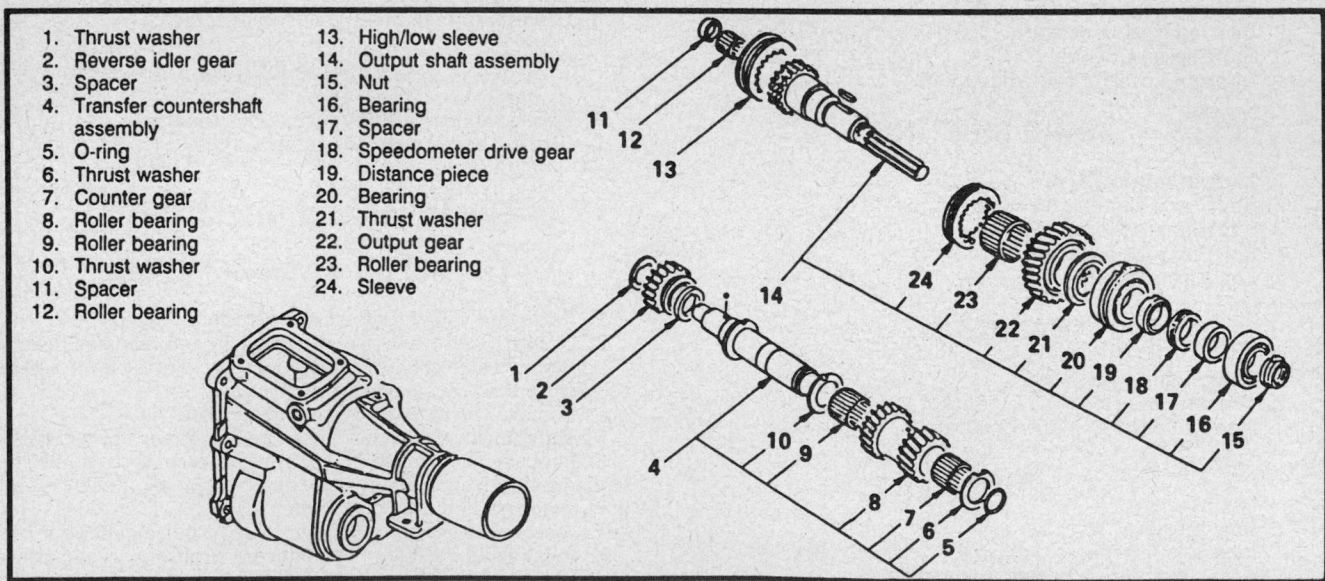

1. Thrust washer
2. Reverse idler gear
3. Spacer
4. Transfer countershaft assembly
5. O-ring
6. Thrust washer
7. Counter gear
8. Roller bearing
9. Roller bearing
10. Thrust washer
11. Spacer
12. Roller bearing
13. High/low sleeve
14. Output shaft assembly
15. Nut
16. Bearing
17. Spacer
18. Speedometer drive gear
19. Distance piece
20. Bearing
21. Thrust washer
22. Output gear
23. Roller bearing
24. Sleeve

Exploded view of transfer case—Isuzu

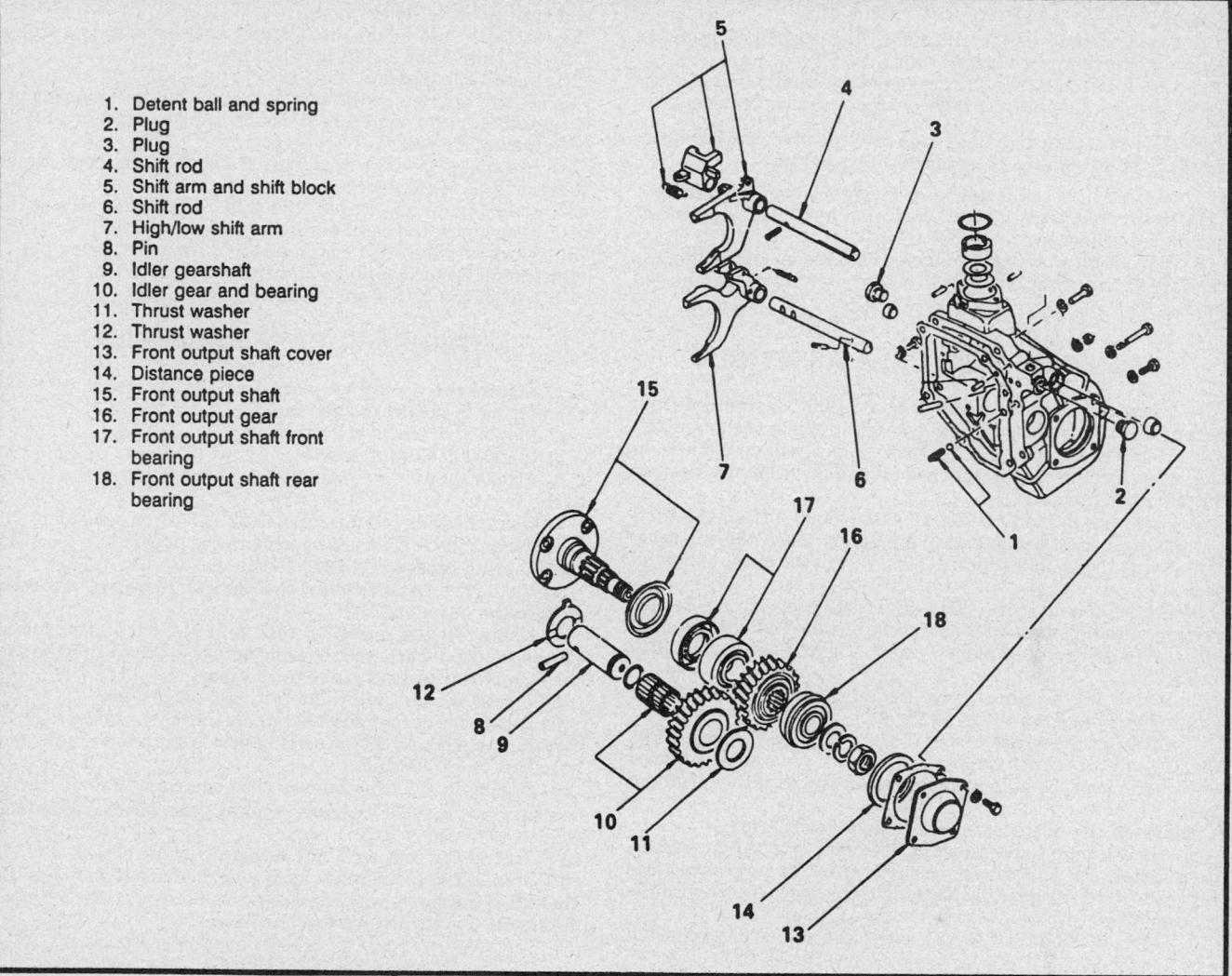

1. Detent ball and spring
2. Plug
3. Plug
4. Shift rod
5. Shift arm and shift block
6. Shift rod
7. High/low shift arm
8. Pin
9. Idler gearshaft
10. Idler gear and bearing
11. Thrust washer
12. Thrust washer
13. Front output shaft cover
14. Distance piece
15. Front output shaft
16. Front output gear
17. Front output shaft front bearing
18. Front output shaft rear bearing

Exploded view of transfer side case—Isuzu

shaft nut spring washer and plain washer.

11. Remove the front output gear.

12. Using special tools J–29040 and J–8092, remove the front output shaft front and rear bearings

CLEANING AND INSPECTION

Cleaning

During overhaul, all components of the transfer case (except bearing assemblies) should be thoroughly cleaned with solvent and dried with air pressure prior to inspection and reassembly. Be sure all gasket sealing material is cleaned off of the case, cover plates and mounting flanges.

Proper cleaning of bearings is of utmost importance. Bearings should always be cleaned separately from other parts.

Soak all bearing assemblies in clean solvent or fuel oil. Bearings should never be cleaned in a hot solution tank. Wash the bearings in solvent until all old lubricant is loosened. Hold races so that bearings will not rotate; then clean bearings with a soft bristled brush until all dirt has been removed. Remove loose particles of dirt by tapping bearing flat against a block of wood. Rinse bearings in clean solvent; then blow bearings dry with air pressure.

— **CAUTION** —
Do not spin bearings while drying.

After drying, rotate each bearing slowly while examining balls or rollers for roughness, damage, or excessive wear. Replace all bearings that are not in first class condition. After cleaning and inspecting bearings lubricate generously with recommended lubricant, then wrap each bearing in clean paper until ready for reassembly.

Inspection

1. Inspect all parts for discoloration or warpage.

2. Examine all gears and splines for chipped, worn, broken or nicked teeth. Small nicks or burrs may be removed with a fine abrasive stone.

3. Inspect the breather assembly to make sure that it is open and not damaged.

4. Check all threaded parts for damaged, stripped, or crossed threads.

5. Replace all gaskets, oil seals and snaprings.

6. Inspect housings, retainers and covers for cracks or other damage. Replace the damaged parts.

7. Inspect keys and keyways for condition and fit.

8. Inspect shift forks for wear, distortion or any other damage.

9. Check detent ball springs for free length, compressed length, distortion or collapsed coils.

10. Check bearing fit on their respective shafts and in their bores or cups. Inspect bearings, shafts and cups for wear.

NOTE: If either the bearings or cups are worn or damaged, it is advisable to replace both parts.

11. Inspect all bearing rollers or balls for pitting or galling.

12. Examine detent balls for corrosion or brinneling. If shift bar detents show wear, replace them.

13. Replace all worn or damaged parts. When assembling the transfer case, coat all moving parts with recommended lubricant.

TRANSFER SIDE CASE ASSEMBLY

1. Using special tools J–29040 and J–8092, install the front output shaft rear bearing deep enough to touch the snapring.

2. Install the output gear, so that the end without splines (on the inner circumference) is turned toward the front side (toward output shaft flange).

3. Using special tools J–29040 and J–8092, install the front output shaft front bearing deep enough to touch the snapring.

4. Using tool J–29037 and J–8092 install the output shaft oil seal.

5. Set the special tool J–8614–01 or equivalent, to the flanged portion of the front output shaft and install. Tighten the shaft nut spring washer and plain washer. Tighten the nut to 101–116 ft. lbs.

6. Install the distance piece. Install the output shaft cover and tighten the bolts to 18–22 ft. lbs.

7. Apply grease to both faces of the idler gear thrust washer, then install the thrust washer, with the oil grooved face turned toward the gear, by aligning the stopper finger with the groove in the case.

8. Install the idler gear and needle roller bearing.

9. Apply grease to both faces of the idler gear thrust washer, then install the 2nd thrust washer, with the oil grooved face turned toward the gear, by aligning the stopper finger with the groove in the case.

10. Coat the idler shaft O-ring with clean engine oil and install the idler gear shaft by aligning the dowel groove in the idler shaft with the dowel pin hole.

11. Install the dowel pin into the case and check that its projection is within 0.355–0.433 in. (9–11mm).

12. Install the high/low shift arm.

13. Attach the range shift arm so that the slit in the spring pin is turned. Attach and secure the shift arm shift rod in position with the spring pin.

14. Assemble the shift arm with the shift block, then attach the gear lock release spring.

15. Insert the interlock pin, the shift rod detent ball and the detent spring in the case. Insert and secure the shift arm, the shift block and the shift rod in position with the spring pin.

16. Install the screw plugs and tighten to 33–40 ft. lbs.

17. Install the detent spring and detent ball.

TRANSFER CASE ASSEMBLY

1. Attach the $4 \times 2/4 \times 4$ sleeve, so that the side with the chamfering is turned to the rear.

2. Install the needle roller bearing.

3. Install the output gear.

4. Attach the thrust washer, so that the oil groove is turned to the front.

5. Using bearing installer tool J–22912–01 or equivalent, attach the output shaft front bearing to the output shaft, so that the snapring groove is turned to the rear.

6. Install the distance piece, speedometer drive gear and spacer onto the output shaft.

7. Using bearing installer tool J–22912–01 or equivalent, press the output shaft rear bearing onto the output shaft so that the face of the seal is turned to the rear.

8. Install the nut and tighten to 101–116 ft. lbs.

9. Install the output shaft assembly into the transfer case, insert the snapring on the transfer case into the groove in the output shaft front bearing.

10. Assemble the components onto the countershaft: thrust washer, needle roller bearing, counter gear, needle roller bearing, thrust washer and O-ring.

11. Install the counter shaft assembly in the case.

12. Install the range shaft sleeve on the output shaft, so that the end of the sleeve with the heavy chamfering on the outer circumference is turned toward the front.

Specifications

TORQUE SPECIFICATIONS

Part	ft. lbs.
Transfer case front cover retaining bolts	13.7
Transfer flange retaining bolt	100
Rear case cover	27.5
Switch assembly	29
Input gear locknut	101.2
Transfercase-to-transmission Retaining bolts	27.5

MAZDA

Trouble Diagnosis

SLIPS OUT OF GEAR (HIGH-LOW)

1. Shifting poppet spring weak.
2. Bearing broken or worn.
3. Shifting fork bent.
4. Improper control rod adjustment.

HARD SHIFTING

1. Lack of lubricant.
2. Shift lever binding on shaft.
3. Shifting poppet ball scored.
4. Shifting fork bent.
5. Low tire pressure.

BACKLASH

1. Companion yoke loose.
2. Transfer case loose on mounts.
3. Internal parts excessively worn.

NOISY

1. Low lubricant level.
2. Bearings improperly adjusted or excessively worn.
3. Gears worn or damaged.
4. Improper alignment of driveshafts or U-joints.

OIL LEAKAGE

1. Excessive amount of lubricant in case.
2. Vent clogged.
3. Gaskets or seals leaking.
4. Bearings loose or damaged.
5. Driveshaft yoke mating surfaces scored.

OVERHEATING

1. Excessive or insufficient amount of lubricant.
2. Bearing adjustment too tight.

Removal and Installation

TRANSFER CASE REMOVAL

1. Raise and safely support the vehicle.
2. Drain the oil from the transmission and transfer case.
3. Remove all electrical connections and shifter lever assemblies from the transmission/transfer case.
4. Remove the exhaust system as needed.
5. Matchmark and remove the front and rear driveshafts.
6. Support the transmission/transfer case with a suitable transmission jack or equivalent and remove all brackets, support members and case protector.
7. Disconnect the speedometer cable or pulse generator.
8. Remove all necessary components to gain access to transmission/transfer case retaining bolts. Remove all retaining bolts and transmission/transfer case assembly.
9. Lower the supported transmission/transfer case assembly and tilt assembly to remove from the vehicle.
10. Remove the transfer case from the transmission assembly.

TRANSFER CASE INSTALLATION

1. Align transfer case with transmission. Install the transfer case assembly to transmission.
2. Torque the transfer case retaining bolts to specifications. Install the supported transmission/transfer case to the vehicle.
3. Install all necessary components that were removed to gain access to transmission/transfer case retaining bolts.
4. Reconnect the speedometer cable or pulse generator.
5. Install all brackets, support members and case protector. Remove the transmission jack or equivalent.
6. Install the front and rear driveshafts in the correct positions.
7. Install the exhaust system as required.
8. Install all electrical connections and shifter lever assembly to the transmission/transfer case assembly.
9. Refill the transmission and transfer case with the correct amount of the specified oil. Lower the vehicle.
10. Road test the vehicle through each gear range to check for proper operation.

Before Disassembly

Cleanliness is an important factor in the overhaul of the transfer case. Before opening up this unit, the entire outside of the transfer case should be cleaned, preferably with a high pressure washer such as a car wash spray unit. During inspection and reassembly all parts should be thoroughly cleaned with solvent then dried with compressed air. Wiping cloths and rags should not be used to dry parts.

Wheel bearing grease, long used to hold thrust washers and lube parts, should not be used. Lube seals with clean transaxle oil and use ordinary unmedicated petroleum jelly to hold the thrust washers and to ease the assembly of seals, since it will not leave a harmful residue as grease often will. Do not use solvent on neoprene seals, if they are to be reused, or thrust washers.

Before installing bolts into aluminum parts, always dip the threads into clean transmission oil. Antiseize compound can also be used to prevent bolts from galling the aluminum and seizing. Always use a torque wrench to keep from stripping the threads. The internal snaprings should be expanded and the external rings should be compressed, if they are to be reused. This will help insure proper seating when installed.

TRANSFER CASE DISASSEMBLY

1. Remove the 2 stopper pins.
2. Hold the companion flange with special tool 49S120710 coupling flange holder and remove the companion flange nut.
3. Remove the companion flange by lightly tapping the backside with a plastic hammer.
4. Remove the 4 × 4 indicator switch, pin, plugs, detent springs and balls.
5. Remove the speedometer drive gear.
6. Remove the snapring from the end of the input shaft.
7. Using special tool 490839425C or equivalent, remove the outer bearing.
8. Position the flat section of the input shaft gear toward the countershaft gear then, remove the input shaft gear and bearing.
9. Using a plastic hammer, separate the chain cover from the transfer case and remove the chain cover.

NOTE: Lift the chain cover vertically to prevent damaging the shift rods.

10. Remove the speedometer drive gear from the output shaft, then, remove the knock pin and bearing.
11. Remove the oil passage by lightly tapping with a plastic hammer.
12. Tap out the spring pin and remove the H–L shift rod, spacer and shift fork.

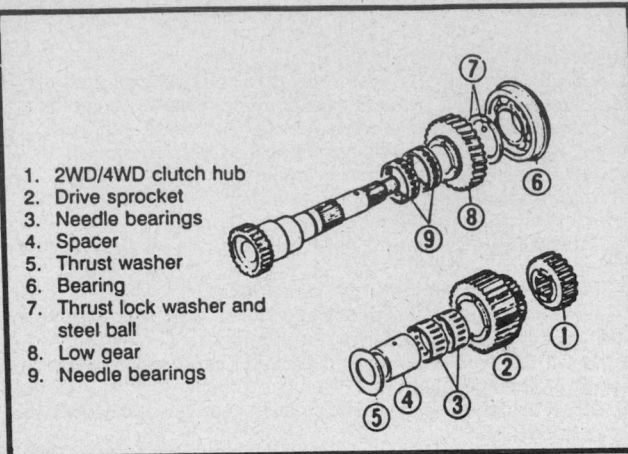

1. 2WD/4WD clutch hub
2. Drive sprocket
3. Needle bearings
4. Spacer
5. Thrust washer
6. Bearing
7. Thrust lock washer and steel ball
8. Low gear
9. Needle bearings

Output shaft components

13. Tap out the spring pin and remove the 2WD–4WD shift rod assembly, spacer and 2WD–4WD shift end.
14. Tap out the spring pins and remove the retainers, 2WD–4WD shift fork, spring and spacer. Remove the pin for the 4 × 4 indicator switch from the rod.
15. Using a magnet, remove the pin and interlock pin from the chain cover.
16. Set the input gear on the output shaft.
17. Remove the output shaft and the front drive sprocket from the transfer case housing by lightly tapping on the input shaft gear and the front drive sprocket with a plastic hammer.
18. Remove the input shaft gear from the transfer case housing.
19. Remove the lock plate.
20. Tap out the countershaft gear support using a punch and hammer.
21. Remove the counter gear and thrust washers.
22. Remove the needle bearings and spacer from the countershaft gear.
23. Remove the O-ring from the countershaft.
24. Using a press and special tool 49G030370, press the output shaft assembly apart.
25. Remove the parts from the output shaft in the sequence shown below.
26. Using bearing puller set 490839425C or equivalent, remove the bearings from both sides of the front drive sprocket.
27. Remove the oil seals.
28. Remove the snapring.
29. Using special tool 49F401331 or equivalent, press the front sprocket bearing out of the housing.

CLEANING AND INSPECTION

Cleaning

During overhaul, all components of the transfer case (except bearing assemblies) should be thoroughly cleaned with solvent and dried with air pressure prior to inspection and reassembly. Be sure all gasket sealing material is cleaned off of the case, cover plates and mounting flanges.

Proper cleaning of bearings is of utmost importance. Bearings should always be cleaned separately from other parts.

Soak all bearing assemblies in clean solvent or fuel oil. Bearings should never be cleaned in a hot solution tank. Wash the bearings in solvent until all old lubricant is loosened. Hold races so that bearings will not rotate; then clean bearings with a soft bristled brush until all dirt has been removed. Remove loose particles of dirt by tapping bearing flat against a block of wood. Rinse bearings in clean solvent; then blow bearings dry with air pressure.

— CAUTION —
Do not spin bearings while drying.

After drying, rotate each bearing slowly while examining balls or rollers for roughness, damage, or excessive wear. Replace all bearings that are not in first class condition. After cleaning and inspecting bearings, lubricate generously with recommended lubricant, then wrap each bearing in clean paper until ready for reassembly.

Inspection

1. Inspect all parts for discoloration or warpage.
2. Examine all gears and splines for chipped, worn, broken or nicked teeth. Small nicks or burrs may be removed with a fine abrasive stone.
3. Inspect the breather assembly to make sure that it is open and not damaged.
4. Check all threaded parts for damaged, stripped, or crossed threads.
5. Replace all gaskets, oil seals and snaprings.
6. Inspect housings, retainers and covers for cracks or other damage. Replace the damaged parts.
7. Inspect keys and keyways for condition and fit.
8. Inspect shift forks for wear, distortion or any other damage.
9. Check detent ball springs for free length, compressed length, distortion or collapsed coils.
10. Check bearing fit on their respective shafts and in their bores or cups. Inspect bearings, shafts and cups for wear.

NOTE: If either the bearings or cups are worn or damaged, it is advisable to replace both parts.

11. Inspect all bearing rollers or balls for pitting or galling.
12. Examine detent balls for corrosion or brinneling. If shift bar detents show wear, replace them.
13. Replace all worn or damaged parts. When assembling the transfer case, coat all moving parts with recommended lubricant.

TRANSFER CASE ASSEMBLY

1. Using tool 490727415 or equivalent, press the front drive sprocket bearing into the transfer case housing. Install the snapring and secure the bearing.
2. Apply oil to the lip of the oil seal and install the seal into the transfer case housing, using tool 490727415 or equivalent.
3. Apply oil to the lip of the oil seal and install the seal into the chain cover, using tool 490727415 or equivalent.
4. Using tool 490727415 or equivalent, press the bearings on both sides of the front drive sprocket. Press the bearings against the drive sprocket stops.
5. Install the lower gear on the output shaft. Lubricate the needle bearing assembly with oil and set it on the shaft.
6. Set the steel ball in the shaft and install the thrust lock washer.
7. Using special tool 490727415 or equivalent, press the bearing on the output shaft.
8. Install the counter gear as follows:
   a. While lubricating the contact surface of the thrust washer and the housing, install the washer so that the dished (convex) part of the washer sets down into the housing.
   b. Lubricate the needle bearings with oil, then install them and the spacer in the counter gear.
   c. Install the couner gear in the housing.
   d. Lubricate a new O-ring with oil and install it on the countershaft.
   e. Center the inside needle bearing and slide the counter shaft into the case.
   f. Install the lock plate and tighten the bolt to 14–19 ft. lbs.
9. Install the input shaft as follows:

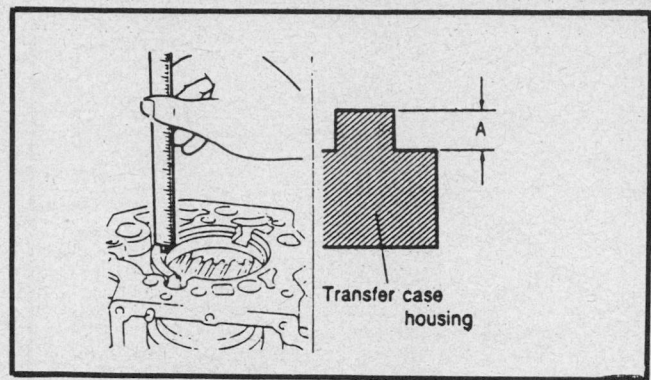
Measuring the bearing bore depth

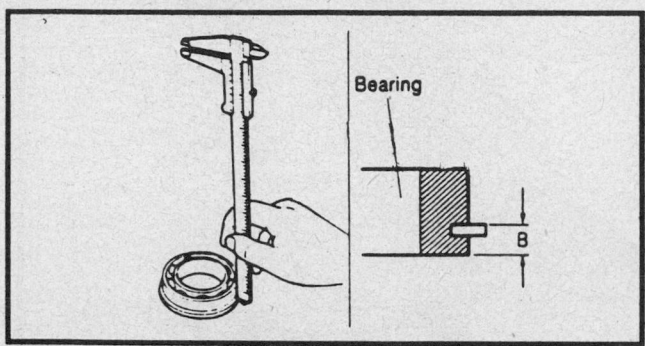
Measuring the bearing height

a. Measure the bearing bore depth **A** of the housing with vernier calipers.

b. Measure the height **B** of the bearing clip with vernier calipers and a surface plate.

c. Calculate the difference between measurement **A** and **B** to determine the clearance. The formula looks like this:

Difference (Clearance) = A - B

d. Select and install the proper shim to obtain a clearance of 0–0.004 in. (0–0.1mm).

e. Using tool 490727415 or equivalent, press the bearing onto the input shaft gear. Install the snapring.

f. Install the input shaft assembly in the housing by lightly tapping the outer race of the bearing with a plastic hammer.

10. Install the needle bearing and the H–L hub sleeve onto the input shaft.

NOTE: To identify the high/low sleeve from the 2WD–4WD sleeve, the thickness of the high/low hub sleeve is 0.83 in. (21mm) and the 2WD–4WD hub sleeve is 0.71 in. (18mm).

11. Install the output shaft in the housing by lightly tapping the outer race of the bearing with a plastic hammer.

12. Set the thrust washer on the output shaft.

13. Lubricate the needle bearings with oil and install them onto the drive sprocket along with the spacer.

14. Install the chain on the drive sprocket assembly and the front drive sprocket and expand the chain using special tool 49S231395 to set the center to center distance for easy installation into the housing.

NOTE: Be careful not to overtighten the chain expansion tool.

15. Install the front drive sprocket assembly into the housing by lightly tapping it with a plastic hammer, while keeping the chain horizontal. After installing, check that the chain rotates smoothly.

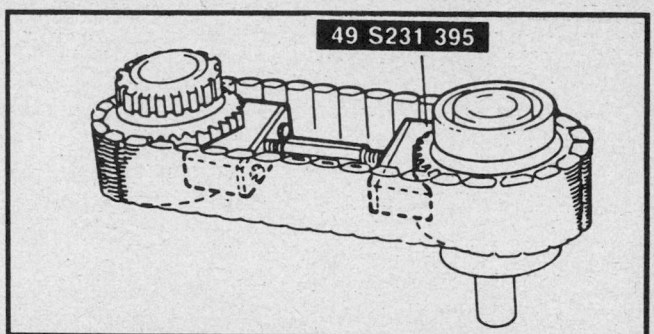
Using tool to install the chain onto the drive sprockets

Measuring for shim selection

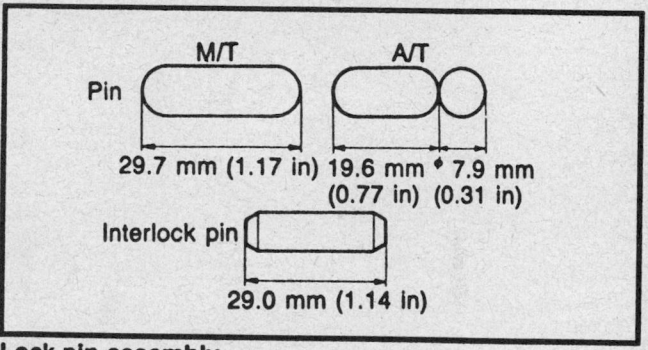
Lock pin assembly

16. Using tool 49 0500 330 or equivalent, tap in the 2WD–4WD clutch hub.

17. Install the 2WD–4WD shift fork onto the shift rod as follows:

a. Slide the retainer on the shift rod and secure it with the spring pin.

b. Install the 0.79 in. (20mm) spacer, spring, 2WD–4WD shift fork and the other retainer.

c. Secure the retainer with the spring pin.

18. Assemble the 2WD–4WD hub sleeve to the shift fork and insert them to the transfer case housing.

19. Set the 2WD–4WD shift fork and the 0.79 in. (20mm) spacer into the case and slide the shift rod assembly through it.

20. Secure the 2WD–4WD shift end to the rod with the spring pin.

21. Install the high/low shift fork, 1.46 in. (37mm) spacer and the rod in the transfer case housing.

22. Secure the high/low shift fork with the spring pin.

23. Install the bearing on the output shaft.

24. Measure the bearing height and the bearing bore depth for

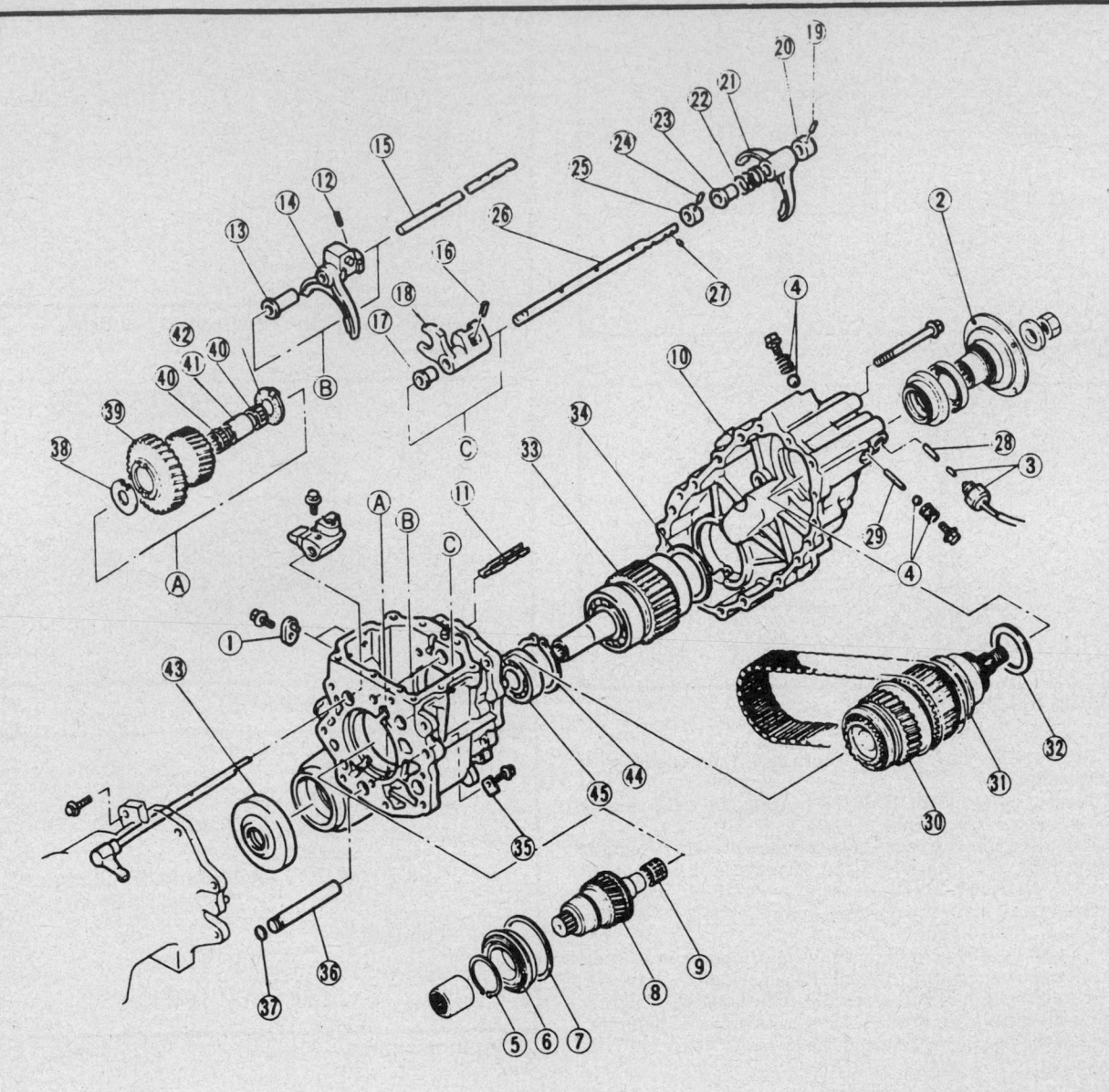

1. Stopper pin
2. Companion flange
3. 4WD indicator switch and pin
4. Detent ball and spring
5. Snapring
6. Bearing
7. Shim
8. Input shaft gear
9. Bearing
10. Chain cover
11. Oil passage
12. Spring pin
13. Spacer
14. H-L shift fork

15. H-L shift rod
16. Pin
17. Spacer
18. 2WD-4WD shift end
19. Pin
20. Retainer
21. 2WD-4WD shift fork
22. Spring
23. Spacer
24. Pin
25. Retainer
26. 2Wd-4WD shift rod
27. Pin
28. Pin
29. Interlock pin
30. Output shaft assembly

31. Chain
32. Shim
33. Front drive sprocket assembly
34. Shim
35. Lock plate
36. Countershaft
37. O-ring
38. Thrust washer
39. Countergear
40. Bearing
41. Spacer
42. Thrust washer
43. Oil seal
44. Snapring
45. Bearing

Exploded view of transfer case – Mazda

the output shaft using the shim selector gauge set tool 49U0173A0.

25. Put the 2 pieces of the gauge set together and measure the clearance.

26. Select the proper adjusting shim to adjust the clearance to 0–0.004 in. (0–0.1mm).

27. Repeat the procedures above and select the correct size shim(s) for the front drive sprocket.

28. Apply grease to the adjusting shims selected and place them in the chain cover.

29. Install the knock pin in the output shaft and install the speedometer drive gear.

30. Install the oil passage in the case.

31. Apply grease to the ball (automatic transmission only), pin and interlock pin and install them in the chain cover.

32. Apply grease to the pin and install it in the 2WD–4WD shift rod.

33. Apply RTV to the mating surface of the chain cover and set the cover on the housing.

34. Apply sealant to the threads of the bolts and tighten to 14–19 ft. lbs.

35. Apply sealant to the threads of the plugs. Install the balls, springs and plugs. Tighten the plugs to 14–19 ft. lbs.

36. Install the pin and the 4 × 4 indicator switch and tighten to tighten to 18–25 ft. lbs.

37. Install the speedometer gear and tighten the hold down bolt to 69–95 inch lbs.

38. Check that the transfer case shifts smoothly using a tool to move the shift forks.

39. Install the companion flanges as follows:
   a. Apply sealant to the splines of the companion flange.
   b. Install the companion flange on the shaft by lightly tapping with a plastic hammer.
   c. Use a new locknut and tighten the flange. Hold the flange with special tool 49S120710 or equivalent, then torque to 94–130 ft lbs.

40. Apply sealant to the contact surfaces of the stopper pins and install them with new O-rings.

Specifications

TORQUE SPECIFICATIONS

Part	ft. lbs.	Nm
Transfer chain cover to housing	14–19	19–26
Plug	14–19	19–26
Indicator switch	18–25	25–34
Speedometer gear	5.8–8.0	7.8–11
Flange retaining nut	94–130	128–177

OUTPUT SHAFT ADJUSTING SHIM THICKNESS SHIM SELECTION

in.	mm
0.020	0.5
0.024	0.6
0.028	0.7
0.031	0.8
0.035	0.9
0.039	1.0
0.043	1.1
0.047	1.2
0.051	1.3
0.055	1.4
0.059	1.5
0.063	1.6
0.067	1.7

INPUT SHAFT ADJUSTING SHIM THICKNESS SHIM SELECTION

in.	mm.
0.28	0.7
0.032	0.8
0.035	0.9
0.039	1.0
0.043	1.1
0.047	1.2

FRONT DRIVE SPROCKET BEARING ADJUSTING SHIM THICKNESS SHIM SELECTION

in.	mm
0.020	0.5
0.024	0.6
0.028	0.7
0.031	0.8
0.035	0.9
0.039	1.0
0.043	1.1
0.047	1.2

NISSAN

Trouble Diagnosis

SLIPS OUT OF GEAR (HIGH-LOW)

1. Shifting poppet spring weak.
2. Bearing broken or worn.
3. Shifting fork bent.
4. Improper control rod adjustment.

HARD SHIFTING

1. Lack of lubricant.
2. Shift lever binding on shaft.
3. Shifting poppet ball scored.
4. Shifting fork bent.
5. Low tire pressure.

BACKLASH

1. Companion yoke loose.
2. Transfer case loose on mounts.
3. Internal parts excessively worn.

NOISY

1. Low lubricant level.
2. Bearings improperly adjusted or excessively worn.
3. Gears worn or damaged.
4. Improper alignment of driveshafts or U-joints.

OIL LEAKAGE

1. Excessive amount of lubricant in case.
2. Vent clogged.
3. Gaskets or seals leaking.
4. Bearings loose or damaged.
5. Driveshaft yoke mating surfaces scored.

OVERHEATING

1. Excessive or insufficient amount of lubricant.
2. Bearing adjustment too tight.

Removal and Installation

TRANSFER CASE REMOVAL

1. Raise and safely support the vehicle.
2. Drain the oil from the transmission and transfer case.
3. Remove all electrical connections and shifter lever assemblies from the transmission/transfer case.
4. Remove the exhaust system as needed.
5. Matchmark and remove the front and rear driveshafts.
6. Support the transmission/transfer case with a suitable transmission jack or equivalent and remove all brackets, support members and case protector.
7. Disconnect the speedometer cable or pulse generator.
8. Remove all necessary components to gain access to transmission/transfer case retaining bolts. Remove all retaining bolts and transmission/transfer case assembly.
9. Lower the supported transmission/transfer case assembly and tilt assembly to remove from the vehicle.
10. Remove the transfer case from the transmission assembly.

TRANSFER CASE INSTALLATION

1. Align transfer case with transmission. Install the transfer case assembly to transmission.
2. Torque the transfer case retaining bolts to specifications. Install the supported transmission/transfer case to the vehicle.
3. Install all necessary components that were removed to gain access to transmission/transfer case retaining bolts.
4. Reconnect the speedometer cable or pulse generator.
5. Install all brackets, support members and case protector. Remove the transmission jack or equivalent.
6. Install the front and rear driveshafts in the correct positions.
7. Install the exhaust system as required.
8. Install all electrical connections and shifter lever assembly to the transmission/transfer case assembly.
9. Refill the transmission and transfer case with the correct amount of the specified oil. Lower the vehicle.
10. Road test the vehicle through each gear range to check for proper operation.

Before Disassembly

Cleanliness is an important factor in the overhaul of the transfer case. Before opening up this unit, the entire outside of the transfer case should be cleaned, preferably with a high pressure washer such as a car wash spray unit. During inspection and reassembly all parts should be thoroughly cleaned with solvent then dried with compressed air. Wiping cloths and rags should not be used to dry parts.

Wheel bearing grease, long used to hold thrust washers and lube parts, should not be used. Lube seals with clean transaxle oil and use ordinary unmedicated petroleum jelly to hold the thrust washers and to ease the assembly of seals, since it will not leave a harmful residue as grease often will. Do not use solvent on neoprene seals, if they are to be reused, or thrust washers.

Before installing bolts into aluminum parts, always dip the threads into clean transmission oil. Antiseize compound can also be used to prevent bolts from galling the aluminum and seizing. Always use a torque wrench to keep from stripping the threads. The internal snaprings should be expanded and the external rings should be compressed, if they are to be reused. This will help insure proper seating when installed.

TRANSFER CASE DISASSEMBLY

Shifting Forks and Fork Rods

1. Wipe off all dirt and grease from the transfer case. Drain the lubricant, if not already done.
2. Move the shift lever to the **4L** and **2H** positions, then remove the driveshaft companion flange locknuts. Remove the companion flanges and the 4WD switch.
3. Remove the front cover from the transfer case. Remove the front driveshaft and needle bearings.
4. Remove the snapring retaining the front shift fork and remove the front shift fork, spacer and coupling sleeve.
5. Remove the snapring retaining the coupling sleeve hub and remove the hub.
6. Remove the bolts that attach the front and back transfer case halves together. Tap the front case half away from the rear with a soft faced hammer. Do not pry the cases apart.
7. Remove the pin that retains the shift cross shaft. The pin is retained by a nut. Remove the nut and carefully drive the pin out with a soft drift. Remove the shift cross shaft and lever.
8. Remove the check ball plug, spring and ball. Drive out the high and low shift fork retaining pin. Tap the rear of the drive-

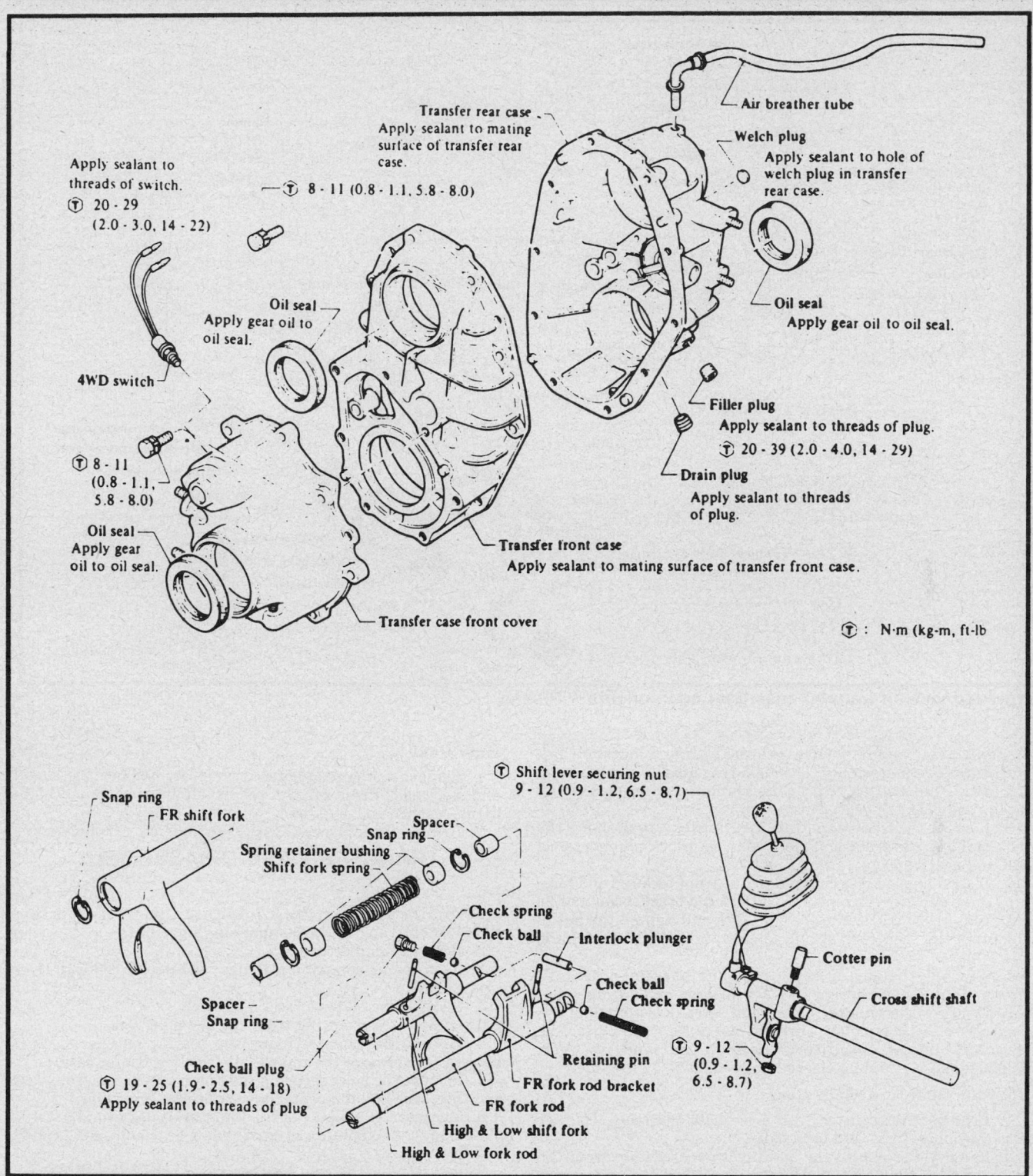

Exploded view of transfer case—Nissan

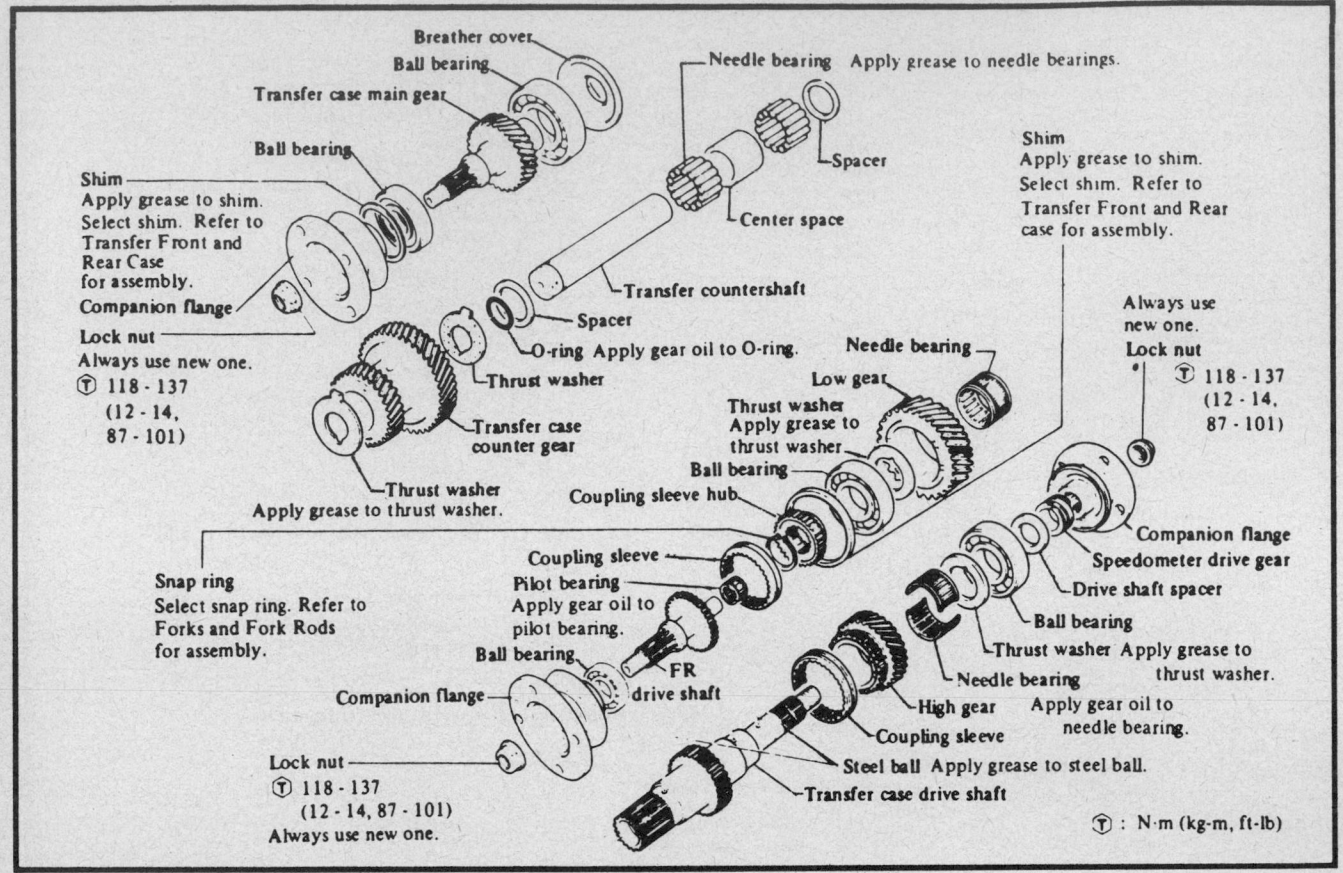

Exploded view of transfer case gear components — Nissan

shaft assembly and remove it with the high and low shift fork and counter gear assembly. The main gear assembly can now be removed. Take care not to drop the counter gear needle bearing when removing the gear.

9. Remove the front shim from the transfer case. Remove the high and low and front shift fork rods, interlock plunger, steel ball and check spring.

10. If servicing is necessary, secure the front fork rod and carefully drive out the retaining pin, the fork rod bracket can now be removed. Insert a bolt into the shift fork and tighten the nut to eliminate the shift fork spring tension. Remove the retaining snapring.

11. Remove the spring retaining bushings and shift fork spring. Separate the spring retainer bushing and spring.

12. Measure the endplay before and after disassembling the shaft. If excessive endplay is present, check for worn parts. The standard endplay specification is high gear and low gear; 0.0039–0.0079. coupling sleeve hub; 0–0.0079.

Counter Gear and Main Gear

1. Remove the transfer case driveshaft assembly, counter gear assembly, forks and fork rods.

2. Remove the main gear and breather assembly from the rear case half. Remove the main gear front bearing and/or rear bearing with a press, if service is necessary. Remove the needle bearings, center spacer and end spacers from the counter gear.

Low Gear

1. Press off the front bearing from the shaft. Remove the thrust washer and steel ball.

2. Remove the low gear and needle bearings.

High Gear

1. Remove the speedometer drive gear. Remove the spacer and steel ball. Press off the rear shaft bearing. Remove the thrust washer and steel ball.

2. Remove the high gear, needle bearings and coupling sleeve.

TRANSFER CASE DISASSEMBLY

1. While holding the companion flange with tool ST38060002, remove the companion flange nut.

2. Remove the rear case.

3. Remove the companion flange with tool ST33051001 or equivalent.

4. Remove the oil cover and oil gutter.

5. Remove the snapring from the 2–4 shift rod.

6. Remove the bolts securing the bearing retainer. This is necessary to remove the mainshaft from the center case.

7. Remove the bolts securing the center case to the front case and then separate the center case from the front case.

8. Measure the endplay of the low gear, if its beyond 0.0079–0.0256 in. (0.2–0.65mm), check the low gear and the L and H hub for wear.

9. Disassemble the center case assembly as follows:

   a. Remove the snapring from the mainshaft.

   b. Pull out the low gear with the L and H hub.

   c. Remove the needle bearing of low gear.

   d. Make sure the direction of the drive chain before removing it. (It must be reinstalled in the same direction.) Check whether the spring part of the drive chain is installed on the front or rear side.

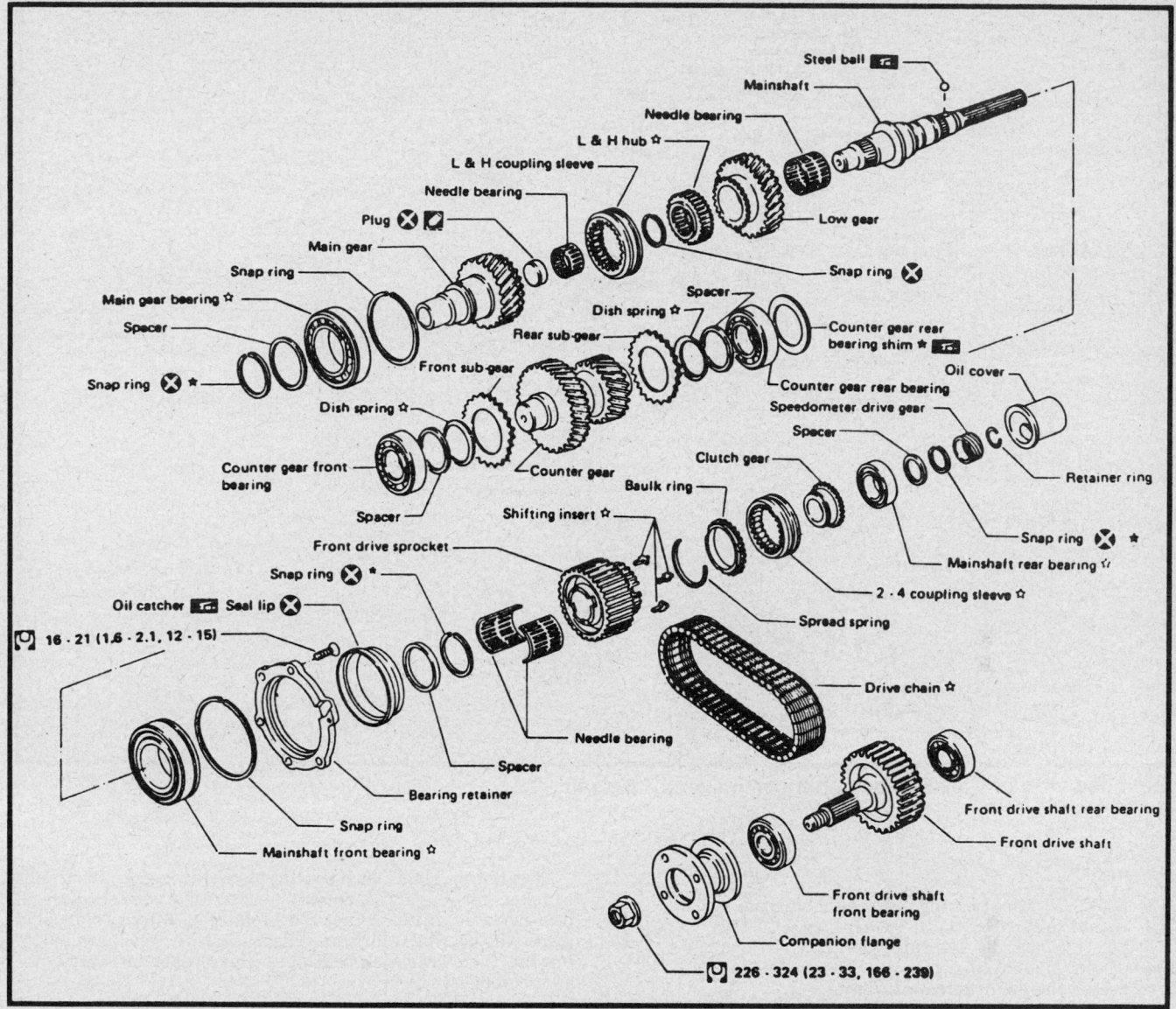

Exploded view of transfer case gear components – Nissan 1986–89

e. Remove the mainshaft, front drive and drive chain as a set by tapping the front end of the mainshaft and the front driveshaft alternately. Be careful not to bend the drive chain.

10. Disassemble the front case assembly as follows:

    a. Remove the switches, check plugs, check springs and check balls.

    b. Remove the outer shift lever.

    c. Remove the lock pin of the inner shift lever and drive out the cross shaft with plug.

    d. Remove the 2–4 shift rod.

    e. Remove the L and H shift rod and fork assembly with coupling sleeve.

    f. Remove the needle bearing from the main gear.

    g. Remove the bolts securing the front case cover and then remove the case.

    h. Remove the counter gear by tapping lighty.

    i. Remove the main gear by tapping lightly.

Unit Disassembly and Assembly

MAINSHAFT

Disassembly

1. Check the endplay of the front drive sprocket with a dial indicator. If the endplay is beyond 0.008–0.020 in. (0.2–0.5mm), check the front drive sprocket and clutch gear for wear.

2. Remove the retaining ring, speedometer drive gear and the steel ball.

3. Remove the snapring and spacer.

4. Press out the front drive sprocket with mainshaft rear bearing and clutch gear together.

5. Remove the needle bearing.

6. Remove the bearing retainer and then remove the snapring and spacer.

7. Press the mainshaft front bearing from the mainshaft.

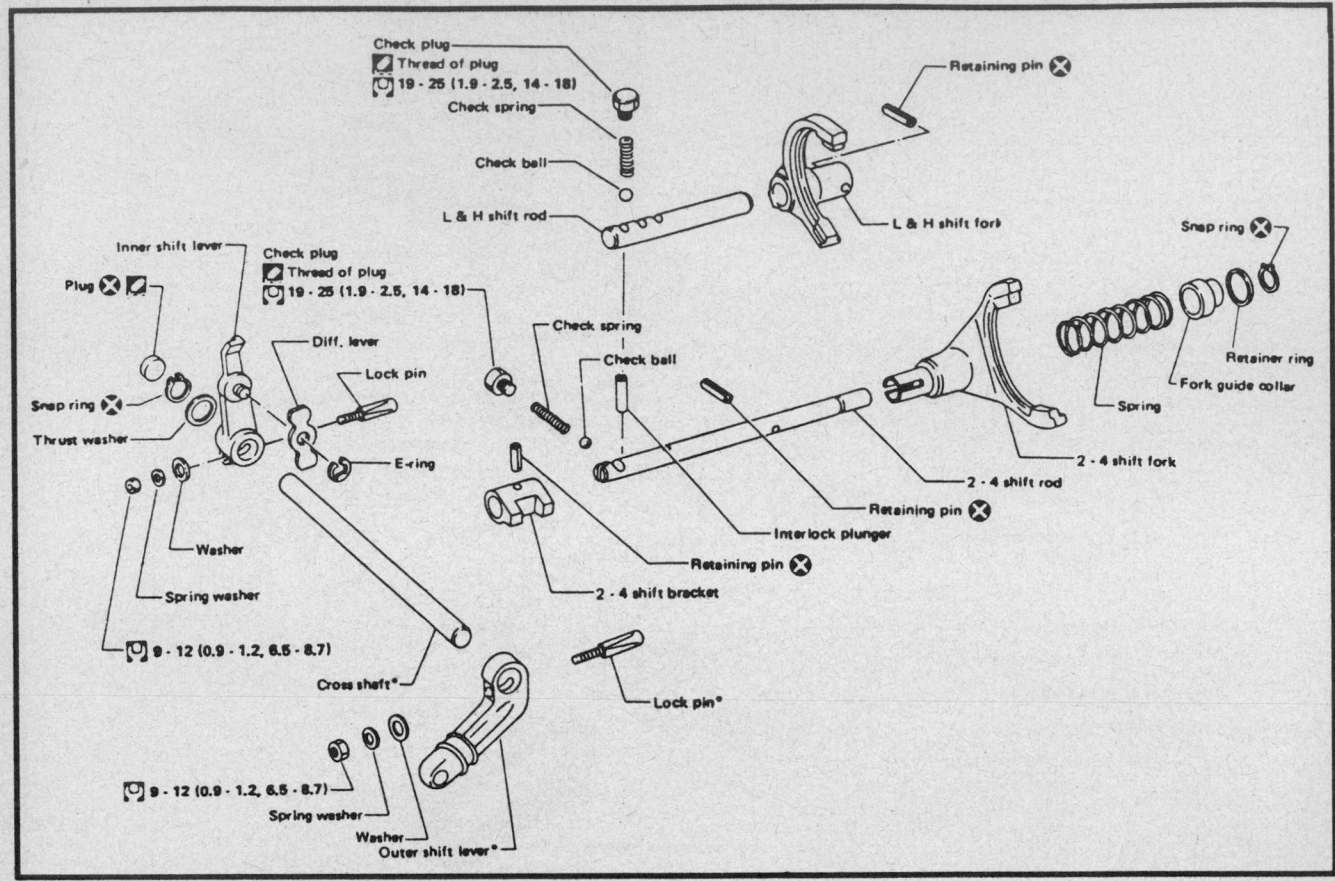

Exploded view of transfer case shift components – Nissan

Assembly

1. Press the front bearing onto the mainshaft.
2. Install the spacer.
3. Select the proper snapring from the chart to allow a clearance of 0–0.0059 in. (0–0.15mm) between the snapring.
4. Install the mainshaft in the case.

CLEANING AND INSPECTION

Cleaning

During overhaul, all components of the transfer case (except bearing assemblies) should be thoroughly cleaned with solvent and dried with air pressure prior to inspection and reassembly. Be sure all gasket sealing material is cleaned off of the case, cover plates and mounting flanges.

Proper cleaning of bearings is of utmost importance. Bearings should always be cleaned separately from other parts.

Soak all bearing assemblies in clean solvent or fuel oil. Bearings should never be cleaned in a hot solution tank. Wash the bearings in solvent until all old lubricant is loosened. Hold races so that bearings will not rotate; then clean bearings with a soft bristled brush until all dirt has been removed. Remove loose particles of dirt by tapping bearing flat against a block of wood. Rinse bearings in clean solvent; then blow bearings dry with air pressure.

— **CAUTION** —

Do not spin bearings while drying.

After drying, rotate each bearing slowly while examining balls or rollers for roughness, damage, or excessive wear. Replace all bearings that are not in first class condition. After cleaning and inspecting bearings lubricate generously with recommended lubricant, then wrap each bearing in clean paper until ready for reassembly.

Inspection

1. Inspect all parts for discoloration or warpage.
2. Examine all gears and splines for chipped, worn, broken or nicked teeth. Small nicks or burrs may be removed with a fine abrasive stone.
3. Inspect the breather assembly to make sure that it is open and not damaged.
4. Check all threaded parts for damaged, stripped, or crossed threads.
5. Replace all gaskets, oil seals and snaprings.
6. Inspect housings, retainers and covers for cracks or other damage. Replace the damaged parts.
7. Inspect keys and keyways for condition and fit.
8. Inspect shift forks for wear, distortion or any other damage.
9. Check detent ball springs for free length, compressed length, distortion or collapsed coils.
10. Check bearing fit on their respective shafts and in their bores or cups. Inspect bearings, shafts and cups for wear.

NOTE: If either the bearings or cups are worn or damaged, it is advisable to replace both parts.

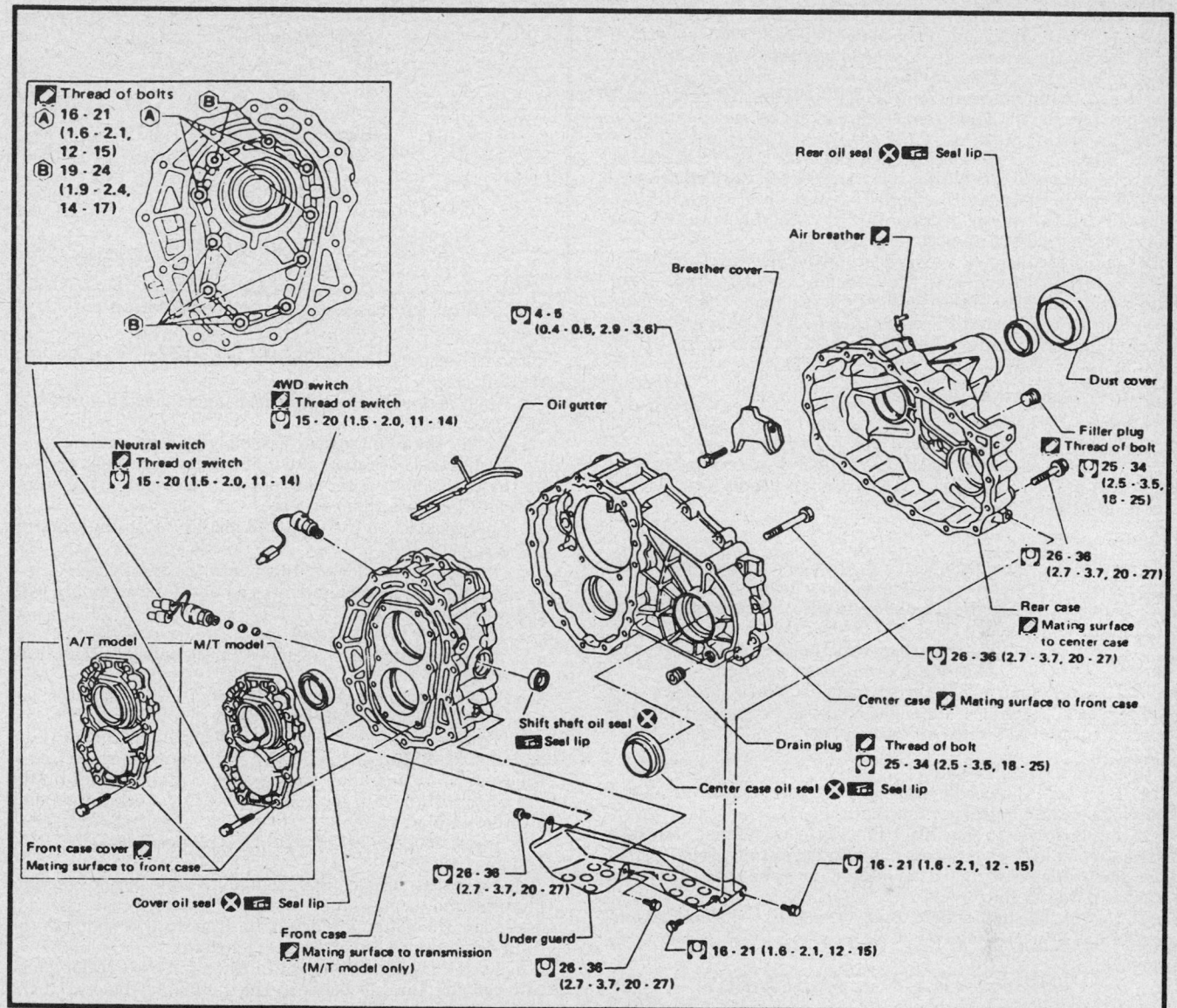

Exploded view of transfer case gear case assembly – Nissan

11. Inspect all bearing rollers or balls for pitting or galling.

12. Examine detent balls for corrosion or brinneling. If shift bar detents show wear, replace them.

13. Replace all worn or damaged parts. When assembling the transfer case, coat all moving parts with recommended lubricant.

TRANSFER CASE ASSEMBLY

Shifting Forks and Fork Rods

1. Install the breather cover (if removed). Install the main gear assembly carefully by tapping into position.

2. Drive out the front shift fork welch plug to enable shift fork installation. Install the check spring and ball in the rear transfer case half. Take care not to lose the check ball as spring pressure will force it out of the bore.

3. Install the high and low shift fork into the coupling sleeve.

Install the retaining pin. Install the front fork rod and the interlocking pin. Secure the front fork rod bracket to the fork rod with the retaining pin.

4. Assemble the snapring, spring retainer bushings and shift fork spring to the front shift fork. Insert an bolt into the bushing and tighten the nut to eliminate spring tension. Install the other retaining snapring and remove the bolt.

5. Lubricate and install a new O-ring to the countershaft and then install the countershaft assembly. Raise the counter gear assembly slightly and install the rear driveshaft assembly making sure the gear teeth mesh.

6. Install the companion flange on the rear end of the shaft assembly and tighten the nut finger tight.

7. Install the high and low fork rod and secure with the retaining pin. Apply sealant to the welch plug bore edges and install a new freeze plug. Install the check ball and spring. Tighten the check ball retaining bolt to 14–18 ft. lbs. after applying sealer to the threads.

8. Install the coupling sleeve hub and snapring. Check endplay. The endplay should be between 0–0.0079 in. snaprings of different thicknesses are available to control the endplay.

9. Install the shift lever. Install the shift cross shaft. Apply grease to the main gear front shims and transfer case thrust washer and install them to the front half of the transfer case. Be sure the mating surfaces of the case halves are clean. Apply a bead of sealant to the mating edge and install the front half of the transfer case. Tap with a soft hammer to seat if necessary.

10. Tighten the mounting bolts to 5–8 ft. lbs.

11. Install the spacer, front shift fork assembly with the coupling sleeve and secure with snapring.

12. Lubricate the pilot needle bearing and place in position. Install the front driveshaft to the transfer case driveshaft. Clean the mating surfaces of the cases. Apply sealant to the extension case surface and install the cover (5–8 ft. lbs.). Install the companion flanges. Tighten the new flange locknuts to 87–101 ft. lbs. Install the 4WD switch to 14–22 ft. lbs.

Counter Gear and Main Gear

1. Press on the front and rear bearings using a suitable press.

2. Install the breather cover and main gear.

3. Apply grease to the needle bearings and spacers and assemble them in the counter gear. Twenty eight needle bearings are used, 14 at each end.

Low Gear

1. Lubricate the needle bearings with gear oil and install the needle bearings, coupling sleeve and low gear.

2. Apply grease to the steel ball and thrust washer and install them on the low gear.

3. Press on the front bearing while holding the low gear so that the trust washer will not drop out of position.

4. If internal parts (i.e. thrust washers, bearings, gears etc.) are replaced, check clearances and adjust as necessary using the correct shim(s) to reduce excessive play.

High Gear

1. Lubricate the needle bearings with gear oil and install the bearings and high gear on the shaft.

2. Apply grease to the steel ball and thrust washer and place them on the high gear. Press the bearing onto the shaft. Hold the gear while pressing on the bearing to make sure the thrust washer does not fall.

3. Install the shaft spacer. Apply grease to the steel ball and install ball and speedometer drive gear.

TRANSFER CASE ASSEMBLY

1. Assemble the front case as follows:
   a. Install the main gear assembly by tapping lightly.
   b. Apply sealant to the mating surface and bolts of the front case cover and install it on the front case. Coat the 10

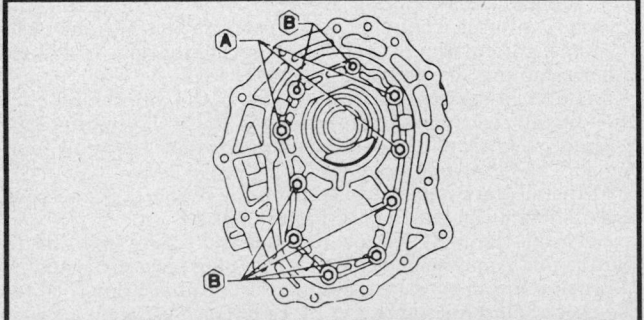

Front cover bolt locations

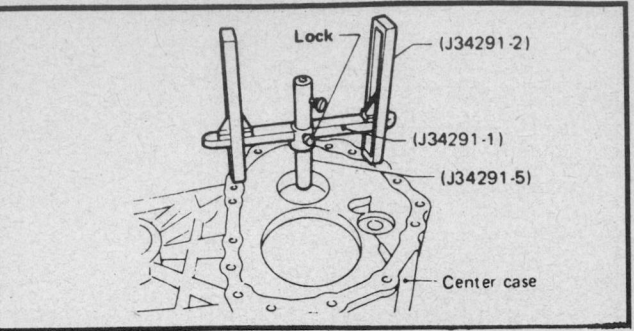

Tool position for countergear shim selection

bolts with sealant, then tighten the bolts: (A) 12–15 ft. lbs. (B) 14–17 ft. lbs.
   c. Apply gear oil to the needle bearing and install it into the main gear.
   d. Install the counter gear assembly by tapping lightly.
   e. Install the cross shaft and inner shift lever. When replacing the cross shaft, outer shift lever or lock pin of the outer shift lever, replace them as a set.
   f. Apply sealant to the plug and install it into the front of the case.
   g. Insert the interlock plunger into the front case.
   h. Install the Low/High shift rod and fork assembly with the coupling sleeve.
   i. Install the 2–4 shift rod.
   j. Apply sealant to the switches, check balls, check springs and plugs.

2. Select the counter gear rear bearing shim as follows:
   a. Seat the counter gear assembly.
   b. Place special tools J34291-1 (bridge), J34291-2 (legs) and J34291-5 (gauging cylinder) on the machined surface of the center case and allow the gauging cylinder to rest on the top portion of the counter gear rear bearing. Lock the gauging cylinder in place.
   c. Insert tool J34291-15 (gauging plunger) into J34291-5 (gauging cylinder).
   d. Place the bridge, legs, gauging cylinder and gauging plunger onto the machined surface of the front case assembly and allow the gauging plunger to drop until it contacts the counter gear rear bearing mating surface.
   e. Lock the gauging plunger in place and use a feeler gauge to meausure the gap between the gauging cylinder and the gauging plunger.
   f. Using the measured distance to obtain the correct shim size. The counter gear endplay should be 0–0.008 in. (0–0.2mm).
   g. Select the counter gear rear bearing shim.

3. Place a suitable shim on the counter gear rear bearing with grease.

4. Apply gear oil to each part of the front case.

5. Assemble the center case assembly as follows:
   a. Apply gear oil to the mainshaft front bearing and install the mainshaft on the center case by tapping lightly.
   b. Install the bearing retainer.
   c. Put the drive chain onto the front drive sprocket and the front driveshaft and then put them in the center case. The chain must be installed in its original position as described during disassembly.
   d. Install the front driveshaft by tapping lightly.
   e. Apply gear oil to the needle bearings and while rotating them install them into the front drive sprocket.
   f. Install the 2–4 coupling sleeve with the 2–4 shift fork.
   g. Insert the shifting inserts and spread spring.
   h. Install the baulk ring and then install the clutch gear and the mainshaft rear bearing.

i. Install the spacer.

j. Select a snapring to obtain the proper clearance of 0–0.0059 in. (0–0.15mm).

k. Install the steel ball, speedometer gear and the retaining ring. The steel ball is the smallest of all the check balls for this unit.

l. Apply gear oil to the needle bearing and then install the low gear and its bearing on the mainshaft.

m. Install the Low/High hub and the snapring to the mainshaft.

n. Check to endplay of low gear, it should be 0.0079–0.0256 in. (0.2–0.65mm).

6. Apply sealant to the mating surface and place the center case assembly onto the front case and tighten the bolts.

7. Install the snapring to the 2–4 shift rod.

8. Install the oil gutter and oil cover.

9. Lubricate all the parts in the center case with gear oil.

10. Apply sealant to the mating surface, install the rear case to the center case and tighten the bolts.

Specifications

TORQUE SPECIFICATIONS

Part	ft. lbs.	Nm
Transfer fixing bolt	23–30	31–41
Second crossmember	43–58	59–78
Guide plate fixing bolt	5.8–8.0	8–11
Control lever bracket	12–15	16–21
Transfer control lever to outer shift lever	18–22	25–30
Transfer unit		
Rear case to center case	20–27	26–36
Center case to front case	20–27	26–36
Front case cover	12–15	16–21
	14–17	19–24
Breather cover fixing bolt	2.9–3.6	4–5
Bearing retainer	12–15	16–21
Companion flange nut	166–239	226–324
Check plug	14–18	19–25
Cross shaft lock pin	6.5–8.7	9–12
4WD switch	11–14	15–20
Neutral switch	11–14	15–20
Drain plug	18–25	25–34
Filler plug	18–25	25–34
Speedometer sleeve	2.2–2.9	3–4

MAINSHAFT REAR BEARING SNAPRING SELECTION CHART

Part No.	Thickness in. (mm)
33138-33G20	0.071 (1.8)
33138-33G21	0.075 (1.9)
33138-33G22	0.079 (2.0)
33138-33G23	0.083 (2.1)
33138-33G24	0.087 (2.2)

MAINSHAFT FRONT BEARING SNAPRING SELECTION CHART

Part No.	Thickness in. (mm)
33138-33G10	0.122 (3.1)
33138-33G11	0.126 (3.2)
33138-33G12	0.130 (3.3)
33138-33G13	0.134 (3.4)

COUNTER GEAR REAR BEARING SHIM SELECTION

Part No.	Thickness in. (mm)
33112-C6900	0.004 (0.1)
33112-C6901	0.008 (0.2)
33112-C6902	0.012 (0.3)
33112-C6903	0.016 (0.4)
33112-33G00	0.020 (0.5)
33112-33G01	0.024 (0.6)

MAIN GEAR BEARING SNAPRING SELECTION CHART

Part No.	Thickness in. (mm)
33114-33G00	0.102 (2.6)
33114-33G01	0.106 (2.7)
33114-33G02	0.110 (2.8)
33114-33G03	0.114 (2.9)

SUZUKI

Trouble Diagnosis

SLIPS OUT OF GEAR (HIGH-LOW)

1. Shifting poppet spring weak.
2. Bearing broken or worn.
3. Shifting fork bent.
4. Improper control rod adjustment.

HARD SHIFTING

1. Lack of lubricant.
2. Shift lever binding on shaft.
3. Shifting poppet ball scored.
4. Shifting fork bent.
5. Low tire pressure.

BACKLASH

1. Companion yoke loose.
2. Transfer case loose on mounts.
3. Internal parts excessively worn.

NOISY

1. Low lubricant level.
2. Bearings improperly adjusted or excessively worn.
3. Gears worn or damaged.
4. Improper alignment of driveshafts or U-joints.

OIL LEAKAGE

1. Excessive amount of lubricant in case.
2. Vent clogged.
3. Gaskets or seals leaking.
4. Bearings loose or damaged.
5. Driveshaft yoke mating surfaces scored.

OVERHEATING

1. Excessive or insufficient amount of lubricant.
2. Bearing adjustment too tight.

Removal and Installation

TRANSFER CASE REMOVAL

1. Raise and support the vehicle.
2. Remove all driveshafts from the transfer gear box.
3. Remove the retaining clamp and boot from the shifter assembly.
4. Remove the shifter lever by twisting control lever guide counterclockwise while pushing it down.
5. Drain oil from the transfer gear box.
6. Disconnect the speedometer cable from the transfer gear box.
7. Disconnect the 4WD switch electrical connection.
8. While suitable supporting transfer gear box remove the transfer gear box retaining bolts. Remove the transfer gear box from the vehicle.

TRANSFER CASE INSTALLATION

1. Install transfer gear box to the vehicle. Torque the retaining bolts to specifications.

2. Reconnect the 4WD switch electrical connection.
3. Connect the speedometer cable to the transfer gear box.
4. Install the shifter lever by twisting control lever guide clockwise while pushing it down.
5. Install the boot and retaining clamp to the shifter assembly.
6. Install all driveshafts to the transfer gear box.
7. Lower the vehicle. Refill the transfer case with the correct amount of the specified oil.
8. Road test the vehicle through each gear range to check for proper operation.

Before Disassembly

Cleanliness is an important factor in the overhaul of the transfer case. Before opening up this unit, the entire outside of the transfer case should be cleaned, preferably with a high pressure washer such as a car wash spray unit. During inspection and reassembly all parts should be thoroughly cleaned with solvent then dried with compressed air. Wiping cloths and rags should not be used to dry parts.

Wheel bearing grease, long used to hold thrust washers and lube parts, should not be used. Lube seals with clean transaxle oil and use ordinary unmedicated petroleum jelly to hold the thrust washers and to ease the assembly of seals, since it will not leave a harmful residue as grease often will. Do not use solvent on neoprene seals, if they are to be reused, or thrust washers.

Before installing bolts into aluminum parts, always dip the threads into clean transmission oil. Antiseize compound can also be used to prevent bolts from galling the aluminum and seizing. Always use a torque wrench to keep from stripping the threads. The internal snaprings should be expanded and the external rings should be compressed, if they are to be reused. This will help insure proper seating when installed.

TRANSFER CASE DISASSEMBLY

1. Remove the 3 flanges; one from the input shaft, one from the front and rear output shafts. Lock the flange with special tool No. 09930–40113, so that it will not turn and loosen and remove the nut holding the flange to the shaft. Draw the flange off the shaft.
2. Loosen the speedometer drive gear case bolt and remove the speedometer drive gear case with the gear.
3. Remove the indicator light switch from the front case.

NOTE: Be careful not to lose the switch ball. The ball is larger than the interlock ball and the locating balls.

4. Remove the bolts securing the transfer front case and take off the case.
5. By tapping the front output shaft with a plastic hammer, remove the output shaft from the front case.
6. After removing the oil seal, remove the circlip and drive the bearing out of the front case by using the bearing installer tool No. 09913–76010.
7. Remove the bolts fastening the center case and the rear case together. By tapping the rear case and the output rear shaft with a plastic hammer, separate the center and rear case.

NOTE: Do not loosen bolt No. 1 at this point.

8. Disassemble the components of the center case as follows:
   a. Loosen the gear shift locating spring plug and take out the spring and locating ball.
   b. Using spring pin remover, tool 09922–85811 or equivalent, drive the 2 spring pins out of the front drive shift shaft No.1 and the reduction shift shaft No.2.
   c. Remove the forks and shift shafts.

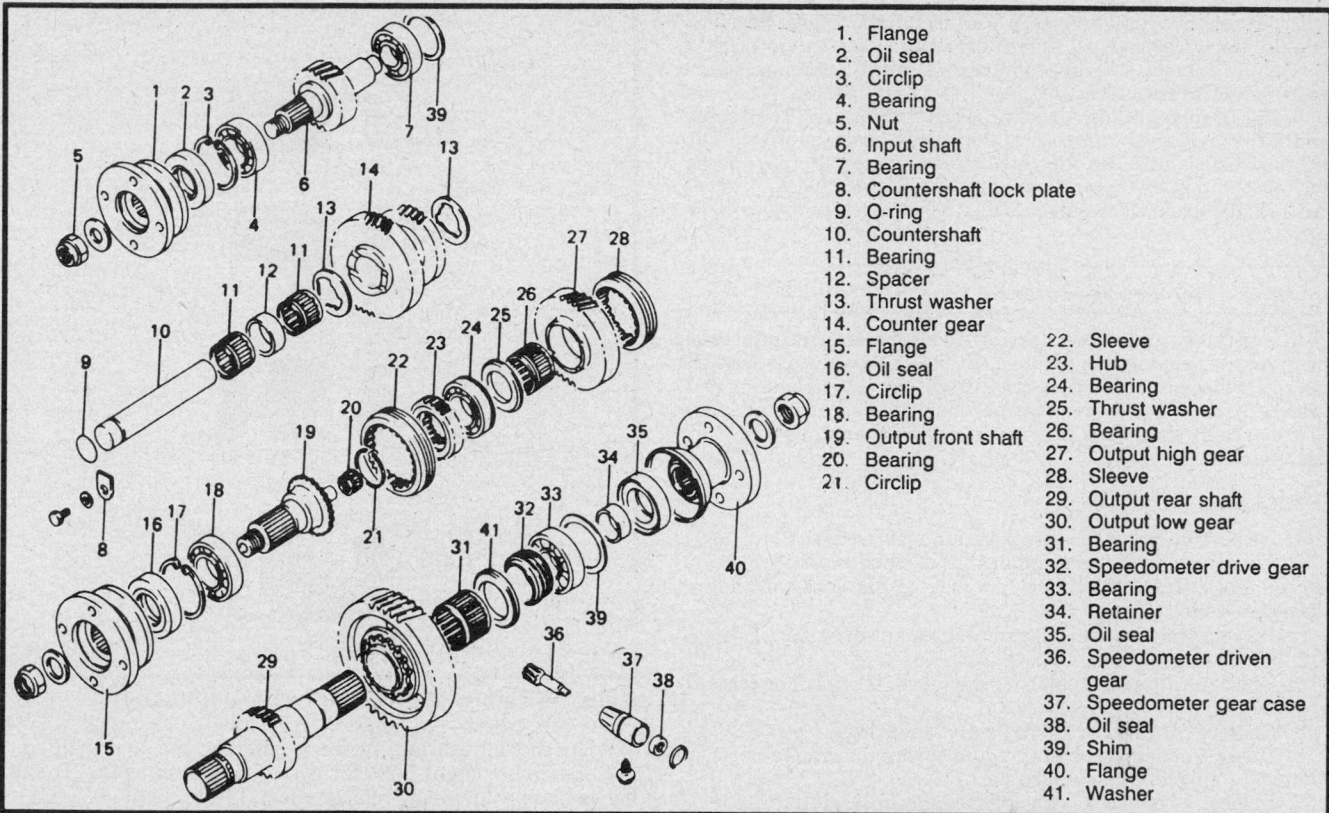

1. Flange
2. Oil seal
3. Circlip
4. Bearing
5. Nut
6. Input shaft
7. Bearing
8. Countershaft lock plate
9. O-ring
10. Countershaft
11. Bearing
12. Spacer
13. Thrust washer
14. Counter gear
15. Flange
16. Oil seal
17. Circlip
18. Bearing
19. Output front shaft
20. Bearing
21. Circlip
22. Sleeve
23. Hub
24. Bearing
25. Thrust washer
26. Bearing
27. Output high gear
28. Sleeve
29. Output rear shaft
30. Output low gear
31. Bearing
32. Speedometer drive gear
33. Bearing
34. Retainer
35. Oil seal
36. Speedometer driven gear
37. Speedometer gear case
38. Oil seal
39. Shim
40. Flange
41. Washer

Exploded view of transfer case — Suzuki

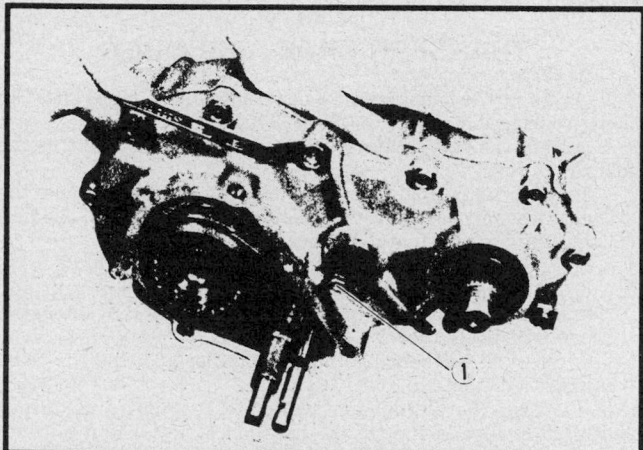

Location of No. 1 bolt on the center case

d. Hammer the rear output shaft with a plastic hammer to drive it out of the center case.

e. Pull out the counter gear, bearings and spacer. Remove the counter shaft from the center case by loosening the counter shaft lock plate bolt.

f. Remove the input shaft from the center case by hammering the thick part of the case or the input shaft center with a plastic hammer.

g. Remove the output shaft rear bearing and retainer together by using a bearing puller. After removing the bearing, speedometer gear, thrust washer, the output low gear and the needle roller bearing can be removed.

h. Remove the front drive clutch hub circlip and pull the clutch hub off the shaft by using a bearing puller and puller attachment, special tool 09926–58010 or equivalent.

NOTE: Be careful to prevent damage to the needle roller bearing in the output rear shaft when removing the clutch hub.

i. Remove the front bearing by using the bearing puller and puller attachment, special tool 09926–58010 or equivalent.

NOTE: Be careful to prevent damage to the needle roller bearing in the output rear shaft when removing the clutch hub.

j. When the input shaft is removed or the center case and rear case are separated, the input bearings may come off. In such a case, the bearings can be removed from the shaft by using a bearing puller.

k. When the input shaft is removed, the front bearing may be left in the case. In this case, after removing the oil seal and circlip, the bearing can be taken out of the case using the bearing installer tool No. 09913–75810.

9. When the center case and the rear case are separated, the input shaft may be left in the rear case. In this case, remove the input shaft from the rear case by hammering the thick part of the case with a plastic hammer.

CLEANING AND INSPECTION

Cleaning

During overhaul, all components of the transfer case (except bearing assemblies) should be thoroughly cleaned with solvent and dried with air pressure prior to inspection and reassembly. Be sure all gasket sealing material is cleaned off of the case, cover plates and mounting flanges.

Proper cleaning of bearings is of utmost importance. Bearings should always be cleaned separately from other parts.

Soak all bearing assemblies in clean solvent or fuel oil. Bearings should never be cleaned in a hot solution tank. Wash the bearings in solvent until all old lubricant is loosened. Hold races so that bearings will not rotate; then clean bearings with a soft bristled brush until all dirt has been removed. Remove loose particles of dirt by tapping bearing flat against a block of wood. Rinse bearings in clean solvent; then blow bearings dry with air pressure.

— CAUTION —

Do not spin bearings while drying.

After drying, rotate each bearing slowly while examining balls or rollers for roughness, damage, or excessive wear. Replace all bearings that are not in first class condition. After cleaning and inspecting bearings lubricate generously with recommended lubricant, then wrap each bearing in clean paper until ready for reassembly.

Inspection

1. Inspect all parts for discoloration or warpage.
2. Examine all gears and splines for chipped, worn, broken or nicked teeth. Small nicks or burrs may be removed with a fine abrasive stone.
3. Inspect the breather assembly to make sure that it is open and not damaged.
4. Check all threaded parts for damaged, stripped, or crossed threads.
5. Replace all gaskets, oil seals and snaprings.
6. Inspect housings, retainers and covers for cracks or other damage. Replace the damaged parts.
7. Inspect keys and keyways for condition and fit.
8. Inspect shift forks for wear, distortion or any other damage.
9. Check detent ball springs for free length, compressed length, distortion or collapsed coils.
10. Check bearing fit on their respective shafts and in their bores or cups. Inspect bearings, shafts and cups for wear.

NOTE: If either the bearings or cups are worn or damaged, it is advisable to replace both parts.

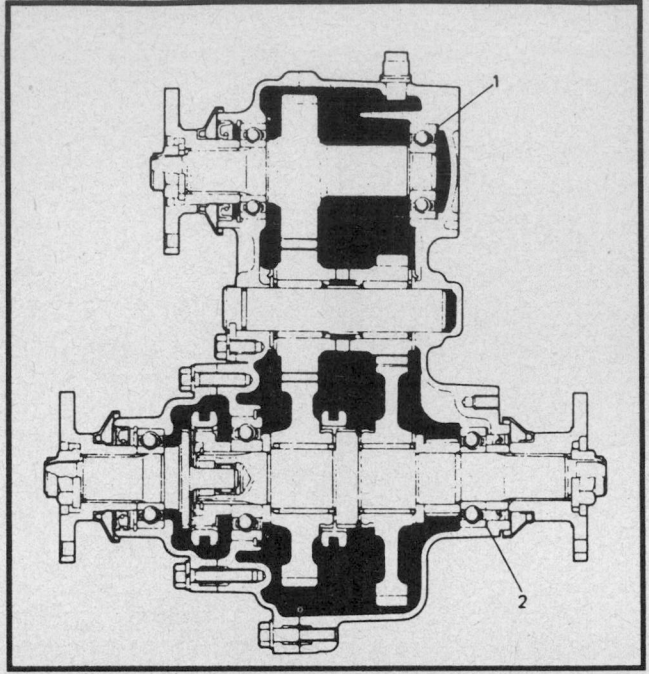

Shim locations fot the input and output shafts

11. Inspect all bearing rollers or balls for pitting or galling.
12. Examine detent balls for corrosion or brinneling. If shift bar detents show wear, replace them.
13. Replace all worn or damaged parts. When assembling the transfer case, coat all moving parts with recommended lubricant.

TRANSFER CASE ASSEMBLY

1. Press fit the bearings onto both sides of the input shaft by using bearing installer No. 09913–84510.
2. Install the component parts onto the output shaft in the following order:
   a. After installing the (long) bearing, high gear and the thrust washer, press- fit the bearing and then install the hub using the bearing installer, tool No. 09913–84510.
   b. Fit the circlip securely to the groove in the shaft.
   c. After installing the sleeve, (short) bearing, low gear and the thrust washer, press fit the speedometer gear by using the bearing installer tool No. 09913–84510.
   d. Press fit the bearing and the retainer by using the bearing installer tool No. 09913–84510.
3. Perform the shim adjustment of the input and output shafts. Clearance in the thrust direction of both the input and output shafts is adjusted by putting shims between the input shaft rear bearing and the rear case for the input shaft and between the output shaft rear bearing and the rear case for the output shaft.

As the thrust clearance is specified as follows, determine the shim thickness to meet specification according to the following procedures.

Thrust clearance specification:
0.002–0.006 in. (0.05–0.15mm)

4. Make the input shaft measurements as follows:
   a. With vernier calipers and a straight edge, take measurement **A** of the rear case.
   b. Take measurement **B** of the center case with the bearing circlip installed.
   c. Take measurement **C** (between the bearing inner races) of the input shaft with the bearings installed.

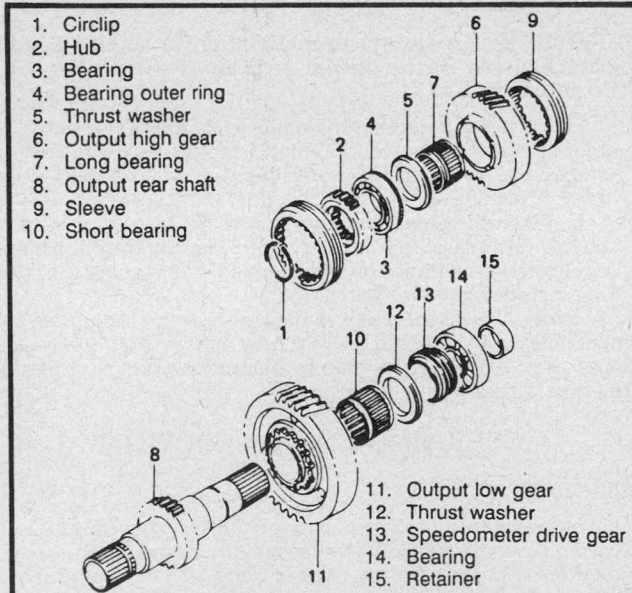

1. Circlip
2. Hub
3. Bearing
4. Bearing outer ring
5. Thrust washer
6. Output high gear
7. Long bearing
8. Output rear shaft
9. Sleeve
10. Short bearing

11. Output low gear
12. Thrust washer
13. Speedometer drive gear
14. Bearing
15. Retainer

Output shaft components

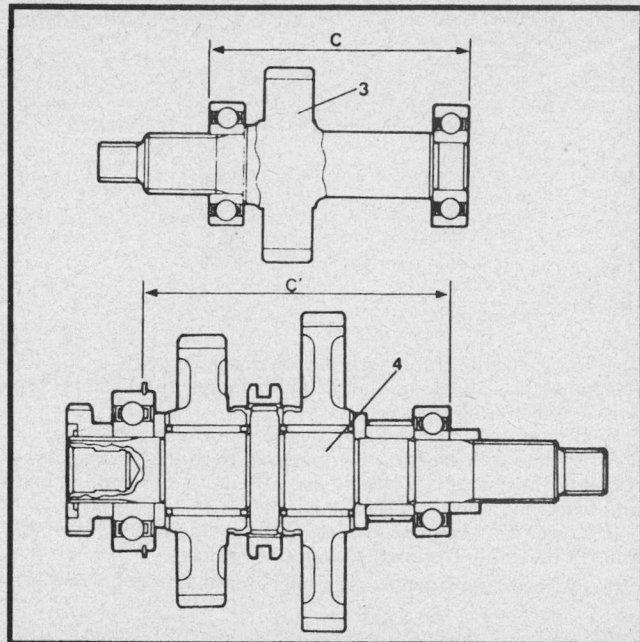

Input and output shaft measurements

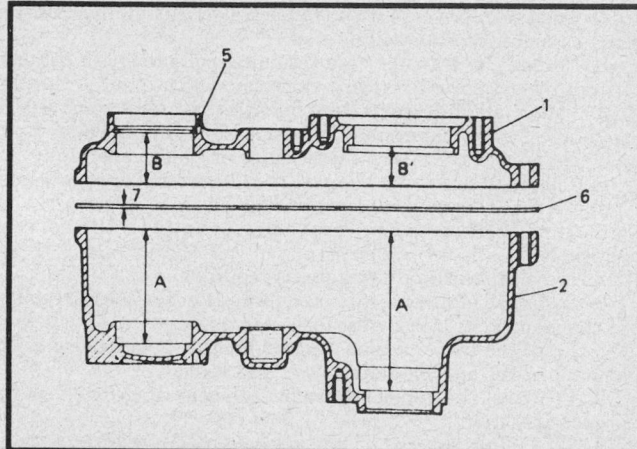

Transfer case measurements

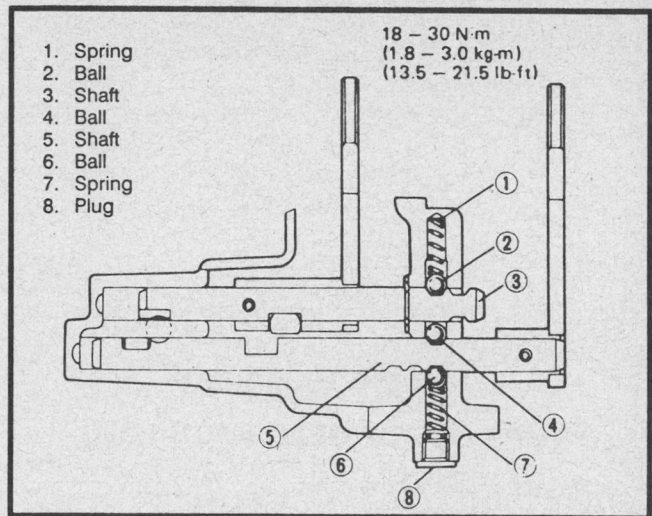

1. Spring
2. Ball
3. Shaft
4. Ball
5. Shaft
6. Ball
7. Spring
8. Plug

18 – 30 N·m
(1.8 – 3.0 kg-m)
(13.5 – 21.5 lb-ft)

Front shift shaft assembly

d. Using measurements obtained in steps a thru c and the equation described below, calculate shim thickness which is necessary for the proper thrust clearance.

Thrust clearance =

$(A + B + \text{Gasket thickness}) - C$

As the above equation holds for the thrust clearance and gasket thickness is specified as 0.3mm and the thrust clearance as 0.05–0.15mm, the shim thickness is calculated by the following equation:

Shim thickness =

$. (A + B + 0.3mm) - (C + 0.05 - 0.15mm)$

e. When the proper thickness is determined, select the proper shim(s) from among the following shim sizes and use them between the input shaft and the rear bearing and the rear case when matching the center case and the rear case.
Avaiable shim thickness: 0.1, 0.3, 0.5mm

5. Shim the output shaft the same as the input shaft, take measurements of **A**, **B** and **C** as indicated in the illustration. Calculate the shim thickness and install the proper shim(s) be-

tween the output shaft rear bearing and the rear case when matching the center case and rear case

6. Install the oil seal in the rear case and apply grease to the oil seal lip.

7. Install the counter shaft thrust washer to the rear case, bringing its face without depressions against the case and fit its bent portion securely into the groove in the case.

8. Install the input shaft front bearing, circlip and the oil seal in the center case.

NOTE: Apply an ample amount of grease to both surfaces of the washer to retain it in position.

9. Install the input shaft to the center case.

10. After greasing the O-ring on the counter shaft, insert the shaft into the center case and secure the shaft with the lock plate and bolt.

11. Install the counter shafty thrust washer to the center case. For installation, apply an ample amount of grease to both faces of the washer so as to lubricate the sliding surfaces and prevent it from moving out of place or slipping off and bring its face without depressions against the center case and install its bent portion into the groove in the case securely.

12. Install the needle roller bearings, spacer and the counter gear on the counter shaft.

13. Install the output shaft assembly to the center case.

14. When installing the front drive shift shaft and the reduction shift shaft in the center case, install the spring, ball, shaft, ball, shaft, ball, spring and plug in that order.

15. Fit the forks on the shift shafts and lock them with spring pins. Forks should be fitted in their original positions.

16. Check the center case (or the rear case) to ensure that it is provided with 2 dowel pins.

17. Put the gasket on the center case. Bring the rear case and the center case into alignment and apply uniform force gradually all around the rear case with a plastc hammer. Tighten the center case securing bolts to 9.5–16.5 ft. lbs.

18. Apply grease to the front output shaft rear bearing.

19. Install the bearing, circlip and oil seal to the front case. Apply grease to the oil seal lip and install the front output shaft using the bearing installer tool No. 09913–76010.

20. Put a new gasket on the center case.

21. Check that the 2 dowel pins are posioned in the front case.

22. Install the front case to the center case.

23. When installing the speedometer gear and its gear case in

the rear case, apply grease to the O-ring and the oil seal lip and align the bolt holes in the rear case and the drive gear case.

24. Install the 4WD ball and switch. Then clamp the switch lead wire properly.

25. Install the propeller shaft flanges and tighten the nuts to 80–108 ft. lbs., then caulk the nuts to prevent them from loosening.

TOYOTA

Trouble Diagnosis

SLIPS OUT OF GEAR (HIGH-LOW)

1. Shifting poppet spring weak.
2. Bearing broken or worn.
3. Shifting fork bent.
4. Improper control rod adjustment.

HARD SHIFTING

1. Lack of lubricant.
2. Shift lever binding on shaft.
3. Shifting poppet ball scored.
4. Shifting fork bent.
5. Low tire pressure.

BACKLASH

1. Companion yoke loose.
2. Transfer case loose on mounts.
3. Internal parts excessively worn.

NOISY

1. Low lubricant level.
2. Bearings improperly adjusted or excessively worn.
3. Gears worn or damaged.
4. Improper alignment of driveshafts or U-joints.

OIL LEAKAGE

1. Excessive amount of lubricant in case.
2. Vent clogged.
3. Gaskets or seals leaking.
4. Bearings loose or damaged.
5. Driveshaft yoke mating surfaces scored.

OVERHEATING

1. Excessive or insufficient amount of lubricant.
2. Bearing adjustment too tight.

Removal and Installation

TRANSFER CASE REMOVAL

1. Raise and safely support the vehicle.
2. Drain the oil from the transmission and transfer case.
3. Remove all electrical connections and shifter lever assemblies from the transmission/transfer case.
4. Remove the exhaust system as needed.
5. Matchmark and remove the front and rear driveshafts.

6. Support the transmission/transfer case with a suitable transmission jack or equivalent and remove all brackets, support members and case protector.
7. Disconnect the speedometer cable or pulse generator.
8. Remove all necessary components to gain access to transmission/transfer case retaining bolts. Remove all retaining bolts and transmission/transfer case assembly.
9. Lower the supported transmission/transfer case assembly and tilt assembly to remove from the vehicle.
10. Remove the transfer case from the transmission assembly.

TRANSFER CASE INSTALLATION

1. Align transfer case with transmission. Install the transfer case assembly to transmission.
2. Torque the transfer case retaining bolts to specifications. Install the supported transmission/transfer case to the vehicle.
3. Install all necessary components that were removed to gain access to transmission/transfer case retaining bolts.
4. Reconnect the speedometer cable or pulse generator.
5. Install all brackets, support members and case protector. Remove the transmission jack or equivalent.
6. Install the front and rear driveshafts in the correct positions.
7. Install the exhaust system as required.
8. Install all electrical connections and shifter lever assembly to the transmission/transfer case assembly.
9. Refill the transmission and transfer case with the correct amount of the specified oil. Lower the vehicle.
10. Road test the vehicle through each gear range to check for proper operation.

Before Disassembly

Cleanliness is an important factor in the overhaul of the transfer case. Before opening up this unit, the entire outside of the transfer case should be cleaned, preferably with a high pressure washer such as a car wash spray unit. During inspection and reassembly all parts should be thoroughly cleaned with solvent then dried with compressed air. Wiping cloths and rags should not be used to dry parts.

Wheel bearing grease, long used to hold thrust washers and lube parts, should not be used. Lube seals with clean transaxle oil and use ordinary unmedicated petroleum jelly to hold the thrust washers and to ease the assembly of seals, since it will not leave a harmful residue as grease often will. Do not use solvent on neoprene seals, if they are to be reused, or thrust washers.

Before installing bolts into aluminum parts, always dip the threads into clean transmission oil. Antiseize compound can also be used to prevent bolts from galling the aluminum and seizing. Always use a torque wrench to keep from stripping the threads. The internal snaprings should be expanded and the ex-

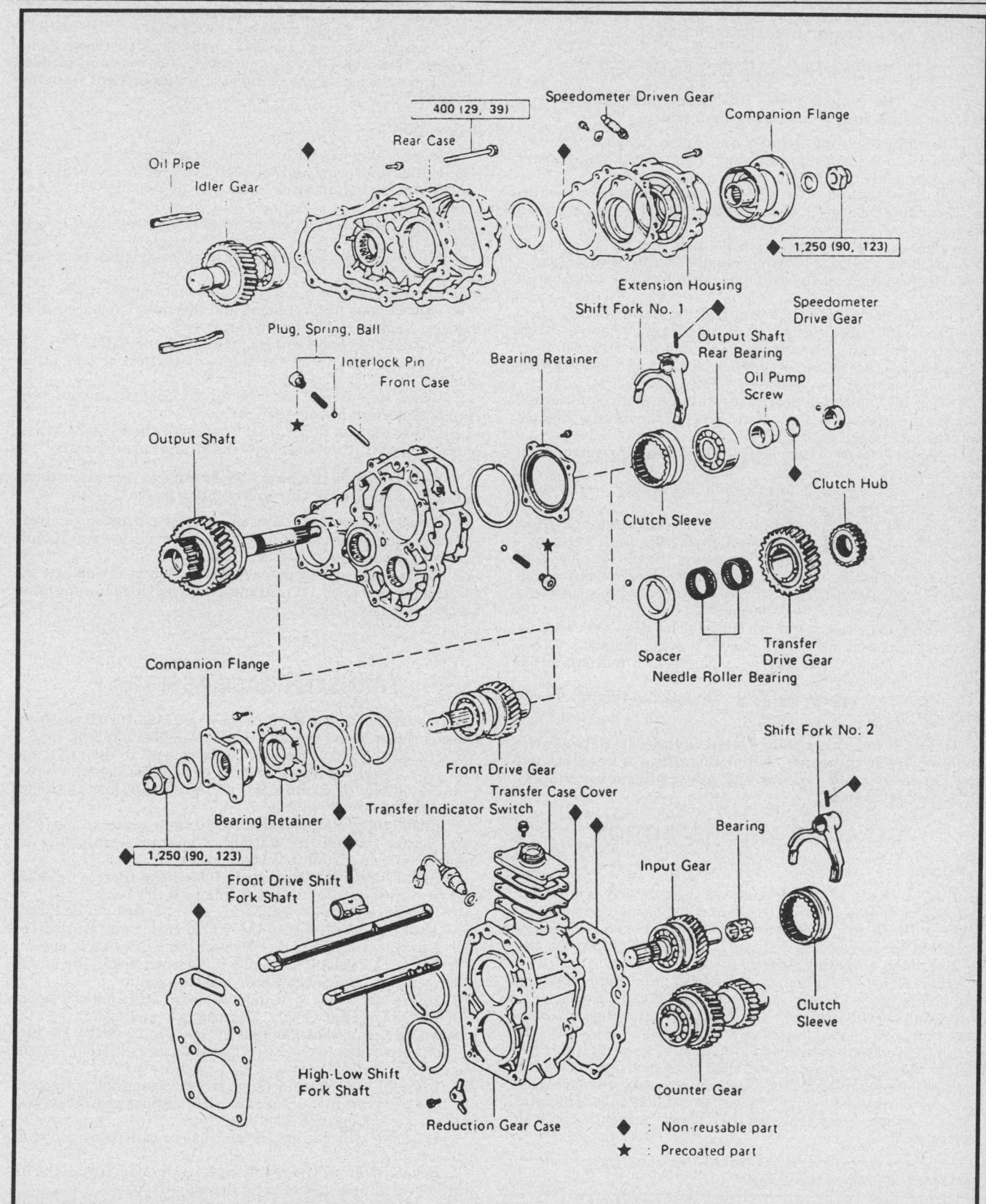

400 (29, 39)

Oil Pipe
Idler Gear
Rear Case
Speedometer Driven Gear
Companion Flange

1,250 (90, 123)

Plug, Spring, Ball
Interlock Pin
Front Case
Bearing Retainer
Extension Housing
Shift Fork No. 1
Output Shaft
Rear Bearing
Speedometer
Drive Gear
Oil Pump
Screw

Output Shaft
Clutch Sleeve
Clutch Hub

Companion Flange
Spacer
Needle Roller Bearing
Transfer
Drive Gear

Bearing Retainer
Shift Fork No. 2
1,250 (90, 123)
Front Drive Shift
Fork Shaft
Transfer Indicator Switch
Front Drive Gear
Transfer Case Cover
Input Gear
Bearing
Clutch
Sleeve

High-Low Shift
Fork Shaft
Counter Gear
Reduction Gear Case

◆ : Non-reusable part
★ : Precoated part

Exploded view of transfer case—Toyota

ternal rings should be compressed, if they are to be reused. This will help insure proper seating when installed.

TRANSFER CASE DISASSEMBLY

NOTE: The transfer case has been removed from the transmission in the following procedure.

1. Remove the front and rear companion flanges.
2. Remove the extension housing. Remove the speedometer drive gear, steel ball, oil pump screw and bearing.
3. Remove the rear case half with the idler gear in position while holding the front half so that the clutch hub and steel ball do not fall out.
4. Remove the idler gear from the rear case.
5. Remove the front bearing retainer and front drive gear.
6. Remove the 2 oil pipes. Remove shift fork No. 1 and clutch sleeve.
7. Remove the clutch hub and transfer drive gear. Remove the needle roller bearing, No. 2 spacer and steel ball. On some models, remove the transfer case cover and shift lever retainer.
8. Remove the screw cover plugs, springs and locking balls from both sides of the case.
9. Remove the spring pins that retain the shifting forks and remove the front drive fork shaft. Remove the interlocking pin and the high-low fork.
10. Remove the front case, tap lightly with a plastic hammer if necessary.
11. Remove the No. 2 fork, clutch sleeve and needle roller bearing from the input shaft.
12. Remove the input gear and counter gear from the reduction gear case. Remove the output shaft from the front case.
13. Check the oil and thrust clearance of the transfer low gear: Oil clearance between the gear and shaft with needle bearing installed; 0.0004–0.0022 in. Thrust clearance with spacer and bearing installed; 0.0039–0.0098 in.
14. Check the clearance of the thrust drive gear: Oil clearance between gear and shaft with needle bearing installed: 0.004–0.0020 in. Thrust clearance with clutch hub and spacer installed: 0.0035–0.0106 in.
15. Measure the clearance of the shift forks and clutch sleeves: Max. is 0.039 in.

NOTE: If bearing replacement is indicated, press the bearing from the shaft. When installing a bearing, use the thickest snapring that will allow minimum endplay 0.0059 in. (0.15mm).

CLEANING AND INSPECTION

Cleaning

During overhaul, all components of the transfer case (except bearing assemblies) should be thoroughly cleaned with solvent and dried with air pressure prior to inspection and reassembly. Be sure all gasket sealing material is cleaned off of the case, cover plates and mounting flanges.

Proper cleaning of bearings is of utmost importance. Bearings should always be cleaned separately from other parts.

Soak all bearing assemblies in clean solvent or fuel oil. Bearings should never be cleaned in a hot solution tank. Wash the bearings in solvent until all old lubricant is loosened. Hold races so that bearings will not rotate; then clean bearings with a soft bristled brush until all dirt has been removed. Remove loose particles of dirt by tapping bearing flat against a block of wood. Rinse bearings in clean solvent; then blow bearings dry with air pressure.

────────── **CAUTION** ──────────
Do not spin bearings while drying.

After drying, rotate each bearing slowly while examining balls or rollers for roughness, damage, or excessive wear. Replace all bearings that are not in first class condition. After cleaning and inspecting bearings lubricate generously with recommended lubricant, then wrap each bearing in clean paper until ready for reassembly.

Inspection

1. Inspect all parts for discoloration or warpage.
2. Examine all gears and splines for chipped, worn, broken or nicked teeth. Small nicks or burrs may be removed with a fine abrasive stone.
3. Inspect the breather assembly to make sure that it is open and not damaged.
4. Check all threaded parts for damaged, stripped, or crossed threads.
5. Replace all gaskets, oil seals and snaprings.
6. Inspect housings, retainers and covers for cracks or other damage. Replace the damaged parts.
7. Inspect keys and keyways for condition and fit.
8. Inspect shift forks for wear, distortion or any other damage.
9. Check detent ball springs for free length, compressed length, distortion or collapsed coils.
10. Check bearing fit on their respective shafts and in their bores or cups. Inspect bearings, shafts and cups for wear.

NOTE: If either the bearings or cups are worn or damaged, it is advisable to replace both parts.

11. Inspect all bearing rollers or balls for pitting or galling.
12. Examine detent balls for corrosion or brinelling. If shift bar detents show wear, replace them.
13. Replace all worn or damaged parts. When assembling the transfer case, coat all moving parts with recommended lubricant.

TRANSFER CASE ASSEMBLY

1. Install the output shaft to the front case. Install the front bearing retainer and torque the mounting bolts to 9 ft. lbs.
2. Install the input gear and counter gear to the reduction gear case. Install the roller bearing on the input shaft.
3. Install the No. 2 hub sleeve and No. 2 shift fork on the input shaft.
4. Install the reduction gear case and new gasket to the front case. Torque the bolts to 29 ft. lbs. 2 different length bolts are used, be sure to install in correct position.
5. Install the front drive gear. Install the bearing retainer and new gasket. Torque the bolts to 14 ft. lbs.
6. Install the high-low shift fork, the interlock pin and front drive shift fork shaft. Install the slotted spring pins. Install the balls, springs and side plugs. Tighten the plugs to 9 ft. lbs.
7. Install the locking ball and No. 2 spacer. Install the needle roller bearing, transfer low gear and clutch hub.
8. Install No. 1 shift fork and hub sleeve. Install the oil pipes.
9. Install the idler gear to the rear case and install the rear case with a new gasket. Tighten the bolts to 29 ft. lbs. Be sure the bolts are install in the correct position as 2 different lengths are used.
10. Install the bearing, oil; pump screw, locking ball and speedometer drive gear. Install the extension housing with a new gasket. Torque the bolts to 29 ft. lbs.
11. On some vehicles, install the transfer case cover and shift lever retainer.
12. Install the front and rear flanges (90 ft. lbs.). Install the indicator switch and speedometer driven gear.

BORG WARNER 1356 ELECTRONIC SHIFT TRANSFER CASE

General Description

The Borg Warner 1356 electronic shift transfer case is a 3 piece magnesium part time transfer case. It transfers power from the transmission to the rear axle and when electronically actuated, also to the front drive axle. The unit is lubricated by a positive displacement oil pump that channels oil flow through drilled holes in the rear output shaft. The pump turns with the rear output shaft and allows towing of the vehicle at maximum legal road speeds for extended distances without disconnecting the front and/or rear driveshaft.

The electronic system consists of a 2 rocker switch control system, an electronic control module, an electric shift motor with an integral shift position sensor and a speed sensor. The 2 rocker control switches are located on the lower right hand coner of the instrument panel for fingertip shift control. The electronic control module is located on the right hand cowl side. The electronic control module, controls the operation of the transfer case in response to inputs to the push button control by the vehicle operator.

The speed sensor, is mounted to the rear of the transfer case, the sensor tells the control module the proper speed to shift the transfer case. The shift position sensor, is an integral part of the electric shift motor, tells the control module the shift position of the transfer case.

The electronic shift motor mounted externally at the rear of the transfer case, drives a rotary helical cam which moves the 2WD–4WD shift fork and 4H–4L reduction shift fork to the selected vehicle drive position.

The transfer case is equipped with a magnetic clutch, similar to an air conditioning compressor clutch, which is located inside the transfer case adjacent to the 2WD–4WD shift collar. The clutch is used to spin up the front drive system from zero to vehicle speed in milliseconds. This spin up allows the shift between 2H and 4H to be made at any vehicle speed. When the transfer case rear and front output shafts reach synchronous speed, the spring loaded shift collar mechanically engages the mainshaft hub to the chain drive sprocket and the magnetic clutch is deactivated.

Shifts between 4H and 4L can only occur with the clutch interlock or transmission safety switches closed. The vehicle's speed must also be within specified limits as determined by the transfer case speed sensor (3 mph or under).

When the operator selects the drive combination through the push button control, an electric motor turns a helical cam, which is linked to the high low and 2WD–4WD shift forks through fork mounted roller bushing assemblies. As the electric motor turns the helical cam, the high low fork bushing rides in a slotted lobe in the cam to make low high or high low range changes; and the 2WD–4WD for bushing rides on lobes at the end of the cam to make the 2WD–4WD or 4WD–2WD shift.

Trouble Diagnosis

CHILTON'S THREE C'S TRANSFER CASE DIAGNOSIS

Condition	Cause	Correction
Slips out of gear	a) Shifting poppet spring weak	a) Replace the shifting poppet spring
	b) Bearing broken or worn	b) Replace the bearing
	c) Shifter fork bent	c) Replace shifter fork
	d) Improper control rod adjustment	d) Adjust the control rod
Hard shifting	a) Lack of lubricant	a) Add the recommended fluid to the proper level
	b) Shift lever binding on shaft	b) Repair and adjust the shift lever
	c) Shifting poppet ball scored	c) Replace the shifting poppet ball
	d) Shifter fork bent	d) Replace shifter fork
	e) Low tire pressure	e) Inflate tires to the correct pressure
Backlash	a) Companion yoke loose	a) Torque the companion yoke to specifications
	b) Transfer case loose on mounts	b) Torque the mount bolts to specification
	c) Internal parts excessively worn	c) Rebuild the transfer case
Noisy	a) Low lubricant level	a) Add the recommended fluid to the proper level
	b) Bearings improperly adjusted or excessively worn	b) Adjust or replace the bearing
	c) Gears worn or damaged	c) Replace the gear in question
	d) Improper alignment of driveshafts or U-joint	d) Realign the driveshaft and U-joint
Oil leakage	a) Excessive amount of oil in the case	a) Drain the fluid to the proper level
	b) Oil vent clogged	b) Clean oil vent
	c) Gaskets or seals leaking	c) Replace leaking gaskets or seals
	d) Bearings improperly adjusted or excessively worn	d) Adjust or replace the bearing
	e) Driveshaft yoke mating surfaces scored	e) Machine the driveshaft yoke mating surface

CHILTON'S THREE C'S TRANSFER CASE DIAGNOSIS

Condition	Cause	Correction
Overheating	a) Excessive amount of oil in the case	a) Drain the fluid to the proper level
	b) Low lubricant level	b) Add the recommended fluid to the proper level
	c) Bearing adjustment too tight	c) Adjust or replace the bearing

Electronic Controls

DIAGNOSIS AND TESTING

The battery feed circuit, through a circuit breaker provides memory capability for the electronic control module. The ignition **RUN** and **ACC** feed circuits through a fuse, provide power for the switches and the electric shift motor. The headlamp dimmer circuit provides the power for night time illumination of the overhead roof console vehicle graphics.

CONTROL MODULE

Self Test

The electronic control module has a diagnostic capability of its own circuitry. The self test procedures are as follows:
1. Remove the 5 wire connector and the 8 wire connector from the electronic control module.
2. Turn the ignition switch to the **RUN** position.
3. Activate the self test switch and note the results.
4. A flashing indicator lamp (approximately one flash per second) indicates that the control module is functioning properly.
5. A steady indicator light indicates that the control module is inoperative and must be replaced.

CONTROL MODULE CIRCUIT

There are 3 wiring harness connected to the electronic control module, the 8 wire pigtail harness connector, the 5 wire harness connector and the 8 wire harness connector. To check the integrity of these circuits, disconnect the harness from the electronic control module and perform the following test.

8 Wire Pigtail Harness Connector Test

1. Remove the 8 wire pigtail harness connector and connect a suitable voltmeter between terminal 8 and the ground. The voltmeter should indicate battery (12 volts) voltage at all times.
2. Connect the voltmeter between terminal 7 and ground. Turn the ignition switch to the **RUN** position. The voltmeter should indicate battery (12 volts) voltage.

NOTE: In the following test where the usage of an ohmmeter is specified, always remember that an ohmmeter should never be connected into a live or powered circuit. If an ohmmeter is connected to a powered circuit, severe damage will be done to the instrument. The vehicle's battery should be disconnected before disconnecting any circuit with an ohmmeter to prevent any accidental damage to the instrument.

3. Connect an ohmmeter between terminal 6 and ground. The ohmmeter should indicate a low resistance valve of less than 10 ohms.
4. Connect an ohmmeter between terminal 4 and 5. The ohmmeter should indicate a low resistance valve of less than 10 ohms.
5. Connect an ohmmeter between terminal 3 and ground. The ohmmeter should indicate a 0 ohms.
6. Connect an ohmmeter between terminal 2 and ground. The ohmmeter should indicate a 0 ohms.

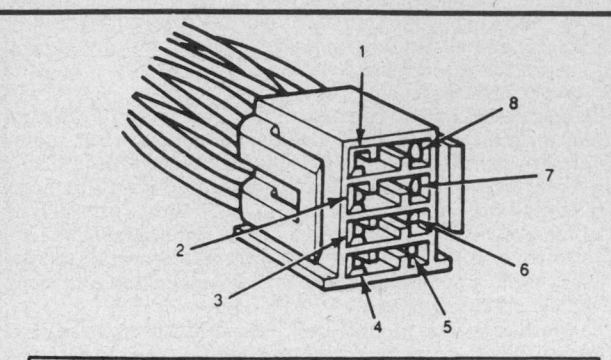

Position	Circuit Number	Color Code	Function
1	OPEN		
2	57	Blk	Ground
	57A	Blk	Ground
3	396	Blk/Org	Logic Ground
4	778	Org	Transfer Case Motor Control (Clockwise) 2H-4H-4L
5	777	Yel	Transfer Case Motor Control (Counterclockwise) 4L-4H-2H
6	79	Brn	Electro-Magnetic Clutch (Feed)
7	296	Wht/Ppl	Ignition Run and Accessory Feed (Fused)
8	517	Blk/Wht	Battery Feed (Circuit Breaker)

Testing the 8 wire pigtail harness connector

5 Wire Harness Connector Test

1. Remove the 5 wire connector and connect a suitable ohmmeter between terminal 1 and 2. Then depress the 4WD (2H–4H) switch in the overhead roof console. The ohmmeter should indicate a very low resistance valve (less than 50 ohms) while the switch is being depressed.
2. Connect a suitable ohmmeter between terminal 1 and 3. Then depress the low range switch in the overhead roof console. The ohmmeter should indicate a very low resistance valve (less than 50 ohms) while the switch is being depressed.
3. Connect a test lead between terminal 4 and ground. Then turn the ignition switch to the **RUN** position and observe the overhead roof console. The light in the console low range bar should illuminate.
4. Connect a test lead between terminal 5 and ground. Then turn the ignition switch to the **RUN** position and observe the overhead roof console. The light in the console 4WD bar should illuminate.

8 Wire Harness Connector Test

1. Remove the 8 wire connector and connect a suitable ohmmeter between terminal 1 and ground. Then depress the clutch pedal and observe the ohmmeter. The ohmmeter should indicate a very low resistance valve (less than 50 ohms) while the clutch pedal is being depressed.

2. If the vehicle is equipped with a automatic transmission, connect a suitable ohmmeter between terminal 1 and ground. Then shift the transmission into the **N** position and observe the ohmmeter. The ohmmeter should indicate a very low resistance valve (less than 50 ohms) while in the **N** position.

3. Connect a suitable ohmmeter between terminal 2 and 3. The ohmmeter should indicate a very low resistance valve (200–350 ohms).

4. This will check the continuity of the speed sensor that is located in the transfer case. The speed sensor picks up the rotat-

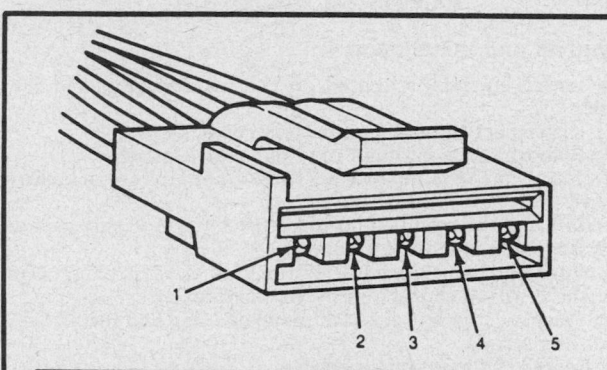

Testing the 5 wire harness connector

Position	Circuit Number	Color Code	Function
1	465	Wht/Lt Blu	Switch Feed
2	780	Dk Blu	4x4 Switch
3	781	Org/Lt Blu	Low Range Switch
4	782	Brn/Wht	Low Range Light
5	783	Gry	4x4 Light

OHMMETER READINGS FOR SHIFT MOTOR POSITION SENSOR

Ohmmeter Connection	Transfer Case Gear Position		
	2 High	4 High	4 Low
Meter Reading From Terminal #8 to #4	Short	Open	Short
Meter Reading From Terminal #8 to #5	Open	Open	Short
Meter Reading From Terminal #8 to #6	Short	Short	Open
Meter Reading From Terminal #8 to #7	Open	Short	Open

NOTE: SHORT is a "low" resistance reading on the ohmmeter (zero ohms).
OPEN is a "high" resistance reading on the ohmmeter (infinity).

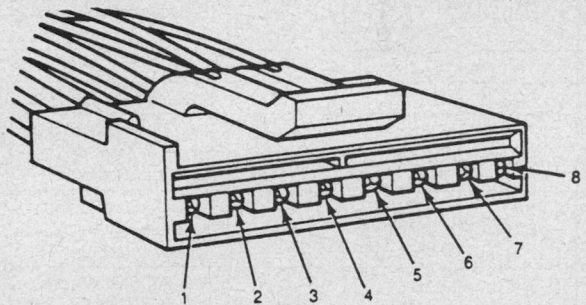

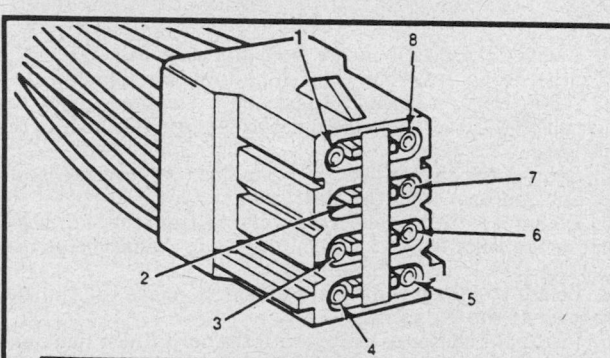

Main feed connector terminal pin identification

Position	Circuit Number	Color Code	Function
1	782	Red/Yel	Ignition Run and Accessory Feed (Fused)
2 (Used Only on Auto Trans)	463	Red/Wht	Automatic Transmission Neutral Safety Switch
3	296	Wht/Ppl	Ignition Run and Accessory Feed (Fused)
4	57	Blk	Ground
5	780	Lt Blu/Red	Side Marker Lamp (Feed)
6	783	Lt Gm/Yel	Dome Lamp (Feed)
7 (Used Only on Manual Trans)	463	Red/Lt Blu	Manual Transmission Clutch Interlock Switch
8	517	Blk/Wht	Battery Feed (Circuit Breaker)

Testing the 8 wire harness connector

Position	Circuit Number	Color Code	Function
1	32	Red/Lt Blu	Manual Transmission Clutch Interlock Switch˙˙
	463	Red/Wht	Automatic Transmission Neutral Safety Switch
2	774	Lt Grn	Speed Sensor (Feed)
3	772	Lt Blu	Speed Sensor Return
4	771	Violet	Wire #5, Contact Plate Position Sensor in Transfer Case
5	770	Wht	Wire #4, Contact Plate Position Sensor in Transfer Case
6	764	Brn/Wht	Wire #3, Contact Plate Position Sensor in Transfer Case
7	763	Org/Wht	Wire #2, Contact Plate Position Sensor in Transfer Case
8	762	Yel/Wht	Wire #1, Contact Plate Position Sensor in Transfer Case

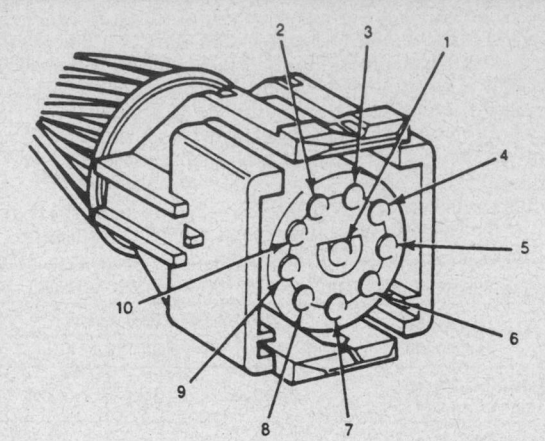

Position	Circuit Number	Color Code	Function
1	779	Brn	Electro-Magnetic Clutch (Feed)
2	778	Org	Transfer Case Motor Control (Clockwise) 2H-4H-4L
3	777	Yel	Transfer Case Motor Control (Counterclockwise) 4L-4H-2H
4	774	Lt Grn	Speed Sensor (Feed)
5	772	Lt Blu	Speed Sensor (Return)
6	771	Violet	Wire #5, Shift Position Sensor in Transfer Case (Output to Module)
7	770	Wht	Wire #4, Shift Position Sensor in Transfer Case (Output to Module)
8	764	Brn/Wht	Wire #3, Shift Position Sensor in Transfer Case (Output to Module)
9	763	Org/Wht	Wire #2, Shift Position Sensor in Transfer Case (Output to Module)
10	762	Yel/Wht	Wire #1, Shift Position Sensor in Transfer Case (Input from Module)

Electronic transfer case feed 10 pin connector terminal pin identification

ing speed of the output shaft from 2 notches that are cut in opposite sides of the outer ring of the clutch housing assembly.

5. Connect an ohmmeter between terminal 8 and terminals 4, 5, 6 and 7, respectively. Use the chart provided for the ohmmeter reading in each transfer case position.

On Vehicle Services

4WD SHIFT SWITCH

Removal and Installation

1. Disconnect the negative battery cable. Remove the instrument panel assembly.

2. Remove switch mounting screw and remove the switch from the panel.
3. When installing the switch, position the switch in the panel and retain it with the mounting screw.
4. Install the instrument panel assembly.

CONTROL MODULE

Removal and Installation

The control module is located on the inside right hand cowl panel.
1. Disconnect the negative battery cable.
2. Remove the right hand cowl panel kick panel.
3. Remove the 2 module to instrument panel attaching screws.
4. Lift out the module and disconnect the 3 wiring connectors. Remove the module assembly.
5. Position the new module to the kick panel opening. Connect the 3 wiring connectors to the module.
6. Place module into the kick panel opening and install the 2 mounting screws.
7. Install the kick panel pad.

SHIFT LEVER

Removal and Installation

NOTE: Remove the shift ball only if the shift ball, boot or lever have to be replaced. If any of these parts are not being replaced, remove the shift ball, boot and lever as an assembly.

1. Remove the plastic insert from the shift ball. Warm the ball with a heat gun or equivalent until it reaches approximately 140–180°F. Using a block of wood and a hammer, knock the shift ball off the lever. Be careful not to damage the finish on the shift lever.
2. Remove the rubber boot with the floor pan cover. Disconnect the vent hose from the shift lever.
3. Disconnect the transfer case shift rod from the shift lever. Remove the bolts holding the shift lever to transfer case. Remove the shift lever and bushings.
4. Before installing the shifter assembly, move the transfer case lever to the **4L** position.
5. Install the shifter assembly with the bolts finger tight, and move the cam plate rearward until the bottom chamfered corner of the neutral lug just contact the forward right edge of the shift lever.
6. Hold the cam plate in the position mentioned above and tighten the bolts to 71–90 ft. lbs. (95–122 Nm).
7. Move the transfer case in-cab shift lever to all positions to check for positive engagement. There should be clearance between the shift lever and the cam plate in the **2H** front, and **4H** rear (clearance should not exceed 2.0mm), and the **4L** shift positions.
8. Attach the shift lever to the control lever and tighten to 23–32 ft. lbs. (31–43 Nm).
9. Install the vent assembly so the white marking on the housing is in the position in the notch in the shifter. Install the rubber boot and the floor pan cover.
10. Warm the ball with a heat gun or equivalent until it reaches approximately 140–180°F. Using a $^7/_{16}$ in. socket and a mallet, tap the ball on to the lever and install the plastic shift pattern insert.
11. Check the transfer case for proper shifting and operation.

REAR OR FRONT OUTPUT SHAFT WITH FIXED YOKES OIL SEAL

Removal and Installation

1. Raise and support the vehicle safely.
2. Place a drain pan under transfer case, remove the drain plug and drain fluid from the transfer case.
3. Disconnect the front or rear driveshaft from the transfer case output shaft yoke. Wire the driveshaft out of the way.
4. Remove the oil seal by removing the 30mm nut, steel washer and rubber seal from the front or rear output shaft and remove the yokes.
5. Remove the oil seal from the front of the rear output housing bore with a suitable seal remover and slide hammer. Remove the oil slinger from each yoke.
6. Make sure that the housing face and bore are free from nicks and burrs. Coat the seal with a suitable lubricant. Position the oil seal into the front or rear output housing bore, making sure the oil seal is not cocked in the bore. Drive the new seal into the housing with a suitable seal installer. Install a new oil seal slinger on each yoke.
7. Install the yoke, rubber seal, steel washer and locknut on the front or rear output shafts. Torque the locknut to 150–180 ft. lbs. (203–244 Nm).
8. Connect the front or rear driveshaft to the output yoke and torque the bolts to 61–87 ft. lbs. (83–118 Nm).
10. Fill the transfer case with 6.5 pints of Dexron®II transmission fluid or equivalent. Torque the fill plug to 14–22 ft. lbs. (19–32 Nm). Lower the vehicle. Start the engine and check the transfer case for correct operation. Stop the engine and check the fluid level, add as necessary.

Removal and Installation

TRANSFER CASE REMOVAL

The catalytic converter is located beside the transfer case. Be careful when working around the catalytic converter because of the extremely high temperatures generated by the converter.

1. Raise and support the vehicle safely. Drain the gear fluid from the transfer case into a suitable drain pan.
2. Disconnect the 4WD indicator switch connector at the transfer case and if so equipped, remove the skid plate from the frame.
3. Remove the wire connector from the feed wire harness at the rear of the transfer case. Be sure to squeeze the locking tabs, then pull the connectors apart.
4. Disconnect the front driveshaft from the front output yoke. Disconnect the rear driveshaft from the rear output yoke.
5. Disconnect the speedometer driven gear from the transfer case rear cover. Disconnect the vent hose from the mounting bracket.
6. Using a suitable transmission jack, support the transfer case. Remove the bolts that hold the transfer case to the transmission.
7. Slide the transfer case rearward off the transmission output shaft and lower the transfer case from the vehicle. Remove the old gasket between the transfer case and the adapter.

TRANSFER CASE INSTALLATION

1. Install the heat shield onto the transfer case and place a new gasket between the transfer case and adapter.
2. Raise the transfer case with a suitable transmission jack or equivalent, raise it high enough so that the transmission output shaft aligns with the splined transfer case input shaft.
3. Slide the transfer case forward on to the transmission output shaft and onto the dowel pin. Install transfer case retaining

bolts and torque them to 26–43 ft. lbs. (36–58 Nm). Remove the transmission jack from the transfer case.
4. Install the vent hose so that the white marking on the hose aligns with the mounting bracket. Connect the speedometer driven gear to the transfer case rear cover. Torque the screw to 20–25 inch lbs. (27–35 Nm).
5. Connect the rear driveshaft to the rear output shaft yoke and torque the retaining bolts to 20–28 ft. lbs.(27–38 Nm).
6. Connect the front driveshaft to the front output yoke and torque the yoke nut to 20–28 ft. lbs. (27–38 Nm). Attach the heat shield to the engine mounting bracket and mounting lug on the transfer case.
7. Install the skid plate to the frame. Install the transfer case drain plug and torque the plug to 6–14 ft. lbs. (8–19 Nm).
8. Fill the transfer case with 6.5 pints of Dexron®II transmission fluid or equivalent. Torque the fill plug to 15–25 ft. lbs. (11–35 Nm). Lower the vehicle. Start the engine and check the transfer case for correct operation. Stop the engine and check the fluid level, add as necessary.

Before Disassembly

Cleanliness during disassembly and assembly is necessary to avoid further transfer case trouble after overhaul. Before removing any of the transfer case subassemblies, plug all the openings and clean the outside of the of the transfer case thoroughly. Steam cleaning or car wash type high pressure equipment is preferable. During disassembly, clean all parts in suitable solvent and dry each part. Do not use cloth or paper towels to dry parts. Use compressed air only.

Transfer Case Disassembly

1. Remove the transfer case from the vehicle.
2. Remove the transfer case drain plug with a ⅜ in. drive ratchet and drain the fluid.
3. Remove the rear output shaft yoke by removing the 30mm nut, steel washer and rubber seal from the output shaft. Remove the front and rear output shaft yoke seals using special tool T74P–77248–A and T50L–100–A or equivalents. Remove the input shaft seals using the same tools.
4. Remove the wire connector assembly from the mounting bracket on the rear cover. If required, remove the 2 bolts and remove the bracket.
Form a small hook at the end of a paper clip or safety pin. Remove the locking sleeve from the wire connector by hooking the paper clip or safety pin and pulling it up from the bottom. Be sure not to damage the wire connector locking sleeve.
5. Remove the brown wire from the No. 1 center position in the connector. If required, remove the speed sensor green wire from the No. 4 connector position and blue wire from the No. 5 connector position.
6. Remove the 4 No. 50 Torx® head bolts securing the rear bearing retainer to the cover. Pry the rear bearing retainer from the cover using a ½ in. drive breaker bar between the pry bosses and separate and remove the bearing retainer from the cover. Remove all traces of RTV gasket sealant from the mating surfaces of the cover and the bearing retainer.

NOTE: When removing the RTV sealer, be careful not to damage the mating surfaces of the magnesium cases.

7. Lift the rear output shaft and using a small prybar, remove the speedometer gear retaining clip. Slide the speedometer gear forward and remove the ball with a small magnet. The speedometer gear can now be removed off of the rear output shaft. Remove the speed sensor from the rear cover.
8. Remove the 4 bolts retaining the shift motor to the rear cover and remove the motor. Note the position of the triangular shaft extending out of the rear cover and the triangular slot in the motor.

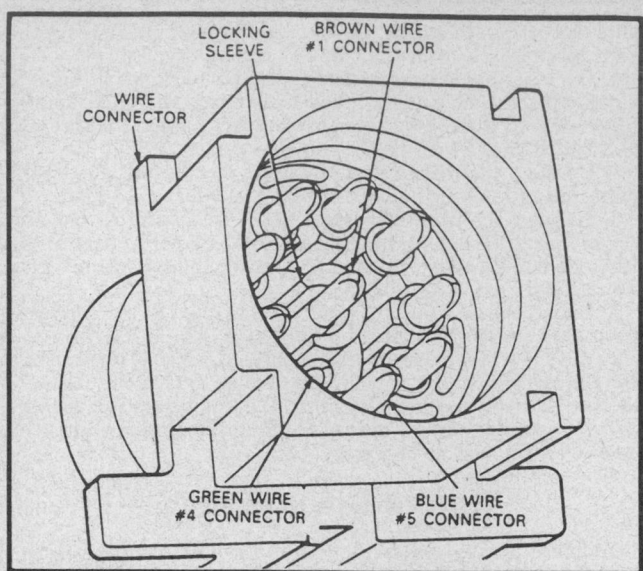

Rear wiring connector terminal pin identification

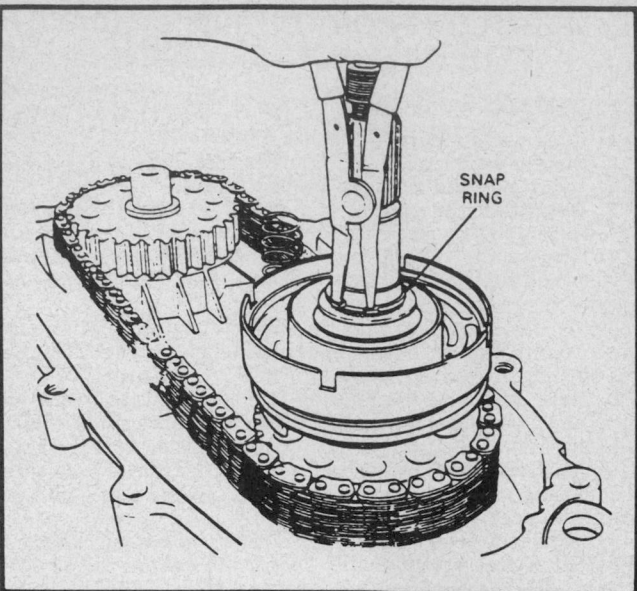

Removing the clutch housing retaining snapring

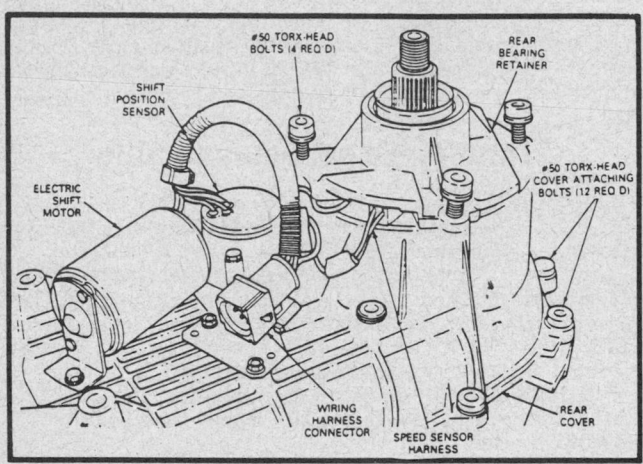

Removing the rear bearing retainer

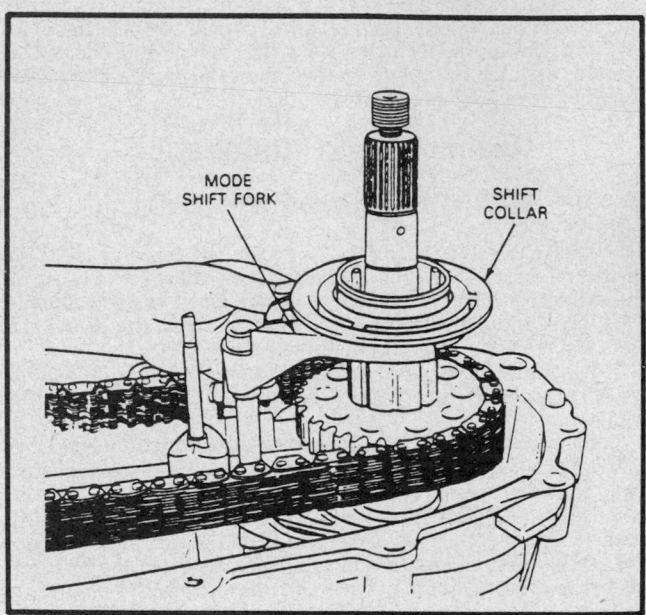

Removing the mode shift fork and shift collar

NOTE: The motor is serviced as a complete assembly. Do not remove the screws that secure the rear cover to the motor gear housing.

9. Remove the snapring on the output shaft retaining the upper rear ball bearing using a suitable tool.

10. Remove the 12 No. 50 Torx® bolts that retain the front case to the rear cover. Insert a ½ in. drive breaker bar between the pry bosses and separate. Lift the front case from the rear cover. Remove all traces of RTV gasket sealant from the mating surfaces of the cover and the bearing retainer.

NOTE: When removing the RTV sealer, be careful not to damage the mating surfaces of the magnesium cases.

11. Remove the front output shaft inner needle bearing from the rear cover with special slide hammer tool T50T–100–A and D80L–100–T, collet from D80L–100–A blind hole puller set or equivalents.

12. Drive out the rear output shaft bearing from the inside of the case using the appropriate tools.

13. Remove the snapring on the output shaft securing the clutch hub. Slide the 4WD hub off of the output shaft.

14. Remove the spring from the shift rail and lift the mode shift fork complete with the shifting collar from the upper sprocket spline.

15. Disassemble the 2WD–4WD lockup assembly by removing the internal snapring and pull the lockup hub and spring from the collar.

16. Remove the snapring retaining the lower sprocket to the lower output shaft. Grasp the upper and lower sprocket complete with the chain and lift them at the same time from the upper and lower output shafts.

17. Remove the snapring retaining the lower sprocket complete with the chain and lift them at the same time from the upper and lower output shafts.

18. Remove the shift rail by sliding it straight out from the shift fork.

19. Remove the high and low shift fork by first rotating it until the roller is free from the cam then sliding out of the engagement from the shift hub.

20. Remove the chip collecting magnet from its slot in the case.

21. Lift out the pump screen and remove the output shaft assembly with the pump assembled on it. If the pump is to be disassembled, remove the 4 bolts from the pump body. Note the position of the pump front body, pins, spring, rear cover and pump retainer as removed.

22. Remove the high low shift fork by rotating it until the roller is free from the cam then sliding out the engagement from the shifting hub. Remove the helical cam assembly from the front case. If required, remove the helical cam, torsion spring and sleeve from the shaft. Remove the external snapring and thrust washer that retains the drive sprocket to the front output shaft.

NOTE: If it is necessary to disassemble the helical cam assembly care should be execised as the cam is slid rearward to disengage it from the spring. The spring is energized and can release violently. The spring must be removed from the helical cam and the shaft finger. Do not get your fingers in the way of the disengaging spring. It will rotate to the point that the spring ends will be roughly 180 degrees apart.

23. Remove the front output shaft from the case.

24. Turn the front case over and remove the front oil seal from the case using tool T74P-77248-A and T50T-100-A or equivalents.

25. Reaching through the front opening with a pair of snapring pliers, expand the snapring on the input shaft allowing it to drop out of the bearing. The carrier assembly, including the input shaft is serviced as an assembly only. If the bearing or bushing is to be replaced, drive out both of them through the input spline using suitable tools.

26. Remove the ring gear by prying out the internal snapring and lift out the gear.

27. Remove the power take off drive gear from the input shaft carrier assembly, if equipped using appropriate tools.

28. Remove the internal snapring securing the input shaft bearing to the case and drive it out from the outside of the case using tool T73T-1202-A and T80T-4000-W or equivalents.

29. Remove the internal snapring securing the front output shaft bearing in the magnesium housing and drive the bearing out from the front of the case using tool T73T-1202-B and T80T-4000-W or equivalents.

30. Remove the shift cam by removing the retaining clip and sliding the shift shaft out of the case.

31. Remove the shift shaft seal by carefully prying it out of the case, being careful not to damage the case.

32. Remove the shift cam, assist spring, and the assist spring bushing from the case.

CLEANING AND INSPECTION

Cleaning

During overhaul, all components of the transfer case (except bearing assemblies) should be thoroughly cleaned with solvent and dried with air pressure prior to inspection and reassembly.

1. Clean the bearing assemblies as follows:

NOTE: Proper cleaning of bearings is of utmost importance. Bearings should always be cleaned separately from other parts.

   a. Soak all bearing assemblies in clean solvent or fuel oil. Bearings should never be cleaned in a hot solution tank.

   b. Slush bearings in solvent until all old lubricant is loosened. Hold races so that bearings will not rotate; then clean bearings with a soft bristled brush until all dirt has been removed. Remove loose particles of dirt by tapping bearing flat against a block of wood.

   c. Rinse bearings in clean solvent; then blow bearings dry with air pressure.

--- CAUTION ---
Do not spin bearings while drying.

   d. After drying, rotate each bearing slowly while examining balls or rollers for roughness, damage, or excessive wear. Replace all bearings that are not in first class condition.

NOTE: After cleaning and inspecting bearings, lubricate generously with recommended lubricant, then wrap each bearing in clean paper until ready for reassembly.

2. Remove all portions of old gaskets from parts, using a stiff brush or scraper.

Inspection

1. Inspect all parts for discoloration or warpage.

2. Examine all gears and splines for chipped, worn, broken or nicked teeth. Small nicks or burrs may be removed with a fine abrasive stone.

3. Inspect the breather assembly to make sure that it is open and not damaged.

4. Check all threaded parts for damaged, stripped, or crossed threads.

5. Replace all gaskets, oil seals and snaprings.

6. Inspect housings, retainers and covers for cracks or other damage. Replace the damaged parts.

7. Inspect keys and keyways for condition and fit.

8. Inspect shift forks for wear, distortion or any other damage.

9. Check detent ball springs for free length, compressed length, distortion or collapsed coils.

10. Check bearing fit on their respective shafts and in their bores or cups. Inspect bearings, shafts and cups for wear.

NOTE: If either bearings or cups are worn or damaged, it is advisable to replace both parts.

11. Inspect all bearing rollers or balls for pitting or galling.

12. Examine detent balls for corrosion or brinelling. If shift bar detents show wear, replace them.

13. Replace all worn or damaged parts. When assembling the transfer case, coat all moving parts with recommended lubricant.

Transfer Case Assembly

NOTE: Before starting the assembly procedure, lubricate all the internal parts, with Dexron®II transmission fluid or equivalent.

1. Install the input shaft and the front output shaft bearings in the case using the appropriate tools. Install the internal snaprings retaining the bearings in the case.

2. Drive the front output shaft seal into the case unit until it is fully seated against the case using tool T86T-7034-CH or equivalent.

3. Install the front output shaft through the lower bearing. The front output shaft is held in place in the case by the front output yoke and oil seal slinger assembly. Install the front yoke assembly onto the front output shaft then the rubber seal, flat washer and 30mm locknut. Torque the yoke locknut to 130-180 ft. lbs. (176-244 Nm).

4. Press the power take-off drive gear onto the input shaft assembly if it was removed.

5. Press the needle bearing and bronze bushing into the input shaft with the appropriate tools.

6. Install the ring gear into the slots in the case and retain it with the large internal snapring making sure that it is fully seated.

7. Install the input shaft and carrier assembly in the case through the input shaft bearing being careful not to damage the gear teeth when aligning them with the ring gear teeth.

8. While supporting the carrier assembly in position, install a new spring on the front side of the input bearing making sure that it is fully seated in the snapring groove of the input shaft.

9. Install the upper input shaft oil seal into the case using an appropriate tool until it is fully seated against the case.

10. Install a new shifter shaft seal into the case using an appropriate tool.

11. Assemble the shift cam assembly into the case by sliding the shift shaft and lever assembly through the case and seal into engagement with the shift cam. Secure the shift cam with the retaining clip.

12. Install the shift cam assist spring in position in the bushing of the shift cam and in the recess in the case.

13. Assemble the pump and output shaft as follows: Place the oil pump cover with the word **TOP** facing the front of the front case. Install the 2 pins (with the flats facing upwards) with the spring between the pins and place the assembly in the oil pump bore in the output shaft. Place the oil pump body and the pick up tube over the shaft and make sure that the pins are riding against the inside of the pump body. Place the oil pump rear cover with the words **TOP REAR** facing the rear of the case. The word **TOP** on the front cover and the rear cover should be on the same side. Install the pump retainer with the tabs facing the front of the transfer case. Install the 4 retaining bolts and rotate the output shaft while tightening the bolts to prevent the pump from binding. Tighten the bolts to 36–40 inch lbs. Lubricate the assembly with automatic transmission fluid.

NOTE: The output shaft must turn freely within the oil pump. If binding occurs, loosen the 4 bolts and retighten again.

14. Install the high low shift hub. Install the high low shift fork by engaging it with the shift hub flange and rotating it until the roller is engaged with the lower groove of the cam.

15. Install the shift rail through the high low fork bore and into the rail bore in the case.

16. Install the output shaft and oil pump assembly in the input shaft. Make certain that the external splines of the output shaft engage the internal splines of the high low shift hub. Make sure that the oil pump retainer and oil filter leg are in the groove and notch of the front case. Install the collector magnet in the notch in the front case.

17. Assemble the upper and lower sprockets with the chain and place them as an assembly over the upper and lower output shafts. Install the washer and snapring which retain the lower sprocket to the front output shaft.

18. Assemble the 2WD–4WD lockup assembly by installing the tapered compression spring in the lockup collar with the small end installed first. Place the lockup hub over the spring and compress the spring while installing the internal snapring which holds the lockup assembly together.

19. Install the lockup assembly and its shift fork over the external splines of the upper sprocket and the shift rail with the long boss of the shift rail facing foreward.

20. Assemble the 4WD return spring over the shift rail and against the shift fork.

21. Place the 4WD hub over the external splines of the output shaft and secure with the appropriate snapring. Make sure that the snapring is fully seated in the snapring groove.

22. Press the lower output needle bearing in its bore in the rear cover using an appropriate tool.

23. Press the rear output shaft bearing into position in the cover. Install the bearing snapring retainer in the cover.

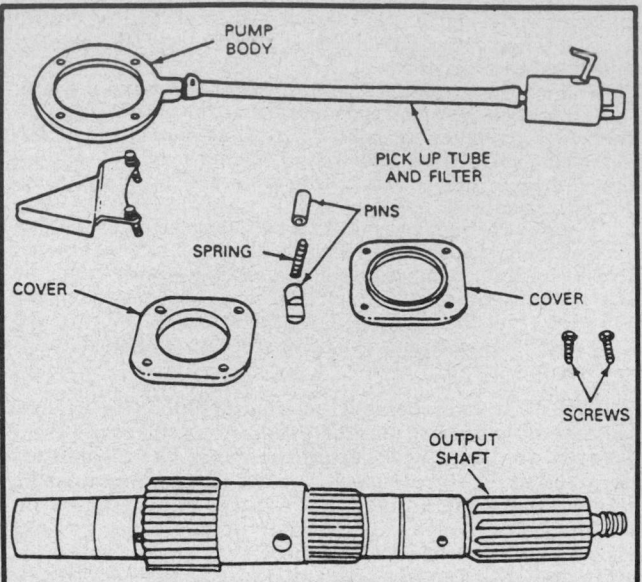

Exploded view of the rear output shaft and oil pump assembly

24. Install the rear output shaft oil seal in the bearing retainer using the appropriate tool making sure it is fully seated.

25. Coat the mating surface of the front case with a bead of RTV.

26. Place the cover on the case making sure that the lower output shaft, shift shaft and the shift rail are aligned. Install and torque the 12 No. 50 Torx® head case to cover bolts to 22–36 ft. lbs. (30–49 Nm).

27. Install the bearing retainer snapring on the output shaft making sure that the snapring is fully seated in the groove on the shaft.

28. Place the speedometer drive gear over the shaft with the slot aligned with the hole for the drive ball. The gear should go completely against the snapring which retains the output shaft. Place the ball in the hole and pull the speedometer gear over the ball. Snap the retaining clip between the snapring and the speedometer gear. Install the speed sensor in its bore in the cover.

29. Apply a bead of RTV to the face of the rear bearing retainer or to the rear slip yoke extension housing.

30. Place the rear bearing retainer or the rear slip yoke extension housing in its position and secure with the 4 Torx® head bolts.

31. On the transfer case with the slip yoke bearing retainer housing remove the extension oil seal using tool T74P-77248-A and T50T-100-A or equivalents. Remove the extension housing bushing using tool T85-7034-AH or equivalent. Install a new bushing using tool T85T-7034-BH and T80T-4000-W or equivalent. Install a new seal using tool T61L-7657-B. or equivalent.

32. Install the rear output shaft yoke and slinger assembly onto the rear splines of the output shaft. Install the rubber seal, flat steel washer and 30mm locknut on the output shaft and torque to 150–180 ft. lbs. (203–244 Nm).

33. Using a pair of pliers equipped with copper or wood jaws, rotate the triangular shaft so that it aligns with the triangular slot in the motor. Install the motor and torque the retaining bolts to 6–8 ft. lbs. (8–11 Nm).

NOTE: If the shaft will not stay in 4H position, rotate the shaft to the 2H position. Install the motor and rotate

the counterclockwise until the motor is aligned with the mounting holes.

34. Install the brown clutch coil wire to the No. 1 center terminal and if removed, the speed sensor green wire to the No. 4 connector position and the blue wire to the No. 5 connector position. Install the locking sleeve.

35. Position the wire connector mounting bracket on the rear cover. Install the bolts and torque them to 5–7 ft. lbs. (6–10 Nm). Install the wiring connector to the mounting bracket.

36. Install the drain plug and tighten to 14–22 ft. lbs. (19–32 Nm).

37. Place a ⅜ in. drive ratchet in the fill plug and remove the plug. Fill the transfer case with 64 oz. of Dexron®II transmission fluid.

38. Install the fill plug and tighten to 14–22 ft. lbs.

39. Install the transfer case. Lower the vehicle.

40. Start the engine, check the transfer case for proper operation. Stop the engine and check the fluid level. The fluid should drip out of the level hole. If the fluid flows out of the level hole, the oil pump may not be funtioning properly.

Specifications
TORQUE SPECIFICATIONS
1356 Electronic Shift Transfer Case

Description	ft. lbs.	Nm
Case half attaching bolts	35–40	48–54
Four wheel drive indicator switch	8–12	11–16
Front and rear output yokes to transfer case	120–150	163–203
Drain plug	14–22	19–30
Fill plug	14–22	19–30
Transfer case to transmission adapter	25–43	34–58
Heat shield to transfer case	40–45	54–61
Skid plate to frame	15–20	20–27
Front driveshaft to front output yoke	8–15	11–20

TORQUE SPECIFICATIONS
1356 Electronic Shift Transfer Case

Description	ft. lbs.	Nm
Rear driveshaft to rear output yoke—bolt—Bronco	20–28	28–33
Rear driveshaft to rear output yoke—Nut—F150-F350 4×4	8–15	11–20

Special Tools

Number	Description
T50T-100-A	Impact slide hammer—2½ lb.
D80L-100-A	Blind hole puller set
D80L-100-T	Blind hole puller
D80L-100-H	Actuator pin
TOOL-1175-AC	Seal remover
T80T-7127-B	Output bearing replacer—front
T80T-7127-C	Output bearing replacer—rear
T80T-4000-P	Bearing installer
T74P-77248-A	Oil seal remover
T61L-7657-B	Oil seal installer
T86L-7034-AH	Extension housing bushing remover
T85T-7034-BH	Extension housing bushing installer
T80T-4000-W	Bearing installer
T86T-7034-CH	Oil seal installer
T73T-1202-B	Bearing installer
T73T-1202-A	Bearing installer

NEW PROCESS 231 TRANSFER CASE

General Description

The NP231 is a part time unit with a built-in low range reduction gear system. It has 3 operating ranges plus a Neutral position. The low-range system provides a 2.72:1 gear reduction ratio for increased low-speed torque capacity. The unit has a 2 piece aluminum housing assembly. On the front case half, the front output shaft, front input shaft, 4WD indicator switch and shift lever assembly are located. On the rear case half, the rear output shaft, bearing retainer and drain and fill plugs are located.

Trouble Diagnosis

CHILTON'S THREE C's TRANSFER CASE DIAGNOSIS

Condition	Cause	Correction
Transfer case difficult to shift or will not shift into desired range	a) Vehicle speed too great to permit shifting	a) Stop vehicle and shift into desired range. Or reduce speed to 2–3 mph (3–4 km/h) before attempting to shift
	b) If vehicle was operated for extended period in 4H mode on dry paved surface, driveline torque load may cause difficult shifting	b) Stop vehicle, shift transmission to neutral, shift transfer case to 2H mode and operate vehicle in 2H on dry paved surfaces
	c) Transfer case external shift linkage binding	c) Lubricate or repair or replace linkage, or tighten loose components as necessary
	d) Insufficient or incorrect lubricant	d) Drain and refill to edge of fill hole with Dexron®II only

	e) Internal components binding, worn or damaged	e) Disassemble unit and replace worn or damaged components as necessary
Transfer case noisy in all drive modes	a) Insufficient or incorrect lubricant	a) Drain and refill to edge of fill hole with Dexron®II only. Check for leaks and repair if necessary. Note: If unit is still noisy after drain and refill, disassembly and inspection may be required to locate source of noise
Noisy in—or jumps out of four wheel drive low range	a) Transfer case not completely engaged in 4L position	a) Stop vehicle, shift transfer case in Neutral, then shift back into 4L position
	b) Shift linkage loose or binding	b) Tighten, lubricate or repair linkage as necessary
	c) Range fork cracked, inserts worn, or fork is binding on shift rail	c) Disassemble unit and repair as necessary
	d) Annulus gear or lockplate worn or damaged	d) Disassemble unit and repair as necessary
Lubricate leaking from output shaft seals or from vent	a) Transfer case overfilled	a) Drain to correct level
	b) Vent closed or restricted	b) Clear or replace vent if necessary
	c) Output shaft seals damaged or installed incorrectly	c) Replace seals. Be sure seal lip faces interior of case when installed. Also be sure yoke seal surfaces are not scored or nicked. Remove scores, nicks with fine sandpaper or replace yoke(s) if necessary
Abnormal tire wear	a) Extended operation on dry hard surface (paved) roads in 4H range	a) Operate in 2H on hard surface (paved) roads

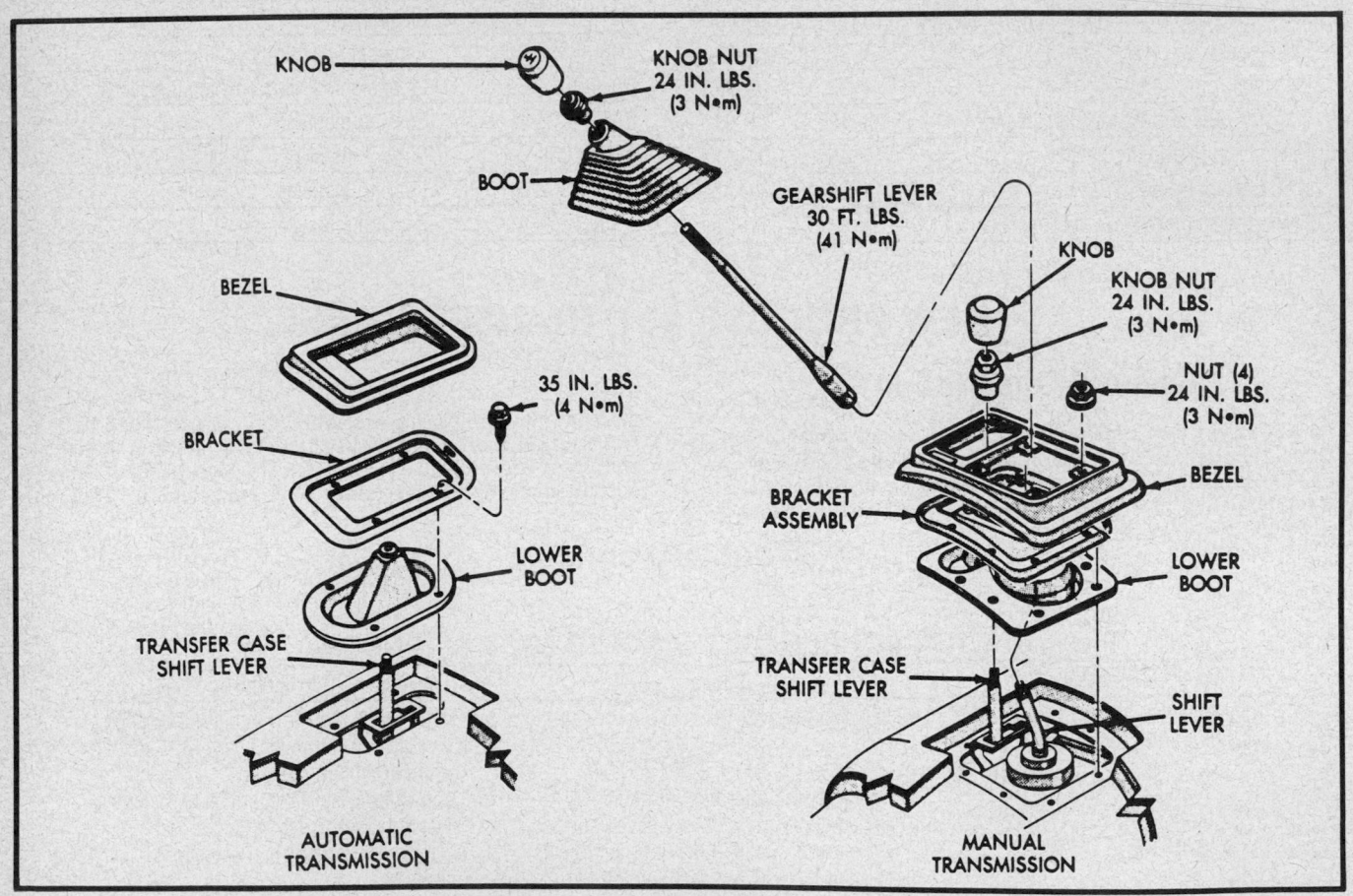

Exploded view of the transfer case shift linkage — Dodge Dakota

On Vehicle Services

SHIFT LINKAGE

Adjustment

DODGE DAKOTA

1. Place the shift lever in the **4H** position.
2. Remove the screws attaching the shift lever boot to the floorpan. Slide the boot upward to provide access to the shift gate.
3. Insert a ⅛ in. (3mm) spacer between the shift lever and the forward edge of the shift lever gate. Secure the lever and spacer in position with tape or wire.
4. Raise and support the vehicle safely. Loosen the adjusting link enough to allow the linkage to slide freely in the link.
5. Move the tranfer case range lever to the **4H** position. Position the linkage so it is a free fir in the range lever. Tighten the setscrew, in adjusting link, securely.
6. Lower the vehicle. Remove the shift lever spacer and install the boot to the floorpan.

GENERAL MOTORS S–10 AND S–15 SERIES TRUCKS

1. Remove the console assembly. Raise the upper boot on the shift lever.
2. Loosen the shift assembly lock bolt. Loosen the pivot bolt. Place the transfer case shifter lever in the **4HI** position.
3. Insert a ⅝ (8mm) drill bit through the shifter into the bracket.
4. Install a bolt at the lower transfer case shift lever. This will lock the transfer case in the **4HI** position.
5. Remove the bolt from the lower transfer case shift lever. Remove the drill bit.
6. Install the shift assembly lock bolt and torque it to 30 ft. lbs. Torque the shift lever through bolt with the grease fitting on it to 96 ft. lbs.
7. Install the upper boot and the console assembly.

JEEP CHEROKEE, COMANCHE AND WAGONEER

1. Remove the shift lever boot. Place the shift lever in the **4L** position.
2. Insert a 0.157 in. (4mm) spacer between the shift lever and

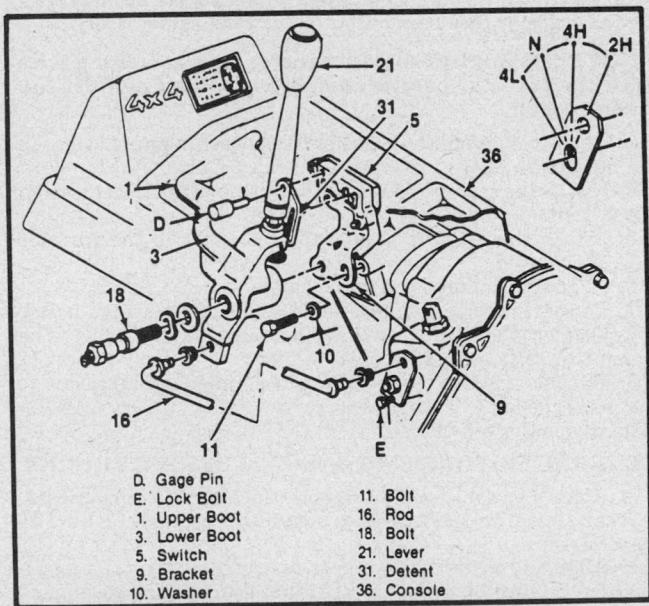

Exploded view of the transfer case shift linkage— General Motors S–10, S–15 and light trucks

D. Gage Pin
E. Lock Bolt
1. Upper Boot
3. Lower Boot
5. Switch
9. Bracket
10. Washer
11. Bolt
16. Rod
18. Bolt
21. Lever
31. Detent
36. Console

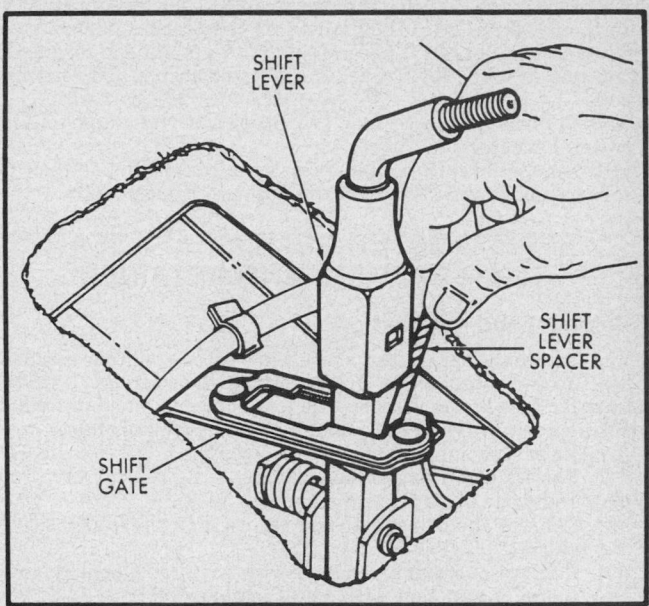

Installing the shift lever spacer — Jeep Wrangler

the forward edge of the shift lever gate. Secure the lever and spacer in position with tape or wire.
3. Raise and support the vehicle safely. Loosen the trunnion lock bolt. The linkage rod should now slide freely in the trunnion.
4. Be sure that the tranfer case range lever is still in the **4L** position. Position the linkage so it is a free fit in the range lever. Tighten the trunnion locknut.
5. Lower the vehicle. Remove the shift lever spacer and install the boot and bezel.

JEEP WRANGLER

1. Remove the transfer case shift knob locknut and remove the knob. Remove the shift lever boot. Place the shift lever in the **4L** position.
2. Insert a ⅛ in. (3mm) spacer between the shift lever and the forward edge of the shift lever gate. Secure the lever and spacer in position with tape or wire.
3. Raise and support the vehicle safely. Loosen the trunnion lock bolt. The linkage rod should now slide freely in the trunnion.
4. Be sure that the tranfer case range lever is still in the **4L** position. Position the linkage so it is a free fit in the range lever. Tighten the trunnion locknut.
5. Lower the vehicle. Remove the shift lever spacer and install the boot and shift knob.

SHIFT LEVER AND SELECTOR SWITCH

Removal and Installation
GENERAL MOTORS S–10 AND S–15 SERIES TRUCKS

1. Disconnect the negative battery cable.
2. Remove the console assembly and shift boot. Loosen the jam nut at the shift lever.
3. Disconnect the selector switch wiring harness and front axle switch wiring harness. Remove the selector switch retaining bolt and remove the switch.
4. Raise and support the vehicle safely.
5. Remove the shift rod from the shifter assembly.
6. Remove the pivot bolt, adjusting bolt and remove the shift lever assembly.
7. Install the shift lever assembly, pivot bolt and adjusting bolt. Install the shift rod into the shifter assembly. Adjust the shift linkage.

8. Lower the vehicle. Install the shift lever by screwing the shift lever down until the pawl clears the bracket. Then turn it down an additional 1½ turns. Install the jam nut and torque the jam nut to 18 ft. lbs. Install the selector switch and retaining bolt.

9. Connect the front axle switch wire harness and selector switch harness.

10. Install the shift boot and retaining screws. Install the console assembly and reconnect the negative battery cable.

SPEEDOMETER GEAR, SHAFT SEAL, REAR BEARING AND RETAINER

Removal and Installation

The front and rear output shaft seals, extension, rear retainer, bearing and speedometer drive gear can all be serviced with the transfer case in the vehicle. The following combined procedure outlines removal and installation of these components.

1. Raise and support the vehicle safely.
2. Place a drain pan under transfer case, remove the drain plug and drain fluid from the transfer case.
3. Remove the driveshaft and secure it to the under side of the vehicle.
4. Remove the extension seal with a suitable seal removal tool. Install a new seal with a seal installer tool.
5. Remove the extension housing. Remove the speedometer gear from the rear retainer. Mark the retainer for assembly alignment reference.
6. Remove the retainer attaching bolts and remove the retainer. Pry the retainer with a suitable tool to remove it.
7. Completely clean off all the old RTV sealant. If the retainer or bearing are to be replaced, remove the bearing retainer snapring from the rear retainer and remove the bearing.
8. Install the rear output bearing in the rear retainer. Apply a ⅛ in. bead or RTV sealant to the mating surface of the rear retainer. Align the retainer case reference marks and install the rear retainer on the case. Torque the rear retainer bolts to 18 ft. lbs.
9. Install the output shaft seal. Install the speedometer driven gear.
10. Fill the transfer case to the edge of the fill plug opening with the recommended lubricant. Install the speedometer driven gear. Install the drain plug to 35 ft. lbs.
11. Install the driveshaft and tighten the clamp strap bolts to 170 inch lbs. (19 Nm). Lower the vehicle.

Removal and Installation

TRANSFER CASE REMOVAL

EXCEPT GENERAL MOTORS S–10 AND S–15 SERIES TRUCKS

1. Raise the vehicle and support safely.
2. Remove the drain plug and drain the fluid from the transfer case.
3. Mark the transfer case front and rear output shaft yokes and driveshafts for assembly alignment and reference.
4. Disconnect the speedometer cable and vacuum switch hoses.
5. Disconnect the shift lever link from the operating lever.
6. Place a support stand under the transmission and remove the rear crossmember.
7. Mark the transfer case front and rear output shaft yokes and driveshafts for assembly alignment reference.
8. Disconnect the front and rear driveshafts at the transfer case yokes. Secure the shafts to the frame rails with wire.

NOTE: Do not allow the shafts to hang.

9. Remove the bolts attaching the exhaust pipe support bracket to the transfer case, if necessary.

10. Remove the transfer case-to-transmission nuts.
11. Move the transfer case assembly rearward until free of the transmission output shaft and remove the assembly.
12. Remove all the gasket material from the rear of the transmission adapter housing.

GENERAL MOTORS S–10 AND S–15 SERIES TRUCKS

1. Shift the vehicle into the **4HI** position. Raise the vehicle and support safely.
2. Remove the drain plug and drain the fluid from the transfer case.
3. Mark the transfer case front and rear output shaft yokes and driveshafts for assembly alignment and reference.
4. Remove the skid plate. Remove the front and rear driveshafts and secure them to the frame.
5. Disconnect the speedometer cable, electrical connections and vacuum harness.
6. Remove the shift lever from the case. Remove the catalytic converter hanger bolts at the converter.
7. Place a suitable transmission jack under the transmission and transfer case assembly. Remove the transmission mounting bolts and raise the transmission assembly.
8. Remove the catalytic converter hanger. Lower the transmission assembly.
9. Suport the transfer case with a suitable stand and remove the transfer case to transmission case bolts. On vehicles with automatic transmissions, remove the shift lever bracket mounting bolts from the adapter to permit the removal of the upper left transfer attaching bolts.
10. Remove the transfer case from the adpater or the the extension housing.

TRANSFER CASE INSTALLTION

EXCEPT GENERAL MOTORS S–10 AND S–15 SERIES TRUCKS

1. Apply a suitable sealant to both sides of the transfer case-to-transmission gasket and position the gasket on the transmission.
2. Align and install the transfer case assembly on the transmission. Be sure the transfer case input gear splines are aligned with the transmission output shaft. Align the splines by rotating the transfer case rear output shaft yoke as necessary.

NOTE: Do not install any transfer case attaching nuts until the transfer case is completely seated against the transmission.

3. Align and install the transfer case attaching nuts. Tighten the nuts to 35 ft. lbs (48 Nm).
4. Install the rear crossmember and remove the transmission support stand.
5. Attach the exhaust pipe support bracket to the transfer case, if removed.
6. Align and connect the driveshafts.
7. Connect the speedometer cable and vacuum switch hoses.
8. Connect the shift lever to the operating lever. Tighten the locknut to 18 ft. lbs. (23 Nm).
9. Fill the transfer case with the recommended lubricant to the proper level.
10. Lower the vehicle.

GENERAL MOTORS S–10 AND S–15 SERIES TRUCKS

1. Apply a suitable sealant to both sides of the transfer case-to-transmission gasket and position the gasket on the transmission.
2. Align and install the transfer case assembly on the transmission. Be sure the transfer case input gear splines are aligned with the transmission output shaft. Align the splines by rotating the transfer case rear output shaft yoke as necessary.

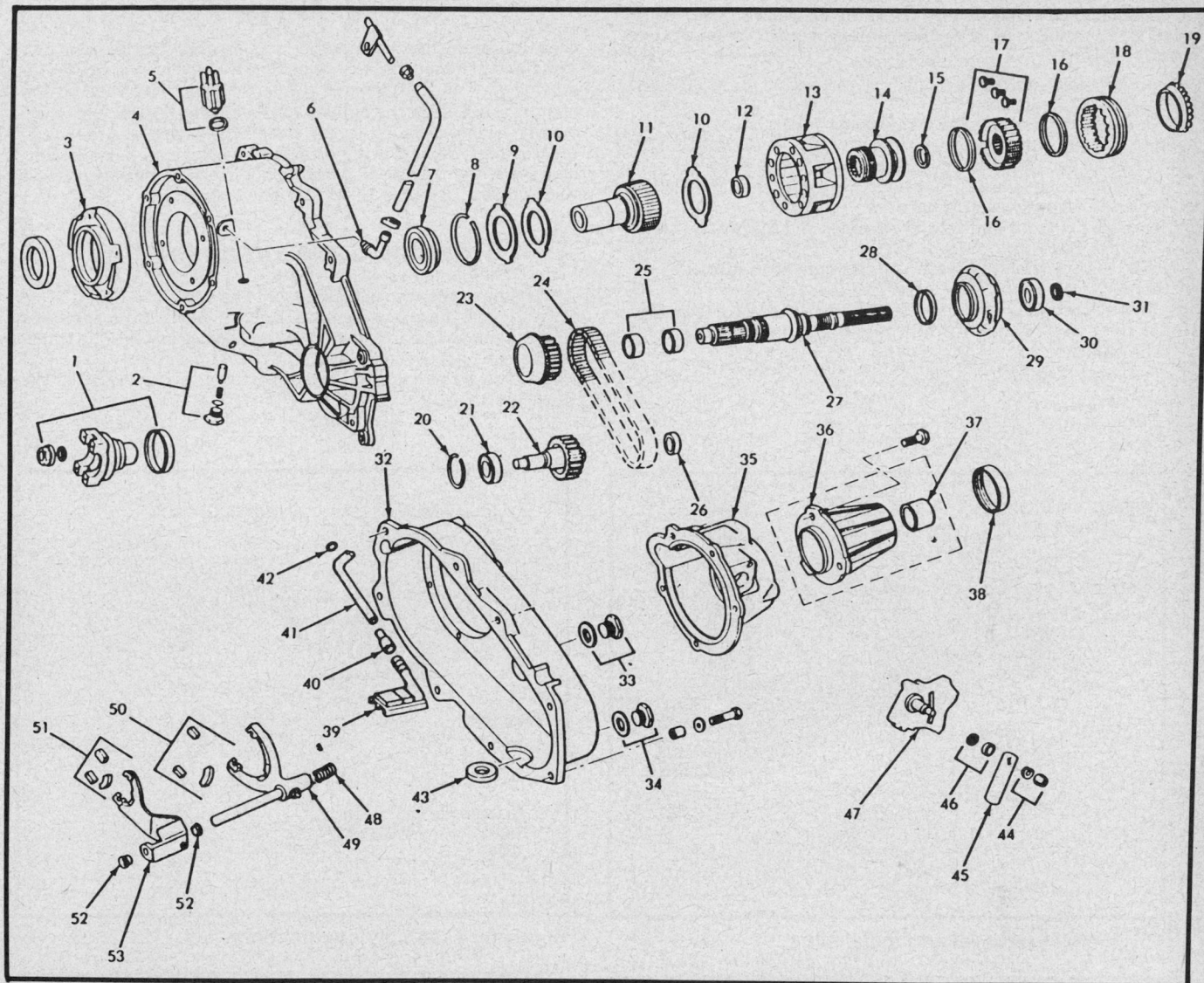

Exploded view of the NP231 Transfer case

1. Front yoke nut, seal washer, yoke, and oil seal
2. Shift detent plug, spring, and pin
3. Front retainer and seal
4. Front case
5. Vacuum switch and seal
6. Vent assembly
7. Input gear bearing and snap ring
8. Low range gear snap ring
9. Input gear retainer
10. Low range gear thrust washers
11. Input gear
12. Input gear pilot bearing
13. Low range gear
14. Range fork shift hub
15. Synchronizer hub snap ring
16. Synchronizer hub springs
17. Synchronizer hub and inserts
18. Synchronizer sleeve
19. Synchronizer stop ring
20. Snap ring
21. Output shaft front bearing
22. Output shaft (front)
23. Drive sprocket
24. Drive chain
25. Drive sprocket bearings
26. Output shaft rear bearing
27. Mainshaft
28. Oil seal
29. Oil pump assembly
30. Rear bearing
31. Snap ring
32. Rear case
33. Fill plug and gasket
34. Drain plug and gasket
35. Rear retainer
36. Extension housing
37. Bushing
38. Oil seal
39. Oil pickup screen
40. Tube connector
41. Oil pickup tube
42. Pickup tube O-ring
43. Magnet
44. Range lever nut and washer
45. Range lever
46. O-ring and seal
47. Sector
48. Mode spring
49. Mode fork
50. Mode fork inserts
51. Range fork inserts
52. Range fork bushings
53. Range fork

NOTE: Do not install any transfer case attaching nuts until the transfer case is completely seated against the transmission.

3. Align and install the transfer case attaching nuts. Tighten the nuts to 23 ft. lbs.

4. Install the transmission mount and the catalytic converter hanger. Torque the tranmission mount bolts to 22 ft. lbs. (29 Nm) and the converter hanger bolts to 40 ft. lbs. (54 Nm).

5. Install the shift lever. Reconnect the speedometer, electrical connections and vacuum harness.

6. Install the front and rear driveshafts and torque the bolts to 15 ft. lbs. (20 Nm).

7. Fill the transfer case with the recommended lubricant to the proper level.

8. Install the skid plate and torque the bolts to 21 ft. lbs. (28 Nm). Lower the Vehicle. Install the negative battery and road test the vehicle.

Before Disassembly

Cleanliness during disassembly and assembly is necessary to avoid further transfer case trouble after overhaul. Before removing any of the transfer case subassemblies, plug all the openings and clean the outside of the of the transfer case thoroughly. Steam cleaning or car wash type high pressure equipment is preferable. During disassembly, clean all parts in suitable solvent and dry each part. Do not use cloth or paper towels to dry parts. Use compressed air only.

Transfer Case Disassembly

1. Remove the transfer case from the vehicle.

2. Remove the attaching nuts from the front and rear output yokes. Remove the yokes and sealing washers. Move the transfer case selector lever rearward to the **4L** position.

3. Remove the bolts and tap the extension housing off of the

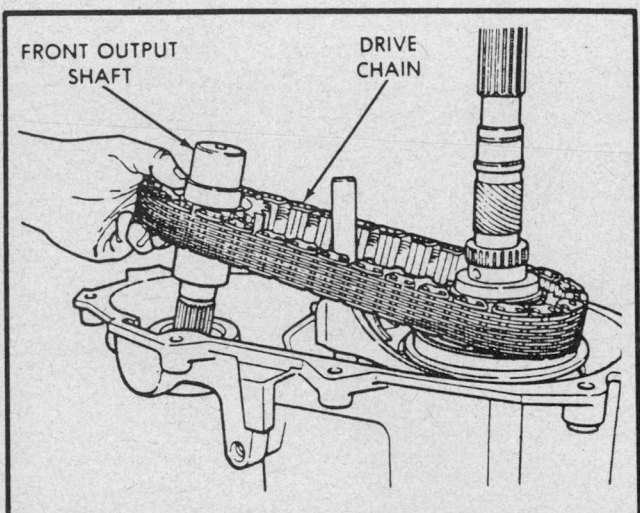

Drive chain removal and Installation

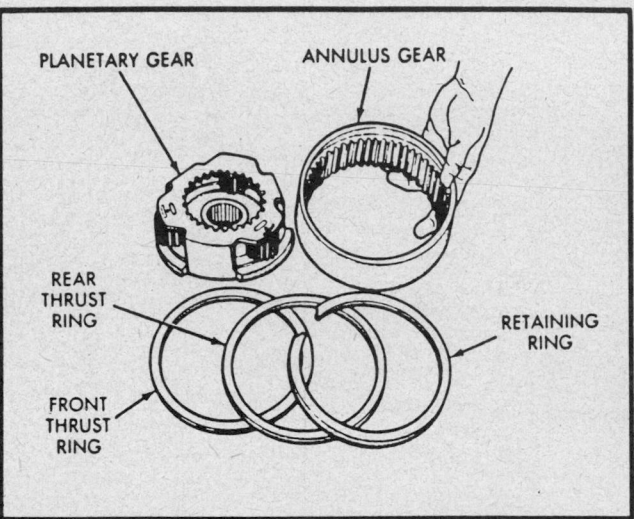

Planetary assembly components

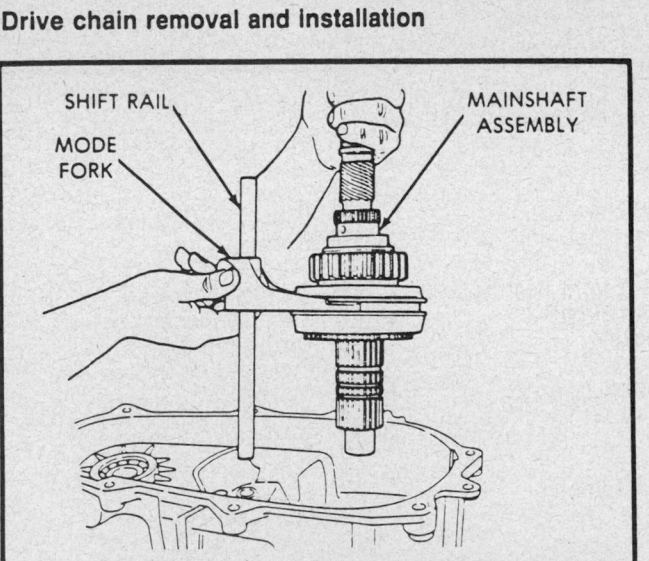

Mainshaft assembly removal

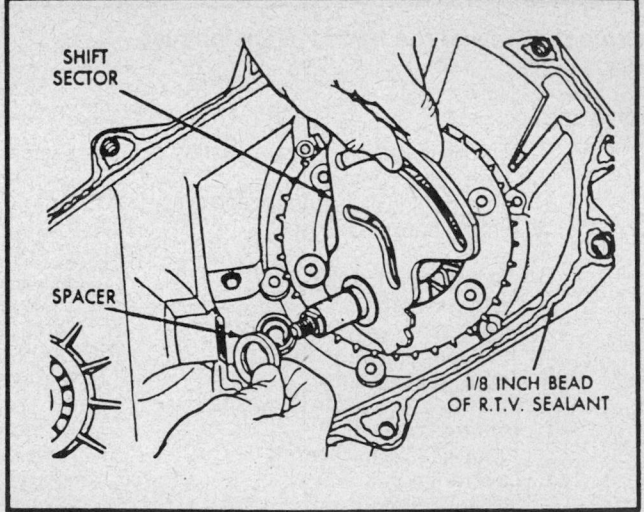

Shift selector removal

rear retainer. Tap the extension housing in the clockwise direction to break the sealer bead, then remove the housing.

NOTE: To avoid damaging the sealing surfacee of the extension housing and rear retainer, do not attempt to pry or wedge the housing off of the retainer.

4. Remove the snapring from the rear bearing, then, remove the 4 bolts and separate the rear bearing retainer from the rear case half.
5. Remove the rear retainer, position a pry bar under each of the tabs on the retainer housing and carefully pry the retainer upward and off the rear case. Remove the bolts attaching the rear case to the front case. Separate the rear case from the front case.
6. Remove the oil pump and rear case as an assembly. Slide the oil screen out of the case pocket. Disconnect the screen from the pickup tube and remove the screen. Remove the pickup tube from the oil pump and remove the oil pump from the rear case.
7. Remove the pickup tube O-ring from the oil pump and mark the oil pump housing for assembly reference.
8. Remove the screws that attach the 2 halves of the pump. Remove the feed housing from the gear housing. Be sure to note the position of the pump gears and remove them from the housing.
9. Remove the mode spring from the shift rail. Tap the front output shaft upward to free it from the shaft bearing. Remove the front output shaft and drive chain as an assembly.
10. Remove the mainshaft, mode fork and spring rail assembly from the front case half. Remove the mode fork and shift rail from the synchro sleeve. Remove the synchro sleeve from the mainshaft.
11. Remove the synchro hub snapring, hub and stop ring. Remove the drive sprocket.
12. Slide the range fork pin out of the shift selector. Remove the range fork and shift hub. Remove the transfer case range lever from the sector shaft. Remove the shift sector.
13. Remove the sector shaft bushing and O-ring. Remove the shift detent pin, spring and plug.
14. Turn the front case over and remove the front bearing retainer bolts. Remove the front bearing retainer. Remove the input gear snapring.
15. Press the input low range gear assembly out of the input bearing with a suitable arbor press. Remove the low range gear snapring. Remove the retainer, thrust washers and input gear from the low range gear.
16. Remove the oil seals from the retainer, rear extension housing, oil pump feed housing and case halves. Remove the magnet from the front of the case.
17. Remove the speedometer driven gear, seals and adaptor.

CLEANING AND INSPECTION

Cleaning

During overhaul, all components of the transfer case (except bearing assemblies) should be thoroughly cleaned with solvent and dried with air pressure prior to inspection and reassembly.
1. Clean the bearing assemblies as follows:

NOTE: Proper cleaning of bearings is of utmost importance. Bearings should always be cleaned separately from other parts.

a. Soak all bearing assemblies in clean solvent or fuel oil. Bearings should never be cleaned in a hot solution tank.
b. Slush bearings in solvent until all old lubricant is loosened. Hold races so that bearings will not rotate; then clean bearings with a soft bristled brush until all dirt has been removed. Remove loose particles of dirt by tapping bearing flat against a block of wood.
c. Rinse bearings in clean solvent; then blow bearings dry with air pressure.

CAUTION
Do not spin bearings while drying.
---

d. After drying, rotate each bearing slowly while examining balls or rollers for roughness, damage, or excessive wear. Replace all bearings that are not in first class condition.

NOTE: After cleaning and inspecting bearings, lubricate generously with recommended lubricant, then wrap each bearing in clean paper until ready for reassembly.

2. Remove all portions of old gaskets from parts, using a stiff brush or scraper.

Inspection

1. Inspect all parts for discoloration or warpage.
2. Examine all gears and splines for chipped, worn, broken or nicked teeth. Small nicks or burrs may be removed with a fine abrasive stone.
3. Inspect the breather assembly to make sure that it is open and not damaged.
4. Check all threaded parts for damaged, stripped, or crossed threads.
5. Replace all gaskets, oil seals and snaprings.
6. Inspect housings, retainers and covers for cracks or other damage. Replace the damaged parts.
7. Inspect keys and keyways for condition and fit.
8. Inspect shift forks for wear, distortion or any other damage.
9. Check detent ball springs for free length, compressed length, distortion or collapsed coils.
10. Check bearing fit on their respective shafts and in their bores or cups. Inspect bearings, shafts and cups for wear.

NOTE: If either bearings or cups are worn or damaged, it is advisable to replace both parts.

11. Inspect all bearing rollers or balls for pitting or galling.
12. Examine detent balls for corrosion or brinneling. If shift bar detents show wear, replace them.
13. Replace all worn or damaged parts. When assembling the transfer case, coat all moving parts with recommended lubricant.

Transfer Case Assembly

Before assembly, lubricate all parts with the recommended lubricant. The bearing bores in the various transfer case components contain oil feed holes. Be sure the replace bearings do not block these feed holes.
1. Remove the input gear pilot bearing with a suitable slide hammmer and seal removal tool.
2. Install a new input gear pilot bearing into the input gear.
3. Assemble the low range gear, input gear thrust washers, input gear and input gear retainer.
4. Install the low range gear snapring. Lubricate the input gear with automatic transmission fluid. Start the input gear into the front bearing. Press the input gear into the front bearing.

NOTE: Use a proper size tool to press the input gear into the front bearing. An incorrect tool could push the input gear pilot bearing too far into the gear bore. Also, do not press against the end faces of the low range gear. The gear cae and thrust washers could be damaged.

5. Install a new input gear snapring. Install a new oil seal in the front bearing retainer. Apply a ⅛ in. (3mm) wide bead of RTV sealant to the front bearing retainer seal surface. Install the front bearing retainer on the front case. Torque the retainer bolts to 16 ft. lbs. (21 Nm).

6. Install a new sector shaft O-ring and bushing. Install the shift sector in the case. Install the range lever and lever attaching nut on the shift sector. Torque the attaching nut to 22 ft. lbs. (32 Nm).

7. Install the detent pin, spring and plug. Torque the plug to 15 ft. lbs. (20 Nm). Install new pads and shift rail bushings in the range fork. Assemble the range fork and shift hub. Engage the range fork pin in the sector slot.

8. If the drive sprocket bearings are to be replaced install them as follows:
   a. Press both bearings out of the sprockets simultaneously.
   b. Install a new front bearing by pressing the bearing flush with the edge of the bore.
   c. Install the rear bearing by pressing the bearing in until it is $\frac{3}{16}$ in. (4.6mm) below the edge of the bore.

NOTE: Do not press the bearings any farther into the sprocket than specified. The bearings could block the mainshaft oil feed hole pressed too deeply into the sprocket.

9. Install the synchro hub springs struts and spring. Lubricate the drive sprocket bearings, the stop ring and synchro hub with the recommended fluid. Install the sprocket, stop ring and synchro hub on the mainshaft. Be sure to seat the hub struts on the stop ring lugs.

10. Install the synchro hub snapring. Install the sleeve on the synchro hub. Be sure the sleeve is installed with the beveled spline ends facing the stop ring. Install the new pads on the mode fork and install the shift rail in the fork.

11. Engage the mode fork in the synchro sleeve. Install the mode fork mainshaft assembly in the case. Be sure the mode fork rail is seated in both of the range fork bushings.

12. Assemble and install the output shaft and drive chain. Lift the mainshaft slightly to ease the chain and shaft installation. Install the mode spring on the shift rail.

13. Install a new output shaft rear bearing. Remove the bearing with an internal type puller and slide hammer. Seat the new bearing in the case with a suitable seal installer.

14. Install a new seal in the oil pump feed housing. Assemble the oil pump. Lubricate and install the 2 gears in the gear housing. Align and install the feed housing on the gear housing. Install and tighten the oil pump screws to 14 inch lbs.

15. Install the pickup tube O-ring in the oil pump. Insert the oil pickup tube in the oil pump. Attach the oil screen and connecting hose to the pickup tube. Install thre assembled oil pump, pickup tube and screen in the rear case. Be sure that the screen isseated in the case slot. Install the magnet in the front case.

16. Apply a ⅛ in. (3mm) wide bead of RTV sealant to the sealing surface of the front case. Align and install the rear case on the front case. Be sure the case locating dowels are in place and the mainshaft splines are engaged in the oil pump inner gear.

17. Install and torque the front case to rear case attaching bolts to 22 ft. lbs. (32 Nm). Be sure to install a washer under each of the bolts use at each case dowel locations.

18. Apply a ⅛ in. (3mm) wide bead of RTV sealant to the flange surface of the rear retainer. Install the locating dowel in the rear retainer and install the retainer on the case. Torque the retainer bolts to 18 ft. lbs. (23 Nm). Install a new rear bearing snapring. Lift the mainshaft slightly to seat the snapring in the shaft groove.

19. Install a new seal in the extension housing. Apply a ⅛ in. (3mm) wide bead of RTV sealant to the flange surface of the extension housing. Install the exstension housing on the case, torque the retaining bolt to 30 ft. lbs. (41 Nm).

20. Install the front yoke. Secure the yoke with a replacement seal washer and nut. Torque the nut to 110 ft. lbs. (149 Nm).

21. Install a replacement gasket on the vacuum switch and install the switch in the case.

22. Install the speedometer driven gear, seals and adapter. Refill the transfer case with the recommended fluid to the proper level. Install and torque the drain plug to 35 ft. lbs. (48 Nm).

Specifications

TORQUE SPECIFICATIONS
New Process 231 Transfer Case

Description	Ft. Lbs.	N•m
Bolt, Low Range Lock Plate	25	34
Vacuum Switch	20	27
Nut, Range Lever	18	24
Bolt, Front Case-to-Rear Case	22	30
Bolt, Rear Retainer	18	24
Bolt, Extension Housing	22	30
Plug, Drain/Fill	35	47
Bolt, Adapter-to-Transfer Case	24	33
Nut, Transfer Case-to-Adapter	26	35
U-Joint Clamp Strap Bolts	14	19

NEW PROCESS 242 TRANSFER CASE

General Description

The NP242 is a part time unit with a built-in low range reduction gear system. It has 4 operating ranges plus a Neutral position. The low-range system provides a 2.72:1 gear reduction ratio for increased low-speed torque capacity. The unit has a 2 piece aluminum housing assembly. On the front case half, the front output shaft, front input shaft, 4WD indicator switch and shift lever assembly are located. On the rear case half, the rear output shaft, bearing retainer and drain and fill plugs are located.

The NP242 transfer case provides a 2WD and a full time 4WD drive operation. An interaxle differential is used to control the torque transfer to the front and rear axles. The differential has a locking mechanism to undifferentiated 4WD in the high and low ranges.

On Vehicle Services

SHIFT LINKAGE

ADJUSTMENT

1. Remove the shift lever boot. Place the shift lever in the **4L** position.
2. Insert a 0.157 in. (4mm) spacer between the shift lever and the forward edge of the shift lever gate. Secure the lever and spacer in position with tape or wire.
3. Raise and support the vehicle safely. Loosen the trunnion lock bolt. The linkage rod should now slide freely in the trunnion.
4. Be sure that the transfer case range lever is still in the **4L** position. Position the linkage so it is a free fit in the range lever. Tighten the trunnion locknut.
5. Lower the vehicle. Remove the shift lever spacer and install the boot and bezel.

SPEEDOMETER GEAR, SHAFT SEAL, REAR BEARING AND RETAINER

Removal and Installation

The front and rear output shaft seals, extension, rear retainer, bearing and speedometer drive gear can all be serviced with the transfer case in the vehicle. The following combined procedure outlines removal and installation of these components.

1. Raise and support the vehicle safely.
2. Place a drain pan under transfer case, remove the drain plug and drain fluid from the transfer case.
3. Remove the driveshaft and secure it to the under side of the vehicle.
4. Remove the extension seal with a suitable seal removal tool. Install a new seal with a seal installer tool.
5. Remove the extension housing. Remove the speedometer gear from the rear retainer. Mark the retainer for assembly alignment reference.
6. Remove the retainer attaching bolts and remove the retainer. Pry the retainer with a suitable tool to remove it.
7. Completely clean off all the old RTV sealant. If the retainer or bearing are to be replaced, remove the bearing retainer snapring from the rear retainer and remove the bearing.

8. Install the rear output bearing in the rear retainer. Apply a ⅛ in. bead or RTV sealant to the mating surface of the rear retainer. Align the retainer case reference marks and install the rear retainer on the case. Torque the rear retainer bolts to 18 ft. lbs. (23 Nm).
9. Install the output shaft seal. Install the speedometer driven gear.
10. Fill the transfer case to the edge of the fill plug opening with the recommended lubricant. Install the speedometer driven gear.Install the drain plug to 35 ft. lbs. (48 Nm).
11. Install the driveshaft and tighten the clamp strap bolts to 170 inch lbs. (19 Nm). Lower the vehicle.

Removal and Installation

TRANSFER CASE REMOVAL

1. Raise the vehicle and support safely.
2. Remove the drain plug and drain the fluid from the transfer case.
3. Mark the transfer case front and rear output shaft yokes and driveshafts for assembly alignment and reference.
4. Disconnect the speedometer cable and vacuum switch hoses.
5. Disconnect the shift lever link from the operating lever.
6. Place a support stand under the transmission and remove the rear crossmember.
7. Mark the transfer case front and rear output shaft yokes and driveshafts for assembly alignment reference.
8. Disconnect the front and rear driveshafts at the transfer case yokes. Secure the shafts to the frame rails with wire.

NOTE: Do not allow the shafts to hang.

9. Remove the bolts attaching the exhaust pipe support bracket to the transfer case, if necessary.
10. Remove the transfer case-to-transmission nuts.
11. Move the transfer case assembly rearward until free of the transmission output shaft and remove the assembly.
12. Remove all the gasket material from the rear of the transmission adapter housing.

TRANSFER CASE INSTALLATION

1. Apply a suitable sealant to both sides of the transfer case-to-transmission gasket and position the gasket on the transmission.
2. Align and install the transfer case assembly on the transmission. Be sure the transfer case input gear splines are aligned with the transmission output shaft. Align the splines by rotating the transfer case rear output shaft yoke as necessary.

NOTE: Do not install any transfer case attaching nuts until the transfer case is completely seated against the transmission.

3. Align and install the transfer case attaching nuts. Tighten the nuts to 26 ft. lbs. (35 Nm).
4. Install the rear crossmember and torque the rear crossmember bolts to 30 ft. lbs. (41 Nm). Remove the transmission support stand.
5. Attach the exhaust pipe support bracket to the transfer case, if removed.
6. Align and connect the driveshafts.
7. Connect the speedometer cable and vacuum switch hoses.

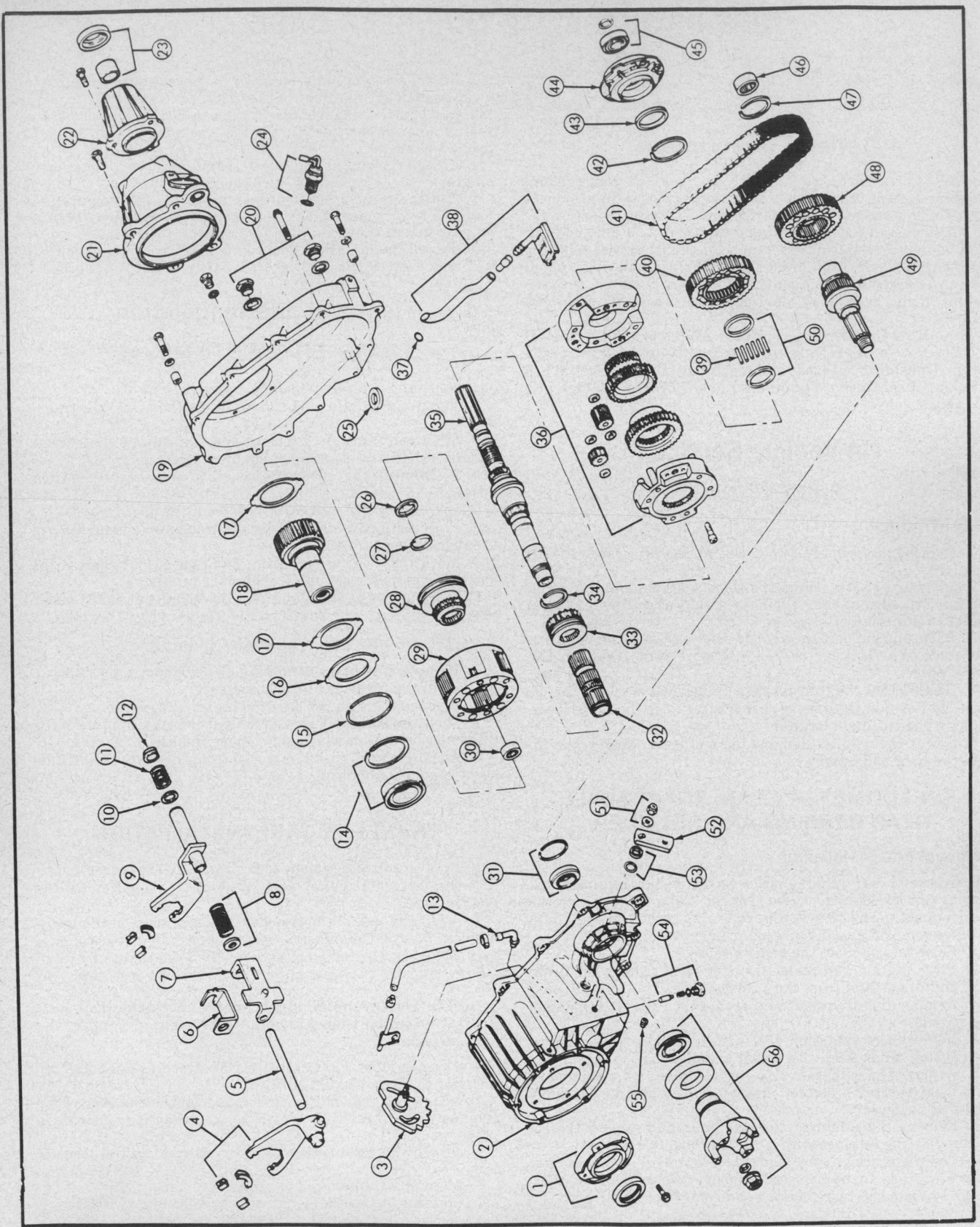

Exploded view of the view of the NP242 transfer case assembly

Trouble Diagnosis
CHILTON'S THREE C'S TRANSFER CASE DIAGNOSIS

Condition	Cause	Correction
Transfer case difficult to shift or will not shift into desired range	a) Vehicle speed too great to permit shifting	a) Stop vehicle and shift into desired range. Or reduce speed to 2–3 mph (3–4 km/h) before attempting to shift
	b) If vehicle was operated for extended period in 4H mode on dry paved surface, driveline torque load may cause difficulty	b) Stop vehicle, shift transmission to neutral, shift transfer case to 2H mode and operate vehicle on 2H on dry paved surfaces
	c) Transfer case external shift linkage binding	c) Lubricate, repair or replace linkage, or tighten loose components as necessary
	d) Insufficient or incorrect lubricant	d) Drain and refill to edge of fill hole
	e) Internal components binding, worn or damaged	e) Disassemble unit and replace worn or damaged components as necessary
Transfer case noisy in all drive modes	a) Insufficient or incorrect lubricant	a) Drain and refill to edge of fill hole. If unit is still noisy after drain and refill, disassembly and inspection may be required to locate source of noise
Noisy in—or jumps out of the four-wheel-drive low range	a) Transfer case not completely engaged in 4L position	a) Stop vehicle, shift transfer case to Neutral, then shift back into 4L position
	b) Shift linkage loose or binding	b) Tighten, lubricate, or repair linkage as necessary
	c) Range fork cracked, inserts worn, or fork is binding on shift rail	c) Disassemble unit and repair as necessary
	d) Annulus gear or lockplate worn or damaged	d) Disassemble unit and repair as necessary
Lubricant leaking from output shaft seals or from vent	a) Transfer case overfilled	a) Drain to correct level
	b) Vent closed or restricted	b) Clear or replace vent if necessary
	c) Output shaft seals damaged or installed incorrectly	c) Replace seals. Be sure seal lip faces interior of case when installed. Also be sure yoke seal surfaces are not scored or nicked. Remove scores and nicks with fine sandpaper or replace yoke(s) if necessary

1 FRONT BEARING RETAINER AND SEAL
2 FRONT CASE
3 SHIFT SECTOR
4 LOW RANGE FORK AND INSERTS
5 SHIFT RAIL
6 SHIFT BRACKET
7 SLIDER BRACKET
8 BUSHING AND SPRING
9 MODE FORK AND INSERTS
10 BUSHING
11 FORK SPRING
12 BUSHING
13 VENT TUBE ASSEMBLY
14 INPUT GEAR BEARING AND SNAP RING
15 LOW RANGE GEAR SNAP RING
16 RETAINER, LOW RANGE GEAR
17 THRUST WASHER, LOW RANGE GEAR
18 INPUT GEAR
19 REAR CASE
20 DRAIN/FILL PLUGS
21 REAR BEARING RETAINER
22 EXTENSION HOUSING
23 BUSHING AND OIL SEAL
24 VACUUM SWITCH
25 MAGNET
26 THRUST RING
27 SNAP RING
28 SHIFT SLEEVE
29 LOW RANGE GEAR
30 PILOT BUSHING (INPUT GEAR/MAINSHAFT)
31 FRONT OUTPUT SHAFT FRONT BEARING AND SNAP RING
32 INTERMEDIATE CLUTCH SHAFT
33 SHIFT SLEEVE
34 SNAP RING
35 MAINSHAFT
36 DIFFERENTIAL ASSEMBLY
37 OIL PUMP TUBE O-RING
38 OIL PUMP PICKUP TUBE AND SCREEN
39 MAINSHAFT BEARING ROLLERS
40 DRIVE SPROCKET
41 DRIVE CHAIN
42 SNAP RING
43 OIL PUMP SEAL
44 OIL PUMP
45 REAR BEARING AND SNAP RING
46 FRONT OUTPUT SHAFT REAR BEARING
47 SNAP RING
48 DRIVEN SPROCKET
49 FRONT OUTPUT SHAFT
50 MAINSHAFT BEARING SPACERS
51 SHIFT LEVER WASHER AND NUT
52 SHIFT LEVER
53 SECTOR O-RING AND SEAL
54 DETENT PIN, SPRING AND PLUG
55 SEAL PLUG
56 FRONT YOKE NUT, SEAL WASHER, YOKE, SLINGER AND OIL SEAL

8. Connect the shift lever to the operating lever. Tighten the locknut to 18 ft. lbs. (23 Nm).

9. Fill the transfer case with the recommended lubricant to the proper level.

10. Lower the vehicle.

Before Disassembly

Cleanliness during disassembly and assembly is necessary to avoid further transfer case trouble after overhaul. Before removing any of the transfer case subassemblies, plug all the openings and clean the outside of the of the transfer case thoroughly. Steam cleaning or car wash type high pressure equipment is preferable. During disassembly, clean all parts in suitable solvent and dry each part. Do not use cloth or paper towels to dry parts. Use compressed air only.

Transfer Case Disassembly

1. Place the transfer case into a suitable holding fixture.

2. Remove the attaching nuts from the front and rear output yokes. Remove the yokes and sealing washers. Move the transfer case selector lever rearward to the 4L position.

3. Remove the bolts and tap the extension housing off of the rear retainer. Tap the extension housing in the clockwise direction to break the sealer bead, then remove the housing.

NOTE: To avoid damaging the sealing surface of the extension housing and rear retainer, do not attempt to pry or wedge the housing off of the retainer.

4. Remove the snapring from the rear bearing, then, remove the 4 bolts and separate the rear bearing retainer from the rear case half.

5. Remove the rear retainer, position a pry bar under each of the tabs on the retainer housing and carefully pry the retainer upward and off the rear case. Remove the bolts attaching the rear case to the front case. Separate the rear case from the front case.

6. Remove the oil pump and rear case as an assembly. Slide the oil screen out of the case pocket. Disconnect the screen from the pickup tube and remove the screen. Remove the pickup tube from the oil pump and remove the oil pump from the rear case.

7. Remove the pickup tube O-ring from the oil pump and mark the oil pump housing for assembly reference.

8. Remove the screws that attach the 2 halves of the pump. Remove the feed housing from the gear housing. Be sure to note the position of the pump gears and remove them from the housing.

9. Remove the mode spring from the shift rail. Tap the front output shaft upward to free it from the shaft bearing. Remove the front output shaft and drive chain as an assembly.

10. Remove the transfer case shift lever nut and lever. Remove the shift detent plug, spring and pin.

11. Remove the seal plug from the low range fork lockpin access hole. Move the shift selector to align the low range fork lockpin with the access hole. Remove the range fork lockpin with a size No. 1 easy out* tool or equivalent. Grip the easy out with a locking pliers and remove the pin with a counterclockwise, twist and pull motion. Remove the shift rail by pulling it strait up and out of the fork.

12. Remove the mainshaft, mode fork and spring rail assembly from the front case half. Remove the mode fork and shift rail from the synchro sleeve. Remove the synchro sleeve from the mainshaft.

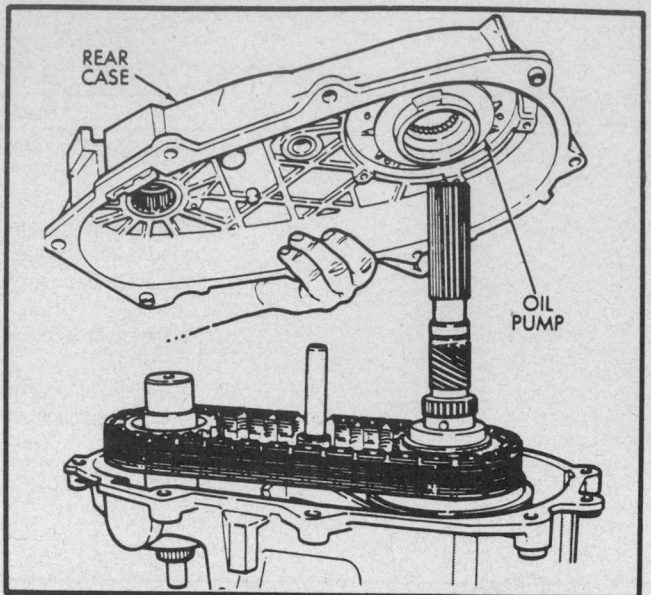

Removing the rear case and oil pump assembly

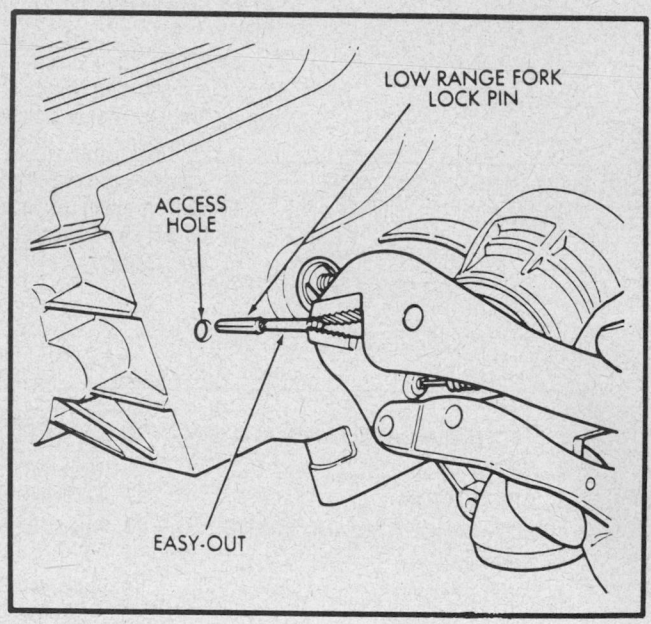

Removing the low range fork lockpin

13. Remove the intermediate clutch shaft snapring, the clutch shaft thrust ring, intermediate clutch shaft, differential snapring and remove the differential.

14. Remove the differential needle bearings and the 2 needle bearing thrust washers from the mainshaft.

15. Slide the range fork pin out of the shift selector. Remove the range fork and shift hub. Remove the transfer case range lever from the sector shaft. Remove the shift sector.

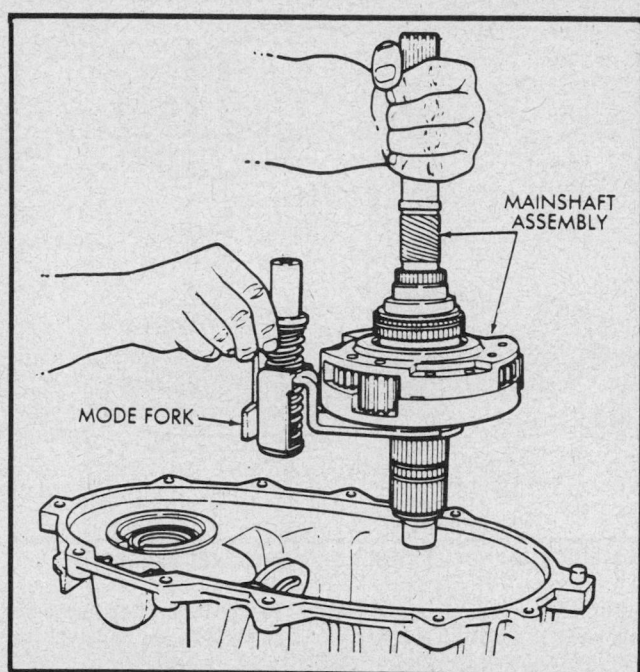

Removing the mode fork and mainshaft

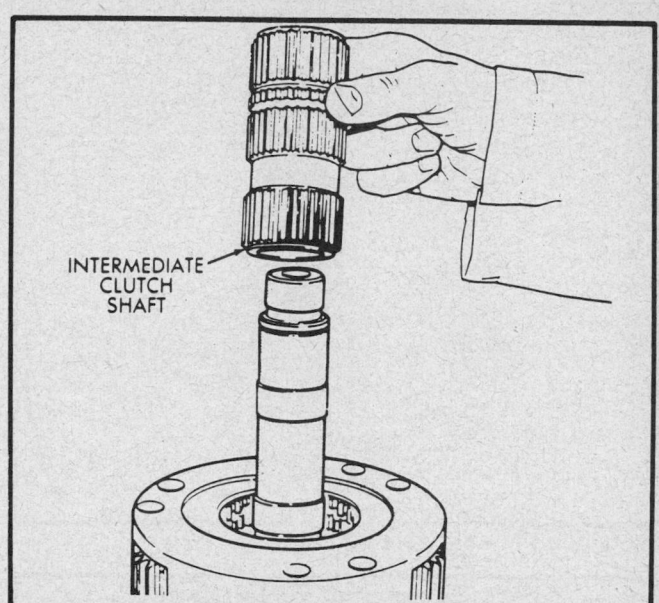

Removing the intermediate clutch shaft

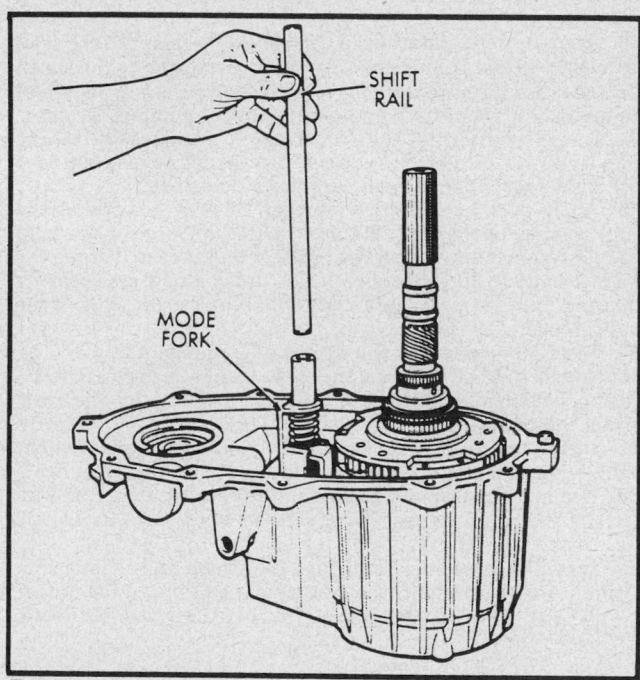

Removing the shift rail

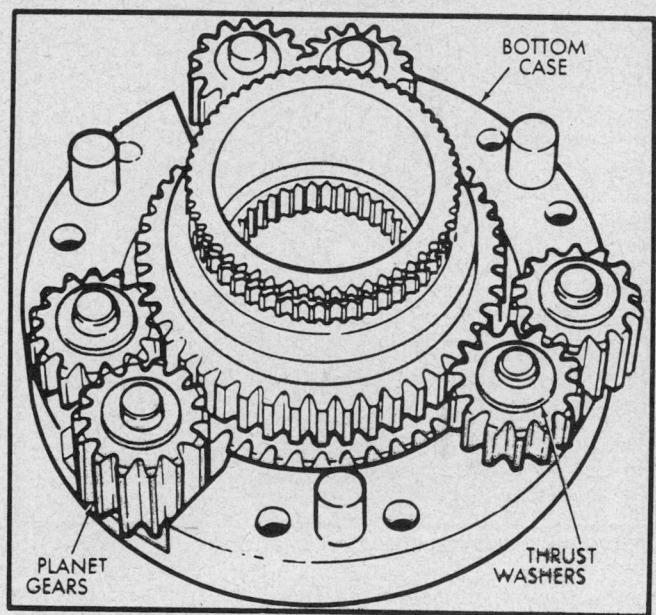

Removing the planet gears and carrier

16. Remove the sector shaft bushing and O-ring. Remove the shift detent pin, spring and plug.

17. Turn the front case over and remove the front bearing retainer bolts. Remove the front bearing retainer. Remove the input gear snapring.

18. Press the input low range gear assembly out of the input bearing with a suitable arbor press. Remove the low range gear snapring. Remove the retainer, thrust washers and input gear from the low range gear.

NOTE: The gear is not a serviceable component. If it is damaged, replace the gear and front case as an assembly.

19. Remove the oil seals from the retainer, rear extension housing, oil pump feed housing and case halves. Remove the magnet from the front of the case.

20. Remove the speedometer driven gear, seals and adaptor.

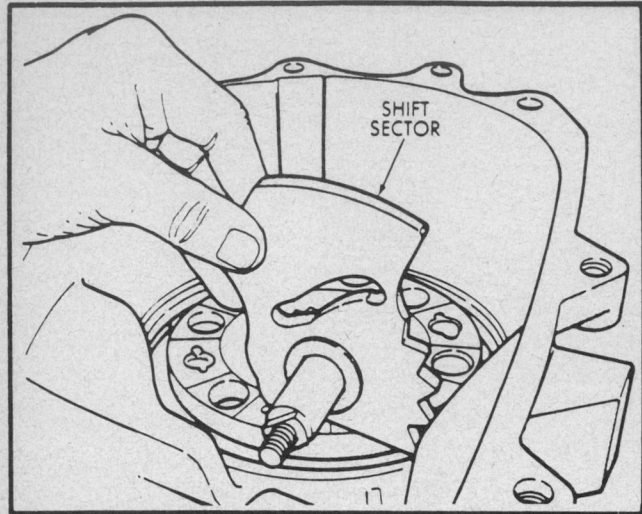

Installing the shift selector

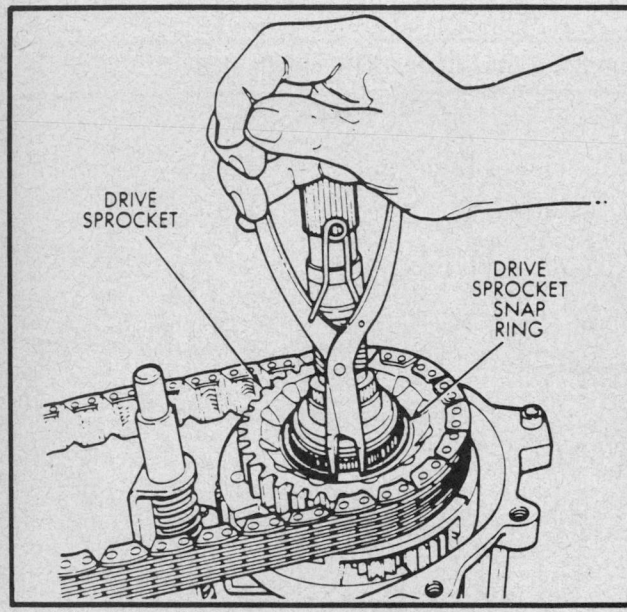

Installing the drive sprocket snapring

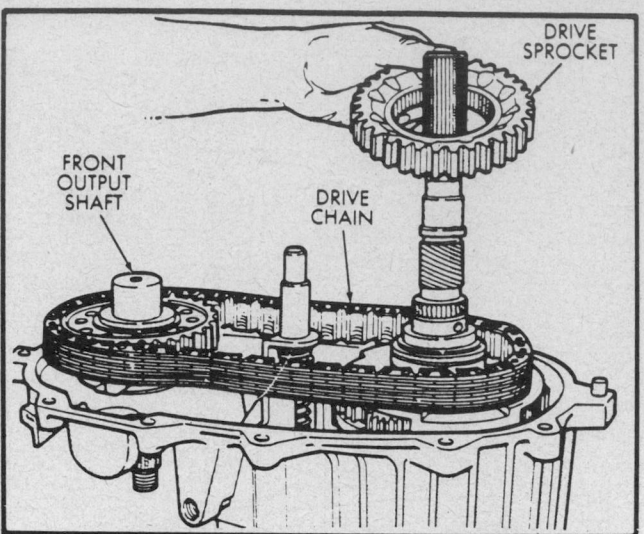

Installing the drive chain and sprocket assembly

the chain and shaft installation. Install the drive sprocket. Engage the drive sprocket with the chain. Engage the sprocket splines with the mainshaft splines. Install a new drive socket snapring.

20. Install a new output shaft rear bearing. Remove the bearing with an internal type puller and slide hammer. Seat the new bearing in the case with a suitable seal installer.

21. Install a new seal in the oil pump feed housing. Assemble

the oil pump. Lubricate and install the 2 gears in the gear housing. Align and install the feed housing on the gear housing. Install and tighten the oil pump screws to 14 inch lbs.

22. Install the pickup tube O-ring in the oil pump. Insert the oil pickup tube in the oil pump. Attach the oil screen and connecting hose to the pickup tube. Install thre assembled oil pump, pickup tube and screen in the rear case. Be sure that the screen isseated in the case slot. Install the magnet in the front case.

23. Apply a ⅛ in. (3mm) wide bead of RTV sealant to the sealing surface of the front case. Align and install the rear case on the front case. Be sure the case locating dowels are in place and the mainshaft splines are engaged in the oil pump inner gear.

24. Install and torque the front case to rear case attaching bolts to 30 ft. lbs. (41 Nm).Be sure to install a washer under each of the bolts use at each case dowel locations.

25. Apply a ⅛ in. (3mm) wide bead of RTV sealant to the flange surface of the rear retainer. Install the locating dowel in the rear retainer and install the retainer on the case. Torque the retainer bolts to 30 ft. lbs. (41 Nm). Install a new rear bearing snapring. Lift the mainshaft slightly to seat the snapring in the shaft groove.

26. Install a new seal in the extension housing. Apply a ⅛ in. (3mm) wide bead of RTV sealant to the flange surface of the extension housing. Install the exstension housing on the case, torque the retaining bolt to 30 ft. lbs. (41 Nm).

27. Install the front yoke. Secure the yoke with a replacement seal washer and nut. Torque the nut to 110 ft. lbs. (169 Nm).

28. Install a replacement gasket on the vacuum switch and install the switch in the case. Torque the switch to 20 ft. lbs. (27 Nm).

29. Install the speedometer driven gear, seals and adapter. Refill the transfer case with the recommended fluid to the proper level. Install and torque the drain plug to 35 ft. lbs. (48 Nm).

Specifications

TORQUE SPECIFICATIONS
NP242 Transfer Case

Component	ft. lbs.	Nm
Extension housing bolt	30	41
Rear retainer bolt	30	41
Front case-to-rear case bolt	30	41
Front yoke nut	110	149
Front bearing retainer bolt	16	21
Differential housing bolt	N/A	N/A
Shift lever nut	22	30
Switch	20	27
Detent spring cover	15	20
Drain and fill plug	35	47
Oil pump screw	14	1.6

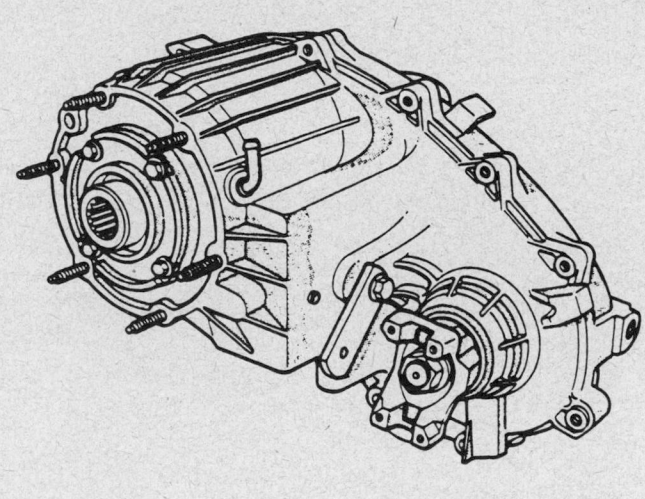

Model 242 Transfer Case

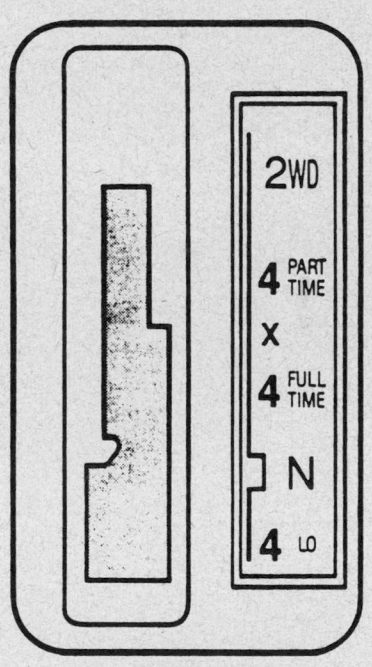

Shift Pattern

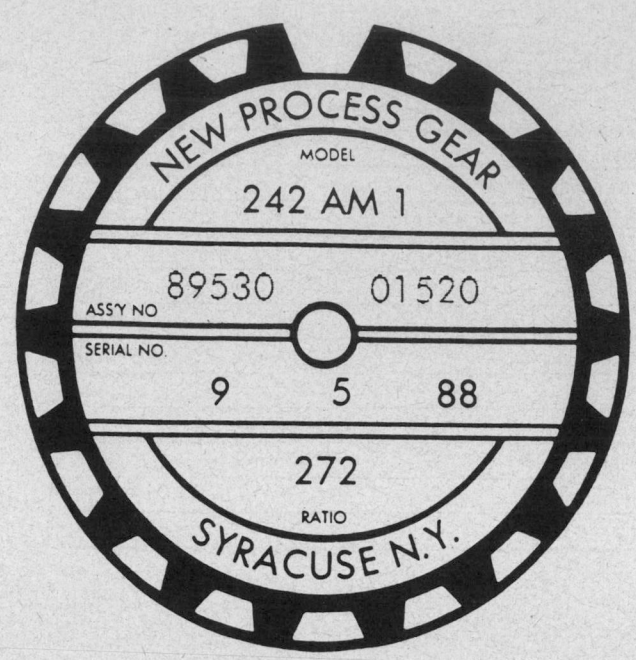

Transfer Case I.D. Tag

GROUP INDEX

ALPHABETICAL INDEX

LABOR — 1 TUNE UP 1 — LABOR

	Chilton Time
Compression Test	
All models	.6

Engine Tune Up, (Electronic Ignition)
Includes: Test battery and clean connections. Tighten manifold and carburetor mounting bolts. Check engine compression, clean and adjust or renew spark plugs. Test resistance of spark plug cables. Inspect distributor cap and rotor. Adjust air gap. Check vacuum advance operation. Reset ignition timing. Adjust idle mixture and idle speed. Service air cleaner. Inspect and adjust drive belts. Inspect choke operation and adjust or free up. Check operation of EGR valve.

	Chilton Time
All models	1.5

LABOR — 2 IGNITION SYSTEM 2 — LABOR

GASOLINE ENGINES

	Chilton Time
Spark Plugs, Clean and Reset or Renew	
All models	.5
Ignition Timing, Reset	
All models	.4
Distributor, Renew	
Includes: Reset ignition timing.	
All models	.6
Distributor Reluctor, Renew	
Includes: R&R distributor and reset ignition timing and dwell.	
All models	1.0
Vacuum Control Unit, Renew	
Includes: R&R distributor and reset ignition timing and dwell.	
All models	.9

	Chilton Time
Pick-Up Set, Renew	
Includes: R&R distributor and reset ignition timing.	
All models	1.1
Ignitor Set, Renew	
Includes: R&R distributor and reset ignition timing.	
All models	1.0
Distributor Cap and/or Rotor, Renew	
All models	.4
Electronic Ignition Control Unit, Renew	
All models	.8
Ignition Cables, Renew	
All models	.5
Ignition Coil, Renew	
All models	.6

	Chilton Time
Ignition Switch, Renew	
All models	.7
Electronic Ignition Ballast Resistor, Renew	
All models	.3

DIESEL ENGINE

	Chilton Time
Glow Plugs, Renew	
All models	
one or all	.5
Glow Plug Relay, Renew	
All models	.4
Glow Plug Control Unit, Renew	
All models	.4

LABOR — 3 FUEL SYSTEM 3 — LABOR

GASOLINE ENGINES

	Chilton Time
Fuel Pump, Test	
Includes: Disconnect line at carburetor, attach pressure gauge.	
All models	.3
Carburetor Air Cleaner, Service	
All models	.2
Carburetor, Adjust (On Truck)	
All models	.6
Propane enrichment	1.2
Automatic Choke Cover/Float Chamber, Renew	
All models	1.5
Dash Pot, Renew	
(w/Manual Trans)	
All models	.4
Engine Speed Sensor, Renew	
All models	.6
Accelerator Pump, Renew	
All models	.5
Needle Valve and Seat, Renew	
Includes: Renew float, reset idle speed.	
All models	1.7
Enrichment Body Assembly, Renew	
All models	1.5

	Chilton Time
Vacuum Throttle Opener, Renew	
All models	.8
Fuel Cut-Off Solenoid, Renew	
All models	.4
Carburetor Sub-EGR Valve, Renew	
All models	.7
Fuel Filter, Renew	
All models	.4
Carburetor, Renew	
Includes: All necessary adjustments.	
All models	1.5
Carburetor, R&R and Clean or Recondition	
Includes: All necessary adjustments.	
All models	2.9
Fuel Pump, Renew	
All models	1.2
Add pump test if performed.	
Fuel Tank, Renew	
Includes: Drain and refill tank.	
All models	1.5
Fuel Gauge (Dash), Renew	
All models	1.2
Fuel Gauge (Tank), Renew	
All models	1.4

	Chilton Time
Intake Manifold or Gasket, Renew	
All models	4.1

DIESEL ENGINE

	Chilton Time
Injection Pump Timing, Adjust	
All models	.6
Fuel Injection Pump Assy., Renew	
All models	2.0
Injection Nozzles, R&R or Renew	
All models-one	.6
each adtnl	.4
Clean or recond add-each	.3
Fuel Filter Bleed Pump, Renew	
All models	.4
Fuel Temperature Sensor, Renew	
All models	.7
Water Level Sensor, Renew	
All models	.7
Turbocharger Assy., R&R or Renew	
Includes: Renew gasket.	
All models	1.5
Intake and Exhaust Manifold Gaskets, Renew	
All models	1.8

LABOR 3A EMISSION CONTROLS 3A LABOR

	Chilton Time		Chilton Time		Chilton Time
Fuel Vapor Canister, Renew		**Aspirator, Renew**		**Secondary Air Supply Reed Valve, Renew**	
All models	.3	All models	.4	All models	.4
Fuel Vapor Separator, Renew		**Pulse Air Feeder or Aspirator Tube, Renew**		**Enrichment Solenoid Valve, Renew**	
All models-one or both	1.4	All models	1.0	All models	.4
E.G.R. Valve, Renew		**P.C.V. Valve, Renew**		**Jet Mixture Solenoid Valve, Renew**	
All models	.5	All models	.2	All models	.4
Coolant Control Valve (CCEGR), Renew		**Oxygen Sensor, Renew**		**Deceleration Solenoid Valve, Renew**	
All models	.5	All models	.6	All models	.4
Pulse Air Feeder, Renew		**High Altitude Compensator, Renew**			
All models	1.2	All models	.6		

LABOR 4 ALTERNATOR AND REGULATOR 4 LABOR

	Chilton Time		Chilton Time		Chilton Time
Alternator Circuits, Test		**Alternator, R&R and Recondition**		**Alternator Gauge, Renew**	
Includes: Test battery, regulator and alternator output.		Includes: Test and disassemble.		All models	.7
All models	.6	All models	2.5		
Alternator, Renew		**Alternator, R&R and Renew Bearings**		**Instrument Cluster Voltage Limiter, Renew**	
Includes: Transfer pulley if required.		All models	1.7	All models	.9
All models	1.4	**Voltage Regulator, Test and Renew**			
Add circuit test if performed.		All models	1.6		

LABOR 5 STARTING SYSTEM 5 LABOR

	Chilton Time		Chilton Time		Chilton Time
Starter Draw Test (On Truck)		**Starter, R&R and Recondition**		**Starter Drive, Renew**	
All models	.3	Includes: Test starter relay, starter solenoid and amperage draw. Turn down armature.		Includes: R&R starter.	
		All models	2.3	All models	1.2
		Renew field coils add	.5	**Battery Cables, Renew**	
Starter, Renew		**Starter Solenoid, Renew**		All models-each	.4
Includes: Test starter relay, starter solenoid and amperage draw.		Includes: R&R starter.		**Battery Terminals, Clean**	
All models	1.0	All models	1.1	All models	.3

LABOR 6 BRAKE SYSTEM 6 LABOR

	Chilton Time
Brakes, Adjust (Minor)	
Includes: Adjust brake shoes, fill master cylinder.	
two wheels	.4
Bleed Brakes (Four Wheels)	
Includes: Fill master cylinder.	
All models	.6
Brake Shoes and/or Pads, Renew	
Includes: Install new or exchange brake shoes or pads. Adjust service and hand brake. Bleed system.	
front-disc	.9
rear-drum	1.4
all four wheels	2.2
Resurface disc rotor, add-each	.9
Resurface brake drum, add-each	.5
Brake Drum, Renew (One)	
All models	.4

Combinations
Add to Brakes, Renew

	Chilton Time		Chilton Time
RENEW WHEEL CYLINDER		**RENEW BRAKE HOSE**	
Each	.2	Each	.3
REBUILD WHEEL CYLINDER		**RENEW REAR WHEEL INNER OIL SEAL**	
Each	.3	Each	.3
REBUILD CALIPER ASSEMBLY		**REPACK FRONT WHEEL BEARINGS (BOTH WHEELS)**	
Each	.5	All models	.6
RENEW MASTER CYLINDER		**RENEW DISC BRAKE ROTOR**	
All models	.6	Each	.3
REBUILD MASTER CYLINDER		**DISC BRAKE ROTOR STUDS, RENEW**	
All models	.6	Each	.1

BRAKE HYDRAULIC SYSTEM

	Chilton Time		Chilton Time		Chilton Time
Wheel Cylinder, Renew		**Wheel Cylinder, R&R and Rebuild**		**Master Cylinder, Renew**	
Includes: Bleed system.		Includes: Hone cylinder and bleed system.		Includes: Bleed system.	
All models-one	.9	All models-one	1.2	All models	1.0
both	1.7	both	2.3		

LABOR — 6 BRAKE SYSTEM 6 — LABOR

Master Cylinder, R&R and Rebuild
Includes: Hone cylinder and bleed system.
All models 1.6

Brake Hose, Renew (Flex)
Includes: Bleed system.
All models-one 6
each adtnl 3

Brake System Combination Valve, Renew
Includes: Bleed system.
All models 1.2

POWER BRAKES

Power Brake Booster, Renew
All models 1.1

Check Valve, Renew
All models 2

DISC BRAKES

Disc Brake Pads, Renew
Includes: Install new disc brake pads only.
All models 9

Disc Brake Rotor, Renew (Disc Only)
All models-one 1.0
both 1.9

Disc Brake Hub Assy., Renew
Includes: Renew inner and outer bearings if required.
All models-one 1.3
both 2.5

Caliper Assembly, Renew
Includes: Bleed system.
All models-one 8
both 1.5

Caliper Assy., R&R and Recondition
Includes: Bleed system.
All models-one 1.3
both 2.5

PARKING BRAKE

Parking Brake, Adjust
All models 3

Parking Brake Control, Renew
All models 7

Parking Brake Cable, Renew
All models-one 1.0

Parking Brake Warning Lamp Switch, Renew
All models 3

LABOR — 7 COOLING SYSTEM 7 — LABOR

Winterize Cooling System
Includes: Run engine to check for leaks, tighten all hose connections. Test radiator and pressure cap, drain radiator and engine block. Add antifreeze and refill system.
All models 5

Thermostat, Renew
All models 5

Radiator Assembly, R&R or Renew
Includes: Drain and refill cooling system.
All models 7
w/A.T. add 2

ADD THESE OPERATIONS TO RADIATOR R&R

Boil & Repair 1.5
Rod Clean 1.9
Repair Core 1.3
Renew Tank 1.6
Renew Trans. Oil Cooler 1.9
Recore Radiator 1.7

Radiator Hoses, Renew
upper 4
lower 4
both 6

Water Pump, Renew
All models
Gas
chain drive 1.4
belt drive 2.0
Diesel 1.7
w/P.S. add 4

Fan Blades, Renew
All models 5
w/A.C. add 2
w/P.S. add 1

Fan and Alternator Belt, Renew
All models 3

Fan and Alternator Belt, Adjust
All models 2

Fluid Fan Drive Unit, Renew
All models 5
w/A.C. add 2
w/P.S. add 1

Temperature Gauge (Dash Unit), Renew
All models 1.2

Temperature Gauge (Engine Unit), Renew
All models 4

Transmission Auxiliary Oil Cooler, Renew
All models 1.0

Heater Core, R&R or Renew
Raider 1.7
Ram 50 .... 5.5

ADD THESE OPERATIONS TO HEATER CORE R&R

Boil & Repair 1.2
Repair Core 9
Recore 1.2

Heater Water Valve, Renew
All models 9
w/A.C. add 1

Heater Control Assembly, Renew
All models 9

Heater Blower Motor Switch, Renew
All models 6

Heater Blower Motor, Renew
All models 1.0

Heater Blower Motor Resistor, Renew
All models 4

LABOR — 8 EXHAUST SYSTEM 8 — LABOR

Muffler, Renew
All models 6

Exhaust Pipe, Renew
All models 7

Catalytic Converter, Renew
All models 1.0

Exhaust Manifold or Gasket, Renew
All models-Gas 1.2
Diesel 1.8

LABOR — 9 FRONT SUSPENSION 9 — LABOR

Note: On all front suspension operations alignment charges must be added if performed. Time given does not include alignment.

Wheel, Renew
one 5

Wheels, Rotate (All)
All models 5

Wheels, Balance
one 3
each adtnl 2

Toe-In, Adjust
All models 6

Align Front End
Includes: Adjust front wheel bearings.
Raider 1.7
Ram 50 .... 1.4

Front Wheel Bearings, Clean and Repack (Both Wheels)
All models 1.2

LABOR 9 FRONT SUSPENSION 9 LABOR

	Chilton Time
Front Wheel Bearings and Cups, Renew	
Includes: Renew dust seal.	
All models-one side	.8
both sides	1.5
Renew axle shaft outer seal & brg add	.7
Steering Knuckle, Renew	
Add alignment charges.	
4X2 models-one	1.6
both	3.0
4X4 models-one	1.8
both	3.5
Steering Knuckle Arm, Renew	
4X2 models-one	1.0
both	1.8
4X4 models-one	1.5
both	2.9
Lower Control Arm Assy., Renew	
Add alignment charges.	
4X2 models-one	2.1
both	4.0
4X4 models-one	1.6
both	3.0
Lower Ball Joint, Renew	
Add alignment charges.	
4X2 models-one	1.8
both	3.5
4X4 models-one	1.3
both	2.5
Lower Control Arm Strut Bar or Bushings, Renew	
All models-one side	.9
both sides	1.5
Lower Control Arm Bushings, Renew	
Add alignment charges.	
4X2 models-one side	2.0
both sides	3.7
4X4 models-one side	1.7
both sides	3.3

	Chilton Time
Upper Control Arm Assy., Renew	
Includes: Align front end.	
All models-one	2.5
both	4.3
Upper Ball Joint, Renew	
Add alignment charges.	
4X2 models-one	1.5
both	2.8
4X4 models-one	1.6
both	3.0
Front Coil Spring, Renew	
All models-one	1.9
both	3.5
Front Shock Absorbers, Renew	
All models-one	.7
both	1.1
Front Sway Bar, Renew	
All models	1.5
Front Sway Bar Bushings, Renew	
All models-one or all	.5
Front Torsion Bars, Renew	
All models-one	.5
both	.8
Torsion Bar Anchor/Adjusting Bolt, Renew	
All models-one	.6
both	1.0
4 WHEEL DRIVE FRONT AXLE	
Front Differential, Drain & Refill	
All models	.6
Front Axle Housing Cover or Gasket, Renew	
All models	.6
Drive Pinion Oil Seal, Renew	
All models	.8
Front Axle Propeller Shaft Flange, Renew	
All models	.6
Axle Shaft Boot, Renew (One)	
Includes: Clean and lubricate C/V joint.	
All models	1.9

	Chilton Time
Front Axle Shaft, Renew (One)	
Includes: Renew outer wheel bearings if required.	
1986-87	
outer-w/Joint	2.0
inner	1.6
1988-90	
outer-w/Joint	1.2
inner	1.6
Locking Hub Assy., Renew or Recondition	
All models-each	.5
Axle Shaft C.V. Joint, Renew	
All models-inner	1.8
Front Propeller Shaft, Renew	
All models	
transfer case to ft axle	.6
Differential Side Bearings, Renew	
Includes: R&R ring gear and pinion, renew axle housing oil seals and adjust bearing preload and backlash.	
All models	4.9
Differential Side Gears, Renew	
Includes: Renew axle housing oil seals if required.	
All models	4.7
Differential Case, Renew	
Includes: R&R ring gear and pinion, renew bearings and gears, renew pinion and axle housing seals. Adjust backlash.	
All models	5.1
Ring Gear and Pinion Set, Renew	
Includes: Renew pinion bearing, side bearings and all seals. Adjust bearing preload and backlash.	
All models	5.6
Renew diff case add	.2
Front Axle Housing, Renew	
Includes: Renew oil seals. Transfer axle shafts, differential and brake assemblies.	
All models	5.7

LABOR 10 STEERING LINKAGE 10 LABOR

	Chilton Time
Tie Rods or Tie Rod Ends, Renew	
Includes: Reset toe-in.	
All models-one side	1.0
both sides	1.7
Idler Arm, Renew	
All models	.5

	Chilton Time
Center Link (Relay Rod), Renew	
All models	.6
Pitman Arm, Renew	
All models	.6

LABOR 11 STEERING GEAR 11 LABOR

	Chilton Time
MANUAL STEERING	
Steering Wheel, Renew	
All models	.5
Horn Contact Ring or Cable, Renew	
All models	.4
Steering Column Flex Coupling, Renew	
All models	1.3
w/P.S. add	.3
Steering Column Mast Jacket, Renew	
Does not include painting.	
All models	1.5

	Chilton Time
Steering Column Upper Mast Jacket Bearing, Renew	
All models	1.6
Steering Gear, Adjust (On Truck)	
All models	.5
Steering Gear Assy., R&R or Renew	
All models	1.0
Steering Gear, R&R and Recondition	
Includes: Disassemble, renew parts as required, reassemble and adjust.	
All models	1.9

	Chilton Time
Sector Shaft Oil Seal, Renew	
All models	.8
POWER STEERING	
Power Steering Pump Pressure Check	
All models	.5
Pump Drive Belt, Renew	
All models	.3
Power Steering Gear, R&R or Renew	
All models	2.0

LABOR   11 STEERING GEAR 11   LABOR

	Chilton Time
Power Steering Gear, R&R and Recondition	
Includes: Disassemble, renew all parts as required, reassemble and adjust.	
All models	2.7
Steering Gear Sector Shaft, Adjust	
All models	.6
Sector Shaft Oil Seals, Renew	
Includes: Renew inner and outer seals.	
All models	2.1
Gear Control Valve Assy., Renew	
All models	3.1

	Chilton Time
Power Steering Pump, Test and Renew	
Includes: Transfer or renew pulley as required.	
All models	1.0
Power Steering Pump, R&R and Recondition	
All models	1.9
Pump Flow Control Valve, Test and Clean or Renew	
All models	.9
Power Steering Pump Reservoir, Renew	
Includes: Renew seals.	
All models	.6

	Chilton Time
Pump Drive Shaft Oil Seal, Renew	
All models	1.6
Power Steering Hoses, Renew	
All models	
pressure	.9
return	.9
supply	.4

LABOR   12 CYLINDER HEAD & VALVE SYSTEM 12   LABOR

	Chilton Time
GASOLINE ENGINE	
Compression Test	
All models	.6
Cylinder Head Gasket, Renew	
Includes: Clean carbon. Minor tune up.	
All models	3.5
Cylinder Head, Renew	
Includes: Reface and adjust valves, clean carbon. Minor tune up.	
All models	6.5
Clean Carbon and Grind Valves	
Includes: R&R cylinder head, reface valves and seats. Minor tune up.	
All models	6.2
Jet Valve, Renew	
All models-one or all	1.1
Cylinder Head Cover Gasket, Renew	
All models	.6

	Chilton Time
Valve Rocker Arms, Renew	
All models	
all-one side	1.4
all-both sides	2.3
Valve Tappets, Renew (Lifters)	
All models	
2.6L eng-one or all	1.1
Valve Springs or Valve Stem Oil Seals, Renew (Head on Car)	
All models-one cyl	1.3
all cyls	3.0
Valve Clearance, Adjust	
All models	1.5
DIESEL ENGINE	
Compression Test	
All models	.6
Cylinder Head Gasket, Renew	
Includes: Clean carbon. Make all necessary adjustments.	
All models	3.5

	Chilton Time
Cylinder Head, Renew	
Includes: Reface and adjust valves, clean carbon. Make all necessary adjustments.	
All models	6.2
Clean Carbon and Grind Valves	
Includes: R&R cylinder head, reface valves and seats. Make all necessary adjustments.	
All models	5.5
Cylinder Head Cover Gasket, Renew	
All models	.6
Valve Rocker Arms, Renew	
All models	1.1
Valve Springs and/or Valve Stem Oil Seals, Renew (All)	
All models	4.2
Valve Clearance, Adjust	
All models	1.5

LABOR   13 ENGINE ASSEMBLY & MOUNTS 13   LABOR

	Chilton Time
GASOLINE ENGINES	
Note: All engine operations listed in this group are for assemblies as supplied by the original equipment manufacturer. Time to replace assemblies from independent rebuilders may vary.	
Engine Assembly, Remove and Install	
Does not include transfer of any parts or equipment.	
All models	5.9
w/A.C. add	.6
4X4 add	1.7
Short Engine Assembly, Renew (w/All Internal Parts Less Head and Oil Pan)	
Includes: R&R engine, transfer all necessary parts not supplied with replacement engine.	

	Chilton Time
Minor tune up.	
All models	12.6
w/A.C. add	.6
4X4 add	1.7
Recond valves add	2.5
Engine Assy., R&R and Recondition	
Includes: Rebore block, install new pistons, pins, rings, rod and main bearings. Clean carbon, grind valves. Tune engine.	
All models	20.8
w/A.C. add	.6
4X4 add	1.7
Engine Mounts, Renew	
All models-front	.7
rear	.6

	Chilton Time
DIESEL ENGINE	
Engine Assembly, Remove and Install	
Does not include transfer of any parts or equipment.	
All models	5.1
w/A.C. add	.6
Short Engine Assembly, Renew (w/All Internal Parts Less Cyl. Head and Oil Pan)	
Includes: R&R engine assy. Transfer all necessary parts not supplied with replacement engine. Clean carbon, grind valves. Make all necessary adjustments.	
All models	14.7
w/A.C. add	.6
Engine Mounts, Renew	
All models-one	.5
both	.7

LABOR 14 PISTONS, RINGS & BEARINGS 14 LABOR

GASOLINE ENGINES

Rings, Renew
Includes: Replace connecting rod bearings, deglaze cylinder walls, remove cylinder top ridge, clean carbon from cylinder head. Minor tune up.

Ram 50	5.8
one cyl	5.8
all cyls	7.7
4X4 add	2.3
Raider	
one cyl	7.4
all cyls	10.0

Pistons or Connecting Rods, Renew
Includes: Replace connecting rod bearings, deglaze cylinder walls, remove cylinder top ridge, replace piston rings. Clean carbon from cylinder head. Minor tune up.

Ram 50	
one cyl	6.1
all cyls	8.9
4X4 add	2.3
Raider	
one cyl	7.7
all cyls	11.2

Connecting Rod Bearings, Renew

Ram 50	2.5
4X4 add	2.4
Raider	4.9

COMBINATIONS

DRAIN, EVACUATE & RECHARGE AIR CONDITIONING SYSTEM All models	1.0	**RECONDITION CYLINDER HEAD (HEAD REMOVED)** All models	2.5
DISTRIBUTOR, RECONDITION All models	1.0	**MAIN BEARINGS, RENEW (PAN REMOVED)** All models	1.5
CARBURETOR, RECONDITION All models	1.6	**PLASTIGAUGE BEARINGS** Each	.1
DEGLAZE CYLINDER WALLS Each	.1	**RENEW OIL PUMP** All models	1.7
REMOVE CYLINDER TOP RIDGE Each	.1	**OIL FILTER ELEMENT, RENEW** All models	.2

DIESEL ENGINE

Chilton Time

Rings, Renew
Includes: Replace connecting rod bearings, deglaze cylinder walls, remove cylinder top ridge, clean carbon from cylinder head. Make all necessary adjustments.

All models	7.1

Chilton Time

Pistons or Connecting Rods, Renew
Includes: Replace connecting rod bearings, deglaze cylinder walls, remove cylinder top ridge, replace piston rings. Clean carbon from cylinder head. Make all necessary adjustments.

All models	8.3

Connecting Rod Bearings, Renew

All models	3.1

LABOR 15 CRANKSHAFT & DAMPER 15 LABOR

GASOLINE ENGINES

Chilton Time

Crankshaft and Main Bearings, Renew
Includes: R&R engine assembly.

Ram 50	12.5
4X4 add	1.7
Raider	14.2
w/A.C. add	.6
w/P.S. add	.1

Main Bearings, Renew
Includes: Replace pan gasket and oil seals, plastigauge all bearings.

Ram 50	4.0
4X4 add	1.7
Raider	5.7

Main and Rod Bearings, Renew
Includes: Replace pan gasket and oil seals, plastigauge all bearings.

Ram 50	5.2
4X4 add	1.7
Raider	6.9

Chilton Time

Crankshaft Rear Main Oil Seal, Renew (Complete)

Ram 50	
w/M.T.	3.9
w/A.T.	4.7
4X4 add	1.7
Raider	
w/M.T.	5.9
w/A.T.	6.4

Crankshaft Front Oil Seal, Renew

All models	
2.0L eng	1.9
w/A.C. add	.6
w/P.S. add	.1

Crankshaft Pulley, Renew

All models	.6
w/A.C. add	.2
w/P.S. add	.1

Chilton Time

DIESEL ENGINE

Crankshaft and Main Bearings, Renew
Includes: R&R engine assembly.

All models	10.5
w/A.C. add	.6

Main Bearings, Renew
Includes: Plastigauge all bearings.

All models	3.4

Main and Rod Bearings, Renew
Includes: Plastigauge all bearings.

All models	4.6

Crankshaft Pulley, Renew

All models	.6
w/A.C. add	.1
w/P.S. add	.1

Crankshaft Front Oil Seal, Renew

All models	1.7
w/A.C. add	.6

LABOR 16 CAMSHAFT & TIMING GEARS 16 LABOR

GASOLINE ENGINES

Chilton Time

Timing Belt, Renew

All models	
cam drive	1.7
shaft drive	1.8
w/P.S. add	.1
w/A.C. add	.6

Timing Belt Tensioner, Renew

All models	
cam drive	1.8
shaft drive	1.9
w/P.S. add	.1
w/A.C. add	.6

Chilton Time

Timing Belt Cover, Renew

All models	
upper	.3
lower	1.0
w/A.C. add	.6

Timing Chain Cover Gasket, Renew

All models	4.4

Renew timing chain guide

add-each	.2
w/A.C. add	.6

Chilton Time

Timing Chain, Renew
Includes: Renew cover oil seal.

All models	
cam drive	5.4
silent shaft drive	4.9
w/A.C. add	.6

Timing Chain Tensioner, Renew
Includes: Renew cover oil seal.

All models	5.5
w/A.C. add	.6

Timing Chain Cover Oil Seal, Renew

All models	1.1
w/A.C. add	.6

LABOR 16 CAMSHAFT & TIMING GEARS 16 LABOR

	Chilton Time
Camshaft, Renew	
All models	3.0
Camshaft Sprocket, Renew	
Includes: Renew crankshaft gear and timing chain if required.	
All models	
chain driven	5.0
belt driven	1.8
w/A.C. add	.6
Silent Shaft or Bearings, Renew	
All models	
chain drive	
right	5.3
left	4.9
both	5.5
belt drive	
one	4.0
all	4.2
Renew shaft brg add	
each	.2
w/A.C. add	.6

	Chilton Time
Silent Shaft Oil Seals, Renew	
Ram 50	
2.0L eng	1.9
w/A.C. add	.6
w/P.S. add	.1
DIESEL ENGINE	
Timing Belt Cover, Renew	
All models	
upper	.3
lower	1.0
Timing Belt, Renew	
All models	
cam drive	1.6
silent shaft drive	1.8
w/A.C. add	.6
Timing Belt Tensioner, Renew	
All models	
cam drive	1.7
silent shaft drive	1.9
w/A.C. add	.6

	Chilton Time
Camshaft, Renew	
All models	2.0
Silent Shaft, Renew	
All models	
right side	2.5
left side	4.0
both sides	4.5
w/A.C. add	.6
Silent Shaft Oil Seal, Renew	
All models	1.9
w/A.C. add	.6

LABOR 17 ENGINE OILING SYSTEM 17 LABOR

	Chilton Time
GASOLINE ENGINES	
Oil Pan or Gasket, Renew	
4X2 models	1.9
4X4 models	3.6
Pressure Test Engine Bearings (Pan Off)	
All models	1.0
Oil Pump, Renew	
2.0L eng	4.2

	Chilton Time
2.6L eng	
Ram 50	5.0
4X4 add	1.7
Raider	6.7
w/P.S. add	.1
Oil Pressure Sending Unit, Renew	
All models	.5
Oil Pressure Gauge, Renew	
All models	.6

	Chilton Time
Oil Filter Element, Renew	
All models	.3
DIESEL ENGINE	
Oil Pan and/or Gasket, Renew	
All models	1.6
Oil Pump, Renew	
All models	3.4
Oil Filter Element, Renew	
All models	.3

LABOR 18 CLUTCH & FLYWHEEL 18 LABOR

Clutch Pedal Free Play, Adjust	
All models	.4
Clutch Release Bearing, Renew	
Includes: R&R trans and adjust clutch pedal free play.	
All models	
4X2	2.8
4X4	4.7
Renew clutch fork add	.2

Clutch Master Cylinder, Renew	
Includes: Bleed system.	
All models	1.0
Clutch Assembly, Renew	
Includes: R&R trans and adjust clutch pedal free play.	
All models	
4X2	3.0
4X4	5.3
Renew input shaft seal add	.2

Clutch Slave Cylinder, Renew	
Includes: Bleed system.	
All models	.7
Clutch Release Cable, Renew	
All models	.5
Flywheel, Renew	
Includes: R&R transmission.	
All models	
4X2	3.3
4X4	5.6
Renew ring gear add	.4

LABOR 19 STANDARD TRANSMISSION 19 LABOR

	Chilton Time
Transmission Assy., R&R and Recondition	
Includes: Complete disassembly, clean and inspect or renew all parts. Install new gaskets and seals.	
All models	
4 Speed	
4X2	5.6
4X4	8.0
5 Speed	
4X2	8.7
4X4	11.0

	Chilton Time
Speedometer Driven Pinion, Renew	
Includes: Renew oil seal.	
All models	.4
Transmission Assembly, R&R or Renew	
All models	
4X2	2.7
4X4	5.0
Renew trans add	.6
Extension Housing Oil Seal, Renew	
5 Speed	.7

LABOR 20 TRANSFER CASE 20 LABOR

TRANSFER CASE

	Chilton Time
Transfer Case Assy., Remove & Reinstall	
All models	3.9
Renew assy add	.8
Transfer Case, R&R and Recondition	
All models	6.9
Transfer Case Drive Chain, Renew	
All models	6.4

LABOR 21 SHIFT LINKAGE 21 LABOR

MANUAL

	Chilton Time
Gearshift Lever, Renew	
All models	.6
Gearshift Lever Boot, Renew	
All models	.3

AUTOMATIC

	Chilton Time
Shift Linkage, Adjust	
All models	.4
Throttle Linkage, Adjust	
All models	.3

	Chilton Time
Gearshift Lever, Renew	
All models	.7
Gear Selector Indicator Assy., Renew	
All models	.6

LABOR 23 AUTOMATIC TRANSMISSION 23 LABOR

ON CAR SERVICES

	Chilton Time
Drain & Refill Unit	
All models	1.0
Oil Pressure Check	
All models	.9
Check Unit For Oil Leaks	
Includes: Clean and dry outside of case and run unit to determine point of leak.	
All models	.9
Neutral Safety Switch, Renew	
All models	.4
Throttle Linkage, Adjust	
All models	.3
Throttle Valve Lever Shaft Seal, Renew	
All models	.6
Valve Body Manual Level Shaft Seal, Renew	
All models	1.0
Extension Housing Oil Seal, Renew	
All models	.9
Extension Housing Gasket, Renew	
All models	2.0
Renew bushing add	.3
Governor Assy., Renew or Recondition	
Includes: R&R extension housing.	
All models	2.4
Parking Lock Sprag, Renew	
Includes: R&R extension housing.	
All models	2.2

	Chilton Time
Oil Pan Gasket, Renew	
All models	.8
Oil Filter, Renew	
All models	1.0
Accumulator Piston, Renew or Recondition	
Includes: R&R oil pan.	
All models	1.6
Servo's, Renew or Recondition	
Includes: R&R oil pan and adjust band.	
All models	
kickdown	1.5
reverse	1.4
Valve Body Assembly, Renew	
Includes: R&R oil pan.	
All models	1.5
Valve Body Assy., R&R and Recondition	
Includes: R&R oil pan and replace filter. Disassemble, clean, inspect, free all valves. Replace parts as required.	
All models	3.0
Bands, Adjust	
Includes: R&R oil pan.	
All models	
kickdown	1.2
reverse	1.2
both	1.9

SERVICES REQUIRING R&R

	Chilton Time
Transmission Assembly, R&R or Renew	
Includes: Drain and refill unit.	
All models	
4X2	3.2

	Chilton Time
4X4	5.6
Renew trans add	.6
Flush converter and cooler	
lines add	.7
Transmission Assembly, Reseal	
Includes: R&R trans and renew all seals and gaskets.	
All models	
4X2	6.0
4X4	8.4
Transmission and Converter, R&R and Recondition	
Includes: Disassemble trans including valve body, clean, inspect and replace all parts as required.	
All models	
4X2	9.5
4X4	12.0
Torque Converter or Drive Plate, Renew	
Includes: R&R trans.	
All models	
4X2	3.6
4X4	5.8
Front Pump Assy., and/or Bushing, Renew	
Includes: R&R trans.	
All models	
4X2	4.0
4X4	6.4
Front Pump Oil Seal, Renew	
Includes: R&R trans.	
All models	
4X2	3.5
4X4	5.8

LABOR 25 U-JOINTS & DRIVESHAFT 25 LABOR

	Chilton Time
Center Bearing, Renew	
All models	1.3
Driveshaft, Renew	
All models	
trans to rear	.8
center brg to rear	1.2
transfer case to ft. axle	.8
transfer case to rear axle	.7
trans to center brg	1.6

	Chilton Time
Universal Joints, Renew	
Single Piece Shaft	
trans to rear axle	.9
transfer case to rear axle	.8
at front axle	.9
Two Piece Shaft	
trans to center brg	1.0
center brg to rear axle	1.0
at rear axle	1.0

LABOR 26 DRIVE AXLE 26 LABOR

REAR DIFFERENTIAL

Axle Shaft and/or Bearing, Renew
Includes: Renew oil seal.
All models-one	2.1
both	3.0

Axle Shaft Oil Seal, Renew
All models-one	1.3
both	2.4

Axle Shaft Wheel Mounting Studs, Renew
All models-one	.5
each adtnl	.1

Pinion Shaft Oil Seal, Renew
All models	.7

Differential Carrier Gasket, Renew
All models	2.9

Differential Carrier Assy., R&R or Renew
All models	3.3

Differential Side Bearings, Renew
Includes: Renew pinion oil seal and adjust backlash.
All models	4.3

Differential Side Gears, Renew
Includes: Renew axle shaft oil seals.
All models	4.8

Ring Gear and Pinion Set, Renew
Includes: Renew axle shaft and pinion seals. Make all necessary adjustments.
All models	5.5

Rear Axle Housing, Renew
Includes: Renew pinion oil seal, inner and outer axle shaft seals and gaskets. Bleed brakes.
All models	4.1

FRONT DIFFERENTIAL

Front Axle Housing Cover, Renew or Reseal
All models	.6

Drive Pinion Oil Seal, Renew
All models	.8

Front Axle Shaft, Renew
1986-87
outer-w/Joint	2.0
inner	1.6
1988-90
outer-w/Joint	1.2
inner	1.6

Axle Shaft Boot, Renew
All models-one side	1.9

Axle Shaft C/V Joint, Renew
All models-inner	1.8

Differential Side Bearings, Renew
All models	4.9

Ring Gear and Pinion Set, Renew
All models	5.6
Renew diff case add	.2

LABOR 27 REAR SUSPENSION 27 LABOR

Rear Spring, Renew
All models-one	1.1
both	2.0

Rear Spring Front Eye Bushing, Renew
All models-one	1.0
both	1.8

Rear Spring Shackle or Bushing, Renew
All models-one side	.9
both sides	1.5

Rear Shock Absorbers, Renew
All models-one	.4
both	.6

LABOR 28 AIR CONDITIONING 28 LABOR

Note: If more than one item requires replacement where evacuation and discharging the system is already included in the operation, deduct 1.0 hour for each additional item to the times listed.

Drain, Evacuate, Leak Test & Charge System
All models	1.0

Flush Refrigerant System, Complete
To be used in conjunction with component replacement which could contaminate system.
All models	1.3

Partial Charge
Includes: Leak test.
All models	.6

Compressor Drive Belt, Renew
All models	.3

Compressor Assembly, Renew
Includes: Pressure test and charge system.
All models	3.0

Compressor Clutch Assy., Renew
All models	.6

Expansion Valve, Renew
Includes: Pressure test and charge system.
All models	3.1
Renew receiver drier add	.2

Receiver-Drier, Renew
Includes: Add partial charge, leak test and charge system.
All models	1.5

High Pressure Cut-Off Switch, Renew
All models	.4

Thermostatic Control Clutch Cycling Switch, Renew
All models	1.0

Condenser Assembly, Renew
Includes: Add partial charge, leak test and charge system.
All models	2.3
Renew receiver drier add	.2

Water Valve, Renew (With Air Conditioning)
All models	1.0

Temperature Control Assy., Renew
All models	1.5

Blower Motor Switch, Renew
All models	.6

Blower Motor, Renew
All models	1.6

Blower Motor Resistor, Renew
All models	1.1

Evaporator Core, Renew
Includes: Add partial charge, leak test and charge system.
All models	3.9

Air Conditioning Hoses, Renew
Includes: Add partial charge, leak test and charge system.
All models-suction	1.7
discharge	1.7
Renew receiver drier add	.2

LABOR 29 LOCKS, HINGES & WIND. REGULATORS 29 LABOR

Hood Hinge, Renew (One)
Does not include painting.
All models	.8

Hood Latch, Renew
All models	.6

Door Handle (Outside), Renew
All models	.5

Hood Lock Release Cable, Renew
All models	.9

Door Lock Remote Control, Renew
All models	.6

Lock Striker Plate, Renew
All models	.3

Door and Ignition Lock Cylinders, Renew
Includes: R&R both door lock cylinders and ignition lock to renew or recode.
All models	1.5

Window Regulator, Renew
All models-one	.9

LABOR　30　HEAD AND PARKING LAMPS　30　LABOR

	Chilton Time		Chilton Time		Chilton Time
Aim Headlamps All models	.4	Parking Lamp Lens or Bulb, Renew All models	.3	Side Marker Lamp Assy., Renew All models	.4
Head Lamp Sealed Beam Bulb, Renew All models–each	.3	Tail Lamp Lens or Bulb, Renew All models	.3	License Lamp Assembly, Renew All models	.3

LABOR　31　WINDSHIELD WIPER & SPEEDOMETER　31　LABOR

	Chilton Time		Chilton Time		Chilton Time
Windshield Wiper Motor, Renew All models	.7	Washer Pump, Renew All models front rear	.5 .6	Speedometer Cable (Inner), Renew or Lubricate All models	.7
Wiper Switch, Renew 1986	.4	Windshield Wiper Linkage, Renew All models	.7	Speedometer Driven Pinion, Renew Includes: Renew oil seal. All models	.4
Speedometer Cable and Casing, Renew All models	.9	Speedometer Head, R&R or Renew Does not include reset odometer. All models	1.2	Radio, R&R Ram 50 Raider	.5 .8
Combination Switch Assembly, Renew 1987-90	1.0				

LABOR　32　LIGHT SWITCHES & WIRING　32　LABOR

	Chilton Time		Chilton Time		Chilton Time
Headlamp Switch, Renew 1986	.4	Neutral Safety (w/Back-Up Lamp) Switch, Renew All models	.4	Combination Switch (Turn Signal/Dimmer), Renew All models	1.0
Headlamp Dimmer Switch, Renew 1986	.4	Parking Brake Warning Lamp Switch, Renew All models	.3	Turn Signal, Washer/Wiper Lever Assy., Renew All models	1.0
				Turn Signal or Hazard Warning Flasher, Renew All models	.3
Horn Switch, Renew All models	.4	Stop Light Switch, Renew All models	.3	Horn, Renew All models	.3

LABOR　34　CRUISE CONTROL　34　LABOR

	Chilton Time		Chilton Time		Chilton Time
Speed Control Servo/Motor Assy., Renew All models	.7	Speed Control Clutch Safety Cut-Out Switch, Renew All models	.5	Combination Switch Assembly, Renew 1987-90	1.0
Speed Control Valve Body, Renew All models	.5	Speed Control and Turn Signal Lever Switch, Renew 1986	.4	Speed Control Vacuum Actuator, Renew All models	.3
				Speed Control Module, Renew All models	.3

GROUP INDEX

ALPHABETICAL INDEX

LABOR   1   TUNE UP   1   LABOR

	Chilton Time
Compression Test	
Four	.6
V-6	.8

Engine Tune Up, (Electronic Ignition)
Includes: Test battery and clean connections. Tighten manifold and carburetor mounting bolts. Check engine compression, clean and adjust or renew spark plugs. Test resistance of spark plug cables. Inspect distributor cap and rotor. Check vacuum advance operation. Reset ignition timing. Adjust idle mixture and idle speed. Service air cleaner. Inspect and adjust drive belts. Inspect choke operation and adjust or free up. Check operation of EGR valve.

	Chilton Time
Four	1.5
V-6	1.8

LABOR   2   IGNITION SYSTEM   2   LABOR

GASOLINE ENGINE

	Chilton Time
Spark Plugs, Clean and Reset or Renew	
Four	.5
V-6	.7
Ignition Timing, Reset	
Four	.4
V-6	.6
Distributor, Renew	
Includes: Reset ignition timing.	
Four	.6
V-6	.7
Distributor, R&R and Recondition	
Includes: Reset ignition timing.	
Four	1.5
V-6	1.6

	Chilton Time
Distributor Cap and/or Rotor, Renew	
Four	.4
V-6	.6
Ignition Coil, Renew	
Includes: Test coil.	
Four	.4
V-6	.5
Renew igniter add	.1
Vacuum Control Unit, Renew	
Includes: Reset ignition timing and dwell.	
All models	.7
Ignition Cables, Renew	
All models	.4
Ignition Switch, Renew	
All models	.5

	Chilton Time
Ignition Switch Lock Cylinder, Renew	
Includes: Recode cylinder.	
All models	1.0

DIESEL ENGINE

	Chilton Time
Glow Plugs, Renew	
All models-one	.5
all	.8
Glow Plug Control Switch, Renew	
All models	.3
Coolant Fast Idle Temperature Switch, Renew	
All models	.3
Glow Plug Relay, Renew	
All models-one	.3

LABOR   3   FUEL SYSTEM   3   LABOR

GASOLINE ENGINE

	Chilton Time
Fuel Pump, Test	
Includes: Disconnect line at carburetor, attach pressure gauge.	
All models	.3
Fuel Filter, Renew	
All models	.3
Carburetor Air Cleaner, Service	
All models	.2
Air Cleaner Vacuum Motor, Renew	
All models	.4
Air Cleaner Temperature Sensor, Renew	
All models	.5
Carburetor, Adjust (On Truck)	
Includes: Adjust curb and fast idle speed, choke and choke vacuum break adjustments.	
All models	.5
Choke Assembly, Renew	
All models	.8
Accelerator Pump, Renew	
All models	.8
Float or Needle Valve and Seat, Renew	
All models	1.0
Carburetor, Renew	
Includes: All necessary adjustments.	
All models	1.1
Carburetor, R&R and Clean or Recondition	
Includes: All necessary adjustments.	
All models	2.9
Anti-Dieseling or Idle Stop Solenoid, Renew	
All models	.6

	Chilton Time
Fuel Gauge (Dash), Renew	
P/up	1.0
Trooper	.7
Fuel Gauge (Tank), Renew	
Includes: Drain and refill tank.	
All models	.7
Fuel Tank, Renew	
Includes: Drain and refill tank.	
All models	1.7
Fuel Pump, Renew	
P/up	
1986-87	.9
1988-90	*1.8
Trooper II	
wo/4ZD1 eng	.9
w/4ZD1 eng	*1.8
*Includes R&R intake manifold.	
Add pump test if performed.	
Fuel Pump Relay, Renew	
All models	.3
Intake Manifold or Gasket, Renew	
Four	
w/Carb	1.5
w/F.I.	2.5
V-6	4.5
w/A.T. add	.2
Renew manif add	.5

DIESEL ENGINE

	Chilton Time
Air Cleaner, Service	
All models	.3
Idle Speed, Adjust	
All models	.3

	Chilton Time
Injection Pump Timing, Adjust	
All models	.9
w/A.C. add	.2
w/Turbo add	.7
Vacuum Pump, Renew	
All models	.6
Recond pump add	.4
Vacuum Pump Valve, Renew	
All models	.5
High Pressure Fuel Lines, Renew	
All models-one	.5
all	.9
Fuel Injection Nozzles and/or Seals, Renew	
All models-one	.6
all	1.0
Clean nozzles add-each	.2
Fuel Injection Pump, Renew	
All models	3.5
w/A.C. add	.3
w/Turbo add	.7
Intake Manifold or Gasket, Renew	
All models	1.1
w/A.C. add	.2
w/P.S. add	.1
w/Turbo add	.2

TURBOCHARGER

	Chilton Time
Turbocharger Assy., R&R or Renew	
All models	2.4
Turbocharger Wastegate Actuator, Renew	
All models	.4

FUEL INJECTION

	Chilton Time
Control Unit, Renew	
All models	.4

LABOR   3 FUEL SYSTEM 3   LABOR

	Chilton Time
Idle Speed, Adjust	
Trooper II	.5
Throttle Valve Unit, Renew	
All models	.9
Renew gskt or seal add	.3
w/A.T. add	.2
Fuel Pressure Regulator, Renew	
Four	.5
V-6	.6

	Chilton Time
Fuel Injectors, Renew	
Four-all	2.2
w/A.T. add	.2
V-6-one	.8
Clean and test injectors add-	
each	.2
Air Regulator, Renew	
All models	.6
Resistor, Renew	
All models	.3

	Chilton Time
Throttle Valve Switch, Renew	
All models	.4
Air Flow Sensor, Renew	
All models	.4
Electric Fuel Pump, Renew (In Tank)	
All models	2.0
Air Injection Manifold, Renew	
All models	1.8
w/A.T. add	.2

LABOR   3A EMISSION CONTROLS 3A   LABOR

	Chilton Time
CLOSED LOOP EMISSION CONTROL	
Oxygen Sensor, Renew	
All models	
Four	.5
V-6	.4
Coolant Temperature Sensor, Renew	
All models	
Four	.4
V-6	.3
Electronic Control Module, Renew	
All models	.8
Idle and Wide Open Throttle Switch, Renew	
All models	.5
Solenoid and Vacuum Regulator Assy., Renew	
All models	.4
Barometric Switch, Renew	
All models	.3
EGR Temperature Sensor, Renew	
P/up	.6
Duty Solenoid and Vacuum Regulator Assy., Renew	
P/up	.4
Map Sensor, Renew	
P/up	.4
Trooper II	.3
CRS SYSTEM	
Engine Speed Sensor, Renew	
All models	.4
Accelerator Switch, Renew	
All models	.4

	Chilton Time
Clutch Switch, Renew	
All models	.4
Neutral Switch, Renew	
All models	.5
AIR INJECTION SYSTEM	
Air Pump, Renew	
All models	
Four	.8
V-6	1.0
Air Manifold Check Valve, Renew	
All models	.4
Air Injection Manifold, Renew	
All models	1.2
Air Switching Valve, Renew	
All models	.4
Mixture Control Valve, Renew	
All models	.6
Vacuum Switching Valve, Renew	
All models	.4
EGR SYSTEM	
EGR Valve, Renew	
All models	
Four	.8
V-6	.5
Thermal Vacuum Valve, Renew	
All models	.4
Back Pressure Tranducer, Renew	
All models	.5
EFE SYSTEM	
EFE Heater, Renew	
All models	1.1

	Chilton Time
EFE Temperature Switch, Renew	
All models	.4
EVAPORATIVE EMISSIONS	
Charcoal Canister, Renew	
All models	.4
Fuel Vapor Separator, Renew	
All models	.4
Check and Relief Valve, Renew	
All models	.3
Evaporator Control Valve, Renew	
All models	.4
HEATED AIR INLET SYSTEM	
Air Cleaner Vacuum Motor, Renew	
All models	.4
Air Cleaner Temperature Sensor, Renew	
All models	.5
Idle Compensator, Renew	
All models	.5
DIESEL EMISSION CONTROLS	
EGR Controller, Renew	
All models	.4
EGR Valve or Gasket, Renew	
All models	.6
Vacuum Switching Valve, Renew	
All models	.4
Thermal Vacuum Valve, Renew	
All models	.4
Vacuum Regulator Valve, Renew	
All models	.3
Mass Air Flow Sensor, Renew	
All models	.4

LABOR   4 ALTERNATOR AND REGULATOR 4   LABOR

	Chilton Time
Alternator Circuits, Test	
Includes: Test battery, regulator and alternator output.	
All models	.5
Alternator, Renew	
Includes: Transfer pulley and fan.	
Four	
Gas	.7
Diesel	1.0
V-6	.8
Add circuit test if performed.	

	Chilton Time
Alternator, R&R and Recondition	
Includes: Complete disassembly, inspect, test, replace parts as required, reassemble.	
Four	
Gas	2.2
Diesel	2.5
V-6	2.3
Voltage Regulator, Test and Renew	
All models	
External	.6
Internal	1.7

	Chilton Time
Alternator Bearings, Renew	
Includes: R&R alternator, separate end frames.	
Four	
Gas	1.0
Diesel	1.6
V-6	1.1
Voltmeter, Renew	
P/up	
1986-87	.4
1988-90	1.0

LABOR 5 STARTING SYSTEM 5 LABOR

	Chilton Time
Starter Draw Test (On Truck)	
All models	.3
Starter, Renew	
Four	
P/up	
1988-90	.5
All other models	
4X2	1.0
4X4	1.3
V-6	.8
Add draw test if performed.	
Battery Terminals, Clean	
All models	.3
Battery Cables, Renew	
All models-each	.4

	Chilton Time
Starter, R&R and Recondition	
Four	
P/up	
1988-90	2.0
All other models	
4X2	2.0
4X4	2.3
V-6	2.0
Renew field coils add	.4
Add draw test if performed.	
Starter Drive, Renew	
Includes: R&R starter.	
Four	
P/up	
1988-90	.7

	Chilton Time
All other models	
4X2	1.2
4X4	1.5
V-6	1.0
Starter Solenoid, Renew	
Includes: R&R starter.	
Four	
P/up	
1988-90	.7
All other models	
4X2	1.2
4X4	1.5
V-6	1.0
Starter Relay, Renew	
All models	.3

LABOR 6 BRAKE SYSTEM 6 LABOR

	Chilton Time
Brake Pedal Free Play, Adjust	
All models	.3
Brakes, Adjust (Minor)	
Includes: Adjust brake shoes and fill master cylinder.	
two wheels	.4
four wheels	.7
Bleed Brakes (Four Wheels)	
Includes: Fill master cylinder.	
All models	.6
Brake Shoes, Renew	
Includes: Install new or exchange brake shoes, adjust service and hand brake. Bleed system.	
front	1.3
rear	1.7
all four wheels	2.9
Resurface brake drum, add-each	.5
Brake Shoes and/or Pads, Renew	
Includes: Install new or exchange brake shoes or pads, adjust service and hand brake. Bleed system.	
front-disc	.8
rear-drum	1.7
all four wheels	2.3
Resurface brake rotor, add-each	.9
Resurface brake drum, add-each	.5
Brake Drum, Renew	
front-one	.7
rear-one	.5
Free Up or Renew Brake Self Adjusting Units	
one	.7
each adtnl	.4
Brake Combination Valve, Renew	
Includes: Bleed system.	
All models	.7
BRAKE HYDRAULIC SYSTEM	
Wheel Cylinder, Renew	
Includes: Bleed system.	
front-one	.9
both	1.8
rear-one	.9
both	1.8
all four wheels	3.5
Wheel Cylinder, R&R and Rebuild	
Includes: Bleed system.	
front-one	1.2
both	2.4
rear-one	1.2

COMBINATIONS

	Chilton Time
RENEW WHEEL CYLINDER	
Each	.2
REBUILD WHEEL CYLINDER	
Each	.3
REBUILD CALIPER ASSEMBLY	
Front	.5
Rear	.3
RENEW MASTER CYLINDER	
All models	.5
REBUILD MASTER CYLINDER	
All models	.8
RENEW BRAKE HOSE	
Each	.3
REPACK FRONT WHEEL BEARINGS (Both Wheels)	
Drum brakes	.4
Disc brakes	.6
RENEW BRAKE DRUM	
Each	.1
RENEW DISC BRAKE ROTOR	
Each	.2

	Chilton Time
both	2.4
all four wheels	4.7
Master Cylinder, Renew	
Includes: Bleed system.	
All models	.9
Master Cylinder, R&R and Rebuild	
Includes: Hone cylinder and bleed system.	
All models	1.5
Brake Hose, Renew (Flex)	
Includes: Bleed system.	
front-one	.7
both	1.1
rear	.6
DISC BRAKES	
Disc Brake Pads, Renew	
Includes: Install new disc brake pads only.	
front	.8
rear	.8
all four whls	1.5

	Chilton Time
Caliper Assembly, Renew	
Includes: Bleed system.	
All models	
Front	
one	1.0
both	1.7
Rear	
one	.9
both	1.6
all four whls	3.0
Caliper Assy., R&R and Recondition	
Includes: Bleed system.	
All models	
Front	
one	1.5
both	2.7
Rear	
one	1.2
both	2.2
all four whls	4.5
Disc Brake Rotor, Renew	
All models	
Front	
one	1.2
both	2.1
Rear	
one	.8
both	1.3
all four whls	3.1
POWER BRAKES	
Power Brake Cylinder, Renew	
All models	1.0
Power Brake Cylinder, R&R and Recondition	
All models	2.0
Check Valve, Renew	
All models	.3
PARKING BRAKE	
Parking Brake, Adjust	
All models	.5
Parking Brake Warning Lamp Switch, Renew	
All models	.4
Parking Brake Control, Renew	
All models	.8
Parking Brake Cables, Renew	
front	1.1
rear-both	2.0
center	.9

LABOR 7 COOLING SYSTEM 7 LABOR

Winterize Cooling System
Includes: Run engine to check for leaks, tighten all hose connections. Test radiator and pressure cap, drain radiator and engine block. Add anti-freeze and refill system.
All models...................................... .5

Thermostat, Renew
All models
Gas 5
Diesel.. .8

Radiator Assy., R&R or Renew
Includes: Drain and refill cooling system.
All models
w/Carb.. .9
w/F.I. 1.4
w/A.C. add 1

ADD THESE OPERATIONS TO RADIATOR R&R
Boil & Repair...................................... 1.5
Rod Clean 1.9
Repair Core....................................... 1.3
Renew Tank 1.6
Renew Trans. Oil Cooler...................... 1.9
Recore Radiator.................................. 1.7

Radiator Hoses, Renew
Four-each 4
V-6
upper.. .3
lower.. .7

Fan Blade, Renew
All models
Four... .5
V-6 8

Fan Clutch, Renew
All models
Four... .6
V-6 9

Drive Belt, Renew
Four-one 4
V-6-one 3
each adtnl 1

Drive Belt, Adjust
All models-one 2
each adtnl 1

Water Pump, Renew
Four
Gas
1.8-2.0L engs 1.4
2.3L eng 4.0
2.6L eng 1.9
Diesel................................... 1.2
V-6 .... 1.9
w/A.C. add 3
w/P.S. add 3
w/A.T. add 4

Water Jacket Expansion Plugs, Renew (Side of Block)
each 5
Note: If necessary to R&R any component to gain access to plug, add appropriate time.

Temperature Gauge (Dash Unit), Renew
P/up.. 1.0
Trooper 7

Temperature Gauge (Engine Unit), Renew
All models.. .5

Heater Core, R&R or Renew
All models 5.5

ADD THESE OPERATIONS TO HEATER CORE R&R
Boil & Repair...................................... 1.2
Repair Core.. .9
Recore 1.2

Heater Blower Motor, Renew
All models 7

Blower Motor Resistor, Renew
All models 4

Temperature Control Assy., Renew
All models 7

Heater Hose, Renew
All models 4

LABOR 8 EXHAUST SYSTEM 8 LABOR

Muffler, Renew
Amigo... .9
All other models 1.0

Exhaust Pipe Packing, Renew
All models.. 1.0

Front Exhaust Pipe, Renew
Amigo... 1.3
P/up-Trooper II
Four... 1.0
V-6
right... .7
left.. .6
both... 1.1

Catalytic Converter, Renew
Four... 1.1
V-6 8

Catalytic Converter Catalyst, Renew
All models.. .9

Intermediate Exhaust Pipe, Renew
All models.. .8

Exhaust Pipe and Resonator, Renew
All models.. 1.0

Rear Exhaust Pipe, Renew
All models.. .8

Tail Pipe, Renew
All models.. .7

Exhaust Manifold or Gasket, Renew
All models
Four
w/Carb.. 1.0
w/F.I. 1.4
Diesel... *1.2
*w/A.C. add 2
*w/P.S. add 1
*w/Turbo add 2
V-6
right... 2.1
left.. 1.2
both... 3.3

LABOR 9 FRONT SUSPENSION 9 LABOR

Note: On all front suspension operations alignment charges must be added if performed. Time given does not include alignment.

Wheel, Renew
one.. .5

Wheels, Rotate (All)
All models... .5

Wheel, Balance
one.. .3
each adtnl 2

Check Alignment of Front End
All models... .5
Note: Deduct if alignment is performed.

Toe-In, Adjust
All models... .6

Align Front End
All models.. 1.4

Torsion Bars, Adjust
All models
one side 4
both sides 6

Front Wheel Grease Seals, Renew
P/up-Trooper II
4x2 models
1986-87
one 5
both 8
1988-90
one 8
both 1.4
4x4 models
one 6
both 1.0

Amigo
one 7
both 1.3

Front Wheel Bearings and Cups, Renew (Inner & Outer)
P/up-Trooper II
4x2 models
1986-87
one side....................................... .6
both sides 1.0
1988-90
one side....................................... 1.0
both sides 1.8
4x4 models
one side....................................... 1.9
both sides 3.6
Amigo
one side....................................... 1.9
both sides 3.6

LABOR 9 FRONT SUSPENSION 9 LABOR

	Chilton Time
Front Shock Absorbers, Renew	
All models-one	.5
both	.7
Front Strut Bar or Bushing, Renew	
All models-one	.4
both	.7
Renew bushing add	.3
Front Stabilizer Bar, Renew	
All models	.5
Renew bushings add	.3
Steering Knuckle Assy., Renew	
Add alignment charges.	
P/up-Trooper II	
4x2 models	
one	1.5
both	2.8
4x4 models	
one	1.7
both	3.2
Amigo	
one	1.8
both	3.4
Rebuild knuckle add-each	.5
Upper Ball Joints, Renew	
Add alignment charges.	
P/up-Trooper II	
4x2 models	
one	1.0
both	1.7
Amigo	
one	.7
both	1.2

	Chilton Time
Lower Ball Joint, Renew	
Add alignment charges.	
P/up-one	1.0
Trooper-one	1.5
Amigo-one	.8
Upper & Lower Ball Joints, Renew (One Side)	
Add alignment charges.	
P/up-Amigo	1.6
Trooper	2.0
Front Torsion Bar, Renew	
All models-one	.8
both	1.2
Upper Control Arm Assy., Renew	
Add alignment charges.	
P/up-Trooper II	
1986-87	
one	1.2
both	1.9
1988-90	
one	1.7
both	3.2
Amigo	
one	2.2
both	4.1
Renew bushings add, each	.3
Lower Control Arm Assy., Renew	
Add alignment charges.	
P/up-Trooper II	
one	2.5
both	4.5

	Chilton Time
Amigo	
one	2.8
both	5.2
Renew bushings add-each	.3
Locking Hub Cam and/or Clutch Assy., Renew	
auto lock-one	.6
manual lock-one	.9
Front Hub Oil Seal, Renew (4X4)	
All models-each	.9
4 WHEEL DRIVE FRONT AXLE	
Front Axle Shaft Oil Seal, Renew	
All models-one	1.2
both	2.3
Front Axle Shaft Bearing, Renew	
Includes: Renew oil seal.	
All models-one	1.3
both	2.5
Front Axle Shaft Assy., R&R or Renew	
All models	
one or both	4.6
Renew shaft assy add-each	.3
Renew inner shaft add-each	.5
Renew outer shaft add-each	.4
Renew shaft boot(s) add-each	.4
Repack outer joint add-each	.4
Renew D.O. Joint add-each	.4
Renew inner seal add-each	.2

LABOR 10 STEERING LINKAGE 10 LABOR

	Chilton Time
Relay Rod, Renew	
Includes: Reset toe-in.	
All models	1.4
Pitman Arm, Renew	
All models	.6

	Chilton Time
Tie Rod or Tie Rod End, Renew	
Includes: Reset toe-in.	
All models-one side	1.0
both sides	1.4

	Chilton Time
Idler Arm, Renew	
All models	.7
Center Tie Rod Assy., Renew	
Includes: Reset toe-in.	
All models	1.2

LABOR 11 STEERING GEAR 11 LABOR

	Chilton Time
MANUAL STEERING	
Steering Wheel, Renew	
All models	.4
Flexible Coupling, Renew	
All models	.6
Steering Column, R&R or Renew	
All models	1.3
Steering Gear, Adjust (On Truck)	
All models	.6
Steering Gear, R&R or Renew	
All models	1.1
Steering Gear, R&R and Recondition	
Includes: Disassemble, renew necessary parts, reassemble and adjust.	
All models	2.8

	Chilton Time
POWER STEERING	
Trouble Shoot Power Steering	
Includes: Test pump and system pressure. Check pounds pull on steering wheel and check for leaks.	
All models	.5
Power Steering Gear, Adjust (On Truck)	
All models	.6
Pump Drive Belt, Renew	
All models	.3
Power Steering Gear, R&R or Renew	
All models	1.5
Power Steering Hoses, Renew	
All models	
pressure	.6
return	.5

	Chilton Time
Power Steering Gear, R&R and Recondition	
Includes: Disassemble, renew necessary parts, reassemble and adjust.	
All models	2.7
Power Steering Pump, R&R or Renew	
Four	.9
V-6	1.1
Power Steering Pump, R&R and Recondition	
Four	1.6
V-6	1.8
Pump Shaft Oil Seal, Renew	
All models	1.0
Power Steering Reservoir, Renew	
All models	.4

LABOR 12 CYLINDER HEAD & VALVE SYSTEM 12 LABOR

GASOLINE ENGINE

Compression Test
	Chilton Time
Four	.6
V-6	.8

Cylinder Head Gasket, Renew
Includes: Clean carbon and make all necessary adjustments.
Four	
w/Carb	4.2
w/F.I.	7.7
w/A.C. add	.3
w/P.S. add	.3
V-6	
right	6.7
left	6.4
both	8.5

Cylinder Head, Renew
Includes: Transfer all component parts, reface valves, clean carbon, make all necessary adjustments.
Four	
w/Carb	5.2
w/F.I.	8.7
w/A.C. add	.3
w/P.S. add	.3
V-6	
right	7.7
left	7.4
both	10.0

Clean Carbon and Grind Valves
Includes: R&R cylinder head, grind valves and seats. Minor tune up.
Four	
w/Carb	6.7
w/F.I.	9.2
w/A.C. add	.3
w/P.S. add	.3
V-6	
right	8.1
left	7.8
both	11.0

Rocker Arm Cover or Gasket, Renew
Four	
w/Carb	.6
w/F.I.	.9
w/A.T. add	.2
V-6	
right	1.7
left	.8
both	2.4

Hydraulic Valve Lifters, Renew
V-6	
one cyl	4.9
each adtnl cyl	.3

Valve Push Rod, Renew
V-6	
right side	2.1
left side	1.1

Rocker Arms, Renew
Four-one cyl	1.3
all cyls	1.6
w/A.T. add	.2

Rocker Arm Shafts, Renew
Four-one or both	1.2
w/A.T. add	.2
V-6	
right side	2.1
left side	1.2
Renew rocker arms add–each side	.3

Valve Spring and/or Valve Stem Oil Seals, Renew (Head on Car)
Four	
w/Carb-one cyl	1.5
each adtnl cyl	.3
If nec to R&R head add	3.0
w/F.I.-all	3.6
V-6	
one cyl-right side	2.5
one cyl-left side	1.7
all cyls-both sides	6.2

Valves, Adjust
Four	
w/Carb	1.0
w/F.I.	1.2
w/A.T. add	.2
V-6	2.5

DIESEL ENGINE

Compression Test
	Chilton Time
All models	1.0

Cylinder Head Gasket, Renew
Includes: Clean carbon and make all necessary adjustments.
All models	5.2
w/A.C. add	.3
w/P.S. add	.2
w/Turbo add	.7

Cylinder Head, Renew
Includes: Transfer parts as required. Make all necessary adjustments.
All models	5.8
w/A.C. add	.3
w/P.S. add	.2
w/Turbo add	.7

Clean Carbon and Grind Valves
Includes: R&R cylinder head, reface valves and seats. Make all necessary adjustments.
All models	6.2
w/A.C. add	.3
w/P.S. add	.2
w/Turbo add	.7

Rocker Arm Cover and/or Gasket, Renew
All models	.6

Rocker Arms and/or Push Rods, Renew
All models-one cyl	1.3
all cyls	1.6

Rocker Arm Shaft, Renew
All models	
one or both	1.2

Valve Clearance, Adjust
All models	1.0

Valve Springs and/or Valve Stem Oil Seals, Renew (Head on Truck)
All models	
one cyl	1.5
each adtnl cyl	.3
If necc to R&R head add	3.0

Valve Lifters, Renew (All)
Includes: R&R engine assy.
4X2 models	10.9
4X4 models	14.4

LABOR 13 ENGINE ASSEMBLY & MOUNTS 13 LABOR

GASOLINE ENGINE
Note: All engine operations listed in this group are for assemblies as supplied by the original equipment manufacturer. Time to replace assemblies from independent rebuilders may vary.

Engine Assembly, Remove & Install
Does not include transfer of any parts or equipment.
	Chilton Time
Four	
w/Carb	
4X2 models	6.3
4X4 models	9.8
w/A.C. add	.3
w/P.S. add	.3
w/A.T. add	.2
w/F.I.	
4X2 models	8.5
4X4 models	10.0
w/A.C. add	.4
w/P.S. add	.3

	Chilton Time
w/A.T. add	1.2
V-6	9.0

Engine Assembly, Renew (Short Block)
Includes: R&R engine assy., transfer all component parts not supplied with replacement engine. Tune engine.
Four	
w/Carb	
4X2 models	13.3
4X4 models	16.8
w/A.C. add	.3
w/P.S. add	.3
w/A.T. add	.2
w/F.I.	
4X2 models	15.2
4X4 models	16.8
w/A.C. add	.4
w/P.S. add	.3
w/A.T. add	1.2
V-6	19.0

Engine Assy., R&R and Recondition
Includes: Rebore block, install new pistons, rings, rod and main bearings, clean carbon, grind valves. Tune engine.
	Chilton Time
Four	
w/Carb	
4X2 models	24.6
4X4 models	28.1
w/A.C. add	.3
w/P.S. add	.3
w/A.T. add	.2
w/F.I.	
4X2 models	26.8
4X4 models	28.3
w/A.C. add	.4
w/P.S. add	.3
w/A.T. add	1.2
V-6	31.7

LABOR 13 ENGINE ASSEMBLY & MOUNTS 13 LABOR

Engine Mounts, Renew
Four

exc 2.6L eng
Front
one 7
both 1.0
Rear 7

2.6L eng
right........................ .9
left.......................... .9
rear 1.0

V-6
right........................ 1.0
left.......................... 1.0
rear 6

DIESEL ENGINE

Engine Assembly, Remove & Install
Does not include transfer of any parts or equipment.
4X2 models 7.4
4X4 models 10.9
w/A.T. add 3
w/A.C. add 3
w/P.S. add 3
w/Turbo add 2

Engine Assembly, Renew (Partial)
Includes: R&R engine assy. Transfer all component parts not supplied with replacement engine. Clean carbon, grind valves. Make all necessary adjustments.
4X2 models 16.0
4X4 models 17.9

w/A.T. add 3
w/A.C. add 3
w/P.S. add 3
w/Turbo add 7

Engine Assy., R&R and Recondition
Includes: Install new pistons, pins, rings, rod and main bearings. Clean carbon, grind valves. Make all necessary adjustments.
4X2 models 27.3
4X4 models 28.7
w/A.T. add 3
w/A.C. add 3
w/P.S. add 3
w/Turbo add 7

Engine Mounts, Renew
Front-one 7
both 1.0
Rear.................................... .7

LABOR 14 PISTONS, RINGS & BEARINGS 14 LABOR

GASOLINE ENGINE

Piston Rings, Renew (All)
Includes: R&R engine assy. Remove cylinder top ridge, deglaze cylinder walls. Clean piston and ring grooves. Minor tune up.
Four
w/Carb
4X2 models 10.5
4X4 models 14.0
w/A.C. add 3
w/P.S. add 3
w/A.T. add 3
w/F.I.
4X2 models 11.6
4X4 models 13.1
w/A.C. add 4
w/P.S. add 3
w/A.T. add 1.2
V-6 .... 21.4

Pistons or Connecting Rods, Renew (All)
Includes: R&R engine assy. Remove cylinder top ridge, deglaze cylinder walls. Minor tune up.
Four
w/Carb
4X2 models 11.7
4X4 models 15.2
w/A.C. add 3
w/P.S. add 3
w/A.T. add 3
w/F.I.
4X2 models 12.8
4X4 models 14.3
w/A.C. add 4
w/P.S. add 3
w/A.T. add 1.2
V-6 .... 23.2

COMBINATIONS

DRAIN, EVACUATE & RECHARGE AIR CONDITIONING SYSTEM
All models.......................... 1.0
CARBURETOR, RECONDITION
All models.......................... 1.2
REMOVE CYLINDER TOP RIDGE
Each 3
DEGLAZE CYLINDER WALLS
Each 1
RECONDITION CYLINDER HEAD (HEAD REMOVED)
All models.......................... 2.9
VALVE GUIDES, RENEW
Each 2
VALVE SEAT, RENEW
Each 2
OIL FILTER ELEMENT, RENEW
All models.......................... .3

Connecting Rod Bearings, Renew (All)
Includes: R&R engine.
w/Carb
4X2 models 7.2
4X4 models 10.7
w/A.C. add 3
w/P.S. add 3
w/A.T. add 3
w/F.I.
4X2 models 9.3
4X4 models 10.9

w/A.C. add 4
w/P.S. add 3
w/A.T. add 1.2
V-6 .... 16.1

DIESEL ENGINE

Piston Rings, Renew (All)
Includes: R&R engine assy. Remove cylinder top ridge, deglaze cylinder walls, clean piston and ring grooves. Make all necessary adjustments.
4X2 models 9.8
4X4 models 15.0
w/A.C. add 3
w/P.S. add 3
w/A.T. add 3
w/Turbo add 7

Pistons or Connecting Rods, Renew (All)
Includes: R&R engine assy. Remove cylinder top ridge, deglaze cylinder walls. Make all necessary adjustments.
4X2 models 11.0
4X4 models 16.2
w/A.C. add 3
w/P.S. add 3
w/A.T. add 3
w/Turbo add 7

Connecting Rod Bearings, Renew (All)
Includes: R&R engine assy.
4X2 models 7.8
4X4 models 12.2
w/A.C. add 3
w/P.S. add 3
w/A.T. add 3
w/Turbo add 7

LABOR 15 CRANKSHAFT & DAMPER 15 LABOR

GASOLINE ENGINE

Crankshaft and Main Bearings, Renew
Includes: R&R engine assy., and cylinder head. Plastigauge all bearings.
Four
w/Carb
4X2 models 8.9
4X4 models 12.4
w/A.C. add 8

w/P.S. add 3
w/A.T. add 3
w/F.I.
4X2 models 10.9
4X4 models 12.4
w/A.C. add 4
w/P.S. add 3
w/A.T. add 1.2
V-6 .... 15.0

Main and Rod Bearings, Renew
Includes: R&R engine assy. Plastigauge all bearings.
w/Carb
4X2 models 10.1
4X4 models 13.6
w/P.S. add 3
w/A.T. add 3
w/F.I.
4X2 models 12.1

LABOR 15 CRANKSHAFT & DAMPER 15 LABOR

	Chilton Time
4X4 models	13.6
w/A.C. add	.4
w/P.S. add	.3
w/A.T. add	1.2

Rear Main Bearing Oil Seal, Renew
Includes: R&R transmission.
Four

	Chilton Time
w/Carb	
4X2 models	3.8
4X4 models	5.3
A.T. add	.2
w/F.I.	
4X2 models	5.6
4X4 models	7.1
w/A.T. add	1.1
V-6	8.4

Crankshaft Pulley or Damper, Renew

	Chilton Time
All models	1.5
w/A.C. add	.1
w/P.S. add	.3

Crankshaft Front Oil Seal, Renew

	Chilton Time
All models	3.5

Crankshaft Front Oil Seal, Renew
Four

	Chilton Time
1.8-2.0L engs	2.3
2.3L eng	4.0
w/A.C. add	.3
w/P.S. add	.3
w/A.T. add	.3
2.6L eng	2.2
w/A.C. add	.4
w/P.S. add	.3
w/A.T. add	.3
V-6	2.7

DIESEL ENGINE

Crankshaft and Main Bearings, Renew
Includes: R&R engine assy. Check all bearing clearances.

	Chilton Time
4X2 models	9.3
4X4 models	12.9
w/A.C. add	.8
w/P.S. add	.3
w/A.T. add	.3
w/Turbo add	.7

Main Bearings, Renew
Includes: R&R engine assy.

	Chilton Time
4X2 models	11.4
4X4 models	12.9
w/A.C. add	.8
w/P.S. add	.3
w/A.T. add	.3
w/Turbo add	.7

Main and Rod Bearings, Renew
Includes: R&R engine assy.

	Chilton Time
4X2 models	12.6
4X4 models	14.1
w/A.C. add	.8
w/P.S. add	.3
w/A.T. add	.3
w/Turbo add	.7

Rear Main Bearing Oil Seal, Renew
Includes: R&R trans.

	Chilton Time
4X2 models	3.8
4X4 models	5.1
w/A.T. add	.3

Crankshaft Pulley or Damper, Renew

	Chilton Time
All models	1.5
w/A.C. or P.S. add	.2

LABOR 16 CAMSHAFT & TIMING GEARS 16 LABOR

GASOLINE ENGINE

Timing Chain Cover and/or Gasket, Renew
Includes: R&R engine, renew cover oil seal on Four cyl engines.

Four

	Chilton Time
4X2 models	10.5
4X4 models	13.7
V-6	2.5
w/A.C. add	.3
w/A.T. add	.3
w/P.S. add	.3

Timing Chain, Renew
Includes: R&R engine, renew cover oil seal on Four cyl engines.
Four

	Chilton Time
4X2 models	11.6
4X4 models	14.6
V-6	2.8
w/A.C. add	.3
w/A.T. add	.3
w/P.S. add	.3

Camshaft, Renew
Four

	Chilton Time
w/Carb	1.5
w/F.I.	3.0
w/A.T. add	.2
Renew front seal add	.2
V-6	8.8

Timing Belt Cover, R&R or Renew
Includes: Renew front cover oil seal.
All models

	Chilton Time
2.3L eng	3.2
w/A.C. add	.3
w/A.T. add	.3
w/P.S. add	.3
2.6L eng	1.5
w/A.C. add	.4
w/P.S. add	.3
w/A.T. add	.3

Timing Belt, Renew
Includes: R&R front cover, renew cover oil seal.
All models

	Chilton Time
2.3L eng	3.5
w/A.C. add	.3
w/A.T. add	.3
w/P.S. add	.3

	Chilton Time
2.6L eng	1.7
w/A.C. add	.4
w/P.S. add	.3
w/A.T. add	.3

DIESEL ENGINE

Timing Cover and/or Oil Seal, Renew
Includes: R&R pulleys and renew timing belt.

	Chilton Time
All models	3.2

Timing Belt, Renew
Includes: R&R pulley housing.

	Chilton Time
All models	2.8
Renew tensioner add	.2

Timing Gears, Renew
Includes: Renew crankshaft and/or camshaft gears.

	Chilton Time
All models	4.2

Camshaft and Lifters, Renew
Includes: R&R engine assy.

	Chilton Time
4X2 models	10.9
4X4 models	14.4
w/A.C. add	.8
w/P.S. add	.3
w/A.T. add	.3

LABOR 17 ENGINE OILING SYSTEM 17 LABOR

GASOLINE ENGINE

Oil Pan or Gasket, Renew (Except 4X4 w/2.3L eng)
Includes: R&R engine assy.

	Chilton Time
4X2 models	6.5
4X4 models	10.0
w/A.C. add	.3
w/P.S. add	.3
w/A.T. add	.3

Pressure Test Engine Bearings (Pan Off)

	Chilton Time
All models	1.0

Oil Pump, Renew (Except 4X4 w/2.3L eng)
Includes: R&R engine assy.
Four

	Chilton Time
4X2 models	6.7
Trooper 4X4 models	10.2
w/A.C. add	.8
w/P.S. add	.3
w/A.T. add	.3
V-6	9.9

Sub Oil Pan or Gasket, Renew (4X4 w/2.3L & 2.6L engs)

	Chilton Time
All models	.8

Oil Pump, Renew (4X4 w/2.3L eng)
Includes: R&R timing belt cover and timing belt.

	Chilton Time
All models	3.9
w/A.C. add	.3
w/A.T. add	.3
w/P.S. add	.3

Oil Pan and/or Gasket, Renew (2.6L eng)

	Chilton Time
4X2 models	9.1
4X4 models	10.6
w/A.C. add	.4
w/P.S. add	.3
w/A.T. add	1.2

LABOR 17 ENGINE OILING SYSTEM 17 LABOR

Chilton Time

Oil Pressure Gauge (Dash Unit), Renew
P/up... 1.0
Trooper 7

Oil Pressure Sending Unit, Renew
All models.................................... .5

Oil Filter Element, Renew
All models.................................... .4

DIESEL ENGINE

Oil Pan or Gasket, Renew
Includes: R&R engine assy.
4X2 models 7.8
4X4 models 11.0
w/A.C. add 3
w/P.S. add 3
w/A.T. add 3
w/Turbo add 7

Pressure Test Engine Bearings (Pan Off)
All models.................................... 1.0

Oil Pump, Renew
Includes: R&R engine assy.
4X2 models 8.0
4X4 models 11.2
w/A.C. add 3
w/P.S. add 3
w/A.T. add 3
w/Turbo add 7
Recond pump add 2

Oil Pressure Sending Unit, Renew
All models.................................... .4

Oil Filter Element, Renew
All models.................................... .3

LABOR 18 CLUTCH & FLYWHEEL 18 LABOR

Chilton Time

Clutch Pedal Free Play, Adjust
All models.................................... .3

Clutch Hydraulic System, Bleed
All models.................................... .3

Clutch Control Cable, Renew
Includes: Adjust cable.
All models.................................... 1.0

Flywheel, Renew
Includes: R&R trans.
1986-87
4X2 models 3.6
4X4 models 4.6
1988-90
4X2 models 5.3
4X4 models 6.9
Long bed add............................... .2
V-6 .... 8.2
Renew ring gear add...................... .5

Clutch Assembly, Renew
Includes: R&R trans and adjust linkage.
Four
1986-87
4X2 models 3.3
4X4 models 4.3
1988-90
4X2 models 5.0
4X4 models 6.5
Long bed add............................... .2
V-6 .... 7.9

Clutch Master Cylinder, Renew
Includes: Bleed system.
All models.................................... 1.0

Clutch Slave Cylinder, Renew
Includes: Bleed system.
All models.................................... .6

Clutch Release Bearing, Fork and/or Ball Stud, Renew
Includes: R&R trans and adjust linkage.
Four
1986-87
4X2 models 3.0
4X4 models 4.0
1988-90
4X2 models 4.7
4X4 models 6.2
Long bed add............................... .2
V-6 .... 7.6

Clutch Slave Cylinder, R&R and Recondition
Includes: Bleed system.
All models.................................... 1.0

Clutch Master Cylinder, R&R and Recondition
Includes: Bleed system.
All models.................................... 1.5

LABOR 19 STANDARD TRANSMISSION 19 LABOR

Chilton Time

Transmission Assy., R&R or Renew
Four
1986-87
4X2 models 2.7
4X4 models 3.7
1988-90
4X2 models 4.5
4X4 models 6.0
V-6 .... 7.4
Renew trans add 5

Speedometer Drive Gear, Renew
Includes: R&R and disassemble trans on 1981 thru 1987 models. R&R extension housing on later models.
1986-87
4X2 models 3.0
4X4 models 4.0
1988-90
4X2 models 3.2
4X4 models 4.5

Extension Housing Oil Seal, Renew
1986-87 7
1988-90 .... 1.0

Transmission Assy., R&R and Recondition
Includes: Complete disassembly, clean and inspect or renew all parts. Install new gaskets and seals.
Four
1986-87
4X2 models 10.1
4X4 models 11.4
1988-90
4X2 models 10.1
4X4 models 15.7
V-6 .... 11.9

Speedometer Driven Gear, Renew
All models.................................... .5

LABOR — 20 TRANSFER CASE 20 — LABOR

	Chilton Time		Chilton Time		Chilton Time
Transfer Case Lever and/or Boot, Renew		**Transfer Case Assy, and/or Gasket, Renew**		**Transfer Case Assy., R&R and Recondition (Complete)**	
All models	.4	P/up		P/up	
		1986-87	1.0	1986-87	3.6
		1988-90	6.3	1988-90	10.0
		Trooper		Trooper	
Rear Cover and/or Gasket, Renew		1986-90	1.0	1986-90	3.6
All models	.5	Renew output shaft oil seal, add	.3		

LABOR — 21 SHIFT LINKAGE 21 — LABOR

	Chilton Time		Chilton Time		Chilton Time
MANUAL		**Shift Control Lever, Renew**		**Transfer Case Position Switch, Renew**	
Gearshift Control Lever, Renew		All models	.5	All models	.4
All models	.5	**Shift Control Assembly, Renew**		**Speed Sensor, Renew**	
w/Console add	.1	All models	1.0	All models	.4
Transfer Case Control Lever, Renew		**Shift Control Rods, Renew**			
All models	.5	All models	.7	**Transmission Controller (ECT), Renew**	
AUTOMATIC		**Shift Control Rods, Adjust**		All models	.3
Shift Linkage, Adjust		All models	.3	**Overdrive Control Switch, Renew**	
Includes: Adjust linkage and neutral safety switch.		**Transfer Case Linkage, Adjust**		(On Shift Lever)	
All models	.6	All models	.4	All models	.3

LABOR — 23 AUTOMATIC TRANSMISSION 23 — LABOR

	Chilton Time		Chilton Time		Chilton Time
THM-200		**Parking Pawl, Renew**		**Front Pump Seal, Renew**	
ON TRUCK SERVICES		Includes: R&R oil pan.		Includes: R&R trans.	
		All models	1.9	All models	3.9
Drain & Refill Unit		**Intermediate Servo, Renew**		**Flywheel (Flexplate), Renew**	
All models	.7	Includes: Renew cover and 'O' rings.		Includes: R&R trans.	
Oil Pressure Check		All models	.9	All models	4.0
All models	.5	**Intermediate Accumulator, Renew**		**Converter Assy., Renew**	
Check Unit for Oil Leaks		Includes: R&R oil pan, valve body and accumulator.		Includes: R&R trans, pressure check converter and check end play.	
Includes: Clean and dry outside of case, run unit to determine point of leak.		All models	1.7	All models	4.4
All models	.9	**Pressure Regulator Valve, Renew**		**Front Oil Pump, Renew**	
Linkage Adjust		Includes: R&R oil pan.		Includes: R&R trans, converter and pump seal.	
Includes: Adjust neutral safety switch, indicator needle and detent rod, cable or switch.		All models	1.5	All models	4.6
All models	.6	**Valve Body Assy., R&R or Renew**		Recond pump add	.9
Shift Control Rod, Adjust		Includes: R&R oil pan and filter.		**AW-55**	
All models	.5	All models	1.7	**ON TRUCK SERVICES**	
Detent Cable, Adjust		**Valve Body Assy., R&R and Recondition**		**Drain & Refill Unit**	
All models	.3	Includes: R&R oil pan and filter. Disassemble, clean, inspect, free all valves. Replace parts as required.		1986-87	.6
Detent Cable, Renew				1988-90	
Includes: Adjust.		All models	2.8	P/up	1.4
All models	.7			Trooper	1.6
Speedometer Driven Gear and/or Oil Seal, Renew		**SERVICES REQUIRING R&R**		**Oil Pressure Check**	
All models	.5	**Transmission Assy., R&R or Renew**		All models	.5
Governor Assy., R&R or Renew		All models	3.8	**Check Unit for Oil Leaks**	
All models	1.0	Leak check converter add	.4	Includes: Clean and dry outside of case and run unit to determine point of leak.	
Governor Assy., R&R and Recondition		Renew trans add	.5	All models	.9
All models	1.6	**Transmission and Converter Assy., R&R and Recondition**		**Neutral Safety Switch, Renew**	
Renew governor gear add	.3	Includes: Drain and pressure test converter, recondition all assemblies. Make all necessary adjustments.		All models	.5
Extension Housing Rear Oil Seal, Renew				w/Console add	.1
Includes: R&R driveshaft.		All models	10.7	**Throttle Cable, Adjust**	
All models	.8	**Transmission Assy., Reseal**		All models	.5
Oil Pan Gasket, Renew		Includes: R&R trans. Renew all seals and gaskets.		**Throttle Cable, Renew**	
Includes: Clean oil pan and service screen.		All models	6.0	All models	
All models	.9			1986-87	2.2
				1988-90	3.0

LABOR 23A AUTOMATIC TRANSMISSION (RWD) 23A LABOR

	Chilton Time
Extension Housing and/or Gasket, Renew	
1986-87	2.2
1988-90	
P/up	2.9
Trooper	2.5
Extension Housing Oil Seal, Renew	
1986-87	.8
1988-90	1.3
Governor Assy., Renew	
Includes: R&R extension housing.	
1986-87	2.4
1988-90	3.0
Oil Pan and/or Gasket, Renew	
1986-87	.6
1988-90	
P/up	1.4
Trooper	1.6
Transfer Case Oil Pan and/or Gasket, Renew	
1988-90	.6
Valve Body Assy., Renew	
Includes: R&R oil pan.	
1986-87	1.5
1988-90	2.8
Valve Body Assy., R&R and Recondition	
Includes: R&R oil pan and filter. Dissassemble, clean, inspect, free all valves. Replace parts as required.	
1986-87	3.0
1988-90	4.9

	Chilton Time
Throttle Valve and Kick Down Cam, Renew	
Includes: R&R oil pan.	
1986-87	1.2
1988-90	3.0
Speedometer Driven Gear, Renew	
All models	.5
Manual Valve Lever and/or Seal, Renew	
1986-87	3.7
1988-90	
P/up	3.7
Trooper	4.7
Parking Pawl, Renew	
1986-87	3.7
1988-90	
P/up	3.7
Trooper	4.7
Transfer Case Valve Body Assy., R&R or Renew	
1988-90	1.6
Transfer Case Valve Body Assy., R&R and Recondition	
1988-90	2.4
SERVICES REQUIRING R&R	
Transmission Assy., R&R or Renew	
1986-87	3.8
1988-90	
P/up	7.0
Trooper	8.0
Long bed add	.2
Renew trans add	.5

	Chilton Time
Transmission and Converter Assy., R&R and Recondition	
Includes: Drain and pressure test converter, recondition all assemblies. Make all necessary adjustments.	
1986-87	10.5
1988-90	
P/up	
4X2	25.5
4X4	36.8
Trooper	29.6
Long bed add	.2
Torque Converter, Renew	
Includes: R&R trans.	
1986-87	4.0
1988-90	
P/up	7.2
Trooper	8.2
Long bed add	.2
Front Pump Assy., Renew	
Includes: R&R trans.	
1986-87	4.2
1988-90	
P/up	7.4
Trooper	8.4
Renew front seal add	.2
Long bed add	.2
Flywheel (Flexplate), Renew	
Includes: R&R trans.	
1986-87	4.0
1988-90	
P/up	7.3
Trooper	8.3
Long bed add	.2

LABOR 25 U-JOINTS & DRIVESHAFT 25 LABOR

	Chilton Time
Drive Shaft, Renew	
One piece shaft	.6
Two piece shaft	
front	.7
rear	.5

	Chilton Time
Universal Joint, Renew	
Includes: Disconnect driveshaft.	
All models-one	.8
each adtnl	.4

	Chilton Time
Center Bearing, Renew	
All models	.9
R&R second shaft add	.3

LABOR 26 DRIVE AXLE 26 LABOR

	Chilton Time
REAR DIFFERENTIAL ASSY.	
Axle Shaft Assy., Renew	
All models-one	1.3
both	2.4
Axle Shaft Bearing and/or Oil Seal, Renew	
All models-one	1.2
both	2.3
Axle Tube Oil Seal, Renew	
All models-one	1.2
both	2.2
Pinion Shaft Oil Seal, Renew	
All models	.9
Differential Carrier Case, Renew	
Includes: R&R carrier and renew case.	
All models	4.3
Ring Gear and Pinion Set, Renew	
All models	5.1
Renew pinion brgs add	.4
Renew side brgs add	.6
Pinion Gear Bearings, Renew	
All models	5.5

	Chilton Time
Side Carrier Bearings, Renew	
All models	3.5
Side Carrier and Pinion Bearings, Renew	
All models	3.2
Rear Axle Housing, Renew	
All models	5.2
Differential Carrier Assy., Renew	
All models	2.8
Rear Axle Housing Cover Gasket, Renew	
All models	2.5
FRONT DIFFERENTIAL ASSY	
Front Propeller Shaft, R&R or Renew	
All models	.5
Front Axle Shaft Oil Seal, Renew	
All models-one	1.2
both	2.3
Front Axle Shaft Bearing, Renew	
Includes: Renew oil seal.	
All models-one	1.3
both	2.5

	Chilton Time
Front Axle Shaft Assy., R&R or Renew	
All models	
one or both	4.6
Renew shaft assy add-each	.3
Renew inner shaft add-each	.5
Renew outer shaft add-each	.4
Renew shaft boot(s) add-each	.4
Repack outer joint add-each	.4
Renew D.O. Joint add-each	.4
Renew inner seal add-each	.2
Front Pinion Shaft Oil Seal, Renew	
All models	.9
Front Differential Carrier Assy., R&R or Renew Gasket	
All models	5.6
w/Skid plate add	.3
Front Pinion Shafts and/or Side and Pinion Gears, Renew	
Includes: R&R front carrier assy.	
All models	7.4
w/Skid plate add	.3

LABOR   26   DRIVE AXLE   26   LABOR

	Chilton Time		Chilton Time		Chilton Time
Side Bearings, Renew Includes: R&R front carrier assy.		**Pinion Bearings, Renew** Includes: R&R front carrier assy.		**Ring Gear and Pinion Assy., Renew** Includes: R&R front carrier assy.	
All models	6.3	All models	6.9	All models	7.7
w/Skid plate add	.3	w/Skid plate add	.3	w/Skid plate add	.3

LABOR   27   REAR SUSPENSION   27   LABOR

	Chilton Time		Chilton Time		Chilton Time
Rear Spring, Renew		**Rear Spring Shackle, Renew**		**Rear Shock Absorbers, Renew**	
All models-one	1.0	All models-one	.6	All models-one	.5
both	1.8	both	1.0	both	.7
Renew bushings add-each	.3	Renew bushings add-each	.2		

LABOR   28   AIR CONDITIONING   28   LABOR

	Chilton Time		Chilton Time		Chilton Time
Note: If more than one item requires replacement where evacuation and discharging the system is already included in the operation, deduct 1.0 hour for each additional item to the times listed.		**Compressor Assembly, Renew** Includes: Transfer parts as required. Evacuate and charge system.		**Expansion Valve, Renew** Includes: Evacuate and charge system.	
		Four	2.0	All models	3.0
		V-6	1.5	**Evaporator Core, Renew** Includes: Evacuate and charge system.	
Drain, Evacuate and Recharge System		**Compressor Assy., R&R and Recondition** Includes: Completely disassemble compressor. Clean, inspect and renew all parts as required. Evacuate and charge system.		All models	3.0
All models	1.0			**Condenser Assembly, Renew** Includes: Evacuate and charge system.	
Flush Refrigerant System, Complete To be used in conjunction with component replacement which could contaminate system.		Four	3.5	All models	2.0
		V-6	3.0	**Condenser Pressure Switch, Renew**	
All models	1.3	**Clutch Hub and Drive Plate, Renew**		Trooper II	1.4
Leak Check Includes: Check all lines and connections.		All models	2.0	**Blower Motor, Renew**	
		Compressor Pulley and/or Bearing, Renew		All models	.7
All models	.5	All models	2.0	**Blower Motor Resistor, Renew**	
		Compressor Shaft Seal Kit, Renew Includes: Evacuate and charge system.		All models	.4
Refrigerant, Add (Partial Charge)				**Temperature Control Unit, Renew**	
All models	.6	All models	2.1	All models	.7
		Receiver-Dehydrator, Renew Includes: Evacuate and charge system.		**Air Conditioning Hoses, Renew** Includes: Evacuate and charge system.	
Compressor Belt, Renew				All models-exc below-one	1.7
All models	.3	All models	1.4	evaporator liquid line	3.0
				each adtnl	.5

LABOR   29   LOCKS, HINGES & WIND. REGULATORS   29   LABOR

	Chilton Time		Chilton Time		Chilton Time
Front Door Window Regulator, Renew		**Door Lock Cylinder Assy., Renew**		**Lock Striker Plate, Renew**	
All models	.9	All models	.5	All models	.3
Door Handle (Outside), Renew		Recode cyl add	.3		
All models	.5	**Front Door Window Regulator Motor, Renew**		**Hood Hinge, Renew (One)**	
Front Door Lock Assembly, Renew		P/up	1.5	All models	.4
All models	.8	Trooper II	.7	**Hood Latch Assembly, Renew**	
Rear Door Lock Assy., Renew		**Rear Door Window Regulator Motor, Renew**		All models	.4
Trooper	.6				
Rear Door Window Regulator, Renew		Trooper II	.8	**Hood Release Cable, Renew**	
Trooper	.8			All models	.6

LABOR   30   HEAD AND PARKING LAMPS   30   LABOR

	Chilton Time		Chilton Time		Chilton Time
Aim Headlamps		**Composite (Halogen) Headlamp Bulb, Renew**		**Side Marker Lamp Lens or Bulb, Renew**	
All models	.4	Trooper-each	.3	All models	.3
				Tail or Stop Lamp Lens or Bulb, Renew	
		Turn Signal or Parking Lamp Lens or Bulb, Renew		All models	.3
Headlamp Sealed Beam Bulb, Renew				**License Lamp Assembly, Renew**	
All models-each	.5	All models	.3	All models	.2

LABOR 31 WINDSHIELD WIPER & SPEEDOMETER 31 LABOR

	Chilton Time
Windshield Wiper Motor, Renew	
All models	.9
Windshield Wiper Switch, Renew	
All models	.9
Windshield Washer Pump Valve, Renew	
All models	.3
Wiper Transmission Assy., Renew	
All models	1.5

	Chilton Time
Windshield Washer Pump, Renew	
All models	.3
Rear Window Wiper and Washer Switch, Renew	
Trooper	.5
Rear Window Wiper Motor, Renew	
Trooper	.9
Rear Window Washer Motor, Renew	
Trooper	.3

	Chilton Time
Speedometer Head, R&R or Renew	
P/up	1.0
Trooper	.7
Speedometer Cable and Casing, Renew	
All models	.8
Speedometer Cable (Inner), Renew or Lubricate	
All models	.6
Radio, R&R	
All models	.5

LABOR 32 LIGHT SWITCHES & WIRING 32 LABOR

	Chilton Time
Headlamp Switch, Renew	
All models	.4
Headlamp Dimmer Switch, Renew	
All models	.6
Combination Switch Assy., Renew	
All models	.9
Light Switch Assy., Renew	
All models	.9
Turn Signal and Hazard Warning Switch Assy., Renew	
All models	.7

	Chilton Time
Parking Brake Lamp Switch, Renew	
All models	.3
Stop Light Switch, Renew	
All models	.3
Starter Safety Switch, Renew	
All models	.4
Back-Up Lamp Switch, Renew	
All models-w/M.T.	.3
w/A.T.	.4

	Chilton Time
Flasher/Turn Signal Relay, Renew	
Trooper II	.3
Horn Assembly, Renew (One)	
P/up	.3
Trooper	.5
each adtnl	.1
Horn Relay, Renew	
All models	.3
Turn Signal or Hazard Warning Flasher, Renew	
All models	.3

LABOR 34 CRUISE CONTROL 34 LABOR

	Chilton Time
Control Unit, Renew	
Trooper II	.3
Actuator Cable, Renew	
Trooper II	.5

	Chilton Time
Cruise Control Actuator, Renew	
Trooper II	.6
Cruise Control Relay, Renew	
All models	.3

LABOR — 1 TUNE UP 1 — LABOR

	Chilton Time
Compression Test	
Four	.5
V-6	.6
Engine Tune Up, (Electronic Ignition)	

Includes: Test battery and clean connections. Tighten manifold and carburetor mounting bolts. Check engine compression, clean and adjust or renew spark plugs. Test resistance of spark plug cables. Inspect distributor cap and rotor. Check vacuum advance operation. Reset ignition timing. Change fuel filter. Inspect and adjust drive belts. Check operation of EGR valve.

	Chilton Time
Four	1.5
V-6	1.8

LABOR — 2 IGNITION SYSTEM 2 — LABOR

GASOLINE ENGINES

	Chilton Time
Spark Plugs, Clean and Reset or Renew	
Four	.5
V-6	.6
Ignition Timing, Reset	
All models	.3
Distributor, Renew	
Includes: Reset ignition timing.	
All models	.8
Distributor, R&R and Recondition	
Includes: Reset ignition timing.	
All models	1.9

	Chilton Time
Vacuum Control Unit, Renew	
Includes: R&R distributor cap.	
All models	.5
Pick-Up Coil, Renew	
All models	1.1
Ignition Coils, Renew	
All models—one	.3
both	.4
Ignition Cables, Renew	
All models	.4
Distributor Cap and/or Rotor, Renew	
All models	.3

	Chilton Time
Ignition Switch, Renew	
MPV	.6
All other models	1.0
Igniter Set, Renew	
All models	1.1

DIESEL ENGINE

	Chilton Time
Glow Plugs, Renew	
B2200 models—one	.4
all	.6
Glow Plug Relay, Renew	
B2200 models	.3
Glow Plug Control Unit, Renew	
B2200 models	.4

LABOR — 3 FUEL SYSTEM 3 — LABOR

GASOLINE ENGINES

	Chilton Time
Fuel Pump, Test	
Includes: Disconnect fuel line, attach pressure gauge.	
All models	.3
Air Cleaner, Service	
All models	.2
Carburetor, Adjust	
Includes: R&R carburetor.	
All models	1.7
Float Level, Adjust	
All models	1.5
Carburetor, Renew	
Includes: All necessary adjustments.	
All models	1.7
Carburetor, R&R and Clean or Recondition	
Includes: All necessary adjustments.	
All models	2.8
Fuel Filter, Renew	
All models	.3
Fuel Pump, Renew	
B2000-2200 models	
w/M.T.	.5
w/A.T.	1.0
B2600 models	1.0
MPV	1.0
Add pump test if performed.	
Fuel Tank, Renew	
Includes: Drain and refill tank. Transfer sending unit.	
MPV	1.5
All other models	1.2
Fuel Gauge (Dash Unit), Renew	
All models	1.1

	Chilton Time
Fuel Gauge (Tank Unit), Renew	
Includes: R&R fuel tank.	
All models	1.1
Intake Manifold or Gasket, Renew	
B2000-2200 models	2.0
B2600 models	2.3
MPV	
Four	2.8
V-6	2.1
Renew manif add	.5

FUEL INJECTION (MPV)

	Chilton Time
Throttle Body, Renew	
All models	1.2
Throttle Body Lever Set, Renew	
All models	.6
By-Pass Air Control Valve, Renew	
All models	.3
Solenoid Valves, Renew	
All models	.5
Fuel Rail(s), Renew	
Four	1.2
V-6	
one	1.6
both	1.8
Fuel Injectors, Renew	
Four	1.4
V-6	
one side	1.8
both sides	2.0
Fuel Pressure Regulator, Renew	
Four	.5
V-6	1.0
Pulsation Damper, Renew	
All models	.9
System Relay, Renew	
All models	.4

	Chilton Time
Fuel Hoses, Renew	
All models	.5
Air Flow Meter, Renew	
All models	.6

DIESEL ENGINE

	Chilton Time
both sides	2.0
Injection Pump and/or Gasket, Renew	
B2200 models	1.8
Injection Pump, R&R and Recondition	
B2200 models	4.5
Governor Cover and/or Seal Ring, Renew	
B2200 models	.6
Governor Assembly, Renew	
B2200 models	2.6
Load Limiter, Renew	
B2200 models	2.9
Distributor Head Assy., and/or 'O' Ring, Renew	
B2200 models	3.5
Fuel Injection Nozzles, Renew	
B2200 models—one	.5
all	1.5
Fuel Filter, Renew	
B2200 models	.5
Fuel Gauge (Dash Unit), Renew	
B2200 models	1.4
Fuel Gauge (Tank Unit), Renew	
Includes: R&R fuel tank.	
B2200 models	1.1
Fuel Tank, Renew	
Includes: Drain and refill tank.	
B2200 models	1.4
Intake Manifold Gasket, Renew	
B2200 models	1.9
Renew manif add	.4

LABOR 3A EMISSION CONTROLS 3A LABOR

	Chilton Time		Chilton Time		Chilton Time
Positive Crankcase Ventilation Valve, Renew		**Air Manifold, Renew**		**Check/Cut Valve(s), Renew**	
All models	.2	All models	.6	MPV	.5
Air Control Valve, Renew		**Air Injection Nozzles, Renew (All)**		**Air Temperature Sensor, Renew**	
1986-90—one	.4	All models	.6	MPV	.6
Air Cleaner Control Valve, Renew		**Charcoal Canister or Filter, Renew**		**Throttle Sensor, Renew**	
1986-90	.4	All models	.2	MPV	.6
Hot Idle Compensator, Renew		**Solenoid Valve(s), Renew**		**Coolant Temperature Sensor, Renew**	
1986-90	.4	MPV	.4	MPV	.6
Altitude Compensator, Renew		**Check Valve(s), Renew**		**Oxygen Sensor, Renew**	
All models	.4	MPV	.3	MPV	.4
E.G.R. Control Valve, Renew		**Three Way Solenoid Valve, Renew**		**EGI Control Unit, Renew**	
1986-90	.6	MPV	.4	MPV	.5

LABOR 4 ALTERNATOR AND REGULATOR 4 LABOR

	Chilton Time		Chilton Time		Chilton Time
Alternator Circuits, Test		**Alternator Drive Belt, Renew**		**Alternator Bearings, Renew**	
Includes: Test battery, regulator and alternator output.		All models	.4	Includes: R&R alternator, separate end frames.	
All models	.4			Diesel models—front	1.6
				rear	2.0
Alternator, Renew		**Alternator, R&R and Recondition**		Gas models—front	.9
Diesel models	1.1	Includes: Disassemble, clean and test all parts. Renew parts as required, reassemble.		rear	1.5
Gas models	.6	Diesel models	2.5	**Voltage Regulator, Test and Renew**	
Add circuit test if performed.		Gas models	2.0	All models—external	.4
				internal	1.5

LABOR 5 STARTING SYSTEM 5 LABOR

	Chilton Time		Chilton Time		Chilton Time
Starter Draw Test (On Truck)		Diesel models	2.5	**Starter Drive, Renew**	
All models	.3	MPV		Includes: R&R starter.	
Starter, Renew		2 WD	2.3	B2000-2200-2600	
B2000-2200-2600		4 WD	4.7	Gas models	1.6
Gas models	.7			Diesel models	1.8
Diesel models	.8			MPV	
MPV				2 WD	1.2
2 WD	1.0	**Magnetic Switch (Solenoid), Renew**		4 WD	3.6
4 WD	3.4	Includes: R&R starter.			
Add draw test if performed.		B2000-2200-2600			
		Gas models	.9		
Starter, R&R and Recondition		Diesel models	1.1	**Battery Cables, Renew**	
Includes: Turn down armature.		MPV		All models	
B2000-2200-2600		2 WD	1.1	positive	.5
Gas models	2.2	4 WD	3.5	negative	.2

LABOR 6 BRAKE SYSTEM 6 LABOR

	Chilton Time		Chilton Time		Chilton Time
Brakes, Adjust (Minor)		MPV		MPV—one side	1.5
Includes: Fill master cylinder.		front-disc	.6	both sides	2.4
two wheels	.4	rear-drum	1.1		
four wheels	.6	all four wheels	1.6	**Wheel Cylinders, R&R and Rebuild**	
		Resurface brake rotor, add-each	.9	Includes: Bleed system.	
Bleed Brakes (Four Wheels)		Resurface brake drum, add-each	.5	B2000-2200-2600	1.2
Includes: Fill master cylinder.				both	2.3
All models	.6	**Rear Brake Drum, Renew**		MPV—one side	1.7
		B2000 models—one	.6	both sides	2.8
Brake Pedal Free Play, Adjust		both	.9		
All models	.3	B2200-2600 models—one	.9	**Master Cylinder, Renew**	
		both	1.7	Includes: Bleed system.	
Brake Shoes and/or Pads, Renew		MPV—one	1.0	B2000-2200-2600	1.3
Includes: Install new or exchange brake shoes or pads. Adjust service and hand brake. Bleed system.		both	1.9	MPV	1.1
B2000-2200-2600		**BRAKE HYDRAULIC SYSTEM**			
front-disc	.8			**Master Cylinder, R&R and Rebuild**	
rear-drum	1.2	**Wheel Cylinders, Renew**		Includes: Bleed system.	
all four wheels	1.9	Includes: Bleed system.		B2000-2200-2600	1.8
		B2000-2200-2600	1.0	MPV	1.5
		both	1.9		

LABOR 6 BRAKE SYSTEM 6 LABOR

	Chilton Time
Brake Hose, Renew (Flex)	
Includes: Bleed system.	
All models–front-one	.6
rear-one	.6
each adtnl	.3
DISC BRAKES	
Disc Brake Pads, Renew	
Includes: Install new disc brake pads only.	
B2000-2200-2600	.8
MPV	.6
Resurface brake rotor, add-each	.9
Caliper Assembly, Renew	
Includes: Bleed system.	
B2000-2200-2600-one	1.0
both	1.5
MPV-one	.7
both	1.0
Caliper Assy., R&R and Recondition	
Includes: Bleed system.	
B2000-2200-2600-one	1.4
both	2.3
MPV-one	1.1
both	1.8
Disc Brake Rotor, Renew	
B2000-2200-2600	
4X2 models-one	.9
both	1.7
4X4 models-one	1.2
both	2.2
MPV-one	.8
both	1.3

COMBINATIONS

	Chilton Time
WHEEL CYLINDER, RENEW	
Each	.3
WHEEL CYLINDER, REBUILD	
Each	.4
CALIPER ASSEMBLY, REBUILD	
Each	.4
MASTER CYLINDER, REBUILD	
All models	.4
BRAKE HOSE, RENEW	
Each	.3
FRONT WHEEL BEARINGS, CLEAN AND REPACK (BOTH WHEELS)	
All models	.6
DISC BRAKE ROTOR, RENEW	
Each	.3
BRAKE DRUM, RENEW	
Each	.1

	Chilton Time
Proportioning Valve, Renew	
Includes: Bleed system.	
All models	1.1

	Chilton Time
POWER BRAKES	
Power Brake Booster, Renew	
Includes: R&R master cylinder and bleed system.	
MPV	
Four	1.5
V-6	1.7
All other models	1.4
Power Brake Booster, R&R and Recondition	
Includes: R&R master cylinder and bleed system.	
B2000-2200-2600	1.7
Vacuum Check Valve, Renew	
All models	.2
PARKING BRAKE	
Parking Brake, Adjust	
All models	.3
Parking Brake Control, Renew	
MPV	.5
All other models	.6
Parking Brake Cables, Renew	
Includes: Adjust cables.	
MPV	
front	.9
rear-one	1.3
both	2.0
All other models-front	1.0
rear-one	1.1
both	1.7

LABOR 7 COOLING SYSTEM 7 LABOR

	Chilton Time
Winterize Cooling System	
Includes: Run engine to check for leaks, tighten all hose connections. Test radiator and pressure cap, drain radiator and engine block. Add antifreeze and refill system.	
All models	.5
Thermostat, Renew	
B2000-2200 models	.7
B2600 models	.7
MPV	.8
Radiator Assy., R&R or Renew	
Includes: Drain and refill cooling system.	
All models	1.2
w/A.T. add	.2
ADD THESE OPERATIONS TO RADIATOR R&R	
Boil & Repair	1.5
Rod Clean	1.9
Repair Core	1.3
Renew Tank	1.6
Renew Trans. Oil Cooler	1.9
Recore Radiator	1.7
Radiator Hoses, Renew	
All models	
upper	.4
lower	.4

	Chilton Time
Fan Belt, Renew	
All models	.3
Cooling Fan or Drive Assy., Renew	
All models	.6
Water Pump Assy., Renew	
Includes: R&R radiator where required. Drain and refill cooling system.	
GAS	
B2000-2200 models	2.5
B2600 models	.8
MPV	
Four	.8
V-6	2.4
w/A.C. add	.1
w/P.S. add	.1
DIESEL	
All models	1.5
w/A.C. & P.S. add	.2
Cooling System Hoses, Renew	
All models-each	.3
Temperature Gauge (Dash Unit), Renew	
B2000 models	1.2
B2200 models	1.4
MPV	.9
Temperature Gauge (Engine Unit), Renew	
All models	.5

	Chilton Time
Heater Control Assembly, Renew	
All models	.7
Heater Blower Motor, Renew	
B2000-2200-2600	1.0
MPV	.6
Heater Water Valve, Renew	
All models	.5
Heater Core, R&R or Renew	
B2000-2200-2600	4.5
MPV	
front	3.0
rear	1.7
ADD THESE OPERATIONS TO HEATER CORE R&R	
Boil & Repair	1.2
Repair Core	.9
Recore	1.2
Heater Hoses, Renew	
All models-one side	.6
both sides	1.0
Heater Blower Motor Resistor, Renew	
1986-90	.5
Cooling Fan Relay, Renew	
MPV	.4

LABOR · 8 EXHAUST SYSTEM 8 · LABOR

	Chilton Time		Chilton Time		Chilton Time
Front Exhaust Pipe, Renew		**Monolith Converter, Renew**		**Catalytic Converter, Renew**	
MPV	.7	1986-90	1.5	B2000-2200-2600	.7
B2000-2200-2600	.9			MPV	.8
Center Exhaust Pipe, Renew		**Muffler, Renew**		**Exhaust Manifold or Gaskets, Renew**	
MPV	1.3	MPV	.6	B2000-2200-2600	1.5
B2000-2200-2600	.9	B2000-2200-2600	.8	MPV	
				Four	.8
Pre-Muffler, Renew		**Tail Pipe, Renew**		V-6–left	1.1
B2000 models	1.3	MPV	.4	right	1.3
		B2000-2200-2600	.5	both	2.1

LABOR · 9 FRONT SUSPENSION 9 · LABOR

	Chilton Time		Chilton Time		Chilton Time
Wheel, Renew		**Front Hub Assy., Renew**		MPV	
one	.5	B2000-2200-2600		one side	.9
Wheels, Balance		4X2 models–one	1.1	both sides	1.2
one	.3	both	2.0	**Front Stabilizer Bar and/or Bushings,**	
each adtnl	.2	4X4 models	1.5	**Renew**	
Wheels, Rotate (All)		both	2.7	B2000-2200-2600	.8
All models	.5	MPV		MPV	.6
Toe-In, Adjust		4X2		**Steering Knuckles, Renew**	
All models	.6	one side	.8	Includes: Align front end.	
		both side	1.2	B2000-2200-2600	
Caster, Camber and Toe-In, Check and		4X4		4X2 models–one side	2.4
Adjust		one side	1.2	both sides	4.0
All models	1.5	both sides	1.7	4X4 models–one side	2.8
				both sides	4.2
Front Wheel Bearings, Clean and Repack		**Front Shock Absorbers or Rubber**		MPV	
B2000-2200-2600		**Bushings, Renew**		4X2	
4X2 models–one side	.8	B2000-2200-2600–one	.4	one side	1.3
both sides	1.5	both	.7	both sides	1.7
4X4 models–one side	1.2	MPV–one	1.0	4X4	
both sides	2.3	both	1.5	one side	1.8
		Front Coil Springs, Renew		both sides	2.6
Front Wheel Bearings, Renew		B2000-2200-2600–one side	1.4	**Torsion Rods and/or Bushings, Renew**	
B2000-2200-2600		both sides	2.6	Includes: Reset car height.	
4X2 models–one side	.9	MPV–one	.9	1986–one side	1.0
both sides	1.7	both	1.4	both sides	1.9
4X4 models–one side	1.3	**Upper Control Arm and/or Bushings,**		**Torsion Bar Spring, Renew**	
both sides	2.5	**Renew**		Includes: Reset car height.	
MPV		Add alignment charges.		1986–one side	1.1
4X2		B2000-2200-2600–one side	1.4	both sides	1.5
one side	1.3	both sides	2.3	**Torsion Arm, Renew**	
both sides	1.8			Includes: Reset car height.	
4X4		**Lower Control Arm and/or Bushings,**		1986–one side	1.1
one side	1.7	**Renew**		both sides	1.6
both sides	2.2	Includes: Align front end.		**Steering Knuckle Oil Seals, Renew**	
		B2000-2200-2600		B2600	
Front Hub Oil Seal, Renew		4X2 models–one side	1.7	4X4 models–one side	1.1
B2000-2200-2600		both sides	3.1	both sides	2.0
4X2 models–one side	.7	4X4 models–one side	1.9	**Steering Knuckle Bearings, Renew**	
both sides	1.3	both sides	3.3	B2600	
4X4 models–one side	.9	MPV		4X4 models–one side	1.5
both sides	1.7	one side	1.5	both sides	2.7
MPV		both sides	2.3	**Four Wheel Drive Locking Hubs, Renew**	
4X2		**Ball Joints, Renew (Upper or Lower)**		B2600 models–one	.5
one side	.8	Add alignment charges.		both	.7
both sides	1.2	B2000-2200-2600–one	.9		
4X4		both–one side	1.5		
one side	1.2	all–both sides	2.9		
both sides	1.7				

LABOR · 10 STEERING LINKAGE 10 · LABOR

	Chilton Time		Chilton Time		Chilton Time
Tie Rod, Renew		**Tie Rod End, Renew**		**Idler Arm Assembly, Renew**	
Includes: Reset toe-in.		Includes: Reset toe-in.		All models	.8
All models–one side	.7	All models–one side	1.0	Renew bushing add	.2
both sides	1.1	both sides	1.5		
Renew seal add–each	.1	**Center Link, Renew**		**Steering Knuckle Arms, Renew**	
Pitman Arm, Renew		Includes: Reset toe-in.		Includes: Reset toe-in.	
All models	.6	All models	1.2	All models–one side	1.1
				both sides	1.8

LABOR   11   STEERING GEAR   11   LABOR

MANUAL STEERING

	Chilton Time
Horn Button, Renew	
All models....................	.4
Steering Wheel, Renew	
All models....................	.3
Steering Column Support Bushing, Renew	
All models....................	.9
Steering Gear, Adjust (On Truck)	
All models....................	.5
Steering Gear, R&R or Renew	
B2000-2200-2600....................	.9
Steering Gear, R&R and Recondition	
Includes: Disassemble, renew necessary parts, reassemble and adjust.	
B2000-2200-2600....................	2.0
Steering Gear Side Cover Gasket, Renew (On Truck)	
Includes: Adjust steering gear.	
B2000-2200 models....................	.5
B2600 models....................	.8

	Chilton Time
Sector Shaft and/or Oil Seal, Renew	
Includes: Disconnect center link. R&R pitman arm and side cover.	
B2000-2200 models....................	1.1
B2600 models....................	1.3

POWER STEERING

	Chilton Time
Power Steering Gear, R&R or Renew	
B2000-2200 models....................	1.1
B2600 models....................	1.3
MPV	
4X2	2.0
4X4	3.1
Power Steering Gear, R&R and Recondition	
B2000-2200 models....................	2.4
B2600 models....................	2.6
MPV	
4X2	4.2
4X4	5.3

	Chilton Time
Power Steering Pump, R&R or Renew	
B2000-2200-2600	
wo/A.C....................	1.2
w/A.C....................	1.9
MPV....................	1.1
Power Steering Pump, R&R and Recondition	
B2000-2200-2600	
wo/A.C....................	2.0
w/A.C....................	2.7
MPV....................	1.6
Power Steering Hoses, Renew	
B2000-2200-2600	
Pressure hose	
wo/A.C....................	.8
w/A.C....................	1.3
Return hose....................	.8
Return pipes	
each....................	.6
MPV	
Pressure....................	1.8
Return....................	.8

LABOR   12   CYLINDER HEAD & VALVE SYSTEM   12   LABOR

GASOLINE ENGINES

	Chilton Time
Compression Test	
Four....................	.5
V-6....................	.6
Cylinder Head Gasket, Renew	
Includes: Clean carbon. Make all necessary adjustments.	
B2000-2200 models....................	6.5
B2600 models....................	6.3
w/A.C. & P.S. add....................	.2
MPV	
Four....................	5.3
V-6	
right side....................	5.1
left side....................	5.4
both sides....................	7.1
w/A.C. add....................	.1
w/P.S. add....................	.1
Cylinder Head, Renew	
Includes: Clean carbon. Transfer parts as required. Reface valves. Make all necessary adjustments.	
B2000-2200 models....................	11.3
B2600 models....................	10.5
w/A.C. & P.S. add....................	.2
Clean Carbon and Grind Valves	
Includes: R&R cylinder head, clean carbon, reface valves and seats. Minor tune up.	
B2000-2200 models....................	9.9
B2600 models....................	9.2
w/A.C. & P.S. add....................	.2
MPV	
Four....................	11.9
V-6	
right side....................	11.4
left side....................	11.7
both sides....................	19.7
w/A.C. add....................	.1
w/P.S. add....................	.1
Rocker Arm Cover Gasket(s), Renew	
B2000-2200-2600....................	.5
MPV	
Four....................	.7
V-6	
right....................	.5
left....................	.6
both....................	1.0

	Chilton Time
Rocker Arm(s) or Shaft(s), Renew (One or All)	
B2000-2200 models....................	2.4
B2600 models....................	2.1
MPV	
Four....................	1.8
V-6	
right side....................	1.4
left side....................	1.5
both sides....................	1.8
Valve Springs and/or Valve Stem Oil Seals, Renew (Head on Truck)	
B2000-2200 models....................	5.0
B2600 models....................	4.5
MPV	
Four....................	7.7
V-6	
right side....................	5.4
left side....................	5.6
both sides....................	10.9
w/A.C. add....................	.1
w/P.S. add....................	.1
Cylinder Head Oil Seals, Renew	
Includes: R&R valve cover.	
All models....................	.4
Hydraulic Valve Lash Adjustors, Renew	
B2200 models	
one....................	2.6
all....................	2.8
B2600 models	
one....................	1.8
all....................	2.0
MPV	
Four....................	2.5
V-6	
right side....................	1.8
left side....................	1.9
both sides....................	2.1
Jet Valves, Renew	
B2600 models	
one....................	1.9
all....................	2.1
Valves, Adjust	
All models....................	1.0
Cylinder Head, Retorque	
All models....................	1.3

DIESEL ENGINE

	Chilton Time
Compression Test	
B2200 models....................	1.4
Cylinder Head Gasket, Renew	
Includes: Clean carbon. Make all necessary adjustments.	
B2200 models....................	6.7
Cylinder Head, Renew	
Includes: Clean carbon. Transfer parts as required. Reface valves. Make all necessary adjustments.	
B2200 models....................	9.8
Clean Carbon and Grind Valves	
Includes: R&R cylinder head, clean carbon, reface valves and seats. Make all necessary adjustments.	
B2200 models....................	9.5
Rocker Arm Cover Gasket, Renew	
B2200 models....................	.5
Valve Push Rods, Renew (One or All)	
B2200 models....................	2.3
Rocker Arms or Shaft, Renew (One or All)	
B2200 models....................	2.1
Valve Tappets, Renew	
Includes: R&R engine and trans.	
B2200 models....................	6.0
Valve Springs and/or Valve Stem Oil Seals, Renew	
Includes: R&R cylinder head.	
B2200 models–one cyl....................	7.0
all cyls....................	8.2
Valve Clearance, Adjust	
B2200 models....................	1.0

LABOR 13 ENGINE ASSEMBLY & MOUNTS 13 LABOR

GASOLINE ENGINES

Note: All engine operations listed in this group are for assemblies as supplied by the original equipment manufacturer. Time to replace assemblies from independent rebuilders may vary.

Engine Assembly, Remove and Install

Does not include transfer of any parts or equipment.

	Chilton Time
B2000-2200 models	
4X2	5.6
4X4	6.1
B2600 models	
w/M.T.	6.0
w/A.T.	
4X2	6.5
4X4	7.4
w/A.C. & P.S. add	.4
MPV	
w/M.T.	
Four	8.5
V-6	9.1
w/A.T.	
4X2	
Four	9.3
V-6	9.5
4X4	9.9
w/A.C. add	.4
w/P.S. add	.4

Cylinder Assy. (Short Block), Renew

Includes: R&R engine assy. Transfer all component parts not supplied with replacement engine. Minor tune up.

	Chilton Time
B2000-2200 models	
4X2	14.4
4X4	14.9

	Chilton Time
B2600 models	
w/M.T.	13.3
w/A.T.	
4X2	13.8
4X4	14.7
w/A.C. & P.S. add	.4
MPV	
w/M.T.	
Four	16.5
V-6	18.4
w/A.T.	
4X2	
Four	17.3
V-6	18.9
4X4	19.3
w/A.C. add	.4
w/P.S. add	.4

Engine Assy., R&R and Recondition

Includes: Install new pistons, pins, rings, rod and main bearings. Clean carbon, grind valves. Tune engine.

	Chilton Time
B2000-2200 models	
4X2	21.9
4X4	22.5
B2600 models	
w/M.T.	23.1
w/A.T.	
4X2	23.6
4X4	24.5
w/A.C. & P.S. add	.4
MPV	
w/M.T.	
Four	26.0
V-6	27.0

	Chilton Time
w/A.T.	
4X2	
Four	26.8
V-6	27.4
4X4	27.8
w/A.C. add	.4
w/P.S. add	.4

Engine Mounts, Renew

	Chilton Time
All models-front-one	.5
both	.8
rear	.6

DIESEL ENGINE

Engine Assembly, Remove and Install

Does not include transfer of any parts or equipment.

	Chilton Time
B2200 models	4.8

Cylinder Assembly, Renew (Short Block)

Includes: R&R engine assy. Transfer all component parts not supplied with replacement engine. Make all necessary adjustments.

	Chilton Time
B2200 models	21.2
Renew cyl liners add	.8

Engine Assy., R&R and Recondition

Includes: Install new pistons, pins, rings, rod and main bearings. Clean carbon, grind valves. Make all necessary adjustments.

	Chilton Time
B2200 models	26.0

Engine Mounts, Renew

	Chilton Time
B2200 models	
front-one	.6
both	1.0

LABOR 14 PISTONS, RINGS & BEARINGS 14 LABOR

GASOLINE ENGINES

Rings, Renew (All)

Includes: Remove cylinder top ridge, deglaze cylinder walls. Clean carbon from cylinder head. Minor tune up.

	Chilton Time
B2000-2200 models	11.6
B2600 models	
4X2	10.7
4X4	13.9
w/A.C. & P.S. add	.8
MPV	
Four	10.3
V-6	
4X2	14.2
4X4	14.5
w/A.C. add	.1
w/P.S. add	.1

Pistons or Connecting Rods, Renew

Includes: Remove cylinder top ridge, deglaze cylinder walls. Clean carbon from cylinder head. Replace rod bearings. Minor tune up.

	Chilton Time
B2000-2200 models	12.8
B2600 models	
4X2	11.9
4X4	15.1
w/A.C. & P.S. add	.8
MPV	
Four	11.5

COMBINATIONS

	Chilton Time
DISTRIBUTOR, RECONDITION	
All models	1.0
CARBURETOR, RECONDITION	
All models	1.4
OIL PUMP, RECONDITION	
All models	.4
WATER PUMP, RECONDITION	
All models	1.0
PLASTIGAUGE BEARINGS	
Each	.1
REMOVE CYLINDER TOP RIDGE	
Each	.3
DEGLAZE CYLINDER WALLS	
Each	.1
OIL FILTER ELEMENT, RENEW	
All models	.3

	Chilton Time
V-6	
4X2	16.0
4X4	16.3
w/A.C. add	.1
w/P.S. add	.1

Connecting Rod Bearings, Renew

Includes: R&R oil pan.

	Chilton Time
B2000-2200 models	4.5
B2600 models	
4X2	6.9
4X4	7.5
MPV	
Four	4.2
V-6	
4X2	5.3
4X4	5.7
w/A.C. add	.1
w/P.S. add	.1

DIESEL ENGINE

Rings, Renew (All)

Includes: Remove cylinder top ridge, deglaze cylinder walls. Clean carbon from cylinder head. Make all necessary adjustments.

	Chilton Time
B2200 models	11.5

Pistons or Connecting Rods, Renew

Includes: Remove cylinder top ridge, deglaze cylinder walls. Clean carbon from cylinder head. Make all necessary adjustments.

	Chilton Time
B2200 models	12.7

Connecting Rod Bearings, Renew

Includes: R&R oil pan.

	Chilton Time
B2200 models	3.2

LABOR 15 CRANKSHAFT & DAMPER 15 LABOR

GASOLINE ENGINES

Crankshaft and Main Bearings, Renew
Includes: R&R engine assy. Check all bearing clearances.

	Chilton Time
B2000-2200 models	
4X2	19.6
4X4	20.1
B2600 models	
4X2	
w/M.T.	19.1
w/A.T.	19.8
4X4	
w/M.T.	19.3
w/A.T.	20.7
w/A.C. & P.S. add	.8
MPV	
w/M.T.	
Four	18.2
V-6	21.5
w/A.T.	
4X2	
Four	19.0
V-6	21.9
4X4	22.4
w/A.C. add	.4
w/P.S. add	.4

Crankshaft Rear Oil Seal, Renew
Includes: R&R transmission.

	Chilton Time
B2000-2200 models	
w/M.T.	4.0
w/A.T.	4.0
B2600 models	
w/M.T.	
4X2	4.0
4X4	4.6
w/A.T.	
4X2	4.0
4X4	5.8
MPV	
w/M.T.	4.9
w/A.T.	
4X2	
Four	6.1
V-6	5.6
4X4	6.0

Crankshaft Front Oil Seal, Renew

	Chilton Time
B2600 models	1.0
w/A.C. & P.S. add	.1

Crankshaft Pulley, Renew

	Chilton Time
B2000-2200-2600	.7
w/A.C. & P.S. add	.1
MPV	1.0

DIESEL ENGINE

Crankshaft and Main Bearings, Renew
Includes: R&R engine assy. Check all bearing clearances.

	Chilton Time
B2200 models	19.7

Crankshaft Front Oil Seal, Renew

	Chilton Time
B2200 models	2.2

Crankshaft Rear Oil Seal, Renew
Includes: R&R trans.

	Chilton Time
B2200 models	3.1

Crankshaft Pulley, Renew

	Chilton Time
B2200 models	2.0

LABOR 16 CAMSHAFT & TIMING GEARS 16 LABOR

GASOLINE ENGINES

Timing Chain Cover Gaskets, Renew
Includes: R&R cylinder head, radiator, water and air pumps, where required.

	Chilton Time
B2600 models	
4X2	3.4
4X4	7.4
w/A.C. & P.S. add	.5
MPV	
Four	8.7
w/A.C. add	.4
w/P.S. add	.3
Renew cover add	.5

Timing Chain and/or Sprockets, Renew
Includes: R&R front cover.

	Chilton Time
B2600 models	
4X2	3.9
4X4	7.9
w/A.C. & P.S. add	.5
MPV	
Four	9.6
w/A.C. add	.4
w/P.S. add	.3

Timing Chain Tensioner, Renew
Includes: Reset ignition timing.

	Chilton Time
B2600 models	
4X2	3.9
4X4	7.9
w/A.C. & P.S. add	.5
MPV	
Four	9.4
w/A.C. add	.4
w/P.S. add	.3

Vibration Damper and/or Chain Guide, Renew
Includes: R&R front cover.

	Chilton Time
B2600 models	
4X2	3.9
4X4	7.9
w/A.C. & P.S. add	.5
MPV	
Four	9.4
w/A.C. add	.4
w/P.S. add	.3

Balance Shafts, Renew

	Chilton Time
B2600 models	
4X2	
w/M.T.-one	8.8
two	9.0
w/A.T.-one	9.4
two	9.6
4X4	
w/M.T.-one	9.0
two	9.2
w/A.T.-one	10.2
two	10.4
w/A.C. & P.S. add	.5
MPV	
Four	
w/M.T.	11.0
w/A.T.	11.9
w/A.C. add	.4
w/P.S. add	.4
Renew brgs add–each	.2

Timing Belt Cover and/or Gasket, Renew

	Chilton Time
B2200	
upper	.6
lower	1.4
w/A.C. & P.S. add	.2
MPV	
V-6	1.0
w/A.C. add	.1
w/P.S. add	.1

Timing Belt Cover Oil Seal, Renew

	Chilton Time
1986-90	2.0
w/A.C. & P.S. add	.2

Timing Belt Pulley (Crank Sprocket), Renew
Includes: R&R timing belt.

	Chilton Time
B2200	3.2
w/A.C. & P.S. add	.2
MPV	
V-6	1.7
w/A.C. add	.1
w/P.S. add	.1

Timing Belt, Renew

	Chilton Time
B2200	3.0
w/A.C. & P.S. add	.2
MPV	
V-6	1.8
w/A.C. add	.1
w/P.S. add	.1

Timing Belt Tensioner, Renew

	Chilton Time
B2200	1.5
w/A.C. & P.S. add	.2
MPV	
V-6	1.8
w/A.C. add	.1
w/P.S. add	.1

Camshaft Pulley (Sprocket), Renew

	Chilton Time
B2200	1.9
w/A.C. & P.S. add	.2
MPV	
Four	1.7
V-6	
right side	1.3
left side	1.4
both sides	1.6
w/A.C. add	.1
w/P.S. add	.1

Camshaft, Renew

	Chilton Time
B2000-2200 models	3.6
B2600 models	3.4
w/A.C. & P.S. add	.2
MPV	
Four	1.8
V-6	
right side	2.6
left side	2.8
both sides	3.7
w/A.C. add	.1
w/P.S. add	.1

DIESEL ENGINE

Timing Case Cover and/or Gasket, Renew

	Chilton Time
B2200 models	3.0

Timing Gear, Renew
Includes: Renew idler gear and/or bushing.

	Chilton Time
B2200 models	4.0

Timing Gear Case Assy., and/or Gasket, Renew
Includes: R&R injection pump and idler gear. R&R cam gear and oil pan. Reset injection timing.

	Chilton Time
B2200 models	5.5

Camshaft, Renew
Includes: Renew thrust plate and cam sprocket. Adjust valve clearance and injection timing.

	Chilton Time
B2200 models	6.0

LABOR 17 ENGINE OILING SYSTEM 17 LABOR

	Chilton Time
GASOLINE ENGINES	
Oil Pan and/or Gasket, Renew	
B2000-2200-2600	
4X2	2.6
4X4	5.8
MPV	
Four	2.4
V-6	
4X2	2.1
4X4	2.5
Pressure Test Engine Bearings (Pan Off)	
All models	1.0
Oil Pump, Renew	
B2000-2200 models	4.0
B2600 models	
4X2	4.2
4X4	8.4
w/A.C. & P.S. add	.5
MPV	
Four	8.9
w/A.C. add	.4
w/P.S. add	.3

	Chilton Time
V-6	
4X2	2.3
4X4	2.7
w/A.C. add	.1
w/P.S. add	.1
Oil Pump, R&R and Recondition	
B2000-2200 models	4.3
B2600 models	
4X2	4.5
4X4	8.7
w/A.C. & P.S. add	.5
MPV	
Four	9.1
w/A.C. add	.4
w/P.S. add	.3
V-6	
4X2	3.7
4X4	4.2
w/A.C. add	.1
w/P.S. add	.1
Oil Pressure Switch, Renew	
All models	.4

	Chilton Time
Oil Filter Element, Renew	
All models	.3
DIESEL ENGINE	
Oil Pan and/or Gasket, Renew	
B2200 models	2.0
Pressure Test Engine Bearings (Pan Off)	
B2200 models	1.0
Oil Pump, Renew	
Includes: R&R oil pan.	
B2200 models	2.3
Oil Pump, R&R and Recondition	
Includes: R&R oil pan.	
B2200 models	2.6
Oil Cooler, Renew	
B2200 models	1.0
Oil Filter Element, Renew	
B2200 models	.3

LABOR 18 CLUTCH & FLYWHEEL 18 LABOR

	Chilton Time
Clutch Pedal Free Play, Adjust	
All models	.3
Bleed Clutch Hydraulic System	
All models	.3
Clutch Master Cylinder, Renew	
Includes: Bleed system.	
All models	.6
Clutch Master Cylinder, R&R and Recondition	
Includes: Bleed system.	
All models	1.0
Clutch Slave Cylinder, Renew	
Includes: Bleed system.	
All models	.5

	Chilton Time
Clutch Slave Cylinder, R&R and Recondition	
Includes: Bleed system.	
All models	.7
Clutch Release Bearing and/or Fork, Renew	
Includes: R&R trans and adjust clutch pedal free play.	
B2000-2200-2600	
4X2	3.6
4X4	4.1
MPV	
4X2	3.0
4X4	4.9
Clutch Assembly, Renew	
Includes: R&R trans and adjust clutch pedal free play.	
B2000-2200-2600	
4X2	3.9

	Chilton Time
4X4	4.4
MPV	
4X2	3.3
4X4	5.2
Flywheel, Renew	
Includes: R&R trans and clutch. Adjust clutch pedal free play.	
B2000-2200-2600	
4X2	4.2
4X4	4.7
MPV	
4X2	3.6
4X4	5.5
Renew ring gear add	.4
Renew pilot brg add	.2

LABOR 19A MANUAL TRANSMISSION (RWD) 19A LABOR

	Chilton Time
Transmission Assembly, Remove & Install	
B2000-2200-2600	
4X2	3.3
4X4	3.9
MPV	
4X2	2.8
4X4	5.0
Speedometer Driven Gear, Renew	
All models	.5

	Chilton Time
Transmission Assy., R&R and Recondition	
Includes: Clean and inspect all parts. Install all new parts as required. Install new gaskets and seals.	
B2000 models	
4 Speed	8.0
5 Speed	9.0
B2200 models	
5 Speed	7.5
B2600 models	
4X2	7.1
4X4	9.0

	Chilton Time
MPV	
4X2	6.5
4X4	9.5
Extension Housing and/or Gasket, Renew	
B2000-2200-2600	
4X2	2.7
4X4	5.0
MPV	3.1
Extension Housing Oil Seal, Renew	
All models	.7

LABOR 20 TRANSFER CASE 20 LABOR

	Chilton Time
Transfer Case Assy., R&R or Renew	
B2600 models	
w/M.T.	4.5
w/A.T.	5.6
MPV	4.8

	Chilton Time
Transfer Case Assy., R&R and Recondition	
B2600 models	
w/M.T.	6.8
w/A.T.	8.0
MPV	7.7

	Chilton Time
Transfer Case Chain Cover, R&R or Renew	
B2600 models	2.5
Transfer Case Rear Flange Oil Seal, Renew	
B2600 models	.8

LABOR   21 SHIFT LINKAGE 21   LABOR

MANUAL

Gear Shift Lever, Renew
All models 4

Gear Shift Housing, Renew
All models
  4X2 7
  4X4 .... 4.0

AUTOMATIC

Shift Linkage, Adjust
All models 4

Selector Lever, Renew
All models 6

LABOR   23A AUTOMATIC TRANSMISSION (RWD) 23A LABOR

ON CAR SERVICES

Drain & Refill Unit
All models 8

Pressure Check
All models 8

Check Unit For Oil Leaks
Includes: Clean and dry outside of case and run unit to determine point of leak.
All models 9

Vacuum Control Unit, Renew
All models 5

Neutral Safety Switch, Renew
All models 5

Oil Pan Gasket, Renew
All models 8

Valve Body Assembly, Renew
Includes: R&R oil pan.
  B2000-2200-2600 .... 1.7
  MPV
    Four 1.4
    V-6 .... 4.7

Valve Body Assy., R&R and Recondition
Includes: R&R oil pan, clean, inspect, free all valves. Replace parts as required.
  B2000-2200-2600 .... 3.0
  MPV
    Four 2.5
    V-6 .... 6.5

Speedometer Driven Gear, Renew
All models 5

SERVICES REQUIRING R&R

Transmission Assembly, Remove & Install
Includes: Drain and refill unit, adjust linkage. Road test.
  B2000-2200-2600
    4X2 .... 3.3
    4X4 .... 5.1
  MPV
    Four 4.0
    V-6
      4X2 .... 3.5
      4X4 .... 6.3

Transmission Assy., R&R and Recondition
Includes: Disassemble complete unit, renew or recondition all parts. Reassemble, make all necessary adjustments. Road test.
  B2000-2200-2600
    4X2 .... 10.2
    4X4 .... 13.0
  MPV
    Four 11.2
    V-6
      4X2 .... 11.0
      4X4 .... 11.4

Extension Housing Gasket, Renew
Includes: R&R transmission where required.
  B2000-2200-2600
    4X2 .... 2.9
    4X4 .... 6.7
  MPV
    Four 3.6
    V-6
      4X2 .... 3.2
      4X4 .... 3.6

Governor Assembly, Renew
Includes: R&R trans and extension housing.
  B2000-2200-2600
    4X2 .... 4.2

    4X4 .... 7.0
  MPV
    Four 4.7
    V-6
      4X2 .... 4.2
      4X4 .... 7.0
  Recond governor add 4

Front Pump Oil Seal, Renew
Includes: R&R transmission.
  B2000-2200-2600
    4X2 .... 4.9
    4X4 .... 6.2
  MPV
    Four 4.7
    V-6
      4X2 .... 4.4
      4X4 .... 6.4

Torque Converter, Renew
Includes: R&R transmission.
  B2000-2200-2600
    4X2 .... 3.3
    4X4 .... 5.1
  MPV
    Four 4.0
    V-6
      4X2 .... 3.5
      4X4 .... 6.7

Drive Plate (Flywheel), Renew
Includes: R&R transmission.
  B2000-2200-2600
    4X2 .... 3.6
    4X4 .... 5.4
  MPV
    Four 4.4
    V-6
      4X2 .... 3.9
      4X4 .... 7.1

LABOR   25 U-JOINTS & DRIVESHAFT 25   LABOR

Driveshaft, Renew
  B2000-2200-2600 7
4X4 add 2
  MPV
    4X2 6
    4X4
      front 6
      rear 7

Universal Joints, Renew or Recondition
Includes: R&R driveshaft.
  B2000-2200-2600
    one 1.3
  MPV
    one 1.0
    two 1.3
    three 1.8

Center Bearing or Seals, Renew
Includes: R&R driveshaft.
  B2000-2200-2600 .... 1.5
4X4 add 2
  MPV 1.0

LABOR   26 DRIVE AXLE 26   LABOR

	Chilton Time
REAR DIFFERENTIAL ASSEMBLY	
Differential, Drain & Refill	
All models	.6
Axle Shaft Assembly, Renew	
Includes: Renew outer oil seals. Bleed rear brake lines.	
B2000-2200-2600	
one side	1.5
both sides	2.6
MPV	
one	1.5
both	2.4
Rear Axle Inner Oil Seals, Renew	
Includes: R&R axle shafts. Bleed rear brake lines.	
B2000-2200-2600	
one side	1.2
both sides	2.2
MPV	
one side	1.5
both sides	2.4
Rear Axle Bearings and/or Bearing Housing, Renew	
Includes: R&R axle shafts, renew oil seals. Bleed rear brake lines.	
B2000-2200-2600	
one side	1.6
both sides	2.8
MPV	
one side	1.5
both sides	2.4

	Chilton Time
Pinion Shaft Oil Seal, Renew	
All models	1.0
Differential Carrier Assy., Remove & Install	
Includes: R&R axle shafts, disconnect brake lines and parking brake cable. Bleed rear brake lines.	
B2000-2200-2600	3.0
MPV	2.7
Differential Carrier Assy., R&R and Recondition	
Includes: R&R axle shafts. Disconnect brake lines and parking brake cable. Recondition carrier assy. Make all necessary adjustments. Bleed rear brake lines.	
B2000-2200-2600	5.0
MPV	4.9
Rear Axle Housing, R&R or Renew	
Includes: Disconnect all attaching parts. Transfer carrier assy. Make all necessary adjustments. Bleed rear brake lines.	
B2000-2200-2600	4.5
MPV	4.3
FRONT DIFFERENTIAL ASSEMBLY	
Front Propeller Shaft, R&R or Renew	
All models	.6
Front Drive Axle Shaft, R&R or Renew	
All models-one	1.2
both	2.1

	Chilton Time
Drive Shaft Boots, Renew	
B2600 models-one side	1.5
both sides	2.8
Inner or Outer C.V. Joints, Renew or Recondition	
All models-one side	1.6
both sides	3.0
Pinion Shaft Oil Seal, Renew	
All models	.8
Front Differential Assy., R&R or Reseal	
B2600 models	3.7
MPV	3.5
Front Differential Assy., R&R and Recondition	
B2600 models	6.1
MPV	5.7
Ring Gear and Pinion Set, Renew	
B2600 models	6.0
MPV	5.0
Drive Pinion Gears, Renew	
B2600 models	5.1
MPV	4.2
Limited Slip Clutch Plates, Renew	
B2600 models	3.2
Axle Housing Oil Seals and/or Bearings, Renew	
B2600 models-right side	1.2
left side	1.4
both sides	2.4
MPV	5.0

LABOR   27 REAR SUSPENSION 27   LABOR

	Chilton Time
Rear Shock Absorbers or Rubber Bushings, Renew	
All models-one	.6
both	.9
Rear Spring Shackles or Bushings, Renew	
B2000-2200-2600	
one side	.6
both sides	1.0

	Chilton Time
Rear Springs, Renew	
B2000-2200-2600	
one	1.3
both	2.1
MPV	
one	.7
both	1.3
Recond spring add, each	.5

	Chilton Time
Lateral Rod, Renew	
MPV	.5
Lower Arms/Links, Renew	
MPV	
one	.6
both	1.1
Upper Links, Renew	
MPV	
one	.5
both	.9

LABOR 29 LOCKS, HINGES & WIND. REGULATORS 29 LABOR

	Chilton Time
Hood Hinge, Renew	
All models-one	.4
both	.5
Hood Lock, Renew	
All models	.3
Hood Release Cable, Renew	
All models	.6

	Chilton Time
Lock Striker Plate, Renew	
All models	.2
Door Lock Assembly, Renew	
Includes: R&R trim panel.	
All models	.7
Door Lock Cylinder, Renew	
All models	.6

	Chilton Time
Recode cyl add	.3
Door Window Regulator, Renew	
Includes: R&R trim panel.	
All models-manual	1.0
power	1.1

LABOR 30 HEAD AND PARKING LAMPS 30 LABOR

	Chilton Time
Aim Headlamps	
All models-one side	.4
both sides	.6
Headlamp Sealed Beam Bulb, Renew	
B2000-2200-2600-one side	.6
both sides	.8

	Chilton Time
Halogen Headlamp Bulb, Renew	
MPV-each	.2
Front Turn Signal Lamp Lens or Bulb, Renew	
All models	.2

	Chilton Time
Side Marker Lamp Lens or Bulb, Renew	
All models	.2
Rear Combination Lamp Lens or Bulb, Renew	
All models-each	.3
License Lamp Assembly, Renew	
All models-each	.2

LABOR 31 WINDSHIELD WIPER & SPEEDOMETER 31 LABOR

	Chilton Time		Chilton Time		Chilton Time
Wiper Motor, Renew		**Wiper Link, Renew**		**Speedometer Head, R&R or Renew**	
B2000-2200-2600	.6	All models................................	.7	B2000-2200-2600	
MPV		**Wiper and Washer Switch, Renew**		Gas models	1.1
front...................................	.6	B2000	.9	Diesel models	1.4
rear....................................	.6	MPV	.8	MPV	.9
Windshield Wiper Motor, R&R and Recondition		**Washer Motor, Renew**		**Speedometer Cable, Renew**	
All models...........................	1.2	All models..............................	.3	All models................................	.8

LABOR 32 LIGHT SWITCHES & WIRING 32 LABOR

	Chilton Time		Chilton Time		Chilton Time
Combination Switch Assy., Renew		**Back-Up Lamp Switch, Renew**		**Parking Brake Lamp Switch, Renew**	
All models...........................	.8	All models–w/4 spd	.4	All models................................	.3
Turn Signal or Hazard Flasher, Renew		w/5 spd	.9	**Horn Relay, Renew**	
All models...........................	.3	**Stop Lamp Switch, Renew**		All models................................	.2
Headlamp Switch, Renew		All models..............................	.4	**Horns, Renew**	
All models...........................	.9	**Clutch Switch, Renew**		All models–one........................	.3
		All models..............................	.4	both......................................	.4

LABOR 34 CRUISE CONTROL 34 LABOR

	Chilton Time		Chilton Time
Cruise Control Switch, Renew		**Cruise Control Cut-Out Switch, Renew**	
1986-90	.9	1986-90	.4
Cruise Control Actuator, Renew		**Electronic Control Unit, Renew**	
1986-90	.6	1986-90	.8

GROUP INDEX

ALPHABETICAL INDEX

LABOR 1 TUNE UP 1 LABOR

	Chilton Time
Compression Test	
Four	.6
V-6	.7

Engine Tune Up, (Electronic Ignition)
Includes: Test battery and clean connections. Check engine compression, clean and adjust or renew spark plugs. Test resistance of spark plug

cables. Inspect distributor cap and rotor. Set ignition timing. Check vacuum advance operation. Inspect and adjust all drive belts. Set carburetor idle mixture and idle speed. Check operation of EGR valve.

	Chilton Time
Four	
Truck-Montero	1.5
Van-Wagon	1.7
V-6	2.0

LABOR 2 IGNITION SYSTEM 2 LABOR

GASOLINE ENGINES

	Chilton Time
Spark Plugs, Clean and Reset or Renew	
Four	.5
V-6	.6
Ignition Timing, Reset	
All models	.4
Distributor Assy., Renew	
Includes: Reset ignition timing.	
Four	
Truck-Montero	.9
Van-Wagon	1.0
V-6	1.0
Distributor, R&R and Recondition	
Includes: Reset ignition timing.	
Four	
Truck-Montero	1.5
Van-Wagon	1.6
V-6	1.6
Distributor Reluctor, Renew	
Includes: R&R distributor and reset ignition timing.	
Truck-Montero	1.2
Van-Wagon	1.3

	Chilton Time
Vacuum Control Unit, Renew	
Includes: R&R distributor and reset ignition timing.	
Truck-Montero	1.1
Van-Wagon	1.2
Distributor Pick-Up Set, Renew	
Includes: R&R distributor.	
Four	1.1
Distributor Ignitor Set, Renew	
Includes: R&R distributor.	
Four	1.2
V-6	1.3
Distributor Cap and/or Rotor, Renew	
All models	.4
Electronic Ignition Control Unit, Renew	
All models	.7
Ignition Coil, Renew	
Four	
Truck	.6
Montero	.5
Van-Wagon	.6
V-6	.7

	Chilton Time
Ballast Resistor, Renew	
All models	.4
Ignition Cables, Renew	
All models	.4
Ignition Switch, Renew	
All models	.7

DIESEL ENGINE

	Chilton Time
Glow Plugs, Renew	
All models	
one or all	.5
Glow Plug Relay, Renew	
All models	.4
Glow Plug Control Unit, Renew	
All models	.4

LABOR 3 FUEL SYSTEM 3 LABOR

GASOLINE ENGINES

	Chilton Time
Fuel Pump, Test	
Includes: Disconnect line at carburetor, attach pressure gauge.	
All models	.3
Carburetor, Adjust (On Truck)	
All models	.6
Carburetor Air Cleaner, Service	
All models	.2
Carburetor Assy., Renew	
Includes: All necessary adjustments.	
All models	1.0
Carburetor, R&R and Clean or Recondition	
Includes: All necessary adjustments.	
All models	2.9
Accelerator Pump, Renew	
All models	.6
Coasting Air Valve, Renew	
All models	.4
Air Switching Valve, Renew	
All models	.4
Jet Air Control Valve, Renew	
All models	.6
Enrichment Body Assembly, Renew	
All models	.4
Vacuum Throttle Opener, Renew	
All models	.8

	Chilton Time
Fuel Cut-Off Solenoid, Renew	
All models	.4
Carburetor Sub-EGR Valve, Renew	
1983-86	.7
Dash Pot, Renew	
All models	.4
Throttle Position Sensor, Renew	
All models	.5
Fuel Filter, Renew	
All models	.4
Mechanical Fuel Pump, Renew	
All models	.8
Fuel Tank, Renew	
Montero	1.6
Truck	
1986	1.6
1987-90	.8
Van-Wagon	1.4
Fuel Gauge (Tank Unit), Renew	
Montero	1.5
Truck	
1986	1.5
1987-90	.7
Van-Wagon	.6
Fuel Gauge (Dash Unit), Renew	
Montero	1.2
Truck	
1986	1.2
1987-90	.6

	Chilton Time
Van-Wagon	.9
Intake Manifold and/or Gasket, Renew	
Four	
Truck-Montero	4.1
Van-Wagon	*2.1
V-6	3.2
*Renew manif add	.6

DIESEL ENGINE

	Chilton Time
Injection Pump Timing, Adjust	
All models	.6
Fuel Injection Pump Assy., Renew	
All models	2.0
Injection Nozzles, R&R or Renew	
All models-one	.6
each adtnl	.4
Clean or recond add-each	.3
High Pressure Fuel Lines, Renew	
All models-one	.6
each adtnl	.3
Fuel Pump, Renew	
All models	.8
Turbocharger Assy., R&R or Renew	
Includes: Renew gasket.	
All models	1.5
Recond add	1.0

LABOR 3 FUEL SYSTEM 3 LABOR

FUEL INJECTION

	Chilton Time
Fuel Injectors, Clean (On Car) (w/TBI or MPI) Includes: Hook up pressurized fuel injection cleaning equipment.	
All models	.5
Fuel Filter, Renew (In Tank) Four	
Truck	.8
Montero	1.3
Van-Wagon	1.5
V-6	.9
Idle Speed Control Servo, Renew	
Van-Wagon	.6

	Chilton Time
Throttle Body, Renew Van-Wagon	.8
Fuel Injectors, Renew Van-Wagon	
one	.8
all	.9
Surge Tank, Renew (Intake Plenum) Van-Wagon	.6
Throttle Position Sensor, Renew Van-Wagon	.4
Fuel Pressure Regulator, Renew Van-Wagon	.4
Electric Fuel Pump, Renew Van-Wagon	1.5

LABOR 3A EMISSION CONTROLS 3A LABOR

	Chilton Time
PCV Valve, Renew All models	.2
Fuel Vapor Canister, Renew All models	.3
Fuel Vapor Separator, Renew (One)	
Truck	.6
Montero	1.4
Purge Control Valve, Renew All models	.3
E.G.R. Valve, Renew All models	
Gas or Diesel	.5

	Chilton Time
E.G.R. Coolant Valve, Renew All models	.5
Vacuum Time Delay Solenoid, Renew All models	.4
High Altitude Compensator, Renew All models	.6
E.G.R. Vacuum Reducer Valve, Renew All models	
Diesel	.4
E.G.R. Control Valve, Renew All models	
Diesel	.4

	Chilton Time
Vacuum Regulator Valve, Renew All models	
Diesel	.4
Oxygen Sensor, Renew	
Truck	.4
Montero-Van-Wagon	.5
Purge Control Solenoid, Renew Van-Wagon	.7

LABOR 4 ALTERNATOR AND REGULATOR 4 LABOR

	Chilton Time
Alternator Circuits, Test Includes: Test battery, regulator and alternator output.	
All models	.6
Alternator Assy., Renew Includes: Circuit test. Transfer pulley if required.	
Truck	1.4
Montero-Van-Wagon	1.2

	Chilton Time
Alternator, R&R and Recondition Includes: Complete disassembly, inspect, test, replace parts as required, reassemble.	
Truck	2.4
Montero-Van-Wagon	2.2
Alternator Front Bearing, Renew Includes: R&R alternator, separate end frames.	
All models	1.1
Renew rear brg add	.2

	Chilton Time
Voltage Regulator, Test and Renew All models	
internal type	1.6
Alternator Gauge, Renew	
All models	.7

LABOR 5 STARTING SYSTEM 5 LABOR

	Chilton Time
Starter Drive, Renew Includes: R&R starter. All models	
Four	1.2
V-6	2.5
Starter Assy., Renew Includes: Test relay, starter solenoid and amperage draw. All models	
Four	1.1
V-6	2.2

	Chilton Time
Starter, R&R and Recondition Includes: Test relay, starter solenoid and amperage draw. Turn down armature. All models	
Four	2.3
V-6	3.4
Renew field coils add	.5
Starter Draw Test (On Truck) All models	.3

	Chilton Time
Starter Solenoid, Renew Includes: R&R starter. All models	
Four	1.2
V-6	2.3
Neutral Safety and/or Back-Up Lamp Switch, Renew All models	.4
Battery Cables, Renew All models	
positive	.4
negative	.4

LABOR 6 BRAKE SYSTEM 6 LABOR

	Chilton Time
Brake Pedal Free Play, Adjust	
All models	.3
Brakes, Adjust (Minor)	
Includes: Adjust brake shoes, fill master cylinder.	
two wheels	.4
Bleed Brakes (Four Wheels)	
Includes: Fill master cylinder.	
All models	.5
Brake Shoes and/or Pads, Renew	
Includes: Install new or exchange brake shoes or pads. Adjust service and hand brake. Bleed system.	
All models	
front-disc	.9
rear-drum	1.5
all four wheels	2.3
Resurface disc rotor add-each	.9
Resurface brake drum add-each	.5
Rear Brake Drum, Renew (One)	
All models	.6

BRAKE HYDRAULIC SYSTEM

	Chilton Time
Wheel Cylinder, Renew	
Includes: Bleed brake system.	
Van-Wagon-one	1.0
both	1.9
All other models-one	.9
both	1.7
Wheel Cylinder, R&R and Rebuild	
Includes: Bleed brake system.	
Van-Wagon-one	1.3
both	2.5
All other models-one	1.2
both	2.3
Master Cylinder, Renew	
Includes: Bleed brake system.	
Truck-Montero	.9
Van-Wagon	1.4
Master Cylinder, R&R and Rebuild	
Includes: Bleed brake system.	
Truck-Montero	1.6
Van-Wagon	2.1
Master Cylinder Reservoir, Renew	
Includes: Bleed brake system.	
All models	1.0

COMBINATIONS

Add to Brakes, Renew	Chilton Time
RENEW WHEEL CYLINDER	
Each	.2
REBUILD WHEEL CYLINDER	
Each	.3
RENEW BRAKE HOSE	
Each	.3
RENEW MASTER CYLINDER	
All models	.7
REBUILD MASTER CYLINDER	
All models	1.4
REBUILD CALIPER ASSEMBLY	
Each	.5
RENEW DISC BRAKE ROTOR	
Each	.3
CLEAN AND REPACK FRONT WHEEL BEARINGS (BOTH WHEELS)	
All models	.6
RENEW BRAKE DRUM	
Each	.1
RENEW DISC BRAKE ROTOR STUDS	
Each	.1

	Chilton Time
Brake Hose (Flexible), Renew	
Includes: Bleed system.	
All models-one	.6
each adtnl	.3
Brake System, Flush and Refill	
All models	1.2

DISC BRAKES

	Chilton Time
Disc Brake Pads, Renew	
Includes: Install new disc brake pads only.	
All models	
front	.9
rear	.9
all four wheels	1.7
Resurface disc rotor add-each	.9
Caliper Assembly, Renew	
Includes: Bleed brake system.	
Van-Wagon-one	1.0
both	1.9

	Chilton Time
All other models-one	.8
two	1.5
all four wheels	2.9
Caliper Assy., R&R and Recondition	
Includes: Bleed brake system.	
Van-Wagon-one	1.5
both	2.9
All other models-one	1.3
two	2.5
all four wheels	4.9
Disc Brake Rotor, Renew	
FRONT	
2 WD models	.6
4 WD models	1.2
REAR	
All models	.8
Front Disc Brake Hub, Renew	
2 WD models	.8
4 WD models	1.2
Brake System Combination Valve, Renew	
Includes: Bleed brake system.	
All models	1.2
Load Sensing Proportioning Valve, Renew	
Includes: Adjust valve and bleed brake system.	
All models	1.0

POWER BRAKES

	Chilton Time
Power Brake Booster, Renew	
Truck-Montero	1.1
Van-Wagon	2.5
Power Brake Booster Check Valve, Renew	
All models	.3

PARKING BRAKE

	Chilton Time
Parking Brake, Adjust	
All models	.3
Parking Brake Cable, Renew	
Front	
All models	.8
Rear	
Truck-Montero-each	1.0
Van-Wagon-each	1.8
Parking Brake Control, Renew	
All models	.7
Parking Brake Warning Lamp Switch, Renew	
Montero	.6
Truck	
1986	.6
1987-90	.3
Van-Wagon	.5

LABOR 7 COOLING SYSTEM 7 LABOR

	Chilton Time
Winterize Cooling System	
Includes: Run engine to check for leaks, tighten all hose connections. Test radiator and pressure cap, drain radiator and engine block. Add anti-freeze and refill system.	
All models	.5
Thermostat, Renew	
Includes: Drain and refill cooling system.	
All models	.5
Radiator Assy., R&R or Renew	
Includes: Drain and refill cooling system.	
Truck-Montero	.7
Van-Wagon	1.2
w/A.T. add	.2

	Chilton Time
ADD THESE OPERATIONS TO RADIATOR R&R	
Boil & Repair	1.5
Rod Clean	1.9
Repair Core	1.3
Renew Tank	1.6
Renew Trans. Oil Cooler	1.9
Recore Radiator	1.7
Drive Belt, Adjust	
All models-one	.2
each adtnl	.1
Drive Belt, Renew	
All models-one	.3
each adtnl	.1

	Chilton Time
Fluid Fan Drive Unit, Renew	
All models	.5
w/A.C. add	.1
Radiator Hoses, Renew	
Upper	.3
Lower	
Truck-Montero	.4
Van-Wagon	.8
Water Pump and/or Gasket, Renew	
Includes: Drain and refill cooling system.	
Four	
Truck-Montero	
Gas	1.4
Diesel	1.7
Van-Wagon	2.0

LABOR   7 COOLING SYSTEM 7   LABOR

	Chilton Time
V-6	4.2
w/A.C. add	.3
w/P.S. add	.2
Engine Oil Cooler, Renew	
All models	.7
Temperature Gauge (Dash Unit), Renew	
Truck	
1986	1.2
1987-90	.5
Van-Wagon	.9
Fuel and Temperature Gauge Assy., Renew	
Montero	
1986-90	1.2
Temperature Gauge Sending Unit, Renew	
All models	.4
Water Jacket Expansion Plugs, Renew (Cylinder Block)	
Right side	
front	1.2
center or rear	1.2

	Chilton Time
Left side	
upper front	1.3
lower front	1.4
rear	3.0
Rear of Engine	3.5
Heater Hose, Renew	
1986	1.0
1987-90	.8
Front Heater Water Valve, Renew	
Truck	.6
Montero	3.5
Front Heater Blower Motor Switch, Renew	
Truck-Montero	1.2
Van-Wagon	.8
Front Heater Blower Motor, Renew	
Truck	
1986	1.0
1987-90	.6
Montero-Van-Wagon	.6
Front Heater Blower Motor Resistor, Renew	
Truck	
1986	.7
1987-90	.6
Montero-Van-Wagon	.6

	Chilton Time
Front Heater Core, R&R or Renew	
Truck	
1986	1.7
1987-90	2.3
Montero-Van-Wagon	3.5
ADD THESE OPERATIONS TO HEATER CORE R&R	
Boil & Repair	1.2
Repair Core	.9
Recore	1.2
Rear Heater Core, R&R or Renew	
Montero	1.5
Van-Wagon	1.1
Rear Heater Water Valve, Renew	
Montero	1.5
Rear Heater Blower Motor, Renew	
Montero	1.5
Van-Wagon	.5
Rear Heater Blower Motor Resistor, Renew	
Montero-Van-Wagon	.5
Rear Heater Switch, Renew	
Van-Wagon	.4

LABOR   8 EXHAUST SYSTEM 8   LABOR

	Chilton Time
Front Exhaust Pipe, Renew	
All models	.7
Center Exhaust Pipe, Renew	
All models	.7
Tail Pipe, Renew	
All models	.6

	Chilton Time
Muffler, Renew	
All models	.6
Catalytic Converter, Renew	
Manif Mount	
2 WD	1.0
4 WD	1.2
Ex Mount	
All models	.8

	Chilton Time
Exhaust Manifold and/or Gasket, Renew	
All models	
Four	
Gas	
Truck-Montero	1.2
Van-Wagon	1.6
Diesel	2.0
V-6	
front	1.4
rear	1.5

LABOR   9 FRONT SUSPENSION 9   LABOR

	Chilton Time
Note: On all front suspension operations alignment charges must be added if performed. Time given does not include alignment.	
Wheel, Renew	
one	.5
Wheels, Rotate (All)	
All models	.5
Wheel, Balance	
one	.3
each adtnl	.2
Toe-In, Adjust	
All models	.6
Align Front End	
Includes: Adjust caster, camber and toe. Adjust front wheel bearings.	
All models	1.5
Front Wheel Bearings and Cups, Renew	
Includes: Renew dust seal.	
All models	
one side	.8
both sides	1.5
Front Wheel Grease Seal, Renew	
All models-one side	.8

	Chilton Time
Steering Knuckle, Renew (One)	
2 WD models	1.6
4 WD models	1.8
Renew tie rod, add	
each	.3
Renew whl brgs, add	
each side	.5
Lower Control Arm, Renew (One)	
Includes: Reset toe-in.	
2 WD models	2.1
4 WD models	1.6
Lower Control Arm Bushings, Renew (One Side)	
Add alignment charges.	
2 WD models	2.0
4 WD models	1.7
Lower Ball Joint or Ball Socket, Renew (One Side)	
Add alignment charges.	
2 WD models	1.8
4 WD models	1.3
Lower Control Arm Strut, Renew (One Side)	
Add alignment charges.	
2 WD models	1.0

	Chilton Time
Upper Control Arm, Renew (One)	
Includes: Alignment charges.	
Truck-Montero	2.5
Van-Wagon	2.0
Upper Ball Joint or Ball Socket, Renew (One Side)	
Add alignment charges.	
2 WD models	1.5
4 WD models	1.6
Front Shock Absorbers, Renew	
All models-one	.7
both	1.1
Front Sway Bar, Renew	
Truck-Montero	1.5
Van-Wagon	1.2
Front Sway Bar Link and/or Bushings, Renew	
All models-one side	.5
Front Torsion Bars, Renew	
2 WD models	
one side	1.0
both sides	1.8
4 WD models	
one side	.5
both sides	.8

LABOR　　10　STEERING LINKAGE　10　　LABOR

	Chilton Time
Torsion Bar Anchor or Adjusting Bolt, Renew	
4 WD models	
each	.6
Front Coil Springs, Renew	
2 WD models-one	1.9
both	3.5

4 WHEEL DRIVE FRONT AXLE

	Chilton Time
Front Differential, Drain & Refill	
All models	.6
Front Axle Housing Cover or Gasket, Renew	
All models	.6
Drive Pinion Oil Seal, Renew	
All models	.8
Front Axle Propeller Shaft Flange, Renew	
All models	.6

	Chilton Time
Front Axle Shaft, Renew (One)	
Includes: Renew outer wheel bearings if required.	
All models	
outer-w/Joint	2.0
inner	1.6
Drive Shaft Boot, Renew (One)	
Includes: Clean and lubricate C/V joint.	
All models	1.9
Front Wheel Drive Shaft, Renew (w/M.T. or A.T.)	
All models-one	1.6
both	3.0
Inner C.V. Joint, Renew	
All models-one	1.8
Locking Hub Assy., Renew or Recondition	
All models-one	.9
both	1.7
Front Propeller Shaft, Renew	
All models	
transfer case to ft axle	.6

	Chilton Time
Differential Side Bearings, Renew	
Includes: R&R ring gear and pinion, renew axle housing oil seals and adjust bearing preload and backlash.	
All models	4.9
Differential Side Gears, Renew	
Includes: Renew axle housing oil seals if required.	
All models	4.7
Differential Case, Renew	
Includes: R&R ring gear and pinion, renew bearings and gears, renew pinion and axle housing seals. Adjust backlash.	
All models	5.1
Ring Gear and Pinion Set, Renew	
Includes: Renew pinion bearing, side bearings and all seals. Adjust bearing preload and backlash.	
All models	5.6
Renew diff case add	.2
Front Axle Housing, Renew	
Includes: Renew oil seals. Transfer axle shafts, differential and brake assemblies.	
All models	5.7

LABOR　　11　STEERING GEAR　11　　LABOR

	Chilton Time
Tie Rod End, Renew	
Includes: Reset toe-in.	
Truck-Montero	1.0
Van-Wagon	1.3
Tie Rod End Boot, Renew	
All models-one	.8
Steering Center Link, Renew	
Add alignment charges.	
All models	.6
Steering Wheel, Renew	
All models	.4
Idler Arm, Renew	
All models	.6
Pitman Arm, Renew	
Truck-Montero	.6
Steering Column Flex Coupling, Renew	
Truck	1.3

MANUAL STEERING

	Chilton Time
Steering Gear, Adjust (On Truck)	
All models	.5
Sector Shaft Oil Seal, Renew	
Truck	.8

	Chilton Time
Steering Gear Assy., R&R or Renew	
Truck	1.0
Van-Wagon	1.4
Steering Gear Assy., R&R and Recondition	
Includes: Disassemble, renew necessary parts, reassemble and adjust.	
Truck	1.9
Van-Wagon	2.9

POWER STEERING

	Chilton Time
Power Steering Drive Belt, Renew	
All models	.3
Power Steering Gear, Adjust	
All models	.5
Power Steering Gear, R&R or Renew	
All models	2.0
Power Steering Gear, R&R and Recondition	
Includes: Disassemble, renew necessary parts, reassemble and adjust.	
All models	2.7
Steering Gear Sector Shaft, Adjust	
All models	.6

	Chilton Time
Sector Shaft Oil Seals, Renew (Inner and Outer)	
All models	2.1
Gear Control Valve Assy., Renew	
All models	3.1
Power Steering Pump, Renew	
All models	1.0
Power Steering Pump, R&R and Recondition	
All models	1.9
Pump Flow Control Valve, Clean and Test or Renew	
All models	.9
Pump Reservoir, Renew	
Includes: Renew seals.	
All models	.6
Pump Drive Shaft Oil Seal, Renew	
All models	1.6
Power Steering Hoses, Renew	
All models	
pressure	.9
return	.9
supply	.4

LABOR　　12　CYLINDER HEAD & VALVE SYSTEM　12　　LABOR

	Chilton Time
### GASOLINE ENGINE	
Compression Test	
Four	.6
V-6	.7
Cylinder Head Gasket, Renew	
Includes: Clean carbon, minor tune up.	
Four	3.6
V-6	
front	9.4
rear	8.3
both	10.1

	Chilton Time
Clean Carbon and Grind Valves	
Includes: R&R cylinder head, reface valves and seats. Tune engine.	
Four	
2.0-2.4L engs	
Truck	5.6
Van-Wagon	7.2
2.6L eng	7.2
V-6	
front	10.9
rear	9.7
both	13.0

	Chilton Time
Cylinder Head Cover Gasket, Renew	
Four	.6
V-6-front	1.0
rear	1.9
Valve Rocker Arms and/or Shaft, Renew	
Includes: Renew shaft if required.	
Four	
one shaft	1.4
both shafts	2.3
V-6	
one side	1.4
both sides	2.5

LABOR 12 CYLINDER HEAD & VALVE SYSTEM 12 LABOR

Cylinder Head, Renew
Includes: Reface and adjust valves, clean carbon. Minor tune up.

	Chilton Time
Four	8.9
V-6	
front	11.2
rear	10.4
both	12.7

Jet Valve, Renew
(One or All)

Four	2.1

Valve Springs and/or Valve Stem Oil Seals, Renew
Four
2.0-2.4L engs

1986	
one cyl	1.3
all cyls	3.0
1987-90	
Truck	
one cyl	4.2
all cyls	4.5

	Chilton Time
Van-Wagon	
one cyl	4.7
all cyls	5.0
2.6L eng	
one cyl	5.6
all cyls	6.0

Valve Clearance, Adjust

V-6	
front	10.9
rear	9.6
both	13.0
All models	1.5

Valve Lash Adjustors, Renew

Four	1.5
V-6–front	1.3
rear	2.4

DIESEL ENGINE

Compression Test

All models	.6

	Chilton Time
Cylinder Head Gasket, Renew	

Includes: Clean carbon. Make all necessary adjustments.

All models	3.5

Cylinder Head, Renew
Includes: Reface and adjust valves, clean carbon. Make all necessary adjustmets.

All models	6.2

Clean Carbon and Grind Valves
Includes: R&R cylinder head. Reface valves and seats. Make all necessary adjustments.

All models	5.5

Cylinder Head Cover Gasket, Renew

All models	.6

Valve Rocker Arms, Renew

All models	1.1

Valve Springs and/or Valve Stem Oil Seals, Renew (All)

All models	4.2

Valve Clearance, Adjust

All models	1.5

LABOR 13 ENGINE ASSEMBLY & MOUNTS 13 LABOR

GASOLINE ENGINE

Note: All engine operations listed in this group are for assemblies as supplied by the original equipment manufacturer. Time to replace assemblies from independent rebuilders may vary.

Engine Assembly, Remove & Install
Does not include transfer of any parts or equipment.

	Chilton Time
Four	8.0
V-6	9.0
w/A.C. add	.3
w/P.S. add	.2

Short Engine Assembly, Renew
(w/All Internal Parts Less Head and Oil Pan)
Includes: R&R engine assy. Transfer all necessary parts not supplied with replacement engine. Minor tune up.

Four	14.5

	Chilton Time
V-6	19.6
w/A.C. add	.3
w/P.S. add	.2
Recond valves add	
Four	3.5
V-6	3.6

Engine Assy., R&R and Recondition (Complete)
Includes: Rebore block, install new pistons, rings, rod and main bearings. Clean carbon, grind valves. Tune engine.

Four	26.0
V-6	31.7
w/A.C. add	.3
w/P.S. add	.2

Engine Support, Renew

All models-one	.7
both	1.1

DIESEL ENGINE

Engine Assembly, Remove & Install
Does not include transfer of any parts or equipment.

	Chilton Time
All models	5.1
w/A.C. add	.6

Short Engine Assembly, Renew
(w/All Internal Parts Less Head and Oil Pan)
Includes: R&R engine assy. Transfer all necessary parts not supplied with replacement engine. Clean carbon, grind valves. Make all necessary adjustments.

All models	14.7
w/A.C. add	.6

Engine Mount, Renew

All models-one	.5
both	.7

LABOR 14 PISTONS, RINGS & BEARINGS 14 LABOR

GASOLINE ENGINE

Rings, Renew (All)
Includes: Replace connecting rod bearings, deglaze cylinder walls, remove cylinder top ridge. Clean carbon from cylinder head. Minor tune up.

	Chilton Time
Four	7.5
V-6	20.8
w/P.S. add	.3

Pistons or Connecting Rods, Renew
Includes: Replace connecting rod bearings, deglaze cylinder walls, remove cylinder top ridge, clean carbon from cylinder head. Minor tune up.

Four	8.7
V-6	22.6
w/P.S. add	.3

Connecting Rod Bearings, Renew (All)

Four	4.0
V-6	9.5

COMBINATIONS

	Chilton Time
DRAIN, EVACUATE & RECHARGE AIR CONDITIONING SYSTEM	
All models	1.0
DISTRIBUTOR, RECONDITION	
All models	1.0
CARBURETOR, RECONDITION	
All models	1.6
DEGLAZE CYLINDER WALLS	
Each	.1
REMOVE CYLINDER TOP RIDGE	
Each	.3
CYLINDER HEAD, R&R (ENGINE REMOVED)	
Four	1.0
V-6	
one	1.0

	Chilton Time
both	1.9
RECONDITION CYLINDER HEAD (HEAD REMOVED)	
Four	3.5
V-6	3.6
CONNECTING ROD, RENEW (ENGINE DISASSEMBLED)	
Each	.4
PLASTIGAUGE BEARINGS	
Each	.1
ROD BEARINGS, RENEW (PAN REMOVED)	
Four	1.2
V-6	1.8
OIL FILTER ELEMENT, RENEW	
All models	.2

LABOR 14 PISTONS, RINGS & BEARINGS 14 LABOR

DIESEL ENGINE

Rings, Renew (All)
Includes: Replace connecting rod bearings, deglaze cylinder walls, remove cylinder top ridge, clean carbon from cylinder head. Make all necessary adjustments.
All models 7.1

Pistons or Connecting Rods, Renew (All)
Includes: Replace connecting rod bearings, deglaze cylinder walls, remove cylinder top ridge, replace piston rings. Clean carbon from cylinder head. Make all necessary adjustments.
All models 8.3

Connecting Rod Bearings, Renew (All)
All models 3.1

LABOR 15 CRANKSHAFT & DAMPER 15 LABOR

GASOLINE ENGINE

Crankshaft and Main Bearings, Renew
Includes: R&R engine assembly.
Four 17.3
V-6 .... 17.3
w/A.C. add 1.0

Main Bearings, Renew
Includes: R&R engine.
Four 17.3
V-6 .... 17.3
w/A.C. add 1.0

Main and Rod Bearings, Renew
Includes: R&R engine.
Four 18.5
V-6 .... 18.5
w/A.C. add 1.0

Crankshaft Pulley, Renew
All models 6
w/A.C. add 1

Rear Main Bearing Oil Seal, Renew (Complete)
Four
w/M.T. 3.5
w/A.T. 3.8
V-6 .... 7.5
4X4 add 6

DIESEL ENGINE

Crankshaft and Main Bearings, Renew
Includes: R&R engine assembly.
All models 7.7
w/A.C. add 6

Main Bearings, Renew
All models 3.4

Main and Rod Bearings, Renew
All models 4.6

Crankshaft Pulley, Renew
All models 6
w/A.C. add 1
w/P.S. add 1

Crankshaft Front Oil Seal, Renew
All models 1.7
w/A.C. add 6

LABOR 16 CAMSHAFT & TIMING GEARS 16 LABOR

GASOLINE ENGINE

Camshaft, Renew
Includes: Renew valve lifters and adjust valve clearance.
Four
1986-88
2.0-2.4L engs 2.1
2.6L eng 3.0
1989-90 .... 1.5
V-6
front 1.4
rear 2.5

Camshaft Oil Seal, Renew
Four 2.0
V-6
front 3.5
rear 4.3

Timing Belt, Renew
Four
Truck-Montero 2.1
Van-Wagon 3.5
w/A.C. add 3
w/P.S. add 2
V-6 .... 3.6
w/A.C. add 4
w/P.S. add 2

Timing Chain, Renew
Four
cam drive 5.4
silent shaft drive 4.9
w/A.C. add 7

Timing Chain Tensioner, Renew
Includes: Renew cover oil seal.
Four 5.2
w/A.C. add 7

Timing Belt Tensioner, Renew
Four
Truck-Montero 2.1
Van-Wagon 3.5

Timing Chain or Belt Case/Cover Gasket, Renew
Includes: Renew oil seal.
Four
2.6L eng 4.3
2.0-2.4L engs
upper-outer 4
upper-inner 8
lower-outer 1.4
lower-inner 1.8
w/A.C. add 7

Timing Chain Case/Cover Oil Seal, Renew
All models 2.3
w/A.C. add 7

Silent Shaft Oil Seal, Renew
All models 4.4
w/A.C. add 5
w/P.S. add 2

Silent Shaft, Renew
Four
2.6L eng
1986-88
right 7.7
left 7.2
both 8.1
1989-90
one or both 10.5
2.0-2.4L engs
1986-88
right 6.4
left 6.8
both 7.4

1989-90
one or both 8.3
w/A.C. add 7
w/P.S. add 1

DIESEL ENGINE

Timing Belt Cover, Renew
All models
upper 3
lower 1.0

Timing Belt, Renew
All models
cam drive 1.6
silent shaft drive 1.8
w/A.C. add 6

Timing Belt Tensioner, Renew
All models
cam drive 1.7
silent shaft drive 1.9
w/A.C. add 6

Camshaft, Renew
All models 2.0

Silent Shaft, Renew
All models
right side 2.5
left side 4.0
both sides 4.5
w/A.C. add 6

Silent Shaft Oil Seal, Renew
All models 1.9
w/A.C. add 6

LABOR 17 ENGINE OILING SYSTEM 17 LABOR

GASOLINE ENGINE

	Chilton Time
Oil Pan and/or Gasket, Renew	
Four	
Truck-Montero	1.5
Van-Wagon	1.7
V-6	6.4
Oil Pump, Renew	
Four	
Truck-Montero	5.0
Van-Wagon	7.2
V-6	10.0

	Chilton Time
Pressure Test Engine Bearings (Pan Off)	
All models	1.0
Oil Pressure Gauge (Dash), Renew	
Truck	.6
Oil Pressure Sending Unit, Renew	
All models	.5
Oil Filter Element, Renew	
All models	.3

DIESEL ENGINE

	Chilton Time
Oil Pan and/or Gasket, Renew	
All models	1.6
Oil Pump, Renew	
All models	3.4
Oil Filter Element, Renew	
All models	.3

LABOR 18 CLUTCH & FLYWHEEL 18 LABOR

	Chilton Time
Clutch Release Bearing, Renew	
All models	
Four	
2 WD	3.6
4 WD	4.1
V-6	5.8
Renew fork add	.3
Clutch Cable, Adjust	
All models	.4
Clutch Release Cable, Renew	
All models	.5

	Chilton Time
Clutch Assembly, Renew	
All models	
Four	
2 WD	3.9
4 WD	4.4
V-6	6.1
Clutch Slave Cylinder, Renew	
Includes: Bleed system.	
All models	1.0

	Chilton Time
Flywheel, Renew	
All models	
Four	
2 WD	4.2
4 WD	4.7
V-6	6.4
Renew ring gear add	.4
Clutch Master Cylinder, Renew	
Includes: Bleed system.	
All models	1.0

LABOR 19A MANUAL TRANSMISSION (RWD) 19A LABOR

	Chilton Time
Transmission Assy., R&R or Renew	
All models	
4 spd	3.7
5 spd	
KM 132	3.7
V5MT-1	5.8
Renew assy add	.6
4X4 add	.6

	Chilton Time
Transmission Assy., R&R and Recondition	
Includes: Disassemble, clean and inspect or renew all parts. Install all new gaskets and seals.	
All models	
4 spd	6.7
5 spd	
KM 132	9.0
V5MT-1	10.3
4X4 add	.6

	Chilton Time
Extension Housing Oil Seal, Renew	
5 Spd models	.7

LABOR 20 TRANSFER CASE 20 LABOR

	Chilton Time
Transfer Case Adaptor Gasket, Renew	
All models	4.1
Transfer Case Shift Lever Boot, Renew	
All models	.5
Transfer Case Shifter, Renew	
All models	.8

	Chilton Time
Rear Output Shaft Housing, Renew	
All models	1.0
Rear Output Shaft Seal, Renew	
All models	.6
Front Output Rear Bearing Gasket, Renew	
All models	.4
Speedometer Drive Pinion, Renew	
All models	.3

	Chilton Time
Transfer Case Assy., Remove & Install	
All models	6.5
Renew assy add	.8
Renew rear housing add	1.9
Renew front housing add	2.8
Renew drive chain add	2.5
Transfer Case Assy., R&R and Recondition (Complete)	
All models	9.5

LABOR 23A AUTOMATIC TRANSMISSION (RWD) 23A LABOR

3 SPEED
ON CAR SERVICES

	Chilton Time
Drain & Refill Unit	
All models	.8
Oil Pressure Check	
All models	.9

	Chilton Time
Check Unit for Oil Leaks	
Includes: Clean and dry outside of case and run unit to determine point of leak.	
All models	.9
Neutral Safety Switch, Renew	
All models	.4
Throttle Linkage, Adjust	
All models	.4

	Chilton Time
Throttle Valve Lever Shaft Seal, Renew	
All models	.6
Valve Body Manual Lever Shaft Seal, Renew	
All models	1.0
Kickdown Band, Adjust (External)	
All models	.5
Extension Housing Oil Seal, Renew	
All models	.8

LABOR 23A AUTOMATIC TRANSMISSION (RWD) 23A LABOR

	Chilton Time
Governor Assy., Renew or Recondition	
Includes: R&R extension housing and renew bearing.	
All models	2.4
Governor Support and Parking Gear, Renew	
Includes: R&R extension housing and renew bearing.	
All models	2.4
Parking Lock Sprag, Renew	
Includes: R&R extension housing.	
All models	2.2
Oil Pan and/or Gasket, Renew	
All models	.7
Bands, Adjust	
Includes: R&R oil pan.	
All models	
kickdown	1.2
reverse	1.2
Valve Body Assy., Renew	
Includes: R&R oil pan and renew filter.	
All models	1.5
Valve Body Assy., R&R and Recondition	
Includes: R&R oil pan and renew filter. Disassemble, clean, inspect, free all valves. Replace parts as required.	
All models	3.0
SERVICES REQUIRING R&R	
Transmission Assy., R&R or Renew	
All models	3.5
Renew assy add	.6
4X4 add	.6
Transmission Assy., R&R and Recondition (Complete)	
All models	9.0
Flush cooler lines add	.2
4X4 add	.6
Transmission Assembly, Reseal	
Includes: R&R trans and renew all gaskets and seals.	
All models	6.0
4X4 add	.6

	Chilton Time
Torque Converter, Renew	
Includes: R&R transmission.	
All models	3.6
4X4 add	.6
Front Pump Oil Seal, Renew	
Includes: R&R transmission.	
All models	3.6
4X4 add	.6
Front Pump Assy., Renew	
Includes: R&R transmission.	
All models	4.2
4X4 add	.6
4 SPEED	
ON CAR SERVICES	
Drain and Refill Unit	
All models	1.5
Oil Pressure Check	
All models	.9
Check Unit for Oil Leaks	
Includes: Clean and dry outside of case and run unit to determine point of leak.	
All models	.9
Throttle Linkage, Adjust	
All models	.3
Gearshift Control Cable, Renew	
All models	.8
Extension Housing Oil Seal, Renew	
All models	.7
Throttle Cable, Renew	
All models	2.3
Extension Housing Gasket, Renew	
4X2 models	1.7
4X4 models	2.4
Governor Assembly, Renew	
Includes: R&R extension housing.	
4X2 models	2.2
4X4 models	3.0
Transmission Solenoid Valve, Renew	
All models	1.8

	Chilton Time
Oil Pan Gasket, Renew	
All models	1.5
Valve Body Assy., Renew or Recondition	
All models	5.0
SERVICES REQUIRING R&R	
Transmission Assy., R&R or Renew	
Four	
4X2 models	3.2
4X4 models	5.6
Van-Wagon	2.0
V-6	9.6
Renew assy add	.6
Transmission Assy., R&R and Recondition (Complete)	
Four	
4X2 models	9.5
4X4 models	12.0
Van-Wagon	8.6
V-6	13.4
Transmission Assembly, Reseal	
Includes: R&R trans and renew all gaskets and seals.	
Four	
4X2 models	6.0
4X4 models	8.4
Van-Wagon	5.5
Torque Converter, Renew	
Includes: R&R transmission.	
4X2 models	3.6
4X4 models	5.8
Van-Wagon	2.2
Front Pump Oil Seal, Renew	
Includes: R&R transmission.	
Four	
4X2 models	3.5
4X4 models	5.7
Van-Wagon	2.5
Front Pump Assy., Renew	
Includes: R&R transmission.	
Four	
4X2 models	4.0
4X4 models	6.4
Van-Wagon	2.3

LABOR 25 U-JOINTS & DRIVESHAFT 25 LABOR

	Chilton Time
Drive Shaft Center Bearing, Renew	
All models	1.3
Drive Shaft Assy., R&R or Renew	
Trans to Rear Axle	
Truck-Montero	.8
Van-Wagon	.5

	Chilton Time
Center Brg to Rear Axle	
Truck	1.2
Transfer Case to Front Axle	
Truck-Montero	.6
Trans to Center Brg	
Truck	1.6

	Chilton Time
Universal Joints, R&R and Recondition	
2 Joint Type	
one	1.0
3 Joint Type	
one	1.1
all	2.8

LABOR 26 DRIVE AXLE 26 LABOR

	Chilton Time
REAR DIFFERENTIAL	
Axle Shaft or Bearing, Renew (One)	
All models	2.1
Axle Shaft Oil Seal, Renew (One)	
All models	1.3
Differential Carrier Gasket, Renew	
All models	2.9

	Chilton Time
Differential Side Bearings, Renew	
Includes: Adjust backlash and renew axle shaft oil seals.	
All models	4.3
Differential Side Gears, Renew	
Includes: Adjust backlash and renew axle shaft oil seal.	
All models	4.8

	Chilton Time
Ring Gear and Pinion Set, Renew	
Includes: Renew axle shaft oil seals and pinion bearings.	
All models	5.5
Pinion Shaft Oil Seal, Renew	
All models	1.0

LABOR   26   DRIVE AXLE   26   LABOR

FRONT DIFFERENTIAL

	Chilton Time
Front Differential, Drain & Refill	
All models	.6
Front Axle Housing Cover or Gasket, Renew	
All models	.6
Drive Pinion Oil Seal, Renew	
All models	.8
Front Axle Propeller Shaft Flange, Renew	
All models	.6
Front Axle Shaft, Renew (One)	
Includes: Renew outer wheel bearings if required.	
All models	
outer-w/Joint	2.0
inner	1.6

	Chilton Time
Drive Shaft Boot, Renew (One)	
Includes: Clean and lubricate C/V joint.	
All models	1.9
Drive Shaft C.V. Joint, Renew	
All models	1.8
Front Propeller Shaft, Renew	
All models	
transfer case to ft axle	.6
Differential Side Bearings, Renew	
Includes: R&R ring gear and pinion, renew axle housing oil seals and adjust bearing preload and backlash.	
All models	4.9
Differential Side Gears, Renew	
Includes: Renew axle housing oil seals if required.	
All models	4.7

	Chilton Time
Differential Case, Renew	
Includes: R&R ring gear and pinion, renew bearings and gears, renew pinion and axle housing seals. Adjust backlash.	
All models	5.1
Ring Gear and Pinion Set, Renew	
Includes: Renew pinion bearing, side bearings and all seals. Adjust bearing preload and backlash.	
All models	5.6
Renew diff case add	.2
Front Axle Housing, Renew	
Includes: Renew oil seals. Transfer axle shafts, differential and brake assemblies.	
All models	5.7

LABOR   27   REAR SUSPENSION   27   LABOR

	Chilton Time
Rear Shock Absorbers, Renew	
All models-one	.4
both	.6
Rear Springs, Renew (w/Bushings)	
All models-one	1.1
both	2.0

	Chilton Time
Rear Spring Front Eye Bushing, Renew	
All models-one	1.0
Rear Spring Shackle and/or Bushing, Renew	
All models	.9

LABOR   28   AIR CONDITIONING   28   LABOR

	Chilton Time
Note: If more than one item requires replacement where evacuation and discharging the system is already included in the operation, deduct 1.0 hour for each additional item to the times listed.	
Drain, Evacuate, Leak Test & Charge System	
All models	1.0
Flush Refrigerant System, Complete	
To be used in conjunction with component replacement which could contaminate system.	
All models	1.3
Partial Charge System	
All models	.6
Compressor Drive Belt, Renew	
All models	.4
Compressor Assembly, Renew	
Includes: Pressure test and charge system.	
Truck	2.5
Montero	2.0
Van-Wagon	2.2
Compressor Crankshaft Seal, Renew	
Includes: Pressure test and charge system.	
Truck	3.2
Montero-Van-Wagon	2.3
Compressor Clutch Assy., Renew	
Truck	2.8
Montero-Van-Wagon	2.3

	Chilton Time
Expansion Valve, Renew	
Includes: Pressure test and charge system.	
Truck-Montero	4.0
Van-Wagon	
front	2.0
rear	1.6
Receiver Drier, Renew	
Includes: Pressure test and charge system.	
Truck-Montero	1.5
Van-Wagon	1.3
High Pressure Cut-Off Switch, Renew	
Includes: Pressure test and charge system.	
1986-90	1.2
Condenser Assembly, Renew	
Includes: Pressure test and charge system.	
Truck	2.0
Montero	1.6
Van-Wagon	1.4
Evaporator Core, Renew	
Includes: Pressure test and charge system.	
Truck-Montero	3.9
Van-Wagon	
front	3.5
rear	2.0
Air Conditioning Switch, Renew	
Truck	
1986	1.2
1987-90	1.0
Montero	1.2
Van	
front	.6
rear	.5

	Chilton Time
A.C. Blower Motor Relay, Renew	
Montero-Truck	.5
A.C. Blower Motor Resistor, Renew	
Truck	
1986	.7
1987-90	.6
Montero	.6
Van	
front	.6
rear	.5
Air Conditioning Hoses, Renew	
Includes: Pressure test and charge system.	
All models-one	1.7
each adtnl	.5
A.C. Blower Motor, Renew	
Truck	
1986	1.0
1987-90	.6
Montero	.6
Van	
front	.6
rear	.5
A.C. Blower Motor Switch, Renew	
Truck-Montero	1.2
Van	.7

LABOR   29   LOCKS, HINGES & WIND. REGULATORS   29   LABOR

	Chilton Time		Chilton Time		Chilton Time
Hood Hinge, Renew (One) Does not include painting. Truck	.8	**Lock Striker Plate, Renew** All models	.3	**Door Handle (Outside), Renew** All models	.6
Hood Release Cable, Renew All models	.9	**Door Lock Remote Control, Renew** Truck	.6	**Front Door Window Regulator, Renew** All models	
		Van-Wagon-Montero	.5	manual	.9
				electric	1.0

LABOR   30   HEAD AND PARKING LAMPS   30   LABOR

	Chilton Time		Chilton Time		Chilton Time
Aim Headlamps All models	.4	**License Lamp Assembly, Renew** All models	.3	**Tail, Stop and Turn Signal Lamp Assy., Renew** All models	.3
Head Lamp Sealed Beam Bulb, Renew Does not include aiming. All models	.3	**Park and Turn Signal Lamp Assy., Renew** All models	.3	**Side Marker Lamp Assy., Renew** All models	.4

LABOR   31   WINDSHIELD WIPER & SPEEDOMETER   31   LABOR

	Chilton Time		Chilton Time		Chilton Time
Windshield Wiper Motor, Renew All models	.7	**Speedometer Head, R&R or Renew** All models	1.2	**Rear Window Wiper Switch, Renew** Van-Wagon	.4
Windshield Wiper and Washer Switch, Renew All models	.8	**Speedometer Cable and Casing, Renew** All models	.9	**Rear Window Washer Pump, Renew** Van-Wagon	.4
Windshield Washer Pump, Renew All models	.5	**Speedometer Cable (Inner), Renew or Lubricate** All models	.4	**Radio, R&R** Truck	
Windshield Wiper Link Assy., Renew Truck-Montero	7			1986	1.0
Van-Wagon	2.3	**Rear Window Wiper Motor, Renew** Van-Wagon	.6	1987-90	.5
				Montero	1.1
				Van-Wagon	.6

LABOR   32   LIGHT SWITCHES & WIRING   32   LABOR

	Chilton Time		Chilton Time		Chilton Time
Headlamp Switch, Renew All models	.6	**Parking Brake Warning Lamp Switch, Renew** All models	.6	**Turn Signal, Washer/Wiper Lever Assy., Renew** All models	.8
Back-Up Lamp Switch, Renew (w/Manual Trans) All models	.4	**Hazard Warning Switch, Renew** All models	.4		
Neutral Safety and/or Back-Up Lamp Switch, Renew All models	.4	**Column Switch Assy., Renew** Truck-Montero	.9	**Horn, Renew** Truck-Montero–one	.3
		Van-Wagon	.8	Van-Wagon	.5
Stop Lamp Switch, Renew All models	.4	**Turn Signal or Hazard Warning Flasher, Renew** All models	.3		
w/Cruise control add	.1			**Horn Switch, Renew** All models	.4

LABOR   34   CRUISE CONTROL   34   LABOR

	Chilton Time		Chilton Time		Chilton Time
Speed Control Vacuum Pump, Renew Truck	1.0	**Speed Control Vacuum Hoses, Renew** Truck-Van-Wagon	.4	**Speed Control Vacuum Pump Relay, Renew** Truck-Van-Wagon	.4
Van-Wagon	.4				
Speed Control Vacuum Switch, Renew Truck-Van-Wagon	.3	**Speed Control Clutch Release Switch, Renew** Truck-Van-Wagon	.5		
Speed Control Actuator, Renew Truck	.9	**Speed Control Control Unit, Renew** Truck-Van-Wagon	.4	**Speed Control Vacuum Check Valve, Renew** Truck-Van-Wagon	.3
Van-Wagon	.6				

GROUP INDEX

ALPHABETICAL INDEX

LABOR 1 TUNE UP 1 LABOR

	Chilton Time
Compression Test	
Four	.7
Van add	.1
V-6	.9

Engine Tune Up, (Electronic Ignition)
Includes: Test battery and clean connections. Tighten manifold and carburetor mounting bolts. Check engine compression, clean and adjust or renew spark plugs. Test resistance of spark plug cables. Inspect distributor cap and rotor. Adjust air gap. Check vacuum advance operation. Reset ignition timing. Adjust idle mixture and idle speed. Service air cleaner. Inspect and adjust drive belts. Inspect choke operation and adjust or free up. Check operation of E.G.R. valve.

	Chilton Time
Four	2.4
Van add	.1
V-6	3.0
w/A.C. add	.4

LABOR 2 IGNITION SYSTEM 2 LABOR

GASOLINE ENGINES

	Chilton Time
Spark Plugs, Clean and Reset or Renew	
All models Four	.6
Van add	.1
V-6	.8
w/A.C. add	.4
Ignition Timing, Reset All models	.3
Distributor, Renew Includes: Reset ignition timing. All models Four	.6
V-6	.7
Distributor, R&R and Recondition Includes: Reset ignition timing. All models Four	1.7
V-6	1.8

	Chilton Time
Distributor Reluctor and/or Pick-Up Coil, Renew Includes: Reset ignition timing. All models	.7
Distributor Cap and/or Rotor, Renew All models	.5
Vacuum Control Unit, Renew All models	.6
Transistorized Ignition Control Unit(s), Renew Does not include test. All models	.6
w/A.C. add	.2
Integrated Circuit Ignition Unit, Renew All models	.6
Spark Plug Cables, Renew All models Four	.5
V-6	.6

	Chilton Time
Ignition Coil/Power Transistor, Renew All models	.4
Axxess add	.1
Van add	.1
Ignition Switch, Renew All models	.6
Steering Lock Assembly, Renew Includes: R&R ignition switch. All models	1.2

DIESEL ENGINE

	Chilton Time
Glow Plugs, Renew All models	.6
After Glow Timer, Renew All models	.4
Glow Plug Relay, Renew All models	.4

LABOR 3 FUEL SYSTEM 3 LABOR

GASOLINE ENGINE

	Chilton Time
Fuel Pump, Test Includes: Disconnect fuel line, attach pressure gauge. All models	.3
Carburetor Air Cleaner, Service All models	.3
Air Cleaner Vacuum Motor, Renew All models	.5
Air Cleaner Temperature Sensor, Renew All models	.5
Anti-Dieseling Solenoid, Renew (Dash Pot) All models	.6
Fuel Shut-Off Vacuum Switch, Renew All models	.4
Automatic Choke Relay, Renew All models	.6
Needle Valve and Seat, Renew Includes: Renew and/or reset float. All models	.8
Carburetor, Renew Includes: All necessary adjustments. All models	1.2
Carburetor, R&R and Recondition Includes: All necessary adjustments. All models	3.0

	Chilton Time
Electric Fuel Pump, Renew	
D21 models	1.3
720 models	.7
Recond pump add	.4
Electric Fuel Pump Control Unit, Renew All models	.4
Mechanical Fuel Pump, Renew	
Axxess	.8
720 models	.5
Fuel Tank, Renew Includes: Drain and refill tank.	
D21 models	1.2
720 models	.9
Axxess	
4X2	1.2
4X4	2.2
Van	.7
Fuel Gauge (Tank Unit), Renew	
D21 models	1.4
720 models	1.0
Axxess	.8
Van	.7
Fuel Gauge (Dash Unit), Renew	
D21 models	.7
720 models	1.5
Axxess	.9
Van	1.0

	Chilton Time
Intake and Exhaust Manifold and/or Gaskets, Renew	
Four	
D21 models	2.0
720 models	2.5
Axxess	4.2
Van	4.0
V-6	3.5
Renew exhaust manif or gskt add	
D21 models	1.0
720 models	.7

AXXESS (MPI)

	Chilton Time
Fuel Injectors, Renew (All) All models	.9
Pressure Regulator Valve, Renew All models	.4
Throttle Chamber, Renew All models	.8
Throttle Valve Switch, Renew All models	.8
Air Regulator, Renew All models	.6
Coolant Temperature Sensor, Renew All models	.4
Fuel Pump Relay, Renew All models	.3

LABOR   3 FUEL SYSTEM 3   LABOR

	Chilton Time
Crank Angle Sensor, Renew	
All models	.6
Pressure Regulator Control Solenoid Valve, Renew	
All models	.7
FUEL INJECTION (TBI)	
Fuel Injection Unit, R&R or Renew	
Van	2.4
All other models	.8
Renew injectors add	.2
Fuel Pressure Regulator, Renew	
Van	1.1
All other models	.6
Air Flow Meter, Renew	
Van	1.1
All other models	.6
Throttle Value Switch, Renew	
Van	2.5
All other models	.7
Solenoid Valve, Renew	
Van	.8
All other models	.6
Electronic Control Unit, Renew	
All models	.5

	Chilton Time
Fuel Pump Relay, Renew	
All models	.5
Mixture Heater Relay, Renew	
All models	.4
Coolant Temperature Sensor, Renew	
All models	.5
Fuel Pump Control Unit, Renew	
All models	.5
DIESEL ENGINE	
Air Cleaner, Service	
All models	.3
Injection Pump Timing, Adjust	
All models	1.0
Primary Fuel Filter, Renew	
All models	.4
Air Control Valves, Renew	
All models	.3
Injection Pump Controller, Renew	
All models	.6
Control Relay, Renew	
All models	.3
Automatic Timer, Renew	
All models	1.0

	Chilton Time
Altitude Compensator, Renew	
All models	.5
Fuel Injection Nozzles, Renew	
All models	1.2
Clean and test add— each	.2
Fuel Injection Pump, Renew	
Includes: R&R timing cover and automatic timer.	
All models	1.8
Fuel Supply Pump, Renew	
Includes: Bleed fuel system.	
All models	.5
Fuel Supply Pump, R&R and Recondition	
Includes: Bleed fuel system.	
All models	1.5
Vacuum Pump, Renew	
All models	.7
Recond add	.4
Intake Manifold and/or Gasket, Renew	
All models	1.5
Renew manif add	.5

LABOR   3A EMISSION CONTROLS 3A   LABOR

	Chilton Time
GASOLINE ENGINE	
POSITIVE CRANKCASE VENTILATION SYSTEM	
P.C.V. Valve, Renew	
All models	.5
HEATED AIR SYSTEM	
Air Cleaner Vacuum Motor, Renew	
All models	.4
Air Cleaner Temperature Sensor, Renew	
All models	.4
Altitude Compensator, Renew	
All models	.4
BOOST CONTROLLED DECELERATION DEVICE (B.C.D.D.)	
B.C.D.D. Assembly, Renew	
All models	.6
B.C.D.D. Control Valve Assy., Renew	
All models	.4
ALTITUDE COMPENSATOR	
Altitude Compensator, Renew	
All models	.5
SPARK TIMING CONTROL	
Vacuum Solenoid Valve, Renew	
All models	.4
Thermal Vacuum Valve, Renew	
All models	.4
Spark Delay Valve, Renew	
All models	.3
Vacuum Control Valve, Renew	
All models	.4
DETONATION CONTROL SYSTEM	
Fuel Cut-Off Solenoid, Renew	
All models	.5

	Chilton Time
Throttle Valve Switch, Renew	
All models	.5
Fuel Shut-Off Clutch Switch, Renew	
All models	.4
Fuel Shut-Off Vacuum Switch, Renew	
All models	.3
Detonation Sensor, Renew	
All models	.6
Detonation Control Unit, Renew	
All models	.4
EVAPORATIVE EMISSION CONTROL SYSTEM	
Vapor/Liquid Separator, Renew	
All models	.8
Charcoal Canister, Renew	
All models	.3
Canister Filter, Renew	
All models	.4
AIR INJECTION SYSTEM	
Air Pump Assembly, Renew	
All models	.7
Air Pump Drive Belt, Renew	
All models	.6
w/A.C. add	.3
Anti-Backfire Valve, Renew	
All models	.5
Air Control Valve, Renew	
Axxess	.6
All other models	.5
Air Control Solenoid Valve, Renew	
All models	.5
E.C.C. SYSTEM	
E.C.C. Control Unit, Renew	
All models	.5

	Chilton Time
E.C.C. Relay, Renew	
All models	.4
Air-Fuel Control Solenoid, Renew	
All models	1.2
EXHAUST GAS RECIRCULATION SYSTEM	
E.G.R. Valve, Renew	
Van	.8
All other models	.6
E.G.R. Solenoid Valve, Renew	
Axxess	.4
All other models	.3
E.G.R. Thermal Vacuum Valve, Renew	
All models	.5
Back Pressure Transducer, Renew	
All models	.5
Oxygen Sensor, Renew	
All models	.5
E.G.R. Control Unit, Renew	
Axxess	.4
DIESEL ENGINE	
Venturi Vacuum Transducer Valve, Renew	
All models	.4
Vacuum Amplifier, Renew	
All models	.5
Check Valve, Renew	
All models	.3
Thermal Vacuum Valve, Renew	
All models	.6
Venturi Assembly, Renew	
All models	.6
Venturi Assy., R&R and Recondition	
All models	1.1
E.G.R. Control Valve, Renew	
All models	.6

LABOR 4 ALTERNATOR AND REGULATOR 4 LABOR

	Chilton Time
Alternator Circuits, Test	
Includes: Test battery, regulator and alternator output.	
All models	.6
Alternator Assembly, Renew	
Axxess	.6
All other models	.9
Add circuit test if performed.	

	Chilton Time
Alternator, R&R and Recondition	
Includes: Complete disassembly, inspect, test, replace parts as required, reassemble.	
Axxess	2.0
All other models	2.5
Alternator Bearings, Renew	
Includes: R&R alternator.	
Axxess	1.0
All other models	1.3

	Chilton Time
Voltage Regulator, Test and Renew	
Axxess	1.0
All other models	1.3
Ammeter or Voltmeter, Renew	
D21 models	.7
720 models	1.5
Axxess	.9
Van	1.0

LABOR 5 STARTING SYSTEM 5 LABOR

	Chilton Time
Starter Draw Test (On Truck)	
All models	.3
Starter, Renew	
All models	.8
Axxess add	.1
Add draw test if performed.	
Starter, R&R and Recondition	
Includes: Turn down armature.	
All models	2.5
Axxess add	.1

	Chilton Time
Renew field coils add	.5
Add draw test if performed.	
Starter Solenoid, Renew	
Includes: R&R starter.	
All models	1.0
Axxess add	.1
Starter Drive, Renew	
Includes: R&R starter.	
All models	1.1
Axxess add	.1

	Chilton Time
Starter Relay, Renew	
D21 models	.4
Ignition Switch, Renew	
All models	.6
Battery Cables, Renew	
All models-each	.4
Axxess add	.1

LABOR 6 BRAKE SYSTEM 6 LABOR

	Chilton Time
Brake Pedal Free Play, Adjust	
All models	.3
Bleed Brakes (Four Wheels)	
Includes: Fill master cylinder.	
All models	1.0
Brake Shoes, Renew	
Includes: Install new or exchange brake shoes, Adjust service and hand brake. Bleed system.	
All models	
front	1.4
rear	
w/Single rear whls	1.1
w/Dual rear whls	3.0
Resurface brake drum add-each	.5
Brake Drum, Renew (One)	
All models	.5
w/Dual rear whls add	.5

BRAKE HYDRAULIC SYSTEM

	Chilton Time
Wheel Cylinder, Renew	
Includes: Bleed system.	
Front	
all models-one	.9
both	1.7
Rear	
w/Single rear whls	
one	.9
both	1.7
w/Dual rear whls	
one	1.9
both	3.6
Wheel Cylinder, R&R and Rebuild	
Includes: Bleed system.	
Front	
all models-one	1.1
both	2.0
Rear	
w/Single rear whls	
one	1.1
both	2.0

COMBINATIONS

	Chilton Time
RENEW WHEEL CYLINDER	
Each	.3
REBUILD WHEEL CYLINDER	
Each	.4
REBUILD CALIPER ASSEMBLY	
Each	.4
RENEW MASTER CYLINDER	
All models	.5
REBUILD MASTER CYLINDER	
All models	1.0
RENEW BRAKE HOSE	
Each	.3
RENEW BRAKE DRUM	
Each	.1
RENEW DISC BRAKE ROTOR	
Each	.2
REPACK FRONT WHEEL BEARINGS (BOTH WHEELS)	
Drum brakes	.3
Disc brakes	.6

	Chilton Time
w/Dual rear whls	
one	2.0
both	3.8
Master Cylinder, Renew	
Includes: Bleed system.	
All models	.8
Axxess add	.1
Master Cylinder, R&R and Rebuild	
Includes: Bleed system.	
All models	1.5
Axxess add	.1

	Chilton Time
Brake Hose, Renew (Flex)	
Includes: Bleed system.	
All models-one	.6
each adtnl	.3
Proportioning Valve, Renew	
Includes: Bleed system.	
All models	.7

DISC BRAKES

	Chilton Time
Disc Brake Pads, Renew	
Includes: Install new disc brake pads only.	
Front	
Axxess	.6
Van	.5
D21-720 models	.8
Rear	
All models	.8
Caliper Assembly, Renew	
Includes: Bleed system.	
Front	
2 WD-one	.8
both	1.5
4 WD	
Nissan-one	.8
both	1.5
Datsun-one	1.9
both	3.7
Rear	
one	1.0
both	1.9
Recond caliper add, each	.4
Disc Brake Rotor, Renew	
Front	
2 WD-one	.8
both	1.5
4 WD	
Nissan-one	.8
both	1.5
Datsun-one	1.9
both	3.7
Axxess-one	1.4

LABOR — 6 BRAKE SYSTEM 6 — LABOR

	Chilton Time
Van	
one	.9
both	1.7
Rear	
one	1.0
both	1.9
Resurface rotor add-each	.5

POWER BRAKES

Power Brake Booster, Renew
Includes: Bleed system.

	Chilton Time
D21-720 models	1.0
Axxess	1.6
Van	3.1

	Chilton Time
Brake Booster Check Valve, Renew	
Van	2.5
All other models	.3
Vacuum Pump, R&R or Renew	
Diesel models	.7
Recond pump add	.4

PARKING BRAKE

	Chilton Time
Parking Brake, Adjust	
All models	.4
Parking Brake Control, Renew	
D21-720 models	.7
Axxess	.5

	Chilton Time
Van	.8
Parking Brake Equalizer, Renew	
All models	.6
Parking Brake Cable, Renew (One)	
Includes: Adjust cable.	
Front	
Axxess	.5
Van	.9
D21-720 models	.6
Rear	
Van	1.9
Axxess	.5
D21-720 models	.6

LABOR — 7 COOLING SYSTEM 7 — LABOR

Winterize Cooling System
Includes: Run engine to check for leaks, tighten all hose connections. Test radiator and pressure cap, drain radiator and engine block. Add anti-freeze and refill system.

	Chilton Time
All models	.5

Thermostat, Renew

	Chilton Time
Four	
D21-720 models	.5
Axxess	1.6
Van	1.4
V-6	1.3

Radiator Assembly, R&R or Renew
Includes: Drain and refill coolant.

	Chilton Time
D21 models	.8
720 models	1.0
Axxess	1.0
Van	2.4

ADD THESE OPERATIONS TO RADIATOR R&R

	Chilton Time
Boil & Repair	1.5
Rod Clean	1.9
Repair Core	1.3
Renew Tank	1.6
Renew Trans. Oil Cooler	1.9
Recore Radiator	1.7

Radiator Hoses, Renew

	Chilton Time
Van	
upper	1.7
lower	1.6
All other models–each	.4

Drive Belt, Renew

	Chilton Time
Axxess	.6
All other models	.5

Drive Belts, Adjust

	Chilton Time
All models	.4

Coolant Temperature Sensor, Renew

	Chilton Time
Four	
D21-720 models	.4
Axxess	.4
Van	1.3
V-6	.8

Fluid Fan Coupling, Renew

	Chilton Time
2 WD models	.9
4 WD models	1.3

Temperature Gauge Sending Unit, Renew

	Chilton Time
All models	.4

Temperature Gauge (Dash Unit), Renew

	Chilton Time
D21 models	.7
720 models	1.5
Axxess	.9
Van	1.0

Water Pump, Renew
Includes: R&R radiator, Drain and refill coolant.

	Chilton Time
Gas	
Four	
D21-720 models	1.5
Axxess	4.2
Van	2.9
V-6	2.5
Diesel	1.2
w/A.C. or P.S. add	.2

Radiator Fan and/or Motor, Renew

	Chilton Time
Axxess	.6

Cooling Fan Relay, Renew

	Chilton Time
Axxess	.4

Fan Blade or Pulley, Renew

	Chilton Time
Axxess	.3
D21 models	.7
720 models	1.0
Axxess	.6
Van	2.5

Heater Core, R&R or Renew

	Chilton Time
D21 models	*4.5
720 models	2.7
Axxess	4.0
Van	3.2
*w/A.C. add	2.5

ADD THESE OPERATIONS TO HEATER CORE R&R

	Chilton Time
Boil & Repair	1.2
Repair Core	.9
Recore	1.2

Heater Blower Motor Relay, Renew

	Chilton Time
Axxess	.3
Van	.4

Heater Blower Motor Assy., Renew

	Chilton Time
D21 models	1.2
720 models	.5
Axxess	.5
Van	1.0

Heater Hoses, Renew (All)

	Chilton Time
D21 models	2.5
720 models-wo/A.C.	.8
w/A.C.	1.9
Axxess	.8
Van	3.0

Heater Temperature Control Assy., Renew

	Chilton Time
D21 models	1.4
720 models	1.0
Axxess	.8
Van	.8

Blower Motor Switch, Renew

	Chilton Time
D21 models	1.6
720 models	1.2
Axxess	1.0
Van	1.0

Blower Motor Resistor, Renew

	Chilton Time
All models	.4

REAR HEATER

Rear Heater Core, R&R or Renew

	Chilton Time
Van	2.0

Rear Heater Blower Motor, Renew
Includes: R&R heater core.

	Chilton Time
Van	2.2
Renew blower motor resistor, add	.2

Rear Heater Hoses, Renew

	Chilton Time
Van	.7

Rear Heater Control Assy., Renew

	Chilton Time
Van	.5

Rear Heater Relay, Renew

	Chilton Time
Van	.4

LABOR — 8 EXHAUST SYSTEM 8 — LABOR

Front Exhaust Pipe, Renew

	Chilton Time
D21-720 models	1.3
Van-Axxess	.8

Muffler and Rear Pipe, Renew

	Chilton Time
All models	.9

Intermediate Exhaust Pipe, Renew

	Chilton Time
All models	1.0

Catalytic Converter, Renew

	Chilton Time
D21-720 models	1.2
Axxess	.5

	Chilton Time
Van	.8
E.F.E. Valve (Heat Riser), Renew	
All models	1.3

LABOR 8 EXHAUST SYSTEM 8 LABOR

Intake and Exhaust Manifolds and/or Gaskets, Renew
Four
- D21 models 2.0
- 720 models 2.5
- V-6 .... 3.5

Renew exhaust manif or gskt add
- D21 models 1.0
- 720 models 7

Diesel
- All models 1.3

Renew manif. add 4

Exhaust Manifold Gaskets, Renew
Four
- D21 models 1.7
- 720 models 1.5
- Van 1.5

Axxess
- 2 WD 1.0
- 4 WD 1.3

- V-6-right 2.5
- left 3.5

LABOR 9 FRONT SUSPENSION 9 LABOR

Chilton Time

Note: On all front suspension operations alignment charges must be added if performed. Time given does not include alignment.

Wheel, Renew
- one 5

Wheels, Rotate (All)
- All models 5

Wheels, Balance
- one 3
- each adtnl 2

Toe-In, Adjust
- All models 6

Front Strut Assy., R&R or Renew
- Axxess-one 6
- both 1.1

Front Strut Shock Absorbers, Renew
- Axxess-one 1.0
- both 1.9

Front Hub Assembly, Renew
Includes: Renew wheel bearings and seals.
- Axxess-one 1.9
- both 3.7

Lower Ball Joints, Renew
Add alignment charges.
- Axxess-one 1.2
- both 2.3

Steering Knuckle Arm, Renew
Add alignment charges.
- Axxess-one 1.5
- both 2.9

Lower Control Arm Assy., Renew
Add alignment charges.
- Axxess-one 1.2
- both 2.3
Renew bushings add-each side 2

Front Stabilizer Bar, Renew
- Axxess 8

Halfshaft Assy., R&R or Renew
Includes: Renew C.V. joint boot.
Axxess
- w/M.T.-one 1.0
- both 1.9
- w/A.T.-one 2.0
- both 3.0
Recond C.V. joint add-each 6
Renew center brg add 3

LABOR 9 FRONT SUSPENSION 9 LABOR

Note: On all front suspension operations alignment charges must be added if performed. Time given does not include alignment.

Wheel, Renew
- one 5

Wheels, Rotate (All)
- All models 5

Wheel, Balance
- one 3
- each adtnl 2

Toe-In, Adjust
- All models 6

Align Front End
Includes: Adjust front wheel bearings.
- All models 1.5

D21-720 models

Steering Knuckle Spindle, Renew
Add alignment charges.
- All models-one 2.1
- both 4.0

Front Wheel Hub, Renew
Includes: Renew bearings and seals.
- All models-one 1.5
- both 2.9

Upper Ball Joint, Renew
Add alignment charges.
- All models-one side 1.0
- both sides 1.9

Lower Ball Joint, Renew
Add alignment charges.
- All models-one side 1.1
- both sides 2.0

Steering Knuckle Arm, Renew
- All models-one 6
- both 1.0

Upper Control Arm Assy., Renew
Add alignment charges.
- All models-one side 1.6
- both sides 3.0
Renew bushings add-each side 4

Lower Control Arm Assy., Renew
Add alignment charges.
- All models-one side 1.6
- both sides 3.0
Renew bushings add-each side 4

Front Torsion Bar, Renew
All models
- one side 1.2
- both sides 1.9

Front Stabilizer Bar and Bushings, Renew
- All models 9

Front Shock Absorbers or Rubber Bushings, Renew
- All models-one 5
- both 8

VAN

Steering Knuckle, Upper or Lower Ball Joints, Renew
Add alignment charges.
- All models-one side 2.0
- both sides 3.9

Front Wheel Bearings or Hub, Renew
- All models-one side 1.2
- both sides 2.3

Upper Ball Joints, Renew
Add alignment charges.
- All models-one 1.1
- both 2.1

Front Stabilizer Bar, Renew
- All models 7

Upper Control Arms, Renew
Add alignment charges.
- All models-one 1.7
- both 3.3

Lower Control Arms, Renew
Add alignment charges.
- All models-one 1.8
- both 3.5

Front Shock Absorbers, Renew
- All models-one 5
- both 8

Front Leaf Spring, Renew
- All models-one 2.7
Recond spring add 5

LABOR 9A FRONT SUSPENSION (RWD) 9A LABOR

	Chilton Time		Chilton Time		Chilton Time
4 WHEEL DRIVE FRONT AXLE		Datsun models		both sides	.8
		one side	1.9		
Steering Knuckle Spindle, Renew		both sides	3.7	**Upper Ball Joint, Renew**	
Add alignment charges.		**Front Drive Shafts, Renew**		Add alignment charges.	
All models–one	2.1	All models–one side	1.4	All models–one side	1.0
both	4.0	both sides	2.7	both sides	1.9
		Front Drive Shaft Boot, Renew			
Front Wheel Hub Assy., Renew		All models–one	2.0	**Steering Knuckle Arms, Renew**	
Includes: Renew bearings and seals.		both	3.9	Add alignment charges.	
Nissan models		**Free-Running Hubs, Renew**		All models–one side	.6
one side	.9	All models–one side	.5	both sides	1.0
both sides	1.7				

LABOR 10 STEERING LINKAGE 10 LABOR

	Chilton Time		Chilton Time		Chilton Time
Tie Rod or Tie Rod Ends, Renew		**Idler Arm Assembly, Renew**		**Cross Rod Assembly, Renew**	
Includes: Reset toe-in.		Includes: Reset toe-in.		Includes: Reset toe-in.	
All models–one side	.8	All models	.8	Van	.6
both sides	1.5	**Pitman Arm, Renew**		All other models	1.0
		Includes: Reset toe-in.			
Steering Damper, Renew		All models	.8		
4 WD models	.6				

LABOR 11 STEERING GEAR 11 LABOR

	Chilton Time		Chilton Time		Chilton Time
MANUAL STEERING		**Power Steering Oil Pressure Switch, Renew**		**POWER STEERING RACK AND PINION TYPE**	
Steering Gear, Adjust (On Truck)		All models	.4		
All models	.5	**Power Steering Pump Drive Belt, Renew**		**Power Steering Pump Drive Belt, Renew**	
Steering Gear Assy., R&R or Renew		All models	.4	Axxess	.4
All models	1.2				
Sector Shaft and/or Oil Seal, Renew		**Power Steering Gear, Renew**		**Power Rack and Pinion Assy., R&R or Renew**	
Includes: R&R steering gear and make all necessary adjustments.		All models	1.8	Includes: Reset toe-in.	
All models	1.7	**Power Steering Pump, Renew**		Axxess	3.2
		D21 models	.9		
Steering Gear Assy., R&R and Recondition		720 models	1.7	**Power Rack and Pinion Assy., R&R and Recondition**	
Includes: Disassemble, renew necessary parts, reassemble and adjust.		Van	1.4	Includes: Reset toe-in.	
All models	3.0	**Power Steering Pump, R&R and Recondition**		Axxess	4.0
		D21 models	2.0		
Steering Column Upper Bushing, Renew		720 models	2.7	**Outer Tie Rods and/or Rack End Boots, Renew**	
Van	1.6	Van	2.3	Axxess–one side	1.0
All other models	1.4			both sides	1.9
Steering Column Flex Coupler, Renew		**Sector Shaft Oil Seals, Renew**		**Power Steering Oil Pump, Renew**	
Axxess	1.1	All models	2.2	Axxess	1.0
All other models	.6	**Power Steering Oil Pressure Switch, Renew**			
Steering Column Lock Assy., Renew		All models	.4	**Power Steering Oil Pump, R&R and Recondition**	
Axxess	.8			Axxess	2.0
All other models	1.2	**Power Steering Hoses, Renew**			
		Includes: Bleed system.		**Power Steering Hoses, Renew**	
POWER STEERING		D21 models	.6	Includes: Bleed system.	
WORM & SECTOR TYPE		720 models	1.1	Axxess	1.4
Power Steering Pump Drive Belt, Adjust		Van	3.2		
All models	.3				

LABOR 12 CYLINDER HEAD & VALVE SYSTEM 12 LABOR

	Chilton Time		Chilton Time		Chilton Time
GASOLINE ENGINES		**Cylinder Head Gasket, Renew**		V-6	
Compression Test		Includes: Clean carbon and make all necessary adjustments.		right side	7.6
Four	.7	Four		left side	8.1
V-6	.9	D21-720 models	4.4	both sides	10.0
		Axxess	6.0	w/A.C. add	.2
		Van	6.3	w/P.S. add	.3

LABOR 12 CYLINDER HEAD & VALVE SYSTEM 12 LABOR

Clean Carbon and Grind Valves
Includes: R&R cylinder heads. Reface valves and seats. Clean carbon and make all necessary adjustments.

	Chilton Time
Four	
D21-720 models	8.9
Axxess	11.0
Van	10.5
V-6	17.6
w/A.C. add	.2
w/P.S. add	.3

Cylinder Head, Renew
Includes: R&R cylinder head, transfer all necessary component parts. Clean carbon, grind valves. Make all necessary adjustments.

Four	
D21-720 models	9.4
Axxess	11.5
Van	11.0
V-6	
right side	8.6
left side	9.1
both sides	19.6
w/A.C. add	.2
w/P.S. add	.3

Rocker Arm Cover Gasket, Renew
Four	
D21-720 models	.6
Axxess	.4
Van	2.2

	Chilton Time
V-6-one side	.7
both sides	1.0

Valve Springs or Valve Stem Oil Seals, Renew (Head On Truck)
Four	
D21-720 models-all	3.3
Axxess-all	2.7
Van-all	3.6
V-6-one side	2.0
both sides	3.0

Valve Rocker Arm Pivots, Springs and Arms, Renew (All)
Four	
D21-720 models	1.2
Axxess	.8
Van	2.7

Valve Rocker Arms/Shafts and/or Lifters, Renew
V-6-one side	1.2
both sides	2.0

Valve Clearance, Adjust
Four	
D21-720 models	1.0
Van	2.3

DIESEL ENGINE
Compression Test
All models	1.4

Cylinder Head Gasket, Renew
Includes: Clean carbon. Make all necessary adjustments.

	Chilton Time
All models	3.4
w/A.C. add	.4

Cylinder Head, Renew
Includes: Clean carbon. Transfer parts as required. Reface valves. Make all necessary adjustments.

All models	5.3
w/A.C. add	.4

Clean Carbon and Grind Valves
Includes: R&R cylinder head. Recondition valves and seats. Make all necessary adjustments.

All models	7.2
w/A.C. add	.4

Rocker Arm Cover or Gasket, Renew
All models	.6

Valve Springs and/or Valve Stem Oil Seals, Renew (Head on Truck)
All models-one cyl	1.0
each adtnl cyl	.3

Valve Push Rods, Renew
All models	1.3
w/A.C. add	.4

Valve Rocker Arm Assy., Renew
All models	1.4

LABOR 13 ENGINE ASSEMBLY & MOUNTS 13 LABOR

GASOLINE ENGINES
Note: All engine operations listed in this group are for assemblies as supplied by the original equipment manufacturer. Time to replace assemblies from independent rebuilders may vary.

Engine Assembly, Remove & Install
Does not include transfer of any parts or equipment.

	Chilton Time
Four	
D21 models	
4X2	7.1
4X4	9.1
720 models	
4X2	7.8
4X4	10.4
Axxess	
4X2	10.1
4X4	14.0
Van	11.0
w/A.C. add	.7
V-6	
4X2	7.4
4X4	10.5
w/A.C. or P.S. add	.4

Cylinder Assy. (Short Block), Renew
Includes: R&R engine assy. Transfer all component parts not supplied with replacement engine. Tune engine.

Four	
D21 models	
4X2	9.7
4X4	11.8
720 models	
4X2	11.0
4X4	13.9

	Chilton Time
Axxess	
4X2	16.7
4X4	17.6
Van	13.8
w/A.C. add	.7
V-6	
4X2	10.0
4X4	15.5
w/A.C. or P.S. add	.4

Engine Assy., R&R and Recondition
Includes: Rebore block, install new pistons, pins, rings, rod and main bearings. Clean carbon, grind valves. Tune engine.

Four	
D21 models	
4X2	21.3
4X4	27.3
720 models	
4X2	23.4
4X4	31.2
Axxess	
4X2	25.8
4X4	26.8
Van	31.1
w/A.C. add	.7
V-6	
4X2	22.2
4X4	31.5
w/A.C. or P.S. add	.4

Engine Mounts, Renew
Front	
D21-720 models	1.0
Axxess-Van	1.4
Rear	
2 WD	.8
4 WD	
D21 models	.8

	Chilton Time
720 models	1.0
Axxess	1.0

DIESEL ENGINE
Engine Assembly, Remove & Install
Does not include transfer of any parts or equipment.

All models	5.9
w/A.C. add	.4
w/P.S. add	.3

Cylinder Block, Renew
Includes: R&R engine assy. Transfer all component parts not supplied with replacement engine. Clean carbon, grind valves. Make all necessary adjustments.

All models	16.6
w/A.C. add	.4
w/P.S. add	.3

Short Block Assy., Renew
Includes: R&R engine assy. Transfer all component parts not supplied with replacement engine. Clean carbon, grind valves. Make all necessary adjustments.

All models	13.3
w/A.C. add	.4
w/P.S. add	.3

Engine Assy., R&R and Recondition
Includes: Install new pistons, rings, pins, rod and main bearings. Renew cylinder liners. Clean carbon, grind valves. Make all necessary adjustments.

All models	25.0
w/A.C. add	.4

Engine Mounts, Renew
All models-front	1.0
rear	.8

LABOR 14 PISTONS, RINGS & BEARINGS 14 LABOR

GASOLINE ENGINES

	Chilton Time
Pistons or Connecting Rods, Renew (All)	
Includes: R&R cylinder head and oil pan on all models. Remove cylinder top ridge and deglaze cylinder walls. Renew piston rings and rod bearings.	
Four	
D21 models	
4X2 models	11.8
4X4 models	14.2
720 models	
4X2 models	9.1
4X4 models	13.7
Axxess	9.1
Van	13.7
V-6	
4X2	12.1
4X4	14.5
w/A.C. add	1.0
w/P.S. add	.3
Connecting Rod Bearings, Renew	
Includes: R&R oil pan on all models. R&R engine assy. on 4X4 models where required.	
4X2	2.5
4X4	
D21 models	6.9

COMBINATIONS

	Chilton Time
DRAIN, EVACUATE & RECHARGE AIR CONDITIONING SYSTEM	
All models	1.0
DISTRIBUTOR, RECONDITION	
All models	.9
CARBURETOR, RECONDITION	
All models	2.5
VALVE GUIDE OR SEAT, RENEW	
Each	.5
OIL PUMP DRIVING GEAR, RENEW	
All models	.2
DEGLAZE CYLINDER WALLS	
Each	.1
REMOVE CYLINDER TOP RIDGE	
Each	.1
PLASTIGAUGE BEARINGS	
Each	.1
OIL FILTER ELEMENT, RENEW	
All models	.3

	Chilton Time
720 models	*10.5
*w/A.C. add	1.0
*w/P.S. add	.3
Axxess	
4X2	3.2
4X4	2.9
Van	2.6

DIESEL ENGINE

	Chilton Time
Pistons or Connecting Rods, Renew (All)	
Includes: R&R cylinder head and oil pan.	
All models	9.9
Renew cyl liner add	
each	.3
w/A.C. add	.2
Piston Rings, Renew (All)	
Includes: R&R cylinder head and oil pan.	
All models	8.7
Renew cyl liner add	
each	.3
w/A.C. add	.2
Connecting Rod Bearings, Renew	
Includes: R&R oil pan.	
All models	2.7

LABOR 15 CRANKSHAFT & DAMPER 15 LABOR

GASOLINE ENGINES

	Chilton Time
Crankshaft and Main Bearings, Renew	
Includes: R&R engine assy. Plastigauge all bearing clearances.	
Four	
D21 models	
4X2	9.5
4X4	11.8
720 models	
4X2	11.1
4X4	13.3
Axxess	
4X2	12.6
4X4	13.6
Van	14.5
w/A.C. add	.7
V-6	
4X2	8.9
4X4	19.5
w/A.C. or P.S. add	.4
Crankshaft Rear Main Oil Seal, Renew	
Four	
D21 models	
4X2	12.4

	Chilton Time
4X4	14.7
720 models	
4X2	5.0
4X4	8.2
Axxess	
4X2	5.8
4X4	8.5
Van	11.7
V-6	
4X2	12.7
4X4	15.0
w/A.C. or P.S. add	.4
Crankshaft Pulley, Renew	
Includes: R&R radiator.	
All models	1.4
Renew front crankshaft seal add	.2
w/A.C. add	.2

DIESEL ENGINE

	Chilton Time
Crankshaft and Main Bearings, Renew	
Includes: R&R engine assembly. Plastigauge all bearing clearances.	
All models	10.8
w/A.C. add	.4

	Chilton Time
w/P.S. add	.3
Crankshaft Rear Main Bearing Oil Seal, Renew	
Includes: R&R engine and trans, where required.	
All models	
SD 22 eng	13.0
SD 25 eng	6.3
w/A.C. add	.4
w/P.S. add	.3
Crankshaft Pulley, Renew	
Includes: R&R radiator assy.	
All models	1.0
w/A.C. add	.2
Crankshaft Front Oil Seal, Renew	
Includes: R&R radiator assy.	
All models	1.4
w/A.C. add	.2

LABOR 16 CAMSHAFT & TIMING GEARS 16 LABOR

GASOLINE ENGINES

	Chilton Time
Timing Chain Cover or Gasket, Renew	
Includes: R&R radiator, loosen oil pan on all models.	
720 models	
4X2	5.0
4X4	5.7
w/P.S. add	.2
w/A.C. add	.2
Axxess	7.2
Van	7.0
Timing Chain, Crankshaft and Cam Sprockets, Renew	
720 models	
4X2	5.5

	Chilton Time
4X4	6.2
w/P.S. add	.2
w/A.C. add	.2
Axxess	7.7
Van	7.5
Camshaft and Lifters, Renew	
Four	
D21-720 models	3.4
Axxess	1.1
Van	4.2
Camshaft Sprocket or Gear, Renew	
Four	1.0
Timing Belt Cover and/or Gasket, Renew	
Four	4.0

	Chilton Time
Renew timing belt add	.2
Renew cam or crank gears	
add	.4
Camshafts, Renew	
V-6—right side	8.8
left side	9.3
Camshaft Oil Seals, Renew	
V-6	4.8

DIESEL ENGINE

	Chilton Time
Timing Gear Cover or Gasket, Renew	
All models	.7
Renew inj. pump drive gear	
add	.4
w/A.C. add	.2

LABOR 16 CAMSHAFT & TIMING GEARS 16 LABOR

	Chilton Time
Engine Front Cover, Renew	
All models	2.9
w/A.C. add	.2

	Chilton Time
Crankshaft and Timing Gears, Renew	
All models	3.4
w/A.C. add	.2

	Chilton Time
Camshaft and Lifters, Renew	
Includes: R&R engine assembly.	
All models	8.5
Renew cam bushings add	1.0
w/A.C. add	.4

LABOR 17 ENGINE OILING SYSTEM 17 LABOR

GASOLINE ENGINES

	Chilton Time
Oil Pan and/or Gasket, Renew	
Includes: R&R engine assy. on 4X4 models, where required.	
Four	
D21 models	
4X2	1.6
4X4	5.9
720 models	
4X2	1.6
4X4	9.5
Axxess	
4X2	2.4
4X4	2.1
Van	1.6
V-6	
4X2	1.8
4X4	3.2
w/A.C. or P.S. add	.4
Oil Pump Assembly, Renew	
Four	
D21 models	
4X2	1.3
4X4	2.1

	Chilton Time
720 models	
4X2	1.1
4X4	1.9
Axxess	
4X2	6.3
4X4	6.0
Van	1.2
V-6	
4X2	11.4
4X4	12.3
Recond oil pump add	.4
Oil Pump Regulator or Relief Valve, Renew	
All models	.6
Oil Pressure Gauge (Dash Unit), Renew	
D21 models	.7
720 models	1.5
Axxess	.9
Van	1.0
Oil Pressure Sending Unit, Renew	
All models	.5

	Chilton Time
Oil Pressure Switch, Renew	
Van	.8
Axxess	.6
D21-720 models	.5
Oil Filter Element, Renew	
All models	.4

DIESEL ENGINE

	Chilton Time
Oil Pan and/or Gasket, Renew	
All models	1.5
Oil Pump, Renew	
All models	1.7
Oil Pump, R&R and Recondition	
All models	2.1
Oil Pump Regulator or Relief Valve, Renew	
All models	.6
Oil Filter Element, Renew	
All models	.4

LABOR 18 CLUTCH & FLYWHEEL 18 LABOR

	Chilton Time
Clutch Pedal Free Play, Adjust	
All models	.3
Bleed Clutch Hydraulic System	
All models	.4
Clutch Damper, Renew	
Includes: Bleed system.	
All models	.6
Clutch Damper, R&R and Recondition	
Includes: Bleed system.	
All models	.9
Clutch Master Cylinder, Renew	
Includes: Bleed system.	
All models	.9
Clutch Master Cylinder, R&R and Recondition	
Includes: Bleed system.	
All models	1.5

	Chilton Time
Clutch Slave Cylinder, Renew	
Includes: Bleed system.	
All models	.7
Clutch Slave Cylinder, R&R and Recondition	
Includes: Bleed system.	
All models	1.0
Clutch Assembly, Renew	
Includes: R&R trans.	
D21 models	
4X2	3.7
4X4	6.6
720 models	
4X2	4.1
4X4	7.0
Axxess	
4X2	4.6
4X4	7.3
Van	3.2
Renew pilot brg add	.3

	Chilton Time
Clutch Release Bearing, Renew	
Includes: R&R trans.	
D21 models	
4X2	3.5
4X4	6.4
720 models	
4X2	4.0
4X4	6.8
Axxess	
4X2	4.4
4X4	7.1
Van	3.0
Flywheel, Renew	
Includes: R&R trans.	
D21 models	
4X2	4.0
4X4	6.9
720 models	
4X2	4.4
4X4	7.4
Axxess	
4X2	4.9
4X4	7.6
Van	3.5
Renew ring gear add	.5
Renew rear main seal add	.3

LABOR — 19 MANUAL TRANSAXLE (FWD) 19 — LABOR

	Chilton Time
Manual Trans/Axle Assy., Remove & Install	
Axxess	
2 WD	4.3
4 WD	7.0
Manual Trans/Axle Assy., R&R and Recondition	
Axxess	
2 WD	7.8
4 WD	12.3

	Chilton Time
Differential Case Assy., R&R and Recondition w/Manual Trans/Axle	
Axxess	10.2
Speedometer Pinion, Renew	
Axxess	.4
Differential Side Oil Seals, Renew	
Axxess-one	1.0
both	1.9

	Chilton Time
Halfshaft Assy., R&R or Renew	
Includes: Renew C.V. joint boots.	
Axxess-one	1.0
both	1.9
Recond joint add-each	.6
Renew center brg add	.3

LABOR — 19A MANUAL TRANSMISSION (RWD) 19A — LABOR

	Chilton Time
Transmission Assy., R&R or Renew	
D21 models	
4X2	3.4
4X4	6.2
720 models	
4X2	3.5
4X4	6.6
Van	2.9
Renew front cover, gasket or seal add	.4

	Chilton Time
Rear Extension Housing and/or Gasket, Renew	
Includes: R&R trans.	
D21 models	
4X2	4.3
4X4	6.7
720 models	
4X2	4.0
4X4	6.8
Van	3.2
Renew rear oil seal add	.2
Speedometer Pinion, Renew	
All models	.4

	Chilton Time
Transmission Assy., R&R and Recondition	
Includes: Completely disassemble, clean, inspect, renew all parts as required. Install all new gaskets and seals.	
4 Speed	
720 models	10.9
5 Speed	
D21 models	
4X2	6.6
4X4	
Four	12.0
V-6	13.0
720 models	
4X2	7.1
4X4	10.5
Van	10.6

LABOR — 20 TRANSFER CASE 20 — LABOR

	Chilton Time
720 MODELS	
Transfer Case Assembly, Remove & Install	
720 models	1.7
Transfer Case Housings, Renew	
Includes: R&R transfer case assy.	
720 models	3.6
Companion Flanges, Renew (Front or Rear)	
720 models	.7
Transmission Side Flange, Renew	
Includes: R&R transfer case assy.	
720 models	2.0
Speedometer Drive Gear, Renew	
Includes: Renew rear drive shaft oil seal.	
720 models	1.2
Front or Rear Cover Oil Seals, Renew	
Includes: R&R companion flange.	
720 models	.9
Transfer Case Front Cover, R&R or Renew	
Includes: R&R transfer case assy.	
720 models	3.4

	Chilton Time
Transfer Case Front Oil Seal, Renew	
Includes: R&R transfer case assy.	
720 models	2.0
Transfer Case Assy., R&R and Recondition	
Includes: Complete disassembly, clean, inspect, renew all parts as required. Install all new gaskets and seals.	
720 models	4.5
Transfer Case Mount and Insulator, Renew	
Includes: Disconnect transfer case as required.	
720 models	1.6
D21 MODELS	
Transfer Case Assy., R&R or Renew	
D21 models	4.5
Transfer Case Assy., R&R and Recondition	
D21 models	8.6
Transfer Case Front Cover, Renew	
D21 models	4.7
Renew front case add	.4
Rear or Center Case Oil Seals, Renew	
D21 models	.8

	Chilton Time
Transfer Case Front Cover Oil Seal, Renew	
D21 models	5.4
Speedometer Drive Gear, Renew	
D21 models	1.0
Companion Flange, Renew	
D21 models	.6
Transfer Case Drive Chain, Renew	
D21 models	2.0
AXXESS	
Transfer Case Assy., Remove & Install	
Axxess	
w/M.T.	8.8
w/A.T.	7.5
Transfer Case Assy., R&R and Recondition	
Axxess	
w/M.T.	12.7
w/A.T.	11.4
Transfer Case Front Oil Seal, Renew	
Axxess	
w/M.T.	1.4
w/A.T.	2.4
Companion Flange, Renew	
Axxess	.6

LABOR 23 AUTOMATIC TRANSAXLE (FWD) 23 LABOR

ON CAR SERVICES

	Chilton Time
Speedometer Pinion, Renew	
Axxess	
2 WD models	.4
4 WD models	1.0
Throttle Cable, Renew	
Axxess	1.5
Differential Side Oil Seals, Renew	
Axxess	
one	1.0
both	1.9
Neutral Safety Switch, Renew	
Axxess	.5
Valve Body Assembly, Renew	
Includes: R&R oil pan.	
Axxess	1.5
Valve Body Assy., R&R and Recondition	
Includes: R&R oil pan.	
Axxess	3.5

	Chilton Time
Overdrive Cancel Solenoid, Renew	
Axxess	1.7
Overdrive Cancel/Power Switch, Renew	
Axxess	.4
Lock-Up Solenoid, Renew	
Axxess	1.7
SERVICES REQUIRING R&R	
Automatic Trans/Axle Assy., Remove & Install	
Axxess	
2 WD models	5.6
4 WD models	7.5
Automatic Trans/Axle Assy., R&R and Recondition	
Axxess	
2 WD models	15.6
4 WD models	17.7

	Chilton Time
Flywheel (Flexplate) Renew	
Includes: R&R trans/axle.	
Axxess	
2 WD models	5.9
4 WD models	7.8
Torque Converter, Renew	
Includes: R&R trans/axle.	
Axxess	
2 WD models	6.1
4 WD models	8.0
Parking Pawl, Renew	
Includes: R&R trans/axle.	
Axxess	
2 WD models	6.5
4 WD models	8.4
Differential Case, Recondition	
Includes: R&R trans/axle.	
Axxess	
2 WD models	8.1
4 WD models	10.1

LABOR 23 AUTOMATIC TRANSMISSION 23 LABOR

ON TRUCK SERVICES

	Chilton Time
Drain & Refill Unit	
All models	.8
Oil Pressure Check	
All models	.7
Check Unit For Oil Leaks	
Includes: Clean and dry outside of case and run unit to determine point of leak.	
All models	.9
Vacuum Diaphragm Assy., Renew	
All models	.5
Kickdown Switch, Renew	
All models	.5
Downshift Solenoid, Renew	
All models	.8
Neutral Safety Switch, Renew	
All models	.6
Speedometer Pinion, Renew	
Includes: Renew oil seal.	
All models	.5
Overdrive Cancel Solenoid, Renew	
All models	.6
Overdrive Indicator Switch, Renew	
All models	.6
Overdrive Cancel/Power Switch, Renew	
All models	.6
Lock-Up Solenoid, Renew	
All models	.6
Extension Housing Oil Seal, Renew	
All models	1.0
Oil Pan Gasket, Renew	
All models	.8
Valve Body Assembly, Renew	
Includes: R&R oil pan.	
All models	1.7
Valve Body Assy., R&R and Recondition	
Includes: R&R oil pan. Clean, inspect, free all valves. Replace parts as required.	
All models	3.0

	Chilton Time
SERVICES REQUIRING R&R	
Transmission and Torque Converter Assy., Remove & Install	
Includes: Drain and refill unit.	
Van	4.5
All other models	
4X2	4.0
4X4	7.8
Transmission and Torque Converter Assy., R&R and Recondition	
Includes: Completely disassemble trans, including valve body. Clean, inspect, replace all parts as required. Make all necessary adjustments. Road test.	
All models	
4X2	14.7
4X4	18.0
Pressure check add	.8
Torque Converter, Renew	
Includes: R&R trans.	
Van	4.7
All other models	
4X2	4.2
4X4	8.0
Renew flywheel add	.4
Governor Assy., R&R or Renew	
Includes: R&R trans.	
Van	5.0
All other models	
4X2	5.0
4X4	8.8
Recond gover add	.4
Front Oil Pump, Renew or Recondition	
Includes: R&R trans. Renew pump seals and gaskets.	
Van	5.1
All other models	
4X2	4.7
4X4	8.5

ELECTRONIC AUTOMATIC TRANS

ON CAR SERVICES

	Chilton Time
Drain & Refill Unit	
All models	1.0

	Chilton Time
Check Unit for Oil Leaks	
Includes: Clean and dry outside of case and run unit to determine point of leak.	
All models	.9
Lock-Up Solenoid, Renew	
All models	1.2
Control Unit, Renew	
All models	.5
Control Solenoids and/or Seals, Renew	
All models	2.0
Speed Sensor, Renew	
All models	.6
Dropping Resistor, Renew	
All models	.5
Oil Pan and/or Gasket, Renew	
All models	1.0
Valve Body Assembly, Renew	
Includes: R&R oil pan.	
All models	1.8
Valve Body Assy., R&R and Recondition	
Includes: R&R oil pan.	
All models	3.5

SERVICES REQUIRING R&R

	Chilton Time
Front Pump Assy., R&R and Recondition	
Includes: R&R transmission.	
All models	8.6
Reverse and High Clutch Assy., Recondition	
Includes: R&R transmission.	
All models	9.8
Forward and Overrunning Clutches, Recondition	
Includes: R&R transmission.	
All models	11.4
Brake Band and Servo Assy., Recondition	
Includes: R&R transmission.	
All models	8.8
Transmission Assembly, R&R and Recondition (Complete)	
All models	20.0

LABOR 25 U-JOINTS & DRIVESHAFT 25 LABOR

	Chilton Time
Driveshaft, Renew	
2 Joint Shaft	
All models	.5
3 Joint Shaft	
Axxess	.6
All other models	.6

	Chilton Time
Universal Joint, Renew or Recondition (One)	
Includes: R&R driveshaft.	
2 Joint Shaft	
All models	.9
3 Joint Shaft	
Axxess	1.2
All other models	1.0

	Chilton Time
Center Bearing, Renew	
Includes: R&R driveshaft.	
Axxess	1.2
All other models	1.0

LABOR 26 DRIVE AXLE 26 LABOR

REAR DIFFERENTIAL ASSY.
INTEGRAL CARRIER

	Chilton Time
Rear Axle Shaft and/or Bearing, Renew	
Includes: Renew oil seal.	
With Single Rear Whls	
one side	1.4
both sides	2.7
With Dual Rear Whls	
one side	.6
both sides	1.2
Rear Wheel Hub Assy., Renew	
With Dual Rear Wheels	
All models-one	1.0
both	1.9
Axle Shaft Oil Seal, Renew	
All models-one	.9
both	1.7
Drive Pinion Oil Seal, Renew	
All models	
Four	5.3
V-6	1.3
Rear Differential Carrier Assy., Remove and Install	
All models	2.5
Ring Gear and Pinion Set, Renew	
Includes: R&R carrier assy. and make all necessary adjustments.	
All models	3.8
Differential Side Bearings, Renew	
Includes: R&R carrier assy. and make all necessary adjustments.	
All models	2.6
Rear Differential Carrier Assy., R&R and Recondition	
All models	4.8

FRONT DIFFERENTIAL

	Chilton Time
Differential, Drain & Refill	
All models	1.1
Rear Cover Gasket, Renew	
All models	1.1
Differential Assy., Remove & Install	
D21 models	4.5
720 models	1.5

	Chilton Time
Differential Assy., R&R and Recondition	
D21 models	8.6
720 models	6.0
Ring and Pinion Set, Renew	
Includes: R&R differential.	
D21 models	7.5
720 models	5.0
Side Flange or Oil Seals, Renew	
All models-one	1.6
both	3.1
Drive Pinion Oil Seal, Renew	
All models	1.7
Front Drive Shaft Assy., R&R or Renew	
All models	.6
Renew U-Joint add-each	.3
Primary Drive Shaft, Renew	
All models	.8
Renew U-Joint add-each	.3
Front Wheel Hub Assy., Renew	
Includes: Renew bearings and seals.	
Nissan models	
one side	.9
both sides	1.7
Datsun models	
one side	1.9
both sides	3.7
Front Drive Axle Assy., Renew	
720 models-one	1.4
both	2.7
Front Drive Shaft Boot, Renew	
All models-one	2.0
both	3.9

DUAL WHEEL DIFFERENTIAL

	Chilton Time
Drain & Refill Unit	
All models	.6
Rear Cover Gasket, Renew	
All models	.6
Drive Pinion Oil Seal, Renew	
Includes: R&R carrier assy.	
All models	5.3
Differential Side Bearings and Seals, Renew	
All models	5.3

	Chilton Time
Ring Gear and Pinion Set, Renew	
All models	7.1
Renew pinion gears add	.5

REMOVABLE CARRIER

	Chilton Time
Differential Cover Gasket, Renew	
All models	.6
Ring Gear and Pinion Assy., Renew	
All models	4.9
Differential Side Gears, Renew	
All models	3.2
Pinion Oil Seal, Renew	
Van	2.8
D21 models	5.3
Rear Axle Shaft and/or Bearings, Renew	
All models-one	1.5
both	2.9
Axle Shaft Oil Seals, Renew	
D21 models	
one side	1.2
both sides	2.3
Van	
one side	.8
both sides	1.5

AXXESS

	Chilton Time
Rear Differential Assy., Remove & Install	
All models	1.9
Rear Differential Assy., R&R and Recondition	
All models	6.0
Ring Gear and Pinion Assy., Renew	
All models	4.6
Differential Side Bearings, Renew	
All models	3.0
Drive Pinion Oil Seal, Renew	
All models	4.7
Side Flange Oil Seals, Renew	
All models-one	.8
both	1.5
Rear Cover Gasket, Renew	
All models	2.0

LABOR 27 REAR SUSPENSION 27 LABOR

LEAF SPRING SUSPENSION

	Chilton Time
Rear Leaf Spring, Renew	
All models-one	1.8
both	3.5

	Chilton Time
Rear Spring Shackle and/or Bushings, Renew	
With Single Rear Whls	
All models-one side	.6
both sides	1.1
With Dual Rear Whls	
All models-one side	.9

	Chilton Time
both sides	1.7
Rear Spring Front Eye Mount and/or Bushings, Renew	
All models-one side	1.0
both sides	1.9

LABOR 27 REAR SUSPENSION 27 LABOR

	Chilton Time
Rear Shock Absorber or Rubber Bushing, Renew	
D21 models-one	.5
both	.7
720 models-one	.7
both	1.1

LINK TYPE SUSPENSION

	Chilton Time
Rear Shock Absorbers, Renew	
All models-one	.4
both	.6
Upper Link and/or Bushings, Renew	
All models-one	.4
both	.6
Lower Link and/or Bushings, Renew	
All models-one	.4
both	.6
Rear Coil Springs, Renew	
All models-one	1.3
both	2.5

	Chilton Time
Rear Stabilizer Bar or Connecting Rod, Renew	
Van	.8
D21 models	.7

INDEPENDENT REAR SUSPENSION

	Chilton Time
Rear Halfshaft Assy., R&R or Renew	
All models-one	.8
both	1.5

Rear Halfshaft Assy., R&R and Recondition
Includes: Renew boots and renew or recondition C.V. joints.

	Chilton Time
All models-one side	1.4
both sides	2.7
Lower Link or Bracket, Renew	
2 WD models	.6
4 WD models	.5
Parrallel Rods, Renew	
2 WD models	.5
4 WD models	.6

	Chilton Time
Rear Strut Assy., R&R or Renew	
2 WD models	
one	1.8
both	3.5
4 WD models	
one	1.0
both	1.9
Rear Axle Shaft Oil Seals, Renew	
2 WD models	
one	.8
both	1.5
4 WD models	
one	1.6
both	3.1
Rear Axle Bearings, Renew	
All models-one side	1.9
both sides	3.7
Rear Stabilizer Bar and/or Bushings, Renew	
All models	.6
Rear Knuckle Spindle, Renew	
All models	2.3
Rear Wheel Hub, Renew	
All models	.8

LABOR 28 AIR CONDITIONING 28 LABOR

	Chilton Time
Note: If more than one item requires replacement where evacuation and discharging the system is already included in the operation, deduct 1.0 hour for each additional item to the times listed.	
Drain, Evacuate & Recharge System	
All models	1.0

Flush Refrigerant System, Complete
To be used in conjunction with component replacement which could contaminate system.

	Chilton Time
All models	1.3
Compressor Drive Belt, Renew	
Axxess	.6
All other models	.7

Compressor Assembly, Renew
Includes: Transfer parts as required. Evacuate and charge system.

	Chilton Time
Van-D21 models	2.3
Axxess-720 models	2.5

Compressor Shaft Seal, Renew
Includes: R&R compressor. Evacuate and charge system.

	Chilton Time
D21 models	3.0
720 models	3.2
Van-Axxess	3.2
Compressor Relay, Renew	
All models	.5
A.C. Relay, Renew	
D21 models	.4

Compressor Assembly, R&R and Recondition
Includes: Completely disassemble compressor. Clean, inspect and renew all parts as required. Evacuate and charge system.

	Chilton Time
Van-D21 models	3.6
Axxess-720 models	3.8
Condenser Fan and Motor Assy., Renew	
Van-one	1.7
both	2.5
Axxess	1.3
Low Pressure Switch, Renew	
All models	.4

Expansion Valve, Renew
Includes: R&R evaporate. Evacuate and charge system.

	Chilton Time
D21 models	3.6
720 models	2.4
Axxess	2.1
Van	2.2
Blower Motor, Renew	
D21 models	2.5
720 models	.5
Axxess	.5
Van	1.0
A.C. Temperature Control Assy., Renew	
D21 models	1.4
720 models	1.0
Axxess	.8
Van	.8
Renew fan switch add	.2

Evaporator Assembly, Renew
Includes: Evacuate and charge system.

	Chilton Time
D21 models	3.6
720 models	2.4
Axxess	2.1
Van	2.2
Renew thermo switch add	.3

Receiver-Drier Assembly, Renew
Includes: Evacuate and charge system.

	Chilton Time
All models	1.8

Condenser Assembly, Renew
Includes: Evacuate and charge system.

	Chilton Time
D21 models	2.0
720 models	2.4
Axxess	2.4
Van	1.8

Air Conditioning Hoses, Renew
Includes: Evacuate and charge system.

	Chilton Time
All models-one	1.9
each adtnl	.5

Rear A.C. Evaporator Assy., Renew
Includes: Evacuate and charge system.

	Chilton Time
Van	3.0

Rear A.C. Blower Motor, Renew
Add time to evacuate and charge system if required.

	Chilton Time
Van	1.2

LABOR 29 LOCKS, HINGES & WIND. REGULATORS 29 LABOR

	Chilton Time
Hood Hinge, Renew (One)	
All models	.6
Hood Lock, Renew	
All models	.6

	Chilton Time
Hood Release Cable Assy., Renew	
Axxess	.9
All other models	.7
Door Window Regulator, Renew	
Includes: R&R window glass.	
D21 models	1.5

	Chilton Time
720 models	1.3
Axxess	.8
Van	.9
Power Window Regulator Motor, Renew	
Axxess	1.0
Van	1.7

LABOR 29 LOCKS, HINGES & WIND. REGULATORS 29 LABOR

	Chilton Time		Chilton Time		Chilton Time
D21-720 models	1.5	**Door Lock Assembly, Renew (One)**		**Door Lock Remote Control Rod, Renew (One)**	
		Van-D21 models	.7	D21 models	.6
		720 models	.9	720 models	.8
Door Handle (Outside), Renew		Axxess	.6	Axxess	.6
D21 models	.6	**Door Lock Cylinder, Renew (One)**		Van	.7
720 models	.8	Van	.7	**Lock Striker Plate, Renew**	
		All other models	.5	All models	.4

LABOR 30 HEAD AND PARKING LAMPS 30 LABOR

	Chilton Time		Chilton Time		Chilton Time
Aim Headlamps		**Turn Signal or Parking Lamp Lens or Bulb, Renew**		**Back-Up Lamp Assembly, Renew**	
two	.4	All models-each	.3	All models-each	.3
four	.6			**Rear Combination Lamp Assy., Renew**	
Headlamp Sealed Beam Bulb, Renew (One)		**Stop and Tail Lamp Lens or Bulb, Renew**		All models-each	.4
All models	.3	All models-each	.3	**License Lamp Assembly, Renew**	
Halogen Headlamp Bulb, Renew		**Side Marker Lamp Lens or Bulb, Renew**		All models	.3
Van	.4	All models-each	.3	**High Mount Stop Lamp Assy., Renew**	
D21 models	.3			Axxess	.4

LABOR 31 WINDSHIELD WIPER & SPEEDOMETER 31 LABOR

	Chilton Time		Chilton Time		Chilton Time
Windshield Wiper Motor, Renew		**Rear Window Wiper and Washer Switch, Renew**		Axxess	.9
All models	.7	All models	.4	Van	1.0
Axxess add	.1	**Rear Window Wiper Motor, Renew**		**Speedometer Cable and Casing, Renew**	
Windshield Wiper Rods or Pivots, Renew		Van-Axxess	.5	D21 models	.9
All models	.8	D21 models	.8	720 models	.7
Axxess add	.1	**Rear Window Washer Motor, Renew**		Van	1.3
Intermittent Wiper Amplifier, Renew		Van	.3	**Radio, R&R**	
All models	.4	Axxess	.7	D21 models	1.0
Windshield Washer Motor, Renew		D21 models	.4	720 models	1.5
D21-720 models	.4	**Rear Window Intermittent Wiper Relay, Renew**		Axxess	1.0
Axxess	.6	D21 models	.4	Van	1.3
Van	.5	**Speedometer Head, R&R or Renew**		**Antenna, Renew**	
Windshield Wiper/Washer Switch, Renew		D21 models	.7	Axxess	.4
All models	.6	720 models	1.5	Van	.4
				D21 models	.3
				720 models	.4

LABOR 32 LIGHT SWITCHES & WIRING 32 LABOR

	Chilton Time		Chilton Time		Chilton Time
Hazard Warning Switch, Renew		**Stop Lamp Switch, Renew**		**Turn Signal or Hazard Warning Flasher Unit, Renew**	
All models	.6	All models	.5	All models	.3
Wiper/Washer Switch Assy., Renew		**Back-Up Lamp Switch, Renew (w/Manual Trans.)**		**Horn Assembly, Renew**	
All models	.6	All models	.5	Van-one	.6
Combination Switch Assy., Renew		**Parking Brake Warning Lamp Switch, Renew**		All other models-one	.3
Axxess	.2	All models	.4	**Horn Relay, Renew**	
All other models	.9			All models	.4

LABOR 34 CRUISE CONTROL 34 LABOR

	Chilton Time		Chilton Time		Chilton Time
Cruise Control Circuits, Test		**Solenoid or Servo Valve, Renew**		**Controller Assembly, Renew**	
All models	1.0	All models	.5	All models	.6
Cruise Control Cable, Renew				**Cruise Control Clutch Switch, Renew**	
All models	.6			All models	.4
Actuator Assembly, Renew		**Cruise Control Speed Switch, Renew (Sensor)**		**Cruise Control Stop Switch, Renew**	
All models	.5	Van	.6	All models	.4
Cruise Control Master Switch, Renew		D21 models	.6	**Cruise Control Relay, Renew**	
All models	.5	720 models	.8	All models	.6

GROUP INDEX

ALPHABETICAL INDEX

LABOR — 1 TUNE UP 1 — LABOR

Compression Test
All models 6

Engine Tune Up, (Electronic Ignition)
Includes: Test battery and clean connections. Tighten manifold and carburetor mounting bolts. Check engine compression, clean and adjust or renew spark plugs. Test resistance of spark plug cables. Inspect distributor cap and rotor. Check vacuum advance operation. Reset ignition timing. Adjust idle mixture and idle speed. Service air cleaner. Inspect and adjust drive belts. Inspect choke operation and adjust or free up. Check operation of EGR valve.
All models 1.5

LABOR — 2 IGNITION SYSTEM 2 — LABOR

Spark Plugs, Clean and Reset or Renew
Samuri 5
Swift 6
Sidekick 5

Ignition Timing, Reset
All models 4

Distributor, Renew
Includes: Reset ignition timing.
Samuri 8
Swift 7
Sidekick 8

Distributor, R&R and Recondition
Samuri 1.3
Swift 1.2
Sidekick 1.3

Distributor Cap and/or Rotor, Renew
All models 3

Ignition Coil, Renew
Includes: Test coil.
All models 4

Ignition Switch Lock Cylinder, Renew
All models 1.2

Vacuum Control Unit, Renew
Includes: Reset ignition timing.
Samuri 1.1
Swift 1.0
Sidekick 1.1

Igniter Assembly, Renew (Signal Generator)
Samuri 1.1
Swift 1.0
Sidekick 1.1

Ignition Cables, Renew
All models 4

LABOR — 3 FUEL SYSTEM 3 — LABOR

Fuel Pump, Test
Includes: Disconnect line at carburetor, attach pressure gauge.
All models 3

Carburetor Air Cleaner, Service
All models 2

Air Cleaner Vacuum Motor, Renew
All models 4

Air Cleaner Temperature Sensor, Renew
All models 5

Fuel Filter, Renew
Samuri 4
Sidekick 4

Carburetor, Renew
Includes: All necessary adjustments.
All models 1.8

Carburetor, R&R and Recondition
Includes: All necessary adjustments.
All models 3.0

Needle Valve and Seat, Renew
Includes: Renew or adjust float.
All models 2.3

Choke System, Adjust
Sidekick 5

Fuel Gauge (Tank), Renew
Samuri 1.5
Swift 1.0
Sidekick 1.3

Fuel Gauge (Dash Unit), Renew
Samuri 1.1
Swift 1.1
Sidekick 1.4

Fuel Tank, Renew
Includes: Drain and refill tank.
Samuri 1.5
Swift 1.4
Sidekick 1.5

Mechanical Fuel Pump, Renew
Samuri 5
Sidekick 5

Intake Manifold or Gasket, Renew
Samuri 1.8
Swift
SOHC eng 2.2
DOHC eng 2.2
Sidekick 2.9
Renew manif add 5

FUEL INJECTION (SWIFT)

Fuel Injectors, Clean (On Car)
Includes: Hook up pressurized fuel injection cleaning equipment.
All models 5

Fuel Filter Assembly, Renew
All models 8

Electric Fuel Pump, Renew (In Tank)
All models 1.4

Fuel Rail, R&R or Renew
All models 1.6

Fuel Injectors, R&R or Renew (All)
All models 1.9
Clean and test add-each 2

Air Flow Meter and/or Gasket, Renew
All models 8

Throttle Body and/or Gasket, Renew
All models 1.0

Throttle Position Sensor, Renew
All models 8

Fuel Injector Assy., Renew (TBI)
All models 7

FUEL INJECTION (SIDEKICK)

Fuel Injectors, Clean (On Car)
Includes: Hook up pressurized fuel injection cleaning equipment.
All models 5

Fuel Filter Assembly, Renew
All models 7

Electric Fuel Pump, Renew (In Tank)
All models 1.3

Throttle Body and/or Gasket, Renew
All models 1.7

Mixture Control Assy., and/or Gasket, Renew
All models 1.9

Fuel Injector Assembly, Renew
All models 9

Solenoid Assembly, Renew
All models 7

Fuel Pressure Regulator, Renew
All models 5

Throttle Valve Body Assy., Renew
All models 2.0

LABOR 3A EMISSION CONTROLS 3A LABOR

	Chilton Time		Chilton Time		Chilton Time
Emission Control Computer, Renew		**PCV Valve, Renew**		**EGR Valve, Renew**	
Swift	.7	Samuri	.3	All models	.6
Sidekick	.6	Swift	.5	**EGR Modulator Valve, Renew**	
Samuri	.5	Sidekick	.4	Swift	.4
Oxygen Sensor, Renew		**Vacuum Delay Valve, Renew**		Samuri-Sidekick	.3
Swift	.7	All models	.3	**Charcoal Canister, Renew**	
Samuri-Sidekick	.4	**Vacuum Switching Valve, Renew**		Samuri	.3
Coolant Temperature Sensor, Renew		Sidekick	.3	Swift-Sidekick	.4
All models	.4	**Mixture Control Valve, Renew**		**Fuel Vapor Separator, Renew**	
Solenoid and Vacuum Regulator Assy., Renew		Samuri	.3	All models	.4
		Barometric Pressure Sensor, Renew		**Hot Idle Compensator, Renew**	
All models	.5	Swift	.4	Samuri	.4
		Sidekick	.4	Sidekick	.5

LABOR 4 ALTERNATOR AND REGULATOR 4 LABOR

	Chilton Time		Chilton Time		Chilton Time
Alternator Circuits, Test		**Alternator, R&R and Recondition**		Swift	1.4
Includes: Test battery, regulator and alternator output.		Includes: Complete disassembly, inspect, test, replace parts as required, reassemble.		Sidekick	1.2
All models	.5	Samuri	2.0		
Alternator Assy., Renew		Swift	2.1	**Voltage Regulator, Test and Renew**	
Includes: Transfer pulley or fan.		Sidekick	1.9	Samuri	1.4
Samuri	1.0			Swift	1.5
Swift	1.1			Sidekick	1.3
Sidekick	.9	**Alternator Bearings, Renew**		**Voltmeter, Renew**	
Add circuit test if performed.		Includes: R&R alternator, separate end frames.		Sidekick	.9
		Samuri	1.3		

LABOR 5 STARTING SYSTEM 5 LABOR

	Chilton Time		Chilton Time		Chilton Time
Starter Draw Test (On Truck)		**Starter Drive, Renew**		**Battery Cables, Renew**	
All models	.3	Includes: R&R starter.		Samuri	.4
Starter Assy., Renew		Samuri	1.0	each	.4
Samuri	.6	Swift	1.5	Swift	
Swift	1.1	Sidekick	1.5	positive	.4
Sidekick	1.1			negative	.3
Add draw test if performed.				Sidekick	
Starter, R&R and Recondition				each	.4
Includes: Turn down armature.		**Starter Solenoid, Renew**			
Samuri	2.0	Includes: R&R starter.		**Battery Terminals, Clean**	
Swift	2.4	Samuri	.9	All models	.3
Sidekick	2.3	Swift	1.4		
Renew field coils add	.5	Sidekick	1.4		

LABOR 6 BRAKE SYSTEM 6 LABOR

	Chilton Time		Chilton Time		Chilton Time
Brake Pedal Free Play, Adjust		Rear-Drum		**Wheel Cylinders, R&R and Rebuild**	
All models	.3	Samuri-Sidekick	1.8	Includes: Bleed system.	
Brakes, Adjust (Minor)		Swift	1.5	Samuri-Sidekick	
Includes: Adjust brake shoes and fill master cylinder.		Resurface brake rotor, add-each	.5	one	1.9
All models	.4	Resurface brake drum, add-each	.5	both	3.0
Bleed Brakes (Four Wheels)		**Rear Brake Drum, Renew (One)**		Swift	
Includes: Fill master cylinder.		Samuri-Sidekick	.9	one	1.8
All models	.6	Swift	1.0	both	2.6
Brake Shoes and/or Pads, Renew				**Master Cylinder, Renew**	
Includes: Install new or exchange brake shoes or pads, adjust service and hand brake. Bleed system.		**BRAKE HYDRAULIC SYSTEM**		Includes: Bleed system.	
		Wheel Cylinders, Renew		Samuri	.9
Front-Disc		Includes: Bleed system.		Swift	1.0
Samuri-Sidekick	1.5	Samuri-Sidekick		Sidekick	1.3
Swift	1.2	one	1.7		
		both	2.6	**Master Cylinder, R&R and Rebuild**	
		Swift		Includes: Bleed system.	
		one	1.6	Samuri	1.3
		both	2.2	Swift	1.4

LABOR   6 BRAKE SYSTEM 6   LABOR

	Chilton Time
Sidekick	1.7

Brake Hose, Renew (Flex)
Includes: Bleed system.

	Chilton Time
Samuri	
front-one	.9
rear-one	.9
Swift	
front-one	1.1
rear-one	1.1
Sidekick	
front-one	.9
rear-one	.9
each adtnl	.3

Proportioning Valve, Renew
Includes: Bleed system.

	Chilton Time
Samuri	1.3
Swift	1.6
Sidekick	1.3

DISC BRAKES

Disc Brake Pads, Renew
Includes: Install new disc brake pads only.

	Chilton Time
Samuri-Sidekick	1.5
Swift	
front	1.2
rear	1.2
all four wheels	2.2

Caliper Assy., Renew
Includes: Bleed system.

	Chilton Time
Samuri-Sidekick	
one	1.2
both	1.8
Swift	
front-one	1.2
both	1.9
rear-one	1.5
both	2.0
all four wheels	3.7

COMBINATIONS

	Chilton Time
RENEW WHEEL CYLINDER	
Each	.2
REBUILD WHEEL CYLINDER	
Each	.2
REBUILD CALIPER ASSEMBLY	
Each	.4
RENEW MASTER CYLINDER	
All models	.5
REBUILD MASTER CYLINDER	
All models	.8
RENEW BRAKE HOSE	
Each	.3
REPACK FRONT WHEEL BEARINGS (BOTH WHEELS)	
All models	.6
RENEW BRAKE DRUM	
Each	.1
RENEW DISC BRAKE ROTOR	
Each	.2

Caliper Assy., R&R and Recondition
Includes: Bleed system.

	Chilton Time
Samuri-Sidekick	
one	1.6
both	2.6
Swift	
front-one	1.6
both	2.7
rear-one	1.9
both	2.8
all four wheels	5.0

Disc Brake Rotor, Renew

	Chilton Time
Samuri-Sidekick	
one	.9
both	1.3
Swift	
front-one	1.2
both	2.1
rear-one	.9
both	1.5
all four wheels	3.4

POWER BRAKES

Power Brake Booster, Renew

	Chilton Time
Samuri	1.4
Swift	1.5
Sidekick	1.7
Recond booster add	.5

Vacuum Check Valve, Renew

	Chilton Time
All models	.3

PARKING BRAKE

Parking Brake, Adjust

	Chilton Time
All models	.5

Parking Brake Lever Assy., Renew

	Chilton Time
Samuri	.5
Swift	.6
Sidekick	.8

Parking Brake Cables, Renew

	Chilton Time
Samuri	
front	.8
rear	.8
Swift	
one or one side	1.3
both sides	1.7
Sidekick	
one	1.3
both	1.7

LABOR   7 COOLING SYSTEM 7   LABOR

Winterize Cooling System
Includes: Run engine to check for leaks, tighten all hose connections. Test radiator and pressure cap, drain radiator and engine block. Add antifreeze and refill system.

	Chilton Time
All models	.5

Thermostat, Renew

	Chilton Time
Samuri	.4
Swift	.6
Sidekick	.5

Radiator Assy., R&R or Renew
Includes: Drain and refill cooling system.

	Chilton Time
Samuri	1.4
Swift	1.2
w/A.C. add	.7
Sidekick	1.3

ADD THESE OPERATIONS TO RADIATOR R&R

	Chilton Time
Boil & Repair	1.5
Rod Clean	1.9
Repair Core	1.3
Renew Tank	1.6
Renew Trans. Oil Cooler	1.9
Recore Radiator	1.7

Radiator Hoses, Renew

	Chilton Time
All models	
upper	.5
lower	.7

Fan Blades or Clutch Assy., Renew

	Chilton Time
Samuri	1.0
Swift	.9
Sidekick	1.4

Water Pump Drive Belt, Renew

	Chilton Time
Samuri	.8
Swift	.6
Sidekick	.6

Water Pump Drive Belt, Adjust

	Chilton Time
All models	.3

Cooling Fan and/or Motor, Renew

	Chilton Time
Samuri	1.3
Swift	1.0
Sidekick	1.3

Water Pump By-Pass Hose, Renew

	Chilton Time
Samuri	.5
Sidekick	.6

Water Pump, Renew
Includes: Drain and refill cooling system.

	Chilton Time
Samuri	3.2
Swift	3.0
Sidekick	3.6

Cooling Fan Switch, Renew

	Chilton Time
Swift	.5

Water Jacket Expansion Plugs, Renew (Side of Block)

	Chilton Time
each	.5

Note: If necessary to R&R any component to gain access to plug, add appropriate time.

Heater Water Control Valve, Renew

	Chilton Time
Samuri	.8

Temperature Gauge Sending Unit, Renew

	Chilton Time
Samuri	.5
Swift	.5
Sidekick	.4

Heater Core, R&R or Renew
Includes: Drain and refill cooling system.

	Chilton Time
Samuri	4.5
Swift	2.8
Sidekick	
wo/A.C.	4.5
w/A.C.	5.8

ADD THESE OPERATIONS TO HEATER CORE R&R

	Chilton Time
Boil & Repair	1.2
Repair Core	.9
Recore	1.2

Heater Blower Motor, Renew

	Chilton Time
Samuri	4.3
Swift	.6

Heater Blower Motor Resistor, Renew

	Chilton Time
Samuri	4.2
Swift	.6
Sidekick	.5

Heater Blower Motor Switch, Renew

	Chilton Time
Samuri	1.0
Sidekick	.6

LABOR   7   COOLING SYSTEM   7   LABOR

	Chilton Time		Chilton Time		Chilton Time
Temperature Control Assy., Renew		**Heater Hoses, Renew**		**Temperature Gauge (Dash Unit), Renew**	
Samuri	2.2	Samuri-each	.4	Samuri	1.1
Swift	1.9	Swift-each	.6	Swift	1.1
Sidekick	2.9	Sidekick-each	.5	Sidekick	1.4

LABOR   8   EXHAUST SYSTEM   8   LABOR

	Chilton Time		Chilton Time		Chilton Time
Muffler, Renew		**Exhaust Pipes, Renew**		**Exhaust Manifold and/or Gasket, Renew**	
Samuri	.9	Samuri		Samuri	1.3
Swift	.8	center	.8	Swift	
Sidekick	.8	Swift		SOHC eng	1.5
Catalytic Converter, Renew		each	.7	DOHC eng	1.5
All models	1.0	Sidekick		Sidekick	1.4
		center	.9		

LABOR   9   FRONT SUSPENSION & HALFSHAFTS (FWD)   9   LABOR

	Chilton Time		Chilton Time		Chilton Time
Note: On all front suspension operations alignment charges must be added if performed. Time given does not include alignment.		**Front Strut Shock Absorbers, Renew**		**Front Wheel Bearings, Renew**	
		All models-one	1.2	All models-one side	2.0
		both	1.8	both sides	3.3
		Renew springs add-each	.1	**Front Wheel Grease Seals, Renew**	
Wheel, Renew		**Steering Knuckle, Renew**		All models-one side	1.9
one	.5	All models-one	1.9	both sides	3.1
Wheels, Rotate (All)		both	3.1		
All models	.5			**FRONT DRIVE AXLE**	
Wheels, Balance		**Lower Control Arm Assy., Renew**		**Halfshaft Assembly, R&R or Renew**	
one	.3	All models-one	1.4	All models-one	1.2
each adtnl	.2	both	1.9	both	2.1
		Renew bushings add-each side	.2	**C.V. Joints, Renew or Recondition**	
Check Alignment of Front End				Includes: R&R halfshaft.	
All models	.5	**Front Stabilizer Bar, Renew**		All models	
Note: Deduct if alignment is performed.		All models	.8	inner & outer	
				one side	1.8
Toe-In, Adjust		**Stabilizer Ball Joints, Renew (All)**		both sides	3.2
All models	.6	All models	.8	**C.V. Joint Boots, Renew**	
Align Front End		**Front Wheel Hub, Renew**		Includes: R&R halfshaft.	
All models	1.4	All models-one	1.3	All models	
		both	2.1	inner & outer	
				one side	1.6

LABOR   9A   FRONT SUSPENSION (RWD)   9A   LABOR

	Chilton Time		Chilton Time		Chilton Time
Note: On all front suspension operations alignment charges must be added if performed. Time given does not include alignment.		**LEAF SPRING SUSPENSION**		**STRUT TYPE SUSPENSION**	
		Front Shock Absorbers, Renew		**Front Strut Assy., R&R or Renew**	
		All models-one	.5	All models-one	1.1
Wheel, Renew		both	.8	both	1.6
one	.5			Renew strut spring add-each	.1
Wheels, Rotate (All)		**Front Stabilizer Bar, Renew**		**Steering Knuckle, Renew**	
All models	.5	All models	1.0	All models-one	2.0
Wheels, Balance		**Front Spring, Renew**		both	3.2
one	.3	All models-one	1.3	**Lower Control Arms, Renew**	
each adtnl	.2	both	2.5	All models-one	1.5
		Recond spring add-each	.5	both	2.6
Check Alignment of Front End		**Front Stabilizer Bar Bushings, Renew**		**Front Stabilizer Bar, Renew**	
All models	.5	All models-one	.4	All models	.8
Note: Deduct if alignment is performed.		both	.5	**Lower Ball Joints, Renew**	
		Spring Shackle Bushings, Renew		All models-one	1.5
Toe-In, Adjust		All models		both	2.3
All models	.6	front-one side	.6	**Stabilizer Ball Joints, Renew (All)**	
		both sides	.9	All models	.6
Align Front End		rear-one side	.8	**Front Coil Springs, Renew**	
All models	1.4	both sides	1.5	All models-one	1.0
				both	1.5

LABOR   9A   FRONT SUSPENSION (RWD)   9A   LABOR

4 WHEEL DRIVE FRONT AXLE

SAMURI

	Chilton Time
Axle Shaft Assy., R&R or Renew	
All models	1.9
Axle Shaft Oil Seal, Renew	
All models-one side	2.0
both sides	3.1
Front Spindle Assy., Renew	
All models-one side	1.7
both sides	2.6
Renew bushing add-each	.1
Front Wheel Hub, Renew	
All models-one	1.4
both	2.1
Renew oil seal add-each	.1
Renew hub brg add-each	.1
Steering Knuckle, Renew	
All models-one	3.9

	Chilton Time
Steering Knuckle Pivot (King Pin), Renew	
All models-one side	1.9
both sides	3.4
Steering Knuckle Bearings, Renew	
All models-one side	3.4
both	6.0
Steering Knuckle Retainer Oil Seals, Renew	
All models-one side	.9
both sides	1.4
Locking Hub, Renew or Recondition	
All models-one	.4
both	.7
SIDEKICK	
Front Drivershaft Assy., R&R or Renew	
All models-one	1.1
both	1.7

	Chilton Time
C.V. Joints, Renew or Recondition	
Includes: R&R driveshaft.	
All models	
inner & outer	
one side	1.8
both sides	3.1
C.V. Joint Boots, Renew	
Includes: R&R driveshaft.	
All models	
inner & outer	
one side	1.6
both sides	2.7
Front Hub, Bearing or Seal, Renew	
All models-one side	1.2
both sides	2.0
Locking Hub, Renew or Recondition	
All models-one	.7
both	1.1

LABOR   10   STEERING LINKAGE   10   LABOR

	Chilton Time
Tie Rod or Tie Rod End, Renew	
Includes: Reset toe-in.	
All models-one	1.2
each adtnl	.3

	Chilton Time
Pitman Arm, Renew	
All models	.9
Center Tie Rod Assy., Renew	
Includes: Reset toe-in.	
All models	1.2

	Chilton Time
Steering Damper, Renew	
Samuri	.4
Idler Arm, Renew	
Sidekick	.8

LABOR   11   STEERING GEAR   11   LABOR

	Chilton Time
Steering Wheel, Renew	
Samuri	.4
Swift	.5
Sidekick	.4
Horn Button or Pad, Renew	
All models	.2
Steering Column, R&R or Renew	
Samuri	1.3
Swift	1.2
Sidekick	1.6
MANUAL STEERING	
WORM AND SECTOR TYPE	
Manual Steering Gear, R&R or Renew	
Samuri	1.3
Sidekick	1.3

	Chilton Time
POWER STEERING	
WORM AND SECTOR TYPE	
Power Steering Pump Drive Belt, Renew	
Sidekick	.5
Power Steering Gear, R&R or Renew	
Sidekick	1.9
Power Steering Pump, Renew	
Sidekick	1.5
Power Steering Pump, R&R and Recondition	
Sidekick	2.0
Power Steering Hoses, Renew	
Sidekick	
pressure	.8
return	.6

	Chilton Time
MANUAL RACK AND PINION TYPE	
Manual Rack and Pinion Assy., R&R or Renew	
Swift	3.0
Inner Tie Rod Ends, Renew	
Includes: R&R rack assy.	
Swift-one side	2.5
both sides	2.8
Outer Tie Rod Ends, Renew	
Swift-one side	1.2
both sides	1.7
Tie Rod End Boots, Renew	
Swift-one	1.1
both	1.6
Steering Rack Boot, Renew	
Swift-one	1.5

LABOR   12   CYLINDER HEAD & VALVE SYSTEM   12   LABOR

	Chilton Time
Compression Test	
All models	.6
Cylinder Head Gasket, Renew	
Includes: Clean carbon and make all necessary adjustments.	
Samari	4.5
Swift	
SOHC eng	4.4
DOHC eng	5.6
w/A.C. add	.4
Sidekick	6.1
w/A.C. add	.2

	Chilton Time
Cylinder Head, Renew (wo/Valves)	
Includes: Transfer all component parts, reface valves, clean carbon, make all necessary adjustments.	
Samari	7.5
Swift	
SOHC eng	7.5
DOHC eng	10.9
w/A.C. add	.4
Sidekick	8.8
w/A.C. add	.2

	Chilton Time
Clean Carbon and Grind Valves	
Includes: R&R cylinder head, grind valves and seats. Minor tune up.	
Samari	8.8
Swift	
SOHC eng	9.2
DOHC eng	14.5
w/A.C. add	.4
Sidekick	9.4
w/A.C. add	.2
Rocker Arm Cover Gasket, Renew	
Samari	.5
Swift	.6
Sidekick	.6

LABOR 12 CYLINDER HEAD & VALVE SYSTEM 12 LABOR

	Chilton Time
Rocker Arms and/or Shafts, Renew	
Samari	3.2
Swift	2.1
w/A.C. add	.8
Sidekick	3.8
w/A.C. add	.1

	Chilton Time
Valve Springs and/or Valve Stem Oil Seals, Renew	
Samari	6.3
Swift	
SOHC eng	7.0
DOHC eng	10.0
w/A.C. add	.4
Sidekick	8.3
w/A.C. add	.2

	Chilton Time
Valve Lash Adjustors, Renew	
Swift	3.9
w/A.C. add	.5
Valve Clearance, Adjust	
Swift	1.0
Sidekick	1.1

LABOR 13 ENGINE ASSEMBLY & MOUNTS 13 LABOR

Note: All engine operations listed in this group are for assemblies as supplied by the original equipment manufacturer. Time to replace assemblies from independent rebuilders may vary.

	Chilton Time
Engine Assembly, Remove & Install	
Does not include transfer of any parts or equipment.	
Samari	6.1
Swift	6.7
w/A.C. add	1.0
Sidekick	6.8
w/A.C. add	.2

	Chilton Time
Cylinder Block, Renew (w/All Internal Parts Less Head and Oil Pan)	
Includes: R&R engine assy., transfer all component parts not supplied with replacement engine. Clean carbon, grind valves. Tune engine.	
Samari	11.0
Swift	
SOHC eng	11.6
DOHC eng	13.0
w/A.C. add	1.0
w/A.T. add	1.0
Sidekick	11.7
w/A.C. add	.4

	Chilton Time
Engine Assy., R&R and Recondition	
Includes: Rebore block, install new pistons, pins, rings, rod and main bearings. Clean carbon, grind valves. Tune engine.	
Samari	20.4
Swift	
SOHC eng	23.8
DOHC eng	29.9
w/A.C. add	1.0
Sidekick	21.1
w/A.C. add	.4
Engine Mounts, Renew	
Front	
Samari-one	.8
Sidekick	1.1

LABOR 14 PISTONS, RINGS & BEARINGS 14 LABOR

	Chilton Time
Piston Rings, Renew (All)	
Includes: Remove cylinder top ridge, deglaze cylinder walls. Clean piston and ring grooves. Minor tune up.	
Samari	7.7
Swift	
SOHC eng	6.8
DOHC eng	8.2
w/A.C. add	.5
Sidekick	10.9
w/A.C. add	.2
Pistons or Connecting Rods, Renew (All)	
Includes: Remove cylinder top ridge, deglaze cylinder walls. Minor tune up.	
Samari	8.9
Swift	
SOHC eng	8.0
DOHC eng	9.4
Sidekick	12.1
w/A.C. add	.2
Connecting Rod Bearings, Renew (All)	
Samari	2.7
Swift	2.9
Sidekick	4.9

COMBINATIONS	Chilton Time
DRAIN, EVACUATE & RECHARGE AIR CONDITIONING SYSTEM	
All models	1.0
CARBURETOR, RECONDITION	
All models	1.2
REMOVE CYLINDER TOP RIDGE	
Each	.1
DEGLAZE CYLINDER WALLS	
Each	.1
RECONDITION CYLINDER HEAD (HEAD REMOVED)	
All models	1.5
VALVE GUIDES, RENEW	
Each	.2
OIL FILTER ELEMENT, RENEW	
All models	.3

LABOR 15 CRANKSHAFT & DAMPER 15 LABOR

	Chilton Time
Crankshaft and Main Bearings, Renew	
Includes: R&R engine assy. Check all bearing clearances.	
Samari	11.2
Swift	
w/M.T.	12.2
w/A.T.	13.3
w/A.C. add	.8
Sidekick	12.2
w/A.C. add	.3

	Chilton Time
Rear Main Oil Seal, Renew	
Samari	5.3
Swift	
w/M.T.	8.2
w/A.T.	9.5
Sidekick	8.5
Crankshaft Pulley, Renew	
Samari	.9
Swift	.9
Sidekick	1.0

	Chilton Time
Crankshaft Front Oil Seal, Renew	
Samari	5.4
Swift	4.8
w/A.C. add	.6
Sidekick	7.4
w/A.C. add	.4

LABOR 16 CAMSHAFT & TIMING GEARS 16 LABOR

	Chilton Time		Chilton Time		Chilton Time
Camshaft and/or Oil Seal, Renew		**Timing Belt and/or Tensioner, Renew**		**Timing Belt Covers, R&R or Renew**	
Samari	5.0	Includes: Renew pulleys.		Samari	2.1
Swift	3.9	Samari	3.0	Sidekick	2.2
w/A.C. add	.5	Swift	2.7		
Sidekick	6.9	Sidekick	3.4		
w/A.C. add	.2				

LABOR 17 ENGINE OILING SYSTEM 17 LABOR

	Chilton Time		Chilton Time		Chilton Time
Oil Pan and/or Gasket, Renew		**Engine Oil Pump, Renew (Front Cover)**		**Oil Pressure Sending Unit, Renew**	
Samari	1.7	Samari	5.4	Samari	.4
Swift	1.7	Swift	4.9	Swift	.7
Sidekick	3.8	w/A.C. add	.6	Sidekick	.6
Oil Filter Element, Renew		Sidekick	7.4		
All models	.4	w/A.C. add	.4	**Oil Pressure Gauge (Dash), Renew**	
		Recond pump add	.4	Sidekick	.9

LABOR 18 CLUTCH & FLYWHEEL 18 LABOR

	Chilton Time		Chilton Time		Chilton Time
Clutch Pedal Free Play, Adjust		**Clutch Assembly, Renew**		**Flywheel, Renew**	
All models	.3	Includes: R&R trans and adjust linkage.		Includes: R&R trans and adjust linkage.	
Clutch Release Bearing, Renew		Samuri	3.5	Samuri	3.8
Includes: R&R trans and adjust linkage.		Swift	7.1	Swift	7.4
Samauri	3.2	Sidekick	5.0	Sidekick	5.3
Swift	6.8	**Clutch Cable Assy., Renew**			
Sidekick	4.7	All models	.7		

LABOR 19 MANUAL TRANSAXLE (FWD) 19 LABOR

	Chilton Time		Chilton Time		Chilton Time
Manual Trans/Axle Assy., R&R or Renew		**Differential Carrier, Renew or Recondition**		**Inner Half Shaft, R&R or Renew**	
Swift	6.8	Swift	9.8	Swift-one	1.5
Manual Trans/Axle Assy., R&R and Recondition		**Axle Shaft Oil Seals, Renew**		Recond shaft add	.4
Swift	11.3	Swift-one side	1.6	**Speedometer Driven Gear, Renew**	
		both sides	2.4	Swift	.5

LABOR 19A MANUAL TRANSMISSION (RWD) 19A LABOR

	Chilton Time		Chilton Time		Chilton Time
Transmission Assy., R&R or Renew		**Transmission Assy., R&R and Recondition**		**Extension Housing Oil Seal, Renew**	
Samuri	3.2	Includes: Complete disassembly, clean and inspect all parts. Renew parts as required. Install new gaskets and seals.		Samuri	3.0
Sidekick	4.7	Samuri	7.8	**Speedometer Driven Gear, Renew**	
		Sidekick	9.1	All models	.5

LABOR 20 TRANSFER CASE 20 LABOR

	Chilton Time		Chilton Time		Chilton Time
Transfer Case Assy., Remove & Install		**Speedometer Drive Gear, Renew**		**Front Cover and/or Gasket, Renew**	
Samuri	3.2	Samuri	.8	Samuri	1.8
Sidekick		Sidekick	.7	Sidekick	
w/M.T.	4.9			w/M.T.	5.6
w/A.T.	2.9	**Output Shaft Oil Seals, Renew**		w/A.T.	3.9
		Sidekick			
		front	.9		
Transfer Case Assy., R&R and Recondition		rear	.9	**Transfer Case Mount, Renew**	
Samuri	5.0			Samuri-one	.7
Sidekick		**4 Wheel Drive Switch, Renew**			
w/M.T.	8.4	Samuri	.5		
w/A.T.	6.8	Sidekick	.6		

LABOR 20 TRANSFER CASE 20 LABOR

ON CAR SERVICES

	Chilton Time
Drain & Refill Unit	
All models	1.3
Oil Pressure Check	
All models	.5
Check Unit for Oil Leaks	
Includes: Clean and dry outside of case and run unit to determine point of leak.	
All models	.9
Manual Shaft Oil Seal, Renew	
All models	.8
Oil Pressure Control Valve Cable, Renew	
All models	1.7
Oil Pan and/or Gasket, Renew	
All models	1.3
Solenoids, Renew	
All models	
2 nd brake	1.5
direct clutch	1.5

	Chilton Time
Differential Oil Seals, Renew	
All models-one	1.5
both	2.1
Speedometer Driven Gear, Renew	
All models	.6
Valve Body, R&R and Recondition	
All models	3.0
Inner Half Shaft, R&R or Renew	
All models-one	1.5
Recond shaft add	.4

SERVICES REQUIRING R&R

	Chilton Time
Automatic Trans/Axle Assy., Remove & Install	
All models	7.5
Automatic Trans/Axle Assy., R&R and Recondition	
Includes: Recondition transmission and differential assemblies.	
All models	15.1

	Chilton Time
Torque Converter, Renew	
Includes: R&R trans/axle.	
All models	7.5
Flywheel (Flexplate), Renew	
Includes: R&R trans/axle.	
All models	7.7
Oil Pump Assy., R&R or Renew	
Includes: R&R trans/axle.	
All models	7.9
Recond pump add	.5
Ring Gear and Pinion Assy., Renew	
Includes: R&R trans/axle, renew ring gear and pinion, side bearings and speedometer drive gear.	
All models	9.5
Renew diff carrier add	.4

LABOR 23 AUTOMATIC TRANSMISSION 23 LABOR

ON CAR SERVICES

	Chilton Time
Drain & Refill Unit	
All models	1.3
Oil Pressure Check	
All models	.5
Check Unit for Oil Leaks	
Includes: Clean and dry outside of case and run unit to determine point of leak.	
All models	.9
Oil Pan and/or Gasket, Renew	
All models	1.3
Solenoid Assembly, Renew	
Includes: R&R oil pan.	
All models	1.7

	Chilton Time
Modulator Assembly, Renew	
All models	4.2
Valve Body Assembly, Recondition.	
Includes: R&R oil pan.	
All models	2.6
Transfer Case Adapter Gasket, Renew	
All models	3.4

SERVICES REQUIRING R&R

	Chilton Time
Transmission Assembly, Remove & Install	
All models	6.2
Transmission Assy., R&R and Recondition	
All models	11.0

	Chilton Time
Flywheel (Flexplate), Renew	
Includes: R&R trans.	
All models	6.3
Torque Converter, Renew	
Includes: R&R trans.	
All models	6.4
Torque Converter Front Seal, Renew	
Includes: R&R trans.	
All models	6.5
Oil Pump Assy., R&R or Renew	
Includes: R&R trans.	
All models	7.0
Recond pump add	.5

LABOR 25 U-JOINTS & DRIVESHAFT 25 LABOR

	Chilton Time
Propeller Shaft, Renew	
Includes: Renew boot.	
Samuri	.9
Sidekick	.8

	Chilton Time
Universal Joint, Renew or Recondition	
Includes: Disconnect drive shaft.	
Samuri-one	1.2
Sidekick-one	1.1
each adtnl	.4

LABOR 26 DRIVE AXLE 26 LABOR

FRONT DIFFERENTIAL ASSY

	Chilton Time
Differential Carrier, Remove & Install	
Samuri	4.0
Sidekick	3.5
Differential Carrier Assy., R&R and Recondition	
Samuri	6.8
Sidekick	6.4
Ring Gear and Pinion Assy., Renew	
Samuri	6.3
Sidekick	5.9
Pinion Oil Seal, Renew	
All models	1.1

	Chilton Time
Front Drive Shaft, Renew	
Sidekick	1.0
Front Drive Shaft Oil Seals, Renew	
Sidekick-one	1.1
both	1.7

REAR DIFFERENTIAL

	Chilton Time
Rear Axle Shaft, Renew	
Samuri-Sidekick	
one	2.2
both	3.3
Axle Shaft Bearing and/or Oil Seal, Renew	
Samuri-Sidekick	
one	2.2
both	3.3

	Chilton Time
Differential Carrier, R&R or Renew	
Includes: Renew gasket.	
Samuri	3.4
Sidekick	3.5
Ring Gear and Pinion Assy., Renew	
Samuri	6.0
Sidekick	6.1
Recond diff assy add	.5
Rear Axle Housing, Renew	
Includes: Transfer parts as required. Bleed brakes.	
Samuri	4.9
Sidekick	4.5
Pinion Shaft Oil Seal, Renew	
All models	1.0

LABOR 27 REAR SUSPENSION 27 LABOR

	Chilton Time
LEAF SPRING SUSPENSION	
Rear Spring, Renew	
Samuri-one	1.3
both	2.5
Recond spring add-each	.5
Rear Spring Front Eye Bushings, Renew	
Samuri-one side	.8
both side	1.4
Rear Spring Shackle, Renew	
Samuri-one	.6
both	.8
Rear Shock Absorbers, Renew	
Samuri-one	.5
both	.8
COIL SPRING SUSPENSION	
Trailing Arm or Bushings, Renew	
Sidekick-one side	1.1
both sides	1.8

	Chilton Time
Rear Shock Absorbers, Renew	
Sidekick-one	.5
both	.7
Upper Control Arm Assy., Renew	
Sidekick-one	1.4
Renew bushings add	.2
STRUT TYPE SUSPENSION	
Rear Strut Assy., Renew	
Swift-one	1.1
both	1.8
Rear Coil Springs, Renew	
Swift-one	.8
both	1.2
Rear Knuckle Assy., Renew	
Swift-one	1.6
both	2.6

	Chilton Time
Lower Control Arm Assy., Renew	
Swift-one	1.1
both	1.8
Control Arm Bushings, Renew	
Swift-one side	.8
both sides	1.2
Rear Control Rods, Renew	
Swift-one	1.0
both	1.4
Rear Stabilizer Bar and/or Joints, Renew	
Swift	.8
Rear Wheel Bearings, Renew	
Swift-one side	1.1
both sides	1.5
Rear Wheel hub, Renew	
Swift-one	1.2
both	1.8

LABOR 28 AIR CONDITIONING 28 LABOR

	Chilton Time
Note: If more than one item requires replacement where evacuation and discharging the system is already included in the operation, deduct 1.0 hour for each additional item to the times listed.	
Drain, Evacuate and Recharge System	
All models	1.0
Flush Refrigerant System, Complete	
To be used in conjunction with component replacement which could contaminate system.	
All models	1.3
Leak Check	
Includes: Check all lines and connections.	
All models	.5
Refrigerant, Add (Partial Charge)	
All models	.6
Compressor Drive Belt, Renew	
Samuri	.4
Swift	1.3
Sidekick	.4
Condenser Motor, Renew	
Samuri	.9
Swift	3.0

	Chilton Time
Compressor Assembly, Renew	
Includes: Transfer parts as required. Evacuate and charge system.	
Samuri	2.0
Swift	3.0
Sidekick	2.3
Compressor Clutch Assembly, Renew	
Includes: R&R compressor. Evacuate and charge system.	
Samuri	2.3
Swift	3.2
Sidekick	2.6
Compressor Shaft Seal Kit, Renew	
Includes: Evacuate and charge system.	
Samuri	2.8
Swift	3.6
Sidekick	3.1
Receiver–Dehydrator, Renew	
Includes: Evacuate and charge system.	
Samuri	1.4
Swift	3.0
Sidekick	1.5
Blower Motor Resistor, Renew	
All models	.4

	Chilton Time
Expansion Valve, Renew	
Includes: Evacuate and charge system.	
Samuri	2.7
Swift	3.6
Sidekick	4.5
Evaporator Core, Renew	
Includes: Evacuate and charge system.	
Samuri	2.4
Swift	3.5
Sidekick	4.3
Condensor Assembly, Renew	
Includes: Evacuate and charge system.	
Samuri	2.4
Swift	3.3
Sidekick	2.5
Air Conditioning Switch, Renew	
Samuri	.7
Swift	.5
Sidekick	.5
Air Conditioning Hoses, Renew	
Includes: Evacuate and charge system.	
Samuri-one	1.7
Swift-one	1.6
Sidekick-one	1.6

LABOR 29 LOCKS, HINGES & WIND. REGULATORS 29 LABOR

	Chilton Time
Hood Rlease Cable, Renew	
Samuri	.6
Swift	.9
Sidekick	.9
Hood Latch Assembly, Renew	
Samuri	.4
Swift	.3
Sidekick	.4
Hood Hinges, Renew (both)	
All models	.4
Samuri	.5
Swift	.6
Sidekick	.6
Door Handle (Outside), Renew	
Samuri	.6
Swift	.6
Sidekick	.9

	Chilton Time
Lock Striker Plate, Renew	
All models	.3
Door Lock Assembly, Renew	
Samuri	1.1
Swift	.9
Sidekick	.8
Door Lock Cylinder Assy., Renew	
Samuri	.8
Swift	.7
Sidekick	.9
Recode cyl add	.3
Door Window Regulator, Renew	
Samuri	.9
Swift	.9
Sidekick	1.0

LABOR   30   HEAD AND PARKING LAMPS   30   LABOR

	Chilton Time
Aim Headlamps	
All models	.4
Headlamp Sealed Beam Bulb, Renew	
Samuri	.5
Halogen Headlamp Bulb, Renew	
Swift	.3
Sidekick	.3
Turn Signal or Parking Lamp Lens or Bulb, Renew	
All models	.3
Side Marker Lamp Lens or Bulb, Renew	
All models	.3

	Chilton Time
Tail or Stop Lamp Lens or Bulb, Renew	
All models	.3
Front Combination Lamp Assy., Renew	
Samuri	.4
Turn Signal Lamp Assy., Renew	
Swift	.3
Sidekick	.5
Side Marker and Reflector Assy., Renew	
Samuri	.3
Sidekick	.3
Clearance Lamp Assy., Renew	
Swift	1.1

	Chilton Time
Rear Combination Lamp Assy., Renew	
Samuri	.4
Swift	.6
Sidekick	.3
License Lamp Assy., Renew	
Samuri	.3
Swift	.3
Sidekick	.4
High Mount Stop Lamp Assy., Renew	
Swift	.4

LABOR   31   WINDSHIELD WIPER & SPEEDOMETER   31   LABOR

	Chilton Time
Windshield Wiper Motor, Renew	
Samuri	
soft top	1.1
hard top	2.9
Swift	.7
Sidekick	1.0
Wiper Transmission Assy., Renew	
Samuri	
soft top	1.3
hard top	3.2
Swift	.9
Sidekick	3.8

	Chilton Time
Windshield Washer Pump, Renew	
Samuri	.3
Swift	1.0
Sidekick	.4
Rear Window Wiper Motor, Renew	
Swift	.6
Sidekick	.8
Rear Washer Pump, Renew	
Swift	1.0
Sidekick	.5
Rear Wiper/Washer Switch, Renew	
Swift	.4
Sidekick	.7

	Chilton Time
Speedometer Head, R&R or Renew	
Samuri	1.0
Swift	.9
Sidekick	.7
Speedometer Cable and Casing, Renew	
Samuri	.9
Swift	1.0
Sidekick	1.2
Radio, R&R	
Samuri	1.0
Swift	2.5
Sidekick	1.4

LABOR   32   LIGHT SWITCHES & WIRING   32   LABOR

	Chilton Time
Headlamp Switch, Renew	
All models	.5
Combination Switch, Renew	
Samuri	1.2
Swift	.6
Sidekick	.7
Parking Brake Warning Lamp Switch, Renew	
All models	.4
Stop Light Switch, Renew	
All models	.4

	Chilton Time
Starter Safety Switch, Renew	
All models	.5
Back-Up Lamp Switch, Renew	
Samuri	.5
Swift	.4
Sidekick	3.6
Turn Signal or Hazard Warning Flasher, Renew (Relay)	
Samuri	.2
Swift	.4
Sidekick	.2
Horn Assembly, Renew	
All models	.3

LABOR   34   CRUISE CONTROL   34   LABOR

	Chilton Time
Cruise Control Cable Assy., Renew	
Sidekick	.6

	Chilton Time
Cruise Control Main Switch, Renew	
Sidekick	.5

	Chilton Time
Cruise Control Actuator Assy., Renew	
Sidekick	.7
Cruise Control Stop Switch, Renew	
Sidekick	1.3

GROUP INDEX

ALPHABETICAL INDEX

LABOR — 1 TUNE UP 1 — LABOR

	Chilton Time
Compression Test	
Four	
Van	.7
All other models	.6
V-6	.8

Engine Tune Up, (Electronic Ignition)
Includes: Test battery and clean connections. Tighten manifold mounting bolts. Check engine compression, clean and adjust or renew spark plugs. Test resistance of spark plug cables. Inspect distributor cap and rotor. Check vacuum advance operation. Reset ignition timing. Adjust idle mixture and idle speed. Service air cleaner. Inspect and adjust drive belts. Inspect choke operation and adjust or free up. Check operation of EGR valve.

	Chilton Time
Van	2.3
All other models	1.5
Adjust valves add	
Four	.5
Six	.8

LABOR — 2 IGNITION SYSTEM 2 — LABOR

	Chilton Time
Spark Plugs, Clean and Reset or Renew	
Four	
Van	.6
All other models	.5
V-6	.7
Ignition Timing, Reset	
Van	1.0
All other models	.4
Distributor Assy. or Cam Position Sensor, Renew	
Includes: Reset ignition timing.	
Four	
Van	1.4
All other models	.8
V-6	1.1

	Chilton Time
Distributor Assy., R&R and Recondition	
Includes: Reset ignition timing.	
Four	
Van	2.0
All other models	1.3
V-6	1.6
Distributor Cap and/or Rotor, Renew	
Four	
Van	1.0
All other models	.4
V-6	.5
Vacuum Advance Unit, Renew	
Includes: Reset ignition timing.	
Four	
Van	1.1
All other models	.5

	Chilton Time
Signal Generator Assy., Renew	
Van	1.9
All other models	.7
Spark Plug Cables, Renew	
Van	.5
All other models	.4
Ignition Coil or Igniter, Renew	
Van	1.7
All other models	.4
Ignition Switch, Renew	
Van	.7
All other models	.6

LABOR — 3 FUEL SYSTEM 3 — LABOR

	Chilton Time
Fuel Pump, Test	
Includes: Disconnect line at carburetor, attach pressure gauge.	
All models	.3
Carburetor Air Cleaner, Service	
All models	.2
Carburetor Idle Speed, Adjust	
All models	.4
Float Level, Adjust	
All models	1.0
Carburetor Assembly, Renew	
Includes: All necessary adjustments.	
All models	1.5
Carburetor, R&R and Clean or Recondition	
Includes: All necessary adjustments.	
All models	3.0
Needle Valve and Seat, Renew	
Includes: Reset float level.	
All models	1.5
Fuel Pump, Renew	
All models	
mechanical	.6
electric	1.0
Fuel Tank, Renew	
Includes: Drain and refill tank.	
Van	1.3
P/up-4 Runner	
1986-88	2.0
1989-90	1.6
Land Cruiser	
H/T	2.5
Wagon	2.3
Fuel Gauge (Dash Unit), Renew	
Van	.9
All other models	1.0

	Chilton Time
Fuel Gauge (Tank Unit), Renew	
Van	1.2
P/up-4 Runner	
1986-88	2.0
1989-90	1.5
Land Cruiser	
H/T	1.0
Wagon	.5
Intake Manifold Gasket, Renew	
Van	3.7
P/up-4 Runner	1.8
w/Fuel inj or E.F.I. add	1.0
Land Cruiser	2.3
Intake and Exhaust Manifold Gaskets, Renew	
Land Cruiser	4.0
ELECTRONIC FUEL INJECTION	
Fuel Injectors, Clean (On Car) (w/TBI or MPI)	
Includes: Hook up pressurized fuel injection cleaning equipment.	
All models	.5
Throttle Body and/or Gasket, Renew	
All models	1.4
Electric Fuel Pump, Renew	
All models	
Four	1.7
V-6	1.7
Fuel Filter, Renew	
All models	.9
Fuel Injection Computer, Renew	
All models	.9
Water Temperature Sensor, Renew	
Van	1.2

	Chilton Time
All other models	
Four	1.1
V-6	.9
Start Injector Time Switch, Renew	
Van	1.2
All other models	
Four	1.1
V-6	.6
Oxygen Sensor, Renew	
Van	.8
All other models	1.1
Air Flow Meter, Renew	
Van	1.1
All other models	1.2
Fuel Pressure Regulator, Renew	
All models	1.4
Fuel Injectors, Renew (All)	
Van	4.0
All other models	
Four	3.2
V-6	2.6
Cold Start Injector Assy., Renew	
Van	.7
All other models	.6
Air Valve Assembly, Renew	
Van	2.4
All other models	
Four	1.2
V-6	1.0
Intake Manifold and/or Gasket, Renew	
Van	3.7
All other models	
Four	3.4
V-6	3.6
Renew manif add	.5

LABOR   3 FUEL SYSTEM 3   LABOR

DIESEL ENGINE

	Chilton Time
Air Cleaner, Service	
All models	.2
Glow Plugs, Renew	
All models-one	.4
all	.8
Glow Plug Relay, Renew	
All models	.5
Starter Relay, Renew	
All models	.4
Fuel Injection Pump, R&R or Renew	
P/up	4.0
Land Cruiser	
H/T	2.0
Wagon	3.2

	Chilton Time
Fuel Injection Pump, R&R and Recondition	
P/up	9.1
Land Cruiser	
H/T	6.1
Wagon	8.0
Delivery Valve and/or Gasket, Renew	
P/up	1.3
Land Cruiser	
H/T	1.4
Wagon	2.2
Fuel Injection Nozzles, Renew (All)	
All models	1.3
Fuel Injection Lines, Renew	
All models-one	.5
each adtnl	.2
Fuel Filter, Renew	
All models	.4

	Chilton Time
Fuel Tank, Renew	
All models	1.9
Fuel Gauge (Tank), Renew	
All models	1.9
Intake Manifold and/or Gasket, Renew	
All models	1.7
TURBOCHARGER	
Turbocharger Assembly, Renew	
All models	
Gas	2.9
Diesel	1.5
Turbo to Exhaust Manifold Gasket, Renew	
All models	
Gas	2.5
Diesel	1.2

LABOR   3A EMISSION CONTROLS 3A   LABOR

POSITIVE CRANKCASE VENTILATION SYSTEM

	Chilton Time
PCV Valve, Renew	
All models	.3
AIR INJECTION SYSTEM	
Air Pump, Renew	
P/up	.6
Land Cruiser	.7
Air Pump Drive Belt, Renew	
P/up	.4
Land Cruiser	.5
Air Injection Manifold, Renew	
Four	
P/up	1.3
Land Cruiser	.6
V-6	.4
Air Injection Check Valve, Renew	
Four	
P/up	1.4
Land Cruiser	.4
Air By-Pass Valve, Renew	
Land Cruiser	.4

	Chilton Time
Air Switching Valve, Renew	
P/up	.4
Air Control Valve, Renew	
P/up	.6
Land Cruiser	.7
EXHAUST GAS RECIRCULATION SYSTEM	
E.G.R. Valve, Renew	
Van	1.1
P/up	.6
Land Cruiser	.5
E.G.R. Vacuum Modulator Valve, Renew	
Van	.4
P/up	.3
Land Cruiser	.4
Thermo Sensor, Renew	
Land Cruiser	.3
COMBUSTION SYSTEM	
Vacuum Switching Valve, Renew	
All models	.3
Thermo Sensor, Renew	
All models	.7

	Chilton Time
Throttle Positioner, Renew	
Van	.7
Computer, Renew	
All models	.5
Vacuum Control Valve, Renew	
All models	.3
Vacuum Transmitting Valve, Renew	
All models	.3
Bimetal Vacuum Switching Valve, Renew	
Four	.9
V-6	.4
Mixture Control Valve, Renew	
All models	.4
Check Valve, Renew	
All models	.3
Vacuum Switch, Renew	
All models	.4
High Altitude Compensator Valve, Renew	
All models	.3
Charcoal Canister, Renew	
All models	.3

LABOR   4 ALTERNATOR AND REGULATOR 4   LABOR

	Chilton Time
Alternator Circuits, Test	
Includes: Test battery, regulator and alternator output.	
All models	.3
Alternator Assembly, Renew	
Four	
Van	1.5
P/up-4 Runner	*1.0
All other models	1.1
*w/Diesel eng add	.1
V-6	.8
Add circuit test if performed.	

	Chilton Time
Alternator Assy., R&R and Recondition	
Includes: Disassemble, clean and test. Renew parts as required, reassemble.	
Four	
Van	3.0
P/up-4 Runner	*2.0
All other models	2.3
*w/Diesel eng add	.3
V-6	2.0
Alternator Bearing, Renew	
Four	
Van	2.0

	Chilton Time
P/up-4 Runner	*1.4
All other models	1.6
*w/Diesel eng add	.2
V-6	1.3
Voltage Regulator, Test and Renew	
All models-external	.5
internal	1.5
Ammeter, Renew	
All models	.8

LABOR 5 STARTING SYSTEM 5 LABOR

	Chilton Time
Starter Draw Test (On Truck)	
All models	.3
Starter Assembly, Renew	
All models	.7
Add draw test if performed.	
Starter Assy., R&R and Recondition	
Includes: Turn down armature.	
All models	2.0
Renew field coils add	.5
Add draw test if performed.	

	Chilton Time
Starter Solenoid, Renew	
Includes: R&R starter.	
All models	.8
REDUCTION TYPE	
Starter Assembly, Renew	
All models	.7
Add draw test if performed.	
Starter Assy., R&R and Recondition	
Includes: Turn down armature.	
All models	1.5

	Chilton Time
Starter Solenoid, Renew	
Includes: R&R starter.	
All models	.9
Battery Cables, Renew	
Van	
each	.6
All other models	
positive	.4
negative	.3

LABOR 6 BRAKE SYSTEM 6 LABOR

	Chilton Time
Bleed Brakes	
Includes: Fill master cylinder.	
two wheels	.6
four wheels	1.0
Brakes, Adjust (Minor)	
two wheels	.4
four wheels	.7
Brake Shoes, Renew	
Includes: Install new or exchange brake shoes.	
Adjust service and hand brake. Bleed system.	
Van	2.5
All other models	2.0
w/Dual whls add	1.0
Resurface brake drum add-each	.5
Rear Brake Drum, Renew (One)	
Van	1.5
All other models	1.2
w/Dual whls add	.5

BRAKE HYDRAULIC SYSTEM

	Chilton Time
Wheel Cylinders, Renew	
Includes: Bleed system.	
Van-one side	1.9
All other models	
one side	1.5
w/Dual whls add	.5
Wheel Cylinders, R&R and Rebuild	
Includes: Bleed system.	
Van-one side	2.3
All other models	
one side	1.9
w/Dual whls add	.5
Master Cylinder, Renew	
Includes: Bleed system.	
Van	2.2
All other models	1.8
Master Cylinder, R&R and Rebuild	
Includes: Bleed system.	
Van	2.6
All other models	2.2
Brake Hose, Renew (Flex)	
Includes: Bleed system.	
All models	
front-one	.8
rear-one	.9

COMBINATIONS

	Chilton Time
RENEW WHEEL CYLINDER	
one side	.2
REBUILD WHEEL CYLINDER	
One side	.4
REBUILD MASTER CYLINDER	
All models	.5
REBUILD CALIPER ASSEMBLY	
Each	.4
RENEW BRAKE HOSE	
Each	.3
RENEW BRAKE DRUM	
2WD	.2
4WD	.4
RENEW DISC BRAKE ROTOR	
2WD	.2
4WD	.4

	Chilton Time
Load Sensing Proportioning Valve, Renew	
Includes: Bleed system.	
Van	1.6
All other models	1.9
Brake System, Flush and Refill	
All models	1.2

DISC BRAKES

	Chilton Time
Disc Brake Pads, Renew	
Includes: Install new disc brake pads only.	
Van-P/up-4 Runner	1.1
Land Cruiser	1.3
Disc Brake Rotor, Renew (One)	
Van	1.4
4X4 add	.1
P/up-4 Runner	
2WD	1.5
4WD	2.3
Land Cruiser	2.2
Caliper Assembly, Renew (One)	
Includes: Bleed system.	
Van	1.2
P/up-4 Runner	1.3
Land Cruiser	1.4

	Chilton Time
Caliper Assy., R&R and Rebuild (One)	
Includes: Bleed system.	
Van	1.6
P/up-4 Runner	1.7
Land Cruiser	1.8
Proportioning and By-Pass Valve, Renew	
Includes: Bleed system.	
All models	1.1

POWER BRAKES

	Chilton Time
Brake Booster Assembly, Renew	
Includes: Bleed system.	
Van	3.0
P/up-4 Runner	
1986-88	2.5
1989-90	1.8
Land Cruiser	2.2
Brake Booster, R&R and Recondition	
Includes: Bleed system.	
Van	3.6
P/up-4 Runner	
1986-88	3.1
1989-90	2.2
Land Cruiser	2.9
Vacuum Check Valve, Renew	
Van-P/up-4 Runner	.4
Land Cruiser	.5
Vacuum Pump, Renew (w/Diesel eng)	
All models	.7
Recond pump add	.4

PARKING BRAKE

	Chilton Time
Parking Brake, Adjust	
All models	.3
Parking Brake Control, Renew	
All models	1.0
Parking Brake Cables, Renew	
Front	
All models	1.0
Rear	
Van	1.9
All other models	
4X2	2.1
4X4	1.1

LABOR 7 COOLING SYSTEM 7 LABOR

Winterize Cooling System
Includes: Run engine to check for leaks, tighten all hose connections. Test radiator and pressure cap, drain radiator and engine block. Add anti-freeze and refill system.

	Chilton Time
All models	.5

Thermostat, Renew
Four
Van	1.0
All other models	.7
V-6	.8

Radiator Assy., R&R or Renew
Includes: Drain and refill cooling system.
Van	1.9
P/up-4 Runner	1.2
Land Cruiser	1.4

ADD THESE OPERATIONS TO RADIATOR R&R
Boil & Repair	1.5
Rod Clean	1.9
Repair Core	1.3
Renew Tank	1.6
Renew Trans. Oil Cooler	1.9
Recore Radiator	1.7

Radiator Hoses, Renew
UPPER
Van	1.1
P/up-4 Runner	.7
Land Cruiser	.5

LOWER
All models	.8

By-Pass Hose, Renew
Four
P/up-4 Runner	.9
Land Cruiser	.5
V-6	.5

Fan Blades or Fluid Coupling, Renew
Van	1.5
All other models	.6

Fan Belt, Renew
Van	.6
All other models	.4

Fan Belt, Adjust
All models	.3

Water Pump, Renew
Four
Van	2.3
All other models	
Gas	1.4
Diesel	2.1
V-6	4.0

Temperature Gauge (Dash Unit), Renew
Van	1.2
P/up-4 Runner	1.0
Land Cruiser	1.1

Temperature Gauge Sending Unit, Renew
All models	.6

Heater Blower Motor, Renew
Van
wo/A.C.	1.4
w/A.C.	2.6

P/up-4 Runner
1986-88	.9
1989-90	
wo/A.C.	.5
w/A.C.	1.5

Land Cruiser
H/T	.9
Wagon	.5

Heater Core, R&R or Renew
Van	2.4

P/up-4 Runner
wo/A.C.	2.1
w/A.C.	4.5

Land Cruiser
H/T	3.0
Wagon	3.6
w/A.C. add	1.0

ADD THESE OPERATIONS TO HEATER CORE R&R
Boil & Repair	1.2
Repair Core	.9
Recore	1.2

Heater Control Assembly, Renew
Van	.8
P/up-4 Runner	1.0

Land Cruiser
H/T	1.2
Wagon	.9

Heater Blower Motor Switch, Renew
1986-88	.5
1989-90	
P/up-4 Runner	.8
Van	.5
Land Cruiser	.6

Heater Blower Motor Resistor, Renew
Van	.8
All other models	.4

Heater Water Valve, Renew
Van	1.2

P/up-4 Runner
1986-88	.6
1989-90	.8
Land Cruiser	.9

Heater Hose, Renew (One)
Van	1.2
P/up-4 Runner	.5
Land Cruiser	.7

LABOR 8 EXHAUST SYSTEM 8 LABOR

Muffler and Tail Pipe Assy., Renew
Van	1.0
All other models	.6

Front Exhaust Pipe, Renew
Van	1.0
P/up-4 Runner	.6

Land Cruiser
H/T	.9
Wagon	.6

Intermediate Pipe, Renew
Land Cruiser	.9

Catalytic Converter, Renew
Van
1986-88	1.0
1989-90	.6
P/up-4 Runner	.8

Exhaust Manifold or Gasket, Renew
Four
Van	3.6

All other models
Gas	1.3
Diesel	1.7
V-6-both sides	2.5

Intake and Exhaust Manifold or Gaskets, Renew
P/up-4 Runner
Gas	1.7
Diesel	1.8

Land Cruiser
H/T	1.9
Wagon	2.2
w/E.F.I. or Turbo add	1.0

LABOR 9 FRONT SUSPENSION 9 LABOR

Note: On all front suspension operations alignment charges must be added if performed. Time given does not include alignment.

Wheel, Renew (One)
All models	.5

Wheels, Rotate (All)
All models	.5

Wheels, Balance
one	.3
each adtnl	.2

Toe-In, Adjust
All models	.4

Align Front End
All models	1.4

CONTROL ARM SUSPENSION

Upper Control Arm Assy., Renew (One Side)
Add alignment charges.
Van	2.8

P/up-4 Runner
4X2	2.3
4X4	2.7

Upper Control Arm Shaft and Bushings, Renew (One Side)
Add alignment charges.
Van	3.1

P/up-4 Runner
4X2	2.6
4X4	3.3

LABOR   9 · FRONT SUSPENSION 9   LABOR

	Chilton Time
Lower Control Arm Assy., Renew (One)	
Add alignment charges.	
Van..	2.3
P/up-4 Runner	
4X2..	3.2
4X4..	2.4
Torsion Bar, Renew (One Side)	
Van..	.8
P/up-4 Runner	
4X2..	1.2
4X4..	1.3
Front Shock Absorbers, Renew	
Van-one..	.5
both..	.7
P/up-4 Runner	
one...	.8
both..	1.0
Upper Ball Joint, Renew (One Side)	
Add alignment charges.	
Van..	1.8
P/up-4 Runner	
4X2..	2.2
4X4..	2.7
Lower Ball Joint, Renew (One Side)	
Add alignment charges.	
Van..	1.7
P/up-4 Runner......................................	2.3

	Chilton Time
Front Axle Hub, Renew (One Side)	
Van..	1.5
P/up-4 Runner	
4X2..	1.7
4X4..	2.4
Front Wheel Bearings, Renew (One Side)	
Van..	1.3
P/up-4 Runner	
4X2..	1.4
4X4..	1.9
Front Wheel Grease Seals, Renew (One Side)	
Van..	1.0
P/up-4 Runner	
4X2..	1.2
4X4..	1.9
Steering Knuckle, Renew	
Add alignment charges.	
Van..	2.2
P/up-4 Runner	
4X2..	3.2
4X4..	3.4
LEAF SPRING SUSPENSION	
Front Spring, Renew (One)	
All models..	1.5
Front Spring, R&R and Recondition (One)	
All models..	2.0
Front Spring Shackle Assy., Renew (One Side)	
All models..	.8

	Chilton Time
Front Shock Absorber, Renew (One Side)	
All models..	.6
4 WHEEL DRIVE FRONT AXLE	
Front Axle, Hub, Renew (One)	
Van..	1.9
P/up...	2.4
Land Cruiser..	2.2
Front Hub Oil Seal, Renew (One Side)	
P/up...	1.9
Land Cruiser..	1.6
Front Hub Bearings, Renew (One Side)	
Van..	1.8
P/up...	1.9
Land Cruiser..	1.7
Steering Knuckle, Renew (One)	
Add alignment charges.	
P/up...	3.4
Land Cruiser..	3.0
Renew brg add.....................................	.2
Front Drive Shaft, Renew	
Van..	1.5
All other models...................................	1.9
Front Drive Shaft Boot, Renew	
Includes: Renew or recondition C.V. joints.	
Van..	2.1
All other models...................................	2.4
Free Wheeling Hub Assy., Renew (One)	
All models..	.8

LABOR   10 STEERING LINKAGE 10   LABOR

	Chilton Time
Pitman Arm, Renew	
All models..	.9
Idler Arm, Renew	
Van..	.9
All other models...................................	1.0

	Chilton Time
Tie Rod, Renew (One Side)	
Land Cruiser	
1986..	2.0
All other models...................................	1.2
Tie Rod End, Renew (One Side)	
Land Cruiser	
1986..	1.4
All other models...................................	1.0

	Chilton Time
Center Arm Bracket, Renew	
Van..	1.0
Recond add..	.5
Steering Damper, Renew	
All models..	.8

LABOR   11 STEERING GEAR 11   LABOR

	Chilton Time
Horn Button or Contact Plate, Renew	
All models..	.5
Steering Wheel, Renew	
All models..	.4
Upper Mast Jacket Bearing, Renew	
Van-Land Cruiser..................................	1.7
All other models...................................	2.1
Flex Coupling, Renew	
All models	
wo/Tilt whl...	1.2
w/Tilt whl...	.6
MANUAL STEERING	
WORM & SECTOR TYPE	
Steering Gear, Adjust (On Truck)	
All models..	.5
Steering Gear, R&R or Renew	
Van..	1.0
P/up-4 Runner......................................	1.2
Land Cruiser..	1.4

	Chilton Time
Steering Gear, R&R and Recondition	
Includes: Disassemble, renew parts as required, reassemble and adjust.	
Van..	1.8
P/up-4 Runner......................................	2.0
Land Cruiser..	2.5
RACK & PINION TYPE	
Manual Rack and Pinion Assy., R&R or Renew	
Van..	1.6
Manual Rack and Pinion Assy., R&R and Recondition	
Van..	3.1
Steering Rack End, Renew (One Side)	
Van..	1.8
Steering Rack End Boot, Renew (One Side)	
Van..	1.3
Tie Rod End, Renew	
Van-manual or power..............................	1.2

	Chilton Time
POWER STEERING	
WORM & SECTOR TYPE	
Power Steering Pump Drive Belt, Renew	
Van..	1.5
All other models	
Four...	.4
V-6..	.6
Power Steering Gear, R&R or Renew	
Van..	1.6
All other models...................................	2.0
Power Steering Pump, Renew	
Land Cruiser-H/T..................................	2.0
Van..	1.7
All other models...................................	1.5
Power Steering Pump, R&R and Recondition	
Land Cruiser-H/T..................................	3.4
Van..	2.7
All other models...................................	2.5

LABOR 11 STEERING GEAR 11 LABOR

	Chilton Time
Power Steering Hoses, Renew	
Pressure	
Van	1.6
All other models	1.1
Return	
Van	2.3
Land Cruiser	1.1
All other models	.5
RACK & PINION TYPE	
Power Steering Pump Drive Belt, Renew	
Van	1.5

	Chilton Time
Power Rack and Pinion Assy., R&R or Renew	
Van	2.3
Power Rack and Pinion Assy., R&R and Reseal	
Van	3.6
Power Steering Rack End Boot, Renew (One Side)	
Van	1.3

	Chilton Time
Power Steering Pump, Renew	
Van	1.7
Power Steering Pump, R&R and Recondition	
Van	2.9
Power Steering Hoses, Renew	
Van	
Pressure	1.6
Return	2.3

LABOR 12 CYLINDER HEAD & VALVE SYSTEM 12 LABOR

	Chilton Time
GASOLINE ENGINES	
Compression Test	
Four	
Van	.7
All other models	.6
V-6	.8
Cylinder Head Gasket, Renew	
Includes: Clean carbon. Make all necessary adjustments.	
Four	
Van	5.6
P/up-4 Runner	
wo/F.I.	4.7
w/F.I.	5.5
w/Turbo	6.5
Land Cruiser	
H/T	4.3
Wagon	5.1
w/P.S. add	.5
V-6-both	10.3
Cylinder Head, Renew	
Includes: R&R cylinder head. Reface valves and seats. Make all necessary adjustments.	
Four	
Van	7.7
P/up-4 Runner	
wo/F.I.	7.3
w/F.I.	8.2
w/Turbo	9.3
Land Cruiser	
H/T	7.0
Wagon	8.6
w/P.S. add	.5
V-6-both	17.4
Clean Carbon and Grind Valves	
Includes: R&R cylinder head(s). Reface valves and seats. Make all necessary adjustments.	
Four	
Van	8.7
P/up-4 Runner	
wo/F.I.	8.7
w/F.I.	9.7
w/Turbo	10.8

	Chilton Time
Land Cruiser	
H/T	8.3
Wagon	10.3
w/P.S. add	.5
V-6-both	17.4
Cylinder Head Cover Gasket, Renew	
Four	
Van	.8
P/up-4 Runner	.9
Land Cruiser	.7
V-6-both	2.2
Valve Springs and/or Valve Stem Oil Seals, Renew (All)	
Four	
Van	6.4
P/up-4 Runner	
wo/F.I.	5.5
w/F.I.	6.5
w/Turbo	7.5
Land Cruiser	
H/T	5.5
Wagon	6.0
w/P.S. add	.5
V-6	13.1
Valve Push Rods, Renew (All)	
Four	
Van	1.0
Land Cruiser	1.5
Valve Lifters, Renew (All)	
Four	
Van	1.1
Land Cruiser	
H/T	3.2
Wagon	2.3
V-6	7.6
Rocker Arms, Shafts and Supports, Renew (All)	
Four	
Van	1.5
P/up-4 Runner	2.3
Land Cruiser	
H/T	2.0
Wagon	2.3

	Chilton Time
Valve Clearance, Adjust	
Four	1.5
V-6	3.2
DIESEL ENGINE	
Compression Test	
All models	1.0
Cylinder Head Gasket, Renew	
Includes: Clean carbon. Make all necessary adjustments.	
All models	6.0
w/Turbo add	.5
Cylinder Head, Renew	
Includes: Transfer parts as required. Clean carbon. Make all necessary adjustments.	
All models	8.5
w/Turbo add	.5
Clean Carbon and Grind Valves	
Includes: R&R cylinder head. Resurface valves and seats. Make all necessary adjustments.	
All models	9.8
w/Turbo add	.5
Cylinder Head Cover Gasket, Renew	
All models	.7
w/Turbo add	.2
Valve Springs and/or Valve Stem Oil Seals, Renew (All)	
Includes: R&R cylinder head.	
All models	7.0
w/Turbo add	.5
Valve Rocker Arms and/or Shafts, Renew (All)	
All models	2.5
w/Turbo add	.2
Valve Clearance, Adjust	
All models	1.5
w/Turbo add	.2

LABOR 13 ENGINE ASSEMBLY & MOUNTS 13 LABOR

	Chilton Time
GASOLINE ENGINES	
Note: All engine operations listed in this group are for assemblies as supplied by the original equipment manufacturer. Time to replace assemblies from independent rebuilders may vary.	

	Chilton Time
Engine Assembly, Remove & Install	
Does not include transfer of any parts or equipment.	
Four	
Van	9.9
P/up-4 Runner	
4X2	
wo/F.I.	5.2

	Chilton Time
w/F.I.	6.0
4X4	
wo/F.I.	7.3
w/F.I.	7.7
Land Cruiser	5.5
w/A.C. add	.7
w/P.S. add	.7

LABOR 13 ENGINE ASSEMBLY & MOUNTS 13 LABOR

V-6

	Chilton Time
4X2	11.5
4X4	13.8
w/A.C. add	.4

Cylinder Assy., (Short Block), Renew
Includes: R&R engine assy. Transfer all component parts not supplied with replacement engine. Tune up.

Four

Van	15.9
P/up-4 Runner	
4X2	
wo/F.I.	10.2
w/F.I.	11.7
4X4	
wo/F.I.	12.3
w/F.I.	13.5
Land Cruiser	14.0
w/A.C. add	.7
w/P.S. add	.7

V-6

4X2	17.5
4X4	19.8
w/A.C. add	.4

Engine Assy., R&R and Recondition
Includes: Install new pistons, pins, rings, rod and main bearings. Clean carbon, grind valves. Tune engine.

Four

Van	21.9

P/up-4 Runner

4X2	
wo/F.I.	21.7
w/F.I.	22.6
4X4	
wo/F.I.	22.4
w/F.I.	24.6
Land Cruiser	26.6
w/A.C. add	.7
w/P.S. add	.7

V-6

4X2	33.3
4X4	35.8
w/A.C. add	.4

Engine Mounts, Renew
Front-one side

Van	.8
P/up-4 Runner	.6
Land Cruiser	.7

Rear

Van	.9
P/up-4 Runner	.7
Land Cruiser	.9

DIESEL ENGINE

Engine Assembly, Remove & Install
Does not include transfer of any parts or equipment.

All models

4X2	5.6
4X4	6.8
w/A.C. add	.7

w/P.S. add	.7
w/Turbo add	.2

Cylinder Assembly, Renew (Short Block)
Includes: R&R engine assy. Transfer all component parts not supplied with replacement engine. Clean carbon, grind valves. Make all necessary adjustments.

All models

4X2	13.9
4X4	15.1
w/A.C. add	.7
w/P.S. add	.7
w/Turbo add	.2

Engine Assembly, R&R and Recondition
Includes: Install new pistons, pins and rings. Renew cylinder liners and seals. Renew main and connecting rod bearings. Clean carbon, grind valves. Make all necessary adjustments.

All models

4X2	20.2
4X4	22.6
w/A.C. add	.7
w/P.S. add	.7
w/Turbo add	.2

Front Engine Mount, Renew

All models-one side	.5

Rear Engine Mount, Renew

All models	.6

LABOR 14 PISTONS, RINGS & BEARINGS 14 LABOR

GASOLINE ENGINES

Pistons or Connecting Rods, Renew (All)
Includes: R&R cylinder head and oil pan. Clean carbon. Make all necessary adjustments.

Four

Van	9.4
P/up-4 Runner	
wo/F.I.	9.7
w/F.I.	
4X2	10.6
4X4	12.4
w/Turbo	10.3
Land Cruiser	
H/T	7.9
Wagon	9.7
w/P.S. add	.5

V-6

4X2	14.8
4X4	17.2

Piston Rings, Renew (All)
Includes: R&R cylinder head and oil pan. Clean carbon. Make all necessary adjustments.

Four

Van	10.3
P/up-4 Runner	
wo/F.I.	8.5
w/F.I.	
4X2	10.1
4X4	12.0
w/Turbo	11.1
Land Cruiser	
H/T	8.3
Wagon	10.4
w/P.S. add	.5

COMBINATIONS

DRAIN, EVACUATE & RECHARGE AIR CONDITIONING SYSTEM

All models	1.0

CARBURETOR, RECONDITION

All models	1.5

WATER PUMP, RECONDITION

Four	.5

CYLINDER HEAD, RECONDITION (HEAD REMOVED)

Four

P/up	3.5
Land Cruiser	4.5

OIL PUMP, RECONDITION

Four

Van	.4
All other models	1.0

VALVE GUIDES, RENEW (ALL) (CYL HEAD STRIPPED)

Four

Van	1.0
All other models	1.6

PLASTIGAUGE BEARINGS

Each	.1

REMOVE CYLINDER TOP RIDGE

Each	.3

DEGLAZE CYLINDER WALLS

Each	.1

OIL FILTER ELEMENT, RENEW

All models	.3

V-6

4X2	15.2
4X4	17.5

Connecting Rod Bearings, Renew
Includes: R&R oil pan.

Four

Van	3.2
P/up-4 Runner	
4X2	3.7
4X4	6.8
Land Cruiser	3.5

V-6

4X2	4.8
4X4	7.2

DIESEL ENGINE

Piston Rings, Renew (All)
Includes: R&R cylinder head and oil pan.

All models	10.5
w/Turbo add	.2

Pistons or Connecting Rods, Renew (All)
Includes: R&R cylinder head and oil pan.

All models	11.7
w/Turbo add	.2

Connecting Rod Bearings, Renew

All models	3.7

Cylinder Liners and/or 'O' Rings, Renew
Includes: R&R engine assembly.

All models	17.0
w/A.C. add	.7
w/Turbo add	.2

LABOR 15 CRANKSHAFT & DAMPER 15 LABOR

GASOLINE ENGINES

	Chilton Time
Crankshaft and Main Bearings, Renew	
Includes: R&R engine assembly.	
Four	
Van..	16.5
P/up-4 Runner	
4X2	
wo/F.I.	12.0
w/F.I.	13.0
4X4	
wo/F.I.	13.4
w/F.I.	14.8
Land Cruiser	15.5
w/A.C. add	.7
w/P.S. add	.7
V-6	
4X2	18.6
4X4	20.8
w/A.C. add	.2
Crankshaft Pulley, Renew	
Four	
Van..	1.7
P/up-4 Runner..........................	1.6
Land Cruiser	
H/T	1.0
Wagon	1.5
w/A.C. add	.2
w/P.S. add	.2
V-6	1.6
w/A.C. add	.2

	Chilton Time
Crankshaft Front Oil Seal, Renew	
Four	
Van..	1.8
P/up-4 Runner..........................	1.6
Land Cruiser	1.3
w/A.C. add	.2
w/P.S. add	.2
V-6	5.2
Crankshaft Rear Oil Seal, Renew	
Four	
Van	
w/M.T.	
4X2	3.6
4X4	4.6
w/A.T.	
4X2	3.2
4X4	4.5
P/up-4 Runner	
4X2	
w/M.T.	4.8
w/A.T.	5.2
4X4	
w/M.T.	5.8
w/A.T.	6.2
Land Cruiser	
w/M.T.	5.0
w/A.T.	7.5
V-6	
w/M.T.	5.5
w/A.T.	6.5

DIESEL ENGINE

	Chilton Time
Crankshaft and Main Bearings, Renew	
Includes: R&R engine assembly.	
All models	
4X2	12.6
4X4	13.9
w/A.C. add	.7
w/P.S. add	.7
w/Turbo add	.5
Crankshaft Pulley, Renew	
All models.................................	.8
w/A.C. add	.1
w/P.S. add	.1
Crankshaft Front Oil Seal, Renew	
All models.................................	5.5
w/A.C. add	.1
w/P.S. add	.1
Crankshaft Rear Oil Seal, Renew	
Includes: R&R transmission.	
All models	
4X2	4.2
4X4	5.2

LABOR 16 CAMSHAFT & TIMING GEARS 16 LABOR

GASOLINE ENGINES

	Chilton Time
Timing Chain Cover and/or Gasket, Renew	
Four	
Van..	1.9
P/up-4 Runner	
wo/F.I....................................	8.4
w/F.I.	
4X2	9.0
4X4	11.6
Land Cruiser	1.8
w/A.C. add	.7
w/P.S. add	.5
Timing Chain or Tensioner, Renew	
Includes: All necessary adjustments.	
Four	
Van..	2.9
P/up-4 Runner	
wo/F.I....................................	8.8
w/F.I.	
4X2	9.4
4X4	12.0
w/A.C. add	.7
w/P.S. add	.5
Timing Belt Cover, R&R or Renew	
V-6	2.3
Timing Belt, Renew	
V-6	3.5

	Chilton Time
Camshaft Gear or Sprocket, Renew	
Includes: All necessary adjustments.	
Four	
Van..	2.9
P/up-4 Runner..........................	1.2
w/P.S. add	.1
Land Cruiser	
H/T	4.7
Wagon	4.1
w/A.C. add	.1
w/P.S. add	.1
V-6	3.7
w/A.C. add	.4
Crankshaft Gear or Sprocket, Renew	
Includes: All necessary adjustments.	
Four	
Van..	2.9
P/up-4 Runner	
wo/F.I....................................	8.1
w/F.I.	
4X2	9.7
4X4	12.3
Land Cruiser	1.9
w/A.C. add	.3
w/P.S. add	.5
V-6	3.7
w/A.C. add	.4

DIESEL ENGINE

	Chilton Time
Camshaft(s), Renew	
Includes: All necessary adjustments.	
Four	
Van..	4.9
w/A.C. add	1.9
w/P.S. add	.4
P/up-4 Runner..........................	3.0
w/P.S. add	.5
Land Cruiser	
H/T	4.7
Wagon	6.6
w/A.C. add	1.1
V-6	7.5
w/A.C. add	.4

DIESEL ENGINE

	Chilton Time
Camshaft, Renew	
All models.................................	4.1
w/A.C. add	.7
w/Turbo add	.2
Camshaft Timing Gear or Sprocket, Renew	
All models.................................	1.5
Renew crank gear add..................	.3
w/A.C. add	.7
Timing Belt and/or Idler, Renew	
All models.................................	1.5
w/A.C. add	.7
Timing Gear Cover and/or Gasket, Renew	
All models.................................	1.7
w/A.C. add	.7
w/P.S. add	.1

LABOR 17 ENGINE OILING SYSTEM 17 LABOR

GASOLINE ENGINES

	Chilton Time
Oil Pan and/or Gasket, Renew	
Four	
Van	
4X2	2.4
4X4	3.2
P/up-4 Runner	
4X2	3.2
4X4	5.2
Land Cruiser	
H/T	2.0
Wagon	2.3
V-6	
4X2	3.4
4X4	5.1
Pressure Test Engine Bearings (Pan Off)	
All models	1.0
Oil Pump, Renew	
Four	
Van	
4X2	2.6
4X4	3.4
P/up-4 Runner	2.5
Land Cruiser	
H/T	6.5
Wagon	7.4
V-6	
4X2	6.2
4X4	8.0
Oil Pump, R&R and Recondition	
Four	
Van	
4X2	2.8
4X4	3.6
P/up-4 Runner	2.7
Land Cruiser	
H/T	6.7
Wagon	7.6
V-6	
4X2	6.4
4X4	8.2
Oil Pressure Sending Unit, Renew	
All models	.5
Oil Pressure Gauge (Dash Unit), Renew	
All models	1.0
Oil Filter Element, Renew	
All models	.3

DIESEL ENGINE

	Chilton Time
Oil Pan and/or Gasket, Renew	
All models	2.5
Pressure Test Engine Bearings (Pan Off)	
All models	1.0
Oil Pump, Renew	
All models	5.3
Oil Cooler Assembly, Renew	
All models	1.9
Oil Pressure Sending Unit, Renew	
All models	.3
Oil Filter Element, Renew	
All models	.3

LABOR 18 CLUTCH & FLYWHEEL 18 LABOR

	Chilton Time
Bleed Clutch Hydraulic System	
All models	.4
Clutch Master Cylinder, Renew	
Includes: Bleed system.	
Van	1.5
All other models	1.3
Clutch Master Cylinder, R&R and Recondition	
Includes: Bleed system.	
Van	1.8
All other models	1.6
Clutch Slave Cylinder, Renew	
Includes: Bleed system.	
All models	.9
Clutch Slave Cylinder, R&R and Recondition	
Includes: Bleed system.	
All models	1.2
Clutch Assembly, Renew	
Van	
4X2	3.3
4X4	4.0
P/up-4 Runner	
4X2	4.2
4X4	4.0
Land Cruiser	4.5
Renew throw out brg add	.1
Renew pilot brg add	.1
Flywheel, Renew	
Van	
4X2	3.7
4X4	4.4
P/up-4 Runner	
4X2	4.8
4X4	4.6
Land Cruiser	5.3

LABOR 19 STANDARD TRANSMISSION 19 LABOR

4 SPEED

	Chilton Time
Transmission Assy., Remove & Install	
All models	
Gas	3.6
Diesel	4.0
Transmission Assy., R&R and Recondition	
Includes: Complete disassembly, clean and inspect or renew all parts. Install new gaskets and seals.	
All models	
Gas	8.2
Diesel	9.3
Extension Housing Gasket, Renew	
All models	
Gas	2.9
Diesel	1.8
Extension Housing Rear Oil Seal, Renew	
All models	
Gas	1.3
Diesel	1.0
Rear Engine Mount, Renew	
All models	.6
Speedometer Driven Gear, Renew	
Land Cruiser	.6
All other models	.5

5 SPEED

	Chilton Time
Transmission Assy., Remove & Install	
Van	
4X2	3.0
4X4	3.7
P/up-4 Runner	
Four	
4X2	3.6
4X4	3.7
V-6	
4X2	3.6
4X4	4.1
Land Cruiser	
H/T	7.4
Wagon	6.9
Rear Engine Mount, Renew	
Van	1.0
All other models	.6
Transmission Assy., R&R and Recondition	
Includes: Complete disassembly, clean and inspect or renew all parts. Install new gaskets and seals.	
Van	
4X2	7.8
4X4	8.1
P/up-4 Runner	
Four	
4X2	
Gas	7.6
Diesel	9.5
4X4	7.8
V-6	
4X2	7.6
4X4	8.0
Land Cruiser	
H/T	12.1
Wagon	11.5
Extension Housing Gasket, Renew	
Van	1.8
P/up-4 Runner	2.7
Extension Housing Rear Oil Seal, Renew	
Van	1.0
P/up-4 Runner	1.4

LABOR   19A   MANUAL TRANSMISSION (RWD)   19A   LABOR

	Chilton Time
Transfer Case Assy., Remove & Install	
Van	2.1
P/up-4 Runner	
w/M.T.	
Four	4.2
V-6	4.4
w/A.T.	
Four	9.3
V-6	9.6
Land Cruiser	5.9

	Chilton Time
Transfer Case Assy., R&R and Recondition	
Van	5.7
P/up-4 Runner	
w/M.T.	
Four	8.1
V-6	8.4
w/A.T.	
Four	13.2
V-6	13.4
Land Cruiser	8.9
Front Driveshaft Oil Seal, Renew	
Van	1.2

	Chilton Time
P/up-4 Runner	1.7
Land Cruiser	
H/T	1.5
Wagon	1.3
Output Shaft Bearing Retainer and/or Oil Seal, Renew	
Van	1.4
P/up-4 Runner	1.1
Land Cruiser	
H/T	1.5
Wagon	1.6

LABOR   21   SHIFT LINKAGE   21   LABOR

MANUAL	Chilton Time
Gear Shift Lever, Renew	
Van	.6
P/up-4 Runner	.7
Land Cruiser-H/T	.6
Sta Wagon	.9
Gearshift Lever Retainer, Renew	
All models	.8

AUTOMATIC	Chilton Time
Selector Lever, Renew	
Van	.6
P/up-4 Runner	
4X2	1.1
4X4	1.6
Land Cruiser	.8

	Chilton Time
Selector Lever Boot and/or Retainer, Renew	
P/up-4 Runner	
4X2	.8
4X4	1.8
Selector Lever Indicator Bulb, Renew	
All models	
4X2	.5
4X4	.7

LABOR   23   AUTOMATIC TRANSMISSION   23   LABOR

A-30
ON CAR SERVICES

	Chilton Time
Drain & Refill Unit	
All models	.8
Check Unit For Oil Leaks	
Includes: Clean and dry outside of case and run unit to determine point of leak.	
All models	.9
Oil Pressure Test	
All models	1.0
Throttle Rod or Cable, Adjust	
All models	.4
Throttle Valve Lever Seal, Renew	
All models	1.9
Parking Lock Rod, Renew	
All models	.6
Extension Housing Rear Oil Seal, Renew	
All models	1.3
Extension Housing Gasket, Renew	
All models	2.7
Governor Assembly, Renew	
Includes: R&R extension housing.	
All models	2.9
Oil Pan or Gasket, Renew	
All models	1.2
Valve Body Assembly, Renew	
Includes: R&R oil pan.	
All models	2.5
Valve Body Assy., R&R and Recondition	
Includes: R&R oil pan. Disassemble, clean, inspect, free all valves. Replace parts as required.	
All models	3.5

SERVICES REQUIRING R&R

	Chilton Time
Transmission Assembly, Renew	
All models	4.7

	Chilton Time
Transmission Assy., R&R and Recondition	
Includes: Complete disassembly, including valve body. Clean and inspect or renew all parts. Reassemble, make all necessary adjustments.	
All models	11.0
Torque Converter, Renew	
Includes: R&R transmission.	
All models	4.9
Front Pump Oil Seal, Renew	
Includes: R&R transmission.	
All models	5.1
Flywheel and Drive Plate, Renew	
Includes: R&R transmission.	
All models	5.1

A-40–A43D–A340E–A340H
ON CAR SERVICES

	Chilton Time
Drain and Refill Unit	
All models	.8
Check Unit For Oil Leaks	
Includes: Clean and dry outside of case and run unit to determine point of leak.	
All models	.9
Oil Pressure Test	
All models	1.5
Throttle Rod or Cable, Adjust	
All models	.4
Manual Valve Lever Shaft Seal, Renew	
Van	2.5
P/up-4 Runner	
4X2	5.9
4X4	6.6
Land Cruiser	3.1
Throttle Cable, Renew	
Van-P/up	2.1
Land Cruiser	3.4

	Chilton Time
Overdrive Solenoid, Renew	
Van	1.2
All other models	
4X2	.9
4X4	2.0
Extension Housing Rear Oil Seal, Renew	
Van-P/up	1.1
Extension Housing Gasket, Renew	
Van	2.5
P/up	2.9
Speedometer Cable and Casing, Renew	
Van-P/up	1.3
Land Cruiser	
H/T	.7
Wagon	1.0
Governor Assembly, Renew	
Van-P/up	3.1
Land Cruiser	7.4
Valve Body Assembly, Renew	
Van	2.5
All other models	3.7

SERVICES REQUIRING R&R

	Chilton Time
Transmission Assy., R&R or Renew	
Van	
4X2	4.2
4X4	5.2
P/up-4 Runner	
4X2	5.6
4X4	6.0
Land Cruiser	7.3
Transmission Assy., R&R and Recondition	
Includes: Complete disassembly, including valve body. Clean and inspect or renew all parts. Reassemble and adjust.	
Van	
4X2	16.3
4X4	16.9
P/up-4 Runner	
4X2	13.5
4X4	14.0
Land Cruiser	20.7

LABOR 23A AUTOMATIC TRANSMISSION (RWD) 23A LABOR

	Chilton Time
Torque Converter, Renew	
Includes: R&R trans.	
Van	
4X2	4.3
4X4	5.3
P/up-4 Runner	
4X2	5.7
4X4	6.2
Land Cruiser	7.4
Front Pump Oil Seal, Renew	
Includes: R&R trans.	
Van	
4X2	4.9

	Chilton Time
4X4	5.9
P/up-4 Runner	
4X2	5.8
4X4	6.3
Land Cruiser	7.5
Flywheel and Flex Plate, Renew	
Includes: R&R trans.	
Van	
4X2	4.3
4X4	5.3

	Chilton Time
P/up-4 Runner	
4X2	5.8
4X4	6.5
Land Cruiser	7.7
Transfer Case, R&R and Recondition	
Includes: R&R transmission.	
Van	8.8
P/up-4 Runner	12.3
Land Cruiser	12.8

LABOR 25 U-JOINTS & DRIVESHAFT 25 LABOR

	Chilton Time
Rear Driveshaft, R&R or Renew	
Van	.8
All other models	1.1
Intermediate Driveshaft, R&R or Renew	
P/up-4 Runner	1.2

	Chilton Time
Universal Spider Joint, Renew or Rebuild (One)	
Van	1.3
All other models	1.8
Center Bearing, Renew	
P/up-4 Runner	1.3

	Chilton Time
U-Joint Yoke, Renew	
Van	1.3
P/up-4 Runner	1.3
Land Cruiser	1.6

LABOR 26 DRIVE AXLE 26 LABOR

	Chilton Time
REAR DIFFERENTIAL ASSEMBLY	
Rear Axle Shaft, Renew (One)	
Van	1.6
P/up-4 Runner	
w/Single rear whls	1.7
w/Dual rear whls	.7
Land Cruiser	1.8
Rear Axle Shaft Bearing, Renew (One Side)	
Van	1.5
P/up-4 Runner	
w/Single rear whls	1.7
w/Dual rear whls	2.0
Land Cruiser	1.7
Rear Axle Shaft Oil Seal, Renew (One Side)	
Van	1.0
P/up-4 Runner	
w/Single rear whls	1.5
w/Dual rear whls	.7
Land Cruiser	1.4
Differential Rear Cover Gasket, Renew	
Land Cruiser	.9
Pinion Shaft Oil Seal, Renew	
Van	1.0
P/up-4 Runner	1.7
Land Cruiser	
H/T	1.5
Wagon	1.0
Differential Carrier Assy., R&R or Renew Gasket	
Van	2.6
P/up-4 Runner	
w/Single rear whls	2.6
w/Dual rear whls	2.5
Land Cruiser	3.1

	Chilton Time
Differential Carrier Assy., R&R and Recondition	
Van	6.0
P/up-4 Runner	
w/Single rear whls	6.6
w/Dual rear whls	5.7
Land Cruiser	6.9
Ring Gear and Pinion Set, Renew	
Van	5.5
P/up-4 Runner	
w/Single rear whls	6.1
w/Dual rear whls	5.2
Land Cruiser	6.4
Differential Side Bearings, Renew (Both Sides)	
Van	3.5
P/up-4 Runner	
w/Single rear whls	3.7
w/Dual rear whls	3.1
Land Cruiser	4.1
FRONT DIFFERENTIAL ASSEMBLY	
Front Axle Inner Shaft, Renew (One)	
P/up-4 Runner	1.9
Land Cruiser	2.0
Universal Joint Flange, Renew	
Van	2.4
P/up-4 Runner	1.9
Land Cruiser	.9
Pinion Shaft Oil Seal, Renew	
Van	2.4
P/up-4 Runner	1.9
Land Cruiser	
H/T	1.5
Wagon	1.0

	Chilton Time
Differential Carrier Assy., R&R or Renew Gasket	
Van	2.5
P/up-4 Runner	3.2
Land Cruiser	4.9
Ring Gear and Pinion Set, Renew	
Van	6.6
P/up-4 Runner	7.9
Land Cruiser	
H/T	8.1
Wagon	7.4
Differential Side Bearings, Renew	
Van	4.8
All other models	5.9
Pinion Bearings, Renew	
Van	6.1
P/up-4 Runner	7.1
Land Cruiser	6.7
Front Differential Assy., R&R and Recondition	
Van	7.6
P/up-4 Runner	8.7
Land Cruiser	8.3
Front Drive Shaft, Renew	
Van	1.4
All other models	1.9
Front Drive Shaft Boot, Renew	
Includes: Renew or recondition C.V. joints.	
Van	2.0
All other models	2.4

LABOR 27 REAR SUSPENSION 27 LABOR

LEAF TYPE

	Chilton Time
Rear Leaf Spring, Renew (One)	
Van	1.2
All other models	1.4
Rear Leaf Spring, R&R and Recondition	
Van	1.7
All other models	1.9

	Chilton Time
Rear Spring Shackle, Renew (One Side)	
All models	.8
Rear Shock Absorbers, Renew	
All models–one	.5
both	.7

LINK TYPE

	Chilton Time
Lower Control Arm, Renew (One)	
Van	.7
Rear Coil Spring, Renew (One)	
Van	.7
Rear Shock Absorbers, Renew	
Van–one	.7
both	.9

LABOR 28 AIR CONDITIONING 28 LABOR

FACTORY INSTALLED SYSTEM

Note: If more than one item requires replacement where evacuation and discharging the system is already included in the operation, deduct 1.0 hour for each additional item to the times listed.

	Chilton Time
Drain, Evacuate & Recharge System	
All models	1.0
Flush Refrigerant System, Complete	
To be used in conjunction with component replacement which could contaminate system.	
All models	1.3
Compressor Drive Belt, Renew	
Van	1.0
All other models	.5
Compressor Assembly, Renew	
Includes: Transfer parts as required. Evacuate and charge system.	
Van	2.3
All other models	1.7
Condenser Assembly, Renew	
Includes: Evacuate and charge system.	
Van	2.4
All other models	1.7
Receiver-Drier, Renew	
Includes: Evacuate and charge system.	
Van	2.0
All other models	1.4

	Chilton Time
Compressor Clutch Assembly, Renew	
Van	2.4
P/up-4 Runner	
Gas	1.8
Diesel	1.8
Land Cruiser	.7
Expansion Valve, Renew	
Includes: Evacuate and charge system.	
Van	3.0
All other models	2.1
Evaporator Coil, Renew	
Includes: Evacuate and charge system.	
Van	3.0
All other models	2.3
Pressure Cut Off Switch, Renew	
Includes: Evacuate and charge system.	
Van	2.9
All other models	1.8
A.C. Blower Motor, Renew	
Van	3.7
P/up-4 Runner	
1986-88	.9
1989-90	1.5
Land Cruiser	.5

DEALER INSTALLED SYSTEM

	Chilton Time
Drain, Evacuate & Recharge System	
All models	1.0

	Chilton Time
Compressor Drive Belt, Renew	
All models	.6
Compressor Assembly, Renew	
Includes: Transfer parts as required. Evacuate and charge system.	
All models	2.0
Compressor Clutch Assy., or Bearing, Renew	
All models	.9
Condenser Assembly, Renew	
Includes: Evacuate and charge system.	
All models	1.9
Receiver-Drier, Renew	
Includes: Evacuate and charge system.	
All models	1.4
Expansion Valve, Renew	
Includes: Evacuate and charge system.	
All models	1.7
Evaporator Coil, Renew	
Includes: Evacuate and charge system.	
All models	2.3
Blower Motor, Renew	
All models	2.0
Blower Motor Resistor, Renew	
All models	2.2

LABOR 29 LOCKS, HINGES & WIND. REGULATORS 29 LABOR

	Chilton Time
Hood Hinges, Renew (Both)	
All models	.8
Hood Lock, Renew	
All models	.4
Hood Release Cable, Renew	
All models	.8
Front Door Lock Assy., Renew (One Side)	
All models	.6

	Chilton Time
Rear Door Lock Assy., Renew	
All models	.8
Lock Striker Plate, Renew	
All models	.3
Door Handle (Outside), Renew	
All models–front	.6
rear	.7

	Chilton Time
Door Window Regulator, Renew	
All models–front	.8
rear	.9
w/Pwr windows add	.2
Tail Gate Lock Assy., Renew	
All models	.5
Tail Gate Window Regulator, Renew	
Land Cruiser	1.0

LABOR 30 HEAD AND PARKING LAMPS 30 LABOR

	Chilton Time
Aim Headlamps	
two	.4
four	.6
Headlamp Sealed Beam Bulb, Renew	
All models	.6
Turn Signal Lamp Lens or Bulb, Renew	
All models	.3

	Chilton Time
Parking Lamp Lens or Bulb, Renew	
All models	.3
Side Marker Lamp Lens or Bulb, Renew	
All models	.4
Back-Up Lamp Lens or Bulb, Renew	
All models	.4

	Chilton Time
Rear Combination Lamp Lens or Bulb, Renew	
All models	.4
License Lamp Lens or Bulb, Renew	
All models	.3

LABOR 31 WINDSHIELD WIPER & SPEEDOMETER 31 LABOR

	Chilton Time
Windshield Wiper Motor, Renew	
Van	2.7
All other models	.5
Wiper Link Assy., Renew	
Van	2.8
Land Cruiser-H/T	1.0
All other models	.7
Washer Motor and Pump Assy., Renew	
Van	.7
All other models	.4
Speedometer Head, R&R or Renew	
Van	1.1
All other models	1.0

	Chilton Time
Speedometer Cable and Casing, Renew (w/Manual Trans.)	
Van P/up-4 Runner	1.3
Land Cruiser-H/T	.7
Wagon	1.0
Windshield Wiper Switch Assy., Renew	
Van	1.1
P/up-4 Runner	.8
Land Cruiser	
H/T	1.0
Wagon	.5
Rear Window Wiper Switch, Renew	
All models	.4

	Chilton Time
Rear Window Wiper Motor, Renew	
Van	.6
P/up-4 Runner	.7
Land Cruiser	
H/T	.9
Wagon	.5
Rear Window Washer Motor and Pump, Renew	
Van	1.0
P/up-4 Runner	.3
Land Cruiser	
H/T	.5
Wagon	.4
Radio, R&R	
Van	.6
All other models	.8

LABOR 32 LIGHT SWITCHES & WIRING 32 LABOR

	Chilton Time
Stop Light Switch, Renew	
All models	.7
Back-Up Lamp Switch, Renew	
Van-P/up-4 Runner	.5
Land Cruiser	
H/T	.5
Wagon	1.0
Neutral Safety Switch, Renew	
All models	.7

	Chilton Time
Turn Signal Switch Assy., Renew	
Van	.9
P/up-4 Runner	.7
Land Cruiser	.8
Turn Signal Flasher, Renew	
All models	.3
Hazard Warning Switch, Renew	
P/up-4 Runner	.3
Van	1.0
Land Cruiser	1.0

	Chilton Time
Parking Brake Warning Lamp Switch, Renew	
Van-P/up-4 Runner	.4
Land Cruiser	.5
Headlamp Switch, Renew	
Van	1.1
P/up-4 Runner	.8
Land Cruiser	1.0
Horns, Renew	
All models	.4

LABOR 34 CRUISE CONTROL 34 LABOR

	Chilton Time
Cruise Control Computer, Renew	
Van	.9
P/up-4 Runner	.9

	Chilton Time
Cruise Control Switch, Renew	
Van	.4
P/up-4 Runner	.5

	Chilton Time
Cruise Control Actuator, Renew	
Van	.8
P/up-4 Runner	.6

GROUP INDEX

ALPHABETICAL INDEX

LABOR   1   TUNE UP   1   LABOR

	Chilton Time
Compression Test	
All models	.6
w/A.C. add	.2
Engine Tune Up, (Electronic Ignition)	

Includes: Test battery and clean connections. Tighten manifold mounting bolts. Check engine compression, clean and adjust or renew

spark plugs. Inspect distributor cap and rotor. Check vacuum advance operation. Reset ignition timing. Adjust idle mixture and idle speed. Service air cleaner. Inspect crankcase ventilation system. Inspect and adjust drive belts. Inspect choke operation and adjust or free up. Check operation of EGR valve.

	Chilton Time
All models	1.5

LABOR   2   IGNITION SYSTEM   2   LABOR

POINT TYPE IGNITION	Chilton Time
Spark Plugs, Clean and Reset or Renew	
All models	.5
Ignition Timing, Reset	
All models	.4
Distributor, Renew	
Includes: Reset ignition timing and dwell.	
All models	.6
Distributor Cap and/or Rotor, Renew	
All models	.3

	Chilton Time
Vacuum Advance Unit, Renew	
Includes: R&R distributor and reset ignition timing and dwell.	
All models	.8
Ignition Coil, Renew	
All models	.4
Ignition Cables, Renew	
All models	.6
Ignition Switch, Renew	
All models	.9

ELECTRONIC IGNITION	Chilton Time
Control Unit, Renew	
All models	.4
Pick-Up Coil, Renew (Hall Generator)	
All models	.6
Glow Plugs, Renew	
All models-one	.5
all	.8
Glow Plug Relay, Renew	
All models	.4

LABOR   3   FUEL SYSTEM   3   LABOR

	Chilton Time
Fuel Injectors, Clean (On Car) (w/TBI or MPI)	
Includes: Hook up pressurized fuel injection cleaning equipment.	
All models	.5
ELECTRONIC FUEL INJECTION	
Fuel Injection System, Test and Adjust	
All models	1.4
Fuel Injectors, Renew	
All models-one side	.6
both sides	.9
Clean and test add-each	.2
Throttle Valve Housing, Renew	
Includes: Transfer or renew throttle valve switch and adjust.	
All models	.9
Throttle Valve Switch, Renew or Adjust	
All models	.5
Intake Air Sensor, Renew	
All models	.4
Intake Air Distributor, Renew	
All models	1.5
Intake Pipes, Renew	
Includes: R&R injector and retainer.	
All models-one side	1.2
both sides	2.0

	Chilton Time
Auxiliary Air Regulator, Renew	
All models	.6
Temperature Sensor, Renew	
All models	.5
Thermo Switch, Renew	
All models	.6
Pressure Sensor, Renew	
All models	.3
Pressure Regulator, R&R or Renew	
All models	.8
Cold Start Valve, Renew	
All models	.6
Temperature Sensor (In Head), Renew	
All models	.6
Electronic Control Unit, Renew	
All models	.4
Deceleration Valve, Renew	
All models	.4
Oxygen Sensor, Renew	
All models	.4
Voltage Supply Relay, Renew	
All models	.4
Electric Fuel Pump, Renew	
All models	.6
Fuel Tank, Renew	
Includes: Drain and refill tank.	
All models	
4X2	2.0
4X4	4.0

	Chilton Time
Fuel Gauge (Tank Unit), Renew	
All models	
4X2	2.4
4X4	1.8
Fuel Gauge (Dash Unit), Renew	
All models	1.5
DIESEL FUEL INJECTION	
Fuel Filter, Renew	
All models	.4
Idle Speed, Adjust	
All models	.5
Injection Timing, Check and Adjust	
All models	1.0
Advance Cable, Renew	
All models	3.9
Air Cleaner, Service	
All models	.3
Injection Pump, Renew	
All models	3.6
Fuel Injection Lines, Renew	
All models-all	.8
Fuel Injectors, Renew	
All models-one	.4
all	.9
Clean and test add, each	.3
Fuel Shut-Off Solenoid, Renew	
All models	.4
Intake Manifold and/or Gasket, Renew	
All models	1.5

LABOR 3A EMISSION CONTROLS 3A LABOR

	Chilton Time
E.G.R. Valve, Renew	
All models	.5
E.G.R. Filter, Renew	
All models	.4
Check Valve, Renew	
All models	.3

	Chilton Time
Diverter Valve, Renew	
All models	.3
Catalytic Converter Temperature Sensor, Renew	
All models	.4
Oxygen Sensor, Renew	
All models	.4

	Chilton Time
Charcoal Filter, Renew	
All models	.3
Deceleration Valve, Renew	
All models	.3
Anti-Backfire Valve, Renew	
All models	.3

LABOR 4 ALTERNATOR AND REGULATOR 4 LABOR

	Chilton Time
Alternator Circuits, Test	
Includes: Test battery, regulator and alternator output.	
All models	.5
Alternator Assembly, Renew	
Includes: Circuit test.	
All models	
Air cooled eng	1.4
Water cooled eng	.6
Diesel eng	1.1

	Chilton Time
Alternator, R&R and Recondition	
Includes: Disassemble alternator completely, renew parts as required, reassemble and test.	
All models	
Air cooled eng	3.1
Water cooled eng	2.3
Diesel eng	2.8
Voltage Regulator, Test and Renew	
All models	.8

	Chilton Time
Alternator Bearings, Renew	
Includes: R&R alternator.	
All models	
Air cooled eng	1.8
Water cooled eng	1.0
Diesel eng	1.5

LABOR 5 STARTING SYSTEM 5 LABOR

	Chilton Time
Starter Draw Test (On Vehicle)	
All models	.3
Starter Assembly, Renew	
All models	
Gas	1.0
Diesel	1.6
Add draw test if performed.	

	Chilton Time
Starter, R&R and Recondition	
Includes: Turn down armature.	
All models	
Gas	2.9
Diesel	3.6
Renew field coils add	.5
Starter Solenoid, Renew	
Includes: R&R starter.	
All models	
Gas	1.2
Diesel	1.9

	Chilton Time
Starter Drive, Renew	
Includes: R&R starter.	
All models	
Gas	1.8
Diesel	2.4
Battery Cables, Renew	
All models	
positive	.8
negative	.3

LABOR 6 BRAKE SYSTEM 6 LABOR

	Chilton Time
Brakes, Adjust (Minor)	
Includes: Fill master cylinder.	
two wheels	.4
Bleed Brakes (Four Wheels)	
Includes: Fill master cylinder.	
All models	.5
Brake Shoes and/or Pads, Renew	
Includes: Install new or exchange brake shoes or pads. Adjust service and hand brake. Bleed system.	
All models	
front-disc	.9
rear-drum	2.0
all four wheels	2.7
Resurface disc brake rotor, add-each	.9
Resurface brake drum, add-each	.5
Rear Brake Drum, Renew (One)	
All models	1.0

BRAKE HYDRAULIC SYSTEM

	Chilton Time
Wheel Cylinders, Renew	
Includes: Bleed system.	
All models-one	1.4
both	2.7

COMBINATIONS

	Chilton Time
RENEW WHEEL CYLINDER	
Each	.3
REBUILD WHEEL CYLINDER	
Each	.4
REBUILD MASTER CYLINDER	
All models	.5
RENEW BRAKE HOSE	
Each	.3
REBUILD CALIPER ASSEMBLY	
Each	.5
CLEAN AND REPACK FRONT WHEEL BEARINGS (BOTH WHEELS)	
All models	.6
RENEW BRAKE DRUM	
Each	.2
RENEW DISC BRAKE ROTOR	
Each	.2

	Chilton Time
Wheel Cylinders, R&R and Rebuild	
Includes: Bleed system.	
All models-one	1.8
both	3.5
Master Cylinder, Renew	
Includes: Bleed system.	
All models	2.4
Master Cylinder, R&R and Rebuild	
Includes: Bleed system.	
All models	3.0
Brake Hose, Renew (Flex)	
Includes: Bleed system.	
All models-one	.6
Brake Pressure Limiting Valve, Renew	
Includes: Bleed system.	
All models	1.0
Brake System, Flush and Refill	
All models	1.2

DISC BRAKES

	Chilton Time
Disc Brake Pads, Renew	
Includes: Install new disc brake pads only.	
All models	.9

LABOR   6   BRAKE SYSTEM   6   LABOR

	Chilton Time
Disc Brake Rotor, Renew	
All models-one	1.1
both	2.0
Caliper Assembly, Renew	
Includes: Bleed system.	
All models-one	1.0
both	1.9
Caliper Assy., R&R and Recondition	
Includes: Bleed system.	
All models-one	1.5
both	2.9

	Chilton Time
POWER BRAKES	
Power Brake Booster, Renew	
Includes: R&R master cylinder and bleed system.	
All models	3.0
Brake Booster Check Valve, Renew	
All models	.3
Vacuum Pump, Renew	
All models	.6
Recond pump add	.4

	Chilton Time
PARKING BRAKE	
Parking Brake, Adjust	
All models	.5
Parking Brake Control, Renew	
All models	.9
Parking Brake Cables, Renew	
All models	
one	1.0
both	1.5

LABOR   7   COOLING SYSTEM   7   LABOR

	Chilton Time
AIR COOLED ENGINE	
Air Cooling Fan, Renew	
All models	1.5
Air Cooled Thermostat, Renew	
All models	.8
Fresh Air Blower Motor, Renew	
All models	3.1
Fan Housing, Remove & Install	
Includes: R&R engine assy.	
All models	4.4
w/A.C. add	1.5
Heater Control Cable, Renew (One)	
All models	1.5
Heat Exchanger, Renew (One)	
Includes: R&R heater.	
All models	2.6
WATER COOLED ENGINES	
Thermostat, Renew	
All models	
Gas eng	
1986-90	.4
Diesel eng	1.4

	Chilton Time
Radiator Assembly, R&R or Renew	
All models	2.4
Radiator Hose, Renew	
All models-one	.8
Electric Fan, Renew	
All models	1.4
Electric Fan Relay, Renew	
All models	.3
Fan Thermo Switch, Renew	
All models	1.4
Water Pump, Renew	
All models	
Gas eng	2.4
Diesel eng	2.0
w/A.C. add	.5
w/P.S. add	.2
Water Pump/Alternator Belt, Renew	
All models	
w/Diesel eng	1.1
Water Pump/Alternator Belt, Adjust	
All models	
w/Diesel eng	.6

	Chilton Time
Temperature Gauge (Engine Unit), Renew	
All models	.6
Temperature Gauge (Dash Unit), Renew	
All models	1.5
Heater Valve, Renew	
All models	
w/Diesel eng	.5
Heater Core, R&R or Renew	
All models	4.5
ADD THESE OPERATIONS TO HEATER CORE R&R	
Boil & Repair	1.2
Repair Core	.9
Recore	1.2
Rear Heater Core, Renew	
All models	
Gas	.8
Diesel	1.0
Heater Blower Motor, Renew	
All models	
Gas	4.0
Diesel	5.0
Renew resistor add	.2

LABOR   8   EXHAUST SYSTEM   8   LABOR

	Chilton Time
Front Exhaust Pipe, Renew	
All models	.8
Muffler, Renew	
All models	1.2
w/Diesel eng add	.1

	Chilton Time
Tail Pipe, Renew	
All models	.4
w/Diesel eng add	.1
Catalytic Converter, Renew	
All models	1.0

	Chilton Time
Exhaust Manifolds, Renew	
All models	
Air Cooled eng	
one	1.1
both	1.8
Water Cooled eng	
one	.9
both	2.4
Diesel eng	1.1

LABOR   9A   FRONT SUSPENSION (RWD)   9A   LABOR

	Chilton Time
Note: On all front suspension operations alignment charges must be added if performed. Time given does not include alignment.	
Wheel, Renew	
one	.5
Wheels, Rotate (All)	
All models	.5

	Chilton Time
Wheel, Balance	
one	.3
each adtnl	.2
Toe-In, Adjust	
All models	.6
Align Front End	
Includes: Adjust camber, toe-in and front wheel bearings.	
All models	1.5

	Chilton Time
Radias Rod, Renew (One)	
Includes: Adjust.	
All models	1.0
Upper Control Arms, Renew	
Add alignment charges.	
All models	
one side	.9
both sides	1.7
Renew bushings, add-each side	.3

LABOR 9A FRONT SUSPENSION (RWD) 9A LABOR

	Chilton Time		Chilton Time		Chilton Time
Lower Control Arms, Renew		**Steering Knuckles, Renew**		**Front Coil Spring, Renew (One)**	
Add alignment charges.		Add alignment charges.		Includes: Alignment charges.	
All models		All models		All models	1.8
one side	2.4	one side	2.1		
both sides	4.4	both sides	3.8	**Front Stabilizer Bar, Renew**	
Renew bushings, add-each side	.3	**Front Wheel Bearings, Clean and Repack (Both Wheels)**		All models	1.0
		All models		**Front Shock Absorbers, Renew**	
Upper Ball Joints, Renew		4X2	1.2	4X2-one	.6
Add alignment charges.		4X4	2.0	both	1.0
All models		**Front Wheel Bearings, Renew (One Side)**		4X4-one	1.1
one side	.9	All models		both	2.0
both sides	1.4	4X2	1.2		
		4X4	2.0	**Half Shaft, R&R or Renew**	
Lower Ball Joints, Renew		**Front Wheel Hubs, Renew**		All models-one	1.5
Add alignment charges.		All models		Renew or Recond C.V. Joint or boot add	
All models		one	1.2	inner or outer-one	.4
one side	1.7	both	2.0	inner and outer-one side	.6
both sides	3.0				

LABOR 11 STEERING GEAR 11 LABOR

	Chilton Time		Chilton Time		Chilton Time
MANUAL STEERING		**Manual Rack and Pinion Assy., R&R or Renew**		**Power Steering Pump Drive Belt, Adjust**	
Steering Wheel, Renew		Add alignment charges.		All models	.2
All models	.4	All models	1.1	**Power Steering Pump, Renew**	
		Tie Rods or Tie Rod Ends, Renew		All models	1.0
Upper Mast Jacket Bearing, Renew		Includes: Reset toe-in. Renew boots.		**Power Rack and Pinion Assy., R&R or Renew**	
All models	1.0	All models-one side	.7	Add alignment charges.	
		both sides	1.2	All models	1.2
Coupling Disc, Renew		**POWER STEERING**		**Power Steering Hoses, Renew**	
All models	.6	**Power Steering Pump Drive Belt, Renew**		All models	
		All models	.3	pressure	.7
				return	.5

LABOR 12 CYLINDER HEAD & VALVE SYSTEM 12 LABOR

	Chilton Time		Chilton Time		Chilton Time
AIR COOLED ENGINE		w/A.T.-one side	9.0	**Cylinder Head Gasket, Renew**	
Compression Test		both sides	11.7	All models-one	6.0
All models	.6	w/A.C. add	1.5	both	8.2
w/A.C. add	.2	Renew valve guides, add-each	.3	w/A.C. add	.8
Cylinder Head Gasket, Renew		**Valve Cover Gasket, Renew**		**Cylinder Head, Renew**	
Includes: R&R engine assy. Make all necessary		All models-one	.4	Includes: Transfer parts. Reface valves to seats. Make all necessary adjustments.	
adjustments.		both	.6	All models-one	6.6
All models		**Rocker Arms, Renew**		both	9.4
w/M.T.-one side	6.4	Includes: Adjust valve clearance.		w/A.C. add	.8
both sides	8.1	All models-one side	1.0		
w/A.T.-one side	7.8	both sides	1.6	**Clean Carbon and Grind Valves**	
both sides	9.4	**Valve Push Rods, Renew**		Includes: Reface valves and seats. Inspect valve guides. Make all necessary adjustments.	
w/A.C. add	1.5	Includes: R&R rocker arms and adjust valve		All models-one	7.2
Cylinder Head, Renew		clearance.		both	10.5
Includes: R&R engine assy. Transfer parts as required. Reface valves. Make all necessary adjustments.		All models-one side	1.4	w/A.C. add	.8
		both sides	2.0	Renew valve guides add, each	.3
All models		**Push Rod Tubes, Reseal**		**Valve Cover Gaskets, Renew**	
w/M.T.-one side	7.0	Includes: Adjust valve clearance.		All models-one	.4
both sides	9.3	All models-one side	1.6	both	.6
w/A.T.-one side	8.4	both sides	2.4	**Push Rod Tubes, Reseal (Head on Car)**	
both sides	10.6	**Valve Springs, Renew (Head Installed)**		All models	
w/A.C. add	1.5	All models-one	1.2	one side	1.4
Clean Carbon and Grind Valves		all	2.8	**Hydraulic Valve Lifters, Renew**	
Includes: R&R engine assy. and cylinder head(s). Reface valves and seats. Inspect valve guides. Make all necessary adjustments.		**Hydraulic Valve Lifters, Renew**		All models-one side	1.7
		All models-one side	1.5		
All models		**WATER COOLED ENGINE**		**DIESEL ENGINE**	
w/M.T.-one side	7.6	**Compression Test**		**Compression Test**	
both sides	10.3	All models	.6	All models	1.0

LABOR 12 CYLINDER HEAD & VALVE SYSTEM 12 LABOR

	Chilton Time
Cylinder Head Gasket, Renew	
Includes: Clean carbon. Make all necessary adjustments.	
All models	4.9
Cylinder Head, Renew (Exchange)	
Includes: Transfer parts as required. Make all necessary adjustments.	
All models	5.0

	Chilton Time
Clean Carbon and Grind Valves	
Includes: R&R cylinder head. Reface valves and seats. Renew valve stem oil seals. Make all necessary adjustments.	
All models	10.5
Valve Cover and/or Gasket, Renew	
All models	.5
Valve Clearance, Adjust	
All models	1.0

	Chilton Time
Cam Followers, Renew	
All models	2.4
Valve Stem Oil Seals, Renew (Head on Car)	
All models	3.3
Cylinder Head, Retorque	
Includes: Adjust valve clearance.	
All models	1.5

LABOR 13 ENGINE ASSEMBLY & MOUNTS 13 LABOR

	Chilton Time
AIR COOLED ENGINE	
Engine Assembly, Remove & Install	
Does not include transfer of any parts or equipment.	
All models	
w/M.T.	2.4
w/A.T.	3.7
w/A.C. add	1.5
Engine Assembly, Renew (Exchange)	
Includes: R&R engine assy. Transfer all component parts not supplied with replacement engine. Tune engine.	
All models	
w/M.T.	8.4
w/A.T.	9.9
w/A.C. add	1.5
Engine Assy., R&R and Recondition	
Includes: Install new cylinder assemblies, pistons, rings, pins, rod and main bearings. Clean	

	Chilton Time
carbon, grind valves. Reseal crankcase. Tune engine.	
All models	
w/M.T.	20.0
w/A.T.	21.5
w/A.C. add	1.5
Engine Support Pads, Renew	
Includes: R&R muffler and heat exchanger.	
All models	2.5
WATER COOLED ENGINE	
Engine Assembly, Remove & Install	
Does not include transfer of any parts or equipment.	
All models	4.3
w/A.C. add	.8
Engine Assembly, Renew (Exchange)	
Includes: R&R engine assy. Transfer all component parts not supplied with replacement en-	

	Chilton Time
gine.	
All models	10.3
w/A.C. add	.8
Engine Carrier, Renew	
Includes: Renew or transfer engine mounting support pads.	
All models	2.5
DIESEL ENGINE	
Engine Assembly, Remove & Install	
Does not include transfer of any parts or equipment.	
All models	4.3
Cylinder Assy. (Short Block), Renew	
Includes: R&R engine assy. Transfer all component parts not supplied with replacement engine, clean carbon, grind valves. Make all necessary adjustments.	
All models	15.4
Engine Mounts, Renew	
All models-one	1.2

LABOR 14 PISTONS, RINGS & BEARINGS 14 LABOR

	Chilton Time
AIR COOLED ENGINE	
Piston and Cylinder Assy,s. Renew	
Includes: R&R engine assy. and cylinder head(s). Install new cylinder assemblies with pistons and rings. Install new rod bearings. Make all necessary adjustments.	
All models	
w/M.T.-one side	6.9
both sides	9.4
w/A.T.-one side	8.2
both sides	10.8
w/A.C. add	1.5
Piston Rings, Renew	
Includes: R&R engine assy. and cylinder head(s). Remove pistons and install new rings. Make all necessary adjustments.	
All models	
w/M.T.-one side	7.3
both sides	11.2

	Chilton Time
w/A.T.-one side	8.7
both sides	12.6
w/A.C. add	1.5
WATER COOLED ENGINE	
Piston and Cylinder Assy's, renew	
All models	
one side	8.2
both sides	11.4
w/A.C. add	.8
Piston Rings, Renew	
Includes: Remove pistons and install new rings. Make all necessary adjustments.	
All models	
one side	9.1
both sides	12.6
w/A.C. add	.8

	Chilton Time
DIESEL ENGINE	
Pistons or Connecting Rods, Renew (All)	
Includes: R&R cylinder head and oil pan.	
All models	8.4
Piston Rings, Renew (All)	
Includes: R&R cylinder head and oil pan.	
All models	9.0
Connecting Rod Bearings, Renew	
Includes: R&R oil pan.	
All models	3.0

LABOR 15 CRANKSHAFT & DAMPER 15 LABOR

AIR COOLED ENGINE

Crankshaft and Main Bearings, Renew
Includes: R&R engine assy. Make all necessary adjustments.
	Chilton Time
All models	
w/M.T.	18.1
w/A.T.	19.5
w/A.C. add	1.5

Crankcase Joining Surfaces, Reseal
Includes: R&R engine assy.
All models	12.7
w/A.C. add	.8

Crankshaft Rear Oil Seal, Renew
Includes: R&R engine assy.
All models	
w/M.T.	3.4
w/A.T.	4.5
w/A.C. add	1.5

Crankshaft Pulley Seal, Renew
Includes: R&R engine assy.
	Chilton Time
All models	
w/M.T.	4.2
w/A.T.	5.5
w/A.C. add	1.5

Crankshaft Pulley, Renew
All models	.8
w/A.C. add	.8

WATER COOLED ENGINE

Crankshaft and Main Bearings, Renew
Includes: R&R engine assy. Make all necessary adjustments.
All models	17.4
w/A.C. add	.8

Crankcase Joining Surfaces, Reseal
Includes: R&R engine assy.
	Chilton Time
All models	12.7
w/A.C. add	.8

Crankshaft Front Oil Seal, Renew
All models	2.4

DIESEL ENGINE

Crankshaft and Main Bearings, Renew
Includes: R&R engine assy.
All models	8.7

Rear Main Bearing Oil Seal, Renew
Includes: R&R transmission.
All models	5.4

Front Crankshaft Flange and/or Gasket, Renew
All models	2.4

Crankshaft Front Oil Seal, Renew
All models	3.0

LABOR 16 CAMSHAFT & TIMING GEARS 16 LABOR

AIR COOLED ENGINE

Camshaft, Renew
Includes: R&R engine assy. Inspect or renew camshaft bearings. Make all necessary adjustments.
	Chilton Time
All models	
w/M.T.	15.1
w/A.T.	16.5
w/A.C. add	1.5

Hydraulic Cam Followers, Renew
All models-one side	1.5
both sides	2.4

WATER COOLED ENGINE

Camshaft, Renew
Includes: R&R engine assy. Inspect or renew camshaft bearings. Make all necessary adjustments.
	Chilton Time
All models	15.4
w/A.C. add	.8

Hydraulic Cam Followers, Renew
All models-one side	1.7

DIESEL ENGINE

Camshaft, Renew
All models	3.0

Camshaft Oil Seal, Renew
	Chilton Time
All models	2.0

Intermediate Shaft, Renew
All models	2.2

Timing Belt (Spur Belt) Cover, Renew
All models	.5

Timing Belt (Spur Belt), Renew
All models	2.4

Timing Belt (Spur Belt) Sprocket, Renew
All models	1.5

Timing Belt, Adjust
All models	.6

LABOR 17 ENGINE OILING SYSTEM 17 LABOR

AIR COOLED ENGINE

Oil Pressure Test
	Chilton Time
All models	.6

Oil Pressure Switch, Renew
All models	.5

Oil Pump and Gaskets, Renew
Includes: R&R engine assy., muffler and fan housing.
All models	
w/M.T.	5.1
w/A.T.	6.4
w/A.C. add	1.5

Oil Sump Cover and Gaskets, Renew
	.7

Oil Filter Element, Renew
	.3

Oil Cooler, Renew
Includes: R&R engine assy.
	Chilton Time
All models	
w/M.T.	4.9
w/A.T.	6.3
w/A.C. add	1.5

WATER COOLED ENGINE

Oil Pump Pressure, Test
All models	.6

Oil Pressure Switch, Renew
All models	.5

Oil Pump and Gaskets, Renew
Includes: R&R engine support.
All models	3.7

Oil Filter Element, Renew
	Chilton Time
All models	.3

DIESEL ENGINE

Oil Pan and/or Gasket, Renew
All models	3.0

Pressure Test Engine Bearing (Pan Off)
All models	1.0

Oil Pump, Renew
All models	3.2

Oil Pressure Switch, Renew
All models	.6

Oil Filter Element, Renew
All models	.3

LABOR 18 CLUTCH & FLYWHEEL 18 LABOR

Clutch Pedal Free Play, Adjust
	Chilton Time
All models	.4

Bleed Clutch Hydraulic System
All models	.5

Clutch Master Cylinder, Renew
Includes: Bleed system.
	Chilton Time
All models	1.2

Clutch Slave Cylinder, Renew
Includes: Bleed system.
	Chilton Time
All models	1.2

LABOR 18 CLUTCH & FLYWHEEL 18 LABOR

	Chilton Time
Clutch Release Bearing, Renew	
Includes: R&R engine assy.	
All models-Gas	
Air Cooled	2.5
Water Cooled	4.3
Diesel	4.3
w/A.C. add	1.5

	Chilton Time
Clutch Assembly, Renew	
Includes: R&R engine assy.	
All models-Gas	
Air Cooled	2.8
Water Cooled	4.6
Diesel	4.6
w/A.C. add	1.5

	Chilton Time
Flywheel, Renew	
Includes: R&R engine assy.	
All models-Gas	
Air Cooled	3.2
Water Cooled	5.0
Diesel	4.9
w/A.C. add	1.5

LABOR 19 STANDARD TRANSMISSION 19 LABOR

	Chilton Time
Transmission Assembly, Remove & Install	
Includes: R&R engine assy.	
All models-Gas	2.6
Diesel	3.5
Syncro	3.5
w/A.C. add	1.5

	Chilton Time
Transmission Assy., R&R and Recondition	
Includes: R&R engine and trans. Disassemble trans. Clean and inspect all parts. Renew parts as required, install new gaskets and seals.	
All models-Gas	11.3
Diesel	11.7

	Chilton Time
Syncro	11.7
w/A.C. add	1.5
Front Transmission Mount, Renew	
All models	.7

LABOR 21 SHIFT LINKAGE 21 LABOR

	Chilton Time
MANUAL	
Shift Linkage, Adjust	
All models	.6
Gear Shift Lever, Renew	
All models	.9
Shift Lever Boot, Renew	
All models	.4

	Chilton Time
Front Shift Rod, Renew	
All models	1.5
AUTOMATIC	
Selector Lever, Renew	
All models	1.0

	Chilton Time
Selector Cable, Renew	
Includes: Adjust cable.	
All models	1.1
Selector Cable, Adjust	
All models	.4

LABOR 23 AUTOMATIC TRANSMISSION 23 LABOR

	Chilton Time
ON CAR SERVICES	
Drain & Refill Unit	
All models	.8
Check Unit For Oil Leaks	
Includes: Clean and dry outside of case and run unit to determine point of leak.	
All models	.9
Performance Test	
Includes: Inspect fluid level, perform stall speed and pressure test.	
All models	1.0
Neutral Safety Switch, Renew	
All models	1.2
Governor, Renew	
All models	.5
Oil Pan or Gasket, Renew	
All models	.8

	Chilton Time
Valve Body Assembly, Renew	
Includes: R&R oil pan.	
All models	.9
Valve Body, R&R and Recondition	
Includes: R&R oil pan. Clean, inspect, free all valves. Replace parts as required.	
All models	2.5
Valve Body Electro Magnet, Renew	
Includes: R&R oil pan and valve body.	
All models	2.0
Vacuum Modulator, Renew	
All models	.6
Kick-Down Switch, Renew	
Includes: R&R accelerator pedal.	
All models	.5

	Chilton Time
SERVICES REQUIRING R&R	
Transmission Assembly, Remove & Install	
Includes: R&R engine assy.	
All models	
Air cooled eng	2.5
Water cooled eng	4.3
w/A.C. add	1.5
Torque Converter, Renew	
Includes: R&R engine assy.	
All models	
Air cooled eng	2.7
Water cooled eng	4.5
w/A.C. add	1.5
Renew seal add	.2
Transmission Assy., R&R and Recondition	
Includes: R&R engine and transmission. Disassemble trans completely. Clean and inspect all parts. Renew parts as required. Reassemble and adjust.	
All models	
Air cooled eng	10.6
Water cooled eng	12.6
w/A.C. add	1.5

LABOR 26 DRIVE AXLE 26 LABOR

	Chilton Time
Rear Half Shaft Assy., R&R or Renew	
All models-one	1.0
both	1.9
Recond shafts, add-each	.5
Note: Includes renew or recondition C.V. Joint, or renew boot.	

	Chilton Time
Stub Axle Shaft, Renew	
Includes: R&R brake drum, CV joint, wheel bearings and seal. Renew parts as required.	
All models-one	2.2
both	4.2

	Chilton Time
Rear Wheel Bearing or Seal, Renew (One Side)	
All models	2.4

LABOR   26 DRIVE AXLE 26   LABOR

SERVICES REQUIRING R&R

w/MANUAL TRANS

Drive Shaft Flange, R&R or Renew
Includes: R&R transmission.
All models

	Chilton Time
Gas	3.4
Diesel	4.2
Syncro	4.2

Drive Shaft Flange Oil Seal, Renew
Includes: R&R transmission.
All models

Gas	3.6
Diesel	4.4
Syncro	4.4

Ring Gear and Pinion Set, Renew
Includes: R&R engine and trans. Partially disassemble trans. Adjust ring gear and pinion and bearing pre-load.
All models

Gas	10.0
Diesel	10.5
Syncro	10.5
w/A.C. add	1.5

Differential Housing and Cover, Renew
Includes: R&R engine and trans. R&R differential. Adjust ring gear and pinion and bearing pre-load.
All models

Gas	7.5
Diesel	8.0
Syncro	8.0
w/A.C. add	1.5

Differential Bearings, Renew
Includes: R&R engine and trans. R&R differential. Adjust ring gear and pinion and bearing pre-load.
All models

	Chilton Time
Gas	7.0
Diesel	7.5
Syncro	7.5
w/A.C. add	1.5

Differential Side Gears, Renew
Includes: R&R engine and trans. R&R differential carrier. Check ring gear adjustment.
All models

Gas	6.5
Diesel	7.0
Syncro	7.0
w/A.C. add	1.5

w/AUTO TRANS

Drive Shaft Flange, R&R or Renew
Includes: R&R transmission.
All models

Air cooled eng	2.9
Water cooled eng	4.7

Drive Shaft Flange Oil Seal, Renew
Includes: R&R transmission.
All models

Air cooled eng	3.1
Water cooled eng	4.9

Ring Gear and Pinion Set, Renew
Includes: R&R engine and trans. Partially disassemble final drive and differential carrier.

Adjust ring gear and pinion and bearing pre-load.
All models

	Chilton Time
Air cooled eng	9.5
Water cooled eng	9.4
w/A.C. add	1.5

Differential Housing and Cover, Renew
Includes: R&R engine and trans. Partially disassemble final drive and differential carrier. Adjust ring gear and pinion and bearing pre-load.
All models

Air cooled eng	7.0
Water cooled eng	8.5
w/A.C. add	1.5

Differential Carrier Pinion Seal, Renew
Includes: R&R engine and trans. Partially disassemble final drive and differential carrier.
All models

Air cooled eng	3.0
Water cooled eng	4.6
w/A.C. add	1.5

SYNCRO

Propeller Shaft, R&R or Renew	
Syncro	1.0
Front or Rear Prop Shaft Seal, Renew	
Syncro	1.1
Final Drive Assembly, R&R or Renew	
Syncro	2.4

LABOR   27 REAR SUSPENSION 27   LABOR

Rear Wheels, Align

	Chilton Time
All models	.8

Front and Rear Wheel Alignment, Check
Does not include any adjustments.

All models	1.4

Rear Control Arms, Renew

	Chilton Time
All models-one	2.1
both	4.0
Renew bushings, add-each side	.5

Rear Coil Spring, Renew (One)

All models	1.1

Rear Shock Absorbers, Renew

	Chilton Time
All models-one	.5
both	.8

Rear Wheel Hub, Renew (One)

All models	1.0

LABOR   28 AIR CONDITIONING 28   LABOR

Note: If more than one item requires replacement where evacuation and discharging the system is already included in the operation, deduct 1.0 hour for each additional item to the times listed.

Drain, Evacuate & Recharge System

	Chilton Time
All models	1.0

Flush Refrigerant System, Complete
To be used in conjunction with component replacement which could contaminate system.

All models	1.3

Leak Check
Includes: Check all hoses and connections.

All models	.5

Compressor Drive Belt, Renew
All models

	Chilton Time
Idler pulley to comp	.9
crank to idler pulley	1.2

Compressor Clutch Assy., Renew

All models	.5

Compressor Front Seal, Renew
Includes: R&R clutch assy. Evacuate and charge system.

All models	2.2

Compressor Assembly, Renew
Includes: Transfer parts as required. Evacuate and charge system.

All models	2.2

Condenser Assembly, Renew
Includes. Evacuate and charge system.

	Chilton Time
All models	1.5

Condenser Fan and Motor, Renew

All models-one	.6

Evaporator Coil, Renew
Includes: R&R evaporator assy. Transfer or renew expansion valve. Evacuate and charge system.

All models	3.6
Renew blower motor add	.1

Expansion Valve, Renew
Includes: R&R evaporator assy. Evacuate and charge system.

1986-90	4.0

Air Conditioning Hoses, Renew
Includes: Evacuate and charge system.
All models

suction	3.5
discharge	2.4